WEBSTER'S
NEW
EXPLORER
DICTIONARY
AND
THESAURUS

NEW EDITION

WEBSTER'S NEW EXPLORER DICTIONARY AND THESAURUS

NEW EDITION

Created in Cooperation with the Editors of
MERRIAM-WEBSTER

FEDERAL STREET PRESS

A Division of Merriam-Webster, Incorporated
Springfield, Massachusetts

This edition published by Federal Street Press,
a Division of Merriam-Webster, Incorporated
P.O. Box 281
Springfield, MA 01102

Federal Street Press books are available for bulk purchase for sales promotion
and premium use. For details write the manager of special sales,
Federal Street Press, P.O. Box 281, Springfield, MA 01102

ISBN 10   1-892859-78-5

ISBN 13   978-892859-78-5

Printed in the United States of America

05   06   07   08   09   5   4   3   2   1

CONTENTS

A 48 page full-color world atlas follows page 686

PREFACE

This new edition of *Webster's New Explorer Dictionary and Thesaurus* contains the language reference features people most want in a single volume. It has been edited in cooperation with the editors of Merriam-Webster, the premier name in dictionaries, and everything in it has been updated for the 21st century.

Every entry in the dictionary has been reviewed and updated, and its 75,000 definitions cover the core of the English vocabulary. Additionally, the dictionary has reference features most sought after by students and by those new to the English language.

Following the A-Z section of the dictionary are sections identifying the most often looked-up names of individuals and of places, information on foreign words and phrases that often appear in English writing, and special sections on common questions of usage, grammar, and word roots. The Handbook of Style and Documentation of Sources sections provide valuable guidance for writers. The thesaurus section also has been completely re-edited to make it more relevant to the needs of the student as well as the casual adult user. Each section has its own explanation on the styling of entries, to help with more efficient use of the references.

A special feature of *Webster's New Explorer Dictionary and Thesaurus* is the 48-page full-color atlas of the world. The maps, created and updated specially for this edition by the editors of Encyclopædia Britannica, are a useful resource for classwork, business projects, and a more complete understanding of world events.

We offer this work in the confidence that users will turn to it often for answers to their questions about the language.

DICTIONARY

PREFACE

The editors of this new edition have created it with the same careful, serious attention given its predecessor. This edition preserves the best aspects of the preceding edition and at the same time offers much that is new. Every entry and every section have been reexamined and revised in light of the most current information available. Definitions have been based on millions of citations of actual use from a wide range of printed sources.

The 75,000 definitions in this dictionary cover the most frequently used words in the language. The heart of the dictionary is the A-Z vocabulary section, where readers will find information about meaning, spelling, pronunciation, etymology, and synonyms. This section is followed by others that users have long found useful. For example, the section Foreign Words and Phrases covers words and phrases from other languages that often occur in English texts but have not become part of the English vocabulary; the section Biographical Names identifies individuals from history and contemporary culture, as well as biblical, legendary, and mythological characters; the section Geographical Names identifies places of importance in the United States and the world, along with current population figures.

This dictionary has been created by the editors of Merriam-Webster, a company that has been publishing dictionaries for more than 150 years. The editors, a professional staff of experienced lexicographers, believe it will serve well those who want a handy guide to the English language of today.

EXPLANATORY NOTES

The dictionary contains so much information that it is necessary to condense much of it to accommodate the limitations of the printed page. This section provides information on the conventions used throughout the dictionary, from the styling of entries and pronunciation to how we present information on usage and meaning. An understanding of the information contained in these notes will make the dictionary both easier and more rewarding to use.

ENTRIES

A boldface letter or a combination of such letters, including punctuation marks and diacritics where needed, that is set flush with the left-hand margin of each column of type is a main entry. The main entry may consist of letters set solid, of letters joined by a hyphen or a diagonal, or of letters separated by one or more spaces:

> **alone** . . . *adj*
> **avant–garde** . . . *n*
> **and/or** . . . *conj*
> **assembly language** *n*
> **av·a·lanche** . . . *n*

The material in lightface type that follows each main entry on the same line and on succeeding indented lines presents information about the main entry.

The main entries follow one another in alphabetical order letter by letter: *bill of attainder* follows *billion; Day of Atonement* follows *daylight saving time*. Those containing an Arabic numeral are alphabetized as if the numeral were spelled out: *4-H* comes between *fourfold* and *Four Hundred; 3-D* comes between *three* and *three-dimensional*. Those that often begin with the abbreviation *St.* in common usage have the abbreviation spelled out: *Saint Valentine's Day*. Main entries that begin with *Mc* are alphabetized just as they are spelled.

A pair of guide words is printed at the top of each page. These indicate that the entries falling alphabetically between the words at the top of the outer column of each page are found on that page.

The guide words are usually the alphabetically first and the alphabetically last entries on the page:

> **alpha rhythm • ambition**

Occasionally the last printed entry is not the alphabetically last entry. Any boldface word—a main entry with definition, a variant, an inflected form, a defined or undefined run-on, or a run-in entry—may be used as a guide word.

On page 27, for example, *ascertain* is the last main entry, but *ascertainable*, an undefined run-on entry at *ascertain*, is the alphabetically last entry and is therefore the second guide word. The alphabetically last entry is not used, however, if it follows alphabetically the first guide word on the succeeding page. Thus on page 41 *bears* is not a guide word because it follows alphabetically the entry *bear* which is the first guide word on page 42.

When one main entry has exactly the same written form as another, the two are distinguished by superscript numerals preceding each word:

> **¹melt** . . . *vb*
> **²melt** *n*
> **¹pine** . . . *n*
> **²pine** *vb*

Full words come before parts of words made up of the same letters; solid compounds come before hyphenated compounds; hyphenated compounds come before open compounds; and lowercase entries come before those with an initial capital:

> **²super** *n*
> **super-** . . . *prefix*
> **run·down** . . . *n*
> **run–down** . . . *adj*
> **run down** *vb*
> **dutch** . . . *adv*
> **Dutch** . . . *n*

The centered dots within entry words indicate division points at which a hyphen may be put at the end of a line of print or writing. Thus the noun *cap·puc·ci·no* may be ended on one line and continued on the next in this manner:

> cap-
> puccino
>
> cappuc-
> cino
>
> cappucci-
> no

Centered dots are not shown after a single initial letter or before a single terminal letter because typesetters seldom cut off a single letter:

> **abyss** . . . *n*
> **flighty** . . . *adj*
> **idea** . . . *n*

Nor are they usually shown at the second and succeeding homographs unless they differ among themselves:

> ¹**sig·nal** . . . *n*
> ²**signal** *vb*
> ³**signal** *adj*
>   *but*
> ¹**min·ute** . . . *n*
> ²**mi·nute** . . . *adj*

There are acceptable alternative end-of-line divisions just as there are acceptable variant spellings and pronunciations, but no more than one division is shown for any entry in this dictionary.

A double hyphen at the end of a line in this dictionary (as in the definition at ¹**pug 1**) stands for a hyphen that is retained when the word is written as a unit on one line. This kind of fixed hyphen is always represented in boldface words in this dictionary with an en dash, longer than an ordinary hyphen.

When a main entry is followed by the word *or* and another spelling, the two spellings are equal variants. Both are standard, and either one may be used according to personal inclination:

> **ocher** *or* **ochre**

If two variants joined by *or* are out of alphabetical order, they remain equal variants. The one printed first is, however, slightly more common than the second:

> ¹**plow** *or* **plough**

When another spelling is joined to the main entry by the word *also*, the spelling after *also* is a secondary variant and occurs less frequently than the first:

> **absinthe** *also* **absinth**

Secondary variants belong to standard usage and may be used according to personal inclination. Once the word *also* is used to signal a secondary variant, all following secondary variants are joined by *or*:

> ²**wool·ly** *also* **wool·ie** *or* **wooly**

Variants whose spelling puts them alphabetically more than a column away from the main entry are entered at their own alphabetical places as well as at the applicable main entry:

> ²**gage** *var of* GAUGE
> ¹**gauge** *also* **gage**
> ²**gauge** *also* **gage**

Variants having a usage label appear only at their own alphabetical places:

> **me·tre** . . . *chiefly Brit var of* METER

To show all the stylings that are found for English compounds would require space that can be better used for other information. So this dictionary limits itself to a single styling for a compound:

> **peace·mak·er**
> **pell–mell**
> **boom box**

When a compound is widely used and one styling predominates, that styling is shown. When a compound is uncommon or when the evidence indicates that two or three stylings are approximately equal in frequency, the styling shown is based on the comparison of other similar compounds.

A main entry may be followed by one or more derivatives or by a homograph with a different functional label. These are run-on entries. Each is introduced by a long dash and each has a functional label. They are not defined, however, since their meanings are readily understood from the meaning of the root word:

> **fear·less** . . . *adj* . . . — **fear·less·ly** *adv* —
>   **fear·less·ness** *n*
> **hic·cup** . . . *n* . . . — **hiccup** *vb*

A main entry may be followed by one or more phrases containing the entry word or an inflected form of it. These are also run-on entries. Each is introduced by a long dash but there is no functional label. They are, however, defined since their meanings are more than the sum of the meanings of their elements:

> ¹**set** . . . *vb* . . . — **set sail** : . . .
> ¹**hand** . . . *n* . . . — **at hand** : . . .

Defined phrases of this sort are run on at the entry defining the first major word in the phrase. When there are variants, however, the run-on appears at the entry defining the first major invariable word in the phrase:

> ¹**seed** . . . *n* . . . — **go to seed** *or* **run to seed**
>   **1** : . . .

Boldface words that appear within parentheses (as **co·ca** at **co·caine** and **jet engine** and **jet propulsion** at **jet–propelled**) are run-in entries.

Attention is called to the definition of *vocabulary entry* on page 556. The term *dictionary entry* includes all vocabulary entries as well as all boldface entries in the back sections headed "Foreign Words & Phrases," "Biographical Names," and "Geographical Names."

PRONUNCIATION

The matter between a pair of reversed slashes \ \ following the entry word indicates the pronunciation. The symbols used are explained in the chart at the end of this section.

A hyphen is used in the pronunciation to show syllabic division. These hyphens sometimes coincide with the centered dots in the entry word that indicate end-of-line division:

> **ab·sen·tee** \ˌab-sən-ˈtē\

Sometimes they do not:

> **met·ric** \ˈme-trik\

A high-set mark ˈ indicates major (primary) stress or accent; a low-set mark ˌ indicates minor (secondary) stress or accent:

> **heart·beat** \ˈhärt-ˌbēt\

The stress mark stands at the beginning of the syllable that receives the stress.

A syllable with neither a high-set mark nor a low-set mark is unstressed:

> ¹**struc·ture** \ˈstrək-chər\

The presence of variant pronunciations indicates that not all educated speakers pronounce words the same way. A second-place variant is not to be regarded as less acceptable than the pronunciation that is given first. It may, in fact, be used by as many educated speakers as the first variant, but the requirements of the printed page are such that one must precede the other:

> **apri·cot** \ˈa-prə-ˌkät, ˈā-\
> **fore·head** \ˈfȯr-əd, ˈfȯr-ˌhed\

Symbols enclosed by parentheses represent elements that are present in the pronunciation of some speakers but are absent from the pronunciation of other speakers, or elements that are present in some but absent from other utterances of the same speaker:

> ¹**om·ni·bus** \ˈäm-ni-(ˌ)bəs\
> **ad·di·tion·al** \ə-ˈdi-sh(ə-)nəl\

Thus, the above parentheses indicate that some people say \ˈäm-ni-ˌbəs\ and others say \ˈäm-ni-bəs\; some \ə-ˈdi-shə-nəl\, others \ə-ˈdi-shnəl\.

When a main entry has less than a full pronunciation, the missing part is to be supplied from a pronunciation in a preceding entry or within the same pair of reversed slashes:

> **cham·pi·on·ship** \-ˌship\
> **pa·la·ver** \pə-ˈla-vər, -ˈlä-\

The pronunciation of the first three syllables of *championship* is found at the main entry *champion*. The hyphens before and after \ˈlä\ in the pronunciation of *palaver* indicate that both the first and the last parts of the pronunciation are to be taken from the immediately preceding pronunciation.

In general, no pronunciation is indicated for open compounds consisting of two or more English words that have own-place entry:

> **witch doctor** *n*

Only the first entry in a sequence of numbered homographs is given a pronunciation if their pronunciations are the same:

> ¹**re·ward** \ri-ˈwȯrd\ *vb*
> ²**reward** *n*

The absent but implied pronunciation of derivatives and compounds run on after a main entry is a combination of the pronunciation at the main entry and the pronunciation of the other element as given at its alphabetical place in the vocabulary:

> — **quick·ness** *n*
> — **hold with**

Thus, the pronunciation of *quickness* is the sum of the pronunciations given at *quick* and *-ness;* that of *hold with*, the sum of the pronunciations of the two elements that make up the phrase.

FUNCTIONAL LABELS

An italic label indicating a part of speech or another functional classification follows the pronunciation or, if no pronunciation is given, the main entry. The eight traditional parts of speech are indicated as follows:

> **bold** . . . *adj*
> **forth·with** . . . *adv*
> ¹**but** . . . *conj*

> **ge·sund·heit** . . . *interj*
> **bo·le·ro** . . . *n*
> ²**un·der** . . . *prep*
> ¹**it** . . . *pron*
> **slap** . . . *vb*

Other italicized labels used to indicate functional classifications that are not traditional parts of speech include:

AT *abbr*
self- *comb form*
un- . . . *prefix*
-ial *adj suffix*
²**-ly** *adv suffix*
²**-er** . . . *n suffix*

-ize *vb suffix*
Fe *symbol*
may . . . *verbal auxiliary*

Functional labels are sometimes combined:

afloat . . . *adj or adv*

INFLECTED FORMS

NOUNS

The plurals of nouns are shown in this dictionary when suffixation brings about a change of final -*y* to -*i*-, when the noun ends in a consonant plus -*o* or in -*ey*, when the noun ends in -*oo*, when the noun has an irregular plural or an uninflected plural or a foreign plural, when the noun is a compound that pluralizes any element but the last, when a final consonant is doubled, when the noun has variant plurals, and when it is believed that the dictionary user might have reasonable doubts about the spelling of the plural or when the plural is spelled in a way contrary to what is expected:

²**spy** *n, pl* **spies**
si·lo . . . *n, pl* **silos**
val·ley . . . *n, pl* **valleys**
²**shampoo** *n, pl* **shampoos**
mouse . . . *n, pl* **mice**
moose . . . *n, pl* **moose**
cri·te·ri·on . . . *n, pl* **-ria**
son–in–law . . . *n, pl* **sons–in–law**
¹**quiz** . . . *n, pl* **quiz·zes**
¹**fish** . . . *n, pl* **fish** *or* **fish·es**

pi . . . *n, pl* **pis**
³**dry** *n, pl* **drys**

Cutback inflected forms are used when the noun has three or more syllables:

ame·ni·ty . . . *n, pl* **-ties**

The plurals of nouns are usually not shown when the base word is unchanged by suffixation, when the noun is a compound whose second element is readily recognizable as a regular free form entered at its own place, or when the noun is unlikely to occur in the plural:

night . . . *n*
fore·foot . . . *n*
mo·nog·a·my . . . *n*

Nouns that are plural in form and that are regularly construed as plural are labeled *n pl*:

munch·ies . . . *n pl*

Nouns that are plural in form but that are not always construed as plurals are appropriately labeled:

lo·gis·tics . . . *n sing or pl*

VERBS

The principal parts of verbs are shown in this dictionary when suffixation brings about a doubling of a final consonant or an elision of a final -*e* or a change of final -*y* to -*i*-, when final -*c* changes to -*ck* in suffixation, when the verb ends in -*ey*, when the inflection is irregular, when there are variant inflected forms, and when it is believed that the dictionary user might have reasonable doubts about the spelling of an inflected form or when the inflected form is spelled in a way contrary to what is expected:

²**snag** *vb* **snagged; snag·ging**
¹**move** . . . *vb* **moved; mov·ing**
¹**cry** . . . *vb* **cried; cry·ing**
¹**frol·ic** . . . *vb* **frol·icked; frol·ick·ing**
¹**sur·vey** . . . *vb* **sur·veyed; sur·vey·ing**
¹**drive** . . . *vb* **drove** . . . **driv·en** . . . **driv·ing**
²**bus** *vb* **bused** *or* **bussed; bus·ing** *or* **bus·sing**

²**visa** *vb* **vi·saed** . . . **vi·sa·ing**
²**chagrin** *vb* **cha·grined** . . . **cha·grin·ing**

The principal parts of a regularly inflected verb are shown when it is desirable to indicate the pronunciation of one of the inflected forms:

learn . . . *vb* **learned** \'lərnd, 'lərnt\; **learning**
¹**al·ter** \'ȯl-tər\ *vb* **al·tered; al·ter·ing** \-t(ə-)riŋ\

Cutback inflected forms are usually used when the verb has three or more syllables, when it is a two-syllable word that ends in -*l* and has variant spellings, and when it is a compound whose second element is readily recognized as an irregular verb:

elim·i·nate . . . *vb* **-nat·ed; -nat·ing**
²**quarrel** *vb* **-reled** *or* **-relled; -rel·ing** *or* **-rel·ling**
¹**re·take** . . . *vb* **-took** . . . **-tak·en** . . . **-tak·ing**

The principal parts of verbs are usually not shown when the base word is unchanged by suffixation or when the verb is a compound whose second element is readily recognizable as a regular free form entered at its own place:

¹jump . . . *vb*
pre·judge . . . *vb*

Another inflected form of English verbs is the third person singular of the present tense, which is regularly formed by the addition of -*s* or -*es* to the base form of the verb. This inflected form is not shown except at a handful of entries (as *have* and *do*) for which it is in some way unusual.

ADJECTIVES & ADVERBS

The comparative and superlative forms of adjectives and adverbs are shown in this dictionary when suffixation brings about a doubling of a final consonant or an elision of a final -*e* or a change of final -*y* to -*i*-, when the word ends in -*ey*, when the inflection is irregular, and when there are variant inflected forms:

¹red . . . *adj* **red·der; red·dest**
¹tame . . . *adj* **tam·er; tam·est**
¹kind·ly . . . *adj* **kind·li·er; -est**
hors·ey *also* **horsy** . . . *adj* **hors·i·er; -est**
¹good . . . *adj* **bet·ter** . . . **best**
¹far . . . *adv* **far·ther** . . . *or* **fur·ther** . . .
    far·thest *or* **fur·thest** . . .

The superlative forms of adjectives and adverbs of two or more syllables are usually cut back:

³fancy *adj* **fan·ci·er; -est**
¹ear·ly . . . *adv* **ear·li·er; -est**

The comparative and superlative forms of regularly inflected adjectives and adverbs are shown when it is desirable to indicate the pronunciation of the inflected forms:

¹young \'yəŋ\ *adj* **youn·ger** \'yəŋ-gər\; **youn-gest** \'yəŋ-gəst\

The inclusion of inflected forms in -*er* and -*est* at adjective and adverb entries means nothing more about the use of *more* and *most* with these adjectives and adverbs than that their comparative and superlative degrees may be expressed in either way: *lazier* or *more lazy; laziest* or *most lazy.*

At a few adjective entries only the superlative form is shown:

²mere *adj, superlative* **mer·est**

The absence of the comparative form indicates that there is no evidence of its use.

The comparative and superlative forms of adjectives and adverbs are usually not shown when the base word is unchanged by suffixation, when the inflected forms of the word are identical with those of a preceding homograph, or when the word is a compound whose second element is readily recognizable as a regular free form entered at its own place:

¹near . . . *adv*
³good *adv*
un·wor·thy . . . *adj*

Inflected forms are not shown at undefined run-ons.

CAPITALIZATION

Most entries in this dictionary begin with a lowercase letter. A few of these have an italicized label *often cap*, which indicates that the word is as likely to be capitalized as not and that it is as acceptable with an uppercase initial as it is with one in lowercase. Some entries begin with an uppercase letter, which indicates that the word is usually capitalized. The absence of an initial capital or of an *often cap* label indicates that the word is not ordinarily capitalized:

salm·on . . . *n*
gar·gan·tuan . . . *adj, often cap*
Mo·hawk . . . *n*

The capitalization of entries that are open or hyphenated compounds is similarly indicated by the form of the entry or by an italicized label:

dry goods . . . *n pl*
french fry *n, often cap 1st F*
un–Amer·i·can . . . *adj*
Par·kin·son's disease . . . *n*
lazy Su·san . . . *n*
Jack Frost *n*

A word that is capitalized in some senses and lowercase in others shows variations from the form of the main entry by the use of italicized labels at the appropriate senses:

Trin·i·ty . . . *n* . . . **2** *not cap*
To·ry . . . *n* . . . **3** *often not cap*
ti·tan . . . *n* **1** *cap*
re·nais·sance . . . *n* . . . **1** *cap* . . . **2** *often cap*

ETYMOLOGY

This dictionary gives the etymologies for a number of the vocabulary entries. These etymologies are inside square brackets preceding the definition. Meanings given in roman type within these brackets are not definitions of the entry, but are meanings of the Middle English, Old English, or non-English words within the brackets.

The etymology gives the language from which words borrowed into English have come. It also gives the form of the word in that language or a representation of the word in our alphabet if the form in that language differs from that in English:

   philo·den·dron . . . [NL, fr. Gk, neut. of *philo-dendros* loving trees . . .]
   ¹**sav·age** . . . [ME, *sauvage,* fr. AF, *salvage, savage,* LL *salvaticus,* alter. of L *silvaticus* of the woods, wild . . .]

An etymology beginning with the name of a language (including ME or OE) and not giving the foreign (or Middle English or Old English) form indicates that this form is the same as the form of the entry word:

   le·gume . . . [F]
   ¹**jour·ney** . . . [ME, fr. OF . . .]

An etymology beginning with the name of a language (including ME or OE) and not giving the foreign (or Middle English or Old English) meaning indicates that this meaning is the same as the meaning expressed in the first definition in the entry:

   ug·ly . . . *adj* . . . [ME, fr. ON *uggligr* . . .] 1 : FRIGHTFUL, DIRE

USAGE

Three types of status labels are used in this dictionary—temporal, regional, and stylistic—to signal that a word or a sense of a word is not part of the standard vocabulary of English.

The temporal label *obs* for "obsolete" means that there is no evidence of use since 1755:

   ³**post** *n* 1 *obs*

The label *obs* is a comment on the word being defined. When a thing, as distinguished from the word used to designate it, is obsolete, appropriate orientation is usually given in the definition:

   cat·a·pult . . . *n* 1 : an ancient military machine for hurling missiles

The temporal label *archaic* means that a word or sense once in common use is found today only sporadically or in special contexts:

   ¹**mete** . . . *vb* . . . 1 *archaic*
   ¹**thou** . . . *pron, archaic*

A word or sense limited in use to a specific region of the U.S. has an appropriate label. The adverb *chiefly* precedes a label when the word has some currency outside the specified region, and a double label is used to indicate considerable currency in each of two specific regions:

   ²**wash** *n* . . . 8 *West*
   do·gie . . . *n, chiefly West*
   crul·ler . . . *n* . . . 2 *Northern & Midland*

Words current in all regions of the U.S. have no label.

A word or sense limited in use to one of the other countries of the English-speaking world has an appropriate regional label:

   chem·ist . . . *n* . . . 2 *Brit*
   loch . . . *n, Scot*
   ²**wireless** *n* . . . 2 *chiefly Brit*

The label *dial* for "dialect" indicates that the pattern of use of a word or sense is too complex for summary labeling: it usually includes several regional varieties of American English or of American and British English:

   ²**mind** *vb* 1 *chiefly dial*

The stylistic label *slang* is used with words or senses that are especially appropriate in contexts of extreme informality:

   ³**can** . . . *vb* . . . 2 *slang*
   ²**grand** *n* . . . *slang*

There is no satisfactory objective test for slang, especially with reference to a word out of context. No word, in fact, is invariably slang, and many standard words can be given slang applications.

The stylistic labels *offensive* and *disparaging* are used for those words or senses that in common use are intended to hurt or that are likely to give offense even when they are used without such an intent:

   dumb . . . *adj* 1 *often offensive*
   half–breed . . . *n, often disparaging*

Definitions are sometimes followed by verbal illustrations that show a typical use of the word in context. These illustrations are enclosed in angle brackets, and the word being illustrated is usually replaced by a lightface swung dash. The swung dash stands for the boldface entry word, and it may be followed by an italicized suffix:

> **¹jump** . . . *vb* . . . **5** . . . ⟨~ town⟩
> **all–around** . . . *adj* **1** . . . ⟨best ~ performance⟩
> **¹can·on** . . . *n* . . . **3** . . . ⟨the ~s of good taste⟩
> **en·joy** . . . *vb* . . . **2** . . . ⟨~*ed* the concert⟩

The swung dash is not used when the form of the boldface entry word is changed in suffixation, and it is not used for compounds:

> **²deal** *vb* . . **2** . . . ⟨*dealt* him a blow⟩
> **drum up** *vb* **1** . . . ⟨*drum up* business⟩

Definitions are sometimes followed by usage notes that give supplementary information about such matters as idiom, syntax, and semantic relationship. A usage note is introduced by a lightface dash:

> **²cry** *n* . . . **5** . . . — usu. used in the phrase *a far cry*
> **²drum** *vb* . . . **4** . . . — usu. used with *out*
> **¹jaw** . . . *n* . . . **2** . . . — usu. used in pl.
> **¹ada·gio** . . . *adv or adj* . . . — used as a direction in music
> **hajji** . . . *n* . . . — often used as a title

Sometimes a usage note is used in place of a definition. Some function words (as conjunctions and prepositions) have chiefly grammatical meaning and little or no lexical meaning; most interjections express feelings but are otherwise untranslatable into lexical meaning; and some other words (as honorific titles) are more amenable to comment than to definition:

> **or** . . . *conj* — used as a function word to indicate an alternative
> **¹at** . . . *prep* **1** — used to indicate a point in time or space
> **auf Wie·der·seh·en** . . . *interj* . . . — used to express farewell
> **sir** . . . *n* . . . **2** — used as a usu. respectful form of address

SENSE DIVISION

A boldface colon is used in this dictionary to introduce a definition:

> **equine** . . . *adj* . . . : of or relating to the horse

It is also used to separate two or more definitions of a single sense:

> **no·ti·fy** . . . *vb* . . . **1** : to give notice of : report the occurrence of

Boldface Arabic numerals separate the senses of a word that has more than one sense:

> **add** . . . *vb* **1** : to join to something else so as to increase in number or amount **2** : to say further . . . **3** : to combine (numbers) into one sum

A particular semantic relationship between senses is sometimes suggested by the use of one of the two italic sense dividers *esp* or *also*.

The sense divider *esp* (for *especially*) is used to introduce the most common meaning included in the more general preceding definition:

> **crys·tal** . . . *n* . . . **2** : something resembling crystal (as in transparency); *esp* : a clear colorless glass of superior quality

The sense divider *also* is used to introduce a meaning related to the preceding sense by an easily understood extension of that sense:

> **chi·na** . . . *n* . . . : porcelain ware; *also* : domestic pottery in general

The order of senses is historical: the sense known to have been first used in English is entered first. This is not to be taken to mean, however, that each sense of a multisense word developed from the immediately preceding sense. It is altogether possible that sense 1 of a word has given rise to sense 2 and sense 2 to sense 3, but frequently sense 2 and sense 3 may have developed independently of one another from sense 1.

When an italicized label follows a boldface numeral, the label applies only to that specific numbered sense. It does not apply to any other boldface numbered senses:

> **craft** . . . *n* . . . **3** *pl usu* **craft**
> **¹fa·ther** . . . *n* . . . **2** *cap* . . . **5** *often cap*
> **dul·ci·mer** . . . *n* . . . **2** *or* **dul·ci·more** \-ˌmȯr\
> **²lift** *n* . . . **5** *chiefly Brit*

At *craft* the *pl* label applies to sense 3 but to none of the other numbered senses. At *father* the *cap* label applies only to sense 2 and the *often cap* label only to sense 5. At *dulcimer* the variant spelling and pronunciation apply only to sense 2, and the *chiefly Brit* label at *lift* applies only to sense 5.

CROSS-REFERENCE

Four different kinds of cross-references are used in this dictionary: directional, synonymous, cognate, and inflectional. In each instance the cross-reference is readily recognized by the lightface small capitals in which it is printed.

A cross-reference following a lightface dash and beginning with *see* is a directional cross-reference. It directs the dictionary user to look elsewhere for further information:

eu·ro . . . *n* . . . —see MONEY table

A cross-reference following a boldface colon is a synonymous cross-reference. It may stand alone as the only definition for an entry or for a sense of an entry; it may follow an analytical definition; it may be one of two or more synonymous cross-references separated by commas:

pa·pa . . . *n* : FATHER
¹**par·tic·u·lar** . . . *adj* . . . **4** : attentive to details
  : PRECISE
²**main** *adj* **1** : CHIEF, PRINCIPAL
¹**fig·ure** . . . *n* . . . **6** : SHAPE, FORM, OUTLINE

A synonymous cross-reference indicates that an entry, a definition at the entry, or a specific sense at the entry cross-referred to can be substituted as a definition for the entry or the sense in which the cross-reference appears.

A cross-reference following an italic *var of* ("variant of") is a cognate cross-reference:

pick·a·back . . . *var of* PIGGYBACK

Occasionally a cognate cross-reference has a limiting label preceding *var of* as an indication that the variant is not standard American English:

aero·plane . . . *chiefly Brit var of* AIRPLANE

A cross-reference following an italic label that identifies an entry as an inflected form (as of a noun or verb) is an inflectional cross-reference:

calves *pl of* CALF
woven *past part of* WEAVE

Inflectional cross-references appear only when the inflected form falls at least a column away from the entry cross-referred to.

SYNONYMS

A bold italic Synonyms preceded by a small black diamond figure near the end of an entry introduces words that are synonymous with the word being defined:

alone . . . *adj* . . . ♦ *Synonyms* LONELY, LONESOME, LONE, SOLITARY

Synonyms are not definitions although they may often be substituted for each other in context.

COMBINING FORMS, PREFIXES, & SUFFIXES

An entry that begins or ends with a hyphen is a word element that forms part of an English compound:

-wise . . . *adv comb form* . . . ⟨slant*wise*⟩
ex- . . . *prefix* . . . **2** . . . ⟨*ex*-president⟩
-let *n suffix* **1** . . . ⟨book*let*⟩

Combining forms, prefixes, and suffixes are entered in this dictionary for two reasons: to make understandable the meaning of many undefined run-ons and to make recognizable the meaningful elements of words that are not entered in the dictionary.

LISTS OF UNDEFINED WORDS

Many words that begin with the prefixes or combining forms *anti-, in-, non-, over-, re-, self-, semi-, sub-, super-,* and *un-* are self-explanatory combinations of the prefix or combining form and a word entered elsewhere in the dictionary, and they are listed undefined at the bottom of the page or spread on which they would normally appear if defined.

ABBREVIATIONS & SYMBOLS

Abbreviations and symbols for chemical elements are included as main entries in the vocabulary:

RSVP *abbr* . . . please reply
Ca *symbol* calcium

Abbreviations have been normalized to one form. In practice, however, there is considerable variation in the use of periods and in capitalization (as *vhf, v.h.f.,* and *V.H.F.* for the entry VHF), and stylings other than those given in this dictionary are often acceptable.

ABBREVIATIONS IN THIS WORK

ab	about	*G, Ger*	German	*OIt*	Old Italian
abbr	abbreviation	*Gk*	Greek	*ON*	Old Norse
abl	ablative	*Gmc*	Germanic	*OPers*	Old Persian
acc	accusative	*Heb*	Hebrew	*orig*	originally
A.D.	anno Domini	*Hung*	Hungarian	*part*	participle
adj	adjective	*Icel*	Icelandic	*Pers*	Persian
adv	adverb	*imit*	imitative	*perh*	perhaps
AF	Anglo-French	*imper*	imperative	*Pg*	Portuguese
alter	alteration	*interj*	interjection	*pl*	plural
Am, Amer	American	*Ir*	Irish	*Pol*	Polish
AmerF	American French	*irreg*	irregular	*pp*	past participle
AmerInd	American Indian	*It, Ital*	Italian	*prep*	preposition
AmerSp	American Spanish	*Jp*	Japanese	*pres*	present, president
Ar	Arabic	*K*	Kelvin	*prob*	probably
Aram	Aramaic	*km*	kilometers	*pron*	pronoun,
B.C.	before Christ	*L*	Latin		pronunciation
Brit	British	*LaF*	Louisiana French	*prp*	present participle
C	Celsius	*LG*	Low German	*pseud*	pseudonym
ca	circa	*LGk*	Late Greek	*r*	reigned
Calif	California	*LHeb*	Late Hebrew	*Russ*	Russian
Canad	Canadian	*lit*	literally	*Sc*	Scotch, Scots
CanF	Canadian French	*LL*	Late Latin	*Scand*	Scandinavian
cap	capital, capitalized	*m*	meters	*ScGael*	Scottish Gaelic
Celt	Celtic	*masc*	masculine	*Scot*	Scottish
cen	central	*MD*	Middle Dutch	*sing*	singular
cent	century	*ME*	Middle English	*Skt*	Sanskrit
Chin	Chinese	*MexSp*	Mexican Spanish	*Slav*	Slavic
comb	combining	*MF*	Middle French	*So*	South
compar	comparative	*MGk*	Middle Greek	*Sp, Span*	Spanish
conj	conjunction	*mi*	miles	*St*	Saint
D	Dutch	*ML*	Medieval Latin	*superl*	superlative
Dan	Danish	*modif*	modification	*Sw*	Swedish
dat	dative	*MS*	manuscript	*syn*	synonym, synonymy
deriv	derivative	*Mt*	Mount	*trans*	translation
dial	dialect	*n*	noun	*Turk*	Turkish
dim	diminutive	*neut*	neuter	*US*	United States
E	English	*NewEng*	New England	*USSR*	Union of Soviet
Egypt	Egyptian	*NGk*	New Greek		Socialist Republics
Eng	English	*NHeb*	New Hebrew	*usu*	usually
esp	especially	*NL*	New Latin	*var*	variant
est	estimated	*No*	North	*vb*	verb
F	Fahrenheit, French	*Norw*	Norwegian	*vi*	verb intransitive
fem	feminine	*n pl*	noun plural	*VL*	Vulgar Latin
fl	flourished	*obs*	obsolete	*vt*	verb transitive
fr	from	*OE*	Old English	*W*	Welsh
ft	feet	*OF*	Old French		

PRONUNCIATION SYMBOLS

ə	abut, collect, suppose
ˈə, ˌə	humdrum
ə	(in ᵊl, ᵊn) battle, cotton; (in lᵊ, mᵊ, rᵊ) French table, prisme, titre
ər	operation, further
a	map, patch
ā	day, fate
ä	bother, cot, father
är	car, heart
aù	now, out
b	baby, rib
ch	chin, catch
d	did, adder
e	set, red
er	bare, fair
ē	beat, easy
f	fifty, cuff
g	go, big
h	hat, ahead
hw	whale
i	tip, banish
ir	near, deer
ī	site, buy
j	job, edge
k	kin, cook
k̲	German Bach, Scots loch
l	lily, cool
m	murmur, dim
n	nine, own
ⁿ	indicates that a preceding vowel is pronounced through both nose and mouth, as in French bon \bōⁿ\
ŋ	sing, singer, finger, ink
ō	bone, hollow
ȯ	saw
ȯr	boar, port
œ	French bœuf, feu, German Hölle, Höhle

ȯi	toy
p	pepper, lip
r	rarity
s	source, less
sh	shy, mission
t	tie, attack
th	thin, ether
t̲h̲	then, either
ü	boot, few \ˈfyü\
ù	put, pure \ˈpyùr\
ùr	boor, tour
ᴦ	French rue, German füllen, fühlen
v	vivid, give
w	we, away
y	yard, cue \ˈkyü\
ʸ	indicates that a preceding \l\, \n\, or \w\ is modified by having the tongue approximate the position for \y\, as in French digne \dēnʸ\
z	zone, raise
zh	vision, pleasure
\	slant line used in pairs to mark the beginning and end of a transcription: \ˈpen\
ˈ	mark at the beginning of a syllable that has primary (strongest) stress: \ˈshə-fəl-ˌbȯrd\
ˌ	mark at the beginning of a syllable that has secondary (next-strongest) stress: \ˈshə-fəl-ˌbȯrd\
-	mark of a syllable division in pronunciations (the mark of end-of-line division in boldface entries is a centered dot ·)
( )	indicate that what is symbolized between sometimes occurs and sometimes does not occur in the pronunciation of the word: **bakery** \ˈbā-k(ə-)rē\ = \ˈbā-kə-rē, ˈbā-krē\

¹a \'ā\ *n, pl* **a's** *or* **as** \'āz\ *often cap* **1** : the 1st letter of the English alphabet **2** : a grade rating a student's work as superior

²a \ə, (')ā\ *indefinite article* : ONE, SOME — used to indicate an unspecified or unidentified individual ⟨there's ∼ man outside⟩

³a *abbr, often cap* **1** absent **2** acre **3** alto **4** answer **5** are **6** area

AA *abbr* **1** Alcoholics Anonymous **2** antiaircraft **3** associate in arts

AAA *abbr* American Automobile Association

A and M *abbr* agricultural and mechanical

A and R *abbr* artists and repertory

aard·vark \'ärd-ˌvärk\ *n* [obs. Afrikaans, fr. Afrikaans *aard* earth + *vark* pig] : a large burrowing African mammal that feeds on ants and termites with its long sticky tongue

aardvark

¹ab \'ab\ *n* : an abdominal muscle

²ab *abbr* about

AB *abbr* **1** able-bodied seaman **2** airman basic **3** [NL *artium baccalaureus*] bachelor of arts

ABA *abbr* American Bar Association

aback \ə-'bak\ *adv* : by surprise ⟨taken ∼⟩

aba·cus \'a-bə-kəs\ *n, pl* **aba·ci** \-ˌsī, -ˌkē\ *or* **aba·cus·es** : an instrument for making calculations by sliding counters along rods or grooves

¹abaft \ə-'baft\ *prep* : to the rear of

²abaft *adv* : toward or at the stern : AFT

ab·a·lo·ne \ˌa-bə-'lō-nē, 'a-bə-ˌ\ *n* : any of a genus of large edible sea mollusks with a flattened slightly spiral shell with holes along the edge

¹aban·don \ə-'ban-dən\ *vb* [ME *abandounen*, fr. AF *abanduner*, fr. (*mettre*) *a bandun* to hand over, put in someone's control] : to give up completely : FORSAKE, DESERT — **aban·don·ment** *n*

²abandon *n* : a thorough yielding to natural impulses; *esp* : EXUBERANCE

aban·doned \ə-'ban-dənd\ *adj* : morally unrestrained
♦ *Synonyms* PROFLIGATE, DISSOLUTE, REPROBATE

abase \ə-'bās\ *vb* **abased; abas·ing** : HUMBLE, DEGRADE — **abase·ment** *n*

abash \ə-'bash\ *vb* : to destroy the composure of : EMBARRASS — **abash·ment** *n*

abate \ə-'bāt\ *vb* **abat·ed; abat·ing** **1** : to put an end to ⟨∼ a nuisance⟩ **2** : to decrease in amount, number, or degree

abate·ment \ə-'bāt-mənt\ *n* **1** : DECREASE **2** : an amount abated; *esp* : a deduction from a tax

ab·at·toir \'a-bə-ˌtwär\ *n* [F] : SLAUGHTERHOUSE

ab·ba·cy \'a-bə-sē\ *n, pl* **-cies** : the office or term of office of an abbot or abbess

ab·bé \a-'bā, 'a-ˌ\ *n* : a member of the French secular clergy — used as a title

ab·bess \'a-bəs\ *n* : the superior of a convent for nuns

ab·bey \'a-bē\ *n, pl* **abbeys** **1** : MONASTERY **2** : CONVENT **3** : an abbey church

ab·bot \'a-bət\ *n* [ME *abbod*, fr. OE, fr. LL *abbat-*, *abbas*, fr. LGk *abbas*, fr. Aramaic *abbā* father] : the superior of a monastery for men

abbr *abbr* abbreviation

ab·bre·vi·ate \ə-'brē-vē-ˌāt\ *vb* **-at·ed; -at·ing** : SHORTEN, CURTAIL; *esp* : to reduce to an abbreviation

ab·bre·vi·a·tion \ə-ˌbrē-vē-'ā-shən\ *n* **1** : the act or result of abbreviating **2** : a shortened form of a word or phrase used for brevity esp. in writing

¹ABC \ˌā-(ˌ)bē-'sē\ *n, pl* **ABC's** *or* **ABCs** \-'sēz\ **1** : ALPHABET — usu. used in pl. **2** : RUDIMENTS — usu. used in pl.

²ABC *abbr* American Broadcasting Company

Ab·di·as \ab-'dī-əs\ *n* : OBADIAH

ab·di·cate \'ab-di-ˌkāt\ *vb* **-cat·ed; -cat·ing** : to give up (as a throne) formally — **ab·di·ca·tion** \ˌab-di-'kā-shən\ *n*

ab·do·men \'ab-də-mən, ab-'dō-\ *n* **1** : the cavity in or area of the body between the chest and the pelvis **2** : the part of the body posterior to the thorax in an arthropod — **ab·dom·i·nal** \ab-'dä-mə-nᵊl\ *adj* — **ab·dom·i·nal·ly** *adv*

ab·duct \ab-'dəkt\ *vb* : to take away (a person) by force : KIDNAP — **ab·duc·tion** \-'dək-shən\ *n* — **ab·duc·tor** \-tər\ *n*

abeam \ə-'bēm\ *adv or adj* : on a line at right angles to a ship's keel

abed \ə-'bed\ *adv or adj* : in bed

Abe·na·ki \ˌa-bə-'nä-kē\ *also* **Ab·na·ki** \ab-'nä-kē\ *n, pl* **Abenaki** *or* **Abenakis** *also* **Abnaki** *or* **Abnakis** : a member of a group of American Indian peoples of northern New England and southern Quebec

ab·er·ra·tion \ˌa-bə-'rā-shən\ *n* **1** : deviation esp. from a moral standard or normal state **2** : failure of a mirror or lens to produce exact point-to-point correspondence between an object and its image **3** : unsoundness of mind : DERANGEMENT — **ab·er·rant** \a-'ber-ənt\ *adj*

abet \ə-'bet\ *vb* **abet·ted; abet·ting** [ME *abetten*, fr. AF *abeter*, fr. *beter* to bait] **1** : INCITE, ENCOURAGE **2** : to assist or support in the achievement of a purpose ⟨∼ a fugitive⟩ — **abet·tor** *or* **abet·ter** \-'be-tər\ *n*

abey·ance \ə-'bā-əns\ *n* : a condition of suspended activity — **abey·ant** \-ənt\ *adj*

ab·hor \ab-'hor, əb-\ *vb* **ab·horred; ab·hor·ring** [ME *abhorren*, fr. L *abhorrēre*, fr. *ab-* + *horrēre* to shudder] : LOATHE, DETEST — **ab·hor·rence** \-əns\ *n*

ab·hor·rent \-ənt\ *adj* : LOATHSOME, DETESTABLE ⟨∼ crimes⟩

abide \ə-'bīd\ *vb* **abode** \-'bōd\ *or* **abid·ed; abid·ing** **1** : BEAR, ENDURE **2** : DWELL, REMAIN, LAST — **abide by** : to conform or acquiesce to ⟨*abide by* the law⟩

abil·i·ty \ə-'bi-lə-tē\ *n, pl* **-ties** : the quality of being able : POWER, SKILL

-ability *also* **-ibility** *n suffix* : capacity, fitness, or tendency to act or be acted on in a (specified) way ⟨flamm*ability*⟩

ab·ject \'ab-ˌjekt, ab-'jekt\ *adj* : low in spirit, hope, or state ⟨∼ poverty⟩ — **ab·jec·tion** \ab-'jek-shən\ *n* — **ab·ject·ly** *adv* — **ab·ject·ness** *n*

ab·jure \ab-'jùr\ *vb* **ab·jured; ab·jur·ing** **1** : to renounce solemnly : RECANT **2** : to abstain from — **ab·ju·ra·tion** \ˌab-jə-'rā-shən\ *n*

abl *abbr* ablative

ab·late \a-'blāt\ *vb* **ab·lat·ed; ab·lat·ing** : to remove or become removed esp. by cutting, abrading, or vaporizing

ab·la·tion \a-'blā-shən\ *n* **1** : surgical cutting and removal **2** : loss of a part (as the outside of a nose cone) by melting or vaporization

ab·la·tive \'ab-lə-tiv\ *adj* : of, relating to, or constituting a grammatical case (as in Latin) expressing typically the relation of separation and source — **ablative** *n*

ablaze \ə-'blāz\ *adj or adv* : being on fire : BLAZING

able \'ā-bəl\ *adj* **abler** \-b(ə-)lər\; **ablest** \-b(ə-)ləst\ [ME, fr. AF, fr. L *habilis* apt, fr. *habēre* to hold, possess] **1** : having sufficient power, skill, or resources to accomplish an object **2** : marked by skill or efficiency — **ably** \-blē\ *adv*

-able *also* **-ible** *adj suffix* **1** : capable of, fit for, or worthy of (being so acted upon or toward) 〈breakable〉 〈collectible〉 **2** : tending, given, or liable to 〈knowledgeable〉 〈perishable〉

able–bod·ied \ˌā-bəl-'bä-dēd\ *adj* : having a sound strong body

abloom \ə-'blüm\ *adj* : BLOOMING

ab·lu·tion \ə-'blü-shən, a-\ *n* : the washing of one's body or part of it

ABM \ˌā-(ˌ)bē-'em\ *n, pl* **ABM's** *or* **ABMs** : ANTIBALLISTIC MISSILE

Abnaki *var of* ABENAKI

ab·ne·gate \'ab-ni-ˌgāt\ *vb* **-gat·ed; -gat·ing** **1** : DENY, RENOUNCE **2** : SURRENDER, RELINQUISH 〈~ her powers〉 — **ab·ne·ga·tion** \ˌab-ni-'gā-shən\ *n*

ab·nor·mal \ab-'nȯr-məl\ *adj* : deviating from the normal or average — **ab·nor·mal·i·ty** \ˌab-nȯr-'ma-lə-tē\ *n* — **ab·nor·mal·ly** *adv*

¹aboard \ə-'bȯrd\ *adv* **1** : ALONGSIDE **2** : on, onto, or within a car, ship, or aircraft **3** : in or into a group or association 〈welcome new workers ~〉

²aboard *prep* : ON, ONTO, WITHIN

abode \ə-'bōd\ *n* **1** : STAY, SOJOURN **2** : HOME, RESIDENCE

abol·ish \ə-'bä-lish\ *vb* : to do away with : ANNUL 〈~ slavery〉 — **ab·o·li·tion** \ˌa-bə-'li-shən\ *n*

ab·o·li·tion·ism \ˌa-bə-'li-shə-ˌni-zəm\ *n* : advocacy of the abolition of slavery — **ab·o·li·tion·ist** \-'li-sh(ə-)nist\ *n or adj*

A–bomb \'ā-ˌbäm\ *n* : ATOMIC BOMB — **A–bomb** *vb*

abom·i·na·ble \ə-'bä-mə-nə-bəl\ *adj* : ODIOUS, LOATHSOME, DETESTABLE

abominable snow·man \-'snō-mən, -ˌman\ *n, often cap A&S* : a mysterious creature with human or apelike characteristics reported to exist in the high Himalayas

abom·i·nate \ə-'bä-mə-ˌnāt\ *vb* **-nat·ed; -nat·ing** [L *abominari*, lit., to deprecate as an ill omen, fr. *ab-* away + *omen* omen] : LOATHE, DETEST

abom·i·na·tion \ə-ˌbä-mə-'nā-shən\ *n* **1** : something abominable **2** : DISGUST, LOATHING

ab·orig·i·nal \ˌa-bə-'ri-jə-nəl\ *adj* : ORIGINAL, INDIGENOUS, PRIMITIVE

ab·orig·i·ne \ˌa-bə-'ri-jə-nē\ *n* : a member of the original race of inhabitants of a region : NATIVE

aborn·ing \ə-'bȯr-niŋ\ *adv* : while being born or produced

¹abort \ə-'bȯrt\ *vb* **1** : to cause or undergo abortion **2** : to terminate prematurely 〈~ a spaceflight〉 — **abor·tive** \-'bȯr-tiv\ *adj*

²abort *n* : the premature termination of a mission of or a procedure relating to an aircraft or spacecraft

abor·tion \ə-'bȯr-shən\ *n* : the spontaneous or induced termination of a pregnancy after, accompanied by, resulting in, or closely followed by the death of the embryo or fetus

abor·tion·ist \-sh(ə-)nist\ *n* : one who induces abortions

abound \ə-'baund\ *vb* **1** : to be plentiful : TEEM **2** : to be fully supplied

¹about \ə-'baut\ *adv* **1** : reasonably close to; *also* : on the verge of 〈~ to join the army〉 **2** : on all sides **3** : NEARBY

²about *prep* **1** : on every side of **2** : near to **3** : CONCERNING

about–face \-'fās\ *n* : a reversal of direction or attitude — **about–face** *vb*

¹above \ə-'bəv\ *adv* **1** : in the sky; *also* : in or to heaven **2** : in or to a higher place; *also* : higher on the same page or on a preceding page

²above *prep* **1** : in or to a higher place than : OVER 〈storm clouds ~ the bay〉 **2** : superior to 〈he thought her far ~ him〉 **3** : more than : EXCEEDING **4** : as distinct from 〈~ the noise〉

above·board \-ˌbȯrd\ *adv or adj* : without concealment or deception : OPENLY

abp *abbr* archbishop

abr *abbr* abridged; abridgment

ab·ra·ca·dab·ra \ˌa-brə-kə-'da-brə\ *n* **1** : a magical charm or incantation against calamity **2** : GIBBERISH

abrade \ə-'brād\ *vb* **abrad·ed; abrad·ing** **1** : to wear away by friction **2** : to wear down in spirit : IRRITATE — **abra·sion** \-'brā-zhən\ *n*

¹abra·sive \ə-'brā-siv\ *n* : a substance (as pumice) for abrading, smoothing, or polishing

²abrasive *adj* **1** : tending to abrade : causing irritation 〈~ relationships〉 — **abra·sive·ly** *adv* — **abra·sive·ness** *n*

abreast \ə-'brest\ *adv or adj* **1** : side by side **2** : up to a standard or level esp. of knowledge 〈kept ~ of the news〉

abridge \ə-'brij\ *vb* **abridged; abridg·ing** [ME *abregen*, fr. AF *abreger*, fr. LL *abbreviare*, fr. L *ad* to + *brevis* short] : to lessen in length or extent : SHORTEN — **abridg·ment** *or* **abridge·ment** *n*

abroad \ə-'brȯd\ *adv or adj* **1** : over a wide area **2** : away from one's home **3** : outside one's country

ab·ro·gate \'a-brə-ˌgāt\ *vb* **-gat·ed; -gat·ing** : ANNUL, REVOKE — **ab·ro·ga·tion** \ˌa-brə-'gā-shən\ *n*

abrupt \ə-'brəpt\ *adj* **1** : broken or as if broken off **2** : SUDDEN, HASTY 〈an ~ turn〉 **3** : so quick as to seem rude 〈an ~ reply〉 **4** : DISCONNECTED **5** : STEEP — **abrupt·ly** *adv*

abs *abbr* absolute

ab·scess \'ab-ˌses\ *n, pl* **ab·scess·es** [L *abscessus,* lit., act of going away, fr. *abscedere* to go away, fr. *abs-, ab-* away + *cedere* to go] : a localized collection of pus surrounded by inflamed tissue — **ab·scessed** \-ˌsest\ *adj*

ab·scis·sa \ab-'si-sə\ *n, pl* **abscissas** *also* **ab·scis·sae** \-'si-(ˌ)sē\ : the horizontal coordinate of a point in a plane coordinate system obtained by measuring parallel to the x-axis

ab·scis·sion \ab-'si-zhən\ *n* **1** : the act or process of cutting off **2** : the natural separation of flowers, fruits, or leaves from plants — **ab·scise** \ab-'sīz\ *vb*

ab·scond \ab-'skänd\ *vb* : to depart secretly and hide oneself

ab·sence \'ab-səns\ *n* **1** : the state or time of being absent **2** : WANT, LACK **3** : INATTENTION

¹ab·sent \'ab-sənt\ *adj* **1** : not present **2** : LACKING **3** : INATTENTIVE

²ab·sent \ab-'sent\ *vb* : to keep (oneself) away

³ab·sent \'ab-sənt\ *prep* : in the absence of : WITHOUT

ab·sen·tee \ˌab-sən-'tē\ *n* : one that is absent or keeps away

absentee ballot *n* : a ballot submitted (as by mail) in advance of an election by a voter who is unable to be present at the polls

ab·sen·tee·ism \ˌab-sən-'tē-ˌi-zəm\ *n* : chronic absence (as from work or school)

ab·sent·mind·ed \ˌab-sənt-'mīn-dəd\ *adj* : unaware of one's surroundings or actions : INATTENTIVE — **ab·sent·mind·ed·ly** *adv* — **ab·sent·mind·ed·ness** *n*

ab·sinthe *also* **ab·sinth** \'ab-ˌsinth\ *n* [F] : a liqueur flavored esp. with wormwood and anise

ab·so·lute \'ab-sə-ˌlüt, ˌab-sə-'lüt\ *adj* **1** : free from imperfection or mixture **2** : free from control, restriction, or qualification 〈~ power〉 **3** : lacking grammatical connection with any other word in a sentence 〈~ construction〉 **4** : POSITIVE 〈~ proof〉 **5** : relating to the fundamental units of length, mass, and time **6** : FUNDAMENTAL, ULTIMATE — **ab·so·lute·ly** *adv*

absolute pitch *n* **1** : the position of a tone in a standard scale independently determined by its rate of vibration **2** : the ability to sing a note asked for or to name a note heard

absolute value *n* : a nonnegative number equal to a given real number with any negative sign removed

absolute zero *n* : a theoretical temperature marked by a complete absence of heat and motion and equivalent to exactly -273.15°C or -459.67°F

ab·so·lu·tion \ˌab-sə-'lü-shən\ *n* : the act of absolving; *esp* : a remission of sins pronounced by a priest in the sacrament of reconciliation

ab·so·lut·ism \'ab-sə-ˌlü-ˌti-zəm\ *n* **1** : the theory that a ruler or government should have unlimited power **2** : government by an absolute ruler or authority

ab·solve \əb-'zälv, -'sälv\ *vb* **ab·solved; ab·solv·ing** : to set free from an obligation or the consequences of guilt

ab·sorb \əb-'sȯrb, -'zȯrb\ *vb* **1** : to take in and make part of an existent whole **2** : to suck up or take in in the manner of a sponge **3** : to engage (one's attention) : ENGROSS **4** : to receive without recoil or echo 〈a ceiling that ~s sound⟩ **5** : ASSUME, BEAR ⟨~ all costs⟩ **6** : to transform (radiant energy) into a different form esp. with a resulting rise in temperature — **ab·sorb·ing** *adj* — **ab·sorb·ing·ly** *adv*

ab·sor·bent *also* **ab·sor·bant** \əb-'sȯr-bənt, -'zȯr-\ *adj* : able to absorb ⟨~ cotton⟩ — **ab·sor·ben·cy** \-bən-sē\ *n* — **absorbent** *also* **absorbant** *n*

ab·sorp·tion \əb-'sȯrp-shən, -'zȯrp-\ *n* **1** : a process of absorbing or being absorbed **2** : concentration of attention — **ab·sorp·tive** \-tiv\ *adj*

ab·stain \əb-'stān\ *vb* : to refrain from an action or practice — **ab·stain·er** *n* — **ab·sten·tion** \-'sten-chən\ *n*

ab·ste·mi·ous \ab-'stē-mē-əs\ *adj* : sparing in use of food or drink : TEMPERATE — **ab·ste·mi·ous·ly** *adv* — **ab·ste·mi·ous·ness** *n*

ab·sti·nence \'ab-stə-nəns\ *n* : voluntary refraining esp. from eating certain foods, drinking liquor, or engaging in sexual intercourse — **ab·sti·nent** \-nənt\ *adj*

abstr *abbr* abstract

¹ab·stract \'ab-ˌstrakt, 'ab-'strakt\ *adj* **1** : considered apart from a particular instance **2** : expressing a quality apart from an object ⟨*whiteness* is an ~ word⟩ **3** : having only intrinsic form with little or no pictorial representation ⟨~ painting⟩ — **ab·stract·ly** *adv* — **ab·stract·ness** *n*

²ab·stract \'ab-ˌstrakt; 2 *also* ab-'strakt\ *n* **1** : SUMMARY, EPITOME **2** : an abstract thing or state

³ab·stract \ab-'strakt, 'ab-ˌstrakt; 2 *usu* 'ab-ˌstrakt\ *vb* **1** : REMOVE, SEPARATE **2** : to make an abstract of : SUMMARIZE **3** : to draw away the attention of **4** : STEAL — **ab·stract·ed** \-'strak-təd-lē, 'ab-ˌstrak-\ *adv*

abstract expressionism *n* : art that expresses the artist's attitudes and emotions through abstract forms — **abstract expressionist** *n*

ab·strac·tion \ab-'strak-shən\ *n* **1** : the act of abstracting : the state of being abstracted **2** : an abstract idea **3** : an abstract work of art

ab·struse \ab-'strüs\ *adj* : hard to understand : RECONDITE — **ab·struse·ly** *adv* — **ab·struse·ness** *n*

ab·surd \əb-'sərd, -'zərd\ *adj* [MF *absurde*, fr. L *absurdus*, fr. *ab-* from + *surdus* deaf, stupid] : RIDICULOUS, UNREASONABLE — **ab·sur·di·ty** \-'sər-də-tē, -'zər-\ *n* — **ab·surd·ly** *adv*

abun·dant \ə-'bən-dənt\ *adj* [ME, fr. AF, fr. L *abundant-, abundans*, prp. of *abundare* to abound, fr. *ab-* from + *unda* wave] : more than enough : amply sufficient ◆ **Synonyms** COPIOUS, PLENTIFUL, AMPLE, BOUNTIFUL — **abun·dance** \-dəns\ *n* — **abun·dant·ly** *adv*

¹abuse \ə-'byüs\ *n* **1** : a corrupt practice **2** : MISUSE ⟨drug ~⟩ **3** : coarse and insulting speech **4** : MISTREATMENT ⟨child ~⟩

²abuse \ə-'byüz\ *vb* **abused; abus·ing 1** : to put to a wrong use : MISUSE **2** : to use excessively ⟨~ alcohol⟩ **3** : MISTREAT **4** : to attack in words : REVILE — **abus·er** *n* — **abu·sive** \-'byü-siv\ *adj* — **abu·sive·ly** *adv* — **abu·sive·ness** *n*

abut \ə-'bət\ *vb* **abut·ted; abut·ting** : to touch along a border : border on

abut·ment \ə-'bət-mənt\ *n* : the part of a structure (as a bridge) that supports weight or withstands lateral pressure

abut·ter \ə-'bə-tər\ *n* : one that abuts; *esp* : the owner of a contiguous property

abuzz \ə-'bəz\ *adj* : filled or resounding with activity or excitement ⟨an office ~ with rumors⟩

abys·mal \ə-'biz-məl\ *adj* **1** : immeasurably deep : BOTTOMLESS **2** : absolutely wretched ⟨~ living conditions of the poor⟩ — **abys·mal·ly** *adv*

abyss \ə-'bis\ *n* **1** : the bottomless pit in old accounts of the universe **2** : an immeasurable depth

abys·sal \ə-'bi-səl\ *adj* : of or relating to the bottom waters of the ocean depths

ac *abbr* account

-ac *n suffix* : one affected with ⟨hypochondri*ac*⟩

Ac *symbol* actinium

AC *abbr* **1** air-conditioning **2** alternating current **3** [L *ante Christum*] before Christ **4** [L *ante cibum*] before meals **5** area code

aca·cia \ə-'kā-shə\ *n* : any of a genus of leguminous trees or shrubs with round white or yellow flower clusters and often feathery leaves

acad *abbr* academic; academy

ac·a·deme \'a-kə-ˌdēm, ˌa-kə-'\ *n* : SCHOOL; *also* : academic environment

¹ac·a·dem·ic \ˌa-kə-'de-mik\ *n* : a person who is academic in background, outlook, or methods

²academic *adj* **1** : of, relating to, or associated with schools or colleges **2** : literary or general rather than technical **3** : theoretical rather than practical — **ac·a·dem·i·cal·ly** \-mi-k(ə-)lē\ *adv*

ac·a·de·mi·cian \ˌa-kə-də-'mi-shən, ə-ˌka-də-\ *n* **1** : a member of a society of scholars or artists **2** : ACADEMIC

ac·a·dem·i·cism \ˌa-kə-'de-mə-ˌsi-zəm\ *also* **acad·e·mism** \ə-'ka-də-ˌmi-zəm\ *n* **1** : a formal academic quality **2** : purely speculative thinking

acad·e·my \ə-'ka-də-mē\ *n, pl* **-mies** [Gk *Akadēmeia*, school of philosophy founded by Plato, fr. *Akadēmeia*, gymnasium where Plato taught, fr. *Akadēmos* Greek mythological hero] **1** : a school above the elementary level; *esp* : a private high school **2** : a society of scholars or artists

acan·thus \ə-'kan-thəs\ *n, pl* **acanthus 1** : any of a genus of prickly herbs of the Mediterranean region **2** : an ornamentation (as on a column) representing the leaves of the acanthus

a cap·pel·la *also* **a ca·pel·la** \ˌä-kə-'pe-lə\ *adv or adj* [It *a cappella* in chapel style] : without instrumental accompaniment

acc *abbr* accusative

ac·cede \ak-'sēd\ *vb* **ac·ced·ed; ac·ced·ing 1** : to become a party to an agreement **2** : to express approval **3** : to enter upon an office ◆ **Synonyms** AGREE, ACQUIESCE, ASSENT, CONSENT, SUBSCRIBE

ac·cel·er·ate \ik-'se-lə-ˌrāt, ak-\ *vb* **-at·ed; -at·ing 1** : to bring about earlier **2** : to speed up : QUICKEN — **ac·cel·er·a·tion** \-ˌse-lə-'rā-shən\ *n*

ac·cel·er·a·tor \ik-'se-lə-ˌrā-tər, ak-\ *n* **1** : one that accelerates **2** : a pedal for controlling the speed of a motor-vehicle engine **3** : an apparatus for imparting high velocities to charged particles

ac·cel·er·om·e·ter \ik-ˌse-lə-'rä-mə-tər, ak-\ *n* : an instrument for measuring acceleration or vibrations

¹ac·cent \'ak-ˌsent, ak-'sent\ *vb* : STRESS, EMPHASIZE

²ac·cent \'ak-ˌsent\ *n* **1** : prominence given to one syllable of a word esp. by stress **2** : a distinctive manner of pronunciation ⟨a foreign ~⟩ **3** : a mark (as ´, `, ˆ) over a vowel used usu. to indicate a difference in pronunciation from a vowel not so marked — **ac·cen·tu·al** \ak-'sen-chə-wəl\ *adj*

ac·cen·tu·ate \ak-'sen-chə-ˌwāt\ *vb* **-at·ed; -at·ing** : STRESS, EMPHASIZE — **ac·cen·tu·a·tion** \-ˌsen-chə-'wā-shən\ *n*

ac·cept \ik-'sept, ak-\ *vb* **1** : to receive willingly **2** : to agree to **3** : to assume an obligation to pay

ac·cept·able \ik-'sep-tə-bəl, ak-\ *adj* : capable or worthy of being accepted — **ac·cept·abil·i·ty** \ik-ˌsep-tə-'bi-lə-tē, ak-\ *n*

ac·cep·tance \ik-'sep-təns, ak-\ *n* **1** : the act of accepting **2** : the state of being accepted or acceptable **3** : an accepted bill of exchange

ac·cep·ta·tion \ˌak-ˌsep-'tā-shən\ *n* : the generally understood meaning of a word

¹ac·cess \'ak-ˌses\ *n* **1** : capacity to enter or approach **2** : a way of approach : ENTRANCE

²access *vb* : to get at : gain access to

ac·ces·si·ble \ik-'se-sə-bəl, ak-, ek-\ *adj* **1** : capable of being reached ⟨~ by train⟩ **2** : capable of being used or seen ⟨~ archives⟩ **3** : capable of being understood ⟨an ~ film⟩ — **ac·ces·si·bil·i·ty** \-ˌse-sə-'bi-lə-tē\ *n*

ac·ces·sion \ik-'se-shən, ak-\ *n* **1** : increase by something added **2** : something added **3** : the act of coming to a high office or position

ac·ces·so·ry *also* **ac·ces·sa·ry** \ik-'se-sə-rē, ak-\ *n, pl* **-ries 1** : a person who though not present abets or assists in the commission of an offense **2** : something helpful but not essential ◆ **Synonyms** APPURTENANCE, ADJUNCT, APPENDAGE, APPENDIX — **accessory** *adj*

ac·ci·dent \'ak-sə-dənt\ *n* **1** : an event occurring by chance or unintentionally **2** : CHANCE ⟨met by ~⟩ **3** : a nonessential property

¹ac·ci·den·tal \ˌak-sə-'den-t°l\ *adj* **1** : happening unexpectedly or by chance **2** : happening without intent or through carelessness ◆ **Synonyms** CASUAL, FORTU-

ITOUS, INCIDENTAL, CHANCE — **ac·ci·den·tal·ly** \-'den-t³l-ē\ *also* **ac·ci·dent·ly** \-'dent-lē\ *adv*

²**accidental** *n* : a musical note foreign to a key indicated by a signature

ac·claim \ə-'klām\ *vb* **1** : APPLAUD, PRAISE **2** : to declare by acclamation ✦ *Synonyms* EXTOL, LAUD, COMMEND, HAIL — **acclaim** *n*

ac·cla·ma·tion \ˌa-klə-'mā-shən\ *n* **1** : loud eager applause **2** : an overwhelming affirmative vote by shouting or applause rather than by ballot

ac·cli·mate \'a-klə-ˌmāt, ə-'klī-mət\ *vb* **-mat·ed; -mat·ing** : to accustom or become accustomed to a new climate or situation — **ac·cli·ma·tion** \ˌa-klə-'mā-shən, -ˌklī-\ *n*

ac·cli·ma·tise *Brit var of* ACCLIMATIZE

ac·cli·ma·tize \ə-'klī-mə-ˌtīz\ *vb* **-tized; -tiz·ing** : ACCLIMATE — **ac·cli·ma·ti·za·tion** \-ˌklī-mə-tə-'zā-shən\ *n*

ac·cliv·i·ty \ə-'kli-və-tē\ *n, pl* **-ties** : an ascending slope

ac·co·lade \'a-kə-ˌlād\ *n* [F, fr. *accoler* to embrace, ultim. fr. L *ad-* to + *collum* neck] : an expression of praise : AWARD

ac·com·mo·date \ə-'kä-mə-ˌdāt\ *vb* **-dat·ed; -dat·ing 1** : to make fit or suitable : ADAPT, ADJUST **2** : HARMONIZE, RECONCILE **3** : to provide with something needed **4** : to hold without crowding **5** : to undergo visual accommodation

ac·com·mo·dat·ing *adj* : OBLIGING

ac·com·mo·da·tion \ə-ˌkä-mə-'dā-shən\ *n* **1** : something supplied to satisfy a need; *esp* : LODGINGS — usu. used in pl. **2** : the act of accommodating : ADJUSTMENT **3** : the automatic adjustment of the eye for seeing at different distances

ac·com·pa·ni·ment \ə-'kəm-pə-nē-mənt, -'kəmp-nē-\ *n* : something that accompanies another; *esp* : subordinate music to support a principal voice or instrument

ac·com·pa·ny \-nē\ *vb* **-nied; -ny·ing 1** : to go or occur with : ATTEND **2** : to play an accompaniment for — **ac·com·pa·nist** \-nist\ *n*

ac·com·plice \ə-'käm-pləs, -'kəm-\ *n* : an associate in wrongdoing

ac·com·plish \ə-'käm-plish, -'kəm-\ *vb* : to bring to completion ✦ *Synonyms* ACHIEVE, EFFECT, EXECUTE, PERFORM — **ac·com·plish·er** *n*

ac·com·plished \-plisht\ *adj* **1** : EXPERT, SKILLED ⟨an ∼ pianist⟩ **2** : established beyond doubt ⟨an ∼ fact⟩

ac·com·plish·ment \ə-'käm-plish-mənt, -'kəm-\ *n* **1** : COMPLETION **2** : something completed or effected **3** : an acquired excellence or skill

¹**ac·cord** \ə-'kȯrd\ *vb* [ME, fr. AF *acorder*, fr. VL **accordare*, fr. L *ad-* to + *cord-, cor* heart] **1** : GRANT, CONCEDE **2** : AGREE, HARMONIZE — **ac·cor·dant** \-'kȯr-d³nt\ *adj*

²**accord** *n* **1** : AGREEMENT, HARMONY **2** : willingness to act ⟨gave of their own ∼⟩

ac·cor·dance \ə-'kȯr-d³ns\ *n* **1** : ACCORD **2** : the act of granting

ac·cord·ing·ly \ə-'kȯr-diŋ-lē\ *adv* **1** : in accordance **2** : CONSEQUENTLY, SO

according to *prep* **1** : in conformity with ⟨paid *according to* ability⟩ **2** : as stated or attested by ⟨*according to* you⟩

¹**ac·cor·di·on** \ə-'kȯr-dē-ən\ *n* [G *Akkordion*, fr. *Akkord* chord] : a portable keyboard instrument with a bellows and reeds — **ac·cor·di·on·ist** \-ə-nist\ *n*

²**accordion** *adj* : folding like the bellows of an accordion ⟨∼ pleats⟩

ac·cost \ə-'kȯst\ *vb* [MF *accoster*, ultim. fr. L *ad-* to + *costa* rib, side] : to approach and speak to esp. aggressively

¹**ac·count** \ə-'kaůnt\ *n* **1** : a statement of business transactions **2** : a formal business arrangement for regular dealings or services **3** : a statement of reasons, causes, or motives **4** : VALUE, IMPORTANCE **5** : a sum of money deposited in a bank and subject to withdrawal by the depositor — **on account of** : BECAUSE OF — **on no account** : under no circumstances — **on one's own account** : on one's own behalf

²**account** *vb* **1** : CONSIDER ⟨I ∼ him lucky⟩ **2** : to give an explanation — used with *for*

ac·count·able \ə-'kaůn-tə-bəl\ *adj* **1** : ANSWERABLE, RESPONSIBLE **2** : EXPLICABLE — **ac·count·abil·i·ty** \-ˌkaůn-tə-'bi-lə-tē\ *n*

ac·coun·tant \ə-'kaůn-t³nt\ *n* : a person skilled in accounting — **ac·coun·tan·cy** \-t³n-sē\ *n*

account executive *n* : a business executive in charge of a client's account

ac·count·ing \ə-'kaůn-tiŋ\ *n* : the art or system of keeping and analyzing financial records

ac·cou·tre *or* **ac·cou·ter** \ə-'kü-tər\ *vb* **-cou·tred** *or* **-cou·tered; -cou·tring** *or* **-cou·ter·ing** \-'kü-t(ə-)riŋ\ : EQUIP, OUTFIT

ac·cou·tre·ment *or* **ac·cou·ter·ment** \ə-'kü-trə-mənt, -'kü-tər-\ *n* [F] **1** : an accessory item — usu. used in pl. **2** : an identifying characteristic

ac·cred·it \ə-'kre-dət\ *vb* **1** : to endorse or approve officially **2** : CREDIT — **ac·cred·i·ta·tion** \-ˌkre-də-'tā-shən\ *n*

ac·cre·tion \ə-'krē-shən\ *n* **1** : growth or enlargement esp. by addition from without **2** : a product of accretion

accretion disk *n* : a disk of usu. gaseous matter surrounding and gradually accumulating onto a massive celestial object

ac·crue \ə-'krü\ *vb* **ac·crued; ac·cru·ing 1** : to come by way of increase **2** : to be added by periodic growth — **ac·cru·al** \-əl\ *n*

acct *abbr* account; accountant

ac·cul·tur·a·tion \ə-ˌkəl-chə-'rā-shən\ *n* : cultural modification of an individual or group by borrowing and adapting traits from another culture

ac·cu·mu·late \ə-'kyü-myə-ˌlāt\ *vb* **-lat·ed; -lat·ing** [L *accumulare*, fr. *ad-* to + *cumulare* to heap up] : to heap or pile up ✦ *Synonyms* AMASS, GATHER, COLLECT, STOCKPILE — **ac·cu·mu·la·tion** \-ˌkyü-myə-'lā-shən\ *n* — **ac·cu·mu·la·tive** \-'kyü-myə-lə-tiv\ *adj* — **ac·cu·mu·la·tor** \-'kyü-myə-ˌlā-tər\ *n*

ac·cu·rate \'a-kyə-rət\ *adj* : free from error : EXACT, PRECISE — **ac·cu·ra·cy** \-rə-sē\ *n* — **ac·cu·rate·ly** *adv* — **ac·cu·rate·ness** *n*

ac·cursed \ə-'kərst, -'kər-səd\ *or* **ac·curst** \ə-'kərst\ *adj* **1** : being under a curse **2** : DAMNABLE, EXECRABLE

ac·cus·al \ə-'kyü-zəl\ *n* : ACCUSATION

ac·cu·sa·tive \ə-'kyü-zə-tiv\ *adj* : of, relating to, or being a grammatical case marking the direct object of a verb or the object of a preposition — **accusative** *n*

ac·cu·sa·to·ry \ə-'kyü-zə-ˌtȯr-ē\ *adj* : expressing accusation ⟨an ∼ tone⟩

ac·cuse \ə-'kyüz\ *vb* **ac·cused; ac·cus·ing** : to charge with an offense : BLAME — **ac·cu·sa·tion** \ˌa-kyə-'zā-shən\ *n* — **ac·cus·er** *n*

ac·cused \ə-'kyüzd\ *n, pl* **accused** : the defendant in a criminal case

ac·cus·tom \ə-'kəs-təm\ *vb* : to make familiar through use or experience

ac·cus·tomed \ə-'kəs-təmd\ *adj* : USUAL, CUSTOMARY ⟨with ∼ grace⟩; *also* : being in the habit ⟨∼ed to winning⟩

¹**ace** \'ās\ *n* [ME *as* a die face marked with one spot, fr. AF, fr. L, unit, a copper coin] **1** : a playing card bearing a single large pip in its center **2** : a point (as in tennis) won on a serve that goes untouched **3** : a golf score of one stroke on a hole **4** : a combat pilot who has downed five or more enemy planes **5** : one that excels **6** : the best pitcher on a baseball team

²**ace** *vb* **aced; ac·ing 1** : to score an ace against (an opponent) or on (a golf hole) **2** : to defeat decisively **3** : to perform extremely well in or on ⟨*aced* the quiz⟩

³**ace** *adj* : of first rank or quality

ACE inhibitor \ˌā-ˌsē-'ē-in-'hi-bə-tər, 'ās-\ *n* : any of a group of drugs that lower blood pressure by relaxing the arteries

acer·bic \ə-'sər-bik, a-\ *adj* : acid in temper, mood, or tone ⟨∼ wit⟩

acer·bi·ty \ə-'sər-bə-tē\ *n, pl* **-ties** : SOURNESS, BITTERNESS

acet·amin·o·phen \ə-ˌsē-tə-'mi-nə-fən\ *n* : a crystalline compound used in chemical synthesis and in medicine to relieve pain and fever

ac·e·tate \'a-sə-ˌtāt\ *n* **1** : a salt or ester of acetic acid **2** : a textile fiber made from cellulose and acetic acid; *also* : a fabric or plastic made of this fiber

ace·tic acid \ə-'sē-tik-\ *n* : a colorless pungent liquid acid that is the chief acid of vinegar and is used esp. in making chemical compounds

ac·e·tone \'a-sə-ˌtōn\ *n* : a volatile flammable fragrant liquid compound used in making other chemical compounds and as a solvent

ace·tyl·cho·line \ə-ˌsē-t³l-ˈkō-ˌlēn\ *n* : a compound that is released at nerve endings of the autonomic nervous system and is active in the transmission of nerve impulses

acet·y·lene \ə-ˈse-t³l-ən, -t³l-ˌēn\ *n* : a colorless flammable gas used as a fuel (as in welding and soldering)

ace·tyl·sal·i·cyl·ic acid \ə-ˌsē-t³l-ˌsa-la-ˌsi-lik-\ *n* : ASPIRIN 1

ache \ˈāk\ *vb* **ached; ach·ing** 1 : to suffer a usu. dull persistent pain ⟨an *aching* back⟩ 2 : LONG, YEARN ⟨*aching* to go home⟩ — **ache** *n* — **ach·ing·ly** \ˈā-kiŋ-lē\ *adv*

achieve \ə-ˈchēv\ *vb* **achieved; achiev·ing** [ME *acheven*, fr. AF *achever* to finish, fr. *a-* to (fr. L *ad-*) + *chef* end, head, fr. L *caput*] : to gain by work or effort ◆ *Synonyms* ACCOMPLISH, ATTAIN, REALIZE — **achiev·able** \-ˈchē-və-bəl\ *adj* — **achieve·ment** *n* — **achiev·er** *n*

Achil·les' heel \ə-ˌki-lēz-\ *n* [fr. the story that the Greek warrior Achilles was vulnerable only in the heel] : a vulnerable point

Achil·les tendon \ə-ˌki-lēz-\ *n* : the tendon joining the muscles in the calf of the leg to the bone of the heel

ach·ro·mat·ic \ˌa-krə-ˈma-tik\ *adj* : giving an image almost free from extraneous colors ⟨∼ lens⟩

achy \ˈā-kē\ *adj* **ach·i·er; ach·i·est** : afflicted with aches — **ach·i·ness** *n*

¹**ac·id** \ˈa-səd\ *adj* 1 : sour or biting to the taste; *also* : sharp or sour in manner 2 : of or relating to an acid — **acid·i·ty** \ə-ˈsi-də-tē\ *n* — **acid·ly** *adv*

²**acid** *n* 1 : a sour substance 2 : a usu. water-soluble chemical compound that has a sour taste, reacts with a base to form a salt, and reddens litmus 3 : LSD — **acid·ic** \ə-ˈsi-dik\ *adj*

acid·i·fy \ə-ˈsi-də-ˌfī\ *vb* **-fied; -fy·ing** 1 : to make or become acid 2 : to change into an acid — **acid·i·fi·ca·tion** \-ˌsi-də-fə-ˈkā-shən\ *n*

ac·i·do·sis \ˌa-sə-ˈdō-səs\ *n, pl* **-do·ses** \-ˌsēz\ : an abnormal state of reduced alkalinity of the blood and body tissues

acid precipitation *n* : precipitation with above normal acidity that is caused esp. by atmospheric pollutants

acid rain *n* : acid precipitation in the form of rain

acid test *n* : a severe or crucial test

acid·u·lous \ə-ˈsi-jə-ləs\ *adj* : somewhat acid or harsh in taste or manner

ack *abbr* acknowledge; acknowledgment

ac·knowl·edge \ik-ˈnä-lij, ak-\ *vb* **-edged; -edg·ing** 1 : to recognize the rights or authority of 2 : to admit as true 3 : to express thanks for; *also* : to report receipt of ⟨∼ a letter⟩ 4 : to recognize as valid — **ac·knowl·edg·ment** *or* **ac·knowl·edge·ment** *n*

ACL \ˌā-ˌsē-ˈel\ *n* : ANTERIOR CRUCIATE LIGAMENT

ACLU *abbr* American Civil Liberties Union

ac·me \ˈak-mē\ *n* [Gk *akmē*] : the highest point

ac·ne \ˈak-nē\ *n* [Gk *aknē*, MS var. of *akmē*, lit., point] : a skin disorder marked by inflammation of skin glands and hair follicles and by pimple formation esp. on the face

ac·o·lyte \ˈa-kə-ˌlīt\ *n* 1 : one who assists a member of the clergy in a liturgical service 2 : FOLLOWER

ac·o·nite \ˈa-kə-ˌnīt\ *n* 1 : MONKSHOOD 2 : the dried root of a common Eurasian monkshood used formerly as a drug

acorn \ˈā-ˌkȯrn, -kərn\ *n* : the nut of the oak

acorn: three different kinds of oak tree

acorn squash *n* : an acorn-shaped dark green winter squash with a ridged surface and yellow to orange flesh

acous·tic \ə-ˈkü-stik\ *or* **acous·ti·cal** \-sti-kəl\ *adj* 1 : of or relating to the sense or organs of hearing, to sound, or to the science of sounds 2 : deadening sound ⟨∼ tile⟩ 3 : operated by or utilizing sound waves 4 : having a sound that is not electronically modified ⟨∼ guitar⟩ — **acous·ti·cal·ly** \-k(ə-)lē\ *adv*

acous·tics \ə-ˈkü-stiks\ *n sing or pl* 1 : the science of sound 2 : the qualities in a room that make it easy or hard for a person in it to hear distinctly

ac·quaint \ə-ˈkwānt\ *vb* [ME, ultim. fr. L *ad-* + *cognoscere* to know] 1 : to cause to know personally 2 : INFORM

ac·quain·tance \ə-ˈkwān-t³ns\ *n* 1 : personal knowledge 2 : a person with whom one is acquainted — **ac·quain·tance·ship** *n*

acquaintance rape *n* : rape committed by someone known to the victim

ac·qui·esce \ˌa-kwē-ˈes\ *vb* **-esced; -esc·ing** : to accept, comply, or submit without open opposition ◆ *Synonyms* CONSENT, AGREE, ASSENT, ACCEDE — **ac·qui·es·cence** \-ˈe-s³ns\ *n* — **ac·qui·es·cent** \-s³nt\ *adj* — **ac·qui·es·cent·ly** *adv*

ac·quire \ə-ˈkwī(-ə)r\ *vb* **ac·quired; ac·quir·ing** : to gain possession of : GET — **ac·quir·able** \-ˈkwī-rə-bəl\ *adj*

acquired *adj* 1 : gained by or as a result of effort or experience 2 : caused by environmental forces and not passed from parent to offspring in the genes ⟨∼ characteristics⟩

acquired immune deficiency syndrome *n* : AIDS

acquired immunodeficiency syndrome *n* : AIDS

ac·quire·ment \ə-ˈkwī(-ə)r-mənt\ *n* 1 : ATTAINMENT, ACCOMPLISHMENT 2 : the act of acquiring

ac·qui·si·tion \ˌa-kwə-ˈzi-shən\ *n* 1 : ACQUIREMENT 2 : something acquired

ac·quis·i·tive \ə-ˈkwi-zə-tiv\ *adj* : eager to acquire : GREEDY — **ac·quis·i·tive·ly** *adv* — **ac·quis·i·tive·ness** *n*

ac·quit \ə-ˈkwit\ *vb* **ac·quit·ted; ac·quit·ting** 1 : to pronounce not guilty 2 : to conduct (oneself) usu. satisfactorily — **ac·quit·tal** \ə-ˈkwi-t³l\ *n*

acre \ˈā-kər\ *n* 1 *pl* : LANDS, ESTATE 2 — see WEIGHT table

acre·age \ˈā-k(ə-)rij\ *n* : area in acres

ac·rid \ˈa-krəd\ *adj* 1 : sharp and biting in taste or odor 2 : deeply bitter : CAUSTIC — **acrid·i·ty** \a-ˈkri-də-tē\ *n* — **ac·rid·ly** *adv* — **ac·rid·ness** *n*

ac·ri·mo·ny \ˈa-krə-ˌmō-nē\ *n, pl* **-nies** : harsh or biting sharpness of language or feeling — **ac·ri·mo·ni·ous** \ˌa-krə-ˈmō-nē-əs\ *adj* — **ac·ri·mo·ni·ous·ly** *adv* — **ac·ri·mo·ni·ous·ness** *n*

ac·ro·bat \ˈa-krə-ˌbat\ *n* [F *acrobate*, fr. Gk *akrobatēs*, fr. *akros* topmost + *bainein* to go] : a performer of gymnastic feats — **ac·ro·bat·ic** \ˌa-krə-ˈba-tik\ *adj* — **ac·ro·bat·i·cal·ly** \-ti-k(ə-)lē\ *adv*

ac·ro·bat·ics \ˌa-krə-ˈba-tiks\ *n sing or pl* : the performance of an acrobat

ac·ro·nym \ˈa-krə-ˌnim\ *n* : a word (as *radar*) or abbreviation (as *FBI*) formed from the initial letter or letters of each of the successive parts or major parts of a compound term

ac·ro·pho·bia \ˌa-krə-ˈfō-bē-ə\ *n* : abnormal dread of being in a high place : fear of heights

acrop·o·lis \ə-ˈkrä-pə-ləs\ *n* [Gk *akropolis*, fr. *akros* topmost + *polis* city] : the upper fortified part of an ancient Greek city

¹**across** \ə-ˈkrȯs\ *adv* 1 : to or on the opposite side 2 : so as to be understandable ⟨get the point ∼⟩

²**across** *prep* 1 : to or on the opposite side of ⟨ran ∼ the street⟩ 2 : on so as to cross or pass at an angle ⟨a log ∼ the road⟩

across–the–board *adj* 1 : placed to win if a competitor wins, places, or shows ⟨an ∼ bet⟩ 2 : including all classes or categories ⟨an ∼ wage increase⟩

acros·tic \ə-ˈkrȯs-tik\ *n* : a composition usu. in verse in which the initial or final letters of the lines taken in order form a word or phrase — **acrostic** *adj*

acryl·ic \ə-ˈkri-lik\ *n* 1 : ACRYLIC RESIN 2 : a paint in which the vehicle is acrylic resin 3 : a quick-drying synthetic textile fiber

acrylic resin *n* : a glassy thermoplastic used for cast and molded parts or as coatings and adhesives

¹**act** \ˈakt\ *n* 1 : a thing done : DEED 2 : STATUTE, DECREE 3 : a main division of a play; *also* : an item on a va-

riety program **4** : an instance of insincere behavior
: PRETENSE
²**act** \ *vb* **1** : to perform by action esp. on the stage; *also*
: FEIGN, SIMULATE, PRETEND **2** : to take action **3** : to
conduct oneself : BEHAVE **4** : to perform a specified
function **5** : to produce an effect
³**act** *abbr* **1** active **2** actual
ACT *abbr* Australian Capital Territory
actg *abbr* acting
ACTH \ˌā-(ˌ)sē-(ˌ)tē-ˈāch\ *n* : a protein hormone of the pituitary gland that stimulates the adrenal cortex
act·ing \ˈak-tiŋ\ *adj* : doing duty temporarily or for another ⟨~ president⟩
ac·tin·i·um \ak-ˈti-nē-əm\ *n* : a radioactive metallic chemical element
ac·tion \ˈak-shən\ *n* **1** : a legal proceeding **2** : the manner or method of performing **3** : ACTIVITY **4** : ACT,
DEED **5** : the accomplishment of a thing usu. over a period of time, in stages, or with the possibility of repetition **6** *pl* : CONDUCT **7** : COMBAT, BATTLE **8** : the
events of a literary plot **9** : an operating mechanism ⟨the
~ of a gun⟩; *also* : the way it operates ⟨stiff ~⟩
ac·tion·able \ˈak-sh(ə-)nə-bəl\ *adj* : affording ground for
an action or suit at law — **ac·tion·ably** \-blē\ *adv*
ac·ti·vate \ˈak-tə-ˌvāt\ *vb* **-vat·ed; -vat·ing** **1** : to spur into
action; *also* : to make active, reactive, or radioactive **2**
: to treat (as carbon) so as to improve adsorptive properties **3** : to set up (a military unit) formally; *also* : to call
to active duty — **ac·ti·va·tion** \ˌak-tə-ˈvā-shən\ *n* — **ac·ti-
va·tor** \ˈak-tə-ˌvā-tər\ *n*
ac·tive \ˈak-tiv\ *adj* **1** : causing or involving action or
change **2** : asserting that the grammatical subject performs the action represented by the verb ⟨~ voice⟩ **3**
: BRISK, LIVELY **4** : erupting or likely to erupt ⟨~ vol-
cano⟩ **5** : presently in operation or use **6** : tending to
progress or to cause degeneration ⟨~ tuberculosis⟩ —
active *n* — **ac·tive·ly** *adv* — **ac·tive·ness** *n*
ac·tive–ma·trix \ˈak-tiv-ˌmā-triks\ *adj* : of, relating to, or
being an LCD in which each pixel is individually controlled
ac·tive·wear \ˈak-tiv-ˌwer\ *n* : clothing designed for recreation or informal wear
ac·tiv·ism \ˈak-ti-ˌvi-zəm\ *n* : a doctrine or practice that
emphasizes vigorous action for political ends — **ac·tiv·ist**
\-vist\ *n or adj*
ac·tiv·i·ty \ak-ˈti-və-tē\ *n, pl* **-ties** **1** : the quality or state
of being active **2** : forceful or energetic action **3** : an occupation in which one is engaged
ac·tor \ˈak-tər\ *n* : a person who acts in a play or motion
picture
ac·tress \ˈak-trəs\ *n* : a woman who is an actor
Acts \ˈakts\ *or* **Acts of the Apostles** *n* — see BIBLE table
ac·tu·al \ˈak-chə-wəl, -shə-\ *adj* : really existing : REAL —
ac·tu·al·i·ty \ˌak-chə-ˈwa-lə-tē, -shə-\ *n* — **ac·tu·al·i·za-
tion** \ˌak-chə-wə-lə-ˈzā-shən, -shə-\ *n* — **ac·tu·al·ize** \ˈak-
chə-wə-ˌlīz, -shə-\ *vb*
ac·tu·al·ly \ˈak-chə-wə-lē, -shə-\ *adv* : in fact or in truth
: REALLY
ac·tu·ary \ˈak-chə-ˌwer-ē, -shə-\ *n, pl* **-ar·ies** : a person
who calculates insurance risks and premiums — **ac·tu·ar-
i·al** \ˌak-chə-ˈwer-ē-əl, -shə-\ *adj*
ac·tu·ate \ˈak-chə-ˌwāt\ *vb* **-at·ed; -at·ing** **1** : to put into
action **2** : to move to action — **ac·tu·a·tion** \ˌak-chə-
ˈwā-shən, -shə-\ *n* — **ac·tu·a·tor** \ˈak-chə-ˌwā-tər, -shə-\ *n*
act up *vb* **1** : MISBEHAVE **2** : to function improperly
acu·ity \ə-ˈkyü-ə-tē\ *n, pl* **-ities** : keenness of perception
acu·men \ə-ˈkyü-mən\ *n* : mental keenness and penetration ✦ *Synonyms* DISCERNMENT, INSIGHT, PERCIPI-
ENCE, PERSPICACITY
acu·pres·sure \ˈa-kyù-ˌpre-shər\ *n* : a finger massage of
those points on the body stimulated in acupuncture
acu·punc·ture \-ˌpəŋk-chər\ *n* : an orig. Chinese practice
of inserting thin needles through the skin at specific
points esp. to cure disease or relieve pain — **acu·punc-
tur·ist** \ˌa-kyù-ˈpəŋk-chə-rist\ *n*
acute \ə-ˈkyüt\ *adj* **acut·er; acut·est** [ME, fr. L *acutus*, pp.
of *acuere* to sharpen, fr. *acus* needle] **1** : SHARP, POINT-
ED **2** : containing less than 90 degrees ⟨an ~ angle⟩ **3**
: sharply perceptive; *esp* : mentally keen **4** : SEVERE ⟨~
distress⟩; *also* : having a sudden onset, sharp rise, and
short duration ⟨~ inflammation⟩ **5** : of, marked by, or

being an accent mark having the form ´ — **acute·ly** *adv*
— **acute·ness** *n*
acy·clo·vir \(ˌ)ā-ˈsī-klō-ˌvir\ *n* : a drug used esp. to treat
the genital form of herpes simplex
ad \ˈad\ *n* : ADVERTISEMENT
AD *abbr* **1** after date **2** [L *anno Domini*] in the year of
our Lord — often printed in small capitals and often
punctuated **3** assistant director **4** athletic director
ad·age \ˈa-dij\ *n* : an old familiar saying : PROVERB,
MAXIM
¹**ada·gio** \ə-ˈdä-j(ē-ˌ)ō, -zh(ē-ˌ)ō\ *adv or adj* [It] : at a slow
tempo — used as a direction in music
²**adagio** *n, pl* **-gios** **1** : an adagio movement **2** : a ballet
duet or trio displaying feats of lifting and balancing
¹**ad·a·mant** \ˈa-də-mənt, -ˌmant\ *n* [ME, fr. AF, fr. L
adamant-, adamas hardest metal, diamond, fr. Gk] : a
stone believed to be impenetrably hard — **ad·a·man·tine**
\ˌa-də-ˈman-ˌtēn, -ˌtīn\ *adj*
²**adamant** *adj* : INFLEXIBLE, UNYIELDING — **ad·a·man·cy**
\ˈa-də-mən-sē\ *n* — **ad·a·mant·ly** *adv*
Ad·am's apple \ˈa-dəmz-\ *n* : the projection in front of the
neck formed by the largest cartilage of the larynx
adapt \ə-ˈdapt\ *vb* **1** : to make suitable or fit (as for a new
use or for a different situation) **2** : to adjust to environmental conditions ✦ *Synonyms* ADJUST, ACCOMMO-
DATE, CONFORM — **adapt·abil·i·ty** \ə-ˌdap-tə-ˈbi-lə-tē\ *n*
— **adapt·able** *adj* — **ad·ap·ta·tion** \ˌa-ˌdap-ˈtā-shən\ *n* —
ad·ap·ta·tion·al \-sh(ə-)nəl\ *adj* — **adap·tive** \ə-ˈdap-tiv\
adj — **ad·ap·tiv·i·ty** \ˌa-ˌdap-ˈti-və-tē\ *n*
adapt·er *also* **adap·tor** \ə-ˈdap-tər\ *n* **1** : one that adapts
2 : a device for connecting two dissimilar parts of an apparatus **3** : an attachment for adapting apparatus for
uses not orig. intended
adaptive optics *n sing or pl* : a telescopic system that im-
proves image resolution by compensating for distortions
from atmospheric turbulence
ADC *abbr* **1** aide-de-camp **2** Aid to Dependent Children
add \ˈad\ *vb* **1** : to join to something else so as to increase
in number or amount **2** : to say further ⟨let me ~ this⟩
3 : to combine (numbers) into one sum
ADD *abbr* attention deficit disorder
ad·dend \ˈa-ˌdend\ *n* : a number to be added to another
ad·den·dum \ə-ˈden-dəm\ *n, pl* **-da** \-də\ [L] : something
added; *esp* : a supplement to a book
¹**ad·der** \ˈa-dər\ *n* [ME, alter. (by false division of *a naddre*)
of *naddre*, fr. OE *næddre*] **1** : a poisonous European
viper or a related snake **2** : any of various harmless No.
American snakes (as the hognose snake)
²**add·er** \ˈa-dər\ *n* : one that adds; *esp* : a device that performs addition
¹**ad·dict** \ə-ˈdikt\ *vb* **1** : to devote or surrender (oneself) to
something habitually or excessively **2** : to cause addiction to a substance in (as a person) — **ad·dic·tive** \-ˈdik-
tiv\ *adj*
²**ad·dict** \ˈa-(ˌ)dikt\ *n* : one who is addicted esp. to a substance
ad·dic·tion \ə-ˈdik-shən\ *n* **1** : the quality or state of
being addicted **2** : compulsive need for and use of a
habit-forming substance (as heroin, nicotine, or alcohol)
characterized by well-defined physiological symptoms
upon withdrawal; *also* : persistent compulsive use of a
substance known by the user to be harmful
ad·di·tion \ə-ˈdi-shən\ *n* **1** : the act or process of adding;
also : something added **2** : the operation of combining
numbers to obtain their sum ✦ *Synonyms* ACCRETION,
INCREMENT, ACCESSION, AUGMENTATION
ad·di·tion·al \ə-ˈdi-sh(ə-)nəl\ *adj* : coming by way of addition : ADDED, EXTRA
ad·di·tion·al·ly \ə-ˈdi-sh(ə-)nə-lē\ *adv* : in or by way of addition : FURTHERMORE
¹**ad·di·tive** \ˈa-də-tiv\ *adj* **1** : of, relating to, or characterized by addition **2** : produced by addition — **ad·di·tiv·i-
ty** \ˌa-də-ˈti-və-tē\ *n*
²**additive** *n* : a substance added to another in small quantities to effect a desired change in properties ⟨food ~*s*⟩
ad·dle \ˈa-dᵊl\ *vb* **ad·dled; ad·dling** **1** : to throw into confusion : MUDDLE **2** : to become rotten ⟨*addled* eggs⟩
addn *abbr* addition
addnl *abbr* additional
add–on \ˈad-ˌón, -ˌän\ *n* : something (as a feature or accessory) added esp. as an enhancement

¹ad·dress \ə-'dres\ *vb* **1** : to direct the attention of (oneself) **2** : to direct one's remarks to : deliver an address to **3** : to mark directions for delivery on **4** : to identify (as a memory location) by an address

²ad·dress \ə-'dres, 'a-,dres\ *n* **1** : skillful management **2** : a formal speech : LECTURE **3** : the place where a person or organization may be communicated with **4** : the directions for delivery placed on mail; *also* : the designation of a computer account from which one can send or receive e-mail **5** : a location (as in a computer's memory) where particular data is stored; *also* : URL

ad·dress·ee \ˌa-ˌdre-'sē, ə-ˌdre-sē\ *n* : one to whom something is addressed

ad·duce \ə-'düs, -'dyüs\ *vb* **ad·duced; ad·duc·ing** : to offer as argument, reason, or proof ◆ *Synonyms* ADVANCE, ALLEGE, CITE, SUBMIT — **ad·duc·er** *n*

-ade *n suffix* **1** : act : action ⟨blockade⟩ **2** : product; *esp* : sweet drink ⟨limeade⟩

ad·e·nine \'a-də-ˌnēn\ *n* : a purine base that codes genetic information in the molecular chain of DNA and RNA

ad·e·noid \'a-də-ˌnȯid, 'ad-ˌnȯid\ *n* : an enlarged mass of tissue near the opening of the nose into the throat — usu. used in pl. — **adenoid** *or* **ad·e·noi·dal** \ˌa-də-'nȯi-d°l\ *adj*

aden·o·sine tri·phos·phate \ə-'de-nə-ˌsēn-trī-'fäs-ˌfāt\ *n* : ATP

ad·e·no·vi·rus \ˌa-dᵊn-ō-'vī-rəs\ *n* : any of a family of viruses causing infections of the respiratory tract, conjunctiva, and gastrointestinal tract

¹ad·ept \'a-ˌdept\ *n* : EXPERT

²adept \ə-'dept\ *adj* : highly skilled : EXPERT — **adept·ly** *adv* — **adept·ness** *n*

ad·e·quate \'a-di-kwət\ *adj* : equal to or sufficient for a specific requirement — **ad·e·qua·cy** \-kwə-sē\ *n* — **ad·e·quate·ly** *adv* — **ad·e·quate·ness** *n*

ad·here \ad-'hir\ *vb* **ad·hered; ad·her·ing** **1** : to give support : maintain loyalty **2** : to stick fast : CLING — **ad·her·ence** \-'hir-əns\ *n* — **ad·her·ent** \-ənt\ *adj or n*

ad·he·sion \ad-'hē-zhən\ *n* **1** : the act or state of adhering **2** : the union of bodily tissues abnormally grown together after inflammation; *also* : the newly formed uniting tissue **3** : the molecular attraction between the surfaces of bodies in contact

¹ad·he·sive \-'hē-siv, -ziv\ *adj* **1** : tending to adhere : STICKY **2** : prepared for adhering

²adhesive *n* : an adhesive substance

adhesive tape *n* : tape coated on one side with an adhesive mixture; *esp* : one used for covering wounds

¹ad hoc \ad-'häk, -'hōk\ *adv* [L, for this] : for the case at hand apart from other applications

²ad hoc *adj* : concerned with or formed for a particular purpose ⟨an *ad hoc* committee⟩ ⟨*ad hoc* solutions⟩

adi·a·bat·ic \ˌa-dē-ə-'ba-tik\ *adj* : occurring without loss or gain of heat — **adi·a·bat·i·cal·ly** \-ti-k(ə-)lē\ *adv*

adieu \ə-'dü, -'dyü\ *n, pl* **adieus** *or* **adieux** \ə-'düz, -'dyüz\ : FAREWELL — often used interjectionally

ad in·fi·ni·tum \ˌad-ˌin-fə-'nī-təm\ *adv or adj* : without end or limit

ad in·ter·im \ad-'in-tə-rəm, -ˌrim\ *adv* : for the intervening time — **ad interim** *adj*

adi·os \ˌa-dē-'ōs, ˌä-\ *interj* [Sp *adiós,* lit., to God] — used to express farewell

ad·i·pose \'a-də-ˌpōs\ *adj* : of or relating to animal fat : FATTY

adj *abbr* **1** adjective **2** adjutant

ad·ja·cent \ə-'jā-sᵊnt\ *adj* : situated near or next ◆ *Synonyms* ADJOINING, CONTIGUOUS, ABUTTING, JUXTAPOSED, CONTERMINOUS — **ad·ja·cent·ly** *adv*

ad·jec·tive \'a-jik-tiv\ *n* : a word that typically serves as a modifier of a noun — **ad·jec·ti·val** \ˌa-jik-'tī-vəl\ *adj* — **ad·jec·ti·val·ly** *adv*

ad·join \ə-'jȯin\ *vb* : to be situated next to

ad·join·ing *adj* : touching or bounding at a point or line

ad·journ \ə-'jərn\ *vb* **1** : to suspend indefinitely or until a stated time **2** : to transfer to another place — **ad·journ·ment** *n*

ad·judge \ə-'jəj\ *vb* **ad·judged; ad·judg·ing** **1** : JUDGE, ADJUDICATE **2** : to hold or pronounce to be : DEEM **3** : to award by judicial decision

ad·ju·di·cate \ə-'jü-di-ˌkāt\ *vb* **-cat·ed; -cat·ing** : to settle judicially — **ad·ju·di·ca·tion** \ə-ˌjü-di-'kā-shən\ *n*

ad·junct \'a-ˌjəŋkt\ *n* : something joined or added to another but not essentially a part of it ◆ *Synonyms* APPENDAGE, APPURTENANCE, ACCESSORY, APPENDIX — **adjunct** *adj*

ad·jure \ə-'jùr\ *vb* **ad·jured; ad·jur·ing** : to command solemnly : urge earnestly ◆ *Synonyms* BEG, BESEECH, IMPLORE — **ad·ju·ra·tion** \ˌa-jə-'rā-shən\ *n*

ad·just \ə-'jəst\ *vb* **1** : to bring to agreement : SETTLE **2** : to cause to conform : ADAPT, FIT **3** : REGULATE ⟨∼ a watch⟩ — **ad·just·able** *adj* — **ad·just·er** *also* **ad·jus·tor** \ə-'jəs-tər\ *n* — **ad·just·ment** \ə-'jəst-mənt\ *n*

ad·ju·tant \'a-jə-tənt\ *n* : one who assists; *esp* : an officer who assists a commanding officer by handling correspondence and keeping records

ad·ju·vant \'a-jə-vənt\ *n* : one that helps or facilitates; *esp* : something that enhances the effectiveness of medical treatment — **adjuvant** *adj*

¹ad–lib \'ad-'lib\ *vb* **ad–libbed; ad–lib·bing** : IMPROVISE — **ad–lib** *n*

²ad–lib *adj* : spoken, composed, or performed without preparation

ad lib \'ad-'lib\ *adv* [NL *ad libitum*] **1** : at one's pleasure **2** : without limit

adm *abbr* administration; administrative

ADM *abbr* admiral

ad·man \'ad-ˌman\ *n* : one who writes, solicits, or places advertisements

admin *abbr* administration; administrative

ad·min·is·ter \ad-'mi-nə-stər\ *vb* **1** : MANAGE, SUPERINTEND **2** : to mete out : DISPENSE ⟨∼ punishment⟩ **3** : to give ritually or remedially ⟨∼ quinine for malaria⟩ **4** : to perform the office of administrator — **ad·min·is·tra·ble** \-strə-bəl\ *adj* — **ad·min·is·trant** \-strənt\ *n*

ad·min·is·tra·tion \ad-ˌmi-nə-'strā-shən\ *n* **1** : the act or process of administering **2** : MANAGEMENT **3** : the officials directing the government of a country **4** : the term of office of an administrative officer or body — **ad·min·is·tra·tive** \ad-'mi-nə-ˌstrā-tiv\ *adj* — **ad·min·is·tra·tive·ly** *adv*

ad·min·is·tra·tor \ad-'mi-nə-ˌstrā-tər\ *n* : one that administers; *esp* : one who settles an intestate estate

ad·mi·ra·ble \'ad-m(ə-)rə-bəl\ *adj* : worthy of admiration : EXCELLENT — **ad·mi·ra·bil·i·ty** \ˌad-m(ə-)rə-'bi-lə-tē\ *n* — **ad·mi·ra·ble·ness** *n* — **ad·mi·ra·bly** \-blē\ *adv*

ad·mi·ral \'ad-m(ə-)rəl\ *n* [ME, ultim. fr. Ar *amīr-al-* commander of the (as in *amīr-al-baḥr* commander of the sea)] : a commissioned officer in the navy ranking next below a fleet admiral

ad·mi·ral·ty \'ad-m(ə-)rəl-tē\ *n* **1** *cap* : a British government department formerly having authority over naval affairs **2** : the court having jurisdiction over questions of maritime law

ad·mire \ad-'mī(-ə)r\ *vb* **ad·mired; ad·mir·ing** [MF *admirer,* fr. L *admirari,* fr. *ad-* to + *mirari* to wonder] : to regard with high esteem — **ad·mi·ra·tion** \ˌad-mə-'rā-shən\ *n* — **ad·mir·er** *n* — **ad·mir·ing·ly** \-'mī-riŋ-lē\ *adv*

ad·mis·si·ble \ad-'mi-sə-bəl\ *adj* : that can be or is worthy to be admitted or allowed : ALLOWABLE ⟨∼ evidence⟩ — **ad·mis·si·bil·i·ty** \-ˌmi-sə-'bi-lə-tē\ *n*

ad·mis·sion \ad-'mi-shən\ *n* **1** : the act of admitting **2** : the privilege of being admitted **3** : a fee paid for admission **4** : the granting of an argument **5** : the acknowledgment of a fact

ad·mit \ad-'mit\ *vb* **ad·mit·ted; ad·mit·ting** **1** : PERMIT, ALLOW **2** : to recognize as genuine or valid **3** : to allow to enter ⟨*admitted* to the club⟩ **4** : to accept into a hospital as an inpatient

ad·mit·tance \ad-'mi-t°ns\ *n* : the act or process of admitting : permission to enter

ad·mit·ted·ly \ad-'mi-təd-lē\ *adv* **1** : as has been or must be admitted **2** : it must be admitted

ad·mix \ad-'miks\ *vb* : to mix in

ad·mix·ture \ad-'miks-chər\ *n* **1** : something added in mixing **2** : MIXTURE

ad·mon·ish \ad-'mä-nish\ *vb* : to warn gently : reprove with a warning ◆ *Synonyms* CHIDE, REPROACH, REBUKE, REPRIMAND, REPROVE — **ad·mon·ish·er** *n* — **ad·mon·ish·ing·ly** *adv* — **ad·mon·ish·ment** *n* — **ad·mo·ni·tion** \ˌad-mə-'ni-shən\ *n* — **ad·mon·i·to·ry** \ad-'mä-nə-ˌtȯr-ē\ *adj*

ad nau·se·am \ad-'nȯ-zē-əm\ *adv* [L] : to a sickening or excessive degree

ado \ə-'dü\ *n* **1** : heightened fuss or concern **2** : TROUBLE

ado·be \ə-'dō-bē\ *n* **1** : sun-dried brick; *also* : clay for making such bricks **2** : a structure made of adobe bricks

ad·o·les·cence \ˌa-də-'les-ᵊns\ *n* : the process or period of growth between childhood and maturity — **ad·o·les·cent** \-ᵊnt\ *adj or n*

adopt \ə-'däpt\ *vb* **1** : to take (a child of other parents) as one's own child **2** : to take up and practice as one's own **3** : to accept formally and put into effect — **adopt·able** \-'däp-tə-bəl\ *adj* — **adopt·er** *n* — **adop·tion** \-'däp-shən\ *n*

adop·tive \ə-'däp-tiv\ *adj* : made or acquired by adoption ⟨the ∼ father⟩ — **adop·tive·ly** *adv*

ador·able \ə-'dór-ə-bəl\ *adj* **1** : worthy of adoration **2** : extremely charming ⟨an ∼ child⟩ — **ador·able·ness** *n* — **ador·ably** \-blē\ *adv*

adore \ə-'dór\ *vb* **adored; ador·ing** [ME *adouren*, fr. AF *aurer, adourer*, fr. L *adorare*, fr. *ad-* to + *orare* to speak, pray] **1** : WORSHIP **2** : to regard with loving admiration ⟨∼s his wife⟩ **3** : to be extremely fond of ⟨∼s pecan pie⟩ — **ad·o·ra·tion** \ˌa-də-'rā-shən\ *n*

adorn \ə-'dórn\ *vb* : to enhance the appearance of esp. with ornaments ⟨blouses ∼ed with sequins⟩ — **adorn·ment** *n*

ad·re·nal \ə-'drē-nᵊl\ *adj* : of, relating to, or being a pair of endocrine organs (**adrenal glands**) that are located near the kidneys and produce several hormones and esp. epinephrine

adren·a·line \ə-'dre-nə-lən\ *n* : EPINEPHRINE

adrift \ə-'drift\ *adv or adj* **1** : afloat without motive power or moorings **2** : without guidance or purpose

adroit \ə-'dróit\ *adj* [F, fr. OF, fr. *a-* to + *droit* right] **1** : dexterous with one's hands **2** : SHREWD, RESOURCEFUL ♦ **Synonyms** CANNY, CLEVER, CUNNING, INGENIOUS — **adroit·ly** *adv* — **adroit·ness** *n*

ad·sorb \ad-'sórb, -'zórb\ *vb* : to take up (as molecules of gases) and hold on the surface of a solid or liquid — **ad·sorp·tion** \-'sórp-shən, -'zórp-\ *n*

ad·u·la·tion \ˌa-jə-'lā-shən\ *n* : excessive admiration or flattery — **ad·u·late** \'a-jə-ˌlāt\ *vb* — **ad·u·la·tor** \-ˌlā-tər\ *n* — **ad·u·la·to·ry** \-lə-ˌtór-ē\ *adj*

¹adult \ə-'dəlt, 'a-ˌ\ *adj* [L *adultus*, pp. of *adolescere* to grow up, fr. *ad-* to + *alescere* to grow] : fully developed and mature — **adult·hood** *n*

²adult *n* : one that is adult; *esp* : a human being after an age (as 18) specified by law

adul·ter·ant \ə-'dəl-tə-rənt\ *n* : something used to adulterate another

adul·ter·ate \ə-'dəl-tə-ˌrāt\ *vb* **-at·ed; -at·ing** [L *adulterare*, fr. *ad-* to + *alter* other] : to make impure by mixing in a foreign or inferior substance — **adul·ter·a·tion** \-ˌdəl-tə-'rā-shən\ *n*

adul·tery \ə-'dəl-t(ə-)rē\ *n, pl* **-ter·ies** : sexual unfaithfulness of a married person — **adul·ter·er** \-tər-ər\ *n* — **adul·ter·ess** \-t(ə-)rəs\ *also* **adul·tress** \-trəs\ *n* — **adul·ter·ous** \-t(ə-)rəs\ *adj*

ad·um·brate \'a-dəm-ˌbrāt\ *vb* **-brat·ed; -brat·ing** **1** : to foreshadow vaguely : INTIMATE **2** : to suggest or disclose partially **3** : SHADE, OBSCURE — **ad·um·bra·tion** \ˌa-dəm-'brā-shən\ *n*

adv *abbr* **1** adverb **2** advertisement

ad va·lor·em \ˌad-və-'lór-əm\ *adj* [L, according to the value] : imposed at a percentage of the value ⟨an *ad valorem* tax⟩

¹ad·vance \əd-'vans\ *vb* **ad·vanced; ad·vanc·ing** **1** : to assist the progress of ⟨∼ a cause⟩ **2** : to bring or move forward ⟨∼ a pawn⟩ **3** : to promote in rank **4** : to make earlier in time **5** : PROPOSE **6** : LEND **7** : to raise in rate : INCREASE — **ad·vance·ment** *n*

²advance *n* **1** : a forward movement **2** : IMPROVEMENT **3** : a rise esp. in price or value **4** : OFFER — **in advance** : BEFOREHAND

³advance *adj* : made, sent, or furnished ahead of time ⟨∼ payment⟩

ad·van·tage \əd-'van-tij\ *n* **1** : superiority of position **2** : BENEFIT, GAIN **3** : the 1st point won in tennis after deuce — **ad·van·ta·geous** \ˌad-van-'tā-jəs\ *adj* — **ad·van·ta·geous·ly** *adv*

ad·vent \'ad-ˌvent\ *n* **1** *cap* : a penitential period beginning four Sundays before Christmas **2** *cap* : the coming of Christ **3** : a coming into being or use

ad·ven·ti·tious \ˌad-vən-'ti-shəs\ *adj* **1** : ACCIDENTAL, INCIDENTAL **2** : arising or occurring sporadically or in other than the usual location ⟨∼ buds⟩ — **ad·ven·ti·tious·ly** *adv*

¹ad·ven·ture \əd-'ven-chər\ *n* **1** : a risky undertaking **2** : a remarkable and exciting experience — **ad·ven·tur·ous** \-ch(ə-)rəs\ *adj*

²adventure *vb* **-ven·tured; -ven·tur·ing** \-'ven-ch(ə-)riŋ\ **1** : RISK, HAZARD ⟨∼ their capital in foreign trade⟩ **2** : to engage in adventure

ad·ven·tur·er \əd-'ven-ch(ə-)rər\ *n* **1** : a person who engages in new and risky undertakings **2** : a person who follows a military career for adventure or profit **3** : a person who tries to gain wealth by questionable means

ad·ven·ture·some \əd-'ven-chər-səm\ *adj* : inclined to take risks

ad·ven·tur·ess \əd-'ven-ch(ə-)rəs\ *n* : a female adventurer

ad·verb \'ad-ˌvərb\ *n* : a word that typically serves as a modifier of a verb, an adjective, or another adverb — **ad·ver·bi·al** \ad-'vər-bē-əl\ *adj* — **ad·ver·bi·al·ly** *adv*

¹ad·ver·sary \'ad-vər-ˌser-ē\ *n, pl* **-sar·ies** : FOE

²adversary *adj* : involving antagonistic parties or interests

ad·verse \ad-'vərs\ *adj* **1** : acting against or in a contrary direction ⟨∼ winds⟩ **2** : UNFAVORABLE ⟨∼ criticism⟩ — **ad·verse·ly** *adv*

ad·ver·si·ty \ad-'vər-sə-tē\ *n, pl* **-ties** : hard times : MISFORTUNE

ad·vert \ad-'vərt\ *vb* : REFER ⟨∼ to a previous remark⟩

ad·ver·tise \'ad-vər-ˌtīz\ *vb* **-tised; -tis·ing** **1** : INFORM, NOTIFY **2** : to call public attention to esp. in order to sell — **ad·ver·tis·er** *n*

ad·ver·tise·ment \ˌad-vər-'tīz-mənt; əd-'vər-təs-mənt\ *n* **1** : the act of advertising **2** : a public notice intended to advertise something

ad·ver·tis·ing \'ad-vər-ˌtī-ziŋ\ *n* : the business of preparing advertisements

ad·vice \əd-'vīs\ *n* **1** : recommendation with regard to a course of action : COUNSEL **2** : INFORMATION, REPORT

ad·vis·able \əd-'vī-zə-bəl\ *adj* : proper to be done : EXPEDIENT ⟨∼ to stay fit⟩ — **ad·vis·abil·i·ty** \-ˌvī-zə-'bi-lə-tē\ *n*

ad·vise \əd-'vīz\ *vb* **ad·vised; ad·vis·ing** **1** : to give advice to : COUNSEL **2** : INFORM, NOTIFY **3** : CONSULT, CONFER ⟨∼ with your friends⟩ — **ad·vis·er** *also* **ad·vi·sor** \-'vī-zər\ *n*

ad·vised \əd-'vīzd\ *adj* : thought out : CONSIDERED ⟨well-*advised*⟩ — **ad·vis·ed·ly** \-'vī-zəd-lē\ *adv*

ad·vise·ment \əd-'vīz-mənt\ *n* **1** : careful consideration ⟨take the matter under ∼⟩ **2** : the act of advising

ad·vi·so·ry \əd-'vī-zə-rē\ *adj* **1** : having or exercising power to advise **2** : containing or giving advice

¹ad·vo·cate \'ad-və-kət, -ˌkāt\ *n* [ultim. fr. L *advocare* to summon, fr. *ad-* to + *vocare* to call] **1** : one who pleads another's cause **2** : one who argues or pleads for a cause or proposal — **ad·vo·ca·cy** \-və-kə-sē\ *n*

²ad·vo·cate \-ˌkāt\ *vb* **-cat·ed; -cat·ing** : to plead in favor of — **ad·vo·ca·tion** \ˌad-və-'kā-shən\ *n*

advt *abbr* advertisement

adze *also* **adz** \'adz\ *n* : a tool with a curved blade set at right angles to the handle that is used in shaping wood

adze

AEC *abbr* Atomic Energy Commission

ae·gis \'ē-jəs\ *n* **1** : SHIELD, PROTECTION ⟨under the ∼ of the constitution⟩ **2** : PATRONAGE, SPONSORSHIP ⟨under the ∼ of the museum⟩

ae·o·li·an harp \ē-'ō-lē-ən-\ *n* : a box with strings that produce musical sounds when the wind blows on them

ae·on *or* **eon** \'ē-ən, -ˌän\ *n* : an indefinitely long time : AGE

aer·ate \'aer-ˌāt\ *vb* **aer·at·ed; aer·at·ing** **1** : to supply, impregnate, or combine with a gas and esp. air **2** : to supply (blood) with oxygen by respiration — **aer·a·tion** \er-'ā-shən\ *n* — **aer·a·tor** \'er-ˌā-tər\ *n*

¹**ae·ri·al** \'er-ē-əl\ *adj* **1** : inhabiting, occurring in, or done in the air **2** : AIRY **3** : of or relating to aircraft

²**aer·i·al** \'er-ē-əl\ *n* : ANTENNA 2

ae·ri·al·ist \'er-ē-ə-list\ *n* : a performer of feats above the ground esp. on a trapeze

ae·rie \'er-ē, 'ir-ē\ *n* : a highly placed nest (as of an eagle)

aer·o·bat·ics \er-ə-'ba-tiks\ *n sing or pl* : spectacular flying feats and maneuvers

aer·o·bic \er-'rō-bik\ *adj* **1** : living or active only in the presence of oxygen ⟨∼ bacteria⟩ **2** : involving or increasing oxygen consumption; *also* : of or relating to aerobics — **aer·o·bi·cal·ly** \-bi-k(ə-)lē\ *adv*

aer·o·bics \-biks\ *n sing or pl* : strenuous exercises that produce a marked temporary increase in respiration and heart rate; *also* : a system of physical conditioning involving these

aero·drome \'er-ˌdrōm\ *n, chiefly Brit* : AIRPORT

aero·dy·nam·ics \er-ō-dī-'na-miks\ *n* : the science dealing with the forces acting on bodies in motion in a gas (as air) — **aero·dy·nam·ic** \-mik\ *also* **aero·dy·nam·i·cal** \-mi-kəl\ *adj* — **aero·dy·nam·i·cal·ly** \-mi-k(ə-)lē\ *adv*

aero·naut \'er-ə-ˌnȯt\ *n* [F *aéronaute*, ultim. fr. Gk *aēr* air + *nautēs* sailor] : one who operates or travels in an airship or balloon

aero·nau·tics \er-ə-'nȯ-tiks\ *n* : the science of aircraft operation — **aero·nau·ti·cal** \-ti-kəl\ *also* **aero·nau·tic** \-tik\ *adj*

aero·pho·bia \er-ō-'fō-bē-ə\ *n* : fear or strong dislike of flying

aero·plane \'er-ə-ˌplān\ *chiefly Brit var of* AIRPLANE

aero·sol \'er-ə-ˌsäl, -ˌsȯl\ *n* **1** : a suspension of fine solid or liquid particles in a gas; *also, pl* : the particles themselves **2** : a substance (as an insecticide) dispensed from a pressurized container as an aerosol

aero·space \'er-ō-ˌspās\ *n* : the earth's atmosphere and the space beyond — **aerospace** *adj*

aery \'er-ē\ *adj* **aer·i·er; -est** : having an aerial quality : ETHEREAL ⟨∼ visions⟩

aes·thete *also* **es·thete** \'es-ˌthēt\ *n* : a person having or affecting sensitivity to beauty esp. in art

aes·thet·ic *also* **es·thet·ic** \es-'the-tik\ *adj* **1** : of or relating to aesthetics : ARTISTIC **2** : appreciative of the beautiful — **aes·thet·i·cal·ly** *also* **es·thet·i·cal·ly** \-ti-k(ə-)lē\ *adv*

aes·thet·ics *also* **es·thet·ics** \-tiks\ *n* : a branch of philosophy dealing with the nature, creation, and appreciation of beauty

ae·ti·ol·o·gy *chiefly Brit var of* ETIOLOGY

AF *abbr* **1** air force **2** audio frequency

¹**afar** \ə-'fär\ *adv* : from, at, or to a great distance

²**afar** *n* : a great distance

AFB *abbr* air force base

AFC *abbr* **1** American Football Conference **2** automatic frequency control

AFDC *abbr* Aid to Families with Dependent Children

af·fa·ble \'a-fə-bəl\ *adj* : courteous and agreeable in conversation — **af·fa·bil·i·ty** \ˌa-fə-'bi-lə-tē\ *n* — **af·fa·bly** \'a-fə-blē\ *adv*

af·fair \ə-'fer\ *n* [ME *afere*, fr. AF fr. *afaire*, fr. *a faire* to do] **1** : something that relates to or involves one : CONCERN **2** : a romantic or sexual attachment of limited duration

¹**af·fect** \ə-'fekt, a-\ *vb* **1** : to be fond of using or wearing **2** : SIMULATE, ASSUME, PRETEND

²**affect** *vb* : to produce an effect on : INFLUENCE

³**af·fect** \'a-ˌfekt\ *n* : EMOTION; *also* : an observable display of emotion ⟨an expressionless ∼⟩

af·fec·ta·tion \ˌa-ˌfek-'tā-shən\ *n* : an attitude or behavior that is assumed by a person but not genuinely felt

af·fect·ed \a-'fek-təd\ *adj* **1** : given to or marked by affectation **2** : artificially assumed to impress others — **af·fect·ed·ly** *adv*

af·fect·ing \a-'fek-tiŋ\ *adj* : arousing pity, sympathy, or sorrow ⟨an ∼ story⟩ — **af·fect·ing·ly** *adv*

af·fec·tion \ə-'fek-shən\ *n* : tender attachment — **af·fec·tion·ate** \-sh(ə-)nət\ *adj* — **af·fec·tion·ate·ly** *adv*

af·fec·tive \a-'fek-tiv\ *adj* : relating to, influencing, or expressing an emotion or feeling : EMOTIONAL ⟨an ∼ disorder⟩

af·fer·ent \'a-fə-rənt, -ˌfer-ənt\ *adj* : bearing or conducting inward toward a more central part and esp. a nerve center (as the central nervous system)

af·fi·ance \ə-'fī-əns\ *vb* **-anced; -anc·ing** : BETROTH, ENGAGE

af·fi·da·vit \ˌa-fə-'dā-vət\ *n* [ML, he has made an oath] : a sworn statement in writing

¹**af·fil·i·ate** \ə-'fi-lē-ˌāt\ *vb* **-at·ed; -at·ing** : to associate as a member or branch — **af·fil·i·a·tion** \-ˌfi-lē-'ā-shən\ *n*

²**af·fil·i·ate** \ə-'fi-lē-ət\ *n* : an affiliated person or organization

af·fin·i·ty \ə-'fi-nə-tē\ *n, pl* **-ties** **1** : KINSHIP, RELATIONSHIP **2** : attractive force : ATTRACTION, SYMPATHY

affinity card *n* : a credit card issued in affiliation with an organization (as a charity or an airline) the use of which benefits the organization or possessor of the card

af·firm \ə-'fərm\ *vb* **1** : CONFIRM **2** : to assert positively **3** : to make a solemn and formal declaration or assertion in place of an oath ♦ *Synonyms* AVER, AVOW, AVOUCH, DECLARE, ASSERT — **af·fir·ma·tion** \ˌa-fər-'mā-shən\ *n*

¹**af·fir·ma·tive** \ə-'fər-mə-tiv\ *adj* : asserting that the fact is so : POSITIVE

²**affirmative** *n* **1** : an expression of affirmation or assent **2** : the side that upholds the proposition stated in a debate

affirmative action *n* : an active effort to improve the employment or educational opportunities of members of minority groups and women

¹**af·fix** \ə-'fiks\ *vb* : ATTACH, ADD

²**af·fix** \'a-ˌfiks\ *n* : one or more sounds or letters attached to the beginning or end of a word that produce a derivative word or an inflectional form

af·fla·tus \ə-'flā-təs\ *n* : divine inspiration

af·flict \ə-'flikt\ *vb* : to cause pain and distress to ♦ *Synonyms* RACK, TRY, TORMENT, TORTURE — **af·flic·tion** \-'flik-shən\ *n*

af·flic·tive \ə-'flik-tiv\ *adj* : causing affliction : DISTRESSING ⟨∼ emotions⟩ — **af·flic·tive·ly** *adv*

af·flu·ence \'a-ˌflü-ən(t)s, a-'flü-\ *n* : abundant supply; *also* : WEALTH, RICHES — **af·flu·ent** \-ənt\ *adj*

af·ford \ə-'fȯrd\ *vb* **1** : to manage to bear or bear the cost of without serious harm or loss **2** : PROVIDE, FURNISH ⟨the roof ∼ed a fine view⟩

af·for·es·ta·tion \a-ˌfȯr-ə-'stā-shən\ *n* : the act or process of establishing a forest — **af·for·est** \a-'fȯr-əst, -'fär-\ *vb*

af·fray \ə-'frā\ *n* : FIGHT, FRAY

af·fright \ə-'frīt\ *vb, archaic* : FRIGHTEN, ALARM — **affright** *n*

af·front \ə-'frənt\ *vb* **1** : INSULT **2** : CONFRONT ⟨∼ death⟩ — **affront** *n*

af·ghan \'af-ˌgan\ *n* **1** *cap* : a native or inhabitant of Afghanistan **2** : a blanket or shawl of colored wool knitted or crocheted in sections — **Afghan** *or* **Af·ghani** \af-'ga-nē, -'gä-\ *adj*

Afghan hound *n* : any of a breed of tall slim swift hunting dogs with a coat of silky thick hair and a long silky top-knot

af·ghani \af-'ga-nē\ *n* — see MONEY table

afi·cio·na·do \ə-ˌfi-sh(ē-)ə-'nä-dō, -sē-ə-\ *n, pl* **-dos** [Sp, fr. pp. of *aficionar* to inspire affection] : DEVOTEE, FAN

afield \ə-'fēld\ *adv or adj* **1** : to, in, or on the field **2** : away from home **3** : out of the way : ASTRAY

afire \ə-'fī(-ə)r\ *adj or adv* : being on fire : BURNING

AFL *abbr* American Football League

aflame \ə-'flām\ *adj or adv* : FLAMING

AFL–CIO *abbr* American Federation of Labor and Congress of Industrial Organizations

afloat \ə-'flōt\ *adj or adv* **1** : borne on or as if on the water **2** : CIRCULATING ⟨rumors were ∼⟩ **3** : ADRIFT

aflut·ter \ə-'flə-tər\ *adj* **1** : FLUTTERING **2** : nervously excited ⟨∼ at the news⟩

afoot \ə-'fut\ *adv or adj* **1** : on foot **2** : in action : in progress

afore·men·tioned \ə-'fȯr-'men-chənd\ *adj* : mentioned previously

afore·said \-ˌsed\ *adj* : said or named before

afore·thought \-ˌthȯt\ *adj* : PREMEDITATED ⟨with malice ∼⟩

a for·ti·o·ri \ˌä-ˌfȯr-tē-ˈȯr-ē\ *adv* [NL, lit., from the stronger (argument)] : with even greater reason

afoul of \ə-ˈfaůl-əv\ *prep* **1** : in or into conflict with **2** : in or into collision or entanglement with

Afr *abbr* Africa; African

afraid \ə-ˈfrād\ *adj* **1** : FRIGHTENED, FEARFUL **2** : filled with concern or regret ⟨∼ I won't be able to go⟩

A–frame \ˈā-ˌfrām\ *n* : a building having triangular front and rear walls with the roof reaching to the ground

afresh \ə-ˈfresh\ *adv* : ANEW, AGAIN

Af·ri·can \ˈa-fri-kən\ *n* **1** : a native or inhabitant of Africa **2** : a person of African ancestry — **African** *adj*

Af·ri·can–Amer·i·can \-ə-ˈmer-ə-kən\ *n* : an American of African and esp. of black African descent — **African–American** *adj*

Af·ri·can·ized bee \ˈa-frə-kə-ˌnīzd-\ *n* : a highly aggressive hybrid honeybee accidentally produced from Brazilian and African stocks that has spread from So. America into Mexico and the southern U.S.

Africanized honeybee *n* : AFRICANIZED BEE

African violet *n* : a tropical African plant widely grown indoors for its velvety fleshy leaves and showy purple, pink, or white flowers

Af·ri·kaans \ˌa-fri-ˈkäns\ *n* : a language developed from 17th century Dutch that is one of the official languages of the Republic of So. Africa

Afro *n, pl* **Afros** : a hairstyle of tight curls in a full evenly rounded shape

Af·ro–Amer·i·can \ˌa-frō-ə-ˈmer-ə-kən\ *n* : AFRICAN–AMERICAN — **Afro–American** *adj*

aft \ˈaft\ *adv* : near, toward, or in the stern of a ship or the tail of an aircraft

AFT *abbr* American Federation of Teachers

¹af·ter \ˈaf-tər\ *adv* : AFTERWARD, SUBSEQUENTLY

²after *prep* **1** : behind in place **2** : later than ⟨∼ dinner⟩ **3** : in pursuit or search of ⟨he's ∼ your job⟩

³after *conj* : following the time when ⟨we will come ∼ we make plans⟩

⁴after *adj* **1** : LATER ⟨in ∼ years⟩ **2** : located toward the rear

af·ter·birth \ˈaf-tər-ˌbərth\ *n* : the placenta and membranes of the fetus that are expelled after childbirth

af·ter·burn·er \-ˌbər-nər\ *n* : a device incorporated in the tail pipe of a turbojet engine for injecting fuel into the hot exhaust gases and burning it to provide extra thrust

af·ter·care \-ˌker\ *n* : the care, nursing, or treatment of a convalescent patient

af·ter·deck \-ˌdek\ *n* : the rear half of the deck of a ship

af·ter·ef·fect \-ə-ˌfekt\ *n* : an effect that follows its cause after an interval

af·ter·glow \-ˌglō\ *n* : a glow remaining where a light has disappeared

af·ter·im·age \-ˌim-ij\ *n* : a usu. visual sensation continuing after the stimulus causing it has ended

af·ter·life \-ˌlif\ *n* : an existence after death

af·ter·math \-ˌmath\ *n* **1** : a second-growth crop esp. of hay **2** : CONSEQUENCES, EFFECTS ♦ *Synonyms* AFTEREFFECT, UPSHOT, RESULT, OUTCOME

af·ter·noon \ˌaf-tər-ˈnün\ *n* : the time between noon and evening

af·ter·shave \ˈaf-tər-ˌshāv\ *n* : a usu. scented lotion for the face after shaving

af·ter·taste \-ˌtāst\ *n* : a sensation (as of flavor) continuing after the stimulus causing it has ended

af·ter–tax \ˈaf-tər-ˈtaks\ *adj* : remaining after payment of taxes and esp. of income tax ⟨an ∼ profit⟩

af·ter·thought \-ˌthȯt\ *n* : an idea occurring later

af·ter·ward \-wərd\ *or* **af·ter·wards** \-wərdz\ *adv* : at a later time

Ag *symbol* [L *argentum*] silver

AG *abbr* **1** adjutant general **2** attorney general

again \ə-ˈgen, -ˈgin\ *adv* **1** : once more : ANEW ⟨come see us ∼⟩ **2** : on the other hand ⟨we may, and ∼ we may not⟩ **3** : in addition : BESIDES

against \ə-ˈgenst\ *prep* **1** : in opposition to **2** : directly opposite to : FACING **3** : as defense from **4** : so as to touch or strike ⟨threw him ∼ the wall⟩; *also* : TOUCHING

¹aga·pe \ä-ˈgä-pā, ˈä-gə-ˌpā\ *n* [LL, fr. Gk *agapē*, lit., love] : unselfish unconditional love for another

²agape \ə-ˈgāp\ *adj or adv* : having the mouth open in wonder or surprise : GAPING

agar \ˈä-ˌgär\ *n* **1** : a jellylike substance extracted from a red alga and used esp. as a gelling and stabilizing agent in foods **2** : a culture medium containing agar

agar–agar \ˌä-ˌgär-ˈä-ˌgär\ *n* : AGAR

ag·ate \ˈa-gət\ *n* **1** : a striped or clouded quartz **2** : a playing marble of agate or of glass

aga·ve \ə-ˈgä-vē\ *n* : any of a genus of spiny-leaved plants (as a century plant) related to the amaryllis

agcy *abbr* agency

¹age \ˈāj\ *n* **1** : the length of time during which a being or thing has lived or existed **2** : the time of life at which some particular qualification is achieved; *esp* : MAJORITY **3** : the latter part of life **4** : a long time **5** : a period in history

²age *vb* **aged; ag·ing** *or* **age·ing** **1** : to grow old or cause to grow old **2** : to become or cause to become mature or mellow

-age *n suffix* **1** : aggregate : collection ⟨track*age*⟩ **2** : action : process ⟨haul*age*⟩ **3** : cumulative result of ⟨break*age*⟩ **4** : rate of ⟨dos*age*⟩ **5** : house or place of ⟨orphan*age*⟩ **6** : state : rank ⟨vassal*age*⟩ **7** : fee : charge ⟨post*age*⟩

aged \ˈā-jəd *for 1;* ˈājd *for 2*\ *adj* **1** : of advanced age **2** : having attained a specified age ⟨a man ∼ 40 years⟩

age·ism \ˈā-ˌji-zəm\ *n* : discrimination against persons of a particular age and esp. the elderly — **age·ist** \-jist\ *n*

age·less \ˈāj-ləs\ *adj* **1** : not growing old or showing the effects of age **2** : TIMELESS, ETERNAL ⟨∼ truths⟩

agen·cy \ˈā-jən-sē\ *n, pl* **-cies** **1** : one through which something is accomplished : INSTRUMENTALITY **2** : the office or function of an agent **3** : an establishment doing business for another **4** : an administrative division (as of a government) ♦ *Synonyms* MEANS, MEDIUM, VEHICLE

agen·da \ə-ˈjen-də\ *n* : a list of things to be done : PROGRAM

agent \ˈā-jənt\ *n* **1** : one that acts **2** : MEANS, INSTRUMENT **3** : a person acting or doing business for another **4** : a computer program designed to automate certain tasks (as gathering information online) ♦ *Synonyms* ATTORNEY, DEPUTY, PROXY, DELEGATE

Agent Orange *n* : an herbicide widely used in the Vietnam War that is composed of 2,4-D and 2,4,5-T and contains a toxic contaminant

agent pro·vo·ca·teur \ˈä-ˌzhäⁿ-prō-ˌvä-kə-ˈtər, ˈä-jənt-\ *n, pl* **agents provocateurs** \ˈä-ˌzhäⁿ-prō-ˌväk-ə-ˈtər, ˈä-jənts-prō-\ [F] : a person hired to infiltrate a group and incite its members to illegal action

age of consent : the age at which one is legally competent to give consent esp. to marriage or to sexual intercourse

age–old \ˈāj-ˈōld\ *adj* : having existed for ages : ANCIENT

ag·er·a·tum \ˌa-jə-ˈrā-təm\ *n, pl* **-tum** *also* **-tums** : any of a genus of tropical American plants that are related to the daisies and have small showy heads of usu. blue or white flowers

age spots *n pl* : benign flat spots of dark pigmentation on the skin occurring esp. among older people

Ag·ge·us \a-ˈgē-əs\ *n* : HAGGAI

¹ag·glom·er·ate \ə-ˈglä-mə-ˌrāt\ *vb* **-at·ed; -at·ing** [L *agglomerare* to heap up, join, fr. *ad-* to + *glomer-, glomus* ball] : to gather into a mass : CLUSTER — **ag·glom·er·a·tion** \-ˌglä-mə-ˈrā-shən\ *n*

²ag·glom·er·ate \-rət\ *n* : rock composed of volcanic fragments

ag·glu·ti·nate \ə-ˈglü-tᵊn-ˌāt\ *vb* **-nat·ed; -nat·ing** **1** : to cause to adhere : gather into a group or mass **2** : to cause (as red blood cells or bacteria) to collect into clumps — **ag·glu·ti·na·tion** \-ˌglü-tᵊn-ˈā-shən\ *n*

ag·gran·dise *Brit var of* AGGRANDIZE

ag·gran·dize \ə-ˈgran-ˌdīz, ˈa-grən-\ *vb* **-dized; -diz·ing** : to make great or greater ⟨∼ an estate⟩ — **ag·gran·dize·ment** \ə-ˈgran-dəz-mənt, -ˌdīz-; ˌa-grən-ˈdīz-\ *n*

ag·gra·vate \ˈa-grə-ˌvāt\ *vb* **-vat·ed; -vat·ing** **1** : to make more severe : INTENSIFY **2** : IRRITATE — **ag·gra·va·tion** \ˌa-grə-ˈvā-shən\ *n*

¹ag·gre·gate \ˈa-gri-gət\ *adj* : formed by the gathering of units into one mass

²ag·gre·gate \-ˌgāt\ *vb* **-gat·ed; -gat·ing** : to collect into one mass

³ag·gre·gate \-gət\ *n* : a mass or body of units or parts somewhat loosely associated with one another; *also* : the whole amount

ag·gre·ga·tion \ˌa-gri-'gā-shən\ n **1** : a group, body, or mass composed of many distinct parts **2** : the collecting of units or parts into a mass or whole

ag·gres·sion \ə-'gre-shən\ n **1** : an unprovoked attack **2** : the practice of making attacks **3** : hostile, injurious, or destructive behavior or outlook esp. when caused by frustration — **ag·gres·sor** \-'gre-sər\ n

ag·gres·sive \ə-'gre-siv\ adj **1** : tending toward or exhibiting aggression; esp : marked by combative readiness **2** : marked by driving energy or initiative : ENTERPRISING **3** : more intensive or comprehensive esp. in dosage or extent — **ag·gres·sive·ly** adv — **ag·gres·sive·ness** n

ag·grieve \ə-'grēv\ vb **ag·grieved; ag·griev·ing 1** : to cause grief to **2** : to inflict injury on : WRONG

ag·gro \'a-ˌgrō\ adj : aggressive or aggressively daring in style or manner ⟨~ music⟩ ⟨~ surfing⟩

aghast \ə-'gast\ adj : struck with amazement or horror

ag·ile \'a-jəl\ adj : able to move quickly and easily — **ag·ile·ly** adv — **agil·i·ty** \ə-'ji-lə-tē\ n

ag·i·ta \'a-jə-tə\ n [southern It dial. pron. of It acido, lit., heartburn, acid] : a feeling of agitation or anxiety

ag·i·tate \'a-jə-ˌtāt\ vb **-tat·ed; -tat·ing 1** : to move with an irregular rapid motion **2** : to stir up : EXCITE **3** : to discuss earnestly **4** : to attempt to arouse public feeling — **ag·i·ta·tion** \ˌa-jə-'tā-shən\ n — **ag·i·ta·tor** \'a-jə-ˌtā-tər\ n

ag·it·prop \'a-jət-ˌpräp\ n [Russ] : political propaganda promulgated esp. through the arts

agleam \ə-'glēm\ adj : GLEAMING ⟨eyes ~ with tears⟩

aglit·ter \ə-'gli-tər\ adj : GLITTERING

aglow \ə-'glō\ adj : GLOWING

ag·nos·tic \ag-'näs-tik\ adj [Gk agnōstos unknown, unknowable, fr. a- un- + gnōstos known] : of or relating to the belief that the existence of any ultimate reality (as God) is unknown and prob. unknowable — **agnostic** n — **ag·nos·ti·cism** \-'näs-tə-ˌsi-zəm\ n

ago \ə-'gō\ adj or adv : earlier than the present time ⟨10 years ~⟩

agog \ə-'gäg\ adj [MF en gogues in mirth] : full of excitement : EAGER

a–go–go \ä-'gō-ˌgō\ adj [Whisky à Gogo, café and disco in Paris, France, fr. F à gogo galore] : GO-GO

ag·o·nise Brit var of AGONIZE

ag·o·nize \'a-gə-ˌnīz\ vb **-nized; -niz·ing** : to suffer or cause to suffer agony — **ag·o·niz·ing·ly** adv

ag·o·ny \'a-gə-nē\ n, pl **-nies** [ME agonie, fr. L agonia, fr. Gk agōnia struggle, anguish, fr. agōn gathering, contest for a prize] : extreme pain of mind or body ♦ Synonyms SUFFERING, DISTRESS, MISERY

ago·ra \ˌä-gə-'rä\ n, pl **ago·rot** \-'rōt\ — see shekel at MONEY table

ag·o·ra·pho·bia \ˌa-gə-rə-'fō-bē-ə\ n : abnormal fear of being in a helpless, embarrassing, or inescapable situation characterized esp. by avoidance of open or public places — **ag·o·ra·pho·bic** \-'fō-bik, -'fä-\ adj or n

agr abbr agricultural; agriculture

agrar·i·an \ə-'grer-ē-ən\ adj **1** : of or relating to land or its ownership ⟨~ reforms⟩ **2** : of or relating to farmers or farming interests — **agrarian** n — **agrar·i·an·ism** n

agree \ə-'grē\ vb **agreed; agree·ing 1** : ADMIT, CONCEDE ⟨~s that he was wrong⟩ **2** : to be similar : CORRESPOND ⟨both copies ~⟩ **3** : to express agreement or approval **4** : to be in harmony **5** : to settle by common consent **6** : to be fitting or healthful : SUIT ⟨this climate ~s with her⟩

agree·able \ə-'grē-ə-bəl\ adj **1** : PLEASING, PLEASANT ⟨an ~ fragrance⟩ **2** : ready to consent ⟨I'm ~ to their proposal⟩ **3** : being in harmony : CONSONANT — **agree·able·ness** n — **agree·ably** \-blē\ adv

agree·ment \ə-'grē-mənt\ n **1** : harmony of opinion or action **2** : mutual understanding or arrangement; also : a document containing such an arrangement

ag·ri·busi·ness \'a-grə-ˌbiz-nəs, -nəz\ n : an industry engaged in the manufacture and sale of farm equipment and supplies and in the production, processing, storage, and sale of farm commodities

agric abbr agricultural; agriculture

ag·ri·cul·ture \'a-gri-ˌkəl-chər\ n : FARMING, HUSBANDRY — **ag·ri·cul·tur·al** \ˌa-gri-'kəl-ch(ə-)rəl\ adj — **ag·ri·cul·tur·ist** \-ch(ə-)rist\ or **ag·ri·cul·tur·al·ist** \-ch(ə-)rə-list\ n

agron·o·my \ə-'grä-nə-mē\ n : a branch of agriculture that deals with the raising of crops and the care of the soil — **ag·ro·nom·ic** \ˌa-grə-'nä-mik\ adj — **agron·o·mist** \ə-'grä-nə-mist\ n

aground \ə-'graünd\ adv or adj : on or onto the bottom or shore ⟨ran ~⟩

agt abbr agent

ague \'ā-gyü\ n : a fever (as malaria) with recurrent chills and sweating

ahead \ə-'hed\ adv or adj **1** : in or toward the front **2** : into or for the future ⟨plan ~⟩ **3** : in or toward a more advantageous position

ahead of prep **1** : in front or advance of **2** : in excess of : ABOVE

ahoy \ə-'hói\ interj — used in hailing ⟨ship ~⟩

AI abbr artificial intelligence

¹aid \'ād\ vb : to provide with what is useful in achieving an end : ASSIST

²aid n **1** : ASSISTANCE **2** : ASSISTANT

AID abbr Agency for International Development

aide \'ād\ n : a person who acts as an assistant; esp : a military officer assisting a superior

aide–de–camp \ˌād-di-'kamp, -'kän\ n, pl **aides–de–camp** \ˌādz-di-\ [F] : AIDE

AIDS \'ādz\ n [acquired immunodeficiency syndrome] : a serious disease of the human immune system that is characterized by severe reduction in the numbers of helper T cells and increased vulnerability to life-threatening illnesses and that is caused by infection with HIV commonly transmitted in infected blood esp. during illicit intravenous drug use and in bodily secretions (as semen) during sexual intercourse

AIDS–related complex n : a group of symptoms (as fever, weight loss, and lymphadenopathy) that is associated with the presence of antibodies to HIV and is followed by the development of AIDS in a certain proportion of cases

AIDS virus n : HIV

ai·grette \ā-'gret, 'ā-ˌ\ n [F, plume, egret] : a plume or decorative tuft for the head

ail \'āl\ vb **1** : to be the matter with : TROUBLE **2** : to be unwell

ai·lan·thus \ā-'lan-thəs\ n : any of a genus of Asian trees or shrubs with pinnate leaves and ill-scented greenish flowers; esp : TREE OF HEAVEN

ai·le·ron \'ā-lə-ˌrän\ n : a movable part of an airplane wing used in banking

ail·ment \'āl-mənt\ n : a bodily disorder

¹aim \'ām\ vb [ME, fr. AF aesmer & esmer; AF aesmer, fr. a- to (fr. L ad-) + esmer to estimate, fr. L aestimare] **1** : to point a weapon at an object **2** : to direct one's efforts : ASPIRE **3** : to direct to or toward a specified object or goal

²aim n **1** : the pointing of a weapon at an object **2** : the ability to hit a target **3** : OBJECT, PURPOSE ⟨my ~ is to win⟩ — **aim·less** \-ləs\ adj — **aim·less·ly** adv — **aim·less·ness** n

AIM abbr American Indian Movement

ain't \'ānt\ **1** : are not **2** : is not **3** : am not — though disapproved by many and more common in less educated speech, used in both speech and writing to catch attention and to gain emphasis

Ai·nu \'ī-nü\ n, pl **Ainu** or **Ainus 1** : a member of an indigenous people of northern Japan **2** : the language of the Ainu people

¹air \'er\ n **1** : the gaseous mixture surrounding the earth **2** : a light breeze **3** : MELODY, TUNE **4** : the outward appearance of a person or thing : MANNER **5** : an artificial manner **6** : COMPRESSED AIR ⟨~ sprayer⟩ **7** : AIRCRAFT ⟨traveled by ~⟩ **8** : AVIATION ⟨~ safety⟩ **9** : the medium of transmission of radio waves; also : RADIO, TELEVISION

²air vb **1** : to expose to the air **2** : to expose to public view

air bag n : a bag designed to inflate automatically to protect automobile occupants in case of collision

air·boat \'er-ˌbōt\ n : a shallow-draft boat driven by an airplane propeller

air·borne \-ˌbórn\ adj : done or being in the air

air brake n **1** : a brake operated by a piston driven by compressed air **2** : a surface projected into the airflow to lower an airplane's speed

air·brush \'er-ˌbrəsh\ n : a device for applying a fine spray (as of paint) by compressed air — **airbrush** vb

air con·di·tion·er \ˌer-kən-'di-sh(ə-)nər\ n : an apparatus for filtering air and controlling its humidity and temperature — **air–con·di·tion** \-'di-shən\ vb

air·craft \'er-ˌkraft\ n, pl **aircraft** : a vehicle for traveling through the air

aircraft carrier n : a warship with a deck on which airplanes can be launched and landed

air·drop \'er-ˌdräp\ n : delivery of cargo or personnel by parachute from an airplane in flight — **air–drop** vb

Aire·dale terrier \'er-ˌdāl-\ n : any of a breed of large terriers with a hard wiry coat

air·fare \'er-ˌfer\ n : fare for travel by airplane

air·field \-ˌfēld\ n : AIRPORT

air·flow \-ˌflō\ n : the motion of air relative to a body in it

air·foil \-ˌfȯi(-ə)l\ n : an airplane surface designed to produce reaction forces from the air through which it moves

air force n : the military organization of a nation for air warfare

air·frame \'er-ˌfrām\ n : the structure of an aircraft, rocket, or missile without the power plant; also : AIRCRAFT

air·freight \-ˌfrāt\ n : freight transport by aircraft in volume; also : the charge for this service

air gun n 1 : a gun operated by compressed air 2 : a hand tool that works by compressed air; esp : AIRBRUSH

air·head \'er-ˌhed\ n : a mindless or stupid person

air lane n : AIRWAY 1

air·lift \'er-ˌlift\ n : transportation (as of supplies or passengers) by aircraft — **airlift** vb

air·line \-ˌlīn\ n : a transportation system using airplanes

air·lin·er \-ˌlī-nər\ n : a large passenger airplane operated by an airline

air lock n : an airtight chamber separating areas of different pressure

air·mail \'er-ˌmāl\ n : the system of transporting mail by aircraft; also : mail so transported — **airmail** vb

air·man \-mən\ n 1 : AVIATOR, PILOT 2 : an enlisted man in the air force in one of the three ranks below sergeant

airman basic n : an enlisted man of the lowest rank in the air force

airman first class n : an enlisted man in the air force with a rank just below that of sergeant

air mass n : a large horizontally homogeneous body of air

air·mo·bile \'er-ˌmō-bəl, -ˌbēl\ adj : of, relating to, or being a military unit whose members are transported to combat areas usu. by helicopter

air·plane \-ˌplān\ n : a powered heavier-than-air aircraft that has fixed wings from which it derives lift

air·play \-ˌplā\ n : the playing of a musical recording on the air by a radio station

air pocket n : a condition of the atmosphere (as a local downdraft) that causes an airplane to drop suddenly

air police n : the military police of an air force

air·port \'er-ˌpȯrt\ n : a place from which aircraft operate that usu. has paved runways and a terminal

air rage n : an airline passenger's uncontrolled anger that is usu. expressed in aggressive or violent behavior

air raid n : an attack by armed airplanes on a surface target

air·ship \'er-ˌship\ n : a lighter-than-air aircraft having propulsion and steering systems

air·sick \-ˌsik\ adj : affected with motion sickness associated with flying — **air·sick·ness** n

air·space \-ˌspās\ n : the space above a nation and under its jurisdiction

air·speed \-ˌspēd\ n : the speed of an object (as an airplane) with relation to the surrounding air

air·strip \-ˌstrip\ n : a runway without normal airport facilities

air·tight \'er-'tīt\ adj 1 : so tightly sealed that no air can enter or escape 2 : leaving no opening for attack

air–to–air adj : launched from one airplane in flight at another; also : involving aircraft in flight

air·waves \'er-ˌwāvz\ n pl : AIR 9

air·way \-ˌwā\ n 1 : a regular route for airplanes 2 : AIRLINE

air·wor·thy \-ˌwər-thē\ adj : fit for operation in the air ⟨~ plane⟩ — **air·wor·thi·ness** n

airy \'er-ē\ adj **air·i·er**; **-est** 1 : LOFTY ⟨~ perches⟩ 2 : lacking in reality : EMPTY 3 : DELICATE 4 : BREEZY

aisle \'ī(-ə)l\ n [ME ile, fr. AF ele, lit., wing, fr. L ala] 1 : the side of a church nave separated by piers from the nave proper 2 : a passage between sections of seats

ajar \ə-'jär\ adj or adv : partly open

AK abbr Alaska

aka abbr also known as

AKC abbr American Kennel Club

akim·bo \ə-'kim-bō\ adj or adv : having the hand on the hip and the elbow turned outward

akin \ə-'kin\ adj 1 : related by blood 2 : similar in kind

Al symbol aluminum

AL abbr 1 Alabama 2 American League 3 American Legion

¹-al adj suffix : of, relating to, or characterized by ⟨directional⟩

²-al n suffix : action : process ⟨rehearsal⟩

Ala abbr Alabama

al·a·bas·ter \'a-lə-ˌbas-tər\ n 1 : a compact fine-textured usu. white and translucent gypsum often carved into objects (as vases) 2 : a hard translucent calcite

à la carte \ˌä-lə-'kärt, ˌä-\ adv or adj [F] : with a separate price for each item on the menu

alac·ri·ty \ə-'la-krə-tē\ n : cheerful readiness : BRISKNESS

à la mode \ˌä-lə-'mōd, ˌä-\ adj [F, according to the fashion] 1 : FASHIONABLE, STYLISH 2 : topped with ice cream

¹alarm \ə-'lärm\ also **ala·rum** \ə-'lär-əm, -'ler-\ n [ME alarme, fr. MF, fr. OIt all'arme, lit., to arms] 1 : a warning signal or device 2 : the terror caused by sudden danger

²alarm also **alarum** vb 1 : to warn of danger 2 : FRIGHTEN

alarm·ist \ə-'lär-mist\ n : a person who alarms others esp. needlessly

alas \ə-'las\ interj — used to express unhappiness, pity, or concern

al·ba·core \'al-bə-ˌkȯr\ n, pl **-core** or **-cores** : a large tuna that is a source of canned tuna

Al·ba·nian \al-'bā-nē-ən\ n : a native or inhabitant of Albania

al·ba·tross \'al-bə-ˌtrȯs, -ˌträs\ n, pl **-tross** or **-tross·es** : any of a family of large web-footed seabirds

al·be·do \al-'bē-(ˌ)dō\ n, pl **-dos** : the fraction of incident radiation that is reflected by a body or surface

al·be·it \ȯl-'bē-ət, al-\ conj : even though : ALTHOUGH

al·bi·no \al-'bī-nō\ n, pl **-nos** : a person or animal lacking coloring matter in the skin, hair, and eyes — **al·bi·nism** \'al-bə-ˌni-zəm\ n

al·bum \'al-bəm\ n 1 : a book with blank pages used for making a collection (as of stamps or photographs) 2 : one or more recordings (as on tape or disk) produced as a single unit

al·bu·men \al-'byü-mən\ n 1 : the white of an egg 2 : ALBUMIN

al·bu·min \al-'byü-mən\ n : any of numerous water-soluble proteins of blood, milk, egg white, and plant and animal tissues

al·bu·min·ous \al-'byü-mə-nəs\ adj : containing or resembling albumen or albumin

al·bu·ter·ol \al-'byü-tə-ˌrȯl, -ˌrōl\ n : a drug used as an aerosol or in tablet form to treat asthma

alc abbr alcohol

al·cal·de \al-'käl-dē\ n : the chief administrative and judicial officer of a Spanish or Spanish-American town

al·ca·zar \al-'kä-zər, -'ka-\ n [Sp alcázar, fr. Ar al-qaṣr the castle] : a Spanish fortress or palace

al·che·my \'al-kə-mē\ n : medieval chemistry chiefly concerned with efforts to turn base metals into gold — **al·che·mist** \'al-kə-mist\ n

al·co·hol \'al-kə-ˌhȯl\ n [NL, fr. ML, powdered antimony, fr. Sp, fr. Ar al-kuḥul the powdered antimony] 1 : a colorless flammable liquid that is the intoxicating agent in fermented and distilled liquors 2 : any of various carbon compounds similar to alcohol 3 : beverages containing alcohol

¹al·co·hol·ic \ˌal-kə-'hȯ-lik, -'hä-\ adj 1 : of, relating to, caused by, or containing alcohol 2 : affected with alcoholism — **al·co·hol·i·cal·ly** \-li-k(ə-)lē\ adv

²alcoholic n : a person affected with alcoholism

al·co·hol·ism \'al-kə-ˌhȯ-ˌli-zəm\ n : continued excessive and usu. uncontrollable use of alcoholic drinks; also : a complex chronic psychological and nutritional disorder associated with such use

al·cove \'al-ˌkōv\ n 1 : a nook or small recess opening off a larger room 2 : a niche or arched opening (as in a wall)

ald *abbr* alderman

al·der \'òl-dər\ *n* : any of a genus of trees or shrubs related to the birches and growing in wet areas

al·der·man \'òl-dər-mən\ *n* : a member of a city legislative body

ale \'āl\ *n* : an alcoholic beverage brewed from malt and hops that is usu. more bitter than beer

ale·a·tor·ic \ˌā-lē-ə-'tòr-ik\ *adj* : characterized by chance or random elements ⟨~ music⟩

ale·a·to·ry \'ā-lē-ə-ˌtòr-ē\ *adj* : ALEATORIC

alee \ə-'lē\ *adv* : on or toward the lee

ale·house \'āl-ˌhaus\ *n* : a place where ale is sold to be drunk on the premises

¹alert \ə-'lərt\ *adj* [It *all' erta*, lit., on the ascent] **1** : watchful against danger **2** : quick to perceive and act — **alert·ly** *adv* — **alert·ness** *n*

²alert *n* **1** : ALARM 1 **2** : the period during which an alert is in effect

³alert *vb* **1** : WARN **2** : to make aware of

Aleut \ə-lē-'üt, ə-'lüt\ *n* **1** : a member of a people of the Aleutian and Shumagin islands and the western part of Alaska Peninsula **2** : the language of the Aleuts

ale·wife \'āl-ˌwīf\ *n, pl* **ale·wives** \-ˌwīvz\ : a food fish related to the herring that is abundant esp. along the Atlantic coast

alewife

Al·ex·an·dri·an \ˌa-lig-'zan-drē-ən\ *adj* **1** : HELLENISTIC **2** : of or relating to Alexander the Great

al·ex·an·drine \-'zan-drən\ *n, often cap* : a line of six iambic feet

al·fal·fa \al-'fal-fə\ *n* : a leguminous plant widely grown for hay and forage

al·fres·co \al-'fres-kō\ *adj or adv* [It] : taking place in the open air

alg *abbr* algebra

al·ga \'al-gə\ *n, pl* **al·gae** \'al-(ˌ)jē\ : any of a group of lower plants having chlorophyll but no vascular system and including seaweeds and related freshwater plants — **al·gal** \-gəl\ *adj*

al·ge·bra \'al-jə-brə\ *n* [ML, fr. Ar *al-jabr*] : a generalization of arithmetic in which letters representing numbers are combined according to the rules of arithmetic — **al·ge·bra·ic** \ˌal-jə-'brā-ik\ *adj* — **al·ge·bra·i·cal·ly** \-'brā-ə-k(ə-)lē\ *adv*

Al·gon·qui·an \al-'gän-kwē-ən, -'gäŋ-\ *or* **Al·gon·quin** \-kwən\ *n* **1** *usu* Algonquin : a member of an American Indian people of the Ottawa River valley **2** *usu* Algonquian : a family of American Indian languages of eastern and central No. America

al·go·rithm \'al-gə-ˌri-thəm\ *n* : a procedure for solving a problem esp. in mathematics or computing — **al·go·rith·mic** \ˌal-gə-'rith-mik\ *adj* — **al·go·rith·mi·cal·ly** \-mi-k(ə-)lē\ *adv*

¹alias \'ā-lē-əs, 'āl-yəs\ *adv* [L, otherwise, fr. *alius* other] : otherwise called

²alias *n* : an assumed name

¹al·i·bi \'a-lə-ˌbī\ *n* [L, elsewhere, fr. *alius* other] **1** : a plea offered by an accused person of not having been at the scene of an offense **2** : an excuse (as for failure)

²alibi *vb* **-bied; -bi·ing** **1** : to furnish an excuse for **2** : offer an excuse

¹alien \'ā-lē-ən, 'āl-yən\ *adj* **1** : belonging to another : FOREIGN **2** : EXOTIC 1

²alien *n* **1** : a foreign-born resident who has not been naturalized **2** : EXTRATERRESTRIAL

alien·able \'āl-yə-nə-bəl, 'ā-lē-ə-nə-\ *adj* : transferable to the ownership of another ⟨~ property⟩

alien·ate \'ā-lē-ə-ˌnāt, 'āl-yə-\ *vb* **-at·ed; -at·ing** **1** : to make hostile : ESTRANGE **2** : to transfer (property) to another — **alien·ation** \ˌā-lē-ə-'nā-shən, ˌāl-yə-\ *n*

alien·ist \'ā-lē-ə-nist, 'āl-yə-\ *n* : PSYCHIATRIST

¹alight \ə-'līt\ *vb* **alight·ed** *also* **alit** \ə-'lit\; **alight·ing** **1** : to get down (as from a vehicle) **2** : to come to rest from the air ♦ **Synonyms** SETTLE, LAND, PERCH

²alight *adj* : lighted up

align *also* **aline** \ə-'līn\ *vb* **1** : to bring into line **2** : to array on the side of or against a cause — **align·er** *n* — **align·ment** *also* **aline·ment** *n*

¹alike \ə-'līk\ *adv* : EQUALLY ⟨denounced by teachers and students ~⟩

²alike *adj* : LIKE ⟨~ in their beliefs⟩ ♦ **Synonyms** AKIN, ANALOGOUS, SIMILAR, COMPARABLE

al·i·ment \'a-lə-mənt\ *n* : NOURISHMENT 1 — **aliment** *vb*

al·i·men·ta·ry \ˌa-lə-'men-t(ə-)rē\ *adj* : of, relating to, or functioning in nourishment or nutrition

alimentary canal *n* : the tube that extends from the mouth to the anus and functions in the digestion and absorption of food and the elimination of residues

al·i·mo·ny \'a-lə-ˌmō-nē\ *n, pl* **-nies** [L *alimonia* sustenance, fr. *alere* to nourish] : an allowance made to one spouse by the other for support pending or after legal separation or divorce

A–line \'ā-ˌlīn\ *adj* : having a flared bottom and a close-fitting top ⟨an ~ skirt⟩

alive \ə-'līv\ *adj* **1** : having life **2** : being in force or operation **3** : SENSITIVE ⟨~ to the danger⟩ **4** : ALERT, BRISK **5** : ANIMATED ⟨streets ~ with traffic⟩ — **alive·ness** *n*

alk *abbr* alkaline

al·ka·li \'al-kə-ˌlī\ *n, pl* **-lies** *or* **-lis** **1** : a substance (as a hydroxide) that has a bitter taste and neutralizes acids **2** : a mixture of salts in the soil of some dry regions in such amount as to make ordinary farming impossible — **al·ka·line** \-kə-lən, -ˌlīn\ *adj* — **al·ka·lin·i·ty** \ˌal-kə-'li-nə-tē\ *n*

al·ka·loid \'al-kə-ˌlòid\ *n* : any of various usu. basic and bitter organic compounds found esp. in seed plants

al·kane \'al-ˌkān\ *n* : a hydrocarbon in which each carbon atom is bonded to 4 other atoms

al·kyd \'al-kəd\ *n* : any of numerous synthetic resins used esp. for protective coatings and in paint

¹all \'òl\ *adj* **1** : the whole of ⟨sat up ~ night⟩ **2** : every member of **3** : EVERY ⟨~ manner of problems⟩ **4** : any whatever ⟨beyond ~ doubt⟩ **5** : nothing but ⟨~ ears⟩ **6** : being more than one person or thing ⟨who ~ is coming⟩

²all *adv* **1** : WHOLLY ⟨sat ~ alone⟩ **2** : selected as the best — used in combination ⟨*all*-state champs⟩ **3** : so much ⟨~ the better for it⟩ **4** : for each side ⟨the score is two ~⟩

³all *pron sing or pl* **1** : the whole number, quantity, or amount ⟨~ of it is gone⟩ **2** : EVERYBODY, EVERYTHING ⟨~ are members⟩ ⟨that is ~⟩

⁴all *n* : the whole of one's resources ⟨gave his ~⟩

Al·lah \'ä-lə, 'a-; 'ä-ˌlä, ä-'lä\ *n* [Ar *allāh*] : GOD 1 — used in Islam

all along *adv* : all the time ⟨knew it *all along*⟩

all–Amer·i·can \ˌòl-ə-'mer-ə-kən\ *adj* **1** : selected as the best in the U.S. **2** : composed wholly of American elements **3** : typical of the U.S. — **all–American** *n*

all–around \ˌòl-ə-'raund\ *adj* **1** : considered in all aspects ⟨best ~ performance⟩ **2** : competent in many fields : VERSATILE ⟨an ~ athlete⟩

al·lay \ə-'lā\ *vb* **1** : ALLEVIATE **2** : CALM ♦ **Synonyms** LIGHTEN, RELIEVE, EASE, ASSUAGE

all clear *n* : a signal that a danger has passed

al·lege \ə-'lej\ *vb* **al·leged; al·leg·ing** **1** : to assert without proof **2** : to offer as a reason — **al·le·ga·tion** \ˌa-li-'gā-shən\ *n* — **al·leged** \ə-'lejd, -'le-jəd\ *adj* — **al·leg·ed·ly** \ə-'le-jəd-lē\ *adv*

al·le·giance \ə-'lē-jəns\ *n* **1** : loyalty owed by a citizen to a government **2** : loyalty to a person or cause

al·le·go·ry \'a-lə-ˌgòr-ē\ *n, pl* **-ries** : the expression through symbolism of truths or generalizations about human experience — **al·le·gor·i·cal** \ˌa-lə-'gòr-i-kəl\ *adj* — **al·le·gor·i·cal·ly** \-k(ə-)lē\ *adv*

¹al·le·gro \ə-'le-grō, -'lā-\ *n, pl* **-gros** : an allegro movement

²allegro *adv or adj* [It, merry] : at a brisk lively tempo — used as a direction in music

al·lele \ə-'lēl\ *n* : any of the alternative forms of a gene that may occur at a given site on a chromosome — **al·le·lic** \-'lē-lik, -'le-\ *adj*

al·le·lu·ia \ˌa-lə-ˈlü-yə\ *interj* : HALLELUJAH

Al·len wrench \ˈa-lən-\ *n* [*Allen* Manufacturing Company, Hartford, Conn.] : an L-shaped hexagonal metal bar of which either end fits the socket of a screw or bolt

al·ler·gen \ˈa-lər-jən\ *n* : something that causes allergy — **al·ler·gen·ic** \ˌa-lər-ˈje-nik\ *adj*

al·ler·gist \ˈa-lər-jist\ *n* : a specialist in allergies

al·ler·gy \ˈa-lər-jē\ *n, pl* **-gies** [G *Allergie*, fr. Gk *allos* other + *ergon* work] : exaggerated or abnormal reaction (as by sneezing) to substances or situations harmless to most people — **al·ler·gic** \ə-ˈlər-jik\ *adj*

al·le·vi·ate \ə-ˈlē-vē-ˌāt\ *vb* **-at·ed; -at·ing** : RELIEVE, LESSEN ⟨~ pain⟩ ◆ *Synonyms* LIGHTEN, MITIGATE, ALLAY — **al·le·vi·a·tion** \ə-ˌlē-vē-ˈā-shən\ *n*

al·ley \ˈa-lē\ *n, pl* **alleys 1** : a garden or park walk **2** : a place for bowling **3** : a narrow passageway esp. between buildings

al·ley–oop \ˌa-lē-ˈyüp\ *n* : a basketball play in which a player catches a pass above the basket and immediately dunks the ball

al·ley·way \ˈa-lē-ˌwā\ *n* : ALLEY 3

all–fired \ˈȯl-ˌfī(-ə)rd\ *adv* : EXTREMELY, EXCESSIVELY ⟨~ stubborn⟩

All·hal·lows \ȯl-ˈha-lōz\ *n, pl* **Allhallows** : ALL SAINTS' DAY

all hours *n pl* : a very late time ⟨stayed up until *all hours*⟩

al·li·ance \ə-ˈlī-əns\ *n* : a union to promote common interests ◆ *Synonyms* LEAGUE, COALITION, CONFEDERACY, FEDERATION

al·li·ga·tor \ˈa-lə-ˌgā-tər\ *n* [Sp *el lagarto* the lizard] : either of two large short-legged reptiles resembling crocodiles but having a shorter and broader snout

alligator pear *n* : AVOCADO

al·lit·er·ate \ə-ˈli-tə-ˌrāt\ *vb* **-at·ed; -at·ing 1** : to form an alliteration **2** : to arrange so as to make alliteration

al·lit·er·a·tion \ə-ˌli-tə-ˈrā-shən\ *n* : the repetition of initial sounds in adjacent words or syllables — **al·lit·er·a·tive** \-ˈli-tə-ˌrā-tiv\ *adj*

al·lo·cate \ˈa-lə-ˌkāt\ *vb* **-cat·ed; -cat·ing** : ALLOT, ASSIGN — **al·lo·ca·tion** \ˌa-lə-ˈkā-shən\ *n*

al·lot \ə-ˈlät\ *vb* **al·lot·ted; al·lot·ting** : to distribute as a share ◆ *Synonyms* ASSIGN, APPORTION, ALLOCATE — **al·lot·ment** *n*

all–out \ˈȯl-ˈaůt\ *adj* : made with maximum effort

¹all over *adv* : EVERYWHERE

²all over *prep* **1** : in eagerly affectionate, attentive, or aggressive pursuit **2** : in or into a state marked by excessive criticism

al·low \ə-ˈlaů\ *vb* **1** : to assign as a share ⟨~ time for rest⟩ **2** : to count as a deduction **3** : to make allowance ⟨~ for expansion⟩ **4** : ADMIT, CONCEDE ⟨~ed that the situation was serious⟩ **5** : PERMIT ⟨~s the dog to roam⟩ — **al·low·able** *adj*

al·low·ance \-əns\ *n* **1** : an allotted share **2** : money given regularly for expenses **3** : a taking into account of extenuating circumstances

al·loy \ˈa-ˌlȯi, ə-ˈlȯi\ *n* **1** : a substance composed of metals melted together **2** : an admixture that lessens value — **al·loy** \ə-ˈlȯi, ˈa-ˌlȯi\ *vb*

all right *adv* **1** — used interjectionally esp. to express agreement or resignation or to indicate the resumption of a discussion ⟨*all right*, let's go⟩ **2** : beyond doubt ⟨SATISFACTORILY ⟨does *all right* in school⟩ — **all right** *adj*

All Saints' Day *n* : a Christian feast on November 1 in honor of all the saints

All Souls' Day *n* : a day of prayer observed by some Christian churches on November 2 for the souls of the faithful departed

all·spice \ˈȯl-ˌspīs\ *n* : the berry of a West Indian tree related to the European myrtle; *also* : the mildly pungent and aromatic spice made from it

all–star \ˈȯl-ˌstär\ *n* : a member of a team of star performers — **all–star** *adj*

all–ter·rain vehicle *n* : a small motor vehicle with three or four wheels for use on a wide range of terrain

all told *adv* : with everything or everyone counted ⟨expecting eight guests *all told*⟩

al·lude \ə-ˈlüd\ *vb* **al·lud·ed; al·lud·ing** [L *alludere*, lit., to play with] : to refer indirectly — **al·lu·sion** \-ˈlü-zhən\ *n* — **al·lu·sive** \-ˈlü-siv\ *adj* — **al·lu·sive·ly** *adv* — **al·lu·sive·ness** *n*

al·lure \ə-ˈlůr\ *vb* **al·lured; al·lur·ing** : CHARM, ENTICE — **allure** *n* — **al·lur·ing·ly** *adv*

al·lu·vi·um \ə-ˈlü-vē-əm\ *n, pl* **-vi·ums** *or* **-via** \-vē-ə\ : soil material (as clay) deposited by running water — **al·lu·vi·al** \-vē-əl\ *adj or n*

all–wheel \ˈȯl-ˌwēl\ *adj* : acting independently on or by means of all four wheels of a vehicle

al·ly \ə-ˈlī, ˈa-ˌlī\ *vb* **al·lied; al·ly·ing** : to enter into an alliance — **al·ly** \ˈa-ˌlī, ə-ˈlī\ *n*

-ally *adv suffix* : ²-LY ⟨specifically⟩

al·ma ma·ter \ˌal-mə-ˈmä-tər\ *n* [L, fostering mother] **1** : an educational institute that one has attended **2** : the song or hymn of an alma mater

al·ma·nac \ˈȯl-mə-ˌnak, ˈal-\ *n* **1** : a publication esp. of astronomical and meteorological data **2** : a usu. annual publication of miscellaneous information

al·man·dite \ˈal-mən-ˌdīt\ *n* : a deep red garnet

al·mighty \ȯl-ˈmī-tē\ *adj* **1** *often cap* : having absolute power over all ⟨*Almighty* God⟩ **2** : relatively unlimited in power — **al·might·i·ness** *n*

Almighty *n* : GOD 1

al·mond \ˈä-mənd, ˈa-, ˈal-\ *n* : a small tree related to the peach; *also* : the edible nutlike kernel of its fruit

al·mo·ner \ˈal-mə-nər, ˈä-mə-\ *n* : a person who distributes alms

al·most \ˈȯl-ˌmōst, ȯl-ˈmōst\ *adv* : very nearly but not exactly

alms \ˈämz, ˈälmz\ *n, pl* **alms** [ME *almesse, almes*, fr. OE *ælmesse, ælms*, fr. L *eleemosyna* alms, fr. Gk *eleēmosynē* pity, alms, fr. *eleēmōn* merciful, fr. *eleos* pity] : something given freely to relieve the poor

alms·house \-ˌhaůs\ *n* : POORHOUSE

al·oe \ˈa-lō\ *n* **1** : any of a large genus of succulent chiefly southern African plants related to the lilies **2** *pl* : the dried juice of the leaves of an aloe used esp. formerly as a laxative

aloe vera \-ˈver-ə, -ˈvir-\ *n* : an aloe with leaves that yield a jellylike emollient extract used esp. in cosmetics; *also* : this extract

aloft \ə-ˈlȯft\ *adv* **1** : high in the air **2** : in flight

alo·ha \ə-ˈlō-ə, ä-ˈlō-hä\ *interj* [Hawaiian] — used to greet or bid farewell

alone \ə-ˈlōn\ *adj* **1** : separated from others **2** : not including anyone or anything else : ONLY ⟨she ~ knows why⟩ ◆ *Synonyms* LONELY, LONESOME, LONE, SOLITARY — **alone** *adv*

¹along \ə-ˈlȯn\ *prep* **1** : in a line matching the direction of ⟨sail ~ the coast⟩ **2** : at a point on or during ⟨stopped ~ the way⟩

²along *adv* **1** : FORWARD, ON ⟨move ~⟩ **2** : as a companion ⟨bring her ~⟩ **3** : at an advanced point ⟨plans are far ~⟩

along·shore \ə-ˈlȯn-ˈshȯr\ *adv or adj* : along the shore or coast ⟨walked ~⟩

¹along·side \-ˌsīd\ *adv* : along or by the side

²alongside *prep* **1** : along or by the side of **2** : in association with

alongside of *prep* : ALONGSIDE

aloof \ə-ˈlüf\ *adj* : removed or distant physically or emotionally — **aloof·ly** *adv* — **aloof·ness** *n*

al·o·pe·cia \ˌa-lə-ˈpē-sh(ē-)ə\ *n* : BALDNESS

aloud \ə-ˈlaůd\ *adv* : with the speaking voice ⟨read ~⟩

alp \ˈalp\ *n* : a high rugged mountain

al·paca \al-ˈpa-kə\ *n* : a domesticated mammal esp. of Peru that is related to the llama; *also* : its woolly hair or a thin cloth made from this hair

al·pha \ˈal-fə\ *n* **1** : the 1st letter of the Greek alphabet — A or α **2** : something first : BEGINNING

al·pha·bet \ˈal-fə-ˌbet\ *n* : the set of letters or characters used in writing a language

al·pha·bet·i·cal \ˌal-fə-ˈbe-ti-kəl\ *or* **al·pha·bet·ic** \-ˈbe-tik\ *adj* **1** : arranged in the order of the letters of the alphabet **2** : of or employing an alphabet — **al·pha·bet·i·cal·ly** \-ti-k(ə-)lē\ *adv*

al·pha·bet·ize \ˈal-fə-bə-ˌtīz\ *vb* **-ized; -iz·ing** : to arrange in alphabetical order — **al·pha·bet·iz·er** *n*

al·pha·nu·mer·ic \ˌal-fə-nů-ˈmer-ik, -nyů-\ *adj* : consisting of letters and numbers and often other symbols ⟨an ~ code⟩; *also* : being a character in an alphanumeric system

alpha particle *n* : a positively charged particle identical with the nucleus of a helium atom that is ejected at high speed in certain radioactive transformations

alpha rhythm *n* : ALPHA WAVE

alpha wave *n* : an electrical rhythm of the brain often associated with a state of wakeful relaxation

Al·pine \'al-,pīn\ *adj* **1** : relating to, located in, or resembling the Alps **2** *often not cap* : of, relating to, or growing on upland slopes above timberline **3** : of or relating to competitive ski events consisting of slalom and downhill racing

al·ready \ol-'re-dē\ *adv* : by this time : PREVIOUSLY

al·right \ol-'rīt\ *adv* : ALL RIGHT

al·so \'ol-sō\ *adv* : in addition : TOO

al·so–ran \-,ran\ *n* **1** : a horse or dog that finishes out of the money in a race **2** : a contestant that does not win

alt *abbr* **1** alternate **2** altitude

Alta *abbr* Alberta

al·tar \'ol-tər\ *n* **1** : a structure on which sacrifices are offered or incense is burned **2** : a table used as a center of ritual or worship

altar server *n* : a boy or girl who assists the celebrant at a church service

¹al·ter \'ol-tər\ *vb* **al·tered; al·ter·ing** \-t(ə-)riŋ\ **1** : to make or become different **2** : CASTRATE, SPAY — **al·ter·able** \'ol-tə-rə-bəl\ *adj* — **al·ter·a·tion** \,ol-tə-'rā-shən\ *n*

²alter *abbr* alteration

al·ter·ca·tion \,ol-tər-'kā-shən\ *n* : a noisy or angry dispute

al·ter ego \,ol-tər-'ē-gō\ *n* [L, lit., second I] : a second self; *esp* : a trusted friend

al·ter·i·ty \ol-'ter-ə-tē\ *n* : the quality or state of being radically alien to the conscious self or a particular cultural orientation

¹al·ter·nate \'ol-tər-nət, 'al-\ *adj* **1** : arranged or succeeding by turns **2** : every other **3** : being an alternative ⟨an ~ route⟩ — **al·ter·nate·ly** *adv*

²al·ter·nate \-,nāt\ *vb* **-nat·ed; -nat·ing** : to occur or cause to occur by turns — **al·ter·na·tion** \,ol-tər-'nā-shən, ,al-\ *n*

³alternate *n* : SUBSTITUTE

alternating current *n* : an electric current that reverses its direction at regular intervals

al·ter·na·tive \ol-'tər-nə-tiv, al-\ *adj* **1** : offering a choice ⟨several ~ plans⟩ **2** : different from the usual or conventional — **alternative** *n*

alternative medicine *n* : any of various systems of healing (as homeopathy) not typically practiced in conventional Western medicine

al·ter·na·tor \'ol-tər-,nā-tər, 'al-\ *n* : an electric generator for producing alternating current

al·though *also* **al·tho** \ol-'thō\ *conj* : in spite of the fact that : even though

al·tim·e·ter \al-'ti-mə-tər, 'al-tə-,mē-tər\ *n* : an instrument for measuring altitude

al·ti·tude \'al-tə-,tüd, -,tyüd\ *n* **1** : angular distance above the horizon **2** : vertical distance : HEIGHT **3** : the perpendicular distance in a geometric figure from the vertex to the base, from the vertex of an angle to the side opposite, or from the base to a parallel side or face

al·to \'al-tō\ *n, pl* **altos** [It, lit., high, fr. L *altus*] : the lower female voice part in a 4-part chorus; *also* : a singer having this voice or part

¹al·to·geth·er \,ol-tə-'ge-thər\ *adv* **1** : WHOLLY ⟨stopped raining ~⟩ **2** : in all ⟨spent $100 ~⟩ **3** : on the whole ⟨~ their efforts were successful⟩

²altogether *n* : NUDE ⟨posed in the ~⟩

al·tru·ism \'al-trü-,i-zəm\ *n* [F *altruisme*, fr. *autrui* other people, fr. OF, oblique case form of *autre* other, fr. L *alter*] : unselfish interest in the welfare of others — **al·tru·ist** \-ist\ *n* — **al·tru·is·tic** \,al-trü-'is-tik\ *adj* — **al·tru·is·ti·cal·ly** \-ti-k(ə-)lē\ *adv*

al·um \'a-ləm\ *n* : either of two colorless crystalline aluminum-containing compounds used esp. as an emetic or as an astringent and styptic

alu·mi·na \ə-'lü-mə-nə\ *n* : the oxide of aluminum occurring in nature as corundum and in bauxite

al·u·min·i·um \,al-yə-'mi-nē-əm\ *n, chiefly Brit* : ALUMINUM

alu·mi·nize \ə-'lü-mə-,nīz\ *vb* **-nized; -niz·ing** : to treat with aluminum

alu·mi·num \ə-'lü-mə-nəm\ *n* : a silver-white malleable ductile light metallic element that is the most abundant metal in the earth's crust

aluminum oxide *n* : ALUMINA

alum·na \ə-'ləm-nə\ *n, pl* **-nae** \-(,)nē\ : a woman graduate or former student of a college or school

alum·nus \ə-'ləm-nəs\ *n, pl* **-ni** \-,nī\ [L, foster son, pupil, fr. *alere* to nourish] : a graduate or former student of a college or school

al·ways \'ol-wēz, -wəz, -(,)wāz\ *adv* **1** : at all times : INVARIABLY **2** : FOREVER

Alz·hei·mer's disease \'älts-,hī-mərz-, 'alts-\ *n* : a degenerative brain disease of unknown cause that is characterized esp. by progressive mental deterioration and memory loss

am *pres 1st sing of* BE

¹Am *abbr* America; American

²Am *symbol* americium

¹AM \'ā-,em\ *n* : a broadcasting system using amplitude modulation; *also* : a radio receiver for broadcasts made by such a system

²AM *abbr* **1** ante meridiem — often not cap. and often punctuated **2** [NL *artium magister*] master of arts

AMA *abbr* American Medical Association

amah \'ä-(,)mä\ *n* : a female servant in eastern Asia; *esp* : a Chinese nurse

amain \ə-'mān\ *adv, archaic* : with full force or speed

amal·gam \ə-'mal-gəm\ *n* **1** : an alloy of mercury with another metal used in making dental cements **2** : a mixture of different elements

amal·gam·ate \ə-'mal-gə-,māt\ *vb* **-at·ed; -at·ing** : to unite or merge into one body — **amal·ga·ma·tion** \-,mal-gə-'mā-shən\ *n*

aman·u·en·sis \ə-,man-yə-'wen-səs\ *n, pl* **-en·ses** \-,sēz\ : one employed to write from dictation or to copy what another has written : SECRETARY

am·a·ranth \'a-mə-,ranth\ *n* **1** : any of a large genus of coarse herbs sometimes grown for their showy flowers **2** : a flower that never fades

am·a·ran·thine \,a-mə-'ran-thən, -,thīn\ *adj* **1** : relating to or resembling an amaranth **2** : UNDYING

am·a·ryl·lis \,a-mə-'ri-ləs\ *n* : any of various plants related to the lilies; *esp* : an autumn-flowering South African bulbous herb widely grown for its large showy red to whitish flowers

amass \ə-'mas\ *vb* : ACCUMULATE

am·a·teur \'a-mə-(,)tər, -,tùr, -,tyùr, -,chùr, -chər\ *n* [F, fr. L *amator* lover, fr. *amare* to love] **1** : a person who engages in a pursuit for pleasure and not as a profession **2** : a person who is not expert — **am·a·teur·ish** \,a-mə-'tər-ish, -'tùr-, -'tyùr-, -'chùr-, -'chər-\ *adj* — **am·a·teur·ism** \'a-mə-(,)tər-i-zəm, -,tùr-, -,tyùr-, -,chùr-, -,chər-\ *n*

am·a·tive \'a-mə-tiv\ *adj* : indicative of love : AMOROUS — **am·a·tive·ly** *adv* — **am·a·tive·ness** *n*

am·a·to·ry \'a-mə-,tòr-ē\ *adj* : of or expressing sexual love

amaze \ə-'māz\ *vb* **amazed; amaz·ing** : to fill with wonder : ASTOUND ✦ **Synonyms** ASTONISH, SURPRISE, DUMBFOUND — **amaze·ment** *n* — **amaz·ing·ly** *adv*

am·a·zon \'a-mə-,zän, -zən\ *n* **1** *cap* : a member of a race of female warriors of Greek mythology **2** : a tall strong often masculine woman — **am·a·zo·ni·an** \,a-mə-'zō-nē-ən\ *adj, often cap*

amb *abbr* ambassador

am·bas·sa·dor \am-'ba-sə-dər\ *n* : a representative esp. of a government — **am·bas·sa·do·ri·al** \-,ba-sə-'dòr-ē-əl\ *adj* — **am·bas·sa·dor·ship** *n*

am·ber \'am-bər\ *n* : a yellowish or brownish fossil resin used esp. for ornamental objects; *also* : the color of this resin

am·ber·gris \'am-bər-,gris, -,grēs\ *n* : a waxy substance from the sperm whale used in making perfumes

am·bi·dex·trous \,am-bi-'dek-strəs\ *adj* : using both hands with equal ease — **am·bi·dex·trous·ly** *adv*

am·bi·ence *or* **am·bi·ance** \'am-bē-əns, äⁿ-'byäⁿs\ *n* : a pervading atmosphere

¹am·bi·ent \'am-bē-ənt\ *adj* : existing on all sides

²ambient *n* : music intended to serve as an unobtrusive accompaniment to other activities

am·big·u·ous \am-'bi-gyə-wəs\ *adj* : capable of being understood in more than one way — **am·bi·gu·i·ty** \,am-bə-'gyü-ə-tē\ *n* — **am·big·u·ous·ly** *adv*

am·bi·tion \am-'bi-shən\ *n* [ME, fr. MF or L; MF, fr. L *ambition-, ambitio*, lit., act of soliciting for votes, fr. *ambire* to go around] : eager desire for success or power

am·bi·tious \-shəs\ *adj* : characterized by ambition — **am·bi·tious·ly** *adv* — **am·bi·tious·ness** *n*

am·biv·a·lence \am-'bi-və-ləns\ *n* : simultaneous attraction toward and repulsion from a person, object, or action — **am·biv·a·lent** \-lənt\ *adj*

¹**am·ble** \'am-bəl\ *vb* **am·bled; am·bling** \-b(ə-)liŋ\ : to go at an amble

²**amble** *n* : an easy gait esp. of a horse

am·bro·sia \am-'brō-zh(ē-)ə\ *n* : the food of the Greek and Roman gods — **am·bro·sial** \-zh(ē-)əl\ *adj*

am·bu·lance \'am-byə-ləns\ *n* : a vehicle equipped for carrying the injured or sick

am·bu·lant \'am-byə-lənt\ *adj* : AMBULATORY

¹**am·bu·la·to·ry** \'am-byə-lə-ˌtȯr-ē\ *adj* **1** : of, relating to, or adapted to walking **2** : able to walk or move about

²**ambulatory** *n, pl* **-ries** : a sheltered place (as in a cloister) for walking

am·bus·cade \'am-bə-ˌskād\ *n* : AMBUSH

am·bush \'am-ˌbu̇sh\ *n* : a trap in which concealed persons wait to attack by surprise — **ambush** *vb*

amdt *abbr* amendment

ameba, ameboid *var of* AMOEBA, AMOEBOID

ame·lio·rate \ə-'mēl-yə-ˌrāt\ *vb* **-rat·ed; -rat·ing** : to make or grow better : IMPROVE — **ame·lio·ra·tion** \-ˌmēl-yə-'rā-shən\ *n*

amen \(ˌ)ā-'men, (ˌ)ä-\ *interj* — used esp. at the end of prayers to affirm or express approval

ame·na·ble \ə-'mē-nə-bəl, -'me-\ *adj* **1** : ANSWERABLE ⟨∼ to the law⟩ **2** : COMPLIANT

amend \ə-'mend\ *vb* **1** : to change for the better : IMPROVE **2** : to alter formally in phraseology — **amend·able** \-'men-də-bəl\ *adj*

amend·ment \ə-'mend-mənt\ *n* **1** : correction of faults **2** : the process of amending a parliamentary motion or a constitution; *also* : the alteration so proposed or made

amends \ə-'mendz\ *n sing or pl* : compensation for injury or loss

ame·ni·ty \ə-'me-nə-tē, -'mē-\ *n, pl* **-ties 1** : AGREEABLE-NESS **2** : a gesture observed in social relationships **3** : something that serves as a comfort or convenience

Amer *abbr* America; American

amerce \ə-'mərs\ *vb* **amerced; amerc·ing 1** : to penalize by a fine determined by the court **2** : PUNISH — **amerce·ment** *n*

Amer·i·ca·na \ə-ˌmer-ə-'ka-nə, -'kä-\ *n pl* : materials concerning or characteristic of America, its civilization, or its culture

American Indian *n* : a member of any of the aboriginal peoples of No. and So. America except the Eskimos

Amer·i·can·ism \ə-'mer-ə-kə-ˌni-zəm\ *n* **1** : a characteristic feature of English as used in the U.S. **2** : attachment or loyalty to the traditions, interests, or ideals of the U.S. **3** : a custom or trait peculiar to the U.S. or to Americans

Amer·i·can·ize \ə-'mer-ə-kə-ˌnīz\ *vb* : to make or become American — **Amer·i·can·i·za·tion** \ə-ˌmer-ə-kə-nə-'zā-shən\ *n*

Amer·i·can·ness \ə-'mer-ə-kən-nəs\ *n* : the quality or state of being American

American plan *n* : a hotel plan whereby the daily rates cover the cost of room and three meals

American Sign Language *n* : a sign language for the deaf in which meaning is conveyed by a system of hand gestures and placement

am·er·i·ci·um \ˌam-ə-'rish-ē-əm, -'ris-\ *n* : a radioactive metallic chemical element produced artificially from plutonium

AmerInd *abbr* American Indian

Am·er·in·di·an \ˌa-mə-'rin-dē-ən\ *n* : AMERICAN INDIAN — **Amerindian** *adj*

am·e·thyst \'a-mə-thəst\ *n* [ME *amatiste*, fr. AF & L; AF, fr. L *amethystus*, fr. Gk *amethystos*, lit., remedy against drunkenness, fr. *a-* not + *methyein* to be drunk, fr. *methy* wine] : a gemstone consisting of clear purple or bluish-violet quartz

ami·a·ble \'ā-mē-ə-bəl\ *adj* **1** : AGREEABLE ⟨an ∼ comedy⟩ **2** : having a friendly and sociable disposition — **ami·a·bil·i·ty** \ˌā-mē-ə-'bi-lə-tē\ *n* — **ami·a·ble·ness** *n* — **ami·a·bly** \'ā-mē-ə-blē\ *adv*

am·i·ca·ble \'a-mi-kə-bəl\ *adj* : FRIENDLY, PEACEABLE ⟨an ∼ settlement of differences⟩ — **am·i·ca·bil·i·ty** \ˌa-mi-kə-'bi-lə-tē\ *n* — **am·i·ca·bly** \'a-mi-kə-blē\ *adv*

amid \ə-'mid\ *or* **amidst** \-'midst\ *prep* : in or into the middle of : AMONG

amid·ships \ə-'mid-ˌships\ *adv* : in or near the middle of a ship

ami·no acid \ə-'mē-nō-\ *n* : any of numerous nitrogen-containing acids that include some which are used by cells to build proteins

amir *var of* EMIR

¹**amiss** \ə-'mis\ *adv* **1** : WRONGLY **2** : ASTRAY ⟨something had gone ∼⟩ **3** : IMPERFECTLY

²**amiss** *adj* **1** : WRONG **2** : out of place

am·i·ty \'a-mə-tē\ *n, pl* **-ties** : FRIENDSHIP; *esp* : friendly relations between nations

am·me·ter \'a-ˌmē-tər\ *n* : an instrument for measuring electric current esp. in amperes

am·mo \'a-mō\ *n* : AMMUNITION

am·mo·nia \ə-'mō-nyə\ *n* [NL, fr. L *sal ammoniacus* sal ammoniac (ammonium chloride), lit., salt of Ammon, fr. Gk *ammōniakos* of Ammon, fr. *Ammōn* Ammon, an Egyptian god near one of whose temples it was extracted] **1** : a colorless gaseous compound of nitrogen and hydrogen used in refrigeration and in the making of fertilizers and explosives **2** : a solution (**ammonia water**) of ammonia in water

am·mo·ni·um \ə-'mō-nē-əm\ *n* : an ion or chemical group derived from ammonia by combination with hydrogen

ammonium chloride *n* : a white crystalline volatile salt used in batteries and as an expectorant

am·mu·ni·tion \ˌam-yə-'ni-shən\ *n* **1** : projectiles fired from guns **2** : explosive items used in war **3** : material for use in attack or defense

Amn *abbr* airman

am·ne·sia \am-'nē-zhə\ *n* **1** : abnormal loss of memory **2** : the selective overlooking of events or acts not favorable to one's purpose — **am·ne·si·ac** \-zhē-ˌak, -zē-\ *or* **am·ne·sic** \-zik, -sik\ *adj or n*

am·nes·ty \'am-nə-stē\ *n, pl* **-ties** : an act granting a pardon to a group of individuals — **amnesty** *vb*

am·nio·cen·te·sis \ˌam-nē-ō-ˌsen-'tē-səs\ *n, pl* **-te·ses** \-ˌsēz\ : the surgical insertion of a hollow needle through the abdominal wall and uterus of a pregnant female esp. to obtain fluid used to check the fetus for chromosomal abnormality and to determine sex

am·ni·ot·ic fluid \ˌam-nē-'ä-tik-\ *n* : the watery fluid in which the embryo or fetus is immersed

amoe·ba *also* **ame·ba** \ə-'mē-bə\ *n, pl* **-bas** *or* **-bae** \-(ˌ)bē\ : any of various tiny one-celled protozoans that lack permanent cell organs and occur esp. in water and soil — **amoe·bic** \-bik\ *adj*

amoe·boid *also* **ame·boid** \-ˌbȯid\ *adj* : resembling an amoeba esp. in moving or readily changing shape

amok \ə-'mək, -'mäk\ *or* **amuck** \-'mək\ *adv* : in a violent, frenzied, or uncontrolled manner ⟨run ∼⟩

among \ə-'məŋ\ *also* **amongst** \-'məŋst\ *prep* **1** : in or through the midst of **2** : in the number, class, or company of **3** : in shares to each of **4** : by common action of

amon·til·la·do \ə-ˌmän-tə-'lä-dō\ *n, pl* **-dos** [Sp] : a medium dry sherry

amor·al \ā-'mȯr-əl\ *adj* **1** : neither moral nor immoral; *esp* : being outside the sphere to which moral judgments apply **2** : lacking moral sensibility — **amor·al·ly** *adv*

am·o·rous \'a-mə-rəs\ *adj* **1** : inclined to love **2** : being in love **3** : of or indicative of love — **am·o·rous·ly** *adv* — **am·o·rous·ness** *n*

amor·phous \ə-'mȯr-fəs\ *adj* **1** : SHAPELESS, FORMLESS **2** : not crystallized

am·or·tize \'a-mər-ˌtīz, ə-'mȯr-\ *vb* **-tized; -tiz·ing** : to extinguish (as a mortgage) usu. by payment on the principal at the time of each periodic interest payment — **amor·ti·za·tion** \ˌa-mər-tə-'zā-shən, ə-ˌmȯr-\ *n*

Amos \'ā-məs\ — see BIBLE table

¹**amount** \ə-'mau̇nt\ *vb* **1** : to be equivalent **2** : to reach a total : add up

²**amount** *n* **1** : the total number or quantity **2** : a principal sum plus the interest on it

amour \ə-'mu̇r, ä-, a-\ *n* **1** : a love affair esp. when illicit **2** : LOVER

amour pro·pre \ˌa-ˌmu̇r-'prȯpr³, ˌä-, -'prȯpr³\ *n* [F] : SELF-ESTEEM

¹**amp** \'amp\ *n* **1** : AMPERE **2** : AMPLIFIER; *also* : a unit consisting of an electronic amplifier and a loudspeaker

²amp *vb* : EXCITE, ENERGIZE ⟨tried to ~ up the crowd⟩

am·per·age \'am-p(ə-)rij\ *n* : the strength of a current of electricity expressed in amperes

am·pere \'am-ˌpir\ *n* : a unit of electric current equivalent to a steady current produced by one volt applied across a resistance of one ohm

am·per·sand \'am-pər-ˌsand\ *n* [alter. of *and per se and*, spoken form of the phrase & *per se and*, lit., (the character) & by itself (stands for the word) *and*] : a character & used for the word *and*

am·phet·amine \am-'fe-tə-ˌmēn, -mən\ *n* : a compound or one of its derivatives that stimulates the central nervous system and is used esp. to treat hyperactive children and to suppress appetite

am·phib·i·an \am-'fi-bē-ən\ *n* **1** : an amphibious organism; *esp* : any of a class of vertebrate animals (as frogs and salamanders) intermediate between fishes and reptiles **2** : an airplane that can land on and take off from either land or water

am·phib·i·ous \am-'fi-bē-əs\ *adj* [Gk *amphibios*, lit., living a double life, fr. *amphi-* on both sides + *bios* mode of life] **1** : able to live both on land and in water **2** : adapted for both land and water **3** : made by joint action of land, sea, and air forces invading from the sea; *also* : trained for such action

am·phi·bole \'am-fə-ˌbōl\ *n* : any of a group of rock-forming minerals of similar crystal structure

am·phi·the·ater \'am-fə-ˌthē-ə-tər\ *n* **1** : an oval or circular structure with rising tiers of seats around an arena **2** : a very large auditorium

am·pho·ra \'am-fə-rə\ *n, pl* **-rae** \-ˌrē\ *or* **-ras** : an ancient Greek jar or vase with two handles that rise almost to the level of the mouth

am·ple \'am-pəl\ *adj* **am·pler** \-plər\; **am·plest** \-pləst\ **1** : LARGE, CAPACIOUS **2** : enough to satisfy : ABUNDANT — **am·ply** \-plē\ *adv*

am·pli·fy \'am-plə-ˌfī\ *vb* **-fied; -fy·ing 1** : to expand by extended treatment **2** : to increase in magnitude or strength; *esp* : to make louder — **am·pli·fi·ca·tion** \ˌam-plə-fə-'kā-shən\ *n* — **am·pli·fi·er** \'am-plə-ˌfī(-ə)r\ *n*

am·pli·tude \-ˌtüd, -ˌtyüd\ *n* **1** : ample extent : FULLNESS **2** : the extent of a vibratory movement (as of a pendulum) **3** : the height or depth of an oscillation (as of an alternating current or a radio wave) compared to its average value

amplitude modulation *n* : modulation of the amplitude of a radio carrier wave in accordance with the strength of the signal; *also* : a broadcasting system using such modulation

am·poule *or* **am·pule** *also* **am·pul** \'am-ˌpyül, -ˌpül\ *n* : a small sealed bulbous glass vessel used to hold a solution for hypodermic injection

am·pu·tate \'am-pyə-ˌtāt\ *vb* **-tat·ed; -tat·ing** : to cut off ⟨~ a leg⟩ — **am·pu·ta·tion** \ˌam-pyə-'tā-shən\ *n*

am·pu·tee \ˌam-pyə-'tē\ *n* : one who has had a limb amputated

AMSLAN *abbr* American Sign Language

amt *abbr* amount

amuck *var of* AMOK

am·u·let \'am-yə-lət\ *n* : an ornament worn as a charm against evil

amuse \ə-'myüz\ *vb* **amused; amus·ing** : to entertain in a light or playful manner : DIVERT — **amuse·ment** *n* — **amusing** *adj* — **amus·ing·ly** *adv*

amusement park *n* : a commercially operated park having various devices (as a roller coaster) for entertainment and booths for selling refreshments

AM·VETS \'am-ˌvets\ *abbr* American Veterans (of World War II)

am·y·lase \'a-mə-ˌlās, -ˌlāz\ *n* : any of several enzymes that accelerate the breakdown of starch and glycogen

an \ən, (ˈ)an\ *indefinite article* : A — used before words beginning with a vowel sound

¹-an *or* **-ian** *also* **-ean** *n suffix* **1** : one that belongs to ⟨American⟩ ⟨crustacean⟩ **2** : one skilled in or specializing in ⟨phonetician⟩

²-an *or* **-ian** *also* **-ean** *adj suffix* **1** : of or belonging to ⟨American⟩ **2** : characteristic of : resembling ⟨Mozartean⟩

AN *abbr* airman (Navy)

an·a·bol·ic steroid \ˌa-nə-'bä-lik-\ *n* : any of a group of

synthetic steroid hormones sometimes abused by athletes in training to increase the size and strength of their muscles

anach·ro·nism \ə-'na-krə-ˌni-zəm\ *n* **1** : the error of placing a person or thing in the wrong period **2** : one that is chronologically out of place — **anach·ro·nis·tic** \ə-ˌna-krə-'nis-tik\ *adj* — **anach·ro·nous** \-'na-krə-nəs\ *adj*

an·a·con·da \ˌa-nə-'kän-də\ *n* : a large So. American snake that suffocates and kills its prey by constriction

anad·ro·mous \ə-'na-drə-məs\ *adj* : ascending rivers from the sea for breeding ⟨shad are ~⟩

anae·mia, anae·mic *chiefly Brit var of* ANEMIA, ANEMIC

an·aer·obe \'a-nə-ˌrōb\ *n* : an anaerobic organism

an·aer·o·bic \ˌa-nə-'rō-bik\ *adj* : living, active, occurring, or existing in the absence of free oxygen

an·aes·the·sia, an·aes·thet·ic *chiefly Brit var of* ANESTHESIA, ANESTHETIC

ana·gram \'a-nə-ˌgram\ *n* : a word or phrase made by transposing the letters of another word or phrase

¹anal \'ā-nᵊl\ *adj* **1** : of, relating to, situated near, or involving the anus **2** : of, relating to, or characterized by the stage of psychosexual development in psychoanalytic theory during which one is concerned esp. with feces **3** : of, relating to, or characterized by personality traits (as frugality and neatness) considered typical of fixation at the anal stage of development — **anal·ly** *adv*

²anal *abbr* **1** analogy **2** analysis; analytic

an·al·ge·sia \ˌa-nᵊl-'jē-zhə\ *n* : insensibility to pain — **an·al·ge·sic** \-'jē-zik, -sik\ *adj*

an·al·ge·sic \-'jē-zik, -sik\ *n* : an agent for producing analgesia

analog computer *n* : a computer that operates with numbers represented by directly measurable quantities (as voltages)

anal·o·gous \ə-'na-lə-gəs\ *adj* : similar in one or more respects — **anal·o·gous·ly** *adv*

an·a·logue *or* **an·a·log** \'a-nə-ˌlóg, -ˌlag\ *n* **1** : something that is analogous to something else **2** : an organ similar in function to one of another animal or plant but different in structure or origin

anal·o·gy \ə-'na-lə-jē\ *n, pl* **-gies 1** : inference that if two or more things agree in some respects they will probably agree in others **2** : a likeness in one or more ways between things otherwise unlike — **an·a·log·i·cal** \ˌa-nə-'lä-ji-kəl\ *adj* — **an·a·log·i·cal·ly** \-k(ə-)lē\ *adv*

anal–re·ten·tive \'ā-nᵊl-ri-'ten-tiv\ *adj* : ANAL 3

an·a·lyse *chiefly Brit var of* ANALYZE

anal·y·sis \ə-'na-lə-səs\ *n, pl* **-y·ses** \-ˌsēz\ [NL, fr. Gk, fr. *analyein* to break up, fr. *ana-* up + *lyein* to loosen] **1** : separation of a thing into the parts or elements of which it is composed **2** : an examination of a thing to determine its parts or elements; *also* : a statement showing the results of such an examination **3** : PSYCHOANALYSIS — **an·a·lyst** \'a-nə-list\ *n* — **an·a·lyt·ic** \ˌa-nə-'li-tik\ *or* **an·a·lyt·i·cal** \-ti-kəl\ *adj* — **an·a·lyt·i·cal·ly** *adv*

an·a·lyte \'a-nə-ˌlīt\ *n* : a chemical substance that is the subject of chemical analysis

an·a·lyze \'a-nə-ˌlīz\ *vb* **-lyzed; -lyz·ing** : to make an analysis of

an·a·pest \'a-nə-ˌpest\ *n* : a metrical foot of two unaccented syllables followed by one accented syllable — **an·a·pes·tic** \ˌa-nə-'pes-tik\ *adj or n*

an·ar·chism \'a-nər-ˌki-zəm\ *n* : the theory that all government is undesirable — **an·ar·chist** \-kist\ *n or adj* — **an·ar·chis·tic** \ˌa-nər-'kis-tik\ *adj*

an·ar·chy \'a-nər-kē\ *n* **1** : a social structure without government or law and order **2** : utter confusion — **an·ar·chic** \a-'när-kik\ *adj* — **an·ar·chi·cal·ly** \-ki-k(ə-)lē\ *adv*

anas·to·mo·sis \ə-ˌnas-tə-'mō-səs\ *n, pl* **-mo·ses** \-ˌsēz\ **1** : the union of parts or branches (as of blood vessels) **2** : NETWORK

anat *abbr* anatomical; anatomy

anath·e·ma \ə-'na-thə-mə\ *n* **1** : a solemn curse **2** : a person or thing accursed; *also* : one intensely disliked

anath·e·ma·tize \-ˌtīz\ *vb* **-tized; -tiz·ing** : to pronounce an anathema against : CURSE

anat·o·mise *Brit var of* ANATOMIZE

anat·o·mize \ə-'na-tə-ˌmīz\ *vb* **-mized; -miz·ing** : to dissect so as to examine the structure and parts; *also* : ANALYZE

anat·o·my \ə-'na-tə-mē\ *n, pl* **-mies** [LL *anatomia* dissection, fr. Gk *anatomē*, fr. *anatemnein* to dissect, fr. *ana-* up + *temnein* to cut] **1** : a branch of science dealing with the structure of organisms **2** : structural makeup esp. of an organism or any of its parts **3** : a separating into parts for detailed study : ANALYSIS — **an·a·tom·i·cal** \‚a-nə-'tä-mi-kəl\ *or* **an·a·tom·ic** \-mik\ *adj* — **an·a·tom·i·cal·ly** \-mi-k(ə-)lē\ *adv* — **anat·o·mist** \ə-'na-tə-mist\ *n*

anc *abbr* ancient

-ance *n suffix* **1** : action or process ⟨further*ance*⟩ : instance of an action or process ⟨perform*ance*⟩ **2** : quality or state : instance of a quality or state ⟨protuber*ance*⟩ **3** : amount or degree ⟨conduct*ance*⟩

an·ces·tor \'an-‚ses-tər\ *n* [ME *ancestre*, fr. AF, fr. L *antecessor* predecessor, fr. *antecedere* to go before, fr. *ante-* before + *cedere* to go] : one from whom an individual is descended

an·ces·tress \'an-‚ses-trəs\ *n* : a female ancestor

an·ces·try \'an-‚ses-trē\ *n* **1** : line of descent : LINEAGE **2** : ANCESTORS — **an·ces·tral** \an-'ses-trəl\ *adj*

an·cho \'än-chō\ *n, pl* **anchos** : a poblano chili pepper esp. when mature and dried to a reddish black

¹an·chor \'an-kər\ *n* **1** : a heavy metal device attached to a ship that catches hold of the bottom and holds the ship in place **2** : something that serves to hold an object firmly **3** : ANCHORPERSON **4** : a large store that attracts customers and other businesses to a shopping mall

anchor 1: different styles

²anchor *vb* : to hold or become held in place by or as if by an anchor

an·chor·age \'an-k(ə-)rij\ *n* : a place suitable for ships to anchor

an·cho·rite \'an-kə-‚rīt\ *n* : HERMIT

an·chor·man \'an-kər-‚man\ *n* **1** : the member of a team who competes last **2** : an anchorperson who is a man

an·chor·per·son \-‚pər-sən\ *n* : a broadcaster who reads the news and introduces the reports of other broadcasters

an·chor·wom·an \-‚wu̇-mən\ *n* **1** : a woman who competes last **2** : an anchorperson who is a woman

an·cho·vy \'an-‚chō-vē, an-'chō-\ *n, pl* **-vies** *or* **-vy** : any of a family of small herringlike fishes often used as food

an·cien ré·gime \‚äⁿs-yaⁿ-rā-'zhēm\ *n* **1** : the political and social system of France before the Revolution of 1789 **2** : a system no longer prevailing

¹an·cient \'ān-shənt\ *adj* **1** : having existed for many years ⟨∼ customs⟩ **2** : belonging to times long past; *esp* : belonging to the period before the Middle Ages

²ancient *n* **1** : an aged person **2** *pl* : the peoples of ancient Greece and Rome; *esp* : the classical authors of Greece and Rome

an·cil·lary \'an-sə-‚ler-ē\ *adj* **1** : SUBORDINATE, SUBSIDIARY ⟨a factory's ∼ plants⟩ **2** : AUXILIARY, SUPPLEMENTARY ⟨∼ evidence⟩ — **ancillary** *n*

-ancy *n suffix* : quality or state ⟨flamboy*ancy*⟩

and \ənd, (')and\ *conj* **1** — used to indicate connection or addition esp. of items within the same class or type or to join words or phrases of the same grammatical rank or function **2** — used to join one finite verb to another so that together they are equivalent to an infinitive of purpose ⟨come ∼ see me⟩

¹an·dan·te \än-'dän-‚tā, -tē\ *adv or adj* [It, lit., going, prp. of *andare* to go] : moderately slow — used as a direction in music

²andante *n* : an andante movement

and·iron \'an-‚dī(-ə)rn\ *n* : one of a pair of metal supports for firewood in a fireplace

and/or \'and-'ȯr\ *conj* — used to indicate that either *and*

or **or** may apply ⟨men ∼ women means men *and* women or men *or* women⟩

an·dro·gen \'an-drə-jən\ *n* : a male sex hormone (as testosterone)

an·drog·y·nous \an-'drä-jə-nəs\ *adj* **1** : having the characteristics of both male and female **2** : suitable for either sex ⟨∼ clothing⟩ — **an·drog·y·ny** \-nē\ *n*

an·droid \'an-‚drȯid\ *n* : a mobile robot usu. with a human form

an·ec·dot·al \‚a-nik-'dō-t³l\ *adj* **1** : relating to or consisting of anecdotes **2** : based on reports of an unscientific nature — **an·ec·dot·al·ly** *adv*

an·ec·dote \'an-ik-‚dōt\ *n, pl* **-dotes** *also* **-dota** \‚a-nik-'dō-tə\ [F, fr. Gk *anekdota* unpublished items, fr. *a-* not + *ekdidonai* to publish] : a brief story of an interesting, amusing, or biographical incident

ane·mia \ə-'nē-mē-ə\ *n* **1** : a condition in which blood is deficient in quantity, in red blood cells, or in hemoglobin and which is marked by pallor, weakness, and irregular heart action **2** : lack of vitality — **ane·mic** \ə-'nē-mik\ *adj*

an·e·mom·e·ter \‚a-nə-'mä-mə-tər\ *n* : an instrument for measuring the force or speed of the wind

anem·o·ne \ə-'ne-mə-nē\ *n* : any of a large genus of herbs related to the buttercups that have showy flowers without petals but with conspicuous often colored sepals

anent \ə-'nent\ *prep* : CONCERNING

an·es·the·sia \‚a-nəs-'thē-zhə\ *n* : loss of bodily sensation

an·es·the·si·ol·o·gy \-‚thē-zē-'ä-lə-jē\ *n* : a branch of medical science dealing with anesthesia and anesthetics — **an·es·the·si·ol·o·gist** \-jist\ *n*

¹an·es·thet·ic \‚a-nəs-'the-tik\ *adj* : of, relating to, or capable of producing anesthesia

²anesthetic *n* : an agent that produces anesthesia

anes·the·tist \ə-'nes-thə-tist\ *n* : one who administers anesthetics

anes·the·tize \ə-'nes-thə-‚tīz\ *vb* **-tized; -tiz·ing** : to subject to anesthesia

an·eu·rysm *also* **an·eu·rism** \'an-yə-‚ri-zəm\ *n* : an abnormal blood-filled bulge of a blood vessel

anew \ə-'nü, -'nyü\ *adv* **1** : over again ⟨begin ∼⟩ **2** : in a new form ⟨this film tells the story ∼⟩

an·gel \'ān-jəl\ *n* [ME, fr. OE *engel* & AF *angele*, both fr. L *angelus*, fr. Gk *angelos*, lit., messenger] **1** : a spiritual being superior to man **2** : an attendant spirit **3** : a winged figure of human form in art **4** : MESSENGER, HARBINGER ⟨∼ of death⟩ **5** : a person held to resemble an angel **6** : a financial backer — **an·gel·ic** \an-'je-lik\ *or* **an·gel·i·cal** \-li-kəl\ *adj* — **an·gel·i·cal·ly** \-k(ə-)lē\ *adv*

an·gel·fish \'ān-jəl-‚fish\ *n* : any of several brightly colored tropical fishes that are flattened from side to side

an·gel·i·ca \an-'je-li-kə\ *n* : a biennial herb related to the carrot whose roots and fruit furnish a flavoring oil

¹an·ger \'aŋ-gər\ *vb* : to make angry

²anger *n* [ME, affliction, anger, fr. ON *angr* grief] : a strong feeling of displeasure ✦ *Synonyms* WRATH, IRE, RAGE, FURY, INDIGNATION

an·gi·na \an-'jī-nə\ *n* : a disorder (as of the heart) marked by attacks of intense pain; *esp* : ANGINA PECTORIS — **an·gi·nal** \an-'jī-n³l\ *adj*

angina pec·to·ris \-'pek-t(ə-)rəs\ *n* : a heart disease marked by brief attacks of sharp chest pain caused by deficient oxygenation of heart muscles

an·gio·gen·e·sis \‚an-jē-ō-'je-nə-səs\ *n* : the formation of blood vessels — **an·gio·gen·ic** \-'je-nik\ *adj*

an·gio·gram \'an-jē-ə-‚gram\ *n* : a radiograph made by angiography

an·gi·og·ra·phy \‚an-jē-'ä-grə-fē\ *n* : the use of radiography to make blood vessels visible after injection of a substance opaque to radiation

an·gio·plas·ty \'an-jē-ə-‚plas-tē\ *n* : surgical repair of a blood vessel esp. by using an inflatable catheter to unblock arteries clogged by atherosclerotic deposits

an·gio·sperm \-‚spərm\ *n* : FLOWERING PLANT

¹an·gle \'aŋ-gəl\ *n* **1** : a sharp projecting corner **2** : the figure formed by the meeting of two lines in a point **3** : a point of view **4** : a special technique or plan : GIMMICK — **an·gled** *adj*

²angle *vb* **an·gled; an·gling** \-g(ə-)liŋ\ : to turn, move, or direct at an angle

³**angle** *vb* **an·gled; an·gling** \-g(ə-)liŋ\ : to fish with a hook and line — **an·gler** \-glər\ *n* — **an·gling** \-gliŋ\ *n*

an·gle·worm \'aŋ-gəl-ˌwərm\ *n* : EARTHWORM

An·gli·can \'aŋ-gli-kən\ *adj* 1 : of or relating to the established episcopal Church of England 2 : of or relating to England or the English nation — **Anglican** *n* — **An·gli·can·ism** \-kə-ˌni-zəm\ *n*

an·gli·cize \'aŋ-glə-ˌsīz\ *vb* **-cized; -ciz·ing** *often cap* 1 : to make English (as in habits, speech, character, or outlook) 2 : to borrow (a foreign word or phrase) into English without changing form or spelling and sometimes without changing pronunciation — **an·gli·ci·za·tion** \ˌaŋ-glə-sə-ˈzā-shən\ *n, often cap*

An·glo \'aŋ-glō\ *n, pl* **Anglos** : a non-Hispanic white inhabitant of the U.S.; *esp* : one of English origin and descent

An·glo·cen·tric \ˌaŋ-glō-ˈsen-trik\ *adj* : centered on or favoring England or things English

An·glo–French \ˌaŋ-glō-ˈfrench\ *n* : the French language used in medieval England

An·glo·phile \'aŋ-glə-ˌfī(-ə)l\ *also* **An·glo·phil** \-ˌfil\ *n* : one who greatly admires England and things English

An·glo·phobe \'aŋ-glə-ˌfōb\ *n* : one who is averse to England and things English

An·glo–Sax·on \ˌaŋ-glō-ˈsak-sən\ *n* 1 : a member of any of the Germanic peoples who invaded England in the 5th century A.D. 2 : a member of the English people 3 : Old English — **Anglo–Saxon** *adj*

an·go·ra \aŋ-ˈgȯr-ə, an-\ *n* 1 : yarn or cloth made from the hair of an Angora goat or rabbit 2 *cap* : any of a breed of cats, goats, or rabbits with a long silky coat

an·gry \'aŋ-grē\ *adj* **an·gri·er; -est** : feeling or showing anger ◆ *Synonyms* ENRAGED, WRATHFUL, IRATE, INDIGNANT, MAD — **an·gri·ly** \-grə-lē\ *adv*

angst \'äŋst\ *n* [G] : a feeling of anxiety

ang·strom \'aŋ-strəm\ *n* : a unit of length equal to one ten-billionth of a meter

an·guish \'aŋ-gwish\ *n* : extreme pain or distress esp. of mind — **an·guished** \-gwisht\ *adj*

an·gu·lar \'aŋ-gyə-lər\ *adj* 1 : sharp-cornered 2 : having one or more angles 3 : being thin and bony — **an·gu·lar·i·ty** \ˌaŋ-gyə-ˈler-ə-tē\ *n*

An·gus \'aŋ-gəs\ *n* : any of a breed of usu. black hornless beef cattle originating in Scotland

an·hy·drous \an-ˈhī-drəs\ *adj* : free from water

an·i·line \'a-nᵊl-ən\ *n* : an oily poisonous liquid used in making dyes, medicines, and explosives

an·i·mad·vert \ˌa-nə-ˌmad-ˈvərt\ *vb* : to remark critically : express censure — **an·i·mad·ver·sion** \-ˈvər-zhən\ *n*

¹**an·i·mal** \'a-nə-məl\ *n* 1 : any of a kingdom of living things typically differing from plants in capacity for active movement, in rapid response to stimulation, and in lack of cellulose cell walls 2 : a lower animal as distinguished from human beings; *also* : MAMMAL

²**animal** *adj* 1 : of, relating to, or derived from animals 2 : of or relating to the physical as distinguished from the mental or spiritual ◆ *Synonyms* CARNAL, FLESHLY, SENSUAL

an·i·mal·cule \ˌa-nə-ˈmal-kyül\ *n* : a tiny animal usu. invisible to the naked eye

¹**an·i·mate** \'a-nə-mət\ *adj* : having life

²**an·i·mate** \-ˌmāt\ *vb* **-mat·ed; -mat·ing** 1 : to impart life to 2 : to give spirit and vigor to 3 : to make appear to move ⟨∼ a cartoon for motion pictures⟩ — **an·i·mat·ed** *adj* — **an·i·mat·ed·ly** *adv*

an·i·ma·tion \ˌa-nə-ˈmā-shən\ *n* 1 : VIVACITY, LIVELINESS 2 : a motion picture made from a series of drawings simulating motions by means of slight progressive changes

an·i·ma·tron·ic \ˌa-nə-mə-ˈträ-nik\ *adj* : of, relating to, or being an electrically animated mechanical figure (as a puppet)

an·i·mism \'a-nə-ˌmi-zəm\ *n* : attribution of conscious life to objects in and phenomena of nature or to inanimate objects — **an·i·mist** \-mist\ *n* — **an·i·mis·tic** \ˌa-nə-ˈmis-tik\ *adj*

an·i·mos·i·ty \ˌa-nə-ˈmä-sə-tē\ *n, pl* **-ties** : ILL WILL, RESENTMENT

an·i·mus \'a-nə-məs\ *n* : deep-seated resentment and hostility

an·ion \'a-ˌnī-ən, -ˌnī-ˌän\ *n* : a negatively charged ion

an·ise \'a-nəs\ *n* : an herb related to the carrot with aromatic seeds (**aniseed** \-ˌsēd\) used in flavoring

an·is·ette \ˌa-nə-ˈset, -ˈzet\ *n* [F] : a usu. colorless sweet liqueur flavored with aniseed

ankh \'äŋk\ *n* : a cross having a loop for its upper vertical arm and serving esp. in ancient Egypt as an emblem of life

an·kle \'aŋ-kəl\ *n* : the joint or region between the foot and the leg

an·kle·bone \'aŋ-kəl-ˌbōn\ *n* : the bone that in human beings bears the weight of the body and with the tibia and fibula forms the ankle joint

an·klet \'aŋ-klət\ *n* 1 : something (as an ornament) worn around the ankle 2 : a short sock reaching slightly above the ankle

ann *abbr* 1 annals 2 annual

an·nals \'a-nᵊlz\ *n pl* 1 : a record of events in chronological order 2 : historical records — **an·nal·ist** \-nᵊl-ist\ *n*

an·neal \ə-ˈnēl\ *vb* 1 : to make (as glass or steel) less brittle by heating and then cooling 2 : STRENGTHEN, TOUGHEN

¹**an·nex** \ə-ˈneks, 'a-ˌneks\ *vb* 1 : to attach as an addition 2 : to incorporate (as a territory) within a political domain — **an·nex·a·tion** \ˌa-ˌnek-ˈsā-shən\ *n*

²**an·nex** \'a-ˌneks, -niks\ *n* : a subsidiary or supplementary structure

an·nexe *chiefly Brit var of* ANNEX

an·ni·hi·late \ə-ˈnī-ə-ˌlāt\ *vb* **-lat·ed; -lat·ing** : to destroy completely — **an·ni·hi·la·tion** \-ˌnī-ə-ˈlā-shən\ *n*

an·ni·ver·sa·ry \ˌa-nə-ˈvər-sə-rē\ *n, pl* **-ries** : the annual return of the date of a notable event and esp. a wedding

an·no Do·mi·ni \ˌa-nō-ˈdä-mə-nē, -ˈdō-, -ˌnī\ *adv, often cap A* [ML, in the year of the Lord] — used to indicate that a time division falls within the Christian era

an·no·tate \'a-nə-ˌtāt\ *vb* **-tat·ed; -tat·ing** : to furnish with notes — **an·no·ta·tion** \ˌa-nə-ˈtā-shən\ *n* — **an·no·ta·tor** \'a-nə-ˌtā-tər\ *n*

an·nounce \ə-ˈnau̇ns\ *vb* **an·nounced; an·nounc·ing** 1 : to make known publicly 2 : to give notice of the arrival or presence of — **an·nounce·ment** *n*

an·nounc·er \ə-ˈnau̇n-sər\ *n* : a person who introduces radio or television programs, makes commercial announcements, or gives station identification

an·noy \ə-ˈnȯi\ *vb* : to disturb or irritate esp. by repeated acts : VEX ◆ *Synonyms* IRK, BOTHER, PESTER, TEASE, HARASS — **an·noy·ing·ly** *adv*

an·noy·ance \ə-ˈnȯi-əns\ *n* 1 : the act of annoying 2 : the state of being annoyed 3 : NUISANCE ⟨the delay was a minor ∼⟩

¹**an·nu·al** \'an-yə-wəl\ *adj* 1 : covering the period of a year ⟨∼ rainfall⟩ 2 : occurring once a year : YEARLY 3 : completing the life cycle in one growing season ⟨∼ plants⟩ — **an·nu·al·ly** *adv*

²**annual** *n* 1 : a publication appearing once a year 2 : an annual plant

annual ring *n* : the layer of wood produced by a single year's growth of a woody plant

an·nu·i·tant \ə-ˈnü-ə-tənt, -ˈnyü-\ *n* : a beneficiary of an annuity

an·nu·i·ty \ə-ˈnü-ə-tē, -ˈnyü-\ *n, pl* **-ties** : an amount payable annually; *also* : the right to receive such a payment

an·nul \ə-ˈnəl\ *vb* **an·nulled; an·nul·ling** : to make legally void — **an·nul·ment** *n*

an·nu·lar \'an-yə-lər\ *adj* : ring-shaped

an·nun·ci·ate \ə-ˈnən-sē-ˌāt\ *vb* **-at·ed; -at·ing** : ANNOUNCE

an·nun·ci·a·tion \ə-ˌnən-sē-ˈā-shən\ *n* 1 *cap* : March 25 observed as a church festival commemorating the announcement of the Incarnation 2 : ANNOUNCEMENT

an·nun·ci·a·tor \ə-ˈnən-sē-ˌā-tər\ *n* : one that annunciates; *specif* : a usu. electrically controlled signal board or indicator

an·ode \'a-ˌnōd\ *n* 1 : the positive electrode of an electrolytic cell 2 : the negative terminal of a battery 3 : the electron-collecting electrode of an electron tube — **an·od·ic** \a-ˈnä-dik\ *also* **an·od·al** \-ˈnō-dᵊl\ *adj*

an·od·ize \'a-nə-ˌdīz\ *vb* **-ized; -iz·ing** : to subject (a metal) to electrolytic action as the anode of a cell in order to coat with a protective or decorative film

an·o·dyne \'a-nə-ˌdīn\ *n* : something that relieves pain : a soothing agent

anoint \ə-ˈnȯint\ vb **1** : to apply oil to esp. as a sacred rite **2** : CONSECRATE — **anoint·ment** n

anom·a·lous \ə-ˈnä-mə-ləs\ adj : deviating from a general rule : ABNORMAL

anom·a·ly \ə-ˈnä-mə-lē\ n, pl **-lies** : something anomalous : IRREGULARITY

¹**anon** \ə-ˈnän\ adv : SOON

²**anon** abbr anonymous; anonymously

anon·y·mous \ə-ˈnä-nə-məs\ adj : of unknown or undeclared origin or authorship — **an·o·nym·i·ty** \ˌa-nə-ˈni-mə-tē\ n — **anon·y·mous·ly** adv

anoph·e·les \ə-ˈnä-fə-ˌlēz\ n [NL, genus name, fr. Gk anōphelēs useless, fr. a- not + ophelos advantage, help] : any of a genus of mosquitoes that includes all mosquitoes which transmit malaria to human beings

an·o·rec·tic \ˌa-nə-ˈrek-tik\ adj : ANOREXIC — **anorectic** n

an·orex·ia \ˌa-nə-ˈrek-sē-ə\ n **1** : loss of appetite esp. when prolonged **2** : ANOREXIA NERVOSA

anorexia ner·vo·sa \-nər-ˈvō-sə\ n : a serious disorder in eating behavior marked esp. by a pathological fear of weight gain leading to faulty eating patterns, malnutrition, and usu. excessive weight loss

an·orex·ic \ˌa-nə-ˈrek-sik\ adj **1** : lacking or causing loss of appetite **2** : affected with or as if with anorexia nervosa — **anorexic** n

¹**an·oth·er** \ə-ˈnə-thər\ adj **1** : some other ⟨do it ∼ time⟩ **2** : being one in addition : one more ⟨∼ piece of pie⟩

²**another** pron **1** : an additional one : one more **2** : one that is different from the first or present one

ans abbr answer

¹**an·swer** \ˈan-sər\ n **1** : something spoken or written in reply to a question **2** : a solution of a problem

²**answer** vb **1** : to speak or write in reply to **2** : to be responsible **3** : to be adequate — **an·swer·er** n

an·swer·able \ˈan-sə-rə-bəl\ adj **1** : subject to taking blame or responsibility **2** : capable of being refuted

answering machine n : a machine that receives telephone calls by playing a recorded message and usu. by recording messages from callers

answering service n : a commercial service that answers telephone calls for its clients

¹**ant** \ˈant\ n : any of a family of small social insects related to the bees and living in communities usu. in earth or wood

²**ant** abbr antonym

Ant abbr Antarctica

ant- — see ANTI-

¹**-ant** n suffix **1** : one that performs or promotes (a specified action) ⟨coolant⟩ **2** : thing that is acted upon (in a specified manner) ⟨inhalant⟩

²**-ant** adj suffix **1** : performing (a specified action) or being (in a specified condition) ⟨propellant⟩ **2** : promoting (a specified action or process) ⟨expectorant⟩

ant·ac·id \ant-ˈa-səd\ n : an agent that counteracts acidity — **antacid** adj

an·tag·o·nism \an-ˈta-gə-ˌni-zəm\ n **1** : active opposition or hostility **2** : opposition in physiological action — **an·tag·o·nis·tic** \-ˌta-gə-ˈnis-tik\ adj

an·tag·o·nist \-nist\ n : ADVERSARY, OPPONENT

an·tag·o·nize \an-ˈta-gə-ˌnīz\ vb **-nized; -niz·ing** : to provoke the hostility of

ant·arc·tic \ant-ˈärk-tik, -ˈär-tik\ adj, often cap : of or relating to the south pole or the region near it

antarctic circle n, often cap A&C : the parallel of latitude that is approximately 66½ degrees south of the equator

¹**an·te** \ˈan-tē\ n : a poker stake put up before the deal to build the pot; also : an amount paid : PRICE

²**ante** vb **an·ted; an·te·ing 1** : to put up (an ante) **2** : PAY

ant·eat·er \ˈant-ˌē-tər\ n : any of several mammals (as an aardvark) that feed mostly on ants or termites

an·te·bel·lum \ˌan-ti-ˈbe-ləm\ adj : existing before a war; esp : existing before the U.S. Civil War of 1861-65

an·te·ced·ent \ˌan-tə-ˈsē-d³nt\ n **1** : a noun, pronoun, phrase, or clause referred to by a personal or relative pronoun **2** : a preceding event or cause **3** pl : the significant conditions of one's earlier life **4** pl : ANCESTORS — **antecedent** adj

an·te·cham·ber \ˈan-ti-ˌchām-bər\ n : ANTEROOM

an·te·date \ˈan-ti-ˌdāt\ vb **1** : to date (a paper) as of an earlier day than that on which the actual writing or signing is done **2** : to precede in time

an·te·di·lu·vi·an \ˌan-ti-də-ˈlü-vē-ən, -dī-\ adj **1** : of the period before the biblical flood **2** : ANTIQUATED

an·te·lope \ˈan-tə-ˌlōp\ n, pl **-lope** or **-lopes** [ME, fabulous heraldic beast, prob. fr. MF antelop savage animal with sawlike horns, fr. ML anthalopus, fr. LGk antholops] **1** : any of various deerlike ruminant mammals that chiefly inhabit Africa and have a slender build and horns extending upward and backward **2** : PRONGHORN

an·te me·ri·di·em \ˈan-ti-mə-ˈri-dē-əm\ adj [L] : being before noon

an·ten·na \an-ˈte-nə\ n, pl **-nae** \-(ˌ)nē\ or **-nas** [ML, fr. L, sail yard] **1** : one of the long slender paired segmented sensory organs on the head of an arthropod (as an insect or crab) **2** pl usu **-nas** : a metallic device (as a rod or wire) for sending out or receiving radio waves

an·te·pe·nult \ˌan-ti-ˈpē-ˌnəlt\ also **an·te·pen·ul·ti·ma** \-pi-ˈnəl-tə-mə\ n : the 3d syllable of a word counting from the end — **an·te·pen·ul·ti·mate** \-pi-ˈnəl-tə-mət\ adj or n

an·te·ri·or \an-ˈtir-ē-ər\ adj **1** : situated before or toward the front **2** : situated near or nearer to the head **3** : coming before in time ◆ **Synonyms** PRECEDING, PREVIOUS, PRIOR, ANTECEDENT

anterior cruciate ligament n : a cross-shaped ligament of the knee that connects the tibia and femur

an·te·room \ˈan-ti-ˌrüm, -ˌrum\ n : a room forming the entrance to another and often used as a waiting room

an·them \ˈan-thəm\ n **1** : a sacred vocal composition **2** : a song or hymn of praise or gladness

an·ther \ˈan-thər\ n : the part of a stamen of a seed plant that produces and contains pollen

ant·hill \ˈant-ˌhil\ n : a mound thrown up by ants or termites in digging their nest

an·thol·o·gy \an-ˈthä-lə-jē\ n, pl **-gies** [NL anthologia collection of epigrams, fr. MGk, fr. Gk, flower gathering, fr. anthos flower + logia collecting, fr. legein to gather] : a collection of literary selections — **an·thol·o·gist** \-jist\ n — **an·thol·o·gize** \-ˌjīz\ vb

an·thra·cite \ˈan-thrə-ˌsīt\ n : a hard glossy coal that burns without much smoke

an·thrax \ˈan-ˌthraks\ n : an infectious and usu. fatal bacterial disease of warm-blooded animals (as cattle and sheep) that is transmissible to humans; also : a bacterium causing anthrax

an·thro·po·cen·tric \ˌan-thrə-pə-ˈsen-trik\ adj : interpreting or regarding the world in terms of human values and experiences

an·thro·poid \ˈan-thrə-ˌpȯid\ n **1** : any of several large tailless apes (as a gorilla) **2** : a person resembling an ape — **anthropoid** adj

an·thro·pol·o·gy \ˌan-thrə-ˈpä-lə-jē\ n : the science of human beings and esp. of their physical characteristics, their origin and ancestry, their environment and social relations, and their culture — **an·thro·po·log·i·cal** \-pə-ˈlä-ji-kəl\ adj — **an·thro·pol·o·gist** \-ˈpä-lə-jist\ n

an·thro·po·mor·phism \ˌan-thrə-pə-ˈmȯr-ˌfi-zəm\ n : an interpretation of what is not human or personal in terms of human or personal characteristics : HUMANIZATION — **an·thro·po·mor·phic** \-fik\ adj

an·ti \ˈan-ˌtī, -tē\ n, pl **antis** : one who is opposed

anti- \ˌan-ti, -tē, ˌtī\ or **ant-** or **anth-** prefix **1** : opposite in kind, position, or action **2** : opposing : hostile toward **3** : counteractive **4** : preventive : curative of

antiaging	antigovernment
anti-AIDS	anti-HIV
antiaircraft	anti-imperialism
antialcohol	anti-imperialist
anti-American	antiknock
antianxiety	antilabor
antiapartheid	antimalarial
antibacterial	antimicrobial
anticapitalist	antinausea
anti-Catholic	antipoverty
anticholesterol	antislavery
anticlerical	antispasmodic
anticolonial	antistatic
anticommunism	antisubmarine
anticommunist	antitank
antidemocratic	antitumor
antidiscrimination	antiviral
antiestablishment	antiwar
antifascist	

an·ti·abor·tion \ˌan-tē-ə-ˈbȯr-shən, ˌan-ˌtī-\ *adj* : opposed to abortion — **an·ti·abor·tion·ist** \-shə-nist\ *n*

an·ti·bal·lis·tic missile \ˌan-ti-bə-ˈlis-tik-, ˌan-ˌtī-\ *n* : a missile for intercepting and destroying ballistic missiles

an·ti·bi·ot·ic \-ˌbī-ˈä-tik, -bē-\ *n* : a substance produced by or derived by chemical alteration of a substance produced by a microorganism (as a fungus or bacterium) that in dilute solution inhibits or kills another microorganism — **antibiotic** *adj*

an·ti·body \ˈan-ti-ˌbä-dē\ *n* : any of a large number of proteins of high molecular weight produced normally by specialized B cells after stimulation by an antigen and acting specifically against the antigen in an immune response

¹**an·tic** \ˈan-tik\ *n* [It *antico* ancient thing or person, fr. *antico* ancient, fr. L *antiquus*] : an often wildly playful or funny act or action

²**antic** *adj* **1** *archaic* : GROTESQUE **2** : PLAYFUL

an·ti·can·cer \ˌan-ti-ˈkan-sər, ˌan-ˌtī-\ *adj* : used against or tending to arrest or prevent cancer ⟨∼ drugs⟩

An·ti·christ \ˈan-ti-ˌkrīst\ *n* **1** : one who denies or opposes Christ **2** : a false Christ

an·tic·i·pate \an-ˈti-sə-ˌpāt\ *vb* **-pat·ed; -pat·ing 1** : to foresee and provide for beforehand ⟨∼s problems⟩ **2** : to look forward to — **an·tic·i·pa·tion** \-ˌti-sə-ˈpā-shən\ *n* — **an·tic·i·pa·to·ry** \-ˈti-sə-pə-ˌtȯr-ē\ *adj*

an·ti·cli·max \ˌan-ti-ˈklī-ˌmaks\ *n* : something (as the ending of a story) that is strikingly less important or dramatic than expected — **an·ti·cli·mac·tic** \-klī-ˈmak-tik\ *adj*

an·ti·cline \ˈan-ti-ˌklīn\ *n* : an arch of layers of rock in the earth's crust

an·ti·co·ag·u·lant \ˌan-ti-kō-ˈa-gyə-lənt\ *n* : a substance that hinders the clotting of blood — **anticoagulant** *adj*

an·ti·cy·clone \ˌan-ti-ˈsī-ˌklōn\ *n* : a system of winds that rotates about a center of high atmospheric pressure — **an·ti·cy·clon·ic** \-sī-ˈklä-nik\ *adj*

an·ti·de·pres·sant \ˌan-ti-di-ˈpres-ᵊnt, ˌan-ˌtī-\ *n* : a drug used to relieve psychic depression — **antidepressant** *adj*

an·ti·dote \ˈan-ti-ˌdōt\ *n* : a remedy to counteract the effects of poison

an·ti·drug \ˈan-ˌtī-ˌdrəg\ *adj* : acting against or opposing illicit drugs

an·ti·fer·til·i·ty \ˌan-ti-fər-ˈti-lə-tē\ *adj* : tending to reduce or destroy fertility : CONTRACEPTIVE ⟨∼ agents⟩

an·ti·freeze \ˈan-ti-ˌfrēz\ *n* : a substance added to a liquid to lower its freezing temperature

an·ti·fun·gal \ˌan-tē-ˈfəŋ-gəl, ˌan-ˌtī-\ *n* : FUNGICIDE — **antifungal** *adj*

an·ti·gen \ˈan-ti-jən\ *n* : any substance (as a toxin) foreign to the body that induces an immune response — **an·ti·gen·ic** \ˌan-ti-ˈje-nik\ *adj* — **an·ti·ge·nic·i·ty** \-jə-ˈni-sə-tē\ *n*

an·ti·grav·i·ty \ˌan-ti-ˈgra-və-tē, ˌan-ˌtī-\ *adj* : reducing or canceling the effect of gravity

an·ti·he·ro \ˈan-ti-ˌhē-rō, ˈan-ˌtī-\ *n* : a protagonist who is notably lacking in heroic qualities (as courage)

an·ti·his·ta·mine \ˌan-ti-ˈhis-tə-mēn, ˌan-ˌtī-, -mən\ *n* : any of various drugs used in treating allergies and colds — **antihistamine** *adj*

an·ti·hy·per·ten·sive \-ˌhī-pər-ˈten-siv\ *n* : a substance that is effective against high blood pressure — **antihypertensive** *adj*

an·ti–in·flam·ma·to·ry \-in-ˈfla-mə-ˌtȯr-ē\ *adj* : counteracting inflammation — **anti–inflammatory** *n*

an·ti–in·tel·lec·tu·al \-ˌin-tə-ˈlek-chə-wəl\ *adj* : opposing or hostile to intellectuals or to an intellectual view or approach

an·ti·lock \ˈan-ti-ˌläk, ˈan-ˌtī-\ *adj* : being a braking system designed to prevent the wheels from locking

an·ti·log·a·rithm \ˌan-ti-ˈlȯ-gə-ˌri-thəm, ˌan-ˌtī-, -ˈlä-\ *n* : the number corresponding to a given logarithm ⟨if the logarithm in base *x* of *a* equals *b* then the antilogarithm in base *x* of *b* equals *a*⟩

an·ti·ma·cas·sar \ˌan-ti-mə-ˈka-sər\ *n* : a cover to protect the back or arms of furniture

an·ti·mat·ter \ˈan-ti-ˌma-tər, ˈan-ˌtī-\ *n* : matter composed of antiparticles

an·ti·mo·ny \ˈan-tə-ˌmō-nē\ *n* : a brittle silvery white metallic chemical element used esp. in alloys

an·ti·neu·tron \ˌan-ti-ˈnü-ˌträn, ˌan-ˌtī-, -ˈnyü-\ *n* : the antiparticle of the neutron

an·ti·no·mi·an \ˌan-ti-ˈnō-mē-ən\ *n* : one who denies the validity of moral laws

an·tin·o·my \an-ˈti-nə-mē\ *n, pl* **-mies** : a contradiction between two seemingly true statements

an·ti·nov·el \ˈan-ti-ˌnä-vəl, ˈan-ˌtī-\ *n* : a work of fiction that lacks all or most of the traditional features of the novel

an·ti·nu·cle·ar \ˌan-ti-ˈnü-klē-ər, -ˈnyü-\ *adj* : opposing the use or production of nuclear power

an·ti·ox·i·dant \ˌan-tē-ˈäk-sə-dənt, ˌan-ˌtī-\ *n* : a substance that inhibits oxidation — **antioxidant** *adj*

an·ti·par·ti·cle \ˈan-ti-ˌpär-ti-kəl, ˈan-ˌtī-\ *n* : a subatomic particle identical to another subatomic particle in mass but opposite to it in electric and magnetic properties

an·ti·pas·to \ˌan-ti-ˈpas-tō, ˌän-ti-ˈpäs-\ *n, pl* **-ti** \-ˌ(ˌ)tē\ : any of various typically Italian hors d'oeuvres

an·tip·a·thy \an-ˈti-pə-thē\ *n, pl* **-thies 1** : settled aversion or dislike **2** : an object of aversion — **an·ti·pa·thet·ic** \ˌan-ti-pə-ˈthe-tik\ *adj*

an·ti·per·son·nel \ˌan-ti-ˌpər-sə-ˈnel, ˌan-ˌtī-\ *adj* : designed for use against military personnel ⟨∼ mine⟩

an·ti·per·spi·rant \-ˈpər-spə-rənt\ *n* : a preparation used to reduce perspiration

an·tiph·o·nal \an-ˈti-fə-nᵊl\ *adj* : performed by two alternating groups — **an·tiph·o·nal·ly** *adv*

an·ti·pode \ˈan-tə-ˌpōd\ *n, pl* **an·tip·o·des** \an-ˈti-pə-ˌdēz\ [ME *antipodes,* pl., persons dwelling at opposite points on the globe, fr. L, fr. Gk, fr. pl. of *antipod-, antipous* with feet opposite, fr. *anti-* against + *pod-, pous* foot] : the parts of the earth diametrically opposite — usu. used in pl. — **an·tip·o·dal** \an-ˈti-pə-dᵊl\ *adj* — **an·tip·o·de·an** \-(ˌ)an-ˌti-pə-ˈdē-ən\ *adj*

an·ti·pol·lu·tion \ˌan-ti-pə-ˈlü-shən\ *adj* : designed to prevent, reduce, or eliminate pollution ⟨∼ laws⟩

an·ti·pope \ˈan-ti-ˌpōp\ *n* : one elected or claiming to be pope in opposition to the pope canonically chosen

an·ti·pro·ton \ˌan-ti-ˈprō-ˌtän\ *n* : the antiparticle of the proton

an·ti·psy·chot·ic \ˌan-tē-sī-ˈkä-tik\ *n* : any of the powerful tranquilizers used to treat psychosis — **antipsychotic** *adj*

an·ti·quar·i·an \ˌan-tə-ˈkwer-ē-ən\ *adj* **1** : of or relating to antiquities **2** : dealing in old books — **antiquarian** *n* — **an·ti·quar·i·an·ism** *n*

an·ti·quary \ˈan-tə-ˌkwer-ē\ *n, pl* **-quar·ies** : a person who collects or studies antiquities

an·ti·quat·ed \ˈan-tə-ˌkwā-təd\ *adj* : OUT-OF-DATE, OLD=FASHIONED

¹**an·tique** \an-ˈtēk\ *n* : an object made in a bygone period

²**antique** *adj* **1** : belonging to antiquity **2** : OLD-FASHIONED **3** : of a bygone style or period

³**antique** *vb* **-tiqued; -tiqu·ing 1** : to finish or refinish in antique style : give an appearance of age to **2** : to shop around for antiques — **an·tiqu·er** *n*

an·tiq·ui·ty \an-ˈti-kwə-tē\ *n, pl* **-ties 1** : ancient times **2** : great age **3** *pl* : relics of ancient times **4** *pl* : matters relating to ancient culture

an·ti·ret·ro·vi·ral \ˌan-tē-ˈre-trō-ˌvī-rəl, ˌan-ˌtī-\ *adj* : effective against retroviruses ⟨∼ drugs⟩ — **antiretroviral** *n*

antis *pl of* ANTI

an·ti–Sem·i·tism \ˌan-ti-ˈse-mə-ˌti-zəm, ˌan-ˌtī-\ *n* : hostility toward Jews as a religious or social minority — **an·ti–Sem·ite** \-ˈse-ˌmīt\ *n* — **an·ti–Se·mit·ic** \-sə-ˈmi-tik\ *adj*

an·ti·sep·tic \ˌan-tə-ˈsep-tik\ *adj* **1** : killing or checking the growth of germs that cause decay or infection **2** : scrupulously clean : ASEPTIC **3** : coldly impersonal ⟨an ∼ greeting⟩ — **antiseptic** *n* — **an·ti·sep·ti·cal·ly** *adv*

an·ti·se·rum \ˈan-ti-ˌsir-əm, ˈan-ˌtī-\ *n* : a serum containing antibodies

an·ti·so·cial \ˌan-ti-ˈsō-shəl\ *adj* **1** : disliking the society of others **2** : contrary or hostile to the well-being of society ⟨crime is ∼⟩; *esp* : deviating sharply from the social norm — **an·ti·so·cial·ly** *adv*

an·tith·e·sis \an-ˈti-thə-səs\ *n, pl* **-e·ses** \-ˌsēz\ **1** : the opposition or contrast of ideas **2** : the direct opposite

an·ti·thet·i·cal \ˌan-tə-ˈthe-ti-kəl\ *also* **an·ti·thet·ic** \-tik\ *adj* : constituting or marked by antithesis — **an·ti·thet·i·cal·ly** \-ti-k(ə-)lē\ *adv*

an·ti·tox·in \ˌan-ti-ˈtäk-sən\ *n* : an antibody that is able to neutralize a particular toxin or disease-causing agent; *also* : an antiserum containing an antitoxin

an·ti·trust \ˌan-ti-ˈtrəst\ *adj* : of or relating to legislation against trusts; *also* : consisting of laws to protect trade and commerce from unlawful restraints and monopolies or unfair business practices

an·ti·ven·in \-ˈve-nən\ *n* : an antitoxin to a venom; *also* : a serum containing such antitoxin

ant·ler \ˈant-lər\ *n* [ME *aunteler,* fr. AF *antiler,* fr. VL *anteocularis located before the eye, fr. L *ante-* before + *oculus* eye] : one of the paired deciduous solid bone processes on the head of a deer; *also* : a branch of this — **ant·lered** \-lərd\ *adj*

ant lion *n* : any of various insects having a long-jawed larva that digs a conical pit in which it lies in wait for insects (as ants) on which it feeds

an·to·nym \ˈan-tə-ˌnim\ *n* : a word of opposite meaning

ant·sy \ˈant-sē\ *adj* **1** : RESTLESS, IMPATIENT ⟨~ children⟩ **2** : APPREHENSIVE ⟨~ investors⟩

anus \ˈā-nəs\ *n* [L] : the lower or posterior opening of the alimentary canal

an·vil \ˈan-vəl\ *n* **1** : a heavy iron block on which metal is shaped **2** : INCUS

anx·i·ety \aŋ-ˈzī-ə-tē\ *n, pl* **-et·ies 1** : painful uneasiness of mind usu. over an anticipated ill **2** : abnormal apprehension and fear often accompanied by physiological signs (as sweating and increased pulse), by doubt about the nature and reality of the threat itself, and by self-doubt

anx·ious \ˈaŋk-shəs\ *adj* **1** : uneasy in mind : WORRIED ⟨~ parents⟩ **2** : earnestly wishing : EAGER ⟨~ to leave⟩ — **anx·ious·ly** *adv*

¹any \ˈe-nē\ *adj* **1** : one chosen at random **2** : of whatever number or quantity

²any *pron* **1** : any one or ones ⟨take ~ of the books you like⟩ **2** : any amount ⟨~ of the money not used is to be returned⟩

³any *adv* : to any extent or degree : AT ALL ⟨could not walk ~ farther⟩

any·body \-ˌbä-dē, -bə-\ *pron* : ANYONE

any·how \-ˌhau̇\ *adv* **1** : in any way **2** : NEVERTHELESS; *also* : in any case

any·more \ˌe-nē-ˈmȯr\ *adv* **1** : any longer ⟨won't bother you ~⟩ **2** : at the present time

any·one \ˈe-nē-(ˌ)wən\ *pron* : any person

any·place \-ˌplās\ *adv* : ANYWHERE 1

any·thing \-ˌthiŋ\ *pron* : any thing whatever

any·time \ˈe-nē-ˌtīm\ *adv* : at any time whatever

any·way \-ˌwā\ *adv* : ANYHOW

any·where \-ˌhwer\ *adv* **1** : in or to any place **2** : to any extent ⟨not ~ near done⟩

any·wise \-ˌwīz\ *adv* : in any way whatever

A–OK \ˌā-ō-ˈkā\ *adv or adj* : very definitely OK

A1 \ˈā-ˈwən\ *adj* : of the finest quality

aor·ta \ā-ˈȯr-tə\ *n, pl* **-tas** *or* **-tae** \-tē\ : the main artery that carries blood from the heart — **aor·tic** \-tik\ *adj*

ap *abbr* **1** apostle **2** apothecaries'

AP *abbr* **1** American plan **2** Associated Press

apace \ə-ˈpās\ *adv* : SWIFTLY

Apache \ə-ˈpa-chē\ *n, pl* **Apache** *or* **Apach·es** \-ˈpa-chēz, -ˈpa-shəz\ : a member of an American Indian people of the southwestern U.S.; *also* : any of the languages of the Apache people — **Apach·e·an** \ə-ˈpa-chē-ən\ *adj or n*

apanage *var of* APPANAGE

apart \ə-ˈpärt\ *adv* **1** : separately in place or time **2** : ASIDE **3** : in two or more parts : to pieces

apart·heid \ə-ˈpär-ˌtāt, -ˌtīt\ *n* [Afrikaans] : a policy of racial segregation formerly practiced in the Republic of So. Africa

apart·ment \ə-ˈpärt-mənt\ *n* : a room or set of rooms occupied as a dwelling; *also* : a building divided into individual dwelling units

ap·a·thy \ˈa-pə-thē\ *n* **1** : lack of emotion **2** : lack of interest : INDIFFERENCE — **ap·a·thet·ic** \ˌa-pə-ˈthe-tik\ *adj* — **ap·a·thet·i·cal·ly** \-ti-k(ə-)lē\ *adv*

ap·a·tite \ˈa-pə-ˌtīt\ *n* : any of a group of minerals that are phosphates of calcium and occur esp. in phosphate rock and in bones and teeth

apato·sau·rus \ə-ˌpa-tə-ˈsȯr-əs\ *n* : BRONTOSAURUS

APB *abbr* all points bulletin

¹ape \ˈāp\ *n* **1** : any of the larger tailless primates (as a baboon or gorilla); *also* : MONKEY **2** : MIMIC, IMITATOR; *also* : a large uncouth person

²ape *vb* **aped; ap·ing** : IMITATE, MIMIC

ape–man \ˈāp-ˌman\ *n* : a primate intermediate in character between Homo sapiens and the higher apes

aper·çu \ˌa-pər-ˈsü\ *n, pl* **aperçus** \-ˈsüz\ : an immediate impression; *esp* : INSIGHT

aper·i·tif \ä-ˌper-ə-ˈtēf\ *n* : an alcoholic drink taken as an appetizer

ap·er·ture \ˈa-pər-ˌchu̇r, -chər\ *n* : OPENING, HOLE

apex \ˈā-ˌpeks\ *n, pl* **apex·es** *or* **api·ces** \ˈā-pə-ˌsēz, ˈa-\ : the highest point : PEAK

apha·sia \ə-ˈfā-zh(ē-)ə\ *n* : loss or impairment of the power to use or comprehend words — **apha·sic** \-zik\ *adj or n*

aph·elion \a-ˈfēl-yən\ *n, pl* **-elia** \-yə\ [NL, fr. *apo-* away from + Gk *hēlios* sun] : the point in an object's orbit most distant from the sun

aphid \ˈā-fəd\ *n* : any of numerous small insects that suck the juices of plants

aphis \ˈā-fəs, ˈa-\ *n, pl* **aphi·des** \-fə-ˌdēz\ : APHID

aph·o·rism \ˈa-fə-ˌri-zəm\ *n* : a short saying stating a general truth : MAXIM — **aph·o·ris·tic** \ˌa-fə-ˈris-tik\ *adj*

aph·ro·di·si·ac \ˌa-frə-ˈdi-zē-ˌak, -ˈdē-zē-\ *n* : an agent that excites sexual desire — **aphrodisiac** *adj*

api·ary \ˈā-pē-ˌer-ē\ *n, pl* **-ar·ies** : a place where bees are kept — **api·a·rist** \-pē-ə-rist\ *n*

api·cal \ˈā-pi-kəl, ˈa-\ *adj* : of, relating to, or situated at an apex — **api·cal·ly** \-k(ə-)lē\ *adv*

apiece \ə-ˈpēs\ *adv* : for each one

aplen·ty \ə-ˈplen-tē\ *adj* : being in plenty or abundance

aplomb \ə-ˈpläm, -ˈpləm\ *n* [F, lit., perpendicularity, fr. MF, fr. *a plomb,* lit., according to the plummet] : complete composure or self-assurance

APO *abbr* army post office

Apoc *abbr* **1** Apocalypse **2** Apocrypha

apoc·a·lypse \ə-ˈpä-kə-ˌlips\ *n* **1** : a writing prophesying a cataclysm in which evil forces are destroyed **2** *cap* — see BIBLE table — **apoc·a·lyp·tic** \-ˌpä-kə-ˈlip-tik\ *also* **apoc·a·lyp·ti·cal** \-ti-kəl\ *adj*

Apoc·ry·pha \ə-ˈpä-krə-fə\ *n* **1** *not cap* : writings of dubious authenticity **2** : books included in the Septuagint and Vulgate but excluded from the Jewish and Protestant canons of the Old Testament — see BIBLE table **3** : early Christian writings not included in the New Testament

apoc·ry·phal \-fəl\ *adj* **1** : not canonical : SPURIOUS **2** *often cap* : of or resembling the Apocrypha — **apoc·ry·phal·ly** *adv* — **apoc·ry·phal·ness** *n*

apo·gee \ˈa-pə-(ˌ)jē\ *n* [F *apogée,* fr. NL *apogaeum,* fr. Gk *apogaion,* fr. *apo* away from + *gē, gaia* earth] : the point at which an orbiting object is farthest from the body being orbited

apo·lit·i·cal \ˌā-pə-ˈli-ti-kəl\ *adj* **1** : having an aversion for or no interest in political affairs **2** : having no political significance — **apo·lit·i·cal·ly** \-k(ə-)lē\ *adv*

apol·o·get·ic \ə-ˌpä-lə-ˈje-tik\ *adj* : expressing apology — **apol·o·get·i·cal·ly** \-ti-k(ə-)lē\ *adv*

ap·o·lo·gia \ˌa-pə-ˈlō-j(ē-)ə\ *n* : APOLOGY; *esp* : an argument in support or justification

apol·o·gise *Brit var of* APOLOGIZE

apol·o·gize \ə-ˈpä-lə-ˌjīz\ *vb* **-gized; -giz·ing** : to make an apology : express regret — **apol·o·gist** \-jist\ *n*

apol·o·gy \ə-ˈpä-lə-jē\ *n, pl* **-gies 1** : a formal justification : DEFENSE **2** : an expression of regret for a wrong

ap·o·plexy \ˈa-pə-ˌplek-sē\ *n* : STROKE 3 — **ap·o·plec·tic** \ˌa-pə-ˈplek-tik\ *adj*

ap·o·pto·sis \ˌa-pəp-ˈtō-səs, -pə-ˈtō-\ *n, pl* **-pto·ses** \-ˌsēz\ : a genetically directed process of cell self-destruction

aport \ə-ˈpȯrt\ *adv* : on or toward the left side of a ship

apos·ta·sy \ə-ˈpäs-tə-sē\ *n, pl* **-sies** : a renunciation or abandonment of a former loyalty (as to a religion) — **apos·tate** \ə-ˈpäs-ˌtāt, -tət\ *adj or n*

a pos·te·ri·o·ri \ˌä-pō-ˌstir-ē-ˈȯr-ē\ *adj* [L, lit., from the latter] : relating to or derived by reasoning from observed facts — **a posteriori** *adv*

apos·tle \ə-ˈpä-səl\ *n* **1** : one of the group composed of Jesus' 12 original disciples and Paul **2** : the first prominent missionary to a region or group **3** : a person who initiates or first advocates a great reform — **apos·tle·ship** *n*

ap·os·tol·ic \ˌa-pəs-ˈtä-lik\ *adj* **1** : of or relating to an apostle or to the New Testament apostles **2** : of or relating to a succession of spiritual authority from the apostles **3** : PAPAL

¹apos·tro·phe \ə-ˈpäs-trə-(ˌ)fē\ *n* : the rhetorical addressing of a usu. absent person or a usu. personified thing (as in "O grave, where is thy victory?")

²**apostrophe** *n* : a punctuation mark ' used esp. to indicate the possessive case or the omission of a letter or figure

apos·tro·phise *Brit var of* APOSTROPHIZE

apos·tro·phize \ə-'päs-trə-ˌfīz\ *vb* **-phized; -phiz·ing** : to address as if present or capable of understanding

apothecaries' weight *n* : a system of weights based on the troy pound and ounce and used chiefly by pharmacists — see WEIGHT table

apoth·e·cary \ə-'pä-thə-ˌker-ē\ *n, pl* **-car·ies** [ME *apothecarie*, fr. ML *apothecarius*, fr. LL, shopkeeper, fr. L *apotheca* storehouse, fr. Gk *apothēkē*, fr. *apotithenai* to put away] : DRUGGIST

ap·o·thegm \'a-pə-ˌthem\ *n* : APHORISM

apo·the·o·sis \ə-ˌpä-thē-'ō-səs, ˌa-pə-'thē-ə-səs\ *n, pl* **-o·ses** \-ˌsēz\ **1** : DEIFICATION **2** : the perfect example

¹**app** \'ap\ *n* : APPLICATION 6

²**app** *abbr* **1** apparatus **2** appendix

ap·pall *also* **ap·pal** \ə-'pól\ *vb* **ap·palled; ap·pall·ing** : to overcome with horror : DISMAY

Ap·pa·loo·sa \ˌa-pə-'lü-sə\ *n* : any of a breed of saddle horses developed in western No. America and usu. having a white or solid-colored coat with small spots

ap·pa·nage *also* **a·pa·nage** \'a-pə-nij\ *n* **1** : provision (as a grant of land) made by a sovereign or legislative body for dependent members of the royal family **2** : a rightful adjunct

ap·pa·ra·tus \ˌa-pə-'ra-təs, -'rä-\ *n, pl* **-tus·es** *or* **-tus** [L] **1** : a set of materials or equipment for a particular use **2** : a complex machine or device : MECHANISM **3** : the organization of a political party or underground movement

¹**ap·par·el** \ə-'per-əl\ *vb* **-eled** *or* **-elled; -el·ing** *or* **-el·ling** **1** : CLOTHE **2** : ADORN

²**apparel** *n* : CLOTHING, DRESS

ap·par·ent \ə-'per-ənt\ *adj* **1** : open to view : VISIBLE **2** : EVIDENT, OBVIOUS **3** : appearing as real or true : SEEMING

ap·par·ent·ly \-lē\ *adv* : it seems apparent

ap·pa·ri·tion \ˌa-pə-'ri-shən\ *n* : a supernatural appearance : GHOST

ap·peal \ə-'pēl\ *vb* **1** : to take steps to have (a case) reheard in a higher court **2** : to plead for help, corroboration, or decision **3** : to arouse a sympathetic response — **appeal** *n*

ap·pear \ə-'pir\ *vb* **1** : to become visible **2** : to come formally before an authority **3** : SEEM **4** : to become evident **5** : to come before the public

ap·pear·ance \ə-'pir-əns\ *n* **1** : outward aspect : LOOK **2** : the act of appearing **3** : PHENOMENON

ap·pease \ə-'pēz\ *vb* **ap·peased; ap·peas·ing** **1** : to cause to subside : ALLAY **2** : PACIFY, CONCILIATE; *esp* : to buy off by concessions — **ap·pease·ment** *n* — **ap·peas·able** \-'pē-zə-bəl\ *adj*

ap·pel·lant \ə-'pe-lənt\ *n* : one who appeals esp. from a judicial decision

ap·pel·late \ə-'pe-lət\ *adj* : having power to review decisions of a lower court

ap·pel·la·tion \ˌa-pə-'lā-shən\ *n* : NAME, DESIGNATION

ap·pel·lee \ˌa-pə-'lē\ *n* : one against whom an appeal is taken

ap·pend \ə-'pend\ *vb* : to attach esp. as something additional : AFFIX

ap·pend·age \ə-'pen-dij\ *n* **1** : something appended to a principal or greater thing **2** : a projecting part (as an antenna) of an animal or plant body; *esp* : an arm, leg, or similar part ♦ *Synonyms* ACCESSORY, ADJUNCT, APPENDIX, APPURTENANCE

ap·pen·dec·to·my \ˌa-pən-'dek-tə-mē\ *n, pl* **-mies** : surgical removal of the intestinal appendix

ap·pen·di·ci·tis \ə-ˌpen-də-'sī-təs\ *n* : inflammation of the intestinal appendix

ap·pen·dix \ə-'pen-diks\ *n, pl* **-dix·es** *or* **-di·ces** \-də-ˌsēz\ [L] **1** : supplementary matter added at the end of a book **2** : a narrow blind tube usu. about three or four inches long that extends from the cecum in the lower right-hand part of the abdomen

ap·per·tain \ˌa-pər-'tān\ *vb* : to belong as a rightful part or privilege

ap·pe·tis·er, ap·pe·tis·ing *Brit var of* APPETIZER, APPETIZING

ap·pe·tite \'a-pə-ˌtīt\ *n* [ME *apetit*, fr. AF, fr. L *appetitus*, fr. *appetere* to strive after, fr. *ad-* to + *petere* to go to] **1** : natural desire for satisfying some want or need esp. for food **2** : TASTE, PREFERENCE

ap·pe·tiz·er \'a-pə-ˌtī-zər\ *n* : a food or drink taken just before a meal to stimulate the appetite

ap·pe·tiz·ing \-zin\ *adj* : tempting to the appetite — **ap·pe·tiz·ing·ly** *adv*

appl *abbr* applied

ap·plaud \ə-'plód\ *vb* : to show approval esp. by clapping

ap·plause \ə-'plòz\ *n* : approval publicly expressed (as by clapping)

ap·ple \'a-pəl\ *n* : a rounded fruit with firm white flesh and a seedy core; *also* : a tree that bears this fruit

ap·ple·jack \-ˌjak\ *n* : a liquor distilled from fermented cider

ap·plet \'a-plət\ *n* : a short computer program esp. for performing a simple specific task

ap·pli·ance \ə-'plī-əns\ *n* **1** : INSTRUMENT, DEVICE **2** : a piece of household equipment (as a stove or toaster) operated by gas or electricity

ap·pli·ca·ble \'a-pli-kə-bəl, ə-'pli-kə-\ *adj* : capable of being applied : RELEVANT — **ap·pli·ca·bil·i·ty** \ˌa-pli-kə-'bi-lə-tē, ə-ˌpli-kə-\ *n*

ap·pli·cant \'a-pli-kənt\ *n* : one who applies ⟨a job ∼⟩

ap·pli·ca·tion \ˌa-plə-'kā-shən\ *n* **1** : the act of applying **2** : assiduous attention **3** : REQUEST; *also* : a form used in making a request **4** : something placed or spread on a surface **5** : capacity for use **6** : a program (as a word processor) that performs one of a computer's major tasks

ap·pli·ca·tor \'a-plə-ˌkā-tər\ *n* : a device for applying a substance (as medicine or polish)

ap·plied \ə-'plīd\ *adj* : put to practical use ⟨∼ art⟩

ap·pli·qué \ˌa-plə-'kā\ *n* [F] : a fabric decoration cut out and fastened to a larger piece of material — **appliqué** *vb*

ap·ply \ə-'plī\ *vb* **ap·plied; ap·ply·ing** **1** : to put to practical use **2** : to place in contact : put or spread on a surface **3** : to employ with close attention **4** : to have reference or connection **5** : to submit a request

ap·point \ə-'póint\ *vb* **1** : to fix or set officially ⟨∼ a day for trial⟩ **2** : to name officially **3** : to fit out : EQUIP

ap·poin·tee \ə-ˌpóin-'tē, ˌa-\ *n* : a person appointed

ap·poin·tive \ə-'póin-tiv\ *adj* : subject to appointment

ap·point·ment \ə-'póint-mənt\ *n* **1** : the act of appointing **2** : an arrangement for a meeting **3** *pl* : FURNISHINGS, EQUIPMENT **4** : a nonelective office or position

ap·por·tion \ə-'pór-shən\ *vb* : to distribute proportionately : ALLOT — **ap·por·tion·ment** *n*

ap·po·site \'a-pə-zət\ *adj* : APPROPRIATE, RELEVANT — **ap·po·site·ly** *adv* — **ap·po·site·ness** *n*

ap·po·si·tion \ˌa-pə-'zi-shən\ *n* : a grammatical construction in which a noun or pronoun is followed by another that has the same referent (as *the poet* and *Burns* in "a biography of the poet Burns")

ap·pos·i·tive \ə-'pä-zə-tiv, a-\ *adj* : of, relating to, or standing in grammatical apposition — **appositive** *n*

ap·praise \ə-'prāz\ *vb* **ap·praised; ap·prais·ing** : to set a value on — **ap·prais·al** \-'prā-zəl\ *n* — **ap·prais·er** *n*

ap·pre·cia·ble \ə-'prē-shə-bəl\ *adj* : large enough to be recognized and measured — **ap·pre·cia·bly** *adv*

ap·pre·ci·ate \ə-'prē-shē-ˌāt\ *vb* **-at·ed; -at·ing** **1** : to value justly **2** : to be aware of **3** : to be grateful for **4** : to increase in value — **ap·pre·ci·a·tion** \-ˌprē-shē-'ā-shən\ *n*

ap·pre·cia·tive \ə-'prē-shə-tiv, -shē-ˌāt-\ *adj* : having or showing appreciation — **ap·pre·cia·tive·ly** *adv*

ap·pre·hend \ˌa-pri-'hend\ *vb* **1** : ARREST **2** : to become aware of **3** : to look forward to with dread **4** : UNDERSTAND — **ap·pre·hen·sion** \-'hen-chən\ *n*

ap·pre·hen·sive \-'hen-siv\ *adj* : viewing the future with anxiety — **ap·pre·hen·sive·ly** *adv* — **ap·pre·hen·sive·ness** *n*

¹**ap·pren·tice** \ə-'pren-təs\ *n* **1** : a person learning a craft under a skilled worker **2** : BEGINNER — **ap·pren·tice·ship** *n*

²**apprentice** *vb* **-ticed; -tic·ing** : to bind or set at work as an apprentice

ap·prise \ə-'prīz\ *vb* **ap·prised; ap·pris·ing** : INFORM ⟨*apprised* him of his rights⟩

ap·proach \ə-'prōch\ *vb* **1** : to move nearer to ⟨∼ the bench⟩ **2** : to be almost the same as **3** : to make advances to esp. for the purpose of creating a desired result **4** : to take preliminary steps toward ⟨~ the subject carefully⟩ — **approach** n — **ap·proach·able** adj

ap·pro·ba·tion \,a-prə-'bā-shən\ n : APPROVAL

¹**ap·pro·pri·ate** \ə-'prō-prē-,āt\ vb **-at·ed; -at·ing 1** : to take possession of **2** : to set apart for a particular use

²**ap·pro·pri·ate** \ə-'prō-prē-ət\ adj : fitted to a purpose or use : SUITABLE ♦ *Synonyms* PROPER, FIT, APT, BEFITTING — **ap·pro·pri·ate·ly** adv — **ap·pro·pri·ate·ness** n

ap·pro·pri·a·tion \ə-,prō-prē-'ā-shən\ n : something (as money) set aside by formal action for a specific use

ap·prov·al \ə-'prü-vəl\ n : an act of approving — **on approval** : subject to a prospective buyer's acceptance or refusal

ap·prove \ə-'prüv\ vb **ap·proved; ap·prov·ing 1** : to have or express a favorable opinion of **2** : to accept as satisfactory : RATIFY ⟨~ the treaty⟩

approx abbr approximate; approximately

¹**ap·prox·i·mate** \ə-'präk-sə-mət\ adj : nearly correct or exact ⟨an ~ count⟩ — **ap·prox·i·mate·ly** adv

²**ap·prox·i·mate** \-,māt\ vb **-mat·ed; -mat·ing** : to come or bring near or close — **ap·prox·i·ma·tion** \ə-,präk-sə-'mā-shən\ n

appt abbr appoint; appointed; appointment

ap·pur·te·nance \ə-'pərt-nəns, -'pər-tə-nəns\ n : something that belongs to or goes with another thing ♦ *Synonyms* ACCESSORY, ADJUNCT, APPENDAGE, APPENDIX — **ap·pur·te·nant** \ə-'pərt-nənt, -'pər-tə-nənt\ adj

Apr abbr April

APR abbr annual percentage rate

apri·cot \'a-prə-,kät, 'ā-\ n [alter. of earlier *abrecock*, ultim. fr. Ar *al-birqūq*, ultim. fr. L (*persicum*) *praecox*, lit., early-ripening (peach)] : an oval orange-colored fruit resembling the related peach and plum in flavor; *also* : a tree bearing apricots

April \'ā-prəl\ n [ME, fr. AF & L; AF *avrill*, fr. L *Aprilis*] : the 4th month of the year

a pri·o·ri \,ä-prē-'ȯr-ē\ adj [L, from the former] **1** : characterized by or derived by reasoning from self-evident propositions **2** : independent of experience — **a priori** adv

apron \'ā-prən\ n [ME, alter. (fr. misdivision of *a napron*) of *napron*, fr. MF *naperon*, dim. of *nape* cloth, modif. of L *mappa* napkin] **1** : a garment tied over the front of the body to protect the clothes **2** : a paved area for parking or handling airplanes — **aproned** adj

¹**ap·ro·pos** \,a-prə-'pō, 'a-prə-,pō\ adv [F *à propos*, lit., to the purpose] **1** : OPPORTUNELY **2** : in passing : INCIDENTALLY

²**apropos** adj : being to the point

apropos of prep : with regard to

apse \'aps\ n : a projecting usu. semicircular and vaulted part of a building (as a church)

¹**apt** \'apt\ adj **1** : well adapted : SUITABLE **2** : having an habitual tendency : LIKELY **3** : quick to learn — **apt·ly** adv — **apt·ness** \'apt-nəs\ n

²**apt** abbr **1** apartment **2** aptitude

ap·ti·tude \'ap-tə-,tüd, -,tyüd\ n **1** : natural ability : TALENT **2** : capacity for learning **3** : APPROPRIATENESS

aqua \'a-kwə, 'ä-\ n : a light greenish blue color

aqua·cul·ture \'a-kwə-,kəl-chər, 'ä-\ n : the cultivation of aquatic organisms (as fish or shellfish) for human use esp. as food — **aqua·cul·tur·ist** \-chə-rist\ n

aqua·ma·rine \,a-kwə-mə-'rēn, ,ä-\ n **1** : a bluish green gem **2** : a pale blue to light greenish blue

aqua·naut \'a-kwə-,nȯt, 'ä-\ n : a person who lives in an underwater shelter for an extended period

aqua·plane \-,plān\ n : a board towed behind a motorboat and ridden by a person standing on it — **aquaplane** vb

aqua re·gia \,a-kwə-'rē-j(ē-)ə\ n [NL, lit., royal water] : a mixture of nitric and hydrochloric acids that dissolves gold or platinum

aquar·i·um \ə-'kwer-ē-əm\ n, pl **-i·ums** or **-ia** \-ē-ə\ **1** : a container (as a glass tank) in which living aquatic animals or plants are kept **2** : a place where aquatic animals and plants are kept and shown

Aquar·i·us \ə-'kwer-ē-əs\ n [L, lit., water carrier] **1** : a zodiacal constellation between Capricorn and Pisces usu. pictured as a man pouring water **2** : the 11th sign of the zodiac in astrology; *also* : one born under this sign

¹**aquat·ic** \ə-'kwä-tik, -'kwa-\ adj **1** : growing or living in or frequenting water **2** : performed in or on water

²**aquatic** n : an aquatic animal or plant

aqua·vit \'ä-kwə-,vēt\ n : a clear liquor flavored with caraway seeds

aqua vi·tae \,a-kwə-'vī-tē, ,ä-\ n [ME, fr. ML, lit., water of life] : a strong alcoholic liquor (as brandy)

aq·ue·duct \'a-kwə-,dəkt\ n **1** : a conduit for carrying running water **2** : a structure carrying a canal over a river or hollow **3** : a passage in a bodily part

aqueduct 2

aque·ous \'ā-kwē-əs, 'a-\ adj **1** : WATERY **2** : made of, by, or with water

aqueous humor n : a clear fluid occupying the space between the lens and the cornea of the eye

aqui·fer \'a-kwə-fər, 'ä-\ n : a water-bearing stratum of permeable rock, sand, or gravel

aq·ui·line \'a-kwə-,līn, -lən\ adj **1** : of or resembling an eagle **2** : hooked like an eagle's beak ⟨an ~ nose⟩

ar abbr arrival; arrive

Ar symbol argon

AR abbr Arkansas

-ar adj suffix : of or relating to ⟨molecular⟩ : being ⟨spectacular⟩ : resembling ⟨oracular⟩

Ar·ab \'a-rəb\ n **1** : a member of a Semitic people of the Arabian peninsula in southwestern Asia **2** : a member of an Arabic-speaking people — **Arab** adj — **Ara·bi·an** \ə-'rā-bē-ən\ adj or n

ar·a·besque \,a-rə-'besk\ n : a design of interlacing lines forming figures of flowers, foliage, and sometimes animals — **arabesque** adj

¹**Ar·a·bic** \'a-rə-bik\ n : a Semitic language of southwestern Asia and northern Africa

²**Arabic** adj **1** : of or relating to the Arabs, Arabic, or the Arabian peninsula in southwestern Asia **2** : expressed in or making use of Arabic numerals

Arabic numeral n : any of the number symbols 0, 1, 2, 3, 4, 5, 6, 7, 8, 9

ar·a·ble \'a-rə-bəl\ adj : fit for or used for the growing of crops ⟨~ land⟩

arach·nid \ə-'rak-nəd\ n : any of a class of usu. 8-legged arthropods comprising the spiders, scorpions, mites, and ticks — **arachnid** adj

Ar·a·ma·ic \,a-rə-'mā-ik\ n : an ancient Semitic language

ar·a·mid \'a-rə-məd, -,mid\ n : any of several light but very strong heat-resistant synthetic materials used esp. in textiles and plastics

Arap·a·ho or **Arap·a·hoe** \ə-'ra-pə-,hō\ n, pl **-ho** or **-hos** or **-hoe** or **-hoes** : a member of an American Indian people of the western U.S.

ar·bi·ter \'är-bə-tər\ n : one having power to decide : JUDGE

ar·bi·trage \'är-bə-,träzh\ n [F, fr. MF, arbitration] : the purchase and sale of the same or equivalent securities in different markets in order to profit from price discrepancies

ar·bi·tra·geur \,är-bə-,trä-'zhər\ or **ar·bi·trag·er** \'är-bə-,trä-zhər\ n : one who practices arbitrage

ar·bit·ra·ment \är-'bi-trə-mənt\ n **1** : the act of deciding a dispute **2** : the judgment given by an arbitrator

ar·bi·trary \'är-bə-,trer-ē\ adj **1** : AUTOCRATIC, DESPOTIC **2** : determined by will or caprice : selected at random — **ar·bi·trari·ly** \,är-bə-'trer-ə-lē\ adv — **ar·bi·trari·ness** \'är-bə-,trer-ē-nəs\ n

ar·bi·trate \'är-bə-,trāt\ vb **-trat·ed; -trat·ing 1** : to act as arbitrator **2** : to act on as arbitrator **3** : to submit for decision to an arbitrator — **ar·bi·tra·tion** \,är-bə-'trā-shən\ n

ar·bi·tra·tor \'är-bə-,trā-tər\ n : one chosen to settle differences between two parties in a controversy

ar·bor \'är-bər\ n [ME *erber*, *herber* garden, fr. AF, fr.

herbe herb, grass] : a shelter formed of or covered with vines or branches

ar·bo·re·al \är-'bȯr-ē-əl\ *adj* **1** : of, relating to, or resembling a tree **2** : living in trees 〈~ monkeys〉

ar·bo·re·tum \,är-bə-'rē-təm\ *n, pl* **-retums** *or* **-re·ta** \-tə\ [L, plantation of trees, fr. *arbor* tree] : a place where trees and plants are grown for scientific and educational purposes

ar·bor·vi·tae \,är-bər-'vī-tē\ *n* : any of various evergreen trees and shrubs with scalelike leaves that are related to the cypresses

ar·bour *chiefly Brit var of* ARBOR

ar·bu·tus \är-'byü-təs\ *n* : TRAILING ARBUTUS

¹arc \'ärk\ *n* **1** : a sustained luminous discharge of electricity (as between two electrodes) **2** : a continuous portion of a curved line (as part of the circumference of a circle)

²arc *vb* **arced** \'ärkt\; **arc·ing** \'är-kiŋ\ : to form an electric arc

ARC *abbr* **1** AIDS-related complex **2** American Red Cross

ar·cade \är-'kād\ *n* **1** : an arched or covered passageway; *esp* : one lined with shops **2** : a row of arches with their supporting columns **3** : an amusement center having coin-operated games

ar·cane \är-'kān\ *adj* : SECRET, MYSTERIOUS

¹arch \'ärch\ *n* **1** : a curved structure spanning an opening (as a door) **2** : something resembling an arch **3** : ARCHWAY

²arch *vb* **1** : to cover with an arch **2** : to form or bend into an arch

³arch *adj* **1** : CHIEF, EMINENT 〈my ~ enemy〉 **2** : ROGUISH, MISCHIEVOUS; *also* : deliberately playful or impudent 〈~ comments〉 — **arch·ly** *adv* — **arch·ness** *n*

⁴arch *abbr* architect; architectural; architecture

ar·chae·ol·o·gy *or* **ar·che·ol·o·gy** \,är-kē-'ä-lə-jē\ *n* : the study of past human life as revealed by relics left by ancient peoples — **ar·chae·o·log·i·cal** \-ə-'lä-ji-kəl\ *adj* — **ar·chae·ol·o·gist** \-'ä-lə-jist\ *n*

ar·cha·ic \är-'kā-ik\ *adj* **1** : having the characteristics of the language of the past and surviving chiefly in specialized uses 〈~ words〉 **2** : belonging to an earlier time : ANTIQUATED — **ar·cha·i·cal·ly** \-i-k(ə-)lē\ *adv*

arch·an·gel \'är-,kān-jəl\ *n* : a chief angel

arch·bish·op \ärch-'bi-shəp\ *n* : a bishop of high rank

arch·bish·op·ric \-shə-(,)prik\ *n* : the jurisdiction or office of an archbishop

arch·con·ser·va·tive \(,)ärch-kən-'sər-və-tiv\ *n* : an extreme conservative — **archconservative** *adj*

arch·dea·con \-'dē-kən\ *n* : a church official who assists a diocesan bishop in ceremonial or administrative functions

arch·di·o·cese \-'dī-ə-səs, -,sēz\ *n* : the diocese of an archbishop

arch·duke \-'dük, -'dyük\ *n* **1** : a sovereign prince **2** : a prince of the imperial family of Austria

Ar·che·an \är-'kē-ən\ *adj* : of, relating to, or being the earliest eon of geologic history — **Archean** *n*

arch·en·e·my \,ärch-'e-nə-mē\ *n, pl* **-mies** : a principal enemy

Ar·cheo·zo·ic \,är-kē-ə-'zō-ik\ *adj* : ARCHEAN — **Archeozoic** *n*

ar·chery \'är-chə-rē\ *n* : the art or practice of shooting with bow and arrows — **ar·cher** \-chər\ *n*

ar·che·type \'är-ki-,tīp\ *n* : the original pattern or model of all things of the same type — **ar·che·typ·al** \,är-kə-'tī-pəl\ *adj*

arch·fiend \,ärch-'fēnd\ *n* : a chief fiend; *esp* : SATAN

ar·chi·epis·co·pal \,är-kē-ə-'pis-kə-pəl\ *adj* : of or relating to an archbishop

ar·chi·man·drite \,är-kə-'man-,drīt\ *n* : a dignitary in an Eastern church ranking below a bishop

ar·chi·pel·a·go \,är-kə-'pe-lə-,gō, ,är-chə-\ *n, pl* **-goes** *or* **-gos** : a group of islands

ar·chi·tect \'är-kə-,tekt\ *n* **1** : a person who plans buildings and oversees their construction **2** : a person who designs and guides a plan or undertaking

ar·chi·tec·ture \'är-kə-,tek-chər\ *n* **1** : the art or science of planning and building structures **2** : a method or style of building **3** : the manner in which the elements (as of a design) or components (of a computer) are arranged or

organized — **ar·chi·tec·tur·al** \,är-kə-'tek-chə-rəl, -'tek-shrəl\ *adj* — **ar·chi·tec·tur·al·ly** *adv*

ar·chi·trave \'är-kə-,trāv\ *n* : the supporting horizontal member just above the columns in a building in the classical style of architecture

ar·chive \'är-,kīv\ *n* **1** : a place for keeping public records; *also* : public records — often used in pl. **2** : a repository esp. of information

ar·chi·vist \'är-kə-vist, -,kī-\ *n* : a person in charge of archives

ar·chon \'är-,kän, -kən\ *n* : a chief magistrate of ancient Athens

arch·ri·val \'ärch-'rī-vəl\ *n* : a principal rival

arch·way \'ärch-,wā\ *n* : a passageway under an arch; *also* : an arch over a passage

arc lamp *n* : a gas-filled electric lamp that produces light when a current arcs between incandescent electrodes

¹arc·tic \'ärk-tik, 'är-tik\ *adj* [ME *artik*, fr. L *arcticus*, fr. Gk *arktikos*, fr. *arktos* bear, Ursa Major, north] **1** *often cap* : of or relating to the north pole or the region near it **2** : FRIGID

²arc·tic \'är-tik, 'ärk-tik\ *n* : a rubber overshoe that reaches to the ankle or above

arctic circle *n, often cap* A&C : the parallel of latitude that is approximately 66½ degrees north of the equator

-ard *also* **-art** *n suffix* : one that is characterized by performing some action, possessing some quality, or being associated with some thing esp. conspicuously or excessively 〈bragg*art*〉 〈dull*ard*〉

ar·dent \'är-d°nt\ *adj* **1** : characterized by warmth of feeling : PASSIONATE **2** : FIERY, HOT 〈an ~ sun〉 **3** : GLOWING 〈~ eyes〉 — **ar·dent·ly** *adv*

ar·dor \'är-dər\ *n* **1** : warmth of feeling : ZEAL **2** : sexual excitement

ar·dour *chiefly Brit var of* ARDOR

ar·du·ous \'är-jə-wəs, -,dyü-wəs\ *adj* : DIFFICULT, LABORIOUS — **ar·du·ous·ly** *adv* — **ar·du·ous·ness** *n*

¹are *pres 2d sing or pres pl of* BE

²are \'er\ *n* — see METRIC SYSTEM table

ar·ea \'er-ē-ə\ *n* **1** : a flat surface or space **2** : the amount of surface included (as within the lines of a geometric figure) **3** : range or extent of some thing or concept : FIELD **4** : REGION

area code *n* : a usu. 3-digit number that identifies each telephone service area in a country (as the U.S. or Canada)

are·na \ə-'rē-nə\ *n* [L *harena, arena* sand, sandy place] **1** : an enclosed area used for public entertainment **2** : a sphere of activity or competition

ar·gen·tite \'är-jən-,tīt\ *n* : a dark gray or black mineral of metallic luster that is an important ore of silver

ar·gon \'är-,gän\ *n* [Gk, neut. of *argos* idle, lazy, fr. *a*- not + *ergon* work; fr. its relative inertness] : a colorless odorless gaseous chemical element found in the air and used for filling electric lamps

ar·go·sy \'är-gə-sē\ *n, pl* **-sies** **1** : a large merchant ship **2** : FLEET

ar·got \'är-gət, -,gō\ *n* : the language of a particular group or class

argu·able \'är-gyü-ə-bəl\ *adj* : open to argument, dispute, or question

ar·gu·ably \'är-gyü-(ə-)blē\ *adv* : as may be argued or shown by argument

ar·gue \'är-gyü\ *vb* **ar·gued; ar·gu·ing** **1** : to give reasons for or against something **2** : to contend in words : DISPUTE **3** : DEBATE **4** : to persuade by giving reasons

ar·gu·ment \'är-gyə-mənt\ *n* **1** : a reason offered in proof **2** : discourse intended to persuade **3** : QUARREL

ar·gu·men·ta·tion \,är-gyə-mən-'tā-shən\ *n* : the art of formal discussion

ar·gu·men·ta·tive \,är-gyə-'men-tə-tiv\ *adj* : inclined to argue

ar·gyle *also* **ar·gyll** \'är-,gī(-ə)l\ *n, often cap* : a geometric knitting pattern of varicolored diamonds on a single background color; *also* : a sock knit in this pattern

aria \'är-ē-ə\ *n* : an accompanied elaborate vocal solo forming part of a larger work

ari·a·ry \,ä-rē-'ä-rē\ *n, pl* **ariary** — see MONEY table

ar·id \'a-rəd\ *adj* : very dry; *esp* : having insufficient rainfall to support agriculture — **arid·i·ty** \ə-'ri-də-tē\ *n*

Ar·ies \'er-,ēz, -ē-,ēz\ *n* [L, lit., ram] **1** : a zodiacal constellation between Pisces and Taurus pictured as a ram **2** : the 1st sign of the zodiac in astrology; *also* : one born under this sign

aright \ə-'rīt\ *adv* : RIGHT, CORRECTLY

arise \ə-'rīz\ *vb* **arose** \-'rōz\; **aris·en** \-'ri-zᵊn\; **aris·ing** \-'rī-ziŋ\ **1** : to get up **2** : ORIGINATE **3** : ASCEND
♦ *Synonyms* RISE, DERIVE, SPRING, ISSUE

ar·is·toc·ra·cy \ˌa-rə-'stä-krə-sē\ *n, pl* **-cies 1** : government by a noble or privileged class; *also* : a state so governed **2** : the governing class of an aristocracy **3** : UPPER CLASS — **aris·to·crat** \ə-'ris-tə-ˌkrat\ *n* — **aris·to·crat·ic** \ə-ˌris-tə-'kra-tik\ *adj*

arith *abbr* arithmetic; arithmetical

arith·me·tic \ə-'rith-mə-ˌtik\ *n* **1** : a branch of mathematics that deals with computations usu. with nonnegative real numbers **2** : COMPUTATION, CALCULATION — **ar·ith·met·ic** \ˌer-ith-'me-tik\ *or* **ar·ith·met·i·cal** \-ti-kəl\ *adj* — **ar·ith·met·i·cal·ly** \-ti-k(ə-)lē\ *adv* — **arith·me·ti·cian** \ə-ˌrith-mə-'ti-shən\ *n*

arithmetic mean *n* : the sum of a set of numbers divided by the number of numbers in the set

Ariz *abbr* Arizona

ark \'ärk\ *n* **1** : a boat held to resemble that of Noah's at the time of the Flood **2** : the sacred chest in a synagogue representing to Hebrews the presence of God; *also* : the repository for the scrolls of the Torah

Ark *abbr* Arkansas

¹**arm** \'ärm\ *n* [ME, fr. OE *earm*] **1** : a human upper limb and esp. the part between the shoulder and wrist; *also* : a corresponding limb of a 2-footed vertebrate **2** : something resembling an arm in shape or position ⟨an ∼ of a chair⟩ ⟨the eight ∼s of an octopus⟩ **3** : POWER, MIGHT ⟨the ∼ of the law⟩ — **armed** \'ärmd\ *adj* — **arm·less** *adj*

²**arm** *vb* [ME, fr. AF *armer*, fr. L *armare*, fr. *arma* weapons, tools] : to furnish with weapons

³**arm** *n* **1** : WEAPON **2** : a branch of the military forces **3** *pl* : the hereditary heraldic devices of a family

ar·ma·da \är-'mä-də, -'mā-\ *n* : a fleet of warships

ar·ma·dil·lo \ˌär-mə-'di-lō\ *n, pl* **-los** [Sp, fr. dim. of *armado* armed one] : any of several small burrowing mammals with the head and body protected by an armor of bony plates

Ar·ma·ged·don \ˌär-mə-'ge-dᵊn\ *n* : a final conclusive battle between the forces of good and evil; *also* : the site or time of this

ar·ma·ment \'är-mə-mənt\ *n* **1** : military strength **2** : arms and equipment (as of a tank or combat unit) **3** : the process of preparing for war

ar·ma·ture \'är-mə-ˌchur, -chər\ *n* **1** : a protective covering or structure (as the spines of a cactus) **2** : the rotating part of an electric generator or motor; *also* : the movable part in an electromagnetic device (as a loudspeaker)

arm·chair \'ärm-ˌcher\ *n* : a chair with armrests

armed forces *n pl* : the combined military, naval, and air forces of a nation

Ar·me·nian \är-'mē-nē-ən\ *n* **1** : a native or inhabitant of Armenia **2** : the Indo-European language of the Armenians

arm·ful \'ärm-ˌful\ *n, pl* **armfuls** *or* **arms·ful** \'ärmz-ˌful\ : as much as the arm or arms can hold

arm·hole \'ärm-ˌhōl\ *n* : an opening for the arm in a garment

ar·mi·stice \'är-mə-stəs\ *n* : temporary suspension of hostilities by mutual agreement : TRUCE

arm·let \'ärm-lət\ *n* : a band worn around the upper arm

ar·mor \'är-mər\ *n* **1** : protective covering **2** : armored forces and vehicles — **ar·mored** \-mərd\ *adj*

ar·mor·er \'är-mər-ər\ *n* **1** : a person who makes arms and armor **2** : a person who services firearms

ar·mo·ri·al \är-'mȯr-ē-əl\ *adj* : of or bearing heraldic arms

ar·mory \'är-mə-rē\ *n, pl* **ar·mor·ies 1** : a place where arms are stored **2** : a factory where arms are made

ar·mour, ar·moury *chiefly Brit var of* ARMOR, ARMORY

arm·pit \'ärm-ˌpit\ *n* : the hollow under the junction of the arm and shoulder

arm·rest \-ˌrest\ *n* : a support for the arm

ar·my \'är-mē\ *n, pl* **armies 1** : a body of men organized for war **2** *often cap* : the complete military organization of a country for land warfare **3** : a great number **4** : a body of persons organized to advance a cause

army ant *n* : any of various nomadic social ants

ar·my·worm \'är-mē-ˌwərm\ *n* : any of numerous moths whose larvae move about destroying crops

aro·ma \ə-'rō-mə\ *n* : a usu. pleasing odor : FRAGRANCE — **ar·o·mat·ic** \ˌar-ə-'ma-tik\ *adj*

aro·ma·ther·a·py \ə-ˌrō-mə-'ther-ə-pē\ *n* : massage with a preparation of fragrant oils extracted from herbs, flowers, and fruits

arose *past of* ARISE

¹**around** \ə-'raund\ *adv* **1** : in a circle or in circumference ⟨a tree five feet ∼⟩ **2** : in or along a circuit ⟨the road goes ∼ by the lake⟩ **3** : on all sides ⟨nothing for miles ∼⟩ **4** : NEARBY ⟨wait ∼ awhile⟩ **5** : from one place to another ⟨travels ∼ on business⟩ **6** : in an opposite direction ⟨turn ∼⟩ **7** — used with some verbs to indicate continued action ⟨joking ∼⟩ **8** : APPROXIMATELY ⟨cost ∼ $5⟩

²**around** *prep* **1** : SURROUNDING ⟨trees ∼ the house⟩ **2** : to or on another side of ⟨∼ the corner⟩ **3** : NEAR ⟨stayed right ∼ home⟩ **4** : along the circuit of ⟨go ∼ the world⟩

arouse \ə-'rauz\ *vb* **aroused; arous·ing 1** : to awaken from sleep **2** : to stir up : EXCITE — **arous·al** \-'rau-zəl\ *n*

ar·peg·gio \är-'pe-jē-ˌō, -'pe-jō\ *n, pl* **-gios** [It fr. *arpeggiare* to play on the harp, fr. *arpa* harp] : a chord whose notes are performed in succession and not simultaneously

arr *abbr* **1** arranged **2** arrival; arrive

ar·raign \ə-'rān\ *vb* **1** : to call before a court to answer to an indictment **2** : to accuse of wrong or imperfection — **ar·raign·ment** *n*

ar·range \ə-'rānj\ *vb* **ar·ranged; ar·rang·ing 1** : to put in order **2** : PLAN ⟨∼ an interview⟩ **3** : to adapt (a musical composition) to voices or instruments other than those for which it was orig. written **4** : to come to an agreement about : SETTLE — **ar·range·ment** *n* — **ar·rang·er** *n*

ar·rant \'a-rənt\ *adj* : being notoriously without moderation : EXTREME

ar·ras \'a-rəs\ *n, pl* **arras 1** : TAPESTRY **2** : a wall hanging or screen of tapestry

¹**ar·ray** \ə-'rā\ *vb* **1** : to dress esp. splendidly **2** : to arrange in order (as in an array)

²**array** *n* **1** : a regular arrangement **2** : rich apparel **3** : a large or varied group

ar·rears \ə-'rirz\ *n pl* **1** : a state of being behind in the discharge of obligations ⟨in ∼ with the rent⟩ **2** : overdue debts

¹**ar·rest** \ə-'rest\ *vb* **1** : STOP, CHECK **2** : to take into legal custody

²**arrest** *n* **1** : the act of stopping; *also* : the state of being stopped **2** : the taking into custody by legal authority

ar·rhyth·mia \ā-'rith-mē-ə\ *n* : an alteration of the heartbeat's rhythm

ar·riv·al \ə-'rī-vəl\ *n* **1** : the act of arriving **2** : one that arrives

ar·rive \ə-'rīv\ *vb* **ar·rived; ar·riv·ing 1** : to reach a destination **2** : to make an appearance ⟨the guests have *arrived*⟩ **3** : to attain success

ar·ro·gant \'er-ə-gənt\ *adj* : offensively exaggerating one's own importance — **ar·ro·gance** \-gəns\ *n* — **ar·ro·gant·ly** *adv*

ar·ro·gate \-ˌgāt\ *vb* **-gat·ed; -gat·ing** : to claim or seize without justification as one's right — **ar·ro·ga·tion** \ˌar-ə-'gā-shən\ *n*

ar·row \'er-ō\ *n* **1** : a missile shot from a bow and usu. having a slender shaft, a pointed head, and feathers at the butt **2** : a pointed mark used to indicate direction

ar·row·head \'er-ō-ˌhed\ *n* : the pointed end of an arrow

arrowhead

ar·row·root \-,rüt, -,rut\ *n* : an edible starch from the roots of any of several tropical American plants; *also* : a plant yielding arrowroot

ar·royo \ə-'rȯi-ə, -ō\ *n, pl* **-royos** [Sp] **1** : a watercourse in a dry region **2** : a water-carved gully or channel

ar·se·nal \'ärs-nəl, 'är-sə-nəl\ *n* [ultim. fr. Ar *dār ṣinā'a* house of manufacture] **1** : a place for making and storing arms and military equipment **2** : STORE, REPERTOIRE

ar·se·nic \'ärs-nik, 'är-sə-nik\ *n* **1** : a solid brittle poisonous chemical element of grayish metallic luster **2** : a very poisonous oxygen compound of arsenic used in making insecticides

ar·son \'är-s°n\ *n* : the willful or malicious burning of property — **ar·son·ist** \-ist\ *n*

¹art \'ärt\ *n* **1** : skill acquired by experience or study **2** : a branch of learning; *esp* : one of the humanities **3** : an occupation requiring knowledge or skill **4** : the use of skill and imagination in the production of things of beauty; *also* : works so produced **5** : ARTFULNESS

²art *adj* : produced as an artistic effort ⟨an ~ film⟩

³art *abbr* **1** article **2** artificial **3** artillery

-art — see -ARD

ar·te·fact *chiefly Brit var of* ARTIFACT

ar·te·ri·al \är-'tir-ē-əl\ *adj* : of or relating to an artery; *also* : relating to or being the oxygenated blood found in most arteries **2** : of, relating to, or being a route for through traffic

ar·te·ri·ole \är-'tir-ē-,ōl\ *n* : any of the small terminal branches of an artery that ends in capillaries — **ar·te·ri·o·lar** \-,tir-ē-'ō-lər\ *adj*

ar·te·rio·scle·ro·sis \är-,tir-ē-ō-sklə-'rō-səs\ *n* : a chronic disease in which arterial walls are abnormally thickened and hardened — **ar·te·rio·scle·rot·ic** \-'rä-tik\ *adj or n*

ar·tery \'är-tə-rē\ *n, pl* **-ter·ies 1** : one of the tubular vessels that carry blood from the heart **2** : a main channel of transportation or communication

ar·te·sian well \är-'tē-zhən-\ *n* : a well from which the water flows to the surface by natural pressure; *also* : a deep well

art·ful \'ärt-fəl\ *adj* **1** : performed with, showing, or using art or skill **2** : CRAFTY — **art·ful·ly** *adv* — **art·ful·ness** *n*

ar·thri·tis \är-'thrī-təs\ *n, pl* **-thri·ti·des** \-'thri-tə-,dēz\ : inflammation of the joints — **ar·thrit·ic** \-'thri-tik\ *adj or n*

ar·thro·pod \'är-thrə-,päd\ *n* : any of a phylum of invertebrate animals comprising those (as insects, spiders, or crabs) with segmented bodies and jointed limbs — **arthropod** *adj*

ar·thros·co·py \är-'thräs-kə-pē\ *n, pl* **-pies** : visual examination of the interior of a joint (as the knee) with a special surgical instrument; *also* : surgery on a joint using arthroscopy — **ar·thro·scope** \'är-thrə-,skōp\ *n* — **ar·thro·scop·ic** \,är-thrə-'skä-pik\ *adj*

ar·ti·choke \'är-tə-,chōk\ *n* [It dial. *articiocco*, ultim. fr. Ar *al-khurshūf*] : a tall thistlelike herb related to the daisies; *also* : its edible flower head

ar·ti·cle \'är-ti-kəl\ *n* [ME, fr. AF, fr. L *articulus* joint, division, dim. of *artus* joint, limb] **1** : a distinct part of a written document **2** : a nonfictional prose composition forming an independent part of a publication **3** : a word (as *an, the*) used with a noun to limit or give definiteness to its application **4** : a member of a class of things; *esp* : COMMODITY

ar·tic·u·lar \är-'ti-kyə-lər\ *adj* : of or relating to a joint ⟨~ cartilage⟩

¹ar·tic·u·late \är-'ti-kyə-lət\ *adj* **1** : divided into meaningful parts : INTELLIGIBLE **2** : able to speak; *also* : expressing oneself readily and effectively ⟨an ~ orator⟩ **3** : JOINTED — **ar·tic·u·late·ly** *adv* — **ar·tic·u·late·ness** *n*

²ar·tic·u·late \-,lāt\ *vb* **-lat·ed; -lat·ing 1** : to utter distinctly **2** : to unite by or as if by joints — **ar·tic·u·la·tion** \-,ti-kyə-'lā-shən\ *n*

ar·ti·fact \'är-tə-,fakt\ *n* : something made or modified by humans usu. for a purpose; *esp* : an object remaining from another time or culture ⟨prehistoric ~s⟩

ar·ti·fice \'är-tə-fəs\ *n* **1** : TRICK; *also* : TRICKERY **2** : an ingenious device; *also* : INGENUITY

ar·ti·fi·cer \är-'ti-fə-sər, 'är-tə-fə-sər\ *n* : a skilled worker

ar·ti·fi·cial \,är-tə-'fi-shəl\ *adj* **1** : produced by art rather than nature; *also* : made by humans to imitate nature **2**

: not genuine : FEIGNED — **ar·ti·fi·ci·al·i·ty** \-,fi-shē-'a-lə-tē\ *n* — **ar·ti·fi·cial·ly** *adv* — **ar·ti·fi·cial·ness** *n*

artificial insemination *n* : introduction of semen into the uterus or oviduct by other than natural means

artificial intelligence *n* : the capability of a machine and esp. a computer to imitate intelligent human behavior

artificial respiration *n* : the rhythmic forcing of air into and out of the lungs of a person whose breathing has stopped

ar·til·lery \är-'ti-lə-rē\ *n, pl* **-ler·ies 1** : crew-served mounted firearms (as guns) **2** : a branch of the army armed with artillery — **ar·til·ler·ist** \-rist\ *n*

ar·ti·san \'är-tə-zən, -sən\ *n* : a worker who practices a trade or handicraft

art·ist \'är-tist\ *n* **1** : one who practices an art; *esp* : one who creates objects of beauty **2** : ARTISTE

ar·tiste \är-'tēst\ *n* : a skilled public performer

ar·tis·tic \är-'tis-tik\ *adj* : showing taste and skill — **ar·tis·ti·cal·ly** \-ti-k(ə-)lē\ *adv*

art·ist·ry \'är-tə-strē\ *n* : artistic quality or ability

art·less \'ärt-ləs\ *adj* **1** : lacking art or skill **2** : free from artificiality : NATURAL **3** : free from guile : SINCERE — **art·less·ly** *adv* — **art·less·ness** *n*

art nou·veau \,är-nü-'vō, ,ärt-\ *n, often cap A&N* [F, lit., new art] : a late 19th century design style characterized by sinuous lines and leaf-shaped forms

art·work \'ärt-,wərk\ *n* : an artistic production or work

arty \'är-tē\ *adj* **art·i·er; -est** : showily or pretentiously artistic — **art·i·ly** \'är-tə-lē\ *adv* — **art·i·ness** *n*

aru·gu·la \ə-'rü-gə-lə\ *n* : a yellowish-flowered herb related to the mustards with edible leaves used esp. in salads

ar·um \'a-rəm\ *n* : any of a family of plants (as the jack-in-the-pulpit or a skunk cabbage) with flowers in a fleshy enclosed spike

ARV *abbr* American Revised Version

¹-ary *n suffix* : thing or person belonging to or connected with ⟨function*ary*⟩

²-ary *adj suffix* : of, relating to, or connected with ⟨budget*ary*⟩

Ary·an \'a-rē-ən, 'er-ē-; 'är-yən\ *adj* **1** : INDO-EUROPEAN **2** : NORDIC — **Aryan** *n*

¹as \əz, (,)az\ *adv* **1** : to the same degree or amount : EQUALLY ⟨~ green as grass⟩ **2** : for instance ⟨various trees, ~ oak or pine⟩ **3** : when considered in a specified relation ⟨my opinion ~ distinguished from his⟩

²as *conj* **1** : in the same amount or degree in which ⟨green ~ grass⟩ **2** : in the same way that ⟨farmed ~ his father before him had farmed⟩ **3** : WHILE, WHEN ⟨spoke to me ~ I was leaving⟩ **4** : THOUGH ⟨improbable ~ it seems⟩ **5** : SINCE, BECAUSE ⟨~ I'm not wanted, I'll go⟩ **6** : that the result is ⟨so guilty ~ to leave no doubt⟩

³as *pron* **1** : THAT — used after *same* or *such* ⟨it's the same price ~ before⟩ **2** : a fact that ⟨he's rich, ~ you know⟩

⁴as *prep* : in the capacity or character of ⟨this will serve ~ a substitute⟩

As *symbol* arsenic

AS *abbr* **1** American Samoa **2** Anglo-Saxon **3** associate in science

asa·fet·i·da *or* **asa·foe·ti·da** \,a-sə-'fe-tə-də, -'fē-\ *n* : an ill-smelling plant gum formerly used in medicine

ASAP *abbr* as soon as possible

as·bes·tos \as-'bes-təs, az-\ *n* : a noncombustible grayish mineral that occurs in fibrous form and has been used as a fireproof material

as·cend \ə-'send\ *vb* **1** : to move upward : MOUNT, CLIMB **2** : to succeed to : OCCUPY ⟨he ~ed the throne⟩

as·cen·dan·cy *also* **as·cen·den·cy** \ə-'sen-dən-sē\ *n* : controlling influence : DOMINATION

¹as·cen·dant *also* **as·cen·dent** \ə-'sen-dənt\ *n* : a dominant position

²ascendant *also* **ascendent** *adj* **1** : moving upward **2** : DOMINANT

as·cen·sion \ə-'sen-chən\ *n* : the act or process of ascending

Ascension Day *n* : the Thursday 40 days after Easter observed in commemoration of Christ's ascension into heaven

as·cent \ə-'sent\ *n* **1** : the act of mounting upward : CLIMB **2** : degree of upward slope

as·cer·tain \,a-sər-'tān\ *vb* : to learn with certainty — **as·cer·tain·able** *adj*

as·cet·ic \ə-'se-tik\ *adj* : practicing self-denial esp. for spiritual reasons : AUSTERE — **ascetic** *n* — **as·cet·i·cism** \-'se-tə-ˌsi-zəm\ *n*

ASCII \'as-kē\ *n* [*American Standard Code for Information Interchange*] : a computer code for representing alphanumeric information

ascor·bic acid \ə-'skȯr-bik-\ *n* : VITAMIN C

as·cot \'as-kət, -ˌkät\ *n* [*Ascot* Heath, racetrack near Ascot, England] : a broad neck scarf that is looped under the chin

as·cribe \ə-'skrīb\ *vb* **as·cribed; as·crib·ing** : to refer to a supposed cause, source, or author : ATTRIBUTE — **as·crib·able** *adj* — **as·crip·tion** \-'skrip-shən\ *n*

asep·tic \ā-'sep-tik\ *adj* : free or freed from disease-causing germs

asex·u·al \ā-'sek-shə-wəl\ *adj* **1** : lacking sex or functional sex organs **2** : occurring or formed without the production and union of two kinds of gametes ⟨∼ reproduction⟩ **3** : devoid of sexuality — **asex·u·al·ly** *adv*

as for *prep* : with regard to : CONCERNING ⟨*as for* the others, they were late⟩

¹**ash** \'ash\ *n* **1** : any of a genus of trees related to the olive and having winged seeds and bark with grooves and ridges **2** : the tough elastic wood of an ash

²**ash** *n* **1** : the solid matter left when material is burned **2** : fine mineral particles from a volcano **3** *pl* : the remains of the dead human body after cremation or disintegration

ashamed \ə-'shāmd\ *adj* **1** : feeling shame **2** : restrained by anticipation of shame ⟨∼ to say anything⟩ — **ashamed·ly** \-'shā-məd-lē\ *adv*

ash·en \'a-shən\ *adj* : resembling ashes (as in color); *esp* : deadly pale

ash·lar \'ash-lər\ *n* : hewn or squared stone; *also* : masonry of such stone

ashore \ə-'shȯr\ *adv* : on or to the shore

as how *conj* : THAT ⟨allowed *as how* she was glad to be here⟩

ash·ram \'äsh-rəm\ *n* : a religious retreat esp. of a Hindu sage

ash·tray \'ash-ˌtrā\ *n* : a receptacle for tobacco ashes

Ash Wednesday *n* : the 1st day of Lent

ashy \'a-shē\ *adj* **ash·i·er; -est** : ASHEN

Asian \'ā-zhən\ *adj* : of, relating to, or characteristic of the continent of Asia or its people — **Asian** *n*

¹**aside** \ə-'sīd\ *adv* **1** : to or toward the side **2** : out of the way : AWAY ⟨putting ∼ savings⟩

²**aside** *n* : an actor's words heard by the audience but supposedly not by other characters on stage

aside from *prep* **1** : BESIDES ⟨*aside from* being pretty, she's intelligent⟩ **2** : with the exception of ⟨*aside from* one D his grades are excellent⟩

as if *conj* **1** : as it would be if ⟨it's *as if* nothing had changed⟩ **2** : as one would if ⟨he acts *as if* he'd never been away⟩ **3** : THAT ⟨it seems *as if* nothing ever happens around here⟩

as·i·nine \'a-sə-ˌnīn\ *adj* [L *asininus*, fr. *asinus* ass] : STUPID, FOOLISH — **as·i·nin·i·ty** \ˌa-sə-'ni-nə-tē\ *n*

ask \'ask\ *vb* **asked** \'askt\; **ask·ing 1** : to call on for an answer ⟨she ∼ed him about his trip⟩ **2** : UTTER ⟨∼ a question⟩ **3** : to make a request of ⟨∼ him for help⟩ **4** : to make a request for ⟨∼ help of her⟩ **5** : to set as a price ⟨∼ed $800 for the car⟩ **6** : INVITE

askance \ə-'skans\ *adv* **1** : with a side glance **2** : with distrust

askew \ə-'skyü\ *adv or adj* : out of line : AWRY

ASL *abbr* American Sign Language

¹**aslant** \ə-'slant\ *adv or adj* : in a slanting direction

²**aslant** *prep* : over or across in a slanting direction

asleep \ə-'slēp\ *adv or adj* **1** : in or into a state of sleep **2** : DEAD **3** : NUMB **4** : INACTIVE

as long as *conj* **1** : provided that ⟨do as you like *as long as* you get home on time⟩ **2** : INASMUCH AS, SINCE ⟨*as long as* you're up, turn on the light⟩

aso·cial \(ˌ)ā-'sō-shəl\ *adj* : ANTISOCIAL

as of *prep* : AT, DURING, FROM, ON ⟨takes effect *as of* July 1⟩

asp \'asp\ *n* : a small poisonous African snake

as·par·a·gus \ə-'sper-ə-gəs\ *n* : a tall branching perennial herb related to the lilies; *also* : its edible young stalks

as·par·tame \'as-pər-ˌtām, ə-'spär-\ *n* : a crystalline low-calorie sweetener

ASPCA *abbr* American Society for the Prevention of Cruelty to Animals

as·pect \'as-ˌpekt\ *n* **1** : a position facing a particular direction **2** : APPEARANCE, LOOK **3** : PHASE

as·pen \'as-pən\ *n* : any of several poplars with leaves that flutter in the slightest breeze

as per \'az-ˌpər\ *prep* : in accordance with ⟨*as per* instructions⟩

as·per·i·ty \a-'sper-ə-tē\ *n, pl* **-ties 1** : ROUGHNESS **2** : harshness of temper

as·per·sion \ə-'spər-zhən\ *n* : a slanderous or defamatory remark

as·phalt \'as-ˌfȯlt\ *also* **as·phal·tum** \as-'fȯl-təm\ *n* : a dark substance found in natural beds or obtained as a residue in petroleum refining and used esp. in paving streets

asphalt jungle *n* : a big city or a specified part of a big city

as·pho·del \'as-fə-ˌdel\ *n* : any of several Old World herbs related to the lilies and bearing flowers in long erect spikes

as·phyx·ia \as-'fik-sē-ə\ *n* : a lack of oxygen or excess of carbon dioxide in the body that results in unconsciousness and often death and is usu. caused by interruption of breathing

as·phyx·i·ate \-sē-ˌāt\ *vb* **-at·ed; -at·ing** : SUFFOCATE — **as·phyx·i·a·tion** \-ˌfik-sē-'ā-shən\ *n*

as·pic \'as-pik\ *n* [F, lit., asp] : a savory meat jelly

as·pi·rant \'as-pə-rənt, ə-'spī-rənt\ *n* : one who aspires
♦ **Synonyms** CANDIDATE, APPLICANT, SEEKER

¹**as·pi·rate** \'as-pə-rət\ *n* **1** : an independent sound \h\ or a character (as the letter *h*) representing it **2** : a consonant having aspiration as its final component

²**as·pi·rate** \'as-pə-ˌrāt\ *vb* **-rat·ed; -rat·ing** : to draw, remove, or take up or into by suction

as·pi·ra·tion \ˌas-pə-'rā-shən\ *n* **1** : the pronunciation or addition of an aspirate; *also* : the aspirate or its symbol **2** : a drawing of something in, out, up, or through by or as if by suction **3** : a strong desire to achieve something noble; *also* : an object of this desire

as·pire \ə-'spī-(ə)r\ *vb* **as·pired; as·pir·ing 1** : to seek to attain or accomplish a particular goal **2** : to rise aloft

as·pi·rin \'as-pə-rən\ *n, pl* **aspirin** *or* **aspirins 1** : a white crystalline drug used to relieve pain and fever **2** : a tablet of aspirin

as regards *also* **as respects** *prep* : in regard to : with respect to

ass \'as\ *n* **1** : any of several long-eared mammals smaller than the related horses; *esp* : one of Africa ancestral to the donkey **2** : a stupid person

as·sail \ə-'sāl\ *vb* : to attack violently — **as·sail·able** *adj* — **as·sail·ant** *n*

as·sas·sin \ə-'sa-sᵊn\ *n* [ML *assassinus*, fr. Ar *ḥashshāshīn*, pl. of *ḥashshāsh* worthless person, lit., hashish-user, fr. *ḥashīsh* hashish] : a murderer esp. for hire or fanatical reasons

as·sas·si·nate \ə-'sa-sə-ˌnāt\ *vb* **-nat·ed; -nat·ing** : to murder by sudden or secret attack — **as·sas·si·na·tion** \-ˌsa-sə-'nā-shən\ *n*

as·sault \ə-'sȯlt\ *n* **1** : a violent attack **2** : an unlawful attempt or threat to do harm to another — **assault** *vb* — **as·sault·ive** \ə-'sȯl-tiv\ *adj*

assault rifle *n* : a military automatic rifle with a large-capacity magazine

¹**as·say** \'a-ˌsā, a-'sā\ *n* : analysis to determine the quantity of one or more components present in a sample (as of an ore or drug)

²**as·say** \a-'sā, 'a-ˌsā\ *vb* **1** : TRY, ATTEMPT **2** : to subject (as an ore or drug) to an assay **3** : JUDGE 3

as·sem·blage \ə-'sem-blij, 3 & 4 also \ˌas-ˌäm-'bläzh\ *n* **1** : a collection of persons or things : GATHERING **2** : the act of assembling **3** : an artistic composition made from scraps, junk, and odds and ends **4** : the art of making assemblages

as·sem·ble \ə-'sem-bəl\ *vb* **-bled; -bling 1** : to collect into one place : CONGREGATE **2** : to fit together the parts of **3** : to meet together : CONVENE

as·sem·bly \ə-'sem-blē\ *n, pl* **-blies 1** : a gathering of persons : MEETING **2** *cap* : a legislative body; *esp* : the lower house of a legislature **3** : a signal for troops to assemble **4** : the fitting together of parts (as of a machine)

assembly language *n* : a computer language consisting of mnemonic codes corresponding to machine-language instructions

as·sem·bly–line \ə-'sem-blē-ˌlīn\ *adj* : made by or as if by an assembly line; *esp* : lacking originality or creativity

assembly line *n* : an arrangement of machines, equipment, and workers in which work passes from operation to operation in a direct line

as·sem·bly·man \ə-'sem-blē-mən\ *n* : a member of a legislative assembly

as·sem·bly·wom·an \-ˌwu̇-mən\ *n* : a woman who is a member of a legislative assembly

as·sent \ə-'sent\ *vb* : AGREE, CONCUR — **assent** *n*

as·sert \ə-'sərt\ *vb* **1** : to state positively **2** : to demonstrate the existence of ✦ *Synonyms* DECLARE, AFFIRM, PROTEST, AVOW, CLAIM — **as·ser·tive** \-'sər-tiv\ *adj* — **as·ser·tive·ly** *adv* — **as·ser·tive·ness** *n*

as·ser·tion \ə-'sər-shən\ *n* : a positive statement

as·sess \ə-'ses\ *vb* **1** : to fix the rate or amount of **2** : to impose (as a tax) at a specified rate **3** : to evaluate for taxation — **as·sess·ment** *n* — **as·ses·sor** \-'se-sər\ *n*

as·set \'a-ˌset\ *n* **1** *pl* : the entire property of a person or company that may be used to pay debts **2** : ADVANTAGE, RESOURCE ⟨my wit is my chief ∼⟩

as·sev·er·ate \ə-'se-və-ˌrāt\ *vb* **-at·ed; -at·ing** : to assert earnestly — **as·sev·er·a·tion** \-ˌse-və-'rā-shən\ *n*

as·sid·u·ous \ə-'si-jə-wəs\ *adj* : steadily attentive : DILIGENT — **as·si·du·i·ty** \ˌa-sə-'dü-ə-tē, -'dyü-\ *n* — **as·sid·u·ous·ly** *adv* — **as·sid·u·ous·ness** *n*

as·sign \ə-'sīn\ *vb* **1** : to transfer (property) to another **2** : to appoint to or as a duty ⟨∼ a lesson⟩ **3** : FIX, SPECIFY ⟨∼ a limit⟩ **4** : ASCRIBE ⟨∼ a reason⟩ — **as·sign·able** *adj*

as·sig·na·tion \ˌa-sig-'nā-shən\ *n* : an appointment for a meeting; *esp* : TRYST

assigned risk *n* : a poor risk (as an accident-prone motorist) that an insurance company is forced to insure by state law

as·sign·ment \ə-'sīn-mənt\ *n* **1** : the act of assigning **2** : something assigned

as·sim·i·late \ə-'si-mə-ˌlāt\ *vb* **-lat·ed; -lat·ing** **1** : to take up and absorb as nourishment; *also* : to absorb into a cultural tradition **2** : COMPREHEND **3** : to make or become similar — **as·sim·i·la·tion** \-ˌsi-mə-'lā-shən\ *n*

¹as·sist \ə-'sist\ *vb* : HELP, AID — **as·sis·tance** \-'sis-təns\ *n*

²assist *n* **1** : an act of assistance **2** : the action of a player who enables a teammate to make a putout (as in baseball) or score a goal (as in hockey or basketball)

as·sis·tant \ə-'sis-tənt\ *n* : a person who assists : HELPER

as·sis·ted living \ə-'sis-təd-\ *n* : a system of housing and limited care for senior citizens who need assistance with daily activities but do not require care in a nursing home

as·sis·tive \ə-'sis-tiv\ *adj* : providing aid or assistance ⟨∼ technology⟩

as·size \ə-'sīz\ *n* [ME *assise*, fr. AF, session, legal action, fr. *asseer, asseoir* to seat, fr. VL **assedēre*, fr. L *assidēre* to sit beside] **1** : a judicial inquest **2** *pl* : the former regular sessions of superior courts in English counties

assn *abbr* association

assoc *abbr* associate; associated; association

¹as·so·ci·ate \ə-'sō-shē-ˌāt, -sē-\ *vb* **-at·ed; -at·ing** **1** : to join in companionship or partnership **2** : to connect in thought

²as·so·ciate \-shē-ət, -sē-; -shət\ *n* **1** : a fellow worker : PARTNER **2** : COMPANION **3** *often cap* : a degree conferred esp. by a junior college ⟨∼ in arts⟩ — **associate** *adj*

as·so·ci·a·tion \ə-ˌsō-shē-'ā-shən, -sē-\ *n* **1** : the act of associating **2** : an organization of persons : SOCIETY

as·so·cia·tive \ə-'sō-shē-ˌā-tiv, -sē-; -shə-tiv\ *adj* **1** : of, relating to, or involved in association esp. of ideas or images **2** : of, having, or being the property of producing the same mathematical value regardless of how an expression's elements are grouped as long as their order is the same

as·so·nance \'a-sə-nəns\ *n* : repetition of vowels esp. as an alternative to rhyme in verse — **as·so·nant** \-nənt\ *adj or n*

as soon as *conj* : immediately at or shortly after the time that ⟨we'll start *as soon as* they arrive⟩

as·sort \ə-'sȯrt\ *vb* **1** : to distribute into like groups : CLASSIFY **2** : HARMONIZE

as·sort·ed \-'sȯr-təd\ *adj* : consisting of various kinds

as·sort·ment \-'sȯrt-mənt\ *n* : a collection of assorted things or persons

asst *abbr* assistant

as·suage \ə-'swāj\ *vb* **as·suaged; as·suag·ing** **1** : to make (as pain or grief) less : EASE **2** : SATISFY ✦ *Synonyms* ALLEVIATE, RELIEVE, LIGHTEN, MITIGATE

as·sume \ə-'süm\ *vb* **as·sumed; as·sum·ing** **1** : to take upon oneself **2** : to pretend to have or be **3** : to take as granted or true though not proved

as·sump·tion \ə-'səmp-shən\ *n* **1** : the taking up of a person into heaven **2** *cap* : August 15 observed in commemoration of the Assumption of the Virgin Mary **3** : a taking upon oneself **4** : PRETENSION **5** : SUPPOSITION

as·sur·ance \ə-'shu̇r-əns\ *n* **1** : PLEDGE **2** *chiefly Brit* : INSURANCE **3** : SECURITY **4** : SELF-CONFIDENCE; *also* : AUDACITY

as·sure \ə-'shu̇r\ *vb* **as·sured; as·sur·ing** **1** : INSURE **2** : to give confidence to **3** : to state confidently to **4** : to make certain the coming or attainment of

as·sured \ə-'shu̇rd\ *n, pl* **assured** *or* **assureds** : INSURED

as·ta·tine \'as-tə-ˌtēn\ *n* : an unstable radioactive chemical element

as·ter \'as-tər\ *n* : any of various mostly fall-blooming leafy-stemmed composite herbs with daisylike purple, white, pink, or yellow flower heads

as·ter·isk \'as-tə-ˌrisk\ *n* [L *asteriscus*, fr. Gk *asteriskos*, lit., little star, dim. of *astēr* star] : a character * used as a reference mark or as an indication of the omission of letters or words

astern \ə-'stərn\ *adv or adj* **1** : in, at, or toward the stern **2** : BACKWARD

as·ter·oid \'as-tə-ˌrȯid\ *n* : any of the numerous small celestial bodies found esp. between Mars and Jupiter

asth·ma \'az-mə\ *n* : a chronic lung disorder marked by recurrent episodes of labored breathing, a feeling of tightness in the chest, and coughing — **asth·mat·ic** \az-'ma-tik\ *adj or n*

as though *conj* : AS IF

astig·ma·tism \ə-'stig-mə-ˌti-zəm\ *n* : a defect in a lens or an eye causing improper focusing and blurred vision — **as·tig·mat·ic** \ˌas-tig-'ma-tik\ *adj*

astir \ə-'stər\ *adj* **1** : being in action : MOVING **2** : being out of bed

as to *prep* **1** : ABOUT, CONCERNING ⟨uncertain *as to* what went on⟩ **2** : ACCORDING TO ⟨graded *as to* size⟩

as·ton·ish \ə-'stä-nish\ *vb* : to strike with sudden and usu. great wonder : AMAZE — **as·ton·ish·ing·ly** *adv* — **as·ton·ish·ment** *n*

as·tound \ə-'staund\ *vb* : to fill with bewilderment or wonder — **as·tound·ing·ly** *adv*

¹astrad·dle \ə-'stra-dᵊl\ *adv* : on or above and extending onto both sides

²astraddle *prep* : ASTRIDE

as·tra·khan \'as-trə-kən, -ˌkan\ *n, often cap* **1** : karakul of Russian origin **2** : a cloth with a usu. wool, curled, and looped pile resembling karakul

as·tral \'as-trəl\ *adj* : of, relating to, or coming from the stars

astray \ə-'strā\ *adv or adj* **1** : off the right path or route **2** : into error

¹astride \ə-'strīd\ *adv* **1** : with one leg on each side **2** : with legs apart

²astride *prep* : with one leg on each side of

¹as·trin·gent \ə-'strin-jənt\ *adj* : able or tending to shrink body tissues — **as·trin·gen·cy** \-jən-sē\ *n*

²astringent *n* : an astringent agent or substance

astrol *abbr* astrologer; astrology

as·tro·labe \'as-trə-ˌlāb\ *n* : an instrument formerly used for observing the positions of celestial bodies

as·trol·o·gy \ə-'strä-lə-jē\ *n* : divination based on the supposed influence of the stars upon human events — **as·trol·o·ger** \-jər\ *n* — **as·tro·log·i·cal** \ˌas-trə-'lä-ji-kəl\ *adj* — **as·tro·log·i·cal·ly** \-kə-lē\ *adv*

astron *abbr* astronomer; astronomy

as·tro·naut \'as-trə-ˌnȯt\ *n* : a traveler in a spacecraft

as·tro·nau·tics \as-trə-'nȯ-tiks\ *n* : the science of the construction and operation of spacecraft — **as·tro·nau·tic** \-tik\ *or* **as·tro·nau·ti·cal** \-ti-kəl\ *adj*

as·tro·nom·i·cal \ˌas-trə-ˈnä-mi-kəl\ *also* **as·tro·nom·ic** \-mik\ *adj* **1** : of or relating to astronomy **2** : extremely large ⟨an ~ amount of money⟩

astronomical unit *n* : a unit of length used in astronomy equal to the mean distance of the earth from the sun or about 93 million miles (150 million kilometers)

as·tron·o·my \ə-ˈsträ-nə-mē\ *n, pl* **-mies** : the science of objects and matter beyond the earth's atmosphere — **as·tron·o·mer** \-mər\ *n*

as·tro·phys·ics \ˌas-trə-ˈfi-ziks\ *n* : astronomy dealing esp. with the physical properties and dynamic processes of celestial objects — **as·tro·phys·i·cal** \-zi-kəl\ *adj* — **as·tro·phys·i·cist** \-ˈfi-zə-sist\ *n*

as·tute \ə-ˈstüt, -ˈstyüt, a-\ *adj* [L *astutus,* fr. *astus* craft] : shrewdly discerning; *also* : WILY — **as·tute·ly** *adv* — **as·tute·ness** *n*

asun·der \ə-ˈsən-dər\ *adv or adj* **1** : into separate pieces ⟨torn ~⟩ **2** : separated in position from each other

ASV *abbr* American Standard Version

¹**as well as** *conj* : and in addition : and moreover ⟨brave *as well as* loyal⟩

²**as well as** *prep* : in addition to : BESIDES ⟨the coach, *as well as* the team, is ready⟩

asy·lum \ə-ˈsī-ləm\ *n* [ME, fr. L, fr. Gk *asylon,* neut. of *asylos* inviolable, fr. *a-* not + *sylon* right of seizure] **1** : a place of refuge **2** : protection given to esp. political fugitives **3** : an institution for the care of the needy or sick and esp. of the insane

asym·met·ri·cal \ˌā-sə-ˈme-tri-kəl\ *or* **asym·met·ric** \-trik\ *adj* : not symmetrical — **asym·met·ri·cal·ly** \-tri-kə-lē\ *adv* — **asym·me·try** \(ˌ)ā-ˈsi-mə-trē\ *n*

asymp·tom·at·ic \ˌā-ˌsimp-tə-ˈma-tik\ *adj* : presenting no symptoms of disease ⟨an ~ infection⟩

as·ymp·tote \ˈa-səmp-ˌtōt\ *n* : a straight line that is approached ever more closely by a curve that never coincides with it — **as·ymp·tot·ic** \ˌa-səmp-ˈtä-tik\ *adj* — **as·ymp·tot·i·cal·ly** \-ti-k(ə-)lē\ *adv*

¹**at** \ət, (ˈ)at\ *prep* **1** — used to indicate a point in time or space ⟨be here ~ 3 o'clock⟩ **2** — used to indicate a goal ⟨swung ~ the ball⟩ **3** — used to indicate position or condition ⟨~ rest⟩ **4** — used to indicate means, cause, or manner ⟨sold ~ auction⟩

²**at** *also* **att** \ˈät\ *n, pl* **at** *also* **att** — see *kip* at MONEY table

At *symbol* astatine

AT *abbr* automatic transmission

at all *adv* : in any way : in any circumstances ⟨not *at all* likely⟩

at·a·vism \ˈa-tə-ˌvi-zəm\ *n* : appearance in an individual of a character typical of an ancestral form; *also* : such an individual or character — **at·a·vis·tic** \ˌa-tə-ˈvis-tik\ *adj*

atax·ia \ə-ˈtak-sē-ə\ *n* : an inability to coordinate muscular movements

ate *past of* EAT

¹**-ate** *n suffix* **1** : one acted upon (in a specified way) ⟨distill*ate*⟩ **2** : chemical compound or complex derived from a (specified) compound or element ⟨acet*ate*⟩

²**-ate** *n suffix* **1** : office : function : rank : group of persons holding a (specified) office or rank ⟨episcop*ate*⟩ **2** : state : dominion : jurisdiction ⟨emir*ate*⟩

³**-ate** *adj suffix* **1** : acted on (in a specified way) : being in a (specified) state ⟨temper*ate*⟩ ⟨degener*ate*⟩ **2** : marked by having ⟨vertebr*ate*⟩

⁴**-ate** *vb suffix* : cause to be modified or affected by ⟨pollin*ate*⟩ : cause to become ⟨activ*ate*⟩ : furnish with ⟨aer*ate*⟩

ate·lier \ˌa-tᵊl-ˈyā\ *n* **1** : an artist's or designer's studio **2** : WORKSHOP

athe·ist \ˈā-thē-ist\ *n* : one who denies the existence of God — **athe·ism** \-ˌi-zəm\ *n* — **athe·is·tic** \ˌā-thē-ˈis-tik\ *adj*

ath·e·nae·um *or* **ath·e·ne·um** \ˌa-thə-ˈnē-əm\ *n* : LIBRARY 1

ath·ero·scle·ro·sis \ˌa-thə-rō-sklə-ˈrō-səs\ *n* : arteriosclerosis characterized by the deposition of fatty substances in and the hardening of the inner layer of the arteries — **ath·ero·scle·rot·ic** \-ˈrä-tik\ *adj*

athirst \ə-ˈthərst\ *adj* **1** *archaic* : THIRSTY **2** : EAGER, LONGING

ath·lete \ˈath-ˌlēt\ *n* [ME, fr. L *athleta,* fr. Gk *athlētēs,* fr. *athlein* to contend for a prize, fr. *athlon* prize, contest] : a person who is trained to compete in athletics

athlete's foot *n* : ringworm of the feet

ath·let·ic \ath-ˈle-tik\ *adj* **1** : of or relating to athletes or athletics **2** : VIGOROUS, ACTIVE **3** : STURDY, MUSCULAR — **ath·let·i·cal·ly** \-ti-kə-lē\ *adv* — **ath·let·i·cism** \-tə-ˌsi-zəm\ *n*

ath·let·ics \ath-ˈle-tiks\ *n sing or pl* : exercises and games requiring physical skill, strength, and endurance

athletic supporter *n* : an elastic pouch used to support the male genitals and worn esp. during athletic activity

¹**athwart** \ə-ˈthwȯrt\ *prep* **1** : ACROSS **2** : in opposition to

²**athwart** *adv* : obliquely across

atilt \ə-ˈtilt\ *adv or adj* **1** : in a tilted position **2** : with lance in hand

-ation *n suffix* : action or process ⟨flirt*ation*⟩ : something connected with an action or process ⟨discolor*ation*⟩

Atl *abbr* Atlantic

at–large \ˈat-ˈlärj\ *adj* : of or being a political representative who is elected to serve an entire area rather than one of its subdivisions

at·las \ˈat-ləs\ *n* : a book of maps

atm *abbr* atmosphere; atmospheric

ATM *n* : a computerized electronic machine that performs basic banking functions

at·mo·sphere \ˈat-mə-ˌsfir\ *n* **1** : the gaseous envelope of a celestial body; *esp* : the mass of air surrounding the earth **2** : a surrounding influence **3** : a unit of pressure equal to the pressure of air at sea level or about 14.7 pounds per square inch (10 newtons per square centimeter) **4** : an intriguing or singular tone, effect, or appeal — **at·mo·spher·ic** \ˌat-mə-ˈsfir-ik, -ˈsfer-\ *adj* — **at·mo·spher·i·cal·ly** \-i-k(ə-)lē\ *adv*

at·mo·spher·ics \ˌat-mə-ˈsfir-iks, -ˈsfer-\ *n pl* : radio noise from atmospheric electrical phenomena

atoll \ˈa-ˌtȯl, -ˌtäl, ˈā-\ *n* : a coral island consisting of a reef surrounding a lagoon

at·om \ˈa-təm\ *n* [ME, fr. L *atomus,* fr. Gk *atomos,* fr. *atomos* indivisible, fr. *a-* not + *temnein* to cut] **1** : a tiny particle : BIT **2** : the smallest particle of a chemical element that can exist alone or in combination

atom·ic \ə-ˈtä-mik\ *adj* **1** : of or relating to atoms; *also* : NUCLEAR 2 ⟨~ energy⟩ **2** : extremely small

atomic bomb *n* : a very destructive bomb utilizing the energy released by splitting the atom

atomic clock *n* : a very precise clock regulated by the natural vibration of atoms or molecules (as of cesium)

atomic number *n* : the number of protons in the nucleus of an element

atomic weight *n* : the mass of one atom of an element

at·om·ise, at·om·is·er *Brit var of* ATOMIZE, ATOMIZER

at·om·ize \ˈa-tə-ˌmīz\ *vb* **-ized; -iz·ing** : to reduce to minute particles

at·om·iz·er \ˈa-tə-ˌmī-zər\ *n* : a device for dispensing a liquid (as perfume) as a mist

atom smasher *n* : ACCELERATOR 3

aton·al \ā-ˈtō-nᵊl\ *adj* : marked by avoidance of traditional musical tonality — **aton·al·i·ty** \ˌā-tō-ˈna-lə-tē\ *n* — **aton·al·ly** \ā-ˈtō-nə-lē\ *adv*

atone \ə-ˈtōn\ *vb* **atoned; aton·ing** **1** : to make amends **2** : EXPIATE

atone·ment \ə-ˈtōn-mənt\ *n* **1** : the reconciliation of God and mankind through the death of Jesus Christ **2** : reparation for an offense : SATISFACTION

¹**atop** \ə-ˈtäp\ *adv or adj* : on, to, or at the top

²**atop** *prep* : on top of

ATP \ˌā-ˌtē-ˈpē\ *n* [adenosine *tri*phosphate] : a compound that occurs widely in living tissue and supplies energy for many cellular processes by undergoing enzymatic hydrolysis

atri·um \ˈā-trē-əm\ *n, pl* **atria** \-trē-ə\ *also* **atri·ums** **1** : the central room of a Roman house; *also* : an open patio or court in the center of a building (as a hotel) **2** : an anatomical cavity or passage; *esp* : one of the chambers of the heart that receives blood from the veins — **atri·al** \-əl\ *adj*

atro·cious \ə-ˈtrō-shəs\ *adj* **1** : savagely brutal, cruel, or wicked **2** : very bad : ABOMINABLE — **atro·cious·ly** *adv* — **atro·cious·ness** *n*

atroc·i·ty \ə-ˈträ-sə-tē\ *n, pl* **-ties** **1** : ATROCIOUSNESS **2** : an atrocious act or object ⟨the *atrocities* of war⟩

at·ro·phy \ˈa-trə-fē\ *n, pl* **-phies** : decrease in size or wasting away of a bodily part or tissue — **atrophy** *vb*

at·ro·pine \ˈa-trə-ˌpēn\ *n* : a drug from belladonna and related plants used esp. to relieve spasms and to dilate the pupil of the eye

¹att *var of* AT

²att *abbr* **1** : attached **2** : attention **3** : attorney

at·tach \ə-'tach\ *vb* **1** : to seize legally in order to force payment of a debt **2** : to bind by personal ties **3** : FASTEN, CONNECT **4** : to be fastened or connected

at·ta·ché \ˌa-tə-'shā, ˌa-ˌta-, ə-ˌta-\ *n* [F] : a technical expert on the diplomatic staff of an ambassador

at·ta·ché case \ə-'ta-shā-, ˌa-tə-'shā-\ *n* : a small thin suitcase used esp. for carrying business papers; *also* : BRIEFCASE

at·tach·ment \ə-'tach-mənt\ *n* **1** : legal seizure of property **2** : connection by ties of affection and regard **3** : a device attached to a machine or implement **4** : a connection by which one thing is attached to another

¹at·tack \ə-'tak\ *vb* **1** : to set upon with force or words : ASSAIL, ASSAULT **2** : to set to work on

²attack *n* **1** : an offensive action **2** : a fit of sickness **3** : a scoring action in a game

³attack *adj* : designed, planned, or used for a military attack

at·tain \ə-'tān\ *vb* **1** : ACHIEVE, ACCOMPLISH **2** : to arrive at : REACH — **at·tain·abil·i·ty** \-ˌtā-nə-'bi-lə-tē\ *n* — **at·tain·able** *adj*

at·tain·der \ə-'tān-dər\ *n* : extinction of the civil rights of a person upon sentence of death or outlawry

at·tain·ment \ə-'tān-mənt\ *n* **1** : the act of attaining **2** : ACCOMPLISHMENT

at·taint \ə-'tānt\ *vb* : to condemn to loss of civil rights

at·tar \'a-tər\ *n* [Pers *'aṭir* perfumed, fr. Ar. fr. *'iṭr* perfume] : a fragrant floral oil

at·tempt \ə-'tempt\ *vb* : to make an effort toward : TRY — **attempt** *n*

at·tend \ə-'tend\ *vb* **1** : to look after : TEND **2** : to be present with **3** : to be present at **4** : to apply oneself **5** : to pay attention **6** : to direct one's attention

at·ten·dance \ə-'ten-dəns\ *n* **1** : the act or fact of attending **2** : the number of persons present; *also* : the number of times a person attends

¹at·ten·dant \ə-'ten-dənt\ *n* : one that attends another to render a service

²attendant *adj* : ACCOMPANYING ⟨∼ circumstances⟩

at·ten·tion \ə-'ten-chən\ *n* **1** : the act or state of applying the mind to an object **2** : CONSIDERATION **3** : an act of courtesy **4** : a position of readiness assumed on command by a soldier — **at·ten·tive** \-'ten-tiv\ *adj* — **at·ten·tive·ly** *adv* — **at·ten·tive·ness** *n*

attention deficit disorder *n* : a behavioral syndrome esp. of children that is marked by hyperactivity, impulsive behavior, and inattention

attention–deficit/hyperactivity disorder *n* : ATTENTION DEFICIT DISORDER

attention span *n* : the length of time during which one is able to concentrate or remain interested

at·ten·u·ate \ə-'ten-yə-ˌwāt\ *vb* **-at·ed; -at·ing** **1** : to make or become thin **2** : WEAKEN ⟨sorrows ∼ with time⟩ — **attenuate** \-wət\ *adj* — **at·ten·u·a·tion** \-ˌten-yə-'wā-shən\ *n*

at·test \ə-'test\ *vb* **1** : to certify as genuine by signing as a witness **2** : MANIFEST ⟨her record ∼s her integrity⟩ **3** : TESTIFY ⟨∼ to a belief⟩ — **at·tes·ta·tion** \ˌa-ˌtes-'tā-shən\ *n*

at·tic \'a-tik\ *n* : the space or room in a building immediately below the roof

¹at·tire \ə-'tī(-ə)r\ *vb* **at·tired; at·tir·ing** : to put garments on : DRESS, ARRAY

²attire *n* : DRESS, CLOTHES

at·ti·tude \'a-tə-ˌtüd, -ˌtyüd\ *n* **1** : POSTURE **2** : a mental position or feeling with regard to a fact or state **3** : the position of something in relation to something else **4** : a negative or hostile state of mind **5** : a cocky or arrogant manner

at·ti·tu·di·nise *Brit var of* ATTITUDINIZE

at·ti·tu·di·nize \ˌa-tə-'tüd-ən-ˌnīz, -'tyü-\ *vb* **-nized; -niz·ing** : to assume an affected mental attitude : POSE

attn *abbr* attention

at·tor·ney \ə-'tər-nē\ *n, pl* **-neys** : a legal agent qualified to act for persons in legal proceedings

attorney general *n, pl* **attorneys general** *or* **attorney generals** : the chief legal representative and adviser of a nation or state

at·tract \ə-'trakt\ *vb* **1** : to draw to or toward oneself : cause to approach **2** : to draw by emotional or aesthetic appeal ◆ *Synonyms* CHARM, FASCINATE, ALLURE, CAPTIVATE, ENCHANT — **at·trac·tive** \-'trak-tiv\ *adj* — **at·trac·tive·ly** *adv* — **at·trac·tive·ness** *n*

at·trac·tant \ə-'trak-tənt\ *n* : a substance (as a pheromone) that attracts specific animals (as insects)

at·trac·tion \ə-'trak-shən\ *n* **1** : the act or power of attracting; *esp* : personal charm **2** : an attractive quality, object, or feature **3** : a force tending to draw particles together

attrib *abbr* attributive

¹at·tri·bute \'a-trə-ˌbyüt\ *n* **1** : an inherent characteristic **2** : a word ascribing a quality; *esp* : ADJECTIVE

²at·trib·ute \ə-'tri-ˌbyüt, -byət\ *vb* **-ut·ed; -ut·ing** **1** : to explain as to cause or origin ⟨∼ the illness to fatigue⟩ **2** : to regard as a characteristic ◆ *Synonyms* ASCRIBE, CREDIT, CHARGE, IMPUTE — **at·trib·ut·able** *adj* — **at·tri·bu·tion** \ˌa-trə-'byü-shən\ *n*

at·trib·u·tive \ə-'trib-yə-tiv\ *adj* : joined directly to a modified noun without a linking verb ⟨*red* in *red hair* is an ∼ adjective⟩ — **attributive** *n* — **at·trib·u·tive·ly** *adv*

at·tri·tion \ə-'tri-shən\ *n* **1** : the act of wearing away by or as if by rubbing **2** : a reduction in numbers as a result of resignation, retirement, or death

at·tune \ə-'tün, -'tyün\ *vb* : to bring into harmony : TUNE — **at·tune·ment** *n*

atty *abbr* attorney

ATV \ˌā-ˌtē-'vē\ *n* : ALL-TERRAIN VEHICLE

atyp·i·cal \ā-'ti-pi-kəl\ *adj* : not typical : IRREGULAR — **atyp·i·cal·ly** \-k(ə-)lē\ *adv*

Au *symbol* [L *aurum*] gold

au·burn \'ò-bərn\ *adj* : reddish brown — **auburn** *n*

au cou·rant \ˌō-kú-'räⁿ\ *adj* [F, lit., in the current] : UP-TO-DATE, STYLISH

¹auc·tion \'òk-shən\ *n* [L *auction-, auctio*, fr. *augēre* to increase] : public sale of property to the highest bidder

²auction *vb* **auc·tioned; auc·tion·ing** \-sh(ə-)niŋ\ : to sell at auction

auc·tion·eer \ˌòk-shə-'nir\ *n* : an agent who conducts an auction

aud *abbr* audit; auditor

au·da·cious \ò-'dā-shəs\ *adj* **1** : DARING, BOLD **2** : INSOLENT — **au·da·cious·ly** *adv* — **au·da·cious·ness** *n* — **au·dac·i·ty** \-'da-sə-tē\ *n*

¹au·di·ble \'ò-də-bəl\ *adj* : capable of being heard — **au·di·bil·i·ty** \ˌò-də-'bi-lə-tē\ *n* — **au·di·bly** \'ò-də-blē\ *adv*

²audible *n* : a play called at the line of scrimmage — **audible** *vb*

au·di·ence \'ò-dē-əns\ *n* **1** : a formal interview **2** : an opportunity of being heard **3** : an assembly of listeners or spectators

¹au·dio \'ò-dē-ˌō\ *adj* **1** : of or relating to frequencies (as of radio waves) corresponding to those of audible sound waves **2** : of or relating to sound or its reproduction and esp. high-fidelity reproduction **3** : relating to or used in the transmission or reception of sound

²audio *n* **1** : the transmission, reception, or reproduction of sound **2** : the section of television or motion-picture equipment that deals with sound

au·di·ol·o·gy \ˌò-dē-'ä-lə-jē\ *n* : a branch of science dealing with hearing and esp. with the treatment of individuals having trouble with hearing — **au·di·o·log·i·cal** \-ə-'lä-ji-kəl\ *adj* — **au·di·ol·o·gist** \-'ä-lə-jist\ *n*

au·dio·phile \'ò-dē-ō-ˌfī(-ə)l\ *n* : one who is enthusiastic about high-fidelity sound reproduction

au·dio·tape \'ò-dē-ō-ˌtāp\ *n* : a tape recording of sound

au·dio·vi·su·al \ˌò-dē-ō-'vi-zhə-wəl\ *adj* : of, relating to, or making use of both hearing and sight

au·dio·vi·su·als \-wəlz\ *n pl* : audiovisual teaching materials (as videotapes)

¹au·dit \'ò-dət\ *n* : a formal examination and verification of financial accounts

²audit *vb* **1** : to perform an audit on or for **2** : to attend (a course) without expecting formal credit

¹au·di·tion \ò-'di-shən\ *n* **1** : HEARING **2** : a trial performance to appraise an entertainer's merits

²audition *vb* **-tioned; -tion·ing** \-'di-shə-niŋ\ : to give an audition to; *also* : to give a trial performance

au·di·tor \'ò-də-tər\ *n* **1** : LISTENER **2** : a person who audits

au·di·to·ri·um \ˌò-də-'tòr-ē-əm\ *n, pl* **-ri·ums** *or* **-ria**

\-rē-ə\ **1** : the part of a public building where an audience sits **2** : a hall or building used for public gatherings

au·di·to·ry \'ȯ-də-ˌtȯr-ē\ *adj* : of or relating to hearing or to the sense or organs of hearing ⟨∼ stimuli⟩

auditory tube *n* : EUSTACHIAN TUBE

auf Wie·der·seh·en \aúf-'vē-dər-ˌzän\ *interj* [G] — used to express farewell

Aug *abbr* August

au·ger \'ȯ-gər\ *n* : a tool for boring

auger

aught \'ȯt, 'ät\ *n* : ZERO, CIPHER

aug·ment \ȯg-'ment\ *vb* : ENLARGE, INCREASE — **aug·men·ta·tion** \ˌȯg-mən-'tā-shən\ *n*

au gra·tin \ō-'gra-tⁿ, ȯ-, -'grä-\ *adj* [F, lit., with the burnt scrapings from the pan] : covered with bread crumbs or grated cheese and browned

¹au·gur \'ȯ-gər\ *n* : DIVINER, SOOTHSAYER

²augur *vb* **1** : to foretell esp. from omens **2** : to give promise of : PRESAGE

au·gu·ry \'ȯ-gyə-rē, -gə-\ *n, pl* **-ries** **1** : divination from omens **2** : OMEN, PORTENT

au·gust \ȯ-'gəst\ *adj* : marked by majestic dignity or grandeur — **au·gust·ly** *adv* — **au·gust·ness** *n*

August \'ȯ-gəst\ *n* [ME, fr. OE, fr. L *Augustus,* fr. *Augustus* Caesar] : the 8th month of the year

au jus \ō-'zhü, -'zhüs, -'jüs; ō-zhⁿ\ *adj* [F] : served in the juice obtained from roasting

auk \'ȯk\ *n* : any of several stocky black-and-white diving seabirds that breed in colder parts of the northern hemisphere

auld \'ȯl, 'ȯld, 'äl, 'äld\ *adj, chiefly Scot* : OLD

aunt \'ant, 'änt\ *n* **1** : the sister of one's father or mother **2** : the wife of one's uncle

aunt·ie \'an-tē, 'än-\ *n* : AUNT

au pair \ō-'per\ *n* [F, on even terms] : a usu. young foreign person who does domestic work for a family in return for room and board and to learn the family's language

au·ra \'ȯr-ə\ *n* **1** : a distinctive atmosphere surrounding a given source **2** : a luminous radiation

au·ral \'ȯr-əl\ *adj* : of or relating to the ear or to the sense of hearing

aurar *pl of* EYRIR

au·re·ole \'ȯr-ē-ˌōl\ *or* **au·re·o·la** \ȯ-'rē-ə-lə\ *n* : HALO, NIMBUS

au re·voir \ˌō-rə-'vwär\ *n* [F, lit., till seeing again] : GOOD-BYE

au·ri·cle \'ȯr-i-kəl\ *n* : an atrium of the heart

au·ric·u·lar \ȯ-'ri-kyə-lər\ *adj* **1** : told privately ⟨∼ confession⟩ **2** : known or recognized by the sense of hearing

au·ro·ra \ə-'rȯr-ə\ *n, pl* **auroras** *or* **au·ro·rae** \ȯ-'rȯr-ē, -ˌī\ : a luminous phenomenon of streamers or arches of light appearing in the upper atmosphere esp. of a planet's polar regions — **au·ro·ral** \-əl\ *adj*

aurora aus·tra·lis \-ȯ-'strā-ləs\ *n* : an aurora that occurs in earth's southern hemisphere

aurora bo·re·al·is \-ˌbȯr-ē-'a-ləs\ *n* : an aurora that occurs in earth's northern hemisphere

AUS *abbr* Army of the United States

aus·pice \'ȯ-spəs\ *n, pl* **aus·pic·es** \-spə-səz, -ˌsēz\ [L *auspicium,* fr. *auspic-, auspex* diviner by birds, fr. *avis* bird + *specere* to look, look at] **1** : observation of birds by an augur **2** *pl* : kindly patronage and protection **3** : a prophetic sign or omen

aus·pi·cious \ȯ-'spi-shəs\ *adj* **1** : promising success

: PROPITIOUS **2** : FORTUNATE, PROSPEROUS ⟨an ∼ year⟩ — **aus·pi·cious·ly** *adv* — **aus·pi·cious·ness** *n*

aus·tere \ȯ-'stir\ *adj* **1** : STERN, SEVERE, STRICT **2** : ABSTEMIOUS **3** : UNADORNED ⟨∼ style⟩ — **aus·tere·ly** *adv* — **aus·ter·i·ty** \-'ster-ə-tē\ *n*

aus·tral \'ȯs-trəl\ *adj* : SOUTHERN

Aus·tro·ne·sian \ˌȯs-trə-'nē-zhən\ *adj* : of, relating to, or constituting a family of languages spoken in the area extending from Madagascar eastward through the Malay Peninsula to Hawaii and Easter Island

auth *abbr* **1** authentic **2** author **3** authorized

au·then·tic \ə-'then-tik, ȯ-\ *adj* : GENUINE, REAL — **au·then·ti·cal·ly** \-ti-k(ə-)lē\ *adv* — **au·then·tic·i·ty** \ˌȯ-ˌthen-'ti-sə-tē\ *n*

au·then·ti·cate \ə-'then-ti-ˌkāt, ȯ-\ *vb* **-cat·ed; -cat·ing** : to prove genuine — **au·then·ti·ca·tion** \-ˌthen-ti-'kā-shən\ *n*

au·thor \'ȯ-thər\ *n* [ME *auctour,* fr. AF *auctor, autor,* fr. L *auctor* originator, author, fr. *augēre* to increase] **1** : one that originates or creates **2** : one that writes or composes a literary work

au·thor·ess \'ȯ-thə-rəs\ *n* : a woman author

au·tho·ri·sa·tion, au·tho·rise *Brit var of* AUTHORIZATION, AUTHORIZE

au·thor·i·tar·i·an \ȯ-ˌthär-ə-'ter-ē-ən, ə-, -ˌthȯr-\ *adj* **1** : characterized by or favoring the principle of blind obedience to authority **2** : characterized by or favoring concentration of political power in an authority not responsible to the people — **authoritarian** *n*

au·thor·i·ta·tive \ȯ-'thär-ə-ˌtā-tiv, ə-, -'thȯr-\ *adj* : supported by, proceeding from, or being an authority — **au·thor·i·ta·tive·ly** *adv* — **au·thor·i·ta·tive·ness** *n*

au·thor·i·ty \ə-'thär-ə-tē, ȯ-, -'thȯr-\ *n, pl* **-ties** **1** : a citation used in support of a statement or in defense of an action; *also* : the source of such a citation **2** : one appealed to as an expert **3** : power to influence thought or behavior **4** : freedom granted : RIGHT **5** : persons in command; *esp* : GOVERNMENT **6** : convincing force

au·tho·rize \'ȯ-thə-ˌrīz\ *vb* **-rized; -riz·ing** **1** : SANCTION ⟨custom *authorized* by time⟩ **2** : to give legal power to — **au·tho·ri·za·tion** \ˌȯ-thə-rə-'zā-shən\ *n*

au·thor·ship \'ȯ-thər-ˌship\ *n* **1** : the state of being an author **2** : the source of a piece of writing, music, or art

au·tism \'ȯ-ˌti-zəm\ *n* : a disorder that appears by age three and is characterized esp. by impaired ability to communicate with others and form normal social relationships and by repetitive patterns of behavior — **au·tis·tic** \ȯ-'tis-tik\ *adj*

¹au·to \'ȯ-tō\ *n, pl* **autos** : AUTOMOBILE

²auto *abbr* automatic

au·to·bahn \'ȯ-tō-ˌbän, 'aú-\ *n* : a German, Swiss, or Austrian expressway

au·to·bi·og·ra·phy \ˌȯ-tə-bī-'ä-grə-fē\ *n* : the biography of a person narrated by that person — **au·to·bi·og·ra·pher** \-fər\ *n* — **au·to·bi·o·graph·i·cal** \-ˌbī-ə-'gra-fi-kəl\ *adj* — **au·to·bi·o·graph·i·cal·ly** \-k(ə-)lē\ *adv*

au·toch·tho·nous \ȯ-'täk-thə-nəs\ *adj* : INDIGENOUS, NATIVE ⟨an ∼ people⟩

au·to·clave \'ȯ-tō-ˌklāv\ *n* : an apparatus (as for sterilizing) using superheated high-pressure steam

au·toc·ra·cy \ȯ-'tä-krə-sē\ *n, pl* **-cies** : government by one person having unlimited power — **au·to·crat** \'ȯ-tə-ˌkrat\ *n* — **au·to·crat·ic** \ˌȯ-tə-'kra-tik\ *adj* — **au·to·crat·i·cal·ly** \-ti-k(ə-)lē\ *adv*

au·to·ex·po·sure \ˌȯ-tō-ik-'spō-zhər\ *n* : a camera system that automatically adjusts the exposure according to ambient light

¹au·to·graph \'ȯ-tə-ˌgraf\ *n* **1** : an original manuscript **2** : a person's signature written by hand

²autograph *vb* : to write one's signature on

au·to·im·mune \ˌȯ-tō-i-'myün\ *adj* : of, relating to, or caused by antibodies or lymphocytes that attack molecules, cells, or tissues of the organism producing them ⟨∼ diseases⟩ — **au·to·im·mu·ni·ty** \-i-'myü-nə-tē\ *n*

au·to·mate \'ȯ-tə-ˌmāt\ *vb* **-mat·ed; -mat·ing** **1** : to operate automatically using mechanical or electronic devices **2** : to convert to automatic operation — **au·to·ma·tion** \ˌȯ-tə-'mā-shən\ *n*

automated teller machine *n* : ATM

¹au·to·mat·ic \ˌȯ-tə-'ma-tik\ *adj* **1** : INVOLUNTARY **2** : made so that certain parts act in a desired manner at the proper time : SELF-ACTING — **au·to·mat·i·cal·ly** \-ti-k(ə-)lē\ *adv*

²automatic *n* : an automatic device; *esp* : an automatic firearm

automatic teller *n* : ATM

automatic teller machine *n* : ATM

au·tom·a·ton \ȯ-'tä-mə-tən, -ˌtän\ *n, pl* **-atons** *or* **-a·ta** \-ə-tə, -ə-ˌtä\ **1** : an automatic machine; *esp* : ROBOT **2** : an individual who acts mechanically

au·to·mo·bile \'ȯ-tə-mō-ˌbēl, ˌȯ-tə-mə-'bēl\ *n* : a usu. 4-wheeled automotive vehicle for passenger transportation

au·to·mo·tive \ˌȯ-tə-'mō-tiv\ *adj* **1** : of or relating to automobiles, trucks, or buses **2** : SELF-PROPELLED

au·to·nom·ic nervous system \ˌȯ-tə-'nä-mik-\ *n* : a part of the vertebrate nervous system that governs involuntary actions and that consists of the sympathetic nervous system and the parasympathetic nervous system

au·ton·o·mous \ȯ-'tä-nə-məs\ *adj* : having the right or power of self-government — **au·ton·o·mous·ly** *adv* — **au·ton·o·my** \-mē\ *n*

au·top·sy \'ȯ-ˌtäp-sē, 'ȯ-təp-\ *n, pl* **-sies** [Gk *autopsia* act of seeing with one's own eyes, fr. *autos* self + *opsis* sight] : examination of a dead body usu. with dissection sufficient to determine the cause of death or extent of change produced by disease — **autopsy** *vb*

au·tumn \'ȯ-təm\ *n* : the season between summer and winter — **au·tum·nal** \ȯ-'təm-nəl\ *adj*

aux *abbr* auxiliary

¹aux·il·ia·ry \ȯg-'zil-yə-rē, -'zi-lə-rē\ *adj* **1** : providing help **2** : functioning in a subsidiary capacity **3** : accompanying a verb form to express person, number, mood, or tense ⟨~ verbs⟩

²auxiliary *n, pl* **-ries** **1** : an auxiliary person, group, or device **2** : an auxiliary verb

aux·in \'ȯk-sən\ *n* : a plant hormone that stimulates growth in length

av *abbr* **1** avenue **2** average **3** avoirdupois

AV *abbr* **1** ad valorem **2** audiovisual **3** Authorized Version

¹avail \ə-'vāl\ *vb* : to be of use or advantage : HELP, BENEFIT

²avail *n* : USE ⟨effort was of no ~⟩

avail·able \ə-'vā-lə-bəl\ *adj* **1** : USABLE ⟨~ resources⟩ **2** : ACCESSIBLE ⟨~ in any drugstore⟩ — **avail·abil·i·ty** \-ˌvā-lə-'bi-lə-tē\ *n*

av·a·lanche \'a-və-ˌlanch\ *n* : a mass of snow, ice, earth, or rock sliding down a mountainside

avant–garde \ˌä-ˌvän-'gärd, -ˌvänt-\ *n* [F, vanguard] : those esp. in the arts who create or apply new or experimental ideas and techniques — **avant–garde** *adj*

av·a·rice \'a-və-rəs\ *n* : excessive desire for wealth : GREED — **av·a·ri·cious** \ˌa-və-'ri-shəs\ *adj*

avast \ə-'vast\ *vb imper* — a nautical command to stop or cease

av·a·tar \'a-və-ˌtär\ *n* [Skt *avatāra* descent] : INCARNATION

avaunt \ə-'vȯnt\ *adv* : AWAY, HENCE

avdp *abbr* avoirdupois

ave *abbr* avenue

Ave Ma·ria \ˌä-ˌvā-mə-'rē-ə\ *n* : HAIL MARY

avenge \ə-'venj\ *vb* **avenged; aveng·ing** : to take vengeance for — **aveng·er** *n*

av·e·nue \'a-və-ˌnü, -ˌnyü\ *n* **1** : a way or route to a place or goal : PATH **2** : a broad street

aver \ə-'vər\ *vb* **averred; aver·ring** : ALLEGE, ASSERT; *also* : DECLARE

¹av·er·age \'a-və-rij, 'a-vrij\ *n* [earlier, proportionally distributed charge for damage at sea, modif. of MF *avarie* damage to ship or cargo, fr. It *avaria*, fr. Ar *'awārīyah* damaged merchandise] **1** : ARITHMETIC MEAN **2** : a ratio of successful tries to total tries esp. in athletics ⟨batting ~ of .303⟩

²average *adj* **1** : equaling or approximating an arithmetic mean **2** : being about midway between extremes **3** : not out of the ordinary : COMMON

³average *vb* **av·er·aged; av·er·ag·ing** **1** : to be at or come to an average **2** : to be, do, or get usually **3** : to find the average of

averse \ə-'vərs\ *adj* : having an active feeling of dislike or reluctance ⟨~ to exercise⟩

aver·sion \ə-'vər-zhən\ *n* **1** : a feeling of repugnance for

something with a desire to avoid it **2** : something decidedly disliked

avert \ə-'vərt\ *vb* **1** : to turn aside or away ⟨~ the eyes⟩ **2** : to ward off

avg *abbr* average

avi·an \'ā-vē-ən\ *adj* [L *avis* bird] : of, relating to, or derived from birds

avi·ary \'ā-vē-ˌer-ē\ *n, pl* **-ar·ies** : a place for keeping birds confined

avi·a·tion \ˌā-vē-'ā-shən, ˌa-\ *n* **1** : the operation of heavier-than-air aircraft **2** : aircraft manufacture, development, and design

avi·a·tor \'ā-vē-ˌā-tər, 'a-\ *n* : an airplane pilot

avi·a·trix \ˌā-vē-'ā-triks, ˌa-\ *n, pl* **-trix·es** \-trik-səz\ *or* **-tri·ces** \-trə-ˌsēz\ : a woman airplane pilot

av·id \'a-vəd\ *adj* **1** : craving eagerly : GREEDY **2** : enthusiastic in pursuit of an interest — **avid·i·ty** \ə-'vi-də-tē, a-\ *n* — **av·id·ly** *adv* — **av·id·ness** *n*

avi·on·ics \ˌā-vē-'ä-niks, ˌa-\ *n pl* : electronics designed for use in aerospace vehicles — **avi·on·ic** \-nik\ *adj*

avo \'a-(ˌ)vü\ *n, pl* **avos** — see *pataca* at MONEY table

av·o·ca·do \ˌa-və-'kä-dō, ˌä-\ *n, pl* **-dos** *also* **-does** [modif. of Sp *aguacate*, fr. Nahuatl *āhuacatl*, avocado, testicle] : a pulpy green- to purple-skinned nutty-flavored fruit of a tropical American tree; *also* : this tree

av·o·ca·tion \ˌa-və-'kä-shən\ *n* : HOBBY

av·o·cet \'a-və-ˌset\ *n* : any of several long-legged shorebirds with webbed feet and slender upward-curving bills

avoid \ə-'vȯid\ *vb* **1** : to keep away from : SHUN **2** : to prevent the occurrence of **3** : to refrain from — **avoid·able** *adj* — **avoid·ably** *adv* — **avoid·ance** \ə-'vȯi-dəns\ *n*

av·oir·du·pois \ˌa-vər-də-'pȯiz\ *n* [ME *avoir de pois* goods sold by weight, fr. AF, lit., goods of weight] **1** : AVOIRDUPOIS WEIGHT **2** : WEIGHT, HEAVINESS; *esp* : personal weight

avoirdupois weight *n* : a system of weights based on a pound of 16 ounces and an ounce of 16 drams (28 grams) — see WEIGHT table

avouch \ə-'vau̇ch\ *vb* **1** : to declare positively : AVER **2** : to vouch for

avow \ə-'vau̇\ *vb* : to declare openly — **avow·al** \-'vau̇(-ə)l\ *n*

avun·cu·lar \ə-'vəŋ-kyə-lər\ *adj* : of, relating to, or resembling an uncle

await \ə-'wāt\ *vb* : to wait for : EXPECT

¹awake \ə-'wāk\ *vb* **awoke** \-'wōk\ *also* **awaked** \-'wākt\; **awo·ken** \-'wō-kən\ *or* **awaked** *also* **awoke; awak·ing** : to bring back to consciousness : wake up

²awake *adj* : not asleep; *also* : ALERT

awak·en \ə-'wā-kən\ *vb* **awak·ened; awak·en·ing** \-'wā-kə-niŋ\ : AWAKE

¹award \ə-'wȯrd\ *vb* **1** : to give by judicial decision ⟨~ damages⟩ **2** : to give in recognition of merit or achievement

²award *n* **1** : a final decision : JUDGMENT **2** : something awarded : PRIZE

aware \ə-'wer\ *adj* : having perception or knowledge : CONSCIOUS, INFORMED — **aware·ness** *n*

awash \ə-'wȯsh, -'wäsh\ *adj* **1** : washed by waves or tide **2** : AFLOAT **3** : FLOODED

¹away \ə-'wā\ *adv* **1** : from this or that place ⟨go ~⟩ **2** : out of the way **3** : in another direction ⟨turn ~⟩ **4** : out of existence ⟨fade ~⟩ **5** : from one's possession ⟨give ~⟩ **6** : without interruption ⟨chatter ~⟩ **7** : at a distance in space or time ⟨far ~⟩ ⟨~ back in 1910⟩

²away *adj* **1** : ABSENT **2** : distant in space or time ⟨a lake 10 miles ~⟩

¹awe \'ȯ\ *n* **1** : profound and reverent dread of the supernatural **2** : respectful fear inspired by authority

²awe *vb* **awed; aw·ing** : to inspire with awe

aweigh \ə-'wā\ *adj* : just clear of the bottom ⟨anchors ~⟩

awe·some \'ȯ-səm\ *adj* **1** : expressive of awe ⟨~ tribute⟩ **2** : inspiring awe

awe·struck \-ˌstrək\ *also* **awe·strick·en** \-ˌstri-kən\ *adj* : filled with awe

aw·ful \'ȯ-fəl\ *adj* **1** : inspiring awe **2** : extremely disagreeable **3** : very great ⟨an ~ lot of money⟩ — **aw·ful·ly** *adv*

awhile \ə-'hwī(-ə)l\ *adv* : for a while

awhirl \ə-'hwərl\ *adj* : being in a whirl

awk·ward \'ȯ-kwərd\ *adj* **1** : CLUMSY ⟨~ with needle and thread⟩ **2** : UNGRACEFUL ⟨∼ writing⟩ **3** : difficult to explain : EMBARRASSING **4** : difficult to deal with — **awk·ward·ly** *adv* — **awk·ward·ness** *n*

awl \'ol\ *n* : a pointed instrument for making small holes

aw·ning \'o-niŋ\ *n* : a rooflike cover (as of canvas) extended over or in front of a place as a shelter

AWOL \'ā-,wol, ,ā-,də-bəl-yü-,ō-'el\ *n* : a person who is absent without leave — **AWOL** *adj or adv*

awry \ə-'rī\ *adv or adj* **1** : ASKEW **2** : AMISS

ax *or* **axe** \'aks\ *n* : a chopping or cutting tool with an edged head fitted parallel to a handle

ax·i·al \'ak-sē-əl\ *adj* **1** : of, relating to, or functioning as an axis **2** : situated around, in the direction of, on, or along an axis — **ax·i·al·ly** *adv*

ax·i·om \'ak-sē-əm\ *n* [L *axioma,* fr. Gk *axiōma,* lit., something worthy, fr. *axioun* to think worthy, fr. *axios* worth, worthy] **1** : a statement generally accepted as true : MAXIM **2** : a proposition regarded as a self-evident truth — **ax·i·om·at·ic** \,ak-sē-ə-'ma-tik\ *adj* — **ax·i·om·at·i·cal·ly** \-ti-k(ə-)lē\ *adv*

ax·is \'ak-səs\ *n, pl* **ax·es** \-,sēz\ **1** : a straight line around which a body rotates **2** : a straight line or structure with respect to which a body or figure is symmetrical **3** : one of the reference lines of a system of coordinates **4** : an alliance between major powers

ax·le \'ak-səl\ *n* : a shaft on which a wheel revolves

ax·on \'ak-,sän\ *n* : the long thin usu. unbranched part of a nerve cell that usu. conducts impulses away from the cell body

ayah \'ī-ə\ *n* [Hindi & Urdu *āyā,* fr. Pg *aia,* fr. L *avia* grandmother] : a nurse or maid native to India

aya·tol·lah \,ī-ə-'tō-lə\ *n* [Pers *āyatollāh,* lit., sign of God, fr. Ar *aya* sign, miracle + *allāh* God] : an Islamic religious leader — used as a title of respect

¹**aye** *also* **ay** \'ā\ *adv* : ALWAYS, EVER

²**aye** *also* **ay** \'ī\ *adv* : YES

³**aye** *also* **ay** \'ī\ *n, pl* **ayes** : an affirmative vote

AZ *abbr* Arizona

aza·lea \ə-'zāl-yə\ *n* : any of numerous rhododendrons with funnel-shaped blossoms and usu. deciduous leaves

az·i·do·thy·mi·dine \ə-,zi-dō-'thī-mə-,dēn\ *n* : AZT

az·i·muth \'a-zə-məth\ *n* : horizontal direction expressed as an angular distance from a fixed point

AZT \,ā-(,)zē-'tē\ *n* : an antiviral drug used to treat AIDS

Az·tec \'az-,tek\ *n* : a member of a Nahuatl-speaking people that founded the Mexican empire and were conquered by Hernan Cortes in 1519 — **Az·tec·an** *adj*

azure \'a-zhər\ *n* : the blue of the clear sky — **azure** *adj*

B

¹**b** \'bē\ *n, pl* **b's** *or* **bs** \'bēz\ *often cap* **1** : the 2d letter of the English alphabet **2** : a grade rating a student's work as good

²**b** *abbr, often cap* **1** bachelor **2** bass **3** bishop **4** book **5** born

B *symbol* boron

Ba *symbol* barium

BA *abbr* **1** bachelor of arts **2** batting average

bab·ble \'ba-bəl\ *vb* **bab·bled; bab·bling** **1** : to talk enthusiastically or excessively **2** : to utter meaningless sounds — **babble** *n* — **bab·bler** \-b(ə-)lər\ *n*

babe \'bāb\ *n* **1** : BABY **2** *slang* : GIRL, WOMAN

ba·bel \'bā-bəl, 'ba-\ *n, often cap* [fr. the Tower of *Babel,* Gen 11:4–9] : a place or scene of noise and confusion; *also* : a confused sound ♦ **Synonyms** HUBBUB, RACKET, DIN, UPROAR, CLAMOR

ba·boon \ba-'bün\ *n* [ME *babewin,* fr. MF *babouin,* fr. *baboue* grimace] : any of several large apes of Asia and Africa with doglike muzzles

ba·bush·ka \bə-'büsh-kə, -'bush-\ *n* [Russ, grandmother, dim. of *baba* old woman] : a kerchief for the head

¹**ba·by** \'bā-bē\ *n, pl* **babies** **1** : a very young child : INFANT **2** : the youngest or smallest of a group **3** : a childish person — **baby** *adj* — **ba·by·hood** *n* — **ba·by·ish** *adj*

²**baby** *vb* **ba·bied; ba·by·ing** : to tend or treat often with excessive care

baby boom *n* : a marked rise in birthrate — **baby boom·er** \-'bü-mər\ *n*

baby's breath *n* : any of a genus of herbs that are related to the pinks and have small delicate flowers

ba·by·sit \'bā-bē-,sit\ *vb* **-sat** \-,sat\; **-sit·ting** : to care for children usu. during a short absence of the parents — **ba·by·sit·ter** *n*

bac·ca·lau·re·ate \,ba-kə-'lor-ē-ət\ *n* **1** : the degree of bachelor conferred by colleges and universities **2** : a sermon delivered to a graduating class

bac·ca·rat \,bä-kə-'rä, ,ba-\ *n* : a card game in which three hands are dealt and players may bet either or both hands against the dealer's

bac·cha·nal \'ba-kə-n°l, ,ba-kə-'nal, ,bä-kə-'näl\ *n* **1** : ORGY **2** : REVELER

bac·cha·na·lia \,ba-kə-'näl-yə\ *n, pl* **bacchanalia** : a drunken orgy — **bac·cha·na·lian** \-'näl-yən\ *adj or n*

bach·e·lor \'bach-lər, 'ba-chə-lər\ *n* **1** : a person who has received the usu. lowest degree conferred by a 4-year college **2** : an unmarried man — **bach·e·lor·hood** *n*

bach·e·lor·ette \,bach-lə-'ret, ,ba-chə-\ *n* : an unmarried woman

bachelor's button *n* : a European plant related to the daisies and having usu. blue, pink, or white flower heads

ba·cil·lus \bə-'si-ləs\ *n, pl* **-li** \-,lī\ [NL, fr. ML, small staff, dim. of L *baculus* staff] : any of a genus of rod-shaped bacteria; *also* : a disease-producing bacterium — **bac·il·lary** \'ba-sə-,ler-ē\ *adj*

¹**back** \'bak\ *n* **1** : the rear or dorsal part of the human body; *also* : the corresponding part of a lower animal **2** : the part or surface opposite the front **3** : a player in the backfield in football — **back·less** \-ləs\ *adj*

²**back** *adv* **1** : to, toward, or at the rear **2** : AGO **3** : so as to be restrained or retarded **4** : to, toward, or in a former place or state **5** : in return or reply

³**back** *adj* **1** : located at or in the back; *also* : REMOTE **2** : OVERDUE ⟨∼ rent⟩ **3** : moving or operating backward **4** : not current ⟨∼ issues of a magazine⟩

⁴**back** *vb* **1** : SUPPORT, UPHOLD **2** : to go or cause to go backward or in reverse **3** : to furnish with a back : form the back of — **back·er** *n*

back·ache \'bak-,āk\ *n* : a pain in the lower back

back–bench·er \-'ben-chər\ *n* : a rank-and-file member of a British legislature

back·bite \-,bīt\ *vb* **-bit** \-,bit\; **-bit·ten** \-,bi-t°n\; **-bit·ing** \-,bī-tiŋ\ : to say mean or spiteful things about someone who is absent — **back·bit·er** *n*

back·board \-,bord\ *n* : a board placed at or serving as the back of something

back·bone \-,bōn\ *n* **1** : the bony column in the back of a vertebrate that is the chief support of the trunk and consists of a jointed series of vertebrae enclosing and protecting the spinal cord **2** : firm resolute character **3** : the primary high-speed hardware and transmission lines of a telecommunication network

back·drop \'bak-,dräp\ *n* : a painted cloth hung across the rear of a stage

back·field \-,fēld\ *n* : the football players whose positions are behind the line

¹**back·fire** \-,fī(-ə)r\ *n* : a loud noise caused by the improperly timed explosion of fuel in the cylinder of an internal combustion engine

²back·fire *vb* **1** : to make or undergo a backfire **2** : to have a result opposite to what was intended

back·flip \-ˌflip\ *n* : a backward somersault esp. in the air

back·gam·mon \ˈbak-ˌga-mən\ *n* : a game played with pieces on a double board in which the moves are determined by throwing dice

back·ground \ˈbak-ˌgraund\ *n* **1** : the scenery behind something **2** : the setting within which something takes place; *also* : the sum of a person's experience, training, and understanding

back·hand \ˈbak-ˌhand\ *n* : a stroke (as in tennis) made with the back of the hand turned in the direction of movement; *also* : the side on which such a stroke is made — **back·hand** *vb*

back·hand·ed \ˈbak-ˌhan-dəd\ *adj* **1** : INDIRECT, DEVIOUS; *esp* : SARCASTIC ⟨a ~ compliment⟩ **2** : using or made with a backhand

back·hoe \ˈbak-ˌhō\ *n* : an excavating machine having a bucket that is drawn toward the machine

back·ing \ˈba-kiŋ\ *n* **1** : something forming a back **2** : SUPPORT, AID; *also* : a body of supporters

back·lash \ˈbak-ˌlash\ *n* **1** : a sudden violent backward movement or reaction **2** : a strong adverse reaction

¹back·log \-ˌlóg, -ˌläg\ *n* **1** : a large log at the back of a hearth fire **2** : an accumulation of tasks unperformed or materials not processed

²backlog *vb* : to accumulate in reserve

back of *prep* : BEHIND

back order *n* : a business order yet to be fulfilled because stock is unavailable — **back–order** *vb*

back out *vb* : to withdraw esp. from a commitment or contest

¹back·pack \ˈbak-ˌpak\ *n* : a camping pack supported by an aluminum frame and carried on the back

²backpack *vb* : to hike with a backpack — **back·pack·er** *n*

back·ped·al \ˈbak-ˌpe-dᵊl\ *vb* : RETREAT

back·rest \-ˌrest\ *n* : a rest for the back

back·side \-ˌsīd\ *n* : BUTTOCKS

back·slap \-ˌslap\ *vb* : to display excessive cordiality — **back·slap·per** *n*

back·slide \-ˌslīd\ *vb* **-slid** \-ˌslid\; **-slid** *or* **-slid·den** \-ˌsli-dᵊn\; **-slid·ing** \-ˌslī-diŋ\ : to lapse morally or in religious practice — **back·slid·er** *n*

back·space \-ˌspās\ *vb* : to move back a space in a text with the press of a key — **backspace** *n*

back·spin \-ˌspin\ *n* : a backward rotary motion of a ball

¹back·stage \ˈbak-ˌstāj\ *adj* **1** : relating to or occurring in the area behind a stage **2** : of or relating to the private lives of theater people **3** : of or relating to the inner working or operation

²back·stage \ˈbak-ˈstāj\ *adv* **1** : in or to a backstage area **2** : SECRETLY ⟨worked ~ to gain support⟩

back·stairs \-ˌsterz\ *adj* : SECRET, FURTIVE; *also* : SORDID, SCANDALOUS

¹back·stop \-ˌstäp\ *n* : something serving as a stop behind something else; *esp* : a screen or fence to keep a ball from leaving the field of play

²backstop *vb* **1** : SUPPORT **2** : to serve as a backstop to

back·sto·ry \-ˌstòr-ē\ *n* : a story that tells what led up to the main story or plot (as of a film)

back·stretch \ˈbak-ˈstrech\ *n* : the side opposite the homestretch on a racecourse

back·stroke \-ˌstrōk\ *n* : a swimming stroke executed on the back — **back·strok·er** \-ˌstrō-kər\ *n*

back talk *n* : impudent, insolent, or argumentative replies

back·track \ˈbak-ˌtrak\ *vb* **1** : to retrace one's course **2** : to reverse a position or stand

back·up \-ˌəp\ *n* **1** : one that serves as a substitute or alternative **2** : a copy of computer data — **back up** *vb*

¹back·ward \ˈbak-wərd\ *or* **back·wards** \-wərdz\ *adv* **1** : toward the back **2** : with the back foremost ⟨ride ~⟩ **3** : in a reverse or contrary direction or way ⟨count ~⟩ **4** : toward the past; *also* : toward a worse state

²backward *adj* **1** : directed, turned, or done backward **2** : DIFFIDENT, SHY **3** : retarded in development — **back·ward·ly** *adv* — **back·ward·ness** *n*

back·wash \ˈbak-ˌwósh, -ˌwäsh\ *n* : a backward flow or movement (as of water or air) produced by a propelling force (as the motion of oars)

back·wa·ter \-ˌwó-tər, -ˌwä-\ *n* **1** : water held or turned back in its course **2** : an isolated or backward place or condition

back·woods \-ˈwudz\ *n pl* **1** : wooded or partly cleared areas far from cities **2** : a remote or isolated place

ba·con \ˈbā-kən\ *n* : salted and smoked meat from the sides or back of a pig

bacteria *pl of* BACTERIUM

bac·te·ri·cid·al \bak-ˌtir-ə-ˈsī-dᵊl\ *adj* : destroying bacteria — **bac·te·ri·cide** \-ˈtir-ə-ˌsīd\ *n*

bac·te·ri·ol·o·gy \bak-ˌtir-ē-ˈä-lə-jē\ *n* **1** : a science dealing with bacteria **2** : bacterial life and phenomena — **bac·te·ri·o·log·ic** \-ə-ˈlä-jik\ *or* **bac·te·ri·o·log·i·cal** \-ə-ˈlä-ji-kəl\ *adj* — **bac·te·ri·ol·o·gist** \-ˈä-lə-jist\ *n*

bac·te·rio·phage \bak-ˈtir-ē-ə-ˌfāj\ *n* : any of various viruses that attack specific bacteria

bac·te·ri·um \bak-ˈtir-ē-əm\ *n, pl* **-ria** \-ē-ə\ [NL, fr. Gk *baktērion* staff] : any of a group of single-celled microorganisms including some that cause disease and others that are valued esp. for their chemical effects (as fermentation) — **bac·te·ri·al** \-ē-əl\ *adj*

bad \ˈbad\ *adj* **worse** \ˈwərs\; **worst** \ˈwərst\ **1** : below standard : POOR; *also* : UNFAVORABLE ⟨a ~ report⟩ **2** : SPOILED, DECAYED **3** : WICKED; *also* : not well-behaved **4** : NAUGHTY **4** : DISAGREEABLE ⟨a ~ taste⟩; *also* : HARMFUL **5** : DEFECTIVE, FAULTY ⟨~ wiring⟩; *also* : not valid ⟨a ~ check⟩ **6** : UNWELL, ILL **7** : SORRY, REGRETFUL ⟨feels ~ about forgetting to call⟩ ♦ *Synonyms* EVIL, WRONG, IMMORAL, INIQUITOUS — **bad·ly** *adv* — **bad·ness** *n*

bade *past and past part of* BID

badge \ˈbaj\ *n* : a device or token usu. worn as a sign of status

¹bad·ger \ˈba-jər\ *n* : any of several sturdy burrowing mammals with long claws on their forefeet

²badger *vb* : to harass or annoy persistently

ba·di·nage \ˌba-də-ˈnäzh\ *n* [F] : playful talk back and forth : BANTER

bad·land \ˈbad-ˌland\ *n* : a region marked by intricate erosional sculpturing and scanty vegetation — usu. used in pl.

bad·min·ton \ˈbad-ˌmi-tᵊn, -ˌmin-tᵊn\ *n* : a court game played with light rackets and a shuttlecock volleyed over a net

bad–mouth \ˈbad-ˌmauth\ *vb* : to criticize severely

Bae·de·ker \ˈbā-di-kər, ˈbe-\ *n* : GUIDEBOOK

¹baf·fle \ˈba-fəl\ *vb* **baf·fled; baf·fling** \-f(ə-)liŋ\ : FRUSTRATE, THWART, FOIL; *also* : PERPLEX — **baf·fle·ment** *n*

²baffle *n* : a device (as a wall or screen) to deflect, check, or regulate flow (as of liquid or sound) — **baf·fled** \ˈba-fəld\ *adj*

¹bag \ˈbag\ *n* **1** : a flexible usu. closable container (as for storing or carrying) **2** : something that bulges and sags like a bag ⟨~s under the eyes⟩

²bag *vb* **bagged; bag·ging** **1** : DISTEND, BULGE **2** : to put in a bag **3** : to get possession of; *esp* : to take in hunting ♦ *Synonyms* TRAP, SNARE, CATCH, CAPTURE, COLLAR

ba·gasse \bə-ˈgas\ *n* [F] : plant residue (as of sugarcane) left after a product (as juice) has been extracted

bag·a·telle \ˌba-gə-ˈtel\ *n* [F] : TRIFLE 1

ba·gel \ˈbā-gəl\ *n* [Yiddish *beygl*] : a firm doughnut-shaped roll usu. made by boiling and then baking

bag·gage \ˈba-gij\ *n* **1** : the traveling bags and personal belongings of a traveler : LUGGAGE **2** : intangible things that get in the way ⟨emotional ~⟩

bag·gies \ˈba-gēz\ *n pl* : baggy pants or shorts

bag·gy \ˈba-gē\ *adj* **bag·gi·er; -est** : puffed out or hanging like a bag — **bag·gi·ly** \-gə-lē\ *adv* — **bag·gi·ness** \-gē-nəs\ *n*

bag·man \ˈbag-mən\ *n* : a person who collects or distributes illicitly gained money on behalf of another

ba·gnio \ˈban-yō\ *n, pl* **bagnios** [It *bagno*, lit., public bath] : BROTHEL

bag of waters : a double-walled fluid-filled sac that encloses and protects the fetus in the womb and that breaks releasing its fluid during the process of birth

bag·pipe \ˈbag-ˌpīp\ *n* : a musical wind instrument consisting of a bag, a tube with valves, and sounding pipes — often used in pl. — **bag·pip·er** \-ˌpī-pər\ *n*

ba·guette \ba-ˈget\ *n* [F, lit., rod] **1** : a gem having the shape of a narrow rectangle; *also* : the shape itself **2** : a long thin loaf of French bread

baht \'bät\ *n, pl* **baht** *also* **bahts** — see MONEY table

¹bail \'bāl\ *n* : a container for ladling water out of a boat

²bail *vb* : to dip and throw out water from a boat — **bail·er** *n*

³bail *n* : security given to guarantee a prisoner's appearance when legally required; *also* : one giving such security or the release secured

⁴bail *vb* : to release under bail; *also* : to procure the release of by giving bail — **bail·able** \'bā-lə-bəl\ *adj*

⁵bail *n* : the arched handle (as of a pail or kettle)

bai·liff \'bā-ləf\ *n* **1** : an aide of a British sheriff who serves writs and makes arrests; *also* : a minor officer of a U.S. court **2** : an estate or farm manager esp. in Britain : STEWARD

bai·li·wick \'bā-li-ˌwik\ *n* : one's special province or domain ♦ *Synonyms* TERRITORY, FIELD, SPHERE

bail·out \'bā-ˌlau̇t\ *n* : a rescue from financial distress

bairn \'bern\ *n, chiefly Scot* : CHILD

¹bait \'bāt\ *vb* **1** : to persecute by continued attacks **2** : to harass with dogs usu. for sport ⟨~ a bear⟩ **3** : to furnish (as a hook) with bait **4** : ALLURE, ENTICE **5** : to give food and drink to (as an animal) ♦ *Synonyms* BADGER, HECKLE, HOUND

²bait *n* **1** : a lure for catching animals (as fish) **2** : LURE, TEMPTATION ♦ *Synonyms* SNARE, TRAP, DECOY, COME-ON, ENTICEMENT

bait·fish \'bāt-ˌfish\ *n* : a small fish that attracts and is a food source for a larger fish; *also* : a fish used for bait

bai·za \'bī-(ˌ)zä\ *n, pl* **baiza** *or* **baizas** — see *rial* at MONEY table

baize \'bāz\ *n* : a coarse feltlike fabric

¹bake \'bāk\ *vb* **baked; bak·ing** **1** : to cook or become cooked in dry heat esp. in an oven **2** : to dry and harden by heat ⟨~ bricks⟩ — **bak·er** *n*

²bake *n* : a social gathering featuring baked food

baker's dozen *n* : THIRTEEN

bak·ery \'bā-k(ə-)rē\ *n, pl* **-er·ies** : a place for baking or selling baked goods

bake sale *n* : a fund-raising event at which usu. homemade foods are sold

bake·shop \'bāk-ˌshäp\ *n* : BAKERY

bake·ware \-ˌwer\ *n* : dishes used for baking and serving food

baking powder *n* : a powder that consists of a carbonate, an acid, and a starch and that makes the dough rise in baking cakes and biscuits

baking soda *n* : SODIUM BICARBONATE

bak·sheesh \'bak-ˌshēsh\ *n* : payment (as a tip or bribe) to expedite service

bal *abbr* balance

bal·a·lai·ka \ˌba-lə-'lī-kə\ *n* [Russ] : a triangular 3-stringed instrument of Russian origin played by plucking or strumming

¹bal·ance \'ba-ləns\ *n* [ME, fr. AF, fr. VL *bilancia*, fr. LL *bilanc-, bilanx* having two scalepans, fr. L *bi* two + *lanc-, lanx* plate] **1** : a weighing device : SCALE **2** : a weight, force, or influence counteracting the effect of another **3** : an oscillating wheel used to regulate a timepiece **4** : a state of equilibrium **5** : REMAINDER, REST; *esp* : an amount in excess esp. on the credit side of an account — **bal·anced** \-lənst\ *adj*

²balance *vb* **bal·anced; bal·anc·ing** **1** : to compute the balance of an account **2** : to arrange so that one set of elements equals another; *also* : to equal or equalize in weight, number, or proportions **3** : WEIGH **4** : to bring or come to a state or position of balance; *also* : to bring into harmony or proportion

bal·boa \bal-'bō-ə\ *n* — see MONEY table

bal·brig·gan \bal-'bri-gən\ *n* : a knitted cotton fabric used esp. for underwear

bal·co·ny \'bal-kə-nē\ *n, pl* **-nies** **1** : a platform projecting from the side of a building and enclosed by a railing **2** : a gallery inside a building

bald \'bȯld\ *adj* **1** : lacking a natural or usual covering (as of hair) **2** : UNADORNED, PLAIN ⟨the ~ truth⟩ ♦ *Synonyms* BARE, BARREN, NAKED, NUDE — **bald·ly** *adv* — **bald·ness** *n*

bal·da·chin \'bȯl-də-kən, 'bal-\ *or* **bal·da·chi·no** \ˌbal-də-'kē-nō\ *n, pl* **-chins** *or* **-chinos** : a canopylike structure over an altar

bald cypress *n* : either of two coniferous trees of southern U.S. swamps; *also* : their hard red wood

bald eagle *n* : a large brown eagle of No. America that when mature has white head and neck feathers and a white tail

bal·der·dash \'bȯl-dər-ˌdash\ *n* : NONSENSE

bald·ing \'bȯl-diŋ\ *adj* : becoming bald

bal·dric \'bȯl-drik\ *n* : a belt worn over the shoulder to carry a sword or bugle

¹bale \'bāl\ *n* : a large or closely packed bundle

²bale *vb* **baled; bal·ing** : to pack in a bale — **bal·er** *n*

ba·leen \bə-'lēn\ *n* : a horny substance attached in plates to the upper jaw of some large whales (**baleen whales**)

bale·ful \'bāl-fəl\ *adj* : DEADLY, HARMFUL; *also* : OMINOUS ♦ *Synonyms* SINISTER, MALEFIC, MALEFICENT, MALIGN

¹balk \'bȯk\ *n* **1** : HINDRANCE, CHECK, SETBACK **2** : an illegal motion of the pitcher in baseball while in position

²balk *vb* **1** : BLOCK, THWART **2** : to stop short and refuse to go on **3** : to commit a balk in sports ♦ *Synonyms* FRUSTRATE, BAFFLE, FOIL, THWART — **balky** \'bȯ-kē\ *adj*

¹ball \'bȯl\ *n* **1** : a rounded body or mass (as an object used in a game or as a missile); *also* : a roundish protuberant part of the body ⟨the ~ of the foot⟩ **2** : a game played with a ball **3** : a pitched baseball that misses the strike zone and is not swung at by the batter **4** : a hit or thrown ball in various games ⟨foul ~⟩ — **on the ball** : COMPETENT, KNOWLEDGEABLE, ALERT

²ball *vb* : to form into a ball

³ball *n* : a large formal dance

bal·lad \'ba-ləd\ *n* **1** : a narrative poem of strongly marked rhythm suitable for singing **2** : a simple song : AIR **3** : a slow romantic song

bal·lad·eer \ˌba-lə-'dir\ *n* : a singer of ballads

¹bal·last \'ba-ləst\ *n* **1** : heavy material used to stabilize a ship or control a balloon's ascent **2** : crushed stone laid in a railroad bed or used in making concrete

²ballast *vb* : to provide with ballast ♦ *Synonyms* BALANCE, STABILIZE, STEADY

ball bearing *n* : a bearing in which the revolving part turns upon steel balls that roll easily in a groove; *also* : one of the balls in such a bearing

ball·car·ri·er \'bȯl-ˌker-ē-ər\ *n* : the football player carrying the ball in an offensive play

ball·er \'bȯ-lər\ *n* : an implement for shaping food into a ball ⟨melon ~⟩

bal·le·ri·na \ˌba-lə-'rē-nə\ *n* : a female ballet dancer

bal·let \'ba-ˌlā, ba-'lā\ *n* **1** : dancing in which fixed poses and steps are combined with light flowing movements often to convey a story; *also* : a theatrical art form using ballet dancing **2** : a company of ballet dancers

bal·let·o·mane \ba-'le-tə-ˌmān\ *n* : a devotee of ballet

bal·lis·tic missile \bə-'lis-tik-\ *n* : a missile that is guided during ascent and that falls freely during descent

bal·lis·tics \-tiks\ *n sing or pl* **1** : the science of the motion of projectiles (as bullets) in flight **2** : the flight characteristics of a projectile — **ballistic** *adj*

ball of fire : an unusually energetic person

¹bal·loon \bə-'lün\ *n* **1** : a bag filled with gas or heated air so as to rise and float in the atmosphere usu. carrying a suspended load **2** : an inflatable bag used as a toy or decoration — **bal·loon·ist** *n*

²balloon *vb* **1** : to swell or puff out **2** : to travel in a balloon **3** : to increase rapidly

balcony 1

¹bal·lot \'ba-lət\ n [It *ballotta* small ball used in secret voting, fr. It dial., dim. of *balla* ball] **1** : a piece of paper used to cast a vote **2** : the action or a system of voting; *also* : the right to vote

²ballot vb : to decide by ballot : VOTE

¹ball·park \'bȯl-ˌpärk\ n : a park in which ball games are played

²ballpark adj : approximately correct ⟨∼ estimate⟩

ball·point \'bȯl-ˌpȯint\ n : a pen whose writing point is a small rotating metal ball that inks itself from an inner container

ball·room \'bȯl-ˌrüm, -ˌrùm\ n : a large room for dances

ballroom dance n : any of various dances (as the tango, two-step, and waltz) in which couples perform set moves

bal·ly·hoo \'ba-lē-ˌhü\ n, pl **-hoos** : extravagant statements and claims made for publicity — **ballyhoo** vb

balm \'bäm, 'bälm\ n **1** : a fragrant healing or soothing lotion or ointment **2** : any of several spicy fragrant herbs of the mint family **3** : something that comforts or soothes

balmy \'bä-mē, 'bäl-\ adj **balm·i·er; -est** **1** : gently soothing : MILD **2** : FOOLISH, ABSURD ✦ *Synonyms* SOFT, BLAND, MILD, GENTLE — **balm·i·ness** n

ba·lo·ney \bə-'lō-nē\ n : NONSENSE

bal·sa \'bȯl-sə\ n : the extremely light strong wood of a tropical American tree; *also* : the tree

bal·sam \'bȯl-səm\ n **1** : a fragrant aromatic and usu. resinous substance oozing from various plants; *also* : a preparation containing or smelling like balsam **2** : a balsam-yielding tree (as balsam fir) **3** : a common garden ornamental plant — **bal·sam·ic** \bȯl-'sa-mik\ adj

balsam fir n : a resinous No. American evergreen tree that is widely used for pulpwood and as a Christmas tree

balsamic vinegar n : an aged Italian vinegar made from white grapes

Balt \'bȯlt\ n : a native or inhabitant of Lithuania, Latvia, or Estonia

Bal·ti·more oriole \'bȯl-tə-ˌmȯr-\ n : a common American oriole in which the male is brightly colored with orange, black, and white

bal·us·ter \'ba-lə-stər\ n [F *balustre*, fr. It *balaustro*, fr. *balaustra* wild pomegranate flower, fr. L *balaustium;* fr. its shape] : an upright support for a rail (as of a staircase)

bal·us·trade \'ba-lə-ˌsträd\ n : a row of balusters topped by a rail

bam·boo \bam-'bü\ n, pl **bamboos** : any of various woody mostly tall tropical grasses including some with strong hollow stems used for building, furniture, or utensils

bamboo curtain n, often cap B&C : a political, military, and ideological barrier in eastern Asia

bam·boo·zle \bam-'bü-zəl\ vb **-boo·zled; -boo·zling** : TRICK, HOODWINK

¹ban \'ban\ vb **banned; ban·ning** : PROHIBIT, FORBID

²ban n **1** : CURSE **2** : a legal or formal prohibition ⟨a ∼ on beef imports⟩

³ban \'bän\ n, pl **ba·ni** \'bä-nē\ — see *leu* at MONEY table

ba·nal \bə-'näl, -'nal; 'bā-nᵊl\ adj [F] : COMMONPLACE, TRITE — **ba·nal·i·ty** \bə-'na-lə-tē\ n

ba·nana \bə-'na-nə\ n : a treelike tropical plant bearing thick clusters of yellow or reddish finger-shaped fruit; *also* : this fruit

¹band \'band\ n **1** : something that binds, ties, or goes around **2** : a strip or stripe that can be distinguished (as by color or texture) from nearby matter **3** : a range of wavelengths (as in radio)

²band vb **1** : to tie up, finish, or enclose with a band **2** : to gather together or unite esp. for some common end — **band·er** n

³band n : a group of persons, animals, or things; *esp* : a group of musicians organized for playing together

¹ban·dage \'ban-dij\ n : a strip of material used esp. in dressing wounds

²bandage vb **ban·daged; ban·dag·ing** : to dress or cover with a bandage

Band–Aid \'ban-ˌdād\ adj : offering, making use of, or serving as a temporary or expedient remedy or solution

ban·dan·na or **ban·dana** \ban-'da-nə\ n : a large colored figured handkerchief

B and B abbr bed-and-breakfast

band·box \'band-ˌbäks\ n : a usu. cylindrical box for carrying clothing

band·ed \'ban-dəd\ adj : having or marked with bands

ban·de·role or **ban·de·rol** \'ban-də-ˌrōl\ n : a long narrow forked flag or streamer

ban·dit \'ban-dət\ n [It *bandito*, fr. *bandire* to banish] **1** pl also **ban·dit·ti** \ban-'di-tē\ : an outlaw who lives by plunder; *esp* : a member of a band of marauders **2** : ROBBER — **ban·dit·ry** \'ban-də-trē\ n

ban·do·lier or **ban·do·leer** \ˌban-də-'lir\ n : a belt slung over the shoulder esp. to carry ammunition

band saw n : a saw in the form of an endless steel belt running over pulleys

band·stand \'band-ˌstand\ n : a usu. roofed platform on which a band or orchestra performs outdoors

b and w abbr black and white

band·wag·on \'band-ˌwa-gən\ n **1** : a wagon carrying musicians in a parade **2** : a movement that attracts growing support

band·width \-'width\ n : the capacity for data transfer of an electronic communication system

¹ban·dy \'ban-dē\ vb **ban·died; ban·dy·ing** **1** : to exchange (as blows or quips) esp. in rapid succession **2** : to use in a glib or offhand way

²bandy adj : curved outward ⟨∼ legs⟩

bane \'bān\ n **1** : POISON **2** : WOE, HARM; *also* : a source of this — **bane·ful** adj

¹bang \'baŋ\ vb **1** : BUMP ⟨fell and ∼ed his knee⟩ **2** : to strike, thrust, or move usu. with a loud noise

²bang n **1** : a resounding blow **2** : a sudden loud noise

³bang adv : DIRECTLY, RIGHT ⟨ran ∼ up against more trouble⟩

⁴bang n : a fringe of hair cut short (as across the forehead) — usu. used in pl.

⁵bang vb : to cut (as hair) to produce bangs

ban·gle \'baŋ-gəl\ n **1** : BRACELET **2** : a loose-hanging ornament

bang·up \'baŋ-ˌəp\ adj : FIRST-RATE, EXCELLENT ⟨a ∼ job⟩

bani pl of ³BAN

ban·ish \'ba-nish\ vb **1** : to require by authority to leave a country **2** : to drive out : EXPEL ✦ *Synonyms* EXILE, OSTRACIZE, DEPORT, RELEGATE — **ban·ish·ment** n

ban·is·ter \'ba-nə-stər\ n **1** : a handrail with its supporting posts **2** : HANDRAIL **3** : BALUSTER

ban·jo \'ban-ˌjō\ n, pl **banjos** also **banjoes** : a musical instrument with a long neck, a drumlike body, and usu. five strings — **ban·jo·ist** \-ist\ n

¹bank \'baŋk\ n **1** : a piled-up mass (as of cloud or earth) **2** : an undersea elevation **3** : rising ground bordering a lake, river, or sea **4** : the sideways slope of a surface along a curve or of a vehicle as it rounds a curve

²bank vb **1** : to form a bank about **2** : to cover (as a fire) with fuel to keep inactive **3** : to build (a curve) with the roadbed or track inclined laterally upward from the inside edge **4** : to pile or heap in a bank; *also* : to arrange in a tier **5** : to incline (an airplane) laterally

³bank n [ME, fr. MF or It; MF *banque*, fr. It *banca*, lit., bench, of Gmc origin] **1** : an establishment concerned esp. with the custody, loan, exchange, or issue of money, the extension of credit, and the transmission of funds **2** : a stock of or a place for holding something in reserve ⟨a blood ∼⟩

⁴bank vb **1** : to conduct the business of a bank **2** : to deposit money or have an account in a bank — **bank·er** n — **bank·ing** n

⁵bank n : a group of objects arranged close together (as in a row or tier) ⟨a ∼ of file drawers⟩

bank·book \'baŋk-ˌbùk\ n : the depositor's book in which a bank records deposits and withdrawals

bank·card \-ˌkärd\ n : a card (as a credit card or an ATM card) issued by a bank

bank·note \-ˌnōt\ n : a promissory note issued by a bank and circulating as money

bank·roll \-ˌrōl\ n : supply of money : FUNDS

¹bank·rupt \'baŋk-(ˌ)rəpt\ n [modif. of MF *banquerote* bankruptcy, fr. It *bancarotta*, fr. *banca* bank + *rotta* broken] : an insolvent person; *esp* : one whose property is turned over by court action to be handled for the benefit of his creditors — **bankrupt** vb

²bankrupt adj **1** : reduced to financial ruin; *esp* : legally declared a bankrupt **2** : wholly lacking in or deprived of some essential ⟨morally ∼⟩ — **bank·rupt·cy** \'baŋk-(ˌ)rəpt-sē\ n

¹ban·ner \'ba-nər\ *n* **1** : a piece of cloth attached to a staff and used by a leader as his standard **2** : FLAG **3** : an advertisement that runs usu. across the top of a Web page

²banner *adj* : distinguished from all others esp. in excellence ⟨a ∼ year⟩

ban·nock \'ba-nək\ *n* : a flat oatmeal or barley cake usu. cooked on a griddle

banns \'banz\ *n pl* : public announcement esp. in church of a proposed marriage

ban·quet \'baŋ-kwət\ *n* [MF, fr. It *banchetto*, fr. dim. of *banca* bench] : a ceremonial dinner — **banquet** *vb*

ban·quette \baŋ-'ket\ *n* : a long upholstered bench esp. along a wall

ban·shee \'ban-shē\ *n* [Ir *bean sídhe* & ScGael *bean sìth*, lit., woman of fairyland] : a female spirit in Gaelic folklore whose wailing warns a family that one of them will soon die

ban·tam \'ban-təm\ *n* **1** : any of numerous small domestic fowls that are often miniatures of standard breeds **2** : a small but pugnacious person

¹ban·ter \'ban-tər\ *vb* : to speak to in a witty and teasing manner

²banter *n* : good-natured witty joking

Ban·tu \'ban-ˌtü\ *n, pl* **Bantu** *or* **Bantus 1** : a group of languages spoken in central and southern Africa **2** : a member of a group of African peoples who speak Bantu

ban·yan \'ban-yən\ *n* : a large tropical Asian tree whose aerial roots grow downward to the ground and form new trunks

ban·zai \bän-'zī\ *n* : a Japanese cheer or cry of triumph

bao·bab \'bau̇-ˌbab, 'bā-ə-\ *n* : a tropical African tree with short swollen trunk and sour edible fruits resembling gourds

bap·tism \'bap-ˌti-zəm\ *n* **1** : a Christian sacrament signifying spiritual rebirth and symbolized by the ritual use of water **2** : an act of baptizing — **bap·tis·mal** \bap-'tiz-məl\ *adj*

baptismal name *n* : GIVEN NAME

Bap·tist \'bap-tist\ *n* : a member of any of several Protestant denominations emphasizing baptism by immersion of believers only

bap·tis·tery *or* **bap·tis·try** \'bap-tə-strē\ *n, pl* **-ter·ies** *or* **-tries** : a place esp. in a church used for baptism

bap·tize \bap-'tīz, 'bap-ˌtīz\ *vb* **bap·tized; bap·tiz·ing** [ME, fr. AF *baptiser*, fr. L *baptizare*, fr. Gk *baptizein* to dip, baptize, fr. *baptein* to dip] **1** : to administer baptism to; *also* : CHRISTEN **2** : to purify esp. by an ordeal

¹bar \'bär\ *n* **1** : a long narrow piece of material (as wood or metal) used esp. for a lever, fastening, or support **2** : BARRIER, OBSTACLE **3** : the railing in a law court at which prisoners are stationed; *also* : the legal profession or the whole body of lawyers **4** : a stripe, band, or line much longer than wide **5** : a counter at which food or esp. drink is served; *also* : BARROOM **6** : a vertical line across the musical staff

²bar *vb* **barred; bar·ring 1** : to fasten, confine, or obstruct with or as if with a bar or bars **2** : to mark with bars : STRIPE **3** : to shut or keep out : EXCLUDE **4** : FORBID, PREVENT

³bar *prep* : EXCEPT ⟨the most popular actor, ∼ none⟩

⁴bar *abbr* barometer; barometric

Bar *abbr* Baruch

barb \'bärb\ *n* **1** : a sharp projection extending backward (as from the point of an arrow) **2** : a biting critical remark — **barbed** \'bärbd\ *adj* — **barb·less** \'bärb-ləs\ *adj*

bar·bar·i·an \bär-'ber-ē-ən\ *adj* **1** : of, relating to, or being a land, culture, or people alien to and usu. believed to be inferior to another's **2** : lacking refinement, learning, or artistic or literary culture — **barbarian** *n* — **bar·bar·i·an·ism** \-ē-ə-ˌni-zəm\ *n*

bar·bar·ic \bär-'ber-ik\ *adj* **1** : BARBARIAN **2** : marked by a lack of restraint : WILD **3** : PRIMITIVE, UNSOPHISTICATED

bar·ba·rism \'bär-bə-ˌri-zəm\ *n* **1** : the social condition of barbarians; *also* : the use or display of barbarian or barbarous acts, attitudes, or ideas **2** : a word or expression that offends standards of correctness or purity

bar·ba·rous \'bär-bə-rəs\ *adj* **1** : lacking culture or refinement **2** : using linguistic barbarisms **3** : mercilessly harsh or cruel — **bar·bar·i·ty** \bär-'ber-ə-tē\ *n* — **bar·ba·rous·ly** *adv* — **bar·ba·rous·ness** *n*

¹bar·be·cue \'bär-bi-ˌkyü\ *vb* **-cued; -cu·ing 1** : to cook on a rack or revolving spit over or before a source of heat **2** : to cook in a highly seasoned vinegar sauce

²barbecue *n* : a social gathering at which barbecued food is served

bar·bell \'bär-ˌbel\ *n* : a bar with adjustable weights attached to each end used for exercise and in weight-lifting competition

bar·ber \'bär-bər\ *n* [ME, fr. AF *barbour*, fr. *barbe* beard, fr. L *barba*] : one whose business is cutting and dressing hair and shaving and trimming beards

bar·ber·ry \'bär-ˌber-ē\ *n* : any of a genus of spiny shrubs bearing yellow flowers and oblong red berries

bar·bi·tu·rate \bär-'bi-chə-rət\ *n* : any of various compounds (as a salt or ester) formed from an organic acid (**bar·bi·tu·ric acid** \ˌbär-bə-'tu̇r-ik-, -'tyu̇r-\); *esp* : one used as a sedative or hypnotic

bar·ca·role *or* **bar·ca·rolle** \'bär-kə-ˌrōl\ *n* : a Venetian boat song characterized by a beat suggesting a rowing rhythm; *also* : a piece of music imitating this

bar chart *n* : BAR GRAPH

bar code *n* : a set of printed and variously spaced bars and sometimes numerals that is designed to be scanned to provide information about the object it labels — **bar–cod·ed** \'bär-ˌkō-dəd\ *adj* — **bar coding** *n*

bard \'bärd\ *n* : POET

¹bare \'ber\ *adj* **bar·er; bar·est 1** : NAKED **2** : UNCONCEALED, EXPOSED **3** : EMPTY **4** : leaving nothing to spare : MERE **5** : PLAIN, UNADORNED ⟨the ∼ facts⟩ ♦ **Synonyms** NUDE, BALD — **bare·ness** *n*

²bare *vb* **bared; bar·ing** : to make or lay bare : UNCOVER

bare·back \-ˌbak\ *or* **bare·backed** \-'bakt\ *adv or adj* : without a saddle

bare·faced \-'fāst\ *adj* **1** : having the face uncovered; *esp* : BEARDLESS **2** : not concealed : OPEN — **bare·faced·ly** \-'fā-səd-lē, -'fāst-lē\ *adv*

bare·foot \-ˌfu̇t\ *or* **bare·foot·ed** \-'fu̇-təd\ *adv or adj* : with bare feet

bare–hand·ed \-'han-dəd\ *adv or adj* **1** : without gloves **2** : without tools or weapons

bare·head·ed \-'he-dəd\ *adv or adj* : without a hat

bare·ly \'ber-lē\ *adv* **1** : PLAINLY, MEAGERLY ⟨a ∼ furnished room⟩ **2** : by a narrow margin : only just ⟨∼ enough money⟩

bar·fly \'bär-ˌflī\ *n* : a drinker who frequents bars

¹bar·gain \'bär-gən\ *n* **1** : AGREEMENT **2** : an advantageous purchase **3** : a transaction, situation, or event regarded in the light of its results

²bargain *vb* **1** : to negotiate over the terms of an agreement; *also* : to come to terms **2** : BARTER

bar·gain–base·ment \'bär-gən-'bās-mənt\ *adj* : markedly inexpensive

¹barge \'bärj\ *n* **1** : a broad flat-bottomed boat usu. moved by towing **2** : a motorboat supplied to a flagship (as for an admiral) **3** : a ceremonial boat elegantly furnished — **barge·man** \-mən\ *n*

²barge *vb* **barged; barg·ing 1** : to carry by barge **2** : to move or thrust oneself clumsily or rudely

bar graph *n* : a graphic technique for comparing amounts by rectangles whose lengths are proportional to the amounts they represent

ba·ris·ta \bə-'rēs-tə\ *n* : a person who makes and serves coffee to the public

bari·tone \'ber-ə-ˌtōn\ *n* [F *baryton* or It *baritono*, fr. Gk *barytonos* deep sounding, fr. *barys* heavy + *tonos* tone] : a male voice between bass and tenor; *also* : a man with such a voice

bar·i·um \'ber-ē-əm\ *n* : a silver-white metallic chemical element that occurs only in combination

¹bark \'bärk\ *vb* **1** : to make the short loud cry of a dog **2** : to speak or utter in a curt loud tone : SNAP

²bark *n* : the sound made by a barking dog

³bark *n* : the tough corky outer covering of a woody stem or root

⁴bark *vb* **1** : to strip the bark from **2** : to rub the skin from : ABRADE

⁵bark *n* : a ship of three or more masts with the aft mast fore-and-aft rigged and the others square-rigged

bar·keep \'bär-ˌkēp\ *also* **bar·keep·er** \-ˌkē-pər\ *n* : BARTENDER

bark·er \\'bär-kər\ *n* : a person who stands at the entrance esp. to a show and tries to attract customers to it

bar·ley \\'bär-lē\ *n* : a cereal grass with seeds used as food and in making malt liquors; *also* : its seed

bar mitz·vah \bär-'mits-və\ *n, often cap B&M* [Heb *bar miṣwāh,* lit., son of the (divine) law] **1** : a Jewish boy who at about 13 years of age assumes religious responsibilities **2** : the ceremony recognizing a boy as a bar mitzvah

barn \\'bärn\ *n* [ME *bern,* fr. OE *bereærn,* fr. *bere* barley + *ærn* house, store] : a building used esp. for storing hay and grain and for housing livestock or farm equipment

bar·na·cle \\'bär-ni-kəl\ *n* : any of numerous small marine crustaceans free-swimming when young but permanently fixed (as to rocks, whales, or ships) when adult

barn·storm \\'bärn-ˌstorm\ *vb* : to travel through the country making brief stops to entertain (as with shows or flying stunts) or to campaign for political office

barn·yard \-ˌyärd\ *n* : a usu. fenced area adjoining a barn

baro·graph \\'ber-ə-ˌgraf\ *n* : a recording barometer

ba·rom·e·ter \bə-'räm-ə-tər\ *n* : an instrument for measuring atmospheric pressure — **baro·met·ric** \ˌbar-ə-'me-trik\ *adj*

bar·on \\'ber-ən\ *n* : a member of the lowest grade of the British peerage — **ba·ro·ni·al** \bə-'rō-nē-əl\ *adj* — **bar·ony** \\'ber-ə-nē\ *n*

bar·on·age \-ə-nij\ *n* : PEERAGE

bar·on·ess \\'ber-ə-nəs\ *n* **1** : the wife or widow of a baron **2** : a woman holding a baronial title in her own right

bar·on·et \\'ber-ə-nət\ *n* : a man holding a rank of honor below a baron but above a knight — **bar·on·et·cy** \-sē\ *n*

ba·roque \bə-'rōk, -'räk\ *adj* : marked by the use of complex forms, bold ornamentation, and the juxtapositioning of contrasting elements

ba·rouche \bə-'rüsh\ *n* [G *Barutsche,* fr. It *biroccio,* ultim. fr. LL *birotus* two-wheeled, fr. L *bi-* two + *rota* wheel] : a 4-wheeled carriage with a high driver's seat in front and a folding top

bar·racks \\'ber-əks\ *n sing or pl* : a building or group of buildings for lodging soldiers

bar·ra·cu·da \ˌber-ə-'kü-də\ *n, pl* **-da** *or* **-das** : any of several large slender predaceous sea fishes including some used for food

bar·rage \bə-'räzh, -'räj\ *n* : a heavy concentration of fire (as of artillery)

barred \\'bärd\ *adj* : STRIPED

¹bar·rel \\'ber-əl\ *n* **1** : a round bulging cask with flat ends of equal diameter **2** : the amount contained in a barrel **3** : a cylindrical or tubular part ⟨gun ∼⟩ — **bar·reled** \-əld\ *adj*

²barrel *vb* **-reled** *or* **-relled; -rel·ing** *or* **-rel·ling** **1** : to pack in a barrel **2** : to travel at high speed

bar·rel·head \-ˌhed\ *n* : the flat end of a barrel — **on the barrelhead** : asking for or granting no credit ⟨paid cash *on the barrelhead*⟩

barrel roll *n* : an airplane maneuver in which a complete revolution about the longitudinal axis is made

¹bar·ren \\'ber-ən\ *adj* **1** : STERILE, UNFRUITFUL **2** : unproductive of results ⟨a ∼ scheme⟩ **3** : lacking interest or charm **4** : lacking inspiration or ideas — **bar·ren·ness** \-nəs\ *n*

²barren *n* : a tract of barren land

bar·rette \bä-'ret, bə-\ *n* : a clasp or bar for holding the hair in place

¹bar·ri·cade \\'ber-ə-ˌkād, ˌber-ə-'kād\ *vb* **-cad·ed; -cad·ing** : to block, obstruct, or fortify with a barricade

²barricade *n* [F, fr. MF, fr. *barriquer* to barricade, fr. *barrique* barrel] **1** : a hastily thrown-up obstruction or fortification **2** : BARRIER, OBSTACLE

bar·ri·er \\'ber-ē-ər\ *n* : something that separates, demarcates, or serves as a barricade ⟨racial ∼s⟩

barrier island *n* : a long broad sandy island lying parallel to a shore

barrier reef *n* : a coral reef roughly parallel to a shore and separated from it usu. by a lagoon

bar·ring \\'bär-iŋ\ *prep* : excluding by exception : EXCEPTING

bar·rio \\'bär-ē-ˌō, 'ber-\ *n, pl* **-ri·os** **1** : a district of a city or town in a Spanish-speaking country **2** : a Spanish-speaking quarter in a U.S. city

bar·ris·ter \\'ber-ə-stər\ *n* : a British counselor admitted to plead in the higher courts

bar·room \\'bär-ˌrüm, -ˌrum\ *n* : a room or establishment whose main feature is a bar for the sale of liquor

¹bar·row \\'ber-ō\ *n* : a large burial mound of earth and stones

²barrow *n* **1** : WHEELBARROW **2** : a cart with a boxlike body and two shafts for pushing it

Bart *abbr* baronet

bar·tend·er \\'bär-ˌten-dər\ *n* : a person who serves liquor at a bar

bar·ter \\'bär-tər\ *vb* : to trade by exchange of goods — **barter** *n* — **bar·ter·er** *n*

Ba·ruch \\'bär-ˌük, bə-'rük\ *n* — see BIBLE table

bas·al \\'bā-səl\ *adj* **1** : situated at or forming the base **2** : BASIC

basal metabolism *n* : the turnover of energy in a fasting and resting organism using energy solely to maintain vital cellular activity, respiration, and circulation as measured by the rate at which heat is given off

ba·salt \bə-'solt, 'bā-ˌsolt\ *n* : a dark fine-grained igneous rock — **ba·sal·tic** \bə-'sol-tik\ *adj*

¹base \\'bās\ *n, pl* **bas·es** \\'bā-səz\ **1** : BOTTOM, FOUNDATION **2** : a side or face on which a geometrical figure stands; *also* : the length of a base **3** : a main ingredient or fundamental part **4** : the point of beginning an act or operation **5** : a place on which a force depends for supplies **6** : a number (as 5 in 5⁷) that is raised to a power; *esp* : a number that when raised to a power equal to the logarithm of a number yields the number itself ⟨the logarithm of 100 to ∼ 10 is 2 since $10^2 = 100$⟩ **7** : the number of units in a given digit's place of a number system that is required to give the numeral 1 in the next higher place ⟨the decimal system uses a ∼ of 10⟩; *also* : such a system using an indicated base ⟨convert from ∼ 10 to ∼ 2⟩ **8** : any of the four stations at the corners of a baseball diamond **9** : a chemical compound (as lime or ammonia) that reacts with an acid to form a salt, has a bitter taste, and turns litmus blue ♦ **Synonyms** BASIS, GROUND, GROUNDWORK, FOOTING, FOUNDATION — **base·less** *adj*

²base *vb* **based; bas·ing** **1** : to form or serve as a base for **2** : ESTABLISH

³base *adj* **1** : of low value and inferior quality : DEBASED, ALLOYED **2** : CONTEMPTIBLE, IGNOBLE **3** : MENIAL, DEGRADING ♦ **Synonyms** LOW, VILE, DESPICABLE, WRETCHED — **base·ly** *adv* — **base·ness** *n*

base·ball \\'bās-ˌbol\ *n* : a game played with a bat and ball by two teams on a field with four bases arranged in a diamond; *also* : the ball used in this game

baseball cap *n* : a cap of the kind worn by baseball players that has a rounded crown and a long visor

base·board \-ˌbord\ *n* : a line of boards or molding covering the joint of a wall and the adjoining floor

base·born \-'born\ *adj* **1** : MEAN, IGNOBLE **2** : of humble birth **3** : of illegitimate birth

base exchange *n* : a post exchange at a naval or air force base

base hit *n* : a hit in baseball that enables the batter to reach base safely with no error made and no base runner forced out

BASE jumping \\'bās-\ *n* [building, antenna, span, earth] : the activity of parachuting from a high structure or cliff

base·line \\'bās-ˌlīn\ *n* **1** : a line serving as a basis esp. to calculate or locate something **2** : the area within which a baseball player must keep when running between bases

base·ment \-mənt\ *n* **1** : the part of a building that is wholly or partly below ground level **2** : the lowest or fundamental part of something

base on balls *n* : an advance to first base given to a baseball player who receives four balls

base runner *n* : a baseball player who is on base or is attempting to reach a base

¹bash \\'bash\ *vb* **1** : to strike violently : HIT **2** : to smash by a blow **3** : to attack physically or verbally

²bash *n* **1** : a heavy blow **2** : a festive social gathering : PARTY

bash·ful \\'bash-fəl\ *adj* : inclined to shrink from public attention — **bash·ful·ly** \-fə-lē\ *adv* — **bash·ful·ness** *n*

ba·sic \\'bā-sik\ *adj* **1** : of, relating to, or forming the base or essence : FUNDAMENTAL **2** : concerned with fundamental scientific principles : not applied **3** : of, relating to, or having the character of a chemical base ◆ *Synonyms* UNDERLYING, BASAL, PRIMARY — **ba·sic·i·ty** \bā-'si-sə-tē\ *n*

BA·SIC \'bā-sik\ *n* [*B*eginner's *A*ll-purpose *S*ymbolic *I*nstruction *C*ode] : a simplified language for programming a computer

ba·si·cal·ly \'bā-si-k(ə-)lē\ *adv* **1** : at a basic level **2** : for the most part **3** : in a basic manner

ba·sil \'bā-zəl, 'ba-, -səl\ *n* : any of several mints with fragrant leaves used in cooking; *also* : the leaves

ba·sil·i·ca \bə-'si-li-kə, -'zi-\ *n* [L, fr. Gk *basilikē*, fr. fem. of *basilikos* royal, fr. *basileus* king] **1** : an early Christian church building consisting of nave and aisles with clerestory and apse **2** : a Roman Catholic church given ceremonial privileges

bas·i·lisk \'ba-sə-,lisk, 'ba-zə-\ *n* [ME, fr. L *basiliscus*, fr. Gk *basiliskos*, fr. dim. of *basileus* king] : a legendary reptile with fatal breath and glance

ba·sin \'bā-sᵊn\ *n* **1** : an open usu. circular vessel with sloping sides for holding liquid (as water) **2** : a hollow or enclosed place containing water; *also* : the region drained by a river

ba·sis \'bā-səs\ *n, pl* **ba·ses** \-,sēz\ **1** : FOUNDATION, BASE **2** : a fundamental principle

bask \'bask\ *vb* **1** : to expose oneself to comfortable heat **2** : to enjoy something warmly comforting ⟨*~ing* in his friends' admiration⟩

bas·ket \'bas-kət\ *n* : a container made of woven material (as twigs or grasses); *also* : any of various lightweight usu. wood containers — **bas·ket·ful** *n*

bas·ket·ball \-,bȯl\ *n* : a game played on a court by two teams who try to throw an inflated ball through a raised goal; *also* : the ball used in this game — **bas·ket·ball·er** \-,bȯ-lər\ *n*

basket case *n* **1** : a person who has all four limbs amputated **2** : a person who is mentally incapacitated or worn out (as from nervous tension)

basket weave *n* : a textile weave resembling the checkered pattern of a plaited basket

bas·ma·ti rice \,bäz-'mä-tē-\ *n* : an aromatic long-grain rice originating in southern Asia

bas mitzvah *var of* BAT MITZVAH

Basque \'bask\ *n* **1** : a member of a people inhabiting a region bordering on the Bay of Biscay in northern Spain and southwestern France **2** : the language of the Basque people — **Basque** *adj*

bas–re·lief \,bä-ri-'lēf\ *n* [F] : a sculpture in relief with the design raised very slightly from the background

bas-relief

¹bass \'bas\ *n, pl* **bass** *or* **bass·es** : any of numerous sport and food bony fishes (as a striped bass)

²bass \'bās\ *adj* : of low pitch

³bass \'bās\ *n* **1** : a deep sound or tone **2** : the lower half of the musical pitch range **3** : the lowest part in a 4-part chorus; *also* : a singer having this voice or part

bas·set hound \'ba-sət-\ *n* : any of an old breed of short-legged hunting dogs of French origin having long ears and a short smooth coat

bas·si·net \,ba-sə-'net\ *n* : a baby's bed that resembles a basket and often has a hood over one end

bas·so \'ba-sō, 'bä-\ *n, pl* **bassos** *or* **bas·si** \'bä-,sē\ [It] : a bass singer

bas·soon \bə-'sün\ *n* : a musical wind instrument lower in pitch than the oboe

bass·wood \'bas-,wùd\ *n* : any of several New World lindens or their wood

bast \'bast\ *n* : BAST FIBER

¹bas·tard \'bas-tərd\ *n* **1** : an illegitimate child **2** : an offensive or disagreeable person

²bastard *adj* **1** : ILLEGITIMATE **2** : of an inferior or nontypical kind, size, or form; *also* : SPURIOUS — **bas·tardy** *n*

bas·tard·ise *Brit var of* BASTARDIZE

bas·tard·ize \'bas-tər-,dīz\ *vb* **-ized; -iz·ing** : to reduce from a higher to a lower state : DEBASE

¹baste \'bāst\ *vb* **bast·ed; bast·ing** : to sew with long stitches so as to keep temporarily in place

²baste *vb* **bast·ed; bast·ing** : to moisten (as meat) at intervals with liquid while cooking

bast fiber *n* : a strong woody plant fiber obtained chiefly from phloem and used esp. in making ropes

bas·ti·na·do \,bas-tə-'nā-dō, -'nä-\ *or* **bas·ti·nade** \,bas-tə-'nād, -'näd\ *n, pl* **-na·does** *or* **-nades** **1** : a blow or beating esp. with a stick **2** : a punishment consisting of beating the soles of the feet

bas·tion \'bas-chən\ *n* : a projecting part of a fortification; *also* : a fortified position

¹bat \'bat\ *n* **1** : a stout stick : CLUB **2** : a sharp blow **3** : an implement (as of wood) used to hit a ball (as in baseball) **4** : a turn at batting — usu. used in the phrase *at bat*

²bat *vb* **bat·ted; bat·ting** : to hit with or as if with a bat

³bat *n* : any of an order of night-flying mammals with fore-limbs modified to form wings

⁴bat *vb* **bat·ted; bat·ting** : WINK, BLINK

batch \'bach\ *n* **1** : a quantity (as of bread) baked at one time **2** : a quantity of material for use at one time or produced at one operation

bate \'bāt\ *vb* **bat·ed; bat·ing** : MODERATE, REDUCE

bath \'bath, 'bäth\ *n, pl* **baths** \'bathz, 'baths, 'bäthz, 'bäths\ **1** : a washing of the body **2** : water for washing the body **3** : a liquid in which objects are immersed so that it can act on them **4** : BATHROOM **5** : a financial loss ⟨took a ~ in the market⟩

bathe \'bāth\ *vb* **bathed; bath·ing** **1** : to wash in liquid and esp. water; *also* : to apply water or a medicated liquid to ⟨*bathed* her eyes⟩ **2** : to take a bath; *also* : to take a swim **3** : to wash along, over, or against so as to wet **4** : to suffuse with or as if with light — **bath·er** *n*

bath·house \'bath-,haùs, 'bäth-\ *n* **1** : a building equipped for bathing **2** : a building containing dressing rooms for bathers

bathing suit *n* : SWIMSUIT

ba·thos \'bā-,thäs\ *n* [Gk, lit., depth] **1** : the sudden appearance of the commonplace in otherwise elevated matter or style **2** : insincere or overdone pathos — **ba·thet·ic** \bə-'the-tik\ *adj*

bath·robe \'bath-,rōb, 'bäth-\ *n* : a loose often absorbent robe worn before and after bathing or as a dressing gown

bath·room \-,rüm, -,rùm\ *n* : a room containing a bathtub or shower and usu. a sink and toilet

bath·tub \-,təb\ *n* : a usu. fixed tub for bathing

ba·tik \bə-'tēk, 'ba-tik\ *n* [Javanese *baṭik*] **1** : an Indonesian method of hand-printing textiles by coating with wax the parts not to be dyed; *also* : a design so executed **2** : a fabric printed by batik

ba·tiste \bə-'tēst\ *n* : a fine sheer fabric of plain weave

bat·man \'bat-mən\ *n* : an orderly of a British military officer

bat mitz·vah \bät-'mits-və\ *also* **bas mitzvah** \bäs-\ *n, often cap B&M* [Heb *bath miṣwāh*, lit., daughter of the (divine) law] **1** : a Jewish girl who at about 13 years of age assumes religious responsibilities **2** : the ceremony recognizing a girl as a bat mitzvah

ba·ton \bə-'tän\ *n* : STAFF, ROD; *esp* : a stick with which the leader directs an orchestra or band

bats·man \'bats-mən\ *n* : a batter esp. in cricket

bat·tal·ion \bə-'tal-yən\ *n* **1** : a large body of troops organized to act together : ARMY **2** : a military unit composed of a headquarters and two or more units (as companies)

¹bat·ten \'ba-tᵊn\ *vb* **1** : to grow or make fat **2** : THRIVE

²batten *n* : a strip of wood used esp. to seal or strengthen a joint

³batten *vb* : to fasten with battens

¹bat·ter \'ba-tər\ *vb* : to beat or damage with repeated blows

²batter n : a soft mixture (as for cake) basically of flour and liquid

³batter n : one that bats; *esp* : the player whose turn it is to bat

battering ram n **1** : an ancient military machine for battering down walls **2** : a heavy metal bar with handles used to batter down doors

bat·tery \'ba-tə-rē\ n, pl **-ter·ies 1** : BEATING; *esp* : unlawful beating or use of force on a person **2** : a grouping of artillery pieces for tactical purposes; *also* : the guns of a warship **3** : a group of electric cells for furnishing electric current; *also* : a single electric cell ⟨a flashlight ∼⟩ **4** : a number of similar items grouped or used as a unit ⟨a ∼ of tests⟩ **5** : the pitcher and catcher of a baseball team

bat·ting \'ba-tiŋ\ n : layers or sheets of cotton or wool (as for lining quilts)

batting cage n : a screen around the back and sides of the home plate area to stop baseballs during practice

¹bat·tle \'ba-t²l\ n [ME *batel*, fr. AF *bataille* battle, battalion, fr. LL *battalia* combat, alter. of *battualia* fencing exercises, fr. L *battuere* to beat] : a general military engagement; *also* : an extended contest or controversy

²battle vb **bat·tled; bat·tling** : to engage in battle : CONTEND, FIGHT

bat·tle–ax *or* **battle–axe** \'ba-t²l-,aks\ n **1** : a long-handled ax formerly used as a weapon **2** : a quarrelsome domineering woman

battle fatigue n : COMBAT FATIGUE

bat·tle·field \'ba-t²l-,fēld\ n : a place where a battle is fought

bat·tle·ment \-mənt\ n : a decorative or defensive parapet on top of a wall

bat·tle·ship \-,ship\ n : a warship of the most heavily armed and armored class

bat·tle·wag·on \-,wa-gən\ n : BATTLESHIP

bat·ty \'ba-tē\ adj **bat·ti·er; -est** : CRAZY, FOOLISH

bau·ble \'bȯ-bəl\ n : TRINKET

baud \'bȯd, *Brit* 'bȯd\ n, pl **baud** *also* **bauds** : a unit of data transmission speed

baulk *chiefly Brit var of* BALK

baux·ite \'bȯk-,sīt\ n : a clayey mixture that is the chief ore of aluminum

bawd \'bȯd\ n **1** : MADAM 2 **2** : PROSTITUTE

bawdy \'bȯ-dē\ adj **bawd·i·er; -est** : OBSCENE, LEWD — **bawd·i·ly** \'bȯ-də-lē\ adv — **bawd·i·ness** \-dē-nəs\ n

¹bawl \'bȯl\ vb : to cry or cry out loudly; *also* : to scold harshly

²bawl n : a long loud cry : BELLOW

¹bay \'bā\ adj : reddish brown

²bay n **1** : a bay-colored animal **2** : a reddish brown color

³bay n **1** : a section or compartment of a building or vehicle **2** : a compartment projecting outward from the wall of a building and containing a window (**bay window**)

⁴bay vb : to bark with deep long tones

⁵bay n **1** : the position of one unable to escape and forced to face danger **2** : a baying of dogs

⁶bay n : an inlet of a body of water (as the sea) usu. smaller than a gulf

⁷bay n : LAUREL; *also* : a shrub or tree resembling the laurel

bay·ber·ry \'bā-,ber-ē\ n : a hardy deciduous shrub of coastal eastern No. America bearing small hard berries coated with a white wax used for candles; *also* : its fruit

bay leaf n : the dried leaf of the European laurel used in cooking

¹bay·o·net \'bā-ə-nət, ,bā-ə-'net\ n : a daggerlike weapon made to fit on the muzzle end of a rifle

²bayonet vb **-net·ed** *also* **-net·ted; -net·ing** *also* **-net·ting** : to use or stab with a bayonet

bay·ou \'bī-yü, -ō\ n [Louisiana French, fr. Choctaw *bayuk*] : a marshy or sluggish body of water

bay rum n : a fragrant liquid used esp. as a cologne or after-shave lotion

ba·zaar \bə-'zär\ n **1** : a group of shops : MARKETPLACE **2** : a fair for the sale of articles usu. for charity

ba·zoo·ka \bə-'zü-kə\ n [*bazooka* (a crude musical instrument made of pipes and a funnel)] : a weapon consisting of a tube that launches an explosive rocket able to pierce armor

¹BB \'bē-(,)bē\ n : a small round shot pellet

²BB *abbr* base on balls

BBB *abbr* Better Business Bureau

BBC *abbr* British Broadcasting Corporation

bbl *abbr* barrel; barrels

BC *abbr* **1** before Christ — often printed in small capitals and often punctuated **2** British Columbia

B cell n [*bone-marrow-derived cell*] : any of the lymphocytes that secrete antibodies when mature

B complex n : VITAMIN B COMPLEX

bd *abbr* **1** board **2** bound

bdl *or* **bdle** *abbr* bundle

bdrm *abbr* bedroom

be \'bē\ vb, *past 1st & 3d sing* **was** \'wəz, 'wäz\; *2d sing* **were** \'wər\; *pl* **were**; *past subjunctive* **were**; *past part* **been** \'bin\; *pres part* **be·ing** \'bē-iŋ\; *pres 1st sing* **am** \əm, 'am\; *2d sing* **are** \ər, 'är\; *3d sing* **is** \'iz, əz\; *pres subjunctive* **be 1** : to equal in meaning or symbolically ⟨God *is* love⟩; *also* : to have a specified qualification or relationship ⟨leaves *are* green⟩ ⟨this fish *is* a trout⟩ **2** : to have objective existence ⟨I think, therefore I *am*⟩; *also* : to have or occupy a particular place ⟨here *is* your pen⟩ **3** : to take place : OCCUR ⟨the meeting *is* tonight⟩ **4** — used with the past participle of transitive verbs as a passive voice auxiliary ⟨the door *was* opened⟩ **5** — used as the auxiliary of the present participle in expressing continuous action ⟨he *is* sleeping⟩ **6** — used as an auxiliary with the past participle of some intransitive verbs to form archaic perfect tenses **7** — used as an auxiliary with *to* and the infinitive to express futurity, prearrangement, or obligation ⟨you *are* to come when called⟩

Be *symbol* beryllium

¹beach \'bēch\ n : a sandy or gravelly part of the shore of an ocean or lake

²beach vb : to run or drive ashore

beach buggy n : DUNE BUGGY

beach·comb·er \'bēch-,kō-mər\ n : a person who searches along a shore for something of use or value

beach·head \'bēch-,hed\ n : a small area on an enemy-held shore occupied in the initial stages of an invasion

bea·con \'bē-kən\ n **1** : a signal fire **2** : a guiding or warning signal (as a lighthouse) **3** : a radio transmitter emitting signals for guidance of aircraft

¹bead \'bēd\ n [ME *bede* prayer, prayer bead, fr. OE *bed, gebed* prayer] **1** *pl* : a series of prayers and meditations made with a rosary **2** : a small piece of material pierced for threading on a line (as in a rosary) **3** : a small globular body **4** : a narrow projecting rim or band — **beading** n — **beady** adj

²bead vb : to form into a bead

bea·dle \'bē-d²l\ n : a usu. English parish officer whose duties include keeping order in church

bea·gle \'bē-gəl\ n : a small short-legged smooth-coated hound

beak \'bēk\ n : the bill of a bird and esp. of a bird of prey; *also* : a pointed projecting part — **beaked** \'bēkt\ adj

bea·ker \'bē-kər\ n **1** : a large widemouthed drinking cup **2** : a widemouthed thin-walled laboratory vessel

¹beam \'bēm\ n **1** : a large long piece of timber or metal **2** : the bar of a balance from which the scales hang **3** : the breadth of a ship at its widest part **4** : a ray or shaft of light **5** : a collection of nearly parallel rays (as X-rays) or particles (as electrons) **6** : a constant radio signal transmitted for the guidance of pilots; *also* : the course indicated by this signal

²beam vb **1** : to send out light **2** : BROADCAST **3** : to transmit (data) electronically **4** : to smile with joy

¹bean \'bēn\ n : the edible seed borne in pods by some leguminous plants; *also* : a plant or a pod bearing beans

²bean vb : to strike on the head with an object

bean·bag \'bēn-,bag\ n : a cloth bag partially filled typically with dried beans and used as a toy

bean·ball \'bēn-,bȯl\ n : a pitch thrown at a batter's head

bean curd n : TOFU

bean·ie \'bē-nē\ n : a small round tight-fitting skullcap

beano \'bē-nō\ n, pl **beanos** : BINGO

¹bear \'ber\ n, pl **bears 1** *or pl* **bear** : any of a family of large heavy mammals with shaggy hair and small tails **2** : a gruff or sullen person **3** : one who sells (as securities) in expectation of a price decline — **bear·ish** adj

²**bear** vb **bore** \'bór\; **borne** \'bórn\ also **born** \'bórn\; **bear·ing** 1 : CARRY 2 : to be equipped with 3 : to give as testimony ⟨~ witness to the facts of the case⟩ 4 : to give birth to; also : PRODUCE, YIELD ⟨a tree that ~s regularly⟩ 5 : ENDURE, SUSTAIN ⟨~ pain⟩ ⟨bore the weight on piles⟩; also : to exert pressure or influence 6 : to go in an indicated direction ⟨~ to the right⟩ — **bear·able** adj — **bear·er** n

¹**beard** \'bird\ n 1 : the hair that grows on the face of a man 2 : a growth of bristly hairs (as on a goat's chin) — **beard·ed** \'bir-dəd\ adj — **beard·less** adj

²**beard** vb : to confront boldly

bearing n 1 : manner of carrying oneself : COMPORTMENT 2 : a supporting object, purpose, or point 3 : a machine part in which another part (as an axle or pin) turns 4 : an emblem in a coat of arms 5 : the position or direction of one point with respect to another or to the compass; also : a determination of position 6 pl : comprehension of one's situation 7 : connection with or influence on something; also : SIGNIFICANCE

bear market n : a market in which securities or commodities are persistently declining in value

bear·skin \'ber-,skin\ n : an article (as a hat) made of the skin of a bear

beast \'bēst\ n 1 : ANIMAL 1; esp : a 4-footed mammal 2 : a contemptible person

¹**beast·ly** \'bēst-lē\ adj **beast·li·er; -est** 1 : BESTIAL 2 : ABOMINABLE, DISAGREEABLE — **beast·li·ness** \-nəs\ n

²**beastly** adv : VERY ⟨a ~ cold day⟩

¹**beat** \'bēt\ vb **beat; beat·en** \'bē-t⁰n\ or **beat; beat·ing** 1 : to strike repeatedly 2 : TREAD 3 : to affect or alter by beating ⟨~ metal into sheets⟩ 4 : to sound (as an alarm) on a drum 5 : OVERCOME; also : SURPASS 6 : to act or arrive before ⟨~ his brother home⟩ 7 : THROB — **beat·er** n

²**beat** n 1 : a single stroke or blow esp. of a series; also : PULSATION 2 : a rhythmic stress in poetry or music or the rhythmic effect of these 3 : a regularly traversed course

³**beat** adj 1 : EXHAUSTED 2 : of or relating to beatniks

⁴**beat** n : BEATNIK

be·atif·ic \,bē-ə-'ti-fik\ adj : giving or indicative of great joy or bliss

be·at·i·fy \bē-'a-tə-,fī\ vb **-fied; -fy·ing** 1 : to make supremely happy 2 : to declare to have attained the blessedness of heaven and authorize the title "Blessed" for — **be·at·i·fi·ca·tion** \-,a-tə-fə-'kā-shən\ n

be·at·i·tude \bē-'a-tə-,tüd, -,tyüd\ n 1 : a state of utmost bliss 2 : any of the declarations made in the Sermon on the Mount (Mt 5:3–12) beginning "Blessed are"

beat·nik \'bēt-nik\ n : a usu. young and artistic person who rejects the mores of established society

beau \'bō\ n, pl **beaux** \'bōz\ or **beaus** [F, fr. beau beautiful, fr. L bellus pretty] 1 : a man of fashion : DANDY 2 : SUITOR, LOVER

beau geste \bō-'zhest\ n, pl **beaux gestes** or **beau gestes** \bō-'zhest\ [F] : a graceful or magnanimous gesture

beau ide·al \,bō-ī-'dē(-ə)l\ n, pl **beau ideals** [F] : the perfect type or model

Beau·jo·lais \,bō-zhō-'lā\ n : a light fruity red wine

beau monde \bō-'mänd, -'mō⁰d\ n, pl **beau mondes** \-'mänz, -'mändz\ or **beaux mondes** \bō-'mō⁰d\ [F] : the world of high society and fashion

beau·te·ous \'byü-tē-əs\ adj : BEAUTIFUL — **beau·te·ous·ly** adv

beau·ti·cian \byü-'ti-shən\ n : COSMETOLOGIST

beau·ti·ful \'byü-ti-fəl\ adj : characterized by beauty : LOVELY ♦ **Synonyms** PRETTY, FAIR, COMELY — **beau·ti·ful·ly** \-f(ə-)lē\ adv

beautiful people n pl, often cap B&P : wealthy or famous people whose lifestyle is usu. expensive and well-publicized

beau·ti·fy \'byü-tə-,fī\ vb **-fied; -fy·ing** : to make more beautiful — **beau·ti·fi·ca·tion** \,byü-tə-fə-'kā-shən\ n — **beau·ti·fi·er** n

beau·ty \'byü-tē\ n, pl **beauties** : qualities that give pleasure to the senses or exalt the mind : LOVELINESS; also : something having such qualities

beauty shop n : an establishment where hairdressing, facials, and manicures are done

beaux arts \bō-'zär\ n pl [F] : FINE ARTS

bea·ver \'bē-vər\ n, pl **beavers** : a large fur-bearing herbivorous rodent that builds dams and underwater houses of mud and sticks; also : its fur

beaver

be·calm \bi-'käm, -'kälm\ vb : to keep (as a ship) motionless by lack of wind

be·cause \bi-'kóz, -'kəz\ conj : for the reason that ⟨ran away ~ they were afraid⟩

because of prep : by reason of

beck \'bek\ n : a beckoning gesture; also : SUMMONS

beck·on \'be-kən\ vb : to summon or signal esp. by a nod or gesture; also : ATTRACT

be·cloud \bi-'klaud\ vb : OBSCURE

be·come \bi-'kəm\ vb **-came** \-'kām\; **-come; -com·ing** 1 : to come to be ⟨~ tired⟩ 2 : to suit or be suitable to ⟨her dress ~s her⟩

becoming adj : SUITABLE, FIT; also : ATTRACTIVE — **be·com·ing·ly** adv

¹**bed** \'bed\ n 1 : an article of furniture to sleep on 2 : a plot of ground prepared for plants 3 : FOUNDATION, BOTTOM 4 : LAYER, STRATUM

²**bed** vb **bed·ded; bed·ding** 1 : to put or go to bed 2 : to fix in a foundation : EMBED 3 : to plant in beds 4 : to lay or lie flat or in layers

bed–and–breakfast n : an establishment offering lodging and breakfast

be·daub \bi-'dób\ vb : SMEAR

be·daz·zle \bi-'da-zəl\ vb : to confuse by or as if by a strong light; also : FASCINATE — **be·daz·zle·ment** n

bed·bug \'bed-,bəg\ n : a wingless bloodsucking bug infesting houses and esp. beds

bed·clothes \'bed-,klōthz\ n pl : materials for making up a bed

bed·ding \'be-diŋ\ n 1 : BEDCLOTHES 2 : FOUNDATION

be·deck \bi-'dek\ vb : ADORN

be·dev·il \bi-'de-vəl\ vb 1 : HARASS, TORMENT 2 : CONFUSE, MUDDLE

be·dew \bi-'dü, -'dyü\ vb : to wet with or as if with dew

bed·fast \'bed-,fast\ adj : BEDRIDDEN

bed·fel·low \-,fe-lō\ n 1 : one sharing the bed of another 2 : a close associate : ALLY

be·di·zen \bi-'dī-z⁰n, -'di-\ vb : to dress or adorn with showy or vulgar finery

bed·lam \'bed-ləm\ n [Bedlam, popular name for the Hospital of St. Mary of Bethlehem, London, an insane asylum, fr. ME Bedlem Bethlehem] 1 often cap : an insane asylum 2 : a scene of uproar and confusion

bed·ou·in also **bed·u·in** \'be-də-wən\ n, pl **bedouin** or **bedouins** also **beduin** or **beduins** often cap [ME Bedoyne, fr. MF bedoïn, fr. Ar badawī desert dweller] : a nomadic Arab of the Arabian, Syrian, or No. African deserts

bed·pan \'bed-,pan\ n : a shallow vessel used by a bedridden person for urination or defecation

bed·post \-,pōst\ n : the post of a bed

be·drag·gled \bi-'dra-gəld\ adj : soiled and disordered as if by being drenched

bed·rid·den \'bed-,ri-d⁰n\ adj : kept in bed by illness or weakness

¹**bed·rock** \-'räk\ n : the solid rock underlying surface materials (as soil)

²**bedrock** adj : solidly fundamental, basic, or reliable ⟨traditional ~ values⟩

bed·roll \'bed-,rōl\ n : bedding rolled up for carrying

bed·room \-,rüm, -,rum\ n : a room containing a bed and used esp. for sleeping

bed·side \-,sīd\ n : the place beside a bed esp. of a sick or dying person

bed·sore \-,sòr\ *n* : an ulceration of tissue deprived of adequate blood supply by prolonged pressure

bed·spread \-,spred\ *n* : a usu. ornamental cloth cover for a bed

bed·stead \-,sted\ *n* : the framework of a bed

bed·time \-,tīm\ *n* : time for going to bed

bed–wet·ting \-,we-tiŋ\ *n* : involuntary discharge of urine esp. in bed during sleep — **bed–wet·ter** *n*

¹**bee** \'bē\ *n* : any of numerous 4-winged insects (as honeybees or bumblebees) that feed on nectar and pollen and that sometimes produce honey or have a painful sting

²**bee** *n* : a gathering of people for a specific purpose ⟨a quilting ∼⟩

beech \'bēch\ *n, pl* **beech·es** *or* **beech** : any of a genus of hardwood trees with smooth gray bark and small sweet triangular nuts; *also* : its wood — **beech·en** \'bē-chən\ *adj*

beech·nut \'bēch-,nət\ *n* : the nut of a beech

¹**beef** \'bēf\ *n, pl* **beefs** \'bēfs\ *or* **beeves** \'bēvz\ **1** : the flesh of a steer, cow, or bull; *also* : the dressed carcass of a beef animal **2** : a steer, cow, or bull esp. when fattened for food **3** : MUSCLE, BRAWN **4** *pl* **beefs** : COMPLAINT

²**beef** *vb* **1** : STRENGTHEN — usu. used with *up* ⟨∼ed up security⟩ **2** : COMPLAIN

beef·eat·er \'bē-,fē-tər\ *n* : a yeoman of the guard of an English monarch

beef·steak \-,stāk\ *n* : a slice of beef suitable for broiling or frying

beefy \'bē-fē\ *adj* **beef·i·er; -est** : THICKSET, BRAWNY

bee·hive \'bē-,hīv\ *n* : HIVE 1, HIVE 3

bee·keep·er \-,kē-pər\ *n* : a person who raises bees — **bee·keep·ing** *n*

bee·line \-,līn\ *n* : a straight direct course

been *past part of* BE

beep·er \'bē-pər\ *n* : PAGER; *esp* : one that beeps

beer \'bir\ *n* : an alcoholic beverage brewed from malt and hops — **beery** *adj*

beer belly *n* : POTBELLY

bees·wax \'bēz-,waks\ *n* : WAX 1

beet \'bēt\ *n* : a garden plant with edible leaves and a thick sweet root used as a vegetable, as a source of sugar, or as forage; *also* : its root

¹**bee·tle** \'bē-t�ᵊl\ *n* : any of an order of insects having four wings of which the stiff outer pair covers the membranous inner pair when not in flight

²**beetle** *vb* **bee·tled; bee·tling** : to jut out : PROJECT

be·fall \bi-'fòl\ *vb* **-fell** \-'fel\; **-fall·en** \-'fò-lən\ : to happen to : OCCUR

be·fit \bi-'fit\ *vb* : to be suitable to

be·fog \bi-'fòg, -'fäg\ *vb* : OBSCURE; *also* : CONFUSE

¹**be·fore** \bi-'fòr\ *adv or adj* **1** : in front **2** : EARLIER

²**before** *prep* **1** : in front of ⟨stood ∼ him⟩ **2** : earlier than ⟨got there ∼ me⟩ **3** : in a more important category than ⟨put quality ∼ quantity⟩

³**before** *conj* **1** : earlier than the time that ⟨he got here ∼ I did⟩ **2** : more willingly than ⟨she'd starve ∼ she'd steal⟩

be·fore·hand \bi-'fòr-,hand\ *adv or adj* : in advance

be·foul \bi-'faù(-ə)l\ *vb* : SOIL

be·friend \bi-'frend\ *vb* : to act as friend to

be·fud·dle \bi-'fə-d⁰l\ *vb* : MUDDLE, CONFUSE

beg \'beg\ *vb* **begged; beg·ging** **1** : to ask as a charity; *also* : ENTREAT **2** : EVADE; *also* : assume as established, settled, or proved ⟨∼ the question⟩

be·get \bi-'get\ *vb* **-got** \-'gät\; **-got·ten** \-'gä-t⁰n\ *or* **-got;** **-get·ting** : to become the father of : SIRE

¹**beg·gar** \'be-gər\ *n* : one that begs; *esp* : a person who begs as a way of life

²**beggar** *vb* : IMPOVERISH

beg·gar·ly \'be-gər-lē\ *adj* **1** : contemptibly mean or inadequate **2** : marked by unrelieved poverty ⟨a ∼ life⟩

beg·gary \'be-gə-rē\ *n* : extreme poverty

be·gin \bi-'gin\ *vb* **be·gan** \-'gan\; **be·gun** \-'gən\; **be·gin·ning** **1** : to do the first part of an action : COMMENCE **2** : to come into being : ARISE; *also* : FOUND **3** : ORIGINATE, INVENT — **be·gin·ner** *n*

beg off *vb* : to ask to be excused from something

be·gone \bi-'gòn\ *vb* : to go away : DEPART — used esp. in the imperative

be·go·nia \bi-'gōn-yə\ *n* : any of a genus of tropical herbs widely grown for their showy leaves and waxy flowers

be·grime \bi-'grīm\ *vb* **be·grimed; be·grim·ing** : to make dirty

be·grudge \bi-'grəj\ *vb* **1** : to give or concede reluctantly **2** : to be reluctant to grant or allow — **be·grudg·ing·ly** \-'grə-jiŋ-lē\ *adv*

be·guile \-'gī(-ə)l\ *vb* **be·guiled; be·guil·ing** **1** : DECEIVE **2** : to while away **3** : to engage the interest of by guile

be·guine \bi-'gēn\ *n* [AmerF *béguine*, fr. F *béguin* flirtation] : a vigorous popular dance of the islands of Saint Lucia and Martinique

be·gum \'bä-gəm, 'bē-\ *n* : a Muslim woman of high rank

be·half \bi-'haf, -'häf\ *n* : BENEFIT, SUPPORT, DEFENSE

be·have \bi-'hāv\ *vb* **be·haved; be·hav·ing** **1** : to bear, comport, or conduct oneself in a particular and esp. a proper way **2** : to act, function, or react in a particular way

be·hav·ior \bi-'hā-vyər\ *n* : way of behaving; *esp* : personal conduct — **be·hav·ior·al** \-vyə-rəl\ *adj* — **be·hav·ior·al·ly** \-rə-lē\ *adv*

be·hav·ior·ism \bi-'hā-vyə-,ri-zəm\ *n* : a school of psychology concerned with the objective evidence of behavior without reference to conscious experience

be·hav·ior·ist \-vyə-rist\ *n* **1** : a person who supports behaviorism **2** : a person who studies behavior

be·hav·iour, be·hav·iour·ism *chiefly Brit var of* BEHAVIOR, BEHAVIORISM

be·head \bi-'hed\ *vb* : to cut off the head of

be·he·moth \bi-'hē-məth, 'bē-ə-,mäth\ *n* : a huge powerful animal described in Job 40:15–24; *also* : something of monstrous size or power

be·hest \bi-'hest\ *n* **1** : COMMAND **2** : an urgent prompting

¹**be·hind** \bi-'hīnd\ *adv or adj* **1** : BACK, BACKWARD ⟨look ∼⟩ **2** : LATE, SLOW

²**behind** *prep* **1** : in or to a place or situation in back of or to the rear of ⟨look ∼ you⟩ ⟨the staff stayed ∼ the troops⟩ **2** : inferior to (as in rank) : BELOW ⟨three games ∼ the first-place team⟩ **3** : in support of : SUPPORTING ⟨we're ∼ you all the way⟩

be·hind·hand \bi-'hīnd-,hand\ *adj* : being in arrears ✦ *Synonyms* TARDY, LATE, OVERDUE, BELATED

be·hold \bi-'hōld\ *vb* **-held** \-'held\; **-hold·ing** **1** : to have in sight : SEE **2** — used imperatively to direct the attention ✦ *Synonyms* VIEW, OBSERVE, NOTICE, ESPY — **be·hold·er** *n*

be·hold·en \bi-'hōl-dən\ *adj* : OBLIGATED, INDEBTED

be·hoove \bi-'hüv\ *vb* **be·hooved; be·hoov·ing** : to be necessary, proper, or advantageous for

be·hove *chiefly Brit var of* BEHOOVE

beige \'bäzh\ *n* : a pale dull yellowish brown — **beige** *adj*

be·ing \'bē-iŋ\ *n* **1** : EXISTENCE; *also* : LIFE **2** : the qualities or constitution of an existent thing **3** : a living thing; *esp* : PERSON

be·la·bor \bi-'lā-bər\ *vb* : to assail (as with words) tiresomely or at length

be·la·bour *chiefly Brit var of* BELABOR

be·lat·ed \bi-'lā-təd\ *adj* : DELAYED, LATE

be·lay \bi-'lā\ *vb* **1** : to wind (a rope) around a pin or cleat in order to hold secure **2** : QUIT, STOP — used in the imperative

belch \'belch\ *vb* **1** : to expel (gas) from the stomach through the mouth **2** : to gush forth ⟨a volcano ∼*ing* lava⟩ — **belch** *n*

bel·dam *or* **bel·dame** \'bel-dəm\ *n* [ME *beldam* grandmother, fr. AF *bel* beautiful + ME *dam* lady, mother] : an old woman

be·lea·guer \bi-'lē-gər\ *vb* **1** : BESIEGE **2** : HARASS ⟨∼ed parents⟩

bel·fry \'bel-frē\ *n, pl* **belfries** : a tower for a bell (as on a church); *also* : the part of the tower in which the bell hangs

Belg *abbr* Belgian; Belgium

Bel·gian endive \'bel-jən\ *n* : the blanched shoot of chicory

Belgian waffle *n* : a waffle having large depressions and usu. topped with fruit and whipped cream

be·lie \bi-'lī\ *vb* **-lied; -ly·ing** **1** : MISREPRESENT **2** : to show (something) to be false **3** : to run counter to

be·lief \bə-'lēf\ *n* **1** : CONFIDENCE, TRUST **2** : something (as a tenet or creed) believed ✦ *Synonyms* CONVICTION, OPINION, PERSUASION, SENTIMENT

be·lieve \bə-'lēv\ vb **be·lieved; be·liev·ing 1** : to have religious convictions **2** : to have a firm conviction about something : accept as true **3** : to hold as an opinion : SUPPOSE — **be·liev·able** \-'lē-və-bəl\ adj — **be·liev·ably** \-blē\ adv — **be·liev·er** n

be·like \bi-'līk\ adv, archaic : PROBABLY

be·lit·tle \bi-'li-t°l\ vb **-lit·tled; -lit·tling** : to make seem little or less; also : DISPARAGE

1bell \'bel\ n **1** : a hollow metallic device that makes a ringing sound when struck **2** : the sounding or stroke of a bell (as on shipboard to tell the time); also : time so indicated **3** : something with the flared form of a typical bell

2bell vb : to provide with a bell

bel·la·don·na \ˌbe-lə-'dä-nə\ n [It, lit., beautiful lady] : a medicinal extract (as atropine) from a poisonous European herb related to the potato; also : this herb

bell–bot·toms \'bel-'bä-təmz\ n pl : pants with wide flaring bottoms — **bell–bottom** adj

bell·boy \'bel-ˌbȯi\ n : BELLHOP

belle \'bel\ n : an attractive and popular girl or woman

belles let·tres \bel-'letr°\ n pl [F] : literature that is an end in itself and not practical or purely informative — **bel·le·tris·tic** \ˌbe-lə-'tris-tik\ adj

bell·hop \'bel-ˌhäp\ n : a hotel or club employee who takes guests to rooms, carries luggage, and runs errands

bel·li·cose \'be-li-ˌkōs\ adj : WARLIKE, PUGNACIOUS ◆ **Synonyms** BELLIGERENT, QUARRELSOME, COMBATIVE, CONTENTIOUS — **bel·li·cos·i·ty** \ˌbe-li-'kä-sə-tē\ n

bel·lig·er·en·cy \bə-'li-jə-rən-sē\ n **1** : the status of a nation engaged in war **2** : BELLIGERENCE, TRUCULENCE

bel·lig·er·ent \-rənt\ adj **1** : waging war **2** : aggressively self-assertive ◆ **Synonyms** BELLICOSE, PUGNACIOUS, COMBATIVE, CONTENTIOUS, WARLIKE — **bel·lig·er·ence** \-rəns\ n — **belligerent** n — **bel·lig·er·ent·ly** adv

bel·low \'be-lō\ vb **1** : to make the deep hollow sound characteristic of a bull **2** : to shout in a deep voice — **bellow** n

bel·lows \-lōz, -ləz\ n sing or pl : a closed device with sides that can be spread apart and then pressed together to draw in air and expel it through a tube

bell·weth·er \'bel-'we-thər, -ˌwe-\ n : one that takes the lead or initiative; also : an indicator of trends

1bel·ly \'be-lē\ n, pl **bellies** [ME bely bellows, belly, fr. OE belg bag, skin] **1** : ABDOMEN 1; also : POTBELLY **2** : the underpart of an animal's body

2belly vb **bel·lied; bel·ly·ing** : BULGE

1bel·ly·ache \'be-lē-ˌāk\ n : pain in the abdomen : STOMACHACHE

2bellyache vb : COMPLAIN

belly button n : the human navel

belly dance n : a usu. solo dance emphasizing movement of the belly — **belly dance** vb — **belly dancer** n

belly laugh n : a deep hearty laugh

be·long \bi-'lȯn\ vb **1** : to be suitable or appropriate; also : to be properly situated ⟨shoes ∼ in the closet⟩ **2** : to be the property ⟨this ∼s to me⟩; also : to be attached (as through birth or membership) ⟨∼ to a club⟩ **3** : to form an attribute or part ⟨this wheel ∼s to the cart⟩ **4** : to be classified ⟨whales ∼ among the mammals⟩

be·long·ings \-'lȯn-inz\ n pl : GOODS, EFFECTS, POSSESSIONS

be·loved \bi-'ləvd, -'lə-vəd\ adj : dearly loved — **beloved** n

1be·low \bi-'lō\ adv **1** : in or to a lower place or rank **2** : on earth **3** : in hell

2below prep **1** : lower than ⟨∼ sea level⟩ **2** : inferior to (as in rank)

be·low·decks \bi-lō-'deks, -'lō-ˌdeks\ adv : inside the superstructure of a boat or down to a lower deck

1belt \'belt\ n **1** : a strip (as of leather) worn about the waist **2** : a flexible continuous band to communicate motion or convey material **3** : a region marked by some distinctive feature; esp : one suited to a particular crop

2belt vb **1** : to encircle or secure with a belt **2** : to beat with or as if with a belt **3** : to mark with an encircling band **4** : to sing loudly

3belt n **1** : a jarring blow : WHACK **2** : DRINK ⟨a ∼ of whiskey⟩

belt·er \'bel-tər\ n : a singer with a powerful voice

belt–tightening n : a reduction in spending

belt·way \'belt-ˌwā\ n : a highway around a city

be·lu·ga \bə-'lü-gə\ n [Russ] **1** : a large white sturgeon of the Black Sea, Caspian Sea, and their tributaries that is a source of caviar; also : caviar from beluga roe **2** : a whale of arctic and subarctic waters that is white when mature

bel·ve·dere \'bel-və-ˌdir\ n [It, lit., beautiful view] : a structure (as a summerhouse) designed to command a view

be·mire \bi-'mī(-ə)r\ vb : to cover or soil with or sink in mire

be·moan \bi-'mōn\ vb : LAMENT, DEPLORE ◆ **Synonyms** BEWAIL, GRIEVE, MOAN, WEEP

be·muse \bi-'myüz\ vb : BEWILDER, CONFUSE

1bench \'bench\ n **1** : a long seat for two or more persons **2** : the seat of a judge in court; also : the office or dignity of a judge **3** : COURT; also : JUDGES **4** : a table for holding work and tools ⟨a carpenter's ∼⟩

2bench vb **1** : to furnish with benches **2** : to seat on a bench **3** : to remove from or keep out of a game

1bench·mark \'bench-ˌmärk\ n **1** usu **bench mark** : a mark on a permanent object serving as an elevation reference in topographical surveys **2** : a point of reference for measurement; also : STANDARD

2benchmark vb : to study (as a competitor's business practices) in order to improve one's own performance

bench press n : an exercise in which a weight is raised by a person lying on a bench — **bench–press** vb

bench warrant n : a warrant issued by a presiding judge or by a court against a person guilty of contempt or indicted for a crime

1bend \'bend\ vb **bent** \'bent\; **bend·ing 1** : to draw (as a bow) taut **2** : to curve or cause a change of shape in ⟨∼ a bar⟩ **3** : to make fast : SECURE **4** : DEFLECT **5** : to turn in a certain direction ⟨bent his steps toward town⟩ **6** : APPLY ⟨bent themselves to the task⟩ **7** : SUBDUE **8** : to curve downward **9** : YIELD, SUBMIT

2bend n **1** : an act or process of bending **2** : something bent; esp : CURVE **3** pl : a painful and sometimes fatal disorder caused by release of gas bubbles in the tissues upon too rapid decrease in air pressure after a stay in a compressed atmosphere

3bend n : a knot by which a rope is fastened (as to another rope)

bend·er \'ben-dər\ n : SPREE ⟨hungover after a weekend ∼⟩

1be·neath \bi-'nēth\ adv : BELOW ⟨the mountains and the town ∼⟩ ◆ **Synonyms** UNDER, UNDERNEATH

2beneath prep **1** : BELOW, UNDER ⟨stood ∼ a tree⟩ **2** : unworthy of ⟨considered such behavior ∼ her⟩ **3** : concealed by ⟨a warm heart ∼ a gruff manner⟩

bene·dic·tion \ˌbe-nə-'dik-shən\ n : the invocation of a blessing esp. at the close of a public worship service

ben·e·fac·tion \-'fak-shən\ n : a charitable donation ◆ **Synonyms** CONTRIBUTION, ALMS, BENEFICENCE, OFFERING

ben·e·fac·tor \'ben-ə-ˌfak-tər\ n : one that confers a benefit and esp. a benefaction

ben·e·fac·tress \-ˌfak-trəs\ n : a woman who is a benefactor

ben·e·fice \'be-nə-fəs\ n : an ecclesiastical office to which the revenue from an endowment is attached

be·nef·i·cence \bə-'ne-fə-səns\ n **1** : beneficent quality **2** : BENEFACTION

be·nef·i·cent \-sənt\ adj : doing or producing good (as by acts of kindness or charity); also : BENEFICIAL

ben·e·fi·cial \ˌbe-nə-'fi-shəl\ adj : being of benefit or help : HELPFUL ◆ **Synonyms** ADVANTAGEOUS, PROFITABLE, FAVORABLE, PROPITIOUS — **ben·e·fi·cial·ly** adv

ben·e·fi·cia·ry \ˌbe-nə-'fi-shē-ˌer-ē, -'fi-shə-rē\ n, pl **-ries** : one that receives a benefit (as the income of a trust or the proceeds of an insurance)

1ben·e·fit \'be-nə-ˌfit\ n **1** : ADVANTAGE ⟨the ∼s of exercise⟩ **2** : useful aid : HELP; also : material aid or service provided or due (as in sickness or unemployment) as a right in addition to regular pay **3** : a performance or event to raise funds

2benefit vb **-fit·ed** \-ˌfi-təd\ also **-fit·ted; -fit·ing** also **-fit·ting 1** : to be useful or profitable to **2** : to receive benefit

be·nev·o·lence \bə-'ne-və-ləns\ n **1** : charitable nature **2**

: an act of kindness : CHARITY — **be·nev·o·lent** \-lənt\ *adj* — **be·nev·o·lent·ly** *adv*

be·night·ed \bi-'nī-təd\ *adj* **1** : overtaken by darkness or night **2** : living in ignorance

be·nign \bi-'nīn\ *adj* [ME *benigne*, fr. AF, fr. L *benignus*] **1** : of a gentle disposition; *also* : showing kindness **2** : of a mild kind; *esp* : not malignant ⟨~ tumors⟩ ♦ **Synonyms** BENIGNANT, KIND, KINDLY, GOOD-HEARTED — **be·nig·ni·ty** \-'nig-nə-tē\ *n* — **be·nign·ly** *adv*

be·nig·nant \-'nig-nənt\ *adj* : BENIGN 1 ♦ **Synonyms** KIND, KINDLY, GOOD-HEARTED

ben·i·son \'be-nə-sən, -zən\ *n* : BLESSING, BENEDICTION

¹**bent** \'bent\ *n* **1** : strong inclination or interest; *also* : TALENT **2** : power of endurance ♦ **Synonyms** TALENT, APTITUDE, GIFT, FLAIR, KNACK, GENIUS

²**bent** *adj* **1** : changed by bending : CROOKED ⟨~ branches⟩ **2** : strongly inclined : DETERMINED ⟨~ on going⟩

bent grass *n* : any of a genus of stiff velvety grasses used esp. for lawns and pastures

ben·thic \'ben-thik\ *adj* : of, relating to, or occurring at the bottom of a body of water

ben·ton·ite \'ben-tə-ˌnīt\ *n* : an absorptive clay used esp. as a filler (as in paper)

bent·wood \'bent-ˌwud\ *adj* : made of wood bent into shape ⟨a ~ rocker⟩

be·numb \bi-'nəm\ *vb* **1** : DULL, DEADEN **2** : to make numb esp. by cold

ben·zene \'ben-ˌzēn\ *n* : a colorless volatile flammable liquid hydrocarbon used in organic synthesis and as a solvent — **ben·ze·noid** \-zə-ˌnoid\ *adj or n*

ben·zine \'ben-ˌzēn\ *n* : any of various flammable petroleum distillates used as solvents or as motor fuels

ben·zo·ate \'ben-zə-ˌwāt\ *n* : a salt or ester of benzoic acid

ben·zo·ic acid \ben-'zō-ik-\ *n* : a white crystalline acid used as a preservative and antiseptic and in synthesizing chemicals

ben·zo·in \'ben-zə-wən, -ˌzoin\ *n* : a balsamic resin from trees of southern Asia used esp. in medicine and perfumes

be·queath \bi-'kwēth, -'kwēth\ *vb* [ME *bequethen*, fr. OE *becwethan*, fr. *be-* + *cwethan* to say] **1** : to leave by will **2** : to hand down

be·quest \bi-'kwest\ *n* **1** : the action of bequeathing **2** : something bequeathed : LEGACY

be·rate \-'rāt\ *vb* : to scold harshly

Ber·ber \'bər-bər\ *n* : a member of any of various peoples living in northern Africa west of Tripoli

ber·ceuse \ber-'sœz, -'süz\ *n, pl* **ber·ceuses** \same *or* -'süzəz\ [F, fr. *bercer* to rock] **1** : LULLABY **2** : a musical composition that resembles a lullaby

¹**be·reaved** \bi-'rēvd\ *adj* : suffering the death of a loved one — **be·reave·ment** *n*

²**bereaved** *n, pl* **bereaved** : one who is bereaved

be·reft \-'reft\ *adj* **1** : deprived of or lacking something — usu. used with *of* **2** : BEREAVED ⟨a ~ mother⟩

be·ret \bə-'rā\ *n* : a round soft cap with no visor

berg \'bərg\ *n* : ICEBERG

beri·beri \ˌber-ē-'ber-ē\ *n* : a deficiency disease marked by weakness, wasting, and nerve damage and caused by lack of thiamine

berke·li·um \'bər-klē-əm\ *n* : an artificially produced radioactive chemical element

berm \'bərm\ *n* : a narrow shelf or path at the top or bottom of a slope; *also* : a mound or bank of earth

Bermuda grass *n* : a creeping grass often used for lawns and pastures

Ber·mu·das \bər-'myü-dəz\ *n pl* : BERMUDA SHORTS

Bermuda shorts *n pl* : knee-length walking shorts

ber·ry \'ber-ē\ *n, pl* **berries** **1** : a small pulpy fruit (as a strawberry) **2** : a simple fruit (as a grape, tomato, or cucumber) with the wall of the ripened ovary thick and pulpy **3** : the dry seed of some plants (as coffee)

ber·serk \bər-'sərk, -'zərk\ *adj* [ON *berserkr* warrior frenzied in battle, prob. fr. *ber-* bear + *serkr* shirt] : FRENZIED, CRAZED — **berserk** *adv*

¹**berth** \'bərth\ *n* **1** : adequate distance esp. for a ship to maneuver **2** : the place where a ship is anchored or a vehicle rests **3** : ACCOMMODATIONS **4** : JOB, POSITION ♦ **Synonyms** POST, SITUATION, OFFICE, APPOINTMENT

²**berth** *vb* **1** : to bring or come into a berth **2** : to allot a berth to

ber·yl \'ber-əl\ *n* : a hard silicate mineral occurring as colorless hexagonal crystals when pure

be·ryl·li·um \bə-'ri-lē-əm\ *n* : a light strong metallic chemical element used as a hardener in alloys

be·seech \bi-'sēch\ *vb* **-sought** \-'sot\ *or* **-seeched**; **-seech·ing** : to beg urgently : ENTREAT ♦ **Synonyms** IMPLORE, PLEAD, SUPPLICATE, IMPORTUNE

be·seem \bi-'sēm\ *vb, archaic* : BEFIT

be·set \-'set\ *vb* **-set; -set·ting** **1** : TROUBLE, HARASS **2** : ASSAIL; *also* : SURROUND

be·set·ting *adj* : persistently present

¹**be·side** \bi-'sīd\ *prep* **1** : by the side of ⟨sit ~ me⟩ **2** : BESIDES **3** : not relevant to ⟨~ the point⟩

²**beside** *adv, archaic* : BESIDES

¹**be·sides** \bi-'sīdz\ *prep* **1** : other than ⟨no one ~ us⟩ **2** : together with

²**besides** *adv* **1** : as well : ALSO **2** : MOREOVER

be·siege \bi-'sēj\ *vb* : to lay siege to; *also* : to press with requests — **be·sieg·er** *n*

be·smear \-'smir\ *vb* : SMEAR

be·smirch \-'smərch\ *vb* : SMIRCH, SOIL

be·som \'bē-zəm\ *n* : BROOM

be·sot \bi-'sät\ *vb* **be·sot·ted; be·sot·ting** **1** : INFATUATE **2** : to make dull esp. by drinking

be·spat·ter \-'spa-tər\ *vb* : SPATTER

be·speak \bi-'spēk\ *vb* **-spoke** \-'spōk\; **-spo·ken** \-'spō-kən\; **-speak·ing** **1** : PREARRANGE **2** : ADDRESS **3** : REQUEST **4** : INDICATE, SIGNIFY **5** : FORETELL

be·sprin·kle \-'spriŋ-kəl\ *vb* : SPRINKLE

¹**best** \'best\ *adj, superlative of* GOOD **1** : excelling all others **2** : most productive (as of good or satisfaction) **3** : LARGEST, MOST

²**best** *adv, superlative of* WELL **1** : in the best way **2** : MOST

³**best** *n* : something that is best

⁴**best** *vb* : to get the better of : OUTDO

bes·tial \'bes-chəl\ *adj* **1** : of or relating to beasts **2** : resembling a beast esp. in brutality or lack of intelligence

bes·ti·al·i·ty \ˌbes-chē-'a-lə-tē, ˌbēs-\ *n, pl* **-ties** **1** : the condition or status of a lower animal **2** : display or gratification of bestial traits or impulses **3** : sexual relations between a human being and a lower animal

bes·ti·ary \'bes-chē-ˌer-ē\ *n, pl* **-ar·ies** : a medieval allegorical or moralizing work on the appearance and habits of animals

be·stir \bi-'stər\ *vb* : to rouse to action

best man *n* : the principal groomsman at a wedding

be·stow \bi-'stō\ *vb* **1** : PUT, PLACE, STOW **2** : to present as a gift — **be·stow·al** *n* — **be·stow·er** *n*

be·stride \bi-'strīd\ *vb* **-strode** \-'strōd\; **-strid·den** \-'strid³n\; **-strid·ing** : to ride, sit, or stand astride

¹**bet** \'bet\ *n* **1** : something that is wagered, risked, or pledged usu. between two parties on the outcome of a contest; *also* : the making of such a bet **2** : OPTION ⟨the back road is your best ~⟩

²**bet** *vb* **bet** *also* **bet·ted; bet·ting** **1** : to stake on the outcome of an issue or a contest ⟨~ $2 on the race⟩ **2** : to make a bet with **3** : to lay a bet

³**bet** *abbr* between

be·ta \'bā-tə\ *n* **1** : the 2d letter of the Greek alphabet — B or β **2** : a nearly complete form of a new product (as software)

beta–block·er \-ˌblä-kər\ *n* : any of a group of drugs that decrease the rate and force of heart contractions and lower high blood pressure

be·ta–car·o·tene \-'ker-ə-ˌtēn\ *n* : an isomer of carotene found in dark green and dark yellow vegetables and fruits

be·take \bi-'tāk\ *vb* **-took** \-'tuk\; **-tak·en** \-'tā-kən\; **-tak·ing** : to cause (oneself) to go

beta particle *n* : a high-speed electron; *esp* : one emitted by a radioactive nucleus

beta ray *n* **1** : BETA PARTICLE **2** : a stream of beta particles

beta test *n* : a field test of the beta version of a product esp. by outside testers and prior to commercial release — **beta test** *vb*

be·tel \'bē-t³l\ *n* : a climbing pepper of southern Asia whose leaves are chewed together with lime and betel nut as a stimulant

betel nut *n* : the astringent seed of an Asian palm that is chewed with betel leaves

bête noire \ˌbet-ˈnwär, ˌbāt-\ *n, pl* **bêtes noires** *same or* -ˈnwärz\ [F, lit., black beast] : a person or thing strongly disliked or avoided

beth·el \ˈbe-thəl\ *n* [Heb *bēth'ēl* house of God] : a place of worship esp. for seamen

be·think \bi-ˈthiŋk\ *vb* **-thought** \-ˈthȯt\; **-think·ing** : REMEMBER; *also* : PONDER

be·tide \bi-ˈtīd\ *vb* : to happen to

be·times \bi-ˈtīmz\ *adv* : in good time : EARLY ✦ *Synonyms* SOON, SEASONABLY, TIMELY

be·to·ken \bi-ˈtō-kən\ *vb* **1** : PRESAGE **2** : to give evidence of ✦ *Synonyms* INDICATE, ATTEST, BESPEAK, TESTIFY

be·tray \bi-ˈtrā\ *vb* **1** : to lead astray; *esp* : SEDUCE **2** : to deliver to an enemy **3** : ABANDON **4** : to prove unfaithful to **5** : to reveal unintentionally; *also* : SHOW, INDICATE ✦ *Synonyms* MISLEAD, DELUDE, DECEIVE, BEGUILE — **be·tray·al** *n* — **be·tray·er** *n*

be·troth \bi-ˈtrȯth, -ˈtrōth\ *vb* : to promise to marry — **be·troth·al** *n*

be·trothed *n* : the person to whom one is betrothed

¹bet·ter \ˈbe-tər\ *adj, comparative of* GOOD **1** : greater than half **2** : improved in health **3** : more attractive, favorable, or commendable **4** : more advantageous or effective ⟨a ∼ solution⟩ **5** : improved in accuracy or performance

²better *vb* **1** : to make or become better **2** : SURPASS, EXCEL

³better *adv, comparative of* WELL **1** : in a superior manner **2** : to a higher or greater degree; *also* : MORE

⁴better *n* **1** : something better; *also* : a superior esp. in merit or rank **2** : ADVANTAGE

⁵better *verbal auxiliary* : had better ⟨you ∼ hurry⟩

better half *n* : SPOUSE

bet·ter·ment \ˈbe-tər-mənt\ *n* : IMPROVEMENT

bet·tor *or* **bet·ter** \ˈbe-tər\ *n* : one that bets

¹be·tween \bi-ˈtwēn\ *prep* **1** : by the common action of ⟨earned $10,000 ∼ the two of them⟩ **2** : in the interval separating ⟨an alley ∼ two buildings⟩; *also* : in intermediate relation to **3** : in point of comparison of ⟨choose ∼ two cars⟩

²between *adv* : in an intervening space or interval

be·twixt \bi-ˈtwikst\ *adv or prep* : BETWEEN

¹bev·el \ˈbe-vəl\ *n* **1** : a device for adjusting the slant of the surfaces of a piece of work **2** : the angle or slant that one surface or line makes with another when not at right angles

²bevel *vb* **-eled** *or* **-elled**; **-el·ing** *or* **-el·ling** **1** : to cut or shape to a bevel **2** : INCLINE, SLANT

bev·er·age \ˈbev-rij\ *n* : a drinkable liquid

bevy \ˈbe-vē\ *n, pl* **bev·ies** **1** : a large group or collection **2** : a group of animals and esp. quail

be·wail \bi-ˈwāl\ *vb* : LAMENT ✦ *Synonyms* DEPLORE, BEMOAN, GRIEVE, MOAN, WEEP

be·ware \-ˈwer\ *vb* : to be on one's guard : be wary of

be·wil·der \bi-ˈwil-dər\ *vb* : PERPLEX, CONFUSE ✦ *Synonyms* MYSTIFY, DISTRACT, PUZZLE — **be·wil·der·ment** *n*

be·witch \-ˈwich\ *vb* **1** : to affect by witchcraft **2** : CHARM, FASCINATE ✦ *Synonyms* ENCHANT, ATTRACT, CAPTIVATE — **be·witch·ment** *n*

bey \ˈbā\ *n* **1** : a former Turkish provincial governor **2** : the former native ruler of Tunis or Tunisia

¹be·yond \bē-ˈänd\ *adv* **1** : FARTHER ⟨extends to the river and ∼⟩ **2** : BESIDES

²beyond *prep* **1** : on or to the farther side of **2** : out of the reach or sphere of **3** : BESIDES

be·zel \ˈbē-zəl, ˈbe-\ *n* **1** : a rim that holds a transparent covering (as on a watch) **2** : the faceted part of a cut gem that rises above the setting

bf *abbr* boldface

BG *or* **B Gen** *abbr* brigadier general

Bh *symbol* bohrium

bhang \ˈbaŋ\ *n* [Hindi *bhāṅg*] : HEMP; *also* : a mildly intoxicating preparation made from hemp leaves

Bi *symbol* bismuth

BIA *abbr* Bureau of Indian Affairs

bi·an·nu·al \(ˌ)bī-ˈan-yə-wəl\ *adj* : occurring twice a year — **bi·an·nu·al·ly** *adv*

¹bi·as \ˈbī-əs\ *n* **1** : a line diagonal to the grain of a fabric **2** : PREJUDICE, BENT

²bias *adv* : on the bias : DIAGONALLY ⟨cut cloth ∼⟩

³bias *vb* **bi·ased** *or* **bi·assed**; **bi·as·ing** *or* **bi·as·sing** : PREJUDICE

bi·ath·lon \bī-ˈath-lən, -ˌlän\ *n* : a composite athletic contest consisting of cross-country skiing and target shooting with a rifle

¹bib \ˈbib\ *n* : a cloth or plastic shield tied under the chin to protect the clothes while eating

²bib *abbr* Bible; biblical

bi·be·lot \ˈbē-bə-ˌlō\ *n, pl* **bibelots** *same or* -ˌlōz\ : a small household ornament or decorative object

bi·ble \ˈbī-bəl\ *n* [ME, fr. OF, fr. ML *biblia*, fr. Gk, pl. of *biblion* book, dim. of *byblos* papyrus, book, fr. *Byblos*, ancient Phoenician city from which papyrus was exported] **1** *cap* : the sacred scriptures of Christians comprising the Old and New Testaments **2** *cap* : the sacred scriptures of Judaism; *also* : those of some other religion **3** : a publication that is considered authoritative for its subject — **bib·li·cal** \ˈbi-bli-kəl\ *adj*

bib·li·og·ra·phy \ˌbi-blē-ˈä-grə-fē\ *n, pl* **-phies** **1** : the history or description of writings or publications **2** : a list of writings (as on a subject or of an author) — **bib·li·og·ra·pher** \-fər\ *n* — **bib·li·o·graph·ic** \-ə-ˈgra-fik\ *also* **bib·li·o·graph·i·cal** \-fi-kəl\ *adj*

bib·lio·phile \ˈbi-blē-ə-ˌfī(-ə)l\ *n* : a lover of books

bib·u·lous \ˈbi-byə-ləs\ *adj* **1** : highly absorbent **2** : fond of alcoholic beverages

bi·cam·er·al \ˈbī-ˈka-mə-rəl\ *adj* : having or consisting of two legislative branches

bicarb \(ˌ)bī-ˈkärb, ˈbī-ˌ\ *n* : SODIUM BICARBONATE

bi·car·bon·ate \(ˌ)bī-ˈkär-bə-ˌnāt, -nət\ *n* : an acid carbonate

bicarbonate of soda : SODIUM BICARBONATE

bi·cen·te·na·ry \ˌbī-sen-ˈte-nə-rē, bī-ˈsen-tᵊn-ˌer-ē\ *n* : BICENTENNIAL — **bicentenary** *adj*

bi·cen·ten·ni·al \ˌbī-sen-ˈte-nē-əl\ *n* : a 200th anniversary or its celebration — **bicentennial** *adj*

bi·ceps \ˈbī-ˌseps\ *n, pl* **biceps** *also* **bi·ceps·es** [NL, fr. L, two-headed, fr. *bi-* two + *caput* head] : a muscle (as in the front of the upper arm) having two points of origin

¹bick·er \ˈbi-kər\ *n* : ALTERCATION

²bicker *vb* : to engage in a petty quarrel

bi·coast·al \bī-ˈkōs-tᵊl\ *adj* : living or working on both the east and west coasts of the U.S.

bi·con·cave \ˌbī-(ˌ)kän-ˈkāv, (ˌ)bī-ˈkän-ˌkāv\ *adj* : concave on both sides

bi·con·vex \ˌbī-(ˌ)kän-ˈveks, (ˌ)bī-ˈkän-ˌveks\ *adj* : convex on both sides

bi·cus·pid \bī-ˈkəs-pəd\ *n* : PREMOLAR

¹bi·cy·cle \ˈbī-ˌsi-kəl\ *n* : a light 2-wheeled vehicle with a saddle, pedals, and handlebars for steering

²bicycle *vb* **-cy·cled**; **-cy·cling** \-ˌsi-k(ə-)liŋ, -ˌsī-\ : to ride a bicycle — **bi·cy·cler** \-k(ə-)lər\ *n* — **bi·cy·clist** \-k(ə-)list\ *n*

¹bid \ˈbid\ *vb* **bade** \ˈbad, ˈbād\ *or* **bid**; **bid·den** \ˈbi-dᵊn\ *or* **bid** *also* **bade**; **bid·ding** **1** : COMMAND, ORDER **2** : INVITE **3** : to give expression to ⟨*bade* a tearful farewell⟩ **4** : to make a bid : OFFER — **bid·der** *n*

²bid *n* **1** : the act of one who bids; *also* : an offer for something **2** : INVITATION **3** : an announcement in a card game of what a player proposes to accomplish **4** : an attempt to win or gain ⟨a ∼ for mayor⟩

bid·da·ble \ˈbi-də-bəl\ *adj* **1** : OBEDIENT, DOCILE **2** : capable of being bid

bid·dy \ˈbi-dē\ *n, pl* **biddies** : HEN; *also* : a young chicken

bide \ˈbīd\ *vb* **bode** \ˈbōd\ *or* **bid·ed**; **bid·ed**; **bid·ing** **1** : to wait for **2** : WAIT, TARRY **3** : DWELL

bi·det \bi-ˈdā\ *n* : a bathroom fixture used esp. for bathing the external genitals and the anal region

bi·di·rec·tion·al \ˌbī-də-ˈrek-sh(ə-)nəl\ *adj* : involving, moving, or taking place in two usu. opposite directions — **bi·di·rec·tion·al·ly** *adv*

bi·en·ni·al \bī-ˈe-nē-əl\ *adj* **1** : taking place once in two years **2** : lasting two years **3** : producing leaves the first year and fruiting and dying the second year — **biennial** *n* — **bi·en·ni·al·ly** *adv*

bi·en·ni·um \bī-ˈe-nē-əm\ *n, pl* **-niums** *or* **-nia** \-ə\ [L, fr. *bi-* two + *annus* year] : a period of two years

bier \ˈbir\ *n* : a stand bearing a coffin or corpse

bi·fo·cal \ˈbī-ˌfō-kəl\ *adj* : having two focal lengths

bifocals \-kəlz\ *n pl* : eyeglasses with lenses that have one

BOOKS OF THE BIBLE

HEBREW BIBLE

LAW	PROPHETS		WRITINGS
Genesis	Joshua	Obadiah	Psalms
Exodus	Judges	Jonah	Proverbs
Leviticus	1 & 2 Samuel	Micah	Job
Numbers	1 & 2 Kings	Nahum	Song of Songs
Deuteronomy	Isaiah	Habakkuk	Ruth
	Jeremiah	Zephaniah	Lamentations
	Ezekiel	Haggai	Ecclesiastes
	Hosea	Zechariah	Esther
	Joel	Malachi	Daniel
	Amos		Ezra
			Nehemiah
			1 & 2 Chronicles

CHRISTIAN CANON—OLD TESTAMENT

ROMAN CATHOLIC	PROTESTANT	ROMAN CATHOLIC	PROTESTANT
Genesis	Genesis	Wisdom	
Exodus	Exodus	Sirach	
Leviticus	Leviticus	Isaiah	Isaiah
Numbers	Numbers	Jeremiah	Jeremiah
Deuteronomy	Deuteronomy	Lamentations	Lamentations
Joshua	Joshua	Baruch	
Judges	Judges	Ezekiel	Ezekiel
Ruth	Ruth	Daniel	Daniel
1 & 2 Samuel	1 & 2 Samuel	Hosea	Hosea
1 & 2 Kings	1 & 2 Kings	Joel	Joel
1 & 2 Chronicles	1 & 2 Chronicles	Amos	Amos
Ezra	Ezra	Obadiah	Obadiah
Nehemiah	Nehemiah	Jonah	Jonah
Tobit		Micah	Micah
Judith		Nahum	Nahum
Esther	Esther	Habakkuk	Habakkuk
Job	Job	Zephaniah	Zephaniah
Psalms	Psalms	Haggai	Haggai
Proverbs	Proverbs	Zechariah	Zechariah
Ecclesiastes	Ecclesiastes	Malachi	Malachi
Song of Songs	Song of Solomon	1 & 2 Maccabees	

PROTESTANT APOCRYPHA

1 & 2 Esdras	Baruch
Tobit	Prayer of Azariah and the Song
Judith	of the Three Holy Children
Additions to Esther	Susanna
Wisdom of Solomon	Bel and the Dragon
Ecclesiasticus or the Wisdom of Jesus	The Prayer of Manasses
Son of Sirach	1 & 2 Maccabees

CHRISTIAN CANON—NEW TESTAMENT

Matthew	Ephesians	James
Mark	Philippians	1 & 2 Peter
Luke	Colossians	1, 2, 3 John
John	1 & 2 Thessalonians	Jude
Acts of the Apostles	1 & 2 Timothy	Revelation *or*
Romans	Titus	Apocalypse
1 & 2 Corinthians	Philemon	
Galatians	Hebrews	

part that corrects for near vision and one for distant vision

bi·fold \'bī-ˌfōld\ *adj* : designed to fold twice ⟨~ doors⟩

bi·fur·cate \'bī-fər-ˌkāt, bī-'fər-\ *vb* **-cat·ed; -cat·ing** : to divide into two branches or parts — **bi·fur·ca·tion** \ˌbī-fər-'kā-shən\ *n*

big \'big\ *adj* **big·ger; big·gest 1** : large in size, amount, or scope **2** : PREGNANT; *also* : SWELLING **3** : IMPORTANT, IMPOSING **4** : NOBLE, GENEROUS **5** : POPULAR — **big·ness** *n* — **big on** : strongly favoring or liking

big·a·my \'bi-gə-mē\ *n* : the act of marrying one person while still legally married to another — **big·a·mist** \-mist\ *n* — **big·a·mous** \-məs\ *adj*

big bang theory *n* : a theory in astronomy: the universe originated in an explosion (**big bang**) from a single point of nearly infinite energy density

big brother *n* **1** : an older brother **2** : a man who befriends a delinquent or friendless boy **3** *cap both Bs* : the leader of an authoritarian state or movement

big cheese *n* : ³BOSS

big crunch *n* : a hypothetical event in which all matter in the universe collapses to a single point of nearly infinite energy density

Big Dipper *n* : the seven principal stars of Ursa Major in a form resembling a dipper

big·foot \'big-ˌfút\ *n* : SASQUATCH

big·horn sheep \'big-ˌhȯrn\ *n* : a wild sheep of mountainous western No. America

bight \'bīt\ *n* **1** : a curve in a coast; *also* : the bay formed by such a curve **2** : a slack part in a rope

big–name \'big-'nām\ *adj* : widely popular ⟨a ~ performer⟩ — **big name** *n*

big·ot \'bi-gət\ *n* : one who regards or treats members of a group with hatred and intolerance ♦ *Synonyms* FANATIC, ENTHUSIAST, ZEALOT — **big·ot·ed** \-gə-təd\ *adj* — **big·ot·ry** \-trē\ *n*

big screen *n* : the motion picture medium as contrasted to television

big shot \'big-ˌshät\ *n* : an important person

big time \-ˌtīm\ *n* **1** : a high-paying vaudeville circuit requiring only two performances a day **2** : the top rank of an activity or enterprise — **big–tim·er** *n*

big top *n* **1** : the main tent of a circus **2** : CIRCUS

big·wig \'big-ˌwig\ *n* : BIG SHOT

bike \'bīk\ *n* **1** : BICYCLE **2** : MOTORCYCLE

bik·er *n* : MOTORCYCLIST; *esp* : one who is a member of an organized gang

bike·way \'bīk-ˌwā\ *n* : a thoroughfare for bicycles

bi·ki·ni \bə-'kē-nē\ *n* [F, fr. *Bikini*, atoll in the Marshall Islands] : a woman's brief 2-piece bathing suit

bi·lat·er·al \bī-'la-tə-rəl\ *adj* **1** : having or involving two sides **2** : affecting reciprocally two sides or parties — **bi·lat·er·al·ism** \-tə-rə-ˌli-zəm\ *n* — **bi·lat·er·al·ly** *adv*

bile \'bī(-ə)l\ *n* **1** : a bitter greenish fluid secreted by the liver that aids in the digestion of fats **2** : an ill-humored mood

bilge \'bilj\ *n* **1** : the part of a ship that lies between the bottom and the point where the sides go straight up **2** : stale or worthless remarks or ideas

bi·lin·gual \bī-'liŋ-gwəl\ *adj* : expressed in, knowing, or using two languages

bil·ious \'bil-yəs\ *adj* **1** : marked by or suffering from disordered liver function **2** : IRRITABLE, ILL-TEMPERED — **bil·ious·ness** *n*

bilk \'bilk\ *vb* : CHEAT, SWINDLE

¹bill \'bil\ *n* : the jaws of a bird together with their horny covering; *also* : a mouthpart (as of a turtle) resembling these — **billed** \'bild\ *adj*

²bill *vb* : to caress fondly

³bill *n* **1** : an itemized statement of particulars; *also* : INVOICE **2** : a written document or note **3** : a printed advertisement (as a poster) announcing an event **4** : a draft of a law presented to a legislature for enactment **5** : a written statement of a legal wrong suffered or of some breach of law **6** : a piece of paper money

⁴bill *vb* **1** : to enter in or prepare a bill; *also* : to submit a bill or account to **2** : to advertise by bills or posters

bill·board \-ˌbȯrd\ *n* : a flat surface on which advertising bills are posted

¹bil·let \'bi-lət\ *n* **1** : an order requiring a person to pro-

vide lodging for a soldier; *also* : quarters assigned by or as if by such an order **2** : POSITION, APPOINTMENT

²billet *vb* : to assign lodging to by billet

bil·let–doux \ˌbi-lā-'dü\ *n, pl* **billets–doux** *same or* -'düz\ [F *billet doux*, lit., sweet letter] : a love letter

bill·fold \'bil-ˌfōld\ *n* : WALLET

bil·liards \'bil-yərdz\ *n* : any of several games played on an oblong table by driving balls against each other or into pockets with a cue

bil·lings·gate \'bi-liŋz-ˌgāt, *Brit usu* -git\ *n* [*Billingsgate*, old gate and fish market, London, England] : coarsely abusive language

bil·lion \'bil-yən\ *n* **1** : a thousand millions **2** *Brit* : a million millions — **billion** *adj* — **bil·lionth** \-yənth\ *adj or n*

bill of attainder : a legislative act that imposes punishment without a trial

bill of health : a usu. favorable report following an examination

bill of sale : a legal document transferring ownership of goods

¹bil·low \'bi-lō\ *n* **1** : WAVE; *esp* : a great wave **2** : a rolling mass (as of fog or flame) like a great wave — **bil·lowy** \'bi-lə-wē\ *adj*

²billow *vb* : to rise and roll in waves; *also* : to swell out ⟨~*ing* sails⟩

bil·ly \'bi-lē\ *n, pl* **billies** : BILLY CLUB

billy club *n* : a heavy usu. wooden club; *esp* : a police officer's club

bil·ly goat \'bi-lē-\ *n* : a male goat

bi·met·al \'bī-ˌme-t³l\ *adj* : BIMETALLIC — **bimetal** *n*

bi·me·tal·lic \ˌbī-mə-'ta-lik\ *adj* : made of two different metals — often used of devices having a bonded expansive part — **bimetallic** *n*

bi·met·al·lism \bī-'me-t³l-ˌi-zəm\ *n* : the use of two metals at fixed ratios to form a standard of value for a monetary system

¹bi·month·ly \bī-'mənth-lē\ *adj* **1** : occurring every two months **2** : occurring twice a month : SEMIMONTHLY — **bimonthly** *adv*

²bimonthly *n* : a bimonthly publication

bin \'bin\ *n* : a box, crib, or enclosure used for storage

bi·na·ry \'bī-nə-rē, -ˌner-ē\ *adj* **1** : consisting of two things or parts **2** : relating to, being, or belonging to a system of numbers having 2 as its base ⟨the ~ digits 0 and 1⟩ **3** : involving a choice between or condition of two alternatives only (as on-off, yes-no) — **binary** *n*

binary star *n* : a system of two stars revolving around each other

binary system *n* : BINARY STAR

bin·au·ral \bī-'nȯr-əl\ *adj* : of or relating to sound reproduction involving the use of two separated microphones and two transmission channels to achieve a stereophonic effect

bind \'bīnd\ *vb* **bound** \'baúnd\; **bind·ing 1** : TIE; *also* : to restrain as if by tying **2** : to put under an obligation; *also* : to constrain with legal authority **3** : BANDAGE **4** : to unite into a mass **5** : to compel as if by a pledge ⟨a handshake ~s the deal⟩ **6** : to strengthen or decorate with a band **7** : to fasten together and enclose in a cover ⟨~ books⟩ **8** : to exert a tying, restraining, or compelling effect — **bind·er** *n*

bind·ing \'bīn-diŋ\ *n* : something (as a ski fastening, a cover, or an edging fabric) used to bind

bin·dle \'bin-d³l\ *n* : a bundle of clothes or bedding

¹binge \'binj\ *n* **1** : SPREE **2** : an act of excessive consumption (as of food)

²binge *vb* **binged; binge·ing** *or* **bing·ing** : to go on a binge — **bing·er** *n*

bin·go \'biŋ-gō\ *n, pl* **bingos** : a game of chance played with cards having numbered squares corresponding to numbered balls drawn at random and won by covering five squares in a row

bin·na·cle \'bi-ni-kəl\ *n* [alter. of ME *bitakle*, fr. Pg or Sp; Pg *bitácola* & Sp *bitácula*, fr. L *habitaculum* dwelling place, fr. *habitare* to inhabit] : a container holding a ship's compass

¹bin·oc·u·lar \bī-'nä-kyə-lər, bə-\ *adj* : of, relating to, or adapted to the use of both eyes — **bin·oc·u·lar·ly** *adv*

²bin·oc·u·lar \bə-'nä-kyə-lər, bī-\ *n* **1** : a binocular optical instrument (as a microscope) **2** : a hand-held optical instrument composed of two telescopes and a focusing device — usu. used in pl.

bi·no·mi·al \bī-'nō-mē-əl\ *n* **1** : a mathematical expression consisting of two terms connected by the sign plus (+) or minus (–) **2** : a biological species name consisting of two terms — **binomial** *adj*

bio·chem·is·try \,bī-ō-'ke-mə-strē\ *n* : chemistry that deals with the chemical compounds and processes occurring in living things — **bio·chem·i·cal** \-mi-kəl\ *adj or n* — **bio·chem·i·cal·ly** \-k(ə-)lē\ *adv* — **bio·chem·ist** \-mist\ *n*

bio·de·grad·able \-di-'grā-də-bəl\ *adj* : capable of being broken down esp. into innocuous products by the actions of living things (as microorganisms) ⟨a ~ detergent⟩ — **bio·de·grad·abil·i·ty** \-,grā-də-'bi-lə-tē\ *n* — **bio·deg·ra·da·tion** \-,de-grə-'dā-shən\ *n* — **bio·de·grade** \-di-'grād\ *vb*

bio·di·ver·si·ty \-də-'vər-sə-tē, -dī-\ *n* : biological diversity in an environment as indicated by numbers of different species of plants and animals

bio·en·gi·neer·ing \-,en-jə-'nir-iŋ\ *n* **1** : the application of engineering principles to medicine and biology **2** : GENETIC ENGINEERING

bio·eth·ics \-'e-thiks\ *n* : the ethics of biological research and its applications esp. in medicine — **bio·eth·i·cal** \-'e-thi-kəl\ *adj* — **bio·eth·i·cist** \-'e-thə-sist\ *n*

bio·feed·back \-'fēd-,bak\ *n* : the technique of making unconscious or involuntary bodily processes (as heartbeats or brain waves) perceptible to the senses (as by use of an oscilloscope) in order to manipulate them by conscious mental control

biog *abbr* biographer; biographical; biography

bio·ge·og·ra·phy \,bī-ō-jē-'ä-grə-fē\ *n* : a science that deals with the geographical distribution of plants and animals — **bio·ge·og·ra·pher** *n*

bi·og·ra·phy \bī-'ä-grə-fē, bē-\ *n, pl* **-phies** : a written history of a person's life; *also* : such writings in general — **bi·og·ra·pher** *n* — **bio·graph·i·cal** \,bī-ə-'gra-fi-kəl\ *also* **bio·graph·ic** \-fik\ *adj*

bio·in·for·mat·ics \,bī-ō-in-fər-'ma-tiks\ *n* : the storage, classification, and analysis of biological information using computers

biol *abbr* biologic; biological; biologist; biology

bi·o·log·i·cal \,bī-ə-'lä-ji-kəl\ *also* **bi·o·log·ic** \-jik\ *adj* **1** : of, relating to, or produced by biology or life and living processes **2** : connected by direct genetic relationship rather than by adoption or marriage ⟨her ~ father⟩ — **bi·o·log·i·cal·ly** \-ji-k(ə-)lē\ *adv*

biological clock *n* : an inherent timing mechanism in a living system that is inferred to exist in order to explain the timing of various physiological and behavioral states and processes

biological warfare *n* : warfare in which harmful living organisms (**biological weapons**) are used against an enemy esp. to cause large-scale death or disease

bi·ol·o·gy \bī-'ä-lə-jē\ *n* [G *Biologie*, fr. Gk *bios* mode of life + *logos* word, discourse] **1** : a science that deals with living beings and life processes **2** : the life processes of an organism or group — **bi·ol·o·gist** \bī-'ä-lə-jist\ *n*

bio·mass \'bī-ō-,mas\ *n* **1** : the amount of living matter (as in a unit area) **2** : plant materials and animal waste used esp. as fuel

bio·med·i·cal \,bī-ō-'me-di-kəl\ *adj* : of, relating to, or involving biological, medical, and physical science

bi·on·ic \bī-'ä-nik\ *adj* : having normal biological capability or performance enhanced by or as if by electronic or mechanical devices

bio·phys·ics \,bī-ō-'fi-ziks\ *n* : a branch of science concerned with the application of physical principles and methods to biological problems — **bio·phys·i·cal** \-zi-kəl\ *adj* — **bio·phys·i·cist** \-'fi-zə-sist\ *n*

bio·pic \'bī-ō-,pik\ *n* : a biographical movie

bi·op·sy \'bī-,äp-sē\ *n, pl* **-sies** : the removal of tissue, cells, or fluids from the living body for examination

bio·rhythm \'bī-ō-,ri-thəm\ *n* : an innately determined rhythmic biological process (as sleep); *also* : the internal mechanism controlling such a process

bio·sci·ence \-'sī-əns\ *n* : BIOLOGY 1; *also* : LIFE SCIENCE

bio·sphere \'bī-ə-,sfir\ *n* **1** : the part of the world in which life can exist **2** : living organisms together with their environment

bio·tech \'bī-ō-,tek\ *n* : BIOTECHNOLOGY

bio·tech·nol·o·gy \,bī-ō-tek-'nä-lə-jē\ *n* : the manipulation (as through genetic engineering) of living organisms to produce useful products; *also* : biological science so applied

bio·ter·ror·ism \-'ter-ər-,i-zəm\ *n* : terrorism involving the use of biological weapons — **bio·ter·ror·ist** \-ist\ *adj or n*

bi·ot·ic \bī-'ä-tik\ *adj* : of, relating to, or caused by living organisms

bi·o·tin \'bī-ə-tən\ *n* : a vitamin of the vitamin B complex found esp. in yeast, liver, and egg yolk and active in growth promotion

bi·o·tite \'bī-ə-,tīt\ *n* : a dark mica containing iron, magnesium, potassium, and aluminum

bi·par·ti·san \bī-'pär-tə-zən\ *adj* : marked by or involving cooperation, agreement, and compromise between two major political parties — **bi·par·ti·san·ship** \-,ship\ *n*

bi·par·tite \-'pär-,tīt\ *adj* **1** : being in two parts **2** : shared by two ⟨~ treaty⟩

bi·ped \'bī-,ped\ *n* : a 2-footed animal — **bi·ped·al** \(,)bī-'pe-dəl\ *adj*

bi·plane \'bī-,plān\ *n* : an aircraft with two wings placed one above the other

bi·po·lar \bī-'pō-lər\ *adj* : having or involving the use of two poles — **bi·po·lar·i·ty** \,bī-pō-'ler-ə-tē\ *n*

bipolar disorder *n* : any of several psychological disorders of mood characterized usu. by alternating episodes of depression and mania

bi·ra·cial \bī-'rā-shəl\ *adj* : of, relating to, or involving members of two races

¹birch \'bərch\ *n* **1** : any of a genus of mostly short-lived deciduous shrubs and trees with membranous outer bark and pale close-grained wood; *also* : this wood **2** : a birch rod or bundle of twigs for flogging — **birch** *or* **birch·en** \'bər-chən\ *adj*

²birch *vb* : WHIP, FLOG

¹bird \'bərd\ *n* : any of a class of warm-blooded egg-laying vertebrates having the body feathered and the forelimbs modified to form wings

²bird *vb* : to observe or identify wild birds in their native habitat — **bird·er** *n*

bird·bath \'bərd-,bath, -,bäth\ *n* : a usu. ornamental basin set up for birds to bathe in

bird·house \-,haus\ *n* : an artificial nesting place for birds; *also* : AVIARY

bird·ie \'bər-dē\ *n* : a score of one under par on a hole in golf

bird·lime \-,līm\ *n* : a sticky substance smeared on twigs to snare small birds

bird of paradise : any of numerous brilliantly colored plumed birds of the New Guinea area

bird of prey : a carnivorous bird that feeds wholly or chiefly on carrion or on meat taken by hunting

bird·seed \'bərd-,sēd\ *n* : a mixture of small seeds (as of hemp or millet) used for feeding birds

bird's—eye \'bərdz-,ī\ *adj* **1** : marked with spots resembling birds' eyes ⟨~ maple⟩ **2** : seen from above as if by a flying bird ⟨~ view⟩; *also* : CURSORY

bi·ret·ta \bə-'re-tə\ *n* : a square cap with three ridges on top worn esp. by Roman Catholic clergymen

birr \'bir, 'bər\ *n, pl* **birr** — see MONEY table

¹birth \'bərth\ *n* **1** : the act or fact of being born or of bringing forth young **2** : LINEAGE, DESCENT **3** : ORIGIN, BEGINNING — **birth** *vb*

²birth *adj* : BIOLOGICAL 2 ⟨~ parents⟩

birth canal *n* : the channel formed by the cervix, vagina, and vulva through which the fetus passes during birth

birth control *n* : control of the number of children born esp. by preventing or lessening the frequency of conception

birth·day \'bərth-,dā\ *n* : the day or anniversary of one's birth

birth defect *n* : a physical or biochemical defect present at birth and inherited or environmentally induced

birth·mark \'bərth-,märk\ *n* : an unusual mark or blemish on the skin at birth

birth·place \-,plās\ *n* : place of birth or origin

birth·rate \-,rāt\ *n* : the number of births per number of individuals in a given area or group during a given time

birth·right \-,rīt\ *n* : a right, privilege, or possession to which one is entitled by birth ◆ **Synonyms** LEGACY, PATRIMONY, HERITAGE, INHERITANCE

birth·stone \-,stōn\ *n* : a gemstone associated symbolically with the month of one's birth

bis·cuit \'bis-kət\ *n* [ME *bisquite,* fr. AF *besquit,* fr. (*pain*) *besquit* twice-cooked bread] 1 : a crisp flat cake; *esp, Brit* : CRACKER 2 2 : a small quick bread made from dough that has been rolled and cut or dropped from a spoon

bi·sect \'bī-,sekt\ *vb* : to divide into two usu. equal parts; *also* : CROSS, INTERSECT — **bi·sec·tion** \'bī-,sek-shən\ *n* — **bi·sec·tor** \-tər\ *n*

bi·sex·u·al \bī-'sek-shə-wəl\ *adj* 1 : possessing characters of or having sexual desire for both sexes 2 : of, relating to, or involving both sexes — **bisexual** *n* — **bi·sex·u·al·i·ty** \,bī-,sek-shə-'wal-ə-tē\ *n*

bish·op \'bi-shəp\ *n* [ME *bisshop,* fr. OE *bisceop,* fr. LL *episcopus,* fr. Gk *episkopos,* lit., overseer, fr. *epi-* on, over + *skeptesthai* to look] 1 : a member of the clergy ranking above a priest and typically governing a diocese 2 : any of various Protestant church officials who superintend other clergy 3 : a chess piece that can move diagonally across any number of adjoining unoccupied squares

bish·op·ric \'bi-shə-prik\ *n* 1 : DIOCESE 2 : the office of bishop

bis·muth \'biz-məth\ *n* : a heavy brittle grayish white metallic chemical element used in alloys and medicine

bi·son \'bī-sᵊn, -zᵊn\ *n, pl* **bison** : BUFFALO 2

bisque \'bisk\ *n* : a thick cream soup

bis·tro \'bēs-trō, 'bis-\ *n, pl* **bistros** [F] 1 : a small or unpretentious restaurant 2 : BAR; *also* : NIGHTCLUB

¹bit \'bit\ *n* 1 : the biting or cutting edge or part of a tool 2 : the part of a bridle that is placed in a horse's mouth

²bit *n* 1 : a morsel of food; *also* : a small piece or quantity of something 2 : a small coin; *also* : a unit of value equal to 12½ cents 3 : something small or trivial 4 : an indefinite usu. small degree or extent ⟨a ~ tired⟩

³bit *n* [*b*inary dig*it*] : a unit of computer information equivalent to the result of a choice between two alternatives; *also* : its physical representation

¹bitch \'bich\ *n* 1 : a female canine; *esp* : a female dog 2 : a malicious, spiteful, or overbearing woman

²bitch *vb* : COMPLAIN

¹bite \'bīt\ *vb* **bit** \'bit\; **bit·ten** \'bi-tᵊn\ *also* **bit**; **bit·ing** \'bī-tiŋ\ 1 : to grip with teeth or jaws; *also* : to wound or sting with or as if with fangs 2 : to cut or pierce with or as if with an edged instrument 3 : to cause to smart or sting 4 : CORRODE 5 : to take bait

²bite *n* 1 : the act or manner of biting 2 : FOOD 3 : a wound made by biting; *also* : a penetrating effect

bite–size \'bīt-,sīz\ *adj* 1 : of a size that can be eaten in one bite 2 : being or made small or brief esp. so as to be easily manageable

biting *adj* : SHARP, CUTTING

bit·map \'bit-,map\ *n* : an array of binary data representing a bitmapped image or display

bit·mapped \'bit-,mapt\ *adj* : of, relating to, or being a digital image or display for which an array of binary data specifies the value of each pixel

bit·ter \'bi-tər\ *adj* 1 : being or inducing the one of the basic taste sensations that is acrid, astringent, or disagreeable and is suggestive of hops 2 : marked by intensity or severity (as of distress or hatred) 3 : extremely harsh or cruel — **bit·ter·ly** *adv* — **bit·ter·ness** *n*

bit·tern \'bi-tərn\ *n* : any of various small or medium-sized herons

bit·ters \'bi-tərz\ *n sing or pl* : a usu. alcoholic solution of bitter and often aromatic plant products used in mixing drinks and as a mild tonic

¹bit·ter·sweet \'bi-tər-,swēt\ *n* 1 : a poisonous nightshade with purple flowers and reddish berries 2 : a woody vine with yellow capsules that open when ripe to show scarlet seed covers

²bittersweet *adj* : being at once both bitter and sweet

bi·tu·mi·nous coal \bə-'tü-mə-nəs, bī-, -'tyü-\ *n* : a coal that when heated yields considerable volatile waste matter

bi·valve \'bī-,valv\ *n* : any of a class of mollusks (as clams or scallops) of two separate parts that open and shut — **bivalve** *adj*

¹biv·ouac \'bi-və-,wak\ *n* [F, fr. LG *biwacht,* fr. *bi* at + *wacht* guard] : a temporary encampment or shelter

²bivouac *vb* **-ouacked; -ouack·ing** : to form a bivouac : CAMP

¹bi·week·ly \,bī-'wē-klē\ *adj* 1 : occurring twice a week 2 : occurring every two weeks : FORTNIGHTLY — **biweekly** *adv*

²biweekly *n* : a biweekly publication

bi·year·ly \-'yir-lē\ *adj* 1 : BIANNUAL 2 : BIENNIAL

bi·zarre \bə-'zär\ *adj* : ODD, ECCENTRIC, FANTASTIC ⟨~ costumes⟩ — **bi·zarre·ly** *adv*

bi·zar·ro \bə-'zär-ō\ *adj* : characterized by a bizarre, fantastic, or unconventional approach

bk *abbr* 1 bank 2 book

Bk *symbol* berkelium

bkg *abbr* banking

bkgd *abbr* background

bks *abbr* barracks

bkt *abbr* 1 basket 2 bracket

bl *abbr* 1 bale 2 barrel 3 blue

blab \'blab\ *vb* **blabbed; blab·bing** : TATTLE, GOSSIP

¹black \'blak\ *adj* 1 : of the color black; *also* : very dark 2 : SWARTHY 3 : of or relating to various groups of dark-skinned people 4 : of or relating to the African-American people or their culture 5 : SOILED, DIRTY 6 : lacking light ⟨a ~ night⟩ 7 : WICKED, EVIL ⟨~ magic⟩ 8 : DISMAL, GLOOMY ⟨a ~ outlook⟩ 9 : SULLEN ⟨a ~ mood⟩ — **black·ish** *adj* — **black·ly** *adv* — **black·ness** *n*

²black *n* 1 : a black pigment or dye; *also* : something (as clothing) that is black 2 : the characteristic color of soot or coal 3 : a person of a dark-skinned race 4 : AFRICAN-AMERICAN

³black *vb* : BLACKEN

black·a·moor \'bla-kə-,mu̇r\ *n* : a dark-skinned person

black–and–blue \,bla-kən-'blü\ *adj* : darkly discolored from blood effused by bruising

black–and–white \,bla-kən-'hwīt\ *n* : SQUAD CAR

black·ball \'blak-,bȯl\ *vb* 1 : to vote against; *esp* : to exclude from membership by casting a negative vote 2 : OSTRACIZE — **black·ball** *n*

black bass *n* : any of several freshwater sunfishes native to eastern and central No. America

black bear *n* : a usu. black-furred bear of No. American forests

¹black belt \'blak-,belt\ *n, often cap both Bs* : an area densely populated by blacks

²black belt \-'belt\ *n* : one who holds the rating of expert (as in judo or karate); *also* : the rating itself

black·ber·ry \-,ber-ē\ *n* : the usu. black or purple juicy but seedy edible fruit of various brambles; *also* : a plant bearing this fruit

black·bird \-,bərd\ *n* : any of various birds (as the red-winged blackbird) of which the male is largely or wholly black

black·board \-,bȯrd\ *n* : a smooth usu. dark surface used for writing or drawing on with chalk

black·body \-'bä-dē\ *n* : a body or surface that completely absorbs incident radiation with no reflection

black box *n* 1 : a usu. complicated electronic device whose components and workings are unknown or mysterious to the user 2 : a device used in aircraft to record cockpit conversations and flight data

black death *n* : an epidemic of bacterial plague and esp. bubonic plague that spread rapidly in Europe and Asia in the 14th century

black·en \'bla-kən\ *vb* **black·ened; black·en·ing** 1 : to make or become black 2 : DEFAME, SULLY ⟨~ed her reputation⟩

black·ened *adj* : coated with spices and quickly seared in a very hot skillet ⟨~ swordfish⟩

black eye *n* : a discoloration of the skin around the eye from bruising

black–eyed Su·san \,blak-,īd-'sü-zᵊn\ *n* : a coarse No. American plant that is related to the daisies and has deep yellow to orange flower heads with dark conical centers

Black·foot \'blak-,fu̇t\ *n, pl* **Black·feet** *or* **Blackfoot** : a member of an American Indian people of Montana, Alberta, and Saskatchewan

black·guard \'bla-gərd, -,gärd\ *n* : SCOUNDREL, RASCAL

black·head \'blak-,hed\ *n* : a small usu. dark oily mass plugging the outlet of a skin gland

black hole *n* : a celestial object with a gravitational field so strong that light cannot escape from it

black·ing \'bla-kiŋ\ *n* : a substance applied to something to make it black

¹black·jack \'blak-ˌjak\ *n*   **1** : a leather-covered club with a flexible handle   **2** : a card game in which the object is to be dealt cards having a higher count than the dealer but not exceeding 21
²blackjack *vb* : to hit with or as if with a blackjack
black light *n* : invisible ultraviolet light
black·list \'blak-ˌlist\ *n* : a list of persons who are disapproved of and are to be punished or boycotted — **blacklist** *vb*
black·mail \'blak-ˌmāl\ *n* : extortion by threats esp. of public exposure; *also* : something so extorted — **blackmail** *vb* — **black·mail·er** *n*
black market *n* : illicit trade in goods; *also* : a place where such trade is carried on
Black Mass *n* : a travesty of the Christian Mass ascribed to worshipers of Satan
Black Muslim *n* : a member of a chiefly black group that professes Islamic religious belief
black nationalist *n, often cap B&N* : a member of a group of militant blacks who advocate separatism from whites and the formation of self-governing black communities — **black nationalism** *n, often cap B&N*
black–on–black *adj* : involving a black person against another black person ⟨∼ crime⟩
black·out \'blak-ˌaůt\ *n*   **1** : a period of darkness due to electrical power failure   **2** : a transitory loss or dulling of vision or consciousness   **3** : the prohibition or restriction of the telecasting of a sports event — **black out** *vb*
black pepper *n* : a spice that consists of the dried berry of a pepper plant ground with the black husk still on
black power *n* : the mobilization of the political and economic power of black Americans esp. to compel respect for their rights and improve their condition
black sheep *n* : a member of a group who is disreputable or not regarded favorably
black·smith \'blak-ˌsmith\ *n* : a smith who forges iron — **black·smith·ing** *n*
black·strap molasses \'blak-ˌstrap-\ *n* : a thick dark molasses obtained from successive processing of raw sugar
black·thorn \-ˌthȯrn\ *n* : a European thorny plum
black–tie \'blak-ˈtī\ *adj* : characterized by or requiring semiformal evening clothes consisting of a usu. black tie and tuxedo for men and a formal dress for women
black·top \'blak-ˌtäp\ *n* : a dark tarry material (as asphalt) used esp. for surfacing roads — **blacktop** *vb*
black widow *n* : a venomous New World spider having the female black with an hourglass-shaped red mark on the underside of the abdomen

black widow

blad·der \'bla-dər\ *n* : a sac in which liquid or gas is stored; *esp* : one in a vertebrate into which urine passes from the kidneys
¹blade \'blād\ *n*   **1** : a leaf of a plant and esp. of a grass; *also* : the flat part of a leaf as distinguished from its stalk   **2** : something (as the flat part of an oar or an arm of a propeller) resembling the blade of a leaf   **3** : the cutting part of an instrument or tool   **4** : SWORD; *also* : SWORDSMAN   **5** : a dashing fellow ⟨a gay ∼⟩   **6** : the runner of an ice skate — **blad·ed** \'blā-dəd\ *adj*
²blade *vb* **blad·ed; blad·ing** : to skate on in-line skates — **blad·er** \'blā-dər\ *n*
blain \'blān\ *n* : an inflammatory swelling or sore
¹blame \'blām\ *vb* **blamed; blam·ing** [ME, fr. AF *blamer*,

blasmer, fr. L *blasphemare* to blaspheme, fr. Gk *blasphēmein*]   **1** : to find fault with   **2** : to hold responsible or responsible for ✦ *Synonyms* CENSURE, DENOUNCE, CONDEMN, CRITICIZE — **blam·able** *adj*
²blame *n*   **1** : CENSURE, REPROOF   **2** : responsibility for fault or error ✦ *Synonyms* GUILT, FAULT, CULPABILITY, ONUS — **blame·less** *adj* — **blame·less·ly** *adv* — **blame·less·ness** *n*
blame·wor·thy \-ˌwər-thē\ *adj* : deserving blame — **blame·wor·thi·ness** *n*
blanch \'blanch\ *vb* : to make or become white or pale : BLEACH
blanc·mange \blə-ˈmänj, -ˈmänᶻh\ *n* : a dessert made from gelatin or a starchy substance and milk usu. sweetened and flavored
bland \'bland\ *adj*   **1** : smooth in manner : SUAVE ⟨a ∼ smile⟩   **2** : gently soothing ⟨a ∼ diet⟩; *also* : INSIPID ✦ *Synonyms* GENTLE, MILD, SOFT, BALMY — **bland·ly** *adv* — **bland·ness** *n*
blan·dish·ment \'blan-dish-mənt\ *n* : flattering or coaxing speech or action : CAJOLERY
¹blank \'blaŋk\ *adj*   **1** : showing or causing an appearance of dazed dismay; *also* : EXPRESSIONLESS   **2** : free from writing or marks; *also* : having spaces to be filled in   **3** : DULL, EMPTY ⟨∼ moments⟩   **4** : ABSOLUTE, DOWNRIGHT ⟨a ∼ refusal⟩   **5** : not shaped in final form — **blank·ly** *adv* — **blank·ness** *n*
²blank *n*   **1** : an empty space   **2** : a form with spaces for the entry of data   **3** : an unfinished form (as of a key)   **4** : a cartridge with propellant and a seal but no projectile
³blank *vb*   **1** : to cover or close up : OBSCURE   **2** : to keep from scoring
blank check *n*   **1** : a signed check with the amount unspecified   **2** : complete freedom of action
¹blan·ket \'blaŋ-kət\ *n*   **1** : a heavy woven often woolen covering   **2** : a covering layer ⟨a ∼ of snow⟩
²blanket *vb* : to cover with a blanket
³blanket *adj* : covering a group or class ⟨∼ insurance⟩; *also* : applicable in all instances ⟨∼ rules⟩
blank verse *n* : unrhymed iambic pentameter
blare \'bler\ *vb* **blared; blar·ing** : to sound loud and harsh; *also* : to proclaim loudly — **blare** *n*
blar·ney \'blär-nē\ *n* [*Blarney stone*, a stone in Blarney Castle, near Cork, Ireland, held to bestow skill in flattery on those who kiss it] : skillful flattery : BLANDISHMENT
bla·sé \blä-ˈzā\ *adj* [F] : apathetic to pleasure or excitement as a result of excessive indulgence; *also* : SOPHISTICATED
blas·pheme \blas-ˈfēm, ˈblas-ˌ\ *vb* **blas·phemed; blas·phem·ing**   **1** : to speak of or address with irreverence   **2** : to utter blasphemy — **blas·phem·er** *n*
blas·phe·my \'blas-fə-mē\ *n, pl* **-mies**   **1** : the act of expressing lack of reverence for God   **2** : irreverence toward something considered sacred — **blas·phe·mous** \-məs\ *adj*
¹blast \'blast\ *n*   **1** : a violent gust of wind; *also* : its effect   **2** : sound made by a wind instrument   **3** : a current of air forced at high pressure through a hole in a furnace (**blast furnace**)   **4** : a sudden withering esp. of plants : BLIGHT   **5** : EXPLOSION; *also* : the shock wave of an explosion
²blast *vb* : to shatter by or as if by an explosive
blast off *vb* : TAKE OFF 4 — used esp. of rocket-propelled vehicles — **blast·off** \'blast-ˌȯf\ *n*
bla·tant \'blā-tᵊnt\ *adj* : offensively obtrusive : vulgarly showy ✦ *Synonyms* VOCIFEROUS, BOISTEROUS, CLAMOROUS, OBSTREPEROUS — **bla·tan·cy** \-tᵊn-sē\ *n* — **bla·tant·ly** *adv*
blath·er \'bla-thər\ *vb* : to talk foolishly at length — **blath·er** *n*
blath·er·skite \'bla-thər-ˌskīt\ *n* : a person who blathers
¹blaze \'blāz\ *n*   **1** : FIRE   **2** : intense direct light accompanied by heat   **3** : something (as a dazzling display or sudden outburst) suggesting fire ⟨a ∼ of autumn leaves⟩ ✦ *Synonyms* GLARE, GLOW, FLAME
²blaze *vb* **blazed; blaz·ing**   **1** : to burn brightly; *also* : to flare up   **2** : to be conspicuously bright : GLITTER
³blaze *vb* **blazed; blaz·ing** : to make public or conspicuous
⁴blaze *n*   **1** : a usu. white stripe on the face of an animal   **2** : a trail marker; *esp* : one made on a tree
⁵blaze *vb* **blazed; blaz·ing** : to mark (as a tree or trail) with blazes

blaze orange *n* : a very bright orange used in clothing for visibility

blaz·er \'blā-zər\ *n* : a sports jacket often with notched collar and pockets that are stitched on

¹**bla·zon** \'blā-zᵊn\ *n* **1** : COAT OF ARMS **2** : ostentatious display

²**blazon** *vb* **1** : to publish widely : PROCLAIM **2** : DECK, ADORN

bldg *abbr* building

bldr *abbr* builder

¹**bleach** \'blēch\ *vb* : WHITEN, BLANCH

²**bleach** *n* : a preparation used in bleaching

bleach·ers \'blē-chərz\ *n sing or pl* : a usu. uncovered stand of tiered seats for spectators

bleak \'blēk\ *adj* **1** : desolately barren and often windswept **2** : lacking warm or cheering qualities — **bleak·ly** *adv* — **bleak·ness** *n*

blear \'blir\ *adj* : dim with water or tears ⟨~ eyes⟩

bleary \'blir-ē\ *adj* **1** : dull or dimmed esp. from fatigue or sleep **2** : poorly outlined or defined ⟨a ~ view⟩

bleat \'blēt\ *n* : the cry of a sheep or goat or a sound like it — **bleat** *vb*

bleed \'blēd\ *vb* **bled** \'bled\; **bleed·ing 1** : to lose or shed blood **2** : to be wounded; *also* : to feel pain or distress **3** : to flow or ooze from a wounded surface; *also* : to draw fluid from ⟨~ a tire⟩ **4** : to extort money from

bleed·er \'blē-dər\ *n* : one that bleeds; *esp* : HEMOPHILIAC

bleeding heart *n* **1** : a garden plant related to the poppies that has usu. deep pink or white drooping heart-shaped flowers **2** : a person who shows extravagant sympathy esp. for an object of alleged persecution

¹**blem·ish** \'ble-mish\ *vb* : to spoil by a flaw : MAR

²**blemish** *n* : a noticeable flaw

¹**blench** \'blench\ *vb* [ME, to deceive, blench, fr. OE *blencan* to deceive] : FLINCH, QUAIL ◆ **Synonyms** SHRINK, RECOIL, WINCE, START

²**blench** *vb* : to grow or make pale

¹**blend** \'blend\ *vb* **blend·ed; blend·ing 1** : to mix thoroughly **2** : to prepare (as coffee) by mixing different varieties **3** : to combine into an integrated whole **4** : HARMONIZE ◆ **Synonyms** FUSE, MERGE, MINGLE, COALESCE — **blend·er** *n*

²**blend** *n* : a product of blending ◆ **Synonyms** COMPOUND, COMPOSITE, ALLOY, MIXTURE

blended family *n* : a family that includes children of a previous marriage of one spouse or both

bless \'bles\ *vb* **blessed** \'blest\ *also* **blest** \'blest\; **bless·ing** [ME, fr. OE *blētsian*, fr. *blōd* blood; fr. the use of blood in consecration] **1** : to consecrate by religious rite or word **2** : to sanctify with the sign of the cross **3** : to invoke divine care for **4** : PRAISE, GLORIFY **5** : to confer happiness upon

bless·ed \'ble-səd\ *also* **blest** \'blest\ *adj* **1** : HOLY **2** : BEATIFIED **3** : DELIGHTFUL — **bless·ed·ly** *adv* — **bless·ed·ness** *n*

bless·ing \'ble-siŋ\ *n* **1** : the act or words of one who blesses; *also* : APPROVAL **2** : a thing conducive to happiness **3** : grace said at a meal

blew *past of* BLOW

¹**blight** \'blīt\ *n* **1** : a plant disease or injury marked esp. by withering and death of parts; *also* : an organism causing blight **2** : an impairing or frustrating influence; *also* : a deteriorated condition ⟨urban ~⟩

²**blight** *vb* : to affect with or suffer from blight

blimp \'blimp\ *n* : an airship that maintains its form by pressure of contained gas

¹**blind** \'blīnd\ *adj* **1** : lacking or grossly deficient in ability to see; *also* : intended for blind persons **2** : not based on reason, evidence, or knowledge ⟨~ faith⟩ **3** : not intelligently controlled or directed ⟨~ chance⟩ **4** : performed solely by using aircraft instruments ⟨a ~ landing⟩ **5** : hard to discern or make out : HIDDEN ⟨a ~ seam⟩ **6** : lacking an opening or outlet ⟨a ~ alley⟩ — **blind·ly** *adv* — **blind·ness** \'blīnd-nəs\ *n*

²**blind** *vb* **1** : to make blind **2** : DAZZLE **3** : DARKEN; *also* : HIDE

³**blind** *n* **1** : something (as a shutter) to hinder vision or keep out light **2** : a place of concealment **3** : SUBTERFUGE

blind date *n* : a date between persons who have not previously met; *also* : either of these persons

blind·er \'blīn-dər\ *n* : either of two flaps on a horse's bridle to prevent it from seeing to the side

blind·fold \'blīnd-ˌfōld\ *vb* : to cover the eyes of with or as if with a bandage — **blindfold** *n*

¹**blink** \'bliŋk\ *vb* **1** : WINK **2** : TWINKLE **3** : EVADE, IGNORE

²**blink** *n* **1** : GLIMMER, SPARKLE **2** : a usu. involuntary shutting and opening of the eye

blink·er \'bliŋ-kər\ *n* : a blinking light used as a signal

blin·tze \'blint-sə\ *or* **blintz** \'blints\ *n* [Yiddish *blintse*] : a thin rolled pancake with a filling usu. of cream cheese

blip \'blip\ *n* **1** : a spot on a radar screen **2** : ABERRATION 1

bliss \'blis\ *n* : complete happiness : JOY ◆ **Synonyms** BEATITUDE, BLESSEDNESS — **bliss·ful** \-fəl\ *adj* — **bliss·ful·ly** *adv*

¹**blis·ter** \'blis-tər\ *n* **1** : a raised area of skin containing watery fluid; *also* : an agent that causes blisters **2** : something (as a raised spot in paint) suggesting a blister **3** : a disease of plants marked by large raised patches on the leaves

²**blister** *vb* : to develop a blister; *also* : to cause blisters

blithe \'blīth, 'blīth\ *adj* **blith·er; blith·est** : happily lighthearted ◆ **Synonyms** MERRY, JOVIAL, JOLLY, JOCUND — **blithe·ly** *adv* — **blithe·some** \-səm\ *adj*

blitz \'blits\ *n* **1** : an intensive series of air raids **2** : a fast intensive campaign **3** : a rush of the passer by the defensive linebackers in football — **blitz** *vb*

blitz·krieg \-ˌkrēg\ *n* [G, fr. *Blitz* lightning + *Krieg* war] : a sudden violent enemy attack

bliz·zard \'bli-zərd\ *n* : a long severe snowstorm

blk *abbr* **1** black **2** block

bloat \'blōt\ *vb* : to swell by or as if by filling with water or air

blob \'bläb\ *n* : a small lump or drop of a thick consistency

bloc \'bläk\ *n* [F, lit., block] : a combination of individuals or groups (as nations) working for a common purpose

¹**block** \'bläk\ *n* **1** : a solid piece of substantial material (as wood or stone) **2** : HINDRANCE, OBSTRUCTION; *also* : interruption of normal function of body or mind ⟨heart ~⟩ **3** : a frame enclosing one or more pulleys and having a hook or strap by which it may be attached **4** : a piece of material with a hand-cut design on its surface from which copies are to be made **5** : a large building divided into separate units (as apartments or offices) **6** : a row of houses or shops **7** : a city square; *also* : the distance along one of the sides of such a square **8** : a quantity of things considered as a unit ⟨a ~ of seats⟩

²**block** *vb* **1** : OBSTRUCT, CHECK **2** : to outline roughly ⟨~ out a design⟩ **3** : to provide or support with a block ◆ **Synonyms** BAR, IMPEDE, HINDER, OBSTRUCT

block·ade \blä-'kād\ *n* : the isolation of a place usu. by troops or ships — **blockade** *vb* — **block·ad·er** *n*

block·age \'blä-kij\ *n* : an act or instance of obstructing : the state of being blocked

block·bust·er \'bläk-ˌbəs-tər\ *n* : one that is very large, successful, expensive, or extravagant ⟨a ~ movie⟩

block·head \'bläk-ˌhed\ *n* : DOLT, DUNCE

block·house \-ˌhaus\ *n* : a small strong building used as a shelter (as from enemy fire) or observation post

¹**blond** *or* **blonde** \'bländ\ *adj* : fair in complexion; *also* : of a light or bleached color ⟨~ mahogany⟩ — **blond·ish** \'blän-dish\ *adj*

²**blond** *or* **blonde** *n* : a person having blond hair

blood \'bləd\ *n* **1** : a usu. red liquid that circulates in the heart, arteries, and veins of animals **2** : LIFEBLOOD; *also* : LIFE **3** : LINEAGE, STOCK **4** : KINSHIP; *also* : KINDRED **5** : the taking of life **6** : TEMPER, PASSION **7** : DANDY 1 — **blood·less** *adj* — **bloody** *adj*

blood·bath \'bləd-ˌbath, -ˌbäth\ *n* : MASSACRE

blood count *n* : the determination of the number of blood cells in a specific volume of blood; *also* : the number of cells so determined

blood·cur·dling \'bləd-kərd-liŋ, -ˌkər-dᵊl-iŋ\ *adj* : arousing fright or horror

blood·ed \'blə-dəd\ *adj* **1** : having blood of a specified kind ⟨warm-*blooded* animals⟩ **2** : entirely or largely purebred ⟨~ horses⟩

blood group *n* : one of the classes into which human beings can be separated by the presence or absence in their blood of specific antigens

blood·hound \'bləd-ˌhȧu̇nd\ *n* : any of a breed of large powerful hounds with long drooping ears, a wrinkled face, and keen sense of smell

blood·let·ting \-ˌle-tiŋ\ *n* **1** : PHLEBOTOMY **2** : BLOODSHED

blood·line \-ˌlīn\ *n* : a sequence of direct ancestors esp. in a pedigree

blood·lust \-ˌləst\ *n* : desire for bloodshed

blood·mo·bile \-mō-ˌbēl\ *n* : a motor vehicle equipped for collecting blood from donors

blood poisoning *n* : invasion of the bloodstream by virulent microorganisms from a focus of infection accompanied esp. by chills, fever, and prostration

blood pressure *n* : pressure of the blood on the walls of blood vessels and esp. arteries

blood·root \'bləd-ˌrüt, -ˌru̇t\ *n* : a plant related to the poppy that has a red root and sap, a solitary leaf, and a white flower in early spring

blood·shed \-ˌshed\ *n* : wounding or taking of life : CARNAGE, SLAUGHTER

blood·shot \-ˌshät\ *adj* : inflamed to redness ⟨~ eyes⟩

blood·stain \-ˌstān\ *n* : a discoloration caused by blood — **blood·stained** \-ˌstānd\ *adj*

blood·stone \-ˌstōn\ *n* : a green quartz sprinkled with red spots

blood·stream \-ˌstrēm\ *n* : the flowing blood in a circulatory system

blood·suck·er \-ˌsə-kər\ *n* : an animal that sucks blood; *esp* : LEECH — **blood·suck·ing** *adj*

blood test *n* : a test of the blood (as to detect disease-causing agents)

blood thinner *n* : a drug used to prevent the clotting of blood

blood·thirsty \'bləd-ˌthər-stē\ *adj* : eager to shed blood — **blood·thirst·i·ly** \-ˌthər-stə-lē\ *adv* — **blood·thirst·i·ness** \-stē-nəs\ *n*

blood type *n* : BLOOD GROUP — **blood–typ·ing** *n*

blood vessel *n* : a vessel (as a vein or artery) in which blood circulates in the body

Bloody Mary \'-ˌmer-ē\ *n, pl* **Bloody Marys** : a drink made essentially of vodka and tomato juice

¹bloom \'blüm\ *n* **1** : FLOWER 1; *also* : flowers or amount of flowers (as of a plant) **2** : the period or state of flowering **3** : a state or time of beauty and vigor **4** : a powdery coating esp. on fruits and leaves **5** : rosy color; *also* : an appearance of freshness or health — **bloomy** *adj*

²bloom *vb* **1** : to produce or yield flowers **2** : MATURE **3** : to glow esp. with healthy color ✦ *Synonyms* FLOWER, BLOSSOM

bloo·mers \'blü-mərz\ *n pl* [Amelia *Bloomer* †1894 Am. reformer] : a woman's garment of short loose pants gathered at the knee

bloop·er \'blü-pər\ *n* **1** : a fly ball hit barely beyond a baseball infield **2** : an embarrassing public blunder

¹blos·som \'blä-səm\ *n* **1** : the flower of a plant **2** : the period or state of flowering

²blossom *vb* : FLOWER, BLOOM

¹blot \'blät\ *n* **1** : SPOT, STAIN ⟨ink ~s⟩ **2** : BLEMISH ✦ *Synonyms* STIGMA, BRAND, SLUR

²blot *vb* **blot·ted; blot·ting** **1** : SPOT, STAIN **2** : OBSCURE, ECLIPSE ⟨~ out the sun⟩ **3** *obs* : MAR; *esp* : DISGRACE **4** : to dry or remove with or as if with an absorbing material **5** : to make a blot

blotch \'bläch\ *n* : a usu. large and irregular spot or mark (as of ink or color) — **blotch** *vb* — **blotchy** *adj*

blot·ter \'blä-tər\ *n* **1** : a piece of blotting paper **2** : a book for preliminary records (as of sales or arrests)

blot·ting paper *n* : a spongy paper used to absorb ink

blouse \'blau̇s, 'blau̇z\ *n* **1** : a loose outer garment like a smock **2** : a usu. loose garment reaching from the neck to about the waist

¹blow \'blō\ *vb* **blew** \'blü\; **blown** \'blōn\; **blow·ing** **1** : to be in motion; *esp* : to move forcibly ⟨the wind *blew*⟩ **2** : to send forth a current of gas (as air) **3** : to act on with a current of gas or vapor; *esp* : to drive with such a current **4** : to clear with a current of air **5** : to sound or cause to sound ⟨~ a horn⟩ **6** : PANT, GASP; *also* : to expel moist air in breathing ⟨the whale *blew*⟩ **7** : BOAST; *also* : BLUSTER **8** : ERUPT, EXPLODE **9** : MELT — used of an electrical fuse **10** : to shape or form by blown or injected air ⟨~ glass⟩ **11** : to shatter or destroy by or as

if by explosion **12** : to make breathless by exertion **13** : to spend recklessly **14** : BOTCH ⟨*blew* her lines⟩ — **blow·er** *n*

²blow *n* **1** : a usu. strong blowing of air : GALE **2** : BOASTING, BRAG **3** : an act or instance of blowing

³blow *vb* **blew** \'blü\; **blown** \'blōn\; **blow·ing** : FLOWER, BLOOM

⁴blow *n* **1** : a forcible stroke ⟨a ~ to the head⟩ **2** : COMBAT ⟨come to ~s⟩ **3** : a severe and usu. unexpected calamity

blow–by–blow *adj* : minutely detailed ⟨~ account⟩

blow–dry \-ˌdrī\ *vb* : to dry and usu. style hair with a blow-dryer

blow–dryer \-ˌdrī(-ə)r\ *n* : a hand-held hair dryer

blow·fly \'blō-ˌflī\ *n* : any of a family of dipteran flies (as a bluebottle) that deposit their eggs or maggots on meat or in wounds

blow·gun \-ˌgən\ *n* : a tube from which an arrow or a dart may be shot by the force of the breath

blow·out \'blō-ˌau̇t\ *n* **1** : a bursting of something (as a tire) because of pressure of the contents (as air) **2** : a depression created by the wind in sand or soil

blow·sy *also* **blow·zy** \'blau̇-zē\ *adj* : DISHEVELED, SLOVENLY

blow·torch \'blō-ˌtȯrch\ *n* : a small portable burner whose flame is made hotter by a blast of air or oxygen

blow–up \'blō-ˌəp\ *n* **1** : EXPLOSION **2** : an outburst of temper **3** : a photographic enlargement

blowy \'blō-ē\ *adj* : WINDY

BLT \ˌbē-ˌel-'tē\ *n* : a bacon, lettuce, and tomato sandwich

¹blub·ber \'blə-bər\ *vb* : to cry noisily

²blubber *n* **1** : the fat of large sea mammals (as whales) **2** : a noisy crying

¹blud·geon \'blə-jən\ *n* : a short often loaded club

²bludgeon *vb* : to strike with or as if with a bludgeon

¹blue \'blü\ *adj* **blu·er; blu·est** [ME, fr. AF *blef, blew,* of Gmc origin] **1** : of the color blue; *also* : BLUISH **2** : MELANCHOLY; *also* : DEPRESSING **3** : PURITANICAL **4** : INDECENT — **blue·ness** *n*

²blue *n* **1** : a color between green and violet in the spectrum : the color of the clear daytime sky **2** : something (as clothing or the sky) that is blue

blue baby *n* : a baby with bluish skin due to faulty circulation caused by a heart defect

blue·bell \-ˌbel\ *n* : any of various plants with blue bell-shaped flowers

blue·ber·ry \'blü-ˌber-ē, -bə-rē\ *n* : the edible blue or blackish berry of various shrubs of the heath family; *also* : one of these shrubs

blue·bird \-ˌbərd\ *n* : any of three small No. American thrushes that are blue above and reddish-brown or pale blue below

blue·bon·net \'blü-ˌbä-nət\ *n* : either of two low-growing annual lupines of Texas with silky foliage and blue flowers

blue·bot·tle \'blü-ˌbä-t²l\ *n* : any of several blowflies with iridescent blue bodies or abdomens

blue cheese *n* : cheese having veins of greenish-blue mold

blue–col·lar \'blü-ˌkä-lər\ *adj* : of, relating to, or being the class of workers whose duties call for work clothes

blue·fish \-ˌfish\ *n* : a marine sport and food fish that is bluish above and silvery below

blue·grass \-ˌgras\ *n* **1** : KENTUCKY BLUEGRASS **2** : country music played on stringed instruments having free improvisation and close harmonies

blue jay \-ˌjā\ *n* : a crested bright blue No. American jay

blue jeans *n pl* : pants usu. made of blue denim

blue·nose \'blü-ˌnōz\ *n* : a person who advocates a rigorous moral code

blue·point \-ˌpȯint\ *n* : a small oyster typically from the south shore of Long Island, New York

blue·print \-ˌprint\ *n* **1** : a photographic print in white on a blue ground used esp. for copying mechanical drawings and architects' plans **2** : a detailed plan of action — **blueprint** *vb*

blues \'blüz\ *n pl* **1** : MELANCHOLY **2** : music in a style marked by recurrent minor intervals and melancholy lyrics

blue screen *n* : a technique in which a subject is filmed in front of a blue background so as to allow the creation of a composite with other footage

blue·stock·ing \'blü-ˌstä-kiŋ\ n : a woman having intellectual interests

blu·et \'blü-ət\ n : a low No. American herb with dainty bluish flowers

blue whale n : a very large baleen whale that may reach a weight of 150 tons (135 metric tons) and a length of 100 feet (30 meters)

¹bluff \'bləf\ adj 1 : having a broad flattened front 2 : rising steeply with a broad flat front 3 : OUTSPOKEN, FRANK ◆ *Synonyms* ABRUPT, BLUNT, BRUSQUE, CURT, GRUFF

²bluff n : a high steep bank : CLIFF

³bluff vb : to frighten or deceive by pretense or a mere show of strength

⁴bluff n : an act or instance of bluffing; *also* : one who bluffs

blu·ing or **blue·ing** \'blü-iŋ\ n : a preparation used in laundering to counteract yellowing of white fabrics

blu·ish \'blü-ish\ adj : somewhat blue

¹blun·der \'blən-dər\ vb 1 : to move clumsily or unsteadily 2 : to make a stupid or needless mistake

²blunder n : an avoidable and usu. serious mistake

blun·der·buss \'blən-dər-ˌbəs\ n [obs. D *donderbus*, fr. D *donder* thunder + obs. D *bus* gun] : an obsolete short-barreled firearm with a flaring muzzle

¹blunt \'blənt\ adj 1 : not sharp : DULL 2 : lacking in tact : BLUFF ⟨~ criticism⟩ ◆ *Synonyms* BRUSQUE, CURT, GRUFF, ABRUPT, CRUSTY — **blunt·ly** adv — **blunt·ness** n

²blunt vb : to make or become dull

¹blur \'blər\ n 1 : a smear or stain that obscures 2 : something vaguely perceived; *esp* : something moving too quickly to be clearly perceived — **blur·ry** \-ē\ adj

²blur vb **blurred**; **blur·ring** : DIM, CLOUD, OBSCURE

blurb \'blərb\ n : a short publicity notice (as on a book jacket)

blurt \'blərt\ vb : to utter suddenly and impulsively

blush \'bləsh\ n 1 : a reddening of the face (as from modesty or confusion) : FLUSH 2 : a cosmetic used to tint the face pink — **blush** vb — **blush·ful** adj

blus·ter \'bləs-tər\ vb 1 : to blow in stormy noisy gusts 2 : to talk or act with noisy swaggering threats — **bluster** n — **blus·tery** \-tə-rē\ adj

blvd abbr boulevard

B lymphocyte n : B CELL

BM abbr bowel movement

B movie n : a cheaply produced motion picture

BO abbr 1 best offer 2 body odor 3 box office 4 branch office

boa \'bō-ə\ n 1 : a large snake (as the **boa con·stric·tor** \-kən-ˈstrik-tər\ or the related anaconda) that suffocates and kills its prey by constriction 2 : a fluffy scarf usu. of fur or feathers

boar \'bōr\ n : a male swine; *also* : WILD BOAR

¹board \'bōrd\ n 1 : the side of a ship 2 : a thin flat length of sawed lumber; *also* : material (as cardboard) or a piece of material formed as a thin flat firm sheet 3 pl : STAGE 1 4 : a table spread with a meal; *also* : daily meals esp. when furnished for pay 5 : a table at which a council or magistrates sit 6 : a group or association of persons organized for a special responsibility (as the management of a business or institution); *also* : an organized commercial exchange 7 : a sheet of insulating material carrying circuit elements and inserted in an electronic device 8 : BULLETIN BOARD

²board vb 1 : to go or put aboard ⟨~ a boat⟩ 2 : to cover with boards 3 : to provide or be provided with meals and often lodging — **board·er** n

board game n : a game of strategy (as checkers or chess) played by moving pieces on a board

board·ing·house \'bōr-diŋ-ˌhaus\ n : a house at which persons are boarded

board·walk \'bōrd-ˌwok\ n : a promenade (as of planking) along a beach

boast \'bōst\ vb 1 : to praise oneself 2 : to mention or assert with excessive pride 3 : to prize as a possession; *also* : HAVE ⟨the house ~s a fireplace⟩ — **boast** n — **boast·ful** \-fəl\ adj — **boast·ful·ly** adv

boat \'bōt\ n : a small vessel for travel on water; *also* : SHIP — **boat** vb

boat·er \'bō-tər\ n 1 : one that travels in a boat 2 : a stiff straw hat

boat·man \'bōt-mən\ n : a man who operates, works on, or deals in boats

boat people n pl : refugees fleeing by boat

boat·swain or **bo·sun** \'bō-sᵊn\ n : a subordinate officer of a ship in charge of the hull and related equipment

¹bob \'bäb\ vb **bobbed**; **bob·bing** 1 : to move up and down jerkily or repeatedly 2 : to emerge, arise, or appear suddenly or unexpectedly

²bob n : a bobbing movement

³bob n 1 : a knob, knot, twist, or curl esp. of ribbons, yarn, or hair 2 : a short haircut of a woman or child 3 : FLOAT 2 4 : a weight hanging from a line

⁴bob vb **bobbed**; **bob·bing** : to cut hair in a bob

⁵bob n, pl **bob** slang Brit : SHILLING

bob·bin \'bä-bən\ n : a cylinder or spindle for holding or dispensing thread (as in a sewing machine)

bob·ble \'bä-bəl\ vb **bob·bled**; **bob·bling** : FUMBLE — **bobble** n

bob·by \'bä-bē\ n, pl **bobbies** [*Bobby*, nickname for Sir *Robert* Peel, who organized the London police force] *Brit* : a police officer

bobby pin n : a flat wire hairpin with prongs that press close together

bob·cat \'bäb-ˌkat\ n : a small usu. rusty-colored No. American lynx

bob·o·link \'bä-bə-ˌliŋk\ n : an American migratory songbird related to the meadowlarks

bob·sled \'bäb-ˌsled\ n 1 : a short sled usu. used as one of a joined pair 2 : a racing sled with two pairs of runners, a steering wheel, and a hand brake — **bobsled** vb

bob·white \(ˌ)bäb-ˈhwīt\ n : any of a genus of quail; *esp* : a popular game bird of eastern and central No. America

boc·cie or **boc·ci** or **boc·ce** \'bä-chē\ n : Italian lawn bowling played on a long narrow court

bock \'bäk\ n : a strong dark beer usu. sold in early spring

bod \'bäd\ n : BODY

¹bode \'bōd\ vb **bod·ed**; **bod·ing** : to indicate by signs : PRESAGE

²bode past of BIDE

bo·de·ga \bō-ˈdā-gə\ n [Sp, fr. L *apotheca* storehouse] : a usu. small store specializing in Hispanic groceries

bod·ice \'bä-dəs\ n [alter. of *bodies*, pl. of *body*] : the usu. close-fitting part of a dress above the waist

bodi·less \'bä-di-ləs\ adj : lacking a body or material form

¹bodi·ly \'bä-dᵊl-ē\ adj : of or relating to the body ⟨~ contact⟩ ⟨~ organs⟩

²bodily adv 1 : in the flesh 2 : as a whole ⟨lifted the crate up ~⟩

bod·kin \'bäd-kən\ n 1 : DAGGER 2 : a pointed implement for punching holes in cloth 3 : a blunt needle for drawing tape or ribbon through a loop or hem

body \'bä-dē\ n, pl **bod·ies** 1 : the physical whole of a living or dead organism; *also* : the trunk or main mass of an organism as distinguished from its appendages 2 : a human being : PERSON 3 : the main part of something 4 : a mass of matter distinct from other masses 5 : GROUP 6 : VISCOSITY, FIRMNESS 7 : richness of flavor — used esp. of wines — **bod·ied** \'bä-dēd\ adj

body·build·ing \'bä-dē-ˌbil-diŋ\ n : the developing of the body through exercise and diet — **body·build·er** \-dər\ n

body English n : bodily motions made in a usu. unconscious effort to influence the movement of a propelled object (as a ball)

body·guard \'bä-dē-ˌgärd\ n : a personal guard; *also* : RETINUE

body language n : movements (as with the hands) or posture used as a means of communication

body stocking n : a sheer close-fitting one-piece garment for the torso that often has sleeves and legs

body·work \'bä-dē-ˌwərk\ n : the making or repairing of vehicle bodies

Boer \'bōr, 'bur\ n [D, lit., farmer] : a South African of Dutch or Huguenot descent

¹bog \'bäg, 'bog\ n : wet, spongy, poorly drained, and usu. acid ground — **bog·gy** adj

²bog vb **bogged**; **bog·ging** : to sink into or as if into a bog

bo·gey also **bo·gie** or **bo·gy** \'bu-gē, 'bō- for 1; 'bō- for 2\ n, pl **bogeys** also **bogies** 1 : SPECTER, HOBGOBLIN; *also* : a source of fear or annoyance 2 : a score of one over par on a hole in golf

bo·gey·man \'bu̇-gē-ˌman, 'bō-, 'bü-\ *n* : an imaginary monster used in threatening children

bog·gle \'bä-gəl\ *vb* **bog·gled; bog·gling** : to overwhelm or be overwhelmed with fright or amazement

bo·gus \'bō-gəs\ *adj* : SPURIOUS, SHAM

Bo·he·mi·an \bō-'hē-mē-ən\ *n* **1** : a native or inhabitant of Bohemia **2** *often not cap* : VAGABOND, WANDERER **3** *often not cap* : a person (as a writer or artist) living an un-conventional life — **bohemian** *adj, often cap*

bohr·i·um \'bȯr-ē-əm\ *n* : an artificially produced radioac-tive chemical element

¹boil \'bȯi(-ə)l\ *n* : an inflamed swelling on the skin con-taining pus

²boil *vb* **1** : to heat or become heated to a temperature (**boil·ing point**) at which vapor is formed and rises in bubbles ⟨water ∼s and changes to steam⟩; *also* : to act on or be acted on by a boiling liquid ⟨∼ eggs⟩ **2** : to be in a state of seething agitation

³boil *n* **1** : the act or state of boiling **2** : a boiled dish (as of seafood) **3** : a gathering where boiled food is served

boil·er \'bȯi-lər\ *n* **1** : a container in which something is boiled **2** : a strong vessel used in making steam **3** : a tank holding hot water

boil·er·mak·er \'bȯi-lər-ˌmā-kər\ *n* : whiskey with a beer chaser

bois·ter·ous \'bȯi-st(ə-)rəs\ *adj* : noisily turbulent or exu-berant — **bois·ter·ous·ly** *adv*

bok choy \'bäk-'chȯi\ *n* : a Chinese vegetable related to the mustards that forms a loose head of green leaves with long thick white stalks

bo·la \'bō-lə\ *or* **bo·las** \-ləs\ *n, pl* **bolas** \-ləz\ *also* **bo·las·es** [AmerSp *bolas,* fr. Sp *bola* ball] : a cord with weights attached to the ends for hurling at and entangling an ani-mal

bold \'bōld\ *adj* **1** : COURAGEOUS, INTREPID **2** : IMPU-DENT **3** : STEEP **4** : ADVENTUROUS, FREE ⟨a ∼ thinker⟩ ✦ *Synonyms* DAUNTLESS, BRAVE, VALIANT — **bold·ly** *adv* — **bold·ness** \'bōld-nəs\ *n*

bold·face \'bōld-ˌfās\ *n* : a heavy-faced type; *also* : print-ing in boldface — **bold–faced** \-'fāst\ *adj*

bole \'bōl\ *n* : the trunk of a tree

bo·le·ro \bə-'ler-ō\ *n, pl* **-ros 1** : a Spanish dance or its music **2** : a short loose jacket open at the front

bo·li·var \bə-'lē-ˌvär, 'bä-lə-vər\ *n, pl* **-va·res** \ˌbä-lə-'vär-ˌās, ˌbō-\ *or* **-vars** — see MONEY table

Bo·liv·i·an \bə-'li-vē-ən\ *n* : a native or inhabitant of Bo-livia — **Bolivian** *adj*

bo·li·vi·a·no \bə-'li-vē-'ä-(ˌ)nō\ *n, pl* **-nos** — see MONEY table

boll \'bōl\ *n* : a seed pod (as of cotton)

boll weevil *n* : a small usu. grayish or brown weevil that infests the cotton plant both as a larva and as an adult

boll·worm \'bōl-ˌwərm\ *n* : any of several moths and esp. the corn earworm whose larvae feed on cotton bolls

bo·lo·gna \bə-'lō-nē\ *n* [short for *Bologna sausage,* fr. *Bologna,* Italy] : a large smoked sausage of beef, veal, and pork

Bol·she·vik \'bōl-shə-ˌvik\ *n, pl* **Bolsheviks** *also* **Bol·she·vi·ki** \ˌbōl-shə-'vi-kē\ [Russ *bol'shevik,* fr. *bol'shiĭ* larger] **1** : a member of the party that seized power in Russia in the revolution of November 1917 **2** : COMMUNIST — **Bolshevik** *adj*

bol·she·vism \'bōl-shə-ˌvi-zəm\ *n, often cap* : the doctrine or program of the Bolsheviks advocating violent over-throw of capitalism

¹bol·ster \'bōl-stər\ *n* : a long pillow or cushion

²bolster *vb* : to support with or as if with a bolster; *also* : REINFORCE

¹bolt \'bōlt\ *n* **1** : a missile (as an arrow) for a crossbow or catapult **2** : a flash of lightning : THUNDERBOLT **3** : a sliding bar used to fasten a door **4** : a roll of cloth or wallpaper of specified length **5** : a rod with a head at one end and a screw thread at the other used with a nut to fas-ten objects together **6** : a metal cylinder that drives the cartridge into the chamber of a firearm

²bolt *vb* **1** : to move suddenly (as in fright or hurry) : START, DASH **2** : to break away (as from association) ⟨∼ from a political platform⟩ **3** : to produce seed pre-maturely **4** : to secure or fasten with a bolt **5** : to swal-low hastily or without chewing

³bolt *n* : an act of bolting

bo·lus \'bō-ləs\ *n, pl* **bo·lus·es 1** : a large pill **2** : a soft mass of chewed food

¹bomb \'bäm\ *n* **1** : a fused explosive device designed to detonate under specified conditions (as impact) **2** : an aerosol or foam dispenser (as of insecticide or hair spray) : SPRAY CAN **3** : FAILURE, FLOP **4** : a long pass, shot, or hit

²bomb *vb* **1** : to attack with bombs **2** : FAIL ⟨∼ed at the audition⟩

bom·bard \bäm-'bärd\ *vb* **1** : to attack esp. with artillery or bombers **2** : to assail persistently **3** : to subject to the impact of rapidly moving particles (as electrons) — **bom·bard·ment** *n*

bom·bar·dier \ˌbäm-bər-'dir\ *n* : a bomber-crew member who releases the bombs

bom·bast \'bäm-ˌbast\ *n* [ME, cotton padding, fr. MF *bombace,* fr. ML *bombax* cotton, alter. of L *bombyx* silk-worm, silk, fr. Gk] : pretentious wordy speech or writing — **bom·bas·tic** \bäm-'bas-tik\ *adj* — **bom·bas·ti·cal·ly** \-ti-k(ə-)lē\ *adv*

bom·ba·zine \ˌbäm-bə-'zēn\ *n* **1** : a twilled fabric with silk warp and worsted filling **2** : a silk fabric in twill weave dyed black

bomb·er \'bä-mər\ *n* : one that bombs; *esp* : an airplane for dropping bombs

bomb·proof \'bäm-ˌprüf\ *adj* : safe against the explosive force of bombs

bomb·shell \'bäm-ˌshel\ *n* **1** : BOMB 1 **2** : one that stuns, amazes, or completely upsets

bona fide \'bō-nə-ˌfīd, 'bä-; ˌbō-nə-'fī-dē, -də\ *adj* [L, in good faith] **1** : made in good faith ⟨a *bona fide* agree-ment⟩ **2** : GENUINE, REAL ⟨a *bona fide* bargain⟩

bo·nan·za \bə-'nan-zə\ *n* [Sp, lit., calm sea, fr. ML *bona-cia,* alter. of L *malacia,* fr. Gk *malakia,* lit., softness, fr. *malakos* soft] **1** : something yielding a rich return **2** : EXTRAVAGANZA

bon·bon \'bän-ˌbän\ *n* : a candy with a creamy center and a soft covering (as of chocolate)

¹bond \'bänd\ *n* **1** : FETTER **2** : a binding or uniting force or tie ⟨∼s of friendship⟩ **3** : an agreement or obligation often made binding by a pledge of money or goods **4** : a person who acts as surety for another **5** : an interest-bearing certificate of public or private indebtedness **6** : the state of goods subject to supervision pending pay-ment of taxes or duties due

²bond *vb* **1** : to assure payment of duties or taxes on (goods) by giving a bond **2** : to insure against losses caused by the acts of ⟨∼ a bank teller⟩ **3** : to make or be-come firmly united as if by bonds ⟨∼ iron to copper⟩ **4** : to form a close relationship ⟨∼ed with her stepmother⟩

bond·age \'bän-dij\ *n* : SLAVERY, SERVITUDE

bond·hold·er \'bänd-ˌhōl-dər\ *n* : one that owns a govern-ment or corporation bond

bond·ing \'bän-diŋ\ *n* **1** : the formation of a close per-sonal relationship esp. through frequent or constant association **2** : the attaching of a material (as porcelain) to a tooth surface esp. for cosmetic purposes

bond·man \'bänd-mən\ *n* : SLAVE, SERF

¹bonds·man \'bändz-mən\ *n* : SURETY 3

²bondsman *var of* BONDMAN

bond·wom·an \'bänd-ˌwu̇-mən\ *n* : a female slave or serf

¹bone \'bōn\ *n* **1** : a hard largely calcareous tissue forming most of the skeleton of a vertebrate animal; *also* : one of the pieces of bone making up a vertebrate skeleton **2** : a hard animal substance (as ivory or baleen) similar to true bone **3** : something made of bone — **bone·less** *adj* — **bony** *also* **bon·ey** \'bō-nē\ *adj*

²bone *vb* **boned; bon·ing** : to free from bones ⟨∼ a chick-en⟩

¹bolt 5: different styles

bone black *n* : the black carbon residue from calcined bones used esp. as a pigment

bone marrow *n* : MARROW

bone·meal \'bōn-ˌmēl\ *n* : crushed or ground bone used esp. as fertilizer or feed

bon·er \'bō-nər\ *n* : a stupid and ridiculous blunder

bone up *vb* **1** : CRAM 3 **2** : to refresh one's memory ⟨*boned up* on the speech before giving it⟩

bon·fire \'bän-ˌfi(-ə)r\ *n* [ME *bonefire* a fire of bones, fr. *bon* bone + *fire*] : a large fire built in the open air

bon·go \'bäŋ-gō\ *n, pl* **bongos** *also* **bongoes** [AmerSp *bongó*] : one of a pair of small tuned drums played with the hands

bon·ho·mie \ˌbä-nə-'mē\ *n* [F *bonhomie*, fr. *bonhomme* good-natured man, fr. *bon* good + *homme* man] : good-natured easy friendliness

bo·ni·to \bə-'nē-tō\ *n, pl* **-tos** *or* **-to** : any of several medium-sized tunas

bon mot \bōⁿ-'mō\ *n, pl* **bons mots** *same*\ *or* **bon mots** *same*\ [F, lit., good word] : a clever remark

bon·net \'bä-nət\ *n* : a covering (as a cap) for the head; *esp* : a hat for a woman or infant tied under the chin

bon·ny \'bä-nē\ *adj* **bon·ni·er; -est** *chiefly Brit* : ATTRACTIVE, FAIR; *also* : FINE, EXCELLENT

bon·sai \bōn-'sī, 'bän-ˌ\ *n, pl* **bonsai** [Jp] : a potted plant (as a tree) dwarfed and trained to an artistic shape; *also* : the art of growing such a plant

bo·nus \'bō-nəs\ *n* : something in addition to what is expected

bon vi·vant \ˌbän-vē-'vänt, ˌbōⁿ-vē-'väⁿ\ *n, pl* **bons vivants** \ˌbän-vē-'vänts, ˌbōⁿ-vē-'väⁿ\ *or* **bon vivants** *same*\ [F, lit., good liver] : a person having cultivated, refined, and sociable tastes esp. in food and drink

bon voy·age \ˌbōⁿ-ˌvȯi-'äzh, ˌbän-; ˌbōⁿ-ˌvwä-'yäzh\ *n* : FAREWELL — often used as an interjection

bony fish *n* : any of a class of fishes (as eels or sturgeons) with a bony rather than a cartilaginous skeleton

bonze \'bänz\ *n* : a Buddhist monk

boo \'bü\ *n, pl* **boos** : a shout of disapproval or contempt — **boo** *vb*

boo·by \'bü-bē\ *n, pl* **boobies** : an awkward foolish person : DOPE

booby hatch *n* : a psychiatric hospital

booby prize *n* : an award for the poorest performance in a contest

booby trap *n* : a trap for the unwary; *esp* : a concealed explosive device set to go off when some harmless-looking object is touched — **booby–trap** *vb*

boo·dle \'bü-dᵊl\ *n* **1** : bribe money **2** : a large amount of money

¹book \'bük\ *n* **1** : a set of sheets bound into a volume **2** : a long written or printed narrative or record **3** : a major division of a long literary work **4** *cap* : BIBLE — **in one's book** : in one's own opinion

²book *vb* **1** : to engage, reserve, or schedule by or as if by writing in a book ⟨∼ seats on a plane⟩ **2** : to enter charges against in a police register

book·case \-ˌkās\ *n* : a piece of furniture consisting of shelves to hold books

book·end \-ˌend\ *n* : a support to hold up a row of books

book·ie \'bu̇-kē\ *n* : BOOKMAKER

book·ish \'bu̇-kish\ *adj* **1** : fond of books and reading **2** : inclined to rely unduly on book knowledge

book·keep·er \'bu̇k-ˌkē-pər\ *n* : a person who records the accounts or transactions of a business — **book·keep·ing** *n*

book·let \'bu̇k-lət\ *n* : PAMPHLET

book·mak·er \'bu̇k-ˌmā-kər\ *n* : a person who determines odds and receives and pays off bets — **book·mak·ing** *n*

book·mark \-ˌmärk\ *or* **book·mark·er** \-ˌmär-kər\ *n* **1** : a marker for finding a place in a book **2** : a shortcut to a previously viewed location (as a Web site) on a computer — **bookmark** *vb*

book·mo·bile \'bu̇k-mō-ˌbēl\ *n* : a truck that serves as a traveling library

book·plate \'bu̇k-ˌplāt\ *n* : a label pasted in a book to show who owns it

book·sell·er \'bu̇k-ˌse-lər\ *n* : one that sells books; *esp* : the proprietor of a bookstore

book·shelf \-ˌshelf\ *n* : a shelf for books

book·worm \'bu̇k-ˌwərm\ *n* : a person unusually devoted to reading and study

¹boom \'büm\ *vb* **1** : to make a deep hollow sound : RESOUND **2** : to grow or cause to grow rapidly esp. in number, value, esteem, or importance

²boom *n* **1** : a booming sound or cry **2** : a rapid expansion or increase esp. of economic activity

³boom *n* [D, tree, beam] **1** : a long spar used to extend the bottom of a sail **2** : a line of floating timbers used to obstruct passage or catch floating objects **3** : a beam projecting from the upright pole of a derrick to support or guide the object lifted **4** : a long usu. horizontal supporting arm (as for a microphone)

boom box *n* : a large portable radio and often tape or CD player

boo·mer·ang \'bü-mə-ˌraŋ\ *n* [Dharuk (an Australian aboriginal language) *bumarin*ⁿ] : a bent or angular club that can be so thrown as to return near the starting point

boom·ing \'bü-miŋ\ *adj* **1** : making a loud deep sound ⟨a ∼ voice⟩ **2** : powerfully executed ⟨hit a ∼ serve⟩

¹boon \'bün\ *n* [ME *bone* prayer, request, the favor requested, fr. ON *bōn* request] : BENEFIT, BLESSING ✦ *Synonyms* FAVOR, GIFT, LARGESS, PRESENT

²boon *adj* [ME *bon*, fr. AF, good] : CONVIVIAL ⟨a ∼ companion⟩

boon·docks \'bün-ˌdäks\ *n pl* [Tagalog (language of the Philippines) *bundok* mountain] **1** : rough country filled with dense brush **2** : a rural area

boon·dog·gle \'bün-ˌdä-gəl, -ˌdȯ-\ *n* : a useless or wasteful project or activity

boor \'bu̇r\ *n* **1** : YOKEL **2** : a rude or insensitive person ✦ *Synonyms* CHURL, LOUT, CLOWN, CLODHOPPER — **boor·ish** *adj*

boost \'büst\ *vb* **1** : to push up from below **2** : INCREASE, RAISE ⟨∼ prices⟩ **3** : AID, PROMOTE ⟨voted a bonus to ∼ morale⟩ — **boost** *n* — **boost·er** *n*

¹boot \'büt\ *n, chiefly dial* : something to equalize a trade — **to boot** : BESIDES

²boot *vb, archaic* : AVAIL, PROFIT

³boot *n* **1** : a covering for the foot and leg **2** : a protective sheath (as of a flower) **3** *Brit* : an automobile trunk **4** : KICK; *also* : discharge from employment **5** : a navy or marine corps trainee

⁴boot *vb* **1** : KICK **2** : to eject or discharge summarily **3** : to load or become loaded into a computer from a disk **4** : to start or become ready for use esp. by booting a program ⟨∼ up the computer⟩

boot·black \'büt-ˌblak\ *n* : a person who shines shoes

boot camp *n* **1** : a navy or marine corps training camp **2** : a facility with a rigorous disciplinary program for young offenders

boo·tee *or* **boo·tie** \'bü-tē\ *n* : an infant's knitted or crocheted sock

booth \'büth\ *n, pl* **booths** \'bü*thz*, 'büths\ **1** : a small enclosed stall (as at a fair) **2** : a small enclosure giving privacy for a person ⟨voting ∼⟩ ⟨telephone ∼⟩ **3** : a restaurant accommodation having a table between backed benches

boot·leg \'büt-ˌleg\ *vb* : to make, transport, or sell (as liquor) illegally — **boot·leg** *adj or n* — **boot·leg·ger** *n*

boot·less \'büt-ləs\ *adj* : USELESS ✦ *Synonyms* FUTILE, VAIN, ABORTIVE, FRUITLESS — **boot·less·ly** *adv* — **boot·less·ness** *n*

¹boo·ty \'bü-tē\ *n, pl* **booties** : PLUNDER, SPOIL

²booty *also* **boo·tie** \'bü-tē\ *n, pl* **booties** *slang* : BUTTOCKS

¹booze \'büz\ *vb* **boozed; booz·ing** : to drink liquor to excess — **booz·er** *n*

²booze *n* : intoxicating liquor — **boozy** *adj*

bop \'bäp\ *vb* **bopped; bop·ping** : HIT, SOCK — **bop** *n*

BOQ *abbr* bachelor officers' quarters

bor *abbr* borough

bo·rate \'bȯr-ˌāt\ *n* : a salt or ester of boric acid

bo·rax \'bȯr-ˌaks\ *n* : a crystalline borate of sodium that occurs as a mineral and is used as a flux and cleanser

bor·del·lo \bȯr-'de-lō\ *n, pl* **-los** [It] : BROTHEL

¹bor·der \'bȯr-dər\ *n* **1** : EDGE, MARGIN **2** : BOUNDARY, FRONTIER ✦ *Synonyms* RIM, BRIM, BRINK, FRINGE, PERIMETER

²border *vb* **bor·dered; bor·der·ing** **1** : to put a border on **2** : ADJOIN **3** : VERGE

border collie *n, often cap B* : any of a British breed of medium-sized long-haired sheepdogs

bor·der·land \'bòr-dər-ˌland\ *n* **1** : territory at or near a border **2** : an outlying or intermediate region often not clearly defined

bor·der·line \-ˌlīn\ *adj* : being in an intermediate position or state; *esp* : not quite up to what is standard or expected ⟨~ intelligence⟩

¹bore \'bòr\ *vb* **bored; bor·ing** **1** : to make a hole in with or as if with a drill **2** : to make (as a well) by boring or digging away material ✦ *Synonyms* PERFORATE, DRILL, PRICK, PUNCTURE — **bor·er** *n*

²bore *n* **1** : a hole made by or as if by boring **2** : a cylindrical cavity **3** : the diameter of a hole or tube; *esp* : the interior diameter of a gun barrel or engine cylinder

³bore *past of* BEAR

⁴bore *n* : a tidal flood with a high abrupt front

⁵bore *n* : one that causes boredom

⁶bore *vb* **bored; bor·ing** : to weary with tedious dullness

bo·re·al \'bòr-ē-əl\ *adj* : of, relating to, or located in northern regions

bore·dom \'bòr-dəm\ *n* : the condition of being bored

bo·ric acid \'bòr-ik-\ *n* : a white crystalline weak acid that contains boron and is used esp. as an antiseptic

born \'bòrn\ *adj* **1** : brought into life by birth **2** : NATIVE ⟨American-*born*⟩ **3** : having special natural abilities or character from birth ⟨a ~ leader⟩

born–again *adj* : having experienced a revival of a personal faith or conviction ⟨a ~ believer⟩ ⟨a ~ liberal⟩

borne *past part of* BEAR

bo·ron \'bòr-ˌän\ *n* : a chemical element that occurs in nature only in combination (as in borax)

bor·ough \'bər-ō\ *n* [ME *burgh*, fr. OE *burg* fortified town] **1** : a British town that sends one or more members to Parliament; *also* : an incorporated British urban area **2** : an incorporated town or village in some U.S. states; *also* : any of the five political divisions of New York City **3** : a civil division of the state of Alaska corresponding to a county in most other states

bor·row \'bär-ō\ *vb* **1** : to take or receive (something) temporarily and with intent to return ⟨~ed my car⟩ **2** : to take into possession or use from another source : DERIVE, APPROPRIATE ⟨~ a metaphor⟩

borscht \'bòrsht\ *or* **borsch** \'bòrsh\ *n* [Yiddish *borsht* & Ukrainian & Russ *borshch*] : a soup made mainly from beets

bosh \'bäsh\ *n* [Turk *boş* empty] : foolish talk or action : NONSENSE

bosky \'bäs-kē\ *adj* : covered with trees or shrubs

¹bos·om \'bu̇-zəm, 'bü-\ *n* **1** : the front of the human chest; *esp* : the female breasts **2** : the seat of secret thoughts and feelings **3** : the part of a garment covering the breast — **bos·omed** \-zəmd\ *adj*

²bosom *adj* : CLOSE, INTIMATE

¹boss \'bäs, 'bòs\ *n* : a knoblike ornament : STUD

²boss *vb* : to ornament with bosses

³boss \'bòs\ *n* **1** : one (as a foreman or manager) exercising control or supervision **2** : a politician who controls votes or dictates policies — **bossy** *adj*

⁴boss \'bòs\ *vb* : to act as or in the manner of a boss

bosun *var of* BOATSWAIN

bot *abbr* botanical; botanist; botany

bot·a·ny \'bä-tə-nē, 'bät-nē\ *n, pl* **-nies** **1** : a branch of biology dealing with plants and plant life **2** : plant life (as of a given region); *also* : the biology of a plant or plant group — **bo·tan·i·cal** \bə-'ta-ni-kəl\ *adj or n* — **bo·tan·i·cal·ly** \-kə-lē\ *adv* — **bot·a·nist** *n* — **bot·a·nize** \'bät-ə-ˌnīz\ *vb*

botch \'bäch\ *vb* : to foul up hopelessly : BUNGLE — **botch** *n*

¹both \'bōth\ *pron* : both ones : the one as well as the other

²both *conj* — used as a function word to indicate and stress the inclusion of each of two or more things specified by coordinated words, phrases, or clauses ⟨~ New York and London⟩

³both *adj* : being the two : affecting the one and the other

both·er \'bä-thər\ *vb* **1** : PESTER, TROUBLE ⟨was ~ed by bees⟩ **2** : to concern oneself : make an effort ⟨didn't ~ asking⟩ ✦ *Synonyms* VEX, ANNOY, IRK, PROVOKE — **bother** *n* — **both·er·some** \-səm\ *adj*

¹bot·tle \'bä-tᵊl\ *n* **1** : a container (as of glass) with a narrow neck and usu. no handles **2** : the quantity held by a bottle **3** : intoxicating liquor

²bottle *vb* **bot·tled; bot·tling** **1** : to confine as if in a bottle : RESTRAIN ⟨*bottled* up his anger⟩ **2** : to put into a bottle

bot·tle·neck \'bä-tᵊl-ˌnek\ *n* **1** : a narrow passage or point of congestion **2** : something that obstructs or impedes

¹bot·tom \'bä-təm\ *n* **1** : an under or supporting surface; *also* : BUTTOCKS **2** : the surface on which a body of water lies **3** : the lowest part or place; *also* : an inferior position ⟨start at the ~⟩ **4** : BOTTOMLAND **5** : BASIS, SOURCE ⟨get to the ~ of this mystery⟩ **6** : a quark with a charge of -⅓ and a measured energy of approximately 5 billion electron volts — **bottom** *adj* — **bot·tom·less** *adj*

²bottom *vb* **1** : to furnish with a bottom **2** : to reach the bottom **3** : to reach a point where a decline is halted or reversed — usu. used with *out*

bot·tom·land \'bä-təm-ˌland\ *n* : low land along a river

bottom line *n* **1** : the essential point : CRUX **2** : the final result : OUTCOME

bot·u·lism \'bä-chə-ˌli-zəm\ *n* : an acute paralytic disease caused by a bacterial toxin (**bot·u·li·num toxin** \ˌbä-chə-'lī-nəm-\) esp. in tainted food

bou·doir \'bü-ˌdwär, 'bu̇-, ˌbü-', ˌbu̇-'\ *n* [F, fr. *bouder* to pout] : a woman's dressing room or bedroom

bouf·fant \bü-'fänt, 'bü-ˌfänt\ *adj* [F] : puffed out ⟨~ hairdos⟩

bough \'bau̇\ *n* : a usu. large or main branch of a tree

bought *past and past part of* BUY

bouil·la·baisse \ˌbü-yə-'bäs\ *n* [F] : a highly seasoned fish stew made with at least two kinds of fish

bouil·lon \'bü-ˌyän; 'bu̇l-ˌyän, -yən\ *n* : a clear soup made usu. from beef

boul·der *also* **bowl·der** \'bōl-dər\ *n* : a large detached rounded or worn mass of rock — **boul·dered** \-dərd\ *adj*

bou·le·vard \'bu̇-lə-ˌvärd, 'bü-\ *n* [F, modif. of MD *bolwerc* bulwark] : a broad often landscaped thoroughfare

bounce \'bau̇ns\ *vb* **bounced; bounc·ing** **1** : to cause to rebound ⟨~ a ball⟩ **2** : to rebound after striking **3** : to issue (a check) from an account with insufficient funds — **bounce** *n* — **bouncy** \'bau̇n-sē\ *adj*

bounc·er \'bau̇n-sər\ *n* : a person employed in a public place to remove disorderly persons

¹bound \'bau̇nd\ *adj* : intending to go

²bound *n* : LIMIT, BOUNDARY — **bound·less** *adj* — **bound·less·ness** *n*

³bound *vb* **1** : to set limits to **2** : to form the boundary of **3** : to name the boundaries of

⁴bound *past and past part of* BIND

⁵bound *adj* **1** : constrained by or as if by bonds : CONFINED, OBLIGED **2** : enclosed in a binding or cover **3** : RESOLVED, DETERMINED; *also* : SURE

⁶bound *n* **1** : LEAP, JUMP **2** : REBOUND, BOUNCE

⁷bound *vb* : SPRING, BOUNCE

bound·ary \'bau̇n-drē\ *n, pl* **-aries** : something that marks or fixes a limit or extent (as of territory) ✦ *Synonyms* BORDER, FRONTIER, MARCH

bound·en \'bau̇n-dən\ *adj* : BINDING

boun·te·ous \'bau̇n-tē-əs\ *adj* **1** : GENEROUS **2** : ABUNDANT — **boun·te·ous·ly** *adv* — **boun·te·ous·ness** *n*

boun·ti·ful \'bau̇n-ti-fəl\ *adj* **1** : giving freely **2** : PLENTIFUL — **boun·ti·ful·ly** *adv* — **boun·ti·ful·ness** *n*

boun·ty \'bau̇n-tē\ *n, pl* **bounties** [ME *bounte* goodness, fr. AF *bunté*, fr. L *bonitas*, fr. *bonus* good] **1** : GENEROSITY **2** : something given liberally **3** : a reward, premium, or subsidy given usu. for doing something

bou·quet \bō-'kā, bü-\ *n* [F, fr. MF, thicket, bunch of flowers, fr. OF (dial. of Normandy and Picardy) *bosquet* thicket, fr. *bosc* forest] **1** : flowers picked and fastened together in a bunch **2** : a distinctive aroma (as of wine) ✦ *Synonyms* SCENT, FRAGRANCE, PERFUME, REDOLENCE

bour·bon \'bər-bən\ *n* : a whiskey distilled from a corn mash

bour·geois \'bu̇rzh-ˌwä, bu̇rzh-'wä\ *n, pl* **bourgeois** *same or* -ˌwäz, -'wäz\ [MF, fr. OF *burgeis* townsman, fr. *burc, borg* town, fr. L *burgus* fortified place, of Gmc origin] : a middle-class person — **bourgeois** *adj*

bour·geoi·sie \ˌbu̇rzh-ˌwä-'zē\ *n* : a social order dominated by bourgeois

bourne *also* **bourn** \'bòrn, 'bu̇rn\ *n* : BOUNDARY; *also* : DESTINATION

bourse \'bùrs\ *n* : a European stock exchange

bout \'baùt\ *n* **1** : CONTEST, MATCH **2** : OUTBREAK, AT-TACK ⟨a ∼ of measles⟩ **3** : SESSION

bou·tique \bü-'tēk\ *n* : a small fashionable specialty shop

bou·ton·niere \,bü-tᵊn-'iər\ *n* : a flower or bouquet worn in a buttonhole

¹**bo·vine** \'bō-,vīn, -,vēn\ *adj* **1** : of or relating to bovines **2** : having qualities (as placidity or dullness) characteristic of oxen or cows

²**bovine** *n* : any of a group of mammals including oxen, buffalo, and their close relatives

bovine spon·gi·form encephalopathy \-'spän-ji-,fòrm-\ *n* : MAD COW DISEASE

¹**bow** \'baù\ *vb* **1** : SUBMIT, YIELD **2** : to bend the head or body (as in submission, courtesy, or assent) **3** : DEBUT ⟨the play ∼s next month⟩

²**bow** *n* : an act or posture of bowing

³**bow** \'bō\ *n* **1** : BEND, ARCH; *esp* : RAINBOW **2** : a weapon for shooting arrows; *also* : ARCHER **3** : a knot formed by doubling a line into two or more loops **4** : a wooden rod strung with horsehairs for playing an instrument of the violin family

⁴**bow** \'bō\ *vb* **1** : BEND, CURVE **2** : to play (an instrument) with a bow

⁵**bow** \'baù\ *n* : the forward part of a ship — **bow** *adj*

bowd·ler·ise *Brit var of* BOWDLERIZE

bowd·ler·ize \'bōd-lə-,rīz, 'baùd-\ *vb* **-ized; -iz·ing** : to expurgate by omitting parts considered vulgar

bow·el \'baù(-ə)l\ *n* **1** : INTESTINE; *also* : one of the divisions of the intestine — usu. used in pl. **2** *pl* : the inmost parts ⟨the ∼s of the earth⟩

bow·er \'baù(-ə)r\ *n* : a shelter of boughs or vines : ARBOR

¹**bowl** \'bōl\ *n* **1** : a concave vessel used to hold liquids **2** : a drinking vessel **3** : a bowl-shaped part or structure — **bowl·ful** \-,fùl\ *n*

²**bowl** *n* **1** : a ball for rolling on a level surface in bowling **2** : a cast of the ball in bowling

³**bowl** *vb* **1** : to play a game of bowling; *also* : to roll a ball in bowling **2** : to travel (as in a vehicle) rapidly and smoothly **3** : to strike or knock down with a moving object

bowlder *var of* BOULDER

bow·legged \'bō-,le-gəd\ *adj* : having legs that bow outward at or below the knee — **bow·leg** \'bō-,leg\ *n*

¹**bowl·er** \'bō-lər\ *n* : a person who bowls

²**bowl·er** \'bō-lər\ *n* : DERBY 3

bow·line \'bō-lən, -,līn\ *n* : a knot used to form a loop that neither slips nor jams

bowl·ing \'bō-liŋ\ *n* : any of various games in which balls are rolled on a green or alley at an object or a group of objects

bow·man \'bō-mən\ *n* : ARCHER

bow·sprit \'baù-,sprit\ *n* : a spar projecting forward from the prow of a ship

bow·string \'bō-,striŋ\ *n* : the cord connecting the two ends of a shooting bow

¹**box** \'bäks\ *n, pl* **box** *or* **box·es** : an evergreen shrub or small tree used esp. for hedges

²**box** *n* **1** : a rigid typically rectangular receptacle often with a cover; *also* : the quantity held by a box **2** : a small compartment (as for a group of theater patrons); *also* : a boxlike receptacle or division **3** : a usu. rectangular space demarcated for a particular purpose ⟨the batter's ∼⟩ **4** : PREDICAMENT — **boxy** \'bäk-sē\ *adj*

³**box** *vb* : to enclose in or as if in a box

⁴**box** *n* : a punch or slap esp. on the ear

⁵**box** *vb* **1** : to strike with the hand **2** : to engage in boxing with

box·car \'bäks-,kär\ *n* : a roofed freight car usu. with sliding doors in the sides

box cutter *n* : a small cutting tool with a retractable razor blade

¹**box·er** \'bäk-sər\ *n* **1** : a person who engages in boxing **2** *pl* : BOXER SHORTS

²**boxer** *n* : any of a German breed of compact medium-sized dogs with a short usu. fawn or brindled coat

boxer shorts *n pl* : men's loose-fitting shorts worn as underwear

box·ing \'bäk-siŋ\ *n* : the sport of fighting with the fists

box office *n* : an office (as in a theater) where admission tickets are sold

box turtle *n* : any of several No. American land turtles able to withdraw completely into their shell

box·wood \'bäks-,wùd\ *n* : the tough hard wood of the box; *also* : a box tree or shrub

boy \'bòi\ *n* **1** : a male child : YOUTH **2** : SON — **boy·hood** \-,hùd\ *n* — **boy·ish** *adj* — **boy·ish·ly** *adv* — **boy·ish·ness** *n*

boy·cott \'bòi-,kät\ *vb* [Charles C. *Boycott* †1897 Eng. land agent in Ireland who was ostracized for refusing to reduce rents] : to refrain from having any dealings with — **boycott** *n*

boy·friend \'bòi-,frend\ *n* **1** : a male friend **2** : a frequent or regular male companion in a romantic relationship

Boy Scout *n* : a member of any of various national scouting programs (as the Boy Scouts of America)

boy·sen·ber·ry \'bòi-zᵊn-,ber-ē, 'bòis-\ *n* : a large reddish-black fruit with a raspberry flavor; *also* ; the hybrid bramble bearing it developed by crossing blackberries and raspberries

bo·zo \'bō-,zō\ *n, pl* **bozos** : a foolish or incompetent person

bp *abbr* **1** bishop **2** birthplace

BP *abbr* **1** batting practice **2** blood pressure **3** boiling point

bpl *abbr* birthplace

BPOE *abbr* Benevolent and Protective Order of Elks

br *abbr* **1** branch **2** brass **3** brown

¹**Br** *abbr* Britain; British

²**Br** *symbol* bromine

BR *abbr* bedroom

bra \'brä\ *n* : BRASSIERE

¹**brace** \'brās\ *vb* **braced; brac·ing** **1** *archaic* : to make fast : BIND **2** : to tighten preparatory to use; *also* : to get ready for : prepare oneself **3** : INVIGORATE **4** : to furnish or support with a brace; *also* : STRENGTHEN **5** : to set firmly **6** : to gain courage or confidence

²**brace** *n, pl* **brac·es** **1** *or pl* **brace** : two of a kind ⟨a ∼ of dogs⟩ **2** : a crank-shaped device for turning a bit **3** : something (as a tie, prop, or clamp) that distributes, directs, or resists pressure or weight **4** *pl* : SUSPENDERS **5** : an appliance for supporting a body part (as the shoulders) **6** *pl* : a dental appliance used to exert pressure to straighten misaligned teeth **7** : one of two marks { } used to connect words or items to be considered together

brace·let \'brā-slət\ *n* [ME, fr. MF, dim. of *bras* arm, fr. L *bracchium*, fr. Gk *brachīon*] : an ornamental band or chain worn around the wrist

bra·ce·ro \brä-'ser-ō\ *n, pl* **-ros** : a Mexican laborer admitted to the U.S. esp. for seasonal farm work

brack·en \'bra-kən\ *n* : a large coarse fern; *also* : a growth of such ferns

¹**brack·et** \'bra-kət\ *n* **1** : a projecting framework or arm designed to support weight; *also* : a shelf on such framework **2** : one of a pair of punctuation marks [ ] used esp. to enclose interpolated matter **3** : a continuous section of a series; *esp* : one of a graded series of income groups

²**bracket** *vb* **1** : to furnish or fasten with brackets **2** : to place within brackets; *also* : to separate or group with or as if with brackets

brack·ish \'bra-kish\ *adj* : somewhat salty — **brack·ish·ness** *n*

bract \'brakt\ *n* : an often modified leaf on or at the base of a flower stalk

brad \'brad\ *n* : a slender nail with a small head

brae \'brā\ *n, chiefly Scot* : a hillside esp. along a river

brag \'brag\ *vb* **bragged; brag·ging** : to talk or assert boastfully — **brag** *n* — **brag·ger** *n*

brag·ga·do·cio \,bra-gə-'dō-shē-,ō, -sē-, -chē-\ *n, pl* **-cios** **1** : BRAGGART, BOASTER **2** : empty boasting **3** : arrogant pretension : COCKINESS

brag·gart \'bra-gərt\ *n* : one who brags

Brah·man *or* **Brah·min** \'brä-mən *for 1;* 'brā-, 'brä-, 'bra-*for 2*\ *n* **1** : a Hindu of the highest caste traditionally assigned to the priesthood **2** : any of a breed of large vigorous humped cattle developed in the southern U.S. from Indian stock **3** *usu* **Brahmin** : a person of high social standing and cultivated intellect and taste

Brah·man·ism \'brä-mə-,ni-zəm\ *n* : orthodox Hinduism

¹**braid** \'brād\ *vb* **1** : to form (strands) into a braid : PLAIT; *also* : to make from braids **2** : to ornament with braid

²**braid** *n* **1** : a length of braided hair **2** : a cord or ribbon

of three or more interwoven strands; *esp* : a narrow ornamental one

braille \'brāl\ *n, often cap* : a system of writing for the blind that uses characters made up of raised dots

braille alphabet

¹brain \'brān\ *n* **1** : the part of the vertebrate central nervous system enclosed in the skull and continuous with the spinal cord that is composed of neurons and supporting structures and is the center of thought and nervous system control; *also* : a centralized mass of nerve tissue in an invertebrate **2** : INTELLECT, INTELLIGENCE — often used in pl. — **brained** \'brānd\ *adj* — **brain·less** *adj* — **brainy** *adj*

²brain *vb* **1** : to kill by smashing the skull **2** : to hit on the head

brain·child \'brān-,chī(-ə)ld\ *n* : a product of one's creative imagination

brain death *n* : final cessation of activity in the central nervous system esp. as indicated by a flat electroencephalogram — **brain-dead** \-,ded\ *adj*

brain drain *n* : the departure of educated or professional people from one country, sector, or field to another usu. for better pay or living conditions

brain·storm \-,stórm\ *n* : a sudden inspiration or idea — **brainstorm** *vb*

brain·teas·er \-,tē-zər\ *n* : a challenging puzzle

brain·wash·ing \'brān-,wó-shiŋ, -,wä-\ *n* **1** : a forcible indoctrination to induce someone to give up basic political, social, or religious beliefs and attitudes and to accept contrasting regimented ideas **2** : persuasion by propaganda or salesmanship — **brain·wash** *vb*

brain wave *n* **1** : BRAINSTORM **2** : rhythmic fluctuations of voltage between parts of the brain; *also* : a current produced by brain waves

braise \'brāz\ *vb* **braised; brais·ing** : to cook slowly in fat and little moisture in a closed pot

¹brake \'brāk\ *n* : a common bracken fern

²brake *n* : rough or wet land heavily overgrown (as with thickets or reeds)

³brake *n* : a device for slowing or stopping motion esp. by friction — **brake·less** *adj*

⁴brake *vb* **braked; brak·ing** **1** : to slow or stop by or as if by a brake **2** : to apply a brake

brake·man \'brāk-mən\ *n* : a train crew member who inspects the train and assists the conductor

bram·ble \'bram-bəl\ *n* : any of a large genus of prickly shrubs (as a blackberry) related to the roses; *also* : any rough prickly shrub or vine — **bram·bly** \-b(ə-)lē\ *adj*

bran \'bran\ *n* : the edible broken husks of cereal grain sifted from flour or meal

¹branch \'branch\ *n* [ME, fr. AF *branche,* fr. LL *branca* paw] **1** : a natural subdivision (as a bough or twig) of a plant stem **2** : a division (as of an antler or a river) related to a whole like a plant branch to its stem **3** : a discrete element of a complex system ⟨the executive ∼⟩; *esp* : a division of a family descended from one ancestor — **branched** \'brancht\ *adj*

²branch *vb* **1** : to develop branches **2** : DIVERGE **3** : to extend activities ⟨the business is ∼*ing* out⟩

¹brand \'brand\ *n* **1** : a piece of charred or burning wood **2** : a mark made (as by burning) usu. to identify; *also* : a mark of disgrace : STIGMA **3** : a class of goods identified as the product of a particular firm or producer **4** : a distinctive kind ⟨my own ∼ of humor⟩

²brand *vb* **1** : to mark with a brand **2** : STIGMATIZE ⟨was ∼*ed* a traitor⟩

bran·dish \'bran-dish\ *vb* : to shake or wave menacingly ⟨∼ a knife⟩ ♦ **Synonyms** FLOURISH, FLASH, FLAUNT

brand–new \'bran-'nü, -'nyü\ *adj* : conspicuously new and unused

bran·dy \'bran-dē\ *n, pl* **brandies** [short for *brandywine,* fr. D *brandewijn,* fr. MD *brantwijn,* fr. *brant* distilled + *wijn* wine] : a liquor distilled from wine or fermented fruit juice — **brandy** *vb*

brash \'brash\ *adj* **1** : IMPETUOUS, AUDACIOUS **2** : aggressively self-assertive — **brash·ly** *adv* — **brash·ness** *n*

brass \'bras\ *n* **1** : an alloy of copper and zinc; *also* : an object of brass **2** : brazen self-assurance **3** : persons of high rank (as in the military) — **brassy** *adj*

bras·siere \brə-'zir\ *n* : a woman's close-fitting undergarment designed to support the breasts

brat \'brat\ *n* : an ill-behaved child — **brat·ti·ness** *n* — **brat·ty** *adj*

bra·va·do \brə-'vä-dō\ *n, pl* **-does** *or* **-dos** **1** : blustering swaggering conduct **2** : a show of bravery

¹brave \'brāv\ *adj* **brav·er; brav·est** [MF, fr. It & Sp *bravo* courageous, wild, prob. fr. L *barbarus* barbarous] **1** : showing courage **2** : EXCELLENT, SPLENDID ♦ **Synonyms** BOLD, INTREPID, COURAGEOUS, VALIANT — **brave·ly** *adv*

²brave *vb* **braved; brav·ing** : to face or endure bravely

³brave *n* : an American Indian warrior

brav·ery \'brā-və-rē\ *n, pl* **-er·ies** : COURAGE

bra·vo \'brä-vō\ *n, pl* **bravos** : a shout of approval — often used as an interjection in applauding

bra·vu·ra \brə-'vyùr-ə, -'vùr-\ *n* **1** : a florid brilliant musical style **2** : self-assured brilliant performance — **bravura** *adj*

brawl \'bról\ *n* : a noisy quarrel ♦ **Synonyms** FRACAS, ROW, RUMPUS, SCRAP, FRAY, MELEE — **brawl** *vb* — **brawl·er** *n*

brawn \'brón\ *n* : strong muscles; *also* : muscular strength — **brawn·i·ness** *n* — **brawny** *adj*

bray \'brā\ *n* : the characteristic harsh cry of a donkey — **bray** *vb*

braze \'brāz\ *vb* **brazed; braz·ing** : to solder with an alloy (as brass) that melts at a lower temperature than the metals being joined — **braz·er** *n*

¹bra·zen \'brā-z°n\ *adj* **1** : made of brass **2** : sounding harsh and loud **3** : of the color of brass **4** : marked by contemptuous boldness ⟨a ∼ rebuff⟩ — **bra·zen·ly** *adv* — **bra·zen·ness** *n*

²brazen *vb* : to face boldly or defiantly

¹bra·zier \'brā-zhər\ *n* : a worker in brass

²brazier *n* **1** : a vessel holding burning coals (as for heating) **2** : a device on which food is grilled

Bra·zil nut \brə-'zil-\ *n* : a triangular oily edible nut borne in large capsules by a tall So. American tree; *also* : the tree

¹breach \'brēch\ *n* **1** : a breaking of a law, obligation, tie (as of friendship), or standard (as of conduct) **2** : an interruption or opening made by or as if by breaking through ♦ **Synonyms** VIOLATION, TRANSGRESSION, INFRINGEMENT, TRESPASS

²breach *vb* **1** : to make a breach in **2** : to leap out of water ⟨whales ∼*ing*⟩

¹bread \'bred\ *n* **1** : baked food made basically of flour or meal **2** : FOOD

²bread *vb* : to cover with bread crumbs

bread·bas·ket \'bred-,bas-kət\ *n* : a major cereal-producing region

bread·fruit \-,früt\ *n* : a round usu. seedless fruit resembling bread in color and texture when baked; *also* : a tall tropical tree related to the mulberry and bearing breadfruit

bread·stuff \-,stəf\ *n* : GRAIN, FLOUR

breadth \'bredth, 'bretth\ *n* **1** : WIDTH **2** : comprehensive quality : SCOPE ⟨her ∼ of knowledge⟩

bread·win·ner \'bred-,wi-nər\ *n* : a member of a family whose wages supply its livelihood

¹break \'brāk\ *vb* **broke** \'brōk\; **bro·ken** \'brō-kən\; **break·ing** **1** : to separate into parts usu. suddenly or violently; *also* : to render inoperable ⟨*broke* his watch⟩ **2** : TRANSGRESS ⟨∼ a law⟩ **3** : to force a way into, out of, or through **4** : to disrupt the order or unity of ⟨∼ ranks⟩ ⟨∼ up a gang⟩; *also* : to bring to submission or helplessness **5** : EXCEED, SURPASS ⟨∼ a record⟩ **6** : RUIN **7** : to make known ⟨∼ the bad news⟩ **8** : HALT, INTERRUPT; *also* : to act or change abruptly (as a course or activity) **9** : to come esp. suddenly into being or notice ⟨as day ∼s⟩ **10** : to fail under stress **11** : HAPPEN, DEVELOP ⟨report news as it ∼s⟩ — **break·able** *adj or n* — **break into 1** : to begin with a sudden throwing off of restraint ⟨*broke into* tears⟩ **2** : to make entry or entrance into ⟨*break into* show business⟩

²break *n* **1** : an act of breaking **2** : a result of breaking; *esp* : an interruption of continuity ⟨coffee ∼⟩ ⟨a ∼ for the commercial⟩ **3** : a stroke of luck

break·age \'brā-kij\ *n* **1** : loss due to things broken **2** : the action of breaking **3** : articles or amount broken

break·down \'brāk-ˌdau̇n\ *n* **1** : functional failure; *esp* : a physical, mental, or nervous collapse **2** : DISINTEGRATION **3** : DECOMPOSITION **4** : ANALYSIS, CLASSIFICATION — **break down** *vb*

break·er \'brā-kər\ *n* **1** : one that breaks **2** : a wave that breaks into foam (as against the shore)

break·fast \'brek-fəst\ *n* : the first meal of the day — **breakfast** *vb*

break in *vb* **1** : to enter a building by force **2** : INTERRUPT; *also* : INTRUDE **3** : TRAIN — **break–in** \'brāk-ˌin\ *n*

break·neck \'brāk-ˌnek\ *adj* : very fast or dangerous ⟨∼ speed⟩

break out *vb* **1** : to develop or erupt suddenly or with force **2** : to develop a skin rash

break·through \'brāk-ˌthrü\ *n* **1** : an act or instance of breaking through an obstruction or defensive line **2** : a sudden advance in knowledge or technique ⟨a scientific ∼⟩

break·up \-ˌəp\ *n* **1** : DISSOLUTION **2** : a division into smaller units — **break up** *vb*

break·wa·ter \'brāk-ˌwȯ-tər, -ˌwä-\ *n* : a structure protecting a harbor or beach from the force of waves

bream \'brim, 'brēm\ *n, pl* **bream** *or* **breams** : any of various small freshwater sunfishes

breast \'brest\ *n* **1** : either of the pair of mammary glands extending from the front of the chest esp. in pubescent and adult human females **2** : the front part of the body between the neck and the abdomen **3** : the seat of emotion and thought

breast·bone \'brest-ˌbōn\ *n* : STERNUM

breast–feed \-ˌfēd\ *vb* : to feed (a baby) from a mother's breast

breast·plate \-ˌplāt\ *n* : a metal plate of armor for the breast

breast·stroke \-ˌstrōk\ *n* : a swimming stroke executed by extending both arms forward and then sweeping them back with palms out while kicking backward and outward with both legs

breast·work \-ˌwərk\ *n* : a temporary fortification

breath \'breth\ *n* **1** : the act or power of breathing **2** : a slight breeze **3** : air inhaled or exhaled in breathing **4** : spoken sound **5** : SPIRIT — **breath·less** *adj* — **breath·less·ly** *adv* — **breath·less·ness** *n* — **breathy** \'bre-thē\ *adj*

breathe \'brēth\ *vb* **breathed; breath·ing 1** : to inhale and exhale **2** : LIVE **3** : to halt for rest **4** : to utter softly or secretly — **breath·able** *adj*

breath·er \'brē-thər\ *n* **1** : one that breathes **2** : a short rest

breath·tak·ing \'breth-ˌtā-kiŋ\ *adj* **1** : making one out of breath **2** : EXCITING, THRILLING ⟨∼ beauty⟩ — **breath·tak·ing·ly** *adv*

brec·cia \'bre-chē-ə, -chə\ *n* : a rock composed of sharp fragments held in fine-grained material

breech \'brēch\ *n* **1** *pl \usu* 'bri-chəz\ : pants ending near the knee **2** : BUTTOCKS, RUMP **3** : the part of a firearm at the rear of the barrel

¹breed \'brēd\ *vb* **bred** \'bred\; **breed·ing 1** : BEGET; *also* : ORIGINATE **2** : to propagate sexually; *also* : MATE **3** : BRING UP, NURTURE **4** : to produce (fissionable material) from material that is not fissionable ♦ *Synonyms* GENERATE, REPRODUCE, PROCREATE, PROPAGATE — **breed·er** *n*

²breed *n* **1** : a strain of similar and presumably related plants or animals usu. developed in domestication **2** : KIND, SORT, CLASS

breeding *n* **1** : ANCESTRY **2** : training in polite social interaction **3** : sexual propagation of plants or animals

¹breeze \'brēz\ *n* **1** : a light wind **2** : CINCH, SNAP — **breeze·less** *adj*

²breeze *vb* **breezed; breez·ing** : to progress quickly and easily

breeze·way \'brēz-ˌwā\ *n* : a roofed open passage connecting two buildings (as a house and garage)

breezy \'brē-zē\ *adj* **1** : swept by breezes **2** : briskly informal ⟨∼ prose⟩ — **breez·i·ly** \'brē-zə-lē\ *adv* — **breez·i·ness** \-zē-nəs\ *n*

breth·ren \'breth-rən, 'bre-thə-; 'bre-thərn\ *pl of* BROTHER — used esp. in formal or solemn address

Brethren *n pl* : members of one of several Protestant denominations originating chiefly in a German religious movement and stressing personal religious experience

bre·via·ry \'brē-vyə-rē, -vē-ˌer-ē\ *n, pl* **-ries** *often cap* : a book of prayers, hymns, psalms, and readings used by Roman Catholic priests

brev·i·ty \'bre-və-tē\ *n, pl* **-ties 1** : shortness or conciseness of expression **2** : shortness of duration

brew \'brü\ *vb* **1** : to prepare (as beer) by steeping, boiling, and fermenting **2** : to prepare (as tea) by steeping in hot water — **brew** *n* — **brew·er** *n* — **brew·ery** \'brü-ə-rē, 'brü(-ə)r-ē\ *n*

¹bri·ar *also* **bri·er** \'brī-ər\ *n* : a plant (as a bramble or rose) with a thorny or prickly usu. woody stem; *also* : a mass or twig of these — **bri·ary** \'brī-ə-rē\ *adj*

²briar *n* : a tobacco pipe made from the root or stem of a European heath

¹bribe \'brīb\ *n* [ME, morsel given to a beggar, bribe, fr. AF, morsel] : something (as money or a favor) given or promised to a person to influence conduct

²bribe *vb* **bribed; brib·ing** : to influence by offering a bribe — **brib·able** *adj* — **brib·er** *n* — **brib·ery** \'brī-bə-rē\ *n*

bric–a–brac \'bri-kə-ˌbrak\ *n pl* [F] : small ornamental articles

¹brick \'brik\ *n* : a block molded from moist clay and hardened by heat used esp. for building

²brick *vb* : to close, cover, or pave with bricks

brick·bat \'brik-ˌbat\ *n* **1** : a piece of a hard material (as a brick) esp. when thrown as a missile **2** : an uncomplimentary remark

brick·lay·er \'brik-ˌlā-ər\ *n* : a person who builds or paves with bricks — **brick·lay·ing** *n*

¹brid·al \'brī-dʔl\ *n* [ME *bridale*, fr. OE *brydealu*, fr. *bryd* bride + *ealu* ale] : MARRIAGE, WEDDING

²bridal *adj* : of or relating to a bride or a wedding

bride \'brīd\ *n* : a woman just married or about to be married

bride·groom \'brīd-ˌgrüm, -ˌgru̇m\ *n* : a man just married or about to be married

brides·maid \'brīdz-ˌmād\ *n* : a woman who attends a bride at her wedding

¹bridge \'brij\ *n* **1** : a structure built over a depression or obstacle for use as a passageway **2** : something (as the upper part of the nose) resembling a bridge in form or function **3** : a curved piece raising the strings of a musical instrument **4** : the forward part of a ship's superstructure from which it is navigated **5** : an artificial replacement for missing teeth

²bridge *vb* **bridged; bridg·ing** : to build a bridge over — **bridge·able** *adj*

³bridge *n* : a card game for four players developed from whist

bridge·head \-ˌhed\ *n* : an advanced position seized in enemy territory

bridge·work \-ˌwərk\ *n* : dental bridges

¹bri·dle \'brī-dʔl\ *n* **1** : headgear with which a horse is controlled **2** : CURB, RESTRAINT

²bridle *vb* **bri·dled; bri·dling 1** : to put a bridle on; *also* : to restrain with or as if with a bridle **2** : to show hostility or scorn usu. by tossing the head

Brie \'brē\ *n* : a soft cheese with a whitish rind and a pale yellow interior

¹brief \'brēf\ *adj* **1** : short in duration or extent **2** : CONCISE; *also* : CURT — **brief·ly** *adv* — **brief·ness** *n*

²brief *n* **1** : a concise statement or document; *esp* : one summarizing a law client's case or a legal argument **2** *pl* : short snug underpants

³brief *vb* : to give final instructions or essential information to

brief·case \'brēf-ˌkās\ *n* : a flat flexible case for carrying papers

brier *var of* BRIAR

¹**brig** \'brig\ n : a 2-masted square-rigged sailing ship

²**brig** n : the place of confinement for offenders on a naval ship

³**brig** abbr brigade

bri·gade \bri-'gād\ n 1 : a military unit composed of a headquarters, one or more units of infantry or armored forces, and supporting units 2 : a group organized for a particular purpose (as fire fighting)

brig·a·dier general \'bri-gə-,dir-\ n : a commissioned officer (as in the army) ranking next below a major general

brig·and \'bri-gənd\ n : BANDIT — **brig·and·age** \-gən-dij\ n

brig·an·tine \'bri-gən-,tēn\ n : a 2-masted square-rigged ship with a fore-and-aft mainsail

Brig Gen abbr brigadier general

bright \'brīt\ adj 1 : SHINING, RADIANT 2 : ILLUSTRIOUS, GLORIOUS 3 : INTELLIGENT, CLEVER; also : LIVELY, CHEERFUL ♦ **Synonyms** BRILLIANT, LUSTROUS, BEAMING — **bright** adv — **bright·ly** adv — **bright·ness** n

bright·en \'brī-tᵊn\ vb : to make or become bright or brighter — **bright·en·er** n

¹**bril·liant** \'bril-yənt\ adj [F brillant, prp. of briller to shine, fr. It brillare] 1 : very bright 2 : STRIKING, DISTINCTIVE 3 : very intelligent ♦ **Synonyms** RADIANT, LUSTROUS, BEAMING, LUCID, BRIGHT, LAMBENT — **bril·liance** \-yəns\ n — **bril·lian·cy** \-yən-sē\ n — **bril·liant·ly** adv

²**brilliant** n : a gem cut in a particular form with many facets

¹**brim** \'brim\ n : EDGE, RIM ♦ **Synonyms** BRINK, BORDER, VERGE, FRINGE — **brim·less** adj

²**brim** vb brimmed; brim·ming : to be or become full often to overflowing

brim·ful \-'fůl\ adj : full to the brim

brim·stone \'brim-,stōn\ n : SULFUR

brin·dled \'brin-dᵊld\ adj : having dark streaks or flecks on a gray or tawny ground ⟨a ~ Great Dane⟩

brine \'brīn\ n 1 : water saturated with salt 2 : OCEAN — **brin·i·ness** n — **briny** \'brī-nē\ adj

bring \'briŋ\ vb brought \'brȯt\; bring·ing \'briŋ-iŋ\ 1 : to cause to come with one 2 : INDUCE, PERSUADE, LEAD 3 : PRODUCE, EFFECT 4 : to sell for ⟨~ a good price⟩ — **bring·er** n

bring about vb : to cause to take place

bring up vb 1 : to give a parent's fostering care to 2 : to come or bring to a sudden halt 3 : to call to notice

brink \'briŋk\ n 1 : an edge at the top of a steep place 2 : the point of onset

brio \'brē-ō\ n : VIVACITY, SPIRIT

bri·quette or **bri·quet** \bri-'ket\ n : a compacted often brick-shaped mass of fine material ⟨a charcoal ~⟩

bris also **briss** \'bris\ n : the Jewish rite of circumcision

brisk \'brisk\ adj 1 : ALERT, LIVELY 2 : INVIGORATING ⟨~ weather⟩ 3 : highly active ⟨a ~ business⟩ ♦ **Synonyms** AGILE, SPRY, NIMBLE — **brisk·ly** adv — **brisk·ness** n

bris·ket \'bris-kət\ n : the breast or lower chest of a quadruped; also : a cut of beef from the brisket

bris·ling \'briz-liŋ, 'bris-\ n : SPRAT 1

¹**bris·tle** \'bri-səl\ n : a short stiff coarse hair — **bris·tle·like** \'bri-səl-,līk\ adj — **bris·tly** adj

²**bristle** vb bris·tled; bris·tling 1 : to stand stiffly erect 2 : to show angry defiance ⟨bristled at the charges⟩ 3 : to appear as if covered with bristles

Brit abbr Britain; British

Bri·tan·nic \bri-'ta-nik\ adj : BRITISH

britch·es \'bri-chəz\ n pl : BREECHES, TROUSERS

Brit·ish \'bri-tish\ n pl : the people of Great Britain or the Commonwealth — **British** adj — **Brit·ish·ness** n

British thermal unit n : the quantity of heat needed to raise the temperature of one pound of water one degree Fahrenheit

Brit·on \'bri-tᵊn\ n 1 : a member of a people inhabiting Britain before the Anglo-Saxon invasion 2 : a native or inhabitant of Great Britain

brit·tle \'bri-tᵊl\ adj brit·tler; brit·tlest : easily broken : FRAGILE ♦ **Synonyms** CRISP, CRUMBLY, FRIABLE — **brit·tle·ness** n

bro \'brō\ n, pl bros 1 : BROTHER 1 2 : SOUL BROTHER

¹**broach** \'brōch\ n : a pointed tool

²**broach** vb 1 : to pierce (as a cask) in order to draw the contents 2 : to open up (a subject) for discussion

broad \'brȯd\ adj 1 : WIDE 2 : SPACIOUS ⟨the ~ plains⟩ 3 : CLEAR, OPEN ⟨~ daylight⟩ 4 : OBVIOUS ⟨a ~ hint⟩ 5 : COARSE, CRUDE ⟨~ stories⟩ 6 : tolerant in outlook 7 : GENERAL ⟨a ~ rule⟩ 8 : dealing with essential points — **broad·ly** adv — **broad·ness** n

broad·band \'brȯd-,band\ n : a system of high-speed telecommunication in which a frequency range is divided into multiple independent channels for simultaneous transmission of signals

¹**broad·cast** \'brȯd-,kast\ vb broadcast also broad·cast·ed; broad·cast·ing 1 : to scatter or sow broadcast 2 : to make widely known 3 : to transmit a broadcast — **broad·cast·er** n

²**broadcast** adv : to or over a wide area

³**broadcast** n 1 : the transmission of sound or images by radio or television 2 : a single radio or television program

broad·cloth \-,klȯth\ n 1 : a smooth dense woolen cloth 2 : a fine soft cloth of cotton, silk, or synthetic fiber

broad·en \'brȯ-dᵊn\ vb : WIDEN

broad·loom \-,lüm\ adj : woven on a wide loom esp. in a solid color

broad–mind·ed \-'mīn-dəd\ adj : tolerant of varied opinions — **broad–mind·ed·ly** adv — **broad–mind·ed·ness** n

¹**broad·side** \-,sīd\ n 1 : a sheet of paper printed usu. on one side (as an advertisement) 2 : all of the guns on one side of a ship; also : their simultaneous firing 3 : a volley of abuse or denunciation

²**broadside** adv 1 : with one side forward : SIDEWAYS 2 : from the side ⟨the car was hit ~⟩

broad–spectrum adj : effective against a wide range of organisms ⟨~ antibiotics⟩

broad·sword \'brȯd-,sȯrd\ n : a broad-bladed sword

broad·tail \-,tāl\ n : a karakul esp. with flat and wavy fur

bro·cade \brō-'kād\ n : a usu. silk fabric with a raised design

broc·co·li \'brä-kə-lē\ n [It, pl. of broccolo flowering top of a cabbage, dim. of brocco small nail, sprout, fr. L broccus projecting] : the stems and immature usu. green or purple flower heads of either of two garden vegetable plants closely related to the cabbage; also : either of the plants

bro·chette \brō-'shet\ n : SKEWER

bro·chure \brō-'shůr\ n [F, fr. brocher to sew, fr. MF, to prick, fr. OF brochier, fr. broche pointed tool] : PAMPHLET, BOOKLET

bro·gan \'brō-gən, brō-'gan\ n : a heavy shoe

brogue \'brōg\ n : a dialect or regional pronunciation; esp : an Irish accent

broil \'brȯi(-ə)l\ vb : to cook by exposure to radiant heat : GRILL — **broil** n

broil·er \'brȯi-lər\ n 1 : a utensil for broiling 2 : a young chicken fit for broiling

broil·ing \'brȯi(-ə)-liŋ\ adj : extremely hot ⟨a ~ sun⟩

¹**broke** \'brōk\ past of BREAK

²**broke** adj : PENNILESS

¹**bro·ken** \'brō-kən\ past part of BREAK

²**broken** adj 1 : SHATTERED ⟨~ glass⟩ 2 : having gaps or breaks : INTERRUPTED, DISRUPTED 3 : SUBDUED, CRUSHED ⟨a ~ spirit⟩ 4 : BANKRUPT 5 : imperfectly spoken ⟨~ English⟩ — **bro·ken·ly** adv

bro·ken·heart·ed \,brō-kən-'här-təd\ adj : overcome by grief or despair

bro·ker \'brō-kər\ n : an agent who negotiates contracts of purchase and sale — **broker** vb

bro·ker·age \'brō-kə-rij\ n 1 : the business of a broker 2 : the fee or commission charged by a broker

bro·me·li·ad \brō-'mē-lē-,ad\ n : any of several tropical American ornamental plants related to the pineapple that usu. grow on trees

bro·mide \'brō-,mīd\ n : a compound of bromine and another element or chemical group including some (as potassium bromide) used as sedatives

bro·mid·ic \brō-'mi-dik\ adj : TRITE, UNORIGINAL

bro·mine \'brō-,mēn\ n [F brome bromine, fr. Gk brōmos stink] : a deep red liquid corrosive chemical element that gives off an irritating vapor

bronc \'bräŋk\ n : an unbroken or partly broken range horse of western No. America; also : MUSTANG

bron·chi·al \'bräŋ-kē-əl\ adj : of, relating to, or affecting the bronchi or their branches

bron·chi·tis \brän-'kī-təs, bräŋ-\ n : inflammation of the bronchi and their branches — **bron·chit·ic** \-'ki-tik\ adj

bron·chus \'bräŋ-kəs\ *n, pl* **bron·chi** \'bräŋ-ˌkī, -ˌkē\ : either of the main divisions of the trachea each leading to a lung

bronchi

bron·co \'bräŋ-kō\ *n, pl* **broncos** [MexSp, fr. Sp, rough, wild] : BRONC

bron·to·sau·rus \ˌbrän-tə-'sȯr-əs\ *also* **bron·to·saur** \'brän-tə-ˌsȯr\ *n* [NL, fr. Gk *brontē* thunder + *sauros* lizard] : any of a genus of large 4-footed sauropod dinosaurs of the Jurassic

Bronx cheer \'bräŋks-\ *n* : RASPBERRY 2

¹bronze \'bränz\ *vb* **bronzed; bronz·ing** : to give the appearance of bronze to

²bronze *n* **1** : an alloy of copper and tin and sometimes other elements; *also* : something made of bronze **2** : a yellowish brown color — **bronzy** \'brän-zē\ *adj*

brooch \'brōch, 'brüch\ *n* : an ornamental clasp or pin

¹brood \'brüd\ *n* : a family of young animals or children and esp. of birds

²brood *adj* : kept for breeding ⟨a ~ mare⟩

³brood *vb* **1** : to sit on eggs to hatch them; *also* : to shelter (hatched young) with the wings **2** : to think anxiously or gloomily about something — **brood·ing·ly** *adv*

brood·er \'brü-dər\ *n* **1** : one that broods **2** : a heated structure for raising young birds

¹brook \'brük\ *n* : a small natural stream

²brook *vb* : TOLERATE, BEAR ⟨would ~ no interference with his plan⟩

brook·let \'brük-lət\ *n* : a small brook

brook trout *n* : a common speckled cold-water char of No. America

broom \'brüm, 'brüm\ *n* **1** : any of several shrubs of the legume family with long slender branches and usu. yellow flowers **2** : an implement with a long handle (**broomstick** \-ˌstik\) used for sweeping

broth \'brȯth\ *n, pl* **broths** \'brȯths, 'brȯthz\ **1** : liquid in which meat or sometimes vegetable food has been cooked **2** : a fluid culture medium

broth·el \'brä-thəl, 'brȯ-\ *n* : a house of prostitution

broth·er \'brə-thər\ *n, pl* **brothers** *also* **breth·ren** \'breth-rən, 'bre-thə-; 'bre-thərn\ **1** : a male having one or both parents in common with another individual **2** : a man who is a religious but not a priest **3** : KINSMAN; *also* : SOUL BROTHER — **broth·er·li·ness** \-lē-nəs\ *n* — **broth·er·ly** *adj*

broth·er·hood \'brə-thər-ˌhud\ *n* **1** : the state of being brothers or a brother **2** : ASSOCIATION, FRATERNITY **3** : the whole body of persons in a business or profession

broth·er–in–law \'brə-thə-rən-ˌlȯ, 'brə-thərn-ˌlȯ\ *n, pl* **brothers–in–law** \'brə-thər-zən-\ : the brother of one's spouse; *also* : the husband of one's sister or of one's spouse's sister

brougham \'brü-(ə)m, 'brō-(ə)m\ *n* : a light closed horse-drawn carriage with the driver outside in front

brought *past and past part of* BRING

brou·ha·ha \'brü-ˌhä-ˌhä\ *n* : HUBBUB, UPROAR

brow \'braủ\ *n* **1** : the eyebrow or the ridge on which it grows; *also* : FOREHEAD **2** : the projecting upper part of a steep place

brow·beat \'braủ-ˌbēt\ *vb* **-beat; -beat·en** \-ˈbē-t°n\ *or* **-beat; -beat·ing** : to intimidate by sternness or arrogance

¹brown \'braủn\ *adj* : of the color brown; *also* : of dark or tanned complexion

²brown *n* : a color like that of coffee or chocolate that is a blend of red and yellow darkened by black — **brown·ish** *adj*

³brown *vb* : to make or become brown

brown bag·ging \-'ba-giŋ\ *n* : the practice of carrying one's lunch usu. in a brown bag — **brown bag·ger** *n*

brown bear *n* : any of various large typically brown-furred bears including the grizzly bear

brown·ie \'braủ-nē\ *n* **1** : a legendary cheerful elf who performs good deeds at night **2** *cap* : a member of a program of the Girl Scouts for girls in the first through third grades **3** : a small square or rectangle of chocolate cake

brown·nose \'braủn-ˌnōz\ *vb* : to ingratiate oneself with — **brownnose** *n*

brown·out \'braủ-ˌnaủt\ *n* : a period of reduced voltage of electricity caused esp. by high demand and resulting in reduced illumination

brown rice *n* : hulled but unpolished rice that retains most of the bran layers

brown·stone \'braủn-ˌstōn\ *n* : a dwelling faced with reddish-brown sandstone

¹browse \'braủz\ *vb* **browsed; brows·ing** **1** : to feed on browse; *also* : GRAZE **2** : to read or look over something in a casual way **3** : to access (a network) with a browser

²browse *n* : tender shoots, twigs, and leaves fit for food for cattle

brows·er \'braủ-zər\ *n* : a computer program for accessing sites or information on a network (as the World Wide Web)

bru·in \'brü-ən\ *n* : BEAR

¹bruise \'brüz\ *vb* **bruised; bruis·ing** **1** : to inflict a bruise on; *also* : to become bruised **2** : to break down (as leaves or berries) by pounding

²bruise *n* : a surface injury to flesh : CONTUSION

bruis·er \'brü-zər\ *n* : a big husky man

bruit \'brüt\ *vb* : to make widely known by common report ⟨word of his dismissal was ~ed about⟩

brunch \'brənch\ *n* : a meal that combines a late breakfast and an early lunch

bru·net *or* **bru·nette** \brü-'net\ *adj* [F *brunet*, masc., *brunette*, fem., brownish, fr. OF, fr. *brun* brown, of Gmc origin] : having brown or black hair and usu. a relatively dark complexion — **brunet** *or* **brunette** *n*

brunt \'brənt\ *n* : the main shock, force, or stress esp. of an attack; *also* : the greater burden

bru·schet·ta \brü-'she-tə, -'ske-\ *n* : an appetizer of grilled bread with toppings

¹brush \'brəsh\ *n* **1** : BRUSHWOOD **2** : scrub vegetation or land covered with it

²brush *n* **1** : a device composed of bristles set in a handle and used esp. for cleaning or painting **2** : a bushy tail (as of a fox) **3** : an electrical conductor that makes contact between a stationary and a moving part (as of a motor) **4** : a quick light touch in passing

³brush *vb* **1** : to treat (as in cleaning or painting) with a brush **2** : to remove with or as if with a brush; *also* : to dismiss in an offhand manner **3** : to touch gently in passing

⁴brush *n* : SKIRMISH ⟨a ~ with the law⟩ ♦ **Synonyms** ENCOUNTER, RUN-IN

brush fire *n* **1** : a fire involving low-growing plants **2** : a minor conflict or crisis

brush·off \'brəsh-ˌȯf\ *n* : a curt offhand dismissal

brush up *vb* : to renew one's skill

brush·wood \'brəsh-ˌwud\ *n* **1** : small branches of wood esp. when cut **2** : a thicket of shrubs and small trees

brusque \'brəsk\ *adj* [F *brusque*, fr. It *brusco*, fr. ML *bruscus* a plant with stiff twigs used for brooms] : CURT, BLUNT, ABRUPT ⟨a ~ answer⟩ ♦ **Synonyms** GRUFF, BLUFF, CRUSTY, SHORT — **brusque·ly** *adv*

brus·sels sprout \'brəs-əlz-\ *n, often cap B* : one of the edible green heads borne on the stalk of a plant closely related to the cabbage; *also, pl* : this plant

bru·tal \'brü-t°l\ *adj* **1** : befitting a brute : UNFEELING, CRUEL **2** : HARSH, SEVERE ⟨~ weather⟩ **3** : unpleasantly accurate — **bru·tal·i·ty** \brü-'ta-lə-tē\ *n* — **bru·tal·ly** *adv*

bru·tal·ise *Brit var of* BRUTALIZE

bru·tal·ize \'brü-t°l-ˌīz\ *vb* **-ized; -iz·ing** **1** : to make brutal **2** : to treat brutally

¹**brute** \'brüt\ *adj* [ME, fr. MF *brut* rough, fr. L *brutus* brutish, lit., heavy] **1** : of or relating to beasts **2** : BRUTAL **3** : UNREASONING; *also* : purely physical ⟨~ strength⟩

²**brute** *n* **1** : BEAST 1 **2** : a brutal person

brut·ish \'brü-tish\ *adj* **1** : BRUTE 1 **2** : strongly sensual; *also* : showing little intelligence

BS *abbr* bachelor of science

BSA *abbr* Boy Scouts of America

bskt *abbr* basket

Bt *abbr* baronet

btry *abbr* battery

Btu *abbr* British thermal unit

bu *abbr* bushel

¹**bub·ble** \'bə-bəl\ *n* **1** : a globule of gas in a liquid **2** : a thin film of liquid filled with gas **3** : something lacking firmness or solidity — **bub·bly** *adj*

²**bubble** *vb* **bub·bled**; **bub·bling** : to form, rise in, or give off bubbles

bub·kes \'bəp-kəs, 'bùp-\ *n pl* [Yiddish] : the least amount ⟨didn't win ~⟩

bu·bo \'bü-bō, 'byü-\ *n, pl* **buboes** : an inflammatory swelling of a lymph gland

bu·bon·ic plague \bü-'bä-nik-, byü-\ *n* : plague caused by a bacterium transmitted to human beings by flea bites and marked esp. by chills and fever and by buboes usu. in the groin

buc·ca·neer \,bə-kə-'nir\ *n* : PIRATE

¹**buck** \'bək\ *n, pl* **bucks 1** *or pl* **buck** : a male animal (as a deer or antelope) **2** : DANDY **3** : DOLLAR

²**buck** *vb* **1** : to spring with an arching leap ⟨a ~*ing* horse⟩ **2** : to charge against something; *also* : to strive for advancement sometimes without regard to ethical behavior

buck·board \-,bòrd\ *n* : a 4-wheeled horse-drawn wagon with a floor of long springy boards

buck·et \'bə-kət\ *n* **1** : PAIL **2** : an object resembling a bucket in collecting, scooping, or carrying something — **buck·et·ful** *n*

bucket seat *n* : a low separate seat for one person (as in an automobile)

buck·eye \'bə-,kī\ *n* : any of various trees or shrubs related to the horse chestnut; *also* : the large nutlike seed of such a shrub or tree

buck fever *n* : nervous excitement of an inexperienced hunter at the sight of game

¹**buck·le** \'bə-kəl\ *n* : a clasp (as on a belt) for two loose ends

²**buckle** *vb* **buck·led**; **buck·ling 1** : to fasten with a buckle **2** : to apply oneself with vigor **3** : to crumple up : BEND, COLLAPSE

³**buckle** *n* : BEND, FOLD, KINK

buck·ler \'bə-klər\ *n* : SHIELD

buck·ram \'bə-krəm\ *n* : a coarse stiff cloth used esp. for binding books

buck·saw \'bək-,sò\ *n* : a saw set in a usu. H-shaped frame for sawing wood

buck·shot \'bək-,shät\ *n* : lead shot that is from .24 to .33 inch (about 6.1 to 8.4 millimeters) in diameter

buck·skin \-,skin\ *n* **1** : the skin of a buck **2** : a soft usu. suede-finished leather — **buckskin** *adj*

buck·tooth \-'tüth\ *n* : a large protruding front tooth — **buck–toothed** \-'tütht\ *adj*

buck·wheat \-,hwēt\ *n* : either of two plants grown for their triangular seeds which are used as a cereal grain; *also* : these seeds

bu·col·ic \byü-'kä-lik\ *adj* [L *bucolicus*, fr. Gk *boukolikos*, fr. *boukolos* cowherd] : PASTORAL, RURAL

¹**bud** \'bəd\ *n* **1** : an undeveloped plant shoot (as of a leaf or a flower); *also* : a partly opened flower **2** : an asexual reproductive structure that detaches from the parent and forms a new individual **3** : something not yet fully developed ⟨nipped in the ~⟩

²**bud** *vb* **bud·ded**; **bud·ding 1** : to form or put forth buds; *also* : to reproduce by asexual buds **2** : to be or develop like a bud **3** : to reproduce a desired variety (as of peach) by inserting a bud in a plant of a different variety

Bud·dhism \'bü-,di-zəm, 'bù-\ *n* : a religion of eastern and central Asia growing out of the teachings of Gautama Buddha — **Bud·dhist** \'bü-dist, 'bù-\ *n or adj*

bud·dy \'bə-dē\ *n, pl* **buddies 1** : COMPANION; *also* : FRIEND **2** : FELLOW

budge \'bəj\ *vb* **budged**; **budg·ing** : MOVE, SHIFT; *also* : YIELD

bud·ger·i·gar \'bə-jə-rē-,gar\ *n* : a small brightly colored Australian parrot often kept as a pet

¹**bud·get** \'bə-jət\ *n* [ME *bowgette*, fr. MF *bougette*, dim. of *bouge* leather bag, fr. L *bulga*] **1** : STOCK, SUPPLY **2** : a financial report containing estimates of income and expenses; *also* : a plan for coordinating income and expenses **3** : the amount of money available for a particular use — **bud·get·ary** \'bə-jə-,ter-ē\ *adj*

²**budget** *vb* **1** : to allow for in a budget **2** : to draw up a budget

³**budget** *adj* : INEXPENSIVE

bud·gie \'bə-jē\ *n* : BUDGERIGAR

¹**buff** \'bəf\ *n* **1** : a yellow to orange yellow color **2** : FAN, ENTHUSIAST

²**buff** *adj* : of the color buff

³**buff** *vb* : POLISH, SHINE

buf·fa·lo \'bə-fə-,lō\ *n, pl* **-lo** *or* **-loes** *also* **-los 1** : WATER BUFFALO **2** : a large shaggy-maned No. American wild bovine mammal that has short horns and heavy forequarters with a large muscular hump

buffalo soldier *n* : an African-American soldier serving in the western U.S. after the Civil War

¹**buf·fer** \'bə-fər\ *n* : something or someone that protects or shields (as from physical damage or a financial blow)

²**buffer** *n* : one that buffs

¹**buf·fet** \'bə-fət\ *n* : BLOW, SLAP

²**buffet** *vb* **1** : to strike with the hand; *also* : to pound repeatedly **2** : to struggle against or on ♦ *Synonyms* BEAT, BATTER, DRUB, PUMMEL, THRASH

³**buf·fet** \(,)bə-'fā, bü-\ *n* **1** : SIDEBOARD **2** : a counter for refreshments; *also* : a meal at which people serve themselves informally

buff leather *n* : a strong supple oil-tanned leather

buf·foon \(,)bə-'fün\ *n* [MF *bouffon*, fr. It *buffone*] : CLOWN 2 — **buf·foon·ery** \-'fü-nə-rē\ *n* — **buf·foon·ish** \-'fü-nish\ *adj*

¹**bug** \'bəg\ *n* **1** : an insect or other creeping or crawling invertebrate animal; *esp* : an insect pest (as the cockroach or bedbug **2** : any of an order of insects with sucking mouthparts and incomplete metamorphosis that includes many plant pests **3** : an unexpected flaw or imperfection ⟨a ~ in a computer program⟩ **4** : a disease-producing germ; *also* : a disease caused by it **5** : a concealed listening device — **bug·gy** \'bə-gē\ *adj*

²**bug** *vb* **bugged**; **bug·ging 1** : BOTHER, ANNOY **2** : to plant a concealed microphone in

³**bug** *vb* **bugged**; **bug·ging** *of the eyes* : PROTRUDE, BULGE

bug·a·boo \'bə-gə-,bü\ *n, pl* **-boos** : BOGEY 1

bug·bear \'bəg-,ber\ *n* : BOGEY 1; *also* : a source of dread

bug·gy \'bə-gē\ *n, pl* **buggies** : a light horse-drawn carriage; *also* : a carriage for a baby

bu·gle \'byü-gəl\ *n* [ME, buffalo, instrument made of buffalo horn, bugle, fr. AF, fr. L *buculus*, dim. of *bos* head of cattle] : a valveless brass instrument resembling a trumpet and used esp. for military calls — **bu·gler** *n*

bugle

bug out *vb* **1** : to flee in panic **2** : to depart in a hurry

¹**build** \'bild\ *vb* **built** \'bilt\; **build·ing 1** : to form or have formed by ordering and uniting materials ⟨~ a house⟩; *also* : to bring into being or develop **2** : to produce or create gradually ⟨~ an argument on facts⟩ **3** : INCREASE, ENLARGE; *also* : ENHANCE **4** : to engage in building — **build·er** *n*

²**build** *n* : form or mode of structure; *esp* : PHYSIQUE

build·ing \'bil-diŋ\ *n* **1** : a usu. roofed and walled structure (as a house) for permanent use **2** : the art or business of constructing buildings

build·up \'bild-,əp\ *n* : the act or process of building up; *also* : something produced by this

built–in \'bilt-'in\ *adj* **1** : forming an integral part of a structure **2** : INHERENT

bulb \'bəlb\ *n* **1** : an underground resting stage of a plant (as a lily or an onion) consisting of a short stem base bearing one or more buds enclosed in overlapping leaves; *also* : a fleshy plant structure (as a tuber) resembling a bulb **2** : a plant having or growing from a bulb **3** : a rounded more or less bulb-shaped object or part (as for an electric lamp) — **bul·bous** \'bəl-bəs\ *adj*

¹**bulge** \'bəlj\ *vb* **bulged; bulg·ing** : to become or cause to become protuberant

²**bulge** *n* : a swelling projecting part

bu·li·mia \bü-'lē-mē-ə, byü-, -'li-\ *n* **1** : an abnormal and constant craving for food **2** : a serious eating disorder chiefly of females that is characterized by compulsive overeating usu. followed by self-induced vomiting or laxative or diuretic abuse — **bu·lim·ic** \-'lē-mik, -'li-\ *adj or n*

¹**bulk** \'bəlk\ *n* **1** : MAGNITUDE, VOLUME **2** : material that forms a mass in the intestine; *esp* : FIBER 2 **3** : a large mass **4** : the major portion

²**bulk** *vb* **1** : to cause to swell or bulge **2** : to appear as a factor : LOOM

bulk·head \'bəlk-,hed\ *n* **1** : a partition separating compartments **2** : a structure built to cover a shaft or a cellar stairway

bulky \'bəl-kē\ *adj* **bulk·i·er; -est** : having bulk; *esp* : being large and unwieldy

¹**bull** \'bul\ *n* **1** : a male bovine animal; *also* : a usu. adult male of various large animals (as the moose, elephant, or whale) **2** : one who buys securities or commodities in expectation of a price increase — **bull·ish** *adj*

²**bull** *adj* **1** : of, relating to, or suggestive of a bull : MALE **2** : large of its kind ⟨a ∼ lathe⟩

³**bull** *n* [ME *bulle*, fr. ML *bulla*, fr. L, bubble, amulet] **1** : a papal letter **2** : DECREE

⁴**bull** *n, slang* : NONSENSE

⁵**bull** *abbr* bulletin

¹**bull·dog** \'bul-,dóg\ *n* : any of a breed of compact muscular short-haired dogs of English origin

²**bulldog** *vb* : to throw (a steer) by seizing the horns and twisting the neck

bull·doze \-,dōz\ *vb* **1** : to move, clear, or level with a tractor-driven machine (**bull·doz·er**) having a broad blade for pushing **2** : to force as if by using a bulldozer

bul·let \'bu-lət\ *n* [MF *boulette* small ball & *boulet* missile, dims. of *boule* ball, fr. L *bulla* bubble] : a missile to be shot from a firearm

bul·le·tin \'bu-lə-t⁰n\ *n* **1** : a brief public report intended for immediate release on a matter of public interest **2** : a periodical publication (as of a college)

bulletin board *n* **1** : a board for posting notices **2** : a public forum on a computer network in which users write or read messages or download files

bul·let·proof \'bu-lət-,prüf\ *adj* **1** : impenetrable to bullets **2** : not subject to correction, alteration, or modification **3** : INVINCIBLE

bull·fight \'bul-,fīt\ *n* : a spectacle in which people ceremonially fight with and usu. kill bulls in an arena — **bull·fight·er** *n*

bull·frog \-,frog, -,fräg\ *n* : a large deep-voiced frog

bull·head \-,hed\ *n* : any of several common large-headed freshwater catfishes of the U.S.

bull·head·ed \-'he-dəd\ *adj* : stupidly stubborn : HEADSTRONG

bul·lion \'bul-yən\ *n* : gold or silver esp. in bars or ingots

bull market *n* : a market in which securities or commodities are persistently rising in value

bull·ock \'bu-lək\ *n* : a young bull; *also* : STEER

bull pen *n* : a place on a baseball field where pitchers warm up; *also* : the relief pitchers of a baseball team

bull session *n* : an informal discussion

bull's–eye \'bulz-,ī\ *n, pl* **bull's–eyes** : the center of a target; *also* : a shot that hits the bull's-eye

¹**bul·ly** \'bu-lē\ *n, pl* **bullies** : a person habitually cruel to others who are weaker

²**bully** *adj* : EXCELLENT, FIRST-RATE — often used interjectionally ⟨∼ for you⟩

³**bully** *vb* **bul·lied; bul·ly·ing** : to behave as a bully toward : DOMINEER ♦ *Synonyms* BROWBEAT, INTIMIDATE, HECTOR

bul·rush \'bul-,rəsh\ *n* : any of several large rushes or sedges of wetlands

bul·wark \'bul-(,)wərk, -,wórk; 'bəl-(,)wərk\ *n* **1** : a wall-like defensive structure **2** : a strong support or protection

¹**bum** \'bəm\ *adj* **1** : of poor quality ⟨∼ advice⟩ **2** : disabled by damage or injury ⟨a ∼ knee⟩

²**bum** *vb* **bummed; bum·ming** **1** : to spend time unemployed and wandering; *also* : LOAF **2** : to obtain by begging

³**bum** *n* **1** : LOAFER **2** : one whose time is devoted to a recreational activity ⟨a ski ∼⟩ **3** : TRAMP 1

bum·ble \'bəm-bəl\ *vb* **bum·bled; bum·bling** **1** : to speak in a stuttering and faltering manner **2** : to proceed unsteadily **3** : BUNGLE

bum·ble·bee \'bəm-bəl-,bē\ *n* : any of numerous large hairy social bees

bum·mer \'bə-mər\ *n* **1** : an unpleasant experience **2** : FAILURE

¹**bump** \'bəmp\ *n* **1** : a local bulge; *esp* : a swelling of tissue **2** : a sudden forceful blow or impact — **bumpy** *adj*

²**bump** *vb* **1** : to strike or knock forcibly; *also* : to move by or as if by bumping **2** : to collide with

¹**bum·per** \'bəm-pər\ *n* **1** : a cup or glass filled to the brim **2** : something unusually large — **bumper** *adj*

²**bump·er** \'bəm-pər\ *n* : a device for absorbing shock or preventing damage; *esp* : a usu. metal bar at either end of an automobile

bump·kin \'bəmp-kən\ *n* : an awkward and unsophisticated country person

bump·tious \'bəmp-shəs\ *adj* : obtusely and often noisily self-assertive

bun \'bən\ *n* : a sweet biscuit or roll

¹**bunch** \'bənch\ *n* **1** : SWELLING **2** : CLUSTER, GROUP — **bunchy** *adj*

²**bunch** *vb* : to form into a group or bunch

bun·co *or* **bun·ko** \'bəŋ-kō\ *n, pl* **buncos** *or* **bunkos** : a swindling scheme — **bunco** *vb*

¹**bun·dle** \'bən-d⁰l\ *n* **1** : several items bunched and fastened together; *also* : something wrapped for carrying **2** : a considerable amount : LOT **3** : a small band of mostly parallel nerve or muscle fibers **4** : a package offering related products or services at a single price

²**bundle** *vb* **bun·dled; bun·dling** : to gather or tie in a bundle

bundling *n* : a former custom of a courting couple's occupying the same bed without undressing

bung \'bəŋ\ *n* : the stopper in the bunghole of a cask

bun·ga·low \'bəŋ-gə-,lō\ *n* [Hindi & Urdu *banglā*, lit., (house) in the Bengal style] : a one-storied house with a low-pitched roof

bun·gee cord \'bən-jē-\ *n* : a long elastic cord used esp. as a fastening or shock-absorbing device

bungee jump *vb* : to jump from a height while attached to a bungee cord — **bungee jumper** *n*

bung·hole \'bəŋ-,hōl\ *n* : a hole for emptying or filling a cask

bun·gle \'bəŋ-gəl\ *vb* **bun·gled; bun·gling** : to do badly : BOTCH — **bungle** *n* — **bun·gler** *n*

bun·ion \'bən-yən\ *n* : an inflamed swelling of the first joint of the big toe

¹**bunk** \'bəŋk\ *n* : BED; *esp* : a built-in bed that is often one of a tier

²**bunk** *n* : BUNKUM, NONSENSE

bunk bed *n* : one of two single beds usu. placed one above the other

bun·ker \'bəŋ-kər\ *n* **1** : a bin or compartment for storage (as for coal on a ship) **2** : a protective embankment or dugout **3** : a sand trap or embankment constituting a hazard on a golf course

bun·kum *or* **bun·combe** \'bəŋ-kəm\ *n* [*Buncombe* County, N.C.; fr. a remark made by its congressman, who defended an irrelevant speech by claiming that he was speaking to Buncombe] : insincere or foolish talk

bun·ny \'bə-nē\ *n, pl* **-nies** : RABBIT

bunny slope *n* : a gentle incline used by novice skiers — called also *bunny hill*

Bun·sen burner \'bən-sən-\ *n* : a gas burner usu. consisting of a straight tube with air holes at the bottom

¹**bunt** \'bənt\ *vb* **1** : ¹BUTT **2** : to push or tap a baseball lightly without swinging the bat

²**bunt** *n* : an act or instance of bunting; *also* : a bunted ball

¹bun·ting \'bən-tiŋ\ *n* : any of numerous small stout-billed finches

²bunting *n* : a thin fabric used esp. for flags; *also* : FLAGS

¹buoy \'bü-ē, 'bȯi\ *n* **1** : a floating object anchored in water to mark something (as a channel) **2** : a float consisting of a ring of buoyant material to support a person who has fallen into the water

²buoy *vb* **1** : to mark by a buoy **2** : to keep afloat **3** : to raise the spirits of

buoy·an·cy \'bȯi-ən-sē, 'bü-yən-\ *n* **1** : the tendency of a body to float or rise when submerged in a fluid **2** : the power of a fluid to exert an upward force on a body placed in it **3** : resilience of spirit — **buoy·ant** \-ənt, -yənt\ *adj*

¹bur *var of* BURR

²bur *abbr* bureau

burbs \'bərbz\ *n pl* : SUBURBS

¹bur·den \'bər-d²n\ *n* **1** : LOAD; *also* : CARE, RESPONSIBILITY **2** : something oppressive : ENCUMBRANCE **3** : CARGO; *also* : capacity for cargo

²burden *vb* : LOAD, OPPRESS — **bur·den·some** \-səm\ *adj*

³burden *n* **1** : REFRAIN, CHORUS **2** : a main theme or idea : GIST

bur·dock \'bər-ˌdäk\ *n* : any of a genus of coarse composite herbs with globe-shaped flower heads surrounded by prickly bracts

bu·reau \'byu̇r-ō\ *n, pl* **bureaus** *also* **bu·reaux** \-ōz\ [F, desk, cloth covering for desks, fr. OF *burel* woolen cloth, ultim. fr. L *burra* shaggy cloth] **1** : a chest of drawers **2** : an administrative unit (as of a government department) **3** : a branch of a publication or wire service in an important news center

bu·reau·cra·cy \byu̇-'rä-krə-sē\ *n, pl* **-cies** **1** : a body of appointive government officials **2** : government marked by specialization of functions under fixed rules and a hierarchy of authority; *also* : an unwieldy administrative system burdened with excessive complexity and lack of flexibility — **bu·reau·crat** \'byu̇r-ə-ˌkrat\ *n* — **bu·reau·crat·ic** \ˌbyu̇r-ə-'kra-tik\ *adj*

bur·geon \'bər-jən\ *vb* : to put forth fresh growth (as from buds) : grow vigorously : FLOURISH

burgh \'bər-ō\ *n* : a Scottish town

bur·gher \'bər-gər\ *n* **1** : TOWNSMAN **2** : a prosperous solid citizen

bur·glary \'bər-glə-rē\ *n, pl* **-glar·ies** : forcible entry into a building esp. at night with the intent to commit a crime (as theft) — **bur·glar** \-glər\ *n* — **bur·glar·ize** \'bər-glə-ˌrīz\ *vb*

bur·gle \'bər-gəl\ *vb* **bur·gled; bur·gling** : to commit burglary on

bur·go·mas·ter \'bər-gə-ˌmas-tər\ *n* : the chief magistrate of a town in some European countries

bur·gun·dy \'bər-gən-dē\ *n, pl* **-dies** *often cap* **1** : a red or white table wine from the Burgundy region of France **2** : a blended red wine

buri·al \'ber-ē-əl\ *n* : the act or process of burying

bur·ka *or* **bur·qa** \'bu̇r-kə\ *n* : a loose garment that covers the face and body and is worn in public by certain Muslim women

burl \'bərl\ *n* : a hard woody often flattened hemispherical outgrowth on a tree

bur·lap \'bər-ˌlap\ *n* : a coarse fabric usu. of jute or hemp used esp. for bags

¹bur·lesque \(ˌ)bər-'lesk\ *n* [*burlesque*, adj., comic, droll, fr. F, fr. It *burlesco*, fr. *burla* joke, fr. Sp] **1** : a witty or derisive literary or dramatic imitative work **2** : broadly humorous theatrical entertainment consisting of several items (as songs, skits, or dances)

²burlesque *vb* **bur·lesqued; bur·lesqu·ing** : to make ludicrous by burlesque ✦ *Synonyms* CARICATURE, PARODY, TRAVESTY

bur·ly \'bər-lē\ *adj* **bur·li·er; -est** : strongly and heavily built : HUSKY ✦ *Synonyms* MUSCULAR, BRAWNY, BEEFY, HEFTY

¹burn \'bərn\ *vb* **burned** \'bərnd, 'bərnt\ *or* **burnt** \'bərnt\; **burn·ing** **1** : to be on fire **2** : to feel or look as if on fire **3** : to alter or become altered by or as if by the action of fire or heat **4** : to use as fuel 〈~ coal〉; *also* : to destroy by fire 〈~ trash〉 **5** : to cause or make by fire 〈~ a hole〉; *also* : to affect as if by heat **6** : to record digital data or music on (an optical disk) using a laser 〈~ a CD〉

²burn *n* : an injury or effect produced by or as if by burning

burn·er \'bər-nər\ *n* : the part of a fuel-burning or heat-producing device where the flame or heat is produced

bur·nish \'bər-nish\ *vb* : to make shiny esp. by rubbing : POLISH — **bur·nish·er** *n* — **bur·nish·ing** *adj or n*

bur·noose *or* **bur·nous** \(ˌ)bər-'nüs\ *n* : a hooded cloak worn esp. by Arabs

burn·out \'bərn-ˌau̇t\ *n* **1** : the cessation of operation of a jet or rocket engine **2** : exhaustion of one's physical or emotional strength; *also* : a person suffering from burnout

burp \'bərp\ *n* : an act of belching — **burp** *vb*

burp gun *n* : a small submachine gun

burr \'bər\ *n* **1** *usu* **bur** : a rough or prickly envelope of a fruit; *also* : a plant that bears burs **2** : roughness left in cutting or shaping metal **3** : a trilled \r\ as used by some speakers in northern England and Scotland **4** : WHIR — **bur·ry** *adj*

bur·ri·to \bə-'rē-tō\ *n* [AmerSp, fr. Sp, little donkey, dim. of *burro*] : a flour tortilla rolled around a filling and baked

bur·ro \'bər-ō, 'bu̇r-\ *n, pl* **burros** [Sp] : a usu. small donkey

¹bur·row \'bər-ō\ *n* : a hole in the ground made by an animal (as a rabbit)

²burrow *vb* **1** : to form by tunneling; *also* : to make a burrow **2** : to progress by or as if by digging — **bur·row·er** *n*

bur·sar \'bər-sər\ *n* : a treasurer esp. of a college

bur·si·tis \(ˌ)bər-'sī-təs\ *n* : inflammation of the serous sac (**bur·sa** \'bər-sə\) of a joint (as the elbow or shoulder)

¹burst \'bərst\ *vb* **burst** *or* **burst·ed; burst·ing** **1** : to fly apart or into pieces **2** : to show one's feelings suddenly; *also* : PLUNGE 〈~ into song〉 **3** : to enter or emerge suddenly : SPRING **4** : to be filled to the breaking point

²burst *n* **1** : a sudden outbreak : SPURT **2** : EXPLOSION **3** : result of bursting

bury \'ber-ē\ *vb* **bur·ied; bury·ing** **1** : to deposit in the earth; *also* : to inter with funeral ceremonies **2** : CONCEAL, HIDE **3** : SUBMERGE, ENGROSS — usu. used with *in* 〈*buried* himself in work〉

¹bus \'bəs\ *n, pl* **bus·es** *also* **bus·ses** [short for *omnibus*, fr. F, fr. L, for all, dat. pl. of *omnis* all] : a large motor vehicle for carrying passengers

²bus *vb* **bused** *or* **bussed; bus·ing** *or* **bus·sing** **1** : to travel or transport by bus **2** : to work as a busboy

³bus *abbr* business

bus·boy \'bəs-ˌbȯi\ *n* : a waiter's helper

bus·by \'bəz-bē\ *n, pl* **busbies** : a military full-dress fur hat

bush \'bu̇sh\ *n* **1** : SHRUB **2** : rough uncleared country **3** : a thick tuft 〈a ~ of hair〉 — **bushy** *adj*

bushed \'bu̇sht\ *adj* : TIRED, EXHAUSTED

bush·el \'bu̇-shəl\ *n* — see WEIGHT table

bush·ing \'bu̇-shiŋ\ *n* : a usu. removable cylindrical lining for an opening of a mechanical part to limit the size of the opening, resist wear, or serve as a guide

bush·mas·ter \'bu̇sh-ˌmas-tər\ *n* : a large venomous pit viper of Central and So. America

bush·whack \-ˌhwak\ *vb* **1** : AMBUSH **2** : to clear a path through esp. by chopping down bushes and branches — **bush·whack·er** *n*

busi·ness \'biz-nəs, -nəz\ *n* **1** : OCCUPATION; *also* : TASK, MISSION **2** : a commercial or industrial enterprise; *also* : TRADE 〈~ is good〉 **3** : AFFAIR, MATTER **4** : personal concern

busi·ness·man \-ˌman\ *n* : a man engaged in business esp. as an executive

busi·ness·per·son \-ˌpər-s²n\ *n* : a businessman or businesswoman

busi·ness·wom·an \-ˌwu̇-mən\ *n* : a woman engaged in business esp. as an executive

bus·kin \'bəs-kən\ *n* **1** : a laced boot reaching halfway to the knee **2** : tragic drama

buss \'bəs\ *n* : KISS — **buss** *vb*

¹bust \'bəst\ *n* [F *buste*, fr. It *busto*, fr. L *bustum* tomb] **1** : sculpture representing the upper part of the human figure **2** : the part of the human torso between the neck and the waist; *esp* : the breasts of a woman

²bust *vb* **bust·ed** *also* **bust; bust·ing** **1** : BREAK, SMASH; *also* : BURST **2** : to ruin financially **3** : TAME **4** : DEMOTE **5** *slang* : ARREST; *also* : RAID

³bust *n* **1** : a drinking session **2** : a complete failure : FLOP **3** : a business depression **4** : PUNCH, SOCK **5** *slang* : a police raid; *also* : ARREST

¹bus·tle \'bə-səl\ *vb* **bus·tled; bus·tling** : to move or work in a brisk busy manner

²**bustle** *n* : briskly energetic activity

³**bustle** *n* : a pad or frame worn to support the fullness at the back of a woman's skirt

¹**busy** \'bi-zē\ *adj* **busi·er; -est** **1** : engaged in action : not idle **2** : being in use ⟨~ telephones⟩ **3** : full of activity ⟨~ streets⟩ **4** : MEDDLING — **busi·ly** \'bi-zə-lē\ *adv*

²**busy** *vb* **bus·ied; busy·ing** : to make or keep busy : OCCUPY

busy·body \'bi-zē-,bä-dē\ *n* : MEDDLER

busy·work \-,wərk\ *n* : work that appears productive but only keeps one occupied

¹**but** \'bət\ *conj* **1** : except for the fact ⟨would have protested ~ that he was afraid⟩ **2** : THAT ⟨there's no doubt ~ he won⟩ **3** : without the certainty that ⟨never rains ~ it pours⟩ **4** : on the contrary ⟨not one, ~ two job offers⟩ **5** : YET ⟨poor ~ proud⟩ **6** : with the exception of ⟨none ~ the strongest attempt it⟩

²**but** *prep* : other than : EXCEPT ⟨this letter is nothing ~ an insult⟩; *also* : with the exception of ⟨no one here ~ me⟩

bu·tane \'byü-,tān\ *n* : either of two gaseous hydrocarbons used as a fuel

butch \'bůch\ *adj* : notably masculine in appearance or manner

¹**butch·er** \'bů-chər\ *n* [ME *bocher*, fr. AF, fr. *buc* he-goat] **1** : one who slaughters animals or dresses their flesh; *also* : a dealer in meat **2** : one that kills brutally or needlessly **3** : one that botches — **butch·ery** \-chə-rē\ *n*

²**butcher** *vb* **1** : to slaughter and dress for meat ⟨~ hogs⟩ **2** : to kill barbarously **3** : BOTCH

but·ler \'bət-lər\ *n* [ME *buteler*, fr. AF *butiller*, † fr. OF *botele* bottle] : the chief male servant of a household

¹**butt** \'bət\ *vb* : to strike with the head or horns

²**butt** *n* : a blow or thrust with the head or horns

³**butt** *n* : a large cask

⁴**butt** *n* **1** : TARGET **2** : an object of abuse or ridicule

⁵**butt** *n* **1** : BUTTOCKS **2** : a large, thicker, or bottom end of something

⁶**butt** *vb* **1** : ABUT — used with *on* or *against* **2** : to place or join edge to edge without overlapping

butte \'byüt\ *n* : an isolated steep hill

¹**but·ter** \'bə-tər\ *n* [ME, fr. OE *butere*, fr. L *butyrum* butter, fr. Gk *boutyron*, fr. *bous* cow + *tyros* cheese] **1** : a solid edible emulsion of fat obtained from cream by churning **2** : a substance resembling butter — **but·tery** *adj*

²**butter** *vb* : to spread with or as if with butter

but·ter–and–eggs \,bə-tər-ən-'negz\ *n sing or pl* : a common perennial herb related to the snapdragon that has showy yellow and orange flowers

butter bean *n* **1** : LIMA BEAN **2** : WAX BEAN **3** : a green shell bean

but·ter·cream \'bə-tər-,krēm\ *n* : a sweet butter-based mixture used esp. as a filling or frosting

but·ter·cup \'bə-tər-,kəp\ *n* : any of a genus of herbs having usu. yellow flowers with five petals and sepals

but·ter·fat \-,fat\ *n* : the natural fat of milk and chief constituent of butter

but·ter·fin·gered \-,fiŋ-gərd\ *adj* : likely to let things fall or slip through the fingers — **but·ter·fin·gers** \-gərz\ *n sing or pl*

but·ter·fly \-,flī\ *n* : any of a group of slender day-flying insects with broad often brightly-colored wings

but·ter·milk \-,milk\ *n* : the liquid remaining after butter is churned

but·ter·nut \-,nət\ *n* : the sweet egg-shaped nut of an American tree related to the walnut; *also* : this tree

butternut squash *n* : a smooth buff-colored cylindrical winter squash

but·ter·scotch \-,skäch\ *n* : a candy made from brown sugar, corn syrup, and water; *also* : the flavor of such candy

but·tock \'bə-tək\ *n* **1** : the back of a hip that forms one of the fleshy parts on which a person sits **2** *pl* : the seat of the body : RUMP

¹**but·ton** \'bə-tⁿn\ *n* **1** : a small knob secured to an article (as of clothing) and used as a fastener by passing it through a buttonhole or loop **2** : something that resembles a button **3** : PUSH BUTTON **4** : a hidden sensitivity that can be manipulated to produce a desired response **5** : a usu. box-shaped computer icon that initiates a software function

²**button** *vb* : to close or fasten with or as if with buttons

¹**but·ton·hole** \'bə-tⁿn-,hōl\ *n* : a slit or loop for a button to pass through

²**buttonhole** *vb* : to detain in conversation by or as if by holding on to the outer garments of

²**but·tress** \'bə-trəs\ *n* [ME *butres*, fr. AF (*arche*) *boteraz* thrusting (arch), ultim. fr. *buter* to thrust] **1** : a projecting structure to support a wall **2** : PROP, SUPPORT

²**buttress** *vb* : PROP, SUPPORT

bu·tut \bů-'tüt\ *n, pl* **bututs** *or* **butut** — see *dalasi* at MONEY table

bux·om \'bək-səm\ *adj* : healthily plump; *esp* : full-bosomed

¹**buy** \'bī\ *vb* **bought** \'bȯt\; **buy·ing** **1** : to obtain for a price : PURCHASE; *also* : BRIBE **2** : to accept as true — **buy·er** *n*

²**buy** *n* **1** : PURCHASE 1, 2 **2** : an exceptional value : BARGAIN

¹**buzz** \'bəz\ *vb* **1** : to make a buzz **2** : to fly fast and close to

²**buzz** *n* **1** : a low humming sound **2** : RUMOR, GOSSIP

buz·zard \'bə-zərd\ *n* : any of various usu. large birds of prey and esp. the turkey vulture

buzz·er \'bə-zər\ *n* : a device that signals with a buzzing sound

buzz saw *n* : CIRCULAR SAW

buzz·word \'bəz-,wərd\ *n* : a voguish word or phrase often from technical jargon

BVM *abbr* Blessed Virgin Mary

BWI *abbr* British West Indies

bx *abbr* box

BX *abbr* base exchange

¹**by** \'bī, bə\ *prep* **1** : NEAR ⟨stood ~ the window⟩ **2** : through or through the medium of : VIA ⟨left ~ the door⟩ **3** : PAST ⟨drove ~ the house⟩ **4** : DURING, AT ⟨studied ~ night⟩ **5** : no later than ⟨get here ~ 3 p.m.⟩ **6** : through the means or direct agency of ⟨~ force⟩ **7** : in conformity with; *also* : ACCORDING TO ⟨did it ~ the book⟩ **8** : with respect to ⟨a doctor ~ profession⟩ **9** : to the amount or extent of ⟨won ~ a nose⟩ **10** — used to express relationship in multiplication, in division, and in measurements ⟨divide *a* ~ *b*⟩ ⟨multiply ~ 6⟩ ⟨15 feet ~ 20 feet⟩

²**by** \'bī\ *adv* **1** : near at hand; *also* : IN ⟨stop ~⟩ **2** : PAST ⟨saw him go ~⟩ **3** : ASIDE, APART

bye \'bī\ *n* : a position of a participant in a tournament who advances to the next round without playing

by–elec·tion *also* **bye–election** \'bī-ə-,lek-shən\ *n* : a special election held between regular elections in order to fill a vacancy

by·gone \'bī-,gȯn\ *adj* : gone by : PAST — **bygone** *n*

by·law *also* **bye·law** \'bī-,lȯ\ *n* : a rule adopted by an organization for managing its internal affairs

by–line \'bī-,līn\ *n* : a line at the beginning of a news story or magazine article giving the writer's name

BYO *abbr* bring your own

BYOB *abbr* bring your own beer; bring your own booze; bring your own bottle

¹**by·pass** \'bī-,pas\ *n* : a passage to one side or around a blocked or congested area; *also* : a surgical procedure establishing this ⟨a coronary ~⟩

²**bypass** *vb* : to avoid by means of a bypass

by·path \-,path, -,päth\ *n* : BYWAY

by·play \'bī-,plā\ *n* : action engaged in on the side (as of a stage) while the main action proceeds

by–prod·uct \-,prä-(,)dəkt\ *n* : a sometimes unexpected product or result produced in addition to the main product or result

by·stand·er \-,stan-dər\ *n* : one present but not participating ✦ *Synonyms* ONLOOKER, WITNESS, SPECTATOR, EYEWITNESS

byte \'bīt\ *n* : a unit of computer information consisting of a group of 8 bits

by·way \'bī-,wā\ *n* **1** : a little-traveled side road **2** : a secondary aspect

by·word \-,wərd\ *n* **1** : PROVERB **2** : one that is noteworthy or notorious

Byz·an·tine \'biz-ⁿn-,tēn, 'bī-, -,tīn; bə-'zan-, bī-\ *adj* **1** : of, relating to, or characteristic of the ancient city of Byzantium or the Byzantine Empire **2** *often not cap* : intricately involved and often devious

DICTIONARY

¹**c** \'sē\ *n, pl* **c's** *or* **cs** \'sēz\ *often cap* **1** : the 3d letter of the English alphabet **2** : one hundred in Roman numerals **3** *slang* : a sum of $100 **4** : a grade rating a student's work as fair

²**c** *abbr, often cap* **1** calorie **2** carat **3** Celsius **4** cent **5** centigrade **6** centimeter **7** century **8** chapter **9** circa **10** cocaine **11** copyright

C *symbol* carbon

ca *abbr* circa

Ca *symbol* calcium

CA *abbr* **1** California **2** chartered accountant **3** chief accountant **4** chronological age

cab \'kab\ *n* **1** : a light closed horse-drawn carriage **2** : TAXICAB **3** : the covered compartment for the engineer and controls of a locomotive; *also* : a similar compartment (as on a truck) — **cab** *vb*

CAB *abbr* Civil Aeronautics Board

ca·bal \kə-'bäl, -'bal\ *n* [F *cabale*, fr. ML *cabbala* cabala, fr. Heb *qabbālāh*, lit., received (lore)] **1** : a secret group of plotters or political conspirators **2** : CLUB, GROUP ⟨a ∼ of artists⟩

cabala *var of* KABALLAH

ca·bana \kə-'ban-yə, -'ba-nə\ *n* : a shelter at a beach or swimming pool

cab·a·ret \ˌka-bə-'rā\ *n* : NIGHTCLUB

cab·bage \'ka-bij\ *n* [ME *caboche*, fr. MF dial., lit., head, noggin] : a vegetable related to the mustard with a dense head of leaves

cab·bie *or* **cab·by** \'ka-bē\ *n, pl* **cabbies** : a driver of a cab

cab·er·net sau·vi·gnon \ˌka-bər-'nā-sō-vē-'nyōⁿ\ *n* : a dry red wine made from a single variety of black grape

cab·in \'ka-bən\ *n* **1** : a private room on a ship; *also* : a compartment below deck on a boat for passengers or crew **2** : an aircraft or spacecraft compartment for passengers, crew, or cargo **3** : a small simple one-story house

cabin boy *n* : a boy working as servant on a ship

cabin class *n* : a class of accommodations on a passenger ship superior to tourist class and inferior to first class

cabin cruiser *n* : CRUISER 3

cab·i·net \'kab-nit\ *n* **1** : a case or cupboard for holding or displaying articles **2** : the advisory council of a head of state (as a president or sovereign)

cab·i·net·mak·er \-ˌmā-kər\ *n* : a woodworker who makes fine furniture — **cab·i·net·mak·ing** *n*

cab·i·net·work \-ˌwərk\ *n* : the finished work of a cabinet-maker

¹**ca·ble** \'kā-bəl\ *n* **1** : a very strong rope, wire, or chain **2** : a bundle of insulated wires usu. twisted around a central core **3** : CABLEGRAM **4** : CABLE TELEVISION

²**cable** *vb* **ca·bled; ca·bling** : to telegraph by cable

cable car *n* : a vehicle moved by an endless cable

ca·ble·cast \'kā-bəl-ˌkast\ *n* : a cable television transmission — **cablecast** *vb*

ca·ble·gram \'kā-bəl-ˌgram\ *n* : a message sent by a submarine telegraph cable

cable modem *n* : a modem for connecting a computer to a network over a cable television line

cable television *n* : a system of television reception in which signals from distant stations are sent by cable to the receivers of paying subscribers

cab·o·chon \'ka-bə-ˌshän\ *n* : a gem or bead cut in convex form and highly polished but not given facets; *also* : this style of cutting — **cabochon** *adv*

ca·boose \kə-'büs\ *n* : a car usu. at the rear of a freight train for the use of the train crew and railroad workers

cab·ri·o·let \ˌka-brē-ə-'lā\ *n* [F] **1** : a light 2-wheeled one-horse carriage **2** : a convertible coupe

cab·stand \'kab-ˌstand\ *n* : a place where cabs wait for passengers

ca·cao \kə-'kaù, -'kā-ō\ *n, pl* **cacaos** [Sp, fr. Nahuatl *cacahuatl*] : a So. American tree whose seeds (**cacao beans**)

are the source of cocoa and chocolate; *also* : its dried fatty seeds

cac·cia·to·re \ˌkä-chə-'tōr-ē\ *adj* [It] : cooked with tomatoes and herbs ⟨chicken ∼⟩

cache \'kash\ *n* [F] **1** : a hiding place esp. for preserving provisions; *also* : something hidden or stored in a cache — **cache** *vb*

ca·chet \ka-'shā\ *n* [F] **1** : a seal used esp. as a mark of official approval **2** : a feature or quality conferring prestige; *also* : PRESTIGE **3** : a design, inscription, or advertisement printed or stamped on mail

cack·le \'ka-kəl\ *vb* **cack·led; cack·ling** **1** : to make the sharp broken cry characteristic of a hen **2** : to laugh or chatter noisily — **cackle** *n* — **cack·ler** *n*

ca·coph·o·ny \ka-'kä-fə-nē\ *n, pl* **-nies** : harsh or discordant sound — **ca·coph·o·nous** \-nəs\ *adj*

cac·tus \'kak-təs\ *n, pl* **cac·ti** \-ˌtī\ *or* **cac·tus·es** *also* **cactus** : any of a large family of drought-resistant flowering plants with succulent stems and with leaves replaced by scales or prickles

cad \'kad\ *n* : a man who deliberately disregards another's feelings — **cad·dish** \'ka-dish\ *adj* — **cad·dish·ly** *adv* — **cad·dish·ness** *n*

ca·dav·er \kə-'da-vər\ *n* : a dead body

ca·dav·er·ous \kə-'da-və-rəs\ *adj* : suggesting a corpse esp. in gauntness or pallor ♦ **Synonyms** WASTED, EMACIATED, GAUNT — **ca·dav·er·ous·ly** *adv*

cad·die *or* **cad·dy** \'ka-dē\ *n, pl* **caddies** [Sc, errand boy, modif. of F *cadet* military cadet] : a person who assists a golfer esp. by carrying the clubs — **caddie** *or* **caddy** *vb*

cad·dy \'ka-dē\ *n, pl* **caddies** [Malay *kati* a unit of weight] : a small box, can, or chest; *esp* : one to keep tea in

ca·dence \'kād-ᵊns\ *n* : the measure or beat of a rhythmical flow : RHYTHM — **ca·denced** \-ᵊnst\ *adj*

ca·den·za \kə-'den-zə\ *n* [It] : a brilliant sometimes improvised passage usu. toward the close of a musical composition

ca·det \kə-'det\ *n* [F, fr. Occitan (Gascony) *capdet* chief, fr. L *capitellum*, fr. L *caput* head] **1** : a younger son or brother **2** : a student in a service academy

Ca·dette \kə-'det\ *n* : a member of a Girl Scout program for girls in sixth through ninth grades

cadge \'kaj\ *vb* **cadged; cadg·ing** : SPONGE, BEG ⟨∼ a free meal⟩ — **cadg·er** *n*

cad·mi·um \'kad-mē-əm\ *n* : a bluish-white metallic chemical element used esp. in protective platings

ca·dre \'ka-ˌdrā, 'kä-, -drē\ *n* [F] **1** : FRAMEWORK **2** : a central unit esp. of trained personnel able to assume control and train others **3** : a group of indoctrinated leaders active in promoting the interests of a revolutionary party

ca·du·ceus \kə-'dü-sē-əs, -'dyü-, -shəs\ *n, pl* **-cei** \-sē-ˌī\ [L] **1** : the staff of a herald; *esp* : a representation of a staff with two entwined snakes and two wings at the top **2** : an insignia bearing a caduceus and symbolizing a physician

cae·cum *var of* CECUM

Cae·sar \'sē-zər\ *n* **1** : any of the Roman emperors succeeding Augustus Caesar — used as a title **2** *often not cap* : a powerful ruler : AUTOCRAT, DICTATOR; *also* : the civil or temporal power

caesarean *also* **caesarian** *var of* CESAREAN

cae·si·um *chiefly Brit var of* CESIUM

cae·sura \si-'zhùr-ə\ *n, pl* **-suras** *or* **-su·rae** \-'zhùr-(ˌ)ē\ : a break in the flow of sound usu. in the middle of a line of verse

ca·fé \ka-'fā\ *n* [F, lit., coffee] **1** : RESTAURANT **2** : BARROOM **3** : NIGHTCLUB

ca·fé au lait \(ˌ)ka-ˌfā-ō-'lā\ *n* : coffee with hot milk in about equal parts

caf·e·te·ria \ˌka-fə-'tir-ē-ə\ *n* [AmerSp *cafetería* coffeehouse] : a restaurant in which the customers serve themselves or are served at a counter

caf·feine \ka-ˈfēn, ˈka-ˌfēn\ *n* : a stimulating alkaloid found esp. in coffee and tea

caf·fein·at·ed \ˈka-fə-ˌnā-təd\ *adj* **1** : stimulated by or as if by caffeine **2** : containing caffeine

caf·fe lat·te \ˈkä-fā-ˈlä-tā\ *n* [It] : espresso mixed with hot or steamed milk

caf·tan \kaf-ˈtan, ˈkaf-ˌtan\ *n* [Russ *kaftan,* fr. Turk, fr. Pers *qaftān*] : an ankle-length garment with long sleeves worn in countries of the eastern Mediterranean

¹cage \ˈkāj\ *n* **1** : an openwork enclosure for confining an animal **2** : something resembling a cage

²cage *vb* **caged; cag·ing** : to put or keep in or as if in a cage

ca·gey *also* **ca·gy** \ˈkā-jē\ *adj* **ca·gi·er; -est** : wary of being trapped or deceived : SHREWD ⟨a ~ dealer⟩ — **ca·gi·ly** \-jə-lē\ *adv* — **ca·gi·ness** \-jē-nəs\ *n*

CAGS *abbr* Certificate of Advanced Graduate Study

ca·hoot \kə-ˈhüt\ *n* : PARTNERSHIP, LEAGUE — usu. used in pl. ⟨officials in ~s with the underworld⟩

cai·man *also* **cayman** \ˈkā-mən; kā-ˈman, kī-\ *n* : any of several Central and So. American reptiles closely related to alligators and crocodiles

cairn \ˈkarn\ *n* : a heap of stones serving as a memorial or a landmark

cais·son \ˈkā-ˌsän, ˈkās-ᵊn\ *n* **1** : a usu. 2-wheeled vehicle for artillery ammunition **2** : a watertight chamber used in underwater construction work or as a foundation

caisson disease *n* : ²BEND 3

cai·tiff \ˈkā-təf\ *adj* [ME *caitif,* fr. AF *caitif, chaitif* wretched, despicable, fr. L *captivus* captive] : being base, cowardly, or despicable — **caitiff** *n*

ca·jole \kə-ˈjōl\ *vb* **ca·joled; ca·jol·ing** [F *cajoler*] : to persuade or coax esp. with flattery or false promises — **ca·jole·ment** *n* — **ca·jol·ery** \-ˈjō-lə-rē\ *n*

Ca·jun \ˈkā-jən\ *n* : a Louisianian descended from French-speaking immigrants from Acadia (Nova Scotia) — **Cajun** *adj*

¹cake \ˈkāk\ *n* **1** : a baked or fried breadlike food usu. in a small flat shape **2** : a sweet baked food made from batter or dough usu. containing flour, sugar, shortening, and a leaven (as baking powder) **3** : a hardened or compacted substance ⟨a ~ of soap⟩ **4** : something easily done ⟨the quiz was ~⟩

²cake *vb* **caked; cak·ing** **1** : ENCRUST **2** : to form or harden into a cake

cake·walk \ˈkāk-ˌwòk\ *n* **1** : a stage dance typically involving a high prance with backward tilt **2** : a one-sided contest or an easy task

cal *abbr* **1** calendar **2** caliber

Cal *abbr* **1** California **2** calorie

cal·a·bash \ˈka-lə-ˌbash\ *n* : the fruit of a gourd; *also* : a utensil made from its hard shell

cal·a·boose \ˈka-lə-ˌbüs\ *n* [Sp *calabozo* dungeon] : JAIL

ca·la·di·um \kə-ˈlā-dē-əm\ *n* : any of a genus of tropical American ornamental plants related to the arums

cal·a·mari \ˌkä-lə-ˈmär-ē\ *n* [It] : squid used as food

cal·a·mine \ˈka-lə-ˌmīn\ *n* : a lotion of oxides of zinc and iron

ca·lam·i·ty \kə-ˈla-mə-tē\ *n, pl* **-ties** **1** : great distress or misfortune **2** : an event causing great harm or loss and affliction : DISASTER ⟨an economic ~⟩ — **ca·lam·i·tous** \-təs\ *adj* — **ca·lam·i·tous·ly** *adv* — **ca·lam·i·tous·ness** *n*

calc *abbr* calculate; calculated

cal·car·e·ous \kal-ˈkar-ē-əs\ *adj* : resembling calcium carbonate in hardness; *also* : containing calcium or calcium carbonate

cal·cif·er·ous \kal-ˈsi-fə-rəs\ *adj* : producing or containing calcium carbonate

cal·ci·fy \ˈkal-sə-ˌfī\ *vb* **-fied; -fy·ing** : to make or become calcareous — **cal·ci·fi·ca·tion** \ˌkal-sə-fə-ˈkā-shən\ *n*

cal·ci·mine \ˈkal-sə-ˌmīn\ *n* : a thin water paint used esp. on plastered surfaces — **calcimine** *vb*

cal·cine \kal-ˈsīn\ *vb* **cal·cined; cal·cin·ing** : to heat to a high temperature but without fusing to drive off volatile matter and often to reduce to powder — **cal·ci·na·tion** \ˌkal-sə-ˈnā-shən\ *n*

cal·cite \ˈkal-ˌsīt\ *n* : a crystalline mineral consisting of calcium carbonate — **cal·cit·ic** \kal-ˈsi-tik\ *adj*

cal·ci·um \ˈkal-sē-əm\ *n* : a silver-white soft metallic chemical element occurring only in combination

calcium carbonate *n* : a substance found in nature as limestone and marble and in plant ashes, bones, and shells

cal·cu·late \ˈkal-kyə-ˌlāt\ *vb* **-lat·ed; -lat·ing** [L *calculare,* fr. *calculus* pebble (used in reckoning)] **1** : to determine by mathematical processes : COMPUTE **2** : to reckon by exercise of practical judgment : ESTIMATE **3** : to design or adapt for a purpose **4** : COUNT, RELY — **cal·cu·la·ble** \-lə-bəl\ *adj* — **cal·cu·la·tor** \-ˌlā-tər\ *n*

cal·cu·lat·ed \-ˌlā-təd\ *adj* **1** : undertaken after estimating the chance of success or failure ⟨a ~ risk⟩ **2** : planned purposefully : DELIBERATE ⟨a ~ strategy⟩

cal·cu·lat·ing \-ˌlā-tiŋ\ *adj* : marked by shrewd consideration esp. of self-interest — **cal·cu·lat·ing·ly** *adv*

cal·cu·la·tion \ˌkal-kyə-ˈlā-shən\ *n* **1** : the process or an act of calculating **2** : the result of an act of calculating **3** : studied care; *also* : cold heartless planning to promote self-interest

cal·cu·lus \ˈkal-kyə-ləs\ *n, pl* **-li** \-ˌlī\ *also* **-lus·es** [L, pebble (used in reckoning)] **1** : a method of computation or calculation in a special notation (as of logic) **2** : a branch of mathematics concerned with the rate of change of functions and with methods of finding lengths, areas, and volumes **3** : a concretion usu. of mineral salts esp. in hollow organs or ducts

cal·de·ra \kal-ˈder-ə, kòl-, -ˈdir-\ *n* [Sp, lit., cauldron] : a large crater usu. formed by the collapse of a volcanic cone

cal·dron *var of* CAULDRON

¹cal·en·dar \ˈka-lən-dər\ *n* **1** : an arrangement of time into days, weeks, months, and years; *also* : a sheet or folder containing such an arrangement for a period **2** : an orderly list

²calendar *vb* : to enter in a calendar

¹cal·en·der \ˈka-lən-dər\ *vb* : to press (as cloth or paper) between rollers or plates so as to make smooth or glossy or to thin into sheets

²calender *n* : a machine for calendering

ca·lends \ˈka-ləndz, ˈkā-\ *n sing or pl* : the first day of the ancient Roman month

ca·len·du·la \kə-ˈlen-jə-lə\ *n* : any of a genus of yellow-flowered herbs related to the daisies

¹calf \ˈkaf, ˈkȧf\ *n, pl* **calves** \ˈkavz, ˈkȧvz\ **1** : the young of the domestic cow; *also* : the young of various large mammals (as the elephant or whale) **2** : CALFSKIN

²calf *n, pl* **calves** \ˈkavz, ˈkȧvz\ : the fleshy back of the leg below the knee

calf·skin \ˈkaf-ˌskin, ˈkȧf-\ *n* : leather made of the skin of a calf

cal·i·ber *or* **cal·i·bre** \ˈka-lə-bər\ *n* [MF *calibre,* fr. It *calibro,* fr. Ar *qālib* shoemaker's last] **1** : degree of mental capacity, excellence, or importance **2** : the diameter of a projectile **3** : the diameter of the bore of a gun

cal·i·brate \ˈka-lə-ˌbrāt\ *vb* **-brat·ed; -brat·ing** : to adjust precisely

cal·i·bra·tion \ˌka-lə-ˈbrā-shən\ *n* : a set of graduated marks indicating values or positions — usu. used in pl.

cal·i·co \ˈka-li-ˌkō\ *n, pl* **-coes** *or* **-cos** **1** : printed cotton fabric **2** : a mottled or spotted animal — **calico** *adj*

Calif *abbr* California

Cal·i·for·nia poppy \ˌka-lə-ˈfòr-nyə-\ *n* : a widely cultivated herb with usu. yellow or orange flowers that is related to the poppies

cal·i·for·ni·um \ˌka-lə-ˈfòr-nē-əm\ *n* : an artificially prepared radioactive chemical element

cal·i·per \ˈka-lə-pər\ *n* **1** : any of various instruments having two arms, legs, or jaws used esp. to measure diameter or thickness — usu. used in pl. **2** : a device for pressing a frictional material against the sides of a rotating wheel or disk

ca·liph \ˈkā-ləf, ˈka-\ *n* : a successor of Muhammad as head of Islam — used as a title — **ca·liph·ate** \-lə-ˌfāt, -fət\ *n*

cal·is·then·ics \ˌka-ləs-ˈthe-niks\ *n sing or pl* [Gk *kalos* beautiful + *sthenos* strength] : bodily exercises usu. done without apparatus — **cal·is·then·ic** *adj*

calk \ˈkòk\ *var of* CAULK

¹call \ˈkòl\ *vb* **1** : SHOUT, CRY; *also* : to utter a characteristic note or cry **2** : to utter in a loud clear voice ⟨~ed out my name⟩ **3** : to announce authoritatively **4** : SUMMON ⟨was *~ed* to testify⟩ **5** : to make a request or demand ⟨*~ for* an investigation⟩ **6** : to halt (as a baseball game) because of unsuitable conditions **7** : to demand payment of (a loan); *also* : to demand surrender of (as a bond) for redemption **8** : to get or try to get in communication by telephone **9** : to make a brief visit **10** : to speak of or address by name : give a name to **11** : to estimate or consider for practical purposes ⟨*~ it* ten miles⟩ **12** : to temporarily transfer control of computer processing to (as a subroutine or procedure) — **call·er** *n*

²**call** *n* **1** : SHOUT **2** : the cry of an animal (as a bird) **3** : a request or a command to come or assemble : INVITATION, SUMMONS **4** : DEMAND, CLAIM; *also* : REQUEST **5** : a brief usu. formal visit **6** : an act of calling on the telephone **7** : DECISION ⟨a tough *~*⟩ **8** : a temporary transfer of control of computer processing to a particular set of instructions

cal·la lily \'ka-lə-\ *n* : a plant related to the arums and grown for its large white lilylike bract that surrounds a fleshy spike of small yellow flowers

call·back \'kȯl-ˌbak\ *n* : a calling back; *esp* : RECALL 5

call–board \-ˌbȯrd\ *n* : a board for posting notices (as of rehearsal calls)

call down *vb* : REPRIMAND

call girl *n* : a prostitute with whom appointments are made by phone

cal·lig·ra·phy \kə-'li-grə-fē\ *n* : artistic or elegant handwriting; *also* : the art of producing such writing — **cal·lig·ra·pher** \-fər\ *n* — **cal·li·graph·ic** \ˌka-lə-'graf-ik\ *adj*

call–in \'kȯl-ˌin\ *adj* : allowing listeners to engage in broadcast telephone conversations ⟨a *~* show⟩

call in *vb* **1** : to order to return or be returned **2** : to summon to one's aid **3** : to report by telephone

call·ing \'kȯ-liŋ\ *n* **1** : a strong inner impulse toward a particular course of action **2** : the activity in which one customarily engages as an occupation

cal·li·ope \kə-'lī-ə-(ˌ)pē, 'ka-lē-ˌōp\ *n* [fr. *Calliope,* chief of the Muses, fr. L, fr. Gk *Kalliopē*] : a keyboard musical instrument similar to an organ and made up of a series of whistles

cal·li·per *chiefly Brit var of* CALIPER

call number *n* : a combination of characters assigned to a library book to indicate its place on a shelf

call off *vb* : CANCEL ⟨*called off* the trip⟩

cal·los·i·ty \ka-'lä-sə-tē\ *n, pl* **-ties** **1** : the quality or state of being callous **2** : CALLUS 1

¹**cal·lous** \'ka-ləs\ *adj* **1** : being thickened and hardened ⟨*~* skin⟩ **2** : feeling no emotion or sympathy — **cal·lous·ly** *adv* — **cal·lous·ness** *n*

²**callous** *vb* : to make callous

cal·low \'ka-lō\ *adj* [ME *calu* bald, fr. OE] : lacking adult sophistication ⟨a *~* youth⟩ — **cal·low·ness** *n*

call–up \'kȯ-ˌləp\ *n* : an order to report for active military service

call up *vb* : to summon for active military duty

cal·lus \'ka-ləs\ *n* **1** : a callous area on skin or bark **2** : tissue that is converted into bone in the healing of a bone fracture — **callus** *vb*

call–waiting *n* : a telephone service by which during a call in progress an incoming call is signaled (as by a click)

¹**calm** \'käm, 'kälm\ *n* **1** : a period or a condition free from storms, high winds, or rough water **2** : complete or almost complete absence of wind **3** : a state of tranquillity

²**calm** *vb* : to make or become calm

³**calm** *adj* : marked by calm : STILL, UNRUFFLED — **calm·ly** *adv* — **calm·ness** *n*

cal·o·mel \'ka-lə-məl, -ˌmel\ *n* : a chloride of mercury used esp. as a fungicide

ca·lor·ic \kə-'lȯr-ik\ *adj* **1** : of or relating to heat **2** : of, relating to, or containing calories — **ca·lo·ric·al·ly** \-i-k(ə-)lē\ *adv*

cal·o·rie *also* **cal·o·ry** \'ka-lə-rē\ *n, pl* **-ries** : a unit for measuring heat; *esp* : one for measuring the value of foods for producing heat and energy in the human body equivalent to the amount of heat required to raise the temperature of one kilogram of water one degree Celsius

cal·o·rim·e·ter \ˌka-lə-'ri-mə-tər\ *n* : an apparatus for measuring quantities of heat — **cal·o·rim·e·try** \-trē\ *n*

cal·u·met \'kal-yə-ˌmet, -mət\ *n* : an American Indian ceremonial pipe

calumet

ca·lum·ni·ate \kə-'ləm-nē-ˌāt\ *vb* **-at·ed; -at·ing** : to make false and malicious statements about **♦ Synonyms** DEFAME, MALIGN, LIBEL, SLANDER, TRADUCE — **ca·lum·ni·a·tion** \-ˌləm-nē-'ā-shən\ *n* — **ca·lum·ni·a·tor** \-'ləm-nē-ˌā-tər\ *n*

cal·um·ny \'ka-ləm-nē\ *n, pl* **-nies** : false and malicious accusation — **ca·lum·ni·ous** \kə-'ləm-nē-əs\ *adj*

calve \'kav, 'kàv\ *vb* **calved; calv·ing** : to give birth to a calf

calves *pl of* CALF

Cal·vin·ism \'kal-və-ˌni-zəm\ *n* : the theological system of John Calvin and his followers — **Cal·vin·ist** \-nist\ *n or adj* — **Cal·vin·is·tic** \ˌkal-və-'nis-tik\ *adj*

ca·lyp·so \kə-'lip-sō\ *n, pl* **-sos** : a style of music originating in the British West Indies and having lyrics that usu. satirize local personalities and events

ca·lyx \'kā-liks, 'ka-\ *n, pl* **ca·lyx·es** *or* **ca·ly·ces** \'kā-lə-ˌsēz, 'ka-\ : the usu. green or leaflike outer part of a flower consisting of sepals

cal·zo·ne \kal-'zōn, -'zō-nē\ *n* : a baked or fried turnover of pizza dough stuffed with cheese and various fillings

¹**cam** \'kam\ *n* : a rotating or sliding piece in a mechanical linkage by which rotary motion is transformed into linear motion or vice versa

²**cam** *n* : CAMERA

ca·ma·ra·de·rie \ˌkäm-'rä-də-rē, ˌkam-, -'ra-\ *n* [F] : friendly feeling and goodwill among comrades

cam·bi·um \'kam-bē-əm\ *n, pl* **-bi·ums** *or* **-bia** \-bē-ə\ : a thin cellular layer between xylem and phloem of most higher plants from which new tissues develop — **cam·bi·al** \-əl\ *adj*

Cam·bri·an \'kam-brē-ən, 'käm-\ *adj* : of, relating to, or being the earliest period of the Paleozoic era — **Cambrian** *n*

cam·bric \'kām-brik\ *n* : a fine thin white linen or cotton fabric

cam·cord·er \'kam-ˌkȯr-dər\ *n* : a small portable combined camera and VCR

came *past of* COME

cam·el \'ka-məl\ *n* : either of two large hoofed cud-chewing mammals used esp. in desert regions of Asia and Africa for carrying and riding

camel hair *also* **camel's hair** *n* **1** : the hair of a camel or a substitute for it **2** : cloth made of camel hair or of camel hair and wool

ca·mel·lia \kə-'mēl-yə\ *n* : any of a genus of shrubs and trees related to the tea plant and grown in warm regions and greenhouses for their showy roselike flowers

Cam·em·bert \'ka-məm-ˌber\ *n* : a soft cheese with a grayish rind and yellow interior

cam·eo \'ka-mē-ˌō\ *n, pl* **-eos** **1** : a gem carved in relief; *also* : a small medallion with a profiled head in relief **2** : a brief appearance esp. by a well-known actor in a play or movie

cam·era \'kam-rə, 'ka-mər-ə\ *n* : a device with a lightproof chamber fitted with a lens through which the image of an object is projected onto a surface for recording (as on film) or for conversion into electrical signals (as for television broadcast) — **cam·era·man** \-ˌman, -mən\ *n* — **cam·era·wom·an** *n*

cam·i·sole \'ka-mə-ˌsōl\ *n* : a short sleeveless garment for women

camomile *var of* CHAMOMILE

cam·ou·flage \'ka-mə-ˌfläzh, -ˌfläj\ *n* [F] **1** : the disguising of military equipment with paint, nets, or foliage; *also* : the disguise itself **2** : deceptive behavior — **camouflage** *vb*

¹**camp** \'kamp\ *n* **1** : a place where tents or buildings are erected for usu. temporary shelter **2** : a collection of

tents or other shelters **3** : a program offering recreational activities (as boating and hiking) for a limited time ⟨summer ~⟩ **4** : a body of persons encamped **5** : a training session for athletes outside of the regular season — **camp·ground** \-ˌgrau̇nd\ n — **camp·site** \-ˌsīt\ n

²camp vb **1** : to make or occupy a camp **2** : to live in a camp or outdoors

³camp n **1** : exaggerated effeminate mannerisms **2** : something so outrageous, inappropriate, or theatrical as to be considered amusing — **camp** adj — **camp·i·ly** \'kam-pə-lē\ adv — **camp·i·ness** \-pē-nəs\ n — **campy** \-pē\ adj

⁴camp vb : to engage in camp : exhibit the qualities of camp

cam·paign \kam-'pān\ n **1** : a series of military operations forming one distinct stage in a war **2** : a series of activities designed to bring about a particular result ⟨advertising ~⟩ — **campaign** vb — **cam·paign·er** n

cam·pa·ni·le \ˌkam-pə-'nē-lē\ n, pl **-ni·les** or **-ni·li** \-'nē-lē\ : a usu. freestanding bell tower

cam·pa·nol·o·gy \ˌkam-pə-'nä-lə-jē\ n : the art of bell ringing — **cam·pa·nol·o·gist** \-jist\ n

camp·er \'kam-pər\ n **1** : one who camps **2** : a portable dwelling (as a specially equipped vehicle) for use during casual travel and camping

Camp Fire Girl n : a member of a national organization of girls from ages 5 to 18

camp follower n **1** : a civilian (as a prostitute) who follows a military unit to attend or exploit its personnel **2** : a follower of a group who is not an adherent; esp : a politician who joins a movement for personal gain

cam·phor \'kam-fər\ n : a gummy volatile aromatic compound obtained from an evergreen Asian tree (**camphor tree**) and used esp. in medicine

camp meeting n : a series of evangelistic meetings usu. held outdoors

camp·o·ree \ˌkam-pə-'rē\ n : a gathering of Boy Scouts or Girl Scouts from a given geographic area

cam·pus \'kam-pəs\ n [L, plain] : the grounds and buildings of a college or school; also : grounds resembling a campus ⟨hospital ~⟩

cam·shaft \'kam-ˌshaft\ n : a shaft to which a cam is fastened

¹can \kən, 'kan\ vb, past **could** \kəd, 'ku̇d\; pres sing & pl **can** **1** : be able to **2** : may perhaps ⟨~ he still be alive⟩ **3** : be permitted by conscience or feeling to ⟨you ~ hardly blame her⟩ **4** : have permission to ⟨you ~ go now⟩

²can \'kan\ n **1** : a usu. cylindrical container or receptacle ⟨garbage ~⟩ ⟨coffee ~⟩ **2** : JAIL **3** : TOILET

³can \'kan\ vb **canned; can·ning** **1** : to put in a can : preserve by sealing in airtight cans or jars **2** slang : to discharge from employment **3** slang : to put a stop or an end to — **can·ner** n

Can or **Canad** abbr Canada; Canadian

Can·a·da goose \'ka-nə-də-\ n : a common wild goose of No. America

ca·naille \kə-'nī, -'nāl\ n [F, fr. It canaglia, fr. cane dog] : RABBLE, RIFFRAFF

ca·nal \kə-'nal\ n **1** : a tubular passage in the body : DUCT **2** : an artificial waterway (as for boats or irrigation)

can·a·lize \'kan-əl-ˌīz\ vb **-lized; -liz·ing** **1** : to provide with a canal or make into or like a channel **2** : to provide with an outlet; esp : to direct into preferred channels — **ca·nal·i·za·tion** \ˌkan-əl-ə-'zā-shən\ n

can·a·pé \'ka-nə-pē, -ˌpā\ n [F, lit., sofa, fr. ML canopeum, canapeum mosquito net] : a piece of bread or toast or a cracker topped with a savory food

ca·nard \kə-'närd\ n : a false or unfounded report, story or belief

ca·nary \kə-'ner-ē\ n, pl **ca·nar·ies** [fr. the Canary islands] **1** : a usu. sweet wine similar to Madeira **2** : a usu. yellow or greenish finch often kept in a cage as a pet

ca·nas·ta \kə-'nas-tə\ n [Sp, lit., basket] : rummy played with two full decks of cards plus four jokers

canc abbr canceled

can·can \'kan-ˌkan\ n : a woman's dance of French origin characterized by high kicking

¹can·cel \'kan-səl\ vb **-celed** or **-celled; -cel·ing** or **-cel·ling** [ME cancellen, fr. AF canceller, chanceller, fr. LL cancellare, fr. L, to make like a lattice, fr. cancelli lattice] **1** : to destroy the force or validity of : ANNUL **2**

: to match in force or effect : OFFSET **3** : to cross out : DELETE **4** : to remove (a common divisor) from a numerator and denominator; also : to remove (equivalents) on opposite sides of an equation or account **5** : to mark (a postage stamp or check) so that it cannot be reused **6** : to neutralize each other's strength or effect — **can·cel·la·tion** \ˌkan-sə-'lā-shən\ n — **can·cel·er** or **can·cel·ler** n

²cancel n **1** : CANCELLATION **2** : a deleted part

can·cer \'kan-sər\ n [L, lit., crab] **1** cap : a zodiacal constellation between Gemini and Leo usu. pictured as a crab **2** cap : the 4th sign of the zodiac in astrology; also : one born under this sign **3** : a malignant tumor that tends to spread in the body; also : an abnormal state marked by such tumors **4** : a malignant evil that spreads destructively — **can·cer·ous** \-sə-rəs\ adj — **can·cer·ous·ly** adv

can·de·la·bra \ˌkan-də-'lä-brə, -'la-\ n : an ornamental branched candlestick or lamp with several lights

can·de·la·brum \-brəm\ n, pl **-bra** also **-brums** : CANDELABRA

can·did \'kan-dəd\ adj **1** : FRANK, STRAIGHTFORWARD ⟨a ~ critique⟩ **2** : relating to photography of subjects acting naturally or spontaneously without being posed — **can·did·ly** adv — **can·did·ness** n

can·di·da·cy \'kan-də-də-sē\ n, pl **-cies** : the state of being a candidate

can·di·date \'kan-də-ˌdāt, 'ka-nə-, -dət\ n [L candidatus, fr. candidatus clothed in white, fr. candidus white; fr. the white toga worn by office seekers in ancient Rome] : one who seeks or is proposed for an office, honor, or membership ⟨a ~ for governor⟩

can·di·da·ture \'kan-də-də-ˌchu̇r, 'ka-nə-\ n, chiefly Brit : CANDIDACY

can·died \'kan-dēd\ adj : preserved in or encrusted with sugar

¹can·dle \'kan-dəl\ n : a usu. slender mass of tallow or wax molded around a wick that is burned to give light

²candle vb **can·dled; can·dling** : to examine (as eggs) by holding between the eye and a light — **can·dler** n

can·dle·light \'kan-dəl-ˌlīt\ n **1** : the light of a candle; also : any soft artificial light **2** : the time when candles are lit : TWILIGHT

can·dle·lit \-ˌlit\ adj : illuminated by candlelight ⟨a ~ dinner⟩

Can·dle·mas \'kan-dəl-məs\ n : February 2 observed as a church festival in commemoration of the presentation of Christ in the temple

can·dle·stick \-ˌstik\ n : a holder with a socket for a candle

can·dle·wick \-ˌwik\ n : a soft cotton yarn; also : embroidery made with this yarn usu. in tufts

can·dor \'kan-dər\ n : FRANKNESS, OUTSPOKENNESS

can·dour chiefly Brit var of CANDOR

C and W abbr country and western

¹can·dy \'kan-dē\ n, pl **candies** [ME sugre candy, fr. MF sucre candi, fr. OF sucre sugar + Ar qandī candied, fr. qand crystallized sugar] **1** : a confection made from sugar often with flavoring and filling **2** : something that appeals in a light or frivolous way

²candy vb **can·died; can·dy·ing** : to encrust in sugar often by cooking in a syrup

candy strip·er \-'strī-pər\ n : a teenage volunteer worker at a hospital

¹cane \'kān\ n **1** : a slender hollow or pithy stem (as of a reed or bramble) **2** : a tall woody grass or reed (as sugarcane or sorghum) **3** : a walking stick; also : a rod for flogging

²cane vb **caned; can·ing** **1** : to beat with a cane **2** : to weave or make with cane — **can·er** n

cane·brake \'kān-ˌbrāk\ n : a thicket of cane

¹ca·nine \'kā-ˌnīn\ n **1** : a pointed tooth between the outer incisor and the first premolar **2** : a canine mammal (as a domestic dog)

²canine adj [L caninus, fr. canis dog] : of or relating to dogs or to the family to which they belong

can·is·ter \'ka-nə-stər\ n : an often cylindrical container

can·ker \'kaŋ-kər\ n : a spreading sore that eats into tissue — **can·ker·ous** \-kə-rəs\ adj

can·ker·worm \-ˌwərm\ n : either of two moths and esp. their larvae that are pests of fruit and shade trees

can·na \'ka-nə\ n : any of a genus of tropical herbs with large leaves and racemes of bright-colored flowers

can·na·bis \'ka-nə-bəs\ *n* : any of the psychoactive preparations (as marijuana) or chemicals (as THC) derived from hemp; *also* : HEMP

canned \'kand\ *adj* : prepared in standardized form for general use or wide distribution ⟨∼ music⟩

can·nery \'ka-nə-rē\ *n, pl* **-ner·ies** : a factory for the canning of foods

can·ni·bal \'ka-nə-bəl\ *n* [NL *Canibalis* a member of a Caribbean Indian people, fr. Sp *Caníbal*] : one that eats the flesh of its own kind — **can·ni·bal·ism** \-bə,li-zəm\ *n* — **can·ni·bal·is·tic** \-bə-'lis-tik\ *adj*

can·ni·bal·ise *Brit var of* CANNIBALIZE

can·ni·bal·ize \'ka-nə-bə-,līz\ *vb* **-ized; -iz·ing** **1** : to take usable parts from (as an inoperative machine) to construct or repair another machine **2** : to practice cannibalism

can·non \'ka-nən\ *n, pl* **cannons** *or* **cannon** [ME *canon,* fr. AF, fr. It *cannone,* lit., large tube, fr. *canna* reed, tube, fr. L, cane, reed] : a large heavy gun; *esp* : one mounted on a carriage

can·non·ade \,ka-nə-'nād\ *n* : a heavy fire of artillery — **cannonade** *vb*

can·non·ball \'ka-nən-,bȯl\ *n* : a usu. round solid missile for a cannon

can·non·eer \,ka-nə-'nir\ *n* : an artillery gunner

can·not \'ka-,nät; kə-'nät\ : can not — **cannot but** : to be unable to do otherwise than ⟨*we cannot but* wonder why⟩

can·nu·la \'kan-yə-lə\ *n, pl* **-las** *or* **-lae** \-,lē\ : a small tube for insertion into a body cavity or into a duct or vessel

can·ny \'ka-nē\ *adj* **can·ni·er; -est** : PRUDENT, SHREWD — **can·ni·ly** \'kan-ə¹-lē\ *adv* — **can·ni·ness** \'ka-nē-nəs\ *n*

ca·noe \kə-'nü\ *n* : a light narrow boat with sharp ends and curved sides that is usu. propelled by paddles — **canoe** *vb* — **ca·noe·ist** *n*

ca·no·la \kə-'nō-lə\ *n* : a rape plant producing seeds that are low in a toxic acid and yield an edible oil (**canola oil**) high in monounsaturated fatty acids; *also* : this oil

¹can·on \'ka-nən\ *n* **1** : a regulation decreed by a church council; *also* : a provision of canon law **2** : an official or authoritative list (as of works of literature) **3** : an accepted principle ⟨the ∼s of good taste⟩

²canon *n* : a member of the clergy on the staff of a cathedral

ca·non·i·cal \kə-'nä-ni-kəl\ *adj* **1** : of, relating to, or forming a canon **2** : conforming to a general rule or acceptable procedure : ORTHODOX **3** : of or relating to a canon of a cathedral — **ca·non·i·cal·ly** \-k(ə-)lē\ *adv*

can·on·ize \'ka-nə-,nīz\ *vb* **can·on·ized** \-,nīzd\; **can·on·iz·ing** **1** : to declare (a deceased person) an officially recognized saint **2** : GLORIFY, EXALT — **can·on·i·za·tion** \,ka-nə-nə-'zā-shən\ *n*

canon law *n* : the law governing a church

can·o·py \'ka-nə-pē\ *n, pl* **-pies** [ME *canope,* fr. ML *canopeum* mosquito net, fr. L *conopeum,* fr. Gk *kōnōpion,* fr. *kōnōps* mosquito] **1** : an overhanging cover, shelter, or shade **2** : the uppermost spreading layer of a forest **3** : a transparent cover for an airplane cockpit **4** : the fabric part of a parachute — **canopy** *vb*

¹cant \'kant\ *vb* : to give a slant to

²cant *n* **1** : an oblique or slanting surface **2** : TILT, SLANT

³cant *vb* **1** : to beg in a whining manner **2** : to talk hypocritically

⁴cant *n* **1** : the special idiom of a profession or trade : JARGON **2** : insincere speech; *esp* : insincerely pious words or statements

Cant *abbr* Canticle of Canticles

can·ta·bi·le \kän-'tä-bə-,lā\ *adv or adj* [It] : in a singing manner — used as a direction in music

can·ta·loupe *also* **can·ta·loup** \'kant-ə¹-,ōp\ *n* : MUSKMELON; *esp* : one with orange flesh and rough skin

can·tan·ker·ous \kan-'taŋ-kə-rəs\ *adj* : difficult to deal with : ILL-NATURED ⟨a ∼ mule⟩ — **can·tan·ker·ous·ly** *adv* — **can·tan·ker·ous·ness** *n*

can·ta·ta \kən-'tä-tə\ *n* [It] : a choral composition usu. sung to instrumental accompaniment

can·teen \kan-'tēn\ *n* [F *cantine* bottle case, canteen (store), fr. It *cantina* wine cellar] **1** : a flask for carrying liquids **2** : a place of recreation and entertainment for military personnel **3** : a small cafeteria or counter at which snacks are served

can·ter \'kan-tər\ *n* : a horse's 3-beat gait resembling but smoother and slower than a gallop — **canter** *vb*

Can·ter·bury bell \'kant-ər-,ber-ē-\ *n* : any of several plants related to the bluebell that are cultivated for their showy flowers

can·ti·cle \'kan-ti-kəl\ *n* : SONG; *esp* : any of several liturgical songs taken from the Bible

Canticle of Canticles *n* : SONG OF SONGS

¹can·ti·le·ver \'kant-ə¹-,ē-vər\ *n* : a projecting beam or structure supported only at one end; *also* : either of a pair of such structures projecting toward each other so that when joined they form a bridge

²cantilever *vb* **1** : to support by a cantilever ⟨a ∼ed shelf⟩ **2** : to build as a cantilever **3** : to project as a cantilever

can·tle \'kant-ə¹\ *n* : the upwardly projecting rear part of a saddle

can·to \'kan-,tō\ *n, pl* **cantos** [It, fr. L *cantus* song] : one of the major divisions of a long poem

can·ton \'kant-ə¹n, 'kan-,tän\ *n* : a small territorial division of a country; *esp* : one of the political divisions of Switzerland — **can·ton·al** \'kant-ə¹n-əl, kan-'tän-ə¹\ *adj*

can·ton·ment \kan-'tōn-mənt, -'tän-\ *n* : usu. temporary quarters for troops

can·tor \'kan-tər\ *n* **1** : a choir leader **2** : a synagogue official who sings liturgical music and leads the congregation in prayer

can·vas *also* **can·vass** \'kan-vəs\ *n* **1** : a strong cloth formerly much used for making tents and sails **2** : a set of sails **3** : a group of tents **4** : a piece of cloth prepared as a surface for a painting; *also* : a painting on this surface **5** : the canvas-covered floor of a boxing or wrestling ring

can·vas·back \'kan-vəs-,bak\ *n* : a No. American wild duck with red head and gray back

¹can·vass *also* **can·vas** \'kan-vəs\ *vb* **can·vassed; can·vas·sing** : to go through (a district) or to (persons) to solicit votes or orders for goods or to determine public opinion or sentiment — **can·vass·er** *n*

²canvass *n* : an act or instance of canvassing

can·yon \'kan-yən\ *n* : a deep narrow valley with high steep sides

¹cap \'kap\ *n* **1** : a covering for the head esp. with a visor and no brim; *also* : something resembling such a covering esp. on a tip, knob or end ⟨a bottle ∼⟩ **2** : a container holding an explosive charge (as for a toy gun) **3** : an upper limit (as on expenditures)

²cap *vb* **capped; cap·ping** **1** : to provide or protect with a cap **2** : to form a cap over : CROWN **3** : OUTDO, SURPASS **4** : to bring to a conclusion ⟨∼ off dinner with coffee⟩

³cap *abbr* **1** capacity **2** capital **3** capitalize; capitalized

CAP *abbr* Civil Air Patrol

ca·pa·ble \'kā-pə-bəl\ *adj* : having ability, capacity, or power to do something : ABLE, COMPETENT — **ca·pa·bil·i·ty** \,kā-pə-'bi-lə-tē\ *n* — **ca·pa·bly** *adv*

ca·pa·cious \kə-'pā-shəs\ *adj* : able to contain much — **ca·pa·cious·ly** *adv* — **ca·pa·cious·ness** *n*

ca·pac·i·tance \kə-'pa-sə-təns\ *n* : the property of an electric nonconductor that permits the storage of energy

ca·pac·i·tor \kə-'pa-sə-tər\ *n* : an electronic circuit device for temporary storage of electrical energy

¹ca·pac·i·ty \kə-'pa-sə-tē\ *n, pl* **-ties** **1** : legal qualification or fitness ⟨∼ to stand trial⟩ **2** : the ability to contain, receive, or accommodate ⟨seating ∼⟩ **3** : the maximum amount or number that can be contained — see METRIC SYSTEM table, WEIGHT table **4** : ABILITY **5** : position or character assigned or assumed

²capacity *adj* : equaling maximum capacity ⟨a ∼ crowd⟩

cap-a-pie *or* **cap-à-pie** \,ka-pə-'pē\ *adv* [MF] : from head to foot : at all points

ca·par·i·son \kə-'par-ə-sən\ *n* **1** : an ornamental covering for a horse **2** : TRAPPINGS, ADORNMENT — **caparison** *vb*

¹cape \'kāp\ *n* **1** : a point of land jutting out into water **2** *often cap* : CAPE COD COTTAGE

²cape *n* : a sleeveless garment hanging from the neck over the shoulders — **caped** *adj*

Cape Cod cottage \'kāp-'käd-\ *n* : a compact rectangular dwelling of one or one-and-a-half stories usu. with a steep gable roof

¹ca·per \'kā-pər\ *n* : the greenish flower bud or young berry of a Mediterranean shrub pickled for use as a relish; *also* : this shrub

²**caper** *vb* **ca·pered; ca·per·ing** : to leap about in a playful manner

³**caper** *n* **1** : a frolicsome leap **2** : a capricious escapade **3** : an illegal or questionable act

cape·skin \'kāp-ˌskin\ *n* : a light flexible leather made from sheepskins

cap·ful \'kap-ˌfȯl\ *n, pl* **cap·fuls** *also* **caps·ful** \'kaps-\ : as much as a cap will hold

cap·il·lar·i·ty \ˌka-pə-'lar-ə-tē\ *n, pl* **-ties** : the action by which the surface of a liquid where it is in contact with a solid (as in a slender tube) is raised or lowered depending on the relative attraction of the molecules of the liquid for each other and for those of the solid

¹**cap·il·lary** \'ka-pə-ˌler-ē\ *adj* **1** : resembling a hair **2** : having a very small bore ⟨~ tube⟩ **3** : of or relating to capillaries or to capillarity

²**capillary** *n, pl* **-lar·ies** : any of the tiny thin-walled blood vessels that carry blood between the smallest arteries and their corresponding veins

¹**cap·i·tal** \'ka-pət-ᵊl\ *n* : the top part or piece of an architectural column

¹**capital: different styles**

²**capital** *adj* **1** : conforming to the series A, B, C rather than a, b, c ⟨~ letters⟩ ⟨~ G⟩ **2** : punishable by death ⟨a ~ crime⟩ **3** : most serious ⟨a ~ error⟩ **4** : first in importance or position : CHIEF; *also* : being the seat of government ⟨the ~ city⟩ **5** : of or relating to capital ⟨~ expenditures⟩; *esp* : relating to or being assets that add to the long-term net worth of a corporation **6** : FIRST-RATE, EXCELLENT

³**capital** *n* **1** : accumulated wealth esp. as used to produce more wealth **2** : the total face value of shares of stock issued by a company **3** : persons holding capital **4** : ADVANTAGE, GAIN **5** : a letter larger than the ordinary small letter and often different in form **6** : the capital city of a state, province or country; *also* : a city preeminent in some activity ⟨the fashion ~⟩

capital gain *n* : the increase in value of an asset (as stock or real estate) between the time it is bought and the time it is sold

capital goods *n pl* : machinery, tools, factories, and commodities used in the production of goods

cap·i·tal·ise *Brit var of* CAPITALIZE

cap·i·tal·ism \'ka-pət-ᵊl-ˌi-zəm\ *n* : an economic system characterized by private or corporate ownership of capital goods and by prices, production, and distribution of goods that are determined mainly by competition in a free market

¹**cap·i·tal·ist** \-ist\ *n* **1** : a person who has capital esp. invested in business **2** : a person of great wealth : PLUTOCRAT **3** : a believer in capitalism

²**capitalist** *or* **cap·i·tal·is·tic** \ˌka-pət-ᵊl-'is-tik\ *adj* **1** : owning capital **2** : practicing or advocating capitalism **3** : marked by capitalism — **cap·i·tal·is·ti·cal·ly** \-ti-k(ə-)lē\ *adv*

cap·i·tal·iza·tion \ˌka-pət-ᵊl-ə-'zā-shən\ *n* **1** : the act or process of capitalizing **2** : the total amount of money used as capital in a business

cap·i·tal·ize \'ka-pət-ᵊl-ˌīz\ *vb* **-ized; -iz·ing** **1** : to write or print with an initial capital or in capitals **2** : to convert into or use as capital **3** : to supply capital for **4** : to gain by turning something to advantage : PROFIT

cap·i·tal·ly \'ka-pət-ᵊl-ē\ *adv* : ADMIRABLY, EXCELLENTLY

cap·i·ta·tion \ˌka-pə-'tā-shən\ *n* : a direct uniform tax levied on each person

cap·i·tol \'ka-pət-ᵊl\ *n* : the building in which a legislature holds its sessions

ca·pit·u·late \kə-'pi-chə-ˌlāt\ *vb* **-lat·ed; -lat·ing** **1** : to surrender esp. on conditions agreed upon **2** : to cease resisting : ACQUIESCE ♦ *Synonyms* SUBMIT, YIELD, SUCCUMB, CAVE, DEFER — **ca·pit·u·la·tion** \-ˌpi-chə-'lā-shən\ *n*

ca·pon \'kā-ˌpän, -pən\ *n* : a castrated male chicken

cap·puc·ci·no \ˌka-pə-'chē-nō, ˌkä-\ *n* [It., lit., Capuchin; fr. the likeness of its color to that of a Capuchin's habit] : espresso mixed with foamy hot milk or cream and often flavored with cinnamon

ca·pric·cio \kə-'prē-chē-ˌō, -chō\ *n, pl* **-cios** [It., lit., whim, prank] : an instrumental piece in free form usu. lively in tempo and brilliant in style

ca·price \kə-'prēs\ *n* [F, fr. It *capriccio*] **1** : a sudden whim or fancy **2** : an inclination to do things impulsively **3** : CAPRICCIO — **ca·pri·cious** \-'pri-shəs\ *adj* — **ca·pri·cious·ly** *adv* — **ca·pri·cious·ness** *n*

Cap·ri·corn \'ka-pri-ˌkȯrn\ *n* **1** : a zodiacal constellation between Sagittarius and Aquarius usu. pictured as a goat **2** : the 10th sign of the zodiac in astrology; *also* : one born under this sign

cap·ri·ole \'ka-prē-ˌōl\ *n* : ³CAPER 1; *also* : an upward leap of a horse with a backward kick at the height of the leap — **capriole** *vb*

caps *abbr* **1** capitals **2** capsule

cap·sa·i·cin \kap-'sā-ə-sən\ *n* : a colorless compound found in various capsicums that gives hot peppers their hotness

cap·si·cum \'kap-si-kəm\ *n* : PEPPER 2

cap·size \'kap-ˌsīz, kap-'sīz\ *vb* **cap·sized; cap·siz·ing** : UPSET, OVERTURN

cap·stan \'kap-stən, -ˌstan\ *n* **1** : a machine for moving or raising heavy weights that consists of a vertical drum which can be rotated and around which cable is turned **2** : a rotating shaft that drives recorder tape

cap·su·lar \'kap-sə-lər\ *adj* : of, relating to, or resembling a capsule

cap·su·lat·ed \-ˌlā-təd\ *adj* : enclosed in a capsule

¹**cap·sule** \'kap-səl, -sül\ *n* **1** : a membrane or sac enclosing a body part (as of a joint) **2** : a case bearing spores or seeds **3** : a shell usu. of gelatin that is used for packaging something (as a drug); *also* : such a shell together with its contents **4** : a small pressurized compartment or vehicle (as for space flight)

²**capsule** *adj* **1** : very brief **2** : very compact

Capt *abbr* captain

¹**cap·tain** \'kap-tən\ *n* **1** : a commander of a body of troops **2** : a commissioned officer in the army, air force, or marine corps ranking next below a major **3** : an officer in charge of a ship **4** : a commissioned officer in the navy ranking next below a rear admiral or a commodore **5** : a leader of a side or team **6** : a dominant figure — **cap·tain·cy** *n*

²**captain** *vb* : to be captain of : LEAD

cap·tion \'kap-shən\ *n* **1** : a heading esp. of an article or document : TITLE **2** : the explanatory matter accompanying an illustration **3** : a motion-picture subtitle — **caption** *vb*

cap·tious \'kap-shəs\ *adj* : marked by an inclination to find fault — **cap·tious·ly** *adv* — **cap·tious·ness** *n*

cap·ti·vate \'kap-tə-ˌvāt\ *vb* **-vat·ed; -vat·ing** : to attract and hold irresistibly by some special charm or art — **cap·ti·va·tion** \ˌkap-tə-'vā-shən\ *n* — **cap·ti·va·tor** \'kap-tə-ˌvā-tər\ *n*

cap·tive \'kap-tiv\ *adj* **1** : made prisoner esp. in war **2** : kept within bounds : CONFINED **3** : held under control — **captive** *n* — **cap·tiv·i·ty** \kap-'ti-və-tē\ *n*

cap·tor \'kap-tər\ *n* : one that captures

¹**cap·ture** \'kap-chər\ *n* **1** : the act of capturing **2** : one that has been captured

²**capture** *vb* **cap·tured; cap·tur·ing** **1** : to take captive : WIN, GAIN ⟨~ the crown⟩ **2** : to preserve in a relatively permanent form ⟨~ the moment on film⟩

Ca·pu·chin \'ka-pyə-shən\ *n* : a member of an austere branch of the order of St. Francis of Assisi engaged in missionary work and preaching

car \'kär\ *n* **1** : a vehicle moving on wheels **2** : the compartment of an elevator **3** : the part of a balloon or airship that carries passengers or equipment

car·a·cole \'kar-ə-ˌkōl\ *n* : a half turn to right or left executed by a mounted horse — **caracole** *vb*

car·a·cul \'kar-ə-kəl\ *n* : the pelt of a karakul lamb after the curl begins to loosen

ca·rafe \kə-'raf, -'räf\ *n* **1** : a bottle with a flaring lip used esp. to hold wine **2** : a usu. glass pitcher for pouring coffee

car·am·bo·la \,kar-əm-'bō-lə\ n **1** : a 5-angled green to yellow edible tropical fruit of star-shaped cross section **2** : a tropical Asian tree widely cultivated for carambolas

car·a·mel \'kar-ə-məl, 'kär-məl\ n **1** : an amorphous substance obtained by heating sugar and used for flavoring and coloring **2** : a firm chewy candy

car·a·pace \'kar-ə-,pās\ n : a protective case or shell on the back of some animals (as turtles or crabs)

¹carat var of KARAT

²car·at \'kar-ət\ n : a unit of weight for precious stones equal to 200 milligrams

car·a·van \'kar-ə-,van\ n **1** : a group of travelers journeying together through desert or hostile regions **2** : a group of vehicles traveling in a file

car·a·van·sa·ry \,kar-ə-'van-sə-rē\ or **car·a·van·se·rai** \-sə-,rī\ n, pl **-ries** or **-rais** or **-rai** [Pers kārvānsarāī, fr. kārvān caravan + sarāī palace, inn] **1** : an inn in eastern countries where caravans rest at night **2** : HOTEL, INN

car·a·vel \'kar-ə-,vel\ n : a small 15th and 16th century ship with a broad bow, high narrow poop, and usu. three masts

car·a·way \'kar-ə-,wā\ n : an aromatic herb related to the carrot with fruits **(caraway seed)** used in seasoning and medicine; also : its fruit

car·bide \'kär-,bīd\ n : a compound of carbon with another element

car·bine \'kär-,bēn, -,bīn\ n : a short-barreled lightweight rifle

car·bo·hy·drate \,kär-bō-'hī-,drāt, -drət\ n : any of various compounds composed of carbon, hydrogen, and oxygen (as sugars and starches)

car·bol·ic acid \,kär-'bä-lik-\ n : PHENOL

car·bon \'kär-bən\ n **1** : a nonmetallic chemical element occurring in nature esp. as diamond and graphite and as a constituent of coal, petroleum, and limestone **2** : a sheet of carbon paper; also : CARBON COPY 1 — **car·bon·less** \-ləs\ adj

car·bo·na·ceous \,kär-bə-'nā-shəs\ adj : relating to, containing, or composed of carbon

¹car·bon·ate \'kär-bə-,nāt, -nət\ n : a salt or ester of carbonic acid

²car·bon·ate \-,nāt\ vb **-at·ed; -at·ing** : to combine or infuse with carbon dioxide ⟨carbonated beverages⟩ — **car·bon·ation** \,kär-bə-'nā-shən\ n

carbon black n : any of various black substances consisting chiefly of carbon and used esp. as pigments

carbon copy n **1** : a copy made by carbon paper **2** : DUPLICATE

carbon dating n : the determination of the age of old material (as an archaeological specimen) by its content of carbon 14

carbon dioxide n : a heavy colorless gas that does not support combustion and is formed in animal respiration and in the combustion and decomposition of organic substances

carbon 14 n : a heavy radioactive form of carbon used esp. in dating old materials (as archaeological specimens)

car·bon·ic acid \kär-'bä-nik-\ n : a weak acid that decomposes readily into water and carbon dioxide

car·bon·if·er·ous \,kär-bə-'ni-fə-rəs\ adj **1** : producing or containing carbon or coal **2** cap : of, relating to, or being the period of the Paleozoic era between the Devonian and the Permian — **Carboniferous** n

carbon monoxide n : a colorless odorless very poisonous gas formed by the incomplete burning of carbon

carbon paper n : a thin paper coated with a pigment and used for making copies

carbon tet·ra·chlo·ride \-,te-trə-'klōr-,īd\ n : a colorless nonflammable toxic liquid used esp. as a solvent

carbon 12 n : the most abundant isotope of carbon having a nucleus of 6 protons and 6 neutrons and used as a standard for measurements of atomic weight

car·boy \'kär-,bói\ n [Pers qarāba, fr. Ar qarrāba demijohn] : a large container for liquids

car·bun·cle \'kär-,bəŋ-kəl\ n : a painful inflammation of the skin and underlying tissue that discharges pus from several openings

car·bu·re·tor \'kär-bə-,rā-tər, -byə-\ n : an apparatus for premixing vaporized fuel and air and supplying the mixture to an internal combustion engine

car·bu·ret·tor also **car·bu·ret·ter** \,kär-byə-'re-tər, 'kär-byə-,\ chiefly Brit var of CARBURETOR

car·case Brit var of CARCASS

car·cass \'kär-kəs\ n : a dead body; esp : one of an animal dressed for food

car·cin·o·gen \kär-'si-nə-jən\ n : a substance or agent causing cancer — **car·ci·no·gen·ic** \,kärs-ᵊn-ō-'je-nik\ adj — **car·ci·no·ge·nic·i·ty** \-jə-'ni-sə-tē\ n

car·ci·no·ma \,kärs-ᵊn-'ō-mə\ n, pl **-mas** also **-ma·ta** \-tə\ : a malignant tumor of epithelial origin — **car·ci·no·ma·tous** \-təs\ adj

¹card \'kärd\ vb : to comb with a card : cleanse and untangle before spinning — **card·er** n

²card n : an instrument for combing fibers (as wool or cotton)

³card n **1** : PLAYING CARD **2** pl : a game played with playing cards; also : card playing **3** : an emotional issue used to one's advantage (as in a political campaign) **4** : a usu. clownishly amusing person : WAG **5** : a flat stiff usu. small piece of paper, cardboard, or plastic often bearing pictures or information **6** : PROGRAM; esp : a sports program — **in the cards** : INEVITABLE

⁴card vb **1** : to list or schedule on a card **2** : SCORE **3** : to ask for identification (as at a bar)

⁵card abbr cardinal

car·da·mom \'kär-də-məm\ n : the aromatic capsular fruit of an Indian herb related to the ginger whose seeds are used as a spice or condiment and in medicine; also : this plant

card·board \'kärd-,bōrd\ n : a material thicker than paper and made from cellulose fiber

card–car·ry·ing \'kärd-,kar-ē-iŋ\ adj : being a regularly enrolled member of an organization (as a political party)

card catalog n : a catalog (as of books) in which the entries are arranged systematically on cards

car·di·ac \'kär-dē-,ak\ adj [L cardiacus, fr. Gk kardiakos, fr. kardia heart] **1** : of, relating to, or located near the heart **2** : of, relating to, or affected with heart disease ⟨~ patients⟩

car·di·gan \'kär-di-gən\ n : a sweater or jacket usu. without a collar and with a full-length opening in the front

¹car·di·nal \'kärd-nəl, 'kär-dᵊn-əl\ n **1** : an ecclesiastical official of the Roman Catholic Church ranking next below the pope **2** : a crested No. American finch that is nearly completely red in the male

²cardinal adj [ME, fr. LL cardinalis, fr. L serving as a hinge, fr. cardo hinge] **1** : of basic importance : CHIEF, MAIN, PRIMARY **2** : very serious ⟨a ~ sin⟩ — **car·di·nal·ly** adv

car·di·nal·ate \'kärd-nə-lət, -'kärd-ᵊn-ə-let, -,lāt\ n : the office, rank, or dignity of a cardinal

cardinal flower n : a No. American plant that bears a spike of brilliant red flowers

cardinal number n : a number (as 1, 5, 82, 357) that is used in simple counting and answers the question "how many?" — compare ORDINAL NUMBER

cardinal point n : one of the four principal compass points north, south, east, and west

car·dio \'kär-dē-ō\ adj : CARDIOVASCULAR 2

car·di·ol·o·gy \,kär-dē-'ä-lə-jē\ n : the study of the heart and its action and diseases — **car·di·ol·o·gist** \-jist\ n

car·dio·pul·mo·nary resuscitation \,kär-dē-ō-'púl-mə-,ner-ē-\ n : a procedure to restore normal breathing after cardiac arrest that includes the clearance of air passages to the lungs, mouth-to-mouth method of artificial respiration, and heart massage by the exertion of pressure on the chest

car·dio·vas·cu·lar \-'vas-kyə-lər\ adj **1** : of or relating to the heart and blood vessels **2** : causing a temporary increase in heart rate ⟨a ~ workout⟩

card·sharp \-,shärp\ or **card·sharp·er** \'kärd-,shär-pər\ n : a cheater at cards

¹care \'ker\ n **1** : a disquieted state of uncertainty and responsibility : ANXIETY **2** : watchful attention : HEED **3** : CHARGE, SUPERVISION ⟨under a doctor's ~⟩ **4** : a person or thing that is an object of anxiety or solicitude

²care vb **cared; car·ing 1** : to feel anxiety **2** : to feel interest **3** : to give care **4** : to have a liking, fondness, taste, or inclination **5** : to be concerned about ⟨~ what happens⟩

CARE abbr Cooperative for American Relief to Everywhere

ca·reen \kə-'rēn\ vb **1** : to put (a ship or boat) on a beach esp. in order to clean or repair its hull **2** : to sway from side to side **3** : CAREER

¹ca·reer \kə-'rir\ *n* [MF *carrière,* fr. Old Occitan *carriera* street, fr. ML *carraria* road for vehicles, fr. L *carrus* car] **1** : COURSE, PASSAGE; *also* : speed in a course 〈ran at full ~〉 **2** : an occupation or profession followed as a life's work

²career *vb* : to go at top speed esp. in a headlong manner

care·free \'ker-,frē\ *adj* : free from care or worry

care·ful \-fəl\ *adj* **care·ful·ler; care·ful·lest** **1** : using or taking care : VIGILANT **2** : marked by solicitude, caution, or prudence — **care·ful·ly** *adv* — **care·ful·ness** *n*

care·giv·er \-,gi-vər\ *n* : a person who provides direct care (as for children, elderly people, or the chronically ill)

care·less \-ləs\ *adj* **1** : free from care : UNTROUBLED **2** : UNCONCERNED, INDIFFERENT 〈~ of the consequences〉 **3** : not taking care **4** : not showing or receiving care — **care·less·ly** *adv* — **care·less·ness** *n*

care package *n* : a package of useful or pleasurable items given as a gift to another

¹ca·ress \kə-'res\ *vb* : to touch or stroke tenderly or lovingly — **ca·ress·er** *n*

²caress *n* : a tender or loving touch or embrace

car·et \'ker-ət\ *n* [L, there is lacking, fr. *carēre* to lack, be without] : a mark ^ used to indicate the place where something is to be inserted

care·tak·er \'ker-,tā-kər\ *n* **1** : one in charge usu. as occupant in place of an absent owner **2** : one temporarily fulfilling the functions of an office

care·worn \-,wòrn\ *adj* : showing the effects of grief or anxiety

car·fare \'kär-,fer\ *n* : passenger fare (as on a streetcar or bus)

car·go \'kär-gō\ *n, pl* **cargoes** *or* **cargos** : the goods carried in a ship, airplane, or vehicle : FREIGHT

Ca·rib·be·an \,ker-ə-'bē-ən, kə-'ri-bē-ən\ *adj* : of or relating to the eastern and southern West Indies or the Caribbean Sea

car·i·bou \'ker-ə-,bü\ *n, pl* **caribou** *or* **caribous** : a large circumpolar gregarious deer of northern taiga and tundra that usu. has large branched antlers usu. in both sexes — used esp. for one of the New World

car·i·ca·ture \'ker-i-kə-,chùr\ *n* **1** : distorted representation to produce a ridiculous effect **2** : a representation esp. in literature or art having the qualities of caricature — **caricature** *vb* — **car·i·ca·tur·ist** \-ist\ *n*

car·ies \'ker-ēz\ *n, pl* **caries** : tooth decay

car·il·lon \'ker-ə-,län\ *n* : a set of tuned bells sounded by hammers controlled from a keyboard

car·i·ous \'ker-ē-əs\ *adj* : affected with caries

car·jack·ing \'kär-ja-kiŋ\ *n* : the theft of an automobile by force or intimidation — **car·jack·er** *n*

car·load \'kär-,lōd\ *n* : a load that fills a car

car·mi·na·tive \kär-'mi-nə-tiv\ *adj* : expelling gas from the stomach or intestines — **carminative** *n*

car·mine \'kär-mən, -,mīn\ *n* : a vivid red

car·nage \'kär-nij\ *n* : great destruction of life : SLAUGHTER

car·nal \'kär-n²l\ *adj* [ME, fr. LL *carnalis,* fr. L *carn-, caro* flesh] **1** : of or relating to the body **2** : relating to or given to sensual pleasures and appetites — **car·nal·i·ty** \kär-'na-lə-tē\ *n* — **car·nal·ly** *adv*

car·na·tion \kär-'nā-shən\ *n* : a cultivated pink of any of numerous usu. double-flowered varieties derived from an Old World species

car·nau·ba wax \kär-'nò-bə-, -'naù-; ,kär-nə-'ü-bə-\ *n* : a brittle yellowish wax from a Brazilian palm that is used esp. in polishes

car·ne·lian \kär-'nēl-yən\ *n* : a hard red chalcedony used as a gem

car·ni·val \'kär-nə-vəl\ *n* [It *carnevale,* alter. of *carnelevare,* lit., removal of meat] **1** : a season of merrymaking just before Lent **2** : a boisterous merrymaking **3** : a traveling enterprise offering amusements **4** : an organized program of entertainment

car·ni·val·esque \,kär-nə-və-'lesk\ *adj* : suggestive of a carnival

car·ni·vo·ra \kär-'ni-və-rə\ *n pl* : carnivorous mammals

car·ni·vore \'kär-nə-,vòr\ *n* : a flesh-eating animal; *esp* : any of an order of mammals (as dogs, cats, bears, minks, and seals) feeding mostly on animal flesh

car·niv·o·rous \kär-'ni-və-rəs\ *adj* **1** : feeding on animal tissues **2** : of or relating to the carnivores — **car·niv·o·rous·ly** *adv* — **car·niv·o·rous·ness** *n*

car·ny *or* **car·ney** *or* **car·nie** \'kär-nē\ *n, pl* **carnies** *or* **carneys** **1** : CARNIVAL 3 **2** : one who works with a carnival

car·ol \'ker-əl\ *n* : a song of joy or devotion — **carol** *vb* — **car·ol·er** *or* **car·ol·ler** *n*

car·om \'ker-əm\ *n* **1** : a shot in billiards in which the cue ball strikes two other balls **2** : a rebounding esp. at an angle — **carom** *vb*

car·o·tene \'ker-ə-,tēn\ *n* : any of several orange to red pigments (as beta-carotene) formed esp. in plants and used as a source of vitamin A

ca·rot·en·oid \kə-'rä-tə-,nòid\ *n* : any of various usu. yellow to red pigments (as carotenes) found widely in plants and animals

ca·rot·id \kə-'rä-təd\ *adj* : of, relating to, or being the chief artery or pair of arteries that pass up the neck and supply the head — **carotid** *n*

ca·rous·al \kə-'raù-zəl\ *n* : CAROUSE

ca·rouse \kə-'raùz\ *n* [MF *carrousse,* fr. *carous,* adv., all out (in *boire carous* to empty the cup), fr. G *garaus*] : a drunken revel — **carouse** *vb* — **ca·rous·er** *n*

car·ou·sel *also* **car·rou·sel** \,ker-ə-'sel, 'kar-ə-,sel\ *n* **1** : MERRY-GO-ROUND **2** : a circular conveyor

¹carp \'kärp\ *vb* : to find fault : CAVIL, COMPLAIN — **carp** *n* — **carp·er** *n*

²carp *n, pl* **carp** *or* **carps** : a large variable Asian freshwater fish of sluggish waters often raised for food

¹car·pal \'kär-pəl\ *adj* : of or relating to the wrist or the bones of the wrist

²carpal *n* : a carpal element or bone

carpal tunnel syndrome *n* : a condition characterized esp. by weakness, pain, and disturbances of sensation (as numbness) in the hand and fingers and caused by compression of a nerve in the wrist

car·pe di·em \'kär-pe-'dē-,em, -'dī-\ *n* [L, lit., pluck the day] : enjoyment of the present without concern for the future

car·pel \'kär-pəl\ *n* : one of the highly modified leaves that together form the ovary of a flower of a seed plant

car·pen·ter \'kär-pən-tər\ *n* : one who builds or repairs wooden structures — **carpenter** *vb* — **car·pen·try** \-trē\ *n*

car·pet \'kär-pət\ *n* : a heavy fabric used as a floor covering — **carpet** *vb*

car·pet·bag \-,bag\ *n* : a traveling bag common in the 19th century

car·pet·bag·ger \-,ba-gər\ *n* : a Northerner in the South after the American Civil War usu. seeking private gain under the reconstruction governments

car·pet·ing \'kär-pə-tiŋ\ *n* : material for carpets; *also* : CARPETS

car pool *n* : an arrangement in which a group of people commute together by car; *also* : a group having this arrangement — **car·pool** \-,pül\ *vb*

car·port \'kär-,pòrt\ *n* : an open-sided automobile shelter

car·pus \'kär-pəs\ *n* : the wrist or its bones

car·ra·geen·an *or* **car·ra·geen·in** \,ker-ə-'gē-nən\ *n* : a colloid extracted esp. from a dark purple branching seaweed and used in foods esp. to stabilize and thicken them

car·rel \'ker-əl\ *n* : a table often partitioned or enclosed for individual study in a library

car·riage \'ker-ij\ *n* **1** : the act of carrying **2** : manner of holding the body **3** : a wheeled vehicle **4** *Brit* : a railway passenger coach **5** : a movable part of a machine for supporting some other moving part 〈a typewriter ~〉

carriage trade *n* : trade from well-to-do or upper-class people

car·ri·er \'ker-ē-ər\ *n* **1** : one that carries **2** : a person or organization in the transportation business **3** : AIRCRAFT CARRIER **4** : one whose system carries the causative agents of a disease but who is immune to the disease **5** : an individual having a gene for a trait or condition that is not expressed outwardly **6** : an electromagnetic wave whose amplitude or frequency is varied in order to convey a radio or television signal

carrier pigeon *n* : a pigeon used esp. to carry messages

car·ri·on \'ker-ē-ən\ *n* : dead and decaying flesh

car·rot \'ker-ət\ *n* : the elongated usu. orange root of a common garden plant that is eaten as a vegetable; *also* : this plant

carrousel *var of* CAROUSEL

¹**car·ry** \ka-rē, 'ker-ē\ *vb* **car·ried; car·ry·ing** [ME *carien*, fr. AF *carier*, fr. *carre* vehicle, fr. L *carrus*] **1** : to move while supporting : TRANSPORT, CONVEY, TAKE **2** : to influence by mental or emotional appeal **3** : to get possession or control of : CAPTURE, WIN **4** : to transfer from one place (as a column) to another ⟨∼ a number in adding⟩ **5** : to have or wear on one's person; *also* : to bear within one **6** : INVOLVE, IMPLY **7** : to hold or bear (oneself) in a specified way **8** : to keep in stock for sale **9** : to sustain the weight or burden of : SUPPORT **10** : to prolong in space, time, or degree **11** : to keep on one's books as a debtor **12** : to succeed in (an election) **13** : to win adoption (as in a legislature) **14** : PUBLISH, PRINT **15** : to reach or penetrate to a distance

²**carry** *n* **1** : the range of a gun or projectile or of a struck or thrown ball **2** : PORTAGE **3** : an act or method of carrying ⟨fireman's ∼⟩

car·ry·all \-ˌȯl\ *n* : a capacious bag or case

carry away *vb* : to arouse to a high and often excessive degree of emotion

carrying charge *n* : a charge added to the price of merchandise sold on the installment plan

car·ry·on \-ˌȯn, -ˌän\ *n* : a piece of luggage suitable for being carried aboard an airplane by a passenger — **carry-on** *adj*

carry on *vb* **1** : CONDUCT, MANAGE **2** : to behave in a foolish, excited, or improper manner **3** : to continue in spite of hindrance or discouragement

carry out *vb* **1** : to bring to a successful conclusion **2** : to put into execution

car·sick \'kär-ˌsik\ *adj* : affected with motion sickness esp. in an automobile — **car sickness** *n*

¹**cart** \'kärt\ *n* **1** : a heavy 2-wheeled wagon **2** : a small wheeled vehicle

²**cart** *vb* : to convey in or as if in a cart — **cart·er** *n*

cart·age \'kär-tij\ *n* : the act of or rate charged for carting

carte blanche \'kärt-'blänsh\ *n, pl* **cartes blanches** *same or* -'blän-shəz\ [F, lit., blank document] : full discretionary power

car·tel \kär-'tel\ *n* : a combination of independent business enterprises designed to limit competition ♦ **Synonyms** POOL, SYNDICATE, MONOPOLY, TRUST

car·ti·lage \'kär-tə-lij\ *n* : a usu. translucent somewhat elastic tissue that composes most of the skeleton of young vertebrate embryos and later is mostly converted to bone in higher vertebrates — **car·ti·lag·i·nous** \ˌkär-tə-'la-jə-nəs\ *adj*

cartilaginous fish *n* : any of a class of fishes (as a shark or ray) having the skeleton wholly or largely composed of cartilage

car·tog·ra·phy \kär-'tä-grə-fē\ *n* : the making of maps — **car·tog·ra·pher** *n* — **car·to·graph·ic** \ˌkär-tə-'gra-fik\ *adj*

car·ton \'kär-tᵊn\ *n* : a cardboard box or container

car·toon \kär-'tün\ *n* **1** : a preparatory sketch (as for a painting) **2** : a drawing intended as humor, caricature, or satire **3** : COMIC STRIP — **cartoon** *vb* — **car·toon·ist** *n*

car·tridge \'kär-trij\ *n* **1** : a tube containing a complete charge for a firearm **2** : a container of material for insertion into an apparatus **3** : a small case containing a phonograph needle and transducer that is attached to a tonearm **4** : a case containing a magnetic tape or disk **5** : a case for holding integrated circuits containing a computer program

cart·wheel \'kärt-ˌhwēl\ *n* **1** : a large coin (as a silver dollar) **2** : a lateral handspring with arms and legs extended

carve \'kärv\ *vb* **carved; carv·ing** **1** : to cut with care or precision : shape by cutting **2** : to cut into pieces or slices **3** : to slice and serve meat at table — **carv·er** *n*

cary·at·id \ˌker-ē-'a-təd\ *n, pl* **-ids** *or* **-i·des** \-'a-tə-ˌdēz\ : a sculptured draped female figure used as an architectural column

CAS *abbr* certificate of advanced study

ca·sa·ba \kə-'sä-bə\ *n* : any of several muskmelons with a yellow rind and sweet flesh

¹**cas·cade** \kas-'kād\ *n* **1** : a steep usu. small waterfall **2** : something arranged in a series or succession of stages so that each stage derives from or acts upon the product of the preceding

²**cas·cade** *vb* **cas·cad·ed; cas·cad·ing** : to fall, pass, or connect in or as if in a cascade

cas·cara \ka-'ska-rə\ *n* : the dried bark of a small Pacific coastal tree of the U.S. and southern Canada used as a laxative; *also* : this tree

¹**case** \'kās\ *n* [ME *cas*, fr. AF, fr. L *casus* fall, chance, fr. *cadere* to fall] **1** : a particular instance or situation **2** : an inflectional form of a noun, pronoun, or adjective indicating its grammatical relation to other words; *also* : such a relation whether indicated by inflection or not **3** : what actually exists or happens : FACT **4** : a suit or action in law : CAUSE **5** : a convincing argument **6** : an instance of disease or injury; *also* : PATIENT **7** : INSTANCE, EXAMPLE — **in case** : as a precaution — **in case of** : in the event of

²**case** *n* [ME *cas*, fr. AF *case*, *chase*, fr. L *capsa*] **1** : a box or container for holding something; *also* : a box with its contents **2** : an outer covering **3** : a divided tray for holding printing type **4** : CASING 2

³**case** *vb* **cased; cas·ing** **1** : to enclose in or cover with a case **2** : to inspect esp. with intent to rob

ca·sein \'kā-ˌsēn, kā-'\ *n* : any of several phosphorus-containing proteins occurring in or produced from milk

case·ment \'kās-mənt\ *n* : a window that opens like a door

case·work \-ˌwərk\ *n* : social work that involves the individual person or family — **case·work·er** *n*

¹**cash** \'kash\ *n* [MF or It; MF *casse* money box, fr. It *cassa*, fr. L *capsa* chest, case] **1** : ready money **2** : money or its equivalent paid at the time of purchase or delivery

²**cash** *vb* : to pay or obtain cash for

ca·shew \'ka-shü, kə-'shü\ *n* : an edible kidney-shaped nut of a tropical American tree related to the sumacs; *also* : the tree

¹**ca·shier** \ka-'shir\ *vb* : to dismiss from service; *esp* : to dismiss in disgrace

²**cash·ier** \ka-'shir\ *n* **1** : a bank official responsible for moneys received and paid out **2** : a person who receives and records payments

cashier's check *n* : a check drawn by a bank upon its own funds and signed by its cashier

cash in *vb* **1** : to convert into cash ⟨*cash in* bonds⟩ **2** : to settle accounts and withdraw from a gambling game or business deal **3** : to obtain financial profit or advantage

cash·less \'kash-ləs\ *adj* : relying on monetary transactions that use electronic means rather than cash

cash·mere \'kazh-ˌmir, 'kash-\ *n* : fine wool from the undercoat of an Indian goat (**cashmere goat**) or a yarn spun of this; *also* : a soft twilled fabric orig. woven from this yarn

cash out *vb* : to convert noncash assets into cash

cash register *n* : a business machine that usu. has a money drawer, indicates each sale, and records the money received

cash–strapped \'kash-ˌstrapt\ *adj* : lacking sufficient money

cas·ing \'kā-siŋ\ *n* **1** : something that encases **2** : the frame of a door or window

ca·si·no \kə-'sē-nō\ *n, pl* **-nos** [It, fr. *casa* house] **1** : a building or room for social amusements; *esp* : one used for gambling **2** *also* **cas·si·no** : a card game in which players win cards by matching those on the table

cask \'kask\ *n* : a barrel-shaped container usu. for liquids; *also* : the quantity held by such a container

cas·ket \'kas-kət\ *n* **1** : a small box (as for jewels) **2** : COFFIN

casque \'kask\ *n* : HELMET

cas·sa·va \kə-'sä-və\ *n* : any of several tropical spurges with rootstocks yielding a nutritious starch from which tapioca is prepared; *also* : the rootstock or its starch

cas·se·role \'ka-sə-ˌrōl\ *n* **1** : a dish in which food may be baked and served **2** : food cooked and served in a casserole

cas·sette *also* **ca·sette** \kə-'set\ *n* **1** : a lightproof container for photographic plates or film **2** : a plastic case containing magnetic tape

cas·sia \'ka-shə\ *n* **1** : a dried coarse cinnamon bark **2** : any of a genus of leguminous herbs, shrubs, and trees of warm regions including several which yield senna

cas·sit·er·ite \kə-'si-tə-ˌrīt\ *n* : a dark mineral that is the chief tin ore

cas·sock \'ka-sək\ *n* : an ankle-length garment worn esp. by Roman Catholic and Anglican clergy

cas·so·wary \'ka-sə-ˌwer-ē\ *n, pl* **-war·ies** : any of a genus of large flightless birds closely related to the emu

¹**cast** \'kast\ *vb* **cast; cast·ing** 1 : THROW, FLING 2 : DIRECT ⟨∼ a glance⟩ 3 : to deposit (a ballot) formally 4 : to throw off, out, or away : DISCARD, SHED 5 : COMPUTE; *esp* : to add up 6 : to assign the parts of (a play) to actors; *also* : to assign to a role or part 7 : to shape (a substance) by pouring in liquid or plastic form into a mold and letting harden without pressure 8 : to make (as a knot or stitch) by looping or catching up

²**cast** *n* 1 : THROW, FLING 2 : a throw of dice 3 : the set of actors in a dramatic production 4 : something formed in or as if in a mold; *also* : a rigid surgical casing (as for protecting and supporting a fractured bone) 5 : TINGE, HUE 6 : APPEARANCE, LOOK ⟨features of delicate ∼⟩ 7 : something thrown out or off, shed, or expelled ⟨worm ∼s⟩

cas·ta·net \ˌkas-tə-'net\ *n* [Sp *castañeta*, fr. *castaña* chestnut, fr. L *castanea*] : a rhythm instrument consisting of two small wooden, ivory, or plastic shells held in the hand and clicked together

cast·away \'kas-tə-ˌwā\ *adj* 1 : thrown away : REJECTED 2 : cast adrift or ashore as a survivor of a shipwreck — **castaway** *n*

caste \'kast\ *n* [Pg *casta*, lit., race, lineage, fr. fem. of *casto* pure, chaste, fr. L *castus*] 1 : one of the hereditary social classes in Hinduism 2 : a division of a society based on wealth, inherited rank, or occupation 3 : social position : PRESTIGE 4 : a system of rigid social stratification

cas·tel·lat·ed \'kas-tə-ˌlā-təd\ *adj* : having battlements like a castle

cast·er \'kas-tər\ *n* 1 **or cas·tor** : a small container to hold salt or pepper at the table 2 : a small wheel that turns freely and is used to support and move furniture, trucks, and equipment

cas·ti·gate \'kas-tə-ˌgāt\ *vb* **-gat·ed; -gat·ing** : to punish or criticize severely — **cas·ti·ga·tion** \ˌkas-tə-'gā-shən\ *n* — **cas·ti·ga·tor** \'kas-tə-ˌgā-tər\ *n*

cast·ing \'kas-tiŋ\ *n* 1 : CAST 7 2 : something cast in a mold

casting vote *n* : a deciding vote cast by a presiding officer to break a tie

cast iron *n* : a hard brittle alloy of iron, carbon, and silicon cast in a mold

cas·tle \'ka-səl\ *n* 1 : a large fortified building or set of buildings 2 : a large or imposing house 3 : ³ROOK

castle in the air : an impracticable project

cast–off \'kast-ˌȯf\ *adj* : thrown away or aside — **cast-off** *n*

cas·tor oil \'kas-tər-\ *n* : a thick yellowish oil extracted from the poisonous seeds of an herb (**castor–oil plant**) and used as a lubricant and purgative

cas·trate \'kas-ˌtrāt\ *vb* **cas·trat·ed; cas·trat·ing** : to deprive of sex glands and esp. testes — **cas·tra·tion** \kas-'trā-shən\ *n* — **cas·tra·tor** \-ər\ *n*

ca·su·al \'ka-zhə-wəl\ *adj* 1 : resulting from or occurring by chance 2 : OCCASIONAL, INCIDENTAL ⟨∼ employment⟩ 3 : OFFHAND, NONCHALANT ⟨a ∼ approach to cooking⟩ 4 : designed for informal use ⟨∼ clothing⟩ — **ca·su·al·ly** *adv* — **ca·su·al·ness** *n*

ca·su·al·ty \'ka-zhəl-tē, 'ka-zhə-wəl-\ *n, pl* **-ties** 1 : serious or fatal accident 2 : a military person lost through death, injury, sickness, or capture or through being missing in action 3 : a person or thing injured, lost, or destroyed

ca·su·ist·ry \'ka-zhə-wə-strē\ *n, pl* **-ries** : specious argument : RATIONALIZATION — **ca·su·ist** \-wist\ *n* — **ca·su·is·tic** \ˌka-zhə-'wis-tik\ *or* **ca·su·is·ti·cal** \-ti-kəl\ *adj*

ca·sus bel·li \ˌkä-səs-'be-ˌlē, ˌkä-səs-'be-ˌlī\ *n, pl* **ca·sus belli** \ˌkä-ˌsüs-, ˌkä-\ [NL, occasion of war] : a cause or pretext for a declaration of war

¹**cat** \'kat\ *n* 1 : a carnivorous mammal long domesticated as a pet and for catching rats and mice 2 : any of a family of animals (as the lion, lynx, or leopard) including the domestic cat 3 : a malicious woman 4 : GUY

²**cat** *abbr* catalog

ca·tab·o·lism \kə-'ta-bə-ˌli-zəm\ *n* : destructive metabolism involving the release of energy and resulting in the breakdown of complex materials — **cat·a·bol·ic** \ˌka-tə-'bä-lik\ *adj*

cat·a·clysm \'ka-tə-ˌkli-zəm\ *n* : a violent change or up-

heaval — **cat·a·clys·mal** \ˌka-tə-'kliz-məl\ *or* **cat·a·clys·mic** \-'kliz-mik\ *adj*

cat·a·comb \'ka-tə-ˌkōm\ *n* : an underground burial place with galleries and recesses for tombs

cat·a·falque \'ka-tə-ˌfalk, -ˌfȯlk, -ˌfȯk\ *n* : an ornamental structure sometimes used in solemn funerals to hold the body

cat·a·lep·sy \'ka-tə-ˌlep-sē\ *n, pl* **-sies** : a trancelike state characterized esp. by loss of voluntary motion — **cat·a·lep·tic** \ˌka-tə-'lep-tik\ *adj or n*

¹**cat·a·log** *or* **cat·a·logue** \'ka-tə-ˌlȯg\ *n* 1 : LIST, REGISTER 2 : a systematic list of items with descriptive details; *also* : a book containing such a list

²**catalog** *or* **catalogue** *vb* **-loged** *or* **-logued; -log·ing** *or* **-logu·ing** 1 : to make a catalog of 2 : to enter in a catalog — **cat·a·log·er** *or* **cat·a·logu·er** *n*

ca·tal·pa \kə-'tal-pə\ *n* : any of a genus of broad-leaved trees with showy flowers and long slim pods

ca·tal·y·sis \kə-'ta-lə-səs\ *n, pl* **-y·ses** \-ˌsēz\ : a change and esp. increase in the rate of a chemical reaction brought about by a substance (**cat·a·lyst** \'ka-tə-list\) that is itself unchanged at the end of the reaction — **cat·a·lyt·ic** \ˌka-tə-'li-tik\ *adj* — **cat·a·lyt·i·cal·ly** \-ti-k(ə-)lē\ *adv*

catalytic converter *n* : an automobile exhaust-system component in which a catalyst changes harmful gases into mostly harmless products

cat·a·lyze \'ka-tə-ˌlīz\ *vb* **-lyzed; -lyz·ing** : to bring about the catalysis of (a chemical reaction)

cat·a·ma·ran \ˌka-tə-mə-'ran\ *n* [Tamil (a language of southern India) *kaṭṭumaram*, fr. *kaṭṭu* to tie + *maram* tree] : a boat with twin hulls

cat·a·mount \'ka-tə-ˌmaůnt\ *n* : COUGAR; *also* : LYNX

cat·a·pult \'ka-tə-ˌpəlt, -ˌpůlt\ *n* 1 : an ancient military machine for hurling missiles 2 : a device for launching an airplane (as from an aircraft carrier) — **catapult** *vb*

cat·a·ract \'ka-tə-ˌrakt\ *n* 1 : a cloudiness of the lens of the eye obstructing vision 2 : a large waterfall; *also* : steep rapids in a river

ca·tarrh \kə-'tär\ *n* : inflammation of a mucous membrane esp. of the nose and throat — **ca·tarrh·al** \-əl\ *adj*

ca·tas·tro·phe \kə-'tas-trə-(ˌ)fē\ *n* [Gk *katastrophē*, fr. *katastrephein* to overturn, fr. *kata-* down + *strephein* to turn] 1 : a great disaster or misfortune 2 : utter failure — **cat·a·stroph·ic** \ˌka-tə-'strä-fik\ *adj* — **cat·a·stroph·i·cal·ly** \-fi-k(ə-)lē\ *adv*

cat·a·ton·ic \ˌka-tə-'tä-nik\ *adj* : of, relating to, or marked by schizophrenia characterized esp. by stupor, negativism, rigidity, purposeless excitement, and bizarre posturing — **catatonic** *n*

cat·bird \'kat-ˌbərd\ *n* : an American songbird with a catlike mewing call

cat·boat \'kat-ˌbōt\ *n* : a single-masted sailboat with a single large sail extended by a long boom

cat·call \-ˌkȯl\ *n* : a loud cry made esp. to express disapproval — **catcall** *vb*

¹**catch** \'kach, 'kech\ *vb* **caught** \'kȯt\; **catch·ing** [ME *cacchen*, fr. AF *cacher, chacher, chacer* to hunt, ultim. fr. L *captare* to chase] 1 : to capture esp. after pursuit 2 : TRAP 3 : to discover unexpectedly ⟨*caught* in the act⟩ 4 : to become suddenly aware of 5 : to take hold of : SNATCH ⟨∼ at a straw⟩ 6 : INTERCEPT 7 : to get entangled 8 : to become affected with or by ⟨∼ fire⟩ ⟨∼ cold⟩ 9 : to seize and hold firmly; *also* : FASTEN 10 : OVERTAKE 11 : to be in time for ⟨∼ a train⟩ 12 : to take in and retain 13 : to look at or listen to

²**catch** *n* 1 : something caught 2 : the act of catching; *also* : a game consisting of throwing and catching a ball 3 : something that catches or checks or holds immovable ⟨a door ∼⟩ 4 : one worth catching esp. as a mate 5 : FRAGMENT, SNATCH 6 : a concealed difficulty or complication

catch·all \'kach-ˌȯl, 'kech-\ *n* : something to hold a variety of odds and ends

catch–as–catch–can *adj* : using any means available

catch·er \'ka-chər, 'ke-\ *n* : one that catches; *esp* : a player positioned behind home plate in baseball

catch·ing *adj* 1 : INFECTIOUS, CONTAGIOUS 2 : ALLURING, CATCHY

catch·ment \'kach-mənt, 'kech-\ *n* 1 : something that catches water 2 : the action of catching water

catch on *vb* 1 : UNDERSTAND 2 : to become popular

catch·pen·ny \'kach-ˌpe-nē, 'kech-\ *adj* : using sensationalism or cheapness for appeal ⟨a ∼ newspaper⟩

catch·phrase \-ˌfrāz\ *n* : a word or expression frequently used to represent or characterize a person, group, idea, or point of view

catch–22 \-ˌtwen-tē-'tü\ *n, pl* **catch–22's** *or* **catch–22s** *often cap* C [fr. *Catch-22*, a paradoxical rule found in the novel *Catch-22* (1961) by Joseph Heller] : a problematic situation for which the only solution is denied by a circumstance inherent in the problem or by a rule; *also* : the circumstance or rule that denies a solution

catchup *var of* KETCHUP

catch up *vb* : to travel or work fast enough to overtake or complete

catch·word \'kach-ˌwərd, 'kech-\ *n* **1** : GUIDE WORD **2** : CATCHPHRASE

catchy \'ka-chē, 'ke-\ *adj* **catch·i·er; -est 1** : likely to catch the interest or attention **2** : TRICKY ⟨a ∼ question⟩

cat·e·chism \'ka-tə-ˌki-zəm\ *n* : a summary or test (as of religious doctrine) usu. in the form of questions and answers — **cat·e·chist** \-kist\ *n* — **cat·e·chize** \-ˌkīz\ *vb*

cat·e·chu·men \ˌka-tə-'kyü-mən\ *n* : a religious convert receiving training before baptism

cat·e·gor·i·cal \ˌka-tə-'gor-i-kəl\ *adj* **1** : ABSOLUTE, UNQUALIFIED ⟨a ∼ denial⟩ **2** : of, relating to, or constituting a category — **cat·e·gor·i·cal·ly** \-i-k(ə-)lē\ *adv*

cat·e·go·rise *Brit var of* CATEGORIZE

cat·e·go·rize \'ka-ti-gə-ˌrīz\ *vb* **-rized; -riz·ing** : to put into a category : CLASSIFY — **cat·e·go·ri·za·tion** \ˌka-ti-gə-rə-'zā-shən\ *n*

cat·e·go·ry \'ka-tə-ˌgor-ē\ *n, pl* **-ries** : a division used in classification; *also* : CLASS, GROUP, KIND

ca·ter \'kā-tər\ *vb* [obs. *cater* buyer of provisions, fr. ME *catour*, short for *acatour*, fr. AF, fr. *acater*, *achater* to buy] **1** : to provide a supply of food **2** : to supply what is wanted — **ca·ter·er** *n*

catercorner *or* **cater–cornered** *var of* KITTY-CORNER

cat·er·pil·lar \'ka-tər-ˌpi-lər\ *n* [ME *catyrpel*, fr. OF *catepelose*, lit., hairy cat] : a wormlike often hairy insect larva esp. of a butterfly or moth

caterpillar

cat·er·waul \'ka-tər-ˌwol\ *vb* : to make a harsh cry — **caterwaul** *n*

cat·fish \'kat-ˌfish\ *n* : any of an order of chiefly freshwater stout-bodied fishes with slender tactile processes around the mouth

cat·gut \-ˌgət\ *n* : a tough cord made usu. from sheep intestines

ca·thar·sis \kə-'thär-səs\ *n, pl* **ca·thar·ses** \-ˌsēz\ **1** : an act of purging or purification **2** : elimination of a complex by bringing it to consciousness and affording it expression

¹ca·thar·tic \kə-'thär-tik\ *adj* : of, relating to, or producing catharsis

²cathartic *n* : PURGATIVE

ca·the·dral \kə-'thē-drəl\ *n* : the principal church of a diocese

cath·e·ter \'ka-thə-tər\ *n* : a tube for insertion into a bodily passage or cavity usu. for injecting or drawing off material or for keeping a passage open

cath·e·ter·i·za·tion \ˌka-thə-tə-rə-'zā-shən\ *n* : the use of or introduction of a catheter — **cath·e·ter·ize** \'ka-thə-tə-ˌrīz\ *vb*

cath·ode \'ka-ˌthōd\ *n* **1** : the negative electrode of an electrolytic cell **2** : the positive terminal of a battery **3** : the electron-emitting electrode of an electron tube — **cath·od·al** \'ka-ˌthō-d²l\ *adj* — **ca·thod·ic** \ka-'thä-dik\ *adj*

cathode–ray tube *n* : a vacuum tube in which a beam of electrons is projected on a phosphor-coated screen to produce a luminous spot

cath·o·lic \'kath-lik, 'ka-thə-\ *adj* [ME *catholik* relating to the church universal, ultim. fr. Gk *katholikos* universal,

general, fr. *katholou* in general] **1** *cap* : of or relating to Catholics and esp. Roman Catholics **2** : GENERAL, UNIVERSAL

Cath·o·lic \'kath-lik, 'ka-thə-\ *n* : a member of a church claiming historical continuity from the ancient undivided Christian church; *esp* : a member of the Roman Catholic Church — **Ca·thol·i·cism** \kə-'thä-lə-ˌsi-zəm\ *n*

cath·o·lic·i·ty \ˌka-thə-'li-sə-tē\ *n, pl* **-ties 1** *cap* : the character of being in conformity with a Catholic church **2** : liberality of sentiments or views **3** : comprehensive range

cat·ion \'kat-ˌī-ən\ *n* : the ion in an electrolyte that migrates to the cathode; *also* : a positively charged ion

cat·kin \'kat-kən\ *n* : a long flower cluster (as of a willow) bearing crowded flowers and prominent bracts

cat·like \-ˌlīk\ *adj* : resembling a cat or its behavior; *esp* : STEALTHY

cat·nap \-ˌnap\ *n* : a very short light nap — **catnap** *vb*

cat·nip \-ˌnip\ *n* : an aromatic mint that is esp. attractive to cats

cat–o'–nine–tails \ˌka-tə-'nīn-ˌtālz\ *n, pl* **cat–o'–nine–tails** : a whip made of usu. nine knotted cords fastened to a handle

CAT scan \'kat-\ *n* [computerized *a*xial *t*omography] : an image made by computed tomography

CAT scanner *n* : a medical instrument consisting of integrated X-ray and computing equipment that is used to make CAT scans

cat's cradle *n* : a game played with a string looped on the fingers in such a way as to resemble a small cradle

cat's–eye \'kats-ˌī\ *n, pl* **cat's–eyes** : any of various iridescent gems

cat's–paw \-ˌpò\ *n, pl* **cat's–paws** : a person used by another as a tool

cat·suit \'kat-ˌsüt\ *n* : a close-fitting one-piece garment that covers the torso and the legs

catsup *var of* KETCHUP

cat·tail \'kat-ˌtāl\ *n* : any of a genus of tall reedlike marsh plants with furry brown spikes of tiny flowers

cat·tle \'ka-t²l\ *n pl* : LIVESTOCK; *esp* : domestic bovines (as cows, bulls, or calves) — **cat·tle·man** \-mən, -ˌman\ *n*

cat·ty \'ka-tē\ *adj* **cat·ti·er, -est** : slyly spiteful — **cat·ti·ly** \'ka-tə-lē\ *adv* — **cat·ti·ness** *n*

catty–corner *or* **catty–cornered** *var of* KITTY-CORNER

CATV *abbr* community antenna television

cat·walk \'kat-ˌwok\ *n* : a narrow walk (as along a bridge)

Cau·ca·sian \kò-'kā-zhən\ *adj* : of or relating to the white race of humankind — **Caucasian** *n* — **Cau·ca·soid** \'kò-kə-ˌsòid\ *adj or n*

cau·cus \'kò-kəs\ *n* : a meeting of a group of persons belonging to the same political party or faction usu. to decide upon policies and candidates — **caucus** *vb*

cau·dal \'kò-d²l\ *adj* : of, relating to, or located near the tail or the hind end of the body — **cau·dal·ly** *adv*

cau·di·llo \kaù-'thē-(ˌ)yō, -'thēl-\ *n, pl* **-llos** : a Spanish or Latin-American military dictator

caught \'kòt\ *past and past part of* CATCH

caul \'kòl\ *n* : the inner fetal membrane of higher vertebrates esp. when covering the head at birth

caul·dron \'kòl-drən\ *n* : a large kettle

cau·li·flow·er \'kò-li-ˌflaù(-ə)r\ *n* [It *cavolfiore*, fr. *cavolo* cabbage + *fiore* flower] : a garden plant closely related to cabbage and grown for its compact edible head of undeveloped flowers; *also* : this head used as a vegetable

cauliflower ear *n* : an ear deformed from injury and excessive growth of scar tissue

¹caulk *or* **calk** \'kòk\ *vb* [ME, fr. AF *cauker*, *calcher* to trample, fr. L *calcare*, fr. *calx* heel] : to stop up and make tight against leakage (as a boat or its seams) — **caulk·er** *n*

²caulk *or* **calk** *also* **caulk·ing** *or* **calk·ing** *n* : material used to caulk

caus·al \'kò-zəl\ *adj* **1** : expressing or indicating cause **2** : relating to or acting as a cause — **cau·sal·i·ty** \kò-'za-lə-tē\ *n* — **caus·al·ly** *adv*

cau·sa·tion \kò-'zā-shən\ *n* **1** : the act or process of causing **2** : the means by which an effect is produced

¹cause \'kòz\ *n* **1** : REASON, MOTIVE **2** : something that brings about a result; *esp* : a person or thing that is the agent of bringing something about **3** : a suit or action in court : CASE **4** : a question or matter to be decided **5** : a principle or movement earnestly supported — **cause-less** *adj*

²**cause** *vb* **caused; caus·ing** : to be the cause or occasion of — **caus·a·tive** \'kȯ-zə-tiv\ *adj* — **caus·er** *n*

cause cé·lè·bre \ˌkȯz-sā-'lebrᵊ, ˌkȯz-\ *n, pl* **causes célèbres** *same*\ [F, lit., celebrated case] **1** : a legal case that excites widespread interest **2** : a notorious person, thing, incident, or episode

cau·se·rie \ˌkȯz-'rē, ˌkō-zə-\ *n* [F] **1** : an informal conversation : CHAT **2** : a short informal essay

cause·way \'kȯz-ˌwā\ *n* : a raised way or road across wet ground or water

¹**caus·tic** \'kȯ-stik\ *adj* **1** : CORROSIVE **2** : SHARP, INCISIVE ⟨~ wit⟩

²**caustic** *n* **1** : a substance that burns or destroys organic tissue by chemical action **2** : SODIUM HYDROXIDE

cau·ter·ize \'kȯ-tə-ˌrīz\ *vb* **-ized; -iz·ing** : to burn or sear usu. to prevent infection or bleeding — **cau·ter·i·za·tion** \ˌkȯ-tə-rə-'zā-shən\ *n*

¹**cau·tion** \'kȯ-shən\ *n* **1** : ADMONITION, WARNING **2** : prudent forethought to minimize risk **3** : one that astonishes — **cau·tion·ary** \-shə-ˌner-ē\ *adj*

²**caution** *vb* : to advise caution to

cau·tious \'kȯ-shəs\ *adj* : marked by or given to caution : CAREFUL — **cau·tious·ly** *adv* — **cau·tious·ness** *n*

cav *abbr* **1** cavalry **2** cavity

cav·al·cade \ˌka-vəl-'kād\ *n* **1** : a procession of riders or carriages; *also* : a procession of vehicles **2** : a dramatic sequence or procession

¹**cav·a·lier** \ˌka-və-'lir\ *n* [MF, fr. It *cavaliere*, fr. Old Occitan *cavalier*, fr. LL *caballarius* horseman, fr. L *caballus* horse] **1** : a mounted soldier : KNIGHT **2** *cap* : an adherent of Charles I of England **3** : GALLANT

²**cavalier** *adj* **1** : DEBONAIR **2** : DISDAINFUL, HAUGHTY ⟨a ~ attitude toward money⟩ — **cav·a·lier·ly** *adv*

cav·al·ry \'ka-vəl-rē\ *n, pl* **-ries** : troops mounted on horseback or moving in motor vehicles — **cav·al·ry·man** \-mən, -ˌman\ *n*

¹**cave** \'kāv\ *n* : a natural underground chamber open to the surface

²**cave** *vb* **caved; cav·ing** **1** : to collapse or cause to collapse **2** : to cease to resist : SUBMIT — usu. used with *in*

ca·ve·at \'ka-vē-ˌät, -ˌat; 'kä-vē-ˌät\ *n* [L, let him beware] : WARNING

caveat emp·tor \-'emp-tər, -ˌtȯr\ *n* [NL, let the buyer beware] : a principle in commerce: without a warranty the buyer takes a risk

cave–in \'kā-ˌvin\ *n* **1** : the action of caving in **2** : a place where earth has caved in

cave·man \'kāv-ˌman\ *n* **1** : a cave dweller esp. of the Stone Age **2** : a man who acts in a rough or crude manner

cav·ern \'ka-vərn\ *n* : CAVE; *esp* : one of large or unknown size — **cav·ern·ous** *adj* — **cav·ern·ous·ly** *adv*

cav·i·ar *also* **cav·i·are** \'ka-vē-ˌär, 'kä-\ *n* : the salted roe of a large fish (as sturgeon) used as an appetizer

cav·il \'ka-vəl\ *vb* **-iled** *or* **-illed; -il·ing** *or* **-il·ling** : to make frivolous objections or raise trivial objections to — **cavil** *n* — **cav·il·er** *or* **cav·il·ler** *n*

cav·ing \'kā-viŋ\ *n* : the sport of exploring caves : SPELUNKING

cav·i·ta·tion \ˌka-və-'tā-shən\ *n* : the formation of partial vacuums in a liquid by a swiftly moving solid body (as a propeller) or by high-intensity sound waves

cav·i·ty \'ka-və-tē\ *n, pl* **-ties** **1** : an unfilled space within a mass : a hollow place **2** : an area of decay in a tooth

ca·vort \kə-'vȯrt\ *vb* : PRANCE, CAPER

ca·vy \'kā-vē\ *n, pl* **cavies** : GUINEA PIG 1

caw \'kȯ\ *vb* : to utter the harsh call of the crow or a similar cry — **caw** *n*

cay \'kē, 'kā\ *n* : ⁴KEY

cay·enne pepper \ˌkī-'en-, ˌkā-\ *n* : a condiment consisting of ground dried fruits or seeds of a hot pepper

cayman *var of* CAIMAN

Ca·yu·ga \kā-'ü-gə, kī-\ *n, pl* **Cayuga** *or* **Cayugas** : a member of an American Indian people of New York

Cay·use \'kī-ˌyüs, kī-'\ *n* **1** *pl* **Cayuse** *or* **Cayuses** : a member of an American Indian people of Oregon and Washington **2** *pl* **cayuses**, *not cap West* : a native range horse

Cb *symbol* columbium

CB \ˈsē-'bē\ *n* : CITIZENS BAND; *also* : the radio set used for citizens-band communications

CBC *abbr* Canadian Broadcasting Corporation

CBD *abbr* cash before delivery

CBS *abbr* Columbia Broadcasting System

CBW *abbr* chemical and biological warfare

cc *abbr* cubic centimeter

CC *abbr* **1** carbon copy **2** community college **3** country club

CCD \ˌsē-ˌsē-'dē\ *n* : CHARGE-COUPLED DEVICE

CCTV *abbr* closed-circuit television

CCU *abbr* **1** cardiac care unit **2** coronary care unit **3** critical care unit

ccw *abbr* counterclockwise

cd *abbr* cord

Cd *symbol* cadmium

¹**CD** \ˌsē-'dē\ *n* : CERTIFICATE OF DEPOSIT

²**CD** *n* : a small optical disk usu. containing recorded music or computer data; *also* : the content of a CD

³**CD** *abbr* Civil Defense

CDR *abbr* commander

CD–ROM \ˌsē-ˌdē-'räm\ *n* : a CD containing computer data that cannot be altered

CDT *abbr* central daylight (saving) time

Ce *symbol* cerium

CE *abbr* **1** chemical engineer **2** civil engineer **3** Corps of Engineers

cease \'sēs\ *vb* **ceased; ceas·ing** : to come or bring to an end : STOP

cease–fire \'sēs-'fī(-ə)r\ *n* : a suspension of active hostilities

cease·less \'sēs-ləs\ *adj* : being without pause or stop : CONTINUOUS — **cease·less·ly** *adv* — **cease·less·ness** *n*

ce·cum *also* **cae·cum** \'sē-kəm\ *n, pl* **ce·ca** \-kə\ : the blind pouch at the beginning of the large intestine into which the small intestine opens — **ce·cal** *also* **cae·cal** \-kəl\ *adj*

ce·dar \'sē-dər\ *n* : any of numerous coniferous trees (as a juniper) noted for their fragrant durable wood; *also* : this wood

cede \'sēd\ *vb* **ced·ed; ced·ing** **1** : to yield or give up esp. by treaty **2** : ASSIGN, TRANSFER — **ced·er** *n*

ce·di \'sā-dē\ *n* — see MONEY table

ce·dil·la \si-'di-lə\ *n* : a mark placed under the letter *c* (as ç) to show that the *c* is to be pronounced like *s*

ceil·ing \'sē-liŋ\ *n* **1** : the overhead inside lining of a room **2** : the height above the ground of the base of the lowest layer of clouds when over half of the sky is obscured **3** : the greatest height at which an airplane can operate efficiently **4** : a prescribed upper limit ⟨price ~⟩

cel·an·dine \'se-lən-ˌdīn, -ˌdēn\ *n* : a yellow-flowered herb related to the poppies

cel·e·brant \'se-lə-brənt\ *n* : one who celebrates; *esp* : a priest officiating at the Eucharist

cel·e·brate \'se-lə-ˌbrāt\ *vb* **-brat·ed; -brat·ing** **1** : to perform (as a sacrament) with appropriate rites **2** : to honor (as a holiday) by solemn ceremonies or by refraining from ordinary business **3** : to observe a notable occasion with festivities **4** : EXTOL — **cel·e·bra·tion** \ˌse-lə-'brā-shən\ *n* — **cel·e·bra·tor** \'se-lə-brā-tər\ *n* — **cel·e·bra·to·ry** \-brə-ˌtȯr-ē, ˌse-lə-'brā-tə-rē\ *adj*

celebrated *adj* : widely known and often referred to ⟨a ~ author⟩ ◆ **Synonyms** DISTINGUISHED, RENOWNED, NOTED, FAMOUS, ILLUSTRIOUS, NOTORIOUS

ce·leb·ri·ty \sə-'le-brə-tē\ *n, pl* **-ties** **1** : the state of being celebrated : RENOWN **2** : a celebrated person

ce·ler·i·ty \sə-'ler-ə-tē\ *n* : SPEED, RAPIDITY

cel·ery \'se-lə-rē\ *n, pl* **-er·ies** : a European herb related to the carrot and widely grown for the crisp edible stems of its leaves

celery cabbage *n* : CHINESE CABBAGE 2

ce·les·ta \sə-'les-tə\ *or* **ce·leste** \sə-'lest\ *n* : a keyboard instrument with hammers that strike steel plates

ce·les·tial \sə-'les-chəl\ *adj* **1** : HEAVENLY, DIVINE **2** : of or relating to the sky — **ce·les·tial·ly** *adv*

celestial navigation *n* : navigation by observation of the positions of stars

celestial sphere *n* : an imaginary sphere of infinite radius against which the celestial bodies appear to be projected

cel·i·ba·cy \'se-lə-bə-sē\ *n* **1** : the state of being unmarried; *esp* : abstention by vow from marriage **2** : abstention from sexual intercourse

cel·i·bate \'se-lə-bət\ *n* : one who lives in celibacy — **celibate** *adj*

cell \'sel\ *n* **1** : a small room (as in a convent or prison) usu. for one person; *also* : a small compartment, cavity, or bounded space **2** : a tiny mass of protoplasm that usu. contains a nucleus, is enclosed by a membrane, and forms the smallest structural unit of living matter capable of functioning independently **3** : a container holding an electrolyte either for generating electricity or for use in electrolysis **4** : a single unit in a device for converting radiant energy into electrical energy — **celled** \'seld\ *adj*

cel·lar \'se-lər\ *n* **1** : BASEMENT 1 **2** : the lowest place in the standings (as in an athletic league) **3** : a stock of wines

cel·lar·ette *or* **cel·lar·et** \ˌse-lə-'ret\ *n* : a case or cabinet for a few bottles of wine or liquor

cell body *n* : the nucleus-containing central part of a neuron exclusive of its processes

cel·lo \'che-lō\ *n, pl* **cellos** : a bass member of the violin family tuned an octave below the viola — **cel·list** \-list\ *n*

cel·lo·phane \'se-lə-ˌfān\ *n* : a thin transparent material made from cellulose and used as a wrapping

cell phone *n* : a portable cordless telephone for use in a cellular system

cel·lu·lar \'sel-yə-lər\ *adj* **1** : of, relating to, or consisting of cells ⟨∼ proteins⟩ **2** : of, relating to, or being a radiotelephone system in which a geographical area is divided into small sections each served by a transmitter of limited range

cel·lu·lite \'sel-yə-ˌlīt\ *n* : deposits of lumpy fat within connective tissue (as in the thighs, hips, and buttocks)

cel·lu·lose \'sel-yə-ˌlōs\ *n* : a complex carbohydrate of the cell walls of plants used esp. in making paper or rayon — **cel·lu·los·ic** \ˌsel-yə-'lō-sik\ *adj or n*

Cel·si·us \'sel-sē-əs\ *adj* : relating to or having a scale for measuring temperature on which the interval between the triple point and the boiling point of water is divided into 99.99 degrees with 0.01° being the triple point and 100.00° the boiling point; *also* : CENTIGRADE

Celt \'kelt, 'selt\ *n* : a member of any of a group of peoples (as the Irish or Welsh) of western Europe — **Celt·ic** *adj*

cem·ba·lo \'chem-bə-ˌlō\ *n, pl* **-ba·li** \-ˌlē\ *or* **-balos** [It] : HARPSICHORD

¹ce·ment \si-'ment\ *n* **1** : CONCRETE; *also* : a powder that is produced from a burned mixture chiefly of clay and limestone and that is used in mortar and concrete **2** : a binding element or agency **3** : CEMENTUM; *also* : a substance for filling cavities in teeth

²cement *vb* **1** : to unite by or as if by cement **2** : to cover with concrete — **ce·ment·er** *n*

ce·men·tum \si-'men-təm\ *n* : a specialized external bony layer covering the dentin of the part of a tooth normally within the gum

cem·e·tery \'se-mə-ˌter-ē\ *n, pl* **-ter·ies** [ME *cimitery*, fr. AF *cimiterie*, fr. LL *coemeterium*, fr. Gk *koimētērion* sleeping chamber, burial place, fr. *koiman* to put to sleep] : a burial ground : GRAVEYARD

cen·o·bite \'se-nə-ˌbīt\ *n* : a member of a religious group living together in a monastic community — **cen·o·bit·ic** \ˌse-nə-'bi-tik\ *adj*

ceno·taph \'se-nə-ˌtaf\ *n* [F *cénotaphe*, fr. L *cenotaphium*, fr. Gk *kenotaphion*, fr. *kenos* empty + *taphos* tomb] : a tomb or a monument erected in honor of a person whose body is elsewhere

Ce·no·zo·ic \ˌsē-nə-'zō-ik, ˌse-\ *adj* : of, relating to, or being the era of geologic history that extends from about 65 million years ago to the present — **Cenozoic** *n*

cen·ser \'sen-sər\ *n* : a vessel for burning incense (as in a religious ritual)

¹cen·sor \'sen-sər\ *n* **1** : a person who inspects printed matter or motion pictures with power to suppress anything objectionable **2** : one of two early Roman magistrates whose duties included taking the census — **cen·so·ri·al** \sen-'sòr-ē-əl\ *adj*

²censor *vb* : to subject to censorship

cen·so·ri·ous \sen-'sōr-ē-əs\ *adj* : marked by or given to censure : CRITICAL — **cen·so·ri·ous·ly** *adv* — **cen·so·ri·ous·ness** *n*

cen·sor·ship \'sen-sər-ˌship\ *n* **1** : the action of a censor esp. in stopping the transmission or publication of matter considered objectionable **2** : the office of a Roman censor

¹cen·sure \'sen-chər\ *n* **1** : the act of blaming or condemning sternly **2** : an official reprimand

²censure *vb* **cen·sured; cen·sur·ing** : to find fault with and criticize as blameworthy — **cen·sur·able** *adj* — **cen·sur·er** *n*

cen·sus \'sen-səs\ *n* **1** : a periodic governmental count of population **2** : COUNT, TALLY — **cen·sus** *vb*

¹cent \'sent\ *n* [F, hundred, fr. L *centum*] **1** : a monetary unit equal to ¹⁄₁₀₀ of a basic unit of value — see *birr, dollar, euro, gulden, leone, lilangeni, lira, nakfa, pound, rand, rupee, shilling* at MONEY table **2** : a coin, token, or note representing one cent **3** : a former monetary unit equal to ¹⁄₁₀₀ Dutch gulden

²cent *abbr* **1** centigrade **2** central **3** century

cen·tas \'sen-ˌtäs\ *n, pl* **cen·tai** \-ˌtī\ *or* **cen·tu** \-ˌtü\ — see *litas* at MONEY table

cen·taur \'sen-ˌtòr\ *n* : any of a race of creatures in Greek mythology half man and half horse

¹cen·ta·vo \sen-'tä-(ˌ)vō\ *n, pl* **-vos** — see *boliviano, colón, cordoba, lempira, peso, quetzal, sucre* at MONEY table

²cen·ta·vo \-'tä-(ˌ)vü, -(ˌ)vō\ *n, pl* **-vos** **1** — see *escudo, metical, real* at MONEY table **2** : a former monetary unit equal to ¹⁄₁₀₀ Portuguese escudo

cen·te·nar·i·an \ˌsen-tə-'ner-ē-ən\ *n* : a person who is 100 or more years old

cen·te·na·ry \sen-'te-nə-rē, 'sen-tə-ˌner-ē\ *n, pl* **-ries** : CENTENNIAL — **centenary** *adj*

cen·ten·ni·al \sen-'te-nē-əl\ *n* : a 100th anniversary or its celebration — **centennial** *adj*

¹cen·ter \'sen-tər\ *n* **1** : the point that is equally distant from all points on the circumference of a circle or surface of a sphere; *also* : MIDDLE 1 **2** : the point about which an activity concentrates or from which something originates **3** : a region of concentrated population **4** : a middle part **5** *often cap* : political figures holding moderate views esp. between those of conservatives and liberals **6** : a player occupying a middle position (as in football or basketball)

²center *vb* **1** : to place or fix at or around a center or central area **2** : to give a central focus or basis : CONCENTRATE **3** : to have a center : FOCUS

cen·ter·board \'sen-tər-ˌbòrd\ *n* : a retractable keel used esp. in sailboats

cen·ter·piece \-ˌpēs\ *n* **1** : an object in a central position; *esp* : an adornment in the center of a table **2** : one that is of central importance or interest in a larger whole

cen·tes·i·mal \sen-'te-sə-məl\ *adj* : marked by or relating to division into hundredths

¹cen·tes·i·mo \chen-'te-zə-ˌmō\ *n, pl* **-mi** \-(ˌ)mē\ : a former monetary unit equal to ¹⁄₁₀₀ Italian lira

²cen·tes·i·mo \sen-'te-sə-ˌmō\ *n, pl* **-mos** — see *balboa, peso* at MONEY table

cen·ti·grade \'sen-tə-ˌgrād, 'sän-\ *adj* : relating to, conforming to, or having a thermometer scale on which the interval between the freezing and boiling points of water is divided into 100 degrees with 0° representing the freezing point and 100° the boiling point ⟨10° ∼⟩ — compare CELSIUS

cen·ti·gram \-ˌgram\ *n* — see METRIC SYSTEM table

cen·ti·li·ter \'sen-ti-ˌlē-tər\ *n* — see METRIC SYSTEM table

cen·time \'sän-ˌtēm\ *n* **1** : a former monetary unit of any of several countries (as Belgium, France, and Luxembourg) equal to ¹⁄₁₀₀ franc **2** — see *dinar, dirham, franc, gourde* at MONEY table

cen·ti·me·ter \'sen-tə-ˌmē-tər, 'sän-\ *n* — see METRIC SYSTEM table

centimeter–gram–second *adj* : of, relating to, or being a system of units based on the centimeter as the unit of length, the gram as the unit of mass, and the second as the unit of time

cen·ti·mo \'sen-tə-ˌmō\ *n, pl* **-mos** **1** — see *bolivar, colón, dobra, guarani, sol* at MONEY table **2** : a former monetary unit equal to ¹⁄₁₀₀ peseta

cen·ti·pede \'sen-tə-ˌpēd\ *n* [L *centipeda*, fr. *centum* hundred + *pes* foot] : any of a class of long flattened segmented arthropods with one pair of legs on each segment except the first which has a pair of poison fangs

centipede

¹cen·tral \'sen-trəl\ *adj* **1** : constituting a center **2** : ESSENTIAL, PRINCIPAL ⟨the novel's ~ character⟩ **3** : situated at, in, or near the center **4** : centrally placed and superseding separate units ⟨~ heating⟩ — **cen·tral·ly** *adv*
²central *n* : a central controlling office
cen·tral·ise *Brit var of* CENTRALIZE
cen·tral·ize \'sen-trə-ˌlīz\ *vb* **-ized; -iz·ing** : to bring to a central point or under central control — **cen·tral·i·za·tion** \ˌsen-trə-lə-'zā-shən\ — **cen·tral·iz·er** \'sen-trə-ˌlī-zər\ *n*
central nervous system *n* : the part of the nervous system which integrates nervous function and activity and which in vertebrates consists of the brain and spinal cord
cen·tre *chiefly Brit var of* CENTER
cen·trif·u·gal \sen-'tri-fyə-gəl, -fi-\ *adj* [NL *centrifugus,* fr. *centr-* center + L *fugere* to flee] **1** : proceeding or acting in a direction away from a center or axis **2** : using or acting by centrifugal force
centrifugal force *n* : the apparent force felt by an object moving in a curved path and acting outward from a center of rotation
cen·tri·fuge \'sen-trə-ˌfyüj\ *n* : a machine using centrifugal force (as for separating substances of different densities or for removing moisture)
cen·trip·e·tal \sen-'tri-pə-t⁰l\ *adj* [NL *centripetus,* fr. *centr-* center + L *petere* seek] : proceeding or acting in a direction toward a center or axis
centripetal force *n* : the force needed to keep an object revolving about a point moving in a circular path
cen·trist \'sen-trist\ *n* **1** *often cap* : a member of a center party **2** : one who holds moderate views
cen·tu·ri·on \sen-'tùr-ē-ən, -'tyùr-\ *n* : an officer commanding a Roman century
cen·tu·ry \'sen-chə-rē\ *n, pl* **-ries** **1** : a subdivision of a Roman legion **2** : a group or sequence of 100 like things **3** : a period of 100 years
century plant *n* : a Mexican agave maturing and flowering only once in many years and then dying
CEO \ˌsē-(ˌ)ē-'ō\ *n* : the executive with the chief decision-making authority in an organization or business
ce·phal·ic \sə-'fa-lik\ *adj* **1** : of or relating to the head **2** : directed toward or situated on or in or near the head
ce·ram·ic \sə-'ra-mik\ *n* **1** *pl* : the art or process of making articles from a nonmetallic mineral (as clay) by firing **2** : a product produced by ceramics — **ceramic** *adj*
ce·ra·mist \sə-'ra-mist\ *or* **ce·ram·i·cist** \sə-'ra-mə-sist\ *n* : one who engages in ceramics
¹ce·re·al \'sir-ē-əl\ *adj* [L *cerealis,* fr. *Ceres,* the Roman goddess of agriculture] : relating to grain or to the plants that produce it; *also* : made of grain
²cereal *n* **1** : a grass (as wheat) yielding grain suitable for food; *also* : its grain **2** : a food and esp. a breakfast food prepared from the grain of a cereal
cer·e·bel·lum \ˌser-ə-'be-ləm\ *n, pl* **-bellums** *or* **-bel·la** \-lə\ [ML, fr. L, dim. of *cerebrum* brain] : a part of the brain that projects over the medulla and is concerned esp. with coordination of muscular action and with bodily balance — **cer·e·bel·lar** \-lər\ *adj*
ce·re·bral \sə-'rē-brəl, 'ser-ə-\ *adj* **1** : of or relating to the brain, intellect, or cerebrum **2** : appealing to or involving the intellect — **ce·re·bral·ly** *adv*
cerebral cortex *n* : the surface layer of gray matter of the cerebrum that functions chiefly in coordination of sensory and motor information
cerebral palsy *n* : a disorder caused by brain damage usu. before, during, or shortly after birth and marked esp. by defective muscle control
cer·e·brate \'ser-ə-ˌbrāt\ *vb* **-brat·ed; -brat·ing** : THINK — **cer·e·bra·tion** \ˌser-ə-'brā-shən\ *n*
ce·re·brum \sə-'rē-brəm, 'ser-ə-\ *n, pl* **-brums** *or* **-bra**

\-brə\ [L, brain] : the enlarged front and upper part of the brain that contains the higher nervous centers
cere·ment \'ser-ə-mənt, 'sir-mənt\ *n* : a shroud for the dead
¹cer·e·mo·ni·al \ˌser-ə-'mō-nē-əl\ *adj* : of, relating to, or forming a ceremony; *also* : stressing careful attention to form and detail — **cer·e·mo·ni·al·ly** *adv*
²ceremonial *n* : a ceremonial act or system : RITUAL, FORM
cer·e·mo·ni·ous \ˌser-ə-'mō-nē-əs\ *adj* **1** : devoted to forms and ceremony **2** : CEREMONIAL **3** : according to formal usage or procedure **4** : marked by ceremony — **cer·e·mo·ni·ous·ly** *adv* — **cer·e·mo·ni·ous·ness** *n*
cer·e·mo·ny \'ser-ə-ˌmō-nē\ *n, pl* **-nies** **1** : a formal act or series of acts prescribed by law, ritual, or convention **2** : a conventional act of politeness **3** : a mere outward form with no deeper significance **4** : FORMALITY
ce·re·us \'sir-ē-əs\ *n* : any of various cacti of the western U.S. and tropical America
ce·rise \sə-'rēs\ *n* [F, lit., cherry] : a moderate red color
ce·ri·um \'sir-ē-əm\ *n* : a malleable metallic chemical element used esp. in alloys
cer·met \'sər-ˌmet\ *n* : a strong alloy of a heat-resistant compound and a metal used esp. for turbine blades
cert *abbr* certificate; certification; certified; certify
¹cer·tain \'sər-t⁰n\ *adj* **1** : FIXED, SETTLED **2** : of a specific but unspecified character ⟨~ people in authority⟩ **3** : DEPENDABLE, RELIABLE **4** : INDISPUTABLE, UNDENIABLE **5** : assured in mind or action — **cer·tain·ly** *adv*
²certain *pron* : certain ones
cer·tain·ty \-tē\ *n, pl* **-ties** **1** : something that is certain **2** : the quality or state of being certain
cer·tif·i·cate \sər-'ti-fi-kət\ *n* **1** : a document testifying to the truth of a fact **2** : a document testifying that one has fulfilled certain requirements (as of a course) **3** : a document giving evidence of ownership or debt ⟨a stock ~⟩
certificate of deposit : a money-market bond redeemable without penalty only on maturity
cer·ti·fi·ca·tion \ˌsər-tə-fə-'kā-shən\ *n* **1** : the act of certifying : the state of being certified **2** : a certified statement
certified mail *n* : first class mail for which proof of delivery may be secured but no indemnity value is claimed
certified public accountant *n* : an accountant who has met the requirements of a state law and has been granted a certificate
cer·ti·fy \'sər-tə-ˌfī\ *vb* **-fied; -fy·ing** **1** : VERIFY, CONFIRM **2** : to endorse officially **3** : to guarantee (a bank check) as good by a statement to that effect stamped on its face **4** : to recognize as having met specific qualifications within a field ⟨*certified* teachers⟩ ♦ **Synonyms** ACCREDIT, APPROVE, SANCTION, ENDORSE — **cer·ti·fi·able** \-ə-bəl\ *adj* — **cer·ti·fi·ably** \-blē\ *adv* — **cer·ti·fi·er** *n*
cer·ti·tude \'sər-tə-ˌtüd, -ˌtyüd\ *n* : the state of being or feeling certain
ce·ru·le·an \sə-'rü-lē-ən\ *adj* : AZURE
ce·ru·men \sə-'rü-mən\ *n* : EARWAX
cer·vi·cal \'sər-vi-kəl\ *adj* : of or relating to a neck or cervix
cervical cap *n* : a contraceptive device in the form of a thimble-shaped molded cap that fits snugly over the uterine cervix and blocks sperm from entering the uterus
cer·vix \'sər-viks\ *n, pl* **cer·vi·ces** \-və-ˌsēz\ *or* **cer·vix·es** **1** : NECK; *esp* : the back part of the neck **2** : a constricted portion of an organ or part; *esp* : the narrow outer end of the uterus
ce·sar·e·an *or* **cae·sar·e·an** *also* **ce·sar·i·an** *or* **cae·sar·i·an** \si-'zer-ē-ən\ *n, often cap* : CESAREAN SECTION — **ce·sar·ean** *or* **caesarean** *also* **cesarian** *or* **caesarian** *adj*
cesarean section *also* **caesarean section** *n, often cap C* [fr. the legendary association of such a delivery with the Roman cognomen *Caesar*] : surgical incision of the walls of the abdomen and uterus for delivery of offspring
ce·si·um \'sē-zē-əm\ *n* : a silver-white soft ductile chemical element
ces·sa·tion \se-'sā-shən\ *n* : a temporary or final ceasing (as of action)
ces·sion \'se-shən\ *n* : a yielding (as of rights) to another
cess·pool \'ses-ˌpül\ *n* **1** : an underground pit or tank for receiving household sewage **2** : a filthy or corrupt situation
ce·ta·cean \si-'tā-shən\ *n* : any of an order of aquatic

mostly marine mammals that includes whales, porpoises, dolphins, and related forms — **cetacean** *adj*

cf *abbr* [L *confer*] compare

Cf *symbol* californium

CF *abbr* cystic fibrosis

CFC *abbr* chlorofluorocarbon

cg *abbr* centigram

CG *abbr* **1** coast guard **2** commanding general

cgs *abbr* centimeter-gram-second

ch *abbr* **1** chain **2** champion **3** chapter **4** church

CH *abbr* **1** clearinghouse **2** courthouse **3** customhouse

Cha·blis \sha-ˈblē, shə-, shä-; ˈsha-ˌblē\ *n, pl* **Cha·blis** \-ˈblēz, -(ˌ)blēz\ **1** : a dry sharp white Burgundy wine **2** : a white California wine

cha–cha \ˈchä-ˌchä\ *n* : a fast rhythmic ballroom dance of Latin American origin

chafe \ˈchāf\ *vb* **chafed; chaf·ing** **1** : IRRITATE, VEX **2** : FRET **3** : to warm by rubbing **4** : to rub so as to wear away; *also* : to make sore by rubbing

cha·fer \ˈchā-fər\ *n* : any of various scarab beetles

¹chaff \ˈchaf\ *n* **1** : debris (as husks) separated from grain in threshing **2** : something comparatively worthless — **chaffy** *adj*

²chaff *n* : light jesting talk : BANTER

³chaff *vb* : to tease good-naturedly

chaf·fer \ˈcha-fər\ *vb* : BARGAIN, HAGGLE — **chaf·fer·er** *n*

chaf·finch \ˈcha-ˌfinch\ *n* : a common European finch with a cheerful song

chaf·ing dish \ˈchā-fiŋ-\ *n* : a utensil for cooking food at the table

¹cha·grin \shə-ˈgrin\ *n* : mental uneasiness or annoyance caused by failure, disappointment, or humiliation

²chagrin *vb* **cha·grined** \-ˈgrind\; **cha·grin·ing** : to cause to feel chagrin

¹chain \ˈchān\ *n* [ME *cheyne*, fr. AF *chaene*, fr. L *catena*] **1** : a flexible series of connected links **2** : a chainlike surveying instrument; *also* : a unit of length equal to 66 feet (about 20 meters) **3** *pl* : BONDS, FETTERS **4** : a series of things linked together ⟨mountain ∼s⟩; *also* : a group of usu. identical enterprises with a single owner ⟨fast-food ∼s⟩ ♦ **Synonyms** TRAIN, STRING, SEQUENCE, SUCCESSION, SERIES

²chain *vb* : to fasten, bind, or connect with a chain; *also* : FETTER

chain gang *n* : a gang of convicts chained together

chain letter *n* : a letter sent to several persons with a request that each send copies to an equal number of persons

chain mail *n* : flexible armor of interlocking metal rings

chain reaction *n* **1** : a series of events in which each event initiates the succeeding one **2** : a chemical or nuclear reaction yielding products that cause further reactions of the same kind

chain saw *n* : a portable power saw that has teeth linked together to form an endless chain — **chain·saw** \ˈchān-ˌsȯ\ *vb*

chain–smoke \ˈchān-ˈsmōk\ *vb* : to smoke esp. cigarettes continuously

¹chair \ˈcher\ *n* [ME *chaiere*, fr. AF, fr. L *cathedra*, fr. Gk *kathedra*, fr. *kata-* down + *hedra* seat] **1** : a seat with a back for one person **2** : ELECTRIC CHAIR **3** : an official seat; *also* : an office or position of authority or dignity **4** : CHAIRMAN

²chair *vb* : to act as chairman of

chair·lift \ˈcher-ˌlift\ *n* : a motor-driven conveyor for skiers consisting of seats hung from a moving cable

chair·man \-mən\ *n* : the presiding officer of a meeting, committee, or event — **chair·man·ship** *n*

chair·per·son \-ˌpər-sən\ *n* : CHAIRMAN

chair·wom·an \-ˌwu̇-mən\ *n* : a woman who serves as chairman

chaise \ˈshāz\ *n* : a 2-wheeled horse-drawn carriage with a folding top

chaise longue \ˈshāz-ˈlȯŋ\ *n, pl* **chaise longues** *same or* -ˈlȯŋz\ [F, lit., long chair] : a long reclining chair

chaise lounge \-ˈlau̇nj\ *n* : CHAISE LONGUE

chal·ced·o·ny \kal-ˈse-dᵊn-ē\ *n, pl* **-nies** : a translucent quartz of various colors

chal·co·py·rite \ˌkal-kə-ˈpī-ˌrīt\ *n* : a yellow mineral constituting an important copper ore

cha·let \sha-ˈlā\ *n* **1** : a herdsman's cabin in the Swiss mountains **2** : a building in the style of a Swiss cottage with a wide roof overhang

chal·ice \ˈcha-ləs\ *n* : a drinking cup; *esp* : the eucharistic cup

¹chalk \ˈchȯk\ *n* **1** : a soft limestone **2** : chalk or chalky material esp. when used as a crayon — **chalky** *adj*

²chalk *vb* **1** : to rub or mark with chalk **2** : to record with or as if with chalk — usu. used with *up*

chalk·board \ˈchȯk-ˌbȯrd\ *n* : BLACKBOARD

chalk up *vb* **1** : ASCRIBE, CREDIT **2** : ATTAIN, ACHIEVE ⟨*chalk up* a victory⟩

¹chal·lenge \ˈcha-lənj\ *vb* **chal·lenged; chal·leng·ing** [ME *chalengen* to accuse, fr. AF *chalenger*, fr. L *calumniari* to accuse falsely, fr. *calumnia* calumny] **1** : to order to halt and prove identity **2** : to take exception to : DISPUTE ⟨∼ a ruling⟩ **3** : to issue an invitation to compete ⟨*challenged* me to another game⟩ **4** : to stimulate by presenting difficulties ⟨a job that ∼s her⟩ — **chal·leng·er** *n*

²challenge *n* **1** : a summons to a duel **2** : an invitation to compete in a sport **3** : a calling into question **4** : an exception taken to a juror **5** : a sentry's command to halt and prove identity **6** : a stimulating or interesting task or problem

challenged *adj* : presented with difficulties (as by a disability)

chal·lis \ˈsha-lē\ *n, pl* **chal·lises** \-lēz\ : a lightweight clothing fabric of wool, cotton, or synthetic yarns

cham·ber \ˈchām-bər\ *n* **1** : ROOM; *esp* : BEDROOM **2** : an enclosed space or cavity **3** : a hall for meetings of a legislative body **4** : a judge's consultation room — usu. used in pl. **5** : a legislative or judicial body; *also* : a council for a business purpose **6** : the part of a firearm that holds the cartridge or powder charge during firing — **cham·bered** \-bərd\ *adj*

cham·ber·lain \ˈchām-bər-lən\ *n* **1** : a chief officer in the household of a king or nobleman **2** : TREASURER

cham·ber·maid \-ˌmād\ *n* : a maid who takes care of bedrooms

chamber music *n* : music intended for performance by a few musicians before a small audience

chamber of commerce : an association of businesspeople for promoting commercial and industrial interests in the community

cham·bray \ˈsham-ˌbrā\ *n* : a lightweight clothing fabric of white and colored threads

cha·me·leon \kə-ˈmēl-yən\ *n* [ME *camelion*, fr. MF, fr. L *chamaeleon*, fr. Gk *chamaileōn*, fr. *chamai* on the ground + *leōn* lion] : a small lizard whose skin changes color esp. according to its surroundings

chameleon

¹cham·fer \ˈcham-fər\ *vb* **1** : to cut a furrow in (as a column) : GROOVE **2** : to make a chamfer on : BEVEL

²chamfer *n* : a beveled edge

cham·ois \ˈsha-mē\ *n, pl* **cham·ois** *same or* -mēz\ **1** : a small goatlike ruminant mammal of Europe and the Caucasus region of Russia **2** *also* **cham·my** \ˈsha-mē\ : a soft leather made esp. from the skin of the sheep or goat **3** : a cotton fabric made in imitation of chamois leather

cham·o·mile *or* **cam·o·mile** \ˈka-mə-ˌmī(-ə)l, -ˌmēl\ *n* : any of a genus of strong-scented herbs related to the daisies and having flower heads that yield a bitter substance used esp. in tonics and teas

¹champ \ˈchamp, ˈchämp\ *vb* **1** : to chew noisily **2** : to show impatience of delay or restraint

²champ \ˈchamp\ *n* : CHAMPION

cham·pagne \sham-ˈpān\ *n* : a white effervescent wine

¹**cham·pi·on** \'cham-pē-ən\ *n* **1** : a militant advocate or defender **2** : one that wins first prize or place in a contest **3** : one that is acknowledged to be better than all others

²**champion** *vb* : to protect or fight for as a champion ✦ **Synonyms** BACK, ADVOCATE, UPHOLD, SUPPORT

cham·pi·on·ship \-,ship\ *n* **1** : the position or title of a champion **2** : the act of championing : DEFENSE **3** : a contest held to determine a champion

¹**chance** \'chans\ *n* **1** : something that happens without apparent cause **2** : the unpredictable element in existence : LUCK, FORTUNE **3** : OPPORTUNITY **4** : the likelihood of a particular outcome in an uncertain situation : PROBABILITY **5** : RISK **6** : a raffle ticket — **chance** *adj* — **by chance** : in the haphazard course of events

²**chance** *vb* **chanced; chanc·ing** **1** : to take place by chance : HAPPEN **2** : to come casually and unexpectedly — used with *upon* **3** : to leave to chance **4** : to accept the risk of

chan·cel \'chan-səl\ *n* : the part of a church including the altar and choir

chan·cel·lery *or* **chan·cel·lory** \'chan-sə-lə-rē\ *n, pl* **-ler·ies** *or* **-lor·ies** **1** : the position or office of a chancellor **2** : the building or room where a chancellor works **3** : the office or staff of an embassy or consulate

chan·cel·lor \'chan-sə-lər\ *n* **1** : a high state official in various countries **2** : the head of a university **3** : a judge in the equity court in various states of the U.S. **4** : the chief minister of state in some European countries — **chan·cel·lor·ship** *n*

chan·cery \'chan-sə-rē\ *n, pl* **-cer·ies** **1** : a record office for public or diplomatic archives **2** : any of various courts of equity in the U.S. and Britain **3** : a chancellor's court or office **4** : the office of an embassy **5** : the business office of a diocese

chan·cre \'shaŋ-kər\ *n* [F, fr. OF, fr. L *cancer*] : a primary sore or ulcer at the site of entry of an infective agent (as of syphilis)

chan·croid \'shaŋ-,krȯid\ *n* : a sexually transmitted disease caused by a bacterium and characterized by chancres that differ from those of syphilis in lacking hardened margins

chancy \'chan-sē\ *adj* **chanc·i·er; -est** **1** *Scot* : AUSPICIOUS **2** : RISKY

chan·de·lier \,shan-də-'lir\ *n* : a branched lighting fixture suspended from a ceiling

chan·dler \'chand-lər\ *n* [ME *chandeler* a maker or seller of candles, fr. AF, fr. *chandele* candle, fr. L *candela*] : a dealer in provisions and supplies of a specified kind ⟨ship's ~⟩ — **chan·dlery** *n*

¹**change** \'chānj\ *vb* **changed; chang·ing** **1** : to make or become different : ALTER **2** : to replace with another **3** : to give or receive an equivalent sum in notes or coins of usu. smaller denominations or of another currency **4** : to put fresh clothes or covering on ⟨~ a bed⟩ **5** : to put on different clothes **6** : EXCHANGE — **change·able** *adj* — **chang·er** *n*

²**change** *n* **1** : the act, process, or result of changing **2** : a fresh set of clothes **3** : money given in exchange for other money of higher denomination **4** : money returned when a payment exceeds the sum due **5** : coins esp. of small denominations — **change·ful** *adj*

change·ling \'chānj-liŋ\ *n* : a child secretly exchanged for another in infancy

change of life *n* : MENOPAUSE

change·over \'chānj-,ō-vər\ *n* : CONVERSION, TRANSITION

change ringing *n* : the art or practice of ringing a set of tuned bells in continually varying order

¹**chan·nel** \'cha-nⁿl\ *n* **1** : the bed of a stream **2** : the deeper part of a waterway **3** : STRAIT **4** : a means of passage or transmission **5** : a range of frequencies of sufficient width for a single radio or television transmission **6** : a usu. tubular enclosed passage : CONDUIT **7** : a long gutter, groove, or furrow

²**channel** *vb* **-neled** *or* **-nelled; -neling** *or* **-nel·ling** **1** : to make a channel in **2** : to direct into or through a channel

chan·nel·ize \'cha-nə-,līz\ *vb* **-ized; -iz·ing** : CHANNEL — **chan·nel·i·za·tion** \,cha-nə-lə-'zā-shən\ *n*

chan·son \shäⁿ-'sōⁿ\ *n, pl* **chan·sons** *same or* -'sōⁿz\ : SONG; *esp* : a cabaret song

¹**chant** \'chant\ *vb* **1** : SING; *esp* : to sing a chant **2** : to utter or recite in the manner of a chant **3** : to celebrate or praise in song — **chant·er** *n*

²**chant** *n* **1** : a repetitive melody in which several words are sung to one tone : SONG; *esp* : a liturgical melody **2** : a manner of singing or speaking in musical monotones

chan·te·relle \,shan-tə-'rel\ *n* : a fragrant edible mushroom

chan·teuse \shäⁿ-'tərz, shan-'tüz\ *n, pl* **chan·teuses** *same or* -'tər-zəz, -'tü-zəz\ [F] : a woman who is a concert or nightclub singer

chan·tey *or* **chan·ty** \'shan-tē, 'chan-\ *n, pl* **chanteys** *or* **chanties** : a song sung by sailors in rhythm with their work

chan·ti·cleer \,chan-tə-'klir, ,shan-\ *n* : ROOSTER

Chanukah *var of* HANUKKAH

cha·os \'kā-,äs\ *n* **1** *often cap* : the confused unorganized state existing before the creation of distinct forms **2** : the inherent unpredictability in the behavior of a complex natural system (as the atmosphere or the beating heart) **3** : complete disorder ✦ **Synonyms** CONFUSION, JUMBLE, SNARL, MUDDLE, DISARRAY — **cha·ot·ic** \kā-'ä-tik\ *adj* — **cha·ot·i·cal·ly** \-ti-k(ə-)lē\ *adv*

chaos theory *n* : a branch of mathematical and physical theory concerned with chaotic systems

¹**chap** \'chap\ *vb* **chapped; chap·ping** : to dry and crack open usu. from wind and cold ⟨*chapped* lips⟩

²**chap** *n* : a jaw with its fleshy covering — usu. used in pl.

³**chap** *n, chiefly Brit* : FELLOW

⁴**chap** *abbr* chapter

chap·ar·ral \,sha-pə-'ral\ *n* **1** : a dense impenetrable thicket of shrubs or dwarf trees **2** : an ecological community esp. of southern California composed of shrubby plants

chap·book \'chap-,bůk\ *n* : a small book of ballads, tales, or tracts

cha·peau \sha-'pō\ *n, pl* **cha·peaus** \-'pōz\ *or* **cha·peaux** \-'pō, -'pōz\ [MF] : HAT

cha·pel \'cha-pəl\ *n* [ME, fr. AF *chapele*, fr. ML *cappella*, fr. LL *cappa* cloak; fr. the cloak of St. Martin of Tours preserved as a sacred relic in a chapel built for that purpose] **1** : a private or subordinate place of worship **2** : an assembly at an educational institution usu. including devotional exercises **3** : a place of worship used by a Christian group other than an established church

¹**chap·er·one** *or* **chap·er·on** \'sha-pə-,rōn\ *n* [F *chaperon*, lit., hood, fr. MF, head covering, fr. *chape* cape, fr. LL *cappa*] **1** : a person (as a matron) who accompanies young unmarried women in public for propriety **2** : an older person who accompanies young people at a social gathering to ensure proper behavior

²**chaperone** *or* **chaperon** *vb* **-oned; -on·ing** **1** : ESCORT, GUIDE **2** : to act as a chaperone to or for ⟨~ a dance⟩ ⟨~ teenagers⟩ — **chap·er·on·age** \-,rō-nij\ *n*

chap·fall·en \'chap-,fȯ-lən, 'chäp-\ *adj* **1** : having the lower jaw hanging loosely **2** : DEJECTED, DEPRESSED

chap·lain \'cha-plən\ *n* **1** : a member of the clergy officially attached to a special group (as the army) **2** : a person chosen to conduct religious exercises (as for a club) — **chap·lain·cy** \-sē\ *n*

chap·let \'cha-plət\ *n* **1** : a wreath for the head **2** : a string of beads : NECKLACE

chap·man \'chap-mən\ *n, Brit* : an itinerant dealer : PEDDLER

chaps \'shaps, 'chaps\ *n pl* [MexSp *chaparreras*] : leather leggings resembling pants without a seat that are worn esp. by western ranch hands

chap·ter \'chap-tər\ *n* **1** : a main division of a book **2** : a body of canons (as of a cathedral) **3** : a local branch of a society or fraternity

¹**char** \'chär\ *n, pl* **char** *or* **chars** : any of a genus of trouts (as the common brook trout) with small scales

²**char** *vb* **charred; char·ring** **1** : to burn or become burned to charcoal **2** : SCORCH

³**char** *vb* **charred; char·ring** : to work as a cleaning woman

char·ac·ter \'ker-ik-tər\ *n* [ME *caracter*, fr. L *character* mark, distinctive quality, fr. Gk *charaktēr*, fr. *charassein* to scratch, engrave] **1** : a graphic symbol (as a letter) used in writing or printing **2** : a symbol that represents information; *also* : a representation of such a character that may be accepted by a computer **3** : a distinguishing feature : ATTRIBUTE **4** : the complex of mental and ethical traits marking a person or a group **5** : a person marked by conspicuous often peculiar traits **6** : one of the persons in a novel or play **7** : REPUTATION **8** : moral excellence

¹**char·ac·ter·is·tic** \ˌker-ik-tə-ˈris-tik\ *n* : a distinguishing trait, quality, or property

²**characteristic** *adj* : serving to mark individual character ◆ **Synonyms** INDIVIDUAL, PECULIAR, DISTINCTIVE — **char·ac·ter·is·ti·cal·ly** \-ti-k(ə-)lē\ *adv*

char·ac·ter·ize \ˈker-ik-tə-ˌrīz\ *vb* **-ized; -iz·ing** **1** : to describe the character of **2** : to be characteristic of — **char·ac·ter·i·za·tion** \ˌker-ik-tə-rə-ˈzā-shən\ *n*

cha·rades \shə-ˈrādz\ *n sing or pl* : a game in which some of the players try to guess a word or phrase from the actions of another player who may not speak

char·coal \ˈchär-ˌkōl\ *n* **1** : a porous carbon prepared from vegetable or animal substances **2** : a piece of fine charcoal used in drawing; *also* : a drawing made with charcoal

chard \ˈchärd\ *n* : SWISS CHARD

char·don·nay \ˌshär-dᵊn-ˈā\ *n, often cap* [F] : a dry white wine made from a single variety of white grape

¹**charge** \ˈchärj\ *n* **1** : a quantity (as of fuel or ammunition) required to fill something to capacity **2** : a store or accumulation of force **3** : an excess or deficiency of electrons in a body **4** : THRILL, KICK **5** : a task or duty imposed **6** : CARE, RESPONSIBILITY **7** : one given into another's care **8** : instructions from a judge to a jury **9** : COST, EXPENSE, PRICE; *also* : a debit to an account **10** : ACCUSATION, INDICTMENT **11** : ATTACK, ASSAULT

²**charge** *vb* **charged; charg·ing** **1** : to load or fill to capacity **2** : to give an electric charge to; *also* : to restore the activity of (a storage battery) by means of an electric current **3** : to impose a task or responsibility on **4** : COMMAND, ORDER **5** : ACCUSE **6** : to rush against : rush forward in assault **7** : to make liable for payment; *also* : to record a debt or liability against **8** : to fix as a price — **charge·able** *adj*

charge–coupled device *n* : a semiconductor device used esp. as an optical sensor

char·gé d'af·faires \shär-ˌzhā-də-ˈfer\ *n, pl* **chargés d'affaires** \-ˌzhā-, -ˌzhāz-\ [F] : a diplomat who substitutes for an ambassador or minister

¹**char·ger** \ˈchär-jər\ *n* : a large platter

²**charg·er** *n* **1** : a device or a worker that charges something **2** : WARHORSE 1

char·i·ot \ˈcher-ē-ət\ *n* : a 2-wheeled horse-drawn vehicle of ancient times used esp. in war and in races — **char·i·o·teer** \ˌcher-ē-ə-ˈtir\ *n*

cha·ris·ma \kə-ˈriz-mə\ *n* : a personal quality of leadership arousing popular loyalty or enthusiasm — **char·is·mat·ic** \ˌkar-əz-ˈma-tik\ *adj*

char·i·ta·ble \ˈcher-ə-tə-bəl\ *adj* **1** : liberal in giving to needy people **2** : merciful or lenient in judging others ◆ **Synonyms** BENEVOLENT, PHILANTHROPIC, ALTRUISTIC, HUMANITARIAN — **char·i·ta·ble·ness** *n* — **char·i·ta·bly** \-blē\ *adv*

char·i·ty \ˈcher-ə-tē\ *n, pl* **-ties** **1** : goodwill toward or love of humanity **2** : an act or feeling of generosity **3** : the giving of aid to the poor; *also* : ALMS **4** : an institution engaged in relief of the poor **5** : leniency in judging others ◆ **Synonyms** MERCY, CLEMENCY, LENITY

char·la·tan \ˈshär-lə-tən\ *n* : a person making usu. showy pretenses to knowledge or ability : FRAUD, FAKER

Charles·ton \ˈchärl-stən\ *n* : a lively dance in which the knees are swung in and out and the heels are turned sharply outward on each step

char·ley horse \ˈchär-lē-ˌhȯrs\ *n* : a muscular pain, cramping, or stiffness from a strain or bruise

¹**charm** \ˈchärm\ *n* [ME *charme*, fr. AF, fr. L *carmen* song, fr. *canere* to sing] **1** : a practice or expression believed to have magic power **2** : something worn about the person to ward off evil or bring good fortune : AMULET **3** : a trait that fascinates or allures **4** : physical grace or attraction **5** : a small ornament worn on a bracelet or chain **6** : a quark with a charge of +⅔ and a measured energy of approximately 1.5 billion electron volts

²**charm** *vb* **1** : to affect by or as if by a magic spell **2** : to protect by or as if by charms **3** : FASCINATE, ENCHANT

◆ **Synonyms** ALLURE, CAPTIVATE, BEWITCH, ATTRACT — **charm·er** *n*

charmed \ˈchärmd\ *adj* : extremely lucky or prosperous ⟨a ∼ life⟩

charm·ing \ˈchär-miŋ\ *adj* : PLEASING, DELIGHTFUL — **charm·ing·ly** *adv*

char·nel house \ˈchär-nᵊl-\ *n* : a building or chamber in which bodies or bones are deposited

¹**chart** \ˈchärt\ *n* **1** : MAP **2** : a sheet giving information in the form of a table, list, or diagram; *also* : GRAPH

²**chart** *vb* **1** : PLAN ⟨∼ a course⟩ **2** : to make a chart of **3** : CHRONICLE ⟨∼ed his adventures⟩

¹**char·ter** \ˈchär-tər\ *n* **1** : an official document granting rights or privileges (as to a colony, town, or college) from a sovereign or a governing body **2** : CONSTITUTION **3** : a written instrument from a society creating a branch **4** : a mercantile lease of a ship

²**charter** *vb* **1** : to grant a charter to **2** *Brit* : CERTIFY ⟨∼ed engineer⟩ **3** : to hire, rent, or lease for temporary use ⟨∼ a bus⟩ — **char·ter·er** *n*

charter member *n* : an original member of an organization

char·treuse \shär-ˈtrüz, -ˈtrüs\ *n* : a brilliant yellow green

char·wom·an \ˈchär-ˌwu̇-mən\ *n* : a cleaning woman esp. in large buildings

chary \ˈcher-ē\ *adj* **chari·er; -est** [ME, sorrowful, dear, fr. OE *cearig* sorrowful, fr. *caru* sorrow] **1** : CAUTIOUS, CIRCUMSPECT **2** : SPARING — **char·i·ly** \-ə-lē\ *adv*

¹**chase** \ˈchās\ *n* **1** : PURSUIT; *also* : HUNTING **2** : QUARRY **3** : a tract of unenclosed land used as a game preserve

²**chase** *vb* **chased; chas·ing** **1** : to follow rapidly : PURSUE **2** : HUNT **3** : to seek out ⟨*chasing* down clues⟩ **4** : to cause to depart or flee : drive away **5** : RUSH, HASTEN

³**chase** *vb* **chased; chas·ing** : to decorate (a metal surface) by embossing or engraving

⁴**chase** *n* : FURROW, GROOVE

chas·er \ˈchā-sər\ *n* **1** : one that chases **2** : a mild drink (as beer) taken after hard liquor

chasm \ˈka-zəm\ *n* : GORGE 2

chas·sis \ˈcha-sē, ˈsha-sē\ *n, pl* **chas·sis** \-sēz\ : the supporting frame of a structure (as an automobile or television set)

chaste \ˈchāst\ *adj* **chast·er; chast·est** **1** : innocent of unlawful sexual intercourse : VIRTUOUS, PURE **2** : CELIBATE **3** : pure in thought : MODEST **4** : severe or simple in design — **chaste·ly** *adv* — **chaste·ness** *n*

chas·ten \ˈchā-sᵊn\ *vb* : to correct through punishment or suffering : DISCIPLINE; *also* : PURIFY — **chas·ten·er** *n*

chas·tise \chas-ˈtīz\ *vb* **chas·tised; chas·tis·ing** [ME *chastisen*, alter. of *chasten*] **1** : to punish esp. bodily **2** : to censure severely : CASTIGATE — **chas·tise·ment** \-mənt, ˈchas-təz-\ *n*

chas·ti·ty \ˈchas-tə-tē\ *n* : the quality or state of being chaste; *esp* : sexual purity

cha·su·ble \ˈcha-zə-bəl, -sə-\ *n* : the outer vestment of the priest at mass

chat \ˈchat\ *n* **1** : light familiar informal talk **2** : online discussion in a chat room — **chat** *vb*

châ·teau \sha-ˈtō\ *n, pl* **châ·teaus** \-ˈtōz\ *or* **châ·teaux** \-ˈtō, -ˈtōz\ [F, fr. OF *chastel*, fr. L *castellum* castle, dim. of *castra* camp] **1** : a feudal castle in France **2** : a large country house **3** : a French vineyard estate

chat·e·laine \ˈshat-tə-ˌlān\ *n* **1** : the mistress of a chateau **2** : a clasp or hook for a watch, purse, or keys

chat room *n* : a real-time online interactive discussion group

chat·tel \ˈcha-tᵊl\ *n* **1** : an item of tangible property other than real estate **2** : SLAVE, BONDMAN

chat·ter \ˈcha-tər\ *vb* **1** : to utter speechlike but meaningless sounds **2** : to talk idly, incessantly, or fast **3** : to click repeatedly or uncontrollably — **chatter** *n* — **chat·ter·er** *n*

chat·ter·box \ˈcha-tər-ˌbäks\ *n* : one who talks incessantly

chat·ty \ˈcha-tē\ *adj* **chat·ti·er; -est** : TALKATIVE — **chat·ti·ly** \-tə-lē\ *adv* — **chat·ti·ness** \-tē-nəs\ *n*

¹**chauf·feur** \ˈshō-fər, shō-ˈfər\ *n* [F, lit., stoker, fr. *chauffer* to heat] : a person employed to drive an automobile

²**chauffeur** *vb* **1** : to do the work of a chauffeur **2** : to transport in the manner of a chauffeur ⟨∼ed the kids to school⟩

chaunt *var of* CHANT

chau·vin·ism \'shō-və-ˌni-zəm\ *n* [F *chauvinisme*, fr. Nicolas *Chauvin*, fictional soldier of excessive patriotism and devotion to Napoleon] **1** : excessive or blind patriotism **2** : an attitude of superiority toward members of the opposite sex — **chau·vin·ist** \-nist\ *n or adj* — **chau·vin·is·tic** \ˌshō-və-'nis-tik\ *adj* — **chau·vin·is·ti·cal·ly** \-ti-k(ə-)lē\ *adv*

cheap \'chēp\ *adj* **1** : INEXPENSIVE **2** : costing little effort to obtain ⟨∼ tickets⟩ **3** : worth little : SHODDY, TAWDRY ⟨∼ workmanship⟩ **4** : worthy of scorn **5** : STINGY — **cheap** *adv* — **cheap·ly** *adv* — **cheap·ness** *n*

cheap·en \'chē-pən\ *vb* **1** : to make or become cheap or cheaper in price or value **2** : to make tawdry

cheap·skate \'chēp-ˌskāt\ *n* : a miserly or stingy person; *esp* : one who tries to avoid paying a fair share of costs

¹cheat \'chēt\ *vb* **1** : to deprive of something through fraud or deceit ⟨∼ed workers of their pay⟩ **2** : to practice fraud or trickery **3** : to violate rules dishonestly ⟨∼ at cards⟩ **4** : to be sexually unfaithful — **cheat·er** *n*

²cheat *n* **1** : the act of deceiving : FRAUD, DECEPTION **2** : one that cheats : a dishonest person

¹check \'chek\ *n* **1** : exposure of a chess king to an attack **2** : a sudden stoppage of progress **3** : a sudden pause or break **4** : something that stops or restrains **5** : a standard for testing or evaluation **6** : EXAMINATION, INVESTIGATION **7** : the act of testing or verifying **8** : a written order to a bank to pay money **9** : a ticket or token showing ownership or identity **10** : a slip indicating an amount due **11** : a pattern in squares; *also* : a fabric in such a pattern **12** : a mark typically ✓ placed beside an item to show that it has been noted **13** : CRACK, SPLIT

²check *vb* **1** : to put (a chess king) in check **2** : to slow down or stop : BRAKE **3** : to restrain the action or force of : CURB **4** : to compare with a source, original, or authority : VERIFY **5** : to inspect or test for satisfactory condition **6** : to mark with a check as examined **7** : to consign for shipment for one holding a passenger ticket **8** : to leave or accept for safekeeping in a checkroom **9** : to prove to be consistent or truthful **10** : to prove to be consistent or truthful **11** : CRACK, SPLIT

check·book \'chek-ˌbuk\ *n* : a book containing blank checks

¹check·er \'che-kər\ *n* : a piece in the game of checkers

²checker *vb* **1** : to variegate with different colors or shades **2** : to vary with contrasting elements ⟨a ∼ed career⟩ **3** : to mark into squares

³checker *n* : one that checks; *esp* : an employee who checks out purchases in a store

check·er·ber·ry \'che-kər-ˌber-ē\ *n* : WINTERGREEN 1; *also* : the spicy red fruit of this plant

check·er·board \-ˌbord\ *n* : a board of 64 squares of alternate colors used in various games

check·ered \'che-kərd\ *adj* : marked by inconsistent fortune or recurring problems ⟨his ∼ past⟩

check·ers \'che-kərz\ *n* : a checkerboard game for 2 players each with 12 pieces

check in *vb* : to report one's presence or arrival (as at a hotel)

check·list \'chek-ˌlist\ *n* : a list of things to be checked or done; *also* : a comprehensive list

check·mate \'chek-ˌmāt\ *vb* [ME *chekmaten*, fr. *chekmate*, interj. used to announce checkmate, fr. AF *eschec mat*, fr. Ar *shāh māt*, fr. Pers, lit., the king is left unable to escape] **1** : to thwart completely : DEFEAT, FRUSTRATE **2** : to attack (an opponent's king) in chess so that escape is impossible — **checkmate** *n*

check·off \'chek-ˌof\ *n* : the deduction of union dues from a worker's paycheck by the employer

check·out \'chek-ˌaut\ *n* **1** : the action or an instance of checking out **2** : a counter at which checking out is done **3** : the process of examining and testing something as to readiness for intended use

check out *vb* **1** : to settle one's account (as at a hotel) and leave **2** : to total or have totaled the cost of purchases in a store and to make or receive payment for them

check·point \'chek-ˌpoint\ *n* : a point at which a check is performed

check·room \-ˌrüm, -ˌrum\ *n* : a room at which baggage, parcels, or clothing is left for safekeeping

checks and balances *n pl* : a system allowing each branch of a government to restrict the actions of another branch (as by a veto)

check·up \'chek-ˌəp\ *n* : EXAMINATION; *esp* : a general physical examination

ched·dar \'che-dər\ *n, often cap* : a hard mild to sharp white or yellow cheese of smooth texture

cheek \'chēk\ *n* **1** : the fleshy side part of the face **2** : IMPUDENCE, BOLDNESS, AUDACITY **3** : BUTTOCK 1 — **cheeked** \'chēkt\ *adj*

cheek·bone \'chēk-ˌbōn\ *n* : the bone or bony ridge below the eye

cheeky \'chē-kē\ *adj* **cheek·i·er; -est** : IMPUDENT, SAUCY — **cheek·i·ly** \-kə-lē\ *adv* — **cheek·i·ness** \-kē-nəs\ *n*

cheep \'chēp\ *vb* : to utter faint shrill sounds : PEEP — **cheep** *n*

¹cheer \'chir\ *n* [ME *chere* face, cheer, fr. AF, face, fr. ML *cara*, prob. fr. Gk *kara* head, face] **1** : state of mind or heart : SPIRIT **2** : ANIMATION, GAIETY **3** : hospitable entertainment : WELCOME **4** : food and drink for a feast **5** : something that gladdens **6** : a shout of applause or encouragement

²cheer *vb* **1** : to give hope or courage to : COMFORT **2** : to make glad **3** : to urge on esp. by shouts **4** : to applaud with shouts **5** : to grow or be cheerful — usu. used with *up* — **cheer·er** *n*

cheer·ful \'chir-fəl\ *adj* **1** : having or showing good spirits **2** : conducive to good spirits : pleasant and bright — **cheer·ful·ly** *adv* — **cheer·ful·ness** *n*

cheer·lead·er \'chir-ˌlē-dər\ *n* : a person who directs organized cheering esp. at a sports event — **cheer·lead·ing** *n*

cheer·less \'chir-ləs\ *adj* : BLEAK, DISPIRITING ⟨a ∼ office⟩ — **cheer·less·ly** *adv* — **cheer·less·ness** *n*

cheery \'chir-ē\ *adj* **cheer·i·er; -est** : CHEERFUL ⟨∼ music⟩ — **cheer·i·ly** \-ə-lē\ *adv* — **cheer·i·ness** \-ē-nəs\ *n*

cheese \'chēz\ *n* : the curd of milk usu. pressed into cakes and cured for use as food

cheese·burg·er \-ˌbər-gər\ *n* : a hamburger topped with cheese

cheese·cake \-ˌkāk\ *n* **1** : a dessert consisting of a creamy filling usu. containing cheese baked in a shell **2** : photographs of shapely scantily clad women

cheese·cloth \-ˌkloth\ *n* : a lightweight coarse cotton gauze

cheese·par·ing \-ˌper-iŋ\ *n* : miserly economizing — **cheeseparing** *adj*

cheese·steak \-ˌstāk\ *n* : a sandwich of thinly sliced beef topped with melted cheese

cheesy \'chē-zē\ *adj* **chees·i·er; -est** **1** : resembling, suggesting, or containing cheese **2** : CHEAP 3 ⟨∼ motels⟩

chee·tah \'chē-tə\ *n* [Hindi *cītā* leopard, fr. Skt *citraka*, fr. *citra* bright, variegated] : a large long-legged swift-moving spotted cat of Africa and southwestern Asia

chef \'shef\ *n* : COOK; *esp* : one who manages a kitchen (as of a restaurant)

chef d'oeu·vre \shā-'dœvrᵊ\ *n, pl* **chefs d'oeuvre** *same*\ : MASTERPIECE

chem *abbr* chemical; chemist; chemistry

¹chem·i·cal \'ke-mi-kəl\ *adj* **1** : of, relating to, used in, or produced by chemistry ⟨∼ reactions⟩ **2** : acting or operated or produced by chemicals — **chem·i·cal·ly** \-k(ə-)lē\ *adv*

²chemical *n* **1** : a substance obtained by a chemical process or producing a chemical effect **2** : DRUG

chemical engineering *n* : engineering dealing with the industrial application of chemistry — **chemical engineer** *n*

chemical warfare *n* : warfare using incendiary mixtures, smokes, or irritant, burning, or asphyxiating gases

chemical weapon *n* : a weapon used in chemical warfare

che·mise \shə-'mēz\ *n* **1** : a woman's one-piece undergarment **2** : a loose straight-hanging dress

chem·ist \'ke-mist\ *n* **1** : one trained in chemistry **2** *Brit* : PHARMACIST

chem·is·try \'ke-mə-strē\ *n, pl* **-tries** **1** : the science that deals with the composition, structure, and properties of substances and of the changes they undergo **2** : chemical composition or properties ⟨the ∼ of gasoline⟩ **3** : a strong mutual attraction; *also* : harmonious interaction among people (as on a team)

che·mo \'kē-mō\ *n* : CHEMOTHERAPY

che·mo·ther·a·py \,kē-mō-'ther-ə-pē\ *n* : the use of chemicals in the treatment or control of disease — che·mo·ther·a·peu·tic \-,ther-ə-'pyü-tik\ *adj*

che·nille \shə-'nēl\ *n* [F, lit., caterpillar, fr. OF, fr. L *canicula,* dim. of *canis* dog] : a fabric with a deep fuzzy pile often used for bedspreads and rugs

cheque *chiefly Brit var of* ¹CHECK 7

che·quer *chiefly Brit var of* CHECKER

cher·ish \'cher-ish\ *vb* 1 : to hold dear : treat with care and affection 2 : to keep deeply in mind ⟨~ a memory⟩ — cher·ish·able *adj* — cher·ish·er *n*

Cher·o·kee \'cher-ə-(,)kē\ *n, pl* Cherokee *or* Cherokees : a member of an American Indian people orig. of Tennessee and No. Carolina; *also* : their language

che·root \shə-'rüt\ *n* : a cigar cut square at both ends

cher·ry \'cher-ē\ *n, pl* cherries [ME *chery,* fr. AF *cherise, cirice* (taken as a plural), fr. LL *ceresia,* fr. L *cerasus* cherry tree, fr. Gk *kerasos*] 1 : the small fleshy pale yellow to deep blackish red fruit of a tree related to the roses; *also* : the tree or its wood 2 : a moderate red

chert \'chərt, 'chat\ *n* : a rock resembling flint and consisting essentially of fine crystalline quartz and fibrous chalcedony — cherty *adj*

cher·ub \'cher-əb\ *n* 1 *pl* cher·u·bim \'cher-ə-,bim\ : an angel of the 2d highest rank 2 *pl* cherubs : a chubby rosy person — che·ru·bic \chə-'rü-bik\ *adj*

chess \'ches\ *n* : a game for 2 played on a chessboard with each player having 16 pieces — chess·man \-,man, -mən\ *n*

chess·board \'ches-,bȯrd\ *n* : a checkerboard used in the game of chess

chest \'chest\ *n* 1 : a box, case, or boxlike receptacle for storage or shipping 2 : the part of the body enclosed by the ribs and sternum — chest·ed \'ches-təd\ *adj* — chest·ful \'chest-,fül\ *n*

ches·ter·field \'ches-tər-,fēld\ *n* : an overcoat with a velvet collar

chest·nut \'ches-(,)nət\ *n* 1 : the edible nut of any of a genus of trees related to the beeches and oaks; *also* : this tree or its wood 2 : a grayish to reddish brown 3 : an old joke or story

chet·rum \'che-trəm\ *n, pl* chetrums *or* chetrum — see *ngultrum* at MONEY table

che·val glass \shə-'val-\ *n* : a full-length mirror that may be tilted in a frame

che·va·lier \,she-və-'lir, shə-'val-,yā\ *n* : a member of one of various orders of knighthood or of merit

chev·i·ot \'she-vē-ət\ *n, often cap* 1 : a twilled fabric with a rough nap 2 : a sturdy soft-finished cotton fabric

chev·ron \'she-vrən\ *n* : a sleeve badge of one or more V-shaped or inverted V-shaped stripes worn to indicate rank or service (as in the armed forces)

¹chew \'chü\ *vb* : to crush or grind with the teeth — chew·able *adj* — chew·er *n* — chewy \'chü-ē\ *adj* — chew on : to think about : PONDER ⟨*chew on* the proposals⟩ — chew the fat : to make conversation : CHAT

²chew *n* 1 : an act of chewing 2 : something for chewing

Chey·enne \shī-'an, -'en\ *n, pl* Cheyenne *or* Cheyennes [AmerF, fr. Dakota *šahíyena*] : a member of an American Indian people of the western plains of the U.S.; *also* : their language

chg *abbr* 1 change 2 charge

chi \'kī\ *n* : the 22d letter of the Greek alphabet — X or χ

Chi·an·ti \kē-'än-tē, -'an-\ *n* : a dry usu. red wine

chiar·oscu·ro \kē-,är-ə-'skür-ō, -'skyùr-\ *n, pl* -ros [It, fr. *chiaro* clear, light + *oscuro* obscure, dark] 1 : pictorial representation in terms of light and shade without regard to color 2 : the arrangement or treatment of light and dark parts in a pictorial work of art

¹chic \'shēk\ *n* : STYLISHNESS

²chic *adj* : cleverly stylish : SMART; *also* : currently fashionable

Chi·ca·na \chi-'kä-nə *also* shi-\ *n* : an American woman or girl of Mexican descent — Chicana *adj*

chi·cane \shi-'kān\ *n* : CHICANERY

chi·ca·nery \-'kā-nə-rē\ *n, pl* -ner·ies : TRICKERY, DECEPTION

Chi·ca·no \chi-'kä-nō\ *n, pl* -nos : a usu. male American of Mexican descent — Chicano *adj*

chi·chi \'shē-(,)shē, 'chē-(,)chē\ *adj* [F] 1 : SHOWY, FRILLY 2 : ARTY, PRECIOUS 3 : CHIC — chichi *n*

chick \'chik\ *n* 1 : a young chicken; *also* : a young bird 2 *slang* : GIRL, WOMAN

chick·a·dee \'chi-kə-(,)dē\ *n* : any of several small grayish American birds with black or brown caps

Chick·a·saw \'chi-kə-,sȯ\ *n, pl* Chickasaw *or* Chickasaws : a member of an American Indian people of Mississippi and Alabama

¹chick·en \'chi-kən\ *n* 1 : a common domestic fowl esp. when young; *also* : its flesh used as food 2 : COWARD

²chicken *adj* 1 : COWARDLY 2 *slang* : insistent on petty esp. military discipline

chicken feed *n, slang* : an insignificant sum of money

chick·en·heart·ed \,chi-kən-'här-təd\ *adj* : TIMID, COWARDLY

chicken out *vb* : to lose one's courage

chicken pox *n* : an acute contagious viral disease esp. of children characterized by a low fever and blisters

chicken wire *n* : a light wire netting of hexagonal mesh

chick·pea \'chik-,pē\ *n* : an Asian herb of the legume family cultivated for its short pods with one or two edible seeds; *also* : its seed

chick·weed \'chik-,wēd\ *n* : any of several low-growing small-leaved weeds related to the pinks

chi·cle \'chi-kəl\ *n* : a gum from the latex of a tropical tree used as the chief ingredient of chewing gum

chic·o·ry \'chi-kə-rē\ *n, pl* -ries : a usu. blue-flowered herb related to the daisies and grown for its root and for use in salads; *also* : its dried ground root used to flavor or adulterate coffee

chide \'chīd\ *vb* chid \'chid\ *or* chid·ed \'chī-dəd\; chid *or* chid·den \'chid-ᵊn\ *or* chided; chid·ing : to speak disapprovingly to ✦ *Synonyms* REPROACH, REPROVE, REPRIMAND, ADMONISH, SCOLD, REBUKE

¹chief \'chēf\ *adj* 1 : highest in rank 2 : most important ✦ *Synonyms* PRINCIPAL, MAIN, LEADING, MAJOR — chief·ly *adv*

²chief *n* 1 : the leader of a body or organization : HEAD 2 : the principal or most valuable part — chief·dom *n*

chief master sergeant *n* : a noncommissioned officer of the highest rank in the air force

chief of staff 1 : the ranking officer of a staff in the armed forces 2 : the ranking office of the army or air force

chief of state : the formal head of a national state as distinguished from the head of the government

chief petty officer *n* : an enlisted man in the navy ranking next below a senior chief petty officer

chief·tain \'chēf-tən\ *n* : a chief esp. of a band, tribe, or clan — chief·tain·cy \-sē\ *n* — chief·tain·ship *n*

chief warrant officer *n* : a warrant officer of senior rank

chif·fon \shi-'fän, 'shi-,\ *n* [F, lit., rag, fr. *chiffe* old rag] : a sheer fabric esp. of silk

chif·fo·nier \,shi-fə-'nir\ *n* : a high narrow chest of drawers

chig·ger \'chi-gər\ *n* : a bloodsucking larval mite that causes intense itching

chi·gnon \'shēn-,yän\ *n* [F, fr. MF *chaignon* chain, collar, nape] : a knot of hair worn at the back of the head

Chi·hua·hua \chə-'wä-,wä\ *n* : any of a breed of very small large-eared dogs that originated in Mexico

Chihuahua

chil·blain \'chil-,blān\ *n* : a sore or inflamed swelling (as on the feet or hands) caused by exposure to cold

child \'chī(-ə)ld\ *n, pl* **chil·dren** \'chil-drən\ **1** : an unborn or recently born person **2** : a young person between the periods of infancy and youth **3** : a male or female offspring : SON, DAUGHTER **4** : one strongly influenced by another or by a place or state of affairs — **child·ish** *adj* — **child·ish·ly** *adv* — **child·ish·ness** *n* — **child·less** *adj* — **child·less·ness** *n* — **child·like** *adj*

child·bear·ing \'chīld-,ber-iŋ\ *n* : CHILDBIRTH — **childbearing** *adj*

child·birth \-,bərth\ *n* : the act or process of giving birth to offspring

child·hood \-,hůd\ *n* : the state or time of being a child

¹child·proof \-,prüf\ *adj* **1** : made to prevent opening or use by children ⟨~ lighters⟩ **2** : made safe for children

²childproof *vb* : to make childproof ⟨~ a house⟩

child's play *n* : a simple task or act

chili *also* **chile** *or* **chil·li** \'chil-lē\ *n, pl* **chil·ies** *also* **chil·es** *or* **chilis** *or* **chil·lies** **1** : any of various pungent peppers related to the tomato **2** : a thick sauce of meat and chilies **3** : CHILI CON CARNE

chili con car·ne \,chi-lē-kän-'kär-nē\ *n* [AmerSp *chile con carne* chili with meat] : a spiced stew of ground beef and chilies or chili powder usu. with beans

chili powder *n* : a seasoning made of ground chilies and other spices

chili sauce *n* : a spiced tomato sauce usu. made with red and green peppers

¹chill \'chil\ *n* **1** : a feeling of coldness accompanied by shivering **2** : moderate coldness **3** : a check to enthusiasm or warmth of feeling

²chill *adj* **1** : moderately cold **2** : COLD, RAW **3** : DISTANT, FORMAL ⟨a ~ reception⟩ **4** : DEPRESSING, DISPIRITING

³chill *vb* **1** : to make or become cold or chilly **2** : to make cool esp. without freezing **3** : RELAX — **chill·er** *n*

chill·ing \'chi-liŋ\ *adj* : gravely disturbing or frightening ⟨a ~ scene⟩

chilly \'chi-lē\ *adj* **chill·i·er; -est** **1** : noticeably cold **2** : unpleasantly affected by cold **3** : lacking warmth of feeling ⟨a ~ reception⟩ — **chill·i·ness** *n*

chimaera *chiefly Brit var of* CHIMERA

¹chime \'chīm\ *n* **1** : a set of bells musically tuned **2** : the sound of a set of bells — usu. used in pl. **3** : a musical sound suggesting bells

²chime *vb* **chimed; chim·ing** **1** : to make bell-like sounds **2** : to indicate (as the time of day) by chiming **3** : to be or act in accord : be in harmony

chime in *vb* : to break into or join in a conversation

chi·me·ra \kī-'mir-ə, kə-\ *n* [L *chimaera*, fr. Gk *chimaira* she-goat, chimera] **1** : an imaginary monster made up of incongruous parts **2** : an illusion or fabrication of the mind; *esp* : an impossible dream

chi·me·ri·cal \kī-'mer-i-kəl\ *also* **chi·me·ric** \-ik\ *adj* **1** : FANTASTIC, IMAGINARY **2** : inclined to fantastic schemes

chim·ney \'chim-nē\ *n, pl* **chimneys** **1** : a vertical structure extending above the roof of a building for carrying off smoke **2** : a glass tube around a lamp flame

chimp \'chimp\ *n* : CHIMPANZEE

chim·pan·zee \,chim-,pan-'zē, chim-'pan-zē\ *n* : an African ape related to the much larger gorilla

¹chin \'chin\ *n* : the part of the face below the lower lip including the prominence of the lower jaw — **chin·less** *adj*

²chin *vb* **chinned; chin·ning** : to raise (oneself) while hanging by the hands until the chin is level with the support

chi·na \'chī-nə\ *n* : porcelain ware; *also* : domestic pottery in general

Chi·na·town \-,taůn\ *n* : the Chinese quarter of a city

chinch bug \'chinch-\ *n* : a small black and white bug destructive to cereal grasses

chin·chil·la \chin-'chi-lə\ *n* **1** : either of two small So. American rodents with soft pearl-gray fur; *also* : this fur **2** : a heavy long-napped woolen cloth

chine \'chīn\ *n* : BACKBONE, SPINE; *also* : a cut of meat including all or part of the backbone

Chi·nese \chī-'nēz, -'nēs\ *n, pl* **Chinese** **1** : a native or inhabitant of China **2** : any of a group of related languages of China — **Chinese** *adj*

Chinese cabbage *n* **1** : BOK CHOY **2** : an Asian garden plant related to the cabbage and widely grown in the U.S. for its tight elongate cylindrical heads of pale green to cream-colored leaves

Chinese checkers *n* : a game in which each player in turn transfers a set of marbles from a home point to the opposite point of a pitted 6-pointed star

Chinese gooseberry *n* : a subtropical vine that bears kiwifruit; *also* : KIWIFRUIT

Chinese lantern *n* : a collapsible translucent cover for a light

¹chink \'chiŋk\ *n* : a small crack or fissure

²chink *vb* : to fill the chinks of : stop up

³chink *n* : a slight sharp metallic sound

⁴chink *vb* : to make a slight sharp metallic sound

chi·no \'chē-nō\ *n, pl* **chinos** **1** : a usu. khaki cotton twill **2** *pl* : an article of clothing made of chino

Chi·nook \shə-'nůk, chə-'nůk\ *n, pl* **Chinook** *or* **Chinooks** : a member of an American Indian people of Oregon

chintz \'chints\ *n* : a usu. glazed printed cotton cloth

chintzy \'chint-sē\ *adj* **chintz·i·er; -est** **1** : decorated with or as if with chintz **2** : GAUDY, CHEAP **3** : STINGY — **chintz·i·ness** *n*

chin·up \'chin-,əp\ *n* : the act of chinning oneself

¹chip \'chip\ *n* **1** : a small usu. thin and flat piece (as of wood) cut or broken off **2** : a thin crisp morsel of food **3** : a counter used in games (as poker) **4** *pl, slang* : MONEY **5** : a flaw left after a chip is broken off **6** : INTEGRATED CIRCUIT **7** : a very small slice of silicon containing electronic circuits — **chip off the old block** : a child that resembles his or her parent

²chip *vb* **chipped; chip·ping** **1** : to cut or break chips from **2** : to break off in small pieces at the edges **3** : to play a chip shot

chip in *vb* : CONTRIBUTE

chip·munk \'chip-,məŋk\ *n* [earlier *chitmunk*, prob. fr. Ojibwa *ačitamoˀnˀ?* red squirrel] : any of a genus of small striped No. American and Asian rodents closely related to the squirrels and marmots

chi·pot·le \chə-'pōt-lā\ *n* : a smoked and usu. dried jalapeño pepper

chipped beef \'chipt-\ *n* : smoked dried beef sliced thin

¹chip·per \'chi-pər\ *n* : one that chips

²chipper *adj* : LIVELY, CHEERFUL

Chip·pe·wa \'chi-pə-,wȯ, -,wä, -,wā, -wə\ *n, pl* **Chippewa** *or* **Chippewas** : OJIBWA

chip shot *n* : a short usu. low shot to the green in golf

chi·rog·ra·phy \kī-'rä-grə-fē\ *n* : HANDWRITING, PENMANSHIP — **chi·ro·graph·ic** \,kī-rə-'gra-fik\ *adj*

chi·rop·o·dy \kə-'rä-pə-dē, shə-\ *n* : PODIATRY — **chi·rop·o·dist** \-dist\ *n*

chi·ro·prac·tic \'kī-rə-,prak-tik\ *n* : a system of therapy based esp. on manipulation of body structures — **chi·ro·prac·tor** \-tər\ *n*

chirp \'chərp\ *n* : a short sharp sound characteristic of a small bird or cricket — **chirp** *vb* — **chirpy** \'chər-pē\ *adj*

¹chis·el \'chi-zəl\ *n* : a metal tool with a sharpened edge at one end used to chip, carve, or cut into a solid material (as wood or stone)

²chisel *vb* **-eled** *or* **-elled; -el·ing** *or* **-el·ling** **1** : to work with or as if with a chisel **2** : to obtain by shrewd often unfair methods; *also* : CHEAT — **chis·el·er** *n*

¹chit \'chit\ *n* [ME *chitte* kitten, cub] **1** : CHILD **2** : a pert young woman

²chit *n* [Hindi *ciṭṭhī* letter, note] : a signed voucher for a small debt

chit·chat \'chit-,chat\ *n* : casual or trifling conversation — **chitchat** *vb*

chi·tin \'kī-t³n\ *n* : a sugar polymer that forms part of the hard outer integument esp. of insects — **chi·tin·ous** *adj*

chit·ter·lings *or* **chit·lins** \'chit-lənz\ *n pl* : the intestines of hogs esp. when prepared as food

chi·val·ric \shə-'val-rik\ *adj* : relating to chivalry : CHIVALROUS

chiv·al·rous \'shi-vəl-rəs\ *adj* **1** : of or relating to chivalry **2** : marked by honor, courtesy, and generosity **3** : marked by especial courtesy to women — **chiv·al·rous·ly** *adv* — **chiv·al·rous·ness** *n*

chiv·al·ry \'shi-vəl-rē\ *n, pl* **-ries** **1** : mounted men-at-arms **2** : the system or practices of knighthood **3** : the spirit or character of the ideal knight

chive \'chīv\ *n* : an herb related to the onion that has slender leaves used for flavoring; *also* : its leaves

chla·myd·ia \klə-'mi-dē-ə\ *n, pl* **-i·ae** \-dē-,ē\ **1** : any of a genus of bacteria that cause various diseases of the eye and urogenital tract **2** : a disease or infection caused by chlamydiae

chlo·ral hydrate \'klȯr-əl-\ *n* : a white crystalline compound used as a hypnotic and sedative

chlor·dane \'klȯr-,dān\ *n* : a highly chlorinated persistent insecticide

chlo·ride \'klȯr-,īd\ *n* : a compound of chlorine with another element or group

chlo·ri·nate \'klȯr-ə-,nāt\ *vb* **-nat·ed; -nat·ing** : to treat or combine with chlorine or a chlorine compound — **chlo·ri·na·tion** \,klȯr-ə-'nā-shən\ *n* — **chlo·ri·na·tor** \'klȯr-ə-,nā-tər\ *n*

chlo·rine \'klȯr-,ēn\ *n* : a nonmetallic chemical element that is found alone as a strong-smelling greenish-yellow irritating gas and is used as a bleach, oxidizing agent, and disinfectant

chlorine monoxide *n* : a reactive radical that plays a major role in stratospheric ozone depletion

chlo·rite \'klȯr-,īt\ *n* : a usu. green mineral found with and resembling mica

chlo·ro·flu·o·ro·car·bon \,klȯr-ə-'flȯr-ə-,kär-bən, -'flȯr-\ *n* : any of several gaseous compounds that contain carbon, chlorine, fluorine, and sometimes hydrogen and are used esp. as solvents, refrigerants, and aerosol propellants

¹chlo·ro·form \'klȯr-ə-,fȯrm\ *n* : a colorless heavy fluid with etherlike odor used as a solvent

²chloroform *vb* : to treat with chloroform to produce anesthesia or death

chlo·ro·phyll \-,fil\ *n* : the green coloring matter of plants that functions in photosynthesis

chlo·ro·plast \'klȯr-ə-,plast\ *n* : a cytoplasmic organelle that contains chlorophyll and is the site of photosynthesis

chm *abbr* chairman

chock \'chäk\ *n* : a wedge for steadying something or for blocking the movement of a wheel — **chock** *vb*

chock·a·block \'chä-kə-,bläk\ *adj* : very full : CROWDED

chock–full \'chək-'fu̇l, 'chäk-\ *adj* : full to the limit : CRAMMED

choc·o·late \'chä-k(ə-)lət, 'chȯ-\ *n* [Sp, fr. Nahuatl *chocolātl*] **1** : a food prepared from ground roasted cacao beans; *also* : a drink prepared from this **2** : a candy made of or with a coating of chocolate **3** : a dark brown color — **choc·o·laty** *or* **choc·o·lat·ey** \-k(ə-)lə-tē\ *adj*

Choc·taw \'chäk-,tȯ\ *n, pl* **Choctaw** *or* **Choctaws** : a member of an American Indian people of Mississippi, Alabama, and Louisiana; *also* : their language

¹choice \'chȯis\ *n* **1** : the act of choosing : SELECTION **2** : the power or opportunity of choosing : OPTION **3** : the best part **4** : a person or thing selected **5** : a variety offered for selection

²choice *adj* **choic·er; choic·est** **1** : worthy of being chosen **2** : selected with care **3** : of high quality

choir \'kwī-(ə-)r\ *n* **1** : an organized company of singers (as in a church service) **2** : the part of a church occupied by the singers or by the clergy

choir·boy \'kwī-(ə)r-,bȯi\ *n* : a boy member of a choir

choir·mas·ter \-,mas-tər\ *n* : the director of a choir (as in a church)

¹choke \'chōk\ *vb* **choked; chok·ing** **1** : to hinder breathing (as by obstructing the trachea) : STRANGLE **2** : to check the growth or action of **3** : CLOG, OBSTRUCT **4** : to enrich the fuel mixture of (a motor) by restricting the carburetor air intake **5** : to perform badly in a critical situation

²choke *n* **1** : the act of choking **2** : a narrowing in size toward the muzzle in the bore of a gun **3** : a valve for choking a gasoline engine

choke hold *n* **1** : a hold that involves strong choking pressure **2** : absolute control

chok·er \'chō-kər\ *n* : something (as a necklace) worn tightly around the neck

cho·ler \'kä-lər, 'kō-\ *n* : a tendency toward anger : IRASCIBILITY

chol·era \'kä-lə-rə\ *n* : any of several bacterial diseases usu. marked by severe vomiting and dysentery

chol·er·ic \'kä-lə-rik, kə-'ler-ik\ *adj* **1** : IRASCIBLE **2** : ANGRY, IRATE

cho·les·ter·ol \kə-'les-tə-,rȯl\ *n* : a physiologically important waxy steroid alcohol found in animal tissues and in high concentrations implicated as a cause of arteriosclerosis

chomp \'chämp, 'chȯmp\ *vb* : to chew or bite on something heavily

chon \'chän\ *n, pl* **chon** — see **won** at MONEY table

choose \'chüz\ *vb* **chose** \'chōz\; **cho·sen** \'chō-z³n\; **choos·ing** \'chü-ziŋ\ **1** : to select esp. after consideration **2** : DECIDE **3** : to have a preference for — **chooser** *n*

choosy *or* **choos·ey** \'chü-zē\ *adj* **choos·i·er; -est** : very particular in making choices

¹chop \'chäp\ *vb* **chopped; chop·ping** **1** : to cut by repeated blows **2** : to cut into small pieces : MINCE **3** : to strike (a ball) with a short quick downward stroke

²chop *n* **1** : a sharp downward blow or stroke **2** : a small cut of meat often including part of a rib **3** : a short abrupt motion (as of a wave)

³chop *n* **1** : an official seal or stamp **2** : a mark on goods to indicate quality or kind; *also* : QUALITY, GRADE

chop·house \'chäp-,haus\ *n* : RESTAURANT

chop·per \'chä-pər\ *n* **1** : one that chops **2** *pl, slang* : TEETH **3** : HELICOPTER

chop·pi·ness \'chä-pē-nəs\ *n* : the quality or state of being choppy

¹chop·py \'chä-pē\ *adj* **chop·pi·er; -est** **1** : rough with small waves **2** : JERKY, DISCONNECTED — **chop·pi·ly** \-pə-lē\ *adv*

²choppy *adj* **chop·pi·er; -est** : CHANGEABLE, VARIABLE ⟨a ~ wind⟩

chops \'chäps\ *n pl* **1** : the fleshy covering of the jaws **2** : expertise in a particular field or activity ⟨acting ~⟩

chop·stick \'chäp-,stik\ *n* : one of a pair of sticks used chiefly in Asian countries for lifting food to the mouth

chop su·ey \chäp-'sü-ē\ *n, pl* **chop sueys** : a dish made of vegetables (as bean sprouts, bamboo shoots, water chestnuts, onions, mushrooms) and meat or fish and served with rice

cho·ral \'kȯr-əl\ *adj* : of, relating to, or sung by a choir or chorus or in chorus — **cho·ral·ly** *adv*

cho·rale \kə-'ral, -'räl\ *n* **1** : a hymn or psalm sung in church; *also* : a harmonization of a traditional melody **2** : CHORUS, CHOIR

¹chord \'kȯrd\ *n* [alter. of ME *cord*, short for *accord*] : three or more musical tones sounded simultaneously

²chord *n* **1** : CORD 2 **2** : a straight line joining two points on a curve

chore \'chȯr\ *n* [ME *char* turn, piece of work, fr. OE *chierr*] **1** *pl* : the daily light work of a household or farm **2** : a routine task or job **3** : a difficult or disagreeable task

cho·rea \kə-'rē-ə\ *n* : any of various nervous disorders marked by spasmodic uncontrolled movements

cho·re·og·ra·phy \,kȯr-ē-'ä-grə-fē\ *n, pl* **-phies** : the art of composing and arranging dances and esp. ballets — **cho·reo·graph** \'kȯr-ē-ə-,graf\ *vb* — **cho·re·og·ra·pher** \,kȯr-ē-'ä-grə-fər\ *n* — **cho·reo·graph·ic** \,kȯr-ē-ə-'gra-fik\ *adj* — **cho·reo·graph·i·cal·ly** \-fi-k(ə-)lē\ *adv*

cho·ris·ter \'kȯr-ə-stər\ *n* : a singer in a choir

chor·tle \'chȯr-t³l\ *vb* **chor·tled; chor·tling** : to laugh or chuckle esp. in satisfaction or exultation — **chortle** *n*

¹cho·rus \'kȯr-əs\ *n* **1** : an organized company of singers : CHOIR **2** : a group of dancers and singers (as in a musical comedy) **3** : a part of a song repeated at intervals **4** : a composition to be sung by a chorus; *also* : group singing **5** : sounds uttered by a number of persons or animals together ⟨a ~ of boos⟩

²chorus *vb* : to sing or utter in chorus

chose *past of* CHOOSE

cho·sen \'chō-z³n\ *adj* : selected or marked for special favor or privilege

chou·croute \shü-'krüt\ *n* **1** : SAUERKRAUT **2** *or* **choucroute gar·nie** \-gär-'nē\ : sauerkraut cooked and served with meat

¹chow \'chau̇\ *n* : FOOD

²chow *vb* : EAT — often used with *down*

³chow *n* : CHOW CHOW

chow·chow \'chau̇-,chau̇\ *n* : chopped mixed pickles in mustard sauce

chow chow \'chaù-ˌchaù\ *n* : any of a breed of thick-coated muscular dogs of Chinese origin with a blue-black tongue and a short tail curled close to the back

chow·der \'chaù-dər\ *n* : a soup or stew made from seafood or vegetables and containing milk or tomatoes

chow mein \'chaù-'mān\ *n* : a seasoned stew of shredded or diced meat, mushrooms, and vegetables that is usu. served with fried noodles

chrism \'kri-zəm\ *n* : consecrated oil used esp. in baptism, confirmation, and ordination

Christ \'krīst\ *n* [ME *Crist*, fr. OE, fr. L *Christus*, fr. Gk *Christos*, lit., anointed] : Jesus esp. as the Messiah — **Christ·like** *adj* — **Christ·ly** *adj*

chris·ten \'kri-sᵊn\ *vb* 1 : BAPTIZE 2 : to name at baptism 3 : to name or dedicate (as a ship) by a ceremony suggestive of baptism — **chris·ten·ing** *n*

Chris·ten·dom \'kri-sᵊn-dəm\ *n* 1 : CHRISTIANITY 2 : the part of the world in which Christianity prevails

¹Chris·tian \'kris-chən\ *n* : an adherent of Christianity

²Christian *adj* 1 : of or relating to Christianity 2 : based on or conforming with Christianity 3 : of or relating to a Christian 4 : professing Christianity

Chris·ti·an·i·ty \ˌkris-chē-'a-nə-tē\ *n* : the religion derived from Jesus Christ, based on the Bible as sacred scripture, and professed by Christians

Chris·tian·ize \'kris-chə-ˌnīz\ *vb* **-ized; -iz·ing** : to make Christian

Christian name *n* : GIVEN NAME

Christian Science *n* : a religion and system of healing founded by Mary Baker Eddy and taught by the Church of Christ, Scientist — **Christian Scientist** *n*

chris·tie *or* **chris·ty** \'kris-tē\ *n, pl* **christies** : a skiing turn made by shifting body weight forward and skidding into a turn with parallel skis

Christ·mas \'kris-məs\ *n* : December 25 celebrated as a church festival in commemoration of the birth of Christ and observed as a legal holiday

Christmas club *n* : a savings account in which regular deposits are made to provide money for Christmas shopping

Christ·mas·tide \'kris-məs-ˌtīd\ *n* : the season of Christmas

chro·mat·ic \krō-'ma-tik\ *adj* 1 : of or relating to color 2 : proceeding by half steps of the musical scale — **chro·mat·i·cism** \-tə-ˌsi-zəm\ *n*

chro·mato·graph \krō-'ma-tə-ˌgraf\ *n* : an instrument used in chromatography

chro·ma·tog·ra·phy \ˌkrō-mə-'tä-grə-fē\ *n* : the separation of a complex mixture into its component compounds as a result of the different rates at which the compounds travel through or over a stationary substance due to differing affinities for the substance — **chro·mato·graph·ic** \krō-ˌma-tə-'gra-fik\ *adj* — **chro·mato·graph·i·cal·ly** \-fi-k(ə-)lē\ *adv*

chrome \'krōm\ *n* 1 : CHROMIUM 2 : a chromium pigment 3 : something plated with an alloy of chromium

chro·mi·um \'krō-mē-əm\ *n* : a bluish white metallic element used esp. in alloys and chrome plating

chro·mo·some \'krō-mə-ˌsōm, -ˌzōm\ *n* [G *Chromosom*, fr. Gk *chrōma* color, pigment + *sōma* body] : any of the rod-shaped or threadlike DNA-containing structures of cellular organisms that contain most or all of the genes of the organism — **chro·mo·som·al** \ˌkrō-mə-'sō-məl, -'zō-\ *adj*

chro·mo·sphere \'krō-mə-ˌsfir\ *n* : the lower part of a star's atmosphere

chron *abbr* 1 chronicle 2 chronological; chronology

Chron *abbr* Chronicles

chron·ic \'krä-nik\ *adj* : marked by long duration or frequent recurrence ⟨a ~ disease⟩; *also* : HABITUAL ⟨a ~ grumbler⟩ — **chron·i·cal·ly** \-ni-k(ə-)lē\ *adv*

chronic fatigue syndrome *n* : a disorder of unknown cause that is characterized by persistent profound fatigue

¹chron·i·cle \'krä-ni-kəl\ *n* : HISTORY, NARRATIVE

²chronicle *vb* **-cled; -cling** : to record in or as if in a chronicle — **chron·i·cler** *n*

Chronicles *n* — see BIBLE table

chro·no·graph \'krä-nə-ˌgraf\ *n* : an instrument for measuring and recording time intervals with accuracy — **chro·no·graph·ic** \ˌkrä-nə-'gra-fik\ *adj* — **chro·nog·ra·phy** \krə-'nä-grə-fē\ *n*

chro·nol·o·gy \krə-'nä-lə-jē\ *n, pl* **-gies** 1 : the science that deals with measuring time and dating events 2 : a chronological list or table 3 : arrangement of events in the order of their occurrence — **chron·o·log·i·cal** \ˌkrän-ᵊl-'ä-ji-kəl\ *adj* — **chron·o·log·i·cal·ly** \-k(ə-)lē\ *adv* — **chro·nol·o·gist** \krə-'nä-lə-jist\ *n*

chro·nom·e·ter \krə-'nä-mə-tər\ *n* : a very accurate timepiece

chrys·a·lid \'kri-sə-ləd\ *n* : CHRYSALIS

chrys·a·lis \'kri-sə-ləs\ *n, pl* **chry·sal·i·des** \kri-'sa-lə-ˌdēz\ *or* **chrys·a·lis·es** : an insect pupa in a firm case without a cocoon

chry·san·the·mum \kri-'san-thə-məm\ *n* [L, fr. Gk *chrysanthemon*, fr. *chrysos* gold + *anthemon* flower] : any of various plants related to the daisies including some grown for their showy brightly colored flowers or for medicinal products or insecticides; *also* : a flower of a chrysanthemum

chub \'chəb\ *n, pl* **chub** *or* **chubs** : any of various small freshwater fishes related to the carp

chub·by \'chə-bē\ *adj* **chub·bi·er; -est** : PLUMP ⟨a ~ child⟩ — **chub·bi·ness** *n*

¹chuck \'chək\ *vb* 1 : to give a pat or tap 2 : TOSS 3 : DISCARD; *also* : EJECT 4 : to have done with ⟨~ed his job⟩

²chuck *n* 1 : a light pat under the chin 2 : TOSS

³chuck *n* 1 : a cut of beef including most of the neck and the parts around the shoulder blade and the first three ribs 2 : a device for holding work or a tool in a machine (as a lathe)

chuck·hole \'chək-ˌhōl\ *n* : POTHOLE

chuck·le \'chə-kəl\ *vb* **chuck·led; chuck·ling** : to laugh in a quiet hardly audible manner — **chuckle** *n*

chuck wagon *n* : a wagon equipped with a stove and food supplies

¹chug \'chəg\ *n* : a dull explosive sound made by or as if by a laboring engine

²chug *vb* **chugged; chug·ging** : to move or go with chugs

chuk·ka \'chə-kə\ *n* : a usu. ankle-length leather boot

chuk·ker \'chə-kər\ *also* **chuk·ka** \'chə-kə\ *n* : a playing period of a polo game

¹chum \'chəm\ *n* : a close friend

²chum *vb* **chummed; chum·ming** 1 : to room together 2 : to be a close friend

chum·my \'chə-mē\ *adj* **chum·mi·er; -est** : quite friendly — **chum·mi·ly** \-mə-lē\ *adv* — **chum·mi·ness** \-mē-nəs\ *n*

chump \'chəmp\ *n* : FOOL, BLOCKHEAD

chunk \'chəŋk\ *n* 1 : a short thick piece 2 : a sizable amount

chunky \'chəŋ-kē\ *adj* **chunk·i·er; -est** 1 : STOCKY 2 : containing chunks

church \'chərch\ *n* [ME *chirche*, fr. OE *cirice*, ultim. fr. LGk *kyriakon*, fr. Gk, neut. of *kyriakos* of the lord, fr. *kyrios* lord, master] 1 : a building esp. for Christian public worship 2 *often cap* : the whole body of Christians 3 : DENOMINATION 4 : CONGREGATION 5 : public divine worship

church·go·er \'chərch-ˌgō-ər\ *n* : one who habitually attends church — **church·go·ing** *adj or n*

church·less \'chərch-ləs\ *adj* : not affiliated with a church

church·man \'chərch-mən\ *n* 1 : CLERGYMAN 2 : a member of a church

church·war·den \'chərch-ˌwȯr-dᵊn\ *n* : WARDEN 5

church·yard \-ˌyärd\ *n* : a yard that belongs to a church and is often used as a burial ground

churl \'chərl\ *n* 1 : a medieval peasant 2 : RUSTIC 3 : a rude ill-bred person — **churl·ish** *adj* — **churl·ish·ly** *adv* — **churl·ish·ness** *n*

¹churn \'chərn\ *n* : a container in which milk or cream is agitated in making butter

²churn *vb* 1 : to stir in a churn; *also* : to make (butter) by such stirring 2 : to shake around violently

churn out *vb* : to produce mechanically or in large quantity

chute \'shüt\ *n* 1 : an inclined surface, trough, or passage down or through which something may pass ⟨a coal ~⟩ ⟨a mail ~⟩ 2 : PARACHUTE

chut·ney \'chət-nē\ *n, pl* **chutneys** : a thick sauce containing fruits, vinegar, sugar, and spices

chutz·pah \'hut-spə, 'kut-, -(ˌ)spä\ *n* : supreme self-confidence

DICTIONARY

CIA *abbr* Central Intelligence Agency

cía *abbr* [Sp *compañía*] company

ciao \'chaù\ *interj* — used to express greeting or farewell

ci·ca·da \sə-'kā-də\ *n* : any of a family of stout-bodied insects related to the aphids and having wide blunt heads and large transparent wings

ci·ca·trix \'si-kə-ˌtriks\ *n, pl* **ci·ca·tri·ces** \ˌsi-kə-'trī-ˌsēz\ [L] : a scar resulting from formation and contraction of fibrous tissue in a wound

ci·ce·ro·ne \ˌsi-sə-'rō-nē, ˌchē-chə-\ *n, pl* **-ni** \-(ˌ)nē\ : a guide who conducts sightseers

CID *abbr* Criminal Investigation Department

ci·der \'sī-dər\ *n* : juice pressed from fruit (as apples) and used as a beverage, vinegar, or flavoring

cie *abbr* [F *compagnie*] company

ci·gar \si-'gär\ *n* [Sp *cigarro*] : a roll of tobacco for smoking

cig·a·rette \ˌsi-gə-'ret, 'si-gə-ˌret\ *n* [F, dim. of *cigare* cigar] : a slender roll of cut tobacco enclosed in paper for smoking

cig·a·ril·lo \ˌsi-gə-'ri-lō, -'rē-ō\ *n, pl* **-los** [Sp] 1 : a very small cigar 2 : a cigarette wrapped in tobacco rather than paper

ci·lan·tro \si-'län-trō, -'lan-\ *n* : leaves of coriander used as a flavoring or garnish; *also* : the coriander plant

cil·i·ate \'si-lē-ˌāt\ *n* : any of a group of protozoans characterized by cilia

cil·i·um \'si-lē-əm\ *n, pl* **cil·ia** \-lē-ə\ 1 : a minute short hairlike process; *esp* : one of a cell 2 : EYELASH

C in C *abbr* commander in chief

cinch \'sinch\ *n* 1 : a girth for a pack or saddle 2 : a sure or an easy thing — **cinch** *vb*

cin·cho·na \siŋ-'kō-nə\ *n* : any of a genus of So. American trees related to the madder; *also* : the bitter quinine-containing bark of a cinchona

cinc·ture \'siŋk-chər\ *n* : BELT, SASH

cin·der \'sin-dər\ *n* 1 : SLAG 2 *pl* : ASHES 3 : a hot piece of partly burned wood or coal 4 : a fragment of lava from an erupting volcano — **cin·dery** *adj*

cinder block *n* : a building block made of cement and coal cinders

cin·e·ma \'si-nə-mə\ *n* 1 : a motion-picture theater 2 : MOVIES — **cin·e·mat·ic** \ˌsi-nə-'ma-tik\ *adj*

cin·e·ma·theque \ˌsi-nə-mə-'tek\ *n* : a small movie house specializing in avant-garde films

cin·e·ma·tog·ra·phy \ˌsi-nə-mə-'tä-grə-fē\ *n* : motion-picture photography — **cin·e·ma·tog·ra·pher** *n* — **cin·e·mat·o·graph·ic** \-ˌma-tə-'gra-fik\ *adj*

cine·phile \'si-nə-ˌfī(-ə)l\ *n* : a lover of motion pictures

cin·e·plex \'si-nə-ˌpleks\ *n* : a complex that houses several movie theaters

cin·er·ar·i·um \ˌsi-nə-'rer-ē-əm\ *n, pl* **-ia** \-ē-ə\ : a place to receive the ashes of the cremated dead — **cin·er·ary** \'si-nə-ˌrer-ē\ *adj*

cin·na·bar \'si-nə-ˌbär\ *n* 1 : a red mineral that is the only important ore of mercury 2 : a deep vivid red

cin·na·mon \'si-nə-mən\ *n* : a spice prepared from the highly aromatic bark of any of several Asian trees related to the true laurel; *also* : a tree that yields cinnamon

cinque·foil \'siŋk-ˌfói(-ə)l, 'saŋk-\ *n* : any of a genus of plants related to the roses with leaves having five lobes

¹**ci·pher** \'sī-fər\ *n* [ME, fr. ML *cifra*, fr. Ar *ṣifr* empty, zero] 1 : ZERO, NAUGHT 2 : a method of secret writing

²**cipher** *vb* : to compute arithmetically

cir *or* **circ** *abbr* circular

cir·ca \'sər-kə\ *prep* : ABOUT ⟨~ 1600⟩

cir·ca·di·an \ˌsər-'kā-dē-ən\ *adj* : being, having, characterized by, or occurring in approximately 24-hour intervals (as of biological activity)

¹**cir·cle** \'sər-kəl\ *n* 1 : a closed curve every point of which is equally distant from a fixed point within it 2 : something circular 3 : an area of action or influence 4 : CYCLE 5 : a group bound by a common tie ⟨sewing ~⟩

²**circle** *vb* **cir·cled; cir·cling** 1 : to enclose in a circle 2 : to move or revolve around; *also* : to move in a circle

cir·clet \'sər-klət\ *n* : a small circle; *esp* : a circular ornament

cir·cuit \'sər-kət\ *n* 1 : a boundary around an enclosed space 2 : a course around a periphery 3 : a regular tour (as by a judge) around an assigned territory 4 : the com-

plete path of an electric current; *also* : an assemblage of electronic components 5 : LEAGUE; *also* : a chain of theaters

circuit board *n* : BOARD 7

circuit breaker *n* : a switch that automatically interrupts the current of an overloaded circuit

circuit court *n* : a court that sits at two or more places within one judicial district

cir·cu·i·tous \ˌsər-'kyü-ə-təs\ *adj* 1 : having a circular or winding course 2 : not being forthright or direct in language or action

cir·cuit·ry \'sər-kə-trē\ *n, pl* **-ries** : the plan or the components of an electric circuit

cir·cu·ity \ˌsər-'kyü-ə-tē\ *n, pl* **-ities** : INDIRECTION

¹**cir·cu·lar** \'sər-kyə-lər\ *adj* 1 : having the form of a circle : ROUND 2 : moving in or around a circle 3 : CIRCUITOUS 4 : intended for circulation ⟨a ~ letter⟩ — **cir·cu·lar·i·ty** \ˌsər-kyə-'ler-ə-tē\ *n*

²**circular** *n* : a paper (as a leaflet) intended for wide distribution

cir·cu·lar·ise *Brit var of* CIRCULARIZE

cir·cu·lar·ize \'sər-kyə-lə-ˌrīz\ *vb* **-ized; -iz·ing** 1 : to send circulars to 2 : to poll by questionnaire 3 : to make circular

circular saw *n* : a power saw with a round cutting blade

cir·cu·late \'sər-kyə-ˌlāt\ *vb* **-lat·ed; -lat·ing** 1 : to move or cause to move in a circle, circuit, or orbit 2 : to pass from place to place or from person to person — **cir·cu·la·tion** \ˌsər-kyə-'lā-shən\ *n*

cir·cu·la·to·ry \'sər-kyə-lə-ˌtòr-ē\ *adj* : of or relating to circulation or the circulatory system

circulatory system *n* : the system of blood, blood vessels, lymphatic vessels, and heart concerned with the circulation of the blood and lymph

cir·cum·am·bu·late \ˌsər-kəm-'am-byə-ˌlāt\ *vb* **-lat·ed; -lat·ing** : to circle on foot esp. as part of a ritual

cir·cum·cise \'sər-kəm-ˌsīz\ *vb* **-cised; -cis·ing** [ME, fr. L *circumcisus*, pp. of *circumcidere*, lit., to cut around, fr. *circum* around + *caedere* to cut] : to cut off the foreskin of — **cir·cum·ci·sion** \ˌsər-kəm-'si-zhən\ *n*

cir·cum·fer·ence \sər-'kəm-f(ə-)rəns\ *n* 1 : the perimeter of a circle 2 : the external boundary or surface of a figure or object

cir·cum·flex \'sər-kəm-ˌfleks\ *n* : the mark ˆ over a vowel

cir·cum·lo·cu·tion \ˌsər-kəm-lō-'kyü-shən\ *n* : the use of unnecessary words in expressing an idea

cir·cum·lu·nar \-'lü-nər\ *adj* : revolving about or surrounding the moon

cir·cum·nav·i·gate \-'na-və-ˌgāt\ *vb* : to go completely around (as the earth) esp. by water — **cir·cum·nav·i·ga·tion** \-ˌna-və-'gā-shən\ *n*

cir·cum·po·lar \-'pō-lər\ *adj* 1 : continually visible above the horizon ⟨a ~ star⟩ 2 : surrounding or found near a pole of the earth ⟨a ~ current⟩

cir·cum·scribe \'sər-kəm-ˌskrīb\ *vb* 1 : to constrict the range or activity of 2 : to draw a line around — **cir·cum·scrip·tion** \ˌsər-kəm-'skrip-shən\ *n*

cir·cum·spect \'sər-kəm-ˌspekt\ *adj* : careful to consider all circumstances and consequences : PRUDENT — **cir·cum·spec·tion** \ˌsər-kəm-'spek-shən\ *n*

cir·cum·stance \'sər-kəm-ˌstans\ *n* 1 : a fact or event that must be considered along with another fact or event 2 : surrounding conditions 3 : CHANCE, FATE 4 *pl* : situation with regard to wealth 5 : CEREMONY

cir·cum·stan·tial \ˌsər-kəm-'stan-chəl\ *adj* 1 : consisting of or depending on circumstances 2 : INCIDENTAL 3 : containing full details — **cir·cum·stan·tial·ly** *adv*

cir·cum·vent \ˌsər-kəm-'vent\ *vb* : to check or defeat esp. by stratagem — **cir·cum·ven·tion** \'vent-shən\ *n*

cir·cus \'sər-kəs\ *n* 1 : a usu. traveling show that features feats of physical skill, wild animal acts, and performances by clowns 2 : a circus performance; *also* : the equipment, livestock, and personnel of a circus

cirque \'sərk\ *n* : a deep steep-walled mountain basin usu. forming the blunt end of a valley

cir·rho·sis \sə-'rō-səs\ *n, pl* **-rho·ses** \-ˌsēz\ [NL, fr. Gk *kirrhos* orange-colored] : fibrosis of the liver — **cir·rhot·ic** \-'rä-tik\ *adj or n*

cir·rus \'sir-əs\ *n, pl* **cir·ri** \'sir-ˌī\ : a wispy white cloud usu. of minute ice crystals at high altitudes

cis·lu·nar \(ˌ)sis-ˈlü-nər\ *adj* : lying between the earth and the moon or the moon's orbit

cis·sy *Brit var of* SISSY

cis·tern \ˈsis-tərn\ *n* : an often underground tank for storing water

cit *abbr* **1** citation; cited **2** citizen

cit·a·del \ˈsi-tə-dəl, -ˌdel\ *n* **1** : a fortress commanding a city **2** : STRONGHOLD

ci·ta·tion \sī-ˈtā-shən\ *n* **1** : an official summons to appear (as before a court) **2** : QUOTATION **3** : a formal statement of the achievements of a person; *also* : a specific reference in a military dispatch to meritorious performance of duty

cite \ˈsīt\ *vb* **cit·ed; cit·ing** **1** : to summon to appear before a court **2** : QUOTE **3** : to refer to esp. in commendation or praise

cit·i·fied \ˈsi-ti-ˌfīd\ *adj* : of, relating to, or characterized by an urban style of living

cit·i·zen \ˈsi-tə-zən\ *n* **1** : an inhabitant of a city or town **2** : a person who owes allegiance to a government and is entitled to its protection — **cit·i·zen·ship** *n*

cit·i·zen·ry \-rē\ *n, pl* **-ries** : a whole body of citizens

citizens band *n* : a range of radio frequencies set aside for private radio communications

cit·ric acid \ˈsi-trik-\ *n* : a sour organic acid obtained from lemon and lime juices or by fermentation of sugars and used chiefly as a flavoring

cit·ron \ˈsi-trən\ *n* **1** : the oval lemonlike fruit of a citrus tree; *also* : the tree **2** : a small hard-fleshed watermelon used esp. in pickles and preserves

cit·ro·nel·la \ˌsi-trə-ˈne-lə\ *n* : a lemon-scented oil obtained from a fragrant grass of southern Asia and used in perfumes and as an insect repellent

cit·rus \ˈsi-trəs\ *n, pl* **citrus** *or* **cit·rus·es** : any of a genus of often thorny evergreen trees or shrubs grown in warm regions for their fruits (as the orange, lemon, lime, and grapefruit); *also* : the fruit

city \ˈsi-tē\ *n, pl* **cit·ies** [ME *citie* large or small town, fr. AF *cité*, fr. ML *civitas*, fr. L, citizenship, state, city of Rome, fr. *civis* citizen] **1** : an inhabited place larger or more important than a town **2** : a municipality in the U.S. governed under a charter granted by the state; *also* : an incorporated municipal unit of the highest class in Canada

city manager *n* : an official employed by an elected council to direct the administration of a city government

city–state \ˈsi-tē-ˌstāt\ *n* : an autonomous state consisting of a city and surrounding territory

civ *abbr* **1** civil; civilian **2** civilization

civ·et \ˈsi-vət\ *n* : a yellowish strong-smelling substance obtained from a catlike Old World mammal (**civet cat**) and used in making perfumes

civ·ic \ˈsi-vik\ *adj* : of or relating to a city, citizenship, or civil affairs

civ·ics \-viks\ *n* : a social science dealing with the rights and duties of citizens

civ·il \ˈsi-vəl\ *adj* **1** : of or relating to citizens or to the state as a political body **2** : COURTEOUS, POLITE **3** : of or relating to legal proceedings in connection with private rights and obligations ⟨the ∼ code⟩ **4** : of or relating to the general population : not military or ecclesiastical

civil defense *n* : protective measures and emergency relief activities conducted by civilians in case of enemy attack or natural disaster

civil disobedience *n* : refusal to obey governmental commands esp. as a nonviolent means of protest

civil engineer *n* : an engineer whose training or occupation is in the design and construction esp. of public works (as roads or harbors) — **civil engineering** *n*

ci·vil·ian \sə-ˈvil-yən\ *n* : a person not on active duty in a military, police, or fire-fighting force

civ·i·li·sa·tion, civ·i·lise *chiefly Brit var of* CIVILIZATION, CIVILIZE

ci·vil·i·ty \sə-ˈvi-lə-tē\ *n, pl* **-ties** **1** : POLITENESS, COURTESY **2** : a polite act or expression

civ·i·li·za·tion \ˌsi-və-lə-ˈzā-shən\ *n* **1** : a relatively high level of cultural and technological development **2** : the culture characteristic of a time or place — **civ·i·li·za·tion·al** \-shə-nᵊl\ *adj*

civ·i·lize \ˈsi-və-ˌlīz\ *vb* **-lized; -liz·ing** **1** : to raise from a primitive state to an advanced and ordered stage of cultural development **2** : REFINE — **civ·i·lized** *adj*

civil liberty *n* : freedom from arbitrary governmental interference specifically by denial of governmental power — usu. used in pl.

civ·il·ly \ˈsi-vəl-lē\ *adv* **1** : in terms of civil rights, matters, or law ⟨∼ dead⟩ **2** : in a civil manner : POLITELY

civil rights *n pl* : the nonpolitical rights of a citizen; *esp* : those guaranteed by the 13th and 14th amendments to the Constitution and by acts of Congress

civil servant *n* : a member of a civil service

civil service *n* : the administrative service of a government

civil war *n* : a war between opposing groups of citizens of the same country

civ·vies \ˈsi-vēz\ *n pl* : civilian clothes as distinguished from a military uniform

CJ *abbr* chief justice

ck *abbr* **1** cask **2** check

cl *abbr* **1** centiliter **2** class

Cl *symbol* chlorine

¹clack \ˈklak\ *vb* **1** : CHATTER, PRATTLE **2** : to make or cause to make a clatter

²clack *n* **1** : rapid continuous talk : CHATTER **2** : a sound of clacking ⟨the ∼ of a typewriter⟩

clad \ˈklad\ *adj* **1** : CLOTHED, COVERED **2** : being or consisting of coins made of outer layers of one metal bonded to a core of a different metal

¹claim \ˈklām\ *vb* [ME, fr. AF *claimer, clamer*, fr. L *clamare* to cry out, shout] **1** : to ask for as one's own; *also* : to take as the rightful owner **2** : to call for : REQUIRE **3** : to state as a fact : MAINTAIN

²claim *n* **1** : a demand for something due ⟨an insurance ∼⟩ **2** : a right to something usu. in another's possession **3** : an assertion open to challenge **4** : something claimed (as a tract of land)

claim·ant \ˈklā-mənt\ *n* : a person making a claim

clair·voy·ant \klar-ˈvȯi-ənt\ *adj* [F, fr. *clair* clear + *voyant* seeing] **1** : able to see beyond the range of ordinary perception **2** : having the power of discerning objects not present to the senses — **clair·voy·ance** \-əns\ *n* — **clairvoyant** *n*

clam \ˈklam\ *n* **1** : any of numerous bivalve mollusks including many that are edible **2** : DOLLAR

clam 1

clam·bake \-ˌbāk\ *n* : a party or gathering (as at the seashore) at which food is cooked usu. on heated rocks covered by seaweed

clam·ber \ˈklam-bər\ *vb* : to climb awkwardly — **clam·ber·er** *n*

clam·my \ˈkla-mē\ *adj* **clam·mi·er; -est** : being damp, soft, sticky, and usu. cool — **clam·mi·ness** *n*

clam·or \ˈkla-mər\ *n* **1** : a noisy shouting **2** : a loud continuous noise **3** : insistent public expression (as of support or protest) — **clamor** *vb* — **clam·or·ous** *adj*

clam·our *chiefly Brit var of* CLAMOR

¹clamp \ˈklamp\ *n* : a device that holds or presses parts together firmly

²clamp *vb* : to fasten with or as if with a clamp

clamp down *vb* : to impose restrictions : become repressive — **clamp·down** \ˈklamp-ˌdaun\ *n*

clam·shell \ˈklam-ˌshel\ *n* **1** : the shell of a clam **2** : a bucket or grapnel (as on a dredge) having two hinged jaws

clam up *vb* : to become silent

clan \ˈklan\ *n* [ME, fr. ScGael *clann* offspring, clan, fr. Old Irish *cland* plant, offspring, fr. L *planta* plant] : a group (as in the Scottish Highlands) made up of households whose heads claim descent from a common ancestor — **clan·nish** *adj* — **clan·nish·ness** *n*

clan·des·tine \klan-'des-tən\ *adj* : held in or conducted with secrecy

clang \'klaŋ\ *n* : a loud metallic ringing sound — **clang** *vb*

clan·gor \'klaŋ-ər, -gər\ *n* : a resounding clang or medley of clangs

clan·gour *chiefly Brit var of* CLANGOR

clank \'klaŋk\ *n* : a sharp brief metallic ringing sound — **clank** *vb*

¹**clap** \'klap\ *vb* **clapped; clap·ping** 1 : to strike noisily 2 : APPLAUD

²**clap** *n* 1 : a loud noisy crash 2 : the noise made by clapping the hands

³**clap** *n* : GONORRHEA

clap·board \'kla-bərd, -,bȯrd; 'klap-,bȯrd\ *n* : a narrow board thicker at one edge than the other used for siding — **clap·board** *vb*

clap·per \'kla-pər\ *n* : one that claps; *esp* : the tongue of a bell

clap·trap \'klap-,trap\ *n* : pretentious nonsense

claque \'klak\ *n* [F, fr. *claquer* to clap] 1 : a group hired to applaud at a performance 2 : a group of sycophants

clar·et \'kler-ət\ *n* [ME, fr. AF (*vin*) *claret* clear wine] : a dry red wine

clar·i·fy \'kler-ə-,fī\ *vb* -**fied; -fy·ing** : to make or become clear — **clar·i·fi·ca·tion** \,kler-ə-fə-'kā-shən\ *n*

clar·i·net \,kler-ə-'net\ *n* : a single-reed woodwind instrument in the form of a cylindrical tube with a moderately flaring end — **clar·i·net·ist** *or* **clar·i·net·tist** \-'ne-tist\ *n*

clar·i·on \'kler-ē-ən\ *adj* : brilliantly clear ⟨a ~ call⟩

clar·i·ty \'kler-ə-tē\ *n* : CLEARNESS

¹**clash** \'klash\ *vb* 1 : to make or cause to make a clash 2 : CONFLICT, COLLIDE

²**clash** *n* 1 : a noisy usu. metallic sound of collision 2 : a hostile encounter 3 : a sharp conflict ⟨a ~ of opinions⟩

clasp \'klasp\ *n* 1 : a device (as a hook) for holding objects or parts together 2 : EMBRACE, GRASP — **clasp** *vb*

¹**class** \'klas\ *n* [F *classe*, fr. L *classis* group called to military service, fleet, class] 1 : a group of students meeting regularly in a course; *also* : a group graduating together 2 : a course of instruction; *also* : the period when such a course is taught 3 : social rank; *also* : high quality 4 : a group of the same general status or nature; *esp* : a major category in biological classification that is above the order and below the phylum 5 : a division or rating based on grade or quality — **class·less** *adj*

²**class** *vb* : CLASSIFY

class action *n* : a legal action undertaken in behalf of the plaintiffs and all others having an identical interest in the alleged wrong

¹**clas·sic** \'kla-sik\ *adj* 1 : serving as a standard of excellence; *also* : TRADITIONAL 2 : CLASSICAL 2 3 : notable esp. as the best example 4 : AUTHENTIC ⟨a ~ folk dance⟩

²**classic** *n* 1 : a work of enduring excellence and esp. of ancient Greece or Rome; *also* : its author 2 : a traditional event ⟨a football ~⟩

clas·si·cal \'kla-si-kəl\ *adj* 1 : CLASSIC 2 : of or relating to the ancient Greek and Roman classics 3 : of or relating to a form or system of primary significance before modern times ⟨~ economics⟩ 4 : concerned with a general study of the arts and sciences — **clas·si·cal·ly** \-k(ə-)lē\ *adv*

clas·si·cism \'kla-sə-,si-zəm\ *n* 1 : the principles or style of the literature or art of ancient Greece and Rome 2 : adherence to traditional standards believed to be universally valid — **clas·si·cist** \-sist\ *n*

clas·si·fied \'kla-sə-,fīd\ *adj* : withheld from general circulation for reasons of national security

clas·si·fieds \-,fīdz\ *n pl* : advertisements grouped by subject

clas·si·fy \'kla-sə-,fī\ *vb* -**fied; -fy·ing** : to arrange in or assign to classes — **clas·si·fi·able** *adj* — **clas·si·fi·ca·tion** \,kla-sə-fə-'kā-shən\ *n* — **clas·si·fi·er** *n*

class·mate \'klas-,māt\ *n* : a member of the same class (as in a college)

class·room \-,rüm, -,rùm\ *n* : a place where classes meet

classy \'kla-sē\ *adj* **class·i·er; -est** : ELEGANT, STYLISH ⟨a ~ clientele⟩ — **class·i·ness** *n*

clat·ter \'kla-tər\ *n* : a rattling sound ⟨the ~ of dishes⟩ — **clatter** *vb*

clause \'klȯz\ *n* 1 : a group of words having its own subject and predicate but forming only part of a compound or complex sentence 2 : a separate part of an article or document

claus·tro·pho·bia \,klȯ-strə-'fō-bē-ə\ *n* : abnormal dread of being in closed or narrow spaces — **claus·tro·pho·bic** \-'bik\ *adj*

clav·i·chord \'kla-və-,kȯrd\ *n* : an early keyboard instrument in use before the piano

clav·i·cle \'kla-vi-kəl\ *n* [F *clavicule*, fr. NL *clavicula*, fr. L, dim. of L *clavis* key] : COLLARBONE

cla·vier \klə-'vir; 'klā-vē-ər\ *n* 1 : the keyboard of a musical instrument 2 : an early keyboard instrument

¹**claw** \'klȯ\ *n* 1 : a sharp usu. curved nail on the toe of an animal 2 : a sharp curved process (as on the foot of an insect); *also* : a pincerlike organ at the end of a limb of some arthropods (as a lobster) — **clawed** \'klȯd\ *adj*

²**claw** *vb* : to rake, seize, or dig with or as if with claws

clay \'klā\ *n* 1 : an earthy material that is plastic when moist but hard when fired and is used in making pottery; *also* : finely divided soil consisting largely of such clay 2 : EARTH, MUD 3 : a plastic substance used for modeling 4 : the mortal human body — **clay·ey** \'klā-ē\ *adj*

clay·more \'klā-,mȯr\ *n* : a large 2-edged sword formerly used by Scottish Highlanders

clay pigeon *n* : a saucer-shaped target thrown from a trap in trapshooting

¹**clean** \'klēn\ *adj* 1 : free from dirt, disease, or pollution ⟨~ air⟩ 2 : PURE ⟨the ~ thrill of one's first flight⟩; *also* : HONORABLE 3 : THOROUGH ⟨made a ~ sweep⟩ 4 : TRIM ⟨a ~ edge⟩ ⟨a ship with ~ lines⟩; *also* : EVEN 5 : habitually neat — **clean** *adv* — **clean·ly** \'klēn-lē\ *adv* — **clean·ness** \'klēn-nəs\ *n*

²**clean** *vb* : to make or become clean — **clean·able** \'klē-nə-bəl\ *adj* — **clean·er** *n*

clean–cut \'klēn-'kət\ *adj* 1 : cut so that the surface or edge is smooth and even 2 : sharply defined or outlined 3 : giving an effect of wholesomeness

clean·ly \'klen-lē\ *adj* **clean·li·er; -est** 1 : careful to keep clean 2 : habitually kept clean — **clean·li·ness** *n*

clean room \'klēn-,rüm, -,rùm\ *n* : an uncontaminated room maintained for the manufacture or assembly of objects (as precision parts)

cleanse \'klenz\ *vb* **cleansed; cleans·ing** : to make clean — **cleans·er** *n*

¹**clean·up** \'klēn-,əp\ *n* 1 : an act or instance of cleaning 2 : a very large profit

²**cleanup** *adj* : being 4th in the batting order of a baseball team — **cleanup** *adv*

clean up *vb* : to make a spectacular business profit

¹**clear** \'klir\ *adj* [ME *clere*, fr. AF *cler*, fr. L *clarus*] 1 : BRIGHT, LUMINOUS; *also* : UNTROUBLED, SERENE 2 : CLOUDLESS 3 : CLEAN, PURE; *also* : TRANSPARENT 4 : easily heard, seen, or understood 5 : capable of sharp discernment; *also* : free from doubt 6 : INNOCENT ⟨a ~ conscience⟩ 7 : free from restriction, obstruction, or entanglement — **clear** *adv* — **clear·ness** *n*

²**clear** *vb* 1 : to make or become clear 2 : to go away : DISPERSE 3 : to free from accusation or blame; *also* : to certify as trustworthy 4 : EXPLAIN 5 : to get free from obstruction 6 : SETTLE 7 : NET ⟨~ed a profit⟩ 8 : to get rid of : REMOVE 9 : to jump or go by without touching; *also* : PASS ⟨the bill ~ed the legislature⟩

³**clear** *n* : a clear space or part

clear·ance \'klir-əns\ *n* 1 : an act or process of clearing 2 : the distance by which one object clears another 3 : AUTHORIZATION

clear–cut \'klir-'kət\ *adj* 1 : sharply outlined 2 : DEFINITE, UNEQUIVOCAL ⟨a ~ victory⟩

clear–cut·ting \-,kə-tiŋ\ *n* : removal of all the trees in a stand of timber — **clear–cut** \-'kət\ *vb*

clear·head·ed \-'he-dəd\ *adj* : having a clear understanding : PERCEPTIVE

clear·ing \'klir-iŋ\ *n* 1 : a tract of land cleared of wood and brush 2 : the passage of checks and claims through a clearinghouse

clear·ing·house \-,haùs\ *n* : an institution maintained by banks for making an exchange of checks and claims held by each bank against other banks; *also* : an informal channel for information or assistance

clear·ly \'klir-lē\ *adv* 1 : in a clear manner 2 : it is clear

cleat \'klēt\ *n* : a piece of wood or metal fastened on or projecting from something to give strength, provide a grip, or prevent slipping

cleat

cleav·age \'klē-vij\ *n* 1 : a splitting apart : SPLIT 2 : the depression between a woman's breasts esp. when exposed by a low-cut dress
¹**cleave** \'klēv\ *vb* **cleaved** \'klēvd\ *or* **clove** \'klōv\; **cleaved**; **cleav·ing** : ADHERE, CLING
²**cleave** *vb* **cleaved** \'klēvd\ *also* **cleft** \'kleft\ *or* **clove** \'klōv\; **cleaved** *also* **cleft** *or* **clo·ven** \'klō-vən\; **cleav·ing** 1 : to divide by force : split asunder 2 : DIVIDE
cleav·er \'klē-vər\ *n* : a heavy chopping knife for cutting meat
clef \'klef\ *n* : a sign placed on the staff in music to show what pitch is represented by each line and space
cleft \'kleft\ *n* : FISSURE, CRACK
cleft lip *n* : a birth defect in which the upper lip is vertically split
cleft palate *n* : a split in the roof of the mouth that appears as a birth defect
clem·a·tis \'kle-mə-təs; kli-'ma-təs\ *n* : any of a genus of vines or herbs related to the buttercups that have showy usu. white or purple flowers
clem·en·cy \'kle-mən-sē\ *n, pl* **-cies** 1 : disposition to be merciful 2 : mildness of weather
clem·ent \'kle-mənt\ *adj* 1 : MERCIFUL, LENIENT ⟨a ∼ judge⟩ 2 : TEMPERATE, MILD ⟨∼ weather for this time of year⟩
clem·en·tine \'kle-mən-ˌtēn\ *n* : a small citrus fruit that is probably a hybrid between a tangerine and an orange
clench \'klench\ *vb* 1 : CLINCH 1 2 : to hold fast 3 : to set or close tightly
clere·sto·ry \'klir-ˌstȯr-ē\ *n* : an outside wall of a room or building that rises above an adjoining roof and contains windows
cler·gy \'klər-jē\ *n* : a body of religious officials authorized to conduct services
cler·gy·man \-mən\ *n* : a member of the clergy
cler·gy·per·son \-ˌpər-s³n\ *n* : a member of the clergy
cler·ic \'kler-ik\ *n* : a member of the clergy
cler·i·cal \'kler-i-kəl\ *adj* 1 : of or relating to the clergy 2 : of or relating to a clerk
cler·i·cal·ism \'kler-i-kə-ˌli-zəm\ *n* : a policy of maintaining or increasing the power of a religious hierarchy
clerk \'klərk, *Brit* 'klärk\ *n* 1 : CLERIC 2 : an official responsible for correspondence, records, and accounts; *also* : a person employed to perform general office work 3 : a store salesperson — **clerk** *vb* — **clerk·ship** *n*
clev·er \'kle-vər\ *adj* 1 : showing skill or resourcefulness 2 : marked by wit or ingenuity — **clev·er·ly** *adv* — **clev·er·ness** *n*
clev·is \'kle-vəs\ *n* : a U-shaped shackle used for fastening
¹**clew** \'klü\ *n* 1 : CLUE 2 : a metal loop on a lower corner of a sail
²**clew** *vb* : to haul (a sail) up or down by ropes through the clews
cli·ché \kli-'shā\ *n* [F] : a trite phrase or expression — **cli·chéd** \-'shād\ *adj*
¹**click** \'klik\ *vb* 1 : to make or cause to make a click 2 : to fit or work together smoothly 3 : to select or make a selection on a computer by pressing a button on a control device (as a mouse) — **click·able** \'kli-kə-bəl\ *adj*
²**click** *n* 1 : a slight sharp noise 2 : an instance of clicking ⟨a mouse ∼⟩
click·er \'kli-kər\ *n* : REMOTE CONTROL 2
cli·ent \'klī-ənt\ *n* 1 : DEPENDENT 2 : a person who engages the professional services of another; *also* : PATRON,

CUSTOMER 3 : a computer in a network that uses the services (as access to files) provided by a server
cli·en·tele \ˌklī-ən-'tel, ˌklē-\ *n* : a body of clients and esp. customers
cliff \'klif\ *n* : a high steep face of rock, earth, or ice
cliff–hang·er \-ˌhaŋ-ər\ *n* 1 : an adventure serial or melodrama usu. presented in installments each of which ends in suspense 2 : a contest whose outcome is in doubt up to the very end
cli·mac·ter·ic \klī-'mak-tə-rik\ *n* 1 : a major turning point or critical stage 2 : MENOPAUSE; *also* : a corresponding period in the male
cli·mate \'klī-mət\ *n* [ME *climat*, fr. MF, fr. LL *clima*, fr. Gk *klima* inclination, latitude, climate, fr. *klinein* to lean] 1 : a region having specific climatic conditions 2 : the average weather conditions at a place over a period of years 3 : the prevailing set of conditions (as temperature and humidity) indoors 4 : a prevailing atmosphere or environment ⟨the ∼ of opinion⟩ — **cli·mat·ic** \klī-'ma-tik\ *adj* — **cli·mat·i·cal·ly** \-ti-k(ə-)lē\ *adv*
cli·ma·tol·o·gy \ˌklī-mə-'tä-lə-jē\ *n* : the science that deals with climates — **cli·ma·to·log·i·cal** \-mə-tə-'lä-ji-kəl\ *adj* — **cli·ma·to·log·i·cal·ly** \-k(ə-)lē\ *adv* — **cli·ma·tol·o·gist** \-mə-'tä-lə-jist\ *n*
¹**cli·max** \'klī-ˌmaks\ *n* [L, fr. Gk *klimax*, lit., ladder, fr. *klinein* to lean] 1 : a series of ideas or statements so arranged that they increase in force and power from the first to the last; *also* : the last member of such a series 2 : the highest point 3 : ORGASM — **cli·mac·tic** \klī-'mak-tik\ *adj*
²**climax** *vb* : to come or bring to a climax
¹**climb** \'klīm\ *vb* 1 : to rise to a higher point 2 : to go up or down esp. by use of hands and feet; *also* : to ascend in growing — **climb·er** *n*
²**climb** *n* 1 : a place where climbing is necessary 2 : the act of climbing : ascent by climbing
clime \'klīm\ *n* : CLIMATE
¹**clinch** \'klinch\ *vb* 1 : to turn over or flatten the end of something sticking out ⟨∼ a nail⟩; *also* : to fasten by clinching 2 : to make final : SETTLE 3 : to hold a boxing opponent 4 : to hold fast or firmly
²**clinch** *n* 1 : a fastening by means of a clinched nail, rivet, or bolt 2 : an act or instance of clinching in boxing
clinch·er \'klin-chər\ *n* : one that clinches; *esp* : a decisive fact, argument, act, or remark
cling \'kliŋ\ *vb* **clung** \'kləŋ\; **cling·ing** 1 : to adhere as if glued; *also* : to hold or hold on tightly 2 : to have a strong emotional attachment — **clingy** \'kliŋ-ē\ *adj*
cling·stone \'kliŋ-ˌstōn\ *n* : any of various fruits (as some peaches) whose flesh adheres strongly to the pit
clin·ic \'kli-nik\ *n* 1 : a medical class in which patients are examined and discussed 2 : a group meeting for teaching a certain skill and working on individual problems ⟨a reading ∼⟩ 3 : a facility (as of a hospital) for diagnosis and treatment of outpatients
clin·i·cal \'kli-ni-kəl\ *adj* 1 : of, relating to, or typical of a clinic; *esp* : involving direct observation of the patient ⟨∼ studies⟩ 2 : scientifically dispassionate — **clin·i·cal·ly** \-k(ə-)lē\ *adv*
cli·ni·cian \kli-'ni-shən\ *n* : a person qualified in the clinical practice of medicine, psychiatry, or psychology as distinguished from one specializing in laboratory or research techniques or in theory
¹**clink** \'kliŋk\ *vb* : to make or cause to make a sharp short metallic sound
²**clink** *n* : a clinking sound
clin·ker \'kliŋ-kər\ *n* : stony matter fused together : SLAG
¹**clip** \'klip\ *vb* **clipped**; **clip·ping** : to fasten with a clip
²**clip** *n* 1 : a device that grips, clasps, or hooks 2 : a cartridge holder for a rifle
³**clip** *vb* **clipped**; **clip·ping** 1 : to cut or cut off with shears 2 : CURTAIL, DIMINISH 3 : HIT, PUNCH 4 : to illegally block (an opponent) in football
⁴**clip** *n* 1 : a 2-bladed instrument for cutting esp. the nails 2 : a sharp blow 3 : a rapid pace
clip art *n* : ready-made usu. copyright-free illustrations
clip·board \'klip-ˌbȯrd\ *n* 1 : a small writing board with a spring clip at the top for holding papers 2 : a section of computer memory that temporarily stores data esp. to facilitate its movement or duplication

clip joint *n, slang* : an establishment (as a nightclub) that makes a practice of defrauding its customers

clip·per \'kli-pər\ *n* **1** : an implement for clipping esp. the hair or nails — usu. used in pl. **2** : a fast sailing ship

clip·ping \'kli-piŋ\ *n* : a piece clipped from something (as a newspaper)

clique \'klēk, 'klik\ *n* [F] : a small exclusive group of people : COTERIE — **cliqu·ey** \'klē-kē, 'kli-\ *adj* — **cliqu·ish** \-kish\ *adj*

cli·to·ris \'kli-tə-rəs\ *n, pl* **cli·to·ris·es** : a small erectile organ at the anterior or ventral part of the vulva homologous to the penis — **cli·to·ral** \-rəl\ *adj*

clk *abbr* clerk

clo *abbr* clothing

¹cloak \'klōk\ *n* **1** : a loose outer garment **2** : something that conceals

²cloak *vb* : to cover or hide with a cloak

cloak–and–dagger *adj* : involving or suggestive of espionage

clob·ber \'klä-bər\ *vb* **1** : to pound mercilessly; *also* : to hit with force : SMASH **2** : to defeat overwhelmingly

cloche \'klōsh\ *n* [F, lit., bell] : a woman's small close-fitting hat

¹clock \'kläk\ *n* : a timepiece not intended to be carried on the person

²clock *vb* **1** : to time (a person or a performance) by a timing device **2** : to register (as speed) on a mechanical recording device — **clock·er** *n*

³clock *n* : an ornamental figure on a stocking or sock

clock·wise \'kläk-₁wīz\ *adv* : in the direction in which the hands of a clock move — **clockwise** *adj*

clock·work \-₁wərk\ *n* **1** : the machinery that runs a mechanical device (as a clock or toy) **2** : the precision or regularity associated with a clock

clod \'kläd\ *n* **1** : a lump esp. of earth or clay **2** : a dull or insensitive person

clod·hop·per \-₁hä-pər\ *n* **1** : an uncouth rustic **2** : a large heavy shoe

¹clog \'kläg\ *n* **1** : a weight attached esp. to an animal to impede motion **2** : a thick-soled shoe

²clog *vb* **clogged; clog·ging** **1** : to impede with a clog : HINDER **2** : to obstruct passage through **3** : to become filled with extraneous matter

cloi·son·né \₁klói-zə-'nā\ *adj* : a colored decoration made of enamels poured into the divided areas in a design outlined with wire or metal strips

¹clois·ter \'klói-stər\ *n* [ME *cloistre*, fr. AF, fr. ML *claustrum*, fr. L, bar, bolt, fr. *claudere* to close] **1** : a monastic establishment **2** : a covered usu. colonnaded passage on the side of a court — **clois·tral** \-strəl\ *adj*

²cloister *vb* : to shut away from the world

clone \'klōn\ *n* [Gk *klōn* twig, slip] **1** : the collection of genetically identical cells or organisms produced asexually from a single ancestral cell or organism; *also* : an individual grown from a single cell and genetically identical to it ⟨a sheep ∼⟩ **2** : a group of replicas of a biological molecule (as DNA) **3** : one that appears to be a copy of an original form — **clon·al** \'klō-n°l\ *adj* — **clone** *vb*

clop \'kläp\ *n* : a sound made by or as if by a hoof or wooden shoe against pavement — **clop** *vb*

¹close \'klōz\ *vb* **closed; clos·ing** **1** : to bar passage through : SHUT **2** : to suspend the operations (as of a school) **3** : END, TERMINATE **4** : to bring together the parts or edges of; *also* : to fill up **5** : GRAPPLE ⟨∼ with the enemy⟩ **6** : to enter into an agreement — **clos·able** *or* **close·able** *adj*

²close \'klōz\ *n* : CONCLUSION, END

³close \'klōs\ *adj* **clos·er; clos·est** **1** : having no openings **2** : narrowly restricting or restricted **3** : limited to a privileged class **4** : SECLUDED; *also* : SECRETIVE **5** : RIGOROUS ⟨keep ∼ watch⟩ **6** : SULTRY, STUFFY **7** : STINGY **8** : having little space between items or units **9** : fitting tightly; *also* : SHORT ⟨∼ haircut⟩ **10** : NEAR ⟨at ∼ range⟩ **11** : INTIMATE ⟨∼ friends⟩ **12** : ACCURATE **13** : decided by a narrow margin ⟨a ∼ game⟩ — **close** *adv* — **close·ly** *adv* — **close·ness** *n*

closed–circuit \'klōzd-'sər-kət\ *adj* : used in, shown on, or being a television installation in which the signal is transmitted by wire to a limited number of receivers

closed shop *n* : an establishment having only members of a labor union on the payroll

close-fist·ed \'klōz-'fis-təd, 'klōs-\ *adj* : STINGY

close-knit \'klōs-'nit\ *adj* : closely bound together by social, cultural, economic, or political ties

close-mouthed \'klōz-'maúthd, 'klōs-'maútht\ *adj* : cautious or reticent in speaking

close-out \'klōz-₁aút\ *n* : a sale of a business's entire stock at low prices

close out *vb* **1** : to dispose of by a closeout **2** : to dispose of a business : SELL OUT

clos·er \'klō-zər\ *n* : one that closes; *esp* : a relief pitcher who specializes in finishing games

¹clos·et \'klä-zət, 'klò-\ *n* **1** : a small room for privacy **2** : a small compartment for household utensils or clothing **3** : a state or condition of secrecy ⟨came out of the ∼⟩

²closet *vb* : to take into a private room for an interview

close-up \'klōs-₁əp\ *n* **1** : a photograph or movie shot taken at close range **2** : an intimate view or examination

clo·sure \'klō-zhər\ *n* **1** : an act of closing : the condition of being closed **2** : something that closes **3** : CLOTURE

clot \'klät\ *n* : a mass formed by a portion of liquid (as blood) thickening and sticking together — **clot** *vb*

cloth \'klòth\ *n, pl* **cloths** \'klòthz, 'klòths\ **1** : a pliable fabric made usu. by weaving or knitting natural or synthetic fibers and filaments **2** : TABLECLOTH **3** : distinctive dress of the clergy; *also* : CLERGY

clothe \'klōth\ *vb* **clothed** *or* **clad** \'klad\; **cloth·ing** **1** : DRESS; *also* : to provide with clothes **2** : to express by suitably significant language ⟨policies *clothed* in rhetoric⟩

clothes \'klōthz, 'klōz\ *n pl* **1** : CLOTHING **2** : BEDCLOTHES

clothes·horse \-₁hòrs\ *n* **1** : a frame on which to hang clothes **2** : a conspicuously dressy person

¹clothes·line \-₁līn\ *n* : a rope or cord on which clothes are hung to dry

²clothesline *vb* : to knock down by catching by the neck with one's outstretched arm

clothes moth *n* : any of several small pale moths whose larvae eat wool, fur, and feathers

clothes·pin \'klōthz-₁pin, 'klōz-\ *n* : a device for fastening clothes on a line

clothes·press \-₁pres\ *n* : a receptacle for clothes

cloth·ier \'klōth-yər, 'klō-thē-ər\ *n* : a maker or seller of clothing

cloth·ing \'klō-thiŋ\ *n* : garments in general

clo·ture \'klō-chər\ *n* : the closing or limitation (as by calling for a vote) of debate in a legislative body

¹cloud \'klaúd\ *n* [ME, rock, cloud, fr. OE *clūd*] **1** : a visible mass of particles of condensed vapor (as water or ice) suspended in the atmosphere **2** : a usu. visible mass of minute airborne particles; *also* : a mass of obscuring matter in interstellar space **3** : CROWD, SWARM ⟨a ∼ of mosquitoes⟩ **4** : something having a dark or threatening aspect ⟨a ∼ of suspicion⟩ **5** : something that obscures or blemishes ⟨a ∼ of ambiguity⟩ — **cloud·i·ness** \'klaú-dē-nəs\ *n* — **cloud·less** *adj* — **cloudy** *adj*

²cloud *vb* **1** : to darken or hide with or as if with a cloud **2** : OBSCURE ⟨∼ed in mystery⟩ **3** : TAINT, SULLY ⟨a ∼ed reputation⟩

cloud·burst \-₁bərst\ *n* : a sudden heavy rainfall

cloud·let \-lət\ *n* : a small cloud

cloud nine *n* : a feeling of extreme well-being or elation — usu. used with *on*

¹clout \'klaút\ *n* **1** : a blow esp. with the hand **2** : PULL, INFLUENCE

²clout *vb* : to hit forcefully

¹clove \'klōv\ *n* : one of the small bulbs that grows at the base of the scales of a large bulb ⟨a ∼ of garlic⟩

²clove *past of* CLEAVE

³clove *n* [ME *clowe*, fr. AF *clou (de girofle)*, lit., nail of clove, fr. L *clavus* nail] : the dried flower bud of a tropical tree used esp. as a spice

clo·ven \'klō-vən\ *past part of* CLEAVE

cloven foot *n* : CLOVEN HOOF — **cloven–foot·ed** \-'fú-təd\ *adj*

cloven hoof *n* : a foot (as of a sheep) with the front part divided into two parts — **cloven–hoofed** \-'hüft, -'hüvd\ *adj*

clo·ver \'klō-vər\ *n* : any of a genus of leguminous herbs with usu. 3-parted leaves and dense flower heads

clo·ver·leaf \-₁lēf\ *n, pl* **cloverleafs** \-₁lēfs\ *or* **clo·ver-**

leaves \-,lēvz\ : an interchange between two major highways that from above resembles a 4-leaf clover

¹clown \'klaün\ n 1 : BOOR 2 : a fool or comedian in an entertainment (as a circus) 3 : a person given to joking and buffoonery — **clown·ish** adj — **clown·ish·ly** adv — **clown·ish·ness** n

²clown vb : to act like a clown

cloy \'klói\ vb : to disgust or nauseate with excess of something orig. pleasing — **cloy·ing·ly** adv

clr abbr clear

¹club \'kləb\ n 1 : a heavy wooden stick or staff used as a weapon; also : BAT 2 : any of a suit of playing cards marked with a black figure resembling a clover leaf 3 : a group of persons associated for a common purpose; also : the meeting place of such a group 4 : CLUB SANDWICH

²club vb clubbed; club·bing 1 : to strike with a club 2 : to unite or combine for a common cause 3 : to patronize nightclubs

club·foot \'kləb-,füt\ n : a misshapen foot twisted out of position from birth; also : this deformed condition — **club·foot·ed** \-'fü-təd\ adj

club·house \'kləb-,haüs\ n 1 : a house occupied by a club 2 : locker rooms used by an athletic team 3 : a building at a golf course with locker rooms and usu. a pro shop and a restaurant

club sandwich n : a sandwich of three slices of bread with two layers of meat (as turkey) and lettuce, tomato, and mayonnaise

club soda n : SODA WATER

cluck \'klək\ n : the call of a hen esp. to her chicks — **cluck** vb

¹clue \'klü\ n 1 : something that guides through an intricate procedure or maze; esp : a piece of evidence leading to the solution of a problem 2 : IDEA, NOTION ⟨has no ~ what he's doing⟩

²clue vb clued; clue·ing or clu·ing : to provide with a clue; also : to give information to ⟨~ me in⟩

¹clump \'kləmp\ n 1 : a group of things clustered together 2 : a heavy tramping sound

²clump vb : to tread clumsily and noisily

clum·sy \'kləm-zē\ adj clum·si·er; -est 1 : lacking dexterity, nimbleness, or grace 2 : not tactful or subtle — **clum·si·ly** \-zə-lē\ adv — **clum·si·ness** \-zē-nəs\ n

clung past and past part of CLING

clunk·er \'kləŋ-kər\ n 1 : a dilapidated automobile 2 : a notable failure

¹clus·ter \'kləs-tər\ n : GROUP, BUNCH

²cluster vb : to grow or gather in a cluster

¹clutch \'kləch\ vb : to grasp with or as if with the hand

²clutch n 1 : the claws or a hand in the act of grasping; also : CONTROL, POWER 2 : a device for gripping an object 3 : a coupling used to connect and disconnect a driving and a driven part of a mechanism; also : a lever or pedal operating such a coupling 4 : a crucial situation

³clutch adj : made, done, or successful in a crucial situation

⁴clutch n 1 : a nest or batch of eggs; also : a brood of chicks 2 : GROUP, BUNCH

¹clut·ter \'klə-tər\ vb : to fill or cover with a disorderly scattering of things

²clutter n : a crowded mass

cm abbr centimeter

Cm symbol curium

CM abbr [Commonwealth of the Northern Mariana Islands] Northern Mariana Islands

cmdr abbr commander

cml abbr commercial

CMSgt abbr chief master sergeant

CNO abbr chief of naval operations

CNS abbr central nervous system

co abbr 1 company 2 county

Co symbol cobalt

CO abbr 1 Colorado 2 commanding officer 3 conscientious objector

c/o abbr care of

¹coach \'kōch\ n [MF coche, ultim. fr. Hung kocsi (szekér), lit., (wagon) of Kocs (town in Hungary)] 1 : a large closed 4-wheeled carriage with an elevated outside front seat for the driver 2 : a railroad passenger car esp. for day travel 3 : BUS 4 : a private tutor; also : one who instructs or trains ⟨an acting ~⟩ ⟨a soccer ~⟩

²coach vb : to instruct, direct, or prompt as a coach

coach·man \-mən\ n : a man who drives a coach or carriage

co·ad·ju·tor \,kō-ə-'jü-tər, kō-'a-jə-tər\ n : ASSISTANT; esp : an assistant bishop having the right of succession

co·ag·u·lant \kō-'a-gyə-lənt\ n : something that produces coagulation

co·ag·u·late \-,lāt\ vb -lat·ed; -lat·ing : CLOT — **co·ag·u·la·tion** \kō-,a-gyə-'lā-shən\ n

¹coal \'kōl\ n 1 : EMBER 2 : a black solid combustible mineral used as fuel

²coal vb 1 : to supply with coal 2 : to take in coal

co·a·lesce \,kō-ə-'les\ vb co·a·lesced; co·a·lesc·ing : to grow together; also : FUSE ✦ **Synonyms** MERGE, BLEND, MINGLE, MIX — **co·a·les·cence** \-'ns\ n

coal·field \'kōl-,fēld\ n : a region rich in coal deposits

coal gas n : gas from coal; esp : gas distilled from bituminous coal and used for heating

co·a·li·tion \,kō-ə-'li-shən\ n : UNION; esp : a temporary union for a common purpose — **co·a·li·tion·ist** n

coal oil n : KEROSENE

coal tar n : tar distilled from bituminous coal and used in dyes and drugs

co–an·chor \'kō-,aŋ-kər\ n : a newscaster who shares the duties of head broadcaster

coarse \'kórs\ adj coars·er; coars·est 1 : of ordinary or inferior quality 2 : composed of large parts or particles ⟨~ sand⟩ 3 : CRUDE ⟨~ manners⟩ 4 : ROUGH, HARSH — **coarse·ly** adv — **coarse·ness** n

coars·en \'kór-s°n\ vb : to make or become coarse

¹coast \'kōst\ n [ME cost, fr. AF coste, fr. L costa rib, side] 1 : SEASHORE 2 : a slide down a slope 3 : the immediate area of view — used in the phrase the coast is clear — **coast·al** adj

²coast vb 1 : to sail along the shore 2 : to move (as downhill on a sled) without effort

coast·er n 1 : one that coasts 2 : a shallow container or a plate or mat to protect a surface

coaster brake n : a brake in the hub of the rear wheel of a bicycle

coast guard n : a military force employed in guarding or patrolling a coast — **coast·guards·man** \'kōst-,gärdz-mən\ n

coast·line \'kōst-,līn\ n : the outline or shape of a coast

¹coat \'kōt\ n 1 : an outer garment for the upper part of the body 2 : an external growth (as of fur or feathers) on an animal 3 : a covering layer ⟨a ~ of paint⟩ — **coat·ed** \'kō-təd\ adj

²coat vb : to cover usu. with a finishing or protective coat

coat·ing \'kō-tiŋ\ n : COAT, COVERING

coat of arms : the heraldic bearings (as of a person) usu. depicted on an escutcheon

coat of mail : a garment of metal scales or rings worn as armor

co·au·thor \'kō-'ó-thər\ n : a joint or associate author — **coauthor** vb

coax \'kōks\ vb : WHEEDLE; also : to gain by gentle urging or flattery

co·ax·i·al \'kō-'ak-sē-əl\ adj : having coincident axes — **co·ax·i·al·ly** adv

coaxial cable n : a cable that consists of a tube of electrically conducting material surrounding a central conductor

cob \'käb\ n 1 : a male swan 2 : CORN-COB 3 : a short-legged stocky horse

co·balt \'kō-,bólt\ n [G Kobalt, alter. of Kobold, lit., goblin; fr. its occurrence in silver ore, believed to be due to goblins] : a tough shiny silver-white magnetic metallic chemical element found with iron and nickel

cob·ble \'kä-bəl\ vb cob·bled; cob·bling : to make or put together roughly or hastily ⟨~ together a solution⟩

cob·bler \'kä-blər\ n 1 : a mender or maker of shoes 2 : a deep-dish fruit pie with a thick crust

cob·ble·stone \'kä-bəl-,stōn\ n : a naturally rounded stone larger than a pebble and smaller than a boulder

co·bra \'kō-brə\ n [Pg cobra (de capello), lit., hooded snake] : any of several venomous snakes of Asia and Africa that when excited expand the skin of the neck into a broad hood

cob·web \'käb-,web\ n [ME coppeweb, fr. coppe spider, fr. OE ātorcoppe] 1 : SPIDERWEB; also : a thread spun by a spider or insect larva **2** : something flimsy or entangling — **cob·web·by** \-ˌwe-bē\ adj

co·caine \kō-ˈkān, ˈkō-ˌkān\ n : a drug obtained from the leaves of a So. American shrub (**co·ca** \ˈkō-kə\) that can result in severe psychological dependence and is sometimes used in medicine as a local anesthetic and illegally as a stimulant of the central nervous system

coc·cus \ˈkä-kəs\ n, pl **coc·ci** \ˈkäk-ˌsī\ : a spherical bacterium

coc·cyx \ˈkäk-siks\ n, pl **coc·cy·ges** \ˈkäk-sə-ˌjēz\ also **coc·cyx·es** \ˈkäk-sik-səz\ : the end of the spinal column beyond the sacrum esp. in humans

co·chi·neal \ˈkä-chə-ˌnēl\ n : a red dye made from the dried bodies of females of a tropical American insect (**cochineal insect**)

co·chlea \ˈkō-klē-ə, ˈkä-\ n, pl **co·chle·as** or **co·chle·ae** \-klē-ˌē, -ˌī\ : the usu. spiral part of the inner ear containing nerve endings which carry information about sound to the brain — **co·chle·ar** \-klē-ər\ adj

¹**cock** \ˈkäk\ n **1** : the adult male of a bird and esp. of the common domestic chicken **2** : VALVE, FAUCET **3** : LEADER **4** : the hammer of a firearm; also : the position of the hammer when ready for firing

²**cock** vb **1** : to draw back the hammer of a firearm **2** : to set or draw back in readiness for some action ⟨~ your arm to throw⟩ **3** : to turn or tilt usu. to one side ⟨~ one's head⟩

³**cock** n : a small pile (as of hay)

cock·ade \kä-ˈkād\ n : an ornament worn on the hat as a badge

cock·a·tiel \ˌkä-kə-ˈtēl\ n : a small crested gray parrot often kept as a cage bird

cock·a·too \ˈkä-kə-ˌtü\ n, pl **-toos** [D kaketoe, fr. Malay kakatua] : any of various large noisy crested parrots chiefly of Australia

cock·a·trice \ˈkä-kə-trəs, -ˌtrīs\ n : a legendary serpent with a deadly glance

cock·crow \ˈkäk-ˌkrō\ n : DAWN

cocked hat \ˈkäkt-\ n : a hat with the brim turned up on two or three sides

cock·er·el \ˈkä-kə-rəl\ n : a young male domestic chicken

cock·er spaniel \ˈkä-kər-\ n [cocking woodcock hunting] : any of a breed of small spaniels with long ears, square muzzle, and silky coat

cock·eyed \ˈkä-ˈkīd\ adj **1** : turned or tilted to one side **2** : slightly crazy : FOOLISH

cock·fight \ˈkäk-ˌfīt\ n : a contest of gamecocks usu. fitted with metal spurs

¹**cock·le** \ˈkä-kəl\ n : any of several weedy plants related to the pinks

²**cockle** n : a bivalve mollusk with a heart-shaped shell

cock·le·shell \-ˌshel\ n **1** : the shell of a cockle **2** : a light flimsy boat

cock·ney \ˈkäk-nē\ n, pl **cockneys** : a native of London and esp. of the East End of London; also : the dialect of a cockney

cock·pit \ˈkäk-ˌpit\ n **1** : a pit for cockfights **2** : a space or compartment in a vehicle from which it is steered, piloted, or driven

cock·roach \ˈkäk-ˌrōch\ n [Sp cucaracha] : any of an order or suborder of active nocturnal insects including some which infest houses and ships

cock·sure \ˈkäk-ˈshùr\ adj **1** : perfectly sure : CERTAIN **2** : COCKY

cock·tail \ˈkäk-ˌtāl\ n **1** : an iced drink made of liquor and flavoring ingredients **2** : an appetizer (as tomato juice) served as a first course of a meal

cocky \ˈkä-kē\ adj **cock·i·er; -est** : marked by overconfidence : PERT, CONCEITED — **cock·i·ly** \-kə-lē\ adv — **cock·i·ness** \-kē-nəs\ n

co·coa \ˈkō-kō\ n **1** : CACAO **2** : chocolate deprived of some of its fat and powdered; also : a drink made of this heated with water or milk

cocoa butter n : a pale vegetable fat obtained from cacao beans

co·co·nut \ˈkō-kə-(ˌ)nət\ n : a large edible hard-shelled fruit produced by a tall tropical palm (**coconut palm**)

co·coon \kə-ˈkün\ n **1** : a case usu. of silk formed by some insect larvae for protection during the pupal stage **2** : something that offers protection or isolation

cod \ˈkäd\ n, pl **cod** also **cods** : a bottom-dwelling bony fish of the North Atlantic that is an important food fish; also : a related fish of the Pacific Ocean

COD abbr **1** cash on delivery **2** collect on delivery

co·da \ˈkō-də\ n : a closing section in a musical composition that is formally distinct from the main structure

cod·dle \ˈkä-dᵊl\ vb **cod·dled; cod·dling 1** : to cook slowly in water below the boiling point **2** : PAMPER

¹**code** \ˈkōd\ n [ME, fr. MF, fr. L caudex, codex trunk of a tree, document formed orig. from wooden tablets] **1** : a systematic statement of a body of law **2** : a system of principles or rules ⟨moral ~⟩ **3** : a system of signals **4** : a system of symbols (as in secret communication) with special meanings **5** : GENETIC CODE

²**code** vb **cod·ed; cod·ing** : to put into the form or symbols of a code

co·deine \ˈkō-ˌdēn\ n : a narcotic drug obtained from opium and used esp. as an analgesic and cough suppressant

co·dex \ˈkō-ˌdeks\ n, pl **co·di·ces** \ˈkō-də-ˌsēz, ˈkä-\ : a manuscript book (as of the Scriptures or classics)

cod·fish \ˈkäd-ˌfish\ n : COD

cod·ger \ˈkä-jər\ n : an odd or cranky and usu. elderly fellow

cod·i·cil \ˈkä-də-səl, -ˌsil\ n : a legal instrument modifying an earlier will

cod·i·fy \ˈkä-də-ˌfī, ˈkō-\ vb **-fied; -fy·ing** : to arrange in a systematic form — **cod·i·fi·ca·tion** \ˌkä-də-fə-ˈkä-shən, ˌkō-\ n

co·ed \ˈkō-ˌed\ n : a female student in a coeducational institution — **coed** adj

co·ed·u·ca·tion \ˌkō-ˌe-jə-ˈkä-shən\ n : the education of male and female students at the same institution — **co·ed·u·ca·tion·al** \-shə-nəl\ adj — **co·ed·u·ca·tion·al·ly** adv

co·ef·fi·cient \ˌkō-ə-ˈfi-shənt\ n **1** : a constant factor as distinguished from a variable in a mathematical term **2** : a number that serves as a measure of some property (as of a substance, device, or process)

coe·len·ter·ate \si-ˈlen-tə-ˌrāt, -rət\ n : any of a phylum of radially symmetrical invertebrate animals including the corals, sea anemones, and jellyfishes

co·equal \kō-ˈē-kwəl\ adj : equal with another — **coequal** n — **co·equal·i·ty** \ˌkō-ē-ˈkwä-lə-tē\ n — **co·equal·ly** adv

co·erce \kō-ˈərs\ vb **co·erced; co·erc·ing 1** : RESTRAIN, REPRESS **2** : COMPEL **3** : ENFORCE — **co·er·cion** \-ˈər-zhən, -shən\ n — **co·er·cive** \-ˈər-siv\ adj

co·eval \kō-ˈē-vəl\ adj : of the same age — **coeval** n

co·ex·ist \ˌkō-ig-ˈzist\ vb **1** : to exist together or at the same time **2** : to live in peace with each other — **co·ex·is·tence** \-ˈzis-təns\ n

co·ex·ten·sive \ˌkō-ik-ˈsten-siv\ adj : having the same scope or extent in space or time

C of C abbr Chamber of Commerce

cof·fee \ˈkò-fē\ n [It & Turk; It caffè, fr. Turk kahve, fr. Ar qahwa] : a drink made from the roasted and ground seeds of a fruit of a tropical shrub or tree; also : these seeds (**coffee beans**) or a plant producing them

cof·fee·house \-ˌhaùs\ n : a place where refreshments (as coffee) are sold

coffee klatch \-ˌklach\ n : KAFFEE-KLATSCH

cof·fee·pot \-ˌpät\ n : a pot for brewing or serving coffee

coffee shop n : a small restaurant

coffee table n : a low table customarily placed in front of a sofa

cof·fer \ˈkò-fər\ n : a chest or box used esp. for valuables

cof·fer·dam \-ˌdam\ n : a watertight enclosure from which water is pumped to expose the bottom of a body of water and permit construction

cof·fin \ˈkò-fən\ n : a box or chest for burying a corpse

C of S abbr chief of staff

¹**cog** \ˈkäg\ n : a tooth on the rim of a wheel or gear — **cogged** \ˈkägd\ adj

²**cog** abbr cognate

co·gen·er·a·tion \ˌkō-je-nə-ˈrā-shən\ n : the simultaneous generation of electricity and heat from the same fuel

co·gent \ˈkō-jənt\ adj : having power to compel or constrain : CONVINCING ⟨a ~ argument⟩ — **co·gen·cy** \-jən-sē\ n

cog·i·tate \ˈkä-jə-ˌtāt\ vb **-tat·ed; -tat·ing** : THINK, PONDER — **cog·i·ta·tion** \ˌkä-jə-ˈtā-shən\ n — **cog·i·ta·tive** \ˈkä-jə-ˌtā-tiv\ adj

co·gnac \'kōn-ˌyak\ *n* : a French brandy

cog·nate \'käg-ˌnāt\ *adj* **1** : of the same or similar nature **2** : RELATED; *esp* : related by descent from the same ancestral language — **cognate** *n*

cog·ni·tive \'käg-nə-tiv\ *adj* : of, relating to, or being conscious intellectual activity (as thinking, remembering, reasoning, or using language) — **cog·ni·tion** \käg-'ni-shən\ *n* — **cog·ni·tive·ly** *adv*

cog·ni·zance \'käg-nə-zəns\ *n* **1** : apprehension by the mind : AWARENESS **2** : NOTICE, HEED — **cog·ni·zant** \'käg-nə-zənt\ *adj*

cog·no·men \käg-'nō-mən, 'käg-nə-\ *n, pl* **cognomens** *or* **cog·no·mi·na** \käg-'nä-mə-nə, -'nō-\ : NAME; *esp* : NICKNAME

co·gno·scen·te \ˌkän-yə-'shen-tē\ *n, pl* **-scen·ti** \-tē\ [obs. It] : CONNOISSEUR

cog·wheel \'käg-ˌhwēl\ *n* : a wheel with cogs or teeth

co·hab·it \kō-'ha-bət\ *vb* : to live together as a couple — **co·hab·i·ta·tion** \-ˌha-bə-'tā-shən\ *n*

co·here \kō-'hir\ *vb* **co·hered; co·her·ing** : to stick together

co·her·ent \kō-'hir-ənt\ *adj* **1** : having the quality of cohering **2** : logically consistent ⟨a ~ explanation⟩ — **co·her·ence** \-əns\ *n* — **co·her·ent·ly** *adv*

co·he·sion \kō-'hē-zhən\ *n* **1** : a sticking together **2** : molecular attraction by which the particles of a body are united — **co·he·sive** \-siv\ *adj* — **co·he·sive·ly** *adv* — **co·he·sive·ness** *n*

co·ho \'kō-ˌhō\ *n, pl* **cohos** *or* **coho** : a rather small Pacific salmon with light-colored flesh

co·hort \'kō-ˌhòrt\ *n* **1** : a group of warriors or followers **2** : COMPANION, ACCOMPLICE

coif \'kòif; *2 usu* 'kwäf\ *n* **1** : a close-fitting hat **2** : COIFFURE

coif·feur \kwä-'fər\ *n* [F] : HAIRDRESSER

coif·feuse \kwä-'fərz, -'fəz, -'füz, -'fyüz\ *n* : a female hairdresser

coif·fure \kwä-'fyùr\ *n* : a manner of arranging the hair

¹coil \'kòi(-ə)l\ *vb* : to wind in a spiral shape

²coil *n* : a series of rings or loops (as of coiled rope, wire, or pipe) : RING, LOOP

¹coin \'kòin\ *n* [ME, wedge, corner, image on a coin, fr. AF *coing*, fr. L *cuneus* wedge] **1** : a piece of metal issued by government authority as money **2** : metal money

²coin *vb* **1** : to make (a coin) esp. by stamping : MINT **2** : CREATE, INVENT ⟨~ a phrase⟩ — **coin·er** *n*

coin·age \'kòi-nij\ *n* **1** : the act or process of coining **2** : COINS

co·in·cide \ˌkō-ən-'sīd, 'kō-ən-ˌsīd\ *vb* **-cid·ed; -cid·ing** **1** : to occupy the same place in space or time **2** : to correspond or agree exactly

co·in·ci·dence \kō-'in-sə-dəns\ *n* **1** : exact agreement **2** : occurrence together apparently without reason; *also* : an event that so occurs

co·in·ci·dent \-sə-dənt\ *adj* **1** : of similar nature **2** : occupying the same space or time — **co·in·ci·den·tal** \kō-ˌin-sə-'den-tᵊl\ *adj*

co·i·tus \'kō-ə-təs\ *n* [L, fr. *coire* to come together] : SEXUAL INTERCOURSE 1 — **co·i·tal** \-tᵊl\ *adj*

¹coke \'kōk\ *n* : a hard gray porous fuel made by heating soft coal to drive off most of its volatile material

²coke *n* : COCAINE

¹col *abbr* **1** colonial; colony **2** column

²col *or* **coll** *abbr* **1** collect, collected, collection **2** college, collegiate

Col *abbr* **1** colonel **2** Colorado **3** Colossians

COL *abbr* **1** colonel **2** cost of living

co·la \'kō-lə\ *n* : a carbonated soft drink usu. containing sugar, caffeine, caramel, and special flavoring

col·an·der \'kə-lən-dər, 'kä-\ *n* : a perforated utensil for draining food

¹cold \'kōld\ *adj* **1** : having a low or decidedly subnormal temperature **2** : lacking warmth of feeling **3** : suffering or uncomfortable from lack of warmth — **cold·ly** *adv* — **cold·ness** *n* — **in cold blood** : with premeditation : DELIBERATELY

²cold *n* **1** : a condition marked by low temperature; *also* : cold weather **2** : a chilly feeling **3** : a bodily disorder popularly associated with chilling; *esp* : COMMON COLD

³cold *adv* **1** : TOTALLY, FINALLY ⟨stopped them ~⟩ **2** : without notice or preparation

cold–blood·ed \'kōld-'blə-dəd\ *adj* **1** : lacking normal human feelings **2** : having a body temperature not internally regulated but close to that of the environment **3** : sensitive to cold

cold cuts *n pl* : sliced assorted cold cooked meats

cold feet *n pl* : doubt or fear that prevents action

cold front *n* : an advancing edge of a cold air mass

cold shoulder *n* : cold or unsympathetic behavior — **cold–shoul·der** *vb*

cold sore *n* : a group of fluid-filled blisters appearing in or about the mouth in the oral form of herpes simplex

cold sweat *n* : concurrent perspiration and chill usu. associated with fear, pain, or shock

¹cold turkey *n* : abrupt complete cessation of the use of an addictive drug

²cold turkey *adv* **1** : without a period of adjustment **2** : without preparation

cold war *n* : a conflict characterized by the use of means short of sustained overt military action

cole·slaw \'kōl-ˌslò\ *n* [D *koolsla*, fr. *kool* cabbage + *sla* salad] : a salad made of raw cabbage

col·ic \'kä-lik\ *n* **1** : sharp sudden abdominal pain **2** : a condition marked by recurrent episodes of crying and irritability in an otherwise healthy infant — **col·icky** \'kä-li-kē\ *adj*

col·i·se·um \ˌkä-lə-'sē-əm\ *n* : a large structure esp. for athletic contests

co·li·tis \kō-'lī-təs\ *n* : inflammation of the colon

col·lab·o·rate \kə-'la-bə-ˌrāt\ *vb* **-rat·ed; -rat·ing** **1** : to work jointly with others (as in writing a book) **2** : to cooperate with an enemy force occupying one's country — **col·lab·o·ra·tion** \-ˌla-bə-'rā-shən\ *n* — **col·lab·o·ra·tive** \-'la-bə-ˌrā-tiv, -b(ə-)rə-\ *adj* — **col·lab·o·ra·tor** \-'la-bə-ˌrā-tər\ *n*

col·lage \kə-'läzh\ *n* [F, lit., gluing] : an artistic composition of fragments (as of printed matter) pasted on a surface; *also* : a work that combines various elements into a cohesive whole

col·la·gen \'kä-lə-jən\ *n* : any of a group of fibrous proteins widely found in vertebrate connective tissue

¹col·lapse \kə-'laps\ *vb* **col·lapsed; col·laps·ing** **1** : to shrink together abruptly **2** : DISINTEGRATE; *also* : to fall in : give way **3** : to break down physically or mentally; *esp* : to fall helpless or unconscious **4** : to fold down compactly — **col·laps·ible** *adj*

²collapse *n* : BREAKDOWN

¹col·lar \'kä-lər\ *n* **1** : a band, strip, or chain worn around the neck or the neckline of a garment **2** : something resembling a collar — **col·lar·less** *adj*

²collar *vb* : to seize by the collar; *also* : ARREST, GRAB ⟨~ a fugitive⟩

col·lar·bone \-ˌbōn\ *n* : the bone of the shoulder that joins the breastbone and the shoulder blade

col·lard \'kä-lərd\ *n* : a stalked smooth-leaved kale — usu. used in pl.

col·late \kə-'lāt; 'kä-ˌlāt, 'kō-\ *vb* **col·lat·ed; col·lat·ing** **1** : to compare (as two texts) carefully and critically **2** : to assemble in proper order

¹col·lat·er·al \kə-'la-tə-rəl\ *adj* **1** : associated but of secondary importance **2** : descended from the same ancestors but not in the same line **3** : PARALLEL **4** : of, relating to, or being collateral used as security; *also* : secured by collateral

²collateral *n* : property (as stocks) used as security for the repayment of a loan

col·la·tion \kä-'lā-shən, kō-\ *n* **1** : a light meal **2** : the act, process, or result of collating

col·league \'kä-ˌlēg\ *n* : an associate esp. in a profession

¹col·lect \'kä-likt, -ˌlekt\ *n* : a short prayer comprising an invocation, petition, and conclusion

²col·lect \kə-'lekt\ *vb* **1** : to bring or come together into one body or place : GATHER **2** : to accumulate (as coins) as a hobby **3** : to gain control of ⟨~ his thoughts⟩ **4** : to receive payment of — **col·lect·ible** *or* **col·lect·able** *adj or n* — **col·lec·tor** \-'lek-tər\ *n*

³col·lect \kə-'lekt\ *adv or adj* : to be paid for by the receiver

col·lect·ed \kə-'lek-təd\ *adj* **1** : gathered together ⟨his ~ poems⟩ **2** : SELF-POSSESSED, CALM

col·lec·tion \kə-'lek-shən\ *n* **1** : the act or process of collecting ⟨garbage ∼⟩ **2** : something collected ⟨a stamp ∼⟩ **3** : GROUP, AGGREGATE

¹**col·lec·tive** \kə-ˈlek-tiv\ *adj* **1** : of, relating to, or denoting a group of individuals considered as a whole **2** : involving all members of a group as distinct from its individuals ⟨∼ action⟩ **3** : shared or assumed by all members of the group ⟨a ∼ groan⟩ — **col·lec·tive·ly** *adv*

²**collective** *n* **1** : GROUP **2** : a cooperative unit or organization

collective bargaining *n* : negotiation between an employer and a labor union

col·lec·tiv·ise *chiefly Brit var of* COLLECTIVIZE

col·lec·tiv·ism \kə-ˈlek-ti-ˌvi-zəm\ *n* : a political or economic theory advocating collective control esp. over production and distribution

col·lec·tiv·ize \-ˌvīz\ *vb* **-ized; -iz·ing** : to organize under collective control — **col·lec·tiv·i·za·tion** \-ˌlek-ti-və-ˈzā-shən\ *n*

col·leen \kä-ˈlēn, ˈkä-ˌlēn\ *n* : an Irish girl

col·lege \ˈkä-lij\ *n* [ME, endowed body of clergy or scholars, fr. AF, fr. L *collegium* society, fr. *collega* colleague, fr. *com-* with + *legare* to depute] **1** : a building used for an educational or religious purpose **2** : an institution of higher learning or division of a university granting a bachelor's degree; *also* : an institution offering instruction esp. in a vocational or technical field ⟨barber ∼⟩ **3** : an organized body of persons having common interests or duties ⟨∼ of cardinals⟩ — **col·le·giate** \kə-ˈlē-jət\ *adj*

col·le·gi·al·i·ty \kə-ˌlē-jē-ˈa-lə-tē\ *n* : the relationship of colleagues

col·le·gian \kə-ˈlē-jən\ *n* : a college student or recent college graduate

col·le·gi·um \kə-ˈle-gē-əm, -ˈlā-\ *n, pl* **-gia** \-gē-ə\ *or* **-giums** : a group in which each member has approximately equal power

col·lide \kə-ˈlīd\ *vb* **col·lid·ed; col·lid·ing** **1** : to come together with solid impact **2** : to come into conflict : CLASH

col·lid·er \kə-ˈlī-dər\ *n* : a particle accelerator in which two beams of particles are made to collide

col·lie \ˈkä-lē\ *n* : any of a breed of large dogs developed in Scotland for herding sheep that occur in rough-coated and smooth-coated varieties

col·lier \ˈkäl-yər\ *n* **1** : a coal miner **2** : a ship for carrying coal

col·liery \ˈkäl-yə-rē\ *n, pl* **-lier·ies** : a coal mine and its associated buildings

col·li·mate \ˈkä-lə-ˌmāt\ *vb* **-mat·ed; -mat·ing** : to make (as light rays) parallel

col·li·sion \kə-ˈli-zhən\ *n* : an act or instance of colliding

col·lo·ca·tion \ˌkä-lə-ˈkā-shən\ *n* : the act or result of placing or arranging together; *esp* : a noticeable arrangement or conjoining of linguistic elements (as words)

col·loid \ˈkä-ˌlȯid\ *n* : a substance in the form of submicroscopic particles that when in solution or suspension do not settle out; *also* : such a substance together with the medium in which it is dispersed — **col·loi·dal** \kə-ˈlȯi-dᵊl\ *adj*

colloq *abbr* colloquial

col·lo·qui·al \kə-ˈlō-kwē-əl\ *adj* : of, relating to, or characteristic of conversation and esp. of familiar and informal conversation

col·lo·qui·al·ism \-ˈlō-kwē-ə-ˌli-zəm\ *n* : a colloquial expression

col·lo·qui·um \kə-ˈlō-kwē-əm\ *n, pl* **-qui·ums** *or* **-quia** \-ə\ : CONFERENCE, SEMINAR

col·lo·quy \ˈkä-lə-kwē\ *n, pl* **-quies** : a usu. formal conversation or conference

col·lu·sion \kə-ˈlü-zhən\ *n* : secret agreement or cooperation for an illegal or deceitful purpose — **col·lu·sive** \-siv\ *adj*

Colo *abbr* Colorado

co·logne \kə-ˈlōn\ *n* [*Cologne,* Germany] : a perfumed liquid — **co·logned** \-ˈlōnd\ *adj*

Co·lom·bi·an \kə-ˈləm-bē-ən\ *n* : a native or inhabitant of Colombia — **Colombian** *adj*

¹**co·lon** \ˈkō-lən\ *n, pl* **colons** *or* **co·la** \-lə\ : the part of the large intestine extending from the cecum to the rectum — **co·lon·ic** \kō-ˈlä-nik\ *adj*

²**colon** *n, pl* **colons** : a punctuation mark : used esp. to direct attention to following matter (as a list)

co·lón *also* **co·lone** \kə-ˈlōn\ *n, pl* **co·lo·nes** \-ˈlō-ˌnäs\ — see MONEY table

col·o·nel \ˈkər-nᵊl\ *n* [alter. of *coronel,* fr. MF, fr. It *colonnello* column of soldiers, colonel, ultim. fr. L *columna* column] : a commissioned officer (as in the army) ranking next below a brigadier general

¹**co·lo·nial** \kə-ˈlō-nē-əl\ *adj* **1** : of, relating to, or characteristic of a colony; *also* : possessing or composed of colonies **2** *often cap* : of or relating to the original 13 colonies forming the U.S.

²**colonial** *n* **1** : a member or inhabitant of a colony **2** : a house built in the style of the American colonial period

co·lo·nial·ism \-ə-ˌli-zəm\ *n* : control by one power over a dependent area or people; *also* : a policy advocating or based on such control — **co·lo·nial·ist** \-list\ *n or adj*

col·o·nise *Brit var of* COLONIZE

col·o·nist \ˈkä-lə-nist\ *n* **1** : COLONIAL **2** : one that colonizes or settles in a new country

col·o·nize \ˈkä-lə-ˌnīz\ *vb* **-nized; -niz·ing** **1** : to establish a colony in or on **2** : SETTLE — **col·o·ni·za·tion** \ˌkä-lə-nə-ˈzā-shən\ *n* — **col·o·niz·er** *n*

col·on·nade \ˌkä-lə-ˈnād\ *n* : an evenly spaced row of columns usu. supporting the base of a roof structure

colonnade

co·lo·nos·co·py \ˌkō-lə-lə-ˈnäs-kə-pē\ *n, pl* **-pies** : endoscopic examination of the colon — **co·lon·o·scope** \kō-ˈlä-nə-ˌskōp\ *n*

col·o·ny \ˈkä-lə-nē\ *n, pl* **-nies** **1** : a body of people living in a new territory; *also* : the territory inhabited by these people **2** : a localized population of organisms ⟨a ∼ of bees⟩ **3** : a group with common interests situated in close association ⟨a writers' ∼⟩; *also* : the area occupied by such a group

co·lo·phon \ˈkä-lə-fən, -ˌfän\ *n* **1** : an inscription placed at the end of a book with facts relative to its production **2** : a distinctive symbol used by a printer or publisher

¹**col·or** \ˈkə-lər\ *n* **1** : a phenomenon of light (as red or blue) or visual perception that enables one to differentiate otherwise identical objects; *also* : a hue as contrasted with black, white, or gray **2** : APPEARANCE **3** : complexion tint **4** *pl* : FLAG; *also* : military service ⟨a call to the ∼s⟩ **5** : VIVIDNESS, INTEREST — **col·or·ful** *adj* — **col·or·less** *adj*

²**color** *vb* **1** : to give color to; *also* : to change the color of **2** : BLUSH

Col·o·ra·do potato beetle \ˌkä-lə-ˈra-dō-, -ˈrä-\ *n* : a black-and-yellow striped beetle that feeds on the leaves of the potato

col·or·ation \ˌkə-lə-ˈrā-shən\ *n* : use or arrangement of colors

col·o·ra·tu·ra \ˌkä-lə-rə-ˈtu̇r-ə, -ˈtyu̇r-\ *n* **1** : elaborate ornamentation in vocal music **2** : a soprano specializing in coloratura

col·or·blind \ˈkə-lər-ˌblīnd\ *adj* **1** : partially or totally unable to distinguish one or more chromatic colors **2** : not influenced by differences of race — **color blindness** *n*

co·lo·rec·tal \ˌkō-lō-ˈrek-tᵊl\ *adj* : relating to or affecting the colon and rectum ⟨∼ cancer⟩

col·ored \ˈkə-lərd\ *adj* **1** : having color **2** : SLANTED, BIASED

col·or·fast \ˈkə-lər-ˌfast\ *adj* : having color that does not fade or run — **col·or·fast·ness** *n*

col·or·ize \ˈkə-lə-ˌrīz\ *vb* **-ized; -iz·ing** : to add color to by means of a computer — **col·or·i·za·tion** \ˌkə-lə-rə-ˈzā-shən\ *n*

co·los·sal \kə-ˈlä-səl\ *adj* : of very great size or degree ⟨a ∼ feat⟩

Co·los·sians \kə-ˈlä-shənz\ *n* — see BIBLE table

co·los·sus \kə-'lä-səs\ *n, pl* **co·los·si** \-ˌsī\ [L] : a gigantic statue; *also* : something of immense size or power

col·our *chiefly Brit var of* COLOR

col·por·teur \'käl-ˌpȯr-tər\ *n* [F] : a peddler of religious books

colt \'kōlt\ *n* : FOAL; *also* : a young male horse, ass, or zebra — **colt·ish** *adj*

col·um·bine \'kä-ləm-ˌbīn\ *n* [ME, fr. AF, fr. ML *columbina,* fr. L, fem. of *columbinus* dovelike, fr. *columba* dove] : any of a genus of plants with showy spurred flowers that are related to the buttercups

co·lum·bi·um \kə-'ləm-bē-əm\ *n* : NIOBIUM

Columbus Day \kə-'ləm-bəs-\ *n* : the 2d Monday in October or formerly October 12 observed as a legal holiday in many states in commemoration of the landing of Columbus

col·umn \'kä-ləm\ *n* **1** : one of two or more vertical sections of a printed page; *also* : one in a usu. regular series of articles (as in a newspaper) **2** : a supporting pillar; *esp* : one consisting of a usu. round shaft, a capital, and a base **3** : something resembling a column ⟨a ∼ of water⟩ **4** : a long row (as of soldiers) **5** : a statistical category tracked vertically (as on a spreadsheet) — **co·lum·nar** \kə-'ləm-nər\ *adj*

col·um·nist \'kä-ləm-nist\ *n* : a person who writes a newspaper or magazine column

com *abbr* **1** comedy; comic **2** comma **3** commercial organization

co·ma \'kō-mə\ *n* : a state of deep unconsciousness caused by disease, injury, or poison — **co·ma·tose** \'kō-mə-ˌtōs, 'kä-\ *adj*

Co·man·che \kə-'man-chē\ *n, pl* **Comanche** *or* **Comanches** : a member of an American Indian people ranging from Wyoming and Nebraska south into New Mexico and Texas

¹comb \'kōm\ *n* **1** : a toothed instrument for arranging the hair or for separating and cleaning textile fibers **2** : a fleshy crest on the head of a fowl **3** : HONEYCOMB

²comb *vb* **1** : to pass a comb through **2** : to search through systematically

³comb *abbr* combination; combining

com·bat \kəm-'bat, 'käm-ˌbat\ *vb* **-bat·ed** *or* **-bat·ted; -bat·ing** *or* **-bat·ting** **1** : FIGHT, CONTEND **2** : to struggle against : OPPOSE — **com·bat** \'käm-ˌbat\ *n* — **com·bat·ant** \kəm-'ba-tᵊnt, 'käm-bə-tənt\ *n* — **com·bat·ive** \kəm-'ba-tiv\ *adj*

combat fatigue *n* : a traumatic psychological reaction occurring under wartime conditions (as combat) that cause intense stress

comb·er \'kō-mər\ *n* **1** : one that combs **2** : a long curling wave of the sea

com·bi·na·tion \ˌkäm-bə-'nā-shən\ *n* **1** : a result or product of combining **2** : a sequence of letters or numbers chosen in setting a lock **3** : the act or process of combining; *also* : the quality or state of being combined

¹com·bine \kəm-'bīn\ *vb* **com·bined; com·bin·ing** : to become one : UNITE

²com·bine \'käm-ˌbīn\ *n* **1** : a combination esp. of business or political interests **2** : a machine that harvests and threshes grain while moving over a field

comb·ings \'kō-miŋz\ *n pl* : loose hairs or fibers removed by a comb

combining form *n* : a linguistic form that occurs only in compounds or derivatives

com·bo \'käm-bō\ *n, pl* **combos** : a small jazz or dance band

comb–over \'kōm-ˌō-vər\ *n* : a hairstyle in which hair from the side of the head is combed over a bald spot

com·bus·ti·ble \kəm-'bəs-tə-bəl\ *adj* **1** : capable of being burned **2** : easily excited — **com·bus·ti·bil·i·ty** \-ˌbəs-tə-'bi-lə-tē\ *n* — **combustible** *n*

com·bus·tion \kəm-'bəs-chən\ *n* **1** : an act or instance of burning **2** : slow oxidation (as in the animal body)

comdg *abbr* commanding

comdr *abbr* commander

comdt *abbr* commandant

come \'kəm\ *vb* **came** \'kām\; **come; com·ing** \'kə-miŋ\ **1** : APPROACH **2** : ARRIVE **3** : to reach the point of being or becoming ⟨∼ to a boil⟩ **4** : AMOUNT ⟨the bill *came* to $10⟩ **5** : to take place **6** : ORIGINATE, ARISE ⟨wine ∼s from grapes⟩ **7** : to be available ⟨∼s in three sizes⟩ **8** : REACH, EXTEND ⟨grass that ∼s to our knees⟩ — **come across 1** : to make a specified impression ⟨*came across* as rude⟩ **2** : to find esp. by chance ⟨*came across* an intriguing story⟩ — **come clean** : CONFESS — **come into** : ACQUIRE, ACHIEVE — **come of age** : MATURE — **come to grips with** : to meet or deal with frankly — **come to pass** : HAPPEN — **come to terms** : to reach an agreement

come·back \'kəm-ˌbak\ *n* **1** : RETORT **2** : a return to a former position or condition — **come back** *vb*

co·me·di·an \kə-'mē-dē-ən\ *n* **1** : an actor in comedy **2** : a comic person; *esp* : an entertainer specializing in comedy

co·me·di·enne \-ˌmē-dē-'en\ *n* : a woman who is a comedian

come·down \'kəm-ˌdau̇n\ *n* : a descent in rank or dignity

com·e·dy \'kä-mə-dē\ *n, pl* **-dies** [ME, narrative that ends happily, fr. ML *comoedia,* fr. L, play with a happy ending, fr. Gk *kōmōidia,* fr. *kōmos* revel + *aeidein* to sing] **1** : a light amusing play with a happy ending **2** : a literary work treating a comic theme or written in a comic style **3** : humorous entertainment — **co·me·dic** \kə-'mē-dik\ *adj*

come·ly \'kəm-lē\ *adj* **come·li·er; -est** : ATTRACTIVE, HANDSOME — **come·li·ness** *n*

come off *vb* **1** : APPEAR, SEEM ⟨*comes off* as crass⟩ **2** : SUCCEED **3** : to have recently ended ⟨is *coming off* surgery⟩

come–on \'kə-ˌmȯn, -ˌmän\ *n* : INDUCEMENT, LURE

come out *vb* **1** : to come into public view **2** : to declare oneself **3** : TURN OUT **6** ⟨everything *came out* all right⟩ — **come out with** : SAY 1

com·er \'kə-mər\ *n* **1** : one that comes ⟨all ∼s⟩ **2** : a promising beginner

¹co·mes·ti·ble \kə-'mes-tə-bəl\ *adj* : EDIBLE

²comestible *n* : FOOD — usu. used in pl.

com·et \'kä-mət\ *n* [ME *comete,* fr. OE *cometa,* fr. L, fr. Gk *kometēs,* lit., long-haired, fr. *komē* hair] : a small bright celestial body that develops a long tail when near the sun

come to *vb* : to regain consciousness

come·up·pance \kə-'mə-pəns\ *n* : a deserved rebuke or penalty

com·fit \'kəm-fət\ *n* : a candied fruit or nut

¹com·fort \'kəm-fərt\ *vb* **1** : to give strength and hope to **2** : CONSOLE

²comfort *n* **1** : CONSOLATION **2** : freedom from pain, trouble, or anxiety; *also* : something that gives such freedom

com·fort·able \'kəm-fər-tə-bəl, 'kəmf-tər-\ *adj* **1** : providing comfort or security **2** : feeling at ease — **com·fort·ably** \-blē\ *adv*

com·fort·er \'kəm-fər-tər\ *n* **1** : one that comforts **2** : QUILT

com·frey \'kəm-frē\ *n, pl* **comfreys** : any of a genus of perennial herbs that have coarse hairy leaves and are often used in herbal remedies

com·fy \'kəm-fē\ *adj* : COMFORTABLE

¹com·ic \'kä-mik\ *adj* **1** : relating to comedy or comic strips **2** : provoking laughter or amusement ♦ *Synonyms* LAUGHABLE, FUNNY, FARCICAL — **com·i·cal** *adj*

²comic *n* **1** : COMEDIAN **2** *pl* : the part of a newspaper devoted to comic strips

comic book *n* : a magazine containing sequences of comic strips

comic strip *n* : a group of cartoons in narrative sequence

coming *adj* **1** : APPROACHING, NEXT **2** : gaining importance ⟨the ∼ trend⟩

co·mi·ty \'kä-mə-tē, 'kō-\ *n, pl* **-ties** : friendly civility : COURTESY

coml *abbr* commercial

comm *abbr* **1** command; commander **2** commerce; commercial **3** commission; commissioner **4** committee **5** common **6** commonwealth

com·ma \'kä-mə\ *n* : a punctuation mark, used esp. as a mark of separation within the sentence

¹com·mand \kə-'mand\ *vb* **1** : to direct authoritatively : ORDER **2** : DOMINATE, CONTROL, GOVERN **3** : to overlook from a strategic position

²command *n* **1** : an order given **2** : ability to control : MASTERY **3** : the act of commanding **4** : a signal that actuates a device (as a computer); *also* : the activation of a device by means of a signal **5** : a body of troops under a commander; *also* : an area or position that one commands **6** : a position of highest authority

com·man·dant \'kä-mən-ˌdant, -ˌdänt\ *n* : an officer in command

com·man·deer \ˌkä-mən-'dir\ *vb* : to take possession of by force

com·mand·er \kə-'man-dər\ *n* **1** : LEADER, CHIEF; *esp* : an officer commanding an army or subdivision of an army **2** : a commissioned officer in the navy ranking next below a captain

commander in chief : the supreme commander of the armed forces

com·mand·ment \kə-'mand-mənt\ *n* : COMMAND, ORDER; *esp* : any of the Ten Commandments

command module *n* : a space vehicle module designed to carry the crew and reentry equipment

com·man·do \kə-'man-dō\ *n, pl* **-dos** *or* **-does** : a member of a military unit trained for surprise raids

command sergeant major *n* : a noncommissioned officer in the army ranking above a sergeant major

com·mem·o·rate \kə-'me-mə-ˌrāt\ *vb* **-rat·ed; -rat·ing 1** : to call or recall to mind **2** : to serve as a memorial of — **com·mem·o·ra·tion** \-ˌme-mə-'rā-shən\ *n*

com·mem·o·ra·tive \kə-'mem-rə-tiv, -'me-mə-ˌrā-tiv\ *adj* : intended to commemorate an event ⟨a ∼ stamp⟩

com·mence \kə-'mens\ *vb* **com·menced; com·menc·ing** : BEGIN, START

com·mence·ment \-mənt\ *n* **1** : the act or time of a beginning **2** : the graduation exercises of a school or college

com·mend \kə-'mend\ *vb* **1** : to commit to one's care **2** : RECOMMEND **3** : PRAISE — **com·mend·able** \-'men-də-bəl\ *adj* — **com·mend·ably** \-blē\ *adv* — **com·men·da·tion** \ˌkä-mən-'dā-shən, -ˌmen-\ *n* — **com·mend·er** *n*

com·men·su·ra·ble \kə-'men-sə-rə-bəl\ *adj* : having a common measure or a common divisor

com·men·su·rate \kə-'men-sə-rət, -'men-chə-\ *adj* : equal in measure or extent; *also* : PROPORTIONAL, CORRESPONDING ⟨a job ∼ with her abilities⟩

com·ment \'kä-ˌment\ *n* **1** : an expression of opinion **2** : an explanatory, illustrative, or critical note or observation : REMARK — **comment** *vb*

com·men·tary \'kä-mən-ˌter-ē\ *n, pl* **-tar·ies** : a systematic series of comments

com·men·ta·tor \-ˌtā-tər\ *n* : one who comments; *esp* : a person who discusses news events on radio or television

com·merce \'kä-(ˌ)mərs\ *n* : the buying and selling of commodities : TRADE

¹**com·mer·cial** \kə-'mər-shəl\ *adj* : having to do with commerce; *also* : designed for profit or for mass appeal — **com·mer·cial·ly** *adv*

²**commercial** *n* : an advertisement broadcast on radio or television

com·mer·cial·ise *Brit var of* COMMERCIALIZE

com·mer·cial·ism \kə-'mər-shə-ˌli-zəm\ *n* **1** : a spirit, method, or practice characteristic of business **2** : excessive emphasis on profit

com·mer·cial·ize \-ˌlīz\ *vb* **-ized; -iz·ing 1** : to manage on a business basis for profit **2** : to exploit for profit

com·mi·na·tion \ˌkä-mə-'nā-shən\ *n* : DENUNCIATION — **com·mi·na·to·ry** \'kä-mə-nə-ˌtȯr-ē\ *adj*

com·min·gle \kə-'miŋ-gəl\ *vb* : MINGLE, BLEND

com·mis·er·ate \kə-'mi-zə-ˌrāt\ *vb* **-at·ed; -at·ing** : to feel or express pity : SYMPATHIZE — **com·mis·er·a·tion** \-ˌmi-zə-'rā-shən\ *n*

com·mis·sar \'kä-mə-ˌsär\ *n* [Russ *komissar*] : a Communist party official

com·mis·sar·i·at \ˌkä-mə-'ser-ē-ət\ *n* **1** : a system for supplying troops with food **2** : a department headed by a commissar

com·mis·sary \'kä-mə-ˌser-ē\ *n, pl* **-sar·ies** : a store for equipment and provisions esp. for military personnel

¹**com·mis·sion** \kə-'mi-shən\ *n* **1** : a warrant granting certain powers and imposing certain duties **2** : a certificate conferring military rank and authority **3** : authority to act as agent for another; *also* : something to be done by an agent **4** : a body of persons charged with performing a duty **5** : the doing of some act ⟨∼ of a crime⟩; *also* : the thing done **6** : the allowance made to an agent for transacting business for another

²**commission** *vb* **1** : to give a commission to **2** : to order to be made ⟨∼ a portrait⟩ **3** : to put (a ship) into a state of readiness for service

commissioned officer *n* : an officer of the armed forces holding rank by a commission from the president

com·mis·sion·er \kə-'mi-shə-nər\ *n* **1** : a member of a commission **2** : an official in charge of a department of public service ⟨a police ∼⟩ **3** : the administrative head of a professional sport — **com·mis·sion·er·ship** *n*

com·mit \kə-'mit\ *vb* **com·mit·ted; com·mit·ting 1** : to put into charge or trust : ENTRUST **2** : to put in a prison or mental institution **3** : TRANSFER, CONSIGN **4** : to carry into action : PERPETRATE ⟨∼ a crime⟩ **5** : to pledge or assign to some particular course or use — **com·mit·ment** *n* — **com·mit·tal** *n*

com·mit·tee \kə-'mi-tē\ *n* : a body of persons selected to consider and act or report on some matter — **com·mit·tee·man** \-mən\ *n* — **com·mit·tee·wom·an** \-ˌwu̇-mən\ *n*

commo *abbr* commodore

com·mode \kə-'mōd\ *n* [F, fr. *commode*, adj., suitable, convenient, fr. L *commodus*, fr. *com-* with + *modus* measure] **1** : a movable washstand with cupboard below **2** : TOILET **3**

com·mo·di·ous \kə-'mō-dē-əs\ *adj* : comfortably spacious : ROOMY

com·mod·i·ty \kə-'mä-də-tē\ *n, pl* **-ties 1** : a product of agriculture or mining **2** : an article of commerce **3** : something useful or valued ⟨that valuable ∼ patience⟩

com·mo·dore \'kä-mə-ˌdȯr\ *n* **1** : a commissioned officer in the navy ranking next below a rear admiral **2** : an officer commanding a group of merchant ships **3** : the chief officer of a yacht club

¹**com·mon** \'kä-mən\ *adj* **1** : belonging to or serving the community : PUBLIC **2** : shared by a number in a group **3** : widely or generally known, found, or observed : FAMILIAR ⟨∼ knowledge⟩ **4** : VERNACULAR **3** ⟨∼ names of plants⟩ **5** : not above the average esp. in social status ♦ **Synonyms** UNIVERSAL, GENERAL, GENERIC — **com·mon·ly** *adv*

²**common** *n* **1** *pl* : the common people **2** *pl* : a dining hall **3** *pl, cap* : the lower house of the British and Canadian parliaments **4** : a piece of land subject to common use — **in common** : shared together

com·mon·al·ty \'kä-mə-nºl-tē\ *n, pl* **-ties** : the common people

common cold *n* : a contagious respiratory disease caused by a virus and characterized by a sore, swollen, and inflamed nose and throat, usu. by much mucus, and by coughing and sneezing

common denominator *n* **1** : a common multiple of the denominators of a group of fractions **2** : a common trait or theme

common divisor *n* : a number or expression that divides two or more numbers or expressions without remainder

com·mon·er \'kä-mə-nər\ *n* : one of the common people : a person having no rank of nobility

common fraction *n* : a fraction (as ½ or ¾) in which the numerator and denominator are both integers and are separated by a horizontal or slanted line

common law *n* : a group of legal practices and traditions based on judges' decisions and social customs and usu. having the same force as laws passed by legislative bodies

common logarithm *n* : a logarithm whose base is 10

common market *n* : an economic association formed to remove trade barriers among members

common multiple *n* : a multiple of each of two or more numbers or expressions

¹**com·mon·place** \'kä-mən-ˌplās\ *n* : something that is ordinary or trite

²**commonplace** *adj* : ORDINARY

common sense *n* : ordinary good sense and judgment — **com·mon·sen·si·cal** \ˌkä-mən-'sen-si-kəl\ *adj*

com·mon·weal \'kä-mən-ˌwēl\ *n* **1** *archaic* : COMMONWEALTH **2** : the general welfare

com·mon·wealth \-ˌwelth\ *n* **1** : the body of people politically organized into a state : STATE; *also* : an association or federation of autonomous states

com·mo·tion \kə-'mō-shən\ *n* **1** : DISTURBANCE, UPRISING **2** : AGITATION

com·mu·nal \kə-'myü-nºl, 'käm-yə-nºl\ *adj* **1** : of or relating to a commune or community **2** : marked by collective ownership and use of property **3** : shared or used in common

¹com·mune \kə-'myün\ *vb* com·muned; com·mun·ing : to communicate intimately ⟨∼ with nature⟩

²com·mune \'käm-ˌyün; kə-'myün\ *n* **1** : the smallest administrative district in some European countries **2** : a community organized on a communal basis

com·mu·ni·ca·ble \kə-'myü-ni-kə-bəl\ *adj* : capable of being communicated ⟨∼ diseases⟩ — com·mu·ni·ca·bil·i·ty \-ˌmyü-ni-kə-'bi-lə-tē\ *n*

com·mu·ni·cant \-'myü-ni-kənt\ *n* **1** : a church member entitled to receive Communion **2** : one that communicates; *esp* : INFORMANT

com·mu·ni·cate \kə-'myü-nə-ˌkāt\ *vb* -cat·ed; -cat·ing **1** : to make known **2** : to pass from one to another : TRANSMIT **3** : to receive Communion **4** : to be in communication **5** : JOIN, CONNECT — com·mu·ni·ca·tor \-ˌkā-tər\ *n*

com·mu·ni·ca·tion \kə-ˌmyü-nə-'kā-shən\ *n* **1** : an act of transmitting **2** : MESSAGE **3** : exchange of information or opinions **4** : a means of communicating — com·mu·ni·ca·tive \-'myü-nə-ˌkā-tiv, -ni-kə-tiv\ *adj*

com·mu·nion \kə-'myü-nyən\ *n* **1** : a sharing of something with others **2** *cap* : a Christian sacrament in which bread and wine are consumed as the substance or symbols of Christ's body and blood in commemoration of the death of Christ **3** : intimate fellowship or rapport **4** : a body of Christians having a common faith and discipline

com·mu·ni·qué \kə-'myü-nə-ˌkā, -ˌmyü-nə-'kā\ *n* : BULLETIN 1

com·mu·nism \'käm-yə-ˌni-zəm\ *n* **1** : social organization in which goods are held in common **2** : a theory of social organization advocating common ownership of means of production and a distribution of products of industry based on need **3** *cap* : a political doctrine based on revolutionary Marxist socialism that was the official ideology of the U.S.S.R. and some other countries; *also* : a system of government in which one party controls state-owned means of production — com·mu·nist \-nist\ *n or adj, often cap* — com·mu·nis·tic \ˌkäm-yə-'nis-tik\ *adj, often cap*

com·mu·ni·ty \kə-'myü-nə-tē\ *n, pl* -ties **1** : a body of people living in the same place under the same laws; *also* : a natural population of plants and animals that interact ecologically and live in one place (as a pond) **2** : society at large **3** : joint ownership ⟨∼ of goods⟩ **4** : SIMILARITY, LIKENESS ⟨∼ of interests⟩

community college *n* : a 2-year government-supported college that offers an associate degree

community property *n* : property held jointly by husband and wife

com·mu·ta·tion \ˌkäm-yə-'tā-shən\ *n* : substitution of one form of payment or penalty for another

com·mu·ta·tive \'käm-yə-ˌtā-tiv, kə-'myü-tə-\ *adj* : of, having, or being the property that the result obtained using a mathematical operation on any two elements of a set does not differ with the order in which the elements are used ⟨a x b = b x a because multiplication is ∼⟩ — com·mu·ta·tiv·i·ty \kə-ˌmyü-tə-'ti-və-tē, ˌkäm-yə-tə-\ *n*

com·mu·ta·tor \'käm-yə-ˌtā-tər\ *n* : a device (as on a generator or motor) for changing the direction of electric current

¹com·mute \kə-'myüt\ *vb* com·mut·ed; com·mut·ing **1** : EXCHANGE **2** : to revoke (a sentence) and impose a milder penalty **3** : to travel back and forth regularly — com·mut·er *n*

²commute *n* : a trip made in commuting

comp *abbr* **1** comparative; compare **2** compensation **3** compiled; compiler **4** composition; compositor **5** compound **6** comprehensive **7** comptroller

¹com·pact \kəm-'pakt, 'käm-ˌpakt\ *adj* **1** : SOLID, DENSE **2** : BRIEF, SUCCINCT **3** : occupying a small volume by efficient use of space ⟨∼ camera⟩ — com·pact·ly *adv* — com·pact·ness *n*

²compact *vb* : to pack together : COMPRESS — com·pac·tor \kəm-'pak-tər, 'käm-ˌpak-\ *n*

³com·pact \'käm-ˌpakt\ *n* **1** : a small case for cosmetics **2** : a small automobile

⁴com·pact \'käm-ˌpakt\ *n* : AGREEMENT, COVENANT

com·pact disc \'käm-ˌpakt-\ *n* : CD

com·pa·dre \kəm-'pä-drā\ *n* : a close friend : BUDDY

¹com·pan·ion \kəm-'pan-yən\ *n* [ME *compainoun*, fr. AF *cumpaing, cumpaignun,* fr. LL *companion-, companio,* fr. L *com-* together + *panis* bread] **1** : an intimate friend or associate : COMRADE **2** : one that is closely connected with something similar **3** : a celestial body that appears close to another but that may not be associated with it in space — com·pan·ion·able *adj* — com·pan·ion·ship *n*

²companion *n* : COMPANIONWAY

com·pan·ion·way \-ˌwā\ *n* : a ship's stairway from one deck to another

com·pa·ny \'kəm-pə-nē\ *n, pl* -nies **1** : association with others : FELLOWSHIP; *also* : COMPANIONS **2** : GUESTS **3** : a group of persons or things **4** : an infantry unit consisting of two or more platoons and normally commanded by a captain **5** : a group of musical or dramatic performers **6** : the officers and crew of a ship **7** : an association of persons for carrying on a business ♦ **Synonyms** PARTY, BAND, TROOP, TROUPE, CORPS, OUTFIT

com·pa·ra·ble \'käm-pə-rə-bəl, -prə-\ *adj* : capable of being compared ⟨singers of ∼ talent⟩ ♦ **Synonyms** PARALLEL, SIMILAR, LIKE, ALIKE, CORRESPONDING — com·pa·ra·bil·i·ty \ˌkäm-pə-rə-'bi-lə-tē\ *n*

¹com·par·a·tive \kəm-'per-ə-tiv\ *adj* **1** : of, relating to, or constituting the degree of grammatical comparison that denotes increase in quality, quantity, or relation **2** : RELATIVE ⟨a ∼ stranger⟩ — com·par·a·tive·ly *adv*

²comparative *n* : the comparative degree or form in a language

¹com·pare \kəm-'per\ *vb* com·pared; com·par·ing **1** : to represent as similar : LIKEN **2** : to examine for likenesses and differences **3** : to inflect or modify (an adjective or adverb) according to the degrees of comparison

²compare *n* : the possibility of comparing ⟨beauty beyond ∼⟩

com·par·i·son \kəm-'per-ə-sən\ *n* **1** : the act of comparing **2** : change in the form of an adjective or adverb to show different levels of quality, quantity, or relation

com·part·ment \kəm-'pärt-mənt\ *n* **1** : a separate division **2** : a section of an enclosed space : ROOM

com·part·men·tal·ise *Brit var of* COMPARTMENTALIZE

com·part·men·tal·ize \kəm-ˌpärt-'men-tᵊl-ˌīz\ *vb* -ized; -iz·ing : to separate into compartments

¹com·pass \'kəm-pəs, 'käm-\ *vb* [ME, fr. AF *cumpasser* to measure, fr. VL **compassare* to pace off, fr. L *com-* + *passus* pace] **1** : CONTRIVE, PLOT **2** : ENCIRCLE, ENCOMPASS **3** : BRING ABOUT, ACHIEVE

²compass *n* **1** : BOUNDARY, CIRCUMFERENCE **2** : an enclosed space **3** : RANGE, SCOPE **4** : a device for determining direction by means of a magnetic needle swinging freely and pointing to the magnetic north; *also* : a nonmagnetic device that indicates direction **5** : an instrument for drawing circles or transferring measurements consisting of two legs joined by a pivot

com·pas·sion \kəm-'pa-shən\ *n* : sympathetic feeling : PITY, MERCY — com·pas·sion·ate \-shə-nət\ *adj* — com·pas·sion·ate·ly *adv*

com·pat·i·ble \kəm-'pa-tə-bəl\ *adj* : able to exist or act together harmoniously ⟨∼ colors⟩ ⟨∼ drugs⟩ ♦ **Synonyms** CONSONANT, CONGENIAL, SYMPATHETIC — com·pat·i·bil·i·ty \-ˌpa-tə-'bi-lə-tē\ *n*

com·pa·tri·ot \kəm-'pā-trē-ət, -ˌät\ *n* : a fellow countryman

com·peer \'käm-ˌpir\ *n* : EQUAL, PEER

com·pel \kəm-'pel\ *vb* com·pelled; com·pel·ling : to drive or urge with force

com·pen·di·ous \kəm-'pen-dē-əs\ *adj* : concise and comprehensive; *also* : COMPREHENSIVE ⟨a ∼ almanac⟩

com·pen·di·um \kəm-'pen-dē-əm\ *n, pl* -di·ums *or* -dia \-ə\ **1** : a brief summary of a larger work or of a field of knowledge **2** : COLLECTION

com·pen·sate \'käm-pən-ˌsāt\ *vb* -sat·ed; -sat·ing **1** : to be equivalent to : make up for **2** : PAY, REMUNERATE ♦ **Synonyms** BALANCE, OFFSET, COUNTERBALANCE, COUNTERPOISE — com·pen·sa·tion \ˌkäm-pən-'sā-shən\ *n* — com·pen·sa·to·ry \kəm-'pen-sə-ˌtȯr-ē\ *adj*

com·pete \kəm-'pēt\ *vb* com·pet·ed; com·pet·ing : CONTEND, VIE ⟨∼ for the title⟩ ⟨∼ for customers⟩

com·pe·tence \'käm-pə-təns\ *n* **1** : adequate means for subsistence **2** : FITNESS, ABILITY

com·pe·ten·cy \-tən-sē\ *n, pl* -cies : COMPETENCE

com·pe·tent \-tənt\ *adj* : CAPABLE, FIT, QUALIFIED ⟨a ∼ mechanic⟩ ⟨a ∼ juror⟩

com·pe·ti·tion \ˌkäm-pə-'ti-shən\ *n* **1** : the act of competing : RIVALRY **2** : CONTEST, MATCH; *also* : one's competitors — **com·pet·i·tive** \kəm-'pe-tə-tiv\ *adj* — **com·pet·i·tive·ly** *adv* — **com·pet·i·tive·ness** *n*

com·pet·i·tor \kəm-'pe-tə-tər\ *n* : one that competes : RIVAL

com·pile \kəm-'pī(-ə)l\ *vb* **com·piled; com·pil·ing** [ME, fr. AF *compiler*, fr. L *compilare* to plunder] **1** : to compose out of materials from other documents **2** : to collect and edit into a volume **3** : to translate (a computer program) with a compiler **4** : to build up gradually ⟨~ a record of four wins and two losses⟩ — **com·pi·la·tion** \ˌkäm-pə-'lā-shən\ *n*

com·pil·er \kəm-'pī-lər\ *n* : one that compiles **2** : a computer program that translates any program correctly written in a specific programming language into machine language

com·pla·cence \kəm-'plā-s°ns\ *n* : COMPLACENCY — **com·pla·cent** \-s°nt\ *adj* — **com·pla·cent·ly** *adv*

com·pla·cen·cy \-s°n-sē\ *n, pl* **-cies** : SATISFACTION; *esp* : SELF-SATISFACTION

com·plain \kəm-'plān\ *vb* **1** : to express grief, pain, or discontent **2** : to make a formal accusation — **com·plain·ant** *n* — **com·plain·er** *n*

com·plaint \kəm-'plānt\ *n* **1** : expression of grief, pain, or dissatisfaction **2** : a bodily ailment or disease **3** : a formal accusation against a person

com·plai·sance \kəm-'plā-s°ns, ˌkäm-plā-'zans\ *n* [F] : disposition to please — **com·plai·sant** \-s°nt, -'zant\ *adj* — **com·plai·sant·ly** *adv*

com·pleat \kəm-'plēt\ *adj* : PROFICIENT

com·plect·ed \kəm-'plek-təd\ *adj* : having a specified facial complexion ⟨dark-*complected*⟩

¹com·ple·ment \'käm-plə-mənt\ *n* **1** : something that fills up or completes; *also* : the full quantity, number, or amount that makes a thing complete **2** : an added word by which a predicate is made complete **3** : a group of proteins in blood that combines with antibodies to destroy antigens — **com·ple·men·ta·ry** \ˌkäm-plə-'men-t(ə-)rē\ *adj*

²com·ple·ment \-ˌment\ *vb* : to be complementary to : fill out

complementary medicine *n* : ALTERNATIVE MEDICINE

¹com·plete \kəm-'plēt\ *adj* **com·plet·er; -est** **1** : having all parts or elements **2** : brought to an end **3** : fully carried out; *also* : ABSOLUTE **2** ⟨~ silence⟩ — **com·plete·ly** *adv* — **com·plete·ness** *n* — **com·ple·tion** \-'plē-shən\ *n*

²complete *vb* **com·plet·ed; com·plet·ing** **1** : FINISH, CONCLUDE **2** : to make whole or perfect ⟨the hat ~s the outfit⟩

com·plet·ist \kəm-'plē-tist\ *n* : one who wants to make something (as a collection) complete

¹com·plex \'käm-ˌpleks\ *n* **1** : a whole made up of or involving intricately interrelated elements **2** : a group of repressed desires and memories that exert a dominating influence on one's personality and behavior ⟨a guilt ~⟩

²com·plex \käm-'pleks, 'käm-ˌpleks\ *adj* **1** : composed of two or more parts **2** : consisting of a main clause and one or more subordinate clauses ⟨~ sentence⟩ **3** : hard to separate, analyze, or solve — **com·plex·i·ty** \käm-'plek-sə-tē\ *n* — **com·plex·ly** *adv*

complex fraction *n* : a fraction with a fraction or mixed number in the numerator or denominator or both

com·plex·ion \kəm-'plek-shən\ *n* **1** : the hue or appearance of the skin esp. of the face **2** : overall appearance — **com·plex·ioned** \-shənd\ *adj*

complex number *n* : a number of the form $a + b \sqrt{-1}$ where *a* and *b* are real numbers

com·pli·ance \kəm-'plī-əns\ *n* **1** : the act of complying to a demand or proposal **2** : a disposition to yield — **com·pli·ant** \-ənt\ *adj*

com·pli·cate \'käm-plə-ˌkāt\ *vb* **-cat·ed; -cat·ing** : to make or become complex or intricate

com·pli·cat·ed \'käm-plə-ˌkā-təd\ *adj* **1** : consisting of parts intricately combined **2** : difficult to analyze, understand, or explain — **com·pli·cat·ed·ly** *adv*

com·pli·ca·tion \ˌkäm-plə-'kā-shən\ *n* **1** : the quality or state of being complicated; *also* : a complex feature **2** : a disease or condition that develops during and affects the course of a primary disease or condition

com·plic·i·ty \kəm-'pli-sə-tē\ *n, pl* **-ties** : the state of being an accomplice

¹com·pli·ment \'käm-plə-mənt\ *n* **1** : an expression of approval or admiration; *esp* : a flattering remark **2** *pl* : best wishes : REGARDS

²com·pli·ment \-ˌment\ *vb* : to pay a compliment to

com·pli·men·ta·ry \ˌkäm-plə-'men-t(ə-)rē\ *adj* **1** : containing or expressing a compliment **2** : given free as a courtesy ⟨~ ticket⟩

com·ply \kəm-'plī\ *vb* **com·plied; com·ply·ing** : CONFORM, YIELD

¹com·po·nent \kəm-'pō-nənt, 'käm-ˌpō-\ *n* : a component part ◆ *Synonyms* INGREDIENT, ELEMENT, FACTOR, CONSTITUENT

²component *adj* : serving to form a part of : CONSTITUENT

com·port \kəm-'pōrt\ *vb* **1** : AGREE, ACCORD ⟨actions that ~ with policy⟩ **2** : CONDUCT ⟨~ oneself with dignity⟩ ◆ *Synonyms* BEHAVE, ACQUIT, DEPORT — **com·port·ment** *n*

com·pose \kəm-'pōz\ *vb* **com·posed; com·pos·ing** **1** : to form by putting together : FASHION **2** : to produce (as pages of type) by composition **3** : ADJUST, ARRANGE **4** : CALM, QUIET **5** : to practice composition ⟨~ music⟩ — **com·pos·er** *n*

¹com·pos·ite \käm-'pä-zət\ *adj* **1** : made up of distinct parts or elements **2** : of, relating to, or being a large family of flowering plants (as a daisy or aster) that bear many small flowers united into compact heads resembling single flowers

²composite *n* **1** : something composite **2** : a plant of the composite family ◆ *Synonyms* BLEND, COMPOUND, MIXTURE, AMALGAMATION

com·po·si·tion \ˌkäm-pə-'zi-shən\ *n* **1** : the act or process of composing; *esp* : arrangement esp. in artistic form **2** : the arrangement or production of type for printing **3** : general makeup **4** : a product of mixing various elements or ingredients **5** : a literary, musical, or artistic product; *esp* : ESSAY

com·po·si·tion·ist \-'zi-shə-nist\ *n* : a teacher of writing

com·pos·i·tor \kəm-'pä-zə-tər\ *n* : one who sets type

com·post \'käm-ˌpōst\ *n* : a fertilizing material consisting largely of decayed organic matter — **compost** *vb*

com·po·sure \kəm-'pō-zhər\ *n* : CALMNESS, SELF-POSSESSION

com·pote \'käm-ˌpōt\ *n* **1** : fruits cooked in syrup **2** : a bowl (as of glass) usu. with a base and stem for serving esp. fruit or compote

¹com·pound \käm-'paund, 'käm-ˌ\ *vb* [ME *compounen*, fr. AF *cumpundre*, fr. L *componere*, fr. *com-* together + *ponere* to put] **1** : COMBINE **2** : to form by combining parts ⟨~ a medicine⟩ **3** : SETTLE ⟨~ a dispute⟩; *also* : to refrain from prosecuting (an offense) in return for a consideration **4** : to increase (as interest) by an amount that can itself vary; *also* : to add to

²com·pound \'käm-ˌpaund\ *adj* **1** : made up of individual parts **2** : composed of united similar parts esp. of a kind usu. independent ⟨a ~ plant ovary⟩ **3** : formed by the combination of two or more otherwise independent elements ⟨~ sentence⟩

³com·pound \'käm-ˌpaund\ *n* **1** : a word consisting of parts that are words **2** : something formed from a union of elements or parts; *esp* : a distinct substance formed by the union of two or more chemical elements ◆ *Synonyms* MIXTURE, COMPOSITE, BLEND, ADMIXTURE, ALLOY

⁴com·pound \'käm-ˌpaund\ *n* [by folk etymology fr. Malay *kampung* group of buildings, village] : an enclosure containing buildings

compound interest *n* : interest computed on the sum of an original principal and accrued interest

com·pre·hend \ˌkäm-pri-'hend\ *vb* **1** : UNDERSTAND **2** : INCLUDE — **com·pre·hen·si·ble** \-'hen-sə-bəl\ *adj* — **com·pre·hen·sion** \-'hen-chən\ *n*

com·pre·hen·sive \ˌkäm-pri-'hen-siv\ *adj* : covering completely or broadly ⟨~ insurance⟩ — **com·pre·hen·sive·ly** *adv* — **com·pre·hen·sive·ness** *n*

¹com·press \kəm-'pres\ *vb* **1** : to squeeze together **2** : to reduce in size as if by squeezing ◆ *Synonyms* CONSTRICT, CONTRACT, SHRINK — **com·pres·sor** \-'pre-sər\ *n*

²com·press \'käm-ˌpres\ *n* : a folded pad or cloth used to press upon a body part

compressed air *n* : air under pressure greater than that of the atmosphere

com·pres·sion \kəm-'pre-shən\ n 1 : the act or process of compressing 2 : the process of compressing the fuel mixture in an internal combustion engine 3 : conversion (as of data) in order to reduce the space occupied or the bandwidth required

com·prise \kəm-'prīz\ vb **com·prised; com·pris·ing 1** : INCLUDE, CONTAIN 2 : to be made up of 3 : COMPOSE, CONSTITUTE

¹**com·pro·mise** \'käm-prə-ˌmīz\ n : a settlement of differences reached by mutual concessions

²**compromise** vb **-mised; -mis·ing 1** : to settle by compromise 2 : to expose to suspicion or loss of reputation

comp·trol·ler \kən-'trō-lər, 'kämp-ˌtrō-\ n : an official who audits and supervises expenditures and accounts

com·pul·sion \kəm-'pəl-shən\ n 1 : an act of compelling 2 : a force that compels 3 : an irresistible persistent impulse to perform an act ♦ *Synonyms* CONSTRAINT, FORCE, VIOLENCE, DURESS — **com·pul·sive** \-siv\ adj — **com·pul·sive·ly** adv — **com·pul·so·ry** \-sə-rē\ adj

com·punc·tion \kəm-'pəŋk-shən\ n : anxiety arising from guilt : REMORSE

com·pute \kəm-'pyüt\ vb **com·put·ed; com·put·ing** : CALCULATE, RECKON — **com·pu·ta·tion** \ˌkäm-pyü-'tā-shən\ n — **com·pu·ta·tion·al** adj

computed tomography n : radiography in which a three-dimensional image of a body structure is constructed by computer from a series of plane cross-sectional images made along an axis

com·put·er \kəm-'pyü-tər\ n : a programmable electronic device that can store, retrieve, and process data

com·put·er·ise *chiefly Brit var of* COMPUTERIZE

com·put·er·ize \kəm-'pyü-tə-ˌrīz\ vb **-ized; -iz·ing 1** : to carry out, control, or produce by means of a computer 2 : to provide with computers 3 : to store in a computer; *also* : put into a form that a computer can use — **com·put·er·i·za·tion** \-ˌpyü-tə-rə-'zā-shən\ n

computerized axial tomography n : COMPUTED TOMOGRAPHY

com·rade \'käm-ˌrad\ n [MF *camarade* group sleeping in one room, roommate, companion, fr. Sp *camarada*, fr. *cámara* room, fr. LL *camera*] : COMPANION, ASSOCIATE — **com·rade·ly** adj — **com·rade·ship** n

¹**con** \'kän\ vb **conned; con·ning 1** : MEMORIZE 2 : STUDY

²**con** adv : in opposition : AGAINST

³**con** n : an opposing argument, person, or position ⟨pros and ~s⟩

⁴**con** vb **conned; con·ning 1** : SWINDLE 2 : PERSUADE, CAJOLE

⁵**con** n : CONVICT

conc abbr concentrated

con·cat·e·nate \kän-'ka-tə-ˌnāt\ vb **-nat·ed; -nat·ing** : to link together in a series or chain — **con·cat·e·na·tion** \(ˌ)kän-ˌka-tə-'nā-shən\ n

con·cave \kän-'kāv, 'kän-ˌ\ adj : curved or rounded inward like the inside of a bowl — **con·cav·i·ty** \kän-'ka-və-tē\ n

con·ceal \kən-'sēl\ vb : to place out of sight : HIDE — **con·ceal·er** n — **con·ceal·ment** n

con·cede \kən-'sēd\ vb **con·ced·ed; con·ced·ing 1** : to admit to be true 2 : GRANT, YIELD ♦ *Synonyms* ALLOW, ACKNOWLEDGE, AVOW, CONFESS

con·ceit \kən-'sēt\ n 1 : excessively high opinion of one's self or ability : VANITY 2 : an elaborate or strained metaphor — **con·ceit·ed** adj — **con·ceit·ed·ly** adv — **con·ceit·ed·ness** n

con·ceive \kən-'sēv\ vb **con·ceived; con·ceiv·ing 1** : to become pregnant or pregnant with ⟨~ a child⟩ 2 : to form an idea of : THINK, IMAGINE — **con·ceiv·able** \-'sē-və-bəl\ adj — **con·ceiv·ably** \-blē\ adv

con·cel·e·brant \kən-'se-lə-brənt\ n : one that jointly participates in celebrating the Eucharist

¹**con·cen·trate** \'kän-sən-ˌtrāt\ vb **-trat·ed; -trat·ing 1** : to gather into one body, mass, or force 2 : to make less dilute 3 : to fix one's powers, efforts, or attentions

²**concentrate** n : something concentrated

con·cen·tra·tion \ˌkän-sən-'trā-shən\ n 1 : the act or process of concentrating : the state of being concentrated; *esp* : direction of attention on a single object 2 : the amount of a component in a given area or volume

concentration camp n : a camp where persons (as prisoners of war or political prisoners) are confined

con·cen·tric \kən-'sen-trik\ adj 1 : having a common center ⟨~ circles⟩ 2 : COAXIAL

¹**con·cept** \'kän-ˌsept\ n : THOUGHT, NOTION, IDEA — **con·cep·tu·al** \kən-'sep-chə-wəl\ adj — **con·cep·tu·al·ly** adv

²**concept** adj 1 : organized around a main idea or theme ⟨a ~ album⟩ 2 : created to illustrate a concept ⟨a ~ car⟩

con·cep·tion \kən-'sep-shən\ n 1 : the process of conceiving or being conceived 2 : the power to form or understand ideas or concepts 3 : IDEA, CONCEPT 4 : the originating of something

con·cep·tu·al·ise *Brit var of* CONCEPTUALIZE

con·cep·tu·al·ize \-'sep-chə-wə-ˌlīz\ vb **-ized; -iz·ing** : to form a conception of

¹**con·cern** \kən-'sərn\ vb 1 : to relate to 2 : to be the business of : INVOLVE 3 : ENGAGE, OCCUPY

²**concern** n 1 : INTEREST, ANXIETY 2 : AFFAIR, MATTER 3 : a business organization ♦ *Synonyms* CARE, WORRY, DISQUIET, UNEASE

con·cerned \-'sərnd\ adj 1 : ANXIOUS, UNEASY ⟨~ for their safety⟩ 2 : INVOLVED

con·cern·ing \-'sər-niŋ\ prep : relating to : REGARDING

con·cern·ment \kən-'sərn-mənt\ n 1 : something in which one is concerned 2 : IMPORTANCE, CONSEQUENCE

¹**con·cert** \'kän-(ˌ)sərt\ n 1 : agreement in a plan or design 2 : a public performance (as of music)

²**con·cert** \kən-'sərt\ vb : to plan together

con·cert·ed \kən-'sər-təd\ adj : mutually agreed on; *also* : performed in unison

con·cer·ti·na \ˌkän-sər-'tē-nə\ n : an instrument of the accordion family

concertina wire n : a coiled wire with sharp points for use as an obstacle

con·cert·mas·ter \'kän-sərt-ˌmas-tər\ *or* **con·cert·meis·ter** \-ˌmī-stər\ n : the leader of the first violins of an orchestra and assistant to the conductor

con·cer·to \kən-'cher-tō\ n, pl **-ti** \-(ˌ)tē\ *or* **-tos** [It] : a piece for one or more solo instruments and orchestra in three movements

con·ces·sion \kən-'se-shən\ n 1 : an act of conceding or yielding 2 : something yielded 3 : a grant by a government of land or of a right to use it 4 : a grant of a portion of premises for some specific purpose; *also* : the activities or enterprise carried on — **con·ces·sion·ary** \-'se-shə-ˌner-ē\ adj

con·ces·sion·aire \kən-ˌse-shə-'ner\ n : one that owns or operates a concession

conch \'käŋk, 'känch\ n, pl **conchs** \'käŋks\ *or* **conch·es** \'kän-chəz\ : a large spiral-shelled marine gastropod mollusk; *also* : its shell

conch

con·cierge \kōⁿ-'syerzh\ n, pl **con·cierges** *same or* -'syer-zhəz\ [F] 1 : a resident in an apartment building who performs services for the tenants 2 : a usu. multilingual hotel staff member who usu. handles mail and reservations

con·cil·i·ate \kən-'si-lē-ˌāt\ vb **-at·ed; -at·ing 1** : to bring into agreement : RECONCILE 2 : to gain the goodwill of — **con·cil·i·a·tion** \-ˌsi-lē-'ā-shən\ n — **con·cil·i·a·tor** \-'si-lē-ˌā-tər\ n — **con·cil·i·a·to·ry** \-'si-lē-ə-ˌtōr-ē\ adj

con·cise \kən-'sīs\ adj : expressing much in few words : BRIEF — **con·cise·ly** adv — **con·cise·ness** n

con·clave \'kän-ˌklāv\ n [ME, fr. ML, fr. L, room that can be locked, fr. *com-* together + *clavis* key] : a private gathering; *also* : CONVENTION

con·clude \kən-'klüd\ *vb* **con·clud·ed; con·clud·ing** **1** : to bring to a close : END **2** : DECIDE, JUDGE **3** : to bring about as a result ◆ *Synonyms* CLOSE, FINISH, TERMINATE, COMPLETE, HALT

con·clu·sion \kən-'klü-zhən\ *n* **1** : the logical consequence of a reasoning process **2** : TERMINATION, END **3** : OUTCOME, RESULT — **con·clu·sive** \-siv\ *adj* — **con·clu·sive·ly** *adv* — **con·clu·sive·ness** *n*

con·coct \kən-'käkt, kän-\ *vb* **1** : to prepare by combining raw materials **2** : DEVISE — **con·coc·tion** \-'käk-shən\ *n*

con·com·i·tant \-'kä-mə-tənt\ *adj* : ACCOMPANYING, ATTENDING — **concomitant** *n*

con·cord \'kän-,kȯrd, 'käŋ-\ *n* : AGREEMENT, HARMONY

con·cor·dance \kən-'kȯr-dᵊns\ *n* **1** : an alphabetical index of words in a book or in an author's works with the passages in which they occur **2** : AGREEMENT, COVENANT

con·cor·dant \-dᵊnt\ *adj* : HARMONIOUS, AGREEING

con·cor·dat \kən-'kȯr-,dat\ *n* : CONCORDANCE 2

con·course \'kän-,kȯrs\ *n* **1** : a spontaneous coming together : GATHERING **2** : an open space or hall (as in a bus terminal) where crowds gather

¹con·crete \'kän-,krēt, 'kän-,krēt\ *adj* **1** : naming a real thing or class of things : not abstract **2** : not theoretical : ACTUAL **3** : made of or relating to concrete

²con·crete \'kän-,krēt, kän-'krēt\ *vb* **con·cret·ed; con·cret·ing** **1** : SOLIDIFY **2** : to cover with concrete

³con·crete \'kän-,krēt, kän-'krēt\ *n* : a hard building material made by mixing cement, sand, and gravel with water

con·cre·tion \kän-'krē-shən\ *n* : a hard mass esp. when formed abnormally in the body

con·cu·bine \'kän-kyu̇-,bīn\ *n* [ME, fr. AF, fr. L *concubina,* fr. *com-* with + *cubare* to lie] : a woman who is not legally a wife but lives with a man and sometimes has a recognized position in his household; *also* : MISTRESS — **con·cu·bi·nage** \kän-'kyü-bə-nij\ *n*

con·cu·pis·cence \kän-'kyü-pə-səns\ *n* : ardent sexual desire : LUST

con·cur \kən-'kər\ *vb* **con·curred; con·cur·ring** **1** : to act together **2** : AGREE **3** : COINCIDE ◆ *Synonyms* UNITE, COMBINE, COOPERATE, BAND, JOIN

con·cur·rence \-'kər-əns\ *n* **1** : agreement in action or opinion **2** : occurrence together : CONJUNCTION

con·cur·rent \-'kər-ənt\ *adj* **1** : happening or operating at the same time **2** : joint and equal in authority

con·cus·sion \kən-'kə-shən\ *n* **1** : a hard blow or collision; *also* : bodily injury (as to the brain) resulting from a sudden jar **2** : AGITATION, SHAKING

con·demn \kən-'dem\ *vb* **1** : to declare to be wrong **2** : to convict of guilt **3** : to sentence judicially **4** : to pronounce unfit for use ⟨~ a building⟩ **5** : to declare forfeited or taken for public use ◆ *Synonyms* DENOUNCE, CENSURE, BLAME, CRITICIZE, REPREHEND — **con·dem·na·tion** \,kän-,dem-'nā-shən\ *n* — **con·dem·na·to·ry** \kən-'dem-nə-,tȯr-ē\ *adj*

con·den·sate \'kän-dən-,sāt, kən-'den-\ *n* : a product of condensation

con·dense \kən-'dens\ *vb* **con·densed; con·dens·ing** **1** : to make or become more compact or dense : CONCENTRATE **2** : to change from vapor to liquid ◆ *Synonyms* CONTRACT, SHRINK, COMPRESS, CONSTRICT — **con·den·sa·tion** \,kän-den-'sā-shən\ *n*

con·dens·er \kən-'den-sər\ *n* **1** : one that condenses **2** : CAPACITOR

con·de·scend \,kän-di-'send\ *vb* : to assume an air of superiority — **con·de·scend·ing·ly** \-'sen-diŋ-lē\ *adv* — **con·de·scen·sion** \-'sen-chən\ *n*

con·dign \kən-'dīn, 'kän-,dīn\ *adj* : DESERVED, APPROPRIATE ⟨~ punishment⟩

con·di·ment \'kän-də-mənt\ *n* : something used to make food savory; *esp* : a pungent seasoning (as pepper)

¹con·di·tion \kən-'di-shən\ *n* **1** : something essential to the occurrence of some other thing **2** : state of being **3** : social status **4** *pl* : state of affairs : CIRCUMSTANCES **5** : a bodily state in which something is wrong ⟨a heart ~⟩ **6** : a state of health, fitness, or working order ⟨in good ~⟩

²condition *vb* **1** : to put into proper condition for action or use **2** : to adapt, modify, or mold to respond in a particular way **3** : to modify so that an act or response previously associated with one stimulus becomes associated with another

con·di·tion·al \kən-'di-shə-nəl\ *adj* : containing, implying, or depending on a condition — **con·di·tion·al·ly** *adv*

con·di·tioned \-'di-shənd\ *adj* : determined or established by conditioning

con·di·tion·er \-'di-shə-nər\ *n* : a preparation used to improve the condition of hair

con·do \'kän-(,)dō\ *n* : CONDOMINIUM 3

con·dole \kən-'dōl\ *vb* **con·doled; con·dol·ing** : to express sympathetic sorrow — **con·do·lence** \kən-'dō-ləns\ *n*

con·dom \'kän-dəm, 'kən-\ *n* : a usu. rubber sheath worn over the penis (as to prevent pregnancy or venereal infection during sexual intercourse)

con·do·min·i·um \,kän-də-'mi-nē-əm\ *n, pl* **-ums** **1** : joint sovereignty (as by two or more nations) **2** : a politically dependent territory under condominium **3** : individual ownership of a unit (as an apartment) in a multiunit structure; *also* : a unit so owned

con·done \kən-'dōn\ *vb* **con·doned; con·don·ing** : to overlook or forgive esp. by treating (an offense) as harmless or trivial ◆ *Synonyms* EXCUSE, PARDON, FORGIVE, REMIT — **con·do·na·tion** \,kän-də-'nā-shən\ *n*

con·dor \'kän-dər, -,dȯr\ *n* [Sp *cóndor,* fr. Quechua *kuntur*] : a very large American vulture of the high Andes; *also* : a related nearly extinct vulture of southern California now resident only in captivity

con·duce \kən-'düs, -'dyüs\ *vb* **con·duced; con·duc·ing** : to lead or contribute to a particular result — **con·du·cive** *adj*

¹con·duct \'kän-(,)dəkt\ *n* **1** : MANAGEMENT, DIRECTION **2** : BEHAVIOR

²con·duct \kən-'dəkt\ *vb* **1** : GUIDE, ESCORT **2** : MANAGE, DIRECT **3** : to act as a medium for conveying or transmitting **4** : BEHAVE — **con·duc·tion** \-'dək-shən\ *n*

con·duc·tance \kən-'dək-təns\ *n* : the readiness with which a conductor transmits an electric current

con·duc·tive \kən-'dək-tiv\ *adj* : having the power to conduct (as heat or electricity) — **con·duc·tiv·i·ty** \,kän-,dək-'ti-və-tē\ *n*

con·duc·tor \kən-'dək-tər\ *n* **1** : one that conducts; *esp* : a material that permits an electric current to flow easily **2** : a collector of fares in a public conveyance **3** : the leader of a musical ensemble

con·duit \'kän-,dü-ət, -,dyü-, -dwət\ *n* **1** : a channel for conveying fluid **2** : a tube or trough for protecting electric wires or cables **3** : a means of transmitting or distributing

con·dyle \'kän-,dī(-ə)l, -dᵊl\ *n* : an articular prominence of a bone — **con·dy·lar** \-də-lər\ *adj*

cone \'kōn\ *n* **1** : the scaly usu. ovate fruit of trees of most conifers **2** : a solid figure formed by rotating a right triangle about one of its legs **3** : a solid figure that slopes evenly to a point from a usu. circular base **4** : any of the conical light-sensitive receptor cells of the retina that function in color vision **5** : something shaped like a cone

cone·flow·er \'kōn-,flau̇(-ə)r\ *n* : any of several composite plants having cone-shaped flower disks

Con·es·to·ga wagon \,kä-nə-'stō-gə-\ *n* : a broad-wheeled covered wagon used esp. for transporting freight across the prairies

Conestoga wagon

co·ney *or* **co·ny** \'kō-nē\ *n, pl* **coneys** *or* **conies** **1** : RABBIT; *also* : its fur **2** : PIKA

conf *abbr* **1** conference **2** confidential

con·fab \'kän-,fab, kən-'fab\ *n* : CONFABULATION 1

con·fab·u·la·tion \kən-ˌfab-yə-ˈlā-shən\ n 1 : CHAT; also : CONFERENCE 2 : a filling in of gaps in memory by fabrication — **con·fab·u·late** \-ˈfa-byə-ˌlāt\ vb

con·fec·tion \kən-ˈfek-shən\ n 1 : something put together from varied material 2 : a fancy dish or sweet; also : CANDY — **con·fect** \kən-ˈfekt\ vb

con·fec·tion·er \-sh(ə-)nər\ n : a maker of or dealer in confections

con·fec·tion·ery \-shə-ˌner-ē\ n, pl **-er·ies** 1 : sweet foods 2 : a confectioner's place of business

Confed abbr Confederate

con·fed·er·a·cy \kən-ˈfe-də-rə-sē\ n, pl **-cies** 1 : LEAGUE, ALLIANCE 2 cap : the 11 southern states that seceded from the U.S. in 1860 and 1861

¹con·fed·er·ate \kən-ˈfe-də-rət\ adj 1 : united in a league : ALLIED 2 cap : of or relating to the Confederacy

²confederate n 1 : ALLY, ACCOMPLICE 2 cap : an adherent of the Confederacy

³con·fed·er·ate \-ˈfe-də-ˌrāt\ vb **-at·ed; -at·ing** : to unite in a confederacy

con·fed·er·a·tion \kən-ˌfe-də-ˈrā-shən\ n 1 : an act of confederating : ALLIANCE 2 : LEAGUE

con·fer \kən-ˈfər\ vb **con·ferred; con·fer·ring** 1 : GRANT, BESTOW 2 : to exchange views : CONSULT — **con·fer·ee** \ˌkän-fə-ˈrē\ n

con·fer·ence \ˈkän-f(ə-)rəns\ n 1 : an interchange of views; also : a meeting for this purpose 2 : an association of athletic teams

con·fer·enc·ing \ˈkän-f(ə-)rən-siŋ\ n : the holding of conferences esp. by means of electronic devices

con·fess \kən-ˈfes\ vb 1 : to acknowledge or disclose one's misdeed, fault, or sin 2 : to acknowledge one's sins to God or to a priest 3 : to receive the confession of a (penitent) ♦ **Synonyms** ADMIT, OWN, AVOW, CONCEDE, GRANT

con·fessed·ly \-ˈfe-səd-lē\ adv : by confession : ADMITTEDLY

con·fes·sion \-ˈfe-shən\ n 1 : an act of confessing (as in the sacrament of penance) 2 : an acknowledgment of guilt 3 : a formal statement of religious beliefs 4 : a religious body having a common creed — **con·fes·sion·al** adj

con·fes·sion·al \-ˈfe-shə-nəl\ n : a place where a priest hears confessions

con·fes·sor \kən-ˈfe-sər\ n 1 : one that confesses 2 : a priest who hears confessions

con·fet·ti \kən-ˈfe-tē\ n [It, pl. of confetto sweetmeat, fr. ML confectum, fr. L, neut. of confectus, pp. of conficere to prepare] : bits of colored paper or ribbon for throwing (as at weddings)

con·fi·dant \ˈkän-fə-ˌdänt, -ˌdant\ n : one to whom secrets are confided

con·fi·dante \-ˌdänt, -ˌdant\ n : CONFIDANT; esp : one who is a woman

con·fide \kən-ˈfīd\ vb **con·fid·ed; con·fid·ing** 1 : to have or show faith : TRUST ⟨~ in a friend⟩ 2 : to tell confidentially ⟨~ a secret⟩ 3 : ENTRUST

¹con·fi·dence \ˈkän-fə-dəns\ n 1 : TRUST, RELIANCE 2 : SELF-ASSURANCE, BOLDNESS 3 : a state of trust or intimacy 4 : SECRET 2 — **con·fi·dent** \-dənt\ adj — **con·fi·dent·ly** adv

²confidence adj : of or relating to swindling by false promises ⟨a ~ game⟩

con·fi·den·tial \ˌkän-fə-ˈden-shəl\ adj 1 : SECRET, PRIVATE ⟨~ information⟩ 2 : entrusted with confidences ⟨~ clerk⟩ — **con·fi·den·ti·al·i·ty** \-ˌden-shē-ˈa-lə-tē\ n — **con·fi·den·tial·ly** \-ˈden-shə-lē\ adv

con·fig·u·ra·tion \kən-ˌfi-gyə-ˈrā-shən\ n : structural arrangement of parts : SHAPE

con·fig·ure \kən-ˈfi-gyər\ vb **-ured; -ur·ing** : to set up for operation esp. in a particular way

con·fine \kən-ˈfīn\ vb **con·fined; con·fin·ing** 1 : to hold within a location; also : IMPRISON 2 : to keep within limits ⟨will ~ my remarks to one subject⟩ — **con·fine·ment** n — **con·fin·er** n

con·fines \ˈkän-ˌfīnz\ n pl : BOUNDS, BORDERS

con·firm \kən-ˈfərm\ vb 1 : to give approval to : RATIFY 2 : to make firm or firmer 3 : to administer the rite of confirmation to 4 : VERIFY, CORROBORATE — **con·fir·ma·to·ry** \-ˈfər-mə-ˌtȯr-ē\ adj

con·fir·ma·tion \ˌkän-fər-ˈmā-shən\ n 1 : a religious cere-

mony admitting a person to full membership in a church or synagogue 2 : an act of ratifying or corroborating; also : PROOF

con·fis·cate \ˈkän-fə-ˌskāt\ vb **-cat·ed; -cat·ing** [L confiscare, fr. com- with + fiscus treasury] : to take possession of by or as if by public authority — **con·fis·ca·tion** \ˌkän-fə-ˈskā-shən\ n — **con·fis·ca·to·ry** \kən-ˈfis-kə-ˌtȯr-ē\ adj

con·fit \kȯn-ˈfē\ n : a garnish of fruit or vegetables cooked in a seasoned liquid

con·fla·gra·tion \ˌkän-flə-ˈgrā-shən\ n : FIRE; esp : a large disastrous fire

¹con·flict \ˈkän-ˌflikt\ n 1 : WAR 2 : a clash between hostile or opposing elements, ideas, or forces

²con·flict \kən-ˈflikt\ vb : to show opposition or irreconcilability : CLASH

con·flu·ence \ˈkän-ˌflü-əns, kən-ˈflü-\ n 1 : a coming together at one point 2 : the meeting or place of meeting of two or more streams — **con·flu·ent** \-ənt\ adj

con·flux \ˈkän-ˌfləks\ n : CONFLUENCE

con·form \kən-ˈfȯrm\ vb 1 : to be similar or identical; also : AGREE 2 : to obey customs or standards; also : COMPLY — **con·form·able** adj — **con·form·ist** \-ˈfȯr-mist\ adj

con·for·mance \kən-ˈfȯr-məns\ n : CONFORMITY

con·for·ma·tion \ˌkän-fȯr-ˈmā-shən\ n : a forming into a whole by arranging parts

con·for·mi·ty \kən-ˈfȯr-mə-tē\ n, pl **-ties** 1 : HARMONY, AGREEMENT 2 : COMPLIANCE, OBEDIENCE

con·found \kən-ˈfaùnd, kän-\ vb 1 : to throw into disorder or confusion 2 : CONFUSE 2 ♦ **Synonyms** BEWILDER, PUZZLE, PERPLEX, BEFOG

con·fra·ter·ni·ty \ˌkän-frə-ˈtər-nə-tē\ n : a society devoted esp. to a religious or charitable cause

con·frere \ˈkän-ˌfrer, ˈkōⁿ-\ n : COLLEAGUE, COMRADE

con·front \kən-ˈfrənt\ vb 1 : to face esp. in challenge : OPPOSE; also : to deal unflinchingly with ⟨~ed the issue⟩ 2 : to cause to face or meet — **con·fron·ta·tion** \ˌkän-frən-ˈtā-shən\ n — **con·fron·ta·tion·al** \-shə-nᵊl\ adj

Con·fu·cian \kən-ˈfyü-shən\ adj : of or relating to the Chinese philosopher Confucius or his teachings — **Con·fu·cian·ism** \-shə-ˌni-zəm\ n

con·fuse \kən-ˈfyüz\ vb **con·fused; con·fus·ing** 1 : to make mentally unclear or uncertain; also : to disturb the composure of 2 : to mix up : JUMBLE ♦ **Synonyms** MUDDLE, BEFUDDLE, ADDLE, FLUSTER — **con·fus·ed·ly** \-ˈfyü-zəd-lē\ adv — **con·fus·ing·ly** \-ˈfyü-ziŋ-lē\ adv

con·fu·sion \-ˈfyü-zhən\ n 1 : an act or instance of confusing 2 : the quality or state of being confused

con·fute \kən-ˈfyüt\ vb **con·fut·ed; con·fut·ing** : to overwhelm by argument : REFUTE — **con·fu·ta·tion** \ˌkän-fyù-ˈtā-shən\ n

cong abbr congress; congressional

con·ga \ˈkäŋ-gə\ n : a Cuban dance of African origin performed by a group usu. in single file

con·geal \kən-ˈjēl\ vb 1 : FREEZE 2 : to make or become hard or thick

con·gee \ˈkän-jē\ n : porridge made from rice

con·ge·ner \ˈkän-jə-nər\ n : one related to another; esp : a plant or animal of the same taxonomic genus as another — **con·ge·ner·ic** \ˌkän-jə-ˈner-ik\ adj

con·ge·nial \kən-ˈjē-nyəl\ adj 1 : KINDRED, SYMPATHETIC ⟨~ companions⟩ 2 : suited to one's taste or nature : AGREEABLE — **con·ge·ni·al·i·ty** \-ˌjē-nē-ˈa-lə-tē\ n — **con·ge·nial·ly** adv

con·gen·i·tal \kən-ˈje-nə-tᵊl\ adj : existing at or dating from birth ⟨~ deafness⟩ ♦ **Synonyms** INBORN, INNATE, NATURAL

con·ger eel \ˈkäŋ-gər-\ n : a large edible marine eel of the Atlantic

con·ge·ries \ˈkän-jə-(ˌ)rēz\ n, pl **congeries** : AGGREGATION, COLLECTION

con·gest \kən-ˈjest\ vb 1 : to cause excessive fullness of the blood vessels of (as a lung) 2 : to obstruct by overcrowding — **con·ges·tion** \-ˈjes-chən\ n — **con·ges·tive** \-ˈjes-tiv\ adj

congestive heart failure n : heart failure in which the heart is unable to keep enough blood circulating in the tissues or is unable to pump out the blood returned to it by the veins

¹con·glom·er·ate \kən-ˈglä-mə-rət\ adj [L conglomerare to roll together, fr. *com-* together + *glomerare* to wind into a ball, fr. *glomer-*, *glomus* ball] : made up of parts from various sources

²**con·glom·er·ate** \-ˌrāt\ *vb* **-at·ed; -at·ing** : to form into a mass — **con·glom·er·a·tion** \-ˌglä-mə-ˈrā-shən\ *n*

³**con·glom·er·ate** \-rət\ *n* **1** : a mass formed of fragments from various sources; *esp* : a rock composed of fragments varying from pebbles to boulders held together by a cementing material **2** : a widely diversified corporation

con·grat·u·late \kən-ˈgra-chə-ˌlāt\ *vb* **-lat·ed; -lat·ing** : to express sympathetic pleasure to on account of success or good fortune : FELICITATE — **con·grat·u·la·tion** \-ˌgra-chə-ˈlā-shən\ *n* — **con·grat·u·la·to·ry** \-ˈgra-chə-lə-ˌtōr-ē\ *adj*

con·gre·gate \ˈkäŋ-gri-ˌgāt\ *vb* **-gat·ed; -gat·ing** [ME, fr. L *congregatus*, pp. of *congregare*, fr. *com-* together + *greg-*, *grex* flock] : ASSEMBLE

con·gre·ga·tion \ˌkäŋ-gri-ˈgā-shən\ *n* **1** : an assembly of persons met esp. for worship; *also* : a group that habitually so meets **2** : a religious community or order **3** : the act or an instance of congregating

con·gre·ga·tion·al \-shə-nəl\ *adj* **1** : of or relating to a congregation **2** *cap* : observing the faith and practice of certain Protestant churches which recognize the independence of each congregation in church matters — **con·gre·ga·tion·al·ism** \-nə-ˌli-zəm\ *n, often cap* — **con·gre·ga·tion·al·ist** \-list\ *n, often cap*

con·gress \ˈkäŋ-grəs\ *n* **1** : an assembly esp. of delegates for discussion and usu. action on some question **2** : the body of senators and representatives constituting a nation's legislature — **con·gres·sio·nal** \kən-ˈgre-shə-nəl\ *adj*

con·gress·man \ˈkäŋ-grəs-mən\ *n* : a member of a congress

con·gress·wom·an \-ˌwu̇-mən\ *n* : a woman who is a member of a congress

con·gru·ence \kən-ˈgrü-əns, ˈkäŋ-grü-\ *n* : the quality of agreeing or coinciding : CONGRUITY — **con·gru·ent** \kən-ˈgrü-ənt, ˈkäŋ-grü-\ *adj*

con·gru·en·cy \-sē\ *n, pl* **-cies** : CONGRUENCE

con·gru·ity \kän-ˈgrü-ə-tē\ *n, pl* **-ities** : correspondence between things — **con·gru·ous** \ˈkäŋ-grü-əs\ *adj*

con·ic \ˈkä-nik\ *adj* **1** : of or relating to a cone **2** : CONICAL

con·i·cal \ˈkä-ni-kəl\ *adj* : resembling a cone esp. in shape

co·ni·fer \ˈkä-nə-fər, ˈkō-\ *n* : any of an order of shrubs or trees (as the pines) that usu. are evergreen and bear cones — **co·nif·er·ous** \kō-ˈni-fə-rəs\ *adj*

conj *abbr* conjunction

con·jec·ture \kən-ˈjek-chər\ *n* : GUESS, SURMISE — **con·jec·tur·al** \-chə-rəl\ *adj* — **conjecture** *vb*

con·join \kən-ˈjȯin\ *vb* : to join together — **con·joint** \-ˈjȯint\ *adj*

con·ju·gal \ˈkän-ji-gəl\ *adj* : of or relating to marriage : MATRIMONIAL

¹**con·ju·gate** \ˈkän-ji-gət, -jə-ˌgāt\ *adj* **1** : united esp. in pairs : COUPLED **2** : of kindred origin and meaning ⟨*sing* and *song* are ∼⟩ — **con·ju·gate·ly** *adv*

²**con·ju·gate** \-jə-ˌgāt\ *vb* **-gat·ed; -gat·ing** **1** : INFLECT ⟨∼ a verb⟩ **2** : to join together : COUPLE

con·ju·ga·tion \ˌkän-jə-ˈgā-shən\ *n* **1** : an arrangement of the inflectional forms of a verb **2** : the act of conjugating : the state of being conjugated

con·junct \kän-ˈjəŋkt\ *adj* : JOINED, UNITED

con·junc·tion \kən-ˈjəŋk-shən\ *n* **1** : COMBINATION **2** : occurrence at the same time **3** : a word that joins together sentences, clauses, phrases, or words

con·junc·ti·va \ˌkän-jəŋk-ˈtī-və\ *n, pl* **-vas** *or* **-vae** \-(ˌ)vē\ : the mucous membrane lining the inner surface of the eyelids and continuing over the forepart of the eyeball

con·junc·tive \kən-ˈjəŋk-tiv\ *adj* **1** : CONNECTIVE **2** : CONJUNCT ⟨the ∼ operation of different factors⟩ **3** : being or functioning like a conjunction

con·junc·ti·vi·tis \kən-ˌjəŋk-ti-ˈvī-təs\ *n* : inflammation of the conjunctiva

con·junc·ture \kən-ˈjəŋk-chər\ *n* **1** : CONJUNCTION, UNION **2** : JUNCTURE 3

con·jun·to \kōn-ˈhün-tō\ *n* : Mexican-American music influenced by the music of German immigrants to Texas

con·jure \ˈkän-jər, ˈkən- *for 1, 2;* kən-ˈju̇r *for 3*\ *vb* **con·jured; con·jur·ing** **1** : to implore earnestly or solemnly

2 : to practice magic; *esp* : to summon (as a devil) by sorcery **3** : to practice sleight of hand — **con·ju·ra·tion** \ˌkän-ju̇-ˈrā-shən, ˌkən-\ *n* — **con·jur·er** *or* **con·ju·ror** \ˈkän-jər-ər, ˈkən-\ *n*

conk \ˈkäŋk\ *vb* : BREAK DOWN; *esp* : STALL ⟨the motor ∼ed out⟩

Conn *abbr* Connecticut

con·nect \kə-ˈnekt\ *vb* **1** : JOIN, LINK **2** : to associate in one's mind **3** : to establish a communications connection ⟨∼ to the Internet⟩ — **con·nect·able** *adj* — **con·nec·tor** *n*

con·nec·tion \kə-ˈnek-shən\ *n* **1** : JUNCTION, UNION **2** : logical relationship : COHERENCE; *esp* : relation of a word to other words in a sentence **3** : family relationship **4** : BOND, LINK **5** : a person related by blood or marriage **6** : relationship in social affairs or in business **7** : an association of persons; *esp* : a religious denomination **8** : a means of communication or transport ⟨a telephone ∼⟩

¹**con·nec·tive** \kə-ˈnek-tiv\ *adj* : serving to connect — **con·nec·tiv·i·ty** \ˌkä-ˌnek-ˈti-və-tē\ *n*

²**connective** *n* : a word (as a conjunction) that connects words or word groups

connective tissue *n* : a tissue (as bone or cartilage) that forms a supporting framework for the body or its parts

con·nex·ion *chiefly Brit var of* CONNECTION

con·ning tower \ˈkä-niŋ-\ *n* : a raised structure on the deck of a submarine

con·nip·tion \kə-ˈnip-shən\ *n* : a fit of rage, hysteria, or alarm

con·nive \kə-ˈnīv\ *vb* **con·nived; con·niv·ing** [F or L; F *conniver*, fr. L *conivēre* to close the eyes, connive] **1** : to pretend ignorance of something one ought to oppose as wrong **2** : to cooperate secretly : give secret aid — **con·niv·ance** *n* — **con·niv·er** *n*

con·nois·seur \ˌkä-nə-ˈsər\ *n* : a critical judge in matters of art or taste

con·no·ta·tion \ˌkä-nə-ˈtā-shən\ *n* : a meaning in addition to or apart from the thing explicitly named or described by a word

con·no·ta·tive \ˈkä-nə-ˌtā-tiv, kə-ˈnō-tə-\ *adj* **1** : connoting or tending to connote **2** : relating to connotation

con·note \kə-ˈnōt\ *vb* **con·not·ed; con·not·ing** : to suggest or mean as a connotation

con·nu·bi·al \kə-ˈnü-bē-əl, -ˈnyü-\ *adj* : of or relating to marriage : CONJUGAL

con·quer \ˈkäŋ-kər\ *vb* **1** : to gain by force of arms : WIN **2** : to get the better of : OVERCOME ♦ *Synonyms* DEFEAT, SUBJUGATE, SUBDUE, OVERTHROW, VANQUISH — **con·quer·or** \-ər\ *n*

con·quest \ˈkän-ˌkwest, ˈkäŋ-\ *n* **1** : an act of conquering : VICTORY **2** : something conquered

con·quis·ta·dor \kȯn-ˈkēs-tə-ˌdȯr, kän-ˈkwis-\ *n, pl* **-do·res** \-ˌkēs-tə-ˈdȯr-ēz, -ˌkwis-\ *or* **-dors** : CONQUEROR; *esp* : a leader in the Spanish conquest of the Americas in the 16th century

cons *abbr* consonant

con·san·guin·i·ty \ˌkän-san-ˈgwi-nə-tē, -ˌsaŋ-\ *n, pl* **-ties** : blood relationship — **con·san·guin·e·ous** \-nē-əs\ *adj*

con·science \ˈkän-chəns\ *n* : consciousness of the moral right and wrong of one's own acts or motives — **con·sci·ence·less** *adj*

con·sci·en·tious \ˌkän-chē-ˈen-chəs\ *adj* : guided by one's own sense of right and wrong ♦ *Synonyms* SCRUPULOUS, HONORABLE, HONEST, UPRIGHT, JUST — **con·sci·en·tious·ly** *adv*

conscientious objector *n* : a person who refuses to serve in the armed forces or to bear arms on moral or religious grounds

¹**con·scious** \ˈkän-chəs\ *adj* **1** : AWARE **2** : known or felt by one's inner self **3** : mentally awake or alert : not asleep or unconscious **4** : done with awareness or purpose ⟨a ∼ decision⟩ — **con·scious·ly** *adv* — **con·scious·ness** *n*

²**conscious** *n* : the upper level of mental life of which a person is aware : CONSCIOUSNESS

con·script \kən-ˈskript\ *vb* : to enroll by compulsion for military or naval service — **conscript** \ˈkän-ˌskript\ *n* — **con·scrip·tion** \kən-ˈskrip-shən\ *n*

con·se·crate \ˈkän-sə-ˌkrāt\ *vb* **-crat·ed; -crat·ing** [ME, fr. L *consecratus*, pp. of *consecrare*, fr. *com-* together +

sacrare to set aside as sacred, fr. *sacer* sacred] **1** : to in-duct (as a bishop) into an office with a religious rite **2** : to make or declare sacred ⟨~ a church⟩ **3** : to devote solemnly to a purpose — **con·se·cra·tion** \ˌkän-sə-ˈkrā-shən\ *n*

con·sec·u·tive \kən-ˈse-kyə-tiv\ *adj* : following in regular order : SUCCESSIVE — **con·sec·u·tive·ly** *adv*

con·sen·su·al \kən-ˈsen-chə-wəl\ *adj* : involving or based on mutual consent

con·sen·sus \kən-ˈsen-səs\ *n* **1** : agreement in opinion, testimony, or belief **2** : collective opinion

¹con·sent \kən-ˈsent\ *vb* : to give assent or approval

²consent *n* : approval or acceptance of something done or proposed by another

con·se·quence \ˈkän-sə-ˌkwens\ *n* **1** : RESULT **2** : IM-PORTANCE ✦ *Synonyms* EFFECT, OUTCOME, AFTER-MATH, UPSHOT

con·se·quent \-kwənt, -ˌkwent\ *adj* : following as a result or effect

con·se·quen·tial \ˌkän-sə-ˈkwen-chəl\ *adj* **1** : having sig-nificant consequences **2** : showing self-importance

con·se·quent·ly \ˈkän-sə-ˌkwent-lē, -kwənt-\ *adv* : as a re-sult : ACCORDINGLY

con·ser·van·cy \kən-ˈsər-vən-sē\ *n, pl* **-cies** : an organiza-tion or area designated to conserve natural resources

con·ser·va·tion \ˌkän-sər-ˈvā-shən\ *n* : PRESERVATION; *esp* : planned management of natural resources

con·ser·va·tion·ist \-shə-nist\ *n* : a person who advocates conservation esp. of natural resources

con·ser·va·tism \kən-ˈsər-və-ˌti-zəm\ *n* : disposition to keep to established ways : opposition to change

¹con·ser·va·tive \kən-ˈsər-və-tiv\ *adj* **1** : PRESERVATIVE **2** : disposed to maintain existing views, conditions, or in-stitutions **3** : MODERATE, CAUTIOUS ⟨a ~ invest\ment⟩ — **con·ser·va·tive·ly** *adv*

²conservative *n* : a person who is conservative esp. in pol-itics

con·ser·va·tor \kən-ˈsər-və-tər, ˈkän-sər-ˌvā-\ *n* **1** : PRO-TECTOR, GUARDIAN **2** : one named by a court to protect the interests of an incompetent (as a child)

con·ser·va·to·ry \kən-ˈsər-və-ˌtȯr-ē\ *n, pl* **-ries** **1** : GREENHOUSE **2** : a place of instruction in one of the fine arts (as music)

¹con·serve \kən-ˈsərv\ *vb* **con·served; con·serv·ing** : to keep from losing or wasting : PRESERVE

²con·serve \ˈkän-ˌsərv\ *n* **1** : CONFECTION 2; *esp* : a can-died fruit **2** : PRESERVE; *esp* : one prepared from a mix-ture of fruits

con·sid·er \kən-ˈsi-dər\ *vb* [ME, fr. AF *considerer*, fr. L *considerare* to observe, think about, fr. *com-* together + *sider-, sidus* heavenly body] **1** : THINK, PONDER **2** : HEED, REGARD **3** : JUDGE, BELIEVE — **con·sid·ered** *adj*

con·sid·er·able \-ˈsi-dər-ə-bəl, -ˈsi-drə-bəl\ *adj* **1** : IMPOR-TANT **2** : large in extent, amount, or degree — **con·sid-er·ably** \-blē\ *adv*

con·sid·er·ate \kən-ˈsi-də-rət\ *adj* : observant of the rights and feelings of others ✦ *Synonyms* THOUGHTFUL, AT-TENTIVE

con·sid·er·ation \kən-ˌsi-də-ˈrā-shən\ *n* **1** : careful thought : DELIBERATION **2** : a matter taken into ac-count **3** : thoughtful attention **4** : JUDGMENT, OPIN-ION **5** : RECOMPENSE

con·sid·er·ing \-ˈsi-d(ə-)riŋ\ *prep* : in view of : taking into account ⟨did well ~ his limitations⟩

con·sign \kən-ˈsīn\ *vb* **1** : ENTRUST, COMMIT **2** : to de-liver formally **3** : to send (goods) to an agent for sale — **con·sign·ee** \ˌkän-sə-ˈnē, -ˌsī-; kən-ˌsī-\ *n* — **con·sign·or** \ˌkän-sə-ˈnȯr, -ˌsī-; kən-ˌsī-\ *n*

con·sign·ment \kən-ˈsīn-mənt\ *n* : something consigned esp. in a single shipment

con·sil·ience \kən-ˈsil-yəns\ *n* : the linking together of principles from different disciplines when forming a com-prehensive theory

con·sist \kən-ˈsist\ *vb* **1** : to be inherent : LIE — usu. used with *in* **2** : to be composed or made up — usu. used with *of*

con·sis·tence \kən-ˈsis-təns\ *n* : CONSISTENCY

con·sis·ten·cy \-tən-sē\ *n, pl* **-cies** **1** : COHESIVENESS, FIRMNESS **2** : agreement or harmony in parts or of dif-

ferent things **3** : UNIFORMITY ⟨~ of behavior⟩ — **con-sis·tent** \-tənt\ *adj* — **con·sis·tent·ly** *adv*

con·sis·to·ry \kən-ˈsis-tə-rē\ *n, pl* **-ries** : a solemn assem-bly (as of Roman Catholic cardinals)

consol *abbr* consolidated

¹con·sole \ˈkän-ˌsōl\ *n* [F] **1** : the desklike part of an organ at which the organist sits **2** : the combination of displays and controls of a device or system **3** : a cabinet for a radio or television set resting directly on the floor **4** : a small storage cabinet between bucket seats in an auto-mobile

²con·sole \kən-ˈsōl\ *vb* **con·soled; con·sol·ing** : to soothe the grief of : COMFORT, SOLACE — **con·so·la·tion** \ˌkän-sə-ˈlā-shən\ *n* — **con·so·la·to·ry** \kən-ˈsō-lə-ˌtȯr-ē, -ˈsä-\ *adj*

con·sol·i·date \kən-ˈsä-lə-ˌdāt\ *vb* **-dat·ed; -dat·ing** **1** : to unite or become united into one whole : COMBINE **2** : to make firm or secure **3** : to form into a compact mass — **con·sol·i·da·tion** \-ˌsä-lə-ˈdā-shən\ *n* — **con·sol·i·da·tor** \-ˈsä-lə-ˌdā-tər\ *n*

con·som·mé \ˌkän-sə-ˈmā\ *n* [F] : a clear soup made from well-seasoned stock

con·so·nance \ˈkän-sə-nəns\ *n* **1** : AGREEMENT, HARMO-NY **2** : repetition of consonants esp. as an alternative to rhyme in verse

¹con·so·nant \-nənt\ *adj* : having consonance, harmony, or agreement ✦ *Synonyms* CONSISTENT, COMPATIBLE, CONGRUOUS, CONGENIAL, SYMPATHETIC — **con·so-nant·ly** *adv*

²consonant *n* **1** : a speech sound (as \p\, \g\, \n\, \l\, \s\, \r\) characterized by constriction or closure at one or more points in the breath channel **2** : a letter other than *a, e, i, o,* and *u* — **con·so·nan·tal** \ˌkän-sə-ˈnan-tᵊl\ *adj*

¹con·sort \ˈkän-ˌsȯrt\ *n* **1** : a ship accompanying another **2** : SPOUSE, MATE

²con·sort \kən-ˈsȯrt\ *vb* **1** : to keep company **2** : AC-CORD, HARMONIZE

con·sor·tium \kən-ˈsȯr-shəm, -shē-əm, -tē-\ *n, pl* **-sor·tia** \-shə-; -shē-ə, -tē-\ [L, fellowship] : an agreement or com-bination (as of companies) formed to undertake a large enterprise

con·spec·tus \kən-ˈspek-təs\ *n* **1** : a brief survey or sum-mary **2** : SUMMARY

con·spic·u·ous \kən-ˈspi-kyə-wəs\ *adj* : attracting atten-tion : PROMINENT, STRIKING ✦ *Synonyms* NOTICEABLE, REMARKABLE, OUTSTANDING — **con·spic·u·ous·ly** *adv*

con·spir·a·cy \kən-ˈspir-ə-sē\ *n, pl* **-cies** : an agreement among conspirators : PLOT

con·spir·a·tor \kən-ˈspir-ə-tər\ *n* : one who conspires — **con·spir·a·to·ri·al** \-ˌspir-ə-ˈtȯr-ē-əl\ *adj*

con·spire \kən-ˈspī(-ə)r\ *vb* **conspired; con·spir·ing** [ME, fr. AF *conspirer,* fr. L *conspirare* to be in harmony, con-spire, fr. *com-* together + *spirare* to breathe] : to plan se-cretly an unlawful act : PLOT

const *abbr* **1** constant **2** constitution; constitutional

con·sta·ble \ˈkän-stə-bəl, ˈkən-\ *n* [ME *conestable,* fr. AF, fr. LL *comes stabuli,* lit., officer of the stable] : a public officer responsible for keeping the peace

con·stab·u·lary \kən-ˈsta-byə-ˌler-ē\ *n, pl* **-lar·ies** **1** : the police of a particular district or country **2** : a police force organized like the military

con·stan·cy \ˈkän-stən-sē\ *n, pl* **-cies** **1** : firmness of mind **2** : STABILITY

¹con·stant \-stənt\ *adj* **1** : STEADFAST, FAITHFUL **2** : FIXED, UNCHANGING ⟨a ~ flow⟩ **3** : continually re-curring : REGULAR ⟨a ~ annoyance⟩ — **con·stant·ly** *adv*

²constant *n* : something unchanging

con·stel·la·tion \ˌkän-stə-ˈlā-shən\ *n* **1** : any of 88 groups of stars forming patterns **2** : a group of usu. related per-sons, qualities, or things

con·ster·na·tion \ˌkän-stər-ˈnā-shən\ *n* : amazed dismay and confusion

con·sti·pa·tion \ˌkän-stə-ˈpā-shən\ *n* : abnormally difficult or infrequent bowel movements — **con·sti·pate** \ˈkän-stə-ˌpāt\ *vb*

con·stit·u·en·cy \kən-ˈsti-chə-wən-sē\ *n, pl* **-cies** : a body of constituents; *also* : an electoral district

¹con·stit·u·ent \-wənt\ *n* **1** : a person entitled to vote for a representative for a district **2** : a component part

²constituent *adj* **1** : COMPONENT ⟨~ parts⟩ **2** : having power to create a government or frame or amend a constitution

con·sti·tute \'kän-stə-ˌtüt, -ˌtyüt\ *vb* **-tut·ed; -tut·ing** **1** : to appoint to an office or duty **2** : SET UP, ESTABLISH ⟨~ a law⟩ **3** : MAKE UP, COMPOSE

con·sti·tu·tion \ˌkän-stə-'tü-shən, -'tyü-\ *n* **1** : an established law or custom **2** : the physical makeup of the individual **3** : the structure, composition, or makeup of something ⟨~ of the sun⟩ **4** : the basic law in a politically organized body; *also* : a document containing such law

¹con·sti·tu·tion·al \-shə-nəl\ *adj* **1** : of or relating to the constitution of body or mind **2** : being in accord with the constitution of a state or society; *also* : of or relating to such a constitution — **con·sti·tu·tion·al·ly** *adv*

²constitutional *n* : an exercise (as a walk) taken for one's health

con·sti·tu·tion·al·i·ty \-ˌtü-shə-'na-lə-tē, -ˌtyü-\ *n* : the quality or state of being constitutional

con·sti·tu·tive \'kän-stə-ˌtü-tiv, -ˌtyü-, kən-'sti-chə-tiv\ *adj* **1** : CONSTRUCTIVE **2** : CONSTITUENT, ESSENTIAL

constr *abbr* construction

con·strain \kən-'strān\ *vb* **1** : COMPEL, FORCE **2** : CONFINE **3** : RESTRAIN

con·straint \-'strānt\ *n* **1** : COMPULSION; *also* : RESTRAINT **2** : repression of one's natural feelings

con·strict \kən-'strikt\ *vb* : to draw together : SQUEEZE — **con·stric·tion** \-'strik-shən\ *n* — **con·stric·tive** \-'strik-tiv\ *adj*

con·stric·tor \kən-'strik-tər\ *n* : a snake that coils around and compresses its prey

con·struct \kən-'strəkt\ *vb* : BUILD, MAKE — **con·struc·tor** \-'strək-tər\ *n*

con·struc·tion \kən-'strək-shən\ *n* **1** : INTERPRETATION **2** : the art, process, or manner of building; *also* : something built, created, or established : STRUCTURE **3** : syntactical arrangement of words in a sentence — **con·struc·tive** \-tiv\ *adj*

con·struc·tion·ist \-shə-nist\ *n* : a person who construes a legal document (as the U.S. Constitution) in a specific way ⟨a strict ~⟩

con·strue \kən-'strü\ *vb* **con·strued; con·stru·ing** **1** : to analyze the mutual relations of words in a sentence; *also* : TRANSLATE **2** : EXPLAIN, INTERPRET — **con·stru·able** \-'strü-əl\ *adj* — **con·stru·al** \-'strü-əl\ *n*

con·sub·stan·ti·a·tion \ˌkän-səb-ˌstan-chē-'ā-shən\ *n* : the actual substantial presence and combination of the body and blood of Christ with the eucharistic bread and wine

con·sul \'kän-səl\ *n* **1** : a chief magistrate of the Roman republic **2** : an official appointed by a government to reside in a foreign country to care for the commercial interests of the appointing government's citizens — **con·sul·ar** \-sə-lər\ *adj* — **con·sul·ate** \-lət\ *n* — **con·sul·ship** *n*

con·sult \kən-'səlt\ *vb* **1** : to ask the advice or opinion of **2** : CONFER — **con·sul·tant** \-'səl-tᵊnt\ *n* — **con·sul·ta·tion** \ˌkän-səl-'tā-shən\ *n*

con·sume \kən-'süm\ *vb* **con·sumed; con·sum·ing** **1** : DESTROY ⟨*consumed* by fire⟩ **2** : to spend wastefully **3** : to eat up : DEVOUR **4** : to absorb the attention of : ENGROSS — **con·sum·able** *adj* — **con·sum·er** *n*

con·sum·er·ism \kən-'sü-mə-ˌri-zəm\ *n* : the promotion of consumers' interests (as against false advertising)

consumer price index *n* : an index measuring the change in the cost of widely purchased goods and services from the cost in some base period

¹con·sum·mate \'kän-sə-mət, kən-'sə\ *adj* : PERFECT ⟨a ~ team player⟩ ◆ **Synonyms** FINISHED, ACCOMPLISHED

²con·sum·mate \'kän-sə-ˌmāt\ *vb* **-mat·ed; -mat·ing** : to make complete : FINISH, ACHIEVE — **con·sum·ma·tion** \ˌkän-sə-'mā-shən\ *n*

con·sump·tion \kən-'səmp-shən\ *n* **1** : progressive bodily wasting away; *also* : TUBERCULOSIS **2** : the act of consuming or using up **3** : the use of economic goods

¹con·sump·tive \-'səmp-tiv\ *adj* **1** : tending to consume **2** : relating to or affected with consumption

²consumptive *n* : a person who has consumption

cont *abbr* **1** containing **2** contents **3** continent; continental **4** continued **5** control

¹con·tact \'kän-ˌtakt\ *n* **1** : a touching or meeting of bodies **2** : ASSOCIATION, RELATIONSHIP; *also* : CONNECTION,

COMMUNICATION **3** : a person serving as a go-between or source of information **4** : CONTACT LENS

²contact *vb* **1** : to come or bring into contact : TOUCH **2** : to get in communication with

contact lens *n* : a thin lens fitting over the cornea usu. to correct vision

con·ta·gion \kən-'tā-jən\ *n* [ME, fr. L *contagio*, fr. *contingere* to have contact with, pollute, fr. *com-* together + *tangere* to touch] **1** : a contagious disease; *also* : the transmission of such a disease **2** : a disease-producing agent (as a virus) **3** : transmission of an influence on the mind or emotions

con·ta·gious \-jəs\ *adj* **1** : able to be passed by contact between individuals ⟨colds are ~⟩ ⟨~ disease⟩; *also* : capable of passing on a contagious disease **2** : communicated or transmitted like a contagious disease; *esp* : exciting similar emotion or conduct in others

con·tain \kən-'tān\ *vb* **1** : RESTRAIN **2** : to have within : HOLD **3** : COMPRISE, INCLUDE — **con·tain·able** \-'tā-nə-bəl\ *adj* — **con·tain·ment** \-'tān-mənt\ *n*

con·tain·er \kən-'tā-nər\ *n* : RECEPTACLE

con·tam·i·nant \kən-'ta-mə-nənt\ *n* : something that contaminates

con·tam·i·nate \kən-'ta-mə-ˌnāt\ *vb* **-nat·ed; -nat·ing** : to soil, stain, or infect by contact or association — **con·tam·i·na·tion** \-ˌta-mə-'nā-shən\ *n*

contd *abbr* continued

con·temn \kən-'tem\ *vb* : to view or treat with contempt : DESPISE

con·tem·plate \'kän-təm-ˌplāt\ *vb* **-plat·ed; -plat·ing** [L *contemplari*, fr. *com-* with + *templum* space marked out for observation of auguries] **1** : to view or consider with continued attention **2** : INTEND — **con·tem·pla·tion** \ˌkän-təm-'plā-shən\ *n* — **con·tem·pla·tive** \kən-'tem-plə-tiv, 'kän-təm-ˌplā-\ *adj*

con·tem·po·ra·ne·ous \kən-ˌtem-pə-'rā-nē-əs\ *adj* : CONTEMPORARY 1

con·tem·po·rary \kən-'tem-pə-ˌrer-ē\ *adj* **1** : occurring or existing at the same time **2** : marked by characteristics of the present period — **contemporary** *n*

con·tempt \kən-'tempt\ *n* **1** : the act of despising : the state of mind of one who despises **2** : the state of being despised **3** : disobedience to or open disrespect of a court or legislature

con·tempt·ible \kən-'temp-tə-bəl\ *adj* : deserving contempt : DESPICABLE — **con·tempt·ibly** \-blē\ *adv*

con·temp·tu·ous \-'temp-chə-wəs\ *adj* : feeling or expressing contempt — **con·temp·tu·ous·ly** *adv*

con·tend \kən-'tend\ *vb* **1** : to strive against rivals or difficulties **2** : ARGUE **3** : MAINTAIN, ASSERT — **con·tend·er** *n*

¹con·tent \kən-'tent\ *adj* : SATISFIED

²content *vb* : SATISFY; *esp* : to limit (oneself) in requirements or actions

³content *n* : CONTENTMENT ⟨ate to his heart's ~⟩

⁴con·tent \'kän-ˌtent\ *n* **1** : something contained ⟨~s of a room⟩ **2** : subject matter or topics treated (as in a book) **3** : material (as text or music) offered by a Web site **4** : MEANING, SIGNIFICANCE **5** : the amount of material contained

con·tent·ed \kən-'ten-təd\ *adj* : SATISFIED — **con·tent·ed·ly** *adv* — **con·tent·ed·ness** *n*

con·ten·tion \kən-'ten-chən\ *n* **1** : CONTEST, STRIFE **2** : an idea or point for which a person argues — **con·ten·tious** \-chəs\ *adj* — **con·ten·tious·ly** *adv*

con·tent·ment \kən-'tent-mənt\ *n* : ease of mind : SATISFACTION

con·ter·mi·nous \kän-'tər-mə-nəs\ *adj* : having the same or a common boundary — **con·ter·mi·nous·ly** *adv*

¹con·test \kən-'test\ *vb* **1** : to engage in a struggle or competition : COMPETE, VIE **2** : CHALLENGE, DISPUTE ⟨~ the accusations⟩ — **con·tes·tant** \-'tes-tənt\ *n*

²con·test \'kän-ˌtest\ *n* : STRUGGLE, COMPETITION

con·text \'kän-ˌtekst\ *n* [ME, fr. L *contextus* connection of words, coherence, fr. *contexere* to weave together] : the parts of a discourse that surround a word or passage and help to explain its meaning; *also* : the circumstances surrounding an act or event ⟨the ~ of the war⟩ — **con·tex·tu·al·ly** *adv*

con·tig·u·ous \kən-'ti-gyə-wəs\ *adj* : being in contact

: TOUCHING; *also* : NEXT, ADJOINING — **con·ti·gu·i·ty**
\ˌkän-tə-'gyü-ə-tē\ *n*
con·ti·nence \'kän-tə-nəns\ *n* **1** : SELF-RESTRAINT; *esp* : a
refraining from sexual intercourse **2** : the ability to retain urine or feces voluntarily
¹**con·ti·nent** \'kän-tə-nənt\ *adj* : exercising continence
²**continent** *n* **1** : any of the great divisions of land on the
globe **2** *cap* : the continent of Europe
¹**con·ti·nen·tal** \ˌkän-tə-'nen-tᵊl\ *adj* **1** : of or relating to a
continent; *esp, often cap* : of or relating to the continent
of Europe **2** *often cap* : of or relating to the colonies
later forming the U.S. **3** : of or relating to cuisine based
on classical European cooking
²**continental** *n* **1** *often cap* : a soldier in the Continental
army **2** : EUROPEAN
continental drift *n* : a slow movement of the continents
over a fluid layer deep within the earth
continental shelf *n* : a shallow submarine plain forming a
border to a continent
continental slope *n* : a comparatively steep slope from a
continental shelf to the ocean floor
con·tin·gen·cy \kən-'tin-jən-sē\ *n, pl* **-cies** : a chance or
possible event
¹**con·tin·gent** \-jənt\ *adj* **1** : liable but not certain to happen : POSSIBLE **2** : happening by chance : not planned **3**
: dependent on something that may or may not occur **4**
: CONDITIONAL ♦ *Synonyms* ACCIDENTAL, CASUAL, IN-
CIDENTAL, ODD
²**contingent** *n* : a quota (as of troops) supplied from an
area or group
con·tin·u·al \kən-'tin-yə-wəl\ *adj* **1** : CONTINUOUS, UN-
BROKEN **2** : steadily recurring — **con·tin·u·al·ly** *adv*
con·tin·u·ance \-yə-wəns\ *n* **1** : unbroken succession **2**
: the extent of continuing : DURATION **3** : adjournment
of legal proceedings
con·tin·u·a·tion \kən-ˌtin-yə-'wā-shən\ *n* **1** : extension or
prolongation of a state or activity **2** : resumption after
an interruption; *also* : something that carries on after a
pause or break
con·tin·ue \kən-'tin-yü\ *vb* **-tin·ued; -tinu·ing** **1** : to
maintain without interruption **2** : ENDURE, LAST ⟨the
tradition ∼s⟩ **3** : to remain in a place or condition ⟨∼
at this job⟩ **4** : to resume (as a story) after an intermission **5** : EXTEND ⟨∼ a subscription⟩; *also* : to persist in
⟨will ∼ to remind you⟩ **6** : to allow to remain **7** : to
keep (a legal case) on the calendar or undecided
con·ti·nu·i·ty \ˌkän-tə-'nü-ə-tē, -'nyü-\ *n, pl* **-ties** **1** : the
state of being continuous **2** : something (as a film script)
that has or provides continuity
con·tin·u·ous \kən-'tin-yə-wəs\ *adj* : continuing without
interruption — **con·tin·u·ous·ly** *adv*
con·tin·u·um \-yə-wəm\ *n, pl* **-ua** \-yə-wə\ *also* **-u·ums**
: something that is the same throughout or consists of a
series of variations or of a sequence of things in regular
order
con·tort \kən-'tòrt\ *vb* : to twist out of shape ⟨a ∼ed face⟩
⟨∼ the truth⟩ — **con·tor·tion** \-'tòr-shən\ *n*
con·tor·tion·ist \-'tòr-shə-nist\ *n* : an acrobat able to twist
the body into unusual postures
con·tour \'kän-ˌtùr\ *n* [F, fr. It *contorno* fr. *contornare* to
round off, fr. ML, to turn around, fr. L *com-* together +
tornare to turn on a lathe, fr. *tornus* lathe] **1** : OUTLINE
2 : SHAPE, FORM — often used in pl. ⟨the ∼s of a statue⟩
contr *abbr* contract; contraction
con·tra·band \'kän-trə-ˌband\ *n* : goods legally prohibited
in trade; *also* : smuggled goods
con·tra·cep·tion \ˌkän-trə-'sep-shən\ *n* : intentional prevention of conception and pregnancy — **con·tra·cep·tive**
\-'sep-tive\ *adj or n*
¹**con·tract** \'kän-ˌtrakt\ *n* **1** : a binding agreement; *also* : a
document stating its terms **2** : an undertaking to win a
specified number of tricks in bridge — **contract** *adj* —
con·trac·tu·al \kən-'trak-chə-wəl\ *adj* — **con·trac·tu·al·
ly** *adv*
²**con·tract** \kən-'trakt, *2 usu* 'kän-ˌtrakt\ *vb* **1** : to become
affected with ⟨∼ a disease⟩ **2** : to establish or undertake
by contract **3** : SHRINK, LESSEN; *esp* : to draw together
esp. so as to shorten ⟨∼ a muscle⟩ **4** : to shorten (a word)
by omitting letters or sounds in the middle — **con·tract·
ible** \kən-'trak-tə-bəl, 'kän-ˌ\ *adj* — **con·trac·tion** \kən-
'trak-shən\ *n* — **con·trac·tor** \'kän-ˌtrak-tər, kən-'trak-\ *n*

con·trac·tile \kən-'trak-tᵊl\ *adj* : able to contract — **con-
trac·til·i·ty** \ˌkän-ˌtrak-'ti-lə-tē\ *n*
con·tra·dict \ˌkän-trə-'dikt\ *vb* : to assert the contrary of
: deny the truth of ⟨∼ a rumor⟩ — **con·tra·dic·tion**
\-'dik-shən\ *n* — **con·tra·dic·to·ry** \-'dik-tə-rē\ *adj*
con·tra·dis·tinc·tion \ˌkän-trə-dis-'tiŋk-shən\ *n* : distinction by contrast
con·trail \'kän-ˌtrāl\ *n* : a streak of condensed water vapor
created by an airplane or rocket at high altitudes
con·tra·in·di·cate \ˌkän-trə-'in-də-ˌkāt\ *vb* : to make (a
treatment or procedure) inadvisable — **con·tra·in·di·ca·
tion** \-ˌin-də-'kā-shən\ *n*
con·tral·to \kən-'tral-tō\ *n, pl* **-tos** : the lowest female
voice; *also* : a singer having such a voice
con·trap·tion \kən-'trap-shən\ *n* : CONTRIVANCE, DEVICE
con·tra·pun·tal \ˌkän-trə-'pən-tᵊl\ *adj* : of or relating to
counterpoint
con·tra·ri·ety \ˌkän-trə-'rī-ə-tē\ *n, pl* **-eties** : the state of
being contrary : DISAGREEMENT, INCONSISTENCY
con·trari·wise \'kän-ˌtrer-ē-ˌwīz, kən-'trer-\ *adv* **1** : on
the contrary **2** : VICE VERSA
con·trary \'kän-ˌtrer-ē; *4 often* kən-'trer-ē\ *adj* **1** : opposite in nature or position **2** : COUNTER, OPPOSED **3**
: UNFAVORABLE — used of wind or weather **4** : unwilling to accept control or advice — **con·trar·i·an** \kən-
'trer-ē-ən, kän-\ *n or adj* — **con·trari·ly** \'kän-ˌtrer-ə-lē,
kən-'trer-\ *adv* — **con·trary** *n is* 'kän-ˌtrer-ē, *adv is like
adj*\ *n or adv*
¹**con·trast** \kən-'trast\ *vb* [F *contraster,* fr. MF, to oppose,
resist, fr. VL *contrastare,* fr. L *contra-* against + *stare* to
stand] **1** : to show differences when compared **2** : to
compare in such a way as to show differences
²**con·trast** \'kän-ˌtrast\ *n* **1** : diversity of adjacent parts in
color, emotion, tone, or brightness ⟨the ∼ of a photo-
graph⟩ **2** : unlikeness as shown when things are compared : DIFFERENCE
con·tra·vene \ˌkän-trə-'vēn\ *vb* **-vened; -ven·ing** **1** : to
go or act contrary to ⟨∼ a law⟩ **2** : CONTRADICT ⟨∼ a
claim⟩
con·tre·temps \'kän-trə-ˌtän, kōⁿ-trə-'täⁿ\ *n, pl* **con·tre·
temps** \-ˌtäⁿ, -ˌtäⁿz\ [F] : an inopportune or embarrassing
occurrence
contrib *abbr* contribution; contributor
con·trib·ute \kən-'tri-byət\ *vb* **-ut·ed; -ut·ing** : to give
along with others (as to a fund); *also* : HELP, ASSIST —
con·tri·bu·tion \ˌkän-trə-'byü-shən\ *n* — **con·trib·u·tor**
\kən-'tri-byə-tər\ *n* — **con·trib·u·to·ry** \-byə-ˌtòr-ē\ *adj*
con·trite \'kän-ˌtrīt, kən-'trīt\ *adj* : PENITENT, REPENTANT
— **con·trite·ly** *adv* — **con·tri·tion** \kən-'tri-shən\ *n*
con·triv·ance \kən-'trī-vəns\ *n* **1** : a mechanical device **2**
: SCHEME, PLAN
con·trive \kən-'trīv\ *vb* **con·trived; con·triv·ing** **1**
: PLAN, DEVISE **2** : FRAME, MAKE **3** : to bring about
with difficulty — **con·triv·er** *n*
con·trived \-'trīvd\ *adj* : lacking in natural quality ⟨a ∼
plot⟩
¹**con·trol** \kən-'trōl\ *vb* **con·trolled; con·trol·ling** [ME
countrollen to verify, fr. AF *countrerouler,* fr. *countreroule*
copy of an account, audit, fr. ML *contrarotulus,* fr. L *contra* against + ML *rotulus* roll] **1** : to exercise restraining
or directing influence over : REGULATE **2** : DOMINATE,
RULE — **con·trol·la·ble** \-'trō-lə-bəl\ *adj*
²**control** *n* **1** : power to direct or regulate **2** : RESERVE,
RESTRAINT **3** : a device for regulating a mechanism
con·trol·ler \kən-'trō-lər, 'kän-ˌtrō-lər\ *n* **1** : COMPTROL-
LER **2** : a person or thing that controls ⟨an air traffic ∼⟩
⟨a game ∼⟩
con·tro·ver·sy \'kän-trə-ˌvər-sē\ *n, pl* **-sies** : a clash of opposing views : DISPUTE — **con·tro·ver·sial** \ˌkän-trə-
ˌvər-shəl, -sē-əl\ *adj*
con·tro·vert \'kän-trə-ˌvərt, ˌkän-trə-'vərt\ *vb* : DENY,
CONTRADICT — **con·tro·vert·ible** *adj*
con·tu·ma·cious \ˌkän-tü-'mā-shəs, -tyü-\ *adj* : stubbornly disobedient ♦ *Synonyms* REBELLIOUS, INSUBOR-
DINATE, SEDITIOUS — **con·tu·ma·cy** \kən-'tü-mə-sē,
-tyü-; 'kän-tyə-\ *n* — **con·tu·ma·cious·ly** *adv*
con·tu·me·ly \kən-'tü-mə-lē, -'tyü-; 'kän-tə-ˌmē-lē, -tyə-\
n, pl **-lies** : contemptuous treatment : INSULT
con·tu·sion \kən-'tü-zhən, -'tyü-\ *n* : BRUISE — **con·tuse**
\-'tüz, -'tyüz\ *vb*
co·nun·drum \kə-'nən-drəm\ *n* : RIDDLE

conv *abbr* **1** convention **2** convertible

con·va·lesce \ˌkän-və-ˈles\ *vb* **-lesced; -lesc·ing** : to recover health gradually — **con·va·les·cence** \-ˈle-sᵊns\ *n* — **con·va·les·cent** \-sᵊnt\ *adj or n*

con·vec·tion \kən-ˈvek-shən\ *n* : circulatory motion in a fluid due to warmer portions rising and cooler denser portions sinking; *also* : the transfer of heat by such motion — **con·vec·tion·al** \-shə-nəl\ *adj* — **con·vec·tive** \-ˈvek-tiv\ *adj*

convection oven *n* : an oven with a fan that circulates hot air uniformly and continuously around the food

con·vene \kən-ˈvēn\ *vb* **con·vened; con·ven·ing** : ASSEMBLE, MEET

con·ve·nience \kən-ˈvē-nyəns\ *n* **1** : SUITABLENESS **2** : a laborsaving device **3** : a suitable time ⟨at your ∼⟩ **4** : personal comfort : EASE

convenience store *n* : a small market that is open long hours

con·ve·nient \-nyənt\ *adj* **1** : suited to personal comfort or ease **2** : placed near at hand — **con·ve·nient·ly** *adv*

con·vent \ˈkän-vənt, -ˌvent\ *n* [ME *covent*, fr. AF, fr. ML *conventus*, fr. L, assembly, fr. *convenire* to come together] : a local community or house of a religious order esp. of nuns — **con·ven·tu·al** \kän-ˈven-chə-wəl\ *adj*

con·ven·ti·cle \kən-ˈven-ti-kəl\ *n* : MEETING; *esp* : a secret meeting for worship

con·ven·tion \kən-ˈven-chən\ *n* **1** : an agreement esp. between states on a matter of common concern **2** : MEETING, ASSEMBLY **3** : an assembly of persons convened for some purpose **4** : generally accepted custom, practice, or belief

con·ven·tion·al \-chə-nəl\ *adj* **1** : sanctioned by general custom **2** : COMMONPLACE, ORDINARY — **con·ven·tion·al·i·ty** \-ˌven-chə-ˈna-lə-tē\ *n* — **con·ven·tion·al·ize** \-ˈven-chə-nə-ˌlīz\ *vb* — **con·ven·tion·al·ly** *adv*

con·verge \kən-ˈvərj\ *vb* **con·verged; con·verg·ing** : to approach one common center or single point ⟨*converging* paths⟩ — **con·ver·gence** \kən-ˈvər-jəns\ *n* — **con·ver·gent** \-jənt\ *adj*

con·ver·sant \kən-ˈvər-sᵊnt\ *adj* : having knowledge and experience — used with *with*

con·ver·sa·tion \ˌkän-vər-ˈsā-shən\ *n* : an informal talking together — **con·ver·sa·tion·al** \-shə-nᵊl\ *adj* — **con·ver·sa·tion·al·ly** *adv*

con·ver·sa·tion·al·ist \-shə-nᵊl-ist\ *n* : a person who converses a great deal or who excels in conversation

¹con·verse \ˈkän-ˌvərs\ *n* : CONVERSATION

²con·verse \kən-ˈvərs\ *vb* **con·versed; con·vers·ing** : to engage in conversation

³con·verse \ˈkän-ˌvərs\ *n* : a statement related to another statement by having its hypothesis and conclusion or its subject and predicate reversed or interchanged

⁴con·verse \kən-ˈvərs, ˈkän-ˌvərs\ *adj* : reversed in order or relation — **con·verse·ly** *adv*

con·ver·sion \kən-ˈvər-zhən\ *n* **1** : a change in nature or form **2** : an experience associated with a decisive adoption of religion

¹con·vert \kən-ˈvərt\ *vb* **1** : to turn from one belief or party to another **2** : TRANSFORM, CHANGE **3** : MISAPPROPRIATE **4** : EXCHANGE — **con·vert·er** *or* **con·ver·tor** \-ˈvər-tər\ *n*

²con·vert \ˈkän-ˌvərt\ *n* : a person who has undergone religious conversion

¹con·vert·ible \kən-ˈvər-tə-bəl\ *adj* : capable of being converted

²convertible *n* : an automobile with a top that may be lowered or removed

con·vex \kän-ˈveks, ˈkän-ˌveks\ *adj* : curved or rounded outward like the exterior of a sphere or circle — **con·vex·i·ty** \kän-ˈvek-sə-tē\ *n*

con·vey \kən-ˈvā\ *vb* **1** : CARRY, TRANSPORT ⟨a river ∼*ing* logs⟩ **2** : TRANSFER, COMMUNICATE ⟨∼ a message⟩ — **con·vey·or** *also* **con·vey·er** \-ər\ *n*

con·vey·ance \-ˈvā-əns\ *n* **1** : the act of conveying **2** : a legal paper transferring ownership of property **3** : VEHICLE

¹con·vict \kən-ˈvikt\ *vb* : to prove or find guilty

²con·vict \ˈkän-ˌvikt\ *n* : a person serving a prison sentence

con·vic·tion \kən-ˈvik-shən\ *n* **1** : the act of convicting esp. in a court **2** : the state of being convinced : BELIEF

con·vince \kən-ˈvins\ *vb* **con·vinced; con·vinc·ing** : to bring (as by argument) to belief or action — **con·vinc·ing** *adj* — **con·vinc·ing·ly** *adv*

con·viv·ial \kən-ˈvi-vē-əl\ *adj* [LL *convivialis*, fr. L *convivium* banquet, fr. *com-* together + *vivere* to live] : enjoying companionship and the pleasures of feasting and drinking : JOVIAL, FESTIVE — **con·viv·i·al·i·ty** \-ˌvi-vē-ˈa-lə-tē\ *n* — **con·viv·ial·ly** *adv*

con·vo·ca·tion \ˌkän-və-ˈkā-shən\ *n* **1** : a ceremonial assembly (as of the clergy) **2** : the act of convoking

con·voke \kən-ˈvōk\ *vb* **con·voked; con·vok·ing** : to call together to a meeting

con·vo·lut·ed \ˈkän-və-ˌlü-təd\ *adj* **1** : folded in curved or tortuous windings **2** : INVOLVED, INTRICATE

con·vo·lu·tion \ˌkän-və-ˈlü-shən\ *n* : a tortuous or winding structure; *esp* : one of the ridges of the brain

¹con·voy \ˈkän-ˌvȯi, kän-ˈvȯi\ *vb* : to accompany for protection

²con·voy \ˈkän-ˌvȯi\ *n* **1** : one that convoys; *esp* : a protective escort (as for ships) **2** : the act of convoying **3** : a group of moving vehicles

con·vulse \kən-ˈvəls\ *vb* **con·vulsed; con·vuls·ing** : to agitate violently

con·vul·sion \kən-ˈvəl-shən\ *n* **1** : an abnormal and violent involuntary contraction or series of contractions of muscle **2** : a violent disturbance — **con·vul·sive** \-siv\ *adj* — **con·vul·sive·ly** *adv*

cony *var of* CONEY

coo \ˈkü\ *n* : a soft low sound made by doves or pigeons; *also* : a sound like this — **coo** *vb*

COO *abbr* chief operating officer

¹cook \ˈku̇k\ *n* : a person who prepares food for eating

²cook *vb* **1** : to prepare food for eating **2** : to subject to heat or fire **3** : CONCOCT, FABRICATE — usu. used with *up* ⟨∼ up a scheme⟩ — **cook·er** *n* — **cook·ware** \-ˌwer\ *n*

cook·book \-ˌbu̇k\ *n* : a book of cooking directions and recipes

cook·ery \ˈku̇-kə-rē\ *n, pl* **-er·ies** : the art or practice of cooking

cook·ie *or* **cooky** \ˈku̇-kē\ *n, pl* **cook·ies** [D *koekje*, dim. of *koek* cake] **1** : a small sweet flat cake **2** *cookie* : a file containing information about a Web site user created and read by a Web site server and stored on the user's computer

cookie–cutter *adj* : marked by a lack of originality or distinction ⟨∼ malls⟩

cook·out \ˈku̇k-ˌau̇t\ *n* : an outing at which a meal is cooked and served in the open

¹cool \ˈkül\ *adj* **1** : moderately cold **2** : not excited : CALM **3** : not friendly **4** : IMPUDENT **5** : protecting from heat **6** *slang* : very good **7** *slang* : FASHIONABLE ✦ *Synonyms* UNFLAPPABLE, COMPOSED, COLLECTED, UNRUFFLED, NONCHALANT — **cool·ly** *adv* — **cool·ness** *n*

²cool *vb* : to make or become cool

³cool *n* **1** : a cool time or place **2** : INDIFFERENCE; *also* : SELF-ASSURANCE, COMPOSURE ⟨kept his ∼⟩

cool·ant \ˈkü-lənt\ *n* : a usu. fluid cooling agent

cool·er \ˈkü-lər\ *n* **1** : a container for keeping food or drink cool **2** : JAIL, PRISON **3** : a tall iced drink

coo·lie \ˈkü-lē\ *n* [Hindi & Urdu *qulī*] : an unskilled laborer usu. in or from the Far East

coon \ˈkün\ *n* : RACCOON

coon·hound \-ˌhau̇nd\ *n* : a sporting dog trained to hunt raccoons

coon·skin \-ˌskin\ *n* : the pelt of a raccoon; *also* : something (as a cap) made of this

¹coop \ˈküp, ˈku̇p\ *n* : a small enclosure or building usu. for poultry

²coop *vb* : to confine in or as if in a coop — usu. used with *up*

co–op \ˈkō-ˌäp\ *n* : COOPERATIVE

coo·per \ˈkü-pər, ˈku̇-\ *n* : one who makes or repairs barrels or casks — **cooper** *vb* — **coo·per·age** \-pə-rij\ *n*

co·op·er·ate \kō-ˈä-pə-ˌrāt\ *vb* : to act jointly or in compliance with others — **co·op·er·a·tion** \-ˌä-pə-ˈrā-shən\ *n* — **co·op·er·a·tor** \-ˈä-pə-ˌrā-tər\ *n*

¹co·op·er·a·tive \kō-ˈä-pra-tiv, -ˈä-pə-ˌrā-\ *adj* **1** : willing to work with others **2** : of or relating to an association formed to enable its members to buy or sell to better advantage by eliminating middlemen's profits

²**cooperative** *n* : a cooperative association

co·opt \kō-'äpt\ *vb* **1** : to choose or elect as a colleague **2** : ABSORB, ASSIMILATE; *also* : TAKE OVER ⟨a style *~ed* by advertisers⟩

¹**co·or·di·nate** \kō-'ȯr-də-nət\ *adj* **1** : equal in rank or order **2** : of equal rank in a compound sentence ⟨*~* clause⟩ **3** : joining words or word groups of the same rank — **co·or·di·nate·ly** *adv*

²**co·or·di·nate** \-'ȯr-də-ˌnāt\ *vb* **-nat·ed; -nat·ing** **1** : to make or become coordinate ⟨*~* our schedules⟩ **2** : to work or act together harmoniously ⟨a *coordinated* wardrobe⟩ — **co·or·di·na·tion** \-ˌȯr-də-'nā-shən\ *n* — **co·or·di·na·tor** \-'ȯr-də-ˌnā-tər\ *n*

³**co·or·di·nate** \-'ȯr-də-nət\ *n* **1** : one of a set of numbers used in specifying the location of a point on a surface or in space **2** *pl* : articles (as of clothing) designed to be used together and to attain their effect through pleasing contrast

coot \'küt\ *n* **1** : a dark-colored ducklike bird related to the rails **2** : any of several No. American sea ducks **3** : a harmless simple person

coo·tie \'kü-tē\ *n* : a body louse

¹**cop** \'käp\ *n* : POLICE OFFICER

²**cop** *vb* **1** *slang* : STEAL ⟨*~* a glance⟩ **2** *slang* : ADMIT — used with *to* ⟨*~* to the charges⟩ **3** : ADOPT ⟨*~* an attitude⟩

co–pay \'kō-ˌpā\ *n* : CO-PAYMENT

co–pay·ment \'kō-ˌpā-mənt, ˌkō-'\ *n* : a fixed fee required of a patient by a health insurer (as an HMO) at the time of each outpatient service or filling of a prescription

¹**cope** \'kōp\ *n* : a long cloaklike ecclesiastical vestment

²**cope** *vb* **coped; cop·ing** : to struggle to overcome problems or difficulties ⟨*~* with tragedy⟩

copi·er \'kä-pē-ər\ *n* : one that copies; *esp* : a machine for making copies

co·pi·lot \'kō-ˌpī-lət\ *n* : an assistant pilot of an aircraft or spacecraft

cop·ing \'kō-piŋ\ *n* : the top layer of a wall

co·pi·ous \'kō-pē-əs\ *adj* : LAVISH, ABUNDANT ⟨a *~* harvest⟩ — **co·pi·ous·ly** *adv* — **co·pi·ous·ness** *n*

cop–out \'käp-ˌaȯt\ *n* : an excuse for copping out; *also* : an act of copping out

cop out *vb* : to back out (as of an unwanted responsibility)

cop·per \'kä-pər\ *n* **1** : a malleable reddish metallic chemical element that is one of the best conductors of heat and electricity **2** : a coin or token made of copper — **cop·pery** *adj*

cop·per·head \'kä-pər-ˌhed\ *n* : a largely coppery brown pit viper esp. of the eastern and central U.S.

cop·pice \'kä-pəs\ *n* : THICKET

co·pra \'kō-prə\ *n* : dried coconut meat yielding coconut oil

copse \'käps\ *n* : THICKET

cop·ter \'käp-tər\ *n* : HELICOPTER

cop·u·la \'kä-pyə-lə\ *n* : LINKING VERB — **cop·u·la·tive** \-lə-tiv, -ˌlā-\ *adj*

cop·u·late \'kä-pyə-ˌlāt\ *vb* **-lat·ed; -lat·ing** : to engage in sexual intercourse — **cop·u·la·tion** \ˌkä-pyə-'lā-shən\ *n* — **cop·u·la·to·ry** \'kä-pyə-lə-ˌtȯr-ē\ *adj*

¹**copy** \'kä-pē\ *n, pl* **cop·ies** **1** : an imitation or reproduction of an original work **2** : material to be set in type **3** : DUPLICATE ◆ **Synonyms** DUPLICATE, REPRODUCTION, FACSIMILE, REPLICA

²**copy** *vb* **cop·ied; copy·ing** **1** : to make a copy of **2** : IMITATE — **copy·ist** *n*

copy·book \'kä-pē-ˌbu̇k\ *n* : a book formerly used to teach handwriting containing examples to be copied

copy·boy \-ˌbȯi\ *n* : a person who carries copy and runs errands (as in a newspaper office)

copy·cat \-ˌkat\ *n* : a slavish imitator

copy·desk \-ˌdesk\ *n* : the desk at which newspaper copy is edited

copy editor *n* : one who edits or prepares copy (as headlines) esp. for a newspaper

copy·read·er \-ˌrē-dər\ *n* : COPY EDITOR

¹**copy·right** \-ˌrīt\ *n* : the sole right to reproduce, publish, sell, or distribute a literary or artistic work

²**copyright** *vb* : to secure a copyright on

copy·writ·er \'kä-pē-ˌrī-tər\ *n* : a writer of advertising copy

co·quet *or* **co·quette** \kō-'ket\ *vb* **co·quet·ted; co·quet·ting** : FLIRT — **co·quet·ry** \'kō-kə-trē, kō-'ke-trē\ *n*

co·quette \kō-'ket\ *n* [F, fem. of *coquet*, flirtatious man, dim. of *coq* cock] : FLIRT — **co·quett·ish** *adj*

cor *abbr* corner

Cor *abbr* Corinthians

cor·a·cle \'kȯr-ə-kəl\ *n* [W *corwgl*] : a boat made of a frame covered usu. with hide or tarpaulin

cor·al \'kȯr-əl\ *n* **1** : a stony or horny material that forms the skeleton of colonies of tiny sea polyps and includes a red form used in jewelry; *also* : a coral-forming polyp or polyp colony **2** : a deep pink color — **coral** *adj*

coral snake *n* : any of several venomous chiefly tropical New World snakes brilliantly banded in red, black, and yellow or white

cor·bel \'kȯr-bəl\ *n* : a bracket-shaped architectural member that projects from a wall and supports a weight

¹**cord** \'kȯrd\ *n* **1** : a usu. heavy string consisting of several strands woven or twisted together **2** : a long slender anatomical structure (as a tendon or nerve) **3** : a small flexible insulated electrical cable used to connect an appliance with a receptacle **4** : a cubic measure used esp. for firewood and equal to a stack 4×4×8 feet **5** : a rib or ridge on cloth

²**cord** *vb* **1** : to tie or furnish with a cord **2** : to pile (wood) in cords

cord·age \'kȯr-dij\ *n* : ROPES, CORDS; *esp* : ropes in the rigging of a ship

¹**cor·dial** \'kȯr-jəl\ *adj* [ME, fr. ML *cordialis*, fr. L *cord-, cor* heart] : warmly receptive or welcoming : HEARTFELT, HEARTY — **cor·di·al·i·ty** \ˌkȯr-jē-'a-lə-tē, kȯr-'ja-\ *n* — **cor·dial·ly** *adv*

²**cordial** *n* **1** : a stimulating medicine or drink **2** : LIQUEUR

cor·dil·le·ra \ˌkȯr-dəl-'yer-ə, -də-'ler-\ *n* [Sp] : a series of parallel mountain ranges

cord·less \'kȯrd-ləs\ *adj* : having no cord; *esp* : powered by a battery ⟨a *~* phone⟩ — **cord·less** *n*

cor·do·ba \'kȯr-də-bə, -və\ *n* — see MONEY table

cor·don \'kȯr-dᵊn\ *n* **1** : an ornamental cord or ribbon **2** : an encircling line (as of troops or police) — **cordon** *vb*

cor·do·van \'kȯr-də-vən\ *n* : a soft fine-grained leather

cor·du·roy \'kȯr-də-ˌrȯi\ *n, pl* **-roys** : a heavy ribbed fabric; *also, pl* : pants of this material

cord·wain·er \'kȯrd-ˌwā-nər\ *n* : SHOEMAKER

¹**core** \'kȯr\ *n* **1** : the central usu. inedible part of some fruits (as the apple); *also* : an inmost part of something **2** : GIST, ESSENCE

²**core** *vb* **cored; cor·ing** : to take out the core of — **cor·er** *n*

CORE \'kȯr\ *abbr* Congress of Racial Equality

co·re·op·sis \ˌkȯr-ē-'äp-səs\ *n, pl* **coreopsis** : any of a genus of widely cultivated composite herbs with showy often yellow flower heads

co·re·spon·dent \ˌkō-ri-'spän-dənt\ *n* : a person named as guilty of adultery with the defendant in a divorce suit

co·ri·an·der \'kȯr-ē-ˌan-dər\ *n* : an herb related to the carrot; *also* : its aromatic dried fruit used as a flavoring

Cor·in·thi·ans \kə-'rin-thē-ənz\ *n* — see BIBLE table

¹**cork** \'kȯrk\ *n* **1** : the tough elastic bark of a European oak (**cork oak**) used esp. for stoppers and insulation; *also* : a stopper of this **2** : a tissue of a woody plant making up most of the bark — **corky** *adj*

²**cork** *vb* : to furnish with or stop up with cork or a cork ⟨*~* a bottle⟩

cork·screw \'kȯrk-ˌskrü\ *n* : a device for drawing corks from bottles

corm \'kȯrm\ *n* : a solid bulblike underground part of a stem (as of the crocus or gladiolus)

cor·mo·rant \'kȯr-mə-rənt, -ˌrant\ *n* [ME *cormeraunt*, fr. MF *cormorant*, fr. OF *cormareng*, fr. *corp* raven + *marenc* of the sea, fr. L *marinus*] : any of various dark-colored water birds with a long neck, hooked bill, and distensible throat pouch

¹**corn** \'kȯrn\ *n* **1** : the seeds of a cereal grass and esp. of the chief cereal crop of a region (as wheat in Britain and Indian corn in the U.S.); *also* : a cereal grass **2** : sweet corn served as a vegetable

²**corn** *vb* : to salt (as beef) in brine and preservatives

³**corn** *n* : a local hardening and thickening of skin (as on a toe)

¹**corn·ball** \'korn-ˌbol\ *n* : an unsophisticated person; *also*
: something corny

²**cornball** *adj* : CORNY ⟨∼ humor⟩

corn bread *n* : bread made with cornmeal

corn·cob \-ˌkäb\ *n* : the woody core on which the kernels
of Indian corn are arranged

corn·crib \-ˌkrib\ *n* : a crib for storing ears of Indian corn

cor·nea \'kor-nē-ə\ *n* : the transparent part of the coat of
the eyeball covering the iris and the pupil — **cor·ne·al**
adj

corn ear·worm \-'ir-ˌwərm\ *n* : a moth whose larva is destructive esp. to Indian corn

¹**cor·ner** \'kor-nər\ *n* [ME, fr. AF *cornere*, fr. *corne* horn,
corner, fr. L *cornu* horn, point] **1** : the point or angle
formed by the meeting of lines, edges, or sides **2** : the
place where two streets come together **3** : a quiet secluded place **4** : a position from which retreat or escape
is impossible **5** : control of enough of the available supply (as of a commodity) to permit manipulation of the
price — **cor·nered** *adj* — **around the corner** : IMMI-
NENT ⟨has a birthday just *around the corner*⟩

²**cor·ner** *vb* **1** : to drive into a corner **2** : to get a corner
on ⟨∼ the wheat market⟩ **3** : to turn a corner

cor·ner·stone \'kor-nər-ˌstōn\ *n* **1** : a stone forming part
of a corner in a wall; *esp* : such a stone laid at a formal
ceremony **2** : something of basic importance

cor·net \kor-'net\ *n* : a brass band instrument resembling
the trumpet

cornet

corn flour *n, Brit* : CORNSTARCH

corn·flow·er \'korn-ˌflau̇(-ə)r\ *n* : BACHELOR'S BUTTON

cor·nice \'kor-nəs\ *n* : the horizontal projecting part
crowning the wall of a building

corn·meal \'korn-ˌmēl\ *n* : meal ground from corn

corn·row \-ˌrō\ *n* : a section of hair braided flat to the
scalp in rows — **cornrow** *vb*

corn·stalk \-ˌstok\ *n* : a stalk of Indian corn

corn·starch \-ˌstärch\ *n* : a starch made from corn and
used in cookery as a thickening agent

corn syrup *n* : a sweet syrup obtained from cornstarch

cor·nu·co·pia \ˌkor-nə-'kō-pē-ə, -nyə-\ *n* [LL, fr. L *cornu
copiae* horn of plenty] **1** : a horn-shaped container filled
with fruits and grain emblematic of abundance **2**
: ABUNDANCE

corny \'kor-nē\ *adj* **corn·i·er; -est** : tiresomely simple or
sentimental

co·rol·la \kə-'rä-lə, -'rō-\ *n* : the petals of a flower

cor·ol·lary \'kor-ə-ˌler-ē\ *n, pl* **-lar·ies 1** : a deduction
from a proposition already proved true **2** : CONSE-
QUENCE, RESULT

co·ro·na \kə-'rō-nə\ *n* **1** : a colored circle often seen
around and close to a luminous body (as the sun or
moon) **2** : the outermost part of the atmosphere of a star
(as the sun) — **co·ro·nal** \'kor-ə-nᵊl, kə-'rō-\ *adj*

cor·o·nal \'kor-ə-nᵊl\ *n* : a circlet for the head

¹**cor·o·nary** \'kor-ə-ˌner-ē\ *adj* : of or relating to the heart
or its blood vessels

²**coronary** *n, pl* **-nar·ies 1** : a coronary blood vessel **2**
: CORONARY THROMBOSIS; *also* : HEART ATTACK

coronary thrombosis *n* : the blocking by a thrombus of
one of the arteries supplying the heart tissues

cor·o·na·tion \ˌkor-ə-'nā-shən\ *n* : the act or ceremony of
crowning a monarch

cor·o·ner \'kor-ə-nər\ *n* [ME, an officer of the crown, fr.
AF, fr. *corone* crown, fr. L *corona*] : a public official who
investigates causes of deaths possibly not due to natural
causes

cor·o·net \ˌkor-ə-'net\ *n* **1** : a small crown **2** : an ornamental band worn around the temples

corp *abbr* **1** corporal **2** corporation

¹**cor·po·ral** \'kor-p(ə-)rəl\ *adj* : of or relating to the body
⟨∼ punishment⟩

²**corporal** *n* : a noncommissioned officer (as in the army)
ranking next below a sergeant

cor·po·rate \'kor-p(ə-)rət\ *adj* **1** : INCORPORATED; *also*
: belonging to an incorporated body **2** : of or relating to
large-scale business ⟨∼ mergers⟩ **3** : combined into one
body

cor·po·ra·tion \ˌkor-pə-'rā-shən\ *n* **1** : the municipal authorities of a town or city **2** : a legal creation authorized
to act with the rights and liabilities of a person; *also*
: COMPANY

cor·po·rat·ize \'kor-pə-rə-ˌtīz\ *vb* **ized; -iz·ing** : to subject
to corporate control ⟨∼ education⟩

cor·po·re·al \kor-'pōr-ē-əl\ *adj* **1** : PHYSICAL, MATERIAL
2 *archaic* : BODILY — **cor·po·re·al·i·ty** \kor-ˌpōr-ē-'a-lə-
tē\ *n* — **cor·po·re·al·ly** *adv*

corps \'kor\ *n, pl* **corps** \'korz\ [F, fr. OF *cors*, fr. L *corpus*
body] **1** : an organized subdivision of a country's military
forces **2** : a group acting under common direction

corpse \'korps\ *n* : a dead body

corps·man \'kor-mən, 'korz-\ *n* : an enlisted man trained
to give first aid

cor·pu·lence \'kor-pyə-ləns\ *n* : excessive fatness : OBESI-
TY

cor·pu·lent \-lənt\ *adj* : OBESE

cor·pus \'kor-pəs\ *n, pl* **cor·po·ra** \-pə-rə\ [ME, fr. L] **1**
: BODY; *esp* : CORPSE **2** : a body of writings or works

cor·pus·cle \'kor-pə-səl, -ˌpə-\ *n* **1** : a minute particle **2**
: a living cell (as in blood or cartilage) not aggregated into
continuous tissues — **cor·pus·cu·lar** \kor-'pəs-kyə-lər\
adj

cor·pus de·lic·ti \ˌkor-pəs-di-'lik-ˌtī, -tē\ *n, pl* **corpora
delicti** [NL, lit., body of the crime] **1** : the substantial
fact proving that a crime has been committed **2** : the
body of a victim of murder

corr *abbr* **1** correct; corrected; correction **2** correspondence; correspondent; corresponding

cor·ral \kə-'ral\ *n* [Sp] : an enclosure for confining or capturing animals; *also* : an enclosure of wagons for defending a camp — **corral** *vb*

¹**cor·rect** \kə-'rekt\ *vb* **1** : to make right ⟨∼ an error⟩ **2**
: REPROVE, CHASTISE ⟨∼ed the child⟩ — **cor·rect·able**
\-'rek-tə-bəl\ *adj* — **cor·rec·tion** \-'rek-shən\ *n* — **cor·
rec·tion·al** \-'rek-sh(ə-)nəl\ *adj* — **cor·rec·tive** \-'rek-tiv\
adj

²**correct** *adj* **1** : conforming to a conventional standard ⟨∼
behavior⟩ **2** : agreeing with fact or truth ⟨a ∼ answer⟩
3 : conforming to the standards of a specific ideology ⟨en-
vironmentally ∼⟩ — **cor·rect·ly** *adv* — **cor·rect·ness** *n*

cor·re·late \'kor-ə-ˌlāt\ *vb* **-lat·ed; -lat·ing** : to connect in a
systematic way : establish the mutual relations of — **cor·
re·late** \-lət, -ˌlāt\ *n* — **cor·re·la·tion** \ˌkor-ə-'lā-shən\ *n*

cor·rel·a·tive \kə-'re-lə-tiv\ *adj* **1** : reciprocally related **2**
: regularly used together (as *either* and *or*) — **correlative**
n — **cor·rel·a·tive·ly** *adv*

cor·re·spond \ˌkor-ə-'spänd\ *vb* **1** : to be in agreement
: SUIT, MATCH **2** : to communicate by letter — **cor·re·
spond·ing·ly** *adv*

cor·re·spon·dence \-'spän-dəns\ *n* **1** : agreement between particular things **2** : communication by letters;
also : the letters exchanged

¹**cor·re·spon·dent** \-dənt\ *adj* **1** : SIMILAR **2** : FITTING,
CONFORMING

²**correspondent** *n* **1** : something that corresponds **2** : a
person with whom one communicates by letter **3** : a person employed to contribute news regularly from a place
⟨a war ∼⟩

cor·ri·dor \'kor-ə-dər, -ˌdor\ *n* **1** : a passageway into
which compartments or rooms open (as in a hotel or
school) **2** : a narrow strip of land esp. through foreign-
held territory **3** : a densely populated strip of land including two or more major cities **4** : an area identified
by a common characteristic or purpose ⟨a ∼ of liberal-
ism⟩

cor·ri·gen·dum \ˌkor-ə-'jen-dəm\ *n, pl* **-da** \-də\ [L] : an
error in a printed work discovered after printing and
shown with its correction on a separate sheet

cor·ri·gi·ble \'kor-ə-jə-bəl\ *adj* : CORRECTABLE

cor·rob·o·rate \kə-'rä-bə-ˌrāt\ *vb* **-rat·ed; -rat·ing** [L *cor-
roborare*, fr. *robur* strength] : to support with evidence

: CONFIRM — **cor·rob·o·ra·tion** \-ˌrä-bə-'rā-shən\ n —
cor·rob·o·ra·tive \-'rä-bə-ˌrā-tiv, -'rä-brə-\ adj — **cor·rob·o·ra·to·ry** \-'rä-bə-rə-ˌtȯr-ē\ adj

cor·rode \kə-'rōd\ vb **cor·rod·ed; cor·rod·ing** : to wear or be worn away gradually (as by chemical action) — **cor·ro·sion** \-'rō-zhən\ n — **cor·ro·sive** \-'rō-siv\ adj or n

cor·ru·gate \'kȯr-ə-ˌgāt\ vb **-gat·ed; -gat·ing** : to form into wrinkles or ridges and grooves — **cor·ru·gat·ed** adj — **cor·ru·ga·tion** \ˌkȯr-ə-'gā-shən\ n

¹cor·rupt \kə-'rəpt\ vb **1** : to make evil : DEPRAVE; esp : BRIBE **2** : ROT, SPOIL — **cor·rupt·ible** adj — **cor·rup·tion** \-'rəp-shən\ n

²corrupt adj : morally degenerate; also : characterized by improper conduct ⟨~ officials⟩

cor·sage \kȯr-'säzh, -'säj\ n [F, bust, bodice, fr. OF, bust, fr. L cors body, fr. L corpus] **1** : the waist or bodice of a dress **2** : a bouquet to be worn or carried

cor·sair \'kȯr-ˌser\ n : PIRATE

cor·set \'kȯr-sət\ n : a stiffened undergarment worn for support or to give shape to the waist and hips

cor·tege also **cor·tège** \kȯr-'tezh, 'kȯr-ˌtezh\ n [F] : PROCESSION; esp : a funeral procession

cor·tex \'kȯr-ˌteks\ n, pl **cor·ti·ces** \'kȯr-tə-ˌsēz\ or **cor·tex·es** : an outer or covering layer of an organism or one of its parts ⟨the adrenal ~⟩ ⟨~ of a plant stem⟩; esp : CEREBRAL CORTEX — **cor·ti·cal** \'kȯr-ti-kəl\ adj

cor·ti·co·ste·roid \ˌkȯr-ti-kō-'stir-ˌȯid, -'ster-\ n : any of various steroids made in the adrenal cortex and used medically as anti-inflammatory agents

cor·ti·sone \'kȯr-tə-ˌsōn, -ˌzōn\ n : a corticosteroid used esp. in treating rheumatoid arthritis

co·run·dum \kə-'rən-dəm\ n : a very hard aluminum-containing mineral used as an abrasive or as a gem

cor·us·cate \'kȯr-ə-ˌskāt\ vb **-cat·ed; -cat·ing** : FLASH, SPARKLE — **cor·us·ca·tion** \ˌkȯr-ə-'skā-shən\ n

cor·vette \kȯr-'vet\ n **1** : a naval sailing ship smaller than a frigate **2** : an armed escort ship smaller than a destroyer

co·ry·za \kə-'rī-zə\ n : an inflammatory disorder of the upper respiratory tract; esp : COMMON COLD

cos abbr cosine

COS abbr **1** cash on shipment **2** chief of staff

co·sig·na·to·ry \kō-'sig-nə-ˌtȯr-ē\ n : a joint signer

co·sign·er \'kō-ˌsī-nər\ n : COSIGNATORY; esp : a joint signer of a promissory note

co·sine \'kō-ˌsīn\ n : the trigonometric function that is the ratio between the side next to an acute angle in a right triangle and the hypotenuse

¹cos·met·ic \käz-'me-tik\ adj [Gk kosmētikos skilled in adornment, fr. kosmein to arrange, adorn, fr. kosmos order, ornament, universe] **1** : intended to beautify the hair or complexion **2** : correcting physical defects esp. to improve appearance ⟨~ dentistry⟩ **3** : SUPERFICIAL — **cos·met·i·cal·ly** \-ti-k(ə-)lē\ adv

²cosmetic n : a cosmetic preparation

cos·me·tol·o·gist \ˌkäz-mə-'tä-lə-jist\ n : one who gives beauty treatments — **cos·me·tol·o·gy** \-jē\ n

cos·mic \'käz-mik\ also **cos·mi·cal** \-mi-kəl\ adj **1** : of or relating to the cosmos **2** : VAST, GRAND **3** : of or relating to spiritual or metaphysical ideas ⟨a ~ thinker⟩ — **cos·mi·cal·ly** adv

cosmic ray n : a stream of very penetrating atomic nuclei that enter the earth's atmosphere from outer space

cos·mog·o·ny \käz-'mä-gə-nē\ n, pl **-nies** : the origin or creation of the world or universe

cos·mol·o·gy \-'mä-lə-jē\ n, pl **-gies** : a branch of astronomy dealing with the origin and structure of the universe — **cos·mo·log·i·cal** \ˌkäz-mə-'lä-ji-kəl\ adj — **cos·mol·o·gist** \käz-'mä-lə-jist\ n

cos·mo·naut \'käz-mə-ˌnȯt\ n : a Soviet or Russian astronaut

cos·mo·pol·i·tan \ˌkäz-mə-'pä-lə-tən\ adj : belonging to all the world : not local ✦ Synonyms UNIVERSAL, GLOBAL, CATHOLIC — **cosmopolitan** n

cos·mos \'käz-məs, 1 also -ˌmōs, -ˌmäs\ n **1** : UNIVERSE **2** : a tall garden herb related to the daisies

co·spon·sor \'kō-ˌspän-sər, -'spän-\ n : a joint sponsor — **cosponsor** vb

Cos·sack \'kä-ˌsak, -sək\ n [Pol & Ukrainian kozak, of Turkic origin] : a member of one of several autonomous communities drawn from various ethnic groups in southern Russia; also : a mounted soldier from one of these communities

¹cost \'kȯst\ n **1** : the amount paid or charged for something : PRICE **2** : the loss or penalty incurred in gaining something **3** pl : expenses incurred in a law suit — **at all costs** : regardless of consequences ⟨win at all costs⟩

²cost vb **cost; cost·ing** **1** : to require a specified amount in payment **2** : to cause to pay, suffer, or lose

co–star \'kō-ˌstär\ n : one of two leading players in a motion picture or play — **co–star** vb

cos·tive \'käs-tiv\ adj : affected with or causing constipation

cost·ly \'kȯst-lē\ adj **cost·li·er; -est** **1** : of great cost or value ⟨~ gems⟩ **2** : done at great expense or sacrifice ⟨a ~ error⟩ ✦ Synonyms DEAR, VALUABLE, EXPENSIVE — **cost·li·ness** n

cos·tume \'käs-ˌtüm, -ˌtyüm\ n [F, fr. It, custom, dress, fr. L consuetudo custom] **1** : the style of attire characteristic of a period or country **2** : a special or fancy dress ⟨Halloween ~s⟩ — **cos·tum·er** \'käs-ˌtü-mər, -ˌtyü-\ n

costume jewelry n : inexpensive jewelry

cosy chiefly Brit var of COZY

¹cot \'kät\ n : a small house : COTTAGE

²cot n : a small often collapsible bed

cote \'kōt, 'kät\ n : a small shed or coop (as for sheep or doves)

co·te·rie \'kō-tə-ˌrē, ˌkō-tə-'rē\ n [F] : an intimate often exclusive group of persons with a common interest

co·ter·mi·nous \ˌko-'tər-mə-nəs\ adj : having the same scope or duration

co·til·lion \kō-'til-yən, kə-\ n : a formal ball

cot·tage \'kä-tij\ n : a small house — **cot·tag·er** n

cottage cheese n : a soft uncured cheese made from soured skim milk

cot·tar or **cot·ter** \'kä-tər\ n : a peasant or farm laborer occupying a cottage and often a small holding

cotter pin n : a metal strip bent into a pin whose ends can be spread apart after insertion through a hole or slot

cot·ton \'kä-tᵊn\ n [ME coton, fr. AF cotun, fr. Ar quṭun] **1** : a soft fibrous usu. white substance composed of hairs attached to the seeds of various tropical plants related to the mallow; also : this plant **2** : thread or cloth made of cotton — **cot·tony** adj

cotton candy n : a candy made of spun sugar

cot·ton·mouth \'kä-tᵊn-ˌmau̇th\ n : WATER MOCCASIN

cot·ton·seed \-ˌsēd\ n : the seed of the cotton plant yielding a protein-rich meal and a fatty oil (**cottonseed oil**) used esp. in cooking

cot·ton·tail \-ˌtāl\ n : a No. American rabbit with a white-tufted tail

cot·ton·wood \-ˌwu̇d\ n : a poplar having seeds with cottony hairs

cot·y·le·don \ˌkä-tə-'lē-dᵊn\ n : the first leaf or one of the first pair or whorl of leaves developed by a seed plant

¹couch \'kau̇ch\ vb **1** : to lie or place on a couch **2** : to phrase in a specified manner ⟨proposals ~ed in jargon⟩

²couch n : a piece of furniture (as a bed or sofa) that one can sit or lie on

couch·ant \'kau̇-chənt\ adj : lying down with the head raised ⟨coat of arms with lion ~⟩

couch potato n : one who spends a great deal of time watching television

cou·gar \'kü-gər\ n, pl **cougars** also **cougar** [F couguar, fr. NL cuguacuarana, modif. of Tupi (a Brazilian Indian language) siwasuarána, fr. siwásu deer + -ran resembling] : a large powerful tawny brown wild American cat

cougar

cough \\'kof\\ *vb* : to force air from the lungs with short sharp noises; *also* : to expel by coughing — **cough** *n*

could \\kəd, 'kŭd\\ *past of* CAN — used as an auxiliary in the past or as a polite or less forceful alternative to *can* in the present

cou·lee \\'kü-lē\\ *n* **1** : a small stream **2** : a dry streambed **3** : GULLY

cou·lomb \\'kü-,läm, -,lōm\\ *n* : a unit of electric charge equal to the electricity transferred by a current of one ampere in one second

coun·cil \\'kaůn-səl\\ *n* **1** : ASSEMBLY, MEETING **2** : an official body of lawmakers ⟨city ∼⟩ — **coun·cil·lor** *or* **coun·cil·or** \\-sə-lər\\ *n* — **coun·cil·man** \\-səl-mən\\ *n* — **coun·cil·wom·an** \\-,wŭ-mən\\ *n*

¹coun·sel \\'kaůn-səl\\ *n* **1** : ADVICE **2** : a plan of action **3** : deliberation together **4** *pl* **counsel** : LAWYER

²counsel *vb* **-seled** *or* **-selled; -sel·ing** *or* **-sel·ling** **1** : ADVISE **2** : CONSULT

coun·sel·or *or* **coun·sel·lor** \\'kaůn-sə-lər\\ *n* **1** : ADVISER **2** : LAWYER **3** : one who has supervisory duties at a summer camp

¹count \\'kaůnt\\ *vb* [ME, fr. AF *cunter, counter,* fr. L *computare,* fr. *com-* + *putare* to consider] **1** : to name or indicate one by one in order to find the total number **2** : to recite numbers in order **3** : CONSIDER, ACCOUNT **4** : RELY ⟨you can ∼ on me⟩ **5** : to be of value or account ⟨∼s toward your grade⟩ — **count·able** *adj*

²count *n* **1** : the act of counting; *also* : the total obtained by counting **2** : a particular charge in an indictment or legal declaration ⟨two ∼s of murder⟩

³count *n* [ME, fr. AF *cunte,* fr. LL *comes,* fr. L, companion, one of the imperial court, fr. *com-* with + *ire* to go] : a European nobleman whose rank corresponds to that of a British earl

count·down \\'kaůnt-,daůn\\ *n* : a backward counting in fixed units (as seconds) to indicate the time remaining before an event (as the launching of a rocket) — **count down** *vb*

¹coun·te·nance \\'kaůn-tⁿn-əns\\ *n* **1** : the human face **2** : FAVOR, APPROVAL

²countenance *vb* **-nanced; -nanc·ing** : SANCTION, TOLERATE

¹count·er \\'kaůn-tər\\ *n* **1** : a piece (as of metal or plastic) used in reckoning or in games **2** : a level surface over which business is transacted, food is served, or work is conducted

²count·er *n* : a device for recording a number or amount

³coun·ter *vb* : to act in opposition to

⁴coun·ter *adv* : in an opposite direction : CONTRARY

⁵coun·ter *n* **1** : OPPOSITE, CONTRARY **2** : an answering or offsetting force or blow

⁶coun·ter *adj* : CONTRARY, OPPOSITE

coun·ter·act \\,kaůn-tər-'akt\\ *vb* : to lessen the force of : OFFSET — **coun·ter·ac·tive** \\-'ak-tiv\\ *adj*

coun·ter·at·tack \\'kaůn-tər-ə-,tak\\ *n* : an attack made to oppose an enemy's attack — **counterattack** *vb*

¹coun·ter·bal·ance \\'kaůn-tər-,ba-ləns\\ *n* : a weight or influence that balances another

²counterbalance \\,kaůn-tər-'ba-ləns\\ *vb* : to oppose with equal weight or influence

coun·ter·claim \\'kaůn-tər-,klām\\ *n* : an opposing claim esp. in law

coun·ter·clock·wise \\,kaůn-tər-'kläk-,wīz\\ *adv* : in a direction opposite to that in which the hands of a clock rotate — **counterclockwise** *adj*

coun·ter·cul·ture \\'kaůn-tər-,kəl-chər\\ *n* : a culture with values and mores that run counter to those of established society

coun·ter·es·pi·o·nage \\,kaůn-tər-'es-pē-ə-,näzh, -nij\\ *n* : activities intended to discover and defeat enemy espionage

¹coun·ter·feit \\'kaůn-tər-,fit\\ *adj* : SHAM, SPURIOUS; *also* : FORGED ⟨∼ money⟩

²counterfeit *vb* **1** : to copy or imitate in order to deceive **2** : PRETEND, FEIGN — **coun·ter·feit·er** *n*

³counterfeit *n* : something counterfeit : FORGERY ♦ **Synonyms** FRAUD, SHAM, FAKE, IMPOSTURE, DECEIT, DECEPTION

coun·ter·in·sur·gen·cy \\,kaůn-tər-in-'sər-jən-sē\\ *n* : military activity designed to deal with insurgents

coun·ter·in·tel·li·gence \\-in-'te-lə-jəns\\ *n* : organized activities of an intelligence service designed to counter the activities of an enemy's intelligence service

coun·ter·in·tu·i·tive \\-in-'tü-ə-tiv, -'tyü-\\ *adj* : contrary to what would intuitively be expected

count·er·man \\'kaůn-tər-,man, -mən\\ *n* : one who tends a counter

coun·ter·mand \\'kaůnt-ər-,mand\\ *vb* : to withdraw (an order already given) by a contrary order

coun·ter·mea·sure \\-,me-zhər\\ *n* : an action or device designed to counter another

coun·ter·of·fen·sive \\-ə-,fen-siv\\ *n* : a large-scale counterattack

coun·ter·pane \\-,pān\\ *n* : BEDSPREAD

coun·ter·part \\-,pärt\\ *n* : a person or thing very closely like or corresponding to another person or thing

coun·ter·point \\-,pȯint\\ *n* : music in which one melody is accompanied by one or more other melodies all woven into a harmonious whole

coun·ter·poise \\-,pȯiz\\ *n* : COUNTERBALANCE

coun·ter·rev·o·lu·tion \\,kaůn-tər-,re-və-'lü-shən\\ *n* : a revolution opposed to a current or earlier one — **coun·ter·rev·o·lu·tion·ary** \\-shə-,ner-ē\\ *adj or n*

coun·ter·sign \\'kaůn-tər-,sīn\\ *n* **1** : a confirmatory signature added to a writing already signed by another person **2** : a military secret signal that must be given by a person who wishes to pass a guard — **countersign** *vb*

coun·ter·sink \\-,siŋk\\ *vb* **-sunk** \\-,səŋk\\; **-sink·ing** **1** : to form a funnel-shaped enlargement at the outer end of a drilled hole **2** : to set the head of (as a screw) at or below the surface — **countersink** *n*

coun·ter·spy \\-,spī\\ *n* : a spy engaged in counterespionage

coun·ter·ten·or \\-,te-nər\\ *n* : a tenor with an unusually high range

coun·ter·vail \\,kaůn-tər-'vāl\\ *vb* : COUNTERACT

coun·ter·weight \\'kaůn-tər-,wāt\\ *n* : COUNTERBALANCE

count·ess \\'kaůn-təs\\ *n* **1** : the wife or widow of a count or an earl **2** : a woman holding the rank of a count or an earl in her own right

count·ing·house \\'kaůn-tiŋ-,haůs\\ *n* : a building or office for keeping books and conducting business

count·less \\'kaůnt-ləs\\ *adj* : INNUMERABLE

coun·tri·fied *also* **coun·try·fied** \\'kən-tri-,fīd\\ *adj* **1** : RURAL, RUSTIC **2** : UNSOPHISTICATED **3** : played or sung in the manner of country music

¹coun·try \\'kən-trē\\ *n, pl* **countries** [ME *contree,* fr. AF *cuntree, contré,* fr. ML *contrata,* fr. L *contra* against, on the opposite side] **1** : REGION, DISTRICT **2** : FATHERLAND **3** : a nation or its territory **4** : rural regions as opposed to towns and cities **5** : COUNTRY MUSIC

²country *adj* **1** : RURAL **2** : of or relating to country music ⟨a ∼ singer⟩

country and western *n* : COUNTRY MUSIC

country club *n* : a suburban club for social life and recreation; *esp* : one having a golf course — **country-club** *adj*

coun·try–dance \\'kən-trē-,dans\\ *n* : an English dance in which partners face each other esp. in rows

coun·try·man \\'kən-trē-mən, *2 often* -,man\\ *n* **1** : an inhabitant of a specified country **2** : COMPATRIOT **3** : one raised or living in the country : RUSTIC

country music *n* : music derived from or imitating the folk style of the southern U.S. or of the Western cowboy

coun·try·side \\'kən-trē-,sīd\\ *n* : a rural area or its people

coun·ty \\'kaůn-tē\\ *n, pl* **counties** **1** : the domain of a count **2** : a territorial division of a country or state for purposes of local government

coup \\'kü\\ *n, pl* **coups** \\'küz\\ [F, blow, stroke] **1** : a brilliant sudden stroke or stratagem **2** : COUP D'ÉTAT

coup de grace \\,kü-də-'gräs\\ *n, pl* **coups de grace** *same*\\ [F *coup de grâce,* lit., stroke of mercy] : DEATHBLOW; *also* : a final decisive stroke or event

coup d'état \\,kü-dā-'tä\\ *n, pl* **coups d'état** *same or* -'täz\\ [F, lit., stroke of state] : a sudden violent overthrow of a government by a small group

cou·pé *or* **coupe** \\kü-'pā, *2 often* 'küp\\ *n* [F *coupé,* fr. *couper* to cut] **1** : a closed horse-drawn carriage for two persons inside with an outside seat for the driver **2** *usu* **coupe** : a 2-door automobile with an enclosed body

¹cou·ple \\'kə-pəl\\ *n* **1** : two persons married, engaged, or otherwise romantically paired **2** : PAIR **3** : BOND, TIE **4** : an indefinite small number : FEW ⟨a ∼ of days ago⟩

²couple *vb* **cou·pled; cou·pling** : to link together

cou·plet \'kə-plət\ n : two successive rhyming lines of verse

coup·ling \'kə-pliŋ (*usual for 2*), -pə-liŋ\ n **1** : CONNECTION **2** : a device for connecting two parts or things

cou·pon \'kü-ˌpän, 'kyü-\ n **1** : a statement attached to a bond showing interest due and designed to be cut off and presented for payment **2** : a form surrendered in order to obtain an article, service, or accommodation **3** : a printed document or slip used to submit orders or inquiries or to obtain a discount on merchandise or services

cour·age \'kər-ij\ n : ability to conquer fear or despair : BRAVERY, VALOR — **cou·ra·geous** \kə-'rā-jəs\ adj — **cou·ra·geous·ly** adv

cou·ri·er \'kur-ē-ər, 'kər-ē-\ n : one who bears messages or information esp. for the diplomatic or military services

¹course \'kors\ n **1** : PROGRESS, PASSAGE; *also* : direction of progress **2** : the ground or path over which something moves **3** : method of procedure : CONDUCT, BEHAVIOR **4** : an ordered series of acts or proceedings : sequence of events **5** : a series of instruction periods dealing with a subject **6** : the series of studies leading to graduation from a school or college **7** : the part of a meal served at one time — **of course** : as might be expected

²course vb **coursed; cours·ing** **1** : to hunt with dogs **2** : to run or go speedily

cours·er \'kor-sər\ n : a swift or spirited horse

¹court \'kort\ n [ME, fr. AF, fr. L *cohort-, cohors* enclosure, group, retinue, cohort] **1** : the residence of a sovereign or similar dignitary **2** : a sovereign's formal assembly of officials and advisers as a governing power **3** : an assembly of the retinue of a sovereign **4** : an open space enclosed by a building or buildings **5** : a space walled. or marked off for playing a game (as tennis or basketball) **6** : the place where justice is administered; *also* : a judicial body or a meeting of a judicial body **7** : attention intended to win favor

²court vb **1** : to try to gain the favor of **2** : WOO **3** : ATTRACT, TEMPT

cour·te·ous \'kər-tē-əs\ adj : marked by respect for others : CIVIL, POLITE — **cour·te·ous·ly** adv

cour·te·san \'kor-tə-zən, -ˌzan\ n : PROSTITUTE

cour·te·sy \'kər-tə-sē\ n, pl **-sies** **1** : courteous behavior : POLITENESS **2** : a favor courteously performed

court·house \'kort-ˌhaus\ n : a building in which courts of law are held or county offices are located

court·ier \'kor-tē-ər\ n : a person in attendance at a royal court

court·ly \'kort-lē\ adj **court·li·er; -est** : REFINED, ELEGANT, POLITE ♦ **Synonyms** GALLANT, GRACIOUS — **court·li·ness** n

court–mar·tial \'kort-ˌmär-shəl\ n, pl **courts–martial** : a military or naval court for trial of offenses against military or naval law; *also* : a trial by this court — **court–martial** vb

court·room \-ˌrüm, -ˌrum\ n : a room in which a court of law is held

court·ship \-ˌship\ n : the act of courting : WOOING

court·yard \-ˌyärd\ n : an enclosure next to a building

cous·cous \'küs-ˌküs\ n : a No. African dish of steamed semolina usu. served with meat or vegetables; *also* : the semolina itself

cous·in \'kə-zən\ n [ME *cosin*, fr. AF, fr. L *consobrinus*, fr. *com-* with + *sobrinus* second cousin, fr. *soror* sister] : a child of one's uncle or aunt

cou·ture \kü-'tur, -'tuer\ n [F] : the business of designing fashionable custom-made women's clothing; *also* : the designers and establishments engaged in this business

cou·tu·ri·er \kü-'tur-ē-ər, -ē-ˌā\ n [F, dressmaker] : the owner of an establishment engaged in couture

cove \'kōv\ n : a small sheltered inlet or bay

co·ven \'kə-vən\ n : an assembly or band of witches

cov·e·nant \'kə-və-nənt\ n : a formal binding agreement : COMPACT — **cov·e·nant** \-nənt, -ˌnant\ vb

¹cov·er \'kə-vər\ vb **1** : to bring or hold within range of a firearm **2** : PROTECT, GUARD ⟨~ed by insurance⟩ **3** : to get to third base **3** : HIDE, CONCEAL ⟨~ up a crime⟩ **4** : to place something over or upon **5** : INCLUDE, COMPRISE **6** : to have as one's field of activity ⟨one salesman ~s the state⟩ **7** : to buy (stocks) in order to have them for delivery on a previous short sale

²cover n **1** : something that protects or shelters **2** : LID, TOP **3** : CASE, BINDING **4** : TABLECLOTH **5** : a cloth used on a bed **6** : SCREEN, DISGUISE **7** : an envelope or wrapper for mail

cov·er·age \'kə-və-rij\ n **1** : the act or fact of covering **2** : the total group covered : SCOPE

cov·er·all \'kə-vər-ˌol\ n : a one-piece outer garment worn to protect one's clothes — usu. used in pl.

cover charge n : a charge made by a restaurant or nightclub in addition to the charge for food and drink

cover crop n : a crop planted to prevent soil erosion and to provide humus

cov·er·let \'kə-vər-lət\ n : BEDSPREAD

¹co·vert \'kō-ˌvərt, 'kə-vərt\ adj **1** : HIDDEN, SECRET ⟨a ~ operation⟩ **2** : SHELTERED — **co·vert·ly** adv

²co·vert \'kə-vərt, 'kō-\ n **1** : a secret or sheltered place; *esp* : a thicket sheltering game **2** : a feather covering the bases of the quills of the wings and tail of a bird

cov·er–up \'kə-vər-ˌəp\ n **1** : a device for masking or concealing **2** : a usu. concerted effort to keep an illegal or unethical act or situation from being made public

cov·et \'kə-vət\ vb : to desire enviously (what belongs to another) — **cov·et·ous** adj — **cov·et·ous·ness** n

cov·ey \'kə-vē\ n, pl **coveys** [ME, fr. AF *covee* sitting (of a hen), fr. *cover* to sit on, brood over, fr. L *cubare* to lie] **1** : a bird with her brood of young **2** : a small flock (as of quail) **3** : GROUP 1

¹cow \'kau\ n **1** : the mature female of cattle or of an animal (as the moose, elephant, or whale) of which the male is called *bull* **2** : any domestic bovine animal irrespective of sex or age

²cow vb : INTIMIDATE, DAUNT, OVERAWE

cow·ard \'kau-(ə)rd\ n [ME, fr. AF *cuard*, fr. *cue, coe* tail, fr. L *cauda*] : one who lacks courage or shows shameful fear or timidity — **coward** adj — **cow·ard·ice** \'kau-ər-dəs\ n — **cow·ard·ly** adv or adj

cow·bird \'kau-ˌbərd\ n : a small No. American blackbird that lays its eggs in the nests of other birds

cow·boy \-ˌboi\ n : one (as a mounted ranch hand) who tends cattle or horses

cow·er \'kau-(ə)r\ vb : to shrink or crouch down from fear or cold : QUAIL

cow·girl \'kau-ˌgərl\ n : a girl or woman who tends cattle or horses

cow·hand \'kau-ˌhand\ n : COWBOY

cow·herd \-ˌhərd\ n : one who tends cows

cow·hide \-ˌhīd\ n **1** : the hide of a cow; *also* : leather made from it **2** : a coarse whip of braided rawhide

cowl \'kaul\ n : a monk's hood

cow·lick \'kau-ˌlik\ n : a turned-up tuft of hair that resists control

cowl·ing \'kau-liŋ\ n : a usu. metal covering for the engine or another part of an airplane

cow·man \'kau-mən, -ˌman\ n : COWBOY; *also* : a cattle owner or rancher

co·work·er \'kō-ˌwər-kər\ n : a fellow worker

cow·poke \'kau-ˌpōk\ n : COWBOY

cow pony n : a strong and agile horse trained for herding cattle

cow·pox \'kau-ˌpäks\ n : a mild disease of the cow that when communicated to humans protects against smallpox

cow·punch·er \-ˌpən-chər\ n : COWBOY

cow·slip \'kau-ˌslip\ n **1** : a yellow-flowered European primrose **2** : MARSH MARIGOLD

cox·comb \'käks-ˌkōm\ n : a conceited foolish person : FOP

cox·swain \'käk-sən, -ˌswān\ n : the steersman of a ship's boat or a racing shell

coy \'koi\ adj [ME, quiet, shy, fr. AF *quei, quoi, koi* quiet, fr. L *quietus*] **1** : BASHFUL, SHY **2** : marked by artful playfulness : COQUETTISH — **coy·ly** adv — **coy·ness** n

coy·ote \'kī-ˌōt, kī-'ō-tē\ n, pl **coyotes** or **coyote** : a mammal of No. America smaller than the related wolves

coy·pu \'koi-pü\ n : NUTRIA 2

coz·en \'kə-z²n\ vb : CHEAT, DEFRAUD — **coz·en·age** \-ij\ n — **coz·en·er** n

¹co·zy \'kō-zē\ adj **co·zi·er; -est** : SNUG, COMFORTABLE ⟨a ~ cabin⟩ — **co·zi·ly** \-zə-lē\ adv — **co·zi·ness** \-zē-nəs\ n

²cozy n, pl **co·zies** : a padded covering for a vessel (as a teapot) to keep the contents hot

cp abbr **1** compare **2** coupon

CP *abbr* **1** cerebral palsy **2** chemically pure **3** command post **4** communist party

CPA *abbr* certified public accountant

CPB *abbr* Corporation for Public Broadcasting

cpd *abbr* compound

CPI *abbr* consumer price index

Cpl *abbr* corporal

CPO *abbr* chief petty officer

CPOM *abbr* master chief petty officer

CPOS *abbr* senior chief petty officer

CPR *abbr* cardiopulmonary resuscitation

CPT *abbr* captain

CPU \ˌsē-ˌpē-'yü\ *n* [*central processing unit*] : the part of a computer that performs its basic operations, manages its components, and exchanges data with memory or peripherals

CQ *abbr* charge of quarters

cr *abbr* credit; creditor

Cr *symbol* chromium

¹crab \'krab\ *n, pl* **crabs** *also* **crab** : any of various crustaceans with a short broad shell and small abdomen

²crab *n* : an ill-natured person

³crab *vb* **crabbed; crab·bing** : COMPLAIN, GROUSE

crab apple *n* : a small often highly colored sour apple; *also* : a tree that produces crab apples

crab·bed \'kra-bəd\ *adj* **1** : MOROSE, PEEVISH ⟨a ~ view of human nature⟩ **2** : CRAMPED, IRREGULAR ⟨~ handwriting⟩

crab·by \'kra-bē\ *adj* **crab·bi·er; -est** : CROSS, ILL-NATURED

crab·grass \'krab-ˌgras\ *n* : a weedy grass with creeping or sprawling stems that root freely at the nodes

crab louse *n* : a louse infesting the pubic region in humans

¹crack \'krak\ *vb* **1** : to break with a sharp sudden sound **2** : to break with or without completely separating into parts **3** : to fail in tone or become harsh ⟨her voice ~ed⟩ **4** : to subject (as a petroleum oil) to heat for breaking down into lighter products (as gasoline)

²crack *n* **1** : a sudden sharp noise **2** : a witty or sharp remark **3** : a narrow break or opening : FISSURE **4** : a sharp blow **5** : ATTEMPT, TRY **6** : a potent form of cocaine in small chips used illicitly for smoking

³crack *adj* : extremely proficient

crack·down \'krak-ˌdau̇n\ *n* : an act or instance of taking positive disciplinary action ⟨a ~ on gambling⟩ — **crack down** *vb*

crack·er \'kra-kər\ *n* **1** : FIRECRACKER **2** : a dry thin crispy baked bread product made of flour and water

crack·er·jack \-ˌjak\ *n* : something excellent — **crackerjack** *adj*

crack·le \'kra-kəl\ *vb* **crack·led; crack·ling 1** : to make small sharp snapping noises **2** : to develop fine cracks in a surface — **crackle** *n* — **crack·ly** \-k(ə-)lē\ *adj*

crack·pot \'krak-ˌpät\ *n* : an eccentric person

crack–up \'krak-ˌəp\ *n* : CRASH, WRECK; *also* : BREAKDOWN

crack up *vb* **1** : PRAISE ⟨isn't all it's *cracked up* to be⟩ **2** : to laugh or cause to laugh out loud **3** : to crash a vehicle

¹cra·dle \'krā-dᵊl\ *n* **1** : a baby's bed or cot **2** : a framework or support (as for a telephone receiver) **3** : INFANCY ⟨from ~ to the grave⟩ **4** : a place of origin

²cradle *vb* **cra·dled; cra·dling 1** : to place in or as if in a cradle **2** : SHELTER, REAR

craft \'kraft\ *n* **1** : ART, SKILL; *also* : an occupation requiring special skill **2** : CUNNING, GUILE **3** *pl usu* **craft** : a boat esp. of small size; *also* : AIRCRAFT, SPACECRAFT

crafts·man \'krafts-mən\ *n* : a skilled artisan — **craftsman·ship** *n*

crafty \'kraf-tē\ *adj* **craft·i·er; -est** : CUNNING, DECEITFUL, SUBTLE — **craft·i·ly** \-tə-lē\ *adv* — **craft·i·ness** \-tē-nəs\ *n*

crag \'krag\ *n* : a steep rugged cliff or rock — **crag·gy** *adj*

cram \'kram\ *vb* **crammed; cram·ming 1** : to pack in tight : JAM **2** : to eat greedily **3** : to study rapidly under pressure for an examination

¹cramp \'kramp\ *n* **1** : a sudden painful contraction of muscle **2** : sharp abdominal pain — usu. used in pl.

²cramp *vb* **1** : to affect with a cramp or cramps **2** : to restrain from free action : HAMPER

cran·ber·ry \'kran-ˌber-ē, -bə-rē\ *n* : the red acid berry of any of several trailing plants related to the heaths; *also* : one of these plants

¹crane \'krān\ *n* **1** : any of a family of tall wading birds related to the rails; *also* : any of several herons **2** : a machine for lifting and carrying heavy objects

²crane *vb* **craned; cran·ing** : to stretch one's neck to see better

crane fly *n* : any of a family of long-legged slender dipteran flies that resemble large mosquitoes but do not bite

cranial nerve *n* : any of the nerves that arise in pairs from the lower surface of the brain and pass through openings in the skull to the periphery of the body

cra·ni·um \'krā-nē-əm\ *n, pl* **-ni·ums** *or* **-nia** \-ə\ : SKULL; *esp* : the part enclosing the brain — **cra·ni·al** \-əl\ *adj*

¹crank \'kraŋk\ *n* **1** : a bent part of an axle or shaft or an arm at right angles to the end of a shaft by which circular motion is imparted to or received from it **2** : an eccentric person **3** : a bad-tempered person : GROUCH

²crank *vb* : to start or operate by or as if by turning a crank

crank·case \'kraŋk-ˌkās\ *n* : the housing of a crankshaft

crank out *vb* : to produce in a mechanical manner

crank·shaft \'kraŋk-ˌshaft\ *n* : a shaft turning or driven by a crank

cranky \'kraŋ-kē\ *adj* **crank·i·er; -est 1** : IRRITABLE **2** : operating uncertainly or imperfectly ⟨a ~ old tractor⟩

cran·ny \'kra-nē\ *n, pl* **crannies** : CREVICE, CHINK

craps \'kraps\ *n* : a gambling game played with two dice

crap·shoot·er \'krap-ˌshü-tər\ *n* : a person who plays craps

¹crash \'krash\ *vb* **1** : to break noisily : SMASH **2** : to damage an airplane in landing **3** : to enter or attend without invitation or without paying ⟨~ a party⟩ **4** : to suffer a sudden major failure usu. with loss of data ⟨my computer ~ed⟩

²crash *n* **1** : a loud sound (as of things smashing) **2** : an instance of crashing ⟨a plane ~⟩; *also* : COLLISION **3** : a sudden failure (as of a business)

³crash *adj* : marked by concentrated effort over the shortest possible time ⟨a ~ diet⟩

⁴crash *n* : coarse linen fabric used for towels and draperies

crash–land \'krash-'land\ *vb* : to land an aircraft or spacecraft under emergency conditions usu. with damage to the craft — **crash landing** *n*

crass \'kras\ *adj* : GROSS, INSENSITIVE ⟨~ ignorance⟩ — **crass·ly** *adv* — **crass·ness** *n*

crate \'krāt\ *n* : a container often of wooden slats — **crate** *vb*

cra·ter \'krā-tər\ *n* [L, mixing bowl, crater, fr. Gk *kratēr*, fr. *kerannynai* to mix] **1** : the depression around the opening of a volcano **2** : a depression formed by the impact of a meteorite or by the explosion of a bomb or shell

cra·vat \krə-'vat\ *n* : NECKTIE

crave \'krāv\ *vb* **craved; crav·ing 1** : to ask for earnestly : BEG **2** : to long for : DESIRE

cra·ven \'krā-vən\ *adj* : COWARDLY — **craven** *n* — **cra·ven·ly** *adv*

crav·ing \'krā-viŋ\ *n* : an urgent or abnormal desire

craw·fish \'krȯ-ˌfish\ *n* **1** : CRAYFISH 1 **2** : SPINY LOBSTER

¹crawl \'krȯl\ *vb* **1** : to move slowly by drawing the body along the ground **2** : to advance feebly, cautiously, or slowly **3** : to be swarming with or feel as if swarming with creeping things ⟨a place ~ing with ants⟩ ⟨her flesh ~ed⟩

²crawl *n* **1** : a very slow pace **2** : a prone speed swimming stroke

cray·fish \'krā-ˌfish\ *n* **1** : any of numerous freshwater crustaceans usu. much smaller than the related lobsters **2** : SPINY LOBSTER

crayfish 1

cray·on \'krā-ˌän, -ən\ n : a stick of chalk or wax used for writing, drawing, or coloring; *also* : a drawing made with such material — **crayon** *vb*

¹craze \'krāz\ *vb* **crazed; craz·ing** [ME *crasen* to crush, craze, of Scand origin] : to make or become insane

²craze n : FAD, MANIA

cra·zy \'krā-zē\ *adj* **cra·zi·er; -est** **1** : mentally disordered : INSANE **2** : wildly impractical ⟨a ~ plan⟩; *also* : ERRATIC ⟨~ drivers⟩ — **cra·zi·ly** \-zə-lē\ *adv* — **cra·zi·ness** \-zē-nəs\ n

CRC *abbr* Civil Rights Commission

creak \'krēk\ *vb* : to make a prolonged squeaking or grating sound — **creak** n — **creaky** *adj*

¹cream \'krēm\ n **1** : the yellowish fat-rich part of milk **2** : a thick smooth sauce, confection, or cosmetic **3** : the choicest part **4** : a pale yellow color — **creamy** *adj*

²cream *vb* **1** : to prepare with a cream sauce **2** : to beat or blend into creamy consistency **3** : to defeat decisively

cream cheese n : a cheese made from whole milk enriched with cream

cream·ery \'krē-mə-rē\ n, pl **-er·ies** : an establishment where butter and cheese are made or milk and cream are prepared for sale

crease \'krēs\ n : a mark or line made by or as if by folding — **crease** *vb*

cre·ate \krē-'āt\ *vb* **cre·at·ed; cre·at·ing** : to bring into being : cause to exist : MAKE, PRODUCE — **cre·a·tive** \-'ā-tiv\ *adj* — **cre·a·tive·ness** n — **cre·a·tiv·i·ty** \krē-(ˌ)ā-'ti-və-tē\ n

cre·a·tion \krē-'ā-shən\ n **1** : the act of creating or producing ⟨~ of the world⟩ **2** : something that is created **3** : all created things : WORLD

cre·a·tion·ism \krē-'ā-shə-ˌni-zəm\ n : a doctrine or theory holding that matter, the various forms of life, and the world were created by God out of nothing — **cre·a·tion·ist** \-nist\ n or *adj*

cre·a·tor \krē-'ā-tər\ n **1** : one that creates : MAKER, AUTHOR **2** *cap* : GOD 1

crea·ture \'krē-chər\ n : a lower animal; *also* : a human being

crèche \'kresh\ n [F, manger, crib, fr. OF *creche*, of Gmc origin] : a representation of the Nativity scene

cre·dence \'krē-d°ns\ n : mental acceptance as true or real

cre·den·tial \kri-'den-chəl\ n : something that gives a basis for credit or confidence

cre·den·za \kri-'den-zə\ n [It, lit., belief, confidence] : a sideboard, buffet, or bookcase usu. without legs

cred·i·ble \'kre-də-bəl\ *adj* : TRUSTWORTHY, BELIEVABLE — **cred·i·bil·i·ty** \ˌkre-də-'bi-lə-tē\ n — **cred·i·bly** \'kre-də-blē\ *adv*

¹cred·it \'kre-dət\ n [MF, fr. It *credito*, fr. L *creditum* something entrusted to another, loan, fr. *credere* to believe, entrust] **1** : the balance (as in a bank) in a person's favor **2** : time given for payment for goods sold on trust **3** : an accounting entry of payment received **4** : BELIEF, FAITH **5** : financial trustworthiness **6** : ESTEEM **7** : a source of honor or distinction **8** : a unit of academic work

²credit *vb* **1** : BELIEVE **2** : to give credit to

cred·it·able \'kre-də-tə-bəl\ *adj* : worthy of esteem or praise — **cred·it·ably** \-blē\ *adv*

credit card n : a card authorizing purchases on credit

cred·i·tor \'kre-də-tər\ n : a person to whom money is owed

cre·do \'krē-dō, 'krā-\ n, pl **credos** [ME, fr. L, I believe] : CREED

cred·u·lous \'kre-jə-ləs\ *adj* : inclined to believe esp. on slight evidence — **cred·u·lous·ly** *adv* — **cre·du·li·ty** \kri-'dü-lə-tē, -'dyü-\ n

Cree \'krē\ n, pl **Cree** or **Crees** : a member of an American Indian people of Canada

creed \'krēd\ n [ME *crede*, fr. OE *crēda*, fr. L *credo* I believe, first word of the Apostles' and Nicene Creeds] : a statement of the essential beliefs of a religious faith

creek \'krēk, 'krik\ n **1** *chiefly Brit* : a small inlet **2** : a stream smaller than a river and larger than a brook

Creek \'krēk\ n : a member of an American Indian people of Alabama, Georgia, and Florida

creel \'krēl\ n : a wicker basket esp. for carrying fish

creep \'krēp\ *vb* **crept** \'krept\; **creep·ing** **1** : CRAWL **2** : to feel as though insects were crawling on the skin **3**

: to spread or grow over a surface like ivy — **creep** n — **creep·er** n

creep·ing \'krē-piŋ\ *adj* : developing or advancing by imperceptible degrees

creepy \'krē-pē\ *adj* **creep·i·er; -est** : having or producing a nervous shivery fear

cre·mate \'krē-ˌmāt\ *vb* **cre·mat·ed; cre·mat·ing** : to reduce (a dead body) to ashes with fire — **cre·ma·tion** \kri-'mā-shən\ n

cre·ma·to·ry \'krē-mə-ˌtȯr-ē, 'kre-\ n, pl **-ries** : a furnace for cremating; *also* : a structure containing such a furnace

crème or **creme** \'krem, 'krēm\ n, pl **crèmes** or **cremes** \same or 'kremz, 'krēmz\ [F, lit., cream] : a sweet liqueur

cren·el·lat·ed or **cren·el·at·ed** \'kre-nə-lā-təd\ *adj* : having battlements — **cren·el·la·tion** \ˌkre-nə-'lā-shən\ n

Cre·ole \'krē-ˌōl\ n **1** : a descendant of early French or Spanish settlers of the U.S. Gulf states preserving their speech and culture; *also* : a person of mixed French or Spanish and black descent speaking a dialect of French or Spanish **2** *not cap* : a language that has evolved from a pidgin but serves as the native language of a speech community

cre·o·sote \'krē-ə-ˌsōt\ n : an oily liquid obtained by distillation of coal tar and used in preserving wood

crepe or **crêpe** \'krāp\ n : a light crinkled fabric of any of various fibers

crêpe su·zette \ˌkrāp-sü-'zet\ n, pl **crêpes suzette** \same or ˌkrāps-\ or **crêpe suzettes** \-sü-'zets\ *often cap S* : a thin folded or rolled pancake in a hot orange-butter sauce that is sprinkled with a liqueur and set ablaze for serving

cre·pus·cu·lar \kri-'pəs-kyə-lər\ *adj* **1** : of, relating to, or resembling twilight **2** : occurring or active during twilight ⟨~ insects⟩

cre·scen·do \krə-'shen-dō\ *adv or adj* [It] : increasing in loudness — used as a direction in music — **crescendo** n

cres·cent \'kre-s°nt\ n [ME *cressant*, fr. AF fr. prp. of *crestre* to grow, increase, fr. L *crescere*] : the moon at any stage between new moon and first quarter and between last quarter and new moon; *also* : something shaped like the figure of the crescent moon with a convex and a concave edge — **cres·cen·tic** \kre-'sen-tik\ *adj*

cress \'kres\ n : any of several salad plants related to the mustards

¹crest \'krest\ n **1** : a tuft or process on the head of an animal (as a bird) **2** : a heraldic device **3** : an upper part, edge, or limit ⟨the ~ of a hill⟩ — **crest·ed** \'kres-təd\ *adj* — **crest·less** *adj*

²crest *vb* **1** : CROWN **2** : to reach the crest of **3** : to rise to a crest

crest·fall·en \'krest-ˌfȯ-lən\ *adj* : DISPIRITED, DEJECTED

Cre·ta·ceous \kri-'tā-shəs\ *adj* : of, relating to, or being the latest period of the Mesozoic era marked by great increase in flowering plants, diversification of mammals, and extinction of the dinosaurs — **Cretaceous** n

cre·tin \'krē-t°n\ n [F *crétin*, fr. F dial. *cretin*, lit., wretch, innocent victim, fr. L *christianus* Christian] **1** : one affected with cretinism **2** : a stupid person

cre·tin·ism \-ˌi-zəm\ n : a usu. congenital abnormal condition characterized by physical stunting and mental retardation

cre·tonne \'krē-ˌtän\ n : a strong unglazed cotton cloth for curtains and upholstery

cre·vasse \kri-'vas\ n : a deep fissure esp. in a glacier

crev·ice \'kre-vəs\ n : a narrow fissure

¹crew \'krü\ *chiefly Brit past of* CROW

²crew n [ME *crue*, fr. MF, reinforcement, lit., increase, fr. *croistre* to grow, fr. L *crescere*] **1** : a body of people trained to work together for certain purposes **2** : a group of people who operate a ship, train, aircraft, or spacecraft **3** : the rowers and coxswain of a racing shell; *also* : the sport of rowing engaged in by a crew — **crew·man** \-mən\ n

crew cut n : a very short bristly haircut

crew·el \'krü-əl\ n : slackly twisted worsted yarn used for embroidery — **crew·el·work** \-ˌwərk\ n

¹crib \'krib\ n **1** : a manger for feeding animals **2** : a child's bedstead with high sides **3** : a building or bin for storage (as of grain) **4** : something used for cheating in an exam

²crib *vb* **cribbed; crib·bing** **1** : to put in a crib **2** : STEAL, PLAGIARIZE — **crib·ber** n

DICTIONARY

crib·bage \'kri-bij\ *n* : a card game usu. played by two players and scored on a board (**cribbage board**)

crib death *n* : SUDDEN INFANT DEATH SYNDROME

crick \'krik\ *n* : a painful spasm of muscles (as of the neck)

¹**crick·et** \'kri-kət\ *n* [ME *criket*, fr. AF, of imit. origin] : any of a family of leaping insects related to the grasshoppers and noted for the chirping noises of the male

²**cricket** *n* [MF *criquet* goal stake in a bowling game] : a game played with a bat and ball by two teams on a field centering upon two wickets each defended by a batsman

cri·er \'kri(-ə)r\ *n* : one who calls out proclamations and announcements

crime \'krīm\ *n* : a serious offense against the public law

¹**crim·i·nal** \'kri-mə-nᵊl\ *adj* **1** : involving or being a crime **2** : relating to crime or its punishment — **crim·i·nal·i·ty** \,kri-mə-'na-lə-tē\ *n* — **crim·i·nal·ly** *adv*

²**criminal** *n* : one who has committed a crime

crim·i·nol·o·gy \,kri-mə-'nä-lə-jē\ *n* : the scientific study of crime and criminals — **crim·i·no·log·i·cal** \-mə-nə-'lä-ji-kəl\ *adj* — **crim·i·nol·o·gist** \,kri-mə-'nä-lə-jist\ *n*

¹**crimp** \'krimp\ *vb* : to cause to become crinkled, wavy, or bent

²**crimp** *n* : something (as a curl in hair) produced by or as if by crimping

crim·son \'krim-zən\ *n* : a deep purplish red color — **crimson** *adj*

cringe \'krinj\ *vb* **cringed**; **cring·ing** : to shrink in fear : WINCE, COWER

crin·kle \'kriŋ-kəl\ *vb* **crin·kled**; **crin·kling** : to form many short bends or curves; *also* : WRINKLE — **crinkle** *n* — **crin·kly** \-kə-lē\ *adj*

crin·o·line \'kri-nə-lən\ *n* **1** : an open-weave cloth used for stiffening and lining **2** : a full stiff skirt or underskirt made of crinoline

¹**crip·ple** \'kri-pəl\ *n* : one that is disabled or deficient in a specified manner ⟨a social ∼⟩

²**cripple** *vb* **crip·pled**; **crip·pling** **1** : to make lame **2** : to make useless or imperfect — **crip·pler** \'kri-p(ə-)lər\ *n*

cri·sis \'krī-səs\ *n, pl* **cri·ses** \-,sēz\ [ME, fr. L, fr. Gk *krisis*, lit., decision, fr. *krinein* to decide] **1** : the turning point for better or worse in an acute disease or fever **2** : a decisive or critical moment

crisp \'krisp\ *adj* **1** : CURLY, WAVY **2** : BRITTLE ⟨a ∼ potato chip⟩ **3** : FIRM, FRESH ⟨∼ lettuce⟩ **4** : being sharp and clear ⟨a ∼ photo⟩ **5** : LIVELY, SPARKLING **6** : FROSTY, SNAPPY; *also* : INVIGORATING — **crisp** *vb* — **crisp·ly** *adv* — **crisp·ness** *n* — **crispy** *adj*

¹**criss·cross** \'kris-,krȯs\ *vb* **1** : to mark with crossed lines **2** : to go or pass back and forth

²**crisscross** *adj* : marked or characterized by crisscrossing — **crisscross** *adv*

³**crisscross** *n* : a pattern formed by crossed lines

crit *abbr* critical; criticism

cri·te·ri·on \krī-'tir-ē-ən\ *n, pl* **-ria** \-ē-ə\ : a standard on which a judgment may be based

crit·ic \'kri-tik\ *n* **1** : a person who judges literary or artistic works **2** : one inclined to find fault

crit·i·cal \'kri-ti-kəl\ *adj* **1** : being or relating to a condition or disease involving danger of death ⟨∼ care⟩ **2** : being a crisis **3** : inclined to criticize **4** : relating to criticism or critics **5** : requiring careful judgment ⟨∼ thinking⟩ — **crit·i·cal·ly** \-k(ə-)lē\ *adv*

crit·i·cise *Brit var of* CRITICIZE

crit·i·cism \'kri-tə-,si-zəm\ *n* **1** : the act of criticizing; *esp* : CENSURE **2** : a judgment or review **3** : the art of judging works of literature or art

crit·i·cize \'kri-tə-,sīz\ *vb* **-cized**; **-ciz·ing** **1** : to judge as a critic : EVALUATE **2** : to find fault : express criticism ♦ *Synonyms* BLAME, CENSURE, CONDEMN

cri·tique \krə-'tēk\ *n* : a critical estimate or discussion

crit·ter \'kri-tər\ *n* : CREATURE

croak \'krōk\ *n* : a hoarse harsh cry (as of a frog) — **croak** *vb*

croak·er \'krō-kər\ *n* **1** : an animal that croaks **2** : a fish that produces croaking or grunting noises

Croat \'krō-,at\ *n* : CROATIAN

Cro·atian \krō-'ā-shən\ *n* **1** : a native or inhabitant of Croatia **2** : a Slavic language spoken by Croatians — **Croatian** *adj*

cro·chet \krō-'shā\ *n* : needlework done with a single thread and hooked needle — **crochet** *vb*

crock \'kräk\ *n* : a thick earthenware pot or jar

crock·ery \'krä-kə-rē\ *n* : EARTHENWARE

croc·o·dile \'krä-kə-,dī(-ə)l\ *n* [ME & L; ME *cocodrille*, fr. AF, fr. ML *cocodrillus*, alter. of L *crocodilus*, fr. Gk *krokodilos* lizard, crocodile, fr. *krokē* shingle, pebble + *drillos* worm] : any of several thick-skinned long-bodied carnivorous reptiles of tropical and subtropical waters

cro·cus \'krō-kəs\ *n, pl* **cro·cus·es** *also* **crocus** *or* **cro·ci** \-,kī\ : any of a large genus of low herbs related to the irises and having brightly colored flowers borne singly in early spring

Crohn's disease \'krōnz\ *n* : a chronic inflammatory disease of the gastrointestinal tract and esp. the ileum

crois·sant \krȯ-'sänt, krwä-'säⁿ\ *n, pl* **croissants** *same or* -'sänts, -'säⁿz\ : a rich crescent-shaped roll

Cro–Ma·gnon \krō-'mag-nən, -'man-yən\ *n* : a hominid of a tall erect race known from skeletal remains found in southern France and usu. classified as the same species as present-day humans — **Cro–Magnon** *adj*

crone \'krōn\ *n* : HAG

cro·ny \'krō-nē\ *n, pl* **cronies** : a close friend esp. of long standing

¹**crook** \'krúk\ *vb* : to curve or bend sharply

²**crook** *n* **1** : a bent or curved implement **2** : a bent or curved part; *also* : BEND, CURVE **3** : SWINDLER, THIEF

crook·ed \'krú-kəd\ *adj* **1** : having a crook : BENT, CURVED **2** : DISHONEST — **crook·ed·ly** *adv* — **crook·ed·ness** *n*

croon \'krün\ *vb* : to sing or hum in a gentle murmuring voice — **croon·er** *n*

¹**crop** \'kräp\ *n* **1** : the handle of a whip; *also* : a short riding whip **2** : a pouch in the throat of many birds and insects where food is received **3** : something (as a plant product) that can be harvested; *also* : the yield at harvest

²**crop** *vb* **cropped**; **crop·ping** **1** : to remove the tips of : cut off short; *also* : TRIM **2** : to feed on by cropping **3** : to devote (land) to crops **4** : to appear unexpectedly

crop duster *n* : a person who uses an airplane to spray crops with insecticidal dusts; *also* : an airplane so used

crop·land \-,land\ *n* : land devoted to the production of plant crops

crop·per \'krä-pər\ *n* : a raiser of crops; *esp* : SHARECROPPER

cro·quet \krō-'kā\ *n* : a game in which mallets are used to drive wooden balls through a series of wickets set out on a lawn

cro·quette \krō-'ket\ *n* [F] : a small often rounded mass of minced meat, fish, or vegetables fried in deep fat

cro·sier *or* **cro·zier** \'krō-zhər\ *n* : a staff carried by bishops and abbots

¹**cross** \'krȯs\ *n* **1** : a structure consisting of an upright beam and a crossbar used esp. by the ancient Romans for execution **2** : a figure of the cross on which Christ was crucified used as a Christian symbol **3** : a hybridizing of unlike individuals or strains; *also* : a product of this **4** : a punch delivered with a circular motion over an opponent's lead

²**cross** *vb* **1** : to lie or place across; *also* : INTERSECT **2** : to cancel by marking a cross on or by lining through **3** : THWART, OBSTRUCT **4** : to go or extend across : TRAVERSE **5** : HYBRIDIZE **6** : to meet and pass on the way

³**cross** *adj* **1** : lying across **2** : CONTRARY, OPPOSED **3** : marked by bad temper **4** : HYBRID — **cross·ly** *adv*

cross·bar \'krȯs-,bär\ *n* : a transverse bar or piece

cross·bow \-,bō\ *n* : a short bow mounted crosswise at the end of a wooden stock that shoots short arrows

cross·breed \'krȯs-,brēd, -'brēd\ *vb* **-bred** \-'bred\; **-breed·ing** : HYBRIDIZE

cross–coun·try \-'kən-trē\ *adj* **1** : extending or moving across a country **2** : proceeding over the countryside (as fields and woods) and not by roads **3** : of or relating to racing or skiing over the countryside instead of over a track or run — **cross–country** *adv*

cross·cur·rent \-'kər-ənt\ *n* **1** : a current running counter to another **2** : a conflicting tendency — usu. used in pl.

¹**cross·cut** \-,kət\ *vb* : to cut or saw crosswise esp. of the grain of wood

²**crosscut** *adj* **1** : made or used for crosscutting ⟨a ∼ saw⟩ **2** : cut across the grain

³**crosscut** *n* : something that cuts through transversely

cross·ex·am·ine \ˌkrȯs-ig-ˈza-mən\ *vb* : to examine with questions to check the answers to previous questions — **cross·ex·am·i·na·tion** \-ˌza-mə-ˈnā-shən\ *n* — **cross·ex·am·in·er** *n*

cross-eyed \ˈkrȯs-ˌsīd\ *adj* : having one or both eyes turned inward toward the nose

cross·fer·til·i·za·tion \-ˌfər-tə-lə-ˈzā-shən\ *n* 1 : fertilization between sex cells produced by separate individuals or sometimes by individuals of different kinds; *also* : CROSS-POLLINATION 2 : a broadening or productive interchange (as between cultures) — **cross·fer·til·ize** \-ˈfərt-tə-ˌlīz\ *vb*

cross fire *n* 1 : crossing lines of fire in combat 2 : rapid or angry interchange

cross·hair \ˈkrȯs-ˌher\ *n* : a fine wire or thread in the eyepiece of an optical instrument used as a reference line

cross·hatch \ˈkrȯs-ˌhach\ *vb* : to mark with two series of parallel lines that intersect — **cross·hatch·ing** *n*

cross·ing \ˈkrȯ-siŋ\ *n* 1 : a place or structure for crossing something (as a river) 2 : a point of intersection (as of a street and a railroad track)

cross·over \ˈkrȯs-ˌō-vər\ *n* 1 : CROSSING 2 : a member of a political party who votes in the primary of the other party 3 : a broadening of the popular appeal of an artist (as a musician) by a change in the artist's style, genre, or medium 4 : an instance of breaking into another category

cross over *vb* : to achieve broader popularity by a change of medium or style

cross·piece \ˈkrȯs-ˌpēs\ *n* : a horizontal member

cross·pol·li·na·tion \ˌkrȯs-ˌpä-lə-ˈnā-shən\ *n* : transfer of pollen from one flower to the stigma of another — **cross·pol·li·nate** \ˈkrȯs-ˈpä-lə-ˌnāt\ *vb*

cross·pur·pose \ˈkrȯs-ˈpər-pəs\ *n* : a purpose contrary to another purpose ⟨working at ∼s⟩

cross·ques·tion \-ˈkwes-chən\ *vb* : CROSS-EXAMINE — **cross·question** *n*

cross·re·fer \ˌkrȯs-ri-ˈfər\ *vb* : to refer by a notation or direction from one place to another (as in a book or list) — **cross·ref·er·ence** \ˈkrȯs-ˈre-frəns\ *n*

cross·road \ˈkrȯs-ˌrōd\ *n* 1 : a road that crosses a main road or runs between main roads 2 : a place where roads meet — usu. used in pl. 3 : a crucial point where a decision must be made — usu. used in pl.

cross section *n* 1 : a section cut across something; *also* : a representation made by or as if by such cutting 2 : a number of persons or things selected from a group that show the general nature of the whole group — **cross·sec·tion·al** *adj*

cross·walk \ˈkrȯs-ˌwȯk\ *n* : a marked path for pedestrians crossing a street

cross·ways \-ˌwāz\ *adv* : CROSSWISE

cross·wind \-ˌwind\ *n* : a wind not parallel to a course (as of an airplane)

cross·wise \-ˌwīz\ *adv* : so as to cross something : ACROSS — **crosswise** *adj*

cross·word \ˈkrȯs-ˌwərd\ *n* : a puzzle in which words are put into a pattern of numbered squares in answer to clues

cros·ti·ni \krȯ-ˈstē-nē\ *n pl* : small slices of toasted bread served with a topping

crotch \ˈkräch\ *n* : an angle or area formed by the parting of two legs, branches, or members

crotch·et \ˈkrä-chət\ *n* : an odd notion : WHIM — **crotch·ety** *adj*

crouch \ˈkraùch\ *vb* 1 : to stoop or bend low 2 : CRINGE, COWER — **crouch** *n*

croup \ˈkrüp\ *n* : laryngitis esp. of infants marked by a hoarse ringing cough and difficult breathing — **croupy** *adj*

crou·pi·er \ˈkrü-pē-ər, -pē-ˌā\ *n* [F, lit., rider on the rump of a horse, fr. *croupe* rump] : an employee of a gambling casino who collects and pays bets at a gaming table

crou·ton \ˈkrü-ˌtän\ *n* [F *croûton*, dim. of *croûte* crust] : a small cube of bread toasted or fried crisp

¹**crow** \ˈkrō\ *n* 1 : any of various large glossy black birds related to the jays 2 *cap* : a member of an American Indian people of a region in Montana and Wyoming; *also* : the language of the Crow people

²**crow** *vb* 1 : to make the loud shrill sound characteristic of the cock 2 : to utter a sound expressive of pleasure 3 : EXULT, GLOAT; *also* : BRAG, BOAST

³**crow** *n* : the cry of the cock

crow·bar \ˈkrō-ˌbär\ *n* : a metal bar usu. wedge-shaped at the end for use as a pry or lever

¹**crowd** \ˈkraùd\ *vb* 1 : to press close 2 : to collect in numbers : THRONG 3 : CRAM, STUFF

²**crowd** *n* : a large number of people gathered together at random : THRONG

¹**crown** \ˈkraùn\ *n* 1 : a mark of victory or honor; *esp* : the title of a champion in a sport 2 : a royal headdress 3 : the top of the head; *also* : the part of a hat that covers the top of the head 4 : the highest part (as of a tree or tooth) 5 *often cap* : sovereign power; *also* : MONARCH 6 : a formerly used British silver coin — **crowned** \ˈkraùnd\ *adj*

²**crown** *vb* 1 : to place a crown on 2 : HONOR 3 : TOP, SURMOUNT 4 : to fit (a tooth) with an artificial crown

crown vetch *n* : a Eurasian leguminous herb with umbels of pink-and-white flowers and sharp-angled pods

crow's-foot \ˈkrōz-ˌfùt\ *n, pl* **crow's-feet** \-ˌfēt\ : any of the wrinkles around the outer corners of the eyes — usu. used in pl.

crow's nest *n* : a partly enclosed platform high on a ship's mast for use as a lookout

crozier *var of* CROSIER

¹**CRT** \ˌsē-(ˌ)är-ˈtē\ *n, pl* **CRTs** *or* **CRT's** : CATHODE-RAY TUBE; *also* : a display device incorporating a cathode-ray tube

²**CRT** *abbr* carrier route

cru·cial \ˈkrü-shəl\ *adj* : DECISIVE ⟨a ∼ step⟩; *also* : IMPORTANT, SIGNIFICANT ⟨a ∼ question⟩

cru·ci·ate \ˈkrü-shē-ˌāt\ *adj* : CRUCIFORM

cru·ci·ble \ˈkrü-sə-bəl\ *n* : a heat-resistant container in which material can be subjected to great heat

cru·ci·fix \ˈkrü-sə-ˌfiks\ *n* : a representation of Christ on the cross

cru·ci·fix·ion \ˌkrü-sə-ˈfik-shən\ *n* 1 *cap* : the crucifying of Christ 2 : the act of crucifying

cru·ci·form \ˈkrü-sə-ˌfȯrm\ *adj* : shaped like a cross

cru·ci·fy \ˈkrü-sə-ˌfī\ *vb* **-fied; -fy·ing** 1 : to put to death by nailing or binding the hands and feet to a cross 2 : MORTIFY 1 3 : TORTURE, PERSECUTE

¹**crude** \ˈkrüd\ *adj* **crud·er; crud·est** 1 : not refined : RAW ⟨∼ oil⟩ ⟨∼ statistics⟩ 2 : lacking grace, taste, tact, or polish : RUDE — **crude·ly** *adv* — **crude·ness** — **cru·di·ty** \ˈkrü-də-tē\ *n*

²**crude** *n* : unrefined petroleum

cru·el \ˈkrü-əl\ *adj* **cru·el·er** *or* **cru·el·ler; cru·el·est** *or* **cru·el·lest** [ME, fr. AF, fr. L *crudelis*, fr. *crudus* crude] : causing pain and suffering to others : MERCILESS — **cru·el·ly** *adv* — **cru·el·ty** \-tē\ *n*

cru·et \ˈkrü-ət\ *n* : a small usu. glass bottle for vinegar, oil, or sauce

cruise \ˈkrüz\ *vb* **cruised; cruis·ing** [D *kruisen* to make a cross, cruise] 1 : to sail about touching at a series of ports 2 : to travel for enjoyment 3 : to travel about the streets at random 4 : to travel at the most efficient operating speed ⟨the *cruising* speed of an airplane⟩ 5 : SURF 2 — **cruise** *n*

cruis·er \ˈkrü-zər\ *n* 1 : SQUAD CAR 2 : a large fast moderately armored and gunned warship 3 : a motorboat equipped for living aboard

cruis·er·weight \-ˌwāt\ *n* : a boxer weighing no more than 190 pounds

crul·ler \ˈkrə-lər\ *n* 1 : a small sweet cake in the form of a twisted strip fried in deep fat 2 *Northern & Midland* : an unraised doughnut

¹**crumb** \ˈkrəm\ *n* : a small fragment

²**crumb** *vb* 1 : to break into crumbs 2 : to cover with crumbs

crum·ble \ˈkrəm-bəl\ *vb* **crum·bled; crum·bling** : to break into small pieces : DISINTEGRATE — **crum·bly** *adj*

crum·my *also* **crumby** \ˈkrə-mē\ *adj* **crum·mi·er** *also* **crumb·i·er; -est** : very poor or inferior : LOUSY

crum·pet \ˈkrəm-pət\ *n* : a small round unsweetened bread cooked on a griddle

crum·ple \ˈkrəm-pəl\ *vb* **crum·pled; crum·pling** 1 : to crush together : RUMPLE 2 : COLLAPSE

¹**crunch** \ˈkrənch\ *vb* : to chew with a grinding noise; *also* : to grind or press with a crushing noise

²**crunch** *n* 1 : an act of or a sound made by crunching 2 : a tight or critical situation — **crunchy** *adj*

cru·sade \krü-ˈsād\ *n* 1 *cap* : any of the expeditions in the 11th, 12th, and 13th centuries undertaken by Christian countries to take the Holy Land from the Muslims **2** : a reforming enterprise undertaken with zeal — **crusade** *vb* — **cru·sad·er** *n*

cruse \'krüz, 'krüs\ *n* : a jar for water or oil

¹**crush** \'krəsh\ *vb* **1** : to squeeze out of shape **2** : HUG, EMBRACE **3** : to grind or pound to small bits **4** : OVERWHELM, SUPPRESS

²**crush** *n* **1** : an act of crushing **2** : a violent crowding **3** : INFATUATION

crust \'krəst\ *n* **1** : the outside part of bread; *also* : a piece of old dry bread **2** : the cover of a pie **3** : a hard or brittle surface layer — **crust·al** *adj*

crus·ta·cean \,krəs-'tā-shən\ *n* : any of a large class of mostly aquatic arthropods (as lobsters or crabs) having a firm crustlike shell — **crustacean** *adj*

crusty \'krəs-tē\ *adj* **crust·i·er; -est 1** : having or being a crust **2** : CROSS, GRUMPY

crutch \'krəch\ *n* : a supporting device; *esp* : a support fitting under the armpit for use by the disabled in walking

crux \'krəks, 'krüks\ *n, pl* **crux·es** [L, cross, torture] **1** : a puzzling or difficult problem **2** : a crucial point

¹**cry** \'krī\ *vb* **cried; cry·ing 1** : to call out : SHOUT **2** : to proclaim publicly : ADVERTISE **3** : WEEP

²**cry** *n, pl* **cries 1** : a loud outcry **2** : APPEAL, ENTREATY **3** : a fit of weeping **4** : the characteristic sound uttered by an animal **5** : DISTANCE — usu. used in the phrase *a far cry*

cry·ba·by \'krī-,bā-bē\ *n* : one who cries easily or often

cryo·gen·ic \,krī-ə-'je-nik\ *adj* : of or relating to the production of very low temperatures; *also* : involving the use of a very low temperature — **cryo·gen·i·cal·ly** \-ni-k(ə-)lē\ *adv*

cryo·gen·ics \-niks\ *n* : a branch of physics that relates to the production and effects of very low temperatures

cryo·lite \'krī-ə-,līt\ *n* : a usu. white mineral formerly used in making aluminum

crypt \'kript\ *n* : a chamber wholly or partly underground

cryp·tic \'krip-tik\ *adj* : meant to be puzzling or mysterious ⟨~ messages⟩

cryp·to·gram \'krip-tə-,gram\ *n* : a communication in cipher or code

cryp·tog·ra·phy \krip-'tä-grə-fē\ *n* : the coding and decoding of secret messages — **cryp·tog·ra·pher** \-fər\ *n*

cryp·to·sys·tem \'krip-tō-'sis-təm\ *n* : a method for coding and decoding messages

crys·tal \'kris-t³l\ *n* [ME *cristal*, fr. AF, fr. L *crystallum*, fr. Gk *krystallos* ice, crystal] **1** : transparent quartz **2** : something resembling crystal (as in transparency); *esp* : a clear colorless glass of superior quality **3** : a body that is formed by solidification of a substance and has a regular repeating arrangement of atoms and often of external plane faces ⟨a salt ~⟩ **4** : the transparent cover of a watch dial

crystal 3: snowflake crystals

crystal clear *adj* : perfectly or transparently clear

crys·tal·line \'kris-tə-lən\ *adj* **1** : made of or resembling crystal **2** : very clear or sparkling

crys·tal·lise *Brit var of* CRYSTALLIZE

crys·tal·lize \'kris-tə-,līz\ *vb* **-lized; -liz·ing 1** : to assume or cause to assume a crystalline form **2** : to take or cause to take a definite form — **crys·tal·li·za·tion** \,kris-tə-lə-'zā-shən\ *n*

crys·tal·log·ra·phy \,kris-tə-'lä-grə-fē\ *n* : the science dealing with the forms and structures of crystals — **crys·tal·log·ra·pher** *n*

cs *abbr* case; cases

Cs *symbol* cesium

CS *abbr* **1** civil service **2** county seat

CSA *abbr* Confederate States of America

C–section \'sē-,sek-shən\ *n* : CESAREAN SECTION

CSM *abbr* command sergeant major

CST *abbr* central standard time

ct *abbr* **1** carat **2** cent **3** count **4** county **5** court

CT *abbr* **1** central time **2** Connecticut

ctn *abbr* carton

ctr *abbr* **1** center **2** counter

CT scan \,sē-'tē\ *n* : CAT SCAN

cu *abbr* cubic

Cu *symbol* [L *cuprum*] copper

cub \'kəb\ *n* : a young individual of some animals (as a fox, bear, or lion)

cub·by·hole \'kə-bē-,hōl\ *n* : a snug place (as for storing things)

Cu·ban sandwich \'kyü-bən-\ *n* : a usu. grilled and pressed sandwich served on a long split roll

¹**cube** \'kyüb\ *n* **1** : a solid having 6 equal square sides **2** : the result of raising a number to the third power ⟨the ~ of 3 is 27⟩

²**cube** *vb* **cubed; cub·ing 1** : to raise to the third power **2** : to form into a cube **3** : to cut into cubes

cube root *n* : a number whose cube is a given number

cu·bic \'kyü-bik\ *also* **cu·bi·cal** *adj* **1** : having the form of a cube **2** : being the volume of a cube whose edge is a specified unit **3** : having length, width, and height

cu·bi·cle \'kyü-bi-kəl\ *n* : a small separate space (as for sleeping, studying, or working)

cubic measure *n* : a unit (as cubic inch) for measuring volume — see METRIC SYSTEM table, WEIGHT table

cubic zir·co·nia \-,zər-'kō-nē-ə\ *also* **cubic zirconium** *n* : a synthetic gemstone resembling a diamond made from an oxide of zirconium

cub·ism \'kyü-,bi-zəm\ *n* : a style of art characterized by the abstraction of natural forms into fragmented geometric shapes — **cub·ist** \-bist\ *n or adj*

cu·bit \'kyü-bət\ *n* : an ancient unit of length equal to about 18 inches (46 centimeters)

Cub Scout *n* : a member of the program of the Boy Scouts for boys in the first through fifth grades in school

cuck·old \'kə-kəld, 'kü-\ *n* : a man whose wife is unfaithful — **cuckold** *vb*

¹**cuck·oo** \'kü-kü, 'kú-\ *n, pl* **cuckoos** : a largely grayish brown European bird that lays its eggs in the nests of other birds for them to hatch

²**cuckoo** *adj* : SILLY, FOOLISH

cu·cum·ber \'kyü-(,)kəm-bər\ *n* : the long fleshy many=seeded fruit of a vine of the gourd family that is grown as a garden vegetable; *also* : this vine

cud \'kəd\ *n* : food brought up into the mouth by some animals (as cows) from the rumen to be chewed again

cud·dle \'kə-d³l\ *vb* **cud·dled; cud·dling** : to lie close : SNUGGLE

cud·gel \'kə-jəl\ *n* : a short heavy club — **cudgel** *vb*

¹**cue** \'kyü\ *n* **1** : a word, phrase, or action in a play serving as a signal for the next actor to speak or act **2** : HINT — **cue** *vb*

²**cue** *n* : a tapered rod for striking the balls in billiards or pool

cue ball *n* : the ball a player strikes with a cue in billiards or pool

¹**cuff** \'kəf\ *n* **1** : a part (as of a sleeve or glove) encircling the wrist **2** : the folded hem of a trouser leg

²**cuff** *vb* : to strike esp. with the open hand : SLAP

³**cuff** *n* : a blow with the hand esp. when open

cui·sine \kwi-'zēn\ *n* : style of cooking; *also* : the food prepared

cuke \'kyük\ *n* : CUCUMBER

cul–de–sac \,kəl-di-'sak, ,kúl-\ *n, pl* **culs–de–sac** *same or* ,kəlz-, ,kúlz\ *also* **cul–de–sacs** \,kəl-də-'saks, ,kúl-\ [F, lit., bottom of the bag] : a street or passage closed at one end

cu·li·nary \'kə-lə-,ner-ē, 'kyü-\ *adj* : of or relating to the kitchen or cookery

¹**cull** \'kəl\ *vb* : to pick out from a group

²**cull** *n* : something rejected from a group or lot as worthless or inferior

cul·mi·nate \'kəl-mə-,nāt\ *vb* **-nat·ed; -nat·ing** : to reach the highest point — **cul·mi·na·tion** \,kəl-mə-'nā-shən\ *n*

cu·lotte \'kü-,lät, kyü-, kü-,lät, kyü-\ *n* [F, breeches, fr. dim. of *cul* backside] : a divided skirt; *also* : a garment having a divided skirt — often used in pl.

cul·pa·ble \'kəl-pə-bəl\ *adj* : deserving blame — **cul·pa·bil·i·ty** \,kəl-pə-'bi-lə-tē\ *n*

cul·prit \'kəl-prət\ n [AF cul. (abbr. of culpable guilty) + prest, prit ready (i.e., to prove it), fr. L praestus] : one accused or guilty of a crime

cult \'kəlt\ n 1 : formal religious veneration 2 : a religious system; also : its adherents 3 : faddish devotion; also : a group of persons showing such devotion — **cult·ish** \'kəl-tish\ adj — **cult·ist** \-tist\ n

cul·ti·va·ble \'kəl-tə-və-bəl\ adj : capable of being cultivated

cul·ti·var \'kəl-tə-ˌvär, -ˌvär\ n : a plant variety originating and persisting under cultivation

cul·ti·vate \'kəl-tə-ˌvāt\ vb **-vat·ed; -vat·ing** 1 : to prepare for the raising of crops 2 : to foster the growth of by tilling or by labor and care ⟨~ vegetables⟩ 3 : REFINE, IMPROVE 4 : ENCOURAGE, FURTHER — **cul·ti·va·tion** \ˌkəl-tə-'vā-shən\ n — **cul·ti·va·tor** \'kəl-tə-ˌvā-tər\ n

cul·ture \'kəl-chər\ n 1 : TILLAGE, CULTIVATION 2 : the act of developing by education and training 3 : refinement of intellectual and artistic taste 4 : the customary beliefs, social forms, and material traits of a racial, religious, or social group — **cul·tur·al** \'kəl-chə-rəl\ adj — **cul·tur·al·ly** adv — **cul·tured** \-chərd\ adj

cul·vert \'kəl-vərt\ n : a drain crossing under a road or railroad

cum abbr cumulative

cum·ber \'kəm-bər\ vb : to weigh down : BURDEN, HINDER

cum·ber·some \'kəm-bər-səm\ adj : hard to handle or manage because of size or weight — **cum·ber·some·ly** adv

cum·brous \'kəm-brəs\ adj : CUMBERSOME — **cum·brous·ly** adv — **cum·brous·ness** n

cum·in \'kə-mən, 'kyü-\ n : the seedlike fruit of a small annual herb related to the carrot that is used as a spice; also : this herb

cum·mer·bund \'kə-mər-ˌbənd, 'kəm-bər-\ n [Hindi & Urdu kamarband, fr. Pers, fr. kamar waist + band band] : a broad sash worn as a waistband

cu·mu·la·tive \'kyü-myə-lə-tiv, -ˌlā-\ adj : increasing in force or value by successive additions

cu·mu·lo·nim·bus \ˌkyü-myə-lō-'nim-bəs\ n : an anvil-shaped cumulus cloud extending to great heights

cu·mu·lus \'kyü-myə-ləs\ n, pl **-li** \-ˌlī, -ˌlē\ : a dense puffy cloud having a flat base and rounded outlines

cu·ne·i·form \kyü-'nē-ə-ˌfȯrm\ adj 1 : wedge-shaped 2 : composed of wedge-shaped characters

cun·ni·lin·gus \ˌkə-ni-'liŋ-gəs\ also **cun·ni·linc·tus** \-'liŋk-təs\ n : oral stimulation of the vulva or clitoris

¹**cun·ning** \'kə-niŋ\ adj 1 : SKILLFUL, DEXTEROUS 2 : marked by wiliness and trickery ⟨~ schemes⟩ 3 : CUTE ⟨a ~ kitten⟩ — **cun·ning·ly** adv

²**cunning** n 1 : SKILL 2 : SLYNESS

¹**cup** \'kəp\ n 1 : a small bowl-shaped drinking vessel 2 : the contents of a cup 3 : the consecrated wine of the Communion 4 : something resembling a cup : a small bowl or hollow 5 : a half pint — **cup·ful** n — **cup·like** \-ˌlīk\ adj

²**cup** vb **cupped; cup·ping** : to curve into the shape of a cup

cup·board \'kə-bərd\ n : a small closet with shelves for food or dishes

cup·cake \'kəp-ˌkāk\ n : a small cake baked in a cuplike mold

cu·pid \'kyü-pəd\ n : a winged naked figure of an infant often with a bow and arrow that represents the god Cupid

cu·pid·i·ty \kyü-'pi-də-tē\ n, pl **-ties** : excessive desire for money

cu·po·la \'kyü-pə-lə, -ˌlō\ n : a small structure on top of a roof or building

¹**cur** \'kər\ n : a mongrel dog

²**cur** abbr 1 currency 2 current

cu·rate \'kyùr-ət\ n 1 : a member of the clergy who is in charge of a parish 2 : a member of the clergy who assists a rector or vicar — **cu·ra·cy** \-ə-sē\ n

cu·ra·tive \-ə-tiv\ adj : relating to or used in the cure of diseases ⟨~ therapy⟩ ⟨~ powers⟩ — **curative** n

cu·ra·tor \'kyùr-ˌā-tər, kyù-'rā-\ n : CUSTODIAN; esp : one in charge of a place of exhibit (as a museum or zoo)

¹**curb** \'kərb\ n 1 : a bit that exerts pressure on a horse's jaws 2 : CHECK, RESTRAINT 3 : a raised edging (as of stone or concrete) along a paved street

²**curb** vb : to hold in or back : RESTRAIN

curb·ing \'kər-biŋ\ n 1 : the material for a curb 2 : CURB

curd \'kərd\ n : the thick protein-rich part of coagulated milk

cur·dle \'kər-dᵊl\ vb **cur·dled; cur·dling** : to form curds; also : SPOIL, SOUR

¹**cure** \'kyùr\ n 1 : spiritual care 2 : recovery or relief from disease 3 : a curative agent : REMEDY 4 : a course or period of treatment

²**cure** vb **cured; cur·ing** 1 : to restore to health : HEAL, REMEDY; also : to become cured 2 : to process for storage or use ⟨~ bacon⟩ — **cur·able** adj

cu·ré \kyù-'rā\ n [F] : a parish priest

cure-all \'kyùr-ˌȯl\ n : a remedy for all ills : PANACEA

cu·ret·tage \ˌkyùr-ə-'täzh\ n : a surgical scraping or cleaning of a body part (as the uterus)

cur·few \'kər-ˌfyü\ n [ME, fr. AF covrefeu, signal given to bank the hearth fire, curfew, fr. coverir to cover + fu, feu fire, fr. L focus hearth] : a regulation that specified persons (as children) be off the streets at a set hour of the evening; also : the sounding of a signal (as a bell) at this hour

cu·ria \'kyùr-ē-ə, 'kùr-\ n, pl **cu·ri·ae** \'kyùr-ē-ˌē, 'kùr-ē-ˌī\ often cap : the body of congregations, tribunals, and offices through which the pope governs the Roman Catholic Church

cu·rie \'kyùr-ē\ n : a unit of radioactivity equal to 37 billion disintegrations per second

cu·rio \'kyùr-ē-ˌō\ n, pl **cu·ri·os** : an object or article valued because it is strange or rare

cu·ri·ous \'kyùr-ē-əs\ adj 1 : having a desire to investigate and learn 2 : STRANGE, UNUSUAL, ODD ⟨a ~ coincidence⟩ — **cu·ri·os·i·ty** \ˌkyùr-ē-'ä-sə-tē\ n — **cu·ri·ous·ness** n

cu·ri·ous·ly adv 1 : in a curious manner 2 : as is curious

cu·ri·um \'kyùr-ē-əm\ n : a metallic radioactive element produced artificially

¹**curl** \'kərl\ vb 1 : to form into ringlets 2 : CURVE, COIL — **curl·er** n

²**curl** n 1 : a lock of hair that coils : RINGLET 2 : something having a spiral or twisted form — **curly** adj

cur·lew \'kər-lü, 'kərl-yü\ n, pl **curlews** or **curlew** : any of various long-legged brownish birds that have a down-curved bill and are related to the sandpipers and snipes

curli·cue \'kər-li-ˌkyü\ n : a fancifully curved or spiral figure

cur·rant \'kər-ənt\ n 1 : a small seedless raisin 2 : the acid berry of various shrubs related to the gooseberry; also : this plant

cur·ren·cy \'kər-ən-sē\ n, pl **-cies** 1 : general use or acceptance 2 : something that is in circulation as a medium of exchange : MONEY

¹**cur·rent** \'kər-ənt\ adj 1 : occurring in or belonging to the present ⟨the ~ crisis⟩ 2 : used as a medium of exchange 3 : generally accepted or practiced

²**current** n 1 : the part of a body of fluid moving continuously in a certain direction; also : the swiftest part of a stream 2 : a flow of electric charge; also : the rate of such flow

cur·ric·u·lum \kə-'ri-kyə-ləm\ n, pl **-la** \-lə\ also **-lums** [L, running, course, fr. currere to run] : the courses offered by an educational institution

¹**cur·ry** \'kər-ē\ vb **cur·ried; cur·ry·ing** 1 : to clean the coat of (a horse) with a currycomb 2 : to treat (tanned leather) esp. by incorporating oil or grease — **curry favor** : to seek to gain favor by flattery or attention

²**cur·ry** n, pl **cur·ries** : a powder of pungent spices used in cooking; also : a food seasoned with curry

cur·ry·comb \-ˌkōm\ n : a comb used esp. to curry horses — **currycomb** vb

¹**curse** \'kərs\ n 1 : a prayer for harm to come upon one 2 : something that is cursed 3 : evil or misfortune coming as if in response to a curse

²**curse** vb **cursed; curs·ing** 1 : to call on divine power to send injury upon 2 : BLASPHEME 3 : AFFLICT ♦ **Synonyms** EXECRATE, DAMN, ANATHEMATIZE, OBJURGATE

cur·sive \'kər-siv\ adj : written with the strokes of the letters joined together and the angles rounded

cur·sor \'kər-sər\ n : a visual cue (as a pointer) on a computer screen that indicates position (as for data entry)

cur·so·ry \'kər-sə-rē\ adj : rapidly and often superficially done : HASTY ⟨a ~ reading of the report⟩ — **cur·so·ri·ly** \-rə-lē\ adj

curt \'kərt\ adj : rudely short or abrupt — **curt·ly** adv — **curt·ness** n

cur·tail \(ˌ)kər-'tāl\ vb : to cut off the end of : SHORTEN — **cur·tail·ment** n

cur·tain \'kər-t°n\ n **1** : a hanging screen that can be drawn back esp. at a window **2** : the screen between the stage and auditorium of a theater — **curtain** vb

curt·sy also **curt·sey** \'kərt-sē\ n, pl **curtsies** or **curtseys** : a courteous bow made by women chiefly by bending the knees — **curtsy** also **curtsey** vb

cur·va·ceous also **cur·va·cious** \ˌkər-'vā-shəs\ adj : having curves suggestive of a well-proportioned feminine figure

cur·va·ture \'kər-və-ˌchúr\ n : a measure or amount of curving : BEND

¹curve \'kərv\ vb **curved; curv·ing** : to bend from a straight line or course

²curve n **1** : a line esp. when curved **2** : something that bends or curves without angles ⟨a ~ in the road⟩ **3** : a baseball pitch thrown so that it swerves esp. downward and to one side

cur·vet \(ˌ)kər-'vet\ n : a prancing leap of a horse — **curvet** vb

¹cush·ion \'kù-shən\ n [ME cusshin, fr. AF cussin, quissin, fr. VL *coxinus, fr. L coxa hip] **1** : a soft pillow or pad to rest on or against **2** : the springy pad inside the rim of a billiard table **3** : something soft that prevents discomfort or protects against injury

²cushion vb **1** : to provide (as a seat) with a cushion **2** : to soften or lessen the force or shock of

cusp \'kəsp\ n : a pointed end or part (as of a tooth)

cus·pid \'kəs-pəd\ n : a canine tooth

cus·pi·dor \'kəs-pə-ˌdòr\ n : SPITTOON

cus·tard \'kəs-tərd\ n : a sweetened cooked mixture of milk and eggs

cus·to·di·al \ˌkəs-'tō-dē-əl\ adj : marked by watching and protecting rather than seeking to cure ⟨~ care⟩

cus·to·di·an \ˌkəs-'tō-dē-ən\ n : one who has custody (as of a building)

cus·to·dy \'kəs-tə-dē\ n, pl **-dies** : immediate charge and control

¹cus·tom \'kəs-təm\ n **1** : habitual course of action : recognized usage **2** pl : taxes levied on imports **3** : business patronage

²custom adj **1** : made to personal order **2** : doing work only on order

cus·tom·ary \'kəs-tə-ˌmer-ē\ adj **1** : based on or established by custom **2** : commonly practiced or observed : HABITUAL — **cus·tom·ar·i·ly** adv

cus·tom–built \'kəs-təm-'bilt\ adj : built to individual order

cus·tom·er \'kəs-tə-mər\ n : BUYER, PURCHASER; esp : a regular or frequent buyer

cus·tom·house \'kəs-təm-ˌhaùs\ n : the building where customs are paid

cus·tom·ise Brit var of CUSTOMIZE

cus·tom·ize \'kəs-tə-ˌmīz\ vb **-ized; -iz·ing** : to build, fit, or alter according to individual specifications

cus·tom–made \'kəs-təm-'mād\ adj : made to individual order

¹cut \'kət\ vb **cut; cut·ting** **1** : to penetrate or divide with a sharp edge : CLEAVE, GASH; also : to experience the growth of (a tooth) through the gum **2** : to hurt the feelings of **3** : to strike sharply **4** : SHORTEN, REDUCE **5** : to remove by severing or paring **6** : INTERSECT, CROSS **7** : to divide into parts **8** : to go quickly or change direction abruptly **9** : to cause to stop

²cut n **1** : something made by cutting : GASH, CLEFT **2** : SHARE **3** : a segment or section of a meat carcass **4** : an excavated channel or roadway **5** : BAND **6** : a sharp stroke or blow **7** : REDUCTION ⟨a ~ in wages⟩ **8** : the shape or manner in which a thing is cut

cut–and–dried \ˌkət-°n-'drīd\ also **cut–and–dry** \-'drī\ adj : according to a plan, set procedure, or formula

cu·ta·ne·ous \kyú-'tā-nē-əs\ adj : of, relating to, or affecting the skin

cut·back \'kət-ˌbak\ n **1** : something cut back **2** : REDUCTION

cute \'kyüt\ adj **cut·er; cut·est** [short for acute] **1** : CLEVER, SHREWD **2** : daintily attractive : PRETTY

cu·ti·cle \'kyü-ti-kəl\ n **1** : an outer layer (as of skin or a leaf) **2** : dead or horny epidermis esp. around a fingernail — **cu·tic·u·lar** \kyù-'ti-kyə-lər\ adj

cut in vb **1** : to thrust oneself between others **2** : to interrupt a dancing couple and take one as one's partner

cut·lass \'kət-ləs\ n : a short heavy curved sword

cut·ler \'kət-lər\ n [ME, fr. AF cuteler, fr. LL cultellarius, fr. L cultellus knife] : one who makes, deals in, or repairs cutlery

cut·lery \'kət-lə-rē\ n : edged or cutting tools; esp : implements for cutting and eating food

cut·let \'kət-lət\ n : a slice of meat (as veal) for broiling or frying

cut·off \'kət-ˌòf\ n **1** : the channel formed when a stream cuts through the neck of an oxbow; also : SHORTCUT **2** : a device for cutting off **3** pl : shorts orig. made from jeans with the legs cut off at the knees or higher

cut·out \'kət-ˌaùt\ n : something cut out or prepared for cutting out from something else

cut out vb **1** : to determine or assign through necessity ⟨had her work cut out for her⟩ **2** : DISCONNECT **3** : to cease operating ⟨the engine cut out⟩ **4** : ELIMINATE ⟨cut out unnecessary expense⟩

cut–rate \'kət-'rāt\ adj : relating to or dealing in goods sold at reduced rates

cut·ter \'kə-tər\ n **1** : a tool or a machine for cutting **2** : a ship's boat for carrying stores and passengers **3** : a small armed vessel in government service **4** : a light sleigh

¹cut·throat \'kət-ˌthrōt\ n : MURDERER

²cutthroat adj **1** : MURDEROUS, CRUEL **2** : RUTHLESS ⟨~ competition⟩

cutthroat trout n : a large American trout with a red mark under the jaw

¹cut·ting \'kə-tiŋ\ n : a piece of a plant able to grow into a new plant

²cutting adj **1** : SHARP, EDGED **2** : marked by piercing cold **3** : likely to hurt the feelings : SARCASTIC ⟨a ~ remark⟩

cut·tle·fish \'kə-t°l-ˌfish\ n : any of various marine mollusks having eight arms and two usu. longer tentacles and an internal shell (**cut·tle·bone** \-ˌbōn\) composed of calcium compounds

cut·up \'kət-ˌəp\ n : a person who clowns or acts boisterously — **cut up** vb

cut·worm \-ˌwərm\ n : any of various smooth-bodied moth larvae that feed on plants at night

cw abbr clockwise

CWO abbr **1** cash with order **2** chief warrant officer

cwt abbr hundredweight

-cy \sē\ n suffix **1** : action : practice ⟨mendancy⟩ **2** : rank : office ⟨chaplaincy⟩ **3** : body : class ⟨constituency⟩ **4** : state : quality ⟨accuracy⟩

cy·an \'sī-ˌan, -ən\ n : a greenish blue color

cy·a·nide \'sī-ə-ˌnīd, -nəd\ n : a poisonous compound of carbon and nitrogen with another element (as potassium)

cy·ber \'sī-bər\ adj : of, relating to, or involving computers or computer networks

cyber- comb form : computer : computer network

cy·ber·ca·fe \'sī-bər-ka-ˌfā\ n : a small restaurant offering use of computers with Internet access

cy·ber·net·ics \ˌsī-bər-'ne-tiks\ n : the science of communication and control theory that is concerned esp. with the comparative study of automatic control systems — **cy·ber·net·ic** adj

cy·ber·punk \'sī-bər-ˌpəŋk\ n **1** : science fiction dealing with computer-dominated future societies **2** : HACKER **3**

cy·ber·sex \'sī-bər-ˌseks\ n **1** : online sex-oriented conversations **2** : sex-oriented material available on a computer

cy·ber·space \'sī-bər-ˌspās\ n : the online world of the Internet

cy·cla·men \'sī-klə-mən\ n : any of a genus of plants related to the primroses and having showy nodding flowers

¹cy·cle \'sī-kəl\ n **1** : a period of time occupied by a series of events that repeat themselves regularly and in the same order **2** : a recurring round of operations or events **3** : one complete occurrence of a periodic process (as a vibration or current alternation) **4** : a circular or spiral arrangement **5** : a long period of time : AGE **6** : BICYCLE **7** : MOTORCYCLE — **cy·clic** \'sī-klik, 'si-\ or **cy·cli·cal** \kli-kəl\ adj — **cy·cli·cal·ly** \-k(ə-)lē\ also **cy·clic·ly** adv

²**cy·cle** \'sī-kəl\ *vb* **cy·cled; cy·cling** : to ride a cycle — **cy·clist** \'sī-klist, -kə-list\ *n*

cy·clone \'sī-ˌklōn\ *n* **1** : a storm or system of winds that rotates about a center of low atmospheric pressure and advances at 20 to 30 miles (about 30 to 50 kilometers) an hour **2** : TORNADO — **cy·clon·ic** \sī-'klä-nik\ *adj*

cy·clo·pe·dia *also* **cy·clo·pae·dia** \ˌsī-klə-'pē-dē-ə\ *n* : ENCYCLOPEDIA

cy·clo·tron \'sī-klə-ˌträn\ *n* : a device for giving high speed to charged particles by magnetic and electric fields

cy·der *Brit var of* CIDER

cyg·net \'sig-nət\ *n* : a young swan

cyl *abbr* cylinder

cyl·in·der \'si-lən-dər\ *n* : the solid figure formed by turning a rectangle about one side as an axis; *also* : a body or space of this form ⟨an engine ∼⟩ ⟨a bullet in the ∼ of a revolver⟩ — **cy·lin·dri·cal** \sə-'lin-dri-kəl\ *adj*

cym·bal \'sim-bəl\ *n* : a concave brass plate that produces a brilliant clashing sound

cyn·ic \'si-nik\ *n* : one who attributes all actions to selfish motives — **cyn·i·cal** \-ni-kəl\ *adj* — **cyn·i·cal·ly** \-k(ə-)lē\ *adv* — **cyn·i·cism** \si-nə-ˌsi-zəm\ *n*

cy·no·sure \'sī-nə-ˌshu̇r, 'si-\ *n* [MF & L; MF, Ursa Minor, guide, fr. L *cynosura* Ursa Minor, fr. Gk *kynosoura*, fr. *kynos oura*, lit., dog's tail] : a center of attraction

CYO *abbr* Catholic Youth Organization

cy·pher *chiefly Brit var of* CIPHER

cy·press \'sī-prəs\ *n* **1** : any of a genus of scaly-leaved evergreen trees and shrubs **2** : BALD CYPRESS **3** : the wood of a cypress

cyst \'sist\ *n* : an abnormal closed bodily sac usu. containing liquid — **cys·tic** \'sis-tik\ *adj*

cystic fibrosis *n* : a common hereditary disease marked esp. by deficiency of pancreatic enzymes, by respiratory symptoms, and by excessive loss of salt in the sweat

cy·tol·o·gy \sī-'tä-lə-jē\ *n* : a branch of biology dealing with cells — **cy·to·log·i·cal** \ˌsī-tə-'lä-ji-kəl\ *or* **cy·to·log·ic** \-jik\ *adj* — **cy·tol·o·gist** \sī-'tä-lə-jist\ *n*

cy·to·plasm \'sī-tə-ˌpla-zəm\ *n* : the protoplasm of a cell that lies external to the nucleus — **cy·to·plas·mic** \ˌsī-tə-'plaz-mik\ *adj*

cy·to·sine \'sī-tə-ˌsēn\ *n* : a chemical base that is a pyrimidine coding genetic information in DNA and RNA

CZ *abbr* Canal Zone

czar *also* **tsar** \'zär, 'tsär\ *n* [NL, fr. Russ *tsar'*, ultim. fr. L *Caesar* Caesar] : the ruler of Russia until 1917; *also* : one having great authority — **czar·ist** *also* **tsar·ist** \-ist\ *n or adj*

cza·ri·na \zä-'rē-nə\ *n* : the wife of a czar

Czech \'chek\ *n* **1** : a native or inhabitant of Czechoslovakia or the Czech Republic **2** : the language of the Czechs — **Czech** *adj*

D

¹**d** \'dē\ *n, pl* **d's** *or* **ds** \'dēz\ *often cap* **1** : the 4th letter of the English alphabet **2** : five hundred in Roman numerals **3** : a grade rating a student's work as poor **4** : DEFENSE

²**d** *abbr, often cap* **1** date **2** daughter **3** day **4** dead **5** deceased **6** degree **7** Democrat **8** [L *denarius, denarii*] penny; pence **9** depart; departure **10** diameter

D *symbol* deuterium

d *symbol* — used after the figure 2 or 3 to indicate the ordinal number second or third

DA *abbr* **1** deposit account **2** district attorney **3** don't answer

¹**dab** \'dab\ *n* **1** : a sudden blow or thrust : POKE; *also* : PECK **2** : a gentle touch or stroke : PAT

²**dab** *vb* **dabbed; dab·bing 1** : to strike or touch gently : PAT **2** : to apply lightly or irregularly : DAUB — **dab·ber** *n*

³**dab** *n* **1** : DAUB **2** : a small amount

dab·ble \'da-bəl\ *vb* **dab·bled; dab·bling 1** : to wet by splashing : SPATTER **2** : to paddle or play in or as if in water **3** : to work or involve oneself without serious effort — **dab·bler** *n*

da capo \dä-'kä-(ˌ)pō\ *adv or adj* [It] : from the beginning — used as a direction in music to repeat

dace \'dās\ *n, pl* **dace** : any of various small No. American freshwater fishes related to the carp

da·cha \'dä-chə\ *n* [Russ] : a Russian country house

dachs·hund \'däks-ˌhu̇nt\ *n* [G, fr. *Dachs* badger + *Hund* dog] : any of a breed of long-bodied short-legged dogs of German origin

dachshund

dac·tyl \'dak-t²l\ *n* [ME *dactile*, fr. L *dactylus*, fr. Gk *daktylos*, lit., finger; fr. the fact that the three syllables have the first one longest like the joints of the finger] : a metrical foot of one accented syllable followed by two unaccented syllables — **dac·tyl·ic** \dak-'ti-lik\ *adj or n*

dad \'dad\ *n* : FATHER 1

Da·da \'dä-(ˌ)dä\ *n* : a movement in art and literature based on deliberate irrationality and negation of traditional artistic values — **da·da·ism** \-ˌi-zəm\ *n, often cap* — **da·da·ist** \-ist\ *n or adj, often cap*

dad·dy \'da-dē\ *n, pl* **daddies** : FATHER 1

dad·dy long·legs \ˌda-dē-'lȯn-ˌlegz\ *n, pl* **daddy longlegs** : any of an order of arachnids resembling the true spiders but having small rounded bodies and long slender legs

daemon *var of* DEMON

daf·fo·dil \'da-fə-ˌdil\ *n* : any of various bulbous herbs with usu. large flowers having a trumpetlike center

daf·fy \'da-fē\ *adj* **daf·fi·er; -est** : DAFT

daft \'daft\ *adj* : FOOLISH; *also* : INSANE — **daft·ness** *n*

dag *abbr* dekagram

dag·ger \'da-gər\ *n* **1** : a sharp pointed knife for stabbing **2** : a character † used as a reference mark or to indicate a death date

da·guerre·o·type \də-'ger-(ē-)ə-ˌtīp\ *n* : an early photograph produced on a silver or a silver-covered copper plate

dahl·ia \'dal-yə, 'däl-\ *n* : any of a genus of tuberous herbs related to the daisies and having showy flowers

¹**dai·ly** \'dā-lē\ *adj* **1** : occurring, done, or used every day or every weekday **2** : of or relating to every day ⟨∼ visitors⟩ **3** : computed in terms of one day ⟨∼ wages⟩ ♦ *Synonyms* DIURNAL, QUOTIDIAN — **dai·li·ness** \-lē-nəs\ *n* — **daily** *adv*

²**daily** *n, pl* **dailies** : a newspaper published every weekday

daily double *n* : a system of betting on races in which the bettor must pick the winners of two stipulated races in order to win

¹**dain·ty** \'dān-tē\ *n, pl* **dainties** [ME *deinte* high esteem, delight, fr. AF *deinté*, fr. L *dignitas* dignity, worth] : something delicious or pleasing to the taste : DELICACY

²**dainty** *adj* **dain·ti·er; -est 1** : pleasing to the taste **2** : delicately pretty **3** : having or showing delicate taste;

also : FASTIDIOUS ♦ *Synonyms* CHOICE, DELICATE, EX-QUISITE, RARE, RECHERCHÉ — **dain·ti·ly** \-ti-lē\ *adv* — **dain·ti·ness** \-tē-nəs\ *n*

dai·qui·ri \'da-kə-rē, 'dī-\ *n* [*Daiquirí,* Cuba] : a cocktail made usu. of rum, lime juice, and sugar

dairy \'der-ē\ *n, pl* **dair·ies** [ME *deyerie,* fr. *deye* dairymaid, fr. OE *dæge* kneader of bread] **1** : CREAMERY **2** : a farm specializing in milk production

dairy·ing \'der-ē-iŋ\ *n* : the business of operating a dairy

dairy·maid \-,mād\ *n* : a woman employed in a dairy

dairy·man \-mən, -,man\ *n* : a person who operates a dairy farm or works in a dairy

da·is \'dā-əs\ *n* : a raised platform usu. above the floor of a hall or large room

dai·sy \'dā-zē\ *n, pl* **daisies** [ME *dayeseye,* fr. OE *dægesēage,* fr. *dæg* day + *ēage* eye] : any of numerous composite plants having flower heads in which the marginal flowers resemble petals

dai·sy–chain \-,chān\ *vb* : to link (as computer components) together in series — **daisy chain** *n*

daisy wheel *n* : a disk with spokes bearing type that serves as the printing element of an electric typewriter or printer; *also* : a printer that uses such a disk

Da·ko·ta \də-'kō-tə\ *n, pl* **Dakotas** *also* **Dakota** : a member of an American Indian people of the northern Mississippi valley; *also* : their language

dal *abbr* dekaliter

da·la·si \dä-'lä-sē\ *n, pl* **dalasi** *or* **dalasis** — see MONEY table

dale \'dāl\ *n* : VALLEY

dal·ly \'da-lē\ *vb* **dal·lied; dal·ly·ing** **1** : to act playfully; *esp* : to play amorously **2** : to waste time **3** : LINGER, DAWDLE ♦ *Synonyms* FLIRT, COQUET, TOY, TRIFLE — **dal·li·ance** \-lē-əns\ *n*

dal·ma·tian \dal-'mā-shən\ *n, often cap* : any of a breed of medium-sized dogs having a white short-haired coat with many black or brown spots

¹dam \'dam\ *n* : the female parent of an animal and esp. of a domestic animal

²dam *n* : a barrier (as across a stream) to stop the flow of water — **dam** *vb*

³dam *abbr* dekameter

¹dam·age \'da-mij\ *n* **1** : loss or harm due to injury to persons, property, or reputation **2** *pl* : compensation in money imposed by law for loss or injury ⟨bring a suit for ~s⟩

²damage *vb* **dam·aged; dam·ag·ing** : to cause damage to ⟨~ the furniture⟩

dam·a·scene \'da-mə-,sēn\ *vb* **-scened; -scen·ing** : to ornament (as iron or steel) with wavy patterns or with inlaid work of precious metals

dam·ask \'da-məsk\ *n* **1** : a firm lustrous reversible figured fabric used for household linen **2** : a tough steel having decorative wavy lines

dame \'dām\ *n* **1** : a woman of rank, station, or authority **2** : an elderly woman **3** : WOMAN

damn \'dam\ *vb* [ME *dampnen,* fr. AF *dampner,* fr. L *damnare,* fr. *damnum* damage, loss, fine] **1** : to condemn esp. to hell **2** : CURSE — **damned** *adj*

dam·na·ble \'dam-nə-bəl\ *adj* **1** : liable to or deserving punishment **2** : DETESTABLE ⟨~ weather⟩ — **dam·na·bly** \-blē\ *adv*

dam·na·tion \dam-'nā-shən\ *n* **1** : the act of damning **2** : the state of being damned

¹damp \'damp\ *n* **1** : a noxious gas **2** : MOISTURE

²damp *vb* : DAMPEN

³damp *adj* : MOIST — **damp·ness** *n*

damp·en \'dam-pən\ *vb* **1** : to check or diminish in activity or vigor ⟨~ enthusiasm⟩ **2** : to make or become damp ⟨~ a sponge⟩

damp·er \'dam-pər\ *n* **1** : a dulling or deadening influence ⟨put a ~ on the party⟩ **2** : one that damps; *esp* : a valve or movable plate (as in the flue of a stove, furnace, or fireplace) to regulate the draft

dam·sel \'dam-zəl\ *n* : MAIDEN, GIRL

dam·sel·fly \-,flī\ *n* : any of a group of insects that are closely related to the dragonflies but fold their wings above the body when at rest

dam·son \'dam-zən\ *n* : a plum with acid purple fruit; *also* : its fruit

Dan *abbr* Daniel

¹dance \'dans\ *vb* **danced; danc·ing** **1** : to glide, step, or move through a set series of movements usu. to music **2** : to move quickly up and down or about **3** : to perform or take part in as a dancer — **danc·er** *n*

²dance *n* **1** : an act or instance of dancing **2** : a social gathering for dancing **3** : a piece of music (as a waltz) by which dancing may be guided **4** : the art of dancing

D & C *n* [*dilation and curettage*] : a surgical procedure that involves stretching the cervix and scraping the inside walls of the uterus (as to test for cancer or to perform an abortion)

dan·de·li·on \'dan-də-,lī-ən, -dē-\ *n* [ME *dendelyoun,* fr. AF *dent de lion,* lit., lion's tooth] : any of a genus of common yellow-flowered composite herbs

dan·der \'dan-dər\ *n* : ANGER, TEMPER

dan·di·fy \'dan-di-,fī\ *vb* **-fied; -fy·ing** : to cause to resemble a dandy

dan·dle \'dan-d²l\ *vb* **dan·dled; dan·dling** : to move up and down in one's arms or on one's knee in affectionate play ♦ *Synonyms* CARESS, FONDLE, LOVE, PET

dan·druff \'dan-drəf\ *n* : scaly white or grayish flakes of dead skin cells that come off the scalp — **dan·druffy** \-drə-fē\ *adj*

¹dan·dy \'dan-dē\ *n, pl* **dandies** **1** : a man unduly attentive to personal appearance **2** : something excellent in its class ♦ *Synonyms* FOP, COXCOMB, POPINJAY

²dandy *adj* **dan·di·er; -est** : very good : FIRST-RATE

Dane \'dān\ *n* **1** : a native or inhabitant of Denmark **2** : GREAT DANE

dan·ger \'dān-jər\ *n* [ME *daunger* control, resistance, peril, fr. AF *dangier,* fr. VL **dominiarium,* fr. L *dominium* ownership] **1** : exposure or liability to injury, harm, or evil **2** : something that may cause injury or harm ♦ *Synonyms* PERIL, HAZARD, RISK, JEOPARDY

dan·ger·ous \'dān-jə-rəs\ *adj* **1** : HAZARDOUS, PERILOUS ⟨a ~ slope⟩ **2** : able or likely to inflict injury ⟨a ~ man⟩ — **dan·ger·ous·ly** *adv*

dan·gle \'daŋ-gəl\ *vb* **dan·gled; dan·gling** **1** : to hang loosely esp. with a swinging motion : SWING **2** : to be a hanger-on or dependent **3** : to be left without proper grammatical connection in a sentence ⟨a *dangling* participle⟩ **4** : to keep hanging uncertainly **5** : to offer as an inducement

Dan·iel \'dan-yəl\ *n* — see BIBLE table

Dan·ish \'dā-nish\ *n* : the language of the Danes — **Danish** *adj*

Danish pastry *n* : a pastry made of a rich yeast-raised dough

dank \'daŋk\ *adj* : disagreeably wet or moist : DAMP — **dank·ness** *n*

dan·seuse \dän-'sərz, -'səz; dän-'süz\ *n* [F] : a female ballet dancer

dap·per \'da-pər\ *adj* **1** : SPRUCE, TRIM **2** : being alert and lively in movement and manners : JAUNTY

dap·ple \'da-pəl\ *vb* **dap·pled; dap·pling** : to mark with different-colored spots

DAR *abbr* Daughters of the American Revolution

¹dare \'der\ *vb* **dared; dar·ing** **1** : to have sufficient courage : be bold enough to **2** : CHALLENGE ⟨*dared* him to jump⟩ **3** : to confront boldly

²dare *n* : an act or instance of daring : CHALLENGE

dare·dev·il \-,de-vəl\ *n* : a recklessly bold person — **dare·devil** *adj*

dar·ing \'der-iŋ\ *n* : venturesome boldness — **daring** *adj* — **dar·ing·ly** *adv*

¹dark \'därk\ *adj* **1** : being without light or without much light **2** : not light in color ⟨a ~ suit⟩ **3** : GLOOMY ⟨a ~ outlook⟩ **4** *often cap* : being a period of stagnation or decline ⟨the *Dark* Ages⟩ **5** : SECRETIVE ⟨~ dealings⟩ ♦ *Synonyms* DIM, DUSKY, MURKY, TENEBROUS — **dark·ly** *adv* — **dark·ness** *n*

²dark *n* **1** : absence of light : DARKNESS; *esp* : NIGHT **2** : a dark or deep color — **in the dark** **1** : in secrecy **2** : in ignorance ⟨kept *in the dark* about the plans⟩

dark·en \'där-kən\ *vb* **1** : to make or grow dark or darker **2** : DIM **3** : BESMIRCH, TARNISH **4** : to make or become gloomy or forbidding

dark horse *n* : a contestant or a political figure whose abilities and chances as a contender are not known

dark·ling \'där-kliŋ\ *adj* **1** : DARK ⟨a ~ plain⟩ **2** : MYSTERIOUS

dark·room \'därk-ˌrüm, -ˌrüm\ *n* : a lightproof room in which photographic materials are processed

¹dar·ling \'där-liŋ\ *n* 1 : a dearly loved person 2 : FAVORITE

²darling *adj* 1 : dearly loved : FAVORITE 2 : very pleasing : CHARMING

darm·stadt·i·um \ˌdärm-'sta-tē-əm\ *n* : a short-lived radioactive chemical element produced artificially

¹darn \'därn\ *vb* : to mend with interlacing stitches — **darn·er** *n*

²darn *or* **darned** \'därnd\ *adv* : VERY, EXTREMELY ⟨a ~ good job⟩

darning needle *n* 1 : a needle for darning 2 : DRAGONFLY

¹dart \'därt\ *n* 1 : a small missile with a point on one end and feathers on the other; *also, pl* : a game in which darts are thrown at a target 2 : something causing a sudden pain 3 : a stitched tapering fold in a garment 4 : a quick movement

²dart *vb* 1 : to throw with a sudden movement 2 : to thrust or move suddenly or rapidly ⟨~ed across the street⟩ 3 : to shoot with a dart containing a usu. tranquilizing drug

dart·er \'där-tər\ *n* : any of numerous small No. American freshwater fishes related to the perches

Dar·win·ism \'där-wə-ˌni-zəm\ *n* : a theory explaining the origin and continued existence of new species of plants and animals by means of natural selection acting on chance variations — **Dar·win·ist** \-nist\ *n or adj*

¹dash \'dash\ *vb* 1 : SMASH 2 : to knock, hurl, or thrust violently 3 : SPLASH, SPATTER 4 : RUIN 5 : DEPRESS, SADDEN 6 : to perform or finish hastily ⟨~ off a letter⟩ 7 : to move with sudden speed ⟨~ed down the hall⟩

²dash *n* 1 : a sudden burst or splash 2 : a stroke of a pen 3 : a punctuation mark — that is used esp. to indicate a break in the thought or structure of a sentence 4 : a small addition ⟨a ~ of salt⟩ 5 : flashy showiness 6 : animation in style and action 7 : a sudden rush or attempt ⟨made a ~ for the door⟩ 8 : a short foot race 9 : DASHBOARD

dash·board \-ˌbȯrd\ *n* : a panel in an automobile or aircraft below the windshield usu. containing dials and controls

dash·er \'da-shər\ *n* : a device (as in a churn) for agitating something

da·shi·ki \də-'shē-kē\ *also* **dai·shi·ki** \dī-\ *n* [modif. of Yoruba (an African language) *dàṣíkí*] : a usu. brightly colored loose-fitting pullover garment

dash·ing \'da-shiŋ\ *adj* 1 : marked by vigorous action 2 : marked by smartness esp. in dress and manners ◆ **Synonyms** STYLISH, CHIC, FASHIONABLE, MODISH, SMART, SWANK

das·tard \'das-tərd\ *n* 1 : COWARD 2 : a person who acts treacherously — **das·tard·ly** *adj*

dat *abbr* dative

da·ta \'dā-tə, 'da-, 'dä-\ *n sing or pl* [L, pl. of *datum*] : factual information (as measurements or statistics) used as a basis for reasoning, discussion, or calculation

da·ta·base \-ˌbās\ *n* : a usu. large collection of data organized esp. for rapid search and retrieval (as by a computer) — **database** *vb*

data processing *n* : the action or process of supplying a computer with information and having the computer use it to produce a desired result

¹date \'dāt\ *n* [ME, fr. AF, ultim. fr. L *dactylus*, fr. Gk *daktylos*, lit., finger] : the oblong edible fruit of a tall palm; *also* : this palm

²date *n* [ME, fr. AF, fr. LL *data*, fr. *data* (as in *data Romae* given at Rome), fem. of L *datus*, pp. of *dare* to give] 1 : the day, month, or year of an event 2 : a statement giving the time of execution or making (as of a coin or check) 3 : the period to which something belongs 4 : APPOINTMENT; *esp* : a social engagement between two persons that often has a romantic character 5 : a person with whom one has a usu. romantic date — **to date** : up to the present moment

³date *vb* **dat·ed; dat·ing** 1 : to record the date of or on 2 : to determine, mark, or reveal the date, age, or period of 3 : go on a date or dates with ⟨~ed her for a year⟩ 4 : ORIGINATE ⟨~s from ancient times⟩ 5 : EXTEND ⟨*dating* back to childhood⟩ 6 : to show qualities typical of a past period

dat·ed \'dā-təd\ *adj* 1 : provided with a date 2 : OLD-FASHIONED ⟨a ~ custom⟩ ◆ **Synonyms** ANTIQUATED, ARCHAIC, OLD HAT, OUTDATED, OUTMODED, PASSÉ

date·less \'dāt-ləs\ *adj* 1 : ENDLESS 2 : having no date 3 : too ancient to be dated 4 : TIMELESS

date·line \'dāt-ˌlīn\ *n* : a line in a publication giving the date and place of composition or issue — **dateline** *vb*

date rape *n* : rape committed by the victim's date

da·tive \'dā-tiv\ *adj* : of, relating to, or constituting a grammatical case marking typically the indirect object of a verb — **dative** *n*

da·tum \'dā-təm, 'da-, 'dä-\ *n, pl* **da·ta** \-tə\ *or* **datums** : a single piece of data : FACT

dau *abbr* daughter

¹daub \'dȯb\ *vb* 1 : to cover with soft adhesive matter 2 : SMEAR, SMUDGE 3 : to paint crudely — **daub·er** *n*

²daub *n* 1 : something daubed on : SMEAR 2 : a crude picture

daugh·ter \'dȯ-tər\ *n* 1 : a female offspring esp. of human beings 2 : a female adopted child 3 : a human female descendant — **daughter** *adj* — **daugh·ter·less** \-ləs\ *adj*

daugh·ter-in-law \'dȯ-tə-rən-ˌlȯ\ *n, pl* **daugh·ters-in-law** \-tər-zən-\ : the wife of one's son

daunt \'dȯnt\ *vb* [ME, fr. AF *danter, daunter*, fr. L *domitare* to tame] : to lessen the courage of : INTIMIDATE, OVERWHELM

daunt·ing \'dȯn-tiŋ\ *adj* : tending to overwhelm or intimidate ⟨a ~ task⟩

daunt·less \-ləs\ *adj* : FEARLESS, UNDAUNTED ◆ **Synonyms** BRAVE, BOLD, COURAGEOUS, LIONHEARTED — **daunt·less·ly** *adv*

dau·phin \'dȯ-fən\ *n, often cap* : the eldest son of a king of France

DAV *abbr* Disabled American Veterans

dav·en·port \'da-vən-ˌpȯrt\ *n* : a large upholstered sofa

da·vit \'dā-vət, 'da-\ *n* : a small crane on a ship used in pairs esp. to raise or lower boats

daw·dle \'dȯ-dᵊl\ *vb* **daw·dled; daw·dling** 1 : to spend time wastefully or idly 2 : LOITER — **daw·dler** *n*

¹dawn \'dȯn\ *vb* 1 : to begin to grow light as the sun rises 2 : to begin to appear or develop 3 : to begin to be understood ⟨the solution ~ed on him⟩

²dawn *n* 1 : the first appearance of light in the morning 2 : a first appearance : BEGINNING ⟨the ~ of a new era⟩

day \'dā\ *n* 1 : the period of light between one night and the next; *also* : DAYLIGHT, DAYTIME 2 : the period of rotation of a planet (as earth) or a moon on its axis 3 : a period of 24 hours beginning at midnight 4 : a specified day or date ⟨wedding ~⟩ 5 : a specified time or period : AGE ⟨in olden ~s⟩ 6 : the conflict or contention of the day 7 : the time set apart by usage or law for work ⟨the 8-hour ~⟩

day·bed \'dā-ˌbed\ *n* : a couch that can be converted into a bed

day·book \-ˌbùk\ *n* : DIARY, JOURNAL

day·break \-ˌbrāk\ *n* : DAWN

day care *n* : supervision of and care for children or disabled adults provided during the day; *also* : a program offering day care

day·dream \'dā-ˌdrēm\ *n* : a pleasant reverie — **daydream** *vb*

day·light \'dā-ˌlīt\ *n* 1 : the light of day 2 : DAYTIME 3 : DAWN 4 : understanding of something that has been obscure 5 *pl* : CONSCIOUSNESS; *also* : WITS 6 : a perceptible space, gap, or difference

daylight saving time *n* : time usu. one hour ahead of standard time

Day of Atonement : YOM KIPPUR

day school *n* : a private school without boarding facilities

day student *n* : a student who attends regular classes at a college or preparatory school but does not live there

day·time \'dā-ˌtīm\ *n* : the period of daylight

daze \'dāz\ *vb* **dazed; daz·ing** 1 : to stupefy esp. by a blow 2 : DAZZLE — **daze** *n* — **da·zed·ly** \'dā-zəd-lē\ *adv*

daz·zle \'da-zəl\ *vb* **daz·zled; daz·zling** 1 : to overpower with light 2 : to impress greatly or confound with brilliance ⟨*dazzled* by her wit⟩ — **dazzle** *n*

dB *abbr* decibel

Db *symbol* dubnium

d/b/a *abbr* doing business as

dbl *or* **dble** *abbr* double

DC *abbr* **1** [It *da capo*] from the beginning **2** direct current **3** District of Columbia **4** doctor of chiropractic

DD *abbr* **1** days after date **2** demand draft **3** dishonorable discharge **4** doctor of divinity

D–day *n* [*D*, abbr. for *day*] : a day set for launching an operation (as an invasion)

DDS *abbr* doctor of dental surgery

DDT \ˌdē-ˌdē-ˈtē\ *n* : a persistent insecticide poisonous to many higher animals

DE *abbr* Delaware

dea·con \ˈdē-kən\ *n* [ME *dekene*, fr. OE *dēacon*, fr. LL *diaconus*, fr. Gk *diakonos*, lit., servant] : a subordinate officer in a Christian church

dea·con·ess \ˈdē-kə-nəs\ *n* : a woman chosen to assist in the church ministry

de·ac·ti·vate \dē-ˈak-tə-ˌvāt\ *vb* : to make inactive or ineffective

¹**dead** \ˈded\ *adj* **1** : LIFELESS **2** : DEATHLIKE, DEADLY ⟨in a ~ faint⟩ **3** : NUMB **4** : very tired **5** : UNRESPONSIVE **6** : EXTINGUISHED ⟨~ coals⟩ **7** : INANIMATE, INERT **8** : no longer active or functioning ⟨a ~ battery⟩ **9** : lacking power, significance, or effect ⟨a ~ custom⟩ **10** : OBSOLETE ⟨a ~ language⟩ **11** : lacking in gaiety or animation ⟨a ~ party⟩ **12** : QUIET, IDLE, UNPRODUCTIVE ⟨~ capital⟩ **13** : lacking elasticity ⟨a ~ tennis ball⟩ **14** : not circulating : STAGNANT ⟨~ air⟩ **15** : lacking warmth, vigor, or taste ⟨~ wine⟩ **16** : absolutely uniform ⟨~ level⟩ **17** : UNERRING, EXACT ⟨a ~ shot⟩ **18** : ABRUPT ⟨a ~ stop⟩ **19** : COMPLETE ⟨a ~ loss⟩

²**dead** *n, pl* **dead 1** : one that is dead — usu. used collectively ⟨the living and the ~⟩ **2** : the time of greatest quiet ⟨the ~ of the night⟩

³**dead** *adv* **1** : UTTERLY ⟨~ right⟩ **2** : in a sudden and complete manner ⟨stopped ~⟩ **3** : DIRECTLY ⟨~ ahead⟩

dead·beat \-ˌbēt\ *n* : a person who persistently fails to pay personal debts or expenses

dead duck *n* : GONER

dead·en \ˈde-dᵊn\ *vb* **1** : to impair in vigor or sensation : BLUNT ⟨~ pain⟩ **2** : to lessen the luster or spirit of **3** : to make (as a wall) soundproof

dead end *n* **1** : an end (as of a street) without an exit **2** : a position, situation, or course of action that leads to nothing further — **dead–end** \ˌded-ˌend\ *adj*

dead heat *n* : a contest in which two or more contestants tie (as by crossing the finish line simultaneously)

dead horse *n* : an exhausted topic or issue

dead letter *n* **1** : something that has lost its force or authority without being formally abolished **2** : a letter that cannot be delivered or returned

dead·line \ˈded-ˌlīn\ *n* : a date or time before which something must be done

dead·lock \ˈded-ˌläk\ *n* **1** : a stoppage of action because neither faction in a struggle will give in **2** : a tie score — **deadlock** *vb*

¹**dead·ly** \ˈded-lē\ *adj* **dead·li·er; -est 1** : likely to cause or capable of causing death **2** : HOSTILE, IMPLACABLE **3** : very accurate : UNERRING **4** : tending to deprive of force or vitality ⟨a ~ habit⟩ **5** : suggestive of death **6** : very great : EXTREME — **dead·li·ness** *n*

²**deadly** *adv* **1** : suggesting death ⟨~ pale⟩ **2** : EXTREMELY ⟨~ dull⟩

deadly sin *n* : one of seven sins of pride, covetousness, lust, anger, gluttony, envy, and sloth held to be fatal to spiritual progress

dead meat *n* : one that is doomed

¹**dead·pan** \ˈded-ˌpan\ *adj* : marked by an impassive manner or expression ⟨~ humor⟩ — **deadpan** *vb* — **deadpan** *adv*

²**deadpan** *n* : a completely expressionless face

dead reckoning *n* : the determination of the position of a ship or aircraft solely from the record of the direction and distance of its course

dead·weight \ˈded-ˈwāt\ *n* **1** : the unrelieved weight of an inert mass **2** : a ship's load including the weight of cargo, fuel, crew, and passengers

dead·wood \-ˌwu̇d\ *n* **1** : wood dead on the tree **2** : useless personnel or material

deaf \ˈdef\ *adj* **1** : unable to hear **2** : unwilling to hear or listen ⟨~ to all suggestions⟩ — **deaf·ness** *n*

deaf·en \ˈde-fən\ *vb* : to make deaf

¹**deal** \ˈdēl\ *n* **1** : a usu. large or indefinite quantity or degree ⟨a great ~ of support⟩ **2** : the act or right of distributing cards to players in a card game; *also* : HAND

²**deal** *vb* **dealt** \ˈdelt\; **deal·ing 1** : DISTRIBUTE; *esp* : to distribute playing cards to players in a game **2** : ADMINISTER, DELIVER ⟨*dealt* him a blow⟩ **3** : to concern itself : TREAT ⟨the book ~s with crime⟩ **4** : to take action in regard to something ⟨~ with offenders⟩ **5** : TRADE; *also* : to sell or distribute something as a business ⟨~ in used cars⟩ **6** : to reach a state of acceptance ⟨~ with her child's death⟩ — **deal·er** *n*

³**deal** *n* **1** : BARGAINING, NEGOTIATION **2** : TRANSACTION; *esp* : an agreement by contract **3** : treatment received ⟨a raw ~⟩ **4** : an often secret agreement or arrangement for mutual advantage **5** : BARGAIN

⁴**deal** *n* : wood or a board of fir or pine

deal·er·ship \ˈdē-lər-ˌship\ *n* : an authorized sales agency ⟨an auto ~⟩

deal·ing \ˈdē-liŋ\ *n* **1** : a way of acting or of doing business **2** *pl* : friendly or business transactions

dean \ˈdēn\ *n* [ME *deen*, fr. AF *deien*, fr. LL *decanus*, lit., chief of ten, fr. Gk *dekanos*, fr. *deka* ten] **1** : a clergyman who is head of a group of canons or of joint pastors of a church **2** : the head of a division, faculty, college, or school of a university **3** : a college or secondary school administrator in charge of counseling and disciplining students **4** : DOYEN ⟨the ~ of a diplomatic corps⟩ — **dean·ship** *n*

dean·ery \ˈdē-nə-rē\ *n, pl* **-er·ies** : the office, jurisdiction, or official residence of a clerical dean

¹**dear** \ˈdir\ *adj* **1** : highly valued : PRECIOUS **2** : AFFECTIONATE, FOND **3** : EXPENSIVE **4** : HEARTFELT — **dear·ly** *adv* — **dear·ness** *n*

²**dear** *n* : a loved one : DARLING

Dear John \-ˈjän\ *n* : a letter (as to a soldier) in which a woman breaks off a marital or romantic relationship

dearth \ˈdərth\ *n* **1** : SCARCITY, FAMINE **2** : an inadequate supply : LACK ⟨a ~ of jobs⟩

death \ˈdeth\ *n* **1** : the end of life **2** : the cause of loss of life **3** : a cause of ruin **4** : the state of being dead **5** : DESTRUCTION, EXTINCTION **6** : SLAUGHTER — **death·like** *adj*

death·bed \-ˌbed\ *n* **1** : the bed in which a person dies **2** : the last hours of life

death·blow \-ˌblō\ *n* : a destructive or killing stroke or event

death grip *n* : an extremely tight grip or hold

death·less \-ləs\ *adj* : IMMORTAL, IMPERISHABLE ⟨~ fame⟩

death·ly \-lē\ *adj* **1** : FATAL **2** : of, relating to, or suggestive of death ⟨a ~ pallor⟩ — **deathly** *adv*

death rattle *n* : a sound produced by air passing through mucus in the lungs and air passages of a dying person

death's–head \ˈdeths-ˌhed\ *n* : a human skull emblematic of death

death·watch \ˈdeth-ˌwäch\ *n* : a vigil kept over the dead or dying

deb \ˈdeb\ *n* : DEBUTANTE

de·ba·cle \di-ˈbä-kəl, -ˈba-\ *also* **dé·bâ·cle** *same or* dā-ˈbäk\ *n* [F *débâcle*] : DISASTER, FAILURE, ROUT ⟨stock market ~⟩

de·bar \di-ˈbär\ *vb* : to bar from having or doing something : PRECLUDE

de·bark \di-ˈbärk\ *vb* : DISEMBARK — **de·bar·ka·tion** \ˌdē-ˌbär-ˈkā-shən\ *n*

de·base \di-ˈbās\ *vb* : to lower in character, quality, or value ◆ **Synonyms** DEGRADE, CORRUPT, DEPRAVE — **de·base·ment** *n*

de·bate \di-ˈbāt\ *vb* **de·bat·ed; de·bat·ing 1** : to discuss a question by considering opposed arguments **2** : to take part in a debate — **de·bat·able** *adj* — **debate** *n* — **de·bat·er** *n*

de·bauch \di-ˈbȯch\ *vb* : SEDUCE, CORRUPT ◆ **Synonyms** DEBASE, DEMORALIZE, DEPRAVE, PERVERT — **de·bauch·ery** \-ˈbȯ-chə-rē\ *n*

de·ben·ture \di-ˈben-chər\ *n* : BOND; *esp* : one secured by the general credit of the issuer rather than a lien on particular assets

de·bil·i·tate \di-ˈbi-lə-ˌtāt\ *vb* **-tat·ed; -tat·ing** : to impair the health or strength of ◆ **Synonyms** WEAKEN, DISABLE, ENFEEBLE, UNDERMINE

de·bil·i·ty \di-'bi-lə-tē\ *n, pl* **-ties** : an infirm or weakened state

¹**deb·it** \'de-bət\ *vb* : to enter as a debit : charge with or as a debit

²**debit** *n* **1** : an entry in an account showing money paid out or owed **2** : DISADVANTAGE, SHORTCOMING

debit card *n* : a card by which money may be withdrawn or the cost of purchases paid directly from the holder's bank account

deb·o·nair \,de-bə-'ner\ *adj* [ME *debonere*, fr. AF *deboneire*, fr. *de bon aire* of good family or nature] : SUAVE, URBANE; *also* : LIGHTHEARTED

de·bouch \di-'baùch, -'büsh\ *vb* [F *déboucher*, fr. *dé-* out of + *bouche* mouth] : to come out into an open area : EMERGE

de·brief \di-'brēf\ *vb* **1** : to question (as a pilot back from a mission) in order to obtain useful information **2** : to review carefully upon completion

de·bris \də-'brē, dā-; 'dā-,brē\ *n, pl* **debris** \-'brēz, -,brēz\ **1** : the remains of something broken down or destroyed **2** : an accumulation of rock fragments : RUBBISH

debt \'det\ *n* **1** : SIN, TRESPASS **2** : something owed : OBLIGATION **3** : a condition of owing

debt·or \'de-tər\ *n* **1** : one guilty of neglect or violation of duty **2** : one that owes a debt

de·bug \(,)dē-'bəg\ *vb* : to eliminate errors in ⟨∼ a computer program⟩

de·bunk \dē-'bəŋk\ *vb* : to expose the sham or falseness of ⟨∼ a legend⟩

¹**de·but** \'dā-,byü, dā-'byü\ *n* **1** : a first appearance **2** : a formal entrance into society

²**debut** *vb* : to make a debut; *also* : INTRODUCE

deb·u·tante \'de-byù-,tänt\ *n* : a young woman making her formal entrance into society

dec *abbr* **1** deceased **2** decrease

Dec *abbr* December

dec·ade \'de-,kād, de-'kād\ *n* : a period of 10 years

dec·a·dence \'de-kə-dəns, di-'kā-d°ns\ *n* : DETERIORATION, DECLINE — **dec·a·dent** \'de-kə-dənt, di-'kā-d°nt\ *adj or n*

de·caf \'dē-,kaf\ *n* : decaffeinated coffee

de·caf·fein·at·ed \(,)dē-'ka-fə-nā-təd\ *adj* : having the caffeine removed ⟨∼ coffee⟩

deca·gon \'de-kə-,gän\ *n* : a plane polygon of 10 angles and 10 sides

de·cal \'dē-,kal\ *n* : a picture, design, or label made to be transferred (as to glass) from specially prepared paper

de·cal·co·ma·nia \di-,kal-kə-'mā-nē-ə\ *n* [F *décalcomanie*, fr. *décalquer* to copy by tracing (fr. *calquer* to trace, fr. It *calcare*, lit., to tread, fr. L) + *manie* mania, fr. LL *mania*] : DECAL

Deca·logue \'de-kə-,lóg\ *n* : TEN COMMANDMENTS

de·camp \di-'kamp\ *vb* **1** : to break up a camp **2** : to depart suddenly ✦ *Synonyms* ESCAPE, ABSCOND, FLEE

de·cant \di-'kant\ *vb* : to pour (as wine) from one vessel into another

de·cant·er \di-'kan-tər\ *n* : an ornamental glass bottle for serving wine

de·cap·i·tate \di-'ka-pə-,tāt\ *vb* **-tat·ed; -tat·ing** : BEHEAD — **de·cap·i·ta·tion** \-,ka-pə-'tā-shən\ *n* — **de·cap·i·ta·tor** \-'ka-pə-,tā-tər\ *n*

deca·syl·lab·ic \,de-kə-sə-'la-bik\ *adj* : having or composed of verses having 10 syllables — **decasyllabic** *n*

de·cath·lon \di-'kath-lən, -,län\ *n* : a 10-event athletic contest

de·cay \di-'kā\ *vb* **1** : to decline from a sound or prosperous condition ⟨a ∼*ing* town⟩ **2** : to cause or undergo decomposition ⟨radium ∼s slowly⟩; *esp* : to break down while spoiling : ROT ⟨∼*ing* teeth⟩ — **decay** *n*

decd *abbr* deceased

de·cease \di-'sēs\ *n* : DEATH

¹**de·ceased** \-'sēst\ *adj* : no longer living; *esp* : recently dead

²**deceased** *n, pl* **deceased** : a dead person

de·ce·dent \di-'sē-d°nt\ *n* : a deceased person

de·ceit \di-'sēt\ *n* **1** : DECEPTION **2** : TRICK **3** : DECEITFULNESS ✦ *Synonyms* DISSIMULATION, DUPLICITY, GUILE

de·ceit·ful \-fəl\ *adj* **1** : practicing or tending to practice deceit **2** : MISLEADING, DECEPTIVE ⟨a ∼ answer⟩ — **de·ceit·ful·ly** *adv* — **de·ceit·ful·ness** *n*

de·ceive \di-'sēv\ *vb* **de·ceived; de·ceiv·ing** **1** : to cause to believe an untruth **2** : to use or practice deceit ✦ *Synonyms* BEGUILE, BETRAY, DELUDE, MISLEAD — **de·ceiv·er** *n*

de·cel·er·ate \dē-'se-lə-,rāt\ *vb* **-at·ed; -at·ing** : to slow down

De·cem·ber \di-'sem-bər\ *n* [ME *Decembre*, fr. OE or AF, both fr. L *December* (tenth month), fr. *decem* ten] : the 12th month of the year

de·cen·cy \'dē-s°n-sē\ *n, pl* **-cies** **1** : PROPRIETY **2** : conformity to standards of taste, propriety, or quality **3** : standard of propriety — usu. used in pl.

de·cen·ni·al \di-'se-nē-əl\ *adj* **1** : consisting of 10 years **2** : happening every 10 years ⟨∼ census⟩

de·cent \'dē-s°nt\ *adj* **1** : conforming to standards of propriety, good taste, or morality **2** : modestly clothed **3** : free from immodesty or obscenity **4** : ADEQUATE ⟨∼ housing⟩ — **de·cent·ly** *adv*

de·cen·tral·i·za·tion \dē-,sen-trə-lə-'zā-shən\ *n* **1** : the distribution of powers from a central authority to regional and local authorities **2** : the redistribution of population and industry from urban centers to outlying areas — **de·cen·tral·ize** \-'sen-trə-,līz\ *vb*

de·cep·tion \di-'sep-shən\ *n* **1** : the act of deceiving **2** : the fact or condition of being deceived **3** : FRAUD, TRICK — **de·cep·tive** \-'sep-tiv\ *adj* — **de·cep·tive·ly** *adv* — **de·cep·tive·ness** *n*

deci·bel \'de-sə-,bel, -bəl\ *n* : a unit for measuring the relative loudness of sounds

de·cide \di-'sīd\ *vb* **de·cid·ed; de·cid·ing** [ME, fr. L *cidere*, lit., to cut off, fr. *de-* off + *caedere* to cut] **1** : make a final choice or judgment **2** : to bring to a definitive end ⟨one blow *decided* the fight⟩ **3** : to induce to come to a choice

de·cid·ed \di-'sī-dəd\ *adj* **1** : UNQUESTIONABLE **2** : FIRM, DETERMINED — **de·cid·ed·ly** *adv*

de·cid·u·ous \di-'si-jə-wəs\ *adj* **1** : falling off or out usu. at the end of a period of growth or function ⟨∼ leaves⟩ ⟨a ∼ tooth⟩ **2** : having deciduous parts ⟨∼ trees⟩

deci·gram \'de-sə-,gram\ *n* — see METRIC SYSTEM table

deci·li·ter \-,lē-tər\ *n* — see METRIC SYSTEM table

¹**dec·i·mal** \'de-sə-məl\ *adj* : based on the number 10 : reckoning by tens

²**decimal** *n* : any number expressed in base 10; *esp* : DECIMAL FRACTION

decimal fraction *n* : a fraction or mixed number in which the denominator is a power of 10 and that is usu. expressed with a decimal point ⟨the *decimal fraction* .25 is equivalent to the common fraction ²⁵/₁₀₀⟩

decimal place *n* : the position of a digit as counted to the right of the decimal point in a decimal fraction

decimal point *n* : a period, centered dot, or in some countries a comma at the left of a decimal fraction (as .678) less than one or between a whole number and a decimal fraction in a mixed number (as 3.678)

dec·i·mate \'de-sə-,māt\ *vb* **-mat·ed; -mat·ing** **1** : to take or destroy the 10th part of **2** : to cause great destruction or harm to ⟨factories *decimated* by fire⟩

dec·i·me·ter \'de-sə-,mē-tər\ *n* — see METRIC SYSTEM table

de·ci·pher \di-'sī-fər\ *vb* **1** : DECODE **2** : to make out the meaning of despite indistinctness — **de·ci·pher·able** *adj*

de·ci·sion \di-'si-zhən\ *n* **1** : the act or result of deciding **2** : promptness and firmness in deciding : DETERMINATION

de·ci·sive \-'sī-siv\ *adj* **1** : having the power to decide ⟨the ∼ vote⟩ **2** : RESOLUTE, DETERMINED **3** : CONCLUSIVE ⟨a ∼ victory⟩ — **de·ci·sive·ly** *adv* — **de·ci·sive·ness** *n*

¹**deck** \'dek\ *n* **1** : a floorlike platform of a ship; *also* : something resembling the deck of a ship **2** : a pack of playing cards

²**deck** *vb* **1** : ARRAY ⟨men ∼*ed* out in suits⟩ **2** : DECORATE **3** : to furnish with a deck **4** : KNOCK DOWN, FLOOR

deck·hand \'dek-,hand\ *n* : a sailor who performs manual duties

deck·le edge \'dek-əl-\ *n* : the rough untrimmed edge of paper — **deck·le-edged** \-'ejd\ *adj*

de·claim \di-'klām\ *vb* : to speak or deliver in the manner of a formal speech ⟨an actor ∼*ing* his lines⟩ — **dec·la-**

ma·tion \ˌde-klə-ˈmā-shən\ *n* — **de·clam·a·to·ry** \di-ˈkla-mə-ˌtȯr-ē\ *adj*

de·clar·a·tive \di-ˈkler-ə-tiv\ *adj* : making a declaration ⟨∼ sentence⟩

de·clare \di-ˈkler\ *vb* **de·clared; de·clar·ing 1** : to make known formally, officially, or explicitly : ANNOUNCE ⟨∼ war⟩ **2** : to state emphatically : AFFIRM **3** : to make a full statement of ◆ *Synonyms* BLAZON, BROADCAST, PROCLAIM, PUBLISH — **dec·la·ra·tion** \ˌde-klə-ˈrā-shən\ *n* — **de·clar·a·to·ry** \di-ˈkler-ə-ˌtȯr-ē\ *adj* — **de·clar·er** *n*

de·clas·si·fy \dē-ˈkla-sə-ˌfī\ *vb* : to remove the security classification of ⟨∼ documents⟩ — **de·clas·si·fi·ca·tion** \-ˌkla-sə-fə-ˈkā-shən\ *n*

de·clen·sion \di-ˈklen-chən\ *n* **1** : the inflectional forms of a noun, pronoun, or adjective **2** : DECLINE, DETERIORATION **3** : DESCENT, SLOPE

¹de·cline \di-ˈklīn\ *vb* **de·clined; de·clin·ing 1** : to slope downward : DESCEND **2** : DROOP **3** : RECEDE ⟨morale *declined*⟩ **4** : WANE **5** : to withhold consent; *also* : REFUSE, REJECT ⟨∼ an invitation⟩ ⟨∼ to answer⟩ **6** : INFLECT **2** ⟨∼ a noun⟩ — **de·clin·able** *adj* — **dec·li·na·tion** \ˌde-klə-ˈnā-shən\ *n*

²decline *n* **1** : a gradual sinking and wasting away **2** : a change to a lower state or level **3** : the time when something is approaching its end ⟨an empire in ∼⟩ **4** : a descending slope

de·cliv·i·ty \di-ˈkli-və-tē\ *n, pl* **-ties** : a steep downward slope

de·code \dē-ˈkōd\ *vb* : to convert (a coded message) into ordinary language — **de·cod·er** *n*

dé·col·le·tage \dā-ˌkä-lə-ˈtäzh\ *n* : the low-cut neckline of a dress

dé·col·le·té \dā-ˌkäl-ˈtā\ *adj* [F] **1** : wearing a strapless or low-necked gown **2** : having a low-cut neckline

de·com·mis·sion \ˌdē-kə-ˈmi-shən\ *vb* : to remove from service

de·com·pose \ˌdē-kəm-ˈpōz\ *vb* **1** : to separate into constituent parts **2** : to break down in decay : ROT — **de·com·po·si·tion** \dē-ˌkäm-pə-ˈzi-shən\ *n*

de·com·press \ˌdē-kəm-ˈpres\ *vb* : to release from pressure or compression — **de·com·pres·sion** \-ˈpre-shən\ *n*

decompression sickness *n* : ²BEND **3**

de·con·ges·tant \ˌdē-kən-ˈjes-tənt\ *n* : an agent that relieves congestion (as of mucous membranes)

de·con·struc·tion \ˌdē-kən-ˈstrək-shən\ *n* : the analysis of something (as language or literature) by the separation and individual examination of its basic elements — **de·con·struct** \-ˈstrəkt\ *vb*

de·con·tam·i·nate \ˌdē-kən-ˈta-mə-ˌnāt\ *vb* : to rid of contamination (as radioactive material) — **de·con·tam·i·na·tion** \-ˌta-mə-ˈnā-shən\ *n*

de·con·trol \ˌdē-kən-ˈtrōl\ *vb* : to end control of ⟨∼ prices⟩ — **decontrol** *n*

de·cor *or* **dé·cor** \dā-ˈkȯr, ˈdā-ˌkȯr\ *n* : DECORATION; *esp* : the style and layout of interior furnishings

dec·o·rate \ˈde-kə-ˌrāt\ *vb* **-rat·ed; -rat·ing 1** : to furnish with something ornamental ⟨∼ a room⟩ **2** : to award a mark of honor (as a medal) to ⟨*decorated* soldiers⟩ ◆ *Synonyms* ADORN, BEAUTIFY, BEDECK, GARNISH, ORNAMENT

dec·o·ra·tion \ˌde-kə-ˈrā-shən\ *n* **1** : the act or process of decorating **2** : ORNAMENT **3** : a badge of honor

dec·o·ra·tive \ˈde-kə-rə-tiv\ *adj* : ORNAMENTAL

dec·o·ra·tor \ˈde-kə-ˌrā-tər\ *n* : one that decorates; *esp* : a person who designs or executes interiors and their furnishings

dec·o·rous \ˈde-kə-rəs, di-ˈkȯr-əs\ *adj* : PROPER, SEEMLY, CORRECT

de·co·rum \di-ˈkȯr-əm\ *n* [L] **1** : conformity to accepted standards of conduct **2** : ORDERLINESS, PROPRIETY

¹de·coy \ˈdē-ˌkȯi, di-ˈkȯi\ *n* [prob. fr. D *de kooi,* lit., the cage] **1** : something that lures or entices; *esp* : an artificial bird used to attract live birds within shot **2** : something used to draw attention away from another

²de·coy \di-ˈkȯi, ˈdē-ˌkȯi\ *vb* : to lure by or as if by a decoy : ENTICE

¹de·crease \di-ˈkrēs\ *vb* **de·creased; de·creas·ing** : to grow or cause to grow less : DIMINISH

²de·crease \ˈdē-ˌkrēs\ *n* **1** : the process of decreasing **2** : REDUCTION

¹de·cree \di-ˈkrē\ *n* **1** : ORDER, EDICT **2** : a judicial decision

²decree *vb* **de·creed; de·cree·ing 1** : COMMAND **2** : to determine or order judicially ◆ *Synonyms* DICTATE, ORDAIN, PRESCRIBE

dec·re·ment \ˈde-krə-mənt\ *n* **1** : gradual decrease **2** : the quantity lost by diminution or waste

de·crep·it \di-ˈkre-pət\ *adj* : broken down with age : WORN-OUT — **de·crep·i·tude** \-pə-ˌtüd, -ˌtyüd\ *n*

de·cre·scen·do \ˌdā-krə-ˈshen-dō\ *adv or adj* : with a decrease in volume — used as a direction in music

de·crim·i·nal·ize \dē-ˈkri-mə-nə-ˌlīz\ *vb* : to remove or reduce the criminal status of

de·cry \di-ˈkrī\ *vb* : to express strong disapproval of ⟨∼ welfare policies⟩

ded·i·cate \ˈde-di-ˌkāt\ *vb* **-cat·ed; -cat·ing 1** : to devote to the worship of a divine being esp. with sacred rites **2** : to set apart for a definite purpose **3** : to inscribe or address as a compliment ⟨∼ a novel⟩ — **ded·i·ca·tion** \ˌde-di-ˈkā-shən\ *n* — **ded·i·ca·tor** \ˈde-di-ˌkā-tər\ *n* — **ded·i·ca·to·ry** \-kə-ˌtȯr-ē\ *adj*

de·duce \di-ˈdüs, -ˈdyüs\ *vb* **de·duced; de·duc·ing 1** : to derive by reasoning : INFER **2** : to trace the course of — **de·duc·ible** *adj*

de·duct \di-ˈdəkt\ *vb* : SUBTRACT — **de·duct·ible** *adj*

de·duc·tion \di-ˈdək-shən\ *n* **1** : SUBTRACTION **2** : something that is or may be subtracted **3** : the deriving of a conclusion by reasoning : the conclusion so reached — **de·duc·tive** \-ˈdək-tiv\ *adj* — **de·duc·tive·ly** *adv*

¹deed \ˈdēd\ *n* **1** : something done **2** : FEAT, EXPLOIT **3** : a document containing some legal transfer, bargain, or contract

²deed *vb* : to convey or transfer by deed

dee·jay \ˈdē-ˌjā\ *n* : DISC JOCKEY

deem \ˈdēm\ *vb* : THINK, JUDGE ◆ *Synonyms* CONSIDER, ACCOUNT, RECKON, REGARD, VIEW

de—em·pha·size \dē-ˈem-fə-ˌsīz\ *vb* : to reduce in relative importance; *also* : to attach little importance to — **de—em·pha·sis** \-səs\ *n*

¹deep \ˈdēp\ *adj* **1** : extending far down, back, within, or outward ⟨a ∼ well⟩ **2** : having a specified extension downward or backward ⟨3 feet ∼⟩ **3** : difficult to understand; *also* : MYSTERIOUS, OBSCURE ⟨a ∼ dark secret⟩ **4** : WISE **5** : ENGROSSED, INVOLVED ⟨∼ in thought⟩ **6** : INTENSE, PROFOUND ⟨∼ sleep⟩ **7** : dark and rich in color ⟨a ∼ red⟩ **8** : having a low musical pitch or range ⟨a ∼ voice⟩ **9** : situated well within **10** : covered, enclosed, or filled often to a specified degree — **deep·ly** *adv*

²deep *adv* **1** : DEEPLY **2** : far on : LATE ⟨∼ in the night⟩

³deep *n* **1** : an extremely deep place or part; *esp* : OCEAN **2** : the middle or most intense part ⟨the ∼ of winter⟩

deep·en \ˈdē-pən\ *vb* : to make or become deep or deeper

deep—freeze \ˈdēp-ˈfrēz\ *vb* **-froze** \-ˈfrōz\; **-fro·zen** \-ˈfrō-z°n\ : QUICK-FREEZE

deep—fry *vb* : to cook in enough oil to cover the food being fried

deep pocket *n* **1** : one having substantial financial resources **2** *pl* : substantial financial resources

deep—root·ed \ˈdēp-ˈrü-təd, -ˈrü-\ *adj* : deeply implanted or established

deep—sea \ˈdēp-ˈsē\ *adj* : of, relating to, or occurring in the deeper parts of the sea ⟨∼ fishing⟩

deep—seat·ed \ˈdēp-ˈsē-təd\ *adj* **1** : situated far below the surface **2** : firmly established ⟨∼ convictions⟩

deer \ˈdir\ *n, pl* **deer** [ME, deer, animal, fr. OE *dēor* beast] : any of numerous ruminant mammals with cloven hoofs and usu. antlers esp. in the males

deer·fly \-ˌflī\ *n* : any of numerous small horseflies

deer·skin \-ˌskin\ *n* : leather made from the skin of a deer; *also* : a garment of such leather

deer tick *n* : a tick that transmits the bacterium causing Lyme disease

de·es·ca·late \dē-ˈes-kə-ˌlāt\ *vb* : to decrease in extent, volume, or scope : LIMIT — **de·es·ca·la·tion** \-ˌes-kə-ˈlā-shən\ *n*

deet \ˈdēt\ *n, often all cap* : a colorless oily liquid insect and tick repellent

¹def \ˈdef\ *adj* **def·fer; def·fest** *slang* : very good : COOL

²def *abbr* **1** defendant **2** definite **3** definition

de·face \di-'fās\ *vb* : to destroy or mar the face or surface of ⟨~ a desk⟩ — **de·face·ment** *n* — **de·fac·er** *n*

de fac·to \di-'fak-tō, dā-\ *adj or adv* 1 : existing though not formally recognized ⟨a *de facto* recession⟩ 2 : actually exercising power ⟨*de facto* government⟩

de·fal·ca·tion \ˌdē-ˌfal-'kā-shən, -ˌfol-; ˌde-fəl-\ *n* : EMBEZZLEMENT

de·fame \di-'fām\ *vb* **de·famed; de·fam·ing** : to injure or destroy the reputation of by libel or slander ✦ *Synonyms* CALUMNIATE, DENIGRATE, LIBEL, MALIGN, SLANDER, VILIFY — **def·a·ma·tion** \ˌde-fə-'mā-shən\ *n* — **de·fam·a·to·ry** \di-'fa-mə-ˌtor-ē\ *adj*

de·fault \di-'folt\ *n* 1 : failure to do something required by duty or law; *also* : failure to appear for a legal proceeding 2 : failure to compete in or to finish an appointed contest ⟨lose a race by ~⟩ 3 : a choice made without active consideration due to lack of viable alternatives 4 : a selection made automatically by a computer in the absence of a choice by the user — **default** *vb* — **de·fault·er** *n*

¹**de·feat** \di-'fēt\ *vb* 1 : FRUSTRATE, NULLIFY 2 : to win victory over : BEAT — **de·feat·able** \-'fē-tə-bəl\ *adj*

²**defeat** *n* 1 : FRUSTRATION 2 : an overthrow of an army in battle 3 : loss of a contest

de·feat·ism \-'fē-ˌti-zəm\ *n* : acceptance of or resignation to defeat — **de·feat·ist** \-tist\ *n or adj*

def·e·cate \'de-fi-ˌkāt\ *vb* **-cat·ed; -cat·ing** 1 : to free from impurity or corruption 2 : to discharge feces from the bowels — **def·e·ca·tion** \ˌde-fi-'kā-shən\ *n*

¹**de·fect** \'dē-ˌfekt, di-'fekt\ *n* : BLEMISH, FAULT, IMPERFECTION

²**de·fect** \di-'fekt\ *vb* : to desert a cause, party, or nation esp. in order to espouse another — **de·fec·tion** \-'fek-shən\ *n* — **de·fec·tor** \-'fek-tər\ *n*

de·fec·tive \di-'fek-tiv\ *adj* : FAULTY, DEFICIENT — **defective** *n*

de·fence *chiefly Brit var of* DEFENSE

de·fend \di-'fend\ *vb* [ME, fr. AF *defendre*, fr. L *defendere*, fr. *de-* from + *-fendere* to strike] 1 : to repel danger or attack from ⟨~ the fort⟩ 2 : to act as attorney for 3 : to oppose the claim of another in a lawsuit : CONTEST 4 : to maintain against opposition ⟨~ an idea⟩ 5 : to try to retain against a challenge ⟨~ed his title⟩ — **de·fend·er** *n*

de·fen·dant \di-'fen-dənt\ *n* : a person required to make answer in a legal action or suit

de·fense \di-'fens\ *n* 1 : the act of defending : resistance against attack 2 : means, method, or capability of defending 3 : an argument in support 4 : the answer made by the defendant in a legal action 5 : a defending party, group, or team — **de·fense·less** *adj* — **de·fen·si·ble** *adj*

defense mechanism *n* : an often unconscious mental process (as repression) that assists in reaching compromise solutions to personal problems

¹**de·fen·sive** \di-'fen-siv\ *adj* 1 : serving or intended to defend or protect 2 : of or relating to the attempt to keep an opponent from scoring (as in a game) — **de·fen·sive·ly** *adv* — **de·fen·sive·ness** *n*

²**defensive** *n* : a defensive position

¹**de·fer** \di-'fər\ *vb* **de·ferred; de·fer·ring** [ME *deferren, differren*, fr. MF *differer*, fr. L *differre* to postpone, be different] : POSTPONE, PUT OFF

²**defer** *vb* **deferred; deferring** [ME *deferren, differren*, fr. MF *deferer, defferer*, fr. LL *deferre*, fr. L, to bring down, bring, fr. *de-* down + *ferre* to carry] : to submit or yield to the opinion or wishes of another — **de·fer·ral** \-əl\ *n*

def·er·ence \'de-fər-əns\ *n* : courteous, respectful, or ingratiating regard for another's wishes ✦ *Synonyms* HONOR, HOMAGE, OBEISANCE, REVERENCE — **def·er·en·tial** \ˌde-fə-'ren-chəl\ *adj*

de·fer·ment \di-'fər-mənt\ *n* : the act of delaying; *esp* : official postponement of military service

de·fi·ance \di-'fī-əns\ *n* 1 : CHALLENGE 2 : disposition to resist or contend

de·fi·ant \-ənt\ *adj* : full of defiance : BOLD, IMPUDENT — **de·fi·ant·ly** *adv*

de·fi·bril·la·tor \dē-'fi-brə-ˌlā-tər\ *n* : an electronic device that applies an electric shock to restore the rhythm of a fibrillating heart — **de·fi·bril·late** \-ˌlāt\ *vb* — **de·fi·bril·la·tion** \-ˌfi-brə-'lā-shən\ *n*

deficiency disease *n* : a disease (as scurvy or beriberi) caused by a lack of essential dietary elements and esp. a vitamin or mineral

de·fi·cient \di-'fi-shənt\ *adj* : lacking in something necessary; *also* : not up to a normal standard — **de·fi·cien·cy** \-shən-sē\ *n*

def·i·cit \'de-fə-sət\ *n* : a deficiency in amount; *esp* : an excess of expenditures over revenue

¹**de·file** \di-'fī(-ə)l\ *vb* **de·filed; de·fil·ing** 1 : to make filthy 2 : CORRUPT 3 : to violate the chastity of 4 : to violate the sanctity of : DESECRATE 5 : DISHONOR ✦ *Synonyms* CONTAMINATE, POLLUTE, SOIL, TAINT — **de·file·ment** *n*

²**de·file** \di-'fī(-ə)l, 'dē-ˌfī(-ə)l\ *n* : a narrow passage or gorge

de·fine \di-'fīn\ *vb* **de·fined; de·fin·ing** 1 : to set forth the meaning of ⟨~ a word⟩ 2 : to fix or mark the limits of 3 : to clarify in outline or character — **de·fin·able** *adj* — **de·fin·er** *n*

def·i·nite \'de-fə-nət\ *adj* 1 : having distinct limits : FIXED 2 : clear in meaning 3 : typically designating an identified or immediately identifiable person or thing ⟨a ~ article⟩ — **def·i·nite·ly** *adv* — **def·i·nite·ness** *n*

def·i·ni·tion \ˌde-fə-'ni-shən\ *n* 1 : an act of determining or settling 2 : a statement of the meaning of a word or word group; *also* : the action or process of defining 3 : the action or the power of making definite and clear : CLARITY, DISTINCTNESS

de·fin·i·tive \di-'fi-nə-tiv\ *adj* 1 : DECISIVE, CONCLUSIVE 2 : authoritative and apparently exhaustive ⟨a ~ edition⟩ 3 : serving to define or specify precisely ⟨~ laws⟩

de·flate \di-'flāt\ *vb* **de·flat·ed; de·flat·ing** 1 : to release air or gas from 2 : to reduce in size, importance, or effectiveness; *also* : to reduce from a state of inflation 3 : to become deflated

de·fla·tion \-'flā-shən\ *n* 1 : an act or instance of deflating : the state of being deflated 2 : reduction in the volume of available money or credit resulting in a decline of the general price level

de·flect \di-'flekt\ *vb* : to turn aside — **de·flec·tion** \-'flek-shən\ *n*

de·flo·ra·tion \ˌdē-flə-'rā-shən\ *n* : rupture of the hymen

de·flow·er \dē-'flaú(-ə)r\ *vb* : to deprive of virginity

de·fog \dē-'fog, -'fäg\ *vb* : to remove fog or condensed moisture from ⟨~ a windshield⟩ — **de·fog·ger** *n*

de·fo·li·ant \dē-'fō-lē-ənt\ *n* : a chemical spray or dust used to defoliate plants

de·fo·li·ate \-ˌāt\ *vb* : to deprive of leaves esp. prematurely — **de·fo·li·a·tion** \dē-ˌfō-lē-'ā-shən\ *n* — **de·fo·li·a·tor** \dē-'fō-lē-ˌā-tər\ *n*

de·for·es·ta·tion \dē-ˌfor-ə-'stā-shən\ *n* : the action or process of clearing an area of forests; *also* : the state of having been cleared of forests — **de·for·est** \(ˌ)dē-'for-əst, -'fär-\ *vb*

de·form \di-'form\ *vb* 1 : DISFIGURE, DEFACE 2 : to make or become misshapen or changed in shape — **de·for·ma·tion** \ˌdē-ˌfor-'mā-shən, ˌde-fər-\ *n*

de·for·mi·ty \di-'for-mə-tē\ *n, pl* **-ties** 1 : the state of being deformed 2 : a physical blemish or distortion

de·fraud \di-'frod\ *vb* : CHEAT

de·fray \di-'frā\ *vb* : to provide for the payment of : PAY — **de·fray·al** *n*

de·frock \(ˌ)dē-'fräk\ *vb* : to deprive (as a priest) of the right to exercise the functions of office

de·frost \di-'frost\ *vb* 1 : to thaw out 2 : to free from ice — **de·frost·er** *n*

deft \'deft\ *adj* : quick and neat in action — **deft·ly** *adv* — **deft·ness** *n*

de·funct \di-'fəŋkt\ *adj* : DEAD, EXTINCT ⟨a ~ language⟩

de·fuse \dē-'fyüz\ *vb* 1 : to remove the fuse from (as a bomb) 2 : to make less harmful, potent, or tense

de·fy \di-'fī\ *vb* **de·fied; de·fy·ing** [ME, to renounce faith in, challenge, fr. AF *desfier, defier*, fr. *de-* from + *fier* to entrust, ultim. fr. L *fidere* to trust] 1 : CHALLENGE, DARE 2 : to refuse boldly to obey or to yield to : DISREGARD ⟨~ the law⟩ 3 : WITHSTAND, BAFFLE ⟨a scene that *defies* description⟩

deg *abbr* degree

de·gas \dē-'gas\ *vb* : to remove gas from

de·gen·er·a·cy \di-'je-nə-rə-sē\ *n, pl* **-cies** 1 : the state of being degenerate 2 : the process of becoming degenerate 3 : PERVERSION

¹**de·gen·er·ate** \di-'je-nə-rət\ *adj* : fallen or deteriorated from a former, higher, or normal condition — **de·gen·er-**

a·tion \-je-nə-'rā-shən\ n — **de·gen·er·a·tive** \-'je-nə-ˌrā-tiv\ adj

²**de·gen·er·ate** \di-'je-nə-ˌrāt\ vb : to undergo deterioration (as in morality, intelligence, structure, or function)

³**de·gen·er·ate** \-rət\ n : a degenerate person; esp : a sexual pervert

de·grad·able \di-'grā-də-bəl\ adj : capable of being chemically degraded

de·grade \di-'grād\ vb **1** : to reduce from a higher to a lower rank or degree **2** : DEBASE, CORRUPT **3** : DECOMPOSE — **deg·ra·da·tion** \ˌde-grə-'dā-shən\ n

de·gree \di-'grē\ n [ME, fr. AF degré, fr. VL *degradus, fr. L de- down + gradus step, grade] **1** : a step in a series **2** : a rank or grade of official, ecclesiastical, or social position; also : the civil condition of a person **3** : the extent, intensity, or scope of something esp. as measured by a graded series **4** : one of the forms or sets of forms used in the comparison of an adjective or adverb **5** : a title conferred upon students by a college, university, or professional school on completion of a program of study **6** : a line or space of the musical staff; also : a note or tone of a musical scale **7** : a unit of measure for angles that is equal to an angle with its vertex at the center of a circle and its sides cutting off ¹⁄₃₆₀ of the circumference; also : a unit of measure for arcs of a circle that is equal to the amount of arc extending ¹⁄₃₆₀ of the circumference **8** : any of various units for measuring temperature

degree 7

de·horn \dē-'hórn\ vb : to deprive of horns

de·hu·man·ize \dē-'hyü-mə-ˌnīz\ vb : to deprive of human qualities, personality, or spirit — **de·hu·man·i·za·tion** \ˌdē-ˌhyü-mə-nə-'zā-shən\ n

de·hu·mid·i·fy \ˌdē-hyü-'mi-də-ˌfī\ vb : to remove moisture from (as the air) — **de·hu·mid·i·fi·er** n

de·hy·drate \dē-'hī-ˌdrāt\ vb : to remove water from; also : to lose liquid — **de·hy·dra·tion** \ˌdē-hī-'drā-shən\ n

de·hy·dro·ge·na·tion \ˌdē-(ˌ)hī-ˌdrä-jə-'nā-shən, -drə-\ n : the removal of hydrogen from a chemical compound — **de·hy·dro·ge·nate** \ˌdē-(ˌ)hī-'drä-jə-ˌnāt, dē-'hī-drə-jə-\ vb

de·ice \dē-'īs\ vb : to keep free or rid of ice ⟨~ a lock⟩ — **de·ic·er** n

de·i·fy \'dē-ə-ˌfī, 'dā-\ vb -**fied**; -**fy·ing 1** : to make a god of **2** : WORSHIP, GLORIFY — **de·i·fi·ca·tion** \ˌdē-ə-fə-'kā-shən, ˌdā-\ n

deign \'dān\ vb [ME, fr. AF deigner, fr. L dignare, dignari, fr. dignus worthy] : CONDESCEND

de·ion·ize \dē-'ī-ə-ˌnīz\ vb : to remove ions from

de·ism \'dē-ˌi-zəm, 'dā-\ n, often cap : a system of thought advocating natural religion based on human morality and reason rather than divine revelation — **de·ist** \-ist\ n, often cap — **de·is·tic** \dē-'is-tik, dā-\ adj

de·i·ty \'dē-ə-tē, 'dā-\ n, pl -**ties 1** : DIVINITY 2 **2** cap : GOD 1 **3** : a god or goddess

dé·jà vu \ˌdā-ˌzhä-'vü\ n [F, adj., already seen] : the feeling that one has seen or heard something before

de·ject·ed \di-'jek-təd\ adj : low in spirits : SAD — **de·ject·ed·ly** adv

de·jec·tion \di-'jek-shən\ n : lowness of spirits

de ju·re \dē-'jùr-ē\ adv or adj [ML] : by legal right

deka·gram \'de-kə-ˌgram\ n — see METRIC SYSTEM table

deka·li·ter \-ˌlē-tər\ n — see METRIC SYSTEM table

deka·me·ter \-ˌmē-tər\ n — see METRIC SYSTEM table

del abbr delegate; delegation

Del abbr Delaware

Del·a·ware \'de-lə-ˌwer\ n, pl **Delaware** or **Delawares** : a member of an American Indian people orig. of the Delaware valley; also : their language

¹**de·lay** \di-'lā\ n **1** : the act of delaying : the state of being delayed **2** : the time for which something is delayed

²**delay** vb **1** : POSTPONE, PUT OFF **2** : to stop, detain, or hinder for a time **3** : to move or act slowly

de·lec·ta·ble \di-'lek-tə-bəl\ adj **1** : highly pleasing : DELIGHTFUL **2** : DELICIOUS

de·lec·ta·tion \ˌdē-ˌlek-'tā-shən\ n : DELIGHT, PLEASURE, DIVERSION

¹**del·e·gate** \'de-li-gət, -ˌgāt\ n **1** : DEPUTY, REPRESENTATIVE **2** : a member of the lower house of the legislature of Maryland, Virginia, or West Virginia

²**del·e·gate** \-ˌgāt\ vb -**gat·ed**; -**gat·ing 1** : to entrust to another ⟨~ authority⟩ **2** : to appoint as one's delegate

del·e·ga·tion \ˌde-li-'gā-shən\ n **1** : the act of delegating **2** : one or more persons chosen to represent others

de·le·git·i·mize \ˌdē-lə-'ji-tə-ˌmīz\ vb : to diminish or destroy the legitimacy, prestige, or authority of

de·lete \di-'lēt\ vb **de·let·ed**; **de·let·ing** [L deletus, pp. of delēre to wipe out, destroy] : to eliminate esp. by blotting out, cutting out, or erasing ⟨~ a computer file⟩ — **de·le·tion** \-'lē-shən\ n

del·e·te·ri·ous \ˌde-lə-'tir-ē-əs\ adj : HARMFUL, NOXIOUS

delft \'delft\ n **1** : a Dutch pottery with an opaque white glaze and predominantly blue decoration **2** : glazed pottery esp. when blue and white

delft·ware \-ˌwer\ n : DELFT

deli \'de-lē\ n, pl **del·is** : DELICATESSEN

¹**de·lib·er·ate** \di-'li-bə-ˌrāt\ vb -**at·ed**; -**at·ing** : to consider carefully — **de·lib·er·a·tion** \-ˌli-bə-'rā-shən\ n — **de·lib·er·a·tive** \-'li-bə-ˌrā-tiv, -brə-tiv\ adj — **de·lib·er·a·tive·ly** adv

²**de·lib·er·ate** \di-'li-bə-rət, -'li-brət\ adj **1** : determined after careful thought **2** : done or said intentionally **3** : UNHURRIED, SLOW — **de·lib·er·ate·ly** adv — **de·lib·er·ate·ness** n

del·i·ca·cy \'de-li-kə-sē\ n, pl -**cies 1** : something pleasing to eat and considered rare or luxurious **2** : FINENESS, DAINTINESS; also : FRAILTY **3** : nicety or expressiveness of touch **4** : precise perception and discrimination : SENSITIVITY **5** : sensibility in feeling or conduct; also : SQUEAMISHNESS **6** : the quality or state of requiring delicate handling

del·i·cate \'de-li-kət\ adj **1** : pleasing to the senses of taste or smell esp. in a mild or subtle way **2** : marked by daintiness or charm : EXQUISITE **3** : FASTIDIOUS, SQUEAMISH ⟨a person of ~ tastes⟩ **4** : easily damaged : FRAGILE; also : SICKLY **5** : requiring skill or tact **6** : marked by care, skill, or tact **7** : marked by minute precision : very sensitive ⟨a ~ instrument⟩ — **del·i·cate·ly** adv

del·i·ca·tes·sen \ˌde-li-kə-'te-sᵊn\ n pl [G, pl. of Delicatesse delicacy, fr. F délicatesse] **1** : ready-to-eat food products (as cooked meats and prepared salads) **2** sing, pl **delicatessens** : a store where delicatessen are sold

de·li·cious \di-'li-shəs\ adj : affording great pleasure : DELIGHTFUL; esp : very pleasing to the taste or smell — **de·li·cious·ly** adv — **de·li·cious·ness** n

¹**de·light** \di-'līt\ n **1** : great pleasure or satisfaction : JOY **2** : something that gives great pleasure — **de·light·ful** \-fəl\ adj — **de·light·ful·ly** adv

²**delight** vb **1** : to take great pleasure **2** : to satisfy greatly : PLEASE

de·light·ed adj : highly pleased : GRATIFIED — **de·light·ed·ly** adv

de·lim·it \di-'li-mət\ vb : to fix the limits of

de·lin·eate \di-'li-nē-ˌāt\ vb -**eat·ed**; -**eat·ing 1** : SKETCH, PORTRAY **2** : to picture in words : DESCRIBE — **de·lin·ea·tion** \-ˌli-nē-'ā-shən\ n

de·lin·quen·cy \di-'liŋ-kwən-sē\ n, pl -**cies** : the quality or state of being delinquent

¹**de·lin·quent** \-kwənt\ n : a delinquent person

²**delinquent** adj **1** : offending by neglect or violation of duty or law **2** : being overdue in payment

del·i·quesce \ˌde-li-'kwes\ vb -**quesced**; -**quesc·ing** : MELT, DISSOLVE — **del·i·ques·cent** \-'kwe-sᵊnt\ adj

de·lir·i·um \di-'lir-ē-əm\ n [L, fr. delirare to be crazy, lit., to leave the furrow (in plowing), fr. de- from + lira furrow] : mental disturbance marked by confusion, disordered speech, and hallucinations; also : frenzied excitement — **de·lir·i·ous** \-ē-əs\ adj — **de·lir·i·ous·ly** adv

delirium tre·mens \-'trē-mənz, -'tre-\ n : a violent delirium with tremors that is induced by excessive and prolonged use of alcoholic liquors

de·liv·er \di-'li-vər\ vb -**ered**; -**er·ing 1** : to set free : SAVE **2** : CONVEY, TRANSFER ⟨~ a letter⟩ **3** : to assist in giving birth or at the birth of; also : to give birth to **4** : UTTER, COMMUNICATE **5** : to send to an intended target or destination — **de·liv·er·able** \-'li-v(ə-)rə-bəl\ *adj* — **de·liv·er·ance** \-v(ə-)rəns\ *n* — **de·liv·er·er** *n*

de·liv·ery \di-'li-və-rē\ *n, pl* **-er·ies** : the act of delivering something; *also* : something delivered — **de·liv·ery·man** \-,man\ *n*

dell \'del\ *n* : a small secluded valley

de·louse \dē-'laús\ *vb* : to remove lice from

del·phin·i·um \del-'fi-nē-əm\ *n* : any of a genus of mostly perennial herbs related to the buttercups with tall branching spikes of irregular flowers

del·ta \'del-tə\ *n* **1** : the 4th letter of the Greek alphabet — Δ or δ **2** : something shaped like a capital Δ; *esp* : the triangular silt-formed land at the mouth of a river — **del·ta·ic** \del-'tā-ik\ *adj*

del·toid \'del-,tóid\ *n* : a large triangular muscle that covers the shoulder joint and raises the arm laterally

de·lude \di-'lüd\ *vb* **de·lud·ed; de·lud·ing** : MISLEAD, DECEIVE, TRICK

¹**del·uge** \'del-,yüj\ *n* **1** : a flooding of land by water **2** : a drenching rain **3** : a great amount or number ⟨a ~ of mail⟩

²**deluge** *vb* **del·uged; del·ug·ing 1** : INUNDATE, FLOOD **2** : to overwhelm as if with a deluge

de·lu·sion \di-'lü-zhən\ *n* : a deluding or being deluded; *esp* : a persistent false psychotic belief — **de·lu·sion·al** \-'lü-zhə-nəl\ *adj* — **de·lu·sive** \-'lü-siv\ *adj*

de·luxe \di-'lúks, -'ləks, -'lúks\ *adj* : notably luxurious or elegant

delve \'delv\ *vb* **delved; delv·ing 1** : DIG **2** : to seek laboriously for information

dely *abbr* delivery

Dem *abbr* Democrat; Democratic

de·mag·ne·tize \dē-'mag-nə-,tīz\ *vb* : to cause to lose magnetic properties — **de·mag·ne·ti·za·tion** \dē-,mag-nə-tə-'zā-shən\ *n*

dem·a·gogue *also* **dem·a·gog** \'de-mə-,gäg\ *n* [Gk *dēmagōgos*, fr. *dēmos* people + *agōgos* leading, fr. *agein* to lead] : a person who appeals to the emotions and prejudices of people esp. in order to gain political power — **dem·a·gogu·ery** \-,gä-gə-rē\ *n* — **dem·a·gogy** \-,gä-gē, -,gä-jē\ *n*

¹**de·mand** \di-'mand\ *n* **1** : an act of demanding; *also* : something claimed as due or just **2** : the ability and desire to buy goods or services; *also* : the quantity of goods wanted at a stated price **3** : a seeking or being sought after : urgent need **4** : a pressing need or requirement

²**demand** *vb* **1** : to ask for with authority : claim as due or just **2** : to ask earnestly or in the manner of a command **3** : REQUIRE, NEED ⟨a patient who ~s constant care⟩

de·mar·cate \di-'mär-,kāt, 'dē-,mär-\ *vb* **-cat·ed; -cat·ing 1** : DELIMIT **2** : to set apart : DISTINGUISH — **de·mar·ca·tion** \,dē-,mär-'kā-shən\ *n*

dé·marche *or* **de·marche** \dā-'märsh\ *n* : a course of action : MANEUVER

¹**de·mean** \di-'mēn\ *vb* **de·meaned; de·mean·ing** : to behave or conduct (oneself) usu. in a proper manner

²**demean** *vb* **de·meaned; de·mean·ing** : DEGRADE, DEBASE

de·mean·or \di-'mē-nər\ *n* : CONDUCT, BEARING

de·mean·our *Brit var of* DEMEANOR

de·ment·ed \di-'men-təd\ *adj* : MAD, INSANE — **de·ment·ed·ly** *adv*

de·men·tia \di-'men-chə\ *n* **1** : deterioration of cognitive functioning (as in Alzheimer's disease) **2** : INSANITY

de·mer·it \di-'mer-ət\ *n* **1** : FAULT **2** : a mark placed against a person's record for some fault or offense

de·mesne \di-'mān, -'mēn\ *n* **1** : REALM **2** : manorial land actually possessed by the lord and not held by free tenants **3** : ESTATE **4** : REGION

demi·god \'de-mi-,gäd\ *n* : a mythological being with more power than a mortal but less than a god

demi·john \'de-mi-,jän\ *n* [F *dame-jeanne*, lit., Lady Jane] : a large narrow-necked bottle usu. enclosed in wickerwork

de·mil·i·ta·rize \dē-'mi-lə-tə-,rīz\ *vb* : to strip of military forces, weapons, or fortifications — **de·mil·i·tar·i·za·tion** \dē-,mi-lə-tə-rə-'zā-shən\ *n*

demi·mon·daine \,de-mi-,män-'dān\ *n* : a woman of the demimonde

demi·monde \'de-mi-,mänd\ *n* [F *demi-monde*, fr. *demi-* half + *monde* world] **1** : a class of women on the fringes

of respectable society supported by wealthy lovers **2** : a distinct isolated group having low reputation or prestige

de·min·er·al·ize \dē-'mi-nə-rə-,līz\ *vb* : to remove the mineral matter from — **de·min·er·al·i·za·tion** \-,mi-nə-rə-lə-'zā-shən\ *n*

de·mise \di-'mīz\ *n* **1** : LEASE **2** : transfer of sovereignty to a successor ⟨~ of the crown⟩ **3** : DEATH **4** : loss of status

demi·tasse \'de-mi-,tas\ *n* : a small cup of black coffee; *also* : the cup used to serve it

demo \'de-mō\ *n, pl* **demos 1** : DEMONSTRATION **2** : a product used to show performance or merits to prospective buyers **3** : a recording used to show off a song or performer

de·mo·bi·lize \di-'mō-bə-,līz, dē-\ *vb* **1** : DISBAND **2** : to discharge from military service — **de·mo·bi·li·za·tion** \di-,mō-bə-lə-'zā-shən, dē-\ *n*

de·moc·ra·cy \di-'mä-krə-sē\ *n, pl* **-cies** [MF *democratie*, fr. LL *democratia*, fr. Gk *dēmokratia*, fr. *dēmos* people + *kratos* strength, power] **1** : government by the people; *esp* : rule of the majority **2** : a government in which the supreme power is held by the people **3** : a political unit that has a democratic government **4** *cap* : the principles and policies of the Democratic party in the U.S. **5** : the common people esp. when constituting the source of political authority **6** : the absence of hereditary or arbitrary class distinctions or privileges

dem·o·crat \'de-mə-,krat\ *n* **1** : one who believes in or practices democracy **2** *cap* : a member of the Democratic party of the U.S.

dem·o·crat·ic \,de-mə-'kra-tik\ *adj* **1** : of, relating to, or favoring democracy **2** *often cap* : of or relating to one of the two major political parties in the U.S. associated in modern times with policies of broad social reform and internationalism **3** : relating to or appealing to the common people ⟨~ art⟩ **4** : not snobbish — **dem·o·crat·i·cal·ly** \-ti-k(ə-)lē\ *adv*

de·moc·ra·tize \di-'mä-krə-,tīz\ *vb* **-tized; -tiz·ing** : to make democratic

dé·mo·dé \,dā-mō-'dā\ *adj* [F] : no longer fashionable : OUT-OF-DATE

de·mo·graph·ics \,de-mə-'gra-fiks, ,dē-\ *n pl* : the statistical characteristics of human populations

de·mog·ra·phy \di-'mä-grə-fē\ *n* : the statistical study of human populations and esp. their size and distribution and the number of births and deaths — **de·mog·ra·pher** \-fər\ *n* — **de·mo·graph·ic** \,de-mə-'gra-fik, ,dē-\ *adj* — **de·mo·graph·i·cal·ly** \-fi-k(ə-)lē\ *adv*

dem·oi·selle \,dem-wə-'zel\ *n* [F] : a young woman

de·mol·ish \di-'mä-lish\ *vb* **1** : to destroy by breaking apart : RAZE **2** : SMASH **3** : to put an end to

de·mo·li·tion \,de-mə-'li-shən, ,dē-\ *n* : the act of demolishing; *esp* : destruction by means of explosives

de·mon *or* **dae·mon** \'dē-mən\ *n* **1** : an evil spirit : DEVIL **2** *usu* **daemon** : an attendant power or spirit **3** : one that has unusual drive or effectiveness ⟨a ~ for work⟩

de·mon·e·tize \dē-'mä-nə-,tīz, -'mə-\ *vb* : to stop using as money or as a monetary standard ⟨~ silver⟩ — **de·mon·e·ti·za·tion** \dē-,mä-nə-tə-'zā-shən, -,mə-\ *n*

de·mo·ni·ac \di-'mō-nē-,ak\ *also* **de·mo·ni·a·cal** \,dē-mə-'nī-ə-kəl\ *adj* **1** : possessed or influenced by a demon **2** : DEMONIC

de·mon·ic \di-'mä-nik\ *also* **de·mon·i·cal** \-ni-kəl\ *adj* : DEVILISH, FIENDISH ⟨~ cruelty⟩

de·mon·ize \'dē-mə-,nīz\ *vb* **-ized; iz·ing 1** : to convert into a demon **2** : to characterize or treat as evil or harmful

de·mon·ol·o·gy \,dē-mə-'nä-lə-jē\ *n* **1** : the study of demons **2** : belief in demons

de·mon·stra·ble \di-'män-strə-bəl\ *adj* **1** : capable of being demonstrated **2** : APPARENT, EVIDENT — **de·mon·stra·bly** \-blē\ *adv*

dem·on·strate \'de-mən-,strāt\ *vb* **-strat·ed; -strat·ing 1** : to show clearly **2** : to prove or make clear by reasoning or evidence **3** : to explain esp. with many examples **4** : to show publicly ⟨~ a new car⟩ **5** : to make a public display ⟨~ in protest⟩ — **dem·on·stra·tion** \,de-mən-'strā-shən\ *n.* — **dem·on·stra·tor** \'de-mən-,strā-tər\ *n*

¹**de·mon·stra·tive** \di-'män-strə-tiv\ *adj* **1** : demonstrating as real or true **2** : characterized by demonstration **3**

: pointing out the one referred to and distinguishing it from others of the same class ⟨∼ pronoun⟩ **4** : marked by display of feeling : EFFUSIVE — **de·mon·stra·tive·ly** *adv* — **de·mon·stra·tive·ness** *n*

²demonstrative *n* : a demonstrative word and esp. a pronoun

de·mor·al·ize \di-ˈmȯr-ə-ˌlīz\ *vb* **1** : to corrupt in morals **2** : to weaken in discipline or spirit : DISORGANIZE — **de·mor·al·i·za·tion** \di-ˌmȯr-ə-lə-ˈzā-shən\ *n*

de·mote \di-ˈmōt\ *vb* **de·mot·ed; de·mot·ing** : to reduce to a lower grade or rank — **de·mo·tion** \-ˈmō-shən\ *n*

de·mot·ic \di-ˈmä-tik\ *adj* : COMMON, POPULAR ⟨∼ idiom⟩

de·mur \di-ˈmər\ *vb* **de·murred; de·mur·ring** [ME *demuren, demeren* to linger, fr. AF *demurer, demoerer,* fr. L *demorari,* fr. *morari* to linger, fr. *mora* delay] : to take exception — OBJECT — **de·mur** *n*

de·mure \di-ˈmyu̇r\ *adj* **1** : quietly modest : DECOROUS **2** : affectedly modest, reserved, or serious : PRIM ♦ **Synonyms** SHY, BASHFUL, COY, DIFFICULT, RETIRING, UNASSERTIVE — **de·mure·ly** *adv*

de·mur·rer \di-ˈmər-ər\ *n* : a claim by the defendant in a legal action that the plaintiff does not have sufficient grounds to proceed

den \ˈden\ *n* **1** : LAIR 1 **2** : HIDEOUT ⟨a robber's ∼⟩; *also* : a place like a hideout or a center of secret activity ⟨opium ∼⟩ ⟨a ∼ of iniquity⟩ **3** : a cozy private little room

Den *abbr* Denmark

de·nar \ˈde-ˌnär, ˈdä-\ — see MONEY table

de·na·ture \dē-ˈnā-chər\ *vb* **de·na·tured; de·na·tur·ing** : to remove or change the natural qualities of; *esp* : to make (alcohol) unfit for drinking

den·drol·o·gy \den-ˈdrä-lə-jē\ *n* : the study of trees — **den·drol·o·gist** \-jist\ *n*

den·gue \ˈdeŋ-gē, -ˌgā\ *n* [Sp] : an acute infectious disease characterized by headache, severe joint pain, and rash

de·ni \ˈde-ˌnē, ˈdä-\ *n pl* — see *denar* at MONEY table

de·ni·al \di-ˈnī-(ə)l\ *n* **1** : rejection of a request **2** : refusal to admit the truth of a statement or charge; *also* : assertion that something alleged is false **3** : DISAVOWAL **4** : restriction on one's own activity or desires

de·nier \ˈden-yər\ *n* : a unit of fineness for yarn

den·i·grate \ˈde-ni-ˌgrāt\ *vb* **-grat·ed; -grat·ing** [L *denigrare,* fr. *nigrare* to blacken, fr. *niger* black] : to cast aspersions on : DEFAME — **den·i·gra·tion** \ˌde-ni-ˈgrā-shən\ *n*

den·im \ˈde-nəm\ *n* [F *(serge) de Nîmes* serge of Nîmes, France] **1** : a firm durable twilled usu. cotton fabric woven with colored warp and white filling threads **2** *pl* : overalls or pants of usu. blue denim

den·i·zen \ˈde-nə-zən\ *n* : INHABITANT

de·nom·i·nate \di-ˈnä-mə-ˌnāt\ *vb* : to give a name to : DESIGNATE

de·nom·i·na·tion \di-ˌnä-mə-ˈnā-shən\ *n* **1** : an act of denominating **2** : a value or size of a series of related values (as of money) **3** : NAME, DESIGNATION; *esp* : a general name for a category **4** : a religious organization uniting local congregations in a single body — **de·nom·i·na·tion·al** \-shə-nəl\ *adj*

de·nom·i·na·tor \di-ˈnä-mə-ˌnā-tər\ *n* : the part of a fraction that is below the line indicating division

de·no·ta·tive \ˈdē-nō-ˌtā-tiv, di-ˈnō-tə-tiv\ *adj* **1** : denoting or tending to denote **2** : relating to denotation

de·note \di-ˈnōt\ *vb* **1** : to mark out plainly : INDICATE **2** : to make known **3** : MEAN, NAME — **de·no·ta·tion** \ˌdē-nō-ˈtā-shən\ *n*

de·noue·ment \ˌdā-ˌnü-ˈmäⁿ\ *n* [F *dénouement,* lit., untying] : the final outcome of the dramatic complications in a literary work

de·nounce \di-ˈnau̇ns\ *vb* **de·nounced; de·nounc·ing** **1** : to pronounce esp. publicly to be blameworthy or evil **2** : to inform against : ACCUSE **3** : to announce formally the termination of (as a treaty) — **de·nounce·ment** *n*

de no·vo \di-ˈnō-vō\ *adv or adj* [L] : over again : ANEW ⟨a case tried ∼⟩

dense \ˈdens\ *adj* **dens·er; dens·est** **1** : marked by compactness or crowding together of parts : THICK ⟨∼ forest⟩ ⟨a ∼ fog⟩ **2** : DULL, STUPID — **dense·ly** *adv* — **dense·ness** *n*

den·si·ty \ˈden-sə-tē\ *n, pl* **-ties** **1** : the quality of state of

being dense **2** : the quantity of something per unit volume, unit area, or unit length

dent \ˈdent\ *n* **1** : a small depressed place made by a blow or by pressure **2** : an impression or weakening effect made usu. against resistance **3** : initial progress — **dent** *vb*

den·tal \ˈden-tᵊl\ *adj* : of or relating to teeth or dentistry — **den·tal·ly** *adv*

dental floss *n* : a thread used to clean between the teeth

dental hygienist *n* : a person licensed to clean and examine teeth

den·tate \ˈden-ˌtāt\ *adj* : having pointed projections : NOTCHED

den·ti·frice \ˈden-tə-frəs\ *n* [ME *dentifricie,* fr. L *dentifricium,* fr. *dent-, dens* tooth + *fricare* to rub] : a powder, paste, or liquid for cleaning the teeth

den·tin \ˈden-tᵊn\ *or* **den·tine** \ˈden-ˌtēn, den-ˈtēn\ *n* : a calcareous material like bone but harder and denser that composes the principal mass of a tooth

den·tist \ˈden-tist\ *n* : a person licensed in the care, treatment, and replacement of teeth — **den·tist·ry** *n*

den·ti·tion \den-ˈti-shən\ *n* : the number, kind, and arrangement of teeth (as of a person or animal); *also* : TEETH

den·ture \ˈden-chər\ *n* : a set of teeth; *esp* : a partial or complete set of false teeth

de·nude \di-ˈnüd, -ˈnyüd\ *vb* **de·nud·ed; de·nud·ing** : to strip the covering from — **de·nu·da·tion** \ˌdē-nü-ˈdā-shən, -nyü-\ *n*

de·nun·ci·a·tion \di-ˌnən-sē-ˈā-shən\ *n* : the act of denouncing; *esp* : a public condemnation — **de·nun·ci·a·to·ry** \-ˈnən-sē-ə-ˌtȯr-ē\ *adj*

de·ny \di-ˈnī\ *vb* **de·nied; de·ny·ing** **1** : to declare untrue **2** : to refuse to recognize or acknowledge : DISAVOW **3** : to refuse to grant ⟨∼ a request⟩ **4** : to reject as false ⟨∼ a theory⟩

de·o·dar \ˈdē-ə-ˌdär\ *n* [Hindi & Urdu *devadār, deodār,* fr. Skt *devadāru,* fr. *deva* god + *dāru* wood] : a Himalayan cedar

de·odor·ant \dē-ˈō-də-rənt\ *n* : a preparation that destroys or masks unpleasant odors

de·odor·ize \dē-ˈō-də-ˌrīz\ *vb* : to eliminate the offensive odor of

de·ox·i·dize \dē-ˈäk-sə-ˌdīz\ *vb* : to remove esp. elemental oxygen from

de·oxy·ri·bo·nu·cle·ic acid \dē-ˈäk-si-ˌrī-bō-nú-ˌklē-ik-, -nyü-\ *n* : DNA

de·oxy·ri·bose \dē-ˈäk-si-ˈrī-ˌbōs\ *n* : a sugar with five carbon and four oxygen atoms in each molecule that is part of DNA

dep *abbr* **1** depart; departure **2** deposit **3** deputy

de·part \di-ˈpärt\ *vb* **1** : to go away : go away from : LEAVE **2** : DIE **3** : to turn aside : DEVIATE

de·part·ee \di-ˌpär-ˈtē\ *n* : a person who is departing or who has departed

de·part·ment \di-ˈpärt-mənt\ *n* **1** : a distinct sphere or category esp. of an activity or attribute **2** : a functional or territorial division (as of a government, business, or college) — **de·part·men·tal** \di-ˌpärt-ˈmen-tᵊl, ˌdē-\ *adj* — **de·part·men·tal·ly** *adv*

department store *n* : a store having separate sections for a wide variety of goods

de·par·ture \di-ˈpär-chər\ *n* **1** : the act of going away **2** : a starting out (as on a journey) **3** : DIVERGENCE ⟨a ∼ from tradition⟩

de·pend \di-ˈpend\ *vb* **1** : to be determined, based, or contingent ⟨life ∼s on food⟩ **2** : TRUST, RELY ⟨you can ∼ on me⟩ **3** : to be dependent esp. for financial support **4** : to hang down ⟨a vine ∼ing from a tree⟩

de·pend·able \di-ˈpen-də-bəl\ *adj* : TRUSTWORTHY, RELIABLE — **de·pend·abil·i·ty** \-ˌpen-də-ˈbi-lə-tē\ *n*

de·pen·dence *also* **de·pen·dance** \di-ˈpen-dəns\ *n* **1** : the quality or state of being dependent; *esp* : the quality or state of being influenced by or subject to another **2** : RELIANCE, TRUST **3** : something on which one relies **4** : drug addiction; *also* : HABITUATION 2

de·pen·den·cy \-dən-sē\ *n, pl* **-cies** **1** : DEPENDENCE **2** : a territory under the jurisdiction of a nation but not formally annexed by it

¹de·pen·dent \-dənt\ *adj* **1** : hanging down **2** : determined or conditioned by another; *also* : affected with drug dependence **3** : relying on another for support **4** : subject to another's jurisdiction **5** : SUBORDINATE 4 ⟨~ clauses⟩

²**dependent** *also* **de·pen·dant** \-dənt\ *n* : one that is dependent; *esp* : a person who relies on another for support

dependent variable *n* : a variable whose value is determined by that of one or more other variables in a function

de·pict \di-'pikt\ *vb* **1** : to represent by a picture **2** : to describe in words — **de·pic·tion** \-'pik-shən\ *n*

de·pil·a·to·ry \di-'pi-lə-ˌtȯr-ē\ *n, pl* **-ries** : a preparation for removing hair, wool, or bristles

de·plane \dē-'plān\ *vb* : to get out of an airplane

de·plete \di-'plēt\ *vb* **de·plet·ed; de·plet·ing** : to exhaust esp. of strength or resources — **de·ple·tion** \-'plē-shən\ *n*

de·plor·able \di-'plȯr-ə-bəl\ *adj* **1** : LAMENTABLE ⟨a ~ death⟩ **2** : WRETCHED — **de·plor·ably** *adv*

de·plore \-'plȯr\ *vb* **de·plored; de·plor·ing** **1** : to feel or express grief for **2** : to regret strongly **3** : to consider unfortunate or deserving of disapproval

de·ploy \di-'plȯi\ *vb* : to spread out (as troops or ships) in order for battle — **de·ploy·ment** \-mənt\ *n*

de·po·nent \di-'pō-nənt\ *n* : one who gives evidence

de·pop·u·late \dē-'pä-pyə-ˌlāt\ *vb* : to reduce greatly the population of — **de·pop·u·la·tion** \-ˌpä-pyə-'lā-shən\ *n*

de·port \di-'pȯrt\ *vb* **1** : CONDUCT, BEHAVE **2** : BANISH, EXILE — **de·por·ta·tion** \ˌdē-ˌpȯr-'tā-shən\ *n*

de·port·ment \di-'pȯrt-mənt\ *n* : BEHAVIOR, BEARING

de·pose \di-'pōz\ *vb* **de·posed; de·pos·ing** **1** : to remove from high office (as of king) **2** : to testify under oath or by affidavit

¹**de·pos·it** \di-'pä-zət\ *vb* **de·pos·it·ed** \-zə-təd\; **de·pos·it·ing** **1** : to place for safekeeping or as a pledge; *esp* : to put money in a bank **2** : to lay down : PLACE **3** : to let fall or sink ⟨silt ~ed by a flood⟩ — **de·pos·i·tor** \-zə-tər\ *n*

²**deposit** *n* **1** : the state of being deposited ⟨money on ~⟩ **2** : something placed for safekeeping; *esp* : money deposited in a bank **3** : money given as a pledge **4** : an act of depositing **5** : something laid down ⟨a ~ of silt⟩ **6** : a natural accumulation (as of a mineral)

de·po·si·tion \ˌde-pə-'zi-shən, ˌdē-\ *n* **1** : an act of removing from a position of authority **2** : TESTIMONY **3** : the process of depositing **4** : DEPOSIT

de·pos·i·to·ry \di-'pä-zə-ˌtȯr-ē\ *n, pl* **-ries** : a place where something is deposited esp. for safekeeping

de·pot *1, 2 usu* 'de-pō, *3 usu* 'dē-\ *n* **1** : a place for storing goods or vehicles **2** : a place where military supplies or replacements are kept or assembled **3** : a building for railroad or bus passengers

depr *abbr* depreciation

de·prave \di-'prāv\ *vb* **de·praved; de·prav·ing** [ME, fr. AF *depraver*, fr. L *depravare* to pervert, fr. *pravus* crooked, bad] : CORRUPT, PERVERT — **de·praved** *adj* — **de·prav·i·ty** \-'pra-və-tē\ *n*

dep·re·cate \'de-pri-ˌkāt\ *vb* **-cat·ed; -cat·ing** [L *deprecari* to avert by prayer, fr. *precari* to pray] **1** : to express disapproval of **2** : BELITTLE — **dep·re·ca·tion** \ˌde-pri-'kā-shən\ *n*

dep·re·ca·to·ry \'de-pri-kə-ˌtȯr-ē\ *adj* **1** : APOLOGETIC **2** : serving to deprecate : DISAPPROVING

de·pre·ci·ate \di-'prē-shē-ˌāt\ *vb* **-at·ed; -at·ing** [ME, fr. LL *depreciatus*, pp. of *depretiare*, fr. L *pretium* price] **1** : BELITTLE, DISPARAGE **2** : to lessen in price or value — **de·pre·cia·ble** \-shə-bəl\ *adj* — **de·pre·ci·a·tion** \-ˌprē-shē-'ā-shən\ *n*

dep·re·da·tion \ˌde-prə-'dā-shən\ *n* : a laying waste or plundering — **dep·re·date** \'de-prə-ˌdāt\ *vb*

de·press \di-'pres\ *vb* **1** : to press down : cause to sink to a lower position **2** : to lessen the activity or force of **3** : SADDEN, DISCOURAGE **4** : to lessen in price or value — **de·pres·sor** \-'pre-sər\ *n*

de·pres·sant \di-'pre-sᵊnt\ *n* : one that depresses; *esp* : a chemical substance (as a drug) that reduces bodily functional activity — **depressant** *adj*

de·pressed \-'prest\ *adj* **1** : low in spirits; *also* : affected with psychological depression **2** : suffering from economic depression

de·pres·sion \di-'pre-shən\ *n* **1** : an act of depressing : a state of being depressed **2** : a pressing down : LOWERING **3** : a state of feeling sad **4** : a psychological disorder marked esp. by sadness, inactivity, difficulty in think-ing and concentration, and feelings of dejection **5** : a depressed area or part **6** : a period of low general economic activity with widespread unemployment

¹**de·pres·sive** \di-'pre-siv\ *adj* **1** : tending to depress **2** : characterized or affected by psychological depression

²**depressive** *n* : a person affected with or prone to psychological depression

de·pres·sur·ize \(ˌ)dē-'pre-shə-ˌrīz\ *vb* : to release pressure from

dep·ri·va·tion \ˌde-prə-'vā-shən\ *n* **1** : an act or instance of depriving : LOSS **2** : PRIVATION 2

de·prive \di-'prīv\ *vb* **de·prived; de·priv·ing** **1** : to take something away from **2** : to stop from having something

deprived *adj* : marked by deprivation esp. of the necessities of life

de·pro·gram \(ˌ)dē-'prō-ˌgram, -grəm\ *vb* : to dissuade from convictions usu. of a religious nature often by coercive means

dept *abbr* department

depth \'depth\ *n, pl* **depths** \'depths\ **1** : something that is deep; *esp* : the deep part of a body of water **2** : a part that is far from the outside or surface; *also* : the middle or innermost part **3** : ABYSS **4** : a profound or intense state ⟨the ~s of reflection⟩; *also* : the worst part ⟨during the ~s of the depression⟩ **5** : a reprehensibly low condition **6** : the distance from top to bottom or from front to back **7** : the quality of being deep **8** : the degree of intensity

depth charge *n* : an explosive device for use underwater esp. against submarines

dep·u·ta·tion \ˌde-pyə-'tā-shən\ *n* **1** : the act of appointing a deputy **2** : DELEGATION

de·pute \di-'pyüt\ *vb* **de·put·ed; de·put·ing** : DELEGATE

dep·u·tize \'de-pyə-ˌtīz\ *vb* **-tized; -tiz·ing** : to appoint or act as deputy

dep·u·ty \'de-pyə-tē\ *n, pl* **-ties** **1** : a person appointed to act for or in place of another **2** : an assistant empowered to act as a substitute in the absence of a superior **3** : a member of a lower house of a legislative assembly

der *or* **deriv** *abbr* derivation; derivative

de·rail \di-'rāl\ *vb* : to leave or cause to leave the rails — **de·rail·ment** *n*

de·rail·leur \di-'rā-lər\ *n* [F *dérailleur*] : a device for shifting gears on a bicycle by moving the chain from one set of exposed gears to another

de·range \di-'rānj\ *vb* **de·ranged; de·rang·ing** **1** : DISARRANGE, UPSET **2** : to make insane — **de·range·ment** *n*

der·by \'dər-bē, *Brit* 'där-\ *n, pl* **derbies** **1** : a horse race usu. for three-year-olds held annually **2** : a race or contest open to all **3** : a stiff felt hat with dome-shaped crown and narrow brim

derby 3

de·reg·u·la·tion \(ˌ)dē-ˌre-gyù-'lā-shən\ *n* : the act of removing restrictions or regulations — **de·reg·u·late** \-'re-gyù-ˌlāt\ *vb*

¹**der·e·lict** \'der-ə-ˌlikt\ *adj* **1** : abandoned by the owner or occupant **2** : NEGLIGENT ⟨~ in his duty⟩

²**derelict** *n* **1** : something voluntarily abandoned; *esp* : a ship abandoned on the high seas **2** : a destitute homeless social misfit : VAGRANT, BUM

der·e·lic·tion \ˌder-ə-'lik-shən\ *n* **1** : the act of abandoning : the state of being abandoned **2** : intentional neglect ⟨~ of duty⟩

de·ride \di-'rīd\ *vb* **de·rid·ed; de·rid·ing** [L *deridēre*, fr. *ridēre* to laugh] : to laugh at scornfully : RIDICULE

de ri·gueur \də-rē-'gər\ *adj* [F] : prescribed or required by fashion, etiquette, or custom : PROPER

de·ri·sion \də-'ri-zhən\ *n* : RIDICULE — **de·ri·sive** \-'rī-siv\ *adj* — **de·ri·sive·ly** *adv* — **de·ri·sive·ness** *n* — **de·ri·so·ry** \-'rī-sə-rē\ *adj*

der·i·va·tion \ˌder-ə-'vā-shən\ *n* **1** : the formation of a word from an earlier word or root; *also* : an act of ascertaining or stating the derivation of a word **2** : ETYMOLOGY **3** : SOURCE, ORIGIN; *also* : DESCENT **4** : an act or process of deriving

de·riv·a·tive \di-'ri-və-tiv\ *n* **1** : a word formed by derivation **2** : something derived **3** : the limit of the ratio of the change of a function's value to the change in its independent variable as the latter change approaches zero — **derivative** *adj*

de·rive \di-'rīv\ *vb* **de·rived; de·riv·ing** [ME, fr. AF *deriver*, fr. L *derivare*, lit., to draw off (water), fr. *de-* from + *rivus* stream] **1** : to receive or obtain from a source **2** : to obtain from a parent substance **3** : INFER, DEDUCE **4** : to trace the derivation of **5** : to come from a certain source

der·mal \'dər-məl\ *adj* : of or relating to the skin : CUTANEOUS

der·ma·ti·tis \ˌdər-mə-'tī-təs\ *n, pl* **-tit·i·des** \-'ti-tə-ˌdēz\ or **-ti·tis·es** : inflammation of the skin

der·ma·tol·o·gy \-'tä-lə-jē\ *n* : a branch of medical science dealing with the structure, functions, and diseases of the skin — **der·ma·tol·o·gist** \-jist\ *n*

der·mis \'dər-məs\ *n* : the sensitive vascular inner layer of the skin

der·o·gate \'der-ə-ˌgāt\ *vb* **-gat·ed; -gat·ing** **1** : to cause to seem inferior : DISPARAGE **2** : DETRACT — **der·o·ga·tion** \ˌder-ə-'gā-shən\ *n* — **de·rog·a·tive** \di-'rä-gə-tiv\ *adj*

de·rog·a·to·ry \di-'rä-gə-ˌtȯr-ē\ *adj* : intended to lower the reputation of a person or thing : DISPARAGING — **de·rog·a·to·ri·ly** \-ˌrä-gə-'tȯr-ə-lē\ *adv*

der·rick \'der-ik\ *n* [obs. *derrick* hangman, gallows, fr. *Derick*, name of 17th cent. Eng. hangman] **1** : a hoisting apparatus : CRANE **2** : a framework over a drill hole (as for oil) for supporting machinery

der·ri·ere *or* **der·ri·ère** \ˌder-ē-'er\ *n* : BUTTOCKS

der·ring–do \ˌder-iŋ-'dü\ *n* : DARING

der·rin·ger \'der-ən-jər\ *n* : a short-barreled pocket pistol

der·vish \'dər-vish\ *n* [Turk *derviş*, lit., beggar, fr. Pers *darvīsh*] : a member of a Muslim religious order noted for devotional exercises (as bodily movements leading to a trance)

de·sal·i·nate \dē-'sa-lə-ˌnāt\ *vb* **-nat·ed; -nat·ing** : DESALT — **de·sal·i·na·tion** \-ˌsa-lə-'nā-shən\ *n*

de·sal·i·nize \dē-'sa-lə-ˌnīz\ *vb* **-nized; -niz·ing** : DESALT — **de·sal·i·ni·za·tion** \-ˌsa-lə-nə-'zā-shən\ *n*

de·salt \dē-'sȯlt\ *vb* : to remove salt from ⟨~ seawater⟩ — **de·salt·er** *n*

des·cant \'des-ˌkant\ *vb* **1** : to sing or play part music : SING **2** : to discourse or write at length

de·scend \di-'send\ *vb* **1** : to pass from a higher to a lower place or level : pass, move, or climb down or down along **2** : DERIVE ⟨~ed from royalty⟩ **3** : to pass by inheritance or transmission **4** : to incline, lead, or extend downward **5** : to swoop down or appear suddenly (as in an attack)

¹de·scen·dant *also* **de·scen·dent** \di-'sen-dənt\ *adj* **1** : DESCENDING **2** : proceeding from an ancestor or source

²descendant *also* **descendent** *n* **1** : one descended from another or from a common stock **2** : one deriving directly from a precursor or prototype

de·scent \di-'sent\ *n* **1** : ANCESTRY, BIRTH, LINEAGE **2** : the act or process of descending **3** : SLOPE **4** : a descending way (as a downgrade) **5** : a sudden hostile raid or assault **6** : a downward step (as in station or value) : DECLINE

de·scram·ble \dē-'skram-bəl\ *vb* : UNSCRAMBLE 2 — **de·scram·bler** \-b(ə-)lər\ *n*

de·scribe \di-'skrīb\ *vb* **de·scribed; de·scrib·ing** **1** : to represent or give an account of in words **2** : to trace the outline of — **de·scrib·able** *adj*

de·scrip·tion \di-'skrip-shən\ *n* **1** : an account of something; *esp* : an account that presents a picture to a person who reads or hears it **2** : KIND, SORT — **de·scrip·tive** \-'skrip-tiv\ *adj*

de·scry \di-'skrī\ *vb* **de·scried; de·scry·ing** **1** : to catch sight of **2** : to discover by observation or investigation

des·e·crate \'de-si-ˌkrāt\ *vb* **-crat·ed; -crat·ing** : PROFANE — **des·e·cra·tion** \ˌde-si-'krā-shən\ *n*

de·seg·re·gate \dē-'se-gri-ˌgāt\ *vb* : to eliminate segregation in; *esp* : to free of any law or practice requiring isolation on the basis of race — **de·seg·re·ga·tion** \-ˌse-gri-'gā-shən\ *n*

de·sen·si·tize \dē-'sen-sə-ˌtīz\ *vb* : to make (a sensitized or hypersensitive individual) insensitive or nonreactive to a sensitizing agent — **de·sen·si·ti·za·tion** \-ˌsen-sə-tə-'zā-shən\ *n*

¹des·ert \'de-zərt\ *n* : dry land with few plants and little rainfall

²des·ert \'de-zərt\ *adj* : of, relating to, or resembling a desert; *esp* : being barren and without life ⟨a ~ island⟩

³de·sert \di-'zərt\ *n* **1** : the quality or fact of deserving reward or punishment **2** : a just reward or punishment

⁴de·sert \di-'zərt\ *vb* **1** : to withdraw from **2** : ABANDON, FORSAKE — **de·sert·er** *n* — **de·ser·tion** \-'zər-shən\ *n*

de·serve \di-'zərv\ *vb* **de·served; de·serv·ing** : to be worthy of : MERIT — **de·serv·ing** *adj*

de·serv·ed·ly \-'zər-vəd-lē\ *adv* : according to merit : JUSTLY

deshabille *var of* DISHABILLE

des·ic·cate \'de-si-ˌkāt\ *vb* **-cat·ed; -cat·ing** : DRY, DEHYDRATE — **des·ic·ca·tion** \ˌde-si-'kā-shən\ *n* — **des·ic·ca·tor** \'de-si-ˌkā-tər\ *n*

de·sid·er·a·tum \di-ˌsi-də-'rä-təm, -ˌzi-, -'rā-\ *n, pl* **-ta** \-tə\ [L] : something desired as essential

¹de·sign \di-'zīn\ *vb* **1** : to conceive and plan out in the mind **3** : INTEND **3** : to devise for a specific function or end **4** : to make a pattern or sketch of **5** : to conceive and draw the plans for

²design *n* **1** : a particular purpose : deliberate planning **2** : a mental project or scheme : PLAN **3** : a secret project or scheme : PLOT **4** *pl* : aggressive or evil intent — used with *on* or *against* **5** : a preliminary sketch or plan **6** : an underlying scheme that governs functioning, developing, or unfolding : MOTIF ⟨the general ~ of the epic⟩ **7** : the arrangement of elements or details in a product or a work of art **8** : a decorative pattern ⟨a floral ~⟩ **9** : the art of executing designs

¹des·ig·nate \'de-zig-ˌnāt, -nət\ *adj* : chosen but not yet installed ⟨ambassador ~⟩

²des·ig·nate \-ˌnāt\ *vb* **-nat·ed; -nat·ing** **1** : to appoint and set apart for a special purpose **2** : to mark or point out : INDICATE; *also* : SPECIFY, STIPULATE **3** : to call by a name or title — **des·ig·na·tion** \ˌde-zig-'nā-shən\ *n*

designated driver *n* : a person chosen to abstain from alcohol so as to transport others safely

designated hitter *n* : a baseball player designated at the start of the game to bat in place of the pitcher without causing the pitcher to be removed from the game

de·sign·er \di-'zī-nər\ *n* **1** : one who creates plans for a project or structure **2** : one who designs and manufactures high-fashion clothing — **designer** *adj*

designer drug *n* : a synthetic version of an illicit drug that has been chemically altered to avoid its prohibition

de·sign·ing \di-'zī-nin\ *adj* : CRAFTY, SCHEMING

de·sir·able \di-'zī-rə-bəl\ *adj* **1** : PLEASING, ATTRACTIVE **2** : ADVISABLE ⟨~ legislation⟩ — **de·sir·abil·i·ty** \-ˌzī-rə-'bi-lə-tē\ *n* — **de·sir·able·ness** *n* — **de·sir·ably** \-'zī-rə-blē\ *adv*

¹de·sire \di-'zī(-ə)r\ *vb* **de·sired; de·sir·ing** [ME, fr. AF *desirer*, fr. L *desiderare*, fr. *sider-, sidus* heavenly body] **1** : to long or hope for : exhibit or feel desire for **2** : REQUEST

²desire *n* **1** : a strong wish : LONGING, CRAVING **2** : sexual urge or appetite **3** : a usu. formal request for action **4** : something desired

de·sir·ous \di-'zī(-ə)r-əs\ *adj* : eagerly wishing : DESIRING ⟨~ of fame⟩

de·sist \di-'zist, -'sist\ *vb* : to cease to proceed or act

desk \'desk\ *n* [ME *deske*, fr. ML *desca*, fr. It *desco* table, fr. L *discus* dish, disc] **1** : a table, frame, or case esp. for writing and reading **2** : a counter, stand, or booth at which a person performs duties **3** : a specialized division of an organization (as a newspaper) ⟨city ~⟩

desk·top publishing \'desk-ˌtäp-\ *n* : the production of printed matter by means of a microcomputer

¹des·o·late \'de-sə-lət, -zə-\ *adj* **1** : DESERTED, ABANDONED **2** : FORSAKEN, LONELY **3** : DILAPIDATED **4**

: BARREN, LIFELESS ⟨a ~ landscape⟩ 5 : CHEERLESS, GLOOMY ⟨~ memories⟩ — **des·o·late·ly** *adv* — **des·o·late·ness** *n*

²**des·o·late** \-ˌlāt\ *vb* **-lat·ed; -lat·ing** : to make desolate : lay waste : make wretched

des·o·la·tion \ˌde-sə-ˈlā-shən, -zə-\ *n* 1 : the action of desolating 2 : GRIEF, SADNESS 3 : LONELINESS 4 : DEVASTATION, RUIN 5 : barren wasteland

des·oxy·ri·bo·nu·cle·ic acid \dē-ˌzäk-sē-ˈrī-bō-nú-ˌklē-ik-, -nyú-\ *n* : DNA

¹**de·spair** \di-ˈsper\ *vb* : to lose all hope or confidence — **de·spair·ing** \-iŋ\ *adj* — **de·spair·ing·ly** *adv*

²**despair** *n* 1 : utter loss of hope 2 : a cause of hopelessness

des·patch *chiefly Brit var of* DISPATCH

des·per·a·do \ˌdes-pə-ˈrä-dō, -ˈrā-\ *n, pl* **-does** *or* **-dos** : a bold or reckless criminal

des·per·ate \ˈdes-pə-rət, -prət\ *adj* 1 : being beyond or almost beyond hope : causing despair 2 : RASH ⟨a ~ attempt⟩ 3 : extremely intense — **des·per·ate·ly** *adv* — **des·per·ate·ness** *n*

des·per·a·tion \ˌdes-pə-ˈrā-shən\ *n* 1 : a loss of hope and surrender to despair 2 : a state of hopelessness leading to rashness

de·spi·ca·ble \di-ˈspi-kə-bəl, ˈdes-pi-\ *adj* : deserving to be despised — **de·spi·ca·bly** \-blē\ *adv*

de·spise \di-ˈspīz\ *vb* **de·spised; de·spis·ing** 1 : to look down on with contempt or aversion : DISDAIN, DETEST 2 : to regard as negligible, worthless, or distasteful

de·spite \di-ˈspīt\ *prep* : in spite of

de·spoil \di-ˈspói(-ə)l\ *vb* : to strip of belongings, possessions, or value — **de·spoil·er** *n* — **de·spoil·ment** *n*

de·spo·li·a·tion \di-ˌspō-lē-ˈā-shən\ *n* : the act of plundering : the state of being despoiled

¹**de·spond** \di-ˈspänd\ *vb* : to become discouraged or disheartened

²**despond** *n* : DESPONDENCY

de·spon·den·cy \-ˈspän-dən-sē\ *n* : DEJECTION, HOPELESSNESS — **de·spon·dent** \-dənt\ *adj* — **de·spon·dent·ly** *adv*

des·pot \ˈdes-pət, -ˌpät\ *n* [MF *despote,* fr. Gk *despotēs* master, lord, autocrat] 1 : a ruler with absolute power and authority 2 : a person exercising power tyrannically — **des·pot·ic** \des-ˈpä-tik\ *adj* — **des·po·tism** \ˈdes-pə-ˌti-zəm\ *n*

des·sert \di-ˈzərt\ *n* : a course of sweet food, fruit, or cheese served at the close of a meal

de·stig·ma·tize \dē-ˈstig-mə-ˌtīz\ *vb* : to remove associations of shame or disgrace from

des·ti·na·tion \ˌdes-tə-ˈnā-shən\ *n* 1 : a purpose for which something is destined 2 : an act of appointing, setting aside for a purpose, or predetermining 3 : a place to which one is journeying or to which one is sent

des·tine \ˈdes-tən\ *vb* **des·tined; des·tin·ing** 1 : to settle in advance 2 : to designate, assign, or dedicate in advance 3 : to direct or set apart for a specific purpose or place

des·ti·ny \ˈdes-tə-nē\ *n, pl* **-nies** 1 : something to which a person or thing is destined : FATE, FORTUNE 2 : a predetermined course of events

des·ti·tute \ˈdes-tə-ˌtüt, -ˌtyüt\ *adj* 1 : lacking something needed or desirable 2 : suffering extreme poverty — **des·ti·tu·tion** \ˌdes-tə-ˈtü-shən, -ˈtyü-\ *n*

de·stroy \di-ˈstrói\ *vb* 1 : to put an end to : RUIN 2 : KILL

de·stroy·er \di-ˈstrói-ər\ *n* 1 : one that destroys 2 : a small speedy warship

de·struc·ti·ble \di-ˈstrək-tə-bəl\ *adj* : capable of being destroyed — **de·struc·ti·bil·i·ty** \-ˌstrək-tə-ˈbi-lə-tē\ *n*

de·struc·tion \di-ˈstrək-shən\ *n* 1 : RUIN 2 : the action or process of destroying something 3 : a destroying agency

de·struc·tive \di-ˈstrək-tiv\ *adj* 1 : causing destruction : RUINOUS 2 : designed or tending to hurt or destroy — **de·struc·tive·ly** *adv* — **de·struc·tive·ness** *n*

de·sue·tude \ˈde-swi-ˌtüd, -ˌtyüd\ *n* : DISUSE

des·ul·to·ry \ˈde-səl-ˌtór-ē\ *adj* : passing aimlessly from one thing or subject to another : DISCONNECTED

det *abbr* 1 detached; detachment 2 detail

de·tach \di-ˈtach\ *vb* 1 : to separate esp. from a larger mass 2 : DISENGAGE, WITHDRAW — **de·tach·able** *adj*

de·tached \di-ˈtacht\ *adj* 1 : not joined or connected : SEPARATE 2 : ALOOF, IMPARTIAL ⟨a ~ attitude⟩

de·tach·ment \di-ˈtach-mənt\ *n* 1 : SEPARATION 2 : the dispatching of a body of troops or part of a fleet from the main body for special service; *also* : the portion so dispatched 3 : a small permanent military unit of special composition 4 : indifference to worldly concerns : ALOOFNESS 5 : IMPARTIALITY

¹**de·tail** \di-ˈtāl, ˈdē-ˌtāl\ *n* [F *détail,* fr. OF *detail* slice, piece, fr. *detaillier* to cut in pieces, fr. *taillier* to cut] 1 : a dealing with something item by item ⟨go into ~⟩; *also* : ITEM, PARTICULAR ⟨the ~s of a story⟩ 2 : selection (as of soldiers) for special duty; *also* : the persons thus selected

²**detail** *vb* 1 : to report in particulars : SPECIFY 2 : to assign to a special duty

de·tailed \di-ˈtāld, ˈdē-ˌtāld\ *adj* : marked by abundant detail

de·tail·ing \ˈdē-ˌtāl-iŋ\ *n* : the meticulous cleaning and refurbishing of an automobile

de·tain \di-ˈtān\ *vb* 1 : to hold in or as if in custody 2 : STOP, DELAY

de·tect \di-ˈtekt\ *vb* : to discover the nature, existence, presence, or fact of — **de·tect·able** *adj* — **de·tec·tion** \-ˈtek-shən\ *n* — **de·tec·tor** \-ˈtek-tər\ *n*

¹**de·tec·tive** \di-ˈtek-tiv\ *adj* 1 : fitted or used for detection 2 : of or relating to detectives

²**detective** *n* : a person employed or engaged in detecting lawbreakers or getting information that is not readily accessible

dé·tente *or* **de·tente** \dā-ˈtänt\ *n* [F] : a relaxation of strained relations or tensions (as between nations)

de·ten·tion \di-ˈten-chən\ *n* 1 : the act or fact of detaining : CONFINEMENT; *esp* : a period of temporary custody prior to disposition by a court 2 : a forced delay

de·ter \di-ˈtər\ *vb* **de·terred; de·ter·ring** [L *deterrēre,* fr. *terrēre* to frighten] 1 : to turn aside, discourage, or prevent from acting (as by fear) 2 : INHIBIT

de·ter·gent \di-ˈtər-jənt\ *n* : a cleansing agent; *esp* : a chemical product similar to soap in its cleaning ability

de·te·ri·o·rate \di-ˈtir-ē-ə-ˌrāt\ *vb* **-rat·ed; -rat·ing** : to make or become worse in quality or condition — **de·te·ri·o·ra·tion** \-ˌtir-ē-ə-ˈrā-shən\ *n*

de·ter·min·able \-ˈtər-mə-nə-bəl\ *adj* : capable of being determined; *esp* : ASCERTAINABLE

de·ter·mi·nant \-mə-nənt\ *n* 1 : something that determines or conditions 2 : GENE

de·ter·mi·nate \di-ˈtər-mə-nət\ *adj* 1 : having fixed limits : DEFINITE ⟨a ~ period of time⟩ 2 : definitely settled ⟨in ~ order⟩ — **de·ter·mi·nate·ness** *n*

de·ter·mi·na·tion \di-ˌtər-mə-ˈnā-shən\ *n* 1 : the act of coming to a decision; *also* : the decision or conclusion reached 2 : a fixing of the extent, position, or character of something 3 : accurate measurement (as of length or volume) 4 : firm or fixed purpose — **de·ter·mi·na·tive** \-ˈtər-mə-ˌnā-tiv, -ˈtər-mə-nə-\ *adj*

de·ter·mine \di-ˈtər-mən\ *vb* **-mined; -min·ing** 1 : to fix conclusively or authoritatively 2 : to come to a decision : SETTLE, RESOLVE 3 : to fix the form or character of beforehand : ORDAIN; *also* : REGULATE 4 : to find out the limits, nature, dimensions, or scope of ⟨~ a position at sea⟩ 5 : to bring about as a result

de·ter·mined \-ˈtər-mənd\ *adj* 1 : firmly resolved 2 : characterized by or showing determination — **de·ter·mined·ly** \-mənd-lē, -mə-nəd-lē\ *adv* — **de·ter·mined·ness** *n*

de·ter·min·ism \di-ˈtər-mə-ˌni-zəm\ *n* : a doctrine that acts of the will, natural events, or social changes are determined by preceding events or natural causes — **de·ter·min·ist** \-nist\ *n or adj*

de·ter·rence \di-ˈtər-əns\ *n* : the inhibition of criminal behavior by fear esp. of punishment

de·ter·rent \-ənt\ *adj* 1 : serving to deter 2 : relating to deterrence — **deterrent** *n*

de·test \di-ˈtest\ *vb* [L *detestari,* lit., to curse while calling a deity to witness, fr. *de-* from + *testari* to call to witness, fr. *testis* witness] : LOATHE, HATE — **de·test·able** *adj* — **de·tes·ta·tion** \ˌdē-ˌtes-ˈtā-shən\ *n*

de·throne \di-ˈthrōn\ *vb* : to remove from a throne : DEPOSE — **de·throne·ment** *n*

det·o·nate \ˈde-tᵊn-ˌāt\ *vb* **-nat·ed; -nat·ing** : to explode or cause to explode with violence — **det·o·na·tion** \ˌde-tᵊn-ˈā-shən\ *n*

det·o·na·tor \'de-t³n-ˌā-tər\ *n* : a device for detonating an explosive

¹de·tour \'dē-ˌtu̇r\ *n* : an indirect way replacing part of a route

²detour *vb* : to go by detour

de·tox \'dē-ˌtäks, di-ˈtäks\ *n* : detoxification from an intoxicating or addictive substance — **detox** *vb*

de·tox·i·fy \dē-ˈtäk-sə-ˌfī\ *vb* **-fied; -fy·ing** **1** : to remove a poison or toxin or the effect of such from **2** : to free (as a drug user) from an intoxicating or addictive substance or from dependence on it — **de·tox·i·fi·ca·tion** \dē-ˌtäk-sə-fə-ˈkā-shən\ *n*

de·tract \di-ˈtrakt\ *vb* **1** : to take away or diminish the value or effect of something — **de·trac·tion** \-ˈtrak-shən\ *n* — **de·trac·tor** \-ˈtrak-tər\ *n*

de·train \dē-ˈtrān\ *vb* : to leave or cause to leave a railroad train

det·ri·ment \'de-trə-mənt\ *n* : INJURY, DAMAGE; *also* : a cause of injury or damage — **det·ri·men·tal** \ˌde-trə-ˈment-ᵊl\ *adj* — **det·ri·men·tal·ly** *adv*

de·tri·tus \di-ˈtrī-təs\ *n, pl* **de·tri·tus** : fragments resulting from disintegration (as of rocks) : DEBRIS

deuce \'düs, 'dyüs\ *n* **1** : a two in cards or dice **2** : a tie in a tennis game with both sides at 40 **3** : DEVIL — used chiefly as a mild oath

Deut *abbr* Deuteronomy

deu·te·ri·um \dü-ˈtir-ē-əm, dyü-\ *n* : an isotope of hydrogen that has twice the mass of ordinary hydrogen

Deu·ter·on·o·my \ˌdü-tə-ˈrä-nə-mē, ˌdyü-\ *n* — see BIBLE table

deut·sche mark \'dȯi-chə-ˌmärk\ *n* : a former basic monetary unit of Germany

dev *abbr* deviation

de·val·ue \dē-ˈval-yü\ *vb* : to reduce the international exchange value of ⟨∼ a currency⟩ — **de·val·u·a·tion** \-ˌval-yə-ˈwā-shən\ *n*

dev·as·tate \'de-və-ˌstāt\ *vb* **-tat·ed; -tat·ing** **1** : to bring to ruin **2** : to reduce to chaos or helplessness — **dev·as·tat·ing·ly** *adv* — **dev·as·ta·tion** \ˌde-və-ˈstā-shən\ *n*

de·vel·op \di-ˈve-ləp\ *vb* **1** : to unfold gradually or in detail **2** : to place (exposed photographic material) in chemicals to produce a visible image **3** : to bring out the possibilities of **4** : to make more available or usable ⟨∼ land⟩ **5** : to acquire gradually ⟨∼ a taste for olives⟩ **6** : to go through a natural process of growth, differentiation, or evolution **7** : to come into being gradually — **de·vel·op·er** *n* — **de·vel·op·ment** *n* — **de·vel·op·men·tal** \-ˌve-lə-ˈmen-tᵊl\ *adj* — **de·vel·op·men·tal·ly** \-tᵊl-ē\ *adv*

de·vi·ant \'dē-vē-ənt\ *adj* : deviating esp. from some accepted norm ⟨∼ behavior⟩ — **de·vi·ance** \-əns\ *n* — **de·vi·an·cy** \-ən-sē\ *n* — **deviant** *n*

de·vi·ate \'dē-vē-ˌāt\ *vb* **-at·ed; -at·ing** [LL *deviare*, fr. L *de-* from + *via* way] : to turn aside from a course, standard, principle, or topic — **de·vi·ate** \-vē-ət, -vē-ˌāt\ *n* — **de·vi·a·tion** \ˌdē-vē-ˈā-shən\ *n*

de·vice \di-ˈvīs\ *n* **1** : SCHEME, STRATAGEM **2** : a piece of equipment or a mechanism for a special purpose **3** : DESIRE, INCLINATION ⟨left to my own ∼s⟩ **4** : an emblematic design

¹dev·il \'de-vəl\ *n* [ME *devel*, fr. OE *dēofol*, fr. LL *diabolus*, fr. Gk *diabolos*, lit., slanderer, fr. *diaballein* to throw across, slander, fr. *dia-* across + *ballein* to throw] **1** *often cap* : the personal supreme spirit of evil **2** : DEMON **3** : a wicked person **4** : an energetic, reckless, or dashing person **5** : FELLOW ⟨poor ∼⟩ ⟨lucky ∼⟩

²devil *vb* **-iled** *or* **-illed; -il·ing** *or* **-il·ling** **1** : to season highly ⟨∼ed eggs⟩ **2** : TEASE, ANNOY

dev·il·ish \'de-və-lish\ *adj* **1** : befitting a devil : EVIL; *also* : MISCHIEVOUS **2** : EXTREME ⟨in a ∼ hurry⟩ — **dev·il·ish·ly** *adv* — **dev·il·ish·ness** *n*

dev·il·ment \'de-vəl-mənt, -ˌment\ *n* : MISCHIEF

dev·il·ry \-rē\ *or* **dev·il·try** \-trē\ *n, pl* **-il·ries** *or* **-il·tries** **1** : action performed with the help of the devil **2** : MISCHIEF

de·vi·ous \'dē-vē-əs\ *adj* **1** : deviating from a straight line : ROUNDABOUT **2** : ERRANT **3** **3** : TRICKY, CUNNING

¹de·vise \di-ˈvīz\ *vb* **de·vised; de·vis·ing** [ME, fr. AF *deviser* to divide, distinguish, invent, fr. VL *divisare*, fr. L *dividere* to divide] **1** : INVENT **2** : PLOT **3** : to give (real estate) by will

²devise *n* **1** : a disposing of real property by will **2** : a will

or clause of a will disposing of real property **3** : property given by will

de·vi·tal·ize \dē-ˈvīt-ᵊl-ˌīz\ *vb* : to deprive of life or vitality

de·void \di-ˈvȯid\ *adj* : being without : VOID ⟨a book ∼ of interest⟩

de·voir \də-ˈvwär\ *n* **1** : DUTY **2** : a formal act of civility or respect

de·volve \di-ˈvälv\ *vb* **de·volved; de·volv·ing** : to pass (as rights or responsibility) from one to another usu. by succession or transmission — **dev·o·lu·tion** \ˌde-və-ˈlü-shən, ˌdē-\ *n*

De·vo·ni·an \di-ˈvō-nē-ən\ *adj* : of, relating to, or being the period of the Paleozoic era between the Silurian and the Mississippian — **Devonian** *n*

de·vote \di-ˈvōt\ *vb* **de·vot·ed; de·vot·ing** **1** : to commit to wholly or chiefly **2** : to set apart for a special purpose : DEDICATE

de·vot·ed \-ˈvō-təd\ *adj* : characterized by loyalty and devotion : FAITHFUL

dev·o·tee \ˌde-və-ˈtē, -ˈtā\ *n* : an ardent follower, supporter, or enthusiast

de·vo·tion \di-ˈvō-shən\ *n* **1** : religious fervor **2** : an act of prayer or private worship — usu. used in pl. **3** : a religious exercise for private use **4** : the fact or state of being dedicated and loyal ⟨∼ to music⟩; *also* : the act of devoting — **de·vo·tion·al** \-shə-nəl\ *adj*

de·vour \di-ˈvau̇(-ə)r\ *vb* **1** : to eat up greedily or ravenously **2** : WASTE, ANNIHILATE **3** : to enjoy avidly ⟨∼ a book⟩ — **de·vour·er** *n*

de·vout \di-ˈvau̇t\ *adj* **1** : devoted to religion : PIOUS **2** : expressing devotion or piety **3** : EARNEST, SERIOUS ⟨a ∼ baseball fan⟩ — **de·vout·ly** *adv* — **de·vout·ness** *n*

dew \'dü, 'dyü\ *n* : moisture that condenses on the surfaces of cool bodies at night — **dewy** *adj*

dew·ber·ry \'dü-ˌber-ē, 'dyü-\ *n* : any of several sweet edible berries related to and resembling blackberries; *also* : a trailing bramble bearing these

dew·claw \-ˌklȯ\ *n* : a digit on the foot of a mammal that does not reach the ground; *also* : its claw or hoof

dew·lap \-ˌlap\ *n* : loose skin hanging under the neck of an animal

dew point *n* : the temperature at which the moisture in the air begins to condense

dex·ter·i·ty \dek-ˈster-ə-tē\ *n, pl* **-ties** **1** : mental skill or quickness **2** : readiness and grace in physical activity; *esp* : skill and ease in using the hands

dex·ter·ous \'dek-strəs\ *adj* **1** : CLEVER **2** : done with skillfulness **3** : skillful and competent with the hands — **dex·ter·ous·ly** *adv*

dex·trose \'dek-ˌstrōs\ *n* : the naturally occurring form of glucose found in plants and blood

DFC *abbr* Distinguished Flying Cross

dg *abbr* decigram

DG *abbr* **1** [LL *Dei gratia*] by the grace of God **2** director general

DH \ˌdē-ˈāch\ *n* : DESIGNATED HITTER

dhow \'dau̇\ *n* : an Arab sailing ship usu. having a long overhang forward and a high poop

DI *abbr* drill instructor

dia *abbr* diameter

di·a·be·tes \ˌdī-ə-ˈbē-tēz, -təs\ *n* : an abnormal state marked by passage of excessive amounts of urine; *esp* : one (**diabetes mel·li·tus** \-ˈme-lə-təs\) characterized by deficient insulin, by excess sugar in the blood and urine, and by thirst, hunger, and loss of weight — **di·a·bet·ic** \-ˈbe-tik\ *adj or n*

di·a·bol·i·cal \ˌdī-ə-ˈbä-li-kəl\ *or* **di·a·bol·ic** \-lik\ *adj* : DEVILISH ⟨a ∼ plot⟩ — **di·a·bol·i·cal·ly** \-k(ə-)lē\ *adv*

di·a·crit·ic \ˌdī-ə-ˈkri-tik\ *n* : a mark accompanying a letter and indicating a sound value different from that of the same letter when unmarked — **di·a·crit·i·cal** \-ti-kəl\ *adj*

di·a·dem \'dī-ə-ˌdem\ *n* : CROWN; *esp* : a royal headband

di·aer·e·sis *or* **di·er·e·sis** \dī-ˈer-ə-səs\ *n, pl* **-e·ses** \-ˌsēz\ : a mark ¨ placed over a vowel to show that it is pronounced in a separate syllable (as in *naïve*)

diag *abbr* **1** diagonal **2** diagram

di·ag·no·sis \ˌdī-ig-ˈnō-səs\ *n, pl* **-no·ses** \-ˌsēz\ : the art or act of identifying a disease from its signs and symptoms; *also* : the decision reached by diagnosis — **di·ag·nose** \'dī-ig-ˌnōs\ *vb* — **di·ag·nos·tic** \ˌdī-ig-ˈnäs-tik\ *adj* — **di·ag·nos·ti·cian** \-ˌnäs-ˈti-shən\ *n*

¹**di·ag·o·nal** \dī-'a-gə-nəl\ *adj* **1** : extending from one corner to the opposite corner in a 4-sided figure **2** : running in a slanting direction ⟨∼ stripes⟩ **3** : having slanting markings or parts ⟨a ∼ weave⟩ — **di·ag·o·nal·ly** *adv*

²**diagonal** *n* **1** : a diagonal line **2** : a diagonal row, pattern, or direction **3** : SLASH 3

¹**di·a·gram** \'dī-ə-ˌgram\ *n* : a design and esp. a drawing that makes something easier to understand — **di·a·gram·ma·ble** \-ˌgra-mə-bəl\ *adj* — **di·a·gram·mat·ic** \ˌdī-ə-grə-'ma-tik\ *adj* — **di·a·gram·mat·i·cal·ly** \-ti-k(ə-)lē\ *adv*

²**diagram** *vb* **-grammed** *or* **-gramed** \-ˌgramd\; **-gram·ming** *or* **-gram·ing** : to represent by a diagram

¹**di·al** \'dī(-ə)l\ *n* [ME *dyal*, fr. ML *dialis* clock wheel revolving daily, fr. L *dies* day] **1** : the face of a sundial **2** : the face of a timepiece **3** : a face with a pointer and numbers that indicate something ⟨the ∼ of a gauge⟩ **4** : a device used for making electrical connections or for regulating operation (as of a radio)

²**dial** *vb* **di·aled** *or* **di·alled**; **di·al·ing** *or* **di·al·ling** **1** : to manipulate a dial so as to operate or select **2** : to make a telephone call or connection

³**dial** *abbr* dialect

di·a·lect \'dī-ə-ˌlekt\ *n* : a regional variety of a language

di·a·lec·tic \ˌdī-ə-'lek-tik\ *n* : the process or art of reasoning by discussion of conflicting ideas; *also* : the tension between opposing elements — **di·a·lec·ti·cal** \-ti-kəl\ *adj*

dialog box *n* : a window on a computer screen for choosing options or inputting information

di·a·logue \'dī-ə-ˌlòg\ *n* **1** : a conversation between two or more parties **2** : the parts of a literary or dramatic work that represent conversation

di·al·y·sis \dī-'a-lə-səs\ *n, pl* **-y·ses** \-ˌsēz\ **1** : the separation of substances from solution by means of their unequal diffusion through semipermeable membranes **2** : the medical procedure of removing blood from an artery, purifying it by dialysis, and returning it to a vein

diam *abbr* diameter

di·am·e·ter \dī-'a-mə-tər\ *n* [ME *diametre*, fr. MF, fr. L *diametros*, fr. Gk, fr. *dia-* through + *metron* measure] **1** : a straight line passing through the center of a figure or body; *esp* : one that divides a circle in half **2** : the length of a diameter

di·a·met·ric \ˌdī-ə-'me-trik\ *or* **di·a·met·ri·cal** \-tri-kəl\ *adj* **1** : of, relating to, or constituting a diameter **2** : completely opposed or opposite — **di·a·met·ri·cal·ly** \-k(ə-)lē\ *adv*

di·a·mond \'dī-mənd, 'dī-ə-\ *n* **1** : a hard brilliant mineral that consists of crystalline carbon and is used as a gem **2** : a flat figure having four equal sides, two acute angles, and two obtuse angles **3** : any of a suit of playing cards marked with a red diamond **4** : INFIELD; *also* : the entire playing field in baseball

di·a·mond·back rattlesnake \-ˌbak-\ *n* : either of two large and deadly rattlesnakes of the southern U.S.

di·an·thus \dī-'an-thəs\ *n* : ¹PINK 1

di·a·pa·son \ˌdī-ə-'pā-z²n, -s²n\ *n* **1** : the organ stop governing the flue pipes that form the primary basis of organ tone **2** : the entire range of musical tones

¹**di·a·per** \'dī-pər, 'dī-ə-\ *n* **1** : a cotton or linen fabric woven in a simple geometric pattern **2** : a garment for a baby drawn up between the legs and fastened about the waist

²**diaper** *vb* **1** : to ornament with diaper designs **2** : to put a diaper on

di·aph·a·nous \dī-'a-fə-nəs\ *adj* : of so fine a texture as to be transparent

di·a·pho·ret·ic \ˌdī-ə-fə-'re-tik\ *adj* : having the power to increase perspiration — **diaphoretic** *n*

di·a·phragm \'dī-ə-ˌfram\ *n* **1** : a sheet of muscle between the chest and abdominal cavities of a mammal **2** : a vibrating disk (as in a microphone) **3** : a cup-shaped device usu. of thin rubber fitted over the uterine cervix to act as a mechanical contraceptive barrier — **di·a·phrag·mat·ic** \ˌdī-ə-frəg-'ma-tik, -ˌfrag-\ *adj*

di·a·rist \'dī-ə-rist\ *n* : one who keeps a diary

di·a·ris·tic \ˌdī-ə-'ris-tik\ *adj* : of, relating to, or characteristic of a diary

di·ar·rhea \ˌdī-ə-'rē-ə\ *n* [ME *diaria*, fr. LL *diarrhoea*, fr. Gk *diarrhoia*, fr. *diarrhein* to flow through, fr. *dia-* through + *rhein* to flow] : abnormally frequent and watery bowel movements — **di·ar·rhe·al** \-'rē-əl\ *adj*

di·ar·rhoea *chiefly Brit var of* DIARRHEA

di·a·ry \'dī-ə-rē\ *n, pl* **-ries** : a daily record esp. of personal experiences; *also* : a book used as a diary

di·as·po·ra \dī-'as-pə-rə\ *n* **1** *cap* : the settling of scattered colonies of Jews outside Palestine after the Babylonian exile **2** *cap* : the Jews living outside Palestine or modern Israel **3** : the migration or scattering of a people away from an ancestral homeland

di·as·to·le \dī-'as-tə-(ˌ)lē\ *n* : the stretching of the chambers of the heart during which they fill with blood — **di·a·stol·ic** \ˌdī-ə-'stä-lik\ *adj*

di·a·ther·my \'dī-ə-ˌthər-mē\ *n* : the generation of heat in tissue by electric currents for medical purposes

di·a·tom \'dī-ə-ˌtäm\ *n* : any of a class of planktonic one-celled or colonial algae with skeletons of silica

di·atom·ic \ˌdī-ə-'tä-mik\ *adj* : having two atoms in the molecule

di·a·tribe \'dī-ə-ˌtrīb\ *n* : biting or abusive speech or writing

di·az·e·pam \dī-'a-zə-ˌpam\ *n* : a tranquilizer used esp. to relieve anxiety, tension, and muscle spasms

dib·ble \'di-bəl\ *n* : a pointed hand tool for making holes (as for planting bulbs) in the ground — **dibble** *vb*

¹**dice** \'dīs\ *n, pl* **dice** : DIE 1

²**dice** *vb* **diced**; **dic·ing** **1** : to cut into small cubes ⟨∼ carrots⟩ **2** : to play games with dice

di·chot·o·my \dī-'kä-tə-mē\ *n, pl* **-mies** : a division or the process of dividing into two esp. mutually exclusive or contradictory groups — **di·chot·o·mous** \-məs\ *adj*

dick·er \'di-kər\ *vb* : BARGAIN, HAGGLE

dick·ey *or* **dicky** \'di-kē\ *n, pl* **dickeys** *or* **dick·ies** : a small fabric insert worn to fill in the neckline

di·cot·y·le·don \ˌdī-ˌkä-tə-'lēd-²n\ *n* : any of a group of seed plants having an embryo with two cotyledons — **di·cot·y·le·don·ous** *adj*

dict *abbr* dictionary

¹**dic·tate** \'dik-ˌtāt\ *vb* **dic·tat·ed**; **dic·tat·ing** **1** : to speak or read for a person to transcribe or for a machine to record **2** : COMMAND, ORDER — **dic·ta·tion** \dik-'tā-shən\ *n*

²**dic·tate** \'dik-ˌtāt\ *n* : an authoritative rule, prescription, or injunction : COMMAND ⟨the ∼s of conscience⟩

dic·ta·tor \'dik-ˌtā-tər\ *n* **1** : a person ruling absolutely and often brutally and oppressively **2** : one that dictates

dic·ta·to·ri·al \ˌdik-tə-'tòr-ē-əl\ *adj* : of, relating to, or characteristic of a dictator or a dictatorship

dic·ta·tor·ship \dik-'tā-tər-ˌship, 'dik-ˌtā-\ *n* **1** : the office of a dictator **2** : autocratic rule, control, or leadership **3** : a government or country in which absolute power is held by a dictator or a small clique

dic·tion \'dik-shən\ *n* **1** : choice of words esp. with regard to correctness, clearness, or effectiveness : WORDING **2** : ENUNCIATION

dic·tio·nary \'dik-shə-ˌner-ē\ *n, pl* **-nar·ies** : a reference book containing words usu. alphabetically arranged along with information about their forms, pronunciations, functions, etymologies, meanings, and syntactical and idiomatic uses

dic·tum \'dik-təm\ *n, pl* **dic·ta** \-tə\ *also* **dictums** : a noteworthy, formal, or authoritative statement or observation

did *past of* DO

di·dac·tic \dī-'dak-tik\ *adj* **1** : intended to instruct, inform, or teach a moral lesson **2** : making moral observations

di·do \'dī-dō\ *n, pl* **didoes** *or* **didos** : a mischievous act : PRANK

¹**die** \'dī\ *vb* **died**; **dy·ing** \'dī-iŋ\ [ME *dien*, fr. or akin to ON *deyja* to die] **1** : to stop living : EXPIRE **2** : to pass out of existence ⟨a *dying* race⟩ **3** : SUBSIDE 4 ⟨the wind *died* down⟩ **4** : to long keenly ⟨*dying* to go⟩ **5** : STOP ⟨the motor *died*⟩

²**die** \'dī\ *n* [ME *dee*, fr. AF *dé*] **1** *pl* **dice** \'dīs\ : a small cube marked on each face with one to six spots and used usu. in pairs in games and gambling **2** *pl* **dies** \'dīz\ : a device used to shape, finish, or impress an object

die·hard \'dī-ˌhärd\ *n* : one who is strongly devoted or determined — **die–hard** *adj*

dieresis *var of* DIAERESIS

die·sel \'dē-zəl, -səl\ *n* **1** : DIESEL ENGINE **2** : a vehicle driven by a diesel engine **3** : DIESEL FUEL

diesel engine *n* : an internal combustion engine in whose cylinders air is compressed to a temperature sufficiently high to ignite the fuel

diesel fuel *n* : a heavy mineral oil used as fuel in diesel engines

die·sel·ing \'dē-zə-liŋ\ *n* : the continued operation of an internal combustion engine after the ignition has been turned off

¹di·et \'dī-ət\ *n* [ME *diete*, fr. AF, fr. L *diaeta*, fr. Gk *diaita*, lit., manner of living, fr. *diaitasthai* to lead one's life] **1** : food and drink regularly consumed : FARE **2** : an allowance of food prescribed for a special reason (as to lose weight) — **di·e·tary** \-ə-ˌter-ē\ *adj or n*

²diet *vb* : to eat or cause to eat or drink less or according to a prescribed rule — **di·et·er** *n*

dietary supplement *n* : a product taken orally that contains ingredients (as vitamins or amino acids) intended to supplement one's diet

di·e·tet·ics \ˌdī-ə-'te-tiks\ *n sing or pl* : the science or art of applying the principles of nutrition to diet — **di·e·tet·ic** *adj*

di·e·ti·tian *or* **di·e·ti·cian** \ˌdī-ə-'ti-shən\ *n* : a specialist in dietetics

dif *or* **diff** *abbr* difference

dif·fer \'di-fər\ *vb* **dif·fered; dif·fer·ing** **1** : to be unlike **2** : VARY **3** : DISAGREE

dif·fer·ence \'di-frəns, 'di-fə-rəns\ *n* **1** : UNLIKENESS ⟨~ in their looks⟩ **2** : distinction or discrimination in preference **3** : DISAGREEMENT; *also* : an instance or cause of disagreement ⟨unable to settle their ~s⟩ **4** : the amount by which one number or quantity differs from another

dif·fer·ent \'di-frənt, 'di-fə-rənt\ *adj* **1** : unlike in nature or quality **2** : DISTINCT ⟨~ age groups⟩; *also* : VARIOUS ⟨~ members of the club⟩ **3** : ANOTHER ⟨try a ~ channel⟩ **4** : UNUSUAL, SPECIAL — **dif·fer·ent·ly** *adv*

¹dif·fer·en·tial \ˌdi-fə-'ren-chəl\ *adj* : showing, creating, or relating to a difference

²differential *n* **1** : the amount or degree by which things differ **2** : an arrangement of gears in an automobile that allows one wheel to turn faster than another (as in rounding curves)

differential gear *n* : DIFFERENTIAL 2

dif·fer·en·ti·ate \ˌdi-fə-'ren-chē-ˌāt\ *vb* **-at·ed; -at·ing** **1** : to make or become different **2** : to attain a specialized adult form and function during development **3** : to recognize or state the difference ⟨~ between them⟩ — **dif·fer·en·ti·a·tion** \-ˌren-chē-'ā-shən\ *n*

dif·fi·cult \'di-fi-(ˌ)kəlt\ *adj* **1** : hard to do or make ⟨a ~ climb⟩ **2** : hard to understand or deal with ⟨~ reading⟩ ⟨a ~ child⟩

dif·fi·cul·ty \-(ˌ)kəl-tē\ *n, pl* **-ties** [ME *difficulte*, fr. AF *difficulté*, fr. L *difficilis* not easy, fr. *dis-* not + *facilis* easy] **1** : difficult nature ⟨the ~ of a task⟩ **2** : DISAGREEMENT ⟨settled their *difficulties*⟩ **3** : OBSTACLE ⟨overcome *difficulties*⟩ **4** : TROUBLE ⟨in financial *difficulties*⟩ ◆ *Synonyms* HARDSHIP, RIGOR, VICISSITUDE

dif·fi·dent \'di-fə-dənt\ *adj* **1** : lacking confidence **2** : RESERVED **1** — **dif·fi·dence** \-dəns\ *n* — **dif·fi·dent·ly** *adv*

dif·frac·tion \di-'frak-shən\ *n* : the bending or spreading of waves (as of light) esp. when passing through narrow slits

¹dif·fuse \di-'fyüs\ *adj* **1** : VERBOSE, WORDY ⟨~ writing⟩ **2** : not concentrated or localized ⟨~ light⟩

²dif·fuse \di-'fyüz\ *vb* **dif·fused; dif·fus·ing** **1** : to pour out or spread widely **2** : to undergo or cause to undergo diffusion **3** : to break up light by diffusion

dif·fu·sion \di-'fyü-zhən\ *n* **1** : a diffusing or a being diffused **2** : movement of particles (as of a gas) from a region of high to one of lower concentration **3** : the reflection of light from a rough surface or the passage of light through a translucent material

¹dig \'dig\ *vb* **dug** \'dəg\; **dig·ging** **1** : to turn up the soil (as with a spade) **2** : to hollow out or form by removing earth ⟨~ a hole⟩ **3** : to uncover or seek by turning up earth ⟨~ potatoes⟩ **4** : DISCOVER ⟨~ up information⟩ **5** : POKE, THRUST ⟨~ a person in the ribs⟩ **6** : to work hard **7** : UNDERSTAND, APPRECIATE; *also* : LIKE, ADMIRE

²dig *n* **1** : THRUST, POKE; *also* : a cutting remark : GIBE **2** *pl* : living or working accommodations

³dig *abbr* digest

¹di·gest \'dī-ˌjest\ *n* : a summarized or shortened version esp. of a literary work

²di·gest \dī-'jest, də-\ *vb* **1** : to think over and arrange in

the mind **2** : to convert (food) into simpler forms that can be absorbed by the body **3** : to compress into a short summary — **di·gest·ibil·i·ty** \-ˌjes-tə-'bi-lə-tē\ *n* — **di·gest·ible** *adj* — **di·ges·tion** \-'jes-chən\ *n* — **di·ges·tive** \-'jes-tiv\ *adj*

di·ges·tif \ˌdē-zhes-'tēf\ *n* : an alcoholic drink taken after a meal

dig in *vb* **1** : to take a defensive stand esp. by digging trenches **2** : to firmly set to work **3** : to begin eating

dig·it \'di-jət\ *n* [ME, fr. L *digitus* finger, toe] **1** : any of the Arabic numerals 1 to 9 and usu. the symbol 0 **2** : FINGER, TOE

dig·i·tal \'di-jə-tᵊl\ *adj* **1** : of, relating to, or done with a finger or toe **2** : of, relating to, or using calculation by numerical methods or by discrete units **3** : relating to or employing communications signals in the form of binary digits ⟨a ~ broadcast⟩ **4** : providing a readout in numerical digits ⟨a ~ watch⟩ **5** : ELECTRONIC; *also* : characterized by computerized technology ⟨the ~ age⟩ — **dig·i·tal·ly** *adv*

digital camera *n* : a camera that records images as digital data instead of on film

dig·i·tal·is \ˌdi-jə-'ta-ləs\ *n* : a drug from the common foxglove that is a powerful heart stimulant; *also* : FOXGLOVE

digital versatile disc *n* : DVD

digital video disc *n* : DVD

dig·ni·fied \'dig-nə-ˌfīd\ *adj* : showing or expressing dignity

dig·ni·fy \-ˌfī\ *vb* **-fied; -fy·ing** : to give dignity, distinction, or attention to

dig·ni·tary \'dig-nə-ˌter-ē\ *n, pl* **-tar·ies** : a person of high position or honor

dig·ni·ty \'dig-nə-tē\ *n, pl* **-ties** **1** : the quality or state of being worthy, honored, or esteemed **2** : high rank, office, or position **3** : formal reserve of manner, language, or appearance

di·graph \'dī-ˌgraf\ *n* : a group of two successive letters whose phonetic value is a single sound (as *ea* in *bread*)

di·gress \dī-'gres, də-\ *vb* : to turn aside esp. from the main subject or argument — **di·gres·sion** \-'gre-shən\ *n* — **di·gres·sive** \-'gre-siv\ *adj*

Di·jon mustard \'dē-ˌzhän-, di-'zhän-\ *n* : a mustard made from dark mustard seeds, white wine, and spices

dike \'dīk\ *n* : a bank of earth constructed to control water : LEVEE

dil *abbr* dilute

di·lap·i·dat·ed \də-'la-pə-ˌdā-təd\ *adj* : fallen into partial ruin or decay — **di·lap·i·da·tion** \-ˌla-pə-'dā-shən\ *n*

di·late \dī-'lāt, 'dī-ˌlāt\ *vb* **di·lat·ed; di·lat·ing** : SWELL, DISTEND, EXPAND — **dil·a·ta·tion** \ˌdi-lə-'tā-shən\ *n* — **di·la·tion** \dī-'lā-shən\ *n*

dil·a·to·ry \'di-lə-ˌtȯr-ē\ *adj* **1** : DELAYING **2** : TARDY, SLOW

di·lem·ma \də-'le-mə\ *n* **1** : a usu. undesirable or unpleasant choice; *also* : a situation involving such a choice **2** : PREDICAMENT

dil·et·tante \ˌdi-lə-'tänt, -'tänt\ *n, pl* **-tantes** *or* **-tan·ti** \-'tän-tē, -'tan-\ [It, fr. prp. of *dilettare* to delight, fr. L *dilectare*] : a person having a superficial interest in an art or a branch of knowledge

dil·i·gent \'di-lə-jənt\ *adj* : characterized by steady, earnest, and energetic effort : PAINSTAKING — **dil·i·gence** \-jəns\ *n* — **dil·i·gent·ly** *adv*

dill \'dil\ *n* : an herb related to the carrot with aromatic leaves and seeds used as a seasoning and in pickles

dil·ly \'di-lē\ *n, pl* **dil·lies** : one that is remarkable or outstanding

dil·ly·dal·ly \'di-lē-ˌda-lē\ *vb* : to waste time by loitering or delaying

¹di·lute \dī-'lüt, də-\ *vb* **di·lut·ed; di·lut·ing** : to lessen the consistency or strength of by mixing with something else — **di·lu·tion** \-'lü-shən\ *n*

²dilute *adj* : DILUTED, WEAK

¹dim \'dim\ *adj* **dim·mer; dim·mest** **1** : LUSTERLESS, DULL ⟨~ colors⟩ **2** : not bright or distinct : OBSCURE, FAINT **3** : not seeing or understanding clearly — **dim·ly** *adv* — **dim·ness** *n*

²dim *vb* **dimmed; dim·ming** **1** : to make or become dim or lusterless **2** : to reduce the light from

³dim *abbr* **1** dimension **2** diminished **3** diminutive

dime \'dīm\ *n* [ME, tenth part, tithe, fr. AF *disme*, *dime*, fr.

L *decima,* fr. fem. of *decimus* tenth, fr. *decem* ten] : a U.S. coin worth ¹/₁₀ dollar

di·men·sion \də-'men-chən, dī-\ *n* **1** : the physical property of length, breadth, or thickness; *also* : a measure of this **2** : EXTENT, SCOPE, PROPORTIONS — usu. used in pl. — **di·men·sion·al** \-'men-chə-nəl\ *adj* — **di·men·sion·al·i·ty** \-,men-chə-'na-lə-tē\ *n*

di·min·ish \də-'mi-nish\ *vb* **1** : to make less or cause to appear less **2** : BELITTLE **3** : DWINDLE **4** : TAPER — **dim·i·nu·tion** \,di-mə-'nü-shən, -'nyü-\ *n*

di·min·u·en·do \də-,min-yə-'wen-dō\ *adv or adj* : DECRESCENDO

¹di·min·u·tive \də-'min-yə-tiv\ *n* **1** : a diminutive word or affix **2** : a diminutive individual

²diminutive *adj* **1** : indicating small size and sometimes the state or quality of being lovable, pitiable, or contemptible ⟨the ∼ suffixes *-ette* and *-ling*⟩ **2** : extremely small : TINY

dim·i·ty \'di-mə-tē\ *n, pl* **-ties** : a thin usu. corded cotton fabric

dim·mer \'di-mər\ *n* : a device for controlling the amount of light from an electric lighting unit

di·mor·phic \(,)dī-'mȯr-fik\ *adj* : occurring in two distinct forms — **di·mor·phism** \-,fi-zəm\ *n*

¹dim·ple \'dim-pəl\ *n* : a small depression esp. in the cheek or chin

²dimple *vb* **dim·pled; dim·pling** : to form dimples (as in smiling)

din \'din\ *n* : a loud confused mixture of noises

di·nar \di-'när\ *n* **1** — see MONEY table **2** — see *rial* at MONEY table

dine \'dīn\ *vb* **dined; din·ing** [ME, fr. AF *disner, diner* to eat, have a meal, fr. VL *disjejunare* to break one's fast, ultim. fr. L *jejunus* fasting] **1** : to eat dinner **2** : to give a dinner to

din·er \'dī-nər\ *n* **1** : one that dines **2** : a railroad dining car **3** : a restaurant usu. resembling a dining car

di·nette \dī-'net\ *n* : an alcove or small room used for dining

ding \'diŋ\ *vb* : to cause minor damage to a surface — **ding** *n*

din·ghy \'diŋ-ē\ *n, pl* **dinghies** **1** : a small boat **2** : LIFE RAFT

din·gle \'diŋ-gəl\ *n* : a small wooded valley

din·go \'diŋ-gō\ *n, pl* **dingoes** : a reddish brown wild dog of Australia

din·gus \'diŋ-gəs, -əs\ *n* : DOODAD

din·gy \'diŋ-jē\ *adj* **din·gi·er; -est** : DIRTY, UNCLEAN; *also* : SHABBY — **din·gi·ness** *n*

dink \'diŋk\ *n, often all cap* [double income, no kids] : a couple with two incomes and no children; *also* : a member of such a couple

din·ky \'diŋ-kē\ *adj* **din·ki·er; -est** : overly small ⟨a ∼ apartment⟩

din·ner \'di-nər\ *n* : the main meal of the day; *also* : a formal banquet

din·ner·ware \'di-nər-,wer\ *n* : tableware other than flatware

di·no \'dī-nō\ *n, pl* **dinos** : DINOSAUR

di·no·fla·gel·late \,dī-nō-'fla-jə-lət, -,lāt\ *n* : any of an order of planktonic plantlike unicellular flagellates of which some cause red tide

di·no·saur \'dī-nə-,sȯr\ *n* [ultim. fr. Gk *deinos* terrifying + *sauros* lizard] : any of a group of extinct long-tailed Mesozoic reptiles often of huge size

dint \'dint\ *n* **1** : FORCE ⟨by ∼ of sheer grit⟩ **2** : DENT

di·o·cese \'dī-ə-səs, -,sēz, -,sēs\ *n, pl* **-ces·es** \-s-səz, -,sē-zəz, -,sē-səz\ : the territorial jurisdiction of a bishop — **di·oc·e·san** \dī-'ä-sə-sən, ,dī-ə-'sē-z²n\ *adj or n*

di·ode \'dī-,ōd\ *n* : an electronic device with two electrodes or terminals used esp. as a rectifier

di·ox·in \dī-'äk-sən\ *n* : a persistent toxic hydrocarbon that occurs esp. as a by-product of industrial processes and waste incineration

¹dip \'dip\ *vb* **dipped; dip·ping** **1** : to plunge temporarily or partially under the surface (as of a liquid) **2** : to thrust in a way to suggest immersion **3** : to scoop up or out : LADLE **4** : to lower and then raise quickly ⟨∼ a flag in salute⟩ **5** : to drop or slope down esp. suddenly ⟨the moon *dipped* below the crest⟩ **6** : to decrease moderately and usu. temporarily ⟨prices *dipped*⟩ **7** : to reach inside

or as if inside or below a surface ⟨*dipped* into their savings⟩ **8** : to delve casually into something; *esp* : to read superficially ⟨∼ into a book⟩

²dip *n* **1** : an act of dipping; *esp* : a short swim **2** : inclination downward : DROP **3** : something obtained by or used in dipping **4** : a sauce or soft mixture into which food may be dipped **5** : a liquid into which something may be dipped (as for cleansing or coloring)

diph·the·ria \dif-'thir-ē-ə\ *n* : an acute contagious bacterial disease marked by fever and by coating of the air passages with a membrane that interferes with breathing

diph·thong \'dif-,thȯŋ, 'dip-\ *n* : two vowel sounds joined in one syllable to form one speech sound (as *ou* in *out*)

dip·loid \'di-,plȯid\ *adj* : having two haploid sets of chromosomes ⟨∼ somatic cells⟩ — **diploid** *n*

di·plo·ma \də-'plō-mə\ *n* : an official record of graduation from or of a degree conferred by a school

di·plo·ma·cy \də-'plō-mə-sē\ *n* **1** : the art and practice of conducting negotiations between nations **2** : TACT

dip·lo·mat \'di-plə-,mat\ *n* : one employed or skilled in diplomacy — **dip·lo·mat·ic** \,di-plə-'ma-tik\ *adj*

di·plo·ma·tist \də-'plō-mə-tist\ *n* : DIPLOMAT

dip·per \'di-pər\ *n* **1** : any of a genus of birds that are related to the thrushes and are skilled in diving **2** : something (as a ladle or scoop) that dips or is used for dipping **3** *cap* : BIG DIPPER **4** *cap* : LITTLE DIPPER

dipper 2

dip·so·ma·nia \,dip-sə-'mā-nē-ə\ *n* : an uncontrollable craving for alcoholic liquors — **dip·so·ma·ni·ac** \-nē-,ak\ *n*

dip·stick \'dip-,stik\ *n* : a graduated rod for indicating depth

dip·ter·an \'dip-tə-rən\ *adj* : of, relating to, or being a fly (sense 2) — **dipteran** *n* — **dip·ter·ous** \-rəs\ *adj*

dir *abbr* **1** direction **2** director

di·ram \dē-'ram\ *n* — see *somoni* at MONEY table

dire \'dī-(-ə)r\ *adj* **dir·er; dir·est** **1** : very horrible : DREADFUL ⟨∼ suffering⟩ **2** : warning of disaster **3** : EXTREME ⟨∼ poverty⟩

¹di·rect \də-'rekt, dī-\ *vb* **1** : ADDRESS ⟨∼ a letter⟩; *also* : to impart orally : AIM ⟨∼ a remark to the gallery⟩ **2** : to regulate the activities or course of : guide the supervision, organizing, or performance of **3** : to cause to turn, move, or point or to follow a certain course **4** : to point, extend, or project in a specified line or course **5** : to request or instruct with authority **6** : to show or point out the way

²direct *adj* **1** : stemming immediately from a source ⟨∼ result⟩ **2** : being or passing in a straight line of descent : LINEAL ⟨∼ ancestor⟩ **3** : leading from one point to another in time or space without turn or stop : STRAIGHT **4** : NATURAL, STRAIGHTFORWARD ⟨a ∼ manner⟩ **5** : operating without an intervening agency or step ⟨∼ action⟩ **6** : effected by the action of the people or the electorate and not by representatives ⟨∼ democracy⟩ **7** : consisting of or reproducing the exact words of a speaker or writer — **direct** *adv* — **di·rect·ly** *adv* — **di·rect·ness** *n*

direct broadcast satellite *n* : a television broadcasting system in which satellite transmissions are received at the viewing location

direct current *n* : an electric current flowing in one direction only

direct deposit *n* : a method of payment in which money is transferred to the payee's account without the use of checks or cash

di·rec·tion \də-'rek-shən, dī-\ *n* **1** : MANAGEMENT, GUIDANCE **2** : COMMAND, ORDER, INSTRUCTION **3** : the course or line along which something moves, lies, or points   **4** : TENDENCY, TREND — **di·rec·tion·al** \-shə-nəl\ *adj*

di·rec·tive \də-'rek-tiv, dī-\ *n* : something that directs and usu. impels toward an action or goal; *esp* : an order issued by a high-level body or official

direct mail *n* : printed matter used for soliciting business or contributions and mailed direct to individuals

di·rec·tor \də-'rek-tər, dī-\ *n*   **1** : one that directs : MANAGER, SUPERVISOR, CONDUCTOR   **2** : one of a group of persons who direct the affairs of an organized body — **di·rec·to·ri·al** \-ˌrek-'tȯr-ē-əl\ *adj* — **di·rec·tor·ship** *n*

di·rec·tor·ate \-tə-rət\ *n*   **1** : the office or position of director   **2** : a board of directors; *also* : membership on such a board   **3** : an executive staff

director's cut *n* : a version of a motion picture that is edited according to the director's wishes

di·rec·to·ry \-tə-rē\ *n, pl* **-ries**   **1** : an alphabetical or classified list esp. of names and addresses   **2** : FOLDER 4

dire·ful \'dī(-ə)r-fəl\ *adj* : DREADFUL; *also* : OMINOUS

dirge \'dərj\ *n* [ME *dirige* church service for the dead, fr. the first word of a LL anthem, fr. L, imper. of *dirigere* to direct] : a song of lamentation; *also* : a slow mournful piece of music

dir·ham \'dir-həm\ *n*   **1** — see MONEY table   **2** — see *dinar, riyal* at MONEY table

di·ri·gi·ble \'dir-ə-jə-bəl, də-'ri-jə-\ *n* : AIRSHIP

dirk \'dərk\ *n* : DAGGER 1

dirndl \'dərn-dᵊl\ *n* [short for G *Dirndlkleid,* fr. G dial. *Dirndl* girl + G *Kleid* dress] : a full skirt with a tight waistband

dirt \'dərt\ *n*   **1** : a filthy or soiling substance (as mud, dust, or grime)   **2** : loose or packed earth : SOIL   **3** : moral uncleanness   **4** : scandalous gossip   **5** : embarrassing or incriminating information

¹dirty \'dər-tē\ *adj* **dirt·i·er; -est**   **1** : SOILED, FILTHY   **2** : INDECENT, SMUTTY ⟨∼ jokes⟩   **3** : BASE, UNFAIR ⟨a ∼ trick⟩   **4** : STORMY, FOGGY ⟨∼ weather⟩   **5** : not clear in color : DULL ⟨∼ red⟩ — **dirt·i·ness** *n* — **dirty** *adv*

²dirty *vb* **dirt·ied; dirty·ing** : to make or become dirty

dis·able \di-'sā-bəl\ *vb* **dis·abled; dis·abling**   **1** : to disqualify legally   **2** : to make unable to perform by or as if by illness, injury, or malfunction — **dis·abil·i·ty** \ˌdi-sə-'bi-lə-tē\ *n*

dis·abled *adj* : incapacitated by illness or injury; *also* : physically or mentally impaired

dis·abuse \ˌdi-sə-'byüz\ *vb* : to free from error, fallacy, or misconception

dis·ad·van·tage \ˌdi-səd-'van-tij\ *n*   **1** : loss or damage esp. to reputation or finances   **2** : an unfavorable, inferior, or prejudicial condition, quality, or circumstance — **dis·ad·van·ta·geous** \di-ˌsad-vən-'tā-jəs, -vən-\ *adj*

dis·ad·van·taged \-tijd\ *adj* : lacking in basic resources or conditions believed necessary for an equal position in society

dis·af·fect \ˌdi-sə-'fekt\ *vb* : to alienate the affection or loyalty of — **dis·af·fec·tion** \-'fek-shən\ *n*

dis·agree \ˌdi-sə-'grē\ *vb*   **1** : to fail to agree   **2** : to differ in opinion   **3** : to cause discomfort or distress ⟨fried foods ∼ with her⟩ — **dis·agree·ment** *n*

dis·agree·able \-ə-bəl\ *adj*   **1** : causing discomfort : UNPLEASANT, OFFENSIVE ⟨a ∼ odor⟩   **2** : ILL-TEMPERED, PEEVISH — **dis·agree·able·ness** *n* — **dis·agree·ably** \-blē\ *adv*

dis·al·low \ˌdis-ə-'laú\ *vb* : to refuse to admit or recognize : REJECT ⟨∼ a claim⟩ — **dis·al·low·ance** *n*

dis·ap·pear \ˌdis-ə-'pir\ *vb*   **1** : to pass out of sight   **2** : to cease to be : become lost — **dis·ap·pear·ance** *n*

dis·ap·point \ˌdis-ə-'pȯint\ *vb* : to fail to fulfill the expectation or hope of — **dis·ap·point·ment** *n*

dis·ap·pro·ba·tion \dis-ˌa-prə-'bā-shən\ *n* : DISAPPROVAL

dis·ap·prov·al \ˌdis-ə-'prü-vəl\ *n* : adverse judgment : CENSURE

dis·ap·prove \-'prüv\ *vb*   **1** : CONDEMN   **2** : to feel or express disapproval ⟨∼s of smoking⟩   **3** : REJECT — **dis·ap·prov·ing·ly** \-'prü-viŋ-lē\ *adv*

dis·arm \dis-'ärm\ *vb*   **1** : to take arms or weapons from   **2** : to reduce the size and strength of the armed forces of a country   **3** : to make harmless, peaceable, or friendly : win over ⟨a ∼ing smile⟩ — **dis·ar·ma·ment** \-'är-mə-mənt\ *n*

dis·ar·range \ˌdis-ə-'rānj\ *vb* : to disturb the arrangement or order of — **dis·ar·range·ment** *n*

dis·ar·ray \-'rā\ *n*   **1** : DISORDER, CONFUSION   **2** : disorderly or careless dress

dis·as·sem·ble \ˌdis-ə-'sem-bəl\ *vb* : to take apart

dis·as·so·ci·ate \-'sō-shē-ˌāt, -sē-\ *vb* : to detach from association

di·sas·ter \di-'zas-tər, -'sas-\ *n* [MF *desastre,* fr. It *disastro,* fr. *astro* star, fr. L *astrum*] : a sudden or great misfortune — **di·sas·trous** \-'zas-trəs\ *adj* — **di·sas·trous·ly** *adv*

dis·avow \ˌdis-ə-'vaú\ *vb* : to deny responsibility for : REPUDIATE — **dis·avow·al** \-'vaú(-ə)l\ *n*

dis·band \dis-'band\ *vb* : to break up the organization of : DISPERSE

dis·bar \dis-'bär\ *vb* : to expel from the legal profession — **dis·bar·ment** *n*

dis·be·lieve \ˌdis-bə-'lēv\ *vb*   **1** : to hold not worthy of belief : not believe   **2** : to withhold or reject belief — **dis·be·lief** \-'lēf\ *n* — **dis·be·liev·er** *n*

dis·bur·den \dis-'bər-dᵊn\ *vb* : to rid of a burden

dis·burse \dis-'bərs\ *vb* **dis·bursed; dis·burs·ing**   **1** : to pay out : EXPEND   **2** : DISTRIBUTE — **dis·burse·ment** *n*

¹disc *var of* DISK

²disc *abbr* discount

dis·card \dis-'kärd, 'dis-ˌkärd\ *vb*   **1** : to let go a playing card from one's hand; *also* : to play (a card) from a suit other than a trump but different from the one led   **2** : to get rid of as unwanted — **dis·card** \'dis-ˌkärd\ *n*

disc brake *n* : a brake that operates by the friction of a pair of plates pressing against the sides of a rotating disc

dis·cern \di-'sərn, -'zərn\ *vb*   **1** : to detect with the eyes : DISTINGUISH   **2** : DISCRIMINATE   **3** : to come to know or recognize mentally — **dis·cern·ible** *adj* — **dis·cern·ment** *n*

dis·cern·ing *adj* : revealing insight and understanding

¹dis·charge \dis-'chärj, 'dis-ˌchärj\ *vb*   **1** : to relieve of a charge, load, or burden : UNLOAD; *esp* : to remove the electrical energy from ⟨∼ a storage battery⟩   **2** : to let or put off ⟨∼ passengers⟩   **3** : SHOOT ⟨∼ an arrow⟩   **4** : to set free ⟨∼ a prisoner⟩   **5** : to dismiss from service or employment ⟨∼ a soldier⟩   **6** : to get rid of by paying or doing ⟨∼ a debt⟩   **7** : to give forth fluid ⟨the river ∼s into the ocean⟩

²dis·charge \'dis-ˌchärj, dis-'chärj\ *n*   **1** : the act of discharging, unloading, or releasing   **2** : something that discharges; *esp* : a certification of release or payment   **3** : a firing off (as of a gun)   **4** : a flowing out (as of blood from a wound); *also* : something that is emitted ⟨a purulent ∼⟩   **5** : release or dismissal esp. from an office or employment; *also* : complete separation from military service   **6** : a flow of electricity (as through a gas)

dis·ci·ple \di-'sī-pəl\ *n* [ultim. fr. LL *discipulus* follower of Jesus in his lifetime, fr. L, pupil]   **1** : one who accepts and helps to spread the teachings of another; *also* : a convinced adherent   **2** *cap* : a member of the Disciples of Christ

dis·ci·pli·nar·i·an \ˌdi-sə-plə-'ner-ē-ən\ *n* : one who enforces order

dis·ci·plin·ary \'di-sə-plə-ˌner-ē\ *adj* : of or relating to discipline; *also* : CORRECTIVE ⟨take ∼ action⟩

¹dis·ci·pline \'di-sə-plən\ *n*   **1** : PUNISHMENT   **2** : a field of study : SUBJECT   **3** : training that corrects, molds, or perfects   **4** : control gained by obedience or training : orderly conduct   **5** : a system of rules governing conduct

²discipline *vb* **-plined; -plin·ing**   **1** : PUNISH   **2** : to train or develop by instruction and exercise esp. in self-control   **3** : to bring under control ⟨∼ troops⟩; *also* : to impose order upon

disc jockey *or* **disk jockey** *n* : an announcer of a radio show of popular recorded music

dis·claim \dis-'klām\ *vb* : DENY, DISAVOW — **dis·claim·er** *n*

dis·close \dis-'klōz\ *vb* : to expose to view — **dis·clo·sure** \-'klō-zhər\ *n*

dis·co \'dis-kō\ *n, pl* **discos**   **1** : a nightclub for dancing to live or recorded music   **2** : popular dance music characterized by hypnotic rhythm, repetitive lyrics, and electronically produced sounds

dis·col·or \dis-'kə-lər\ *vb* : to alter or change in hue or color esp. for the worse — **dis·col·or·ation** \-ˌkə-lə-'rā-shən\ *n*

dis·com·bob·u·late \dis-kəm-'bä-byù-ˌlāt\ *vb* **-lat·ed; -lat·ing** : UPSET, CONFUSE

dis·com·fit \dis-'kəm-fət, *esp Southern* ˌdis-kəm-'fit\ *vb* : UPSET, FRUSTRATE — **dis·com·fi·ture** \dis-'kəm-fə-ˌchùr\ *n*

¹**dis·com·fort** \dis-'kəm-fərt\ *vb* : to make uncomfortable or uneasy

²**discomfort** *n* : mental or physical uneasiness

dis·com·mode \ˌdis-kə-'mōd\ *vb* **-mod·ed; -mod·ing** : INCONVENIENCE, TROUBLE

dis·com·pose \-kəm-'pōz\ *vb* **1** : to destroy the calmness or peace of **2** : DISARRANGE — **dis·com·po·sure** \-'pō-zhər\ *n*

dis·con·cert \ˌdis-kən-'sərt\ *vb* : CONFUSE, UPSET

dis·con·nect \ˌdis-kə-'nekt\ *vb* : to undo the connection of — **dis·con·nec·tion** \-'nek-shən\ *n*

dis·con·nect·ed *adj* : not connected; *also* : INCOHERENT — **dis·con·nect·ed·ly** *adv* — **dis·con·nect·ed·ness** *n*

dis·con·so·late \dis-'kän-sə-lət\ *adj* **1** : CHEERLESS **2** : hopelessly sad — **dis·con·so·late·ly** *adv*

dis·con·tent \ˌdis-kən-'tent\ *n* : uneasiness of mind : DISSATISFACTION — **dis·con·tent·ed** *adj*

dis·con·tin·ue \ˌdis-kən-'tin-yü\ *vb* **1** : to break the continuity of : cease to operate, use, or take **2** : END — **dis·con·tin·u·ance** \-yə-wəns\ *n* — **dis·con·ti·nu·i·ty** \dis-ˌkän-tə-'nü-ə-tē, -'nyü-\ *n* — **dis·con·tin·u·ous** \ˌdis-kən-'tin-yə-wəs\ *adj*

dis·cord \'dis-ˌkòrd\ *n* **1** : lack of agreement or harmony : DISSENSION, CONFLICT **2** : a harsh combination of musical sounds **3** : a harsh or unpleasant sound — **dis·cor·dant** \dis-'kòr-d°nt\ *adj* — **dis·cor·dant·ly** *adv*

dis·co·theque *or* **discothèque** \'dis-kə-ˌtek\ *n* : DISCO 1

¹**dis·count** \'dis-ˌkaùnt\ *n* **1** : a reduction made from a regular or list price **2** : a deduction of interest in advance when lending money

²**dis·count** \'dis-ˌkaùnt, dis-'kaùnt\ *vb* **1** : to deduct from the amount of a bill, debt, or charge usu. for cash or prompt payment; *also* : to sell or offer for sale at a discount **2** : to lend money after deducting the discount ⟨∼ a note⟩ **3** : DISREGARD; *also* : MINIMIZE **4** : to make allowance for bias or exaggeration **5** : to take into account (as a future event) in present calculations — **count·able** *adj* — **dis·count·er** *n*

³**dis·count** \'dis-ˌkaùnt\ *adj* : selling goods or services at a discount; *also* : sold at or reflecting a discount

dis·coun·te·nance \dis-'kaùn-tə-nənts\ *vb* **1** : EMBARRASS, DISCONCERT **2** : to look with disfavor on

dis·cour·age \dis-'kər-ij\ *vb* **-aged; -ag·ing** **1** : to deprive of courage or confidence : DISHEARTEN **2** : to hinder by disfavoring **3** : to attempt to dissuade — **dis·cour·age·ment** *n* — **dis·cour·ag·ing·ly** *adv*

¹**dis·course** \'dis-ˌkòrs\ *n* [ME *discours*, fr. ML & LL *discursus;* ML, argument, fr. LL, conversation, fr. L, act of running about, fr. *discurrere* to run about, fr. *currere* to run] **1** : CONVERSATION **2** : formal and usu. extended expression of thought on a subject

²**dis·course** \dis-'kòrs\ *vb* **dis·coursed; dis·cours·ing** **1** : to express oneself in esp. oral discourse **2** : TALK, CONVERSE

dis·cour·te·ous \(ˌ)dis-'kər-tē-əs\ *adj* : lacking courtesy : UNCIVIL, RUDE — **dis·cour·te·ous·ly** *adv*

dis·cour·te·sy \-'kər-tə-sē\ *n* : RUDENESS; *also* : a rude act

dis·cov·er \dis-'kə-vər\ *vb* **1** : to make known or visible **2** : to obtain sight or knowledge of for the first time; *also* : FIND OUT — **dis·cov·er·er** *n*

dis·cov·ery \dis-'kə-və-rē\ *n, pl* **-er·ies** **1** : the act or process of discovering **2** : something discovered **3** : the disclosure usu. before a civil trial of pertinent facts or documents

¹**dis·cred·it** \(ˌ)dis-'kre-dət\ *vb* **1** : DISBELIEVE **2** : to cause disbelief in the accuracy or authority of **3** : DISGRACE — **dis·cred·it·able** *adj*

²**discredit** *n* **1** : loss of reputation **2** : lack or loss of belief or confidence

dis·creet \dis-'krēt\ *adj* : showing good judgment; *esp* : capable of observing prudent silence — **dis·creet·ly** *adv*

dis·crep·an·cy \dis-'kre-pən-sē\ *n, pl* **-cies** **1** : DIFFERENCE, DISAGREEMENT **2** : an instance of being discrepant

dis·crep·ant \-pənt\ *adj* [ME *discrepaunt*, fr. L *discrepans,* prp. of *discrepare* to sound discordantly, fr. *crepare* to rat-

tle, creak] : being at variance : DISAGREEING ⟨∼ conclusions⟩

dis·crete \dis-'krēt, 'dis-ˌkrēt\ *adj* **1** : individually distinct ⟨several ∼ sections⟩ **2** : NONCONTINUOUS

dis·cre·tion \dis-'kre-shən\ *n* **1** : the quality of being discreet : PRUDENCE **2** : individual choice or judgment ⟨left the decision to his ∼⟩ **3** : power of free decision or latitude of choice — **dis·cre·tion·ary** *adj*

dis·crim·i·nate \dis-'kri-mə-ˌnāt\ *vb* **-nat·ed; -nat·ing** **1** : DISTINGUISH, DIFFERENTIATE **2** : to make a difference in treatment on a basis other than individual merit — **dis·crim·i·na·tion** \-ˌkri-mə-'nā-shən\ *n*

dis·crim·i·nat·ing *adj* : marked by discrimination; *esp* : DISCERNING, JUDICIOUS — **dis·crim·i·nat·ing·ly** *adv*

dis·crim·i·na·to·ry \dis-'kri-mə-nə-ˌtòr-ē\ *adj* : marked by esp. unjust discrimination ⟨∼ treatment⟩

dis·cur·sive \dis-'kər-siv\ *adj* : passing from one topic to another : RAMBLING — **dis·cur·sive·ly** *adv* — **dis·cur·sive·ness** *n*

dis·cus \'dis-kəs\ *n, pl* **dis·cus·es** : a heavy disk that is hurled for distance in a track-and-field contest

dis·cuss \di-'skəs\ *vb* [ME, fr. AF *discusser,* fr. L *discussus,* pp. of *discutere* to disperse, fr. *dis-* apart + *quatere* to shake] **1** : to argue or consider carefully by presenting the various sides **2** : to talk about — **dis·cus·sion** \-'skə-shən\ *n*

dis·cus·sant \di-'skə-s°nt\ *n* : one who takes part in a formal discussion

¹**dis·dain** \dis-'dān\ *n* : CONTEMPT, SCORN — **dis·dain·ful** \-fəl\ *adj* — **dis·dain·ful·ly** *adv*

²**disdain** *vb* **1** : to look on with scorn **2** : to reject or refrain from because of disdain

dis·ease \di-'zēz\ *n* : an abnormal bodily condition that impairs normal functioning and can usu. be recognized by signs and symptoms : SICKNESS — **dis·eased** \-'zēzd\ *adj*

dis·em·bark \ˌdi-səm-'bärk\ *vb* : to go or put ashore from a ship — **dis·em·bar·ka·tion** \di-ˌsem-ˌbär-'kā-shən\ *n*

dis·em·body \ˌdi-səm-'bä-dē\ *vb* : to deprive of bodily existence

dis·em·bow·el \-'baù(-ə)l\ *vb* : EVISCERATE 1 — **dis·em·bow·el·ment** *n*

dis·em·power \ˌdis-im-'paù(-ə)r\ *vb* : to deprive of power, authority, or influence

dis·en·chant \ˌdis-in-'chant\ *vb* : DISILLUSION — **dis·en·chant·ment** \-mənt\ *n*

dis·en·chant·ed \-'chan-təd\ *adj* : DISAPPOINTED, DISSATISFIED

dis·en·cum·ber \ˌdis-°n-'kəm-bər\ *vb* : to free from something that burdens

dis·en·fran·chise \ˌdis-in-'fran-ˌchīz\ *vb* : to deprive of a franchise, a legal right, or a privilege; *esp* : to deprive of the right to vote — **dis·en·fran·chise·ment** *n*

dis·en·gage \ˌdis-°n-'gāj\ *vb* : RELEASE, EXTRICATE, DISENTANGLE — **dis·en·gage·ment** *n*

dis·en·gaged \-'gājd\ *adj* : IMPARTIAL, DETACHED ⟨a ∼ observer⟩

dis·en·tan·gle \ˌdis-in-'taŋ-gəl\ *vb* : to free from entanglement : UNRAVEL

dis·equi·lib·ri·um \dis-ˌē-kwə-'li-brē-əm\ *n* : loss or lack of equilibrium

dis·es·tab·lish \ˌdis-ə-'sta-blish\ *vb* : to end the establishment of; *esp* : to deprive of the status of an established church — **dis·es·tab·lish·ment** *n*

dis·es·teem \ˌdis-ə-'stēm\ *n* : lack of esteem : DISFAVOR, DISREPUTE

dis·fa·vor \(ˌ)dis-'fā-vər\ *n* **1** : DISAPPROVAL, DISLIKE **2** : the state or fact of being no longer favored

dis·fig·ure \dis-'fi-gyər\ *vb* : to spoil the appearance of ⟨*disfigured* by a scar⟩ — **dis·fig·ure·ment** *n*

dis·fran·chise \dis-'fran-ˌchīz\ *vb* : DISENFRANCHISE — **dis·fran·chise·ment** *n*

disfunction *var of* DYSFUNCTION

dis·gorge \-'gòrj\ *vb* : VOMIT; *also* : to discharge forcefully or confusedly

¹**dis·grace** \di-'skrās, dis-'grās\ *vb* : to bring reproach or shame to

²**disgrace** *n* **1** : SHAME, DISHONOR; *also* : a cause of shame **2** : the condition of being out of favor : loss of respect — **dis·grace·ful** \-fəl\ *adj* — **dis·grace·ful·ly** *adv*

dis·grun·tle \dis-'grən-t°l\ *vb* **dis·grun·tled; dis·grun·tling** : to put in bad humor

¹**dis·guise** \dis-ˈgīz\ vb **dis·guised; dis·guis·ing 1** : to change the appearance of so as to conceal the identity or to resemble another **2** : HIDE, CONCEAL

²**disguise** n **1** : clothing put on to conceal one's identity or counterfeit another's **2** : an outward appearance that hides what something really is

¹**dis·gust** \dis-ˈgəst\ n : AVERSION, REPUGNANCE — **dis·gust·ful** \-fəl\ adj

²**disgust** vb : to provoke to loathing, repugnance, or aversion : be offensive to — **dis·gust·ed·ly** adv — **dis·gust·ing** \-ˈgəs-tin\ adj — **dis·gust·ing·ly** adv

¹**dish** \ˈdish\ n [ME, fr. OE disc plate, fr. L discus quoit, disk, dish, fr. Gk diskos, fr. dikein to throw] **1** : a vessel used for serving food **2** : the food served in a dish ⟨a ~ of berries⟩ **3** : food prepared in a particular way **4** : something resembling a dish esp. in being shallow and concave **5** : SATELLITE DISH **6** : GOSSIP 2

²**dish** vb **1** : to put into a dish **2** : to make concave like a dish **3** : GOSSIP

dis·ha·bille \ˌdi-sə-ˈbēl\ or **des·ha·bille** \ˌde-\ n [F déshabillé] : the state of being dressed in a casual or careless manner

dis·har·mo·ny \(ˌ)dis-ˈhär-mə-nē\ n : lack of harmony — **dis·har·mo·ni·ous** \ˌdis-(ˌ)här-ˈmō-nē-əs\ adj

dish·cloth \ˈdish-ˌklȯth\ n : a cloth for washing dishes

dis·heart·en \dis-ˈhär-t³n\ vb : DISCOURAGE, DEJECT

dished \ˈdisht\ adj : CONCAVE

di·shev·el \di-ˈshe-vəl\ vb **-shev·eled** or **-shev·elled; -shev·el·ing** or **-shev·el·ling** [ME discheveled bareheaded, with disordered hair, fr. AF deschevelé, fr. des- apart + chevoil hair, fr. L capillus] : to throw into disorder or disarray — **di·shev·eled** or **di·shev·elled** adj — **di·shev·el·ment** \-mənt\ n

dis·hon·est \di-ˈsä-nəst\ adj : not honest : UNTRUSTWORTHY, DECEITFUL — **dis·hon·est·ly** adv — **dis·hon·es·ty** \-nə-stē\ n

¹**dis·hon·or** \dis-ˈä-nər\ n **1** : lack or loss of honor **2** : SHAME, DISGRACE **3** : a cause of disgrace **4** : the act of dishonoring a negotiable instrument when presented for payment — **dis·hon·or·able** \dis-ˈä-nə-rə-bəl\ adj — **dis·hon·or·ably** \-blē\ adv

²**dishonor** vb **1** : DISGRACE **2** : to refuse to accept or pay ⟨~ a check⟩

dish out vb : to give freely

dish·rag \ˈdish-ˌrag\ n : DISHCLOTH

dish·wash·er \-ˌwȯ-shər, -ˌwä-\ n : a person or machine that washes dishes

dish·wa·ter \-ˌwȯ-tər, -ˌwä-\ n : water used for washing dishes

dis·il·lu·sion \ˌdis-ə-ˈlü-zhən\ vb : to free from illusion — **dis·il·lu·sion·ment** n

dis·il·lu·sioned adj : DISAPPOINTED, DISSATISFIED

dis·in·cli·na·tion \dis-ˌin-klə-ˈnā-shən\ n : a preference for avoiding something : slight aversion

dis·in·cline \ˌdis-in-ˈklīn\ vb : to make unwilling

dis·in·clined adj : unwilling because of dislike or disapproval

dis·in·fect \ˌdis-in-ˈfekt\ vb : to cleanse of infection-causing germs — **dis·in·fec·tant** \-ˈfek-tənt\ n — **dis·in·fec·tion** \-ˈfek-shən\ n

dis·in·for·ma·tion \-ˌin-fər-ˈmā-shən\ n : false information deliberately and often covertly spread

dis·in·gen·u·ous \ˌdis-in-ˈjen-yə-wəs\ adj : lacking in candor; also : giving a false appearance of simple frankness

dis·in·her·it \ˌdis-in-ˈher-ət\ vb : to deprive of the right to inherit

dis·in·te·grate \dis-ˈin-tə-ˌgrāt\ vb **1** : to break or decompose into constituent parts or small particles **2** : to destroy the unity or integrity of — **dis·in·te·gra·tion** \-ˌin-tə-ˈgrā-shən\ n

dis·in·ter \ˌdis-in-ˈtər\ vb **1** : to take from the grave or tomb **2** : UNEARTH

dis·in·ter·est·ed \(ˌ)dis-ˈin-tə-rəs-təd, -ˌres-\ adj **1** : not interested **2** : free from selfish motive or interest : UNBIASED — **dis·in·ter·est·ed·ness** n

dis·join \(ˌ)dis-ˈjȯin\ vb : SEPARATE

dis·joint \(ˌ)dis-ˈjȯint\ vb : to disturb the orderly arrangement of; also : to separate at the joints

dis·joint·ed adj **1** : INCOHERENT ⟨~ conversation⟩ **2** : separated at or as if at the joint

disk or **disc** \ˈdisk\ n **1** : something round and flat; esp : a flat rounded anatomical structure (as the central part of the flower head of a composite plant or a pad of cartilage between vertebrae) **2** usu disc : a phonograph record **3** : a round flat plate coated with a magnetic substance on which data for a computer is stored **4** usu disc : OPTICAL DISK

disk drive n : a device for accessing or storing data on a magnetic disk

dis·kette \ˌdis-ˈket\ n : FLOPPY DISK

disk jockey var of DISC JOCKEY

¹**dis·like** \(ˌ)dis-ˈlīk\ n : a feeling of aversion or disapproval

²**dislike** vb : to regard with dislike : DISAPPROVE

dis·lo·cate \ˈdis-lō-ˌkāt, dis-ˈlō-\ vb **1** : to put out of place; esp : to displace (a bone or joint) from normal connections ⟨~ a shoulder⟩ **2** : DISRUPT — **dis·lo·ca·tion** \ˌdis-(ˌ)lō-ˈkā-shən\ n

dis·lodge \(ˌ)dis-ˈläj\ vb : to force out of a place esp. of rest, hiding, or defense

dis·loy·al \(ˌ)dis-ˈlȯi-(ə)l\ adj : lacking in loyalty — **dis·loy·al·ty** n

dis·mal \ˈdiz-məl\ adj [ME, fr. dismal, n., days marked as unlucky in medieval calendars, fr. AF, fr. ML dies mali, lit., evil days] **1** : showing or causing gloom or depression **2** : lacking merit — **dis·mal·ly** adv

dis·man·tle \(ˌ)dis-ˈman-t³l\ vb **-tled; -tling 1** : to take apart **2** : to strip of furniture and equipment — **dis·man·tle·ment** n

dis·may \dis-ˈmā\ vb : to cause to lose courage or resolution from alarm or fear : DAUNT — **dismay** n — **dis·may·ing·ly** adv

dis·mem·ber \dis-ˈmem-bər\ vb **1** : to cut off or separate the limbs or parts of **2** : to break up or tear into pieces — **dis·mem·ber·ment** n

dis·miss \dis-ˈmis\ vb **1** : to send away **2** : DISCHARGE **5** : **3** : to put aside or out of mind **4** : to put out of judicial consideration ⟨~ed all charges⟩ — **dis·miss·al** n — **dis·mis·sive** \-ˈmi-siv\ adj — **dis·mis·sive·ly** adv

dis·mount \dis-ˈmaunt\ vb **1** : to get down from something (as a horse or bicycle) **2** : UNHORSE **3** : DISASSEMBLE

dis·obe·di·ence \ˌdis-ə-ˈbē-dē-əns\ n : neglect or refusal to obey — **dis·obe·di·ent** \-ənt\ adj

dis·obey \ˌdis-ə-ˈbā\ vb : to fail to obey : be disobedient

dis·oblige \ˌdis-ə-ˈblīj\ vb **1** : to go counter to the wishes of **2** : INCONVENIENCE

¹**dis·or·der** \dis-ˈȯr-dər\ vb **1** : to disturb the order of **2** : to disturb the regular or normal functions of

²**disorder** n **1** : lack of order : CONFUSION **2** : breach of the peace or public order : TUMULT **3** : an abnormal physical or mental condition : AILMENT

dis·or·der·ly \-lē\ adj **1** : offensive to public order **2** : marked by disorder ⟨a ~ desk⟩ — **dis·or·der·li·ness** n

dis·or·ga·nize \dis-ˈȯr-gə-ˌnīz\ vb : to break up the regular system of : throw into disorder — **dis·or·ga·ni·za·tion** \dis-ˌȯr-gə-nə-ˈzā-shən\ n

dis·ori·ent \dis-ˈȯr-ē-ˌent\ vb : to cause to be confused or lost — **dis·ori·en·ta·tion** \dis-ˌȯr-ē-ən-ˈtā-shən\ n

dis·own \dis-ˈōn\ vb : REPUDIATE, RENOUNCE, DISCLAIM

dis·par·age \di-ˈsper-ij\ vb **-aged; -ag·ing** [ME to degrade by marriage below one's class, disparage, fr. AF desparager to marry below one's class, fr. parage equality, lineage, fr. per peer] **1** : to lower in rank or reputation : DEGRADE **2** : BELITTLE — **dis·par·age·ment** n — **dis·par·ag·ing·ly** adv

dis·pa·rate \ˈdis-pə-rət, di-ˈsper-ət\ adj : distinct in quality or character — **dis·par·i·ty** \di-ˈsper-ə-tē\ n

dis·pas·sion·ate \(ˌ)dis-ˈpa-shə-nət\ adj : not influenced by strong feeling : CALM, IMPARTIAL — **dis·pas·sion** \-ˈpa-shən\ n — **dis·pas·sion·ate·ly** adv

¹**dis·patch** \di-ˈspach\ vb **1** : to send off or away with promptness or speed esp. on official business **2** : to put to death **3** : to attend to rapidly or efficiently **4** : DEFEAT — **dis·patch·er** n

²**dis·patch** \di-ˈspach, ˈdis-ˌpach\ n **1** : MESSAGE **2** : a news item sent in by a correspondent to a newspaper **3** : the act of dispatching; esp : SHIPMENT **4** : the act of putting to death **5** : promptness and efficiency in performing a task

dis·pel \di-ˈspel\ vb **dis·pelled; dis·pel·ling** : to drive away by scattering : DISSIPATE

dis·pens·able \di-'spen-sə-bəl\ *adj* : capable of being dispensed with

dis·pen·sa·ry \di-'spen-sə-rē\ *n, pl* **-ries** : a place where medicine or medical or dental aid is dispensed

dis·pen·sa·tion \dis-pən-'sā-shən\ *n* **1** : a system of rules for ordering affairs **2** : a particular arrangement or provision esp. of nature **3** : an exemption from a rule or from a vow or oath **4** : the act of dispensing **5** : something dispensed or distributed

dis·pense \di-'spens\ *vb* **dis·pensed; dis·pens·ing** **1** : to portion out **2** : ADMINISTER ⟨∼ justice⟩ **3** : EXEMPT **4** : to make up and give out (remedies) — **dis·pens·er** *n* — **dispense with 1** : SUSPEND **2** : to do without

dis·perse \di-'spərs\ *vb* **dis·persed; dis·pers·ing** : to break up and scatter about : SPREAD — **dis·per·sal** \-'spər-səl\ *n* — **dis·per·sion** \-'spər-zhən\ *n*

dis·pir·it \dis-'pir-ət\ *vb* : DEPRESS, DISCOURAGE, DISHEARTEN

dis·place \dis-'plās\ *vb* **1** : to remove from the usual or proper place; *esp* : to expel or force to flee from home or native land ⟨*displaced* persons⟩ **2** : to move out of position ⟨water *displaced* by a floating object⟩ **3** : to take the place of : REPLACE

dis·place·ment \-mənt\ *n* **1** : the act of displacing : the state of being displaced **2** : the volume or weight of a fluid (as water) displaced by a floating body (as a ship) **3** : the difference between the initial position of an object and a later position

¹dis·play \di-'splā\ *vb* [ME, fr. AF *desplaier, desploier*, lit., to unfold, fr. *des*- un- + *ploier, plier* to fold, fr. L *plicare*] : to present to view : make evident

²display *n* **1** : a displaying of something **2** : an electronic device (as a cathode-ray tube) that gives information in visual form; *also* : the visual information

dis·please \(ˌ)dis-'plēz\ *vb* **1** : to arouse the disapproval and dislike of **2** : to be offensive to : give displeasure

dis·plea·sure \-'ple-zhər\ *n* : a feeling of dislike and irritation

dis·port \di-'spórt\ *vb* **1** : DIVERT, AMUSE **2** : FROLIC **3** : DISPLAY

dis·pos·able \di-'spō-zə-bəl\ *adj* **1** : remaining after deduction of taxes ⟨∼ income⟩ **2** : designed to be used once and then thrown away ⟨∼ diapers⟩ — **disposable** *n*

dis·pos·al \di-'spō-zəl\ *n* **1** : CONTROL, COMMAND **2** : an orderly arrangement **3** : a getting rid of **4** : MANAGEMENT, ADMINISTRATION **5** : presenting or bestowing something ⟨∼ of favors⟩ **6** : a device used to reduce waste matter (as by grinding)

dis·pose \di-'spōz\ *vb* **dis·posed; dis·pos·ing** **1** : to give a tendency to : INCLINE ⟨*disposed* to accept⟩ **2** : to put in place : ARRANGE ⟨troops *disposed* for withdrawal⟩ **3** : SETTLE — **dis·pos·er** *n* — **dispose of 1** : to transfer to the control of another **2** : to get rid of **3** : to deal with conclusively

dis·po·si·tion \ˌdis-pə-'zi-shən\ *n* **1** : the act or power of disposing : DISPOSAL **2** : RELINQUISHMENT **3** : ARRANGEMENT **4** : TENDENCY, INCLINATION **5** : natural attitude toward things ⟨a cheerful ∼⟩

dis·pos·sess \ˌdis-pə-'zes\ *vb* : to put out of possession or occupancy — **dis·pos·ses·sion** \-'ze-shən\ *n*

dis·praise \(ˌ)dis-'prāz\ *vb* : DISPARAGE — **dispraise** *n* — **dis·prais·er** *n*

dis·pro·por·tion \ˌdis-prə-'pór-shən\ *n* : lack of proportion, symmetry, or proper relation — **dis·pro·por·tion·ate** \-shə-nət\ *adj*

dis·prove \(ˌ)dis-'prüv\ *vb* : to prove to be false — **dis·proof** \-'prüf\ *n*

dis·pu·tant \di-'spyü-tᵊnt, 'dis-pyə-tənt\ *n* : one that is engaged in a dispute

dis·pu·ta·tion \ˌdis-pyù-'tā-shən\ *n* **1** : DEBATE **2** : an oral defense of an academic thesis

dis·pu·ta·tious \-shəs\ *adj* : inclined to dispute : ARGUMENTATIVE

¹dis·pute \di-'spyüt\ *vb* **dis·put·ed; dis·put·ing** **1** : ARGUE, DEBATE **2** : WRANGLE **3** : to deny the truth or rightness of **4** : to struggle against or over : OPPOSE — **dis·put·able** \di-'spyü-tə-bəl, 'dis-pyə-tə-bəl\ *adj* — **dis·put·er** *n*

²dispute *n* **1** : DEBATE **2** : QUARREL

dis·qual·i·fy \(ˌ)dis-'kwä-lə-ˌfī\ *vb* : to make or declare

unfit or not qualified — **dis·qual·i·fi·ca·tion** \-ˌkwä-lə-fə-'kā-shən\ *n*

¹dis·qui·et \(ˌ)dis-'kwī-ət\ *vb* : to make uneasy or restless : DISTURB — **dis·qui·et·ing** *adj*

²disquiet *n* : lack of peace or tranquillity : ANXIETY

dis·qui·etude \(ˌ)dis-'kwī-ə-ˌtüd, -ˌtyüd\ *n* : AGITATION, ANXIETY

dis·qui·si·tion \ˌdis-kwə-'zi-shən\ *n* : a formal inquiry or discussion

¹dis·re·gard \ˌdis-ri-'gärd\ *vb* : to pay no attention to : treat as unworthy of notice or regard

²disregard *n* : the act of disregarding : the state of being disregarded : NEGLECT — **dis·re·gard·ful** *adj*

dis·re·pair \ˌdis-ri-'per\ *n* : the state of being in need of repair

dis·rep·u·ta·ble \dis-'re-pyù-tə-bəl\ *adj* : having a bad reputation

dis·re·pute \ˌdis-ri-'pyüt\ *n* : lack or decline of reputation : low esteem

dis·re·spect \ˌdis-ri-'spekt\ *n* : DISCOURTESY — **dis·re·spect·ful** *adj*

dis·robe \dis-'rōb\ *vb* : UNDRESS

dis·rupt \dis-'rəpt\ *vb* **1** : to break apart **2** : to throw into disorder **3** : INTERRUPT — **dis·rup·tion** \-'rəp-shən\ *n* — **dis·rup·tive** \-'rəp-tiv\ *adj*

dis·sat·is·fac·tion \di-ˌsa-təs-'fak-shən\ *n* : DISCONTENT

dis·sat·is·fy \di-'sa-təs-ˌfī\ *vb* : to fail to satisfy : DISPLEASE

dis·sect \dī-'sekt, di-\ *vb* **1** : to divide into parts esp. for examination and study **2** : ANALYZE — **dis·sec·tion** \-'sek-shən\ *n* — **dis·sec·tor** \-'sek-tər\ *n*

dis·sect·ed *adj* : cut deeply into narrow lobes ⟨a ∼ leaf⟩

dis·sem·ble \di-'sem-bəl\ *vb* **-bled; -bling** **1** : to hide under or put on a false appearance : conceal facts, intentions, or feelings under some pretense **2** : SIMULATE — **dis·sem·bler** *n*

dis·sem·i·nate \di-'se-mə-ˌnāt\ *vb* **-nat·ed; -nat·ing** : to spread abroad as if sowing seed ⟨∼ ideas⟩ — **dis·sem·i·na·tion** \-ˌse-mə-'nā-shən\ *n*

dis·sen·sion \di-'sen-chən\ *n* : disagreement in opinion : DISCORD

¹dis·sent \di-'sent\ *vb* **1** : to withhold assent **2** : to differ in opinion

²dissent *n* **1** : difference of opinion; *esp* : religious nonconformity **2** : a written statement in which a justice disagrees with the opinion of the majority

dis·sent·er \di-'sen-tər\ *n* **1** : one that dissents **2** *cap* : an English Nonconformist

dis·ser·ta·tion \ˌdi-sər-'tā-shən\ *n* : an extended usu. written treatment of a subject; *esp* : one submitted for a doctorate

dis·ser·vice \di-'sər-vəs\ *n* : INJURY, HARM, MISCHIEF

dis·sev·er \di-'se-vər\ *vb* : SEPARATE, DISUNITE

dis·si·dent \'di-sə-dənt\ *adj* [L *dissidens*, prp. of *dissidēre* to sit apart, disagree, fr. *dis*- apart + *sedēre* to sit] : disagreeing esp. with an established religious or political system, organization, or belief — **dis·si·dence** \-dəns\ *n* — **dissident** *n*

dis·sim·i·lar \di-'si-mə-lər\ *adj* : UNLIKE — **dis·sim·i·lar·i·ty** \di-ˌsi-mə-'ler-ə-tē\ *n*

dis·sim·u·late \di-'si-myə-ˌlāt\ *vb* : to hide under a false appearance : DISSEMBLE — **dis·sim·u·la·tion** \di-ˌsi-myə-'lā-shən\ *n*

dis·si·pate \'di-sə-ˌpāt\ *vb* **-pat·ed; -pat·ing** **1** : to break up and drive off : DISPERSE, SCATTER ⟨the breeze *dissipated* the fog⟩ **2** : SQUANDER **3** : to break up and vanish **4** : to be dissolute; *esp* : to drink alcoholic beverages to excess — **dis·si·pat·ed** *adj* — **dis·si·pa·tion** \di-sə-'pā-shən\ *n*

dis·so·ci·ate \di-'sō-shē-ˌāt\ *vb* **-at·ed; -at·ing** : DISCONNECT, DISUNITE — **dis·so·ci·a·tion** \di-ˌsō-shē-'ā-shən\ *n* — **dis·so·cia·tive** \di-'sō-shē-ˌā-tiv\ *adj*

dis·so·lute \'di-sə-ˌlüt\ *adj* : loose in morals or conduct — **dis·so·lute·ly** *adv* — **dis·so·lute·ness** *n*

dis·so·lu·tion \ˌdi-sə-'lü-shən\ *n* **1** : the action or process of dissolving **2** : separation of a thing into its parts **3** : DECAY; *also* : DEATH **4** : the termination or breaking up of (as an assembly)

dis·solve \di-'zälv\ *vb* **1** : to separate into component parts **2** : to pass or cause to pass into solution ⟨sugar ∼s in water⟩ **3** : TERMINATE, DISPERSE ⟨∼ parliament⟩ **4**

: to waste or fade away ⟨his courage *dissolved*⟩ **5** : to be overcome emotionally ⟨∼ in tears⟩ **6** : to resolve itself as if by dissolution

dis·so·nance \'di-sə-nəns\ *n* : DISCORD — **dis·so·nant** \-nənt\ *adj*

dis·suade \di-'swād\ *vb* **dis·suad·ed; dis·suad·ing** : to advise against a course of action : persuade or try to persuade not to do something — **dis·sua·sion** \-'swā-zhən\ *n* — **dis·sua·sive** \-'swā-siv\ *adj*

dist *abbr* **1** distance **2** district

¹dis·taff \'dis-ˌtaf\ *n, pl* **distaffs** \-ˌtafs, -ˌtavz\ [ME *distaf,* fr. OE *distæf,* fr. *dis-* bunch of flax + *stæf* stick, staff] **1** : a staff for holding the flax, tow, or wool in spinning **2** : a woman's work or domain **3** : the female branch or side of a family

²distaff *adj* **1** : MATERNAL **2** ⟨the ∼ side of the family⟩ **2** : FEMALE **1** ⟨∼ executives⟩

dis·tal \'dis-t⁹l\ *adj* **1** : situated away from the point of attachment or origin esp. on the body **2** : of, relating to, or being the surface of a tooth that is farthest from the middle of the front of the jaw — **dis·tal·ly** *adv*

¹dis·tance \'dis-təns\ *n* **1** : measure of separation in space or time **2** : EXPANSE **3** : the full length ⟨go the ∼⟩ **4** : spatial remoteness **5** : COLDNESS, RESERVE **6** : DIFFERENCE, DISPARITY **7** : a distant point

²distance *vb* **dis·tanced; dis·tanc·ing** : to leave far behind : OUTSTRIP

³distance *adj* : taking place via electronic media linking instructors and students ⟨∼ learning⟩

dis·tant \'dis-tənt\ *adj* **1** : separate in space : AWAY **2** : FAR-OFF ⟨a ∼ galaxy⟩ **3** : far apart or behind **4** : not close in relationship ⟨a ∼ cousin⟩ **5** : different in kind **6** : RESERVED, ALOOF, COLD ⟨∼ politeness⟩ **7** : going a long distance ⟨∼ voyages⟩ — **dis·tant·ly** *adv* — **dis·tant·ness** *n*

dis·taste \ˌ(ˌ)dis-'tāst\ *n* : DISINCLINATION, DISLIKE — **dis·taste·ful** *adj*

dis·tem·per \ˌ(ˌ)dis-'tem-pər\ *n* : a bodily disorder usu. of a domestic animal; *esp* : a contagious often fatal virus disease of dogs

dis·tend \di-'stend\ *vb* : EXPAND, SWELL — **dis·ten·si·ble** \-'sten-sə-bəl\ *adj* — **dis·ten·sion** *or* **dis·ten·tion** \-chən\ *n*

dis·tich \'dis-ˌ(ˌ)tik\ *n* : a unit of two lines of poetry

dis·till *also* **dis·til** \di-'stil\ *vb* **dis·tilled; dis·till·ing** **1** : to fall or let fall in drops **2** : to obtain or purify by distillation — **dis·till·er** *n* — **dis·till·ery** \-'sti-lə-rē\ *n*

dis·til·late \'dis-tə-ˌlāt, -lət\ *n* : a liquid product condensed from vapor during distillation

dis·til·la·tion \ˌdis-tə-'lā-shən\ *n* : the process of purifying a liquid by successive evaporation and condensation

dis·tinct \di-'stiŋkt\ *adj* **1** : SEPARATE, INDIVIDUAL ⟨a ∼ cultural group⟩ **2** : presenting a clear unmistakable impression — **dis·tinct·ly** *adv* — **dis·tinct·ness** *n*

dis·tinc·tion \di-'stiŋk-shən\ *n* **1** : the distinguishing of a difference; *also* : the difference distinguished **2** : something that distinguishes **3** : special honor or recognition

dis·tinc·tive \di-'stiŋk-tiv\ *adj* **1** : serving to distinguish ⟨the ∼ flight of the crane⟩ **2** : having or giving style or distinction — **dis·tinc·tive·ly** *adv* — **dis·tinc·tive·ness** *n*

dis·tin·guish \di-'stiŋ-gwish\ *vb* [alter. of ME *distinguen,* fr. AF *distinguer,* fr. L *distinguere,* lit., to separate by pricking] **1** : to recognize by some mark or characteristic **2** : to hear or see clearly : DISCERN **3** : to make distinctions ⟨∼ between right and wrong⟩ **4** : to give prominence or distinction to; *also* : to take special notice of — **dis·tin·guish·able** *adj*

dis·tin·guished \-gwisht\ *adj* **1** : marked by eminence or excellence **2** : befitting an eminent person

dis·tort \di-'stȯrt\ *vb* **1** : to twist out of the true meaning **2** : to twist out of a natural, normal, or original shape or condition **3** : to cause to be perceived unnaturally — **dis·tor·tion** \-'stȯr-shən\ *n*

distr *abbr* distribute; distribution

dis·tract \di-'strakt\ *vb* **1** : to draw (the attention or mind) to a different object : DIVERT **2** : to stir up or confuse with conflicting emotions or motives — **dis·trac·tion** \-'strak-shən\ *n*

dis·trait \di-'strā\ *adj* : DISTRAUGHT 1

dis·traught \di-'strȯt\ *adj* **1** : agitated with doubt or mental conflict or pain **2** : INSANE

dis·tress \di-'stres\ *n* **1** : suffering of body or mind : PAIN, ANGUISH **2** : TROUBLE, MISFORTUNE **3** : a condition of danger or desperate need — **dis·tress·ful** *adj*

²distress *vb* **1** : to subject to great strain or difficulties **2** : UPSET

dis·tress·ed \-'strest\ *adj* : experiencing economic decline or difficulty

dis·trib·ute \di-'stri-byüt\ *vb* **-ut·ed; -ut·ing** **1** : to divide among several or many **2** : to spread out : SCATTER; *also* : DELIVER **3** : CLASSIFY — **dis·tri·bu·tion** \ˌdis-trə-'byü-shən\ *n*

dis·trib·u·tive \di-'stri-byü-tiv\ *adj* **1** : of or relating to distribution **2** : of, having, or being the property of producing the same value when an operation is carried out on a whole expression and when it is carried out on each part of an expression with the results then collected together ⟨$a(b + c) = ab + ac$ because multiplication is ∼⟩ — **dis·trib·u·tive·ly** *adv*

dis·trib·u·tor \di-'stri-byü-tər\ *n* **1** : one that distributes **2** : one that markets goods **3** : a device for directing current to the spark plugs of an engine

dis·trict \'dis-ˌ(ˌ)trikt\ *n* **1** : a fixed territorial division (as for administrative or electoral purposes) **2** : an area, region, or section with a distinguishing character

district attorney *n* : the prosecuting attorney of a judicial district

¹dis·trust \dis-'trəst\ *n* : a lack or absence of trust — **dis·trust·ful** \-fəl\ *adj* — **dis·trust·ful·ly** *adv*

²distrust *vb* : to have no trust or confidence in

dis·turb \di-'stərb\ *vb* **1** : to interfere with : INTERRUPT **2** : to alter the position or arrangement of; *also* : to upset the natural and esp. the ecological balance of **3** : to destroy the tranquillity or composure of : make uneasy **4** : to throw into disorder **5** : INCONVENIENCE — **dis·tur·bance** \-'stər-bəns\ *n* — **dis·turb·er** *n* — **dis·turb·ing·ly** \-'stər-biŋ-lē\ *adv*

dis·turbed \-'stərbd\ *adj* : showing symptoms of emotional illness

dis·unite \ˌdis-yü-'nīt\ *vb* : DIVIDE, SEPARATE

dis·uni·ty \dis-'yü-nə-tē\ *n* : lack of unity; *esp* : DISSENSION

dis·use \-'yüs\ *n* : a cessation of use or practice

dis·used \-'yüzd\ *adj* : no longer used or occupied

¹ditch \'dich\ *n* : a long narrow channel or trench dug in the earth

²ditch *vb* **1** : to enclose with a ditch; *also* : to dig a ditch in **2** : to get rid of : DISCARD **3** : to make a forced landing of an airplane on water

dith·er \'di-thər\ *n* : a highly nervous, excited, or agitated state

dit·to \'di-tō\ *n, pl* **dittos** [It *ditto, detto,* pp. of *dire* to say, fr. L *dicere*] **1** : a thing mentioned previously or above — used to avoid repeating a word **2** : a mark " or " used as a symbol for the word *ditto*

dit·ty \'di-tē\ *n, pl* **ditties** : a short simple song

dit·zy *or* **dit·sy** \'dit-sē\ *adj* **ditz·i·er** *or* **dits·i·er; -est** : eccentrically silly, giddy, or inane

di·uret·ic \ˌdī-yə-'re-tik\ *adj* : tending to increase urine flow — **diuretic** *n*

di·ur·nal \dī-'ər-n⁹l\ *adj* **1** : DAILY ⟨a ∼ chore⟩ **2** : of, relating to, occurring, or active in the daytime ⟨∼ animals⟩

div *abbr* **1** divided **2** dividend **3** division **4** divorced

di·va \'dē-və\ *n, pl* **divas** *or* **di·ve** \-ˌvä\ [It, lit., goddess, fr. L, fem. of *divus* divine, god] **1** : PRIMA DONNA **2** : a usu. glamorous and successful female performer or personality

di·va·gate \'dī-və-ˌgāt\ *vb* **-gat·ed; -gat·ing** : to wander or stray from a course or subject : DIVERGE — **di·va·ga·tion** \ˌdī-və-'gā-shən\ *n*

di·van \'dī-ˌvan, di-'van\ *n* : COUCH, SOFA

¹dive \'dīv\ *vb* **dived** \'dīvd\ *or* **dove** \'dōv\; **dived; div·ing** **1** : to plunge into water headfirst **2** : SUBMERGE **3** : to come or drop down precipitously **4** : to descend in an airplane at a steep angle **5** : to plunge into some matter or activity **6** : DART, LUNGE — **div·er** *n*

²dive *n* **1** : the act or an instance of diving **2** : a sharp decline **3** : a disreputable bar or place of amusement

di·verge \də-'vərj, dī-\ *vb* **di·verged; di·verg·ing** **1** : to move or extend in different directions from a common point : draw apart **2** : to differ in character, form, or opinion **3** : DEVIATE **4** : DEFLECT — **di·ver·gence** \-'vər-jəns\ *n* — **di·ver·gent** \-jənt\ *adj*

di·vers \'dī-vərz\ *adj* : VARIOUS

di·verse \dī-'vərs, də-, 'dī-,vərs\ *adj* **1** : UNLIKE **2** : composed of distinct forms or qualities — **di·verse·ly** *adv*

di·ver·si·fy \də-'vər-sə-,fī, dī-\ *vb* **-fied; -fy·ing** : to make different or various in form or quality — **di·ver·si·fi·ca·tion** \-,vər-sə-fə-'kā-shən\ *n*

di·ver·sion \də-'vər-zhən, dī-\ *n* **1** : a turning aside from a course, activity, or use : DEVIATION **2** : something that diverts or amuses : PASTIME

di·ver·si·ty \də-'vər-sə-tē, dī-\ *n, pl* **-ties 1** : the condition of being diverse : VARIETY **2** : an instance of being diverse

di·vert \də-'vərt, dī-\ *vb* **1** : to turn from a course or purpose : DEFLECT **2** : DISTRACT **3** : ENTERTAIN, AMUSE

di·vert·ing \-'vər-tiŋ\ *adj* : providing amusement or entertainment

di·vest \dī-'vest, də-\ *vb* **1** : to deprive or dispossess esp. of property, authority, or rights **2** : to strip esp. of clothing, ornament, or equipment

¹di·vide \də-'vīd\ *vb* **di·vid·ed; di·vid·ing 1** : SEPARATE; *also* : CLASSIFY **2** : CLEAVE, PART ⟨a ship *dividing* the waves⟩ **3** : DISTRIBUTE, APPORTION **4** : to possess or make use of in common : share in **5** : to cause to be separate, distinct, or apart from one another **6** : to separate into opposing sides or parties **7** : to mark divisions on **8** : to subject to or use in mathematical division; *also* : to be used as a divisor with respect to **9** : to branch out

²divide *n* : WATERSHED 1

div·i·dend \'di-və-,dend\ *n* **1** : an individual share of something distributed **2** : BONUS **3** : a number to be divided **4** : a sum or fund to be divided or distributed

di·vid·er \də-'vī-dər\ *n* **1** : one that divides (as a partition) ⟨room ~⟩ **2** *pl* : COMPASS 5

div·i·na·tion \,di-və-'nā-shən\ *n* **1** : the art or practice of using omens or magic powers to foretell the future **2** : unusual insight or intuitive perception

¹di·vine \də-'vīn\ *adj* **di·vin·er; -est 1** : of, relating to, or being God or a god **2** : supremely good : SUPERB; *also* : HEAVENLY — **di·vine·ly** *adv*

²divine *n* **1** : CLERGYMAN **2** : THEOLOGIAN

³divine *vb* **di·vined; di·vin·ing 1** : INFER, CONJECTURE **2** : PROPHESY **3** : DOWSE — **di·vin·er** *n*

divining rod *n* : a forked rod believed to reveal the presence of water or minerals by dipping downward when held over a vein

di·vin·i·ty \də-'vi-nə-tē\ *n, pl* **-ties 1** : THEOLOGY **2** : the quality or state of being divine **3** : a divine being; *esp* : GOD 1

di·vis·i·ble \də-'vi-zə-bəl\ *adj* : capable of being divided — **di·vis·i·bil·i·ty** \-,vi-zə-'bi-lə-tē\ *n*

di·vi·sion \də-'vi-zhən\ *n* **1** : DISTRIBUTION, SEPARATION **2** : one of the parts or groupings into which a whole is divided **3** : DISAGREEMENT, DISUNITY **4** : something that divides or separates **5** : the mathematical operation of finding how many times one number is contained in another **6** : a large self-contained military unit **7** : an administrative or operating unit of a governmental, business, or educational organization — **di·vi·sion·al** \-'vi-zhə-nəl\ *adj*

di·vi·sive \də-'vī-siv, -'vi-siv, -'vi-ziv\ *adj* : creating disunity or dissension — **di·vi·sive·ly** *adv* — **di·vi·sive·ness** *n*

di·vi·sor \də-'vī-zər\ *n* : the number by which a dividend is divided

di·vorce \də-'vȯrs\ *n* **1** : an act or instance of legally dissolving a marriage **2** : SEPARATION, SEVERANCE — **divorce** *vb* — **di·vorce·ment** *n*

di·vor·cé \də-,vȯr-'sā\ *n* [F] : a divorced man

di·vor·cée \də-,vȯr-'sā, -'sē\ *n* : a divorced woman

div·ot \'di-vət\ *n* : a piece of turf dug from a golf fairway in making a stroke

di·vulge \də-'vəlj, dī-\ *vb* **di·vulged; di·vulg·ing** : REVEAL, DISCLOSE

Dix·ie·land \'dik-sē-,land\ *n* : jazz music in duple time played in a style developed in New Orleans

diz·zy \'di-zē\ *adj* **diz·zi·er; -est** [ME *disy*, fr. OE *dysig* stupid] **1** : FOOLISH, SILLY **2** : having a sensation of whirling : GIDDY **3** : causing or caused by giddiness — **diz·zi·ly** \-zə-lē\ *adv* — **diz·zi·ness** \-zē-nəs\ *n*

DJ *n, often not cap* : DISC JOCKEY

dk *abbr* **1** dark **2** deck **3** dock

dl *abbr* deciliter

DLitt *or* **DLit** *abbr* [NL *doctor litterarum*] doctor of letters; doctor of literature

DLO *abbr* dead letter office

dm *abbr* decimeter

DMD *abbr* [NL *dentariae medicinae doctor*] doctor of dental medicine

DMZ *abbr* demilitarized zone

dn *abbr* down

DNA \,dē-(,)en-'ā\ *n* : any of various nucleic acids that are usu. the molecular basis of heredity and are localized esp. in cell nuclei

DNR *abbr* do not resuscitate

¹do \'dü\ *vb* **did** \'did\; **done** \'dən\; **do·ing; does** \'dəz\ **1** : to bring to pass : ACCOMPLISH **2** : ACT, BEHAVE ⟨~ as I say⟩ **3** : to be active or busy ⟨up and ~*ing*⟩ **4** : HAPPEN ⟨what's ~*ing*?⟩ **5** : to be engaged in the study or practice of : work at ⟨he *does* tailoring⟩ **6** : COOK ⟨steak *done* rare⟩ **7** : to put in order (as by cleaning or arranging) ⟨~ the dishes⟩ **8** : DECORATE ⟨*did* the hall in blue⟩ **9** : GET ALONG ⟨~ well in school⟩ **10** : CARRY ON, MANAGE **11** : RENDER ⟨sleep will ~ you good⟩ **12** : FINISH ⟨when he had *done*⟩ **13** : EXERT ⟨*did* my best⟩ **14** : PRODUCE ⟨*did* a poem⟩ **15** : to play the part of **16** : CHEAT ⟨*did* him out of his share⟩ **17** : TRAVERSE, TOUR **18** : TRAVEL **19** : to spend or serve out a period of time ⟨*did* ten years in prison⟩ **20** : SUFFICE, SUIT **21** : to be fitting or proper **22** : USE ⟨doesn't ~ drugs⟩ **23** — used as an auxiliary verb (1) before the subject in an interrogative sentence ⟨*does* he work?⟩ and after some adverbs ⟨never *did* she say so⟩, (2) in a negative statement ⟨I *don't* know⟩, (3) for emphasis ⟨you ~ know⟩, and (4) as a substitute for a preceding predicate ⟨he works harder than I ~⟩ — **do·able** \'dü-ə-bəl\ *adj* — **do away with 1** : to put an end to **2** : DESTROY, KILL — **do by** : to deal with : TREAT ⟨*did* right by her⟩ — **do for** *chiefly Brit* : to bring about the death or ruin of — **do the trick** : to produce a desired result

²do *n* **1** : AFFAIR, PARTY **2** : a command or entreaty to do something ⟨list of ~s and don'ts⟩ **3** : HAIRSTYLE

³do *abbr* ditto

DOA *abbr* dead on arrival

DOB *abbr* date of birth

dob·bin \'dä-bən\ *n* [*Dobbin*, nickname for *Robert*] **1** : a farm horse **2** : a quiet plodding horse

Do·ber·man pin·scher \'dō-bər-mən-'pin-chər\ *n* : any of a German breed of short-haired medium-sized dogs

do·bra \'dō-brə\ *n* — see MONEY table

¹doc \'däk\ *n* : DOCTOR

²doc *abbr* document

do·cent \'dō-sᵊnt, dōt-'sent\ *n* [obs. G (now *Dozent*), fr. L *docens*, prp. of *docēre* to teach] : TEACHER, LECTURER; *also* : a person who leads a guided tour

doc·ile \'dä-səl\ *adj* [L *docilis*, fr. *docēre* to teach] : easily taught, led, or managed : TRACTABLE — **do·cil·i·ty** \dä-'si-lə-tē\ *n*

¹dock \'däk\ *n* : any of a genus of coarse weedy herbs related to buckwheat

²dock *vb* **1** : to cut off the end of : cut short **2** : to take away a part of : deduct from ⟨~ a worker's wages⟩

³dock *n* **1** : an artificial basin to receive ships **2** : ²SLIP 2 **3** : a wharf or platform for loading or unloading materials or for mooring a boat

⁴dock *vb* **1** : to bring or come into dock **2** : to join (as two spacecraft) mechanically in space

⁵dock *n* : the place in a court where a prisoner stands or sits during trial

dock·age \'dä-kij\ *n* : docking facilities

dock·et \'dä-kət\ *n* **1** : a formal abridged record of the proceedings in a legal action; *also* : a register of such records **2** : a list of legal causes to be tried **3** : a calendar of matters to be acted on : AGENDA **4** : a label attached to a document containing identification or directions — **docket** *vb*

dock·hand \'däk-,hand\ *n* : LONGSHOREMAN

dock·work·er \-,wər-kər\ *n* : LONGSHOREMAN

dock·yard \-,yärd\ *n* : SHIPYARD

¹doc·tor \'däk-tər\ *n* [ME *doctour* teacher, doctor, fr. AF & ML; AF, fr. ML *doctor*, fr. L, teacher, fr. *docēre* to teach] **1** : a person holding one of the highest academic degrees (as a PhD) conferred by a university **2** : a person skilled in healing arts; *esp* : one (as a physician, dentist, or veterinarian) academically and legally qualified to practice **3** : a person who restores or repairs things — **doc·tor·al** \-tə-rəl\ *adj*

²**doctor** *vb* **1** : to give medical treatment to **2** : to practice medicine **3** : REPAIR **4** : to adapt or modify for a desired end **5** : to alter deceptively

doc·tor·ate \'däk-tə-rət\ *n* : the degree, title, or rank of a doctor

doc·tri·naire \,däk-trə-'ner\ *n* [F] : one who attempts to put an abstract theory into effect without regard to practical difficulties — **doctrinaire** *adj*

doc·trine \'däk-trən\ *n* **1** : something that is taught **2** : DOGMA, TENET — **doc·tri·nal** \-trə-nᵊl\ *adj*

docu·dra·ma \'dä-kyə-,drä-mə, -,dra-\ *n* : a drama made for television, motion pictures, or theater that deals freely with historical events

doc·u·ment \'dä-kyə-mənt\ *n* **1** : a paper that furnishes information, proof, or support of something else **2** : a computer file containing information input by a computer user usu. via a word processor — **doc·u·ment** \-,ment\ *vb* — **doc·u·men·ta·tion** \,dä-kyə-mən-'tā-shən\ *n* — **doc·u·ment·er** *n*

doc·u·men·ta·ry \,dä-kyə-'men-tə-rē\ *adj* **1** : consisting of documents; *also* : being in writing ⟨∼ proof⟩ **2** : giving a factual presentation in artistic form ⟨a ∼ movie⟩ — **documentary** *n*

DOD *abbr* Department of Defense

¹**dod·der** \'dä-dər\ *n* : any of a genus of leafless parasitic twining vines that are highly deficient in chlorophyll

²**dodder** *vb* **dod·dered; dod·der·ing** **1** : to tremble or shake usu. from age **2** : to progress feebly and unsteadily

¹**dodge** \'däj\ *n* **1** : an act of evading by sudden bodily movement **2** : an artful device to evade, deceive, or trick **3** : EXPEDIENT

²**dodge** *vb* **dodged; dodg·ing** **1** : to evade usu. by trickery **2** : to move suddenly aside; *also* : to avoid or evade by so doing — **dodg·er** *n*

do·do \'dō-dō\ *n, pl* **dodoes** *or* **dodos** [Pg *doudo*, fr. *doudo* silly, stupid] **1** : an extinct heavy flightless bird of the island of Mauritius related to the pigeons and larger than a turkey **2** : one hopelessly behind the times; *also* : a stupid person

doe \'dō\ *n, pl* **does** *or* **doe** : an adult female of various mammals (as a deer, rabbit, or kangaroo) of which the male is called *buck*

DOE *abbr* Department of Energy

do·er \'dü-ər\ *n* : one that does

does *pres 3d sing of* DO, *pl of* DOE

doff \'däf\ *vb* [ME, fr. *don* to do + *of* off] **1** : to take off (the hat) in greeting or as a sign of respect **2** : to rid oneself of

¹**dog** \'dȯg\ *n* **1** : a flesh-eating domestic mammal related to the wolves; *esp* : a male of this animal **2** : a worthless or contemptible person **3** : FELLOW, CHAP ⟨you lucky ∼⟩ **4** : a mechanical device for holding something **5** : uncharacteristic or affected stylishness or dignity ⟨put on the ∼⟩ **6** *pl* : RUIN ⟨gone to the ∼s⟩

²**dog** *vb* **dogged; dog·ging** **1** : to hunt or track like a hound **2** : to worry as if by pursuit with dogs : PLAGUE

dog·bane \'dȯg-,bān\ *n* : any of a genus of mostly poisonous herbs with milky juice and often showy flowers

dog·cart \-,kärt\ *n* : a light one-horse carriage with two seats back to back

dog·catch·er \-,ka-chər, -,ke-\ *n* : a community official assigned to catch and dispose of stray dogs

dog–ear \'dȯg-,ir\ *n* : the turned-down corner of a leaf of a book — **dog–ear** *vb* — **dog–eared** \-,ird\ *adj*

dog·fight \'dȯg-,fīt\ *n* : a fight between fighter planes at close range

dog·fish \-,fish\ *n* : any of various small usu. bottom-dwelling sharks

dog·ged \'dȯ-gəd\ *adj* : stubbornly determined : TENACIOUS — **dog·ged·ly** *adv* — **dog·ged·ness** *n*

dog·ger·el \'dȯ-gə-rəl\ *n* : verse that is loosely styled and irregular in measure esp. for comic effect

dog·gie bag *or* **doggy bag** \'dȯ-gē-\ *n* : a container for carrying home leftover food from a restaurant meal

¹**dog·gy** *or* **dog·gie** \'dȯ-gē\ *n, pl* **doggies** : a small dog

²**dog·gy** *adj* **dog·gi·er; -est** : of or resembling a dog ⟨a ∼ odor⟩

dog·house \'dȯg-,haůs\ *n* : a shelter for a dog — **in the doghouse** : in a state of disfavor

do·gie \'dō-gē\ *n, chiefly West* : a motherless calf in a range herd

dog·leg \'dȯg-,leg\ *n* : a sharp bend or angle (as in a road or golf fairway) — **dogleg** *vb*

dog·ma \'dȯg-mə\ *n, pl* **dogmas** *also* **dog·ma·ta** \-mə-tə\ [L, fr. Gk, fr. *dokein* to think, have an opinion] **1** : a tenet or code of tenets **2** : a doctrine or body of doctrines formally proclaimed by a church

dog·ma·tism \'dȯg-mə-,ti-zəm\ *n* : positiveness in stating matters of opinion esp. when unwarranted or arrogant — **dog·mat·ic** \dȯg-'ma-tik\ *adj* — **dog·mat·i·cal·ly** \-ti-k(ə-)lē\ *adv*

do–good·er \'dü-,gů-dər\ *n* : an earnest often naive humanitarian or reformer

dog·tooth violet \'dȯg-,tüth-\ *n* : any of a genus of small spring-flowering bulbous herbs related to the lilies

dog·trot \'dȯg-,trät\ *n* : a gentle trot — **dogtrot** *vb*

dog·wood \'dȯg-,wůd\ *n* : any of a genus of trees and shrubs having heads of small flowers often with showy white, pink, or red bracts

doi·ly \'dȯi-lē\ *n, pl* **doilies** : a small often decorative mat

do in *vb* **1** : RUIN **2** : KILL **3** : TIRE, EXHAUST ⟨the climb *did* him *in*⟩ **4** : CHEAT

do·ings \'dü-iŋz\ *n pl* : GOINGS-ON

do–it–yourself *n* : the activity of doing or making something without professional training or help — **do–it–your·self·er** *n*

dol *abbr* dollar

dol·drums \'dōl-drəmz, 'däl-\ *n pl* **1** : a spell of listlessness or despondency **2** *often cap* : a part of the ocean near the equator known for calms **3** : a state or period of inactivity, stagnation, or slump

¹**dole** \'dōl\ *n* **1** : a distribution esp. of food, money, or clothing to the needy; *also* : something so distributed **2** : a grant of government funds to the unemployed

²**dole** *vb* **doled; dol·ing** : to give or distribute as a charity — usu. used with *out*

dole·ful \'dōl-fəl\ *adj* : full of grief : SAD — **dole·ful·ly** *adv*

dole out *vb* **1** : to give or deliver in small portions **2** : DISH OUT

doll \'däl, 'dȯl\ *n* **1** : a small figure of a human being used esp. as a child's plaything **2** : a pretty woman **3** : an attractive person — **doll·ish** \'dä-lish, 'dȯ-\ *adj*

dol·lar \'dä-lər\ *n* [Dutch or LG *daler*, fr. G *Taler*, short for *Joachimstaler*, fr. Sankt *Joachimsthal*, Bohemia, where talers were first made] **1** : any of various basic monetary units (as in the U.S. and Canada) — see MONEY table **2** : a coin, note, or token representing one dollar **3** : RINGGIT

dol·lop \'dä-ləp\ *n* **1** : LUMP, GLOB **2** : PORTION 1 — **dollop** *vb*

doll up *vb* **1** : to dress elegantly or extravagantly **2** : to make more attractive **3** : to get dolled up

dol·ly \'dä-lē\ *n, pl* **dollies** : a small cart or wheeled platform (as for a television or movie camera)

dol·men \'dōl-mən, 'däl-\ *n* : a prehistoric monument consisting of two or more upright stones supporting a horizontal stone slab

dolmen

do·lo·mite \'dō-lə-,mīt, 'dä-\ *n* : a mineral found in broad layers as a compact limestone

do·lor \'dō-lər, 'dä-\ *n* : mental suffering or anguish : SORROW — **do·lor·ous** *adj* — **do·lor·ous·ly** *adv*

do·lour *chiefly Brit var of* DOLOR

dol·phin \'däl-fən\ *n* **1** : any of various small whales with conical teeth and an elongated beaklike snout **2** : either of two active food fishes of tropical and temperate seas

dolt \'dōlt\ *n* : a stupid person — **dolt·ish** \'dōl-tish\ *adj* — **dolt·ish·ness** *n*

dom *abbr* **1** domestic **2** dominant **3** dominion

-dom *n suffix* **1** : dignity : office ⟨duke*dom*⟩ **2** : realm : jurisdiction ⟨king*dom*⟩ **3** : state or fact of being ⟨free-*dom*⟩ **4** : those having a (specified) office, occupation, interest, or character ⟨official*dom*⟩

do·main \dō-'mān\ *n* **1** : complete and absolute ownership of land **2** : land completely owned **3** : a territory over which dominion is exercised **4** : a sphere of knowledge, influence, or activity ⟨the ~ of science⟩ **5** : a subdivision of the Internet made up of computers whose URLs share a characteristic abbreviation (as *com* or *gov*)

domain name *n* : a sequence of characters (as Merriam-Webster.com) that specifies a group of online resources and forms part of its URL

dome \'dōm\ *n* **1** : a large hemispherical roof or ceiling **2** : a structure or natural formation that resembles the dome of a building **3** : a roofed sports stadium — **dome** *vb*

¹do·mes·tic \də-'mes-tik\ *adj* **1** : living near or about human habitations **2** : TAME, DOMESTICATED **3** : relating and limited to one's own country or the country under consideration **4** : of or relating to the household or the family **5** : devoted to home duties and pleasures **6** : INDIGENOUS — **do·mes·ti·cal·ly** \-ti-k(ə-)lē\ *adv*

²domestic *n* : a household servant

do·mes·ti·cate \də-'mes-ti-ˌkāt\ *vb* **-cat·ed; -cat·ing** : to adapt to life in association with and to the use of humans — **do·mes·ti·ca·tion** \-ˌmes-ti-'kā-shən\ *n*

do·mes·tic·i·ty \ˌdō-ˌmes-ti-sə-tē, də-\ *n, pl* **-ties** **1** : the quality or state of being domestic or domesticated **2** : domestic activities or life

domestic violence *n* : the inflicting of injury by one family or household member on another

do·mi·cile \'dä-mə-ˌsī(-ə)l, 'dō-; 'dä-mə-səl\ *n* : a dwelling place : HOME — **domicile** *vb* — **dom·i·cil·i·ary** \ˌdä-mə-'si-lē-ˌer-ē, ˌdō-\ *adj*

dom·i·nance \'dä-mə-nəns\ *n* **1** : AUTHORITY, CONTROL **2** : the property of one of a pair of alleles or traits that suppresses expression of the other when both are present

¹dom·i·nant \-nənt\ *adj* **1** : controlling or prevailing over all others **2** : overlooking from a high position **3** : exhibiting genetic dominance

²dominant *n* : a dominant gene or trait

dom·i·nate \'dä-mə-ˌnāt\ *vb* **-nat·ed; -nat·ing** **1** : RULE, CONTROL **2** : to have a commanding position or controlling power over **3** : to rise high above in a position suggesting power to dominate — **dom·i·na·tor** \-ˌnā-tər\ *n*

dom·i·na·tion \ˌdä-mə-'nā-shən\ *n* **1** : supremacy or preeminence over another **2** : exercise of mastery, ruling power, or preponderant influence

do·mi·na·trix \ˌdä-mə-'nā-triks\ *n, pl* **-trices** \-'nā-trə-ˌsēz, -nə-'trī-sēz\ : a woman who dominates her sexual partner; *also* : a dominating woman

dom·i·neer \ˌdä-mə-'nir\ *vb* **1** : to rule in an arrogant manner **2** : to be overbearing

do·mi·nie *1 usu* 'dä-mə-nē, *2 usu* 'dō-\ *n* **1** *chiefly Scot* : SCHOOLMASTER **2** : CLERGYMAN

do·min·ion \də-'min-yən\ *n* **1** : DOMAIN **2** : supreme authority : SOVEREIGNTY **3** *often cap* : a self-governing nation of the Commonwealth

dom·i·no \'dä-mə-ˌnō\ *n, pl* **-noes** *or* **-nos** **1** : a long loose hooded cloak usu. worn with a half mask as a masquerade costume **2** : a flat rectangular block used as a piece in a game (**dominoes**)

¹don \'dän\ *vb* **donned; don·ning** [ME, fr. *don* to do + *on*] : to put on (as clothes)

²don *n* [Sp, fr. L *dominus* lord, master] **1** : a Spanish nobleman or gentleman — used as a title prefixed to the Christian name **2** : a head, tutor, or fellow in an English university

do·ña \'dō-nyə\ *n* : a Spanish woman of rank — used as a title prefixed to the Christian name

do·nate \'dō-ˌnāt\ *vb* **do·nat·ed; do·nat·ing** **1** : to make a gift of : CONTRIBUTE **2** : to make a donation

do·na·tion \dō-'nā-shən\ *n* **1** : the making of a gift esp. to a charity **2** : a free contribution : GIFT

¹done \'dən\ *past part of* DO

²done *adj* **1** : doomed to failure, defeat, or death **2** : gone by : OVER ⟨when day is ~⟩ **3** : cooked sufficiently **4** : conformable to social convention

done deal *n* : FAIT ACCOMPLI

dong \'doŋ, 'däŋ\ *n* — see MONEY table

don·key \'däŋ-kē, 'dəŋ-\ *n, pl* **donkeys** **1** : a sturdy and patient domestic mammal classified with the asses **2** : a stupid or obstinate person

don·ny·brook \'dä-nē-ˌbrùk\ *n, often cap* [*Donnybrook Fair,* annual Irish event known for its brawls] : an uproarious brawl

do·nor \'dō-nər\ *n* : one that gives, donates, or presents

donut *var of* DOUGHNUT

doo·dad \'dü-ˌdad\ *n* : an often small article whose common name is unknown or forgotten

doo·dle \'dü-dᵊl\ *vb* **doo·dled; doo·dling** : to draw or scribble aimlessly while occupied with something else — **doodle** *n* — **doo·dler** *n*

doom \'düm\ *n* **1** : JUDGMENT; *esp* : a judicial condemnation or sentence **2** : DESTINY **3** : RUIN, DEATH — **doom** *vb*

dooms·day \'dümz-ˌdā\ *n* : JUDGMENT DAY

door \'dōr\ *n* **1** : a barrier by which an entry is closed and opened; *also* : a similar part of a piece of furniture **2** : DOORWAY **3** : a means of access or participation : OPPORTUNITY

door·keep·er \-ˌkē-pər\ *n* : a person who tends a door

door·knob \-ˌnäb\ *n* : a knob that when turned releases a door latch

door·man \-ˌman, -mən\ *n* : a usu. uniformed attendant at the door of a building (as a hotel)

door·mat \-ˌmat\ *n* : a mat placed before or inside a door for wiping dirt from the shoes

door·plate \-ˌplāt\ *n* : a nameplate on a door

door·step \-ˌstep\ *n* : a step or series of steps before an outer door

door·way \-ˌwā\ *n* **1** : the opening that a door closes **2** : DOOR 3

do·pa \'dō-pə\ *n* : a form of an amino acid that is used esp. in the treatment of Parkinson's disease

do·pa·mine \'dō-pə-ˌmēn\ *n* : an organic compound that occurs esp. as a neurotransmitter in the brain

¹dope \'dōp\ *n* **1** : a preparation for giving a desired quality **2** : an illicit, habit-forming, or narcotic drug; *esp* : MARIJUANA **3** : a stupid person **4** : INFORMATION

²dope *vb* **doped; dop·ing** **1** : to treat with dope; *esp* : to give a narcotic to **2** : FIGURE OUT — usu. used with *out* **3** : to take dope — **dop·er** *n*

dop·ey *also* **dopy** \'dō-pē\ *adj* **dop·i·er; -est** **1** : dulled by alcohol or a narcotic **2** : SLUGGISH **3** : STUPID — **dop·i·ness** *n*

doping *n* : the use of a substance or technique to illegally improve athletic performance

Dopp·ler effect \'dä-plər-\ *n* : a change in the frequency at which waves (as of sound) reach an observer from a source in motion with respect to the observer

do–rag \'dü-ˌrag\ *n* : a kerchief worn esp. to cover the hair

dork \'dörk\ *n, slang* : NERD; *also* : JERK 2

dorm \'dörm\ *n* : DORMITORY

dor·mant \'dör-mənt\ *adj* : INACTIVE; *esp* : not actively growing or functioning ⟨~ buds⟩ — **dor·man·cy** \-mən-sē\ *n*

dor·mer \'dör-mər\ *n* [MF *dormeor* dormitory, fr. L *dormitorium,* fr. *dormire* to sleep] : a window built upright in a sloping roof; *also* : the roofed structure containing such a window

dor·mi·to·ry \'dör-mə-ˌtòr-ē\ *n, pl* **-ries** **1** : a room for sleeping; *esp* : a large room containing a number of beds **2** : a residence hall providing sleeping rooms

dor·mouse \'dör-ˌmaùs\ *n* : any of numerous Old World rodents that resemble small squirrels

dor·sal \'dör-səl\ *adj* : of, relating to, or located near or on the surface of the body that in humans is the back but in most other animals is the upper surface — **dor·sal·ly** *adv*

do·ry \'dòr-ē\ *n, pl* **dories** : a flat-bottomed boat with high flaring sides and a sharp bow

DOS *abbr* disk operating system

¹dose \'dōs\ *n* [ME, fr. MF, fr. LL *dosis,* fr. Gk, lit., act of giving, fr. *didonai* to give] **1** : a measured quantity (as of medicine) to be taken or administered at one time **2** : the quantity of radiation administered or absorbed — **dos·age** \'dō-sij\ *n*

²dose *vb* **dosed; dos·ing** **1** : to give in doses **2** : to give medicine to

do·sim·e·ter \dō-'si-mə-tər\ *n* : a device for measuring doses of radiations (as X-rays) — **do·sim·e·try** \-mə-trē\ *n*

dos·sier \'dòs-,yā, 'dò-sē-,ā\ *n* [F, bundle of documents labeled on the back, dossier, fr. *dos* back, fr. OF, fr. L *dorsum*] : a file containing detailed records on a particular person or subject

¹**dot** \'dät\ *n* **1** : a small spot : SPECK **2** : a small round mark **3** : a precise point esp. in time ⟨be here on the ∼⟩

²**dot** *vb* **dot·ted; dot·ting** **1** : to mark with a dot ⟨∼ an *i*⟩ **2** : to cover with or as if with dots — **dot·ter** *n*

DOT *abbr* Department of Transportation

dot·age \'dō-tij\ *n* : feebleness of mind esp. in old age : SENILITY

dot·ard \-tərd\ *n* : a person in dotage

dot–com \'dät-,käm\ *n* : a company that markets its products or services usu. exclusively via a Web site

dote \'dōt\ *vb* **dot·ed; dot·ing** **1** : to be feebleminded esp. from old age **2** : to be lavish or excessive in one's attention, affection, or fondness ⟨*doted* on her niece⟩

dot matrix *n* : a rectangular arrangement of dots from which alphanumeric characters can be formed (as by a computer printer)

Dou·ay Version \dü-'ā-\ *n* : an English translation of the Vulgate used by Roman Catholics

¹**dou·ble** \'də-bəl\ *adj* [ME, fr. AF, fr. L *duplus*, fr. *duo* two + *-plus* multiplied by] **1** : TWOFOLD, DUAL ⟨serving a ∼ function⟩ **2** : consisting of two members or parts **3** : being twice as great or as many **4** : folded in two **5** : having more than one whorl of petals ⟨∼ roses⟩

²**double** *vb* **dou·bled; dou·bling** **1** : to make, be, or become twice as great or as many **2** : to make a call in bridge that increases the trick values and penalties of (an opponent's bid) **3** : FOLD **4** : CLENCH **5** : to be or cause to be bent over **6** : to take the place of another **7** : to hit a double **8** : to turn sharply and suddenly; *esp* : to turn back on one's course

³**double** *adv* **1** : DOUBLY **2** : two together ⟨sleep ∼⟩

⁴**double** *n* **1** : something twice another in size, strength, speed, quantity, or value **2** : a base hit that enables the batter to reach second base **3** : COUNTERPART, DUPLICATE; *esp* : a person who closely resembles another **4** : UNDERSTUDY, SUBSTITUTE **5** : a sharp turn : REVERSAL **6** : FOLD **7** : a combined bet placed on two different contests **8** *pl* : a game between two pairs of players **9** : an act of doubling in a card game

double bond *n* : a chemical bond in which two atoms in a molecule share two pairs of electrons

double cross *n* : an act of betraying or cheating esp. an associate — **dou·ble–cross** \,də-bəl-'kròs\ *vb* — **dou·ble–cross·er** *n*

dou·ble–deal·ing \,də-bəl-'dē-liŋ\ *n* : DUPLICITY — **dou·ble–deal·er** \-'dē-lər\ *n* — **double–dealing** *adj*

dou·ble–deck·er \-'de-kər\ *n* : something having two decks, levels, or layers — **dou·ble–deck** \-,dek\ *or* **dou·ble–decked** \-,dekt\ *adj*

dou·ble–dig·it \,də-bəl-'di-jət\ *adj* : amounting to 10 percent or more

dou·ble en·ten·dre \,düb-ᵊl-äⁿ-'täⁿd, ,də-bəl-, -'täⁿd-rᵊ\ *n, pl* **double entendres** *same or* -'tän-drəz\ [obs. F, lit., double meaning] : a word or expression capable of two interpretations with one usu. risqué

dou·ble·head·er \,də-bəl-'he-dər\ *n* : two games played consecutively on the same day

double helix *n* : a helix or spiral consisting of two strands (as of DNA) in the surface of a cylinder which coil around its axis

dou·ble–hung \,də-bəl-'həŋ\ *adj, of a window* : having an upper and a lower sash that can slide past each other

dou·ble–joint·ed \-'jòin-təd\ *adj* : having a joint that permits an exceptional degree of freedom of motion of the parts joined ⟨a ∼ finger⟩

dou·ble–park \,də-bəl-'pärk\ *vb* : to park a vehicle beside a row of vehicles already parked parallel to the curb

double play *n* : a play in baseball by which two players are put out

double pneumonia *n* : pneumonia affecting both lungs

double standard *n* : a set of principles that applies differently and usu. more rigorously to one group of people or circumstances than to another

dou·blet \'də-blət\ *n* **1** : a man's close-fitting jacket worn in Europe esp. in the 16th century **2** : one of two similar or identical things

dou·ble take \'də-bəl-,tāk\ *n* : a delayed reaction to a surprising or significant situation after an initial failure to notice anything unusual

dou·ble–talk \-,tòk\ *n* : language that appears to be meaningful but in fact is a mixture of sense and nonsense

double up *vb* : to share accommodations designed for one

double whammy *n* : a combination of two usu. adverse forces, circumstances, or effects

dou·bloon \,də-'blün\ *n* : a former gold coin of Spain and Spanish America

dou·bly \'də-blē\ *adv* **1** : in a twofold manner **2** : to twice the degree ⟨∼ glad⟩

¹**doubt** \'daùt\ *vb* **1** : to be uncertain about **2** : to lack confidence in : DISTRUST **3** : to consider unlikely — **doubt·able** *adj* — **doubt·er** *n*

²**doubt** *n* **1** : uncertainty of belief or opinion **2** : a condition causing uncertainty, hesitation, or suspense ⟨the outcome was in ∼⟩ **3** : DISTRUST **4** : an inclination not to believe or accept

doubt·ful \'daùt-fəl\ *adj* **1** : QUESTIONABLE ⟨∼ they knew what happened⟩ **2** : UNDECIDED ⟨the outcome of the election is ∼⟩ — **doubt·ful·ly** *adv* — **doubt·ful·ness** *n*

¹**doubt·less** \'daùt-ləs\ *adv* **1** : without doubt **2** : PROBABLY

²**doubtless** *adj* : free from doubt : CERTAIN — **doubt·less·ly** *adv*

douche \'düsh\ *n* [F] **1** : a jet of fluid (as water) directed against a part or into a cavity of the body; *also* : a cleansing with a douche **2** : a device for giving douches — **douche** *vb*

dough \'dō\ *n* **1** : a mixture that consists of flour or meal and a liquid (as milk or water) and is stiff enough to knead or roll **2** : something resembling dough esp. in consistency **3** : MONEY — **doughy** \'dō-ē\ *adj*

dough·boy \-,bòi\ *n* : an American infantryman esp. in World War I

dough·nut *also* **do·nut** \-(,)nət\ *n* : a small usu. ring-shaped cake fried in fat

dough·ty \'daù-tē\ *adj* **dough·ti·er; -est** : ABLE, VALIANT ⟨a ∼ warrior⟩

Doug·las fir \'də-gləs-\ *n* : a tall evergreen timber tree of the western U.S.

dou·la \'dü-lə\ *n* : a woman who provides assistance to a mother before, during, and just after childbirth

do up *vb* **1** : to prepare (as by cleaning) for use **2** : to wrap up **3** : CLOTHE, DECORATE **4** : FASTEN

dour \'daù(-ə)r, 'dùr\ *adj* [ME, fr. L *durus* hard] **1** : STERN, HARSH **2** : OBSTINATE **3** : SULLEN — **dour·ly** *adv*

douse \'daùs, 'daùz\ *vb* **doused; dous·ing** **1** : to plunge into water **2** : DRENCH **3** : EXTINGUISH ⟨∼ a match⟩

¹**dove** \'dəv\ *n* **1** : any of numerous pigeons; *esp* : a small wild pigeon **2** : an advocate of peace or of a peaceful policy — **dov·ish** \'də-vish\ *adj*

²**dove** \'dōv\ *past of* DIVE

¹**dove·tail** \'dəv-,tāl\ *n* : something that resembles a dove's tail; *esp* : a flaring tenon and a mortise into which it fits tightly

dovetail: with mortises and tenons

²**dovetail** *vb* **1** : to join by means of dovetails **2** : to fit skillfully together to form a whole ⟨our plans ∼ nicely⟩

dow·a·ger \'daù-i-jər\ *n* **1** : a widow owning property or a title from her deceased husband **2** : a dignified elderly woman

dowdy \'daù-dē\ *adj* **dowd·i·er; -est** : lacking neatness and charm : SHABBY, UNTIDY; *also* : lacking smartness

dow·el \'daù(-ə)l\ *n* **1** : a pin used for fastening together two pieces of wood   2 : a round rod (as of wood) — **dowel** vb

¹**dow·er** \'daú(-ə)r\ n [ME dowere, fr. AF dower, douaire, fr. ML dotarium, fr. L dot-, dos gift, marriage portion]   1 : the part of a deceased husband's real estate which the law gives for life to his widow   2 : DOWRY

²**dower** vb : to supply with a dower : ENDOW

dow·itch·er \'daú-i-chər\ n : any of several long-billed wading birds related to the sandpipers

¹**down** \'daún\ adv [ME doun, fr. OE dūne, short for adūne, of dūne, lit., from (the) hill]   1 : toward or in a lower physical position   2 : to a lying or sitting position   3 : toward or to the ground, floor, or bottom   4 : as a down payment ⟨paid $5 ∼⟩   5 : on paper ⟨put ∼ what he says⟩   6 : in a direction that is the opposite of up   7 : SOUTH   8 : to or in a lower or worse condition or status   9 : from a past time   10 : to or in a state of less activity   11 : into defeat ⟨voted the motion ∼⟩

²**down** prep : down in, on, along, or through : toward the bottom of ⟨fell ∼ a hole⟩ ⟨lives ∼ the road⟩

³**down** vb   1 : to go or cause to go or come down ⟨∼ed a warplane⟩   2 : DEFEAT   3 : to cause (a football) to be out of play   4 : CONSUME 3 ⟨∼ed two beers⟩

⁴**down** adj   1 : occupying a low position; esp : lying on the ground   2 : directed or going downward   3 : being in a state of reduced or low activity   4 : DEPRESSED, DEJECTED   5 : SICK ⟨∼ with a cold⟩   6 : FINISHED, DONE   7 : completely mastered ⟨got her lines ∼⟩   8 : being on record ⟨you're ∼ for two tickets⟩

⁵**down** n   1 : a low or falling period (as in activity, emotional life, or fortunes)   2 : one of a series of attempts to advance a football   3 : a quark with a charge of -⅓ that is one of the constituents of the proton and neutron

⁶**down** n : a rolling usu. treeless upland with sparse soil — usu. used in pl

⁷**down** n   1 : a covering of soft fluffy feathers; also : such feathers   2 : a downlike covering or material

down·beat \'daún-ˌbēt\ n : the downward stroke of a conductor indicating the principally accented note of a measure of music

down·burst \-ˌbərst\ n : a powerful downdraft usu. associated with a thunderstorm that is a hazard for low-flying aircraft; also : MICROBURST

down·cast \-ˌkast\ adj   1 : DEJECTED   2 : directed down ⟨a ∼ glance⟩

down·draft \-ˌdraft\ n : a downward current of gas (as air)

down·er \'daú-nər\ n   1 : a depressant drug; esp : BARBITURATE   2 : someone or something depressing

down·fall \'daún-ˌfol\ n   1 : a sudden fall (as from high rank)   2 : something that causes a downfall — **down·fall·en** \-ˌfo-lən\ adj

¹**down·grade** \'daún-ˌgrād\ n   1 : a downward slope (as of a road)   2 : a decline toward a worse condition

²**downgrade** vb : to lower in quality, value, extent, or status

down·heart·ed \-'här-təd\ adj : DEJECTED

¹**down·hill** \'daún-'hil\ adv : toward the bottom of a hill — **downhill** \-ˌhil\ adj

²**down·hill** \-ˌhil\ n : the sport of skiing downhill usu. in a race against time

¹**down·load** \'daún-ˌlōd\ n : an act or instance of downloading something; also : the item downloaded

²**download** vb : to transfer (data) from a computer to another device — **down·load·able** \-ˌlō-də-bəl\ adj

down payment n : a part of the full price paid at the time of purchase or delivery with the balance to be paid later

down·play \'daún-ˌplā\ vb : DE-EMPHASIZE ⟨∼ed the allegations⟩

down·pour \'daún-ˌpór\ n : a heavy rain

down·range \-'rānj\ adv : away from a launching site

¹**down·right** \-ˌrīt\ adv : THOROUGHLY

²**downright** adj   1 : ABSOLUTE, UTTER ⟨a ∼ lie⟩   2 : PLAIN, BLUNT ⟨a ∼ man⟩

down·shift \-ˌshift\ vb : to shift an automotive vehicle into a lower gear

down·size \-ˌsīz\ vb : to reduce or undergo reduction in size or numbers

down·spout \-ˌspaút\ n : a vertical pipe used to drain rainwater from a roof

Down syndrome \'daún-\ or **Down's syndrome** \'daúnz-\ n : a birth defect characterized by mental retardation,

slanting eyes, a broad short skull, broad hands with short fingers, and the presence of an extra chromosome

down·stage \'daún-'stāj\ adv or adj : toward or at the front of a theatrical stage — **down·stage** \-ˌstāj\ n

down·stairs \-'sterz\ adv : on or to a lower floor and esp. the main or ground floor — **down·stairs** \-ˌsterz\ adj or n

down·stream \-'strēm\ adv or adj : in the direction of flow of a stream

down·stroke \-ˌstrōk\ n : a downward stroke

down·swing \-ˌswiŋ\ n   1 : a swing downward   2 : DOWNTURN

down–to–earth adj : PRACTICAL, REALISTIC

down·town \'daún-ˌtaún\ n : the main business district of a town or city — **downtown** \'daún-'taún\ adj or adv

down·trod·den \'daún-'trä-d°n\ adj : suffering oppression

down·turn \-ˌtərn\ n : a downward turn esp. in economic activity

¹**down·ward** \'daún-wərd\ or **down·wards** \-wərdz\ adv   1 : from a higher to a lower place or condition   2 : from an earlier time   3 : from an ancestor or predecessor

²**downward** adj : directed toward or situated in a lower place or condition

down·wind \'daún-'wind\ adv or adj : in the direction that the wind is blowing

downy \'daú-nē\ adj **down·i·er; -est** : resembling or covered with down

downy mildew n : any of various parasitic fungi producing whitish masses esp. on the underside of plant leaves; also : a plant disease caused by downy mildew

downy woodpecker n : a small black-and-white woodpecker of No. America

dow·ry \'daú(-ə)r-ē\ n, pl **dowries** [ME dowarie, fr. AF, alter. of dower, douaire dower] : the property that a woman brings to her husband in marriage

dowse \'daúz\ vb **dowsed; dows·ing** : to use a divining rod esp. to find water — **dows·er** n

dox·ol·o·gy \däk-'sä-lə-jē\ n, pl **-gies** : a usu. short hymn of praise to God

doy·en \'dói-ən, 'dwä-ˌyaⁿ\ n : the senior or most experienced person in a group

doy·enne \dói-'yen, dwä-'yen\ n : a woman who is a doyen

doy·ley chiefly Brit var of DOILY

doz abbr   dozen

doze \'dōz\ vb **dozed; doz·ing** : to sleep lightly — **doze** n

doz·en \'də-z°n\ n, pl **dozens** or **dozen** [ME dozeine, fr. AF duzeine, fr. duze twelve, fr. L duodecim, fr. duo two + decem ten] : a group of twelve — **doz·enth** \-z°nth\ adj

¹**DP** \ˌdē-'pē\ n, pl **DP's** or **DPs**   1 : a displaced person   2 : DOUBLE PLAY

²**DP** abbr   data processing

dpt abbr   department

DPT abbr   diphtheria-pertussis-tetanus (vaccines)

dr abbr   1 debtor   2 dram   3 drive   4 drum

Dr abbr   doctor

DR abbr   1 dead reckoning   2 dining room

drab \'drab\ adj **drab·ber; drab·best**   1 : being of a light olive-brown color   2 : DULL, MONOTONOUS, CHEERLESS — **drab·ly** adv — **drab·ness** n

drach·ma \'drak-mə\ n, pl **drach·mas** or **drach·mai** \-ˌmī\ or **drach·mae** \-(ˌ)mē\ : the former basic monetary unit of Greece

dra·co·ni·an \drā-'kō-nē-ən, drə-\ adj, often cap : CRUEL; also : SEVERE

¹**draft** \'draft, 'dräft\ n   1 : the act of drawing or hauling   2 : the act or an instance of drinking or inhaling; also : the portion drunk or inhaled in one such act   3 : DOSE, POTION   4 : DELINEATION, PLAN, DESIGN; also : a preliminary sketch, outline, or version ⟨a rough ∼ of a speech⟩   5 : the act of drawing (as from a cask); also : a portion of liquid so drawn   6 : the depth of water a ship draws esp. when loaded   7 : a system for or act of selecting persons (as for sports teams or compulsory military service); also : the persons so selected   8 : an order for the payment of money drawn by one person or bank on another   9 : a heavy demand : STRAIN   10 : a current of air; also : a device to regulate air supply (as in a stove) — **on draft** : ready to be drawn from a receptacle ⟨beer on draft⟩

²**draft** adj   1 : used or adapted for drawing loads ⟨∼ horses⟩   2 : being or having been on draft ⟨∼ beer⟩

³**draft** vb   1 : to select usu. on a compulsory basis; esp : to

conscript for military service   **2** : to draw the preliminary sketch, version, or plan of   **3** : COMPOSE, PREPARE   **4** : to draw off or away

draft·ee \draf-'tē, 'dräf-\ *n* : a person who is drafted

drafts·man \'draft-smən, 'dräft-\ *n* : a person who draws plans (as for buildings or machinery) — **drafts·man·ly** \-lē\ *adj*

drafty \'draf-tē, 'dräf-\ *adj* **draft·i·er; -est** : exposed to or abounding in drafts of air ⟨a ~ room⟩

¹**drag** \'drag\ *n* **1** : a device pulled along under water for detecting or gathering   **2** : something (as a harrow or sledge) that is dragged along over a surface   **3** : the act or an instance of dragging   **4** : something that hinders progress; *also* : something boring ⟨thinks school is a ~⟩   **5** : STREET ⟨the main ~⟩   **6** : clothing typical of one sex worn by a member of the opposite sex

²**drag** *vb* **dragged; drag·ging   1** : HAUL   **2** : to move or proceed with slowness or difficulty ⟨*dragged* himself out of bed⟩ ⟨the lecture *dragged* on⟩   **3** : to force into or out of some situation, condition, or course of action   **4** : PROTRACT ⟨~ a story out⟩   **5** : to hang or lag behind   **6** : to explore, search, or fish with a drag   **7** : to trail along on the ground   **8** : DRAW, PUFF ⟨~ on a cigarette⟩   **9** : to move (items on a computer screen) esp. by using a mouse — **drag·ger** *n* — **drag one's feet** *also* **drag one's heels** : to act slowly or with hesitation

drag·net \-ˌnet\ *n* **1** : NET, TRAWL   **2** : a network of planned actions for pursuing and catching ⟨a police ~⟩

drag·o·man \'dra-gə-mən\ *n, pl* **-mans** *or* **-men** \-mən\ : an interpreter employed esp. in the Near East

drag·on \'dra-gən\ *n* [ME, fr. AF *dragun*, fr. L *dracon-, draco* serpent, dragon, fr. Gk *drakōn* serpent] : a fabulous animal usu. represented as a huge winged scaly serpent with a crested head and large claws

drag·on·fly \-ˌflī\ *n* : any of a group of large harmless 4-winged insects that hold the wings horizontal and unfolded in repose

¹**dra·goon** \drə-'gün, dra-\ *n* [F *dragon* dragon, dragoon, fr. MF] **1** : a heavily armed mounted soldier   **2** : CAVALRYMAN

²**dragoon** *vb* : to force or attempt to force into submission : COERCE

drag race *n* : an acceleration contest between vehicles — **drag racer** *n*

drag·ster \'drag-stər\ *n* : a usu. high-powered vehicle used in a drag race

drag strip *n* : a site for drag races

¹**drain** \'drān\ *vb* **1** : to draw off or flow off gradually or completely   **2** : to exhaust physically or emotionally ⟨~ed by the work⟩   **3** : to make or become gradually dry or empty ⟨~ a swamp⟩   **4** : to carry away the surface water of : discharge surface or surplus water   **5** : EMPTY, EXHAUST ⟨~ed our savings⟩ — **drain·er** *n*

²**drain** *n* **1** : a means (as a channel or sewer) of draining   **2** : the act of draining   **3** : a gradual outflow; *also* : something causing an outflow ⟨a ~ on our savings⟩

drain·age \'drā-nij\ *n* **1** : the act or process of draining; *also* : something that is drained off   **2** : a means for draining : DRAIN, SEWER   **3** : an area drained

drain·pipe \'drān-ˌpīp\ *n* : a pipe for drainage

drake \'drāk\ *n* : a male duck

¹**dram** \'dram\ *n* **1** — see WEIGHT table   **2** : FLUID DRAM   **3** : a small drink

²**dram** \'dräm\ *n* — see MONEY table

dra·ma \'drä-mə, 'dra-\ *n* [LL, fr. Gk, deed, drama, fr. *dran* to do, act] **1** : a literary composition designed for theatrical presentation; *also* : a production (as a film) with a serious tone or subject   **2** : dramatic art, literature, or affairs   **3** : a series of events involving conflicting forces — **dra·mat·ic** \drə-'ma-tik\ *adj* — **dra·mat·i·cal·ly** \-ti-k(ə-)lē\ *adv* — **dra·ma·tist** \'dra-mə-tist, 'drä-\ *n*

dram·a·ti·sa·tion, dra·ma·tise *Brit var of* DRAMATIZATION, DRAMATIZE

dra·ma·tize \'dra-mə-ˌtīz, 'drä-\ *vb* **-tized; -tiz·ing   1** : to adapt for or be suitable for theatrical presentation   **2** : to present or represent in a dramatic manner — **dram·a·ti·za·tion** \ˌdra-mə-tə-'zā-shən, ˌdrä-\ *n*

dra·me·dy \'drä-mə-ˌdē, 'dra-\ *n* : a comedy having dramatic moments

drank *past and past part of* DRINK

¹**drape** \'drāp\ *vb* **draped; drap·ing   1** : to cover or adorn

with or as if with folds of cloth ⟨kings *draped* in robes⟩   **2** : to cause to hang or stretch out loosely or carelessly   **3** : to arrange or become arranged in flowing lines or folds

²**drape** *n* **1** : CURTAIN   **2** : arrangement in or of folds   **3** : the cut or hang of clothing

drap·er \'drā-pər\ *n, chiefly Brit* : a dealer in cloth and sometimes in clothing and dry goods

drap·ery \'drā-pə-rē\ *n, pl* **-er·ies   1** *Brit* : DRY GOODS   **2** : a decorative fabric esp. when hung loosely and in folds; *also* : hangings of heavy fabric used as a curtain

dras·tic \'dras-tik\ *adj* : HARSH, RIGOROUS, SEVERE ⟨~ punishment⟩ — **dras·ti·cal·ly** \-ti-k(ə-)lē\ *adv*

draught \'draft\, **draughty** \'dräf-tē\ *chiefly Brit var of* DRAFT, DRAFTY

draughts \'dräfts\ *n, Brit* : CHECKERS

draughts·man *chiefly Brit var of* DRAFTSMAN

Dra·vid·i·an \drə-'vi-dē-ən\ *n* : a language family of south Asia that includes the major literary languages of southern India

¹**draw** \'drò\ *vb* **drew** \'drü\; **drawn** \'dròn\; **draw·ing   1** : to cause to move toward a force exerted   **2** : to cause to go in a certain direction ⟨*drew* him aside⟩   **3** : to move or go steadily or gradually ⟨night ~s near⟩   **4** : ATTRACT, ENTICE   **5** : PROVOKE, ROUSE ⟨*drew* enemy fire⟩   **6** : INHALE ⟨~ a deep breath⟩   **7** : to bring or pull out ⟨*drew* a gun⟩   **8** : to cause to come out of a container or source ⟨~ blood⟩ ⟨~ water for a bath⟩   **9** : EVISCERATE   **10** : to require (a specified depth) to float in   **11** : ACCUMULATE, GAIN ⟨~ing interest⟩   **12** : to take money from a place of deposit : WITHDRAW   **13** : to receive regularly ⟨~ a salary⟩   **14** : to take (cards) from a stack or the dealer   **15** : to receive or take at random ⟨~ a winning number⟩   **16** : to bend (a bow) by pulling back the string   **17** : WRINKLE, SHRINK   **18** : to change shape by or as if by pulling or stretching ⟨a face *drawn* with sorrow⟩   **19** : to leave (a contest) undecided : TIE   **20** : DELINEATE, SKETCH   **21** : to write out in due form : DRAFT ⟨~ up a will⟩   **22** : FORMULATE ⟨~ comparisons⟩   **23** : INFER ⟨~ a conclusion⟩   **24** : to spread or elongate (metal) by hammering or by pulling through dies   **25** : to produce or allow a draft or current of air ⟨the chimney ~s well⟩   **26** : to swell out in a wind ⟨all sails ~ing⟩ — **draw a blank** : to be unable to think of something — **draw the line** *or* **draw a line** : to fix an arbitrary boundary usu. between two things

²**draw** *n* **1** : the act, process, or result of drawing   **2** : a lot or chance drawn at random   **3** : a contest left undecided or deadlocked : TIE   **4** : one that draws attention or patronage : ATTRACTION

draw·back \'drò-ˌbak\ *n* : DISADVANTAGE 2

draw·bridge \-ˌbrij\ *n* : a bridge made to be raised, lowered, or turned to permit or deny passage

draw·er \'dròr, 'drò-ər\ *n* **1** : one that draws   **2** *pl* : an undergarment for the lower part of the body   **3** : a sliding boxlike compartment (as in a table or desk)

draw·ing \'drò-iŋ\ *n* **1** : an act or instance of drawing; *esp* : an occasion when something is decided by drawing lots ⟨tonight's lottery ~⟩   **2** : the act or art of making a figure, plan, or sketch by means of lines   **3** : a representation made by drawing : SKETCH

drawing card *n* : DRAW 4

drawing room *n* : a formal reception room

drawl \'dròl\ *vb* : to speak or utter slowly with vowels greatly prolonged — **drawl** *n*

draw on *vb* : APPROACH ⟨night *draws on*⟩

draw out *vb* **1** : PROLONG   **2** : to cause to speak freely

draw·string \'drò-ˌstriŋ\ *n* : a string, cord, or tape for use in closing a bag or controlling fullness in garments or curtains

draw up *vb* **1** : to prepare a draft or version of   **2** : to pull oneself erect   **3** : to bring or come to a stop

dray \'drā\ *n* : a strong low cart for carrying heavy loads

¹**dread** \'dred\ *vb* **1** : to fear greatly   **2** : to feel extreme reluctance to meet or face

²**dread** *n* : great fear esp. of some harm to come

³**dread** *adj* **1** : causing great fear or anxiety   **2** : inspiring awe

dread·ful \'dred-fəl\ *adj* **1** : inspiring dread or awe : FRIGHTENING   **2** : extremely distasteful, unpleasant, or shocking — **dread·ful·ly** *adv*

dread·locks \'dred-ˌläks\ *n pl* : long braids of hair over the entire head

dread·nought \'dred-ˌnȯt\ *n* : BATTLESHIP

¹**dream** \'drēm\ *n* [ME *dreem,* fr. OE *drēam* noise, joy, and ON *draumr* dream] **1** : a series of thoughts, images, or emotions occurring during sleep **2** : a dreamlike vision : DAYDREAM, REVERIE **3** : something notable for its beauty, excellence, or enjoyable quality **4** : IDEAL — **dream·like** \-ˌlīk\ *adj* — **dreamy** *adj*

²**dream** \'drēm\ *vb* **dreamed** \'dremt, 'drēmd\ *or* **dreamt** \'dremt\; **dream·ing 1** : to have a dream of **2** : to indulge in daydreams or fantasies : pass (time) in reverie or inaction **3** : IMAGINE — **dream·er** *n*

dream·boat \'drēm-ˌbōt\ *n, slang* : something highly desirable; *esp* : a very attractive person

dream·land \'drēm-ˌland\ *n* : an unreal delightful country that exists in imagination or in dreams

dream up *vb* : INVENT, CONCOCT

dream·world \-ˌwərld\ *n* : a world of illusion or fantasy

drear \'drir\ *adj* : DREARY

drea·ry \'drir-ē\ *adj* **drea·ri·er; -est** [ME *drery,* fr. OE *drēorig* sad, bloody, fr. *drēor* gore] **1** : DOLEFUL, SAD **2** : DISMAL, GLOOMY — **drea·ri·ly** \-ə-lē\ *adv*

¹**dredge** \'drej\ *vb* **dredged; dredg·ing** : to gather or search with or as if with a dredge — **dredg·er** *n*

²**dredge** *n* : a machine or barge for removing earth or silt

³**dredge** *vb* **dredged; dredg·ing** : to coat (food) by sprinkling (as with flour)

dregs \'dregz\ *n pl* **1** : SEDIMENT 1 **2** : the most undesirable part ⟨the ∼ of humanity⟩

drench \'drench\ *vb* : to wet thoroughly

¹**dress** \'dres\ *vb* [ME, fr. AF *drescer* to direct, put right, fr. VL **directiare,* fr. L *directus* direct] **1** : to make or set straight : ALIGN **2** : to prepare for use; *esp* : BUTCHER **3** : TRIM, EMBELLISH ⟨∼ a store window⟩ **4** : to put clothes on : CLOTHE; *also* : to put on or wear formal or fancy clothes **5** : to apply dressings or medicine to ⟨∼ a wound⟩ **6** : to arrange (the hair) by combing, brushing, or curling **7** : to apply fertilizer to ⟨∼ a field⟩ **8** : SMOOTH, FINISH ⟨∼ leather⟩

²**dress** *n* **1** : APPAREL, CLOTHING ⟨casual ∼⟩ **2** : a garment usu. consisting of a one-piece bodice and skirt — **dress·mak·er** \-ˌmā-kər\ *n* — **dress·mak·ing** \-ˌmā-kiŋ\ *n*

³**dress** *adj* : suitable for a formal occasion; *also* : requiring formal dress

dres·sage \drə-'säzh\ *n* [F] : the execution by a trained horse of complex movements in response to barely perceptible signals from its rider

dress down *vb* : to scold severely

¹**dress·er** \'dre-sər\ *n* : a chest of drawers or bureau with a mirror

²**dresser** *n* : one that dresses

dress·ing \'dre-siŋ\ *n* **1** : the act or process of one who dresses **2** : a sauce for adding to a dish (as a salad) **3** : a seasoned mixture usu. used as stuffing **4** : material used to cover an injury (as a wound)

dressing gown *n* : a loose robe worn esp. while dressing or resting

dressy \'dre-sē\ *adj* **dress·i·er; -est 1** : showy in dress **2** : STYLISH, SMART

drew *past of* DRAW

¹**drib·ble** \'dri-bəl\ *vb* **drib·bled; drib·bling 1** : to fall or flow in drops : TRICKLE **2** : DROOL **3** : to propel by successive slight taps or bounces

²**dribble** *n* **1** : a small trickling stream or flow **2** : a drizzling shower **3** : the dribbling of a ball or puck

drib·let \'dri-blət\ *n* **1** : a trifling amount **2** : a drop of liquid

dri·er *or* **dry·er** \'drī-ər\ *n* **1** : a substance that speeds drying (as of paint or ink) **2** *usu* **dryer** : a device for drying

¹**drift** \'drift\ *n* **1** : the motion or course of something drifting; *also* : a gradual shift of position **2** : a mass of matter (as snow or sand) piled up esp. by wind **3** : earth, gravel, and rock deposited by a glacier **4** : a general underlying design or tendency : MEANING ⟨catch my ∼⟩

²**drift** *vb* **1** : to float or be driven along by or as if by a current of water or air ⟨∼ing logs⟩ **2** : to become piled up by wind or water ⟨∼ing snow⟩

drift·er \'drif-tər\ *n* : a person who moves about aimlessly

drift net *n* : a fishing net often miles in extent arranged to drift with the tide or current

drift·wood \'drift-ˌwu̇d\ *n* : wood drifted or floated by water

¹**drill** \'dril\ *n* **1** : a tool for boring holes **2** : the training of soldiers in marching and the handling of arms **3** : a regularly practiced exercise ⟨a shooting ∼⟩

²**drill** *vb* **1** : to instruct and exercise by repetition **2** : to train in or practice military drill **3** : to bore with a drill ⟨∼ a hole⟩ — **drill·er** *n*

³**drill** *n* **1** : a shallow furrow or trench in which seed is sown **2** : an agricultural implement for making furrows and dropping seed into them

⁴**drill** *n* : a firm cotton twilled fabric

drill·mas·ter \'dril-ˌmas-tər\ *n* : an instructor in military drill

drill press *n* : an upright drilling machine in which the drill is pressed to the work usu. by a hand lever

drily *var of* DRYLY

¹**drink** \'driŋk\ *vb* **drank** \'draŋk\; **drunk** \'drəŋk\ *or* **drank**; **drink·ing 1** : to swallow liquid : IMBIBE **2** : ABSORB **3** : to take in through the senses ⟨∼ in the beautiful scenery⟩ **4** : to give or join in a toast **5** : to drink alcoholic beverages esp. to excess — **drink·able** *adj* — **drink·er** *n*

²**drink** *n* **1** : BEVERAGE; *also* : an alcoholic beverage **2** : a draft or portion of liquid **3** : excessive consumption of alcoholic beverages

¹**drip** \'drip\ *vb* **dripped; drip·ping 1** : to fall or let fall in drops **2** : to let fall drops of moisture or liquid ⟨a *dripping* faucet⟩ **3** : to overflow with or as if with moisture ⟨clothes *dripping* with sweat⟩ ⟨stories *dripping* with irony⟩

²**drip** *n* **1** : a falling in drops **2** : liquid that falls, overflows, or is extruded in drops **3** : the sound made by or as if by falling drops

¹**drive** \'drīv\ *vb* **drove** \'drōv\; **driv·en** \'dri-vən\; **driv·ing 1** : to urge, push, or force onward **2** : to carry through strongly ⟨∼ a bargain⟩ **3** : to set or keep in motion or operation **4** : to direct the movement or course of **5** : to convey in a vehicle ⟨*drove* her to school⟩ **6** : to bring into a specified condition ⟨the noise ∼s me crazy⟩ **7** : FORCE, COMPEL ⟨*driven* by hunger to steal⟩ **8** : to project, inject, or impress forcefully ⟨*drove* the lesson home⟩ **9** : to produce by opening a way ⟨∼ a well⟩ **10** : to progress with strong momentum ⟨a *driving* rain⟩ **11** : to propel an object of play (as a golf ball) by a hard blow — **driv·er** *n*

²**drive** *n* **1** : a trip in a carriage or automobile **2** : a driving or collecting of animals ⟨a cattle ∼⟩ **3** : the guiding of logs downstream to a mill **4** : the act of driving a ball; *also* : the flight of a ball **5** : DRIVEWAY **6** : a public road for driving (as in a park) **7** : the state of being hurried and under pressure **8** : an intensive campaign ⟨membership ∼⟩ **9** : the apparatus by which motion is imparted to a machine **10** : an offensive or aggressive move : a military attack **11** : NEED, LONGING ⟨the ∼ to succeed⟩ **12** : dynamic quality **13** : a device for reading and writing on magnetic media (as magnetic tape or disks)

drive–in \'drī-ˌvin\ *adj* : accommodating patrons while they remain in their automobiles — **drive–in** *n*

¹**driv·el** \'dri-vəl\ *vb* **-eled** *or* **-elled; -el·ing** *or* **-el·ling 1** : DROOL, SLAVER **2** : to talk or utter stupidly, carelessly, or in an infantile way — **driv·el·er** *n*

²**drivel** *n* : NONSENSE

drive·shaft \'drīv-ˌshaft\ *n* : a shaft that transmits mechanical power

drive–through *also* **drive–thru** \'drīv-ˌthrü\ *adj* : designed for the service of patrons remaining in their automobiles — **drive–through** *also* **drive–thru** *n*

drive·way \-ˌwā\ *n* : a short private road leading from the street to a house, garage, or parking lot

¹**driz·zle** \'dri-zəl\ *n* : a fine misty rain

²**drizzle** *vb* **driz·zled; driz·zling** : to rain in very small drops

drogue \'drōg\ *n* : a small parachute for slowing down or stabilizing something (as a space capsule)

droll \'drōl\ *adj* [F *drôle,* fr. *drôle* scamp, fr. MF *drolle,* fr. MD, imp] : having a humorous, whimsical, or odd quality ⟨a ∼ expression⟩ — **droll·ery** \'drō-lə-rē\ *n* — **drol·ly** *adv*

drom·e·dary \'drä-mə-ˌder-ē\ *n, pl* **-dar·ies** [ME *drome-*

darie, fr. MF *dromedaire,* fr. LL *dromedarius,* fr. L *dromad-, dromas,* fr. Gk, running] : CAMEL; *esp* : a domesticated one-humped camel of western Asia and northern Africa

¹drone \'drōn\ *n* 1 : a male honeybee 2 : one that lives on the labors of others : PARASITE 3 : an unmanned aircraft or ship guided by remote control 4 : DRUDGE

²drone *vb* **droned; dron·ing** : to sound with a low dull monotonous murmuring sound : speak monotonously

³drone *n* : a deep monotonous sound ⟨the ∼ of engines⟩

drool \'drül\ *vb* 1 : to let liquid flow from the mouth 2 : to talk foolishly — **drool** *n*

droop \'drüp\ *vb* 1 : to hang or incline downward 2 : to sink gradually — LANGUISH — **droop** *n* — **droopy** *adj*

¹drop \'dräp\ *n* 1 : the quantity of fluid that falls in one spherical mass 2 *pl* : a dose of medicine measured by drops 3 : a small quantity of drink 4 : the smallest practical unit of liquid measure 5 : something (as a pendant or a small round candy) that resembles a liquid drop 6 : FALL 7 : a decline in quantity or quality 8 : a descent by parachute 9 : the distance through which something drops 10 : a slot into which something is to be dropped 11 : something that drops or has dropped

²drop *vb* **dropped; drop·ping** 1 : to fall or let fall in drops 2 : to let fall : LOWER ⟨∼ a glove⟩ ⟨*dropped* his voice⟩ 3 : SEND ⟨∼ me a note⟩ 4 : to let go : DISMISS ⟨∼ the subject⟩ 5 : MENTION ⟨∼ a suggestion⟩ 6 : to knock down : cause to fall 7 : to go lower : become less ⟨prices *dropped*⟩ 8 : SPEND, LOSE ⟨∼ $20⟩ ⟨*dropped* ten pounds⟩ 9 : to come or go unexpectedly or informally ⟨a friend *dropped* in⟩ 10 : to pass from one state into a less active one ⟨∼ off to sleep⟩ 11 : to move downward or with a current 12 : QUIT ⟨*dropped* out of the race⟩ — **drop back** : to move toward the rear — **drop behind** : to fail to keep up

drop–down \'dräp-ˌdau̇n\ *adj* : PULL-DOWN

drop·kick \-ˈkik\ *n* : a kick made by dropping a ball to the ground and kicking it at the moment it starts to rebound — **drop–kick** *vb*

drop·let \'drä-plət\ *n* : a tiny drop

drop–off \'dräp-ˌȯf\ *n* 1 : a steep or perpendicular descent 2 : a marked decline ⟨a ∼ in attendance⟩ 3 : an act or instance of delivering or depositing something ⟨∼ points along the route⟩

drop off *vb* : to fall asleep

drop out *vb* : to withdraw from participation or membership; *esp* : to leave school before graduation — **drop·out** \'dräp-ˌau̇t\ *n*

drop·per \'drä-pər\ *n* 1 : one that drops 2 : a short glass tube with a rubber bulb used to measure out liquids by drops

drop·pings *n pl* : MANURE, DUNG

drop·sy \'dräp-sē\ *n* [ME *dropesie,* short for *ydropesie,* fr. AF, fr. L *hydropisis,* fr. Gk *hydrōps,* fr. *hydōr* water] : EDEMA — **drop·si·cal** \-si-kəl\ *adj*

drop–top \'dräp-ˌtäp\ *n* : CONVERTIBLE

dross \'dräs\ *n* 1 : the scum that forms on the surface of a molten metal 2 : waste matter : REFUSE

drought \'drau̇t\ *also* **drouth** \'drau̇th\ *n* : a long spell of dry weather

¹drove \'drōv\ *n* 1 : a group of animals driven or moving in a body 2 : a large number : CROWD — usu. used in pl. ⟨tourists arriving in ∼s⟩

²drove *past of* DRIVE

drov·er \'drō-vər\ *n* : one who drives domestic animals usu. to market

drown \'drau̇n\ *vb* **drowned** \'drau̇nd\; **drown·ing** 1 : to suffocate by submersion esp. in water 2 : to become drowned 3 : to cover with water 4 : to cause to be muted (as a sound) by a loud noise 5 : OVERPOWER, OVERWHELM

drowse \'drau̇z\ *vb* **drowsed; drows·ing** : DOZE — **drowse** *n*

drowsy \'drau̇-zē\ *adj* **drows·i·er; -est** 1 : ready to fall asleep 2 : making one sleepy ⟨∼ music⟩ — **drows·i·ly** \-zə-lē\ *adv* — **drows·i·ness** \-zē-nəs\ *n*

drub \'drəb\ *vb* **drubbed; drub·bing** 1 : to beat severely 2 : to berate critically 3 : to defeat decisively

drudge \'drəj\ *vb* **drudged; drudg·ing** : to do hard, menial, or monotonous work — **drudge** *n* — **drudg·ery** \'drə-jə-rē\ *n*

¹drug \'drəg\ *n* 1 : a substance used as a medicine or in making medicine 2 : a substance (as heroin or marijuana) that can cause addiction, habituation, or a marked change in mental status

²drug *vb* **drugged; drug·ging** : to affect with or as if with drugs; *esp* : to stupefy with a narcotic

drug·gist \'drə-gist\ *n* : a dealer in drugs and medicines; *also* : PHARMACIST

drug·store \'drəg-ˌstȯr\ *n* : a retail shop where medicines and miscellaneous articles are sold

dru·id \'drü-əd\ *n, often cap* : one of an ancient Celtic priesthood appearing in Irish, Welsh, and Christian legends as magicians and wizards

¹drum \'drəm\ *n* 1 : a percussion instrument usu. consisting of a hollow cylinder with a skin or plastic head stretched over one or both ends that is beaten with the hands or with a stick 2 : the sound of a drum; *also* : a similar sound 3 : a drum-shaped object (as a structure or container)

²drum *vb* **drummed; drum·ming** 1 : to beat a drum 2 : to sound rhythmically : THROB, BEAT 3 : to summon or enlist by or as if by beating a drum ⟨*drummed* into service⟩ 4 : EXPEL — usu. used with *out* 5 : to drive or force by steady effort ⟨∼ the facts into memory⟩ 6 : to strike or tap repeatedly so as to produce rhythmic sounds

drum·beat \'drəm-ˌbēt\ *n* : a stroke on a drum or its sound

drum major *n* : the leader of a marching band

drum ma·jor·ette \-ˌmā-jə-ˈret\ *n* : a girl or woman who leads a marching band; *also* : a baton twirler who accompanies a marching band

drum·mer \'drə-mər\ *n* 1 : one that plays a drum 2 : a traveling salesman

drum·stick \'drəm-ˌstik\ *n* 1 : a stick for beating a drum 2 : the lower segment of a fowl's leg

drum up *vb* 1 : to bring about by persistent effort ⟨*drum up* business⟩ 2 : INVENT, ORIGINATE

¹drunk *past part of* DRINK

²drunk \'drəŋk\ *adj* 1 : having the faculties impaired by alcohol ⟨∼ drivers⟩ 2 : dominated by an intense feeling ⟨∼ with power⟩ 3 : of, relating to, caused by, or characterized by intoxication

³drunk *n* 1 : a period of excessive drinking 2 : a drunken person

drunk·ard \'drəŋ-kərd\ *n* : one who is habitually drunk

drunk·en \'drəŋ-kən\ *adj* 1 : DRUNK 2 : given to habitual excessive use of alcohol 3 : of, relating to, or resulting from intoxication ⟨a ∼ brawl⟩ 4 : unsteady or lurching as if from intoxication ⟨walked with a ∼ shuffle⟩ — **drunk·en·ly** *adv* — **drunk·en·ness** *n*

drupe \'drüp\ *n* : a partly fleshy fruit (as a plum or cherry) having one seed enclosed in a hard inner shell

¹dry \'drī\ *adj* **dri·er** \'drī-ər\; **dri·est** \-əst\ 1 : free or freed from water or liquid ⟨∼ fruits⟩; *also* : not being in or under water 2 : characterized by lack of water or moisture ⟨∼ climate⟩ 3 : lacking freshness : STALE 4 : devoid of natural moisture; *also* : THIRSTY 5 : no longer liquid or sticky ⟨the ink is ∼⟩ 6 : not giving milk ⟨a ∼ cow⟩ 7 : marked by the absence of alcoholic beverages ⟨a ∼ dormitory⟩ 8 : prohibiting the making or distributing of alcoholic beverages 9 : not sweet ⟨∼ wine⟩ 10 : solid as opposed to liquid ⟨∼ groceries⟩ 11 : containing or employing no liquid 12 : SEVERE; *also* : UNINTERESTING, WEARISOME 13 : not productive ⟨a writer's ∼ spell⟩ 14 : marked by a matter-of-fact, ironic, or terse manner of expression ⟨∼ humor⟩ — **dri·ly** *or* **dry·ly** *adv* — **dry·ness** *n*

²dry *vb* **dried; dry·ing** : to make or become dry

³dry *n, pl* **drys** : PROHIBITIONIST

dry·ad \'drī-əd, -ˌad\ *n* : WOOD NYMPH

dry cell *n* : a battery whose contents are not spillable

dry–clean \'drī-ˌklēn\ *vb* : to clean (fabrics) chiefly with solvents other than water — **dry cleaning** *n*

dry dock \'drī-ˌdäk\ *n* : a dock that can be kept dry during ship construction or repair

dryer *var of* DRIER

dry farm·ing *n* : farming without irrigation in areas of limited rainfall — **dry–farm** *vb* — **dry farm·er** *n*

dry goods \'drī-ˌgu̇dz\ *n pl* : cloth goods (as fabrics, ribbon, and ready-to-wear clothing)

dry ice *n* : solid carbon dioxide

dry measure *n* : a series of units of capacity for dry commodities — see METRIC SYSTEM table, WEIGHT table

dry rot *n* : decay of timber in which fungi consume the wood's cellulose

dry run *n* : REHEARSAL, TRIAL

dry·wall \'drī-ˌwȯl\ *n* : a wallboard consisting of fiberboard, paper, or felt over a plaster core

Ds *symbol* darmstadtium

DSC *abbr* 1 Distinguished Service Cross 2 doctor of surgical chiropody

DSM *abbr* Distinguished Service Medal

DST *abbr* daylight saving time

DTP *abbr* diphtheria, tetanus, pertussis (vaccines)

d.t.'s \ˌdē-'tēz\ *n pl, often cap D&T* : DELIRIUM TREMENS

du·al \'dü-əl, 'dyü-\ *adj* 1 : TWOFOLD, DOUBLE 2 : having a double character or nature — **du·al·ism** \-ə-ˌli-zəm\ *n* — **du·al·i·ty** \dü-'a-lə-tē, dyü-\ *n*

¹dub \'dəb\ *vb* **dubbed; dub·bing** 1 : to confer knighthood upon 2 : NAME, NICKNAME

²dub *n* : a clumsy person : DUFFER

³dub *vb* **dubbed; dub·bing** : to add (sound effects) to a motion picture or to a radio or television production

du·bi·ety \dü-'bī-ə-tē, dyü-\ *n, pl* **-eties** 1 : UNCERTAINTY 2 : a matter of doubt

du·bi·ous \'dü-bē-əs, 'dyü-\ *adj* 1 : UNCERTAIN 2 : QUESTIONABLE 3 : feeling doubt : UNDECIDED — **du·bi·ous·ly** *adv* — **du·bi·ous·ness** *n*

dub·ni·um \'düb-nē-əm, 'dəb-\ *n* : a short-lived radioactive chemical element produced artificially

du·cal \'dü-kəl, 'dyü-\ *adj* : of or relating to a duke or dukedom

duc·at \'də-kət\ *n* : a gold coin formerly used in various European countries

duch·ess \'də-chəs\ *n* 1 : the wife or widow of a duke 2 : a woman holding the rank of duke in her own right

duchy \'də-chē\ *n, pl* **duch·ies** : the territory of a duke or duchess : DUKEDOM

¹duck \'dək\ *n, pl* **ducks** : any of various swimming birds related to but smaller than geese and swans

¹duck

²duck *vb* 1 : to thrust or plunge under water 2 : to lower the head or body suddenly : BOW; *also* : DODGE 3 : to evade a duty, question, or responsibility ⟨~ the issue⟩

³duck *n* 1 : a durable closely woven usu. cotton fabric 2 *pl* : light clothes made of duck

duck·bill \'dək-ˌbil\ *n* : PLATYPUS

duck·ling \-liŋ\ *n* : a young duck

duck·pin \-ˌpin\ *n* 1 : a small bowling pin shorter and wider in the middle than a tenpin 2 *pl but sing in constr* : a bowling game using duckpins

duck sauce *n* : a thick sweet sauce made with fruits and seasonings and used in Chinese cuisine

duct \'dəkt\ *n* 1 : a tube or canal for conveying a bodily fluid 2 : a pipe or tube through which a fluid (as air) flows — **duct·less** *adj*

duc·tile \'dək-t²l\ *adj* 1 : capable of being drawn out into wire or thread 2 : easily led : DOCILE — **duc·til·i·ty** \ˌdək-'ti-lə-tē\ *n*

ductless gland *n* : an endocrine gland

duct tape *n* : a cloth adhesive tape orig. designed for sealing certain ducts and joints — **duct tape** *vb*

dud \'dəd\ *n* 1 *pl* : CLOTHING 2 : one that fails completely; *also* : a bomb or missile that fails to explode

dude \'düd, 'dyüd\ *n* 1 : DANDY 1 2 : a city dweller; *esp* : an Easterner in the West 3 : FELLOW, GUY — sometimes used as an informal form of address

dude ranch *n* : a vacation resort offering activities (as horseback riding) typical of western ranches

dud·geon \'də-jən\ *n* : a fit or state of indignation ⟨in high ~⟩

¹due \'dü, 'dyü\ *adj* [ME, fr. AF *deu*, pp. of *dever* to owe, fr. L *debēre*] 1 : owed or owing as a debt 2 : owed or owing as a right ⟨is ~ a fair trial⟩ 3 : APPROPRIATE, FITTING ⟨with all ~ respect⟩ 4 : SUFFICIENT, ADEQUATE 5 : REGULAR, LAWFUL ⟨~ process of law⟩ 6 : ATTRIBUTABLE, ASCRIBABLE ⟨~ to negligence⟩ 7 : PAYABLE ⟨a bill ~ today⟩ 8 : SCHEDULED ⟨~ to arrive soon⟩

²due *n* 1 : something that rightfully belongs to one ⟨give everyone their ~⟩ 2 : DEBT 3 *pl* : FEES, CHARGES

³due *adv* : DIRECTLY, EXACTLY ⟨~ north⟩

du·el \'dü-əl, 'dyü-\ *n* : a combat between two persons; *esp* : one fought with weapons in front of witnesses — **duel** *vb* — **du·el·ist** \-ə-list\ *n*

du·en·de \dü-'en-dā\ *n* [Sp dial., charm, fr. Sp, ghost, goblin, fr. *duen de casa*, prob. fr. *dueño de casa* owner of a house] : the power to attract through personal magnetism and charm

du·en·na \dü-'e-nə, dyü-\ *n* 1 : an elderly woman in charge of the younger ladies in a Spanish or Portuguese family 2 : CHAPERONE

du·et \dü-'et, dyü-\ *n* : a musical composition for two performers

due to *prep* : BECAUSE OF

duf·fel bag \'də-fəl-\ *n* : a soft oblong bag for personal belongings

duf·fer \'də-fər\ *n* : an incompetent or clumsy person

dug *past and past part of* DIG

dug·out \'dəg-ˌaut\ *n* 1 : a boat made by hollowing out a log 2 : a shelter dug in the ground 3 : a low shelter facing a baseball diamond that contains the players' bench

DUI *n* : the act or crime of driving while under the influence of alcohol

duke \'dük, 'dyük\ *n* 1 : a sovereign ruler of a continental European duchy 2 : a nobleman of the highest rank; *esp* : a member of the highest grade of the British peerage 3 *slang* : FIST 1 ⟨put up your ~s⟩ — **duke·dom** *n*

dul·cet \'dəl-sət\ *adj* 1 : pleasing to the ear 2 : AGREEABLE, SOOTHING

dul·ci·mer \'dəl-sə-mər\ *n* 1 : a stringed instrument of trapezoidal shape played with light hammers held in the hands 2 *or* **dul·ci·more** \-ˌmȯr\ : an American folk instrument with three or four strings that is held on the lap and played by plucking or strumming

¹dull \'dəl\ *adj* 1 : mentally slow : STUPID 2 : slow in perception or sensibility 3 : LISTLESS 4 : slow in action : SLUGGISH ⟨a ~ market⟩ 5 : lacking intensity ⟨a ~ pain⟩; *also* : not resonant or ringing 6 : BLUNT 7 : lacking brilliance or luster ⟨a ~ finish⟩ 8 : low in saturation and lightness ⟨~ color⟩ 9 : CLOUDY, OVERCAST ⟨~ weather⟩ 10 : TEDIOUS, UNINTERESTING ⟨a ~ lecture⟩ — **dull·ness** *also* **dul·ness** *n* — **dul·ly** *adv*

²dull *vb* : to make or become dull

dull·ard \'də-lərd\ *n* : a stupid person

du·ly \'dü-lē, 'dyü-\ *adv* : in a due manner or time

dumb \'dəm\ *adj* 1 *often offensive* : lacking the power of speech 2 : SILENT 3 : STUPID — **dumb·ly** *adv*

dumb·bell \'dəm-ˌbel\ *n* 1 : a bar with weights at the end used for exercise 2 : one who is stupid

dumb down *vb* : to lower the level of intelligence or intellectual content of

dumb·found *also* **dum·found** \ˌdəm-'faund\ *vb* : ASTONISH, AMAZE — **dumb·found·ing·ly** \-'faun-diŋ-lē\ *adv*

dumb·wait·er \'dəm-ˌwā-tər\ *n* : a small elevator for conveying food and dishes from one floor to another

dum·my \'də-mē\ *n, pl* **dummies** 1 : a person who cannot speak; *also* : a stupid person 2 : the exposed hand in bridge played by the declarer in addition to that player's own hand; *also* : a bridge player whose hand is a dummy 3 : an imitative substitute for something; *also* : MANNEQUIN 4 : one seeming to act alone but really acting for another 5 : a mock-up of matter to be reproduced esp. by printing

¹dump \'dəmp\ *vb* : to let fall in a pile ⟨~ laundry on the floor⟩; *also* : to get rid of carelessly ⟨~ed her boyfriend⟩

²dump *n* 1 : a place for dumping something (as refuse) 2 : a reserve supply; *also* : a place where such supplies are kept ⟨an ammunition ~⟩ 3 : a messy or objectionable place

dump·ing \'dəm-piŋ\ *n* : the selling of goods in quantity at below market price

dump·ling \'dəm-pliŋ\ *n* **1** : a small mass of boiled or steamed dough **2** : a dessert of fruit baked in biscuit dough

dumps \'dəmps\ *n pl* : a gloomy state of mind : low spirits ⟨in the ∼⟩

dump truck *n* : a truck for transporting and dumping bulk material

dumpy \'dəm-pē\ *adj* **dump·i·er; -est 1** : short and thick in build **2** : SHABBY

¹dun \'dən\ *n* : a brownish dark gray

²dun *vb* **dunned; dun·ning 1** : to make persistent demands for payment **2** : PLAGUE, PESTER — **dun** *n*

dunce \'dəns\ *n* [John *Duns* Scotus, whose once accepted writings were ridiculed in the 16th cent.] : a slow stupid person

dun·der·head \'dən-dər-ˌhed\ *n* : DUNCE, BLOCKHEAD

dune \'dün, 'dyün\ *n* : a hill or ridge of sand piled up by the wind

dune buggy *n* : a motor vehicle with oversize tires for use on sand

¹dung \'dəŋ\ *n* : MANURE

²dung *vb* : to dress (land) with dung

dun·ga·ree \ˌdəŋ-gə-'rē\ *n* **1** : a heavy coarse cotton twill; *esp* : blue denim **2** *pl* : clothes made of blue denim

dun·geon \'dən-jən\ *n* [ME *dongeoun* fortress, prison, fr. AF *donjun*, fr. VL *domnion-, *domnio* keep, mastery, fr. L *dominus* lord] : a dark prison commonly underground

dung·hill \'dəŋ-ˌhil\ *n* : a manure pile

dunk \'dəŋk\ *vb* **1** : to dip or submerge temporarily in liquid **2** : to submerge oneself in water **3** : to shoot a basketball into the basket from above the rim

duo \'dü-(ˌ)ō, 'dyü-\ *n, pl* **du·os 1** : DUET **2** : PAIR 3

duo·dec·i·mal \ˌdü-ə-'de-sə-məl, ˌdyü-\ *adj* : of, relating to, or being a system of numbers with a base of 12

du·o·de·num \ˌdü-ə-'dē-nəm, ˌdyü-, dù-'ä-də-nəm, dyü-\ *n, pl* **-de·na** \-'dē-nə, -də-nə\ *or* **-denums** : the first part of the small intestine extending from the stomach to the jejunum — **du·o·de·nal** \-'dē-nᵊl, -də-nəl\ *adj*

dup *abbr* **1** duplex **2** duplicate

¹dupe \'düp, 'dyüp\ *n* : one who is easily deceived or cheated : FOOL

²dupe *vb* **duped; dup·ing** : to make a dupe of : DECEIVE, FOOL

du·ple \'dü-pəl, 'dyü-\ *adj* : having two beats or a multiple of two beats to the measure ⟨∼ time⟩

¹du·plex \'dü-ˌpleks, 'dyü-\ *adj* : DOUBLE

²duplex *n* : something duplex; *esp* : a 2-family house

¹du·pli·cate \'dü-pli-kət, 'dyü-\ *adj* **1** : consisting of or existing in two corresponding or identical parts or examples **2** : being the same as another

²du·pli·cate \'dü-pli-ˌkāt, 'dyü-\ *vb* **-cat·ed; -cat·ing 1** : to make double or twofold **2** : to make a copy of — **du·pli·ca·tion** \ˌdü-pli-'kā-shən, ˌdyü-\ *n*

³du·pli·cate \-kət\ *n* : a thing that exactly resembles another in appearance, pattern, or content : COPY

du·pli·ca·tor \'dü-pli-ˌkā-tər, 'dyü-\ *n* : COPIER

du·plic·i·ty \dù-'pli-sə-tē, dyü-\ *n, pl* **-ties** : the disguising of true intentions by deceptive words or action — **du·plic·i·tous** \-təs\ *adj* — **du·plic·i·tous·ly** *adv*

du·ra·ble \'dùr-ə-bəl, 'dyùr-\ *adj* : able to exist for a long time without significant deterioration ⟨∼ goods⟩ — **du·ra·bil·i·ty** \ˌdùr-ə-'bi-lə-tē, ˌdyùr-\ *n*

du·rance \'dùr-əns, 'dyùr-\ *n* : restraint by or as if by physical force ⟨held in ∼ vile⟩

du·ra·tion \dù-'rā-shən, dyü-\ *n* : the time during which something exists or lasts

du·ress \dù-'res, dyü-\ *n* : compulsion by threat ⟨confession made under ∼⟩

dur·ing \'dùr-iŋ, 'dyùr-\ *prep* **1** : THROUGHOUT ⟨swims every day ∼ the summer⟩ **2** : at some point in ⟨broke in ∼ the night⟩

dusk \'dəsk\ *n* **1** : the darker part of twilight esp. at night **2** : partial darkness

dusky \'dəs-kē\ *adj* **dusk·i·er; -est 1** : somewhat dark in color **2** : SHADOWY — **dusk·i·ly** \-kə-lē\ *adv* — **dusk·i·ness** *n*

¹dust \'dəst\ *n* **1** : fine particles of matter **2** : the particles into which something disintegrates **3** : something worth-

less **4** : the surface of the ground — **dust·less** *adj* — **dusty** *adj*

²dust *vb* **1** : to make free of or remove dust ⟨∼ the furniture⟩ **2** : to sprinkle with fine particles ⟨popcorn ∼ed with salt⟩ **3** : to sprinkle in the form of dust **4** : to defeat badly

dust bowl *n* : a region suffering from long droughts and dust storms

dust devil *n* : a small whirlwind containing sand or dust

dust·er \'dəs-tər\ *n* **1** : one that removes dust **2** : a dress-length housecoat **3** : one that scatters fine particles; *esp* : a device for applying insecticides to crops

dust·pan \'dəst-ˌpan\ *n* : a flat-ended pan for sweepings

dust storm *n* : a violent wind carrying dust across a dry region

dutch \'dəch\ *adv, often cap* : with each person paying his or her own way ⟨go ∼⟩

Dutch \'dəch\ *n* **1 Dutch** *pl* : the people of the Netherlands **2** : the language of the Netherlands — **Dutch** *adj* — **Dutch·man** \-mən\ *n*

Dutch elm disease *n* : a fungus disease of elms characterized by yellowing of the foliage, defoliation, and death

dutch treat *n, often cap D* : an entertainment (as a meal) for which each person pays his or her own way — **dutch treat** *adv, often cap D*

du·te·ous \'dü-tē-əs, 'dyü-\ *adj* : DUTIFUL, OBEDIENT

du·ti·able \'dü-tē-ə-bəl, 'dyü-\ *adj* : subject to a duty ⟨∼ imports⟩

du·ti·ful \'dü-ti-fəl, 'dyü-\ *adj* **1** : motivated by a sense of duty ⟨a ∼ son⟩ **2** : coming from or showing a sense of duty ⟨∼ affection⟩ — **du·ti·ful·ly** *adv* — **du·ti·ful·ness** *n*

du·ty \'dü-tē, 'dyü-\ *n, pl* **duties 1** : conduct or action required by one's occupation or position **2** : assigned service or business; *esp* : active military service **3** : a moral or legal obligation **4** : TAX **5** : the service required (as of a machine) : USE ⟨a heavy-*duty* tire⟩

DV *abbr* **1** [L *Deo volente*] God willing **2** Douay Version

DVD \ˌdē-ˌvē-'dē\ *n* [*d*igital *v*ideo *d*isk] : a high-capacity optical disk format; *also* : an optical disk using such a format

DVM *abbr* doctor of veterinary medicine

¹dwarf \'dwórf\ *n, pl* **dwarfs** \'dwórfs\ *also* **dwarves** \'dwórvz\ : one that is much below normal size — **dwarf·ish** *adj* — **dwarf·ism** \'dwór-ˌfi-zəm\ *n*

²dwarf *vb* **1** : to restrict the growth or development of : STUNT **2** : to cause to appear smaller ⟨*dwarfed* by comparison⟩

dwell \'dwel\ *vb* **dwelt** \'dwelt\ *or* **dwelled** \'dweld, 'dwelt\; **dwell·ing** [ME, fr. OE *dwellan* to go astray, hinder] **1** : ABIDE, REMAIN **2** : RESIDE, EXIST **3** : to keep the attention directed **4** : to write or speak insistently — used with *on* or *upon* — **dwell·er** *n*

dwell·ing \'dwe-liŋ\ *n* : RESIDENCE

DWI \ˌdē-ˌdəb-əl-(ˌ)yü-'ī\ *n* [*d*riving *w*hile *i*ntoxicated] : DUI

dwin·dle \'dwin-dᵊl\ *vb* **dwin·dled; dwin·dling** : to make or become steadily less : DIMINISH

dwt *abbr* pennyweight

Dy *symbol* dysprosium

dyb·buk \'di-bək\ *n, pl* **dyb·bu·kim** \ˌdi-bù-'kēm\ *also* **dybbuks** : a wandering soul believed in Jewish folklore to enter and possess a person

¹dye \'dī\ *n* **1** : color produced by dyeing **2** : material used for coloring or staining

²dye *vb* **dyed; dye·ing 1** : to impart a new color to esp. by impregnating with a dye **2** : to take up or impart color in dyeing — **dy·er** \'dī(-ə)r\ *n*

dye·stuff \'dī-ˌstəf\ *n* : DYE 2

dying *pres part of* DIE

dyke *chiefly Brit var of* DIKE

dy·nam·ic \dī-'na-mik\ *also* **dy·nam·i·cal** \-mi-kəl\ *adj* : of or relating to physical force producing motion : ENERGETIC, FORCEFUL

¹dy·na·mite \'dī-nə-ˌmīt\ *n* : an explosive made of nitroglycerin absorbed in a porous material; *also* : an explosive made without nitroglycerin

²dynamite *vb* **-mit·ed; -mit·ing** : to blow up with dynamite

³dynamite *adj* : TERRIFIC, WONDERFUL

dy·na·mo \'dī-nə-ˌmō\ *n, pl* **-mos 1** : an electrical generator **2** : a forceful energetic individual

dy·na·mom·e·ter \ˌdī-nə-'mä-mə-tər\ *n* : an instrument for measuring mechanical power (as of an engine)

dy·nas·ty \'dī-nəs-tē, -ˌnas-\ *n, pl* **-ties 1** : a succession of rulers of the same family **2** : a powerful group or family that maintains its position for a long time — **dy·nas·tic** \dī-'nas-tik\ *adj*

dys·en·tery \'di-sᵊn-ˌter-ē\ *n, pl* **-ter·ies** : a disease marked by diarrhea with blood and mucus in the feces; *also* : DIARRHEA

dys·func·tion *also* **dis·func·tion** \dis-'fəŋk-shən\ *n* **1** : impaired or abnormal functioning ⟨liver ∼⟩ **2** : abnormal or unhealthy behavior within a group ⟨family ∼⟩ — **dys·func·tion·al** \-shə-nəl\ *adj*

dys·lex·ia \dis-'lek-sē-ə\ *n* : a learning disability marked by difficulty in reading, writing, and spelling — **dys·lex·ic** \-sik\ *adj or n*

dys·pep·sia \dis-'pep-shə, -sē-ə\ *n* : INDIGESTION — **dys·pep·tic** \-'pep-tik\ *adj or n*

dys·pla·sia \dis-'plā-zh(ē-)ə\ *n* : abnormal growth or development

dys·pro·si·um \dis-'prō-zē-əm\ *n* : a metallic chemical element that forms highly magnetic compounds

dys·tro·phy \'dis-trə-fē\ *n, pl* **-phies** : a disorder involving atrophy of muscular tissue; *esp* : MUSCULAR DYSTROPHY

dz *abbr* dozen

¹e \'ē\ *n, pl* **e's** *or* **es** \'ēz\ *often cap* **1** : the 5th letter of the English alphabet **2** : the base of the system of natural logarithms having the approximate value 2.71828 **3** : a grade rating a student's work as poor or failing

²e *abbr, often cap* **1** east; eastern **2** error **3** excellent

e- *comb form* : electronic ⟨*e*-commerce⟩

ea *abbr* each

¹each \'ēch\ *adj* : being one of the class named ⟨∼ player⟩

²each *pron* : every individual one

³each *adv* : APIECE ⟨cost five cents ∼⟩

each other *pron* : each of two or more in reciprocal action or relation ⟨looked at *each other*⟩

ea·ger \'ē-gər\ *adj* : marked by urgent or enthusiastic desire or interest ⟨∼ to learn⟩ ✦ **Synonyms** AVID, ANXIOUS, ARDENT, KEEN — **ea·ger·ly** *adv* — **ea·ger·ness** *n*

¹ea·gle \'ē-gəl\ *n* **1** : a large bird of prey related to the hawks **2** : a score of two under par on a hole in golf

²eagle *vb* **ea·gled; ea·gling** : to score an eagle on a golf hole

ea·glet \'ē-glət\ *n* : a young eagle

-ean — see -AN

E and OE *abbr* errors and omissions excepted

¹ear \'ir\ *n* **1** : the organ of hearing; *also* : the outer part of this in a vertebrate **2** : something resembling a mammal's ear in shape, position, or function **3** : an ability to understand and appreciate something heard ⟨a good ∼ for music⟩ **4** : sympathetic attention

²ear *n* : the fruiting spike of a cereal (as wheat or Indian corn)

ear·ache \-ˌāk\ *n* : an ache or pain in the ear

ear·drum \-ˌdrəm\ *n* : a thin membrane that receives and transmits sound waves in the ear

eared \'ird\ *adj* : having ears esp. of a specified kind or number ⟨a long-*eared* dog⟩

ear·ful \'ir-ˌfúl\ *n* : a verbal outpouring (as of news, gossip, or complaint)

earl \'ərl\ *n* [ME *erl*, fr. OE *eorl* warrior, nobleman] : a member of the British peerage ranking below a marquess and above a viscount — **earl·dom** \-dəm\ *n*

ear·lobe \'ir-ˌlōb\ *n* : the pendent part of the ear

¹ear·ly \'ər-lē\ *adv* **ear·li·er; -est** : at an early time (as in a period or series)

²early *adj* **ear·li·er; -est** **1** : of, relating to, or occurring near the beginning **2** : ANCIENT, PRIMITIVE ⟨∼ tools⟩ **3** : occurring before the usual time ⟨an ∼ breakfast⟩; *also* : occurring in the near future

¹ear·mark \'ir-ˌmärk\ *n* : an identification mark (as on the ear of an animal); *also* : a distinguishing mark ⟨∼s of poverty⟩

²earmark *vb* **1** : to mark with an earmark **2** : to designate for a specific purpose ⟨money ∼ed for education⟩

ear·muff \-ˌməf\ *n* : one of a pair of ear coverings worn to protect against cold

earn \'ərn\ *vb* **1** : to receive as a return for service **2** : DESERVE, MERIT ✦ **Synonyms** GAIN, SECURE, GET, OBTAIN, ACQUIRE, WIN — **earn·er** *n*

earned run *n* : a run in baseball that scores without benefit of an error before the fielding team has had a chance to make the third putout of the inning

earned run average *n* : the average number of earned runs per game scored against a pitcher in baseball

¹ear·nest \'ər-nəst\ *n* : an intensely serious state of mind ⟨spoke in ∼⟩

²earnest *adj* **1** : seriously intent and sober ⟨an ∼ face⟩ ⟨an ∼ attempt⟩ **2** : GRAVE, IMPORTANT ✦ **Synonyms** SOLEMN, SEDATE, STAID — **ear·nest·ly** *adv* — **ear·nest·ness** *n*

³earnest *n* **1** : something of value given by a buyer to a seller to bind a bargain **2** : PLEDGE

earn·ings \'ər-niŋz\ *n pl* **1** : something (as wages) earned **2** : the balance of revenue after deduction of costs and expenses

ear·phone \'ir-ˌfōn\ *n* : a device that reproduces sound and is worn over or in the ear

ear·piece \-ˌpēs\ *n* : a part of an instrument which is placed against or in the ear; *esp* : EARPHONE

ear·plug \-ˌpləg\ *n* : a protective device for insertion into the opening of the ear

ear·ring \-ˌriŋ\ *n* : an ornament for the earlobe

ear·shot \-ˌshät\ *n* : range of hearing

ear·split·ting \-ˌspli-tiŋ\ *adj* : intolerably loud or shrill

earth \'ərth\ *n* **1** : SOIL, DIRT **2** : LAND, GROUND **3** *often cap* : the planet on which we live that is 3d in order from the sun — see PLANET table

earth·en \'ər-thən\ *adj* : made of earth or baked clay

earth·en·ware \-ˌwer\ *n* : slightly porous opaque pottery fired at low heat

earth·ling \'ərth-liŋ\ *n* : an inhabitant of the earth

earth·ly \'ərth-lē\ *adj* : having to do with the earth esp. as distinguished from heaven — **earth·li·ness** *n*

earth·quake \-ˌkwāk\ *n* : a shaking or trembling of a portion of the earth

earth science *n* : any of the sciences (as geology or meteorology) that deal with the earth or one of its parts

earth·shak·ing \'ərth-ˌshā-kiŋ\ *adj* : of great importance : MOMENTOUS

earth·ward \-wərd\ *also* **earth·wards** \-wərdz\ *adv* : toward the earth

earth·work \'ərth-ˌwərk\ *n* : an embankment or fortification of earth

earth·worm \-ˌwərm\ *n* : a long segmented worm found in damp soil

earthy \'ər-thē\ *adj* **earth·i·er; -est** **1** : of, relating to, or consisting of earth; *also* : suggesting earth ⟨∼ flavors⟩ **2** : PRACTICAL **4** **3** : COARSE, GROSS ⟨∼ humor⟩ — **earth·i·ness** *n*

ear·wax \'ir-ˌwaks\ *n* : the yellow waxy secretion from the ear

ear·wig \-ˌwig\ *n* : any of numerous insects with slender antennae and a pair of appendages resembling forceps at the end of the body

¹ease \'ēz\ *n* **1** : comfort of body or mind **2** : naturalness of manner **3** : freedom from difficulty or effort ✦ **Synonyms** RELAXATION, REST, REPOSE, LEISURE

²ease *vb* **eased; eas·ing** **1** : to relieve from distress **2** : to lessen the pressure or tension of **3** : to make or become less difficult ⟨∼ credit⟩

ea·sel \'ē-zəl\ *n* [Dutch *ezel*, lit., ass] : a frame for supporting something (as an artist's canvas)

¹east \'ēst\ *adv* : to or toward the east

²east *adj* **1** : situated toward or at the east ⟨an ~ window⟩ **2** : coming from the east ⟨an ~ wind⟩

³east *n* **1** : the general direction of sunrise **2** : the compass point directly opposite to west **3** *cap* : regions or countries east of a specified or implied point — **east·er·ly** \'ē-stər-lē\ *adv or adj* — **east·ward** *adv or adj* — **eastwards** *adv*

Eas·ter \'ē-stər\ *n* : a church feast observed on a Sunday in March or April in commemoration of Christ's resurrection

east·ern \'ē-stərn\ *adj* **1** *often cap* : of, relating to, or characteristic of a region designated East **2** *cap* : of, relating to, or being the Christian churches originating in the Church of the Eastern Roman Empire **3** : lying toward or coming from the east — **East·ern·er** *n*

easy \'ē-zē\ *adj* **eas·i·er; -est 1** : marked by ease ⟨an ~ life⟩; *esp* : not causing distress or difficulty ⟨~ tasks⟩ **2** : MILD, LENIENT ⟨be ~ on him⟩ **3** : GRADUAL ⟨an ~ slope⟩ **4** : LEISURELY ⟨an ~ pace⟩ **5** : free from pain, trouble, or worry **6** : COMFORTABLE ⟨an ~ chair⟩ **7** : showing ease : NATURAL ⟨an ~ manner⟩ — **eas·i·ly** \'ē-zə-lē\ *adv* — **eas·i·ness** \-zē-nəs\ *n*

easy·go·ing \ē-zē-'gō-iŋ\ *adj* : relaxed and casual in style or manner

eat \'ēt\ *vb* **ate** \'āt\; **eat·en** \'ēt-ᵊn\; **eat·ing 1** : to take in as food : take food **2** : to use up : DEVOUR **3** : CORRODE — **eat·able** *adj or n* — **eat·er** *n*

eat·ery \'ē-tə-rē\ *n, pl* **-er·ies** : LUNCHEONETTE, RESTAURANT

eaves \'ēvz\ *n pl* : the overhanging lower edge of a roof

eaves·drop \'ēvz-ˌdräp\ *vb* : to listen secretly — **eaves·drop·per** *n*

¹ebb \'eb\ *n* **1** : the flowing back from shore of water brought in by the tide **2** : a point or state of decline

²ebb *vb* **1** : to recede from the flood **2** : DECLINE ⟨his fortunes ~ed⟩

EBCDIC \'eb-sə-ˌdik\ *n* [*extended binary coded decimal interchange code*] : a computer code for representing alphanumeric information

Ebo·la \ē-bō-lə\ *n* : an often fatal hemorrhagic fever caused by a virus (**Ebola virus**) of African origin

¹eb·o·ny \'e-bə-nē\ *n, pl* **-nies** : a hard heavy blackish wood of various tropical trees related to the persimmon

²ebony *adj* **1** : made of or resembling ebony **2** : BLACK, DARK

ebul·lient \i-'bu̇l-yənt, -'bəl-\ *adj* **1** : BOILING, AGITATED **2** : EXUBERANT — **ebul·lience** \-yəns\ *n*

EC *abbr* European Community

ec·cen·tric \ik-'sen-trik\ *adj* **1** : deviating from a usual or accepted pattern **2** : deviating from a circular path ⟨~ orbits⟩ **3** : set with axis or support off center ⟨an ~ cam⟩; *also* : being off center ✦ *Synonyms* ERRATIC, QUEER, SINGULAR, CURIOUS, ODD — **eccentric** *n* — **ec·cen·tri·cal·ly** \-tri-k(ə-)lē\ *adv* — **ec·cen·tric·i·ty** \ˌek-ˌsen-'tri-sə-tē\

Eccles *abbr* Ecclesiastes

Ec·cle·si·as·tes \i-ˌklē-zē-'as-tēz\ *n* — see BIBLE table

ec·cle·si·as·tic \i-ˌklē-zē-'as-tik\ *n* : CLERGYMAN

ec·cle·si·as·ti·cal \-ti-kəl\ *or* **ec·cle·si·as·tic** \-tik\ *adj* : of or relating to a church esp. as an institution ⟨~ art⟩ — **ec·cle·si·as·ti·cal·ly** \-ti-k(ə-)lē\ *adv*

Ec·cle·si·as·ti·cus \i-ˌklē-zē-'as-ti-kəs\ *n* — see BIBLE table

Ecclus *abbr* Ecclesiasticus

ECG *abbr* electrocardiogram

ech·e·lon \'e-shə-ˌlän\ *n* [F *échelon*, lit., rung of a ladder] **1** : a steplike arrangement (as of troops or airplanes) **2** : a level (as of authority or responsibility) within an organization

ech·i·na·cea \ˌe-ki-'nā-sē-ə, -shə\ *n* : the dried root of three composite herbs that is used primarily in herbal remedies to boost the immune system; *also* : any of these herbs

echi·no·derm \i-'kī-nə-ˌdərm\ *n* : any of a phylum of marine animals (as starfishes and sea urchins) having similar body parts (as the arms of a starfish) arranged around a central axis and often having a calcium-containing outer skeleton

echo \'e-kō\ *n, pl* **ech·oes** *also* **ech·os** : repetition of a sound caused by a reflection of the sound waves; *also* : the reflection of a radar signal by an object — **echo** *vb* — **echo·ic** \e-'kō-ik\ *adj*

echo·lo·ca·tion \ˌe-kō-lō-'kā-shən\ *n* : a process for locating distant or invisible objects by sound waves reflected back to the sender (as a bat) from the objects

echt \'ekt\ *adj* [G] : TRUE, GENUINE ⟨an ~ New Yorker⟩

éclair \ā-'kler\ *n* [F, lit., lightning] : an oblong shell of light pastry with whipped cream or custard filling

éclat \ā-'klä\ *n* [F] **1** : a dazzling effect or success **2** : ACCLAIM

eclec·tic \e-'klek-tik\ *adj* : selecting or made up of what seems best of varied sources — **eclectic** *n* — **eclec·ti·cism** \-'klek-tə-ˌsi-zəm\ *n*

¹eclipse \i-'klips\ *n* **1** : the total or partial obscuring of one heavenly body by another; *also* : a passing into the shadow of a heavenly body **2** : a falling into obscurity or decline

²eclipse *vb* **eclipsed; eclips·ing** : to cause an eclipse of; *also* : SURPASS

eclip·tic \i-'klip-tik\ *n* : the great circle of the celestial sphere that is the apparent path of the sun

ec·logue \'ek-ˌlȯg, -ˌläg\ *n* : a pastoral poem

ECM *abbr* European Common Market

ecol *abbr* ecological; ecology

E. coli \ˌē-'kō-ˌlī\ *n, pl* **E. coli** : a rod-shaped bacterium that sometimes causes intestinal illness

ecol·o·gy \i-'kä-lə-jē, e-\ *n, pl* **-gies** [G *Ökologie*, fr. Gk *oikos* house + *logos* word] **1** : a branch of science concerned with the relationships between organisms and their environment **2** : the pattern of relations between one or more organisms and the environment — **eco·log·i·cal** \ˌē-kə-'lä-ji-kəl, ˌe-\ *also* **eco·log·ic** \-jik\ *adj* — **eco·log·i·cal·ly** \-ji-k(ə-)lē\ *adv* — **ecol·o·gist** \i-'kä-lə-jist, e-\ *n*

e—com·merce \'ē-ˌkä-(ˌ)mərs\ *n* : commerce conducted via the Internet

econ *abbr* economics; economist; economy

eco·nom·ic \ˌe-kə-'nä-mik, ˌē-\ *adj* : of or relating to the production, distribution, and consumption of goods and services

eco·nom·i·cal \-'nä-mi-kəl\ *adj* **1** : THRIFTY **2** : operating with little waste or at a saving ✦ *Synonyms* FRUGAL, SPARING, PROVIDENT — **eco·nom·i·cal·ly** \-k(ə-)lē\ *adv*

eco·nom·ics \ˌe-kə-'nä-miks, ˌē-\ *n sing or pl* : a social science dealing with the production, distribution, and consumption of goods and services — **econ·o·mist** \i-'kä-nə-mist\ *n*

econ·o·mise *Brit var of* ECONOMIZE

econ·o·mize \i-'kä-nə-ˌmīz\ *vb* **-mized; -miz·ing** : to practice economy : be frugal — **econ·o·miz·er** *n*

¹econ·o·my \i-'kä-nə-mē\ *n, pl* **-mies** [MF *yconomie*, fr. ML *oeconomia*, fr. Gk *oikonomia*, fr. *oikonomos* household manager, fr. *oikos* house + *nemein* to manage] **1** : thrifty and efficient use of resources; *also* : an instance of this **2** : manner of arrangement or functioning : ORGANIZATION **3** : an economic system ⟨a money ~⟩

²economy *adj* : ECONOMICAL ⟨~ cars⟩

eco·sys·tem \'ē-kō-ˌsis-təm, 'e-\ *n* : the complex of an ecological community and its environment functioning as a unit in nature

eco·tour·ism \ˌē-kō-'tu̇r-ˌi-zəm, ˌe-\ *n* : the touring of natural habitats in a manner meant to minimize ecological impact — **eco·tour·ist** \-'tu̇r-ist\ *n*

ecru \'e-krü, 'ā-\ *n* [F *écru*, lit., unbleached] : BEIGE — **ecru** *adj*

ec·sta·sy \'ek-stə-sē\ *n, pl* **-sies 1** : extreme and usu. rapturous emotional excitement **2** *often cap* : an illicit drug with hallucinogenic properties that is chemically related to amphetamine — **ec·stat·ic** \ek-'sta-tik, ik-\ *adj* — **ec·stat·i·cal·ly** \-ti-k(ə-)lē\ *adv*

Ecua *abbr* Ecuador

ec·u·men·i·cal \ˌe-kyu̇-'me-ni-kəl\ *adj* **1** : general in extent or influence **2** : promoting or tending toward worldwide Christian unity — **ec·u·men·i·cal·ly** \-k(ə-)lē\ *adv*

ec·ze·ma \ig-'zē-mə, 'eg-zə-mə, 'ek-sə-\ *n* : an itching skin inflammation with oozing and then crusted lesions — **ec·zem·a·tous** \ig-'ze-mə-təs\ *adj*

ed *abbr* **1** edited; edition; editor **2** education

¹-ed \d *after a vowel or* b, g, j, l, m, n, ŋ, r, *th*, v, z, zh; əd, id *after* d, t; t *after other sounds*\ *vb suffix or adj suffix* **1** —

used to form the past participle of regular weak verbs ⟨end*ed*⟩ ⟨fad*ed*⟩ ⟨tri*ed*⟩ ⟨patt*ed*⟩ **2** : having : character-ized by ⟨cultur*ed*⟩ ⟨2-legg*ed*⟩; *also* : having the character-istics of ⟨bigot*ed*⟩

²-ed *vb suffix* — used to form the past tense of regular weak verbs ⟨judg*ed*⟩ ⟨deni*ed*⟩ ⟨dropp*ed*⟩

Edam \ˈē-dəm, -ˌdam\ *n* : a yellow Dutch pressed cheese made in balls

ed·dy \ˈe-dē\ *n, pl* **eddies** : WHIRLPOOL — **eddy** *vb*

edel·weiss \ˈā-dᵊl-ˌwīs, -ˌvīs\ *n* [G, fr. *edel* noble + *weiss* white] : a small perennial woolly composite herb that grows high in the Alps

ede·ma \i-ˈdē-mə\ *n* : abnormal accumulation of watery fluid in connective tissue or in a serous cavity — **edem-a·tous** \-ˈde-mə-təs\ *adj*

Eden \ˈē-dᵊn\ *n* : PARADISE 2

¹edge \ˈej\ *n* **1** : the cutting side of a blade **2** : SHARP-NESS; *also* : FORCE, EFFECTIVENESS **3** : the line where something begins or ends; *also* : the area adjoining such an edge **4** : ADVANTAGE ⟨has an ∼ on the competition⟩ — **edged** \ˈejd\ *adj*

²edge *vb* **edged; edg·ing 1** : to give or form an edge **2** : to move or force gradually ⟨∼ into a crowd⟩ **3** : to defeat by a small margin ⟨*edged* out her opponent⟩ — **edg·er** *n*

edge·wise \ˈej-ˌwīz\ *adv* : SIDEWAYS

edg·ing \ˈe-jiŋ\ *n* : something that forms an edge or border ⟨a lace ∼⟩

edgy \ˈe-jē\ *adj* **edg·i·er; -est 1** : SHARP ⟨an'∼ tone⟩ **2** : TENSE, NERVOUS **3** : having a bold, provocative, or un-conventional quality — **edg·i·ness** *n*

ed·i·ble \ˈe-də-bəl\ *adj* : fit or safe to be eaten — **ed·i·bil-i·ty** \ˌe-də-ˈbi-lə-tē\ *n* — **edible** *n*

edict \ˈē-ˌdikt\ *n* : ORDER, DECREE

ed·i·fi·ca·tion \ˌe-də-fə-ˈkā-shən\ *n* : instruction and im-provement esp. in morality — **ed·i·fy** \ˈe-də-ˌfī\ *vb*

ed·i·fice \ˈe-də-fəs\ *n* : a usu. large building

ed·it \ˈe-dət\ *vb* **1** : to revise, assemble, or prepare for publication or release (as a motion picture) **2** : to direct the publication and policies of (as a newspaper) **3** : DELETE — **ed·i·tor** \ˈe-də-tər\ *n* — **ed·i·tor·ship** *n* — **ed·i·tress** \-trəs\ *n*

edi·tion \i-ˈdi-shən\ *n* **1** : the form in which a text is pub-lished **2** : the total number of copies (as of a book) pub-lished at one time **3** : VERSION

¹ed·i·to·ri·al \ˌe-də-ˈtȯr-ē-əl\ *adj* **1** : of or relating to an ed-itor or editing **2** : being or resembling an editorial — **ed-i·to·ri·al·ly** *adv*

²editorial *n* : an article (as in a newspaper) giving the views of the editors or publishers; *also* : an expression of opin-ion resembling an editorial ⟨a television ∼⟩

ed·i·to·ri·al·ize \ˌe-də-ˈtȯr-ē-ə-ˌlīz\ *vb* **-ized; -iz·ing 1** : to express an opinion in an editorial **2** : to introduce opin-ions into factual reporting **3** : to express an opinion — **ed·i·to·ri·al·i·za·tion** \-ˌtȯr-ē-ə-lə-ˈzā-shən\ *n* — **ed·i·to·ri-al·iz·er** *n*

EDP *abbr* electronic data processing

EDT *abbr* Eastern daylight (saving) time

educ *abbr* education; educational

ed·u·ca·ble \ˈe-jə-kə-bəl\ *adj* : capable of being educated

ed·u·cate \ˈe-jə-ˌkāt\ *vb* **-cat·ed; -cat·ing** [ME, to rear, fr. L *educatus,* pp. of *educare,* fr. *educere* to lead forth, draw out] **1** : to provide with schooling **2** : to develop men-tally and morally; *also* : to provide with information **♦ Synonyms** TRAIN, DISCIPLINE, SCHOOL, INSTRUCT, TEACH — **ed·u·ca·tor** \-ˌkā-tər\ *n*

ed·u·ca·tion \ˌe-jə-ˈkā-shən\ *n* **1** : the action or process of educating or being educated **2** : a field of study dealing with methods of teaching and learning — **ed·u·ca·tion·al** \-shə-nəl\ *adj* — **ed·u·ca·tion·al·ly** *adv*

educational television *n* **1** : television that provides edu-cational programming (as for students) **2** : television (as public television) that receives support from contribu-tors

educe \i-ˈdüs, -ˈdyüs\ *vb* **educed; educ·ing 1** : ELICIT, EVOKE **2** : DEDUCE **♦ Synonyms** EXTRACT, EVINCE, EXTORT

ed·u·tain·ment \ˌe-jə-ˈtān-mənt\ *n* : entertainment that is designed to be educational

¹-ee \ˈē, (ˌ)ē\ *n suffix* **1** : one that receives or benefits from (a specified action or thing) ⟨grant*ee*⟩ ⟨patent*ee*⟩ **2** : a person who does (a specified action) ⟨escap*ee*⟩

²-ee *n suffix* **1** : a particular esp. small kind of ⟨boot*ee*⟩ **2** : one resembling or suggestive of ⟨goat*ee*⟩

EE *abbr* electrical engineer

EEC *abbr* European Economic Community

EEG *abbr* **1** electroencephalogram **2** electroencephalo-graph

eel \ˈēl\ *n* : any of numerous snakelike bony fishes with a smooth slimy skin

EEO *abbr* equal employment opportunity

ee·rie *also* **ee·ry** \ˈir-ē\ *adj* **ee·ri·er; -est** : WEIRD, UNCAN-NY — **ee·ri·ly** \ˈir-ə-lē\ *adv*

eff *abbr* efficiency

ef·face \i-ˈfās, e-\ *vb* **ef·faced; ef·fac·ing** : to obliterate or obscure by or as if by rubbing out **♦ Synonyms** ERASE, DELETE, ANNUL, CANCEL, EXPUNGE — **ef·face·able** *adj* — **ef·face·ment** *n*

¹ef·fect \i-ˈfekt\ *n* **1** : MEANING, INTENT **2** : RESULT **3** : APPEARANCE **4** : INFLUENCE **5** *pl* : GOODS, POSSES-SIONS **6** : the quality or state of being operative : OPER-ATION **♦ Synonyms** CONSEQUENCE, OUTCOME, UPSHOT, AFTERMATH, ISSUE

²effect *vb* : to cause to happen ⟨∼ repairs⟩ ⟨∼ changes⟩

ef·fec·tive \i-ˈfek-tiv\ *adj* **1** : producing a decisive or de-sired effect **2** : IMPRESSIVE, STRIKING **3** : ready for service or action ⟨∼ manpower⟩ **4** : being in effect — **ef·fec·tive·ly** *adv* — **ef·fec·tive·ness** *n*

ef·fec·tu·al \i-ˈfek-chə-wəl\ *adj* : producing an intended ef-fect : ADEQUATE — **ef·fec·tu·al·ly** *adv*

ef·fec·tu·ate \i-ˈfek-chə-ˌwāt\ *vb* **-at·ed; -at·ing** : BRING ABOUT, EFFECT

ef·fem·i·nate \ə-ˈfe-mə-nət\ *adj* : marked by qualities more typical of women than men — **ef·fem·i·na·cy** \-nə-sē\ *n*

ef·fen·di \e-ˈfen-dē\ *n* [Turk *efendi* master, fr. ModGk *aphentēs,* alter. of Gk *authentēs*] : a man of property, au-thority, or education in an eastern Mediterranean country

ef·fer·ent \ˈe-fə-rənt\ *adj* : bearing or conducting outward from a more central part ⟨∼ nerves⟩

ef·fer·vesce \ˌe-fər-ˈves\ *vb* **-vesced; -vesc·ing 1** : to bubble and hiss as gas escapes **2** : to show liveliness or exhilaration — **ef·fer·ves·cence** \-ˈve-sᵊns\ *n* — **ef·fer-ves·cent** \-sᵊnt\ *adj* — **ef·fer·ves·cent·ly** *adv*

ef·fete \e-ˈfēt\ *adj* **1** : having lost character, vitality, or strength; *also* : DECADENT **2** : EFFEMINATE

ef·fi·ca·cious \ˌe-fə-ˈkā-shəs\ *adj* : producing an intended effect ⟨∼ remedies⟩ **♦ Synonyms** EFFECTUAL, EFFEC-TIVE, EFFICIENT — **ef·fi·ca·cy** \ˈe-fi-kə-sē\ *n*

ef·fi·cient \i-ˈfi-shənt\ *adj* : productive of desired effects esp. without waste — **ef·fi·cien·cy** \-shən-sē\ *n* — **ef·fi-cient·ly** *adv*

ef·fi·gy \ˈe-fə-jē\ *n, pl* **-gies** : IMAGE; *esp* : a crude figure of a hated person

ef·flo·res·cence \ˌe-flə-ˈre-sᵊns\ *n* **1** : the period or state of flowering **2** : the action or process of developing **3** : fullness of development : FLOWERING

ef·flu·ence \ˈe-ˌflü-əns\ *n* : something that flows out

ef·flu·ent \ˈe-ˌflü-ənt\ *n* : something that flows out; *esp* : a fluid (as sewage) discharged as waste — **effluent** *adj*

ef·flu·vi·um \e-ˈflü-vē-əm\ *n, pl* **-via** \-vē-ə\ *also* **-vi·ums** [L, outflow] **1** : a usu. unpleasant emanation **2** : a by-product usu. in the form of waste

ef·fort \ˈe-fərt\ *n* **1** : EXERTION, ENDEAVOR; *also* : a prod-uct of effort **2** : active or applied force — **ef·fort·less** *adj* — **ef·fort·less·ly** *adv*

ef·fron·tery \i-ˈfrən-tə-rē\ *n, pl* **-ter·ies** : shameless bold-ness : IMPUDENCE **♦ Synonyms** TEMERITY, AUDACITY, BRASS, GALL, NERVE, CHUTZPAH

ef·ful·gence \i-ˈfu̇l-jəns, -ˈfəl-\ *n* : radiant splendor : BRIL-LIANCE — **ef·ful·gent** \-jənt\ *adj*

ef·fu·sion \i-ˈfyü-zhən, e-\ *n* : a gushing forth; *also* : unre-strained utterance — **ef·fuse** \-ˈfyüz, e-\ *vb* — **ef·fu·sive** \i-ˈfyü-siv, e-\ *adj* — **ef·fu·sive·ly** *adv*

eft \ˈeft\ *n* : NEWT

EFT *or* **EFTS** *abbr* electronic funds transfer (system)

e.g. *abbr* [L *exempli gratia*] for example

Eg *abbr* Egypt; Egyptian

egal·i·tar·i·an·ism \i-ˌga-lə-ˈter-ē-ə-ˌni-zəm\ *n* : a belief in human equality esp. in social, political, and economic af-fairs — **egal·i·tar·i·an** *adj or n*

¹egg \ˈeg\ *vb* [ME, fr. ON *eggja;* akin to OE *ecg* edge] : to urge to action — usu. used with *on*

²egg *n* [ME *egge,* fr. ON *egg;* akin to OE *ǣg* egg, L *ovum*] **1**

: a rounded usu. hard-shelled reproductive body esp. of birds and reptiles from which the young hatches; *also* : the egg of the common domestic chicken as an article of food **2** : a germ cell produced by a female

egg·beat·er \'eg-₁bē-tər\ *n* : a hand-operated kitchen utensil for beating, stirring, or whipping

egg cell *n* : EGG 2

egg foo yong *or* **egg foo young** *or* **egg foo yung** \-'fü-'yəŋ\ : a fried egg patty

egg·head \-₁hed\ *n* : INTELLECTUAL, HIGHBROW

egg·nog \-₁näg\ *n* : a drink consisting of eggs beaten with sugar, milk or cream, and often alcoholic liquor

egg·plant \-₁plant\ *n* : the edible usu. large and dark purplish fruit of a plant related to the potato; *also* : the plant

egg roll *n* : a thin egg-dough casing filled with minced vegetables and often bits of meat and usu. deep-fried

egg·shell \'eg-₁shel\ *n* : the hard exterior covering of an egg

egis *var of* AEGIS

eg·lan·tine \'e-glən-₁tīn, -₁tēn\ *n* : SWEETBRIAR

ego \'ē-gō\ *n, pl* **egos** [L, I] **1** : the self as distinguished from others **2** : the one of the three divisions of the psyche in psychoanalytic theory that is the organized conscious mediator between the person and reality

ego·cen·tric \₁ē-gō-'sen-trik\ *adj* : concerned or overly concerned with the self; *esp* : SELF-CENTERED

ego·ism \'ē-gō-₁i-zəm\ *n* **1** : a doctrine holding self-interest to be the motive or the valid end of action **2** : excessive concern for oneself with or without exaggerated feelings of self-importance — **ego·ist** \-ist\ *n* — **ego·is·tic** \₁ē-gō-'is-tik\ *adj* — **ego·is·ti·cal·ly** *adv*

ego·tism \'ē-gə-₁ti-zəm\ *n* **1** : the practice of talking about oneself too much **2** : an exaggerated sense of self-importance : CONCEIT — **ego·tist** \-tist\ *n* — **ego·tis·tic** \₁ē-gə-'tis-tik\ *or* **ego·tis·ti·cal** \-ti-kəl\ *adj* — **ego·tis·ti·cal·ly** *adv*

ego trip *n* : an act that enhances and satisfies one's ego

egre·gious \i-'grē-jəs\ *adj* [L *egregius* outstanding, fr. *ex, e* out of + *greg-, grex* flock, herd] : notably bad : FLAGRANT — **egre·gious·ly** *adv* — **egre·gious·ness** *n*

egress \'ē-₁gres\ *n* : a way out : EXIT

egret \'ē-grət, i-'gret\ *n* : any of various herons that bear long plumes during the breeding season

egret

Egyp·tian \i-'jip-shən\ *n* **1** : a native or inhabitant of Egypt **2** : the language of the ancient Egyptians from earliest times to about the 3d century A.D. — **Egyptian** *adj*

ei·der \'ī-dər\ *n* : any of several northern sea ducks that yield a soft down

ei·der·down \-₁daùn\ *n* **1** : the down of the eider **2** : a comforter filled with eiderdown

ei·do·lon \ī-'dō-lən\ *n, pl* **-lons** *or* **-la** \-lə\ **1** : PHANTOM **2** : IDEAL

eight \'āt\ *n* **1** : one more than seven **2** : the 8th in a set or series **3** : something having eight units — **eight** *adj or pron* — **eighth** \'ātth\ *adj or adv or n*

eight ball *n* : a black pool ball numbered 8 — **behind the eight ball** : in a highly disadvantageous position

eigh·teen \'āt-'tēn\ *n* : one more than 17 — **eighteen** *adj or pron* — **eigh·teenth** \-'tēnth\ *adj or n*

eighty \'ā-tē\ *n, pl* **eight·ies** : eight times 10 — **eight·i·eth** \'ā-tē-əth\ *adj or n* — **eighty** *adj or pron*

ein·stei·ni·um \īn-'stī-nē-əm\ *n* : an artificially produced radioactive element

ei·re·nic *chiefly Brit var of* IRENIC

¹ei·ther \'ē-thər, 'ī-\ *adj* **1** : being the one and the other of two : EACH ⟨trees on ~ side⟩ **2** : being the one or the other of two ⟨take ~ road⟩

²either *pron* : the one or the other

³either *conj* — used as a function word before the first of two or more words or word groups of which the last is preceded by *or* to indicate that they represent alternatives ⟨a statement is ~ true or false⟩

ejac·u·late \i-'ja-kyə-₁lāt\ *vb* **-lat·ed; -lat·ing** **1** : to eject a fluid (as semen) **2** : to utter suddenly : EXCLAIM — **ejac·u·la·tion** \-₁ja-kyə-'lā-shən\ *n* — **ejac·u·la·to·ry** \-'ja-kyə-lə-₁tòr-ē\ *adj*

eject \i-'jekt\ *vb* : to drive or throw out or off ♦ *Synonyms* EXPEL, OUST, EVICT, DISMISS — **ejec·tion** \-'jek-shən\ *n*

eke \'ēk\ *vb* **eked; ek·ing** : to gain, supplement, or extend usu. with effort — usu. used with *out* ⟨~ out a living⟩

EKG *abbr* [G *Elektrokardiogramm*] electrocardiogram; electrocardiograph

el *abbr* elevation

¹elab·o·rate \i-'la-bə-rət, -'la-brət\ *adj* **1** : planned or carried out with great care **2** : being complex and usu. ornate — **elab·o·rate·ly** *adv* — **elab·o·rate·ness** *n*

²elab·o·rate \i-'la-bə-₁rāt\ *vb* **-rat·ed; -rat·ing** **1** : to build up from simpler ingredients **2** : to work out in detail : develop fully — **elab·o·ra·tion** \-₁la-bə-'rā-shən\ *n*

élan \ā-'läⁿ\ *n* [F] : ARDOR, SPIRIT

eland \'ē-lənd, -₁land\ *n, pl* **eland** *also* **elands** [Afrikaans] : either of two large African antelopes with spirally twisted horns in both sexes

elapse \i-'laps\ *vb* **elapsed; elaps·ing** : to slip by : PASS

¹elas·tic \i-'las-tik\ *adj* **1** : SPRINGY **2** : FLEXIBLE, PLIABLE ⟨an ~ bandage⟩ **3** : ADAPTABLE ⟨an ~ plan⟩ ♦ *Synonyms* RESILIENT, SUPPLE, STRETCH — **elas·tic·i·ty** \-₁las-'ti-sə-tē, ₁ē-₁las-\ *n*

²elastic *n* **1** : elastic material **2** : a rubber band

elate \i-'lāt\ *vb* **elat·ed; elat·ing** : to fill with joy — **ela·tion** \-'lā-shən\ *n*

¹el·bow \'el-₁bō\ *n* [ME *elbowe*, fr. OE *elboga*, fr. *el-* (akin to *eln* ell) + *boga* bow] **1** : the joint of the arm; *also* : the outer curve of the bent arm **2** : a bend or joint resembling an elbow in shape

²elbow *vb* : to push aside with the elbow; *also* : to make one's way by elbowing

el·bow room \'el-₁bō-₁rüm, -₁rùm\ *n* : enough space for work or operation

¹el·der \'el-dər\ *n* : ELDERBERRY 2

²elder *adj* **1** : OLDER **2** : EARLIER, FORMER **3** : of higher rank : SENIOR

³elder *n* **1** : an older individual : SENIOR **2** : one having authority by reason of age and experience **3** : a church officer

el·der·ber·ry \'el-dər-₁ber-ē\ *n* **1** : the edible black or red fruit of a shrub or tree related to the honeysuckle and bearing flat clusters of small white or pink flowers **2** : a tree or shrub bearing elderberries

el·der·ly \'el-dər-lē\ *adj* **1** : rather old; *esp* : past middle age **2** : of, relating to, or characteristic of later life

el·dest \'el-dəst\ *adj* : of the greatest age

El Do·ra·do \₁el-də-'rä-dō, -'rā-\ *n* [Sp, lit., the gilded one] : a place of vast riches, abundance, or opportunity

elec *abbr* electric; electrical; electricity

¹elect \i-'lekt\ *adj* **1** : CHOSEN, SELECT **2** : elected but not yet installed in office (the president-*elect*)

²elect *n, pl* **elect** **1** : a selected person **2** *pl* : a select or exclusive group

³elect *vb* **1** : to select by vote (as for office or membership) **2** : CHOOSE, PICK

elec·tion \i-'lek-shən\ *n* **1** : an act or process of electing **2** : the fact of being elected

elec·tion·eer \i-₁lek-shə-'nir\ *vb* : to work for the election of a candidate or party

¹elec·tive \i-'lek-tiv\ *adj* **1** : chosen or filled by election **2** : permitting a choice : OPTIONAL

²elective *n* : an elective course or subject of study

elec·tor \i-'lek-tər\ *n* **1** : one qualified to vote in an election **2** : one elected to an electoral college — **elec·tor·al** \i-'lek-tə-rəl\ *adj*

electoral college *n* : a body of electors who elect the president and vice president of the U.S.

elec·tor·ate \i-ˈlek-tə-rət\ *n* : a body of persons entitled to vote

elec·tric \i-ˈlek-trik\ *adj* [NL *electricus* produced from amber by friction, electric, fr. ML, of amber, fr. L *electrum* amber, fr. Gk *ēlektron*] **1** *or* **elec·tri·cal** \-tri-kəl\ : of, relating to, operated by, or produced by electricity **2** : ELECTRIFYING, THRILLING ⟨an ~ performance⟩ — **elec·tri·cal·ly** *adv*

electrical storm *n* : THUNDERSTORM

electric chair *n* : a chair used to carry out the death penalty by electrocution

electric eye *n* : PHOTOELECTRIC CELL

elec·tri·cian \i-ˌlek-ˈtri-shən\ *n* : a person who installs, operates, or repairs electrical equipment

elec·tric·i·ty \i-ˌlek-ˈtri-sə-tē\ *n, pl* **-ties** **1** : a form of energy that occurs naturally (as in lightning) or is produced (as in a generator) and that is expressed in terms of the movement and interaction of electrons **2** : electric current

elec·tri·fy \i-ˈlek-trə-ˌfī\ *vb* **-fied; -fy·ing** **1** : to charge with electricity **2** : to equip for use of electric power **3** : THRILL — **elec·tri·fi·ca·tion** \i-ˌlek-trə-fə-ˈkā-shən\ *n*

elec·tro·car·dio·gram \i-ˌlek-trō-ˈkär-dē-ə-ˌgram\ *n* : the tracing made by an electrocardiograph

elec·tro·car·dio·graph \-ˌgraf\ *n* : a device for recording the changes of electrical potential occurring during the heartbeat — **elec·tro·car·dio·graph·ic** \-ˌkär-dē-ə-ˈgra-fik\ *adj* — **elec·tro·car·di·og·ra·phy** \-dē-ˈä-grə-fē\ *n*

elec·tro·chem·is·try \-ˈke-mə-strē\ *n* : a branch of chemistry that deals with the relation of electricity to chemical changes — **elec·tro·chem·i·cal** \-ˈke-mi-kəl\ *adj*

elec·tro·cute \i-ˈlek-trə-ˌkyüt\ *vb* **-cut·ed; -cut·ing** **1** : to kill (a criminal) by electricity **2** : to kill by electric shock — **elec·tro·cu·tion** \-ˌlek-trə-ˈkyü-shən\ *n*

elec·trode \i-ˈlek-ˌtrōd\ *n* : a conductor used to establish electrical contact with a nonmetallic part of a circuit

elec·tro·en·ceph·a·lo·gram \i-ˌlek-trō-in-ˈse-fə-lə-ˌgram\ *n* : the tracing made by an electroencephalograph

elec·tro·en·ceph·a·lo·graph \-ˌgraf\ *n* : an apparatus for detecting and recording brain waves — **elec·tro·en·ceph·a·lo·graph·ic** \-ˌse-fə-lə-ˈgra-fik\ *adj* — **elec·tro·en·ceph·a·log·ra·phy** \-ˈlä-grə-fē\ *n*

elec·trol·o·gist \i-ˌlek-ˈträ-lə-jist\ *n* : one that uses electrical means to remove hair, warts, moles, and birthmarks from the body

elec·trol·y·sis \i-ˌlek-ˈträ-lə-səs\ *n* **1** : the production of chemical changes by passage of an electric current through an electrolyte **2** : the destruction of hair roots with an electric current — **elec·tro·lyt·ic** \-trə-ˈli-tik\ *adj*

elec·tro·lyte \i-ˈlek-trə-ˌlīt\ *n* : a nonmetallic electric conductor in which current is carried by the movement of ions; *also* : a substance whose solution or molten form is such a conductor

elec·tro·mag·net \i-ˌlek-trō-ˈmag-nət\ *n* : a core of magnetic material (as iron) surrounded by a coil of wire through which an electric current is passed to magnetize the core

elec·tro·mag·net·ic \-mag-ˈne-tik\ *adj* : of, relating to, or produced by electromagnetism — **elec·tro·mag·net·i·cal·ly** *adv*

electromagnetic radiation *n* : energy in the form of electromagnetic waves; *also* : a series of electromagnetic waves

electromagnetic wave *n* : a wave (as a radio wave, an X-ray, or a wave of visible light) that consists of associated electric and magnetic effects and that travels at the speed of light

elec·tro·mag·ne·tism \i-ˌlek-trō-ˈmag-nə-ˌti-zəm\ *n* **1** : magnetism developed by a current of electricity **2** : a natural force responsible for interactions between charged particles which result from their charge

elec·tro·mo·tive force \i-ˌlek-trə-ˈmō-tiv-\ *n* : the potential difference derived from an electrical source per unit quantity of electricity passing through the source

elec·tron \i-ˈlek-ˌträn\ *n* : a negatively charged elementary particle

elec·tron·ic \i-ˌlek-ˈträ-nik\ *adj* **1** : of or relating to electrons or electronics **2** : involving a computer — **elec·tron·i·cal·ly** \-ni-k(ə-)lē\ *adv*

electronic mail *n* : E-MAIL

elec·tron·ics \i-ˌlek-ˈträ-niks\ *n* **1** : the physics of electrons and electronic devices **2** : electronic components, devices, or equipment

electron microscope *n* : an instrument in which a beam of electrons is used to produce an enlarged image of a minute object

electron tube *n* : a device in which electrical conduction by electrons takes place within a sealed container and which is used for the controlled flow of electrons

electron volt *n* : a unit of energy equal to 1.60×10^{-19} joule

elec·tro·pho·re·sis \i-ˌlek-trə-fə-ˈrē-səs\ *n* : the movement of suspended particles through a medium (as paper or gel) by an electromotive force — **elec·tro·pho·ret·ic** \-ˈrē-tik\ *adj*

elec·tro·plate \i-ˈlek-trə-ˌplāt\ *vb* : to coat (as with metal) by electrolysis

elec·tro·shock therapy \i-ˈlek-trō-ˌshäk-\ *n* : the treatment of mental disorder by applying electric current to the head and inducing convulsions

elec·tro·stat·ics \i-ˌlek-trə-ˈsta-tiks\ *n* : physics dealing with the interactions of stationary electric charges

el·ee·mos·y·nary \ˌe-li-ˈmäs-sə-ˌner-ē\ *adj* : CHARITABLE

el·e·gance \ˈe-li-gəns\ *n* **1** : refined gracefulness; *also* : tasteful richness (as of design) **2** : something marked by elegance — **el·e·gant** \-gənt\ *adj* — **el·e·gant·ly** *adv*

ele·giac \ˌe-lə-ˈjī-ək, -ˌak\ *adj* : of or relating to an elegy

el·e·gy \ˈe-lə-jē\ *n, pl* **-gies** : a song, poem, or speech expressing grief for one who is dead; *also* : a reflective poem usu. melancholy in tone

elem *abbr* elementary

el·e·ment \ˈe-lə-mənt\ *n* **1** *pl* : weather conditions; *esp* : severe weather ⟨boards exposed to the ~s⟩ **2** : natural environment ⟨in her ~⟩ **3** : a constituent part **4** *pl* : the simplest principles (as of an art or science) : RUDIMENTS **5** : a member of a mathematical set **6** : any of the fundamental substances that consist of atoms of only one kind ♦ *Synonyms* COMPONENT, INGREDIENT, CONSTITUENT — **el·e·men·tal** \ˌe-lə-ˈment-ᵊl\ *adj*

el·e·men·ta·ry \ˌe-lə-ˈmen-trē, -tə-rē\ *adj* : SIMPLE, RUDIMENTARY; *also* : of, relating to, or teaching the basic subjects of education

elementary particle *n* : a subatomic particle of matter and energy that does not appear to be made up of other smaller particles

elementary school *n* : a school usu. including the first six or the first eight grades

el·e·phant \ˈe-lə-fənt\ *n, pl* **elephants** *also* **elephant** : any of a family of huge thickset nearly hairless mammals that have the snout lengthened into a trunk and two long curving pointed ivory tusks

el·e·phan·ti·a·sis \ˌe-lə-fən-ˈtī-ə-səs\ *n, pl* **-a·ses** \-ˌsēz\ : enlargement and thickening of tissues in response esp. to infection by minute parasitic worms

el·e·phan·tine \ˌe-lə-ˈfan-ˌtēn, -ˌtīn, ˈe-lə-fən-\ *adj* **1** : of great size or strength **2** : CLUMSY, PONDEROUS ⟨~ verse⟩

elev *abbr* elevation

el·e·vate \ˈe-lə-ˌvāt\ *vb* **-vat·ed; -vat·ing** **1** : to lift up : RAISE **2** : EXALT, ENNOBLE **3** : ELATE

el·e·va·tion \ˌe-lə-ˈvā-shən\ *n* **1** : the height to which something is raised (as above sea level) **2** : a lifting up **3** : something (as a hill or swelling) that is elevated

el·e·va·tor \ˈe-lə-ˌvā-tər\ *n* **1** : a cage or platform for conveying people or things from one level to another **2** : a building for storing and discharging grain **3** : a movable surface on an airplane to produce motion up or down

elev·en \i-ˈle-vən\ *n* **1** : one more than 10 **2** : the 11th in a set or series **3** : something having 11 units; *esp* : a football team — **eleven** *adj or pron* — **elev·enth** \-vənth\ *adj or n*

elf \ˈelf\ *n, pl* **elves** \ˈelvz\ : a mischievous fairy — **elf·ish** \ˈel-fish\ *adj*

ELF *abbr* extremely low frequency

elf·in \ˈel-fən\ *adj* : of, relating to, or resembling an elf

elic·it \i-ˈli-sət\ *vb* : to draw out or forth ♦ *Synonyms* EVOKE, EDUCE, EXTRACT, EXTORT

elide \i-ˈlīd\ *vb* **elid·ed; elid·ing** : to suppress or alter by elision

el·i·gi·ble \ˈe-lə-jə-bəl\ *adj* : qualified to participate or to be chosen — **el·i·gi·bil·i·ty** \ˌe-lə-jə-ˈbi-lə-tē\ *n* — **eligible** *n*

CHEMICAL ELEMENTS

ELEMENT NAME	SYMBOL & ATOMIC NUMBER	ATOMIC WEIGHT[1]	ELEMENT NAME	SYMBOL & ATOMIC NUMBER	ATOMIC WEIGHT[1]
actinium	(Ac = 89)	227.0277	meitnerium	(Mt = 109)	(268)
aluminum	(Al = 13)	26.98154	mendelevium	(Md = 101)	(258)
americium	(Am = 95)	(243)	mercury	(Hg = 80)	200.59
antimony	(Sb = 51)	121.760	molybdenum	(Mo = 42)	95.94
argon	(Ar = 18)	39.948	neodymium	(Nd = 60)	144.24
arsenic	(As = 33)	74.92160	neon	(Ne = 10)	20.180
astatine	(At = 85)	(210)	neptunium	(Np = 93)	(237)
barium	(Ba = 56)	137.33	nickel	(Ni = 28)	58.6934
berkelium	(Bk = 97)	(247)	niobium	(Nb = 41)	92.90638
beryllium	(Be = 4)	9.012182	nitrogen	(N = 7)	14.0067
bismuth	(Bi = 83)	208.98038	nobelium	(No = 102)	(259)
bohrium	(Bh = 107)	(264)	osmium	(Os = 76)	190.23
boron	(B = 5)	10.81	oxygen	(O = 8)	15.9994
bromine	(Br = 35)	79.904	palladium	(Pd = 46)	106.42
cadmium	(Cd = 48)	112.41	phosphorus	(P = 15)	30.973761
calcium	(Ca = 20)	40.078	platinum	(Pt = 78)	195.078
californium	(Cf = 98)	(251)	plutonium	(Pu = 94)	(244)
carbon	(C = 6)	12.011	polonium	(Po = 84)	(209)
cerium	(Ce = 58)	140.116	potassium	(K = 19)	39.0983
cesium	(Cs = 55)	132.90545	praseodymium	(Pr = 59)	140.90765
chlorine	(Cl = 17)	35.453	promethium	(Pm = 61)	(145)
chromium	(Cr = 24)	51.996	protactinium	(Pa = 91)	(231)
cobalt	(Co = 27)	58.93320	radium	(Ra = 88)	(226)
copper	(Cu = 29)	63.546	radon	(Rn = 86)	(222)
curium	(Cm = 96)	(247)	rhenium	(Re = 75)	186.207
darmstadtium	(Ds = 110)	(269)	rhodium	(Rh = 45)	102.90550
dubnium	(Db = 105)	(262)	rubidium	(Rb = 37)	85.4678
dysprosium	(Dy = 66)	162.50	ruthenium	(Ru = 44)	101.07
einsteinium	(Es = 99)	(252)	rutherfordium	(Rf = 104)	(261)
erbium	(Er = 68)	167.259	samarium	(Sm = 62)	150.36
europium	(Eu = 63)	151.964	scandium	(Sc = 21)	44.95591
fermium	(Fm = 100)	(257)	seaborgium	(Sg = 106)	(266)
fluorine	(F = 9)	18.998403	selenium	(Se = 34)	78.96
francium	(Fr = 87)	(223)	silicon	(Si = 14)	28.0855
gadolinium	(Gd = 64)	157.25	silver	(Ag = 47)	107.8682
gallium	(Ga = 31)	69.723	sodium	(Na = 11)	22.989770
germanium	(Ge = 32)	72.64	strontium	(Sr = 38)	87.62
gold	(Au = 79)	196.96655	sulfur	(S = 16)	32.07
hafnium	(Hf = 72)	178.49	tantalum	(Ta = 73)	180.9479
hassium	(Hs = 108)	(277)	technetium	(Tc = 43)	(98)
helium	(He = 2)	4.002602	tellurium	(Te = 52)	127.60
holmium	(Ho = 67)	164.93032	terbium	(Tb = 65)	158.92534
hydrogen	(H = 1)	1.0079	thallium	(Tl = 81)	204.3833
indium	(In = 49)	114.818	thorium	(Th = 90)	232.0381
iodine	(I = 53)	126.90447	thulium	(Tm = 69)	168.93421
iridium	(Ir = 77)	192.217	tin	(Sn = 50)	118.71
iron	(Fe = 26)	55.845	titanium	(Ti = 22)	47.867
krypton	(Kr = 36)	83.80	tungsten	(W = 74)	183.84
lanthanum	(La = 57)	138.9055	uranium	(U = 92)	(238)
lawrencium	(Lr = 103)	(262)	vanadium	(V = 23)	50.9415
lead	(Pb = 82)	207.2	xenon	(Xe = 54)	131.29
lithium	(Li = 3)	6.941	ytterbium	(Yb = 70)	173.04
lutetium	(Lu = 71)	174.967	yttrium	(Y = 39)	88.90585
magnesium	(Mg = 12)	24.305	zinc	(Zn = 30)	65.39
manganese	(Mn = 25)	54.93805	zirconium	(Zr = 40)	91.224

[1] Weights are based on the naturally occurring isotope compositions and scaled to $^{12}C = 12$. For elements lacking stable isotopes, the mass number of the most stable nuclide is shown in parentheses.

elim·i·nate \i-'li-mə-ˌnāt\ vb -nat·ed; -nat·ing [L eliminatus, pp. of eliminare, fr. limen threshold] **1** : REMOVE, ERADICATE **2** : to pass (wastes) from the body **3** : to leave out : IGNORE — elim·i·na·tion \-ˌli-mə-'nā-shən\ n

eli·sion \i-'li-zhən\ n : the omission of a final or initial sound or a word; esp : the omission of an unstressed vowel or syllable in a verse to achieve a uniform rhythm

elite \ā-'lēt, ē-\ n [F élite] **1** : the choice part; also : a superior group **2** : a typewriter type providing 12 characters to the inch — elite adj

elit·ism \-'lē-ˌti-zəm\ n : leadership or rule by an elite; also : advocacy of such elitism — elit·ist \-tist\ n or adj

elix·ir \i-'lik-sər\ n [ME, fr. ML, fr. Ar al-iksīr the elixir, fr. al the + iksīr elixir] **1** : a substance held capable of prolonging life indefinitely; also : PANACEA **2** : a sweetened alcoholic medicinal solution

Eliz·a·be·than \i-ˌli-zə-'bē-thən\ adj : of, relating to, or characteristic of Elizabeth I of England or her times

elk \'elk\ n, pl elk or elks **1** : MOOSE — used for one of the Old World **2** : a large gregarious deer of No. America, Europe, Asia, and northwestern Africa with curved antlers having many branches

elk 2

¹ell \'el\ n [ME eln, fr. OE; akin to L ulna forearm, Gk ōlenē elbow] : a former English cloth measure of 45 inches

²ell n : an extension at right angles to a building

el·lipse \i-'lips, e-\ n : a closed curve of oval shape

el·lip·sis \i-'lip-səs, e-\ n, pl el·lip·ses \-ˌsēz\ **1** : omission from an expression of a word clearly implied **2** : marks (as . . .) to show omission

el·lip·soid \i-'lip-ˌsȯid, e-\ n : a surface all plane sections of which are circles or ellipses — el·lip·soi·dal \-ˌlip-'sȯi-dᵊl\ also ellipsoid adj

el·lip·ti·cal \i-'lip-ti-kəl, e-\ or el·lip·tic \-tik\ adj **1** : of, relating to, or shaped like an ellipse **2** : of, relating to, or marked by ellipsis — el·lip·ti·cal·ly \-ti-k(ə-)lē\ adv

elm \'elm\ n : any of a genus of large trees that have toothed leaves and nearly circular one-seeded winged fruits and are often grown as shade trees; also : the wood of an elm

El Ni·ño \el-'nē-nyō\ n : a flow of unusually warm Pacific Ocean water moving toward and along the west coast of So. America

el·o·cu·tion \ˌe-lə-'kyü-shən\ n : the art of effective public speaking — el·o·cu·tion·ist \-sha-nist\ n

elon·gate \i-'lȯŋ-ˌgāt\ vb -gat·ed; -gat·ing : to make or grow longer ✦ Synonyms EXTEND, LENGTHEN, PROLONG, PROTRACT — elon·ga·tion \ˌ(ˌ)ē-ˌlȯŋ-'gā-shən\ n

elope \i-'lōp\ vb eloped; elop·ing : to run away esp. to be married — elope·ment n — elop·er n

el·o·quent \'e-lə-kwənt\ adj **1** : having or showing clear and forceful expression **2** : clearly showing some feeling or meaning — el·o·quence \-kwəns\ n — el·o·quent·ly adv

¹else \'els\ adv **1** : in a different or additional manner or place or at a different or additional time ⟨where ~ can we meet⟩ **2** : OTHERWISE ⟨obey or ~ you'll be sorry⟩

²else adj : OTHER; esp : being in addition ⟨what ~ do you want⟩

else·where \-ˌhwer\ adv : in or to another place ⟨took my business ~⟩

elu·ci·date \i-'lü-sə-ˌdāt\ vb -dat·ed; -dat·ing : to make clear usu. by explanation ✦ Synonyms CLARIFY, EXPLAIN, ILLUMINATE — elu·ci·da·tion \-ˌlü-sə-'dā-shən\ n

elude \ē-'lüd\ vb elud·ed; elud·ing **1** : EVADE **2** : to escape the notice of

elu·sive \ē-'lü-siv\ adj : tending to elude : EVASIVE — elu·sive·ly adv — elu·sive·ness n

el·ver \'el-vər\ n [alter. of eelfare migration of eels] : a young eel

elves pl of ELF

Ely·si·um \i-'li-zhē-əm, -zē-\ n, pl -si·ums or -sia \-zhē-ə, -zē-\ : PARADISE **2** — Ely·sian \-'li-zhən\ adj

em \'em\ n : a length approximately the width of the letter M

EM abbr **1** electromagnetic **2** electron microscope **3** enlisted man

ema·ci·ate \i-'mā-shē-ˌāt\ vb -at·ed; -at·ing : to become or cause to become very thin — ema·ci·a·tion \-ˌmā-shē-'ā-shən, -sē-\ n

e–mail \'ē-ˌmāl\ n **1** : a system for transmitting messages between computers on a network **2** : a message or messages sent and received through an e-mail system

emalangeni pl of LILANGENI

em·a·nate \'e-mə-ˌnāt\ vb -nat·ed; -nat·ing : to come out from a source ✦ Synonyms PROCEED, SPRING, RISE, ARISE, ORIGINATE — em·a·na·tion \ˌe-mə-'nā-shən\ n

eman·ci·pate \i-'man-sə-ˌpāt\ vb -pat·ed; -pat·ing : to set free ✦ Synonyms LIBERATE, RELEASE, DELIVER, DISCHARGE — eman·ci·pa·tion \-ˌman-sə-'pā-shən\ n — eman·ci·pa·tor \-'man-sə-ˌpā-tər\ n

emas·cu·late \i-'mas-kyu-ˌlāt\ vb -lat·ed; -lat·ing : to deprive of virility : CASTRATE; also : WEAKEN — emas·cu·la·tion \-ˌmas-kyu-'lā-shən\ n

em·balm \im-'bäm, -'bälm\ vb : to treat (a corpse) so as to protect from decay — em·balm·er n

em·bank·ment \im-'baŋk-mənt\ n : a raised structure (as of earth) to hold back water or carry a roadway

em·bar·go \im-'bär-gō\ n, pl -goes [Sp, fr. embargar to bar] : a prohibition on commerce — embargo vb

em·bark \im-'bärk\ vb **1** : to put or go on board a ship or airplane **2** : to make a start — em·bar·ka·tion \ˌem-ˌbär-'kā-shən\ n

em·bar·rass \im-'ber-əs\ vb **1** : CONFUSE, DISCONCERT **2** : to involve in financial difficulties **3** : to cause to experience self-conscious distress **4** : HINDER, IMPEDE — em·bar·rass·ing·ly adv — em·bar·rass·ment n

em·bas·sy \'em-bə-sē\ n, pl -sies **1** : a group of representatives headed by an ambassador **2** : the function, position, or mission of an ambassador **3** : the official residence and offices of an ambassador

em·bat·tle \im-'ba-tᵊl\ vb : to arrange in order for battle; also : FORTIFY

em·bat·tled adj **1** : engaged in battle, conflict, or controversy **2** : being a site of battle, conflict, or controversy **3** : characterized by conflict or controversy ⟨an ~ presidency⟩

em·bed \im-'bed\ vb em·bed·ded; em·bed·ding **1** : to enclose closely in a surrounding mass **2** : to make something an integral part of

em·bel·lish \im-'be-lish\ vb **1** : ADORN, DECORATE **2** : to add ornamental details to ✦ Synonyms BEAUTIFY, DECK, BEDECK, GARNISH, ORNAMENT, DRESS — em·bel·lish·er n — em·bel·lish·ment n

em·ber \'em-bər\ n **1** : a glowing or smoldering fragment from a fire **2** pl : the smoldering remains of a fire

em·bez·zle \im-'be-zəl\ vb -zled; -zling : to steal (as money) by falsifying records — em·bez·zle·ment n — em·bez·zler n

em·bit·ter \im-'bi-tər\ vb **1** : to arouse bitter feelings in **2** : to make bitter

em·bla·zon \-'blā-zᵊn\ vb **1** : to adorn with heraldic devices **2** : to display conspicuously

em·blem \'em-bləm\ n : something (as an object or picture) suggesting another object or an idea : SYMBOL — em·blem·at·ic \ˌem-blə-'ma-tik\ also em·blem·at·i·cal \-ti-kəl\ adj

em·body \im-'bä-dē\ vb em·bod·ied; em·body·ing **1** : INCARNATE **2** : to express in definite form **3** : to incorporate into a system or body **4** : PERSONIFY ✦ Syno-

nyms COMBINE, INTEGRATE — **em·bodi·ment** \-di-mənt\ n

em·bold·en \im-'bōl-dən\ vb : to inspire with courage

em·bo·lism \'em-bə-ˌli-zəm\ n : the obstruction of a blood vessel by a foreign or abnormal particle

em·bon·point \äⁿ-bōⁿ-'pwaⁿ\ n [F] : plumpness of person : STOUTNESS

em·boss \im-'bäs, -'bȯs\ vb : to ornament with raised work

em·bou·chure \'äm-bù-ˌshùr, ˌäm-bù-'shùr\ n [F, ultim. fr. *bouche* mouth] : the position and use of the lips, tongue, and teeth in playing a wind instrument

em·bow·er \im-'baù-(ə)r\ vb : to shelter or enclose in a bower

¹**embrace** \im-'brās\ vb **em·braced; em·brac·ing 1** : to clasp in the arms; *also* : CHERISH, LOVE **2** : ENCIRCLE **3** : TAKE UP, ADOPT ⟨*embraced* the cause⟩; *also* : WELCOME ⟨*embraced* the opportunity⟩ **4** : INCLUDE **5** : to participate in an embrace ✦ **Synonyms** COMPREHEND, INVOLVE, ENCOMPASS, EMBODY

²**embrace** n : an encircling with the arms

em·bra·sure \im-'brā-zhər\ n **1** : an opening in a wall through which a cannon is fired **2** : a recess of a door or window

em·bro·ca·tion \ˌem-brə-'kā-shən\ n : LINIMENT

em·broi·der \im-'brȯi-dər\ vb **1** : to ornament with or do needlework **2** : to elaborate with exaggerated detail

em·broi·dery \im-'brȯi-də-rē\ n, pl **-der·ies 1** : the forming of decorative designs with needlework **2** : something embroidered

em·broil \im-'brȯi(-ə)l\ vb **1** : to throw into confusion or disorder **2** : to involve in conflict or difficulties — **em·broil·ment** n

em·bryo \'em-brē-ˌō\ n, pl **embryos** : a living thing in its earliest stages of development — **em·bry·on·ic** \ˌem-brē-'ä-nik\ adj

em·bry·ol·o·gy \ˌem-brē-'ä-lə-jē\ n : a branch of biology dealing with embryos and their development — **em·bry·o·log·i·cal** \-brē-ə-'lä-ji-kəl\ adj — **em·bry·ol·o·gist** \-brē-'ä-lə-jist\ n

em·cee \ˌem-'sē\ n : MASTER OF CEREMONIES — **emcee** vb

emend \ē-'mend\ vb : to correct usu. by altering the text of ✦ **Synonyms** RECTIFY, REVISE, AMEND — **emen·da·tion** \ˌē-ˌmen-'dā-shən\ n

emer abbr emeritus

¹**em·er·ald** \'em-rəld, 'e-mə-\ n : a green beryl prized as a gem

²**emerald** adj : brightly or richly green

emerge \i-'mərj\ vb **emerged; emerg·ing** : to rise, come forth, or come out into view — **emer·gence** \-'mər-jəns\ n — **emer·gent** \-jənt\ adj

emer·gen·cy \i-'mər-jən-sē\ n, pl **-cies** : an unforeseen event or condition requiring prompt action ✦ **Synonyms** EXIGENCY, CONTINGENCY, CRISIS, JUNCTURE

emergency room n : a hospital room for receiving and treating persons needing immediate medical care

emer·i·ta \i-'mer-ə-tə\ adj : EMERITUS — used of a woman

emer·i·tus \i-'mer-ə-təs\ adj [L] : retired from active duty ⟨professor ∼⟩

em·ery \'e-mə-rē\ n, pl **em·er·ies** : a dark granular mineral consisting primarily of corundum and used as an abrasive

emet·ic \i-'me-tik\ n : an agent that induces vomiting — **emetic** adj

emf n [electromotive force] : POTENTIAL DIFFERENCE

em·i·grate \'e-mə-ˌgrāt\ vb **-grat·ed; -grat·ing** : to leave a place (as a country) to settle elsewhere — **em·i·grant** \-mi-grənt\ n — **em·i·gra·tion** \ˌe-mə-'grā-shən\ n

émi·gré also **emi·gré** \'e-mi-ˌgrā, ˌe-mi-'grā\ n [F] : a person who emigrates esp. because of political conditions

em·i·nence \'e-mə-nəns\ n **1** : high rank or position; *also* : a person of high rank or attainments **2** : a lofty place

em·i·nent \'e-mə-nənt\ adj **1** : CONSPICUOUS, EVIDENT **2** : DISTINGUISHED, PROMINENT ⟨an ∼ physician⟩ — **em·i·nent·ly** adv

eminent domain n : a right of a government to take private property for public use

emir or **amir** \ə-'mir, ā-\ n [Ar *amīr* commander] : a ruler, chief, or commander in Islamic countries — **emir·ate** \'e-mər-ət\ n

em·is·sary \'e-mə-ˌser-ē\ n, pl **-sar·ies** : AGENT; *esp* : a secret agent

emis·sion \ē-'mi-shən\ n : something emitted; *esp* : substances discharged into the air

emit \ē-'mit\ vb **emit·ted; emit·ting 1** : to give off or out ⟨∼ light⟩; *also* : EJECT **2** : EXPRESS, UTTER — **emit·ter** n

emol·lient \i-'mäl-yənt\ adj : making soft or supple; *also* : soothing esp. to the skin or mucous membrane ⟨an ∼ hand lotion⟩ — **emollient** n

emol·u·ment \i-'mäl-yə-mənt\ n [ME, fr. L *emolumentum* advantage, fr. *emolere* to produce by grinding] : the product (as salary or fees) of an employment

emote \i-'mōt\ vb **emot·ed; emot·ing** : to give expression to emotion in or as if in a play

emo·ti·con \i-'mō-ti-ˌkän\ n : a group of keyboard characters (as :)) that represents a facial expression esp. in online communications

emo·tion \i-'mō-shən\ n : a usu. intense feeling (as of love, hate, or despair) — **emo·tion·al** \-shə-nəl\ adj — **emo·tion·al·ly** adv

emo·tive \i-'mō-tiv\ adj **1** : of or relating to the emotions **2** : appealing to or expressing emotion

emp abbr emperor; empress

empanel var of IMPANEL

em·pa·thy \'em-pə-thē\ n : the experiencing as one's own of the feelings of another; *also* : the capacity for this — **em·path·ic** \em-'pa-thik\ adj

em·pen·nage \ˌäm-pə-'näzh, ˌem-\ n [F] : the tail assembly of an airplane

em·per·or \'em-pər-ər\ n : the sovereign male ruler of an empire

em·pha·sis \'em-fə-səs\ n, pl **-pha·ses** \-ˌsēz\ : particular prominence given (as to a syllable in speaking or to a phase of action)

em·pha·sise Brit var of EMPHASIZE

em·pha·size \-ˌsīz\ vb **-sized; -siz·ing** : to place emphasis on : STRESS

em·phat·ic \im-'fa-tik, em-\ adj : uttered with emphasis : STRESSED — **em·phat·i·cal·ly** \-'ti-k(ə-)lē\ adv

em·phy·se·ma \ˌem-fə-'zē-mə, -'sē-\ n : a condition marked esp. by abnormal expansion of the air spaces of the lungs resulting in severe breathlessness

em·pire \'em-ˌpī(-ə)r\ n **1** : a large state or a group of states under a single sovereign who is usu. an emperor; *also* : something resembling a political empire **2** : imperial sovereignty or dominion

em·pir·i·cal \im-'pir-i-kəl\ also **em·pir·ic** \-ik\ adj : based on observation; *also* : subject to verification by observation or experiment ⟨∼ laws⟩ — **em·pir·i·cal·ly** \-i-k(ə-)lē\ adv

em·pir·i·cism \im-'pir-ə-ˌsi-zəm, em-\ n : the practice of relying on observation and experiment esp. in the natural sciences — **em·pir·i·cist** \-sist\ n

em·place·ment \im-'plās-mənt\ n **1** : a prepared position for weapons or military equipment **2** : PLACEMENT

¹**em·ploy** \im-'plȯi\ vb **1** : to make use of **2** : to use the services of **3** : OCCUPY, DEVOTE — **em·ploy·er** n

²**em·ploy** \im-'plȯi, 'im-ˌplȯi, 'em-\ n : EMPLOYMENT

em·ploy·ee also **em·ploye** \im-ˌplȯi-'ē, ˌem-; im-'plȯi-ˌē, em-\ n : a person who works for another

em·ploy·ment \im-'plȯi-mənt\ n **1** : OCCUPATION, ACTIVITY **2** : the act of employing : the condition of being employed

em·po·ri·um \im-'pȯr-ē-əm, em-\ n, pl **-ri·ums** also **-ria** \-ē-ə\ [L, fr. Gk *emporion*, fr. *emporos* traveler, trader] : a commercial center; *esp* : a store carrying varied articles

em·pow·er \im-'paù-(ə)r\ vb : to give authority or power to; *also* : ENABLE — **em·pow·er·ment** \-mənt\ n

em·press \'em-prəs\ n **1** : the wife or widow of an emperor **2** : a sovereign female ruler of an empire

¹**emp·ty** \'emp-tē\ adj **emp·ti·er; -est** [ME, fr. OE *æmettig* unoccupied, fr. *æmetta* leisure] **1** : containing nothing ⟨∼ shelves⟩ **2** : UNOCCUPIED, UNINHABITED ⟨an ∼ building⟩ **3** : lacking value, force, sense, or purpose ✦ **Synonyms** VACANT, BLANK, VOID, STARK, VACUOUS — **emp·ti·ness** n

²**empty** vb **emp·tied; emp·ty·ing 1** : to make or become empty **2** : to discharge contents; *also* : to remove from what holds or encloses

³**empty** n, pl **empties** : an empty bottle or can

emp·ty–hand·ed \ˌemp-tē-ˈhan-dəd\ *adj* **1** : having or bringing nothing **2** : having acquired or gained nothing

em·py·re·an \ˌem-ˌpī-ˈrē-ən, -pə-\ *n* **1** : the highest heaven; *also* : FIRMAMENT **2** : an ideal place or state

EMT \ˌē-(ˌ)em-ˈtē\ *n* [*e*mergency *m*edical *t*echnician] : a specially trained medical technician certified to provide basic medical services before and during transport to a hospital

¹**emu** \ˈē-myü, -mü\ *n* : a swift-running flightless Australian bird smaller than the related ostrich

²**emu** *abbr* electromagnetic unit

em·u·late \ˈem-yə-ˌlāt\ *vb* **-lat·ed; -lat·ing** : to strive to equal or excel : IMITATE — **em·u·la·tion** \ˌem-yə-ˈlā-shən\ *n* — **em·u·lous** \ˈem-yə-ləs\ *adj*

emul·si·fi·er \i-ˈməl-sə-ˌfī(-ə)r\ *n* : a substance (as a soap) that helps to form and stabilize an emulsion

emul·si·fy \-ˌfī\ *vb* **-fied; -fy·ing** : to disperse (as an oil) in an emulsion — **emul·si·fi·ca·tion** \i-ˌməl-sə-fə-ˈkā-shən\ *n*

emul·sion \i-ˈməl-shən\ *n* **1** : a mixture of mutually insoluble liquids in which one is dispersed in droplets throughout the other ⟨an ~ of oil in water⟩ **2** : a light-sensitive coating on photographic film or paper

en \ˈen\ *n* : a length approximately half the width of the letter *M*

¹**-en** *also* **-n** *adj suffix* : made of : consisting of ⟨earth*en*⟩

²**-en** *vb suffix* **1** : become or cause to be ⟨sharp*en*⟩ **2** : cause or come to have ⟨length*en*⟩

en·able \i-ˈnā-bəl\ *vb* **en·abled; en·abling** **1** : to make able or feasible ⟨wings that ~ one to fly⟩ **2** : to give legal power, capacity, or sanction to

en·act \i-ˈnakt\ *vb* **1** : to make into law **2** : to act out — **en·act·ment** *n*

enam·el \i-ˈna-məl\ *n* **1** : a glasslike substance used to coat the surface of metal or pottery **2** : the hard outer layer of a tooth **3** : a usu. glossy paint that forms a hard coat — **enamel** *vb*

enam·el·ware \-ˌwer\ *n* : metal utensils coated with enamel

en·am·or \i-ˈna-mər\ *vb* : to inflame with love

en·am·our *chiefly Brit var of* ENAMOR

en bloc \äⁿ-ˈbläk\ *adv or adj* : as a whole : in a mass

enc *or* **encl** *abbr* enclosure

en·camp \in-ˈkamp\ *vb* : to make camp — **en·camp·ment** *n*

en·cap·su·late \in-ˈkap-sə-ˌlāt\ *vb* **-lat·ed; -lat·ing** **1** : to encase or become encased in a capsule **2** : SUMMARIZE — **en·cap·su·la·tion** \-ˌkap-sə-ˈlā-shən\ *n*

en·case \in-ˈkās\ *vb* : to enclose in or as if in a case — **en·case·ment** \-ˈkā-smənt\ *n*

-ence *n suffix* **1** : action or process ⟨emerg*ence*⟩ : instance of an action or process ⟨refer*ence*⟩ **2** : quality or state ⟨depend*ence*⟩

en·ceinte \äⁿ-ˈsant\ *adj* : PREGNANT 1

en·ceph·a·li·tis \in-ˌse-fə-ˈlī-təs\ *n, pl* **-lit·i·des** \-ˈli-tə-ˌdēz\ : inflammation of the brain — **en·ceph·a·lit·ic** \-ˈli-tik\ *adj*

en·ceph·a·lop·a·thy \in-ˌse-fə-ˈlä-pə-thē\ *n, pl* **-thies** : a disease of the brain

en·chain \in-ˈchān\ *vb* : FETTER, CHAIN

en·chant \in-ˈchant\ *vb* **1** : BEWITCH **2** : ENRAPTURE, FASCINATE ⟨was ~*ed* by his poetry⟩ — **en·chant·er** *n* — **en·chant·ing·ly** *adv* — **en·chant·ment** *n* — **en·chant·ress** \-ˈchan-trəs\ *n*

en·chi·la·da \ˌen-chə-ˈlä-də\ *n* : a tortilla rolled around a filling, covered with chili sauce, and usu. baked

en·ci·pher \in-ˈsī-fər, en-\ *vb* : ENCODE

en·cir·cle \in-ˈsər-kəl\ *vb* : to pass completely around : SURROUND — **en·cir·cle·ment** *n*

en·clave \ˈen-ˌklāv; ˈän-ˌklāv\ *n* : a distinct territorial, cultural, or social unit enclosed within or as if within foreign territory

en·close \in-ˈklōz\ *vb* **1** : to shut up or in; *esp* : to surround with a fence **2** : to include along with something else in a parcel or envelope ⟨~ a check⟩ — **en·clo·sure** \-ˈklō-zhər\ *n*

en·code \in-ˈkōd, en-\ *vb* : to convert (a message) into code

en·co·mi·um \en-ˈkō-mē-əm\ *n, pl* **-mi·ums** *also* **-mia** \-mē-ə\ : high or glowing praise

en·com·pass \in-ˈkəm-pəs\ *vb* **1** : ENCIRCLE **2** : ENVELOP, INCLUDE

en·core \ˈän-ˌkȯr\ *n* **1** : a demand for repetition or reappearance **2** : a further performance or appearance demanded by an audience **3** : a second achievement that usu. surpasses the first — **encore** *vb*

¹**en·coun·ter** \in-ˈkaun-tər\ *vb* **1** : to meet as an enemy : FIGHT **2** : to meet usu. unexpectedly ⟨~ problems⟩

²**encounter** *n* **1** : a hostile usu. violent meeting **2** : a chance meeting **3** : an experience shared with another ⟨a romantic ~⟩

en·cour·age \in-ˈkər-ij\ *vb* **-aged; -ag·ing** **1** : to inspire with courage and hope **2** : STIMULATE, INCITE ⟨tax cuts to ~ spending⟩ **3** : FOSTER — **en·cour·age·ment** *n* — **en·cour·ag·ing·ly** *adv*

en·croach \in-ˈkrōch\ *vb* [ME *encrochen* to seize, fr. AF *encrocher*, fr. *croche* hook] : to enter gradually or stealthily upon another's property or rights — **en·croach·er** *n* — **en·croach·ment** *n*

en·crust *also* **in·crust** \in-ˈkrəst\ *vb* : to provide with or form a crust

en·crus·ta·tion \(ˌ)in-ˌkrəs-ˈtā-shən, ˌen-\ *var of* INCRUSTATION

en·cum·ber \in-ˈkəm-bər\ *vb* **1** : to weigh down : BURDEN **2** : to hinder the function or activity of ⟨relations ~*ed* by mistrust⟩ — **en·cum·brance** \-brəns\ *n*

ency *or* **encyc** *abbr* encyclopedia

-en·cy *n suffix* : quality or state ⟨despond*ency*⟩

¹**en·cyc·li·cal** \in-ˈsi-kli-kəl, en-\ *adj* : addressed to all the individuals of a group

²**encyclical** *n* : an encyclical letter; *esp* : a papal letter to the bishops of the church

en·cy·clo·pae·dia, en·cy·clo·pae·dic *chiefly Brit var of* ENCYCLOPEDIA, ENCYCLOPEDIC

en·cy·clo·pe·dia *n* [ML *encyclopaedia* course of general education, fr. Gk *enkyklios paideia* general education] : a work treating the various branches of learning — **en·cy·clo·pe·dic** \-ˈpē-dik\ *adj*

en·cyst \in-ˈsist, en-\ *vb* : to form or become enclosed in a cyst — **en·cyst·ment** *n*

¹**end** \ˈend\ *n* **1** : the part of an area that lies at the boundary; *also* : a point which marks the extent or limit of something or at which something ceases to exist **2** : a ceasing of a course (as of action or activity); *also* : DEATH **3** : the ultimate state; *also* : RESULT, ISSUE **4** : REMNANT **5** : PURPOSE, OBJECTIVE **6** : a player stationed at the extremity of a line (as in football) **7** : a share, operation, or aspect of an undertaking

²**end** *vb* **1** : to bring or come to an end **2** : DESTROY; *also* : DIE **3** : to form or be at the end of ✦ **Synonyms** CLOSE, CONCLUDE, TERMINATE, FINISH, COMPLETE

en·dan·ger \in-ˈdān-jər\ *vb* : to bring into danger; *also* : to create danger

en·dan·gered *adj* : being or relating to an endangered species

endangered species *n* : a species threatened with extinction

en·dear \in-ˈdir\ *vb* : to cause to become beloved or admired

en·dear·ment \-mənt\ *n* : a sign of affection : CARESS

en·deav·or \in-ˈde-vər\ *vb* : TRY, ATTEMPT — **endeavor** *n*

en·deav·our *chiefly Brit var of* ENDEAVOR

en·dem·ic \en-ˈde-mik, in-\ *adj* : restricted to a particular place ⟨~ plants⟩ ⟨an ~ disease⟩ — **endemic** *nm*

end·ing \ˈen-diŋ\ *n* : something that forms an end; *esp* : SUFFIX

en·dive \ˈen-ˌdīv\ *n* **1** : an herb related to chicory and grown as a salad plant **2** : the blanched shoot of chicory

end·less \ˈend-ləs\ *adj* **1** : having or seeming to have no end : ETERNAL ⟨~ debates⟩ **2** : united at the ends : CONTINUOUS ⟨an ~ belt⟩ ✦ **Synonyms** INTERMINABLE, EVERLASTING, UNCEASING, CEASELESS, UNENDING — **end·less·ly** *adv*

end·most \-ˌmōst\ *adj* : situated at the very end

end·note \-ˌnōt\ *n* : a note placed at the end of a text

en·do·crine \ˈen-də-krən, -ˌkrīn, -ˌkrēn\ *adj* : producing secretions that are distributed by way of the bloodstream ⟨~ glands⟩ — **endocrine** *n* — **en·do·cri·nol·o·gist** \-kri-ˈnä-lə-jist\ *n* — **en·do·cri·nol·o·gy** \-jē\ *n*

en·dog·e·nous \en-ˈdä-jə-nəs\ *adj* : caused or produced by factors inside the organism or system ⟨~ depression⟩ — **en·dog·e·nous·ly** *adv*

en·do·me·tri·um \ˌen-dō-ˈmē-trē-əm\ *n, pl* **-tria** \-trē-ə\

: the mucous membrane lining the uterus — **en·do·me·tri·al** \-trē-əl\ *adj*

en·dor·phin \en-'dòr-fən\ *n* : any of a group of endogenous morphinelike proteins found esp. in the brain

en·dorse *also* **in·dorse** \in-'dòrs\ *vb* **en·dorsed; en·dorsing** [ME *endosen*, fr. AF *endosser* to put on, don, write on the back of, fr. *dos* back, fr. L *dorsum*] **1** : to sign one's name on the back of (as a check) **2** : APPROVE, SANCTION **3** : to recommend (as a product) usu. for financial compensation — **en·dorse·ment** *also* **in·dorse·ment** *n*

en·do·scope \'en-də-ˌskōp\ *n* : an illuminated usu. fiberoptic instrument for visualizing the interior of a hollow organ or part (as the colon or esophagus) — **en·do·scop·ic** \ˌen-də-'skä-pik\ *adj* — **en·dos·co·py** \en-'däs-kə-pē\ *n*

en·do·ther·mic \ˌen-də-'thər-mik\ *adj* : characterized by or formed with absorption of heat

en·dow \in-'daù\ *vb* **1** : to furnish with funds for support ⟨~ a school⟩ **2** : to furnish with something freely or naturally — **en·dow·ment** *n*

en·due \in-'dü, -'dyü\ *vb* **en·dued; en·du·ing** : PROVIDE, ENDOW

en·dur·ance \in-'dùr-əns, -'dyùr-\ *n* **1** : DURATION **2** : the ability to withstand hardship or stress : FORTITUDE

en·dure \in-'dùr, -'dyùr\ *vb* **en·dured; en·dur·ing** **1** : LAST, PERSIST **2** : to suffer firmly or patiently : BEAR **3** : TOLERATE — **en·dur·able** *adj*

end·ways \'end-ˌwāz\ *adv or adj* **1** : LENGTHWISE **2** : with the end forward **3** : on end

end·wise \-ˌwīz\ *adv or adj* : ENDWAYS

ENE *abbr* east-northeast

en·e·ma \'e-nə-mə\ *n, pl* **enemas** *also* **ene·ma·ta** \ˌe-nə-'mä-tə, 'e-nə-mə-tə\ : injection of liquid into the rectum; *also* : material so injected

en·e·my \'e-nə-mē\ *n, pl* **-mies** [ME *enemi*, fr. AF, fr. L *inimicus*, fr. *in-* not + *amicus* friend] : one that attacks or tries to harm another : FOE; *esp* : a military opponent

en·er·get·ic \ˌe-nər-'je-tik\ *adj* : marked by energy : ACTIVE, VIGOROUS ✦ *Synonyms* STRENUOUS, LUSTY, DYNAMIC, VITAL — **en·er·get·i·cal·ly** \-ti-k(ə-)lē\ *adv*

en·er·gise *Brit var of* ENERGIZE

en·er·gize \'e-nər-ˌjīz\ *vb* **-gized; -giz·ing** : to give energy to

en·er·gy \'e-nər-jē\ *n, pl* **-gies** **1** : vigorous action : EFFORT **2** : capacity for action **3** : a fundamental entity of nature usu. regarded as the capacity for performing work **4** : usable power (as heat or electricity); *also* : the resources for producing such power

energy level *n* : one of the stable states of constant energy that may be assumed by a physical system (as the electrons in an atom)

en·er·vate \'e-nər-ˌvāt\ *vb* **-vat·ed; -vat·ing** : to lessen the strength or vigor of : weaken in mind or body — **en·er·vat·ing·ly** \-ˌvā-tiŋ-lē\ *adv* — **en·er·va·tion** \ˌe-nər-'vā-shən\ *n*

en·fee·ble \in-'fē-bəl\ *vb* **-bled; -bling** : to make feeble ✦ *Synonyms* WEAKEN, DEBILITATE, SAP, UNDERMINE, CRIPPLE — **en·fee·ble·ment** *n*

en·fi·lade \'en-fə-ˌlād, -ˌläd\ *n* : gunfire directed along the length of an enemy battle line — **enfilade** *vb*

en·fold \in-'fōld\ *vb* **1** : ENVELOP **2** : EMBRACE

en·force \in-'fòrs\ *vb* **1** : COMPEL ⟨~ obedience by threats⟩ **2** : to execute effectively ⟨~ the law⟩ — **en·force·able** *adj* — **en·force·ment** *n*

en·forc·er \in-'fòr-sər\ *n* : one that enforces; *esp* : a player (as in ice hockey) known for rough play

en·fran·chise \in-'fran-ˌchīz\ *vb* **-chised; -chis·ing** **1** : to set free (as from slavery) **2** : to admit to citizenship; *also* : to grant the vote to — **en·fran·chise·ment** \-ˌchīz-mənt, -chəz-\ *n*

eng *abbr* engine; engineer; engineering

Eng *abbr* England; English

en·gage \in-'gāj\ *vb* **en·gaged; en·gag·ing** **1** : PLEDGE; *esp* : to bind by a pledge to marry **2** : EMPLOY, HIRE **3** : to attract and hold esp. by interesting; *also* : to cause to participate **4** : to commence or take part in a venture ⟨*engaged* in shady deals⟩ **5** : to bring or enter into conflict ⟨~ the enemy⟩ **6** : to connect or interlock with : MESH; *also* : to cause to mesh

en·gage·ment \in-'gāj-mənt\ *n* **1** : APPOINTMENT **2** : EMPLOYMENT **3** : a mutual promise to marry : BETROTHAL **4** : a hostile encounter

en·gag·ing *adj* : ATTRACTIVE ⟨an ~ smile⟩ — **en·gag·ing·ly** *adv*

en·gen·der \in-'jen-dər\ *vb* **1** : BEGET **2** : BRING ABOUT, CREATE ⟨~ controversy⟩ ✦ *Synonyms* GENERATE, BREED, OCCASION, PRODUCE

en·gine \'en-jən\ *n* [ME *engin*, fr. AF, fr. L *ingenium* natural disposition, talent] **1** : a mechanical device **2** : a machine for converting energy into mechanical motion **3** : LOCOMOTIVE **4** : software that performs a fundamental function esp. of a larger program — **en·gine·less** *adj*

¹en·gi·neer \ˌen-jə-'nir\ *n* **1** : a member of a military unit specializing in engineering work **2** : a designer or builder of engines **3** : one trained in engineering **4** : one that operates an engine

²engineer *vb* **1** : to lay out or manage as an engineer **2** : to guide the course of ⟨~ a rally⟩ ✦ *Synonyms* PILOT, LEAD, STEER

en·gi·neer·ing *n* : the practical applications of scientific and mathematical principles

En·glish \'iŋ-glish\ *n* **1** : the language of England, the U.S., and many areas now or formerly under British rule **2** **English** *pl* : the people of England **3** : spin imparted to a ball that is driven or rolled — **English** *adj* — **En·glish·man** \-mən\ *n* — **En·glish·wom·an** \-ˌwù-mən\ *n*

English horn *n* : a woodwind instrument longer than and having a range lower than the oboe

English horn

English setter *n* : any of a breed of hunting dogs with a flat silky coat of white or white with color

English sparrow *n* : HOUSE SPARROW

English system *n* : a system of weights and measures in which the foot is the principal unit of length and the pound is the principal unit of weight

engr *abbr* **1** engineer **2** engraved

en·gram \'en-ˌgram\ *n* : a hypothetical change in neural tissue postulated in order to account for persistence of memory

en·grave \in-'grāv\ *vb* **en·graved; en·grav·ing** **1** : to produce (as letters or lines) by incising a surface **2** : to cut figures, letters, or designs on for printing; *also* : to print from an engraved plate ⟨~ an invitation⟩ **3** : PHOTOENGRAVE — **en·grav·er** *n*

en·grav·ing \in-'grā-viŋ\ *n* **1** : the art of one who engraves **2** : an engraved plate; *also* : a print made from it

en·gross \in-'grōs\ *vb* : to take up the whole interest or attention of ✦ *Synonyms* MONOPOLIZE, ABSORB, CONSUME

en·gulf \in-'gəlf\ *vb* : to flow over and enclose : OVERWHELM ⟨~ed in flames⟩

en·hance \in-'hans\ *vb* **en·hanced; en·hanc·ing** : to increase or improve (as in value or desirability) ✦ *Synonyms* HEIGHTEN, INTENSIFY, MAGNIFY — **en·hance·ment** *n*

enig·ma \i-'nig-mə\ *n* [L *aenigma*, fr. Gk *ainigma*, fr. *ainissesthai* to speak in riddles, fr. *ainos* fable] : something obscure or hard to understand

enig·mat·ic \ˌen-ig-'ma-tik\ *adj* : resembling an enigma ✦ *Synonyms* OBSCURE, CRYPTIC, MYSTIFYING — **en·ig·mat·i·cal·ly** \-ti-k(ə-)lē\ *adv*

en·join \in-'jòin\ *vb* **1** : COMMAND, ORDER ⟨~ed us to desist⟩ **2** : FORBID ✦ *Synonyms* DIRECT, BID, CHARGE, COMMAND, INSTRUCT

en·joy \in-'jòi\ *vb* **1** : to have for one's benefit or use ⟨~ good health⟩ **2** : to take pleasure or satisfaction in ⟨~ed the concert⟩ — **en·joy·able** *adj* — **en·joy·ment** *n*

enl *abbr* **1** enlarged **2** enlisted

en·large \in-'lärj\ vb en·larged; en·larg·ing 1 : to make or grow larger 2 : ELABORATE ◆ Synonyms INCREASE, AUGMENT, MULTIPLY, EXPAND — en·large·ment n

en·light·en \in-'lī-tᵊn\ vb 1 : INSTRUCT, INFORM 2 : to give spiritual insight to — en·light·en·ment n

en·list \in-'list\ vb 1 : to secure the aid or support of 2 : to engage for service in the armed forces — en·list·ee \-ˌlis-'tē\ n — en·list·ment \-'list-mənt\ n

en·list·ed \in-'lis-təd\ adj : of, relating to, or forming the part of a military force below commissioned or warrant officers

enlisted man n : a man or woman in the armed forces ranking below a commissioned or warrant officer

en·liv·en \in-'lī-vən\ vb : to give life, action, or spirit to : ANIMATE

en masse \äⁿ-'mas\ adv [F] : in a body : as a whole

en·mesh \in-'mesh\ vb : to catch or entangle in or as if in meshes

en·mi·ty \'en-mə-tē\ n, pl -ties : ILL WILL; esp : mutual hatred ◆ Synonyms HOSTILITY, ANTIPATHY, ANIMOSITY, RANCOR, ANTAGONISM

en·no·ble \i-'nō-bəl\ vb -bled; -bling : EXALT, ELEVATE; esp : to raise to noble rank — en·no·ble·ment n

en·nui \ˌän-'wē\ n [F] : BOREDOM

enor·mi·ty \i-'nȯr-mə-tē\ n, pl -ties 1 : an outrageous, vicious, or immoral act 2 : great wickedness 3 : IMMENSITY

enor·mous \i-'nȯr-məs\ adj [L enormis, fr. e, ex out of + norma rule] 1 : exceedingly wicked 2 : great in size, number, or degree : HUGE ◆ Synonyms IMMENSE, VAST, GIGANTIC, COLOSSAL, MAMMOTH, ELEPHANTINE — enor·mous·ly adv

¹enough \i-'nəf\ adj : SUFFICIENT

²enough adv 1 : SUFFICIENTLY 2 : FULLY, QUITE 3 : TOLERABLY

³enough pron : a sufficient number, quantity, or amount

en·quire \in-'kwī(-ə)r\, en·qui·ry \'in-ˌkwī(-ə)r-ē, in-'; 'in-kwə-rē, 'iŋ-\ chiefly Brit var of INQUIRE, INQUIRY

en·rage \in-'rāj\ vb : to fill with rage

en·rap·ture \in-'rap-chər\ vb en·rap·tured; en·rap·tur·ing : DELIGHT

en·rich \in-'rich\ vb 1 : to make rich or richer 2 : ORNAMENT, ADORN — en·rich·ment n

en·roll also en·rol \in-'rōl\ vb en·rolled; en·roll·ing 1 : to enter or register on a roll or list 2 : to offer (oneself) for enrolling — en·roll·ment n

en route \än-'rüt, en-\ adv or adj : on or along the way ⟨stalled while en route to work⟩

ENS abbr ensign

en·sconce \in-'skäns\ vb en·sconced; en·sconc·ing 1 : SHELTER, CONCEAL 2 : to settle snugly or securely ◆ Synonyms SECRETE, HIDE, CACHE, STASH

en·sem·ble \än-'säm-bəl\ n [F, fr. ensemble together, fr. L insimul at the same time] : a group (as of singers, dancers, or players) or a set (as of clothes) producing a single effect

en·sheathe \in-'shēth\ vb : to cover with or as if with a sheath

en·shrine \in-'shrīn\ vb 1 : to enclose in or as if in a shrine 2 : to cherish as sacred — en·shrine·ment \-mənt\ n

en·shroud \in-'shraud\ vb : SHROUD, OBSCURE

en·sign \'en-sən, 1 also 'en-ˌsīn\ n 1 : FLAG; also : BADGE, EMBLEM 2 : a commissioned officer in the navy ranking next below a lieutenant junior grade

en·slave \in-'slāv\ vb : to make a slave of — en·slave·ment n

en·snare \in-'sner\ vb : SNARE, TRAP ◆ Synonyms ENTRAP, BAG, CATCH, CAPTURE

en·sue \in-'sü\ vb en·sued; en·su·ing : to follow in time or as a result ⟨the birds escaped and chaos ensued⟩

en·sure \in-'shur\ vb en·sured; en·sur·ing : INSURE, GUARANTEE

en·tail \in-'tāl\ vb 1 : to limit the inheritance of (property) to the owner's lineal descendants or to a class thereof 2 : to include or involve as a necessary step or result ⟨the sacrifices that parenting ∼s⟩ — en·tail·ment n

en·tan·gle \in-'taŋ-gəl\ vb : TANGLE, CONFUSE — en·tan·gle·ment n

en·tente \än-'tänt\ n [F] : an understanding providing for joint action; also : parties linked by such an entente

en·ter \'en-tər\ vb 1 : to go or come in or into 2 : to become a member of : JOIN ⟨∼ the ministry⟩ 3 : BEGIN 4 : to take part in : CONTRIBUTE 5 : to go into or upon and take possession 6 : to set down (as in a list) : REGISTER ⟨∼ the data⟩ 7 : to place (a complaint) before a court; also : to put on record ⟨∼ a complaint⟩

en·ter·i·tis \ˌen-tə-'rī-təs\ n : intestinal inflammation; also : a disease marked by this

en·ter·prise \'en-tər-ˌprīz\ n 1 : UNDERTAKING, PROJECT 2 : readiness for daring action : INITIATIVE 3 : a business organization

en·ter·pris·ing \-ˌprī-ziŋ\ adj : bold and vigorous in action : ENERGETIC

en·ter·tain \ˌen-tər-'tān\ vb 1 : to treat or receive as a guest 2 : AMUSE, DIVERT ⟨∼ed us with jokes⟩ 3 : to hold in mind ⟨∼ed thoughts of retirement⟩ ◆ Synonyms HARBOR, SHELTER, LODGE, HOUSE, BILLET — en·ter·tain·er n — en·ter·tain·ment n

en·thrall or en·thral \in-'thrȯl\ vb en·thralled; en·thrall·ing 1 : ENSLAVE 2 : to hold spellbound

en·throne \in-'thrōn\ vb 1 : to seat on or as if on a throne 2 : EXALT

en·thuse \in-'thüz, -'thyüz\ vb en·thused; en·thus·ing 1 : to make enthusiastic 2 : to show enthusiasm

en·thu·si·asm \in-'thü-zē-ˌa-zəm, -'thyü-\ n [Gk enthousiasmos, fr. enthousiazein to be inspired, irreg. fr. entheos inspired, fr. theos god] 1 : strong warmth of feeling : keen interest : FERVOR 2 : a cause of fervor — en·thu·si·ast \-ˌast, -əst\ n — en·thu·si·as·tic \in-ˌthü-zē-'as-tik, -ˌthyü-\ adj — en·thu·si·as·ti·cal·ly \-ti-k(ə-)lē\ adv

en·tice \in-'tīs\ vb en·ticed; en·tic·ing : ALLURE, TEMPT — en·tice·ment n

en·tire \in-'tī(-ə)r\ adj : COMPLETE, WHOLE ◆ Synonyms SOUND, PERFECT, INTACT, UNDAMAGED — en·tire·ly adv

en·tire·ty \in-'tī-rə-tē, -'tī(-ə)r-tē\ n, pl -ties 1 : COMPLETENESS 2 : WHOLE, TOTALITY

en·ti·tle \in-'tī-tᵊl\ vb en·ti·tled; en·ti·tling 1 : NAME, DESIGNATE 2 : to give a right or claim to ⟨entitled to a fair trial⟩

en·ti·tle·ment \in-'tī-tᵊl-mənt\ n : a government program providing benefits to members of a specified group

en·ti·ty \'en-tə-tē\ n, pl -ties 1 : EXISTENCE, BEING 2 : something with separate and real existence

en·tomb \in-'tüm\ vb : to place in a tomb : BURY — en·tomb·ment n

en·to·mol·o·gy \ˌen-tə-'mä-lə-jē\ n : a branch of zoology that deals with insects — en·to·mo·log·i·cal \-mə-'lä-ji-kəl\ adj — en·to·mol·o·gist \-jist\ n

en·tou·rage \ˌän-tü-'räzh\ n [F] : RETINUE

en·tr acte \'äⁿ-ˌtrakt\ n [F] 1 : something (as a dance) performed between two acts of a play 2 : the interval between two acts of a play

en·trails \'en-ˌtrālz\ n pl : VISCERA; esp : INTESTINES

¹en·trance \'en-trəns\ n 1 : permission or right to enter 2 : the act of entering 3 : a means or place of entry

²en·trance \in-'trans\ vb en·tranced; en·tranc·ing : CHARM, DELIGHT

en·trant \'en-trənt\ n : one that enters esp. as a competitor

en·trap \in-'trap\ vb : ENSNARE, TRAP — en·trap·ment n

en·treat \in-'trēt\ vb : to ask urgently : BESEECH ◆ Synonyms BEG, IMPLORE, PLEAD, SUPPLICATE — en·treaty \-'trē-tē\ n

en·trée or en·tree \'än-ˌtrā\ n [F entrée] 1 : freedom of entry or access 2 : the main course of a meal in the U.S. ◆ Synonyms ADMISSION, ADMITTANCE, ENTRANCE

en·trench \in-'trench\ vb 1 : to place within or surround with a trench esp. for defense; also : to establish solidly ⟨∼ed customs⟩ 2 : ENCROACH, TRESPASS — en·trench·ment n

en·tre·pre·neur \ˌän-trə-prə-'nər, -'nur, -'nyur\ n [F, fr. OF, fr. entreprendre to undertake] : one who organizes and assumes the risk of a business or enterprise — en·tre·pre·neur·ial \-'nur-ē-əl, -'nyur-, -'nər-\ adj — en·tre·pre·neur·ship \-ˌship\ n

en·tro·py \'en-trə-pē\ n, pl -pies 1 : the degree of disorder in a system 2 : an ultimate state of inert uniformity

en·trust \in-'trəst\ vb 1 : to commit something to as a trust 2 : to commit to another with confidence ◆ Synonyms CONFIDE, CONSIGN, RELEGATE, COMMEND

en·try \'en-trē\ n, pl entries 1 : ENTRANCE 2 2 : ENTRANCE 3; also : VESTIBULE 1 3 : an entering in a record;

also : an item so entered   **4** : a headword with its definition or identification; *also* : VOCABULARY ENTRY   **5** : one entered in something (as a contest or market)

en·twine \in-'twīn\ *vb* : to twine together or around

enu·mer·ate \i-'nü-mə-ˌrāt, -'nyü-\ *vb* **-at·ed; -at·ing** **1** : to determine the number of : COUNT   **2** : LIST — **enu·mer·a·tion** \-ˌnü-mə-'rā-shən, -ˌnyü-\ *n*

enun·ci·ate \ē-'nən-sē-ˌāt\ *vb* **-at·ed; -at·ing** **1** : to state definitely; *also* : ANNOUNCE, PROCLAIM   **2** : PRONOUNCE, ARTICULATE — **enun·ci·a·tion** \-ˌnən-sē-'ā-shən\ *n*

en·ure·sis \ˌen-yù-'rē-səs\ *n* : involuntary discharge of urine : BED-WETTING

env *abbr* envelope

en·vel·op \in-'ve-ləp\ *vb* : to enclose completely with or as if with a covering — **en·vel·op·ment** *n*

en·ve·lope \'en-və-ˌlōp, 'än-\ *n* **1** : a usu. paper container for a letter   **2** : WRAPPER, COVERING   **3** : a conventionally accepted limit ⟨fashions that push the ∼⟩

en·ven·om \in-'ve-nəm\ *vb* **1** : to make poisonous   **2** : EMBITTER

en·vi·able \'en-vē-ə-bəl\ *adj* : highly desirable — **en·vi·ably** \-blē\ *adv*

en·vi·ous \'en-vē-əs\ *adj* : feeling or showing envy — **en·vi·ous·ly** *adv* — **en·vi·ous·ness** *n*

en·vi·ron·ment \in-'vī-rən-mənt, -'vī(-ə)rn-\ *n* **1** : SURROUNDINGS   **2** : the whole complex of factors (as soil, climate, and living things) that influence the form and the ability to survive of a plant or animal or ecological community — **en·vi·ron·men·tal** \-ˌvī-rən-'men-tᵊl, -ˌvīrn-\ *adj* — **en·vi·ron·men·tal·ly** \-tᵊl-ē\ *adv*

en·vi·ron·men·tal·ist \-ˌvī-rən-'men-tᵊl-ist, -ˌvīr(-ə)n-\ *n* : a person concerned about environmental quality esp. with respect to control of pollution — **en·vi·ron·men·tal·ism** \-ˌvī-rən-'men-tə-ˌli-zəm, -ˌvī(-ə)rn-\

en·vi·rons \in-'vī-rənz\ *n pl* **1** : SUBURBS   **2** : SURROUNDINGS; *also* : VICINITY

en·vis·age \in-'vi-zij\ *vb* **-aged; -ag·ing** : to have a mental picture of

en·vi·sion \in-'vi-zhən, en-\ *vb* : to picture to oneself ⟨∼s world peace⟩

en·voy \'en-ˌvoi, 'än-\ *n* **1** : a diplomatic agent   **2** : REPRESENTATIVE, MESSENGER

¹en·vy \'en-vē\ *n, pl* **envies** [ME *envie*, fr. AF, fr. L *invidia*, fr. *invidus* envious, fr. *invidēre* to look askance at, envy, fr. *vidēre* to see] : painful or resentful awareness of another's advantages; *also* : an object of envy

²envy *vb* **en·vied; en·vy·ing** : to feel envy toward or on account of

en·zyme \'en-ˌzīm\ *n* : any of various complex proteins produced by living cells that catalyze specific biochemical reactions at body temperatures — **en·zy·mat·ic** \ˌen-zə-'ma-tik\ *adj*

Eo·cene \'ē-ə-ˌsēn\ *adj* : of, relating to, or being the epoch of the Tertiary between the Paleocene and the Oligocene — **Eocene** *n*

EOE *abbr* equal opportunity employer

eo·lian \ē-'ō-lē-ən\ *adj* : borne, deposited, or produced by the wind

EOM *abbr* end of month

eon *var of* AEON

EP *abbr* European plan

EPA *abbr* Environmental Protection Agency

ep·au·let *also* **ep·au·lette** \ˌe-pə-'let\ *n* [F *épaulette*, dim. of *épaule* shoulder] : a shoulder ornament esp. on a coat or military uniform

épée \'e-ˌpā, ā-'pā\ *n* [F] : a fencing or dueling sword

Eph *or* **Ephes** *abbr* Ephesians

ephed·rine \i-'fe-drən\ *n* : a stimulant drug used to treat asthma and nasal congestion

ephem·era \i-'fe-mər-ə\ *n pl* : paper items (as posters or tickets) of little original value collected usu. as a hobby

ephem·er·al \i-'fe-mə-rəl\ *adj* [Gk *ephēmeros* lasting a day, daily, fr. *epi*-on +*hēmera* day] : SHORT-LIVED, TRANSITORY ♦ **Synonyms** PASSING, FLEETING, TRANSIENT, EVANESCENT — **ephem·er·al·i·ty** \i-ˌfe-mə-'ra-lə-tē\ *n*

Ephe·sians \i-'fē-zhənz\ *n* — see BIBLE table

ep·ic \'e-pik\ *n* : a long poem in elevated style narrating the deeds of a hero — **epic** *adj*

epi·cen·ter \'e-pi-ˌsen-tər\ *n* : the point on the earth's surface directly above the point of origin of an earthquake

ep·i·cure \'e-pi-ˌkyùr\ *n* : a person with sensitive and discriminating tastes esp. in food and wine

ep·i·cu·re·an \ˌe-pi-kyù-'rē-ən, -'kyùr-ē-\ *n* : EPICURE — **epicurean** *adj*

¹ep·i·dem·ic \ˌe-pə-'de-mik\ *adj* : affecting many persons at one time ⟨∼ disease⟩; *also* : excessively prevalent

²epidemic *n* : an epidemic outbreak esp. of disease

ep·i·de·mi·ol·o·gy \ˌep-ə-ˌdē-mē-'ä-lə-jē\ *n* : the study of the incidence, distribution, and control of disease in a population — **ep·i·de·mi·o·log·i·cal** \-ˌdē-mē-ə-'lä-ji-kəl\ *also* **ep·i·de·mi·o·log·ic** \-jik\ *adj* — **ep·i·de·mi·ol·o·gist** \-'ä-lə-jist\ *n*

epi·der·mis \ˌe-pə-'dər-məs\ *n* : an outer layer esp. of skin — **epi·der·mal** \-məl\ *adj*

epi·du·ral \ˌe-pi-'d(y)ùr-əl\ *adj* : administered into the space outside the membrane that envelops the spinal cord ⟨∼ anesthesia⟩ — **epidural** *n*

epi·glot·tis \ˌe-pə-'glä-təs\ *n* : a thin plate of flexible tissue protecting the tracheal opening during swallowing

ep·i·gram \'e-pə-ˌgram\ *n* : a short witty poem or saying — **ep·i·gram·mat·ic** \ˌe-pə-grə-'ma-tik\ *adj*

ep·i·lep·sy \'e-pə-ˌlep-sē\ *n, pl* **-sies** [ultim. fr. Gk *epilēpsia*, fr. *epilambanein* to seize] : a disorder marked by abnormal electrical discharges in the brain and typically manifested by sudden periods of diminished consciousness or by convulsions — **ep·i·lep·tic** \ˌe-pə-'lep-tik\ *adj or n*

ep·i·logue *also* **ep·i·log** \'e-pə-ˌlóg, -ˌläg\ *n* **1** : a concluding section of a literary work   **2** : a speech addressed to the spectators by an actor at the end of a play

epi·neph·rine \ˌe-pə-'ne-frən\ *n* : an adrenal hormone used medicinally esp. as a heart stimulant, a muscle relaxant, and a vasoconstrictor

epiph·a·ny \i-'pi-fə-nē\ *n, pl* **-nies** **1** *cap* : January 6 observed as a church festival in commemoration of the coming of the Magi to Jesus at Bethlehem   **2** : a sudden striking understanding of something

epis·co·pa·cy \i-'pis-kə-pə-sē\ *n, pl* **-cies** **1** : government of a church by bishops   **2** : EPISCOPATE

epis·co·pal \i-'pis-kə-pəl\ *adj* **1** : of or relating to a bishop or episcopacy   **2** *cap* : of or relating to the Protestant Episcopal Church

Epis·co·pa·lian \i-ˌpis-kə-'pāl-yən\ *n* : a member of the Protestant Episcopal Church

epis·co·pate \i-'pis-kə-pət, -ˌpāt\ *n* **1** : the rank, office, or term of a bishop   **2** : a body of bishops

ep·i·sode \'e-pə-ˌsōd\ *n* [Gk *epeisodion*, fr. *epeisodios* coming in besides, fr. *eisodios* coming in, fr. *eis* into + *hodos* road, journey] **1** : a unit of action in a dramatic or literary work   **2** : an incident in a course of events : OCCURRENCE ⟨a feverish ∼⟩ — **ep·i·sod·ic** \ˌe-pə-'sä-dik\ *adj*

epis·tle \i-'pi-səl\ *n* **1** *cap* : one of the letters of the New Testament   **2** : LETTER — **epis·to·lary** \i-'pis-tə-ˌler-ē\ *adj*

ep·i·taph \'e-pə-ˌtaf\ *n* : an inscription in memory of a dead person

ep·i·tha·la·mi·um \ˌe-pə-thə-'lā-mē-əm\ *or* **ep·i·tha·la·mi·on** \-mē-ən\ *n, pl* **-mi·ums** *or* **-mia** \-mē-ə\ : a song or poem in honor of a bride and bridegroom

ep·i·the·li·um \ˌe-pə-'thē-lē-əm\ *n, pl* **-lia** \-lē-ə\ : a cellular membrane covering a bodily surface or lining a cavity — **ep·i·the·li·al** \-lē-əl\ *adj*

ep·i·thet \'e-pə-ˌthet, -thət\ *n* : a characterizing and often abusive word or phrase ⟨a racial ∼⟩

epit·o·me \i-'pi-tə-mē\ *n* **1** : ABSTRACT, SUMMARY   **2** : EMBODIMENT — **epit·o·mize** \-ˌmīz\ *vb*

ep·och \'e-pək, -ˌpäk\ *n* : a usu. extended period : ERA, AGE — **ep·och·al** \-pə-kəl, -ˌpä-\ *adj*

ep·onym \'e-pə-ˌnim\ *n* **1** : one for whom something is or is believed to be named   **2** : a name (as of a disease) based on or derived from an eponym — **epon·y·mous** \i-'pä-nə-məs\ *adj*

ep·oxy \i-'päk-sē\ *vb* **ep·ox·ied** *or* **ep·oxyed; ep·oxy·ing** : to glue, fill, or coat with epoxy resin

epoxy resin *n* : a synthetic resin used in coatings and adhesives

ep·si·lon \'ep-sə-ˌlän, -lən\ *n* : the 5th letter of the Greek alphabet — E or ε

Ep·som salts \'ep-səm-\ *n* : a bitter colorless or white magnesium salt with cathartic properties

eq *abbr* **1** equal   **2** equation

equa·ble \'e-kwə-bəl, 'ē-\ *adj* : UNIFORM, EVEN; *esp* : free from unpleasant extremes — **eq·ua·bil·i·ty** \,e-kwə-'bi-lə-tē, ,ē-\ *n* — **eq·ua·bly** \'e-kwə-blē, 'ē-\ *adv*

¹equal \'ē-kwəl\ *adj* **1** : of the same measure, quantity, value, quality, number, degree, or status as another ⟨~ opportunity⟩ **2** : IMPARTIAL **3** : free from extremes **4** : able to cope with a situation or task — **equal·i·ty** \i-'kwä-lə-tē\ *n* — **equal·ly** *adv*

²equal *vb* **equaled** *or* **equalled**; **equal·ing** *or* **equal·ling** : to be or become equal to; *also* : to be identical in value to

³equal *n* : one that is equal

equal·ise, equal·is·er *Brit var of* EQUALIZE, EQUALIZER

equal·ize \'ē-kwə-,līz\ *vb* **-ized; -iz·ing** : to make equal, uniform, or constant — **equal·i·za·tion** \,ē-kwə-lə-'zā-shən\ *n* — **equal·iz·er** *n*

equals sign *or* **equal sign** *n* : a sign = indicating equivalence

equa·nim·i·ty \,ē-kwə-'ni-mə-tē, ,e-\ *n, pl* **-ties** : COMPOSURE

equate \i-'kwāt\ *vb* **equat·ed; equat·ing** : to make, treat, or regard as equal or comparable ⟨~s liars with thieves⟩

equa·tion \i-'kwā-zhən\ *n* **1** : an act of equating : the state of being equated **2** : a usu. formal statement of equivalence esp. of mathematical expressions

equa·tor \i-'kwā-tər, 'ē-\ *n* : an imaginary circle around the earth that is everywhere equally distant from the two poles — **equa·to·ri·al** \,ē-kwə-'tòr-ē-əl, ,e-\ *adj*

equer·ry \'e-kwə-rē, i-'kwer-ē\ *n, pl* **-ries 1** : an officer in charge of the horses of a prince or noble **2** : a personal attendant of a member of the British royal family

¹eques·tri·an \i-'kwes-trē-ən\ *adj* : of or relating to horseback riding ⟨~ competition⟩; *also* : representing a person on horseback ⟨an ~ statue⟩

²equestrian *n* : one who rides a horse

eques·tri·enne \i-,kwes-trē-'en\ *n* : a female rider on horseback

equi·dis·tant \,ē-kwə-'dis-tənt\ *adj* : equally distant

equi·lat·er·al \,ē-kwə-'la-tə-rəl\ *adj* : having all sides or faces equal ⟨~ triangles⟩

equi·lib·ri·um \,ē-kwə-'li-brē-əm, ,e-\ *n, pl* **-ri·ums** *or* **-ria** \-brē-ə\ : a state of intellectual or emotional balance; *also* : a state of balance between opposing forces or actions ♦ *Synonyms* POISE, BALANCE, EQUIPOISE

equine \'ē-,kwīn, 'e-\ *adj* [L *equinus*, fr. *equus* horse] : of or relating to the horse — **equine** *n*

equi·noc·tial \,ē-kwə-'näk-shəl, ,e-\ *adj* : relating to an equinox

equi·nox \'ē-kwə-,näks, 'e-\ *n* : either of the two times each year when the sun appears directly overhead at the equator and day and night are everywhere on earth of equal length

equip \i-'kwip\ *vb* **equipped; equip·ping** [AF *eskiper* to load on board a ship, outfit, man, of Gmc origin] **1** : to supply with needed resources **2** : to make ready : PREPARE

eq·ui·page \'e-kwə-pij\ *n* : a horse-drawn carriage usu. with its servants

equip·ment \i-'kwip-mənt\ *n* **1** : things used in equipping : SUPPLIES, OUTFIT **2** : the equipping of a person or thing : the state of being equipped

equi·poise \'e-kwə-,pòiz, 'ē-\ *n* **1** : BALANCE, EQUILIBRIUM **2** : COUNTERBALANCE

eq·ui·ta·ble \'e-kwə-tə-bəl\ *adj* : JUST, FAIR — **eq·ui·ta·bly** \-blē\ *adv*

eq·ui·ta·tion \,e-kwə-'tā-shən\ *n* : the act or art of riding on horseback

eq·ui·ty \'e-kwə-tē\ *n, pl* **-ties 1** : JUSTNESS, IMPARTIALITY **2** : value of a property or of an interest in it in excess of claims against it

equiv *abbr* equivalent

equiv·a·lent \i-'kwi-və-lənt\ *adj* : EQUAL; *also* : virtually identical — **equiv·a·lence** \-ləns\ *n* — **equivalent** *n*

equiv·o·cal \i-'kwi-və-kəl\ *adj* **1** : AMBIGUOUS **2** : UNCERTAIN, UNDECIDED **3** : SUSPICIOUS, DUBIOUS ⟨~ behavior⟩ ♦ *Synonyms* OBSCURE, DARK, VAGUE, ENIGMATIC — **equiv·o·cal·ly** *adv*

equiv·o·cate \i-'kwi-və-,kāt\ *vb* **-cat·ed; -cat·ing 1** : to use misleading language **2** : to avoid giving a definite answer — **equiv·o·ca·tion** \-,kwi-və-'kā-shən\ *n*

¹-er \ər\ *adj suffix or adv suffix* — used to form the comparative degree of adjectives and adverbs of one or two syllables ⟨hott*er*⟩ ⟨dri*er*⟩ ⟨silli*er*⟩ and sometimes of longer ones

²-er \ər\ *also* **-ier** \ē-ər, yər\ *or* **-yer** \yər\ *n suffix* **1** : a person occupationally connected with ⟨furri*er*⟩ ⟨lawy*er*⟩ **2** : a person or thing belonging to or associated with ⟨old-tim*er*⟩ **3** : a native of : resident of ⟨New Zealand*er*⟩ **4** : one that has ⟨double-deck*er*⟩ **5** : one that produces or yields ⟨pork*er*⟩ **6** : one that does or performs (a specified action) ⟨batt*er*⟩ **7** : one that is a suitable object of (a specified action) ⟨broil*er*⟩ **8** : one that is ⟨foreign*er*⟩

Er *symbol* erbium

ER *abbr* emergency room

era \'er-ə, 'e-rə, 'ir-ə\ *n* [LL *aera*, fr. L, counters, pl. of *aes* copper, money] **1** : a chronological order or system of notation reckoned from a given date as basis **2** : a period identified by some special feature ⟨the ~ of industrialization⟩ **3** : any of the four major divisions of geologic time ♦ *Synonyms* AGE, EPOCH, PERIOD, TIME

ERA *abbr* **1** earned run average **2** Equal Rights Amendment

erad·i·cate \i-'ra-də-,kāt\ *vb* **-cat·ed; -cat·ing** [L *eradicatus*, pp. of *eradicare*, fr. *e-* out + *radix* root] : UPROOT, ELIMINATE ♦ *Synonyms* EXTERMINATE, ANNIHILATE, ABOLISH, EXTINGUISH — **erad·i·ca·ble** \-di-kə-bəl\ *adj* — **erad·i·ca·tion** \-,ra-də-'kā-shən\ *n*

erase \i-'rās\ *vb* **erased; eras·ing** : to rub or scratch out (as written words); *also* : OBLITERATE ♦ *Synonyms* CANCEL, EFFACE, DELETE, EXPUNGE — **eras·er** *n* — **era·sure** \i-'rā-shər\ *n*

er·bi·um \'ər-bē-əm\ *n* : a rare metallic element found with yttrium

¹ere \'er\ *prep* : BEFORE

²ere *conj* : BEFORE

¹erect \i-'rekt\ *adj* **1** : not leaning or lying down : UPRIGHT **2** : being in a state of physiological erection

²erect *vb* **1** : BUILD **2** : to fix or set in an upright position ⟨~ an antenna⟩ **3** : SET UP; *also* : ESTABLISH, DEVELOP

erec·tile \i-'rek-t³l, -'rek-,tī(-ə)l\ *adj* : capable of becoming erect ⟨~ tissue⟩ ⟨~ feathers of a bird⟩

erec·tion \i-'rek-shən\ *n* **1** : the turgid state of a previously flaccid bodily part when it becomes dilated with blood **2** : CONSTRUCTION

ere·long \er-'lòn\ *adv* : before long

er·e·mite \'er-ə-,mīt\ *n* : HERMIT

er·go \'er-gō, 'ər-\ *adv* [L] : THEREFORE

er·go·nom·ics \,ər-gə-'nä-miks\ *n sing or pl* : an applied science concerned with designing and arranging things people use in order to improve efficiency and safety — **er·go·nom·ic** \-mik\ *adj*

er·got \'ər-gət, -,gät\ *n* **1** : a disease of rye and other cereals caused by a fungus; *also* : this fungus **2** : a medicinal compound or preparation derived from an ergot fungus

er·mine \'ər-mən\ *n, pl* **ermines 1** : any of several weasels with winter fur mostly white; *also* : this white fur **2** : a rank or office whose official robe is ornamented with ermine

ermine 1

erode \i-'rōd\ *vb* **erod·ed; erod·ing** : to diminish or destroy by degrees; *esp* : to gradually eat into or wear away ⟨soil *eroded* by wind and water⟩ — **erod·ible** *also* **erod·able** \-'rō-də-bəl\ *adj*

erog·e·nous \i-'rä-jə-nəs\ *adj* **1** : sexually sensitive ⟨~ zones⟩ **2** : of, relating to, or arousing sexual feelings

ero·sion \i-'rō-zhən\ *n* : the process or state of being eroded — **ero·sion·al** \-'rō-zhə-nəl\ *adj* — **ero·sion·al·ly** *adv*

ero·sive \i-'rō-siv\ *adj* : tending to erode — **ero·sive·ness** *n*

erot·ic \i-'rä-tik\ *adj* : relating to or dealing with sexual love : AMATORY ⟨∼ art⟩ — **erot·i·cal·ly** \-ti-k(ə-)lē\ *adv* — **erot·i·cism** \-tə-ˌsi-zəm\ *n*

err \'er, 'ər\ *vb* : to be or do wrong

er·rand \'er-ənd\ *n* : a short trip taken to do something; *also* : the object or purpose of such a trip

er·rant \'er-ənt\ *adj* **1** : WANDERING ⟨an ∼ knight⟩ **2** : straying outside proper bounds ⟨an ∼ throw⟩ **3** : behaving wrongly ⟨an ∼ child⟩

er·ra·ta \e-'rä-tə\ *n* : a list of corrigenda

er·rat·ic \i-'ra-tik\ *adj* **1** : having no fixed course **2** : INCONSISTENT ⟨∼ dieting⟩; *also* : ECCENTRIC — **er·rat·i·cal·ly** \-ti-k(ə-)lē\ *adv*

er·ra·tum \e-'rä-təm\ *n, pl* **-ta** \-tə\ : CORRIGENDUM

er·ro·ne·ous \i-'rō-nē-əs, e-'rō-\ *adj* : INCORRECT — **er·ro·ne·ous·ly** *adv*

er·ror \'er-ər\ *n* **1** : a usu. ignorant or unintentional deviating from accuracy or truth ⟨made an ∼ in adding⟩ **2** : a defensive misplay in baseball **3** : the state of one that errs ⟨to be in ∼⟩ **4** : a product of mistake ⟨a typographical ∼⟩ — **er·ror·less** *adj*

er·satz \'er-ˌzäts\ *adj* [G *ersatz-*, fr. *Ersatz*, n., substitute] : being usu. an artificial and inferior substitute

erst \'ərst\ *adv, archaic* : ERSTWHILE

¹**erst·while** \-ˌhwī(-ə)l\ *adv* : in the past : FORMERLY

²**erstwhile** *adj* : FORMER, PREVIOUS

er·u·di·tion \ˌer-ə-'di-shən, ˌer-yə-\ *n* : SCHOLARSHIP, LEARNING — **er·u·dite** \'er-ə-ˌdīt, 'er-yə-\ *adj*

erupt \i-'rəpt\ *vb* **1** : to burst forth or cause to burst forth : EXPLODE **2** : to break through a surface ⟨teeth ∼*ing* through the gum⟩ **3** : to break out with or as if with a skin rash — **erup·tion** \-'rəp-shən\ *n* — **erup·tive** \-tiv\ *adj*

-ery *n suffix* **1** : qualities collectively : character : -NESS ⟨snobb*ery*⟩ **2** : art : practice ⟨cook*ery*⟩ **3** : place of doing, keeping, producing, or selling (the thing specified) ⟨fish*ery*⟩ ⟨bak*ery*⟩ **4** : collection : aggregate ⟨fin*ery*⟩ **5** : state or condition ⟨slav*ery*⟩

ery·sip·e·las \ˌer-ə-'si-pə-ləs, ˌir-\ *n* : an acute bacterial disease marked by fever and severe skin inflammation

er·y·the·ma \ˌer-ə-'thē-mə\ *n* : abnormal redness of the skin due to capillary congestion (as in inflammation)

eryth·ro·cyte \i-'ri-thrə-ˌsīt\ *n* : RED BLOOD CELL

Es *symbol* einsteinium

¹**-es** \əz, iz *after* s, z, sh, ch; z *after* v *or a vowel*\ *n pl suffix* — used to form the plural of most nouns that end in *s* ⟨glass*es*⟩, *z* ⟨fuzz*es*⟩, *sh* ⟨bush*es*⟩, *ch* ⟨peach*es*⟩, or a final *y* that changes to *i* ⟨lad*ies*⟩ and of some nouns ending in *f* that changes to *v* ⟨loav*es*⟩

²**-es** *vb suffix* — used to form the third person singular present of most verbs that end in *s* ⟨bless*es*⟩, *z* ⟨fizz*es*⟩, *sh* ⟨hush*es*⟩, *ch* ⟨catch*es*⟩, or a final *y* that changes to *i* ⟨defi*es*⟩

es·ca·late \'es-kə-ˌlāt\ *vb* **-lat·ed; -lat·ing** : to increase in extent, volume, number, intensity, or scope — **es·ca·la·tion** \ˌes-kə-'lā-shən\ *n*

es·ca·la·tor \'es-kə-ˌlā-tər\ *n* : a moving set of stairs

escallop *var of* SCALLOP

es·ca·pade \'es-kə-ˌpād\ *n* [F, action of escaping] : a mischievous adventure

¹**es·cape** \is-'kāp\ *vb* **es·caped; es·cap·ing** [ME, fr. AF *escaper, eschaper*, fr. VL *excappare*, fr. L *ex-* out + LL *cappa* head covering, cloak] **1** : to get free or away **2** : to avoid a threatening evil **3** : AVOID 2 ⟨∼ injury⟩ **4** : ELUDE ⟨his name ∼*s* me⟩ **5** : to be produced or uttered involuntarily ⟨let a sob ∼ him⟩

²**escape** *n* **1** : flight from or avoidance of something unpleasant **2** : LEAKAGE **3** : a means of escape

³**escape** *adj* : providing a means or way of escape

es·cap·ee \is-ˌkā-'pē, ˌes-(ˌ)kā-\ *n* : one that has escaped esp. from prison

escape velocity *n* : the minimum velocity needed by a body (as a rocket) to escape from the gravitational field of a celestial body (as the earth)

es·cap·ism \is-'kā-ˌpi-zəm\ *n* : diversion of the mind to imaginative activity as an escape from routine — **es·cap·ist** \-pist\ *adj or n*

es·car·got \ˌes-ˌkär-'gō\ *n, pl* **-gots** \-'gō(z)\ : a snail prepared for use as food

es·ca·role \'es-kə-ˌrōl\ *n* : ENDIVE 1

es·carp·ment \es-'kärp-mənt\ *n* **1** : a steep slope in front of a fortification **2** : a long cliff

es·chew \is-'chü\ *vb* : SHUN, AVOID

¹**es·cort** \'es-ˌkȯrt\ *n* : one (as a person or warship) accompanying another esp. as a protection or courtesy

²**es·cort** \is-'kȯrt, es-\ *vb* : to accompany as an escort

es·crow \'es-ˌkrō\ *n* [AF *escrowe* scroll, strip of parchment] : something (as a deed or a sum of money) delivered by one person to another to be delivered to a third party only upon the fulfillment of a condition; *also* : a fund or deposit serving as an escrow

es·cu·do \is-'kü-dō\ *n, pl* **-dos** **1** : the former basic monetary unit of Portugal **2** — see MONEY table

es·cutch·eon \is-'kə-chən\ *n* : the usu. shield-shaped surface on which a coat of arms is shown

Esd *abbr* Esdras

Es·dras \'ez-drəs\ *n* — see BIBLE table

ESE *abbr* east-southeast

Es·ki·mo \'es-kə-ˌmō\ *n* **1** : a member of a group of peoples of northern Canada, Greenland, Alaska, and eastern Siberia **2** : any of the languages of the Eskimo peoples

Eskimo dog *n* : a sled dog of American origin

ESL *abbr* English as a second language

esoph·a·gus \i-'sä-fə-gəs\ *n, pl* **-gi** \-ˌgī, -ˌjī\ : a muscular tube that leads from the cavity behind the mouth to the stomach — **esoph·a·geal** \-ˌsä-fə-'jē-əl\ *adj*

es·o·ter·ic \ˌe-sə-'ter-ik\ *adj* **1** : designed for or understood only by the specially initiated **2** : PRIVATE, SECRET

esp *abbr* especially

ESP \ˌē-(ˌ)es-'pē\ *n* : EXTRASENSORY PERCEPTION

es·pa·drille \'es-pə-ˌdril\ *n* [F] : a flat sandal usu. having a fabric upper and a flexible sole

es·pal·ier \is-'pal-yər, -ˌyā\ *n* : a plant (as a fruit tree) trained to grow flat against a support — **espalier** *vb*

es·pe·cial \is-'pe-shəl\ *adj* : SPECIAL, PARTICULAR — **es·pe·cial·ly** *adv*

Es·pe·ran·to \ˌes-pə-'rän-tō, -'rän-\ *n* : an artificial international language based esp. on words common to the chief European languages

es·pi·o·nage \'es-pē-ə-ˌnäzh, -nij\ *n* [F *espionnage*] : the practice of spying

es·pla·nade \'es-plə-ˌnäd\ *n* : a level open stretch or area; *esp* : one for walking or driving along a shore

es·pous·al \i-'spaú-zəl\ *n* **1** : BETROTHAL; *also* : WEDDING **2** : a taking up (as of a cause) as a supporter ⟨∼ of human rights⟩ — **es·pouse** \-'spaúz\ *vb*

espres·so \e-'spre-sō\ *n, pl* **-sos** : coffee brewed by forcing steam or hot water through finely ground darkly roasted coffee beans

es·prit \i-'sprē\ *n* : sprightly wit

es·prit de corps \i-ˌsprē-də-'kȯr\ *n* [F] : the common spirit existing in the members of a group

es·py \i-'spī\ *vb* **es·pied; es·py·ing** : to catch sight of

◆ *Synonyms* BEHOLD, SEE, VIEW, DESCRY

Esq *or* **Esqr** *abbr* esquire

es·quire \'es-ˌkwī(-ə)r\ *n* [ME, fr. AF *esquier* squire, fr. LL *scutarius*, fr. L *scutum* shield] **1** : a man of the English gentry ranking next below a knight **2** : a candidate for knighthood serving as attendant to a knight **3** — used as a title of courtesy

-ess \əs, ˌes\ *n suffix* : female ⟨author*ess*⟩

¹**es·say** \e-'sā, 'e-ˌsā\ *vb* : ATTEMPT, TRY

²**es·say** *n* **1** \'e-ˌsā, e-'sā\ : ATTEMPT **2** \'e-ˌsā\ : a literary composition usu. dealing with a subject from a limited or personal point of view — **es·say·ist** \'e-ˌsā-ist\ *n*

es·sence \'e-sⁿns\ *n* **1** : fundamental nature or quality **2** : a substance distilled or extracted from another substance (as a plant or drug) and having the special qualities of the original substance **3** : PERFUME **4** : the most significant element or aspect of something ⟨the ∼ of the issue⟩

¹**es·sen·tial** \i-'sen-chəl\ *adj* **1** : of, relating to, or constituting an essence ⟨voting is an ∼ right of citizenship⟩ ⟨∼ oils⟩ **2** : of the utmost importance : INDISPENSABLE **3** : being a substance that must be obtained from the diet because it is not sufficiently produced by the body ⟨∼ amino acids⟩ ◆ *Synonyms* IMPERATIVE, NECESSARY, NECESSITOUS — **es·sen·tial·ly** *adv*

²**essential** *n* : something essential

est *abbr* **1** established **2** estimate; estimated

EST *abbr* eastern standard time

¹**-est** \əst, ist\ *adj suffix or adv suffix* — used to form the superlative degree of adjectives and adverbs of one or two

syllables ⟨fatt*est*⟩ ⟨lat*est*⟩ ⟨lucki*est*⟩ ⟨often*est*⟩ and less often of longer ones

²est \əst, ist\ *or* **-st** \st\ *vb suffix* — used to form the archaic second person singular of English verbs (with *thou*) ⟨did*st*⟩

es·tab·lish \i-'sta-blish\ *vb* **1** : to institute permanently ⟨∼ a law⟩ **2** : FOUND ⟨∼ a settlement⟩; *also* : EFFECT **3** : to make firm or stable **4** : to put on a firm basis : SET UP ⟨∼ a son in business⟩ **5** : to gain acceptance or recognition of ⟨the movie ∼*ed* her as a star⟩; *also* : PROVE

es·tab·lish·ment \-mənt\ *n* **1** : something established **2** : a place of residence or business with its furnishings and staff **3** : an established ruling or controlling group ⟨the literary ∼⟩ **4** : the act or state of establishing or being established

es·tate \i-'stāt\ *n* **1** : STATE, CONDITION; *also* : social standing : STATUS **2** : a social or political class ⟨the three ∼s of nobility, clergy, and commons⟩ **3** : a person's possessions : FORTUNE **4** : a landed property

¹es·teem \i-'stēm\ *n* : high regard

²esteem *vb* **1** : REGARD **2** : to set a high value on ✦ *Synonyms* RESPECT, ADMIRE, REVERE

es·ter \'es-tər\ *n* : an often fragrant organic compound formed by the reaction of an acid and an alcohol

Esth *abbr* Esther

Es·ther \'es-tər\ *n* — see BIBLE table

esthete, esthetic, esthetically, esthetics *var of* AESTHETE, AESTHETIC, AESTHETICALLY, AESTHETICS

es·ti·ma·ble \'es-tə-mə-bəl\ *adj* : worthy of esteem ⟨an ∼ adversary⟩

¹es·ti·mate \'es-tə-ˌmāt\ *vb* **-mat·ed; -mat·ing** **1** : to give or form an approximation (as of value, size, or cost) **2** : JUDGE, CONCLUDE ✦ *Synonyms* EVALUATE, VALUE, RATE, APPRAISE, ASSAY, ASSESS — **es·ti·ma·tor** \-ˌmā-tər\ *n*

²es·ti·mate \'es-tə-mət\ *n* **1** : OPINION, JUDGMENT **2** : a rough or approximate calculation **3** : a statement of the cost of work to be done

es·ti·ma·tion \ˌes-tə-'mā-shən\ *n* **1** : JUDGMENT, OPINION **2** : ESTIMATE **3** : ESTEEM, HONOR

es·ti·vate \'es-tə-ˌvāt\ *vb* **-vat·ed; -vat·ing** : to pass the summer in an inactive or resting state — **es·ti·va·tion** \ˌes-tə-'vā-shən\ *n*

es·trange \i-'strānj\ *vb* **es·tranged; es·trang·ing** : to alienate the affections or confidence of — **es·trange·ment** *n*

es·tro·gen \'es-trə-jən\ *n* : a steroid (as a sex hormone) that tends to cause estrus and the development of female secondary sex characteristics — **es·tro·gen·ic** \ˌes-trə-'je-nik\ *adj*

estrous cycle *n* : the cycle of changes in the endocrine and reproductive systems of a female mammal from the beginning of one period of estrus to the beginning of the next

es·trus \'es-trəs\ *n* : a periodic state of sexual excitability during which the female of most mammals is willing to mate with the male and is capable of becoming pregnant : HEAT — **es·trous** \-trəs\ *adj*

es·tu·ary \'es-chə-ˌwer-ē\ *n, pl* **-ar·ies** : an arm of the sea at the mouth of a river — **es·tu·a·rine** \-wə-ˌrīn, -ˌrēn, -rin\ *adj*

ET *abbr* eastern time

eta \'ā-tə\ *n* : the 7th letter of the Greek alphabet — H or η

ETA *abbr* estimated time of arrival

et al \et-'al\ *abbr* [L *et alii* (masc.), *et aliae* (fem.), or *et alia* (neut.)] and others

etc *abbr* et cetera

et cet·era \et-'se-tə-rə, -'se-trə\ [L] and others esp. of the same kind

etch \'ech\ *vb* [D *etsen,* fr. G *ätzen* to etch, corrode, fr. OHG *azzen* to feed] **1** : to produce (as a design) on a hard material by corroding its surface (as by acid) **2** : to delineate clearly — **etch·er** *n*

etch·ing *n* **1** : the action, process, or art of etching **2** : a design produced on or print made from an etched plate

ETD *abbr* estimated time of departure

eter·nal \i-'tər-n³l\ *adj* : EVERLASTING, PERPETUAL — **eter·nal·ly** *adv*

eter·ni·ty \i-'tər-nə-tē\ *n, pl* **-ties** **1** : infinite duration **2** : IMMORTALITY

¹-eth \əth, ith\ *or* **-th** \th\ *vb suffix* — used to form the archaic third person singular present of verbs ⟨do*th*⟩

²-eth — see ²-TH

eth·ane \'e-ˌthān\ *n* : a colorless odorless gaseous hydrocarbon found in natural gas and used esp. as a fuel

eth·a·nol \'e-thə-ˌnȯl\ *n* : ALCOHOL 1

ether \'ē-thər\ *n* **1** : the upper regions of space; *also* : the gaseous element formerly held to fill these regions **2** : a light flammable liquid used as an anesthetic and solvent

ethe·re·al \i-'thir-ē-əl\ *adj* **1** : CELESTIAL, HEAVENLY **2** : exceptionally delicate : AIRY, DAINTY — **ethe·re·al·ly** *adv* — **ethe·re·al·ness** *n*

Ether·net \'ē-thər-ˌnet\ *n* : a computer network architecture for local area networks

eth·i·cal \'e-thi-kəl\ *adj* **1** : of or relating to ethics **2** : conforming to accepted and esp. professional standards of conduct ✦ *Synonyms* VIRTUOUS, MORAL, PRINCIPLED — **eth·i·cal·ly** *adv*

eth·ics \'e-thiks\ *n sing or pl* **1** : a discipline dealing with good and evil and with moral duty **2** : moral principles or practice

¹eth·nic \'eth-nik\ *adj* [ME, heathen, fr. LL *ethnicus,* fr. Gk *ethnikos* national, gentile, fr. *ethnos* nation, people] : of or relating to races or large groups of people classed according to common traits and customs — **eth·ni·cal·ly** *adv*

²ethnic *n* : a member of a minority ethnic group who retains its customs, language, or social views

eth·nol·o·gy \eth-'nä-lə-jē\ *n* : a science dealing with the races of human beings, their origin, distribution, characteristics, and relations — **eth·no·log·i·cal** \ˌeth-nə-'lä-ji-kəl\ *adj* — **eth·nol·o·gist** \eth-'nä-lə-jist\ *n*

ethol·o·gy \ē-'thä-lə-jē\ *n* : the scientific and objective study of animal behavior — **etho·log·i·cal** \ˌē-thə-'lä-ji-kəl, ˌe-\ *adj* — **ethol·o·gist** \ē-'thä-lə-jist\ *n*

ethos \'ē-ˌthäs\ *n* : the distinguishing character, sentiment, moral nature, or guiding beliefs of a person, group, or institution

ethyl alcohol *n* : ALCOHOL 1

eth·yl·ene \'e-thə-ˌlēn\ *n* : a colorless flammable gas found in coal gas or obtained from petroleum

eti·ol·o·gy \ˌē-tē-'ä-lə-jē\ *n* : the causes of a disease or abnormal condition; *also* : a branch of medicine concerned with the causes and origins of diseases — **eti·o·log·ic** \ˌē-tē-ə-'lä-jik\ *or* **eti·o·log·i·cal** \-ji-kəl\ *adj*

et·i·quette \'e-ti-kət, -ˌket\ *n* [F *étiquette,* lit., label, list] : the forms prescribed by custom or authority to be observed in social, official, or professional life ✦ *Synonyms* PROPRIETY, DECORUM, DECENCY, DIGNITY

Etrus·can \i-'trəs-kən\ *n* **1** : the language of the Etruscans **2** : an inhabitant of ancient Etruria — **Etruscan** *adj*

et seq *abbr* [L *et sequens*] and the following one; [L *et sequentes* (masc. & fem. pl.) or *et sequentia* (neut. pl.)] and the following ones

-ette \'et, ˌet, ət, it\ *n suffix* **1** : little one ⟨din*ette*⟩ **2** : female ⟨usher*ette*⟩

étude \'ā-ˌtüd, -ˌtyüd\ *n* [F, lit., study] : a musical composition for practice to develop technical skill

et·y·mol·o·gy \ˌe-tə-'mä-lə-jē\ *n, pl* **-gies** **1** : the history of a linguistic form (as a word) shown by tracing its development and relationships **2** : a branch of linguistics dealing with etymologies — **et·y·mo·log·i·cal** \-mə-'lä-ji-kəl\ *adj* — **et·y·mol·o·gist** \-'mä-lə-jist\ *n*

Eu *symbol* europium

eu·ca·lyp·tus \ˌyü-kə-'lip-təs\ *n, pl* **-ti** \-ˌtī\ *or* **-tus·es** : any of a genus of mostly Australian evergreen trees widely grown for shade or their wood, oils, resins, and gums

Eu·cha·rist \'yü-kə-rəst\ *n* : COMMUNION 2 — **eu·cha·ris·tic** \ˌyü-kə-'ris-tik\ *adj, often cap*

¹eu·chre \'yü-kər\ *n* : a card game in which the side naming the trump must take three of five tricks to win

²euchre *vb* **eu·chred; eu·chring** : CHEAT, TRICK

eu·clid·e·an *also* **eu·clid·i·an** \yü-'kli-dē-ən\ *adj, often cap* : of or relating to the geometry of Euclid or a geometry based on similar axioms

eu·gen·ics \yu̇-'je-niks\ *n* : a science dealing with the improvement (as by selective breeding) of hereditary qualities esp. of human beings — **eu·gen·ic** \-nik\ *adj*

eu·lo·gy \'yü-lə-jē\ *n, pl* **-gies** **1** : a speech in praise of some person or thing esp. in honor of a deceased person **2** : high praise — **eu·lo·gis·tic** \ˌyü-lə-'jis-tik\ *adj* — **eu·lo·gize** \'yü-lə-ˌjīz\ *vb* eu·nuch \'yü-nək\ *n* : a castrated man

eu·phe·mism \'yü-fə-ˌmi-zəm\ *n* [Gk *euphēmismos,* fr. *euphēmos* auspicious, sounding good, fr. *eu-* good + *phēmē* speech] : the substitution of a mild or pleasant expression for one offensive or unpleasant; *also* : the expression substituted — **eu·phe·mis·tic** \ˌyü-fə-'mis-tik\ *adj* — **eu·phe·mis·ti·cal·ly** \-'ti-k(ə-)lē\ *adv*

eu·pho·ni·ous \yu-'fō-nē-əs\ *adj* : pleasing to the ear — **eu·pho·ni·ous·ly** *adv*

eu·pho·ny \'yü-fə-nē\ *n, pl* **-nies** : the effect produced by words so combined as to please the ear

eu·pho·ria \yu-'fōr-ē-ə\ *n* : a marked feeling of well-being or elation — **eu·phor·ic** \-'fōr-ik\ *adj*

Eur *abbr* Europe; European

Eur·asian \yu-'rā-zhən, -shən\ *adj* **1** : of mixed European and Asian origin **2** : of or relating to Europe and Asia — **Eurasian** *n*

eu·re·ka \yu-'rē-kə\ *interj* [Gk *heurēka* I have found, fr. *heuriskein* to find; fr. the exclamation attributed to Archimedes on discovering a method for determining the purity of gold] — used to express triumph on a discovery

eu·ro \'yur-ō\ *n, pl* **euros** : the common basic monetary unit of most countries of the European Union — see MONEY table

Eu·ro–Amer·i·can \ˌyur-ō-ə-'mer-ə-kən\ *n* **1** : a person of mixed European and American ancestry **2** : CAUCASIAN

Eu·ro·bond \'yur-ō-ˌbänd\ *n* : a bond of a U.S. corporation that is sold outside the U.S. but that is valued and paid for in dollars and yields interest in dollars

Eu·ro·cur·ren·cy \ˌyur-ō-'kər-ən-sē\ *n* : moneys (as of the U.S. and Japan) held outside their countries of origin and used in the money markets of Europe

Eu·ro·dol·lar \'yur-ō-ˌdä-lər\ *n* : a U.S. dollar held as Eurocurrency

Eu·ro·pe·an \ˌyur-ə-'pē-ən\ *n* **1** : a native or inhabitant of Europe **2** : a person of European descent — **European** *adj* — **Eu·ro·pe·an·ize** \-ə-ˌnīz\ *vb*

European–American *n* : EURO-AMERICAN

Eu·ro·pe·an·ism \ˌyur-ō-'pē-ə-ni-zəm\ *n* **1** : allegiance to the traditions, interests, or ideals of Europeans **2** : advocacy of political and economic integration of Europe — **eu·ro·pe·an·ist** \-nist\ *n*

European plan *n* : a hotel plan whereby the daily rates cover only the cost of the room

eu·ro·pi·um \yu-'rō-pē-əm\ *n* : a rare metallic chemical element

eu·sta·chian tube \yu-'stā-shən-\ *n, often cap E* : a tube connecting the inner cavity of the ear with the throat and equalizing air pressure on both sides of the eardrum

eu·tha·na·sia \ˌyü-thə-'nā-zhə\ *n* [Gk, easy death, fr. *eu-* good + *thanatos* death] : the act or practice of killing or permitting the death of hopelessly sick or injured persons or animals with as little pain as possible for reasons of mercy

EVA *abbr* extravehicular activity

evac·u·ate \i-'va-kyə-ˌwāt\ *vb* **-at·ed; -at·ing** **1** : EMPTY **2** : to discharge wastes from the body **3** : to remove or withdraw from : VACATE — **evac·u·a·tion** \-ˌva-kyə-'wā-shən\ *n*

evac·u·ee \i-ˌva-kyə-'wē\ *n* : a person removed from a dangerous place

evade \i-'vād\ *vb* **evad·ed; evad·ing** : to manage to avoid esp. by dexterity or slyness : ELUDE, ESCAPE

eval·u·ate \i-'val-yu-ˌwāt\ *vb* **-at·ed; -at·ing** : APPRAISE, VALUE — **eval·u·a·tion** \-ˌval-yu-'wā-shən\ *n*

ev·a·nes·cent \ˌe-və-'ne-s°nt\ *adj* : tending to vanish like vapor ⟨∼ pleasures⟩ ♦ *Synonyms* PASSING, TRANSIENT, TRANSITORY, MOMENTARY — **ev·a·nes·cence** \-s°ns\ *n*

evan·gel·i·cal \ˌē-ˌvan-'je-li-kəl, ˌe-vən-\ *adj* [LL *evangelium* gospel, fr. Gk *evangelion,* fr. *euangelos* bringing good news, fr. *eu-* good + *angelos* messenger] **1** : of or relating to the Christian gospel esp. as presented in the four Gospels **2** : of or relating to certain Protestant churches emphasizing the authority of Scripture and the importance of preaching as contrasted with ritual **3** : ZEALOUS ⟨∼ fervor⟩ — **Evangelical** *n* — **Evan·gel·i·cal·ism** \-kə-ˌli-zəm\ *n* — **evan·gel·i·cal·ly** *adv*

evan·ge·lism \i-'van-jə-ˌli-zəm\ *n* **1** : the winning or revival of personal commitments to Christ **2** : militant or crusading zeal — **evan·ge·lis·tic** \-ˌvan-jə-'lis-tik\ *adj* — **evan·ge·lis·ti·cal·ly** *adv*

evan·ge·list \i-'van-jə-list\ *n* **1** *often cap* : the writer of any of the four Gospels **2** : a person who evangelizes; *esp* : a Protestant minister or layman who preaches at special services

evan·ge·lize \i-'van-jə-ˌlīz\ *vb* **-lized; -liz·ing** **1** : to preach the gospel **2** : to convert to Christianity

evap *abbr* evaporate

evap·o·rate \i-'va-pə-ˌrāt\ *vb* **-rat·ed; -rat·ing** **1** : to pass off or cause to pass off in vapor **2** : to disappear quickly **3** : to drive out the moisture from (as by heat) — **evap·o·ra·tion** \-ˌva-pə-'rā-shən\ *n* — **evap·o·ra·tor** \-ˌrā-tər\ *n*

evap·o·rite \i-'va-pə-ˌrīt\ *n* : a sedimentary rock that originates by the evaporation of seawater in an enclosed basin

eva·sion \i-'vā-zhən\ *n* **1** : a means of evading **2** : an act or instance of evading — **eva·sive** \i-'vā-siv\ *adj* — **eva·sive·ness** *n*

eve \'ēv\ *n* **1** : EVENING **2** : the period just before some important event

¹even \'ē-vən\ *adj* **1** : LEVEL, FLAT **2** : REGULAR, SMOOTH **3** : EQUAL, FAIR ⟨an ∼ exchange⟩ **4** : BALANCED; *also* : fully revenged **5** : divisible by two **6** : EXACT ⟨an ∼ dollar⟩ — **even·ly** *adv* — **even·ness** *n*

²even *adv* **1** : EXACTLY, PRECISELY **2** : FULLY, QUITE **3** : at the very time **4** — used as an intensive to stress identity ⟨∼ I know that⟩ **5** — used as an intensive to emphasize something extreme or highly unlikely ⟨so simple ∼ a child can do it⟩ **6** — used as an intensive to stress the comparative degree ⟨did ∼ better⟩ **7** — used as an intensive to indicate a small or minimum degree ⟨didn't ∼ try⟩

³even *vb* : to make or become even

even·hand·ed \ˌē-vən-'han-dəd\ *adj* : FAIR, IMPARTIAL — **even·hand·ed·ly** *adv*

eve·ning \'ēv-niŋ\ *n* **1** : the end of the day and early part of the night **2** *chiefly Southern & Midland* : AFTERNOON

evening primrose *n* : a coarse biennial herb with yellow flowers that open in the evening

evening star *n* : a bright planet (as Venus) seen esp. in the western sky at or after sunset

even·song \'ē-vən-ˌsȯŋ\ *n, often cap* **1** : VESPERS **2** : evening prayer esp. when sung

event \i-'vent\ *n* [MF or L; MF, fr. L *eventus,* fr. *evenire* to happen, fr. *venire* to come] **1** : OCCURRENCE **2** : a noteworthy happening **3** : CONTINGENCY ⟨in the ∼ of rain⟩ **4** : a contest in a program of sports — **event·ful** *adj*

even·tide \'ē-vən-ˌtīd\ *n* : EVENING

even·tu·al \i-'ven-chü-wəl\ *adj* : coming at some later time : ULTIMATE — **even·tu·al·ly** *adv*

even·tu·al·i·ty \i-ˌven-chü-'wa-lə-tē\ *n, pl* **-ties** : a possible event or outcome

even·tu·ate \i-'ven-chü-ˌwāt\ *vb* **-at·ed; -at·ing** : to result finally

ev·er \'e-vər\ *adv* **1** : ALWAYS ⟨∼ faithful⟩ **2** : at any time **3** : in any way : AT ALL

ev·er·glade \'e-vər-ˌglād\ *n* : a low-lying tract of swampy or marshy land

ev·er·green \-ˌgrēn\ *adj* : having foliage that remains green ⟨most coniferous trees are ∼⟩ — **evergreen** *n*

¹ev·er·last·ing \ˌe-vər-'las-tiŋ\ *adj* **1** : enduring forever : ETERNAL **2** : having or being flowers or foliage that retain form or color for a long time when dried — **ev·er·last·ing·ly** *adv*

²everlasting *n* **1** : ETERNITY ⟨from ∼⟩ **2** : a plant with everlasting flowers; *also* : its flower

ev·er·more \ˌe-vər-'mȯr\ *adv* : FOREVER

ev·ery \'ev-rē\ *adj* [ME *everich, every,* fr. OE *ǣfre ǣlc,* fr. *ǣfre* ever + *ǣlc* each] **1** : being each one of a group **2** : all possible ⟨given ∼ chance⟩; *also* : COMPLETE ⟨have ∼ confidence⟩

ev·ery·body \'ev-ri-ˌbä-dē, -bə-\ *pron* : every person

ev·ery·day \'ev-rē-ˌdā\ *adj* : encountered or used routinely : ORDINARY

ev·ery·one \-(ˌ)wən\ *pron* : EVERYBODY

ev·ery·thing \'ev-rē-ˌthiŋ\ *pron* **1** : all that exists **2** : all that is relevant

ev·ery·where \'ev-rē-ˌhwer\ *adv* : in every place or part

evg *abbr* evening

evict \i-'vikt\ *vb* **1** : to put (a person) out from a property by legal process **2** : EXPEL ♦ *Synonyms* EJECT, OUST, DISMISS — **evic·tion** \-'vik-shən\ *n*

¹**ev·i·dence** \'e-və-dəns\ *n* **1** : an outward sign **2** : PROOF, TESTIMONY; *esp* : matter submitted in court to determine the truth of alleged facts

²**evidence** *vb* : PROVE, EVINCE

ev·i·dent \-dənt\ *adj* : clear to the vision and understanding ✦ *Synonyms* MANIFEST, DISTINCT, OBVIOUS, APPARENT, PLAIN

ev·i·dent·ly \'e-və-dənt-lē, ,e-və-'dent-\ *adv* **1** : in an evident manner **2** : on the basis of available evidence

¹**evil** \'ē-vəl\ *adj* **evil·er** *or* **evil·ler; evil·est** *or* **evil·lest 1** : WICKED **2** : causing or threatening distress or harm : PERNICIOUS — **evil·ly** *adv*

²**evil** *n* **1** : the fact of suffering, misfortune, and wrongdoing **2** : a source of sorrow, distress, or calamity

evil·do·er \ē-vəl-'dü-ər\ *n* : one who does evil

evil–mind·ed \-'mīn-dəd\ *adj* : having an evil disposition or evil thoughts — **evil–mind·ed·ly** *adv*

evince \i-'vins\ *vb* **evinced; evinc·ing** : SHOW, REVEAL

evis·cer·ate \i-'vi-sə-,rāt\ *vb* **-at·ed; -at·ing 1** : to remove the entrails of **2** : to deprive of vital content or force — **evis·cer·a·tion** \-,vi-sə-'rā-shən\ *n*

evoke \i-'vōk\ *vb* **evoked; evok·ing** : to call forth or up — **evo·ca·tion** \ē-vō-'kā-shən, ,e-və-\ *n* — **evoc·a·tive** \i-'vä-kə-tiv\ *adj*

evo·lu·tion \,e-və-'lü-shən\ *n* **1** : one of a set of prescribed movements (as in a dance) **2** : a process of change in a particular direction **3** : a theory that the various kinds of plants and animals are descended from other kinds that lived in earlier times and that the differences are due to inherited changes that occurred over many generations — **evo·lu·tion·ary** \-shə-,ner-ē\ *adj* — **evo·lu·tion·ist** \-shə-nist\ *n*

evolve \i-'välv\ *vb* **evolved; evolv·ing** [L *evolvere* to unroll] : to develop or change by or as if by evolution

EW *abbr* enlisted woman

ewe \'yü\ *n* : a female sheep

ew·er \'yü-ər\ *n* : a water pitcher

¹**ex** \'eks\ *prep* [L] : out of : FROM

²**ex** *n* : a former spouse

³**ex** *abbr* **1** example **2** express **3** extra

Ex *abbr* Exodus

ex- \e *also occurs in this prefix where only* i *is shown below (as in "express") and* ks *sometimes occurs where only* gz *is shown (as in "exact")\ prefix* **1** : out of : outside **2** : former ⟨*ex*-president⟩

ex·ac·er·bate \ig-'za-sər-,bāt\ *vb* **-bat·ed; -bat·ing** : to make more violent, bitter, or severe — **ex·ac·er·ba·tion** \-,za-sər-'bā-shən\ *n*

¹**ex·act** \ig-'zakt\ *vb* **1** : to compel to furnish **2** : to call for as suitable or necessary — **ex·ac·tion** \-'zak-shən\ *n*

²**exact** *adj* : precisely accurate or correct — **ex·act·ly** *adv* — **ex·act·ness** *n*

ex·act·ing \ig-'zak-tiŋ\ *adj* **1** : greatly demanding ⟨an ~ taskmaster⟩ **2** : requiring close attention and precision

ex·ac·ti·tude \ig-'zak-tə-,tüd, -,tyüd\ *n* : the quality or state of being exact

ex·ag·ger·ate \ig-'za-jə-,rāt\ *vb* **-at·ed; -at·ing** [L *exaggeratus,* pp. of *exaggerare,* lit., to heap up, fr. *agger* heap] : to enlarge (as a statement) beyond normal : OVERSTATE — **ex·ag·ger·at·ed·ly** *adv* — **ex·ag·ger·a·tion** \-,za-jə-'rā-shən\ *n* — **ex·ag·ger·a·tor** \-'za-jə-,rā-tər\ *n*

ex·alt \ig-'zólt\ *vb* **1** : to raise up esp. in rank, power, or dignity **2** : GLORIFY — **ex·al·ta·tion** \,eg-,zól-'tā-shən, ,ek-,sól-\ *n*

ex·am \ig-'zam\ *n* : EXAMINATION

ex·am·ine \ig-'za-mən\ *vb* **ex·am·ined; ex·am·in·ing 1** : to inspect closely **2** : QUESTION; *esp* : to test by questioning ✦ *Synonyms* INTERROGATE, QUERY, QUIZ, CATECHIZE — **ex·am·i·na·tion** \-,za-mə-'nā-shən\ *n*

ex·am·ple \ig-'zam-pəl\ *n* **1** : something forming a model to be followed or avoided **2** : a representative sample **3** : a problem to be solved in order to show the application of some rule

ex·as·per·ate \ig-'zas-pə-,rāt\ *vb* **-at·ed; -at·ing** : VEX, IRRITATE — **ex·as·per·a·tion** \ig-,zas-pə-'rā-shən\ *n*

exc *abbr* **1** excellent **2** except

ex·ca·vate \'ek-skə-,vāt\ *vb* **-vat·ed; -vat·ing 1** : to hollow out; *also* : to form by hollowing out **2** : to dig out and remove (as earth) **3** : to reveal to view by digging away a covering — **ex·ca·va·tion** \,ek-skə-'vā-shən\ *n* — **ex·ca·va·tor** \'ek-skə-,vā-tər\ *n*

ex·ceed \ik-'sēd\ *vb* **1** : to go or be beyond the limit of **2** : SURPASS — **ex·ceed·ance** \-'sē-d²ns\ *n*

ex·ceed·ing·ly \-'sē-diŋ-lē\ *also* **ex·ceed·ing** *adv* : EXTREMELY, VERY

ex·cel \ik-'sel\ *vb* **ex·celled; ex·cel·ling** : SURPASS, OUTDO

ex·cel·lence \'ek-sə-ləns\ *n* **1** : the quality of being excellent **2** : an excellent or valuable quality : VIRTUE **3** : EXCELLENCY 2

ex·cel·len·cy \-lən-sē\ *n, pl* **-cies 1** : EXCELLENCE **2** — used as a title of honor

ex·cel·lent \-lənt\ *adj* : very good of its kind : FIRST-CLASS — **ex·cel·lent·ly** *adv*

ex·cel·si·or \ik-'sel-sē-ər\ *n* : fine curled wood shavings used esp. for packing fragile items

¹**ex·cept** \ik-'sept\ *also* **ex·cept·ing** *prep* : with the exclusion or exception of ⟨daily ~ Sundays⟩

²**except** *vb* **1** : to take or leave out **2** : OBJECT

³**except** *also* **excepting** *conj* **1** : UNLESS ⟨~ you repent⟩ **2** : ONLY ⟨I'd go, ~ it's too far⟩

ex·cep·tion \ik-'sep-shən\ *n* **1** : the act of excepting **2** : something excepted **3** : OBJECTION

ex·cep·tion·able \ik-'sep-shə-nə-bəl\ *adj* : OBJECTIONABLE

ex·cep·tion·al \ik-'sep-shə-nəl\ *adj* **1** : UNUSUAL ⟨an ~ number of rainy days⟩ **2** : SUPERIOR ⟨~ skill⟩ — **ex·cep·tion·al·ly** *adv*

ex·cerpt \'ek-,sərpt, 'eg-,zərpt\ *n* : a passage selected or copied : EXTRACT — **excerpt** \ek-'sərpt, eg-'zərpt; 'ek-,sərpt, 'eg-,zərpt\ *vb*

ex·cess \ik-'ses, 'ek-,ses\ *n* **1** : SUPERFLUITY, SURPLUS **2** : the amount by which one quantity exceeds another **3** : INTEMPERANCE; *also* : an instance of intemperance — **excess** *adj* — **ex·ces·sive** \ik-'se-siv\ *adj* — **ex·ces·sive·ly** *adv*

exch *abbr* exchange; exchanged

¹**ex·change** \iks-'chānj\ *n* **1** : the giving or taking of one thing in return for another : TRADE **2** : a substituting of one thing for another **3** : interchange of valuables and esp. of bills of exchange or money of different countries **4** : a place where things and services are exchanged; *esp* : a marketplace for securities **5** : a central office in which telephone lines are connected for communication

²**exchange** *vb* **ex·changed; ex·chang·ing** : to transfer in return for some equivalent : BARTER, SWAP — **ex·change·able** \iks-'chān-jə-bəl\ *adj*

ex·che·quer \'eks-,che-kər\ *n* [ME *escheker,* fr. AF, chessboard, counting table, office charged with revenue collection, fr. *eschec* check (in chess), chess] : TREASURY; *esp* : a national treasury

ex·cise \'ek-,sīz\ *n* : a tax on the manufacture, sale, or consumption of a commodity

ex·ci·sion \ik-'si-zhən\ *n* : removal by or as if by cutting out esp. by surgical means — **ex·cise** \ik-'sīz\ *vb*

ex·cit·able \ik-'sī-tə-bəl\ *adj* : easily excited — **ex·cit·abil·i·ty** \-,sī-tə-'bi-lə-tē\ *n*

ex·cite \ik-'sīt\ *vb* **ex·cit·ed; ex·cit·ing 1** : to stir up the emotions of : ROUSE **2** : to increase the activity of : STIMULATE ✦ *Synonyms* PROVOKE, PIQUE, QUICKEN — **ex·ci·ta·tion** \,ek-,sī-'tā-shən, ,ek-sə-\ *n* — **ex·cit·ed·ly** *adv* — **ex·cit·ing·ly** *adv*

ex·cite·ment \ik-'sīt-mənt\ *n* : AGITATION, STIR

ex·claim \iks-'klām\ *vb* : to cry out, speak, or utter sharply or vehemently — **ex·cla·ma·tion** \,eks-klə-'mā-shən\ *n* — **ex·clam·a·to·ry** \iks-'kla-mə-,tór-ē\ *adj*

exclamation point *n* : a punctuation mark ! used esp. after an interjection or exclamation

ex·clude \iks-'klüd\ *vb* **ex·clud·ed; ex·clud·ing 1** : to prevent from using or participating : BAR **2** : to put out : EXPEL — **ex·clu·sion** \-'klü-zhən\ *n* — **ex·clu·sion·ary** \-zhə-,ner-ē\ *adj*

ex·clu·sive \iks-'klü-siv\ *adj* **1** : reserved for particular persons **2** : snobbishly aloof; *also* : STYLISH **3** : SOLE ⟨~ rights⟩; *also* : UNDIVIDED ⟨my ~ attention⟩ ✦ *Synonyms* CHIC, MODISH, SMART, SWANK, FASHIONABLE — **exclusive** *n* — **ex·clu·sive·ly** *adv* — **ex·clu·sive·ness** *n* — **ex·clu·siv·i·ty** \,eks-,klü-si-və-tē, iks-, -zi-\ *n*

exclusive of *prep* : not taking into account

ex·cog·i·tate \ek-'skä-jə-,tāt\ *vb* : to think out : DEVISE

ex·com·mu·ni·cate \,ek-skə-'myü-nə-,kāt\ *vb* : to cut off officially from the rites of the church — **ex·com·mu·ni·ca·tion** \-,myü-nə-'kā-shən\ *n*

ex·co·ri·ate \ek-'skór-ē-ˌāt\ *vb* **-at·ed; -at·ing** : to criticize severely — **ex·co·ri·a·tion** \(ˌ)ek-ˌskór-ē-'ā-shən\ *n*

ex·cre·ment \'ek-skrə-mənt\ *n* : waste discharged from the body; *esp* : FECES — **ex·cre·men·tal** \ˌek-skrə-'men-t°l\ *adj*

ex·cres·cence \ik-'skre-s°ns\ *n* : OUTGROWTH; *esp* : an abnormal outgrowth (as a wart)

ex·cre·ta \ik-'skrē-tə\ *n pl* : waste matter (as feces) separated or eliminated from the body

ex·crete \ik-'skrēt\ *vb* **ex·cret·ed; ex·cret·ing** : to separate and eliminate wastes from the body esp. in urine or sweat — **ex·cre·tion** \-'skrē-shən\ *n* — **ex·cre·to·ry** \'ek-skrə-ˌtór-ē\ *adj*

ex·cru·ci·at·ing \ik-'skrü-shē-ˌā-tiŋ\ *adj* [L *excruciare* to torture, fr. *cruciare* to crucify, fr. *crux* cross] : intensely painful or distressing ✦ *Synonyms* AGONIZING, HARROWING, TORTUROUS — **ex·cru·ci·at·ing·ly** *adv*

ex·cul·pate \'ek-(ˌ)skəl-ˌpāt\ *vb* **-pat·ed; -pat·ing** : to clear from alleged fault or guilt ✦ *Synonyms* ABSOLVE, EXONERATE, ACQUIT, VINDICATE, CLEAR

ex·cur·sion \ik-'skər-zhən\ *n* **1** : EXPEDITION; *esp* : a pleasure trip **2** : DIGRESSION — **ex·cur·sion·ist** \-zhə-nist\ *n*

ex·cur·sive \-'skər-siv\ *adj* : constituting or characterized by digression

¹**ex·cuse** \ik-'skyüz\ *vb* **ex·cused; ex·cus·ing** [ME, fr. AF *excuser*, fr. L *excusare*, fr. *causa* cause, explanation] **1** : to make apology for **2** : PARDON **3** : to release from an obligation **4** : JUSTIFY — **ex·cus·able** *adj*

²**excuse** \ik-'skyüs\ *n* **1** : an act of excusing **2** : something that excuses or is a reason for excusing : JUSTIFICATION

exec *n* : EXECUTIVE

ex·e·cra·ble \'ek-si-krə-bəl\ *adj* **1** : DETESTABLE ⟨∼ crimes⟩ **2** : very bad ⟨∼ spelling⟩

ex·e·crate \'ek-sə-ˌkrāt\ *vb* **-crat·ed; -crat·ing** [L *exsecratus*, pp. of *exsecrari* to put under a curse, fr. *ex-* out of + *sacer* sacred] : to denounce as evil or detestable; *also* : DETEST — **ex·e·cra·tion** \ˌek-sə-'krā-shən\ *n*

ex·e·cute \'ek-si-ˌkyüt\ *vb* **-cut·ed; -cut·ing** **1** : to carry out fully : put completely into effect **2** : to do what is called for by (as a law) **3** : to put to death in accordance with a legal sentence **4** : to produce by carrying out a design **5** : to do what is needed to give validity to ⟨∼ a deed⟩ — **ex·e·cu·tion** \ˌek-si-'kyü-shən\ *n* — **ex·e·cu·tion·er** *n*

¹**ex·ec·u·tive** \ig-'ze-kyə-tiv\ *adj* **1** : of or relating to the enforcement of laws and the conduct of affairs **2** : designed for or related to carrying out plans or purposes

²**executive** *n* **1** : the branch of government with executive duties **2** : one having administrative or managerial responsibility

ex·ec·u·tor \ig-'ze-kyə-tər\ *n* : the person named in a will to execute it

ex·ec·u·trix \ig-'ze-kyə-ˌtriks\ *n, pl* **ex·ec·u·tri·ces** \-ˌze-kyə-'trī-ˌsēz\ *or* **ex·ec·u·trix·es** \-'ze-kyə-ˌtrik-səz\ : a woman who is an executor

ex·e·ge·sis \ˌek-sə-'jē-səs\ *n, pl* **-ge·ses** \-'jē-ˌsēz\ : explanation or critical interpretation of a text

ex·e·gete \'ek-sə-ˌjēt\ *n* : one who practices exegesis — **ex·e·get·i·cal** \ˌek-sə-'je-ti-kəl\ *adj*

ex·em·plar \ig-'zem-ˌplär, -plər\ *n* **1** : one that serves as a model or example; *esp* : an ideal model **2** : a typical instance or example

ex·em·pla·ry \ig-'zem-plə-rē\ *adj* : serving as a pattern; *also* : COMMENDABLE ⟨∼ courage⟩

ex·em·pli·fy \ig-'zem-plə-ˌfī\ *vb* **-fied; -fy·ing** : to illustrate by example : serve as an example of — **ex·em·pli·fi·ca·tion** \-ˌzem-plə-fə-'kā-shən\ *n*

¹**ex·empt** \ig-'zempt\ *adj* : free from some liability to which others are subject ⟨∼ from taxation⟩

²**exempt** *vb* : to make exempt : EXCUSE — **ex·emp·tion** \ig-'zemp-shən\ *n*

¹**ex·er·cise** \'ek-sər-ˌsīz\ *n* **1** : EMPLOYMENT, USE ⟨∼ of authority⟩ **2** : exertion made for the sake of training or physical fitness **3** : a task or problem done to develop skill **4** *pl* : a public exhibition or ceremony

²**exercise** *vb* **-cised; -cis·ing** **1** : EXERT ⟨∼ control⟩ **2** : to train by or engage in exercise **3** : WORRY, DISTRESS — **ex·er·cis·er** *n*

ex·ert \ig-'zərt\ *vb* : to bring or put into action ⟨∼ influence⟩ ⟨∼ed himself⟩ — **ex·er·tion** \-'zər-shən\ *n*

ex·fo·li·ate \eks-'fō-lē-ˌāt\ *vb* **-at·ed; -at·ing** : to cast off in scales, layers, or splinters — **ex·fo·lia·tion** \-ˌfō-lē-'ā-shən\ *n*

ex·hale \eks-'hāl\ *vb* **ex·haled; ex·hal·ing** **1** : to breathe out **2** : to give or pass off in the form of vapor — **ex·ha·la·tion** \ˌeks-hə-'lā-shən\ *n*

¹**ex·haust** \ig-'zóst\ *vb* **1** : to use up wholly **2** : to tire or wear out **3** : to draw off or let out completely; *also* : EMPTY **4** : to develop (a subject) completely

²**exhaust** *n* **1** : the escape of used vapor or gas from an engine; *also* : the gas that escapes **2** : a system of pipes through which exhaust escapes

ex·haus·tion \ig-'zós-chən\ *n* : extreme weariness : FATIGUE

ex·haus·tive \ig-'zó-stiv\ *adj* : covering all possibilities : THOROUGH ⟨an ∼ investigation⟩ — **ex·haus·tive·ly** *adv*

¹**ex·hib·it** \ig-'zi-bət\ *vb* **1** : to display esp. publicly **2** : to present to a court in legal form ✦ *Synonyms* DISPLAY, SHOW, PARADE, FLAUNT — **ex·hi·bi·tion** \ˌek-sə-'bi-shən\ *n* — **ex·hib·i·tor** \ig-'zi-bə-tər\ *n*

²**exhibit** *n* **1** : an act or instance of exhibiting; *also* : something exhibited **2** : something produced and identified in court for use as evidence

ex·hi·bi·tion·ism \ˌek-sə-'bi-shə-ˌni-zəm\ *n* **1** : a perversion marked by a tendency to indecently expose one's genitals **2** : the act or practice of behaving so as to attract attention to oneself — **ex·hi·bi·tion·ist** \-nist\ *n or adj*

ex·hil·a·rate \ig-'zi-lə-ˌrāt\ *vb* **-rat·ed; -rat·ing** : ENLIVEN, STIMULATE — **ex·hil·a·ra·tion** \-ˌzi-lə-'rā-shən\ *n*

ex·hort \ig-'zórt\ *vb* : to urge, advise, or warn earnestly — **ex·hor·ta·tion** \ˌek-ˌsór-tā-shən, ˌeg-ˌzór-, -zər-\ *n*

ex·hume \ig-'züm, iks-'hyüm\ *vb* **ex·humed; ex·hum·ing** [ME fr. ML *exhumare*, fr. L *ex* out of + *humus* earth] : DISINTER — **ex·hu·ma·tion** \ˌeks-hyü-'mā-shən, ˌeg-zü-\ *n*

ex·i·gen·cy \'ek-sə-jən-sē, ig-'zi-jən-\ *n, pl* **-cies** **1** *pl* : REQUIREMENTS **2** : urgent need — **ex·i·gent** \'ek-sə-jənt\ *adj*

ex·ig·u·ous \ig-'zi-gyə-wəs\ *adj* : scanty in amount — **ex·i·gu·i·ty** \ˌeg-zi-'gyü-ə-tē\ *n*

¹**ex·ile** \'eg-ˌz(-ə)l, 'ek-ˌsī(-ə)l\ *n* **1** : BANISHMENT; *also* : voluntary absence from one's country or home **2** : a person driven from his or her native place

²**exile** *vb* **ex·iled; ex·il·ing** : BANISH, EXPEL ✦ *Synonyms* EXPATRIATE, DEPORT, OSTRACIZE

ex·ist \ig-'zist\ *vb* **1** : to have being **2** : to continue to be : LIVE

ex·is·tence \ig-'zis-təns\ *n* **1** : continuance in living **2** : actual or present occurrence ⟨∼ of a state of war⟩ — **ex·is·tent** \-tənt\ *adj*

ex·is·ten·tial \ˌeg-zis-'ten-chəl, ˌek-sis-\ *adj* **1** : of or relating to existence **2** : EMPIRICAL **3** : having being in time and space **4** : of or relating to existentialism or existentialists

ex·is·ten·tial·ism \ˌeg-zis-'ten-chə-ˌli-zəm\ *n* : a philosophy centered on individual existence and personal responsibility for acts of free will in the absence of certain knowledge of what is right or wrong — **ex·is·ten·tial·ist** \-list\ *adj or n*

ex·it \'eg-zət, 'ek-sət\ *n* **1** : a departure from a stage **2** : a going out or away; *also* : DEATH **3** : a way out of an enclosed space **4** : a point of departure from an expressway — **exit** *vb*

exo·bi·ol·o·gy \ˌek-sō-bī-'ä-lə-jē\ *n* : biology concerned with life originating or existing outside the earth or its atmosphere — **exo·bi·ol·o·gist** \-jist\ *n*

exo·crine gland \'ek-sə-krən, -ˌkrīn-, -ˌkren-\ *n* : a gland (as a salivary gland) that releases a secretion externally by means of a canal or duct

Exod *abbr* Exodus

ex·o·dus \'ek-sə-dəs\ *n* **1** *cap* — see BIBLE table **2** : a mass departure : EMIGRATION

ex of·fi·cio \ˌek-sə-'fi-shē-ˌō\ *adv or adj* : by virtue of or because of an office ⟨*ex officio* chairman⟩

ex·og·e·nous \ek-'sä-jə-nəs\ *adj* : caused or produced by factors outside the organism or system — **ex·og·e·nous·ly** *adv*

ex·on·er·ate \ig-'zä-nə-ˌrāt\ *vb* **-at·ed; -at·ing** [ME, fr. L *exoneratus*, pp. of *exonerare* to unburden, fr. *ex-* out + *onus* load] : to free from blame ✦ *Synonyms* ACQUIT,

ABSOLVE, EXCULPATE, VINDICATE — **ex·on·er·a·tion** \-,zä-nə-'rā-shən\ n

ex·or·bi·tant \ig-'zór-bə-tənt\ adj : exceeding what is usual or proper

ex·or·cise \'ek-,sòr-,sīz, -sər-\ vb **-cised; -cis·ing** 1 : to get rid of by or as if by solemn command 2 : to free of an evil spirit — **ex·or·cism** \-,si-zəm\ n — **ex·or·cist** \-,sist\ n

exo·sphere \'ek-sō-,sfir\ n : the outermost region of the atmosphere

exo·ther·mic \,ek-sō-'thər-mik\ adj : characterized by or formed with evolution of heat

ex·ot·ic \ig-'zä-tik\ adj 1 : introduced from another country ⟨∼ plants⟩ 2 : strikingly, excitingly, or mysteriously different or unusual ⟨∼ flavors⟩ — **exotic** n — **ex·ot·i·cal·ly** \-ti-k(ə-)lē\ adv — **ex·ot·i·cism** \-tə-,si-zəm\ n

exp abbr 1 expense 2 experiment 3 export 4 express

ex·pand \ik-'spand\ vb 1 : to open up : UNFOLD 2 : ENLARGE 3 : to develop in detail ♦ **Synonyms** AMPLIFY, SWELL, DISTEND, INFLATE, DILATE — **ex·pand·able** \-'span-də-bəl\ adj — **ex·pand·er** n

ex·panse \ik-'spans\ n : a broad extent (as of land or sea)

ex·pan·sion \ik-'span-chən\ n 1 : the act or process of expanding 2 : the quality or state of being expanded 3 : an expanded part or thing

expansion slot n : a socket on a motherboard for a circuit board (**expansion card**) offering additional capabilities

ex·pan·sive \ik-'span-siv\ adj 1 : tending to expand or to cause expansion 2 : warmly benevolent, generous, or ready to talk 3 : of large extent or scope — **ex·pan·sive·ly** adv — **ex·pan·sive·ness** n

ex par·te \eks-'pär-tē\ adv or adj [ML] : from a one-sided point of view

ex·pa·ti·ate \ek-'spā-shē-,āt\ vb **-at·ed; -at·ing** : to talk or write at length — **ex·pa·ti·a·tion** \ek-,spā-shē-'ā-shən\ n

¹**ex·pa·tri·ate** \ek-'spā-trē-,āt\ vb **-at·ed; -at·ing** : EXILE — **ex·pa·tri·a·tion** \ek-,spā-trē-'ā-shən\ n

²**ex·pa·tri·ate** \ek-'spā-trē-,āt, -trē-ət\ adj : living in a foreign country — **expatriate** n

ex·pect \ik-'spekt\ vb 1 : SUPPOSE, THINK 2 : to look forward to : ANTICIPATE 3 : to consider reasonable, due, or necessary 4 : to consider to be obliged

ex·pec·tan·cy \-'spek-tən-sē\ n, pl **-cies** 1 : EXPECTATION 2 : the expected amount (as of years of life)

ex·pec·tant \-tənt\ adj : marked by expectation; esp : expecting the birth of a child — **ex·pec·tant·ly** adv

ex·pec·ta·tion \,ek-,spek-'tā-shən\ n 1 : the act or state of expecting 2 : prospect of inheritance — usu. used in pl. 3 : something expected

ex·pec·to·rant \ik-'spek-tə-rənt\ n : an agent that promotes the discharge or expulsion of mucus from the respiratory tract — **expectorant** adj

ex·pec·to·rate \-,rāt\ vb **-rat·ed; -rat·ing** : SPIT — **ex·pec·to·ra·tion** \-,spek-tə-'rā-shən\ n

ex·pe·di·ence \ik-'spē-dē-əns\ n : EXPEDIENCY

ex·pe·di·en·cy \-ən-sē\ n, pl **-cies** 1 : fitness to some end 2 : use of expedient means and methods; also : something expedient

¹**ex·pe·di·ent** \-ənt\ adj [ME, fr. AF or L; AF, fr. L expediens, prp. of expedire to extricate, prepare, be useful, fr. ex- out + ped-, pes foot] 1 : adapted for achieving a particular end 2 : marked by concern with what is advantageous; esp : governed by self-interest

²**expedient** n : something expedient; esp : a temporary means to an end

ex·pe·dite \'ek-spə-,dīt\ vb **-dit·ed; -dit·ing** : to carry out promptly; also : to speed up

ex·pe·dit·er \-,dī-tər\ n : one that expedites; esp : one employed to ensure efficient movement of goods or supplies in a business

ex·pe·di·tion \,ek-spə-'di-shən\ n 1 : a journey for a particular purpose; also : the persons making it 2 : efficient promptness

ex·pe·di·tion·ary \-'di-shə-,ner-ē\ adj : of, relating to, or constituting an expedition; also : sent on military service abroad

ex·pe·di·tious \-'di-shəs\ adj : marked by or acting with prompt efficiency ♦ **Synonyms** SWIFT, FAST, RAPID, SPEEDY

ex·pel \ik-'spel\ vb **ex·pelled; ex·pel·ling** : to drive or force out : EJECT

ex·pend \ik-'spend\ vb 1 : to pay out : SPEND 2 : UTILIZE; also : USE UP — **ex·pend·able** adj

ex·pen·di·ture \ik-'spen-di-chər, -,chúr\ n 1 : the act or process of expending 2 : something expended

ex·pense \ik-'spens\ n 1 : EXPENDITURE 2 : COST 3 : a cause of expenditure 4 : SACRIFICE ⟨had a laugh at my ∼⟩

ex·pen·sive \ik-'spen-siv\ adj : COSTLY, DEAR — **ex·pen·sive·ly** adv

¹**ex·pe·ri·ence** \ik-'spir-ē-əns\ n 1 : observation of or participation in events resulting in or tending toward knowledge 2 : knowledge, practice, or skill derived from observation or participation in events; also : the length of such participation 3 : something encountered, undergone, or lived through (as by a person or community)

²**experience** vb **-enced; -enc·ing** 1 : FIND OUT, DISCOVER 2 : to have experience of : UNDERGO

ex·pe·ri·enced adj : made capable through experience ⟨an ∼ pilot⟩

¹**ex·per·i·ment** \ik-'sper-ə-mənt\ n : a controlled procedure carried out to discover, test, or demonstrate something; also : the process of testing — **ex·per·i·men·tal** \-,sper-ə-'men-tᵊl\ adj — **ex·per·i·men·tal·ly** \-'men-tᵊl-ē\ adv

²**ex·per·i·ment** \-,ment\ vb : to make experiments — **ex·per·i·men·ta·tion** \ik-,sper-ə-mən-'tā-shən\ n — **ex·per·i·ment·er** n

¹**ex·pert** \'ek-,spərt\ adj : showing special skill or knowledge — **ex·pert·ly** adv — **ex·pert·ness** n

²**ex·pert** \'ek-,spərt\ n : an expert person : SPECIALIST

ex·per·tise \,ek-(,)spər-'tēz\ n : the skill of an expert

expert system n : computer software that attempts to mimic the reasoning of a human specialist

ex·pi·ate \'ek-spē-,āt\ vb **-at·ed; -at·ing** : to give satisfaction for : ATONE — **ex·pi·a·tion** \,ek-spē-'ā-shən\ n

ex·pi·a·to·ry \'ek-spē-ə-,tòr-ē\ adj : serving to expiate

expiration date n 1 : the date after which something is no longer in effect 2 : the date after which a product is expected to decline in quality or effectiveness

ex·pire \ik-'spī(-ə)r, ek-\ vb **ex·pired; ex·pir·ing** 1 : to breathe one's last breath : DIE 2 : to come to an end 3 : to breathe out from or as if from the lungs — **ex·pi·ra·tion** \,ek-spə-'rā-shən\ n

ex·plain \ik-'splān\ vb [ME explanen, fr. L explanare, lit., to make level, fr. planus level, flat] 1 : to make clear 2 : to give the reason for — **ex·pla·na·tion** \,ek-splə-'nā-shən\ n — **ex·plan·a·to·ry** \ik-'spla-nə-,tòr-ē\ adj

ex·ple·tive \'ek-splə-tiv\ n : a usu. profane exclamation

ex·pli·ca·ble \ek-'spli-kə-bəl, 'ek-(,)spli-\ adj : capable of being explained

ex·pli·cate \'ek-splə-,kāt\ vb **-cat·ed; -cat·ing** : to give a detailed explanation of — **ex·pli·ca·tion** \,ek-spli-'kā-shən\ n

ex·plic·it \ik-'spli-sət\ adj : clearly and precisely expressed — **ex·plic·it·ly** adv — **ex·plic·it·ness** n

ex·plode \ik-'splōd\ vb **ex·plod·ed; ex·plod·ing** [L explodere to drive off the stage by clapping, fr. ex- out + plaudere to clap] 1 : DISCREDIT ⟨∼ a belief⟩ 2 : to burst or cause to burst violently and noisily ⟨∼ a bomb⟩ ⟨the boiler exploded⟩ 3 : to undergo a rapid chemical or nuclear reaction with production of heat and violent expansion of gas ⟨dynamite ∼s⟩ 4 : to give forth a sudden strong and noisy outburst of emotion 5 : to increase rapidly ⟨the city's population exploded⟩

exploded adj : showing the parts separated but in correct relationship to each other ⟨an ∼ view of a carburetor⟩

¹**ex·ploit** \'ek-,splòit\ n : DEED; esp : a notable or heroic act

²**ex·ploit** \ik-'splòit\ vb 1 : to make productive use of : UTILIZE 2 : to use unfairly for one's own advantage — **ex·ploi·ta·tion** \,ek-,splòi-'tā-shən\ n

ex·plore \ik-'splōr\ vb **ex·plored; ex·plor·ing** 1 : to look into or travel over thoroughly 2 : to examine carefully ⟨∼ a wound⟩ — **ex·plo·ra·tion** \,ek-splə-'rā-shən\ n — **ex·plor·a·to·ry** \ik-'splōr-ə-,tòr-ē\ adj — **ex·plor·er** n

ex·plo·sion \ik-'splō-zhən\ n : the act or an instance of exploding

ex·plo·sive \ik-'splō-siv\ adj 1 : relating to or able to cause explosion 2 : tending to explode — **explosive** n — **ex·plo·sive·ly** adv

ex·po \'ek-,spō\ n, pl **expos** : EXPOSITION 2

ex·po·nent \ik-'spō-nənt, 'ek-,spō-\ n 1 : a symbol written above and to the right of a mathematical expression (as ³ in *a*³) to signify how many times it is to be used as a factor **2** : INTERPRETER, EXPOUNDER **3** : ADVOCATE, CHAMPION — **ex·po·nen·tial** \ˌek-spə-ˈnen-chəl\ *adj* — **ex·po·nen·tial·ly** *adv*

ex·po·nen·ti·a·tion \ˌek-spə-ˌnen-chē-ˈā-shen\ *n* : the mathematical operation of raising a quantity to a power

¹ex·port \ek-ˈspȯrt, ˈek-ˌspȯrt\ *vb* : to send (as merchandise) to foreign countries — **ex·por·ta·tion** \ˌek-ˌspȯr-ˈtā-shən, -spər-\ *n* — **ex·port·er** *n*

²ex·port \ˈek-ˌspȯrt\ *n* **1** : something exported esp. for trade **2** : the act of exporting

ex·pose \ik-ˈspōz\ *vb* **ex·posed; ex·pos·ing** **1** : to deprive of shelter or protection **2** : to submit or subject to an action or influence; *esp* : to subject (as photographic film) to radiant energy (as light) **3** : to bring to light : DISCLOSE **4** : to cause to be open to view

ex·po·sé \ˌek-spō-ˈzā\ *n* : an exposure of something discreditable

ex·po·si·tion \ˌek-spə-ˈzi-shən\ *n* **1** : a setting forth of the meaning or purpose (as of a writing); *also* : discourse designed to convey information **2** : a public exhibition

ex·pos·i·tor \ik-ˈspä-zə-tər\ *n* : one who explains : COMMENTATOR

ex post fac·to \ˌeks-ˈpōst-ˌfak-tō\ *adv or adj* : after the fact

ex·pos·tu·late \ik-ˈspäs-chə-ˌlāt\ *vb* : to reason earnestly with a person esp. in dissuading : REMONSTRATE — **ex·pos·tu·la·tion** \-ˌspäs-chə-ˈlā-shən\ *n*

ex·po·sure \ik-ˈspō-zhər\ *n* **1** : the fact or condition of being exposed **2** : the act or an instance of exposing **3** : the length of time for which a film is exposed **4** : a section of a photographic film for one picture

ex·pound \ik-ˈspau̇nd\ *vb* **1** : STATE **2** : INTERPRET, EXPLAIN — **ex·pound·er** *n*

¹ex·press \ik-ˈspres\ *adj* **1** : EXPLICIT; *also* : EXACT, PRECISE **2** : SPECIFIC ⟨this ∼ purpose⟩ **3** : traveling at high speed and esp. with few stops ⟨an ∼ train⟩; *also* : adapted to high speed use ⟨∼ roads⟩ — **ex·press·ly** *adv*

²express *adv* : by express ⟨ship it ∼⟩

³express *n* **1** : a system for the prompt transportation of goods; *also* : a company operating such a service or the shipments so transported **2** : an express vehicle

⁴express *vb* **1** : to make known : SHOW, STATE ⟨∼ regret⟩; *also* : SYMBOLIZE **2** : to squeeze out : extract by pressing **3** : to send by express **4** : to manifest or produce by a genetic process

ex·pres·sion \ik-ˈspre-shən\ *n* **1** : UTTERANCE **2** : something that represents or symbolizes : SIGN; *esp* : a mathematical symbol or combination of signs and symbols representing a quantity or operation **3** : the detectable effect of a gene **4** : a significant word or phrase; *also* : manner of expressing (as in writing or music) **5** : facial aspect or vocal intonation indicative of feeling — **ex·pres·sion·less** *adj*

ex·pres·sion·ism \ik-ˈspre-shə-ˌni-zəm\ *n* : a theory or practice in art of seeking to depict the artist's subjective responses to objects and events — **ex·pres·sion·ist** \-nist\ *n or adj* — **ex·pres·sion·is·tic** \-ˌspre-shə-ˈnis-tik\ *adj*

ex·pres·sive \ik-ˈspre-siv\ *adj* **1** : of or relating to expression **2** : serving to express — **ex·pres·sive·ly** *adv* — **ex·pres·sive·ness** *n*

ex·press·way \ik-ˈspres-ˌwā\ *n* : a divided superhighway with limited access

ex·pro·pri·ate \ek-ˈsprō-prē-ˌāt\ *vb* **-at·ed; -at·ing** : to deprive of possession or the right to own — **ex·pro·pri·a·tion** \(ˌ)ek-ˌsprō-prē-ˈā-shən\ *n*

expt *abbr* experiment

ex·pul·sion \ik-ˈspəl-shən\ *n* : an expelling or being expelled : EJECTION

ex·punge \ik-ˈspənj\ *vb* **ex·punged; ex·pung·ing** [L *pungere* to mark for deletion by dots, fr. *ex-* out + *pungere* to prick] : OBLITERATE, ERASE

ex·pur·gate \ˈek-spər-ˌgāt\ *vb* **-gat·ed; -gat·ing** : to clear (as a book) of objectionable passages — **ex·pur·ga·tion** \ˌek-spər-ˈgā-shən\ *n*

ex·qui·site \ek-ˈskwi-zət, ˈek-(ˌ)skwi-\ *adj* [ME *exquisit*, fr. L *exquisitus*, pp. of *exquirere* to search out, fr. *ex* out + *quaerere* to seek] **1** : marked by flawless form or workmanship **2** : keenly appreciative or sensitive **3** : pleasingly beautiful or delicate **4** : INTENSE ⟨∼ pain⟩

ext *abbr* **1** extension **2** exterior **3** external **4** extra **5** extract

ex·tant \ˈek-stənt; ek-ˈstant\ *adj* : EXISTENT; *esp* : not lost or destroyed

ex·tem·po·ra·ne·ous \ek-ˌstem-pə-ˈrā-nē-əs\ *adj* : not planned beforehand : IMPROMPTU — **ex·tem·po·ra·ne·ous·ly** *adv*

ex·tem·po·rary \ik-ˈstem-pə-ˌrer-ē\ *adj* : EXTEMPORANEOUS

ex·tem·po·re \ik-ˈstem-pə-(ˌ)rē\ *adv* : EXTEMPORANEOUSLY

ex·tem·po·rise *Brit var of* EXTEMPORIZE

ex·tem·po·rize \ik-ˈstem-pə-ˌrīz\ *vb* **-rized; -riz·ing** : to do something extemporaneously

ex·tend \ik-ˈstend\ *vb* **1** : to spread or stretch forth or out (as in reaching) **2** : to exert or cause to exert to full capacity **3** : PROFFER ⟨∼ credit⟩ **4** : PROLONG ⟨∼ a note⟩ **5** : to make greater or broader ⟨∼ knowledge⟩ ⟨∼ a business⟩ **6** : to stretch out or reach across a distance, space, or time ✦ *Synonyms* LENGTHEN, ELONGATE, PROTRACT — **ex·tend·able** *also* **ex·tend·ible** \-ˈsten-də-bəl\ *adj*

ex·ten·sion \ik-ˈsten-chən\ *n* **1** : an extending or being extended **2** : a program that geographically extends the educational resources of an institution **3** : an additional part; *also* : an extra telephone connected to a line

ex·ten·sive \ik-ˈsten-siv\ *adj* : of considerable extent : FAR-REACHING, BROAD — **ex·ten·sive·ly** *adv*

ex·tent \ik-ˈstent\ *n* **1** : the range or space over which something extends ⟨a property of large ∼⟩ **2** : the point or degree to which something extends ⟨to the fullest ∼ of the law⟩

ex·ten·u·ate \ik-ˈsten-yù-ˌwāt\ *vb* **-at·ed; -at·ing** : to lessen the seriousness of — **ex·ten·u·a·tion** \-ˌsten-yù-ˈwā-shən\ *n*

¹ex·te·ri·or \ek-ˈstir-ē-ər\ *adj* **1** : EXTERNAL **2** : suitable for use on an outside surface ⟨∼ paint⟩

²exterior *n* : an exterior part or surface

ex·ter·mi·nate \ik-ˈstər-mə-ˌnāt\ *vb* **-nat·ed; -nat·ing** : to get rid of completely usu. by killing off ✦ *Synonyms* EXTIRPATE, ERADICATE, ABOLISH, ANNIHILATE — **ex·ter·mi·na·tion** \-ˌstər-mə-ˈnā-shən\ *n* — **ex·ter·mi·na·tor** \-ˈstər-mə-ˌnā-tər\ *n*

¹ex·ter·nal \ek-ˈstər-n°l\ *adj* **1** : outwardly perceivable; *also* : SUPERFICIAL **2** : of, relating to, or located on the outside or an outer part **3** : arising or acting from without; *also* : FOREIGN ⟨∼ affairs⟩ — **ex·ter·nal·ly** *adv*

²external *n* : an external feature

ex·tinct \ik-ˈstiŋkt\ *adj* **1** : EXTINGUISHED; *also* : no longer active ⟨an ∼ volcano⟩ **2** : no longer existing or in use ⟨dinosaurs are ∼⟩ ⟨∼ languages⟩ — **ex·tinc·tion** \ik-ˈstiŋk-shən\ *n*

ex·tin·guish \ik-ˈstiŋ-gwish\ *vb* : to cause to stop burning; *also* : to bring to an end (as by destroying) — **ex·tin·guish·able** *adj* — **ex·tin·guish·er** *n*

ex·tir·pate \ˈek-stər-ˌpāt\ *vb* **-pat·ed; -pat·ing** [L *exstirpatus*, pp. of *exstirpare*, fr. *ex-* out + *stirps* trunk, root] **1** : to destroy completely **2** : UPROOT ✦ *Synonyms* EXTERMINATE, ERADICATE, ABOLISH, ANNIHILATE — **ex·tir·pa·tion** \ˌek-stər-ˈpā-shən\ *n*

ex·tol *also* **ex·toll** \ik-ˈstōl\ *vb* **ex·tolled; ex·tol·ling** : to praise highly : GLORIFY

ex·tort \ik-ˈstȯrt\ *vb* [L *extortus*, pp. of *extorquēre* to wrench out, extort, fr. *ex-* out + *torquēre* to twist] : to obtain by force or improper pressure (as a bribe) — **ex·tor·tion** \-ˈstȯr-shən\ *n* — **ex·tor·tion·er** *n* — **ex·tor·tion·ist** *n*

ex·tor·tion·ate \ik-ˈstȯr-shə-nət\ *adj* : EXCESSIVE, EXORBITANT ⟨∼ prices⟩ — **ex·tor·tion·ate·ly** *adv*

¹ex·tra \ˈek-strə\ *adj* **1** : ADDITIONAL ⟨∼ work⟩ **2** : SUPERIOR ⟨∼ quality⟩

²extra *n* **1** : a special edition of a newspaper **2** : an added charge **3** : an additional worker or performer (as in a motion picture)

³extra *adv* : beyond what is usual ⟨∼ large⟩

¹ex·tract \ik-ˈstrakt, *esp for 3* ˈek-ˌstrakt\ *vb* **1** : to draw out; *esp* : to pull out forcibly ⟨∼ a tooth⟩ **2** : to withdraw (as a juice or a constituent) by a physical or chemical process **3** : to select for citation : QUOTE — **ex·tract·able** *adj* — **ex·trac·tion** \ik-ˈstrak-shən\ *n* — **ex·trac·tor** \-tər\ *n*

²**ex·tract** \'ek-ˌstrakt\ *n* **1** : EXCERPT, CITATION **2** : a product (as a juice or concentrate) obtained by extracting

ex·tra·cur·ric·u·lar \ˌek-strə-kə-'ri-kyə-lər\ *adj* : lying outside the regular curriculum; *esp* : of or relating to school-connected activities (as sports) usu. carrying no academic credit

ex·tra·dite \'ek-strə-ˌdīt\ *vb* **-dit·ed; -dit·ing** : to obtain by or deliver up to extradition

ex·tra·di·tion \ˌek-strə-'di-shən\ *n* : the surrender of an alleged criminal to a different jurisdiction for trial

ex·tra·mar·i·tal \ˌek-strə-'ma-rə-t³l\ *adj* : of or relating to sexual intercourse by a married person with someone other than his or her spouse

ex·tra·mu·ral \-'myùr-əl\ *adj* : existing or functioning beyond the bounds of an organized unit

ex·tra·ne·ous \ek-'strā-nē-əs\ *adj* **1** : coming from without ⟨∼ light⟩ **2** : not forming a vital part; *also* : IRRELEVANT — **ex·tra·ne·ous·ly** *adv*

ex·tra·net \'ek-strə-ˌnet\ *n* : a network like an intranet but also allowing access by certain outside parties

ex·traor·di·nary \ik-'strȯr-də-ˌner-ē, ˌek-strə-'ȯr-\ *adj* **1** : notably unusual or exceptional **2** : employed on special service ⟨an ambassador ∼⟩ — **ex·traor·di·nari·ly** \-ˌstrȯr-də-'ner-ə-lē, ˌek-strə-ȯr-\ *adv*

ex·trap·o·late \ik-'stra-pə-ˌlāt\ *vb* **-lat·ed; -lat·ing** : to infer (unknown data) from known data — **ex·trap·o·la·tion** \-ˌstra-pə-'lā-shən\ *n*

ex·tra·sen·so·ry \ˌek-strə-'sen-sə-rē\ *adj* : not acting or occurring through the known senses

extrasensory perception *n* : perception (as in telepathy) of events external to the self not gained through the senses and not deducible from previous experience

ex·tra·so·lar \-'sō-lər\ *adj* : originating or existing outside the solar system

ex·tra·ter·res·tri·al \-tə-'res-trē-əl\ *adj* : originating or existing outside the earth or its atmosphere ⟨∼ life⟩ — **extraterrestrial** *n*

ex·tra·ter·ri·to·ri·al \-ˌter-ə-'tȯr-ē-əl\ *adj* : existing or taking place outside the territorial limits of a jurisdiction

ex·tra·ter·ri·to·ri·al·i·ty \-ˌtȯr-ē-'a-lə-tē\ *n* : exemption from the application or jurisdiction of local law or tribunals ⟨diplomats enjoy ∼⟩

ex·trav·a·gant \ik-'stra-vi-gənt\ *adj* **1** : EXCESSIVE ⟨∼ claims⟩ **2** : unduly lavish : WASTEFUL **3** : too costly ♦ **Synonyms** IMMODERATE, EXORBITANT, EXTREME, INORDINATE, UNDUE — **ex·trav·a·gance** \-gəns\ *n* — **ex·trav·a·gant·ly** *adv*

ex·trav·a·gan·za \ik-ˌstra-və-'gan-zə\ *n* **1** : a literary or musical work marked by extreme freedom of style and structure **2** : a spectacular show

ex·tra·ve·hic·u·lar \ˌek-strə-vē-'hi-kyə-lər\ *adj* : taking place outside a vehicle (as a spacecraft) ⟨∼ activity⟩

¹**ex·treme** \ik-'strēm\ *adj* **1** : very great or intense ⟨∼ cold⟩ **2** : very severe or radical ⟨∼ measures⟩ **3** : going to great lengths or beyond normal limits ⟨politically ∼⟩ **4** : most remote ⟨the ∼ end⟩ **5** : UTMOST; *also* : MAXIMUM — **ex·treme·ly** *adv*

²**extreme** *n* **1** : something located at one end or the other of a range or series **2** : EXTREMITY 4

extremely low frequency *n* : a radio frequency in the lowest range of the radio spectrum

ex·trem·ism \ik-'strē-ˌmi-zəm\ *n* : the quality or state of being extreme; *esp* : advocacy of extreme political measures — **ex·trem·ist** \-mist\ *n or adj*

ex·trem·i·ty \ik-'stre-mə-tē\ *n, pl* **-ties 1** : the most remote part or point **2** : a limb of the body; *esp* : a human hand or foot **3** : the greatest need or danger **4** : the utmost degree **5** : a drastic or desperate measure

ex·tri·cate \'ek-strə-ˌkāt\ *vb* **-cat·ed; -cat·ing** [L *extricatus*, pp. of *extricare*, fr. *ex-* out + *tricae* trifles, perplexities] : to free from an entanglement or difficulty ♦ **Synonyms** DISENTANGLE, UNTANGLE, DISENCUMBER — **ex·tri·ca·ble** \ik-'stri-kə-bəl, ek-; 'ek-(ˌ)stri-\ *adj* — **ex·tri·ca·tion** \ˌek-strə-'kā-shən\ *n*

ex·trin·sic \ek-'strin-zik, -sik\ *adj* **1** : not forming part of or belonging to a thing **2** : EXTERNAL — **ex·trin·si·cal·ly** \-zi-k(ə-)lē, -si-\ *adv*

ex·tro·vert *also* **ex·tra·vert** \'ek-strə-ˌvərt\ *n* : a gregarious and unreserved person — **ex·tro·ver·sion** *or* **ex·tra·ver·sion** \ˌek-strə-'vər-zhən\ *n* — **ex·tro·vert·ed** *also* **ex·tra·vert·ed** *adj*

ex·trude \ik-'strüd\ *vb* **ex·trud·ed; ex·trud·ing 1** : to force, press, or push out **2** : to shape (as plastic) by forcing through a die — **ex·tru·sion** \-'strü-zhən\ *n* — **ex·trud·er** *n*

ex·u·ber·ant \ig-'zü-bə-rənt\ *adj* **1** : unrestrained in enthusiasm or style **2** : PROFUSE ⟨∼ vegetation⟩ — **ex·u·ber·ance** \-rəns\ *n* — **ex·u·ber·ant·ly** *adv*

ex·ude \ig-'züd\ *vb* **ex·ud·ed; ex·ud·ing** [L *exsudare*, fr. *ex-* out + *sudare* to sweat] **1** : to discharge slowly through pores or cuts : OOZE **2** : to display conspicuously or abundantly ⟨∼s charm⟩ — **ex·u·date** \'ek-sù-ˌdāt, -syù-\ *n* — **ex·u·da·tion** \ˌek-sù-'dā-shən, -syù-\ *n*

ex·ult \ig-'zəlt\ *vb* : REJOICE, GLORY — **ex·ul·tant** \-'zəl-t³nt\ *adj* — **ex·ul·tant·ly** *adv* — **ex·ul·ta·tion** \ˌek-(ˌ)səl-'tā-shən, eg-(ˌ)zəl-\ *n*

ex·urb \'ek-ˌsərb, 'eg-ˌzərb\ *n* : a region outside a city and its suburbs inhabited chiefly by well-to-do families — **ex·ur·ban** \ek-'sər-bən, eg-'zər-\ *adj*

ex·ur·ban·ite \ek-'sər-bə-ˌnīt; eg-'zər-\ *n* : one who lives in an exurb

ex·ur·bia \ek-'sər-bē-ə, eg-'zər-\ *n* : the generalized region of exurbs

-ey — see -Y

¹**eye** \'ī\ *n* **1** : an organ of sight typically consisting in vertebrates of a globular structure that is located in a socket of the skull, is lined with a sensitive retina, and is normally paired **2** : VISION, PERCEPTION; *also* : faculty of discrimination ⟨an ∼ for bargains⟩ **3** : POINT OF VIEW, JUDGMENT — often used in pl. ⟨in the ∼s of the law⟩ **4** : something suggesting an eye (as the hole of a needle or the bud of a potato) **5** : the calm center of a cyclone — **eyed** \'īd\ *adj*

²**eye** *vb* **eyed; eye·ing** *or* **ey·ing** : to look at : WATCH

¹**eye·ball** \'ī-ˌbȯl\ *n* : the globular capsule of the vertebrate eye

²**eyeball** *vb* : to look at intently

eye·brow \-ˌbraù\ *n* : the ridge over the eye or the hair growing on it

eye·drop·per \-ˌdrä-pər\ *n* : DROPPER 2

eye·glass \-ˌglas\ *n* : a lens worn to aid vision; *also, pl* : GLASSES

eye·lash \-ˌlash\ *n* **1** : the fringe of hair edging the eyelid — usu. used in pl. **2** : a single hair of the eyelashes

eye·let \-lət\ *n* **1** : a small hole intended for ornament or for passage of a cord or lace **2** : a typically metal ring for reinforcing an eyelet : GROMMET

eye·lid \-ˌlid\ *n* : either of the movable folds of skin and muscle that can be closed over the eyeball

eye·lin·er \-ˌlī-nər\ *n* : makeup used to emphasize the contour of the eyes

eye-open·er \-ˌō-pə-nər\ *n* : something startling or surprising — **eye-open·ing** *adj*

eye·piece \-ˌpēs\ *n* : the lens or combination of lenses at the eye end of an optical instrument

eye shadow *n* : a colored cosmetic applied to the eyelids to accent the eyes

eye·sight \-ˌsīt\ *n* : SIGHT, VISION

eye·sore \-ˌsȯr\ *n* : something offensive to view

eye·strain \-ˌstrān\ *n* : weariness or a strained state of the eye

eye·tooth \-'tüth\ *n* : a canine tooth of the upper jaw

eye·wash \-ˌwȯsh, -ˌwäsh\ *n* **1** : an eye lotion **2** : misleading or deceptive statements, actions, or procedures

eye·wit·ness \-'wit-nəs\ *n* : a person who actually sees something happen

ey·rie *chiefly Brit var of* AERIE

ey·rir \'ā-ˌrir\ *n, pl* **au·rar** \'aù-ˌrär\ — see *krona* at MONEY table

Ez *or* **Ezr** *abbr* Ezra

Ezech *abbr* Ezechiel

Eze·chiel \i-'zē-kyəl\ *n* — see BIBLE table

Ezek *abbr* Ezekiel

Eze·kiel \i-'zē-kyəl\ *n* — see BIBLE table

e-zine \'ē-ˌzēn\ *n* : an online magazine

Ez·ra \'ez-rə\ *n* — see BIBLE table

F

¹f \\'ef\\ *n, pl* **f's** *or* **fs** \\'efs\\ *often cap* **1** : the 6th letter of the English alphabet **2** : a grade rating a student's work as failing

²f *abbr, often cap* **1** Fahrenheit **2** false **3** family **4** farad **5** female **6** feminine **7** forte **8** French **9** frequency **10** Friday

³f *symbol* focal length

F *symbol* fluorine

FAA *abbr* Federal Aviation Administration

fab \\'fab\\ *adj* : FABULOUS

Fa·bi·an \\'fā-bē-ən\\ *adj* : of, relating to, or being a society of socialists organized in England in 1884 to spread socialist principles gradually — **Fabian** *n* — **Fa·bi·an·ism** *n*

fa·ble \\'fā-bəl\\ *n* **1** : a legendary story of supernatural happenings **2** : a narration intended to teach a lesson; *esp* : one in which animals speak and act like people **3** : FALSEHOOD

fa·bled \\'fā-bəld\\ *adj* **1** : FICTITIOUS **2** : told or celebrated in fable

fab·ric \\'fa-brik\\ *n* [MF *fabrique*, fr. L *fabrica* workshop, structure] **1** : STRUCTURE, FRAMEWORK ⟨the ~ of society⟩ **2** : CLOTH; *also* : a material that resembles cloth

fab·ri·cate \\'fa-bri-ˌkāt\\ *vb* **-cat·ed; -cat·ing 1** : INVENT, CREATE **2** : to make up for the sake of deception ⟨reporters *fabricating* news stories⟩ **3** : CONSTRUCT, MANUFACTURE — **fab·ri·ca·tion** \\ˌfa-bri-'kā-shən\\ *n*

fab·u·lous \\'fa-byə-ləs\\ *adj* **1** : resembling a fable; *also* : INCREDIBLE, MARVELOUS ⟨had a ~ time⟩ **2** : told in or based on fable — **fab·u·lous·ly** *adv*

fac *abbr* **1** facsimile **2** faculty

fa·cade *also* **fa·çade** \\fə-'säd\\ *n* [F *façade*, fr. It *facciata*, fr. *faccia* face] **1** : the principal face or front of a building **2** : a false, superficial, or artificial appearance ✦ *Synonyms* MASK, DISGUISE, FRONT, GUISE, PRETENSE, VENEER

¹face \\'fās\\ *n* **1** : the front part of the head **2** : PRESENCE ⟨in the ~ of danger⟩ **3** : facial expression : LOOK ⟨put a sad ~ on⟩ **4** : GRIMACE ⟨made a ~⟩ **5** : outward appearance ⟨looks easy on the ~ of it⟩ **6** : CONFIDENCE; *also* : BOLDNESS **7** : DIGNITY, PRESTIGE ⟨afraid to lose ~⟩ **8** : SURFACE; *esp* : a front, principal, bounding, or contacting surface ⟨~ of a cliff⟩ ⟨the ~s of a cube⟩ ⟨the ~ of a golf club⟩ — **faced** \\'fāst, 'fā-səd\\ *adj*

²face *vb* **faced; fac·ing 1** : to confront brazenly **2** : to line near the edge esp. with a different material; *also* : to cover the front or surface of ⟨~ a building with marble⟩ **3** : to meet or bring in direct contact or confrontation ⟨*faced* the problem⟩ **4** : to stand or sit with the face toward ⟨~ the sun⟩ **5** : to have the front oriented toward ⟨a house *facing* the park⟩ **6** : to have as or be a prospect ⟨~ a grim future⟩ **7** : to turn the face or body in a specified direction — **face the music** : to meet the unpleasant consequences of one's actions

face·down \\ˌfās-'daůn\\ *adv* : with the face downward ⟨cards turned ~⟩

face·less \\-ləs\\ *n* **1** : lacking character or individuality **2** : lacking a face

face–lift \\'fās-ˌlift\\ *n* **1** : plastic surgery on the face and neck to remove defects (as wrinkles) typical of aging **2** : MODERNIZATION — **face–lift** *vb*

face–off \\'fās-ˌóf\\ *n* **1** : a method of beginning play by dropping a puck or ball (as in hockey) between two opposing players each of whom attempts to control it **2** : CONFRONTATION — **face off** *vb*

fac·et \\'fa-sət\\ *n* [F *facette*, dim. of *face*] **1** : a small plane surface of a cut gem **2** : ASPECT, PHASE

fa·ce·tious \\fə-'sē-shəs\\ *adj* **1** : joking often inappropriately : JOCULAR, JOCOSE ✦ *Synonyms* WITTY, HUMOROUS — **fa·ce·tious·ly** *adv* — **fa·ce·tious·ness** *n*

¹fa·cial \\'fā-shəl\\ *adj* **1** : of or relating to the face **2** : used to improve the appearance of the face

²facial *n* : a facial treatment

fac·ile \\'fa-səl\\ *adj* **1** : easily accomplished, handled, or attained **2** : SIMPLISTIC **3** : readily manifested and often insincere ⟨~ prose⟩ **4** : READY, FLUENT ⟨a ~ writer⟩

fa·cil·i·tate \\fə-'si-lə-ˌtāt\\ *vb* **-tat·ed; -tat·ing** : to make easier — **fa·cil·i·ta·tion** \\-ˌsi-lə-'tā-shən\\ *n* — **fa·cil·i·ta·tor** \\-'si-lə-ˌtā-tər\\ *n*

fa·cil·i·ty \\fə-'si-lə-tē\\ *n, pl* **-ties 1** : the quality of being easily performed **2** : ease in performance : APTITUDE **3** : PLIANCY **4** : something that makes easier an action, operation, or course of conduct; *also* : REST ROOM — often used in pl. **5** : something (as a hospital) built or installed for a particular purpose

fac·ing \\'fā-siŋ\\ *n* **1** : a lining at the edge esp. of a garment **2** *pl* : the collar, cuffs, and trimmings of a uniform coat **3** : an ornamental or protective layer **4** : material for facing

fac·sim·i·le \\fak-'si-mə-lē\\ *n* [L *fac simile* make similar] **1** : an exact copy **2** : a system of transmitting and reproducing printed matter or pictures by means of signals sent over telephone lines

fact \\'fakt\\ *n* **1** : DEED; *esp* : CRIME ⟨accessory after the ~⟩ **2** : the quality of being actual **3** : something that exists or occurs **4** : a piece of information — **in fact** : in truth

fac·tion \\'fak-shən\\ *n* : a group or combination (as in a government) acting together within and usu. against a larger body : CLIQUE — **fac·tion·al·ism** \\-shə-nə-ˌli-zəm\\ *n*

fac·tious \\'fak-shəs\\ *adj* **1** : of, relating to, or caused by faction **2** : inclined to faction or the formation of factions : causing dissension ✦ *Synonyms* INSUBORDINATE, CONTUMACIOUS, INSURGENT, SEDITIOUS, REBELLIOUS

fac·ti·tious \\fak-'ti-shəs\\ *adj* : ARTIFICIAL, SHAM ⟨a ~ display of grief⟩

fac·toid \\'fak-ˌtóid\\ *n* **1** : an invented fact believed to be true because of its appearance in print **2** : a brief usu. trivial fact

¹fac·tor \\'fak-tər\\ *n* **1** : AGENT **2** : something that actively contributes to a result ⟨a ~ in her decision⟩ **3** : GENE **4** : any of the numbers or symbols in mathematics that when multiplied together form a product; *esp* : any of the integers that divide a given integer without a remainder

²factor *vb* **1** : to work as a factor **2** : to find the mathematical factors of and esp. the prime mathematical factors of

¹fac·to·ri·al \\fak-'tór-ē-əl\\ *adj* : of, relating to, or being a factor

²factorial *n* : the product of all the positive integers from 1 to a given integer *n*

fac·to·ry \\'fak-trē, -tə-rē\\ *n, pl* **-ries 1** : a trading post where resident brokers trade **2** : a building or group of buildings used for manufacturing

fac·to·tum \\fak-'tō-təm\\ *n* [NL, lit., do everything, fr. L *fac* do + *totum* everything] : a person (as a servant) having numerous or varied duties

facet 1

facts of life : the physiological processes and behavior involved in sex and reproduction

fac·tu·al \'fak-chə-wəl\ *adj* : of or relating to facts; *also* : based on fact — **fac·tu·al·ly** *adv*

fac·ul·ty \'fa-kəl-tē\ *n, pl* **-ties** **1** : ability to act or do : POWER; *also* : natural aptitude **2** : one of the powers of the mind or body ⟨the ~ of hearing⟩ **3** : the teachers in a school or college or one of its divisions

fad \'fad\ *n* : a practice or interest followed for a time with exaggerated zeal : CRAZE — **fad·dish** *adj* — **fad·dish·ly** *adv* — **fad·dist** *n*

¹fade \'fād\ *vb* **fad·ed; fad·ing** **1** : WITHER **2** : to lose or cause to lose freshness or brilliance of color **3** : VANISH ⟨a *fading* memory⟩ **4** : to grow dim or faint

²fade *n* : a short haircut in which hair on top of the head stands high

FADM *abbr* fleet admiral

fae·cal, fae·ces *chiefly Brit var of* FECAL, FECES

fa·er·ie *also* **fa·ery** \'fā-rē, 'fer-ē\ *n, pl* **fa·er·ies** **1** : FAIRYLAND **2** : FAIRY

¹fag \'fag\ *vb* **fagged; fag·ging** **1** : DRUDGE **2** : TIRE, EXHAUST ⟨*fagged* by the work⟩

²fag *n* : MENIAL, DRUDGE

³fag *n* : an English public-school boy who acts as servant to another

⁴fag *vb* : to act as a fag

⁵fag *n* : CIGARETTE

fag end *n* **1** : REMNANT **2** : the extreme end **3** : the last part or coarser end of a web of cloth **4** : the untwisted end of a rope

fag·ot *or* **fag·got** \'fa-gət\ *n* : a bundle of sticks or twigs

fag·ot·ing *or* **fag·got·ing** *n* : an embroidery produced by tying threads in hourglass-shaped clusters

Fah *or* **Fahr** *abbr* Fahrenheit

Fahr·en·heit \'fer-ən-ˌhīt\ *adj* : relating to, conforming to, or having a thermometer scale with the boiling point of water at 212 degrees and the freezing point at 32 degrees above zero

fa·ience *or* **fa·ïence** \fā-'äns\ *n* [F] : earthenware decorated with opaque colored glazes

¹fail \'fāl\ *vb* **1** : to become feeble; *esp* : to decline in health **2** : to die away **3** : to stop functioning **4** : to fall short ⟨~*ed* in his duty⟩ **5** : to be or become absent or inadequate **6** : to be unsuccessful esp. in achieving a passing grade **7** : to become bankrupt **8** : DISAPPOINT **9** : NEGLECT ⟨~*ed* to lock the door⟩

²fail *n* : FAILURE ⟨without ~⟩

¹fail·ing \'fā-liŋ\ *n* : WEAKNESS, SHORTCOMING

²failing *prep* : in the absence or lack of

faille \'fī(-ə)l\ *n* : a somewhat shiny closely woven ribbed fabric (as silk)

fail–safe \'fāl-ˌsāf\ *adj* **1** : incorporating a counteractive feature for a possible source of failure **2** : having no chance of failure — **fail–safe** *n*

fail·ure \'fāl-yər\ *n* **1** : a failing to do or perform **2** : a state of inability to perform a normal function adequately ⟨heart ~⟩; *also* : an abrupt cessation of functioning ⟨power ~⟩ **3** : a fracturing or giving way under stress **4** : a lack of success **5** : BANKRUPTCY **6** : DEFICIENCY **7** : DETERIORATION, DECAY **8** : one that has failed

¹fain \'fān\ *adj* **1** *archaic* : GLAD; *also* : INCLINED **2** : being obliged or compelled

²fain *adv* **1** : with pleasure **2** : by preference

¹faint \'fānt\ *adj* [ME *faint, feint*, fr. AF, fr. *faindre, feindre* to feign, lose heart] **1** : COWARDLY, SPIRITLESS **2** : weak, dizzy, and likely to faint **3** : lacking vigor or strength : FEEBLE ⟨~ praise⟩ **4** : hardly perceptible ⟨~ handwriting⟩ — **faint·ly** *adv* — **faint·ness** *n*

²faint *vb* : to lose consciousness

³faint *n* : the action of fainting; *also* : the resulting condition

faint·heart·ed \ˌfānt-'här-təd\ *adj* : lacking courage : TIMID

¹fair \'fer\ *adj* **1** : pleasing in appearance : BEAUTIFUL **2** : superficially pleasing : SPECIOUS **3** : CLEAN, PURE **4** : CLEAR, LEGIBLE **5** : not stormy or cloudy **6** : JUST **7** : conforming with the rules : ALLOWED; *also* : being within the foul lines ⟨~ ball⟩ **8** : open to legitimate pursuit or attack ⟨~ game⟩ **9** : PROMISING, LIKELY ⟨a ~ chance of winning⟩ **10** : favorable to a ship's course ⟨a ~ wind⟩ **11** : light in complexion : BLOND **12** : ADE-

QUATE **13** : significant in size ⟨a ~ amount of traffic⟩ — **fair·ness** *n*

²fair *adv* **1** : in a fair manner ⟨play ~⟩ **2** *chiefly Brit* : FAIRLY **4**

³fair *n* **1** : a gathering of buyers and sellers at a stated time and place for trade **2** : a competitive exhibition (as of farm products) **3** : a sale of assorted articles usu. for a charitable purpose ⟨a book ~⟩ **4** : an exhibition that promotes available services ⟨a job ~⟩

fair·ground \-ˌgraůnd\ *n* : an area where outdoor fairs, circuses, or exhibitions are held

fair·ing \'fer-iŋ\ *n* : a structure for producing a smooth outline and reducing drag (as on an airplane)

fair·ly \'fer-lē\ *adv* **1** : HANDSOMELY **2** : in a manner of speaking ⟨~ bursting with pride⟩ **3** : without bias **4** : to a full degree or extent : PLAINLY, DISTINCTLY **5** : SOMEWHAT, RATHER ⟨a ~ easy job⟩

fair–spo·ken \'fer-'spō-kən\ *adj* : pleasant and courteous in speech

fair–trade \-'trād\ *adj* : of, relating to, or being an agreement between a producer and a seller that branded merchandise will be sold at or above a specified price — **fair–trade** *vb*

fair·way \-ˌwā\ *n* : the mowed part of a golf course between tee and green

fairy \'fer-ē\ *n, pl* **fair·ies** [ME *fairie* fairyland, enchantment, fr. AF *faerie*, fr. *fee* fairy, fr. L *Fata*, goddess of fate, fr. *fatum* fate] : an imaginary being of folklore and romance usu. having diminutive human form and magic powers — **fairy** *adj*

fairy·land \-ˌland\ *n* **1** : the land of fairies **2** : a beautiful or charming place

fairy tale *n* **1** : a children's story usu. about mythical beings (as fairies) **2** : FIB

fait ac·com·pli \ˌfāt-ˌa-kōⁿ-'plē\ *n, pl* **faits accomplis** *same or* -'plēz\ [F, accomplished fact] : a thing accomplished and presumably irreversible

faith \'fāth\ *n, pl* **faiths** \'fāths, 'fāthz\ [ME *feith*, fr. AF *feid, fei*, fr. L *fides*] **1** : allegiance to duty or a person : LOYALTY **2** : belief and trust in God **3** : complete trust **4** : a system of religious beliefs — **faith·ful** \-fəl\ *adj* — **faith·ful·ly** *adv* — **faith·ful·ness** *n*

faith·less \'fāth-ləs\ *adj* **1** : DISLOYAL **2** : not to be relied on ♦ Synonyms FALSE, TRAITOROUS, TREACHEROUS, UNFAITHFUL — **faith·less·ly** *adv* — **faith·less·ness** *n*

fa·ji·ta \fə-'hē-tə\ *n* : a marinated strip usu. of beef or chicken grilled or broiled and served usu. with a flour tortilla and savory fillings

¹fake \'fāk\ *adj* : COUNTERFEIT, SHAM

²fake *n* **1** : IMITATION, FRAUD; *also* : IMPOSTOR **2** : a simulated move in sports (as a pretended pass)

³fake *vb* **faked; fak·ing** **1** : to treat so as to falsify **2** : COUNTERFEIT **3** : to deceive (an opponent) in a sports contest by making a fake — **fak·er** *n*

fa·kir \fə-'kir\ *n* [Ar *faqīr*, lit., poor man] **1** : a Muslim mendicant : DERVISH **2** : a wandering Hindu ascetic

fal·con \'fal-kən, 'fȯl-\ *n* **1** : a hawk trained for use in falconry **2** : any of various swift long-winged long-tailed hawks having a notched beak and usu. inhabiting open areas

fal·con·ry \'fal-kən-rē, 'fȯl-\ *n* **1** : the art of training hawks to hunt in cooperation with a person **2** : the sport of hunting with hawks — **fal·con·er** *n*

¹fall \'fȯl\ *vb* **fell** \'fel\; **fall·en** \'fȯ-lən\; **fall·ing** **1** : to descend freely by the force of gravity **2** : to hang freely **3** : to come or go as if by falling ⟨darkness *fell*⟩ **4** : to become uttered **5** : to lower or become lowered : DROP ⟨her eyes *fell*⟩ **6** : to leave an erect position suddenly and involuntarily **7** : STUMBLE, STRAY **8** : to drop down wounded or dead esp. in battle **9** : to become captured ⟨the city *fell* to the enemy⟩ **10** : to suffer ruin, defeat, or failure **11** : to commit an immoral act **12** : to move or extend in a downward direction **13** : SUBSIDE, ABATE **14** : to decline in quality, activity, quantity, or value **15** : to assume a look of shame or dejection ⟨her face *fell*⟩ **16** : to occur at a certain time **17** : to come by chance **18** : DEVOLVE ⟨the duties *fell* to him⟩ **19** : to have the proper place or station ⟨the accent ~s on the first syllable⟩ **20** : to come within the scope of something **21** : to pass from one condition to another ⟨*fell* ill⟩ **22** : to set about heartily or actively ⟨~ to work⟩ — **fall all over**

oneself *or* **fall over backward** : to display excessive eagerness — **fall flat** : to produce no response or result — **fall for** **1** : to fall in love with **2** : to become a victim of — **fall from grace** : BACKSLIDE — **fall into line** : to comply with a certain course of action — **fall short** **1** : to be deficient **2** : to fail to attain

²**fall** *n* **1** : the act of falling **2** : a falling out, off, or away : DROPPING **3** : AUTUMN **4** : a thing or quantity that falls ⟨a light ∼ of snow⟩ **5** : COLLAPSE, DOWNFALL **6** : the surrender or capture of a besieged place **7** : departure from virtue or goodness **8** : SLOPE **9** : WATERFALL — usu. used in pl. **10** : a decrease in size, quantity, degree, or value ⟨a ∼ in price⟩ **11** : the distance which something falls **12** : an act of forcing a wrestler's shoulders to the mat; *also* : a bout of wrestling

fal·la·cious \fə-'lā-shəs\ *adj* **1** : embodying a fallacy ⟨a ∼ argument⟩ **2** : MISLEADING, DECEPTIVE

fal·la·cy \'fa-lə-sē\ *n, pl* **-cies** **1** : a false or mistaken idea **2** : an often plausible argument using false or illogical reasoning

fall back *vb* : RETREAT, RECEDE

fall guy *n* : SCAPEGOAT

fal·li·ble \'fa-lə-bəl\ *adj* **1** : liable to be erroneous **2** : capable of making a mistake — **fal·li·bly** \-blē\ *adv*

fall·ing—out \ˌfȯ-liŋ-'au̇t\ *n, pl* **fallings—out** *or* **falling—outs** : QUARREL

falling star *n* : METEOR

fal·lo·pi·an tube \fə-'lō-pē-ən-\ *n, often cap F* : either of the pair of anatomical tubes that carry the eggs from the ovary to the uterus

fall·out \'fȯl-ˌau̇t\ *n* **1** : the often radioactive particles that result from a nuclear explosion and descend through the air **2** : a secondary and often lingering effect or result

fall out *vb* : QUARREL

¹**fal·low** \'fa-(ˌ)lō\ *n* : fallow land; *also* : the state or period of being fallow — **fallow** *vb*

²**fallow** *adj* **1** : left without tilling or sowing after plowing **2** : DORMANT, INACTIVE ⟨a writer's ∼ period⟩

false \'fȯls\ *adj* **fals·er; fals·est** **1** : not genuine : ARTIFICIAL ⟨∼ teeth⟩ **2** : intentionally untrue **3** : adjusted or made so as to deceive ⟨∼ scales⟩ **4** : tending to mislead : DECEPTIVE ⟨∼ promises⟩ **5** : not true ⟨∼ concepts⟩ **6** : not faithful or loyal : TREACHEROUS **7** : not essential or permanent ⟨∼ front⟩ **8** : inaccurate in pitch **9** : based on mistaken ideas — **false·ly** *adv* — **false·ness** *n* — **fal·si·ty** \'fȯl-sə-tē\ *n*

false·hood \'fȯls-ˌhu̇d\ *n* **1** : LIE **2** : absence of truth or accuracy **3** : the practice of lying

fal·set·to \fȯl-'se-tō\ *n, pl* **-tos** [It, fr. dim. of *falso* false] : an artificially high voice; *esp* : an artificial singing voice that overlaps and extends above the range of the full voice esp. of a tenor

fal·si·fy \'fȯl-sə-ˌfī\ *vb* **-fied; -fy·ing** **1** : to prove to be false **2** : to alter so as to deceive **3** : LIE; *also* : MISREPRESENT — **fal·si·fi·able** \ˌfȯl-sə-'fī-ə-bəl\ *adj* — **fal·si·fi·ca·tion** \ˌfȯl-sə-fə-'kā-shən\ *n*

fal·ter \'fȯl-tər\ *vb* **1** : to move unsteadily : STUMBLE, TOTTER **2** : to hesitate in speech : STAMMER **3** : to hesitate in purpose or action : WAVER, FLINCH **4** : to lose effectiveness ⟨a ∼ing business⟩ — **fal·ter·ing·ly** *adv*

fam *abbr* **1** familiar **2** family

fame \'fām\ *n* : public reputation : RENOWN — **famed** \'fāmd\ *adj*

fa·mil·ial \fə-'mil-yəl\ *adj* **1** : of, relating to, or suggestive of a family **2** : tending to occur in more members of a family than expected by chance alone ⟨a ∼ disorder⟩

¹**fa·mil·iar** \fə-'mil-yər\ *n* **1** : COMPANION **2** : a spirit held to attend and serve or guard a person **3** : one who frequents a place

²**familiar** *adj* **1** : closely acquainted : INTIMATE **2** : of or relating to a family **3** : INFORMAL **4** : FORWARD, PRESUMPTUOUS **5** : frequently seen or experienced **6** : of everyday occurrence — **fa·mil·iar·ly** *adv*

fa·mil·iar·ise *Brit var of* FAMILIARIZE

fa·mil·iar·i·ty \fə-ˌmil-'yer-ə-tē, -ˌmi-lē-'er-\ *n, pl* **-ties** **1** : close friendship : INTIMACY **2** : INFORMALITY **3** : an unduly bold or forward act or expression : IMPROPRIETY **4** : close acquaintance with something

fa·mil·iar·ize \fə-'mil-yə-ˌrīz\ *vb* **-ized; -iz·ing** **1** : to make known or familiar **2** : to make thoroughly acquainted

fam·i·ly \'fam-lē, 'fa-mə-\ *n, pl* **-lies** [ME *familie*, fr. L *fa-*

milia household, fr. *famulus* servant] **1** : a group of individuals living under one roof and under one head : HOUSEHOLD **2** : a group of persons of common ancestry : CLAN **3** : a group of things having common characteristics; *esp* : a group of related plants or animals ranking in biological classification above a genus and below an order **4** : a social unit usu. consisting of one or two parents and their children

family planning *n* : planning intended to determine the number and spacing of one's children by using birth control

family tree *n* : GENEALOGY; *also* : a genealogical diagram

fam·ine \'fa-mən\ *n* **1** : an extreme scarcity of food **2** : a great shortage

fam·ish \'fa-mish\ *vb* **1** : STARVE **2** : to suffer for lack of something necessary

fa·mous \'fā-məs\ *adj* **1** : widely known **2** : honored for achievement **3** : EXCELLENT, FIRST-RATE ✦ *Synonyms* RENOWNED, CELEBRATED, NOTED, NOTORIOUS, DISTINGUISHED, EMINENT, ILLUSTRIOUS

fa·mous·ly *adv* : SPLENDIDLY, EXCELLENTLY

¹**fan** \'fan\ *n* : a device (as a hand-waved triangular piece or a mechanism with blades) for producing a current of air

²**fan** *vb* **fanned; fan·ning** **1** : to drive away the chaff from grain by winnowing **2** : to move (air) with or as if with a fan **3** : to direct a current of air upon ⟨∼ a fire⟩ **4** : to stir up to activity : STIMULATE **5** : to spread like a fan **6** : to strike out in baseball

³**fan** *n* : an enthusiastic follower or admirer

fa·nat·ic \fə-'na-tik\ *or* **fa·nat·i·cal** \-ti-kəl\ *adj* [L *fanaticus* inspired by a deity, frenzied, fr. *fanum* temple] : marked by excessive enthusiasm and often intense uncritical devotion — **fanatic** *n* — **fa·nat·i·cism** \-tə-ˌsi-zəm\ *n*

fan·ci·er \'fan-sē-ər\ *n* **1** : one that has a special liking or interest **2** : a person who breeds or grows some kind of animal or plant for points of excellence

fan·ci·ful \'fan-si-fəl\ *adj* **1** : marked by, existing in, or given to unrestrained imagination or whim rather than reason **2** : curiously made or shaped ⟨a ∼ design⟩ — **fan·ci·ful·ly** *adv*

¹**fan·cy** \'fan-sē\ *vb* **fan·cied; fan·cy·ing** **1** : LIKE **2** : IMAGINE **3** : to believe without evidence or certainty **4** : to visualize or interpret as

²**fancy** *n, pl* **fancies** [ME *fantasie, fantsy* imagination, image, preference, fr. AF *fantasie* illusion, fr. L *phantasia*, fr. Gk, appearance, imagination] **1** : LIKING, INCLINATION; *also* : LOVE **2** : WHIM, NOTION, IDEA ⟨a passing ∼⟩ **3** : IMAGINATION **4** : TASTE, JUDGMENT ✦ *Synonyms* CAPRICE, CROTCHET, VAGARY

³**fancy** *adj* **fan·ci·er; -est** **1** : WHIMSICAL **2** : not plain : ORNAMENTAL, POSH **3** : of particular excellence **4** : bred esp. for a showy appearance **5** : EXCESSIVE **6** : executed with technical skill and style — **fan·ci·ly** \'fan-sə-lē\ *adv*

fancy dress *n* : a costume (as for a masquerade) chosen to suit a fancy

fan·cy—free \ˌfan-sē-'frē\ *adj* : free from amorous attachment; *also* : free to imagine

fan·cy·work \'fan-sē-ˌwərk\ *n* : ornamental needlework (as embroidery)

fan·dan·go \fan-'daŋ-gō\ *n, pl* **-gos** **1** : a lively Spanish or Spanish-American dance **2** : TOMFOOLERY

fane \'fān\ *n* **1** : TEMPLE **2** : CHURCH

fan·fare \'fan-ˌfer\ *n* **1** : a flourish of trumpets **2** : a showy display

fang \'faŋ\ *n* : a long sharp tooth; *esp* : a grooved or hollow tooth of a venomous snake — **fanged** \'faŋd\ *adj*

fan·light \'fan-ˌlīt\ *n* : a semicircular window with radiating bars like a fan that is set over a door or window

fan·ny \'fa-nē\ *n, pl* **fannies** : BUTTOCKS

fan·tail \'fan-ˌtāl\ *n* **1** : a fan-shaped tail or end **2** : an overhang at the stern of a ship

fan·ta·sia \fan-'tā-zhə, -zhē-ə, -zē-ə; ˌfan-tə-'zē-ə\ *n* : a musical composition free and fanciful in form

fan·ta·sise *Brit var of* FANTASIZE

fan·ta·size \'fan-tə-ˌsīz\ *vb* **-sized; -siz·ing** : IMAGINE, DAYDREAM

fan·tas·tic \fan-'tas-tik\ *also* **fan·tas·ti·cal** \-ti-kəl\ *adj* **1** : IMAGINARY, UNREAL **2** : conceived by unrestrained fancy **3** : exceedingly or unbelievably great **4** : ECCEN-

TRIC ♦ *Synonyms* CHIMERICAL, FANCIFUL, IMAGINARY — **fan·tas·ti·cal·ly** \-ti-k(ə-)lē\ *adv*

fan·ta·sy *also* **phan·ta·sy** \'fan-tə-sē\ *n, pl* **-sies** 1 : IMAGINATION, FANCY 2 : a product of the imagination : ILLUSION 3 : FANTASIA — **fantasy** *vb*

FAQ *abbr* frequently asked question

¹**far** \'fär\ *adv* **farther** \-<u>th</u>ər\ *or* **further** \'fər-\; **farthest** *or* **furthest** \-<u>th</u>əst\ 1 : at or to a considerable distance in space or time ⟨∼ from home⟩ 2 : by a broad interval : WIDELY, MUCH ⟨∼ better⟩ 3 : to or at a definite distance, point, or degree ⟨as ∼ as I know⟩ 4 : to an advanced point or extent ⟨go ∼ in his field⟩ — **by far** : by a considerable margin — **far and away** : DECIDEDLY — **so far** : until now

²**far** *adj* **farther** *or* **further; farthest** *or* **furthest** 1 : remote in space or time 2 : DIFFERENT 3 : LONG ⟨a ∼ journey⟩ 4 : being the more distant of two ⟨on the ∼ side of the lake⟩

far·ad \'fer-ˌad, -əd\ *n* : a unit of capacitance equal to the capacitance of a capacitor having a potential difference of one volt between its plates when it is charged with one coulomb of electricity

far·away \'fär-ə-ˌwä\ *adj* 1 : DISTANT, REMOTE ⟨∼ lands⟩ 2 : DREAMY

farce \'färs\ *n* 1 : a broadly satirical comedy with an improbable plot 2 : the humor characteristic of farce or pretense 3 : a ridiculous or empty display — **far·ci·cal** \'fär-si-kəl\ *adj*

far cry *n* 1 : a long distance 2 : something notably different ⟨a *far cry* from what we expected⟩

¹**fare** \'fer\ *vb* **fared; far·ing** 1 : GO, TRAVEL 2 : GET ALONG, SUCCEED ⟨*fared* well in math⟩ 3 : EAT, DINE

²**fare** *n* 1 : range of food : DIET; *also* : material provided for use, consumption, or enjoyment 2 : the price charged to transport a person 3 : a person paying a fare : PASSENGER

¹**fare·well** \fer-'wel\ *vb imper* : get along well — used interjectionally to or by one departing

²**farewell** *n* 1 : a wish of well-being at parting : GOOD-BYE 2 : LEAVE-TAKING

³**fare·well** \'fer-ˌwel\ *adj* : PARTING, FINAL ⟨a ∼ concert⟩

far–fetched \'fär-'fecht\ *adj* : not easily or naturally deduced or introduced : IMPROBABLE ⟨a ∼ story⟩

far–flung \-'fləŋ\ *adj* : widely spread or distributed ⟨a ∼ empire⟩

fa·ri·na \fə-'rē-nə\ *n* [L, meal, flour] : a fine meal (as of wheat) used in puddings or as a breakfast cereal

far·i·na·ceous \ˌfer-ə-'nā-shəs\ *adj* 1 : having a mealy texture or surface 2 : containing or rich in starch

¹**farm** \'färm\ *n* [ME *ferme* rent, lease, fr. AF, fr. *fermer* to fix, rent, fr. L *firmare* to make firm, fr. *firmus* firm] 1 : a tract of land used for raising crops or livestock 2 : a minor-league subsidiary of a major-league team

²**farm** *vb* : to use (land) as a farm ⟨∼ed 200 acres⟩; *also* : to raise crops or livestock — **farm·er** *n*

farm·hand \'färm-ˌhand\ *n* : a farm laborer

farm·house \-ˌhau̇s\ *n* : a dwelling on a farm

farm·ing \'fär-miŋ\ *n* : the occupation or business of a person who farms

farm·land \'färm-ˌland\ *n* : land used or suitable for farming

farm out *vb* : to turn over (as a task) to another

farm·stead \'färm-ˌsted\ *n* : a farm with its buildings

farm·yard \-ˌyärd\ *n* : land around or enclosed by farm buildings

far–off \'fär-'ȯf\ *adj* : remote in time or space : DISTANT

fa·rouche \fə-'rüsh\ *adj* [F] 1 : WILD 2 : marked by shyness and lack of polish

far–out \'fär-'au̇t\ *adj* : very unconventional ⟨∼ clothes⟩

far·ra·go \fə-'rä-gō, -'rā-\ *n, pl* **-goes** [L, mixed fodder, mixture] : a confused collection : MIXTURE

far–reach·ing \'fär-'rē-chiŋ\ *adj* : having a wide range or effect

far·ri·er \'fer-ē-ər\ *n* [alter. of ME *ferrour*, fr. AF, blacksmith, fr. *ferrer* to shoe (horses)] : a person who shoes horses

¹**far·row** \'fer-ō\ *vb* : to give birth to a litter of pigs

²**farrow** *n* : a litter of pigs

far·see·ing \'fär-ˌsē-iŋ\ *adj* 1 : FARSIGHTED 1 2 : FARSIGHTED 2

far·sight·ed \'fär-ˌsī-təd\ *adj* 1 : seeing or able to see to a

great distance 2 : JUDICIOUS, WISE, SHREWD 3 : affected with an eye condition in which vision is better for distant than near objects — **far·sight·ed·ness** *n*

¹**far·ther** \'fär-<u>th</u>ər\ *adv* 1 : at or to a greater distance or more advanced point 2 : to a greater degree or extent

²**farther** *adj* 1 : more distant 2 : ADDITIONAL

far·ther·most \-ˌmōst\ *adj* : FARTHEST

¹**far·thest** \'fär-<u>th</u>əst\ *adj* : most distant

²**farthest** *adv* 1 : to or at the greatest distance : REMOTEST 2 : to the most advanced point 3 : by the greatest degree or extent : MOST

far·thing \'fär-<u>th</u>iŋ\ *n* 1 : a former British monetary unit equal to $\frac{1}{4}$ of a penny; *also* : a coin representing this unit 2 : something of small value

fas·cia *1 is usu* 'fä-sh(ē-)ə, *2 is usu* 'fa-\ *n, pl* **-ci·ae** \-shē-ˌē\ *or* **-cias** 1 : a flat usu. horizontal part (as a band or board) of or on a building 2 : a sheet of connective tissue covering body structures (as muscles)

fas·ci·cle \'fa-si-kəl\ *n* 1 : a small or slender bundle (as of pine needles or nerve fibers) 2 : one of the divisions of a book published in parts — **fas·ci·cled** \-kəld\ *adj*

fas·ci·nate \'fa-sə-ˌnāt\ *vb* **-nat·ed; -nat·ing** [L *fascinare*, fr. *fascinum* evil spell] 1 : to transfix and hold spellbound by an irresistible power 2 : ALLURE 3 : to be irresistibly attractive — **fas·ci·na·tion** \ˌfa-sə-'nā-shən\ *n*

fas·cism \'fa-ˌshi-zəm\ *n, often cap* : a political philosophy, movement, or regime that exalts nation and often race and stands for a centralized autocratic often militaristic government — **fas·cist** \-shist\ *n or adj, often cap* — **fas·cis·tic** \fa-'shis-tik\ *adj, often cap*

¹**fash·ion** \'fa-shən\ *n* 1 : the make or form of something 2 : MANNER, WAY 3 : a prevailing custom, usage, or style 4 : the prevailing style (as in dress) ♦ *Synonyms* MODE, VOGUE, RAGE, TREND

²**fashion** *vb* 1 : MOLD, CONSTRUCT 2 : FIT, ADAPT

fash·ion·able \'fa-shə-nə-bəl\ *adj* 1 : dressing or behaving according to fashion : STYLISH 2 : of or relating to the world of fashion ⟨∼ resorts⟩ ♦ *Synonyms* CHIC, MODISH, SMART, SWANK — **fash·ion·ably** \-blē\ *adv*

¹**fast** \'fast\ *adj* 1 : firmly fixed 2 : tightly shut 3 : adhering firmly 4 : STUCK 5 : STAUNCH ⟨∼ friends⟩ 6 : characterized by quick motion, operation, or effect ⟨a ∼ trip⟩ 7 : indicating ahead of the correct time ⟨the clock is ∼⟩ 8 : not easily disturbed : SOUND ⟨a ∼ sleep⟩ 9 : permanently dyed; *also* : being proof against fading ⟨colors ∼ to sunlight⟩ 10 : DISSIPATED, WILD 11 : sexually promiscuous ♦ *Synonyms* RAPID, SWIFT, FLEET, QUICK, SPEEDY, HASTY

²**fast** *adv* 1 : in a firm or fixed manner ⟨stuck ∼ in the mud⟩ 2 : SOUNDLY, DEEPLY ⟨∼ asleep⟩ 3 : SWIFTLY 4 : RECKLESSLY

³**fast** *vb* 1 : to abstain from food 2 : to eat sparingly or abstain from some foods

⁴**fast** *n* 1 : the act or practice of fasting 2 : a time of fasting

fast·back \'fast-ˌbak\ *n* : an automobile having a roof with a long slope to the rear

fast·ball \-ˌbȯl\ *n* : a baseball pitch thrown at full speed

fas·ten \'fa-sᵊn\ *vb* 1 : to attach or join by or as if by pinning, tying, or nailing 2 : to make fast : fix securely 3 : to become fixed or joined 4 : to focus attention ⟨∼ed onto the newest trends⟩ — **fas·ten·er** *n*

fas·ten·ing *n* : something that fastens : FASTENER

fast–food \ˌfast-'füd\ *adj* : specializing in food that is prepared and served quickly ⟨a ∼ restaurant⟩

fast–for·ward \-'fȯr-wərd\ *n* 1 : a function of an electronic device that advances a recording rapidly 2 : a state of rapid advancement — **fast–forward** *vb*

fas·tid·i·ous \fa-'sti-dē-əs\ *adj* 1 : overly difficult to please 2 : showing a meticulous or demanding attitude ⟨∼ workmanship⟩ ♦ *Synonyms* NICE, FINICKY, FUSSY, PARTICULAR, PERSNICKETY, SQUEAMISH — **fas·tid·i·ous·ly** *adv* — **fas·tid·i·ous·ness** *n*

fast·ness \'fast-nəs\ *n* 1 : the quality or state of being fast 2 : a fortified or secure place : STRONGHOLD

fast–talk \'fast-ˌtȯk\ *vb* : to influence by persuasive and usu. deceptive talk

fast–track \'fast-ˌtrak\ *vb* : to speed up the processing or production of

fast track *n* : a course leading to rapid advancement or success

¹**fat** \'fat\ *adj* **fat·ter; fat·test** **1** : PLUMP, OBESE **2** : OILY, GREASY **3** : well filled out : BIG **4** : well stocked : ABUNDANT **5** : richly rewarding — **fat·ness** *n*

²**fat** *n* **1** : animal tissue rich in greasy or oily matter **2** : any of various energy-rich esters that occur naturally in animal fats and in plants and are soluble in organic solvents (as ether) but not in water **3** : the best or richest portion ⟨lived on the ∼ of the land⟩ **4** : OBESITY **5** : excess matter

fa·tal \'fāt-ᵊl\ *adj* **1** : FATEFUL ⟨that ∼ day⟩ **2** : causing death or ruin ⟨a ∼ mistake⟩ — **fa·tal·ly** *adv*

fa·tal·ism \-ˌi-zəm\ *n* : the belief that events are determined by fate — **fa·tal·ist** \-ist\ *n* — **fa·tal·is·tic** \ˌfāt-ᵊl-'is-tik\ *adj* — **fa·tal·is·ti·cal·ly** \-ti-k(ə-)lē\ *adv*

fa·tal·i·ty \fā-'ta-lə-tē, fə-\ *n, pl* **-ties 1** : DEADLINESS **2** : FATE **3** : death resulting from a disaster or accident; *also* : one who suffers such a death

fat·back \'fat-ˌbak\ *n* : a fatty strip from the back of the hog usu. cured by salting and drying

fat cat *n* **1** : a wealthy contributor to a political campaign **2** : a wealthy privileged person

fate \'fāt\ *n* [ME, fr. MF or L; MF, fr. L *fatum*, lit., what has been spoken, fr. *fari* to speak] **1** : the cause or will that is held to determine events : DESTINY **2** : LOT, FORTUNE **3** : DISASTER; *esp* : DEATH **4** : END, OUTCOME **5** *pl, cap* : the three goddesses of classical mythology who determine the course of human life

fat·ed \'fā-təd\ *adj* : decreed, controlled, or marked by fate

fate·ful \'fāt-fəl\ *adj* **1** : OMINOUS, PROPHETIC **2** : IMPORTANT, DECISIVE **3** : DEADLY, DESTRUCTIVE **4** : determined by fate — **fate·ful·ly** *adv*

fath *abbr* fathom

fat·head \'fat-ˌhed\ *n* : a stupid person — **fat·head·ed** \-'he-dəd\ *adj*

¹**fa·ther** \'fä-thər\ *n* **1** : a male parent **2** *cap* : God esp. as the first person of the Trinity **3** : FOREFATHER **4** : one deserving the respect and love given to a father **5** *often cap* : an early Christian writer accepted by the church as an authoritative witness to its teaching and practice **6** : ORIGINATOR ⟨the ∼ of modern radio⟩; *also* : SOURCE **7** : PRIEST — used esp. as a title **8** : one of the leading men ⟨city ∼s⟩ — **fa·ther·hood** \-ˌhud\ *n* — **fa·ther·less** *adj* — **fa·ther·ly** *adj*

²**father** *vb* **1** : BEGET **2** : to be the founder, producer, or author of **3** : to treat or care for as a father

father-in-law \'fä-thə-rən-ˌlo\ *n, pl* **fa·thers-in-law** \-thər-zən-\ : the father of one's husband or wife

fa·ther·land \'fä-thər-ˌland\ *n* **1** : the native land of one's ancestors **2** : one's native land

¹**fath·om** \'fa-thəm\ *n* [ME *fadme*, fr. OE *fæthm* length of the outstretched arms] : a unit of length equal to 6 feet (about 1.8 meters) used esp. for measuring the depth of water

²**fathom** *vb* **1** : to measure by a sounding line **2** : PROBE **3** : to penetrate and come to understand — **fath·om·able** \'fa-thə-mə-bəl\ *adj*

fath·om·less \'fa-thəm-ləs\ *adj* : incapable of being fathomed

¹**fa·tigue** \fə-'tēg\ *n* [F] **1** : manual or menial work performed by military personnel **2** *pl* : the uniform or work clothing worn on fatigue and in the field **3** : weariness from labor or stress **4** : the tendency of a material to break under repeated stress

²**fatigue** *vb* **fa·tigued; fa·tigu·ing** : WEARY, TIRE

fat·ten \'fa-tᵊn\ *vb* : to make or grow fat

Fat Tuesday *n* : MARDI GRAS

¹**fat·ty** \'fa-tē\ *adj* **fat·ti·er; -est 1** : containing fat esp. in unusual amounts **2** : GREASY

²**fatty** *n, pl* **fat·ties** : a fat person

fatty acid *n* : any of numerous acids that contain only carbon, hydrogen, and oxygen and that occur naturally in fats and various oils

fa·tu·ity \fə-'tü-ə-tē, -'tyü-\ *n, pl* **-ities** : FOOLISHNESS, STUPIDITY

fat·u·ous \'fa-chù-wəs\ *adj* : FOOLISH, INANE, SILLY — **fat·u·ous·ly** *adv*

fau·bourg \fō-'bùr\ *n* **1** : a suburb esp. of a French city **2** : a city quarter

fau·ces \'fo-ˌsēz\ *n pl* [L, throat] : the narrow passage located between the soft palate and the base of the tongue that joins the mouth to the pharynx

fau·cet \'fo-sət, 'fä-\ *n* : a fixture for drawing off a liquid (as from a pipe)

¹**fault** \'folt\ *n* **1** : a weakness in character : FAILING **2** : IMPERFECTION, IMPAIRMENT, DEFECT **3** : an error esp. in service in a net or racket game **4** : MISDEMEANOR; *also* : MISTAKE **5** : responsibility for something wrong **6** : a fracture in the earth's crust accompanied by a displacement of one side relative to the other — **fault·i·ly** \'fol-tə-lē\ *adv* — **fault·less** *adj* — **fault·less·ly** *adv* — **faulty** *adj*

²**fault** *vb* **1** : to commit a fault : ERR **2** : to fracture so as to produce a geologic fault **3** : to find a fault in

fault·find·er \'folt-ˌfīn-dər\ *n* : a person who tends to find fault or complain ◆ *Synonyms* CRITIC, CARPER, CAVILER, COMPLAINER — **fault·find·ing** *n or adj*

faun \'fon\ *n* : a Roman god similar to but gentler than a satyr

fau·na \'fo-nə\ *n, pl* **faunas** *also* **fau·nae** \-ˌnē, -ˌnī\ [NL, fr. L *Fauna*, sister of Faunus (the Roman god of animals)] : animals or animal life esp. of a region, period, or environment — **fau·nal** \-nəl\ *adj*

fau·vism \'fo-ˌvi-zəm\ *n, often cap* : a movement in painting characterized by vivid colors, free treatment of form, and a vibrant and decorative effect — **fau·vist** \-vist\ *n, often cap*

faux pas \'fō-ˌpä, fo-'\ *n, pl* **faux pas** ⟨*same or* -ˌpäz, -'päz⟩ [F, lit., false step] : BLUNDER; *esp* : a social blunder

fa·va bean \'fä-və-\ *n* : the large flat edible seed of an Old World vetch; *also* : this plant

¹**fa·vor** \'fā-vər\ *n* **1** : friendly regard shown toward another esp. by a superior **2** : APPROVAL **3** : PARTIALITY **4** : POPULARITY **5** : gracious kindness; *also* : an act of such kindness **6** *pl* : effort in one's behalf **7** : a token of love (as a ribbon) usu. worn conspicuously **8** : a small gift or decorative item given out at a party **9** : a special privilege **10** : special privileges — usu. used in pl. **11** *archaic* : LETTER **12** : BEHALF, INTEREST

²**favor** *vb* **1** : to regard or treat with favor **2** : OBLIGE **3** : ENDOW ⟨∼ed by nature⟩ **4** : to treat gently or carefully : SPARE ⟨∼ a lame leg⟩ **5** : PREFER **6** : SUPPORT, SUSTAIN **7** : FACILITATE ⟨darkness ∼s attack⟩ **8** : RESEMBLE ⟨he ∼s his father⟩

fa·vor·able \'fā-və-rə-bəl\ *adj* **1** : APPROVING **2** : HELPFUL, PROMISING, ADVANTAGEOUS ⟨∼ weather⟩ — **fa·vor·ably** \-blē\ *adv*

fa·vor·ite \'fā-və-rət, -vrət\ *n* **1** : a person or a thing that is favored above others **2** : a competitor regarded as most likely to win — **favorite** *adj*

favorite son *n* : a candidate supported by the delegates of his state at a presidential nominating convention

fa·vor·it·ism \'fā-və-rə-ˌti-zəm\ *n* : PARTIALITY, BIAS

fa·vour *chiefly Brit var of* FAVOR

¹**fawn** \'fon, 'fän\ *vb* **1** : to show affection ⟨a dog ∼ing on its master⟩ **2** : to court favor by a cringing or flattering manner ◆ *Synonyms* GROVEL, KOWTOW, TOADY, TRUCKLE

²**fawn** *n* **1** : a young deer **2** : a light grayish brown — **fawny** \'fo-nē, 'fä-\ *adj*

fax \'faks\ *n* **1** : FACSIMILE 2 **2** : a device used to send or receive facsimile communications; *also* : such a communication — **fax** *vb*

fay \'fā\ *n* : FAIRY, ELF — **fay** *adj*

faze \'fāz\ *vb* **fazed; faz·ing** : to disturb the composure or courage of : DAUNT

FBI *abbr* Federal Bureau of Investigation

FCC *abbr* Federal Communications Commission

FD *abbr* fire department

FDA *abbr* Food and Drug Administration

FDIC *abbr* Federal Deposit Insurance Corporation

Fe *symbol* [L *ferrum*] iron

fe·al·ty \'fē(-ə)l-tē\ *n, pl* **-ties** : LOYALTY, ALLEGIANCE ◆ *Synonyms* FIDELITY, DEVOTION, FAITHFULNESS, PIETY

¹**fear** \'fir\ *vb* **1** : to have a reverent awe of ⟨∼ God⟩ **2** : to be afraid of ⟨∼s spiders⟩ **3** : to be apprehensive

²**fear** *n* **1** : an unpleasant often strong emotion caused by expectation or awareness of danger; *also* : an instance of or a state marked by this emotion **2** : anxious concern : SOLICITUDE **3** : profound reverence esp. toward God ◆ *Synonyms* DREAD, FRIGHT, ALARM, PANIC, TERROR, TREPIDATION

fear·ful \-fəl\ *adj* **1** : causing fear **2** : filled with fear **3** : showing or caused by fear **4** : extremely bad, intense, or large — **fear·ful·ly** *adv*

fear·less \-ləs\ *adj* : free from fear : BRAVE — **fear·less·ly** *adv* — **fear·less·ness** *n*

fear·some \-səm\ *adj* **1** : causing fear **2** : TIMID **3** : INTENSE ⟨~ determination⟩

fea·si·ble \'fē-zə-bəl\ *adj* [ME *faisible*, fr. AF *faisable*, fr. *fais-*, stem of *faire* to make, do] **1** : capable of being done or carried out ⟨a ~ plan⟩ **2** : SUITABLE **3** : REASONABLE, LIKELY ◆ **Synonyms** POSSIBLE, PRACTICABLE, VIABLE, WORKABLE — **fea·si·bil·i·ty** \,fē-zə-'bi-lə-tē\ *n* — **fea·si·bly** \'fē-zə-blē\ *adv*

¹**feast** \'fēst\ *n* **1** : an elaborate meal : BANQUET **2** : ABUNDANCE ⟨a ~ of good books⟩ **3** : FESTIVAL 1

²**feast** *vb* **1** : to take part in a feast; *also* : to give a feast for **2** : to enjoy some unusual pleasure or delight **3** : DELIGHT, GRATIFY

feat \'fēt\ *n* : DEED, EXPLOIT, ACHIEVEMENT; *esp* : an act notable for courage, skill, endurance, or ingenuity

¹**feath·er** \'fe-thər\ *n* **1** : any of the light horny outgrowths that form the external covering of the body of a bird **2** : the vane of an arrow **3** : PLUMAGE **4** : KIND, NATURE ⟨birds of a ~⟩ **5** : ATTIRE, DRESS ⟨in full ~⟩ **6** : CONDITION, MOOD ⟨in fine ~⟩ — **feath·ered** \-thərd\ *adj* — **feath·er·less** *adj* — **feath·ery** *adj* — **a feather in one's cap** : a mark of distinction : HONOR

feather 1

²**feather** *vb* **1** : to furnish with a feather ⟨~ an arrow⟩ **2** : to cover, clothe, line, or adorn with or as if with feathers — **feather one's nest** : to provide for oneself financially esp. while exploiting a position of trust

feath·er·bed·ding \'fe-thər-,be-diŋ\ *n* : the requiring of an employer usu. under a union rule or safety statute to employ more workers than are needed

feath·er·edge \-,ej\ *n* : a very thin sharp edge

feath·er·weight \-,wāt\ *n* : one that is very light in weight; *esp* : a boxer weighing more than 118 but not over 126 pounds

¹**fea·ture** \'fē-chər\ *n* [ME *feture*, fr. AF, fr. L *factura* act of making, fr. *facere* to make] **1** : the shape or appearance of the face or its parts **2** : a part of the face : LINEAMENT **3** : a prominent part or characteristic **4** : a special attraction (as in a newspaper) **5** : something offered to the public or advertised as particularly attractive ⟨a new car's ~s⟩ — **fea·ture·less** *adj*

²**feature** *vb* **1** : to picture in the mind : IMAGINE **2** : to give special prominence to ⟨the show ~s new artists⟩ **3** : to play an important part

Feb *abbr* February

fe·brile \'fe-,brī(-ə)l\ *adj* : FEVERISH

Feb·ru·ary \'fe-b(y)ə-,wer-ē, 'fe-brə-\ *n* [ME *Februarie*, fr. L *Februarius*, fr. *Februa*, pl., feast of purification] : the 2d month of the year

fe·ces \'fē-,sēz\ *n pl* : bodily waste discharged from the intestine : EXCREMENT — **fe·cal** \-kəl\ *adj*

feck·less \'fek-ləs\ *adj* **1** : WEAK, INEFFECTIVE **2** : WORTHLESS, IRRESPONSIBLE

fe·cund \'fe-kənd, 'fē-\ *adj* : FRUITFUL, PROLIFIC — **fe·cun·di·ty** \fi-'kən-də-tē, fe-\ *n*

fe·cun·date \'fe-kən-,dāt, 'fē-\ *vb* **-dat·ed; -dat·ing** **1** : to make fecund : IMPREGNATE — **fe·cun·da·tion** \,fe-kən-'dā-shən, ,fē-\ *n*

fed *abbr* federal; federation

fed·er·al \'fe-də-rəl, -drəl\ *adj* **1** : formed by a compact between political units that surrender individual sovereignty to a central authority but retain certain limited powers **2** : of or constituting a form of government in which power is distributed between a central authority and constituent territorial units **3** : of or relating to the central government of a federation **4** *cap* : FEDERALIST **5** *often cap* : of, relating to, or loyal to the federal government or the Union armies of the U.S. in the American Civil War — **fed·er·al·ly** *adv*

Federal *n* : a supporter of the U.S. government in the Civil War; *esp* : a soldier in the federal armies

federal district *n* : a district (as the District of Columbia) set apart as the seat of the central government of a federation

fed·er·al·ism \'fe-də-rə-,li-zəm, -drə-\ *n* **1** *often cap* : the distribution of power in an organization (as a government) between a central authority and the constituent units **2** : support or advocacy of federalism **3** *cap* : the principles of the Federalists

fed·er·al·ist \-list\ *n* **1** : an advocate of federalism **2** *often cap* : an advocate of a federal union between the American colonies after the Revolution and of adoption of the U.S. Constitution **3** *cap* : a member of a major political party in the early years of the U.S. favoring a strong centralized national government — **federalist** *adj, often cap*

fed·er·al·ize \'fe-də-rə-,līz, -drə-\ *vb* **-ized; -iz·ing** **1** : to unite in or under a federal system **2** : to bring under the jurisdiction of a federal government

fed·er·ate \'fe-də-,rāt\ *vb* **-at·ed; -at·ing** : to join in a federation

fed·er·a·tion \,fe-də-'rā-shən\ *n* **1** : a political or societal entity formed by uniting smaller entities **2** : a federal government **3** : a union of organizations **4** : the forming of a federal union

fedn *abbr* federation

fe·do·ra \fi-'dȯr-ə\ *n* : a low soft felt hat with the crown creased lengthwise

fed up *adj* : utterly sated, tired, or disgusted

fee \'fē\ *n* [ME, fr. AF *fé, fief*, of Gmc origin; akin to OE *feoh* cattle, property] **1** : an estate in land held from a feudal lord **2** : an inherited or heritable estate in land **3** : a fixed charge; *also* : a charge for a service

fee·ble \'fē-bəl\ *adj* **fee·bler** \-bə-lər\; **fee·blest** \-bə-ləst\ [ME *feble*, fr. AF, fr. L *flebilis* lamentable, wretched, fr. *flēre* to weep] **1** : DECREPIT, FRAIL **2** : INEFFECTIVE, INADEQUATE ⟨a ~ protest⟩ — **fee·ble·ness** *n* — **fee·bly** \-blē\ *adv*

fee·ble·mind·ed \,fē-bəl-'mīn-dəd\ *adj* : lacking normal intelligence — **fee·ble·mind·ed·ness** *n*

¹**feed** \'fēd\ *vb* **fed** \'fed\; **feed·ing** **1** : to give food to; *also* : to give as food **2** : EAT; *also* : PREY **3** : to furnish what is necessary to the development or function of **4** : to supply for another to use ⟨~ a pass⟩ ⟨fed the actor his lines⟩ — **feed·er** *n*

²**feed** *n* **1** : a usu. large meal **2** : food for livestock **3** : a mechanism for feeding material to a machine

feed·back \'fēd-,bak\ *n* **1** : the return to the input of a part of the output of a machine, system, or process **2** : response esp. to one in authority about an activity or policy **3** : sound (as whistling) resulting from the retransmission of an amplified or broadcast signal

feed·lot \'fēd-,lät\ *n* : land on which cattle are fattened for market

feed·stuff \-,stəf\ *n* : FEED 2

¹**feel** \'fēl\ *vb* **felt** \'felt\; **feel·ing** **1** : to perceive or examine through physical contact : TOUCH, HANDLE **2** : EXPERIENCE; *also* : to suffer from **3** : to ascertain by cautious trial ⟨~ out public sentiment⟩ **4** : to be aware of **5** : to be conscious of an inward impression, state of mind, or physical condition **6** : BELIEVE, THINK ⟨say what you ~⟩ **7** : to search for something with the fingers : GROPE **8** : SEEM ⟨it ~s like spring⟩ **9** : to have sympathy or pity

²**feel** *n* **1** : the sense of touch **2** : SENSATION, FEELING **3** : the quality of a thing as imparted through touch

feel·er \'fē-lər\ *n* **1** : one that feels; *esp* : a tactile organ (as on the head of an insect) **2** : a proposal or remark made to find out the views of other people

¹**feel·ing** \'fē-liŋ\ *n* **1** : the sense of touch; *also* : a sensation perceived by this **2** : a state of mind ⟨a ~ of loneliness⟩ **3** *pl* : general emotional condition : SENSIBILITIES ⟨hurt their ~s⟩ **4** : OPINION, BELIEF **5** : capacity to respond emotionally

²**feeling** *adj* **1** : SENSITIVE; *esp* : easily moved emotionally **2** : expressing emotion or sensitivity — **feel·ing·ly** *adv*

feet *pl of* FOOT

feign \'fān\ *vb* **1** : to give a false appearance of : SHAM ⟨∼ illness⟩ **2** : to assert as if true : PRETEND

feint \'fānt\ *n* : something feigned; *esp* : a mock blow or attack intended to distract attention from the real point of attack — **feint** *vb*

feisty \'fī-stē\ *adj* **feist·i·er; -est** : having or showing a lively aggressiveness ⟨a ∼ heroine⟩

feld·spar \'feld-ˌspär\ *n* : any of a group of crystalline minerals consisting of silicates of aluminum with another element (as potassium or sodium)

fe·lic·i·tate \fi-'li-sə-ˌtāt\ *vb* **-tat·ed; -tat·ing** : CONGRATULATE — **fe·lic·i·ta·tion** \-ˌli-sə-'tā-shən\ *n*

fe·lic·i·tous \fi-'li-sə-təs\ *adj* **1** : well chosen : APT **2** : PLEASANT, DELIGHTFUL — **fe·lic·i·tous·ly** *adv*

fe·lic·i·ty \fi-'li-sə-tē\ *n, pl* **-ties** **1** : the quality or state of being happy; *esp* : great happiness **2** : something that causes happiness **3** : a pleasing manner or quality esp. in art or language **4** : an apt expression

fe·line \'fē-ˌlīn\ *adj* [L *felinus*, fr. *felis* cat] **1** : of or relating to cats or their kin **2** : SLY, TREACHEROUS **3** : STEALTHY — **feline** *n*

¹fell \'fel\ *n* : SKIN, HIDE, PELT

²fell *vb* **1** : to cut, beat, or knock down; *also* : KILL **2** : to sew (a seam) by folding one raw edge under the other

³fell *past of* FALL

⁴fell *adj* : CRUEL, FIERCE; *also* : DEADLY — **in one fell swoop** *also* **at one fell swoop** : all at once : with a single effort

fel·lah \'fe-lə, fə-'lä\ *n, pl* **fel·la·hin** *or* **fel·la·heen** \ˌfe-lə-'hēn\ : a peasant or agricultural laborer in Arab countries (as Egypt or Syria)

fel·la·tio \fə-'lā-shē-ˌō\ *also* **fel·la·tion** \-shən\ *n* : oral stimulation of the penis

fel·low \'fe-lō\ *n* [ME *felawe*, fr. OE *fēolaga*, fr. ON *fēlagi*, fr. *fēlag* partnership (fr. *fē* cattle, money) + *lag* act of laying] **1** : COMRADE, ASSOCIATE **2** : EQUAL, PEER **3** : one of a pair : MATE **4** : a member of an incorporated literary or scientific society **5** : MAN, BOY **6** : BOYFRIEND **7** : a person granted a stipend for advanced study

fellow man *n* : a kindred human being

fel·low·ship \'fe-lō-ˌship\ *n* **1** : the condition of friendly relationship existing among persons : COMRADESHIP **2** : a community of interest or feeling **3** : a group with similar interests **4** : the position of a fellow (as of a university) **5** : the stipend granted a fellow

fellow traveler *n* : a sympathetic supporter of another's cause; *esp* : a person who sympathizes with and often furthers the ideals and program of an organized group (as the Communist party) without joining it

fel·on \'fe-lən\ *n* **1** : one who has committed a felony **2** : WHITLOW

fel·o·ny \'fe-lə-nē\ *n, pl* **-nies** : a serious crime punishable by a heavy sentence — **fe·lo·ni·ous** \fə-'lō-nē-əs\ *adj*

fel·spar *chiefly Brit var of* FELDSPAR

¹felt \'felt\ *n* **1** : a cloth made of wool and fur often mixed with natural or synthetic fibers **2** : a material resembling felt

²felt *past and past part of* FEEL

fem *abbr* **1** female **2** feminine

fe·male \'fē-ˌmāl\ *adj* [ME, alter. of *femel*, fr. AF *femele*, fr. ML *femella*, fr. L, girl, dim. of *femina* woman] **1** : of, relating to, or being the sex that bears young; *also* : PISTILLATE **2** : characteristic of girls or women ⟨∼ voices⟩ ♦ **Synonyms** FEMININE, WOMANLY, WOMANLIKE, WOMANISH, EFFEMINATE — **female** *n*

¹fem·i·nine \'fe-mə-nən\ *adj* **1** : of the female sex; *also* : characteristic of or appropriate or peculiar to women **2** : of, relating to, or constituting the gender that includes most words or grammatical forms referring to females — **fem·i·nin·i·ty** \ˌfe-mə-'ni-nə-tē\ *n*

²feminine *n* : a noun, pronoun, adjective, or inflectional form or class of the feminine gender; *also* : the feminine gender

fem·i·nism \'fe-mə-ˌni-zəm\ *n* **1** : the theory of the political, economic, and social equality of the sexes **2** : organized activity on behalf of women's rights and interests — **fem·i·nist** \-nist\ *n or adj*

femme fa·tale \ˌfem-fə-'tal\ *n, pl* **femmes fa·tales** *same or* -'talz\ [F, lit., disastrous woman] : a seductive woman

fe·mur \'fē-mər\ *n, pl* **fe·murs** *or* **fem·o·ra** \'fe-mə-rə\ : the long leg bone extending from the hip to the knee — **fem·o·ral** \'fe-mə-rəl\ *adj*

¹fen \'fen\ *n* : low swampy land

²fen \'fən\ *n, pl* **fen** — see *yuan* at MONEY table

¹fence \'fens\ *n* [ME *fens*, short for *defens* defense] **1** : a barrier (as of wood or wire) to prevent escape or entry or to mark a boundary **2** : a person who receives stolen goods; *also* : a place where stolen goods are disposed of — **on the fence** : in a position of neutrality or indecision

²fence *vb* **fenced; fenc·ing** **1** : to enclose with a fence **2** : to keep in or out with a fence **3** : to practice fencing **4** : to use tactics of attack and defense esp. in debate — **fenc·er** *n*

fenc·ing *n* **1** : the art or practice of attack and defense with the foil, épée, or saber **2** : the fences of a property or region **3** : material used for building fences

fend \'fend\ *vb* **1** : to keep or ward off : REPEL **2** : SHIFT ⟨∼ for yourself⟩

fend·er \'fen-dər\ *n* : a protective device (as a guard over the wheel of an automobile)

fen·es·tra·tion \ˌfe-nə-'strā-shən\ *n* : the arrangement and design of windows and doors in a building

Fe·ni·an \'fē-nē-ən\ *n* : a member of a secret 19th century Irish and Irish-American organization dedicated to overthrowing British rule in Ireland

fen·nel \'fe-nᵊl\ *n* : a garden plant related to the carrot and grown for its aromatic foliage and seeds

FEPC *abbr* Fair Employment Practices Commission

fe·ral \'fir-əl, 'fer-\ *adj* **1** : SAVAGE **2** : WILD 1 **3** : having escaped from domestication and become wild

fer–de–lance \'fer-də-'lans\ *n, pl* **fer–de–lance** [F, lit., lance iron, spearhead] : a large venomous pit viper of Central and So. America

¹fer·ment \fər-'ment\ *vb* **1** : to cause or undergo fermentation **2** : to be or cause to be in a state of agitation or intense activity

²fer·ment \'fər-ˌment\ *n* **1** : a living organism (as a yeast) causing fermentation by its enzymes; *also* : ENZYME **2** : AGITATION, TUMULT

fer·men·ta·tion \ˌfər-mən-'tā-shən, -ˌmen-\ *n* **1** : chemical decomposition of an organic substance (as in the souring of milk or the formation of alcohol from sugar) by enzymatic action in the absence of oxygen often with formation of gas **2** : FERMENT 2

fer·mi·um \'fer-mē-əm, 'fər-\ *n* : an artificially produced radioactive metallic chemical element

fern \'fərn\ *n* : any of an order of vascular plants resembling seed plants in having roots, stems, and leaflike fronds but reproducing by spores instead of by flowers and seeds

fern·ery \'fər-nə-rē\ *n, pl* **-er·ies** **1** : a place for growing ferns **2** : a collection of growing ferns

fe·ro·cious \fə-'rō-shəs\ *adj* **1** : FIERCE, SAVAGE **2** : extremely intense — **fe·ro·cious·ly** *adv* — **fe·ro·cious·ness** *n*

fe·roc·i·ty \fə-'rä-sə-tē\ *n* : the quality or state of being ferocious

¹fer·ret \'fer-ət\ *n* : a partially domesticated usu. white European mammal related to the weasels

²ferret *vb* **1** : to hunt game with ferrets **2** : to drive out of a hiding place **3** : to find and bring to light by searching ⟨∼ out the truth⟩

fer·ric \'fer-ik\ *adj* : of, relating to, or containing iron

ferric oxide *n* : an oxide of iron found in nature as hematite and as rust and used esp. as a pigment, for polishing, and in magnetic materials

Fer·ris wheel \'fer-əs-\ *n* : an amusement device consisting of a large upright power-driven wheel with seats that remain horizontal around its rim

fer·ro·mag·net·ic \ˌfer-ō-mag-'ne-tik\ *adj* : of or relating to substances that are easily magnetized

fer·rous \'fer-əs\ *adj* : of, relating to, or containing iron

fer·rule \'fer-əl\ *n* : a metal ring or cap around a slender wooden shaft to prevent splitting

¹fer·ry \'fer-ē\ *vb* **fer·ried; fer·ry·ing** [ME *ferien*, fr. OE *ferian* to carry, convey] **1** : to carry by boat across a body of water **2** : to cross by a ferry **3** : to convey from one place to another

²ferry *n, pl* **ferries** **1** : a place where persons or things are ferried **2** : FERRYBOAT

fer·ry·boat \'fer-ē-ˌbōt\ *n* : a boat used in ferrying

fer·tile \'fər-t°l\ *adj* **1** : producing plentifully : PRODUCTIVE ⟨∼ soils⟩ ⟨a ∼ mind⟩ **2** : capable of developing or reproducing ⟨∼ seed⟩ ⟨a ∼ bull⟩ ◆ *Synonyms* FRUITFUL, PROLIFIC, FECUND, PRODUCTIVE — **fer·til·i·ty** \(ˌ)fər-'ti-lə-tē\ *n*

fer·til·ize \'fər-tə-ˌlīz\ *vb* **-ized; -iz·ing** **1** : to unite with in the process of fertilization ⟨a sperm ∼s an egg⟩ **2** : to apply fertilizer to — **fer·til·i·za·tion** \ˌfər-tə-lə-'zā-shən\ *n*

fer·til·iz·er \'fər-tə-ˌlī-zər\ *n* : material (as manure or a chemical mixture) for enriching land

fer·ule \'fer-əl\ *n* : a rod or ruler used to punish children

fer·ven·cy \'fər-vən-sē\ *n, pl* **-cies** : FERVOR

fer·vent \'fər-vənt\ *adj* **1** : very hot : GLOWING **2** : marked by great intensity of feeling ◆ *Synonyms* IMPASSIONED, ARDENT, FERVID, FIERY, PASSIONATE — **fer·vent·ly** *adv*

fer·vid \-vəd\ *adj* **1** : very hot **2** : ARDENT, ZEALOUS — **fer·vid·ly** *adv*

fer·vor \'fər-vər\ *n* **1** : intense heat **2** : intensity of feeling or expression

fer·vour *chiefly Brit var of* FERVOR

fes·cue \'fes-kyü\ *n* : any of a genus of tufted perennial grasses

fes·tal \'fes-t°l\ *adj* : FESTIVE

fes·ter \'fes-tər\ *vb* **1** : to form pus **2** : PUTREFY, ROT **3** : RANKLE

fes·ti·val \'fes-tə-vəl\ *n* **1** : a time of celebration marked by special observances; *esp* : an occasion marked with religious ceremonies **2** : a periodic season or program of cultural events or entertainment ⟨a dance ∼⟩

fes·tive \'fes-tiv\ *adj* **1** : of, relating to, or suitable for a feast or festival **2** : JOYFUL, GAY — **fes·tive·ly** *adv*

fes·tiv·i·ty \fes-'ti-və-tē\ *n, pl* **-ties** **1** : FESTIVAL **2** : the quality or state of being festive **3** : festive activity

¹fes·toon \fes-'tün\ *n* [F *feston,* fr. It *festone,* fr. *festa* festival] **1** : a decorative chain or strip hanging between two points **2** : a carved, molded, or painted ornament representing a decorative chain

²festoon *vb* **1** : to hang or form festoons on **2** : to shape into festoons

fe·ta \'fe-tə\ *n* : a white crumbly Greek cheese made from sheep's or goat's milk

fe·tal \'fē-t°l\ *adj* : of, relating to, or being a fetus

fetch \'fech\ *vb* **1** : to go or come after and bring or take back ⟨teach a dog to ∼ a stick⟩ **2** : to bring in (as a price) **3** : to cause to come : bring out ⟨∼ed tears from the eyes⟩ **4** : to give by striking ⟨∼ him a blow⟩

fetch·ing *adj* : ATTRACTIVE, PLEASING ⟨a ∼ smile⟩ — **fetch·ing·ly** *adv*

¹fete *or* **fête** \'fāt, 'fet\ *n* [F *fête,* fr. OF *feste*] **1** : FESTIVAL **2** : a large elaborate entertainment or party

²fete *or* **fête** *vb* **fet·ed** *or* **fêt·ed; fet·ing** *or* **fêt·ing** **1** : to honor or commemorate with a fete **2** : to pay high honor to

fet·id \'fe-təd\ *adj* : having an offensive smell : STINKING

fe·tish *also* **fe·tich** \'fe-tish\ *n* [F & Pg; F *fétiche,* fr. Pg *feitiço,* fr. *feitiço* artificial, false, fr. L *facticius* factitious] **1** : an object (as an idol or image) believed to have magical powers (as in curing disease) **2** : an object of unreasoning devotion or concern **3** : an object whose real or fantasied presence is psychologically necessary for sexual gratification

fe·tish·ism \-ti-ˌshi-zəm\ *n* **1** : belief in or devotion to fetishes **2** : the pathological transfer of sexual interest and gratification to a fetish — **fe·tish·ist** \-shist\ *n* — **fe·tish·is·tic** \ˌfe-ti-'shis-tik\ *adj*

fe·tish·ize \-ti-ˌshīz\ *vb* **-ized -iz·ing** : to make a fetish of

fet·lock \'fet-ˌläk\ *n* : a projection on the back of a horse's leg above the hoof; *also* : a tuft of hair on this

fet·ter \'fe-tər\ *n* **1** : a chain or shackle for the feet **2** : something that confines : RESTRAINT — **fetter** *vb*

fet·tle \'fe-t°l\ *n* : a state of fitness or order : CONDITION ⟨in fine ∼⟩

fe·tus \'fē-təs\ *n* : an unborn or unhatched vertebrate esp. after its basic structure is laid down; *esp* : a developing human in the uterus from usu. three months after conception to birth

feud \'fyüd\ *n* : a prolonged quarrel; *esp* : a lasting conflict between families or clans marked by violent attacks made for revenge — **feud** *vb*

feu·dal \'fyü-d°l\ *adj* **1** : of, relating to, or having the

characteristics of a medieval fee **2** : of, relating to, or characteristic of feudalism

feu·dal·ism \'fyü-də-ˌli-zəm\ *n* : a system of political organization prevailing in medieval Europe in which a vassal renders service to a lord and receives protection and land in return; *also* : a similar political or social system — **feu·dal·is·tic** \ˌfyü-d°l-'is-tik\ *adj*

¹feu·da·to·ry \'fyü-də-ˌtòr-ē\ *adj* : owing feudal allegiance

²feudatory *n, pl* **-ries** **1** : FIEF **2** : a person who holds lands by feudal law or usage

fe·ver \'fē-vər\ *n* **1** : a rise in body temperature above the normal; *also* : a disease of which this is a chief symptom **2** : a state of heightened emotion or activity **3** : CRAZE — **fe·ver·ish** *adj* — **fe·ver·ish·ly** *adv*

¹few \'fyü\ *pron* : not many : a small number

²few *adj* **1** : consisting of or amounting to a small number **2** : not many but some ⟨caught a ∼ fish⟩ — **few·ness** *n* — **few and far between** : RARE **3**

³few *n* **1** : a small number of units or individuals ⟨a ∼ of them⟩ **2** : a special limited number ⟨among the ∼⟩

few·er \'fyü-ər\ *pron* : a smaller number of persons or things

fey \'fā\ *adj* **1** *chiefly Scot* : fated to die; *also* : marked by a foreboding of death or calamity **2** : able to see into the future : VISIONARY **3** : marked by an otherworldly air or attitude **4** : CRAZY, TOUCHED

fez \'fez\ *n, pl* **fez·zes** *also* **fez·es** : a round red felt hat that has a flat top and a tassel but no brim

ff *abbr* **1** folios **2** [following] and the following ones **3** fortissimo

FHA *abbr* Federal Housing Administration

fi·an·cé \ˌfē-ˌän-'sā\ *n* [F, fr. MF, fr. pp. of *fiancer* to promise, betroth, fr. OF *fiancier,* fr. *fiance* promise, trust, fr. *fier* to trust, ultim. fr. L *fidere*] : a man engaged to be married

fi·an·cée \ˌfē-ˌän-'sā\ *n* : a woman engaged to be married

fi·as·co \fē-'as-kō\ *n, pl* **-coes** [F] : a complete failure

fi·at \'fē-ət, -ˌat, -ˌät; 'fī-ət, -ˌat\ *n* [L, let it be done] : an authoritative and often arbitrary order or decree

¹fib \'fib\ *n* : a trivial or childish lie

²fib *vb* **fibbed; fib·bing** : to tell a fib — **fib·ber** *n*

fi·ber \'fī-bər\ *n* **1** : a threadlike substance or structure (as a muscle cell or fine root); *esp* : a natural (as wool or flax) or artificial (as rayon) filament capable of being spun or woven **2** : indigestible material in food that stimulates the intestine to move its contents along **3** : an element that gives texture or substance **4** : basic toughness : STRENGTH — **fi·brous** \-brəs\ *adj*

fi·ber·board \'fī-bər-ˌbòrd\ *n* : a material made by compressing fibers (as of wood) into stiff sheets

fi·ber·fill \-ˌfil\ *n* : synthetic fibers used as a filling material (as for cushions)

fi·ber·glass \-ˌglas\ *n* : glass in fibrous form used in making various products (as insulation)

fiber optics *n* **1** *pl* : thin transparent fibers of glass or plastic that are enclosed by a less refractive material and that transmit light by internal reflection; *also* : a bundle of such fibers used in an instrument **2** : the technique of the use of fiber optics — **fiber-optic** *adj*

fibre *chiefly Brit var of* FIBER

fi·bril \'fī-brəl, 'fi-\ *n* : a small fiber

fi·bril·la·tion \ˌfi-brə-'lā-shən, ˌfī-\ *n* : rapid irregular contractions of the heart muscle fibers resulting in a lack of synchronism between heartbeat and pulse — **fib·ril·late** \'fi-brə-ˌlāt, 'fī-\ *vb*

fi·brin \'fī-brən\ *n* : a white insoluble fibrous protein formed in the clotting of blood

¹fi·broid \'fī-bròid, 'fi-\ *adj* : resembling, forming, or consisting of fibrous tissue ⟨∼ tumors⟩

²fibroid *n* : a benign tumor of the uterus

fi·bro·my·al·gia \ˌfī-ˌbrō-ˌmī-'al-jə\ *n* : any of a group of rheumatic disorders affecting soft tissues (as muscles or tendons)

fi·bro·sis \fī-'brō-səs\ *n* : a condition marked by abnormal increase of fiber-containing tissue

fib·u·la \'fi-byə-lə\ *n, pl* **-lae** \-lē, -ˌlī\ *or* **-las** : the outer and usu. the smaller of the two bones between the knee and ankle — **fib·u·lar** \-lər\ *adj*

FICA *abbr* Federal Insurance Contributions Act

-fication *n comb form* : making : production ⟨simplification⟩

fiche \'fēsh\ *n, pl* **fiche** : MICROFICHE

fi·chu \'fi-shü\ *n* [F] : a woman's light triangular scarf draped over the shoulders and fastened in front

fick·le \'fi-kəl\ *adj* : not firm or steadfast in disposition or character : INCONSTANT — **fick·le·ness** *n*

fic·tion \'fik-shən\ *n* 1 : something (as a story) invented by the imagination 2 : fictitious literature (as novels) — **fic·tion·al** \-shə-nəl\ *adj* — **fic·tion·al·ly** *adv*

fic·ti·tious \fik-'ti-shəs\ *adj* 1 : of, relating to, or characteristic of fiction : IMAGINARY 2 : FALSE, ASSUMED ⟨a ~ name⟩ 3 : FEIGNED ◆ *Synonyms* CHIMERICAL, FANCIFUL, FANTASTIC, UNREAL

¹**fid·dle** \'fi-dᵊl\ *n* : VIOLIN

²**fiddle** *vb* **fid·dled; fid·dling** 1 : to play on a fiddle 2 : to move the hands or fingers restlessly 3 : PUTTER 4 : MEDDLE, TAMPER — **fid·dler** *n*

fid·dle·head \'fi-dᵊl-,hed\ *n* : one of the young unfurling fronds of some ferns that are often eaten as greens

fiddler crab *n* : any of a genus of burrowing crabs with one claw much enlarged in the male

fiddler crab

fid·dle·stick \'fi-dᵊl-,stik\ *n* 1 : a violin bow 2 *pl* : NONSENSE — used as an interjection

fi·del·i·ty \fə-'de-lə-tē, fī-\ *n, pl* **-ties** 1 : the quality or state of being faithful 2 : ACCURACY ⟨~ in sound reproduction⟩ ◆ *Synonyms* ALLEGIANCE, LOYALTY, DEVOTION, FEALTY

¹**fidg·et** \'fi-jət\ *n* 1 : uneasiness or restlessness as shown by nervous movements — usu. used in pl. 2 : one that fidgets — **fidg·ety** *adj*

²**fidget** *vb* : to move or cause to move or act restlessly or nervously

fi·du·cia·ry \fə-'dü-shē-,er-ē, -'dyü-, -shə-rē\ *adj* 1 : involving a confidence or trust 2 : held or holding in trust for another ⟨~ accounts⟩ — **fiduciary** *n*

fie \'fī\ *interj* — used to express disgust or disapproval

fief \'fēf\ *n* [F, fr. OF] : a feudal estate : FEE

¹**field** \'fēld\ *n* 1 : open country 2 : a piece of cleared land for cultivation or pasture 3 : a piece of land yielding some special product 4 : the place where a battle is fought; *also* : BATTLE 5 : an area, division, or sphere of activity ⟨the ~ of science⟩ ⟨salesmen in the ~⟩ 6 : an area for military exercises 7 : an area for sports 8 : a background on which something is drawn or projected ⟨a flag with white stars on a ~ of blue⟩ 9 : a region or space in which a given effect (as magnetism) exists — **field** *adj*

²**field** *vb* 1 : to handle a batted or thrown baseball while on defense 2 : to put into the field 3 : to answer satisfactorily ⟨~ a tough question⟩ — **field·er** *n*

field day *n* 1 : a day devoted to outdoor sports and athletic competition 2 : a time of extraordinary pleasure or opportunity

field event *n* : a track-and-field event (as weight-throwing) other than a race

field glass *n* : a hand-held binocular telescope — usu. used in pl.

field guide *n* : a manual for identifying natural objects, plants, or animals

field hockey *n* : a field game played between two teams of 11 players each whose object is to knock a ball into the opponent's goal with a curved stick

field marshal *n* : an officer (as in the British army) of the highest rank

field–test \-,test\ *vb* : to test (as a new product) in actual situations reflecting intended use — **field test** *n*

fiend \'fēnd\ *n* 1 : DEVIL 1 2 : DEMON 3 : an extremely wicked or cruel person 4 : a person excessively devoted to a pursuit ⟨a golf ~⟩ 5 : ADDICT ⟨a dope ~⟩ — **fiend·ish** *adj* — **fiend·ish·ly** *adv*

fierce \'firs\ *adj* **fierc·er; fierc·est** 1 : violently hostile or aggressive in temperament 2 : PUGNACIOUS 3 : INTENSE ⟨~ pain⟩ 4 : furiously active or determined 5 : wild or menacing in appearance ◆ *Synonyms* FEROCIOUS, BARBAROUS, SAVAGE, CRUEL — **fierce·ly** *adv* — **fierce·ness** *n*

fi·ery \'fī-ə-rē\ *adj* **fi·er·i·er; -est** 1 : consisting of fire 2 : BURNING, BLAZING 3 : FLAMMABLE 4 : hot like a fire : INFLAMED, FEVERISH 5 : RED ⟨a ~ sunset⟩ 6 : full of emotion or spirit 7 : IRRITABLE — **fi·eri·ness** \-rē-nəs\ *n*

fi·es·ta \fē-'es-tə\ *n* [Sp] : FESTIVAL

fife \'fīf\ *n* [G *Pfeife* pipe, fife] : a small flute

FIFO *abbr* first in, first out

fif·teen \fif-'tēn\ *n* : one more than 14 — **fifteen** *adj or pron* — **fif·teenth** \-'tēnth\ *adj or n*

fifth \'fifth\ *n* 1 : one that is number five in a countable series 2 : one of five equal parts of something 3 : a unit of measure for liquor equal to ¹⁄₅ U.S. gallon (0.757 liter) — **fifth** *adj or adv*

fifth column *n* : a group of secret supporters of a nation's enemy that engage in espionage or sabotage within the country — **fifth columnist** *n*

fifth wheel *n* : one that is unnecessary and often burdensome

fif·ty \'fif-tē\ *n, pl* **fifties** : five times 10 — **fif·ti·eth** \-tē-əth\ *adj or n* — **fifty** *adj or pron*

fif·ty–fif·ty \,fif-tē-'fif-tē\ *adj* 1 : shared equally ⟨a ~ proposition⟩ 2 : half favorable and half unfavorable

¹**fig** \'fig\ *n* : a soft usu. pear-shaped edible fruit of a tree related to the mulberry; *also* : a tree bearing figs

²**fig** *abbr* 1 figurative; figuratively 2 figure

¹**fight** \'fīt\ *vb* **fought** \'fȯt\; **fight·ing** 1 : to contend against another in battle or physical combat 2 : BOX 3 : to put forth a determined effort 4 : STRUGGLE, CONTEND 5 : to attempt to prevent the success or effectiveness of 6 : WAGE 7 : to gain by struggle

²**fight** *n* 1 : a hostile encounter : BATTLE 2 : a boxing match 3 : a verbal disagreement 4 : a struggle for a goal or an objective 5 : strength or disposition for fighting ⟨full of ~⟩

fight·er \'fī-tər\ *n* 1 : one that fights; *esp* : WARRIOR 2 : BOXER 1 3 : a fast maneuverable warplane for destroying enemy aircraft

fig·ment \'fig-mənt\ *n* : something imagined or made up

fig·u·ra·tion \,fi-gyə-'rā-shən, -gə-\ *n* 1 : FORM, OUTLINE 2 : an act or instance of representation in figures and shapes

fig·u·ra·tive \'fi-gyə-rə-tiv, -gə-\ *adj* 1 : EMBLEMATIC 2 : SYMBOLIC, METAPHORICAL ⟨~ language⟩ — **fig·u·ra·tive·ly** *adv*

¹**fig·ure** \'fi-gyər, -gər\ *n* [ME, fr. AF, fr. L *figura,* fr. *fingere* to shape] 1 : NUMERAL 2 *pl* : arithmetical calculations 3 : a written or printed character 4 : PRICE, SUM ⟨sold at a low ~⟩ 5 : a combination of points, lines, or surfaces in geometry ⟨a circle is a closed plane ~⟩ 6 : SHAPE, FORM, OUTLINE 7 : the graphic representation of a form esp. of a person 8 : a diagram or pictorial illustration of textual matter 9 : PATTERN, DESIGN 10 : appearance made or impression produced ⟨they cut quite a ~⟩ 11 : a series of movements (as in a dance) 12 : PERSONAGE

²**figure** *vb* **fig·ured; fig·ur·ing** 1 : to represent by or as if by a figure or outline 2 : to decorate with a pattern 3 : to indicate or represent by numerals 4 : REGARD, CONSIDER 5 : to be or appear important or conspicuous 6 : COMPUTE, CALCULATE

fig·ure·head \'fi-gyər-,hed, -gər-\ *n* 1 : a figure on the bow of a ship 2 : a head or chief in name only

figure of speech : a form of expression (as a simile or metaphor) that often compares or identifies one thing with another to convey meaning or heighten effect

figure out *vb* 1 : FIND OUT, DISCOVER 2 : SOLVE

figure skating *n* : skating that includes various jumps, spins, and dance movements

fig·u·rine \,fi-gyə-'rēn, -gə-\ *n* : a small carved or molded figure

fil·a·ment \'fi-lə-mənt\ *n* : a fine thread or threadlike object, part, or process — **fil·a·men·tous** \,fi-lə-'men-təs\ *adj*

fil·bert \'fil-bərt\ *n* : the sweet thick-shelled nut of either of two European hazels; *also* : a shrub or small tree bearing filberts

filch \'filch\ *vb* : to steal furtively

¹file \'fī(-ə)l\ *n* : a usu. steel tool with a ridged or toothed surface used esp. for smoothing a hard substance

²file *vb* **filed; fil·ing** : to rub, smooth, or cut away with a file

³file *vb* **filed; fil·ing** [ME, fr. ML *filare* to string documents on a string or wire, fr. *filum* file of documents, lit., thread, fr. L] **1** : to arrange in order **2** : to enter or record officially or as prescribed by law ⟨~ a lawsuit⟩ **3** : to send (copy) to a newspaper

⁴file *n* **1** : a device (as a folder or cabinet) by means of which papers may be kept in order **2** : a collection of papers or publications usu. arranged or classified **3** : a collection of data (as text) treated by a computer as a unit

⁵file *n* : a row of persons, animals, or things arranged one behind the other

⁶file *vb* **filed; fil·ing** : to march or proceed in file

fi·let mi·gnon \ˌfi-(ˌ)lā-mēn-ˈyōⁿ, fi-ˌlā-\ *n, pl* **filets mignons** \-(ˌ)lā-mēn-ˈyōⁿz, -ˌlā-\ [F, lit., dainty fillet] : a thick slice of beef cut from the narrow end of a beef tenderloin

fil·ial \'fi-lē-əl, 'fil-yəl\ *adj* : of, relating to, or befitting a son or daughter

fil·i·bus·ter \'fi-lə-ˌbəs-tər\ *n* [Sp *filibustero*, lit., freebooter] **1** : a military adventurer; *esp* : an American engaged in fomenting 19th century Latin American uprisings **2** : the use of delaying tactics (as extremely long speeches) esp. in a legislative assembly; *also* : an instance of this practice — **filibuster** *vb* — **fil·i·bus·ter·er** *n*

fil·i·cide \'fi-lə-ˌsīd\ *n* : the murder of one's own daughter or son

fil·i·gree \'fi-lə-ˌgrē\ *n* [F *filigrane*] : ornamental openwork (as of fine wire) — **fil·i·greed** \-ˌgrēd\ *adj*

fil·ing \'fī-liŋ\ *n* **1** : the act or instance of using a file **2** : a small piece scraped off by a file ⟨iron ~s⟩

Fil·i·pi·no \ˌfi-lə-ˈpē-nō\ *n, pl* **Filipinos** : a native or inhabitant of the Philippines — **Filipino** *adj*

¹fill \'fil\ *vb* **1** : to make or become full **2** : to stop up : PLUG ⟨~ a cavity⟩ **3** : FEED, SATIATE **4** : SATISFY, FULFILL ⟨~ all requirements⟩ **5** : to occupy fully **6** : to spread through ⟨laughter ~ed the room⟩ **7** : OCCUPY ⟨~ the office of president⟩ **8** : to put a person in ⟨~ a vacancy⟩ **9** : to supply as directed ⟨~ a prescription⟩

²fill *n* **1** : a full supply; *esp* : a quantity that satisfies or satiates **2** : material used esp. for filling a low place

¹fill·er \'fi-lər\ *n* **1** : one that fills **2** : a substance added to another substance (as to increase bulk or weight) **3** : a material used for filling cracks and pores in wood before painting

²fil·ler \'fi-ˌler\ *n, pl* **fillers** *or* **filler** — see *forint* at MONEY table

¹fil·let \'fi-lət, in sense 2 fi-ˈlā, 'fi-(ˌ)lā\ *also* **fi·let** \fi-ˈlā, 'fi-(ˌ)lā\ *n* [ME *filet*, fr. AF, dim. of *fil* thread] **1** : a narrow band, strip, or ribbon **2** : a piece or slice of boneless meat or fish; *esp* : the tenderloin of beef

²fil·let \'fi-lət, in sense 2 also fi-ˈlā, 'fi-(ˌ)lā\ *vb* **1** : to bind or adorn with or as if with a fillet **2** : to cut into fillets

fill in *vb* **1** : to provide necessary or recent information **2** : to serve as a temporary substitute

fill·ing \'fi-liŋ\ *n* **1** : material used to fill something ⟨a ~ for a tooth⟩ **2** : the yarn interlacing the warp in a fabric **3** : a food mixture used to fill pastry or sandwiches

filling station *n* : GAS STATION

fil·lip \'fi-ləp\ *n* **1** : a blow or gesture made by a flick or snap of the finger across the thumb **2** : something that serves to arouse or excite — **fillip** *vb*

fill-up \'fil-ˌəp\ *n* : an act or instance of filling something

fil·ly \'fi-lē\ *n, pl* **fillies** : a young female horse usu. less than four years old

¹film \'film\ *n* **1** : a thin skin or membrane **2** : a thin coating or layer **3** : a flexible strip of chemically treated material used in taking pictures **4** : MOTION PICTURE — **filmy** *adj*

²film *vb* **1** : to cover with a film **2** : to make a motion picture of

film·dom \'film-dəm\ *n* : the motion-picture industry

film·og·ra·phy \fil-ˈmä-grə-fē\ *n, pl* **-phies** : a list of motion pictures featuring the work of a film figure or a particular topic

film·strip \'film-ˌstrip\ *n* : a strip of film bearing a sequence of images for projection as still pictures

¹fils \'fēs\ *n* [F] : SON — used after a family name to distinguish a son from his father

²fils \'fils\ *n, pl* **fils** — see *dinar, dirham, rial* at MONEY table

¹fil·ter \'fil-tər\ *n* **1** : a porous material through which a fluid is passed to separate out matter in suspension; *also* : a device containing such material **2** : a device for suppressing waves of certain frequencies; *esp* : one (as for a camera) that absorbs light of certain colors **3** : software for sorting or blocking certain online material

²filter *vb* **1** : to remove by means of a filter **2** : to pass through a filter — **fil·ter·able** *also* **fil·tra·ble** \-tə-rə-bəl, -trə-\ *adj* — **fil·tra·tion** \fil-ˈtrā-shən\ *n*

filth \'filth\ *n* [ME, fr. OE *fylth*, fr. *fūl* foul] **1** : foul matter; *esp* : loathsome dirt or refuse **2** : moral corruption **3** : OBSCENITY — **filth·i·ness** *n* — **filthy** \'fil-thē\ *adj*

filthy *adv* : VERY, EXTREMELY ⟨~ dirty⟩ ⟨~ rich⟩

fil·trate \'fil-ˌtrāt\ *n* : fluid that has passed through a filter

¹fin \'fin\ *n* **1** : a thin external process by which an aquatic animal (as a fish) moves through water **2** : a fin-shaped part (as on an airplane) **3** : FLIPPER 2 — **finned** \'find\ *adj*

²fin *abbr* **1** finance; financial **2** finish

fi·na·gle \fə-ˈnā-gəl\ *vb* **-gled; -gling** **1** : to obtain by indirect or dishonest means : WANGLE **2** : to use devious dishonest methods to achieve one's ends — **fi·na·gler** *n*

¹fi·nal \'fī-nᵊl\ *adj* **1** : not to be altered or undone ⟨all sales are ~⟩ **2** : ULTIMATE **3** : relating to or occurring at the end or conclusion — **fi·nal·i·ty** \fī-ˈna-lə-tē, fə-\ *n* — **fi·nal·ly** *adv*

²final *n* **1** : a deciding match or game — usu. used in pl. **2** : the last examination in a course — often used in pl.

fi·na·le \fə-ˈna-lē, fi-ˈnä-\ *n* : the close or end of something; *esp* : the last section of a musical composition

fi·nal·ise *Brit var of* FINALIZE

fi·nal·ist \'fī-nə-list\ *n* : a contestant in the finals of a competition

fi·nal·ize \'fī-nə-ˌlīz\ *vb* **-ized; -iz·ing** : to put in final or finished form

¹fi·nance \fə-ˈnans, 'fī-ˌnans\ *n* [ME, ending, payment, fr. AF, fr. *finer* to end, pay, fr. *fin* end, fr. L *finis* boundary, end] **1** *pl* : money resources available esp. to a government or business **2** : management of money affairs

²finance *vb* **fi·nanced; fi·nanc·ing** **1** : to raise or provide funds for **2** : to furnish with necessary funds **3** : to sell or supply on credit

finance company *n* : a company that makes usu. small short-term loans usu. to individuals

fi·nan·cial \fə-ˈnan-chəl, fī-\ *adj* : relating to finance or financiers — **fi·nan·cial·ly** *adv*

fi·nan·cials \-shəlz\ *n pl* : financial statistics

fi·nan·cier \ˌfi-nən-ˈsir, ˌfī-ˌnan-\ *n* **1** : a person skilled in managing public moneys **2** : a person who deals with large-scale finance and investment

finch \'finch\ *n* : any of numerous songbirds with strong conical bills

¹find \'fīnd\ *vb* **found** \'faund\; **find·ing** **1** : to meet with either by chance or by searching or study : ENCOUNTER, DISCOVER **2** : to obtain by effort or management ⟨~ time to read⟩ **3** : to arrive at : REACH ⟨the bullet *found* its mark⟩ **4** : EXPERIENCE, FEEL ⟨*found* happiness⟩ **5** : to gain or regain the use of ⟨*found* his voice again⟩ **6** : to determine and make a statement about ⟨~ a verdict⟩

²find *n* **1** : an act or instance of finding **2** : something found; *esp* : a valuable item of discovery

find·er \'fīn-dər\ *n* : one that finds; *esp* : VIEWFINDER

fin de siè·cle \ˌfaⁿ-də-sē-ˈeklᵊ\ *adj* [F, end of century] **1** : of, relating to, or characteristic of the close of the 19th century **2** : of or relating to the end of a century

find·ing \'fīn-diŋ\ *n* **1** : the act of finding **2** : FIND 2 **3** : the result of a judicial proceeding or inquiry

find out *vb* : to learn by study, observation, or search : DISCOVER

¹fine \'fīn\ *n* : money exacted as a penalty for an offense

²fine *vb* **fined; fin·ing** : to impose a fine on : punish by a fine

³fine *adj* **fin·er; fin·est** **1** : free from impurity **2** : very thin in gauge or texture **3** : not coarse ⟨~ sand⟩ **4** : SUBTLE, SENSITIVE ⟨a ~ distinction⟩ **5** : superior in quality or appearance **6** : ELEGANT, REFINED ⟨~ manners⟩ — **fine·ly** *adv* — **fine·ness** *n*

⁴fine *adv* **1** : very well **2** — used to express agreement

fine art *n* : art (as painting, sculpture, or music) concerned primarily with the creation of beautiful objects — usu. used in pl.

fin·ery \'fī-nə-rē\ *n, pl* **-er·ies** : ORNAMENT, DECORATION; *esp* : showy clothing and jewels

fine·spun \'fīn-'spən\ *adj* : developed with extremely or excessively fine delicacy or detail

fi·nesse \fə-'nes\ *n* **1** : refinement or delicacy of workmanship, structure, or texture **2** : CUNNING, SUBTLETY — **finesse** *vb*

fine–tune \'fīn-'tün\ *vb* : to adjust so as to bring to the highest level of performance or effectiveness

fin·fish \'fin-,fish\ *n* : FISH 2

¹fin·ger \'fiŋ-gər\ *n* **1** : any of the five divisions at the end of the hand; *esp* : one other than the thumb **2** : something that resembles or does the work of a finger **3** : a part of a glove into which a finger is inserted

²finger *vb* **fin·gered; fin·ger·ing 1** : to touch or feel with the fingers : HANDLE **2** : to perform with the fingers or with a certain fingering **3** : to mark the notes of a piece of music as a guide in playing **4** : to point out

fin·ger·board \'fiŋ-gər-,bȯrd\ *n* : the part of a stringed instrument against which the fingers press the strings to vary the pitch

finger bowl *n* : a small water bowl for rinsing the fingers at the table

fin·ger·ing \'fiŋ-gə-riŋ\ *n* **1** : handling or touching with the fingers **2** : the act or method of using the fingers in playing an instrument **3** : the marking of the method of fingering

fin·ger·ling \'fiŋ-gər-liŋ\ *n* : a small fish

fin·ger·nail \'fiŋ-gər-,nāl\ *n* : the nail of a finger

fin·ger·print \-,print\ *n* : the pattern of marks made by pressing the tip of a finger or thumb on a surface; *esp* : an ink impression of such a pattern taken for the purpose of identification — **fingerprint** *vb*

fin·ger·tip \-,tip\ *n* : the tip of a finger

fin·i·al \'fi-nē-əl\ *n* : an ornamental projection or end (as on a spire)

fin·ick·ing \'fi-ni-kiŋ\ *adj* : FINICKY

fin·icky \'fi-ni-kē\ *adj* : excessively particular in taste or standards

fi·nis \'fi-nəs\ *n* : END, CONCLUSION

¹fin·ish \'fi-nish\ *vb* **1** : TERMINATE **2** : to use or dispose of entirely **3** : to bring to completion : ACCOMPLISH **4** : to put a final coat or surface on **5** : to come to the end of a course or undertaking — **fin·ish·er** *n*

²finish *n* **1** : END, CONCLUSION **2** : something that completes or perfects **3** : the final treatment or coating of a surface

fi·nite \'fī-,nīt\ *adj* **1** : having definite or definable limits; *also* : having a limited nature or existence **2** : being less than some positive integer in number or measure and greater than its negative **3** : showing distinction of grammatical person and number ⟨a ~ verb⟩

fink \'fiŋk\ *n* **1** : a contemptible person **2** : STRIKEBREAKER **3** : INFORMER

Finn \'fin\ *n* : a native or inhabitant of Finland

fin·nan had·die \,fi-nən-'ha-dē\ *n* : smoked haddock

¹Finn·ish \'fi-nish\ *adj* : of or relating to Finland, the Finns, or Finnish

²Finnish *n* : the language of the Finns

fin·ny \'fi-nē\ *adj* **1** : having or characterized by fins **2** : relating to or being fish

fiord *var of* FJORD

fir \'fər\ *n* : any of a genus of usu. large evergreen trees related to the pines; *also* : the light soft wood of a fir

¹fire \'fī(-ə)r\ *n* **1** : the light or heat and esp. the flame of something burning **2** : ENTHUSIASM, ZEAL **3** : fuel that is burning (as in a stove or fireplace) **4** : destructive burning (as of a house) **5** : the firing of weapons — **fireless** *adj*

²fire *vb* **fired; fir·ing 1** : KINDLE, IGNITE ⟨~ a house⟩ **2** : STIR, ENLIVEN ⟨~ the imagination⟩ **3** : to dismiss from employment **4** : SHOOT ⟨~ a gun⟩ ⟨~ an arrow⟩ **5** : BAKE ⟨firing pottery in a kiln⟩ **6** : to apply fire or fuel to something ⟨~ a furnace⟩

fire ant *n* : either of two small fiercely stinging So. American ants introduced into the southeastern U.S. where they are agricultural pests

fire·arm \'fī(-ə)r-,ärm\ *n* : a weapon (as a pistol) from which a shot is discharged by gunpowder

fire·ball \-,bȯl\ *n* **1** : a ball of fire **2** : a very bright meteor **3** : the highly luminous cloud of vapor and dust created by a nuclear explosion **4** : a highly energetic person

fire·boat \-,bōt\ *n* : a boat equipped for fighting fires

fire·bomb \-,bäm\ *n* : an incendiary bomb — **firebomb** *vb*

fire·box \-,bäks\ *n* **1** : a chamber (as of a furnace) that contains a fire **2** : a box containing a fire alarm

fire·brand \-,brand\ *n* **1** : a piece of burning wood **2** : a person who creates unrest or strife : AGITATOR

fire·break \-,brāk\ *n* : a barrier of cleared or plowed land intended to check a forest or grass fire

fire·bug \-,bəg\ *n* : a person who deliberately sets destructive fires

fire·crack·er \-,kra-kər\ *n* : a usu. paper tube containing an explosive and a fuse and set off to make a noise

fire department *n* : an organization for preventing or extinguishing fires; *also* : its members

fire engine *n* : a motor vehicle with equipment for extinguishing fires

fire escape *n* : a stairway or ladder for escape from a burning building

fire·fight·er \'fī(-ə)r-,fī-tər\ *n* : a person who fights fires; *esp* : a member of a fire department

fire·fly \-,flī\ *n* : any of various small night-flying beetles that produce flashes of light for courtship purposes

firefly

fire·house \-,hau̇s\ *n* : FIRE STATION

fire irons *n pl* : tools for tending a fire esp. in a fireplace

fire·man \'fī(-ə)r-mən\ *n* **1** : STOKER **2** : FIREFIGHTER

fire off *vb* : to write and send

fire·place \-,plās\ *n* **1** : a framed opening made in a chimney to hold an open fire **2** : an outdoor structure of brick or stone for an open fire

fire·plug \-,pləg\ *n* : HYDRANT

fire·pow·er \-,pau̇(-ə)r\ *n* : the ability to deliver gunfire or warheads on a target

¹fire·proof \-'prüf\ *adj* : resistant to fire

²fireproof *vb* : to make fireproof

fire–sale \-,sāl\ *adj* : heavily discounted ⟨~ prices⟩

fire screen *n* : a protective screen before a fireplace

¹fire·side \'fī(-ə)r-,sīd\ *n* **1** : a place near the fire or hearth **2** : HOME

²fireside *adj* : having an informal or intimate quality

fire station *n* : a building housing fire engines and usu. firefighters

fire·storm \'fī(-ə)r-,stȯrm\ *n* **1** : a large destructive very hot fire **2** : a sudden or violent outburst ⟨~ of criticism⟩

fire tower *n* : a tower (as in a forest) from which a watch for fires is kept

fire·trap \'fī(-ə)r-,trap\ *n* : a building or place apt to catch on fire or difficult to escape from in case of fire

fire truck *n* : FIRE ENGINE

fire·wall \-,wȯl\ *n* : computer hardware or software for preventing unauthorized access to data

fire·wa·ter \'fī(-ə)r-,wȯ-tər, -,wä-\ *n* : intoxicating liquor

fire·wood \-,wu̇d\ *n* : wood used for fuel

fire·work \-,wərk\ *n* : a device designed to produce a striking display by the burning of explosive or flammable materials

firing line *n* **1** : a line from which fire is delivered against a target **2** : the forefront of an activity

¹firm \'fərm\ *adj* **1** : securely fixed in place **2** : SOLID, VIGOROUS ⟨a ~ handshake⟩ **3** : having a solid or compact texture **4** : not subject to change or fluctuation

: STEADY ⟨∼ prices⟩ **5** : STEADFAST **6** : indicating firmness or resolution — **firm·ly** adv — **firm·ness** n
²firm vb : to make or become firm
³firm n [G Firma, fr. It, signature, ultim. fr. L firmare to make firm, confirm] **1** : the name under which a company transacts business **2** : a business partnership of two or more persons **3** : a business enterprise
fir·ma·ment \'fər-mə-mənt\ n : the arch of the sky : HEAVENS
firm·ware \'firm-ˌwer\ n : computer programs contained permanently in a hardware device
¹first \'fərst\ adj : preceding all others as in time, order, or importance
²first adv **1** : before any other **2** : for the first time **3** : in preference to something else
³first n **1** : number one in a countable series **2** : something that is first **3** : the lowest forward gear in an automotive vehicle **4** : the winning or highest place in a competition or examination
first aid n : emergency care or treatment given an injured or ill person
first·born \'fərst-'bȯrn\ adj : ELDEST — **firstborn** n
first class n : the best or highest group in a classification — **first–class** adj or adv
first·hand \'fərst-'hand\ adj : coming from direct personal observation or experience — **firsthand** adv
first lady n, often cap F&L : the wife or hostess of the chief executive of a political unit (as a country)
first lieutenant n : a commissioned officer (as in the army) ranking next below a captain
first·ling \'fərst-liŋ\ n : one that comes or is produced first
first·ly \-lē\ adv : in the first place : FIRST
¹first–rate \-'rāt\ adj : of the first order of size, importance, or quality
²first–rate adv : very well
first sergeant n **1** : a noncommissioned officer serving as the chief assistant to the commander of a military unit **2** : a rank in the army below a sergeant major and in the marine corps below a master gunnery sergeant
first strike n : a preemptive nuclear attack
first–string \'fərst-'striŋ\ adj : being a regular as distinguished from a substitute — **first–string·er** \-ˌstriŋ-ər\ n
firth \'fərth\ n [ME, fr. ON fjǫrthr] : ESTUARY
fis·cal \'fis-kəl\ adj [L fiscalis, fr. fiscus basket, treasury] **1** : of or relating to taxation, public revenues, or public debt **2** : of or relating to financial matters — **fis·cal·ly** adv
¹fish \'fish\ n, pl fish or fish·es **1** : a water-dwelling animal — usu. used in combination ⟨star*fish*⟩ ⟨shell*fish*⟩ **2** : any of numerous cold-blooded water-breathing vertebrates with fins, gills, and usu. scales that include the bony fishes and usu. the cartilaginous and jawless fishes **3** : the flesh of fish used as food
²fish vb **1** : to attempt to catch fish **2** : to seek something by roundabout means ⟨∼ for praise⟩ **3** : to search for something underwater **4** : to engage in a search by groping **5** : to draw forth
fish–and–chips n pl : fried fish and french fried potatoes
fish·bowl \'fish-ˌbōl\ n **1** : a bowl for the keeping of live fish **2** : a place or condition that affords no privacy
fish·er \'fish-ər\ n **1** : one that fishes **2** : a dark brown No. American carnivorous mammal related to the weasels
fish·er·man \-mən\ n **1** : a person engaged in fishing **2** : a fishing boat
fish·ery \'fish-ə-rē\ n, pl -er·ies **1** : the business of catching fish **2** : a place for catching fish
fish·hook \'fish-ˌhu̇k\ n : a usu. barbed hook for catching fish
fish ladder n : an arrangement of pools in steps by which fish can pass over a dam in going upstream
fish·net \'fish-ˌnet\ n **1** : netting for catching fish **2** : a coarse open-mesh fabric
fish·tail \-ˌtāl\ vb : to have the rear end slide from side to side out of control while moving forward
fish·wife \-ˌwīf\ n **1** : a woman who sells fish **2** : a vulgar abusive woman
fishy \'fish-ē\ adj fish·i·er; -est **1** : of or resembling fish **2** : QUESTIONABLE ⟨the story sounds ∼ to me⟩
fis·sion \'fish-ən, -zhən\ n [L fissio, fr. findere to split] **1** : a cleaving into parts **2** : a method of reproduction in

which a living cell or body divides into two or more parts each of which grows into a whole new individual **3** : the splitting of an atomic nucleus resulting in the release of large amounts of energy — **fis·sion·able** \'fi-shə-nə-bəl, -zhə-\ adj
fis·sure \'fi-shər\ n : a narrow opening or crack
fist \'fist\ n **1** : the hand with fingers folded into the palm **2** : INDEX 6
fist·ful \'fist-ˌfu̇l\ n : HANDFUL
fist·i·cuffs \'fis-ti-ˌkəfs\ n pl : a fight with the fists
fis·tu·la \'fis-chə-lə\ n, pl -las or -lae : an abnormal passage leading from an abscess or hollow organ — **fis·tu·lous** \-ləs\ adj
¹fit \'fit\ adj fit·ter; fit·test **1** : adapted to a purpose : APPROPRIATE **2** : PROPER, RIGHT ⟨a movie ∼ for children⟩ **3** : PREPARED, READY **4** : physically and mentally sound — **fit·ly** adv — **fit·ness** n
²fit n **1** : a sudden violent attack (as in epilepsy) **2** : a sudden outburst
³fit vb fit·ted also fit; fit·ting **1** : to be suitable for or to **2** : to be correctly adjusted to or shaped for **3** : to insert or adjust until correctly in place **4** : to make a place or room for **5** : to be in agreement or accord with **6** : PREPARE **7** : ADJUST **8** : SUPPLY, EQUIP ⟨fitted out with gear⟩ **9** : BELONG — **fit·ter** n
⁴fit n : the fact, condition, or manner of fitting or being fitted
fit·ful \'fit-fəl\ adj : not regular : INTERMITTENT ⟨∼ sleep⟩ — **fit·ful·ly** adv
¹fit·ting \'fi-tiŋ\ adj : APPROPRIATE, SUITABLE — **fit·ting·ly** adv
²fitting n **1** : the action or act of one that fits; esp : a trying on of clothes being made or altered **2** : a small often standardized part ⟨a plumbing ∼⟩
five \'fīv\ n **1** : one more than four **2** : the 5th in a set or series **3** : something having five units; esp : a basketball team **4** : a 5-dollar bill — **five** adj or pron
¹fix \'fiks\ vb **1** : to make firm, stable, or fast **2** : to give a permanent or final form to **3** : AFFIX, ATTACH **4** : to hold or direct steadily ⟨∼es his eyes on the horizon⟩ **5** : ESTABLISH, SET **6** : ASSIGN ⟨∼ the blame⟩ **7** : to set in order : ADJUST **8** : PREPARE **9** : to make whole or sound again **10** : to get even with **11** : to influence by improper or illegal methods ⟨∼ a race⟩ — **fix·er** n
²fix n **1** : PREDICAMENT **2** : a determination of position (as of a ship) **3** : an accurate determination or understanding **4** : an act of improper influence **5** : a supply or dose of something (as an addictive drug) strongly desired or craved **6** : something that fixes or restores
fix·a·tion \fik-'sā-shən\ n : an obsessive or unhealthy preoccupation or attachment — **fix·ate** \'fik-ˌsāt\ vb
fix·a·tive \'fik-sə-tiv\ n : something that stabilizes or sets
fixed \'fikst\ adj **1** : securely placed or fastened : STATIONARY **2** : not volatile **3** : SETTLED, FINAL **4** : INTENT, CONCENTRATED ⟨a ∼ stare⟩ **5** : supplied with a definite amount of something needed (as money) — **fixed·ly** \'fik-səd-lē\ adv — **fixed·ness** \'fik-səd-nəs\ n
fix·i·ty \'fik-sə-tē\ n, pl -ties : the quality or state of being fixed or stable
fix·ture \'fiks-chər\ n **1** : something firmly attached as a permanent part of some other thing **2** : a familiar feature in a particular setting; esp : a person associated with a place or activity
¹fizz \'fiz\ vb : to make a hissing or sputtering sound
²fizz n : an effervescent beverage
¹fiz·zle \'fi-zəl\ vb fiz·zled; fiz·zling **1** : FIZZ **2** : to fail after a good start — often used with out
²fizzle n : FAILURE
fjord \fē-'ȯrd\ n [Norw] : a narrow inlet of the sea between cliffs or steep slopes
fl abbr **1** [L floruit] flourished **2** fluid
FL or **Fla** abbr Florida
flab \'flab\ n : soft flabby body tissue
flab·ber·gast \'fla-bər-ˌgast\ vb : ASTOUND
flab·by \'fla-bē\ adj flab·bi·er; -est : lacking firmness : FLACCID ⟨∼ muscles⟩ — **flab·bi·ness** \-bē-nəs\ n
flac·cid \'flak-səd\ adj : lacking firmness ⟨∼ muscles⟩
¹flag \'flag\ n : any of various irises; esp : a wild iris
²flag n **1** : a usu. rectangular piece of fabric of distinctive design that is used as a symbol (as of a nation) or as a signaling device **2** : something used like a flag to signal or

attract attention **3** : one of the cross strokes of a musical note less than a quarter note in value

³flag *vb* **flagged; flag·ging 1** : to signal with or as if with a flag; *esp* : to signal to stop ⟨~ a taxi⟩ **2** : to mark or identify with or as if with a flag **3** : to call a penalty on

⁴flag *vb* **flagged; flag·ging 1** : to hang loose or limp **2** : to become unsteady, feeble, or spiritless **3** : to decline in interest or attraction ⟨the topic *flagged*⟩

⁵flag *n* : a hard flat stone suitable for paving

flag·el·late \'fla-jə-ˌlāt\ *vb* **-lat·ed; -lat·ing** : to punish by whipping — **flag·el·la·tion** \ˌfla-jə-'lā-shən\ *n*

fla·gel·lum \flə-'je-ləm\ *n, pl* **-la** \-lə\ *also* **-lums** : a long whiplike process that is the primary organ of motion of many microorganisms — **fla·gel·lar** \-lər\ *adj*

fla·geo·let \ˌfla-jə-'let, -'lā\ *n* [F] : a small woodwind instrument belonging to the flute class

fla·gi·tious \flə-'ji-shəs\ *adj* : grossly wicked : VILLAINOUS

flag·on \'fla-gən\ *n* : a container for liquids usu. with a handle, spout, and lid

flag·pole \'flag-ˌpōl\ *n* : a pole on which to raise a flag

fla·grant \'flā-grənt\ *adj* [L *flagrans*, prp. of *flagrare* to burn] : conspicuously bad ⟨~ abuse of power⟩ — **fla·grant·ly** *adv*

fla·gran·te de·lic·to \flə-ˌgran-tē-di-'lik-tō\ *adv* : IN FLAGRANTE DELICTO

flag·ship \'flag-ˌship\ *n* **1** : the ship that carries the commander of a fleet or subdivision thereof and flies his flag **2** : the most important one of a group

flag·staff \-ˌstaf\ *n* : FLAGPOLE

flag·stone \-ˌstōn\ *n* : ⁵FLAG

¹flail \'flāl\ *n* : a tool for threshing grain by hand

²flail *vb* : to strike or swing with or as if with a flail

flair \'fler\ *n* [F, lit., sense of smell, fr. OF, odor, fr. *flairier* to give off an odor, fr. VL *flagrare*, alter. of L *fragrare*] **1** : ability to appreciate or make good use of something : BENT, TALENT **2** : a unique style

flak \'flak\ *n, pl* **flak** [G, fr. *Fl*iegerabwehr*k*anonen, fr. *Flieger* flyer + *Abwehr* defense + *Kanonen* cannons] **1** : antiaircraft guns or bursting shells fired from them **2** : CRITICISM, OPPOSITION

¹flake \'flāk\ *n* **1** : a small loose mass or bit **2** : a thin flattened piece or layer : CHIP — **flaky** *adj*

²flake *vb* **flaked; flak·ing** : to form or separate into flakes

³flake *n* : a markedly eccentric person : ODDBALL — **flak·i·ness** \'flā-kē-nəs\ *n* — **flaky** *adj*

flam·beau \'flam-ˌbō\ *n, pl* **flambeaux** \-ˌbōz\ *or* **flam·beaus** [F, fr. MF, fr. *flambe* flame] : a flaming torch

flam·boy·ant \flam-'bȯi-ənt\ *adj* : marked by or given to strikingly elaborate or colorful display or behavior — **flam·boy·ance** \-əns\ *n* — **flam·boy·an·cy** \-ən-sē\ *n* — **flam·boy·ant·ly** *adv*

flame \'flām\ *n* **1** : the glowing gaseous part of a fire **2** : a state of blazing combustion **3** : a flamelike condition **4** : burning zeal or passion **5** : BRILLIANCE **6** : SWEETHEART **7** : an angry, hostile, or abusive electronic message — **flame** *vb*

fla·men·co \flə-'meŋ-kō\ *n, pl* **-cos** [Sp, fr. *flamenco* of the Gypsies, lit., Flemish, fr. MD *Vlaminc* Fleming] : a vigorous rhythmic dance style of the Spanish Gypsies

flame·throw·er \'flām-ˌthrō-ər\ *n* : a device that expels from a nozzle a burning stream of liquid or semiliquid fuel under pressure

fla·min·go \flə-'miŋ-gō\ *n, pl* **-gos** *also* **-goes** : any of several long-legged long-necked tropical water birds with scarlet wings and a broad bill bent downward

flam·ma·ble \'fla-mə-bəl\ *adj* : easily ignited and quick-burning — **flam·ma·bil·i·ty** \ˌfla-mə-'bi-lə-tē\ *n* — **flammable** *n*

flan \'flan, 'flän\ *n* **1** : an open pie with a sweet or savory filling **2** : custard baked with a caramel glaze

flange \'flanj\ *n* : a rim used for strengthening or guiding something or for attachment to another object

¹flank \'flaŋk\ *n* **1** : the fleshy part of the side between the ribs and the hip; *also* : the side of a quadruped **2** : SIDE **3** : the right or left of a formation

²flank *vb* **1** : to be situated on the side of : BORDER **2** : to attack or threaten the flank of

flank·er \'flaŋ-kər\ *n* : a football player stationed wide of the formation slightly behind the line of scrimmage as a pass receiver

flan·nel \'fla-nᵊl\ *n* **1** : a soft twilled wool or worsted fab-

ric with a napped surface **2** : a stout cotton fabric napped on one side **3** *pl* : flannel underwear or pants

¹flap \'flap\ *n* **1** : a stroke with something broad : SLAP **2** : something broad, limber, or flat and usu. thin that hangs loose **3** : the motion or sound of something broad and limber as it swings to and fro **4** : a state of excitement or confusion

²flap *vb* **flapped; flap·ping 1** : to beat with something broad and flat **2** : FLING **3** : to move (as wings) with a beating motion **4** : to sway loosely usu. with a noise of striking

flap·jack \'flap-ˌjak\ *n* : PANCAKE

flap·per \'fla-pər\ *n* **1** : one that flaps **2** : a young woman of the 1920s who showed freedom from conventions (as in conduct)

¹flare \'fler\ *n* **1** : a blaze of light used esp. to signal or illuminate; *also* : a device for producing such a blaze **2** : an unsteady glaring light

²flare *vb* **flared; flar·ing 1** : to flame with a sudden unsteady light **2** : to become suddenly excited or angry ⟨after his harangue, I *flared* up⟩ **3** : to spread outward

flare–up \-ˌəp\ *n* : a sudden outburst or intensification

¹flash \'flash\ *vb* **1** : to break forth in or like a sudden flame **2** : to appear or pass suddenly or with great speed **3** : to send out in or as if in flashes ⟨~ a message⟩ **4** : to make a sudden display (as of brilliance or feeling) **5** : to gleam or glow intermittently **6** : to fill by a sudden rush of water **7** : to expose to view very briefly ⟨~ a badge⟩ ◆ **Synonyms** GLANCE, GLINT, SPARKLE, TWINKLE — **flash·er** *n*

²flash *n* **1** : a sudden burst of light **2** : a movement of a flag or light in signaling **3** : a sudden and brilliant burst (as of wit) **4** : a brief time **5** : SHOW, DISPLAY; *esp* : ostentatious display **6** : one that attracts notice; *esp* : an outstanding athlete **7** : GLIMPSE, LOOK **8** : a first brief news report **9** : FLASHLIGHT **10** : a device for producing a brief and very bright flash of light for taking photographs **11** : a quick-spreading flame or momentary intense outburst of radiant heat

³flash *adj* : of sudden origin and short duration ⟨a ~ fire⟩ ⟨a ~ flood⟩

⁴flash *adv* : by very brief exposure to an intense agent (as heat or cold) ⟨~ fry⟩ ⟨~ freeze⟩

flash·back \'flash-ˌbak\ *n* **1** : interruption of the chronological sequence (as of a film or literary work) by an event of earlier occurrence **2** : a past event remembered vividly

flash back *vb* **1** : to vividly remember a past incident **2** : to employ a flashback

flash·bulb \-ˌbəlb\ *n* : an electric bulb that can be used only once to produce a brief and very bright flash of light for taking photographs

flash card *n* : a card bearing words, numbers, or pictures briefly displayed usu. as a learning aid

flash·cube \'flash-ˌkyüb\ *n* : a cubical device incorporating four flashbulbs

flash·gun \-ˌgən\ *n* : a device for producing a bright flash of light for photography

flash·ing \'fla-shiŋ\ *n* : sheet metal used in waterproofing (as at the angle between a chimney and a roof)

flash·light \'flash-ˌlīt\ *n* : a battery-operated portable electric light

flash memory *n* : a computer memory chip not requiring connection to a power source to retain its data

flashy \'fla-shē\ *adj* **flash·i·er; -est 1** : momentarily dazzling **2** : superficially attractive or impressive : SHOWY — **flash·i·ly** \-shə-lē\ *adv* — **flash·i·ness** \-shē-nəs\ *n*

flask \'flask\ *n* : a flattened bottle-shaped container ⟨a whiskey ~⟩

¹flat \'flat\ *adj* **flat·ter; flat·test 1** : spread out along a surface; *also* : being or characterized by a horizontal line **2** : having a smooth, level, or even surface **3** : having a broad smooth surface and little thickness **4** : DOWNRIGHT, POSITIVE ⟨a ~ refusal⟩ **5** : FIXED, UNCHANGING ⟨charge a ~ rate⟩ **6** : EXACT, PRECISE ⟨in four minutes ~⟩ **7** : DULL, UNINTERESTING; *also* : INSIPID **8** : DEFLATED ⟨a ~ tire⟩ **9** : lower than the true pitch; *also* : lower by a half step **10** : free from gloss ⟨a ~ paint⟩ **11** : lacking depth of characterization — **flat·ly** *adv* — **flat·ness** *n*

²flat *n* **1** : a level surface of land : PLAIN **2** : a flat part or surface **3** : a character ♭ that indicates that a specified note is to be lowered by a half step; *also* : the resulting note **4** : something flat **5** : an apartment on one floor **6** : a deflated tire

³**flat** *adv* **1** : FLATLY **2** : COMPLETELY ⟨~ broke⟩ **3** : below the true musical pitch

⁴**flat** *vb* **flat·ted; flat·ting 1** : FLATTEN **2** : to lower in pitch esp. by a half step

flat·bed \'flat-ˌbed\ *n* : a truck or trailer with a body in the form of a platform or shallow box

flat·boat \-ˌbōt\ *n* : a flat-bottomed boat used esp. for carrying bulky freight

flat·car \-ˌkär\ *n* : a railroad freight car without sides or roof

flat·fish \-ˌfish\ *n* : any of an order of flattened marine bony fishes with both eyes on the upper side

flatfish

flat·foot \-ˌfut, -ˈfut\ *n, pl* **flat·feet** \-ˌfēt, -ˈfēt\ : a condition in which the arch of the foot is flattened so that the entire sole rests upon the ground — **flat–foot·ed** \-ˈfu-təd\ *adj*

Flat·head \-ˌhed\ *n, pl* **Flatheads** *or* **Flathead** : a member of an American Indian people of Montana

flat·iron \-ˌī(-ə)rn\ *n* : IRON 3

flat·land \-ˌland\ *n* : land lacking significant variation in elevation

flat–out \'flat-ˌaut\ *adj* **1** : being or going at maximum effort or speed **2** : OUT-AND-OUT, DOWNRIGHT ⟨it was a ~ lie⟩

flat out *adv* **1** : BLUNTLY, DIRECTLY **2** : at top speed **3** *usu* **flat–out** : to the greatest degree : COMPLETELY ⟨is just *flat-out* confusing⟩

flat–panel \-ˈpa-nᵊl\ *adj* : relating to or being a thin flat video display

flat·ten \'fla-tᵊn\ *vb* : to make or become flat

flat·ter \'fla-tər\ *vb* [ME *flateren*, fr. AF *flater* to lap, flatter] **1** : to praise too much or without sincerity **2** : to represent too favorably ⟨the portrait ~s him⟩ **3** : to display to advantage **4** : to judge (oneself) favorably or too favorably — **flat·ter·er** *n*

flat·tery \'fla-tə-rē\ *n, pl* **-ter·ies** : flattering speech or attentions : insincere or excessive praise

flat·top \'flat-ˌtäp\ *n* **1** : AIRCRAFT CARRIER **2** : CREW CUT

flat·u·lent \'fla-chə-lənt\ *adj* **1** : full of gas ⟨a ~ stomach⟩ **2** : INFLATED, POMPOUS — **flat·u·lence** \-ləns\ *n*

fla·tus \'flā-təs\ *n* : gas formed in the intestine or stomach

flat·ware \'flat-ˌwer\ *n* : eating and serving utensils

flat·worm \-ˌwürm\ *n* : any of a phylum of flattened mostly parasitic segmented worms (as trematodes and tapeworms)

flaunt \'flont\ *vb* **1** : to display oneself to public notice **2** : to wave or flutter showily **3** : to display ostentatiously or impudently : PARADE — **flaunt** *n*

flau·ta \'flau-tə\ *n* : a tortilla rolled around a filling and deep-fried

flau·tist \'flo-tist, 'flau-\ *n* [It *flautista*] : FLUTIST

¹**fla·vor** \'flā-vər\ *n* **1** : the quality of something that affects the sense of taste or of taste and smell **2** : a substance that adds flavor **3** : characteristic or predominant quality — **fla·vored** \-vərd\ *adj* — **fla·vor·ful** *adj* — **fla·vor·less** *adj* — **fla·vor·some** *adj*

²**flavor** *vb* : to give or add flavor to

fla·vor·ing *n* : FLAVOR 2

fla·vour *chiefly Brit var of* FLAVOR

flaw \'flo\ *n* : a small often hidden defect — **flaw·less** *adj* — **flaw·less·ly** *adv* — **flaw·less·ness** *n*

flax \'flaks\ *n* : a fiber that is the source of linen; *also* : a blue-flowered plant grown for this fiber and its oily seeds

flax·en \'flak-sən\ *adj* **1** : made of flax **2** : resembling flax esp. in pale soft straw color

flay \'flā\ *vb* **1** : to strip off the skin or surface of **2** : to criticize harshly

fl dr *abbr* fluid dram

flea \'flē\ *n* : any of an order of small wingless leaping bloodsucking insects

flea·bane \'flē-ˌbān\ *n* : any of various plants of the daisy family once believed to drive away fleas

flea–bit·ten \-ˌbi-tᵊn\ *adj* : bitten by or infested with fleas

flea market *n* : a usu. open-air market for secondhand articles and antiques

¹**fleck** \'flek\ *vb* : STREAK, SPOT

²**fleck** *n* **1** : SPOT, MARK **2** : FLAKE, PARTICLE

fledge \'flej\ *vb* **fledged; fledg·ing** : to develop the feathers necessary for flying or independent activity

fledg·ling \'flej-liŋ\ *n* **1** : a young bird just fledged **2** : an immature or inexperienced person

flee \'flē\ *vb* **fled** \'fled\; **flee·ing 1** : to run away often from danger or evil **2** : VANISH **3** : to run away from : SHUN

¹**fleece** \'flēs\ *n* **1** : the woolly coat of an animal and esp. a sheep **2** : a soft or woolly covering — **fleecy** *adj*

²**fleece** *vb* **fleeced; fleec·ing 1** : to strip of money or property by fraud or extortion **2** : SHEAR

¹**fleet** \'flēt\ *vb* : to pass rapidly

²**fleet** *n* [ME *flete*, fr. OE *flēot* ship, fr. *flēotan* to float] **1** : a group of warships under one command **2** : a group (as of ships, planes, or trucks) under one management

³**fleet** *adj* **1** : SWIFT, NIMBLE **2** : not enduring : FLEETING — **fleet·ness** *n*

fleet admiral *n* : an admiral of the highest rank in the navy

fleet·ing \'flē-tiŋ\ *adj* : passing swiftly

Flem·ing \'fle-miŋ\ *n* : a member of a Germanic people inhabiting chiefly northern Belgium

Flem·ish \'fle-mish\ *n* **1** : the Dutch language as spoken by the Flemings **2 Flemish** *pl* : FLEMINGS — **Flemish** *adj*

¹**flesh** \'flesh\ *n* **1** : the soft parts of an animal's body; *esp* : muscular tissue **2** : MEAT **3** : the physical nature of humans as distinguished from the soul **4** : human beings; *also* : living beings **5** : STOCK, KINDRED **6** : fleshy plant tissue (as fruit pulp) — **fleshed** \'flesht\ *adj*

²**flesh** *vb* : to make fuller or more nearly complete — usu. used with *out* ⟨flesh out a schedule⟩

flesh fly *n* : a dipteran fly whose maggots feed on flesh

flesh·ly \'flesh-lē\ *adj* **1** : CORPOREAL, BODILY **2** : not spiritual : WORLDLY **3** : CARNAL, SENSUAL

flesh·pot \'flesh-ˌpät\ *n* **1** *pl* : bodily comfort : LUXURY **2** : a place of lascivious entertainment — usu. used in pl.

fleshy \'fle-shē\ *adj* **flesh·i·er; -est 1** : consisting of or resembling animal flesh **2** : PLUMP, FAT

flew *past of* ¹FLY

flex \'fleks\ *vb* : to bend esp. repeatedly — **flex** *n*

flex·i·ble \'flek-sə-bəl\ *adj* **1** : capable of being flexed : PLIANT **2** : yielding to influence : TRACTABLE **3** : readily changed or changing : ADAPTABLE ♦ **Synonyms** ELASTIC, SUPPLE, RESILIENT, SPRINGY — **flex·i·bil·i·ty** \ˌflek-sə-ˈbi-lə-tē\ *n*

flex·or \'flek-sər, -ˌsȯr\ *n* : a muscle serving to bend a body part

flex·ure \'flek-shər\ *n* : TURN, FOLD

flib·ber·ti·gib·bet \ˌfli-bər-tē-ˈji-bət\ *n* : a silly flighty person

¹**flick** \'flik\ *n* **1** : a light sharp jerky stroke or movement **2** : a sound produced by a flick **3** : ²FLICKER

²**flick** *vb* **1** : to strike lightly with a quick sharp motion **2** : FLUTTER, FLIT

³**flick** *n* : MOVIE

¹**flick·er** \'fli-kər\ *vb* **1** : to move irregularly or unsteadily : FLUTTER **2** : to burn fitfully or with a fluctuating light — **flick·er·ing·ly** *adv*

²**flicker** *n* **1** : an act of flickering **2** : a sudden brief movement ⟨a ~ of an eyelid⟩ **3** : a momentary stirring ⟨a ~ of interest⟩ **4** : a slight indication : HINT **5** : a wavering light

³**flicker** *n* : a large barred and spotted No. American woodpecker with a brown back that occurs as an eastern form

with yellow on the underside of the wings and tail and a western form with red in these areas

flied *past and past part of* ³FLY

fli·er \'flī(-ə)r\ *n* **1** : one that flies; *esp* : PILOT **2** : a reckless or speculative undertaking **3** *usu* **fly·er** : an advertising circular

¹**flight** \'flīt\ *n* **1** : an act or instance of flying **2** : the ability to fly **3** : a passing through air or space **4** : the distance covered in a flight **5** : swift movement **6** : a trip made by or in an airplane or spacecraft **7** : a group of similar individuals (as birds or airplanes) flying as a unit **8** : a passing (as of the imagination) beyond ordinary limits **9** : a series of stairs from one landing to another — **flight·less** *adj*

²**flight** *n* : an act or instance of running away

flight bag *n* **1** : a lightweight traveling bag with zippered outside pockets **2** : a small canvas satchel

flight line *n* : a parking and servicing area for airplanes

flighty \'flī-tē\ *adj* **flight·i·er; -est** **1** : easily upset : VOLATILE **2** : easily excited : SKITTISH **3** : CAPRICIOUS, SILLY — **flight·i·ness** \-tē-nəs\ *n*

flim·flam \'flim-,flam\ *n* : DECEPTION, FRAUD — **flim·flam·mery** \-,fla-mə-re\ *n*

flim·sy \'flim-zē\ *adj* **flim·si·er; -est** **1** : lacking strength or substance **2** : of inferior materials and workmanship **3** : having little worth or plausibility ⟨a ~ excuse⟩ — **flim·si·ly** \-zə-lē\ *adv* — **flim·si·ness** \-zē-nəs\ *n*

flinch \'flinch\ *vb* [MF *flenchir* to bend] : to shrink from or as if from pain : WINCE — **flinch** *n*

¹**fling** \'fliŋ\ *vb* **flung** \'fləŋ\; **fling·ing** **1** : to move hastily, brusquely, or violently ⟨*flung* out of the room⟩ **2** : to kick or plunge vigorously **3** : to throw with force or recklessness; *also* : to cast as if by throwing **4** : to put suddenly into a state or condition

²**fling** *n* **1** : an act or instance of flinging **2** : a casual try : ATTEMPT **3** : a period of self-indulgence

flint \'flint\ *n* **1** : a hard dark quartz that produces a spark when struck by steel **2** : an alloy used for producing a spark in lighters — **flinty** *adj*

flint glass *n* : heavy glass containing an oxide of lead and used in lenses and prisms

flint·lock \'flint-,läk\ *n* **1** : a lock for a gun using a flint to ignite the charge **2** : a firearm fitted with a flintlock

flintlock pistol

¹**flip** \'flip\ *vb* **flipped; flip·ping** **1** : to turn by tossing ⟨~ a coin⟩ **2** : to turn over; *also* : to leaf through **3** : FLICK, JERK ⟨~ a light switch⟩ **4** : to lose self-control — **flip** *n*

²**flip** *adj* : FLIPPANT, IMPERTINENT

flip·pant \'fli-pənt\ *adj* : lacking proper respect or seriousness — **flip·pan·cy** \'fli-pən-sē\ *n*

flip·per \'fli-pər\ *n* **1** : a broad flat limb (as of a seal) adapted for swimming **2** : a paddlelike shoe used in skin diving

flip side *n* : the reverse and usu. less popular side of a phonograph record

¹**flirt** \'flərt\ *vb* **1** : to move erratically : FLIT **2** : to behave amorously without serious intent **3** : to show casual interest ⟨~ed with the idea⟩; *also* : to come close to ⟨~ with danger⟩ — **flir·ta·tion** \,flər-'tā-shən\ *n* — **flir·ta·tious** \-shəs\ *adj*

²**flirt** *n* **1** : an act or instance of flirting **2** : a person who flirts

flit \'flit\ *vb* **flit·ted; flit·ting** : to pass or move quickly or abruptly from place to place : DART — **flit** *n*

flitch \'flich\ *n* : a side of cured meat; *esp* : a side of bacon

fliv·ver \'fli-vər\ *n* : a small cheap usu. old automobile

¹**float** \'flōt\ *n* **1** : something (as a raft) that floats **2** : a cork buoying up the baited end of a fishing line **3** : a hollow ball that floats at the end of a lever in a cistern or tank and regulates the liquid level **4** : a vehicle with a platform to carry an exhibit **5** : a soft drink with ice cream floating in it

²**float** *vb* **1** : to rest on the surface of or be suspended in a fluid **2** : to move gently on or through a fluid **3** : to cause to float **4** : WANDER **5** : to offer (securities) in order to finance an enterprise **6** : to finance by floating an issue of stocks or bonds **7** : to arrange for ⟨~ a loan⟩ — **float·er** *n*

floaty \'flō-tē\ *adj* **float·i·er; -est** **1** : tending to float : BUOYANT **2** : light and billowy

¹**flock** \'fläk\ *n* **1** : a group of animals (as birds or sheep) assembled or herded together **2** : a group of people under the guidance of a leader; *esp* : CONGREGATION **3** : a large number ⟨a ~ of tourists⟩

²**flock** *vb* : to gather or move in a flock ⟨people ~ed to the beach⟩

floe \'flō\ *n* : a flat mass of floating ice

flog \'fläg\ *vb* **flogged; flog·ging** **1** : to beat with or as if with a rod or whip **2** : SELL ⟨~ encyclopedias⟩ — **flog·ger** *n*

¹**flood** \'fləd\ *n* **1** : a great flow of water over the land **2** : the flowing in of the tide **3** : an overwhelming volume

²**flood** *vb* **1** : to cover or become filled with a flood **2** : to fill abundantly or excessively; *esp* : to supply an excess of fuel to **3** : to pour forth in a flood — **flood·er** *n*

flood·gate \'fləd-,gāt\ *n* : a gate for controlling a body of water : SLUICE

flood·light \-,līt\ *n* : a lamp that throws a broad beam of light; *also* : the beam itself — **floodlight** *vb*

flood·plain \-,plān\ *n* : a plain along a river or stream subject to periodic flooding

flood tide *n* **1** : a rising tide **2** : an overwhelming quantity **3** : a high point

flood·wa·ter \'fləd-,wȯ-tər, -,wä-\ *n* : the water of a flood

¹**floor** \'flȯr\ *n* **1** : the bottom of a room on which one stands **2** : a ground surface **3** : a story of a building **4** : a main level space (as in a legislative chamber) distinguished from a platform or gallery **5** : AUDIENCE **6** : the right to address an assembly **7** : a lower limit ⟨put a ~ under wheat prices⟩ — **floor·ing** *n*

²**floor** *vb* **1** : to furnish with a floor **2** : to knock down **3** : AMAZE, DUMBFOUND **4** : to press (a vehicle's accelerator) to the floorboard esp. rapidly

floor·board \-,bȯrd\ *n* **1** : a board in a floor **2** : the floor of an automobile

floor leader *n* : a member of a legislative body who has charge of a party's organization and strategy on the floor

floor show *n* : a series of acts presented in a nightclub

floor·walk·er \'flȯr-,wȯ-kər\ *n* : a person employed in a retail store to oversee the sales force and aid customers

floo·zy *or* **floo·zie** \'flü-zē\ *n, pl* **floozies** : a usu. young woman of loose morals

flop \'fläp\ *vb* **flopped; flop·ping** **1** : FLAP **2** : to throw oneself down heavily, clumsily, or in a relaxed manner ⟨*flopped* into a chair⟩ **3** : FAIL ⟨the show *flopped*⟩ — **flop** *n* — **flop** *adv* — **flop·per** *n*

flop·house \'fläp-,haùs\ *n* : a cheap hotel

¹**flop·py** \'flä-pē\ *adj* **flop·pi·er; -est** : tending to flop; *esp* : soft and flexible — **flop·pi·ly** \-pə-lē\ *adv*

²**floppy** *n, pl* **flop·pies** : FLOPPY DISK

floppy disk *n* : a thin plastic disk with a magnetic coating on which computer data can be stored

flop sweat *n* : sweat caused by the fear of failing

flo·ra \'flȯr-ə\ *n, pl* **floras** *also* **flo·rae** \-,ē, -,ī\ [L *Flora*, Roman goddess of flowers] : plants or plant life esp. of a region or period

flo·ral \'flȯr-əl\ *adj* : of, relating to, or depicting flowers ⟨a ~ design⟩

flo·res·cence \flȯ-'re-s³ns, flə-\ *n* : a state or period of being in bloom or flourishing — **flo·res·cent** \-³nt\ *adj*

flor·id \'flȯr-əd\ *adj* **1** : very flowery in style : ORNATE ⟨~ prose⟩ **2** : tinged with red : RUDDY **3** : marked by emotional or sexual fervor

flo·rin \'flȯr-ən\ *n* **1** : an old gold coin first struck at Florence, Italy, in 1252 **2** : a gold coin of a European country patterned after the florin of Florence **3** : any of several modern silver coins issued in Commonwealth countries **4** : GULDEN

flo·rist \'flȯr-ist\ *n* : a person who sells flowers or ornamental plants

¹**floss** \'fläs\ *n* **1** : soft thread of silk or mercerized cotton for embroidery **2** : DENTAL FLOSS **3** : fluffy fibrous material

²**floss** *vb* : to use dental floss on (one's teeth)

flossy \'flä-sē\ *adj* **floss·i·er; -est 1** : of, relating to, or having the characteristics of floss **2** : STYLISH, GLAMOROUS ⟨∼ hotels⟩ — **floss·i·ly** \-sə-lē\ *adv*

flo·ta·tion \flō-'tā-shən\ *n* : the process or an instance of floating

flo·til·la \flō-'ti-lə\ *n* [Sp, dim. of *flota* fleet] : a fleet esp. of small ships

flot·sam \'flät-səm\ *n* : floating wreckage of a ship or its cargo

¹**flounce** \'flaůns\ *vb* **flounced; flounc·ing 1** : to move with exaggerated jerky or bouncy motions **2** : to go with sudden determination

²**flounce** *n* : an act or instance of flouncing — **flouncy** \'flaůn-sē\ *adj*

³**flounce** *n* : a strip of fabric attached by one edge; *also* : a wide ruffle

¹**floun·der** \'flaůn-dər\ *n, pl* **flounder** *or* **flounders** : FLATFISH; *esp* : any of various important marine food fishes

²**flounder** *vb* **1** : to struggle to move or obtain footing **2** : to proceed clumsily ⟨∼ed through the speech⟩

¹**flour** \'flaů(-ə)r\ *n* [ME, flower, best of anything, flour, fr. AF *flur* flower] : finely ground and sifted meal of a grain (as wheat); *also* : a fine soft powder — **floury** *adj*

²**flour** *vb* : to coat with or as if with flour

¹**flour·ish** \'flər-ish\ *vb* **1** : THRIVE, PROSPER **2** : to be in a state of activity or production ⟨∼ed about 1850⟩ **3** : to reach a height of development or influence **4** : to make bold and sweeping gestures **5** : BRANDISH

²**flourish** *n* **1** : a florid bit of speech or writing; *also* : an ornamental touch or decorative detail **2** : FANFARE **3** : WAVE ⟨with a ∼ of his cane⟩ **4** : showiness in doing something

¹**flout** \'flaůt\ *vb* : to treat with contemptuous disregard ⟨∼ the law⟩ — **flout·er** *n*

²**flout** *n* : TAUNT

¹**flow** \'flō\ *vb* **1** : to issue or move in a stream **2** : RISE ⟨the tide ebbs and ∼s⟩ **3** : ABOUND **4** : to proceed smoothly and readily **5** : to have a smooth continuity **6** : to hang loose and billowing **7** : COME, ARISE **8** : MENSTRUATE

²**flow** *n* **1** : an act of flowing **2** : FLOOD 1, 2 **3** : a smooth uninterrupted movement **4** : STREAM; *also* : a mass of material that has flowed when molten **5** : the quantity that flows in a certain time **6** : MENSTRUATION **7** : a continuous transfer of energy — **flow·age** \'flō-ij\ *n*

flow·chart \'flō-ˌchärt\ *n* : a symbolic diagram showing step-by-step progression through a procedure

flow diagram *n* : FLOWCHART

¹**flow·er** \'flaů(-ə)r\ *n* [ME *flour*, fr. AF *flur, flour*, fr. L *flor-, flos*] **1** : a plant shoot modified for reproduction and bearing leaves specialized into floral organs; *esp* : one of a seed plant consisting of a calyx, corolla, stamens, and carpels **2** : a plant cultivated for its blossoms **3** : the best part or example **4** : the finest most vigorous period **5** : a state of blooming or flourishing — **flow·ered** \'flaů(-ə)rd\ *adj* — **flow·er·less** *adj* — **flow·er·like** \-ˌlīk\ *adj*

²**flower** *vb* **1** : DEVELOP; *also* : FLOURISH **2** : to produce flowers : BLOOM

flower girl *n* : a little girl who carries flowers at a wedding

flower head *n* : a compact cluster of small flowers without stems suggesting a single flower

flowering plant *n* : any of a major group of vascular plants (as magnolias, grasses, or roses) that produce flowers and fruit and have the seeds enclosed in an ovary

flow·er·pot \'flaů(-ə)r-ˌpät\ *n* : a pot in which to grow plants

flow·ery \'flaů(-ə)r-ē\ *adj* **1** : of, relating to, or resembling flowers **2** : full of fine words or phrases — **flow·er·i·ness** \-ē-nəs\ *n*

flown \'flōn\ *past part of* ¹FLY

fl oz *abbr* fluid ounce

flu \'flü\ *n* **1** : INFLUENZA **2** : any of several virus diseases marked esp. by respiratory or intestinal symptoms — **flu-like** \-ˌlīk\ *adj*

flub \'fləb\ *vb* **flubbed; flub·bing** : BOTCH, BLUNDER — **flub** *n*

fluc·tu·ate \'flək-chə-ˌwāt\ *vb* **-at·ed; -at·ing 1** : WAVER **2** : to move up and down or back and forth — **fluc·tu·a·tion** \ˌflək-chə-'wā-shən\ *n*

flue \'flü\ *n* : a passage (as in a chimney) for directing a current (as of smoke or gases)

flu·ent \'flü-ənt\ *adj* **1** : capable of flowing : FLUID **2** : ready or facile in speech ⟨∼ in French⟩; *also* : having or showing mastery in a subject or skill **3** : effortlessly smooth and rapid ⟨∼ speech⟩ — **flu·en·cy** \-ən-sē\ *n* — **flu·ent·ly** *adv*

flue pipe *n* : an organ pipe whose tone is produced by an air current striking the beveled opening of the pipe

¹**fluff** \'fləf\ *n* **1** : ⁷DOWN 1 ⟨∼ from a pillow⟩ **2** : something fluffy **3** : something inconsequential **4** : BLUNDER; *esp* : an actor's lapse of memory

²**fluff** *vb* **1** : to make or become fluffy ⟨∼ up a pillow⟩ **2** : to make a mistake

fluffy \'flə-fē\ *adj* **fluff·i·er; -est 1** : covered with or resembling fluff **2** : being light and soft or airy ⟨a ∼ omelet⟩ **3** : lacking in meaning or substance — **fluff·i·ly** \-fə-lē\ *adv*

¹**flu·id** \'flü-əd\ *adj* **1** : capable of flowing **2** : subject to change or movement **3** : showing a smooth easy style ⟨∼ movements⟩ **4** : available for a different use; *esp* : LIQUID **5** ⟨∼ assets⟩ — **flu·id·i·ty** \flü-'i-də-tē\ *n* — **flu·id·ly** *adv*

²**fluid** *n* : a substance (as a liquid or gas) tending to flow or take the shape of its container

fluid dram *or* **flu·i·dram** \ˌflü-ə-'dram\ *n* — see WEIGHT table

fluid ounce *n* — see WEIGHT table

¹**fluke** \'flük\ *n* : any of various trematode flatworms

²**fluke** *n* **1** : the part of an anchor that fastens in the ground **2** : a lobe of a whale's tail

³**fluke** *n* : a stroke of luck — **fluky** *also* **fluk·ey** \'flü-kē\ *adj*

flume \'flüm\ *n* **1** : an inclined channel for carrying water **2** : a ravine or gorge with a stream running through it

flung *past and past part of* FLING

flunk \'fləŋk\ *vb* : to fail esp. in an examination or course — **flunk** *n*

flun·ky *also* **flun·key** *or* **flun·kie** \'flən-kē\ *n, pl* **flunkies** *also* **flunkeys 1** : a liveried servant; *also* : one performing menial or miscellaneous duties **2** : YES-MAN

fluo·res·cence \flȯ-'re-s²ns\ *n* : luminescence caused by radiation absorption that ceases almost immediately after the incident radiation has stopped; *also* : the emitted radiation — **fluo·resce** \-'res\ *vb* — **fluo·res·cent** \-'res-²nt\ *adj*

fluorescent lamp *n* : a tubular electric lamp in which light is produced by the action of ultraviolet light on a fluorescent material that coats the inner surface of the lamp

fluo·ri·date \'flȯr-ə-ˌdāt\ *vb* **-dat·ed; -dat·ing** : to add a fluoride to (as drinking water) to reduce tooth decay — **fluo·ri·da·tion** \ˌflȯr-ə-'dā-shən\ *n*

fluo·ride \'flȯr-ˌīd\ *n* : a compound of fluorine

fluo·ri·nate \'flȯr-ə-ˌnāt\ *vb* **-nat·ed; -nat·ing** : to treat or cause to combine with fluorine or a compound of fluorine — **fluo·ri·na·tion** \ˌflȯr-ə-'nā-shən\ *n*

fluo·rine \'flȯr-ˌēn, -ən\ *n* : a pale yellowish flammable irritating toxic gaseous chemical element

fluo·rite \'flȯr-ˌīt\ *n* : a mineral that consists of the fluoride of calcium used as a flux and in making glass

fluo·ro·car·bon \ˌflȯr-ō-'kär-bən\ *n* : a compound containing fluorine and carbon used chiefly as a lubricant, refrigerant, or nonstick coating; *also* : CHLOROFLUOROCARBON

fluo·ro·scope \'flȯr-ə-ˌskōp\ *n* : an instrument for observing the internal structure of an opaque object (as the living body) by means of X-rays — **fluo·ro·scop·ic** \ˌflȯr-ə-'skä-pik\ *adj* — **fluo·ros·co·py** \-'ä-skə-pē\ *n*

fluo·ro·sis \ˌflů-'rō-səs, ˌflȯ-\ *n* : an abnormal condition (as spotting of the teeth) caused by fluorine or its compounds

flu·ox·e·tine \flü-'äk-sə-ˌtēn\ *n* : an antidepressant drug that enhances serotonin activity

flur·ry \'flər-ē\ *n, pl* **flurries 1** : a gust of wind **2** : a brief light snowfall **3** : COMMOTION, BUSTLE **4** : a brief outburst of activity ⟨a ∼ of trading⟩ — **flurry** *vb*

¹**flush** \'fləsh\ *vb* : to cause (a bird) to fly away suddenly

²**flush** *n* : a hand of cards all of the same suit

³**flush** *n* **1** : a sudden flow (as of water) **2** : a surge esp. of emotion ⟨a ∼ of triumph⟩ **3** : a tinge of red : BLUSH **4** : a fresh and vigorous state ⟨in the ∼ of youth⟩ **5** : a passing sensation of extreme heat

⁴flush *vb* **1 :** to flow and spread suddenly and freely **2 :** to glow brightly **3 :** BLUSH **4 :** to wash out with a rush of fluid **5 :** INFLAME, EXCITE **6 :** to cause to blush

⁵flush *adj* **1 :** of a ruddy healthy color **2 :** full of life and vigor **3 :** filled to overflowing **4 :** AFFLUENT **5 :** readily available : ABUNDANT **6 :** having an unbroken or even surface **7 :** directly abutting : immediately adjacent **8 :** set even with an edge of a type page or column — **flush·ness** *n*

⁶flush *adv* **1 :** in a flush manner **2 :** SQUARELY ⟨a blow ∼ on the chin⟩

⁷flush *vb* **:** to make flush

flus·ter \'fləs-tər\ *vb* **:** to put into a state of agitated confusion — **fluster** *n*

flute \'flüt\ *n* **1 :** a hollow pipelike musical instrument **2 :** a grooved pleat **3 :** GROOVE — **flute** *vb* — **flut·ed** *adj*

flut·ing *n* **:** fluted decoration

flut·ist \'flü-tist\ *n* **:** a flute player

¹flut·ter \'flə-tər\ *vb* [ME *floteren* to float, flutter, fr. OE *floterian*, fr. *flotian* to float] **1 :** to flap the wings rapidly **2 :** to move with quick wavering or flapping motions **3 :** to vibrate in irregular spasms **4 :** to move about or behave in an agitated aimless manner — **flut·tery** \-tə-rē\ *adj*

²flutter *n* **1 :** an act of fluttering **2 :** a state of nervous confusion **3 :** FLURRY

¹flux \'fləks\ *n* **1 :** an act of flowing **2 :** a state of continuous change **3 :** a substance used to aid in fusing metals

²flux *vb* **:** ¹FUSE

¹fly \'flī\ *vb* **flew** \'flü\; **flown** \'flōn\; **fly·ing** **1 :** to move in or pass through the air with wings **2 :** to move through the air or before the wind **3 :** to float or cause to float, wave, or soar in the air **4 :** FLEE **5 :** to fade and disappear : VANISH **6 :** to move or pass swiftly ⟨time *flies*⟩ **7 :** to become expended or dissipated rapidly **8 :** to operate or travel in an aircraft or spacecraft **9 :** to journey over by flying **10 :** AVOID, SHUN **11 :** to transport by flying

²fly *n, pl* **flies** **1 :** the action or process of flying : FLIGHT **2** *pl* **:** the space over a theater stage **3 :** a garment closing concealed by a fold of cloth **4 :** the length of an extended flag from its staff or support **5 :** a baseball hit high into the air **6 :** the outer canvas of a tent with a double top — **on the fly :** while still in the air

³fly *vb* **flied; fly·ing :** to hit a fly in baseball

⁴fly *n, pl* **flies** **1 :** a winged insect — usu. used in combination ⟨butter*fly*⟩ **2 :** any of a large order of insects mostly with one pair of functional wings and another pair that if present are reduced to balancing organs and often with larvae without a head, eyes, or legs; *esp* **:** one (as a housefly) that is large and stout-bodied **3 :** a fishhook dressed to suggest an insect

fly·able \'flī-ə-bəl\ *adj* **:** suitable for flying or being flown

fly ball *n* **:** ²FLY 5

fly·blown \'flī-ˌblōn\ *adj* **:** not pure : TAINTED, CORRUPT

fly·by \-ˌbī\ *n, pl* **flybys** **1 :** a usu. low-altitude flight by an aircraft over a public gathering **2 :** a flight of a spacecraft past a heavenly body (as Jupiter) close enough to obtain scientific data

fly–by–night \-ˌbī-ˌnīt\ *adj* **1 :** seeking a quick profit usu. by shady acts **2 :** TRANSITORY, PASSING ⟨∼ fashions⟩

fly casting *n* **:** the casting of artificial flies in fly-fishing or as a competitive sport

fly·catch·er \-ˌka-chər, -ˌke-\ *n* **:** any of various passerine birds that feed on insects caught in flight

flyer *var of* FLIER

fly–fish·ing \'flī-ˌfi-shiŋ\ *n* **:** a method of fishing in which an artificial fly is used for bait

flying boat *n* **:** a seaplane with a hull designed for floating

flying buttress *n* **:** a projecting arched structure to support a wall or building

flying fish *n* **:** any of numerous marine bony fishes capable of long gliding flights out of water by spreading their large fins like wings

flying saucer *n* **:** an unidentified flying object reported to be saucer-shaped or disk-shaped

flying squirrel *n* **:** either of two small nocturnal No. American squirrels with folds of skin connecting the forelegs and hind legs that enable them to make long gliding leaps

fly·leaf \'flī-ˌlēf\ *n, pl* **fly·leaves** \-ˌlēvz\ **:** a blank leaf at the beginning or end of a book

fly·pa·per \-ˌpā-pər\ *n* **:** paper poisoned or coated with a sticky substance for killing or catching flies

fly·speck \-ˌspek\ *n* **1 :** a speck of fly dung **2 :** something small and insignificant

fly·way \-ˌwā\ *n* **:** an established air route of migratory birds

fly·wheel \-ˌhwēl\ *n* **:** a heavy wheel for regulating the speed of machinery

fm *abbr* fathom

Fm *symbol* fermium

FM \'ef-ˌem\ *n* **:** a broadcasting system using frequency modulation; *also* **:** a radio receiver of such a system

fn *abbr* footnote

fo *or* **fol** *abbr* folio

FO *abbr* foreign office

¹foal \'fōl\ *n* **:** a young horse or related animal; *esp* **:** one under one year

²foal *vb* **:** to give birth to a foal

¹foam \'fōm\ *n* **1 :** a mass of bubbles formed on the surface of a liquid : FROTH, SPUME **2 :** material (as rubber) in a lightweight cellular form — **foamy** *adj*

²foam *vb* **:** to form foam : FROTH

fob \'fäb\ *n* **1 :** a short strap, ribbon, or chain attached esp. to a pocket watch **2 :** a small ornament worn on a fob

FOB *abbr* free on board

fob off *vb* **1 :** to put off with a trick, excuse, or inferior substitute **2 :** to pass or offer as genuine **3 :** to put aside

FOC *abbr* free of charge

focal length *n* **:** the distance of a focus from a lens or curved mirror

fo'c'sle *var of* FORECASTLE

¹fo·cus \'fō-kəs\ *n, pl* **fo·ci** \-ˌsī\ *also* **fo·cus·es** [NL, fr. L, hearth] **1 :** a point at which rays (as of light, heat, or sound) meet or diverge or appear to diverge; *esp* **:** the point at which an image is formed by a mirror, lens, or optical system **2 :** FOCAL LENGTH **3 :** adjustment (as of eyes or eyeglasses) that gives clear vision **4 :** central point : CENTER — **fo·cal** \'fō-kəl\ *adj* — **fo·cal·ly** *adv*

²focus *vb* **-cused** *also* **-cussed**; **-cus·ing** *also* **-cus·sing** **1 :** to bring or come to a focus ⟨∼ rays of light⟩ **2 :** CENTER ⟨∼ attention on a problem⟩ **3 :** to adjust the focus of

fod·der \'fä-dər\ *n* **1 :** coarse dry food (as cornstalks) for livestock **2 :** available material used to supply a heavy demand

foe \'fō\ *n* [ME *fo*, fr. OE *fāh*, fr. *fāh* hostile] **:** ENEMY

FOE *abbr* Fraternal Order of Eagles

foehn *or* **föhn** \'fərn, 'fœn, 'fān\ *n* [G *Föhn*] **:** a warm dry wind blowing down a mountainside

foe·man \'fō-mən\ *n* **:** FOE

foe·tal, foe·tus *chiefly Brit var of* FETAL, FETUS

¹fog \'fóg, 'fäg\ *n* **1 :** fine particles of water suspended in the lower atmosphere **2 :** mental confusion — **fog·gy** *adj*

²fog *vb* **fogged; fog·ging :** to obscure or be obscured with or as if with fog

fog·horn \'fóg-ˌhórn, 'fäg-\ *n* **:** a horn sounded in a fog to give warning

fo·gy *also* **fo·gey** \'fō-gē\ *n, pl* **fogies** *also* **fogeys :** a person with old-fashioned ideas ⟨an old ∼⟩

foi·ble \'fói-bəl\ *n* **:** a minor failing or weakness in character or behavior

foie gras \'fwä-'grä\ *n* [F, lit., fat liver] **:** the fattened liver of an animal and esp. of a goose usu. served as a pâté

¹foil \'fói(-ə)l\ *vb* [ME, alter. of *fullen* to full cloth, fr. AF *foller*] **1 :** to prevent from attaining an end : DEFEAT **2 :** to bring to naught : THWART

flying fish

²**foil** n [ME, leaf, fr. AF *fuille, foille,* fr. L *folia,* pl. of *folium* leaf] **1** : a very thin sheet of metal ⟨aluminum ∼⟩ **2** : one that serves as a contrast to another ⟨acted as a ∼ for a comedian⟩

³**foil** n : a light fencing sword with a flexible blade tapering to a blunt point

foist \'fȯist\ vb : to pass off (something false or worthless) as genuine

¹**fold** \'fōld\ n **1** : an enclosure for sheep **2** : a group of people with a common faith, belief, or interest

²**fold** vb : to house (sheep) in a fold

³**fold** vb **1** : to lay one part over or against another part **2** : to clasp together **3** : EMBRACE **4** : to bend (as a layer of rock) into folds **5** : to incorporate into a mixture by overturning repeatedly without stirring or beating **6** : to become doubled or pleated **7** : FAIL, COLLAPSE ⟨the business ∼ed⟩

⁴**fold** n **1** : a doubling or folding over **2** : a part doubled or laid over another part

fold·away \'fōld-ə-ˌwā\ adj : designed to fold out of the way or out of sight

fold·er \'fōl-dər\ n **1** : one that folds **2** : a folded printed circular **3** : a folded cover or large envelope for loose papers **4** : an object in a computer operating system used to organize files or other folders

fol·de·rol \'fäl-də-ˌräl\ n **1** : a useless trifle **2** : NONSENSE

fold·out \'fōld-ˌaut\ n : a folded leaf (as in a magazine) larger in some dimension than the page

fo·liage \'fō-lē-ij\ n : a mass of leaves (as of a plant or forest)

fo·li·at·ed \'fō-lē-ˌā-təd\ adj : composed of or separable into layers

fo·lic acid \ˌfō-lik-\ n : a vitamin of the vitamin B complex used esp. to treat nutritional anemias

fo·lio \'fō-lē-ˌō\ n, pl **fo·li·os** **1** : a leaf of a book; *also* : a page number **2** : the size of a piece of paper cut two from a sheet **3** : a book printed on folio pages

¹**folk** \'fōk\ n, pl **folk** or **folks** **1** : the largest number or most characteristic part of a group of people forming a tribe or nation **2** pl : PEOPLE, PERSONS ⟨country ∼⟩ ⟨old ∼s⟩ **3** *folks* pl : the persons of one's own family

²**folk** adj : of, relating to, or originating among the common people ⟨∼ music⟩

folk art n : the traditional anonymous art of usu. untrained people

folk·lore \'fōk-ˌlȯr\ n : customs, beliefs, stories, and sayings of a people handed down from generation to generation — **folk·lor·ic** \-ˌlȯr-ik\ adj — **folk·lor·ist** \-ist\ n

folk mass n : a mass in which traditional liturgical music is replaced by folk music

folk·sing·er \'fōk-ˌsiŋ-ər\ n : a singer of folk songs — **folk·sing·ing** n

folksy \'fōk-sē\ adj **folks·i·er; -est** **1** : SOCIABLE, FRIENDLY **2** : informal, casual, or familiar in manner or style ⟨∼ humor⟩

folk·way \'fōk-ˌwā\ n : a way of thinking, feeling, or acting common to a given group of people; *esp* : a traditional social custom

fol·li·cle \'fä-li-kəl\ n **1** : a small anatomical cavity or gland ⟨a hair ∼⟩ **2** : a small fluid-filled cavity in the ovary of a mammal enclosing a developing egg — **fol·lic·u·lar** \fə-'li-kyə-lər\ adj

fol·low \'fä-lō\ vb **1** : to go or come after **2** : to proceed along ⟨∼ the path⟩ **3** : to engage in as a way of life ⟨∼ the sea⟩ ⟨∼ a profession⟩ **4** : OBEY ⟨∼ instructions⟩ **5** : PURSUE **6** : to come after in order or rank or natural sequence **7** : to keep one's attention fixed on **8** : to result from ♦ *Synonyms* SUCCEED, ENSUE, SUPERVENE — **fol·low·er** n — **follow suit** **1** : to play a card of the same suit as the card led **2** : to follow an example set

¹**fol·low·ing** \'fä-lə-wiŋ\ adj **1** : next after : SUCCEEDING ⟨the ∼ day⟩ **2** : that immediately follows ⟨trains will leave at the ∼ times⟩

²**following** n : a group of followers, adherents, or partisans

³**following** prep : subsequent to : AFTER ⟨∼ the lecture tea was served⟩

follow–up \'fä-lō-ˌəp\ n : a system or instance of pursuing an initial effort by supplementary action

fol·ly \'fä-lē\ n, pl **follies** [ME *folie,* fr. AF, fr. *fol* fool] **1** : lack of good sense **2** : a foolish act or idea : FOOLISH-

NESS **3** : an excessively costly or unprofitable undertaking

fo·ment \fō-'ment\ vb : INCITE

fo·men·ta·tion \ˌfō-mən-'tā-shən, -ˌmen-\ n **1** : a hot moist material (as a damp cloth) applied to the body to ease pain **2** : the act of fomenting : INSTIGATION

fond \'fänd\ adj [ME, fr. *fonne* fool] **1** : FOOLISH, SILLY ⟨∼ pride⟩ **2** : prizing highly : DESIROUS ⟨∼ of praise⟩ **3** : strongly attracted or predisposed ⟨∼ of music⟩ **4** : foolishly tender : INDULGENT; *also* : LOVING, AFFECTIONATE **5** : CHERISHED, DEAR ⟨his ∼est hopes⟩ — **fond·ly** adv — **fond·ness** n

fon·dant \'fän-dənt\ n : a creamy preparation of sugar used as a basis for candies or icings

fon·dle \'fän-dᵊl\ vb **fon·dled; fon·dling** : to touch or handle lovingly : CARESS

fon·due *also* **fon·du** \fän-'dü, -'dyü\ n [F] : a preparation of melted cheese often flavored with white wine

¹**font** \'fänt\ n **1** : a receptacle for baptismal or holy water **2** : FOUNTAIN, SOURCE ⟨a ∼ of information⟩

²**font** n : an assortment of printing type of one style and sometimes one size

food \'füd\ n **1** : material taken into an organism and used for growth, repair, and vital processes and as a source of energy; *also* : organic material produced by green plants and used by them as food **2** : nourishment in solid form **3** : something that nourishes, sustains, or supplies ⟨∼ for thought⟩

food chain n **1** : a hierarchical arrangement of organisms in an ecological community such that each uses the next usu. lower member as a food source **2** : a hierarchy based on power or importance

food court n : an area (as within a shopping mall) set apart for food concessions

food poisoning n : a digestive illness caused by bacteria or by chemicals in food

food·stuff \'füd-ˌstəf\ n : a substance with food value; *esp* : a specific nutrient (as fat or protein)

¹**fool** \'fül\ n [ME, fr. AF *fol,* fr. LL *follis,* fr. L, bellows, bag] **1** : a person who lacks sense or judgment **2** : JESTER **3** : DUPE **4** : IDIOT

²**fool** vb **1** : to spend time idly or aimlessly **2** : to meddle or tamper thoughtlessly or ignorantly **3** : JOKE **4** : DECEIVE **5** : FRITTER ⟨∼ed away his time⟩

fool·ery \'fü-lə-rē\ n, pl **-er·ies** **1** : a foolish act, utterance, or belief **2** : foolish behavior

fool·har·dy \'fül-ˌhär-dē\ adj : foolishly daring : RASH — **fool·har·di·ness** \-dē-nəs\ n

fool·ish \'fü-lish\ adj **1** : showing or arising from folly or lack of judgment **2** : ABSURD, RIDICULOUS **3** : ABASHED — **fool·ish·ly** adv — **fool·ish·ness** n

fool·proof \'fül-ˌprüf\ adj : so simple or reliable as to leave no opportunity for error, misuse, or failure ⟨a ∼ plan⟩

fools·cap \'fül-ˌskap\ n [fr. the watermark of a fool's cap formerly applied to such paper] : a size of paper typically 16×13 inches

fool's gold n : PYRITE

¹**foot** \'fút\ n, pl **feet** \'fēt\ *also* **foot** **1** : the end part of a leg below the ankle of a vertebrate animal **2** — see WEIGHT table **3** : a group of syllables forming the basic unit of verse meter **4** : something resembling an animal's foot in position or use **5** : the lowest part : BOTTOM **6** : the part at the opposite end from the head **7** : the part (as of a stocking) that covers the foot

²**foot** vb **1** : DANCE **2** : to go on foot **3** : to add up **4** : to pay or provide for ⟨foot the bill⟩

foot·age \'fú-tij\ n **1** : length expressed in feet **2** : the length of film used for a scene; *also* : the material contained on such footage

foot–and–mouth disease n : an acute contagious viral disease esp. of cattle

foot·ball \'fút-ˌbȯl\ n **1** : any of several games played by two teams on a rectangular field with goalposts at each end in which the object is to get the ball over the goal line or between goalposts by running, passing, or kicking **2** : the ball used in football

foot·board \-ˌbȯrd\ n **1** : a narrow platform on which to stand or brace the feet **2** : a board forming the foot of a bed

foot·bridge \-ˌbrij\ n : a bridge for pedestrians

foot·ed \'fu̇-təd\ *adj* : having a foot or feet of a specified kind or number ⟨flat-*footed*⟩ ⟨four-*footed*⟩

-foot·er \'fu̇-tər\ *comb form* : one that is a specified number of feet in height, length, or breadth ⟨a six-*footer*⟩

foot·fall \'fu̇t-ˌfȯl\ *n* : the sound of a footstep

foot·hill \-ˌhil\ *n* : a hill at the foot of higher hills or mountains

foot·hold \-ˌhōld\ *n* **1** : a hold for the feet : FOOTING **2** : a position usable as a base for further advance

foot·ing *n* **1** : the placing of one's feet in a stable position **2** : the act of moving on foot **3** : a place or space for standing : FOOTHOLD **4** : position with respect to one another : STATUS **5** : BASIS

foot·less \'fu̇t-ləs\ *adj* **1** : having no feet ⟨∼ tights⟩ **2** : INEPT, INEFFECTUAL

foot·lights \-ˌlīts\ *n pl* **1** : a row of lights along the front of a stage floor **2** : the stage as a profession

foo·tling \'fu̇t-liŋ\ *adj* **1** : INEPT ⟨∼ amateurs⟩ **2** : TRIVIAL

foot·lock·er \'fu̇t-ˌlä-kər\ *n* : a small trunk designed to be placed at the foot of a bed (as in a barracks)

foot·loose \-ˌlüs\ *adj* : having no ties : FREE, UNTRAMMELED

foot·man \-mən\ *n* : a male servant who attends a carriage or waits on table, admits visitors, and runs errands

foot·note \-ˌnōt\ *n* **1** : a note of reference, explanation, or comment placed usu. at the bottom of a page **2** : COMMENTARY

foot·pad \-ˌpad\ *n* : a round somewhat flat foot on the leg of a spacecraft for distributing weight to minimize sinking into a surface

foot·path \-ˌpath, -ˌpȧth\ *n* : a narrow path for pedestrians

foot·print \-ˌprint\ *n* **1** : an impression of the foot **2** : the area on a surface covered by something ⟨a tire with a wide ∼⟩

foot·race \-ˌrās\ *n* : a race run on foot

foot·rest \-ˌrest\ *n* : a support for the feet

foot·sore \-ˌsȯr\ *adj* : having sore or tender feet (as from much walking)

foot·step \-ˌstep\ *n* **1** : the mark of the foot : TRACK **2** : TREAD **3** : distance covered by a step : PACE **4** : a step on which to ascend or descend **5** : a way of life, conduct, or action

foot·stool \-ˌstül\ *n* : a low stool to support the feet

foot·wear \-ˌwer\ *n* : apparel (as shoes or boots) for the feet

foot·work \-ˌwərk\ *n* : the management of the feet (as in boxing)

fop \'fäp\ *n* : DANDY 1 — **fop·pery** \'fä-pə-rē\ *n* — **foppish** *adj*

¹for \fər, 'fȯr\ *prep* **1** : as a preparation toward ⟨dress ∼ dinner⟩ **2** : toward the purpose or goal of ⟨need time ∼ study⟩ ⟨money ∼ a trip⟩ **3** : so as to reach or attain ⟨run ∼ cover⟩ **4** : as being ⟨took him ∼ a fool⟩ **5** : because of ⟨cry ∼ joy⟩ **6** — used to indicate a recipient ⟨a letter ∼ you⟩ **7** : in support of ⟨fought ∼ his country⟩ **8** : directed at : AFFECTING ⟨a cure ∼ what ails you⟩ **9** — used with a noun or pronoun followed by an infinitive to form the equivalent of a noun clause ⟨∼ you to go would be silly⟩ **10** : in exchange as equal to : so as to return the value of ⟨a lot of trouble ∼ nothing⟩ ⟨pay $10 ∼ a hat⟩ **11** : CONCERNING ⟨a stickler ∼ detail⟩ **12** : CONSIDERING ⟨tall ∼ her age⟩ **13** : through the period of ⟨served ∼ three years⟩ **14** : in honor of ⟨named ∼ her grandmother⟩

²for *conj* : BECAUSE

³for *abbr* **1** foreign **2** forestry

fora *pl of* FORUM

¹for·age \'fȯr-ij\ *n* [ME, fr. AF, fr. *fuerre, foer* fodder, straw, of Gmc origin] **1** : food for animals esp. when taken by browsing or grazing **2** : a search for food or supplies

²forage *vb* **for·aged; for·ag·ing 1** : to collect forage from **2** : to search for food or supplies **3** : to get by foraging **4** : to make a search : RUMMAGE

for·ay \'fȯr-ˌā, fȯ-'rā\ *vb* : to raid esp. in search of plunder : PILLAGE — **foray** *n*

¹for·bear \fȯr-'ber\ *vb* **-bore** \-'bȯr\; **-borne** \-'bȯrn\; **-bearing 1** : to refrain from : ABSTAIN **2** : to be patient — **for·bear·ance** \-'ber-əns\ *n*

²forbear *var of* FOREBEAR

for·bid \fər-'bid\ *vb* **-bade** \-'bad, -'bād\ *also* **-bad** \-'bad\;

-bid·den \-'bi-dᵊn\; **-bid·ding 1** : to command against : PROHIBIT **2** : HINDER, PREVENT ✦ **Synonyms** ENJOIN, INTERDICT, INHIBIT, BAN

forbidding *adj* : DISAGREEABLE, REPELLENT ⟨a ∼ task⟩

¹force \'fȯrs\ *n* **1** : strength or energy esp. of an exceptional degree : active power **2** : capacity to persuade or convince **3** : military strength; *also, pl* : the whole military strength (as of a nation) **4** : a body (as of persons or ships) available for a particular purpose **5** : VIOLENCE, COMPULSION **6** : an influence (as a push or pull) that causes motion or a change of motion — **force·ful** \-fəl\ *adj* — **force·ful·ly** *adv* — **in force 1** : in great numbers **2** : VALID, OPERATIVE ⟨the ban remains *in force*⟩

²force *vb* **forced; forc·ing 1** : COMPEL, COERCE **2** : to cause through necessity ⟨*forced* to admit defeat⟩ **3** : to press, attain to, or effect against resistance or inertia ⟨∼ your way through⟩ **4** : to raise or accelerate to the utmost ⟨∼ the pace⟩ **5** : to produce with unnatural or unwilling effort ⟨*forced* a smile⟩ **6** : to hasten (as in growth) by artificial means

for·ceps \'fȯr-səps\ *n, pl* **forceps** [L] : a hand-held instrument for grasping, holding, or pulling objects esp. for delicate operations (as by a surgeon)

forc·ible \'fȯr-sə-bəl\ *adj* **1** : obtained or done by force **2** : showing force or energy : POWERFUL — **forc·i·bly** \-blē\ *adv*

¹ford \'fȯrd\ *n* : a place where a stream may be crossed by wading

²ford *vb* : to cross (a body of water) by wading

¹fore \'fȯr\ *adv* : in, toward, or adjacent to the front : FORWARD

²fore *adj* : being or coming before in time, order, or space

³fore *n* : something that occupies a front position

⁴fore *interj* — used by a golfer to warn anyone within range of the probable line of flight of the ball

fore–and–aft \ˌfȯr-ə-'naft\ *adj* : lying, running, or acting along the length of a structure (as a ship)

¹fore·arm \(ˌ)fȯr-'ärm\ *vb* : to arm in advance : PREPARE

²fore·arm \'fȯr-ˌärm\ *n* : the part of the arm between the elbow and the wrist

fore·bear \-ˌber\ *n* : ANCESTOR, FOREFATHER

fore·bode *also* **for·bode** \fȯr-'bōd\ *vb* **1** : to have a premonition esp. of misfortune **2** : FORETELL, PREDICT ✦ **Synonyms** AUGUR, BODE, FORESHADOW, PORTEND, PROMISE — **fore·bod·ing** *n or adj* — **fore·bod·ing·ly** *adv*

fore·cast \'fȯr-ˌkast\ *vb* **-cast** *also* **-cast·ed; -cast·ing 1** : PREDICT, CALCULATE ⟨∼ weather conditions⟩ **2** : to indicate as likely to occur — **forecast** *n* — **fore·cast·er** *n*

fore·cas·tle *or* **fo'c's'le** \'fōk-səl\ *n* **1** : the forward part of the upper deck of a ship **2** : the crew's quarters usu. in a ship's bow

fore·close \fȯr-'klōz\ *vb* **1** : to shut out : PRECLUDE **2** : to take legal measures to terminate a mortgage and take possession of the mortgaged property

fore·clo·sure \-'klō-zhər\ *n* : the act of foreclosing; *esp* : the legal procedure of foreclosing a mortgage

fore·doom \fȯr-'düm\ *vb* : to doom beforehand

fore·fa·ther \'fȯr-ˌfä-t͟hər\ *n* **1** : ANCESTOR **2** : a person of an earlier period and common heritage

forefend *var of* FORFEND

fore·fin·ger \-ˌfiŋ-gər\ *n* : INDEX FINGER

fore·foot \-ˌfu̇t\ *n* : either of the front feet of a quadruped; *also* : the front part of the human foot

fore·front \-ˌfrənt\ *n* : the foremost part or place

foregather *var of* FORGATHER

¹fore·go \fȯr-'gō\ *vb* **-went** \-'went\; **-gone** \-'gȯn\; **-go·ing** : PRECEDE

²forego *var of* FORGO

foregoing *adj* : PRECEDING ⟨the ∼ statement can be proven⟩

fore·gone \'fȯr-ˌgȯn\ *adj* : determined in advance ⟨a ∼ conclusion⟩

fore·ground \-ˌgrau̇nd\ *n* **1** : the part of a scene or representation that appears nearest to and in front of the spectator **2** : a position of prominence

fore·hand \-ˌhand\ *n* : a stroke (as in tennis) made with the palm of the hand turned in the direction in which the hand is moving; *also* : the side on which such a stroke is made — **forehand** *adj*

fore·hand·ed \(ˌ)fȯr-'han-dəd\ *adj* : mindful of the future : PRUDENT

fore·head \'fȯr-əd, 'fȯr-ˌhed\ *n* : the part of the face above the eyes

for·eign \'fȯr-ən\ *adj* [ME *forein*, fr. AF, fr. LL *foranus* on the outside, fr. L *foris* outside] 1 : situated outside a place or country and esp. one's own country 2 : born in, belonging to, or characteristic of some place or country other than the one under consideration ⟨∼ language⟩ 3 : not connected, pertinent, or characteristically present 4 : related to or dealing with other nations ⟨∼ affairs⟩ 5 : occurring in an abnormal situation in the living body ⟨a ∼ body in the eye⟩

for·eign·er \'fȯr-ə-nər\ *n* : a person belonging to or owing allegiance to a foreign country

foreign minister *n* : a governmental minister for foreign affairs

fore·know \fȯr-'nō\ *vb* **-knew** \-'nü, -'nyü\; **-known** \-'nōn\; **-know·ing** : to have previous knowledge of — **fore·knowl·edge** \'fȯr-ˌnä-lij, fȯr-'nä-\ *n*

fore·la·dy \'fȯr-ˌlā-dē\ *n* : FOREWOMAN

fore·leg \-ˌleg\ *n* : a front leg

fore·limb \-ˌlim\ *n* : a front or upper limb (as a wing, arm, fin, or leg)

fore·lock \-ˌläk\ *n* : a lock of hair growing from the front part of the head

fore·man \-mən\ *n* 1 : a spokesperson of a jury 2 : a person in charge of a group of workers

fore·mast \-ˌmast\ *n* : the mast nearest the bow of a ship

fore·most \-ˌmōst\ *adj* : first in time, place, or order : most important : PREEMINENT — **foremost** *adv*

fore·name \-ˌnām\ *n* : a first name

fore·named \-ˌnāmd\ *adj* : previously named : AFORESAID

fore·noon \-ˌnün\ *n* : MORNING

¹**fo·ren·sic** \fə-'ren-sik\ *adj* [L *forensis* public, forensic, fr. *forum* forum] 1 : belonging to, used in, or suitable to courts of law or to public speaking or debate 2 : relating to the application of scientific knowledge to legal problems ⟨∼ medicine⟩

²**forensic** *n* 1 : an argumentative exercise 2 *pl* : the art or study of argumentative discourse 3 *pl* : scientific analysis of physical evidence (as from a crime scene)

fore·or·dain \ˌfȯr-ȯr-'dān\ *vb* : to ordain or decree beforehand : PREDESTINE

fore·part \'fȯr-ˌpärt\ *n* 1 : the anterior part of something 2 : the earlier part of a period of time

fore·quar·ter \-ˌkwȯr-tər\ *n* : the front half of a lateral half of the body or carcass of a quadruped ⟨a ∼ of beef⟩

fore·run·ner \-ˌrə-nər\ *n* 1 : one that goes before to give notice of the approach of others : HARBINGER 2 : PREDECESSOR, ANCESTOR ♦ *Synonyms* PRECURSOR, HERALD

fore·sail \-ˌsāl, -səl\ *n* 1 : the lowest sail on the foremast of a square-rigged ship or schooner 2 : the principal sail forward of the foremast (as of a sloop)

foresail 1

fore·see \fȯr-'sē\ *vb* **-saw** \-'sȯ\; **-seen** \-'sēn\; **-see·ing** : to see or realize beforehand : EXPECT ♦ *Synonyms* FOREKNOW, DIVINE, APPREHEND, ANTICIPATE — **fore·see·able** *adj*

fore·shad·ow \-'sha-dō\ *vb* : to give a hint or suggestion of beforehand

fore·short·en \fȯr-'shȯr-tᵊn\ *vb* : to shorten (a detail) in a drawing or painting so that it appears to have depth

fore·sight \'fȯr-ˌsīt\ *n* 1 : the act or power of foreseeing 2 : care or provision for the future : PRUDENCE 3 : an act of looking forward; *also* : a view forward — **fore·sight·ed** \-ˌsī-təd\ *adj* — **fore·sight·ed·ly** *adv* — **fore·sight·ed·ness** *n*

fore·skin \-ˌskin\ *n* : a fold of skin enclosing the end of the penis

¹**for·est** \'fȯr-əst\ *n* [ME, fr. AF, fr. LL *forestis (silva)* unenclosed (woodland), fr. L *foris* outside] : a large thick growth of trees and underbrush — **for·est·ed** \'fȯr-ə-stəd\ *adj* — **for·est·land** \'fȯr-əst-ˌland\ *n*

fore·stall \fȯr-'stȯl, fȯr-\ *vb* 1 : to keep out, hinder, or prevent by measures taken in advance 2 : ANTICIPATE

forest ranger *n* : a person in charge of the management and protection of a portion of a forest

for·est·ry \'fȯr-ə-strē\ *n* : the science of growing and caring for forests — **for·est·er** \'fȯr-ə-stər\ *n*

foreswear *var of* FORSWEAR

¹**fore·taste** \'fȯr-ˌtāst\ *n* : an advance indication, warning, or notion

²**fore·taste** \fȯr-'tāst\ *vb* : to taste beforehand : ANTICIPATE

fore·tell \fȯr-'tel\ *vb* **-told** \-'tōld\; **-tell·ing** : to tell of beforehand : PREDICT ♦ *Synonyms* FORECAST, PROPHESY, PROGNOSTICATE

fore·thought \'fȯr-ˌthȯt\ *n* 1 : PREMEDITATION 2 : consideration for the future

fore·to·ken \fȯr-'tō-kən\ *vb* : to indicate in advance

fore·top \'fȯr-ˌtäp\ *n* : a platform near the top of a ship's foremast

for·ev·er \fȯr-'e-vər\ *adv* 1 : for a limitless time 2 : at all times : ALWAYS

for·ev·er·more \-ˌe-vər-'mȯr\ *adv* : FOREVER

fore·warn \fȯr-'wȯrn\ *vb* : to warn beforehand — **fore·warn·ing** \'wȯr-nin\ *n*

forewent *past of* FOREGO

fore·wing \'fȯr-ˌwin\ *n* : either of the anterior wings of a 4-winged insect

fore·wom·an \'fȯr-ˌwù-mən\ *n* : a woman having the responsibilities of a foreman

fore·word \-ˌwərd\ *n* : PREFACE

¹**for·feit** \'fȯr-fət\ *n* [ME *forfait*, fr. AF, fr. pp. of *forfaire*, *forsfaire* to commit a crime, forfeit, fr. *fors* outside + *faire* to do] 1 : something forfeited : PENALTY, FINE 2 : FORFEITURE 3 : something deposited and then redeemed on payment of a fine 4 *pl* : a game in which forfeits are exacted

²**forfeit** *vb* : to lose or lose the right to esp. by some error, offense, or crime

for·fei·ture \'fȯr-fə-ˌchùr\ *n* 1 : the act of forfeiting 2 : something forfeited : PENALTY

for·fend \fȯr-'fend\ *vb* 1 : PREVENT 2 : PROTECT, PRESERVE

for·gath·er *or* **fore·gath·er** \fȯr-'ga-thər\ *vb* 1 : to come together : ASSEMBLE 2 : to meet someone usu. by chance

¹**forge** \'fȯrj\ *n* [ME, fr. AF, fr. L *fabrica*, fr. *faber* smith] : a furnace or shop with its furnace where metal is heated and worked

²**forge** *vb* **forged; forg·ing** 1 : to form (metal) by heating and hammering 2 : FASHION, SHAPE ⟨∼ an agreement⟩ 3 : to make or imitate falsely esp. with intent to defraud ⟨∼ a signature⟩ — **forg·er** *n* — **forg·ery** \'fȯr-jə-rē\ *n*

³**forge** *vb* **forged; forg·ing** : to move ahead steadily but gradually

for·get \fər-'get\ *vb* **-got** \-'gät\; **-got·ten** \-'gät-ᵊn\ *or* **-got**; **-get·ting** 1 : to be unable to think of or recall 2 : to fail to become mindful of at the proper time 3 : NEGLECT, DISREGARD 4 : to give up hope for or expectation of — **for·get·ful** \-'get-fəl\ *adj* — **for·get·ful·ly** *adv* — **for·get·ful·ness** *n*

for·get—me—not \fər-'get-mē-ˌnät\ *n* : any of a genus of small herbs with bright blue or white flowers

forg·ing *n* : a piece of forged work

for·give \fər-'giv\ *vb* **-gave** \-'gāv\; **-giv·en** \-'gi-vən\; **-giv·ing** 1 : to give up resentment of 2 : PARDON, ABSOLVE 3 : to grant relief from payment of — **for·giv·able** *adj* — **for·give·ness** *n* — **for·giv·er** *n*

forgiving *adj* 1 : willing or able to forgive 2 : allowing room for error or weakness

for·go \fȯr-'gō\ *vb* **-went** \-'went\; **-gone** \-'gȯn\; **-go·ing** : to give up the enjoyment or advantage of : do without

fo·rint \'fȯr-int\ *n*, *pl* **forints** *also* **forint** — see MONEY table

¹**fork** \'fȯrk\ *n* 1 : an implement with two or more prongs for taking up (as in eating), pitching, or digging 2 : a forked part, tool, or piece of equipment 3 : a dividing

into branches or a place where something branches; *also* : a branch of such a fork

²**fork** *vb* **1** : to divide into two or more branches **2** : to give the form of a fork to ⟨~*ing* her fingers⟩ **3** : to raise or pitch with a fork ⟨~ hay⟩ **4** : PAY, CONTRIBUTE — used with *over, out,* or *up*

forked \'fórkt, 'fór-kəd\ *adj* : having a fork : shaped like a fork ⟨~ lightning⟩

fork·lift \'fórk-₁lift\ *n* : a machine for lifting heavy objects by means of steel fingers inserted under the load

for·lorn \fər-'lórn, fór-\ *adj* **1** : sad and lonely because of isolation or desertion **2** : WRETCHED **3** : nearly hopeless — **for·lorn·ly** *adv* — **for·lorn·ness** *n*

¹**form** \'fórm\ *n* **1** : SHAPE, STRUCTURE **2** : a body esp. of a person : FIGURE **3** : the essential nature of a thing **4** : established manner of doing or saying something **5** : FORMULA **6** : a document with blank spaces for insertion of information ⟨tax ~⟩ **7** : CEREMONY **8** : manner of performing according to recognized standards **9** : a long seat : BENCH **10** : a model of the human figure used for displaying clothes **11** : MOLD ⟨a ~ for concrete⟩ **12** : type or plates in a frame ready for printing **13** : MODE, KIND, VARIETY ⟨coal is a ~ of carbon⟩ **14** : orderly method of arrangement; *also* : a particular kind or instance of such arrangement ⟨the sonnet ~ in poetry⟩ **15** : the structural element, plan, or design of a work of art **16** : a bounded surface or volume **17** : a grade in a British school or in some American private schools **18** : RACING FORM **19** : known ability to perform; *also* : condition (as of an athlete) suitable for performing **20** : one of the ways in which a word is changed to show difference in use ⟨the plural ~ of a noun⟩ — **form·less** *adj*

²**form** *vb* **1** : to give form or shape to : FASHION, MAKE **2** : TRAIN, INSTRUCT **3** : CONSTITUTE, COMPOSE **4** : DEVELOP, ACQUIRE ⟨~ a habit⟩ **5** : to arrange in order ⟨~ a battle line⟩ **6** : to take form : ARISE ⟨clouds are ~*ing*⟩ **7** : to take a definite form, shape, or arrangement

¹**for·mal** \'fór-məl\ *adj* **1** : according with conventional forms and rules ⟨a ~ dinner party⟩ **2** : done in due or lawful form ⟨a ~ contract⟩ **3** : CEREMONIOUS, PRIM ⟨a ~ manner⟩ **4** : NOMINAL — **for·mal·ly** *adv*

²**formal** *n* : something (as a social event) formal in character

form·al·de·hyde \fór-'mal-də-₁hīd\ *n* : a colorless pungent gas used in water solution as a preservative and disinfectant

for·mal·ise *Brit var of* FORMALIZE

for·mal·ism \'fór-mə-₁li-zəm\ *n* : strict adherence to set forms

for·mal·i·ty \fór-'ma-lə-tē\ *n, pl* **-ties** **1** : compliance with formal or conventional rules **2** : the quality or state of being formal **3** : an established form that is required or conventional

for·mal·ize \'fór-mə-₁līz\ *vb* **-ized; -iz·ing** **1** : to give a certain or definite form to **2** : to make formal; *also* : to give formal status or approval to

¹**for·mat** \'fór-₁mat\ *n* **1** : the general composition or style of a publication **2** : the general plan or arrangement of something **3** : a method of organizing data ⟨various file ~*s*⟩

²**format** *vb* **for·mat·ted; for·mat·ting** : to arrange (as material to be printed) in a particular format — **for·mat·ter** *n*

for·ma·tion \fór-'mā-shən\ *n* **1** : an act of giving form to something : DEVELOPMENT **2** : something that is formed **3** : STRUCTURE, SHAPE **4** : an arrangement of persons or things in a prescribed manner or for a certain purpose

for·ma·tive \'fór-mə-tiv\ *adj* **1** : giving or capable of giving form : CONSTRUCTIVE **2** : of, relating to, or characterized by important growth or formation ⟨a child's ~ years⟩

for·mer \'fór-mər\ *adj* **1** : PREVIOUS, EARLIER **2** : FOREGOING ⟨the ~ part of the chapter⟩ **3** : being first mentioned or in order of two or more things

for·mer·ly \-lē\ *adv* : in time past : PREVIOUSLY

form·fit·ting \'fórm-₁fi-tiŋ\ *adj* : conforming to the outline of the body ⟨a ~ sweater⟩

for·mi·da·ble \'fór-mə-də-bəl, fór-'mi-\ *adj* **1** : exciting fear, dread, or awe ⟨a ~ foe⟩ **2** : imposing serious difficulties ⟨a ~ barrier⟩ — **for·mi·da·bly** \-blē\ *adv*

form letter *n* **1** : a letter on a frequently recurring topic that can be sent to different people at different times **2** : a letter for mass circulation sent out in many printed copies

for·mu·la \'fór-myə-lə\ *n, pl* **-las** *or* **-lae** \-₁lē, -₁lī\ **1** : a set form of words for ceremonial use **2** : RECIPE, PRESCRIPTION **3** : a milk mixture or substitute for a baby **4** : a group of symbols or figures joined to express information concisely **5** : a customary or set form or method

for·mu·late \-₁lāt\ *vb* **-lat·ed; -lat·ing** **1** : to express in a formula **2** : DESIGN, DEVISE ⟨~ a policy⟩ **3** : to prepare according to a formula — **for·mu·la·tion** \₁fór-myə-'lā-shən\ *n*

for·ni·ca·tion \₁fór-nə-'kā-shən\ *n* : consensual sexual intercourse between two persons not married to each other — **for·ni·cate** \'fór-nə-₁kāt\ *vb* — **for·ni·ca·tor** \-₁kā-tər\ *n*

for·sake \fər-'sāk, fór-\ *vb* **for·sook** \-'sùk\; **for·sak·en** \-'sā-kən\; **for·sak·ing** [ME, fr. OE *forsacan,* fr. *sacan* to dispute] : to renounce or turn away from entirely

for·sooth \fər-'süth\ *adv* : in truth : INDEED

for·swear \fór-'swer\ *vb* **-swore** \-'swór\; **-sworn** \-'swórn\; **-swear·ing** **1** : to swear falsely : commit perjury **2** : to renounce earnestly or under oath **3** : to deny under oath

for·syth·ia \fər-'si-thē-ə\ *n, pl* **-ias** *also* **-ia** : any of a genus of shrubs related to the olive and having yellow bell-shaped flowers appearing before the leaves in early spring

fort \'fórt\ *n* [ME *forte,* fr. AF *fort,* fr. *fort* strong, fr. L *fortis*] **1** : a fortified place **2** : a permanent army post

¹**forte** \'fórt, 'fór-₁tā\ *n* [F *fort,* fr. *fort,* adj., strong] : one's strong point

²**for·te** \'fór-₁tā\ *adv or adj* [It, fr. *forte* strong] : LOUD — used as a direction in music

forth \'fórth\ *adv* **1** : FORWARD, ONWARD ⟨from that day ~⟩ **2** : out into view ⟨plants putting ~ leaves⟩

forth·com·ing \fórth-'kə-miŋ\ *adj* **1** : coming or available soon ⟨the ~ holidays⟩ **2** : marked by openness and candor : OUTGOING

forth·right \'fórth-₁rīt\ *adj* : free from ambiguity or evasiveness : going straight to the point ⟨a ~ answer⟩ — **forth·right·ly** *adv* — **forth·right·ness** *n*

forth·with \₁fórth-'with\ *adv* : IMMEDIATELY

for·ti·fy \'fór-tə-₁fī\ *vb* **-fied; -fy·ing** **1** : to strengthen by military defenses **2** : to give physical strength or endurance to **3** : ENCOURAGE **4** : to strengthen or enrich with a material ⟨~ bread with vitamins⟩ — **for·ti·fi·ca·tion** \₁fór-tə-fə-'kā-shən\ *n*

for·tis·si·mo \fór-'ti-sə-₁mō\ *adv or adj* : very loud — used as a direction in music

for·ti·tude \'fór-tə-₁tüd, -₁tyüd\ *n* : strength of mind that enables one to meet danger or bear pain or adversity with courage ♦ *Synonyms* GRIT, BACKBONE, PLUCK, GUTS

fort·night \'fórt-₁nīt\ *n* [ME *fourtenight,* alter. of *fourtene night* fourteen nights] : two weeks — **fort·night·ly** \-lē\ *adj or adv*

for·tress \'fór-trəs\ *n* : FORT 1

for·tu·itous \fór-'tü-ə-təs, -'tyü-\ *adj* **1** : happening by chance **2** : FORTUNATE — **for·tu·itous·ly** *adv*

for·tu·ity \-ə-tē\ *n, pl* **-ities** **1** : the quality or state of being fortuitous **2** : a chance event or occurrence

for·tu·nate \'fór-chə-nət\ *adj* **1** : bringing some good thing not foreseen **2** : LUCKY

for·tu·nate·ly \-lē\ *adv* **1** : in a fortunate manner **2** : it is fortunate that

for·tune \'fór-chən\ *n* **1** : prosperity attained partly through luck; *also* : CHANCE, LUCK **2** : what happens to a person : good or bad luck **3** : FATE, DESTINY **4** : RICHES, WEALTH

fortune hunter *n* : a person who seeks wealth esp. by marriage

for·tune–tell·er \-₁te-lər\ *n* : a person who professes to foretell future events — **for·tune–tell·ing** *n or adj*

for·ty \'fór-tē\ *n, pl* **forties** : four times 10 — **for·ti·eth** \'fór-tē-əth\ *adj or pron*

for·ty–five \₁fór-tē-'fīv\ *n* **1** : a .45 caliber handgun — usu. written .45 **2** : a phonograph record designed to be played at 45 revolutions per minute — usu. written 45

for·ty–nin·er \-'nī-nər\ *n* : a person in the rush to California for gold in 1849

forty winks *n sing or pl* : a short sleep

fo·rum \'fór-əm\ *n, pl* **forums** *also* **fo·ra** \-ə\ [L] **1** : the marketplace or central meeting place of an ancient

Roman city **2** : a medium (as a publication or online service) of open discussion **3** : COURT **4** : a public assembly, lecture, or program involving audience or panel discussion

¹for·ward \'fȯr-wərd\ *adj* **1** : being near or at or belonging to the front **2** : EAGER, READY **3** : BRASH, BOLD **4** : notably advanced or developed : PRECOCIOUS **5** : moving, tending, or leading toward a position in front **6** : EXTREME, RADICAL **7** : of, relating to, or getting ready for the future — **for·ward·ness** *n*

²forward *adv* : to or toward what is ahead or in front

³forward *vb* **1** : to help onward : ADVANCE **2** : to send forward : TRANSMIT **3** : to send or ship onward

⁴forward *n* : a player who plays at the front of a team's offensive formation near the opponent's goal

for·ward·er \-wər-dər\ *n* : one that forwards; *esp* : an agent who forwards goods

for·wards \'fȯr-wərdz\ *adv* : FORWARD

forwent *past of* FORGO

¹fos·sil \'fä-səl\ *adj* [L *fossilis* obtained by digging, fr. *fodere* to dig] **1** : preserved from a past geologic age ⟨~ plants⟩ **2** : of or relating to fossil fuels

²fossil *n* **1** : a trace or impression or the remains of a plant or animal of a past geologic age preserved in the earth's crust **2** : a person whose ideas are out-of-date — **fos·sil·ize** \'fä-sə-ˌlīz\ *vb*

fossil fuel *n* : a fuel (as coal or oil) that is formed in the earth from plant or animal remains

¹fos·ter \'fȯs-tər\ *adj* [ME, fr. OE *fōstor-*, fr. *fōstor* food, feeding] : affording, receiving, or sharing nourishment or parental care though not related by blood or legal ties ⟨~ parent⟩ ⟨~ child⟩

²foster *vb* **1** : to give parental care to : NURTURE **2** : to promote the growth or development of : ENCOURAGE

foster home *n* : a household in which an orphaned, neglected, or delinquent child is placed for care

fos·ter·ling \-tər-liŋ\ *n* : a foster child

Fou·cault pendulum \ˌfü-ˈkō-\ *n* : a device that consists of a heavy weight hung by a long wire and that swings in a constant direction which appears to change showing that the earth rotates

fought *past and past part of* FIGHT

¹foul \'fau̇(-ə)l\ *adj* **1** : offensive to the senses : LOATHSOME; *also* : clogged with dirt **2** : ODIOUS, DETESTABLE ⟨a ~ crime⟩ **3** : OBSCENE, ABUSIVE ⟨~ language⟩ **4** : DISAGREEABLE, STORMY ⟨~ weather⟩ **5** : TREACHEROUS, DISHONORABLE, UNFAIR **6** : marking the bounds of a playing field ⟨~ lines⟩; *also* : being outside the foul line ⟨~ ball⟩ ⟨~ territory⟩ **7** : containing marked-up corrections **8** : ENTANGLED — **foul·ly** *adv* — **foul·ness** *n*

²foul *n* **1** : an entanglement or collision in fishing or sailing **2** : an infraction of the rules in a game or sport; *also* : a baseball hit outside the foul line

³foul *vb* **1** : to make or become foul or filthy **2** : to entangle or become entangled **3** : OBSTRUCT, BLOCK **4** : to collide with **5** : to make or hit a foul

⁴foul *adv* : in a foul manner

fou·lard \fu̇-ˈlärd\ *n* : a lightweight silk of plain or twill weave usu. decorated with a printed pattern

foul·mouthed \'fau̇(-ə)l-ˈmau̇thd, -ˈmau̇tht\ *adj* : given to the use of obscene, profane, or abusive language

foul of *prep* : AFOUL OF

foul play *n* : VIOLENCE; *esp* : MURDER

foul-up \'fau̇(-ə)l-ˌəp\ *n* **1** : a state of being fouled up **2** : a mechanical difficulty

foul up *vb* **1** : to spoil by mistakes or poor judgment **2** : to cause a foul-up : BUNGLE

¹found \'fau̇nd\ *past and past part of* FIND

²found *vb* [ME, fr. AF *funder, fonder*, fr. L *fundare*, fr. *fundus* bottom] **1** : to take the first steps in building **2** : to set or ground on something solid : BASE **3** : to establish (as an institution) often with provision for future maintenance — **found·er** *n*

foun·da·tion \fau̇n-ˈdā-shən\ *n* **1** : the act of founding **2** : a basis upon which something stands or is supported ⟨suspicions without ~⟩ **3** : funds given for the permanent support of an institution : ENDOWMENT; *also* : an institution so endowed **4** : supporting structure : BASE **5** : CORSET — **foun·da·tion·al** \-shə-nəl\ *adj*

foun·der \'fau̇n-dər\ *vb* **1** : to make or become lame ⟨the

horse ~ed⟩ **2** : COLLAPSE **3** : SINK ⟨a ~ing ship⟩ **4** : FAIL

found·ling \'fau̇nd-liŋ\ *n* : an infant found after its unknown parents have abandoned it

found·ry \'fau̇n-drē\ *n, pl* **foundries** : a building or works where metal is cast

fount \'fau̇nt\ *n* : SOURCE, FOUNTAIN

foun·tain \'fau̇n-tᵊn\ *n* **1** : a spring of water **2** : SOURCE **3** : an artificial jet of water **4** : a container for liquid that can be drawn off as needed

foun·tain·head \-ˌhed\ *n* : SOURCE

fountain pen *n* : a pen with a reservoir that feeds the writing point with ink

four \'fȯr\ *n* **1** : one more than three **2** : the 4th in a set or series **3** : something having four units — **four** *adj or pron*

4x4 *also* **four-by-four** \'fȯr-bī-ˌfȯr\ *n* : a four-wheel automobile with four-wheel drive

four-flush \-ˌfləsh\ *vb* : to make a false claim : BLUFF — **four-flush·er** *n*

four·fold \-ˌfōld, -ˈfōld\ *adj* **1** : being four times as great or as many **2** : having four units or members — **four·fold** \-ˈfōld\ *adv*

4-H \'fȯr-ˈāch\ *adj* [fr. the fourfold aim of improving the head, heart, hands, and health] : of or relating to a program set up by the U.S. Department of Agriculture to help young people become productive citizens — **4-H'·er** *n*

Four Hundred *or* **400** *n* : the exclusive social set of a community — used with *the*

four-in-hand \'fȯr-ən-ˌhand\ *n* **1** : a team of four horses driven by one person; *also* : a vehicle drawn by such a team **2** : a necktie tied in a slipknot with long ends overlapping vertically in front

four-o'clock \'fȯr-ə-ˌkläk\ *n* : a garden plant with fragrant yellow, red, or white flowers without petals that open late in the afternoon

four-post·er \ˌfȯr-ˈpō-stər\ *n* : a bed with tall corner posts orig. designed to support curtains or a canopy

four·score \'fȯr-ˈskȯr\ *adj* : being four times twenty : EIGHTY

four·some \'fȯr-səm\ *n* **1** : a group of four persons or things **2** : a golf match between two pairs of partners

four·square \-ˈskwer\ *adj* **1** : SQUARE **2** : marked by boldness and conviction : FORTHRIGHT — **foursquare** *adv*

four·teen \fȯr-ˈtēn\ *n* : one more than 13 — **fourteen** *adj or pron* — **four·teenth** \-ˈtēnth\ *adj or n*

fourth \'fȯrth\ *n* **1** : one that is number four in a countable series **2** : one of four equal parts of something — **fourth** *adj or adv*

fourth estate *n, often cap F&E* : the public press

fourth wall *n* : an imaginary wall that keeps performers from recognizing or directly addressing their audience

4WD *abbr* four-wheel drive

four-wheel \'fȯr-ˌhwēl\ *or* **four-wheeled** \-ˌhwēld\ *adj* : acting on or by means of four wheels of a motor vehicle ⟨~ disc brakes⟩

four-wheel drive *n* : an automotive drive mechanism that acts on all four wheels of the vehicle; *also* : a vehicle with such a drive

¹fowl \'fau̇(-ə)l\ *n, pl* **fowl** *or* **fowls** **1** : BIRD **2** : a cock or hen of the domestic chicken; *also* : the flesh of these used as food

²fowl *vb* : to hunt wildfowl

¹fox \'fäks\ *n, pl* **fox·es** *also* **fox** **1** : any of various flesh-eating mammals related to the wolves but smaller and with shorter legs and a more pointed muzzle; *also* : the fur of a fox **2** : a clever crafty person **3** *cap* : a member of an American Indian people formerly living in what is now Wisconsin

²fox *vb* : TRICK, OUTWIT

fox·glove \'fäks-ˌgləv\ *n* : a common plant related to the snapdragons that is grown for its showy spikes of dotted white or purple tubular flowers and as a source of digitalis

fox·hole \-ˌhōl\ *n* : a pit dug for protection against enemy fire

fox·hound \-ˌhau̇nd\ *n* : any of various large swift powerful hounds used in hunting foxes

fox·ing \'fäk-siŋ\ *n* : brownish spots on old paper

fox terrier *n* : a small lively terrier that occurs in varieties with smooth dense coats or with harsh wiry coats

fox terrier

fox·trot \ˈfäks-ˌträt\ *n* **1** : a short broken slow trotting gait **2** : a ballroom dance in duple time
foxy \ˈfäk-sē\ *adj* **fox·i·er; -est** **1** : resembling or suggestive of a fox **2** : WILY **3** : physically attractive
foy·er \ˈfȯi-(ə)r, ˈfȯi-ˌyā\ *n* [F, lit., fireplace, fr. OF *foier*, fr. VL **focarium*, fr. L *focus* hearth] : LOBBY; *also* : an entrance hallway
fpm *abbr* feet per minute
FPO *abbr* fleet post office
fps *abbr* feet per second
fr *abbr* **1** father **2** franc **3** friar **4** from
¹Fr *abbr* **1** France; French **2** Friday
²Fr *symbol* francium
fra·cas \ˈfrā-kəs, ˈfra-\ *n, pl* **fra·cas·es** \-kə-səz\ [F, din, row, fr. It *fracasso*, fr. *fracassare* to shatter] : BRAWL
frac·tal \ˈfrak-tᵊl\ *n* : an irregular curve or shape that repeats itself at any scale on which it is examined — **fractal** *adj*
frac·tion \ˈfrak-shən\ *n* **1** : a numerical representation (as ¹/₂, ³/₄, or 3.323) indicating the quotient of two numbers **2** : FRAGMENT **3** : PORTION ⟨a small ~ of voters⟩ — **frac·tion·al** \-shə-nəl\ *adj* — **frac·tion·al·ly** *adv*
frac·tious \ˈfrak-shəs\ *adj* **1** : tending to be troublesome : hard to handle or control **2** : QUARRELSOME, IRRITABLE
frac·ture \ˈfrak-chər\ *n* **1** : a breaking of something and esp. a bone **2** : CRACK, CLEFT — **fracture** *vb*
frag·ile \ˈfra-jəl, -ˌjī(-ə)l\ *adj* : easily broken : DELICATE — **fra·gil·i·ty** \frə-ˈji-lə-tē\ *n*
¹frag·ment \ˈfrag-mənt\ *n* : a part broken off, detached, or incomplete
²frag·ment \-ˌment\ *vb* : to break into fragments — **frag·men·ta·tion** \ˌfrag-mən-ˈtā-shən, -ˌmən-\ *n*
frag·men·tary \ˈfrag-mən-ˌter-ē\ *adj* : made up of fragments : INCOMPLETE ⟨a ~ account⟩
fra·grant \ˈfrā-grənt\ *adj* : sweet or agreeable in smell — **fra·grance** \-grəns\ *n* — **fra·grant·ly** *adv*
frail \ˈfrāl\ *adj* [ME, fr. AF *fraile*, fr. L *fragilis* fragile, fr. *frangere* to break] **1** : morally or physically weak **2** : FRAGILE, DELICATE
frail·ty \ˈfrāl-tē\ *n, pl* **frailties** **1** : the quality or state of being frail **2** : a fault due to weakness
¹frame \ˈfrām\ *vb* **framed; fram·ing** **1** : PLAN, CONTRIVE **2** : SHAPE, CONSTRUCT **3** : FORMULATE **4** : DRAW UP ⟨~ a constitution⟩ **5** : to make appear guilty **6** : to fit or adjust for a purpose : ARRANGE **7** : to provide with or enclose in a frame — **fram·er** *n*
²frame *n* **1** : something made of parts fitted and joined together **2** : the physical makeup of the body **3** : an arrangement of structural parts that gives form or support **4** : a supporting or enclosing border or open case (as for a window or picture) **5** : one picture of a series (as on a length of film) **6** : FRAME-UP
³frame *adj* : having a wood frame ⟨~ houses⟩
frame of mind *n* : mental attitude or outlook : MOOD
frame—up \ˈfrā-ˌməp\ *n* **1** : an act or series of actions in which someone is framed **2** : an action that is planned, contrived, or formulated

frame·work \ˈfrām-ˌwərk\ *n* : a basic supporting part or structure
franc \ˈfraŋk\ *n* **1** : any of various former basic monetary units (as of Belgium, France, and Luxembourg) **2** — see MONEY table
fran·chise \ˈfran-ˌchīz\ *n* [ME, fr. AF, fr. *franchir* to free, fr. *franc* free] **1** : a right or license granted to an individual or group ⟨a ~ to operate a ferry⟩ **2** : a constitutional or statutory right or privilege; *esp* : the right to vote **3** : the right of membership in a professional sports league; *also* : a team having such membership
fran·chi·see \ˌfran-ˌchī-ˈzē, -chə-\ *n* : one granted a franchise
fran·chis·er \ˈfran-ˌchī-zər\ *n* **1** : FRANCHISEE **2** : FRANCHISOR
fran·chi·sor \ˌfran-ˌchī-ˈzȯr, -chə-\ *n* : one that grants a franchise
fran·ci·um \ˈfran-sē-əm\ *n* : a radioactive metallic chemical element
Fran·co—Amer·i·can \ˌfraŋ-kō-ə-ˈmer-ə-kən\ *n* : an American of French or esp. French-Canadian descent — **Franco—American** *adj*
fran·gi·ble \ˈfran-jə-bəl\ *adj* : BREAKABLE — **fran·gi·bil·i·ty** \ˌfran-jə-ˈbi-lə-tē\ *n*
¹frank \ˈfraŋk\ *adj* : marked by free, forthright, and sincere expression — **frank·ness** *n*
²frank *vb* : to mark (a piece of mail) with an official sign so that it can be mailed free; *also* : to mail free
³frank *n* **1** : the signature or mark on a piece of mail indicating free or paid postage **2** : the privilege of sending mail free
⁴frank *n* : FRANKFURTER
Fran·ken·stein \ˈfraŋ-kən-ˌstīn\ *n* **1** : a monstrous creation that usu. ruins its originator **2** : a monster in the shape of a man
frank·furt·er \ˈfraŋk-fər-tər, -ˌfər-\ *or* **frank·furt** \-fərt\ *n* : a seasoned sausage (as of beef or beef and pork)
frank·in·cense \ˈfraŋ-kən-ˌsens\ *n* : a fragrant resin burned as incense
frank·ly \ˈfraŋ-klē\ *adv* **1** : in a frank manner **2** : in truth : INDEED ⟨~, I don't know⟩
fran·tic \ˈfran-tik\ *adj* : marked by uncontrolled emotion or disordered anxious activity — **fran·ti·cal·ly** \-ti-k(ə-)lē\ *adv*
frap·pé \fra-ˈpā\ *or* **frappe** *same or* ˈfrap\ *n* [F *frappé*, fr. pp. of *frapper* to strike, chill] **1** : an iced or frozen drink **2** : a thick milk shake — **frap·pé** \fra-ˈpā\ *adj*
fra·ter·nal \frə-ˈtər-nᵊl\ *adj* **1** : of, relating to, or involving brothers **2** : of, relating to, or being a fraternity or society **3** : derived from two ova ⟨~ twins⟩ **4** : FRIENDLY, BROTHERLY — **fra·ter·nal·ly** *adv*
fra·ter·ni·ty \frə-ˈtər-nə-tē\ *n, pl* **-ties** **1** : a social, honorary, or professional group; *esp* : a men's student organization **2** : BROTHERLINESS, BROTHERHOOD **3** : persons of the same class, profession, or tastes
frat·er·nize \ˈfra-tər-ˌnīz\ *vb* **-nized; -niz·ing** **1** : to mingle as friends **2** : to associate on close terms with members of a hostile group — **frat·er·ni·za·tion** \ˌfra-tər-nə-ˈzā-shən\ *n*
frat·ri·cide \ˈfra-trə-ˌsīd\ *n* **1** : one that kills a sibling or countryman **2** : the act of a fratricide — **frat·ri·cid·al** \ˌfra-trə-ˈsī-dᵊl\ *adj*
fraud \ˈfrȯd\ *n* **1** : DECEIT, TRICKERY **2** : TRICK **3** : IMPOSTOR, CHEAT
fraud·ster \ˈfrȯd-stər\ *n, chiefly Brit* : a person who engages in fraud
fraud·u·lent \ˈfrȯ-jə-lənt\ *adj* : characterized by, based on, or done by fraud : DECEITFUL — **fraud·u·lence** \-ləns\ *n* — **fraud·u·lent·ly** *adv*
fraught \ˈfrȯt\ *adj* : full of or accompanied by something specified ⟨~ with danger⟩
¹fray \ˈfrā\ *n* : FIGHT, STRUGGLE; *also* : QUARREL, DISPUTE
²fray *vb* **1** : to wear (as an edge of cloth) by rubbing **2** : to separate the threads at the edge of **3** : STRAIN, IRRITATE ⟨~ed nerves⟩
fraz·zle \ˈfra-zəl\ *vb* **fraz·zled; fraz·zling** **1** : FRAY **2** : to put in a state of extreme physical or nervous fatigue — **frazzle** *n*
¹freak \ˈfrēk\ *n* **1** : WHIM, CAPRICE **2** : a strange, abnormal, or unusual person or thing **3** *slang* : a person who

uses an illicit drug **4** : an ardent enthusiast — **freak·ish** *adj* — **freaky** \'frē-kē\ *adj*

²freak *vb* **1** : to experience the effects (as hallucinations) of taking illicit drugs — often used with *out* **2** : to distress or become distressed — often used with *out* — **freak–out** \'frē-ˌkaut\ *n*

freck·le \'fre-kəl\ *n* : a small brownish spot on the skin — **freckle** *vb*

¹free \'frē\ *adj* **fre·er; fre·est 1** : having liberty **2** : enjoying political or personal independence; *also* : not subject to or allowing slavery **3** : made or done voluntarily : SPONTANEOUS **4** : relieved from or lacking something unpleasant **5** : not subject to a duty, tax, or charge **6** : not obstructed : CLEAR **7** : not being used or occupied ⟨waved with my ∼ hand⟩ **8** : not fastened ⟨the ∼ end of the rope⟩ **9** : LAVISH **10** : OPEN, FRANK **11** : given without charge **12** : not literal or exact ⟨∼ translation⟩ **13** : not restricted by conventional forms ⟨∼ skating⟩ — **free·ly** *adv*

²free *vb* **freed; free·ing 1** : to set free **2** : RELIEVE, RID **3** : DISENTANGLE, CLEAR ♦ *Synonyms* RELEASE, LIBERATE, DISCHARGE, EMANCIPATE, LOOSE

³free *adv* **1** : FREELY **2** : without charge

free·base \'frē-ˌbās\ *n* : purified cocaine smoked as crack or heated to produce vapors for inhalation — **freebase** *vb*

free·bie *or* **free·bee** \'frē-bē\ *n* : something given without charge

free·board \'frē-ˌbȯrd\ *n* : the vertical distance between the waterline and the upper edge of the side of a boat

free·boo·ter \-ˌbü-tər\ *n* [D *vrijbuiter*, fr. *vrijbuit* plunder, fr. *vrij* free + *buit* booty] : PLUNDERER, PIRATE

free·born \-'bȯrn\ *adj* **1** : not born in vassalage or slavery **2** : of, relating to, or befitting one that is freeborn

freed·man \'frēd-mən, -ˌman\ *n* : a person freed from slavery

free·dom \'frē-dəm\ *n* **1** : the quality or state of being free : INDEPENDENCE **2** : EXEMPTION, RELEASE **3** : EASE, FACILITY ⟨spoke the language with ∼⟩ **4** : FRANKNESS **5** : unrestricted use **6** : a political right; *also* : FRANCHISE, PRIVILEGE

freedom fighter *n* : a person who takes part in a resistance movement against an oppressive political or social establishment

free enterprise *n* : freedom of private business to operate with little regulation by the government

free–for–all \'frē-fə-ˌrȯl\ *n* : a competition or fight open to all comers and usu. with no rules : BRAWL — **free–for–all** *adj*

free·hand \-ˌhand\ *adj* : done without mechanical aids or devices

free·hold \'frē-ˌhōld\ *n* : ownership of an estate for life usu. with the right to bequeath it to one's heirs; *also* : an estate thus owned — **free·hold·er** *n*

free·lance \-ˌlans\ *n* : one who pursues a profession (as writing) without a long-term commitment to any one employer — **free·lance** *adj or vb*

free–living \'frē-'li-viŋ\ *adj* **1** : unrestricted in pursuing personal pleasures **2** : being neither parasitic nor symbiotic ⟨∼ organisms⟩

free·load \'frē-ˌlōd\ *vb* : to impose upon another's hospitality — **free·load·er** *n*

free love *n* **1** : the practice of living openly with one of the opposite sex without marriage **2** : sexual relations without any commitments by either partner

free·man \'frē-mən, -ˌman\ *n* **1** : one who has civil or political liberty **2** : one having the full rights of a citizen

Free·ma·son \-ˌmā-s⁰n\ *n* : a member of a secret fraternal society called Free and Accepted Masons — **Free·ma·son·ry** \-rē\ *n*

free radical *n* : an esp. reactive atom or group of atoms with one or more unpaired electrons; *esp* : one that can cause bodily damage (as by altering the chemical structure of cells)

free–range \'frē-ˌrānj\ *adj* : allowed to range and forage with relative freedom ⟨∼ chickens⟩; *also* : produced by free-range animals ⟨∼ eggs⟩

free speech *n* : speech that is protected by the First Amendment to the U.S. Constitution

free spirit *n* : NONCONFORMIST

free·stand·ing \'frē-'stan-diŋ\ *adj* : standing alone or on its own foundation free of support

free·stone \'frē-ˌstōn\ *n* **1** : a stone that may be cut freely without splitting **2** : a fruit stone to which the flesh does not cling; *also* : a fruit (as a peach or cherry) having such a stone

free·think·er \-'thiŋ-kər\ *n* : one who forms opinions on the basis of reason independently of authority; *esp* : one who doubts or denies religious dogma — **free·think·ing** *n or adj*

free trade *n* : trade between nations without restrictions (as high taxes on imports)

free verse *n* : verse whose meter is irregular or whose rhythm is not metrical

free·ware \'frē-ˌwer\ *n* : software that is free or that has a small usu. optional cost

free·way \'frē-ˌwā\ *n* : an expressway without tolls

free·wheel \-'hwēl\ *vb* : to move, live, or play freely or irresponsibly

free·will \'frē-ˌwil\ *adj* : VOLUNTARY

free will *n* : voluntary choice or decision

¹freeze \'frēz\ *vb* **froze** \'frōz\; **fro·zen** \'frō-z⁰n\; **freez·ing 1** : to harden or cause to harden into a solid (as ice) by loss of heat **2** : to withstand freezing **3** : to chill or become chilled with cold **4** : to damage by frost **5** : to adhere solidly by or as if by freezing **6** : to become fixed, motionless, or incapable of speech **7** : to cause to grip tightly **8** : to become clogged with ice **9** : to fix at a certain stage or level ⟨∼ wages⟩

²freeze *n* **1** : an act or instance of freezing **2** : the state of being frozen **3** : a state of weather marked by low temperature

freeze–dry \'frēz-'drī\ *vb* : to dry in a frozen state under vacuum esp. for preservation — **freeze–dried** *adj*

freez·er \'frē-zər\ *n* : a compartment, device, or room for freezing food or keeping it frozen

¹freight \'frāt\ *n* **1** : payment for carrying goods **2** : CARGO **3** : BURDEN **4** : the carrying of goods by a common carrier **5** : a train that carries freight

²freight *vb* **1** : to load with goods for transportation **2** : BURDEN, CHARGE **3** : to ship or transport by freight

freight·er \'frā-tər\ *n* : a ship or airplane used chiefly to carry freight

French \'french\ *n* **1** : the language of France **2** **French** *pl* : the people of France **3** : strong language — **French** *adj* — **French·man** \-mən\ *n* — **French·wom·an** \-ˌwu-mən\ *n*

French door *n* : a door with small panes of glass extending the full length

French dressing *n* **1** : a thin salad dressing usu. made of vinegar and oil with spices **2** : a creamy salad dressing flavored with tomatoes

french fry *n, often cap 1st F* : a strip of potato fried in deep fat until brown — **french fry** *vb, often cap 1st F*

French horn *n* : a curved brass instrument with a funnel⁼ shaped mouthpiece and a flaring bell

French press *n* : a coffeepot in which ground beans are infused and then pressed by a plunger

French toast *n* : bread dipped in a mixture of eggs and milk and fried at a low heat

French twist *n* : a woman's hairstyle in which the hair is coiled at the rear and secured in place

fre·net·ic \fri-'ne-tik\ *adj* : FRANTIC — **fre·net·i·cal·ly** \-ti-k(ə-)lē\ *adv*

fren·zy \'fren-zē\ *n, pl* **frenzies 1** : temporary madness or a violently agitated state **2** : intense often disordered activity — **fren·zied** \-zēd\ *adj*

freq *abbr* frequency; frequent; frequently

fre·quen·cy \'frē-kwən-sē\ *n, pl* **-cies 1** : the fact or condition of occurring frequently **2** : rate of occurrence **3** : the number of cycles per second of an alternating current **4** : the number of waves (as of sound or electromagnetic energy) that pass a fixed point each second

frequency modulation *n* : variation of the frequency of a carrier wave according to another signal; *also* : FM

¹fre·quent \frē-'kwent, 'frē-kwənt\ *vb* : to associate with, be in, or resort to habitually — **fre·quent·er** *n*

²fre·quent \'frē-kwənt\ *adj* **1** : happening often or at short intervals ⟨making ∼ stops⟩ **2** : HABITUAL ⟨a ∼ visitor⟩ — **fre·quent·ly** *adv*

fre·quent–fli·er \'frē-kwənt-'flī-ər\ *adj* : of, relating to, or being an airline program offering awards for specified numbers of air miles traveled

fres·co \'fres-kō\ n, pl **frescoes** [It, fr. fresco fresh] : the art of painting on fresh plaster; also : a painting done by this method

fresh \'fresh\ adj **1** : VIGOROUS, REFRESHED **2** : not stale, sour, or decayed ⟨~ bread⟩ **3** : not faded **4** : not worn or rumpled **5** : not altered by processing (as freezing or canning) **6** : not containing salt **7** : free from taint : PURE **8** : fairly strong : BRISK ⟨~ breeze⟩ **9** : experienced, made, or received newly or anew **10** : ADDITIONAL, ANOTHER ⟨made a ~ start⟩ **11** : ORIGINAL, VIVID ⟨a ~ portrayal⟩ **12** : INEXPERIENCED **13** : newly come or arrived ⟨~ from school⟩ **14** : IMPUDENT — **fresh·ly** adv — **fresh·ness** n

fresh·en \'fre-shən\ vb : to make, grow, or become fresh

fresh·et \'fre-shət\ n : an overflowing of a stream (as by heavy rains)

fresh·man \'fresh-mən\ n **1** : a 1st-year student **2** : BEGINNER, NEWCOMER

fresh·wa·ter \-,wȯ-tər, -,wä-\ n : water that is not salty — **freshwater** adj

¹**fret** \'fret\ vb **fret·ted; fret·ting** [ME, to devour, fret, fr. OE fretan to devour] **1** : WEAR, CORRODE; also : FRAY **2** : RUB, CHAFE **3** : to make by wearing away **4** : to become irritated : WORRY, VEX **5** : GRATE; also : AGITATE

²**fret** n : an irritated or worried state ⟨in a ~ about the interview⟩

³**fret** n : ornamental work esp. of straight lines in symmetrical patterns

⁴**fret** n : one of a series of ridges across the fingerboard of a stringed musical instrument — **fret·ted** adj

fret·ful \'fret-fəl\ adj : IRRITABLE — **fret·ful·ly** adv — **fret·ful·ness** n

fret·saw \-,sȯ\ n : a narrow-bladed handsaw used for cutting curved outlines

fret·work \-,wərk\ n **1** : decoration consisting of frets **2** : ornamental openwork or work in relief

Fri abbr Friday

fri·a·ble \'frī-ə-bəl\ adj : easily crumbled or pulverized ⟨~ soil⟩

fri·ar \'frī(-ə)r\ n [ME frere, fryer, fr. AF frere, friere, lit., brother, fr. L frater] : a member of a religious order that orig. lived by alms

fri·ary \'frī(-ə)r-ē\ n, pl **-ar·ies** : a monastery of friars

¹**fric·as·see** \'fri-kə-,sē, ,fri-kə-'sē\ n : a dish made of meat (as chicken) cut into pieces, stewed in stock, and served in sauce

²**fricassee** vb **-seed; -see·ing** : to cook as a fricassee

fric·tion \'frik-shən\ n **1** : the rubbing of one body against another **2** : the force that resists motion between bodies in contact **3** : clash in opinions between persons or groups : DISAGREEMENT — **fric·tion·al** adj

friction tape n : a usu. cloth adhesive tape impregnated with insulating material and used esp. to protect and insulate electrical conductors

Fri·day \'frī-dē, -(,)dā\ n : the sixth day of the week

fridge \'frij\ n : REFRIGERATOR

fried·cake \'frīd-,kāk\ n : DOUGHNUT, CRULLER

fried rice n : a dish of boiled or steamed rice that is stir-fried with soy sauce and typically includes egg, meat, and vegetables

friend \'frend\ n **1** : one attached to another by respect or affection **2** : ACQUAINTANCE **3** : one who is not hostile **4** : one who supports or favors something ⟨a ~ of art⟩ **5** cap : a member of the Society of Friends : QUAKER — **friend·less** adj — **friend·li·ness** \-lē-nəs\ n — **friend·ly** adj — **friend·ship** \-,ship\ n

frieze \'frēz\ n : an ornamental often sculptured band extending around something (as a building or room)

frig·ate \'fri-gət\ n **1** : a square-rigged warship **2** : a warship smaller than a destroyer

fright \'frīt\ n **1** : sudden terror : ALARM **2** : something that is ugly or shocking

fright·en \'frī-t⁽ə⁾n\ vb **1** : to make afraid **2** : to drive away or out by frightening **3** : to become frightened — **fright·en·ing·ly** adv

fright·ful \'frīt-fəl\ adj **1** : TERRIFYING **2** : STARTLING **3** : EXTREME ⟨~ thirst⟩ — **fright·ful·ly** adv — **fright·ful·ness** n

frig·id \'fri-jəd\ adj **1** : intensely cold **2** : lacking warmth or ardor : INDIFFERENT **3** : abnormally averse to or unable to achieve orgasm during sexual intercourse — used esp. of women — **fri·gid·i·ty** \fri-'ji-də-tē\ n

frigid zone n : the area or region between the arctic circle and the north pole or between the antarctic circle and the south pole

frill \'fril\ n **1** : a gathered, pleated, or ruffled edging **2** : something unessential — **frilly** adj

fringe \'frinj\ n [ME frenge, fr. AF, fr. VL *frimbia, alter. of L fimbriae (pl.)] **1** : an ornamental border consisting of short threads or strips hanging from an edge or band **2** : something that resembles a fringe : EDGE ⟨operated on the ~s of the law⟩ **3** : something that is additional or secondary to an activity, process, or subject — **fringe** vb

fringe benefit n **1** : an employment benefit paid for by an employer without affecting basic wage rates **2** : any additional benefit

frip·pery \'fri-pə-rē\ n, pl **-per·ies** [MF friperie] **1** : FINERY **2** : pretentious display

frisk \'frisk\ vb **1** : to leap, skip, or dance in a lively or playful way : GAMBOL **2** : to search (a person) esp. for concealed weapons by running the hand rapidly over the clothing

frisky \'fris-kē\ adj **frisk·i·er; -est** : PLAYFUL — **frisk·i·ly** \-kə-lē\ adv — **frisk·i·ness** \-kē-nəs\ n

¹**frit·ter** \'fri-tər\ n : a small lump of fried batter often containing fruit or meat

²**fritter** vb **1** : to reduce or waste piecemeal **2** : to break into small fragments

fritz \'frits\ n : a state of disorder or disrepair — used in the phrase on the fritz

friv·o·lous \'fri-və-ləs\ adj **1** : of little importance : TRIVIAL **2** : lacking in seriousness — **fri·vol·i·ty** \fri-'vä-lə-tē\ n — **friv·o·lous·ly** adv

frizz \'friz\ vb : to form into small tight curls — **frizz** n — **frizzy** adj

friz·zies \'fri-zēz\ n pl : hair which has become difficult to manage (as due to humidity)

¹**friz·zle** \'fri-zəl\ vb **friz·zled; friz·zling** : FRIZZ, CURL — **frizzle** n

²**frizzle** vb **friz·zled; friz·zling** **1** : to fry until crisp and curled **2** : to cook with a sizzling noise

fro \'frō\ adv : BACK, AWAY — used in the phrase to and fro

frock \'fräk\ n **1** : an outer garment worn by monks and friars **2** : an outer garment worn esp. by men **3** : a woman's or girl's dress

frock coat n : a man's knee-length usu. double-breasted coat

frog \'frȯg, 'fräg\ n **1** : any of various largely aquatic smooth-skinned tailless leaping amphibians **2** : an ornamental braiding for fastening the front of a garment by a loop through which a button passes **3** : a condition in the throat causing hoarseness **4** : a small holder (as of metal, glass, or plastic) with perforations or spikes that is placed in a bowl or vase to keep cut flowers in position

frog 2

frog·man \'frȯg-,man, 'fräg-, -mən\ n : a swimmer equipped to work underwater for long periods of time

¹**frol·ic** \'frä-lik\ vb **frol·icked; frol·ick·ing** **1** : to make merry **2** : to play about happily : ROMP

²**frolic** n **1** : a playful or mischievous action **2** : FUN, MERRIMENT — **frol·ic·some** \-səm\ adj

from \'frəm, 'främ\ prep **1** — used to show a starting point ⟨a letter ~ home⟩ **2** — used to show removal or separation ⟨subtract 3 ~ 9⟩ **3** — used to show a material, source, or cause ⟨suffering ~ a cold⟩

frond \'fränd\ n : a usu. large divided leaf esp. of a fern or palm tree

¹**front** \'frənt\ n **1** : FOREHEAD; also : the whole face **2** : external and often feigned appearance **3** : a region of active fighting; also : a sphere of activity **4** : a political

coalition **5** : the side of a building containing the main entrance **6** : the forward part or surface **7** : FRONTAGE **8** : a boundary between two dissimilar air masses **9** : a position directly before or ahead of something else **10** : a person, group, or thing used to mask the identity of the actual controlling agent

²front *vb* **1** : to have the principal side adjacent to something **2** : to serve as a front **3** : CONFRONT

front·age \'frən-tij\ *n* **1** : a piece of land lying adjacent (as to a street or the ocean) **2** : the length of a frontage **3** : the front side of a building

front·al \'frən-t³l\ *adj* **1** : of, relating to, or next to the forehead **2** : of, relating to, or directed at the front ⟨a ∼ attack⟩ — **fron·tal·ly** *adv*

fron·tier \'frən-'tir\ *n* **1** : a border between two countries **2** : a region that forms the margin of settled territory **3** : the outer limits of knowledge or achievement ⟨the ∼s of science⟩ — **fron·tiers·man** \-'tirz-mən\ *n*

fron·tis·piece \'frən-tə-,spēs\ *n* : an illustration preceding and usu. facing the title page of a book

front man *n* : a person serving as a front or figurehead

front·ward \'frənt-wərd\ *or* **front·wards** \-wərdz\ *adv or adj* : toward the front

¹frost \'fròst\ *n* **1** : freezing temperature **2** : a covering of tiny ice crystals on a cold surface — **frosty** *adj*

²frost *vb* **1** : to cover with frost **2** : to put icing on (as a cake) **3** : to produce a slightly roughened surface on (as glass) **4** : to injure or kill by frost

¹frost·bite \'fròst-,bīt\ *vb* **-bit** \-,bit\; **-bit·ten** \-,bi-t³n\; **-bit·ing** : to injure by frost or frostbite

²frostbite *n* : the freezing or the local effect of a partial freezing of some part of the body

frost heave *n* : an upthrust of pavement caused by freezing of moist soil

frost·ing \'fròs-tiŋ\ *n* **1** : ICING **2** : dull finish on metal or glass

froth \'fròth\ *n, pl* **froths** \'fròths, 'fròthz\ [ME, fr. ON *frotha*] **1** : bubbles formed in or on a liquid **2** : something light or worthless — **frothy** *adj*

frou-frou \'frü-,frü\ *n* [F] **1** : a rustling esp. of a woman's skirts **2** : showy or frilly ornamentation

fro·ward \'frō-wərd\ *adj* : DISOBEDIENT, WILLFUL

frown \'fraún\ *vb* **1** : to wrinkle the forehead (as in displeasure or thought) **2** : to look with disapproval **3** : to express with a frown — **frown** *n*

frow·sy *or* **frow·zy** \'fraú-zē\ *adj* **frow·si·er** *or* **frow·zi·er**; **-est** : having a slovenly or uncared-for appearance

froze *past of* FREEZE

fro·zen \'frō-z³n\ *adj* **1** : treated, affected, or crusted over by freezing **2** : subject to long and severe cold **3** : incapable of being changed, moved, or undone : FIXED ⟨∼ wages⟩ **4** : not available for present use ⟨∼ capital⟩ **5** : expressing or characterized by cold unfriendliness

FRS *abbr* Federal Reserve System

frt *abbr* freight

fruc·ti·fy \'frək-tə-,fī, 'frúk-\ *vb* **-fied; -fy·ing** **1** : to bear fruit **2** : to make fruitful or productive

fruc·tose \'frək-,tōs, 'frúk-\ *n* : a very sweet soluble sugar that occurs esp. in fruit juices and honey

fru·gal \'frü-gəl\ *adj* : ECONOMICAL, THRIFTY — **fru·gal·i·ty** \frü-'ga-lə-tē\ *n* — **fru·gal·ly** *adv*

¹fruit \'früt\ *n* [ME, fr. AF *frut, fruit*, fr. L *fructus* fruit, use, fr. *frui* to enjoy, have the use of] **1** : a product of plant growth; *esp* : a usu. edible and sweet reproductive body (as a strawberry or apple) of a seed plant **2** : a product of fertilization in a plant; *esp* : the ripe ovary of a seed plant with its contents and appendages **3** : CONSEQUENCE, RESULT — **fruit·ed** \'frü-təd\ *adj*

²fruit *vb* : to bear or cause to bear fruit

fruit·cake \'früt-,kāk\ *n* : a rich cake containing nuts, dried or candied fruits, and spices

fruit fly *n* : any of various small dipteran flies whose larvae feed on fruit or decaying vegetable matter

fruit·ful \'früt-fəl\ *adj* **1** : yielding or producing fruit **2** : very productive; *also* : bringing results ⟨a ∼ idea⟩ — **fruit·ful·ly** *adv* — **fruit·ful·ness** *n*

fru·ition \frü-'i-shən\ *n* **1** : ENJOYMENT **2** : the state of bearing fruit **3** : REALIZATION, ACCOMPLISHMENT ⟨guided the project to ∼⟩

fruit·less \'früt-ləs\ *adj* **1** : not bearing fruit **2** : UNSUCCESSFUL ⟨a ∼ attempt⟩ — **fruit·less·ly** *adv*

fruity \'frü-tē\ *adj* **fruit·i·er; -est** : resembling a fruit esp. in flavor

frumpy \'frəm-pē\ *adj* **frump·i·er; -est** : DOWDY, DRAB

frus·trate \'frəs-,trāt\ *vb* **frus·trat·ed; frus·trat·ing** **1** : to balk or defeat in an endeavor **2** : to induce feelings of insecurity, discouragement, or dissatisfaction in **3** : to bring to nothing — **frus·trat·ing·ly** *adv* — **frus·tra·tion** \,frəs-'trā-shən\ *n*

frus·tum \'frəs-təm\ *n, pl* **frustums** *or* **frus·ta** \-tə\ : the part of a cone or pyramid formed by cutting off the top by a plane parallel to the base

frwy *abbr* freeway

¹fry \'frī\ *vb* **fried; fry·ing** [ME *frien*, fr. AF *frire*, fr. L *frigere* to roast] **1** : to cook in a pan or on a griddle over heat esp. with the use of fat **2** : to undergo frying **3** : to damage or destroy by overheating esp. by high voltage

²fry *n, pl* **fries** **1** : a social gathering where fried food is eaten **2** : a dish of something fried; *esp, pl* : FRENCH FRIES

³fry *n, pl* **fry** [ME, fr. AF *frie*, fr. *freier, frier* to rub, spawn, fr. L *fricare* to rub] **1** : recently hatched fishes; *also* : very small adult fishes **2** : members of a group or class ⟨small ∼⟩

fry·er \'frī(-ə)r\ *n* **1** : something (as a young chicken) suitable for frying **2** : a deep utensil for frying foods

FSLIC *abbr* Federal Savings and Loan Insurance Corporation

ft *abbr* **1** feet; foot **2** fort

FTC *abbr* Federal Trade Commission

FTP \,ef-,tē-'pē\ *n* [*f*ile *t*ransfer *p*rotocol] : a system for transferring computer files esp. via the Internet — **FTP** *vb*

fuch·sia \'fyü-shə\ *n* **1** : any of a genus of shrubs related to the evening primrose and grown for their showy nodding often red or purple flowers **2** : a vivid reddish purple color

fud·dle \'fə-d³l\ *vb* **fud·dled; fud·dling** : MUDDLE, CONFUSE

fud·dy–dud·dy \'fə-dē-,də-dē\ *n, pl* **-dies** : one that is old-fashioned, unimaginative, or conservative

¹fudge \'fəj\ *vb* **fudged; fudg·ing** **1** : to exceed the proper bounds of something **2** : CHEAT; *also* : FALSIFY **3** : to fail to come to grips with

²fudge *n* **1** : NONSENSE **2** : a soft candy of milk, sugar, butter, and flavoring

¹fu·el \'fyü-əl, 'fyül\ *n* : a material used to produce heat or power by burning; *also* : a material from which nuclear energy can be liberated

²fuel *vb* **-eled** *or* **-elled; -el·ing** *or* **-el·ling** : to provide with or take in fuel

fuel cell *n* : a device that continuously changes the chemical energy of a fuel directly into electrical energy

fuel injection *n* : a system for injecting a precise amount of atomized fuel into an internal combustion engine — **fuel–in·ject·ed** \'fyü-in-'jek-təd\ *adj*

¹fu·gi·tive \'fyü-jə-tiv\ *adj* **1** : running away or trying to escape **2** : likely to vanish suddenly : not fixed or lasting

²fugitive *n* **1** : one who flees or tries to escape **2** : something elusive or hard to find

fugue \'fyüg\ *n* **1** : a musical composition in which different parts successively repeat the theme **2** : a disturbed state of consciousness characterized by acts that are not recalled upon recovery

füh·rer *or* **rueh·rer** \'fyúr-ər, 'fir-\ *n* [G] : LEADER; *esp* : TYRANT

¹-ful \fəl\ *adj suffix, sometimes* **-ful·ler;** *sometimes* **-ful·lest** **1** : full of ⟨pride*ful*⟩ **2** : characterized by ⟨peace*ful*⟩ **3** : having the qualities of ⟨master*ful*⟩ **4** : tending, given, or liable to ⟨help*ful*⟩

²-ful \,fúl\ *n suffix* : number or quantity that fills or would fill ⟨room*ful*⟩

ful·crum \'fúl-krəm, 'fəl-\ *n, pl* **ful·crums** *or* **ful·cra** \-krə\ [LL, fr. L, bedpost] : the support on which a lever turns

ful·fill *or* **ful·fil** \fúl-'fil\ *vb* **ful·filled; ful·fill·ing** **1** : to put into effect **2** : to bring to an end **3** : SATISFY — **ful·fill·ment** *or* **ful·fil·ment** *n*

¹full \'fúl\ *adj* **1** : FILLED **2** : complete esp. in detail, number, or duration **3** : having all the distinguishing characteristics ⟨a ∼ member⟩ **4** : MAXIMUM ⟨∼ strength⟩ **5** : rounded in outline ⟨a ∼ figure⟩ **6** : possessing or containing an abundance ⟨∼ of wrinkles⟩ **7** : having an abundance of material ⟨a ∼ skirt⟩ **8** : satisfied esp. with food or drink **9** : having volume or depth of sound **10** : completely occupied with a thought or plan — **full·ness** also **ful·ness** n

²**full** adv **1** : VERY, EXTREMELY **2** : ENTIRELY ⟨fill a glass ∼⟩ **3** : STRAIGHT, SQUARELY ⟨hit him ∼ in the face⟩

³**full** n **1** : the highest or fullest state or degree **2** : the utmost extent — **in full** : to the requisite or complete amount

⁴**full** vb : to shrink and thicken (woolen cloth) by moistening, heating, and pressing — **full·er** n

full·back \'fu̇l-ˌbak\ n : a football back stationed between the halfbacks

full–blood·ed \'fu̇l-'blə-dəd\ adj : of unmixed ancestry : PUREBRED

full–blown \-'blōn\ adj **1** : being at the height of bloom **2** : fully mature or developed

full–bod·ied \-'bä-dēd\ adj : marked by richness and fullness

full dress n : the style of dress worn for ceremonial or formal occasions

full–fledged \'fu̇l-'flejd\ adj **1** : fully developed **2** : having attained complete status ⟨a ∼ lawyer⟩

full house n : a poker hand containing three of a kind and a pair

full moon n : the moon with its whole disk illuminated

full–on \-ˌȯn, -ˌän\ adj : COMPLETE, FULL-FLEDGED

full–scale \'fu̇l-'skāl\ adj **1** : identical to an original in proportion and size ⟨∼ drawing⟩ **2** : involving full use of available resources ⟨a ∼ revolt⟩

full–term \-ˌtərm\ adj : retained in the uterus for the normal period of gestation before birth ⟨a ∼ baby⟩

full tilt adv : at high speed

full–time \'fu̇l-'tīm\ adj or adv : involving or working a normal or standard schedule

ful·ly \'fu̇-lē\ adv **1** : in a full manner or degree : COMPLETELY **2** : at least ⟨∼ nine tenths of us⟩

ful·mi·nate \'fu̇l-mə-ˌnāt, 'fəl-\ vb **-nat·ed; -nat·ing** [ME, fr. ML fulminatus, pp. of fulminare, fr. L, to strike (of lightning), fr. fulmen lightning] : to utter or send out censure or invective : condemn severely — **ful·mi·na·tion** \ˌfu̇l-mə-'nā-shən, ˌfəl-\ n

ful·some \'fu̇l-səm\ adj **1** : COPIOUS, ABUNDANT ⟨∼ detail⟩ **2** : generous in amount or extent ⟨a ∼ victory⟩ **3** : excessively flattering ⟨∼ praise⟩

fu·ma·role \'fyü-mə-ˌrōl\ n : a hole in a volcanic region from which hot gases issue

fum·ble \'fəm-bəl\ vb **fum·bled; fum·bling 1** : to grope about clumsily **2** : to fail to hold, catch, or handle properly — **fumble** n

¹**fume** \'fyüm\ n : a usu. irritating smoke, vapor, or gas

²**fume** vb **fumed; fum·ing 1** : to treat with fumes **2** : to give off fumes **3** : to express anger or annoyance

fu·mi·gant \'fyü-mi-gənt\ n : a substance used for fumigation

fu·mi·gate \'fyü-mə-ˌgāt\ vb **-gat·ed; -gat·ing** : to treat with fumes to disinfect or destroy pests — **fu·mi·ga·tion** \ˌfyü-mə-'gā-shən\ n — **fu·mi·ga·tor** \'fyü-mə-ˌgā-tər\ n

¹**fun** \'fən\ n [E dial. fun to hoax] **1** : something that provides amusement or enjoyment **2** : ENJOYMENT

²**fun** adj : full of fun ⟨a ∼ person⟩ ⟨had a ∼ time⟩

¹**func·tion** \'fəŋk-shən\ n **1** : OCCUPATION **2** : special purpose **3** : the particular purpose for which a person or thing is specially fitted or used or for which a thing exists ⟨the ∼ of a hammer⟩; also : the natural or proper action of a bodily part in a living thing ⟨the ∼ of the heart⟩ **4** : a formal ceremony or social affair **5** : a mathematical relationship that assigns to each element of a set one and only one element of the same or another set **6** : a variable (as a quality, trait, or measurement) that depends on and varies with another ⟨height is a ∼ of age in children⟩ **7** : a computer subroutine that performs a calculation with variables provided by a program — **func·tion·al** \-shə-nəl\ adj — **func·tion·al·ly** adv

²**function** vb : to have or carry on a function

func·tion·ary \'fəŋk-shə-ˌner-ē\ n, pl **-ar·ies** : one who performs a certain function; esp : OFFICIAL

function word n : a word (as a preposition, auxiliary verb, or conjunction) expressing the grammatical relationship between other words

¹**fund** \'fənd\ n [L fundus bottom, country estate] **1** : a sum of money or resources intended for a special pur-

pose **2** : STORE, SUPPLY **3** pl : available money **4** : an organization administering a special fund

²**fund** vb **1** : to provide funds for **2** : to convert (a short-term obligation) into a long-term interest-bearing debt — **fund·er** n

fun·da·men·tal \ˌfən-də-'men-t³l\ adj **1** : serving as an origin : PRIMARY **2** : BASIC, ESSENTIAL **3** : RADICAL ⟨∼ change⟩ **4** : of central importance : PRINCIPAL ⟨∼ purpose⟩ — **fundamental** n — **fun·da·men·tal·ly** adv

fun·da·men·tal·ism \-tə-ˌli-zəm\ n **1** often cap : a Protestant religious movement emphasizing the literal infallibility of the Bible **2** : a movement or attitude stressing strict adherence to a set of basic principles — **fun·da·men·tal·ist** \-list\ adj or n

¹**fu·ner·al** \'fyü-nə-rəl\ adj **1** : of, relating to, or constituting a funeral **2** : FUNEREAL 2

²**funeral** n : the ceremonies held for a dead person usu. before burial

fu·ner·ary \'fyü-nə-ˌrer-ē\ adj : of, used for, or associated with burial

fu·ne·re·al \fyu̇-'nir-ē-əl\ adj **1** : of or relating to a funeral **2** : suggesting a funeral

fun·gi·cide \'fən-jə-ˌsīd, 'fəŋ-gə-\ n : an agent that kills or checks the growth of fungi — **fun·gi·cid·al** \ˌfən-jə-'sī-d³l, ˌfəŋ-gə-\ adj

fun·gus \'fəŋ-gəs\ n, pl **fun·gi** \'fən-ˌjī, 'fəŋ-ˌgī\ also **fun·gus·es** \'fəŋ-gə-səz\ : any of a kingdom of parasitic spore-producing organisms (as molds, mildews, and mushrooms) formerly classified as plants — **fun·gal** \-gəl\ adj — **fun·gous** \-gəs\ adj

fu·nic·u·lar \fyu̇-'ni-kyə-lər, fə-\ n : a cable railway ascending a mountain

¹**funk** \'fəŋk\ n : a strong offensive smell

²**funk** n : a depressed state of mind

funky \'fəŋ-kē\ adj **funk·i·er; -est 1** : having an earthy unsophisticated style and feeling; esp : having the style and feeling of older black American music **2** : odd or quaint in appearance or style — **funk·i·ness** n

¹**fun·nel** \'fə-n³l\ n **1** : a cone-shaped utensil with a tube used for catching and directing a downward flow (as of liquid) **2** : FLUE, SMOKESTACK

²**funnel** vb **-neled** also **-nelled; -nel·ing** also **-nel·ling 1** : to pass through or as if through a funnel **2** : to move to a central point or into a central channel

fun·nies \'fə-nēz\ n pl : a comic strip or a comic section (as of a newspaper) — used with the

fun·ny \'fə-nē\ adj **fun·ni·er; -est 1** : AMUSING **2** : FACETIOUS **3** : PECULIAR **4** : UNDERHANDED — **funny** adv

funny bone n : a place at the back of the elbow where a blow easily compresses a nerve and causes a painful tingling sensation

fun·plex \'fən-ˌpleks\ n : a center containing various entertainment facilities

¹**fur** \'fər\ n **1** : an article of clothing made of or with fur **2** : the hairy coat of a mammal esp. when fine, soft, and thick; also : this coat dressed for use — **fur** adj — **furred** \'fərd\ adj

²**fur** abbr furlong

fur·be·low \'fər-bə-ˌlō\ n **1** : FLOUNCE, RUFFLE **2** : showy trimming

fur·bish \'fər-bish\ vb **1** : to make lustrous : POLISH **2** : to give a new look to : RENOVATE

fu·ri·ous \'fyu̇r-ē-əs\ adj **1** : FIERCE, ANGRY, VIOLENT **2** : BOISTEROUS **3** : INTENSE ⟨∼ growth⟩ — **fu·ri·ous·ly** adv

furl \'fərl\ vb **1** : to wrap or roll (as a sail or a flag) close to or around something **2** : to curl in furls — **furl** n

fur·long \'fər-ˌlȯŋ\ n [ME, fr. OE furlang, fr. furh furrow + lang long] : a unit of distance equal to 220 yards (about 201 meters)

fur·lough \'fər-lō\ n [D verlof, lit., permission] : a leave of absence from duty granted esp. to a soldier — **furlough** vb

fur·nace \'fər-nəs\ n : an enclosed structure in which heat is produced

fur·nish \'fər-nish\ vb **1** : to provide with what is needed : EQUIP **2** : SUPPLY, GIVE ⟨∼ed them with food⟩

fur·nish·ings \-ni-shiŋz\ n pl **1** : articles or accessories of dress **2** : FURNITURE

fur·ni·ture \'fər-ni-chər\ n : equipment that is necessary or desirable; esp : movable articles (as chairs or beds) for a room

fu·ror \'fyuṙ-ȯr\ *n* 1 : ANGER, RAGE 2 : a contagious excitement; *esp* : a fashionable craze 3 : UPROAR

fu·rore \-ȯr\ *n* [It] : FUROR 2, 3

fur·ri·er \'fər-ē-ər\ *n* : one who prepares or deals in fur

fur·ring \'fər-iŋ\ *n* : wood or metal strips applied to a wall or ceiling to form a level surface or an air space

fur·row \'fər-ō\ *n* 1 : a trench in the earth made by a plow 2 : a narrow groove or wrinkle — **furrow** *vb*

fur·ry \'fər-ē\ *adj* **fur·ri·er; -est** 1 : resembling or consisting of fur 2 : covered with fur

¹fur·ther \'fər-thər\ *adv* 1 : FARTHER 1 2 : in addition : MOREOVER 3 : to a greater extent or degree

²further *vb* : to help forward — **fur·ther·ance** \'fər-thə-rəns\ *n*

³further *adj* 1 : FARTHER 1 2 : ADDITIONAL ⟨~ education⟩

fur·ther·more \'fər-thər-ˌmȯr\ *adv* : in addition to what precedes : BESIDES

fur·ther·most \-ˌmōst\ *adj* : most distant : FARTHEST

fur·thest \'fər-thəst\ *adv or adj* : FARTHEST

fur·tive \'fər-tiv\ *adj* [F or L; F *furtif*, fr. L *furtivus*, fr. *furtum* theft, fr. *fur* thief] : done by stealth : SLY — **fur·tive·ly** *adv* — **fur·tive·ness** *n*

fu·ry \'fyuṙ-ē\ *n, pl* **furies** 1 : intense and often destructive rage 2 : extreme fierceness or violence 3 : FRENZY

furze \'fərz\ *n* : GORSE

¹fuse \'fyüz\ *vb* **fused; fus·ing** 1 : MELT 2 : to unite by or as if by melting together — **fus·ible** *adj*

²fuse *n* : an electrical safety device having a metal wire or strip that melts and interrupts the circuit when the current becomes too strong

³fuse *n* 1 : a cord or cable that is set afire to ignite an explosive charge 2 *usu* **fuze** : a mechanical or electrical device for setting off the explosive charge of a projectile, bomb, or torpedo

⁴fuse *also* **fuze** \'fyüz\ *vb* **fused** *also* **fuzed; fus·ing** *also* **fuz·ing** : to equip with a fuse

fu·se·lage \'fyü-sə-ˌläzh, -zə-\ *n* : the central body portion of an aircraft

fu·sil·lade \'fyü-sə-ˌläd, -ˌlad\ *n* : a number of shots fired simultaneously or in rapid succession

fu·sion \'fyü-zhən\ *n* 1 : the act or process of melting or making plastic by heat 2 : union by or as if by melting 3 : the union of light atomic nuclei to form heavier nuclei with the release of huge quantities of energy

¹fuss \'fəs\ *n* 1 : needless bustle or excitement : COMMOTION 2 : effusive praise 3 : a state of agitation 4 : OBJECTION, PROTEST 5 : DISPUTE

²fuss *vb* : to make a fuss

fuss·bud·get \'fəs-ˌbə-jət\ *n* : one who fusses or is fussy about trifles

fussy \'fə-sē\ *adj* **fuss·i·er; -est** 1 : IRRITABLE 2 : overly decorative ⟨a ~ wallpaper pattern⟩ 3 : requiring or giving close attention or concern to details or niceties — **fuss·i·ly** \-sə-lē\ *adv* — **fuss·i·ness** \-sē-nəs\ *n*

fus·tian \'fəs-chən\ *n* 1 : a strong usu. cotton fabric 2 : pretentious writing or speech — **fustian** *adj*

fus·ty \'fəs-tē\ *adj* **fus·ti·er; -est** [prob. alter. of ME *foisted*, *foist* musty, fr. *foist* wine cask, fr. AF *fust* wood, tree trunk, cask] 1 : MUSTY 2 : OLD-FASHIONED

fut *abbr* future

fu·tile \'fyü-t²l, 'fyü-ˌtī(-ə)l\ *adj* 1 : USELESS, VAIN 2 : FRIVOLOUS, TRIVIAL — **fu·tile·ly** *adv* — **fu·til·i·ty** \fyü-'ti-lə-tē\ *n*

fu·ton \'fü-ˌtän\ *n* [Jp] : a usu. cotton-filled mattress used on the floor or in a frame as a bed, couch, or chair

¹fu·ture \'fyü-chər\ *adj* 1 : of, relating to, or constituting a verb tense that expresses time yet to come 2 : coming after the present

²future *n* 1 : time that is to come 2 : what is going to happen 3 : an expectation of advancement or progressive development 4 : the future tense; *also* : a verb form in it

fu·tur·ism \'fyü-chə-ˌri-zəm\ *n* : a modern movement in art, music, and literature that tries esp. to express the energy and activity of mechanical processes — **fu·tur·ist** \'fyü-chə-rist\ *n*

fu·tur·is·tic \ˌfyü-chə-'ris-tik\ *adj* : of or relating to the future or to futurism; *also* : very modern

fu·tu·ri·ty \fyü-'tu̇r-ə-tē, -'tyu̇r-\ *n, pl* **-ties** 1 : FUTURE 2 : the quality or state of being future 3 *pl* : future events or prospects

fuze *var of* FUSE

fuzz \'fəz\ *n* : fine light particles or fibers (as of down or fluff)

fuzzy \'fə-zē\ *adj* **fuzz·i·er; -est** 1 : having or resembling fuzz 2 : INDISTINCT ⟨~ photos⟩ 3 : being or relating to pleasant usu. sentimental emotions ⟨~ feelings⟩ — **fuzz·i·ness** \-zē-nəs\ *n*

fuzzy logic *n* : a system of logic in which a statement can be true, false, or any of a continuum of values in between

fwd *abbr* forward

FWD *abbr* front-wheel drive

FY *abbr* fiscal year

-fy *vb suffix* : make : form into ⟨dand*ify*⟩

FYI *abbr* for your information

¹g \'jē\ *n, pl* **g's** *or* **gs** \'jēz\ *often cap* 1 : the 7th letter of the English alphabet 2 : a unit of force equal to the force exerted by gravity on a body at rest and used to indicate the force to which a body is subjected when accelerated 3 *slang* : a sum of $1000

²g *abbr, often cap* 1 game 2 gauge 3 good 4 gram 5 gravity

ga *abbr* gauge

¹Ga *abbr* Georgia

²Ga *symbol* gallium

GA *abbr* 1 general assembly 2 general average 3 general of the army 4 Georgia

gab \'gab\ *vb* **gabbed; gab·bing** : to talk in a rapid or thoughtless manner : CHATTER — **gab** *n*

gab·ar·dine \'ga-bər-ˌdēn\ *n* 1 : GABERDINE 1 2 : a firm durable twilled fabric having diagonal ribs and made of various fibers; *also* : a garment of gabardine

gab·ble \'ga-bəl\ *vb* **gab·bled; gab·bling** : JABBER, BABBLE

gab·by \'ga-bē\ *adj* **gab·bi·er; -est** : TALKATIVE, GARRULOUS

gab·er·dine \'ga-bər-ˌdēn\ *n* 1 : a long loose outer garment worn in medieval times and associated esp. with Jews 2 : GABARDINE 2

gab·fest \'gab-ˌfest\ *n* 1 : an informal gathering for general talk 2 : an extended conversation

ga·ble \'gā-bəl\ *n* : the vertical triangular end of a building formed by the sides of the roof sloping from the ridge down to the eaves — **ga·bled** \-bəld\ *adj*

gad \'gad\ *vb* **gad·ded; gad·ding** : to be constantly active without specific purpose — usu. used with *about* — **gad·der** *n*

gad·about \'ga-də-ˌbau̇t\ *n* : a person who flits about in social activity

gad·fly \'gad-ˌflī\ *n* 1 : a fly that bites or harasses livestock 2 : a person who annoys esp. by persistent criticism

gad·get \'ga-jət\ *n* : DEVICE, CONTRIVANCE — **gad·get·ry** \'ga-jə-trē\ *n*

gad·o·lin·i·um \ˌga-də-'li-nē-əm\ *n* : a magnetic metallic chemical element

¹Gael \'gāl\ *n* : a Celtic inhabitant of Ireland or Scotland

²Gael *abbr* Gaelic

Gael·ic \'gā-lik\ *adj* : of or relating to the Gaels or their languages — **Gaelic** *n*

gaff \\'gaf\ *n* **1** : a spear used in taking fish or turtles; *also* : a metal hook for holding or lifting heavy fish **2** : the spar supporting the top of a fore-and-aft sail **3** : rough treatment : ABUSE — **gaff** *vb*

gaffe \\'gaf\ *n* : a usu. social blunder

gaf·fer \\'ga-fər\ *n* **1** : an old man **2** : a lighting electrician on a motion-picture or television set

¹gag \\'gag\ *vb* **gagged; gag·ging 1** : to restrict use of the mouth of with a gag **2** : to prevent from speaking freely **3** : to retch or cause to retch **4** : OBSTRUCT, CHOKE **5** : BALK **6** : to make quips — **gag·ger** *n*

²gag *n* **1** : something thrust into the mouth esp. to prevent speech or outcry **2** : an official check or restraint on free speech **3** : a laugh-provoking remark or act **4** : PRANK, TRICK

¹gage \\'gāj\ *n* **1** : a token of defiance; *esp* : a glove or cap cast on the ground as a pledge of combat **2** : SECURITY

²gage *var of* GAUGE

gag·gle \\'ga-gəl\ *n* [ME *gagyll*, fr. *gagelen* to cackle] **1** : a flock of geese **2** : an unorganized group

gai·ety *also* **gay·ety** \\'gā-ə-tē\ *n, pl* **-eties 1** : festive activity : MERRYMAKING **2** : MERRIMENT **3** : FINERY ♦ **Synonyms** MIRTH, FESTIVITY, GLEE, HILARITY, JOLLITY

gai·ly *also* **gay·ly** \\'gā-lē\ *adv* : in a gay manner

¹gain \\'gān\ *n* **1** : PROFIT **2** : ACQUISITION, ACCUMULATION **3** : INCREASE

²gain *vb* **1** : to get possession of : EARN **2** : WIN ⟨~ a victory⟩ **3** : to increase in ⟨~ momentum⟩ **4** : PERSUADE **5** : to arrive at **6** : ACHIEVE ⟨~ strength⟩ **7** : to run fast ⟨the watch ~s a minute a day⟩ **8** : PROFIT **9** : INCREASE **10** : to improve in health ♦ **Synonyms** ACCOMPLISH, ATTAIN, REALIZE — **gain·er** *n*

gain·ful \\'gān-fəl\ *adj* : PROFITABLE ⟨~ employment⟩ — **gain·ful·ly** *adv*

gain·say \\gān-'sā\ *vb* **-said** \-'sād, -'sed\; **-say·ing; -says** \-'sāz, -'sez\ [ME *gainsayen*, fr. *gain-* against + *sayen* to say] **1** : DENY, DISPUTE **2** : to speak against ♦ **Synonyms** CONTRADICT, CONTRAVENE, IMPUGN, NEGATE — **gain·say·er** *n*

gait \\'gāt\ *n* : manner of moving on foot; *also* : a particular pattern or style of such moving — **gait·ed** *adj*

gai·ter \\'gā-tər\ *n* **1** : a leg covering reaching from the instep to ankle, mid-calf, or knee **2** : an overshoe with a fabric upper **3** : an ankle-high shoe with elastic gores in the sides

¹gal \\'gal\ *n* : GIRL

²gal *abbr* gallon

Gal *abbr* Galatians

ga·la \\'gā-lə, 'ga-, 'gä-\ *n* : a festive celebration : FESTIVITY — **gala** *adj*

ga·lac·tic \gə-'lak-tik\ *adj* : of or relating to a galaxy

Ga·la·tians \gə-'lā-shənz\ *n* — see BIBLE table

gal·axy \\'ga-lək-sē\ *n, pl* **-ax·ies** [ME *galaxie, galaxias*, fr. LL *galaxias*, fr. Gk, fr. *galakt-, gala* milk] **1** *often cap* : MILKY WAY GALAXY — used with *the* **2** : a very large group of stars **3** : an assemblage of brilliant or famous persons or things

gale \\'gāl\ *n* **1** : a strong wind **2** : an emotional outburst ⟨~s of laughter⟩

ga·le·na \gə-'lē-nə\ *n* : a lustrous bluish gray mineral that consists of the sulfide of lead and is the chief ore of lead

¹gall \\'gol\ *n* **1** : BILE **2** : something bitter to endure **3** : RANCOR **4** : IMPUDENCE ♦ **Synonyms** EFFRONTERY, BRASS, CHEEK, CHUTZPAH, AUDACITY, PRESUMPTION

²gall *n* : a skin sore caused by chafing

³gall *vb* **1** : CHAFE; *esp* : to become sore or worn by rubbing **2** : VEX, HARASS

⁴gall *n* : an abnormal outgrowth of plant tissue usu. due to parasites

¹gal·lant \gə-'lant, -'länt; 'ga-lənt\ *n* **1** : a young man of fashion **2** : a man who shows a marked fondness for the company of women and who is esp. attentive to them **3** : SUITOR

²gal·lant \\'ga-lənt *(usual for 2, 3, 4);* gə-'lant, -'länt *(usual for 5)*\ *adj* **1** : showy in dress or bearing : SMART **2** : SPLENDID, STATELY **3** : SPIRITED, BRAVE **4** : CHIVALROUS, NOBLE **5** : polite and attentive to women — **gal·lant·ly** *adv*

gal·lant·ry \\'ga-lən-trē\ *n, pl* **-ries 1** *archaic* : gallant appearance **2** : an act of marked courtesy **3** : courteous

attention to a woman **4** : conspicuous bravery ♦ **Synonyms** HEROISM, VALOR, PROWESS

gall·blad·der \\'gol-,bla-dər\ *n* : a membranous muscular sac attached to the liver and serving to store bile

gal·le·on \\'ga-lē-ən\ *n* : a large square-rigged sailing ship formerly used esp. by the Spanish

gal·le·ria \,ga-lə-'rē-ə\ *n* [It] : a roofed and usu. glass-enclosed promenade or court

gal·lery \\'ga-lə-rē\ *n, pl* **-ler·ies 1** : an outdoor balcony; *also* : PORCH, VERANDA **2** : a long narrow passage, apartment, or hall **3** : a narrow passage (as one made underground by a miner or through wood by an insect) **4** : a room where works of art are exhibited; *also* : an organization dealing in works of art **5** : a balcony in a theater, auditorium, or church; *esp* : the highest one in a theater **6** : the spectators at a sporting event (as a tennis or golf match) **7** : a photographer's studio — **gal·ler·ied** \-rēd\ *adj*

gal·ley \\'ga-lē\ *n, pl* **galleys 1** : a long low ship propelled esp. by oars and formerly used esp. in the Mediterranean Sea **2** : the kitchen esp. of a ship or airplane **3** : a proof of typeset matter esp. in a single column

galley 1

Gal·lic \\'ga-lik\ *adj* : of or relating to Gaul or France

gal·li·mau·fry \,ga-lə-'mò-frē\ *n, pl* **-fries** [MF *galimafree* stew] : HODGEPODGE

gal·li·nule \\'ga-lə-,nül, -,nyül\ *n* : any of several aquatic birds related to the rails

gal·li·um \\'ga-lē-əm\ *n* : a bluish-white metallic chemical element used esp. in semiconductors

gal·li·vant \\'ga-lə-,vant\ *vb* : to travel, roam, or move about for pleasure

gal·lon \\'ga-lən\ *n* — see WEIGHT table

¹gal·lop \\'ga-ləp\ *vb* **1** : to go or cause to go at a gallop **2** : to run fast — **gal·lop·er** *n*

²gallop *n* **1** : a bounding gait of a quadruped; *esp* : a fast 3-beat gait of a horse **2** : a ride or run at a gallop

gal·lows \\'ga-lōz\ *n, pl* **gallows** *or* **gal·lows·es 1** : a frame usu. of two upright posts and a crosspiece from which criminals are hanged; *also* : the punishment of hanging

gall·stone \\'gol-,stōn\ *n* : an abnormal concretion occurring in the gallbladder or bile passages

gal·lus·es \\'ga-lə-səz\ *n pl* : SUSPENDERS

ga·lore \gə-'lor\ *adj* [Ir *go leor* enough] : ABUNDANT, PLENTIFUL

ga·losh \gə-'läsh\ *n* : a high overshoe

galv *abbr* galvanized

gal·va·nise *Brit var of* GALVANIZE

gal·va·nize \\'gal-və-,nīz\ *vb* **-nized; -niz·ing 1** : to stimulate as if by an electric shock ⟨~ public opinion⟩ **2** : to coat (iron or steel) with zinc — **gal·va·ni·za·tion** \,gal-və-nə-'zā-shən\ *n* — **gal·va·niz·er** *n*

gal·va·nom·e·ter \,gal-və-'nä-mə-tər\ *n* : an instrument for detecting or measuring a small electric current

gam·bit \\'gam-bət\ *n* [It *gambetto*, lit., act of tripping someone, fr. *gamba* leg] **1** : a chess opening in which a player risks one or more minor pieces to gain an advantage in position **2** : a calculated move : STRATAGEM ♦ **Synonyms** TRICK, ARTIFICE, GIMMICK, MANEUVER, PLAY, RUSE

¹gam·ble \\'gam-bəl\ *vb* **gam·bled; gam·bling 1** : to play a game for money or property **2** : BET, WAGER **3** : VENTURE, HAZARD — **gam·bler** *n*

²gamble *n* : a risky undertaking

gam·bol \\'gam-bəl\ *vb* **-boled** *or* **-bolled; -bol·ing** *or* **-bol·ling** : to skip about in play : FRISK — **gambol** *n*

gam·brel roof \'gam-brəl-\ *n* : a roof with a lower steeper slope and an upper flatter one on each side

¹**game** \'gām\ *n* 1 : AMUSEMENT, DIVERSION 2 : SPORT, FUN ⟨made ∼ of the strange boy⟩ 3 : SCHEME, PROJECT 4 : a line of work : PROFESSION 5 : CONTEST 6 : animals hunted for sport or food; *also* : the flesh of a game animal

²**game** *vb* **gamed; gam·ing** 1 : to play for a stake 2 : to take dishonest advantage of

³**game** *adj* : PLUCKY, RESOLUTE — **game·ly** *adv* — **game·ness** *n*

⁴**game** *adj* : LAME ⟨a ∼ leg⟩

game·cock \'gām-ˌkäk\ *n* : a rooster trained for fighting

game fish *n* : SPORT FISH

game·keep·er \'gām-ˌkē-pər\ *n* : a person in charge of the breeding and protection of game animals or birds on a private preserve

game show *n* : a television program on which contestants compete usu. for prizes in a game

game·some \'gām-səm\ *adj* : MERRY ◆ **Synonyms** PLAYFUL, FROLICSOME, SPORTIVE, ANTIC

game·ster \'gām-stər\ *n* : GAMBLER

gam·ete \'ga-ˌmēt\ *n* : a mature germ cell — **ga·met·ic** \gə-'me-tik\ *adj*

game theory *n* : the analysis of a situation involving conflicting interests (as in business) in terms of gains and losses among opposing players

gam·in \'ga-mən\ *n* [F] 1 : a boy who hangs around on the streets 2 : GAMINE 2

ga·mine \ga-'mēn\ *n* 1 : a girl who hangs around on the streets 2 : a small playfully mischievous girl

gam·ma \'ga-mə\ *n* : the 3d letter of the Greek alphabet — Γ or γ

gamma globulin *n* : a blood protein fraction rich in antibodies; *also* : a solution of this from human blood donors that is given to provide immunity against some infectious diseases (as measles)

gamma ray *n* : a photon emitted by a radioactive substance; *also* : a photon of higher energy than that of an X-ray — usu. used in pl.

gam·mon \'ga-mən\ *n, chiefly Brit* : a cured ham or side of bacon

gam·ut \'ga-mət\ *n* : an entire range or series ◆ **Synonyms** SCALE, SPECTRUM

gamy *or* **gam·ey** \'gā-mē\ *adj* **gam·i·er; -est** 1 : GAME, PLUCKY 2 : having the flavor of game esp. when near tainting 3 : SCANDALOUS; *also* : DISREPUTABLE — **gam·i·ness** \-mē-nəs\ *n*

¹**gan·der** \'gan-dər\ *n* : a male goose

²**gander** *n* : LOOK, GLANCE

¹**gang** \'gaŋ\ *n* 1 : a set of implements or devices arranged to operate together 2 : a group of persons working or associated together; *esp* : a group of criminals or young delinquents

²**gang** *vb* 1 : to attack in a gang — usu. used with *up* 2 : to form into or move or act as a gang

gang·land \'gaŋ-ˌland\ *n* : the world of organized crime

gan·gling \'gaŋ-gliŋ\ *adj* : loosely and awkwardly built : LANKY

gan·gli·on \'gaŋ-glē-ən\ *n, pl* **-glia** \-ə\ *also* **-gli·ons** : a mass of nerve tissue containing cell bodies of neurons outside the central nervous tissue; *also* : NUCLEUS 3 — **gan·gli·on·ic** \ˌgaŋ-glē-'ä-nik\ *adj*

gan·gly \'gaŋ-glē\ *adj* : GANGLING

gang·plank \'gaŋ-ˌplaŋk\ *n* : a movable bridge from a ship to the shore

gang·plow \-ˌplau̇\ *n* : a plow that turns two or more furrows at one time

gan·grene \'gaŋ-ˌgrēn, gaŋ-'grēn\ *n* : the death of soft tissues in a local area of the body due to loss of the blood supply — **gangrene** *vb* — **gan·gre·nous** \'gaŋ-grə-nəs\ *adj*

gang·sta \'gaŋ-stə\ *n* : a member of an urban street gang

gangsta rap *n* : rap music with usu. hostile lyrics portraying urban gang life

gang·ster \'gaŋ-stər\ *n* : a member of a gang of criminals : RACKETEER

gang·way \'gaŋ-ˌwā\ *n* 1 : PASSAGEWAY; *also* : GANGPLANK 2 : clear passage through a crowd

gan·net \'ga-nət\ *n, pl* **gannets** *also* **gannet** : any of several large fish-eating usu. white and black seabirds that breed chiefly on offshore islands

gantlet *var of* GAUNTLET

gan·try \'gan-trē\ *n, pl* **gantries** : a frame structure on side supports over or around something

GAO *abbr* General Accounting Office

gaol \'jāl\, **gaol·er** \'jā-lər\ *chiefly Brit var of* JAIL, JAILER

gap \'gap\ *n* 1 : BREACH, CLEFT 2 : a mountain pass 3 : a blank space; *also* : an incomplete or deficient area 4 : a wide difference in character or attitude 5 : a problem caused by a disparity ⟨credibility ∼⟩

gape \'gāp\ *vb* **gaped; gap·ing** 1 : to open the mouth wide 2 : to open or part widely 3 : to stare with mouth open 4 : YAWN — **gape** *n*

¹**gar** \'gär\ *n* : any of several fishes that have a long body resembling that of a pike and long narrow jaws

²**gar** *abbr* garage

GAR *abbr* Grand Army of the Republic

¹**ga·rage** \gə-'räzh, -'räj\ *n* [F, act of docking, garage, fr. *garer* to dock, fr. MF *garrer*, prob. ultim. fr. ON *vara* to beware, take care] : a shelter or repair shop for automobiles

²**garage** *vb* **ga·raged; ga·rag·ing** : to keep or put in a garage

garage sale *n* : a sale of used household or personal articles held on the seller's own premises

garb \'gärb\ *n* 1 : style of dress 2 : outward form : APPEARANCE — **garb** *vb*

gar·bage \'gär-bij\ *n* 1 : food waste 2 : unwanted or useless material \-ˌman \-ˌman\ *n*

gar·ble \'gär-bəl\ *vb* **gar·bled; gar·bling** : to distort the meaning of ⟨∼ a story⟩

gar·çon \gär-'sōⁿ\ *n, pl* **garçons** *same or* -'sōⁿz\ [F, boy, servant] : WAITER

¹**gar·den** \'gär-dᵊn\ *n* 1 : a plot for growing fruits, flowers, or vegetables 2 : a public recreation area; *esp* : one for displaying plants or animals

²**garden** *vb* : to lay out or work in a garden — **gar·den·er** *n*

gar·de·nia \gär-'dē-nyə\ *n* [NL, genus name, fr. Alexander *Garden* †1791 Scot. naturalist] : any of a genus of tropical trees or shrubs that are related to the madder and have fragrant white or yellow flowers

garden–variety *adj* : COMMONPLACE, ORDINARY

gar·fish \'gär-ˌfish\ *n* : GAR

gar·gan·tuan \gär-'gan-chə-wən\ *adj, often cap* : tremendous in size, volume, or degree ⟨∼ waterfalls⟩ ◆ **Synonyms** HUGE, COLOSSAL, GIGANTIC, MAMMOTH, MONSTROUS, TITANIC

gar·gle \'gär-gəl\ *vb* **gar·gled; gar·gling** : to rinse the throat with liquid agitated by air forced through it from the lungs — **gargle** *n*

gar·goyle \'gär-ˌgȯi(-ə)l\ *n* 1 : a waterspout in the form of a grotesque human or animal figure projecting from the roof or eaves of a building 2 : a grotesquely carved figure

gar·ish \'ger-ish\ *adj* : FLASHY, GLARING, SHOWY, GAUDY ⟨a ∼ wardrobe⟩

¹**gar·land** \'gär-lənd\ *n* : WREATH, CHAPLET

²**garland** *vb* : to form into or deck with a garland

gar·lic \'gär-lik\ *n* [ME *garlek*, fr. OE *gārlēac*, fr. *gār* spear + *lēac* leek] : an herb related to the lilies and grown for its pungent bulbs used in cooking; *also* : its bulb — **gar·licky** \-li-kē\ *adj*

gar·ment \'gär-mənt\ *n* : an article of clothing

gar·ner \'gär-nər\ *vb* 1 : to gather into storage 2 : to acquire by effort 3 : ACCUMULATE, COLLECT

gar·net \'gär-nət\ *n* [ME *gernet*, fr. AF *gernete*, fr. *gernet* dark red, fr. *pume gernete* pomegranate] : a transparent deep red mineral sometimes used as a gem

gar·nish \'gär-nish\ *vb* 1 : DECORATE, EMBELLISH 2 : to add decorative or savory touches to (food) 3 : GARNISHEE — **garnish** *n*

gar·nish·ee \ˌgär-nə-'shē\ *vb* **-eed; -ee·ing** 1 : to serve with a garnishment 2 : to take (as a debtor's wages) by legal authority

gar·nish·ment \'gär-nish-mənt\ *n* 1 : GARNISH 2 : a legal warning concerning the attachment of property to satisfy a debt; *also* : the attachment of such property

gar·ni·ture \-ni-chər, -ˌchu̇r\ *n* : EMBELLISHMENT, TRIMMING

gar·ret \'ger-ət\ *n* : the part of a house just under the roof : ATTIC

gar·ri·son \'ger-ə-sən\ n [ME *garisoun* protection, fr. AF *garisun* healing, protection, fr. *garir* to heal, protect, of Gmc origin] **1** : a military post; *esp* : a permanent military installation **2** : the troops stationed at a garrison — **garrison** vb

garrison state n : a state organized on a primarily military basis

gar·rote or **ga·rotte** \gə-'rät, -'rōt\ n [Sp *garrote*] **1** : a method of execution by strangulation; *also* : the apparatus used **2** : an implement (as a wire with handles) for strangulation — **garrote** or **garotte** vb

gar·ru·lous \'ger-ə-ləs\ adj : TALKATIVE, WORDY — **gar·ru·li·ty** \gə-'rü-lə-tē\ n — **gar·ru·lous·ly** adv — **gar·ru·lous·ness** n

gar·ter \'gär-tər\ n : a band or strap worn to hold up a stocking or sock

garter snake n : any of a genus of harmless American snakes with longitudinal stripes on the back

¹gas \'gas\ n, pl **gas·es** also **gas·ses** [NL, alter. of L *chaos* space, chaos] **1** : a fluid (as hydrogen or air) that tends to expand indefinitely **2** : a gas or mixture of gases used as a fuel or anesthetic **3** : a substance that can be used to produce a poisonous, asphyxiating, or irritant atmosphere **4** : GASOLINE — **gas·eous** \'ga-sē-əs, -shəs\ adj

²gas vb **gassed; gas·sing 1** : to treat with gas; *also* : to poison with gas **2** : to fill with gasoline ⟨~ up the car⟩

gash \'gash\ n : a deep long cut — **gash** vb

gas·ket \'gas-kət\ n : material (as rubber) or a part used to seal a joint

gas·light \'gas-ˌlīt\ n **1** : light made by burning illuminating gas **2** : a gas flame; *also* : a gas lighting fixture

gas mask n : a mask with a chemical air filter used to protect the face and lungs against poison gas

gas·o·line \'ga-sə-ˌlēn, ˌga-sə-'lēn\ n : a flammable liquid mixture made from petroleum and used esp. as a motor fuel

gasp \'gasp\ vb **1** : to catch the breath audibly (as with shock) **2** : to breathe laboriously : PANT **3** : to utter in a gasping manner — **gasp** n

gas station n : a retail station for servicing and fueling motor vehicles

gas·tric \'gas-trik\ adj : of or relating to the stomach

gastric juice n : the acid digestive secretion of the stomach

gas·tri·tis \gas-'trī-təs\ n : inflammation of the lining of the stomach

gas·tro·en·ter·i·tis \ˌgas-trō-ˌen-tə-'rī-təs\ n : inflammation of the lining membrane of the stomach and intestines

gas·tro·en·ter·ol·o·gy \ˌgas-trō-ˌen-tə-'rä-lə-jē\ n : a branch of medicine concerned with the structure, functions, and diseases of the stomach and intestines — **gas·tro·en·ter·ol·o·gist** \-jist\ n

gas·tro·in·tes·ti·nal \ˌgas-trō-in-'tes-tən-ᵊl\ adj : of, relating to, affecting, or including both the stomach and intestine ⟨~ tract⟩ ⟨~ distress⟩

gas·tron·o·my \gas-'trä-nə-mē\ n [F *gastronomie*, fr. Gk *Gastronomia*, title of a 4th cent. B.C. poem, fr. *gastēr* belly + *-nomia* system of laws] : the art of good eating — **gas·tro·nom·ic** \ˌgas-trə-'nä-mik\ also **gas·tro·nom·i·cal** \-mi-kəl\ adj — **gas·tro·nom·i·cal·ly** \-k(ə-)lē\ adv

gas·tro·pod \'gas-trə-ˌpäd\ n : any of a large class of mollusks (as snails and slugs) with a muscular foot and a spiral shell or none — **gastropod** adj

gas·works \'gas-ˌwərks\ n sing or pl : a plant for manufacturing gas

gate \'gāt\ n **1** : an opening for passage in a wall or fence **2** : a city or castle entrance often with defensive structures **3** : the frame or door that closes a gate **4** : a device (as a valve) for controlling the passage of a fluid or signal **5** : the total admission receipts or the number of people at an event

-gate \ˌgāt\ n comb form [Water*gate*, scandal that resulted in the resignation of President Richard Nixon in 1974] : usu. political scandal often involving the concealment of wrongdoing

gate–crash·er \'gāt-ˌkra-shər\ n : a person who enters without paying admission or attends without invitation

gate·keep·er \-ˌkē-pər\ n : a person who tends or guards a gate

gate·post \-ˌpōst\ n : the post to which a gate is hung or the one against which it closes

gate·way \-ˌwā\ n **1** : an opening for a gate **2** : a means of entrance or exit

¹gath·er \'ga-thər\ vb **1** : to bring together : COLLECT **2** : PICK, HARVEST **3** : to pick up little by little **4** : to scoop up from a resting place ⟨~ed up the child⟩ **5** : to gain or win by gradual increase **6** : ATTRACT, ACCUMULATE ⟨~ dust⟩ **7** : to summon up ⟨~ courage to dive⟩ **8** : to gain control of ⟨~ed his wits⟩ **9** : to draw about or close to something **10** : to pull (fabric) along a line of stitching into puckers **11** : GUESS, DEDUCE, INFER **12** : ASSEMBLE **13** : to swell out and fill with pus **14** : GROW, INCREASE ♦ **Synonyms** CONGREGATE, FORGATHER — **gath·er·er** n

²gather n : a puckering in cloth made by gathering

GATT \'gat\ abbr General Agreement on Tariffs and Trade

gauche \'gōsh\ adj [F, lit., left] **1** : lacking social experience or grace; *also* : not tactful **2** : crudely made or done ♦ **Synonyms** CLUMSY, HEAVY-HANDED, INEPT, MALADROIT

gau·che·rie \ˌgō-shə-'rē\ n : a tactless or awkward action

gau·cho \'gau̇-chō\ n, pl **gauchos** : a cowboy of the So. American pampas

gaud \'gȯd\ n : ORNAMENT, TRINKET

gaudy \'gȯ-dē\ adj **gaud·i·er; -est 1** : ostentatiously or tastelessly ornamented **2** : marked by showiness or extravagance : OUTLANDISH **3** : EXCEPTIONAL ⟨a ~ batting average⟩ ♦ **Synonyms** GARISH, FLASHY, GLARING, TAWDRY — **gaud·i·ly** \-də-lē\ adv — **gaud·i·ness** \-dē-nəs\ n

¹gauge also **gage** \'gāj\ n **1** : measurement according to some standard or system **2** : DIMENSIONS, SIZE **3** usu **gage** : an instrument for measuring, testing, or registering

²gauge also **gage** vb **gauged** also **gaged; gaug·ing** also **gag·ing 1** : MEASURE **2** : to determine the capacity or contents of **3** : ESTIMATE, JUDGE

gaunt \'gȯnt\ adj **1** : excessively thin and angular ⟨a ~ face⟩ **2** : BARREN, DESOLATE ♦ **Synonyms** BONY, LANK, LANKY, LEAN, RAWBONED, SKINNY — **gaunt·ness** n

¹gaunt·let also **gant·let** \'gȯnt-lət\ n **1** : a protective glove **2** : an open challenge (as to combat) **3** : a dress glove extending above the wrist

²gauntlet also **gantlet** n **1** : a double file of men armed with weapons (as clubs) with which to strike at an individual who is made to run between them **2** : ORDEAL **3** : a line or series of something to be greeted or managed

gauss \'gaús\ n : the centimeter-gram-second unit of magnetic flux density that is equal to 1×10^{-4} tesla

gauze \'gȯz\ n : a very thin often transparent fabric used esp. for draperies and surgical dressings

gauzy \'gȯ-zē\ adj **gauz·i·er; -est 1** : made of or resembling gauze **2** : marked by vagueness or fuzziness ⟨a ~ memory⟩

gave past of GIVE

gav·el \'ga-vəl\ n : a mallet used by a presiding officer or auctioneer

ga·votte \gə-'vät\ n : a dance of French peasant origin marked by the raising rather than sliding of the feet

gawk \'gȯk\ vb : to gape or stare stupidly — **gawk·er** n

gawky \'gȯ-kē\ adj **gawk·i·er; -est** : AWKWARD, CLUMSY — **gawk·i·ly** \-kə-lē\ adv — **gawk·i·ness** n

gay \'gā\ adj **1** : MERRY **2** : BRIGHT, LIVELY **3** : brilliant in color **4** : given to social pleasures; *also* : LICENTIOUS **5** : HOMOSEXUAL; *also* : of, relating to, or used by homosexuals ⟨a ~ bar⟩

gayety, gayly var of GAIETY, GAILY

gaz abbr gazette

gaze \'gāz\ vb **gazed; gaz·ing** : to fix the eyes in a steady intent look ♦ **Synonyms** GAPE, GAWK, GLARE, GOGGLE, PEER, STARE — **gaze** n — **gaz·er** n

ga·ze·bo \gə-'zē-bō\ n, pl **-bos 1** : BELVEDERE **2** : a free-standing roofed structure usu. open on the sides

ga·zelle \gə-'zel\ n, pl **gazelles** also **gazelle** : any of numerous small swift graceful antelopes

ga·zette \gə-'zet\ n **1** : NEWSPAPER **2** : an official journal

gaz·et·teer \ˌga-zə-'tir\ n : a geographical dictionary

ga·zil·lion \gə-'zil-yən\ n : ZILLION — **gazillion** adj — **ga·zil·lionth** \-yənth\ adj

gaz·pa·cho \gəz-'pä-(ˌ)chō, gə-'spä-\ n, pl **-chos** [Sp] : a spicy soup usu. made from raw vegetables and served cold

GB *abbr* Great Britain

GCA *abbr* ground-controlled approach

gd *abbr* good

Gd *symbol* gadolinium

GDR *abbr* German Democratic Republic

Ge *symbol* germanium

gear \'gir\ *n* **1** : CLOTHING **2** : movable property : GOODS **3** : EQUIPMENT ⟨fishing ∼⟩ **4** : a mechanism that performs a specific function ⟨steering ∼⟩ **5** : a toothed wheel **6** : working order or adjustment ⟨got her career in ∼⟩ **7** : an adjustment of transmission gears (as of an automobile or bicycle) that determines speed and direction of travel — **gear** *vb*

gear·box \'gir-‚bäks\ *n* : TRANSMISSION 3

gear·shift \-‚shift\ *n* : a mechanism by which transmission gears are shifted

gear·wheel \-‚hwēl\ *n* : GEAR 5

gecko \'ge-kō\ *n, pl* **geck·os** *also* **geck·oes** : any of numerous small chiefly tropical insect-eating lizards

GED *abbr* **1** General Educational Development (tests) **2** general equivalency diploma

geek \'gēk\ *n* : a person of an intellectual bent who is often disliked — **geek·i·ness** *n* — **geeky** *adj*

geese *pl of* GOOSE

gee·zer \'gē-zər\ *n* : an odd or eccentric person usu. of old age

Gei·ger counter \'gī-gər-\ *n* : an electronic instrument for detecting the presence of cosmic rays or radioactive substances

gei·sha \'gā-shə, 'gē-\ *n, pl* **geisha** *or* **geishas** [Jp, fr. *gei* art + *-sha* person] : a Japanese girl or woman who is trained to provide entertaining company for men

gel \'jel\ *n* : a solid jellylike colloid (as gelatin dessert) — **gel** *vb*

gel·a·tin *also* **gel·a·tine** \'je-lə-tən\ *n* : glutinous material and esp. protein obtained from animal tissues by boiling and used as a food, in dyeing, and in photography; *also* : an edible jelly formed with gelatin — **ge·lat·i·nous** \jə-'la-tə-nəs\ *adj*

geld \'geld\ *vb* : CASTRATE

geld·ing *n* : a castrated male horse

gel·id \'je-ləd\ *adj* : extremely cold

gem \'jem\ *n* **1** : JEWEL **2** : a usu. valuable stone cut and polished for ornament **3** : something valued for beauty or perfection

Gem·i·ni \'je-mə-(‚)nē, -‚nī; 'ge-mə-‚nē\ *n* **1** : a zodiacal constellation between Taurus and Cancer usu. pictured as twins sitting together **2** : the 3d sign of the zodiac in astrology; *also* : one born under this sign

gem·ol·o·gy *or* **gem·mol·o·gy** \je-'mä-lə-jē, jə-\ *n* : the science of gems — **gem·olog·i·cal** \‚je-mə-'lä-ji-kəl\ *adj* — **gem·ol·o·gist** *also* **gem·mol·o·gist** \-jist\ *n*

gem·stone \'jem-‚stōn\ *n* : a mineral or petrified material that when cut and polished can be used in jewelry

gen *abbr* **1** general **2** genitive

Gen *abbr* Genesis

Gen AF *abbr* general of the air force

gen·darme \'zhän-‚därm, 'jän-\ *n* [F, intended as sing. of *gensdarmes*, pl. of *gent d'armes*, lit., armed people] : a member of a body of soldiers esp. in France serving as an armed police force

gen·der \'jen-dər\ *n* [ME *gendre*, fr. AF *genre, gendre*, fr. L *gener-, genus* birth, race, kind, gender] **1** : any of two or more divisions within a grammatical class that determine agreement with and selection of other words or grammatical forms **2** : SEX 1

gene \'jēn\ *n* : a part of DNA or RNA that contains chemical information needed to make a particular protein (as an enzyme) controlling or influencing an inherited bodily trait (as eye color) or activity (as metabolism) or that influences or controls the activity of another gene or genes — **gen·ic** \'jē-nik, 'je-\ *adj*

ge·ne·al·o·gy \‚jē-nē-'ä-lə-jē, ‚je-, -'a-\ *n, pl* **-gies** : PEDIGREE, LINEAGE; *also* : the study of family pedigrees — **ge·ne·a·log·i·cal** \‚jē-nē-ə-'lä-ji-kəl, ‚je-\ *adj* — **ge·ne·a·log·i·cal·ly** \-k(ə-)lē\ *adv* — **ge·ne·al·o·gist** \‚jē-nē-'ä-lə-jist, ‚je-; -'a-\ *n*

gene pool *n* : the total genetic information contained in a population of interbreeding organisms

genera *pl of* GENUS

¹gen·er·al \'je-nə-rəl, 'jen-rəl\ *adj* **1** : of or relating to the whole **2** : taken as a whole **3** : relating to or covering all instances **4** : not special or specialized **5** : common to many ⟨a ∼ custom⟩ **6** : not limited in meaning : not specific **7** : holding superior rank ⟨inspector ∼⟩ ✦ *Synonyms* GENERIC, UNIVERSAL

²general *n* **1** : something that involves or is applicable to the whole **2** : a commissioned officer ranking next below a general of the army or a general of the air force **3** : a commissioned officer of the highest rank in the marine corps — **in general** : for the most part

general assembly *n* **1** : a legislative assembly; *esp* : a U.S. state legislature **2** *cap G&A* : the supreme deliberative body of the United Nations

gen·er·al·i·sa·tion, gen·er·al·ise, gen·er·al·ised *Brit var of* GENERALIZATION, GENERALIZE, GENERALIZED

gen·er·al·is·si·mo \‚je-nə-rə-'li-sə-‚mō\ *n, pl* **-mos** [It, fr. *generale* general] : the chief commander of an army

gen·er·al·i·ty \‚je-nə-'ra-lə-tē\ *n, pl* **-ties** **1** : the quality or state of being general **2** : GENERALIZATION 2 **3** : a vague or inadequate statement **4** : the greatest part : BULK

gen·er·al·i·za·tion \‚je-nə-rə-lə-'zā-shən, ‚jen-rə-\ *n* **1** : the act or process of generalizing **2** : a general statement, law, principle, or proposition

gen·er·al·ize \'je-nə-rə-‚līz, 'jen-rə-\ *vb* **-ized; -iz·ing** **1** : to make general **2** : to draw general conclusions from **3** : to reach a general conclusion esp. on the basis of particular instances **4** : to extend throughout the body

gen·er·al·ly \'jen-rə-lē, 'jē-nə-\ *adv* **1** : in a general manner **2** : as a rule

general of the air force : a commissioned officer of the highest rank in the air force

general of the army : a commissioned officer of the highest rank in the army

general practitioner *n* : a physician or veterinarian whose practice is not limited to a specialty

gen·er·al·ship \'je-nə-rəl-‚ship, 'jen-rəl-\ *n* **1** : office or tenure of office of a general **2** : LEADERSHIP **3** : military skill as a high commander

general store *n* : a retail store that carries a wide variety of goods but is not divided into departments

gen·er·ate \'je-nə-‚rāt\ *vb* **-at·ed; -at·ing** : to bring into existence : PRODUCE ⟨∼ electricity⟩ ✦ *Synonyms* CREATE, ORIGINATE, PROCREATE, SPAWN

gen·er·a·tion \‚je-nə-'rā-shən\ *n* **1** : a body of living beings constituting a single step in the line of descent from an ancestor; *also* : the average period between generations **2** : PRODUCTION

Generation X *n* : the generation of Americans born in the 1960s and 1970s

gen·er·a·tive \'je-nə-rə-tiv, -‚rā-tiv\ *adj* : having the power or function of generating, originating, producing, or reproducing ⟨∼ organs⟩

gen·er·a·tor \'je-nə-‚rā-tər\ *n* : one that generates; *esp* : a machine by which mechanical energy is changed into electrical energy

ge·ner·ic \jə-'ner-ik\ *adj* **1** : not specific : GENERAL **2** : not protected by a trademark ⟨a ∼ drug⟩ **3** : of or relating to a biological genus **4** : having no particularly distinctive quality ⟨∼ towns⟩ — **generic** *n* — **ge·ner·i·cal·ly** \-i-k(ə-)lē\ *adv*

gen·er·ous \'je-nə-rəs\ *adj* **1** : free in giving or sharing ⟨∼ donors⟩ **2** : HIGH-MINDED, NOBLE **3** : ABUNDANT, AMPLE, COPIOUS ⟨a ∼ salary⟩ ✦ *Synonyms* LIBERAL, BOUNTIFUL, MUNIFICENT, OPENHANDED — **gen·er·os·i·ty** \‚je-nə-'rä-sə-tē\ *n* — **gen·er·ous·ly** \'je-nə-rəs-lē\ *adv* — **gen·er·ous·ness** *n*

gen·e·sis \'je-nə-səs\ *n, pl* **-e·ses** \-‚sēz\ : the origin or coming into existence of something

Genesis *n* — see BIBLE table

gene-splic·ing \-‚splī-siŋ\ *n* : the process of preparing recombinant DNA

gene therapy *n* : the insertion of normal or altered genes into cells esp. to replace defective genes in the treatment of genetic disorders or to provide a specialized disease-fighting function

ge·net·ic \jə-'ne-tik\ *adj* : of or relating to the origin, development, or causes of something; *also* : of, relating to, or caused by genes or genetics ⟨∼ research⟩ — **ge·net·i·cal·ly** \-ti-k(ə-)lē\ *adv*

genetic code *n* : the chemical code that is the basis of genetic inheritance and consists of units of three linked chemical groups in DNA and RNA which specify particular amino acids used to make proteins or which start or stop the process of making proteins

genetic engineering *n* : the alteration of genetic material esp. by cutting up and joining together DNA from one or more species of organism and inserting the result into an organism — **genetically engineered** *adj*

ge·net·ics \jə-ˈne-tiks\ *n* : a branch of biology dealing with heredity and variation — **ge·net·i·cist** \-tə-sist\ *n*

ge·nial \ˈjē-nyəl, ˈjē-nē-əl\ *adj* **1** : favorable to growth or comfort ⟨~ sunshine⟩ **2** : CHEERFUL, KINDLY ⟨a ~ host⟩ ✦ *Synonyms* AFFABLE, CONGENIAL, CORDIAL, GRACIOUS, SOCIABLE — **ge·nial·i·ty** \jē-nē-ˈa-lə-tē, jēn-ˈya-\ *n* — **ge·nial·ly** *adv*

-gen·ic \ˈje-nik\ *adj comb form* **1** : producing : forming **2** : produced by : formed from **3** : suitable for production or reproduction by (such) a medium

ge·nie \ˈjē-nē\ *n, pl* **ge·nies** *also* **ge·nii** \-nē-ˌī\ [F *génie*, fr. Ar *jinnī*] : a supernatural spirit that often takes human form usu. serving the person who calls on it

gen·i·tal \ˈje-nə-tᵊl\ *adj* **1** : concerned with reproduction ⟨~ organs⟩ **2** : of, relating to, or characterized by the stage of psychosexual development in psychoanalytic theory in which oral and anal impulses are subordinated to adaptive interpersonal mechanisms — **gen·i·tal·ly** *adv*

gen·i·ta·lia \ˌje-nə-ˈtāl-yə\ *n pl* : reproductive organs; *esp* : the external genital organs — **gen·i·tal·ic** \-ˈta-lik, -ˈtā-\ *adj*

gen·i·tals \ˈje-nə-tᵊlz\ *n pl* : GENITALIA

gen·i·tive \ˈje-nə-tiv\ *adj* : of, relating to, or constituting a grammatical case marking typically a relationship of possessor or source — **genitive** *n*

gen·i·to·uri·nary \ˌje-nə-tō-ˈyùr-ə-ˌner-ē\ *adj* : of or relating to the genital and urinary organs or functions

ge·nius \ˈjē-nyəs\ *n, pl* **ge·nius·es** *or* **ge·nii** \-nē-ˌī\ [L, tutelary spirit, natural inclinations, fr. *gignere* to beget] **1** *pl genii* : an attendant spirit of a person or place; *also* : a person who influences another for good or evil **2** : a strong leaning or inclination **3** : a peculiar or distinctive character or spirit (as of a nation or a language) **4** *pl usu genii* : SPIRIT, GENIE **5** *pl usu geniuses* : a single strongly marked capacity or aptitude **6** : extraordinary intellectual power; *also* : a person having such power ✦ *Synonyms* GIFT, FACULTY, FLAIR, KNACK, TALENT

genl *abbr* general

geno·cide \ˈje-nə-ˌsīd\ *n* : the deliberate and systematic destruction of a racial, political, or cultural group

ge·nome \ˈjē-ˌnōm\ *n* **1** : one haploid set of chromosomes **2** : the genetic material of an organism

ge·no·mics \jē-ˈnō-miks\ *n* : a branch of biotechnology concerned esp. with investigating and collecting data about the structure and function of all or part of an organism's genome

-genous \jə-nəs\ *adj comb form* **1** : producing : yielding ⟨erogenous⟩ **2** : having (such) an origin ⟨endogenous⟩

genre \ˈzhän-rə, ˈzhäⁿ-; ˈzhäⁿr; ˈjän-rə\ *n* **1** : a distinctive type or category esp. of literary composition **2** : a style of painting in which everyday subjects are treated realistically

gens \ˈjenz, ˈgens\ *n, pl* **gen·tes** \ˈjen-ˌtēz, ˈgen-ˌtās\ [L] : a Roman clan embracing the families of the same stock in the male line

gent *n* : GENTLEMAN

gen·teel \jen-ˈtēl\ *adj* **1** : ARISTOCRATIC **2** : ELEGANT, STYLISH **3** : POLITE, REFINED **4** : maintaining the appearance of superior social status **5** : marked by false delicacy, prudery, or affectation — **gen·teel·ly** *adv* — **gen·teel·ness** *n*

gen·tian \ˈjen-chən\ *n* : any of numerous herbs with opposite leaves and showy usu. blue flowers in the fall

gen·tile \ˈjen-ˌtī(-ə)l\ *n* [ME, fr. LL *gentilis* heathen, pagan, fr. L *gent-*, *gens* clan, nation] **1** *often cap* : a person who is not Jewish; *esp* : a Christian as distinguished from a Jew **2** : HEATHEN, PAGAN — **gentile** *adj, often cap*

gen·til·i·ty \jen-ˈti-lə-tē\ *n, pl* **-ties** **1** : good birth and family **2** : the qualities characteristic of a well-bred person **3** : good manners **4** : superior social status shown in manners or mode of life

¹gen·tle \ˈjen-tᵊl\ *adj* **gen·tler** \ˈjent-lər, -tᵊl-ər\; **gen·tlest** \ˈjent-ləst, -tᵊl-əst\ **1** : belonging to a family of high social station **2** : of, relating to, or characteristic of a gentleman **3** : KIND, AMIABLE ⟨a ~ pastor⟩ **4** : TRACTABLE, DOCILE ⟨a ~ dog⟩ **5** : not harsh, stern, or violent **6** : SOFT, DELICATE **7** : MODERATE — **gen·tle·ness** *n* — **gen·tly** *adv*

²gentle *vb* **gen·tled; gen·tling** **1** : to make or become mild, docile, soft, or moderate **2** : MOLLIFY, PLACATE

gen·tle·folk \ˈjen-tᵊl-ˌfōk\ *also* **gen·tle·folks** \-ˌfōks\ *n* : persons of good family and breeding

gen·tle·man \-mən\ *n* **1** : a man of good family **2** : a well-bred man **3** : MAN — used in pl. as a form of address — **gen·tle·man·ly** *adj*

gen·tle·wom·an \-ˌwù-mən\ *n* **1** : a woman of good family **2** : a woman attending a lady of rank **3** : a woman with very good manners : LADY

gen·tri·fi·ca·tion \ˌjen-trə-fə-ˈkā-shən\ *n* : the process of renewal accompanying the influx of middle-class people into deteriorating areas that often displaces earlier usu. poorer residents — **gen·tri·fy** \ˈjen-trə-fī\ *vb*

gen·try \ˈjen-trē\ *n, pl* **gentries** **1** : people of good birth, breeding, and education : ARISTOCRACY **2** : the class of English people between the nobility and the yeomanry **3** : persons of a designated class

gen·u·flect \ˈjen-yù-ˌflekt\ *vb* : to bend the knee esp. in worship — **gen·u·flec·tion** \ˌjen-yù-ˈflek-shən\ *n*

gen·u·ine \ˈjen-yə-wən\ *adj* **1** : AUTHENTIC, REAL ⟨a ~ signature⟩ **2** : SINCERE, HONEST ⟨their love is ~⟩ ✦ *Synonyms* BONA FIDE, TRUE, VERITABLE — **gen·u·ine·ly** *adv* — **gen·u·ine·ness** *n*

ge·nus \ˈjē-nəs\ *n, pl* **gen·era** \ˈje-nə-rə\ [L, birth, race, kind] : a category of biological classification that ranks between the family and the species and contains related species

geo·cen·tric \ˌjē-ō-ˈsen-trik\ *adj* **1** : relating to or measured from the earth's center **2** : having or relating to the earth as a center

geo·chem·is·try \-ˈke-mə-strē\ *n* : a branch of geology that deals with the chemical composition of and chemical changes in the earth — **geo·chem·i·cal** \-mi-kəl\ *adj* — **geo·chem·ist** \-mist\ *n*

ge·ode \ˈjē-ˌōd\ *n* : a nodule of stone having a cavity lined with mineral matter

¹geo·de·sic \ˌjē-ə-ˈde-sik\ *adj* : made of light straight structural elements ⟨a ~ dome⟩

²geodesic *n* : the shortest line between two points on a surface

geo·det·ic \ˌjē-ə-ˈde-tik\ *adj* : of, relating to, or being precise measurement of the earth and its features ⟨a ~ survey⟩

geog *abbr* geographic; geographical; geography

ge·og·ra·phy \jē-ˈä-grə-fē\ *n, pl* **-phies** **1** : a science that deals with the natural features of the earth and the climate, products, and inhabitants **2** : the natural features of a region — **ge·og·ra·pher** \-fər\ *n* — **geo·graph·ic** \ˌjē-ə-ˈgra-fik\ *or* **geo·graph·i·cal** \-fi-kəl\ *adj* — **geo·graph·i·cal·ly** \-fi-k(ə-)lē\ *adv*

geol *abbr* geologic; geological; geology

ge·ol·o·gy \jē-ˈä-lə-jē\ *n, pl* **-gies** **1** : a science that deals with the history of the earth and its life esp. as recorded in rocks; *also* : a study of the features of a celestial body (as the moon) **2** : the geologic features of an area — **ge·o·log·ic** \ˌjē-ə-ˈlä-jik\ *or* **ge·o·log·i·cal** \-ji-kəl\ *adj* — **geo·log·i·cal·ly** \-ji-k(ə-)lē\ *adv* — **ge·ol·o·gist** \jē-ˈä-lə-jist\ *n*

geom *abbr* geometric; geometrical; geometry

geo·mag·net·ic \ˌjē-ō-mag-ˈne-tik\ *adj* : of or relating to the magnetism of the earth — **geo·mag·ne·tism** \-ˈmag-nə-ˌti-zəm\ *n*

geometric mean *n* : the *n*th root of the product of *n* numbers; *esp* : a number that is the second term of three consecutive terms of a geometric progression ⟨the *geometric mean* of 9 and 4 is 6⟩

geometric progression *n* : a progression (as 1, ¹/₂, ¹/₄) in which the ratio of a term to its predecessor is always the same

ge·om·e·try \jē-ˈä-mə-trē\ *n, pl* **-tries** [ultim. fr. Gk *geōmetria*, fr. *geōmetrein* to measure the earth, fr. *gē* earth + *metron* measure] : a branch of mathematics dealing with the relations, properties, and measurements of solids, surfaces, lines, points, and angles — **ge·om·e·ter** \-tər\ *n* —

ge·o·met·ric \ˌjē-ə-'me-trik\ *or* **ge·o·met·ri·cal** \-tri-kəl\ *adj*

geo·phys·ics \ˌjē-ō-'fi-ziks\ *n* : the physics of the earth — **geo·phys·i·cal** \-zi-kəl\ *adj* — **geo·phys·i·cist** \-zə-sist\ *n*

geo·pol·i·tics \-'pä-lə-ˌtiks\ *n* : a combination of political and geographic factors relating to a state — **geo·po·lit·i·cal** \-pə-'li-ti-kəl\ *adj*

geo·ther·mal \ˌjē-ō-'thər-məl\ *adj* : of, relating to, or using the heat of the earth's interior

ger *abbr* gerund

Ger *abbr* German; Germany

ge·ra·ni·um \jə-'rā-nē-əm\ *n* [L, fr. Gk *geranion*, fr. *geranos* crane] : any of a genus of herbs with usu. deeply cut leaves and typically pink, purple, or white flowers; *also* : any of a related genus of herbs that are native to southern Africa and are widely grown for their clusters of showy usu. red, pink, or white flowers

ger·bil *also* **ger·bile** \'jər-bəl\ *n* : any of numerous Old World burrowing desert rodents with long hind legs

ge·ri·at·ric \ˌjer-ē-'a-trik\ *adj* **1** : of or relating to geriatrics or the process of aging **2** : of, relating to, or appropriate for elderly people **3** : OLD

ge·ri·at·rics \-triks\ *n* : a branch of medicine dealing with the problems and diseases of old age and aging

germ \'jərm\ *n* **1** : a bit of living matter capable of growth and development (as into an organism) **2** : SOURCE, RUDIMENTS **3** : MICROORGANISM; *esp* : one causing disease

Ger·man \'jər-mən\ *n* **1** : a native or inhabitant of Germany **2** : the language of Germany, Austria, and parts of Switzerland — **German** *adj* — **Ger·man·ic** \jər-'ma-nik\ *adj*

ger·mane \jər-'mān\ *adj* [ME *germain*, lit., having the same parents, fr. AF, fr. L *germanus*, fr. *germen* sprout, bud] : RELEVANT, APPROPRIATE ♦ *Synonyms* APPLICABLE, MATERIAL, PERTINENT

ger·ma·ni·um \jər-'mā-nē-əm\ *n* : a grayish white hard chemical element used esp. in semiconductor and optical materials and as a catalyst

German measles *n sing or pl* : an acute contagious virus disease milder than typical measles but damaging to the fetus when occurring early in pregnancy

German shepherd *n* : any of a breed of intelligent responsive working dogs of German origin often used in police work and as guide dogs for the blind

germ cell *n* : an egg or sperm or one of their antecedent cells

ger·mi·cide \'jər-mə-ˌsīd\ *n* : an agent that destroys germs — **ger·mi·cid·al** \ˌjər-mə-'sī-dᵊl\ *adj*

ger·mi·nal \'jər-mə-nəl\ *adj* : of or relating to a germ or germ cell; *also* : EMBRYONIC

ger·mi·nate \'jər-mə-ˌnāt\ *vb* **-nat·ed; -nat·ing** **1** : cause to develop : begin to develop : SPROUT **2** : to come into being : EVOLVE — **ger·mi·na·tion** \ˌjər-mə-'nā-shən\ *n*

ger·on·tol·o·gy \ˌjer-ən-'tä-lə-jē\ *n* : a scientific study of aging and the problems of the aged — **ge·ron·to·log·i·cal** \jə-ˌrän-tə-'lä-ji-kəl\ *adj* — **ger·on·tol·o·gist** \ˌjer-ən-'tä-lə-jist\ *n*

ger·ry·man·der \'jer-ē-ˌman-dər\ *vb* : to divide into election districts so as to give one political party an advantage — **gerrymander** *n*

ger·und \'jer-ənd\ *n* : a word having the characteristics of both verb and noun

ge·sta·po \gə-'stä-pō\ *n, pl* **-pos** [G, fr. *Geheime Staatspolizei*, lit., secret state police] : a usu. terrorist secret police organization operating against persons suspected of disloyalty

ges·ta·tion \je-'stä-shən\ *n* : PREGNANCY, INCUBATION — **ges·tate** \'jes-ˌtāt\ *vb*

ges·tic·u·late \je-'sti-kyə-ˌlāt\ *vb* **-lat·ed; -lat·ing** : to make gestures esp. when speaking — **ges·tic·u·la·tion** \-ˌsti-kyə-'lā-shən\ *n*

ges·ture \'jes-chər\ *n* **1** : a movement usu. of the body or limbs that expresses or emphasizes an idea, sentiment, or attitude **2** : something said or done by way of formality or courtesy, as a symbol or token, or for its effect on the attitudes of others — **ges·tur·al** \-chə-rəl\ *adj* — **gesture** *vb*

ge·sund·heit \gə-'zùnt-ˌhīt\ *interj* [G, lit., health] — used to wish good health esp. to one who has just sneezed

¹get \'get\ *vb* **got** \'gät\; **got** *or* **got·ten** \'gä-tᵊn\; **get·ting 1** : to gain possession of (as by receiving, acquiring, earning, buying, or winning) : PROCURE, OBTAIN, FETCH **2** : to succeed in coming or going ⟨*got* away to the lake⟩ **3** : to cause to come or go ⟨*got* the car to the station⟩ **4** : BEGET **5** : to cause to be in a certain condition or position ⟨don't ∼ wet⟩ **6** : BECOME ⟨∼ sick⟩ **7** : PREPARE **8** : SEIZE **9** : to move emotionally; *also* : IRRITATE **10** : BAFFLE, PUZZLE **11** : KILL **12** : HIT **13** : to be subjected to ⟨∼ the measles⟩ **14** : to receive as punishment **15** : to find out by calculation **16** : HEAR; *also* : UNDERSTAND ⟨*got* the joke⟩ **17** : PERSUADE, INDUCE **18** : HAVE ⟨he's *got* no money⟩ **19** : to have as an obligation or necessity ⟨you have *got* to come⟩ **20** : to establish communication with **21** : to be able ⟨finally *got* to go to med school⟩ **22** : to come to be ⟨*got* talking about old times⟩ **23** : to leave at once — **get ahead** : to achieve success — **get a move on** : HURRY — **get away with** : to avoid punishment for (as a crime) — **get into** : to become strongly involved or interested in ⟨*got into* music⟩ — **get over** : to reconcile oneself to ⟨*got over* the breakup⟩

²get \'get\ *n* : OFFSPRING, PROGENY

get along *vb* **1** : GET BY **2** : to be on friendly terms

get·away \'ge-tə-ˌwā\ *n* **1** : ESCAPE **2** : START **3** : a usu. brief vacation

get by *vb* : to meet one's needs

get-to·geth·er \'get-tə-ˌge-thər\ *n* : an informal social gathering

get-up \'get-ˌəp\ *n* **1** : OUTFIT, COSTUME **2** : general composition or structure

gew·gaw \'gü-ˌgò, 'gyü-\ *n* : a showy trifle : BAUBLE, TRINKET

gey·ser \'gī-zər\ *n* [Icelandic *Geysir*, hot spring in Iceland] : a spring that intermittently shoots up hot water and steam

g-force \'jē-ˌfòrs\ *n* : the force of gravity or acceleration on a body

ghast·ly \'gast-lē\ *adj* **ghast·li·er; -est 1** : HORRIBLE, SHOCKING **2** : resembling a ghost : DEATHLIKE, PALE ♦ *Synonyms* GRUESOME, GRIM, LURID, GRISLY, MACABRE

ghat \'gòt\ *n* [Hindi & Urdu *ghāṭ*] : a broad flight of steps on an Indian riverbank that provides access to the water

gher·kin \'gər-kən\ *n* **1** : a small prickly fruit of a vine related to the cucumber used to make pickles **2** : an immature cucumber

ghet·to \'ge-tō\ *n, pl* **ghettos** *or* **ghettoes** : a quarter of a city in which members of a minority group live because of social, legal, or economic pressure

¹ghost \'gōst\ *n* **1** : the seat of life : SOUL **2** : a disembodied soul; *esp* : the soul of a dead person believed to be an inhabitant of the unseen world or to appear in bodily form to living people **3** : SPIRIT, DEMON **4** : a faint trace ⟨a ∼ of a smile⟩ **5** : a false image in a photographic negative or on a television screen — **ghost·ly** *adv*

²ghost *vb* : GHOSTWRITE

ghost·write \-ˌrīt\ *vb* **-wrote** \-ˌrōt\; **-writ·ten** \-ˌri-tᵊn\ : to write for and in the name of another — **ghost·writ·er** *n*

ghoul \'gül\ *n* [Ar *ghūl*] : a legendary evil being that robs graves and feeds on corpses — **ghoul·ish** *adj*

GHQ *abbr* general headquarters

gi *abbr* gill

¹GI \ˌjē-'ī\ *adj* [galvanized iron; fr. abbr. used in listing such articles as garbage cans, but taken as abbr. for *government issue*] **1** : provided by an official U.S. military supply department ⟨∼ shoes⟩ **2** : of, relating to, or characteristic of U.S. military personnel **3** : conforming to military regulations or customs ⟨a ∼ haircut⟩

²GI *n, pl* **GIs** *or* **GI's** \-'īz\ : a member or former member of the U.S. armed forces; *esp* : an enlisted man

³GI *abbr* **1** galvanized iron **2** gastrointestinal **3** general issue **4** government issue

gi·ant \'jī-ənt\ *n* **1** : a legendary humanlike being of great size and strength **2** : a living being or thing of extraordinary size or powers — **giant** *adj*

gi·ant·ess \'jī-ən-təs\ *n* : a female giant

giant panda *n* : PANDA 2

gib·ber \'ji-bər\ *vb* : to speak rapidly, inarticulately, and often foolishly

gib·ber·ish \'ji-bə-rish\ *n* : unintelligible or confused speech or language

¹**gib·bet** \'ji-bət\ *n* : GALLOWS

²**gibbet** *vb* **1** : to hang on a gibbet **2** : to expose to public scorn **3** : to execute by hanging

gib·bon \'gi-bən\ *n* : any of several tailless apes of southeastern Asia

gib·bous \'ji-bəs, 'gi-\ *adj* **1** : rounded like the exterior of a sphere or circle **2** : seen with more than half but not all of the apparent disk illuminated ⟨∼ moon⟩ **3** : having a hump : HUMPBACKED

gibe *or* **jibe** \'jīb\ *vb* **gibed** *or* **jibed; gib·ing** *or* **jib·ing** : to utter taunting words : SNEER — **gibe** *or* **jibe** *n*

gib·lets \'jib-ləts\ *n pl* : the edible viscera of a fowl

Gib·son girl \'gib-sən-\ *adj* : of or relating to a style in women's clothing characterized by high necks, full sleeves, and slender waistlines

gid·dy \'gi-dē\ *adj* **gid·di·er; -est** **1** : DIZZY **2** : causing dizziness ⟨a ∼ height⟩ **3** : not serious : FRIVOLOUS, SILLY — **gid·di·ness** \-dē-nəs\ *n*

gid·dy·ap \gi-dē-'ap, -'əp⟩ *or* **gid·dy·up** \-'əp\ *vb imper* — a command (as to a horse) to go ahead or go faster

GIF \'gif, 'jif\ *n* [*g*raphic *i*nterchange *f*ormat] : a computer file format for digital images; *also* : the image itself

gift \'gift\ *n* **1** : a special ability : TALENT **2** : something given : PRESENT **3** : the act or power of giving

gift·ed \'gif-təd\ *adj* : TALENTED

¹**gig** \'gig\ *n* **1** : a long light ship's boat **2** : a light 2-wheeled one-horse carriage

¹gig 2

²**gig** *n* : a pronged spear for catching fish — **gig** *vb*

³**gig** *n* : a job for a specified time; *esp* : an entertainer's engagement

⁴**gig** *n* : a military demerit — **gig** *vb*

giga·byte \'ji-gə-ˌbīt, 'gi-\ *n* : 1024 megabytes or 1,073,741,824 bytes; *also* : one billion bytes

gi·gan·tic \jī-'gan-tik\ *adj* : exceeding the usual (as in size or force)

gig·gle \'gi-gəl\ *vb* **gig·gled; gig·gling** : to laugh with repeated short catches of the breath — **giggle** *n* — **gig·gly** \-gə-lē\ *adj*

GIGO *abbr* garbage in, garbage out

gig·o·lo \'ji-gə-ˌlō\ *n, pl* **-los** **1** : a man supported by a woman usu. in return for his attentions **2** : a professional dancing partner or male escort

Gi·la monster \'hē-lə-\ *n* : a large orange and black venomous lizard of the southwestern U.S.

¹**gild** \'gild\ *vb* **gild·ed** *or* **gilt** \'gilt\; **gild·ing** **1** : to overlay with or as if with a thin covering of gold **2** : to give an attractive but often deceptive appearance to

²**gild** *var of* GUILD

¹**gill** \'jil\ *n* — see WEIGHT table

²**gill** \'gil\ *n* : an organ (as of a fish) for obtaining oxygen from water

¹**gilt** \'gilt\ *adj* : of the color of gold

²**gilt** *n* : gold or a substance resembling gold laid on the surface of an object

³**gilt** *n* : a young female swine

¹**gim·crack** \'jim-ˌkrak\ *n* : a showy object of little use or value

²**gimcrack** *adj* : CHEAP, SHODDY

gim·let \'gim-lət\ *n* : a small tool with screw point and cross handle for boring holes

gim·me cap \'gi-mē-\ *n* : an adjustable visored cap featuring a corporate logo or slogan

gim·mick \'gi-mik\ *n* **1** : CONTRIVANCE, GADGET **2** : an important feature that is not immediately apparent : CATCH **3** : a new and ingenious scheme **4** : a device

used to attract business or attention — **gim·micky** \-mi-kē\ *adj*

gim·mick·ry \'gi-mi-krē\ *n, pl* **-ries** : an array of or the use of gimmicks

gimpy \'gim-pē\ *adj* : LAME 1

¹**gin** \'jin\ *n* [ME *gin*, fr. AF, short for *engin* engine] **1** : TRAP, SNARE **2** : a machine to separate seeds from cotton — **gin** *vb*

²**gin** *n* [by shortening & alter. fr. *geneva*, kind of gin] : a liquor distilled from a grain mash and flavored with juniper berries

gin·ger \'jin-jər\ *n* : the pungent aromatic rootstock of a tropical plant used esp. as a spice and in medicine; *also* : the spice or the plant

ginger ale *n* : a carbonated soft drink flavored with ginger

gin·ger·bread \'jin-jər-ˌbred\ *n* **1** : a cake made with molasses and flavored with ginger **2** : lavish or superfluous ornament esp. in architecture

gin·ger·ly \'jin-jər-lē\ *adj* : very cautious or careful — **gin·gerly** *adv*

gin·ger·snap \-ˌsnap\ *n* : a thin brittle molasses cookie flavored with ginger

ging·ham \'giŋ-əm\ *n* : a clothing fabric usu. of yarn-dyed cotton in plain weave

gin·gi·vi·tis \ˌjin-jə-'vī-təs\ *n* : inflammation of the gums

gink·go *also* **ging·ko** \'giŋ-ˌkō\ *n, pl* **ginkgoes** *or* **ginkgos** *also* **ginkos** *or* **gingkoes** **1** : a tree of eastern China with fan-shaped leaves often grown as a shade tree **2** : GINKGO BILOBA

ginkgo bi·lo·ba \-ˌbī-'lō-bə\ *n* : an extract of the leaves of ginkgo that is held to enhance mental functioning

gin·seng \'jin-ˌseŋ\ *n* : an aromatic root of a Chinese or No. American herb used esp. in Chinese medicine; *also* : one of these herbs

Gip·sy *chiefly Brit var of* GYPSY

gi·raffe \jə-'raf\ *n, pl* **giraffes** [It *giraffa*, fr. Ar *zirāfa*] : an African ruminant mammal with a very long neck and a short coat with dark blotches

gird \'gərd\ *vb* **gird·ed** *or* **girt** \'gərt\; **gird·ing** **1** : to encircle or fasten (as a sword) with or as if with a belt **2** : to invest esp. with power or authority **3** : PREPARE, BRACE

gird·er \'gər-dər\ *n* : a horizontal main supporting beam

gir·dle \'gər-dᵊl\ *n* **1** : something (as a belt or sash) that encircles or confines **2** : a woman's supporting undergarment that extends from the waist to below the hips — **girdle** *vb*

girl \'gərl\ *n* **1** : a female child **2** : a young woman **3** : SWEETHEART — **girl·hood** \-ˌhu̇d\ *n* — **girl·ish** *adj*

girl Friday *n* : a female assistant (as in an office) entrusted with a wide variety of tasks

girl·friend \'gərl-ˌfrend\ *n* **1** : a female friend **2** : a regular female companion in a romantic or sexual relationship

Girl Scout *n* : a member of any of the scouting programs of the Girl Scouts of the United States of America

girth \'gərth\ *n* **1** : a band around an animal by which something (as a saddle) may be fastened on its back **2** : a measure around something

gist \'jist\ *n* [AF, it lies, fr. *gesir* to lie, ultim. fr. L *jacēre*] : the main point or part

git *dial var of* GET

¹**give** \'giv\ *vb* **gave** \'gāv\; **giv·en** \'gi-vən\; **giv·ing** **1** : to make a present of **2** : to bestow by formal action **3** : to accord or yield to another **4** : to yield to force, strain, or pressure **5** : to put into the possession or keeping of another **6** : PROFFER ⟨*gave* her his hand⟩ **7** : DELIVER ⟨*gave* the bride away⟩ **8** : to present in public performance or to view **9** : PROVIDE ⟨∼ a party⟩ **10** : ATTRIBUTE **11** : to make, form, or yield as a product or result ⟨cows ∼ milk⟩ **12** : PAY **13** : to deliver by some bodily action ⟨*gave* me a push⟩ **14** : to offer as a pledge ⟨I ∼ you my word⟩ **15** : DEVOTE **16** : to cause to have or receive

²**give** *n* **1** : capacity or tendency to yield to force or strain **2** : the quality or state of being springy

give–and–take \ˌgiv-ən-'tāk\ *n* **1** : COMPROMISE **2** : a usu. good-natured exchange (as of remarks or ideas)

give·away \'gi-və-ˌwā\ *n* **1** : an unintentional revelation or betrayal **2** : something given away free; *esp* : PREMIUM

give in *vb* : SUBMIT, SURRENDER

¹giv·en \'gi-vən\ *adj* **1** : DISPOSED, INCLINED ⟨~ to swearing⟩ **2** : SPECIFIED, PARTICULAR ⟨at a ~ time⟩

²**given** *n* : something taken for granted : a basic condition or assumption

³**given** *prep* : CONSIDERING

given name *n* : a name that precedes one's surname

give out *vb* **1** : EMIT **2** : BREAK DOWN **3** : to become exhausted : COLLAPSE

give up *vb* **1** : SURRENDER **2** : to abandon (oneself) to a feeling, influence, or activity **3** : QUIT

giz·mo *also* **gis·mo** \'giz-mō\ *n, pl* **gizmos** *also* **gismos** : GADGET

giz·zard \'gi-zərd\ *n* : the muscular usu. horny-lined enlargement of the alimentary canal of a bird used for churning and grinding up food

gla·cial \'glā-shəl\ *adj* **1** : extremely cold **2** : of or relating to glaciers **3** : being or relating to a past period of time when a large part of the earth was covered by glaciers **4** *cap* : PLEISTOCENE **5** : very slow ⟨a ~ pace⟩ — **gla·cial·ly** *adv*

gla·ci·ate \'glā-shē-ˌāt\ *vb* **-at·ed; -at·ing** **1** : to subject to glacial action **2** : to produce glacial effects in or on — **gla·ci·a·tion** \ˌglā-shē-ˈā-shən, -sē-\ *n*

gla·cier \'glā-shər\ *n* [F, fr. MF dial. (Savoy), fr. *glace* ice, fr. L *glacies*] : a large body of ice moving slowly down a slope or spreading outward on a land surface

¹**glad** \'glad\ *adj* **glad·der; glad·dest** **1** : experiencing pleasure, joy, or delight **2** : PLEASED **3** : very willing ⟨was ~ to help⟩ **4** : PLEASANT, JOYFUL **5** : CHEERFUL ⟨a ~ morning⟩ — **glad·ly** *adv* — **glad·ness** *n*

²**glad** *n* : GLADIOLUS

glad·den \'gla-dᵊn\ *vb* : to make glad

glade \'glād\ *n* : a grassy open space surrounded by woods

glad·i·a·tor \'gla-dē-ˌā-tər\ *n* **1** : a person engaged in a fight to the death for public entertainment in ancient Rome **2** : a person engaging in a public fight or controversy; *also* : PRIZEFIGHTER — **glad·i·a·to·ri·al** \ˌgla-dē-ə-ˈtȯr-ē-əl\ *adj*

glad·i·o·lus \ˌgla-dē-ˈō-ləs\ *n, pl* **-oli** \-ˈō-(ˌ)lē, -ˌlī\ *or* **-olus** *also* **-o·lus·es** [L, fr. dim. of *gladius* sword] : any of a genus of chiefly African plants related to the irises and having erect sword-shaped leaves and stalks of bright colored flowers

glad·some \'glad-səm\ *adj* : giving or showing joy : CHEERFUL

glad·stone \'glad-ˌstōn\ *n, often cap* : a suitcase with flexible sides on a rigid frame that opens flat into two compartments

glam \'glam\ *n* : extravagantly showy glamour — **glam** *adj*

glam·or·ise *Brit var of* GLAMORIZE

glam·or·ize *also* **glam·our·ize** \'gla-mə-ˌrīz\ *vb* **-ized; -iz·ing** : to make or look upon as glamorous

glam·our *also* **glam·or** \'gla-mər\ *n* [Sc *glamour* magic spell, alter. of E *grammar;* fr. the popular association of erudition with occult practices] : an exciting and often illusory and romantic attractiveness : *esp* : alluring personal attraction — **glam·or·ous** *also* **glam·our·ous** \-mə-rəs\ *adj*

¹**glance** \'glans\ *vb* **glanced; glanc·ing** **1** : to strike and fly off to one side **2** : GLEAM **3** : to give a quick look

²**glance** *n* **1** : a quick intermittent flash or gleam **2** : a deflected impact or blow **3** : a quick look

gland \'gland\ *n* : a cell or group of cells that prepares and secretes a substance (as saliva or sweat) for further use in or discharge from the body

glan·du·lar \'glan-jə-lər\ *adj* : of, relating to, or involving glands

glans \'glanz\ *n, pl* **glan·des** \'glan-ˌdēz\ [L, lit., acorn] : a conical vascular body forming the extremity of the penis or clitoris

¹**glare** \'gler\ *vb* **glared; glar·ing** **1** : to shine with a harsh dazzling light **2** : to stare fiercely or angrily

²**glare** *n* **1** : a harsh dazzling light **2** : an angry or fierce stare

glaring *adj* : very conspicuous ⟨a ~ error⟩ — **glar·ing·ly** *adv*

glass \'glas\ *n* **1** : a hard brittle amorphous usu. transparent or translucent material consisting typically of silica **2** : something made of glass; *esp* : TUMBLER 2 **3** *pl* : a pair of lenses used to correct defects of vision : SPEC-

TACLES **4** : the quantity held by a glass container — **glass** *adj* — **glass·ful** \-ˌfu̇l\ *n* — **glassy** *adj*

glass·blow·ing \-ˌblō-iŋ\ *n* : the art of shaping a mass of glass that has been softened by heat by blowing air into it through a tube — **glass·blow·er** *n*

glass·ware \-ˌwer\ *n* : articles made of glass

glau·co·ma \glau̇-ˈkō-mə, glȯ-\ *n* : a disease of the eye marked by increased pressure within the eyeball resulting in damage to the retina and gradual loss of vision

¹**glaze** \'glāz\ *vb* **glazed; glaz·ing** **1** : to furnish (as a window frame) with glass **2** : to apply glaze to

²**glaze** *n* : a glassy coating or surface

gla·zier \'glā-zhər\ *n* : a person who sets glass in window frames

¹**gleam** \'glēm\ *n* **1** : a transient subdued or partly obscured light **2** : GLINT **3** : a faint trace ⟨a ~ of hope⟩

²**gleam** *vb* **1** : to shine with subdued light or moderate brightness **2** : to appear briefly or faintly ♦ **Synonyms** FLASH, GLIMMER, GLISTEN, GLITTER, SHIMMER, SPARKLE

glean \'glēn\ *vb* **1** : to gather grain left by reapers **2** : to collect little by little or with patient effort — **glean·able** *adj* — **glean·er** *n*

glean·ings \'glē-niŋz\ *n pl* : things acquired by gleaning

glee \'glē\ *n* [ME, fr. OE *glēo* entertainment, music] **1** : JOY, HILARITY **2** : a part-song for three usu. male voices — **glee·ful** *adj* — **glee·ful·ly** *adv*

glee club *n* : a chorus organized for singing usu. short choral pieces

glen \'glen\ *n* : a narrow hidden valley

glen·gar·ry \glen-ˈga-rē\ *n, pl* **-ries** *often cap* : a woolen cap of Scottish origin

glib \'glib\ *adj* **glib·ber; glib·best** : speaking or spoken with careless ease — **glib·ly** *adv*

glide \'glīd\ *vb* **glid·ed; glid·ing** **1** : to move smoothly and effortlessly **2** : to descend gradually without engine power ⟨~ in an airplane⟩ — **glide** *n*

glid·er \'glī-dər\ *n* **1** : one that glides **2** : an aircraft resembling an airplane but having no engine **3** : a porch seat suspended from an upright frame

¹**glim·mer** \'gli-mər\ *vb* : to shine faintly or unsteadily

²**glimmer** *n* **1** : a faint unsteady light **2** : INKLING **3** : a small amount : HINT

¹**glimpse** \'glimps\ *vb* **glimpsed; glimps·ing** : to take a brief look : see momentarily or incompletely

²**glimpse** *n* **1** : a faint idea : GLIMMER **2** : a short hurried look

glint \'glint\ *vb* **1** : to shine by reflection : SPARKLE, GLITTER, GLEAM **2** : to appear briefly or faintly — **glint** *n*

glis·san·do \gli-ˈsän-(ˌ)dō\ *n, pl* **-di** \-(ˌ)dē\ *or* **-dos** : a rapid sliding up or down the musical scale

¹**glis·ten** \'gli-sᵊn\ *vb* : to shine by reflection with a soft luster or sparkle

²**glisten** *n* : GLITTER, SPARKLE

glis·ter \'glis-tər\ *vb* : GLITTER

glitch \'glich\ *n* : MALFUNCTION; *also* : SNAG 2

¹**glit·ter** \'gli-tər\ *vb* **1** : to shine with brilliant or metallic luster : SPARKLE **2** : to shine with strong emotion : FLASH ⟨eyes ~ing in anger⟩ **3** : to be brilliantly attractive esp. in a superficial way

²**glitter** *n* **1** : sparkling brilliancy, showiness, or attractiveness **2** : small glittering objects used for ornamentation — **glit·tery** \'gli-tə-rē\ *adj*

¹**glitz** \'glits\ *n* : extravagant showiness — **glitzy** \'glit-sē\ *adj*

²**glitz** *vb* : to make flashy or extravagant in appearance — often used with *up*

gloam·ing \'glō-miŋ\ *n* : TWILIGHT, DUSK

gloat \'glōt\ *vb* : to think about something with triumphant and often malicious delight

glob \'gläb\ *n* **1** : a small drop **2** : a large rounded mass

glob·al \'glō-bəl\ *adj* **1** : WORLDWIDE **2** : COMPREHENSIVE, GENERAL — **glob·al·ly** *adv*

glob·al·i·za·tion \ˌglō-bə-lə-ˈzā-shən\ *n* : the development of an increasingly integrated global economy

Global Positioning System *n* : GPS

global warming *n* : an increase in the earth's atmospheric and oceanic temperatures due to an increase in the greenhouse effect

globe \'glōb\ *n* **1** : BALL, SPHERE **2** : EARTH; *also* : a spherical representation of the earth

globe–trot·ter \'glōb-ˌträ-tər\ *n* : a person who travels widely — **globe–trot·ting** *n or adj*

glob·u·lar \'glä-byə-lər\ *adj* : having the shape of a globe or globule

glob·ule \'glä-(ˌ)byül\ *n* : a tiny globe or ball esp. of a liquid

glob·u·lin \'glä-byə-lən\ *n* : any of a class of simple proteins insoluble in pure water but soluble in dilute salt solutions that occur widely in plant and animal tissues

glock·en·spiel \'glä-kən-ˌshpēl, -ˌspēl\ *n* [G, fr. *Glocke* bell + *Spiel* play] : a percussion musical instrument consisting of a series of metal bars played with two hammers

gloom \'glüm\ *n* **1** : partial or total darkness **2** : lowness of spirits : DEJECTION **3** : an atmosphere of despondency — **gloom·i·ly** \'glü-mə-lē\ *adv* — **gloom·i·ness** \-mē-nəs\ *n* — **gloomy** \'glü-mē\ *adj*

Gloomy Gus \-'gəs\ *n, pl* **Gloomy Gus·es** : a person who is habitually gloomy

glop \'gläp\ *n* : a messy mass or mixture

glo·ri·fy \'glȯr-ə-ˌfī\ *vb* **-fied; -fy·ing** **1** : to raise to heavenly glory **2** : to light up brilliantly **3** : EXTOL **4** : to give glory to (as in worship) — **glo·ri·fi·ca·tion** \ˌglȯr-ə-fə-'kā-shən\ *n*

glo·ri·ous \'glȯr-ē-əs\ *adj* **1** : possessing or deserving glory : PRAISEWORTHY **2** : conferring glory **3** : RESPLENDENT, MAGNIFICENT ⟨a ~ sunset⟩ **4** : DELIGHTFUL, WONDERFUL ⟨had a ~ weekend⟩ — **glo·ri·ous·ly** *adv*

¹glo·ry \'glȯr-ē\ *n, pl* **glories** **1** : RENOWN **2** : honor and praise rendered in worship **3** : something that secures praise or renown **4** : a distinguishing quality or asset **5** : RESPLENDENCE, MAGNIFICENCE **6** : heavenly bliss **7** : a height of prosperity or achievement

²glory *vb* **glo·ried; glo·ry·ing** : to rejoice proudly : EXULT

¹gloss \'gläs, 'glȯs\ *n* **1** : LUSTER, SHEEN, BRIGHTNESS **2** : outward show

²gloss *vb* **1** : to give a false appearance of acceptableness to ⟨~ over inadequacies⟩ **2** : to deal with too lightly or not at all

³gloss *n* [alter. of *gloze*, fr. ME *glose*, fr. AF, fr. ML *glosa*, *glossa*, fr. Gk *glōssa*, *glōtta* tongue, language, unusual word] **1** : an explanatory note (as in the margin of a text) **2** : GLOSSARY **3** : an interlinear translation **4** : a continuous commentary accompanying a text

⁴gloss *vb* : to furnish glosses for

glos·sa·ry \'glä-sə-rē, 'glȯ-\ *n, pl* **-ries** : a collection of difficult or specialized terms with their meanings — **glos·sar·i·al** \glä-'ser-ē-əl, glȯ-\ *adj*

glos·so·la·lia \ˌglä-sə-'lā-lē-ə, ˌglȯ-\ *n* [ultim. fr. Gk *glōssa* tongue, language + *lalia* chatter] : TONGUE 6

¹glossy \'glä-sē, 'glȯ-\ *adj* **gloss·i·er; -est** : having a surface luster or brightness — **gloss·i·ly** \-sə-lē\ *adv* — **gloss·i·ness** \-sē-nəs\ *n*

²glossy *n, pl* **gloss·ies** : a photograph printed on smooth shiny paper

glot·tis \'glä-təs\ *n, pl* **glot·tis·es** *or* **glot·ti·des** \-tə-ˌdēz\ : the slitlike opening between the vocal cords in the larynx — **glot·tal** \'glä-tᵊl\ *adj*

glove \'gləv\ *n* **1** : a covering for the hand having separate sections for each finger **2** : a padded leather covering for the hand for use in a sport

¹glow \'glō\ *vb* **1** : to shine with or as if with intense heat **2** : to have a rich warm usu. ruddy color : FLUSH, BLUSH **3** : to feel hot **4** : to show exuberance or elation ⟨~ with pride⟩

²glow *n* **1** : brightness or warmth of color; *esp* : REDNESS **2** : warmth of feeling or emotion **3** : a sensation of warmth **4** : light such as is emitted from a heated substance

glow·er \'glau̇(-ə)r\ *vb* : to stare angrily : SCOWL — **glower** *n*

glow·worm \'glō-ˌwərm\ *n* : any of various insect larvae or adults that give off light

glox·in·ia \gläk-'si-nē-ə\ *n* : any of a genus of tropical herbs related to the African violets; *esp* : one with showy bell-shaped or slipper-shaped flowers

gloze \'glōz\ *vb* **glozed; gloz·ing** : to make appear right or acceptable : GLOSS

glu·cose \'glü-ˌkōs\ *n* **1** : a form of crystalline sugar; *esp* : DEXTROSE **2** : a sweet light-colored syrup made from cornstarch

glue \'glü\ *n* : a jellylike protein substance made from animal materials and used for sticking things together; *also* : any of various other strong adhesives — **glue** *vb* — **glu·ey** \'glü-ē\ *adj*

glum \'gləm\ *adj* **glum·mer; glum·mest** **1** : broodingly morose : SULLEN **2** : DREARY, GLOOMY ⟨a ~ countenance⟩ ♦ *Synonyms* CRABBED, DOUR, SATURNINE, SULKY

¹glut \'glət\ *vb* **glut·ted; glut·ting** **1** : OVERSUPPLY **2** : to fill esp. with food to satiety : SATIATE

²glut *n* : an excessive supply

glu·ten \'glü-tᵊn\ *n* : a gluey protein substance that causes dough to be sticky

glu·ti·nous \'glü-tə-nəs\ *adj* : STICKY

glut·ton \'glə-tᵊn\ *n* : one that eats to excess — **glut·ton·ous** \'glə-tə-nəs\ *adj* — **glut·tony** \'glə-tə-nē\ *n*

glyc·er·in *or* **glyc·er·ine** \'gli-sə-rən\ *n* : GLYCEROL

glyc·er·ol \'gli-sə-ˌrȯl, -ˌrōl\ *n* : a sweet syrupy alcohol usu. obtained from fats and used esp. as a solvent

gly·co·gen \'glī-kə-jən\ *n* : a white tasteless substance that is the chief storage carbohydrate of animals

gm *abbr* gram

GM *abbr* **1** general manager **2** guided missile

G–man \'jē-ˌman\ *n* : a special agent of the Federal Bureau of Investigation

GMT *abbr* Greenwich mean time

gnarled \'närld\ *adj* **1** : KNOTTY ⟨~ hands⟩ **2** : GLOOMY, SULLEN

gnash \'nash\ *vb* : to grind (as teeth) together

gnat \'nat\ *n* : any of various small usu. biting dipteran flies

gnaw \'nȯ\ *vb* **1** : to consume, wear away, or make by persistent biting or nibbling **2** : to affect as if by gnawing — **gnaw·er** *n*

gneiss \'nīs\ *n* : a layered rock similar in composition to granite

gnome \'nōm\ *n* : a dwarf of folklore who lives inside the earth and guards precious ore or treasure — **gnome·like** \-ˌlīk\ *adj* — **gnom·ish** *adj*

GNP *abbr* gross national product

gnu \'nü\ *n, pl* **gnu** *or* **gnus** : WILDEBEEST

¹go \'gō\ *vb* **went** \'went\; **gone** \'gȯn, 'gän\; **go·ing; goes** \'gōz\ **1** : to move on a course : PROCEED ⟨~ slow⟩ **2** : LEAVE, DEPART **3** : to take a certain course or follow a certain procedure ⟨reports ~ through department channels⟩ **4** : EXTEND, RUN ⟨his land ~es to the river⟩; *also* : LEAD ⟨that door ~es to the cellar⟩ **5** : to be habitually in a certain state ⟨~es barefoot⟩ **6** : to become lost, consumed, or spent; *also* : DIE **7** : ELAPSE, PASS **8** : to pass by sale ⟨*went* for a good price⟩ **9** : to become impaired or weakened ⟨his hearing started to ~⟩ **10** : to give way under force or pressure : BREAK **11** : to move along in a specified manner ⟨it *went* well⟩ **12** : to be in general or on an average ⟨cheap, as yachts ~⟩ **13** : to become esp. as the result of a contest ⟨the decision *went* against him⟩ **14** : to put or subject oneself ⟨~ to great expense⟩ **15** : RESORT ⟨*went* to court to recover damages⟩ **16** : to begin or maintain an action or motion **17** : to function properly ⟨the clock doesn't ~⟩ **18** : to be known ⟨~es by an alias⟩ **19** : to be or act in accordance ⟨a good rule to ~ by⟩ **20** : to come to be applied **21** : to pass by award, assignment, or lot **22** : to contribute to a result ⟨qualities that ~ to make a hero⟩ **23** : to be about, intending, or expecting something ⟨is ~ing to leave town⟩ **24** : to arrive at a certain state or condition ⟨~ to sleep⟩ **25** : to come to be ⟨the tire *went* flat⟩ **26** : to be capable of being sung or played ⟨the tune ~es like this⟩ **27** : to be suitable or becoming : HARMONIZE **28** : to be capable of passing, extending, or being contained or inserted ⟨this coat will ~ in the trunk⟩ **29** : to have a usual or proper place or position : BELONG ⟨these books ~ on the top shelf⟩ **30** : to be capable of being divided ⟨3 ~es into 6 twice⟩ **31** : to have a tendency ⟨that ~es to show that he is honest⟩ **32** : to be acceptable, satisfactory, or adequate ⟨any color will ~ with black⟩ **33** : to empty the bladder or bowels **34** : to proceed along or according to : FOLLOW **35** : TRAVERSE **36** : BET, BID ⟨willing to ~ $50⟩ **37** : to assume the function or obligation of ⟨~ bail for a friend⟩ **38** : to participate to the extent of ⟨~ halves⟩ **39** : WEIGH **40** : ENDURE, TOLERATE **41** : AFFORD ⟨can't ~ the price⟩ **42** : SAY — used chiefly in oral narration of speech **43**

go • gondola

212

: to engage in ⟨don't ∼ telling everyone⟩ — **go at** **1** : AT-
TACK, ATTEMPT **2** : UNDERTAKE — **go back on** **1**
: ABANDON **2** : BETRAY **3** : FAIL — **go by the board** : to
be discarded — **go for** **1** : to pass for or serve as **2** : to
try to secure **3** : FAVOR — **go one better** : OUTDO, SUR-
PASS — **go over** **1** : EXAMINE **2** : REPEAT **3** : STUDY,
REVIEW — **go places** : to be on the way to success — **go
steady** : to date one person exclusively — **go to bat for**
: DEFEND, CHAMPION — **go to town** **1** : to work or act
efficiently **2** : to be very successful
²**go** *n, pl* **goes** **1** : the act or manner of going **2** : the height
of fashion ⟨boots are all the ∼⟩ **3** : a turn of affairs : OC-
CURRENCE **4** : ENERGY, VIGOR **5** : ATTEMPT, TRY ⟨give
it a ∼⟩ **6** : a spell of activity ⟨finished the job at one ∼⟩
— **no go** : USELESS, HOPELESS — **on the go** : constantly
active
³**go** *adj* : functioning properly ⟨declared all systems ∼⟩
goad \'gōd\ *n* [ME *gode,* fr. OE *gād* spear, goad] **1** : a
pointed rod used to urge on an animal **2** : something that
urges ✦ *Synonyms* STIMULUS, IMPETUS, INCENTIVE,
SPUR, STIMULANT — **goad** *vb*
go–ahead \'gō-ə-,hed\ *n* : authority to proceed
goal \'gōl\ *n* **1** : the mark set as limit to a race; *also* : an
area to be reached safely in children's games **2** : AIM,
PURPOSE **3** : an area or object toward which play is directed to score; *also* : a successful attempt to score
goal·ie \'gō-lē\ *n* : GOALKEEPER
goal·keep·er \'gōl-,kē-pər\ *n* : a player who defends the
goal in various games
goal·post \-,pōst\ *n* : one of the two vertical posts with a
crossbar that constitute the goal in various games
goat \'gōt\ *n, pl* **goats** *or* **goat** : any of various hollow=
horned ruminant mammals related to the sheep that have
backward-curving horns, a short tail, and usu. straight
hair
goa·tee \gō-'tē\ *n* : a small trim pointed or tufted beard on
a man's chin
goat·herd \'gōt-,hərd\ *n* : a person who tends goats
goat·skin \-,skin\ *n* : the skin of a goat or a leather made
from it
¹**gob** \'gäb\ *n* : LUMP, MASS
²**gob** *n* : SAILOR
gob·bet \'gä-bət\ *n* : LUMP, MASS
¹**gob·ble** \'gä-bəl\ *vb* **gob·bled; gob·bling** **1** : to swallow
or eat greedily **2** : to take eagerly : GRAB
²**gobble** *vb* **gob·bled; gob·bling** : to make the natural guttural noise of a male turkey
gob·ble·dy·gook *also* **gob·ble·de·gook** \'gä-bəl-dē-,gúk,
-,gük\ *n* : generally unintelligible jargon
gob·bler \'gä-blər\ *n* : a male turkey
go–be·tween \'gō-bə-,twēn\ *n* : an intermediate agent
: BROKER
gob·let \'gä-blət\ *n* : a drinking glass with a foot and stem
gob·lin \'gä-blən\ *n* : an ugly or grotesque sprite that is
mischievous and sometimes evil and malicious
go·by \'gō-bē\ *n, pl* **gobies** *also* **goby** : any of numerous
spiny-finned fishes usu. having the pelvic fins united to
form a ventral sucking disk
god \'gäd, 'gòd\ *n* **1** *cap* : the supreme reality; *esp* : the
Being worshiped as the creator and ruler of the universe
2 : a being or object believed to have supernatural attributes and powers and to require worship **3** : a thing of
supreme value **4** : an extraordinarily attractive person
god·child \'gäd-,chī(-ə)ld, 'gòd-\ *n* : a person for whom another person stands as sponsor at baptism
god·daugh·ter \-,dò-tər\ *n* : a female godchild
god·dess \'gä-dəs, 'gò-\ *n* **1** : a female god **2** : a woman
whose charm or beauty arouses adoration
god·fa·ther \'gäd-,fä-thər, 'gòd-\ *n* **1** : a man who sponsors a person at baptism **2** : the leader of an organized
crime syndicate
god·head \-,hed\ *n* **1** : divine nature or essence **2** *cap*
: GOD 1; *also* : the nature of God esp. as existing in three
persons
god·hood \-,húd\ *n* : DIVINITY
god·less \-ləs\ *adj* : not acknowledging a deity or divine
law — **god·less·ness** *n*
god·like \-,līk\ *adj* : resembling or having the qualities of
God or a god
god·ly \-lē\ *adj* **god·li·er; -est** **1** : DIVINE **2** : PIOUS, DE-
VOUT — **god·li·ness** *n*

god·moth·er \-,mə-thər\ *n* : a woman who sponsors a person at baptism
god·par·ent \-,per-ənt\ *n* : a sponsor at baptism
god·send \-,send\ *n* : a desirable or needed thing or event
that comes unexpectedly
god·son \-,sən\ *n* : a male godchild
God·speed \-'spēd\ *n* : a prosperous journey : SUCCESS
⟨bade him ∼⟩
go·fer *or* **go·pher** \'gō-fər\ *n* [alter. of *go for*] : an employee whose duties include running errands
go–get·ter \'gō-,ge-tər\ *n* : an aggressively enterprising
person — **go–get·ting** *adj or n*
gog·gle \'gä-gəl\ *vb* **gog·gled; gog·gling** : to stare with
wide or protuberant eyes
gog·gles \'gä-gəlz\ *n pl* : protective glasses set in a flexible
frame that fits snugly against the face
go–go \'gō-,gō\ *adj* **1** : related to, being, or employed to
entertain in a disco ⟨∼ dancers⟩ **2** : aggressively enterprising and energetic
go·ings–on \,gō-iŋ-'zón, -'zän\ *n pl* : ACTIONS, EVENTS
goi·ter \'gói-tər\ *n* : an abnormally enlarged thyroid gland
visible as a swelling at the base of the neck — **goi·trous**
\-trəs, -tə-rəs\ *adj*
goi·tre *chiefly Brit var of* GOITER
go–kart \'gō-,kärt\ *n* : a small motorized vehicle used esp.
for racing
gold \'gōld\ *n* **1** : a malleable yellow metallic chemical element used esp. for coins and jewelry **2** : gold coins; *also*
: MONEY **3** : a yellow color
gold·brick \'gōld-,brik\ *n* : a person who shirks assigned
work — **goldbrick** *vb*
gold coast *n, often cap G&C* : an exclusive residential district
gold digger *n* : a person who uses charm to extract money
or gifts from others
gold·en \'gōl-dən\ *adj* **1** : made of or relating to gold **2**
: having the color of gold; *also* : BLOND **3** : SHINING,
LUSTROUS **4** : SUPERB **5** : FLOURISHING, PROSPEROUS
6 : radiantly youthful and vigorous **7** : FAVORABLE, AD-
VANTAGEOUS ⟨a ∼ opportunity⟩ **8** : MELLOW, RESO-
NANT ⟨a ∼ tenor⟩
gold·en–ag·er \'gōl-dən-'ā-jər\ *n* : an elderly and often retired person usu. engaging in club activities
golden eagle *n* : a large dark brown eagle with gold-col-
ored feathers on the back of the head and neck
golden hamster *n* : a small tawny hamster often kept as a
pet
golden handcuffs *n pl* : special benefits offered to an employee as an inducement to continue service
golden handshake *n* : a generous severance agreement
given esp. as an inducement to early retirement
golden retriever *n* : any of a breed of retrievers with a flat
golden coat
gold·en·rod \'gōl-dən-,räd\ *n* : any of numerous herbs related to the daisies that have tall slender stalks with many
tiny usu. yellow flower heads
golden years *n pl* : the advanced years in a lifetime
gold·finch \-,finch\ *n* **1** : a small largely red, black, and
yellow Old World finch often kept in a cage **2** : any of
three small related American finches of which the males
usu. become bright yellow and black in summer
gold·fish \-,fish\ *n* : a small usu. golden-orange carp often
kept as an aquarium or pond fish
gold·smith \-,smith\ *n* : a person who makes or deals in
articles of gold
golf \'gälf, 'gòlf\ *n* : a game played with a small ball and
various clubs on a course having 9 or 18 holes — **golf** *vb*
— **golf·er** *n*
-gon \,gän\ *n comb form* : figure having (so many) angles
⟨hexa*gon*⟩
go·nad \'gō-,nad\ *n* : a sperm- or egg-producing gland
: OVARY, TESTIS — **go·nad·al** \gō-'na-d³l\ *adj*
go·nad·o·trop·ic \gō-,na-də-'trä-pik\ *also* **go·nad·o·tro-
phic** \-'trō-fik,-'trä-\ *adj* : acting on or stimulating the gonads
go·nad·o·tro·pin \-'trō-pən\ *also* **go·nad·o·tro·phin** \-fən\
n : a gonadotropic hormone
gon·do·la \'gän-də-lə (*usual for 1*), gän-'dō-\ *n* [It. dial.
(Venice), prob. fr. MGk *kontoura* small vessel] **1** : a long
narrow boat used on the canals of Venice **2** : a railroad
car used for hauling loose freight (as coal) **3** : an enclo-

sure beneath an airship or balloon **4** : an enclosed car suspended from a cable and used esp. for transporting skiers

gon·do·lier \ˌgän-də-ˈlir\ *n* : a person who propels a gondola

¹gone \ˈgȯn\ *past part of* GO

²gone *adj* **1** : LOST, RUINED **2** : DEAD **3** : SINKING, WEAK **4** : INVOLVED, ABSORBED **5** : INFATUATED **6** : PREGNANT **7** : PAST

gon·er \ˈgȯ-nər\ *n* : one whose case is hopeless

gong \ˈgäŋ, ˈgȯŋ\ *n* : a metallic disk that produces a resounding tone when struck

gono·coc·cus \ˌgä-nə-ˈkä-kəs\ *n, pl* -**coc·ci** \-ˈkäk-ˌsī, -ˌsē, -ˈkä-ˌkī, -ˌkē\ : a pus-producing bacterium causing gonorrhea — **gono·coc·cal** \-ˈkä-kəl\ *adj*

gon·or·rhea \ˌgä-nə-ˈrē-ə\ *n* : a contagious sexually transmitted inflammation of the genital tract caused by the gonococcus — **gon·or·rhe·al** \-ˈrē-əl\ *adj*

goo \ˈgü\ *n* **1** : a viscid or sticky substance **2** : sentimental tripe — **goo·ey** \-ē\ *adj*

goo·ber \ˈgü-bər, ˈgü-\ *n, Southern & Midland* : PEANUT

¹good \ˈgu̇d\ *adj* **bet·ter** \ˈbe-tər\; **best** \ˈbest\ **1** : of a favorable character or tendency **2** : BOUNTIFUL, FERTILE ⟨~ land⟩ **3** : COMELY, ATTRACTIVE **4** : SUITABLE, FIT **5** : SOUND, WHOLE ⟨only one ~ arm⟩ **6** : AGREEABLE, PLEASANT ⟨had a ~ time⟩ **7** : SALUTARY, WHOLESOME **8** : CONSIDERABLE, AMPLE ⟨a ~ bit of time⟩ **9** : FULL ⟨waited a ~ hour⟩ **10** : WELL-FOUNDED **11** : TRUE ⟨holds ~ for everybody⟩ **12** : legally valid or effectual **13** : ADEQUATE, SATISFACTORY **14** : conforming to a standard ⟨~ English⟩ **15** : DISCRIMINATING **16** : COMMENDABLE, VIRTUOUS **17** : KIND **18** : UPPER-CLASS **19** : COMPETENT **20** : LOYAL, CLOSE — **good·ish** *adj*

²good *n* **1** : something good **2** : GOODNESS **3** : BENEFIT, WELFARE ⟨for the ~ of mankind⟩ **4** : something that has economic utility **5** *pl* : personal property **6** *pl* : CLOTH **7** *pl* : WARES, MERCHANDISE ⟨canned ~s⟩ **8** : good persons ⟨the ~ die young⟩ **9** *pl* : proof of wrongdoing — **for good** : FOREVER, PERMANENTLY — **to the good** : in a position of net gain or profit ⟨$10 *to the good*⟩

³good *adv* : WELL

good–bye *or* **good–by** \gu̇d-ˈbī, gə-\ *n* : a concluding remark at parting

good cholesterol *n* : HDL

good–for–noth·ing \ˈgu̇d-fər-ˌnə-thiŋ\ *adj* : of no use or value — **good–for–nothing** *n*

Good Friday *n* : the Friday before Easter observed as the anniversary of the crucifixion of Christ

good–heart·ed \ˈgu̇d-ˈhär-təd\ *adj* : having a kindly generous disposition — **good–heart·ed·ly** *adv* — **good–heart·ed·ness** *n*

good–look·ing \ˈgu̇d-ˈlu̇-kiŋ\ *adj* : having an attractive appearance

good·ly \ˈgu̇d-lē\ *adj* **good·li·er; -est** **1** : of pleasing appearance **2** : LARGE, CONSIDERABLE

good·man \ˈgu̇d-mən\ *n, archaic* : MR.

good–na·tured \ˈgu̇d-ˈnā-chərd\ *adj* : of a cheerful disposition — **good–na·tured·ly** \-chərd-lē\ *adv*

good·ness \-nəs\ *n* : EXCELLENCE, VIRTUE

good·wife \-ˌwīf\ *n, archaic* : MRS.

good·will \-ˈwil\ *n* **1** : BENEVOLENCE **2** : the value of the trade a business has built up over time **3** : cheerful consent **4** : willing effort

goody *or* **good·ie** \ˈgu̇-dē\ *n, pl* **good·ies** : something that is good esp. to eat

goody–goody \ˌgu̇-dē-ˈgu̇-dē\ *adj* : affectedly good — **goody–goody** *n*

goof \ˈgüf\ *vb* **1** : to spend time idly or foolishly **2** : BLUNDER — often used with *off* — **goof** *n*

goof·ball \ˈgüf-ˌbȯl\ *n* **1** *slang* : a barbiturate sleeping pill **2** : a goofy person

go off *vb* **1** : EXPLODE **2** : to follow a course ⟨the party *went off* well⟩

goof–off \ˈgüf-ˌȯf\ *n* : one who evades work or responsibility

goofy \ˈgü-fē\ *adj* **goof·i·er; -est** : CRAZY, SILLY — **goof·i·ness** \-fē-nəs\ *n*

goon \ˈgün\ *n* : a man hired to terrorize or kill opponents

go on *vb* **1** : to continue in a course of action **2** : to take place : HAPPEN

goose \ˈgüs\ *n, pl* **geese** \ˈgēs\ **1** : any of numerous long-

necked web-footed birds related to the swans and ducks; *also* : a female goose as distinguished from a gander **2** : a foolish person **3** *pl* **goos·es** : a tailor's smoothing iron

goose·ber·ry \ˈgüs-ˌber-ē, ˈgüz-, -bə-rē\ *n* : the acid berry of any of several shrubs related to the currant and used esp. in jams and pies

goose bumps *n pl* : roughening of the skin caused usu. by cold, fear, or a sudden feeling of excitement

goose·flesh \-ˌflesh\ *n* : GOOSE BUMPS

goose pimples *n pl* : GOOSE BUMPS

go out *vb* **1** : to become extinguished **2** : to become a candidate ⟨*went out* for the football team⟩

go over *vb* : SUCCEED

GOP *abbr* Grand Old Party (Republican)

¹go·pher \ˈgō-fər\ *n* **1** : a burrowing American land tortoise **2** : any of a family of No. American burrowing rodents with large cheek pouches opening beside the mouth **3** : any of several small ground squirrels of the prairie region of No. America

gopher 2

²gopher *var of* GOFER

go·pik \gō-ˈpēk, -ˈpik\ *n, pl* **gopik** — see *manat* at MONEY table

¹gore \ˈgȯr\ *n* : a tapering or triangular piece (as of cloth in a skirt)

²gore *vb* **gored; gor·ing** : to pierce or wound with something pointed

³gore *n* **1** : BLOOD **2** : gruesomeness depicted in vivid detail

¹gorge \ˈgȯrj\ *n* **1** : THROAT **2** : a narrow ravine **3** : a mass of matter that chokes up a passage

²gorge *vb* **gorged; gorg·ing** : to eat greedily : stuff to capacity : GLUT

gor·geous \ˈgȯr-jəs\ *adj* : resplendently beautiful

Gor·gon·zo·la \ˌgȯr-gən-ˈzō-lə\ *n* : a pungent blue cheese of Italian origin

go·ril·la \gə-ˈri-lə\ *n* [NL, fr. Gk *Gorillai*, a tribe of hairy women in an account of a voyage around Africa] : an African anthropoid ape related to but much larger than the chimpanzee

gor·man·dise *chiefly Brit var of* GORMANDIZE

gor·man·dize \ˈgȯr-mən-ˌdīz\ *vb* -**dized; -diz·ing** : to eat ravenously — **gor·man·diz·er** *n*

gorp \ˈgȯrp\ *n* : a snack consisting of high-calorie food (as raisins and nuts)

gorse \ˈgȯrs\ *n* : a spiny yellow-flowered European evergreen shrub of the legume family

gory \ˈgȯr-ē\ *adj* **gor·i·er; -est** **1** : BLOODSTAINED **2** : HORRIBLE, SENSATIONAL

gos·hawk \ˈgäs-ˌhȯk\ *n* : any of several long-tailed hawks with short rounded wings

gos·ling \ˈgäz-liŋ, ˈgȯz-\ *n* : a young goose

¹gos·pel \ˈgäs-pəl\ *n* [ME, fr. OE *gōdspel*, fr. *gōd* good + *spell* message, news] **1** : the teachings of Christ and the apostles **2** *cap* : any of the first four books of the New Testament **3** : something accepted or promoted as infallible truth

²gospel *adj* **1** : of, relating to, or emphasizing the gospel **2** : relating to or being American religious songs associated with evangelism

gos·sa·mer \ˈgä-sə-mər\ *n* [ME *gossomer*, fr. *gos* goose + *somer* summer] **1** : a film of cobwebs floating in the air **2** : something light, delicate, or tenuous

¹gos·sip \ˈgä-səp\ *n* **1** : a person who habitually reveals personal or sensational facts **2** : rumor or report of an intimate nature **3** : an informal conversation — **gos·sipy** *adj*

²gossip *vb* : to spread gossip

got *past and past part of* GET

Goth \'gäth\ *n* : a member of a Germanic people that early in the Christian era overran the Roman Empire

¹**Goth·ic** \'gä-thik\ *adj* **1** : of or relating to the Goths **2** : of or relating to a style of architecture prevalent in western Europe from the middle 12th to the early 16th century

²**Gothic** *n* **1** : the Germanic language of the Goths **2** : the Gothic architectural style or decoration

gotten *past and past part of* GET

Gou·da \'gü-də\ *n* : a mild Dutch milk cheese shaped in balls

¹**gouge** \'gauj\ *n* **1** : a rounded troughlike chisel **2** : a hole or groove made with or as if with a gouge

²**gouge** *vb* **gouged; goug·ing** **1** : to cut holes or grooves in with or as if with a gouge **2** : DEFRAUD, CHEAT

gou·lash \'gü-,läsh, -,lash\ *n* [Hungarian *gulyás*] : a stew made with meat, assorted vegetables, and paprika

go under *vb* : to be overwhelmed, defeated, or destroyed : FAIL

gourd \'gord, 'gurd\ *n* **1** : any of a family of tendril-bearing vines including the cucumber, squash, and melon **2** : the fruit of a gourd; *esp* : any of various inedible hard-shelled fruits used esp. for ornament or implements

gourde \'gurd\ *n* — see MONEY table

gour·mand \'gur-,mänd\ *n* **1** : one who is excessively fond of eating and drinking **2** : GOURMET

gour·met \'gur-,mā, gur-'mā\ *n* [F, fr. MF, alter. of *gromet* boy servant, vintner's assistant] : a connoisseur of food and drink

gout \'gaut\ *n* : a metabolic disease marked by painful inflammation and swelling of the joints — **gouty** *adj*

gov *abbr* **1** government **2** governor **3** governmental institution — used in World Wide Web addresses

gov·ern \'gə-vərn\ *vb* [ME, fr. AF *governer*, fr. L *gubernare* to steer, govern, fr. Gk *kybernan*] **1** : to control and direct the making and administration of policy in : RULE **2** : CONTROL, DIRECT, INFLUENCE **3** : DETERMINE, REGULATE **4** : RESTRAIN — **gov·ern·able** \-vər-nə-bəl\ *adj* — **gov·er·nance** \-vər-nəns\ *n*

gov·ern·ess \'gə-vər-nəs\ *n* : a woman who teaches and trains a child esp. in a private home

gov·ern·ment \'gə-vərn-mənt\ *n* **1** : authoritative direction or control **2** : the making of policy **3** : the organization or agency through which a political unit exercises authority **4** : the complex of institutions, laws, and customs through which a political unit is governed **5** : the governing body — **gov·ern·men·tal** \,gə-vərn-'men-t³l\ *adj* — **gov·ern·men·tal·ly** \-t³l-ē\ *adv*

gov·er·nor \'gə-vər-nər\ *n* **1** : one that governs; *esp* : a ruler, chief executive, or head of a political unit (as a state) **2** : an attachment to a machine for automatic control of speed — **gov·er·nor·ship** *n*

govt *abbr* government

gown \'gaun\ *n* **1** : a loose flowing outer garment **2** : an official robe worn esp. by a judge, clergyman, or teacher **3** : a woman's dress ⟨evening ~s⟩ **4** : a loose robe — **gown** *vb*

gp *abbr* group

GP *abbr* general practitioner

GPO *abbr* **1** general post office **2** Government Printing Office

GPS \,jē-,pē-'es\ *n* [*G*lobal *P*ositioning *S*ystem] : a navigation system that uses satellite signals to fix location; *also* : the signal receiver itself

GQ *abbr* general quarters

gr *abbr* **1** grade **2** grain **3** gram **4** gravity **5** gross

grab \'grab\ *vb* **grabbed; grab·bing** : to take hastily : SNATCH — **grab** *n*

¹**grace** \'grās\ *n* **1** : unmerited help given to people by God (as in overcoming temptation) **2** : freedom from sin through divine grace **3** : a virtue coming from God **4** — used as a title for a duke, a duchess, or an archbishop **5** : a short prayer at a meal **6** : a temporary respite (as from the payment of a debt) **7** : APPROVAL, ACCEPTANCE ⟨in his good ~s⟩ **8** : CHARM **9** : ATTRACTIVENESS, BEAUTY **10** : fitness or proportion of line or expression **11** : ease of movement **12** : a musical trill or ornament — **grace·ful** \-fəl\ *adj* — **grace·ful·ly** *adv* — **grace·ful·ness** *n* — **grace·less** *adj*

²**grace** *vb* **graced; grac·ing** **1** : HONOR **2** : ADORN, EMBELLISH

gra·cious \'grā-shəs\ *adj* **1** : marked by kindness and courtesy ⟨a ~ host⟩ **2** : GRACEFUL **3** : characterized by charm and good taste **4** : MERCIFUL — **gra·cious·ly** *adv* — **gra·cious·ness** *n*

grack·le \'gra-kəl\ *n* : any of several large American blackbirds with glossy iridescent plumage

grad *abbr* graduate; graduated

gra·da·tion \grā-'dā-shən, grə-\ *n* **1** : a series forming successive stages **2** : a step, degree, or stage in a series **3** : an advance by regular degrees **4** : the act or process of grading

¹**grade** \'grād\ *n* [L *gradus* step, degree, fr. *gradi* to step, go] **1** : a position in a scale of rank, quality, or order **2** : a stage in a process or ranking **3** : a division of the school course representing one year's work; *also* : the pupils in such a division **4** : a class of persons or things of the same rank or quality **5** : a mark or rating esp. of accomplishment in school **6** : the degree of slope (as of a road); *also* : SLOPE **7** *pl* : the elementary school system

²**grade** *vb* **grad·ed; grad·ing** **1** : to arrange in grades : SORT **2** : to make level or evenly sloping ⟨a ~ highway⟩ **3** : to give a grade to ⟨~ a pupil in history⟩ **4** : to assign to a grade

grade inflation *n* : the assigning of grades higher than previously assigned for given levels of achievement

grad·er \'grā-dər\ *n* **1** : a machine for leveling earth **2** : a pupil in a school grade

grade school *n* : ELEMENTARY SCHOOL

gra·di·ent \'grā-dē-ənt\ *n* : SLOPE, GRADE

grad·u·al \'gra-jə-wəl\ *adj* : proceeding or changing by steps or degrees — **grad·u·al·ly** *adv*

grad·u·al·ism \-wə-,li-zəm\ *n* : the policy of approaching a desired end gradually

¹**grad·u·ate** \'gra-jə-wət\ *n* **1** : a holder of an academic degree or diploma **2** : a graduated container for measuring contents

²**graduate** *adj* **1** : holding an academic degree or diploma **2** : of or relating to studies beyond the first or bachelor's degree ⟨~ school⟩

³**grad·u·ate** \'gra-jə-,wāt\ *vb* **-at·ed; -at·ing** **1** : to grant or receive an academic degree or diploma **2** : to divide into grades, classes, or intervals **3** : to admit to a particular standing or grade

grad·u·a·tion \,gra-jə-'wā-shən\ *n* **1** : a mark that graduates something **2** : an act or process of graduating **3** : COMMENCEMENT 2

graf·fi·ti \grə-'fē-(,)tē\ *n* : unauthorized writing or drawing on a public surface

graf·fi·to \gra-'fē-tō, grə-\ *n, pl* **-ti** \-(,)tē\ : an inscription or drawing made on a public surface (as a wall)

¹**graft** \'graft\ *n* **1** : a grafted plant; *also* : the point of union in this **2** : material (as skin) used in grafting **3** : the getting of money or advantage dishonestly; *also* : the money or advantage so gained

²**graft** *vb* **1** : to insert a shoot from one plant into another so that they join and grow; *also* : to join one thing to another as in plant grafting ⟨~ skin over a burn⟩ **2** : to get (as money) dishonestly — **graft·er** *n*

gra·ham cracker \'grā-əm-, 'gram-\ *n* : a slightly sweet cracker made chiefly of whole wheat flour

Grail \'grāl\ *n* **1** : the cup or platter used according to medieval legend by Christ at the Last Supper and thereafter the object of knightly quests **2** *not cap* : the object of an extended or difficult quest

grain \'grān\ *n* **1** : a seed or fruit of a cereal grass **2** : seeds or fruits of various food plants and esp. cereal grasses; *also* : a plant (as wheat) producing grain **3** : a small hard particle **4** : a unit of weight based on the weight of a grain of wheat — see WEIGHT table **5** : TEXTURE; *also* : the arrangement of fibers in wood **6** : natural disposition ⟨lying goes against my ~⟩ — **grained** \'grānd\ *adj*

grain alcohol *n* : ALCOHOL 1

grainy \'grā-nē\ *adj* **grain·i·er; -est** **1** : resembling or having some characteristic of grain : not smooth or fine **2** *of a photograph* : appearing to be composed of grain-like particles

¹**gram** \'gram\ *n* [F *gramme*, fr. LL *gramma*, a small weight, fr. Gk *gramma* letter, writing, a small weight, fr. *graphein* to write] : a metric unit of mass and weight equal to $^1/_{1000}$ kilogram — see METRIC SYSTEM table

²gram *abbr* grammar; grammatical

-gram \ˌgram\ *n comb form* : drawing : writing : record ⟨tele*gram*⟩

gram·mar \ˈgra-mər\ *n* **1** : the study of the classes of words, their inflections, and their functions and relations in the sentence **2** : a study of what is to be preferred and what avoided in inflection and syntax **3** : speech or writing evaluated according to its conformity to grammatical rules — **gram·mar·i·an** \grə-ˈmer-ē-ən, -ˈmar-\ *n* — **gram·mat·i·cal** \-ˈma-ti-kəl\ *adj* — **gram·mat·i·cal·ly** \-k(ə-)lē\ *adv*

grammar school *n* **1** : a secondary school emphasizing Latin and Greek in preparation for college; *also* : a British college preparatory school **2** : a school intermediate between the primary grades and high school **3** : ELEMENTARY SCHOOL

gramme \ˈgram\ *chiefly Brit var of* GRAM

gram·o·phone \ˈgra-mə-ˌfōn\ *n* : PHONOGRAPH

gra·na·ry \ˈgrā-nə-rē, ˈgra-\ *n, pl* **-ries** **1** : a storehouse for grain **2** : a region producing grain in abundance

¹grand \ˈgrand\ *adj* **1** : higher in rank or importance : FOREMOST, CHIEF **2** : great in size **3** : INCLUSIVE, COMPLETE ⟨a ~ total⟩ **4** : MAGNIFICENT, SPLENDID **5** : showing wealth or high social standing **6** : IMPRESSIVE, STATELY **7** : very good : FINE ⟨had a ~ time⟩ — **grand·ly** *adv* — **grand·ness** *n*

²grand *n pl* **grand** *slang* : a thousand dollars

gran·dam \ˈgran-ˌdam, -dəm\ *or* **gran·dame** \-ˌdām, -dəm\ *n* : an old woman

grand·child \ˈgrand-ˌchī(-ə)ld\ *n* : a child of one's son or daughter

grand·daugh·ter \ˈgran-ˌdȯ-tər\ *n* : a daughter of one's son or daughter

grande dame \ˈgrän-ˈdäm\ *n, pl* **grandes dames** : a usu. elderly woman of great prestige or ability

gran·dee \gran-ˈdē\ *n* : a high-ranking Spanish or Portuguese nobleman

gran·deur \ˈgran-jər\ *n* **1** : the quality or state of being grand : MAGNIFICENCE **2** : something that is grand

grand·fa·ther \ˈgrand-ˌfä-thər\ *n* : the father of one's father or mother; *also* : ANCESTOR

grandfather clock *n* : a tall clock that stands on the floor

gran·dil·o·quence \gran-ˈdi-lə-kwəns\ *n* : pompous eloquence — **gran·dil·o·quent** \-kwənt\ *adj*

gran·di·ose \ˈgran-dē-ˌōs, ˌgran-dē-ˈōs\ *adj* : IMPRESSIVE, IMPOSING; *also* : affectedly splendid — **gran·di·ose·ly** *adv* — **gran·di·os·i·ty** \ˌgran-dē-ˈä-sə-tē\ *n*

grand jury *n* : a jury that examines accusations of crime against persons and makes formal charges on which the persons are later tried

grand mal \ˈgrän-ˌmäl, ˈgrand-ˌmal\ *n* [F, lit., great illness] : severe epilepsy

grand·moth·er \ˈgrand-ˌmə-thər\ *n* : the mother of one's father or mother; *also* : a female ancestor

grand·par·ent \-ˌper-ənt\ *n* : a parent of one's father or mother

grand piano *n* : a piano with horizontal frame and strings

grand prix \ˈgräⁿ-ˈprē\ *n, pl* **grand prix** *same or* -ˈprēz\ *often cap* G&P : a long-distance auto race over a road course; *also* : a high-level competition in another sport (as sailing)

grand slam *n* **1** : a total victory or success **2** : a home run hit with three runners on base

grand·son \ˈgrand-ˌsən\ *n* : a son of one's son or daughter

grand·stand \-ˌstand\ *n* : a usu. roofed stand for spectators at a racecourse or stadium

grange \ˈgrānj\ *n* **1** : a farm or farmhouse with its various buildings **2** *cap* : one of the lodges of a national association originally made up of farmers; *also* : the association itself — **Grang·er** \ˈgrān-jər\ *n*

gran·ite \ˈgra-nət\ *n* : a hard granular igneous rock used esp. for building — **gra·nit·ic** \grə-ˈni-tik\ *adj*

gran·ite·ware \ˈgra-nət-ˌwer\ *n* : ironware with mottled enamel

gra·no·la \grə-ˈnō-lə\ *n* : a cereal made of rolled oats and usu. raisins and nuts

¹grant \ˈgrant\ *vb* **1** : to consent to : ALLOW, PERMIT **2** : GIVE, BESTOW ⟨~ed land to settlers⟩ **3** : to admit as true — **grant·er** *n* — **grant·or** \ˈgran-tər, -ˌtȯr\ *n*

²grant *n* **1** : the act of granting **2** : something granted; *esp* : a gift for a particular purpose ⟨a ~ for study abroad⟩

3 : a transfer of property by deed or writing; *also* : the instrument by which such a transfer is made **4** : the property transferred by grant — **grant·ee** \gran-ˈtē\ *n*

gran·u·lar \ˈgra-nyə-lər\ *adj* : consisting of or appearing to consist of granules — **gran·u·lar·i·ty** \ˌgra-nyə-ˈlar-ə-tē\ *n*

gran·u·late \ˈgra-nyə-ˌlāt\ *vb* **-lat·ed; -lat·ing** : to form into grains or crystals — **gran·u·la·tion** \ˌgra-nyə-ˈlā-shən\ *n*

gran·ule \ˈgra-nyül\ *n* : a small grain or particle

grape \ˈgrāp\ *n* [ME, fr. AF, grape stalk, bunch of grapes, grape, of Gmc origin] **1** : a smooth-skinned juicy edible greenish white, deep red, or purple berry that is the chief source of wine **2** : any of numerous woody vines widely grown for their bunches of grapes

grape·fruit \ˈgrāp-ˌfrüt\ *n* **1** *pl* **grapefruit** *or* **grapefruits** : a large edible yellow-skinned citrus fruit **2** : a tree bearing grapefruit

grape hyacinth *n* : any of several small bulbous herbs related to the lilies that produce clusters of usu. blue flowers in the spring

grape·shot \ˈgrāp-ˌshät\ *n* : a cluster of small iron balls formerly fired at people from short range by a cannon

grape·vine \-ˌvīn\ *n* **1** : GRAPE 2 **2** : RUMOR; *also* : an informal means of circulating information or gossip

graph \ˈgraf\ *n* : a diagram that usu. by means of dots and lines shows change in one variable factor in comparison with one or more other factors — **graph** *vb*

-graph \ˌgraf\ *n comb form* **1** : something written ⟨auto*graph*⟩ **2** : instrument for making or transmitting records ⟨seismo*graph*⟩

¹graph·ic \ˈgra-fik\ *also* **graph·i·cal** \-fi-kəl\ *adj* **1** : of or relating to the arts (**graphic arts**) of representation, decoration, and printing on flat surfaces **2** : being written, drawn, or engraved **3** : vividly described — **graph·i·cal·ly** \-fi-k(ə-)lē\ *adv*

²graphic *n* **1** : a picture, map, or graph used for illustration **2** : a pictorial image displayed on a computer screen

graphical user interface *n* : a computer program designed to allow easy user interaction esp. by having graphic menus or icons

graph·ics tablet \-fiks-\ *n* : a computer input device for entering pictorial information by drawing or tracing

graph·ite \ˈgra-ˌfīt\ *n* [G *Graphit*, fr. Gk *graphein* to write] : a soft black form of carbon used esp. for lead pencils and lubricants

grap·nel \ˈgrap-nəl\ *n* : a small anchor used esp. to recover a sunken object or to anchor a small boat

¹grap·ple \ˈgra-pəl\ *n* : the act of grappling

²grapple *vb* **grap·pled; grap·pling** **1** : to seize or hold with or as if with a hooked implement **2** : to come to grips with : WRESTLE

¹grasp \ˈgrasp\ *vb* **1** : to make the motion of seizing **2** : to take or seize firmly **3** : to enclose and hold with the fingers or arms **4** : COMPREHEND

²grasp *n* **1** : HANDLE **2** : EMBRACE **3** : HOLD, CONTROL **4** : the reach of the arms **5** : the power of seizing and holding or attaining **6** : COMPREHENSION

grasp·ing *adj* : GREEDY, AVARICIOUS

grass \ˈgras\ *n* **1** : herbage for grazing animals **2** : any of a large family of plants (as wheat, bamboo, or sugarcane) with jointed stems and narrow leaves **3** : grass-covered land **4** : MARIJUANA — **grass·like** \-ˌlīk\ *adj* — **grassy** *adj*

grass·hop·per \-ˌhä-pər\ *n* : any of numerous leaping plant-eating insects

grass·land \-ˌland\ *n* : land covered naturally or under cultivation with grasses and low-growing herbs

grass roots *n pl* : society at the local level as distinguished from the centers of political leadership

¹grate \ˈgrāt\ *vb* **grat·ed; grat·ing** **1** : to pulverize by rubbing against something rough **2** : to grind or rub against with a rasping noise **3** : IRRITATE — **grat·er** *n* — **grat·ing·ly** *adv*

²grate *n* **1** : GRATING **2** : a frame of iron bars for holding fuel while it burns

grate·ful \ˈgrāt-fəl\ *adj* **1** : THANKFUL, APPRECIATIVE; *also* : expressing gratitude **2** : PLEASING — **grate·ful·ly** *adv* — **grate·ful·ness** *n*

grat·i·fy \ˈgra-tə-ˌfī\ *vb* **-fied; -fy·ing** : to afford pleasure to — **grat·i·fi·ca·tion** \ˌgra-tə-fə-ˈkā-shən\ *n*

grat·ing \ˈgrā-tiŋ\ *n* : a framework with parallel bars or crossbars

gra·tis \'gra-təs, 'grā-\ *adv or adj* : without charge or recompense : FREE

grat·i·tude \'gra-tə-ˌtüd, -ˌtyüd\ *n* : THANKFULNESS

gra·tu·itous \grə-'tü-ə-təs, -'tyü-\ *adj* **1** : done or provided without recompense : FREE **2** : UNWARRANTED ⟨a ∼ assumption⟩

gra·tu·ity \-ə-tē\ *n, pl* **-ities** : [10]TIP

gra·va·men \grə-'vā-mən\ *n, pl* **-va·mens** *or* **-vam·i·na** \-'va-mə-nə\ [LL, burden] : the basic or significant part of a grievance or complaint

¹grave \'grāv\ *vb* **graved; grav·en** \'grā-vən\ *or* **graved; grav·ing** : SCULPTURE, ENGRAVE

²grave *n* : an excavation in the earth as a place of burial; *also* : TOMB

³grave \'grāv; 5 *also* 'gräv\ *adj* **1** : IMPORTANT **2** : threatening great harm or danger **3** : DIGNIFIED, SOLEMN **4** : drab in color : SOMBER **5** : of, marked by, or being an accent mark having the form ` — **grave·ly** *adv* — **grave·ness** *n*

grav·el \'gra-vəl\ *n* : pebbles and small pieces of rock larger than grains of sand — **grav·el·ly** *adj*

Graves' disease \'grāvz-\ *n* : hyperthyroidism characterized by goiter and often protrusion of the eyeballs

grave·stone \'grāv-ˌstōn\ *n* : a burial monument

grave·yard \-ˌyärd\ *n* : CEMETERY

grav·id \'gra-vəd\ *adj* [L *gravidus*, fr. *gravis* heavy] : PREGNANT

gra·vi·me·ter \gra-'vi-mə-tər, 'gra-və-ˌmē-\ *n* : a device for measuring variations in a gravitational field

grav·i·tate \'gra-və-ˌtāt\ *vb* **-tat·ed; -tat·ing** : to move or tend to move toward something

grav·i·ta·tion \ˌgra-və-'tā-shən\ *n* **1** : a natural force of attraction that tends to draw bodies together and that occurs because of the mass of the bodies **2** : the action or process of gravitating — **grav·i·ta·tion·al** \-shə-nəl\ *adj* — **grav·i·ta·tion·al·ly** *adv*

grav·i·ty \'gra-və-tē\ *n, pl* **-ties** **1** : IMPORTANCE; *esp* : SERIOUSNESS **2** : [2]MASS 5 **3** : the gravitational attraction of the mass of a celestial object (as earth) for bodies close to it; *also* : GRAVITATION 1

gra·vure \grə-'vyùr\ *n* [F] : PHOTOGRAVURE

gra·vy \'grā-vē\ *n, pl* **gravies** **1** : a sauce made from the thickened and seasoned juices of cooked meat **2** : unearned or illicit gain : GRAFT

¹gray *also* **grey** \'grā\ *adj* **1** : of the color gray; *also* : dull in color **2** : having gray hair **3** : CHEERLESS, DISMAL ⟨a ∼ day⟩ **4** : intermediate in position or character ⟨an ethically ∼ area⟩ — **gray·ish** *adj* — **gray·ness** *n*

²gray *also* **grey** *n* **1** : something of a gray color **2** : a neutral color ranging between black and white

³gray *also* **grey** *vb* : to make or become gray

gray·beard \'grā-ˌbird\ *n* : an old man

gray·ling \'grā-liŋ\ *n, pl* **grayling** *also* **graylings** : any of several slender freshwater food and sport fishes related to the trouts

gray matter *n* **1** : the grayish part of nervous tissue consisting mostly of the cell bodies of neurons **2** : INTELLIGENCE

gray wolf *n* : a large wolf of northern No. America and Asia that is usu. gray

gray wolf

¹graze \'grāz\ *vb* **grazed; graz·ing** [ME *grasen*, fr. OE *grasian*, fr. *græs* grass] **1** : to feed on herbage or pasture **2** : to feed (livestock) on grass or pasture — **graz·er** *n*

²graze *vb* **grazed; graz·ing** **1** : to touch lightly in passing **2** : SCRATCH, ABRADE

¹grease \'grēs\ *n* **1** : rendered animal fat **2** : oily material **3** : a thick lubricant — **greasy** \'grē-sē, -zē\ *adj*

²grease \'grēs, 'grēz\ *vb* **greased; greas·ing** : to smear or lubricate with grease

grease·paint \'grēs-ˌpānt\ *n* : theater makeup

great \'grāt\ *adj* **1** : large in size : BIG **2** : ELABORATE, AMPLE ⟨in ∼ detail⟩ **3** : large in number : NUMEROUS **4** : being beyond the average : MIGHTY, INTENSE ⟨a ∼ weight⟩ ⟨in ∼ pain⟩ **5** : EMINENT, GRAND **6** : long continued ⟨a ∼ while⟩ **7** : MAIN, PRINCIPAL ⟨a reception in the ∼ hall⟩ **8** : more distant in a family relationship by one generation ⟨a *great*-grandfather⟩ **9** : markedly superior in character, quality, or skill ⟨∼ at bridge⟩ **10** : EXCELLENT, FINE ⟨had a ∼ time⟩ — **great·ly** *adv* — **great·ness** *n*

great ape *n* : any of a family of primates including the gorilla, orangutan, and chimpanzees

great blue heron *n* : a large crested grayish blue American heron

great circle *n* : a circle on the surface of a sphere that has the same center as the sphere; *esp* : one on the surface of the earth an arc of which is the shortest travel distance between two points

great·coat \'grāt-ˌkōt\ *n* : a heavy overcoat

Great Dane *n* : any of a breed of very tall powerful smooth-coated dogs

great·heart·ed \'grāt-'här-təd\ *adj* **1** : COURAGEOUS **2** : MAGNANIMOUS

great power *n, often cap G&P* : one of the nations that figure most decisively in international affairs

great white shark *n* : a large and dangerous shark of warm seas that has large saw-edged teeth and is whitish below and bluish or brownish above

grebe \'grēb\ *n* : any of a family of lobe-toed diving birds related to the loons

Gre·cian \'grē-shən\ *adj* : GREEK

greed \'grēd\ *n* : acquisitive or selfish desire beyond reason — **greed·i·ly** \'grē-də-lē\ *adv* — **greed·i·ness** \-dē-nəs\ *n* — **greedy** \'grē-dē\ *adj*

¹Greek \'grēk\ *n* **1** : a native or inhabitant of Greece **2** : the ancient or modern language of Greece

²Greek *adj* **1** : of, relating to, or characteristic of Greece, the Greeks, or Greek **2** : ORTHODOX 3

¹green \'grēn\ *adj* **1** : of the color green **2** : covered with verdure; *also* : consisting of green plants or of the leafy parts of plants ⟨a ∼ salad⟩ **3** : UNRIPE; *also* : IMMATURE **4** : having a sickly appearance **5** : not fully processed or treated ⟨∼ liquor⟩ ⟨∼ hides⟩ **6** : INEXPERIENCED; *also* : NAIVE **7** : concerned with or supporting environmentalism — **green·ish** *adj* — **green·ness** *n*

²green *vb* : to make or become green

³green *n* **1** : a color between blue and yellow in the spectrum : the color of growing fresh grass or of the emerald **2** : something of a green color **3** : green vegetation; *esp, pl* : leafy herbs or leafy parts of a vegetable ⟨collard ∼s⟩ ⟨beet ∼s⟩ **4** : a grassy plot; *esp* : a smooth grassy area around the hole into which the ball must be played in golf

green·back \'grēn-ˌbak\ *n* : a U.S. legal-tender note

green bean *n* : a kidney bean that is used as a snap bean when the pods are colored green

green·belt \'grēn-ˌbelt\ *n* : a belt of parks or farmlands around a community

green card *n* : an identity card attesting the permanent resident status of an alien in the U.S.

green·ery \'grē-nə-rē\ *n, pl* **-er·ies** : green foliage or plants

green–eyed \'grē-ˌnīd\ *adj* : JEALOUS

green·gro·cer \'grēn-ˌgrō-sər\ *n, chiefly Brit* : a retailer of fresh vegetables and fruit

green·horn \-ˌhȯrn\ *n* : an inexperienced person; *also* : NEWCOMER

green·house \-ˌhaüs\ *n* : a glass structure for the growing of tender plants

greenhouse effect *n* : warming of a planet's atmosphere that occurs when the sun's radiation passes through the atmosphere, is absorbed by the planet, and is reradiated as radiation of longer wavelength that can be absorbed by atmospheric gases

green manure *n* : an herbaceous crop (as clover) plowed under when green to enrich the soil

green onion *n* : a young onion pulled before the bulb has enlarged and used esp. in salads; *also* : SCALLION

green pepper *n* : a sweet pepper before it turns red at maturity

green·room \'grēn-ˌrüm, -ˌrùm\ *n* : a room (as in a theater or studio) where performers can relax before, between, or after appearances

green·sward \-ˌswȯrd\ *n* : turf that is green with growing grass

green thumb *n* : an unusual ability to make plants grow

green·wash·ing \'grēn-ˌwȯ-shiŋ, -ˌwä-\ *n* : expressions of environmentalist concerns as a cover for products, policies, or activities deleterious to the environment

Green·wich mean time \'gri-nij-, 'gre-, -nich-\ *n* [*Greenwich*, England] : the time of the meridian of Greenwich used historically as the basis of worldwide standard time

Greenwich time *n* : GREENWICH MEAN TIME

green·wood \'grēn-ˌwùd\ *n* : a forest that is green with foliage

greet \'grēt\ *vb* **1** : to address with expressions of kind wishes **2** : to meet or react to in a specified manner **3** : to be perceived by — **greet·er** *n*

greet·ing *n* **1** : a salutation on meeting **2** *pl* : best wishes : REGARDS

greeting card *n* : a card that bears a message usu. sent on a special occasion

gre·gar·i·ous \gri-'ger-ē-əs\ *adj* [L *gregarius* of a flock or herd, fr. *greg-, grex* flock, herd] **1** : SOCIAL, COMPANIONABLE **2** : tending to flock together — **gre·gar·i·ous·ly** *adv* — **gre·gar·i·ous·ness** *n*

grem·lin \'grem-lən\ *n* : a cause of error or equipment malfunction conceived of as a small gnome

gre·nade \grə-'nād\ *n* [MF, lit., pomegranate, fr. LL *granata*, fr. L, fem. of *granatus* seedy, fr. *granum* grain] : a small bomb that is thrown by hand or launched (as by a rifle)

gren·a·dier \ˌgre-nə-'dir\ *n* : a member of a European regiment formerly armed with grenades

gren·a·dine \ˌgre-nə-'dēn, 'gre-nə-ˌdēn\ *n* : a syrup flavored with pomegranates and used in mixed drinks

grew *past of* GROW

grey *var of* GRAY

grey·hound \'grā-ˌhaùnd\ *n* : any of a breed of tall slender dogs noted for speed and keen sight

grid \'grid\ *n* **1** : GRATING **2** : a network of conductors for distributing electric power **3** : a network of horizontal and perpendicular lines (as for locating points on a map) **4** : GRIDIRON 2; *also* : FOOTBALL

grid·dle \'gri-dᵊl\ *n* : a flat usu. metal surface for cooking food

griddle cake *n* : PANCAKE

grid·iron \'grid-ˌī(-ə)rn\ *n* **1** : a grate for broiling food **2** : a football field

grid·lock \-ˌläk\ *n* : a traffic jam in which an intersection is so blocked that vehicles cannot move

grief \'grēf\ *n* **1** : emotional distress caused by or as if by bereavement; *also* : a cause of such distress **2** : DISASTER; *also* : MISHAP

griev·ance \'grē-vəns\ *n* **1** : a cause of distress affording reason for complaint or resistance **2** : COMPLAINT

grieve \'grēv\ *vb* **grieved; griev·ing** [ME *greven*, fr. AF *grever*, fr. L *gravare* to burden, fr. *gravis* heavy, grave] **1** : to cause grief or sorrow to : DISTRESS **2** : to feel grief : SORROW

griev·ous \'grē-vəs\ *adj* **1** : causing suffering, grief, or sorrow : SEVERE ⟨a ~ wound⟩ **2** : OPPRESSIVE, ONEROUS ⟨~ costs of war⟩ **3** : SERIOUS, GRAVE — **griev·ous·ly** *adv*

¹grill \'gril\ *vb* **1** : to broil on a grill; *also* : to fry or toast on a griddle **2** : to question intensely

²grill *n* **1** : a cooking utensil of parallel bars on which food is grilled **2** : a usu. informal restaurant

grille *or* **grill** \'gril\ *n* : a grating that forms a barrier or screen

grill·work \'gril-ˌwərk\ *n* : work constituting or resembling a grille

grim \'grim\ *adj* **grim·mer; grim·mest** **1** : CRUEL, FIERCE **2** : harsh and forbidding in appearance **3** : ghastly or repellent in character **4** : RELENTLESS — **grim·ly** *adv* — **grim·ness** *n*

gri·mace \'gri-məs, gri-'mās\ *n* : a facial expression usu. of disgust or disapproval — **grimace** *vb*

grime \'grīm\ *n* : soot, smut, or dirt adhering to or embedded in a surface; *also* : accumulated dirtiness and disorder — **grimy** *adj*

grin \'grin\ *vb* **grinned; grin·ning** : to draw back the lips so as to show the teeth esp. in amusement — **grin** *n*

¹grind \'grīnd\ *vb* **ground** \'graùnd\; **grind·ing** **1** : to reduce to small particles **2** : to wear down, polish, or sharpen by friction **3** : OPPRESS **4** : to press with a grating noise : GRIT ⟨~ the teeth⟩ **5** : to operate or produce by turning a crank **6** : DRUDGE; *esp* : to study hard **7** : to move with difficulty or friction ⟨gears ~*ing*⟩

²grind *n* **1** : dreary monotonous labor, routine, or study **2** : one who works or studies excessively

grind·er \'grīn-dər\ *n* **1** : MOLAR **2** *pl* : TEETH **3** : one that grinds **4** : SUBMARINE 2 **5** : an athlete who succeeds through hard work and determination

grind·stone \'grīnd-ˌstōn\ *n* : a flat circular stone of natural sandstone that revolves on an axle and is used for grinding, shaping, or smoothing

¹grip \'grip\ *vb* **gripped; grip·ping** **1** : to seize or hold firmly **2** : to hold the interest of strongly

²grip *n* **1** : GRASP; *also* : strength in gripping **2** : a firm tenacious hold **3** : UNDERSTANDING **4** : a device for gripping **5** : TRAVELING BAG

gripe \'grīp\ *vb* **griped; grip·ing** **1** : IRRITATE, VEX **2** : to cause or experience spasmodic pains in the bowels **3** : COMPLAIN — **gripe** *n*

grippe \'grip\ *n* : INFLUENZA

gris-gris \'grē-ˌgrē\ *n, pl* **gris-gris** \-ˌgrēz\ [F] : an amulet or incantation used chiefly by people of black African ancestry

gris·ly \'griz-lē\ *adj* **gris·li·er; -est** : HORRIBLE, GRUESOME

grist \'grist\ *n* : grain to be ground or already ground

gris·tle \'gri-səl\ *n* : CARTILAGE — **gris·tly** \'gris-lē\ *adj*

grist·mill \'grist-ˌmil\ *n* : a mill for grinding grain

¹grit \'grit\ *n* **1** : a hard sharp granule (as of sand); *also* : material composed of such granules **2** : unyielding courage — **grit·ty** *adj*

²grit *vb* **grit·ted; grit·ting** : GRIND, GRATE

grits \'grits\ *n pl* : coarsely ground hulled grain ⟨hominy ~⟩

griz·zled \'gri-zəld\ *adj* : streaked or mixed with gray; *also* : having gray hair

griz·zly \'griz-lē\ *adj* **griz·zli·er; -est** : GRIZZLED

grizzly bear *n* : a large powerful brownish bear of western No. America

gro *abbr* gross

groan \'grōn\ *vb* **1** : MOAN **2** : to make a harsh sound under sudden or prolonged strain ⟨the chair ~ed under his weight⟩ — **groan** *n*

groat \'grōt\ *n* : an old British coin worth four pennies

gro·cer \'grō-sər\ *n* [ME, fr. AF *groser* wholesaler, fr. *gros* coarse, wholesale, fr. L *grossus* coarse] : a dealer esp. in staple foodstuffs — **gro·cery** \'grōs-rē, 'grōsh-, 'grō-sə-\ *n*

grog \'gräg\ *n* [*Old Grog*, nickname of Edward Vernon †1757 Eng. admiral responsible for diluting the sailors' rum] : alcoholic liquor; *esp* : liquor (as rum) mixed with water

grog·gy \'grä-gē\ *adj* **grog·gi·er; -est** : weak and unsteady on the feet or in action — **grog·gi·ly** \-gə-lē\ *adv* — **grog·gi·ness** \-gē-nəs\ *n*

groin \'grȯin\ *n* **1** : the juncture of the lower abdomen and inner part of the thigh; *also* : the region of this juncture **2** : the curved line or rib on a ceiling along which two vaults meet

grok \'gräk\ *vb* **grokked grok·king** : to understand profoundly and intuitively

grom·met \'grä-mət, 'grə-\ *n* **1** : a ring of rope **2** : an eyelet of firm material to strengthen or protect an opening

¹groom \'grüm, 'grùm\ *n* **1** : a person responsible for the care of horses **2** : BRIDEGROOM

²groom *vb* **1** : to clean and care for (an animal) **2** : to make neat or attractive **3** : PREPARE

grooms·man \'grümz-mən, 'grùmz-\ *n* : a male friend who attends a bridegroom at his wedding

groove \'grüv\ *n* **1** : a long narrow channel **2** : a fixed routine — **groove** *vb*

groovy \'grü-vē\ *adj* **groov·i·er; -est** **1** : EXCELLENT **2** : HIP

grope \'grōp\ *vb* **groped; grop·ing** **1** : to feel about or search for blindly or uncertainly ⟨~ for the right word⟩ **2** : to feel one's way by groping

gros·beak \'grōs-ˌbēk\ *n* : any of several finches of Europe or America with large stout conical bills

gro·schen \'grō-shən\ *n, pl* **groschen** : a former Austrian monetary unit equal to $^1/_{100}$ schilling

gros·grain \'grō-ˌgrān\ *n* [F *gros grain* coarse texture] : a silk or rayon fabric with crosswise cotton ribs

¹**gross** \'grōs\ *adj* 1 : glaringly noticeable 2 : OUT-AND-OUT, UTTER 3 : BIG, BULKY; *esp* : excessively fat 4 : GENERAL, BROAD 5 : consisting of an overall total exclusive of deductions ⟨∼ earnings⟩ 6 : CARNAL, EARTHY ⟨∼ pleasures⟩ 7 : UNREFINED; *also* : crudely vulgar 8 : lacking knowledge — **gross·ly** *adv* — **gross·ness** *n*

²**gross** *n* : an overall total exclusive of deductions — **gross** *vb*

³**gross** *n, pl* **gross** : a total of 12 dozen things ⟨a ∼ of pencils⟩

gross domestic product *n* : the gross national product excluding the value of net income earned abroad

gross national product *n* : the total value of the goods and services produced in a nation during a year

gro·szy \'grò-shē\ *n, pl* **groszy** — see *zloty* at MONEY table

grot \'grät\ *n* : GROTTO

gro·tesque \grō-'tesk\ *adj* 1 : FANCIFUL, BIZARRE 2 : absurdly incongruous 3 : ECCENTRIC — **gro·tesque·ly** *adv*

grot·to \'grä-tō\ *n, pl* **grottoes** *also* **grottos** 1 : CAVE 2 : an artificial cavelike structure

grouch \'graùch\ *n* 1 : a fit of bad temper 2 : a habitually irritable or complaining person — **grouch** *vb* — **grouchy** *adj*

¹**ground** \'graùnd\ *n* 1 : the bottom of a body of water 2 *pl* : sediment at the bottom of a liquid 3 : a basis for belief, action, or argument 4 : BACKGROUND 5 : the surface of the earth; *also* : SOIL 6 : an area with a particular use ⟨fishing ∼s⟩ 7 *pl* : the area about and belonging to a building 8 : a conductor that makes electrical connection with the earth — **ground·less** *adj*

²**ground** *vb* 1 : to bring to or place on the ground 2 : to run or cause to run aground 3 : to provide a reason or justification for 4 : to furnish with a foundation of knowledge 5 : to connect electrically with a ground 6 : to restrict to the ground; *also* : prohibit from some activity

³**ground** *past and past part of* GRIND

ground ball *n* : a batted baseball that rolls or bounces along the ground

ground cover *n* : low plants that grow over and cover the soil; *also* : a plant suitable for use as ground cover

ground·ed \'graùn-dəd\ *adj* : mentally and emotionally stable

ground·er \'graùn-dər\ *n* : GROUND BALL

ground·hog \'graùnd-ˌhóg, -ˌhäg\ *n* : WOODCHUCK

ground·ling \'graùnd-liŋ\ *n* : a spectator in the pit of an Elizabethan theater

ground rule *n* 1 : a sports rule adopted to modify play on a particular field, court, or course 2 : a rule of procedure

ground squirrel *n* : any of various burrowing squirrels of No. America and Eurasia that often live in colonies in open areas

ground swell *n* 1 : a broad deep ocean swell caused by an often distant gale or earthquake 2 *usu* **ground·swell** : a rapid spontaneous growth (as of political opinion)

ground·wa·ter \'graùnd-ˌwò-tər, -ˌwä-\ *n* : water within the earth that supplies wells and springs

ground·work \-ˌwərk\ *n* : FOUNDATION, BASIS

ground zero *n* 1 : the point above, below, or at which a nuclear explosion occurs 2 : the center or origin of rapid, intense, or violent activity

¹**group** \'grüp\ *n* 1 : a number of individuals related by a common factor (as physical association, community of interests, or blood) 2 : a combination of atoms commonly found together in a molecule ⟨a methyl ∼⟩

²**group** *vb* : to associate in groups : CLUSTER, AGGREGATE

grou·per \'grü-pər\ *n, pl* **groupers** *also* **grouper** : any of numerous large solitary bottom fishes of warm seas

group home *n* : a residence for persons requiring care or supervision

group·ie \'grü-pē\ *n* : a fan of a rock group who usu. follows the group around on concert tours; *also* : ENTHUSIAST, FAN

group therapy *n* : therapy in the presence of a therapist in which several patients discuss their personal problems

groupware \'grüp-ˌwer\ *n* : software that enables users to work jointly via a network on projects or files

¹**grouse** \'graùs\ *n, pl* **grouse** *or* **grouses** : any of various chiefly ground-dwelling game birds that have feathered legs and are usu. of reddish brown or other protective color

grouse

²**grouse** *vb* **groused; grous·ing** : COMPLAIN, GRUMBLE

grout \'graùt\ *n* : material (as mortar) used for filling spaces — **grout** *vb*

grove \'grōv\ *n* : a small wood usu. without underbrush

grov·el \'grä-vəl, 'grə-\ *vb* **-eled** *or* **-elled; -el·ing** *or* **-el·ling** 1 : to creep or lie with the body prostrate in fear or humility 2 : to abase oneself

grow \'grō\ *vb* **grew** \'grü\; **grown** \'grōn\; **grow·ing** 1 : to spring up and develop to maturity 2 : to be able to grow : THRIVE 3 : to take on some relation through or as if through growth ⟨tree limbs *grown* together⟩ 4 : INCREASE, EXPAND 5 : to develop from a parent source 6 : BECOME 7 : to have an increasing influence 8 : to cause to grow — **grow·er** *n*

growing pains *n pl* 1 : pains in the legs of growing children having no known relation to growth 2 : the stresses and strains attending a new project or development

growl \'graù(-ə)l\ *vb* 1 : RUMBLE 2 : to utter a deep throaty sound 3 : GRUMBLE — **growl** *n*

grown-up \'grō-ˌnəp\ *adj* : not childish : ADULT — **grown-up** *n*

growth \'grōth\ *n* 1 : stage or condition attained in growing 2 : a process of growing esp. through progressive development or increase 3 : a result or product of growing ⟨a fine ∼ of hair⟩; *also* : an abnormal mass of tissue (as a tumor)

growth hormone *n* : a vertebrate hormone that is secreted by the pituitary gland and regulates growth

growth industry *n* : a business, interest, or activity that is increasingly popular, profitable, or trendy

¹**grub** \'grəb\ *vb* **grubbed; grub·bing** 1 : to clear or root out by digging 2 : to dig in the ground usu. for a hidden object 3 : to search about

²**grub** *n* 1 : a soft thick wormlike insect larva ⟨beetle ∼s⟩ 2 : DRUDGE; *also* : a slovenly person 3 : FOOD

grub·by \'grə-bē\ *adj* **grub·bi·er; -est** : DIRTY, SLOVENLY — **grub·bi·ness** \-bē-nəs\ *n*

grub·stake \'grəb-ˌstāk\ *n* : supplies or funds furnished a mining prospector in return for a share in his finds

¹**grudge** \'grəj\ *vb* **grudged; grudg·ing** : to be reluctant to give : BEGRUDGE

²**grudge** *n* : a feeling of deep-seated resentment or ill will

gru·el \'grü-əl\ *n* : a thin porridge

gru·el·ing *or* **gru·el·ling** \'grü-liŋ, 'grü-ə-\ *adj* : requiring extreme effort : EXHAUSTING

grue·some \'grü-səm\ *adj* [fr. earlier *growsome*, fr. E dial. *grow, grue* to shiver] : inspiring horror or repulsion — **grue·some·ly** *adv* — **grue·some·ness** *n*

gruff \'grəf\ *adj* 1 : rough in speech or manner 2 : being deep and harsh : HOARSE — **gruff·ly** *adv*

grum·ble \'grəm-bəl\ *vb* **grum·bled; grum·bling** 1 : to mutter in discontent 2 : GROWL, RUMBLE — **grum·bler** *n*

grumpy \'grəm-pē\ *adj* **grump·i·er; -est** : moodily cross

: SURLY — **grump·i·ly** \-pə-lē\ *adv* — **grump·i·ness** \-pē-nəs\ *n*

grunge \'grənj\ *n* **1** : one that is grungy **2** : heavy metal rock music expressing alienation and discontent **3** : untidy or tattered clothing typically worn by grunge fans

grun·gy \'grən-jē\ *adj* **grun·gi·er; -est** : shabby or dirty in character or condition

grun·ion \'grən-yən\ *n* : a fish of the California coast which comes inshore to spawn at nearly full moon

grunt \'grənt\ *n* : a deep throaty sound (as that of a hog) — **grunt** *vb*

GSA *abbr* **1** General Services Administration **2** Girl Scouts of America

G suit *n* [gravity] : a suit for a pilot or astronaut designed to counteract the physiological effects of acceleration

GSUSA *abbr* Girl Scouts of the United States of America

gt *abbr* great

Gt Brit *abbr* Great Britain

gtd *abbr* guaranteed

GU *abbr* Guam

gua·ca·mo·le \ˌgwä-kə-'mō-lē\ *n* [MexSp, fr. Nahuatl *āhuacamōlli*, fr. *āhuacatl* avocado + *mōlli* sauce] : mashed and seasoned avocado

gua·nine \'gwä-ˌnēn\ *n* : a purine base that codes genetic information in the molecular chain of DNA and RNA

gua·no \'gwä-nō\ *n* [Sp, fr. Quechua *wanu* fertilizer, dung] : excrement esp. of seabirds or bats; *also* : a fertilizer composed chiefly of this excrement

gua·ra·ni \ˌgwär-ə-'nē\ *n, pl* **guaranies** *also* **guaranis** — see MONEY table

¹guar·an·tee \ˌger-ən-'tē\ *n* **1** : GUARANTOR **2** : GUARANTY 1 **3** : an agreement by which one person undertakes to secure another in the possession or enjoyment of something **4** : an assurance of the quality of or of the length of use to be expected from a product offered for sale **5** : GUARANTY 4

²guarantee *vb* **-teed; -tee·ing 1** : to undertake to answer for the debt, failure to perform, or faulty performance of (another) **2** : to undertake an obligation to establish, perform, or continue **3** : to give security to

guar·an·tor \ˌger-ən-'tȯr\ *n* : one who gives a guarantee

¹guar·an·ty \'ger-ən-tē\ *n, pl* **-ties 1** : an undertaking to answer for another's failure to pay a debt or perform a duty **2** : GUARANTEE 3 : GUARANTOR **4** : PLEDGE, SECURITY

²guaranty *vb* **-tied; -ty·ing** : GUARANTEE

¹guard \'gärd\ *n* **1** : a person or a body of persons on sentinel duty **2** *pl* : troops assigned to protect a sovereign **3** : a defensive position (as in boxing) **4** : the act or duty of protecting or defending **5** : PROTECTION **6** : a protective or safety device **7** : a football lineman playing between center and tackle; *also* : a basketball player stationed toward the rear — **on guard** : WATCHFUL, ALERT

²guard *vb* **1** : PROTECT, DEFEND **2** : to watch over **3** : to be on guard

guard·house \'gärd-ˌhaůs\ *n* **1** : a building occupied by a guard or used as a headquarters by soldiers on guard duty **2** : a military jail

guard·ian \'gär-dē-ən\ *n* **1** : CUSTODIAN **2** : one who has the care of the person or property of another — **guard·ian·ship** *n*

guard·room \'gärd-ˌrüm\ *n* **1** : a room used by a military guard while on duty **2** : a room where military prisoners are confined

guards·man \'gärdz-mən\ *n* : a member of a military body called *guard* or *guards*

gua·va \'gwä-və\ *n* : the sweet yellow or pink acid fruit of a shrubby tropical American tree used esp. for making jam and jelly; *also* : the tree

gu·ber·na·to·ri·al \ˌgü-bər-nə-'tȯr-ē-əl\ *adj* : of or relating to a governor

guer·don \'gər-dᵊn\ *n* : REWARD, RECOMPENSE

Guern·sey \'gərn-zē\ *n, pl* **Guernseys** : any of a breed of usu. reddish brown dairy cattle that produce rich yellowish milk

guer·ril·la *or* **gue·ril·la** \gə-'ri-lə\ *n* [Sp *guerrilla*, fr. dim. of *guerra* war, of Gmc origin] : one who engages in irregular warfare esp. as a member of an independent unit

guess \'ges\ *vb* **1** : to form an opinion from little or no evidence **2** : BELIEVE, SUPPOSE **3** : to conjecture correctly about : DISCOVER — **guess** *n*

guest \'gest\ *n* **1** : a person to whom hospitality (as of a house or a club) is extended **2** : a patron of a commercial establishment (as a hotel) **3** : a person not a regular member of a cast who appears on a program

guest·house \'gest-ˌhaůs\ *n* : a house run as a boarding house or bed-and-breakfast

guf·faw \(ˌ)gə-'fȯ\ *n* : a loud burst of laughter — **guf·faw** *vb*

guid·ance \'gī-dᵊns\ *n* **1** : the act or process of guiding **2** : ADVICE, DIRECTION

¹guide \'gīd\ *n* **1** : one who leads or directs another's course **2** : one who shows and explains points of interest **3** : something that provides guiding information; *also* : SIGNPOST **4** : a device to direct the motion of something

²guide *vb* **guid·ed; guid·ing 1** : to act as a guide to **2** : MANAGE, DIRECT **3** : to superintend the training of — **guid·able** \'gī-də-bəl\ *adj*

guide·book \'gīd-ˌbůk\ *n* : a book of information for travelers

guided missile *n* : a missile whose course may be altered during flight

guide dog *n* : a dog trained to lead the blind

guide·line \'gīd-ˌlīn\ *n* : an indication or outline of policy or conduct

guide word *n* : a term at the head of a page of an alphabetical reference work that indicates the alphabetically first or last word on that page

gui·don \'gī-ˌdän, 'gī-dᵊn\ *n* : a small flag (as of a military unit)

guild \'gild\ *n* : an association of people with common aims and interests; *esp* : a medieval association of merchants or craftsmen — **guild·hall** \-ˌhȯl\ *n*

guil·der \'gil-dər\ *n* : GULDEN

guile \'gī(-ə)l\ *n* : deceitful cunning : DUPLICITY — **guile·ful** *adj* — **guile·less** *adj* — **guile·less·ness** *n*

guil·lo·tine \'gi-lə-ˌtēn, ˌgē-ə-'tēn\ *n* [F, fr. Joseph *Guillotin* †1814 Fr. physician] : a machine for beheading persons — **guillotine** *vb*

guilt \'gilt\ *n* **1** : the fact of having committed an offense esp. against the law **2** : BLAMEWORTHINESS **3** : a feeling of responsibility for wrongdoing — **guilt·less** *adj*

guilt-trip \'gilt-ˌtrip\ *vb* : to cause feelings of guilt in

guilty \'gil-tē\ *adj* **guilt·i·er; -est 1** : having committed a breach of conduct or a crime **2** : suggesting or involving guilt **3** : aware of or suffering from guilt — **guilt·i·ly** \-tə-lē\ *adv* — **guilt·i·ness** \-tē-nəs\ *n*

guin·ea \'gi-nē\ *n* **1** : a British gold coin no longer issued worth 21 shillings **2** : a unit of value equal to 21 shillings

guinea fowl *n* : a gray and white spotted West African bird related to the pheasants and widely raised for food; *also* : any of several related birds

guinea hen *n* : a female guinea fowl; *also* : GUINEA FOWL

guinea pig *n* **1** : a small stocky short-eared and nearly tailless So. American rodent often kept as a pet or used in lab research **2** : a subject of research or testing

guise \'gīz\ *n* **1** : a form or style of dress : COSTUME **2** : external appearance : SEMBLANCE

gui·tar \gi-'tär\ *n* : a musical instrument with usu. six strings plucked with a pick or with the fingers

gulch \'gəlch\ *n* : RAVINE

gul·den \'gül-dən, 'gůl-\ *n, pl* **guldens** *or* **gulden 1** : the basic monetary unit of the Netherlands until 2002 **2** — see MONEY table

gulf \'gəlf\ *n* [ME *goulf*, fr. MF *golfe*, fr. It *golfo*, fr. LL *colpus*, fr. Gk *kolpos* bosom, gulf] **1** : a part of an ocean or sea partly or mostly surrounded by land **2** : ABYSS, CHASM **3** : a wide separation ⟨the ∼ between generations⟩

¹gull \'gəl\ *n* : any of numerous mostly white or gray long-winged web-footed seabirds

²gull *vb* : to make a dupe of : DECEIVE

³gull *n* : DUPE

gul·let \'gə-lət\ *n* : ESOPHAGUS; *also* : THROAT

gull·ible \'gə-lə-bəl\ *adj* : easily duped or cheated

gul·ly \'gə-lē\ *n, pl* **gullies** : a trench worn in the earth by and often filled with running water after rains

gulp \'gəlp\ *vb* **1** : to swallow hurriedly or greedily **2** : SUPPRESS ⟨∼ down a sob⟩ **3** : to catch the breath as if in taking a long drink — **gulp** *n*

¹gum \'gəm\ *n* : the oral tissue that surrounds the necks of the teeth

²**gum** *n* [ME *gomme*, fr. MF, fr. L *cummi, gummi*, fr. Gk *kommi*, fr. Egyptian *qmy.t*] **1** : a sticky plant exudate; *esp* : one that hardens on drying **2** : a sticky substance **3** : a preparation usu. of a plant gum sweetened and flavored and used for chewing — **gum·my** *adj*

gum arabic *n* : a water-soluble gum obtained from several acacias and used esp. in making inks, adhesives, confections, and pharmaceuticals

gum·bo \'gəm-bō\ *n* [AmerF *gombo*, of Bantu origin] : a rich thick soup usu. thickened with okra

gum·drop \'gəm-,dräp\ *n* : a candy made usu. from corn syrup with gelatin and coated with sugar crystals

gump·tion \'gəmp-shən\ *n* **1** *chiefly dial* : shrewd common sense **2** : ENTERPRISE, INITIATIVE ⟨lacked the ~ to try⟩

gum·shoe \'gəm-,shü\ *n* : DETECTIVE — **gumshoe** *vb*

¹**gun** \'gən\ *n* **1** : CANNON **2** : a portable firearm **3** : a discharge of a gun **4** : something suggesting a gun in shape or function **5** : THROTTLE — **gunned** \'gənd\ *adj*

²**gun** *vb* **gunned; gun·ning 1** : to hunt with a gun **2** : SHOOT **3** : to open up the throttle of so as to increase speed

gun·boat \'gən-,bōt\ *n* : a small lightly armed ship for use in shallow waters

gun·fight \-,fīt\ *n* : a duel with guns — **gun·fight·er** *n*

gun·fire \-,fī(-ə)r\ *n* : the firing of guns

gung ho \'gəŋ-'hō\ *adj* : extremely zealous or enthusiastic

gun·man \-mən\ *n* : a man armed with a gun; *esp* : a professional killer

gun·ner \'gə-nər\ *n* **1** : a soldier or airman who operates or aims a gun **2** : one who hunts with a gun

gun·nery \'gə-nə-rē\ *n* : the use of guns; *esp* : the science of the flight of projectiles and effective use of guns

gunnery sergeant *n* : a noncommissioned officer in the marine corps ranking next below a master sergeant

gun·ny·sack \'gə-nē-,sak\ *n* : a sack made of a coarse heavy fabric (as burlap)

gun·point \'gən-,point\ *n* : the muzzle of a gun — **at gunpoint** : under a threat of death by being shot

gun·pow·der \-,paù-dər\ *n* : an explosive powder used in guns and blasting

gun·shot \-,shät\ *n* **1** : shot fired from a gun **2** : the range of a gun ⟨within ~⟩

gun–shy \-,shī\ *adj* **1** : afraid of a loud noise **2** : markedly distrustful

gun·sling·er \-,sliŋ-ər\ *n* : a skilled gunman esp. in the American West

gun·smith \-,smith\ *n* : one who designs, makes, or repairs firearms

gun·wale *also* **gun·nel** \'gə-nᵊl\ *n* : the upper edge of a ship's or boat's side

gup·py \'gə-pē\ *n, pl* **guppies** [R.J.L. *Guppy* †1916 Trinidadian naturalist] : a small brightly colored tropical fish

gur·gle \'gər-gəl\ *vb* **gur·gled; gur·gling** : to make a sound like that of an irregularly flowing or gently splashing liquid — **gurgle** *n*

Gur·kha \'gùr-kə, 'gər-\ *n* : a soldier from Nepal in the British or Indian army

gur·ney \'gər-nē\ *n, pl* **gurneys** : a wheeled cot or stretcher

gu·ru \'gùr-ü\ *n, pl* **gurus** [ultim. Sanskrit *guru*, fr. *guru*, adj., heavy, venerable] **1** : a personal religious and spiritual teacher in Hinduism **2** : a teacher in matters of fundamental concern **3** : EXPERT ⟨a fitness ~⟩

gush \'gəsh\ *vb* **1** : to issue or pour forth copiously or violently : SPOUT **2** : to make an effusive display of affection or enthusiasm

gush·er \'gə-shər\ *n* : one that gushes; *esp* : an oil well with a large natural flow

gushy \'gə-shē\ *adj* **gush·i·er; -est** : marked by effusive sentimentality

gus·set \'gə-sət\ *n* : a triangular insert (as in a seam of a sleeve) to give width or strength — **gusset** *vb*

gus·sy up \'gə-sē-\ *vb* **gus·sied up gus·sy·ing up 1** : in best or formal clothes **2** : to make more attractive, glamorous or fancy

¹**gust** \'gəst\ *n* **1** : a sudden brief rush of wind **2** : a sudden outburst : SURGE — **gusty** *adj*

²**gust** *vb* : to blow in gusts

gus·ta·to·ry \'gəs-tə-,tòr-ē\ *adj* : relating to or associated with the sense of taste

gus·to \'gəs-tō\ *n, pl* **gustoes** : enthusiastic enjoyment; *also* : VITALITY 4

¹**gut** \'gət\ *n* **1** *pl* : BOWELS, ENTRAILS **2** : the alimentary canal or a part of it (as the intestine); *also* : BELLY, ABDOMEN **3** *pl* : the inner essential parts ⟨a car's ~s⟩ **4** *pl* : COURAGE, PLUCK

²**gut** *vb* **gut·ted; gut·ting 1** : EVISCERATE **2** : to destroy the inside of ⟨fire *gutted* the building⟩

gut check *n* : a test of courage, character, or determination

gutsy \'gət-sē\ *adj* **guts·i·er; -est** : marked by courage and determination

gut·ter \'gə-tər\ *n* : a groove or channel for carrying off esp. rainwater

gut·ter·snipe \-,snīp\ *n* : a street urchin

gut·tur·al \'gə-tə-rəl\ *adj* **1** : sounded in the throat **2** : being or marked by an utterance that is strange, unpleasant, or disagreeable — **guttural** *n*

gut·ty \'gə-tē\ *adj* **gut·ti·er; -est 1** : GUTSY **2** : having a vigorous challenging quality

gut–wrench·ing \'gət-,ren-chiŋ\ *adj* : causing emotional anguish

¹**guy** \'gī\ *n* : a rope, chain, or rod attached to something as a brace or guide

²**guy** *vb* : to steady or reinforce with a guy

³**guy** *n* : MAN, FELLOW; *also, pl* : PERSONS ⟨all the ~s came⟩

⁴**guy** *vb* : to make fun of : RIDICULE

guz·zle \'gə-zəl\ *vb* **guz·zled; guz·zling** : to drink greedily

gym \'jim\ *n* : GYMNASIUM

gym·kha·na \jim-'kä-nə\ *n* : a meet featuring sports contests; *esp* : a contest of automobile-driving skill

gym·na·si·um *for 1* 'jim-'nā-zē-əm, -zhəm, *for 2* gim-'nä-zē-əm\ *n, pl* **-si·ums** *or* **-na·sia** \-'nä-zē-ə, -'nä-zhə; -'nä-zē-ə\ [L, exercise ground, school, fr. Gk *gymnasion*, fr. *gymnazein* to exercise naked, fr. *gymnos* naked] **1** : a room or building for indoor sports **2** : a European secondary school that prepares students for the university

gym·nas·tics \jim-'nas-tiks\ *n* : a competitive sport developed from physical exercises designed to demonstrate strength, balance, and body control — **gym·nast** \'jim-,nast\ *n* — **gym·nas·tic** *adj*

gym·no·sperm \'jim-nə-,spərm\ *n* : any of a group of woody vascular seed plants (as conifers) that produce naked seeds not enclosed in an ovary

gyn *or* **gynecol** *abbr* gynecology

gy·nae·col·o·gy *chiefly Brit var of* GYNECOLOGY

gy·ne·col·o·gy \,gī-nə-'kä-lə-jē\ *n* : a branch of medicine dealing with the diseases and hygiene of women — **gy·ne·co·log·ic** \-ni-kə-'lä-jik\ *or* **gy·ne·co·log·i·cal** \-ji-kəl\ *adj* — **gy·ne·col·o·gist** \-nə-'kä-lə-jist\ *n*

gy·no·cen·tric \,gī-nə-'sen-trik\ *adj* : emphasizing feminine interests or a feminine point of view

gyp \'jip\ *n* **1** : CHEAT, SWINDLER **2** : FRAUD, SWINDLE — **gyp** *vb*

gyp·sum \'jip-səm\ *n* : a calcium-containing mineral used in making plaster of paris

Gyp·sy \'jip-sē\ *n, pl* **Gypsies** [by shortening & alter. fr. *Egyptian*] : a member of a traditionally traveling people coming orig. from India and living chiefly in Europe, Asia, and No. America; *also* : the language of the Gypsies

gypsy moth *n* : an Old World moth that was introduced into the U.S. where its caterpillar is a destructive defoliator of many trees

gy·rate \'jī-,rāt\ *vb* **gy·rat·ed; gy·rat·ing 1** : to revolve around a point or axis **2** : to oscillate with or as if with a circular or spiral motion — **gy·ra·tion** \jī-'rā-shən\ *n*

gyr·fal·con \'jər-,fal-kən, -,fòl-\ *n* : an arctic falcon with several color forms that is the largest of all falcons

¹**gy·ro** \'jī-rō\ *n, pl* **gyros** : GYROSCOPE

²**gy·ro** \'yē-,rō, 'zhir-ō\ *n, pl* **gyros** : a sandwich esp. of lamb and beef, tomato, onion, and yogurt sauce on pita bread

gy·ro·scope \'jī-rə-,skōp\ *n* : a wheel or disk mounted to spin rapidly about an axis that is free to turn in various directions

Gy Sgt *abbr* gunnery sergeant

gyve \'jīv, 'gīv\ *n* : FETTER — **gyve** *vb*

¹h \'āch\ *n, pl* **h's** *or* **hs** \'ā-chəz\ *often cap* : the 8th letter of the English alphabet

²h *abbr, often cap* **1** hard; hardness **2** heroin **3** hit **4** husband

H *symbol* hydrogen

¹ha \'hä\ *interj* — used esp. to express surprise or joy

²ha *abbr* hectare

Hab *abbr* Habacuc; Habakkuk

Ha·ba·cuc \'ha-bə-ˌkək, hə-'ba-kək\ *n* : HABAKKUK

Ha·bak·kuk \'ha-bə-ˌkək, hə-'ba-kək\ *n* — see BIBLE table

ha·ba·ne·ra \ˌhä-bə-'ner-ə\ *n* [Sp *(danza) habanera,* lit., dance of Havana] : a Cuban dance in slow time; *also* : the music for this dance

ha·ba·ne·ro *also* **ha·ba·ñe·ro** \ˌ(h)ä-bə-'n(y)er-ō\ *n* : a very hot chili pepper that is usu. orange when mature

ha·be·as cor·pus \'hā-bē-əs-'kȯr-pəs\ *n* [ME, fr. ML, lit., you should have the body (the opening words of the writ)] : a writ issued to bring a party before a court

hab·er·dash·er \'ha-bər-ˌda-shər\ *n* : a dealer in men's clothing and accessories

hab·er·dash·ery \-ˌda-shə-rē\ *n, pl* **-er·ies 1** : goods sold by a haberdasher **2** : a haberdasher's shop

ha·bil·i·ment \hə-'bi-lə-mənt\ *n* **1** *pl* : TRAPPINGS, EQUIPMENT **2** : DRESS; *esp* : the dress characteristic of an occupation or occasion — usu. used in pl.

hab·it \'ha-bət\ *n* **1** : DRESS, GARB **2** : BEARING, CONDUCT **3** : PHYSIQUE **4** : mental makeup **5** : a usual manner of behavior : CUSTOM **6** : a behavior pattern acquired by frequent repetition ⟨has a ~ of swearing⟩ **7** : ADDICTION ⟨a drug ~⟩ **8** : mode of growth or occurrence ⟨trees with a spreading ~⟩

hab·it·able \'ha-bə-tə-bəl\ *adj* : capable of being lived in — **hab·it·abil·i·ty** \ˌha-bə-tə-'bi-lə-tē\ *n*

hab·i·tat \'ha-bə-ˌtat\ *n* [L, it inhabits] : the place or environment where a plant or animal naturally occurs

hab·i·ta·tion \ˌha-bə-'tā-shən\ *n* **1** : OCCUPANCY **2** : a dwelling place : RESIDENCE **3** : SETTLEMENT

hab·it–form·ing \'ha-bət-ˌfȯr-miŋ\ *adj* : causing addiction : ADDICTIVE

ha·bit·u·al \hə-'bi-chə-wəl\ *adj* **1** : CUSTOMARY **2** : doing, practicing, or acting by force of habit **3** : inherent in an individual ⟨~ grace⟩ — **ha·bit·u·al·ly** *adv* — **ha·bit·u·al·ness** *n*

ha·bit·u·ate \hə-'bi-chə-ˌwāt\ *vb* **-at·ed; -at·ing 1** : ACCUSTOM **2** : to cause or undergo habituation

ha·bit·u·a·tion \hə-ˌbi-chə-'wā-shən\ *n* **1** : the process of making habitual **2** : psychological dependence on a drug after a period of use

ha·bi·tué *also* **ha·bi·tue** \hə-'bi-chə-ˌwā\ *n* [F] **1** : one who may be regularly found in or at (as a place of entertainment) **2** : DEVOTEE

ha·ci·en·da \ˌhä-sē-'en-də\ *n* **1** : a large estate in a Spanish-speaking country **2** : the main building of a farm or ranch

¹hack \'hak\ *vb* **1** : to cut or sever with repeated irregular blows **2** : to cough in a short dry manner **3** : to manage successfully; *also* : TOLERATE ⟨can't ~ the pressure⟩ **4** : to gain access to a computer illegally

²hack *n* **1** : an implement for hacking **2** : a short dry cough **3** : a hacking blow

³hack *n* **1** : a horse hired or used for varied work **2** : a horse worn out in service **3** : a light easy often 3-gaited saddle horse **4** : HACKNEY, TAXICAB **5** : a person who works solely for mercenary reasons; *esp* : a writer working solely for commercial success — **hack** *adj*

⁴hack *vb* : to operate a taxicab

hack·er \'ha-kər\ *n* **1** : one that hacks; *also* : a person unskilled at something **2** : an expert at using a computer **3** : a person who illegally gains access to and sometimes tampers with information in a computer system

hack·ie \'ha-kē\ *n* : a taxicab driver

hack·le \'ha-kəl\ *n* **1** : one of the long feathers on the neck or back of a bird **2** *pl* : hairs (as on a dog's neck)

that can be erected **3** *pl* : TEMPER, DANDER

hack·man \'hak-mən\ *n* : HACKIE

¹hack·ney \'hak-nē\ *n, pl* **hackneys 1** : a horse for riding or driving **2** : a carriage or automobile kept for hire

²hackney *vb* : to make trite

hack·neyed \'hak-nēd\ *adj* : lacking in freshness or originality ⟨~ slogans⟩

hack·saw \'hak-ˌsȯ\ *n* : a fine-tooth saw in a frame for cutting metal

hacksaw

hack·work \-ˌwərk\ *n* : work done on order usu. according to a formula

had *past and past part of* HAVE

had·dock \'ha-dək\ *n, pl* **haddock** *also* **haddocks** : an Atlantic food fish usu. smaller than the related cod

Ha·des \'hā-(ˌ)dēz\ *n* **1** : the abode of the dead in Greek mythology **2** *often not cap* : HELL

haem *chiefly Brit var of* HEME

hae·ma·tite *Brit var of* HEMATITE

haf·ni·um \'haf-nē-əm\ *n* : a gray metallic chemical element

haft \'haft\ *n* : the handle of a weapon or tool

hag \'hag\ *n* **1** : an ugly or evil-looking old woman **2** : WITCH 1

Hag *abbr* Haggai

Hag·gai \'ha-gē-ˌī, 'ha-ˌgī\ *n* — see BIBLE table

hag·gard \'ha-gərd\ *adj* : having a worn or emaciated appearance ⟨~ faces⟩ ♦ **Synonyms** CAREWORN, WASTED, DRAWN — **hag·gard·ly** *adv* — **hag·gard·ness** *n*

hag·gis \'ha-gəs\ *n* : a traditionally Scottish dish made of the heart, liver, and lungs of a sheep or a calf minced with suet, onions, oatmeal, and seasonings

hag·gle \'ha-gəl\ *vb* **hag·gled; hag·gling** : to argue in bargaining — **hag·gler** *n*

Ha·gi·og·ra·pha \ˌha-gē-'ä-grə-fə, ˌhā-jē-\ *n pl* — see WRITINGS

ha·gi·o·graph·ic \ˌha-gē-ə-'gra-fik, ˌhā-, -jē-\ *adj* : of or relating to hagiography; *esp* : excessively flattering

ha·gi·og·ra·phy \ˌha-gē-'ä-grə-fē, ˌhā-jē-\ *n* **1** : biography of saints or venerated persons **2** : idealizing or idolizing biography — **ha·gi·og·ra·pher** \-fər\ *n*

hai·ku \'hī-(ˌ)kü\ *n, pl* **haiku** [Jp] : an unrhymed Japanese verse form of three lines containing usu. five, seven, and five syllables respectively; *also* : a poem in this form

¹hail \'hāl\ *n* **1** : precipitation in the form of small lumps of ice **2** : something that gives the effect of falling hail

²hail *vb* **1** : to precipitate hail **2** : to pour down and strike like hail

³hail *interj* [ME, fr. ON *heill,* fr. *heill* healthy] — used to express acclamation

⁴hail *vb* **1** : SALUTE, GREET **2** : SUMMON

⁵hail *n* **1** : an expression of greeting, approval, or praise **2** : hearing distance

Hail Mary *n* : a salutation and prayer to the Virgin Mary

hail·stone \'hāl-ˌstōn\ *n* : a pellet of hail

hail·storm \-ˌstȯrm\ *n* : a storm accompanied by hail

hair \'her\ *n* : a threadlike outgrowth esp. from the skin of a mammal; *also* : a covering or growth of hairs of an animal or a body part — **haired** \'herd\ *adj* — **hair·less** *adj*

hair·breadth \'her-ˌbredth\ *or* **hairs·breadth** \'herz-\ *n* : a very small distance or margin

hair·brush \-ˌbrəsh\ *n* : a brush for the hair

hair·cloth \-ˌklȯth\ *n* : a stiff wiry fabric used esp. for upholstery

hair·cut \-ˌkət\ *n* : the act, process, or style of cutting and shaping the hair

hair·do \-ˌdü\ *n, pl* **hairdos** : HAIRSTYLE

hair·dress·er \-ˌdre-sər\ *n* : a person who dresses or cuts hair — **hair·dress·ing** *n*

hair·line \-ˌlīn\ *n* **1** : a very thin line **2** : the outline of the hair on the head

hair·piece \-ˌpēs\ *n* **1** : supplementary hair (as a switch) used in some women's hairdos **2** : TOUPEE

hair·pin \-ˌpin\ *n* **1** : a U-shaped pin to hold the hair in place **2** : a sharp U-shaped turn in a road — **hairpin** *adj*

hair–rais·ing \ˈher-ˌrā-ziŋ\ *adj* : causing terror or astonishment

hair·split·ter \-ˌspli-tər\ *n* : a person who makes excessively fine distinctions in reasoning — **hair·split·ting** \-ˌspli-tiŋ\ *adj or n*

hair·spray \ˈher-ˌsprā\ *n* : a liquid sprayed onto the hair to hold it in place

hair·style \-ˌstī(-ə)l\ *n* : a way of wearing the hair — **hair·styl·ing** *n*

hair·styl·ist \-ˌstī-list\ *n* : HAIRDRESSER

hair–trigger *adj* : immediately responsive to the slightest stimulus

hairy \ˈher-ē\ *adj* **hair·i·er; -est** **1** : covered with or as if with hair **2** : tending to cause nervous tension ⟨a few ~ moments⟩ **3** : difficult to deal with — **hair·i·ness** \-ē-nəs\ *n*

hairy woodpecker *n* : a common No. American woodpecker with a white back that is larger than the similarly marked downy woodpecker

hajj \ˈhaj\ *n* : the Islamic religious pilgrimage to Mecca

hajji \ˈha-jē\ *n* : one who has made a pilgrimage to Mecca — often used as a title

hake \ˈhāk\ *n* : any of several marine food fishes related to the cod

ha·la·la *or* **ha·la·lah** \hə-ˈlä-lə\ *n, pl* **halala** *or* **halalas** *or* **halalah** *or* **halalahs** — see *riyal* at MONEY table

hal·berd \ˈhal-bərd, ˈhȯl-\ *also* **hal·bert** \-bərt\ *n* : a weapon esp. of the 15th and 16th centuries consisting of a battle-ax and pike on a long handle

hal·cy·on \ˈhal-sē-ən\ *adj* [Gk *halkyōn, alkyōn* a mythical bird believed to nest at sea and to calm the waves] **1** : CALM, PEACEFUL ⟨a ~ lake⟩ **2** : being a time of happiness, success, or prosperity

¹hale \ˈhāl\ *adj* : free from defect, disease, or infirmity ✦ *Synonyms* HEALTHY, SOUND, ROBUST, WELL

²hale *vb* **haled; hal·ing** **1** : HAUL, PULL **2** : to compel to go

ha·ler \ˈhä-lər\ *n, pl* **ha·le·ru** \ˈhä-lə-ˌrü\ — see *koruna* at MONEY table

¹half \ˈhaf, ˈhäf\ *n, pl* **halves** \ˈhavz, ˈhävz\ **1** : either of two equal parts that compose something **2** : one of a pair

²half *adj* **1** : being one of two equal parts **2** : amounting to nearly half **3** : PARTIAL, INCOMPLETE — **half** *adv*

half–and–half \ˌhaf-ᵊn-ˈhaf, ˌhäf-ᵊn-ˈhäf\ *n* : something that is half one thing and half another

half·back \ˈhaf-ˌbak, ˈhäf-\ *n* **1** : a football back stationed on or near the flank **2** : a player stationed immediately behind the forward line

half–baked \-ˈbākt\ *adj* **1** : poorly planned or developed; *also* : lacking common sense **2** : not thoroughly baked

half–breed \-ˌbrēd\ *n, often disparaging* : one of mixed racial descent — **half–breed** *adj, often disparaging*

half brother *n* : a brother related through one parent only

half–caste \ˈhaf-ˌkast, ˈhäf-\ *n* : HALF-BREED — **half–caste** *adj*

half–cocked \ˈhaf-ˈkäkt, ˈhäf-\ *adj* : lacking adequate preparation

half–dol·lar \-ˈdä-lər\ *n* **1** : a coin representing one half of a dollar **2** : the sum of fifty cents

half–heart·ed \-ˈhär-təd\ *adj* : lacking spirit or interest — **half–heart·ed·ly** *adv* — **half–heart·ed·ness** *n*

half–life \-ˌlīf\ *n* : the time required for half of something (as atoms or a drug) to undergo a process

half–mast \-ˈmast\ *n* : a point about halfway down from the top of a mast or staff

half note *n* : a musical note equal in time to one half of a whole note

half·pen·ny \ˈhāp-nē\ *n, pl* **half·pence** \ˈhā-pəns\ *or* **half·pennies** : a former British coin representing one half of a penny

half–pint \ˈhaf-ˌpīnt, ˈhäf-\ *adj* : of less than average size — **half–pint** *n*

half sister *n* : a sister related through one parent only

half sole *n* : a shoe sole extending from the shank forward — **half–sole** *vb*

half–staff \ˈhaf-ˈstaf, ˈhäf-\ *n* : HALF-MAST

half step *n* : a musical interval equivalent to one twelfth of an octave

half·time \ˈhaf-ˌtīm, ˈhäf-\ *n* : an intermission between halves of a game

half–track \-ˌtrak\ *n* : a motor vehicle propelled by an endless chain-track drive system; *esp* : such a vehicle lightly armored for military use

half–truth \-ˌtrüth\ *n* : a statement that is only partially true; *esp* : one that deliberately mixes truth and falsehood

half·way \-ˈwā\ *adj* **1** : midway between two points **2** : PARTIAL 1 — **halfway** *adv*

half–wit \-ˌwit\ *n* : a foolish or imbecilic person — **half–wit·ted** \-ˈwi-təd\ *adj* — **half–wit·ted·ness** *n*

hal·i·but \ˈha-lə-bət\ *n, pl* **halibut** *also* **halibuts** [ME *halybutte,* fr. *haly, holy* holy + *butte* flatfish; fr. its being eaten on holy days] : any of several large edible marine flatfishes

ha·lite \ˈha-ˌlīt, ˈhā-\ *n* : ROCK SALT

hal·i·to·sis \ˌha-lə-ˈtō-səs\ *n* : the condition of having fetid breath

hall \ˈhȯl\ *n* **1** : the residence of a medieval king or noble; *also* : the house of a landed proprietor **2** : a large public building **3** : a college or university building; *also* : DORMITORY **4** : LOBBY; *also* : CORRIDOR **5** : AUDITORIUM

hal·le·lu·jah \ˌha-lə-ˈlü-yə\ *interj* [Heb *hallĕlūyāh* praise (ye) the Lord] — used to express praise, joy, or thanks

hall·mark \ˈhȯl-ˌmärk\ *n* **1** : a mark put on an article to indicate origin, purity, or genuineness **2** : a distinguishing characteristic

hal·low \ˈha-lō\ *vb* **1** : CONSECRATE **2** : REVERE, VENERATE ⟨our ~ed leader⟩ — **hal·lowed** \-lōd, -lə-wəd\ *adj*

Hal·low·een *also* **Hal·low·e'en** \ˌha-lə-ˈwēn, ˌhä-\ *n* : the evening of October 31 observed esp. by children in merrymaking and masquerading

hal·lu·ci·nate \hə-ˈlü-sə-ˌnāt\ *vb* **-nat·ed; -nat·ing** : to have hallucinations or experience as a hallucination

hal·lu·ci·na·tion \hə-ˌlü-sə-ˈnā-shən\ *n* : perception of objects with no reality due usu. to use of drugs (as LSD) or to disorder of the nervous system; *also* : something so perceived ✦ *Synonyms* DELUSION, ILLUSION, MIRAGE — **hal·lu·ci·na·to·ry** \-ˈlü-sə-nə-ˌtȯr-ē\ *adj*

hal·lu·ci·no·gen \hə-ˈlü-sə-nə-jən\ *n* : a substance that induces hallucinations — **hal·lu·ci·no·gen·ic** \-ˌlü-sə-nə-ˈje-nik\ *adj or n*

hall·way \ˈhȯl-ˌwā\ *n* **1** : an entrance hall **2** : CORRIDOR

ha·lo \ˈhā-lō\ *n, pl* **halos** *or* **haloes** [L *halos,* fr. Gk *halōs* threshing floor, disk, halo] **1** : a circle of light appearing to surround a shining body (as the sun) **2** : the aura of glory surrounding an idealized person or thing

¹hal·o·gen \ˈha-lə-jən\ *n* : any of the five elements fluorine, chlorine, bromine, iodine, and astatine

²hal·o·gen *adj* : containing, using, or being a halogen ⟨a ~ lamp⟩

¹halt \ˈhȯlt\ *adj* : LAME 1

²halt *n* : STOP

³halt *vb* **1** : to stop marching or traveling **2** : DISCONTINUE, END ⟨~ protests⟩

¹hal·ter \ˈhȯl-tər\ *n* **1** : a rope or strap for leading or tying an animal; *also* : HEADSTALL **2** : NOOSE **3** : a brief blouse held in place by straps around the neck and across the back

²halter *vb* **hal·tered; hal·ter·ing** **1** : to catch with or as if with a halter; *also* : to put a halter on (as a horse) **2** : HANG **3** : IMPEDE, RESTRAIN

halt·ing \ˈhȯl-tiŋ\ *adj* : UNCERTAIN, FALTERING — **halt·ing·ly** *adv*

halve \ˈhav, ˈhäv\ *vb* **halved; halv·ing** **1** : to divide into two equal parts **2** : to reduce to one half

halv·ers \ˈha-vərz, ˈhä-\ *n pl* : half shares : HALVES

halves *pl of* HALF

hal·yard \ˈhal-yərd\ *n* : a rope or tackle for hoisting and lowering (as sails)

¹ham \ˈham\ *n* **1** : a buttock with its associated thigh — usu. used in pl. **2** : a cut of meat and esp. pork from the thigh **3** : a showy performer **4** : an operator of an amateur radio station — **ham** *adj*

²**ham** vb **hammed; ham·ming** : to overplay a part : OVER-ACT

ham·burg·er \'ham-ˌbər-gər\ or **ham·burg** \-ˌbərg\ n [G *Hamburger* of Hamburg, Germany] **1** : ground beef **2** : a sandwich consisting of a ground-beef patty in a round roll

ham·let \'ham-lət\ n : a small village

¹**ham·mer** \'ha-mər\ n **1** : a hand tool used for pounding; *also* : something resembling a hammer in form or function **2** : the part of a gun whose striking action causes explosion of the charge **3** : a metal sphere hurled by a flexible handle for distance in a track-and-field event (**hammer throw**) **4** : ACCELERATOR 2

²**hammer** vb **1** : to beat, drive, or shape with repeated blows of a hammer : POUND **2** : to produce or bring about as if by repeated blows — usu. used with *out* **3** : to criticize severely

ham·mer·head \'ha-mər-ˌhed\ n **1** : the striking part of a hammer **2** : any of a family of medium-sized sharks with eyes at the ends of lateral extensions of the flattened head

ham·mer·lock \-ˌläk\ n : a wrestling hold in which an opponent's arm is held bent behind the back

ham·mer·toe \-ˌtō\ n : a toe deformed by having one or more joints permanently flexed

¹**ham·mock** \'ha-mək\ n [Sp *hamaca*, of AmerInd origin] : a swinging couch hung by cords at each end

²**hammock** n : a fertile elevated area of the southern U.S. and esp. Florida with hardwood vegetation and soil rich in humus

¹**ham·per** \'ham-pər\ vb : IMPEDE; *also* : RESTRAIN ✦ **Synonyms** TRAMMEL, CLOG, FETTER, SHACKLE

²**hamper** n : a large usu. lidded basket

ham·ster \'ham-stər\ n [G, fr. OHG *hamustro*, of Slavic origin] : any of a subfamily of small Old World rodents with large cheek pouches

¹**ham·string** \'ham-ˌstriŋ\ n : any of several muscles at the back of the thigh or tendons at the back of the knee

²**hamstring** vb **-strung** \-ˌstrəŋ\; **-string·ing 1** : to make ineffective or powerless ⟨*hamstrung* by guilt⟩ **2** : to cripple by cutting the leg tendons

¹**hand** \'hand\ n **1** : the end of a front limb when modified (as in humans) for grasping **2** : an indicator or pointer on a dial **3** : personal possession — usu. used in pl.; *also* : CONTROL **4** : SIDE 5 **5** : a pledge esp. of betrothal **6** : HANDWRITING **7** : SKILL, ABILITY; *also* : a significant part ⟨had a ∼ in the victory⟩ **8** : ASSISTANCE; *also* : PARTICIPATION ⟨had no ∼ in the affair⟩ **9** : an outburst of applause **10** : a single round in a card game; *also* : the cards held by a player after a deal **11** : WORKER, EMPLOYEE; *also* : a member of a ship's crew — **hand·less** adj — **at hand** : near in time or place — **on hand** : in present possession or readily available — **out of hand** : out of control

²**hand** vb **1** : to lead, guide, or assist with the hand **2** : to give, pass, or transmit with the hand

hand·bag \'hand-ˌbag\ n : a bag for carrying small personal articles and money

hand·ball \-ˌbȯl\ n : a game played by striking a small rubber ball against a wall with the hand

hand·bill \-ˌbil\ n : a small printed sheet for distribution by hand

hand·book \-ˌbuk\ n : a concise reference book : MANUAL

hand·car \-ˌkär\ n : a small 4-wheeled railroad car propelled by hand or by a small motor

hand·clasp \-ˌklasp\ n : HANDSHAKE

hand·craft \-ˌkraft\ vb : to fashion by manual skill

¹**hand·cuff** \-ˌkəf\ n : a metal fastening that can be locked around a wrist and is usu. connected with another such fastening — usu. used in pl.

²**handcuff** vb : MANACLE

hand·ed \'han-dəd\ adj : having or using such or so many hands ⟨a left-*handed* person⟩ — **hand·ed·ness** n

hand·ful \'hand-ˌful\ n, pl **hand·fuls** \-ˌfulz\ *also* **hands-ful** \'handz-ˌful\ **1** : as much or as many as the hand will grasp **2** : a small number **3** : as much as one can manage

hand·gun \-ˌgən\ n : a firearm held and fired with one hand

hand·held \-ˌheld\ adj : designed for use while being held in the hand — **handheld** n

¹**hand·i·cap** \'han-di-ˌkap\ n [obs. E *handicap*, a game in which forfeit money was held in a cap, fr. *hand in cap*] **1** : a contest in which an artificial advantage is given or disadvantage imposed on a contestant to equalize chances of winning; *also* : the advantage given or disadvantage imposed **2** : a disadvantage that makes achievement difficult

²**handicap** vb **-capped; -cap·ping 1** : to give a handicap to **2** : to put at a disadvantage

hand·i·capped adj, *sometimes offensive* : having a physical or mental disability

hand·i·cap·per \-ˌka-pər\ n : a person who predicts the winners in a contest

hand·i·craft \'han-di-ˌkraft\ n **1** : manual skill **2** : an occupation requiring manual skill **3** : the articles fashioned by those engaged in handicraft — **hand·i·craft·er** \-ˌkraf-tər\ n — **hand·i·crafts·man** \-ˌkrafts-mən\ n

hand in glove or **hand and glove** adv : in an extremely close relationship

hand·i·work \'han-di-ˌwərk\ n : work done personally or by the hands

hand·ker·chief \'haŋ-kər-chəf, -ˌchēf\ n, pl **-chiefs** \-chəfs, -ˌchēfs\ *also* **-chieves** \-ˌchēvz\ : a small piece of cloth used for various personal purposes (as the wiping of the face)

¹**han·dle** \'han-dᵊl\ n **1** : a part (as of a tool) designed to be grasped by the hand **2** : NAME; *also* : NICKNAME — **han·dled** \-dᵊld\ adj — **off the handle** : into a state of sudden and violent anger — usu. used with *fly*

²**handle** vb **han·dled; han·dling 1** : to touch, hold, or manage with the hands **2** : to have responsibility for **3** : to deal or trade in **4** : to behave in a certain way when managed or directed ⟨a car that ∼s well⟩ — **han·dler** n

han·dle·bar \'han-dᵊl-ˌbär\ n : a usu. bent bar with a grip at each end (as for steering a bicycle) — usu. used in pl.

hand·made \'hand-'mād\ adj : made by hand or by a hand process

hand·maid·en \-ˌmā-dᵊn\ *also* **hand·maid** \-ˌmād\ n : a female attendant

hand–me–down \-me-ˌdaun\ adj : used by one person after having been used by another — **hand–me–down** n

hand·out \'hand-ˌaut\ n **1** : a portion (as of food) given to a beggar **2** : a piece of printed information for free distribution; *also* : a prepared statement released to the press

hand over vb : to yield control of

hand·pick \'hand-'pik\ vb : to select personally ⟨a ∼ed candidate⟩

hand·rail \-ˌrāl\ n : a narrow rail for grasping as a support

hand·saw \-ˌsȯ\ n : a saw designed to be used with one hand

hands down adv **1** : with little effort **2** : without question

hand·sel \'han-səl\ n **1** : a gift made as a token of good luck **2** : a first installment : earnest money

hand·set \'hand-ˌset\ n : a combined telephone transmitter and receiver mounted on a handheld device

hand·shake \-ˌshāk\ n : a clasping usu. of right hands by two people

hands–off \'handz-'ȯf\ adj : characterized by noninterference

hand·some \'han-səm\ adj **hand·som·er; -est** [ME *handsom* easy to manipulate] **1** : SIZABLE, AMPLE **2** : GENEROUS, LIBERAL **3** : pleasing and usu. impressive in appearance ✦ **Synonyms** BEAUTIFUL, LOVELY, PRETTY, COMELY, FAIR — **hand·some·ly** adv — **hand·some·ness** n

hands–on \'handz-'ȯn, -'än\ adj **1** : being or providing direct practical experience in the operation of something **2** : characterized by active personal involvement ⟨∼ management⟩

hand·spring \'hand-ˌspriŋ\ n : an acrobatic feat in which the body turns in a full circle from a standing position and lands first on the hands and then on the feet

hand·stand \-ˌstand\ n : an act of supporting the body on the hands with the trunk and legs balanced in the air

hand–to–hand adj : involving physical contact or very close range ⟨∼ fighting⟩ — **hand to hand** adv

hand–to–mouth adj : having or providing nothing to spare — **hand to mouth** adv

hand·wo·ven \'hand-'wō-vən\ adj : produced on a hand-operated loom

hand·writ·ing \-ˌrī-tiŋ\ n : writing done by hand; *also* : the form of writing peculiar to a person — **hand·writ·ten** \-ˌri-tᵊn\ adj

handy \'han-dē\ adj **hand·i·er; -est** 1 : conveniently near 2 : easily used 3 : DEXTEROUS — **hand·i·ly** \-də-lē\ adv — **hand·i·ness** \-dē-nəs\ n

handy·man \-ˌman\ n 1 : one who does odd jobs 2 : one competent in a variety of small skills or repair work

¹**hang** \'haŋ\ vb **hung** \'həŋ\ also **hanged; hang·ing** 1 : to fasten or remain fastened to an elevated point without support from below; also : to fasten or be fastened so as to allow free motion on the point of suspension ⟨∼ a door⟩ 2 : to suspend by the neck until dead; also : to die by hanging 3 : DROOP ⟨hung his head in shame⟩ 4 : to fasten to a wall ⟨∼ wallpaper⟩ 5 : to prevent (a jury) from coming to a decision 6 : to display (pictures) in a gallery 7 : to remain stationary in the air 8 : to be imminent 9 : DEPEND 10 : to take hold for support 11 : to be burdensome 12 : to undergo delay 13 : to incline downward; also : to fit or fall from the figure in easy lines 14 : to be raptly attentive 15 : to pass time idly by relaxing or socializing ⟨∼ing at the mall⟩ — often used with around or out — **hang out to dry** : to subject to ruin by abandonment

²**hang** n 1 : the manner in which a thing hangs 2 : an understanding of something ⟨got the ∼ of skiing⟩

han·gar \'haŋ-ər\ n [F] : a covered and usu. enclosed area for housing and repairing aircraft

hang·dog \'haŋ-ˌdȯg\ adj 1 : SAD, DEJECTED 2 : SHEEPISH

hang·er \'haŋ-ər\ n 1 : one that hangs 2 : a device that fits inside or around a garment for hanging from a hook or rod

hang·er–on \'haŋ-ər-ˈȯn, -ˈän\ n, pl **hangers–on** : one who hangs around a person or place esp. for personal gain

hang in vb : to persist tenaciously

hang·ing n 1 : an execution by strangling or snapping the neck by a suspended noose 2 : something hung

hang·man \'haŋ-mən\ n 1 : a public executioner 2 : a game in which players must identify an unknown word by guessing the letters that comprise it within a designated number of chances

hang·nail \-ˌnāl\ n : a bit of skin hanging loose at the edge of a fingernail

hang on vb 1 : to keep hold onto something 2 : HANG IN 3 : to await something desired

hang·out \'haŋ-ˌaút\ n : a favorite place for spending time

hang·over \-ˌō-vər\ n 1 : something that remains from what is past 2 : disagreeable physical effects following heavy drinking or the use of drugs

hang–up \'haŋ-ˌəp\ n : a source of mental or emotional difficulty

hang up vb 1 : to place on a hook or hanger 2 : to end a telephone conversation by breaking the connection 3 : to keep delayed or suspended

hank \'haŋk\ n : COIL, LOOP

han·ker \'haŋ-kər\ vb : to desire strongly or persistently — **han·ker·ing** n

han·kie or **han·ky** \'haŋ-kē\ n, pl **hankies** : HANDKERCHIEF

han·ky–pan·ky \ˌhaŋ-kē-ˈpaŋ-kē\ n 1 : questionable or underhanded activity 2 : sexual dalliance

hansel var of HANDSEL

han·som \'han-səm\ n : a 2-wheeled covered carriage with the driver's seat elevated at the rear

han·ta·virus \'hän-tə-ˌvī-rəs, 'hən-, 'han-\ n : any of a genus of viruses including some transmitted by rodents that cause pneumonia or hemorrhagic fevers

Ha·nuk·kah also **Cha·nu·kah** \'kä-nə-kə, 'hä-\ n [Heb ḥănukkāh dedication] : an 8-day Jewish holiday commemorating the rededication of the Temple of Jerusalem after its defilement by Antiochus of Syria

hap \'hap\ n 1 : HAPPENING 2 : CHANCE, FORTUNE

¹**hap·haz·ard** \hap-ˈha-zərd\ n : CHANCE

²**haphazard** adj : marked by lack of plan or order — **hap·haz·ard·ly** adv — **hap·haz·ard·ness** n

hap·less \'hap-ləs\ adj : UNFORTUNATE — **hap·less·ly** adv — **hap·less·ness** n

hap·loid \'hap-ˌlȯid\ adj : having the number of chromosomes characteristic of gametic cells — **haploid** n

hap·ly \'hap-lē\ adv : by chance

hap·pen \'ha-pən\ vb 1 : to occur by chance 2 : to take place 3 : CHANCE 2

¹**hap·pen·ing** n 1 : OCCURRENCE 2 : an event that is especially interesting, entertaining, or important

²**happening** adj 1 : very fashionable 2 : offering much stimulating activity ⟨a ∼ nightclub⟩

hap·pi·ly \'ha-pə-lē\ adv 1 : LUCKILY 2 : in a happy manner or state ⟨lived ∼ ever after⟩ 3 : APTLY, SUCCESSFULLY

hap·pi·ness \'ha-pē-nəs\ n 1 : a state of well-being and contentment; also : a pleasurable satisfaction 2 : APTNESS

hap·py \'ha-pē\ adj **hap·pi·er; -est** 1 : FORTUNATE 2 : APT, FELICITOUS 3 : enjoying well-being and contentment ⟨a ∼ childhood⟩ 4 : PLEASANT ⟨a ∼ ending⟩; also : PLEASED, GRATIFIED ⟨∼ to meet you⟩ 5 : quick or enthusiastic to use or do something ⟨trigger-happy⟩ ⟨a cliché-happy writer⟩ ♦ **Synonyms** GLAD, CHEERFUL, LIGHTHEARTED, JOYFUL, JOYOUS

hap·py–go–lucky \ˌha-pē-gō-ˈlə-kē\ adj : CAREFREE

happy hour n : a period of time when the price of drinks at a bar is reduced

hara–kiri \ˌha-ri-ˈkir-ē, -ˈka-rē\ n [Jp harakiri, fr. hara belly + kiri cutting] : ritual suicide by disembowelment

ha·rangue \hə-ˈraŋ\ n 1 : a ranting speech or writing 2 : LECTURE — **harangue** vb — **ha·rangu·er** n

ha·rass \hə-ˈras, ˈha-rəs\ vb [F harasser, fr. MF, fr. harer to set a dog on, fr. OF hare, interj. used to incite dogs, of Gmc origin] 1 : EXHAUST, FATIGUE 2 : to worry and impede by repeated raids 3 : to annoy continually 4 : to create an unpleasant or hostile situation for esp. by one's verbal or physical conduct ♦ **Synonyms** HARRY, PLAGUE, PESTER, TEASE, BEDEVIL — **ha·rass·ment** n

har·bin·ger \'här-bən-jər\ n : one that announces or foreshadows what is coming : PRECURSOR; also : PORTENT

¹**har·bor** \'här-bər\ n 1 : a place of security and comfort 2 : a part of a body of water protected and deep enough to furnish anchorage : PORT

²**harbor** vb 1 : to give or take refuge : SHELTER ⟨∼ a fugitive⟩ ⟨∼ed in the barn⟩ 2 : to be the home or habitat of; also : LIVE 3 : to hold a thought or feeling ⟨∼ a grudge⟩

har·bor·age \'här-bə-rij\ n : HARBOR

har·bour chiefly Brit var of HARBOR

hard \'härd\ adj 1 : not easily penetrated : not easily yielding to pressure 2 : high in alcoholic content 3 : containing salts that prevent lathering with soap ⟨∼ water⟩ 4 : stable in value ⟨∼ currency⟩ 5 : physically fit 6 : FIRM, DEFINITE ⟨∼ agreement⟩; also : based on clear fact ⟨∼ evidence⟩ 7 : CLOSE, SEARCHING ⟨a ∼ look⟩ 8 : REALISTIC ⟨good ∼ sense⟩ 9 : OBDURATE, UNFEELING ⟨a ∼ heart⟩ 10 : difficult to bear ⟨∼ times⟩; also : HARSH, SEVERE 11 : RESENTFUL ⟨∼ feelings⟩ 12 : STRICT, UNRELENTING ⟨a ∼ bargain⟩ 13 : INCLEMENT ⟨a ∼ winter⟩ 14 : intense in force or manner ⟨a ∼ gust of wind⟩ 15 : ARDUOUS, STRENUOUS ⟨∼ work⟩ 16 : sounding as in arcing and geese respectively — used of c and g 17 : TROUBLESOME ⟨a ∼ problem⟩ 18 : having difficulty in doing something ⟨∼ of hearing⟩ 19 : addictive and gravely detrimental to health ⟨∼ drugs⟩ 20 : of or relating to the natural sciences and esp. the physical sciences — **hard** adv — **hard·ness** n

hard–and–fast adj : rigidly binding : STRICT ⟨a ∼ rule⟩

hard·back \'härd-ˌbak\ n : a hardcover book

hard·ball \-ˌbȯl\ n 1 : BASEBALL 2 : forceful uncompromising methods

hard–bit·ten \-ˈbi-tᵊn\ adj : SEASONED, TOUGH ⟨∼ campaigners⟩

hard·board \-ˌbȯrd\ n : a very dense fiberboard

hard–boiled \-ˈbȯi(-ə)ld\ adj 1 of an egg : boiled until both white and yolk have solidified 2 : lacking sentiment : TOUGH; also : HARDHEADED 2

hard·bound \-ˌbaúnd\ adj : HARDCOVER

hard copy n : copy of textual or graphic information (as from computer storage) produced on paper

hard–core \'härd-ˈkȯr\ adj 1 : extremely resistant to solution or improvement 2 : being the most determined or dedicated members of a specified group 3 : containing explicit depictions of sex acts — **hard core** n

hard·cov·er \-ˈkə-vər\ adj : having rigid boards on the sides covered in cloth or paper ⟨∼ books⟩

hard disk *n* : a sealed rigid metal disk used as a computer storage device; *also* : HARD DRIVE

hard drive *n* : a data-storage device consisting of a drive and one or more hard disks

hard·en \'här-dᵊn\ *vb* **1** : to make or become hard or harder **2** : to confirm or become confirmed in disposition or action — **hard·en·er** *n*

hard·hack \'härd-ˌhak\ *n* : an American spirea with dense clusters of pink or white flowers and leaves having a hairy rusty yellow underside

hard hat *n* **1** : a protective hat worn esp. by construction workers **2** : a construction worker

hard·head·ed \'härd-'he-dəd\ *adj* **1** : STUBBORN, WILLFUL **2** : SOBER, REALISTIC ⟨some ∼ advice⟩ — **hard·head·ed·ly** *adv* — **hard·head·ed·ness** *n*

hard–heart·ed \-'här-təd\ *adj* : PITILESS, CRUEL — **hard–heart·ed·ly** *adv* — **hard–heart·ed·ness** *n*

har·di·hood \'här-dē-ˌhúd\ *n* **1** : resolute courage and fortitude **2** : VIGOR, ROBUSTNESS

hard–line \'härd-'līn\ *adj* : advocating or involving a rigidly uncompromising course of action — **hard–lin·er** \-'lī-nər\ *n*

hard–luck \-ˌlək\ *adj* : marked by or relating to bad luck ⟨∼ losing teams⟩

hard·ly \'härd-lē\ *adv* **1** : with force **2** : SEVERELY **3** : with difficulty **4** : only just : BARELY ⟨can ∼ tell the difference⟩ **5** : certainly not ⟨is ∼ a friend of mine⟩

hard–nosed \'härd-'nōzd\ *adj* : TOUGH, UNCOMPROMISING; *also* : HARDHEADED 2

hard palate *n* : the bony anterior part of the palate forming the roof of the mouth

hard·pan \'härd-ˌpan\ *n* : a compact layer in soil that is impenetrable by roots

hard–pressed \-'prest\ *adj* : HARD PUT; *esp* : being under financial strain

hard put *adj* **1** : barely able **2** : faced with difficulty or perplexity

hard rock *n* : rock music marked by a heavy beat, high amplification, and usu. frenzied performances

hard–shell \'härd-ˌshel\ *or* **hard–shelled** \-ˌsheld\ *adj* **1** : having a hard shell **2** : HIDEBOUND, UNCOMPROMISING ⟨a ∼ conservative⟩

hard·ship \-ˌship\ *n* **1** : SUFFERING, PRIVATION **2** : something that causes suffering or privation

hard·tack \-ˌtak\ *n* : a saltless hard biscuit, bread, or cracker

hard·top \-ˌtäp\ *n* : an automobile having a permanent rigid top

hard·ware \-ˌwer\ *n* **1** : ware (as cutlery or tools) made of metal **2** : the physical components (as electronic devices) of a vehicle (as a spacecraft) or an apparatus (as a computer)

hard·wired \-ˌwī(-ə)rd\ *adj* **1** : connected or incorporated by or as if by permanent electrical connections **2** : genetically or innately determined or predisposed ⟨∼ reactions⟩ ⟨is ∼ to avoid change⟩

hard·wood \-ˌwùd\ *n* : the wood of a broad-leaved usu. deciduous tree as distinguished from that of a conifer; *also* : such a tree — **hardwood** *adj*

hard·work·ing \-'wər-kiŋ\ *adj* : INDUSTRIOUS, DILIGENT

har·dy \'här-dē\ *adj* **har·di·er; -est** **1** : BOLD, BRAVE **2** : AUDACIOUS, BRAZEN **3** : ROBUST; *also* : able to withstand adverse conditions (as of weather) ⟨∼ shrubs⟩ — **har·di·ly** \-də-lē\ *adv* — **har·di·ness** \-dē-nəs\ *n*

hare \'her\ *n, pl* **hare** *or* **hares** : any of various swift timid long-eared mammals like the related rabbits but born with open eyes and fur

hare·bell \'her-ˌbel\ *n* : a slender herb with bright blue bell-shaped flowers

hare–brained \-'brānd\ *adj* : FOOLISH, ABSURD

hare·lip \-'lip\ *n, sometimes offensive* : cleft lip

ha·rem \'her-əm\ *n* [Ar *ḥarīm*, lit., something forbidden & *ḥaram*, lit., sanctuary] **1** : a house or part of a house allotted to women in a Muslim household **2** : the women and servants occupying a harem **3** : a group of females associated with one male

hark \'härk\ *vb* : LISTEN

harken *var of* HEARKEN

har·le·quin \'här-li-kən, -kwən\ *n* **1** *cap* : a character (as in comedy) with a shaved head, masked face, variegated tights, and wooden sword **2** : CLOWN 2

har·lot \'här-lət\ *n* : PROSTITUTE

¹harm \'härm\ *n* **1** : physical or mental damage : INJURY **2** : MISCHIEF, HURT — **harm·ful** \-fəl\ *adj* — **harm·ful·ly** *adv* — **harm·ful·ness** *n* — **harm·less** *adj* — **harm·less·ly** *adv* — **harm·less·ness** *n*

²harm *vb* : to cause harm to : INJURE

¹har·mon·ic \här-'mä-nik\ *adj* **1** : of or relating to musical harmony or harmonics **2** : pleasing to the ear — **har·mon·i·cal·ly** \-ni-k(ə-)lē\ *adv*

²harmonic *n* : a musical overtone

har·mon·i·ca \här-'mä-ni-kə\ *n* : a small wind instrument in which the sound is produced by metal reeds

har·mo·ni·ous \här-'mō-nē-əs\ *adj* **1** : musically concordant **2** : CONGRUOUS **3** : marked by accord in sentiment or action — **har·mo·ni·ous·ly** *adv* — **har·mo·ni·ous·ness** *n*

har·mo·nise *Brit var of* HARMONIZE

har·mo·ni·um \här-'mō-nē-əm\ *n* : a keyboard wind instrument in which the wind acts on a set of metal reeds

har·mo·nize \'här-mə-ˌnīz\ *vb* **-nized; -niz·ing** **1** : to play or sing in harmony **2** : to be in harmony **3** : to bring into consonance or accord — **har·mo·ni·za·tion** \ˌhär-mə-nə-'zā-shən\ *n*

har·mo·ny \'här-mə-nē\ *n, pl* **-nies** [ME *armony*, fr. AF *armonie*, fr. L *harmonia*, fr. Gk, joint, harmony, fr. *harmos* joint] **1** : musical agreement of sounds; *esp* : the combination of tones into chords and progressions of chords **2** : a pleasing arrangement of parts; *also* : ACCORD **3** : internal calm

¹har·ness \'här-nəs\ *n* **1** : the gear other than a yoke of a draft animal **2** : something that resembles a harness

²harness *vb* **1** : to put a harness on; *also* : YOKE **2** : UTILIZE ⟨∼ one's potential⟩

¹harp \'härp\ *n* : a musical instrument consisting of a triangular frame set with strings plucked by the fingers — **harp·ist** \'här-pist\ *n*

²harp *vb* **1** : to play on a harp **2** : to dwell on a subject tiresomely — **harp·er** *n*

har·poon \här-'pün\ *n* : a barbed spear used esp. in hunting whales — **harpoon** *vb* — **har·poon·er** *n*

harp·si·chord \'härp-si-ˌkórd\ *n* : a keyboard instrument producing tones by the plucking of its strings with quills or with leather or plastic points

har·py \'här-pē\ *n, pl* **harpies** [L *Harpyia*, a malign creature of myth having a woman's head and a bird's body, fr. Gk] **1** : a predatory person : LEECH **2** : a shrewish woman

har·ri·dan \'her-ə-dən\ *n* : SHREW 2

¹har·ri·er \'her-ē-ər\ *n* **1** : any of a breed of medium-sized foxhounds **2** : a runner on a cross-country team

²harrier *n* : a slender long-legged hawk

¹har·row \'her-ō\ *n* : a cultivating tool that has spikes, spring teeth, or disks and is used esp. to pulverize and smooth the soil

²harrow *vb* **1** : to cultivate with a harrow **2** : TORMENT, VEX

har·rumph \hə-'rəmf\ *vb* : to comment disapprovingly as though clearing the throat

har·ry \'her-ē\ *vb* **har·ried; har·ry·ing** **1** : RAID, PILLAGE **2** : to torment by or as if by constant attack ♦ *Synonyms* WORRY, ANNOY, PLAGUE, PESTER

harsh \'härsh\ *adj* **1** : disagreeably rough **2** : causing discomfort or pain **3** : unduly exacting : SEVERE — **harsh·ly** *adv* — **harsh·ness** *n*

harsh·en \'här-shən\ *vb* : to make or become harsh ⟨∼ed his voice⟩

hart \'härt\ *n, chiefly Brit* : STAG

har·um–scar·um \ˌhar-əm-'skar-əm\ *adj* : RECKLESS, IRRESPONSIBLE

¹har·vest \'här-vəst\ *n* **1** : the season for gathering in crops; *also* : the act of gathering in a crop **2** : a mature crop **3** : the product or reward of effort

²harvest *vb* **1** : to gather in a crop : REAP **2** : to gather, hunt, or kill (as deer) for human use or population control **3** : to remove cells, tissues, or organs from a living or recently deceased body esp. for transplanting — **har·vest·er** *n*

has *pres 3d sing of* HAVE

has–been \'haz-ˌbin\ *n* : one that has passed the peak of ability, power, effectiveness, or popularity

¹hash \'hash\ *vb* [F *hacher*, fr. OF *hachier*, fr. *hache* battle-ax, of Gmc origin] **1** : to chop into small pieces **2** : to talk about — often used with *over* or *out*

²hash *n* **1** : chopped meat mixed with potatoes and browned **2** : HODGEPODGE, JUMBLE

³hash *n* : HASHISH

hash browns *n pl* : boiled potatoes that have been diced, mixed with chopped onions and shortening, and fried

hash·ish \'ha-ˌshēsh, ha-'shēsh\ *n* [Ar *ḥashīsh*] : the intoxicating concentrated resin from the flowering tops of the female hemp plant

hasp \'hasp\ *n* : a fastener (as for a door) consisting of a hinged metal strap that fits over a staple and is secured by a pin or padlock

has·si·um \'ha-sē-əm\ *n* : an artificially produced radioactive metallic chemical element

has·sle \'ha-səl\ *n* **1** : WRANGLE; *also* : FIGHT **2** : an annoying or troublesome concern — **hassle** *vb*

has·sock \'ha-sək\ *n* : a cushion that serves as a seat or leg rest; *also* : a cushion to kneel on in prayer

haste \'hāst\ *n* **1** : rapidity of motion or action : SPEED **2** : rash or headlong action **3** : excessive eagerness — **hast·i·ly** \'hā-stə-lē\ *adv* — **hast·i·ness** \-stē-nəs\ *n* — **hasty** \'hā-stē\ *adj*

has·ten \'hā-sᵊn\ *vb* **1** : to urge on **2** : to move or act quickly : HURRY ♦ *Synonyms* SPEED, ACCELERATE, QUICKEN

hat \'hat\ *n* : a covering for the head usu. having a shaped crown and brim — **under one's hat** : SECRET ⟨kept the plans *under his hat*⟩

hat·box \'hat-ˌbäks\ *n* : a round piece of luggage esp. for carrying hats

¹hatch \'hach\ *n* **1** : a small door or opening **2** : a door or cover for access down into a compartment of a ship

²hatch *vb* **1** : to produce by incubation; *also* : INCUBATE **2** : to emerge from an egg or pupa; *also* : to give forth young **3** : ORIGINATE ⟨∼ a scheme⟩ — **hatch·ery** \'ha-chə-rē\ *n*

hatch·back \'hach-ˌbak\ *n* : an automobile with a rear hatch that opens upward

hatch·et \'ha-chət\ *n* **1** : a short-handled ax with a hammerlike part opposite the blade **2** : TOMAHAWK

hatchet man *n* : a person hired for murder, coercion, or unscrupulous attack

hatch·ing \'ha-chiŋ\ *n* : the engraving or drawing of closely spaced fine lines chiefly to give an effect of shading; *also* : the pattern so created

hatch·way \'hach-ˌwā\ *n* : a hatch giving access usu. by a ladder or stairs

¹hate \'hāt\ *n* **1** : intense hostility and aversion **2** : an object of hatred — **hate·ful** \-fəl\ *adj* — **hate·ful·ly** *adv* — **hate·ful·ness** *n*

²hate *vb* **hat·ed; hat·ing** **1** : to express or feel extreme enmity **2** : to find distasteful ♦ *Synonyms* DETEST, ABHOR, ABOMINATE, LOATHE — **hat·er** *n*

ha·tred \'hā-trəd\ *n* : HATE; *also* : prejudiced hostility or animosity

hat·ter \'ha-tər\ *n* : one that makes, sells, or cleans and repairs hats

hau·berk \'hȯ-bərk\ *n* : a coat of mail

haugh·ty \'hȯ-tē\ *adj* **haugh·ti·er; -est** [obs. *haught*, fr. ME *haute*, fr. AF *halt, haut*, lit., high, fr. L *altus*] : disdainfully proud ♦ *Synonyms* INSOLENT, LORDLY, OVERBEARING, ARROGANT — **haugh·ti·ly** \-tə-lē\ *adv* — **haugh·ti·ness** \-tē-nəs\ *n*

¹haul \'hȯl\ *vb* **1** : to exert traction on : DRAW, PULL **2** : to furnish transportation : CART — **haul·er** *n*

²haul *n* **1** : PULL, TUG **2** : the result of an effort to obtain, collect, or win **3** : the length or course of a transportation route; *also* : LOAD

haul·age \'hȯ-lij\ *n* **1** : the act or process of hauling **2** : a charge for hauling

haunch \'hȯnch\ *n* **1** : ²HIP 1 **2** : HINDQUARTER 2 — usu. used in pl. **3** : HINDQUARTER 1

¹haunt \'hȯnt\ *vb* **1** : to visit often : FREQUENT **2** : to have a disquieting effect on ⟨was ∼*ed* by his past⟩; *also* : to reappear continually in **3** : to visit or inhabit as a ghost — **haunt·er** *n* — **haunt·ing·ly** *adv*

²haunt \'hȯnt, *2 is usu* 'hant\ *n* **1** : a place habitually frequented **2** *chiefly dial* : GHOST

haute cou·ture \ˌōt-kü-'tùr\ *n* [F] : the establishments or designers that create exclusive and often trend-setting fashions for women; *also* : the fashions created

haute cui·sine \-kwi-'zēn\ *n* : artful or elaborate cuisine

hau·teur \hȯ-'tər, ō-, hō-\ *n* : ARROGANCE, HAUGHTINESS

¹have \'hav, həv, v; *in sense 2 before "to" usu* 'haf\ *vb* **had** \'had, həd\; **hav·ing; has** \'haz, həz, *in sense 2 before "to" usu* 'has\ **1** : to hold in possession; *also* : to hold in one's use, service, or regard ⟨*has* a good job⟩ **2** : to be compelled or forced ⟨∼ to go now⟩ **3** : to stand in relationship to ⟨*has* many enemies⟩ **4** : OBTAIN; *also* : RECEIVE, ACCEPT **5** : to be marked by ⟨*has* red hair⟩ **6** : SHOW; *also* : USE, EXERCISE ⟨∼ mercy⟩ **7** : EXPERIENCE; *also* : TAKE ⟨∼ a look⟩ **8** : to entertain in the mind ⟨∼ an idea⟩ **9** : to cause to **10** : ALLOW **11** : to be competent in **12** : to hold in a disadvantageous position; *also* : TRICK **13** : BEGET **14** : to partake of **15** — used as an auxiliary with the past participle to form the present perfect, past perfect, or future perfect — **have at** : ATTACK — **have coming** : DESERVE — **have done with** : to be finished with — **have had it** : to have endured all one will permit or can stand — **have to do with** : to have in the way of relation with or effect on

²have \'hav\ *n* : one that has material wealth

ha·ven \'hā-vən\ *n* **1** : HARBOR, PORT **2** : a place of safety **3** : a place offering favorable conditions ⟨an artist's ∼⟩

have–not \'hav-ˌnät, -'nät\ *n* : one that is poor in material wealth

hav·er·sack \'ha-vər-ˌsak\ *n* [F *havresac*, fr. G *Habersack* bag for oats] : a bag similar to a knapsack but worn over one shoulder

hav·oc \'ha-vək\ *n* **1** : wide and general destruction **2** : great confusion and disorder

haw \'hȯ\ *n* : a hawthorn berry; *also* : HAWTHORN

Ha·wai·ian \hə-'wä-yən\ *n* **1** : a native or resident of Hawaii; *esp* : one of Polynesisan ancestry **2** : the Polynesian language of Hawaii

¹hawk \'hȯk\ *n* **1** : any of numerous mostly small or medium-sized day-flying birds of prey (as a falcon or kite) **2** : a supporter of a war or a warlike policy — **hawk·ish** *adj*

hawk 1

²hawk *vb* : to make a harsh coughing sound in or as if in clearing the throat; *also* : to raise by hawking

³hawk *vb* : to offer goods for sale by calling out in the street — **hawk·er** *n*

hawk·weed \'hȯk-ˌwēd\ *n* : any of several plants related to the daisies usu. having yellow flowers

haw·ser \'hȯ-zər\ *n* : a large rope for towing, mooring, or securing a ship

haw·thorn \'hȯ-ˌthȯrn\ *n* : any of a genus of spiny spring-flowering shrubs or small trees related to the apple

¹hay \'hā\ *n* **1** : herbage (as grass) mowed and cured for fodder **2** : REWARD **3** *slang* : BED ⟨hit the ∼⟩ **4** : a small amount of money

²hay *vb* : to cut, cure, and store for hay

hay·cock \'hā-ˌkäk\ *n* : a small conical pile of hay

hay fever *n* : an acute allergic reaction esp. to plant pollen that resembles a cold

hay·loft \'hā-ˌlȯft\ *n* : a loft for hay

hay·mow \-ˌmaù\ *n* : a mow of or for hay

hay·rick \-ˌrik\ *n* : a large sometimes thatched outdoor stack of hay

hay·seed \-ˌsēd\ *n, pl* **hayseed** *or* **hayseeds** **1** : clinging bits of straw or chaff from hay **2** : BUMPKIN, YOKEL

hay·stack \-ˌstak\ *n* : a stack of hay

hay·wire \-ˌwī(-ə)r\ *adj* : being out of order or control : CRAZY ⟨things went ∼⟩

¹haz·ard \'ha-zərd\ *n* [ME, a dice game, fr. AF *hasard,* fr. Sp *azar,* Ar *al-zahr* the die] **1** : a source of danger **2** : CHANCE; *also* : ACCIDENT **3** : an obstacle on a golf course — **haz·ard·ous** *adj*

²hazard *vb* : VENTURE, RISK ⟨~ a guess⟩

¹haze \'hāz\ *n* **1** : fine dust, smoke, or light vapor causing lack of transparency in the air **2** : vagueness of mind or perception

²haze *vb* **hazed; haz·ing** : to harass by abusive and humiliating tricks usu. by way of initiation

ha·zel \'hā-zəl\ *n* **1** : any of a genus of shrubs or small trees related to the birches and bearing edible brown nuts (**ha·zel·nuts** \-ˌnəts\) **2** : a light brown color

hazy \'hā-zē\ *adj* **haz·i·er; -est 1** : obscured or darkened by haze **2** : VAGUE, INDEFINITE ⟨a ~ memory⟩; *also* : UNCERTAIN — **haz·i·ly** \-zə-lē\ *adv* — **haz·i·ness** \-zē-nəs\ *n*

Hb *abbr* hemoglobin

HBM *abbr* Her Britannic Majesty; His Britannic Majesty

H–bomb \'āch-ˌbäm\ *n* : HYDROGEN BOMB

HC *abbr* **1** Holy Communion **2** House of Commons

hd *abbr* head

HD *abbr* heavy-duty

hdbk *abbr* handbook

hdkf *abbr* handkerchief

HDL \ˌāch-(ˌ)dē-'el\ *n* [*h*igh-*d*ensity *l*ipoprotein] : a cholesterol-poor protein-rich lipoprotein of blood plasma correlated with reduced risk of atherosclerosis

hdwe *abbr* hardware

he \'hē\ *pron* **1** : that male one **2** : a person : the person ⟨~ who hesitates is lost⟩

He *symbol* helium

HE *abbr* **1** Her Excellency **2** His Eminence **3** His Excellency

¹head \'hed\ *n* **1** : the front or upper part of the body containing the brain, the chief sense organs, and the mouth **2** : MIND; *also* : natural aptitude ⟨has a ~ for math⟩ **3** : POISE ⟨a level ~⟩ **4** : the obverse of a coin **5** : INDIVIDUAL; *also pl* **head** : one of a number (as of cattle) **6** : the end that is upper or higher or opposite the foot; *also* : either end of something (as a drum) whose two ends need not be distinguished **7** : a compact mass of plant parts (as leaves or flowers) **8** : the source of a stream **9** : DIRECTOR, LEADER; *also* : a leading element (as of a procession) **10** : a projecting part; *also* : the striking part of a weapon **11** : the place of leadership or honor **12** : a separate part or topic **13** : the foam on a fermenting or effervescing liquid **14** : a critical point ⟨events came to a ~⟩ — **head·ed** \'he-dəd\ *adj* — **head·less** *adj* — **over one's head** : beyond one's comprehension or competence

²head *adj* : PRINCIPAL, CHIEF ⟨~ chef⟩

³head *vb* **1** : to provide with or form a head; *also* : to form the head of **2** : LEAD, CONDUCT ⟨~ed the search⟩ **3** : to get in front of esp. so as to stop; *also* : SURPASS **4** : to put or stand at the head **5** : to point or proceed in a certain direction ⟨~ed west⟩

head·ache \'he-ˌdāk\ *n* **1** : pain in the head **2** : a baffling situation or problem — **head·achy** *also* **head·achey** \-ˌā-kē\ *adj*

head·band \'hed-ˌband\ *n* : a band worn on or around the head

head·bang·er \-ˌbaŋ-ər\ *n* : one who performs or enjoys hard rock

head·board \-ˌbȯrd\ *n* : a board forming the head (as of a bed)

head cold *n* : a common cold centered in the nasal passages and adjacent mucous tissues

head·dress \'hed-ˌdres\ *n* : an often elaborate covering for the head

head·first \-'fərst\ *adv* : HEADLONG 1 ⟨dove ~ into the water⟩ — **headfirst** *adj*

head·gear \-ˌgir\ *n* : a covering or protective device for the head

head·hunt·er \-ˌhən-tər\ *n* **1** : one that engages in headhunting **2** : a recruiter of esp. executive personnel

head–hunt·ing \-ˌhən-tiŋ\ *n* : the practice of seeking out and decapitating enemies and preserving their heads as trophies

head·ing \'he-diŋ\ *n* **1** : the compass direction in which the longitudinal axis of a ship or airplane points **2**

: something that appears at the top or beginning of something else (as a document)

head·land \'hed-lənd, -ˌland\ *n* : PROMONTORY

head·light \-ˌlīt\ *n* : a light mounted on the front of a vehicle to illuminate the road ahead

¹head·line \-ˌlīn\ *n* : a head of a newspaper story or article usu. printed in large type

²headline *vb* **1** : to provide with a headline **2** : to publicize highly **3** : to be a leading performer in

head·lock \-ˌläk\ *n* : a wrestling hold in which one encircles the opponent's head with one arm

¹head·long \-'lȯŋ\ *adv* **1** : with the head foremost **2** : RECKLESSLY **3** : without delay

²head·long \-ˌlȯŋ\ *adj* **1** : PRECIPITATE, RASH ⟨~ flight⟩ **2** : plunging with the head foremost

head·man \'hed-ˌman, -ˌman\ *n* : one who is a leader : CHIEF

head·mas·ter \-ˌmas-tər\ *n* : a man who is head of a private school

head·mis·tress \-ˌmis-trəs\ *n* : a woman who is head of a private school

head of stream : strong driving force : MOMENTUM

head–on \'hed-ˈȯn, -ˈän\ *adj* : having the front facing in the direction of initial contact or line of sight ⟨~ collision⟩ — **head–on** *adv*

head·phone \-ˌfōn\ *n* : an earphone held on by a band over the head

head·piece \-ˌpēs\ *n* : a covering for the head

head·pin \-ˌpin\ *n* : a bowling pin that stands foremost in the arrangement of pins

head·quar·ters \-ˌkwȯr-tərz\ *n sing or pl* **1** : a place from which a commander exercises command **2** : the administrative center of an enterprise

head·rest \-ˌrest\ *n* **1** : a support for the head **2** : a pad at the top of the back of an automobile seat

head·room \-ˌrüm, -ˌrum\ *n* : vertical space in which to stand, sit, or move

head–scratcher \-ˌskra-chər\ *n* : PUZZLE, MYSTERY

head·set \-ˌset\ *n* : a pair of headphones

head·ship \-ˌship\ *n* : the position, office, or dignity of a head

heads·man \'hedz-mən\ *n* : EXECUTIONER

head·stall \'hed-ˌstȯl\ *n* : a part of a bridle or halter that encircles the head

head·stone \-ˌstōn\ *n* : a memorial stone at the head of a grave

head·strong \'hed-ˌstrȯŋ\ *adj* **1** : not easily restrained **2** : directed by ungovernable will ♦ *Synonyms* UNRULY, INTRACTABLE, WILLFUL, PERTINACIOUS, REFRACTORY, STUBBORN

heads–up \'hedz-'əp\ *n* : WARNING

head·wait·er \-'wā-tər\ *n* : the head of the dining-room staff of a restaurant or hotel

head·wa·ter \-ˌwȯ-tər, -ˌwä-\ *n* : the source of a stream — usu. used in pl.

head·way \-ˌwā\ *n* : forward motion; *also* : PROGRESS

head·wind \-ˌwind\ *n* : a wind blowing in a direction opposite to a course esp. of a ship or aircraft

head·word \'hed-ˌwərd\ *n* **1** : a word or term placed at the beginning **2** : a word qualified by a modifier

head·work \-ˌwərk\ *n* : mental work or effort : THINKING

heady \'he-dē\ *adj* **head·i·er; -est 1** : WILLFUL, RASH; *also* : IMPETUOUS **2** : INTOXICATING **3** : SHREWD

heal \'hēl\ *vb* **1** : to make or become healthy, sound, or whole **2** : CURE, REMEDY — **heal·er** *n*

health \'helth\ *n* **1** : sound physical or mental condition; *also* : overall condition of the body ⟨in poor ~⟩ **2** : WELL-BEING **3** : a toast to someone's health or prosperity

health care *n* : efforts made to maintain or restore health — usu. hyphenated when used attributively

health club *n* : a commercial establishment providing health and fitness facilities and equipment for members

health·ful \'helth-fəl\ *adj* **1** : beneficial to health **2** : HEALTHY — **health·ful·ly** *adv* — **health·ful·ness** *n*

health maintenance organization *n* : HMO

healthy \'hel-thē\ *adj* **health·i·er; -est 1** : enjoying or typical of good health : WELL **2** : evincing or conducive to health **3** : PROSPEROUS ⟨a ~ economy⟩; *also* : CONSIDERABLE 2 ⟨a ~ savings⟩ — **health·i·ly** \-thə-lē\ *adv* — **health·i·ness** \-thē-nəs\ *n*

¹**heap** \'hēp\ *n* : PILE ⟨rubbish ∼⟩; *also* : LOT 5 ⟨a ∼ of fun⟩

²**heap** *vb* **1** : to throw or lay in a heap **2** : to give in large quantities; *also* : to load heavily

hear \'hir\ *vb* **heard** \'hərd\; **hear·ing** **1** : to perceive by the ear **2** : to gain knowledge of by hearing : LEARN **3** : HEED; *also* : ATTEND **4** : to give a legal hearing to or take testimony from — **hear·er** *n*

hear·ing *n* **1** : the process, function, or power of perceiving sound; *esp* : the special sense by which noises and tones are received as stimuli **2** : EARSHOT **3** : opportunity to be heard **4** : a listening to arguments (as in a court); *also* : a session of (as of a legislative committee) in which testimony is taken from witnesses

hear·ken \'här-kən\ *vb* : to give attention : LISTEN ✦ **Synonyms** HEAR, HARK, HEED

hear·say \'hir-ˌsā\ *n* : RUMOR

hearse \'hərs\ *n* : a vehicle for carrying the dead to the grave

heart \'härt\ *n* **1** : a hollow muscular organ that by rhythmic contraction keeps up the circulation of the blood in the body; *also* : something resembling a heart in shape **2** : any of a suit of playing cards marked with a red figure of a heart; *also, pl* : a card game in which the object is to avoid taking tricks containing hearts **3** : the whole personality; *also* : the emotional or moral as distinguished from the intellectual nature **4** : COURAGE **5** : one's innermost being ⟨knew it in his ∼⟩ **6** : CENTER; *also* : the essential part **7** : the younger central part of a compact leafy cluster (as of lettuce) — **heart·ed** \'här-təd\ *adj* — **by heart** : by rote or from memory

heart·ache \-ˌāk\ *n* : anguish of mind

heart attack *n* : an acute episode of heart disease due to insufficient blood supply to the heart muscle

heart·beat \'härt-ˌbēt\ *n* : one complete pulsation of the heart

heart·break \-ˌbrāk\ *n* : crushing grief

heart·break·ing \-ˌbrā-kiŋ\ *adj* : causing extreme sorrow or distress — **heart·break·er** \-ˌbrā-kər\ *n* — **heart·break·ing·ly** *adv*

heart·bro·ken \-ˌbrō-kən\ *adj* : overcome by sorrow

heart·burn \-ˌbərn\ *n* : a burning distress behind the sternum due esp. to the backward flow of acid from the stomach to the esophagus

heart disease *n* : an abnormal organic condition of the heart or of the heart and circulation

heart·en \'här-tᵊn\ *vb* : ENCOURAGE, CHEER

heart·felt \'härt-ˌfelt\ *adj* : deeply felt : SINCERE

hearth \'härth\ *n* **1** : an area (as of brick) in front of a fireplace; *also* : the floor of a fireplace **2** : HOME

hearth·stone \'härth-ˌstōn\ *n* **1** : stone forming a hearth **2** : HOME

heart·less \'härt-ləs\ *adj* : CRUEL

heart·rend·ing \-ˌren-diŋ\ *adj* : HEARTBREAKING

heart·sick \-ˌsik\ *adj* : very despondent — **heart·sick·ness** *n*

heart–stop·ping \-ˌstä-piŋ\ *adj* : extremely shocking or exciting

heart·strings \-ˌstriŋz\ *n pl* : the deepest emotions or affections

heart·throb \-ˌthräb\ *n* **1** : the throb of a heart **2** : sentimental emotion **3** : SWEETHEART **4** : an entertainer noted for his sex appeal

heart–to–heart *adj* : SINCERE, FRANK

heart·warm·ing \'härt-ˌwȯr-miŋ\ *adj* : inspiring sympathetic feeling

heart·wood \-ˌwu̇d\ *n* : the older harder nonliving and usu. darker wood of the central part of a tree trunk

¹**hearty** \'här-tē\ *adj* **heart·i·er**; **-est** **1** : giving full support; *also* : JOVIAL **2** : vigorously healthy **3** : ABUNDANT; *also* : NOURISHING ✦ **Synonyms** SINCERE, WHOLEHEARTED, UNFEIGNED, HEARTFELT — **heart·i·ly** \-tə-lē\ *adv* — **heart·i·ness** \-tē-nəs\ *n*

²**hearty** *n, pl* **heart·ies** : an enthusiastic jovial fellow; *also* : SAILOR

¹**heat** \'hēt\ *vb* **1** : to make or become warm or hot **2** : EXCITE — **heat·ed·ly** *adv* — **heat·er** *n*

²**heat** *n* **1** : a condition of being hot : WARMTH **2** : a form of energy that when added to a body causes the body to rise in temperature, to fuse, to evaporate, or to expand **3** : high temperature **4** : intensity of feeling; *also* : sexual

excitement esp. in a female mammal **5** : a preliminary race for narrowing the competition **6** : pungency of flavor **7** *slang* : POLICE **8** : PRESSURE, COERCION; *also* : ABUSE, CRITICISM ⟨took ∼ for my mistakes⟩

heat exchanger *n* : a device (as an automobile radiator) for transferring heat from one fluid to another without allowing them to mix

heat exhaustion *n* : a condition marked by weakness, nausea, dizziness, and profuse sweating resulting from physical exertion in a hot environment

heath \'hēth\ *n* **1** : a tract of wasteland **2** : any of a family of often evergreen shrubby plants (as a blueberry or heather) of wet acid soils — **heathy** *adj*

hea·then \'hē-thən\ *n, pl* **heathens** *or* **heathen** **1** : an unconverted member of a people or nation that does not acknowledge the God of the Bible **2** : an uncivilized or irreligious person — **heathen** *adj* — **hea·then·dom** *n* — **hea·then·ish** *adj* — **hea·then·ism** *n*

heath·er \'he-thər\ *n* : a northern and alpine evergreen heath with usu. lavender flowers — **heath·ery** *adj*

heat lightning *n* : flashes of light without thunder ascribed to distant lightning reflected by high clouds

heat·stroke \'hēt-ˌstrōk\ *n* : a disorder marked esp. by high body temperature without sweating and by collapse that follows prolonged exposure to excessive heat

¹**heave** \'hēv\ *vb* **heaved** *or* **hove** \'hōv\; **heav·ing** **1** : to rise or lift upward **2** : THROW **3** : to rise and fall rhythmically; *also* : PANT **4** : RETCH **5** : PULL, PUSH — **heav·er** *n*

²**heave** *n* **1** : an effort to lift or raise **2** : THROW, CAST **3** : an upward motion **4** *pl* : a chronic lung disease of horses marked by difficult breathing and persistent cough

heav·en \'he-vən\ *n* **1** : FIRMAMENT — usu. used in pl. **2** *often cap* : the abode of the Deity and of the blessed dead; *also* : a spiritual state of everlasting communion with God **3** *cap* : GOD 1 **4** : a place of supreme happiness — **heav·en·ly** *adj* — **heav·en·ward** *adv or adj*

¹**heavy** \'he-vē\ *adj* **heavi·er**; **-est** **1** : having great weight **2** : hard to bear **3** : SERIOUS **4** : DEEP, PROFOUND ⟨a ∼ silence⟩ **5** : burdened with something oppressive; *also* : PREGNANT **6** : SLUGGISH **7** : DRAB; *also* : DOLEFUL **8** : DROWSY **9** : greater than the average of its kind or class **10** : very rich and hard to digest; *also* : not properly raised or leavened **11** : producing goods (as steel) used in the production of other goods — **heavi·ly** \-və-lē\ *adv* — **heavi·ness** \-vē-nəs\ *n*

²**heavy** *n, pl* **heav·ies** : a theatrical role representing a dignified or imposing person; *also* : a villain esp. in a story

heavy–du·ty \ˌhe-vē-ˈdü-tē, -ˈdyü-\ *adj* : able to withstand unusual strain

heavy–hand·ed \-ˈhan-dəd\ *adj* **1** : CLUMSY **2** : OPPRESSIVE, HARSH

heavy·heart·ed \-ˈhär-təd\ *adj* : SADDENED, DESPONDENT

heavy lifting *n* : a burdensome or laborious duty

heavy metal *n* : energetic and highly amplified electronic rock music

heavy·set \ˌhe-vē-ˈset\ *adj* : stocky and compact in build

heavy water *n* : water enriched in deuterium

heavy·weight \'he-vē-ˌwāt\ *n* : one above average in weight; *esp* : a boxer in an unlimited weight division

Heb *abbr* Hebrews

He·bra·ism \'hē-brā-ˌi-zəm\ *n* : the thought, spirit, or practice characteristic of the Hebrews — **He·bra·ic** \hi-'brā-ik\ *adj*

He·bra·ist \'hē-ˌbrā-ist\ *n* : a specialist in Hebrew and Hebraic studies

He·brew \'hē-brü\ *n* **1** : the language of the Hebrews **2** : a member of or descendant from a group of Semitic peoples; *esp* : ISRAELITE — **Hebrew** *adj*

He·brews \'hē-(ˌ)brüz\ *n* — see BIBLE table

hec·a·tomb \'he-kə-ˌtōm\ *n* : an ancient Greek and Roman sacrifice of 100 oxen or cattle

heck·le \'he-kəl\ *vb* **heck·led**; **heck·ling** : to harass with questions or gibes : BADGER — **heck·ler** *n*

hect·are \'hek-ˌter\ *n* — see METRIC SYSTEM table

hec·tic \'hek-tik\ *adj* **1** : being hot and flushed **2** : filled with excitement, activity, or confusion — **hec·ti·cal·ly** \-ti-k(ə-)lē\ *adv*

hec·to·gram \'hek-tə-ˌgram\ *n* — see METRIC SYSTEM table

hec·to·li·ter \'hek-tə-ˌlē-tər\ *n* — see METRIC SYSTEM table

hec·to·me·ter \'hek-tə-ˌmē-tər, hek-'tä-mə-tər\ *n* — see METRIC SYSTEM table

hec·tor \'hek-tər\ *vb* [*hector* bully, fr. *Hector*, champion of Troy in Greek legend] **1** : SWAGGER **2** : to intimidate by bluster or personal pressure

¹hedge \'hej\ *n* **1** : a fence or boundary formed of shrubs or small trees **2** : BARRIER **3** : a means of protection (as against financial loss)

²hedge *vb* **hedged; hedg·ing 1** : ENCIRCLE **2** : HINDER **3** : to protect oneself financially by a counterbalancing action **4** : to evade the risk of commitment — **hedg·er** *n*

hedge·hog \'hej-ˌhȯg, -ˌhäg\ *n* : a small Old World insect-eating mammal covered with spines; *also* : PORCUPINE

hedge·hop \-ˌhäp\ *vb* : to fly an airplane very close to the ground

hedge·row \-ˌrō\ *n* : a row of shrubs or trees bounding or separating fields

he·do·nism \'hē-də-ˌni-zəm\ *n* [Gk *hēdonē* pleasure] : the doctrine that pleasure is the chief good in life; *also* : a way of life based on this — **he·do·nist** \-nist\ *n* — **he·do·nis·tic** \ˌhēdə-'ni-stik\ *adj*

¹heed \'hēd\ *vb* : to pay attention

²heed *n* : ATTENTION, NOTICE — **heed·ful** \-fəl\ *adj* — **heed·ful·ly** *adv* — **heed·ful·ness** *n* — **heed·less** *adj* — **heed·less·ly** *adv* — **heed·less·ness** *n*

¹heel \'hēl\ *n* **1** : the hind part of the foot **2** : one of the crusty ends of a loaf of bread **3** : a solid attachment forming the back of the sole of a shoe **4** : a rear, low, or bottom part **5** : a contemptible person

²heel *vb* : to tilt to one side : LIST

¹heft \'heft\ *n* : WEIGHT, HEAVINESS

²heft *vb* : to test the weight of by lifting

hefty \'hef-tē\ *adj* **heft·i·er; -est 1** : marked by bigness, bulk, and usu. strength **2** : impressively large ⟨got a ∼ raise⟩

he·ge·mo·ny \hi-'je-mə-nē\ *n* : preponderant influence or authority over others : DOMINATION

he·gi·ra \hi-'jī-rə\ *n* [the *Hegira*, flight of Muhammad from Mecca in A.D. 622, fr. ML, fr. Ar *hijra*, lit., departure] : a journey esp. when undertaken to escape a dangerous or undesirable environment

heif·er \'he-fər\ *n* : a young cow; *esp* : one that has not had a calf

height \'hīt\ *n* **1** : the highest part or point **2** : the distance from the bottom to the top of something standing upright **3** : ALTITUDE

height·en \'hī-tᵊn\ *vb* **1** : to increase in amount or degree **2** : to make or become high or higher ◆ *Synonyms* ENHANCE, INTENSIFY, AGGRAVATE, MAGNIFY

Heim·lich maneuver \'hīm-lik-\ *n* [Henry J. *Heimlich* b1920 Am. surgeon] : the manual application of sudden upward pressure on the upper abdomen of a choking victim to force a foreign object from the trachea

hei·nous \'hā-nəs\ *adj* [ME, fr. AF *hainus, heinous*, fr. *haine* hate, fr. *hair* to hate] : hatefully or shockingly evil — **hei·nous·ly** *adv* — **hei·nous·ness** *n*

heir \'er\ *n* : one who inherits or is entitled to inherit property, rank, title, or office — **heir·ship** *n*

heir apparent *n, pl* **heirs apparent** : an heir whose right to succeed (as to a title) cannot be taken away if he or she survives the present holder

heir·ess \'er-əs\ *n* : a female heir esp. to great wealth

heir·loom \'er-ˌlüm\ *n* **1** : a piece of personal property that descends by inheritance **2** : something handed on from one generation to another

heir presumptive *n, pl* **heirs presumptive** : an heir whose present right to inherit could be lost through the birth of a nearer relative

heist \'hīst\ *vb* : to commit armed robbery on; *also* : STEAL — **heist** *n*

held *past and past part of* HOLD

he·li·cal \'he-li-kəl, 'hē-\ *adj* : SPIRAL

he·li·cop·ter \'he-lə-ˌkäp-tər, 'hē-\ *n* [F *hélicoptère*, fr. Gk *helik-, helix* spiral + *pteron* wing] : an aircraft that is supported in the air by one or more rotors revolving on substantially vertical axes

he·lio·cen·tric \ˌhē-lē-ō-'sen-trik\ *adj* : having or relating to the sun as center

he·lio·sphere \'hē-lē-ə-ˌsfir, -ō-\ *n* : the region in space influenced by the sun or solar wind

he·lio·trope \'hē-lē-ə-ˌtrōp\ *n* [L *heliotropium*, fr. Gk *hēli-*

otropion, fr. *hēlios* sun + *tropos* turn; fr. its flowers' turning toward the sun] : any of a genus of herbs or shrubs related to the forget-me-nots that have small white or purple flowers

he·li·port \'he-lə-ˌpȯrt\ *n* : a landing and takeoff place for a helicopter

he·li·um \'hē-lē-əm\ *n* [NL, fr. Gk *hēlios* sun] : a very light inert gaseous chemical element occurring in various natural gases

he·lix \'hē-liks\ *n, pl* **he·li·ces** \'he-lə-ˌsēz, 'hē-\ *also* **he·lix·es** \'hē-lik-səz\ : something spiral in form

hell \'hel\ *n* **1** : a nether world in which the dead continue to exist **2** : the realm of the devil in which the damned suffer everlasting punishment **3** : a place or state of torment or destruction — **hell·ish** *adj*

hel·la·cious \he-'lā-shəs\ *adj* **1** : exceptionally powerful or violent **2** : remarkably good **3** : extremely difficult **4** : extraordinarily large

hell–bent \'hel-ˌbent\ *adj* : stubbornly determined

hell·cat \-ˌkat\ *n* **1** : WITCH 2 **2** : a violently temperamental person; *esp* : an ill-tempered woman

hel·le·bore \'he-lə-ˌbȯr\ *n* **1** : any of a genus of poisonous herbs related to the buttercups; *also* : the dried root of a hellebore **2** : a poisonous plant related to the lilies; *also* : its dried roots used in medicine and insecticides

Hel·lene \'he-ˌlēn\ *n* : GREEK

Hel·le·nism \'he-lə-ˌni-zəm\ *n* : a body of humanistic and classical ideals associated with ancient Greece — **Hel·len·ic** \he-'le-nik\ *adj* — **Hel·le·nist** \'he-lə-nist\ *n*

Hel·le·nis·tic \ˌhe-lə-'nis-tik\ *adj* : of or relating to Greek history, culture, or art after Alexander the Great

hell–for–leather *adv* : at full speed

hell·gram·mite \'hel-grə-ˌmīt\ *n* : an aquatic insect larva that is used as bait in fishing

hell·hole \'hel-ˌhōl\ *n* : a place of extreme misery or squalor

hel·lion \'hel-yən\ *n* : a troublesome or mischievous person

hel·lo \hə-'lō, he-\ *n, pl* **hellos** : an expression of greeting — used interjectionally

helm \'helm\ *n* **1** : a lever or wheel for steering a ship **2** : a position of control

hel·met \'hel-mət\ *n* : a protective covering for the head

helmet: ancient battle helmets and modern football helmet

helms·man \'helmz-mən\ *n* : the person at the helm : STEERSMAN

helms·per·son \-ˌpər-sᵊn\ *n* : HELMSMAN

hel·ot \'he-lət\ *n* : SLAVE, SERF

¹help \'help\ *vb* **1** : AID, ASSIST **2** : IMPROVE, RELIEVE **3** : to be of use; *also* : PROMOTE **4** : to change for the better **5** : to refrain from; *also* : PREVENT **6** : to serve with food or drink ⟨∼ yourself⟩ — **help·er** *n*

²help *n* **1** : AID, ASSISTANCE; *also* : a source of aid **2** : REMEDY, RELIEF **3** : one who assists another **4** : EMPLOYEE — **help·ful** \-fəl\ *adj* — **help·ful·ly** *adv* — **help·ful·ness** *n* — **help·less** *adj* — **help·less·ly** *adv* — **help·less·ness** *n*

helper T cell *n* : a T cell that participates in the immune response by recognizing foreign antigens and has a protein on its surface to which HIV attaches

help·ing *n* : a portion of food

help·mate \'help-ˌmāt\ *n* **1** : HELPER **2** : WIFE

help·meet \-ˌmēt\ *n* : HELPMATE

hel·ter–skel·ter \ˌhel-tər-'skel-tər\ *adv* **1** : in undue haste or disorder **2** : HAPHAZARDLY

helve \'helv\ *n* : a handle of a tool or weapon

Hel·ve·tian \hel-'vē-shən\ *adj* : SWISS — **Helvetian** *n*

¹hem \'hem\ *n* **1** : a border of an article (as of cloth) doubled back and stitched down **2** : RIM, MARGIN

²hem *vb* **hemmed; hem·ming 1** : to make a hem in sewing; *also* : BORDER, EDGE **2** : to surround restrictively

he–man \'hē-ˌman\ *n* : a strong virile man

he·ma·tite \'hē-mə-ˌtīt\ *n* : a mineral that consists of an oxide of iron and that constitutes an important iron ore

he·ma·tol·o·gy \ˌhē-mə-'tä-lə-jē\ *n* : a branch of biology that deals with the blood and blood-forming organs — **he·ma·to·log·ic** \-tə-'lä-jik\ *also* **he·ma·to·log·i·cal** \-ji-kəl\ *adj* — **he·ma·tol·o·gist** \-'tä-lə-jist\ *n*

he·ma·to·ma \-'tō-mə\ *n, pl* **-mas** *also* **-ma·ta** \-mə-tə\ : a usu. clotted mass of blood forming as a result of a broken blood vessel

heme \'hēm\ *n* : the deep red iron-containing part of hemoglobin

hemi·sphere \'he-mə-ˌsfir\ *n* **1** : one of the halves of the earth as divided by the equator into northern and southern parts or by a meridian into eastern and western parts **2** : either of two half spheres formed by a plane through the sphere's center — **hemi·spher·ic** \ˌhe-mə-'sfir-ik, -'sfer-\ *or* **hemi·spher·i·cal** \-'sfir-i-kəl, -'sfer-\ *adj*

hem·line \'hem-ˌlīn\ *n* : the line formed by the lower edge of a garment

hem·lock \'hem-ˌläk\ *n* **1** : any of several poisonous herbs related to the carrot **2** : an evergreen tree related to the pines; *also* : its soft light wood

he·mo·glo·bin \'hē-mə-ˌglō-bən\ *n* : an iron-containing compound found in red blood cells that carries oxygen from the lungs to the body tissues

he·mo·phil·ia \ˌhē-mə-'fi-lē-ə\ *n* : a hereditary blood defect usu. of males that slows blood clotting with resulting difficulty in stopping bleeding — **he·mo·phil·i·ac** \-lē-ˌak\ *adj or n*

hem·or·rhage \'hem-rij, 'he-mə-\ *n* : a large discharge of blood from the blood vessels — **hemorrhage** *vb* — **hem·or·rhag·ic** \ˌhe-mə-'ra-jik\ *adj*

hemorrhagic fever *n* : any of a group of virus diseases characterized chiefly by sudden onset, fever, aching, and bleeding in the internal organs

hem·or·rhoid \'hem-ˌròid, 'he-mə-\ *n* : a swollen mass of dilated veins at or just within the anus — usu. used in pl.

hemp \'hemp\ *n* : a tall widely grown Asian herb that is the source of a tough fiber used in rope and of marijuana and hashish from its flowers and leaves; *also* : the fiber — **hemp·en** \'hem-pən\ *adj*

hem·stitch \'hem-ˌstich\ *vb* : to embroider (fabric) by drawing out parallel threads and stitching the exposed threads in groups to form designs

hen \'hen\ *n* : a female chicken esp. over a year old; *also* : a female bird

hence \'hens\ *adv* **1** : AWAY **2** : from this time 〈four years ~〉 **3** : CONSEQUENTLY **4** : from this source or origin

hence·forth \hens-'fòrth\ *adv* : from this point on

hence·for·ward \-'fòr-wərd\ *adv* : HENCEFORTH

hench·man \'hench-mən\ *n* [ME *hengestman* groom, fr. *hengest* stallion] : a trusted follower or supporter

hen·na \'he-nə\ *n* **1** : an Old World tropical shrub with fragrant white flowers; *also* : a reddish brown dye obtained from its leaves and used esp. on hair **2** : the color of henna dye

hen·peck \'hen-ˌpek\ *vb* : to nag and boss one's husband

hep \'hep\ *adj* : HIP

hep·a·rin \'he-pə-rən\ *n* : a compound found esp. in liver that slows the clotting of blood and is used medically

he·pat·ic \hi-'pa-tik\ *adj* : of, relating to, or associated with the liver

he·pat·i·ca \hi-'pa-ti-kə\ *n* : any of a genus of herbs related to the buttercups that have lobed leaves and delicate white, pink, or bluish flowers

hep·a·ti·tis \ˌhe-pə-'tī-təs\ *n, pl* **-tit·i·des** \-'ti-tə-ˌdēz\ : inflammation of the liver; *also* : a virus disease of which this is a feature

hep·tam·e·ter \hep-'ta-mə-tər\ *n* : a line of verse containing seven metrical feet

hep·tath·lon \hep-'tath-lən, -ˌlän\ *n* : a 7-event athletic contest for women

¹her \'hər\ *adj* : of or relating to her or herself

²her *pron, objective case of* SHE

¹her·ald \'her-əld\ *n* **1** : an official crier or messenger **2** : HARBINGER **3** : ANNOUNCER **4** : ADVOCATE

²herald *vb* **1** : to give notice of **2** : HAIL, GREET; *also* : PUBLICIZE

he·ral·dic \he-'ral-dik, hə-\ *adj* : of or relating to heralds or heraldry

her·ald·ry \'her-əl-drē\ *n, pl* **-ries** **1** : the practice of devising and granting armorial insignia and of tracing genealogies **2** : INSIGNIA **3** : PAGEANTRY

herb \'ərb, 'hərb\ *n* **1** : a seed plant that lacks woody tissue and dies to the ground at the end of a growing season **2** : a plant or plant part valued for medicinal or savory qualities — **her·ba·ceous** \ˌər-'bā-shəs, ˌhər-\ *adj*

herb·age \'ər-bij, 'hər-\ *n* : green plants esp. when used or fit for grazing

her·bal \'ər-bəl, 'hər-\ *adj* : of, relating to, utilizing, or made of herbs

herb·al·ist \'ər-bə-list, 'hər-\ *n* **1** : a person who practices healing by the use of herbs **2** : a person who collects or grows herbs

her·bar·i·um \ˌər-'ber-ē-əm, ˌhər-\ *n, pl* **-ia** \-ē-ə\ **1** : a collection of dried plant specimens **2** : a place that houses an herbarium

her·bi·cide \'ər-bə-ˌsīd, 'hər-\ *n* : an agent used to destroy or inhibit plant growth — **her·bi·cid·al** \ˌər-bə-'sī-dᵊl, ˌhər-\ *adj*

her·biv·o·rous \ˌər-'bi-və-rəs, ˌhər-\ *adj* : feeding on plants — **her·bi·vore** \'ər-bə-ˌvòr, 'hər-\ *n*

her·cu·le·an \ˌhər-kyə-'lē-ən, ˌhər-'kyü-lē-\ *adj, often cap* [*Hercules,* hero of Greek myth renowned for his strength] : of extraordinary power, size, or difficulty

¹herd \'hərd\ *n* **1** : a group of animals of one kind kept or living together **2** : a group of people with a common bond 〈a ~ of tourists〉 **3** : MOB

²herd *vb* : to assemble or move in a herd — **herd·er** *n*

herds·man \'hərdz-mən\ *n* : one who manages, breeds, or tends livestock

¹here \'hir\ *adv* **1** : in or at this place; *also* : NOW **2** : at or in this point, particular, or case **3** : in the present life or state **4** : to this place 〈come ~〉

²here *n* : this place 〈get away from ~〉

here·abouts \'hir-ə-ˌbaùts\ *or* **here·about** \-ˌbaùt\ *adv* : in this vicinity

¹here·af·ter \hir-'af-tər\ *adv* **1** : after this in sequence or in time **2** : in some future time or state

²hereafter *n, often cap* **1** : FUTURE **2** : an existence beyond earthly life

here·by \hir-'bī\ *adv* : by means of this

he·red·i·tary \hə-'re-də-ˌter-ē\ *adj* **1** : genetically passed or passable from parent to offspring **2** : passing by inheritance; *also* : having title or possession through inheritance **3** : of a kind established by tradition

he·red·i·ty \-də-tē\ *n* : the characteristics and potentialities genetically derived from one's ancestors; *also* : the passing of these from ancestor to descendant

Her·e·ford \'hər-fərd\ *n* : any of a breed of red-coated beef cattle with white faces and markings

here·in \hir-'in\ *adv* : in this

here·of \-'əv, -'äv\ *adv* : of this

here·on \-'òn, -'än\ *adv* : on this

her·e·sy \'her-ə-sē\ *n, pl* **-sies** [ME *heresie,* fr. AF, fr. LL *haeresis,* fr. LGk *hairesis,* fr. Gk, action of taking, choice, sect, fr. *hairein* to take] **1** : adherence to a religious opinion contrary to church dogma **2** : an opinion or doctrine contrary to church dogma **3** : dissent from a dominant theory, opinion, or practice — **her·e·tic** \-ˌtik\ *n* — **he·ret·i·cal** \hə-'re-ti-kəl\ *adj*

here·to \hir-'tü\ *adv* : to this document

here·to·fore \'hir-tə-ˌfòr\ *adv* : up to this time

here·un·der \hir-'ən-dər\ *adv* : under this or according to this writing

here·un·to \hir-'ən-tü\ *adv* : to this

here·upon \'hir-ə-ˌpòn, -ˌpän\ *adv* : on this or immediately after this

here·with \'hir-'with, -'with\ *adv* **1** : with this **2** : HEREBY

her·i·ta·ble \'her-ə-tə-bəl\ *adj* : capable of being inherited

her·i·tage \'her-ə-tij\ *n* **1** : property that descends to an heir **2** : LEGACY **3** : BIRTHRIGHT

her·maph·ro·dite \(ˌ)hər-'ma-frə-ˌdīt\ *n* : an animal or plant having both male and female reproductive organs — **hermaphrodite** *adj* — **her·maph·ro·dit·ic** \(ˌ)hər-ˌma-frə-'di-tik\ *adj*

her·met·ic \hər-'me-tik\ *also* **her·met·i·cal** \-ti-kəl\ *adj* : AIRTIGHT — **her·met·i·cal·ly** \-ti-k(ə-)lē\ *adv*

her·mit \'hər-mət\ *n* [ME *heremite, eremite,* fr. AF, fr. LL *eremita,* fr. LGk *erēmitēs,* fr. Gk, adj., living in the desert, fr. *erēmia* desert, fr. *erēmos* desolate] : one who lives in solitude esp. for religious reasons

her·mit·age \-mə-tij\ *n* 1 : the dwelling of a hermit 2 : a secluded dwelling

hermit crab *n* : any of numerous crabs that occupy empty mollusk shells

her·nia \'hər-nē-ə\ *n, pl* **-ni·as** *or* **-ni·ae** \-nē-ˌē, -nē-ˌī\ : a protrusion of a bodily part (as a loop of intestine) into a pouch of the weakened wall of a cavity in which it is normally enclosed — **her·ni·ate** \-nē-ˌāt\ *vb* — **her·ni·a·tion** \ˌhər-nē-ˈā-shən\ *n*

he·ro \'hē-rō\ *n, pl* **heroes** 1 : a mythological or legendary figure of great strength or ability 2 : a man admired for his achievements and qualities 3 : the chief male character in a literary or dramatic work 4 *pl usu* **heros** : SUBMARINE 2 — **he·ro·ic** \hi-ˈrō-ik\ *adj* — **he·ro·i·cal·ly** \-i-k(ə-)lē\ *adv*

heroic couplet *n* : a rhyming couplet in iambic pentameter

he·ro·ics \hi-ˈrō-iks\ *n pl* : heroic or showy behavior

her·o·in \'her-ə-wən\ *n* : an illicit addictive narcotic drug made from morphine

her·o·ine \'her-ə-wən\ *n* 1 : a woman admired for her achievements and qualities 2 : the chief female character in a literary or dramatic work

her·o·ism \'her-ə-ˌwi-zəm\ *n* 1 : heroic conduct 2 : the qualities of a hero ♦ *Synonyms* VALOR, PROWESS, GALLANTRY

her·on \'her-ən\ *n, pl* **herons** *also* **heron** : any of various long-legged long-billed wading birds with soft plumage

her·pes \'hər-pēz\ *n* : any of several virus diseases characterized by the formation of blisters on the skin or mucous membranes

herpes sim·plex \-'sim-ˌpleks\ *n* : either of two virus diseases marked in one by watery blisters above the waist (as on the mouth and lips) and in the other on the sex organs

herpes zos·ter \-'zäs-tər\ *n* : SHINGLES

her·pe·tol·o·gy \ˌhər-pə-ˈtä-lə-jē\ *n* : a branch of zoology dealing with reptiles and amphibians — **her·pe·tol·o·gist** \ˌhər-pə-ˈtä-lə-jist\ *n*

her·ring \'her-iŋ\ *n, pl* **herring** *or* **herrings** : a valuable narrow-bodied food fish of the No. Atlantic; *also* : a related fish of the No. Pacific harvested esp. for its roe

her·ring·bone \'her-iŋ-ˌbōn\ *n* : a pattern made up of rows of parallel lines with adjacent rows slanting in reverse directions; *also* : a twilled fabric with this pattern

hers \'hərz\ *pron* : one or the ones belonging to her

her·self \hər-'self\ *pron* : SHE, HER — used reflexively, for emphasis, or in absolute constructions

hertz \'hərts, 'herts\ *n, pl* **hertz** : a unit of frequency equal to one cycle per second

hes·i·tant \'he-zə-tənt\ *adj* : tending to hesitate — **hes·i·tance** \-təns\ *n* — **hes·i·tan·cy** \-tən-sē\ *n* — **hes·i·tant·ly** *adv*

hes·i·tate \'he-zə-ˌtāt\ *vb* **-tat·ed; -tat·ing** 1 : to hold back (as in doubt) 2 : PAUSE ♦ *Synonyms* WAVER, VACILLATE, FALTER, SHILLY-SHALLY — **hes·i·ta·tion** \ˌhe-zə-ˈtā-shən\ *n*

het·er·o·dox \'he-tə-rə-ˌdäks\ *adj* 1 : differing from an acknowledged standard 2 : holding unorthodox opinions — **het·er·o·doxy** \-ˌdäk-sē\ *n*

het·er·o·ge·neous \ˌhe-tə-rə-ˈjē-nē-əs, -nyəs\ *adj* : consisting of dissimilar ingredients or constituents : MIXED — **het·er·o·ge·ne·ity** \-jə-ˈnē-ə-tē\ *n* — **het·er·o·ge·neous·ly** *adv*

het·ero·glos·sia \ˌhe-tə-rō-ˈglä-sē-ə, -ˈglò-\ *n* : a diversity of voices, styles of discourse, or points of view in a literary work

het·ero·sex·ism \ˌhe-tə-rō-ˈsek-si-zəm\ *n* : discrimination or prejudice by heterosexuals against homosexuals

het·ero·sex·u·al \ˌhe-tə-rō-ˈsek-shə-wəl\ *adj* 1 : of, relating to, or marked by sexual interest in the opposite sex; *also* : of, relating to, or involving sexual intercourse between members of opposite sex 2 : of or relating to different sexes — **heterosexual** *n* — **het·ero·sex·u·al·i·ty** \-ˌsek-shə-wa-lə-tē\ *n*

hew \'hyü\ *vb* **hewed; hewed** *or* **hewn** \'hyün\; **hew·ing** 1 : to cut or fell with blows (as of an ax) 2 : to give shape to with or as if with an ax 3 : to conform strictly — **hewer** *n*

HEW *abbr* Department of Health, Education, and Welfare

¹hex \'heks\ *vb* 1 : to practice witchcraft 2 : JINX

²hex *n* : SPELL, JINX

³hex *adj* : HEXAGONAL

⁴hex *abbr* hexagon

hexa·gon \'hek-sə-ˌgän\ *n* [ultim. fr. Gk *hex* six + *gōnia* angle] : a polygon having six angles and six sides — **hex·ag·o·nal** \hek-ˈsa-gən-ᵊl\ *adj*

hex·am·e·ter \hek-ˈsa-mə-tər\ *n* : a line of verse containing six metrical feet

hey \'hā\ *interj* — used esp. to call attention or to express doubt, surprise, or joy

hey·day \'hā-ˌdā\ *n* : a period of greatest strength, vigor, or prosperity

hf *abbr* half

Hf *symbol* hafnium

HF *abbr* high frequency

hg *abbr* hectogram

Hg *symbol* [NL *hydrargyrum*, lit., water silver] mercury

hgt *abbr* height

hgwy *abbr* highway

HH *abbr* 1 Her Highness 2 His Highness 3 His Holiness

HHS *abbr* Department of Health and Human Services

HI *abbr* 1 Hawaii 2 humidity index

hi·a·tus \hī-ˈā-təs\ *n* [L, fr. *hiare* to yawn] 1 : a break in an object : GAP 2 : a period when something is suspended or interrupted

hi·ba·chi \hi-ˈbä-chē\ *n* [Jp] : a charcoal brazier

hi·ber·nate \'hī-bər-ˌnāt\ *vb* **-nat·ed; -nat·ing** : to pass the winter in a torpid or resting state — **hi·ber·na·tion** \ˌhī-bər-ˈnā-shən\ *n* — **hi·ber·na·tor** \'hī-bər-ˌnā-tər\ *n*

hi·bis·cus \hī-ˈbis-kəs, hə-\ *n* : any of a genus of herbs, shrubs, and trees related to the mallows and noted for large showy flowers

hic·cup *also* **hic·cough** \'hi-(ˌ)kəp\ *n* 1 : a spasmodic breathing movement checked by sudden closing of the glottis accompanied by a peculiar sound; *also, pl* : an attack of hiccuping 2 : a slight irregularity, error, or malfunction 3 : a brief minor interruption or change — **hiccup** *vb*

hick \'hik\ *n* [*Hick*, nickname for *Richard*] : an unsophisticated provincial person — **hick** *adj*

hick·o·ry \'hi-kə-rē\ *n, pl* **-ries** : any of a genus of No. American hardwood trees related to the walnuts; *also* : the wood of a hickory — **hickory** *adj*

hi·dal·go \hi-ˈdal-gō\ *n, pl* **-gos** *often cap* [Sp, fr. earlier *fijo dalgo*, lit., son of something] : a member of the lower nobility of Spain

hidden tax *n* 1 : a tax ultimately paid by someone other than the person on whom it is formally levied 2 : an economic injustice that reduces one's income or buying power

¹hide \'hīd\ *vb* **hid** \'hid\; **hid·den** \'hid-ᵊn\ *or* **hid; hid·ing** 1 : to put or remain out of sight 2 : to conceal for shelter or protection; *also* : to seek protection 3 : to keep secret 4 : to turn away in shame or anger — **hider** *n*

²hide *n* : the skin of an animal

hide–and–seek \ˌhīd-ᵊn-ˈsēk\ *n* : a children's game in which everyone hides from one player who tries to find them

hide·away \'hī-də-ˌwā\ *n* : HIDEOUT

hide·bound \'hīd-ˌbaund\ *adj* : being inflexible or conservative

hid·eous \'hi-dē-əs\ *adj* [ME *hidous*, fr. AF *hidus, hisdos*, fr. *hisde, hide* terror] 1 : offensive to one of the senses : UGLY 2 : morally offensive : SHOCKING ♦ *Synonyms* GHASTLY, GRISLY, GRUESOME, HORRIBLE, LURID, MACABRE — **hid·eous·ly** *adv* — **hid·eous·ness** *n*

hide·out \'hīd-ˌaut\ *n* : a place of refuge or concealment

hie \'hī\ *vb* **hied; hy·ing** *or* **hie·ing** : HASTEN

hi·er·ar·chy \'hī-ə-ˌrär-kē\ *n, pl* **-chies** 1 : a ruling body of clergy organized into ranks 2 : persons or things arranged in a graded series — **hi·er·ar·chi·cal** \ˌhī-ə-ˈrär-ki-kəl\ *adj* — **hi·er·ar·chi·cal·ly** \-k(ə-)lē\ *adv*

hi·er·o·glyph·ic \ˌhī-ə-rə-ˈgli-fik\ *n* [MF *hieroglyphique*, adj., ultim. fr. Gk *hieroglyphikos*, fr. *hieros* sacred + *glyphein* to carve] 1 : a character in a system of picture writing (as of the ancient Egyptians) **2** : a symbol or sign difficult to decipher

hieroglyphic 1

hi–fi \'hī-'fī\ *n* **1** : HIGH FIDELITY **2** : equipment for reproduction of sound with high fidelity

hig·gle·dy–pig·gle·dy \,hi-gəl-dē-'pi-gəl-dē\ *adv* : in confusion

¹high \'hī\ *adj* **1** : ELEVATED; *also* : TALL **2** : advanced toward fullness or culmination; *also* : slightly tainted **3** : advanced esp. in complexity ⟨∼*er* mathematics⟩ **4** : long past **5** : SHRILL, SHARP **6** : far from the equator ⟨∼ latitudes⟩ **7** : exalted in character **8** : of greater degree, size, or amount than average ⟨∼ in cholesterol⟩ **9** : of relatively great importance **10** : FORCIBLE, STRONG ⟨∼ winds⟩ **11** : showing elation or excitement **12** : INTOXICATED; *also* : excited or stupefied by or as if by a drug — **high·ly** *adv*

²high *adv* **1** : at or to a high place or degree **2** : LUXURIOUSLY ⟨living ∼⟩

³high *n* **1** : an elevated place **2** : a region of high barometric pressure **3** : a high point or level **4** : the gear of a vehicle giving the highest speed **5** : an excited or stupefied state produced by or as if by a drug

high·ball \'hī-,bȯl\ *n* : a usu. tall drink of liquor mixed with water or a carbonated beverage

high beam *n* : a vehicle headlight with a long-range focus

high·born \'hī-'bȯrn\ *adj* : of noble birth

high·boy \-,bȯi\ *n* : a high chest of drawers mounted on a base with legs

high·bred \-'bred\ *adj* : coming from superior stock

high·brow \-,braȯ\ *n* : a person of superior learning or culture — **highbrow** *adj* — **high·brow·ism** \-,braȯ-i-zəm\ *n*

high–definition *adj* : being or relating to a television system with twice as many scan lines per frame as a conventional system

high–density li·po·pro·tein \-,lī-pō-'prō-tēn, -,li-\ *n* : HDL

high·er–up \,hī-ər-'əp\ *n* : a superior officer or official

high·fa·lu·tin \,hī-fə-'lü-tᵊn\ *adj* : PRETENTIOUS, POMPOUS

high fashion *n* **1** : HIGH STYLE **2** : HAUTE COUTURE

high fidelity *n* : the reproduction of sound or image with a high degree of faithfulness to the original

high five *n* : a slapping of upraised right hands by two people (as in celebration) — **high–five** *vb*

high–flown \'hī-'flōn\ *adj* **1** : EXALTED **2** : BOMBASTIC

high frequency *n* : a radio frequency between 3 and 30 megahertz

high gear *n* **1** : HIGH 4 **2** : a state of intense or maximum activity

high–hand·ed \'hī-'han-dəd\ *adj* : OVERBEARING — **high–hand·ed·ly** *adv* — **high–hand·ed·ness** *n*

high–hat \-'hat\ *adj* : SUPERCILIOUS, SNOBBISH — **high–hat** *vb*

high·land \'hī-lənd\ *n* : elevated or mountainous land

high·land·er \-lən-dər\ *n* **1** : an inhabitant of a highland **2** *cap* : an inhabitant of the Scottish Highlands

high–lev·el \'hī-'le-vəl\ *adj* **1** : being of high importance or rank **2** : being or relating to highly concentrated and environmentally hazardous nuclear waste

¹high·light \-,līt\ *n* : an event or detail of major importance

²highlight *vb* **1** : EMPHASIZE **2** : to constitute a highlight of **3** : to mark (text) with a highlighter **4** : to cause to be displayed in a way that stands out on a computer screen

high·light·er \-,lī-tər\ *n* : a pen with transparent ink used for marking text passages

high–mind·ed \-'mīn-dəd\ *adj* : marked by elevated principles and feelings — **high–mind·ed·ness** *n*

high·ness \'hī-nəs\ *n* **1** : the quality or state of being high **2** — used as a title (as for kings)

high–pres·sure \-'pre-shər\ *adj* : using or involving aggressive and insistent sales techniques

high–rise \-'rīz\ *adj* **1** : having several stories and being equipped with elevators ⟨∼ apartments⟩ **2** : of or relating to high-rise buildings

high road *n* : HIGHWAY

high school *n* : a school usu. including grades 9 to 12 or 10 to 12

high sea *n* : the open sea outside territorial waters — usu. used in pl.

high–sound·ing \'hī-'saȯn-diŋ\ *adj* : POMPOUS, IMPOSING

high–spir·it·ed \-'spir-ə-təd\ *adj* : characterized by a bold or energetic spirit

high–strung \-'strəŋ\ *adj* : having an extremely nervous or sensitive temperament

high style *n* : the newest in fashion or design

high·tail \'hī-,tāl\ *vb* : to retreat at full speed

high tech \-'tek\ *n* : HIGH TECHNOLOGY

high technology *n* : technology involving the use of advanced devices

high–ten·sion \'hī-'ten-chən\ *adj* : having or using a high voltage

high–test \-'test\ *adj* : having a high octane number

high–tick·et \-'ti-kət\ *adj* : EXPENSIVE

high–toned \-'tōnd\ *adj* **1** : high in social, moral, or intellectual quality **2** : PRETENTIOUS, POMPOUS

high·way \'hī-,wā\ *n* : a main direct road

high·way·man \'hī-,wā-mən\ *n* : a thief who robs travelers on a road

hi·jack *also* **high·jack** \'hī-,jak\ *vb* : to steal esp. by stopping a vehicle on the highway; *also* : to commandeer a flying airplane — **hijack** *n* — **hi·jack·er** *n*

¹hike \'hīk\ *vb* **hiked; hik·ing** **1** : to move or raise with a sudden motion **2** : to take a long walk — **hik·er** *n*

²hike *n* **1** : a long walk **2** : RISE, INCREASE ⟨price ∼⟩

hi·lar·i·ous \hi-'ler-ē-əs, hī-\ *adj* : marked by or providing boisterous merriment — **hi·lar·i·ous·ly** *adv* — **hi·lar·i·ty** \-ə-tē\ *n*

hill \'hil\ *n* **1** : a usu. rounded elevation of land **2** : a little heap or mound (as of earth) — **hilly** *adj*

hill·bil·ly \'hil-,bi-lē\ *n, pl* **-lies** : a person from a backwoods area

hill·ock \'hi-lək\ *n* : a small hill

hill·side \'hil-,sīd\ *n* : the part of a hill between the summit and the foot

hill·top \-,täp\ *n* : the top of a hill

hilt \'hilt\ *n* : a handle esp. of a sword or dagger

him \'him\ *pron, objective case of* HE

him·self \him-'self\ *pron* : HE, HIM — used reflexively, for emphasis, or in absolute constructions

¹hind \'hīnd\ *n, pl* **hinds** *also* **hind** : a female of a common Eurasian deer

²hind *adj* : REAR ⟨the dog's ∼ legs⟩

¹hin·der \'hin-dər\ *vb* **1** : to impede the progress of **2** : to hold back ♦ **Synonyms** OBSTRUCT, BLOCK, BAR, IMPEDE

²hind·er \'hīn-dər\ *adj* : HIND

Hin·di \'hin-dē\ *n* : a literary and official language of northern India

hind·most \'hīnd-,mōst\ *adj* : farthest to the rear

hind·quar·ter \-,kwȯr-tər\ *n* **1** : one side of the back half of the carcass of a quadruped **2** *pl* : the part of the body of a quadruped behind the junction of hind limbs and trunk

hin·drance \'hin-drəns\ *n* **1** : the state of being hindered **2** : IMPEDIMENT 1 **3** : the action of hindering

hind·sight \'hīnd-,sīt\ *n* : understanding of an event after it has happened

Hindu–Arabic *adj* : relating to, being, or composed of Arabic numerals

Hin·du·ism \'hin-dü-,i-zəm\ *n* : a body of religious beliefs and practices native to India — **Hin·du** *n or adj*

hind wing *n* : either of the posterior wings of a 4-winged insect

¹hinge \'hinj\ *n* : a jointed device on which a swinging part (as a door, gate, or lid) turns

²hinge *vb* **hinged; hing·ing** **1** : to attach by or furnish with hinges **2** : to be contingent on a single consideration

hint \'hint\ *n* **1** : an indirect or summary suggestion **2** : CLUE **3** : a very small amount ♦ **Synonyms** DASH, SOUPÇON, SUSPICION, TINCTURE, TOUCH — **hint** *vb*

hin·ter·land \'hin-tər-,land\ *n* **1** : a region behind a coast **2** : a region remote from cities

¹hip \'hip\ *n* : the fruit of a rose

²hip *n* **1** : the part of the body on either side below the waist consisting of the side of the pelvis and the upper thigh **2** : HIP JOINT

³**hip** *adj* **hip·per; hip·pest** : keenly aware of or interested in the newest developments or styles — **hip·ness** *n*

⁴**hip** *vb* **hipped; hip·ping** : TELL, INFORM

hip·bone \'hip-ˌbōn, -ˌbōn\ *n* : the large flaring bone that makes a lateral half of the pelvis in mammals

hip–hop \'hip-ˌhäp\ *n* **1** : a subculture esp. of inner-city youths who are devotees of rap music **2** : the stylized rhythmic music that accompanies rap — **hip–hop** *adj*

hip–hug·gers \'hip-ˌhə-gərz\ *n pl* : low-slung close-fitting pants that rest on the hips

hip joint *n* : the articulation between the femur and the hipbone

hipped \'hipt\ *adj* : having hips esp. of a specified kind ⟨broad-*hipped*⟩

hip·pie *or* **hip·py** \'hi-pē\ *n, pl* **hippies** : a usu. young person who rejects established mores and advocates nonviolence; *also* : a long-haired unconventionally dressed young person

hip·po \'hi-pō\ *n, pl* **hippos** : HIPPOPOTAMUS

hip·po·drome \'hi-pə-ˌdrōm\ *n* : an arena for equestrian performances

hip·po·pot·a·mus \ˌhi-pə-'pä-tə-məs\ *n, pl* **-mus·es** *or* **-mi** \-ˌmī\ [L, fr. Gk *hippopotamos*, alter. of *hippos potamios*, lit., river horse] : a large thick-skinned aquatic mammal of sub-Saharan Africa that is related to the swine

¹**hire** \'hī(-ə)r\ *n* **1** : payment for labor or personal services : WAGES **2** : EMPLOYMENT **3** : one who is hired

²**hire** *vb* **hired; hir·ing 1** : to employ for pay **2** : to engage the temporary use of for pay **3** : to take employment

hire·ling \'hī(-ə)r-liŋ\ *n* : a hired person; *esp* : one with mercenary motives

hir·sute \'hər-ˌsüt, 'hir-\ *adj* : HAIRY

¹**his** \'hiz\ *adj* : of or relating to him or himself

²**his** *pron* : one or the ones belonging to him

His·pan·ic \hi-'spa-nik\ *adj* : of, relating to, or being a person of Latin-American descent living in the U.S. — **Hispanic** *n*

hiss \'his\ *vb* : to make a sharp sibilant sound; *also* : to express disapproval of by hissing — **hiss** *n*

hissy fit \'hi-sē-\ *n* : TANTRUM

hist *abbr* historian; historical; history

his·ta·mine \'his-tə-ˌmēn, -mən\ *n* : a compound widespread in animal tissues that plays a major role in allergic reactions (as hay fever)

his·to·gram \'his-tə-ˌgram\ *n* : a representation of statistical data by rectangles whose widths represent class intervals and whose heights usu. represent corresponding frequencies

his·tol·o·gy \his-'tä-lə-jē\ *n, pl* **-gies 1** : a branch of anatomy dealing with tissue structure **2** : tissue structure or organization — **his·to·log·i·cal** \ˌhis-tə-'lä-ji-kəl\ *or* **his·to·log·ic** \-'lä-jik\ *adj* — **his·tol·o·gist** \-'tä-lə-jist\ *n*

his·to·ri·an \hi-'stor-ē-ən\ *n* : a student or writer of history

his·to·ric·i·ty \ˌhis-tə-'ri-sə-tē\ *n* : historical actuality

his·to·ri·og·ra·pher \hi-ˌstor-ē-'ä-grə-fər\ *n* : HISTORIAN

his·to·ry \'his-tə-rē\ *n, pl* **-ries** [ultim. fr. L *historia*, fr. Gk, inquiry, history, fr. *histōr, istōr* knowing, learned] **1** : a chronological record of significant events often with an explanation of their causes **2** : a branch of knowledge that records and explains past events **3** : events that form the subject matter of history **4** : an established record ⟨a convict's ∼ of violence⟩ — **his·tor·ic** \hi-'stor-ik\ *adj* — **his·tor·i·cal** \-i-kəl\ *adj* — **his·tor·i·cal·ly** \-k(ə-)lē\ *adv*

his·tri·on·ic \ˌhis-trē-'ä-nik\ *adj* [LL *histrionicus*, fr. L *histrio* actor] **1** : deliberately affected **2** : of or relating to actors, acting, or the theater — **his·tri·on·i·cal·ly** \-ni-k(ə-)lē\ *adv*

his·tri·on·ics \-niks\ *n pl* **1** : theatrical performances **2** : deliberate display of emotion for effect

¹**hit** \'hit\ *vb* **hit; hit·ting 1** : to reach with a blow : STRIKE; *also* : to arrive with a force like a blow ⟨the storm ∼⟩ **2** : to make or bring into contact : COLLIDE **3** : to affect detrimentally ⟨was ∼ by the flu⟩ **4** : to make a request of **5** : to come upon **6** : to accord with : SUIT **7** : REACH, ATTAIN **8** : to indulge in often to excess — **hit·ter** *n*

²**hit** *n* **1** : an act or instance of hitting or being hit **2** : a great success **3** : BASE HIT **4** : a dose of a drug **5** : a murder committed by a gangster **6** : an instance of connecting to a particular Web site **7** : a successful match in a search (as of the Internet)

¹**hitch** \'hich\ *vb* **1** : to move by jerks **2** : to catch or fasten esp. by a hook or knot **3** : HITCHHIKE

²**hitch** *n* **1** : JERK, PULL **2** : a sudden halt **3** : a connection between something towed and its mover **4** : KNOT

hitch·hike \'hich-ˌhīk\ *vb* : to travel by securing free rides from passing vehicles — **hitch·hik·er** *n*

¹**hith·er** \'hi-thər\ *adv* : to this place

²**hither** *adj* : being on the near or adjacent side

hith·er·to \-ˌtü\ *adv* : up to this time

HIV \ˌāch-(ˌ)ī-'vē\ *n* [*h*uman *i*mmunodeficiency *v*irus] : any of several retroviruses that infect and destroy helper T cells causing the great reduction in their numbers that is diagnostic of AIDS

hive \'hīv\ *n* **1** : a container for housing honeybees **2** : a colony of bees **3** : a place swarming with busy occupants — **hive** *vb*

hives \'hīvz\ *n sing or pl* : an allergic disorder marked by raised itching patches on the skin or mucous membranes

hl *abbr* hectoliter

HL *abbr* House of Lords

hm *abbr* hectometer

HM *abbr* **1** Her Majesty; Her Majesty's **2** His Majesty; His Majesty's

HMO \ˌāch-(ˌ)em-'ō\ *n* [*h*ealth *m*aintenance *o*rganization] : a comprehensive health-care organization financed by periodic fixed payments by voluntarily enrolled individuals and families

HMS *abbr* **1** Her Majesty's ship **2** His Majesty's ship

Ho *symbol* holmium

hoa·gie *also* **hoa·gy** \'hō-gē\ *n, pl* **hoagies** : SUBMARINE 2

hoard \'hōrd\ *n* : a hidden accumulation — **hoard** *vb* — **hoard·er** *n*

hoar·frost \'hōr-ˌfrȯst\ *n* : FROST 2

hoarse \'hȯrs\ *adj* **hoars·er; hoars·est 1** : rough and harsh in sound **2** : having a grating voice — **hoarse·ly** *adv* — **hoarse·ness** *n*

hoary \'hȯr-ē\ *adj* **hoar·i·er; -est 1** : gray or white with or as if with age **2** : ANCIENT — **hoar·i·ness** \'hȯr-ē-nəs\ *n*

hoax \'hōks\ *n* : an act intended to trick or dupe; *also* : something accepted or established by fraud — **hoax** *vb* — **hoax·er** *n*

hob \'häb\ *n* : MISCHIEF, TROUBLE ⟨raising ∼⟩

¹**hob·ble** \'hä-bəl\ *vb* **hob·bled; hob·bling 1** : to limp along; *also* : to make lame **2** : FETTER

²**hobble** *n* **1** : a hobbling movement **2** : something used to hobble an animal

hob·by \'hä-bē\ *n, pl* **hobbies** : a pursuit or interest engaged in for relaxation — **hob·by·ist** \-ist\ *n*

hob·by·horse \'hä-bē-ˌhȯrs\ *n* **1** : a stick with a horse's head on which children pretend to ride **2** : a toy horse mounted on rockers **3** : a topic to which one constantly reverts

hob·gob·lin \'häb-ˌgäb-lən\ *n* **1** : a mischievous goblin **2** : BOGEY 1

hob·nail \-ˌnāl\ *n* : a short large-headed nail for studding shoe soles — **hob·nailed** \-ˌnāld\ *adj*

hob·nob \-ˌnäb\ *vb* **hob·nobbed; hob·nob·bing** : to associate familiarly

ho·bo \'hō-bō\ *n, pl* **hoboes** *also* **hobos** : TRAMP 2

¹**hock** \'häk\ *n* : a joint or region in the hind limb of a quadruped just above the foot and corresponding to the human ankle

²**hock** *n* [D *hok* pen, prison] : ²PAWN 2 ⟨got his watch out of ∼⟩; *also* : DEBT 3 — **hock** *vb*

hock·ey \'hä-kē\ *n* **1** : FIELD HOCKEY **2** : ICE HOCKEY

ho·cus–po·cus \ˌhō-kəs-'pō-kəs\ *n* **1** : SLEIGHT OF HAND **2** : nonsense or sham used to conceal deception

hod \'häd\ *n* : a long-handled carrier for mortar or bricks

hodge·podge \'häj-ˌpäj\ *n* : a heterogeneous mixture : JUMBLE

Hodgkin's disease \'häj-kinz-\ *n* : a neoplastic disease of lymphoid tissue characterized esp. by enlargement of lymph nodes, spleen, and liver

hoe \'hō\ *n* : a long-handled implement with a thin flat blade used esp. for cultivating, weeding, or loosening the earth around plants — **hoe** *vb*

hoe·cake \'hō-ˌkāk\ *n* : a small cornmeal cake

hoe·down \-ˌdau̇n\ *n* **1** : SQUARE DANCE **2** : a gathering featuring hoedowns

¹**hog** \'hȯg, 'häg\ *n, pl* **hogs** *also* **hog 1** : a domestic swine

esp. when grown   **2** : a selfish, gluttonous, or filthy person — **hog·gish** *adj*

²hog *vb* **hogged; hog·ging** : to take or hold selfishly

ho·gan \'hō-ˌgän\ *n* : a Navajo Indian dwelling usu. made of logs and mud

hog·back \'hóg-ˌbak, 'häg-\ *n* : a ridge with a sharp summit and steep sides

hog·nose snake \'hóg-ˌnōz-, 'häg-\ *or* **hog·nosed snake** \-ˌnōzd-\ *n* : any of a genus of rather small harmless stout-bodied No. American snakes that seldom bite but hiss wildly and often play dead when disturbed

hogs·head \'hógz-ˌhed, 'hägz-\ *n* **1** : a large cask or barrel   **2** : a liquid measure equal to 63 U.S. gallons

hog–tie \'hóg-ˌtī, 'häg-\ *vb* **1** : to tie together the feet of ⟨~ a calf⟩   **2** : to make helpless

hog·wash \-ˌwósh, -ˌwäsh\ *n* **1** : SWILL, SLOP   **2** : NONSENSE, BALONEY

hog wild *adj* : lacking in restraint

hoi pol·loi \ˌhói-pə-'lói\ *n pl* [Gk, the many] : the general populace

hoi·sin sauce \'hói-ˌsin-\ *n* : a thick reddish sauce of soybeans, spices, and garlic used in Asian cookery

¹hoist \'hóist\ *vb* : RAISE, LIFT

²hoist *n* **1** : LIFT   **2** : an apparatus for hoisting

hoke \'hōk\ *vb* **hoked; hok·ing** : FAKE — usu. used with *up*

hok·ey \'hō-kē\ *adj* **hok·i·er; -est 1** : CORNY   **2** : PHONY

ho·kum \'hō-kəm\ *n* : NONSENSE

¹hold \'hōld\ *vb* **held** \'held\; **hold·ing 1** : POSSESS; *also* : KEEP   **2** : RESTRAIN   **3** : to have a grasp on   **4** : to support, remain, or keep in a particular situation or position   **5** : SUSTAIN; *also* : RESERVE   **6** : BEAR, COMPORT   **7** : to maintain in being or action : PERSIST   **8** : CONTAIN, ACCOMMODATE   **9** : HARBOR, ENTERTAIN; *also* : CONSIDER, REGARD   **10** : to carry on by concerted action; *also* : CONVOKE   **11** : to occupy esp. by appointment or election   **12** : to be valid   **13** : HALT, PAUSE — **hold·er** *n* — **hold forth** : to speak at length — **hold to** : to adhere to : MAINTAIN — **hold with** : to agree with or approve of

²hold *n* **1** : STRONGHOLD   **2** : CONFINEMENT; *also* : PRISON   **3** : the act or manner of holding : GRIP   **4** : a restraining, dominating, or controlling influence   **5** : something that may be grasped as a support   **6** : an order or indication that something is to be reserved or delayed — **on hold** : in a temporary state of waiting (as during a phone call); *also* : in a state of postponement ⟨plans on hold⟩

³hold *n* **1** : the interior of a ship below decks; *esp* : a ship's cargo deck   **2** : an airplane's cargo compartment

hold·ing *n* **1** : land or other property owned   **2** : a ruling of a court esp. on an issue of law

holding pattern *n* : a course flown by an aircraft waiting to land

hold out *vb* **1** : to continue to fight or work   **2** : to refuse to come to an agreement — **hold·out** \'hōl-ˌdaút\ *n*

hold·over \'hōl-ˌdō-vər\ *n* : one that is held over

hold·up \'hōl-ˌdəp\ *n* **1** : DELAY   **2** : robbery at the point of a gun

hole \'hōl\ *n* **1** : an opening into or through something   **2** : a hollow place (as a pit or cave)   **3** : DEN, BURROW   **4** : a wretched or dingy place   **5** : a unit of play from tee to cup in golf   **6** : an awkward position — **hole** *vb*

hol·i·day \'hä-lə-ˌdā\ *n* [ME, fr. OE *hāligdæg*, fr. *hālig* holy + *dæg* day] **1** : a day set aside for special religious observance   **2** : a day of freedom from work; *esp* : one in commemoration of an event   **3** : VACATION — **holiday** *vb*

ho·li·ness \'hō-lē-nəs\ *n* : the quality or state of being holy — used as a title for various high religious officials

ho·lis·tic \hō-'lis-tik\ *adj* : relating to or concerned with integrated wholes or complete systems rather than with the analysis or treatment of separate parts ⟨~ medicine⟩ ⟨~ ecology⟩

hol·lan·daise \ˌhä-lən-'dāz\ *n* : a rich sauce made basically of butter, egg yolks, and lemon juice or vinegar

hol·ler \'hä-lər\ *vb* : to cry out : SHOUT — **holler** *n*

¹hol·low \'hä-lō\ *n* **1** : CAVITY, HOLE   **2** : a surface depression

²hollow *adj* **hol·low·er** \'hä-lə-wər\; **hol·low·est** \-lə-wəst\ **1** : CONCAVE, SUNKEN   **2** : having a cavity within   **3** : lacking in real value, sincerity, or substance; *also* : FALSE   **4** : MUFFLED ⟨a ~ sound⟩ — **hol·low·ness** *n*

³hollow *vb* : to make or become hollow

hol·low·ware *or* **hol·lo·ware** \'hä-lə-ˌwar\ *n* : vessels (as bowls or cups) with a significant depth and volume

hol·ly \'hä-lē\ *n, pl* **hollies** : either of two trees or shrubs with branches of usu. evergreen glossy spiny-margined leaves and red berries

hol·ly·hock \'hä-lē-ˌhäk, -ˌhók\ *n* [ME *holihoc*, fr. *holi* holy + *hoc* mallow] : a biennial or perennial herb related to the mallows that is widely grown for its tall stalks of showy flowers

hol·mi·um \'hōl-mē-əm\ *n* : a metallic chemical element

ho·lo·caust \'hä-lə-ˌkóst, 'hō-\ *n* **1** : a thorough destruction esp. by fire   **2** *often cap* : the killing of European Jews by the Nazis during World War II; *also* : GENOCIDE

Ho·lo·cene \'hō-lə-ˌsēn\ *adj* : of, relating to, or being the present geologic epoch — **Holocene** *n*

ho·lo·gram \'hō-lə-ˌgram, 'hä-\ *n* : a three-dimensional image produced by an interference pattern of light (as laser light)

ho·lo·graph \'hō-lə-ˌgraf, 'hä-\ *n* : a document wholly in the handwriting of its author

ho·log·ra·phy \hō-'lä-grə-fē\ *n* : the process of making a hologram — **ho·lo·graph·ic** \ˌhō-lə-'gra-fik, ˌhä-\ *adj*

Hol·stein \'hōl-ˌstēn, -ˌstīn\ *n* : any of a breed of large black-and-white dairy cattle that produce large quantities of comparatively low-fat milk

Hol·stein–Frie·sian \-'frē-zhən\ *n* : HOLSTEIN

hol·ster \'hōl-stər\ *n* [D] : a usu. leather case for a firearm

ho·ly \'hō-lē\ *adj* **ho·li·er; -est 1** : worthy of absolute devotion   **2** : SACRED   **3** : having a divine quality ✦ **Synonyms** HALLOWED, BLESSED, SANCTIFIED, CONSECRATED — **ho·li·ly** \-lə-lē\ *adv*

Holy Spirit *n* : the third person of the Christian Trinity

ho·ly·stone \'hō-lē-ˌstōn\ *n* : a soft sandstone used to scrub a ship's wooden decks — **holystone** *vb*

hom·age \'ä-mij, 'hä-\ *n* [ME, fr. AF *homage, omage*, fr. *home* man, vassal, fr. L *homo* human being] : expression of high regard; *also* : TRIBUTE 3

hom·bre \'äm-brā, 'əm-, -brē\ *n* : GUY, FELLOW

hom·burg \'häm-ˌbərg\ *n* [*Homburg*, Germany] : a man's felt hat with a stiff curled brim and a high crown creased lengthwise

homburg

¹home \'hōm\ *n* **1** : one's residence; *also* : HOUSE   **2** : the social unit formed by a family living together   **3** : a congenial environment; *also* : HABITAT   **4** : a place of origin   **5** : the objective in various games

²home *vb* **homed; hom·ing 1** : to go or return home   **2** : to proceed to or toward a source of radiated energy used as a guide

home·body \'hōm-ˌbä-dē\ *n* : one whose life centers on home

home·boy \-ˌbói\ *n* **1** : a boy or man from one's neighborhood, hometown, or region   **2** : a fellow member of a youth gang   **3** : an inner-city youth

home·bred \-'bred\ *adj* : produced at home : INDIGENOUS

home·com·ing \-ˌkə-miŋ\ *n* **1** : a return home   **2** : an annual celebration for alumni at a college or university

home computer *n* : a small inexpensive microcomputer

home economics *n* : the theory and practice of homemaking

home·girl \'hōm-ˌgərl\ *n* **1** : a girl or woman from one's neighborhood, hometown, or region   **2** : a girl or woman who is a member of one's peer group   **3** : an inner-city girl or woman

home·grown \'hōm-'grōn\ *adj* **1** : grown domestically ⟨~ peaches⟩   **2** : LOCAL, INDIGENOUS ⟨a ~ artist⟩

home·land \-ˌland\ *n* **1** : native land **2** : an area set aside to be a state for a people of a particular national, cultural, or racial origin

home·less \-ləs\ *adj* : having no home or permanent residence — **home·less·ness** *n*

home·ly \ˈhōm-lē\ *adj* **home·li·er; -est** **1** : FAMILIAR **2** : unaffectedly natural **3** : lacking beauty or proportion — **home·li·ness** \-lē-nəs\ *n*

home·made \ˈhōm-ˈmād\ *adj* : made in the home, on the premises, or by one's own efforts

home·mak·er \-ˌmā-kər\ *n* : one who manages a household esp. as a wife and mother — **home·mak·ing** \-kiŋ\ *n*

ho·me·op·a·thy \ˌhō-mē-ˈä-pə-thē\ *n* : a system of medical practice that treats disease esp. with minute doses of a remedy that would in healthy persons produce symptoms similar to those of the disease treated — **ho·meo·path** \ˈhō-mē-ə-ˌpath\ *n* — **ho·meo·path·ic** \ˌhō-mē-ə-ˈpa-thik\ *adj*

ho·meo·sta·sis \ˌhō-mē-ō-ˈstā-səs\ *n* : the maintenance of a relatively stable state of equilibrium between interrelated physiological, psychological, or social factors characteristic of an individual or group — **ho·meo·stat·ic** \-ˈsta-tik\ *adj*

home page *n* : the page usu. encountered first at a Web site that usu. contains hyperlinks to the other pages of the site

home plate *n* : a slab at the apex of a baseball diamond that a base runner must touch in order to score

hom·er \ˈhō-mər\ *n* : HOME RUN — **homer** *vb*

home·room \ˈhōm-ˌrüm, -ˌrum\ *n* : a classroom where pupils report at the beginning of each school day

home run *n* : a hit in baseball that enables the batter to go around all the bases and score a run

home·school \ˈhōm-ˌskül\ *vb* : to teach school subjects to one's children at home — **home·school·er** \-ˌskü-lər\ *n*

home·sick \ˈhōm-ˌsik\ *adj* : longing for home and family while absent from them — **home·sick·ness** *n*

home·spun \-ˌspən\ *adj* **1** : spun or made at home; *also* : made of a loosely woven usu. woolen or linen fabric **2** : SIMPLE, HOMELY

¹**home·stead** \-ˌsted\ *n* : the home and land occupied by a family

²**homestead** *vb* : to acquire or settle on public land — **home·stead·er** *n*

home·stretch \-ˈstrech\ *n* **1** : the part of a racecourse between the last curve and the winning post **2** : a final stage (as of a project)

home theater *n* : an entertainment system (as a television with surround sound and a DVD player) for the home

home video *n* : prerecorded videocassettes or videodiscs for home viewing

¹**home·ward** \-wərd\ *or* **home·wards** \-wərdz\ *adv* : toward home

²**homeward** *adj* : being or going toward home

home·work \-ˌwərk\ *n* **1** : an assignment given a student to be completed outside the classroom **2** : preparatory reading or research

¹**hom·ey** \ˈhō-mē\ *adj* **hom·i·er; -est** : characteristic of home

²**homey** *or* **hom·ie** \ˈhō-mē\ *n, pl* **homeys** *or* **homies** : HOMEBOY

ho·mi·cide \ˈhä-mə-ˌsīd, ˈhō-\ *n* [L *homicida* murderer & *homicidium* manslaughter; both fr. *homo* human being + *caedere* to cut, kill] **1** : a person who kills another **2** : a killing of one human being by another — **hom·i·cid·al** \ˌhä-mə-ˈsī-dᵊl\ *adj*

hom·i·ly \ˈhä-mə-lē\ *n, pl* **-lies** : SERMON — **hom·i·let·ic** \ˌhä-mə-ˈle-tik\ *adj*

homing pigeon *n* : a racing pigeon trained to return home

hom·i·nid \ˈhä-mə-nəd, -ˌnid\ *n* : any of a family of primate mammals that comprise all living humans and extinct ancestral and related forms — **hominid** *adj*

hom·i·ny \ˈhä-mə-nē\ *n* : hulled corn with the germ removed

ho·mo·cys·te·ine \ˌhō-mō-ˈsis-tə-ˌēn\ *n* : an amino acid associated with an increased risk of heart disease when occurring at high levels in the blood

ho·mo·erot·ic \ˌhō-mō-i-ˈrä-tik\ *adj* : marked by or portraying homosexual desire — **ho·mo·erot·i·cism** \-ˈrä-tə-ˌsi-zəm\ *n*

ho·mo·ge·neous \ˌhō-mə-ˈjē-nē-əs, -nyəs\ *adj* : of the same or a similar kind; *also* : of uniform structure — **ho·mo·ge·ne·i·ty** \-jə-ˈnē-ə-tē\ *n* — **ho·mo·ge·neous·ly** *adv*

ho·mog·e·ni·sa·tion, ho·mog·e·nise *Brit var of* HOMOGENIZATION, HOMOGENIZE

ho·mog·e·nize \hō-ˈmä-jə-ˌnīz, hə-\ *vb* **-nized; -niz·ing** **1** : to make homogeneous **2** : to reduce the particles in (as milk) to uniform size and distribute them evenly throughout the liquid — **ho·mog·e·ni·za·tion** \-ˌmä-jə-nə-ˈzā-shən\ *n* — **ho·mog·e·niz·er** *n*

ho·mo·graph \ˈhä-mə-ˌgraf, ˈhō-\ *n* : one of two or more words spelled alike but different in origin, meaning, or pronunciation (as the *bow* of a ship, a *bow* and arrow)

ho·mol·o·gy \hō-ˈmä-lə-jē, hə-\ *n, pl* **-gies** **1** : structural likeness between corresponding parts of different plants or animals due to evolution from a common ancestor **2** : structural likeness between different parts of the same individual — **ho·mol·o·gous** \-ˈmä-lə-gəs\ *adj*

hom·onym \ˈhä-mə-ˌnim, ˈhō-\ *n* **1** : HOMOPHONE, HOMOGRAPH **2** : one of two or more words spelled and pronounced alike but different in meaning (as *pool* of water and *pool* the game)

ho·mo·pho·bia \ˈhō-mə-ˈfō-bē-ə\ *n* : irrational fear of, aversion to, or discrimination against homosexuality or homosexuals — **ho·mo·phobe** \ˈhō-mə-ˌfōb\ *n* — **ho·mo·pho·bic** \-ˈfō-bik\ *adj*

ho·mo·phone \ˈhä-mə-ˌfōn, ˈhō-\ *n* : one of two or more words (as *to, too, two*) pronounced alike but different in meaning or derivation or spelling

Ho·mo sa·pi·ens \ˌhō-mō-ˈsā-pē-ənz, -ˈsa-\ *n* : HUMANKIND

ho·mo·sex·u·al \ˌhō-mō-ˈsek-shə-wəl\ *adj* : of, relating to, or marked by sexual interest in the same sex as oneself; *also* : of, relating to, or involving sexual intercourse between members of the same sex — **homosexual** *n* — **ho·mo·sex·u·al·i·ty** \-ˌsek-shə-ˈwa-lə-tē\ *n*

hon *abbr* honor; honorable; honorary

hone \ˈhōn\ *n* : WHETSTONE — **hone** *vb* — **hon·er** *n*

hone in *vb* : to move toward or direct attention to an objective

¹**hon·est** \ˈä-nəst\ *adj* [ME, fr. AF, fr. L *honestus* honorable, fr. *honos, honor* honor] **1** : free from deception : TRUTHFUL; *also* : GENUINE, REAL **2** : REPUTABLE **3** : CREDITABLE ⟨an ~ day's work⟩ **4** : marked by integrity **5** : FRANK ✦ *Synonyms* UPRIGHT, JUST, CONSCIENTIOUS, HONORABLE — **hon·est·ly** *adv* — **hon·es·ty** \-nə-stē\ *n*

²**honest** *adv* : HONESTLY; *also* : with all sincerity ⟨I didn't do it, ~⟩

hon·ey \ˈhə-nē\ *n, pl* **honeys** : a sweet sticky substance made by honeybees from the nectar of flowers — **hon·eyed** \-nēd\ *adj*

hon·ey·bee \ˈhə-nē-ˌbē\ *n* : a honey-producing bee often kept in hives

¹**hon·ey·comb** \-ˌkōm\ *n* : a mass of 6-sided wax cells built by honeybees; *also* : something of similar structure or appearance

²**honeycomb** *vb* : to make or become full of cavities like a honeycomb

hon·ey·dew \-ˌdü, -ˌdyü\ *n* : a sweetish deposit secreted on plants by aphids, scale insects, or fungi

honeydew melon *n* : a smooth-skinned muskmelon with sweet green flesh

honey locust *n* : a tall usu. spiny No. American leguminous tree with hard durable wood and long twisted pods

hon·ey·moon \ˈhə-nē-ˌmün\ *n* **1** : a period of harmony esp. just after marriage **2** : a holiday taken by a newly married couple — **honeymoon** *vb* — **hon·ey·moon·er** *n*

hon·ey·suck·le \ˈhə-nē-ˌsə-kəl\ *n* : any of a genus of shrubs with fragrant tube-shaped flowers rich in nectar

honk \ˈhäŋk, ˈhȯŋk\ *n* : the cry of a goose; *also* : a similar sound (as of a horn) — **honk** *vb* — **honk·er** *n*

honk·y–tonk \ˈhäŋ-kē-ˌtäŋk, ˈhȯŋ-kē-ˌtȯŋk\ *n* : a tawdry nightclub or dance hall — **honky–tonk** *adj*

¹**hon·or** \ˈä-nər\ *n* **1** : good name : REPUTATION; *also* : outward respect **2** : PRIVILEGE **3** : a person of superior standing — used esp. as a title **4** : one who brings respect or fame ⟨an ~ to the class⟩ **5** : an evidence or symbol of distinction **6** : CHASTITY, PURITY **7** : INTEGRITY ✦ *Synonyms* HOMAGE, REVERENCE, DEFERENCE, OBEISANCE

²**honor** *vb* **1** : to regard or treat with honor **2** : to confer honor on **3** : to fulfill the terms of; *also* : to accept as payment — **hon·or·ee** \ˌä-nə-ˈrē\ *n* — **hon·or·er** *n*

hon·or·able \'ä-nə-rə-bəl\ *adj* **1** : deserving of honor **2** : of great renown **3** : accompanied with marks of honor **4** : doing credit to the possessor **5** : characterized by integrity — **hon·or·able·ness** *n* — **hon·or·ably** \-blē\ *adv*

hon·o·rar·i·um \ˌä-nə-'rer-ē-əm\ *n, pl* **-ia** \-ē-ə\ *also* **-i·ums** : a reward usu. for services on which custom or propriety forbids a price to be set

hon·or·ary \'ä-nə-ˌrer-ē\ *adj* **1** : having or conferring distinction **2** : conferred in recognition of achievement without the usual prerequisites ⟨~ degree⟩ **3** : UNPAID, VOLUNTARY ⟨an ~ chairman⟩ — **hon·or·ari·ly** \ˌä-nə-'rer-ə-lē\ *adv*

hon·or·if·ic \ˌä-nə-'ri-fik\ *adj* : conferring or conveying honor ⟨~ titles⟩

hon·our, hon·our·able *chiefly Brit var of* HONOR, HONOR-ABLE

¹hood \'hud\ *n* **1** : a covering for the head and neck and sometimes the face **2** : an ornamental fold (as at the back of an ecclesiastical vestment) **3** : a cover for parts of mechanisms; *esp* : the covering over an automobile engine — **hood·ed** \'hu-dəd\ *adj*

²hood \'hud, 'hud\ *n* : HOODLUM

³hood \'hud\ *n* : an inner-city neighborhood; *also* : INNER CITY

-hood \ˌhud\ *n suffix* **1** : state : condition : quality : character ⟨boy*hood*⟩ ⟨hardi*hood*⟩ **2** : instance of a (specified) state or quality ⟨false*hood*⟩ **3** : individuals sharing a (specified) state or character ⟨brother*hood*⟩

hood·ie \'hu-dē\ *n* : a hooded sweatshirt

hood·lum \'hud-ləm, 'hud-\ *n* **1** : THUG **2** : a young ruffian

hoo·doo \'hu-du\ *n, pl* **hoodoos** **1** : a body of magical practices traditional esp. among blacks in the southern U.S. **2** : something that brings bad luck — **hoodoo** *vb*

hood·wink \'hud-ˌwiŋk\ *vb* : to deceive by false appearance

hoo·ey \'hu-ē\ *n* : NONSENSE

hoof \'huf, 'huf\ *n, pl* **hooves** \'huvz, 'huvz\ *also* **hoofs** : a horny covering that protects the ends of the toes of ungulate mammals (as horses or cattle); *also* : a hoofed foot — **hoofed** \'huft, 'huft\ *adj*

¹hook \'huk\ *n* **1** : a curved or bent device for catching, holding, or pulling **2** : something curved or bent like a hook **3** : a flight of a ball (as in golf) that curves in a direction opposite to the dominant hand of the player propelling it **4** : a short punch delivered with a circular motion and with the elbow bent and rigid

²hook *vb* **1** : CURVE, CROOK **2** : to seize or make fast with a hook **3** : STEAL **4** : to work as a prostitute

hoo·kah \'hu-kə, 'hu-\ *n* [Ar *ḥuqqa* bottle of a water pipe] : WATER PIPE

hook·er \'hu-kər\ *n* **1** : one that hooks **2** : PROSTITUTE

hook·up \'hu-ˌkəp\ *n* : an assemblage (as of apparatus or circuits) used for a specific purpose (as in radio)

hook·worm \'huk-ˌwərm\ *n* : any of several parasitic intestinal nematode worms having hooks or plates around the mouth; *also* : infestation with or disease caused by hookworms

hoo·li·gan \'hu-li-gən\ *n* : RUFFIAN, HOODLUM — **hoo·li·gan·ism** \-gə-ˌni-zəm\ *n*

hoop \'hup, 'hup\ *n* **1** : a circular strip used esp. for holding together the staves of a barrel **2** : a circular figure or object : RING **3** : a circle of flexible material for expanding a woman's skirt **4** : BASKETBALL — usu. used in pl.

hoop·la \'hup-ˌlä, 'hup-\ *n* [F *houp-là*, interj.] : TO-DO; *also* : BALLYHOO

hoop·ster \'hup-stər\ *n* : a basketball player

hoo·ray \hu-'rā\ *interj* — used to express joy, approval, or encouragement

hoose·gow \'hus-ˌgau\ *n* [Sp *juzgado* panel of judges, courtroom] : JAIL

¹hoot \'hut\ *vb* **1** : to shout or laugh usu. in contempt **2** : to make the natural throat noise of an owl — **hoot·er** *n*

²hoot *n* **1** : a sound of hooting **2** : the least bit ⟨don't give a ~⟩ **3** : something or someone amusing ⟨the play is a real ~⟩

hoot·e·nan·ny \'hu-tə-ˌna-nē\ *n, pl* **-nies** : a gathering at which folksingers entertain often with the audience joining in

¹hop \'häp\ *vb* **hopped; hop·ping** **1** : to move by quick springy leaps **2** : to make a quick trip **3** : to ride on esp. surreptitiously and without authorization

²hop *n* **1** : a short brisk leap esp. on one leg **2** : DANCE **3** : a short trip by air

³hop *n* : a vine related to the hemp plant whose ripe dried pistillate catkins are used esp. in flavoring malt liquors; *also, pl* : its pistillate catkins

¹hope \'hōp\ *vb* **hoped; hop·ing** : to desire with expectation of fulfillment

²hope *n* **1** : TRUST, RELIANCE **2** : desire accompanied by expectation of fulfillment; *also* : something hoped for **3** : one that gives promise for the future — **hope·ful** \-fəl\ *adj* — **hope·ful·ness** *n* — **hope·less** *adj* — **hope·less·ly** *adv* — **hope·less·ness** *n*

HOPE *abbr* Health Opportunity for People Everywhere

hope·ful·ly \'hōp-fə-lē\ *adv* **1** : in a hopeful manner **2** : it is hoped

Ho·pi \'hō-pē\ *n, pl* **Hopi** *or* **Hopis** : a member of an American Indian people of Arizona; *also* : the language of the Hopi people

hopped–up \'häpt-'əp\ *adj* **1** : being under the influence of a narcotic; *also* : full of enthusiasm or excitement **2** : having more than usual power ⟨a ~ engine⟩

hop·per \'hä-pər\ *n* **1** : a usu. immature hopping insect (as a grasshopper) **2** : a usu. funnel-shaped container for delivering material (as grain) **3** : a freight car with hinged doors in a sloping bottom **4** : a box into which a bill to be considered by a legislative body is dropped **5** : a tank holding a liquid and having a device for releasing its contents through a pipe

hop·scotch \'häp-ˌskäch\ *n* : a child's game in which a player tosses an object (as a stone) into areas of a figure drawn on the ground and hops through the figure to pick up the object

hor *abbr* horizontal

horde \'hord\ *n* : THRONG, SWARM

ho·ri·zon \hə-'rī-zᵊn\ *n* [ME, fr. LL, fr. Gk *horizont-, horizōn*, fr. prp. of *horizein* to bound, fr. *horos* limit, boundary] **1** : the apparent junction of earth and sky **2** : range of outlook or experience

hor·i·zon·tal \ˌhor-ə-'zän-tᵊl\ *adj* : parallel to the horizon : LEVEL — **horizontal** *n* — **hor·i·zon·tal·ly** *adv*

hor·mon·al \hor-'mō-nᵊl\ *adj* : of, relating to, or effected by hormones — **hor·mon·al·ly** \-nᵊl-ē\ *adv*

hor·mone \'hor-ˌmōn\ *n* [Gk *hormōn*, prp. of *horman* to stir up, fr. *hormē* impulse, assault] : a product of living cells that circulates in body fluids and has a specific effect on the activity of cells remote from its point of origin

horn \'horn\ *n* **1** : one of the hard projections of bone or keratin on the head of many hoofed mammals **2** : something resembling or suggesting a horn **3** : a brass wind instrument **4** : a usu. electrical device that makes a noise ⟨an automobile ~⟩ — **horned** \'hornd\ *adj* — **horn·less** *adj*

horn·book \'horn-ˌbuk\ *n* **1** : a child's primer consisting of a sheet of parchment or paper protected by a sheet of transparent horn **2** : a rudimentary treatise

horned toad *n* : any of several small harmless insect-eating lizards with spines on the head resembling horns and spiny scales on the body

hor·net \'hor-nət\ *n* : any of the larger social wasps

horn in *vb* : to participate without invitation : INTRUDE

horn·pipe \'horn-ˌpīp\ *n* : a lively folk dance of the British Isles

horny \'hor-nē\ *adj* **horn·i·er; -est** **1** : of or made of horn; *also* : HARD, CALLOUS **2** : having horns **3** : desiring sexual gratification; *also* : excited sexually

ho·rol·o·gy \hə-'rä-lə-jē\ *n* : the science of measuring time or constructing time-indicating instruments — **hor·o·log·i·cal** \ˌhor-ə-'lä-ji-kəl\ *adj* — **ho·rol·o·gist** \hə-'rä-lə-jist\ *n*

horo·scope \'hor-ə-ˌskōp\ *n* [ME *horoscopum*, fr. L *horoscopus*, fr. Gk *hōroskopos*, fr. *hōra* hour + *skopos* watcher] **1** : a diagram of the relative positions of planets and signs of the zodiac at a particular time for use by astrologers to foretell events of a person's life **2** : an astrological forecast

hor·ren·dous \hȯ-'ren-dəs\ *adj* : DREADFUL, HORRIBLE

hor·ri·ble \'hor-ə-bəl\ *adj* **1** : marked by or conducive to horror **2** : highly disagreeable — **hor·ri·ble·ness** *n* — **hor·ri·bly** \-blē\ *adv*

hor·rid \'hor-əd\ *adj* **1** : HIDEOUS **2** : REPULSIVE — **hor·rid·ly** *adv*

hor·rif·ic \hȯ-'ri-fik\ *adj* : having the power to horrify — **hor·rif·i·cal·ly** \-fi-k(ə-)lē\ *adv*

hor·ri·fy \'hȯr-ə-ˌfī\ *vb* **-fied; -fy·ing** : to cause to feel horror ✦ *Synonyms* APPALL, DAUNT, DISMAY

hor·ror \'hȯr-ər\ *n* **1** : painful and intense fear, dread, or dismay **2** : intense repugnance **3** : something that horrifies

horror story *n* : an account of an unsettling or unfortunate occurrence

hors de com·bat \ˌȯr-də-kōⁿ-'bä\ *adv or adj* : in a disabled condition

hors d'oeuvre \ȯr-'dərv\ *n, pl* **hors d'oeuvres** *same or* -'dərvz\ *also* **hors d'oeuvre** [F *hors-d'oeuvre,* lit., outside of the work] : any of various savory foods usu. served as appetizers

horse \'hȯrs\ *n, pl* **hors·es** *also* **horse** **1** : a large solid-hoofed herbivorous mammal domesticated as a draft and saddle animal **2** : a supporting framework usu. with legs — **horse·less** *adj*

¹horse·back \'hȯrs-ˌbak\ *n* : the back of a horse

²horseback *adv* : on horseback

horse chestnut *n* : a large tree with palmate leaves, erect conical clusters of showy flowers, and large glossy brown seeds enclosed in a prickly bur; *also* : its seed

horse·flesh \'hȯrs-ˌflesh\ *n* : horses for riding, driving, or racing

horse·fly \-ˌflī\ *n* : any of a family of large dipteran flies with bloodsucking females

horse·hair \-ˌher\ *n* **1** : the hair of a horse esp. from the mane or tail **2** : cloth made from horsehair

horse·hide \-ˌhīd\ *n* **1** : the dressed or raw hide of a horse **2** : the ball used in baseball

horse latitudes *n pl* : either of two calm regions near 30°N and 30°S latitude

horse·laugh \'hȯrs-ˌlaf, -ˌläf\ *n* : a loud boisterous laugh

horse·man \-mən\ *n* **1** : one who rides horseback; *also* : one skilled in managing horses **2** : a breeder or raiser of horses — **horse·man·ship** *n*

horse·play \-ˌplā\ *n* : rough boisterous play

horse·play·er \-ˌər\ *n* : a bettor on horse races

horse·pow·er \'hȯrs-ˌpau̇(-ə)r\ *n* : a unit of power equal in the U.S. to 746 watts

horse·rad·ish \-ˌra-dish\ *n* : a tall white-flowered herb related to the mustards whose pungent root is used as a condiment; *also* : the pungent condiment

horse·shoe \'hȯrs-ˌshü\ *n* **1** : a usu. U-shaped protective metal plate fitted to the rim of a horse's hoof **2** *pl* : a game in which horseshoes are pitched at a fixed object — **horse·shoe** *vb* — **horse·sho·er** *n*

horseshoe crab *n* : any of several marine arthropods with a broad crescent-shaped combined head and thorax

horse·tail \'hȯrs-ˌtāl\ *n* : any of a genus of primitive spore-producing plants with hollow jointed stems and leaves reduced to sheaths about the joints

horse·whip \-ˌhwip\ *vb* : to flog with a whip made to be used on a horse

horse·wom·an \-ˌwu̇-mən\ *n* **1** : a woman skilled in riding horseback or in caring for or managing horses **2** : a woman who breeds or raises horses

hors·ey *also* **horsy** \'hȯr-sē\ *adj* **hors·i·er; -est** **1** : of, relating to, or suggesting a horse **2** : having to do with horses or horse racing

hort *abbr* horticultural; horticulture

hor·ta·tive \'hȯr-tə-tiv\ *adj* : giving exhortation

hor·ta·to·ry \'hȯr-tə-ˌtȯr-ē\ *adj* : HORTATIVE

hor·ti·cul·ture \'hȯr-tə-ˌkəl-chər\ *n* : the science and art of growing fruits, vegetables, flowers, and ornamental plants — **hor·ti·cul·tur·al** \ˌhȯr-tə-'kəl-chə-rəl\ *adj* — **hor·ti·cul·tur·ist** \-rist\ *n*

Hos *abbr* Hosea

ho·san·na \hō-'za-nə, -'zä-\ *interj* [Gk *hōsanna,* fr. Heb *hōshī'āh-nnā* pray, save (us)!] — used as a cry of acclamation and adoration — **hosanna** *n*

¹hose \'hōz\ *n, pl* **hose** *or* **hos·es** **1** *pl* **hose** : STOCKING, SOCK; *also* : a close-fitting garment covering the legs and waist **2** : a flexible tube for conveying fluids (as from a faucet)

²hose *vb* **hosed; hos·ing** : to spray, water, or wash with a hose

Ho·sea \hō-'zā-ə, -'zē-\ *n* — see BIBLE table

ho·siery \'hō-zhə-rē, -zə-\ *n* : STOCKINGS, SOCKS

hosp *abbr* hospital

hos·pice \'häs-pəs\ *n* **1** : a lodging for travelers or for young persons or the underprivileged **2** : a facility or program for caring for dying persons

hos·pi·ta·ble \hä-'spi-tə-bəl, 'häs-(ˌ)pi-\ *adj* **1** : given to generous and cordial reception of guests **2** : readily receptive — **hos·pi·ta·bly** \-blē\ *adv*

hos·pi·tal \'häs-ˌpi-tᵊl\ *n* [ME, fr. AF, fr. ML *hospitale* hospice, guest house, fr. neut. of L *hospitalis* of a guest, fr. *hospit-, hospes* guest, host] : an institution where the sick or injured receive medical or surgical care

hos·pi·tal·ise *Brit var of* HOSPITALIZE

hos·pi·tal·i·ty \ˌhäs-pə-'ta-lə-tē\ *n, pl* **-ties** : hospitable treatment, reception, or disposition

hos·pi·tal·ize \'häs-ˌpi-tə-ˌlīz\ *vb* **-ized; -iz·ing** : to place in a hospital as a patient — **hos·pi·tal·i·za·tion** \ˌhäs-ˌpi-tᵊl-ˌzā-shən\ *n*

¹host \'hōst\ *n* [ME, fr. AF *ost,* fr. LL *hostis,* fr. L, stranger, enemy] **1** : ARMY **2** : MULTITUDE

²host *n* [ME *hoste* host, guest, fr. AF, fr. L *hospit-, hospes*] **1** : one who receives or entertains guests **2** : an animal or plant on or in which a parasite lives **3** : one into which something (as an organ) is transplanted **4** : SERVER 2 — **host** *vb*

³host *n, often cap* [ultim. fr. L *hostia* sacrifice] : the eucharistic bread

hos·tage \'häs-tij\ *n* **1** : a person kept as a pledge pending the fulfillment of an agreement **2** : a person taken by force to secure the taker's demands

hos·tel \'häs-tᵊl\ *n* [ME, fr. AF, fr. ML *hospitale* hospice] **1** : INN **2** : a supervised lodging for youth — **hos·tel·er** *or* **hos·tel·ler** *n*

hos·tel·ry \-rē\ *n, pl* **-ries** : INN, HOTEL

host·ess \'hō-stəs\ *n* : a woman who acts as host

hos·tile \'häs-tᵊl, -ˌtī(-ə)l\ *adj* : marked by usu. overt antagonism : UNFRIENDLY — **hostile** *n* — **hos·tile·ly** *adv*

hos·til·i·ty \hä-'sti-lə-tē\ *n, pl* **-ties** **1** : an unfriendly state or action **2** *pl* : overt acts of war

hos·tler \'häs-lər, 'äs-\ *n* : one who takes care of horses or mules

hot \'hät\ *adj* **hot·ter; hot·test** **1** : marked by a high temperature or an uncomfortable degree of body heat **2** : giving a sensation of heat or of burning **3** : ARDENT, FIERY **4** : sexually excited **5** : EAGER **6** : newly made or received **7** : PUNGENT **8** : unusually lucky or favorable ⟨~ dice⟩ **9** : recently and illegally obtained ⟨~ jewels⟩ — **hot** *adv* — **hot·ly** *adv* — **hot·ness** *n*

hot·bed \-ˌbed\ *n* **1** : a glass-covered bed of soil heated (as by fermenting manure) and used esp. for raising seedlings **2** : an environment that favors rapid growth or development

hot–blood·ed \-'blə-dəd\ *adj* : easily roused or excited

hot·box \-ˌbäks\ *n* : a bearing (as of a railroad car) overheated by friction

hot button *n* : an emotional issue or concern that triggers immediate intense reaction

hot·cake \-ˌkāk\ *n* : PANCAKE

hot dog *n* : a cooked frankfurter usu. served in a long split roll

ho·tel \hō-'tel\ *n* [F *hôtel,* fr. OF *hostel,* fr. ML *hospitale* hospice] : a building where lodging and usu. meals, entertainment, and various personal services are provided for the public

hot flash *n* : a sudden brief flushing and sensation of heat usu. associated with menopausal endocrine imbalance

hot·head·ed \'hät-'he-dəd\ *adj* : FIERY, IMPETUOUS — **hot·head** \-ˌhed\ *n* — **hot·head·ed·ly** *adv* — **hot·head·ed·ness** *n*

hot·house \-ˌhau̇s\ *n* : a heated greenhouse esp. for raising tropical plants

hotline *n* : a telephone line for emergency use (as between governments or to a counseling service)

hot pants *n pl* : very short shorts

hot pepper *n* : a small usu. thin-walled pepper with a pungent taste; *also* : a plant bearing hot peppers

hot plate *n* : a simple portable appliance for heating or for cooking

hot potato *n* : an embarrassing or controversial issue

hot rod *n* : an automobile modified for high speed and fast acceleration — **hot–rod·der** \-'rä-dər\ *n*

hots \'häts\ *n pl* : strong sexual desire — usu. used with *the*

hot seat *n* : a position of anxiety or embarrassment

hot-shot \'hät-,shät\ *n* : a showily skillful person

hot tub *n* : a large tub of hot water for one or more bathers

hot water *n* : TROUBLE, DIFFICULTY

hot-wire \'hät-,wī(-ə)r\ *vb* : to start (an automobile) by short-circuiting the ignition system

¹**hound** \'haùnd\ *n* 1 : : any of various hunting dogs that track prey by scent or sight 2 : FAN, ADDICT

²**hound** *vb* : to pursue relentlessly

hour \'aù(-ə)r\ *n* 1 : the 24th part of a day : 60 minutes 2 : the time of day 3 : a particular or customary time 4 : a class session — **hour·ly** *adv or adj*

hour·glass \'aù(-ə)r-,glas\ *n* : a glass vessel for measuring time in which sand runs from an upper compartment to a lower compartment in an hour

hou·ri \'hùr-ē\ *n* [F, fr. Pers *hūri*, fr. Ar *hūrīya*] : one of the beautiful maidens of the Muslim paradise

¹**house** \'haùs\ *n, pl* **hous·es** \'haù-zəz\ 1 : a building for human habitation 2 : an animal shelter (as a den or nest) 3 : a building in which something is stored 4 : HOUSEHOLD; *also* : FAMILY 5 : a residence for a religious community or for students; *also* : those in residence 6 : a legislative body 7 : a place of business or entertainment 8 : a business organization 9 : the audience in a theater or concert hall — **house·ful** *n*

²**house** \'haùz\ *vb* **housed; hous·ing** 1 : to provide with or take shelter : LODGE 2 : STORE

house·boat \'haùs-,bōt\ *n* : a pleasure boat fitted for use as a dwelling or for leisurely cruising

house·boy \-,bói\ *n* : a boy or man hired to act as a household servant

house·break \-,brāk\ *vb* **–broke; –brok·en; –break·ing** : to train (a pet) in excretory habits acceptable in indoor living

house·break·ing \-,brā-kiŋ\ *n* : the act of breaking into a dwelling with the intent of committing a felony

house·clean \-,klēn\ *vb* : to clean a house and its furniture — **house·clean·ing** *n*

house·coat \-,kōt\ *n* : a woman's often long-skirted informal garment for wear around the house

house·fly \-,flī\ *n* : a dipteran fly that is common about human habitations

¹**house·hold** \-,hōld\ *n* : those who dwell as a family under the same roof — **house·hold·er** *n*

²**household** *adj* 1 : DOMESTIC 2 : FAMILIAR, COMMON ⟨a ~ name⟩

house·keep·er \-,kē-pər\ *n* : a woman employed to take care of a house

house·keep·ing \-,kē-piŋ\ *n* : the care and management of a house or institutional property

house·lights \-,līts\ *n pl* : the lights that illuminate the auditorium of a theater

house·maid \-,mād\ *n* : a girl or woman who is a servant employed to do housework

house·moth·er \-,mə-thər\ *n* : a woman acting as hostess, chaperone, and often housekeeper in a group residence

house·plant \-,plant\ *n* : a plant grown or kept indoors

house sparrow *n* : a Eurasian sparrow widely introduced in urban and agricultural areas

house·top \'haùs-,täp\ *n* : ROOF

house·wares \-,werz\ *n pl* : small articles of household equipment

house·warm·ing \-,wór-miŋ\ *n* : a party to celebrate the taking possession of a house or premises

house·wife \-,wīf\ *n* : a married woman in charge of a household — **house·wife·ly** *adj* — **house·wif·ery** \-,wī-fə-rē\ *n*

house·work \-,wərk\ *n* : the work of housekeeping

¹**hous·ing** \'haù-ziŋ\ *n* 1 : SHELTER; *also* : dwellings provided for people 2 : something that covers or protects

²**housing** *n* : CAPARISON 1

HOV *abbr* high-occupancy vehicle

hove *past and past part of* HEAVE

hov·el \'hə-vəl, 'hä-\ *n* : a small, wretched, and often dirty house : HUT

hov·er \'hə-vər, 'hä-\ *vb* **hov·ered; hov·er·ing** 1 : FLUTTER; *also* : to move to and fro 2 : to be in an uncertain state

hov·er·craft \-,kraft\ *n* : a vehicle that rides on a cushion of air over a surface

¹**how** \'haù\ *adv* 1 : in what way or manner ⟨~ was it done⟩ 2 : with what meaning ⟨~ do we interpret such behavior⟩ 3 : for what reason ⟨~ could you have done such a thing⟩ 4 : to what extent or degree ⟨~ deep is it⟩ 5 : in what state or condition ⟨~ are you⟩ — **how about** : what do you say to or think of ⟨how about coming with me⟩ — **how come** : why is it that

²**how** *conj* 1 : the way or manner in which ⟨remember ~ they fought⟩ 2 : HOWEVER ⟨do it ~ you like⟩

¹**how·be·it** \haù-'bē-ət\ *conj* : ALTHOUGH

²**howbeit** *adv* : NEVERTHELESS

how·dah \'haù-də\ *n* [Hindi &Urdu *hauda*, fr. Ar *haudaj*] : a seat or covered pavilion on the back of an elephant or camel

¹**how·ev·er** \haù-'e-vər\ *conj* : in whatever manner that

²**however** *adv* 1 : in whatever manner; *also* : to whatever degree 2 : in spite of that

how·it·zer \'haù-ət-sər\ *n* : a short cannon that shoots shells at a high angle

howl \'haù(-ə)l\ *vb* 1 : to emit a loud long doleful sound characteristic of dogs 2 : to cry loudly — **howl** *n*

howl·er \'haù-lər\ *n* 1 : one that howls 2 : a humorous and ridiculous blunder

howl·ing *adj* 1 : DESOLATE, WILD 2 : very great ⟨a ~ success⟩

how·so·ev·er \,haù-sə-'we-vər\ *adv* : HOWEVER 1

hoy·den \'hói-d³n\ *n* : a girl or woman of saucy, boisterous, or carefree behavior — **hoy·den·ish** *adj*

hp *abbr* horsepower

HP *abbr* high pressure

HPF *abbr* highest possible frequency

HQ *abbr* headquarters

hr *abbr* 1 here 2 hour

HR *abbr* House of Representatives

HRH *abbr* 1 Her Royal Highness 2 His Royal Highness

hryv·nia \'(h)riv-nē-ə\ *n, pl* **hryvnia** *or* **hryvnias** — see MONEY table

hrzn *abbr* horizon

Hs *symbol* hassium

HS *abbr* high school

HST *abbr* Hawaiian standard time

ht *abbr* height

HT *abbr* 1 Hawaii time 2 high-tension

HTML \,āch-,tē-,em-'el\ *n* [*hypertext markup language*] : a computer language used to create World Wide Web documents

http *abbr* hypertext transfer protocol

hua·ra·che \wə-'rä-chē\ *n* [MexSp] : a sandal with an upper made of interwoven leather strips

hub \'həb\ *n* 1 : the central part of a circular object (as a wheel) 2 : a center of activity; *esp* : an airport or city through which an airline routes most of its traffic

hub·bub \'hə-bəb\ *n* : UPROAR; *also* : TURMOIL

hub·cap \'həb-,kap\ *n* : a removable metal cap over the end of an axle

hu·bris \'hyü-brəs\ *n* : exaggerated pride or self-confidence

huck·le·ber·ry \'hə-kəl-,ber-ē\ *n* 1 : any of a genus of American shrubs of the heath family; *also* : its edible dark blue berry 2 : BLUEBERRY

huck·ster \'hək-stər\ *n* : PEDDLER, HAWKER — **huck·ster·ism** \-stə-,ri-zəm\ *n*

HUD *abbr* Department of Housing and Urban Development

¹**hud·dle** \'hə-d³l\ *vb* **hud·dled; hud·dling** 1 : to crowd together 2 : CONFER

²**huddle** *n* 1 : a closely packed group 2 : MEETING, CONFERENCE

hue \'hyü\ *n* 1 : COLOR; *also* : gradation of color 2 : the attribute of colors that permits them to be classed as red, yellow, green, blue, or an intermediate color — **hued** \'hyüd\ *adj*

hue and cry *n* : a clamor of pursuit or protest

huff \'həf\ *n* : a fit of anger or pique — **huff** *vb* — **huff·i·ly** \'hə-fə-lē\ *adv* — **huffy** \'hə-fē\ *adj*

hug \'həg\ *vb* **hugged; hug·ging** 1 : EMBRACE 2 : to stay close to — **hug** *n*

huge \'hyüj\ *adj* **hug·er; hug·est** : very large or extensive — **huge·ly** *adv* — **huge·ness** *n*

hug·ger–mug·ger \'hə-gər-,mə-gər\ *n* 1 : SECRECY 2 : CONFUSION, MUDDLE

Hu·gue·not \'hyü-gə-ˌnät\ *n* : a French Protestant of the 16th and 17th centuries

hu·la \'hü-lə\ *n* : a sinuous Polynesian dance usu. accompanied by chants

hulk \'həlk\ *n* **1** : a heavy clumsy ship **2** : an old ship unfit for service **3** : a bulky or unwieldy person or thing — **hulk·ing** \'həl-kiŋ\ *adj* : BURLY, MASSIVE

¹hull \'həl\ *n* **1** : the outer covering of a fruit or seed **2** : the frame or body esp. of a ship or boat

²hull *vb* : to remove the hulls of — **hull·er** *n*

hul·la·ba·loo \'hə-lə-bə-ˌlü\ *n, pl* **-loos** : a confused noise : UPROAR

hul·lo \ˌhə-'lō\ *chiefly Brit var of* HELLO

hum \'həm\ *vb* **hummed**; **hum·ming 1** : to utter a sound like that of the speech sound \m\ prolonged **2** : DRONE **3** : to be busily active **4** : to run smoothly **5** : to sing with closed lips — **hum** *n* — **hum·mer** *n*

¹hu·man \'hyü-mən, 'yü-\ *adj* **1** : of, relating to, being, or characteristic of humans **2** : having human form or attributes — **hu·man·ly** *adv* — **hu·man·ness** *n*

²human *n* : any of a species of bipedal primate mammals comprising all living persons and their recent ancestors; *also* : HOMINID — **hu·man·like** \-ˌlīk\ *adj*

hu·mane \hyü-'mān, yü-\ *adj* **1** : marked by compassion, sympathy, or consideration for others **2** : HUMANISTIC — **hu·mane·ly** *adv* — **hu·mane·ness** *n*

human immunodeficiency virus *n* : HIV

hu·man·ism \'hyü-mə-ˌni-zəm, 'yü-\ *n* **1** : devotion to the humanities; *also* : the revival of classical letters characteristic of the Renaissance **2** : a doctrine or way of life centered on human interests or values — **hu·man·ist** \-nist\ *n or adj* — **hu·man·is·tic** \ˌhyü-mə-'nis-tik, ˌyü-\ *adj*

hu·man·i·tar·i·an \hyü-ˌma-nə-'ter-ē-ən, yü-\ *n* : one who practices philanthropy — **humanitarian** *adj* — **hu·man·i·tar·i·an·ism** *n*

hu·man·i·ty \hyü-'ma-nə-tē, yü-\ *n, pl* **-ties 1** : the quality or state of being human or humane **2** *pl* : the branches of learning dealing with human concerns (as philosophy) as opposed to natural processes (as physics) **3** : the human race

hu·man·ize \'hyü-mə-ˌnīz, 'yü-\ *vb* **-ized; -iz·ing** : to make human or humane — **hu·man·i·za·tion** \ˌhyü-mə-nə-'zā-shən, ˌyü-\ *n* — **hu·man·iz·er** *n*

hu·man·kind \'hyü-mən-ˌkīnd, 'yü-\ *n* : the human race

hu·man·oid \'hyü-mə-ˌnȯid, 'yü-\ *adj* : having human form or characteristics — **humanoid** *n*

human papilloma virus \-ˌpa-pə-'lō-mə-\ *n* : any of numerous DNA-containing viruses that cause various human warts

¹hum·ble \'həm-bəl\ *adj* **hum·bler** \-bə-lər\; **hum·blest** \-bə-ləst\ [ME, fr. AF, fr. L *humilis* low, humble, fr. *humus* earth] **1** : not proud or haughty **2** : not pretentious : UNASSUMING **3** : INSIGNIFICANT ✦ *Synonyms* MEEK, MODEST, LOWLY — **hum·ble·ness** *n* — **hum·bly** *adv*

²humble *vb* **hum·bled; hum·bling 1** : to make humble **2** : to destroy the power or prestige of — **hum·bler** *n*

¹hum·bug \'həm-ˌbəg\ *n* **1** : HOAX, FRAUD **2** : NONSENSE

²humbug *vb* **hum·bugged; hum·bug·ging** : DECEIVE

hum·ding·er \'həm-ˌdiŋ-ər\ *n* : a person or thing of striking excellence

hum·drum \'həm-ˌdrəm\ *adj* : MONOTONOUS, DULL — **humdrum** *n*

hu·mer·us \'hyü-mə-rəs\ *n, pl* **hu·meri** \'hyü-mə-ˌrī, -ˌrē\ : the long bone extending from shoulder to elbow

hu·mid \'hyü-məd, 'yü-\ *adj* : containing or characterized by perceptible moisture : DAMP — **hu·mid·ly** *adv*

hu·mid·i·fy \hyü-'mi-də-ˌfī, yü-\ *vb* **-fied; -fy·ing** : to make humid — **hu·mid·i·fi·ca·tion** \-ˌmi-də-fə-'kā-shən\ *n* — **hu·mid·i·fi·er** \-'mi-də-ˌfī-ər\ *n*

hu·mid·i·ty \hyü-'mi-də-tē, yü-\ *n, pl* **-ties** : the amount of atmospheric moisture

hu·mi·dor \'hyü-mə-ˌdȯr, 'yü-\ *n* : a case (as for storing cigars) in which the air is kept properly humidified

hu·mil·i·ate \hyü-'mi-lē-ˌāt, yü-\ *vb* **-at·ed; -at·ing** : to injure the self-respect of : MORTIFY — **hu·mil·i·at·ing·ly** *adv* — **hu·mil·i·a·tion** \-ˌmi-lē-'ā-shən\ *n*

hu·mil·i·ty \hyü-'mi-lə-tē, yü-\ *n* : the quality or state of being humble

hum·ming·bird \'hə-miŋ-ˌbərd\ *n* : any of a family of tiny brightly colored American birds related to the swifts

hum·mock \'hə-mək\ *n* : a rounded mound : KNOLL — **hum·mocky** \-mə-kē\ *adj*

hum·mus \'hə-məs, 'hu̇-\ *n* [Ar *ḥummuṣ* chickpeas] : a paste of pureed chickpeas usu. mixed with sesame oil or paste

hu·mon·gous \hyü-'məŋ-gəs, -'mäŋ-\ *adj* [perh. alter. of *huge + monstrous*] : extremely large

¹hu·mor \'hyü-mər, 'yü-\ *n* **1** : TEMPERAMENT **2** : MOOD **3** : WHIM **4** : a quality that appeals to a sense of the ludicrous or incongruous; *also* : a keen perception of the ludicrous or incongruous **5** : comical or amusing entertainment — **hu·mor·ist** \'hyü-mə-rist, 'yü-\ *n* — **hu·mor·less** \'hyü-mər-ləs, 'yü-\ *adj* — **hu·mor·less·ly** *adv* — **hu·mor·less·ness** *n* — **hu·mor·ous** \'hyü-mə-rəs, 'yü-\ *adj* — **hu·mor·ous·ly** *adv* — **hu·mor·ous·ness** *n*

²humor *vb* : to comply with the wishes or mood of

hu·mour *chiefly Brit var of* HUMOR

hump \'həmp\ *n* **1** : a rounded protuberance (as on the back of a camel) **2** : a difficult phase or obstacle ⟨over the ~⟩ — **humped** *adj*

hump·back \'həmp-ˌbak; *1 also* -'bak\ *n* **1** : HUNCHBACK **2** : HUMPBACK WHALE — **hump·backed** *adj*

humpback whale *n* : a large baleen whale having very long flippers

hu·mus \'hyü-məs, 'yü-\ *n* : the dark organic part of soil formed from decaying matter

Hun \'hən\ *n* : a member of an Asian people that invaded Europe about A.D. 450

¹hunch \'hənch\ *vb* **1** : to thrust oneself forward **2** : to assume or cause to assume a bent or crooked posture

²hunch *n* **1** : PUSH **2** : a strong intuitive feeling about what will happen

hunch·back \'hənch-ˌbak\ *n* : a person with a crooked back; *also* : a back with a hump — **hunch·backed** *adj*

hun·dred \'hən-drəd\ *n, pl* **hundreds** *or* **hundred** : 10 times 10 — **hundred** *adj* — **hun·dredth** \-drədth\ *adj or n*

hun·dred·weight \-ˌwāt\ *n, pl* **hundredweight** *or* **hundredweights** — see WEIGHT table

¹hung *past and past part of* HANG

²hung *adj* : unable to reach a decision or verdict ⟨a ~ jury⟩

Hung *abbr* Hungarian; Hungary

Hun·gar·i·an \ˌhəŋ-'ger-ē-ən\ *n* **1** : a native or inhabitant of Hungary **2** : the language of the Hungarians — **Hungarian** *adj*

hun·ger \'həŋ-gər\ *n* **1** : a craving or urgent need for food **2** : a strong desire — **hunger** *vb* — **hun·gri·ly** *adv* — **hun·gry** *adj*

hung·over \'həŋ-'ō-vər\ *adj* : having a hangover

hung up *adj* **1** : DELAYED **2** : ENTHUSIASTIC; *also* : PREOCCUPIED — usu. used with *on* ⟨hung up on winning⟩

hunk \'həŋk\ *n* **1** : a large piece **2** : an attractive well-built man — **hunky** *adj*

hun·ker \'həŋ-kər\ *vb* **1** : CROUCH, SQUAT — usu. used with *down* **2** : to settle in for a sustained period — used with *down*

hun·ky–do·ry \ˌhəŋ-kē-'dȯr-ē\ *adj* : quite satisfactory : FINE

¹hunt \'hənt\ *vb* **1** : to pursue for food or in sport; *also* : take part in a hunt **2** : to try to find : SEEK **3** : to drive or chase esp. by harrying **4** : to traverse in search of prey — **hunt·er** *n*

²hunt *n* : an act, practice, or instance of hunting

Hun·ting·ton's disease \'hən-tiŋ-tənz-\ *n* : a chorea that usu. begins in middle age and leads to dementia

hunt·ress \'hən-trəs\ *n* : a woman who hunts game

hunts·man \'hənts-mən\ *n* **1** : HUNTER **2** : a person who manages a hunt and looks after the hounds

hur·dle \'hər-d'l\ *n* **1** : a barrier to leap over in a race **2** : OBSTACLE — **hurdle** *vb* — **hur·dler** *n*

hur·dy–gur·dy \ˌhər-dē-'gər-dē, 'hər-dē-ˌgər-dē\ *n, pl* **-gur·dies** : a musical instrument in which the sound is produced by turning a crank

hurl \'hərl\ *vb* **1** : to move or cause to move vigorously **2** : to throw down with violence **3** : FLING; *also* : PITCH — **hurl** *n* — **hurl·er** *n*

hur·ly–bur·ly \ˌhər-lē-'bər-lē\ *n* : UPROAR, TUMULT

Hu·ron \'hyu̇r-ən, 'hyu̇r-ˌän\ *n, pl* **Hurons** *or* **Huron** : a member of a confederacy of American Indian peoples formerly living between Georgian Bay and Lake Ontario

hur·rah \hù-'rȯ, -'rä\ *also* **hur·ray** \hù-'rā\ *interj* — used to express joy, approval, or encouragement

hur·ri·cane \'hər-ə-ˌkān\ *n* [Sp *huracán*, of AmerInd origin] : a tropical cyclone with winds of 74 miles (118 kilometers) per hour or greater that is usu. accompanied by rain, thunder, and lightning

¹**hur·ry** \'hər-ē\ *vb* **hur·ried; hur·ry·ing 1** : to carry or cause to go with haste **2** : to impel to a greater speed **3** : to move or act with haste — **hurried** *adj* — **hur·ried·ly** *adv*

²**hurry** *n* : extreme haste or eagerness

¹**hurt** \'hərt\ *vb* **hurt; hurt·ing 1** : to feel or cause to feel physical or emotional pain **2** : to do harm to : DAMAGE **3** : OFFEND **4** : HAMPER **5** : to be in need — usu. used with *for* — **hurt** *adj*

²**hurt** *n* **1** : a bodily injury or wound **2** : SUFFERING **3** : HARM, WRONG — **hurt·ful** *adj* — **hurt·ful·ness** *n*

hur·tle \'hər-tᵊl\ *vb* **hur·tled; hur·tling 1** : to move rapidly or forcefully **2** : HURL, FLING

¹**hus·band** \'həz-bənd\ *n* [ME *husbonde*, fr. OE *hūsbonda* master of a house, fr. ON *hūsbōndi*, fr. *hūs* house + *bōndi* householder] : a male partner in a marriage

²**husband** *vb* : to manage prudently

hus·band·man \'həz-bənd-mən\ *n* : FARMER

hus·band·ry \'həz-bən-drē\ *n* **1** : the control or judicious use of resources **2** : AGRICULTURE **3** : the production and care of domestic animals

¹**hush** \'həsh\ *vb* **1** : to make or become quiet or calm **2** : SUPPRESS

²**hush** *n* : SILENCE, QUIET

hush-hush \'həsh-ˌhəsh\ *adj* : SECRET, CONFIDENTIAL

¹**husk** \'həsk\ *n* **1** : a usu. thin dry outer covering of a seed or fruit **2** : an outer layer : SHELL

²**husk** *vb* : to strip the husk from — **husk·er** *n*

¹**hus·ky** \'həs-kē\ *adj* **hus·ki·er; -est** : HOARSE — **hus·ki·ly** \-kə-lē\ *adv* — **hus·ki·ness** \-kē-nəs\ *n*

²**husky** *n, pl* **huskies** : a heavy-coated working dog of the New World Arctic **2** : SIBERIAN HUSKY

³**husky** *adj* **1** : BURLY, ROBUST **2** : LARGE

hus·sar \(ˌ)hə-'zär\ *n* [Hung *huszár*] : a member of any of various European cavalry units

hus·sy \'hə-zē, -sē\ *n, pl* **hussies** [alter. of *housewife*] **1** : a lewd or brazen woman **2** : a pert or mischievous girl

hus·tings \'həs-tiŋz\ *n pl* : a place where political campaign speeches are made; *also* : the proceedings in an election campaign

hus·tle \'hə-səl\ *vb* **hus·tled; hus·tling 1** : JOSTLE, SHOVE **2** : HASTEN, HURRY **3** : to work energetically — **hustle** *n* — **hus·tler** \'həs-lər\ *n*

hut \'hət\ *n* : a small and often temporary dwelling : SHACK

hutch \'həch\ *n* **1** : a chest or compartment for storage **2** : a cupboard usu. surmounted with open shelves **3** : a pen or coop for an animal **4** : HUT

huz·zah *or* **huz·za** \(ˌ)hə-'zä\ *n* : a shout of acclaim — often used interjectionally to express joy or approbation

HV *abbr* **1** high velocity **2** high voltage

HVAC *abbr* heating, ventilating and air-conditioning

hvy *abbr* heavy

HW *abbr* hot water

hwy *abbr* highway

hy·a·cinth \'hī-ə-(ˌ)sinth\ *n* : a bulbous Mediterranean herb related to the lilies that is widely grown for its spikes of fragrant bell-shaped flowers

hy·brid \'hī-brəd\ *n* **1** : an offspring of genetically differing parents (as members of different breeds or species) **2** : one of mixed origin or composition — **hybrid** *adj* — **hy·brid·i·za·tion** \ˌhī-brə-də-'zā-shən\ *n* — **hy·brid·ize** \'hī-brə-ˌdīz\ *vb* — **hy·brid·iz·er** *n*

hy·dra \'hī-drə\ *n* : any of numerous small tubular freshwater coelenterates that are polyps having at one end a mouth surrounded by tentacles

hy·dran·gea \hī-'drān-jə\ *n* : any of a genus of shrubs related to the currants and grown for their showy clusters of white, pink, or bluish flowers

hy·drant \'hī-drənt\ *n* : a pipe with a valve and spout at which water may be drawn from a main pipe

hy·drate \'hī-ˌdrāt\ *n* : a compound formed by union of water with some other substance — **hydrate** *vb*

hy·drau·lic \hī-'drȯ-lik\ *adj* [ultim. fr. Gk *hydraulis* pipe organ using water pressure, fr. *hydōr* water + *aulos* reed instrument] **1** : operated, moved, or effected by means of water **2** : of or relating to hydraulics **3** : operated by the resistance offered or the pressure transmitted when a quantity of liquid is forced through a small orifice or through a tube **4** : hardening or setting under water

hy·drau·lics \-liks\ *n* : a science that deals with practical applications of liquid (as water) in motion

hydro \'hī-drō\ *n* : HYDROPOWER

hy·dro·car·bon \'hī-drō-ˌkär-bən\ *n* : an organic compound containing only carbon and hydrogen

hy·dro·ceph·a·lus \ˌhī-drō-'se-fə-ləs\ *n* : abnormal increase in the amount of fluid in the cranial cavity accompanied by enlargement of the skull and atrophy of the brain

hy·dro·chlo·ric acid \ˌhī-drə-'klȯr-ik-\ *n* : a sharp-smelling corrosive acid used in the laboratory and in industry and present in dilute form in gastric juice

hy·dro·dy·nam·ics \ˌhī-drō-dī-'na-miks\ *n* : a science that deals with the motion of fluids and the forces acting on moving bodies immersed in fluids — **hy·dro·dy·nam·ic** *adj*

hy·dro·elec·tric \ˌhī-drō-i-'lek-trik\ *adj* : of or relating to production of electricity by waterpower — **hy·dro·elec·tric·i·ty** \-ˌlek-'tri-sə-tē\ *n*

hy·dro·foil \'hī-drə-ˌfȯi(-ə)l\ *n* : a boat that has fins attached to the bottom by struts for lifting the hull clear of the water to allow faster speeds

hy·dro·gen \'hī-drə-jən\ *n* [F *hydrogène*, fr. Gk *hydōr* water + *-genēs* born; fr. the fact that water is generated by its combustion] : a gaseous colorless odorless highly flammable chemical element that is the lightest of the elements — **hy·drog·e·nous** \hī-'drä-jə-nəs\ *adj*

hy·dro·ge·nate \hī-'drä-jə-ˌnāt, 'hī-drə-\ *vb* **-nat·ed; -nat·ing** : to combine or treat with hydrogen; *esp* : to add hydrogen to the molecule of — **hy·dro·ge·na·tion** \hī-ˌdrä-jə-'nā-shən, ˌhī-drə-\ *n*

hydrogen bomb *n* : a bomb whose violent explosive power is due to the sudden release of atomic energy resulting from the fusion of light nuclei (as of hydrogen atoms)

hydrogen peroxide *n* : an unstable compound of hydrogen and oxygen used esp. as an oxidizing and bleaching agent, an antiseptic, and a propellant

hy·dro·graph·ic \ˌhī-drə-'gra-fik\ *adj* : of or relating to the description and study of bodies of water — **hy·drog·ra·pher** *n* — **hy·drog·ra·phy** \hī-'drä-grə-fē\ *n*

hy·drol·o·gy \hī-'drä-lə-jē\ *n* : a science dealing with the properties, distribution, and circulation of water — **hy·dro·log·ic** \ˌhī-drə-'lä-jik\ *or* **hy·dro·log·i·cal** \-ji-kəl\ *adj* — **hy·drol·o·gist** \hī-'drä-lə-jist\ *n*

hy·dro·ly·sis \hī-'drä-lə-səs\ *n* : a chemical decomposition involving the addition of the elements of water

hy·drom·e·ter \hī-'drä-mə-tər\ *n* : a floating instrument for determining specific gravities of liquids and hence the strength (as of alcoholic liquors)

hy·dro·pho·bia \ˌhī-drə-'fō-bē-ə\ *n* [LL, fr. Gk, fr. *hydōr* water + *phobos* fear] : RABIES

hy·dro·phone \'hī-drə-ˌfōn\ *n* : an underwater listening device

¹**hy·dro·plane** \'hī-drə-ˌplān\ *n* **1** : a powerboat designed for racing that skims the surface of the water **2** : SEAPLANE

²**hydroplane** *vb* : to skid on a wet road due to loss of contact between the tires and road

hy·dro·pon·ics \ˌhī-drə-'pä-niks\ *n* : the growing of plants in nutrient solutions — **hy·dro·pon·ic** *adj*

hy·dro·pow·er \'hī-drə-ˌpau̇(-ə)r\ *n* : hydroelectric power

hy·dro·sphere \'hī-drə-ˌsfir\ *n* : the water (as vapor or lakes) of the earth

hy·dro·stat·ic \ˌhī-drə-'sta-tik\ *adj* : of or relating to fluids at rest or to the pressures they exert or transmit

hy·dro·ther·a·py \ˌhī-drə-'ther-ə-pē\ *n* : the use of water esp. externally in the treatment of disease or disability

hy·dro·ther·mal \ˌhī-drə-'thər-məl\ *adj* : of or relating to hot water

hy·drous \'hī-drəs\ *adj* : containing water

hy·drox·ide \hī-'dräk-ˌsīd\ *n* **1** : a negatively charged ion consisting of one atom of oxygen and one atom of hydrogen **2** : a compound of hydroxide with an element or group

hy·e·na \hī-'ē-nə\ *n* [ME *hyene*, fr. L *hyaena*, fr. Gk *hyaina,* fr. *hys* hog] : any of several large doglike carnivorous mammals of Asia and Africa

hy·giene \'hī-jēn\ *n* **1** : a science concerned with establishing and maintaining good health **2** : conditions or practices conducive to health — **hy·gien·ic** \hī-'je-nik, -'jē-\ *adj* — **hy·gien·i·cal·ly** \-ni-k(ə-)lē\ *adv* — **hy·gien·ist** \hī-'jē-nist, 'hī-jē-, hī-'je-\ *n*

hy·grom·e·ter \hī-'grä-mə-tər\ *n* : any of several instruments for measuring the humidity of the atmosphere

hy·gro·scop·ic \ˌhī-grə-'skä-pik\ *adj* : readily taking up and retaining moisture

hying *pres part of* HIE

hy·men \'hī-mən\ *n* : a fold of mucous membrane partly closing the opening of the vagina

hy·me·ne·al \ˌhī-mə-'nē-əl\ *adj* : NUPTIAL

hymn \'him\ *n* : a song of praise esp. to God — **hymn** *vb*

hym·nal \'him-nəl\ *n* : a book of hymns

hyp *abbr* hypothesis; hypothetical

¹hype \'hīp\ *vb* **hyped; hyp·ing** **1** : STIMULATE — usu. used with *up* **2** : INCREASE — **hyped–up** *adj*

²hype *vb* **hyped; hyping** **1** : DECEIVE **2** : PUBLICIZE

³hype *n* **1** : DECEPTION, PUT-ON **2** : PUBLICITY

hy·per \'hī-pər\ *adj* **1** : HIGH-STRUNG, EXCITABLE **2** : extremely active

hy·per·acid·i·ty \ˌhī-pər-ə-'si-də-tē\ *n* : the condition of containing excessive acid esp. in the stomach — **hy·per·ac·id** \-'a-səd\ *adj*

hy·per·ac·tive \-'ak-tiv\ *adj* : excessively or pathologically active — **hy·per·ac·tiv·i·ty** \-ˌak-'ti-və-tē\ *n*

hy·per·bar·ic \ˌhī-pər-'ber-ik\ *adj* : of, relating to, or utilizing greater than normal pressure (as of oxygen)

hy·per·bo·la \hī-'pər-bə-lə\ *n, pl* **-las** *or* **-lae** \-(ˌ)lē\ : a curve formed by the intersection of a double right circular cone with a plane that cuts both halves of the cone — **hy·per·bol·ic** \ˌhī-pər-'bä-lik\ *adj*

hy·per·bo·le \hī-'pər-bə-(ˌ)lē\ *n* : extravagant exaggeration used as a figure of speech

hy·per·crit·i·cal \ˌhī-pər-'kri-ti-kəl\ *adj* : excessively critical — **hy·per·crit·i·cal·ly** \-k(ə-)lē\ *adv*

hy·per·drive \'hī-pər-ˌdrīv\ *n* : a state of extremely heightened activity

hy·per·ex·tend \ˌhī-pər-ik-'stend\ *vb* : to extend beyond the normal range of motion — **hy·per·ex·ten·sion** \-'sten-shən\ *n*

hy·per·gly·ce·mia \ˌhī-pər-glī-'sē-mē-ə\ *n* : excess of sugar in the blood — **hy·per·gly·ce·mic** \-mik\ *adj*

hy·per·ki·net·ic \-kə-'ne-tik\ *adj* : characterized by fast-paced or frenetic activity

hy·per·link \'hī-pər-ˌliŋk\ *n* : a connecting element (as highlighted text) between one place in a hypertext or hypermedia document and another

hy·per·me·dia \'hī-pər-ˌmē-dē-ə\ *n* : a database format offering direct access to text, sound, or images related to that on display

hy·per·opia \ˌhī-pə-'rō-pē-ə\ *n* : a condition in which visual images come to focus behind the retina resulting esp. in defective vision for near objects — **hy·per·opic** \-'rō-pik, -'rä-\ *adj*

hy·per·sen·si·tive \-'sen-sə-tiv\ *adj* **1** : excessively or abnormally sensitive **2** : abnormally susceptible physiologically to a specific agent (as a drug) — **hy·per·sen·si·tive·ness** *n* — **hy·per·sen·si·tiv·i·ty** \-ˌsen-sə-'ti-və-tē\ *n*

hy·per·ten·sion \'hī-pər-ˌten-chən\ *n* : high blood pressure — **hy·per·ten·sive** \ˌhī-pər-'ten-siv\ *adj or n*

hy·per·text \'hī-pər-ˌtekst\ *n* : a database format in which information related to that on display can be accessed directly from the display

hy·per·thy·roid·ism \ˌhī-pər-'thī-ˌrȯi-ˌdi-zəm\ *n* : excessive activity of the thyroid gland; *also* : the resulting bodily condition — **hy·per·thy·roid** \-'thī-ˌrȯid\ *adj*

hy·per·tro·phy \hī-'pər-trə-fē\ *n, pl* **-phies** : excessive development of a body part — **hy·per·tro·phic** \ˌhī-pər-'trō-fik\ *adj* — **hypertrophy** *vb*

hy·per·ven·ti·late \ˌhī-pər-'ven-tə-ˌlāt\ *vb* : to breathe rapidly and deeply esp. to the point of losing an abnormal amount of carbon dioxide from the blood — **hy·per·ven·ti·la·tion** \-ˌven-tə-'lā-shən\ *n*

hy·phen \'hī-fən\ *n* : a punctuation mark - used esp. to divide or to compound words or word parts — **hyphen** *vb*

hy·phen·ate \'hī-fə-ˌnāt\ *vb* **-at·ed; -at·ing** : to connect or divide with a hyphen — **hy·phen·ation** \ˌhī-fə-'nā-shən\ *n*

hyp·no·sis \hip-'nō-səs\ *n, pl* **-no·ses** \-ˌsēz\ : an induced state that resembles sleep and in which the subject is responsive to suggestions of the inducer (**hyp·no·tist** \'hip-nə-tist\) — **hyp·no·tism** \'hip-nə-ˌti-zəm\ *n* — **hyp·no·tiz·able** \ˌhip-nə-ˌtī-zə-bəl\ *adj* — **hyp·no·tize** \-ˌtīz\ *vb*

¹hyp·not·ic \hip-'nä-tik\ *adj* **1** : inducing sleep : SOPORIFIC **2** : of or relating to hypnosis or hypnotism **3** : readily holding the attention — **hyp·not·i·cal·ly** \-ti-k(ə-)lē\ *adv*

²hypnotic *n* : a sleep-inducing drug

hy·po \'hī-ˌpō\ *n, pl* **hypos** : SODIUM THIOSULFATE; *also* : a solution of sodium thiosulfate

hy·po·al·ler·gen·ic \ˌhī-pō-ˌa-lər-'je-nik\ *adj* : having little likelihood of causing an allergic response

hy·po·cen·ter \'hī-pə-ˌsen-tər\ *n* : the point of origin of an earthquake

hy·po·chon·dria \ˌhī-pə-'kän-drē-ə\ *n* [NL, fr. LL, pl., upper abdomen (formerly regarded as the seat of hypochondria), fr. Gk, lit., the parts under the cartilage (of the breastbone), fr. *hypo-* under + *chondros* cartilage] : depression of mind often centered on imaginary physical ailments — **hy·po·chon·dri·ac** \-drē-ˌak\ *adj or n*

hy·poc·ri·sy \hi-'pä-krə-sē\ *n, pl* **-sies** : a feigning to be what one is not or to believe what one does not; *esp* : the false assumption of an appearance of virtue or religion — **hyp·o·crite** \'hi-pə-ˌkrit\ *n* — **hyp·o·crit·i·cal** \ˌhi-pə-'kri-ti-kəl\ *adj* — **hyp·o·crit·i·cal·ly** \-k(ə-)lē\ *adv*

¹hy·po·der·mic \ˌhī-pə-'dər-mik\ *adj* : administered by or used in making an injection beneath the skin

²hypodermic *n* : HYPODERMIC SYRINGE; *also* : an injection made with this

hypodermic needle *n* : NEEDLE 3; *also* : HYPODERMIC SYRINGE

hypodermic syringe *n* : a small syringe with a hollow needle for injecting material into or through the skin

hypodermic syringe

hy·po·gly·ce·mia \ˌhī-pō-glī-'sē-mē-ə\ *n* : abnormal decrease of sugar in the blood — **hy·po·gly·ce·mic** \-mik\ *adj*

hy·pot·e·nuse \hī-'pä-tə-ˌnüs, -ˌnyüs, -ˌnüz, -ˌnyüz\ *n* : the side of a right triangle that is opposite the right angle; *also* : its length

hy·po·thal·a·mus \ˌhī-pō-'tha-lə-məs\ *n* : a part of the brain that lies beneath the thalamus and is a control center for the autonomic nervous system

hy·poth·e·sis \hī-'pä-thə-səs\ *n, pl* **-e·ses** \-ˌsēz\ : an assumption made esp. in order to test its logical or empirical consequences — **hy·po·thet·i·cal** \ˌhī-pə-'the-ti-kəl\ *adj* — **hy·po·thet·i·cal·ly** \-k(ə-)lē\ *adv*

hy·poth·e·size \-ˌsīz\ *vb* **-sized; -siz·ing** : to adopt as a hypothesis

hy·po·thy·roid·ism \ˌhī-pō-'thī-ˌrȯi-ˌdi-zəm\ *n* : deficient activity of the thyroid gland; *also* : a resultant lowered metabolic rate and general loss of vigor — **hy·po·thy·roid** *adj*

hys·sop \'hi-səp\ *n* : a European mint sometimes used as a potherb

hys·ter·ec·to·my \ˌhis-tə-'rek-tə-mē\ *n, pl* **-mies** : surgical removal of the uterus

hys·te·ria \hi-'ster-ē-ə, -'stir-\ *n* [NL, fr. E *hysteric*, adj., fr. L *hystericus*, fr. Gk *hysterikos*, fr. *hystera* womb; fr. the Greek notion that hysteria was peculiar to women and caused by disturbances in the uterus] **1** : a nervous disorder marked esp. by defective emotional control **2** : unmanageable fear or outburst of emotion — **hys·ter·ic** \-'ster-ik\ *n* — **hys·ter·i·cal** \-'ster-i-kəl\ *also* **hysteric** *adj* — **hys·ter·i·cal·ly** \-k(ə-)lē\ *adv*

hys·ter·ics \-'ster-iks\ *n pl* : a fit of uncontrollable laughter or crying

Hz *abbr* hertz

¹i \ˈī\ n, pl i's or is \ˈīz\ often cap 1 : the 9th letter of the English alphabet 2 : one in Roman numerals
²i abbr, often cap island; isle
³i symbol imaginary unit
¹I \ˈī, ə\ pron : the one speaking or writing
²I abbr interstate
³I symbol iodine
Ia or IA abbr Iowa
-ial adj suffix : ¹-AL ⟨manorial⟩
iamb \ˈī-ˌam\ or iam·bus \ī-ˈam-bəs\ n, pl iambs \ˈī-ˌamz\ or iam·bus·es : a metrical foot of one unaccented syllable followed by one accented syllable — iam·bic \ī-ˈam-bik\ adj or n
-ian — see -AN
-iatric also -iatrical adj comb form : of or relating to (such) medical treatment or healing ⟨pediatric⟩
-iatrics n pl comb form : medical treatment ⟨pediatrics⟩
ib or ibid abbr ibidem
ibex \ˈī-ˌbeks\ n, pl ibex or ibex·es [L] : any of several Old World wild goats with large curved horns
ibi·dem \ˈi-bə-ˌdem, i-ˈbī-dəm\ adv [L] : in the same place
-ibility — see -ABILITY
ibis \ˈī-bəs\ n, pl ibis or ibis·es [L, fr. Gk, fr. Egypt hbw] : any of various wading birds related to the herons but having a downwardly curved bill
-ible — see -ABLE
ibu·pro·fen \ˌī-byü-ˈprō-fən\ n : a nonsteroidal anti-inflammatory drug used to relieve pain and fever
IC \ˌī-ˈsē\ n : INTEGRATED CIRCUIT
¹-ic adj suffix 1 : of, relating to, or having the form of : being ⟨panoramic⟩ 2 : related to, derived from, or containing ⟨alcoholic⟩ 3 : in the manner of : like that of : characteristic of 4 : associated with or dealing with : utilizing ⟨electronic⟩ 5 : characterized by : exhibiting ⟨nostalgic⟩ : affected with ⟨allergic⟩ 6 : caused by 7 : tending to produce ⟨analgesic⟩
²-ic n suffix : one having the character or nature of : one belonging to or associated with : one exhibiting or affected by : one that produces
-ical adj suffix : -IC ⟨symmetrical⟩ ⟨geological⟩ — -ically adv suffix
ICBM \ˌī-ˌsē-(ˌ)bē-ˈem\ n, pl ICBM's or ICBMs \-ˈemz\ : an intercontinental ballistic missile
ICC abbr Interstate Commerce Commission
¹ice \ˈīs\ n 1 : frozen water 2 : a substance resembling ice 3 : a state of coldness (as from formality or reserve) 4 : a flavored frozen dessert; esp : one containing no milk or cream
²ice vb iced; ic·ing 1 : FREEZE 2 : CHILL 3 : to cover with or as if with icing
ice age n : a time of widespread glaciation
ice bag n : a waterproof bag to hold ice for local application of cold to the body
ice·berg \ˈīs-ˌbərg\ n : a large floating mass of ice broken off from a glacier
iceberg lettuce n : any of various crisp light green lettuces that form a compact head like a cabbage
ice·boat \ˈīs-ˌbōt\ n : a boatlike frame on runners propelled on ice by sails
ice·bound \-ˌbaund\ adj : surrounded, obstructed, or covered by ice
ice·box \-ˌbäks\ n : REFRIGERATOR
ice·break·er \-ˌbrā-kər\ n : a ship equipped (as with a reinforced bow) to make a channel through ice
ice cap n : a glacier forming on relatively level land and flowing outward from its center
ice cream n : a frozen food containing sweetened or flavored cream or butterfat
ice hockey n : a game in which two teams of ice-skating players try to shoot a puck into the opponent's goal
ice·house \ˈīs-ˌhaus\ n : a building in which ice is made or stored

¹Ice·lan·dic \īs-ˈlan-dik\ adj : of, relating to, or characteristic of Iceland, the Icelanders, or their language
²Icelandic n : the language of Iceland
ice·man \ˈīs-ˌman\ n : one who sells or delivers ice
ice milk n : a sweetened frozen food made of skim milk
ice pick n : a hand tool ending in a spike for chipping ice
ice–skate \ˈīs-ˌskāt\ vb : to skate on ice — ice–skater n
ice storm n : a storm in which falling rain freezes on contact
ice water n : chilled or iced water esp. for drinking
ich·thy·ol·o·gy \ˌik-thē-ˈä-lə-jē\ n : a branch of zoology dealing with fishes — ich·thy·ol·o·gist \-jist\ n
ici·cle \ˈī-si-kəl\ n [ME isikel, fr. is ice + ikel icicle, fr. OE gicel] : a hanging mass of ice formed by the freezing of dripping water
ic·ing \ˈī-siŋ\ n : a sweet usu. creamy mixture used to coat baked goods
ICJ abbr International Court of Justice
icky \ˈi-kē\ adj ick·i·er; -est : OFFENSIVE, DISTASTEFUL — ick·i·ness n
icon also ikon \ˈī-ˌkän\ n 1 : IMAGE; esp : a religious image painted on a wood panel 2 : a small picture on a computer display that suggests the purpose of an available function — icon·ic \ī-ˈkä-nik\ adj
icon·o·clasm \ī-ˈkä-nə-ˌkla-zəm\ n : the doctrine, practice, or attitude of an iconoclast
icon·o·clast \-ˌklast\ n [ML iconoclastes, fr. MGk eikonoklastēs, lit., image destroyer, fr. Gk eikōn image + klan to break] 1 : one who destroys religious images or opposes their veneration 2 : one who attacks cherished beliefs or institutions
-ics \iks\ n sing or pl suffix 1 : study : knowledge : skill : practice ⟨linguistics⟩ ⟨electronics⟩ 2 : characteristic actions or activities ⟨acrobatics⟩ 3 : characteristic qualities, operations, or phenomena ⟨mechanics⟩
ic·tus \ˈik-təs\ n : the recurring stress or beat in a rhythmic or metrical series of sounds
ICU abbr intensive care unit
icy \ˈī-sē\ adj ic·i·er; -est 1 : covered with, abounding in, or consisting of ice 2 : intensely cold 3 : being cold and unfriendly — ic·i·ly \ˈī-sə-lē\ adv — ic·i·ness \-sē-nəs\ n
¹id \ˈid\ n [L, it] : the part of the psyche in psychoanalytic theory that is completely unconscious and concerned with instinctual needs and drives
²id abbr idem
¹ID \ˈī-ˈdē\ vb ID'd or IDed; ID'ing or IDing : IDENTIFY
²ID abbr 1 Idaho 2 identification
idea \ī-ˈdē-ə\ n 1 : a plan for action : DESIGN 2 : something imagined or pictured in the mind 3 : a central meaning or purpose ♦ Synonyms CONCEPT, CONCEPTION, NOTION, IMPRESSION
¹ide·al \ī-ˈdēl\ adj 1 : existing only in the mind : IMAGINARY; also : lacking practicality 2 : of or relating to an ideal or to perfection : PERFECT
²ideal n 1 : a standard of excellence 2 : one regarded as a model worthy of imitation 3 : GOAL ♦ Synonyms ARCHETYPE, EXAMPLE, EXEMPLAR, PARADIGM, PATTERN
ide·al·ise Brit var of IDEALIZE
ide·al·ism \ī-ˈdē-ə-ˌli-zəm\ n : the practice of forming ideals or living under their influence; also : an idealized representation — ide·al·ist \-list\ n — ide·al·is·tic \ī-ˌdē-ə-ˈlis-tik\ adj — ide·al·is·ti·cal·ly \-ti-k(ə-)lē\ adv
ide·al·ize \ī-ˈdē-ə-ˌlīz\ vb -ized; -iz·ing : to think of or represent as ideal — ide·al·i·za·tion \-ˌdē-ə-lə-ˈzā-shən\ n
ide·al·ly \ī-ˈdē-lē, -ˈdē-ə-lē\ adv 1 : in idea or imagination : MENTALLY 2 : in agreement with an ideal : PERFECTLY
ide·a·tion \ˌī-dē-ˈā-shən\ n : the forming or entertaining of ideas — ide·ate \ˈī-dē-ˌāt\ vb — ide·a·tion·al \ˌī-dē-ˈā-shə-nəl\ adj
idem \ˈī-dem, ˈē-, ˈi-\ pron [L, same] : the same as something previously mentioned
iden·ti·cal \ī-ˈden-ti-kəl\ adj 1 : being the same 2 : essen-

tially alike ♦ *Synonyms* EQUIVALENT, EQUAL, TANTAMOUNT

iden·ti·fi·ca·tion \ī-ˌden-tə-fə-'kā-shən\ *n* **1** : an act of identifying : the state of being identified **2** : evidence of identity **3** : an unconscious psychological process by which an individual models thoughts, feelings, and actions after another person or an object

iden·ti·fy \ī-'den-tə-ˌfī\ *vb* **-fied; -fy·ing 1** : to regard as identical **2** : ASSOCIATE **3** : to establish the identity of **4** : to practice psychological identification — **iden·ti·fi·able** \-ˌden-tə-'fī-ə-bəl\ *adj* — **iden·ti·fi·ably** \-blē\ *adv* — **iden·ti·fi·er** \-ˌfī-(ə)r\ *n*

iden·ti·ty \ī-'den-tə-tē\ *n, pl* **-ties 1** : sameness of essential character **2** : INDIVIDUALITY **3** : the fact of being the same person or thing as claimed

identity crisis *n* : psychological conflict esp. in adolescence involving confusion about one's social role and one's personality

identity theft *n* : the illegal use of someone else's personal information to obtain money or credit

ideo·gram \'ī-dē-ə-ˌgram, 'i-\ *n* **1** : a picture or symbol used in a system of writing to represent a thing or an idea **2** : a character or symbol used in a system of writing to represent an entire word

ideo·logue *also* **idea·logue** \'ī-dē-ə-ˌlȯg\ *n* : a partisan advocate or adherent of a particular ideology

ide·ol·o·gy \ˌī-dē-'ä-lə-jē, ˌi-\ *also* **ide·al·o·gy** \-'a-lə-jē, -'a-\ *n, pl* **-gies 1** : the body of ideas characteristic of a particular individual, group, or culture **2** : the assertions, theories, and aims that constitute a political, social, and economic program — **ide·o·log·i·cal** \ˌī-dē-ə-'lä-ji-kəl, ˌi-\ *adj* — **ideo·log·i·cal·ly** \-'lä-ji-k(ə-)lē\ *adv* — **ide·ol·o·gist** \-dē-'ä-lə-jist\ *n*

ides \'īdz\ *sing or pl* : the 15th day of March, May, July, or October or the 13th day of any other month in the ancient Roman calendar

id·i·o·cy \'i-dē-ə-sē\ *n, pl* **-cies 1** *usu offensive* : extreme mental retardation **2** : something notably stupid or foolish

id·i·om \'i-dē-əm\ *n* **1** : the language peculiar to a person or group **2** : the characteristic form or structure of a language **3** : an expression that cannot be understood from the meanings of its separate words (as *give way*) — **id·i·o·mat·ic** \ˌi-dē-ə-'ma-tik\ *adj* — **id·i·o·mat·i·cal·ly** \-ti-k(ə-)lē\ *adv*

id·i·o·path·ic \ˌi-dē-ə-'pa-thik\ *adj* : arising spontaneously or from an obscure or unknown cause ⟨an ∼ disease⟩

id·i·o·syn·cra·sy \ˌi-dē-ə-'siŋ-krə-sē\ *n, pl* **-sies** : personal peculiarity — **id·i·o·syn·crat·ic** \ˌi-dē-ō-sin-'kra-tik\ *adj* — **id·i·o·syn·crat·i·cal·ly** \-'kra-ti-k(ə-)lē\ *adv*

id·i·ot \'i-dē-ət\ *n* [ME, fr. AF *ydiote*, fr. L *idiota* ignorant person, fr. Gk *idiōtēs* one in a private station, layman, ignorant person, fr. *idios* one's own, private] **1** *usu offensive* : a person affected with idiocy **2** : a foolish or stupid person — **id·i·ot·ic** \ˌi-dē-'ä-tik\ *adj* — **id·i·ot·i·cal·ly** \-ti-k(ə-)lē\ *adv*

id·i·ot·proof \'i-dē-ət-ˌprüf\ *adj* : extremely easy to operate or maintain

¹idle \'ī-dᵊl\ *adj* **idler** \'ī-də-lər\; **idlest** \'ī-də-ləst\ **1** : GROUNDLESS, WORTHLESS, USELESS ⟨∼ talk⟩ **2** : not occupied or employed : INACTIVE **3** : LAZY — **idle·ness** *n* — **idly** \'īd-lē\ *adv*

²idle *vb* **idled; idling 1** : to spend time doing nothing **2** : to make idle **3** : to run without being connected so that power is not used for useful work — **idler** *n*

idol \'ī-dᵊl\ *n* **1** : an image worshipped as a god; *also* : a false god **2** : an object of passionate devotion

idol·a·ter *or* **idol·a·tor** \ī-'dä-lə-tər\ *n* : a worshiper of idols

idol·a·try \-trē\ *n, pl* **-tries 1** : the worship of a physical object as a god **2** : excessive devotion — **idol·a·trous** \-trəs\ *adj*

idol·ize \'ī-də-ˌlīz\ *vb* **-ized; -iz·ing** : to make an idol of — **idol·i·za·tion** \ˌī-də-lə-'zā-shən\ *n*

idyll \'ī-dᵊl\ *n* **1** : a simple work of writing or poetry that describes country life or suggests a peaceful setting **2** : a fit subject for an idyll — **idyl·lic** \ī-'di-lik\ *adj*

i.e. \'ī-'ē\ *abbr* [L *id est*] that is

IE *abbr* industrial engineer

-ier — see -ER

if \'if\ *conj* **1** : in the event that ⟨∼ he stays, I leave⟩ **2** : WHETHER ⟨ask ∼ he left⟩ **3** — used as a function word to introduce an exclamation expressing a wish ⟨∼ it would only rain⟩ **4** : even though ⟨an interesting ∼ untenable argument⟩ **5** : and perhaps not even ⟨few ∼ any changes are expected⟩

IF *abbr* intermediate frequency

if·fy \'i-fē\ *adj* : full of contingencies or unknown conditions

-i·fy \ə-ˌfī\ *vb suffix* : -FY

IG *abbr* inspector general

ig·loo \'i-glü\ *n, pl* **igloos** [Inuit (an Eskimo language) *iglu* house] : an Eskimo house or hut often made of snow blocks and in the shape of a dome

ig·ne·ous \'ig-nē-əs\ *adj* **1** : FIERY **2** : formed by solidification of molten rock

ig·nite \ig-'nīt\ *vb* **ig·nit·ed; ig·nit·ing** : to set afire or catch fire — **ig·nit·able** \-'nī-tə-bəl\ *adj*

ig·ni·tion \ig-'ni-shən\ *n* **1** : a setting on fire **2** : the process or means (as an electric spark) of igniting the fuel mixture in an engine **3** : a device that activates an ignition system

ig·no·ble \ig-'nō-bəl\ *adj* **1** : of common birth **2** : not honorable : BASE, MEAN ♦ *Synonyms* DESPICABLE, SCURVY, SORDID, VILE, WRETCHED — **ig·no·bly** *adv*

ig·no·min·i·ous \ˌig-nə-'mi-nē-əs\ *adj* **1** : DISHONORABLE **2** : DESPICABLE **3** : HUMILIATING, DEGRADING ♦ *Synonyms* DISREPUTABLE, DISCREDITABLE, DISGRACEFUL, INGLORIOUS — **ig·no·min·i·ous·ly** *adv* — **ig·no·mi·ny** \'ig-nə-ˌmi-nē, ig-'nä-mə-nē\ *n*

ig·no·ra·mus \ˌig-nə-'rā-məs\ *n, pl* **-mus·es** *also* **-mi** \-mē\ [*Ignoramus*, ignorant lawyer in *Ignoramus* (1615), play by George Ruggle] : an utterly ignorant person

ig·no·rance \'ig-nə-rəns\ *n* : the state of being ignorant

ig·no·rant \'ig-nə-rənt\ *adj* **1** : lacking knowledge **2** : resulting from or showing lack of knowledge or intelligence **3** : UNAWARE, UNINFORMED ♦ *Synonyms* BENIGHTED, ILLITERATE, UNEDUCATED, UNLETTERED, UNTUTORED — **ig·no·rant·ly** *adv*

ig·nore \ig-'nȯr\ *vb* **ig·nored; ig·nor·ing** : to refuse to take notice of ♦ *Synonyms* OVERLOOK, SLIGHT, NEGLECT

igua·na \i-'gwä-nə\ *n* : any of various large tropical American lizards

iguana

ihp *abbr* indicated horsepower

IHS \ˌī-ˌāch-'es\ [LL, part transliteration of Gk IHΣ, abbr. for IHΣΟΥΣ *Iēsous* Jesus] — used as a Christian symbol and monogram for *Jesus*

ikon *var of* ICON

IL *abbr* Illinois

il·e·itis \ˌi-lē-'ī-təs\ *n* : inflammation of the ileum

il·e·um \'i-lē-əm\ *n, pl* **il·ea** \-lē-ə\ : the part of the small intestine between the jejunum and the large intestine

il·i·ac \'i-lē-ˌak\ *adj* : of, relating to, or located near the ilium

il·i·um \'i-lē-əm\ *n, pl* **il·ia** \-lē-ə\ : the uppermost and largest of the three bones making up either side of the pelvis

ilk \'ilk\ *n* : SORT, KIND

¹ill \'il\ *adj* **worse** \'wərs\; **worst** \'wərst\ **1** : attended or caused by an evil intent ⟨∼ deeds⟩ **2** : not normal or sound ⟨∼ health⟩; *also* : not in good health : SICK **3** : BAD, UNLUCKY ⟨an ∼ omen⟩ **4** : not right or proper ⟨∼ manners⟩ **5** : UNFRIENDLY, HOSTILE ⟨∼ feeling⟩

²ill *adv* **worse; worst 1** : with displeasure **2** : in a harsh manner **3** : HARDLY, SCARCELY ⟨can ∼ afford it⟩ **4** : BADLY, UNLUCKILY **5** : in a faulty way

³ill *n* **1** : EVIL **2** : MISFORTUNE, DISTRESS **3** : AILMENT, SICKNESS; *also* : TROUBLE

⁴ill *abbr* illustrated; illustration; illustrator

Ill *abbr* Illinois

ill—ad·vised \ˌil-əd-ˈvīzd\ *adj* : not well counseled ⟨~ efforts⟩ — **ill—ad·vis·ed·ly** \-ˈvī-zəd-lē\ *adv*

ill—bred \-ˈbred\ *adj* : badly brought up : IMPOLITE

il·le·gal \il-ˈlē-gəl\ *adj* : not lawful; *also* : not sanctioned by official rules ♦ **Synonyms** UNLAWFUL, CRIMINAL, ILLEGITIMATE, ILLICIT, WRONGFUL — **il·le·gal·i·ty** \ˌi-li-ˈga-lə-tē\ *n* — **il·le·gal·ly** *adv*

il·leg·i·ble \il-ˈle-jə-bəl\ *adj* : not legible — **il·leg·i·bil·i·ty** \il-ˌle-jə-ˈbi-lə-tē\ *n* — **il·leg·i·bly** \il-ˈle-jə-blē\ *adv*

il·le·git·i·mate \ˌi-li-ˈji-tə-mət\ *adj* **1** : born of unmarried parents **2** : ILLOGICAL **3** : ILLEGAL — **il·le·git·i·ma·cy** \-ˈji-tə-mə-sē\ *n* — **il·le·git·i·mate·ly** *adv*

ill—fat·ed \ˈil-ˈfā-təd\ *adj* : UNFORTUNATE ⟨an ~ expedition⟩

ill—fa·vored \-ˈfā-vərd\ *adj* : UGLY, UNATTRACTIVE

ill—got·ten \-ˈgä-tᵊn\ *adj* : acquired by improper means ⟨~ gains⟩

ill—hu·mored \-ˈhyü-mərd, -ˈyü-\ *adj* : SURLY, IRRITABLE

il·lib·er·al \il-ˈli-bə-rəl\ *adj* : not liberal : NARROW, BIGOTED

il·lic·it \il-ˈli-sət\ *adj* : not permitted : UNLAWFUL — **il·lic·it·ly** *adv*

il·lim·it·able \il-ˈli-mə-tə-bəl\ *adj* : BOUNDLESS, MEASURELESS — **il·lim·it·ably** \-blē\ *adv*

Il·li·nois \ˌi-lə-ˈnȯi *also* -ˈnȯiz\ *n, pl* **Illinois** : a member of an American Indian people of Illinois, Iowa, and Wisconsin

il·lit·er·ate \il-ˈli-tə-rət\ *adj* **1** : having little or no education; *esp* : unable to read or write **2** : showing a lack of familiarity with the fundamentals of a particular field of knowledge — **il·lit·er·a·cy** \-ˈli-tə-rə-sē\ *n* — **illiterate** *n*

ill—man·nered \ˈil-ˈma-nərd\ *adj* : marked by bad manners : RUDE

ill—na·tured \-ˈnā-chərd\ *adj* : CROSS, SURLY — **ill—na·tured·ly** *adv*

ill·ness \ˈil-nəs\ *n* : SICKNESS

il·log·i·cal \il-ˈlä-ji-kəl\ *adj* : lacking sound reasoning; *also* : SENSELESS — **il·log·i·cal·ly** \-ji-k(ə-)lē\ *adv*

ill—starred \ˈil-ˈstärd\ *adj* : UNLUCKY **1** ⟨an ~ venture⟩

ill—tem·pered \-ˈtem-pərd\ *adj* : CROSS

ill—treat \-ˈtrēt\ *vb* : to treat cruelly or improperly : MALTREAT — **ill—treat·ment** *n*

il·lu·mi·nate \i-ˈlü-mə-ˌnāt\ *vb* **-nat·ed; -nat·ing** **1** : to supply or brighten with light : light up **2** : to make clear : ELUCIDATE; *also* : to bring to the fore **3** : to decorate (as a manuscript) with designs or pictures in gold or colors — **il·lu·mi·nat·ing·ly** *adv* — **il·lu·mi·na·tion** \-ˌlü-mə-ˈnā-shən\ *n* — **il·lu·mi·na·tor** \-ˈlü-mə-ˌnā-tər\ *n*

il·lu·mine \i-ˈlü-mən\ *vb* **-mined; -min·ing** : ILLUMINATE

ill—us·age \ˈil-ˈyü-sij\ *n* : harsh, unkind, or abusive treatment

ill—use \-ˈyüz\ *vb* : MALTREAT, ABUSE

il·lu·sion \i-ˈlü-zhən\ *n* [ME, fr. AF, fr. LL *illusio*, fr. L, action of mocking, fr. *illudere* to mock at, fr. *ludere* to play, mock] **1** : a mistaken idea : MISCONCEPTION **2** : a misleading visual image; *also* : HALLUCINATION

il·lu·sion·ist \i-ˈlü-zhə-nist\ *n* : one that produces illusions; *esp* : a sleight-of-hand performer

il·lu·sive \i-ˈlü-siv\ *adj* : DECEPTIVE

il·lu·so·ry \i-ˈlü-sə-rē, -zə-\ *adj* : DECEPTIVE ⟨~ hopes⟩

illust *or* **illus** *abbr* illustrated; illustration

il·lus·trate \ˈi-ləs-ˌtrāt\ *vb* **-trat·ed; -trat·ing** [L *illustrare*, fr. *lustrare* to purify, make bright] **1** : to explain by use of examples : CLARIFY; *also* : DEMONSTRATE **2** : to provide with pictures or figures that explain or decorate **3** : to serve to explain or decorate — **il·lus·tra·tor** \ˈi-ləs-ˌtrā-tər\ *n*

il·lus·tra·tion \ˌi-lə-ˈstrā-shən\ *n* **1** : the act of illustrating : the condition of being illustrated **2** : an example or instance that helps make something clear **3** : a picture or diagram that explains or decorates

il·lus·tra·tive \i-ˈləs-trə-tiv, ˈi-lə-ˌstrā-\ *adj* : serving, tending, or designed to illustrate — **il·lus·tra·tive·ly** *adv*

il·lus·tri·ous \i-ˈləs-trē-əs\ *adj* : notably outstanding because of rank or achievement ♦ **Synonyms** DISTINGUISHED, EMINENT, FAMOUS, GREAT, NOTABLE, PROMINENT — **il·lus·tri·ous·ness** *n*

ill will *n* : unfriendly feeling

ILS *abbr* instrument landing system

¹im·age \ˈi-mij\ *n* **1** : a likeness or imitation of a person or thing; *esp* : STATUE **2** : a picture of an object formed by a device (as a mirror or lens) **3** : a visual representation of something ⟨a computer ~⟩ **4** : a person strikingly like another person ⟨he is the ~ of his father⟩ **5** : a mental picture or conception : IMPRESSION, IDEA, CONCEPT **6** : a vivid representation or description

²image *vb* **im·aged; im·ag·ing** **1** : to call up a mental picture of **2** : to describe or portray in words **3** : to create a representation of **4** : REFLECT, MIRROR **5** : to make appear : PROJECT

im·ag·ery \ˈi-mij-rē\ *n, pl* **-er·ies** **1** : IMAGES; *also* : the art of making images **2** : figurative language **3** : mental images; *esp* : the products of imagination

imag·in·able \i-ˈma-jə-nə-bəl\ *adj* : capable of being imagined : CONCEIVABLE — **imag·in·ably** *adv*

imag·i·nary \i-ˈma-jə-ˌner-ē\ *adj* **1** : existing only in the imagination **2** : containing or relating to a quantity (**imaginary unit**) that is the positive square root of minus 1 ($\sqrt{-1}$)

imaginary number *n* : a complex number (as $2 + 3i$) with a nonzero term (**imaginary part**) containing the imaginary unit as a factor

imag·i·na·tion \i-ˌma-jə-ˈnā-shən\ *n* **1** : the act or power of forming a mental image of something not present to the senses or not previously known or experienced **2** : creative ability **3** : RESOURCEFULNESS **4** : a mental image : a creation of the mind — **imag·i·na·tive** \i-ˈma-jə-nə-tiv, -ˌnā-\ *adj* — **imag·i·na·tive·ly** *adv*

imag·ine \i-ˈma-jən\ *vb* **imag·ined; imag·in·ing** **1** : to form a mental picture of something not present **2** : THINK, GUESS ⟨I ~ it will rain⟩

imag·in·ings \-ˈmaj-niŋz, -ˈma-jə-\ *n pl* : products of the imagination

im·ag·ism \ˈi-mi-ˌji-zəm\ *n, often cap* : a movement in poetry advocating free verse and the expression of ideas and emotions through clear precise images — **im·ag·ist** \-jist\ *n*

ima·go \i-ˈmā-gō, -ˈmä-\ *n, pl* **imagoes** *or* **ima·gi·nes** \-ˈmā-gə-ˌnēz, -ˈmä-\ [NL, fr. L, image] : an insect in its final adult stage — **ima·gi·nal** \i-ˈmā-gə-nᵊl, -ˈmä-\ *adj*

im·bal·ance \ˈim-ˈba-ləns\ *n* : lack of balance : the state of being out of equilibrium or out of proportion

im·be·cile \ˈim-bə-səl, -ˌsil\ *n* **1** *usu offensive* : a person affected with moderate mental retardation **2** : FOOL, IDIOT — **imbecile** *or* **im·be·cil·ic** \ˌim-bə-ˈsi-lik\ *adj* — **im·be·cil·i·ty** \ˌim-bə-ˈsi-lə-tē\ *n*

imbed *var of* EMBED

im·bibe \im-ˈbīb\ *vb* **im·bibed; im·bib·ing** **1** : to receive and retain in the mind **2** : to drink alcoholic beverages **3** : to take in or up : ABSORB — **im·bib·er** *n*

im·bri·ca·tion \ˌim-brə-ˈkā-shən\ *n* **1** : an overlapping of edges (as of tiles) **2** : a pattern showing imbrication — **im·bri·cate** \ˈim-bri-kət\ *adj*

im·bro·glio \im-ˈbrōl-yō\ *n, pl* **-glios** [It, fr. *imbrogliare* to entangle] **1** : a confused mass **2** : a complicated situation; *also* : a serious or embarrassing misunderstanding

im·brue \im-ˈbrü\ *vb* **im·brued; im·bru·ing** : STAIN ⟨hands *imbrued* with blood⟩

im·bue \-ˈbyü\ *vb* **im·bued; im·bu·ing** **1** : to permeate or influence as if by dyeing **2** : to tinge or dye deeply

IMF *abbr* International Monetary Fund

imit *abbr* imitative

im·i·ta·ble \ˈi-mə-tə-bəl\ *adj* : capable or worthy of being imitated or copied

im·i·tate \ˈi-mə-ˌtāt\ *vb* **-tat·ed; -tat·ing** **1** : to follow as a model : COPY **2** : RESEMBLE **3** : REPRODUCE **4** : MIMIC, COUNTERFEIT — **im·i·ta·tor** \-ˌtā-tər\ *n*

im·i·ta·tion \ˌi-mə-ˈtā-shən\ *n* **1** : an act of imitating **2** : COPY, COUNTERFEIT **3** : a literary work that reproduces the style of another author — **imitation** *adj*

im·i·ta·tive \ˈi-mə-ˌtā-tiv\ *adj* **1** : marked by imitation **2** : inclined to imitate **3** : COUNTERFEIT

im·mac·u·late \i-ˈma-kyə-lət\ *adj* **1** : being without stain or blemish : PURE **2** : spotlessly clean ⟨~ linen⟩ — **im·mac·u·late·ly** *adv*

im·ma·nent \ˈi-mə-nənt\ *adj* **1** INHERENT **2** : being within the limits of experience or knowledge — **im·ma·nence** \-nəns\ *n* — **im·ma·nen·cy** \-nən-sē\ *n*

im·ma·te·ri·al \ˌi-mə-ˈtir-ē-əl\ *adj* **1** : not consisting of matter : SPIRITUAL **2** : UNIMPORTANT, TRIFLING ♦ **Synonyms** BODILESS, DISEMBODIED, INCORPOREAL, INSUB-

STANTIAL, NONPHYSICAL — **im·ma·te·ri·al·i·ty** \-ˌtir-ē-'a-lə-tē\ n

im·ma·ture \ˌi-mə-'tùr, -'tyùr\ adj : lacking complete development : not yet mature — **im·ma·tu·ri·ty** \-'tùr-ə-tē, -'tyùr-\ n

im·mea·sur·able \(ˌ)i-'me-zhə-rə-bəl\ adj : not capable of being measured : indefinitely extensive : ILLIMITABLE — **im·mea·sur·ably** \-blē\ adv

im·me·di·a·cy \i-'mē-dē-ə-sē\ n, pl **-cies** 1 : the quality or state of being immediate 2 : something that is of immediate importance

im·me·di·ate \i-'mē-dē-ət\ adj 1 : acting directly and alone : DIRECT ⟨the ~ cause of death⟩ 2 : being next in line or relation ⟨members of the ~ family⟩ 3 : not distant : CLOSE 4 : made or done at once ⟨an ~ response⟩ 5 : near to or related to the present time ⟨the ~ future⟩ — **im·me·di·ate·ly** adv

im·me·mo·ri·al \ˌi-mə-'mòr-ē-əl\ adj : extending beyond the reach of memory, record, or tradition

im·mense \i-'mens\ adj [ME, fr. MF, fr. L immensus immeasurable, fr. mensus, pp. of metiri to measure] 1 : very great in size or degree : VAST, HUGE 2 : EXCELLENT — **im·mense·ly** adv — **im·men·si·ty** \-'men-sə-tē\ n

im·merse \i-'mərs\ vb **im·mersed**; **im·mers·ing** 1 : to plunge or dip esp. into a fluid 2 : ENGROSS, ABSORB 3 : to baptize by immersing — **im·mer·sion** \-'mər-zhən\ n

im·mi·grant \'i-mi-grənt\ n 1 : a person who immigrates 2 : a plant or animal that becomes established where it did not previously occur

im·mi·grate \'i-mə-ˌgrāt\ vb **-grat·ed**; **-grat·ing** : to come into a foreign country and take up residence — **im·mi·gra·tion** \ˌi-mə-'grā-shən\ n

im·mi·nent \'i-mə-nənt\ adj : ready to take place; esp : hanging threateningly over one's head — **im·mi·nence** \-nəns\ n — **im·mi·nent·ly** adv

im·mis·ci·ble \(ˌ)i-'mi-sə-bəl\ adj : incapable of mixing — **im·mis·ci·bil·i·ty** \-ˌmi-sə-'bi-lə-tē\ n

im·mis·er·a·tion \(ˌ)i-ˌmi-zə-'rā-shən\ n : IMPOVERISHMENT

im·mo·bile \(ˌ)i-'mō-bəl\ adj : incapable of being moved : FIXED — **im·mo·bil·i·ty** \ˌi-mō-'bi-lə-tē\ n

im·mo·bi·lize \i-'mō-bə-ˌliz\ vb : to make immobile — **im·mo·bi·li·za·tion** \i-ˌmō-bə-lə-'zā-shən\ n

im·mod·er·ate \(ˌ)i-'mä-də-rət\ adj : lacking in moderation : EXCESSIVE — **im·mod·er·a·cy** \-rə-sē\ n — **im·mod·er·ate·ly** adv

im·mod·est \(ˌ)i-'mä-dəst\ adj : not modest : BRAZEN, INDECENT ⟨an ~ dress⟩ ⟨~ conduct⟩ — **im·mod·est·ly** adv — **im·mod·es·ty** \-də-stē\ n

im·mo·late \'i-mə-ˌlāt\ vb **-lat·ed**; **-lat·ing** [L immolare, to sprinkle with meal before sacrificing, sacrifice, fr. mola sacrificial barley cake, lit., millstone] : to offer in sacrifice; esp : to kill as a sacrificial victim — **im·mo·la·tion** \ˌi-mə-'lā-shən\ n

im·mor·al \(ˌ)i-'mòr-əl\ adj : not moral — **im·mor·al·ly** adv

im·mo·ral·i·ty \ˌi-mò-'ra-lə-tē, ˌi-mə-\ n 1 : WICKEDNESS; esp : UNCHASTITY 2 : an immoral act or practice

¹**im·mor·tal** \(ˌ)i-'mòr-tᵊl\ adj 1 : not mortal : exempt from death ⟨~ gods⟩ 2 : destined to be remembered forever ⟨those ~ words⟩ — **im·mor·tal·ly** adv

²**immortal** n 1 : one exempt from death 2 pl, often cap : the gods in Greek and Roman mythology 3 : a person whose fame is lasting ⟨an ~ of baseball⟩

im·mor·tal·ise Brit var of IMMORTALIZE

im·mor·tal·i·ty \ˌi-ˌmòr-'ta-lə-tē\ n : the quality or state of being immortal; esp : unending existence

im·mor·tal·ize \i-'mòr-tə-ˌliz\ vb **-ized**; **-iz·ing** : to make immortal

im·mov·able \(ˌ)i-'mü-və-bəl\ adj 1 : firmly fixed, settled, or fastened : FAST, STATIONARY ⟨~ mountains⟩ 2 : STEADFAST, UNYIELDING 3 : IMPASSIVE — **im·mov·abil·i·ty** \-ˌmü-və-'bi-lə-tē\ n — **im·mov·ably** \-blē\ adv

im·mune \i-'myün\ adj 1 : EXEMPT 2 : having a special capacity for resistance (as to a disease) 3 : containing or producing antibodies — **im·mu·ni·ty** \-'myü-nə-tē\ n

immune response n : a response of the body to an antigen resulting in the formation of antibodies and cells designed to react with the antigen and render it harmless

immune system n : the bodily system that protects the body from foreign substances, cells, and tissues by pro-

ducing the immune response and that includes esp. the thymus, spleen, lymph nodes, and lymphocytes

im·mu·nize \'i-myə-ˌnīz\ vb **-nized**; **-niz·ing** : to make immune — **im·mu·ni·za·tion** \ˌi-myə-nə-'zā-shən\ n

im·mu·no·de·fi·cien·cy \ˌi-myə-nō-di-'fi-shən-sē\ n : inability to produce the normal number of antibodies or immunologically sensitized cells esp. in response to specific antigens — **im·mu·no·de·fi·cient** \-'fi-shənt\ adj

im·mu·no·glob·u·lin \ˌi-myə-nō-'glä-byə-lən\ n : ANTIBODY

im·mu·nol·o·gy \ˌi-myə-'nä-lə-jē\ n : a science that deals with the immune system, immunity, and the immune response — **im·mu·no·log·ic** \-nə-'lä-jik\ or **im·mu·no·log·i·cal** \-ji-kəl\ adj — **im·mu·no·log·i·cal·ly** \-ji-k(ə-)lē\ adv — **im·mu·nol·o·gist** \-'nä-lə-jist\ n

im·mu·no·sup·pres·sion \ˌi-myə-nō-sə-'pre-shən\ n : suppression (as by drugs) of natural immune responses — **im·mu·no·sup·press** \-'pres\ vb — **im·mu·no·sup·pres·sant** \-'pre-sᵊnt\ n or adj — **im·mu·no·sup·pres·sive** \-'pre-siv\ adj

im·mu·no·ther·a·py \-'ther-ə-pē\ n : the treatment or prevention of disease by attempting to induce immunity

im·mure \i-'myùr\ vb **im·mured**; **im·mur·ing** 1 : to enclose within or as if within walls 2 : to build into a wall; esp : to entomb in a wall

im·mu·ta·ble \(ˌ)i-'myü-tə-bəl\ adj : UNCHANGEABLE, UNCHANGING — **im·mu·ta·bil·i·ty** \-ˌmyü-tə-'bi-lə-tē\ n — **im·mu·ta·bly** \-'myü-tə-blē\ adv

¹**imp** \'imp\ n 1 : a small demon : FIEND 2 : a mischievous child

²**imp** abbr 1 imperative 2 imperfect 3 imperial 4 import; imported

¹**im·pact** \im-'pakt\ vb 1 : to press together 2 : to have an impact on

²**im·pact** \'im-ˌpakt\ n 1 : a forceful contact, collision, or onset; also : the impetus communicated in or as if in a collision 2 : EFFECT

im·pact·ed \im-'pak-təd\ adj 1 : packed or wedged in 2 : wedged between the jawbone and another tooth

im·pair \im-'per\ vb : to diminish in quantity, value, excellence, or strength : DAMAGE, LESSEN — **im·pair·ment** n

im·paired \-'pärd\ adj : being in a less than perfect or whole condition; esp : disabled or functionally defective — often used in combination ⟨hearing-impaired⟩

im·pa·la \im-'pa-lə\ n, pl **impalas** or **impala** : a large brownish African antelope that in the male has slender curved horns with ridges

im·pale \im-'pāl\ vb **im·paled**; **im·pal·ing** : to pierce with or as if with something pointed — **im·pale·ment** n

im·pal·pa·ble \(ˌ)im-'pal-pə-bəl\ adj 1 : unable to be felt by touch : INTANGIBLE 2 : not easily seen or understood — **im·pal·pa·bly** \-blē\ adv

im·pan·el or **em·pan·el** vb : to enter in or on a panel : ENROLL ⟨~ a jury⟩

im·part \im-'pärt\ vb 1 : to give from one's store or abundance ⟨the sun ~s warmth⟩ 2 : to make known

im·par·tial \(ˌ)im-'pär-shəl\ adj : not partial : UNBIASED, JUST — **im·par·tial·i·ty** \-ˌpär-shē-'a-lə-tē\ n — **im·par·tial·ly** adv

im·pass·able \(ˌ)im-'pa-sə-bəl\ adj : incapable of being passed, traversed, or crossed ⟨~ roads⟩ — **im·pass·ably** \-blē\ adv

im·passe \'im-ˌpas\ n 1 : a predicament from which there is no obvious escape 2 : an impassable road or way

im·pas·si·ble \(ˌ)im-'pa-sə-bəl\ adj : incapable of feeling : IMPASSIVE

im·pas·sioned \im-'pa-shənd\ adj : filled with passion or zeal : showing great warmth or intensity of feeling ✦ **Synonyms** PASSIONATE, ARDENT, FERVENT, FERVID

im·pas·sive \(ˌ)im-'pa-siv\ adj : showing no signs of feeling, emotion, or interest : EXPRESSIONLESS, INDIFFERENT ✦ **Synonyms** STOIC, PHLEGMATIC, APATHETIC, STOLID — **im·pas·sive·ly** adv — **im·pas·siv·i·ty** \ˌim-ˌpa-'si-və-tē\ n

im·pas·to \im-'pas-tō, -'päs-\ n : the thick application of a pigment to a canvas or panel in painting; also : the body of pigment so applied

im·pa·tiens \im-'pā-shənz, -shəns\ n : any of a genus of herbs with usu. spurred flowers and seed capsules that readily split open

im·pa·tient \(ˌ)im-'pā-shənt\ adj 1 : not patient : restless or short of temper esp. under irritation, delay, or opposition **2** : INTOLERANT ⟨~ of poverty⟩ **3** : prompted or marked by impatience ⟨an ~ reply⟩ **4** : ANXIOUS — **im·pa·tience** \-shəns\ *n* — **im·pa·tient·ly** *adv*

im·peach \im-'pēch\ *vb* [ME *empechen* to accuse, fr. AF *empecher, enpechier* to ensnare, impede, prosecute, fr. LL *impedicare* to fetter, fr. L *pedica* fetter, fr. *ped-, pes* foot] **1** : to charge (a public official) before an authorized tribunal with misconduct in office **2** : to challenge the credibility or validity of **3** : to remove from public office for misconduct — **im·peach·ment** *n*

im·pec·ca·ble \(,)im-'pe-kə-bəl\ *adj* **1** : not capable of sinning or wrongdoing **2** : FAULTLESS, IRREPROACHABLE ⟨a man of ~ character⟩ — **im·pec·ca·bil·i·ty** \-,pe-kə-'bi-lə-tē\ *n* — **im·pec·ca·bly** \-'pe-kə-blē\ *adv*

im·pe·cu·nious \,im-pi-'kyü-nyəs, -nē-əs\ *adj* : having little or no money — **im·pe·cu·nious·ness** *n*

im·ped·ance \im-'pē-dᵊns\ *n* : the opposition in an electrical circuit to the flow of an alternating current

im·pede \im-'pēd\ *vb* **im·ped·ed; im·ped·ing** [L *impedire,* fr. *ped-, pes* foot] : to interfere with the progress of

im·ped·i·ment \im-'pe-də-mənt\ *n* **1** : something that impedes, hinders, or obstructs **2** : a speech defect

im·ped·i·men·ta \im-,pe-də-'men-tə\ *n pl* : things that impede

im·pel \im-'pel\ *vb* **im·pelled; im·pel·ling** : to urge or drive forward or on : FORCE; *also* : PROPEL

im·pel·ler *also* **im·pel·lor** \im-'pe-lər\ *n* : a rotor esp. in a pump

im·pend \im-'pend\ *vb* **1** : to hover or hang over threateningly : MENACE **2** : to be about to occur

im·pen·e·tra·ble \(,)im-'pe-nə-trə-bəl\ *adj* **1** : incapable of being penetrated or pierced ⟨an ~ jungle⟩ **2** : incapable of being comprehended : INSCRUTABLE ⟨an ~ mystery⟩ — **im·pen·e·tra·bil·i·ty** \-,pe-nə-trə-'bi-lə-tē\ *n* — **im·pen·e·tra·bly** \-'pe-nə-trə-blē\ *adv*

im·pen·i·tent \(,)im-'pe-nə-tənt\ *adj* : not penitent : not repenting of sin — **im·pen·i·tence** \-təns\ *n*

im·per·a·tive \im-'per-ə-tiv\ *adj* **1** : expressing a command, request, or encouragement ⟨~ sentence⟩ **2** : having power to restrain, control, or direct **3** : NECESSARY ⟨an ~ duty⟩ — **imperative** *n* — **im·per·a·tive·ly** *adv*

im·per·cep·ti·ble \,im-pər-'sep-tə-bəl\ *adj* : not perceptible; *esp* : too slight to be perceived ⟨~ changes⟩ — **im·per·cep·ti·bly** \-blē\ *adv*

im·per·cep·tive \,im-pər-'sep-tiv\ *adj* : not perceptive ⟨an ~ reader⟩

imperf *abbr* imperfect

¹im·per·fect \(,)im-'pər-fikt\ *adj* **1** : not perfect : DEFECTIVE, INCOMPLETE **2** : of, relating to, or being a verb tense used to designate a continuing state or an incomplete action esp. in the past — **im·per·fect·ly** *adv*

²imperfect *n* : the imperfect tense; *also* : a verb form in it

im·per·fec·tion \,im-pər-'fek-shən\ *n* : the quality or state of being imperfect; *also* : FAULT, BLEMISH

im·pe·ri·al \im-'pir-ē-əl\ *adj* **1** : of, relating to, or befitting an empire or an emperor; *also* : of or relating to the United Kingdom or to the Commonwealth or British Empire **2** : ROYAL, SOVEREIGN; *also* : REGAL, IMPERIOUS **3** : of unusual size or excellence

im·pe·ri·al·ism \im-'pir-ē-ə-,li-zəm\ *n* : the policy of seeking to extend the power, dominion, or territories of a nation — **im·pe·ri·al·ist** \-list\ *n or adj* — **im·pe·ri·al·is·tic** \-,pir-ē-ə-'lis-tik\ *adj* — **im·pe·ri·al·is·ti·cal·ly** \-ti-k(ə-)lē\ *adv*

im·per·il \im-'per-əl\ *vb* **-iled** *or* **-illed; -il·ing** *or* **-il·ling** : ENDANGER

im·pe·ri·ous \im-'pir-ē-əs\ *adj* **1** : COMMANDING, LORDLY **2** : ARROGANT, DOMINEERING **3** : IMPERATIVE, URGENT ⟨~ problems⟩ — **im·pe·ri·ous·ly** *adv*

im·per·ish·able \(,)im-'per-i-shə-bəl\ *adj* : not perishable or subject to decay

im·per·ma·nent \(,)im-'pər-mə-nənt\ *adj* : not permanent : TRANSIENT — **im·per·ma·nent·ly** *adv*

im·per·me·able \(,)im-'pər-mē-ə-bəl\ *adj* : not permitting passage (as of a fluid) through its substance

im·per·mis·si·ble \,im-pər-'mi-sə-bəl\ *adj* : not permissible

im·per·son·al \(,)im-'pər-sə-nəl\ *adj* **1** : not referring to any particular person or thing **2** : not involving human emotions — **im·per·son·al·i·ty** \-,pər-sə-'na-lə-tē\ *n* — **im·per·son·al·ly** *adv*

im·per·son·ate \im-'pər-sə-,nāt\ *vb* **-at·ed; -at·ing** : to assume or act the character of — **im·per·son·a·tion** \-,pər-sə-'nā-shən\ *n* — **im·per·son·a·tor** \-'pər-sə-,nā-tər\ *n*

im·per·ti·nent \(,)im-'pər-tə-nənt\ *adj* **1** : IRRELEVANT **2** : not restrained within due or proper bounds : RUDE, INSOLENT, SAUCY — **im·per·ti·nence** \-nəns\ *n* — **im·per·ti·nent·ly** *adv*

im·per·turb·able \,im-pər-'tər-bə-bəl\ *adj* : marked by extreme calm, impassivity, and steadiness : SERENE

im·per·vi·ous \(,)im-'pər-vē-əs\ *adj* **1** : incapable of being penetrated (as by moisture) **2** : not capable of being affected or disturbed ⟨~ to criticism⟩

im·pe·ti·go \,im-pə-'tē-gō, -'tī-\ *n* : a contagious skin disease characterized by vesicles, pustules, and yellowish crusts

im·pet·u·ous \im-'pe-chə-wəs\ *adj* **1** : marked by impulsive vehemence ⟨~ temper⟩ **2** : marked by force and violence ⟨with ~ speed⟩ — **im·pet·u·os·i·ty** \(,)im-,pe-chə-'wä-sə-tē\ *n* — **im·pet·u·ous·ly** *adv*

im·pe·tus \'im-pə-təs\ *n* [L, assault, impetus, fr. *impetere* to attack, fr. *petere* to go to, seek] **1** : a driving force : IMPULSE; *also* : INCENTIVE **2** : MOMENTUM

im·pi·e·ty \(,)im-'pī-ə-tē\ *n, pl* **-ties 1** : the quality or state of being impious **2** : an impious act

im·pinge \im-'pinj\ *vb* **im·pinged; im·ping·ing 1** : to strike or dash esp. with a sharp collision **2** : ENCROACH, INFRINGE — **im·pinge·ment** *n*

im·pi·ous \'im-pē-əs, (,)im-'pī-\ *adj* : not pious : IRREVERENT, PROFANE

imp·ish \'im-pish\ *adj* : of, relating to, or befitting an imp; *esp* : MISCHIEVOUS — **imp·ish·ly** *adv* — **imp·ish·ness** *n*

im·pla·ca·ble \(,)im-'pla-kə-bəl, -'plā-\ *adj* : not capable of being appeased, pacified, mitigated, or changed ⟨an ~ enemy⟩ — **im·pla·ca·bil·i·ty** \-,pla-kə-'bi-lə-tē, -,plā-\ *n* — **im·pla·ca·bly** \-'pla-kə-blē\ *adv*

im·plant \im-'plant\ *vb* **1** : to set firmly or deeply **2** : to fix in the mind or spirit **3** : to insert in living tissue (as for growth or absorption) — **im·plant** \'im-,plant\ *n* — **im·plan·ta·tion** \,im-,plan-'tā-shən\ *n*

im·plau·si·ble \(,)im-'plȯ-zə-bəl\ *adj* : not plausible — **im·plau·si·bil·i·ty** \-,plȯ-zə-'bi-lə-tē\ *n* — **im·plau·si·bly** \-'plȯ-zə-blē\ *adv*

¹im·ple·ment \'im-plə-mənt\ *n* [ME, fr. AF, fr. ML *implementum* item making a full complement, appurtenance, tool, fr. LL, act of filling up, fr. L *implēre* to fill up] : TOOL, UTENSIL, INSTRUMENT

²im·ple·ment \-,ment\ *vb* **1** : CARRY OUT; *esp* : to put into practice **2** : to provide implements for — **im·ple·men·ta·tion** \,im-plə-mən-'tā-shən\ *n*

im·pli·cate \'im-plə-,kāt\ *vb* **-cat·ed; -cat·ing 1** : IMPLY **2** : INVOLVE — **im·pli·ca·tion** \,im-plə-'kā-shən\ *n*

im·plic·it \im-'pli-sət\ *adj* **1** : understood though not directly stated or expressed : IMPLIED; *also* : POTENTIAL **2** : COMPLETE, UNQUESTIONING, ABSOLUTE ⟨~ faith⟩ — **im·plic·it·ly** *adv*

im·plode \im-'plōd\ *vb* **im·plod·ed; im·plod·ing 1** : to burst or collapse inward **2** : SELF-DESTRUCT — **im·plo·sion** \-'plō-zhən\ *n* — **im·plo·sive** \-siv\ *adj*

im·plore \im-'plȯr\ *vb* **im·plored; im·plor·ing** : BESEECH, ENTREAT ✦ *Synonyms* SUPPLICATE, BEG, IMPORTUNE, PLEAD

im·ply \im-'plī\ *vb* **im·plied; im·ply·ing 1** : to involve or indicate by inference, association, or necessary consequence rather than by direct statement ⟨war *implies* fighting⟩ **2** : to express indirectly : hint at : SUGGEST

im·po·lite \,im-pə-'līt\ *adj* : not polite : RUDE, DISCOURTEOUS

im·pol·i·tic \(,)im-'pä-lə-,tik\ *adj* : not politic : UNWISE

im·pon·der·a·ble \(,)im-'pän-də-rə-bəl\ *adj* : incapable of being weighed or evaluated with exactness — **imponderable** *n*

¹im·port \im-'pȯrt\ *vb* **1** : MEAN, SIGNIFY **2** : to bring (as merchandise) into a place or country from a foreign or external source — **im·port·er** *n*

²im·port \'im-,pȯrt\ *n* **1** : IMPORTANCE, SIGNIFICANCE **2** : MEANING, SIGNIFICATION **3** : something (as merchandise) brought in from another country

im·por·tance \im-'pȯr-tᵊns\ *n* : the quality or state of being important : MOMENT, SIGNIFICANCE ✦ *Synonyms* CONSEQUENCE, IMPORT, WEIGHT

im·por·tant \im-ˈpȯr-tᵊnt\ adj **1** : marked by importance : SIGNIFICANT **2** : giving an impression of importance — **im·por·tant·ly** adv

im·por·ta·tion \ˌim-ˌpȯr-ˈtā-shən, -pər-\ n **1** : the act or practice of importing **2** : something imported

im·por·tu·nate \im-ˈpȯr-chə-nət\ adj **1** : troublesomely urgent or persistent **2** : BURDENSOME, TROUBLESOME

im·por·tune \im-pər-ˈtün, -ˈtyün; im-ˈpȯr-chən\ vb **-tuned; -tun·ing** : to urge or beg with troublesome persistence — **im·por·tu·ni·ty** \-pər-ˈtü-nə-tē, -ˈtyü-\ n

im·pose \im-ˈpōz\ vb **im·posed; im·pos·ing 1** : to establish or apply by authority ⟨~ a tax⟩; also : to establish by force ⟨imposed a government⟩ **2** : OBTRUDE ⟨imposed herself on others⟩ **3** : to take unwarranted advantage of something ⟨~ on her good nature⟩ — **im·po·si·tion** \ˌim-pə-ˈzi-shən\ n

im·pos·ing adj : impressive because of size, bearing, dignity, or grandeur — **im·pos·ing·ly** adv

im·pos·si·ble \(ˌ)im-ˈpä-sə-bəl\ adj **1** : incapable of being or of occurring **2** : enormously difficult **3** : extremely undesirable : UNACCEPTABLE — **im·pos·si·bil·i·ty** \-ˌpä-sə-ˈbi-lə-tē\ n — **im·pos·si·bly** \-ˈpä-sə-blē\ adv

¹**im·post** \ˈim-ˌpōst\ n : TAX, DUTY

²**impost** n : a block, capital, or molding from which an arch springs

im·pos·tor or **im·pos·ter** \im-ˈpäs-tər\ n : one that assumes an identity or title not one's own in order to deceive

im·pos·ture \im-ˈpäs-chər\ n : DECEPTION; esp : fraudulent impersonation

im·po·tent \ˈim-pə-tənt\ adj **1** : lacking in power or strength : HELPLESS **2** : unable to copulate; also : STERILE — **im·po·tence** \-təns\ n — **im·po·ten·cy** \-tən-sē\ n — **im·po·tent·ly** adv

im·pound \im-ˈpau̇nd\ vb **1** : CONFINE, ENCLOSE ⟨~ stray dogs⟩ **2** : to seize and hold in legal custody **3** : to collect in a reservoir ⟨~ water⟩ — **im·pound·ment** n

im·pov·er·ish \im-ˈpä-və-rish\ vb : to make poor; also : to deprive of strength, richness, or fertility — **im·pov·er·ish·ment** n

im·prac·ti·ca·ble \(ˌ)im-ˈprak-ti-kə-bəl\ adj : not practicable : incapable of being put into practice or use

im·prac·ti·cal \(ˌ)im-ˈprak-ti-kəl\ adj **1** : not practical **2** : IMPRACTICABLE

im·pre·cate \ˈim-pri-ˌkāt\ vb **-cat·ed; -cat·ing** : CURSE — **im·pre·ca·tion** \ˌim-pri-ˈkā-shən\ n

im·pre·cise \ˌim-pri-ˈsīs\ adj : not precise — **im·pre·cise·ly** adv — **im·pre·cise·ness** n — **im·pre·ci·sion** \-ˈsi-zhən\ n

im·preg·na·ble \im-ˈpreg-nə-bəl\ adj : incapable of being taken by assault : UNCONQUERABLE, UNASSAILABLE — **im·preg·na·bil·i·ty** \(ˌ)im-ˌpreg-nə-ˈbi-lə-tē\ n

im·preg·nate \im-ˈpreg-ˌnāt\ vb **-nat·ed; -nat·ing 1** : to fertilize or make pregnant **2** : to cause to be filled, permeated, or saturated — **im·preg·na·tion** \ˌim-ˌpreg-ˈnā-shən\ n

im·pre·sa·rio \ˌim-prə-ˈsär-ē-ˌō\ n, pl **-ri·os** [It, fr. impresa undertaking, fr. imprendere to undertake] **1** : the manager or conductor of an opera or concert company **2** : one who puts on an entertainment **3** : MANAGER, PRODUCER

¹**im·press** \im-ˈpres\ vb **1** : to apply with or produce (as a mark) by pressure : IMPRINT **2** : to press, stamp, or print in or upon **3** : to produce a vivid impression of **4** : to affect esp. forcibly or deeply — **im·press·ible** adj

²**im·press** \ˈim-ˌpres\ n **1** : a characteristic or distinctive mark **2** : IMPRESSION, EFFECT **3** : an impression or image of something formed by or as if by pressure; also : a product of pressure or influence

³**im·press** \im-ˈpres\ vb **1** : to force into naval service **2** : to get the aid or services of by forcible argument or persuasion — **im·press·ment** n

im·pres·sion \im-ˈpre-shən\ n **1** : a characteristic trait or feature resulting from influence : IMPRESS **2** : a stamp, form, or figure made by impressing : IMPRINT **3** : an esp. marked influence or effect on feeling, sense, or mind **4** : a single print or copy (as from type or from an engraved plate or book) **5** : all the copies of a publication (as a book) printed for one issue : PRINTING **6** : a usu. vague notion or remembrance **7** : an imitation in caricature of a noted personality as a form of entertainment

im·pres·sion·able \im-ˈpre-shə-nə-bəl\ adj : capable of being easily impressed : easily molded or influenced

im·pres·sion·ism \im-ˈpre-shə-ˌni-zəm\ n, often cap : a theory or practice in modern art of depicting the natural appearances of objects by dabs or strokes of primary unmixed colors in order to simulate actual reflected light — **im·pres·sion·is·tic** \-ˌpre-shə-ˈnis-tik\ adj

im·pres·sion·ist \im-ˈpre-shə-nist\ n **1** often cap : a painter who practices impressionism **2** : an entertainer who does impressions

im·pres·sive \im-ˈpre-siv\ adj : making or tending to make a marked impression ⟨an ~ speech⟩ — **im·pres·sive·ly** adv — **im·pres·sive·ness** n

im·pri·ma·tur \ˌim-prə-ˈmä-ˌtu̇r\ n [NL, let it be printed] **1** : a license to print or publish; also : official approval of a publication by a censor **2** : SANCTION, APPROVAL

¹**im·print** \im-ˈprint, ˈim-ˌprint\ vb **1** : to stamp or mark by or as if by pressure : IMPRESS **2** : to fix firmly (as on the memory)

²**im·print** \ˈim-ˌprint\ n **1** : something imprinted or printed **2** : a publisher's name printed at the foot of a title page **3** : an indelible distinguishing effect or influence

im·pris·on \im-ˈpri-zᵊn\ vb : to put in or as if in prison : CONFINE — **im·pris·on·ment** n

im·prob·a·ble \(ˌ)im-ˈprä-bə-bəl\ adj : unlikely to be true or to occur — **im·prob·a·bil·i·ty** \-ˌprä-bə-ˈbi-lə-tē\ n — **im·prob·a·bly** \-ˈprä-bə-blē\ adv

im·promp·tu \im-ˈprämp-tü, -tyü\ adj [F, fr. impromptu extemporaneously, fr. L in promptu in readiness] **1** : made or done on or as if on the spur of the moment **2** : EXTEMPORANEOUS, UNREHEARSED ⟨an ~ speech⟩ — **impromptu** adv or n

im·prop·er \(ˌ)im-ˈprä-pər\ adj **1** : not proper, fit, or suitable **2** : INCORRECT, INACCURATE **3** : not in accord with propriety, modesty, or good manners — **im·prop·er·ly** adv

improper fraction n : a fraction whose numerator is equal to or larger than the denominator

im·pro·pri·e·ty \ˌim-prə-ˈprī-ə-tē\ n, pl **-ties 1** : an improper act or remark; esp : an unacceptable use of a word or of language **2** : the quality or state of being improper

im·prov \ˈim-ˌpräv\ adj : of, relating to, or being an improvised comedy routine — **improv** n

im·prove \im-ˈprüv\ vb **im·proved; im·prov·ing 1** : to enhance or increase in value or quality **2** : to grow or become better ⟨your work is improving⟩ **3** : to make good use of ⟨~ the time by reading⟩ — **im·prov·able** \-ˈprü-və-bəl\ adj

im·prove·ment \im-ˈprüv-mənt\ n **1** : the act or process of improving **2** : increased value or excellence of something **3** : something that adds to the value or appearance of a thing

im·prov·i·dent \(ˌ)im-ˈprä-və-dənt\ adj : not providing for the future — **im·prov·i·dence** \-dəns\ n

im·pro·vise \ˈim-prə-ˌvīz\ vb **-vised; -vis·ing** [F improviser, fr. It improvvisare, fr. improvviso sudden, fr. L improvisus, lit., unforeseen] **1** : to compose, recite, play, or sing on the spur of the moment : EXTEMPORIZE ⟨~ on the piano⟩ **2** : to make, invent, or arrange offhand ⟨~ a sail out of shirts⟩ — **im·pro·vi·sa·tion** \im-ˌprä-və-ˈzā-shən, ˌim-prə-və-\ n — **im·pro·vis·er** or **im·pro·vi·sor** \ˌim-prə-ˈvī-zər, ˈim-prə-ˌvī-\ n

im·pru·dent \(ˌ)im-ˈprü-dᵊnt\ adj : not prudent : lacking discretion, wisdom, or good judgement — **im·pru·dence** \-dᵊns\ n — **im·pru·dent·ly** adv

im·pu·dent \ˈim-pyü-dənt\ adj : marked by contemptuous boldness or disregard of others — **im·pu·dence** \-dəns\ n — **im·pu·dent·ly** adv

im·pugn \im-ˈpyün\ vb [ME, to assail, fr. AF empugner, fr. L inpugnare, fr. pugnare to fight] : to attack by words or arguments : oppose or attack as false or as lacking integrity

im·puis·sance \im-ˈpwi-sᵊns, -ˈpyü-ə-səns\ n [ME, fr. MF] : the quality or state of being powerless : WEAKNESS

im·pulse \ˈim-ˌpəls\ n **1** : a force that starts a body into motion; also : the motion produced by such a force **2** : an arousing of the mind and spirit to some usu. unpremeditated action **3** : NERVE IMPULSE

im·pul·sion \im-ˈpəl-shən\ n **1** : the act of impelling : the state of being impelled **2** : a force that impels **3** : IMPULSE 2; also : COMPULSION 3

im·pul·sive \im-ˈpəl-siv\ adj **1** : having the power of or actually driving or impelling **2** : arising from or prone to act on impulse — **im·pul·sive·ly** *adv* — **im·pul·sive·ness** *n*

im·pu·ni·ty \im-'pyü-nə-tē\ *n* [MF or L; MF *impunité*, fr. L *impunitas*, fr. *impune* without punishment, fr. *poena* penalty, punishment] : exemption from punishment, harm, or loss

im·pure \(,)im-'pyùr\ *adj* **1** : not pure : UNCHASTE, OBSCENE **2** : DIRTY, FOUL ⟨~ water⟩ **3** : ADULTERATED, MIXED — **im·pu·ri·ty** \-'pyùr-ə-tē\ *n*

im·pute \im-'pyüt\ *vb* **im·put·ed; im·put·ing 1** : to lay the responsibility or blame for often falsely or unjustly **2** : to credit to a person or a cause : ATTRIBUTE — **im·put·able** \-'pyü-tə-bəl\ *adj* — **im·pu·ta·tion** \,im-pyü-'tā-shən\ *n*

¹in \'in\ *prep* **1** — used to indicate physical surroundings ⟨swim ~ the lake⟩ **2** : INTO 1 ⟨ran ~ the house⟩ **3** : DURING ⟨~ the summer⟩ **4** : WITH ⟨written ~ pencil⟩ **5** — used to indicate one's situation or state of being ⟨~ luck⟩ ⟨~ love⟩ **6** — used to indicate manner or purpose ⟨~ a hurry⟩ ⟨said ~ reply⟩ **7** : INTO 2 ⟨broke ~ pieces⟩

²in *adv* **1** : to or toward the inside ⟨come ~⟩; *also* : to or toward some destination or place ⟨flew ~ from the South⟩ **2** : at close quarters : NEAR ⟨the enemy closed ~⟩ **3** : into the midst of something ⟨mix ~ the flour⟩ **4** : to or at its proper place ⟨fit a piece ~⟩ **5** : WITHIN ⟨locked ~⟩ **6** : in vogue or season **7** : in one's presence, possession, or control ⟨the results are ~⟩

³in *adj* **1** : located inside or within **2** : that is in position, operation, or power ⟨the ~ party⟩ **3** : directed inward : INCOMING ⟨the ~ train⟩ **4** : keenly aware of and responsive to what is new and fashionable ⟨the ~ crowd⟩; *also* : extremely fashionable ⟨the ~ thing to do⟩

⁴in *n* **1** : one who is in office or power or on the inside **2** : INFLUENCE, PULL ⟨he has an ~ with the owner⟩

⁵in *abbr* **1** inch **2** inlet

In *symbol* indium

IN *abbr* Indiana

in- \(,)in\ *prefix* : not : absence of : NON-, UN-

inaccessibility	indecipherable
inaccessible	indemonstrable
inaccuracy	indestructible
inaccurate	indeterminable
inaction	indiscernible
inactive	indistinguishable
inactivity	inedible
inadmissibility	ineducable
inadmissible	ineffaceable
inadvisability	inefficacious
inadvisable	inefficacy
inapparent	inelastic
inapplicable	inelasticity
inapposite	inequitable
inapproachable	inequity
inappropriate	ineradicable
inaptitude	inerrant
inarguable	inexpedient
inartistic	inexpensive
inattentive	inexpressive
inaudible	inextinguishable
inaudibly	infeasible
inauspicious	inharmonious
inauthentic	inhospitable
incautious	injudicious
incombustible	inoffensive
incomprehension	insanitary
inconclusive	insensitive
incongruent	insensitivity
inconsistency	insignificance
inconsistent	insignificant
incoordination	insolvable
incurious	insusceptible

in·abil·i·ty \,i-nə-'bi-lə-tē\ *n* : the quality or state of being unable

in ab·sen·tia \,in-ab-'sen-chə, -chē-ə\ *adv* : in one's absence

in·ac·ti·vate \(,)i-'nak-tə-,vāt\ *vb* : to make inactive — **in·ac·ti·va·tion** \(,)i-,nak-tə-'vā-shən\ *n*

in·ad·e·quate \(,)i-'na-di-kwət\ *adj* : not adequate : INSUFFICIENT — **in·ad·e·qua·cy** \-kwə-sē\ *n* — **in·ad·e·quate·ly** *adv* — **in·ad·e·quate·ness** *n*

in·ad·ver·tent \,i-nəd-'vər-t³nt\ *adj* **1** : HEEDLESS, INATTENTIVE **2** : UNINTENTIONAL ⟨an ~ omission⟩ — **in·ad·ver·tence** \-t³ns\ *n* — **in·ad·ver·ten·cy** \-t³n-sē\ *n* — **in·ad·ver·tent·ly** *adv*

in·alien·able \(,)i-'nāl-yə-nə-bəl, -'nā-lē-ə-\ *adj* : incapable of being alienated, surrendered, or transferred ⟨~ rights⟩ — **in·alien·abil·i·ty** \(,)i-,nāl-yə-nə-'bi-lə-tē, -,nā-lē-ə-\ *n* — **in·alien·ably** *adv*

in·amo·ra·ta \i-,nä-mə-'rä-tə\ *n* : a woman with whom one is in love

inane \i-'nān\ *adj* **inan·er; -est** : EMPTY, INSUBSTANTIAL; *also* : SHALLOW, SILLY ⟨~ comments⟩ — **inane·ly** *adv* — **inan·i·ty** \i-'na-nə-tē\ *n*

in·an·i·mate \(,)i-'na-nə-mət\ *adj* : not animate or animated : lacking the qualities of living things — **in·an·i·mate·ly** *adv* — **in·an·i·mate·ness** *n*

in·ap·pre·cia·ble \,i-nə-'prē-shə-bəl\ *adj* : too small to be perceived — **in·ap·pre·cia·bly** \-blē\ *adv*

in·apt \(,)i-'napt\ *adj* **1** : not suitable **2** : INEPT — **in·apt·ly** *adv* — **in·apt·ness** *n*

in·ar·tic·u·late \i-när-'ti-kyə-lət\ *adj* **1** : not understandable as spoken words **2** : MUTE **3** : incapable of being expressed by speech ⟨~ fear⟩; *also* : UNSPOKEN **4** : not having the power of distinct utterance or effective expression — **in·ar·tic·u·late·ly** *adv*

in·as·much as \,i-nəz-'məch-\ *conj* : seeing that : SINCE

in·at·ten·tion \,i-nə-'ten-chən\ *n* : failure to pay attention : DISREGARD — **in·at·ten·tive** \-'ten-tiv\ *adj*

¹in·au·gu·ral \i-'nò-gyə-rəl, -gə-\ *adj* **1** : of or relating to an inauguration **2** : marking a beginning

²inaugural *n* **1** : an inaugural address **2** : INAUGURATION

in·au·gu·rate \i-'nò-gyə-,rāt, -gə-\ *vb* **-rat·ed; -rat·ing 1** : to introduce into an office with suitable ceremonies : INSTALL **2** : to dedicate ceremoniously **3** : BEGIN, INITIATE — **in·au·gu·ra·tion** \-,nò-gyə-'rā-shən, -gə-\ *n*

in·board \'in-,bórd\ *adv* **1** : inside the hull of a ship **2** : close or closest to the center line of a vehicle or craft — **inboard** *adj*

in·born \'in-'bórn\ *adj* **1** : present from or as if from birth **2** : HEREDITARY, INHERITED ♦ **Synonyms** INNATE, CONGENITAL, NATIVE

in·bound \'in-,baùnd\ *adj* : inward bound ⟨~ traffic⟩

in-box \'in-,bäks\ *n* : a receptacle for incoming interoffice letters; *also* : a computer folder for incoming e-mail

in·bred \'in-'bred\ *adj* **1** : ingrained in one's nature as deeply as if by heredity **2** : subjected to or produced by inbreeding

in·breed·ing \'in-,brē-diŋ\ *n* **1** : the interbreeding of closely related individuals esp. to preserve and fix desirable characters of and to eliminate unfavorable characters from a stock **2** : confinement to a narrow range or a local or limited field of choice — **in·breed** \-'brēd\ *vb*

inc *abbr* **1** incomplete **2** incorporated **3** increase

In·ca \'iŋ-kə\ *n* [Sp, fr. Quechua *inka* ruler of the Inca empire] **1** : a noble or a member of the ruling family of an Indian empire of Peru, Bolivia, and Ecuador until the Spanish conquest **2** : a member of any people under Inca influence

in·cal·cu·la·ble \(,)in-'kal-kyə-lə-bəl\ *adj* **1** : not capable of being calculated; *esp* : very great **2** : not predictable — **in·cal·cu·la·bly** \-blē\ *adv*

in·can·des·cent \,in-kən-'de-s³nt\ *adj* **1** : glowing with heat **2** : SHINING, BRILLIANT — **in·can·des·cence** \-s³ns\ *n*

incandescent lamp *n* : LIGHT BULB 1

in·can·ta·tion \,in-,kan-'tā-shən\ *n* : a use of spells or verbal charms spoken or sung as a part of a ritual of magic; *also* : a formula of words used in or as if in such a ritual

in·ca·pa·ble \(,)in-'kā-pə-bəl\ *adj* : lacking ability or qualification for a particular purpose; *also* : UNQUALIFIED — **in·ca·pa·bil·i·ty** \-,kā-pə-'bi-lə-tē\ *n*

in·ca·pac·i·tate \,in-kə-'pa-sə-,tāt\ *vb* **-tat·ed; -tat·ing** : to make incapable or unfit

in·ca·pac·i·ty \,in-kə-'pa·sə-tē\ *n, pl* **-ties** : the quality or state of being incapable

in·car·cer·ate \in-'kär-sə-,rāt\ *vb* **-at·ed; -at·ing** : IMPRISON, CONFINE — **in·car·cer·a·tion** \(,)in-,kär-sə-'rā-shən\ *n*

in·car·na·dine \in-'kär-nə-,dīn, -,dēn\ *vb* **-dined; -din·ing** : REDDEN

in·car·nate \in-'kär-nət, -,nāt\ *adj* **1** : having bodily and esp. human form and substance **2** : PERSONIFIED — **in·car·nate** \-,nāt\ *vb*

in·car·na·tion \,in-kär-'nā-shən\ *n* **1** : the embodiment of a deity or spirit in an earthly form **2** *cap* : the union of divine and human natures in Jesus Christ   **3** : a person showing a trait or typical character to a marked degree   **4** : the act of incarnating : the state of being incarnate

in·cen·di·ary \in-'sen-dē-ˌer-ē\ *adj*   **1** : of or relating to a deliberate burning of property   **2** : tending to excite or inflame   **3** : designed to start fires ⟨an ∼ bomb⟩ — **incendiary** *n*

¹in·cense \'in-ˌsens\ *n*   **1** : material used to produce a fragrant odor when burned   **2** : the perfume or smoke from some spices and gums when burned

²in·cense \in-'sens\ *vb* **in·censed; in·cens·ing** : to make extremely angry

in·cen·tive \in-'sen-tiv\ *n* [ME, fr. LL *incentivum*, fr. *incentivus* stimulating, fr. L, setting the tune, fr. *incinere* to play (a tune), fr. *canere* to sing] : something that incites or is likely to incite to determination or action

in·cep·tion \in-'sep-shən\ *n* : BEGINNING, COMMENCEMENT

in·cer·ti·tude \(ˌ)in-'sər-tə-ˌtüd, -ˌtyüd\ *n*   **1** : UNCERTAINTY, DOUBT, INDECISION   **2** : INSECURITY, INSTABILITY

in·ces·sant \(ˌ)in-'se-sᵊnt\ *adj* : continuing or flowing without interruption ⟨∼ rains⟩ — **in·ces·sant·ly** *adv*

in·cest \'in-ˌsest\ *n* [ME, fr. L *incestus* sexual impurity, fr. *incestus* impure, fr. *castus* pure] : sexual intercourse between persons so closely related that marriage is illegal — **in·ces·tu·ous** \in-'ses-chù-wəs\ *adj*

¹inch \'inch\ *n* [ME, fr. OE *ynce*, fr. L *uncia* twelfth part, inch, ounce] — see WEIGHT table

²inch *vb* : to move by small degrees

in·cho·ate \in-'kō-ət, 'in-kə-ˌwāt\ *adj* : being only partly in existence or operation : INCOMPLETE, INCIPIENT

inch·worm \'inch-ˌwərm\ *n* : LOOPER

in·ci·dence \'in-sə-dəns\ *n* : rate of occurrence or effect

¹in·ci·dent \-dənt\ *n*   **1** : OCCURRENCE, HAPPENING   **2** : an action likely to lead to grave consequences esp. in diplomatic matters

²incident *adj*   **1** : occurring or likely to occur esp. in connection with some other happening   **2** : falling or striking on something ⟨∼ light rays⟩

¹in·ci·den·tal \ˌin-sə-'den-tᵊl\ *adj*   **1** : subordinate, nonessential, or attendant in position or significance ⟨∼ expenses⟩   **2** : CASUAL, CHANCE

²incidental *n*   **1** *pl* : minor items (as of expense) that are not individually accounted for   **2** : something incidental

in·ci·den·tal·ly \ˌin-sə-'den-tə-lē, -'dent-lē\ *adv*   **1** : in an incidental manner   **2** : by the way

in·cin·er·ate \in-'si-nə-ˌrāt\ *vb* **-at·ed; -at·ing** : to burn to ashes — **in·cin·er·a·tion** \-ˌsi-nə-'rā-shən\ *n*

in·cin·er·a·tor \in-'si-nə-ˌrā-tər\ *n* : a furnace for burning waste

in·cip·i·ent \in-'si-pē-ənt\ *adj* : beginning to be or become apparent

in·cise \in-'sīz\ *vb* **in·cised; in·cis·ing**   **1** : to cut into   **2** : CARVE, ENGRAVE

in·ci·sion \in-'si-zhən\ *n* : CUT, GASH; *esp* : a surgical cut

in·ci·sive \in-'sī-siv\ *adj* : impressively direct and decisive — **in·ci·sive·ly** *adv*

in·ci·sor \in-'sī-zər\ *n* : a front tooth typically adapted for cutting

in·cite \in-'sīt\ *vb* **in·cit·ed; in·cit·ing** : to arouse to action : stir up — **in·cite·ment** *n* — **in·cit·er** *n*

in·ci·vil·i·ty \ˌin-sə-'vi-lə-tē\ *n*   **1** : RUDENESS, DISCOURTESY   **2** : a rude or discourteous act

incl *abbr* include; included; including; inclusive

in·clem·ent \(ˌ)in-'kle-mənt\ *adj* : SEVERE, STORMY ⟨∼ weather⟩ — **in·clem·en·cy** \-mən-sē\ *n*

in·cli·na·tion \ˌin-klə-'nā-shən\ *n*   **1** : PROPENSITY, BENT; *esp* : LIKING   **2** : BOW, NOD ⟨an ∼ of the head⟩   **3** : a tilting of something   **4** : SLANT, SLOPE

¹in·cline \in-'klīn\ *vb* **in·clined; in·clin·ing**   **1** : BOW, BEND   **2** : to be drawn toward an opinion or course of action   **3** : to deviate from the vertical or horizontal : SLOPE   **4** : INFLUENCE, PERSUADE — **in·clin·er** *n*

²in·cline \'in-ˌklīn\ *n* : SLOPE

inclose, inclosure *var of* ENCLOSE, ENCLOSURE

in·clude \in-'klüd\ *vb* **in·clud·ed; in·clud·ing** : to take in or comprise as a part of a whole ⟨the price ∼s tax⟩ — **in·clu·sion** \in-'klü-zhən\ *n*

in·clu·sive \in-'klü-siv\ *adj*   **1** : including stated limits or extremes ⟨from Monday to Friday ∼⟩   **2** : broad in scope; *esp* : covering all items, costs, or services — **in·clu·sive·ly** *adv* — **in·clu·sive·ness** *n*

incog *abbr* incognito

¹in·cog·ni·to \ˌin-ˌkäg-'nē-to, in-'käg-nə-ˌtō\ *adv or adj* [It, fr. L *incognitus* unknown, fr. *cognoscere* to know] : with one's identity concealed

²incognito *n, pl* **-tos**   **1** : one appearing or living incognito   **2** : the state or disguise of an incognito

in·co·her·ent \ˌin-kō-'hir-ənt, -'her-\ *adj*   **1** : not sticking closely or compactly together : LOOSE   **2** : lacking normal clarity or intelligibility in speech or thought — **in·co·her·ence** \-əns\ *n* — **in·co·her·ent·ly** *adv*

in·come \'in-ˌkəm\ *n* : a gain usu. measured in money that derives from labor, business, or property

income tax *n* : a tax on the net income of an individual or business concern

in·com·ing \'in-ˌkə-miŋ\ *adj* : coming in ⟨the ∼ tide⟩ ⟨∼ freshmen⟩

in·com·men·su·rate \ˌin-kə-'men-sə-rət, -'men-chə-\ *adj* : not commensurate; *esp* : INADEQUATE

in·com·mode \ˌin-kə-'mōd\ *vb* **-mod·ed; -mod·ing** : INCONVENIENCE, DISTURB

in·com·mu·ni·ca·ble \ˌin-kə-'myü-ni-kə-bəl\ *adj* : not communicable : not capable of being communicated or imparted; *also* : UNCOMMUNICATIVE

in·com·mu·ni·ca·do \ˌin-kə-ˌmyü-ni-'kä-dō\ *adv or adj* : without means of communication; *also* : in solitary confinement ⟨a prisoner held ∼⟩

in·com·pa·ra·ble \(ˌ)in-'käm-pə-rə-bəl, -prə-\ *adj*   **1** : eminent beyond comparison : MATCHLESS   **2** : not suitable for comparison — **in·com·pa·ra·bly** \-blē\ *adv*

in·com·pat·i·ble \ˌin-kəm-'pa-tə-bəl\ *adj* : incapable of or unsuitable for association or use together ⟨∼ colors⟩ ⟨temperamentally ∼⟩ — **in·com·pat·i·bil·i·ty** \ˌin-kəm-ˌpa-tə-'bi-lə-tē\ *n*

in·com·pe·tent \(ˌ)in-'käm-pə-tənt\ *adj*   **1** : not legally qualified   **2** : not competent : lacking sufficient knowledge, skill, or ability — **in·com·pe·tence** \-təns\ *n* — **in·com·pe·ten·cy** \-tən-sē\ *n* — **incompetent** *n*

in·com·plete \ˌin-kəm-'plēt\ *adj* : lacking a part or parts : UNFINISHED, IMPERFECT — **in·com·plete·ly** *adv* — **in·com·plete·ness** *n*

in·com·pre·hen·si·ble \ˌin-ˌkäm-prē-'hen-sə-bəl\ *adj* : impossible to comprehend : UNINTELLIGIBLE

in·con·ceiv·able \ˌin-kən-'sē-və-bəl\ *adj*   **1** : impossible to comprehend   **2** : UNBELIEVABLE

in·con·gru·ous \(ˌ)in-'käŋ-grü-wəs\ *adj* : not consistent with or suitable to the surroundings or associations — **in·con·gru·i·ty** \ˌin-kən-'grü-ə-tē, -ˌkän-\ *n* — **in·con·gru·ous·ly** *adv*

in·con·se·quen·tial \ˌin-ˌkän-sə-'kwen-chəl\ *adj*   **1** : ILLOGICAL; *also* : IRRELEVANT   **2** : of no significance : UNIMPORTANT — **in·con·se·quence** \(ˌ)in-'kän-sə-ˌkwens\ *n* — **in·con·se·quen·tial·ly** *adv*

in·con·sid·er·able \ˌin-kən-'si-də-rə-bəl\ *adj* : SLIGHT, TRIVIAL ⟨the cost was not ∼⟩

in·con·sid·er·ate \ˌin-kən-'si-də-rət\ *adj* : HEEDLESS, THOUGHTLESS; *esp* : not respecting the rights or feelings of others — **in·con·sid·er·ate·ly** *adv* — **in·con·sid·er·ate·ness** *n*

in·con·sol·able \ˌin-kən-'sō-lə-bəl\ *adj* : incapable of being consoled — **in·con·sol·ably** \-blē\ *adv*

in·con·spic·u·ous \ˌin-kən-'spi-kyə-wəs\ *adj* : not readily noticeable — **in·con·spic·u·ous·ly** *adv*

in·con·stant \(ˌ)in-'kän-stənt\ *adj* : not constant : CHANGEABLE ✦ **Synonyms** FICKLE, CAPRICIOUS, MERCURIAL, UNSTABLE, VOLATILE — **in·con·stan·cy** \-stən-sē\ *n* — **in·con·stant·ly** *adv*

in·con·test·able \ˌin-kən-'tes-tə-bəl\ *adj* : not contestable : INDISPUTABLE — **in·con·test·ably** \-'tes-tə-blē\ *adv*

in·con·ti·nent \(ˌ)in-'känt-ᵊn-ənt\ *adj*   **1** : lacking self-restraint   **2** : unable to retain urine or feces voluntarily — **in·con·ti·nence** \-əns\ *n*

in·con·tro·vert·ible \ˌin-ˌkän-trə-'vər-tə-bəl\ *adj* : not open to question : INDISPUTABLE ⟨∼ evidence⟩ — **in·con·tro·vert·ibly** \-blē\ *adv*

¹in·con·ve·nience \ˌin-kən-'vē-nyəns\ *n*   **1** : something that is inconvenient   **2** : the quality or state of being inconvenient

²inconvenience *vb* **-nienced; -nienc·ing** : to subject to inconvenience

in·con·ve·nient \ˌin-kən-ˈvē-nyənt\ *adj* : not convenient : causing trouble or annoyance : INOPPORTUNE — **in·con·ve·nient·ly** *adv*

in·cor·po·rate \in-ˈkȯr-pə-ˌrāt\ *vb* **-rat·ed; -rat·ing** **1** : to unite closely or so as to form one body : BLEND **2** : to form, form into, or become a corporation **3** : to give material form to : EMBODY — **in·cor·po·ra·tion** \-ˌkȯr-pə-ˈrā-shən\ *n*

in·cor·po·re·al \ˌin-kȯr-ˈpȯr-ē-əl\ *adj* : having no material body or form

in·cor·rect \ˌin-kə-ˈrekt\ *adj* **1** : INACCURATE, FAULTY ⟨an ~ transcription⟩ **2** : not true : WRONG **3** : UNBECOMING, IMPROPER — **in·cor·rect·ly** *adv* — **in·cor·rect·ness** *n*

in·cor·ri·gi·ble \(ˌ)in-ˈkȯr-ə-jə-bəl\ *adj* : incapable of being corrected, amended, or reformed — **in·cor·ri·gi·bil·i·ty** \(ˌ)in-ˌkȯr-ə-jə-ˈbi-lə-tē\ *n* — **in·cor·ri·gi·bly** \-ˈkȯr-ə-jə-blē\ *adv*

in·cor·rupt·ible \ˌin-kə-ˈrəp-tə-bəl\ *adj* **1** : not subject to decay or dissolution **2** : incapable of being bribed or morally corrupted — **in·cor·rupt·ibil·i·ty** \-ˌrəp-tə-ˈbi-lə-tē\ *n* — **in·cor·rupt·ibly** \-ˈrəp-tə-blē\ *adv*

incr *abbr* increase; increased

¹in·crease \in-ˈkrēs, ˈin-ˌkrēs\ *vb* **in·creased; in·creas·ing** [ME *encresen,* fr. AF *encreistre,* fr. L *increscere,* fr. *crescere* to grow] **1** : to become greater : GROW **2** : to multiply by the production of young ⟨rabbits ~ rapidly⟩ **3** : to make greater — **increased** *adj* — **in·creas·ing·ly** \-ˈkrē-siŋ-lē\ *adv*

²in·crease \ˈin-ˌkrēs, in-ˈkrēs\ *n* **1** : addition or enlargement in size, extent, or quantity : GROWTH **2** : something that is added to an original stock or amount (as by growth)

in·cred·i·ble \(ˌ)in-ˈkre-də-bəl\ *adj* : too extraordinary and improbable to be believed; *also* : hard to believe — **in·cred·i·bil·i·ty** \(ˌ)in-ˌkre-də-ˈbi-lə-tē\ *n* — **in·cred·i·bly** \-ˈkre-də-blē\ *adv*

in·cred·u·lous \-ˈkre-jə-ləs\ *adj* **1** : SKEPTICAL **2** : expressing disbelief — **in·cre·du·li·ty** \ˌin-kri-ˈdü-lə-tē, -ˈdyü-\ *n* — **in·cred·u·lous·ly** *adv*

in·cre·ment \ˈiŋ-krə-mənt, ˈin-\ *n* **1** : the action or process of increasing esp. in quantity or value : ENLARGEMENT **2** : something gained or added; *esp* : one of a series of regular consecutive additions — **in·cre·men·tal** \ˌiŋ-krə-ˈmen-tᵊl, ˌin-\ *adj* — **in·cre·men·tal·ly** *adv*

in·crim·i·nate \in-ˈkri-mə-ˌnāt\ *vb* **-nat·ed; -nat·ing** : to charge with or prove involvement in a crime or fault : ACCUSE — **in·crim·i·na·tion** \-ˌkri-mə-ˈnā-shən\ *n* — **in·crim·i·na·to·ry** \-ˈkri-mə-nə-ˌtȯr-ē\ *adj*

incrust *var of* ENCRUST

in·crus·ta·tion \ˌin-ˌkrəs-ˈtā-shən\ *n* **1** : CRUST; *also* : an accumulation (as of habits, opinions, or customs) resembling a crust **2** : the act of encrusting : the state of being encrusted

in·cu·bate \ˈiŋ-kyù-ˌbāt, ˈin-\ *vb* **-bat·ed; -bat·ing** : to sit on (eggs) to hatch by the warmth of the body; *also* : to keep (as an embryo) under conditions favorable for development — **in·cu·ba·tion** \ˌiŋ-kyù-ˈbā-shən, ˌin-\ *n*

in·cu·ba·tor \ˈiŋ-kyù-ˌbāt-ər, ˈin-\ *n* : one that incubates; *esp* : an apparatus providing suitable conditions (as of warmth and moisture) for incubating something (as a premature baby)

in·cu·bus \ˈiŋ-kyə-bəs, ˈin-\ *n, pl* **-bi** \-ˌbī, -ˌbē\ *also* **-bus·es** [ME, fr. LL, fr. L *incubare* to lie on] **1** : a spirit supposed to work evil on persons in their sleep **2** : NIGHTMARE 1 **3** : one that oppresses like a nightmare

in·cul·cate \in-ˈkəl-ˌkāt, ˈin-(ˌ)kəl-\ *vb* **-cat·ed; -cat·ing** [L *inculcare,* lit., to tread on, fr. *calcare* to trample, fr. *calx* heel] : to teach and impress by frequent repetitions or admonitions — **in·cul·ca·tion** \ˌin-(ˌ)kəl-ˈkā-shən\ *n*

in·cul·pa·ble \(ˌ)in-ˈkəl-pə-bəl\ *adj* : free from guilt : INNOCENT

in·cul·pate \in-ˈkəl-ˌpāt, ˈin-(ˌ)kəl-\ *vb* **-pat·ed; -pat·ing** : INCRIMINATE

in·cum·ben·cy \in-ˈkəm-bən-sē\ *n, pl* **-cies** **1** : something that is incumbent **2** : the quality or state of being incumbent **3** : the office or period of office of an incumbent

¹in·cum·bent \in-ˈkəm-bənt\ *n* : the holder of an office or position

²incumbent *adj* **1** : imposed as a duty **2** : occupying a specified office **3** : lying or resting on something else

in·cu·nab·u·lum \ˌin-kyə-ˈna-byə-ləm, ˌiŋ-\ *n, pl* **-la** \-lə\ [NL, fr. L *incunabula,* pl., bands holding the baby in a cradle, fr. *cunae* cradle] : a book printed before 1501

in·cur \in-ˈkər\ *vb* **in·curred; in·cur·ring** : to become liable or subject to : bring down upon oneself

in·cur·able \(ˌ)in-ˈkyûr-ə-bəl\ *adj* **1** : not curable **2** : not likely to be changed — **incurable** *n* — **in·cur·ably** \(ˌ)in-ˈkyûr-ə-blē\ *adv*

in·cur·sion \in-ˈkər-zhən\ *n* **1** : a sudden hostile invasion : RAID **2** : an entering in or into (as an activity)

in·cus \ˈiŋ-kəs\ *n, pl* **in·cu·des** \iŋ-ˈkyü-(ˌ)dēz\ [NL, fr. L, anvil] : the middle bone of a chain of three small bones in the middle ear of a mammal

ind *abbr* **1** independent **2** index **3** industrial; industry

Ind *abbr* **1** Indian **2** Indiana

in·debt·ed \in-ˈde-təd\ *adj* **1** : owing gratitude or recognition to another **2** : owing money — **in·debt·ed·ness** *n*

in·de·cent \(ˌ)in-ˈdē-sᵊnt\ *adj* : not decent; *esp* : grossly improper or offensive — **in·de·cen·cy** \-sᵊn-sē\ *n* — **in·de·cent·ly** *adv*

in·de·ci·sion \ˌin-di-ˈsi-zhən\ *n* : a wavering between two or more possible courses of action : IRRESOLUTION

in·de·ci·sive \ˌin-di-ˈsī-siv\ *adj* **1** : INCONCLUSIVE ⟨an ~ battle⟩ **2** : marked by or prone to indecision **3** : INDEFINITE — **in·de·ci·sive·ly** *adv* — **in·de·ci·sive·ness** *n*

in·de·co·rous \(ˌ)in-ˈde-kə-rəs, ˌin-di-ˈkȯr-əs\ *adj* : conflicting with accepted standards of good conduct or good taste ♦ *Synonyms* IMPROPER, UNSEEMLY, INDECENT, UNBECOMING, INDELICATE — **in·de·co·rous·ly** *adv* — **in·de·co·rous·ness** *n*

in·deed \in-ˈdēd\ *adv* **1** : without any question : TRULY — often used interjectionally to express irony, disbelief, or surprise **2** : in reality **3** : all things considered

in·de·fat·i·ga·ble \ˌin-di-ˈfa-ti-gə-bəl\ *adj* : UNTIRING ⟨an ~ worker⟩ — **in·de·fat·i·ga·bly** \-blē\ *adv*

in·de·fea·si·ble \-ˈfē-zə-bəl\ *adj* : not capable of being annulled or voided — **in·de·fea·si·bly** \-blē\ *adv*

in·de·fen·si·ble \-ˈfen-sə-bəl\ *adj* **1** : incapable of being maintained as right or valid **2** : INEXCUSABLE ⟨~ comments⟩ **3** : incapable of being protected against physical attack

in·de·fin·able \-ˈfī-nə-bəl\ *adj* : incapable of being precisely described or analyzed — **in·de·fin·ably** \-blē\ *adv*

in·def·i·nite \(ˌ)in-ˈde-fə-nət\ *adj* **1** : not defining or identifying ⟨an *is* an ~ article⟩ **2** : not precise : VAGUE **3** : having no fixed limits — **in·def·i·nite·ly** *adv* — **in·def·i·nite·ness** *n*

in·del·i·ble \in-ˈde-lə-bəl\ *adj* [ME, fr. ML *indelibilis,* alter. of L *indelebilis,* fr. *delēre* to delete, destroy] **1** : not capable of being removed or erased **2** : making marks that cannot be erased **3** : LASTING, UNFORGETTABLE — **in·del·i·bly** \in-ˈde-lə-blē\ *adv*

in·del·i·cate \(ˌ)in-ˈde-li-kət\ *adj* : not delicate; *esp* : IMPROPER, COARSE, TACTLESS ♦ *Synonyms* INDECENT, UNSEEMLY, INDECOROUS, UNBECOMING — **in·del·i·ca·cy** \in-ˈde-lə-kə-sē\ *n*

in·dem·ni·fy \in-ˈdem-nə-ˌfī\ *vb* **-fied; -fy·ing** [L *indemnis* unharmed, fr. *in-* not + *damnum* damage] **1** : to secure against hurt, loss, or damage **2** : to make compensation to for hurt, loss, or damage — **in·dem·ni·fi·ca·tion** \-ˌdem-nə-fə-ˈkā-shən\ *n*

in·dem·ni·ty \in-ˈdem-nə-tē\ *n, pl* **-ties** **1** : security against hurt, loss, or damage; *also* : exemption from incurred penalties or liabilities **2** : something that indemnifies

¹in·dent \in-ˈdent\ *vb* [ME, fr. AF *endenter,* fr. *dent* tooth, fr. L *dent-, dens*] **1** : to notch the edge of **2** : INDENTURE **3** : to set (as a line of a paragraph) in from the margin

²indent *vb* **1** : to force inward so as to form a depression **2** : to form a dent in

in·den·ta·tion \ˌin-ˌden-ˈtā-shən\ *n* **1** : NOTCH; *also* : a recess in a surface **2** : the action of indenting : the condition of being indented **3** : DENT **4** : INDENTION 2

in·den·tion \in-ˈden-chən\ *n* **1** : INDENTATION 2 **2** : the blank space produced by indenting

¹in·den·ture \in-ˈden-chər\ *n* **1** : a written certificate or agreement; *esp* : a contract binding one person (as an apprentice) to work for another for a given period of time — often used in pl. **2** : INDENTATION 1 **3** : DENT

²indenture *vb* **in·den·tured; in·den·tur·ing** : to bind (as an apprentice) by indentures

in·de·pen·dence \ˌin-də-ˈpen-dəns\ n : the quality or state of being independent : FREEDOM

Independence Day n : July 4 observed as a legal holiday in the U.S. in commemoration of the adoption of the Declaration of Independence in 1776

in·de·pen·dent \ˌin-də-ˈpen-dənt\ adj 1 : SELF-GOVERNING; also : not affiliated with a larger controlling unit 2 : not requiring or relying on something else or somebody else ⟨an ~ conclusion⟩ ⟨~ of her parents⟩ 3 : not easily influenced : showing self-reliance and personal freedom ⟨an ~ mind⟩ 4 : not committed to a political party ⟨an ~ voter⟩ 5 : MAIN ⟨an ~ clause⟩ — **independent** n — **in·de·pen·dent·ly** adv

independent variable n : a variable whose value is not determined by that of any other variable in a function

in·de·scrib·able \ˌin-di-ˈskrī-bə-bəl\ adj 1 : that cannot be described 2 : being too intense or great for description — **in·de·scrib·ably** \-blē\ adv

in·de·ter·mi·nate \ˌin-di-ˈtər-mə-nət\ adj 1 : VAGUE; also : not known in advance 2 : not limited in advance; also : not leading to a definite end or result — **in·de·ter·mi·na·cy** \-nə-sē\ n — **in·de·ter·mi·nate·ly** adv

¹**in·dex** \ˈin-ˌdeks\ n, pl **in·dex·es** or **in·di·ces** \-də-ˌsēz\ 1 : POINTER 2 : SIGN, INDICATION ⟨an ~ of character⟩ 3 : a guide for facilitating references; esp : an alphabetical list of items treated in a printed work with the page number where each item may be found 4 : a list of restricted or prohibited material 5 pl usu **indices** : a number or symbol or expression (as an exponent) associated with another to indicate a mathematical operation or use or position in an arrangement or expansion 6 : a character ☞ used to direct attention (as to a note) 7 : INDEX NUMBER

²**index** vb 1 : to provide with or put into an index 2 : to serve as an index of 3 : to regulate by indexation

in·dex·ation \ˌin-ˌdek-ˈsā-shən\ n : a system of economic control in which a body of variables (as wages and interest) rise or fall at the same rate as an index of the cost of living

index finger n : the finger next to the thumb

in·dex·ing n : INDEXATION

index number n : a number used to indicate change in magnitude (as of cost) as compared with the magnitude at some specified time

index of refraction n : REFRACTIVE INDEX

in·dia ink \ˈin-dē-ə-\ n, often cap 1st I 1 : a solid black pigment used in drawing 2 : a fluid made from india ink

In·di·an \ˈin-dē-ən\ n 1 : a native or inhabitant of India or of the East Indies; also : a person of Indian descent 2 : AMERICAN INDIAN — **Indian** adj

Indian corn n : a tall widely grown American cereal grass bearing seeds on long ears; also : its ears or seeds

Indian meal n : CORNMEAL

¹**Indian paintbrush** n : any of a genus of herbaceous plants related to the snapdragons that have brightly colored bracts

Indian pipe n : a waxy white leafless saprophytic herb of Asia and the U.S.

Indian summer n : a period of mild weather in late autumn or early winter

In·dia paper \ˈin-dē-ə-\ n 1 : a thin absorbent paper used esp. for taking impressions (as of steel engravings) 2 : a thin tough opaque printing paper

in·di·cate \ˈin-də-ˌkāt\ vb **-cat·ed; -cat·ing** 1 : to point out or to 2 : to show indirectly 3 : to state briefly — **in·di·ca·tion** \ˌin-də-ˈkā-shən\ n — **in·di·ca·tor** \ˈin-də-ˌkā-tər\ n

¹**in·dic·a·tive** \in-ˈdi-kə-tiv\ adj 1 : of, relating to, or being a verb form that represents an act or state as a fact ⟨~ mood⟩ 2 : serving to indicate ⟨actions ~ of fear⟩

²**indicative** n 1 : the indicative mood of a language 2 : a form in the indicative mood

in·di·cia \in-ˈdi-shə, -shē-ə\ n pl 1 : distinctive marks 2 : postal markings often imprinted on mail or mailing labels

in·dict \in-ˈdīt\ vb [alter. of earlier indite, fr. ME, fr. AF to write, point out, indict, ultim. fr. L indicere to make known formally, fr. dicere to say] 1 : to charge with a fault or offense 2 : to charge with a crime by the finding of a jury — **in·dict·able** adj — **in·dict·ment** n

in·die \ˈin-dē\ n 1 : one that is independent; esp : an un-

affiliated record or motion-picture production company 2 : something produced by an indie — **indie** adj

in·dif·fer·ent \in-ˈdi-frənt, -fə-rənt\ adj 1 : UNBIASED, UNPREJUDICED 2 : of no importance one way or the other 3 : marked by no special liking for or dislike of something 4 : being neither excessive nor inadequate 5 : PASSABLE, MEDIOCRE 6 : being neither right nor wrong — **in·dif·fer·ence** \-frəns, -fə-rəns\ n — **in·dif·fer·ent·ly** adv

in·dig·e·nous \in-ˈdi-jə-nəs\ adj : produced, growing, or living naturally in a particular region

in·di·gent \ˈin-di-jənt\ adj : IMPOVERISHED, NEEDY — **in·di·gence** \-jəns\ n

in·di·gest·ible \ˌin-dī-ˈjes-tə-bəl, -də-\ adj : not readily digested

in·di·ges·tion \-ˈjes-chən\ n : inadequate or difficult digestion : DYSPEPSIA

in·dig·nant \in-ˈdig-nənt\ adj : filled with or marked by indignation — **in·dig·nant·ly** adv

in·dig·na·tion \ˌin-dig-ˈnā-shən\ n : anger aroused by something unjust, unworthy, or mean

in·dig·ni·ty \in-ˈdig-nə-tē\ n, pl **-ties** : an offense against personal dignity or self-respect; also : humiliating treatment

in·di·go \ˈin-di-ˌgō\ n, pl **-gos** or **-goes** [It dial., fr. L indicum, fr. Gk indikon, fr. indikos Indic, fr. Indos India] 1 : a blue dye obtained from plants or synthesized 2 : a deep reddish blue color

in·di·rect \ˌin-də-ˈrekt, -dī-\ adj 1 : not straight ⟨an ~ route⟩ 2 : not straightforward and open ⟨~ methods⟩ 3 : not having a plainly seen connection ⟨an ~ cause⟩ 4 : not directly to the point ⟨an ~ answer⟩ — **in·di·rec·tion** \-ˈrek-shən\ n — **in·di·rect·ly** adv — **in·di·rect·ness** n

in·dis·creet \ˌin-di-ˈskrēt\ adj : not discreet : IMPRUDENT — **in·dis·creet·ly** adv

in·dis·cre·tion \ˌin-di-ˈskre-shən\ n 1 : IMPRUDENCE ⟨dietary ~⟩ 2 : something marked by lack of discretion; esp : an act deviating from accepted morality

in·dis·crim·i·nate \ˌin-di-ˈskri-mə-nət\ adj 1 : not marked by discrimination or careful distinction 2 : HAPHAZARD, RANDOM ⟨an ~ application of a law⟩ 3 : UNRESTRAINED 4 : MOTLEY — **in·dis·crim·i·nate·ly** adv

in·dis·pens·able \ˌin-di-ˈspen-sə-bəl\ adj : absolutely essential : REQUISITE — **in·dis·pens·abil·i·ty** \-ˌspen-sə-ˈbi-lə-tē\ n — **indispensable** n — **in·dis·pens·ably** \-ˈspen-sə-blē\ adv

in·dis·posed \-ˈspōzd\ adj 1 : slightly ill 2 : AVERSE — **in·dis·po·si·tion** \(ˌ)in-ˌdis-pə-ˈzi-shən\ n

in·dis·put·able \ˌin-di-ˈspyü-tə-bəl, (ˌ)in-ˈdis-pyə-\ adj : not disputable : UNQUESTIONABLE ⟨~ proof⟩ — **in·dis·put·ably** \-blē\ adv

in·dis·sol·u·ble \ˌin-di-ˈsäl-yə-bəl\ adj : not capable of being dissolved, undone, or broken : PERMANENT ⟨an ~ contract⟩

in·dis·tinct \ˌin-di-ˈstiŋkt\ adj 1 : not sharply outlined or separable : BLURRED, FAINT, DIM 2 : not readily distinguishable : UNCERTAIN — **in·dis·tinct·ly** adv — **in·dis·tinct·ness** n

in·dite \in-ˈdīt\ vb **in·dit·ed; in·dit·ing** : COMPOSE ⟨~ a poem⟩; also : to put in writing ⟨~ a letter⟩

in·di·um \ˈin-dē-əm\ n : a malleable silvery metallic chemical element

indiv abbr individual

¹**in·di·vid·u·al** \ˌin-də-ˈvi-jə-wəl\ adj 1 : of, relating to, or associated with an individual ⟨~ traits⟩ 2 : being an individual : existing as an indivisible whole 3 : intended for one person 4 : SEPARATE ⟨~ copies⟩ 5 : having marked individuality ⟨an ~ style⟩ — **in·di·vid·u·al·ly** adv

²**individual** n 1 : a single member of a category : a particular person, animal, or thing 2 : PERSON ⟨a disagreeable ~⟩

in·di·vid·u·al·ise Brit var of INDIVIDUALIZE

in·di·vid·u·al·ism \ˌin-də-ˈvi-jə-wə-ˌli-zəm\ n 1 : a doctrine that the interests of the individual are primary 2 : a doctrine holding that the individual has political or economic rights with which the state must not interfere 3 : INDIVIDUALITY

in·di·vid·u·al·ist \-list\ n 1 : one that pursues a markedly independent course in thought or action 2 : one that advocates or practices individualism — **individualist** or **in·di·vid·u·al·is·tic** \-ˌvi-jə-wə-ˈlis-tik\ adj

in·di·vid·u·al·i·ty \-ˌvi-jə-'wa-lə-tē\ *n, pl* **-ties** **1** : the sum of qualities that characterize and distinguish an individual from all others; *also* : PERSONALITY **2** : separate or distinct existence **3** : INDIVIDUAL, PERSON

in·di·vid·u·al·ize \-'vi-jə-wə-ˌlīz\ *vb* **-ized; -iz·ing** **1** : to make individual in character **2** : to treat or notice individually : PARTICULARIZE **3** : to adapt to the needs of an individual

individual retirement account *n* : IRA

in·di·vid·u·ate \ˌin-də-'vi-jə-ˌwāt\ *vb* **-at·ed; -at·ing** : to give individuality to : form into an individual — **in·di·vid·u·a·tion** \-ˌvi-jə-'wā-shən\ *n*

in·di·vis·i·ble \ˌin-də-'vi-zə-bəl\ *adj* : impossible to divide or separate — **in·di·vis·i·bil·i·ty** \-ˌvi-zə-'bi-lə-tē\ *n* — **in·di·vis·i·bly** *adv*

In·do-Ar·y·an \ˌin-dō-'er-ē-ən\ *n* : a branch of the Indo-European language family that includes Hindi and other languages of south Asia

in·doc·tri·nate \in-'däk-trə-ˌnāt\ *vb* **-nat·ed; -nat·ing** **1** : to instruct esp. in fundamentals or rudiments : TEACH **2** : to teach the beliefs and doctrines of a particular group — **in·doc·tri·na·tion** \(ˌ)in-ˌdäk-trə-'nā-shən\ *n* — **in·doc·tri·na·tor** *n*

In·do-Eu·ro·pe·an \ˌin-dō-ˌyur-ə-'pē-ən\ *adj* : of, relating to, or constituting a family of languages comprising those spoken in most of Europe and in the parts of the world colonized by Europeans since 1500 and also in Persia, the subcontinent of India, and some other parts of Asia

in·do·lent \'in-də-lənt\ *adj* [LL *indolens* insensitive to pain, fr. L *dolēre* to feel pain] **1** : slow to develop or heal 〈~ ulcers〉 **2** : LAZY — **in·do·lence** \-ləns\ *n* — **in·do·lent·ly** *adv*

in·dom·i·ta·ble \in-'dä-mə-tə-bəl\ *adj* : UNCONQUERABLE 〈~ courage〉 — **in·dom·i·ta·bly** \-blē\ *adv*

in·door \'in-ˌdor\ *adj* **1** : of or relating to the inside of a building **2** : living, located, or carried on within a building

in·doors \in-'dorz\ *adv* : in or into a building

indorse, indorsement *var of* ENDORSE, ENDORSEMENT

in·du·bi·ta·ble \(ˌ)in-'dü-bə-tə-bəl, -'dyü-\ *adj* : UNQUESTIONABLE — **in·du·bi·ta·bly** \-blē\ *adv*

in·duce \in-'düs, -'dyüs\ *vb* **in·duced; in·duc·ing** **1** : PERSUADE, INFLUENCE **2** : BRING ABOUT **3** : to produce (as an electric current) by induction **4** : to determine by induction; *esp* : to infer from particulars — **in·duc·er** *n*

in·duce·ment \-mənt\ *n* **1** : something that induces : MOTIVE **2** : the act or process of inducing

in·duct \in-'dəkt\ *vb* **1** : to place in office **2** : to admit as a member **3** : to enroll for military training or service — **in·duct·ee** \-ˌdək-'tē\ *n*

in·duc·tance \in-'dək-təns\ *n* : a property of an electric circuit by which a varying current produces an electromotive force in that circuit or in a nearby circuit; *also* : the measure of this property

in·duc·tion \in-'dək-shən\ *n* **1** : the act or process of inducting; *also* : INITIATION **2** : the formality by which a civilian is inducted into military service **3** : inference of a generalized conclusion from particular instances; *also* : a conclusion so reached **4** : the act of causing or bringing on or about **5** : the process by which an electric current, an electric charge, or magnetism is produced in a body by the proximity of an electric or magnetic field

in·duc·tive \in-'dək-tiv\ *adj* : of, relating to, or employing induction

in·duc·tor \in-'dək-tər\ *n* : an electrical component that acts upon another or is itself acted upon by induction

in·dulge \in-'dəlj\ *vb* **in·dulged; in·dulg·ing** **1** : to give free rein to : GRATIFY **2** : HUMOR **3** : to gratify one's taste or desire for 〈~ in alcohol〉

in·dul·gence \in-'dəl-jəns\ *n* **1** : remission of temporal punishment due in Roman Catholic doctrine for sins whose eternal punishment has been remitted by reception of the sacrifice of penance **2** : the act of indulging : the state of being indulgent **3** : an indulgent act **4** : the thing indulged in **5** : SELF-INDULGENCE — **in·dul·gent** \-jənt\ *adj* — **in·dul·gent·ly** *adv*

in·du·rat·ed \'in-dyu̇-ˌrā-təd, -du̇-\ *adj* : physically or emotionally hardened — **in·du·ra·tion** \ˌin-dyu̇-'rā-shən, -du̇-\ *n*

in·dus·tri·al \in-'dəs-trē-əl\ *adj* **1** : of or relating to industry **2** : HEAVY-DUTY 〈an ~ zipper〉 **3** : characterized by highly developed industries — **in·dus·tri·al·ly** *adv*

in·dus·tri·al·ise *Brit var of* INDUSTRIALIZE

in·dus·tri·al·ist \-ə-list\ *n* : a person owning or engaged in the management of an industry

in·dus·tri·al·ize \in-'dəs-trē-ə-ˌlīz\ *vb* **-ized; -iz·ing** : to make or become industrial — **in·dus·tri·al·i·za·tion** \-ˌdəs-trē-ə-lə-'zā-shən\ *n*

in·dus·tri·ous \in-'dəs-trē-əs\ *adj* : DILIGENT, BUSY — **in·dus·tri·ous·ly** *adv* — **in·dus·tri·ous·ness** *n*

in·dus·try \'in-(ˌ)dəs-trē\ *n, pl* **-tries** **1** : DILIGENCE **2** : a department or branch of a craft, art, business, or manufacture; *esp* : one that employs a large personnel and capital **3** : a distinct group of productive enterprises **4** : manufacturing activity as a whole

in·dwell \(ˌ)in-'dwel\ *vb* : to exist within as an activating spirit or force

In·dy car \'in-dē-\ *n* : a single-seat, open-cockpit racing car with the engine in the rear

¹in·ebri·ate \i-'nē-brē-ˌāt\ *vb* **-at·ed; -at·ing** : to make drunk : INTOXICATE — **in·ebri·a·tion** \-ˌnē-brē-'ā-shən\ *n*

²in·ebri·ate \-ət\ *n* : one that is drunk; *esp* : DRUNKARD

in·ef·fa·ble \(ˌ)in-'e-fə-bəl\ *adj* **1** : incapable of being expressed in words : INDESCRIBABLE 〈~ joy〉 **2** : UNSPEAKABLE 〈~ disgust〉 **3** : not to be uttered : TABOO — **in·ef·fa·bly** \-blē\ *adv*

in·ef·fec·tive \ˌi-nə-'fek-tiv\ *adj* **1** : INEFFECTUAL **2** : not able to perform efficiently or as expected : INCAPABLE — **in·ef·fec·tive·ly** *adv* — **in·ef·fec·tive·ness** *n*

in·ef·fec·tu·al \-'fek-chə-wəl\ *adj* **1** : not producing the proper or usual effect **2** : INEFFECTIVE 2 — **in·ef·fec·tu·al·ly** *adv*

in·ef·fi·cient \ˌi-nə-'fi-shənt\ *adj* **1** : not producing the desired effect **2** : wasteful of time or energy **3** : INCAPABLE, INCOMPETENT — **in·ef·fi·cien·cy** \-'fi-shən-sē\ *n* — **in·ef·fi·cient·ly** *adv*

in·el·e·gant \(ˌ)i-'ne-li-gənt\ *adj* : lacking in refinement, grace, or good taste — **in·el·e·gance** \-gəns\ *n* — **in·el·e·gant·ly** *adv*

in·el·i·gi·ble \(ˌ)i-'ne-lə-jə-bəl\ *adj* : not qualified for an office or position — **in·el·i·gi·bil·i·ty** \(ˌ)i-ˌne-lə-jə-'bi-lə-tē\ *n*

in·eluc·ta·ble \ˌi-ni-'lək-tə-bəl\ *adj* : not to be avoided, changed, or resisted — **in·eluc·ta·bly** \-blē\ *adv*

in·ept \i-'nept\ *adj* **1** : lacking in fitness or aptitude : UNFIT **2** : FOOLISH **3** : being out of place : INAPPROPRIATE **4** : generally incompetent : BUNGLING — **in·ept·ly** *adv* — **in·ept·ness** *n*

in·ep·ti·tude \(ˌ)i-'nep-ti-ˌtüd, -ˌtyüd\ *n* : the quality or state of being inept; *esp* : INCOMPETENCE

in·equal·i·ty \ˌi-ni-'kwä-lə-tē\ *n* **1** : the quality of being unequal or uneven; *also* : UNEVENNESS, DISPARITY **2** : an instance of being unequal

in·ert \i-'nərt\ *adj* [L *inert-, iners* unskilled, idle, fr. *art-, ars* skill] **1** : powerless to move **2** : SLUGGISH **3** : lacking in active properties 〈chemically ~〉 — **in·ert·ly** *adv* — **in·ert·ness** *n*

in·er·tia \i-'nər-shə, -shē-ə\ *n* **1** : a property of matter whereby it remains at rest or continues in uniform motion unless acted upon by some outside force **2** : INERTNESS, SLUGGISHNESS — **in·er·tial** \-shəl\ *adj*

in·es·cap·able \ˌi-nə-'skā-pə-bəl\ *adj* : incapable of being escaped : INEVITABLE — **in·es·cap·ably** \-blē\ *adv*

in·es·ti·ma·ble \(ˌ)i-'nes-tə-mə-bəl\ *adj* **1** : incapable of being estimated or computed 〈~ errors〉 **2** : too valuable or excellent to be fully appreciated — **in·es·ti·ma·bly** \-blē\ *adv*

in·ev·i·ta·ble \i-'ne-və-tə-bəl\ *adj* : incapable of being avoided or evaded : bound to happen — **in·ev·i·ta·bil·i·ty** \(ˌ)i-ˌne-və-tə-'bi-lə-tē\ *n*

in·ev·i·ta·bly \-blē\ *adv* **1** : in an inevitable way **2** : as is to be expected

in·ex·act \ˌi-nig-'zakt\ *adj* **1** : not precisely correct or true : INACCURATE **2** : not rigorous and careful — **in·ex·act·ly** *adv* — **in·ex·act·ness** *n*

in·ex·cus·able \ˌi-nik-'skyü-zə-bəl\ *adj* : impossible to excuse or justify — **in·ex·cus·ably** \-blē\ *adv*

in·ex·haust·ible \ˌi-nig-'zȯ-stə-bəl\ *adj* **1** : incapable of being used up 〈an ~ supply〉 **2** : UNTIRING 〈an ~ hiker〉 — **in·ex·haust·ibly** \-blē\ *adv*

in·ex·o·ra·ble \(ˌ)i-ˈnek-sə-rə-bəl\ adj : not to be persuaded, moved, or stopped : RELENTLESS — **in·ex·o·ra·bly** adv

in·ex·pe·ri·ence \ˌi-nik-ˈspir-ē-əns\ n : lack of experience or of knowledge gained by experience — **in·ex·pe·ri·enced** \-ənst\ adj

in·ex·pert \(ˌ)i-ˈnek-ˌspərt\ adj : not expert : UNSKILLED — **in·ex·pert·ly** adv

in·ex·pi·a·ble \(ˌ)i-ˈnek-spē-ə-bəl\ adj : not capable of being atoned for

in·ex·pli·ca·ble \ˌi-nik-ˈspli-kə-bəl, (ˌ)i-ˈnek-(ˌ)spli-\ adj : incapable of being explained or accounted for — **in·ex·pli·ca·bly** \-blē\ adv

in·ex·press·ible \-ˈspre-sə-bəl\ adj : not capable of being expressed — **in·ex·press·ibly** \-blē\ adv

in ex·tre·mis \ˌin-ik-ˈstrā-məs, -ˈstrē-\ adv : in extreme circumstances; esp : at the point of death

in·ex·tri·ca·ble \ˌi-nik-ˈstri-kə-bəl, (ˌ)i-ˈnek-(ˌ)stri-\ adj 1 : forming a maze or tangle from which it is impossible to get free 2 : incapable of being disentangled or untied — **in·ex·tri·ca·bly** \-blē\ adv

inf abbr 1 infantry 2 infinitive

in·fal·li·ble \(ˌ)in-ˈfa-lə-bəl\ adj 1 : incapable of error : UNERRING 2 : SURE, CERTAIN ⟨an ~ remedy⟩ — **in·fal·li·bil·i·ty** \(ˌ)in-ˌfa-lə-ˈbi-lə-tē\ n — **in·fal·li·bly** \(ˌ)in-ˈfa-lə-blē\ adv

in·fa·mous \ˈin-fə-məs\ adj 1 : having a reputation of the worst kind 2 : DISGRACEFUL — **in·fa·mous·ly** adv

in·fa·my \-mē\ n, pl **-mies** 1 : evil reputation brought about by something grossly criminal, shocking, or brutal 2 : an extreme and publicly known criminal or evil act 3 : the state of being infamous

in·fan·cy \ˈin-fən-sē\ n, pl **-cies** 1 : early childhood 2 : a beginning or early period of existence

in·fant \ˈin-fənt\ n [ME enfaunt, fr. AF enfant, fr. L infant-, infans, adj., incapable of speech, young, fr. fant-, fans, prp. of fari to speak] : BABY; also : a person who is a legal minor

in·fan·ti·cide \in-ˈfan-tə-ˌsīd\ n : the killing of an infant

in·fan·tile \ˈin-fən-ˌtī(-ə)l, -tˀl, -ˌtēl\ adj : of or relating to infants; also : CHILDISH

infantile paralysis n : POLIOMYELITIS

in·fan·try \ˈin-fən-trē\ n, pl **-tries** [MF & It; MF infanterie, fr. It infanteria, fr. infante boy, foot soldier] : soldiers trained, armed, and equipped to fight on foot — **in·fan·try·man** \-mən\ n

in·farct \ˈin-ˌfärkt\ n [L infarctus, pp. of infarcire to stuff] : an area of dead tissue (as of the heart wall) caused by blocking of local blood circulation — **in·farc·tion** \in-ˈfärk-shən\ n

in·fat·u·ate \in-ˈfa-chə-ˌwāt\ vb **-at·ed; -at·ing** : to inspire with a foolish or extravagant love or admiration — **in·fat·u·a·tion** \-ˌfa-chə-ˈwā-shən\ n

in·fect \in-ˈfekt\ vb 1 : to contaminate with disease-producing matter 2 : to communicate a pathogen or disease to 3 : to cause to share one's feelings ⟨~ed us with his enthusiasm⟩

in·fec·tion \in-ˈfek-shən\ n 1 : a disease or condition caused by a germ or parasite; also : such a germ or parasite 2 : an act or process of infecting — **in·fec·tious** \-shəs\ adj — **in·fec·tive** \-ˈfek-tiv\ adj

infectious mononucleosis n : an acute infectious disease characterized by fever, swelling of lymph glands, and increased numbers of lymph cells in the blood

in·fe·lic·i·tous \ˌin-fi-ˈli-sə-təs\ adj : not appropriate in application or expression — **in·fe·lic·i·ty** \-sə-tē\ n

in·fer \in-ˈfər\ vb **in·ferred; in·fer·ring** 1 : to derive as a conclusion from facts or premises 2 : GUESS, SURMISE 3 : to lead to as a conclusion or consequence 4 : HINT, SUGGEST ♦ **Synonyms** DEDUCE, CONCLUDE, JUDGE, GATHER — **in·fer·ence** \ˈin-frəns, -fə-rəns\ n — **in·fer·en·tial** \ˌin-fə-ˈren-chəl\ adj

in·fe·ri·or \in-ˈfir-ē-ər\ adj 1 : situated lower down 2 : of low or lower degree or rank 3 : of lesser quality 4 : of little or less importance, value, or merit — **inferior** n — **in·fe·ri·or·i·ty** \(ˌ)in-ˌfir-ē-ˈor-ə-tē\ n

in·fer·nal \in-ˈfər-nˀl\ adj 1 : of or relating to hell 2 : HELLISH, FIENDISH ⟨~ schemes⟩ 3 : DAMNABLE ⟨an ~ pest⟩ — **in·fer·nal·ly** adv

in·fer·no \in-ˈfər-nō\ n, pl **-nos** [It, hell, fr. LL infernus, fr.

L, lower] : a place or a state that resembles or suggests hell; also : intense heat

in·fer·tile \(ˌ)in-ˈfər-tˀl\ adj : not fertile or productive : BARREN — **in·fer·til·i·ty** \ˌin-fər-ˈti-lə-tē\ n

in·fest \in-ˈfest\ vb : to trouble by spreading or swarming in or over; also : to live in or on as a parasite — **in·fes·ta·tion** \ˌin-ˌfes-ˈtā-shən\ n

in·fi·del \ˈin-fə-dˀl, -fə-ˌdel\ n 1 : one who is not a Christian or opposes Christianity 2 : an unbeliever esp. with respect to a particular religion

in·fi·del·i·ty \ˌin-fə-ˈde-lə-tē, -fī-\ n, pl **-ties** 1 : lack of belief in a religion 2 : unfaithfulness or an instance of it esp. in marriage

in·field \ˈin-ˌfēld\ n : the part of a baseball field inside the baselines — **in·field·er** n

in·fight·ing \ˈin-ˌfī-tiŋ\ n 1 : fighting at close quarters 2 : dissension or rivalry among members of a group

in·fil·trate \in-ˈfil-ˌtrāt, ˈin-(ˌ)fil-\ vb **-trat·ed; -trat·ing** 1 : to enter or filter into or through something 2 : to pass into or through by or as if by filtering or permeating — **in·fil·tra·tion** \ˌin-(ˌ)fil-ˈtrā-shən\ n — **in·fil·tra·tor** n

in·fi·nite \ˈin-fə-nət\ adj 1 : LIMITLESS, BOUNDLESS, ENDLESS ⟨~ space⟩ ⟨~ patience⟩ 2 : VAST, IMMENSE; also : INEXHAUSTIBLE ⟨~ wealth⟩ 3 : greater than any preassigned finite value however large ⟨~ number of positive integers⟩; also : extending to infinity ⟨~ plane surface⟩ — **infinite** n — **in·fi·nite·ly** adv

in·fin·i·tes·i·mal \(ˌ)in-ˌfi-nə-ˈte-sə-məl\ adj : immeasurably or incalculably small — **in·fin·i·tes·i·mal·ly** adv

in·fin·i·tive \in-ˈfi-nə-tiv\ n : a verb form having the characteristics of both verb and noun and in English usu. being used with to

in·fin·i·tude \in-ˈfi-nə-ˌtüd, -ˌtyüd\ n 1 : the quality or state of being infinite 2 : something that is infinite esp. in extent

in·fin·i·ty \in-ˈfi-nə-tē\ n, pl **-ties** 1 : the quality of being infinite 2 : unlimited extent of time, space, or quantity : BOUNDLESSNESS 3 : an indefinitely great number or amount

in·firm \in-ˈfərm\ adj 1 : deficient in vitality; esp : feeble from age 2 : weak of mind, will, or character : IRRESOLUTE 3 : not solid or stable : INSECURE

in·fir·ma·ry \in-ˈfər-mə-rē\ n, pl **-ries** : a place for the care of the infirm or sick

in·fir·mi·ty \in-ˈfər-mə-tē\ n, pl **-ties** 1 : FEEBLENESS 2 : DISEASE, AILMENT 3 : a personal failing : FOIBLE

infl abbr influenced

in fla·gran·te de·lic·to \ˌin-flə-ˈgrän-tē-di-ˈlik-tō, -ˈgran-\ adv 1 : in the very act of committing a misdeed 2 : in the midst of sexual activity

in·flame \in-ˈflām\ vb **in·flamed; in·flam·ing** 1 : KINDLE 2 : to excite to excessive or uncontrollable action or feeling; also : INTENSIFY 3 : to affect or become affected with inflammation

in·flam·ma·ble \in-ˈfla-mə-bəl\ adj 1 : FLAMMABLE 2 : easily inflamed, excited, or angered : IRASCIBLE

in·flam·ma·tion \ˌin-flə-ˈmā-shən\ n : a bodily response to injury in which an affected area becomes red, hot, and painful and congested with blood

in·flam·ma·to·ry \in-ˈfla-mə-ˌtor-ē\ adj 1 : tending to excite the senses or to arouse anger, disorder, or tumult : SEDITIOUS 2 : causing or accompanied by inflammation ⟨an ~ disease⟩

in·flate \in-ˈflāt\ vb **in·flat·ed; in·flat·ing** 1 : to swell with air or gas ⟨~ a balloon⟩ 2 : to puff up : ELATE ⟨~ one's ego⟩ 3 : to expand or increase abnormally ⟨~ prices⟩ — **in·flat·able** adj

in·fla·tion \in-ˈflā-shən\ n 1 : an act of inflating : the state of being inflated 2 : empty pretentiousness : POMPOSITY 3 : a continuing rise in the general price level usu. attributed to an increase in the volume of money and credit

in·fla·tion·ary \-shə-ˌner-ē\ adj : of, characterized by, or productive of inflation

in·flect \in-ˈflekt\ vb 1 : to turn from a direct line or course : CURVE 2 : to vary a word by inflection 3 : to change or vary the pitch of the voice

in·flec·tion \in-ˈflek-shən\ n 1 : the act or result of curving or bending 2 : a change in pitch or loudness of the voice 3 : the change of form that words undergo to mark case, gender, number, tense, person, mood, or voice — **in·flec·tion·al** \-shə-nəl\ *adj*

in·flex·i·ble \(ˌ)in-ˈflek-sə-bəl\ *adj* **1** : UNYIELDING **2** : RIGID **3** : incapable of change — **in·flex·i·bil·i·ty** \-ˌflek-sə-ˈbi-lə-tē\ *n* — **in·flex·i·bly** \-ˈflek-sə-blē\ *adv*

in·flex·ion \in-ˈflek-shən\ *chiefly Brit var of* INFLECTION

in·flict \in-ˈflikt\ *vb* : AFFLICT; *also* : to give by or as if by striking — **in·flic·tion** \-ˈflik-shən\ *n*

in·flo·res·cence \ˌin-flə-ˈres-ᵊns\ *n* : the manner of development and arrangement of flowers on a stem; *also* : a flowering stem with its appendages : a flower cluster

in·flow \ˈin-ˌflō\ *n* : a flowing in

¹in·flu·ence \ˈin-ˌflü-əns\ *n* **1** : the act or power of producing an effect without apparent force or direct authority **2** : the power or capacity of causing an effect in indirect or intangible ways **3** : one that exerts influence — **in·flu·en·tial** \ˌin-flü-ˈen-chəl\ *adj* — **under the influence** : affected by alcohol

²influence *vb* **-enced; -enc·ing** **1** : to affect or alter by influence : SWAY **2** : to have an effect on the condition or development of : MODIFY

in·flu·en·za \ˌin-flü-ˈen-zə\ *n* [It., lit., influence, fr. ML *influentia;* fr. the belief that epidemics were due to the influence of the stars] : an acute and highly contagious virus disease marked by fever, prostration, aches and pains, and respiratory inflammation; *also* : any of various feverish usu. virus diseases typically with respiratory symptoms

in·flux \ˈin-ˌfləks\ *n* : a coming in

in·fo \ˈin-(ˌ)fō\ *n* : INFORMATION

in·fold \in-ˈfōld\ *vb* **1** : ENFOLD **2** : to fold inward or toward one another

in·fo·mer·cial \ˈin-fō-ˌmər-shəl\ *n* : a television program that is an extended advertisement often including a discussion or demonstration

in·form \in-ˈfȯrm\ *vb* **1** : to communicate knowledge to : TELL **2** : to give information or knowledge **3** : to act as an informer ♦ *Synonyms* ACQUAINT, APPRISE, ADVISE, NOTIFY

in·for·mal \(ˌ)in-ˈfȯr-məl\ *adj* **1** : conducted or carried out without formality or ceremony ⟨an ~ party⟩ **2** : characteristic of or appropriate to ordinary, casual, or familiar use ⟨~ clothes⟩ — **in·for·mal·i·ty** \ˌin-fȯr-ˈma-lə-tē, -fər-\ *n* — **in·for·mal·ly** \(ˌ)in-ˈfȯr-mə-lē\ *adv*

in·for·mant \in-ˈfȯr-mənt\ *n* : a person who gives information : INFORMER

in·for·ma·tion \ˌin-fər-ˈmā-shən\ *n* **1** : the communication or reception of knowledge or intelligence **2** : knowledge obtained from investigation, study, or instruction : FACTS, DATA **3** : the attribute communicated by one of two or more alternative sequences of something (as nucleotides in DNA or binary digits in a computer program) — **in·for·ma·tion·al** \-shə-nəl\ *adj*

information superhighway *n* : INTERNET

in·for·ma·tive \in-ˈfȯr-mə-tiv\ *adj* : imparting knowledge : INSTRUCTIVE

in·formed \in-ˈfȯrmd\ *adj* **1** : having or based on information ⟨an ~ decision⟩ **2** : EDUCATED, KNOWLEDGEABLE

informed consent *n* : consent to a medical procedure by someone who understands what is involved

in·form·er \-ˈfȯr-mər\ *n* : one that informs; *esp* : a person who informs against others for illegalities esp. for financial gain

in·fo·tain·ment \ˌin-fō-ˈtān-mənt\ *n* : a television program that presents information (as news) in a manner intended to be entertaining

in·frac·tion \in-ˈfrak-shən\ *n* [ME, fr. ML *infractio,* fr. L, subduing, fr. *infringere* to break, crush] : the act of infringing : VIOLATION

in·fra dig \ˌin-frə-ˈdig\ *adj* [short for L *infra dignitatem*] : being beneath one's dignity

in·fra·red \ˌin-frə-ˈred\ *adj* : being, relating to, or using radiation having wavelengths longer than those of red light — **infrared** *n*

in·fra·struc·ture \ˈin-frə-ˌstrək-chər\ *n* **1** : the underlying foundation or basic framework (as of a system or organization) **2** : the system of public works of a country, state, or region; *also* : the resources (as buildings or equipment) required for an activity

in·fre·quent \(ˌ)in-ˈfrē-kwənt\ *adj* **1** : seldom happening : RARE **2** : placed or occurring at wide intervals in space

or time ♦ *Synonyms* UNCOMMON, SCARCE, SPORADIC — **in·fre·quent·ly** *adv*

in·fringe \in-ˈfrinj\ *vb* **in·fringed; in·fring·ing** **1** : VIOLATE, TRANSGRESS ⟨~ a patent⟩ **2** : ENCROACH, TRESPASS ⟨~ on our rights⟩ — **in·fringe·ment** *n*

in·fu·ri·ate \in-ˈfyu̇r-ē-ˌāt\ *vb* **-at·ed; -at·ing** : to make furious : ENRAGE — **in·fu·ri·at·ing·ly** *adv*

in·fuse \in-ˈfyüz\ *vb* **in·fused; in·fus·ing** **1** : to instill a principle or quality in ⟨*infused* the team with confidence⟩ **2** : INSPIRE, ANIMATE **3** : to steep (as tea) without boiling — **in·fu·sion** \-ˈfyü-zhən\ *n*

¹-ing \iŋ\ *n suffix* **1** : action or process ⟨sleep*ing*⟩ : instance of an action or process ⟨a meet*ing*⟩ **2** : product or result of an action or process ⟨an engrav*ing*⟩ ⟨earn*ings*⟩ **3** : something used in an action or process ⟨a bed cover*ing*⟩ **4** : something connected with, consisting of, or used in making (a specified thing) ⟨scaffold*ing*⟩ **5** : something related to (a specified concept) ⟨off*ing*⟩

²-ing *n suffix* : one of a (specified) kind

³-ing *vb suffix or adj suffix* — used to form the present participle ⟨sail*ing*⟩ and sometimes to form an adjective resembling a present participle but not derived from a verb ⟨swashbuckl*ing*⟩

in·ga·ther \ˈin-ˌga-thər\ *vb* : to gather in : ASSEMBLE

in·ge·nious \in-ˈjēn-yəs\ *adj* **1** : marked by special aptitude at discovering, inventing, or contriving **2** : marked by originality, resourcefulness, and cleverness in conception or execution — **in·ge·nious·ly** *adv* — **in·ge·nious·ness** *n*

in·ge·nue *or* **in·gé·nue** \ˈan-jə-ˌnü, ˈän-; ˈaⁿ-zhə-, ˈäⁿ-\ *n* : a naive girl or young woman; *esp* : an actress portraying such a person

in·ge·nu·i·ty \ˌin-jə-ˈnü-ə-tē, -ˈnyü-\ *n, pl* **-ties** : skill or cleverness in planning or inventing : INVENTIVENESS

in·gen·u·ous \in-ˈjen-yə-wəs\ *adj* [L *ingenuus* native, freeborn, fr. *gignere* to beget] **1** : innocently straightforward ⟨her ~ curiosity⟩ **2** : lacking craft or subtlety ⟨~ comments⟩ — **in·gen·u·ous·ly** *adv* — **in·gen·u·ous·ness** *n*

in·gest \in-ˈjest\ *vb* : to take in for or as if for digestion — **in·ges·tion** \-ˈjes-chən\ *n*

in·gle·nook \ˈiŋ-gəl-ˌnu̇k\ *n* : a nook by a large open fireplace; *also* : a bench occupying this nook

in·glo·ri·ous \(ˌ)in-ˈglȯr-ē-əs\ *adj* **1** : SHAMEFUL **2** : not glorious : lacking fame or honor — **in·glo·ri·ous·ly** *adv*

in·got \ˈiŋ-gət\ *n* : a mass of metal cast in a form convenient for storage or transportation

¹in·grain \(ˌ)in-ˈgrān\ *vb* : to work indelibly into the natural texture or mental or moral constitution — **in·grained** *adj*

²in·grain \ˈin-ˌgrān\ *adj* **1** : made of fiber that is dyed before being spun into yarn **2** : made of yarn that is dyed before being woven or knitted **3** : INNATE — **in·grain** *n*

in·grate \ˈin-ˌgrāt\ *n* : an ungrateful person

in·gra·ti·ate \in-ˈgrā-shē-ˌāt\ *vb* **-at·ed; -at·ing** : to gain favor by deliberate effort

in·gra·ti·at·ing *adj* **1** : capable of winning favor : PLEASING ⟨an ~ smile⟩ **2** : FLATTERING ⟨an ~ manner⟩

in·grat·i·tude \(ˌ)in-ˈgra-tə-ˌtüd, -ˌtyüd\ *n* : lack of gratitude : UNGRATEFULNESS

in·gre·di·ent \in-ˈgrē-dē-ənt\ *n* : one of the substances that make up a mixture or compound : CONSTITUENT

in·gress \ˈin-ˌgres\ *n* : ENTRANCE, ACCESS — **in·gres·sion** \in-ˈgre-shən\ *n*

in·grow·ing \ˈin-ˌgrō-iŋ\ *adj* : growing or tending inward

in·grown \-ˌgrōn\ *adj* : grown in; *esp* : having the free tip or edge embedded in the flesh ⟨an ~ toenail⟩

in·gui·nal \ˈiŋ-gwə-nᵊl\ *adj* : of, relating to, or situated in or near the region of the groin ⟨an ~ hernia⟩

in·hab·it \in-ˈha-bət\ *vb* : to live or dwell in ⟨spiders that ~ caves⟩ — **in·hab·it·able** *adj* — **in·hab·i·ta·tion** \in-ˌha-bə-ˈtā-shən\ *n*

in·hab·i·tant \in-ˈha-bə-tənt\ *n* : a permanent resident in a place

in·hal·ant \in-ˈhā-lənt\ *n* : something (as a medicine) that is inhaled

in·ha·la·tor \ˈin-hə-ˌlā-tər\ *n* : a device that provides a mixture of carbon dioxide and oxygen for breathing

in·hale \in-ˈhāl\ *vb* **in·haled; in·hal·ing** : to breathe in — **in·ha·la·tion** \ˌin-hə-ˈlā-shən\ *n*

in·hal·er \in-ˈhā-lər\ *n* : a device by means of which medicinal material is inhaled

in·here \in-ʹhir\ *vb* **in·hered; in·her·ing** : to be inherent

in·her·ent \in-ʹhir-ənt, -ʹher-\ *adj* : established as an essential part of something : INTRINSIC ⟨risks ∼ in the venture⟩ — **in·her·ent·ly** *adv*

in·her·it \in-ʹher-ət\ *vb* **1** : to receive esp. from one's ancestors **2** : to receive by genetic transmission — **in·her·it·able** \-ə-tə-bəl\ *adj* — **in·her·i·tance** \-ə-təns\ *n* — **in·her·i·tor** \-ə-tər\ *n*

in·hib·it \in-ʹhi-bət\ *vb* **1** : PROHIBIT, FORBID **2** : to hold in check : RESTRAIN — **in·hib·i·tor** \-bə-tər\ *n* — **in·hib·i·to·ry** \-bə-ʹtȯr-ē\ *adj*

in·hi·bi·tion \ˌin-hə-ʹbi-shən\ *n* **1** : PROHIBITION, RESTRAINT **2** : a usu. inner check on free activity, expression, or functioning

in–house \ʹin-ˌhau̇s, -ʹhau̇s\ *adj* : existing, originating, or carried on within a group or organization

in·hu·man \(ˌ)in-ʹhyü-mən, -ʹyü-\ *adj* **1** : lacking pity, kindness, or mercy : SAVAGE ⟨an ∼ tyrant⟩ **2** : COLD, IMPERSONAL **3** : not worthy of or conforming to the needs of human beings ⟨∼ living conditions⟩ **4** : of or suggesting a nonhuman class of beings — **in·hu·man·ly** *adv* — **in·hu·man·ness** *n*

in·hu·mane \ˌin-hyü-ʹmān, -yü-\ *adj* : not humane : INHUMAN 1

in·hu·man·i·ty \-ʹma-nə-tē\ *n, pl* **-ties** **1** : the quality or state of being cruel or barbarous **2** : a cruel or barbarous act

in·im·i·cal \i-ʹni-mi-kəl\ *adj* **1** : being adverse often by reason of hostility ⟨forces ∼ to change⟩ **2** : HOSTILE, UNFRIENDLY ⟨∼ factions⟩ — **in·im·i·cal·ly** *adv*

in·im·i·ta·ble \(ˌ)i-ʹni-mə-tə-bəl\ *adj* : not capable of being imitated

in·iq·ui·ty \i-ʹni-kwə-tē\ *n, pl* **-ties** [ME *iniquite*, fr. AF *iniquité*, fr. L *iniquitas*, fr. *iniquus* uneven, fr. *aequus* equal] **1** : WICKEDNESS **2** : a wicked act — **in·iq·ui·tous** \-təs\ *adj*

¹ini·tial \i-ʹni-shəl\ *adj* **1** : of or relating to the beginning : INCIPIENT ⟨my ∼ reaction⟩ **2** : being at the beginning — **ini·tial·ly** *adv*

²initial *n* : the first letter of a word or name

³initial *vb* **-tialed** *or* **-tialled; -tial·ing** *or* **-tial·ling** : to affix an initial to

¹ini·ti·ate \i-ʹni-shē-ˌāt\ *vb* **-at·ed; -at·ing** **1** : START, BEGIN **2** : to induct into membership by or as if by special ceremonies **3** : to instruct in the rudiments or principles of something — **ini·ti·a·tion** \-ˌni-shē-ʹā-shən\ *n*

²ini·ti·ate \i-ʹni-shē-ət\ *n* **1** : a person who is undergoing or has passed an initiation **2** : a person who is instructed or adept in some special field

ini·tia·tive \i-ʹni-shə-tiv\ *n* **1** : an introductory step **2** : self-reliant enterprise ⟨showed great ∼⟩ **3** : a process by which laws may be introduced or enacted directly by vote of the people

ini·tia·to·ry \i-ʹni-shē-ə-ˌtȯr-ē\ *adj* **1** : INTRODUCTORY **2** : tending or serving to initiate ⟨∼ rites⟩

in·ject \in-ʹjekt\ *vb* **1** : to force into something ⟨∼ serum with a needle⟩ **2** : to introduce as an element into some situation or subject ⟨∼ a note of suspicion⟩ — **in·jec·tion** \-ʹjek-shən\ *n*

in·junc·tion \in-ʹjəŋk-shən\ *n* **1** : ORDER, ADMONITION **2** : a court writ whereby one is required to do or to refrain from doing a specified act

in·jure \ʹin-jər\ *vb* **in·jured; in·jur·ing** **1** : WRONG **2** : to damage or hurt esp. physically ♦ *Synonyms* HARM, IMPAIR, MAR, SPOIL

in·ju·ry \ʹin-jə-rē\ *n, pl* **-ries** **1** : an act that damages or hurts : WRONG **2** : hurt, damage, or loss sustained — **in·ju·ri·ous** \in-ʹju̇r-ē-əs\ *adj*

in·jus·tice \(ˌ)in-ʹjəs-təs\ *n* **1** : violation of a person's rights : UNFAIRNESS **2** : an unjust act or deed : WRONG

¹ink \ʹiŋk\ *n* [ME *enke*, fr. AF *encre, enke*, fr. LL *encaustum*, fr. L *encaustus* burned in, fr. Gk *enkaustos*, fr. *enkaiein* to burn in] : a usu. liquid and colored material for writing and printing — **inky** *adj*

²ink *vb* : to put ink on; *esp* : SIGN

ink-blot test \ʹiŋk-ˌblät-\ *n* : any of several psychological tests based on the interpretation of irregular figures

ink·horn \-ˌhȯrn\ *n* : a small bottle (as of horn) for holding ink

in–kind \ʹin-ʹkīnd\ *adj* : consisting of something (as goods) other than money

ink–jet *n* : a computer printer that sprays electrically charged droplets of ink onto paper — **ink–jet** *adj*

in·kling \ʹiŋ-kliŋ\ *n* **1** : HINT, INTIMATION **2** : a vague idea

ink·stand \ʹiŋk-ˌstand\ *n* : INKWELL; *also* : a pen and ink stand

ink·well \-ˌwel\ *n* : a container for ink

in·laid \ʹin-ʹlād\ *adj* : decorated with material set into a surface

¹in·land \ʹin-ˌland, -lənd\ *adj* **1** *chiefly Brit* : not foreign : DOMESTIC ⟨∼ revenue⟩ **2** : of or relating to the interior of a country ⟨the ∼ states⟩

²inland *n* : the interior of a country

³inland *adv* : into or toward the interior

in–law \ʹin-ˌlȯ\ *n* : a relative by marriage

¹in·lay \(ˌ)in-ʹlā, ʹin-ˌlā\ *vb* **in·laid** \-ʹlād\; **in·lay·ing** : to set (a material) into a surface or ground material esp. for decoration

²in·lay \ʹin-ˌlā\ *n* **1** : inlaid work **2** : a shaped filling cemented into a tooth

in·let \ʹin-ˌlet, -lət\ *n* **1** : a small or narrow bay **2** : an opening for intake esp. of a fluid

in–line skate *n* : a roller skate whose four wheels are set in a straight line — **in–line skater** *n* — **in–line skating** *n*

in·mate \ʹin-ˌmāt\ *n* : any of a group occupying a single place of residence; *esp* : a person confined (as in a hospital or prison)

in me·di·as res \in-ˌmā-dē-əs-ʹrās\ *adv* [L, lit., into the midst of things] : in or into the middle of a narrative or plot

in me·mo·ri·am \ˌin-mə-ʹmȯr-ē-əm\ *prep* [L] : in memory of

in·most \ʹin-ˌmōst\ *adj* : deepest within : INNERMOST

inn \ʹin\ *n* : HOTEL, TAVERN

in·nards \ʹi-nərdz\ *n pl* [alter. of *inwards*] **1** : the internal organs of a human being or animal; *esp* : VISCERA **2** : the internal parts of a structure or mechanism

in·nate \i-ʹnāt\ *adj* **1** : existing in, belonging to, or determined by factors present in an individual from birth : NATIVE **2** : INHERENT, INTRINSIC — **in·nate·ly** *adv*

in·ner \ʹi-nər\ *adj* **1** : situated farther in ⟨the ∼ bark⟩ **2** : near a center esp. of influence ⟨the ∼ circle⟩ **3** : of or relating to the mind or spirit ⟨an ∼ voice⟩ **4** : being a usu. repressed part of one's psychological makeup ⟨the ∼ child⟩

inner city *n* : the usu. older, poorer, and more densely populated section of a city — **inner–city** *adj*

in·ner–di·rect·ed \ˌi-nər-də-ʹrek-təd, -(ˌ)dī-\ *adj* : directed in thought and action by one's own scale of values as opposed to external norms

inner ear *n* : the part of the ear that is most important for hearing, is located in a cavity in the temporal bone, and contains sense organs of hearing and of awareness of position in space

in·ner·most \ʹi-nər-ˌmōst\ *adj* : farthest inward : INMOST

in·ner·sole \ʹi-nər-ʹsōl\ *n* : INSOLE

in·ner·spring \ʹi-nər-ʹspriŋ\ *adj* : having coil springs inside a padded casing ⟨an ∼ mattress⟩

inner tube *n* : an airtight rubber tube inside a tire to hold air under pressure

in·ning \ʹi-niŋ\ *n* **1** *sing or pl* : a division of a cricket match **2** : a baseball team's turn at bat; *also* : a division of a baseball game consisting of a turn at bat for each team

inn·keep·er \ʹin-ˌkē-pər\ *n* **1** : a proprietor of an inn **2** : a hotel manager

in·no·cence \ʹi-nə-səns\ *n* **1** : BLAMELESSNESS; *also* : freedom from legal guilt **2** : GUILELESSNESS, SIMPLICITY; *also* : IGNORANCE

in·no·cent \-sənt\ *adj* [ME, fr. AF, fr. L *innocens*, fr. *nocens* wicked, fr. *nocēre* to harm] **1** : free from guilt or sin : BLAMELESS **2** : harmless in effect or intention; *also* : CANDID ⟨an ∼ remark⟩ **3** : free from legal guilt or fault : LAWFUL **4** : INGENUOUS **5** : UNAWARE — **innocent** *n* — **in·no·cent·ly** *adv*

in·noc·u·ous \i-ʹnä-kyə-wəs\ *adj* **1** : HARMLESS **2** : not offensive; *also* : INSIPID ⟨∼ jokes⟩

in·nom·i·nate \i-ʹnä-mə-nət\ *adj* : having no name; *also* : ANONYMOUS

in·no·vate \ʹi-nə-ˌvāt\ *vb* **-vat·ed; -vat·ing** : to introduce as or as if new : make changes — **in·no·va·tive** \-ˌvā-tiv\ *adj* — **in·no·va·tor** \-ˌvā-tər\ *n*

in·no·va·tion \ˌi-nə-'vā-shən\ *n* **1** : the introduction of something new **2** : a new idea, method, or device

in·nu·en·do \ˌin-yə-'wen-dō\ *n, pl* **-dos** *or* **-does** [L, by nodding, fr. *innuere* to nod to, make a sign to, fr. *nuere* to nod] : HINT, INSINUATION; *esp* : a veiled reflection on character or reputation

in·nu·mer·a·ble \i-'nü-mə-rə-bəl, -'nyü-\ *adj* : too many to be numbered

in·oc·u·late \i-'nä-kyə-lāt\ *vb* **-lat·ed; -lat·ing** [ME, to insert a bud in a plant, fr. L *inoculare*, fr. *oculus* eye, bud] : to introduce something into; *esp* : to introduce a serum or antibody into (an organism) to treat or prevent a disease — **in·oc·u·la·tion** \-ˌnä-kyə-'lā-shən\ *n*

in·op·er·a·ble \(ˌ)in-'ä-pə-rə-bəl\ *adj* **1** : not suitable for surgery ⟨an ∼ tumor⟩ **2** : not operable ⟨∼ vehicles⟩

in·op·er·a·tive \-'ä-pə-rə-tiv, -'ä-pə-ˌrā-\ *adj* : not functioning

in·op·por·tune \(ˌ)in-ˌä-pər-'tün, -'tyün\ *adj* : INCONVENIENT, INAPPROPRIATE — **in·op·por·tune·ly** *adv*

in·or·di·nate \in-'ȯr-d³n-ət\ *adj* : exceeding reasonable limits : IMMODERATE ⟨drank an ∼ amount of water⟩ — **in·or·di·nate·ly** *adv*

in·or·gan·ic \ˌin-ˌȯr-'ga-nik\ *adj* : being or composed of matter of other than plant or animal origin : MINERAL

in·pa·tient \'in-ˌpā-shənt\ *n* : a hospital patient who receives lodging and food as well as treatment

in·put \'in-ˌpu̇t\ *n* **1** : something put in **2** : power or energy put into a machine or system **3** : information fed into a computer or data processing system **4** : ADVICE, OPINION — **input** *vb*

in·quest \'in-ˌkwest\ *n* **1** : an official inquiry or examination esp. before a jury **2** : INQUIRY, INVESTIGATION

in·qui·etude \(ˌ)in-'kwī-ə-ˌtüd, -ˌtyüd\ *n* : UNEASINESS, RESTLESSNESS

in·quire \in-'kwī(-ə)r\ *vb* **in·quired; in·quir·ing** **1** : to ask about : ASK **2** : INVESTIGATE, EXAMINE — **in·quir·er** *n* — **in·quir·ing·ly** *adv*

in·qui·ry \'in-ˌkwī(-ə)r-ē, in-'kwī(-ə)r-ē; 'in-kwə-rē, 'iŋ-\ *n, pl* **-ries** **1** : a request for information; *also* : RESEARCH **2** : a systematic investigation of a matter of public interest

in·qui·si·tion \ˌin-kwə-'zi-shən, ˌiŋ-\ *n* **1** : a judicial or official inquiry usu. before a jury **2** *cap* : a former Roman Catholic tribunal for the discovery and punishment of heresy **3** : a severe questioning — **in·quis·i·tor** \in-'kwi-zə-tər\ *n* — **in·quis·i·to·ri·al** \-ˌkwi-zə-'tȯr-ē-əl\ *adj*

in·quis·i·tive \in-'kwi-zə-tiv\ *adj* **1** : given to examination or investigation **2** : unduly curious — **in·quis·i·tive·ly** *adv* — **in·quis·i·tive·ness** *n*

in re \in-'rā, -'rē\ *prep* : in the matter of

INRI *abbr* [L *Iesus Nazarenus Rex Iudaeorum*] Jesus of Nazareth, King of the Jews

in·road \'in-ˌrōd\ *n* **1** : INVASION, RAID **2** : an advance made usu. at the expense of another ⟨made ∼s toward getting the job⟩

in·rush \'in-ˌrəsh\ *n* : a crowding or flooding in

ins *abbr* **1** inches **2** insurance

INS *abbr* Immigration and Naturalization Service

in·sa·lu·bri·ous \ˌin-sə-'lü-brē-əs\ *adj* : UNWHOLESOME, NOXIOUS

ins and outs *n pl* **1** : characteristic peculiarities **2** : RAMIFICATIONS

in·sane \(ˌ)in-'sān\ *adj* **1** : exhibiting serious and debilitating mental disorder; *also* : used by or for the insane **2** : ABSURD **3** : greatly exceeding the ordinary, usual, or expected — **in·sane·ly** *adv* — **in·san·i·ty** \in-'sa-nə-tē\ *n*

in·sa·tia·ble \(ˌ)in-'sā-shə-bəl\ *adj* : incapable of being satisfied ⟨an ∼ thirst⟩ — **in·sa·tia·bil·i·ty** \(ˌ)in-ˌsā-shə-'bi-lə-tē\ *n* — **in·sa·tia·bly** *adv*

in·sa·ti·ate \(ˌ)in-'sā-shē-ət, -shət\ *adj* : INSATIABLE — **in·sa·ti·ate·ly** *adv*

in·scribe \in-'skrīb\ *vb* **1** : to write, engrave, or print as a lasting record **2** : ENROLL **3** : to write, engrave, or print characters upon **4** : to dedicate to someone **5** : to draw within a figure so as to touch in as many places as possible — **in·scrip·tion** \-'skrip-shən\ *n*

in·scru·ta·ble \in-'skrü-tə-bəl\ *adj* : not readily comprehensible : MYSTERIOUS — **in·scru·ta·bly** \-blē\ *adv*

in·seam \'in-ˌsēm\ *n* : the seam on the inside of the leg of a pair of pants; *also* : the length of this seam

in·sect \'in-ˌsekt\ *n* [L *insectum*, fr. *insectus*, pp. of *insecare* to cut into, fr. *secare* to cut] : any of a class of small usu. winged arthropod animals (as flies, bees, beetles, and moths) with usu. three pairs of legs as adults

in·sec·ti·cide \in-'sek-tə-ˌsīd\ *n* : an agent for destroying insects — **in·sec·ti·cid·al** \(ˌ)in-ˌsek-tə-'sīd-³l\ *adj*

in·sec·tiv·o·rous \ˌin-sek-'ti-və-rəs\ *adj* : feeding on insects

in·se·cure \ˌin-si-'kyu̇r\ *adj* **1** : UNCERTAIN **2** : not protected : UNSAFE ⟨an ∼ investment⟩ **3** : LOOSE, SHAKY ⟨an ∼ hinge⟩ **4** : not highly stable ⟨an ∼ marriage⟩; *also* : lacking assurance : ANXIOUS, FEARFUL — **in·se·cure·ly** *adv* — **in·se·cu·ri·ty** \-'kyu̇r-ə-tē\ *n*

in·sem·i·nate \in-'se-mə-ˌnāt\ *vb* **-nat·ed; -nat·ing** : to introduce semen into the genital tract of (a female) — **in·sem·i·na·tion** \-ˌse-mə-'nā-shən\ *n*

in·sen·sate \(ˌ)in-'sen-ˌsāt, -sət\ *adj* **1** : lacking sense or understanding; *also* : FOOLISH **2** : INANIMATE **3** : BRUTAL, INHUMAN ⟨∼ rage⟩

in·sen·si·ble \(ˌ)in-'sen-sə-bəl\ *adj* **1** : IMPERCEPTIBLE; *also* : SLIGHT, GRADUAL **2** : INANIMATE **3** : UNCONSCIOUS **4** : lacking sensory perception or ability to react ⟨∼ to pain⟩ **5** : APATHETIC, INDIFFERENT; *also* : UNAWARE ⟨∼ of their danger⟩ **6** : MEANINGLESS **7** : lacking delicacy or refinement — **in·sen·si·bil·i·ty** \-ˌsen-sə-'bi-lə-tē\ *n* — **in·sen·si·bly** \-'sen-sə-blē\ *adv*

in·sen·tient \(ˌ)in-'sen-chē-ənt\ *adj* : lacking perception, consciousness, or animation — **in·sen·tience** \-chē-əns\ *n*

in·sep·a·ra·ble \(ˌ)in-'se-prə-bəl, -pə-rə-\ *adj* **1** : incapable of being separated or disjoined **2** : very close or intimate ⟨∼ friends⟩ — **in·sep·a·ra·bil·i·ty** \-ˌse-prə-'bi-lə-tē, -pə-rə-\ *n* — **inseparable** *n* — **in·sep·a·ra·bly** \-'se-prə-blē, -pə-rə-\ *adv*

¹in·sert \in-'sərt\ *vb* **1** : to put or thrust in ⟨∼ a key in a lock⟩ ⟨∼ a comma⟩ **2** : INTERPOLATE **3** : to set in (as a piece of fabric) and make fast

²in·sert \'in-ˌsərt\ *n* : something that is inserted or is for insertion; *esp* : written or printed material inserted (as between the leaves of a book)

in·ser·tion \in-'sər-shən\ *n* **1** : something that is inserted **2** : the act or process of inserting

in·set \'in-ˌset\ *vb* **inset** *or* **in·set·ted; in·set·ting** : to set in : INSERT — **inset** *n*

¹in·shore \'in-'shȯr\ *adj* **1** : situated, living, or carried on near shore **2** : moving toward shore ⟨an ∼ current⟩

²inshore *adv* : to or toward shore

¹in·side \in-'sīd, 'in-ˌsīd\ *n* **1** : an inner side or surface : INTERIOR **2** : inward nature, thoughts, or feeling **3** *pl* : VISCERA, ENTRAILS **4** : a position of power, trust, or familiarity — **inside** *adj*

²inside *adv* **1** : on the inner side **2** : in or into the interior

³inside *prep* **1** : in or into the inside of ⟨∼ the house⟩ **2** : WITHIN ⟨∼ an hour⟩

inside of *prep* : INSIDE

inside out *adv* **1** : in such a manner that the inner surface becomes the outer ⟨turned the shirt *inside out*⟩ **2** : in a state of disarray or reorganization ⟨turned her life *inside out*⟩

in·sid·er \in-'sī-dər\ *n* : a person who is in a position of power or has access to confidential information

in·sid·i·ous \in-'si-dē-əs\ *adj* [L *insidiosus*, fr. *insidiae* ambush, fr. *insidēre* to sit in, sit on, fr. *sedēre* to sit] **1** : SLY, TREACHEROUS **2** : SEDUCTIVE **3** : having a gradual and cumulative effect : SUBTLE — **in·sid·i·ous·ly** *adv* — **in·sid·i·ous·ness** *n*

in·sight \'in-ˌsīt\ *n* : the power, act, or result of seeing into a situation : UNDERSTANDING, PENETRATION — **in·sight·ful** \-'sīt-fəl, in-'sīt-\ *adj*

in·sig·nia \in-'sig-nē-ə\ *also* **in·sig·ne** \-(ˌ)nē\ *n, pl* **-nia** *or* **-ni·as** : a distinguishing mark esp. of authority or honor : BADGE

in·sin·cere \ˌin-sin-'sir\ *adj* : not sincere : HYPOCRITICAL — **in·sin·cere·ly** *adv* — **in·sin·cer·i·ty** \-'ser-ə-tē\ *n*

in·sin·u·ate \in-'sin-yə-ˌwāt\ *vb* **-at·ed; -at·ing** [L *insinuare*, fr. *sinuare* to bend, curve, fr. *sinus* curve] **1** : to introduce gradually or in a subtle, indirect, or artful way **2** : to imply in a subtle or devious way — **in·sin·u·a·tion** \(ˌ)in-ˌsin-yə-'wā-shən\ *n*

in·sin·u·at·ing *adj* **1** : winning favor and confidence by im·per·cep·ti·ble degrees **2** : tending gradually to cause doubt, distrust, or change of outlook

in·sip·id \in-'si-pəd\ *adj* **1** : lacking taste or savor **2** : DULL, FLAT — **in·si·pid·i·ty** \ˌin-sə-'pi-də-tē\ *n*

in·sist \in-'sist\ *vb* [MF or L; MF *insister*, fr. L *insistere* to stand upon, persist, fr. *sistere* to take a stand] : to take a resolute stand ⟨~ed on paying⟩

in·sis·tence \in-'sis-təns\ *n* : the act of insisting; *also* : an insistent attitude or quality : URGENCY

in·sis·tent \in-'sis-tənt\ *adj* : disposed to insist — **in·sis·tent·ly** *adv*

in si·tu \in-'sī-tü, -'sē-\ *adv or adj* [L, in position] : in the natural or original position ⟨an *in situ* cancer⟩

in·so·far as \ˌin-sə-'fär-\ *conj* : to the extent or degree that

insol *abbr* insoluble

in·so·la·tion \ˌin-(ˌ)sō-'lā-shən\ *n* : solar radiation that has been received

in·sole \'in-ˌsōl\ *n* **1** : an inside sole of a shoe **2** : a loose thin strip placed inside a shoe for warmth or comfort

in·so·lent \'in-sə-lənt\ *adj* : contemptuous, rude, disrespectful, or bold in behavior or language — **in·so·lence** \-ləns\ *n*

in·sol·u·ble \(ˌ)in-'säl-yə-bəl\ *adj* **1** : having or admitting of no solution or explanation **2** : difficult or impossible to dissolve — **in·sol·u·bil·i·ty** \ˌsäl-yə-'bi-lə-tē\ *n*

in·sol·vent \(ˌ)in-'säl-vənt\ *adj* **1** : unable or insufficient to pay all debts ⟨an ~ estate⟩ **2** : IMPOVERISHED, DEFICIENT — **in·sol·ven·cy** \-vən-sē\ *n*

in·som·nia \in-'säm-nē-ə\ *n* : prolonged and usu. abnormal sleeplessness — **in·som·ni·ac** \-nē-ˌak\ *n*

in·so·much as \ˌin-sə-'məch-\ *conj* : INASMUCH AS

insomuch that *conj* : to such a degree that : SO

in·sou·ci·ance \in-'sü-sē-əns, aⁿ-'süs-'yäⁿs\ *n* [F] : lighthearted unconcern — **in·sou·ci·ant** \in-'sü-sē-ənt, aⁿ-'süs-'yäⁿ\ *adj*

insp *abbr* inspector

in·spect \in-'spekt\ *vb* : to view closely and critically : EXAMINE ⟨~ the gem for flaws⟩ — **in·spec·tion** \-'spek-shən\ *n* — **in·spec·tor** \-tər\ *n*

inspector general *n* : the head of a system of inspection (as of an army)

in·spi·ra·tion \ˌin-spə-'rā-shən\ *n* **1** : the act or power of moving the intellect or emotions **2** : INHALATION **3** : the quality or state of being inspired; *also* : something that is inspired **4** : an inspiring agent or influence — **in·spi·ra·tion·al** \-shə-nəl\ *adj*

in·spire \in-'spīr\ *vb* **in·spired; in·spir·ing** **1** : to influence, move, or guide by divine or supernatural inspiration **2** : to exert an animating, enlivening, or exalting influence upon ⟨a painter *inspired* by cubism⟩; *also* : AFFECT **3** : to communicate to an agent supernaturally; *also* : bring out or about **4** : INHALE **5** : INCITE **6** : to spread by indirect means — **in·spir·er** *n*

in·spir·it \in-'spir-ət\ *vb* : ENCOURAGE, HEARTEN

inst *abbr* **1** instant **2** institute; institution; institutional

in·sta·bil·i·ty \ˌin-stə-'bi-lə-tē\ *n* : lack of steadiness; *esp* : lack of emotional or mental stability

in·stal *chiefly Brit var of* INSTALL

in·stall \in-'stȯl\ *vb* **1** : to place formally in office : induct into an office, rank, or order **2** : to establish in an indicated place, condition, or status **3** : to set up for use or service — **in·stal·la·tion** \ˌin-stə-'lā-shən\ *n*

¹in·stall·ment *also* **in·stal·ment** \in-'stȯl-mənt\ *n* : INSTALLATION

²installment *also* **instalment** *n* **1** : one of the parts into which a debt or sum is divided for payment **2** : one of several parts presented at intervals

¹in·stance \'in-stəns\ *n* **1** : INSTIGATION, REQUEST **2** : EXAMPLE ⟨for ~⟩ **3** : an event or step that is part of a process or series ♦ **Synonyms** CASE, ILLUSTRATION, SAMPLE, SPECIMEN

²instance *vb* **in·stanced; in·stanc·ing** : to mention as a case or example

¹in·stant \'in-stənt\ *n* **1** : MOMENT ⟨the ~ we met⟩ **2** : the present or current month

²instant *adj* **1** : URGENT **2** : PRESENT, CURRENT **3** : IMMEDIATE ⟨~ relief⟩ **4** : premixed or precooked for easy final preparation ⟨~ cake mix⟩; *also* : immediately soluble in water ⟨~ coffee⟩

in·stan·ta·neous \ˌin-stən-'tā-nē-əs\ *adj* : done or occur-

ring in an instant or without delay ⟨an ~ chemical reaction⟩ — **in·stan·ta·neous·ly** *adv*

in·stan·ter \in-'stan-tər\ *adv* : at once

in·stan·ti·ate \in-'stan-chē-ˌāt\ *vb* **-at·ed; -at·ing** : to represent (an abstraction) by a concrete example — **in·stan·ti·a·tion** \-ˌstan-chē-'ā-shən\ *n*

in·stant·ly \'in-stənt-lē\ *adv* : at once : IMMEDIATELY

in·state \in-'stāt\ *vb* : to establish in a rank or office : INSTALL

in·stead \in-'sted\ *adv* **1** : as a substitute or equivalent **2** : as an alternative : RATHER

instead of *prep* : as a substitute for or alternative to ⟨use glue *instead of* paste⟩

in·step \'in-ˌstep\ *n* : the arched part of the human foot in front of the ankle joint; *esp* : its upper surface

in·sti·gate \'in-stə-ˌgāt\ *vb* **-gat·ed; -gat·ing** : to goad or urge forward : PROVOKE, INCITE ⟨~ a revolt⟩ — **in·sti·ga·tion** \ˌin-stə-'gā-shən\ *n* — **in·sti·ga·tor** \'in-stə-ˌgā-tər\ *n*

in·stil *chiefly Brit var of* INSTILL

in·still \in-'stil\ *vb* **1** : to cause to enter drop by drop **2** : to impart gradually

¹in·stinct \'in-ˌstiŋkt\ *n* **1** : a natural aptitude **2** : a largely inheritable and unalterable tendency of an organism to make a complex and specific response to environmental stimuli without involving reason; *also* : behavior originating below the conscious level — **in·stinc·tive** \in-'stiŋk-tiv\ *adj* — **in·stinc·tive·ly** *adv*

²in·stinct \in-'stiŋkt, 'in-ˌstiŋkt\ *adj* : IMBUED, INFUSED

in·stinc·tu·al \in-'stiŋk-chə-wəl\ *adj* : of, relating to, or based on instinct

¹in·sti·tute \'in-stə-ˌtüt, -ˌtyüt\ *vb* **-tut·ed; -tut·ing** **1** : to establish in a position or office **2** : ORGANIZE **3** : INAUGURATE, INITIATE

²institute *n* **1** : an elementary principle recognized as authoritative; *also, pl* : a collection of such principles and precepts **2** : an organization for the promotion of a cause : ASSOCIATION **3** : an educational institution **4** : a brief course of instruction on a particular field

in·sti·tu·tion \ˌin-stə-'tü-shən, -'tyü-\ *n* **1** : an act of originating, setting up, or founding **2** : an established practice, law, or custom **3** : a society or corporation esp. of a public character ⟨a charitable ~⟩; *also* : ASYLUM **3** — **in·sti·tu·tion·al** \-'tü-shə-nəl, -'tyü-\ *adj* — **in·sti·tu·tion·al·ize** \-nə-ˌlīz\ *vb* — **in·sti·tu·tion·al·ly** *adv*

instr *abbr* **1** instructor **2** instrument; instrumental

in·struct \in-'strəkt\ *vb* [ME, fr. L *instructus*, pp. of *instruere*, fr. *struere* to build] **1** : TEACH **2** : INFORM **3** : to give an order or a command to

in·struc·tion \in-'strək-shən\ *n* **1** : LESSON, PRECEPT **2** : COMMAND, ORDER **3** *pl* : DIRECTIONS **4** : the action, practice, or profession of a teacher — **in·struc·tion·al** \-shə-nəl\ *adj*

in·struc·tive \in-'strək-tiv\ *adj* : carrying a lesson : ENLIGHTENING

in·struc·tor \in-'strək-tər\ *n* : one that instructs; *esp* : a college teacher below professorial rank — **in·struc·tor·ship** *n*

in·stru·ment \'in-strə-mənt\ *n* **1** : a device used to produce music **2** : a means by which something is done **3** : a device for doing work and esp. precision work ⟨a drafting ~⟩ **4** : a legal document (as a deed) **5** : a device used in navigating an airplane — **in·stru·ment** \-ˌment\ *vb*

in·stru·men·tal \ˌin-strə-'men-t°l\ *adj* **1** : acting as a crucial agent or means ⟨was ~ in arranging the deal⟩ **2** : of, relating to, or done with an instrument **3** : relating to, composed for, or performed on a musical instrument

in·stru·men·tal·ist \-'men-tə-list\ *n* : a player on a musical instrument

in·stru·men·tal·i·ty \ˌin-strə-mən-'ta-lə-tē, -ˌmen-\ *n, pl* **-ties** **1** : the quality or state of being instrumental **2** : MEANS, AGENCY

in·stru·men·ta·tion \ˌin-strə-mən-'tā-shən, -ˌmen-\ *n* **1** : ORCHESTRATION **2** : instruments for a particular purpose

instrument panel *n* : DASHBOARD

in·sub·or·di·nate \ˌin-sə-'bȯr-də-nət\ *adj* : disobedient to authority — **in·sub·or·di·na·tion** \-ˌbȯr-də-'nā-shən\ *n*

in·sub·stan·tial \ˌin-səb-'stan-chəl\ *adj* **1** : lacking substance or reality **2** : lacking firmness or solidity

in·suf·fer·able \(ˌ)in-ˈsə-fə-rə-bəl\ *adj* : not to be endured : INTOLERABLE ⟨an ~ bore⟩ — **in·suf·fer·ably** \-blē\ *adv*

in·suf·fi·cient \ˌin-sə-ˈfi-shənt\ *adj* : not sufficient ⟨~ funds⟩; *also* : lacking capacity — **in·suf·fi·cien·cy** \-shən-sē\ *n* — **in·suf·fi·cient·ly** *adv*

in·su·lar \ˈin-sə-lər, -syə-\ *adj* 1 : of, relating to, or forming an island 2 : dwelling or situated on an island 3 : NARROW-MINDED — **in·su·lar·i·ty** \ˌin-sə-ˈlar-ə-tē, -syə-\ *n*

in·su·late \ˈin-sə-ˌlāt\ *vb* **-lat·ed; -lat·ing** [L *insula* island] : ISOLATE; *esp* : to separate a conductor of electricity, heat, or sound from other conducting bodies by means of a nonconductor — **in·su·la·tion** \ˌin-sə-ˈlā-shən\ *n* — **in·su·la·tor** \ˈin-sə-ˌlā-tər\ *n*

in·su·lin \ˈin-sə-lən\ *n* : a pancreatic hormone essential esp. for the metabolism of carbohydrates and the regulation of glucose levels in the blood

¹**in·sult** \in-ˈsəlt\ *vb* [MF or L; MF *insulter,* fr. L *insultare,* lit., to spring upon, fr. *saltare* to leap] : to treat with insolence or contempt : AFFRONT — **in·sult·ing·ly** *adv*

²**in·sult** \ˈin-ˌsəlt\ *n* : a gross indignity

in·su·per·a·ble \(ˌ)in-ˈsü-pə-rə-bəl\ *adj* : incapable of being surmounted, overcome, passed over, or solved — **in·su·per·a·bly** \-blē\ *adv*

in·sup·port·able \ˌin-sə-ˈpȯr-tə-bəl\ *adj* 1 : UNENDURABLE 2 : UNJUSTIFIABLE

in·sur·able \in-ˈshùr-ə-bəl\ *adj* : capable of being or proper to be insured

in·sur·ance \in-ˈshùr-əns\ *n* 1 : the business of insuring persons or property 2 : coverage by contract whereby one party agrees to guarantee another against a specified loss 3 : the sum for which something is insured 4 : a means of guaranteeing protection or safety

in·sure \in-ˈshùr\ *vb* **in·sured; in·sur·ing** 1 : to provide or obtain insurance on or for : UNDERWRITE 2 : to make certain : ENSURE

in·sured \in-ˈshùrd\ *n* : a person whose life or property is insured

in·sur·er \in-ˈshùr-ər\ *n* : one that insures; *esp* : an insurance company

in·sur·gent \in-ˈsər-jənt\ *n* 1 : a person who revolts against civil authority or an established government : REBEL 2 : a member of a political party who rebels against it — **in·sur·gence** \-jəns\ *n* — **in·sur·gen·cy** \-jən-sē\ *n* — **in·sur·gent** *adj*

in·sur·mount·able \ˌin-sər-ˈmaùn-tə-bəl\ *adj* : INSUPERABLE ⟨~ problems⟩ — **in·sur·mount·ably** \-blē\ *adv*

in·sur·rec·tion \ˌin-sə-ˈrek-shən\ *n* : an act or instance of revolting against civil authority or an established government — **in·sur·rec·tion·ist** \-shə-nist\ *n*

int *abbr* 1 interest 2 interior 3 intermediate 4 internal 5 international 6 intransitive

in·tact \in-ˈtakt\ *adj* : untouched esp. by anything that harms or diminishes

in·ta·glio \in-ˈtal-yō\ *n, pl* **-glios** [It] : an engraving cut deeply into the surface of a hard material (as stone)

in·take \ˈin-ˌtāk\ *n* 1 : an opening through which fluid enters 2 : the act of taking in 3 : something taken in

¹**in·tan·gi·ble** \(ˌ)in-ˈtan-jə-bəl\ *adj* : incapable of being touched : IMPALPABLE — **in·tan·gi·bly** \-blē\ *adv*

²**intangible** *n* 1 : an incorporeal asset 2 : an abstract quality or attribute

in·te·ger \ˈin-ti-jər\ *n* [L, adj., whole, entire] : a number (as 1, 2, 3, 12, 432) that is not a fraction and does not include a fraction, is the negative of such a number, or is 0

¹**in·te·gral** \ˈin-ti-grəl\ *adj* 1 : essential to completeness ⟨~ to the company⟩ 2 : formed as a unit with another part 3 : composed of parts that make up a whole 4 : ENTIRE

²**integral** *n* : the result of a mathematical integration

in·te·grate \ˈin-tə-ˌgrāt\ *vb* **-grat·ed; -grat·ing** 1 : to find a function that has a given derivative 2 : to form, coordinate, or blend into a functioning whole : UNITE 3 : to incorporate into a larger unit 4 : to end the segregation of and bring into equal membership in society or an organization; *also* : DESEGREGATE — **in·te·gra·tion** \ˌin-tə-ˈgrā-shən\ *n*

integrated circuit *n* : a group of tiny electronic components and their connections that is produced in or on a small slice of material (as silicon)

in·teg·ri·ty \in-ˈte-grə-tē\ *n* 1 : adherence to a code of values : INCORRUPTIBILITY 2 : SOUNDNESS 3 : COMPLETENESS

in·teg·u·ment \in-ˈte-gyə-mənt\ *n* : a covering layer (as a skin or cuticle) of an organism or one of its parts

in·tel·lect \ˈin-tə-ˌlekt\ *n* 1 : the power of knowing : the capacity for knowledge 2 : the capacity for rational or intelligent thought esp. when highly developed 3 : a person with great intellectual powers

in·tel·lec·tu·al \ˌin-tə-ˈlek-chə-wəl\ *adj* 1 : of, relating to, or performed by the intellect : RATIONAL 2 : given to study, reflection, and speculation ⟨~ games⟩ 3 : engaged in activity requiring the creative use of the intellect — **intellectual** *n* — **in·tel·lec·tu·al·ly** *adv*

in·tel·lec·tu·al·ism \-chə-wə-ˌli-zəm\ *n* : devotion to the exercise of intellect or to intellectual pursuits

in·tel·li·gence \in-ˈte-lə-jəns\ *n* 1 : ability to learn and understand or to deal with new or trying situations 2 : mental acuteness 3 : INFORMATION, NEWS 4 : an agency engaged in obtaining information esp. concerning an enemy or possible enemy; *also* : the information so gained

intelligence quotient *n* : IQ

in·tel·li·gent \in-ˈte-lə-jənt\ *adj* [L *intelligens,* fr. *intelligere* to understand, fr. *inter* between + *legere* to select] : having or showing intelligence or intellect — **in·tel·li·gent·ly** *adv*

in·tel·li·gen·tsia \in-ˌte-lə-ˈjent-sē-ə, -ˈgent-\ *n* [Russ *intelligentsiya,* fr. L *intelligentia* intelligence] : intellectuals forming a vanguard or elite

in·tel·li·gi·ble \in-ˈte-lə-jə-bəl\ *adj* : capable of being understood or comprehended — **in·tel·li·gi·bil·i·ty** \-ˌte-lə-jə-ˈbi-lə-tē\ *n* — **in·tel·li·gi·bly** \-ˈte-lə-jə-blē\ *adv*

in·tem·per·ance \(ˌ)in-ˈtem-pə-rəns\ *n* : lack of moderation; *esp* : habitual or excessive drinking of intoxicants — **in·tem·per·ate** \-pə-rət\ *adj* — **in·tem·per·ate·ness** *n*

in·tend \in-ˈtend\ *vb* [ME *entenden, intenden,* fr. AF *entendre,* fr. L *intendere* to stretch out, direct, aim at, fr. *tendere* to stretch] 1 : to have in mind as a purpose or aim ⟨~s to retire⟩ 2 : to design for a specified use or future ⟨programs ~ed to help students⟩

in·ten·dant \in-ˈten-dənt\ *n* : an official (as a governor) esp. under the French, Spanish, or Portuguese monarchies

¹**in·tend·ed** *adj* 1 : expected to be such in the future; *esp* : BETROTHED 2 : INTENTIONAL ⟨an ~ pun⟩

²**intended** *n* : an engaged person

in·tense \in-ˈtens\ *adj* 1 : existing in an extreme degree ⟨~ pain⟩ 2 : marked by great zeal, energy, or eagerness ⟨~ effort⟩ 3 : showing strong feeling; *also* : deeply felt — **in·tense·ly** *adv*

in·ten·si·fy \in-ˈten-sə-ˌfī\ *vb* **-fied; -fy·ing** 1 : to make or become intense or more intensive 2 : to make more acute : SHARPEN ♦ *Synonyms* AGGRAVATE, HEIGHTEN, ENHANCE, MAGNIFY — **in·ten·si·fi·ca·tion** \-ˌten-sə-fə-ˈkā-shən\ *n*

in·ten·si·ty \in-ˈten-sə-tē\ *n, pl* **-ties** 1 : the quality or state of being intense; *esp* : degree of strength, energy, or force

¹**in·ten·sive** \in-ˈten-siv\ *adj* 1 : highly concentrated 2 : serving to give emphasis — **in·ten·sive·ly** *adv*

²**intensive** *n* : an intensive word, particle, or prefix

intensive care *n* : continuous monitoring and treatment of seriously ill patients; *also* : an area of a hospital providing this treatment

¹**in·tent** \in-ˈtent\ *n* 1 : the state of mind with which an act is done : VOLITION 2 : PURPOSE, AIM ⟨the artist's ~⟩ 3 : MEANING, SIGNIFICANCE

²**intent** *adj* 1 : directed with keen attention ⟨an ~ gaze⟩ 2 : ENGROSSED; *also* : DETERMINED ⟨~ on winning⟩ — **in·tent·ly** *adv* — **in·tent·ness** *n*

in·ten·tion \in-ˈten-chən\ *n* 1 : a determination to act in a certain way 2 : PURPOSE, AIM, END ♦ *Synonyms* INTENT, DESIGN, OBJECT, OBJECTIVE, GOAL

in·ten·tion·al \in-ˈten-chə-nəl\ *adj* : done by intention or design : INTENDED — **in·ten·tion·al·ly** *adv*

in·ter \in-ˈtər\ *vb* **in·terred; in·ter·ring** : BURY

in·ter·ac·tion \ˌin-tər-ˈak-shən\ *n* : mutual or reciprocal action or influence — **in·ter·act** \-ˈakt\ *vb*

in·ter·ac·tive \-ˈak-tiv\ *adj* 1 : mutually or reciprocally active 2 : involving the actions or input of a user ⟨~ exhibits⟩ 3 : allowing two-way electronic communications (as between a person and a computer) — **in·ter·ac·tive·ly** *adv* — **in·ter·ac·tiv·i·ty** \-ˌak-ˈti-və-tē\ *n*

in·ter alia \ˌin-tər-ˈā-lē-ə, -ˈä-\ *adv* : among other things

in·ter·atom·ic \ˌin-tər-ə-ˈtä-mik\ *adj* : existing or acting between atoms

in·ter·breed \-ˈbrēd\ *vb* **-bred** \-ˈbred\; **-breed·ing** : to breed together

in·ter·ca·la·ry \in-ˈtər-kə-ˌler-ē\ *adj* **1** : INTERCALATED ⟨February 29 is an ∼ day⟩ **2** : INTERPOLATED

in·ter·ca·late \-ˌlāt\ *vb* **-lat·ed; -lat·ing 1** : to insert (as a day) in a calendar **2** : to insert between or among existing elements or layers — **in·ter·ca·la·tion** \-ˌtər-kə-ˈlā-shən\ *n*

in·ter·cede \ˌin-tər-ˈsēd\ *vb* **-ced·ed; -ced·ing** : to act between parties with a view to reconciling differences

¹**in·ter·cept** \ˌin-tər-ˈsept\ *vb* **1** : to stop or interrupt the progress or course of **2** : to include (as part of a curve or solid) between two points, curves, or surfaces **3** : to gain possession of (an opponent's pass) — **in·ter·cep·tion** \-ˈsep-shən\ *n*

²**in·ter·cept** \ˈin-tər-ˌsept\ *n* : INTERCEPTION; *esp* : the interception of a target by an interceptor or missile

in·ter·cep·tor \ˌin-tər-ˈsep-tər\ *n* : a fighter plane designed for defense against attacking bombers

in·ter·ces·sion \ˌin-tər-ˈse-shən\ *n* **1** : MEDIATION **2** : prayer or petition in favor of another — **in·ter·ces·sor** \-ˈse-sər\ *n* — **in·ter·ces·so·ry** \-ˈse-sə-rē\ *adj*

¹**in·ter·change** \ˌin-tər-ˈchānj\ *vb* **1** : to put each in the place of the other **2** : EXCHANGE **3** : to change places mutually — **in·ter·change·able** \-ˈchān-jə-bəl\ *adj* — **in·ter·change·ably** \-blē\ *adv*

²**in·ter·change** \ˈin-tər-ˌchānj\ *n* **1** : EXCHANGE **2** : a highway junction that by separated levels permits passage between highways without crossing traffic streams

in·ter·col·le·giate \ˌin-tər-kə-ˈlē-jət\ *adj* : existing or carried on between colleges ⟨∼ sports⟩

in·ter·com \ˈin-tər-ˌkäm\ *n* : a two-way system for localized communication

in·ter·con·nect \ˌin-tər-kə-ˈnekt\ *vb* : to connect with one another — **in·ter·con·nec·tion** \-ˈnek-shən\ *n*

in·ter·con·ti·nen·tal \ˌin-tər-ˌkän-tə-ˈnent-ᵊl\ *adj* **1** : extending among or carried on between continents ⟨∼ trade⟩ **2** : capable of traveling between continents ⟨∼ ballistic missiles⟩

in·ter·course \ˈin-tər-ˌkȯrs\ *n* **1** : connection or dealings between persons or nations **2** : physical sexual contact between individuals that involves the genitalia of at least one person ⟨anal ∼⟩; *esp* : SEXUAL INTERCOURSE

in·ter·de·nom·i·na·tion·al \ˌin-tər-di-ˌnä-mə-ˈnā-shə-nəl\ *adj* : involving different denominations

in·ter·de·part·men·tal \ˌin-tər-di-ˌpärt-ˈmen-tᵊl, -ˌdē-\ *adj* : carried on between or involving different departments (as of a college)

in·ter·de·pen·dent \ˌin-tər-di-ˈpen-dənt\ *adj* : dependent upon one another — **in·ter·de·pen·dence** \-dəns\ *n*

in·ter·dict \ˌin-tər-ˈdikt\ *vb* **1** : to prohibit by decree **2** : to destroy, cut off, or damage (as an enemy line of supply) **3** : INTERCEPT ⟨∼ed drug shipments⟩ — **in·ter·dic·tion** \-ˈdik-shən\ *n*

in·ter·dis·ci·plin·ary \-ˈdi-sə-plə-ˌner-ē\ *adj* : involving two or more academic, scientific, or artistic disciplines

¹**in·ter·est** \ˈin-trəst; ˈin-tə-rəst, -ˌrest\ *n* **1** : right, title, or legal share in something **2** : a charge for borrowed money that is generally a percentage of the amount borrowed; *also* : the return received by capital on its investment **3** : WELFARE, BENEFIT; *also* : SELF-INTEREST **4** : CURIOSITY, CONCERN **5** : readiness to be concerned with or moved by an object or class of objects **6** : a quality in a thing that arouses interest

²**interest** *vb* **1** : to persuade to participate or engage **2** : to engage the attention of

in·ter·est·ing *adj* : holding the attention — **in·ter·est·ing·ly** *adv*

¹**in·ter·face** \ˈin-tər-ˌfās\ *n* **1** : a surface forming a common boundary of two bodies, spaces, or phases ⟨an oil=water ∼⟩ **2** : the place at which two independent systems meet and act on or communicate with each other ⟨the man-machine ∼⟩ **3** : the means by which interaction or communication is achieved at an interface — **in·ter·fa·cial** \ˌin-tər-ˈfā-shəl\ *adj*

²**interface** *vb* **-faced; -fac·ing 1** : to connect by means of an interface **2** : to serve as an interface

in·ter·faith \ˌin-tər-ˈfāth\ *adj* : involving persons of different religious faiths

in·ter·fere \ˌin-tər-ˈfir\ *vb* **-fered; -fer·ing** [ME *enterferen*, fr. AF *(s')entreferir* to strike one another, fr. *entre* between, among + *ferir* to strike, fr. L *ferire*] **1** : to come in collision or be in opposition : CLASH **2** : to enter into the affairs of others **3** : to affect one another

in·ter·fer·ence \-ˈfir-əns\ *n* **1** : the act or process of interfering **2** : something that interferes : OBSTRUCTION **3** : the mutual effect on meeting of two waves resulting in areas of increased and decreased amplitude **4** : the blocking of an opponent in football to make way for the ballcarrier **5** : the illegal hindering of an opponent in sports

in·ter·fer·om·e·ter \ˌin-tər-fə-ˈrä-mə-tər\ *n* : an apparatus that uses the interference of waves (as of light) for making precise measurements — **in·ter·fer·om·e·try** \-fə-ˈrä-mə-trē\ *n*

in·ter·fer·on \ˌin-tər-ˈfir-ˌän\ *n* : any of a group of antiviral proteins of low molecular weight produced usu. by animal cells in response to a virus, a parasite in the cell, or a chemical

in·ter·ga·lac·tic \ˌin-tər-gə-ˈlak-tik\ *adj* : relating to or situated in the spaces between galaxies

in·ter·gen·er·a·tion·al \-ˌje-nə-ˈrā-shə-nəl\ *adj* : existing or occurring between generations

in·ter·gla·cial \-ˈglā-shəl\ *n* : a warm period between successive glaciations

in·ter·gov·ern·men·tal \-ˌgə-vərn-ˈmen-tᵊl\ *adj* : existing or occurring between two governments or levels of government

in·ter·im \ˈin-tə-rəm\ *n* [L, adv., meanwhile, fr. *inter* between] : a time intervening : INTERVAL — **interim** *adj*

¹**in·te·ri·or** \in-ˈtir-ē-ər\ *adj* **1** : lying, occurring, or functioning within the limiting boundaries : INSIDE, INNER **2** : remote from the surface, border, or shore : INLAND

²**interior** *n* **1** : the inland part (as of a country) **2** : INSIDE **3** : the internal affairs of a state or nation **4** : a scene or view of the interior of a building

interior decoration *n* : INTERIOR DESIGN — **interior decorator** *n*

interior design *n* : the art or practice of planning and supervising the design and execution of architectural interiors and their furnishings — **interior designer** *n*

interj *abbr* interjection

in·ter·ject \ˌin-tər-ˈjekt\ *vb* : to throw in between or among other things

in·ter·jec·tion \ˌin-tər-ˈjek-shən\ *n* : an exclamatory word (as *ouch*) — **in·ter·jec·tion·al·ly** \-shə-nə-lē\ *adv*

in·ter·lace \ˌin-tər-ˈlās\ *vb* **1** : to unite by or as if by lacing together : INTERWEAVE **2** : INTERSPERSE

in·ter·lard \ˌin-tər-ˈlärd\ *vb* : to vary by inserting or interjecting something

in·ter·leave \ˌin-tər-ˈlēv\ *vb* **-leaved; -leav·ing** : to arrange in alternate layers

in·ter·leu·kin \ˌin-tər-ˈlü-kən\ *n* : any of several proteins of low molecular weight that are produced by cells of the body and regulate the immune system and immune responses

¹**in·ter·line** \ˌin-tər-ˈlīn\ *vb* : to insert between lines already written or printed

²**interline** *vb* : to provide (as a coat) with an interlining

in·ter·lin·ear \ˌin-tər-ˈli-nē-ər\ *adj* : inserted between lines already written or printed ⟨an ∼ translation of a text⟩

in·ter·lin·gual \ˌin-tər-ˈliŋ-gwəl\ *adj* : of, relating to, or existing between two or more languages

in·ter·lin·ing \ˈin-tər-ˌlī-niŋ\ *n* : a lining (as of a coat) between the ordinary lining and the outside fabric

in·ter·link \ˌin-tər-ˈliŋk\ *vb* : to link together

in·ter·lock \ˌin-tər-ˈläk\ *vb* **1** : to engage or interlace together : lock together : UNITE **2** : to connect so that action of one part affects action of another part — **in·ter·lock** \ˈin-tər-ˌläk\ *n*

in·ter·loc·u·tor \ˌin-tər-ˈlä-kyə-tər\ *n* : one who takes part in dialogue or conversation

in·ter·loc·u·to·ry \-ˌtȯr-ē\ *adj* : made during the progress of a legal action and not final or definite ⟨an ∼ decree⟩

in·ter·lope \ˌin-tər-ˈlōp\ *vb* **-loped; -lop·ing 1** : to encroach on the rights (as in trade) of others **2** : INTRUDE, INTERFERE — **in·ter·lop·er** *n*

in·ter·lude \ˈin-tər-ˌlüd\ *n* **1** : a usu. short simple play or dramatic entertainment **2** : an intervening period, space, or event **3** : a piece of music inserted between the parts of a longer composition or a religious service

in·ter·mar·riage \ˌin-tər-ˈmer-ij\ *n* **1** : marriage within one's own group as required by custom **2** : marriage between members of different groups

in·ter·mar·ry \-ˈmer-ē\ *vb* **1** : to marry each other **2** : to marry within a group **3** : to become connected by intermarriage

¹in·ter·me·di·ary \ˌin-tər-ˈmē-dē-ˌer-ē\ *adj* **1** : INTERMEDIATE **2** : acting as a mediator

²intermediary *n, pl* **-ar·ies** : MEDIATOR, GO-BETWEEN

¹in·ter·me·di·ate \ˌin-tər-ˈmē-dē-ət\ *adj* : being or occurring at the middle place or degree or between extremes

²intermediate *n* **1** : one that is intermediate **2** : INTERMEDIARY

intermediate school *n* **1** : JUNIOR HIGH SCHOOL **2** : a school usu. comprising grades 4–6

in·ter·ment \in-ˈtər-mənt\ *n* : BURIAL

in·ter·mez·zo \ˌin-tər-ˈmet-sō, -ˈmed-zō\ *n, pl* **-zi** \-sē, -zē\ *or* **-zos** [It, ultim. fr. L *intermedius* intermediate] : a short movement connecting major sections of an extended musical work (as a symphony); *also* : a short independent instrumental composition

in·ter·mi·na·ble \(ˌ)in-ˈtər-mə-nə-bəl\ *adj* : ENDLESS; *esp* : wearisomely protracted — **in·ter·mi·na·bly** \-blē\ *adv*

in·ter·min·gle \ˌin-tər-ˈmiŋ-gəl\ *vb* : to mingle or mix together

in·ter·mis·sion \ˌin-tər-ˈmi-shən\ *n* **1** : INTERRUPTION, BREAK **2** : a temporary halt esp. in a public performance

in·ter·mit \-ˈmit\ *vb* **-mit·ted; -mit·ting** : DISCONTINUE; *also* : to be intermittent

in·ter·mit·tent \-ˈmi-tᵊnt\ *adj* : coming and going at intervals ♦ **Synonyms** RECURRENT, PERIODIC, ALTERNATE — **in·ter·mit·tent·ly** *adv*

in·ter·mix \ˌin-tər-ˈmiks\ *vb* : to mix together : INTERMINGLE — **in·ter·mix·ture** \-ˈmiks-chər\ *n*

in·ter·mo·lec·u·lar \-mə-ˈle-kyə-lər\ *adj* : existing or acting between molecules

in·ter·mon·tane \ˌin-tər-ˈmän-ˌtān\ *adj* : situated between mountains

¹in·tern \ˈin-ˌtərn, in-ˈtərn\ *vb* : to confine or impound esp. during a war — **in·tern·ee** \(ˌ)in-ˌtər-ˈnē\ *n* — **in·tern·ment** \in-ˈtərn-mənt\ *n*

²in·tern *also* **in·terne** \ˈin-ˌtərn\ *n* : an advanced student or recent graduate (as in medicine) gaining supervised practical experience — **in·tern·ship** *n*

³in·tern \ˈin-ˌtərn\ *vb* : to work as an intern

in·ter·nal \in-ˈtər-nᵊl\ *adj* **1** : INWARD, INTERIOR **2** : relating to or located in the inside of the body ⟨~ pain⟩ **3** : of, relating to, or occurring within the confines of an organized structure ⟨~ affairs⟩ **4** : of, relating to, or existing within the mind **5** : INTRINSIC, INHERENT ⟨~ evidence⟩ — **in·ter·nal·ly** *adv*

internal combustion engine *n* : an engine in which the fuel is ignited within the engine cylinder

in·ter·nal·ise *Brit var of* INTERNALIZE

in·ter·nal·ize \in-ˈtər-nə-ˌlīz\ *vb* **-ized; -iz·ing** : to incorporate (as values) within the self through learning or socialization — **in·ter·nal·i·za·tion** \-ˌtər-nə-lə-ˈzā-shən\ *n*

internal medicine *n* : a branch of medicine that deals with the diagnosis and treatment of diseases not requiring surgery

¹in·ter·na·tion·al \ˌin-tər-ˈna-shə-nəl\ *adj* **1** : common to or affecting two or more nations ⟨~ trade⟩ **2** : of, relating to, or constituting a group having members in two or more nations — **in·ter·na·tion·al·ly** *adv*

²international *n* : one that is international; *esp* : an organization of international scope

in·ter·na·tion·al·ise *Brit var of* INTERNATIONALIZE

in·ter·na·tion·al·ism \-ˈna-shə-nə-ˌli-zəm\ *n* : a policy of cooperation among nations; *also* : an attitude favoring such a policy — **in·ter·na·tion·al·ist** \-ˌlist\ *n or adj*

in·ter·na·tion·al·ize \-ˈna-shə-nə-ˌlīz\ *vb* : to make international; *esp* : to place under international control

International System of Units *n* : a system of units based on the metric system and used by international convention esp. for scientific work

in·ter·ne·cine \ˌin-tər-ˈne-ˌsēn, -ˈnē-ˌsīn\ *adj* [L *internecinus*, fr. *internecare* to destroy, kill, fr. *necare* to kill, fr.

nec-, nex violent death] **1** : DEADLY; *esp* : mutually destructive **2** : of, relating to, or involving conflict within a group ⟨~ feuds⟩

In·ter·net \ˈin-tər-ˌnet\ *n* : an electronic communications network that connects computer networks worldwide

in·ter·nist \ˈin-ˌtər-nist\ *n* : a physician who specializes in internal medicine

in·ter·nun·cio \ˌin-tər-ˈnən-sē-ˌō, -ˈnún-\ *n* [It *internunzio*] : a papal legate of lower rank than a nuncio

in·ter·of·fice \-ˈȯ-fəs\ *adj* : functioning or communicating between the offices of an organization

in·ter·per·son·al \-ˈpər-sə-nəl\ *adj* : being, relating to, or involving relations between persons — **in·ter·per·son·al·ly** *adv*

in·ter·plan·e·tary \ˌin-tər-ˈpla-nə-ˌter-ē\ *adj* : existing, carried on, or operating between planets ⟨~ space⟩

in·ter·play \ˈin-tər-ˌplā\ *n* : INTERACTION

in·ter·po·late \in-ˈtər-pə-ˌlāt\ *vb* **-lat·ed; -lat·ing** **1** : to change (as a text) by inserting new or foreign matter **2** : to insert (as words) into a text or into a conversation **3** : to estimate values of (data or a function) between two known values — **in·ter·po·la·tion** \-ˌtər-pə-ˈlā-shən\ *n*

in·ter·pose \ˌin-tər-ˈpōz\ *vb* **-posed; -pos·ing** **1** : to place between **2** : to thrust in : INTRUDE, INTERRUPT **3** : to inject between parts of a conversation or argument **4** : to come or be between ♦ **Synonyms** INTERFERE, INTERCEDE, INTERMEDIATE, INTERVENE — **in·ter·po·si·tion** \-pə-ˈzi-shən\ *n*

in·ter·pret \in-ˈtər-prət\ *vb* **1** : to explain the meaning of; *also* : to act as an interpreter : TRANSLATE **2** : to understand according to individual belief, judgment, or interest **3** : to represent artistically — **in·ter·pret·er** *n* — **in·ter·pre·tive** \-ˈtər-prə-tiv\ *adj*

in·ter·pre·ta·tion \in-ˌtər-prə-ˈtā-shən\ *n* **1** : EXPLANATION **2** : an instance of artistic interpretation in performance or adaptation — **in·ter·pre·ta·tive** \-ˈtər-prə-ˌtā-tiv\ *adj*

in·ter·ra·cial \-ˈrā-shəl\ *adj* : of, involving, or designed for members of different races

in·ter·reg·num \ˌin-tə-ˈreg-nəm\ *n, pl* **-nums** *or* **-na** \-nə\ **1** : the time during which a throne is vacant between two successive reigns or regimes **2** : a pause in a continuous series

in·ter·re·late \ˌin-tər-ri-ˈlāt\ *vb* : to bring into or have a mutual relationship — **in·ter·re·lat·ed·ness** \-ˈlā-təd-nəs\ *n* — **in·ter·re·la·tion** \-ˈlā-shən\ *n* — **in·ter·re·la·tion·ship** *n*

interrog *abbr* interrogative

in·ter·ro·gate \in-ˈter-ə-ˌgāt\ *vb* **-gat·ed; -gat·ing** : to question esp. formally and systematically — **in·ter·ro·ga·tion** \-ˌter-ə-ˈgā-shən\ *n* — **in·ter·ro·ga·tor** \-ˈter-ə-ˌgā-tər\ *n*

in·ter·rog·a·tive \ˌin-tə-ˈrä-gə-tiv\ *adj* : asking a question ⟨~ sentence⟩ — **interrogative** *n* — **in·ter·rog·a·tive·ly** *adv*

in·ter·rog·a·to·ry \ˌin-tə-ˈrä-gə-ˌtȯr-ē\ *adj* : INTERROGATIVE

in·ter·rupt \ˌin-tə-ˈrəpt\ *vb* **1** : to stop or hinder by breaking in **2** : to break the uniformity or continuity of **3** : to break in by speaking while another is speaking — **in·ter·rupt·er** *n* — **in·ter·rup·tion** \-ˈrəp-shən\ *n* — **in·ter·rup·tive** \-ˈrəp-tiv\ *adv*

in·ter·scho·las·tic \ˌin-tər-skə-ˈlas-tik\ *adj* : existing or carried on between schools

in·ter·sect \ˌin-tər-ˈsekt\ *vb* **1** : to divide by passing through or across **2** : to meet and cross (as at a point); *also* : OVERLAP — **in·ter·sec·tion** \-ˈsek-shən\ *n*

in·ter·sperse \ˌin-tər-ˈspərs\ *vb* **-spersed; -spers·ing** **1** : to place something at intervals in or among **2** : to insert at intervals among other things — **in·ter·sper·sion** \-ˈspər-zhən\ *n*

¹in·ter·state \ˌin-tər-ˈstāt\ *adj* : relating to, including, or connecting two or more states esp. of the U.S.

²in·ter·state \ˈin-tər-ˌstāt\ *n* : an interstate highway

in·ter·stel·lar \ˌin-tər-ˈste-lər\ *adj* : located or taking place among the stars

in·ter·stice \in-ˈtər-stəs\ *n, pl* **-stic·es** \-stə-ˌsēz, -stə-səz\ : a space that intervenes between things : CHINK — **in·ter·sti·tial** \ˌin-tər-ˈsti-shəl\ *adj*

in·ter·tid·al \ˌin-tər-ˈtī-dᵊl\ *adj* : of, relating to, or being the area that is above low-tide mark but exposed to tidal flooding ⟨life in the ~ mud⟩

in·ter·twine \-'twīn\ *vb* : to twine or cause to twine about one another : INTERLACE — **in·ter·twine·ment** *n*

in·ter·twist \-'twist\ *vb* : INTERTWINE

in·ter·ur·ban \-'ər-bən\ *adj* : connecting cities or towns

in·ter·val \'in-tər-vəl\ *n* [ME *intervalle*, fr. AF & L; AF *entreval*, fr. L *intervallum* space between ramparts, interval, fr. *inter-* between + *vallum* rampart] **1** : a space of time between events or states : PAUSE **2** : a space between objects, units, or states **3** : the difference in pitch between two tones

in·ter·vene \ˌin-tər-'vēn\ *vb* **-vened; -ven·ing 1** : to occur, fall, or come between points of time or between events **2** : to enter or appear as an unrelated feature or circumstance ⟨rain *intervened* and we postponed the trip⟩ **3** : to come in or between in order to stop, settle, or modify ⟨~ in a quarrel⟩ **4** : to occur or lie between two things — **in·ter·ven·tion** \-'ven-chən\ *n*

in·ter·ven·tion·ism \-'ven-chə-ˌni-zəm\ *n* : interference by one country in the political affairs of another — **in·ter·ven·tion·ist** \-'ven-chə-nist\ *n or adj*

in·ter·view \'in-tər-ˌvyü\ *n* **1** : a formal consultation usu. to evaluate qualifications **2** : a meeting at which a writer or reporter obtains information from a person; *also* : the recorded or written account of such a meeting — **interview** *vb* — **in·ter·view·ee** \ˌin-tər-(ˌ)vyü-'ē\ *n* — **in·ter·view·er** *n*

in·ter·vo·cal·ic \ˌin-tər-vō-'ka-lik\ *adj* : immediately preceded and immediately followed by a vowel

in·ter·weave \ˌin-tər-'wēv\ *vb* **-wove** \-'wōv\ *also* **-weaved; -wo·ven** \-'wō-vən\ *also* **-weaved; -weav·ing** : to weave or blend together : INTERTWINE, INTERMINGLE — **interwoven** *adj*

in·tes·tate \in-'tes-ˌtāt, -tət\ *adj* **1** : having made no valid will ⟨died ~⟩ **2** : not disposed of by will ⟨~ estate⟩

in·tes·tine \in-'tes-tən\ *n* : the tubular part of the alimentary canal that extends from stomach to anus and consists of a long narrow upper part (**small intestine**) followed by a broader shorter lower part (**large intestine**) — **in·tes·ti·nal** \-tə-nᵊl\ *adj*

in·ti·fa·da \ˌin-tə-'fä-də\ *n* : an armed uprising of Palestinians against Israeli occupation of the West Bank and Gaza Strip

¹in·ti·mate \'in-tə-ˌmāt\ *vb* **-mat·ed; -mat·ing** [LL *intimare* to put in, announce, fr. L *intimus* innermost] **1** : ANNOUNCE, NOTIFY **2** : to communicate indirectly : HINT — **in·ti·ma·tion** \ˌin-tə-mā-shən\ *n*

²in·ti·mate \'in-tə-mət\ *adj* **1** : INTRINSIC; *also* : INNERMOST **2** : marked by very close association, contact, or familiarity **3** : marked by a warm friendship **4** : suggesting informal warmth or privacy **5** : of a very personal or private nature — **in·ti·ma·cy** \'in-tə-mə-sē\ *n* — **in·ti·mate·ly** *adv*

³in·ti·mate \'in-tə-mət\ *n* : an intimate friend, associate, or confidant

in·tim·i·date \in-'ti-mə-ˌdāt\ *vb* **-dat·ed; -dat·ing** : to make timid or fearful : FRIGHTEN; *esp* : to compel or deter by or as if by threats ✦ *Synonyms* COW, BULLDOZE, BULLY, BROWBEAT — **in·tim·i·dat·ing·ly** *adv* — **in·tim·i·da·tion** \-ˌti-mə-'dā-shən\ *n*

intl *or* **intnl** *abbr* international

in·to \'in-tü\ *prep* **1** : to the inside of ⟨ran ~ the house⟩ **2** : to the state, condition, or form of ⟨got ~ trouble⟩ **3** : AGAINST ⟨ran ~ a wall⟩

in·tol·er·a·ble \(ˌ)in-'tä-lə-rə-bəl\ *adj* **1** : UNBEARABLE ⟨~ pain⟩ **2** : EXCESSIVE — **in·tol·er·a·bly** \-blē\ *adv*

in·tol·er·ant \(ˌ)in-'tä-lə-rənt\ *adj* **1** : unable or unwilling to endure **2** : unwilling to grant equality, freedom, or other social rights : BIGOTED — **in·tol·er·ance** \-rəns\ *n*

in·to·na·tion \ˌin-tō-'nā-shən\ *n* **1** : something that is intoned **2** : the act of intoning and esp. of chanting **3** : the manner of singing, playing, or uttering tones; *esp* : the rise and fall in pitch of the voice in speech

in·tone \in-'tōn\ *vb* **in·toned; in·ton·ing** : to utter in musical or prolonged tones : CHANT

in to·to \in-'tō-tō\ *adv* [L, on the whole] : TOTALLY, ENTIRELY

in·tox·i·cant \in-'täk-si-kənt\ *n* : something that intoxicates; *esp* : an alcoholic drink — **intoxicant** *adj*

in·tox·i·cate \-sə-ˌkāt\ *vb* **-cat·ed; -cat·ing 1** : to affect by a drug (as alcohol or cocaine) esp. to the point of physical or mental impairment **2** : to excite to enthusiasm or frenzy — **in·tox·i·ca·tion** \-ˌtäk-sə-'kā-shən\ *n*

in·trac·ta·ble \(ˌ)in-'trak-tə-bəl\ *adj* : not easily controlled

in·tra·mu·ral \-'myùr-əl\ *adj* : being or occurring within the walls or limits (as of a city or college) ⟨~ sports⟩

in·tra·mus·cu·lar \-'məs-kyə-lər\ *adj* : situated within, occurring in, or administered by entering a muscle — **in·tra·mus·cu·lar·ly** *adv*

in·tra·net \'in-trə-ˌnet\ *n* : a network similar to the World Wide Web but having access limited to certain authorized users

intrans *abbr* intransitive

in·tran·si·gent \-jənt\ *adj* : UNCOMPROMISING ⟨an ~ attitude⟩ — **in·tran·si·gence** \-jəns\ *n* — **intransigent** *n*

in·tran·si·tive \(ˌ)in-'tran-sə-tiv, -zə-\ *adj* : not transitive; *esp* : not having or containing an object ⟨an ~ verb⟩ — **in·tran·si·tive·ly** *adv* — **in·tran·si·tive·ness** *n*

in·tra·state \ˌin-trə-'stāt\ *adj* : existing or occurring within a state

in·tra·uter·ine device \-'yü-tə-rən-, -ˌrīn-\ *n* : a device inserted into and left in the uterus to prevent pregnancy

in·tra·ve·nous \ˌin-trə-'vē-nəs\ *adj* : being within or entering by way of the veins ⟨~ feeding⟩; *also* : used in or using intravenous procedures ⟨~ needles⟩ — **in·tra·ve·nous·ly** *adv*

intrench *var of* ENTRENCH

in·trep·id \in-'tre-pəd\ *adj* : characterized by resolute fearlessness, fortitude, and endurance — **in·tre·pid·i·ty** \ˌin-trə-'pi-də-tē\ *n*

in·tri·cate \'in-tri-kət\ *adj* [ME, fr. L *intricatus*, pp. of *intricare* to entangle, fr. *tricae* trifles, complications] **1** : having many complexly interrelated parts : COMPLICATED **2** : difficult to follow, understand, or solve — **in·tri·ca·cy** \-tri-kə-sē\ *n* — **in·tri·cate·ly** *adv*

¹in·trigue \'in-ˌtrēg, in-'trēg\ *n* **1** : a secret scheme : MACHINATION **2** : a clandestine love affair

²in·trigue \in-'trēg\ *vb* **in·trigued; in·trigu·ing 1** : to accomplish by intrigue **2** : to carry on an intrigue; *esp* : PLOT, SCHEME **3** : to arouse the interest, desire, or curiosity of — **in·trigu·ing·ly** *adv*

in·trin·sic \in-'trin-zik, -sik\ *adj* : belonging to the essential nature or constitution of a thing — **in·trin·si·cal·ly** \-zi-k(ə-)lē, -si-\ *adv*

introd *abbr* introduction

in·tro·duce \ˌin-trə-'düs, -'dyüs\ *vb* **-duced; -duc·ing 1** : to lead or bring in esp. for the first time **2** : to bring into practice or use **3** : to cause to be acquainted **4** : to present for discussion **5** : PLACE, INSERT ✦ *Synonyms* INSINUATE, INTERPOLATE, INTERPOSE, INTERJECT — **in·tro·duc·tion** \-'dək-shən\ *n* — **in·tro·duc·to·ry** \-'dək-tə-rē\ *adj*

in·troit \'in-ˌtrȯit, -ˌtrō-ət\ *n* **1** *often cap* : the first part of the traditional proper of the Mass **2** : a piece of music sung or played at the beginning of a worship service

in·tro·spec·tion \-'spek-shən\ *n* : a reflective looking inward : an examination of one's own thoughts or feelings — **in·tro·spect** \ˌin-trə-'spekt\ *vb* — **in·tro·spec·tive** \-'spek-tiv\ *adj* — **in·tro·spec·tive·ly** *adv*

in·tro·vert \'in-trə-ˌvərt\ *n* : a reserved or shy person — **in·tro·ver·sion** \ˌin-trə-'vər-zhən\ *n* — **introvert** *adj* — **in·tro·vert·ed** \'in-trə-ˌvər-təd\ *adj*

in·trude \in-'trüd\ *vb* **in·trud·ed; in·trud·ing 1** : to thrust, enter, or force in or upon **2** : ENCROACH, TRESPASS — **in·trud·er** *n* — **in·tru·sion** \-'trü-zhən\ *n* — **in·tru·sive** \-'trü-siv\ *adj* — **in·tru·sive·ness** *n*

intrust *var of* ENTRUST

in·tu·it \in-'tü-ət, -'tyü-\ *vb* : to know, sense, or understand by intuition

in·tu·ition \ˌin-tù-'wi-shən, -tyü-\ *n* **1** : quick and ready insight **2** : the power or faculty of knowing things without conscious reasoning — **in·tu·i·tive** \in-'tü-ə-tiv, -'tyü-\ *adj* — **in·tu·i·tive·ly** *adv*

In·u·it \'i-nü-wət, 'in-yü-\ *n* [Inuit *inuit*, pl. of *inuk* person] **1** *pl* **Inuit** *or* **Inuits** : a member of the Eskimo people of No. America and Greenland **2** : the language of the Inuit people

in·un·date \'i-nən-ˌdāt\ *vb* **-dat·ed; -dat·ing** : to cover with or as if with a flood : OVERFLOW — **in·un·da·tion** \ˌi-nən-ˈdā-shən\ *n*

in·ure \i-ˈnu̇r, -ˈnyu̇r\ *vb* **in·ured; in·ur·ing** [ME *enuren,* fr. *in ure* customary, fr. *putten in ure* to use, put into practice, part trans. of AF *mettre en ovre, en uevre*] **1** : to accustom to accept something undesirable **2** : to become of advantage

in utero \in-ˈyü-tə-ˌrō\ *adv or adj* [L] : in the uterus : before birth

inv *abbr* **1** inventor **2** invoice

in vac·uo \in-ˈva-kyu̇-ˌwō\ *adv* [L] : in a vacuum

in·vade \in-ˈvād\ *vb* **in·vad·ed; in·vad·ing** **1** : to enter for conquest or plunder **2** : to encroach upon **3** : to spread through and usu. harm ⟨germs ∼ the tissues⟩ — **in·vad·er** *n*

¹in·val·id \(ˌ)in-ˈva-ləd\ *adj* : being without foundation or force in fact, reason, or law — **in·va·lid·i·ty** \ˌin-və-ˈli-də-tē\ *n* — **in·val·id·ly** *adv*

²in·va·lid \ˈin-və-ləd\ *adj* : being in ill health : SICKLY

³invalid \ˈin-və-ləd\ *n* : a person in usu. chronic ill health — **in·va·lid·ism** \-lə-ˌdi-zəm\ *n*

⁴in·va·lid \ˈin-və-ləd, -ˌlid\ *vb* **1** : to remove from active duty by reason of sickness or disability **2** : to make sickly or disabled

in·val·i·date \(ˌ)in-ˈva-lə-ˌdāt\ *vb* : to make invalid; *esp* : to weaken or make valueless — **in·val·i·da·tion** \in-ˌva-lə-ˈdā-shən\ *n*

in·valu·able \-ˈval-yə-bəl, -yə-wə-bəl\ *adj* : valuable beyond estimation

in·vari·able \-ˈver-ē-ə-bəl\ *adj* : not changing or capable of change : CONSTANT — **in·vari·ably** \-blē\ *adv*

in·va·sion \in-ˈvā-zhən\ *n* : an act or instance of invading; *esp* : entry of an army into a country for conquest

in·va·sive \in-ˈvā-siv, -ziv\ *adj* **1** : tending to spread ⟨∼ cancer cells⟩ **2** : involving entry into the living body (as by surgery) ⟨∼ therapy⟩

in·vec·tive \in-ˈvek-tiv\ *n* **1** : an abusive expression or speech **2** : abusive language — **invective** *adj*

in·veigh \in-ˈvā\ *vb* : to protest or complain bitterly or vehemently : RAIL

in·vei·gle \in-ˈvā-gəl, -ˈvē-\ *vb* **in·vei·gled; in·vei·gling** [AF *enveegler, aveogler* to blind, hoodwink, fr. *avogle, enveugle* blind, fr. ML *ab oculis,* lit., lacking eyes] **1** : to win over by flattery : ENTICE **2** : to acquire by ingenuity or flattery

in·vent \in-ˈvent\ *vb* **1** : to think up **2** : to create or produce for the first time — **in·ven·tor** \-ˈven-tər\ *n*

in·ven·tion \in-ˈven-chən\ *n* **1** : INVENTIVENESS **2** : a creation of the imagination; *esp* : a false conception **3** : a device, contrivance, or process originated after study and experiment **4** : the act or process of inventing

in·ven·tive \in-ˈven-tiv\ *adj* **1** : CREATIVE, INGENIOUS ⟨an ∼ composer⟩ **2** : characterized by invention ⟨an ∼ turn of mind⟩ — **in·ven·tive·ness** *n*

in·ven·to·ry \ˈin-vən-ˌtȯr-ē\ *n, pl* **-ries** **1** : an itemized list of current goods or assets **2** : SURVEY, SUMMARY **3** : STOCK, SUPPLY **4** : the act or process of taking an inventory — **inventory** *vb*

¹in·verse \(ˌ)in-ˈvərs, ˈin-ˌvərs\ *adj* : opposite in order, nature, or effect : REVERSED — **in·verse·ly** *adv*

²inverse *n* : something inverse or resulting in or from inversion : OPPOSITE

in·ver·sion \in-ˈvər-zhən\ *n* **1** : a reversal of position, order, or relationship; *esp* : an increase of temperature with altitude through a layer of air **2** : the act or process of inverting

in·vert \in-ˈvərt\ *vb* **1** : to reverse in position, order, or relationship **2** : to turn upside down or inside out **3** : to turn inward

in·ver·te·brate \(ˌ)in-ˈvər-tə-brət, -ˌbrāt\ *adj* : lacking a backbone; *also* : of or relating to invertebrate animals — **invertebrate** *n*

¹in·vest \in-ˈvest\ *vb* **1** : to install formally in an office or honor **2** : to furnish with power or authority : VEST **3** : to cover completely : ENVELOP **4** : CLOTHE, ADORN **5** : BESIEGE **6** : to endow with a quality or characteristic

²invest *vb* **1** : to commit (money) in order to earn a financial return **2** : to expend for future benefits or advantages **3** : to make an investment — **in·ves·tor** \-ˈves-tər\ *n*

in·ves·ti·gate \in-ˈves-tə-ˌgāt\ *vb* **-gat·ed; -gat·ing** [L *investigare* to track, investigate, fr. *vestigium* footprint, track]

: to study by close examination and systematic inquiry — **in·ves·ti·ga·tion** \-ˌves-tə-ˈgā-shən\ *n* — **in·ves·ti·ga·tive** \-ˈves-tə-ˌgā-tiv\ *adj* — **in·ves·ti·ga·tor** \-ˌgā-tər\ *n*

in·ves·ti·ture \in-ˈves-tə-ˌchu̇r, -chər\ *n* **1** : the act of ratifying or establishing in office **2** : something that covers or adorns

¹in·vest·ment \in-ˈvest-mənt\ *n* **1** : an outer layer : ENVELOPE **2** : INVESTITURE 1 **3** : BLOCKADE, SIEGE

²investment *n* : the outlay of money for income or profit; *also* : the sum invested or the property purchased

in·vet·er·ate \in-ˈve-tə-rət\ *adj* **1** : firmly established by age or long persistence **2** : confirmed in a habit

in·vi·able \(ˌ)in-ˈvī-ə-bəl\ *adj* : incapable of surviving

in·vid·i·ous \in-ˈvi-dē-əs\ *adj* **1** : tending to cause discontent, animosity, or envy **2** : ENVIOUS **3** : OBNOXIOUS ⟨∼ remarks⟩ — **in·vid·i·ous·ly** *adv*

in·vig·o·rate \in-ˈvi-gə-ˌrāt\ *vb* **-rat·ed; -rat·ing** : to give life and energy to : ANIMATE — **in·vig·o·ra·tion** \-ˌvi-gə-ˈrā-shən\ *n*

in·vin·ci·ble \(ˌ)in-ˈvin-sə-bəl\ *adj* : incapable of being conquered, overcome, or subdued — **in·vin·ci·bil·i·ty** \-ˌvin-sə-ˈbi-lə-tē\ *n* — **in·vin·ci·bly** \-ˈvin-sə-blē\ *adv*

in·vi·o·la·ble \-ˈvī-ə-lə-bəl\ *adj* **1** : safe from violation or profanation **2** : UNASSAILABLE ⟨∼ borders⟩ — **in·vi·o·la·bil·i·ty** \-ˌvī-ə-lə-ˈbi-lə-tē\ *n*

in·vi·o·late \-ˈvī-ə-lət\ *adj* : not violated or profaned : PURE

in·vis·i·ble \-ˈvi-zə-bəl\ *adj* **1** : incapable of being seen ⟨∼ to the naked eye⟩ **2** : HIDDEN **3** : IMPERCEPTIBLE, INCONSPICUOUS — **in·vis·i·bil·i·ty** \-ˌvi-zə-ˈbi-lə-tē\ *n* — **in·vis·i·bly** \-ˈvi-zə-blē\ *adv*

invisible hand *n* : a hypothetical economic force that works for the benefit of all

in·vi·ta·tion·al \ˌin-və-ˈtā-shə-nəl\ *adj* : limited to invited participants ⟨an ∼ tournament⟩ — **invitational** *n*

in·vite \in-ˈvīt\ *vb* **in·vit·ed; in·vit·ing** **1** : ENTICE, TEMPT **2** : to increase the likelihood of ⟨∼ trouble⟩ **3** : to request the presence or participation of : ASK **4** : to request formally **5** : ENCOURAGE ⟨∼ suggestions⟩ — **in·vi·ta·tion** \ˌin-və-ˈtā-shən\ *n*

in·vit·ing *adj* : ATTRACTIVE, TEMPTING

in vi·tro \in-ˈvē-trō, -ˈvī-, -ˈvi-\ *adv or adj* [NL, lit., in glass] : outside the living body and in an artificial environment ⟨*in vitro* fertilization⟩

in·vo·ca·tion \ˌin-və-ˈkā-shən\ *n* **1** : SUPPLICATION; *esp* : a prayer at the beginning of a service **2** : a formula for conjuring : INCANTATION

¹in·voice \ˈin-ˌvȯis\ *n* [modif. of MF *envois,* pl. of *envoi* message] : an itemized list of goods shipped usu. specifying the price and the terms of sale : BILL

²invoice *vb* **in·voiced; in·voic·ing** : to send an invoice to or for : BILL

in·voke \in-ˈvōk\ *vb* **in·voked; in·vok·ing** **1** : to petition for help or support **2** : to appeal to or cite as authority ⟨∼ a law⟩ **3** : to call forth by incantation : CONJURE ⟨∼ spirits⟩ **4** : to make an earnest request for : SOLICIT **5** : to put into effect or operation **6** : to bring about : CAUSE

in·vol·un·tary \(ˌ)in-ˈvä-lən-ˌter-ē\ *adj* **1** : done contrary to or without choice **2** : COMPULSORY ⟨∼ servitude⟩ **3** : not controlled by the will : REFLEX ⟨∼ contractions⟩ — **in·vol·un·tari·ly** \-ˌvä-lən-ˈter-ə-lē\ *adv*

in·vo·lute \ˈin-və-ˌlüt\ *adj* : INVOLVED, INTRICATE

in·vo·lu·tion \ˌin-və-ˈlü-shən\ *n* **1** : the act or an instance of enfolding or entangling **2** : COMPLEXITY, INTRICACY

in·volve \in-ˈvälv\ *vb* **in·volved; in·volv·ing** **1** : to draw in as a participant **2** : ENVELOP **3** : to occupy (as oneself) absorbingly; *esp* : to commit oneself emotionally **4** : to relate closely : CONNECT **5** : to have as part of itself : INCLUDE **6** : ENTAIL, IMPLY **7** : ²AFFECT — **in·volve·ment** *n*

in·volved \-ˈvälvd\ *adj* : INTRICATE, COMPLEX ⟨an ∼ plot⟩

in·vul·ner·a·ble \(ˌ)in-ˈvəl-nə-rə-bəl\ *adj* **1** : incapable of being wounded, injured, or damaged **2** : immune to or proof against attack — **in·vul·ner·a·bil·i·ty** \-ˌvəl-nə-rə-ˈbi-lə-tē\ *n* — **in·vul·ner·a·bly** \-ˈvəl-nə-rə-blē\ *adv*

¹in·ward \ˈin-wərd\ *adj* **1** : situated on the inside **2** : MENTAL; *also* : SPIRITUAL **3** : directed toward the interior

²inward *or* **in·wards** \-wərdz\ *adv* **1** : toward the inside, center, or interior **2** : toward the inner being ⟨turned his thoughts ∼⟩

in·ward·ly \ˈin-wərd-lē\ *adv* **1** : MENTALLY, SPIRITUALLY **2** : INTERNALLY ⟨bled ∼⟩ **3** : to oneself ⟨cursed ∼⟩

IOC *abbr* International Olympic Committee

io·dide \'ī-ə-ˌdīd\ *n* : a compound of iodine with another element or group

io·dine \'ī-ə-ˌdīn, -d°n\ *n* **1** : a nonmetallic chemical element used esp. in medicine and photography **2** : a solution of iodine used as a local antiseptic

io·dise *Brit var of* IODIZE

io·dize \'ī-ə-ˌdīz\ *vb* **io·dized; io·diz·ing** : to treat with iodine or an iodide

ion \'ī-ən, 'ī-ˌän\ *n* [Gk, neut. of *iōn*, prp. of *ienai* to go; so called because in electrolysis it goes to one of the two poles] : an electrically charged particle, atom, or group of atoms — **ion·ic** \ī-'ä-nik\ *adj*

-ion *n suffix* : act, process, state, or condition ⟨valid*ation*⟩

ion·ise *Brit var of* IONIZE

ion·ize \'ī-ə-ˌnīz\ *vb* **ion·ized; ion·iz·ing** **1** : to convert wholly or partly into ions **2** : to become ionized — **ion·iz·able** \ˌī-ə-'nī-zə-bəl\ *adj* — **ion·i·za·tion** \ˌī-ə-nə-'zā-shən\ *n* — **ion·iz·er** \'ī-ə-ˌnī-zər\ *n*

ion·o·sphere \ī-'ä-nə-ˌsfir\ *n* : the part of the earth's atmosphere extending from about 30 miles (50 kilometers) to the exosphere that contains ionized atmospheric gases — **ion·o·spher·ic** \ī-ˌä-nə-'sfir-ik, -'sfer-\ *adj*

IOOF *abbr* Independent Order of Odd Fellows

io·ta \ī-'ō-tə\ *n* [L, fr. Gk *iōta*] **1** : the 9th letter of the Greek alphabet — I or ι **2** : a very small quantity : JOT

IOU \ˌī-(ˌ)ō-'yü\ *n* : an acknowledgement of a debt

IP *abbr* innings pitched

IP address \'ī-ˌpē-\ *n* [*Internet protocol*] : the numeric address of a computer on the Internet

ip·e·cac \'i-pi-ˌkak\ *n* [Pg *ipecacuanha*] : an emetic and expectorant drug used esp. as a syrup in treating accidental poisoning; *also* : either of two tropical American plants or their rhizomes and roots used to make ipecac

IPO \ˌī-ˌpē-'ō\ *n, pl* **IPOs** : an initial public offering of a company's stock

ip·so fac·to \ˌip-sō-'fak-tō\ *adv* [NL, lit., by the fact itself] : by the very nature of the case

iq *abbr* [L *idem quod*] the same as

IQ \'ī-ˌkyü\ *n* : a number used to express a person's relative intelligence as determined by a standardized test

¹Ir *abbr* Irish

²Ir *symbol* iridium

IR *abbr* infrared

¹IRA \ˌī-(ˌ)är-'ā; 'ī-rə\ *n* [*individual retirement account*] : a retirement savings account in which income taxes are deferred until withdrawals are made

²IRA *abbr* Irish Republican Army

irai·mbi·la·nja \ē-ˌrīm-bē-'län(d)-zə\ *n, pl* **iraimbilanja** — see *ariary* at MONEY table

iras·ci·ble \i-'ra-sə-bəl\ *adj* : marked by hot temper and easily provoked anger ♦ *Synonyms* CHOLERIC, TESTY, TOUCHY, CRANKY, CROSS — **iras·ci·bil·i·ty** \-ˌra-sə-'bi-lə-tē\ *n*

irate \ī-'rāt\ *adj* **1** : roused to ire **2** : arising from anger — **irate·ly** *adv*

ire \'ī(-ə)r\ *n* : ANGER, WRATH — **ire·ful** *adj*

Ire *abbr* Ireland

ire·nic \ī-'re-nik\ *adj* : favoring, conducive to, or operating toward peace or conciliation

ir·i·des·cence \ˌir-ə-'de-s°ns\ *n* : a rainbowlike play of colors — **ir·i·des·cent** \-s°nt\ *adj*

irid·i·um \ir-'i-dē-əm\ *n* : a hard brittle heavy metallic chemical element

iris \'ī-rəs\ *n, pl* **iris·es** *also* **iri·des** \'ī-rə-ˌdēz, 'ir-ə-\ [ME, fr. L *iris* rainbow, iris plant, fr. Gk, rainbow, iris plant, iris of the eye] **1** : the colored part around the pupil of the eye **2** : any of a large genus of plants with linear basal leaves and large showy flowers

Irish \'ī-rish\ *n* **1 Irish** *pl* : the people of Ireland **2** : the Celtic language of Ireland — **Irish** *adj* — **Irish·man** \-mən\ *n* — **Irish·wom·an** \-ˌwu̇-mən\ *n*

Irish bull *n* : an incongruous statement (as "it was hereditary in his family to have no children")

Irish coffee *n* : hot sugared coffee with Irish whiskey and whipped cream

Irish moss *n* : the dried and bleached plants of a red alga that is a source of carrageenan; *also* : this red alga

Irish setter *n* : any of a breed of hunting dogs with a mahogany-red coat

irk \'ərk\ *vb* : to make weary, irritated, or bored : ANNOY

irk·some \'ərk-səm\ *adj* : tending to irk : ANNOYING — **irk·some·ly** *adv*

¹iron \'ī(-ə)rn\ *n* [ME, fr. OE *īsern, īren*] **1** : a heavy malleable magnetic metallic chemical element that rusts easily and is vital to biological processes **2** : something made of metal and esp. iron; *also* : something (as handcuffs) used to bind or restrain ⟨put them in ~s⟩ **3** : a household device with a flat base that is heated and used for pressing cloth **4** : STRENGTH, HARDNESS

²iron *vb* **1** : to press or smooth with or as if with a heated iron **2** : to remove (as wrinkles) by ironing — **iron·er** *n*

¹iron·clad \-'klad\ *adj* **1** : sheathed in iron armor **2** : so firm or secure as to be unbreakable

²iron·clad \-ˌklad\ *n* : an armored naval vessel esp. of the 19th century

iron curtain *n* : a political, military, and ideological barrier that isolates an area; *esp, often cap* : one formerly isolating an area under Soviet control

iron·ic \ī-'rä-nik\ *also* **iron·i·cal** \-ni-kəl\ *adj* **1** : of, relating to, or marked by irony **2** : given to irony

iron·i·cal·ly \-ni-k(ə-)lē\ *adv* **1** : in an ironic manner **2** : it is ironic

iron·ing *n* : clothes ironed or to be ironed

iron lung *n* : a device for artificial respiration that encloses the chest in a chamber in which changes of pressure force air into and out of the lungs

iron out *vb* : to remove or lessen difficulties in or extremes of

iron oxide *n* : FERRIC OXIDE

iron·stone \'ī(-ə)rn-ˌstōn\ *n* **1** : a hard iron-rich sedimentary rock **2** : a hard heavy durable pottery developed in England in the 19th century

iron·ware \-ˌwer\ *n* : articles made of iron

iron·weed \-ˌwēd\ *n* : any of a genus of mostly weedy plants related to the asters that have terminal heads of red, purple, or white flowers

iron·wood \-ˌwu̇d\ *n* : any of numerous trees or shrubs with exceptionally hard wood; *also* : the wood

iron·work \-ˌwərk\ *n* **1** : work in iron **2** *pl* : a mill or building where iron or steel is smelted or heavy iron or steel products are made — **iron·work·er** *n*

iro·ny \'ī-rə-nē\ *n, pl* **-nies** [L *ironia*, fr. Gk *eirōnia*, fr. *eirōn* dissembler] **1** : the use of words to express the opposite of what one really means **2** : incongruity between the actual result of a sequence of events and the expected result

Ir·o·quois \'ir-ə-ˌkwȯi\ *n, pl* **Iroquois** *same or* -ˌkwȯiz\ **1** *pl* : an American Indian confederacy orig. of New York that consisted of the Cayuga, Mohawk, Oneida, Onondaga, and Seneca and later included the Tuscarora **2** : a member of any of the Iroquois peoples

ir·ra·di·ate \i-'rā-dē-ˌāt\ *vb* **-at·ed; -at·ing** **1** : ILLUMINATE **2** : ENLIGHTEN **3** : to treat by exposure to radiation **4** : RADIATE — **ir·ra·di·a·tion** \-ˌrā-dē-'ā-shən\ *n*

¹ir·ra·tio·nal \(ˌ)i-'ra-shə-nəl\ *adj* **1** : incapable of reasoning ⟨~ beasts⟩; *also* : defective in mental power ⟨~ with fever⟩ **2** : not based on reason ⟨~ fears⟩ **3** : being or numerically equal to an irrational number — **ir·ra·tio·nal·i·ty** \(ˌ)i-ˌra-shə-'na-lə-tē\ *n* — **ir·ra·tio·nal·ly** *adv*

²irrational *n* : IRRATIONAL NUMBER

irrational number *n* : a real number that cannot be expressed as the quotient of two integers

ir·rec·on·cil·able \(ˌ)i-ˌre-kən-'sī-lə-bəl, -'re-kən-ˌsī-\ *adj* : impossible to reconcile, adjust, or harmonize — **ir·rec·on·cil·abil·i·ty** \(ˌ)i-ˌre-kən-ˌsī-lə-'bi-lə-tē\ *n*

ir·re·cov·er·able \ˌir-i-'kə-və-rə-bəl\ *adj* : not capable of being recovered or rectified : IRREPARABLE ⟨an ~ loss⟩ — **ir·re·cov·er·ably** \-blē\ *adv*

ir·re·deem·able \ˌir-i-'dē-mə-bəl\ *adj* **1** : not redeemable; *esp* : not terminable by payment of the principal ⟨an ~ bond⟩ **2** : not convertible into gold or silver at the will of the holder **3** : being beyond remedy : HOPELESS

ir·re·den·tism \-'den-ˌti-zəm\ *n* : a principle or policy directed toward the incorporation of a territory historically or ethnically part of another into that other — **ir·re·den·tist** \-tist\ *n or adj*

ir·re·duc·ible \ˌir-i-'dü-sə-bəl, -'dyü-\ *adj* : not reducible — **ir·re·duc·ibly** \-blē\ *adv*

ir·re·fut·able \ˌir-i-'fyü-tə-bəl, (ˌ)i-'re-fyət-\ *adj* : impossible to refute

irreg *abbr* irregular

ir·reg·u·lar \(ˌ)i-ˈre-gyə-lər\ *adj* **1** : not regular : not natural or uniform **2** : not conforming to the normal or usual manner of inflection ⟨∼ verbs⟩ **3** : not belonging to a regular or organized army ⟨∼ troops⟩ — **irregular** *n* — **ir·reg·u·lar·ly** *adv*

ir·reg·u·lar·i·ty i-ˌre-gyə-ˈla-rə-tē\ *n, pl* **-ties 1** : something that is irregular **2** : the quality or state of being irregular **3** : occasional constipation

ir·rel·e·vant \(ˌ)i-ˈre-lə-vənt\ *adj* : not relevant — **ir·rel·e·vance** \-vəns\ *n*

ir·re·li·gious \ˌi-ri-ˈli-jəs\ *adj* : lacking religious emotions, doctrines, or practices

ir·re·me·di·a·ble \ˌir-i-ˈmē-dē-ə-bəl\ *adj* : impossible to remedy or correct

ir·re·mov·able \-ˈmü-və-bəl\ *adj* : not removable

ir·rep·a·ra·ble \(ˌ)i-ˈre-pə-rə-bəl\ *adj* : impossible to make good, undo, repair, or remedy ⟨∼ damage⟩

ir·re·place·able \ˌir-i-ˈplā-sə-bəl\ *adj* : not replaceable ⟨∼ antiques⟩

ir·re·press·ible \-ˈpre-sə-bəl\ *adj* : impossible to repress or control

ir·re·proach·able \-ˈprō-chə-bəl\ *adj* : not reproachable : BLAMELESS

ir·re·sist·ible \ˌir-i-ˈzis-tə-bəl\ *adj* : impossible to successfully resist — **ir·re·sist·ibly** \-blē\ *adv*

ir·res·o·lute \(ˌ)i-ˈre-zə-ˌlüt\ *adj* : uncertain how to act or proceed : VACILLATING — **ir·res·o·lute·ly** \-ˌlüt-lē, (ˌ)i-ˌre-zə-ˈlüt-\ *adv* — **ir·res·o·lu·tion** \(ˌ)i-ˌre-zə-ˈlü-shən\ *n*

ir·re·spec·tive of \ˌir-i-ˈspek-tiv-\ *prep* : without regard to

ir·re·spon·si·ble \-ˈspän-sə-bəl\ *adj* : not responsible — **ir·re·spon·si·bil·i·ty** \-ˌspän-sə-ˈbi-lə-tē\ *n* — **ir·re·spon·si·bly** \-ˈspän-sə-blē\ *adv*

ir·re·triev·able \ˌir-i-ˈtrē-və-bəl\ *adj* : not retrievable : IRRECOVERABLE

ir·rev·er·ence \(ˌ)i-ˈre-və-rəns\ *n* **1** : lack of reverence **2** : an irreverent act or utterance — **ir·rev·er·ent** \-rənt\ *adj* — **ir·rev·er·ent·ly** *adv*

ir·re·vers·ible \ˌir-i-ˈvər-sə-bəl\ *adj* : incapable of being reversed

ir·rev·o·ca·ble \(ˌ)i-ˈre-və-kə-bəl\ *adj* : incapable of being revoked or recalled — **ir·rev·o·ca·bly** \-blē\ *adv*

ir·ri·gate \ˈir-ə-ˌgāt\ *vb* **-gat·ed; -gat·ing** : to supply (as land) with water by artificial means; *also* : to flush with liquid — **ir·ri·ga·tion** \ˌir-ə-ˈgā-shən\ *n*

ir·ri·ta·bil·i·ty \ˌir-ə-tə-ˈbi-lə-tē\ *n* **1** : the property of living things and of protoplasm that enables reaction to stimuli **2** : the quality or state of being irritable; *esp* : readiness to become annoyed or angry

ir·ri·ta·ble \ˈir-ə-tə-bəl\ *adj* : capable of being irritated; *esp* : readily or easily irritated — **ir·ri·ta·bly** \-blē\ *adv*

ir·ri·tate \ˈir-ə-ˌtāt\ *vb* **-tat·ed; -tat·ing 1** : to excite to anger : EXASPERATE **2** : to make sore or inflamed — **ir·ri·tant** \ˈir-ə-tənt\ *adj or n* — **ir·ri·tat·ing·ly** *adv* — **ir·ri·ta·tion** \ˌir-ə-ˈtā-shən\ *n*

ir·rupt \(ˌ)i-ˈrəpt\ *vb* **1** : to rush in forcibly or violently **2** : to increase suddenly in numbers ⟨rabbits ∼ in cycles⟩ — **ir·rup·tion** \-ˈrəp-shən\ *n*

IRS *abbr* Internal Revenue Service

is *pres 3d sing of* BE

Isa *or* **Is** *abbr* Isaiah

Isa·iah \ī-ˈzā-ə\ *n* — see BIBLE table

Isa·ias \ī-ˈzā-əs\ *n* : ISAIAH

ISBN *abbr* International Standard Book Number

is·che·mia \is-ˈkē-mē-ə\ *n* : deficient supply of blood to a body part (as the brain) — **is·che·mic** \-mik\ *adj*

-ish *adj suffix* **1** : of, relating to, or being ⟨Finn*ish*⟩ **2** : characteristic of ⟨boy*ish*⟩ ⟨mul*ish*⟩ **3** : inclined or liable to ⟨book*ish*⟩ **4** : having a touch or trace of : somewhat ⟨purpl*ish*⟩ **5** : having the approximate age of ⟨forty*ish*⟩

isin·glass \ˈī-zⁿ-ˌglas, ˈī-ziŋ-\ *n* **1** : a gelatin obtained from various fish **2** : mica esp. in thin sheets

isl *abbr* island

Is·lam \is-ˈläm, iz-, -ˈlam, ˈis-ˌ, ˈiz-ˌ\ *n* [Ar *islām* submission (to the will of God)] : the religious faith of Muslims including belief in Allah as the sole deity and in Muhammad as his prophet; *also* : the civilization built on this faith — **Is·lam·ic** \is-ˈlä-mik, iz-, -ˈla-\ *adj*

is·land \ˈī-lənd\ *n* [ME *iland*, fr. OE *īgland*, fr. *īg* island + *land* land] **1** : a body of land smaller than a continent surrounded by water **2** : something resembling an island in its isolation

is·land·er \ˈī-lən-dər\ *n* : a native or inhabitant of an island

isle \ˈī(-ə)l\ *n* : ISLAND; *esp* : a small island

is·let \ˈī-lət\ *n* : a small island

ism *n* : a distinctive doctrine, cause, or theory

-ism \ˌi-zəm\ *n suffix* **1** : act : practice : process ⟨criti*cism*⟩ **2** : manner of action or behavior characteristic of a (specified) person or thing ⟨fanatic*ism*⟩ **3** : state : condition : property ⟨dual*ism*⟩ **4** : abnormal state or condition ⟨alcohol*ism*⟩ **5** : doctrine : theory : cult ⟨Buddh*ism*⟩ **6** : adherence to a set of principles ⟨stoic*ism*⟩ **7** : prejudice or discrimination on the basis of a (specified) attribute ⟨rac*ism*⟩ ⟨sex*ism*⟩ **8** : characteristic or peculiar feature or trait ⟨colloquial*ism*⟩

iso·bar \ˈī-sə-ˌbär\ *n* : a line on a map connecting places of equal barometric pressure — **iso·bar·ic** \ˌī-sə-ˈbär-ik, -ˈber-\ *adj*

isobars

iso·late \ˈī-sə-ˌlāt\ *vb* **-lat·ed; -lat·ing** [fr. *isolated* set apart, fr. F *isolé*, fr. It *isolato*, fr. *isola* island, fr. L *insula*] : to place or keep by itself : separate from others — **iso·la·tion** \ˌī-sə-ˈlā-shən\ *n*

isolated *adj* **1** : occurring alone or once : UNIQUE **2** : SPORADIC

iso·la·tion·ism \ˌī-sə-ˈlā-shə-ˌni-zəm\ *n* : a policy of national isolation by abstention from international political and economic relations — **iso·la·tion·ist** \-shə-nist\ *n or adj*

iso·mer \ˈī-sə-mər\ *n* : any of two or more chemical compounds that contain the same numbers of atoms of the same elements but differ in structural arrangement and properties — **iso·mer·ic** \ˌī-sə-ˈmer-ik\ *adj* — **isom·er·ism** \ī-ˈsä-mə-ˌri-zəm\ *n*

iso·met·rics \ˌī-sə-ˈme-triks\ *n sing or pl* : exercise involving a series of brief and intense contractions of muscles against each other or against an immovable resistance — **iso·met·ric** *adj*

iso·prene \ˈī-sə-ˌprēn\ *n* : a hydrocarbon used esp. in making synthetic rubber

isos·ce·les \ī-ˈsä-sə-ˌlēz\ *adj* : having two equal sides ⟨an ∼ triangle⟩

iso·therm \ˈī-sə-ˌthərm\ *n* : a line on a map connecting points having the same temperature

iso·ther·mal \ˌī-sə-ˈthər-məl\ *adj* : of, relating to, or marked by equality of temperature

iso·tope \ˈī-sə-ˌtōp\ *n* [Gk *isos* equal + *topos* place] : any of the forms of a chemical element that differ chiefly in the number of neutrons in an atom — **iso·to·pic** \ˌī-sə-ˈtä-pik, -ˈtō-\ *adj* — **iso·to·pi·cal·ly** \-ˈtä-pi-k(ə-)lē, -ˈtō-\ *adv*

Isr *abbr* Israel; Israeli

Is·ra·el·ite \ˈiz-rē-ə-ˌlīt\ *n* : a member of the Hebrew people descended from Jacob

is·su·ance \ˈi-shü-wəns\ *n* : the act of issuing or giving out esp. officially

¹is·sue \ˈi-shü\ *n* [ME, exit, proceeds, fr. AF, fr. *issir* to come out, go out, fr. L. *exire*, fr. *ire* to go] **1** : the action of going, coming, or flowing out : EGRESS, EMERGENCE **2** : EXIT, OUTLET, VENT **3** : OFFSPRING, PROGENY **4** : OUTCOME, RESULT **5** : a point of debate or controversy; *also* : the point at which an unsettled matter is ready for a decision **6** : a discharge (as of blood) from the body **7** : something coming forth from a specified source **8** : the act of officially giving out or printing : PUBLICATION; *also* : the quantity of things given out at one time

²issue *vb* **is·sued; is·su·ing 1** : to go, come, or flow out **2** : to come forth or cause to come forth : EMERGE, DISCHARGE, EMIT **3** : ACCRUE **4** : to descend from a specified parent or ancestor **5** : to result in **6** : to put forth or distribute officially **7** : PUBLISH **8** : EMANATE, RESULT — **is·su·er** *n*

¹-ist *n suffix* **1** : one that performs a (specified) action ⟨cyclist⟩ : one that makes or produces ⟨novelist⟩ **2** : one that plays a (specified) musical instrument ⟨harpist⟩ **3** : one that operates a (specified) mechanical instrument or contrivance ⟨machinist⟩ **4** : one that specializes in a (specified) art or science or skill ⟨geologist⟩ **5** : one that adheres to or advocates a (specified) doctrine or system or code of behavior ⟨socialist⟩ or that of a (specified) individual ⟨Darwinist⟩

²-ist *adj suffix* : -ISTIC

isth·mi·an \'is-mē-ən\ *adj* : of, relating to, or situated in or near an isthmus

isth·mus \'is-məs\ *n* : a narrow strip of land connecting two larger portions of land

¹it \'it, ət\ *pron* **1** : that one — used of a lifeless thing, a plant, a person or animal, or an abstract entity ⟨∼'s a big building⟩ ⟨∼'s a shade tree⟩ ⟨who is ∼⟩ ⟨beauty is everywhere and ∼ is a source of joy⟩ **2** — used as a subject of an impersonal verb that expresses a condition or action without reference to an agent ⟨∼ is raining⟩ **3** — used as an anticipatory subject or object ⟨∼'s good to see you⟩

²it \'it\ *n* : the player in a game who performs the principal action of the game (as trying to find others in hide-and-seek)

It *abbr* Italian; Italy

ital *abbr* italic; italicized

Ital *abbr* Italian

Ital·ian \i-'tal-yən\ *n* **1** : a native or inhabitant of Italy **2** : the language of Italy — **Italian** *adj*

ital·ic \i-'ta-lik, ī-\ *adj* : relating to type in which the letters slope up toward the right (as in "*italic*") — **italic** *n*

ital·i·cise *Brit var of* ITALICIZE

ital·i·cize \i-'ta-lə-,sīz, ī-\ *vb* **-cized; -ciz·ing** : to print in italics — **ital·i·ci·za·tion** \-,ta-lə-sə-'zā-shən\ *n*

itch \'ich\ *n* **1** : an uneasy irritating skin sensation that evokes a desire to scratch the affected area **2** : a skin disorder accompanied by an itch **3** : a persistent desire — **itch** *vb* — **itchy** *adj*

-ite *n suffix* **1** : native : resident ⟨suburbanite⟩ **2** : adherent : follower ⟨Leninite⟩ **3** : product ⟨metabolite⟩ **4** : mineral : rock ⟨quartzite⟩

item \'ī-təm\ *n* [L, likewise, also] **1** : a separate particular in a list, account, or series : ARTICLE **2** : a separate piece of news (as in a newspaper)

item·ise *Brit var of* ITEMIZE

item·ize \'ī-tə-,mīz\ *vb* **-ized; -iz·ing** : to set down in detail : LIST — **item·i·za·tion** \,ī-tə-mə-'zā-shən\ *n*

it·er·ate \'i-tə-,rāt\ *vb* **-at·ed; -at·ing** : REITERATE, REPEAT

it·er·a·tion \,i-tə-'rā-shən\ *n* **1** : REPETITION; *esp* : a computational process in which a series of operations is repeated until a condition is met **2** : one repetition of the series of operations in iteration **3** : VERSION

itin·er·ant \ī-'ti-nə-rənt, ə-\ *adj* : traveling from place to place; *esp* : covering a circuit ⟨an ∼ preacher⟩

itin·er·ary \ī-'ti-nə-,rer-ē, ə-\ *n, pl* **-ar·ies 1** : the route of a journey or the proposed outline of one **2** : a travel diary **3** : GUIDEBOOK

its \'its\ *adj* : of or relating to it or itself

it·self \it-'self\ *pron* : that identical one — used reflexively, for emphasis, or in absolute constructions

-ity *n suffix* : quality : state : degree ⟨alkalinity⟩

IUD \,ī-(,)yü-'dē\ *n* : INTRAUTERINE DEVICE

IV \,ī-'vē\ *n, pl* **IVs** [*intravenous*] : an apparatus used to administer a fluid (as of nutrients) intravenously; *also* : a fluid administered by IV

-ive *adj suffix* : that performs or tends toward an (indicated) action ⟨corrective⟩

ivo·ry \'ī-vrē, -və-rē\ *n, pl* **-ries** [ME *ivorie*, fr. AF *ivoire, ivurie*, fr. L *eboreus* of ivory, fr. *ebur* ivory] **1** : the hard creamy-white material composing the tusks of an elephant or walrus **2** : a pale yellow color **3** : something made of ivory or of a similar substance

ivory tower *n* **1** : an impractical lack of concern with urgent problems **2** : a place of learning

ivy \'ī-vē\ *n, pl* **ivies** : a trailing woody evergreen vine with small black berries that is related to ginseng

IWW *abbr* Industrial Workers of the World

-ize *vb suffix* **1** : cause to be or conform to or resemble ⟨Americanize⟩ : cause to be formed into ⟨unionize⟩ **2** : subject to a (specified) action ⟨satirize⟩ **3** : saturate, treat, or combine with ⟨macadamize⟩ **4** : treat like ⟨idolize⟩ **5** : become : become like ⟨crystallize⟩ **6** : be productive in or of : engage in a (specified) activity ⟨philosophize⟩ **7** : adopt or spread the manner of activity or the teaching of ⟨Christianize⟩

J

¹j \'jā\ *n, pl* **j's** *or* **js** \jāz\ *often cap* : the 10th letter of the English alphabet

²j *abbr, often cap* **1** jack **2** journal **3** judge **4** justice

¹jab \'jab\ *vb* **jabbed; jab·bing** : to thrust quickly or abruptly : POKE

²jab *n* : a usu. short straight punch

jab·ber \'ja-bər\ *vb* : to talk rapidly, indistinctly, or unintelligibly : CHATTER — **jabber** *n* — **jab·ber·er** *n*

jab·ber·wocky \'ja-bər-,wä-kē\ *n* : meaningless speech or writing

ja·bot \zha-'bō, 'ja-,bō\ *n* : a ruffle worn down the front of a dress or shirt

jac·a·ran·da \,ja-kə-'ran-də\ *n* : any of a genus of pinnate-leaved tropical American trees with clusters of showy blue flowers

¹jack \'jak\ *n* **1** : a mechanical device; *esp* : one used to raise a heavy body a short distance **2** : a male donkey **3** : a small target ball in lawn bowling **4** : a small national flag flown by a ship **5** : a small 6-pointed metal object used in a game (**jacks**) **6** : a playing card bearing the figure of a soldier or servant **7** : a socket into which a plug is inserted for connecting electric circuits

²jack *vb* **1** : to raise by means of a jack **2** : INCREASE ⟨∼ up prices⟩

jack·al \'ja-kəl\ *n* [Turk *çakal*, fr. Pers *shaqāl*] : any of several mammals of Asia and Africa related to the wolves

jack·a·napes \'ja-kə-,nāps\ *n* **1** : MONKEY, APE **2** : an impudent or conceited person

jack·ass \'jak-,as\ *n* **1** : DONKEY; *esp* : a male donkey **2** : a stupid person : FOOL

jack·boot \-,büt\ *n* **1** : a heavy military boot of glossy black leather extending above the knee **2** : a laceless military boot reaching to the calf

jack·daw \'jak-,do\ *n* : a black and gray Old World crow-like bird

jack·et \'ja-kət\ *n* [ME *jaket*, fr. AF *jackés*, pl., dim. of MF *jaque* short jacket, fr. *jacques* peasant, fr. the name *Jacques* James] **1** : a garment for the upper body usu. having a front opening, collar, and sleeves **2** : an outer covering or casing ⟨a book ∼⟩

Jack Frost *n* : frost or frosty weather personified

jack·ham·mer \'jak-,ha-mər\ *n* : a pneumatic percussion tool for drilling rock or breaking pavement

jack–in–the–box *n, pl* **jack–in–the–boxes** *or* **jacks–in–the–box** : a toy consisting of a small box out of which a figure springs when the lid is raised

jack–in–the–pulpit *n, pl* **jack–in–the–pulpits** *also* **jacks–in–the–pulpit** : a No. American spring-flowering woodland herb having an upright club-shaped spadix arched over by a green and purple spathe

¹jack·knife \'jak-,nīf\ *n* **1** : a large pocketknife **2** : a dive in which the diver bends from the waist and touches the ankles before straightening out

DICTIONARY

²jackknife *vb* : to fold like a jackknife ⟨the trailer truck *jackknifed*⟩

jack·leg \'jak-,leg\ *adj* **1** : lacking skill or training **2** : MAKESHIFT

jack–of–all–trades *n, pl* **jacks–of–all–trades** : one who is able to do passable work at various tasks

jack–o'–lan·tern \'ja-kə-,lan-tərn\ *n* : a lantern made of a pumpkin cut to look like a human face

jack·pot \'jak-,pät\ *n* **1** : a large sum of money formed by the accumulation of stakes from previous play (as in poker) **2** : an impressive and often unexpected success or reward

jack·rab·bit \-,ra-bət\ *n* : any of several large hares of western No. America with very long ears and hind legs

Jack Russell terrier \'jak-'rə-səl-\ *n* : any of a breed of small terriers having a white coat with dark markings

jack·straw \-,strò\ *n* **1** *pl* : a game in which straws or thin sticks are let fall in a heap and each player in turn tries to remove them one at a time without disturbing the rest **2** : one of the pieces used in jackstraws

jack–tar \-'tär\ *n, often cap* : SAILOR

Ja·cob's ladder \'jā-kəbz-\ *n* : any of several perennial herbs related to phlox that have pinnate leaves and blue or white bell-shaped flowers

jac·quard \'ja-,kärd\ *n, often cap* : a fabric of intricate var-iegated weave or pattern

¹jade \'jād\ *n* **1** : a broken-down, vicious, or worthless horse **2** : a disreputable woman

²jade *vb* **jad·ed; jad·ing 1** : to wear out by overwork or abuse **2** : to become weary ♦ *Synonyms* EXHAUST, FA-TIGUE, TIRE

³jade *n* [F, fr. obs. Sp (*piedra de la*) *ijada,* lit., loin stone; fr. the belief that jade cures renal colic] : a usu. green gem-stone that takes a high polish

jad·ed *adj* : made dull, apathetic, or cynical by experience or by surfeit

¹jag \'jag\ *n* : a sharp projecting part

²jag *n* : SPREE ⟨a crying ∼⟩

jag·ged \'ja-gəd\ *adj* : sharply notched

jag·uar \'ja-,gwär\ *n* : a black-spotted tropical American cat that is larger and stockier than the Old World leopard

jaguar

jai alai \'hī-,lī\ *n* [Sp, fr. Basque, fr. *jai* festival + *alai* merry] : a court game played by usu. two or four players with a ball and a curved wicker basket strapped to the wrist

jail \'jāl\ *n* [ME *jaiole,* fr. AF *gaiole, jaiole,* fr. LL *caveola,* dim. of L *cavea* cage] : PRISON; *esp* : one for persons held in lawful custody — **jail** *vb*

jail·bird \-,bərd\ *n* : a habitual criminal

jail·break \-,brāk\ *n* : a forcible escape from jail

jail·er *also* **jail·or** \'jā-lər\ *n* : a keeper of a jail

jal·ap \'ja-ləp, 'jä-\ *n* : a powdered purgative drug from the root of a Mexican plant related to the morning glory; *also* : this root or plant

ja·la·pe·ño \,hä-lə-'pān-(,)yō\ *n* : a small plump dark green chili pepper

ja·lopy \jə-'lä-pē\ *n, pl* **ja·lop·ies** : a dilapidated vehicle (as an automobile)

jal·ou·sie \'ja-lə-sē\ *n* [F, lit., jealousy] : a blind, window, or door with adjustable horizontal slats or louvers

¹jam \'jam\ *vb* **jammed; jam·ming 1** : to press into a close or tight position **2** : to cause to become wedged so as to be unworkable; *also* : to make or become unworkable through the jamming of a movable part **3** : to push forc-

ibly ⟨∼ on the brakes⟩ **4** : CRUSH, BRUISE ⟨*jammed* a finger in the door⟩ **5** : to make unintelligible by sending out interfering signals or messages **6** : to take part in a jam session — **jam·mer** *n*

²jam *n* **1** : a crowded mass that impedes or blocks ⟨traffic ∼⟩ **2** : a difficult state of affairs

³jam *n* : a food made by boiling fruit and sugar to a thick consistency

Jam *abbr* Jamaica

jamb \'jam\ *n* [ME *jambe,* fr. AF *jambe, gambe,* lit., leg] : an upright piece forming the side of an opening (as of a door)

jam·ba·laya \,jəm-bə-'lī-ə\ *n* [LaF] : rice cooked with ham, sausage, chicken, shrimp, or oysters and seasoned with herbs

jam·bo·ree \,jam-bə-'rē\ *n* : a large festive gathering

James \'jāmz\ *n* — see BIBLE table

jam–pack \'jam-'pak\ *vb* : to pack tightly or to excess

jam session *n* : an impromptu performance esp. by jazz musicians

Jan *abbr* January

jan·gle \'jaŋ-gəl\ *vb* **jan·gled; jan·gling** : to make a harsh or discordant sound — **jangle** *n*

jan·i·tor \'ja-nə-tər\ *n* [L, doorkeeper, fr. *janus* arch, gate] : a person who has the care of a building — **jan·i·to·ri·al** \,ja-nə-'tòr-ē-əl\ *adj*

Jan·u·ary \'ja-nyə-,wer-ē\ *n* [ME *Januarie,* fr. L *Januarius,* first month of the ancient Roman year, fr. *Janus,* two-faced god of gates and beginnings] : the 1st month of the year

¹ja·pan \jə-'pan\ *n* : a varnish giving a hard brilliant finish

²japan *vb* **ja·panned; ja·pan·ning** : to cover with a coat of japan

Jap·a·nese \,ja-pə-'nēz, -'nēs\ *n, pl* **Japanese 1** : a native or inhabitant of Japan **2** : the language of Japan — **Japanese** *adj*

Japanese beetle *n* : a small metallic green and brown scarab beetle introduced from Japan that is a pest on the roots of grasses as a grub and on foliage and fruits as an adult

¹jape \'jāp\ *vb* **japed; jap·ing 1** : JOKE **2** : MOCK

²jape *n* : JEST, GIBE

¹jar \'jär\ *vb* **jarred; jar·ring 1** : to make a harsh or dis-cordant sound **2** : to have a harsh or disagreeable effect **3** : VIBRATE, SHAKE

²jar *n* **1** : a state of conflict **2** : a harsh discordant sound **3** : JOLT **4** : a painful effect : SHOCK

³jar *n* : a widemouthed container usu. of glass or earthen-ware

jar·di·niere \,jär-də-'nir\ *n* : an ornamental stand for plants or flowers

jar·gon \'jär-gən\ *n* **1** : confused unintelligible language **2** : the special vocabulary of a particular group or activi-ty **3** : obscure and often pretentious language

Jas *abbr* James

jas·mine \'jaz-mən\ *also* **jes·sa·mine** \'jes-mən, 'je-sə-\ *n* [MF *jasmin,* fr. Ar *yāsamīn,* fr. Pers] : any of various climbing shrubs with fragrant flowers

jas·per \'jas-pər\ *n* : a usu. red, yellow, or brown opaque quartz

jaun·dice \'jòn-dəs\ *n* : yellowish discoloration of skin, tis-sues, and body fluids by bile pigments; *also* : an abnormal condition marked by jaundice

jaun·diced \-dəst\ *adj* **1** : affected with or as if with jaun-dice **2** : exhibiting envy, distaste, or hostility

jaunt \'jònt\ *n* : a short trip usu. for pleasure

jaun·ty \'jòn-tē\ *adj* **jaun·ti·er; -est** : sprightly in manner or appearance : LIVELY — **jaun·ti·ly** \-tə-lē\ *adv* — **jaun·ti·ness** \-tē-nəs\ *n*

jav·e·lin \'ja-və-lən\ *n* **1** : a light spear **2** : a slender shaft thrown for distance in a track-and-field contest

¹jaw \'jò\ *n* **1** : either of the bony or cartilaginous struc-tures that support the soft tissues enclosing the mouth and that usu. bear teeth **2** : the parts forming the walls of the mouth and serving to open and close it — usu. used in pl. **3** : one of a pair of movable parts for holding or crushing something — **jawed** \'jòd\ *adj*

²jaw *vb* : to talk abusively, indignantly, or at length

¹jaw·bone \-,bōn\ *n* : JAW 1

²jawbone *vb* : to talk forcefully and persuasively

jaw·break·er \-ˌbrā-kər\ *n* **1** : a word difficult to pronounce **2** : a round hard candy

jaw–drop·ping \ˈjȯ-ˌdrä-piŋ\ *adj* : causing great surprise or astonishment

jaw·less fish \ˈjȯ-ləs-\ *n* : any of a group of primitive vertebrates (as lampreys) without jaws

jay \ˈjā\ *n* : any of various noisy brightly colored often largely blue birds smaller than the related crows

jay·bird \ˈjā-ˌbərd\ *n* : JAY

jay·vee \ˈjā-ˈvē\ *n* **1** : JUNIOR VARSITY **2** : a member of a junior varsity team

jay·walk \ˈjā-ˌwȯk\ *vb* : to cross a street carelessly without regard for traffic regulations — **jay·walk·er** *n*

¹**jazz** \ˈjaz\ *n* **1** : American music characterized by improvisation, syncopated rhythms, and contrapuntal ensemble playing **2** : empty talk **3** : similar but unspecified things : STUFF

²**jazz** *vb* : ENLIVEN ⟨∼ things up⟩

jazzy \ˈja-zē\ *adj* **jazz·i·er**; **-est** **1** : having the characteristics of jazz **2** : marked by unrestraint, animation, or flashiness

JCS *abbr* joint chiefs of staff

jct *abbr* junction

JD *abbr* **1** [L *juris doctor*] doctor of jurisprudence; doctor of law **2** [L *jurum doctor*] doctor of laws **3** justice department **4** juvenile delinquent

jeal·ous \ˈje-ləs\ *adj* **1** : demanding complete devotion **2** : suspicious of a rival or of one believed to enjoy an advantage **3** : VIGILANT — **jeal·ous·ly** *adv* — **jeal·ou·sy** \-lə-sē\ *n*

jeans \ˈjēnz\ *n pl* [pl. of *jean* twilled cloth, short for *jean fustian*, fr. ME *Gene* Genoa, Italy] : pants made of durable twilled cotton cloth

jeep \ˈjēp\ *n* : a small four-wheel drive general-purpose motor vehicle used in World War II

¹**jeer** \ˈjir\ *vb* : to speak or cry out in derision : MOCK

²**jeer** *n* : TAUNT

Je·ho·vah \ji-ˈhō-və\ *n* : GOD 1

je·hu \ˈjē-hü, -hyü\ *n* : a driver of a coach or cab

je·june \ji-ˈjün\ *adj* [L *jejunus* empty of food, hungry, meager] : lacking interest or significance : DULL

je·ju·num \ji-ˈjü-nəm\ *n* [L] : the section of the small intestine between the duodenum and the ileum — **je·ju·nal** \-ˈjü-nᵊl\ *adj*

jell \ˈjel\ *vb* **1** : to come to the consistency of jelly **2** : to take shape ⟨my idea began to ∼⟩

jel·ly \ˈje-lē\ *n, pl* **jellies** **1** : a food with a soft elastic consistency due usu. to the presence of gelatin or pectin; *esp* : a fruit product made by boiling sugar and the juice of a fruit **2** : a substance resembling jelly — **jelly** *vb* — **jel·ly·like** *adj*

jelly bean *n* : a bean-shaped candy

jel·ly·fish \ˈje-lē-ˌfish\ *n* : a marine coelenterate with a nearly transparent jellylike body and stinging tentacles

jen·net \ˈje-nət\ *n* **1** : a small Spanish horse **2** : a female donkey

jen·ny \ˈje-nē\ *n, pl* **jennies** : a female bird or donkey

jeop·ar·dy \ˈje-pər-dē\ *n* [ME *jeopardie*, fr. AF *juparti, jeuparti* alternative, lit., divided game] : exposure to death, loss, or injury ✦ *Synonyms* PERIL, HAZARD, RISK, DANGER — **jeop·ar·dize** \-ˌdīz\ *vb*

Jer *abbr* Jeremiah; Jeremias

jer·e·mi·ad \ˌjer-ə-ˈmī-əd, -ˌad\ *n* : a prolonged lamentation or complaint; *also* : a cautionary or angry harangue

Jer·e·mi·ah \ˌjer-ə-ˈmī-ə\ *n* — see BIBLE table

Jer·e·mi·as \ˌjer-ə-ˈmī-əs\ *n* : JEREMIAH

¹**jerk** \ˈjərk\ *n* **1** : a short quick pull or twist : TWITCH **2** : an annoyingly stupid or foolish person — **jerk·i·ly** \ˈjər-kə-lē\ *adv* — **jerky** \ˈjər-kē\ *adj*

²**jerk** *vb* **1** : to give a sharp quick push, pull, or twist **2** : to move in short abrupt motions

jer·kin \ˈjər-kən\ *n* : a close-fitting usu. sleeveless jacket

jerk·wa·ter \ˈjərk-ˌwȯ-tər, -ˌwä-\ *adj* [fr. *jerkwater* rural train] : of minor importance : INSIGNIFICANT ⟨∼ towns⟩

jer·ry–built \ˈjer-ē-ˌbilt\ *adj* : built cheaply and flimsily

jer·ry–rigged \-ˌrigd\ *adj* : organized or constructed in a crude or improvised manner

jer·sey \ˈjər-zē\ *n, pl* **jerseys** [*Jersey*, one of the Channel islands] **1** : a plain weft-knitted fabric **2** : a close-fitting knitted shirt **3** *often cap* : any of a breed of small usu. fawn-colored dairy cattle

Jersey barrier *n* : a concrete slab that is used with others to block or reroute traffic or to divide a highway

Je·ru·sa·lem artichoke \jə-ˈrü-sə-ləm-\ *n* : a No. American sunflower widely grown for its edible tubers that are used as a vegetable; *also* : its tubers

jess \ˈjes\ *n* : a leg strap by which a captive bird of prey may be controlled

jessamine *var of* JASMINE

jest \ˈjest\ *n* **1** : an act intended to provoke laughter **2** : a witty remark **3** : a frivolous mood ⟨said in ∼⟩ — **jest** *vb*

jest·er \ˈjes-tər\ *n* : a retainer formerly kept to provide casual entertainment

¹**jet** \ˈjet\ *n* : a velvet-black coal that takes a good polish and is often used for jewelry

²**jet** *vb* **jet·ted; jet·ting** : to spout or emit in a stream

³**jet** *n* **1** : a forceful rush (as of liquid or gas) through a narrow opening; *also* : a nozzle for a jet of fluid **2** : a jet-propelled airplane

⁴**jet** *vb* **jet·ted; jet·ting** : to travel by jet

jet lag *n* : a condition that is marked esp. by fatigue and irritability and occurs following a long flight through several time zones — **jet–lagged** *adj*

jet·lin·er \ˈjet-ˌlī-nər\ *n* : a jet-propelled airliner

jet·port \-ˌpȯrt\ *n* : an airport designed to handle jets

jet–pro·pelled \ˌjet-prə-ˈpeld\ *adj* : driven by an engine (**jet engine**) that produces propulsion (**jet propulsion**) by the rearward discharge of a jet of fluid (as heated air and exhaust gases)

jet·sam \ˈjet-səm\ *n* : jettisoned goods; *esp* : such goods washed ashore

jet set *n* : an international group of wealthy people who frequent fashionable resorts

jet stream *n* : a long narrow high-altitude current of high-speed winds blowing generally from the west

jet·ti·son \ˈje-tə-sən\ *vb* **1** : to throw (goods) overboard to lighten a ship or aircraft in distress **2** : DISCARD — **jettison** *n*

jet·ty \ˈje-tē\ *n, pl* **jetties** **1** : a pier built to influence the current or to protect a harbor **2** : a landing wharf

jeu d'es·prit \zhœ-des-ˈprē\ *n, pl* **jeux d'esprit** *same*\ [F, lit., play of the mind] : a witty comment or composition

Jew \ˈjü\ *n* **1** : ISRAELITE **2** : one whose religion is Judaism — **Jew·ish** *adj*

¹**jew·el** \ˈjü-əl\ *n* [ME *juel*, fr. AF, dim. of *ju, jeu* game, play, fr. L *jocus* game, joke] **1** : an ornament of precious metal **2** : GEMSTONE, GEM

²**jewel** *vb* **-eled** *or* **-elled; -el·ing** *or* **-el·ling** : to adorn or equip with jewels

jewel box *n* : a thin plastic case for a CD or DVD

jew·el·er *or* **jew·el·ler** \ˈjü-ə-lər\ *n* : a person who makes or deals in jewelry and related articles

jew·el·lery *chiefly Brit var of* JEWELRY

jew·el·ry \ˈjü-əl-rē\ *n* : JEWELS; *esp* : objects of precious metal set with gems and worn for personal adornment

Jew·ry \ˈjür-ē, ˈjü-ər-ē, ˈjü-rē\ *n* : the Jewish people

jg *abbr* junior grade

¹**jib** \ˈjib\ *n* : a triangular sail set on a line running from the bow to the mast

²**jib** *vb* **jibbed; jib·bing** : to refuse to proceed further

¹**jibe** *var of* GIBE

²**jibe** \ˈjīb\ *vb* **jibed; jib·ing** : to be in accord : AGREE

ji·ca·ma \ˈhē-kə-mə\ *n* : an edible starchy tuber of a tropical American vine of the legume family

jif·fy \ˈji-fē\ *n, pl* **jiffies** : MOMENT, INSTANT ⟨I'll be ready in a ∼⟩

¹**jig** \ˈjig\ *n* **1** : a lively dance in triple rhythm **2** : TRICK, GAME ⟨the ∼ is up⟩ **3** : a device used to hold work during manufacture or assembly

²**jig** *vb* **jigged; jig·ging** : to dance a jig

jig·ger \ˈji-gər\ *n* : a measure usu. holding 1 to 2 ounces (30 to 60 milliliters) used in mixing drinks

jig·gle \ˈji-gəl\ *vb* **jig·gled; jig·gling** : to move with quick little jerks — **jiggle** *n*

jig·saw \ˈjig-ˌsȯ\ *n* : SCROLL SAW 2

jigsaw puzzle *n* : a puzzle consisting of small irregularly cut pieces to be fitted together to form a picture

ji·had \ji-ˈhäd, -ˈhad\ *n* **1** : a Muslim holy war **2** : CRUSADE 2

¹**jilt** \ˈjilt\ *vb* : to drop (as a lover) capriciously or unfeelingly

²jilt *n* : one who jilts a lover

jim crow \'jim-'krō\ *n, often cap J&C* : discrimination against blacks esp. by legal enforcement or traditional sanctions — **jim crow** *adj, often cap J&C* — **jim crow·ism** \-'krō-ˌi-zəm\ *n, often cap J&C*

jim–dan·dy \'jim-'dan-dē\ *n* : something excellent of its kind — **jim–dandy** *adj*

jim·mies \'ji-mēz\ *n pl* : tiny rod-shaped bits of usu. chocolate-flavored candy often sprinkled on ice cream

¹jim·my \'ji-mē\ *n, pl* **jimmies** : a small crowbar

²jimmy *vb* **jim·mied; jim·my·ing** : to force open with a jimmy

jim·son·weed \'jim-sən-ˌwēd\ *n, often cap* : a coarse poisonous weed related to the tomato that has large trumpet-shaped white or violet flowers

¹jin·gle \'jiŋ-gəl\ *vb* **jin·gled; jin·gling** : to make a light clinking or tinkling sound

²jingle *n* **1** : a light clinking or tinkling sound **2** : a short verse or song with catchy repetition

jin·go·ism \'jiŋ-gō-ˌi-zəm\ *n* : extreme chauvinism or nationalism marked esp. by a belligerent foreign policy — **jin·go·ist** \-ist\ *n* — **jin·go·is·tic** \ˌjiŋ-gō-'is-tik\ *adj*

jin·rik·sha \jin-'rik-ˌshö\ *n* : RICKSHA

¹jinx \'jiŋks\ *n* : one that brings bad luck

²jinx *vb* : to foredoom to failure or misfortune

jit·ney \'jit-nē\ *n, pl* **jitneys** : a small bus that serves a regular route on a flexible schedule

jit·ter·bug \'ji-tər-ˌbəg\ *n* : a dance in which couples two-step, balance, and twirl vigorously in standardized patterns — **jitterbug** *vb*

jit·ters \'ji-tərz\ *n pl* : extreme nervousness — **jit·tery** \-tə-rē\ *adj*

¹jive \'jīv\ *n* **1** : swing music or dancing performed to it **2** : glib, deceptive, or foolish talk **3** : the jargon of jazz enthusiasts

²jive *vb* **jived; jiv·ing** **1** : KID, TEASE **2** : to dance to or play jive

Jn *or* **Jno** *abbr* John

Jo *abbr* Joel

¹job \'jäb\ *n* **1** : a piece of work **2** : something that has to be done : TASK **3** : a regular remunerative position — **job·less** *adj*

²job *vb* **jobbed; job·bing** **1** : to do occasional pieces of work for hire **2** : to hire or let by the job

Job \'jōb\ *n* — see BIBLE table

job action *n* : a protest action by workers to force compliance with demands

job·ber \'jä-bər\ *n* **1** : a person who buys goods and then sells them to other dealers : MIDDLEMAN **2** : a person who does work by the job

job·hold·er \'jäb-ˌhōl-dər\ *n* : one having a regular job

jock \'jäk\ *n* [*jockstrap*] : ATHLETE; *esp* : a school or college athlete

¹jock·ey \'jä-kē\ *n, pl* **jockeys** : one who rides a horse esp. as a professional in a race

²jockey *vb* **jock·eyed; jock·ey·ing** : to maneuver or manipulate by adroit or devious means

jock·strap \'jäk-ˌstrap\ *n* [E slang *jock* penis] : ATHLETIC SUPPORTER

jo·cose \jō-'kōs\ *adj* **1** : MERRY **2** : HUMOROUS ♦ **Synonyms** JOCULAR, FACETIOUS, WITTY

joc·u·lar \'jä-kyə-lər\ *adj* : marked by jesting : PLAYFUL — **joc·u·lar·i·ty** \ˌjäk-yə-'lar-ə-tē\ *n* — **joc·u·lar·ly** *adv*

jo·cund \'jä-kənd\ *adj* : marked by mirth or cheerfulness

jodh·pur \'jäd-pər\ *n* **1** *pl* : riding breeches loose above the knee and tight-fitting below **2** : an ankle-high boot fastened with a strap

Joe Blow \'jō-\ *n* : an average or ordinary man

Jo·el \'jō-əl\ *n* — see BIBLE table

Joe Six–Pack \'jō-\ *n* : a blue-collar worker

¹jog \'jäg\ *vb* **jogged; jog·ging** **1** : to give a slight shake or push to **2** : to go at a slow monotonous pace **3** : to run or ride at a slow trot — **jog·ger** *n*

²jog *n* **1** : a slight shake **2** : a jogging movement or pace

³jog *n* **1** : a projecting or retreating part of a line or surface **2** : a brief abrupt change in direction

jog·gle \'jä-gəl\ *vb* **jog·gled; jog·gling** : to shake slightly — **joggle** *n*

john \'jän\ *n* **1** : TOILET **2** : a prostitute's client

John \'jän\ *n* — see BIBLE table

john·ny \'jä-nē\ *n, pl* **johnnies** : a short-sleeved gown opening in the back that is worn by hospital patients

John·ny–jump–up \ˌjä-nē-'jəmp-ˌəp\ *n* : any of various small-flowered cultivated pansies

joie de vi·vre \ˌzhwä-də-'vēvrᵊ\ *n* [F] : keen enjoyment of life

join \'join\ *vb* **1** : to come or bring together so as to form a unit **2** : to come or bring into close association **3** : to become a member of **4** : ADJOIN **5** : to take part in a collective activity

join·er \'joi-nər\ *n* **1** : a worker who constructs articles by joining pieces of wood **2** : a gregarious person who joins many organizations

¹joint \'joint\ *n* **1** : the point of contact between bones of an animal skeleton with the parts that surround and support it **2** : a cut of meat suitable for roasting **3** : a place where two things or parts are connected **4** : ESTABLISHMENT; *esp* : a shabby or disreputable establishment **5** : a marijuana cigarette — **joint·ed** *adj*

²joint *adj* **1** : UNITED **2** : common to two or more — **joint·ly** *adv*

³joint *vb* **1** : to unite by or provide with a joint **2** : to separate the joints of

joist \'joist\ *n* : any of the small beams ranged parallel from wall to wall in a building to support a floor or ceiling

floor joists

¹joke \'jōk\ *n* : something said or done to provoke laughter; *esp* : a brief narrative with a humorous climax

²joke *vb* **joked; jok·ing** : to make jokes — **jok·ing·ly** *adv*

jok·er \'jō-kər\ *n* **1** : a person who jokes **2** : an extra card used in some card games **3** : a misleading part of an agreement that works to one party's disadvantage

jol·li·fi·ca·tion \ˌjä-li-fə-'kā-shən\ *n* : a festive celebration

jol·li·ty \'jä-lə-tē\ *n, pl* **-ties** : GAIETY, MERRIMENT

jol·ly \'jä-lē\ *adj* **jol·li·er; -est** : full of high spirits : MERRY

¹jolt \'jōlt\ *vb* **1** : to give a quick hard knock or blow to **2** : to move with a sudden jerky motion — **jolt·er** *n*

²jolt *n* **1** : an abrupt jerky blow or movement **2** : a sudden shock

Jon *abbr* Jonah; Jonas

Jo·nah \'jō-nə\ *n* — see BIBLE table

Jo·nas \'jō-nəs\ *n* : JONAH

¹jones \'jōnz\ *n* **1** *slang* : addiction to heroin **2** *slang* : HEROIN **3** *slang* : a craving for something

²jones *vb, slang* : to have a craving for something

jon·gleur \zhōⁿ-'glər\ *n* : an itinerant medieval minstrel

jon·quil \'jän-kwəl\ *n* [F *jonquille*, fr. Sp *junquillo*, dim. of *junco* reed, fr. L *juncus*] : a narcissus with fragrant clustered white or yellow flowers

josh \'jäsh\ *vb* : TEASE, JOKE

Josh *abbr* Joshua

Josh·ua \'jä-shə-wə\ *n* — see BIBLE table

Joshua tree *n* : a tall branched yucca of the southwestern U.S.

jos·tle \'jä-səl\ *vb* **jos·tled; jos·tling** **1** : to come in contact or into collision **2** : to make one's way by pushing and shoving

Jos·ue \'jä-shü-ē\ *n* : JOSHUA

¹jot \'jät\ *n* : the least bit : IOTA

²jot *vb* **jot·ted; jot·ting** : to write briefly and hurriedly

jot·ting \'jä-tiŋ\ *n* : a brief note

joule \'jül\ *n* : a unit of work or energy equal to the work done by a force of one newton acting through a distance of one meter

jounce \'jauns\ *vb* **jounced; jounc·ing** : JOLT — **jounce** *n*

jour *abbr* **1** journal **2** journeyman

jour·nal \'jər-nᵊl\ *n* [ME, service book containing the day hours, fr. AF *jurnal,* fr. *jurnal* daily, fr. L *diurnalis,* fr. *dies* day] **1** : a brief account of daily events **2** : a record of proceedings (as of a legislative body) **3** : a periodical (as a newspaper) dealing esp. with current events **4** : the part of a rotating axle or spindle that turns in a bearing

jour·nal·ese \ˌjər-nə-ˈlēz, -ˈlēs\ *n* : a style of writing held to be characteristic of newspapers

jour·nal·ism \ˈjər-nə-ˌli-zəm\ *n* **1** : the business of writing for, editing, or publishing periodicals (as newspapers) **2** : writing designed for or characteristic of newspapers — **jour·nal·ist** \-list\ *n* — **jour·nal·is·tic** \ˌjər-nə-ˈlis-tik\ *adj*

¹jour·ney \ˈjər-nē\ *n, pl* **journeys** [ME, fr. OF *journee* day's journey, fr. *jour* day] : a traveling from one place to another

²journey *vb* **jour·neyed; jour·ney·ing** : to go on a journey : TRAVEL

jour·ney·man \-mən\ *n* **1** : a worker who has learned a trade and works for another person **2** : an experienced reliable worker

¹joust \ˈjaust\ *vb* : to engage in a joust

²joust *n* : a combat on horseback between two knights with lances esp. as part of a tournament

jo·vial \ˈjō-vē-əl\ *adj* : marked by good humor — **jo·vi·al·i·ty** \ˌjō-vē-ˈa-lə-tē\ *n* — **jo·vi·al·ly** *adv*

¹jowl \ˈjaù-(ə)l\ *n* : loose flesh about the lower jaw or throat

²jowl *n* **1** : the lower jaw **2** : CHEEK

¹joy \ˈjòi\ *n* [ME, fr. AF *joie,* fr. L *gaudia*] **1** : a feeling of happiness that comes from success, good fortune, or a sense of well-being **2** : a source of happiness ♦ *Synonyms* BLISS, DELIGHT, ENJOYMENT, PLEASURE — **joy·less** *adj*

²joy *vb* : REJOICE

joy·ful \-fəl\ *adj* : experiencing, causing, or showing joy — **joy·ful·ly** *adv*

joy·ous \ˈjòi-əs\ *adj* : JOYFUL — **joy·ous·ly** *adv* — **joy·ous·ness** *n*

joy·ride \ˈjòi-ˌrīd\ *n* : a ride for pleasure often marked by reckless driving — **joyride** *vb* — **joy·rid·er** *n* — **joy·rid·ing** *n*

joy·stick \-ˌstik\ *n* : a control device (as for a computer) consisting of a lever capable of motion in two or more directions

JP *abbr* **1** jet propulsion **2** justice of the peace

JPEG \ˈjā-ˌpeg\ *n* [*Joint Photographic Experts Group*] : a computer file format for usu. high-quality digital images

Jr *abbr* junior

jt *or* **jnt** *abbr* joint

ju·bi·lant \ˈjü-bə-lənt\ *adj* [L *jubilans,* prp. of *jubilare* to rejoice] : EXULTANT — **ju·bi·lant·ly** *adv*

ju·bi·la·tion \ˌjü-bə-ˈlā-shən\ *n* : EXULTATION

ju·bi·lee \ˈjü-bə-ˌlē, ˌjü-bə-ˈlē\ *n* [ME, fr. AF & LL; AF *jubilé,* fr. LL *jubilaeus,* fr. LGk *iōbēlaios,* fr. Heb *yōbhēl* ram's horn, trumpet, jubilee] **1** : a 50th anniversary **2** : a season or occasion of celebration

ju·co \ˈjü-ˌkō\ *n, pl* **jucos** : JUNIOR COLLEGE; *also* : an athlete at a junior college

Jud *abbr* Judith

Ju·da·ic \jü-ˈdā-ik\ *also* **Ju·da·ical** \-ˈdā-ə-kəl\ *adj* : of, relating to, or characteristic of Jews or Judaism

Ju·da·ism \ˈjü-də-ˌi-zəm, -ˌdā-, -ˌdē-\ *n* : a religion developed among the ancient Hebrews and marked by belief in one God and by the moral and ceremonial laws of the Old Testament and the rabbinic tradition

Jude \ˈjüd\ *n* — see BIBLE table

Judg *abbr* Judges

¹judge \ˈjəj\ *vb* **judged; judg·ing** **1** : to form an authoritative opinion **2** : to decide as a judge : TRY **3** : to form an estimate or evaluation about something : THINK ♦ *Synonyms* CONCLUDE, DEDUCE, GATHER, INFER

²judge *n* **1** : a public official authorized to decide questions brought before a court **2** : UMPIRE **3** : one who gives an authoritative opinion : CRITIC — **judge·ship** *n*

Judges *n* — see BIBLE table

judg·ment *or* **judge·ment** \ˈjəj-mənt\ *n* **1** : a decision or opinion given after judging; *esp* : a formal decision given by a court **2** *cap* : the final judging of mankind by God **3** : the process of forming an opinion by discerning and comparing **4** : the capacity for judging : DISCERNMENT

judg·men·tal \ˌjəj-ˈmen-təl\ *adj* **1** : of, relating to, or involving judgment **2** : characterized by a tendency to judge harshly — **judg·men·tal·ly** *adv*

judgment call *n* : a subjective decision, ruling, or opinion

Judgment Day *n* : the day of the final judging of all human beings by God

ju·di·ca·ture \ˈjü-di-kə-ˌchûr\ *n* **1** : the administration of justice **2** : JUDICIARY 1

ju·di·cial \jù-ˈdi-shəl\ *adj* **1** : of or relating to the administration of justice or the judiciary **2** : ordered or enforced by a court **3** : CRITICAL — **ju·di·cial·ly** *adv*

ju·di·cia·ry \jù-ˈdi-shē-ˌer-ē, -shə-rē\ *n* **1** : a system of courts of law; *also* : the judges of these courts **2** : a branch of government in which judicial power is vested — **judiciary** *adj*

ju·di·cious \jù-ˈdi-shəs\ *adj* : having, exercising, or characterized by sound judgment ♦ *Synonyms* PRUDENT, SAGE, SANE, SENSIBLE, WISE — **ju·di·cious·ly** *adv*

Ju·dith \ˈjü-dəth\ *n* — see BIBLE table

ju·do \ˈjü-dō\ *n* [Jp, fr. *jū* weakness, gentleness + *dō* art] : a sport derived from jujitsu that emphasizes the use of quick movement and leverage to throw an opponent — **ju·do·ist** \-ist\ *n*

ju·do·ka \ˈjü-dō-ˌkä\ *n, pl* **judoka** *or* **judokas** : one who participates in judo

¹jug \ˈjəg\ *n* **1** : a large deep container with a narrow mouth and a handle **2** : JAIL, PRISON

²jug *vb* **jugged; jug·ging** : JAIL, IMPRISON

jug–eared \ˈjəg-ˌird\ *adj* : having protuberant ears

jug·ger·naut \ˈjə-gər-ˌnòt\ *n* [Hindi *Jagannāth,* title of Vishnu (a Hindu god), lit., lord of the world] : a massive inexorable force or object that crushes everything in its path

jug·gle \ˈjə-gəl\ *vb* **jug·gled; jug·gling** **1** : to keep several objects in motion in the air at the same time **2** : to manipulate esp. in order to achieve a desired and often fraudulent end — **jug·gler** \ˈjə-glər\ *n*

jug·u·lar \ˈjə-gyə-lər\ *adj* : of, relating to, or situated in or on the throat or neck ⟨the ∼ veins⟩

juice \ˈjüs\ *n* **1** : the extractable fluid contents of cells or tissues **2** *pl* : the natural fluids of an animal body **3** : something that supplies power; *esp* : ELECTRICITY 2

juic·er \ˈjü-sər\ *n* : an appliance for extracting juice (as from fruit)

juice up *vb* : to give life, energy, or spirit to

juicy \ˈjü-sē\ *adj* **juic·i·er; -est** **1** : SUCCULENT **2** : rich in interest; *also* : RACY — **juic·i·ly** \-sə-lē\ *adv* — **juic·i·ness** \-sē-nəs\ *n*

ju·jit·su *also* **ju·jut·su** *or* **jiu·jit·su** \jü-ˈjit-sü\ *n* : an art of fighting employing holds, throws, and paralyzing blows

ju·ju \ˈjü-jü\ *n* : a style of African music characterized by a rapid beat, use of percussion instruments, and vocal harmonies

ju·jube \ˈjü-ˌjüb, ˈjü-jù-ˌbē\ *n* : a fruit-flavored gumdrop or lozenge

juke·box \ˈjük-ˌbäks\ *n* : a coin-operated machine that automatically plays selected recordings

Jul *abbr* July

ju·lep \ˈjü-ləp\ *n* [ME, sweetened water, fr. MF, fr. Ar *julāb,* fr. Pers *gulāb,* fr. *gul* rose + *āb* water] : a drink made of bourbon, sugar, and mint served over crushed ice

Ju·ly \jù-ˈlī\ *n* [ME *Julie,* fr. OE *Julius,* fr. L, fr. Gaius *Julius* Caesar] : the 7th month of the year

¹jum·ble \ˈjəm-bəl\ *vb* **jum·bled; jum·bling** : to mix in a confused mass

²jumble *n* : a disorderly mass or pile

jum·bo \ˈjəm-bō\ *n, pl* **jumbos** [*Jumbo,* a huge elephant exhibited by P.T. Barnum] : a very large specimen of its kind — **jumbo** *adj*

¹jump \ˈjəmp\ *vb* **1** : to spring into the air : leap over **2** : to give a start **3** : to rise or increase suddenly or sharply **4** : to make a sudden attack **5** : to leave hurriedly and often furtively ⟨∼ town⟩ **6** : to act or move before (as a signal) — **jump bail** : to abscond after being released from custody on bail — **jump ship** **1** : to leave the company of a ship without authority **2** : to desert a cause — **jump the gun** : to begin something before the proper time

²jump *n* **1** : a spring into the air; *esp* : one made for height or distance in a track meet **2** : a sharp sudden increase **3** : an initial advantage

¹jump·er \ˈjəm-pər\ *n* : one that jumps

²jumper *n* **1** : a loose blouse **2** : a sleeveless one-piece dress worn usu. with a blouse **3** *pl* : a child's sleeveless coverall

jumping bean *n* : a seed of any of several Mexican shrubs that tumbles about because of the movements of a small moth larva inside it

jumping–off place *n* **1** : a remote or isolated place **2** : a place from which an enterprise is launched

jump·mas·ter \'jəmp-ˌmas-tər\ *n* : a person who supervises parachutists

jump–start \'jəmp-ˌstärt\ *vb* : to start (an engine or vehicle) by connection to an external power source

jump·suit \'jəmp-ˌsüt\ *n* **1** : a coverall worn by parachutists in jumping **2** : a one-piece garment consisting of a blouse or shirt with attached pants or shorts

jumpy \'jəm-pē\ *adj* **jump·i·er; -est** : NERVOUS, JITTERY

jun *abbr* junior

Jun *abbr* June

junc *abbr* junction

jun·co \'jəŋ-kō\ *n, pl* **juncos** *or* **juncoes** : any of a genus of small common pink-billed No. American finches that are largely gray with conspicuous white tail feathers

junc·tion \'jəŋk-shən\ *n* **1** : an act of joining **2** : a place or point of meeting

junc·ture \'jəŋk-chər\ *n* **1** : JOINT, CONNECTION **2** : UNION **3** : a critical time or state of affairs

June \'jün\ *n* [ME, fr. L *Junius*] : the 6th month of the year

jun·gle \'jəŋ-gəl\ *n* [Hindi & Urdu *jangal* forest] **1** : a thick tangled mass of tropical vegetation; *also* : a tract overgrown with vegetation **2** : a place of ruthless struggle for survival

¹ju·nior \'jü-nyər\ *adj* **1** : YOUNGER **2** : lower in rank ⟨a ∼ partner⟩ **3** : of or relating to juniors

²junior *n* **1** : a person who is younger or of lower rank than another **2** : a student in the next-to-last year before graduating

junior college *n* : a school that offers studies corresponding to those of the 1st two years of college

junior high school *n* : a school usu. including grades 7–9

junior varsity *n* : a team whose members lack the experience or qualifications required for the varsity

ju·ni·per \'jü-nə-pər\ *n* : any of numerous coniferous shrubs or trees with leaves like needles or scales and female cones like berries

¹junk \'jəŋk\ *n* **1** : old iron, glass, paper, or waste; *also* : discarded articles **2** : a shoddy product **3** : something of little meaning, worth, or significance **4** *slang* : NARCOTICS; *esp* : HEROIN — **junky** *adj*

²junk *vb* : DISCARD, SCRAP

³junk *n* : a ship of eastern Asia with a high stern and 4-cornered sails

junk·er \'jəŋ-kər\ *n* : something (as an old automobile) ready for scrapping

Jun·ker \'yùn-kər\ *n* [G] : a member of the Prussian landed aristocracy

jun·ket \'jəŋ-kət\ *n* **1** : a pudding of sweetened flavored milk set by rennet **2** : a trip made by an official at public expense

junk food *n* : food that is high in calories but low in nutritional content

junk·ie *also* **junky** \'jəŋ-kē\ *n, pl* **junkies** **1** : a narcotics peddler or addict **2** : one that derives inordinate pleasure from or is dependent on something ⟨a sugar ∼⟩

jun·ta \'hùn-tə, 'jən-, 'hən-\ *n* [Sp, fr. *junto* joined, fr. L *junctus*, pp. of *jungere* to join] : a group of persons controlling a government esp. after a revolutionary seizure of power

Ju·pi·ter \'jü-pə-tər\ *n* : the largest of the planets and the one 5th in order of distance from the sun — see PLANET table

Ju·ras·sic \jù-'ra-sik\ *adj* : of, relating to, or being the period of the Mesozoic era between the Triassic and the Cretaceous that is marked esp. by the presence of dinosaurs — **Jurassic** *n*

ju·rid·i·cal \jù-'ri-di-kəl\ *also* **ju·rid·ic** \-dik\ *adj* **1** : of or relating to the administration of justice **2** : LEGAL — **ju·rid·i·cal·ly** \-di-k(ə-)lē\ *adv*

ju·ris·dic·tion \ˌjùr-əs-'dik-shən\ *n* **1** : the power, right, or authority to interpret and apply the law **2** : the authority of a sovereign power **3** : the limits or territory within which authority may be exercised — **ju·ris·dic·tion·al** \-shə-nəl\ *adj*

ju·ris·pru·dence \-'prü-dᵊns\ *n* **1** : the science or philosophy of law **2** : a system of laws

ju·rist \'jùr-ist\ *n* : one having a thorough knowledge of law; *esp* : JUDGE

ju·ris·tic \jù-'ris-tik\ *adj* **1** : of or relating to a jurist or jurisprudence **2** : of, relating to, or recognized in law

ju·ror \'jùr-ər, -ˌȯr\ *n* : a member of a jury

¹ju·ry \'jùr-ē\ *n, pl* **juries** **1** : a body of persons sworn to inquire into a matter submitted to them and to give their verdict **2** : a committee for judging and awarding prizes

²jury *adj* : improvised for temporary use esp. in an emergency ⟨a ∼ mast⟩

jury nullification *n* : the acquitting of a defendant by a jury in disregard of the judge's instructions and contrary to the jury's findings of fact

jury–rig \'jùr-ē-ˌrig\ *vb* : to construct or arrange in a makeshift fashion

¹just \'jəst\ *adj* **1** : having a basis in or conforming to fact or reason : REASONABLE ⟨∼ comment⟩ **2** : CORRECT, PROPER ⟨∼ proportions⟩ **3** : morally or legally right ⟨a ∼ title⟩ **4** : DESERVED, MERITED ⟨∼ punishment⟩ ♦ **Synonyms** UPRIGHT, HONORABLE, CONSCIENTIOUS, HONEST — **just·ly** *adv* — **just·ness** *n*

²just \'jəst, 'jist\ *adv* **1** : EXACTLY ⟨∼ right⟩ **2** : very recently ⟨has ∼ left⟩ **3** : BARELY ⟨∼ too late⟩ **4** : DIRECTLY ⟨∼ west of here⟩ **5** : ONLY ⟨∼ last year⟩ **6** : QUITE ⟨∼ wonderful⟩ **7** : POSSIBLY ⟨it ∼ might work⟩

jus·tice \'jəs-təs\ *n* **1** : the administration of what is just (as by assigning merited rewards or punishments) **2** : JUDGE **3** : the administration of law **4** : FAIRNESS; *also* : RIGHTEOUSNESS

justice of the peace : a local magistrate empowered chiefly to try minor cases, to administer oaths, and to perform marriages

jus·ti·fy \'jəs-tə-ˌfī\ *vb* **-fied; -fy·ing** **1** : to prove to be just, right, or reasonable **2** : to pronounce free from guilt or blame **3** : to adjust spaces in a line of printed text so the margins are even — **jus·ti·fi·able** *adj* — **jus·ti·fi·ca·tion** \ˌjəs-tə-fə-'kā-shən\ *n*

jut \'jət\ *vb* **jut·ted; jut·ting** : PROJECT, PROTRUDE

jute \'jüt\ *n* : a strong glossy fiber from either of two tropical plants used esp. for making sacks and twine

juv *abbr* juvenile

¹ju·ve·nile \'jü-və-ˌnī(-ə)l, -nəl\ *adj* **1** : showing incomplete development **2** : of, relating to, or characteristic of children or young people

²juvenile *n* **1** : a young person; *esp* : one below the legally established age of adulthood **2** : a young animal (as a fish or a bird) or plant **3** : an actor or actress who plays youthful parts

juvenile delinquency *n* : violation of the law or antisocial behavior by a juvenile — **juvenile delinquent** *n*

jux·ta·pose \'jək-stə-ˌpōz\ *vb* **-posed; -pos·ing** : to place side by side — **jux·ta·po·si·tion** \ˌjək-stə-pə-'zi-shən\ *n*

JV *abbr* junior varsity

DICTIONARY

¹**k** \\'kā\\ *n, pl* **k's** *or* **ks** \\'kāz\\ **1** *often cap* : the 11th letter of the English alphabet **2** *cap* : STRIKEOUT

²**k** *abbr* **1** karat **2** kitchen **3** knit **4** kosher — often enclosed in a circle

¹**K** *abbr* **1** Kelvin **2** kindergarten

²**K** *symbol* [NL *kalium*] potassium

kab·ba·lah *also* **kab·ba·la** *or* **ka·ba·la** *or* **ca·ba·la** \\kə-'bä-lə, 'ka-bə-lə\\ *n, often cap* **1** : a medieval Jewish mysticism marked by belief in creation through emanation and a cipher method of interpreting Scripture **2** : esoteric or mysterious doctrine

kabob *var of* KEBAB

Ka·bu·ki \\kə-'bü-kē\\ *n* : traditional Japanese popular drama with highly stylized singing and dancing

kad·dish \\'kä-dish\\ *n, often cap* : a Jewish prayer recited in the daily synagogue ritual and by mourners at public services after the death of a close relative

kaf·fee·klatsch \\'kò-fē-ˌklach, 'kä-\\ *n, often cap* [G] : an informal social gathering for coffee and conversation

kai·ser \\'kī-zər\\ *n* : EMPEROR; *esp* : the ruler of Germany from 1871 to 1918

Ka·lash·ni·kov \\kə-'lash-nə-ˌkóf\\ *n* [M. T. *Kalashnikov* b1919 Soviet weapons designer] : a Soviet-designed assault rifle

kale \\'kāl\\ *n* : a hardy cabbage with curled leaves that do not form a head

ka·lei·do·scope \\kə-'lī-də-ˌskōp\\ *n* : a tube containing loose bits of colored material (as glass) and two mirrors at one end that shows many different patterns as it is turned — **ka·lei·do·scop·ic** \\-ˌlī-də-'skä-pik\\ *adj* — **ka·lei·do·scop·i·cal·ly** \\-pi-k(ə-)lē\\ *adv*

ka·ma·ai·na \\ˌkä-mə-'ī-nə\\ *n* [Hawaiian *kama'āina*, fr. *kama* child + *'āina* land] : one who has lived in Hawaii for a long time

kame \\'kām\\ *n* [Sc, lit., comb] : a short ridge or mound of material deposited by water from a melting glacier

ka·mi·ka·ze \\ˌkä-mi-'kä-zē\\ *n* [Jp, lit., divine wind] : a member of a corps of Japanese pilots assigned to make a suicidal crash on a target; *also* : an airplane flown in such an attack

Kan *or* **Kans** *abbr* Kansas

kan·ga·roo \\ˌkaŋ-gə-'rü\\ *n, pl* **-roos** : any of various large leaping marsupial mammals of Australia and adjacent islands with powerful hind legs and a long thick tail used as a support

kangaroo court *n* : a court or an illegal self-appointed tribunal characterized by irresponsible, perverted, or irregular procedures

ka·o·lin \\'kā-ə-lən\\ *n* : a fine usu. white clay used in ceramics and refractories and for the treatment of diarrhea

ka·pey·ka \\kä-'pā-kä\\ *n, pl* **ka·pe·ek** \\kä-'pā-ək\\ — see *rubel* at MONEY table

ka·pok \\'kā-ˌpäk\\ *n* : silky fiber from the seeds of a tropical tree used esp. as a filling (as for life preservers)

Kap·o·si's sar·co·ma \\'ka-pə-sēz-sär-'kō-mə\\ *n* : a neoplastic disease associated esp. with AIDS that affects esp. the skin and mucous membranes and is characterized usu. by the formation of pink to reddish-brown or bluish plaques

kap·pa \\'ka-pə\\ *n* : the 10th letter of the Greek alphabet — K or κ

ka·put *also* **ka·putt** \\kä-'pút, kə-, -'pút\\ *adj* [G, fr. F *capot* not having made a trick at piquet] **1** : utterly defeated or destroyed **2** : unable to function : USELESS

kar·a·kul \\'ker-ə-kəl\\ *n* : the usu. curly glossy black coat of a very young lamb of a hardy Asian breed of sheep

kar·a·o·ke \\ˌker-ē-'ō-kē\\ *n* [Jp] : a device that plays instrumental accompaniments for songs to which the user sings along

kar·at \\'ker-ət\\ *n* : a unit for expressing proportion of gold in an alloy equal to ¹/₂₄ part of pure gold

ka·ra·te \\kə-'rä-tē\\ *n* [Jp, lit., empty hand] : an art of self-defense in which an attacker is disabled by crippling kicks and punches

kar·ma \\'kär-mə\\ *n, often cap* [Skt] : the force generated by a person's actions held in Hinduism and Buddhism to perpetuate reincarnation and to determine the nature of the person's next existence — **kar·mic** \\-mik\\ *adj*

karst \\'kärst\\ *n* [G] : an irregular limestone region with sinks, underground streams, and caverns

ka·ty·did \\'kā-tē-ˌdid\\ *n* : any of several large green tree-dwelling American grasshoppers with long antennae

katydid

kay·ak \\'kī-ˌak\\ *n* : an Eskimo canoe made of a skin-covered frame with a small opening and propelled by a double-bladed paddle; *also* : a similar portable boat — **kay·ak·er** *n*

kayo \\(ˌ)kā-'ō, 'kā-ˌō\\ *n* : KNOCKOUT — **kayo** *vb*

ka·zoo \\kə-'zü\\ *n, pl* **kazoos** : a toy musical instrument consisting of a tube with a membrane sealing one end and a side hole to sing or hum into

KB *abbr* kilobyte

kc *abbr* kilocycle

KC *abbr* **1** Kansas City **2** King's Counsel **3** Knights of Columbus

kc/s *abbr* kilocycles per second

KD *abbr* knocked down

ke·bab *or* **ke·bob** *also* **ka·bob** \\kə-'bäb\\ *n* : cubes of meat cooked with vegetables usu. on a skewer

kedge \\'kej\\ *n* : a small anchor

¹**keel** \\'kēl\\ *n* **1** : the chief structural member of a ship running lengthwise along the center of its bottom **2** : something (as a bird's breastbone) like a ship's keel in form or use — **keeled** \\'kēld\\ *adj*

²**keel** *vb* : FAINT, SWOON — usu. used with *over*

keel·boat \\'kēl-ˌbōt\\ *n* : a shallow covered keeled riverboat for freight that is usu. rowed, poled, or towed

keel·haul \\-ˌhòl\\ *vb* : to haul under the keel of a ship as punishment

¹**keen** \\'kēn\\ *adj* **1** : SHARP ⟨a ~ knife⟩ **2** : SEVERE ⟨a ~ wind⟩ **3** : ENTHUSIASTIC ⟨~ about swimming⟩ **4** : mentally alert ⟨a ~ mind⟩ **5** : STRONG, ACUTE ⟨~ eyesight⟩ **6** : WONDERFUL, EXCELLENT — **keen·ly** *adv* — **keen·ness** *n*

²**keen** *n* : a lamentation for the dead uttered in a loud wailing voice or in a wordless cry — **keen** *vb*

¹**keep** \\'kēp\\ *vb* **kept** \\'kept\\; **keep·ing** **1** : FULFILL, OBSERVE ⟨~ a promise⟩ ⟨~ a holiday⟩ **2** : GUARD ⟨~ us from harm⟩; *also* : to take care of ⟨~ a neighbor's children⟩ **3** : MAINTAIN ⟨~ silence⟩ **4** : to have in one's service or at one's disposal ⟨~ a horse⟩ **5** : to preserve a record in ⟨~ a diary⟩ **6** : to have in stock for sale **7** : to retain in one's possession ⟨~ what you find⟩ **8** : to carry on (as a business) : CONDUCT **9** : HOLD, DETAIN ⟨~ him in jail⟩ **10** : to refrain from revealing ⟨~ a secret⟩ **11** : to continue in good condition ⟨meat will ~ in a freezer⟩ **12** : ABSTAIN, REFRAIN — **keep·er** *n*

²**keep** *n* **1** : FORTRESS **2** : the means or provisions by which one is kept — **for keeps** **1** : with the provision that one keep what one has won ⟨play marbles *for keeps*⟩ **2** : PERMANENTLY ⟨came home *for keeps*⟩

keep–away \\'kēp-ə-ˌwā\\ *n* : a game in which players try to keep an object from one or more other players

keeping *n* : CONFORMITY ⟨in ~ with good taste⟩

keeping room *n* : a common room used for multiple purposes

keep·sake \'kēp-ˌsāk\ *n* : MEMENTO

keep up *vb* **1** : to persevere in **2** : MAINTAIN, SUSTAIN **3** : to keep informed **4** : to continue without interruption

keg \'keg\ *n* : a small cask or barrel

keg·ger \'ke-gər\ *n* : a party featuring one or more kegs of beer

keg·ler \'ke-glər\ *n* : ¹BOWLER

kelp \'kelp\ *n* : any of various coarse brown seaweeds; *also* : a mass of these or their ashes often used as fertilizer

kel·vin \'kel-vən\ *n* : a unit of temperature equal to ¹/₂₇₃.₁₆ of the Kelvin scale temperature of the triple point of water and equal to the Celsius degree

Kelvin *adj* : relating to, conforming to, or being a temperature scale according to which absolute zero is 0 K, the equivalent of –273.15°C

ken \'ken\ *n* **1** : range of vision : SIGHT **2** : range of understanding

ken·nel \'ke-nᵊl\ *n* : a shelter for a dog or cat; *also* : an establishment for the breeding or boarding of dogs or cats — **kennel** *vb*

ke·no \'kē-nō\ *n* : a game resembling bingo

ke·no·sis \kə-'nō-səs\ *n* : the relinquishment of divine attributes by Jesus Christ in becoming human — **ke·not·ic** \-'nä-tik\ *adj*

ken·te cloth \'ken-ˌtā-\ *n* : colorfully patterned cloth traditionally woven by hand in Ghana

Ken·tucky bluegrass \kən-'tə-kē-\ *n* : a valuable pasture and meadow grass of both Europe and America

Ke·ogh plan \'kē-(ˌ)ō-\ *n* [Eugene James *Keogh* †1989 Am. politician] : an individual retirement account for the self-employed

ke·pi \'kā-pē, 'ke-\ *n* [F] : a military cap with a round flat top and a visor

ker·a·tin \'ker-ə-tən\ *n* : any of various sulfur-containing proteins that make up hair and horny tissues

kerb \'kərb\ *n, Brit* : CURB 3

ker·chief \'kər-chəf, -ˌchēf\ *n, pl* **kerchiefs** \-chəfs, -ˌchēfs\ *also* **kerchieves** \-ˌchēvz\ [ME *courchef*, fr. AF *coverchef*, *cuerchief*, fr. *coverir* to cover + *chef* head] **1** : a square of cloth worn esp. as a head covering **2** : HANDKERCHIEF

kerf \'kərf\ *n* : a slit or notch made by a saw or cutting torch

ker·nel \'kər-nᵊl\ *n* **1** : the inner softer part of a seed, fruit stone, or nut **2** : a whole seed of a cereal ⟨a ~ of corn⟩ **3** : a central or essential part : CORE

ker·o·sene *also* **ker·o·sine** \'ker-ə-ˌsēn, ˌker-ə-'sēn\ *n* : a flammable oil produced from petroleum and used for a fuel and as a solvent

kes·trel \'kes-trəl\ *n* : any of various small falcons that usu. hover in the air while searching for prey

ketch \'kech\ *n* : a large fore-and-aft rigged boat with two masts

ketch·up *also* **catch·up** \'ke-chəp, 'ka-\ *or* **cat·sup** \'ke-chəp, 'ka-; 'kat-səp\ *n* : a seasoned tomato puree

ket·tle \'ke-tᵊl\ *n* : a metallic vessel for boiling liquids

ket·tle·drum \-ˌdrəm\ *n* : a brass, copper, or fiberglass drum with calfskin or plastic stretched across the top

¹key \'kē\ *n* **1** : a usu. metal instrument by which the bolt of a lock is turned; *also* : a device having the form or function of a key **2** : a means of gaining or preventing entrance, possession, or control **3** : EXPLANATION, SOLUTION **4** : one of the levers pressed by a finger in operating or playing an instrument **5** : a leading individual or principle **6** : a system of seven tones based on their relationship to a tonic; *also* : the tone or pitch of a voice **7** : a small switch for opening or closing an electric circuit ⟨a telegraph ~⟩

²key *vb* **1** : SECURE, FASTEN **2** : to regulate the musical pitch of **3** : to bring into harmony or conformity **4** : to make nervous — usu. used with *up*

³key *adj* : BASIC, CENTRAL ⟨~ issues⟩

⁴key *n* : a low island or reef (as off the southern coast of Florida)

⁵key *n, slang* ; a kilogram esp. of marijuana or heroin

key·board \-ˌbȯrd\ *n* **1** : a row of keys (as on a piano) **2** : an assemblage of keys for operating a machine

key club *n* : a private club serving liquor and providing entertainment

key·hole \'kē-ˌhōl\ *n* : a hole for receiving a key

¹key·note \-ˌnōt\ *n* **1** : the first and harmonically fundamental tone of a scale **2** : the central fact, idea, or mood

²keynote *vb* **1** : to set the keynote of **2** : to deliver the major address (as at a convention) — **key·not·er** *n*

key·punch \'kē-ˌpənch\ *n* : a machine with a keyboard used to cut holes or notches in punch cards — **keypunch** *vb* — **key·punch·er** *n*

key·stone \-ˌstōn\ *n* : the wedge-shaped piece at the crown of an arch that locks the other pieces in place

key·stroke \-ˌstrōk\ *n* : an act or instance of depressing a key on a keyboard

key word *n* : a word that is a key; *esp usu* **key·word** : a significant word from a title or document used esp. as an indication of the content

kg *abbr* kilogram

KGB *abbr* [Russ *Komitet gosudarstvennoĭ bezopasnosti*] (Soviet) State Security Committee

kha·ki \'ka-kē, 'kä-\ *n* [Hindi & Urdu *khākī* dust-colored, fr. *khāk* dust, fr. Pers] **1** : a light yellowish brown color **2** : a khaki-colored cloth; *also* : a military uniform of this cloth

khan \'kän, 'kan\ *n* : a Mongol leader; *esp* : a successor of Genghis Khan

khe·dive \kə-'dēv\ *n* : a ruler of Egypt from 1867 to 1914 governing as a viceroy of the sultan of Turkey

khoum \'küm\ *n* — see *ouguiya* at MONEY table

kHz *abbr* kilohertz

KIA *abbr* killed in action

kib·ble \'ki-bəl\ *vb* **kib·bled**; **kib·bling** : to grind coarsely — **kibble** *n*

kib·butz \ki-'bu̇ts, -'büts\ *n, pl* **kib·but·zim** \-ˌbu̇t-'sēm, -ˌbüt-\ [ModHeb *qibbūṣ*] : a communal farm or settlement in Israel

ki·bitz·er \'ki-bət-sər, kə-'bit-\ *n* : one who looks on and usu. offers unwanted advice — **kib·itz** \'ki-bəts\ *vb*

ki·bosh \'kī-ˌbäsh\ *n* : something that serves as a check or stop ⟨put the ~ on his plan⟩

¹kick \'kik\ *vb* **1** : to strike out or hit with the foot; *also* : to score by kicking a ball **2** : to object strongly **3** : to recoil when fired — **kick·er** *n*

²kick *n* **1** : a blow or thrust with the foot; *esp* : a propelling of a ball with the foot **2** : the recoil of a gun **3** : a feeling or expression of objection **4** : stimulating effect esp. of pleasure

kick·back \'kik-ˌbak\ *n* **1** : a sharp violent reaction **2** : a secret return of a part of a sum received

kick back *vb* : to assume a relaxed position or attitude

kick·box·ing \'kik-ˌbäk-siŋ\ *n* : boxing in which boxers are permitted to kick with bare feet — **kick·box·er** \-sər\ *n*

kick in *vb* **1** : CONTRIBUTE **2** *slang* : DIE **3** : to begin operating or having an effect

kick·off \'kik-ˌȯf\ *n* **1** : a kick that puts the ball in play (as in football) **2** : COMMENCEMENT ⟨campaign ~⟩

kick off *vb* **1** : to start or resume play with a placekick **2** : to begin proceedings **3** *slang* : DIE

kick over *vb* : to begin or cause to begin to fire — used of an internal combustion engine

kick·shaw \'kik-ˌshȯ\ *n* [modif. of F *quelque chose* something] **1** : DELICACY **2** : TRINKET

kick·stand \'kik-ˌstand\ *n* : a swiveling metal bar attached to a 2-wheeled vehicle for holding it up when not in use

kick·start \'kik-ˌstärt\ *vb* : JUMP-START

kicky \'ki-kē\ *adj* : providing a kick or thrill : EXCITING

¹kid \'kid\ *n* **1** : a young goat **2** : the flesh, fur, or skin of a young goat; *also* : something made of kid **3** : CHILD, YOUNGSTER — **kid·dish** *adj*

²kid *vb* **kid·ded**; **kid·ding** **1** : FOOL **2** : TEASE — **kid·der** *n* — **kid·ding·ly** *adv*

kid·do \'ki-dō\ *n, pl* **kiddos** — used as a familiar form of address ⟨you're okay, ~⟩ **2** : CHILD, KID

kid·nap \'kid-ˌnap\ *vb* **kid·napped** *also* **kid·naped** \-ˌnapt\; **kid·nap·ping** *also* **kid·nap·ing** \-ˌna-piŋ\ : to hold or carry a person away by unlawful force or by fraud and against one's will — **kid·nap·per** *also* **kid·nap·er** \-ˌna-pər\ *n*

kid·ney \'kid-nē\ *n, pl* **kidneys** : either of a pair of organs lying near the backbone that excrete waste products of the body in the form of urine

kidney bean *n* **1** : an edible seed of the common cultivated bean; *esp* : one that is large and dark red **2** : a plant bearing kidney beans

kid·skin \'kid-ˌskin\ *n* : the skin of a young goat used for leather

kiel·ba·sa \kēl-'bä-sə, kil-\ *n, pl* **-basas** *also* **-ba·sy** \-'bä-sē\ [Pol *kielbasa*] : a smoked sausage of Polish origin

¹**kill** \'kil\ *vb* **1** : to deprive of life **2** : to put an end to ⟨∼ competition⟩; *also* : DEFEAT ⟨∼ a proposed amendment⟩ **3** : USE UP ⟨∼ time⟩ **4** : to mark for omission ◆ *Synonyms* SLAY, MURDER, ASSASSINATE, EXECUTE — **kill·er** *n*

²**kill** *n* **1** : an act of killing **2** : an animal or animals killed (as in a hunt); *also* : an aircraft, ship, or vehicle destroyed by military action

kill·deer \'kil-ˌdir\ *n, pl* **killdeers** *or* **killdeer** [imit.] : an American plover with a plaintive penetrating cry

killer app \-'ap\ *n* : a component (as a computer application) that in itself makes something worth having or using

killer bee *n* : AFRICANIZED BEE

killer whale *n* : a small gregarious black and white flesh‗ eating whale with a white oval patch behind each eye

kill·ing *n* : a sudden notable gain or profit

killing field *n* : a scene of mass killing

kill·joy \'kil-ˌjȯi\ *n* : one who spoils the pleasures of others

kiln \'kil, 'kiln\ *n* [ME *kilne*, fr. OE *cyln*, fr. L *culina* kitchen] : a heated enclosure (as an oven) for processing a substance by burning, firing, or drying — **kiln** *vb*

ki·lo \'kē-lō\ *n, pl* **kilos** : KILOGRAM

ki·lo·byte \'ki-lə-ˌbīt, 'kē-\ *n* : 1024 bytes

kilo·cy·cle \'ki-lə-ˌsī-kəl\ *n* : KILOHERTZ

ki·lo·gram \'kē-lə-ˌgram, 'ki-\ *n* **1** : the basic metric unit of mass that is nearly equal to the mass of 1000 cubic centimeters of water at its maximum density — see METRIC SYSTEM table **2** : the weight of a kilogram mass under earth's gravity

ki·lo·hertz \'ki-lə-ˌhərts, 'kē-, -ˌherts\ *n* : 1000 hertz

kilo·li·ter \'ki-lə-ˌlē-tər\ *n* : see METRIC SYSTEM table

ki·lo·me·ter \ki-'lä-mə-tər, 'ki-lə-ˌmē-\ *n* : a metric unit of length equal to 1000 meters — see METRIC SYSTEM table

ki·lo·ton \'ki-lə-ˌtən, 'kē-lō-\ *n* **1** : 1000 tons **2** : an explosive force equivalent to that of 1000 tons of TNT

ki·lo·volt \-ˌvōlt\ *n* : 1000 volts

kilo·watt \'ki-lə-ˌwät\ *n* : 1000 watts

kilowatt–hour *n* : a unit of energy equal to that expended by one kilowatt in one hour

kilt \'kilt\ *n* : a knee-length pleated skirt usu. of tartan worn by men in Scotland

kil·ter \'kil-tər\ *n* : proper condition ⟨out of ∼⟩

ki·mo·no \kə-'mō-nə\ *n, pl* **-nos** **1** : a loose robe with wide sleeves traditionally worn with a wide sash as an outer garment by the Japanese **2** : a loose dressing gown or jacket

kin \'kin\ *n* **1** : an individual's relatives **2** : KINSMAN

ki·na \'kē-nə\ *n, pl* **kina** — see MONEY table

ki·na·ra \kē-'nä-rə\ *n* : a candelabra with seven candlesticks used during Kwanzaa

¹**kind** \'kīnd\ *n* **1** : essential quality or character **2** : a group united by common traits or interests : CATEGORY; *also* : VARIETY **3** : goods or commodities as distinguished from money

²**kind** *adj* **1** : of a sympathetic, forbearing, or pleasant nature **2** : arising from sympathy or forbearance ⟨∼ deeds⟩ ◆ *Synonyms* BENEVOLENT, BENIGN, BENIGNANT, KINDLY — **kind·ness** *n*

kin·der·gar·ten \'kin-dər-ˌgär-tᵊn\ *n* [G, lit., children's garden] : a school or class for children usu. from four to six years old

kin·der·gart·ner \-ˌgärt-nər\ *n* **1** : a kindergarten teacher **2** : a kindergarten pupil

kind·heart·ed \ˌkīnd-'här-təd\ *adj* : marked by a sympathetic nature

kin·dle \'kin-dᵊl\ *vb* **kin·dled; kin·dling** **1** : to set on fire : start burning **2** : to stir up : AROUSE **3** : ILLUMINATE, GLOW

kin·dling \'kind-liŋ, 'kin-lən\ *n* : easily combustible material for starting a fire

¹**kind·ly** \'kīnd-lē\ *adj* **kind·li·er; -est** **1** : of an agreeable or beneficial nature **2** : of a sympathetic or generous nature — **kind·li·ness** *n*

²**kindly** *adv* **1** : READILY ⟨does not take ∼ to criticism⟩ **2** : SYMPATHETICALLY **3** : COURTEOUSLY, OBLIGINGLY

kind of *adv* : to a moderate degree ⟨it's *kind of* late to begin⟩

¹**kin·dred** \'kin-drəd\ *n* **1** : a group of related individuals **2** : one's relatives

²**kindred** *adj* : of a like nature or character

kine \'kīn\ *archaic pl of* COW

kin·e·ma \'ki-nə-mə\ *Brit var of* CINEMA

ki·ne·mat·ics \ˌki-nə-'ma-tiks\ *n* : a science that deals with motion apart from considerations of mass and force — **ki·ne·mat·ic** \-tik\ *or* **ki·ne·mat·i·cal** \-ti-kəl\ *adj*

kin·es·the·sia \ˌki-nəs-'thē-zhə, -zhē-ə\ *or* **kin·es·the·sis** \-'thē-səs\ *n, pl* **-the·sias** *or* **-the·ses** \-ˌsēz\ : a sense that perceives bodily movement, position, and weight and is mediated by nervous receptors in tendons, muscles, and joints; *also* : sensory experience derived from this sense — **kin·es·thet·ic** \-'the-tik\ *adj*

ki·net·ic \kə-'ne-tik\ *adj* : of or relating to the motion of material bodies and the forces and energy (**kinetic energy**) associated with them

ki·net·ics \-tiks\ *n sing or pl* : a science that deals with the effects of forces upon the motions of material bodies or with changes in a physical or chemical system

kin·folk \'kin-ˌfōk\ *or* **kinfolks** *n pl* : RELATIVES

king \'kiŋ\ *n* **1** : a male sovereign **2** : a chief among competitors ⟨home-run ∼⟩ **3** : the principal piece in the game of chess **4** : a playing card bearing the figure of a king **5** : a checker that has been crowned — **king·less** *adj* — **king·ly** *adj* — **king·ship** *n*

king crab *n* **1** : HORSESHOE CRAB **2** : a large crab of the No. Pacific caught commercially for food

king·dom \'kiŋ-dəm\ *n* **1** : a country whose head is a king or queen **2** : a realm or region in which something or someone is dominant ⟨a cattle ∼⟩ **3** : one of the three primary divisions of lifeless material, plants, and animals into which natural objects are grouped; *also* : a biological category that ranks above the phylum

king·fish·er \-ˌfi-shər\ *n* : any of numerous usu. bright‗ colored crested birds that feed chiefly on fish

king·pin \'kiŋ-ˌpin\ *n* **1** : HEADPIN **2** : the leader in a group or undertaking

Kings *n* — see BIBLE table

king–size \'kiŋ-ˌsīz\ *or* **king–sized** \-ˌsīzd\ *adj* **1** : longer than the regular or standard size **2** : unusually large **3** : having dimensions of about 76 by 80 inches (1.9 by 2.0 meters) ⟨a ∼ bed⟩; *also* : of a size that fits a king-size bed

kink \'kiŋk\ *n* **1** : a short tight twist or curl **2** : a mental peculiarity : QUIRK **3** : CRAMP ⟨a ∼ in the back⟩ **4** : an imperfection likely to cause difficulties in operation — **kinky** *adj*

kin·ship \'kin-ˌship\ *n* : RELATIONSHIP

kins·man \'kinz-mən\ *n* : RELATIVE; *esp* : a male relative

kins·wom·an \-ˌwu̇-mən\ *n* : a female relative

ki·osk \'kē-ˌäsk\ *n* **1** : a small structure with one or more open sides **2** : a stand-alone device providing information and services on a computer screen ⟨interactive ∼s at the museum⟩

Ki·o·wa \'kī-ə-ˌwȯ, -ˌwä, -ˌwā\ *n, pl* **Kiowa** *or* **Kiowas** : a member of an American Indian people of Colorado, Kansas, New Mexico, Oklahoma, and Texas

kip \'kip, 'gip\ *n, pl* **kip** *or* **kips** — see MONEY table

kip·per \'ki-pər\ *n* : a fish (as a herring) preserved by salting and drying or smoking — **kipper** *vb*

kirk \'kərk, 'kirk\ *n, chiefly Scot* : CHURCH

kir·tle \'kər-tᵊl\ *n* : a long gown or dress worn by women

kis·met \'kiz-ˌmet, -mət\ *n, often cap* [Turk, fr. Ar *qisma* portion, lot] : FATE

¹**kiss** \'kis\ *vb* **1** : to touch or caress with the lips as a mark of affection or greeting **2** : to touch gently or lightly

²**kiss** *n* **1** : a caress with the lips **2** : a gentle touch or contact **3** : a bite-size candy

kiss·er \'ki-sər\ *n* **1** : one that kisses **2** *slang* : MOUTH **3** *slang* : FACE

kit \'kit\ *n* **1** : a set of articles for personal use; *also* : a set of tools or implements or of parts to be assembled **2** : a container (as a case) for a kit

kitch·en \'ki-chən\ *n* **1** : a room with cooking facilities **2** : the personnel that prepares, cooks, and serves food

kitch·en·ette \ˌki-chə-'net\ *n* : a small kitchen or an alcove containing cooking facilities

kitchen police *n* **1** : KP **2** : the work of KPs

kitch·en·ware \'ki-chən-ˌwer\ *n* : utensils and appliances for kitchen use

kite \'kīt\ *n* **1** : any of various long-winged hawks often with deeply forked tails **2** : a light frame covered with paper or cloth and designed to be flown in the air at the end of a long string

kith \'kith\ *n* [ME, fr. OE *cȳthth*, fr. *cūth* known] : familiar friends, neighbors, or relatives ⟨∼ and kin⟩

kitsch \'kich\ *n* [G] : something often of poor quality that appeals to popular or lowbrow taste — **kitschy** \'ki-chē\ *adj*

kit·ten \'ki-t³n\ *n* : a young cat — **kit·ten·ish** *adj*

¹kit·ty \'ki-tē\ *n, pl* **kitties** : CAT; *esp* : KITTEN

²kitty *n, pl* **kitties** : a fund in a poker game made up of contributions from each pot; *also* : POOL

kit·ty—cor·ner *also* **cat·ty—cor·ner** *or* **cat·er·cor·ner** \'ki-tē-,kȯr-nər, 'ka-; 'ka-tə-\ *or* **kit·ty—cor·nered** *or* **cat·ty—cor·nered** *or* **cat·er·cornered** \-nərd\ *adv or adj* : in a diagonal or oblique position

ki·wi \'kē-(,)wē\ *n* **1** : any of a small genus of flightless New Zealand birds **2** : KIWIFRUIT

ki·wi·fruit \-,früt\ *n* : a brownish hairy egg-shaped fruit of a subtropical vine that has sweet bright green flesh and small edible black seeds

KJV *abbr* King James Version

KKK *abbr* Ku Klux Klan

kl *abbr* kiloliter

klatch *also* **klatsch** \'klach\ *n* [G *Klatsch* gossip] : a gathering marked by informal conversation

klep·toc·ra·cy \klep-'tä-krə-sē\ *n, pl* **-cies** : government by those who seek chiefly status and personal gain at the expense of the governed

klep·to·ma·nia \,klep-tə-'mā-nē-ə\ *n* : a persistent neurotic impulse to steal esp. without economic motive — **klep·to·ma·ni·ac** \-nē-,ak\ *n*

klieg light *or* **kleig light** \'klēg-\ *n* : a very bright lamp used in making motion pictures

klutz \'kləts\ *n* [Yiddish *klots*, lit., wooden beam] : a clumsy person — **klutzy** *adj*

km *abbr* kilometer

kn *abbr* knot

knack \'nak\ *n* **1** : a clever way of doing something **2** : natural aptitude

knap·sack \'nap-,sak\ *n* : a bag (as of canvas) strapped on the back and used esp. for carrying supplies

knave \'nāv\ *n* **1** : ROGUE **2** : JACK 6 — **knav·ery** \'nā-və-rē\ *n* — **knav·ish** \'nā-vish\ *adj*

knead \'nēd\ *vb* : to work and press into a mass with the hands; *also* : MASSAGE — **knead·er** *n*

knee \'nē\ *n* : the joint in the middle part of the leg — **kneed** \'nēd\ *adj*

knee·cap \'nē-,kap\ *n* : a thick flat triangular movable bone forming the front of the knee

knee·hole \-,hōl\ *n* : a space (as under a desk) for the knees

knee—jerk \'nē-,jərk\ *adj* : readily predictable ⟨a ∼ reaction⟩

kneel \'nēl\ *vb* **knelt** \'nelt\ *or* **kneeled; kneel·ing** : to bend the knee : fall or rest on the knees

¹knell \'nel\ *vb* **1** : to ring esp. for a death or disaster **2** : to summon, announce, or proclaim by a knell

²knell *n* **1** : a stroke of a bell esp. when tolled (as for a funeral) **2** : an indication of the end or failure of something

knew *past of* KNOW

knick·ers \'ni-kərz\ *n pl* : loose-fitting short pants gathered at the knee

knick·knack \'nik-,nak\ *n* : a small trivial article intended for ornament

¹knife \'nīf\ *n, pl* **knives** \'nīvz\ **1** : a cutting instrument consisting of a sharp blade fastened to a handle **2** : a sharp cutting tool in a machine

²knife *vb* **knifed; knif·ing** : to stab, slash, or wound with a knife

¹knight \'nīt\ *n* **1** : a mounted warrior of feudal times serving a king **2** : a man honored by a sovereign for merit and in Great Britain ranking below a baronet **3** : a man devoted to the service of a lady **4** : a member of an order or society **5** : a chess piece having an L-shaped move — **knight·ly** *adj*

²knight *vb* : to make a knight of

knight·hood \'nīt-,hůd\ *n* **1** : the rank, dignity, or profession of a knight **2** : CHIVALRY **3** : knights as a class or body

knish \kə-'nish\ *n* [Yiddish] : a small round or square of dough stuffed with a filling (as of meat or fruit) and baked or fried

¹knit \'nit\ *vb* **knit** *or* **knit·ted; knit·ting** **1** : to link firmly or closely **2** : WRINKLE ⟨∼ her brows⟩ **3** : to form a fabric by interlacing yarn or thread in connected loops with needles **4** : to grow together — **knit·ter** *n*

²knit *n* **1** : a basic knitting stitch **2** : a knitted garment or fabric

knit·wear \-,wer\ *n* : knitted clothing

knob \'näb\ *n* **1** : a rounded protuberance; *also* : a small rounded ornament or handle **2** : a rounded usu. isolated hill — **knobbed** \'näbd\ *adj* — **knob·by** \'nä-bē\ *adj*

¹knock \'näk\ *vb* **1** : to strike with a sharp blow **2** : BUMP, COLLIDE **3** : to make a pounding noise; *esp* : to have engine knock **4** : to find fault with

²knock *n* **1** : a sharp blow **2** : a pounding noise; *esp* : one caused by abnormal ignition in an automobile engine

knock·down \'näk-,daůn\ *n* **1** : the action of knocking down **2** : something (as a blow) that knocks down **3** : something that can be easily assembled or disassembled

knock down *vb* **1** : to strike to the ground with or as if with a sharp blow **2** : to take apart : DISASSEMBLE **3** : to receive as income or salary : EARN **4** : to make a reduction in

knock·er \'nä-kər\ *n* : one that knocks; *esp* : a device hinged to a door for use in knocking

knock—knee \'näk-,nē\ *n* : a condition in which the legs curve inward at the knees — **knock—kneed** \-,nēd\ *adj*

knock·off \'näk-,ȯf\ *n* : a copy or imitation of someone or something popular

knock off *vb* **1** : to stop doing something **2** : to do quickly, carelessly, or routinely **3** : to deduct from a price **4** : KILL **5** : ROB **6** : COPY, IMITATE

knock·out \'näk-,aůt\ *n* **1** : a blow that fells and immobilizes an opponent (as in boxing) **2** : something sensationally striking or attractive

knock out *vb* **1** : to defeat by a knockout **2** : to make unconscious or inoperative **3** : to tire out : EXHAUST

knock·wurst *also* **knack·wurst** \'näk-,wərst, -,vůrst\ *n* : a short thick heavily seasoned sausage

knoll \'nōl\ *n* : a small round hill

¹knot \'nät\ *n* **1** : an interlacing (as of string) forming a lump or knob and often used for fastening or tying together **2** : PROBLEM **3** : a bond of union; *esp* : the marriage bond **4** : a protuberant lump or swelling in tissue **5** : a rounded cross-grained area in lumber that is a section through the junction of a tree branch with the trunk; *also* : the woody tissue forming this junction in a tree **6** : GROUP, CLUSTER **7** : an ornamental bow of ribbon **8** : one nautical mile per hour; *also* : one nautical mile — **knot·ty** *adj*

knot 1

²knot *vb* **knot·ted; knot·ting** **1** : to tie in or with a knot **2** : ENTANGLE

knot·hole \-,hōl\ *n* : a hole in a board or tree trunk where a knot has come out

knout \'naůt, 'nüt\ *n* : a whip used for flogging

know \'nō\ *vb* **knew** \'nü, 'nyü\; **known** \'nōn\; **know·ing** **1** : to perceive directly : have understanding or direct cognition of; *also* : to recognize the nature of **2** : to be acquainted or familiar with **3** : to be aware of the truth of **4** : to have a practical understanding of — **know·able** *adj* — **know·er** *n* — **in the know** : possessing confidential information

know—how \'nō-,haů\ *n* : knowledge of how to do something smoothly and efficiently

knowing *adj* **1** : having or reflecting knowledge, intelligence, or information **2** : shrewdly and keenly alert **3** : DELIBERATE ⟨~ interference⟩ ♦ *Synonyms* CLEVER, BRIGHT, SMART — **know·ing·ly** *adv*

knowl·edge \'nä-lij\ *n* **1** : understanding gained by actual experience ⟨a ~ of carpentry⟩ **2** : range of information ⟨to the best of my ~⟩ **3** : clear perception of truth **4** : something learned and kept in the mind

knowl·edge·able \'nä-li-jə-bəl\ *adj* : having or showing knowledge or intelligence

knuck·le \'nə-kəl\ *n* : the rounded knob at a joint and esp. at a finger joint

knuckle down *vb* : to apply oneself earnestly

knuckle under *vb* : SUBMIT, SURRENDER

knurl \'nərl\ *n* **1** : KNOB **2** : one of a series of small ridges on a metal surface to aid in gripping — **knurled** \'nərld\ *adj* — **knurly** *adj*

¹KO \(,)kā-'ō, 'kā-ō\ *n* : KNOCKOUT

²KO *vb* **KO'd; KO'·ing** : to knock out in boxing

ko·ala \kō-'ä-lə\ *n* : a gray furry Australian marsupial that has large hairy ears and feeds on eucalyptus leaves

ko·bo \'kō-(,)bō\ *n, pl* **kobo** — see *naira* at MONEY table

K of C *abbr* Knights of Columbus

kohl·ra·bi \kōl-'rä-bē\ *n, pl* **-bies** [G, fr. It *cavolo rapa*, lit., cabbage turnip] : a cabbage that forms no head but has a swollen fleshy edible stem

koi \'kói\ *n, pl* **koi** [Jp] : a carp bred for large size and a variety of colors and often stocked in ornamental ponds

ko·lin·sky \kə-'lin-skē\ *n, pl* **-skies** : the fur of various Asian minks

Ko·mo·do dragon \kə-'mō-dō-\ *n* [*Komodo* Island, Indonesia] : a carnivorous lizard of Indonesia that is the largest of all known lizards

kook \'kük\ *n* : SCREWBALL 2

kooky *also* **kook·ie** \'kü-kē\ *adj* **kook·i·er; -est** : having the characteristics of a kook : CRAZY, ECCENTRIC — **kook·i·ness** *n*

Koo·te·nai *or* **Ku·te·nai** \'kü-tə-,nā\ *n, pl* **-nai** *or* **-nais** : a member of an American Indian people of the Rocky Mountains in both the U.S. and Canada; *also* : their language

ko·peck *or* **ko·pek** \'kō-,pek\ *n* [Russ *kopeĭka*] — see *ruble* at MONEY table

ko·piy·ka \,kō-'pē-kə\ *n* — see *hryvnia* at MONEY table

ko·ra \'kór-ə\ *n* : a 21-stringed African musical instrument

Ko·ran \kə-'ran, -'rän\ *n* [Ar *qur'ān*] : a sacred book of Islam that contains revelations made to Muhammad by Allah

ko·ru·na \'kór-ə-,nä\ *n, pl* **ko·ru·ny** \-ə-nē\ *or* **korunas** *or* **ko·run** \-ən\ — see MONEY table

ko·sher \'kō-shər\ *adj* [Yiddish, fr. Heb *kāshēr* fit, proper] **1** : ritually fit for use according to Jewish law **2** : selling or serving kosher food

kow·tow \kaú-'taú, 'kaú-,taú\ *vb* [Chin *kòutóu*, fr. *kòu* to knock + *tóu* head] **1** : to show obsequious deference **2** : to kneel and touch the forehead to the ground as a sign of homage or deep respect

KP \,kā-'pē\ *n* **1** : an enlisted man detailed to help the cooks in a military mess **2** : the work of KPs

kph *abbr* kilometers per hour

Kr *symbol* krypton

kraal \'kräl, 'król\ *n* **1** : a native village in southern Africa **2** : an enclosure for domestic animals in southern Africa

kraut \'kraút\ *n* : SAUERKRAUT

Krem·lin \'krem-lən\ *n* : the Russian government

Krem·lin·ol·o·gist \,krem-lə-'nä-lə-jist\ *n* : a specialist in the policies and practices of the government of the Soviet Union

¹kro·na \'krō-nə\ *n, pl* **kro·nor** \-,nór\ [Sw] — see MONEY table

²kro·na \'krō-nə\ *n, pl* **kro·nur** \-nər\ [Icel] — see MONEY table

kro·ne \'krō-nə\ *n, pl* **kro·ner** \-nər\ — see MONEY table

kroon \'krōn\ *n, pl* **kroo·ni** \'krō-nē\ *or* **kroons** — see MONEY table

Kru·ger·rand \'krü-gər-,rand, -,ränd\ *n* : a 1-ounce gold coin of the Republic of South Africa

kryp·ton \'krip-,tän\ *n* : a gaseous chemical element used esp. in electric lamps

KS *abbr* Kansas

kt *abbr* **1** karat **2** knight

ku·do \'kü-dō, 'kyü-\ *n, pl* **kudos** [fr. *kudos* (taken as pl.)] **1** : AWARD, HONOR **2** : COMPLIMENT, PRAISE

ku·dos \'kü-däs, 'kyü-\ *n* : fame and renown resulting from achievement

kud·zu \'kúd-zü, 'kəd-\ *n* [Jp *kuzu*] : a fast-growing weedy leguminous vine used for forage and erosion control

ku·lak \kü-'lak, kyü-, -'läk\ *n* [Russ, lit., fist] **1** : a wealthy peasant farmer in 19th century Russia **2** : a farmer characterized by Communists as too wealthy

kum·quat \'kəm-,kwät\ *n* : any of several small citrus fruits with sweet spongy rind and acid pulp

ku·na \'kü-,nä\ *n, pl* **kuna** *or* **ku·ne** \-nä\ — see MONEY table

kung fu \,kəŋ-'fü, ,kúŋ-\ *n* : a Chinese art of self-defense resembling karate

kung pao \'kəŋ-'paú, 'küŋ-, 'kùŋ-\ *adj* : being stir-fried or deep-fried and served in a spicy hot sauce usu. with peanuts

kur·ta \'kər-tə\ *n* : a long loose-fitting collarless shirt

ku·rus \kə-'rüsh\ *n, pl* **kurus** — see *lira* at MONEY table

kV *abbr* kilovolt

kvell \'kvel\ *vb* : to be extraordinarily proud

kvetch \'kvech, 'kfech\ *vb* : to complain habitually — **kvetch** *n*

kW *abbr* kilowatt

kwa·cha \'kwä-chə\ *n, pl* **kwacha** — see MONEY table

kwan·za \'kwän-zə\ *n, pl* **kwanzas** *or* **kwanza** — see MONEY table

Kwan·zaa *also* **Kwan·za** \'kwän-zə\ *n* [Swahili *kwanza* first] : an African-American cultural festival held from December 26 to January 1

kwash·i·or·kor \,kwä-shē-'ór-kór, -ór-'kór\ *n* : a disease of young children caused by deficient intake of protein

kWh *abbr* kilowatt-hour

Ky *or* **KY** *abbr* Kentucky

kyat \'chät\ *n, pl* **kyats** *or* **kyat** — see MONEY table

ky·bosh *chiefly Brit var of* KIBOSH

¹l \'el\ *n, pl* **l's** *or* **ls** \'elz\ *often cap* **1** : the 12th letter of the English alphabet **2** : fifty in Roman numerals

²l *abbr, often cap* **1** lake **2** large **3** left **4** [L *libra*] pound **5** line **6** liter

¹La *abbr* Louisiana

²La *symbol* lanthanum

LA *abbr* **1** law agent **2** Los Angeles **3** Louisiana

laa·ri \'lä-rē\ *n, pl* **laari** — see *rufiyaa* at MONEY table

lab \'lab\ *n* : LABORATORY

Lab *n* : LABRADOR RETRIEVER

¹la·bel \'lā-bəl\ *n* **1** : a slip attached to something for identification or description **2** : a descriptive or identifying word or phrase **3** : BRAND 3

²label *vb* **-beled** *or* **-belled; -bel·ing** *or* **-bel·ling** **1** : to affix a label to **2** : to describe or name with a label

la·bi·al \'lā-bē-əl\ *adj* : of, relating to, or situated near the lips or labia

la·bia ma·jo·ra \'lā-bē-ə-mə-'jór-ə\ *n pl* : the outer fatty folds of the vulva

labia mi·no·ra \-mə-'nór-ə\ *n pl* : the inner highly vascular folds of the vulva

la·bile \'lā-,bī(-ə)l, -bəl\ *adj* **1** : UNSTABLE **2** : ADAPTABLE

la·bi·um \\'lā-bē-əm\ *n, pl* **la·bia** \-ə\ [NL, fr. L, lip] : any of the folds at the margin of the vulva

¹la·bor \\'lā-bər\ *n* **1** : physical or mental effort; *also* : human activity that provides the goods or services in an economy **2** : the physical efforts of giving birth; *also* : the period of such labor **3** : TASK **4** : those who do manual labor or work for wages; *also* : labor unions or their officials

²labor *vb* **1** : WORK **2** : to move with great effort **3** : to be in the labor of giving birth **4** : to suffer from some disadvantage or distress ⟨~ under a delusion⟩ **5** : to treat or work out laboriously — **la·bor·er** *n*

lab·o·ra·to·ry \\'la-brə-ˌtȯr-ē, -bə-rə-\ *n, pl* **-ries** : a place equipped for making scientific experiments or tests

Labor Day *n* : the 1st Monday in September observed as a legal holiday in recognition of the working people

la·bored \\'lā-bərd\ *adj* : not freely or easily done ⟨~ breathing⟩

la·bo·ri·ous \lə-'bȯr-ē-əs\ *adj* **1** : INDUSTRIOUS **2** : requiring great effort — **la·bo·ri·ous·ly** *adv*

la·bor-sav·ing \\'lā-bər-ˌsā-viŋ\ *adj* : designed to replace or decrease labor

labor union *n* : an organization of workers formed to advance its members' interest in respect to wages and working conditions

la·bour *chiefly Brit var of* LABOR

lab·ra·dor·ite \\'la-brə-ˌdȯr-ˌīt\ *n* : an iridescent feldspar used in jewelry

Lab·ra·dor retriever \\'la-brə-ˌdȯr-\ *n* : any of a breed of strongly built retrievers having a short dense black, yellow, or chocolate coat

la·bur·num \lə-'bər-nəm\ *n* : any of a genus of leguminous shrubs or trees with hanging clusters of yellow flowers

lab·y·rinth \\'la-bə-ˌrinth\ *n* : a place constructed of or filled with confusing intricate passageways : MAZE

lab·y·rin·thine \ˌla-bə-'rin-thən, -ˌthīn, -ˌthēn\ *adj* : INTRICATE, INVOLVED

lac \\'lak\ *n* : a resinous substance secreted by a scale insect and used chiefly in the form of shellac

¹lace \\'lās\ *vb* **laced; lac·ing** **1** : TIE **2** : to adorn with lace **3** : INTERTWINE **4** : BEAT, LASH **5** : to add something that taints (as a drug) or enhances flavor (as a spice) **6** : to criticize sharply — used with *into*

²lace *n* [ME, fr. AF *lace, laz,* fr. L *laqueus* snare] **1** : a cord or string used for drawing together two edges **2** : an ornamental braid **3** : a fine openwork usu. figured fabric made of thread — **lacy** \\'lā-sē\ *adj*

lac·er·ate \\'la-sə-ˌrāt\ *vb* **-at·ed; -at·ing** : to tear roughly — **lac·er·a·tion** \ˌla-sə-'rā-shən\ *n*

lace·wing \\'lās-ˌwiŋ\ *n* : any of various insects with delicate wing veins, long antennae, and often brilliant eyes

lacewing

lach·ry·mal *or* **lac·ri·mal** \\'la-krə-məl\ *adj* **1** *usu* lacrimal : of, relating to, or being glands that produce tears **2** : of, relating to, or marked by tears

lach·ry·mose \\'la-krə-ˌmōs\ *adj* **1** : TEARFUL **2** : MOURNFUL

¹lack \\'lak\ *vb* **1** : to be wanting or missing **2** : to be deficient in

²lack *n* : the fact or state of being wanting or deficient : NEED

lack·a·dai·si·cal \ˌla-kə-'dā-zi-kəl\ *adj* : lacking life, spirit, or zest — **lack·a·dai·si·cal·ly** \-k(ə-)lē\ *adv*

lack·ey \\'la-kē\ *n, pl* **lackeys** **1** : FOOTMAN, SERVANT **2** : TOADY

lack·lus·ter \\'lak-ˌləs-tər\ *adj* : DULL

la·con·ic \lə-'kä-nik\ *adj* [L *laconicus* Spartan, fr. Gk *lakōnikos;* fr. the Spartan reputation for terseness of speech] : sparing of words : TERSE ◆ *Synonyms* CONCISE, CURT, SHORT, SUCCINCT, BRUSQUE — **la·con·i·cal·ly** \-ni-k(ə-)lē\ *adv*

lac·quer \\'la-kər\ *n* : a clear or colored usu. glossy and quick-drying surface coating — **lacquer** *vb*

lac·ri·ma·tion \ˌla-krə-'mā-shən\ *n* : secretion of tears

la·crosse \lə-'krȯs\ *n* [CanF *la crosse,* lit., the crooked stick] : a goal game in which players use a long-handled triangular-headed stick having a mesh pouch for catching, carrying, and throwing the ball

lac·tate \\'lak-ˌtāt\ *vb* **lac·tat·ed; lac·tat·ing** : to secrete milk — **lac·ta·tion** \lak-'tā-shən\ *n*

lac·tic \\'lak-tik\ *adj* **1** : of or relating to milk **2** : obtained from sour milk or whey

lactic acid *n* : a syrupy acid present in blood and muscle tissue and used esp. in food and medicine

lac·tose \\'lak-ˌtōs\ *n* : a sugar present in milk

la·cu·na \lə-'kü-nə, -'kyü-\ *n, pl* **la·cu·nae** \-nē\ *also* **la·cu·nas** [L, pool, pit, gap, fr. *lacus* lake] : a blank space or missing part : GAP, DEFICIENCY

lad \\'lad\ *n* : YOUTH; *also* : FELLOW

lad·der \\'la-dər\ *n* **1** : a structure for climbing that consists of two parallel sidepieces joined at intervals by crosspieces **2** : something resembling a ladder in having ascending steps or stages ⟨a tournament ~⟩

lad·die \\'la-dē\ *n* : a young lad

lad·en \\'lā-dᵊn\ *adj* : LOADED, BURDENED

lad·ing \\'lā-diŋ\ *n* : CARGO, FREIGHT

la·dle \\'lā-dᵊl\ *n* : a deep-bowled long-handled spoon used in taking up and conveying liquids — **ladle** *vb*

la·dy \\'lā-dē\ *n, pl* **ladies** [ME, fr. OE *hlǣfdīge,* fr. *hlāf* bread + *-dīge* (akin to *dǣge* kneader of bread)] **1** : a woman of property, rank, or authority; *also* : a woman of superior social position or of refinement **2** : WOMAN **3** : WIFE

lady beetle *n* : LADYBUG

la·dy·bird \\'lā-dē-ˌbərd\ *n* : LADYBUG

la·dy·bug \-ˌbəg\ *n* : any of various small nearly hemispherical and usu. brightly colored beetles that feed mostly on other insects

la·dy·fin·ger \-ˌfiŋ-gər\ *n* : a small finger-shaped sponge cake

lady-in-waiting *n, pl* **ladies-in-waiting** : a lady appointed to attend or wait on a queen or princess

la·dy·like \\'lā-dē-ˌlīk\ *adj* : WELL-BRED

la·dy·ship \-ˌship\ *n* : the condition of being a lady : rank of lady

lady's slipper *also* **lady slipper** *n* : any of several No. American orchids with slipper-shaped flowers

¹lag \\'lag\ *n* **1** : a slowing up or falling behind; *also* : the amount by which one lags **2** : INTERVAL

²lag *vb* **lagged; lag·ging** **1** : to fail to keep up : stay behind **2** : to slacken gradually ◆ *Synonyms* DAWDLE, DALLY, TARRY, LOITER

la·ger \\'lä-gər\ *n* : a usu. dry beer slowly brewed and matured under refrigeration

lag·gard \\'la-gərd\ *adj* : tending to lag ⟨~ workers⟩ — **laggard** *n* — **lag·gard·ly** *adv or adj* — **lag·gard·ness** *n*

la·gniappe \\'lan-ˌyap\ *n* : something given free esp. with a purchase

la·goon \lə-'gün\ *n* : a shallow sound, channel, or pond near or connected to a larger body of water

laid *past and past part of* LAY

laid-back \\'lād-'bak\ *adj* : having a relaxed style or character ⟨~ music⟩

lain *past part of* ¹LIE

lair \\'ler\ *n* **1** : the resting or living place of a wild animal : DEN **2** : a usu. hidden refuge

laird \\'lerd\ *n, chiefly Scot* : a landed proprietor

lais·ser-faire *chiefly Brit var of* LAISSEZ-FAIRE

lais·sez-faire \ˌle-ˌsā-'fer, ˌlā-, -ˌzā-\ *n* [F *laissez faire* let do] : a doctrine opposing governmental control of economic affairs beyond that necessary to maintain peace and property rights

la·ity \\'lā-ə-tē\ *n* **1** : the people of a religious faith as distinct from its clergy **2** : the mass of people as distinct from those of a particular field

lake \\'lāk\ *n* : an inland body of standing water of considerable size; *also* : a pool of liquid (as lava or pitch)

La·ko·ta \lə-'kō-tə\ *n, pl* **Lakota** *also* **Lakotas** : a member of a western division of the Dakota peoples; *also* : their language

¹lam \'lam\ *vb* **lammed; lam·ming** : to flee hastily — **lam** *n*

²lam *abbr* laminated

Lam *abbr* Lamentations

la·ma \'lä-mə\ *n* : a Buddhist monk of Tibet or Mongolia

la·ma·sery \'lä-mə-ˌser-ē\ *n, pl* **-ser·ies** : a monastery for lamas

¹lamb \'lam\ *n* **1** : a young sheep; *also* : its flesh used as food **2** : an innocent or gentle person

²lamb *vb* : to bring forth a lamb

lam·baste *or* **lam·bast** \lam-'bāst, -'bast\ *vb* **1** : BEAT **2** : EXCORIATE ◆ *Synonyms* CASTIGATE, FLAY, LASH

lamb·da \'lam-də\ *n* : the 11th letter of the Greek alphabet — Λ or λ

lam·bent \'lam-bənt\ *adj* [L *lambens*, prp. of *lambere* to lick] **1** : FLICKERING ⟨a ~ flame⟩ **2** : softly radiant ⟨~ eyes⟩ **3** : marked by lightness or brilliance ⟨~ humor⟩ ◆ *Synonyms* EFFULGENT, INCANDESCENT, LUCENT, LUMINOUS — **lam·ben·cy** \-bən-sē\ *n* — **lam·bent·ly** *adv*

lamb·skin \'lam-ˌskin\ *n* : a lamb's skin or a small fine-grade sheepskin or the leather made from either

¹lame \'lām\ *adj* **lam·er; lam·est** **1** : having a body part and esp. a limb so disabled as to impair freedom of movement; *also* : marked by stiffness and soreness **2** : lacking substance : WEAK ⟨~ excuses⟩ **3** : INFERIOR, PITIFUL — **lame·ly** *adv* — **lame·ness** *n*

²lame *vb* **lamed; lam·ing** : to make lame : DISABLE

la·mé \lä-'mā, la-\ *n* [F] : a brocaded clothing fabric with tinsel filling threads (as of gold or silver)

lame·brain \'lām-ˌbrān\ *n* : DOLT

lame duck *n* : an elected official continuing to hold office between an election and the inauguration of a successor — **lame–duck** *adj*

¹la·ment \lə-'ment\ *vb* **1** : to mourn aloud : WAIL **2** : to express sorrow or regret for : BEWAIL — **lam·en·ta·ble** \'la-mən-tə-bəl, lə-'men-tə-\ *adj* — **lam·en·ta·bly** \-blē\ *adv* — **lam·en·ta·tion** \ˌla-mən-'tā-shən\ *n*

²lament *n* **1** : a crying out in grief : WAIL **2** : DIRGE, ELEGY **3** : COMPLAINT

Lamentations *n* — see BIBLE table

la·mia \'lā-mē-ə\ *n* : a female demon

lam·i·na \'la-mə-nə\ *n, pl* **-nae** \-ˌnē\ *or* **-nas** : a thin plate or scale

¹lam·i·nate \'la-mə-ˌnāt\ *vb* **-nat·ed; -nat·ing** : to make by uniting layers of one or more materials — **lam·i·na·tion** \ˌla-mə-'nā-shən\ *n*

²lam·i·nate \-nət\ *n* : a product manufactured by laminating

lamp \'lamp\ *n* **1** : a vessel with a wick for burning a flammable liquid (as oil) to produce light **2** : a device for producing light or heat

lamp·black \-ˌblak\ *n* : black soot used esp. as a pigment

lamp·light·er \-ˌlī-tər\ *n* : one that lights a lamp

lam·poon \lam-'pün\ *n* : SATIRE; *esp* : a harsh satire directed against an individual — **lampoon** *vb*

lam·prey \'lam-prē\ *n, pl* **lampreys** : any of a family of eel-shaped jawless fishes that have well-developed eyes and a large disk-shaped sucking mouth armed with horny teeth

LAN \'lan, ˌel-ˌā-'en\ *n* : LOCAL AREA NETWORK

la·nai \lə-'nī\ *n* [Hawaiian *lānai*] : PORCH, VERANDA

¹lance \'lans\ *n* **1** : a spear carried by mounted soldiers **2** : any of various sharp-pointed implements; *esp* : LANCET

²lance *vb* **lanced; lanc·ing** : to pierce or open with a lance ⟨~ a boil⟩

lance corporal *n* : an enlisted man in the marine corps ranking above a private first class and below a corporal

lanc·er \'lan-sər\ *n* : a cavalryman of a unit formerly armed with lances

lan·cet \'lan-sət\ *n* : a sharp-pointed and usu. 2-edged surgical instrument

¹land \'land\ *n* **1** : the solid part of the surface of the earth; *also* : a part of the earth's surface ⟨fenced ~⟩ ⟨marshy ~⟩ **2** : NATION **3** : REALM, DOMAIN — **land·less** *adj*

²land *vb* **1** : DISEMBARK; *also* : to touch at a place on shore **2** : to alight or cause to alight on a surface ⟨~ a punch⟩ **3** : to bring to or arrive at a destination **4** : to catch and bring in ⟨~ a fish⟩; *also* : GAIN, SECURE ⟨~ a job⟩

lan·dau \'lan-ˌdau\ *n* : a 4-wheeled carriage with a top divided into two sections that can be lowered, thrown back, or removed

land·ed *adj* : having an estate in land ⟨~ gentry⟩

land·er \'lan-dər\ *n* : a space vehicle designed to land on a celestial body

land·fall \'land-ˌföl\ *n* : a sighting or making of land (as after a voyage); *also* : the land first sighted

land·fill \-ˌfil\ *n* : a low-lying area on which refuse is buried between layers of earth — **landfill** *vb*

land·form \-ˌform\ *n* : a natural feature of a land surface

land·hold·er \-ˌhōl-dər\ *n* : a holder or owner of land — **land·hold·ing** \-diŋ\ *adj or n*

land·ing \'lan-diŋ\ *n* **1** : the action of one that lands **2** : a place for discharging or taking on passengers and cargo **3** : a level part of a staircase

landing gear *n* : the part that supports the weight of an aircraft when it is on the ground

land·la·dy \'land-ˌlā-dē\ *n* : a woman who is a landlord

land·locked \-ˌläkt\ *adj* **1** : enclosed or nearly enclosed by land ⟨a ~ country⟩ **2** : confined to fresh water by some barrier ⟨~ salmon⟩

land·lord \-ˌlord\ *n* **1** : the owner of property leased or rented to another **2** : a person who rents lodgings : INNKEEPER

land·lub·ber \-ˌlə-bər\ *n* : one who knows little of the sea or seamanship

land·mark \-ˌmärk\ *n* **1** : an object that marks a course or boundary or serves as a guide **2** : an event that marks a turning point **3** : a structure of unusual historical and usu. aesthetic interest

land·mass \-ˌmas\ *n* : a large area of land

land mine *n* **1** : a mine placed on or just below the surface of the ground and designed to be exploded by the weight of someone or something passing over it **2** : a trap for the unwary

land·own·er \-ˌō-nər\ *n* : an owner of land

¹land·scape \-ˌskāp\ *n* **1** : a picture of natural inland scenery **2** : a portion of land that can be seen in one glance

²landscape *vb* **land·scaped; land·scap·ing** : to modify (a natural landscape) by grading, clearing, or decorative planting

land·slide \-ˌslīd\ *n* **1** : the slipping down of a mass of rocks or earth on a steep slope; *also* : the mass of material that slides **2** : an overwhelming victory esp. in a political contest

lands·man \'landz-mən\ *n* : a person who lives on land; *esp* : LANDLUBBER

land·ward \'land-wərd\ *adv or adj* : to or toward the land

lane \'lān\ *n* **1** : a narrow passageway (as between fences) **2** : a relatively narrow way or track ⟨traffic ~⟩

lang *abbr* language

lan·guage \'laŋ-gwij\ *n* [ME, fr. AF *langage*, fr. *langue* tongue, language, fr. L *lingua*] **1** : the words, their pronunciation, and the methods of combining them used and understood by a community **2** : form or style of verbal expression ⟨legal ~⟩ **3** : a system of signs and symbols and rules for using them that is used to carry information

lan·guid \'laŋ-gwəd\ *adj* **1** : WEAK **2** : sluggish in character or disposition : LISTLESS **3** : SLOW — **lan·guid·ly** *adv* — **lan·guid·ness** *n*

lan·guish \'laŋ-gwish\ *vb* **1** : to become languid **2** : to become dispirited : PINE **3** : to appeal for sympathy by assuming an expression of grief

lan·guor \'laŋ-gər\ *n* **1** : a languid feeling **2** : listless indolence or inertia ◆ *Synonyms* LETHARGY, LASSITUDE, TORPIDITY, TORPOR — **lan·guor·ous** *adj* — **lan·guor·ous·ly** *adv*

La Ni·ña \lä-'nē-nyə\ *n* : an upwelling of unusually cold ocean water along the west coast of So. America that often follows an El Niño

lank \'laŋk\ *adj* **1** : not well filled out **2** : hanging straight and limp

lanky \'laŋ-kē\ *adj* **lank·i·er; -est** : ungracefully tall and thin

lan·o·lin \'lan-ᵊl-ən\ *n* : the fatty coating of sheep's wool esp. when refined for use in ointments and cosmetics

lan·ta·na \lan-'tä-nə\ *n* : any of a genus of tropical shrubs related to the vervains with showy heads of small bright flowers

lan·tern \'lan-tərn\ *n* [ME *lanterne*, fr. AF, fr. L *lanterna*, fr. Gk *lamptēr*, fr. *lampein* to shine] **1** : a usu. portable light with a protective covering **2** : the chamber in a lighthouse containing the light **3** : a projector for slides

lan·tha·num \'lan-thə-nəm\ *n* : a soft malleable metallic chemical element

lan·yard \'lan-yərd\ *n* : a piece of rope for fastening something in ships; *also* : any of various cords

¹lap \'lap\ *n* **1** : a loose panel of a garment **2** : the clothing that lies on the knees, thighs, and lower part of the trunk when one sits; *also* : the front part of the lower trunk and thighs of a seated person **3** : an environment of nurture ⟨the ∼ of luxury⟩ **4** : CHARGE, CONTROL ⟨in the ∼ of the gods⟩

²lap *vb* **lapped; lap·ping 1** : FOLD **2** : WRAP **3** : to lay over or near so as to partly cover

³lap *n* **1** : the amount by which an object overlaps another; *also* : the part of an object that overlaps another **2** : an act or instance of going over a course (as a track or swimming pool)

⁴lap *vb* **lapped; lap·ping 1** : to scoop up food or drink with the tip of the tongue; *also* : DEVOUR — usu. used with *up* **2** : to splash gently ⟨*lapping* waves⟩

⁵lap *n* **1** : an act or instance of lapping **2** : a gentle splashing sound

lap·a·ros·co·py \ˌla-pə-'räs-kə-pē\ *n, pl* **-pies 1** : visual examination of the abdomen by means of an endoscope; *also* : surgery using laparoscopy — **lap·a·ro·scope** \'la-pə-rə-ˌskōp\ *n* — **lap·a·ro·scop·ic** \ˌla-pə-rə-'skä-pik\ *adj*

lap·dog \'lap-ˌdȯg\ *n* : a small dog that may be held in the lap

la·pel \lə-'pel\ *n* : the fold of the front of a coat that is usu. a continuation of the collar

¹lap·i·dary \'la-pə-ˌder-ē\ *n, pl* **-dar·ies** : a person who cuts, polishes, or engraves precious stones

²lapidary *adj* **1** : of, relating to, or suitable for engraved inscriptions **2** : of, relating to, or suggestive of precious stones or the art of cutting them

lap·in \'la-pən\ *n* : rabbit fur usu. sheared and dyed

la·pis la·zu·li \ˌla-pəs-'la-zə-lē, -zhə-\ *n* : a usu. blue semiprecious stone often having sparkling bits of pyrite

lap·pet \'la-pət\ *n* : a fold or flap on a garment

¹lapse \'laps\ *n* [L *lapsus*, fr. *labi* to slip] **1** : a slight error ⟨a mental ∼⟩ **2** : a fall from a higher to a lower state **3** : the termination of a right or privilege through failure to meet requirements **4** : INTERRUPTION **5** : APOSTASY **6** : a passage of time; *also* : INTERVAL ✦ *Synonyms* BLOOPER, BLUNDER, BONER, GOOF, MISTAKE, SLIP

²lapse *vb* **lapsed; laps·ing 1** : to commit apostasy **2** : SINK, SLIP **3** : CEASE

lap·top \'lap-ˌtäp\ *adj* : of a size that can be used conveniently on one's lap ⟨a ∼ computer⟩ — **laptop** *n*

lap·wing \'lap-ˌwiŋ\ *n* : an Old World crested plover

lar·board \'lär-bərd\ *n* : ⁵PORT

lar·ce·ny \'lär-sə-nē\ *n, pl* **-nies** [ME, fr. AF *larcin* theft, fr. L *latrocinium* robbery, fr. *latro* mercenary soldier] : THEFT — **lar·ce·nous** \-nəs\ *adj*

larch \'lärch\ *n* : any of a genus of trees related to the pines that shed their needles in the fall

¹lard \'lärd\ *vb* **1** : to insert strips of usu. pork fat into (meat) before cooking; *also* : GREASE **2** *obs* : ENRICH

²lard *n* : a soft white fat obtained by rendering fatty tissue of the hog

lar·der \'lär-dər\ *n* : a place where foods (as meat) are kept

large \'lärj\ *adj* **larg·er; larg·est** : having more than usual power, capacity, or scope **2** : exceeding most other things of like kind in quantity or size ✦ *Synonyms* BIG, GREAT, OVERSIZE — **large** *adv* — **large·ness** *n* — **at large 1** : UNCONFINED **2** : as a whole

large·ly \'lärj-lē\ *adv* : to a large extent

lar·gesse *or* **lar·gess** \lär-'zhes, -'jes\ *n* **1** : liberal giving **2** : a generous gift

¹lar·go \'lär-gō\ *adv or adj* [It, slow, broad, fr. L *largus* abundant] : at a very slow tempo — used as a direction in music

²largo *n, pl* **largos** : a largo movement

lari \'lä-rē\ *n, pl* **lari** — see MONEY table

lar·i·at \'lar-ē-ət\ *n* [AmerSp *la reata* the lasso, fr. Sp *la* + AmerSp *reata* lasso, fr. Sp *reatar* to tie again] : a long rope used to catch or tether livestock : LASSO

¹lark \'lärk\ *n* : any of a family of small songbirds; *esp* : SKYLARK

²lark *n* : a source of or quest for fun or adventure

³lark *vb* : to engage in harmless fun or mischief — often used with *about*

lark·spur \'lärk-ˌspər\ *n* : DELPHINIUM; *esp* : any of the widely cultivated annual delphiniums

lar·va \'lär-və\ *n, pl* **lar·vae** \-(ˌ)vē\ *also* **larvas** [NL, fr. L, specter, mask] : the wingless often wormlike form in which insects hatch from the egg; *also* : any young animal (as a tadpole) that is fundamentally unlike its parent — **lar·val** \-vəl\ *adj*

lar·yn·gi·tis \ˌlar-ən-'jī-təs\ *n* : inflammation of the larynx

lar·ynx \'lar-iŋks\ *n, pl* **la·ryn·ges** \lə-'rin-jēz\ *or* **lar·ynx·es** : the upper part of the trachea containing the vocal cords — **la·ryn·ge·al** \lə-'rin-jəl\ *adj*

la·sa·gna \lə-'zän-yə\ *n* [It] : boiled broad flat noodles baked with a sauce usu. of tomatoes, cheese, and meat

las·car \'las-kər\ *n* : an Indian sailor

las·civ·i·ous \lə-'si-vē-əs\ *adj* : LUSTFUL, LEWD ✦ *Synonyms* LICENTIOUS, LECHEROUS, LIBIDINOUS, SALACIOUS — **las·civ·i·ous·ness** *n*

la·ser \'lā-zər\ *n* [*light amplification by stimulated emission of radiation*] **1** : a device that produces an intense monochromatic beam of light **2** : something thrown or directed straight with high speed or intensity

laser disc *n* : OPTICAL DISK; *esp* : one containing a video recording

¹lash \'lash\ *vb* **1** : to move violently or suddenly **2** : WHIP **3** : to attack verbally

²lash *n* **1** : a stroke esp. with a whip; *also* : WHIP **2** : a stinging rebuke **3** : EYELASH

³lash *vb* : to bind with or as if with a line

lass \'las\ *n* : GIRL

lass·ie \'la-sē\ *n* : LASS

las·si·tude \'la-sə-ˌtüd, -ˌtyüd\ *n* **1** : WEARINESS, FATIGUE **2** : LANGUOR

las·so \'la-sō, la-'sü\ *n, pl* **lassos** *or* **lassoes** [Sp *lazo*] : a rope or long leather thong with a noose used for catching livestock — **lasso** *vb*

¹last \'last\ *vb* **1** : to continue in existence or operation **2** : to remain fresh or unimpaired : ENDURE **3** : to manage to continue **4** : to be enough for the needs of

²last *n* : a foot-shaped form on which a shoe is shaped or repaired

³last *vb* : to shape with a last

⁴last *adv* **1** : at the end **2** : most recently **3** : in conclusion

⁵last *adj* **1** : following all the rest : FINAL **2** : next before the present ⟨∼ week⟩ **3** : most up-to-date **4** : farthest from a specified quality, attitude, or likelihood ⟨the ∼ thing we want⟩ **5** : CONCLUSIVE; *also* : SUPREME — **last·ly** *adv*

⁶last *n* : something that is last — **at last** : FINALLY

last–ditch \'last-ˌdich\ *adj* : made as a final effort esp. to avert disaster

last laugh *n* : an ultimate satisfaction or triumph despite previous doubt or criticism

Last Supper *n* : the supper eaten by Jesus and his disciples on the night of his betrayal

lat *abbr* latitude

Lat *abbr* Latin

¹latch \'lach\ *vb* : to catch or get hold

²latch *n* : a catch that holds a door or gate closed

³latch *vb* : to make fast with a latch

latch·et \'la-chət\ *n* : a strap, thong, or lace for fastening a shoe or sandal

latch·key \'lach-ˌkē\ *n* : a key for opening a door latch esp. from the outside

latch·string \-ˌstriŋ\ *n* : a string on a latch that may be left hanging outside the door for raising the latch

¹late \'lāt\ *adj* **lat·er; lat·est 1** : coming or remaining after the due, usual, or proper time **2** : far advanced toward the close or end **3** : recently deceased **4** : made, appearing, or happening just previous to the present : RECENT — **late·ly** *adv* — **late·ness** *n*

²late *adv* **lat·er; lat·est 1** : after the usual or proper time; *also* : at or to an advanced point in time **2** : RECENTLY

late·com·er \'lāt-ˌkə-mər\ *n* : one who arrives late

la·teen \lə-'tēn\ *adj* : relating to or being a triangular sail extended by a long spar slung to a low mast

la·tent \'lāt-ᵊnt\ *adj* : present but not visible or active ✦ *Synonyms* DORMANT, QUIESCENT, POTENTIAL — **la·ten·cy** \-ᵊn-sē\ *n*

¹lat·er·al \'la-tə-rəl\ *adj* : situated on, directed toward, or coming from the side — **lat·er·al·ly** *adv*

²lateral *n* **1** : a branch from the main part **2** : a football pass thrown parallel to the line of scrimmage or away from the opponent's goal

la·tex \'lā-ˌteks\ *n, pl* **la·ti·ces** \'lā-tə-ˌsēz, 'lā-\ *or* **la·tex·es** **1** : a milky juice produced by various plant cells (as of milkweeds, poppies, and the rubber tree) **2** : a water emulsion of a synthetic rubber or plastic used esp. in paint

lath \'lath, 'la_th\ *n, pl* **laths** *or* **lath** : a thin narrow strip of wood used esp. as a base for plaster; *also* : a building material in sheets used for the same purpose — **lath** *vb*

lathe \'lā_th\ *n* : a machine in which a piece of material is held and turned while being shaped by a tool

¹lath·er \'la-_thər\ *n* **1** : a foam or froth formed when a detergent is agitated in water; *also* : foam from profuse sweating (as by a horse) **2** : DITHER

²lather *vb* : to spread lather over; *also* : to form a lather

Lat·in \'lat-ᵊn\ *n* **1** : the language of ancient Rome **2** : a member of any of the peoples whose languages derive from Latin — **Latin** *adj*

La·ti·na \lə-tē-nə\ *n* : a woman or girl who is a native or inhabitant of Latin America; *also* : a woman or girl of Latin-American origin living in the U.S.

Latin American *n* : a native or inhabitant of any of the countries of No., Central, or So. America whose official language is Spanish or Portuguese — **Latin–American** *adj*

La·ti·no \lə-'tē-nō\ *n, pl* **-nos** : a native or inhabitant of Latin America; *also* : a person of Latin-American origin living in the U.S. — **Latino** *adj*

lat·i·tude \'la-tə-ˌtüd, -ˌtyüd\ *n* **1** : angular distance north or south from the earth's equator measured in degrees **2** : a region marked by its latitude **3** : freedom of action or choice

lat·i·tu·di·nar·i·an \ˌla-tə-ˌtü-də-'ner-ē-ən, -ˌtyü-\ *n* : a person who is liberal in religious belief and conduct

la·trine \lə-'trēn\ *n* : TOILET

lats \'läts\ *n, pl* **la·ti** \'lä-tē\ *or* **la·tu** \'lä-tü\ — see MONEY table

lat·ter \'la-tər\ *adj* **1** : more recent; *also* : FINAL **2** : of, relating to, or being the second of two things referred to

lat·ter–day *adj* **1** : of present or recent times **2** : of a later or subsequent time

Latter–day Saint *n* : a member of a religious body founded by Joseph Smith in 1830 and accepting the Book of Mormon as divine revelation : MORMON

lat·ter·ly \'la-tər-lē\ *adv* **1** : LATER **2** : of late : RECENTLY

lat·tice \'la-təs\ *n* **1** : a framework of crossed wood or metal strips; *also* : a window, door, or gate having a lattice **2** : a regular geometrical arrangement

lattice 1

lat·tice·work \-ˌwərk\ *n* : LATTICE; *also* : work made of lattices

Lat·vi·an \'lat-vē-ən\ *n* **1** : a native or inhabitant of Latvia **2** : the language of the Latvians — **Latvian** *adj*

¹laud \'lȯd\ *n* : PRAISE, ACCLAIM

²laud *vb* : PRAISE, EXTOL ♦ *Synonyms* CELEBRATE, EULOGIZE, GLORIFY, MAGNIFY — **laud·able** *adj* — **laud·ably** *adv*

lau·da·num \'lȯd-ᵊn-əm\ *n* : a tincture of opium

lau·da·to·ry \'lȯ-də-ˌtȯr-ē\ *adj* : of, relating to, or expressive of praise

¹laugh \'laf, 'låf\ *vb* [ME, fr. OE *hliehhan*] : to show mirth, joy, or scorn with a chuckle or explosive vocal sound; *also* : to become amused or derisive — **laugh·able** *adj* — **laugh·ing·ly** *adv*

²laugh *n* **1** : the act of laughing **2** : JOKE; *also* : JEER **3** *pl* : SPORT 1

laughing gas *n* : NITROUS OXIDE

laugh·ing·stock \'la-fiŋ-ˌstäk, 'lå-\ *n* : an object of ridicule

laugh·ter \'laf-tər, 'låf-\ *n* : the action or sound of laughing

¹launch \'lȯnch\ *vb* **1** : THROW, HURL; *also* : to send off ⟨∼ a rocket⟩ **2** : to set afloat **3** : to set in operation : START — **launch·er** *n*

²launch *n* : an act or instance of launching

³launch *n* : a small open or half-decked motorboat

launch·pad \'lȯnch-ˌpad\ *n* : a platform from which a rocket is launched

laun·der \'lȯn-dər\ *vb* **1** : to wash or wash and iron clothing and household linens **2** : to transfer (as money of an illegal origin) through an outside party to conceal the true source — **laun·der·er** *n*

laun·dress \'lȯn-drəs\ *n* : a woman who is a laundry worker

laun·dry \'lȯn-drē\ *n, pl* **laundries** [fr. obs. *launder* launderer, fr. AF *lavandere*, fr. ML *lavandarius*, fr. L *lavandus* needing to be washed, fr. *lavare* to wash] **1** : a place where laundering is done **2** : clothes or linens that have been or are to be laundered — **laun·dry·man** \-mən\ *n*

lau·re·ate \'lȯr-ē-ət\ *n* : the recipient of honor for achievement in an art or science — **lau·re·ate·ship** *n*

lau·rel \'lȯ-rəl\ *n* **1** : an evergreen tree or shrub of southern Europe that is related to the sassafras and cinnamon and has glossy aromatic leaves **2** : MOUNTAIN LAUREL **3** : a crown of laurel awarded as an honor — usu. used in pl.

lav *abbr* lavatory

la·va \'lä-və, 'la-\ *n* [It] : melted rock coming from a volcano; *also* : such rock that has cooled and hardened

la·vage \lə-'väzh\ *n* [F] : WASHING; *esp* : the washing out (as of an organ) esp. for medicinal reasons

lav·a·to·ry \'la-və-ˌtȯr-ē\ *n, pl* **-ries** **1** : a fixed washbowl with running water and drainpipe **2** : BATHROOM

lave \'lāv\ *vb* **laved; lav·ing** : WASH

lav·en·der \'la-vən-dər\ *n* **1** : a Mediterranean mint or its dried leaves and flowers used to perfume clothing and bed linen **2** : a pale purple color

¹lav·ish \'la-vish\ *adj* [ME *laves, lavage*, prob. fr. MF *lavasse, lavache* downpour, fr. *laver* to wash] **1** : expending or bestowing profusely **2** : expended or produced in abundance ⟨∼ gifts⟩ **3** : marked by excess ⟨∼ decor⟩ — **lav·ish·ly** *adv* — **lav·ish·ness** *n*

²lavish *vb* : to expend or give freely

law \'lȯ\ *n* **1** : a rule of conduct or action established by custom or laid down and enforced by a governing authority; *also* : the whole body of such rules **2** : the control brought about by enforcing rules **3** *cap* : the revelation of the divine will set forth in the Old Testament; *also* : the first part of the Jewish scriptures — see BIBLE table **4** : a rule or principle of construction or procedure **5** : the science that deals with laws and their interpretation and application **6** : the profession of a lawyer **7** : a rule or principle stating something that always works in the same way under the same conditions

law·break·er \'lȯ-ˌbrā-kər\ *n* : a person who violates the law

law·ful \'lȯ-fəl\ *adj* **1** : permitted by law **2** : RIGHTFUL — **law·ful·ly** *adv*

law·giv·er \-ˌgi-vər\ *n* : LEGISLATOR

law·less \'lȯ-ləs\ *adj* **1** : having no laws **2** : UNRULY, DISORDERLY ⟨a ∼ mob⟩ — **law·less·ly** *adv* — **law·less·ness** *n*

law·mak·er \-ˌmā-kər\ *n* : LEGISLATOR

law·man \'lȯ-mən\ *n* : a law enforcement official (as a sheriff or marshal)

¹lawn \'lȯn\ *n* : ground (as around a house) covered with mowed grass

²lawn *n* : a fine sheer linen or cotton fabric

lawn bowling *n* : a bowling game played on a green with wooden balls which are rolled at a jack

law·ren·ci·um \lȯ-'ren-sē-əm\ *n* : a short-lived radioactive element

law·suit \'lȯ-ˌsüt\ *n* : a suit in law

law·yer \'lȯ-yər\ *n* : one who conducts lawsuits for clients or advises as to legal rights and obligations in other matters — **law·yer·ly** *adj*

lax \'laks\ *adj* **1** : not strict ⟨∼ discipline⟩ **2** : not tense or rigid ♦ *Synonyms* REMISS, NEGLIGENT, NEGLECTFUL, DELINQUENT, DERELICT — **lax·i·ty** \'lak-sə-tē\ *n* — **lax·ly** *adv* — **lax·ness** *n*

¹**lax·a·tive** \'lak-sə-tiv\ *adj* : relieving constipation
²**laxative** *n* : a usu. mild laxative drug
¹**lay** \'lā\ *vb* **laid** \'lād\; **lay·ing 1** : to beat or strike down **2** : to put on or set down : PLACE **3** : to produce and deposit eggs **4** : SETTLE; *also* : ALLAY **5** : SPREAD **6** : PREPARE, CONTRIVE **7** : WAGER **8** : to impose esp. as a duty or burden **9** : to set in order or position **10** : to bring to a specified condition **11** : to put forward : SUBMIT
²**lay** *n* : the way in which something lies or is laid in relation to something else
³**lay** *past of* ¹LIE
⁴**lay** *n* **1** : a simple narrative poem **2** : SONG
⁵**lay** *adj* **1** : of or relating to the laity **2** : not of a particular profession; *also* : lacking extensive knowledge of a particular subject
lay·away \'lā-ə-ˌwā\ *n* : a purchasing agreement by which a retailer agrees to hold merchandise secured by a deposit until the price is paid in full
lay·er \'lā-ər\ *n* **1** : one that lays **2** : one thickness, course, or fold laid or lying over or under another
lay·ette \lā-'et\ *n* [F, fr. MF, dim. of *laye* box] : an outfit of clothing and equipment for a newborn infant
lay·man \'lā-mən\ *n* : a person who is a member of the laity
lay·off \'lā-ˌof\ *n* **1** : a period of inactivity **2** : the act of laying off an employee
lay off *vb* **1** : to cease to employ (a worker) often temporarily **2** : to leave undisturbed **3** : to stop doing something
lay·out \'lā-ˌaut\ *n* : the final arrangement, plan, or design of something
lay·over \-ˌō-vər\ *n* : STOPOVER
lay·per·son \-ˌpər-sən\ *n* : a member of the laity
lay·wom·an \'lā-ˌwu-mən\ *n* : a woman who is a member of the laity
la·zar \'la-zər, 'lā-\ *n* : LEPER
laze \'lāz\ *vb* **lazed; laz·ing** : to pass time in idleness or relaxation
la·zy \'lā-zē\ *adj* **la·zi·er; -est 1** : disliking activity or exertion **2** : encouraging idleness ⟨a ~ day⟩ **3** : SLUGGISH **4** : DROOPY, LAX **5** : not rigorous or strict ⟨~ work habits⟩ — **la·zi·ly** \-zə-lē\ *adv* — **la·zi·ness** \-zē-nəs\ *n*
la·zy·bones \-ˌbōnz\ *n sing or pl* : a lazy person
lazy Su·san \ˌlā-zē-'süz-ᵊn\ *n* : a revolving tray used for serving food
lb *abbr* [L *libra*] pound
lc *abbr* lowercase
LC *abbr* Library of Congress
¹**LCD** \ˌel-(ˌ)sē-'dē\ *n* [*liquid crystal display*] : a display (as of the time in a digital watch) that consists of segments of a liquid crystal whose reflectivity varies with the voltage applied to them
²**LCD** *abbr* least common denominator; lowest common denominator
LCDR *abbr* lieutenant commander
LCM *abbr* least common multiple; lowest common multiple
LCpl *abbr* lance corporal
LCS *abbr* League Championship Series
ld *abbr* **1** load **2** lord
LD *abbr* learning disabled; learning disability
LDC *abbr* less developed country
ldg *abbr* **1** landing **2** loading
LDL \ˌel-(ˌ)dē-'el\ *n* [*low-density lipoprotein*] : a cholesterol-rich protein-poor lipoprotein of blood plasma correlated with increased probability of developing atherosclerosis
L-do·pa \ˌel-'dō-pə\ *n* : an isomer of dopa used esp. in the treatment of Parkinson's disease
LDS *abbr* Latter-day Saints
lea \'lē, 'lā\ *n* : PASTURE, MEADOW
leach \'lēch\ *vb* : to pass a liquid (as water) through to carry off the soluble components; *also* : to dissolve out by such means ⟨~ alkali from ashes⟩
¹**lead** \'lēd\ *vb* **led** \'led\; **lead·ing 1** : to guide on a way **2** : LIVE ⟨~ a quiet life⟩ **3** : to direct the operations, activity, or performance of ⟨~ an orchestra⟩ **4** : to go at the head of : be first ⟨~ a parade⟩ **5** : to begin play with; *also* : BEGIN, OPEN **6** : to tend toward a definite result ⟨study ~*ing* to a degree⟩ — **lead·er** *n* — **lead·er·less** *adj* — **lead·er·ship** *n*

²**lead** \'lēd\ *n* **1** : a position at the front; *also* : a margin by which one leads **2** : the privilege of leading in cards; *also* : the card or suit led **3** : EXAMPLE **4** : one that leads **5** : a principal role (as in a play); *also* : one who plays such a role **6** : INDICATION, CLUE **7** : an insulated electrical conductor
³**lead** \'led\ *n* **1** : a heavy malleable bluish white chemical element **2** : an article made of lead; *esp* : a weight for sounding at sea **3** : a thin strip of metal used to separate lines of type in printing **4** : a thin stick of marking substance in or for a pencil
⁴**lead** \'led\ *vb* **1** : to cover, line, or weight with lead **2** : to fix (glass) in position with lead **3** : to treat or mix with lead or a lead compound
lead·en \'led-ᵊn\ *adj* **1** : made of lead; *also* : of the color of lead **2** : SLUGGISH, DULL
lead off *vb* : OPEN, BEGIN; *esp* : to bat first in an inning — **lead-off** \'lēd-ˌof\ *n or adj*
leaf \'lēf\ *n, pl* **leaves** \'lēvz\ **1** : a usu. flat and green outgrowth of a plant stem that is a unit of foliage and functions esp. in photosynthesis; *also* : FOLIAGE **2** : something (as a page or a flat moving part) that is suggestive of a leaf — **leaf·less** *adj* — **leafy** *adj*
²**leaf** *vb* **1** : to produce leaves **2** : to turn the pages of a book
leaf·age \'lē-fij\ *n* : FOLIAGE
leafed \'lēft\ *adj* : LEAVED
leaf·hop·per \'lēf-ˌhä-pər\ *n* : any of a family of small leaping insects related to the cicadas that suck the juices of plants
leaf·let \'lē-flət\ *n* **1** : a division of a compound leaf **2** : PAMPHLET, FOLDER
leaf mold *n* : a compost or layer composed chiefly of decayed leaves
leaf·stalk \'lēf-ˌstok\ *n* : PETIOLE
¹**league** \'lēg\ *n* : a unit of distance equal to about three miles (five kilometers)
²**league** *n* **1** : an association or alliance (as of nations or sports teams) for a common purpose **2** : CLASS, CATEGORY — **league** *vb* — **leagu·er** \'lē-gər\ *n*
¹**leak** \'lēk\ *vb* **1** : to enter or escape through a leak **2** : to let a substance in or out through an opening **3** : to become or make known ⟨~*ed* the news⟩
²**leak** *n* **1** : a crack or hole that accidentally admits a fluid or light or lets it escape; *also* : something that secretly or accidentally permits the admission or escape of something else **2** : LEAKAGE — **leaky** *adj*
leak·age \'lē-kij\ *n* **1** : the act of leaking **2** : the thing or amount that leaks
¹**lean** \'lēn\ *vb* **1** : to bend from a vertical position : INCLINE **2** : to cast one's weight to one side for support **3** : to rely on for support **4** : to incline in opinion, taste, or desire — **lean** *n*
²**lean** *adj* **1** : lacking or deficient in flesh and esp. in fat ⟨~ meat⟩ **2** : lacking richness or productiveness ⟨~ profits⟩ **3** : low in fuel content — **lean·ness** *n*
leant \'lent\ *chiefly Brit past of* LEAN
lean-to \'lēn-ˌtü\ *n, pl* **lean-tos** \-ˌtüz\ : a wing or extension of a building having a roof of only one slope; *also* : a rough shed or shelter with a similar roof
¹**leap** \'lēp\ *vb* **leapt** \'lept, 'lēpt\ *or* **leaped; leap·ing** : to spring free from a surface or over an obstacle : JUMP
²**leap** *n* : JUMP
leap·frog \'lēp-ˌfrog, -ˌfräg\ *n* : a game in which a player bends down and is vaulted over by another — **leapfrog** *vb*
leap year *n* : a year containing 366 days with February 29 as the extra day
learn \'lərn\ *vb* **learned** \'lərnd, 'lərnt\; **learn·ing 1** : to gain knowledge, understanding, or skill by study or experience; *also* : MEMORIZE **2** : to find out : ASCERTAIN — **learn·er** *n*
learn·ed \'lər-nəd\ *adj* : SCHOLARLY, ERUDITE — **learn·ed·ly** *adv* — **learn·ed·ness** *n*
learn·ing \'lər-niŋ\ *n* : KNOWLEDGE, ERUDITION
learning disability *n* : any of various conditions (as dyslexia) that interfere with a person's ability to learn and so result in impaired functioning (as in language) — **learning disabled** *adj*
learnt \'lərnt\ *chiefly Brit past and past part of* LEARN
¹**lease** \'lēs\ *n* : a contract transferring real estate for a term of years or at will usu. for a specified rent

²**lease** *vb* **leased; leas·ing** [AF *lesser, lescher* to leave, hand over, lease, fr. L *laxare* to loosen, fr. *laxus* slack] **1** : to grant by lease **2** : to hold under a lease ◆ **Synonyms** LET, CHARTER, HIRE, RENT

lease·hold \'lēs-ˌhōld\ *n* **1** : a tenure by lease **2** : land held by lease — **lease·hold·er** *n*

leash \'lēsh\ *n* [ME *lees, leshe,* fr. AF **lesche, lesse* prob. fr. *lesser* to leave, let go] **1** : a line for leading or restraining an animal **2** : a state of restraint ⟨kept spending on a tight ∼⟩ — **leash** *vb*

¹**least** \'lēst\ *adj* **1** : lowest in importance or position **2** : smallest in size or degree **3** : SLIGHTEST

²**least** *n* : one that is least

³**least** *adv* : in the smallest or lowest degree

least common denominator *n* : the least common multiple of two or more denominators

least common multiple *n* : the smallest common multiple of two or more numbers

least·wise \'lēst-ˌwīz\ *adv* : at least

leath·er \'le-thər\ *n* : animal skin dressed for use — **leath·ern** \-thərn\ *adj* — **leath·ery** *adj*

leath·er·back \-ˌbak\ *n* : the largest existing sea turtle with a flexible leathery carapace

leath·er·neck \-ˌnek\ *n* : MARINE

¹**leave** \'lēv\ *vb* **left** \'left\; **leav·ing 1** : to allow or cause to remain behind **2** : to have as a remainder **3** : BEQUEATH **4** : to let stay without interference **5** : to go away : depart from **6** : GIVE UP, ABANDON

²**leave** *n* **1** : PERMISSION; *also* : authorized absence from duty **2** : DEPARTURE

³**leave** *vb* **leaved; leav·ing** : LEAF

leaved \'lēvd\ *adj* : having leaves

¹**leav·en** \'le-vən\ *n* **1** : a substance (as yeast) used to produce fermentation (as in dough) **2** : something that modifies or lightens

²**leaven** *vb* : to raise (dough) with a leaven; *also* : to permeate with a modifying or vivifying element ⟨lectures ∼ed with humor⟩

leav·en·ing *n* : LEAVEN

leaves *pl of* LEAF

leave–tak·ing \'lēv-ˌtā-kiŋ\ *n* : DEPARTURE, FAREWELL

leav·ings \'lē-viŋz\ *n pl* : REMNANT, RESIDUE

lech·ery \'le-chə-rē\ *n* : inordinate indulgence in sexual activity — **lech·er** \'le-chər\ *n* — **lech·er·ous** \'le-chərəs\ *adj* — **lech·er·ous·ly** *adv* — **lech·er·ous·ness** *n*

lec·i·thin \'le-sə-thən\ *n* : any of several waxy phosphoruscontaining substances that are common in animals and plants, form colloidal solutions in water, and have emulsifying and wetting properties

lect *abbr* lecture; lecturer

lec·tern \'lek-tərn\ *n* : a stand to support a book for a standing reader

lec·tor \-tər\ *n* : one whose chief duty is to read the lessons in a church service

lec·ture \'lek-chər\ *n* **1** : a discourse given before an audience esp. for instruction **2** : REPRIMAND — **lec·ture** *vb* — **lec·tur·er** *n* — **lec·ture·ship** *n*

led *past and past part of* LEAD

LED \ˌel-(ˌ)ē-'dē\ *n* [*l*ight-*e*mitting *d*iode] : a semiconductor diode that emits light when a voltage is applied to it and is used esp. for electronic displays

le·der·ho·sen \'lā-dər-ˌhōz-ᵊn\ *n pl* : leather shorts often with suspenders worn esp. in Bavaria

ledge \'lej\ *n* [ME *legge* bar of a gate] **1** : a shelflike projection from a top or an edge **2** : REEF

led·ger \'le-jər\ *n* : a book containing accounts to which debits and credits are transferred in final form

lee \'lē\ *n* **1** : a protecting shelter **2** : the side (as of a ship) that is sheltered from the wind — **lee** *adj*

leech \'lēch\ *n* **1** : any of various bloodsucking segmented usu. freshwater worms that are related to the earthworms and have a sucker at each end **2** : a hanger-on who seeks gain

leek \'lēk\ *n* : an onionlike herb grown for its mildly pungent leaves and stalk

leer \'lir\ *n* : a suggestive, knowing, or malicious look — **leer** *vb*

leery \'lir-ē\ *adj* : SUSPICIOUS, WARY

lees \'lēz\ *n pl* : DREGS

¹**lee·ward** \'lē-wərd, 'lü-ərd\ *n* : the lee side

²**leeward** *adj* : situated away from the wind

lee·way \'lē-ˌwā\ *n* **1** : lateral movement of a ship when under way **2** : an allowable margin of freedom or variation

¹**left** \'left\ *adj* [ME, fr. OE, weak; fr. the left hand's being the weaker in most individuals] **1** : of, relating to, or being the side of the body in which the heart is mostly located; *also* : located nearer to this side than to the right **2** *often cap* : of, adhering to, or constituted by the political left — **left** *adv*

²**left** *n* **1** : the left hand; *also* : the side or part that is on or toward the left side **2** *often cap* : those professing political views marked by desire to reform the established order and usu. to give greater freedom to the common people — **left·ward** \-wərd\ *adv or adj*

³**left** *past and past part of* LEAVE

left–hand *adj* **1** : situated on the left **2** : LEFT-HANDED

left–hand·ed \'left-'han-dəd\ *adj* **1** : using the left hand habitually or more easily than the right **2** : designed for or done with the left hand **3** : INSINCERE, BACKHANDED ⟨a ∼ compliment⟩ **4** : COUNTERCLOCKWISE — **left-handed** *adv* — **left–hand·ed·ness** *n* — **left–hand·er** \-dər\ *n*

left·ism \'lef-ˌti-zəm\ *n* **1** : the principles and views of the left **2** : advocacy of the doctrines of the left — **left·ist** \-tist\ *n or adj*

left·over \'left-ˌō-vər\ *n* : something that remains unused or unconsumed

lefty \'lef-tē\ *n, pl* **left·ies 1** : a left-handed person **2** : an advocate of leftism

¹**leg** \'leg\ *n* **1** : a limb of an animal used esp. for supporting the body and in walking; *also* : the part of the vertebrate leg between knee and foot **2** : something resembling or analogous to an animal leg ⟨table ∼⟩ **3** : the part of an article of clothing that covers the leg **4** : a portion of a trip **5** *pl* : long-term appeal or interest ⟨a musical that has ∼s⟩ — **leg·ged** \'le-gəd\ *adj* — **leg·less** *adj*

²**leg** *vb* **legged; leg·ging** : to use the legs in walking or esp. in running

³**leg** *abbr* **1** legal **2** legislative; legislature

leg·a·cy \'le-gə-sē\ *n, pl* **-cies** : INHERITANCE; *also* : something that has come from a predecessor or the past

le·gal \'lē-gəl\ *adj* **1** : of or relating to law or lawyers **2** : LAWFUL; *also* : STATUTORY **3** : enforced in courts of law — **le·gal·i·ty** \li-'ga-lə-tē\ *n* — **le·gal·ize** \'lē-gə-ˌlīz\ *vb* — **le·gal·ly** *adv*

le·gal·ese \ˌlē-gə-'lēz\ *n* : the specialized language of the legal profession

le·gal·ism \'lē-gə-ˌli-zəm\ *n* **1** : strict, literal, or excessive conformity to the law or to a religious or moral code **2** : a legal term — **le·gal·is·tic** \ˌlē-gə-'lis-tik\ *adj*

le·gate \'le-gət\ *n* : an official representative

le·ga·tee \ˌle-gə-'tē\ *n* : a person to whom a legacy is bequeathed

le·ga·tion \li-'gā-shən\ *n* **1** : a diplomatic mission headed by a minister **2** : the official residence and office of a minister in a foreign country

le·ga·to \li-'gä-tō\ *adv or adj* [It, lit., tied] : in a smooth and connected manner (as of music)

leg·end \'le-jənd\ *n* [ME *legende,* fr. AF & ML; AF *legende,* fr. ML *legenda,* fr. L *legere* to read] **1** : a story coming down from the past; *esp* : one popularly accepted as historical though not verifiable **2** : an inscription on an object; *also* : CAPTION **3** : an explanatory list of the symbols on a map or chart

leg·end·ary \'le-jən-ˌder-ē\ *adj* **1** : of, relating to, or characteristic of a legend **2** : FAMOUS — **leg·en·dari·ly** \-ˌder-ə-lē\ *adv*

leg·er·de·main \ˌle-jər-də-'mān\ *n* [ME, fr. MF *leger de main* light of hand] : SLEIGHT OF HAND

leg·ging *or* **leg·gin** \'le-gən, -giŋ\ *n* : a covering for the leg; *also* : TIGHTS

leg·gy \'le-gē\ *adj* **leg·gi·er; -est 1** : having unusually long legs **2** : having long and attractive legs **3** : SPINDLY — used of a plant

leg·horn \'leg-ˌhòrn, 'le-gərn\ *n* **1** : a fine plaited straw; *also* : a hat made of this straw **2** : any of a Mediterranean breed of small hardy chickens

leg·i·ble \'le-jə-bəl\ *adj* : capable of being read : CLEAR — **leg·i·bil·i·ty** \ˌle-jə-'bi-lə-tē\ *n* — **leg·i·bly** \'le-jə-blē\ *adv*

¹**le·gion** \'lē-jən\ *n* **1** : a unit of the Roman army comprising 3000 to 6000 soldiers **2** : MULTITUDE **3** : an associa-

tion of ex-servicemen — **le·gion·ary** \-jə-ˌner-ē\ *n* — **le·gion·naire** \ˌlē-jə-ˈnar\ *n*

²**legion** *adj* : MANY, NUMEROUS

Legionnaires' disease *also* **Legionnaire's disease** \-ˈnerz-\ *n* : a lobar pneumonia caused by a bacterium

legis *abbr* legislation; legislative; legislature

leg·is·late \ˈle-jəs-ˌlāt\ *vb* **-lat·ed; -lat·ing** : to make or enact laws; *also* : to bring about by legislation — **leg·is·la·tor** \-ˌlā-tər\ *n*

leg·is·la·tion \ˌle-jəs-ˈlā-shən\ *n* 1 : the action of legislating 2 : laws made by a legislative body

leg·is·la·tive \ˈle-jəs-ˌlā-tiv\ *adj* 1 : having the power of legislating 2 : of or relating to a legislature or legislation

leg·is·la·ture \ˈle-jəs-ˌlā-chər\ *n* : an organized body of persons having the authority to make laws

le·git \li-ˈjit\ *adj, slang* : LEGITIMATE

¹**le·git·i·mate** \li-ˈji-tə-mət\ *adj* 1 : lawfully begotten 2 : GENUINE 3 : LAWFUL 4 : conforming to recognized principles or accepted rules or standards — **le·git·i·ma·cy** \-mə-sē\ *n* — **le·git·i·mate·ly** *adv*

²**le·git·i·mate** \-ˌmāt\ *vb* : to make legitimate

le·git·i·mise *Brit var of* LEGITIMIZE

le·git·i·mize \li-ˈji-tə-ˌmīz\ *vb* **-mized; -miz·ing** : LEGITIMATE

leg·man \ˈleg-ˌman\ *n* 1 : a reporter assigned usu. to gather information 2 : an assistant who gathers information and runs errands

le·gume \ˈle-ˌgyüm, li-ˈgyüm\ *n* [F] 1 : any of a large family of plants having fruits that are dry pods and split when ripe and including important food and forage plants (as beans and clover); *also* : the part (as seeds or pods) of a legume used as food 2 : the pod of a legume — **le·gu·mi·nous** \li-ˈgyü-mə-nəs\ *adj*

legume 2

¹**lei** \ˈlā, ˈlā-ˌē\ *n* : a wreath or necklace usu. of flowers

²**lei** \ˈlā\ *pl of* LEU

lei·sure \ˈlē-zhər, ˈle-, ˈlā-\ *n* 1 : time free from work or duties 2 : EASE; *also* : CONVENIENCE ♦ *Synonyms* RELAXATION, REST, REPOSE — **lei·sure·ly** *adj or adv*

leit·mo·tif *also* **leit·mo·tiv** \ˈlīt-mō-ˌtēf\ *n* [G *Leitmotiv*, fr. *leiten* to lead + *Motiv* motive] : a dominant recurring theme

lek \ˈlek\ *n, pl* **leks** *or* **le·ke** *or* **lekë** \ˈle-kə\ — see MONEY table

lem·ming \ˈle-miŋ\ *n* [Norw] : any of various short-tailed rodents found mostly in northern regions and noted for recurrent mass migrations

lem·on \ˈle-mən\ *n* 1 : an acid yellow usu. nearly oblong citrus fruit; *also* : a citrus tree that bears lemons 2 : something (as an automobile) unsatisfactory or defective — **lem·ony** *adj*

lem·on·ade \ˌle-mə-ˈnād\ *n* : a beverage of lemon juice, sugar, and water

lemon curd *n* : a custard made with lemon juice, butter, sugar, and eggs

lem·on·grass \ˈle-mən-ˌgras\ *n* : a tropical Asian grass grown for its lemon-scented foliage used as a seasoning

lem·pi·ra \lem-ˈpir-ə\ *n* — see MONEY table

le·mur \ˈlē-mər\ *n* : any of various arboreal primates largely of Madagascar that have large eyes, very soft woolly fur, and a long furry tail

Len·a·pe \ˈle-nə-pē, lə-ˈnä-pē\ *n, pl* **Lenape** *or* **Lenapes** : DELAWARE

lend \ˈlend\ *vb* **lent** \ˈlent\; **lend·ing** 1 : to give for temporary use on condition that the same or its equivalent be returned 2 : AFFORD, FURNISH 3 : ACCOMMODATE — **lend·er** *n*

lend–lease \-ˈlēs\ *n* : the transfer of goods and services to

an ally to aid in a common cause with payment made by a return of the items or their use in the cause or by a similar transfer of other goods and services

length \ˈleŋth\ *n* 1 : the longer or longest dimension of an object; *also* : a measured distance 2 : duration or extent in time or space 3 : the length of something taken as a unit of measure 4 : a single piece of a series of pieces that may be joined together ⟨a ∼ of pipe⟩ — **at length** 1 : in full 2 : FINALLY

length·en \ˈleŋ-thən\ *vb* : to make or become longer ♦ *Synonyms* EXTEND, ELONGATE, PROLONG, PROTRACT

length·wise \ˈleŋth-ˌwīz\ *adv* : in the direction of the length — **lengthwise** *adj*

lengthy \ˈleŋ-thē\ *adj* **length·i·er; -est** 1 : protracted excessively 2 : EXTENDED, LONG ⟨a ∼ journey⟩

le·nient \ˈlē-nē-ənt, -nyənt\ *adj* : of mild and tolerant disposition or effect ♦ *Synonyms* INDULGENT, FORBEARING, MERCIFUL, TOLERANT — **le·ni·en·cy** \ˈlē-nē-ən-sē, -nyən-sē\ *n* — **le·ni·ent·ly** *adv*

len·i·tive \ˈle-nə-tiv\ *adj* : alleviating pain or harshness

len·i·ty \ˈle-nə-tē\ *n* : LENIENCY

lens \ˈlenz\ *n* [L *lent-, lens* lentil; so called fr. the shape of a convex lens] 1 : a curved piece of glass or plastic used singly or combined in an optical instrument for forming an image; *also* : a device for focusing radiation other than light 2 : a transparent body in the eye that focuses light rays on receptors at the back of the eye

Lent \ˈlent\ *n* : a 40-day period of penitence and fasting observed from Ash Wednesday to Easter by many churches — **Lent·en** \ˈlen-tᵊn\ *adj*

len·til \ˈlen-tᵊl\ *n* : a Eurasian annual legume grown for its flat edible seeds and for fodder; *also* : its seed

Leo \ˈlē-ō\ *n* [L, lit., lion] 1 : a zodiacal constellation between Cancer and Virgo usu. pictured as a lion 2 : the 5th sign of the zodiac in astrology; *also* : one born under this sign

le·one \lē-ˈōn\ *n, pl* **leones** *or* **leone** — see MONEY table

le·o·nine \ˈlē-ə-ˌnīn\ *adj* : of, relating to, or resembling a lion

leop·ard \ˈle-pərd\ *n* : a large usu. tawny and black-spotted cat of southern Asia and Africa

le·o·tard \ˈlē-ə-ˌtärd\ *n* : a close-fitting garment worn esp. by dancers and for exercise

lep·er \ˈle-pər\ *n* 1 : a person affected with leprosy 2 : OUTCAST

lep·re·chaun \ˈle-prə-ˌkän\ *n* : a mischievous elf of Irish folklore

lep·ro·sy \ˈle-prə-sē\ *n* : a chronic bacterial disease marked esp. if not treated by slow-growing swellings with deformity and loss of sensation of affected parts — **lep·rous** \-prəs\ *adj*

lep·tin \ˈlep-tən\ *n* : a hormone that is produced by fat-containing cells and plays a role in body weight regulation

lep·ton \lep-ˈtän\ *n, pl* **lep·ta** \-ˈtä\ : a former monetary unit equal to ¹/₁₀₀ drachma

les·bi·an \ˈlez-bē-ən\ *n* [fr. the reputed homosexual group associated with the poet Sappho of Lesbos] : a woman who is a homosexual — **lesbian** *adj* — **les·bi·an·ism** \-ə-ˌni-zəm\ *n*

lèse ma·jes·té *or* **lese maj·es·ty** \ˈlāz-ˈma-jə-stē, ˈlez-, ˈlēz-\ *n* [MF *lese majesté*, fr. L *laesa majestas*, lit., injured majesty] : an offense violating the dignity of a sovereign

le·sion \ˈlē-zhən\ *n* : an abnormal structural change in the body due to injury or disease; *esp* : one clearly marked off from healthy tissue around it

¹**less** \ˈles\ *adj, comparative of* ¹LITTLE 1 : FEWER ⟨∼ than six⟩ 2 : of lower rank, degree, or importance 3 : SMALLER; *also* : more limited in quantity

²**less** *adv, comparative of* ²LITTLE : to a lesser extent or degree

³**less** *n, pl* **less** 1 : a smaller portion 2 : something of less importance

⁴**less** *prep* : diminished by : MINUS ⟨list price ∼ the discount⟩

-less \ləs\ *adj suffix* 1 : destitute of : not having ⟨child*less*⟩ 2 : unable to be acted on or to act (in a specified way) ⟨daunt*less*⟩

les·see \le-ˈsē\ *n* : a tenant under a lease

les·sen \ˈle-sᵊn\ *vb* : to make or become less ♦ *Synonyms* DECREASE, DIMINISH, DWINDLE, ABATE

less·er \'le-sər\ *adj, comparative of* ¹LITTLE : of less size, quality, or significance

les·son \'le-s²n\ *n* **1** : a passage from sacred writings read in a service of worship **2** : a reading or exercise to be studied by a pupil; *also* : something learned **3** : a period of instruction **4** : an instructive example

les·sor \'le-ˌsȯr, le-'sȯr\ *n* : one who conveys property by a lease

lest \'lest\ *conj* : for fear that

¹let \'let\ *n* [ME *lette*, fr. *letten* to delay, hinder, fr. OE *lettan*] **1** : HINDRANCE, OBSTACLE **2** : a shot or point in racket games that does not count

²let *vb* **let; let·ting** [ME *leten*, fr. OE *lǣtan*] **1** : to cause to : MAKE ⟨~ it be known⟩ **2** : RENT, LEASE; *also* : to assign esp. after bids **3** : ALLOW, PERMIT ⟨~ me go⟩

-let *n suffix* **1** : small one ⟨book*let*⟩ **2** : article worn on ⟨wrist*let*⟩

let·down \'let-ˌdau̇n\ *n* **1** : DISAPPOINTMENT **2** : a slackening of effort

le·thal \'lē-thəl\ *adj* : DEADLY, FATAL — **le·thal·ly** *adv*

leth·ar·gy \'le-thər-jē\ *n* **1** : abnormal drowsiness **2** : the quality or state of being lazy or indifferent ♦ **Synonyms** LANGUOR, LASSITUDE, TORPOR — **le·thar·gic** \li-'thär-jik\ *adj*

let on *vb* **1** : REVEAL 1 **2** : PRETEND

¹let·ter \'le-tər\ *n* **1** : a symbol that stands for a speech sound and constitutes a unit of an alphabet **2** : a written or printed communication **3** *pl* : LITERATURE; *also* : LEARNING **4** : the literal meaning ⟨the ~ of the law⟩ **5** : a single piece of type

²letter *vb* : to mark with letters : INSCRIBE — **let·ter·er** *n*

letter bomb *n* : an explosive device concealed in an envelope and mailed to the intended victim

let·ter·boxed \'le-tər-ˌbäkst\ *adj* : being a video recording formatted to display a frame size proportional to a standard theater screen

let·ter·head \'le-tər-ˌhed\ *n* : stationery with a printed or engraved heading; *also* : the heading itself

let·ter–per·fect \ˌle-tər-'pər-fikt\ *adj* : correct to the smallest detail

let·ter·press \'le-tər-ˌpres\ *n* : printing done directly by impressing the paper on an inked raised surface

letters of marque \-'märk\ : a license granted to a private person by a government to fit out an armed ship to capture enemy shipping

letters patent *n pl* : a written grant from a government to a person in a form readily open for inspection by all

let·tuce \'le-təs\ *n* [ME *letuse*, fr. AF, prob. fr. pl. of *letue* lettuce plant, fr. L *lactuca*, fr. *lac* milk; fr. its milky juice] : a garden composite plant with crisp leaves used esp. in salads

let·up \'let-ˌəp\ *n* : a lessening of effort

leu \'le․u̇\ *n, pl* **lei** \'lā\ — see MONEY table

leu·kae·mia *chiefly Brit var of* LEUKEMIA

leu·ke·mia \lü-'kē-mē-ə\ *n* : a malignant disease characterized by an abnormal increase in the number of white blood cells in the blood-forming tissues — **leu·ke·mic** \-mik\ *adj or n*

leu·ko·cyte \'lü-kə-ˌsīt\ *n* : WHITE BLOOD CELL

lev \'lef\ *n, pl* **le·va** \'le-və\ — see MONEY table

Lev *or* **Levit** *abbr* Leviticus

¹le·vee \'le-vē; lə-'vē, -'vā\ *n* [F *lever* act of arising] : a reception held by or for a person of distinction

²lev·ee \'le-vē\ *n* : an embankment to prevent or confine flooding; *also* : a river landing place

¹lev·el \'le-vəl\ *n* **1** : a device for establishing a horizontal line or plane **2** : horizontal condition **3** : a horizontal position, line, or surface often taken as an index of altitude; *also* : a flat area of ground **4** : height, position, rank, or size in a scale

²level *vb* **-eled** *or* **-elled; -el·ing** *or* **-el·ling** **1** : to make flat or level; *also* : to come to a level **2** : AIM, DIRECT **3** : EQUALIZE **4** : RAZE — **lev·el·er** *n*

³level *adj* **1** : having a flat even surface **2** : HORIZONTAL **3** : of the same height or rank; *also* : UNIFORM **4** : steady and cool in judgment — **lev·el·ly** *adv* — **lev·el·ness** *n*

lev·el·head·ed \ˌle-vəl-'he-dəd\ *adj* : having or showing sound judgment : SENSIBLE

le·ver \'le-vər, 'lē-\ *n* **1** : a bar used for prying or dislodging something; *also* : a means for achieving one's purpose **2** : a rigid piece turning about an axis and used for transmitting and changing force and motion

le·ver·age \'le-vrij, 'lē-, -və-rij\ *n* : the action or mechanical effect of a lever

le·vi·a·than \li-'vī-ə-thən\ *n* **1** : a large sea animal **2** : something large or formidable

lev·i·tate \'le-və-ˌtāt\ *vb* **-tat·ed; -tat·ing** : to rise or cause to rise in the air in seeming defiance of gravitation — **lev·i·ta·tion** \ˌle-və-'tā-shən\ *n*

Le·vit·i·cus \li-'vi-tə-kəs\ *n* — see BIBLE table

lev·i·ty \'le-və-tē\ *n* : lack of seriousness ♦ **Synonyms** LIGHTNESS, FLIPPANCY, FRIVOLITY

levo·do·pa \ˌle-və-'dō-pə\ *n* : L-DOPA

¹levy \'le-vē\ *n, pl* **lev·ies** **1** : the imposition or collection of an assessment; *also* : an amount levied **2** : the enlistment or conscription of men for military service; *also* : troops raised by levy

²levy *vb* **lev·ied; levy·ing** **1** : to impose or collect by legal authority **2** : to enlist for military service **3** : WAGE ⟨~ war⟩ **4** : to seize property

lewd \'lüd\ *adj* [ME *lewed* vulgar, fr. OE *lǣwede* lay, ignorant] **1** : sexually unchaste; *also* : OBSCENE, VULGAR — **lewd·ly** *adv* — **lewd·ness** *n*

lex·i·cog·ra·phy \ˌlek-sə-'kä-grə-fē\ *n* **1** : the editing or making of a dictionary **2** : the principles and practices of dictionary making — **lex·i·cog·ra·pher** \-fər\ *n* — **lex·i·co·graph·i·cal** \-kō-'gra-fi-kəl\ *or* **lex·i·co·graph·ic** \-fik\ *adj*

lex·i·con \'lek-sə-ˌkän\ *n, pl* **lex·i·ca** \-si-kə\ *or* **lexicons** **1** : DICTIONARY **2** : the vocabulary of a language, speaker, or subject

lg *abbr* **1** large **2** long

LH *abbr* **1** left hand **2** lower half

li *abbr* link

Li *symbol* lithium

LI *abbr* Long Island

li·a·bil·i·ty \ˌlī-ə-'bi-lə-tē\ *n, pl* **-ties** **1** : the quality or state of being liable **2** *pl* : DEBTS **3** : DISADVANTAGE

li·a·ble \'lī-ə-bəl\ *adj* **1** : legally obligated : RESPONSIBLE **2** : LIKELY, APT ⟨~ to fall⟩ **3** : SUSCEPTIBLE ⟨~ to disease⟩

li·ai·son \'lē-ə-ˌzän, lē-'ā-\ *n* [F] **1** : a close bond : INTERRELATIONSHIP **2** : an illicit sexual relationship **3** : communication for mutual understanding (as between parts of an armed force); *also* : one that carries on a liaison

li·ar \'lī-(-ə)r\ *n* : a person who lies

¹lib \'lib\ *n* : LIBERATION

²lib *abbr* **1** liberal **2** librarian; library

li·ba·tion \lī-'bā-shən\ *n* **1** : an act of pouring a liquid as a sacrifice (as to a god); *also* : the liquid poured **2** : DRINK

¹li·bel \'lī-bəl\ *n* [ME, written declaration, fr. AF, fr. L *libellus*, dim. of *liber* book] **1** : a spoken or written statement or a representation that gives an unjustly unfavorable impression of a person or thing **2** : the action or crime of publishing a libel — **li·bel·ous** *or* **li·bel·lous** \-bə-ləs\ *adj*

²libel *vb* **-beled** *or* **-belled; -bel·ing** *or* **-bel·ling** : to make or publish a libel — **li·bel·er** *n* — **li·bel·ist** *n*

¹lib·er·al \'li-brəl, -bə-rəl\ *adj* [ME, fr. AF, fr. L *liberalis* suitable for a freeman, generous, fr. *liber* free] **1** : of, relating to, or based on the liberal arts **2** : GENEROUS, BOUNTIFUL ⟨a ~ serving⟩ **3** : not literal **4** : not narrow in opinion or judgment : TOLERANT; *also* : not orthodox **5** : not conservative — **lib·er·al·i·ty** \ˌli-bə-'ra-lə-tē\ *n* — **lib·er·al·i·za·tion** \ˌli-brə-lə-'zā-shən, -bə-rə-\ *n* — **lib·er·al·ize** \'li-brə-ˌlīz, -bə-rə-\ *vb* — **lib·er·al·ly** *adv*

²liberal *n* : a person who holds liberal views

liberal arts *n pl* : the studies (as language, philosophy, history, literature, or abstract science) in a college or university intended to provide chiefly general knowledge and to develop the general intellectual capacities

lib·er·al·ism \'li-brə-ˌli-zəm, -bə-rə-\ *n* : liberal principles and theories

lib·er·ate \'li-bə-ˌrāt\ *vb* **-at·ed; -at·ing** **1** : to free from bondage or restraint; *also* : to raise to equal rights and status **2** : to free (as a gas) from combination — **lib·er·a·tion** \ˌli-bə-'rā-shən\ *n* — **lib·er·a·tor** \'li-bə-ˌrā-tər\ *n*

liberated *adj* : freed from or opposed to traditional social and sexual attitudes or roles ⟨a ~ marriage⟩

lib·er·tar·i·an \ˌli-bər-'ter-ē-ən\ *n* **1** : an advocate of the doctrine of free will **2** : one who upholds the principles of unrestricted liberty

lib·er·tine \'li-bər-ˌtēn\ *n* : a person who leads a dissolute life

lib·er·ty \'li-bər-tē\ *n, pl* **-ties** **1** : FREEDOM **2** : an action going beyond normal limits; *esp* : FAMILIARITY **3** : a short leave from naval duty

li·bid·i·nous \lə-'bi-də-nəs\ *adj* **1** : LASCIVIOUS **2** : LIBIDINAL

li·bi·do \lə-'bē-dō\ *n, pl* **-dos** [NL, fr. L, desire, lust] **1** : psychic energy derived from basic biological urges **2** : sexual drive — **li·bid·i·nal** \lə-'bi-də-nəl\ *adj*

Li·bra \'lē-brə\ *n* [L, lit., scales] **1** : a zodiacal constellation between Virgo and Scorpio usu. pictured as a balance scale **2** : the 7th sign of the zodiac in astrology; *also* : one born under this sign

li·brar·i·an \lī-'brer-ē-ən\ *n* : a specialist in the management of a library

li·brary \'lī-ˌbrer-ē\ *n, pl* **-brar·ies** **1** : a place in which books and related materials are kept for use but not for sale **2** : a collection of books

li·bret·to \lə-'bre-tō\ *n, pl* **-tos** *or* **-ti** \-tē\ [It, dim. of *libro* book, fr. L *liber*] : the text esp. of an opera — **li·bret·tist** \-tist\ *n*

lice *pl of* LOUSE

li·cense *or* **li·cence** \'lī-s⁰ns\ *n* **1** : permission to act **2** : a permission granted by authority to engage in an activity **3** : a document, plate, or tag providing proof of a license **4** : freedom used irresponsibly — **license** *vb*

licensed practical nurse *n* : a specially trained person who is licensed (as by a state) to provide routine care for the sick

li·cens·ee \ˌlī-s⁰n-'sē\ *n* : a licensed person

licente *pl of* SENTE

li·cen·ti·ate \lī-'sen-chē-ət\ *n* : one licensed to practice a profession

li·cen·tious \lī-'sen-chəs\ *adj* : LEWD, LASCIVIOUS — **li·cen·tious·ly** *adv* — **li·cen·tious·ness** *n*

lichee *var of* LITCHI

li·chen \'lī-kən\ *n* : any of various complex plantlike organisms made up of an alga and a fungus growing as a unit on a solid surface — **li·chen·ous** *adj*

lic·it \'li-sət\ *adj* : LAWFUL

¹lick \'lik\ *vb* **1** : to draw the tongue over; *also* : to flicker over like a tongue **2** : THRASH; *also* : DEFEAT

²lick *n* **1** : a stroke of the tongue **2** : a small amount **3** : a hasty careless effort **4** : BLOW **5** : a natural deposit of salt that animals lick

lick·e·ty–split \ˌli-kə-tē-'split\ *adv* : at great speed

lick·spit·tle \'lik-ˌspi-t⁰l\ *n* : a fawning subordinate : TOADY

lic·o·rice \'li-kə-rish, -rəs\ *n* [ME, fr. AF *licoris*, fr. LL *liquiritia*, alter. of L *glycyrrhiza*, fr. Gk *glykyrrhiza*, fr. *glykys* sweet + *rhiza* root] **1** : the dried root of a European leguminous plant; *also* : an extract from it used esp. as a flavoring and in medicine **2** : a candy flavored with licorice **3** : a plant yielding licorice

lid \'lid\ *n* **1** : a movable cover **2** : EYELID **3** : something that confines or suppresses — **lid·ded** \'li-dəd\ *adj*

li·do \'lē-dō\ *n, pl* **lidos** : a fashionable beach resort

¹lie \'lī\ *vb* **lay** \'lā\; **lain** \'lān\; **ly·ing** \'lī-iŋ\ **1** : to be in, stay at rest in, or assume a horizontal position; *also* : to be in a helpless or defenseless state **2** : EXTEND ⟨our route *lay* to the west⟩ **3** : to occupy a certain relative position **4** : to have an effect esp. through mere presence

²lie *n* : the position in which something lies

³lie *vb* **lied**; **ly·ing** \'lī-iŋ\ : to tell a lie

⁴lie *n* : an untrue statement made with intent to deceive

lied \'lēt\ *n, pl* **lie·der** \'lē-dər\ [G] : a German song esp. of the 19th century

lie detector *n* : a polygraph for detecting physiological evidence of the tension that accompanies lying

lief \'lēv, 'lēf\ *adv* : GLADLY, WILLINGLY

¹liege \'lēj\ *adj* : LOYAL, FAITHFUL

²liege *n* **1** : VASSAL **2** : a feudal superior

lien \'lēn, 'lē-ən\ *n* : a legal claim on the property of another for the satisfaction of a debt or duty

lieu \'lü\ *n, archaic* : PLACE, STEAD — **in lieu of** : in the place of

lieut *abbr* lieutenant

lieu·ten·ant \lü-'te-nənt\ *n* [ME, fr. AF *lieu tenant*, fr. *liu,*

lieu place + *tenant* holding, fr. *tenir* to hold, fr. L *tenēre*] **1** : a representative of another in the performance of duty **2** : FIRST LIEUTENANT; *also* : SECOND LIEUTENANT **3** : a commissioned officer in the navy ranking next below a lieutenant commander — **lieu·ten·an·cy** \-nən-sē\ *n*

lieutenant colonel *n* : a commissioned officer (as in the army) ranking next below a colonel

lieutenant commander *n* : a commissioned officer in the navy ranking next below a commander

lieutenant general *n* : a commissioned officer (as in the army) ranking next below a general

lieutenant governor *n* : a deputy or subordinate governor

lieutenant junior grade *n, pl* **lieutenants junior grade** : a commissioned officer in the navy ranking next below a lieutenant

life \'līf\ *n, pl* **lives** \'līvz\ **1** : the quality that distinguishes a vital and functional being from a dead body or inanimate matter; *also* : a state of an organism characterized esp. by capacity for metabolism, growth, reaction to stimuli, and reproduction **2** : the physical and mental experiences of an individual **3** : BIOGRAPHY **4** : a specific phase or period ⟨adult ∼⟩ **5** : the period from birth to death; *also* : a sentence of imprisonment for the remainder of a person's life **6** : a way of living **7** : PERSON ⟨many *lives* were lost in the fire⟩ **8** : ANIMATION, SPIRIT ⟨danced without ∼⟩ **9** : living beings ⟨forest ∼⟩ **10** : animate activity ⟨signs of ∼⟩ **11** : one providing interest and vigor ⟨∼ of the party⟩ — **life·less** *adj* — **life·like** *adj*

life·blood \'līf-ˌbləd\ *n* : a basic source of strength and vitality

life·boat \-ˌbōt\ *n* : a sturdy boat designed for use in saving lives at sea

life·guard \-ˌgärd\ *n* : a usu. expert swimmer employed to safeguard bathers

life·line \-ˌlīn\ *n* **1** : a line to which persons may cling for safety **2** : something considered vital for survival

life·long \-ˌlòŋ\ *adj* : continuing through life

life preserver *n* : a buoyant device designed to save a person from drowning

lif·er \'lī-fər\ *n* **1** : a person sentenced to life imprisonment **2** : a person who makes a career in the armed forces

life raft *n* : a raft for use by people forced into the water

life·sav·ing \'līf-ˌsā-viŋ\ *n* : the skill or practice of saving or protecting lives esp. of drowning persons — **life·sav·er** \-ˌsā-vər\ *n*

life science *n* : a branch of science (as biology, medicine, and sometimes anthropology or sociology) that deals with living organisms and life processes — usu. used in pl. — **life scientist** *n*

¹life·style \'līf-ˌstī(-ə)l\ *n* : a way of living

²lifestyle *adj* : associated with, reflecting, or promoting an enhanced or more desirable lifestyle

life·time \-ˌtīm\ *n* : the duration of an individual's existence

life·work \-'wərk\ *n* : the entire or principal work of one's lifetime; *also* : a work extending over a lifetime

life·world \-ˌwər(-ə)ld\ *n* : the total of an individual's physical surroundings and everyday experiences

LIFO *abbr* last in, first out

¹lift \'lift\ *vb* **1** : RAISE, ELEVATE; *also* : RISE, ASCEND **2** : to put an end to : STOP **3** : to pay off ⟨∼ a mortgage⟩ — **lift·er** *n*

²lift *n* **1** : LOAD **2** : the action or an instance of lifting **3** : HELP; *also* : a ride along one's way **4** : RISE, ADVANCE **5** *chiefly Brit* : ELEVATOR **6** : an elevation of the spirits **7** : the upward force that is developed by a moving airfoil and that opposes the pull of gravity

lift·off \-ˌof\ *n* : a vertical takeoff (as by a rocket)

lift truck *n* : a small truck for lifting and transporting loads

lig·a·ment \'li-gə-mənt\ *n* : a band of tough fibrous tissue that holds bones together or supports an organ in place

li·gate \'lī-ˌgāt\ *vb* **li·gat·ed**; **li·gat·ing** : to tie with a ligature — **li·ga·tion** \lī-'gā-shən\ *n*

lig·a·ture \'li-gə-ˌchùr, -chər\ *n* **1** : something that binds or ties; *also* : a thread used in surgery esp. for tying blood vessels **2** : a printed or written character consisting of two or more letters or characters (as æ) united

¹light \'līt\ *n* **1** : something that makes vision possible : electromagnetic radiation visible to the human eye; *also* : the sensation aroused by stimulation of the visual sense organs **2** : DAYLIGHT **3** : a source of light (as a candle) **4** : ENLIGHTENMENT; *also* : TRUTH **5** : public knowledge ⟨facts brought to ~⟩ **6** : a particular aspect presented to view ⟨saw the matter in a different ~⟩ **7** : WINDOW **8** *pl* : STANDARDS ⟨according to his ~s⟩ **9** : CELEBRITY **10** : LIGHTHOUSE, BEACON; *also* : TRAFFIC LIGHT **11** : a flame for lighting something

²**light** *adj* **1** : having light : BRIGHT **2** : PALE 2 ⟨~ blue⟩ — **light·ness** *n*

³**light** *vb* **lit** \'lit\ *or* **light·ed; light·ing** **1** : to make or become light **2** : to cause to burn : BURN **3** : to conduct with a light **4** : ILLUMINATE

⁴**light** *adj* **1** : not heavy **2** : not serious ⟨~ reading⟩ **3** : SCANTY ⟨~ rain⟩ **4** : easily disturbed ⟨a ~ sleeper⟩ **5** : GENTLE ⟨a ~ blow⟩ **6** : easily endurable ⟨a ~ cold⟩; *also* : requiring little effort ⟨~ exercise⟩ **7** : SWIFT, NIMBLE **8** : FRIVOLOUS **9** : DIZZY **10** : made with lower calorie content or less of some ingredient than usual ⟨~ salad dressing⟩ **11** : producing goods for direct consumption by the consumer ⟨~ industry⟩ — **light·ly** *adv* — **light·ness** *n*

⁵**light** *adv* **1** : LIGHTLY **2** : with little baggage ⟨travel ~⟩

⁶**light** *vb* **lit** \'lit\ *or* **light·ed; light·ing** **1** : SETTLE, ALIGHT **2** : to fall unexpectedly : HAPPEN

light bulb *n* **1** : a lamp in which an electrically heated filament emits light **2** : FLUORESCENT LAMP

light–emitting diode *n* : LED

¹**light·en** \'lī-t³n\ *vb* **1** : ILLUMINATE, BRIGHTEN **2** : to give out flashes of lightning

²**lighten** *vb* **1** : to relieve of a burden **2** : GLADDEN **3** : to become lighter

lighten up *vb* : to take things less seriously

¹**ligh·ter** \'lī-tər\ *n* : a barge used esp. in loading or unloading ships

²**light·er** \'lī-tər\ *n* : one that lights; *esp* : a device for lighting (as a fire or cigarette)

light·face \'līt-,fās\ *n* : a type having light thin lines — **light·faced** \-,fāst\ *adj*

light–head·ed \'līt-,he-dəd\ *adj* **1** : feeling confused or dizzy **2** : lacking maturity or seriousness

light–heart·ed \-,här-təd\ *adj* : free from worry — **light·heart·ed·ly** *adv* — **light·heart·ed·ness** *n*

light·house \-,haùs\ *n* : a structure with a powerful light for guiding sailors

light meter *n* : a usu. hand-held device for indicating correct photographic exposure

¹**light·ning** \'līt-niŋ\ *n* : the flashing of light produced by a discharge of atmospheric electricity; *also* : the discharge itself

²**lightning** *adj* : extremely fast

lightning bug *n* : FIREFLY

lightning rod *n* : a grounded metallic rod set up on a structure to protect it from lightning

light out *vb* : to leave in a hurry

light·proof \'līt-,prüf\ *adj* : impenetrable by light

lights \'līts\ *n pl* : the lungs esp. of a slaughtered animal

light·ship \'līt-,ship\ *n* : a ship with a powerful light moored at a place dangerous to navigation

light show *n* : a kaleidoscopic display (as of colored lights)

light·some \'līt-səm\ *adj* **1** : free from care **2** : NIMBLE

¹**light·weight** \'līt-,wāt\ *n* : one of less than average weight; *esp* : a boxer weighing not over 135 pounds

²**lightweight** *adj* **1** : INCONSEQUENTIAL **2** : of less than average weight

light–year \'līt-,yir\ *n* **1** : an astronomical unit of distance equal to the distance that light travels in one year in a vacuum or about 5.88 trillion miles (9.46 trillion kilometers) **2** : an extremely large measure of comparison ⟨saw it ~s ago⟩

lig·nin \'lig-nən\ *n* : a substance related to cellulose that occurs in the woody cell walls of plants and in the cementing material between them

lig·nite \'lig-,nīt\ *n* : brownish black soft coal

¹**like** \'līk\ *vb* **liked; lik·ing** **1** : ENJOY ⟨~s baseball⟩ **2** : WANT ⟨would ~ a drink⟩ **3** : CHOOSE ⟨does as she ~s⟩ — **lik·able** *or* **like·able** \'lī-kə-bəl\ *adj*

²**like** *n* : PREFERENCE

³**like** *adj* : SIMILAR ♦ *Synonyms* ALIKE, ANALOGOUS, COMPARABLE, PARALLEL, UNIFORM

⁴**like** *prep* **1** : similar or similarly to ⟨seems ~ a dream⟩

2 : typical of **3** : comparable to **4** : as though there would be ⟨looks ~ rain⟩ **5** : such as ⟨a subject ~ physics⟩

⁵**like** *n* **1** : COUNTERPART **2** : one that is similar to another — **and the like** : ET CETERA

⁶**like** *conj* **1** : AS IF ⟨acted ~ they were scared⟩ **2** : in the same way that ⟨do it ~ mom said⟩

-like *adj comb form* : resembling or characteristic of ⟨ladylike⟩ ⟨lifelike⟩

like·li·hood \'lī-klē-,hùd\ *n* : PROBABILITY

¹**like·ly** \'lī-klē\ *adj* **like·li·er; -est** **1** : very probable **2** : BELIEVABLE **3** : PROMISING ⟨a ~ place to fish⟩

²**likely** *adv* : in all probability

lik·en \'lī-kən\ *vb* : COMPARE

like·ness \'līk-nəs\ *n* **1** : COPY, PORTRAIT **2** : SEMBLANCE **3** : RESEMBLANCE

like·wise \-,wīz\ *adv* **1** : in like manner **2** : in addition : ALSO

lik·ing \'lī-kiŋ\ *n* : favorable regard ⟨took a ~ to the newcomer⟩; *also* : TASTE

li·lac \'lī-lək, -,lak, -,läk\ *n* [obs. F (now *lilas*), fr. Ar *līlāk*, fr. Pers *nīlak* bluish, fr. *nīl* blue, fr. Skt *nīla* dark blue] **1** : a shrub related to the olive that produces large clusters of fragrant grayish pink, purple, or white flowers **2** : a moderate purple color

lil·an·ge·ni \,li-lən-'ge-nē\ *n, pl* **em·a·lan·ge·ni** \,e-mə-lən-'ge-nē\ — see MONEY table

lil·li·pu·tian \,li-lə-'pyü-shən\ *adj, often cap* **1** : SMALL, MINIATURE **2** : PETTY

lilt \'lilt\ *n* **1** : a cheerful lively song or tune **2** : a rhythmical swing or flow

lily \'li-lē\ *n, pl* **lil·ies** : any of a genus of tall bulbous herbs with leafy stems and usu. funnel-shaped flowers; *also* : any of various related plants

lily of the valley : a low perennial herb related to the lilies that produces a raceme of fragrant nodding bell-shaped white flowers

li·ma bean \'lī-mə-\ *n* : a bushy or tall-growing bean widely cultivated for its flat edible usu. pale green or whitish seeds; *also* : the seed

limb \'lim\ *n* **1** : one of the projecting paired appendages (as legs, arms, or wings) used by an animal esp. in moving or grasping **2** : a large branch of a tree : BOUGH — **limb·less** *adj*

¹**lim·ber** \'lim-bər\ *adj* **1** : FLEXIBLE, SUPPLE **2** : LITHE, NIMBLE

²**limber** *vb* : to make or become limber

lim·bic \'lim-bik\ *adj* : of, relating to, or being a group of structures of the brain (**limbic system**) concerned esp. with emotion and motivation

¹**lim·bo** \'lim-bō\ *n, pl* **limbos** [ME, fr. ML, abl. of *limbus* limbo, fr. L, border] **1** *often cap* : an abode of souls barred from heaven through no fault of their own **2** : a place or state of confinement, oblivion, or uncertainty

²**limbo** *n, pl* **limbos** : an acrobatic dance or contest that involves passing under a horizontal pole

Lim·burg·er \'lim-,bər-gər\ *n* : a pungent semisoft surface-ripened cheese

¹**lime** \'līm\ *n* : a caustic powdery white solid that consists of calcium and oxygen, is obtained from limestone or shells, and is used in making cement and in fertilizer — **lime** *vb* — **limy** \'lī-mē\ *adj*

²**lime** *n* : a small yellowish green citrus fruit with juicy acid pulp

lime·ade \,līm-'ād, 'lī-,mād\ *n* : a beverage of lime juice, sugar, and water

lime·light \'līm-,līt\ *n* **1** : a device in which flame is directed against a cylinder of lime formerly used in the theater to cast a strong white light on the stage **2** : the center of public attention

lim·er·ick \'li-mə-rik\ *n* : a light or humorous poem of 5 lines

lime·stone \'līm-,stōn\ *n* : a rock that is formed by accumulation of organic remains (as shells), is used in building, and yields lime when burned

¹**lim·it** \'li-mət\ *n* **1** : something that restrains or confines; *also* : the utmost extent **2** : BOUNDARY; *also, pl* : BOUNDS **3** : a prescribed maximum or minimum **4** : a number whose value becomes arbitrarily close to that of a function as its independent variable approaches a given value — **lim·it·less** *adj* — **lim·it·less·ness** *n*

²**limit** *vb* **1** : to set limits to **2** : to reduce in quantity or extent — **lim·i·ta·tion** \ˌli-mə-ˈtā-shən\ *n*

lim·it·ed *adj* **1** : confined within limits **2** : offering faster service esp. by making fewer stops

limn \ˈlim\ *vb* **limned; limn·ing** \ˈli-miŋ, ˈlim-niŋ\ **1** : DRAW; *also* : PAINT **2** : DELINEATE **3** : DESCRIBE

limo \ˈli-(ˌ)mō\ *n, pl* **limos** : LIMOUSINE

li·mo·nite \ˈlī-mə-ˌnīt\ *n* : a ferric oxide that is a major ore of iron — **li·mo·nit·ic** \ˌlī-mə-ˈni-tik\ *adj*

lim·ou·sine \ˈli-mə-ˌzēn, ˌli-mə-ˈzēn\ *n* [F] **1** : a large luxurious often chauffeur-driven sedan **2** : a large vehicle for transporting passengers to and from an airport

¹**limp** \ˈlimp\ *vb* : to walk lamely; *also* : to proceed with difficulty

²**limp** *n* : a limping movement or gait

³**limp** *adj* **1** : having no defined shape; *also* : not stiff or rigid **2** : lacking in strength or firmness — **limp·ly** *adv* — **limp·ness** *n*

lim·pet \ˈlim-pət\ *n* : any of numerous gastropod sea mollusks with a conical shell that clings to rocks or timbers

limpet: shell and bottom view

lim·pid \ˈlim-pəd\ *adj* : CLEAR, TRANSPARENT

lin *abbr* **1** lineal **2** linear

lin·age \ˈlī-nij\ *n* : the number of lines of written or printed matter

linch·pin \ˈlinch-ˌpin\ *n* : a locking pin inserted crosswise (as through the end of an axle)

lin·den \ˈlin-dən\ *n* : any of a genus of trees with large heart-shaped leaves and clustered yellowish flowers; *also* : the light white wood of a linden

¹**line** \ˈlīn\ *n* **1** : CORD, ROPE, WIRE; *also* : a length of material used in measuring and leveling **2** : pipes for conveying a fluid ⟨a gas ∼⟩ **3** : a horizontal row of written or printed characters; *also* : VERSE **4** : NOTE **5** : the words making up a part in a drama — usu. used in pl. **6** : something distinct, long, and narrow; *also* : ROUTE **7** : a state of agreement **8** : a course of conduct, action, or thought; *also* : OCCUPATION **9** : LIMIT **10** : an arrangement of persons or objects of one kind in an orderly series ⟨waiting in ∼⟩ **11** : a transportation system **12 a** : the football players who are stationed on the line of scrimmage **b** : a group of three players who play together as a unit in hockey **13** : a long narrow mark; *also* : EQUATOR **14** : a geometric element that is the path of a moving point **15** : CONTOUR **16** : a general plan ⟨thinking along these ∼s⟩ **17** : an indication based on insight or investigation

²**line** *vb* **lined; lin·ing** **1** : to mark with a line **2** : to place or form a line along **3** : ALIGN

³**line** *vb* **lined; lin·ing** : to cover the inner surface of

lin·eage \ˈli-nē-ij\ *n* : lineal descent from a common progenitor; *also* : FAMILY

lin·eal \ˈli-nē-əl\ *adj* **1** : LINEAR **2** : consisting of or being in a direct line of ancestry; *also* : HEREDITARY

lin·ea·ment \ˈli-nē-ə-mənt\ *n* : an outline, feature, or contour of a body and esp. of a face — usu. used in pl.

lin·ear \ˈli-nē-ər\ *adj* **1** : of, relating to, resembling, or having a graph that is a line and esp. a straight line : STRAIGHT **2** : composed of simply drawn lines with little attempt at pictorial representation ⟨∼ script⟩ **3** : being long and uniformly narrow

line·back·er \ˈlīn-ˌba-kər\ *n* : a defensive football player who lines up just behind the line of scrimmage

line drive *n* : a batted baseball hit in a flatter path than a fly ball

line–item veto *n* : the power of a government executive to veto specific items in an appropriations bill

line·man \ˈlīn-mən\ *n* **1** : a person who sets up or repairs communication or power lines **2** : a player in the line in football

lin·en \ˈli-nən\ *n* **1** : cloth made of flax; *also* : thread or yarn spun from flax **2** : clothing or household articles made of linen cloth or similar fabric

line of scrimmage : an imaginary line in football parallel to the goal lines and tangent to the nose of the ball laid on the ground before a play

¹**lin·er** \ˈlī-nər\ *n* : a ship or airplane of a regular transportation line

²**liner** *n* : one that lines or is used as a lining — **lin·er·less** *adj*

line score *n* : a score of a baseball game giving the runs, hits, and errors made by each team

lines·man \ˈlīnz-mən\ *n* **1** : LINEMAN 1 **2** : an official who assists a referee

line·up \ˈlī-ˌnəp\ *n* **1** : a list of players taking part in a game (as of baseball) **2** : a line of persons arranged esp. for identification by police

ling \ˈliŋ\ *n* : any of various fishes related to the cod

-ling *n suffix* **1** : one associated with ⟨nest*ling*⟩ **2** : young, small, or minor one ⟨duck*ling*⟩

lin·ger \ˈliŋ-gər\ *vb* : TARRY; *also* : PROCRASTINATE — **lin·ger·er** *n*

lin·ge·rie \ˌlän-jə-ˈrā, ˌlaⁿ-zhə-, -ˈrē\ *n* [F, fr. MF, fr. *linge* linen, fr. L *lineus* made of linen, fr. *linum* flax, linen] : women's intimate apparel

lin·go \ˈliŋ-gō\ *n, pl* **lingoes** : a usu. strange or incomprehensible language

lin·gua fran·ca \ˌliŋ-gwə-ˈfraŋ-kə\ *n, pl* **lingua francas** *or* **lin·guae fran·cae** \-gwē-ˈfraŋ-ˌkē\ [It] **1** *often cap* : a common language consisting of Italian mixed with French, Spanish, Greek, and Arabic that was formerly spoken in Mediterranean ports **2** : a common or commercial tongue among speakers of different languages

lin·gual \ˈliŋ-gwəl\ *adj* : of, relating to, or produced by the tongue

lin·gui·ca \liŋ-ˈgwē-sə\ *n* : a spicy Portuguese sausage

lin·guist \ˈliŋ-gwist\ *n* **1** : a person skilled in languages **2** : a person who specializes in linguistics

lin·guis·tics \liŋ-ˈgwis-tiks\ *n* : the study of human speech including the units, nature, structure, and modification of language — **lin·guis·tic** \-tik\ *adj*

lin·i·ment \ˈli-nə-mənt\ *n* : a liquid preparation rubbed on the skin esp. to relieve pain

lin·ing \ˈlī-niŋ\ *n* : material used to line esp. an inner surface

link \ˈliŋk\ *n* **1** : a connecting structure; *esp* : a single ring of a chain **2** : BOND, TIE **3** : HYPERLINK — **link** *vb* — **link·er** *n*

link·age \ˈliŋ-kij\ *n* **1** : the manner or style of being united **2** : the quality or state of being linked **3** : a system of links

linking verb *n* : a word or expression (as a form of *be, become, feel,* or *seem*) that links a subject with its predicate

links \ˈliŋks\ *n pl* : a golf course

link·up \ˈliŋ-ˌkəp\ *n* **1** : MEETING **2** : something that serves as a linking device or factor

lin·net \ˈli-nət\ *n* : an Old World finch

li·no·leum \lə-ˈnō-lē-əm\ *n* [L *linum* flax + *oleum* oil] : a floor covering with a canvas back and a surface of hardened linseed oil and a filler

lin·seed \ˈlin-ˌsēd\ *n* : the seeds of flax yielding a yellowish oil (**linseed oil**) used esp. in paints and linoleum

lin·sey–wool·sey \ˌlin-zē-ˈwùl-zē\ *n* : a coarse sturdy fabric of wool and linen or cotton

lint \ˈlint\ *n* **1** : linen made into a soft fleecy substance **2** : fine ravels and short fibers of yarn or fabric **3** : the fibers that surround cotton seeds and form the cotton staple

lin·tel \ˈlin-tᵊl\ *n* : a horizontal piece across the top of an opening (as of a door) that carries the weight of the structure above it

linz·er torte \ˈlin-sər-, -zər-\ *n, often cap L* : a baked buttery torte made with chopped almonds, sugar, and spices and filled with jam or preserves

li·on \ˈlī-ən\ *n, pl* **lions** : a large heavily-built cat of Africa and southern Asia with a shaggy mane in the male

li·on·ess \ˈlī-ə-nəs\ *n* : a female lion

li·on·heart·ed \ˌlī-ən-ˈhär-təd\ *adj* : COURAGEOUS, BRAVE

li·on·ise *Brit var of* LIONIZE

li·on·ize \'lī-ə-ˌnīz\ *vb* **-ized; -iz·ing** : to treat as an object of great interest or importance — **li·on·i·za·tion** \ˌlī-ə-nə-'zā-shən\ *n*

lion's den *n* : a place or state of extreme disadvantage, antagonism, or hostility

lip \'lip\ *n* **1** : either of the two fleshy folds that surround the mouth; *also* : the margin of the human lip **2** : a part or projection suggesting a lip **3** : the edge of a hollow vessel or cavity — **lipped** \'lipt\ *adj*

li·pa \'lē-ˌpä, -pə\ *n, pl* **lipa** — see *kuna* at MONEY table

lip·id \'li-pəd\ *n* : any of various substances (as fats and waxes) that with proteins and carbohydrates make up the principal structural parts of living cells

lip–lock \'lip-ˌläk\ *n* : a long amorous kiss

li·po·pro·tein \ˌlī-pō-'prō-ˌtēn, ˌli-\ *n* : a protein that is a complex of protein and lipid

li·po·suc·tion \'li-pə-ˌsək-shən, 'lī-\ *n* : surgical removal of local fat deposits (as in the thighs) esp. for cosmetic purposes

lip·read·ing \'lip-ˌrē-diŋ\ *n* : the interpreting of a speaker's words by watching lip and facial movements without hearing the voice

lip service *n* : an avowal of allegiance that is not matched by action

lip·stick \'lip-ˌstik\ *n* : a waxy solid colored cosmetic in stick form for the lips — **lip·sticked** \-ˌstikt\ *adj*

liq *abbr* **1** liquid **2** liquor

liq·ue·fy *also* **liq·ui·fy** \'li-kwə-ˌfī\ *vb* **-fied; -fy·ing** : to make or become liquid — **liq·ue·fi·er** \-ˌfī(-ə)r\ *n*

li·queur \li-'kər\ *n* [F] : a distilled alcoholic liquor flavored with aromatic substances and usu. sweetened

¹liq·uid \'li-kwəd\ *adj* **1** : flowing freely like water **2** : neither solid nor gaseous **3** : shining and clear ⟨large ∼ eyes⟩ **4** : smooth and musical in tone; *also* : smooth and unconstrained in movement **5** : consisting of or capable of ready conversion into cash ⟨∼ assets⟩ — **li·quid·i·ty** \li-'kwi-də-tē\ *n*

²liquid *n* : a liquid substance

liq·ui·date \'li-kwə-ˌdāt\ *vb* **-dat·ed; -dat·ing** **1** : to settle the accounts and distribute the assets of (as a business) **2** : to pay off ⟨∼ a debt⟩ **3** : to get rid of; *esp* : KILL — **liq·ui·da·tion** \ˌli-kwə-'dā-shən\ *n*

liquid crystal *n* : an organic liquid that resembles a crystal in having ordered molecular arrays

liquid crystal display *n* : LCD

liquid measure *n* : a unit or series of units for measuring liquid capacity — see METRIC SYSTEM table,, WEIGHT table

li·quor \'li-kər\ *n* [ME *licour*, fr. AF, fr. L *liquor*, fr. *liquēre* to be fluid] : a liquid substance; *esp* : a distilled alcoholic beverage

li·quo·rice *chiefly Brit var of* LICORICE

li·ra \'lir-ə, 'lē-rä\ *n* **1** *pl* **li·re** \'lē-rā\ : the former basic monetary unit of Italy **2** : the basic monetary unit of Turkey — see MONEY table **3** *pl* **li·ri** \'lē-rē\ : the basic monetary unit of Malta — see MONEY table

lisente *pl of* SENTE

lisle \'lī(-ə)l\ *n* : a smooth tightly twisted thread usu. made of long-staple cotton

lisp \'lisp\ *vb* : to pronounce \s\ and \z\ imperfectly esp. by turning them into \th\ and \t͟h\; *also* : to speak childishly — **lisp** *n* — **lisp·er** *n*

lis·some *also* **lis·som** \'li-səm\ *adj* **1** : easily flexed **2** : LITHE 2 **3** : NIMBLE — **lis·some·ly** *adv*

¹list \'list\ *vb, archaic* : PLEASE; *also* : WISH

²list *vb, archaic* : LISTEN

³list *n* : a leaning to one side : TILT

⁴list *vb* : TILT

⁵list *n* **1** : a simple series of words or numerals; *also* : an official roster **2** : CATALOG, CHECKLIST

⁶list *vb* : to make a list of; *also* : to include on a list — **list·ee** \li-'stē\ *n*

lis·ten \'li-sᵊn\ *vb* **1** : to pay attention in order to hear **2** : HEED — **lis·ten·er** *n*

lis·ten·er·ship \'li-sᵊn-ər-ˌship\ *n* : the audience for a radio program or recording

list·ing \'lis-tiŋ\ *n* **1** : an act or instance of making or including in a list **2** : something that is listed

list·less \'list-ləs\ *adj* : SPIRITLESS, LANGUID ⟨a ∼ performance⟩ — **list·less·ly** *adv* — **list·less·ness** *n*

list price *n* : the price of an item as published in a catalog, price list, or advertisement before being discounted

lists \'lists\ *n pl* : an arena for combat (as jousting)

¹lit \'lit\ *past and past part of* LIGHT

²lit *abbr* **1** liter **2** literal; literally **3** literary **4** literature

lit·a·ny \'li-tə-nē\ *n, pl* **-nies** [ME *letanie*, fr. AF & LL; AF, fr. LL *litania*, fr. LGk *litaneia*, fr. Gk, entreaty, fr. *litanos* suppliant] **1** : a prayer consisting of a series of supplications and responses said alternately by a leader and a group **2** : a lengthy recitation ⟨a ∼ of complaints⟩

li·tas \'lē-ˌtäs\ *n, pl* **li·tai** \-ˌtī\ *or* **li·tu** \-ˌtü\ — see MONEY table

litchi *var of* LYCHEE

lite \'līt\ *adj* **1** : ⁴LIGHT 10 ⟨∼ beer⟩ **2** : lacking in substance or seriousness ⟨∼ news⟩

li·ter \'lē-tər\ *n* — see METRIC SYSTEM table

lit·er·al \'li-tə-rəl\ *adj* **1** : adhering to fact or to the ordinary or usual meaning (as of a word) **2** : UNADORNED; *also* : PROSAIC **3** : VERBATIM

lit·er·al·ism \-rə-ˌli-zəm\ *n* **1** : adherence to the explicit substance (as of an idea) **2** : fidelity to observable fact — **lit·er·al·ist** \-list\ *n* — **lit·er·al·is·tic** \ˌli-tə-rə-'lis-tik\ *adj*

lit·er·al·ly \'li-tə-rə-lē, 'li-trə-\ *adv* **1** : ACTUALLY ⟨was ∼ insane⟩ **2** : VIRTUALLY ⟨∼ poured out new ideas⟩

lit·er·ary \'li-tə-ˌrer-ē\ *adj* **1** : of or relating to literature **2** : WELL-READ

lit·er·ate \'li-tə-rət, -tə-rət\ *adj* **1** : EDUCATED; *also* : able to read and write **2** : LITERARY; *also* : POLISHED, LUCID — **lit·er·a·cy** \'li-tə-rə-sē, -trə-\ *n* — **literate** *n*

li·te·ra·ti \ˌli-tə-'rä-tē\ *n pl* **1** : the educated class **2** : persons interested in literature or the arts

lit·er·a·ture \'li-trə-ˌchúr, -trə-, -chər\ *n* **1** : the production of written works having excellence of form or expression and dealing with ideas of permanent interest **2** : the written works produced in a particular language, country, or age

lithe \'lī͟th, 'līth\ *adj* **1** : SUPPLE **2** : characterized by effortless grace; *also* : athletically slim

lithe·some \'lī͟th-səm, 'līth-\ *adj* : LISSOME

lith·i·um \'li-thē-əm\ *n* : a light silver-white metallic chemical element

li·thog·ra·phy \li-'thä-grə-fē\ *n* : the process of printing from a plane surface (as a smooth stone or metal plate) on which the image to be printed is ink-receptive and the blank area ink-repellent — **lith·o·graph** \'li-thə-ˌgraf\ *vb* — **lithograph** *n* — **li·thog·ra·pher** \li-'thä-grə-fər, 'li-thə-ˌgra-fər\ *n* — **lith·o·graph·ic** \ˌli-thə-'gra-fik\ *adj* — **lith·o·graph·i·cal·ly** \-fi-k(ə-)lē\ *adv*

li·thol·o·gy \li-'thä-lə-jē\ *n, pl* **-gies** : the study of rocks — **lith·o·log·ic** \ˌli-thə-'lä-jik\ *or* **lith·o·log·i·cal** \-ji-kəl\ *adj*

lith·o·sphere \'li-thə-ˌsfir\ *n* : the outer part of the solid earth

Lith·u·a·nian \ˌli-thə-'wā-nē-ən, -thyú-\ *n* **1** : a native or inhabitant of Lithuania **2** : the language of the Lithuanians — **Lithuanian** *adj*

lit·i·gant \'li-ti-gənt\ *n* : a party to a lawsuit — **litigant** *adj*

lit·i·gate \-ˌgāt\ *vb* **-gat·ed; -gat·ing** : to carry on a legal contest by judicial process; *also* : to contest at law — **lit·i·ga·tion** \ˌli-tə-'gā-shən\ *n*

li·ti·gious \lə-'ti-jəs\ *adj* **1** : CONTENTIOUS **2** : prone to engage in lawsuits **3** : of or relating to litigation — **li·ti·gious·ly** *adv* — **li·ti·gious·ness** *n*

lit·mus \'lit-məs\ *n* : a coloring matter from lichens that turns red in acid solutions and blue in alkaline

litmus test *n* : a test in which a single factor (as an attitude) is decisive

Litt D *or* **Lit D** *abbr* [ML *litterarum doctor*] : doctor of letters; doctor of literature

¹lit·ter \'li-tər\ *n* [ME, fr. AF *litere*, fr. *lit* bed, fr. L *lectus*] **1** : a covered and curtained couch with shafts that is used to carry a single passenger; *also* : a device (as a stretcher) for carrying a sick or injured person **2** : material used as bedding for animals; *also* : material used to absorb the urine and feces of animals **3** : the offspring of an animal at one birth **4** : RUBBISH

²litter *vb* **1** : to give birth to young **2** : to strew or mark with scattered objects

lit·ter·bug \'li-tər-ˌbəg\ *n* : one who litters a public area

¹lit·tle \'li-tᵊl\ *adj* **lit·tler** \'li-tᵊl-ər\ *or* **less** \'les\ *or* **less·er** \'le-sər\; **lit·tlest** \'li-tᵊl-əst\ *or* **least** \'lēst\ **1** : not big;

also : YOUNG **2** : not important **3** : PETTY 3 **4** : not much — **lit·tle·ness** *n*

²little *adv* **less** \'les\; **least** \'lēst\ **1** : SLIGHTLY; *also* : not at all **2** : INFREQUENTLY

³little *n* **1** : a small amount or quantity **2** : a short time or distance

Little Dipper *n* : the seven bright stars of Ursa Minor arranged in a form resembling a dipper

little finger *n* : PINKIE

little theater *n* : a small theater for low-cost dramatic productions designed for a limited audience

lit·to·ral \'li-tə-rəl, ˌli-tə-'ral\ *adj* : of, relating to, or growing on or near a shore esp. of the sea — **littoral** *n*

lit·ur·gy \'li-tər-jē\ *n, pl* **-gies** : a rite or body of rites prescribed for public worship — **li·tur·gi·cal** \lə-'tər-ji-kəl\ *adj* — **li·tur·gi·cal·ly** \-k(ə-)lē\ *adv* — **lit·ur·gist** \'li-tər-jist\ *n*

liv·able *also* **live·able** \'li-və-bəl\ *adj* **1** : suitable for living in or with ⟨a ~ house⟩ ⟨~wages⟩ **2** : ENDURABLE — **liv·a·bil·i·ty** \ˌli-və-'bi-lə-tē\ *n*

¹live \'liv\ *vb* **lived; liv·ing** **1** : to be or continue alive ⟨*lived* 80 years⟩ **2** : SUBSIST **3** : RESIDE ⟨~s next door⟩ **4** : to conduct one's life **5** : to remain in human memory or record ⟨his legacy ~s⟩

²live \'līv\ *adj* **1** : having life ⟨~ worms⟩ **2** : ACTUAL ⟨a real ~ celebrity⟩ **3** : BURNING, GLOWING ⟨a ~ cigar⟩ **4** : connected to electric power ⟨a ~ wire⟩ **5** : UNEXPLODED ⟨a ~ bomb⟩ **6** : of continuing interest ⟨a ~ issue⟩ **7** : of or involving the actual presence of real people ⟨~ audience⟩; *also* : broadcast directly at the time of production **8** : being in play ⟨a ~ ball⟩

lived–in \'livd-ˌin\ *adj* : of or suggesting long-term human habitation or use

live down *vb* : to live so as to wipe out the memory or effects of

live in *vb* : to live in one's place of employment — used of a servant — **live–in** \'liv-ˌin\ *adj*

live·li·hood \'līv-lē-ˌhu̇d\ *n* : means of support or subsistence

live·long \'liv-ˌlȯŋ\ *adj* [ME *lef long*, fr. *lef* dear + *long* long] : WHOLE, ENTIRE ⟨the ~ day⟩

live·ly \'līv-lē\ *adj* **live·li·er; -est** **1** : ANIMATED ⟨~ debate⟩ **2** : KEEN, VIVID ⟨~ interest⟩ **3** : showing activity or vigor ⟨a ~ manner⟩ **4** : quick to rebound ⟨a ~ ball⟩ **5** : full of life ♦ *Synonyms* VIVACIOUS, SPRIGHTLY, GAY, SPIRITED — **live·li·ness** *n* — **live·ly** *adv*

liv·en \'lī-vən\ *vb* : ENLIVEN

live oak *n* : any of several American evergreen oaks; *esp* : one of the southeastern U.S. that is often planted as a shade tree

¹liv·er \'li-vər\ *n* **1** : a large glandular organ of vertebrates that secretes bile and is a center of metabolic activity **2** : the liver of an animal (as a calf or chicken) eaten as food

²liver *n* : one that lives esp. in a specified way ⟨a fast ~⟩

liv·er·ish \'li-və-rish\ *adj* **1** : resembling liver in color **2** : BILIOUS **3** : PEEVISH — **liv·er·ish·ness** *adj*

liver spots *n pl* : AGE SPOTS

liv·er·wort \'li-vər-ˌwərt\ *n* : any of a class of flowerless plants resembling the related mosses

liv·er·wurst \-ˌwərst, -ˌwu̇rst\ *n* [part trans. of G *Leberwurst*, fr. *Leber* liver + *Wurst* sausage] : a sausage consisting chiefly of liver

liv·ery \'li-və-rē\ *n, pl* **-er·ies** **1** : a servant's uniform; *also* : distinctive dress **2** : the feeding, care, and stabling of horses for pay; *also* : an establishment (as a stable or business) keeping horses or vehicles for hire — **liv·er·ied** \-rēd\ *adj* — **liv·ery·man** \'li-və-rē-mən\ *n*

lives *pl of* LIFE

live·stock \'līv-ˌstäk\ *n* : farm animals kept for use and profit

live wire *n* : an alert, active, or aggressive person — **live–wire** *adj*

liv·id \'li-vəd\ *adj* [F *livide*, fr. L *lividus*, fr. *livēre* to be blue] **1** : discolored by bruising **2** : ASHEN, PALLID **3** : REDDISH **4** : ENRAGED — **li·vid·i·ty** \li-'vi-də-tē\ *n*

¹liv·ing \'li-viŋ\ *adj* **1** : having life **2** : NATURAL **3** : full of life and vigor; *also* : VIVID ⟨in ~ color⟩

²living *n* **1** : the condition of being alive **2** : LIVELIHOOD **3** : manner of life

living room *n* : a room in a residence used for the common social activities of the occupants

living wage *n* : a wage sufficient to provide an acceptable standard of living

living will *n* : a document requesting that the signer not be kept alive by artificial means unless there is a reasonable expectation of recovery

livre \'lēvrᵊ\ *n* : the pound of Lebanon

liz·ard \'li-zərd\ *n* : any of a group of 4-legged reptiles with long tapering tails

Lk *abbr* Luke

ll *abbr* lines

lla·ma \'lä-mə\ *n* [Sp, fr. Quechua] : any of a genus of wild or domesticated So. American mammals related to the camels but smaller and without a hump

lla·no \'lä-nō\ *n, pl* **llanos** : an open grassy plain esp. of Latin America

LLD *abbr* [NL *legum doctor*] doctor of laws

LNG *abbr* liquefied natural gas

¹load \'lōd\ *n* **1** : PACK; *also* : CARGO **2** : a mass of weight supported by something **3** : something that burdens the mind or spirits **4** : a large quantity — usu. used in pl. **5** : a standard, expected, or authorized burden

²load *vb* **1** : to put a load in or on; *also* : to receive a load **2** : to encumber with an obligation or something heavy or disheartening **3** : to increase the weight of by adding something **4** : to supply abundantly **5** : to put a charge in (as a firearm) **6** : to copy or transfer into a computer's memory esp. from an external source

load·ed *adj* **1** *slang* : HIGH 12 **2** : having a large amount of money **3** : equipped with an abundance of options ⟨a ~ car⟩

load·stone *var of* LODESTONE

¹loaf \'lōf\ *n, pl* **loaves** \'lōvz\ : a shaped or molded mass esp. of bread

²loaf *vb* : to spend time in idleness : LOUNGE

loaf·er \'lō-fər\ *n* **1** : one that loafs : IDLER **2** : a low step-in shoe

loam \'lōm, 'lüm\ *n* : SOIL; *esp* : a loose soil of mixed clay, sand, and silt — **loamy** *adj*

¹loan \'lōn\ *n* **1** : money lent at interest; *also* : something lent for the borrower's temporary use **2** : the grant of temporary use

²loan *vb* : LEND

loan shark *n* : a person who lends money at excessive rates of interest — **loan·shark·ing** \'lōn-ˌshär-kiŋ\ *n*

loan·word \'lōn-ˌwərd\ *n* : a word taken from another language and at least partly naturalized

loath *also* **loth** \'lōth, 'lōth\ *or* **loathe** \'lōth, 'lōth\ *adj* : RELUCTANT

loathe \'lōth\ *vb* **loathed; loath·ing** : to dislike greatly ♦ *Synonyms* ABOMINATE, ABHOR, DETEST, HATE

loath·ing \'lō-thiŋ\ *n* : extreme disgust

loath·some \'lōth-səm, 'lōth-\ *adj* : exciting loathing : REPULSIVE

lob \'läb\ *vb* **lobbed; lob·bing** **1** : to throw, hit, or propel something in a high arc **2** : to direct (as a question) so as to elicit a response — **lob** *n*

¹lob·by \'lä-bē\ *n, pl* **lobbies** **1** : a corridor used esp. as a passageway or waiting room **2** : a group of persons engaged in lobbying

²lobby *vb* **lob·bied; lob·by·ing** : to try to influence public officials and esp. legislators — **lob·by·ist** *n*

lobe \'lōb\ *n* : a curved or rounded part esp. of a bodily organ — **lo·bar** \'lō-bər\ *adj* — **lobed** \'lōbd\ *adj*

lo·be·lia \lō-'bēl-yə\ *n* : any of a genus of plants often grown for their clusters of showy flowers

lo·bot·o·my \lō-'bä-tə-mē\ *n, pl* **-mies** : surgical severance of certain nerve fibers in the brain used esp. formerly to relieve some mental disorders

lob·ster \'läb-stər\ *n* [ME, fr. OE *loppestre*, fr. *loppe* spider] : any of a family of edible marine crustaceans with two large pincerlike claws and four other pairs of legs; *also* : SPINY LOBSTER

¹lo·cal \'lō-kəl\ *adj* **1** : of, relating to, or occupying a particular place **2** : serving a particular limited district; *also* : making all stops ⟨a ~ train⟩ **3** : affecting a small part of the body ⟨a ~ infection⟩ — **lo·cal·ly** *adv*

²local *n* : one that is local

local area network *n* : a network of personal computers in a small area (as an office)

lo·cale \lō-'kal\ *n* : a place that is the setting for a particular event

lo·cal·ise *Brit var of* LOCALIZE

lo·cal·i·ty \lō-'ka-lə-tē\ *n, pl* **-ties** : a particular spot, situation, or location

lo·cal·ize \'lō-kə-ˌlīz\ *vb* **-ized; -iz·ing** : to fix in or confine to a definite place or locality — **lo·cal·i·za·tion** \ˌlō-kə-lə-'zā-shən\ *n*

lo·cate \'lō-ˌkāt, lō-'kāt\ *vb* **lo·cat·ed; lo·cat·ing** **1** : STATION, SETTLE **2** : to determine the site of **3** : to find or fix the place of in a sequence

lo·ca·tion \lō-'kā-shən\ *n* **1** : SITUATION, PLACE **2** : the process of locating **3** : a place outside a studio where a motion picture is filmed

loc cit *abbr* [L *loco citato*] in the place cited

loch \'läk, 'läk\ *n, Scot* : LAKE; *also* : a bay or arm of the sea esp. when nearly landlocked

¹lock \'läk\ *n* : a tuft, strand, or ringlet of hair; *also* : a cohering bunch (as of wool or flax)

²lock *n* **1** : a fastening in which a bolt is operated **2** : the mechanism of a firearm by which the charge is exploded **3** : an enclosure (as in a canal) used in raising or lowering boats from level to level **4** : AIR LOCK **5** : a wrestling hold

³lock *vb* **1** : to fasten the lock of; *also* : to make fast with a lock **2** : to confine or exclude by means of a lock **3** : INTERLOCK **4** : to make or become motionless by the interlocking of parts

lock·er \'lä-kər\ *n* **1** : a drawer, cupboard, or compartment for individual storage use **2** : an insulated compartment for storing frozen food

lock·et \'lä-kət\ *n* : a small usu. metal case for a memento worn suspended from a chain or necklace

lock·jaw \'läk-ˌjò\ *n* : a symptom of tetanus marked by spasms of the jaw muscles and inability to open the jaws; *also* : TETANUS

lock·nut \-ˌnət\ *n* **1** : a nut screwed tight on another to prevent it from slacking back **2** : a nut designed to lock itself when screwed tight

lock·out \-ˌaùt\ *n* : the suspension of work by an employer during a labor dispute in order to make employees accept the terms being offered

lock·smith \-ˌsmith\ *n* : one who makes or repairs locks

lock·step \-ˌstep\ *n* : a mode of marching in step by a body of men moving in a very close single file

lock·up \-ˌəp\ *n* : JAIL

lo·co \'lō-kō\ *adj* [Sp] *slang* : CRAZY, FRENZIED

lo·co·mo·tion \ˌlō-kə-'mō-shən\ *n* **1** : the act or power of moving from place to place **2** : TRAVEL

¹lo·co·mo·tive \ˌlō-kə-'mō-tiv\ *adj* : of or relating to locomotion or a locomotive

²locomotive *n* : a self-propelled vehicle used to move railroad cars

lo·co·mo·tor \ˌlō-kə-'mō-tər\ *adj* : of or relating to locomotion or organs used in locomotion

lo·co·weed \'lō-kō-ˌwēd\ *n* : any of several leguminous plants of western No. America that are poisonous to livestock

lo·cus \'lō-kəs\ *n, pl* **lo·ci** \'lō-ˌsī\ [L] **1** : PLACE, LOCALITY **2** : the set of all points whose location is determined by stated conditions

lo·cust \'lō-kəst\ *n* **1** : a usu. destructive migratory grasshopper **2** : CICADA **3** : any of various leguminous trees; *also* : the wood of a locust

lo·cu·tion \lō-'kyü-shən\ *n* : a particular form of expression; *also* : PHRASEOLOGY

lode \'lōd\ *n* : an ore deposit

lode·stone \-ˌstōn\ *n* : an iron-containing rock with magnetic properties

¹lodge \'läj\ *vb* **lodged; lodg·ing** **1** : to provide quarters for; *also* : to settle in a place **2** : CONTAIN **3** : to come to a rest and remain ⟨*lodged* in his throat⟩ **4** : to deposit for safekeeping **5** : to vest (as authority) in an agent **6** : FILE ⟨~ a complaint⟩

²lodge *n* **1** : a house set apart for residence in a special season or by an employee on an estate; *also* : INN **2** : a den or lair esp. of gregarious animals **3** : the meeting place of a branch of a fraternal organization; *also* : the members of such a branch

lodg·er \'lä-jər\ *n* : a person who occupies a rented room in another's house

lodg·ing \'lä-jiŋ\ *n* **1** : DWELLING **2** : a room or suite of rooms in another's house rented as a dwelling place — usu. used in pl.

lodg·ment *or* **lodge·ment** \'läj-mənt\ *n* **1** : a lodging place **2** : the act or manner of lodging **3** : DEPOSIT

loess \'les, 'ləs\ *n* : a usu. yellowish brown loamy deposit believed to be chiefly deposited by the wind

lo–fi \'lō-ˌfī\ *n* : audio production of rough or unpolished sound quality — **lo–fi** *adj*

¹loft \'lòft\ *n* [ME, fr. OE, air, sky, fr. ON *lopt*] **1** : ATTIC **2** : GALLERY ⟨organ ~⟩ **3** : an upper floor (as in a warehouse or barn) esp. when not partitioned **4** : the thickness of a fabric or insulated material (as of a sleeping bag)

²loft *vb* : to strike or throw a ball so that it rises high in the air

lofty \'lòf-tē\ *adj* **loft·i·er; -est** **1** : NOBLE; *also* : SUPERIOR ⟨~ ideals⟩ **2** : extremely proud **3** : HIGH, TALL — **loft·i·ly** \'lòf-tə-lē\ *adv* — **loft·i·ness** \-tē-nəs\ *n*

¹log \'lòg, 'läg\ *n* **1** : a bulky piece of a cut or fallen tree **2** : an apparatus for measuring a ship's speed **3** : the daily record of a ship's progress; *also* : a regularly kept record of performance or events ⟨a pilot's ~⟩ ⟨a runner's ~⟩

²log *vb* **logged; log·ging** **1** : to cut (trees) for lumber; *also* : to clear (land) of trees in lumbering **2** : to enter in a log **3** : to sail a ship or fly an airplane for (an indicated distance or period of time) **4** : to have (an indicated record) to one's credit : ACHIEVE — **log·ger** \'lò-gər, 'lä-\ *n*

³log *n* : LOGARITHM

lo·gan·ber·ry \'lō-gən-ˌber-ē\ *n* : a red-fruited uprightgrowing dewberry; *also* : its berry

log·a·rithm \'lò-gə-ˌri-thəm, 'lä-\ *n* : the exponent that indicates the power to which a base is raised to produce a given number ⟨the ~ of 100 to base 10 is 2 since $10^2 = 100$⟩ — **log·a·rith·mic** \ˌlò-gə-'rith-mik, ˌlä-\ *adj*

loge \'lōzh\ *n* **1** : a small compartment; *also* : a box in a theater **2** : a small partitioned area; *also* : the forward section of a theater mezzanine **3** : a raised level of seats in a stadium

log·ger·head \'lò-gər-ˌhed, 'lä-\ *n* : a large sea turtle of subtropical and temperate waters — **at loggerheads** : in a state of quarrelsome disagreement

log·gia \'lō-jē-ə, 'lò-jä\ *n, pl* **loggias** \'lō-jē-əz, 'lò-ˌjäz\ : a roofed open gallery

log·ic \'lä-jik\ *n* **1** : a science that deals with the rules and tests of sound thinking and proof by reasoning **2** : sound reasoning **3** : the arrangement of circuit elements for arithmetical computation in a computer — **log·i·cal** \-ji-kəl\ *adj* — **log·i·cal·ly** \-jik(ə-)lē\ *adv* — **lo·gi·cian** \lō-'ji-shən\ *n*

lo·gis·tics \lō-'jis-tiks\ *n sing or pl* : the procurement, maintenance, and transportation of matériel, facilities, and personnel — **lo·gis·tic** \-tik\ *or* **lo·gis·ti·cal** \-ti-kəl\ *adj*

log·jam \'lòg-ˌjam, 'läg-\ *n* **1** : a deadlocked jumble of logs in a watercourse **2** : DEADLOCK — **logjam** *vt*

logo \'lō-gō\ *n, pl* **log·os** \-gōz\ : an identifying symbol (as for advertising)

logo·type \'lò-gə-ˌtīp, 'lä-\ *n* : LOGO

log·roll·ing \-ˌrō-liŋ\ *n* : the trading of votes by legislators to secure favorable action on projects of individual interest

lo·gy \'lō-gē\ *also* **log·gy** \'lò-gē, 'lä-\ *adj* **lo·gi·er; -est** : deficient in vitality : SLUGGISH

loin \'lòin\ *n* [ME *loyne*, fr. AF *loigne*, fr. VL *lumbea*, fr. L *lumbus*] **1** : the part of the body on each side of the spinal column and between the hip and the lower ribs; *also* : a cut of meat from this part of an animal **2** *pl* : the pubic region; *also* : the organs of reproduction

loin·cloth \-ˌklòth\ *n* : a cloth worn about the loins often as the sole article of clothing in warm climates

loi·ter \'lòi-tər\ *vb* **1** : LINGER **2** : to hang around idly
 ✦ *Synonyms* DAWDLE, DALLY, PROCRASTINATE, LAG, TARRY — **loi·ter·er** *n*

loll \'läl\ *vb* **1** : DROOP, DANGLE **2** : LOUNGE

lol·la·pa·loo·za \ˌlä-lə-pə-'lü-zə\ *n* : something extraordinarily impressive or outstanding

lol·li·pop *or* **lol·ly·pop** \'lä-li-ˌpäp\ *n* : a lump of hard candy on a stick

lol·ly·gag \'lä-lē-ˌgag\ *vb* **-gagged; -gag·ging** : DAWDLE

Lond *abbr* London

lone \'lōn\ *adj* **1** : SOLITARY ⟨a ~ sentinel⟩ **2** : SOLE, ONLY ⟨the ~ theater in town⟩ **3** : ISOLATED ⟨a ~ tree⟩

lone·ly \'lōn-lē\ *adj* **lone·li·er; -est** **1** : being without company **2** : UNFREQUENTED ⟨a ~ spot⟩ **3** : LONESOME — **lone·li·ness** *n*

lon·er \'lō-nər\ *n* : one that avoids others

lone·some \'lōn-səm\ *adj* **1** : sad from lack of companionship **2** : REMOTE; *also* : SOLITARY ⟨a ~ road⟩ — **lone·some·ly** *adv* — **lone·some·ness** *n*

¹long \'lȯṅ\ *adj* **lon·ger** \'lȯṅ-gər\; **lon·gest** \'lȯṅ-gəst\ **1** : extending for a considerable distance ⟨a ~ corridor⟩; *also* : TALL, ELONGATED ⟨~ legs⟩ **2** : having a specified length **3** : extending over a considerable time; *also* : TEDIOUS ⟨~ lectures⟩ **4** : containing many items in a series ⟨a ~ list⟩ **5** : being a syllable or speech sound of relatively great duration **6** : extending far into the future **7** : well furnished with something — used with *on*

²long *adv* : for or during a long time

³long *n* : a long period of time

⁴long *vb* **longed; long·ing** \'lȯṅ-iṅ\ : to feel a strong desire or wish ♦ **Synonyms** YEARN, HANKER, PINE, HUNGER, THIRST

⁵long *abbr* longitude

long·boat \'lȯṅ-ˌbōt\ *n* : a large boat usu. carried by a merchant sailing ship

long·bow \-ˌbō\ *n* : a wooden bow drawn by hand and used esp. by medieval English archers

lon·gev·i·ty \län-'je-və-tē\ *n* [LL *longaevitas,* fr. L *longaevus* long-lived, fr. *longus* long + *aevum* age] : a long duration of individual life; *also* : length of life

long·hair \'lȯṅ-ˌher\ *n* **1** : a lover of classical music **2** : HIPPIE **3** : a domestic cat having long outer fur — **long–haired** \-ˌherd\ *or* **long·hair** *adj*

long·hand \-ˌhand\ *n* : HANDWRITING

long·horn \-ˌhȯrn\ *n* : any of the cattle with long horns formerly common in the southwestern U.S.

long hundredweight *n, Brit* — see WEIGHT table

long·ing \'lȯṅ-iṅ\ *n* : a strong desire esp. for something unattainable — **long·ing·ly** *adv*

lon·gi·tude \'län-jə-ˌtüd, -ˌtyüd\ *n* : angular distance expressed usu. in degrees east or west from the prime meridian through Greenwich, England

lon·gi·tu·di·nal \ˌlän-jə-'tü-dᵊn-əl, -'tyüd-\ *adj* **1** : extending lengthwise **2** : of or relating to length — **lon·gi·tu·di·nal·ly** *adv*

long–range \'lȯṅ-'rānj\ *adj* **1** : relating to or fit for long distances **2** : involving a long period of time

long·shore·man \'lȯṅ-ˌshȯr-mən\ *n* : a laborer at a wharf who loads and unloads cargo

long–suf·fer·ing \-'sə-friṅ, -fə-riṅ\ *adj* : patiently enduring lasting offense or hardship

long–term \'lȯṅ-'tərm\ *adj* **1** : extending over or involving a long period of time **2** : constituting a financial obligation based on a term usu. of more than 10 years ⟨~ bonds⟩

long·time \'lȯṅ-'tīm\ *adj* : of long duration ⟨~ friends⟩

long ton *n* — see WEIGHT table

lon·gueur \lōⁿ-'gœr\ *n, pl* **longueurs** *same or* -'gœrz\ [F, lit., length] : a dull tedious portion (as of a book)

long–wind·ed \ˌlȯṅ-'win-dəd\ *adj* : tediously long in speaking or writing

loo·fah \'lü-fə\ *n* : a sponge consisting of the fibrous skeleton of a gourd

¹look \'lu̇k\ *vb* **1** : to exercise the power of vision : SEE ⟨~ what I won⟩ **2** : EXPECT **3** : to have an appearance that befits ⟨~s the part⟩ **4** : SEEM ⟨~s thin⟩ **5** : to direct one's attention : HEED ⟨~ at the sign⟩ **6** : POINT, FACE ⟨~s east⟩ **7** : to show a tendency — **look after** : to take care of — **look at 1** : CONSIDER ⟨*looking at* all possibilities⟩ **2** : CONFRONT, FACE ⟨*looking at* stiff fines⟩ — **look for** : EXPECT — **look forward** : to anticipate with pleasure ⟨*look forward* to summer⟩

²look *n* **1** : the action of looking : GLANCE **2** : EXPRESSION; *also* : physical appearance **3** : ASPECT

look down *vb* : to regard with contempt — used with *on* or *upon*

looking glass *n* : MIRROR

look·out \'lu̇k-ˌau̇t\ *n* **1** : a person assigned to watch (as on a ship) **2** : a careful watch **3** : VIEW **4** : a matter of concern

look up *vb* **1** : IMPROVE ⟨business is *looking up*⟩ **2** : to search for in or as if in a reference work **3** : to seek out esp. for a brief visit

¹loom \'lüm\ *n* : a frame or machine for weaving together threads or yarns into cloth

²loom *vb* **1** : to come into sight in an unnaturally large, indistinct, or distorted form **2** : to appear in an impressively exaggerated form

loon \'lün\ *n* : any of several web-footed black-and-white fish-eating diving birds

loon

loo·ny *or* **loo·ney** \'lü-nē\ *adj* **loo·ni·er; -est** : CRAZY, FOOLISH

loony bin *n* : a psychiatric hospital

loop \'lüp\ *n* **1** : a fold or doubling of a line through which another line or hook can be passed; *also* : a loop-shaped figure or course ⟨a ~ in a river⟩ **2** : a circular airplane maneuver executed in the vertical plane **3** : a continuously repeated segment of film, music, or sound — **loop** *vb*

loop·er \'lü-pər\ *n* : any of numerous rather small hairless moth caterpillars that move with a looping motion

loop·hole \'lüp-ˌhōl\ *n* **1** : a small opening in a wall through which firearms may be discharged **2** : a means of escape; *esp* : an ambiguity or omission that allows one to evade the intent of a law or contract

loopy \'lü-pē\ *adj* **loop·i·er; -est** **1** : having loops **2** : CRAZY, BIZARRE — **loop·i·ly** \-pə-lē\ *adv* — **loop·i·ness** \-pē-nəs\ *n*

¹loose \'lüs\ *adj* **loos·er; loos·est** **1** : not rigidly fastened **2** : free from restraint or obligation **3** : not dense or compact in structure **4** : not chaste : LEWD **5** : SLACK **6** : not precise or exact — **loose·ly** *adv* — **loose·ness** *n*

²loose *vb* **loosed; loos·ing** **1** : RELEASE **2** : UNTIE **3** : DETACH **4** : DISCHARGE **5** : RELAX, SLACKEN

³loose *adv* : LOOSELY

loos·en \'lü-sᵊn\ *vb* **1** : FREE **2** : to make or become loose **3** : to relax the severity of ⟨~ rules⟩

loot \'lüt\ *n* [Hindi & Urdu *lūṭ;* akin to Skt *luṇṭati* he plunders] : goods taken in war or by robbery : PLUNDER — **loot** *vb* — **loot·er** *n*

¹lop \'läp\ *vb* **lopped; lop·ping** : to cut branches or twigs from : TRIM; *also* : to cut off

²lop *vb* **lopped; lop·ping** : to hang downward; *also* : to flop or sway loosely

lope \'lōp\ *n* : an easy bounding gait — **lope** *vb*

lop·sid·ed \'läp-'sī-dəd\ *adj* **1** : leaning to one side **2** : UNSYMMETRICAL — **lop·sid·ed·ly** *adv* — **lop·sid·ed·ness** *n*

lo·qua·cious \lō-'kwā-shəs\ *adj* : excessively talkative — **lo·quac·i·ty** \-'kwa-sə-tē\ *n*

¹lord \'lȯrd\ *n* [ME *loverd, lord,* fr. OE *hlāford,* fr. *hlāf* loaf + *weard* keeper] **1** : one having power and authority over others; *esp* : a person from whom a feudal fee or estate is held **2** *cap* : GOD **1** **3** : a man of rank or high position; *esp* : a British nobleman **4** *pl, cap* : the upper house of the British parliament **5** : a person of great power in some field

²lord *vb* : to act like a lord; *esp* : to put on airs — usu. used with *it*

lord chancellor *n, pl* **lords chancellor** : a British officer of state who presides over the House of Lords, serves as head of the British judiciary, and is usu. a leading member of the cabinet

lord·ly \-lē\ *adj* **lord·li·er; -est** **1** : DIGNIFIED; *also* : NOBLE **2** : HAUGHTY

lord·ship \-ˌship\ *n* **1** : the rank or dignity of a lord — used as a title **2** : the authority or territory of a lord

Lord's Supper *n* : COMMUNION

lore \ˈlȯr\ *n* : KNOWLEDGE; *esp* : traditional knowledge or belief

lor·gnette \lȯrn-ˈyet\ *n* [F, fr. *lorgner* to take a sidelong look at, fr. MF, fr. *lorgne* squinting] : a pair of eyeglasses or opera glasses with a handle

lorn \ˈlȯrn\ *adj* : FORSAKEN, DESOLATE

lor·ry \ˈlȯr-ē\ *n, pl* **lorries** *chiefly Brit* : MOTORTRUCK

lose \ˈlüz\ *vb* **lost** \ˈlȯst\; **los·ing** \ˈlü-ziŋ\ **1** : DESTROY **2** : to miss from a customary place : MISLAY **3** : to suffer deprivation of **4** : to fail to use : WASTE ⟨no time to ∼⟩ **5** : to fail to win or obtain ⟨∼ the game⟩ **6** : to fail to keep or maintain ⟨∼ his balance⟩ **7** : to wander from ⟨∼ her way⟩ **8** : to get rid of ⟨should ∼ the beard⟩ — **los·er** *n* — **lose it 1** : to go crazy **2** : to fail to keep one's composure

loss \ˈlȯs\ *n* **1** : RUIN **2** : the harm resulting from losing **3** : something that is lost **4** *pl* : killed, wounded, or captured soldiers **5** : failure to win **6** : an amount by which the cost exceeds the selling price **7** : decrease in amount or degree

loss leader *n* : an article sold at a loss in order to draw customers

lost \ˈlȯst\ *adj* **1** : not used, won, or claimed **2** : no longer possessed or known **3** : ruined or destroyed physically or morally **4** : DENIED; *also* : HARDENED **5** : unable to find the way; *also* : ABSORBED, RAPT **7** : not appreciated or understood ⟨his jokes were ∼ on me⟩ **8** : made obscure : OVERLOOKED ⟨∼ in translation⟩ **9** : FUTILE ⟨a ∼ cause⟩

lot \ˈlät\ *n* **1** : an object used in deciding something by chance; *also* : the use of lots to decide something **2** : SHARE, PORTION; *also* : FORTUNE, FATE **3** : a plot of land **4** : a group of individuals : SET **5** : a considerable quantity

loth *var of* LOATH

lo·ti \ˈlō-tē\ *n, pl* **ma·lo·ti** \mə-ˈlō-tē\ — see MONEY table

lo·tion \ˈlō-shən\ *n* : a liquid preparation for cosmetic and external medicinal use

lot·tery \ˈlä-tə-rē\ *n, pl* **-ter·ies 1** : a drawing of lots in which prizes are given to the winning names or numbers **2** : a matter determined by chance

lo·tus \ˈlō-təs\ *n* **1** : a fruit held in Greek legend to cause dreamy contentment and forgetfulness **2** : any of various water lilies represented esp. in ancient Egyptian and Hindu art **3** : any of several leguminous forage plants

loud \ˈlau̇d\ *adj* **1** : marked by intensity or volume of sound **2** : CLAMOROUS, NOISY **3** : obtrusive or offensive in color or pattern ⟨a ∼ tie⟩ — **loud** *adv* — **loud·ly** *adv* — **loud·ness** *n*

loud-mouthed \-ˌmau̇tht, -ˌmau̇thd\ *adj* : given to loud offensive talk

loud·speak·er \-ˌspē-kər\ *n* : a device that changes electrical signals into sound

¹lounge \ˈlau̇nj\ *vb* **lounged; loung·ing** : to act or move lazily or listlessly

²lounge *n* **1** : a room with comfortable furniture; *also* : a room (as in a theater) with lounging, smoking, and toilet facilities **2** : a long couch

lour, loury *var of* LOWER, LOWERY

louse \ˈlau̇s\ *n, pl* **lice** \ˈlīs\ **1** : any of various small wingless usu. flattened insects parasitic on warm-blooded animals **2** : a plant pest (as an aphid) **3** *pl* **lous·es** \ˈlau̇-səz\ : a contemptible person

lousy \ˈlau̇-zē\ *adj* **lous·i·er; -est 1** : infested with lice **2** : POOR, INFERIOR **3** : somewhat ill **4** : amply supplied ⟨∼ with money⟩ — **lous·i·ly** \-zə-lē\ *adv* — **lous·i·ness** \-zē-nəs\ *n*

lout \ˈlau̇t\ *n* : a stupid awkward fellow — **lout·ish** *adj* — **lout·ish·ly** *adv*

lou·ver *or* **lou·vre** \ˈlü-vər\ *n* **1** : an opening having parallel slanted slats to allow flow of air but to exclude rain or sun or to provide privacy; *also* : a slat in such an opening **2** : a device with movable slats for controlling the flow of air or light

¹love \ˈləv\ *n* **1** : strong affection **2** : warm attachment ⟨∼ of the sea⟩ **3** : attraction based on sexual desire **4** : a beloved person **5** : unselfish loyal and benevolent concern for others **6** : a score of zero in tennis — **love·less** *adj*

²love *vb* **loved; lov·ing 1** : CHERISH **2** : to feel a passion, devotion, or tenderness for **3** : CARESS **4** : to take plea-

sure in ⟨∼s to play bridge⟩ — **lov·able** *also* **love·able** \ˈlə-və-bəl\ *adj* — **lov·er** *n*

love·bird \ˈləv-ˌbərd\ *n* : any of various small usu. gray or green parrots that seem to show caring behavior for their mates

love·lorn \-ˌlȯrn\ *adj* : deprived of love or of a lover

love·ly \ˈləv-lē\ *adj* **love·li·er; -est** : BEAUTIFUL — **love·li·ly** \ˈləv-lə-lē\ *adv* — **love·li·ness** *n* — **lovely** *adv*

love·mak·ing \-ˌmā-kiŋ\ *n* **1** : COURTSHIP **2** : sexual activity; *esp* : COPULATION

love·sick \-ˌsik\ *adj* **1** : YEARNING **2** : expressing a lover's longing — **love·sick·ness** *n*

lov·ing \ˈlə-viŋ\ *adj* **1** : AFFECTIONATE **2** : PAINSTAKING — **lov·ing·ly** *adv*

¹low \ˈlō\ *vb* : MOO

²low *n* : MOO

³low *adj* **low·er** \ˈlō-ər\; **low·est** \ˈlō-əst\ **1** : not high or tall ⟨∼ wall⟩; *also* : DÉCOLLETÉ **2** : situated or passing below the normal level or surface ⟨∼ ground⟩; *also* : marking a nadir **3** : not loud ⟨∼ voice⟩ **4** : being near the equator **5** : humble in status **6** : WEAK; *also* : DEPRESSED **7** : STRICKEN, PROSTRATE **8** : less than usual in number, amount, or value; *also* : of lesser degree than average **9** : falling short of a standard **10** : UNFAVORABLE — **low** *adv* — **low·ness** *n*

⁴low *n* **1** : something that is low **2** : a region of low barometric pressure **3** : the arrangement of gears in an automobile transmission that gives the slowest speed and greatest power

low·ball \ˈlō-ˌbȯl\ *vb* : to give a deceptively low price, cost estimate, or offer to

low beam *n* : a vehicle headlight beam with short-range focus

low blow *n* : an unprincipled attack

low·brow \ˈlō-ˌbrau̇\ *adj* : having little taste or intellectual interest ⟨∼ humor⟩ — **lowbrow** *n*

low–density lipoprotein *n* : LDL

low·down \-ˌdau̇n\ *n* : pertinent and esp. guarded information

low–down \-ˌdau̇n\ *adj* **1** : MEAN, CONTEMPTIBLE **2** : deeply emotional

low–end \-ˌend\ *adj* : of, relating to, or being the lowest-priced merchandise in a manufacturer's line

¹low·er *also* **lour** \ˈlau̇(-ə)r\ *vb* **1** : FROWN **2** : to become dark, gloomy, and threatening — **lower** *also* **lour** *n*

²low·er \ˈlō-ər\ *adj* **1** : relatively low (as in rank) **2** : SOUTHERN ⟨the ∼ states⟩ **3** : less advanced in the scale of evolutionary development ⟨∼ animals⟩ **4** : situated beneath the earth's surface **5** : constituting the popular and more representative branch of a bicameral legislative body

³low·er \ˈlō-ər\ *vb* **1** : DROP; *also* : DIMINISH **2** : to let descend by its own weight; *also* : to reduce the height of **3** : to reduce in value, number, or amount **4** : DEGRADE; *also* : HUMBLE

low·er·case \ˌlō-ər-ˈkās\ *adj* : being a letter that belongs to or conforms to the series a, b, c, etc., rather than A, B, C, etc. — **lowercase** *n*

lower class *n* : a social class occupying a position below the middle class and having the lowest status in a society — **lower–class** \-ˈklas\ *adj*

low·er·most \ˈlō-ər-ˌmōst\ *adj* : LOWEST

low·ery *also* **loury** \ˈlau̇-(ə-)rē\ *adj* : GLOOMY, LOWERING

lowest common denominator *n* **1** : LEAST COMMON DENOMINATOR **2** : something designed to appeal to a low-brow audience; *also* : such an audience

lowest common multiple *n* : LEAST COMMON MULTIPLE

low–key \ˈlō-ˈkē\ *also* **low–keyed** \-ˈkēd\ *adj* : of low intensity : RESTRAINED

low·land \ˈlō-lənd, -ˌland\ *n* : low and usu. level country

low–lev·el \ˈlō-ˈle-vəl\ *adj* **1** : being of low importance or rank **2** : being or relating to nuclear waste of low concentration

low·life \ˈlō-ˌlīf\ *n, pl* **low·lifes** \-ˌlīfs\ *also* **low·lives** \-ˌlīvz\ : a person of low social status or moral character

low·ly \ˈlō-lē\ *adj* **low·li·er; -est 1** : HUMBLE, MEEK **2** : ranking low in some hierarchy — **low·li·ness** *n*

low–rise \ˈlō-ˈrīz\ *adj* **1** : having few stories and not equipped with elevators ⟨a ∼ building⟩ **2** : of, relating to, or characterized by low-rise buildings

low–slung \'lō-,sləŋ\ *adj* : relatively low to the ground or floor ⟨a ~ building⟩ ⟨~ pants⟩

low–tech \'lō-'tek\ *adj* : technologically simple or unsophisticated

¹lox \'läks\ *n* : liquid oxygen

²lox *n, pl* **lox** *or* **lox·es** : salmon cured in brine and sometimes smoked

loy·al \'loi(-ə)l\ *adj* [MF, fr. OF *leial, leel*, fr. L *legalis* legal] **1** : faithful in allegiance to one's government **2** : faithful esp. to a cause or ideal : CONSTANT — **loy·al·ly** \'loi-ə-lē\ *adv* — **loy·al·ty** \'loi-(ə)l-tē\ *n*

loy·al·ist \'loi-ə-list\ *n* : one who is or remains loyal to a political party, government, or sovereign

loz·enge \'lä-zənj\ *n* **1** : a diamond-shaped figure **2** : a small flat often medicated candy

LP *abbr* low pressure

LPG *abbr* liquefied petroleum gas

LPGA *abbr* Ladies Professional Golf Association

LPN \'el-'pē-'en\ *n* : LICENSED PRACTICAL NURSE

Lr *symbol* Lawrencium

LSD \,el-(,)es-'dē\ *n* [G *Lysergsäure-Diäthylamid* lysergic acid diethylamide] : an illicit and highly potent hallucinogenic drug derived from ergot or produced synthetically

lt *abbr* light

Lt *abbr* lieutenant

LT *abbr* long ton

LTC *or* **Lt Col** *abbr* lieutenant colonel

Lt Comdr *abbr* lieutenant commander

ltd *abbr* limited

LTG *or* **Lt Gen** *abbr* lieutenant general

LTJG *abbr* lieutenant, junior grade

ltr *abbr* letter

Lu *symbol* lutetium

lu·au \'lü-,aù\ *n* : a Hawaiian feast

lub *abbr* lubricant; lubricating

lub·ber \'lə-bər\ *n* **1** : LOUT **2** : an unskilled seaman — **lub·ber·ly** *adj*

lube \'lüb\ *n* : LUBRICANT; *also* : an application of a lubricant

lu·bri·cant \'lü-bri-kənt\ *n* : a material capable of reducing friction when applied between moving parts

lu·bri·cate \'lü-brə-,kāt\ *vb* **-cat·ed; -cat·ing** : to apply a lubricant to — **lu·bri·ca·tion** \,lü-brə-'kā-shən\ *n* — **lu·bri·ca·tor** \'lü-brə-,kā-tər\ *n*

lu·bri·cious \lü-'bri-shəs\ *or* **lu·bri·cous** \'lü-bri-kəs\ *adj* **1** : SMOOTH, SLIPPERY **2** : LECHEROUS; *also* : SALACIOUS — **lu·bric·i·ty** \lü-'bri-sə-tē\ *n*

lu·cent \'lü-s°nt\ *adj* **1** : LUMINOUS **2** : CLEAR, LUCID — **lu·cent·ly** *adv*

lu·cerne \lü-'sərn\ *n, chiefly Brit* : ALFALFA

lu·cid \'lü-səd\ *adj* **1** : SHINING **2** : mentally sound **3** : easily understood — **lu·cid·i·ty** \lü-'si-də-tē\ *n* — **lu·cid·ly** *adv* — **lu·cid·ness** *n*

Lu·ci·fer \'lü-sə-fər\ *n* [ME, the morning star, a fallen rebel archangel, the Devil, fr. OE, fr. L, the morning star, fr. *lucifer* light-bearing] : DEVIL, SATAN

¹luck \'lək\ *n* **1** : CHANCE, FORTUNE **2** : good fortune — **luck·less** *adj*

²luck *vb* **1** : to prosper or succeed esp. through chance or good fortune — usu. used with *out* **2** : to come upon something desirable by chance — usu. used with *out, on, onto,* or *into*

luck·i·ly \'lə-kə-lē\ *adv* **1** : in a lucky manner **2** : FORTUNATELY 2

lucky \'lə-kē\ *adj* **luck·i·er; -est** **1** : favored by luck : FORTUNATE **2** : FORTUITOUS **3** : seeming to bring good luck ⟨a ~ penny⟩ — **luck·i·ness** *n*

lu·cra·tive \'lü-krə-tiv\ *adj* : PROFITABLE ⟨~ business deals⟩ — **lu·cra·tive·ly** *adv* — **lu·cra·tive·ness** *n*

lu·cre \'lü-kər\ *n* [ME, fr. AF, fr. L *lucrum*] : PROFIT; *also* : MONEY

lu·cu·bra·tion \,lü-kyə-'brä-shən, -kə-\ *n* : laborious study : MEDITATION

Ludd·ite \'lə-,dīt\ *n* [perh. fr. Ned *Ludd*, 18th cent. Eng. workman who destroyed a knitting frame] : one who is opposed to technological change

lu·di·crous \'lü-də-krəs\ *adj* : LAUGHABLE, RIDICULOUS — **lu·di·crous·ly** *adv* — **lu·di·crous·ness** *n*

luff \'ləf\ *vb* : to turn the head of a ship toward the wind

¹lug \'ləg\ *vb* **lugged; lug·ging** **1** : DRAG, PULL **2** : to carry laboriously

²lug *n* **1** : a projecting piece (as for fastening, support, or traction) **2** : a nut securing a wheel on an automobile

lug·gage \'lə-gij\ *n* : containers (as suitcases) for carrying personal belongings : BAGGAGE

lu·gu·bri·ous \lù-'gü-brē-əs\ *adj* : mournful often to an exaggerated degree — **lu·gu·bri·ous·ly** *adv* — **lu·gu·bri·ous·ness** *n*

Luke \'lük\ *n* — see BIBLE table

luke·warm \'lük-'wórm\ *adj* **1** : moderately warm : TEPID **2** : not enthusiastic ⟨~ praise⟩ — **luke·warm·ly** *adv*

¹lull \'ləl\ *vb* **1** : SOOTHE, CALM **2** : to cause to relax vigilance

²lull *n* **1** : a temporary calm (as during a storm) **2** : a temporary drop in activity ⟨a ~ in sales⟩

lul·la·by \'lə-lə-,bī\ *n, pl* **-bies** : a song to lull children to sleep

lu·ma \'lü-'mä\ *n* — see *dram* at MONEY table

lum·ba·go \,ləm-'bā-gō\ *n* : acute or chronic pain in the lower back

lum·bar \'ləm-bər, -,bär\ *adj* : of, relating to, or constituting the loins or the vertebrae between the thoracic vertebrae and sacrum ⟨~ region⟩

¹lum·ber \'ləm-bər\ *vb* : to move heavily or clumsily

²lumber *n* **1** : surplus or disused articles that are stored away **2** : timber or logs esp. when dressed for use

³lumber *vb* : to cut logs; *also* : to saw logs into lumber — **lum·ber·man** \-mən\ *n*

lum·ber·jack \-,jak\ *n* : LOGGER

lum·ber·yard \-,yärd\ *n* : a place where lumber is kept for sale

lu·mi·nary \'lü-mə-,ner-ē\ *n, pl* **-nar·ies** **1** : a very famous person **2** : a source of light; *esp* : a celestial body

lu·mi·nes·cence \,lü-mə-'ne-s°ns\ *n* : the low-temperature emission of light (as by a chemical or physiological process); *also* : such light — **lu·mi·nes·cent** \-s°nt\ *adj*

lu·mi·nous \'lü-mə-nəs\ *adj* **1** : emitting light; *also* : LIGHTED **2** : CLEAR, INTELLIGIBLE **3** : ILLUSTRIOUS — **lu·mi·nance** \-nəns\ *n* — **lu·mi·nos·i·ty** \,lü-mə-'nä-sə-tē\ *n* — **lu·mi·nous·ly** *adv*

lum·mox \'lə-məks\ *n* : a clumsy person

¹lump \'ləmp\ *n* **1** : a piece or mass of indefinite size and shape **2** : AGGREGATE, TOTALITY **3** : a usu. abnormal swelling — **lump·ish** *adj* — **lumpy** *adj*

²lump *vb* **1** : to heap together in a lump **2** : to form into lumps

³lump *adj* : not divided into parts ⟨a ~ sum⟩

lump·ec·to·my \,ləm-'pek-tə-mē\ *n, pl* **-mies** : excision of a breast tumor

lu·na·cy \'lü-nə-sē\ *n, pl* **-cies** **1** : INSANITY **2** : extreme folly

lu·nar \'lü-nər\ *adj* : of or relating to the moon

lu·nate \'lü-,nāt\ *adj* : shaped like a crescent

lu·na·tic \'lü-nə-,tik\ *adj* [ME *lunatik*, fr. AF & LL; AF *lunatik*, fr. LL *lunaticus*, fr. L *luna* moon; fr. the belief that lunacy fluctuated with the phases of the moon] **1** : INSANE; *also* : used for insane persons **2** : extremely foolish — **lunatic** *n*

¹lunch \'lənch\ *n* **1** : a light meal usu. eaten in the middle of the day **2** : the food prepared for a lunch

²lunch *vb* : to eat lunch

lun·cheon \'lən-chən\ *n* : a usu. formal lunch

lun·cheon·ette \,lən-chə-'net\ *n* : a small restaurant serving light lunches

lunch·room \'lənch-,rüm, -,rùm\ *n* **1** : LUNCHEONETTE **2** : a room (as in a school) where lunches are sold and eaten or lunches brought from home may be eaten

lu·nette \lü-'net\ *n* : something shaped like a crescent

lung \'ləŋ\ *n* **1** : one of the usu. paired baglike breathing organs in the chest of an air-breathing vertebrate **2** : a mechanical device to promote breathing and make it easier — **lunged** \'ləŋd\ *adj*

lunge \'lənj\ *n* **1** : a sudden thrust or pass (as with a sword) **2** : a sudden forward stride or leap — **lunge** *vb*

lu·pine \'lü-pən\ *n* : any of a genus of leguminous plants with long upright clusters of pealike flowers

lu·pus \'lü-pəs\ *n* [ML, fr. L, wolf] : any of several diseases characterized by skin lesions; *esp* : SYSTEMIC LUPUS ERYTHEMATOSUS

lurch \'lərch\ *n* : a sudden swaying or tipping movement — **lurch** *vb*

¹lure \'lùr\ *n* **1** : ENTICEMENT; *also* : APPEAL **2** : an artificial bait for catching fish

²lure *vb* **lured; lur·ing** : to draw on with a promise of pleasure or gain

lu·rid \'lùr-əd\ *adj* **1** : GRUESOME; *also* : SENSATIONAL **2** : wan and ghostly pale in appearance **3** : shining with the red glow of fire seen through smoke or cloud ◆ *Synonyms* GHASTLY, GRISLY, GRIM, HORRIBLE, MACABRE — **lu·rid·ly** *adv*

lurk \'lərk\ *vb* **1** : to move furtively : SNEAK **2** : to lie concealed

lus·cious \'lə-shəs\ *adj* **1** : having a pleasingly sweet taste or smell **2** : sensually appealing — **lus·cious·ly** *adv* — **lus·cious·ness** *n*

¹lush \'ləsh\ *adj* : having or covered with abundant growth ⟨~ pastures⟩

²lush *n* : a habitual heavy drinker

lust \'ləst\ *n* **1** : usu. intense or unbridled sexual desire : LASCIVIOUSNESS **2** : an intense longing ⟨a ~ to succeed⟩ — **lust** *vb* — **lust·ful** *adj*

lus·ter *or* **lus·tre** \'ləs-tər\ *n* **1** : a shine or sheen esp. from reflected light **2** : BRIGHTNESS, GLITTER **3** : GLORY, SPLENDOR — **lus·ter·less** *adj* — **lus·trous** \-trəs\ *adj*

lus·tral \'ləs-trəl\ *adj* : serving or intended to purify ⟨~ water⟩

lusty \'ləs-tē\ *adj* **lust·i·er; -est** : full of vitality : ROBUST — **lust·i·ly** \'ləs-tə-lē\ *adv* — **lust·i·ness** \-tē-nəs\ *n*

lute \'lüt\ *n* : a stringed musical instrument with a large pear-shaped body and a fretted fingerboard — **lu·te·nist** *or* **lu·ta·nist** \'lüt-ə-nist\ *n*

lu·te·tium *also* **lu·te·cium** \lü-'tē-shē-əm, -shəm\ *n* : a metallic chemical element

Lu·ther·an \'lü-thə-rən\ *n* : a member of a Protestant denomination adhering to the doctrines of Martin Luther — **Lu·ther·an·ism** \-rə-,ni-zəm\ *n*

lux·u·ri·ant \,ləg-'zhùr-ē-ənt, ,lək-'shùr-\ *adj* **1** : yielding or growing abundantly : LUSH, PRODUCTIVE ⟨~ vegetation⟩ **2** : abundantly rich and varied; *also* : FLORID ⟨a ~ fabric⟩ ◆ *Synonyms* EXUBERANT, LAVISH, OPULENT, PRODIGAL, PROFUSE, RIOTOUS — **lux·u·ri·ance** \-ē-əns\ *n* — **lux·u·ri·ant·ly** *adv*

lux·u·ri·ate \-ē-,āt\ *vb* **-at·ed; -at·ing** **1** : to grow profusely **2** : REVEL

lux·u·ry \'lək-shə-rē, 'ləg-zhə-\ *n, pl* **-ries** **1** : great ease and comfort **2** : something adding to pleasure or comfort but not absolutely necessary — **lux·u·ri·ous** \,ləg-'zhùr-ē-əs, ,lək-'shùr-\ *adj* — **lux·u·ri·ous·ly** *adv*

lv *abbr* leave

lwei \lə-'wā\ *n, pl* **lwei** — see *kwanza* at MONEY table

LWV *abbr* League of Women Voters

¹-ly \lē\ *adj suffix* **1** : like in appearance, manner, or nature

⟨queen*ly*⟩ **2** : characterized by regular recurrence in (specified) units of time : every ⟨hour*ly*⟩ ⟨week*ly*⟩

²-ly *adv suffix* **1** : in a (specified) manner ⟨slow*ly*⟩ **2** : from a (specified) point of view ⟨grammatical*ly*⟩

ly·ce·um \lī-'sē-əm, 'lī-sē-\ *n* **1** : a hall for public lectures **2** : an association providing public lectures, concerts, and entertainments

ly·chee *or* **li·tchi** \'lē-chē, 'lī-\ *n* [Ch(Beijing) *lìzhī*] **1** : an oval fruit with a hard scaly outer covering, a small hard seed, and edible flesh **2** : an Asian tree bearing lychees

lye \'lī\ *n* : a corrosive alkaline substance used esp. in making soap

ly·ing \'lī-iŋ\ *adj* : UNTRUTHFUL, FALSE

ly·ing–in \,lī-iŋ-'in\ *n, pl* **lyings–in** *or* **lying–ins** : the state during and consequent to childbirth : CONFINEMENT

Lyme disease \'līm-\ *n* [*Lyme*, Connecticut, where it was first reported] : an acute inflammatory disease that is caused by a spirochete transmitted by ticks, is characterized usu. by chills and fever, and if left untreated may result in joint pain, arthritis, and cardiac and neurological disorders

lymph \'limf\ *n* : a usu. clear fluid consisting chiefly of blood plasma and white blood cells, circulating in thin-walled tubes (**lymphatic vessels**), and bathing the body tissues — **lym·phat·ic** \lim-'fa-tik\ *adj*

lymph·ade·nop·a·thy \,lim-,fa-də-'nä-pə-thē\ *n, pl* **-thies** : abnormal enlargement of the lymph nodes

lymph node *n* : any of the rounded masses of lymphoid tissue surrounded by a capsule of connective tissue

lym·pho·cyte \'lim-fə-,sīt\ *n* : any of the white blood cells arising from lymphoid tissue that are typically found in lymph and blood and that include the cellular mediators (as a B cell or a T cell) of immunity — **lym·pho·cyt·ic** \,lim-fə-'si-tik\ *adj*

lym·phoid \'lim-,fóid\ *adj* **1** : of, relating to, or being tissue (as of the lymph nodes) containing lymphocytes **2** : of, relating to, or resembling lymph

lym·pho·ma \lim-'fō-mə\ *n, pl* **-mas** *also* **-ma·ta** \-mə-tə\ : a usu. malignant tumor of lymphoid tissue

lynch \'linch\ *vb* : to put to death by mob action without legal sanction or due process of law — **lynch·er** *n*

lynx \'liŋks\ *n, pl* **lynx** *or* **lynx·es** : any of several wildcats with a short tail, long legs, and usu. tufted ears

lyre \'lī-(ə)r\ *n* : a stringed musical instrument of the harp class having a U-shaped frame and used by the ancient Greeks

¹lyr·ic \'lir-ik\ *n* **1** : a lyric poem **2** *pl* : the words of a popular song — **lyr·i·cal** \-i-kəl\ *adj*

²lyric *adj* **1** : suitable for singing : MELODIC **2** : expressing direct and usu. intense personal emotion

ly·ser·gic acid di·eth·yl·am·ide \lə-'sər-jik . . . ,dī-,e-thə-'la-,mīd, lī-, -'la-məd\ *n* : LSD

LZ *abbr* landing zone

¹m \'em\ *n, pl* **m's** *or* **ms** \'emz\ *often cap* **1** : the 13th letter of the English alphabet **2** : one thousand in Roman numerals

²m *abbr, often cap* **1** Mach **2** male **3** married **4** masculine **5** medium **6** [L *meridies*] noon **7** meter **8** mile **9** [L *mille*] thousand **10** minute **11** month **12** moon

ma \'mä, 'mò\ *n* : MOTHER

MA *abbr* **1** [ML *magister artium*] master of arts **2** Massachusetts **3** mental age

ma'am \'mam, *after* "yes" *often* əm\ *n* : MADAM

Mac *abbr* Machabees

Mac *or* **Macc** *abbr* Maccabees

ma·ca·bre \mə-'käb; 'kä-brə, -bər\ *adj* [F] **1** : having death as a subject **2** : GRUESOME **3** : HORRIBLE

mac·ad·am \mə-'ka-dəm\ *n* [John L. *McAdam* †1836 Brit. engineer] : a roadway or pavement of small closely packed broken stone — **mac·ad·am·ize** \-də-,mīz\ *vb*

mac·a·da·mia nut \,ma-kə-'dā-mē-ə-\ *n* : a hard-shelled richly-flavored nut of any of several Australian trees

ma·caque \mə-'kak, -'käk\ *n* : any of a genus of short-tailed chiefly Asian monkeys; *esp* : RHESUS MONKEY

mac·a·ro·ni \,ma-kə-'rō-nē\ *n* **1** : pasta made chiefly of wheat flour and shaped in the form of slender tubes **2** *pl* **-nis** *or* **-nies** : FOP, DANDY

mac·a·roon \,ma-kə-'rün\ *n* : a small cookie made chiefly of egg whites, sugar, and ground almonds or coconut

ma·caw \mə-'kò\ *n* : any of numerous parrots of Central and So. America

Mac·ca·bees \'ma-kə-,bēz\ *n* — see BIBLE table

¹mace \'mās\ *n* : a spice made from the fibrous coating of the nutmeg

²mace *n* **1** : a heavy often spiked club used as a weapon esp. in the Middle Ages **2** : an ornamental staff carried as a symbol of authority

mac·er·ate \'ma-sə-ˌrāt\ *vb* **-at·ed; -at·ing 1** : to cause to waste away **2** : to soften by steeping or soaking so as to separate the parts — **mac·er·a·tion** \ˌma-sə-'rā-shən\ *n*

Mac·Guf·fin *or* **Mc·Guf·fin** \mə-'gə-fən\ *n* : an object, event, or character whose main purpose is to advance the plot of a motion picture

mach *abbr* machine; machinery; machinist

Mach \'mäk\ *n* : a speed expressed by a Mach number

Mach·a·bees \'ma-kə-ˌbēz\ *n* : MACCABEES

ma·chete \mə-'she-tē\ *n* : a large heavy knife used for cutting sugarcane and underbrush and as a weapon

Ma·chi·a·vel·lian \ˌma-kē-ə-'ve-lē-ən\ *adj* [Niccolò *Machiavelli*, †1527 Ital. political philosopher] : characterized by cunning, duplicity, and bad faith — **Ma·chi·a·vel·lian·ism** *n*

mach·i·na·tion \ˌma-kə-'nā-shən, ˌma-shə-\ *n* : an act of planning esp. to do harm; *esp* : PLOT — **mach·i·nate** \'ma-kə-ˌnāt, 'ma-shə-\ *vb*

¹ma·chine \mə-'shēn\ *n* **1** : CONVEYANCE, VEHICLE; *esp* : AUTOMOBILE **2** : a combination of mechanical parts that transmit forces, motion, and energy one to another **3** : an instrument (as a lever) for transmitting or modifying force or motion **4** : an electrical, electronic, or mechanical device for performing a task ⟨a sewing ∼⟩ **5** : a highly organized political group under the leadership of a boss or small clique

²machine *vb* **ma·chined; ma·chin·ing** : to shape or finish by machine-operated tools — **ma·chin·able** \-'shē-nə-bəl\ *adj*

machine gun *n* : an automatic gun capable of rapid continuous firing — **machine-gun** *vb* — **machine gunner** *n*

machine language *n* : the set of symbolic instruction codes used to represent operations and data in a machine (as a computer)

machine-readable *adj* : directly usable by a computer

ma·chin·ery \mə-'shē-nə-rē\ *n, pl* **-er·ies 1** : MACHINES; *also* : the working parts of a machine **2** : the means by which something is done

ma·chin·ist \mə-'shē-nist\ *n* : a person who makes or works on machines

ma·chis·mo \mä-'chēz-(ˌ)mō, -'chiz-\ *n* : a strong or exaggerated pride in one's masculinity

Mach number \'mäk-\ *n* : a number representing the ratio of the speed of a body (as an aircraft) to the speed of sound in the surrounding atmosphere

ma·cho \'mä-chō\ *adj* [Sp, lit., male, fr. L *masculus*] : characterized by machismo

mack·er·el \'ma-kə-rəl\ *n, pl* **mackerel** *or* **mackerels** : a No. Atlantic food fish greenish above and silvery below

mack·i·naw \'ma-kə-ˌnô\ *n* : a short heavy plaid coat

mack·in·tosh *also* **mac·in·tosh** \'ma-kən-ˌtäsh\ *n* **1** *chiefly Brit* : RAINCOAT **2** : a lightweight waterproof fabric

mac·ra·mé *also* **mac·ra·me** \'ma-krə-ˌmā\ *n* [ultim. fr. Ar *miqrama* coverlet] : a coarse lace or fringe made by knotting threads or cords in a geometrical pattern

¹mac·ro \'ma-(ˌ)krō\ *adj* : very large; *also* : involving large quantities or being on a large scale

²macro *n, pl* **macros** : a single computer instruction that stands for a sequence of operations

mac·ro·bi·ot·ic \ˌma-krō-bī-'ä-tik, -bē-\ *adj* : relating to or being a very restricted diet (as one containing chiefly whole cereals or grains)

mac·ro·cosm \'ma-krə-ˌkä-zəm\ *n* : the great world : UNIVERSE

ma·cron \'mā-ˌkrän, 'ma-\ *n* : a mark ¯ placed over a vowel (as in \mäk\) to show that the vowel is long

mac·ro·scop·ic \ˌma-krə-'skä-pik\ *adj* : visible to the naked eye — **mac·ro·scop·i·cal·ly** \-pi-k(ə-)lē\ *adv*

mac·u·la \'ma-kyə-lə\ *n, pl* **-lae** \-ˌlē, -ˌlī\ *also* **-las** : an anatomical spot distinguishable from surrounding tissues — **mac·u·lar** \-lər\ *adj*

mad \'mad\ *adj* **mad·der; mad·dest 1** : disordered in mind **2** : INSANE **3** : FURIOUS, ENRAGED **4** : carried away by enthusiasm **5** : RABID **6** : marked by wild gaiety and merriment **7** : FRANTIC — **mad·ly** *adv* — **mad·ness** *n*

mad·am \'ma-dəm\ *n* **1** *pl* **mes·dames** \mā-'däm\ — used as a form of polite address to a woman **2** *pl* **madams** : the female head of a house of prostitution

ma·dame \mə-'dam, *before a surname also* 'ma-dəm\ *n, pl*

mes·dames \mā-'däm\ : MISTRESS — used as a title equivalent to *Mrs.* for a married woman not of English-speaking nationality

mad·cap \'mad-ˌkap\ *adj* : WILD, RECKLESS ⟨a ∼ scheme⟩ — **madcap** *n*

mad cow disease *n* : a fatal encephalopathy of cattle that affects the nervous system causing the brain tissue to resemble a porous sponge

mad·den \'ma-dᵊn\ *vb* : to make mad — **mad·den·ing·ly** *adv*

mad·der \'ma-dər\ *n* : a Eurasian herb with yellow flowers and fleshy red roots; *also* : its root or a dye prepared from it

made *past and past part of* MAKE

Ma·dei·ra \mə-'dir-ə\ *n* : an amber-colored dessert wine

ma·de·moi·selle \ˌma-də-mə-'zel, -mwə-, mam-'zel\ *n, pl* **ma·de·moi·selles** \-'zelz\ *or* **mes·de·moi·selles** \ˌmā-də-me-'zel, -mwə-\ : an unmarried girl or woman — used as a title for an unmarried woman not of English-speaking nationality

made-to-measure *adj* : CUSTOM-MADE

made-up \'mād-'əp\ *adj* **1** : fancifully conceived or falsely devised **2** : marked by the use of makeup

mad·house \'mad-ˌhaus\ *n* **1** : a place for the detention and care of the insane **2** : a place of great uproar

mad·man \'mad-ˌman, -mən\ *n* : LUNATIC

Ma·don·na \mə-'dä-nə\ *n* : a representation (as a picture or statue) of the Virgin Mary

ma·dras \'ma-drəs; ˌmə-'dras, -'dräs\ *n* [*Madras*, India] : a fine usu. cotton fabric with various designs (as plaid)

ma·dras·sa *or* **ma·dra·sa** \mə-'dra-sə, -'drä-\ *n* : a Muslim school, college, or university that is often part of a mosque

mad·ri·gal \'ma-dri-gəl\ *n* [It *madrigale*] **1** : a short lyrical poem in a strict poetic form **2** : an elaborate part-song esp. of the 16th and 17th centuries

mad·wom·an \'mad-ˌwu-mən\ *n* : a woman who is insane

mael·strom \'māl-strəm\ *n* **1** : a violent whirlpool **2** : TUMULT

mae·stro \'mī-strō\ *n, pl* **maestros** *or* **mae·stri** \-ˌstrē\ [It] : a master in an art; *esp* : an eminent composer, conductor, or teacher of music

Ma·fia \'mä-fē-ə\ *n* [It] : a secret criminal society of Sicily or Italy; *also* : a similar organization elsewhere

ma·fi·o·so \ˌmä-fē-'ō-(ˌ)sō\ *n, pl* **-si** \-(ˌ)sē\ : a member of the Mafia

¹mag \'mag\ *n* : MAGAZINE

²mag *abbr* **1** magnetism **2** magneto **3** magnitude

mag·a·zine \'ma-gə-ˌzēn\ *n* [MF, fr. Old Occitan, fr. Ar *makhāzin*, pl. of *makhzan* storehouse] **1** : a storehouse esp. for military supplies **2** : a place for keeping gunpowder in a fort or ship **3** : a publication usu. containing stories, articles, or poems and issued periodically **4** : a container in a gun for holding cartridges; *also* : a chamber (as on a camera) for film

ma·gen·ta \mə-'jen-tə\ *n* : a deep purplish red color

mag·got \'ma-gət\ *n* : the legless wormlike larva of a dipteran fly — **mag·goty** *adj*

ma·gi \'mā-ˌjī\ *n pl, often cap* : the three wise men from the East who paid homage to the infant Jesus

mag·ic \'ma-jik\ *n* **1** : the use of means (as charms or spells) believed to have supernatural power over natural forces **2** : an extraordinary power or influence seemingly from a supernatural force **3** : SLEIGHT OF HAND — **magic** *adj* — **mag·i·cal** \-ji-kəl\ *adj* — **mag·i·cal·ly** \-ji-k(ə-)lē\ *adv*

ma·gi·cian \mə-'ji-shən\ *n* : a person skilled in magic

mag·is·te·ri·al \ˌma-jə-'stir-ē-əl\ *adj* **1** : AUTHORITATIVE **2** : of or relating to a magistrate or a magistrate's office or duties

ma·gis·tral \'ma-jə-strəl\ *adj* : AUTHORITATIVE

mag·is·trate \'ma-jə-ˌstrāt\ *n* : an official entrusted with administration of the laws — **mag·is·tra·cy** \-strə-sē\ *n*

mag·lev \'mag-lev\ *n* **1** : the use of magnetic fields to float an object above a solid surface **2** : a train using maglev technology

mag·ma \'mag-mə\ *n* : molten rock material within the earth — **mag·mat·ic** \mag-'ma-tik\ *adj*

mag·nan·i·mous \mag-'na-nə-məs\ *adj* **1** : showing or suggesting a lofty and courageous spirit **2** : NOBLE, GENEROUS — **mag·na·nim·i·ty** \ˌmag-nə-'ni-mə-tē\ *n* — **mag·nan·i·mous·ly** *adv* — **mag·nan·i·mous·ness** *n*

mag·nate \'mag-ˌnāt\ *n* : a person of rank, influence, or distinction

mag·ne·sia \mag-'nē-shə, -zhə\ *n* [NL, fr. *magnes carneus*, a white earth, lit., flesh magnet] : a light white oxide of magnesium used as a laxative

mag·ne·sium \mag-'nē-zē-əm, -zhəm\ *n* : a silver-white light malleable metallic chemical element

mag·net \'mag-nət\ *n* **1** : LODESTONE **2** : a body that is able to attract iron **3** : something that attracts

mag·net·ic \mag-'ne-tik\ *adj* **1** : having an unusual ability to attract ⟨a ∼ leader⟩ **2** : of or relating to a magnet or magnetism **3** : magnetized or capable of being magnetized — **mag·net·i·cal·ly** \-ti-k(ə-)lē\ *adv*

magnetic disk *n* : DISK 3

magnetic levitation *n* : MAGLEV 1

magnetic north *n* : the northerly direction in the earth's magnetic field indicated by the north-seeking pole of a compass needle

magnetic resonance imaging *n* : a noninvasive diagnostic technique that produces computerized images of internal body tissues based on electromagnetically induced activity of atoms within the body

magnetic tape *n* : a ribbon coated with a magnetic material on which information (as sound) may be stored

mag·ne·tise *Brit var of* MAGNETIZE

mag·ne·tism \'mag-nə-ˌti-zəm\ *n* **1** : the power (as of a magnet) to attract iron **2** : the science that deals with magnetic phenomena **3** : an ability to attract or charm

mag·ne·tite \'mag-nə-ˌtīt\ *n* : a black mineral that is an important iron ore

mag·ne·tize \'mag-nə-ˌtīz\ *vb* **-tized; -tiz·ing 1** : to induce magnetic properties in **2** : to attract like a magnet : CHARM — **mag·ne·tiz·able** *adj* — **mag·ne·ti·za·tion** \ˌmag-nə-tə-'zā-shən\ *n* — **mag·ne·tiz·er** *n*

mag·ne·to \mag-'nē-tō\ *n, pl* **-tos** : a generator used to produce sparks in an internal combustion engine

mag·ne·tom·e·ter \ˌmag-nə-'tä-mə-tər\ *n* : an instrument for measuring the strength of a magnetic field

mag·ne·to·sphere \mag-'nē-tə-ˌsfir, -'ne-\ *n* : a region around a celestial object (as the earth) in which charged particles are trapped by its magnetic field — **mag·ne·to·spher·ic** \-ˌnē-tə-'sfir-ik, -'sfer-\ *adj*

mag·ni·fi·ca·tion \ˌmag-nə-fə-'kā-shən\ *n* **1** : the act of magnifying **2** : the amount by which an optical lens or instrument magnifies

mag·nif·i·cent \mag-'ni-fə-sənt\ *adj* **1** : characterized by grandeur or beauty : SPLENDID **2** : EXALTED, NOBLE ✦ **Synonyms** IMPOSING, STATELY, GRAND, MAJESTIC — **mag·nif·i·cence** \-səns\ *n* — **mag·nif·i·cent·ly** *adv*

mag·nif·i·co \mag-'ni-fi-ˌkō\ *n, pl* **-coes** *or* **-cos 1** : a nobleman of Venice **2** : a person of high position

mag·ni·fy \'mag-nə-ˌfī\ *vb* **-fied; -fy·ing 1** : EXTOL, LAUD; *also* : to cause to be held in greater esteem **2** : INTENSIFY; *also* : EXAGGERATE **3** : to enlarge in fact or in appearance ⟨a microscope *magnifies* an object⟩ — **mag·ni·fi·er** \'mag-nə-ˌfī(-ə)r\ *n*

mag·nil·o·quent \mag-'ni-lə-kwənt\ *adj* : characterized by an exalted and often bombastic style or manner — **mag·nil·o·quence** \-kwəns\ *n*

mag·ni·tude \'mag-nə-ˌtüd, -ˌtyüd\ *n* **1** : greatness of size or extent **2** : SIZE **3** : QUANTITY **4** : a number representing the brightness of a celestial body **5** : a number representing the intensity of an earthquake

mag·no·lia \mag-'nōl-yə\ *n* : any of a genus of usu. spring-flowering shrubs and trees with large often fragrant flowers

mag·num opus \'mag-nəm-'ō-pəs\ *n* [L] : the greatest achievement of an artist or writer

mag·pie \'mag-ˌpī\ *n* : any of various long-tailed often black-and-white birds related to the jays

Mag·yar \'mag-ˌyär, 'mäg-; 'mä-jär\ *n* : a member of the dominant people of Hungary — **Magyar** *adj*

ma·ha·ra·ja *or* **ma·ha·ra·jah** \ˌmä-hə-'rä-jə\ *n* : a Hindu prince ranking above a raja

ma·ha·ra·ni *or* **ma·ha·ra·nee** \-'rä-nē\ *n* **1** : the wife of a maharaja **2** : a Hindu princess ranking above a rani

ma·ha·ri·shi \ˌmä-hə-'rē-shē\ *n* : a Hindu teacher of mystical knowledge

ma·hat·ma \mə-'hät-mə, -'hat-\ *n* [Skt *mahātman*, fr. *mahātman* great-souled, fr. *mahat* great + *ātman* soul] : a person revered for high-mindedness, wisdom, and selflessness

Ma·hi·can \mə-'hē-kən\ *or* **Mo·hi·can** \mō-, mə-\ *n, pl* **-can** *or* **-cans** : a member of an American Indian people of the upper Hudson River valley

ma·hog·a·ny \mə-'hä-gə-nē\ *n, pl* **-nies** : the reddish wood of any of various chiefly tropical trees that is used in furniture; *also* : a tree yielding this wood

ma·hout \mə-'haút\ *n* [Hindi & Urdu *mahāwat, mahāut*] : a keeper and driver of an elephant

maid \'mād\ *n* **1** : an unmarried girl or young woman **2** : MAIDSERVANT; *also* : a woman or girl employed to do domestic work

¹maid·en \'mā-dᵊn\ *n* : MAID 1 — **maid·en·ly** *adj*

²maiden *adj* **1** : UNMARRIED; *also* : VIRGIN **2** : of, relating to, or befitting a maiden **3** : FIRST ⟨a ship's ∼ voyage⟩

maid·en·hair fern \-ˌher-\ *n* : any of a genus of ferns with delicate feathery fronds

maid·en·head \'mā-dᵊn-ˌhed\ *n* **1** : VIRGINITY **2** : HYMEN

maid·en·hood \-ˌhùd\ *n* : the condition or time of being a maiden

maid–in–waiting *n, pl* **maids–in–waiting** : a young woman appointed to attend a queen or princess

maid of honor : a bride's principal unmarried wedding attendant

maid·ser·vant \'mād-ˌsər-vənt\ *n* : a girl or woman who is a servant

¹mail \'māl\ *n* [ME *male* bag, fr. AF, of Gmc origin] **1** : material sent or carried in the postal system **2** : a nation's postal system — often used in pl. **3** : E-MAIL

²mail *vb* : to send by mail

³mail *n* [ME *maille* metal link, mail, fr. AF, fr. L *macula* spot, mesh] : armor made of metal links or plates

mail·box \'māl-ˌbäks\ *n* **1** : a public box for the collection of mail **2** : a private box for the delivery of mail

mail·man \-ˌman\ *n* : a man who delivers mail

maim \'mām\ *vb* : to mutilate, disfigure, or wound seriously

¹main \'mān\ *n* **1** : FORCE ⟨with might and ∼⟩ **2** : MAINLAND; *also* : HIGH SEA **3** : the chief part **4** : a principal pipe, duct, or circuit of a utility system

²main *adj* **1** : CHIEF, PRINCIPAL ⟨the ∼ idea⟩ **2** : fully exerted ⟨∼ force⟩ **3** : expressing the chief predication in a complex sentence ⟨the ∼ clause⟩ — **main·ly** *adv*

main·frame \'mān-ˌfrām\ *n* : a large fast computer

main·land \-ˌland, -lənd\ *n* : a continuous body of land constituting the chief part of a country or continent

main·line \-ˌlīn\ *vb, slang* : to inject a narcotic drug into a vein

main line *n* : a principal highway or railroad line

main·mast \'mān-ˌmast, -məst\ *n* : the principal mast on a sailing ship

main·sail \-ˌsāl, -səl\ *n* : the largest sail on the mainmast

main·spring \-ˌspriŋ\ *n* **1** : the chief spring in a mechanism (as of a watch) **2** : the chief motive, agent, or cause

main·stay \-ˌstā\ *n* **1** : a stay running from the head of the mainmast to the foot of the foremast **2** : a chief support

main·stream \-ˌstrēm\ *n* : a prevailing current or direction of activity or influence — **mainstream** *adj*

main·tain \mān-'tān\ *vb* [ME *mainteinen*, fr. AF *maintenir, mayntener*, fr. ML *manutenēre*, fr. L *manu tenēre* to hold in the hand] **1** : to keep in an existing state (as of repair) **2** : to sustain against opposition or danger **3** : to continue in : CARRY ON **4** : to provide for : SUPPORT **5** : ASSERT ⟨∼ed his innocence⟩ — **main·tain·abil·i·ty** \-ˌtā-nə-'bi-lə-tē\ *n* — **main·tain·able** \-'tā-nə-bəl\ *adj* — **main·te·nance** \'mān-tə-nəns\ *n*

main·top \'mān-ˌtäp\ *n* : a platform at the head of the mainmast of a square-rigged ship

mai·son·ette \ˌmā-zə-'net\ *n* **1** : a small house **2** : an apartment often on two floors

mai tai \'mī-ˌtī\ *n* : a cocktail made with liquors and fruit juices

maî·tre d' *or* **mai·tre d'** \ˌmā-trə-'dē, ˌme-\ *n, pl* **maître d's** *or* **maitre d's** \-'dēz\ : MAÎTRE D'HÔTEL

maî·tre d'hô·tel \ˌmā-trə-dō-'tel, ˌme-\ *n, pl* **maîtres d'hô·tel** *same*\ [F, lit., master of house] **1** : MAJORDOMO **2** : HEADWAITER

maize \'māz\ *n* : INDIAN CORN

Maj *abbr* major

maj·es·ty \'ma-jə-stē\ *n, pl* **-ties** **1** : sovereign power, authority, or dignity; *also* : the person of a sovereign — used as a title **2** : GRANDEUR, SPLENDOR — **ma·jes·tic** \mə-'jes-tik\ *adj* — **ma·jes·ti·cal·ly** \-ti-k(ə-)lē\ *adv*

Maj Gen *abbr* Major General

ma·jol·i·ca \mə-'jä-li-kə\ *also* **ma·iol·i·ca** \-'yä-\ *n* : any of several faiences; *esp* : an Italian tin-glazed pottery

¹ma·jor \'mā-jər\ *adj* **1** : greater in number, extent, or importance ⟨a ∼ poet⟩ **2** : notable or conspicuous in effect or scope ⟨a ∼ improvement⟩ **3** : SERIOUS ⟨a ∼ illness⟩ **4** : having half steps between the 3d and 4th and the 7th and 8th degrees ⟨∼ scale⟩; *also* : based on a major scale ⟨∼ key⟩ ⟨∼ chord⟩

²major *n* **1** : a commissioned officer (as in the army) ranking next below a lieutenant colonel **2** : an academic subject chosen as a field of specialization; *also* : a student specializing in such a field ⟨a history ∼⟩

³major *vb* : to pursue an academic major

ma·jor·do·mo \mā-jər-'dō-mō\ *n, pl* **-mos** [Sp *mayordomo* or obs. It *maiordomo*, fr. ML *major domus*, lit., chief of the house] **1** : a head steward **2** : BUTLER

ma·jor·ette \mā-jə-'ret\ *n* : DRUM MAJORETTE

major general *n* : a commissioned officer (as in the army) ranking next below a lieutenant general

ma·jor·i·ty \mə-'jor-ə-tē\ *n, pl* **-ties** **1** : the age at which full civil rights are accorded; *also* : the status of one who has attained this age **2** : a number greater than half of a total; *also* : the excess of this greater number over the remainder **3** : the rank of a major

ma·jus·cule \'ma-jəs-ˌkyül, mə-'jəs-\ *n* : a large letter (as a capital)

Ma·kah \'mä-kä\ *n, pl* **Makah** *or* **Makahs** : a member of an American Indian people of the northwest coast of No. America

¹make \'māk\ *vb* **made** \'mād\; **mak·ing** **1** : to cause to exist, occur, or appear; *also* : DESTINE ⟨was *made* to be an actor⟩ **2** : FASHION ⟨∼ a dress⟩; *also* : COMPOSE **3** : to formulate in the mind ⟨∼ plans⟩ **4** : CONSTITUTE ⟨house *made* of stone⟩ **5** : to compute to be **6** : to set in order : PREPARE ⟨∼ a bed⟩ **7** : to cause to be or become; *also* : APPOINT **8** : ENACT; *also* : EXECUTE ⟨∼ a will⟩ **9** : CONCLUDE ⟨didn't know what to ∼ of it⟩ **10** : CARRY OUT, PERFORM ⟨∼ a gesture⟩ **11** : COMPEL **12** : to assure the success of ⟨will ∼ us or break us⟩ **13** : amount to in significance ⟨∼s no difference⟩ **14** : to be capable of developing or being fashioned into **15** : REACH, ATTAIN; *also* : GAIN **16** : to start out : GO **17** : to have weight or effect ⟨courtesy ∼s for safer driving⟩ ♦ *Synonyms* FORM, SHAPE, FABRICATE, MANUFACTURE — **mak·er** *n* — **make believe** : PRETEND — **make do** : to manage with the means at hand — **make fun of** : RIDICULE, MOCK — **make good** **1** : INDEMNIFY ⟨*make good* the loss⟩; *also* : to carry out successfully ⟨*make good* his promise⟩ **2** : SUCCEED — **make way** **1** : to give room for passing, entering, or occupying **2** : to make progress

²make *n* **1** : the manner or style of construction; *also* : BRAND **3** **2** : MAKEUP **3** : the action of manufacturing — **on the make** : in search of wealth, social status, or sexual adventure

¹make–be·lieve \'māk-bə-ˌlēv\ *n* : a pretending that what is not real is real

²make–believe *adj* : IMAGINED, PRETENDED

make–do \-ˌdü\ *adj* : MAKESHIFT

make out *vb* **1** : to draw up in writing ⟨*make out* a list⟩ **2** : to find or grasp the meaning of ⟨can you *make* that *out*⟩ **3** : to represent as being **4** : to pretend to be true **5** : DISCERN ⟨*make out* a ship in the fog⟩ **6** : GET ALONG, FARE ⟨*make out* well in life⟩ **7** : to engage in amorous kissing and caressing

make over *vb* : REMAKE, REMODEL — **make·over** \'mā-ˌkō-vər\ *n*

make·shift \'māk-ˌshift\ *n* : a temporary expedient — **makeshift** *adj*

make·up \'mā-ˌkəp\ *n* **1** : the way in which something is put together; *also* : physical, mental, and moral constitution **2** : cosmetics esp. for the face; *also* : materials (as wigs and cosmetics) used in making up

make up *vb* **1** : FORM, COMPOSE **2** : to compensate for a deficiency **3** : SETTLE ⟨*made up* my mind⟩ **4** : INVENT,

IMPROVISE **5** : to become reconciled **6** : to put on makeup (as for a play)

make–work \'māk-ˌwərk\ *n* : BUSYWORK

mak·ings \'mā-kiŋz\ *n pl* : the material from which something is made

Mal *abbr* Malachi

Mal·a·chi \'ma-lə-ˌkī\ *n* — see BIBLE table

Mal·a·chi·as \ˌma-lə-'kī-əs\ *n* : MALACHI

mal·a·chite \'ma-lə-ˌkīt\ *n* : a green mineral that is a carbonate of copper used for making ornamental objects

mal·adapt·ed \ˌma-lə-'dap-təd\ *adj* : poorly suited to a particular use, purpose, or situation

mal·ad·just·ed \ˌma-lə-'jəs-təd\ *adj* : poorly or inadequately adjusted (as to one's environment) — **mal·ad·just·ment** \-'jəst-mənt\ *n*

mal·adroit \ˌma-lə-'droit\ *adj* : not adroit : INEPT

mal·a·dy \'ma-lə-dē\ *n, pl* **-dies** : a disease or disorder of body or mind

mal·aise \mə-'lāz, ma-\ *n* [F] : a hazy feeling of not being well

mal·a·mute \'ma-lə-ˌmyüt\ *n* : a dog often used to draw sleds esp. in northern No. America

mal·a·prop·ism \'ma-lə-ˌprä-ˌpi-zəm\ *n* : a usu. humorous misuse of a word

mal·ap·ro·pos \ˌma-ˌla-prə-'pō, ma-'la-prə-ˌpō\ *adv* : in an inappropriate or inopportune way — **malapropos** *adj*

ma·lar·ia \mə-'ler-ē-ə\ *n* [It, fr. *mala aria* bad air] : a disease marked by recurring chills and fever and caused by a protozoan parasite of the blood that is transmitted by anopheles mosquitoes — **ma·lar·i·al** \-əl\ *adj*

ma·lar·key \mə-'lär-kē\ *n* : insincere or foolish talk

mal·a·thi·on \ˌma-lə-'thī-ən, -ˌän\ *n* : an insecticide with a relatively low toxicity for mammals

Ma·lay \mə-'lā, 'mā-ˌlā\ *n* **1** : a member of a people of the Malay Peninsula and Archipelago **2** : the language of the Malays — **Malay** *adj* — **Ma·lay·an** \mə-'lā-ən, 'mā-ˌlā-\ *n or adj*

mal·con·tent \ˌmal-kən-'tent\ *adj* : marked by a dissatisfaction with the existing state of affairs : DISCONTENTED — **malcontent** *n*

mal de mer \ˌmal-də-'mer\ *n* [F] : SEASICKNESS

¹male \'māl\ *n* : a male individual

²male *adj* **1** : of, relating to, or being the sex that produces germ cells which fertilize the eggs of a female; *also* : STAMINATE **2** : MASCULINE — **male·ness** *n*

male·dic·tion \ˌma-lə-'dik-shən\ *n* : CURSE, EXECRATION

male·fac·tor \'ma-lə-ˌfak-tər\ *n* : EVILDOER; *esp* : one who commits an offense against the law — **mal·e·fac·tion** \ˌma-lə-'fak-shən\ *n*

ma·lef·ic \mə-'le-fik\ *adj* **1** : BALEFUL **2** : MALICIOUS

ma·lef·i·cent \-fə-sənt\ *adj* : working or productive of harm or evil

ma·lev·o·lent \mə-'le-və-lənt\ *adj* : having, showing, or arising from ill will, spite, or hatred ♦ *Synonyms* MALIGNANT, MALIGN, MALICIOUS, SPITEFUL — **ma·lev·o·lence** \-ləns\ *n*

mal·fea·sance \mal-'fē-zᵊns\ *n* : wrongful conduct esp. by a public official

mal·for·ma·tion \ˌmal-fòr-'mā-shən\ *n* : irregular or faulty formation or structure; *also* : an instance of this — **mal·formed** \mal-'fòrmd\ *adj*

mal·func·tion \mal-'fəŋk-shən\ *vb* : to fail to operate normally — **malfunction** *n*

mal·ice \'ma-ləs\ *n* : desire to cause injury or distress to another — **ma·li·cious** \mə-'li-shəs\ *adj* — **ma·li·cious·ly** *adv*

¹ma·lign \mə-'līn\ *adj* **1** : evil in nature, influence, or effect; *also* : MALIGNANT **2** : moved by ill will

²malign *vb* : to speak evil of : DEFAME

ma·lig·nant \mə-'lig-nənt\ *adj* **1** : INJURIOUS, MALIGN **2** : tending to produce death or deterioration ⟨a ∼ tumor⟩ — **ma·lig·nan·cy** \-nən-sē\ *n* — **ma·lig·nant·ly** *adv* — **ma·lig·ni·ty** \-nə-tē\ *n*

ma·lin·ger \mə-'liŋ-gər\ *vb* [F *malingre* sickly] : to pretend illness so as to avoid duty — **ma·lin·ger·er** *n*

mal·i·son \'ma-lə-sən, -zən\ *n* : CURSE

mall \'mòl, 'mal\ *n* **1** : a shaded walk : PROMENADE **2** : an urban shopping area featuring a variety of shops surrounding a concourse **3** : a usu. large enclosed suburban shopping area containing various shops

mal·lard \'ma-lərd\ *n, pl* **mallard** *or* **mallards** : a common wild duck that is the source of domestic ducks

mal·lea·ble \'ma-lē-ə-bəl\ *adj* **1** : capable of being extended or shaped by beating with a hammer or by the pressure of rollers **2** : ADAPTABLE, PLIABLE ✦ *Synonyms* PLASTIC, PLIANT, DUCTILE, SUPPLE — **mal·le·a·bil·i·ty** \,ma-lē-ə-'bi-lə-tē\ *n*

mal·let \'ma-lət\ *n* **1** : a tool with a large head for driving another tool or for striking a surface without marring it **2** : a long-handled hammerlike implement for striking a ball (as in croquet)

mal·le·us \'ma-lē-əs\ *n, pl* **mal·lei** \-lē-,ī, -lē-,ē\ [NL, fr. L, hammer] : the outermost of the three small bones of the mammalian middle ear

mal·low \'ma-lō\ *n* : any of a genus of herbs with lobed leaves, usu. showy flowers, and a disk-shaped fruit

malm·sey \'mälm-zē\ *n, often cap* : the sweetest variety of Madeira

mal·nour·ished \mal-'nər-isht\ *adj* : UNDERNOURISHED

mal·nu·tri·tion \,mal-nü-'tri-shən, -nyü-\ *n* : faulty and esp. inadequate nutrition

mal·oc·clu·sion \,ma-lə-'klü-zhən\ *n* : faulty coming together of teeth in biting

mal·odor·ous \ma-'lō-də-rəs\ *adj* : ill-smelling — **mal·odor·ous·ly** *adv* — **mal·odor·ous·ness** *n*

maloti *pl of* LOTI

mal·prac·tice \mal-'prak-təs\ *n* : a dereliction of professional duty or a failure of professional skill that results in injury, loss, or damage

malt \'molt\ *n* **1** : grain and esp. barley steeped in water until it has sprouted and used in brewing and distilling **2** : liquor made with malt — **malty** *adj*

malted milk \'mol-təd-\ *n* : a powder prepared from dried milk and an extract from malt; *also* : a beverage of this powder in milk or other liquid

Mal·thu·sian \mal-'thü-zhən, -'thyü-\ *adj* : of or relating to a theory that population unless checked (as by war) tends to increase faster than its means of subsistence — **Malthusian** *n* — **Mal·thu·sian·ism** \-zhə-,ni-zəm\ *n*

malt·ose \'mol-,tōs\ *n* : a sugar formed esp. from starch by the action of enzymes

mal·treat \mal-'trēt\ *vb* : to treat cruelly or roughly : ABUSE — **mal·treat·ment** *n*

ma·ma *or* **mam·ma** \'mä-mə\ *n* : MOTHER

mam·bo \'mäm-bō\ *n, pl* **mambos** : a dance of Cuban origin related to the rumba — **mambo** *vb*

mam·mal \'ma-məl\ *n* [NL *Mammalia*, fr. LL, neut. pl. of *mammalis* of the breast, fr. L *mamma* breast] : any of a class of warm-blooded vertebrates that includes humans and all other animals which nourish their young with milk and have the skin more or less covered with hair — **mam·ma·li·an** \mə-'mä-lē-ən, ma-\ *adj or n*

mam·ma·ry \'ma-mə-rē\ *adj* : of, relating to, or being the glands (**mammary glands**) that in female mammals secrete milk

mam·mo·gram \'ma-mə-,gram\ *n* : an X-ray photograph of the breasts

mam·mog·ra·phy \ma-'mä-grə-fē\ *n* : X-ray examination of the breasts (as for early detection of cancer)

mam·mon \'ma-mən\ *n, often cap* : material wealth having a debasing influence

¹mam·moth \'ma-məth\ *n* : any of a genus of large hairy extinct elephants

²mammoth *adj* : of very great size : GIGANTIC ✦ *Synonyms* COLOSSAL, ENORMOUS, IMMENSE, VAST, ELEPHANTINE

¹man \'man\ *n, pl* **men** \'men\ **1** : a human being; *esp* : an adult male **2** : the human race : MANKIND **3** : one possessing in high degree the qualities considered distinctive of manhood **4** : an adult male servant or employee **5** : the individual who can fulfill one's requirements ⟨he's your ∼⟩ **6 a** : one of the pieces with which various games (as chess) are played **b** : one of the players on a team **7** *often cap* : white society or people

²man *vb* **manned; man·ning 1** : to supply with men ⟨∼ a fleet⟩ **2** : FORTIFY, BRACE

³man *abbr* manual

Man *abbr* Manitoba

man–about–town *n, pl* **men–about–town** : a worldly and socially active man

man·a·cle \'ma-ni-kəl\ *n* **1** : a shackle for the hand or wrist **2** : something used as a restraint

man·age \'ma-nij\ *vb* **man·aged; man·ag·ing 1** : HANDLE, CONTROL ⟨∼s her skis well⟩; *also* : to direct or carry on business or affairs **2** : to make and keep compliant **3** : to treat with care : HUSBAND **4** : to achieve one's purpose : CONTRIVE — **man·age·abil·i·ty** \,ma-ni-jə-'bi-lə-tē\ *n* — **man·age·able** \'ma-ni-jə-bəl\ *adj* — **man·age·able·ness** *n* — **man·age·ably** \-blē\ *adv*

managed care *n* : a health-care system that controls costs by limiting doctor's fees and by restricting the patient's choice of doctors

man·age·ment \'ma-nij-mənt\ *n* **1** : the act or art of managing : CONTROL **2** : judicious use of means to accomplish an end **3** : the group of those who manage or direct an enterprise

man·ag·er \'ma-ni-jər\ *n* : one that manages — **man·a·ge·ri·al** \,ma-nə-'jir-ē-əl\ *adj*

ma·ña·na \mən-'yä-nə\ *n* [Sp, lit., tomorrow] : an indefinite time in the future

ma·nat \mä-'nät\ *n, pl* **manat** *or* **manats** — see MONEY table

man–at–arms *n, pl* **men–at–arms** : SOLDIER; *esp* : one who is heavily armed and mounted

man·a·tee \'ma-nə-,tē\ *n* : any of a genus of chiefly tropical plant-eating aquatic mammals having a broad rounded tail

man·ci·ple \'man-sə-pəl\ *n* : a steward or purveyor esp. for a college or monastery

man·da·mus \man-'dä-məs\ *n* [L, we enjoin] : a writ issued by a superior court commanding that an official act or duty be performed

man·da·rin \'man-də-rən\ *n* **1** : a public official of high rank under the Chinese Empire **2** *cap* : the chief dialect group of China **3** : a yellow to reddish orange loose-skinned citrus fruit; *also* : a tree that bears mandarins

man·date \'man-,dāt\ *n* **1** : an authoritative command **2** : an authorization to act given to a representative **3** : a commission granted by the League of Nations to a member nation for governing conquered territory; *also* : a territory so governed

man·da·to·ry \'man-də-,tor-ē\ *adj* **1** : containing or constituting a command : OBLIGATORY **2** : of or relating to a League of Nations mandate

man·di·ble \'man-də-bəl\ *n* **1** : JAW; *esp* : a lower jaw **2** : either segment of a bird's bill — **man·dib·u·lar** \man-'di-byə-lər\ *adj*

man·do·lin \,man-də-'lin, 'man-də-lən\ *n* : a stringed musical instrument with a pear-shaped body and a fretted neck

mandolin

man·drake \'man-,drāk\ *n* **1** : an Old World herb related to the nightshades or its large forked root formerly credited with magical properties **2** : MAYAPPLE

man·drel *also* **man·dril** \'man-drəl\ *n* **1** : an axle or spindle inserted into a hole in a piece of work to support it during machining **2** : a metal bar used as a core around which material may be cast, shaped, or molded

man·drill \'man-drəl\ *n* : a large baboon of western central Africa

mane \'mān\ *n* : long heavy hair growing about the neck of some mammals (as horses) — **maned** \'mānd\ *adj*

man·eat·er \'man-,ē-tər\ *n* : one (as a shark or cannibal) that has or is thought to have an appetite for human flesh — **man·eat·ing** *adj*

ma·nège \ma-'nezh, mə-\ *n* : the art of horsemanship or of training horses

ma·nes \'mä-ˌnās, 'mä-ˌnēz\ *n pl, often cap* : the spirits of the dead and gods of the lower world in ancient Roman belief

ma·neu·ver \mə-'nü-vər, -'nyü-\ *n* [F *manœuvre*, fr. OF *maneuvre* work done by hand, fr. ML *manuopera*, fr. *manu operare* to work by hand] **1** : a military or naval movement; *also* : an armed forces training exercise — often used in pl. **2** : a procedure involving expert physical movement **3** : an evasive movement or shift of tactics; *also* : an action taken to gain a tactical end — **maneuver** *vb* — **ma·neu·ver·abil·i·ty** \-ˌnü-və-rə-'bi-lə-tē, -ˌnyü-\ *n* — **ma·neu·ver·able** \-'nü-və-rə-bəl, -'nyü-\ *adj*

man Friday *n* : an efficient and devoted aide or employee

man·ful \'man-fəl\ *adj* : having or showing courage and resolution — **man·ful·ly** *adv*

man·ga·nese \'maŋ-gə-ˌnēz, -ˌnēs\ *n* : a metallic chemical element resembling iron but not magnetic

mange \'mānj\ *n* : any of several contagious itchy skin diseases esp. of domestic animals — **mangy** \'mān-jē\ *adj*

man·ger \'mān-jər\ *n* : a trough or open box for livestock feed or fodder

¹man·gle \'maŋ-gəl\ *vb* **man·gled; man·gling** **1** : to cut, bruise, or hack with repeated blows **2** : to spoil or injure esp. through ineptitude — **man·gler** *n*

²mangle *n* : a machine with heated rollers for ironing laundry

man·go \'maŋ-gō\ *n, pl* **mangoes** *also* **mangos** [Pg *manga*, prob. fr. Malayalam (Dravidian language of India) *māṅṅa*] : an edible juicy yellowish-red fruit borne by a tropical evergreen tree related to the sumacs; *also* : this tree

man·grove \'man-ˌgrōv\ *n* : any of a genus of tropical maritime trees that send out many prop roots and form dense thickets important in coastal land building

man·han·dle \'man-ˌhan-dᵊl\ *vb* : to handle roughly

man·hat·tan \man-'ha-tᵊn\ *n, often cap* : a cocktail made of whiskey and vermouth

man·hole \'man-ˌhōl\ *n* : a hole through which a person may go esp. to gain access to an underground or enclosed structure

man·hood \-ˌhud\ *n* **1** : the condition of being an adult male **2** : qualities associated with men : MANLINESS **3** : MEN ⟨the nation's ∼⟩

man–hour \-'aù(-ə)r\ *n* : a unit of one hour's work by one person

man·hunt \-ˌhənt\ *n* : an organized hunt for a person and esp. for one charged with a crime

ma·nia \'mā-nē-ə, -nyə\ *n* **1** : excitement manifested by mental and physical hyperactivity, disorganized behavior, and elevated mood **2** : excessive enthusiasm

ma·ni·ac \'mā-nē-ˌak\ *n* : LUNATIC, MADMAN

ma·ni·a·cal \mə-'nī-ə-kəl\ *also* **ma·ni·ac** \'mā-nē-ak\ *adj* **1** : affected with or suggestive of madness **2** : FRANTIC ⟨a ∼ mob⟩

man·ic \'ma-nik\ *adj* : affected with, relating to, characterized by, or resulting from mania — **manic** *n* — **man·i·cal·ly** \-ni-k(ə-)lē\ *adv*

manic depression *n* : BIPOLAR DISORDER

man·ic-de·pres·sive \ˌma-nik-di-'pre-siv\ *adj* : characterized by or affected with either mania or depression or alternating episodes of mania and depression — **manic-depressive** *n*

¹man·i·cure \'ma-nə-ˌkyur\ *n* **1** : MANICURIST **2** : a treatment for the care of the hands and nails

²manicure *vb* **-cured; -cur·ing** **1** : to do manicure work on **2** : to trim closely and evenly

man·i·cur·ist \-ˌkyur-ist\ *n* : a person who gives manicure treatments

¹man·i·fest \'ma-nə-ˌfest\ *adj* [ME, fr. AF or L; AF *manifeste*, fr. L *manifestus*, caught in the act, flagrant, obvious, perh. fr. *manus* hand + *-festus* (akin to L *infestus* hostile)] **1** : readily perceived by the senses and esp. by the sight **2** : easily understood : OBVIOUS — **man·i·fest·ly** *adv*

²manifest *vb* : to make evident or certain by showing or displaying ♦ **Synonyms** EVINCE, DEMONSTRATE, EXHIBIT

³manifest *n* : a list of passengers or an invoice of cargo for a ship or plane

man·i·fes·ta·tion \ˌma-nə-fə-'stā-shən\ *n* : DISPLAY, DEMONSTRATION

man·i·fes·to \ˌma-nə-'fes-tō\ *n, pl* **-tos** *or* **-toes** : a public declaration of intentions, motives, or views

¹man·i·fold \'ma-nə-ˌfōld\ *adj* **1** : marked by diversity or variety **2** : consisting of or operating many of one kind combined

²manifold *n* : a pipe fitting with several lateral outlets for connecting it with other pipes

³manifold *vb* **1** : MULTIPLY **2** : to make a number of copies of (as a letter)

man·i·kin *also* **man·ni·kin** \'ma-ni-kən\ *n* **1** : MANNEQUIN **2** : a little man : DWARF

Ma·nila hemp \mə-'ni-lə-\ *n* : a tough fiber from a Philippine plant related to the banana that is used for cordage

manila paper *n, often cap M* : a tough brownish paper made orig. from Manila hemp

man·i·oc \'ma-nē-ˌäk\ *n* : CASSAVA

ma·nip·u·late \mə-'ni-pyə-ˌlāt\ *vb* **-lat·ed; -lat·ing** **1** : to treat or operate manually or mechanically esp. with skill **2** : to manage or use skillfully **3** : to influence esp. with intent to deceive — **ma·nip·u·la·tion** \mə-ni-pyə-'lā-shən\ *n* — **ma·nip·u·la·tive** \-'ni-pyə-ˌlā-tiv\ *adj* — **ma·nip·u·la·tor** \-ˌlā-tər\ *n*

ma·nip·u·la·tives \mə-'ni-pyə-ˌlā-tivz\ *n pl* : objects that a student is instructed to use in a way that teaches or reinforces a lesson

man·kind *n* **1** \'man-'kīnd\ : the human race **2** \-ˌkīnd\ : men as distinguished from women

¹man·ly \'man-lē\ *adv* : in a manly manner

²manly *adj* **man·li·er; -est** : having qualities appropriate to or generally associated with a man : BOLD, RESOLUTE — **man·li·ness** *n*

man–made \'man-'mād\ *adj* : made by humans rather than nature ⟨∼ systems⟩; *esp* : SYNTHETIC ⟨∼ fibers⟩

man·na \'ma-nə\ *n* **1** : food miraculously supplied to the Israelites in the wilderness **2** : something of value that comes unexpectedly : WINDFALL

manned \'mand\ *adj* : carrying or performed by a person ⟨∼ spaceflight⟩

man·ne·quin \'ma-ni-kən\ *n* **1** : a form representing the human figure used esp. for displaying clothes **2** : a person employed to model clothing

man·ner \'ma-nər\ *n* **1** : KIND, SORT ⟨what ∼ of man is he⟩ **2** : a way of acting or proceeding ⟨worked in a brisk ∼⟩; *also* : normal behavior ⟨spoke bluntly as was his ∼⟩ **3** : a method of artistic execution **4** *pl* : social conduct; *also* : BEARING **5** *pl* : BEHAVIOR ⟨taught the child good ∼s⟩

man·nered \'ma-nərd\ *adj* **1** : having manners of a specified kind ⟨well-*mannered*⟩ **2** : having an artificial character ⟨a highly ∼ style⟩

man·ner·ism \'ma-nə-ˌri-zəm\ *n* **1** : ARTIFICIALITY, PRECIOSITY **2** : a peculiarity of action, bearing, or treatment ♦ **Synonyms** POSE, AIR, AFFECTATION

man·ner·ly \'ma-nər-lē\ *adj* : showing good manners : POLITE — **man·ner·li·ness** *n* — **mannerly** *adv*

man·nish \'ma-nish\ *adj* **1** : resembling or suggesting a man rather than a woman **2** : generally associated with or characteristic of a man — **man·nish·ly** *adv* — **man·nish·ness** *n*

ma·no a ma·no \ˌmä-nō-ä-'mä-nō\ *adv or adj* : in direct competition or conflict

ma·noeu·vre \mə-'nü-vər, -'nyü-\ *chiefly Brit var of* MANEUVER

man–of–war \ˌman-əv-'wor\ *n, pl* **men–of–war** \ˌmen-\ : WARSHIP

ma·nom·e·ter \mə-'nä-mə-tər\ *n* : an instrument for measuring the pressure of gases and vapors — **mano·met·ric** \ˌma-nə-'me-trik\ *adj*

man·or \'ma-nər\ *n* **1** : the house or hall of an estate; *also* : a landed estate **2** : an English estate of a feudal lord — **ma·no·ri·al** \mə-'nor-ē-əl\ *adj* — **ma·no·ri·al·ism** \-ə-ˌli-zəm\ *n*

man power *n* **1** : power available from or supplied by the physical effort of human beings **2** *usu* **man·pow·er** : the total supply of persons available and fitted for service

man·qué \mäⁿ-'kā\ *adj* [F, fr. pp. of *manquer* to lack, fail] : short of or frustrated in the fulfillment of one's aspirations or talents ⟨a poet ∼⟩

man·sard \'man-ˌsärd, -sərd\ *n* : a roof having two slopes on all sides with the lower slope steeper than the upper one

manse \'mans\ *n* : the residence esp. of a Presbyterian minister

man·ser·vant \'man-ˌsər-vənt\ *n, pl* **men·ser·vants** \'men-ˌsər-vənts\ : a male servant

man·sion \'man-chən\ *n* : a large imposing residence; *also* : a separate apartment in a large structure

man–size \'man-ˌsīz\ *or* **man–sized** \-ˌsīzd\ *adj* : suitable for or requiring a man

man·slaugh·ter \-ˌslȯ-tər\ *n* : the unlawful killing of a human being without express or implied malice

man·ta \'man-tə\ *n* : a square piece of cloth or blanket used in southwestern U.S. and Latin America as a cloak or shawl

man·teau \man-'tō\ *n* : a loose cloak, coat, or robe

man·tel \'man-tᵊl\ *n* : a beam, stone, or arch serving as a lintel to support the masonry above a fireplace; *also* : a shelf above a fireplace

man·tel·piece \'man-tᵊl-ˌpēs\ *n* : the shelf of a mantel

man·til·la \man-'tē-yə, -'ti-lə\ *n* : a light scarf worn over the head and shoulders esp. by Spanish and Latin-American women

man·tis \'man-təs\ *n, pl* **man·tis·es** *also* **man·tes** \-ˌtēz\ [NL, fr. Gk, lit., diviner, prophet] : any of a group of large usu. green insect-eating insects that hold their prey in forelimbs folded as if in prayer

man·tis·sa \man-'ti-sə\ *n* : the part of a logarithm to the right of the decimal point

¹man·tle \'man-tᵊl\ *n* **1** : a loose sleeveless garment worn over other clothes **2** : something that covers, enfolds, or envelops **3** : a lacy sheath that gives light by incandescence when placed over a flame **4** : the portion of the earth lying between the crust and the core **5** : MANTEL

²mantle *vb* **man·tled; man·tling** **1** : to cover with a mantle **2** : BLUSH

man·tra \'man-trə\ *n* : a mystical formula of invocation or incantation (as in Hinduism)

¹man·u·al \'man-yə-wəl\ *adj* **1** : of, relating to, or involving the hands; *also* : worked by hand ⟨a ∼ pump⟩ **2** : requiring or using physical skill and energy — **man·u·al·ly** *adv*

²manual *n* **1** : a small book; *esp* : HANDBOOK **2** : the prescribed movements in the handling of a military item and esp. a weapon during a drill or ceremony ⟨the ∼ of arms⟩ **3** : a keyboard esp. of an organ

man·u·fac·to·ry \ˌman-yə-'fak-tə-rē\ *n* : FACTORY

¹man·u·fac·ture \ˌman-yə-'fak-chər\ *n* [MF, fr. ML *manufactura*, L *manu factus* made by hand] **1** : something made from raw materials **2** : the process of making wares by hand or by machinery; *also* : a productive industry using machinery

²manufacture *vb* **-tured; -tur·ing** **1** : to make from raw materials by hand or by machinery; *also* : to engage in manufacture **2** : INVENT, FABRICATE; *also* : CREATE — **man·u·fac·tur·er** *n*

man·u·mit \ˌman-yə-'mit\ *vb* **-mit·ted; -mit·ting** : to free from slavery — **man·u·mis·sion** \-'mi-shən\ *n*

¹ma·nure \mə-'nu̇r, -'nyu̇r\ *vb* **ma·nured; ma·nur·ing** : to fertilize land with manure

²manure *n* : FERTILIZER; *esp* : refuse from stables and barnyards — **ma·nu·ri·al** \-'nu̇r-ē-əl, -'nyu̇r-\ *adj*

man·u·script \'man-yə-ˌskript\ *n* [L *manu scriptus* written by hand] **1** : a written or typewritten composition or document; *also* : a document submitted for publication **2** : writing as opposed to print

Manx \'maŋks\ *n pl* : the people of the Isle of Man — **Manx** *adj*

¹many \'me-nē\ *adj* **more** \'mȯr\; **most** \'mōst\ : consisting of or amounting to a large but indefinite number ⟨∼ years ago⟩

²many *pron* : a large number ⟨∼ are called⟩

³many *n* : a large but indefinite number ⟨a good ∼ of them⟩

many·fold \ˌme-nē-'fōld\ *adv* : by many times

many–sid·ed \-'sī-dəd\ *adj* **1** : having many sides or aspects **2** : VERSATILE

Mao·ism \'mau̇-ˌi-zəm\ *n* : the theory and practice of Communism developed in China chiefly by Mao Zedong — **Mao·ist** \'mau̇-ist\ *n or adj*

Mao·ri \'mau̇-(ə)r-ē\ *n, pl* **Maori** *or* **Maoris** : a member of a Polynesian people native to New Zealand

¹map \'map\ *n* [ML *mappa*, fr. L, napkin, towel] **1** : a representation usu. on a flat surface of the whole or part of an area **2** : a representation of the celestial sphere or part of it

²map *vb* **mapped; map·ping** **1** : to make a map of **2** : to plan in detail ⟨∼ out a program⟩ — **map·pa·ble** \'ma-pə-bəl\ *adj* — **map·per** *n*

MAP *abbr* modified American plan

ma·ple \'mā-pəl\ *n* : any of a genus of trees or shrubs with 2-winged dry fruit and opposite leaves; *also* : the hard light-colored wood of a maple used esp. for floors and furniture

maple sugar *n* : sugar made by boiling maple syrup

maple syrup *n* : syrup made by concentrating the sap of maple trees and esp. the sugar maple

mar \'mär\ *vb* **marred; mar·ring** : to detract from the wholeness or perfection of : SPOIL ◆ **Synonyms** INJURE, HURT, HARM, DAMAGE, IMPAIR, BLEMISH

Mar *abbr* March

ma·ra·ca \mə-'rä-kə, -'ra-\ *n* [Pg *maracá*] : a rattle usu. made from a gourd and used as a percussion instrument

mar·a·schi·no \ˌmer-ə-'skē-nō, -'shē-\ *n, often cap* : a cherry preserved in a sweet liqueur made from the juice of a bitter wild cherry

mar·a·thon \'mer-ə-ˌthän\ *n* [*Marathon*, Greece, site of a victory of Greeks over Persians in 490 B.C. the news of which was carried to Athens by a long-distance runner] **1** : a long-distance race esp. on foot **2** : an endurance contest

mar·a·thon·er \'mer-ə-ˌthä-nər\ *n* : a person who takes part in a marathon — **mar·a·thon·ing** *n*

ma·raud \mə-'rȯd\ *vb* : to roam about and raid in search of plunder : PILLAGE — **ma·raud·er** *n*

mar·ble \'mär-bəl\ *n* **1** : a limestone that can be polished and used in fine building work **2** : something resembling marble (as in coldness) **3** : a small ball (as of glass) used in various games; *also, pl* : a children's game played with these small balls — **marble** *adj*

mar·bling \-bə-liŋ, -bliŋ\ *n* : an intermixture of fat through the lean of a cut of meat

mar·cel \mär-'sel\ *n* : a deep soft wave made in the hair by the use of a heated curling iron — **marcel** *vb*

¹march \'märch\ *n* : a border region : FRONTIER

²march *vb* **1** : to move along in or as if in military formation **2** : to walk in a direct purposeful manner; *also* : PROGRESS, ADVANCE **3** : TRAVERSE ⟨∼ed 10 miles⟩ — **march·er** *n*

³march *n* **1** : the action of marching; *also* : the distance covered (as by a military unit) in a march **2** : a regular measured stride or rhythmic step used in marching **3** : forward movement **4** : a piece of music with marked rhythm suitable for marching to

March *n* [ME, fr. AF, fr. L *martius*, fr. *martius* of Mars, fr. *Mart-, Mars*, Roman god of war] : the 3d month of the year

mar·chio·ness \'mär-shə-nəs\ *n* **1** : the wife or widow of a marquess **2** : a woman holding the rank of a marquess in her own right

Mar·di Gras \'mär-dē-ˌgrä\ *n* [F, lit., fat Tuesday] : the Tuesday before Ash Wednesday often observed with parades and merrymaking

¹mare \'mer\ *n* : an adult female of the horse or a related mammal

²ma·re \'mär-(ˌ)ā\ *n, pl* **ma·ria** \'mär-ē-ə\ : any of several large dark areas on the surface of the moon or Mars

mar·ga·rine \'mär-jə-rən\ *n* : a food product made usu. from vegetable oils churned with skimmed milk and used as a substitute for butter

mar·ga·ri·ta \ˌmär-gə-'rē-tə\ *n* : a cocktail consisting of tequila, lime or lemon juice, and an orange-flavored liqueur

mar·gin \'mär-jən\ *n* **1** : the part of a page outside the main body of printed or written matter **2** : EDGE ⟨continental ∼⟩ **3** : a spare amount, measure, or degree allowed for use if needed **4** : measure or degree of difference ⟨a one-vote ∼⟩

mar·gin·al \-jə-nəl\ *adj* **1** : written or printed in the margin **2** : of, relating to, or situated at a margin or border **3** : close to the lower limit of quality or acceptability **4** : excluded from or existing outside the mainstream of society or a group — **mar·gin·al·ly** *adv*

mar·gi·na·lia \ˌmär-jə-'nā-lē-ə\ *n pl* : marginal notes or embellishments

mar·gin·al·ize \'mär-jə-nᵊl-ˌīz\ *vb* **-ized; -iz·ing** : to relegate to an unimportant position within a society or group

mar·grave \'mär-ˌgrāv\ *n* : the military governor esp. of a medieval German border province

ma·ri·a·chi \ˌmär-ē-'ä-chē, ˌmer-\ *n* : a Mexican street band; *also* : a member of or the music of such a band

mari·gold \'mer-ə-ˌgōld\ *n* : any of a genus of tropical American herbs related to the daisies that are grown for their showy usu. yellow, orange, or maroon flower heads

mar·i·jua·na *also* **mar·i·hua·na** \ˌmer-ə-'wä-nə, -'hwä-\ [MexSp *marihuana*] : the dried leaves and flowering tops of the female hemp plant smoked usu. illegally for their intoxicating effect; *also* : HEMP

ma·rim·ba \mə-'rim-bə\ *n* : a xylophone of southern Africa and Central America; *also* : a modern version of it

marimba

ma·ri·na \mə-'rē-nə\ *n* : a dock or basin providing secure moorings for pleasure boats

mar·i·na·ra \ˌmer-ə-'ner-ə\ *adj* [It *(alla) marinara*, lit., in sailor style] : made with tomatoes, onions, garlic, and spices; *also* : served with marinara sauce

mar·i·nade \ˌmer-ə-'nād\ *n* : a savory usu. acidic sauce in which meat, fish, or a vegetable is soaked to enrich its flavor or to tenderize it

mar·i·nate \'mer-ə-ˌnāt\ *vb* **-nat·ed; -nat·ing** : to steep (as meat or fish) in a marinade

¹ma·rine \mə-'rēn\ *adj* **1** : of or relating to the sea or its navigation or commerce **2** : of or relating to marines

²marine *n* **1** : the mercantile and naval shipping of a country **2** : any of a class of soldiers serving on shipboard or with a naval force

mar·i·ner \'mer-ə-nər\ *n* : SAILOR

mar·i·o·nette \ˌmer-ē-ə-'net\ *n* : a puppet moved by strings or by hand

mar·i·tal \'mer-ə-t⁰l\ *adj* : of or relating to marriage : CONJUGAL ◆ **Synonyms** MATRIMONIAL, CONNUBIAL, NUPTIAL

mar·i·time \'mer-ə-ˌtīm\ *adj* **1** : of, relating to, or bordering on the sea **2** : of or relating to navigation or commerce of the sea

mar·jo·ram \'mär-jə-rəm\ *n* : any of various fragrant mints often used as seasoning

¹mark \'märk\ *n* **1** : something (as a line or fixed object) designed to record position; *also* : the starting line or position in a track event **2** : TARGET; *also* : GOAL, OBJECT **3** : an object of abuse or ridicule **4** : the question under discussion **5** : NORM ⟨not up to the ∼⟩ **6** : a visible sign : INDICATION; *also* : CHARACTERISTIC **7** : a written or printed symbol **8** : GRADE 5 ⟨a ∼ of B+⟩ **9** : IMPORTANCE, DISTINCTION **10** : a lasting impression ⟨made his ∼ in the world⟩; *also* : a damaging impression left on a surface

²mark *vb* **1** : to set apart by a line or boundary **2** : to designate by a mark or make a mark on **3** : CHARACTERIZE ⟨the vehemence that ∼s his speeches⟩; *also* : SIGNALIZE ⟨this year ∼s our 50th anniversary⟩ **4** : to take notice of : OBSERVE — **mark·er** *n*

³mark *n* : DEUTSCHE MARK

Mark \'märk\ *n* — see BIBLE table

mark·down \'märk-ˌdaun\ *n* **1** : a lowering of price **2** : the amount by which an original price is reduced

mark down *vb* : to put a lower price on

marked \'märkt\ *adj* : NOTICEABLE — **mark·ed·ly** \'mär-kəd-lē\ *adv*

¹mar·ket \'mär-kət\ *n* **1** : a meeting together of people for trade by purchase and sale; *also* : a public place where such a meeting is held **2** : the rate or price offered for a commodity or security **3** : the course of commercial activity by which the exchange of commodities is effected **4** : a geographical area of demand for commodities; *also* : extent of demand **5** : a retail establishment usu. of a specific kind

²market *vb* : to go to a market to buy or sell; *also* : SELL — **mar·ket·able** *adj*

mar·ket·place \'mär-kət-ˌplās\ *n* **1** : an open square in a town where markets are held **2** : the world of trade or economic activity

mark·ka \'mär-ˌkä\ *n, pl* **mark·kaa** \'mär-ˌkä\ *or* **markkas** \-ˌkäz\ : the basic monetary unit of Finland from 1917 to 2001

marks·man \'märks-mən\ *n* : a person skillful at hitting a target — **marks·man·ship** *n*

mark·up \'mär-ˌkəp\ *n* **1** : a raising of price **2** : an amount added to the cost price of an article to determine the selling price

mark up *vb* : to put a higher price on

markup language *n* : a system for marking the components and layout of a computer document

marl \'märl\ *n* : an earthy deposit rich in lime used esp. as fertilizer — **marly** \'mär-lē\ *adj*

mar·lin \'mär-lən\ *n* : any of several large oceanic sport fishes related to sailfishes

mar·line·spike *also* **mar·lin·spike** \'mär-lən-ˌspīk\ *n* : a pointed iron tool used to separate strands of rope or wire (as in splicing)

mar·ma·lade \'mär-mə-ˌlād\ *n* : a clear jelly holding in suspension pieces of fruit and fruit rind

mar·mo·re·al \mär-'mȯr-ē-əl\ *adj* : of, relating to, or suggestive of marble

mar·mo·set \'mär-mə-ˌset\ *n* : any of numerous small bushy-tailed monkeys of Central and So. America

mar·mot \'mär-mət\ *n* : any of a genus of stout shortlegged burrowing No. American rodents

¹ma·roon \mə-'rün\ *vb* **1** : to put ashore (as on a desolate island) and leave to one's fate **2** : to leave in isolation and without hope of escape

²maroon *n* : a dark red color

¹mar·quee \mär-'kē\ *n* [modif. of F *marquise*, lit., marchioness] **1** : a large tent set up (as for an outdoor party) **2** : a usu. metal and glass canopy over an entrance (as of a theater) **3** : a sign over the entrance of a theater or arena advertising a performance

²marquee *adj* : having or being a great attraction : PREEMINENT ⟨∼ athletes⟩

mar·quess \'mär-kwəs\ *or* **mar·quis** \'mär-kwəs, mär-'kē\ *n* **1** : a nobleman of hereditary rank in Europe and Japan **2** : a member of the British peerage ranking below a duke and above an earl

mar·que·try \'mär-kə-trē\ *n* : inlaid work of wood, shell, or ivory (as on a table or cabinet)

mar·quise \mär-'kēz\ *n, pl* **mar·quises** *same or* -'kē-zəz\ : MARCHIONESS

mar·riage \'mer-ij\ *n* **1** : the state of being united to another person as a usu. contractual relationship according to law or custom **2** : a wedding ceremony and attendant festivities **3** : a close union ⟨a ∼ of light and shadow⟩ — **mar·riage·able** *adj*

married name *n* : a woman's surname acquired through marriage

mar·row \'mer-ō\ *n* : a soft vascular tissue that fills the cavities of most bones

mar·row·bone \'mer-ə-ˌbōn, 'mer-ō-\ *n* : a bone (as a shinbone) rich in marrow

mar·ry \'mer-ē\ *vb* **mar·ried; mar·ry·ing** **1** : to join in marriage **2** : to take as a spouse : WED **3** : to enter into a close union **4** : COMBINE, UNITE — **mar·ried** *adj or n*

Mars \'märz\ *n* : the planet 4th from the sun and conspicuous for its red color — see PLANET table

marsh \'märsh\ *n* : a tract of soft wet land — **marshy** *adj*

¹mar·shal \'mär-shəl\ *n* [ME, fr. AF *mareschal*, of Gmc origin; akin to OHG *marahscalc* marshal, fr. *marah* horse + *scalc* servant] **1** : a high official in a medieval household; *also* : a person in charge of the ceremonial aspects of a gathering **2** : a general officer of the highest military rank **3** : an administrative officer (as of a U.S. judicial district) having duties similar to a sheriff's **4** : the administrative head of a city police or fire department

²marshal *vb* **mar·shaled** *or* **mar·shalled; mar·shal·ing** *or*

mar·shal·ling 1 : to arrange in order, rank, or position 2 : to bring together 3 : to lead with ceremony : USHER

marsh gas n : METHANE

marsh·mal·low \'märsh-,me-lō, -,ma-\ n : a light spongy confection made from corn syrup, sugar, albumen, and gelatin

marsh marigold n : a swamp herb related to the buttercups that has bright yellow flowers

mar·su·pi·al \mär-'sü-pē-əl\ n : any of an order of primitive mammals (as opossums, kangaroos, or wombats) that bear very immature young which are nourished in a pouch on the abdomen of the female — **marsupial** adj

mart \'märt\ n : MARKET

mar·ten \'mär-tᵊn\ n, pl **marten** or **martens** : a slender mammal that is larger than the related weasels and has soft gray or brown fur; also : this fur

mar·tial \'mär-shəl\ adj [L martialis of Mars, fr. Mart-, Mars Mars, Roman god of war] 1 : of, relating to, or suited for war or a warrior ⟨~ music⟩ 2 : of or relating to an army or military life 3 : WARLIKE

martial law n 1 : the law applied in occupied territory by the occupying military forces 2 : the established law of a country administered by military forces in an emergency when civilian law enforcement agencies are unable to maintain public order and safety

mar·tian \'mär-shən\ adj, often cap : of or relating to the planet Mars or its hypothetical inhabitants — **martian** n, often cap

mar·tin \'mär-tᵊn\ n : any of several swallows and esp. one of No. America with purplish blue plumage

mar·ti·net \,mär-tə-'net\ n : a strict disciplinarian

mar·tin·gale \'mär-tᵊn-,gāl\ n : a strap connecting a horse's girth to the bit or reins so as to hold down its head

mar·ti·ni \mär-'tē-nē\ n : a cocktail made of gin or vodka and dry vermouth

¹**mar·tyr** \'mär-tər\ n [ME, fr. OE, fr. LL, fr. Gk martyr-, martys witness] 1 : a person who dies rather than renounce a religion; also : a person who makes a great sacrifice for the sake of principle 2 : a great or constant sufferer

²**martyr** vb 1 : to put to death for adhering to a belief 2 : TORTURE

mar·tyr·dom \'mär-tər-dəm\ n 1 : the suffering and death of a martyr 2 : TORTURE

¹**mar·vel** \'mär-vəl\ n 1 : one that causes wonder or astonishment 2 : intense surprise or interest

²**marvel** vb **mar·veled** or **mar·velled; mar·vel·ing** or **mar·vel·ling** : to feel surprise, wonder, or amazed curiosity ⟨~ed at the circus act⟩

mar·vel·ous or **mar·vel·lous** \'mär-və-ləs\ adj 1 : causing wonder 2 : of the highest kind or quality — **mar·vel·ous·ly** adv — **mar·vel·ous·ness** n

Marx·ism \'märk-,si-zəm\ n : the political, economic, and social principles and policies advocated by Karl Marx — **Marx·ist** \-sist\ n or adj

mar·zi·pan \'märt-sə-,pän, -,pan; 'mär-zə-,pan\ n [G, fr. It marzapane] : a confection of almond paste, sugar, and egg whites

masc abbr masculine

mas·ca·ra \ma-'sker-ə\ n : a cosmetic esp. for darkening the eyelashes

mas·car·po·ne \,mas-kär-'pō-nā\ n : an Italian cream cheese

mas·cot \'mas-,kät, -kət\ n [F mascotte, fr. Occitan mascoto, fr. masco witch, fr. ML masca] : a person, animal, or object adopted usu. by a group to bring good luck

¹**mas·cu·line** \'mas-kyə-lən\ adj 1 : MALE; also : MANLY 2 : of, relating to, or constituting the gender that includes most words or grammatical forms referring to males — **mas·cu·lin·i·ty** \,mas-kyə-'li-nə-tē\ n

²**masculine** n : a noun, pronoun, adjective, or inflectional form or class of the masculine gender; also : the masculine gender

¹**mash** \'mash\ n 1 : a mixture of ground feeds for livestock 2 : crushed malt or grain steeped in hot water to make wort 3 : a soft pulpy mass

²**mash** vb 1 : to reduce to a soft pulpy state 2 : CRUSH, SMASH ⟨~ a finger⟩ — **mash·er** n

MASH abbr mobile army surgical hospital

¹**mask** \'mask\ n 1 : a cover for the face usu. for disguise or protection 2 : MASQUE 3 : a figure of a head worn on the stage in antiquity 4 : a copy of a face made by means of a mold ⟨death ~⟩ 5 : something that conceals or disguises 6 : the face of an animal

²**mask** vb 1 : to conceal from view : DISGUISE 2 : to cover for protection

mask·er \'mas-kər\ n : a participant in a masquerade

mas·och·ism \'ma-sə-,ki-zəm, 'ma-zə-\ n 1 : a sexual perversion characterized by pleasure in being subjected to pain or humiliation 2 : pleasure in being abused or dominated — **mas·och·ist** \-kist\ n — **mas·och·is·tic** \,ma-sə-'kis-tik, ,ma-zə-\ adj

ma·son \'mā-sᵊn\ n 1 : a skilled worker who builds with stone, brick, or concrete 2 cap : FREEMASON

Ma·son·ic \mə-'sä-nik\ adj : of or relating to Freemasons or Freemasonry

ma·son·ry \'mā-sᵊn-rē\ n, pl **-ries** 1 : something constructed of materials used by masons 2 : the art, trade, or work of a mason 3 cap : FREEMASONRY

masque \'mask\ n 1 : MASQUERADE 2 : a short allegorical dramatic performance (as of the 17th century)

¹**mas·quer·ade** \,mas-kə-'rād\ n 1 : a social gathering of persons wearing masks; also : a costume for wear at such a gathering 2 : DISGUISE

²**masquerade** vb **-ad·ed; -ad·ing** 1 : to disguise oneself : POSE 2 : to take part in a masquerade — **mas·quer·ad·er** n

¹**mass** \'mas\ n 1 cap : a sequence of prayers and ceremonies forming the eucharistic service of the Roman Catholic Church 2 often cap : a celebration of the Eucharist 3 : a musical setting for parts of the Mass

²**mass** n 1 : a quantity or aggregate of matter usu. of considerable size 2 : EXPANSE, BULK; also : MASSIVENESS 3 : the principal part 4 : AGGREGATE, WHOLE 5 : the quantity of matter that a body possesses as measured by its inertia 6 : a large quantity, amount, or number 7 : the great body of people — usu. used in pl. — **massy** adj

³**mass** vb : to form or collect into a mass

Mass abbr Massachusetts

mas·sa·cre \'ma-si-kər\ n 1 : the killing of many persons under cruel or atrocious circumstances 2 : a wholesale slaughter — **massacre** vb

¹**mas·sage** \mə-'säzh, -'säj\ n : manipulation of tissues (as by rubbing and kneading) for therapeutic purposes

²**massage** vb **mas·saged; mas·sag·ing** 1 : to subject to massage 2 : to treat flatteringly; also : MANIPULATE, DOCTOR ⟨~ data⟩

mas·seur \ma-'sər\ n : a man who practices massage

mas·seuse \-'sərz, -'süz\ n : a woman who practices massage

mas·sif \ma-'sēf\ n : a principal mountain mass

mas·sive \'ma-siv\ adj 1 : forming or consisting of a large mass 2 : large in structure, scope, or degree — **mas·sive·ly** adv — **mas·sive·ness** n

mass·less \'mas-ləs\ adj : having no mass ⟨~ particles⟩

mass medium n, pl **mass media** : a medium of communication (as the newspapers or television) that is designed to reach the mass of the people

mass–pro·duce \,mas-prə-'düs, -'dyüs\ vb : to produce in quantity usu. by machinery — **mass production** n

¹**mast** \'mast\ n 1 : a long pole or spar rising from the keel or deck of a ship and supporting the yards, booms, and rigging 2 : a slender vertical structure — **mast·ed** \'mas-təd\ adj

²**mast** n : nuts (as acorns) accumulated on the forest floor and often serving as food for animals (as hogs)

mas·tec·to·my \ma-'stek-tə-mē\ n, pl **-mies** : surgical removal of the breast

¹**mas·ter** \'mas-tər\ n 1 : a male teacher; also : a person holding an academic degree higher than a bachelor's but lower than a doctor's 2 : one highly skilled (as in an art or profession) 3 : one having authority or control 4 : VICTOR, SUPERIOR 5 : the commander of a merchant ship 6 : a youth or boy too young to be called mister — used as a title 7 : an original from which copies are made

²**master** vb 1 : to become master of : OVERCOME 2 : to become skilled or proficient in 3 : to produce a master recording of (as a musical performance)

master chief petty officer n : a petty officer of the highest rank in the navy

mas·ter·ful \'mas-tər-fəl\ adj 1 : inclined and usu. competent to act as master **2** : having or reflecting the skill of a master ⟨∼ verse⟩ — **mas·ter·ful·ly** *adv* — **mas·ter·ful·ness** *n*

master gunnery sergeant *n* : a noncommissioned officer in the marine corps ranking above a master sergeant

master key *n* : a key designed to open several different locks

mas·ter·ly \'mas-tər-lē\ *adj* **1** : indicating thorough knowledge or superior skill ⟨∼ performance⟩ **2** : having the skill of a master ⟨a ∼ writer⟩ — **mas·ter·ly** *adv*

mas·ter·mind \-ˌmīnd\ *n* : a person who directs or provides creative intelligence for a project — **mastermind** *vb*

master of ceremonies : a person who acts as host at a formal event or a program of entertainment

mas·ter·piece \'mas-tər-ˌpēs\ *n* : a work done with extraordinary skill

master plan *n* : an overall plan

mas·ter's \'mas-tərz\ *n* : a master's degree

master sergeant *n* **1** : a noncommissioned officer in the army ranking next below a sergeant major **2** : a noncommissioned officer in the air force ranking next below a senior master sergeant **3** : a noncommissioned officer in the marine corps ranking next below a master gunnery sergeant

mas·ter·stroke \'mas-tər-ˌstrōk\ *n* : a masterly performance or move

mas·ter·work \-ˌwərk\ *n* : MASTERPIECE

mas·tery \'mas-tə-rē\ *n* **1** : DOMINION; *also* : SUPERIORITY **2** : possession or display of great skill or knowledge

mast·head \'mast-ˌhed\ *n* **1** : the top of a mast **2** : the printed matter in a newspaper or periodical giving the title and details of ownership and rates of subscription or advertising

mas·tic \'mas-tik\ *n* : a pasty material used as a coating or cement

mas·ti·cate \'mas-tə-ˌkāt\ *vb* **-cat·ed; -cat·ing** : CHEW — **mas·ti·ca·tion** \ˌmas-tə-'kā-shən\ *n*

mas·tiff \'mas-təf\ *n* : any of a breed of large smooth-coated dogs used esp. as guard dogs

mast·odon \'mas-tə-ˌdän\ *n* [NL, fr. Gk *mastos* breast + *odōn, odous* tooth] : any of numerous huge extinct mammals related to the mammoths

mas·toid \'mas-ˌtȯid\ *n* : a bony prominence behind the ear — **mastoid** *adj*

mas·tur·ba·tion \ˌmas-tər-'bā-shən\ *n* : stimulation of the genital organs apart from sexual intercourse, usu. to orgasm, and esp. by use of one's own hand — **mas·tur·bate** \'mas-tər-ˌbāt\ *vb* — **mas·tur·ba·to·ry** \'mas-tər-bə-ˌtȯr-ē\ *adj*

¹mat \'mat\ *n* **1** : a piece of coarse woven or plaited fabric **2** : something made up of many intertwined strands **3** : a large thick pad used as a surface for wrestling and gymnastics

²mat *vb* **mat·ted; mat·ting** **1** : to provide with a mat **2** : to form into a tangled mass ⟨dirt *matted* her hair⟩

³mat *vb* **mat·ted; mat·ting** **1** *also* **matte** *or* **matt** : to make (as a color) matte **2** : to provide (a picture) with a mat

⁴mat *var of* ²MATTE

⁵mat *or* **matt** *or* **matte** *n* : a border going around a picture between picture and frame or serving as the frame

mat·a·dor \'ma-tə-ˌdȯr\ *n* [Sp, fr. *matar* to kill] : a bullfighter whose role is to kill the bull in a bullfight

¹match \'mach\ *n* **1** : a person or thing equal or similar to another; *also* : one able to cope with another : RIVAL **2** : a suitable pairing of persons or objects **3** : a contest or game between two or more individuals **4** : a marriage union; *also* : a prospective marriage partner — **match·less** *adj*

²match *vb* **1** : to meet as an antagonist; *also* : PIT ⟨∼ wits⟩ **2** : to provide with a worthy competitor; *also* : to set in comparison with **3** : MARRY **4** : to combine suitably or congenially ⟨∼ed the drapes with the rug⟩; *also* : ADAPT, SUIT **5** : to act in harmony ⟨his shoes and belt ∼⟩ **6** : to provide with a counterpart

³match *n* : a short slender piece of flammable material (as wood) tipped with a combustible mixture that ignites through friction

match·book \'mach-ˌbu̇k\ *n* : a small folder containing rows of paper matches

match·lock \-ˌläk\ *n* : a musket with a slow-burning cord lowered over a hole in the breech to ignite the charge

match·mak·er \-ˌmā-kər\ *n* : one who arranges a match and esp. a marriage

match·wood \-ˌwu̇d\ *n* : small pieces of wood

¹mate \'māt\ *vb* **mat·ed; mat·ing** : CHECKMATE — **mate** *n*

²mate *n* **1** : ASSOCIATE, COMPANION; *also* : HELPER **2** : a deck officer on a merchant ship ranking below the captain **3** : one of a pair; *esp* : either member of a married couple or a breeding pair of animals

³mate *vb* **mat·ed; mat·ing** **1** : to join or fit together **2** : to come or bring together as mates **3** : COPULATE

¹ma·te·ri·al \mə-'tir-ē-əl\ *adj* **1** : PHYSICAL ⟨∼ world⟩; *also* : BODILY ⟨∼ needs⟩ **2** : of or relating to matter rather than form ⟨∼ cause⟩; *also* : EMPIRICAL ⟨∼ knowledge⟩ **3** : highly important : SIGNIFICANT **4** : of a physical or worldly nature ⟨∼ progress⟩ — **ma·te·ri·al·ly** *adv*

²material *n* **1** : the elements or substance of which something is composed or made **2** : apparatus necessary for doing or making something

ma·te·ri·al·ise *Brit var of* MATERIALIZE

ma·te·ri·al·ism \mə-'tir-ē-ə-ˌli-zəm\ *n* **1** : a theory that everything can be explained as being or coming from matter **2** : a preoccupation with material rather than intellectual or spiritual things — **ma·te·ri·al·ist** \-list\ *n or adj* — **ma·te·ri·al·is·tic** \-ˌtir-ē-ə-'lis-tik\ *adj* — **ma·te·ri·al·is·ti·cal·ly** \-ti-k(ə-)lē\ *adv*

ma·te·ri·al·ize \mə-'tir-ē-ə-ˌlīz\ *vb* **-ized; -iz·ing** **1** : to give material form to; *also* : to assume bodily form **2** : to make an often unexpected appearance — **ma·te·ri·al·i·za·tion** \mə-ˌtir-ē-ə-lə-'zā-shən\ *n*

ma·té·ri·el *or* **ma·te·ri·el** \mə-ˌtir-ē-'el\ *n* [F *matériel*] : equipment, apparatus, and supplies used by an organization

ma·ter·nal \mə-'tər-n²l\ *adj* **1** : MOTHERLY **2** : related through or inherited or derived from a female parent — **ma·ter·nal·ly** *adv*

¹ma·ter·ni·ty \mə-'tər-nə-tē\ *n, pl* **-ties** **1** : the quality or state of being a mother; *also* : MOTHERLINESS **2** : a hospital facility for the care of women before and during childbirth and for newborn babies

²maternity *adj* **1** : designed for wear during pregnancy ⟨a ∼ dress⟩ **2** : effective for the period close to and including childbirth ⟨∼ leave⟩

¹math \'math\ *n* : MATHEMATICS

²math *abbr* mathematical; mathematician

math·e·mat·ics \ˌma-thə-'ma-tiks\ *n* : the science of numbers and their properties, operations, and relations and with shapes in space and their structure and measurement — **math·e·mat·i·cal** \-'ma-ti-kəl\ *adj* — **math·e·mat·i·cal·ly** \-ti-k(ə-)lē\ *adv* — **math·e·ma·ti·cian** \ˌma-thə-mə-'ti-shən\ *n*

mat·i·nee *or* **mat·i·née** \ˌma-tə-'nā\ *n* [F *matinée*, lit., morning, fr. OF, fr. *matin* morning, fr. L *matutinum*, fr. neut. of *matutinus* of the morning, fr. *Matuta*, goddess of morning] : a musical or dramatic performance in the daytime and esp. the afternoon

mat·ins \'ma-t²nz\ *n pl, often cap* **1** : special prayers said between midnight and 4 a.m. **2** : a morning service of liturgical prayer in Anglican churches

ma·tri·arch \'mā-trē-ˌärk\ *n* : a woman who rules or dominates a family, group, or state — **ma·tri·ar·chal** \ˌmā-trē-'är-kəl\ *adj* — **ma·tri·ar·chy** \'mā-trē-ˌär-kē\ *n*

ma·tri·cide \'ma-trə-ˌsīd, 'mā-\ *n* : the murder of a mother by her child — **ma·tri·cid·al** \ˌma-trə-'sī-d²l, ˌmā-\ *adj*

ma·tric·u·late \mə-'tri-kyə-ˌlāt\ *vb* **-lat·ed; -lat·ing** : to enroll as a member of a body and esp. of a college or university — **ma·tric·u·la·tion** \-ˌtri-kyə-'lā-shən\ *n*

mat·ri·mo·ny \'ma-trə-ˌmō-nē\ *n* [ME, fr. AF *matrimoignie*, fr. L *matrimonium*, fr. *mater* mother, matron] : MARRIAGE — **mat·ri·mo·nial** \ˌma-trə-'mō-nē-əl\ *adj* — **mat·ri·mo·nial·ly** *adv*

ma·trix \'mā-triks\ *n, pl* **ma·tri·ces** \'mā-trə-ˌsēz, 'ma-\ *or* **ma·trix·es** \'mā-trik-səz\ **1** : something within or from which something else originates, develops, or takes form **2** : a mold from which a relief surface (as a piece of type) is made

ma·tron \'mā-trən\ *n* **1** : a married woman usu. of dignified maturity or social distinction **2** : a woman supervisor (as in a school or police station) — **ma·tron·ly** *adj*

Matt *abbr* Matthew

¹matte *or* **matt** *var of* ³MAT

²matte *also* **matt** \'mat\ *adj* : not shiny : DULL

¹mat·ter \'ma-tər\ *n* **1** : a subject of interest or concern **2** *pl* : events or circumstances of a particular situation **3** : the subject of a discourse or writing **4** : TROUBLE, DIFFICULTY ⟨what's the ～⟩ **5** : the substance of which a physical object is composed **6** : PUS **7** : an indefinite amount or quantity ⟨a ～ of a few days⟩ **8** : something written or printed **9** : MAIL — **as a matter of fact** : ACTUALLY — **no matter** : without regard to ⟨will follow *no matter* where you go⟩ — **no matter what** : regardless of the consequences ⟨must win, *no matter what*⟩

²matter *vb* : to be of importance

mat·ter-of-fact \ˌma-tə-rəv-'fakt\ *adj* : adhering to fact; *also* : being plain, straightforward, or unemotional — **mat·ter-of-fact·ly** *adv* — **mat·ter-of-fact·ness** *n*

Mat·thew \'ma-thyü\ *n* — see BIBLE table

mat·tins *often cap chiefly Brit var of* MATINS

mat·tock \'ma-tək\ *n* : a digging and grubbing tool with features of an adze and an ax or pick

mat·tress \'ma-trəs\ *n* **1** : a fabric case filled with resilient material used as or for a bed **2** : an inflatable airtight sack for use as a mattress

mat·u·rate \'ma-chə-ˌrāt\ *vb* **-rat·ed; -rat·ing** : MATURE

mat·u·ra·tion \ˌma-chə-'rā-shən\ *n* **1** : the process of becoming mature **2** : the emergence of personal and behavioral characteristics through growth processes — **mat·u·ra·tion·al** \-shə-nəl\ *adj*

¹ma·ture \mə-'tür, -'tyür\ *adj* **ma·tur·er; -est** **1** : based on slow careful consideration **2** : having attained a final or desired state **3** : of or relating to a condition of full development **4** : suitable only for adults ⟨～ content⟩ **5** : due for payment — **ma·ture·ly** *adv*

²mature *vb* **ma·tured; ma·tur·ing** : to reach or bring to maturity or completion

ma·tu·ri·ty \mə-'tür-ə-tē, -'tyür-\ *n* **1** : the quality or state of being mature; *esp* : full development **2** : the date when a note becomes due for payment

ma·tu·ti·nal \ˌma-chù-'tī-nᵊl; mə-'tü-tə-nəl, -'tyü-\ *adj* : of, relating to, or occurring in the morning : EARLY

mat·zo *or* **mat·zoh** \'mät-sə\ *n, pl* **mat·zoth** \-ˌsōt, -ˌsōth, -sōs\ *or* **mat·zos** *or* **mat·zohs** [Yiddish *matse*, fr. Heb *maṣṣāh*] : unleavened bread eaten esp. at the Passover

maud·lin \'mȯd-lən\ *adj* [alter. of Mary *Magdalene;* fr. her depiction as a weeping, penitent sinner] **1** : drunk enough to be silly **2** : weakly and effusively sentimental

¹maul \'mȯl\ *n* : a heavy hammer often with a wooden head used esp. for driving wedges

²maul *vb* **1** : BEAT, BRUISE; *also* : MANGLE **2** : to handle roughly

maun·der \'mȯn-dər\ *vb* **1** : to wander slowly and idly **2** : to speak indistinctly or disconnectedly

mau·so·le·um \ˌmȯ-sə-'lē-əm, ˌmȯ-zə-\ *n, pl* **-leums** *or* **-lea** \-'lē-ə\ [L, fr. Gk *mausōleion*, fr. *Mausōlos* Mausolus † *ab* 353 B.C. ruler of Caria whose tomb was one of the seven wonders of the ancient world] : a large tomb; *esp* : a usu. stone building for entombment of the dead above ground

mauve \'mōv, 'mȯv\ *n* : a moderate purple, violet, or lilac color

ma·ven *also* **ma·vin** \'mā-vən\ *n* [Yiddish *meyvn*, fr. LHeb *mēbhīn*] : EXPERT

mav·er·ick \'ma-vrik, -və-rik\ *n* [Samuel A. *Maverick* † 1870 Am. pioneer who did not brand his calves] **1** : an unbranded range animal **2** : NONCONFORMIST

maw \'mȯ\ *n* **1** : STOMACH; *also* : the crop of a bird **2** : the throat, gullet, or jaws esp. of a voracious animal

mawk·ish \'mȯ-kish\ *adj* : sickly sentimental — **mawk·ish·ly** *adv* — **mawk·ish·ness** *n*

max *abbr* maximum

maxi \'mak-sē\ *n, pl* **max·is** : a long skirt, dress, or coat

maxi- *comb form* **1** : extra long ⟨*maxi*-kilt⟩ **2** : extra large ⟨*maxi*-problems⟩

max·il·la \mak-'si-lə\ *n, pl* **max·il·lae** \-'si-(ˌ)lē\ *or* **maxil·las** : JAW 1; *esp* : an upper jaw — **max·il·lary** \'mak-sə-ˌler-ē\ *adj*

max·im \'mak-səm\ *n* : a proverbial saying

max·i·mal \'mak-sə-məl\ *adj* : MAXIMUM — **max·i·mal·ly** *adv*

max·i·mise *Brit var of* MAXIMIZE

max·i·mize \'mak-sə-ˌmīz\ *vb* **-mized; -miz·ing** **1** : to increase to a maximum **2** : to make the most of — **max·i·mi·za·tion** \ˌmak-sə-mə-'zā-shən\ *n*

max·i·mum \'mak-sə-məm\ *n, pl* **-ma** \-mə\ *or* **-mums** **1** : the greatest quantity, value, or degree **2** : an upper limit allowed by authority **3** : the largest of a set of numbers — **maximum** *adj*

max out *vb* **1** : to push to or reach a limit or an extreme **2** : to use up all available credit on (a credit card)

may \'mā\ *verbal auxiliary, past* **might** \'mīt\ *pres sing & pl* **may** **1** : have permission or liberty to ⟨you ～ go now⟩ **2** : be in some degree likely to ⟨you ～ be right⟩ **3** — used as an auxiliary to express a wish, purpose, contingency, or concession ⟨～ the best man win⟩

May \'mā\ *n* [ME, fr. OF *mai*, fr. L *Maius*, fr. *Maia*, Roman goddess] : the 5th month of the year

Ma·ya \'mī-ə\ *n, pl* **Maya** *or* **Mayas** : a member of a group of American Indian peoples of Yucatán, Guatemala, and adjacent areas — **Ma·yan** \'mī-ən\ *n or adj*

may·ap·ple \'mā-ˌa-pəl\ *n* : a No. American woodland herb related to the barberry that has a poisonous root, one or two large leaves, and an edible egg-shaped yellow fruit

may·be \'mā-bē, 'me-\ *adv* : PERHAPS

May Day \'mā-ˌdā\ *n* : May 1 celebrated as a springtime festival and in some countries as Labor Day

may·flow·er \'mā-ˌflaú(-ə)r\ *n* : any of several spring blooming herbs (as the trailing arbutus or an anemone)

may·fly \'mā-flī\ *n* : any of an order of insects with an aquatic nymph and a short-lived fragile adult having membranous wings

mayfly

may·hem \'mā-ˌhem, 'mā-əm\ *n* **1** : willful and permanent crippling, mutilation, or disfigurement of a person **2** : needless or willful damage

may·on·naise \'mā-ə-ˌnāz\ *n* [F] : a dressing made of egg yolks, vegetable oil, and vinegar or lemon juice

may·or \'mā-ər\ *n* : an official elected to act as chief executive or nominal head of a city or borough — **may·or·al** \-əl\ *adj* — **may·or·al·ty** \-əl-tē\ *n*

may·pole \'mā-ˌpōl\ *n, often cap* : a tall flower-wreathed pole forming a center for May Day sports and dances

maze \'māz\ *n* : a confusing intricate network of passages — **mazy** *adj*

ma·zur·ka \mə-'zər-kə\ *n* : a Polish dance in moderate triple measure

MB *abbr* Manitoba

MBA *abbr* master of business administration

mc *abbr* megacycle

¹MC *n* : MASTER OF CEREMONIES

²MC *abbr* member of Congress

Mc- \mək; mə *before forms beginning with* k *or* g\ *prefix* : used to indicate a convenient, low-quality version of a specified thing ⟨*Mc*Book⟩

Mc·Coy \mə-'kȯi\ *n* : something that is neither imitation nor substitute ⟨the real ～⟩

McGuffin *var of* MACGUFFIN

MCPO *abbr* master chief petty officer

¹Md *abbr* Maryland

²Md *symbol* mendelevium

MD *abbr* **1** [NL *medicinae doctor*] doctor of medicine **2** Maryland **3** muscular dystrophy

MDMA \ˌem-ˌdē-ˌem-'ā\ *n* : ECSTASY 2

mdnt *abbr* midnight

mdse *abbr* merchandise

MDT *abbr* mountain daylight (saving) time

me \'mē\ *pron, objective case of* I

Me *abbr* Maine

ME *abbr* **1** Maine **2** mechanical engineer **3** medical examiner

¹mead \'mēd\ *n* : an alcoholic beverage brewed from water and honey, malt, and yeast

²mead *n, archaic* : MEADOW

mead·ow \'me-dō\ *n* : land in or mainly in grass; *esp* : a tract of moist low-lying usu. level grassland — **mead·ow·land** \-,land\ *n* — **mead·owy** \'me-də-wē\ *adj*

mead·ow·lark \'me-dō-,lärk\ *n* : any of several American songbirds related to the orioles that are streaked brown above and in northernmost forms have a yellow breast marked with a black crescent

mead·ow·sweet \-,swēt\ *n* : a No. American native or naturalized spirea

mea·ger *or* **mea·gre** \'mē-gər\ *adj* 1 : THIN 2 : lacking richness, fertility, or strength; *also* : POOR ⟨a ∼ income⟩ ♦ **Synonyms** SCANTY, SCANT, SPARE, SPARSE — **mea·ger·ly** *adv* — **mea·ger·ness** *n*

¹meal \'mēl\ *n* 1 : an act or the time of eating a portion of food 2 : the portion of food eaten at a meal

²meal *n* 1 : usu. coarsely ground seeds of a cereal 2 : a product resembling seed meal — **mealy** *adj*

meal·time \'mēl-,tīm\ *n* : the usual time at which a meal is served

mealy·bug \'mē-lē-,bəg\ *n* : any of a family of scale insects with a white cottony or waxy covering that are destructive pests esp. of fruit trees

mealy·mouthed \'mē-lē-,maủthd, -,maủtht\ *adj* : not plain and straightforward : DEVIOUS

¹mean \'mēn\ *vb* **meant** \'ment\; **mean·ing** 1 : to have in the mind as a purpose 2 : to serve to convey, show, or indicate : SIGNIFY ⟨red ∼s stop⟩ 3 : to have importance to the degree of ⟨∼s the world to me⟩ 4 : to direct to a particular individual ⟨a gift *meant* for me⟩

²mean *adj* 1 : HUMBLE 2 : lacking acumen : DULL 3 : SHABBY, CONTEMPTIBLE ⟨no ∼ feat⟩ 4 : IGNOBLE, BASE 5 : STINGY 6 : pettily selfish or malicious 7 : VEXATIOUS 8 : EXCELLENT ⟨throws a ∼ slider⟩ — **mean·ly** *adv* — **mean·ness** *n*

³mean *adj* 1 : occupying a middle position (as in space, order, or time) 2 : being a mean : AVERAGE ⟨a ∼ value⟩

⁴mean *n* 1 : a middle point between extremes 2 *pl* : something helpful in achieving a desired end 3 *pl* : material resources affording a secure life 4 : ARITHMETIC MEAN

¹me·an·der \mē-'an-dər\ *n* [L *maeander*, fr. Gk *maiandros*, fr. *Maiandros* (now *Menderes*), river in Asia Minor] 1 : a winding course 2 : a winding of a stream — **me·an·drous** \-drəs\ *adj*

²meander *vb* 1 : to follow a winding course 2 : to wander aimlessly or casually

mean·ing *n* 1 : the thing one intends to convey esp. by language; *also* : the thing that is thus conveyed 2 : AIM 3 : SIGNIFICANCE; *esp* : implication of a hidden significance 4 : CONNOTATION; *also* : DENOTATION — **mean·ing·ful** \-fəl\ *adj* — **mean·ing·ful·ly** *adv* — **mean·ing·less** *adj*

¹mean·time \'mēn-,tīm\ *n* : the intervening time

²meantime *adv* : MEANWHILE

¹mean·while \-,hwīl\ *n* : MEANTIME

²meanwhile *adv* 1 : during the intervening time 2 : at the same time

meas *abbr* measure

mea·sles \'mē-zəlz\ *n sing or pl* : an acute virus disease marked by fever and an eruption of distinct circular red spots

mea·sly \'mēz-lē, -zə-lē\ *adj* **mea·sli·er; -est** : contemptibly small or insignificant

¹mea·sure \'me-zhər, 'mā-\ *n* 1 : an adequate or moderate portion; *also* : a suitable limit 2 : the dimensions, capacity, or amount of something ascertained by measuring; *also* : an instrument for measuring 3 : a unit of measurement; *also* : a system of such units 4 : the act or process of measuring 5 : rhythmic structure or movement 6 : the part of a musical staff between two bars 7 : CRITERION 8 : a means to an end 9 : a legislative bill — **mea·sure·less** *adj*

²measure *vb* **mea·sured; mea·sur·ing** 1 : to mark or fix in multiples of a specific unit ⟨∼ off five centimeters⟩ 2 : to find out the size, extent, or amount of 3 : to bring into comparison or competition 4 : to serve as a means of measuring 5 : to have a specified measurement — **mea·sur·able** \'me-zhə-rə-bəl, 'mā-\ *adj* — **mea·sur·ably** \-blē\ *adv* — **mea·sur·er** *n*

mea·sure·ment \'me-zhər-mənt, 'mā-\ *n* 1 : the act or process of measuring 2 : a figure, extent, or amount obtained by measuring

measure up *vb* 1 : to have necessary or fitting qualifications 2 : to equal esp. in ability

meat \'mēt\ *n* 1 : FOOD; *esp* : solid food as distinguished from drink 2 : animal and esp. mammal flesh considered as food 3 : the edible part inside a covering (as a shell or rind) — **meaty** *adj*

meat·ball \-,bȯl\ *n* : a small ball of chopped or ground meat

meat loaf *n* : a dish of ground meat seasoned and baked in the form of a loaf

mec·ca \'me-kə\ *n, often cap* [*Mecca*, Saudi Arabia, a destination of pilgrims in the Islamic world] : a center of a specified activity or interest ⟨a shopping ∼⟩

mech *abbr* mechanical; mechanics

¹me·chan·ic \mi-'ka-nik\ *adj* : of or relating to manual work or skill

²mechanic *n* 1 : a manual worker 2 : MACHINIST; *esp* : one who repairs cars

me·chan·i·cal \mi-'ka-ni-kəl\ *adj* 1 : of or relating to machinery, to manual operations, or to mechanics 2 : done as if by a machine : AUTOMATIC ⟨a ∼ response⟩ ♦ **Synonyms** INSTINCTIVE, IMPULSIVE, SPONTANEOUS — **me·chan·i·cal·ly** \-k(ə-)lē\ *adv*

mechanical drawing *n* : drawing done with the aid of instruments

me·chan·ics \mi-'ka-niks\ *n sing or pl* 1 : a branch of physics that deals with energy and forces and their effect on bodies 2 : the practical application of mechanics (as to the operation of machines) 3 : mechanical or functional details ⟨the ∼ of the brain⟩

mech·a·nism \'me-kə-,ni-zəm\ *n* 1 : a piece of machinery; *also* : a process or technique for achieving a result 2 : mechanical operation or action 3 : the fundamental processes involved in or responsible for a natural phenomenon ⟨the visual ∼⟩

mech·a·nis·tic \,me-kə-'nis-tik\ *adj* 1 : mechanically determined ⟨∼ universe⟩ 2 : MECHANICAL — **mech·a·nis·ti·cal·ly** \-ti-k(ə-)lē\ *adv*

mech·a·nize \'me-kə-,nīz\ *vb* **-nized; -niz·ing** 1 : to make mechanical 2 : to equip with machinery esp. in order to replace human or animal labor 3 : to equip with armed and armored motor vehicles — **mech·a·ni·za·tion** \,me-kə-nə-'zā-shən\ *n* — **mech·a·niz·er** *n*

¹med \'med\ *adj* : MEDICAL ⟨∼ school⟩

²med *n* : MEDICINE 1 — usu. used in pl.

³med *abbr* 1 medical; medicine 2 medieval 3 medium

MEd *abbr* master of education

med·al \'me-d²l\ *n* [MF *medaille*, fr. OIt *medaglia* coin worth half a denarius, medal, fr. VL *medalis* half, alter. of LL *medialis* middle, fr. L *medius*] 1 : a small usu. metal object bearing a religious emblem or picture 2 : a piece of metal issued to commemorate a person or event or to award excellence or achievement

med·al·ist *or* **med·al·list** \'me-d²l-ist\ *n* 1 : a designer or maker of medals 2 : a recipient of a medal as an award

me·dal·lion \mə-'dal-yən\ *n* 1 : a large medal 2 : a tablet or panel bearing a portrait or an ornament

med·dle \'me-d²l\ *vb* **med·dled; med·dling** : to interfere without right or propriety — **med·dler** \'me-d²l-ər\ *n*

med·dle·some \'me-d²l-səm\ *adj* : inclined to meddle

med·e·vac *also* **med·i·vac** \'me-də-,vak\ *n* 1 : emergency evacuation of the sick or wounded 2 : a helicopter used for medevac

me·dia \'mē-dē-ə\ *n, pl* **me·di·as** 1 : MEDIUM 4 2 *sing or pl in constr* : MASS MEDIA

me·di·al \'mē-dē-əl\ *adj* : occurring in or extending toward the middle

¹me·di·an \'mē-dē-ən\ *n* 1 : a value in an ordered set of values below and above which there are an equal number of values 2 : MEDIAN STRIP

²median *adj* 1 : being in the middle or in an intermediate position 2 : relating to or constituting a statistical median

median strip *n* : a strip dividing a highway into lanes according to the direction of travel

me·di·ate \'mē-dē-,āt\ *vb* **-at·ed; -at·ing** 1 : to act as an intermediary; *esp* : to work with opposing sides in order to resolve (as a dispute) or bring about (as a settlement) 2 : to bring about, influence, or transmit (as a physical process or effect) by acting as an intermediate or control-ling agent or mechanism ✦ *Synonyms* INTERCEDE, IN-TERVENE, INTERPOSE, INTERFERE — **me·di·a·tion** \ˌmē-dē-ˈā-shən\ *n* — **me·di·a·tor** \ˈmē-dē-ˌā-tər\ *n*

med·ic \ˈme-dik\ *n* : one engaged in medical work; *esp* : CORPSMAN

med·i·ca·ble \ˈme-di-kə-bəl\ *adj* : CURABLE

Med·ic·aid \ˈme-di-ˌkād\ *n* : a program of financial assis-tance for medical care designed for those unable to afford regular medical service and financed jointly by the state and federal governments

med·i·cal \ˈme-di-kəl\ *adj* : of or relating to the science or practice of medicine or the treatment of disease — **med-i·cal·ly** \-k(ə-)lē\ *adv*

medical examiner *n* : a public officer who performs au-topsies on bodies to find the cause of death

med·i·ca·ment \mi-ˈdi-kə-mənt, ˈme-di-kə-\ *n* : a sub-stance used in therapy

Medi·care \ˈme-di-ˌker\ *n* : a government program of fi-nancial assistance for medical care esp. for the aged

med·i·cate \ˈme-də-ˌkāt\ *vb* **-cat·ed; -cat·ing** : to treat with medicine

med·i·ca·tion \ˌme-də-ˈkā-shən\ *n* **1** : the act or process of medicating **2** : MEDICINE 1

me·dic·i·nal \mə-ˈdi-sᵊn-əl\ *adj* : tending or used to cure disease or relieve pain — **me·dic·i·nal·ly** *adv*

med·i·cine \ˈme-də-sən\ *n* **1** : a substance or preparation used in treating disease **2** : a science and art dealing with the prevention, alleviation, and cure of disease

medicine ball *n* : a heavy stuffed leather ball used for con-ditioning exercises

medicine man *n* : a priestly healer or sorcerer esp. among the American Indians : SHAMAN

med·i·co \ˈme-di-ˌkō\ *n, pl* **-cos** : a medical practitioner or student

me·di·e·val *also* **me·di·ae·val** \ˌmē-dē-ˈē-vəl, ˌme-, ˌmē-ˈdē-vəl\ *adj* **1** : of, relating to, or characteristic of the Middle Ages **2** : having a quality (as cruelty) associated with the Middle Ages **3** : extremely outmoded or antiquated — **me·di·e·val·ism** \-və-ˌli-zəm\ *n* — **me·di·e·val·ist** \-list\ *n*

me·di·o·cre \ˌmē-dē-ˈō-kər\ *adj* [MF, fr. L *mediocris*, fr. *medius* middle + *ocris* stony mountain] : of moderate or low quality : ORDINARY — **me·di·oc·ri·ty** \-ˈä-krə-tē\ *n*

med·i·tate \ˈme-də-ˌtāt\ *vb* **-tat·ed; -tat·ing 1** : to muse over : CONTEMPLATE, PONDER **2** : to engage in deep mental exercise directed toward a heightened level of spiritual awareness **3** : INTEND, PLAN — **med·i·ta·tion** \ˌme-də-ˈtā-shən\ *n* — **med·i·ta·tive** \ˈme-də-ˌtā-tiv\ *adj* — **med·i·ta·tive·ly** *adv*

Med·i·ter·ra·nean \ˌme-də-tə-ˈrā-nē-ən, -ˈrā-nyən\ *adj* : of or relating to the Mediterranean Sea or to the lands or people around it

¹me·di·um \ˈmē-dē-əm\ *n, pl* **mediums** *or* **me·dia** \-dē-ə\ [L] **1** : something in a middle position; *also* : a middle position or degree **2** : a means of effecting or conveying something **3** : a surrounding or enveloping substance **4** : a channel or system of communication, information, or entertainment **5** : a mode of artistic expression **6** : an individual held to be a channel of communication be-tween the earthly world and a world of spirits **7** : a con-dition or environment in which something may function or flourish

²medium *adj* : intermediate in amount, quality, position, or degree

me·di·um·is·tic \ˌmē-dē-ə-ˈmis-tik\ *adj* : of, relating to, or being a spiritualistic medium

medivac *var of* MEDEVAC

med·ley \ˈmed-lē\ *n, pl* **medleys 1** : HODGEPODGE **2** : a musical composition made up esp. of a series of songs

me·dul·la \mə-ˈdə-lə\ *n, pl* **-las** *or* **-lae** \-(ˌ)lē, -ˌlī\ : an inner or deep anatomical part; *also* : the posterior part (**medul-la ob·lon·ga·ta** \-ˌä-ˌbloṅ-ˈgä-tə\) of the vertebrate brain that is continuous with the spinal cord

meed \ˈmēd\ *n* : a fitting return

meek \ˈmēk\ *adj* **1** : enduring injury with patience and without resentment **2** : deficient in spirit and courage **3** : MODERATE — **meek·ly** *adv* — **meek·ness** *n*

meer·schaum \ˈmir-shəm, -ˌshȯm\ *n* [G, fr. *Meer* sea + *Schaum* foam] : a tobacco pipe made of a light white clayey mineral

¹meet \ˈmēt\ *vb* **met** \ˈmet\; **meet·ing 1** : to come upon

: FIND **2** : JOIN, INTERSECT **3** : to appear to the percep-tion of **4** : OPPOSE, FIGHT **5** : to join in conversation or discussion; *also* : ASSEMBLE **6** : to conform to **7** : to pay fully **8** : to cope with **9** : to provide for **10** : to be in-troduced to

²meet *n* : an assembling esp. for a hunt or for competitive sports

³meet *adj* : SUITABLE, PROPER

meet·ing \ˈmē-tiṅ\ *n* **1** : an act of coming together : AS-SEMBLY **2** : JUNCTION, INTERSECTION

meet·ing·house \-ˌhau̇s\ *n* : a building for public assem-bly and esp. for Protestant worship

meg \ˈmeg\ *n* : MEGABYTE

mega- *or* **meg-** *comb form* **1** : great : large ⟨*mega*hit⟩ **2** : million ⟨*mega*hertz⟩

mega·byte \ˈme-gə-ˌbīt\ *n* : 1024 kilobytes or 1,048,576 bytes; *also* : one million bytes

mega·cy·cle \-ˌsī-kəl\ *n* : MEGAHERTZ

mega·death \-ˌdeth\ *n* : one million deaths — used as a unit in reference to nuclear warfare

mega·hertz \ˈme-gə-ˌhərts, -ˌherts\ *n* : a unit of frequency equal to one million hertz

mega·lith \ˈme-gə-ˌlith\ *n* : a large stone used in prehis-toric monuments — **mega·lith·ic** \ˌme-gə-ˈli-thik\ *adj*

meg·a·lo·ma·nia \ˌme-gə-lō-ˈmā-nē-ə, -nyə\ *n* : a mental disorder marked by feelings of personal omnipotence and grandeur — **meg·a·lo·ma·ni·ac** \-ˈmā-nē-ˌak\ *adj or n* — **meg·a·lo·ma·ni·a·cal** \-mə-ˈnī-ə-kəl\ *adj*

meg·a·lop·o·lis \ˌme-gə-ˈlä-pə-ləs\ *n* : a very large urban unit

mega·phone \ˈme-gə-ˌfōn\ *n* : a cone-shaped device used to intensify or direct the voice — **megaphone** *vb*

mega·pix·el \ˈme-gə-ˌpik-səl\ *n* : one million pixels

mega·plex \-ˌpleks\ *n* : a cineplex having usu. at least 16 movie theaters

mega·ton \-ˌtən\ *n* : an explosive force equivalent to that of one million tons of TNT

mega·vi·ta·min \-ˌvī-tə-mən\ *adj* : relating to or consisting of very large doses of vitamins — **mega·vi·ta·mins** *n pl*

mei·o·sis \mī-ˈō-səs\ *n* : a process of cell division in gamete-producing cells in which the number of chromo-somes is reduced to one half — **mei·ot·ic** \mī-ˈä-tik\ *adj*

meit·ner·i·um \mīt-ˈnir-ē-əm, -ˈner-\ *n* : an artificially pro-duced radioactive chemical element

mel·an·cho·lia \ˌme-lən-ˈkō-lē-ə\ *n* : a mental condition marked by extreme depression often with delusions

mel·an·chol·ic \ˌme-lən-ˈkä-lik\ *adj* **1** : DEPRESSED **2** : of or relating to melancholia

mel·an·choly \ˈme-lən-ˌkä-lē\ *n, pl* **-chol·ies** [ME *malen-colie*, fr. AF, fr. LL *melancholia*, fr. Gk, fr. *melan-, melas* black + *cholē* bile; so called fr. the former belief that it was caused by an excess of black bile] : depression of spirits : DEJECTION — **melancholy** *adj*

Mel·a·ne·sian \ˌme-lə-ˈnē-zhən\ *n* : a member of the dom-inant native group of the Pacific island grouping of Melanesia — **Melanesian** *adj*

mé·lange \mā-ˈläⁿzh, -ˈlänj\ *n* : a mixture esp. of incon-gruous elements

mel·a·nin \ˈme-lə-nən\ *n* : any of various dark brown pig-ments of animal or plant structures (as skin or hair)

mel·a·nism \ˈme-lə-ˌni-zəm\ *n* : an increased amount of black or nearly black pigmentation

mel·a·no·ma \ˌme-lə-ˈnō-mə\ *n, pl* **-mas** *also* **-ma·ta** \-mə-tə\ : a usu. malignant tumor containing dark pigment

¹meld \ˈmeld\ *vb* : to show or announce for a score in a card game

²meld *n* : a card or combination of cards that is or can be melded

me·lee \ˈmā-ˌlā, mā-ˈlā\ *n* [F *mêlée*] : a confused struggle ✦ *Synonyms* FRACAS, ROW, BRAWL, DONNYBROOK

me·lio·rate \ˈmēl-yə-ˌrāt, ˈmē-lē-ə-\ *vb* **-rat·ed; -rat·ing** : AMELIORATE — **me·lio·ra·tion** \ˌmēl-yə-ˈrā-shən, ˌmē-lē-ə-\ *n* — **me·lio·ra·tive** \ˈmēl-yə-ˌrā-tiv, ˈmē-lē-ə-\ *adj*

mel·lif·lu·ous \me-ˈli-flə-wəs, mə-\ *adj* [ME *mellyfluous*, fr. LL *mellifluus*, fr. L *mel* honey + *fluere* to flow] : sweetly flowing — **mel·lif·lu·ous·ly** *adv* — **mel·lif·lu·ous·ness** *n*

¹mel·low \ˈme-lō\ *adj* **1** : soft and sweet because of ripe-ness; *also* : well aged and pleasingly mild ⟨~ wine⟩ **2** : made gentle by age or experience **3** : being rich and full but not garish or strident ⟨~ colors⟩ **4** : of soft loamy consistency ⟨~ soil⟩ — **mel·low·ness** *n*

²**mellow** vb : to make or become mellow — often used with out

me·lo·di·ous \mə-'lō-dē-əs\ adj : pleasing to the ear — **me·lo·di·ous·ly** adv — **me·lo·di·ous·ness** n

melo·dra·ma \'me-lə-ˌdrä-mə, -ˌdra-\ n 1 : an extravagantly theatrical play in which action and plot predominate over characterization 2 : something having a sensational or theatrical quality — **melo·dra·mat·ic** \ˌme-lə-drə-'ma-tik\ adj — **melo·dra·mat·i·cal·ly** \-ti-k(ə-)lē\ adv — **melo·dra·ma·tist** \ˌme-lə-'dra-mə-tist, -'drä-\ n

mel·o·dy \'me-lə-dē\ n, pl **-dies** 1 : sweet or agreeable sound 2 : a particular succession of notes : TUNE, AIR — **me·lod·ic** \mə-'lä-dik\ adj — **me·lod·i·cal·ly** \-di-k(ə-)lē\ adv

mel·on \'me-lən\ n : any of various typically sweet fruits (as a muskmelon or watermelon) of the gourd family usu. eaten raw

¹**melt** \'melt\ vb 1 : to change from a solid to a liquid state usu. by heat 2 : DISSOLVE, DISINTEGRATE; also : to cause to disperse or disappear 3 : to make or become tender or gentle

²**melt** n : a melted substance

melt·down \'melt-ˌdau̇n\ n 1 : the melting of the core of a nuclear reactor 2 : a collapse of something (as one's self-control)

melting pot n : a place where different races, cultures, or individuals assimilate into a cohesive whole

melt·wa·ter \-ˌwȯ-tər, -ˌwä-\ n : water derived from the melting of ice and snow

mem abbr 1 member 2 memoir 3 memorial

mem·ber \'mem-bər\ n 1 : a part (as an arm, leg, leaf, or branch) of an animal or plant 2 : one of the individuals composing a group 3 : a part of a whole ⟨~s of a set⟩

mem·ber·ship \-ˌship\ n 1 : the state or status of being a member 2 : the body of members

mem·brane \'mem-ˌbrān\ n : a thin pliable layer esp. of animal or plant origin — **mem·bra·nous** \-brə-nəs\ adj

me·men·to \mə-'men-tō\ n, pl **-tos** or **-toes** [ME, fr. L, remember, imper. of meminisse to remember] : something that serves to warn or remind; also : SOUVENIR

memo \'me-mō\ n, pl **mem·os** : MEMORANDUM

mem·oir \'mem-ˌwär\ n 1 : MEMORANDUM 2 : AUTOBIOGRAPHY — usu. used in pl. 3 : an account of something noteworthy; also, pl : the record of the proceedings of a learned society

mem·o·ra·bil·ia \ˌme-mə-rə-'bi-lē-ə, -'bil-yə\ n pl [L] 1 : things worthy of remembrance 2 : things associated with a particular interest and that are usu. collected : MEMENTOS

mem·o·ra·ble \'me-mə-rə-bəl\ adj : worth remembering : NOTABLE — **mem·o·ra·bil·i·ty** \ˌme-mə-rə-'bi-lə-tē\ n — **mem·o·ra·ble·ness** n — **mem·o·ra·bly** \-blē\ adv

mem·o·ran·dum \ˌme-mə-'ran-dəm\ n, pl **-dums** or **-da** \-də\ 1 : an informal record; also : a written reminder 2 : an informal written note

¹**me·mo·ri·al** \mə-'mȯr-ē-əl\ adj : serving to preserve remembrance

²**memorial** n 1 : something designed to keep remembrance alive; esp : MONUMENT 2 : a statement of facts often accompanied with a petition — **me·mo·ri·al·ize** vb

Memorial Day n : the last Monday in May or formerly May 30 observed as a legal holiday in honor of those who died in war

mem·o·rise Brit var of MEMORIZE

mem·o·rize \'me-mə-ˌrīz\ vb **-rized; -riz·ing** : to learn by heart — **mem·o·ri·za·tion** \ˌme-mə-rə-'zā-shən\ n — **mem·o·riz·er** n

mem·o·ry \'me-mə-rē\ n, pl **-ries** 1 : the power or process of remembering 2 : the store of things remembered 3 : COMMEMORATION 4 : something remembered 5 : the time within which past events are remembered 6 : a device (as in a computer) in which information can be stored; esp : RAM 7 : capacity for storing information ⟨512 megabytes of ~⟩ ✦ **Synonyms** REMEMBRANCE, RECOLLECTION, REMINISCENCE

men pl of MAN

¹**men·ace** \'me-nəs\ n 1 : THREAT 2 : DANGER; also : NUISANCE

²**menace** vb **men·aced; men·ac·ing** 1 : THREATEN 2 : ENDANGER — **men·ac·ing·ly** adv

mé·nage \mā-'näzh\ n [F] : HOUSEHOLD

ménage à trois \-ä-'trwä\ n : an arrangement in which three persons share sexual relations esp. while living together

me·nag·er·ie \mə-'na-jə-rē\ n : a collection of wild animals esp. for exhibition

¹**mend** \'mend\ vb 1 : to improve in manners or morals 2 : to put into good shape : REPAIR 3 : to improve in or restore to health : HEAL — **mend·er** n

²**mend** n 1 : an act of mending 2 : a mended place

men·da·cious \men-'dā-shəs\ adj : given to deception or falsehood : UNTRUTHFUL ✦ **Synonyms** DISHONEST, DECEITFUL — **men·da·cious·ly** adv — **men·dac·i·ty** \-'da-sə-tē\ n

men·de·le·vi·um \ˌmen-də-'lē-vē-əm, -'lā-\ n : a radioactive metallic chemical element artificially produced

men·di·cant \'men-di-kənt\ n 1 : BEGGAR 2 often cap : FRIAR — **men·di·can·cy** \-kən-sē\ n — **mendicant** adj

men·folk \'men-ˌfōk\ or **men·folks** \-ˌfōks\ n pl 1 : men in general 2 : the men of a family or community

men·ha·den \men-'hā-dᵊn, mən-\ n, pl **-den** also **-dens** : a marine fish related to the herring that is abundant along the Atlantic coast of the U.S.

¹**me·nial** \'mē-nē-əl, -nyəl\ n : a domestic servant

²**menial** adj 1 : of or relating to servants 2 : HUMBLE, SERVILE ⟨answered in ~ tones⟩ — **me·ni·al·ly** adv

men·in·gi·tis \ˌme-nən-'jī-təs\ n, pl **-git·i·des** \-'ji-tə-ˌdēz\ : inflammation of the membranes enclosing the brain and spinal cord; also : a usu. bacterial disease marked by this

me·ninx \'mē-niŋks, 'me-\ n, pl **me·nin·ges** \mə-'nin-(ˌ)jēz\ : any of the three membranes that envelop the brain and spinal cord — **men·in·ge·al** \ˌme-nən-'jē-əl\ adj

me·nis·cus \mə-'nis-kəs\ n, pl **me·nis·ci** \-'nis-ˌkī, -ˌkē\ also **me·nis·cus·es** 1 : CRESCENT 2 : the curved upper surface of a column of liquid

men·o·pause \'me-nə-ˌpȯz\ n : the period of life when menstruation stops naturally — **men·o·paus·al** \ˌme-nə-'pȯ-zəl\ adj

me·no·rah \mə-'nȯr-ə\ n [Heb měnōrāh candlestick] : a candelabrum that is used in Jewish worship

men·ses \'men-ˌsēz\ n sing or pl : the menstrual flow

menstrual cycle n : the complete cycle of physiological changes from the beginning of one menstrual period to the beginning of the next

men·stru·a·tion \ˌmen-strə-'wā-shən, men-'strā-\ n : a discharging of bloody matter at approximately monthly intervals from the uterus of breeding-age nonpregnant primate females; also : PERIOD 6 — **men·stru·al** \'men-strə-wəl\ adj — **men·stru·ate** \'men-strə-ˌwāt, -ˌstrāt\ vb

men·su·ra·ble \'men-sə-rə-bəl, '-chə-\ adj : MEASURABLE

men·su·ra·tion \ˌmen-sə-'rā-shən, ˌmen-chə-\ n : MEASUREMENT

-ment n suffix 1 : concrete result, object, or agent of a (specified) action ⟨embankment⟩ ⟨entanglement⟩ 2 : concrete means or instrument of a (specified) action ⟨entertainment⟩ 3 : action : process ⟨encirclement⟩ ⟨development⟩ 4 : place of a (specified) action ⟨encampment⟩ 5 : state : condition ⟨amazement⟩

men·tal \'men-tᵊl\ adj 1 : of or relating to the mind 2 : of, relating to, or affected with a disorder of the mind ⟨~ illness⟩ — **men·tal·ly** adv

mental age n : a measure of a child's mental development in terms of the number of years it takes an average child to reach the same level

mental deficiency n : MENTAL RETARDATION

men·tal·i·ty \men-'ta-lə-tē\ n, pl **-ties** 1 : mental power or capacity 2 : mode or way of thought

mental retardation n : subaverage intellectual ability present from infancy that is characterized by an IQ of 70 or less and problems in development, learning, and social adjustment — **mentally retarded** adj

men·tee \men-'tē\ n : PROTÉGÉ

men·thol \'men-ˌthȯl, -ˌthōl\ n : an alcohol occurring esp. in mint oils that has the odor and cooling properties of peppermint — **men·tho·lat·ed** \-thə-ˌlā-təd\ adj

¹**men·tion** \'men-chən\ n 1 : a brief or casual reference 2 : a formal citation for outstanding achievement

²**mention** vb 1 : to refer to : CITE 2 : to cite for superior achievement — **not to mention** : not even yet counting or considering

men·tor \'men-ˌtȯr, -tər\ *n* : a trusted counselor or guide; *also* : TUTOR, COACH — **mentor** *vb*

menu \'men-yü, 'mān-\ *n, pl* **menus** [F, fr. *menu* small, detailed, fr. OF, fr. L *minutus* minute (adj.)] **1** : a list of the dishes available (as in a restaurant) for a meal; *also* : the dishes served **2** : a list of offerings or options

me·ow \mē-ˈaù\ *vb* : to make the characteristic cry of a cat — **meow** *n*

mer *abbr* meridian

mer·can·tile \'mər-kən-ˌtēl, -ˌtī(-ə)l\ *adj* : of or relating to merchants or trading

¹mer·ce·nary \'mər-sə-ˌner-ē\ *n, pl* **-nar·ies** : a person who serves merely for wages; *esp* : a soldier hired into foreign service

²mercenary *adj* **1** : serving merely for pay or gain **2** : hired for service in a foreign army

mer·cer \'mər-sər\ *n, Brit* : a dealer in usu. expensive fabrics

mer·cer·ise *Brit var of* MERCERIZE

mer·cer·ize \'mər-sə-ˌrīz\ *vb* **-ized; -iz·ing** : to treat cotton yarn or cloth with alkali so that it looks silky or takes a better dye

¹mer·chan·dise \'mər-chən-ˌdīz, -ˌdīs\ *n* : the commodities or goods that are bought and sold in business

²mer·chan·dise \-ˌdīz\ *vb* **-dised; -dis·ing** : to buy and sell in business : TRADE — **mer·chan·dis·er** *n*

mer·chant \'mər-chənt\ *n* **1** : a buyer and seller of commodities for profit **2** : STOREKEEPER

mer·chant·able \'mər-chən-tə-bəl\ *adj* : acceptable to buyers : MARKETABLE

mer·chant·man \'mər-chənt-mən\ *n* : a ship used in commerce

merchant marine *n* : the commercial ships of a nation

merchant ship *n* : MERCHANTMAN

mer·ci·ful·ly \'mər-si-fə-lē\ *adv* **1** : in a merciful manner **2** : FORTUNATELY **2** ⟨~ we didn't have to attend⟩

mer·cu·ri·al \ˌmər-ˈkyùr-ē-əl\ *adj* **1** : unpredictably changeable **2** : MERCURIC — **mer·cu·ri·al·ly** *adv* — **mer·cu·ri·al·ness** *n*

mer·cu·ric \ˌmər-ˈkyùr-ik\ *adj* : of, relating to, or containing mercury

mercuric chloride *n* : a poisonous compound of mercury and chlorine used as an antiseptic and fungicide

mer·cu·ry \'mər-kyə-rē\ *n, pl* **-ries** **1** : a heavy silver-white liquid metallic chemical element used esp. in scientific instruments **2** *cap* : the planet nearest the sun — see PLANET table

mer·cy \'mər-sē\ *n, pl* **mercies** [ME, fr. AF *merci*, fr. ML *merced-, merces*, fr. L, price paid, wages, fr. *merc-, merx* merchandise] **1** : compassion shown to an offender; *also* : imprisonment rather than death for first-degree murder **2** : a blessing resulting from divine favor or compassion; *also* : a fortunate circumstance **3** : compassion shown to victims of misfortune — **mer·ci·ful** \-si-fəl\ *adj* — **mer·ci·less** \-si-ləs\ *adj* — **mer·ci·less·ly** *adv* — **mercy** *adj*

mercy killing *n* : EUTHANASIA

¹mere \'mir\ *n* : LAKE, POOL

²mere *adj, superlative* **mer·est** **1** : not diluted : PURE **2** : being nothing more than ⟨a ~ child⟩ — **mere·ly** *adv*

mer·e·tri·cious \ˌmer-ə-ˈtri-shəs\ *adj* [L *meretricius*, fr. *meretrix* prostitute, fr. *merēre* to earn] : tawdrily attractive ⟨~ trinkets⟩; *also* : SPECIOUS — **mer·e·tri·cious·ly** *adv* — **mer·e·tri·cious·ness** *n*

mer·gan·ser \(ˌ)mər-ˈgan-sər\ *n* : any of various fish-eating wild ducks with a usu. crested head and a slender bill hooked at the end and serrated along the margins

merganser

merge \'mərj\ *vb* **merged; merg·ing** **1** : to blend gradually **2** : to combine, unite, or coalesce into one ◆ *Synonyms* MINGLE, AMALGAMATE, FUSE, INTERFUSE, INTERMINGLE

merg·er \'mər-jər\ *n* **1** : the act or process of merging **2** : absorption by a corporation of one or more others

me·rid·i·an \mə-ˈri-dē-ən\ *n* [ME, fr. AF *meridien*, fr. *meridien* of noon, fr. L *meridianus*, fr. *meridies* noon, south, irreg. fr. *medius* mid + *dies* day] **1** : the highest point : CULMINATION **2** : any of the imaginary circles on the earth's surface passing through the north and south poles **3** : any of the pathways along which the body's vital energy flows according to the theory behind acupuncture — **meridian** *adj*

me·ringue \mə-ˈraŋ\ *n* [F] : a baked dessert topping of stiffly beaten egg whites and powdered sugar

me·ri·no \mə-ˈrē-nō\ *n, pl* **-nos** [Sp] **1** : any of a breed of sheep noted for fine soft wool **2** : a fine soft fabric or yarn of wool or wool and cotton

¹mer·it \'mer-ət\ *n* **1** : laudable or blameworthy traits or actions **2** : a praiseworthy quality; *also* : character or conduct deserving reward or honor **3** *pl* : the intrinsic nature of a legal case; *also* : legal significance

²merit *vb* : EARN, DESERVE

mer·i·toc·ra·cy \ˌmer-ə-ˈtä-krə-sē\ *n, pl* **-cies** : a system in which the talented are chosen and moved ahead based on their achievement; *also* : leadership by the talented

mer·i·to·ri·ous \ˌmer-ə-ˈtȯr-ē-əs\ *adj* : deserving honor or esteem — **mer·i·to·ri·ous·ly** *adv* — **mer·i·to·ri·ous·ness** *n*

mer·lin \'mər-lən\ *n* : a small compact falcon of the northern hemisphere

mer·lot \mer-ˈlō, mər-\ *n* : a dry red wine made from a widely grown grape; *also* : the grape itself

mer·maid \'mər-ˌmād\ *n* : a legendary sea creature with a woman's upper body and a fish's tail

mer·man \-ˌman, -mən\ *n* : a legendary sea creature with a man's upper body and a fish's tail

mer·ri·ment \'mer-i-mənt\ *n* **1** : HILARITY **2** : FESTIVITY

mer·ry \'mer-ē\ *adj* **mer·ri·er; -est** **1** : full of gaiety or high spirits **2** : marked by festivity **3** : BRISK ⟨a ~pace⟩ ◆ *Synonyms* BLITHE, JOCUND, JOVIAL, JOLLY, MIRTHFUL — **mer·ri·ly** \'mer-ə-lē\ *adv*

merry-go-round \'mer-ē-gō-ˌraùnd\ *n* **1** : a circular revolving platform with benches and figures of animals on which people sit for a ride **2** : a busy round of activities

mer·ry·mak·ing \'mer-ē-ˌmā-kiŋ\ *n* **1** : jovial or festive activity **2** : a festive occasion — **mer·ry·mak·er** \-ˌmā-kər\ *n*

me·sa \'mā-sə\ *n* [Sp, lit., table, fr. L *mensa*] : a flat-topped hill with steep sides

mes·cal \me-ˈskal, mə-\ *n* **1** : PEYOTE **2** **2** : a usu. colorless liquor distilled from the leaves of an agave; *also* : this agave

mes·ca·line \'mes-kə-lən, -ˌlēn\ *n* : a hallucinatory alkaloid from the peyote cactus

mes·clun \'mes-klən\ *n* : a mixture of young tender greens; *also* : a salad made with mesclun

mesdames *pl of* MADAM, *or of* MADAME, *or of* MRS.

mesdemoiselles *pl of* MADEMOISELLE

¹mesh \'mesh\ *n* **1** : one of the openings between the threads or cords of a net; *also* : one of the similar spaces in a network **2** : the fabric of a net **3** : NETWORK **4** : working contact (as of the teeth of gears) ⟨in ~⟩ — **meshed** \'mesht\ *adj*

²mesh *vb* **1** : to catch in or as if in a mesh **2** : to be in or come into mesh : ENGAGE **3** : to fit together properly

mesh·work \'mesh-ˌwərk\ *n* : NETWORK

me·si·al \'mē-zē-əl, -sē-\ *adj* : of, relating to, or being the surface of a tooth that is closest to the middle of the front of the jaw

mes·mer·ise *Brit var of* MESMERIZE

mes·mer·ize \'mez-mə-ˌrīz\ *vb* **-ized; -iz·ing** : HYPNOTIZE — **mes·mer·ic** \mez-ˈmer-ik\ *adj* — **mes·mer·ism** \'mez-mə-ˌri-zəm\ *n*

Me·so·lith·ic \ˌme-zə-ˈli-thik\ *adj* : of, relating to, or being a transitional period of the Stone Age between the Paleolithic and the Neolithic periods

me·so·sphere \'me-zə-ˌsfir\ *n* : a layer of the atmosphere between the stratosphere and the thermosphere

Me·so·zo·ic \ˌme-zə-ˈzō-ik, ˌmē-\ *adj* : of, relating to, or being the era of geologic history between the Paleozoic and the Cenozoic and extending from about 245 million years ago to about 65 million years ago — **Mesozoic** n

mes·quite \mə-'skēt, me-\ n : any of several spiny leguminous trees and shrubs chiefly of the southwestern U.S. with sugar-rich pods important as fodder; also : mesquite wood used esp. in grilling food

¹**mess** \'mes\ n [ME mes, fr. AF, fr. LL missus course at a meal, fr. missus, pp. of mittere to put, fr. L, to send] 1 : a quantity of food; also : enough food of a specified kind for a dish or meal ⟨a ∼ of beans⟩ 2 : a group of persons who regularly eat together; also : a meal eaten by such a group 3 : a place where meals are regularly served to a group 4 : a confused, dirty, or offensive state — **messy** adj

²**mess** vb 1 : to supply with meals; also : to take meals with a mess 2 : to make dirty or untidy; also : BUNGLE 3 : INTERFERE, MEDDLE ⟨don't ∼ with me⟩ 4 : PUTTER, TRIFLE

mes·sage \'me-sij\ n : a communication sent by one person to another

message board n : BULLETIN BOARD 2

messeigneurs pl of MONSEIGNEUR

mes·sen·ger \'me-sⁿn-jər\ n : one who carries a message or does an errand

messenger RNA n : an RNA that carries the code for a particular protein from DNA in the nucleus to a ribosome in the cytoplasm and acts as a template for the formation of that protein

Mes·si·ah \mə-'sī-ə\ n 1 : the expected king and deliverer of the Jews 2 : Jesus 3 not cap : a professed or accepted leader of a cause — **mes·si·an·ic** \ˌme-sē-'a-nik\ adj

messieurs pl of MONSIEUR

mess·mate \'mes-ˌmāt\ n : a member of a group who eat regularly together

Messrs. \'me-sərz\ pl of MR.

mes·ti·zo \me-'stē-zō\ n, pl **-zos** [Sp] : a person of mixed blood

¹**met** past and past part of MEET

²**met** abbr metropolitan

me·tab·o·lism \mə-'ta-bə-ˌli-zəm\ n : the processes by which the substance of plants and animals incidental to life is built up and broken down; also : the processes by which a substance is handled in the living body ⟨the ∼ of sugar⟩ — **met·a·bol·ic** \ˌme-tə-'bä-lik\ adj — **me·tab·o·lize** \mə-'ta-bə-ˌlīz\ vb

me·tab·o·lite \-ˌlīt\ n 1 : a product of metabolism 2 : a substance essential to the metabolism of a particular organism or to a metabolic process

meta·car·pal \ˌme-tə-'kär-pəl\ n : any of usu. five more or less elongated bones of the part of the hand or forefoot between the wrist and the bones of the digits — **metacarpal** adj

meta·car·pus \-'kär-pəs\ n : the part of the hand or forefoot that contains the metacarpals

met·al \'me-tᵊl\ n 1 : any of various opaque, fusible, ductile, and typically lustrous substances that are good conductors of electricity and heat 2 : METTLE; also : the material out of which a person or thing is made — **me·tal·lic** \mə-'ta-lik\ adj

met·al·lur·gy \'me-tᵊl-ˌər-jē\ n : the science and technology of metals — **met·al·lur·gi·cal** \ˌme-tᵊl-'ər-ji-kəl\ adj — **met·al·lur·gist** \'me-tᵊl-ˌər-jist\ n

met·al·ware \'me-tᵊl-ˌwer\ n : metal utensils for household use

met·al·work \-ˌwərk\ n : work and esp. artistic work made of metal — **met·al·work·er** \-ˌwər-kər\ n — **met·al·work·ing** n

meta·mor·phism \ˌme-tə-'mȯr-ˌfi-zəm\ n : a change in the structure of rock; esp : a change to a more compact and more highly crystalline form produced by pressure, heat, and water — **meta·mor·phic** \-'mȯr-fik\ adj

meta·mor·pho·sis \ˌme-tə-'mȯr-fə-səs\ n, pl **-pho·ses** \-ˌsēz\ 1 : a change of physical form, structure, or substance esp. by supernatural means; also : a striking alteration (as in appearance or character) 2 : a fundamental change in form and often habits of an animal accompanying the transformation of a larva into an adult — **meta·mor·phose** \-ˌfōz, -ˌfōs\ vb

met·a·phor \'me-tə-ˌfȯr\ n : a figure of speech in which a word for one idea or thing is used in place of another to suggest a likeness between them (as in "the ship plows the sea") — **met·a·phor·ic** \ˌme-tə-'fȯr-ik\ or **met·a·phor·i·cal** \ˌme-tə-'fȯr-i-kəl\ adj — **met·a·phor·i·cal·ly** \-i-k(ə-)lē\ adv

meta·phys·ics \ˌme-tə-'fi-ziks\ n [ML Metaphysica, title of Aristotle's treatise on the subject, fr. Gk (ta) meta (ta) physika, lit., the (works) after the physical (works); fr. its position in his collected works] : the philosophical study of the ultimate causes and underlying nature of things — **meta·phys·i·cal** \-'fi-zi-kəl\ adj — **meta·phy·si·cian** \-fə-'zi-shən\ n

me·tas·ta·sis \mə-'tas-tə-səs\ n, pl **-ta·ses** \-ˌsēz\ : the spread of a health-impairing agency (as cancer cells) from the initial or primary site of disease to another part of the body; also : a secondary growth of a malignant tumor — **me·tas·ta·size** \-tə-ˌsīz\ vb — **met·a·stat·ic** \ˌme-tə-'sta-tik\ adj

meta·tar·sal \ˌme-tə-'tär-səl\ n : any of the bones of the foot between the tarsus and the bones of the digits that in humans include five elongated bones — **metatarsal** adj

meta·tar·sus \-'tär-səs\ n : the part of the human foot or the hind foot in quadrupeds that contains the metatarsals

¹**mete** \'mēt\ vb **met·ed; met·ing** 1 archaic : MEASURE 2 : ALLOT — usu. used with out ⟨∼ out punishment⟩

²**mete** n : BOUNDARY ⟨∼s and bounds⟩

me·te·or \'mē-tē-ər, -ˌȯr\ n 1 : a small particle of matter in the solar system directly observable only by its glow from frictional heating on falling into the earth's atmosphere 2 : the streak of light produced by a meteor

me·te·or·ic \ˌmē-tē-'ȯr-ik\ adj 1 : of, relating to, or resembling a meteor 2 : transiently brilliant ⟨a ∼ career⟩ — **me·te·or·i·cal·ly** \-i-k(ə-)lē\ adv

me·te·or·ite \'mē-tē-ə-ˌrīt\ n : a meteor that reaches the surface of the earth

me·te·or·oid \'mē-tē-ə-ˌrȯid\ n : a small particle of matter in the solar system

me·te·o·rol·o·gy \ˌmē-tē-ə-'rä-lə-jē\ n : a science that deals with the atmosphere and its phenomena and esp. with weather forecasting — **me·te·o·ro·log·ic** \ˌmē-tē-ˌȯr-ə-'lä-jik\ or **me·te·o·ro·log·i·cal** \-'lä-ji-kəl\ adj — **me·te·o·rol·o·gist** \ˌmē-tē-ə-'rä-lə-jist\ n

¹**me·ter** \'mē-tər\ n : rhythm in verse or music

²**meter** n : the basic metric unit of length — see METRIC SYSTEM table

³**meter** n : a measuring and sometimes recording instrument

⁴**meter** vb 1 : to measure by means of a meter 2 : to print postal indicia on by means of a postage meter ⟨∼ed mail⟩

meter–kilogram–second adj : of, relating to, or being a system of units based on the meter, the kilogram, and the second

meter maid n : a woman assigned to write tickets for parking violations

meth·a·done \'me-thə-ˌdōn\ also **meth·a·don** \-ˌdän\ n : a synthetic addictive narcotic drug used esp. as a substitute narcotic in the treatment of heroin addiction

meth·am·phet·amine \ˌme-tham-'fe-tə-ˌmēn, -thəm-, -mən\ n : a drug used medically in the form of its hydrochloride in the treatment of obesity and often illicitly as a stimulant

meth·ane \'me-ˌthān\ n : a colorless odorless flammable gas produced by decomposition of organic matter or from coal and used esp. as a fuel

meth·a·nol \'me-thə-ˌnȯl, -ˌnōl\ n : a volatile flammable poisonous liquid alcohol used esp. as a solvent and as an antifreeze

meth·aqua·lone \me-'tha-kwə-ˌlōn\ n : a sedative and hypnotic habit-forming drug that is not a barbiturate

meth·od \'me-thəd\ n [ME, prescribed treatment, fr. L methodus, fr. Gk methodos, fr. meta with + hodos way] 1 : a procedure or process for achieving an end 2 : orderly arrangement : PLAN ◆ **Synonyms** MODE, MANNER, WAY, FASHION, SYSTEM — **me·thod·i·cal** \mə-'thä-di-kəl\ adj — **me·thod·i·cal·ly** \-k(ə-)lē\ adv — **me·thod·i·cal·ness** n

meth·od·ise Brit var of METHODIZE

Meth·od·ist \'me-thə-dist\ n : a member of a Protestant denomination adhering to the doctrines of John Wesley — **Meth·od·ism** \-ˌdi-zəm\ n

meth·od·ize \'me-thə-ˌdīz\ vb **-ized; -iz·ing** : SYSTEMATIZE

meth·od·ol·o·gy \ˌme-thə-'dä-lə-jē\ *n, pl* **-gies** **1** : a body of methods and rules followed in a science or discipline **2** : the study of the principles or procedures of inquiry in a particular field

meth·yl \'me-thəl\ *n* : a chemical radical consisting of carbon and hydrogen

methyl alcohol *n* : METHANOL

meth·yl·mer·cury \ˌme-thəl-'mər-kyə-rē\ *n* : any of various toxic compounds of mercury that often occur as pollutants which accumulate in animals esp. at the top of a food chain

met·i·cal \'me-ti-kəl\ *n, pl* **met·i·cais** \-kī\ *also* **meticals** — see MONEY table

me·tic·u·lous \mə-'ti-kyə-ləs\ *adj* [L *meticulosus* fearful, fr. *metus* fear] : extremely careful in attending to details — **me·tic·u·lous·ly** *adv* — **me·tic·u·lous·ness** *n*

mé·tier \'me-ˌtyā, me-'tyā\ *n* : an area of activity in which one is expert or successful

me·tre \'mē-tər\ *chiefly Brit var of* METER

met·ric \'me-trik\ *adj* **1** : of or relating to measurement; *esp* : of or relating to the metric system **2** : METRICAL 1

met·ri·cal \'me-tri-kəl\ *adj* **1** : of, relating to, or composed in meter **2** : METRIC 1 — **met·ri·cal·ly** \-k(ə-)lē\ *adv*

met·ri·ca·tion \ˌme-tri-'kā-shən\ *n* : the act or process of converting into or expressing in the metric system

met·ri·cize \'me-trə-ˌsīz\ *vb* **-cized; -ciz·ing** : to change into or express in the metric system

metric system *n* : a decimal system of weights and measures based on the meter and on the kilogram
☞ the METRIC SYSTEM table is on page 310

metric ton *n* — see METRIC SYSTEM table

¹me·tro \'me-trō\ *n, pl* **metros** : SUBWAY

²metro *adj* : of, relating to, or characteristic of a metropolis and sometimes including its suburbs

met·ro·nome \'me-trə-ˌnōm\ *n* : an instrument for marking exact time by a regularly repeated tick

me·trop·o·lis \mə-'trä-pə-ləs\ *n* [ME, fr. LL, fr. Gk *mētropolis*, fr. *mētēr* mother + *polis* city] : the chief or capital city of a country, state, or region — **met·ro·pol·i·tan** \ˌme-trə-'pä-lə-tən\ *adj*

met·tle \'me-t³l\ *n* **1** : SPIRIT, COURAGE **2** : quality of temperament

met·tle·some \'me-t³l-səm\ *adj* : full of mettle : COURAGEOUS

MeV *abbr* million electron volts

¹mew \'myü\ *vb* : MEOW — **mew** *n*

²mew *vb* : CONFINE

mews \'myüz\ *n sing or pl, chiefly Brit* : stables usu. with living quarters built around a court; *also* : a narrow street with dwellings converted from stables

Mex *abbr* Mexican; Mexico

mez·za·nine \'me-zə-ˌnēn, ˌme-zə-'\ *n* **1** : a low-ceilinged story between two main stories of a building **2** : the lowest balcony in a theater; *also* : the first few rows of such a balcony

mez·zo for·te \ˌmet-(ˌ)sō-'for-ˌtā, ˌmed-(ˌ)zō-, -tē\ *adj or adv* [It] : moderately loud — used as a direction in music

mez·zo pia·no \-pē-'ä-(ˌ)nō\ *adj or adv* [It] : moderately soft — used as a direction in music

mez·zo-so·pra·no \-sə-'pra-nō, -'prä-\ *n* : a woman's voice having a range between that of the soprano and contralto; *also* : a singer having such a voice

MFA *abbr* master of fine arts

mfr *abbr* manufacture; manufacturer

mg *abbr* milligram

Mg *symbol* magnesium

MG *abbr* **1** machine gun **2** major general **3** military government

mgr *abbr* **1** manager **2** monseigneur **3** monsignor

mgt *or* **mgmt** *abbr* management

MGy Sgt *abbr* master gunnery sergeant

MHz *abbr* megahertz

mi *abbr* **1** mile; mileage **2** mill

MI *abbr* **1** Michigan **2** military intelligence

MIA \ˌem-(ˌ)ī-'ā\ *n* [*missing in action*] : a member of the armed forces whose whereabouts following a combat mission are unknown

Mi·ami \mī-'a-mē, -mə\ *n, pl* **Mi·ami** *or* **Mi·am·is** : a member of an American Indian people orig. of Wisconsin and Indiana

mi·as·ma \mī-'az-mə, mē-\ *n, pl* **-mas** *also* **-ma·ta** \-mə-tə\ **1** : a vapor from a swamp formerly believed to cause disease **2** : a harmful influence or atmosphere — **mi·as·mal** \-məl\ *adj* — **mi·as·mic** \-mik\ *adj*

mic \'mik\ *n* : MICROPHONE

Mic *abbr* Micah

mi·ca \'mī-kə\ *n* [NL, fr. L, grain, crumb] : any of various mineral silicates readily separable into thin transparent sheets

Mi·cah \'mī-kə\ *n* — see BIBLE table

mice *pl of* MOUSE

Mich *abbr* Michigan

Mi·che·as \'mī-kē-əs, mī-'kē-əs\ *n* : MICAH

Mic·mac \'mik-ˌmak\ *n, pl* **Micmac** *or* **Micmacs** : a member of an American Indian people of eastern Canada

micr- *or* **micro-** *comb form* **1** : small : minute ⟨*microcapsule*⟩ **2** : one millionth part of a specified unit ⟨*microsecond*⟩

¹mi·cro \'mī-krō\ *adj* **1** : very small; *esp* : MICROSCOPIC **2** : involving minute quantities or variations

²micro *n* : MICROCOMPUTER

mi·crobe \'mī-ˌkrōb\ *n* : MICROORGANISM; *esp* : one causing disease — **mi·cro·bi·al** \mī-'krō-bē-əl\ *adj*

mi·cro·bi·ol·o·gy \ˌmī-krō-bī-'ä-lə-jē\ *n* : a branch of biology dealing esp. with microscopic forms of life — **mi·cro·bi·o·log·i·cal** \-ˌbī-ə-'lä-ji-kəl\ *adj* — **mi·cro·bi·ol·o·gist** \-bī-'ä-lə-jist\ *n*

mi·cro·brew·ery \'mī-krō-ˌbrü-ə-rē\ *n* : a small brewery making specialty beer in limited quantities

mi·cro·burst \-ˌbərst\ *n* : a violent short-lived localized downdraft that creates extreme wind shears at low altitudes

mi·cro·cap·sule \'mī-krō-ˌkap-səl, -ˌsül\ *n* : a tiny capsule containing material (as a medicine) released when the capsule is broken, melted, or dissolved

mi·cro·chip \-ˌchip\ *n* : INTEGRATED CIRCUIT

mi·cro·cir·cuit \-ˌsər-kət\ *n* : a compact electronic circuit

mi·cro·com·put·er \-kəm-ˌpyü-tər\ *n* : a small computer that uses a microprocessor; *esp* : PERSONAL COMPUTER

mi·cro·cosm \'mī-krə-ˌkä-zəm\ *n* : an individual or community thought of as a miniature world or universe

mi·cro·elec·tron·ics \ˌmī-krō-i-ˌlek-'trä-niks\ *n* : a branch of electronics that deals with the miniaturization of electronic circuits and components — **mi·cro·elec·tron·ic** \-nik\ *adj*

mi·cro·en·cap·su·late \ˌmī-krō-in-'kap-sə-ˌlāt\ *vb* : to enclose (as a drug) in a microcapsule — **mi·cro·en·cap·su·la·tion** \-in-ˌkap-sə-'lā-shən\ *n*

mi·cro·fi·ber \'mī-krō-ˌfī-bər\ *n* : a fine usu. soft polyester fiber; *also* : fabric made from such fibers

mi·cro·fiche \'mī-krō-ˌfēsh, -ˌfish\ *n, pl* **-fiche** *or* **-fiches** *same or* -ˌfē-shəz, -ˌfi-\ : a sheet of microfilm containing rows of images of pages of printed matter

mi·cro·film \-ˌfilm\ *n* : a film bearing a photographic record (as of print) on a reduced scale — **microfilm** *vb*

mi·cro·graph \'mī-krə-ˌgraf\ *n* : a graphic reproduction of the image of an object formed by a microscope

mi·cro·man·age \ˌmī-krō-'ma-nij\ *vb* : to manage esp. with excessive control or attention to details — **mi·cro·man·age·ment** \-mənt\ *n* — **mi·cro·man·ag·er** \-ni-jər\ *n*

mi·cro·me·te·or·ite \ˌmī-krō-'mē-tē-ə-ˌrīt\ *n* : a very small particle in interplanetary space

mi·crom·e·ter \mī-'krä-mə-tər\ *n* : an instrument used with a telescope or microscope for measuring minute distances

mi·cro·min·ia·tur·i·za·tion \ˌmī-krō-ˌmi-nē-ə-ˌchúr-ə-'zā-shən, -ˌmi-ni-ˌchúr-, -chər-\ *n* : the process of producing things in a very small size and esp. in a smaller than one considered miniature — **mi·cro·min·ia·tur·ized** \-'mi-nē-ə-chə-ˌrīzd, -'mi-ni-chə-\ *adj*

mi·cron \'mī-ˌkrän\ *n* : one millionth of a meter

mi·cro·or·gan·ism \ˌmī-krō-'ór-gə-ˌni-zəm\ *n* : an organism (as a bacterium) too tiny to be seen by the unaided eye

mi·cro·phone \'mī-krə-ˌfōn\ *n* : an instrument for converting sound waves into variations of an electric current for transmitting or recording sound

mi·cro·pho·to·graph \ˌmī-krə-'fō-tə-ˌgraf\ *n* : PHOTOMICROGRAPH

mi·cro·pro·ces·sor \ˌmī-krō-'prä-se-sər\ *n* : a computer processor contained on a microchip

mi·cro·scope \'mī-krə-ˌskōp\ *n* : an instrument for mak-

METRIC SYSTEM

LENGTH

UNIT (SYMBOL)	METRIC EQUIVALENT	U.S. EQUIVALENT
kilometer (km)	1,000 meters	0.62 mile
hectometer (hm)	100 meters	328.08 feet
dekameter (dam)	10 meters	32.81 feet
meter (m)	1 meter	39.37 inches
decimeter (dm)	0.1 meter	3.94 inches
centimeter (cm)	0.01 meter	0.39 inch
millimeter (mm)	0.001 meter	0.039 inch
micrometer (μm)	0.000001 meter	0.000039 inch

AREA

UNIT (SYMBOL)	METRIC EQUIVALENT	U.S. EQUIVALENT
square kilometer (sq km *or* km^2)	1,000,000 square meters	0.39 square miles
hectare (ha)	10,000 square meters	2.47 acres
are (a)	100 square meters	119.60 square yards
square centimeter (sq cm *or* cm^2)	0.0001 square meter	0.16 square inch

VOLUME

UNIT (SYMBOL)	METRIC EQUIVALENT	U.S. EQUIVALENT
cubic meter (m^3)		1.31 cubic yards
cubic decimeter (dm^3)	0.001 cubic meter	61.02 cubic inches
cubic centimeter (cu cm *or* cm^3 *also* cc)	0.000001 cubic meter	0.061 cubic inch

MASS AND WEIGHT

UNIT (SYMBOL)	METRIC EQUIVALENT	U.S. EQUIVALENT
metric ton (t)	1,000,000 grams	1.10 short tons
kilogram (kg)	1,000 grams	2.20 pounds
hectogram (hg)	100 grams	3.53 ounces
dekagram (dag)	10 grams	0.35 ounce
gram (g)		0.035 ounce
decigram (dg)	0.1 gram	1.54 grains
centigram (cg)	0.01 gram	0.15 grain
milligram (mg)	0.001 gram	0.015 grain
microgram (μg *or* mcg)	0.000001 gram	0.000015 grain

CAPACITY

UNIT (SYMBOL)	METRIC EQUIVALENT	U.S. EQUIVALENT		
		CUBIC	*DRY*	*LIQUID*
kiloliter (kl)	1,000 liters	1.31 cubic yards	28.38 bushels	264.17 gallons
hectoliter (hl)	100 liters	3.53 cubic feet	2.84 bushels	26.42 gallons
dekaliter (dal)	10 liters	0.35 cubic foot	1.14 pecks	2.64 gallons
liter (l)		61.02 cubic inches	0.91 quart	1.06 quarts
deciliter (dl)	0.1 liter	6.10 cubic inches	0.18 pint	0.21 pint
centiliter (cl)	0.01 liter	0.61 cubic inch		0.34 fluid ounce
milliliter (ml)	0.001 liter	0.061 cubic inch		0.27 fluid dram
microliter (μl)	0.000001 liter	0.000061 cubic inch		0.00027 fluid dram

For metric system equivalents of U.S. system units, see WEIGHTS AND MEASURES table.

ing magnified images of minute objects usu. using light — **mi·cros·co·py** \mī-'kräs-kə-pē\ *n*

mi·cro·scop·ic \ˌmī-krə-'skä-pik\ *also* **mi·cro·scop·i·cal** \-pi-kəl\ *adj* **1** : of, relating to, or involving the use of the microscope **2** : too tiny to be seen without the use of a microscope : very small — **mi·cro·scop·i·cal·ly** \-pi-k(ə-)lē\ *adv*

mi·cro·sec·ond \'mī-krō-ˌse-kənd\ *n* : one millionth of a second

mi·cro·sur·gery \ˌmī-krō-'sər-jə-rē\ *n* : minute dissection or manipulation (as by a laser beam) of living structures or tissue — **mi·cro·sur·gi·cal** \-'sər-ji-kəl\ *adj*

mi·cro·tech·nol·o·gy \-tek-'nä-lə-jē\ *n* : technology on a small or microscopic scale

¹**mi·cro·wave** \'mī-krə-ˌwāv\ *n* **1** : a radio wave between one millimeter and one meter in wavelength **2** : MICROWAVE OVEN

²**microwave** *vb* : to heat or cook in a microwave oven — **mi·cro·wav·able** *or* **mi·cro·wave·able** \ˌmī-krə-'wā-və-bəl\ *adj*

microwave oven *n* : an oven in which food is cooked by the absorption of microwave energy by water molecules in the food

¹**mid** \'mid\ *adj* : MIDDLE

²**mid** *abbr* middle

mid·air \'mid-'er\ *n* : a point or region in the air well above the ground

mid·day \'mid-ˌdā, -'dā\ *n* : NOON

mid·den \'mi-dᵊn\ *n* : a refuse heap

¹**mid·dle** \'mi-dᵊl\ *adj* **1** : equally distant from the extremes : MEDIAL, CENTRAL **2** : being at neither extreme : INTERMEDIATE **3** *cap* : constituting an intermediate period

²**middle** *n* **1** : a middle part, point, or position **2** : WAIST

middle age *n* : the period of life from about 45 to about 64 — **mid·dle–aged** \ˌmi-dᵊl-'ājd\ *adj*

Middle Ages *n pl* : the period of European history from about A.D. 500 to about 1500

mid·dle·brow \'mi-dᵊl-ˌbrau̇\ *n* : a person who is moderately but not highly cultivated — **middlebrow** *adj*

middle class *n* : a social class holding a position between the upper class and the lower class — **middle–class** *adj*

middle ear *n* : a small membrane-lined cavity of the ear through which sound waves are transmitted by a chain of tiny bones

middle finger *n* : the midmost of the five digits of the hand

mid·dle·man \'mi-dᵊl-ˌman\ *n* : INTERMEDIARY; *esp* : one intermediate between the producer of goods and the retailer or consumer

middle–of–the–road *adj* : standing for or following a course of action midway between extremes; *esp* : being neither liberal nor conservative in politics — **mid·dle–of–the–road·er** \-'rō-dər\ *n* — **mid·dle–of–the–road·ism** \-'rō-ˌdi-zəm\ *n*

middle school *n* : a school usu. including grades 5 to 8 or 6 to 8

mid·dle·weight \'mi-dᵊl-ˌwāt\ *n* : one of average weight; *esp* : a boxer weighing not over 160 pounds

mid·dling \'mid-liŋ, -lən\ *adj* **1** : of middle, medium, or moderate size, degree, or quality **2** : MEDIOCRE

mid·dy \'mi-dē\ *n, pl* **middies** : MIDSHIPMAN

midge \'mij\ *n* : a very small fly : GNAT

midg·et \'mi-jət\ *n* **1** : something (as an animal) very small for its kind **2** *sometimes offensive* : a very small person

midi \'mi-dē\ *n* : a calf-length dress, coat, or skirt

MIDI \'mi-dē\ *n* [*musical instrument digital interface*] : a protocol for the transmission of digitally encoded music

mid·land \'mid-lənd, -ˌland\ *n* : the interior or central region of a country

mid·life \'mid-'līf\ *n* : MIDDLE AGE

midlife crisis *n* : a period of emotional turmoil in middle age characterized esp. by a strong desire for change

mid·most \-ˌmōst\ *adj* : being in or near the exact middle — **midmost** *adv*

mid·night \-ˌnīt\ *n* : 12 o'clock at night

mid–ocean ridge \'mid-'ō-shən-\ *n* : an elevation on an ocean floor at the boundary of diverging tectonic plates

mid·point \'mid-ˌpȯint, -'pȯint\ *n* : a point at or near the center or middle

mid·riff \'mi-ˌdrif\ *n* [ME *midrif*, fr. OE *midhrif*, fr. *midde*

mid + *hrif* belly] **1** : DIAPHRAGM 1 **2** : the mid-region of the human torso

mid·sec·tion \-ˌsek-shən\ *n* : a section midway between the extremes; *esp* : MIDRIFF 2

mid·ship·man \'mid-ˌship-mən, (ˌ)mid-'ship-\ *n* : a student in a naval academy

mid·ships \-ˌships\ *adv* : AMIDSHIPS

midst \'midst\ *n* **1** : the interior or central part or point **2** : a position of proximity to the members of a group ⟨in our ∼⟩ **3** : the condition of being surrounded or beset — **midst** *prep*

mid·stream \'mid-'strēm, -ˌstrēm\ *n* : the middle of a stream

mid·sum·mer \-'sə-mər, -ˌsə-\ *n* **1** : the middle of summer **2** : the summer solstice

mid·town \'mid-ˌtau̇n, -'tau̇n\ *n* : a central section of a city; *esp* : one situated between sections called *downtown* and *uptown* — **midtown** *adj*

¹**mid·way** \'mid-ˌwā, -'wā\ *adv* : in the middle of the way or distance

²**mid·way** \-ˌwā\ *n* : an avenue (as at a carnival) for concessions and amusements

mid·week \-ˌwēk\ *n* : the middle of the week — **mid·week·ly** \-ˌwē-klē, -'wē-\ *adj or adv*

mid·wife \'mid-ˌwīf\ *n* : a person who helps women in childbirth — **mid·wife·ry** \-ˌwi-fə-rē\ *n*

mid·win·ter \'mid-ˌwin-tər, -'win-\ *n* **1** : the winter solstice **2** : the middle of winter

mid·year \-ˌyir\ *n* **1** : the middle of a year **2** : a midyear examination — **midyear** *adj*

mien \'mēn\ *n* **1** : air or bearing esp. as expressive of mood or personality : DEMEANOR **2** : APPEARANCE, ASPECT ⟨dresses of formal ∼⟩

miff \'mif\ *vb* : to put into an ill humor

¹**might** \'mīt\ *verbal auxiliary, past of* MAY — used as an auxiliary to express permission or possibility in the past, a present condition contrary to fact, less probability or possibility than *may*, or as a polite alternative to *may*, *ought*, or *should*

²**might** *n* : the power, authority, or resources of an individual or a group

mighty \'mī-tē\ *adj* **might·i·er; -est** **1** : very strong : POWERFUL **2** : GREAT, NOTABLE — **might·i·ly** \'mī-tə-lē\ *adv* — **might·i·ness** \-tē-nəs\ *n* — **mighty** *adv*

mi·gnon·ette \ˌmin-yə-'net\ *n* : an annual garden herb with spikes of tiny fragrant flowers

mi·graine \'mī-ˌgrān\ *n* [ME *mygreyn*, fr. MF *migraine*, fr. LL *hemicrania* pain in one side of the head, fr. Gk *hēmikrania*, fr. *hēmi*- half + *kranion* cranium] : a condition marked by recurrent severe headache and often nausea; *also* : an attack of migraine

mi·grant \'mī-grənt\ *n* : one that migrates; *esp* : a person who moves in order to find work (as picking crops) — **migrant** *adj*

mi·grate \'mī-ˌgrāt\ *vb* **mi·grat·ed; mi·grat·ing** **1** : to move from one country or place to another **2** : to pass usu. periodically from one region or climate to another for feeding or breeding — **mi·gra·tion** \mī-'grā-shən\ *n* — **mi·gra·to·ry** \'mī-grə-ˌtȯr-ē\ *adj*

mi·ka·do \mə-'kä-dō\ *n, pl* **-dos** : an emperor of Japan

mike \'mīk\ *n* : MICROPHONE

¹**mil** \'mil\ *n* : a unit of length equal to ¹/₁₀₀₀ inch

²**mil** *abbr* military

milch \'milk, 'milch\ *adj* : giving milk ⟨∼ cow⟩

mild \'mī(-ə)ld\ *adj* **1** : gentle in nature or behavior **2** : moderate in action or effect **3** : TEMPERATE ⟨∼ weather⟩ ♦ **Synonyms** EASY, COMPLAISANT, AMIABLE, LENIENT — **mild·ly** *adv* — **mild·ness** *n*

mil·dew \'mil-ˌdü, -ˌdyü\ *n* : a superficial usu. whitish growth produced on organic matter and on plants by a fungus; *also* : a fungus producing this growth — **mildew** *vb*

mile \'mī(-ə)l\ *n* [ME, fr. OE *mīl*, fr. L *milia* miles, fr. *milia passuum*, lit., thousands of paces] **1** — see WEIGHT table **2** : NAUTICAL MILE

mile·age \'mī-lij\ *n* **1** : an allowance for traveling expenses at a certain rate per mile **2** : distance in miles traveled (as in a day) **3** : the amount of service yielded (as by a tire) expressed in terms of miles of travel **4** : the average number of miles a motor vehicle will travel on a gallon of gasoline

mile·post \'mī(-ə)l-ˌpōst\ n : a post indicating the distance in miles from a given point

mile·stone \-ˌstōn\ n 1 : a stone serving as a milepost 2 : a significant point in development

mi·lieu \mēl-'yər, -'yü, -'yœ\ n, pl **mi·lieus** or **mi·lieux** \same or -'yərz, -'yüz, -'yœz\ [F] : ENVIRONMENT, SETTING

mil·i·tant \'mi-lə-tənt\ adj 1 : engaged in warfare 2 : aggressively active esp. in a cause — **mil·i·tance** \-təns\ n — **mil·i·tan·cy** \-tən-sē\ n — **militant** n — **mil·i·tant·ly** adv

mil·i·ta·rise Brit var of MILITARIZE

mil·i·ta·rism \'mi-lə-tə-ˌri-zəm\ n 1 : predominance of the military class or its ideals 2 : a policy of aggressive military preparedness — **mil·i·ta·rist** \-rist\ n — **mil·i·ta·ris·tic** \ˌmi-lə-tə-'ris-tik\ adj

mil·i·ta·rize \'mi-lə-tə-ˌrīz\ vb **-rized; -riz·ing** 1 : to equip with military forces and defenses 2 : to give a military character to

¹**mil·i·tary** \'mi-lə-ˌter-ē\ adj 1 : of or relating to soldiers, arms, war, or the army 2 : performed by armed forces; also : supported by armed force ♦ **Synonyms** MARTIAL, WARLIKE — **mil·i·tar·i·ly** \ˌmi-lə-'ter-ə-lē\ adv

²**military** n, pl military also **mil·i·tar·ies** 1 : the military, naval, and air forces of a nation 2 : military persons

military police n : a branch of an army that exercises guard and police functions

mil·i·tate \'mi-lə-ˌtāt\ vb **-tat·ed; -tat·ing** : to have weight or effect ⟨disagreements ∼ against an alliance⟩

mi·li·tia \mə-'li-shə\ n : a part of the organized armed forces of a country liable to call only in emergency — **mi·li·tia·man** \-mən\ n

¹**milk** \'milk\ n 1 : a nutritive usu. whitish fluid secreted by female mammals for feeding their young 2 : a milklike liquid (as a plant juice) — **milk·i·ness** \'mil-kē-nəs\ n — **milky** adj

²**milk** vb 1 : to draw off the milk of ⟨∼ a cow⟩ 2 : to draw something from as if by milking

milk·maid \'milk-ˌmād\ n : DAIRYMAID

milk·man \-ˌman, -mən\ n : a person who sells or delivers milk

milk of magnesia : a milk-white mixture of hydroxide of magnesium and water used as an antacid and a laxative

milk shake n : a thoroughly blended drink made of milk, a flavoring syrup, and often ice cream

milk·sop \'milk-ˌsäp\ n : an unmanly man

milk·weed \-ˌwēd\ n : any of a genus of herbs with milky juice and clustered flowers

Milky Way n 1 : a broad irregular band of light that stretches across the sky and is caused by the light of a very great number of faint stars 2 : MILKY WAY GALAXY

Milky Way galaxy n : the galaxy of which the sun is a member and which includes the stars that create the light of the Milky Way

¹**mill** \'mil\ n 1 : a building with machinery for grinding grain into flour 2 : a machine used in processing (as by grinding, stamping, cutting, or finishing) raw material 3 : FACTORY

²**mill** vb 1 : to process in a mill 2 : to move in a circle or in an eddying mass

³**mill** n : one tenth of a cent

mill·age \'mi-lij\ n : a rate (as of taxation) expressed in mills

mil·len·ni·um \mə-'le-nē-əm\ n, pl **-nia** \-nē-ə\ or **-niums** 1 : a period of 1000 years; also : a 1000th anniversary or its celebration 2 : the 1000 years mentioned in Revelation 20 when holiness is to prevail and Christ is to reign on earth 3 : a period of great happiness or human perfection

mill·er \'mi-lər\ n 1 : one that operates a mill and esp. a flour mill 2 : any of various moths having powdery wings

mil·let \'mi-lət\ n : any of several small-seeded cereal and forage grasses cultivated for grain or hay; also : the grain of a millet

milli– comb form : one thousandth part of

mil·li·am·pere \ˌmi-lē-'am-ˌpir\ n : one thousandth of an ampere

mil·liard \'mil-ˌyärd, 'mi-lē-ˌärd\ n, Brit : a thousand millions

mil·li·bar \'mi-lə-ˌbär\ n : a unit of atmospheric pressure

mil·li·gram \-ˌgram\ n — see METRIC SYSTEM table

mil·li·ter \-ˌlē-tər\ n — see METRIC SYSTEM table

mil·lime \mə-'lēm\ n — see dinar at MONEY table

mil·li·me·ter \'mi-lə-ˌmē-tər\ n — see METRIC SYSTEM table

mil·li·ner \'mi-lə-nər\ n [irreg. fr. Milan, Italy; fr. the importation of women's finery from Italy in the 16th century] : a person who designs, makes, trims, or sells women's hats

mil·li·nery \'mi-lə-ˌner-ē\ n 1 : women's apparel for the head 2 : the business or work of a milliner

mill·ing \'mi-liŋ\ n : a corrugated edge on a coin

mil·lion \'mil-yən\ n, pl **millions** or **million** : a thousand thousands — **million** adj — **mil·lionth** \-yənth\ adj or n

mil·lion·aire \ˌmil-yə-'ner, 'mil-yə-ˌner\ n : one whose wealth is estimated at a million or more (as of dollars or pounds)

mil·li·pede \'mi-lə-ˌpēd\ n : any of a class of arthropods related to the centipedes and having a long segmented body with a hard covering, two pairs of legs on most segments, and no poison fangs

mil·li·sec·ond \-ˌse-kənd\ n : one thousandth of a second

mil·li·volt \-ˌvōlt\ n : one thousandth of a volt

mill·pond \'mil-ˌpänd\ n : a pond made by damming a stream to produce a fall of water for operating a mill

mill·race \-ˌrās\ n : a canal in which water flows to and from a mill wheel

mill·stone \-ˌstōn\ n : either of two round flat stones used for grinding grain

mill·stream \-ˌstrēm\ n : a stream whose flow is used to run a mill; also : the stream in a millrace

mill wheel n : a waterwheel that drives a mill

mill·wright \'mil-ˌrīt\ n : a person who builds mills or sets up or maintains their machinery

milt \'milt\ n : the sperm-containing fluid of a male fish

mime \'mīm\ n 1 : MIMIC 2 : PANTOMIME — **mime** vb

mim·eo·graph \'mi-mē-ə-ˌgraf\ n : a machine for making many copies by means of a stencil through which ink is pressed — **mimeograph** vb

mi·me·sis \mə-'mē-səs, mī-\ n : IMITATION, MIMICRY

mi·met·ic \-'me-tik\ adj 1 : IMITATIVE 2 : relating to, characterized by, or exhibiting mimicry

¹**mim·ic** \'mi-mik\ n : one that mimics

²**mimic** vb **mim·icked** \-mikt\; **mim·ick·ing** 1 : to imitate closely 2 : to ridicule by imitation 3 : to resemble by biological mimicry

mim·ic·ry \'mi-mi-krē\ n, pl **-ries** 1 : an instance of mimicking 2 : a superficial resemblance of one organism to another or to natural objects among which it lives that gives it an advantage (as protection from predation)

mi·mo·sa \mə-'mō-sə, mī-, -zə\ n : any of a genus of trees, shrubs, and herbs of the legume family that occur in warm regions and have ball-shaped heads of small white or pink flowers

min abbr 1 minim 2 minimum 3 mining 4 minister 5 minor 6 minute

min·a·ret \ˌmi-nə-'ret\ n [F, fr. Turk minare, fr. Ar manāra lighthouse] : a tall slender tower of a mosque from which a muezzin calls the faithful to prayer

mi·na·to·ry \'mi-nə-ˌtór-ē, 'mī-\ adj : THREATENING, MENACING

mince \'mins\ vb **minced; minc·ing** [ME, fr. AF mincer, fr. VL *minutiare, fr. L minutia smallness, fr. minutus small, fr. pp. of minuere to lessen] 1 : to cut into very small pieces 2 : to restrain (words) within the bounds of decorum 3 : to walk in a prim affected manner

mince·meat \'mins-ˌmēt\ n : a finely chopped mixture esp. of raisins, apples, spices, and often meat used as a filling for a pie

¹**mind** \'mīnd\ n 1 : MEMORY 2 : the part of an individual that feels, perceives, thinks, wills, and esp. reasons 3 : INTENTION, DESIRE 4 : normal mental condition 5 : OPINION, VIEW 6 : MOOD 7 : mental qualities of a person or group 8 : intellectual ability 9 : ATTENTION ⟨pay him no ∼⟩

²**mind** vb 1 chiefly dial : REMEMBER 2 : to attend to closely 3 : HEED, OBEY 4 : to be concerned about; also : DISLIKE 5 : to be careful or cautious 6 : to take charge of 7 : to regard with attention

mind–bend·ing \'mīnd-ˌben-diŋ\ *adj* : MIND-BLOWING — **mind–bend·ing·ly** *adv*

mind–blow·ing \-ˌblō-iŋ\ *adj* : PSYCHEDELIC 1; *also* : MIND-BOGGLING — **mind·blow·er** \-ˌblō-ər\ *n* — **mind–blow·ing·ly** *adv*

mind–bog·gling \-ˌbä-gə-liŋ\ *adj* : mentally or emotionally exciting or overwhelming

mind·ed \'mīn-dəd\ *adj* 1 : INCLINED, DISPOSED 2 : having a mind of a specified kind or concerned with a specific thing — usu. used in combination ⟨narrow-*minded*⟩ ⟨health-*minded*⟩

mind·ful \'mīnd-fəl\ *adj* : bearing in mind : AWARE — **mind·ful·ly** *adv* — **mind·ful·ness** *n*

mind·less \-ləs\ *adj* 1 : marked by a lack of mind or consciousness; *esp* : marked by no use of the intellect 2 : not mindful : HEEDLESS — **mind·less·ly** *adv* — **mind·less·ness** *n*

¹**mine** \'mīn\ *pron* : that which belongs to me

²**mine** *n* 1 : an excavation in the earth from which minerals are taken; *also* : an ore deposit 2 : an underground passage beneath an enemy position 3 : an explosive device for destroying enemy personnel, vehicles, or ships 4 : a rich source of supply

³**mine** *vb* **mined; min·ing** 1 : to dig a mine 2 : UNDERMINE 3 : to get ore from the earth 4 : to place military mines in — **min·er** *n*

mine·field \'mīn-ˌfēld\ *n* 1 : an area set with mines 2 : something resembling a minefield esp. in having many dangers ⟨a political ∼⟩

mine·lay·er \-ˌlā-ər\ *n* : a naval vessel for laying underwater mines

min·er·al \'mi-nə-rəl\ *n* 1 : a crystalline substance (as diamond or quartz) of inorganic origin 2 : a naturally occurring substance (as coal, salt, or water) obtained usu. from the ground — **mineral** *adj*

min·er·al·ise *Brit var of* MINERALIZE

min·er·al·ize \'mi-nə-rə-ˌlīz\ *vb* **-ized; -iz·ing** 1 : to impregnate or supply with minerals 2 : to change into mineral form — **min·er·al·i·za·tion** \-rə-lə-'zā-shən\ *n*

min·er·al·o·gy \ˌmi-nə-'rä-lə-jē, -'ra-\ *n* : a science dealing with minerals — **min·er·al·og·i·cal** \ˌmi-nə-rə-'lä-ji-kəl\ *adj* — **min·er·al·o·gist** \ˌmi-nə-'rä-lə-jist, -'ra-\ *n*

mineral oil *n* : an oil of mineral origin; *esp* : a refined petroleum oil used as a laxative

mineral water *n* : water infused with mineral salts or gases

min·e·stro·ne \ˌmi-nə-'strō-nē, -'strōn\ *n* [It, fr. *minestra*, fr. *minestrare* to serve, dish up, fr. L *ministrare*, fr. *minister* servant] : a rich thick vegetable soup

mine·sweep·er \'mīn-ˌswē-pər\ *n* : a warship for removing or neutralizing underwater mines

min·gle \'miŋ-gəl\ *vb* **min·gled; min·gling** 1 : to bring or combine together : MIX ⟨*mingling* odors⟩ 2 : ASSOCIATE; *also* : to move about socially ⟨*mingled* with the guests⟩

ming tree \'miŋ-\ *n* : a dwarfed usu. evergreen tree grown as bonsai; *also* : an artificial plant resembling this

mini \'mi-nē\ *n, pl* **min·is** : something small of its kind — **mini** *adj*

mini- *comb form* : smaller or briefer than usual, normal, or standard

min·ia·ture \'mi-nē-ə-ˌchu̇r, 'mi-ni-ˌchu̇r, -chər\ *n* [It *miniatura* art of illuminating a manuscript, fr. ML, fr. L *miniare* to color with red lead, fr. *minium* red lead] 1 : a copy on a much reduced scale; *also* : something small of its kind 2 : a small painting (as on ivory or metal) — **miniature** *adj* — **min·ia·tur·ist** \-ˌchu̇r-ist, -chər-\ *n*

min·ia·tur·ize \'mi-nē-ə-chə-ˌrīz, 'mi-ni-\ *vb* **-ized; -iz·ing** : to design or construct in small size — **min·ia·tur·i·za·tion** \ˌmi-nē-ə-ˌchu̇r-ə-'zā-shən, ˌmi-ni-, -chər-\ *n*

mini·bar \'mi-nē-ˌbär\ *n* : a small refrigerator in a hotel room that is stocked with beverages and snacks

mini·bike \'mi-nē-ˌbīk\ *n* : a small one-passenger motorcycle

mini·bus \-ˌbəs\ *n* : a small bus or van

mini·com·put·er \-kəm-ˌpyü-tər\ *n* : a computer between a mainframe and a microcomputer in size and speed

mini·disc \'mi-nē-ˌdisk\ *n* : a miniature optical disk

min·im \'mi-nəm\ *n* — see WEIGHT table

min·i·mal \'mi-nə-məl\ *adj* 1 : relating to or being a min-imum : LEAST 2 : of or relating to minimalism or minimal art — **min·i·mal·ly** *adv*

minimal art *n* : abstract art consisting primarily of simple geometric forms executed in an impersonal style — **minimal artist** *n*

min·i·mal·ism \'mi-nə-mə-ˌli-zəm\ *n* : MINIMAL ART; *also* : a style (as in music or literature) marked by extreme spareness or simplicity — **min·i·mal·ist** \-list\ *n*

mini·mart \'mi-nē-ˌmärt\ *n* : CONVENIENCE STORE

min·i·mise *Brit var of* MINIMIZE

min·i·mize \'mi-nə-ˌmīz\ *vb* **-mized; -miz·ing** 1 : to reduce or keep to a minimum 2 : to underestimate intentionally ⟨∼ the defects⟩ ♦ **Synonyms** DEPRECIATE, DECRY, DISPARAGE

min·i·mum \'mi-nə-məm\ *n, pl* **-ma** \-mə\ *or* **-mums** 1 : the least quantity assignable, admissible, or possible 2 : the least of a set of numbers 3 : the lowest degree or amount of variation (as of temperature) reached or recorded — **minimum** *adj*

min·ion \'min-yən\ *n* [MF *mignon* darling] 1 : a servile dependent, follower, or underling 2 : one highly favored 3 : a subordinate official

min·is·cule \'mi-nəs-ˌkyül\ *var of* MINUSCULE

mini·se·ries \'mi-nē-ˌsir-ēz\ *n* : a television story presented in sequential episodes

mini·skirt \-ˌskərt\ *n* : a skirt with the hemline several inches above the knee

¹**min·is·ter** \'mi-nə-stər\ *n* 1 : AGENT 2 : a member of the clergy esp. of a Protestant communion 3 : a high officer of state who heads a division of governmental activities 4 : a diplomatic representative to a foreign state — **min·is·te·ri·al** \ˌmi-nə-'stir-ē-əl\ *adj*

²**minister** *vb* 1 : to perform the functions of a minister of religion 2 : to give aid or service — **min·is·tra·tion** \ˌmi-nə-'strā-shən\ *n*

¹**min·is·trant** \'mi-nə-strənt\ *adj, archaic* : performing service as a minister

²**ministrant** *n* : one that ministers

min·is·try \'mi-nə-strē\ *n, pl* **-tries** 1 : MINISTRATION 2 : the office, duties, or functions of a minister; *also* : the period of service or office 3 : CLERGY 4 : AGENCY 5 *often cap* : the body of ministers governing a nation or state; *also* : a government department headed by a minister

mini·tower \'mi-nē-ˌtau̇(-ə)r\ *n* : a computer tower of intermediate size

mini·van \'mi-nē-ˌvan\ *n* : a small van

mink \'miŋk\ *n, pl* **mink** *or* **minks** : either of two slender flesh-eating mammals resembling the related weasels; *also* : the soft lustrous typically dark brown fur of a mink

mink

min·ke whale \'miŋ-kə-\ *n* : a small grayish baleen whale with a whitish underside

Minn *abbr* Minnesota

min·ne·sing·er \'mi-ni-ˌsiŋ-ər, -ˌziŋ-\ *n* [G, fr. Middle High German, fr. *minne* love + *singer* singer] : any of a class of German lyric poets and musicians of the 12th to the 14th centuries

min·now \'mi-nō\ *n, pl* **minnows** *also* **minnow** : any of numerous small freshwater fishes

¹**mi·nor** \'mī-nər\ *adj* 1 : inferior in importance, size, or degree 2 : not having reached majority 3 : having the third, sixth, and sometimes the seventh degrees lowered by a half step ⟨∼ scale⟩; *also* : based on a minor scale ⟨∼ key⟩ 4 : not serious ⟨∼ illness⟩

²**minor** *n* 1 : a person who has not attained majority 2 : a subject of academic study chosen as a secondary field of specialization

³minor *vb* : to pursue an academic minor ⟨~ed in philosophy⟩

mi·nor·i·ty \mə-'nȯr-ə-tē, mī-\ *n, pl* **-ties** **1** : the period or state of being a minor **2** : the smaller in number of two groups; *esp* : a group having less than the number of votes necessary for control **3** : a part of a population differing from others (as in race); *also* : a member of a minority

mi·nox·i·dil \mə-'näk-sə-,dil\ *n* : a drug used orally to treat hypertension and topically in solution to promote hair regrowth in some forms of baldness

min·ster \'min-stər\ *n* : a large or important church

min·strel \'min-strəl\ *n* **1** : a medieval singer of verses; *also* : MUSICIAN, POET **2** : any of a group of performers usu. with blackened faces in a program of black American songs, jokes, and impersonations ⟨a ~ show⟩

min·strel·sy \-sē\ *n* : the singing and playing of a minstrel; *also* : a body of minstrels

¹mint \'mint\ *n* **1** : any of a large family of aromatic square-stemmed herbs and shrubs; *esp* : one (as spearmint) that is fragrant and is the source of a flavoring oil **2** : a mint-flavored piece of candy — **minty** *adj*

²mint *n* **1** : a place where coins are made **2** : a vast sum ⟨worth a ~⟩

³mint *vb* **1** : to make (as coins) out of metal **2** : CREATE; *also* : to give a certain status to ⟨newly ~ed lawyers⟩ — **mint·age** \-ij\ *n* — **mint·er** *n*

⁴mint *adj* : unmarred as if fresh from a mint ⟨in ~ condition⟩

min·u·end \'min-yə-,wend\ *n* : a number from which another is to be subtracted

min·u·et \,min-yə-'wet\ *n* : a slow graceful dance

¹mi·nus \'mī-nəs\ *prep* **1** : diminished by : LESS ⟨seven ~ three equals four⟩ **2** : LACKING, WITHOUT ⟨~ his hat⟩

²minus *n* : a negative quantity or quality

³minus *adj* **1** : algebraically negative ⟨~ quantity⟩ **2** : having a negative quality

¹mi·nus·cule \'mi-nəs-,kyül\ *n* : a lowercase letter

²minuscule *also* **min·is·cule** *adj* : very small

minus sign *n* : a sign – used in mathematics to indicate subtraction or a negative quantity

¹min·ute \'mi-nət\ *n* **1** : the 60th part of an hour or of a degree : 60 seconds **2** : a short space of time **3** *pl* : the official record of the proceedings of a meeting

²mi·nute \mī-'nüt, mə-, -'nyüt\ *adj* **mi·nut·er; -est** **1** : very small **2** : of little importance : TRIFLING **3** : marked by close attention to details ✦ *Synonyms* DIMINUTIVE, TINY, MINIATURE, WEE — **mi·nute·ly** *adv* — **mi·nute·ness** *n*

min·ute·man \'mi-nət-,man\ *n* : a member of a group of armed men pledged to take the field at a minute's notice during and immediately before the American Revolution

mi·nu·tia \mə-'nü-shə, -'nyü-, -shē-ə\ *n, pl* **-ti·ae** \-shē-,ē\ [L] : a minute or minor detail — usu. used in pl.

minx \'miŋks\ *n* : a pert girl

Mio·cene \'mī-ə-,sēn\ *adj* : of, relating to, or being the epoch of the Tertiary between the Oligocene and the Pliocene — **Miocene** *n*

mir·a·cle \'mir-i-kəl\ *n* **1** : an extraordinary event manifesting divine intervention in human affairs **2** : an unusual event, thing, or accomplishment : WONDER, MARVEL — **mi·rac·u·lous** \mə-'ra-kyə-ləs\ *adj* — **mi·rac·u·lous·ly** *adv*

miracle drug *n* : a usu. newly discovered drug that elicits a dramatic response in a patient's condition

mi·rage \mə-'räzh\ *n* **1** : an illusion that often appears as a pool of water or a mirror in which distant objects are seen inverted, is sometimes seen at sea, in the desert, or over a hot pavement, and results from atmospheric conditions **2** : something illusory and unattainable

¹mire \'mī(-ə)r\ *n* : heavy and often deep mud or slush — **miry** *adj*

²mire *vb* **mired; mir·ing** : to stick or sink in or as if in mire

mire·poix \mir-'pwä\ *n, pl* **mirepoix** : a mixture of diced vegetables and sometimes meats used in soups, stews, and sauces

¹mir·ror \'mir-ər\ *n* **1** : a polished or smooth surface (as of glass) that forms images by reflection **2** : a true representation

²mirror *vb* **1** : to reflect in or as if in a mirror **2** : RESEMBLE

mirth \'mərth\ *n* : gladness or gaiety accompanied with laughter ✦ *Synonyms* GLEE, JOLLITY, HILARITY, MERRIMENT — **mirth·ful** \-fəl\ *adj* — **mirth·ful·ly** *adv* — **mirth·ful·ness** *n* — **mirth·less** *adj*

MIRV \'mərv\ *n* [*m*ultiple *i*ndependently targeted *r*eentry *v*ehicle] : an ICBM with multiple warheads that have different targets — **MIRV** *vb*

mis·ad·ven·ture \,mi-səd-'ven-chər\ *n* : MISFORTUNE, MISHAP

mis·aligned \,mi-sə-'līnd\ *adj* : not properly aligned — **mis·align·ment** \-'līn-mənt\ *n*

mis·al·li·ance \,mi-sə-'lī-əns\ *n* : an improper or unsuitable marriage

mis·al·lo·ca·tion \,mi-,sa-lə-'kā-shən\ *n* : faulty or improper allocation

mis·an·dry \'mi-,san-drē\ *n* : a hatred of men — **mis·an·drist** \-drist\ *n or adj*

mis·an·thrope \'mi-sᵊn-,thrōp\ *n* : one who hates mankind — **mis·an·throp·ic** \,mi-sᵊn-'thrä-pik\ *adj* — **mis·an·throp·i·cal·ly** \-pi-k(ə-)lē\ *adv* — **mis·an·thro·py** \mi-'san-thrə-pē\ *n*

mis·ap·ply \,mi-sə-'plī\ *vb* : to apply wrongly — **mis·ap·pli·ca·tion** \,mi-,sa-plə-'kā-shən\ *n*

mis·ap·pre·hend \,mi-,sa-pri-'hend\ *vb* : MISUNDERSTAND — **mis·ap·pre·hen·sion** \-'hen-chən\ *n*

mis·ap·pro·pri·ate \,mi-sə-'prō-prē-,āt\ *vb* : to appropriate wrongly (as by embezzlement) — **mis·ap·pro·pri·a·tion** \-,prō-prē-'ā-shən\ *n*

mis·be·got·ten \-bi-'gä-tᵊn\ *adj* : ILLEGITIMATE; *also* : ill-conceived

mis·be·have \,mis-bi-'hāv\ *vb* : to behave improperly — **mis·be·hav·ior** \-'hā-vyər\ *n*

mis·be·liev·er \-bə-'lē-vər\ *n* : one who holds a false or unorthodox belief

mis·brand \mis-'brand\ *vb* : to brand falsely or in a misleading manner

misc *abbr* miscellaneous

mis·cal·cu·late \mis-'kal-kyə-,lāt\ *vb* : to calculate wrongly — **mis·cal·cu·la·tion** \,mis-,kal-kyə-'lā-shən\ *n*

mis·call \mis-'kȯl\ *vb* : MISNAME

mis·car·riage \-'ker-ij\ *n* **1** : failure in the administration of justice **2** : spontaneous expulsion of a fetus before it is capable of independent life

mis·car·ry \-'ker-ē\ *vb* **1** : to have a miscarriage of a fetus **2** : to go wrong; *also* : to be unsuccessful

mis·ce·ge·na·tion \,mi-se-jə-'nā-shən, ,mi-si-jə-'nā-\ *n* [L *miscēre* to mix + *genus* race] : marriage, cohabitation, or sexual intercourse between persons of different races

mis·cel·la·neous \,mi-sə-'lā-nē-əs\ *adj* **1** : consisting of diverse things or members **2** : having various traits; *also* : dealing with or interested in diverse subjects — **mis·cel·la·neous·ly** *adv* — **mis·cel·la·neous·ness** *n*

mis·cel·la·ny \'mi-sə-,lā-nē\ *n, pl* **-nies** **1** : a collection of writings on various subjects **2** : HODGEPODGE

mis·chance \mis-'chans\ *n* : bad luck; *also* : MISHAP

mis·chief \'mis-chəf\ *n* [ME *meschief*, fr. AF, misfortune, hardship, fr. OF *meschever* to come out badly, fr. *mes-* badly + *chief* head, end] **1** : injury caused by a particular agent **2** : a source of harm or irritation **3** : action that annoys; *also* : MISCHIEVOUSNESS

mis·chie·vous \'mis-chə-vəs\ *adj* **1** : HARMFUL, INJURIOUS **2** : causing annoyance or minor injury **3** : irresponsibly playful — **mis·chie·vous·ly** *adv* — **mis·chie·vous·ness** *n*

mis·ci·ble \'mi-sə-bəl\ *adj* : capable of being mixed

mis·com·mu·ni·ca·tion \,mis-kə-,myü-nə-'kā-shən\ *n* : failure to communicate clearly

mis·con·ceive \,mis-kən-'sēv\ *vb* : to interpret incorrectly — **mis·con·cep·tion** \-'sep-shən\ *n*

mis·con·duct \mis-'kän-(,)dəkt\ *n* **1** : MISMANAGEMENT **2** : intentional wrongdoing **3** : improper behavior; *also* : a penalty in a sport for improper behavior

mis·con·strue \,mis-kən-'strü\ *vb* : MISINTERPRET — **mis·con·struc·tion** \-'strək-shən\ *n*

mis·count \mis-'kaúnt\ *vb* : to count incorrectly : MISCALCULATE

mis·cre·ant \'mis-krē-ənt\ *n* : one who behaves criminally or viciously — **miscreant** *adj*

mis·cue \mis-'kyü\ *n* : MISTAKE, ERROR — **miscue** *vb*

mis·deed \mis-'dēd\ *n* : a wrong deed

mis·de·mean·or \,mis-di-'mē-nər\ *n* **1** : a crime less serious than a felony **2** : MISDEED

mis·di·rect \,mis-də-'rekt, -dī-\ *vb* : to give a wrong direction to — **mis·di·rec·tion** \-'rek-shən\ *n*

mis·do·ing \mis-'dü-iŋ\ *n* : WRONGDOING — **mis·do** \-'dü\ *vb* — **mis·do·er** \-'dü-ər\ *n*

mise–en–scène \,mē-,zän-'sen, -'sän\ *n, pl* **mise–en-scènes** *same or* -'senz, -'sänz\ [F] **1** : the arrangement of the scenery, property, and actors on a stage **2** : SETTING; *also* : ENVIRONMENT

mi·ser \'mī-zər\ *n* [L *miser* miserable] : a person who hoards and is stingy with money — **mi·ser·li·ness** \-lē-nəs\ *n* — **mi·ser·ly** *adj*

mis·er·a·ble \'mi-zə-rə-bəl, 'miz-rə-\ *adj* **1** : wretchedly deficient; *also* : causing extreme discomfort **2** : being in a state of distress **3** : SHAMEFUL — **mis·er·a·ble·ness** *n* — **mis·er·a·bly** \-blē\ *adv*

mis·ery \'mi-zə-rē\ *n, pl* **-er·ies** **1** : suffering and want caused by poverty or affliction **2** : a cause of suffering or discomfort **3** : emotional distress

mis·fea·sance \mis-'fē-z²ns\ *n* : the performance of a lawful action in an illegal or improper manner

mis·file \-'fī(-ə)l\ *vb* : to file in the wrong place

mis·fire \-'fī(-ə)r\ *vb* **1** : to fail to fire **2** : to miss an intended effect — **misfire** *n*

mis·fit \'mis-,fit, *sense 1 also* mis-'fit\ *n* **1** : something that fits badly **2** : a person who is poorly adjusted to a situation or environment

mis·for·tune \mis-'fȯr-chən\ *n* **1** : bad luck **2** : an unfortunate condition or event

mis·giv·ing \-'gi-viŋ\ *n* : a feeling of doubt or suspicion esp. concerning a future event

mis·gov·ern \-'gə-vərn\ *vb* : to govern badly — **mis·gov·ern·ment** *n*

mis·guid·ance \mis-'gī-d²ns\ *n* : faulty guidance — **mis·guide** \-'gīd\ *vb*

mis·guid·ed \-'gī-dəd\ *adj* : led or prompted by wrong or inappropriate motives or ideals — **mis·guid·ed·ly** *adv*

mis·han·dle \-'han-d²l\ *vb* **1** : MALTREAT **2** : to manage wrongly

mis·hap \'mis-,hap\ *n* : an unfortunate accident

mish·mash \'mish-,mash, -,mäsh\ *n* : HODGEPODGE, JUMBLE

mis·in·form \,mis-s²n-'fȯrm\ *vb* : to give false or misleading information to — **mis·in·for·ma·tion** \,mi-,sin-fər-'mā-shən\ *n*

mis·in·ter·pret \,mis-s²n-'tər-prət\ *vb* : to understand or explain wrongly — **mis·in·ter·pre·ta·tion** \-,tər-prə-'tā-shən\ *n*

mis·judge \mis-'jəj\ *vb* **1** : to estimate wrongly **2** : to have an unjust opinion of — **mis·judg·ment** \mis-'jəj-mənt\ *n*

mis·la·bel \-'lā-bəl\ *vb* : to label incorrectly or falsely ⟨was ~*ed* a liar⟩

mis·lay \mis-'lā\ *vb* **-laid** \-'lād\; **-lay·ing** : MISPLACE, LOSE ⟨*mislaid* his keys⟩

mis·lead \mis-'lēd\ *vb* **-led** \-'led\; **-lead·ing** : to lead in a wrong direction or into a mistaken action or belief — **mis·lead·ing·ly** *adv*

mis·like \-'līk\ *vb* : DISLIKE — **mis·like** *n*

mis·man·age \-'ma-nij\ *vb* : to manage badly — **mis·man·age·ment** *n*

mis·match \-'mach\ *vb* : to match unsuitably or badly — **mis·match** \mis-'mach, 'mis-,mach\ *n*

mis·name \-'nām\ *vb* : to name incorrectly : MISCALL

mis·no·mer \mis-'nō-mər\ *n* : a wrong or inappropriate name or designation

mi·so \'mē-sō\ *n* : a high-protein fermented food paste consisting chiefly of soybeans, salt, and usu. grain

mi·sog·y·ny \mə-'sä-jə-nē\ *n* [Gk *misogynia*, fr. *misein* to hate + *gynē* woman] : a hatred of women — **mi·sog·y·nist** \-nist\ *n or adj* — **mi·sog·y·nis·tic** \mə-,sä-jə-'nis-tik\ *adj*

mis·ori·ent \mi-'sȯr-ē-,ent\ *vb* : to orient improperly or incorrectly — **mis·ori·en·ta·tion** \mi-,sȯr-ē-ən-'tā-shən\ *n*

mis·place \mis-'plās\ *vb* **1** : to put in a wrong or unremembered place **2** : to set on a wrong object ⟨~ trust⟩

mis·play \-'plā\ *n* : a wrong or unskillful play — **mis·play** \mis-'plā, 'mis-,plā\ *vb*

mis·print \'mis-,print\ *n* : a mistake in printed matter — **mis·print** \mis-'print\ *vb*

mis·pro·nounce \,mis-prə-'naúns\ *vb* : to pronounce incorrectly — **mis·pro·nun·ci·a·tion** \-prə-,nən-sē-'ā-shən\ *n*

mis·quote \mis-'kwōt\ *vb* : to quote incorrectly — **mis·quo·ta·tion** \,mis-kwō-'tā-shən\ *n*

mis·read \-'rēd\ *vb* **-read** \-'red\; **-read·ing** \-'rē-diŋ\ : to read or interpret incorrectly ⟨~ her expression⟩

mis·rep·re·sent \,mis-,re-pri-'zent\ *vb* : to represent falsely or unfairly ⟨~ the facts⟩ — **mis·rep·re·sen·ta·tion** \-,zen-'tā-shən\ *n*

¹mis·rule \mis-'rül\ *vb* : MISGOVERN

²misrule *n* **1** : MISGOVERNMENT **2** : DISORDER

¹miss \'mis\ *vb* **1** : to fail to hit, reach, or contact **2** : to feel the absence of **3** : to fail to obtain **4** : AVOID ⟨just ~*ed* hitting the other car⟩ **5** : OMIT **6** : to fail to understand ⟨~ the point⟩ **7** : to fail to perform or attend; *also* : MISFIRE

²miss *n* **1** : a failure to hit or to attain a result **2** : MISFIRE

³miss *n* **1** *cap* — used as a title prefixed to the name of an unmarried woman or girl **2** : a young unmarried woman or girl

Miss *abbr* Mississippi

mis·sal \'mi-səl\ *n* : a book containing all that is said or sung at mass during the entire year

mis·send \mis-'send\ *vb* : to send incorrectly (as to a wrong destination)

mis·shap·en \-'shā-pən\ *adj* : badly shaped : having an ugly shape

mis·sile \'mi-səl\ *n* [L, fr. neut. of *missilis* capable of being thrown, fr. *mittere* to let go, send] : an object (as a stone, bullet, or rocket) thrown or projected usu. so as to strike a target

miss·ing \'mi-siŋ\ *adj* : ABSENT; *also* : LOST ⟨~ in action⟩

mis·sion \'mi-shən\ *n* **1** : a group of missionaries; *also* : a place where missionaries work **2** : a group of envoys to a foreign country; *also* : a team of specialists or cultural leaders sent to a foreign country **3** : TASK, OBJECTIVE

¹mis·sion·ary \'mi-shə-,ner-ē\ *adj* : of, relating to, or engaged in missions

²missionary *n, pl* **-ar·ies** : a person commissioned by a church to spread its faith or carry on humanitarian work

mis·sion·er \'mi-shə-nər\ *n* : MISSIONARY

Mis·sis·sip·pi·an \,mi-sə-'si-pē-ən\ *adj* **1** : of or relating to Mississippi, its people, or the Mississippi River **2** : of, relating to, or being the period of the Paleozoic era between the Devonian and the Pennsylvanian — **Mississippian** *n*

mis·sive \'mi-siv\ *n* : LETTER

mis·speak \mis-'spēk\ *vb* : to say imperfectly or incorrectly

mis·spell \-'spel\ *vb* : to spell incorrectly — **mis·spell·ing** *n*

mis·spend \-'spend\ *vb* **-spent** \-'spent\; **-spend·ing** : WASTE, SQUANDER ⟨my *misspent* youth⟩

mis·state \mis-'stāt\ *vb* : to state incorrectly — **mis·state·ment** *n*

mis·step \-'step\ *n* **1** : a wrong step **2** : MISTAKE, BLUNDER

mist \'mist\ *n* **1** : water in the form of particles suspended or falling in the air **2** : something that obscures understanding — **mist** *vb*

mis·tak·able \mə-'stā-kə-bəl\ *adj* : capable of being misunderstood or mistaken

¹mis·take \mi-'stāk\ *vb* **-took** \-'stúk\; **-tak·en** \-'stā-kən\; **-tak·ing** **1** : to blunder in the choice of **2** : MISINTERPRET **3** : to make a wrong judgment of the character or ability of **4** : to confuse with another — **mis·tak·en·ly** *adv* — **mis·tak·er** *n*

²mistake *n* **1** : a wrong judgment : MISUNDERSTANDING **2** : a wrong action or statement : ERROR

¹mis·ter \'mis-tər\ *n* **1** *cap* — used sometimes instead of *Mr.* **2** : SIR — used without a name in addressing a man

²mist·er \'mis-tər\ *n* : a device for spraying mist

mis·tle·toe \'mi-səl-,tō\ *n* : a European parasitic green shrub that grows on trees and has yellowish flowers and waxy white berries

mis·tral \'mis-trəl, mi-'sträl\ *n* [F, fr. Occitan, fr. *mistral* masterful, fr. LL *magistralis* of a teacher, fr. L *magister* master] : a strong cold dry northerly wind of southern France

mis·treat \mis-ˈtrēt\ *vb* : to treat badly : ABUSE — **mis·treat·ment** *n*

mis·tress \ˈmis-trəs\ *n* **1** : a woman who has power, authority, or ownership ⟨∼ of the house⟩ **2** : something personified as female that rules or dominates ⟨when Rome was ∼ of the world⟩ **3** : a woman other than his wife with whom a married man has sexual relations; *also, archaic* : SWEETHEART **4** — used archaically as a title prefixed to the name of a married or unmarried woman

mis·tri·al \ˈmis-ˌtrī(-ə)l\ *n* : a trial that has no legal effect

¹mis·trust \mis-ˈtrəst\ *n* : a lack of confidence : DISTRUST — **mis·trust·ful** \-fəl\ *adj* — **mis·trust·ful·ly** *adv* — **mis·trust·ful·ness** *n*

²mistrust *vb* : to have no trust or confidence in : SUSPECT

misty \ˈmis-tē\ *adj* **mist·i·er; -est 1** : obscured by or as if by mist : INDISTINCT **2** : TEARFUL — **mist·i·ly** \-tə-lē\ *adv* — **mist·i·ness** \-tē-nəs\ *n*

mis·un·der·stand \ˌmi-ˌsən-dər-ˈstand\ *vb* **-stood** \-ˈstud\; **-stand·ing 1** : to fail to understand **2** : to interpret incorrectly

mis·un·der·stand·ing \-ˈstan-diŋ\ *n* **1** : MISINTERPRETATION **2** : DISAGREEMENT, QUARREL

mis·us·age \mis-ˈyü-sij\ *n* **1** : bad treatment : ABUSE **2** : wrong or improper use

mis·use \mis-ˈyüz\ *vb* **1** : to use incorrectly **2** : ABUSE, MISTREAT — **mis·use** \-ˈyüs\ *n*

¹mite \ˈmīt\ *n* : any of numerous tiny arthropod animals related to the spiders that often live and feed on animals or plants

²mite *n* **1** : a small coin or sum of money **2** : a small amount : BIT

¹mi·ter *or* **mi·tre** \ˈmī-tər\ *n* [ME *mitre*, fr. AF, fr. L *mitra* headband, turban, fr. Gk] **1** : a headdress worn by bishops and abbots **2** : MITER JOINT

²miter *or* **mitre** *vb* **mi·tered** *or* **mi·tred; mi·ter·ing** *or* **mi·tring** \ˈmī-tə-riŋ\ **1** : to match or fit together in a miter joint **2** : to bevel the ends of for making a miter joint

miter joint *n* : a usu. perpendicular joint made by fitting together two parts with the ends cut at an angle

miter joints

mit·i·gate \ˈmi-tə-ˌgāt\ *vb* **-gat·ed; -gat·ing 1** : to make less harsh or hostile **2** : to make less severe or painful — **mit·i·ga·tion** \ˌmi-tə-ˈgā-shən\ *n* — **mit·i·ga·tive** \ˈmi-tə-ˌgā-tiv\ *adj*

mi·to·chon·dri·on \ˌmī-tə-ˈkän-drē-ən\ *n, pl* **-dria** \-drē-ə\ : any of various round or long cellular organelles that produce energy for the cell — **mi·to·chon·dri·al** \-drē-əl\ *adj*

mi·to·sis \mī-ˈtō-səs\ *n, pl* **-to·ses** \-ˌsēz\ : a process that takes place in the nucleus of a dividing cell and results in the formation of two new nuclei each of which has the same number of chromosomes as the parent nucleus; *also* : cell division in which mitosis occurs — **mi·tot·ic** \-ˈtä-tik\ *adj*

mitt \ˈmit\ *n* **1** : a baseball catcher's or first baseman's glove **2** *slang* : HAND

mit·ten \ˈmi-tᵊn\ *n* : a covering for the hand having a separate section for the thumb only — **mit·tened** \-tᵊnd\ *adj*

¹mix \ˈmiks\ *vb* **1** : to combine into one mass **2** : ASSOCIATE **3** : to form by mingling components **4** : to produce (a recording) by electronically combining sounds from different sources **5** : HYBRIDIZE **6** : CONFUSE ⟨∼*es* up the facts⟩ **7** : to become involved ♦ **Synonyms** BLEND, MERGE, COALESCE, AMALGAMATE, FUSE — **mix·able** *adj* — **mix it up** : to engage in a fight, contest, or dispute

²mix *n* : a product of mixing; *esp* : a commercially prepared mixture of food ingredients

mixed \ˈmikst\ *adj* **1** : combining features of more than one kind **2** : made up of or involving individuals or items of more than one kind **3** : including or accompanied by different or opposing elements ⟨a ∼ blessing⟩ **4** : resulting from the crossing or breeding of individuals of different races or breeds ⟨a stallion of ∼ blood⟩

mixed number *n* : a number (as $5^2/_3$) composed of an integer and a fraction

mixed–up \ˈmikst-ˈəp\ *adj* : CONFUSED

mix·er \ˈmik-sər\ *n* **1** : one that mixes; *esp* : a machine or device for mixing **2** : an event (as a dance) that encourages meeting and socializing **3** : a nonalcoholic beverage used in a cocktail

mixt *abbr* mixture

mix·ture \ˈmiks-chər\ *n* **1** : the act or process of mixing; *also* : the state of being mixed **2** : a product of mixing

mix–up \ˈmiks-ˌəp\ *n* **1** : an instance of confusion **2** : CONFLICT, FIGHT

miz·zen *also* **miz·en** \ˈmi-zᵊn\ *n* **1** : a fore-and-aft sail set on the mizzenmast **2** : MIZZENMAST — **mizzen** *also* **mizen** *adj*

miz·zen·mast \-ˌmast, -məst\ *n* : the mast aft or next aft of the mainmast

mk *abbr* **1** mark **2** markka

Mk *abbr* Mark

mks *abbr* meter-kilogram-second

mkt *abbr* market

mktg *abbr* marketing

ml *abbr* milliliter

Mlle *abbr* [F] mademoiselle

Mlles *abbr* [F] mesdemoiselles

mm *abbr* millimeter

MM *abbr* [F] messieurs

Mme *abbr* [F] madame

Mmes *abbr* [F] mesdames

Mn *symbol* manganese

MN *abbr* Minnesota

mne·mon·ic \ni-ˈmä-nik\ *adj* : assisting or designed to assist memory; *also* : of or relating to memory

mo *abbr* month

¹Mo *abbr* **1** Missouri **2** Monday

²Mo *symbol* molybdenum

MO *abbr* **1** mail order **2** medical officer **3** Missouri **4** modus operandi **5** money order

moan \ˈmōn\ *n* : a low prolonged sound indicative of pain or grief — **moan** *vb*

moat \ˈmōt\ *n* : a deep wide usu. water-filled trench around a castle

¹mob \ˈmäb\ *n* [L *mobile vulgus* vacillating crowd] **1** : MASSES, RABBLE **2** : a disorderly crowd **3** : a criminal gang

²mob *vb* **mobbed; mob·bing 1** : to crowd about and attack or annoy ⟨*mobbed* by fans⟩ **2** : to crowd into or around ⟨shoppers *mobbed* the stores⟩

¹mo·bile \ˈmō-bəl, -ˌbī(-ə)l, -ˌbēl\ *adj* **1** : capable of moving or being moved **2** : changeable in appearance, mood, or purpose; *also* : ADAPTABLE **3** : having the opportunity for or undergoing a shift in social status **4** : using vehicles for transportation ⟨∼ warfare⟩ **5** : CELLULAR 2 — **mo·bil·i·ty** \mō-ˈbi-lə-tē\ *n*

²mo·bile \ˈmō-ˌbēl\ *n* : a construction or sculpture (as of wire and sheet metal) with parts that can be set in motion by air currents; *also* : a similar structure suspended so that it is moved by air

mobile home *n* : a trailer used as a permanent dwelling

mo·bi·lise *chiefly Brit var of* MOBILIZE

mo·bi·lize \ˈmō-bə-ˌlīz\ *vb* **-lized; -liz·ing 1** : to put into movement or circulation **2** : to assemble and make ready for action ⟨∼ army reserves⟩ — **mo·bi·li·za·tion** \ˌmō-bə-lə-ˈzā-shən\ *n* — **mo·bi·liz·er** \ˈmō-bə-ˌlī-zər\ *n*

mob·ster \ˈmäb-stər\ *n* : a member of a criminal gang

moc·ca·sin \ˈmä-kə-sən\ *n* **1** : a soft leather heelless shoe **2** : WATER MOCCASIN

mo·cha \ˈmō-kə\ *n* [*Mocha*, port in Yemen] **1** : choice coffee grown in Arabia **2** : a mixture of coffee and chocolate or cocoa **3** : a dark chocolate-brown color

¹mock \ˈmäk, ˈmok\ *vb* **1** : to treat with contempt or ridicule **2** : DELUDE **3** : DEFY **4** : to mimic in sport or derision — **mock·er** *n* — **mock·ery** \ˈmä-kə-rē, ˈmo-\ *n* — **mock·ing·ly** *adv*

²mock *adj* : SIMULATED ⟨a ∼ trial⟩

mock·he·ro·ic \ˌmäk-hi-'rō-ik, ˌmȯk-\ *adj* : ridiculing or burlesquing heroic style, character, or action ⟨a ∼ poem⟩

mock·ing·bird \'mä-kiŋ-ˌbərd, 'mȯ-\ *n* : a grayish No. American songbird related to the catbirds and thrashers that mimics the calls of other birds

mock-up \'mä-ˌkəp, 'mȯ-\ *n* **1** : a full-sized structural model built for study, testing, or display ⟨a ∼ of a car⟩ **2** : a working sample (as of a magazine) for review

¹mod \'mäd\ *adj* **1** : of, relating to, or being the style of the 1960s British youth culture **2** : HIP, TRENDY

²mod *abbr* **1** moderate **2** modern **3** modification; modified

mode \'mōd\ *n* **1** : a particular form or variety of something; *also* : STYLE **2** : a manner of doing something **3** : the most frequent value of a set of data — **mod·al** \'mō-dᵊl\ *adj*

¹mod·el \'mä-dᵊl\ *n* **1** : structural design **2** : a miniature representation; *also* : a pattern of something to be made **3** : an example for imitation or emulation **4** : one who poses (as for an artist or to display clothes) **5** : TYPE, DESIGN ⟨a new car ∼⟩

²model *vb* **mod·eled** *or* **mod·elled; mod·el·ing** *or* **mod·el·ling** **1** : SHAPE, FASHION, CONSTRUCT ⟨∼ed in clay⟩ **2** : to work as a fashion model

³model *adj* **1** : serving as or worthy of being a pattern ⟨a ∼ student⟩ **2** : being a miniature representation of something ⟨a ∼ airplane⟩

mo·dem \'mō-dəm, -ˌdem\ *n* : a device that converts signals from one device (as a computer) to a form compatible with another (as a telephone)

¹mod·er·ate \'mä-də-rət\ *adj* **1** : avoiding extremes; *also* : TEMPERATE **2** : AVERAGE; *also* : MEDIOCRE **3** : limited in scope or effect **4** : not expensive — **moderate** *n* — **mod·er·ate·ly** *adv* — **mod·er·ate·ness** *n*

²mod·er·ate \'mä-də-ˌrāt\ *vb* **-at·ed; -at·ing** **1** : to lessen the intensity of : TEMPER **2** : to act as a moderator — **mod·er·a·tion** \ˌmä-də-'rā-shən\ *n*

mod·er·a·tor \'mä-də-ˌrā-tər\ *n* **1** : MEDIATOR **2** : one who presides over an assembly, meeting, or discussion

mod·ern \'mä-dərn\ *adj* [LL *modernus,* fr. L *modo* just now, fr. *modus* measure] : of, relating to, or characteristic of the present or the immediate past : CONTEMPORARY — **modern** *n* — **mo·der·ni·ty** \mə-'dər-nə-tē\ *n* — **mod·ern·ly** *adv* — **mod·ern·ness** *n*

mod·ern·ise, mod·ern·i·sa·tion *Brit var of* MODERNIZE, MODERNIZATION

mod·ern·ism \'mä-dər-ˌni-zəm\ *n* : a practice, movement, or belief peculiar to modern times

mod·ern·ize \'mä-dər-ˌnīz\ *vb* **-ized; -iz·ing** : to make or become modern — **mod·ern·i·za·tion** \ˌmä-dər-nə-'zā-shən\ *n* — **mod·ern·iz·er** *n*

mod·est \'mä-dəst\ *adj* **1** : having a moderate estimate of oneself; *also* : DIFFIDENT **2** : observing the proprieties of dress and behavior **3** : limited in size, amount, or scope ⟨a ∼ income⟩ — **mod·est·ly** *adv* — **mod·es·ty** \-də-stē\ *n*

mod·i·cum \'mä-di-kəm\ *n* : a small amount

modif *abbr* modification

mod·i·fy \'mä-də-ˌfī\ *vb* **-fied; -fy·ing** **1** : MODERATE **2** : to limit the meaning of esp. in a grammatical construction **3** : CHANGE, ALTER — **mod·i·fi·ca·tion** \ˌmä-də-fə-'kā-shən\ *n* — **mod·i·fi·er** \'mä-də-ˌfī-ər\ *n*

mod·ish \'mō-dish\ *adj* : FASHIONABLE, STYLISH — **mod·ish·ly** *adv* — **mod·ish·ness** *n*

mo·diste \mō-'dēst\ *n* : a maker of fashionable dresses and hats

mod·u·lar \'mä-jə-lər\ *adj* : constructed with standardized units

mod·u·lar·ized \'mä-jə-lə-ˌrīzd\ *adj* : containing or consisting of modules

mod·u·late \'mä-jə-ˌlāt\ *vb* **-lat·ed; -lat·ing** **1** : to tune to a key or pitch **2** : to keep in proper measure or proportion : TEMPER **3** : to vary the amplitude or frequency of a carrier wave for the transmission of information (as in radio or television) — **mod·u·la·tion** \ˌmä-jə-'lā-shən\ *n* — **mod·u·la·tor** \'mä-jə-ˌlā-tər\ *n* — **mod·u·la·to·ry** \-lə-ˌtȯr-ē\ *adj*

mod·ule \'mä-jül\ *n* **1** : any in a series of standardized units for use together **2** : an assembly of wired electronic parts for use with other such assemblies **3** : an inde-

pendent unit that constitutes a part of the total structure of a space vehicle ⟨a propulsion ∼⟩

mo·dus ope·ran·di \ˌmō-dəs-ˌä-pə-'ran-dē, -ˌdī\ *n, pl* **mo·di operandi** \ˌmō-ˌdē-, -ˌmō-ˌdī-\ [NL] : a method of procedure

¹mo·gul \'mō-gəl, mō-'gəl\ *n* [fr. *Mogul,* member of a Muslim dynasty ruling northern India] : an important person : MAGNATE ⟨a media ∼⟩

²mogul \'mō-gəl\ *n* : a bump in a ski run

mo·hair \'mō-ˌher\ *n* [modif. of obs. It *mocaiarro,* fr. Ar *mukhayyar,* lit., choice] : a fabric or yarn made wholly or in part from the long silky hair of the Angora goat; *also* : this goat hair

Mo·ham·med·an *also* **Mu·ham·mad·an** \mō-'ha-mə-dən, -'hä-, mü-\ *n* : MUSLIM — **Mo·ham·med·an·ism** *also* **Mu·ham·mad·an·ism** \-də-ˌni-zəm\ *n*

Mo·hawk \'mō-ˌhȯk\ *n, pl* **Mohawk** *or* **Mohawks** **1** : a member of an American Indian people of the Mohawk River valley, New York; *also* : the language of the Mohawk people **2** : a hairstyle with a narrow strip of upright hair down the center and the sides shaved

Mo·he·gan \mō-'hē-gən, mə-\ *or* **Mo·hi·can** \-'hē-kən\ *n, pl* **Mohegan** *or* **Mohegans** *or* **Mohican** *or* **Mohicans** : a member of an American Indian people of southeastern Connecticut

mo·hel \'mō-(h)el, 'mȯi-(ə-)l\ *n, pl* **mohels** *also* **mo·hal·im** \ˌmō-hä-'lēm\ *also* **mo·hel·im** \-(h)e-'lēm\ : a person who performs Jewish circumcisions

Mohican *var of* MAHICAN

moi·e·ty \'mȯi-ə-tē\ *n, pl* **-ties** : one of two equal or approximately equal parts

moil \'mȯi(-ə)l\ *vb* : to work hard : DRUDGE — **moil** *n* — **moil·er** *n*

moi·ré \mȯ-'rā, mwä-\ *or* **moire** *same or* 'mȯir, 'mwär\ *n* : a fabric (as silk) having a watered appearance

moist \'mȯist\ *adj* : slightly or moderately wet — **moist·ly** *adv* — **moist·ness** *n*

moist·en \'mȯi-sᵊn\ *vb* : to make or become moist — **moist·en·er** *n*

mois·ture \'mȯis-chər\ *n* : the small amount of liquid that causes dampness

mois·tur·ise *Brit var of* MOISTURIZE

mois·tur·ize \'mȯis-chə-ˌrīz\ *vb* **-ized; -iz·ing** : to add moisture to ⟨∼ the skin⟩ — **mois·tur·iz·er** *n*

mol *abbr* molecular; molecule

mo·lar \'mō-lər\ *n* [ME *molares,* pl., fr. L *molaris,* fr. *molaris* of a mill, fr. *mola* millstone] : any of the broad teeth adapted to grinding food and located in the back of the jaw — **molar** *adj*

mo·las·ses \mə-'la-səz\ *n* : the thick brown syrup that is separated from raw sugar in sugar manufacture

¹mold \'mōld\ *n* : crumbly soil rich in organic matter

²mold *n* **1** : distinctive nature or character **2** : the frame on or around which something is constructed **3** : a cavity in which something is shaped; *also* : an object so shaped **4** : MOLDING

³mold *vb* **1** : to shape in or as if in a mold **2** : to ornament with molding — **mold·er** *n*

⁴mold *n* : a surface growth of fungus esp. on damp or decaying matter; *also* : a fungus that produces mold — **mold·i·ness** \'mōl-dē-nəs\ *n* — **moldy** *adj*

⁵mold *vb* : to become moldy

mold·board \'mōld-ˌbȯrd\ *n* : a curved iron plate attached above the plowshare to lift and turn the soil

mold·er \'mōl-dər\ *vb* : to crumble into small pieces

mold·ing \'mōl-diŋ\ *n* **1** : an act or process of shaping in a mold; *also* : an object so shaped **2** : a decorative surface, plane, or curved strip

¹mole \'mōl\ *n* : a small often pigmented spot or protuberance on the skin

²mole *n* **1** : any of numerous small burrowing insect-eating mammals related to the shrews and hedgehogs **2** : a spy embedded within an organization

³mole *n* : a massive breakwater or jetty

molecular biology *n* : a branch of biology dealing with the ultimate physical and chemical organization of living matter and esp. with the molecular basis of inheritance and protein synthesis — **molecular biologist** *n*

molecular weight *n* : the mass of a molecule that is equal to the sum of the masses of all atoms contained in the molecule's formula

mol·e·cule \'mä-li-ˌkyül\ *n* : the smallest particle of matter that is the same chemically as the whole mass — **mo·lec·u·lar** \mə-'le-kyə-lər\ *adj*

mole·hill \'mōl-ˌhil\ *n* : a little ridge of earth thrown up by a mole

mole·skin \-ˌskin\ *n* **1** : the skin of the mole used as fur **2** : a heavy durable cotton fabric

mo·lest \mə-'lest\ *vb* **1** : ANNOY, DISTURB **2** : to make annoying sexual advances to; *esp* : to force physical and usu. sexual contact on — **mo·les·ta·tion** \ˌmō-ˌles-'tā-shən\ *n* — **mo·lest·er** *n*

moll \'mäl\ *n* : a gangster's girlfriend

mol·li·fy \'mä-lə-ˌfī\ *vb* **-fied; -fy·ing 1** : to soothe in temper : APPEASE **2** : SOFTEN **3** : to reduce in intensity : ASSUAGE — **mol·li·fi·ca·tion** \ˌmä-lə-fə-'kā-shən\ *n*

mol·lusk *or* **mol·lusc** \'mä-ləsk\ *n* : any of a large phylum of usu. shelled and aquatic invertebrate animals (as snails, clams, and squids) — **mol·lus·can** *also* **mol·lus·kan** \mə-'ləs-kən\ *adj*

¹mol·ly·cod·dle \'mä-lē-ˌkä-dᵊl\ *n* : a pampered man or boy

²mollycoddle *vb* **mol·ly·cod·dled; mol·ly·cod·dling** : PAMPER

Mo·lo·tov cocktail \'mä-lə-ˌtȯf-, 'mȯ-\ *n* [Vyacheslav M. *Molotov* †1986 Soviet foreign minister] : a crude bomb made of a bottle filled usu. with gasoline and fitted with a wick (as a saturated rag) that is ignited just prior to hurling

¹molt \'mōlt\ *vb* : to shed hair, feathers, outer skin, or horns periodically with the cast-off parts being replaced by new growth — **molt·er** *n*

²molt *n* : the act or process of molting

mol·ten \'mōl-tᵊn\ *adj* **1** : fused or liquefied by heat **2** : GLOWING

mo·ly \'mō-lē\ *n* : a mythical herb with black root, white flowers, and magic powers

mo·lyb·de·num \mə-'lib-də-nəm\ *n* : a metallic chemical element used in strengthening and hardening steel

mom \'mäm, 'məm\ *n* : MOTHER

mom–and–pop *adj* : being a small owner-operated business

mo·ment \'mō-mənt\ *n* **1** : a minute portion of time : INSTANT **2** : a time of excellence ⟨he has his ∼s⟩ **3** : IMPORTANCE ♦ **Synonyms** CONSEQUENCE, SIGNIFICANCE, WEIGHT, IMPORT

mo·men·tari·ly \ˌmō-mən-'ter-ə-lē\ *adv* **1** : for a moment **2** *archaic* : INSTANTLY **3** : at any moment : SOON

mo·men·tary \'mō-mən-ˌter-ē\ *adj* **1** : continuing only a moment; *also* : EPHEMERAL **2** : recurring at every moment — **mo·men·tar·i·ness** \-ˌter-ē-nəs\ *n*

mo·men·tous \mō-'men-təs\ *adj* : very important — **mo·men·tous·ly** *adv* — **mo·men·tous·ness** *n*

mo·men·tum \mō-'men-təm\ *n*, *pl* **mo·men·ta** \-'men-tə\ *or* **momentums** : a property that a moving body has due to its mass and motion; *also* : IMPETUS

mom·my \'mä-mē, 'mə-\ *n*, *pl* **mom·mies** : MOTHER

Mon *abbr* Monday

mon·arch \'mä-nərk, -ˌnärk\ *n* **1** : a person who reigns over a kingdom or an empire **2** : one holding preeminent position or power **3** : MONARCH BUTTERFLY — **mo·nar·chi·cal** \mə-'när-ki-kəl\ *also* **mo·nar·chic** \-'när-kik\ *adj*

monarch butterfly *n* : a large orange and black migratory American butterfly whose larva feeds on milkweed

mon·ar·chist \'mä-nər-kist\ *n* : a believer in monarchical government — **mon·ar·chism** \-ˌki-zəm\ *n*

mon·ar·chy \'mä-nər-kē\ *n*, *pl* **-chies** : a nation or state governed by a monarch

mon·as·tery \'mä-nə-ˌster-ē\ *n*, *pl* **-ter·ies** : a house for persons under religious vows (as monks)

mo·nas·tic \mə-'nas-tik\ *adj* : of or relating to monasteries or to monks or nuns — **monastic** *n* — **mo·nas·ti·cal·ly** \-ti-k(ə-)lē\ *adv* — **mo·nas·ti·cism** \-tə-ˌsi-zəm\ *n*

mon·au·ral \mä-'nȯr-əl\ *adj* : MONOPHONIC — **mon·au·ral·ly** *adv*

Mon·day \'mən-dē, -ˌdā\ *n* : the second day of the week

mon·e·tary \'mä-nə-ˌter-ē, 'mə-\ *adj* : of or relating to money or to the mechanisms by which it is supplied and circulated in the economy

mon·ey \'mə-nē\ *n*, *pl* **moneys** *or* **mon·ies** \'mə-nēz\ **1** : something (as metal currency) accepted as a medium of exchange **2** : wealth reckoned in monetary terms **3** : the 1st, 2d, and 3d places in a horse or dog race

mon·eyed \'mə-nēd\ *adj* **1** : having money : WEALTHY **2** : consisting in or derived from money

mon·ey·lend·er \'mə-nē-ˌlen-dər\ *n* : one (as a bank or pawnbroker) whose business is lending money

money market *n* : the trade in short-term negotiable financial instruments

money of account : a denominator of value or basis of exchange used in keeping accounts

money order *n* : an order purchased at a post office, bank, or telegraph office directing another office to pay a sum of money to a party named on it

mon·ger \'məŋ-gər, 'mäŋ-\ *n* **1** : DEALER **2** : one who tries to stir up or spread something — usu. used in combination ⟨war*monger*⟩

mon·go \'mäŋ-(ˌ)gō\ *n*, *pl* **mongo** — see *tugrik* at MONEY table

Mon·gol \'mäŋ-gəl, 'mäŋ-ˌgōl\ *n* : a member of any of several traditionally pastoral peoples of Mongolia — **Mongol** *adj*

Mon·go·lian \män-'gōl-yən, mäŋ-, -'gō-lē-ən\ *n* **1** : a native or inhabitant of Mongolia **2** : a member of the Mongoloid racial stock — **Mongolian** *adj*

Mon·gol·oid \'mäŋ-gə-ˌlȯid\ *adj* : of or relating to a major racial stock native to Asia that includes peoples of northern and eastern Asia, Malaysians, Eskimos, and often American Indians — **Mongoloid** *n*

mon·goose \'mäŋ-ˌgüs, 'mäŋ-\ *n*, *pl* **mon·goos·es** *also* **mon·geese** \-ˌgēs\ : any of a group of small agile Old World mammals that are related to the civet cats and feed chiefly on small animals and fruits

mon·grel \'mäŋ-grəl, 'məŋ-\ *n* : an offspring of parents of different breeds; *esp* : one of uncertain ancestry

mon·i·ker \'mä-ni-kər\ *n* : NAME, NICKNAME

mo·nism \'mō-ˌni-zəm, 'mä-\ *n* : a view that reality is basically one unitary organic whole — **mo·nist** \'mō-nist, 'mä-\ *n*

mo·ni·tion \mō-'ni-shən, mə-\ *n* : WARNING, CAUTION

¹mon·i·tor \'mä-nə-tər\ *n* **1** : a student appointed to assist a teacher **2** : one that monitors; *esp* : a video display screen (as for a computer)

²monitor *vb* : to watch, check, or observe for a special purpose

mon·i·to·ry \'mä-nə-ˌtȯr-ē\ *adj* : giving admonition : WARNING

¹monk \'məŋk\ *n* [ME, fr. OE *munuc*, fr. LL *monachus*, fr. LGk *monachos*, fr. Gk, adj., single, fr. *monos* single, alone] : a man belonging to a religious order and living in a monastery — **monk·ish** *adj*

²monk *n* : MONKEY

¹mon·key \'məŋ-kē\ *n*, *pl* **monkeys** : a nonhuman primate mammal; *esp* : one of the smaller, longer-tailed, and usu. more arboreal primates as contrasted with the apes

²monkey *vb* **mon·keyed; mon·key·ing 1** : FOOL, TRIFLE — often used with *around* **2** : TAMPER — usu. used with *with*

monkey bars *n pl* : a framework of bars on which children can play

mon·key·shine \'məŋ-kē-ˌshīn\ *n* : PRANK — usu. used in pl.

monkey wrench *n* : a wrench with one fixed and one adjustable jaw at right angles to a handle

monkey wrench

monk·fish \'məŋk-ˌfish\ *n* : either of two marine bony fishes that have a large flattened head and are used for food

monks·hood \'məŋks-ˌhu̇d\ *n* : any of a genus of poisonous plants related to the buttercups; *esp* : a tall Eurasian herb with white or purplish flowers

¹mono \'mä-nō\ *adj* : MONOPHONIC

²mono *n* : INFECTIOUS MONONUCLEOSIS

mono·chro·mat·ic \ˌmä-nə-krō-'ma-tik\ *adj* **1** : having or consisting of one color **2** : consisting of radiation (as light) of a single wavelength

MONEY — WORLD CURRENCIES

NAME	SUBDIVISION	COUNTRY	NAME	SUBDIVISION	COUNTRY
afghani	100 puls	Afghanistan	dollar — see RINGGIT, below		
ariary	5 iraimbilanja	Madagascar	dong	100 xu	Vietnam
baht	100 satang	Thailand	dram	100 luma	Armenia
or tical			escudo	100 centavos	Cape Verde
balboa[1]	100 centesimos	Panama	euro[4]	100 cents	Austria,
birr	100 cents	Ethiopia	Belgium, Finland, France, Germany,		
bolivar	100 centimos	Venezuela	Greece, Ireland, Italy, Luxembourg,		
boliviano	100 centavos	Bolivia	Netherlands, Portugal, Spain		
cedi	100 pesewas	Ghana	florin — see GULDEN, below		
colón	100 centimos	Costa Rica	forint	100 fillers	Hungary
colón[1]	100 centavos	El Salvador	franc[5]	100 centimes	Benin,
córdoba	100 centavos	Nicaragua	Burkina Faso, Cameroon, Central		
dalasi	100 bututs	Gambia	African Republic, Chad, Republic		
denar	100 deni[2]	Republic of Macedonia	of the Congo, Equatorial Guinea, Gabon, Guinea-Bissau, Ivory Coast,		
dinar	100 centimes	Algeria	Mali, Niger, Senegal, Togo		
dinar	1000 fils	Bahrain	franc	100 centimes	Burundi
dinar	1000 fils	Iraq	franc	100 centimes	Comoros
dinar	1000 fils	Jordan	franc	100 centimes	Democratic
dinar	1000 fils	Kuwait	Republic of the Congo		
dinar	1000 dirhams	Libya	franc	100 centimes	Djibouti
dinar		Sudan	franc	100 centimes	Guinea
dinar	1000 millimes	Tunisia	franc	100 centimes[2]	Rwanda
dirham	100 centimes	Morocco	franc	100 centimes	Switzerland
dirham	100 fils	United Arab Emirates	*or* rappen		
dobra	100 centimos	São Tomé and Príncipe	gourde	100 centimes	Haiti
			guarani	100 centimos	Paraguay
dollar[3]	100 cents	Antigua and Barbuda, Dominica, Grenada, St. Kitts-Nevis, St. Lucia, St. Vincent and the Grenadines	gulden	100 cents	Suriname
			or florin		
dollar	100 cents	Australia	hryvnia	100 kopiykas	Ukraine
dollar	100 cents	Bahamas	kina	100 toea	Papua New Guinea
dollar	100 cents	Barbados			
dollar	100 cents	Belize	kip	100 at	Laos
dollar	100 cents	Bermuda	koruna	100 haleru	Czech Republic
dollar	100 sen	Brunei	koruna	100 haleru	Slovakia
or cents			krona	100 aurar	Iceland
dollar	100 cents	Canada	(*sing* eyrir)		
dollar	100 cents	Fiji	krona	100 ore	Sweden
dollar	100 cents	Guyana	krone	100 ore	Denmark
dollar	100 cents	Hong Kong	krone	100 ore	Norway
dollar	100 cents	Jamaica	kroon	100 senti	Estonia
dollar	100 cents	Liberia	(*sing* sent)		
dollar	100 cents	Namibia	kuna	100 lipa	Croatia
dollar	100 cents	New Zealand	kwacha	100 tambala	Malawi
dollar	100 cents	Singapore	kwacha	100 ngwee	Zambia
dollar	100 cents	Solomon Islands	kwanza	100 lwei	Angola
			kyat	100 pyas	Myanmar
dollar	100 cents	Taiwan	lari	100 tetri	Republic of Georgia
or yuan					
dollar	100 cents	Trinidad and Tobago	lats	100 santimi	Latvia
			(*sing* santims)		
dollar	100 cents	United States	lek	100 qindarka	Albania
dollar	100 cents	Zimbabwe	(*sing* qintar)		
			lempira	100 centavos	Honduras
			leone	100 cents	Sierra Leone

MONEY — WORLD CURRENCIES

NAME	SUBDIVISION	COUNTRY	NAME	SUBDIVISION	COUNTRY
leu	100 bani (*sing* ban)	Moldova	rial *also* riyal	100 fils	Yemen
leu	100 bani (*sing* ban)	Romania	rial — see RIYAL, below		
lev	100 stotinki	Bulgaria	riel	100 sen	Cambodia
lilangeni (*pl* emalangeni)	100 cents	Swaziland	ringgit *or* dollar	100 sen	Malaysia
lira *or* pound	100 cents	Malta	riyal	100 dirhams	Qatar
lira	100 kurus	Turkey	riyal *also* rial	100 halala	Saudi Arabia
litas	100 centai (*sing* centas)	Lithuania	riyal — see RIAL, above		
livre — see POUND, below			rubel	100 kapeek (*sing* kapeyka)	Belarus
loti	100 licente (*sing* sente)	Lesotho	ruble	100 kopecks	Russia
manat	100 gopik	Azerbaijan	rufiyaa	100 laari	Maldives
manat	100 tennesi	Turkmenistan	rupee	100 paisa	India
metical	100 centavos	Mozambique	rupee	100 cents	Mauritius
naira	100 kobo	Nigeria	rupee	100 paisa	Nepal
nakfa	100 cents	Eritrea	rupee	100 paisa	Pakistan
ngultrum	100 chetrums	Bhutan	rupee	100 cents	Seychelles
ouguiya	5 khoums	Mauritania	rupee	100 cents	Sri Lanka
pa'anga	100 seniti	Tonga	rupiah	100 sen	Indonesia
pataca	100 avos	Macao	shekel	100 agorot	Israel
peso	100 centavos	Argentina	shilling	100 cents	Kenya
peso	100 centavos	Chile	shilling	100 cents	Somalia
peso	100 centavos	Colombia	shilling	100 cents	Tanzania
peso	100 centavos	Cuba	shilling	100 cents	Uganda
peso	100 centavos	Dominican Republic	sol	100 centimos	Peru
			som	100 tyiyn	Kyrgyzstan
peso	100 centavos	Mexico	som	100 tiyin	Uzbekistan
peso *or* piso	100 sentimos *or* centavos	Philippines	somoni	100 dirams	Tajikistan
			sucre[1]	100 centavos	Ecuador
peso	100 centesimos	Uruguay	taka	100 paisa *or* poisha	Bangladesh
pound	100 cents	Cyprus	tala	100 sene	Samoa
pound	100 piastres	Egypt	tenge	100 tyin	Kazakhstan
pound	100 piastres	Lebanon	tical — see BAHT, above		
pound *or* livre			tolar	100 stotinov (*sing* stotin)	Slovenia
pound	100 piastres	Syria	tugrik	100 mongo	Mongolia
pound	100 pence (*sing* penny)	United Kingdom	vatu		Vanuatu
			won	100 chon	North Korea
pound — see LIRA, above					
pula	100 thebe	Botswana	won	100 chon	South Korea
quetzal	100 centavos	Guatemala			
rand	100 cents	South Africa	yen	100 sen[2]	Japan
real	100 centavos	Brazil	yuan	100 fen	China
rial	100 dinars	Iran	yuan — see DOLLAR, above		
rial	1000 baiza	Oman	zloty	100 groszy	Poland

[1] A monetary unit in name only; replaced by the U.S. dollar.
[2] Now a subdivision in name only.
[3] Dollars issued by the Eastern Caribbean Central Bank, established to promote economic cooperation among the member nations.
[4] Replaced the individual monetary units of participating European Union countries Jan. 1, 2002.
[5] Francs issued by the African Financial Community, established to promote economic cooperation among member nations.

mono·chrome \'mä-nə-ˌkrōm\ *adj* : involving or producing visual images in a single color or in varying tones of a single color ⟨~ television⟩

mon·o·cle \'mä-ni-kəl\ *n* : an eyeglass for one eye

mono·clo·nal \ˌmä-nə-ˈklō-nəl\ *adj* : produced by, being, or composed of cells derived from a single cell ⟨~ antibodies⟩

mono·cot·y·le·don \ˌmä-nə-ˌkät-tə-ˈlē-dᵊn\ *n* : any of a class or subclass of chiefly herbaceous seed plants having an embryo with a single cotyledon and usu. parallelveined leaves

mon·o·dy \'mä-nə-dē\ *n, pl* **-dies** : ELEGY, DIRGE — **mo·nod·ic** \mə-ˈnä-dik\ *or* **mo·nod·i·cal** \-di-kəl\ *adj* — **mon·o·dist** \'mä-nə-dist\ *n*

mo·nog·a·my \mə-ˈnä-gə-mē\ *n* **1** : marriage with but one person at a time **2** : the practice of having a single mate during a period of time — **mo·nog·a·mist** \-mist\ *n* — **mo·nog·a·mous** \-məs\ *adj*

mono·gram \'mä-nə-ˌgram\ *n* : a sign of identity composed of the combined initials of a name — **monogram** *vb*

mono·graph \'mä-nə-ˌgraf\ *n* : a learned treatise on a small area of learning

mono·lin·gual \ˌmä-nə-ˈliŋ-gwəl\ *adj* : knowing or using only one language

mono·lith \'mä-nə-lith\ *n* **1** : a single great stone often in the form of a monument or column **2** : something large and powerful that acts as a single unified force — **mono·lith·ic** \ˌmä-nə-ˈli-thik\ *adj*

mono·logue *also* **mono·log** \'mä-nə-ˌlòg\ *n* **1** : a dramatic soliloquy; *also* : a long speech monopolizing conversation **2** : the routine of a stand-up comic — **mono·logu·ist** \-ˌlòg-ist\ *or* **mo·nol·o·gist** \mə-ˈnä-lə-jist; 'mä-nə-ˌlò-gist\ *n*

mono·ma·nia \ˌmä-nə-ˈmā-nē-ə, -nyə\ *n* **1** : mental disorder limited in expression to one area of thought **2** : excessive concentration on a single object or idea — **mono·ma·ni·ac** \-nē-ˌak\ *n or adj*

mono·mer \'mä-nə-mər\ *n* : a simple chemical compound that can be polymerized

mono·nu·cle·o·sis \ˌmä-nō-ˌnü-klē-ˈō-səs, -ˌnyü-\ *n* : INFECTIOUS MONONUCLEOSIS

mono·phon·ic \ˌmä-nə-ˈfä-nik\ *adj* : of or relating to sound recording or reproduction involving a single transmission path

mono·plane \'mä-nə-ˌplān\ *n* : an airplane with only one set of wings

mo·nop·o·ly \mə-ˈnä-pə-lē\ *n, pl* **-lies** [L *monopolium*, fr. Gk *monopōlion*, fr. *monos* single + *pōlein* to sell] **1** : exclusive ownership (as through command of supply) **2** : a commodity controlled by one party **3** : one that has a monopoly — **mo·nop·o·list** \-list\ *n* — **mo·nop·o·lis·tic** \mə-ˌnä-pə-ˈlis-tik\ *adj* — **mo·nop·o·li·za·tion** \-lə-ˈzā-shən\ *n* — **mo·nop·o·lize** \mə-ˈnä-pə-ˌlīz\ *vb*

mono·rail \'mä-nə-ˌrāl\ *n* : a single rail serving as a track for a vehicle; *also* : a vehicle traveling on such a track

monorail

mono·so·di·um glu·ta·mate \ˌmä-nə-ˌsō-dē-əm-ˈglü-tə-ˌmāt\ *n* : a crystalline salt used to enhance the flavor of food

mono·syl·la·ble \'mä-nə-ˌsi-lə-bəl\ *n* : a word of one syllable — **mono·syl·lab·ic** \ˌmä-nə-sə-ˈla-bik\ *adj* — **mono·syl·lab·i·cal·ly** \-bi-k(ə-)lē\ *adv*

mono·the·ism \'mä-nə-(ˌ)thē-ˌi-zəm\ *n* : a doctrine or belief that there is only one deity — **mono·the·ist** \-ˌthē-ist\ *n* — **mono·the·is·tic** \-thē-ˈis-tik\ *adj*

mono·tone \'mä-nə-ˌtōn\ *n* : a succession of syllables, words, or sentences in one unvaried key or pitch

mo·not·o·nous \mə-ˈnä-tə-nəs\ *adj* **1** : uttered or sounded in one unvarying tone **2** : tediously uniform — **mo·not·o·nous·ly** *adv* — **mo·not·o·nous·ness** *n*

mo·not·o·ny \mə-ˈnä-tə-nē\ *n* : tedious sameness or uniformity

mono·un·sat·u·rat·ed \ˌmä-nō-ˌən-ˈsa-chə-ˌrā-təd\ *adj* : containing one double or triple bond per molecule — used esp. of an oil, fat, or fatty acid

mon·ox·ide \mə-ˈnäk-ˌsīd\ *n* : an oxide containing one atom of oxygen in a molecule

mon·sei·gneur \ˌmōⁿ-ˌsān-ˈyər\ *n, pl* **mes·sei·gneurs** \ˌmā-ˌsān-ˈyər, -ˈyərz\ : a French dignitary — used as a title

mon·sieur \məs-ˈyər\ *n, pl* **mes·sieurs** *same or* -ˈyərz\ : a Frenchman of high rank or station — used as a title equivalent to *Mister*

mon·si·gnor \män-ˈsē-nyər\ *n, pl* **monsignors** *or* **mon·si·gno·ri** \ˌmän-ˌsēn-ˈyòr-ē\ [It *monsignore*] : a Roman Catholic prelate — used as a title

mon·soon \män-ˈsün\ *n* [obs. Dutch *monssoen*, fr. Pg *monção*, fr. Ar *mawsim* time, season] **1** : a periodic wind esp. in the Indian Ocean and southern Asia **2** : the season of the southwest monsoon esp. in India **3** : rainfall associated with the monsoon

¹**mon·ster** \'män-stər\ *n* **1** : an abnormally developed plant or animal **2** : an animal of strange or terrifying shape; *also* : one unusually large of its kind **3** : an extremely ugly, wicked, or cruel person — **mon·stros·i·ty** \män-ˈsträ-sə-tē\ *n* — **mon·strous** \'män-strəs\ *adj* — **mon·strous·ly** *adv*

²**monster** *adj* : very large : ENORMOUS

mon·strance \'män-strəns\ *n* : a vessel in which the consecrated Host is exposed for the adoration of the faithful

Mont *abbr* Montana

mon·tage \män-ˈtäzh\ *n* [F] **1** : a composite photograph made by combining several separate pictures **2** : an artistic composition made up of several different kinds of elements **3** : a varied mixture : JUMBLE

month \'mənth\ *n, pl* **months** \'məns, 'mənths\ : one of the 12 parts into which the year is divided — **month·ly** *adv or adj or n*

month·long \'mənth-ˌlòŋ\ *adj* : lasting a month

mon·u·ment \'män-yə-mənt\ *n* **1** : a lasting reminder; *esp* : a structure erected in remembrance of a person or event **2** : NATIONAL MONUMENT

mon·u·men·tal \ˌmän-yə-ˈmen-tᵊl\ *adj* **1** : of or relating to a monument **2** : MASSIVE; *also* : OUTSTANDING ⟨a ~ achievement⟩ **3** : very great — **mon·u·men·tal·ly** *adv*

moo \'mü\ *vb* : to make the natural throat noise of a cow — **moo** *n*

¹**mood** \'müd\ *n* **1** : a conscious state of mind or predominant emotion : FEELING **2** : a prevailing attitude : DISPOSITION **3** : a distinctive atmosphere

²**mood** *n* : distinction of form of a verb to express whether its action or state is conceived as fact or in some other manner (as wish)

moody \'mü-dē\ *adj* **mood·i·er; -est 1** : GLOOMY **2** : subject to moods : TEMPERAMENTAL — **mood·i·ly** \-də-lē\ *adv* — **mood·i·ness** \-dē-nəs\ *n*

¹**moon** \'mün\ *n* **1** : the earth's natural satellite **2** : SATELLITE 2

²**moon** *vb* : to engage in idle reverie

moon·beam \'mün-ˌbēm\ *n* : a ray of light from the moon

¹**moon·light** \-ˌlīt\ *n* : the light of the moon — **moon·lit** \-ˌlit\ *adj*

²**moonlight** *vb* **moon·light·ed; moon·light·ing** : to hold a second job in addition to a regular one — **moon·light·er** *n*

moon·roof \-ˌrüf, -ˌrùf\ *n* : a glass sunroof

moon·scape \-ˌskāp\ *n* : the surface of the moon as seen or as pictured

moon·shine \-ˌshīn\ *n* **1** : MOONLIGHT **2** : empty talk **3** : intoxicating liquor usu. illegally distilled

moon·stone \-ˌstōn\ *n* : a transparent or translucent feldspar of pearly luster used as a gem

moon·struck \-ˌstrək\ *adj* **1** : mentally unbalanced **2** : romantically sentimental **3** : lost in fantasy

¹moor \'mur\ *n* **1** *chiefly Brit* : an expanse of open rolling infertile land **2** : a boggy area; *esp* : one that is peaty and dominated by grasses and sedges

²moor *vb* : to make fast with or as if with cables, lines, or anchors

Moor \'mur\ *n* : one of the Arab and Berber conquerors of Spain — **Moor·ish** *adj*

moor·ing \'mur-iŋ\ *n* **1** : a place where or an object to which a craft can be made fast **2** : an established practice or stabilizing influence — usu. used in pl.

moor·land \-lənd, -,land\ *n* : land consisting of moors

moose \'müs\ *n, pl* **moose** : a large heavy-antlered ruminant mammal related to the deer that has humped shoulders and long legs and inhabits northern forested areas

¹moot \'müt\ *vb* : to bring up for discussion; *also* : DEBATE

²moot *adj* **1** : open to question; *also* : DISPUTED **2** : having no practical significance

¹mop \'mäp\ *n* : an implement made of absorbent material fastened to a handle and used esp. for cleaning floors

²mop *vb* **mopped; mop·ping** : to use a mop on : clean with a mop

mope \'mōp\ *vb* **moped; mop·ing** **1** : to become dull, dejected, or listless **2** : DAWDLE

mo·ped \'mō-,ped\ *n* : a light low-powered motorbike that can be pedaled

mop·pet \'mä-pət\ *n* [obs. E *mop* fool, child] : CHILD

mo·raine \mə-'rān\ *n* : an accumulation of earth and stones left by a glacier

¹mor·al \'mȯr-əl\ *adj* **1** : of or relating to principles of right and wrong **2** : conforming to a standard of right behavior; *also* : capable of right and wrong action **3** : probable but not proved ⟨a ∼ certainty⟩ **4** : perceptual or psychological rather than tangible or practical in nature or effect ⟨a ∼ victory⟩ ♦ **Synonyms** VIRTUOUS, RIGHTEOUS, NOBLE, ETHICAL, PRINCIPLED — **mor·al·ly** *adv*

²moral *n* **1** : the practical meaning (as of a story) **2** *pl* : moral practices or teachings

mo·rale \mə-'ral\ *n* **1** : MORALITY **2** : the mental and emotional attitudes of an individual to the tasks at hand; *also* : ESPRIT DE CORPS

mor·al·ise *Brit var of* MORALIZE

mor·al·ist \'mȯr-ə-list\ *n* **1** : one who leads a moral life **2** : a thinker or writer concerned with morals **3** : one concerned with regulating the morals of others — **mor·al·is·tic** \,mȯr-ə-'lis-tik\ *adj* — **mor·al·is·ti·cal·ly** \-ti-k(ə-)lē\ *adv*

mo·ral·i·ty \mə-'ra-lə-tē\ *n, pl* **-ties** : moral conduct : VIRTUE

mor·al·ize \'mȯr-ə-,līz\ *vb* **-ized; -iz·ing** : to make moral reflections — **mor·al·i·za·tion** \,mȯr-ə-lə-'zā-shən\ *n* — **mor·al·iz·er** \'mȯr-ə-,lī-zər\ *n*

mo·rass \mə-'ras\ *n* [D *moeras*, fr. OF *maresc*, of Gmc origin; akin to OE *mersc* marsh] : SWAMP; *also* : something that entangles, impedes, or confuses

mor·a·to·ri·um \,mȯr-ə-'tȯr-ē-əm\ *n, pl* **-ri·ums** *or* **-ria** \-ē-ə\ [ultim. fr. L *mora* delay] : a suspension of activity

mo·ray eel \'mȯr-,ā-, mȯr-'ā-\ *n* : any of numerous often brightly colored biting eels of warm seas

mor·bid \'mȯr-bəd\ *adj* **1** : of, relating to, or typical of disease; *also* : DISEASED, SICKLY **2** : characterized by gloomy or unwholesome ideas or feelings **3** : GRISLY, GRUESOME ⟨∼ details⟩ — **mor·bid·i·ty** \mȯr-'bi-də-tē\ *n* — **mor·bid·ly** *adv* — **mor·bid·ness** *n*

mor·dant \'mȯr-d³nt\ *adj* **1** : biting or caustic in manner or style **2** : BURNING, PUNGENT — **mor·dant·ly** *adv*

¹more \'mȯr\ *adj* **1** : GREATER ⟨something ∼ than I expected⟩ **2** : ADDITIONAL

²more *adv* **1** : in addition **2** : to a greater or higher degree ⟨∼ evenly matched⟩

³more *n* **1** : a greater quantity, number, or amount ⟨the ∼ the merrier⟩ **2** : an additional amount ⟨costs a little ∼⟩

⁴more *pron* : additional persons or things or a greater amount

mo·rel \mə-'rel\ *n* : any of several pitted edible fungi

more·over \mȯr-'ō-vər\ *adv* : in addition : FURTHER

mo·res \'mȯr-,āz\ *n pl* [L, pl. of *mor-, mos* custom] **1** : the fixed morally binding customs of a group **2** : HABITS, MANNERS

Mor·gan \'mȯr-gən\ *n* : any of an American breed of lightly built horses

morgue \'mȯrg\ *n* : a place where the bodies of dead persons are kept until released for burial or autopsy

mor·i·bund \'mȯr-ə-(,)bənd\ *adj* : being in a dying condition

Mor·mon \'mȯr-mən\ *n* : a member of the Church of Jesus Christ of Latter-day Saints — **Mor·mon·ism** \-mə-,ni-zəm\ *n*

morn \'mȯrn\ *n* : MORNING

morn·ing \'mȯr-niŋ\ *n* **1** : the early part of the day; *esp* : the time from the sunrise to noon **2** : BEGINNING

morn·ing–after pill \,mȯr-niŋ-'af-tər-\ *n* : a contraceptive drug taken up to usu. three days after sexual intercourse

morning glory *n* : any of various twining plants related to the sweet potato that have often showy bell-shaped or funnel-shaped flowers

morning sickness *n* : nausea and vomiting that typically occur in the morning esp. during early pregnancy

morning star *n* : a bright planet (as Venus) seen in the eastern sky before or at sunrise

mo·roc·co \mə-'rä-kō\ *n* : a fine leather made of goatskins tanned with sumac

mo·ron \'mȯr-,än\ *n* **1** *usu. offensive* : a mildly mentally retarded person **2** : a very stupid person — **mo·ron·ic** \mə-'rä-nik\ *adj* — **mo·ron·i·cal·ly** \-ni-k(ə-)lē\ *adv*

mo·rose \mə-'rōs\ *adj* [L *morosus* hard to please, exacting, fr. *mor-, mos* custom, disposition] : having a sullen disposition; *also* : GLOOMY — **mo·rose·ly** *adv* — **mo·rose·ness** *n*

morph \'mȯrf\ *vb* : to change the form or character of : TRANSFORM

mor·pheme \'mȯr-,fēm\ *n* : a meaningful linguistic unit that contains no smaller meaningful parts — **mor·phe·mic** \mȯr-'fē-mik\ *adj*

mor·phia \'mȯr-fē-ə\ *n* : MORPHINE

mor·phine \'mȯr-,fēn\ *n* [F, fr. Gk *Morpheus,* Greek god of dreams] : an addictive drug obtained from opium and used to ease pain or induce sleep

mor·phol·o·gy \mȯr-'fä-lə-jē\ *n* **1** : a branch of biology dealing with the form and structure of organisms **2** : a study and description of word formation in a language — **mor·pho·log·i·cal** \,mȯr-fə-'lä-ji-kəl\ *adj* — **mor·phol·o·gist** \mȯr-'fä-lə-jist\ *n*

mor·ris \'mȯr-əs\ *n* : a vigorous English dance traditionally performed by men wearing costumes and bells

mor·row \'mär-ō\ *n* : the next day

Morse code \'mȯrs-\ *n* : either of two codes consisting of dots and dashes or long and short sounds used for transmitting messages

mor·sel \'mȯr-səl\ *n* [ME, fr. AF, dim. of *mors* bite, fr. L *morsus,* fr. *mordēre* to bite] **1** : a small piece or quantity **2** : a tasty dish

mor·tal \'mȯr-t³l\ *adj* **1** : causing death : FATAL; *also* : leading to eternal punishment ⟨∼ sin⟩ **2** : subject to death ⟨∼ man⟩ **3** : implacably hostile ⟨∼ foe⟩ **4** : very great : EXTREME ⟨∼ fear⟩ **5** : HUMAN ⟨∼ limitations⟩ — **mortal** *n* — **mor·tal·i·ty** \mȯr-'ta-lə-tē\ *n* — **mor·tal·ly** \'mȯr-t³l-ē\ *adv*

¹mor·tar \'mȯr-tər\ *n* **1** : a strong bowl in which substances are pounded or crushed with a pestle **2** : a short-barreled cannon used to fire shells at high angles

²mortar *n* : a building material (as a mixture of lime and cement with sand and water) that is spread between bricks or stones to bind them together as it hardens — **mortar** *vb*

mor·tar·board \'mȯr-tər-,bȯrd\ *n* **1** : a square board for holding mortar **2** : an academic cap with a flat square top

mort·gage \'mȯr-gij\ *n* [ME *morgage,* fr. AF *mortgage,* fr. *mort* dead + *gage* pledge] : a transfer of rights to a piece of property usu. as security for the payment of a loan or debt that becomes void when the debt is paid — **mortgage** *vb* — **mort·gag·ee** \,mȯr-gi-'jē\ *n* — **mort·gag·or** \,mȯr-gi-'jȯr\ *n*

mor·ti·cian \mȯr-'ti-shən\ *n* [L *mort-, mors* death + E *-ician* (as in *physician*)] : UNDERTAKER

mor·ti·fy \'mȯr-tə-,fī\ *vb* **-fied; -fy·ing** **1** : to subdue (as the body) esp. by abstinence or self-inflicted pain **2** : HUMILIATE **3** : to become necrotic or gangrenous — **mor·ti·fi·ca·tion** \,mȯr-tə-fə-'kā-shən\ *n*

mor·tise *also* **mor·tice** \'mȯr-təs\ *n* : a hole cut in a piece of wood into which another piece fits to form a joint

mor·tu·ary \'mȯr-chə-ˌwer-ē\ *n, pl* **-ar·ies** : a place in which dead bodies are kept until burial

mos *abbr* months

mo·sa·ic \mō-'zā-ik\ *n* : a surface decoration made by inlaying small pieces (as of colored glass or stone) to form figures or patterns; *also* : a design made in mosaic — **mosaic** *adj*

mo·sey \'mō-zē\ *vb* **mo·seyed; mo·sey·ing** : SAUNTER

mosh \'mäsh\ *vb* : to engage in rough uninhibited dancing near the stage at a rock concert

mosh pit *n* : an area in front of a stage where rough dancing takes place at a rock concert

Mos·lem \'mäz-ləm\ *var of* MUSLIM

mosque \'mäsk\ *n* : a building used for public worship by Muslims

mos·qui·to \mə-'skē-tō\ *n, pl* **-toes** *also* **-tos** : any of a family of dipteran flies the female of which sucks the blood of animals

mosquito net *n* : a net or screen for keeping out mosquitoes

moss \'mȯs\ *n* : any of a class of green plants that lack flowers but have small leafy stems and often grow in clumps — **mossy** *adj*

moss·back \'mȯs-ˌbak\ *n* : an extremely conservative person : FOGY

¹most \'mōst\ *adj* **1** : GREATEST ⟨the ∼ ability⟩ **2** : the majority of ⟨∼ people⟩

²most *adv* **1** : to the greatest or highest degree ⟨∼ beautiful⟩ **2** : to a very great degree ⟨a ∼ careful driver⟩

³most *n* : the greatest amount ⟨the ∼ I can do⟩

⁴most *pron* : the greatest number or part ⟨∼ became discouraged⟩

-most *adj suffix* : most ⟨inner*most*⟩ : most toward ⟨end*most*⟩

most·ly \'mōst-lē\ *adv* : MAINLY

mot \'mō\ *n, pl* **mots** *same or* \'mōz\ [F, word, saying, fr. LL *muttum* grunt] : a witty saying

mote \'mōt\ *n* : a small particle

mo·tel \mō-'tel\ *n* [blend of *motor* and *hotel*] : a hotel in which the rooms are accessible from the parking area

mo·tet \mō-'tet\ *n* : a choral work on a sacred text for several voices usu. without instrumental accompaniment

moth \'mȯth\ *n, pl* **moths** \'mȯthz, 'mȯths\ : any of various insects belonging to the same order as the butterflies but usu. night-flying and with a stouter body and smaller wings

moth·ball \'mȯth-ˌbȯl\ *n* **1** : a ball (as of naphthalene) used to keep moths out of clothing **2** *pl* : protective storage

¹moth·er \'mə-thər\ *n* **1** : a female parent **2** : the superior of a religious community of women **3** : SOURCE, ORIGIN ⟨necessity is the ∼ of invention⟩ — **moth·er·hood** \-ˌhu̇d\ *n* — **moth·er·less** *adj* — **moth·er·li·ness** \-lē-nəs\ *n* — **moth·er·ly** *adj*

²mother *vb* **1** : to give birth to; *also* : PRODUCE **2** : to care for or protect like a mother

moth·er·board \'mə-thər-ˌbȯrd\ *n* : the main circuit board esp. of a microcomputer

moth·er–in–law \'mə-thər-ən-ˌlȯ\ *n, pl* **mothers–in–law** \'mə-thərz-\ : the mother of one's spouse

moth·er·land \'mə-thər-ˌland\ *n* **1** : the land of origin of something **2** : the native land of one's ancestors

moth·er–of–pearl \ˌmə-thər-əv-'pərl\ *n* : the hard pearly matter forming the inner layer of a mollusk shell

mother ship *n* : a ship serving smaller craft

mo·tif \mō-'tēf\ *n* [F, motive, motif] : a dominant idea or central theme (as in a work of art)

mo·tile \'mōt-ᵊl, 'mō-ˌtī(-ə)l\ *adj* : capable of spontaneous movement — **mo·til·i·ty** \mō-'ti-lə-tē\ *n*

¹mo·tion \'mō-shən\ *n* **1** : an act, process, or instance of moving **2** : a proposal for action (as by a deliberative body) **3** *pl* : ACTIVITIES, MOVEMENTS — **mo·tion·less** *adj* — **mo·tion·less·ly** *adv* — **mo·tion·less·ness** *n*

²motion *vb* : to direct or signal by a movement

motion picture *n* : a series of pictures projected on a screen so rapidly that they produce a continuous picture in which persons and objects seem to move

motion sickness *n* : sickness induced by motion and characterized by nausea

mo·ti·vate \'mō-tə-ˌvāt\ *vb* **-vat·ed; -vat·ing** : to provide with a motive : IMPEL — **mo·ti·va·tion** \ˌmō-tə-'vā-shən\

n — **mo·ti·va·tion·al** \-shə-nəl\ *adj* — **mo·ti·va·tor** \'mō-tə-ˌvā-tər\ *n*

¹mo·tive \'mō-tiv, 2 also mō-'tēv\ *n* **1** : something (as a need or desire) that causes a person to act **2** : a recurrent theme in a musical composition **3** : MOTIF — **mo·tive·less** *adj*

²mo·tive \'mō-tiv\ *adj* **1** : moving to action **2** : of or relating to motion

mot·ley \'mät-lē\ *adj* **1** : variegated in color **2** : made up of diverse often incongruous elements ◆ *Synonyms* HETEROGENEOUS, MISCELLANEOUS, ASSORTED, MIXED, VARIED

¹mo·tor \'mō-tər\ *n* [L, fr. *movēre* to move] **1** : one that imparts motion **2** : a machine that produces motion or power for doing work **3** : AUTOMOBILE

²motor *vb* : to travel or transport by automobile : DRIVE — **mo·tor·ist** *n*

mo·tor·bike \'mō-tər-ˌbīk\ *n* : a small lightweight motorcycle

mo·tor·boat \-ˌbōt\ *n* : a boat propelled by a motor

mo·tor·cade \-ˌkād\ *n* : a procession of motor vehicles

mo·tor·car \-ˌkär\ *n* : AUTOMOBILE

mo·tor·cy·cle \'mō-tər-ˌsī-kəl\ *n* : a 2-wheeled automotive vehicle — **mo·tor·cy·clist** \-k(ə-)list\ *n*

motor home *n* : a large motor vehicle equipped as living quarters

motor inn *n* : MOTEL

mo·tor·ise *Brit var of* MOTORIZE

mo·tor·ize \'mō-tə-ˌrīz\ *vb* **-ized; -iz·ing** **1** : to equip with a motor **2** : to equip with automobiles

mo·tor·man \'mō-tər-mən\ *n* : an operator of a motor-driven vehicle (as a streetcar or subway train)

motor scooter *n* : a low 2- or 3-wheeled automotive vehicle resembling a child's scooter but having a seat

mo·tor·truck \'mō-tər-ˌtrək\ *n* : an automotive truck

motor vehicle *n* : an automotive vehicle (as an automobile) not operated on rails

mot·tle \'mä-tᵊl\ *vb* **mot·tled; mot·tling** : to mark with spots of different color : BLOTCH

mot·to \'mä-tō\ *n, pl* **mottoes** *also* **mottos** [It, fr. LL *muttum* grunt, fr. L *muttire* to mutter] **1** : a sentence, phrase, or word inscribed on something to indicate its character or use **2** : a short expression of a guiding rule of conduct

moue \'mü\ *n* : a little grimace

mould *chiefly Brit var of* MOLD

moult *chiefly Brit var of* MOLT

mound \'maund\ *n* **1** : an artificial bank or hill of earth or stones **2** : KNOLL **3** : HEAP, PILE ⟨a ∼ of work⟩

¹mount \'maunt\ *n* : a high hill

²mount *vb* **1** : to increase in amount or extent; *also* : RISE, ASCEND **2** : to get up on something; *esp* : to seat oneself on (as a horse) for riding **3** : to put in position ⟨∼ artillery⟩ **4** : to set on something that elevates **5** : to attach to a support **6** : to prepare esp. for examination or display — **mount·able** *adj* — **mount·er** *n*

³mount *n* **1** : FRAME, SUPPORT **2** : a means of conveyance; *esp* : SADDLE HORSE

moun·tain \'maun-tᵊn\ *n* : a landmass higher than a hill — **moun·tain·ous** \-tə-nəs\ *adj* — **moun·tainy** \-tᵊn-ē\ *adj*

mountain ash *n* : any of various trees related to the roses that have pinnate leaves and red or orange-red fruits

mountain bike *n* : a bicycle with wide knobby tires, straight handlebars, and 18 or 21 gears that is designed to operate esp. over unpaved terrain

moun·tain·eer \ˌmaun-tə-'nir\ *n* **1** : a native or inhabitant of a mountainous region **2** : one who climbs mountains for sport

mountain goat *n* : a ruminant mammal of mountainous northwestern No. America that resembles a goat

mountain laurel *n* : a No. American evergreen shrub or small tree of the heath family with glossy leaves and clusters of rose-colored or white flowers

mountain lion *n* : COUGAR

moun·tain·side \'maun-tᵊn-ˌsīd\ *n* : the side of a mountain

moun·tain·top \-ˌtäp\ *n* : the summit of a mountain

moun·te·bank \'maun-ti-ˌbaŋk\ *n* [It *montimbanco,* fr. *montare* to mount + *in* in, on + *banco, banca* bench] : QUACK, CHARLATAN

Mount·ie \'maun-tē\ *n* : a member of the Royal Canadian Mounted Police

mount·ing \'maún-tiŋ\ *n* : something that serves as a frame or support

mourn \'mōrn\ *vb* : to feel or express grief or sorrow — **mourn·er** *n*

mourn·ful \-fəl\ *adj* : expressing, feeling, or causing sorrow — **mourn·ful·ly** *adv* — **mourn·ful·ness** *n*

mourn·ing \'mōr-niŋ\ *n* **1** : an outward sign (as black clothes) of grief for a person's death **2** : a period of time during which signs of grief are shown

mouse \'maús\ *n, pl* **mice** \'mīs\ **1** : any of numerous small rodents with pointed snout, long body, and slender tail **2** : a small manual device that controls cursor movement on a computer display

mouse pad *n* : a thin flat pad on which a computer mouse is used

mous·er \'maú-sər\ *n* : a cat proficient at catching mice

mouse·trap \'maús-ˌtrap\ *n* **1** : a trap for catching mice **2** : a stratagem that lures one to defeat or destruction — **mousetrap** *vb*

mousse \'müs\ *n* [F, lit., froth, moss] **1** : a molded chilled dessert made with sweetened and flavored whipped cream or egg whites and gelatin **2** : a foamy preparation used in styling hair — **mousse** *vb*

moustache *var of* MUSTACHE

mousy *or* **mous·ey** \'maú-sē, -zē\ *adj* **mous·i·er; -est 1** : QUIET, STEALTHY **2** : TIMID **3** : grayish brown — **mous·i·ness** \'maú-sē-nəs, -zē-\ *n*

¹mouth \'maúth\ *n, pl* **mouths** \'maúthz, 'maúths\ **1** : the opening through which an animal takes in food; *also* : the cavity that encloses the tongue, lips, and teeth in the typical vertebrate **2** : something resembling a mouth (as in affording entrance) — **mouthed** \'maúthd, 'maútht\ *adj* — **mouth·ful** *n*

²mouth \'maúth\ *vb* **1** : SPEAK; *also* : DECLAIM **2** : to repeat without comprehension or sincerity **3** : to form soundlessly with the lips

mouth harp *n* : HARMONICA

mouth·part \'maúth-ˌpärt\ *n* : a structure or appendage near the mouth (as of an insect) esp. when adapted for eating

mouth·piece \-ˌpēs\ *n* **1** : a part (as of a musical instrument) that goes in the mouth or to which the mouth is applied **2** : SPOKESMAN

mouth–to–mouth *adj* : of, relating to, or being a method of artificial respiration in which air from a rescuer's mouth is forced into a victim's lungs

mouth·wash \-ˌwȯsh, -ˌwäsh\ *n* : a usu. antiseptic liquid preparation for cleaning the mouth and teeth

mou·ton \'mü-ˌtän\ *n* : processed sheepskin that has been sheared or dyed to resemble beaver or seal

¹move \'müv\ *vb* **moved; mov·ing 1** : to change or cause to change position or posture **2** : to go or cause to go from one point to another; *also* : DEPART **3** : to take or cause to take action **4** : to show marked activity **5** : to stir the emotions **6** : to make a formal request, application, or appeal **7** : to change one's residence **8** : EVACUATE **2** — **mov·able** *or* **move·able** \'mü-və-bəl\ *adj*

²move *n* **1** : an act of moving **2** : a calculated step taken to gain an objective **3** : a change of location **4** : an agile action esp. in sports

move·ment \'müv-mənt\ *n* **1** : the act or process of moving : MOVE **2** : a series of organized activities working toward an objective **3** : the moving parts of a mechanism (as of a watch) **4** : RHYTHM **5** : a section of an extended musical composition **6** : an act of voiding the bowels; *also* : STOOL **4**

mov·er \'mü-vər\ *n* : one that moves; *esp* : one that moves the belongings of others from one location to another

mov·ie \'mü-vē\ *n* **1** : MOTION PICTURE **2** *pl* : a showing of a motion picture **3** *pl* : the motion-picture industry

¹mow \'maú\ *n* : the part of a barn where hay or straw is stored

²mow \'mō\ *vb* **mowed; mowed** *or* **mown** \'mōn\; **mow·ing 1** : to cut (as grass) with a scythe or machine **2** : to cut the standing herbage of ⟨~ the lawn⟩ — **mow·er** *n*

mox·ie \'mäk-sē\ *n* **1** : ENERGY, PEP **2** : COURAGE, DETERMINATION

moz·za·rel·la \ˌmät-sə-'re-lə\ *n* [It] : a moist white unsalted unripened mild cheese of a smooth rubbery texture

¹MP \'em-'pē\ *n* **1** : a member of the military police **2** : an elected member of a parliament

²MP *abbr* **1** melting point **2** metropolitan police

mpg *abbr* miles per gallon

mph *abbr* miles per hour

Mr. \'mis-tər\ *n, pl* **Messrs.** \'me-sərz\ — used as a conventional title of courtesy before a man's surname or his title of office

MRI *n* MAGNETIC RESONANCE IMAGING; *also* : the procedure in which magnetic resonance imaging is used

Mr. Right *n* : a man who would make the perfect husband

Mrs. \'mi-səz, -səs, *esp Southern* 'mi-zəz, -zəs\ *n, pl* **Mesdames** \mā-'däm, -'dam\ — used as a conventional title of courtesy before a married woman's surname

Ms. \'miz\ *n, pl* **Mss.** *or* **Mses.** \'mi-zez\ — used instead of *Miss* or *Mrs.*

MS *abbr* **1** manuscript **2** master of science **3** military science **4** Mississippi **5** motor ship **6** multiple sclerosis

msec *abbr* millisecond

msg *abbr* message

MSG *abbr* **1** master sergeant **2** monosodium glutamate

msgr *abbr* **1** monseigneur **2** monsignor

MSgt *abbr* master sergeant

MSS *abbr* manuscripts

MST *abbr* mountain standard time

mt *abbr* mount; mountain

¹Mt *abbr* Matthew

²Mt *symbol* meitnerium

MT *abbr* **1** metric ton **2** Montana **3** mountain time

mtg *abbr* **1** meeting **2** mortgage

mtge *abbr* mortgage

mu \'myü, 'mü\ *n* : the 12th letter of the Greek alphabet — M or μ

¹much \'məch\ *adj* **more** \'mȯr\; **most** \'mōst\ : great in quantity, amount, extent, or degree ⟨~ money⟩

²much *adv* **more; most 1** : to a great degree or extent ⟨~ happier⟩ **2** : ALMOST, NEARLY ⟨looks ~ as he did before⟩

³much *n* **1** : a great quantity, amount, extent, or degree **2** : something considerable or impressive

mu·ci·lage \'myü-sə-lij\ *n* : a watery sticky solution (as of a gum) used esp. as an adhesive — **mu·ci·lag·i·nous** \ˌmyü-sə-'la-jə-nəs\ *adj*

muck \'mək\ *n* **1** : soft moist barnyard manure **2** : FILTH, DIRT **3** : a dark richly organic soil; *also* : MUD, MIRE — **mucky** *adj*

muck·rake \-ˌrāk\ *vb* : to expose publicly real or apparent misconduct of a prominent individual or business — **muck·rak·er** *n*

mu·cus \'myü-kəs\ *n* : a slimy slippery protective secretion of membranes (**mucous membranes**) lining some body cavities — **mu·cous** \-kəs\ *adj*

mud \'məd\ *n* : soft wet earth : MIRE

mud·dle \'mə-dᵊl\ *vb* **mud·dled; mud·dling 1** : to make muddy **2** : to confuse esp. with liquor **3** : to mix up or make a mess of **4** : to think or act in a confused way

mud·dle·head·ed \ˌmə-dᵊl-'he-dəd\ *adj* **1** : mentally confused **2** : INEPT

¹mud·dy \'mə-dē\ *adj* **mud·di·er; -est 1** : full of or covered with mud **2** : suggestive of mud **3** : CLOUDY, OBSCURE — **mud·di·ness** *n*

²muddy *vb* **mud·died; mud·dy·ing 1** : to soil or stain with or as if with mud **2** : to make cloudy or obscure **3** : CONFUSE

mud·flat \'məd-ˌflat\ *n* : a level tract alternately covered and left bare by the tide

mud·guard \'məd-ˌgärd\ *n* : a guard over or a flap behind a wheel of a vehicle to catch or deflect mud

mud·room \-ˌrüm, -ˌrum\ *n* : a room in a house for removing dirty or wet footwear and clothing

mud·sling·er \-ˌsliŋ-ər\ *n* : one who uses invective esp. against a political opponent — **mud·sling·ing** \-ˌsliŋ-iŋ\ *n*

Muen·ster \'mən-stər, 'mün-, 'mun-\ *n* : a semisoft bland cheese

mu·ez·zin \mü-'e-z°n, myü-\ *n* : a Muslim crier who calls the hour of daily prayer

¹muff \'məf\ *n* : a warm tubular covering for the hands

²muff *n* : a bungling performance; *esp* : a failure to hold a ball in attempting a catch — **muff** *vb*

muf·fin \'mə-fən\ *n* : a small soft cake baked in a cup-shaped container

muf·fle \'mə-fəl\ *vb* **muf·fled; muf·fling 1** : to wrap up so as to conceal or protect **2** : to wrap or pad with something to dull the sound of **3** : to keep down : SUPPRESS

muf·fler \'mə-flər\ *n* **1** : a scarf worn around the neck **2** : a device (as on a car's exhaust) to deaden noise

muf·ti \'məf-tē\ *n* : civilian clothes

¹mug \'məg\ *n* : a usu. metal or earthenware cylindrical drinking cup

²mug *vb* **mugged; mug·ging** **1** : to pose or make faces esp. to attract attention or for a camera **2** : PHOTOGRAPH

³mug *vb* **mugged; mug·ging** : to assault usu. with intent to rob — **mug·ger** *n*

mug·gy \'mə-gē\ *adj* **mug·gi·er; -est** : being warm and humid — **mug·gi·ness** \-gē-nəs\ *n*

mug·wump \'məg-ˌwəmp\ *n* [obs. slang *mugwump* kingpin, fr. Massachusett (Algonquian language of New England) *mugquomp* war leader] : an independent in politics

Muhammadan, Muhammadanism *var of* MOHAMMEDAN, MOHAMMEDANISM

mu·ja·hid·een *or* **mu·ja·hed·in** \mü-ja-hi-'dēn, -jä-\ *n pl* [Ar *mujāhidīn*, pl. of *mujāhid*, lit., person who wages jihad] : Islamic guerrilla fighters esp. in the Middle East

muk·luk \'mək-ˌlək\ *n* **1** : an Eskimo boot of sealskin or reindeer skin **2** : a boot with a soft leather sole worn over several pairs of socks

mu·lat·to \mü-'la-tō, myü-, -'lä-\ *n, pl* **-toes** *or* **-tos** [Sp *mulato*, fr. *mulo* mule, fr. L *mulus*] : a first-generation offspring of a black person and a white person; *also* : a person of mixed white and black ancestry

mul·ber·ry \'məl-ˌber-ē\ *n* : any of a genus of trees with edible berrylike fruit and leaves used as food for silkworms; *also* : the fruit

mulch \'məlch\ *n* : a protective covering (as of straw or leaves) spread on the ground esp. to reduce evaporation or control weeds — **mulch** *vb*

¹mulct \'məlkt\ *n* : FINE, PENALTY

²mulct *vb* **1** : FINE **2** : CHEAT, DEFRAUD

¹mule \'myül\ *n* **1** : a hybrid offspring of a male donkey and a female horse **2** : a very stubborn person — **mul·ish** \'myü-lish\ *adj* — **mul·ish·ly** *adv* — **mu·lish·ness** *n*

²mule *n* : a slipper whose upper does not extend around the heel of the foot

mule deer *n* : a long-eared deer of western No. America

mu·le·teer \ˌmyü-lə-'tir\ *n* : one who drives mules

¹mull \'məl\ *vb* : PONDER, MEDITATE

²mull *vb* : to heat, sweeten, and flavor (as wine) with spices

mul·lein \'mə-lən\ *n* : a tall herb related to the snapdragons that has coarse woolly leaves and flowers in spikes

mul·let \'mə-lət\ *n, pl* **mullet** *or* **mullets** : any of a family of largely gray chiefly marine bony fishes including valuable food fishes

mul·li·gan stew \'mə-li-gən-\ *n* : a stew made from whatever ingredients are available

mul·li·ga·taw·ny \ˌmə-li-gə-'tò-nē\ *n* : a soup usu. of chicken stock seasoned with curry

mul·lion \'məl-yən\ *n* : a vertical strip separating windowpanes

multi- *comb form* **1** : many : multiple ⟨*multi*unit⟩ **2** : many times over ⟨*multi*millionaire⟩

mul·ti·col·ored \ˌməl-ti-'kə-lərd\ *adj* : having many colors

mul·ti·cul·tur·al \ˌməl-tē-'kəl-chə-rəl, -ˌtī-\ *adj* : of, relating to, reflecting, or adapted to diverse cultures ⟨a ~ society⟩ — **mul·ti·cul·tur·al·ism** \-rə-ˌli-zəm\ *n* — **mul·ti·cul·tur·al·ist** \-rə-list\ *n or adj*

mul·ti·di·men·sion·al \-ti-də-'men-chə-nəl, -ˌtī-, -dī-\ *adj* : of, relating to, or having many facets or dimensions ⟨a ~ problem⟩ ⟨~ space⟩

mul·ti·eth·nic \-'eth-nik\ *adj* : including, involving, or made up of people of various ethnic groups

mul·ti·fac·et·ed \-'fa-sə-təd\ *adj* : having many facets or aspects

mul·ti·fam·i·ly \-'fam-lē, -'fa-mə-\ *adj* : designed for use by several families

mul·ti·far·i·ous \ˌməl-tə-'fer-ē-əs\ *adj* : having great variety : DIVERSE — **mul·ti·far·i·ous·ness** *n*

mul·ti·form \'məl-ti-ˌfòrm\ *adj* : having many forms or appearances — **mul·ti·for·mi·ty** \ˌməl-ti-'fòr-mə-tē\ *n*

mul·ti·lat·er·al \ˌməl-ti-'la-tə-rəl, -ˌtī-, -'la-trəl\ *adj* : having many sides or participants ⟨~ treaty⟩ — **mul·ti·lat·er·al·ism** \-'la-tə-rə-ˌli-zəm\ *n* — **mul·ti·lat·er·al·ly** *adv*

multilayered \-'lā-ərd, -'lerd\ *or* **multilayer** \-'lā-ər, 'ler\ *adj* : having or involving several distinct layers or levels

mul·ti·lev·el \-'le-vəl\ *adj* : having several levels

mul·ti·lin·gual \-'liŋ-gwəl\ *adj* : knowing or using several languages — **mul·ti·lin·gual·ism** \-gwə-ˌli-zəm\ *n*

¹mul·ti·me·dia \-'mē-dē-ə\ *adj* : using, involving, or encompassing several media ⟨a ~ advertising campaign⟩

²multimedia *n sing or pl* : the technique of using several media (as in art); *also* : something (as software) that uses or facilitates it

mul·ti·mil·lion·aire \ˌməl-ti-ˌmil-yə-'nar, -ˌtī-, -'mil-yə-ˌnar\ *n* : a person worth several million dollars

mul·ti·na·tion·al \-'na-shə-nəl\ *adj* **1** : of or relating to several nationalities **2** : relating to or involving several nations **3** : having divisions in several countries ⟨a ~ corporation⟩ — **multinational** *n*

mul·ti·pack \'məl-tē-ˌpak\ *n* : a package of several individually packed items sold as a unit

¹mul·ti·ple \'məl-tə-pəl\ *adj* **1** : more than one; *also* : MANY ⟨~ achievements⟩ **2** : VARIOUS

²multiple *n* : the product of a quantity by an integer ⟨35 is a ~ of 7⟩

multiple–choice *adj* : having several answers given from which the correct one is to be chosen ⟨a ~ question⟩

multiple personality disorder *n* : a neurosis in which the personality becomes separated into two or more parts each of which controls behavior part of the time

multiple sclerosis *n* : a disease marked by patches of hardened tissue in the brain or spinal cord and associated esp. with partial or complete paralysis and muscular tremor

mul·ti·plex \'məl-tə-ˌpleks\ *n* : CINEPLEX

mul·ti·pli·cand \ˌməl-tə-pli-'kand\ *n* : the number that is to be multiplied by another

mul·ti·pli·ca·tion \ˌməl-tə-plə-'kā-shən\ *n* **1** : INCREASE **2** : a short method of finding the result of adding a figure the number of times indicated by another figure

multiplication sign *n* **1** : TIMES SIGN **2** : a centered dot indicating multiplication

mul·ti·plic·i·ty \ˌməl-tə-'pli-sə-tē\ *n, pl* **-ties** : a great number or variety

mul·ti·pli·er \'məl-tə-ˌplī(-ə)r\ *n* : one that multiplies; *esp* : a number by which another number is multiplied

mul·ti·ply \'məl-tə-ˌplī\ *vb* **-plied; -ply·ing** **1** : to increase in number (as by breeding) **2** : to find the product of by multiplication; *also* : to perform multiplication

mul·ti·pur·pose \ˌməl-ti-'pər-pəs, -ˌtī-\ *adj* : having or serving several purposes

mul·ti·ra·cial \-'rā-shəl\ *adj* : composed of, involving, or representing various races

mul·ti·sense \-ˌsens\ *adj* : having several meanings ⟨~ words⟩

mul·ti·sto·ry \-ˌstòr-ē\ *adj* : having several stories ⟨~ buildings⟩

mul·ti·task·ing \'məl-tē-ˌtas-kiŋ, -ˌtī-\ *n* **1** : the concurrent performance of several jobs by a computer **2** : the performance of multiple tasks at one time — **mul·ti·task** \-ˌtask\ *vb* — **mul·ti·task·er** \-ˌtaskər\ *n*

mul·ti·tude \'məl-tə-ˌtüd, -ˌtyüd\ *n* : a great number — **mul·ti·tu·di·nous** \ˌməl-tə-'tü-d²n-əs, -'tyüd-\ *adj*

mul·ti·unit \ˌməl-ti-'yü-nət, -ˌtī-\ *adj* : having several units

mul·ti·vi·ta·min \-'vī-tə-mən\ *adj* : containing several vitamins and esp. all known to be essential to health — **multivitamin** *n*

¹mum \'məm\ *adj* : SILENT

²mum *chiefly Brit var of* MOM

³mum *n* : CHRYSANTHEMUM

mum·ble \'məm-bəl\ *vb* **mum·bled; mum·bling** : to speak in a low indistinct manner — **mumble** *n* — **mum·bler** *n* — **mum·bly** *adj*

mum·ble·ty–peg \'məm-bəl-tē-ˌpeg\ *also* **mumble–the–peg** \'məm-bəl-thə-\ *n* : a game in which the players try to flip a knife from various positions so that the blade will stick into the ground

mum·bo jum·bo \ˌməm-bō-'jəm-bō\ *n* **1** : a complicated ritual with elaborate trappings **2** : GIBBERISH, NONSENSE

mum·mer \'mə-mər\ *n* **1** : an actor esp. in a pantomime **2** : a person who goes merrymaking in disguise during festivals — **mum·mery** *n*

mum·my \'mə-mē\ *n, pl* **mummies** [ME *mummie* powdered parts of a mummified body used as a drug, fr. AF *mumie*, fr. ML *mumia*, fr. Ar *mūmiya* bitumen, mummy, fr. Per *mūm* wax] : a body embalmed for burial in the manner of the ancient Egyptians — **mum·mi·fi·ca·tion** \ˌmə-mi-fə-ˈkā-shən\ *n* — **mum·mi·fy** \ˈmə-mi-ˌfī\ *vb*

mumps \ˈməmps\ *n sing or pl* [fr. pl. of obs. *mump* grimace] : a virus disease marked by fever and swelling esp. of the salivary glands

mun *or* **munic** *abbr* municipal

munch \ˈmənch\ *vb* : to eat with a chewing action; *also* : to snack on

munch·ies \ˈmən-chēz\ *n pl* 1 : hunger pangs 2 : light snack foods

mun·dane \ˌmən-ˈdān, ˈmən-ˌdān\ *adj* 1 : of or relating to the world 2 : concerned with the practical details of everyday life — **mun·dane·ly** *adv*

mung bean \ˈməŋ-\ *n* : an erect bushy bean widely grown in warm regions for its edible seeds and as the chief source of bean sprouts; *also* : its seed

mu·nic·i·pal \myu̇-ˈni-sə-pəl\ *adj* 1 : of, relating to, or characteristic of a municipality 2 : restricted to one locality — **mu·nic·i·pal·ly** *adv*

mu·nic·i·pal·i·ty \myu̇-ˌni-sə-ˈpa-lə-tē\ *n, pl* **-ties** : an urban political unit with corporate status and usu. powers of self-government

mu·nif·i·cent \myu̇-ˈni-fə-sənt\ *adj* : liberal in giving : GENEROUS — **mu·nif·i·cence** \-səns\ *n*

mu·ni·tion \myu̇-ˈni-shən\ *n* : ARMAMENT, AMMUNITION

¹mu·ral \ˈmyu̇r-əl\ *adj* 1 : of or relating to a wall 2 : applied to and made part of a wall or ceiling surface

²mural *n* : a mural painting — **mu·ral·ist** *n*

¹mur·der \ˈmər-dər\ *n* 1 : the crime of unlawfully killing a person esp. with malice aforethought 2 : something unusually difficult or dangerous

²murder *vb* 1 : to commit a murder; *also* : to kill brutally 2 : to put an end to 3 : to spoil by performing poorly ⟨~ a song⟩ — **mur·der·er** *n*

mur·der·ess \ˈmər-də-rəs\ *n* : a woman who murders

mur·der·ous \ˈmər-də-rəs\ *adj* 1 : having or appearing to have the purpose of murder 2 : marked by or causing murder or bloodshed ⟨~ gunfire⟩ — **mur·der·ous·ly** *adv*

murk \ˈmərk\ *n* : DARKNESS, GLOOM — **murk·i·ly** \ˈmər-kə-lē\ *adv* — **murk·i·ness** \-kē-nəs\ *n* — **murky** *adj*

mur·mur \ˈmər-mər\ *n* 1 : a muttered complaint 2 : a low indistinct often continuous sound — **murmur** *vb* — **mur·mur·er** *n* — **mur·mur·ous** *adj*

mus *abbr* 1 museum 2 music; musical; musician

mus·ca·tel \ˌməs-kə-ˈtel\ *n* : a sweet fortified wine

¹mus·cle \ˈmə-səl\ *n* [ME, fr. L *musculus*, fr. dim. of *mus* mouse] 1 : a body tissue consisting of long cells that contract when stimulated and produce motion; *also* : an organ consisting of this tissue and functioning in moving a body part 2 : STRENGTH, BRAWN — **mus·cled** \-səld\ *adj* — **mus·cu·lar** \ˈməs-kyə-lər\ *adj* — **mus·cu·lar·i·ty** \ˌməs-kyə-ˈlar-ə-tē\ *n*

²muscle *vb* **mus·cled; mus·cling** : to force one's way

mus·cle-bound \ˈmə-səl-ˌbau̇nd\ *adj* : having some of the muscles abnormally enlarged and lacking in elasticity (as from excessive exercise)

mus·cle·man \-ˌman\ *n* : a man with a muscular physique

muscular dystrophy *n* : any of a group of diseases characterized by progressive wasting of muscles

mus·cu·la·ture \ˈməs-kyə-lə-ˌchu̇r\ *n* : the muscles of the body or its parts

muscu·lo·skel·e·tal \ˌməs-kyə-lō-ˈske-lə-t³l\ *adj* : of, relating to, or involving both musculature and skeleton

¹muse \ˈmyüz\ *vb* **mused; mus·ing** [ME, fr. AF *muser* to gape, idle, muse, fr. OF *mus* mouth of an animal, fr. ML *musus*] : to become absorbed in thought — **mus·ing·ly** *adv*

²muse *n* [fr. *Muse* any of the nine sister goddesses of learning and the arts in Greek myth, fr. ME, fr. MF, fr. L *Musa*, fr. Gk *Mousa*] : a source of inspiration

mu·se·um \myu̇-ˈzē-əm\ *n* : an institution devoted to the procurement, care, and display of objects of lasting interest or value

¹mush \ˈməsh\ *n* 1 : cornmeal boiled in water 2 : sentimental drivel

²mush *vb* : to travel esp. over snow with a sled drawn by dogs

¹mush·room \ˈməsh-ˌrüm, -ˌru̇m\ *n* : the fleshy usu.caplike spore-bearing organ of various fungi esp.when edible; *also* : such a fungus

²mushroom *vb* 1 : to spread out : EXPAND 2 : to collect wild mushrooms 3 : to grow rapidly

mushy \ˈmə-shē\ *adj* **mush·i·er; -est** 1 : soft like mush 2 : excessively sentimental

mu·sic \ˈmyü-zik\ *n* 1 : the science or art of combining tones into a composition having structure and continuity; *also* : vocal or instrumental sounds having rhythm, melody, or harmony 2 : an agreeable sound

¹mu·si·cal \ˈmyü-zi-kəl\ *adj* 1 : of or relating to music or musicians 2 : having the pleasing tonal qualities of music 3 : fond of or gifted in music — **mu·si·cal·ly** \-k(ə-)lē\ *adv*

²musical *n* : a film or theatrical production consisting of musical numbers and dialogue based on a unifying plot

mu·si·cale \ˌmyü-zi-ˈkal\ *n* : a usu. private social gathering featuring music

mu·si·cian \myu̇-ˈzi-shən\ *n* : a composer, conductor, or performer of music — **mu·si·cian·ly** *adj* — **mu·si·cian·ship** *n*

mu·si·col·o·gy \ˌmyü-zi-ˈkä-lə-jē\ *n* : the study of music as a field of knowledge or research — **mu·si·co·log·i·cal** \-kə-ˈlä-ji-kəl\ *adj* — **mu·si·col·o·gist** \-ˈkä-lə-jist\ *n*

musk \ˈməsk\ *n* : a substance obtained esp. from a small Asian deer (**musk deer**) and used as a perfume fixative — **musk·i·ness** \ˈməs-kē-nəs\ *n* — **musky** *adj*

mus·keg \ˈməs-ˌkeg\ *n* : BOG; *esp* : a mossy bog in northern No. America

mus·kel·lunge \ˈməs-kə-ˌlənj\ *n, pl* **muskellunge** : a large No. American pike that is a valuable sport fish

mus·ket \ˈməs-kət\ *n* [MF *mousquet*, fr. It *moschetto* small artillery piece, kind of small hawk, fr. dim. of *mosca* fly, fr. L *musca*] : a heavy large-caliber muzzle-loading shoulder firearm — **mus·ke·teer** \ˌməs-kə-ˈtir\ *n*

mus·ket·ry \ˈməs-kə-trē\ *n* 1 : MUSKETS 2 : MUSKETEERS 3 : musket fire

musk·mel·on \ˈməsk-ˌme-lən\ *n* : a small round to oval melon that has usu. a sweet edible green or orange flesh and a musky odor

musk ox *n* : a heavyset shaggy-coated wild ox of Greenland and the arctic tundra of northern No. America

musk·rat \ˈməs-ˌkrat\ *n, pl* **muskrat** *or* **muskrats** : a large No. American aquatic rodent with webbed feet and dark brown fur; *also* : its fur

Mus·lim \ˈməz-ləm\ *n* : an adherent of Islam — **Muslim** *adj*

mus·lin \ˈməz-lən\ *n* : a plain-woven sheer to coarse cotton fabric

¹muss \ˈməs\ *n* : a state of disorder — **muss·i·ly** \ˈmə-sə-lē\ *adv* — **muss·i·ness** \-sē-nəs\ *n* — **mussy** *adj*

²muss *vb* : to make untidy : DISARRANGE

mus·sel \ˈmə-səl\ *n* 1 : a dark edible saltwater bivalve mollusk 2 : any of various freshwater bivalve mollusks of the central U.S. having shells with a pearly lining

¹must \ˈməst\ *vb* — used as an auxiliary esp. to express a command, requirement, obligation, or necessity

²must *n* 1 : an imperative duty 2 : an indispensable item

mus·tache *also* **mous·tache** \ˈməs-ˌtash, (ˌ)məs-ˈtash\ *n* : the hair growing on the human upper lip — **mus·tached** *also* **mous·tached** \-ˌtasht, -ˈtasht\ *adj*

mus·tang \ˈməs-ˌtaŋ\ *n* [MexSp *mestengo*, fr. Sp, stray, fr. *mesteño* strayed, fr. *mesta* annual roundup of cattle that disposed of strays, fr. ML *(animalia) mixta* mixed animals] : a small hardy naturalized horse of the western plains of America; *also* : BRONC

mus·tard \ˈməs-tərd\ *n* 1 : a pungent yellow powder of the seeds of an herb related to the cabbage and used as a condiment or in medicine 2 : a plant that yields mustard; *also* : a closely related plant — **mustardy** *adj*

mustard gas *n* : a poison gas used in warfare that has violent irritating and blistering effects

¹mus·ter \ˈməs-tər\ *n* 1 : an act of assembling (as for military inspection); *also* : critical examination 2 : an assembled group

²muster *vb* [ME *mustren* to show, muster, fr. AF *mustrer*, *monstrer*, fr. L *monstrare* to show, fr. *monstrum* evil omen, monster] 1 : CONVENE, ASSEMBLE; *also* : to call the roll of 2 : ACCUMULATE 3 : to call forth : ROUSE 4 : to amount to : COMPRISE

muster out *vb* : to discharge from military service

musty \ˈməs-tē\ *adj* **mus·ti·er; -est** : MOLDY, STALE; *also* : tasting or smelling of damp or decay — **must·i·ly** \-tə-lē\ *adv* — **must·i·ness** \-tē-nəs\ *n*

mu·ta·ble \'myü-tə-bəl\ *adj* **1** : prone to change : FICKLE **2** : capable of or liable to mutation : VARIABLE — **mu·ta·bil·i·ty** \ˌmyü-tə-'bi-lə-tē\ *n*

mu·tant \'myü-t°nt\ *adj* : of, relating to, or produced by mutation — **mu·tant** *n*

mu·tate \'myü-ˌtāt\ *vb* **mu·tat·ed; mu·tat·ing** : to undergo or cause to undergo mutation — **mu·ta·tive** \'myü-ˌtā-tiv, -tə-tiv\ *adj*

mu·ta·tion \myü-'tā-shən\ *n* **1** : CHANGE **2** : an inherited physical or biochemical change in genetic material; *also* : the process of producing a mutation **3** : an individual, strain, or trait resulting from mutation — **mu·ta·tion·al** *adj*

¹**mute** \'myüt\ *adj* **mut·er; mut·est** **1** : unable to speak **2** : SILENT — **mute·ly** *adv* — **mute·ness** *n*

²**mute** *n* **1** : a person who cannot or does not speak **2** : a device on a musical instrument that reduces, softens, or muffles the tone

³**mute** *vb* **mut·ed; mut·ing** : to muffle, reduce, or eliminate the sound of

mu·ti·late \'myü-tə-ˌlāt\ *vb* **-lat·ed; -lat·ing** **1** : to cut up or alter radically so as to make imperfect **2** : MAIM, CRIPPLE — **mu·ti·la·tion** \ˌmyü-tə-'lā-shən\ *n* — **mu·ti·la·tor** \'myü-tə-ˌlā-tər\ *n*

mu·ti·ny \'myü-tə-nē\ *n, pl* **-nies** : willful refusal to obey constituted authority; *esp* : revolt against a superior officer — **mu·ti·neer** \ˌmyü-tə-'nir\ *n* — **mu·ti·nous** \'myü-tə-nəs\ *adj* — **mu·ti·nous·ly** *adv* — **mutiny** *vb*

mutt \'mət\ *n* : MONGREL, CUR

mut·ter \'mə-tər\ *vb* **1** : to speak indistinctly or with a low voice and lips partly closed **2** : GRUMBLE — **mutter** *n*

mut·ton \'mə-t°n\ *n* [ME *motoun* mutton, sheep, fr. AF *mutun* ram, sheep, mutton] : the flesh of a mature sheep used for food — **mut·tony** *adj*

mut·ton·chops \'mə-t°n-ˌchäps\ *n pl* : whiskers on the side of the face that are narrow at the temple and broad and round by the lower jaws

mu·tu·al \'myü-chə-wəl\ *adj* **1** : given and received in equal amount ⟨~ trust⟩ **2** : having the same feelings one for the other ⟨~ enemies⟩ **3** : COMMON, JOINT ⟨a ~ friend⟩ — **mu·tu·al·ly** *adv*

mutual fund *n* : an investment company that invests money of its shareholders in a usu. diversified group of securities of other corporations

muu-muu \'mü-ˌmü\ *n* : a loose dress of Hawaiian origin

¹**muz·zle** \'mə-zəl\ *n* **1** : the nose and jaws of an animal; *also* : a covering for the muzzle to prevent biting or eating **2** : the mouth of a gun

²**muzzle** *vb* **muz·zled; muz·zling** **1** : to put a muzzle on **2** : to restrain from expression : GAG

mV *abbr* millivolt

MV *abbr* motor vessel

MVP *abbr* most valuable player

MW *abbr* megawatt

my \'mī\ *adj* **1** : of or relating to me or myself **2** — used interjectionally esp. to express surprise

my·col·o·gy \mī-'kä-lə-jē\ *n* : a branch of biology dealing with fungi — **my·co·log·i·cal** \ˌmī-kə-'lä-ji-kəl\ *adj* — **my·col·o·gist** \mī-'kä-lə-jist\ *n*

my·elo·ma \ˌmī-ə-'lō-mə\ *n, pl* **-mas** *or* **-ma·ta** \-mə-tə\ : a primary tumor of the bone marrow

my·nah *or* **my·na** \'mī-nə\ *n* : any of several Asian starlings; *esp* : a dark brown slightly crested bird sometimes taught to mimic speech

my·o·pia \mī-'ō-pē-ə\ *n* : a condition in which visual images come to a focus in front of the retina resulting esp. in defective vision of distant objects — **my·o·pic** \-'ō-pik, -'ä-\ *adj* — **my·o·pi·cal·ly** \-pi-k(ə-)lē\ *adv*

¹**myr·i·ad** \'mir-ē-əd\ *n* [Gk *myriad-, myrias,* fr. *myrioi* countless, ten thousand] : an indefinitely large number

²**myriad** *adj* : consisting of a very great but indefinite number

myr·mi·don \'mər-mə-ˌdän\ *n* : a loyal follower; *esp* : one who executes orders without protest or pity

myrrh \'mər\ *n* : a fragrant aromatic plant gum used in perfumes and formerly for incense

myr·tle \'mər-t°l\ *n* : an evergreen shrub of southern Europe with shiny leaves, fragrant flowers, and black berries; *also* : PERIWINKLE

my·self \mī-'self, mə-\ *pron* : I, ME — used reflexively, for emphasis, or in absolute constructions ⟨I hurt ~⟩ ⟨I ~ did it⟩ ⟨~ busy, I sent him instead⟩

mys·tery \'mis-tə-rē\ *n, pl* **-ter·ies** **1** : a religious truth known by revelation alone **2** : something not understood or beyond understanding **3** : enigmatic quality or character **4** : a work of fiction dealing with the solution of a mysterious crime — **mys·te·ri·ous** \mis-'tir-ē-əs\ *adj* — **mys·te·ri·ous·ly** *adv* — **mys·te·ri·ous·ness** *n*

¹**mys·tic** \'mis-tik\ *adj* **1** : of or relating to mystics or mysticism **2** : MYSTERIOUS; *also* : MYSTIFYING

²**mystic** *n* : a person who follows, advocates, or experiences mysticism

mys·ti·cal \'mis-ti-kəl\ *adj* **1** : SPIRITUAL, SYMBOLIC **2** : of or relating to an intimate knowledge of or direct communion with God (as through contemplation or visions)

mys·ti·cism \'mis-tə-ˌsi-zəm\ *n* : the belief that direct knowledge of God or ultimate reality is attainable through immediate intuition or insight

mys·ti·fy \'mis-tə-ˌfī\ *vb* **-fied; -fy·ing** **1** : to perplex the mind of **2** : to make mysterious — **mys·ti·fi·ca·tion** \ˌmis-tə-fə-'kā-shən\ *n*

mys·tique \mi-'stēk\ *n* [F] **1** : an air or attitude of mystery and reverence developing around something or someone **2** : the special esoteric skill essential in a calling or activity

myth \'mith\ *n* **1** : a usu. legendary narrative that presents part of the beliefs of a people or explains a practice or natural phenomenon **2** : an imaginary or unverifiable person or thing — **myth·i·cal** \'mi-thi-kəl\ *or* **myth·ic** \-thik\ *adj*

my·thol·o·gy \mi-'thä-lə-jē\ *n, pl* **-gies** : a body of myths and esp. of those dealing with the gods and heroes of a people — **myth·o·log·i·cal** \ˌmi-thə-'lä-ji-kəl\ *adj* — **my·thol·o·gist** \mi-'thä-lə-jist\ *n* — **my·thol·o·gize** \-ˌjīz\ *vb*

¹**n** \'en\ *n, pl* **n's** *or* **ns** \'enz\ *often cap* **1** : the 14th letter of the English alphabet **2** : an unspecified quantity

²**n** *abbr, often cap* **1** net **2** neuter **3** noon **4** normal **5** north; northern **6** note **7** noun **8** number

N *symbol* nitrogen

-n — see -EN

Na *symbol* [NL *natrium*] sodium

NA *abbr* **1** no account **2** North America **3** not applicable **4** not available

NAACP \ˌen-ˌdə-bəl-ˌā-ˌsē-'pē, ˌen-ˌā-ˌā-ˌsē-\ *abbr* National Association for the Advancement of Colored People

nab \'nab\ *vb* **nabbed; nab·bing** : SEIZE; *esp* : ARREST

NAB *abbr* New American Bible

na·bob \'nā-ˌbäb\ *n* [Hindi *navāb* & Urdu *nawāb,* provincial governor (in the Mogul empire), fr. Ar *nuwwāb,* pl. of *nā'ib* governor] : a person of great wealth or prominence

na·celle \nə-'sel\ *n* : an enclosure (as for an engine) on an aircraft

na·cho \'nä-chō\ *n, pl* **nachos** [AmerSp] : a tortilla chip topped with melted cheese and often additional savory toppings

na·cre \'nā-kər\ *n* : MOTHER-OF-PEARL — **na·cre·ous** \'nā-krē-əs\ *adj* na·dir \'nā-ˌdir, -dər\ n [ME, fr. MF, fr. Ar naḍhīr oppo-site] 1 : the point of the celestial sphere that is directly opposite the zenith and directly beneath the observer 2 : the lowest point

¹nag \'nag\ n : HORSE; esp : an old or decrepit horse

²nag vb nagged; nag·ging 1 : to find fault incessantly : COMPLAIN 2 : to irritate by constant scolding or urg-ing 3 : to be a continuing source of annoyance ⟨a nag-ging backache⟩

³nag n : one who nags habitually

Nah abbr Nahum

Na·hu·atl \'nä-ˌwä-t²l\ n : a group of American Indian lan-guages of central and southern Mexico

Na·hum \'nā-həm, -əm\ n — see BIBLE table

NAIA abbr National Association of Intercollegiate Ath-letes

na·iad \'nā-əd, 'nī-, -ˌad\ n, pl naiads or na·ia·des \-ə-ˌdēz\ 1 : one of the nymphs in ancient mythology living in lakes, rivers, springs, and fountains 2 : an aquatic young of some insects (as a dragonfly)

¹na·if or na·if \nä-'ēf\ adj : NAIVE

²naïf or naif n : a naive person

¹nail \'nāl\ n 1 : a horny sheath protecting the end of each finger and toe in humans and related primates 2 : a slen-der pointed fastener with a head designed to be pounded in

²nail vb : to fasten with or as if with a nail — nail·er n

nail down vb : to settle or establish clearly and unmis-takably

nain·sook \'nān-ˌsůk\ n : a soft lightweight muslin

nai·ra \'nī-rə\ n — see MONEY table

na·ive or na·ïve \nä-'ēv\ adj na·iv·er; -est [F naïve, fem. of naïf, fr. OF, inborn, natural, fr. L nativus native] 1 : marked by unaffected simplicity : ARTLESS, INGENU-OUS 2 : CREDULOUS ✦ Synonyms NATURAL, INNO-CENT, SIMPLE, UNAFFECTED, UNSOPHISTICATED, UN-STUDIED — na·ive·ly adv — na·ive·ness n

na·ïve·té also na·ive·te or na·ive·té \ˌnä-ˌē-və-'tā, nä-'ē-və-ˌtā\ n 1 : a naive remark or action 2 : the quality or state of being naive

na·ked \'nā-kəd\ adj 1 : having no clothes on : NUDE 2 : UNSHEATHED ⟨a ~ sword⟩ 3 : lacking a usual or nat-ural covering (as of foliage or feathers) 4 : PLAIN, UN-ADORNED ⟨the ~ truth⟩ 5 : not aided by artificial means ⟨seen by the ~ eye⟩ — na·ked·ly adv — na·ked-ness n

nak·fa \'näk-ˌfä\ n, pl nakfa — see MONEY table

nam·by–pam·by \ˌnam-bē-'pam-bē\ adj 1 : INSIPID 2 : WEAK, INDECISIVE ✦ Synonyms BLAND, FLAT, INANE, JEJUNE, VAPID, WISHY-WASHY

¹name \'nām\ n 1 : a word or words by which a person or thing is known 2 : a disparaging epithet ⟨call him ~s⟩ 3 : REPUTATION; esp : distinguished reputation ⟨made a ~ for herself⟩ 4 : FAMILY, CLAN ⟨was a disgrace to their ~⟩ 5 : appearance as opposed to reality ⟨a friend in ~ only⟩

²name vb named; nam·ing 1 : to give a name to : CALL 2 : to mention or identify by name 3 : NOMINATE, AP-POINT 4 : to decide on : CHOOSE 5 : to mention explic-itly : SPECIFY ⟨~ a price⟩ — name·able adj

³name adj 1 : of, relating to, or bearing a name ⟨~ tag⟩ 2 : having an established reputation ⟨~ brands⟩

name day n : the church feast day of the saint after whom one is named

name·less \'nām-ləs\ adj 1 : having no name 2 : not marked with a name ⟨a ~ grave⟩ 3 : not known by name ⟨a ~ hero⟩ 4 : too distressing to be described ⟨~ fears⟩ — name·less·ly adv

name·ly \-lē\ adv : that is to say : AS ⟨the cat family, ~, li-ons, tigers, and similar animals⟩

name·plate \-ˌplāt\ n : a plate or plaque bearing a name (as of a resident)

name·sake \-ˌsāk\ n : one that has the same name as an-other; esp : one named after another

nan·keen \nan-'kēn\ n : a durable brownish yellow cotton fabric orig. woven by hand in China

nan·ny goat \'na-nē-\ n : a female domestic goat

nano·me·ter \'na-nə-ˌmē-tər\ n : one billionth of a meter

nano·scale \-ˌskäl\ adj : having dimensions measured in nanometers

nano·sec·ond \-ˌse-kənd\ n : one billionth of a second

nano·tech·nol·o·gy \ˌna-nō-tek-'nä-lə-jē\ n : the manipu-lation of materials on an atomic or molecular scale

nano·tube \'na-nō-ˌtüb\ n : a microscopic tube (as of car-bon) whose diameter is measured in nanometers

¹nap \'nap\ vb napped; nap·ping 1 : to sleep briefly esp. during the day : DOZE 2 : to be off guard ⟨was caught napping⟩

²nap n : a short sleep esp. during the day

³nap n : a soft downy fibrous surface (as on yarn and cloth) — nap·less adj — napped \'napt\ adj

na·palm \'nā-ˌpälm, -ˌpäm\ n [naphthalene + palmitate, salt of a fatty acid] 1 : a thickener used in jelling gaso-line (as for incendiary bombs) 2 : fuel jelled with na-palm

nape \'nāp, 'nap\ n : the back of the neck

na·pery \'nā-pə-rē\ n : household linen esp. for the table

naph·tha \'naf-thə, 'nap-\ n : any of various liquid hydro-carbon mixtures used chiefly as solvents

naph·tha·lene \-ˌlēn\ n : a crystalline substance used esp. in organic synthesis and as a moth repellent

nap·kin \'nap-kən\ n 1 : a piece of material (as cloth) used at table to wipe the lips or fingers and protect the clothes 2 : a small cloth or towel

na·po·leon \nə-'pōl-yən, -'pō-lē-ən\ n : an oblong pastry with a filling of cream, custard, or jelly

Na·po·le·on·ic \nə-ˌpō-lē-'ä-nik\ adj : of, relating to, or characteristic of Napoleon I or his family

narc also nark \'närk\ n, slang : a person (as a government agent) who investigates narcotics violations

nar·cis·sism \'när-sə-ˌsi-zəm\ n [G Narzissismus, fr. Narziss Narcissus, beautiful youth of Greek mythology who fell in love with his own image] 1 : undue dwelling on one's own self or attainments 2 : love of or sexual de-sire for one's own body — nar·cis·sist \-sist\ n or adj — nar·cis·sis·tic \ˌnär-sə-'sis-tik\ adj

nar·cis·sus \när-'si-səs\ n, pl nar·cis·si \-ˌsī, -ˌsē\ or nar-cis·sus·es or narcissus : DAFFODIL; esp : one with short-tubed flowers usu. borne separately

nar·co·lep·sy \'när-kə-ˌlep-sē\ n, pl -sies : a condition characterized by brief attacks of deep sleep — nar·co-lep·tic \ˌnär-kə-'lep-tik\ adj or n

nar·co·sis \när-'kō-səs\ n, pl -co·ses \-ˌsēz\ : a state of stupor, unconsciousness, or arrested activity produced by the influence of chemicals (as narcotics)

nar·co·ter·ror·ism \'när-kō-'ter-ər-ˌi-zəm\ n : terrorism fi-nanced by profits from illegal drug trafficking

nar·cot·ic \när-'kä-tik\ n [ME narkotik, fr. MF narcotique, fr. narcotique, adj., fr. ML narcoticus, fr. Gk narkōtikos, fr. narkoun to benumb, fr. narkē numbness] 1 : a drug (as opium) that dulls the senses, relieves pain, and induces sleep 2 : an illegal drug (as marijuana or LSD) — nar-cotic adj

nar·co·tize \'när-kə-ˌtīz\ vb -tized; -tiz·ing 1 : to treat with or subject to a narcotic; also : to put into a state of narcosis 2 : to soothe to unconsciousness or un-awareness

nard \'närd\ n : a fragrant ointment of the ancients

na·res \'ner-(ˌ)ēz\ n pl [L] : the pair of openings of the nose

Nar·ra·gan·sett \ˌna-rə-'gan-sət\ n, pl -sett or -setts 1 : a member of an American Indian people of Rhode Island 2 : the Algonquian language of the Narragansett people

nar·rate \'ner-ˌāt\ vb nar·rat·ed; nar·rat·ing : to recite the details of (as a story) : RELATE, TELL — nar·ra·tion \na-'rā-shən\ n — nar·ra·tor \'ner-ˌā-tər\ n

nar·ra·tive \'ner-ə-tiv\ n 1 : something that is narrated : STORY 2 : the art or practice of narrating

¹nar·row \'ner-ō\ adj 1 : of slender or less than standard width 2 : limited in size or scope : RESTRICTED 3 : not liberal in views : PREJUDICED 4 : interpreted or inter-preting strictly 5 : CLOSE ⟨won by a ~ margin⟩; also : barely successful ⟨a ~ escape⟩ — nar·row·ly adv — nar·row·ness n

²narrow vb : to lessen in width or extent

³narrow n : a narrow passage : STRAIT — usu. used in pl.

nar·row–mind·ed \ˌner-ō-'mīn-dəd\ adj : not liberal or broad-minded ✦ Synonyms ILLIBERAL, BIGOTED, HIDE-BOUND, INTOLERANT

nar·whal \'när-ˌhwäl, 'när-wəl\ n : an arctic sea mammal

about 20 feet (6 meters) long that is related to the dolphins and in the male has a long twisted ivory tusk

narwhal

NAS *abbr* naval air station

NASA \'na-sə\ *abbr* National Aeronautics and Space Administration

¹na·sal \'nā-zəl\ *n* **1** : a nasal part **2** : a nasal consonant or vowel

²nasal *adj* **1** : of or relating to the nose **2** : uttered through the nose — **na·sal·ly** *adv*

na·sal·ize \'nā-zə-,līz\ *vb* **-ized; -iz·ing** : to make nasal or pronounce as a nasal sound — **na·sal·i·za·tion** \,nā-zə-lə-'zā-shən\ *n*

na·scent \'na-s°nt, 'nā-\ *adj* : coming into existence : beginning to grow or develop — **na·scence** \-s°ns\ *n*

nas·tur·tium \nə-'stər-shəm, na-\ *n* : either of two widely cultivated watery-stemmed herbs with showy spurred flowers and pungent edible seeds

nas·ty \'nas-tē\ *adj* **nas·ti·er; -est** **1** : FILTHY **2** : INDECENT, OBSCENE **3** : HARMFUL, DANGEROUS ⟨took a ~ fall⟩ **4** : DISAGREEABLE ⟨~ weather⟩ **5** : MEAN, ILL-NATURED ⟨a ~ temper⟩ **6** : DIFFICULT, VEXATIOUS ⟨a ~ problem⟩ **7** : UNFAIR, DIRTY ⟨a ~ trick⟩ — **nas·ti·ly** \'nas-tə-lē\ *adv* — **nas·ti·ness** \-tē-nəs\ *n*

nat *abbr* **1** national **2** native **3** natural

na·tal \'nā-t°l\ *adj* **1** : NATIVE **2** : of, relating to, or present at birth

na·ta·to·ri·um \,nā-tə-'tȯr-ē-əm, ,na-\ *n* : a swimming pool esp. indoors

na·tion \'nā-shən\ *n* [ME *nacioun*, fr. AF *naciun* fr. L *nation-*, *natio* birth, race, nation, fr. *nasci* to be born] **1** : NATIONALITY 5; *also* : a politically organized nationality **2** : a community of people composed of one or more nationalities with its own territory and government **3** : the territory of a nation **4** : a federation of tribes (as of American Indians) — **na·tion·hood** *n*

¹na·tion·al \'na-shə-nəl\ *adj* **1** : of or relating to a nation **2** : comprising or characteristic of a nationality **3** : FEDERAL 3 — **na·tion·al·ly** *adv*

²national *n* **1** : one who owes allegiance to a nation **2** : a competition that is national in scope — usu. used in pl.

national guard *n* **1** : a military force serving as a national constabulary and defense force **2** *cap* : a militia force recruited by each state of the U.S., equipped by the federal government, and jointly maintained subject to the call of either — **national guardsman** *n, often cap*

na·tion·al·ise *chiefly Brit var of* NATIONALIZE

na·tion·al·ism \'na-shə-nə-,li-zəm\ *n* : devotion to national interests, unity, and independence

na·tion·al·ist \-list\ *n* **1** : an advocate of or believer in nationalism **2** : a member of a political party or group advocating national independence or strong national government — **nationalist** *adj* — **na·tion·al·is·tic** \,na-shə-nə-'lis-tik\ *adj*

na·tion·al·i·ty \,na-shə-'na-lə-tē\ *n, pl* **-ties** **1** : national character **2** : a legal relationship involving allegiance of an individual and protection on the part of the state **3** : membership in a particular nation **4** : political independence or existence as a separate nation **5** : a people having a common origin, tradition, and language and capable of forming a state **6** : an ethnic group within a larger unit (as a nation)

na·tion·al·ize \'na-shə-nə-,līz\ *vb* **-ized; -iz·ing** **1** : to make national : make a nation of **2** : to remove from private ownership and place under government control — **na·tion·al·i·za·tion** \,na-shə-nə-lə-'zā-shən\ *n*

national monument *n* : a place of historic, scenic, or scientific interest set aside for preservation usu. by presidential proclamation

national park *n* : an area of special scenic, historical, or scientific importance set aside and maintained by a national government esp. for recreation or study

national seashore *n* : a recreational area adjacent to a seacoast and maintained by the federal government

na·tion·wide \,nā-shən-'wīd\ *adj* : extending throughout a nation

¹na·tive \'nā-tiv\ *adj* **1** : INBORN, NATURAL ⟨~ talents⟩ **2** : born in a particular place or country **3** : belonging to a person because of the place or circumstances of birth ⟨her ~ language⟩ **4** : grown, produced, or originating in a particular place : INDIGENOUS **5** *cap* : NATIVE AMERICAN ♦ **Synonyms** ABORIGINAL, AUTOCHTHONOUS, ENDEMIC

²native *n* : one that is native; *esp* : a person who belongs to a particular country by birth

Native American *n* : a member of any of the aboriginal peoples of No. America and esp. the U.S.

na·tiv·ism \'nā-ti-,vi-zəm\ *n* **1** : a policy of favoring native inhabitants over immigrants **2** : the revival or perpetuation of a native culture esp. in opposition to acculturation

na·tiv·i·ty \nə-'ti-və-tē, nā-\ *n, pl* **-ties** **1** : the process or circumstances of being born : BIRTH **2** *cap* : the birth of Christ

natl *abbr* national

NATO \'nā-(,)tō\ *abbr* North Atlantic Treaty Organization

nat·ty \'na-tē\ *adj* **nat·ti·er; -est** : trimly neat and tidy : SMART — **nat·ti·ly** \-tə-lē\ *adv* — **nat·ti·ness** \-tē-nəs\ *n*

¹nat·u·ral \'na-chə-rəl\ *adj* **1** : determined by nature : INBORN, INNATE ⟨~ ability⟩ **2** : BORN ⟨a ~ fool⟩ **3** : ILLEGITIMATE ⟨a ~ child⟩ **4** : HUMAN **5** : of or relating to nature **6** : not artificial **7** : being simple and sincere : not affected **8** : LIFELIKE **9** : being neither sharp nor flat ♦ **Synonyms** INGENUOUS, NAIVE, UNSOPHISTICATED, ARTLESS, GUILELESS — **nat·u·ral·ness** *n*

²natural *n* **1** : IDIOT **2** : a character ♮ placed on a line or space of the musical staff to nullify the effect of a preceding sharp or flat **3** : one obviously suitable for a purpose **4** : AFRO

natural childbirth *n* : a system of managing childbirth in which the mother prepares to remain conscious and assist in delivery with little or no use of drugs

natural gas *n* : a combustible gaseous mixture of hydrocarbons coming from the earth's crust and used chiefly as a fuel and raw material

natural history *n* **1** : a treatise on some aspect of nature **2** : the study of natural objects esp. from an amateur or popular point of view

nat·u·ral·ise *Brit var of* NATURALIZE

nat·u·ral·ism \'na-chə-rə-,li-zəm\ *n* **1** : action or thought based only on natural desires and instincts **2** : a doctrine that denies a supernatural explanation of the origin or development of the universe and holds that scientific laws account for all of nature **3** : realism in art and literature — **nat·u·ral·is·tic** \,na-chə-rə-'lis-tik\ *adj*

nat·u·ral·ist \-list\ *n* **1** : one that advocates or practices naturalism **2** : a student of animals or plants esp. in the field

nat·u·ral·ize \-,līz\ *vb* **-ized; -iz·ing** **1** : to confer the rights of a citizen on **2** : to become or cause to become established as if native ⟨~ new forage crops⟩ — **nat·u·ral·i·za·tion** \,na-chə-rə-lə-'zā-shən\ *n*

nat·u·ral·ly \'na-chə-rə-lē, 'nach-rə-\ *adv* **1** : by nature : by natural character or ability **2** : as might be expected **3** : without artificial aid; *also* : without affectation **4** : REALISTICALLY

natural science *n* : a science (as physics, chemistry, or biology) that deals with matter, energy, and their interrelations and transformations or with objectively measurable phenomena — **natural scientist** *n*

natural selection *n* : the natural process that results in the survival of individuals or groups best adjusted to their environment

na·ture \'nā-chər\ *n* [ME, fr. MF, fr. L *natura*, fr. *natus*, pp. of *nasci* to be born] **1** : the inherent quality or basic constitution of a person or thing; *also* : DISPOSITION, TEMPERAMENT **2** : KIND, SORT **3** : the physical universe **4** : one's natural instincts or way of life ⟨quirks of human ~⟩; *also* : primitive state ⟨a return to ~⟩ **5** : natural scenery or environment ⟨beauties of ~⟩

¹naught *also* **nought** \'nȯt, 'nät\ *pron* : NOTHING ⟨efforts came to ~⟩

²**naught** *also* **nought** *n* **1** : NOTHINGNESS, NONEXISTENCE **2** : the arithmetical symbol 0 : ZERO

naugh·ty \'nȯ-tē, 'nä-\ *adj* **naugh·ti·er; -est 1** : guilty of disobedience or misbehavior **2** : lacking in taste or propriety — **naugh·ti·ly** \-tə-lē\ *adv* — **naugh·ti·ness** \-tē-nəs\ *n*

nau·sea \'nȯ-zē-ə, -sē-; 'nȯ-zhə, -shə\ *n* [L, seasickness, nausea, fr. Gk *nautia, nausia,* fr. *nautēs* sailor] **1** : sickness of the stomach with a desire to vomit **2** : extreme disgust

nau·se·ate \'nȯ-zē-ˌāt, -sē-, -zhē-, -shē-\ *vb* **-at·ed; -at·ing** : to affect or become affected with nausea — **nau·se·at·ing·ly** *adv*

nau·seous \'nȯ-shəs, -zē-əs\ *adj* **1** : causing nausea or disgust **2** : affected with nausea or disgust

naut *abbr* nautical

nau·ti·cal \'nȯ-ti-kəl\ *adj* : of or relating to sailors, navigation, or ships — **nau·ti·cal·ly** \-k(ə-)lē\ *adv*

nautical mile *n* : a unit of distance equal to about 6080 feet (1852 meters)

nau·ti·lus \'nȯ-tə-l-əs\ *n, pl* **-lus·es** *or* **-li** \ˌlī, -lˌē\ : any of a genus of sea mollusks related to the octopuses but having a spiral chambered shell

nav *abbr* **1** naval **2** navigable; navigation

Na·va·jo *also* **Na·va·ho** \'na-və-ˌhō, 'nä-\ *n, pl* **-jo** *or* **-jos** *also* **-ho** *or* **-hos** : a member of an American Indian people of northern New Mexico and Arizona; *also* : their language

na·val \'nā-vəl\ *adj* : of, relating to, or possessing a navy

naval stores *n pl* : products (as pitch, turpentine, or rosin) obtained from resinous conifers (as pines)

nave \'nāv\ *n* [ML *navis,* fr. L, ship] : the central part of a church running lengthwise

na·vel \'nā-vəl\ *n* : a depression in the middle of the abdomen that marks the point of attachment of fetus and mother

navel–gaz·ing \'nā-vəl-ˈgā-ziŋ\ *n* : useless or excessive self-contemplation

navel orange *n* : a seedless orange having a pit at the blossom end where the fruit encloses a small secondary fruit

nav·i·ga·ble \'na-vi-gə-bəl\ *adj* **1** : capable of being navigated 〈a ∼ river〉 **2** : capable of being steered — **nav·i·ga·bil·i·ty** \ˌna-vi-gə-'bi-lə-tē\ *n*

nav·i·gate \'na-və-ˌgāt\ *vb* **-gat·ed; -gat·ing 1** : to sail on or through 〈∼ the Atlantic Ocean〉 **2** : to steer or direct the course of a ship or aircraft **3** : MOVE; *esp* : WALK 〈could hardly ∼〉 — **nav·i·ga·tion** \ˌna-və-'gā-shən\ *n* — **nav·i·ga·tor** \'na-və-ˌgā-tər\ *n*

na·vy \'nā-vē\ *n, pl* **navies 1** : FLEET; *also* : the warships belonging to a nation **2** *often cap* : a nation's organization for naval warfare

navy yard *n* : a yard where naval vessels are built or repaired

¹**nay** \'nā\ *adv* : NO

²**nay** *n* : a negative vote; *also* : a person casting such a vote

³**nay** *conj* : not merely this but also : not only so but 〈he was happy, ∼, ecstatic〉

nay·say·er \'nā-ˌsā-ər\ *n* : one who denies, refuses, or opposes something

Na·zi \'nät-sē, 'nat-\ *n* [G, fr. *Nationalsozialist,* lit., national socialist] : a member of a German fascist party controlling Germany from 1933 to 1945 under Adolf Hitler — **Nazi** *adj* — **Na·zism** \'nät-ˌsi-zəm, 'nat-\ *also* **Na·zi·ism** \-sē-ˌi-zəm\ *n*

Nb *symbol* niobium

NB *abbr* **1** New Brunswick **2** nota bene

NBA *abbr* **1** National Basketball Association **2** National Boxing Association

NBC *abbr* National Broadcasting Company

NBS *abbr* National Bureau of Standards

NC *abbr* **1** no charge **2** North Carolina

NCAA *abbr* National Collegiate Athletic Association

NCO \ˌen-ˌsē-'ō\ *n* : NONCOMMISSIONED OFFICER

nd *abbr* no date

Nd *symbol* neodymium

ND *abbr* North Dakota

-nd *symbol* — used after the figure 2 to indicate the ordinal number second

N Dak *abbr* North Dakota

Ne *symbol* neon

NE *abbr* **1** Nebraska **2** New England **3** northeast

Ne·an·der·thal \nē-'an-dər-ˌthȯl, nä-'än-dər-ˌtäl\ *n* **1** *or* **Ne·an·der·tal** \-ˌtäl\ : an extinct Old World hominid that lived from about 30,000 to 200,000 years ago **2** : a person who resembles or suggests a caveman — **Neanderthal** *or* **Neandertal** *adj*

neap tide \'nēp-\ *n* : a tide of minimum range occurring at the first and third quarters of the moon

¹**near** \'nir\ *adv* **1** : at, within, or to a short distance or time **2** : ALMOST 〈was ∼ dead〉

²**near** *prep* : close to

³**near** *adj* **1** : closely related or associated; *also* : INTIMATE **2** : not far away; *also* : being the closer or left-hand member of a pair **3** : barely avoided 〈a ∼ accident〉 **4** : DIRECT, SHORT 〈by the ∼est route〉 **5** : STINGY **6** : not real but very like 〈∼ silk〉 — **near·ly** *adv* — **near·ness** *n*

⁴**near** *vb* : APPROACH

near beer *n* : any of various malt liquors low in alcohol

near·by \nir-'bī, 'nir-ˌbī\ *adv or adj* : close at hand

near·sight·ed \'nir-'sī-təd\ *adj* : able to see near things more clearly than distant ones : MYOPIC — **near·sight·ed·ly** *adv* — **near·sight·ed·ness** *n*

neat \'nēt\ *adj* [MF *net,* fr. L *nitidus* bright, neat, fr. *nitēre* to shine] **1** : being orderly and clean **2** : not mixed or diluted 〈∼ brandy〉 **3** : marked by tasteful simplicity **4** : PRECISE, SYSTEMATIC **5** : SKILLFUL, ADROIT **6** : FINE, ADMIRABLE ♦ *Synonyms* SHIPSHAPE, TIDY, TRIG, TRIM — **neat** *adv* — **neat·ly** *adv* — **neat·ness** *n*

neath \'nēth\ *prep, dial* : BENEATH

neat·nik \'nēt-nik\ *n* : a person who is compulsively neat

neb \'neb\ *n* **1** : the beak of a bird or tortoise; *also* : NOSE, SNOUT **2** : NIB

Neb *or* **Nebr** *abbr* Nebraska

NEB *abbr* New English Bible

neb·u·la \'ne-byə-lə\ *n, pl* **-lae** \-ˌlē, -ˌlī\ *also* **-las** [NL, fr. L, mist, cloud] **1** : any of numerous clouds of gas or dust in interstellar space **2** : GALAXY — **neb·u·lar** \-lər\ *adj*

neb·u·liz·er \'ne-byə-ˌlī-zər\ *n* : ATOMIZER

neb·u·lous \'ne-byə-ləs\ *adj* **1** : of or relating to a nebula **2** : HAZY, INDISTINCT

¹**nec·es·sary** \'ne-sə-ˌser-ē\ *adj* **1** : INEVITABLE, INESCAPABLE; *also* : CERTAIN **2** : PREDETERMINED **3** : COMPULSORY **4** : positively needed : INDISPENSABLE ♦ *Synonyms* IMPERATIVE, NECESSITOUS, ESSENTIAL — **nec·es·sar·i·ly** \ˌne-sə-'ser-ə-lē\ *adv*

²**necessary** *n, pl* **-sar·ies** : an indispensable item

ne·ces·si·tate \ni-'se-sə-ˌtāt\ *vb* **-tat·ed; -tat·ing** : to make necessary

ne·ces·si·tous \ni-'se-sə-təs\ *adj* **1** : NEEDY, IMPOVERISHED **2** : URGENT **3** : NECESSARY 〈∼ bargaining〉

ne·ces·si·ty \ni-'se-sə-tē\ *n, pl* **-ties 1** : conditions that cannot be changed **2** : WANT, POVERTY **3** : something that is necessary **4** : very great need

¹**neck** \'nek\ *n* **1** : the part of the body connecting the head and the trunk **2** : the part of a garment covering or near to the neck **3** : a relatively narrow part suggestive of a neck 〈∼ of a bottle〉 〈∼ of land〉 **4** : a narrow margin esp. of victory 〈won by a ∼〉 — **necked** \'nekt\ *adj*

²**neck** *vb* : to kiss and caress amorously

neck and neck *adv or adj* : very close (as in a race)

neck·er·chief \'ne-kər-chəf, -ˌchēf\ *n, pl* **-chiefs** \-chəfs, -ˌchēfs\ *also* **-chieves** \-ˌchēvz\ : a square of cloth worn folded about the neck like a scarf

neck·lace \'ne-kləs\ *n* : an ornament worn around the neck

neck·line \'nek-ˌlīn\ *n* : the outline of the neck opening of a garment

neck·tie \-ˌtī\ *n* : a strip of cloth worn around the neck and tied in front

ne·crol·o·gy \nə-'krä-lə-jē\ *n, pl* **-gies 1** : OBITUARY **2** : a list of the recently dead

nec·ro·man·cy \'ne-krə-ˌman-sē\ *n* **1** : the art or practice of conjuring up the spirits of the dead for purposes of magically revealing the future **2** : MAGIC, SORCERY — **nec·ro·man·cer** \-sər\ *n*

ne·crop·o·lis \nə-'krä-pə-ləs, ne-\ *n, pl* **-lis·es** *or* **-les** \-ˌlēz\ *or* **-leis** \-ˌlās\ *or* **-li** \-ˌlī, -ˌlē\ [LL, fr. Gk *nekropolis,* fr. *nekros* dead body + *polis* city] : CEMETERY; *esp* : a large elaborate cemetery of an ancient city

ne·crop·sy \'ne-ˌkräp-sē\ *n, pl* **-sies** : AUTOPSY; *esp* : an autopsy performed on an animal

ne·cro·sis \nə-'krō-səs, ne-\ *n, pl* **ne·cro·ses** \-ˌsēz\ : usu. local death of body tissue — **ne·crot·ic** \-'krä-tik\ *adj*

nec·tar \'nek-tər\ *n* **1** : the drink of the Greek and Roman gods; *also* : any delicious drink **2** : a sweet plant secretion that is the raw material of honey

nec·tar·ine \,nek-tə-'rēn\ *n* : a smooth-skinned peach

née *or* **nee** \'nā\ *adj* [F, lit., born] — used to identify a woman by her maiden family name

¹need \'nēd\ *n* **1** : OBLIGATION ⟨no ∼ to hurry⟩ **2** : a lack of something requisite, desirable, or useful **3** : a condition requiring supply or relief ⟨when the ∼ arises⟩ **4** : POVERTY ◆ **Synonyms** NECESSITY, EXIGENCY

²need *vb* **1** : to be in want **2** : to have cause or occasion for : REQUIRE ⟨he ∼s advice⟩ **3** : to be under obligation or necessity ⟨we ∼ to know the truth⟩

need·ful \'nēd-fəl\ *adj* : NECESSARY, REQUISITE

¹nee·dle \'nē-d³l\ *n* **1** : a slender pointed usu. steel implement used in sewing **2** : a slender rod (as for knitting, controlling a small opening, or transmitting vibrations to or from a recording) ⟨a phonograph ∼⟩ **3** : a slender hollow instrument by which material is introduced into or withdrawn from the body **4** : a slender indicator on a dial **5** : a needle-shaped leaf (as of a pine)

²needle *vb* **nee·dled; nee·dling** : PROD, GOAD; *esp* : to incite to action by repeated gibes

nee·dle·nose pliers \'nē-d³l-,nōz-\ *n pl* : pliers with long slender jaws for grasping small or thin objects

nee·dle·point \'nē-d³l-,point\ *n* **1** : lace worked with a needle over a paper pattern **2** : embroidery done on canvas across counted threads — **needlepoint** *adj*

need·less \'nēd-ləs\ *adj* : UNNECESSARY ⟨∼ waste⟩ — **need·less·ly** *adv* — **need·less·ness** *n*

nee·dle·wom·an \'nē-d³l-,wu̇-mən\ *n* : a woman who does needlework; *esp* : SEAMSTRESS

nee·dle·work \-,wərk\ *n* : work done with a needle; *esp* : work (as embroidery) other than plain sewing

needs \'nēdz\ *adv* : of necessity : NECESSARILY ⟨must ∼ be recognized⟩

needy \'nē-dē\ *adj* **need·i·er; -est** : being in want : POVERTY-STRICKEN

ne'er \'ner\ *adv* : NEVER

ne'er-do-well \'ner-dü-,wel\ *n* : an idle worthless person — **ne'er-do-well** *adj*

ne·far·i·ous \ni-'fer-ē-əs\ *adj* [L *nefarius*, fr. *nefas* crime, fr. *ne-* not + *fas* right, divine law] : very wicked : EVIL ◆ **Synonyms** BAD, IMMORAL, INIQUITOUS, SINFUL, VICIOUS — **ne·far·i·ous·ly** *adv*

neg *abbr* negative

ne·gate \ni-'gāt\ *vb* **ne·gat·ed; ne·gat·ing** **1** : to deny the existence or truth of **2** : to cause to be ineffective or invalid : NULLIFY

ne·ga·tion \ni-'gā-shən\ *n* **1** : the action or operation of negating or making negative **2** : a negative doctrine or statement

¹neg·a·tive \'ne-gə-tiv\ *adj* **1** : marked by denial, prohibition, or refusal ⟨a ∼ reply⟩ **2** : not positive or constructive; *esp* : not affirming the presence of what is sought or suspected to be present ⟨test results were ∼⟩ **3** : less than zero ⟨a ∼ number⟩ **4** : being, relating to, or charged with electricity of which the electron is the elementary unit **5** : having the light and dark parts opposite to what they were in the original photographic subject — **neg·a·tive·ly** *adv* — **neg·a·tive·ness** *n* — **neg·a·tiv·i·ty** \,ne-gə-'ti-və-tē\ *n*

²negative *n* **1** : a negative word or statement **2** : a negative vote or reply; *also* : REFUSAL **3** : something that is the opposite or negation of something else **4** : a negative number **5** : the side that votes or argues for the opposition (as in a debate) **6** : a negative photographic image on transparent material

³negative *vb* **-tived; -tiv·ing** **1** : to refuse to accept or approve **2** : to vote against **3** : DISPROVE

negative income tax *n* : a system of federal subsidy payments to families with incomes below a stipulated level

neg·a·tiv·ism \'ne-gə-ti-,vi-zəm\ *n* : an attitude of skepticism and denial of nearly everything affirmed or suggested by others

¹ne·glect \ni-'glekt\ *vb* [L *neglectus*, pp. of *neglegere, neclegere*, fr. *nec-* not + *legere* to gather] **1** : DISREGARD **2** : to leave undone or unattended to esp. through carelessness ◆ **Synonyms** OMIT, IGNORE, OVERLOOK, SLIGHT, FORGET, MISS

²neglect *n* **1** : an act or instance of neglecting something **2** : the condition of being neglected — **ne·glect·ful** *adj*

neg·li·gee *also* **neg·li·gé** \,ne-glə-'zhā\ *n* : a woman's long flowing dressing gown

neg·li·gent \'ne-gli-jənt\ *adj* : marked by neglect ◆ **Synonyms** NEGLECTFUL, REMISS, DELINQUENT, DERELICT — **neg·li·gence** \-jəns\ *n* — **neg·li·gent·ly** *adv*

neg·li·gi·ble \'ne-gli-jə-bəl\ *adj* : so small as to be neglected or disregarded

ne·go·ti·ant \ni-'gō-shē-ənt\ *n* : NEGOTIATOR

ne·go·ti·ate \ni-'gō-shē-,āt\ *vb* **-at·ed; -at·ing** [L *negotiari* to carry on business, fr. *negotium* business, fr. *neg-* not + *otium* leisure] **1** : to confer with another so as to arrive at the settlement of some matter; *also* : to arrange for or bring about by such conferences ⟨∼ a treaty⟩ **2** : to transfer to another by delivery or endorsement in return for equivalent value ⟨∼ a check⟩ **3** : to get through, around, or over successfully ⟨∼ a turn⟩ — **ne·go·tia·ble** \-shə-bəl, -shē-ə-\ *adj* — **ne·go·ti·a·tion** \ni-,gō-sē-'ā-shən, -shē-\ *n* — **ne·go·ti·a·tor** \-'gō-shē-,ā-tər\ *n*

ne·gri·tude \'ne-grə-,tüd, -,tyüd, 'nē-\ *n* : a consciousness of and pride in one's African heritage

Ne·gro \'nē-grō\ *n, pl* **Negroes** [Sp *or* Pg, fr. *negro* black] *sometimes offensive* : a member of the human race native to Africa and classified according to physical features (as dark skin pigmentation) — **Negro** *adj, sometimes offensive* — **Ne·groid** \'nē-,groid\ *n or adj, often not cap, sometimes offensive*

Neh *abbr* Nehemiah

Ne·he·mi·ah \,nē-ə-'mī-ə\ *n* — see BIBLE table

neigh \'nā\ *n* : a loud prolonged cry of a horse — **neigh** *vb*

¹neigh·bor \'nā-bər\ *n* **1** : one living or located near another **2** : FELLOW MAN

²neighbor *vb* : to be next to or near to : border on

neigh·bor·hood \'nā-bər-,hu̇d\ *n* **1** : NEARNESS **2** : a place or region near : VICINITY; *also* : a number or amount near ⟨costs in the ∼ of $10⟩ **3** : the people living near one another **4** : a section lived in by neighbors and usu. having distinguishing characteristics

neigh·bor·ly \-lē\ *adj* : befitting congenial neighbors; *esp* : FRIENDLY ⟨a ∼ welcome⟩ — **neigh·bor·li·ness** *n*

neigh·bour *chiefly Brit var of* NEIGHBOR

¹nei·ther \'nē-thər, 'nī-\ *conj* **1** : not either ⟨∼ good nor bad⟩ **2** : NOR ⟨∼ did I⟩

²neither *pron* : neither one : not the one and not the other ⟨∼ of the two⟩

³neither *adj* : not either ⟨∼ hand⟩

nel·son \'nel-sən\ *n* : a wrestling hold in which one applies leverage against an opponent's arm, neck, and head

nem·a·tode \'ne-mə-,tōd\ *n* : any of a phylum of elongated cylindrical worms parasitic in animals or plants or free-living in soil or water

nem·e·sis \'ne-mə-səs\ *n, pl* **-e·ses** \-,sēz\ [L *Nemesis*, goddess of divine retribution, fr. Gk] **1** : one that inflicts retribution or vengeance **2** : a formidable and usu. victorious rival **3** : an act or effect of retribution; *also* : CURSE

neo·clas·sic \,nē-ō-'kla-sik\ *or* **neo·clas·si·cal** \-si-kəl\ *adj* : of or relating to a revival or adaptation of the classical style esp. in literature, art, or music

neo·co·lo·nial·ism \,nē-ō-kə-'lō-nē-ə-,li-zəm\ *n* : the economic and political policies by which a nation indirectly maintains or extends its influence over other areas or peoples — **neo·co·lo·nial** *adj* — **neo·co·lo·nial·ist** \-list\ *n or adj*

neo·con \'nē-ō-,kän\ *n* : NEOCONSERVATIVE

neo·con·ser·va·tive \-kən-'sər-və-tiv\ *n* : a former liberal espousing political conservatism — **neo·con·ser·va·tism** \-və-,ti-zəm\ *n* — **neoconservative** *adj*

neo·dym·i·um \,nē-ō-'di-mē-əm\ *n* : a silver-white to yellow metallic chemical element

neo-im·pres·sion·ism \,nē-ō-im-'pre-shə-,ni-zəm\ *n, often cap N&I* : a late 19th century French art movement that attempted to make impressionism more precise and to use a pointillist painting technique

Neo·lith·ic \,nē-ə-'li-thik\ *adj* : of or relating to the latest period of the Stone Age characterized by polished stone implements

ne·ol·o·gism \nē-'ä-lə-,ji-zəm\ *n* : a new word or expression

ne·on \'nē-,än\ *n* [Gk, neut. of *neos* new] **1** : a gaseous colorless chemical element used in electric lamps **2** : a lamp in which a discharge through neon gives a reddish glow — **neon** *adj*

neo·na·tal \ˌnē-ō-ˈnā-tᵊl\ *adj* : of, relating to, or affecting the newborn ⟨a ∼ infection⟩ — **neo·na·tal·ly** *adv*

ne·o·nate \ˈnē-ə-ˌnāt\ *n* : a newborn child

neo—pa·gan \ˌnē-ō-ˈpā-gən\ *n* : a person who practices a contemporary form of paganism

neo·phyte \ˈnē-ə-ˌfīt\ *n* **1** : a new convert : PROSELYTE **2** : NOVICE **3** : BEGINNER ✦ *Synonyms* APPRENTICE, FRESHMAN, NEWCOMER, ROOKIE, TENDERFOOT, TYRO

neo·plasm \ˈnē-ə-ˌpla-zəm\ *n* : a new growth of tissue serving no useful purpose in the body : TUMOR — **neo·plas·tic** \ˌnē-ə-ˈplas-tik\ *adj*

neo·prene \ˈnē-ə-ˌprēn\ *n* : a synthetic rubber used esp. for special-purpose clothing (as wet suits)

neo·trop·i·cal \ˌnē-ō-ˈträ-pi-kəl\ *adj, often cap* : of or relating to a zoogeographic region of America that extends south from the central plateau of Mexico

ne·pen·the \nə-ˈpen-thē\ *n* **1** : a potion used by the ancients to dull pain and sorrow **2** : something capable of making one forget grief or suffering

neph·ew \ˈne-fyü, *chiefly Brit* -vyü\ *n* [ME *nevew*, fr. AF *neveu*, fr. LL *nepot-*, *nepos*, fr. L grandson, descendant] : a son of one's brother, sister, brother-in-law, or sister-in-law

ne·phrit·ic \ni-ˈfri-tik\ *adj* **1** : RENAL **2** : of, relating to, or affected with nephritis

ne·phri·tis \ni-ˈfrī-təs\ *n, pl* **ne·phrit·i·des** \-ˈfri-tə-ˌdēz\ : kidney inflammation

ne plus ul·tra \ˌnē-ˌpləs-ˈəl-trə\ *n* [NL, (go) no more beyond] : the highest point capable of being attained

nep·o·tism \ˈne-pə-ˌti-zəm\ *n* [F *népotisme*, fr. It *nepotismo*, fr. *nepote* nephew, fr. LL *nepot-*, *nepos*] : favoritism shown to a relative (as in the granting of jobs)

Nep·tune \ˈnep-ˌtün, -ˌtyün\ *n* : the planet 8th in order from the sun — see PLANET table — **Nep·tu·ni·an** \nep-ˈtü-nē-ən, -ˈtyü-\ *adj*

nep·tu·ni·um \nep-ˈtü-nē-əm, -ˈtyü-\ *n* : a short-lived radioactive element

nerd \ˈnərd\ *n* : an unstylish or socially inept person; *esp* : one slavishly devoted to intellectual pursuits — **nerdy** *adj*

Ne·re·id \ˈnir-ē-əd\ *n* : a sea nymph in Greek mythology

¹**nerve** \ˈnərv\ *n* **1** : SINEW, TENDON ⟨strain every ∼⟩ **2** : any of the strands of nervous tissue that carry nerve impulses between the brain and spinal cord and every part of the body **3** : power of endurance or control : FORTITUDE; *also* : BOLDNESS, DARING **4** *pl* : NERVOUSNESS **5** : a vein of a leaf or insect wing — **nerved** \ˈnərvd\ *adj* — **nerve·less** *adj*

nerve 2: cell body at left and nerve ending at right

²**nerve** *vb* **nerved; nerv·ing** : to give strength or courage to

nerve cell *n* : NEURON; *also* : CELL BODY

nerve gas *n* : a chemical weapon damaging esp. to the nervous and respiratory systems

nerve impulse *n* : a physical and chemical change that moves along a process of a neuron after stimulation and carries a record of sensation or an instruction to act

nerve—rack·ing *or* **nerve—wrack·ing** \ˈnərv-ˌra-kiŋ\ *adj* : extremely trying on the nerves

ner·vous \ˈnər-vəs\ *adj* **1** : FORCIBLE, SPIRITED **2** : of, relating to, or made up of neurons or nerves **3** : easily excited or annoyed : JUMPY **4** : TIMID, APPREHENSIVE ⟨a ∼ smile⟩ **5** : UNEASY, UNSTEADY — **ner·vous·ly** *adv* — **ner·vous·ness** *n*

nervous breakdown *n* : an attack of mental or emotional disorder of sufficient severity to be incapacitating esp. when requiring hospitalization

nervous system *n* : a bodily system that in vertebrates is made up of the brain and spinal cord, nerves, ganglia, and

parts of the sense organs and that receives and interprets stimuli and transmits nerve impulses

nervy \ˈnər-vē\ *adj* **nerv·i·er; -est** **1** : showing calm courage **2** : marked by impudence or presumption ⟨a ∼ salesperson⟩ **3** : EXCITABLE, NERVOUS ✦ *Synonyms* BOLD, CHEEKY, FORWARD, FRESH, IMPUDENT, SAUCY

-ness \nəs\ *n suffix* : state : condition : quality : degree ⟨good*ness*⟩

¹**nest** \ˈnest\ *n* **1** : the shelter prepared by a bird for its eggs and young **2** : a place where eggs (as of insects or fish) are laid and hatched **3** : a place of rest, retreat, or lodging **4** : DEN, HANGOUT ⟨a ∼ of thieves⟩ **5** : the occupants of a nest **6** : a series of objects (as bowls or tables) fitting inside or under one another

²**nest** *vb* **1** : to build or occupy a nest **2** : to fit compactly together or within one another

nest egg *n* : a fund of money accumulated as a reserve

nes·tle \ˈne-səl\ *vb* **nes·tled; nes·tling** **1** : to settle snugly or comfortably **2** : to press closely and affectionately : CUDDLE **3** : to settle, shelter, or house as if in a nest

nest·ling \ˈnest-liŋ\ *n* : a bird too young to leave its nest

¹**net** \ˈnet\ *n* **1** : a meshed fabric twisted, knotted, or woven together at regular intervals **2** : a device made all or partly of net and used esp. to catch birds, fish, or insects **3** : something made of net used esp. for protecting, confining, carrying, or dividing ⟨a tennis ∼⟩ **4** : SNARE, TRAP **5** *often cap* : INTERNET

²**net** *vb* **net·ted; net·ting** **1** : to cover or enclose with or as if with a net **2** : to catch in or as if in a net

³**net** *adj* : free from all charges or deductions ⟨∼ profit⟩ ⟨∼ weight⟩

⁴**net** *vb* **net·ted; net·ting** : to gain or produce as profit : CLEAR, YIELD ⟨his business *netted* $50,000 a year⟩

⁵**net** *n* : a net amount, profit, weight, or price

Neth *abbr* Netherlands

neth·er \ˈne-thər\ *adj* : situated down or below ⟨the ∼ regions of the earth⟩

neth·er·most \-ˌmōst\ *adj* : LOWEST

neth·er·world \-ˌwərld\ *n* **1** : the world of the dead **2** : UNDERWORLD

net·i·quette \ˈne-ti-kət, -ˌket\ *n* : etiquette governing communication on the Internet

nett *Brit var of* NET

net·ting *n* **1** : NETWORK **2** : the act or process of making a net or network

¹**net·tle** \ˈne-tᵊl\ *n* : any of a genus of coarse herbs with stinging hairs

²**nettle** *vb* **net·tled; net·tling** : PROVOKE, VEX, IRRITATE

net·tle·some \ˈne-tᵊl-səm\ *adj* : causing vexation : IRRITATING

net·work \ˈnet-ˌwərk\ *n* **1** : NET **2** : a system of elements (as lines or channels) that cross in the manner of the threads in a net **3** : a group or system of related or connected parts; *esp* : a chain of radio or television stations **4** : a system of computers that are connected (as by telephone wires)

net·work·ing \ˈnet-ˌwər-kiŋ\ *n* **1** : the exchange of information or services among individuals, groups, or institutions **2** : the cultivation of productive business relationships

neu·ral \ˈnur-əl, ˈnyur-\ *adj* : of, relating to, or involving a nerve or the nervous system ⟨∼ pathways⟩

neu·ral·gia \nu-ˈral-jə, nyu-\ *n* : acute pain that follows the course of a nerve — **neu·ral·gic** \-jik\ *adj*

neur·as·the·nia \ˌnur-əs-ˈthē-nē-ə, ˌnyur-\ *n* [NL, fr. Gk *neuron* nerve + *asthenia* weakness, fr. *asthenēs* weak, fr. *a-* not + *sthenos* strength] : a psychological disorder marked esp. by fatiguing easily, lack of motivation, feelings of inadequacy, and psychosomatic symptoms — **neur·as·then·ic** \-the-nik, -ˈthē-\ *adj or n*

neu·ri·tis \nu-ˈrī-təs, nyu-\ *n, pl* **-rit·i·des** \-ˈri-tə-ˌdēz\ *or* **-ri·tis·es** : inflammation of a nerve — **neu·rit·ic** \-ˈri-tik\ *adj or n*

neu·ro·bi·ol·o·gy \ˌnur-ō-bī-ˈä-lə-jē\ *n* : a branch of biology that deals with the nervous system — **neu·ro·bi·o·log·i·cal** \-ˌbī-ə-ˈlä-ji-kəl\ *adj* — **neu·ro·bi·ol·o·gist** \-bī-ˈä-lə-jist\ *n*

neu·rol·o·gy \nu-ˈrä-lə-jē, nyu-\ *n* : the scientific study of the nervous system — **neu·ro·log·i·cal** \ˌnur-ə-ˈlä-ji-kəl, ˌnyur-\ *or* **neu·ro·log·ic** \-jik\ *adj* — **neu·ro·log·i·cal·ly** \-ji-k(ə-)lē\ *adv* — **neu·rol·o·gist** \nu-ˈrä-lə-jist, nyu-\ *n*

neu·ro·mus·cu·lar \ˌnu̇r-ō-'məs-kyə-lər, ˌnyu̇r-\ *adj* : of, relating to, or affecting nerves and muscles ⟨a ~ disease⟩

neu·ron \'nu̇-ˌrän, 'nyü-\ *n* : a cell with specialized processes that is the fundamental functional unit of nervous tissue — **neu·ro·nal** \'nu̇r-ə-n³l, 'nyu̇r-\ *adj*

neu·rone \-ˌrōn\ *chiefly Brit var of* NEURON

neu·ro·sci·ence \ˌnu̇r-ō-'sī-əns, ˌnyu̇r-\ *n* : a branch of the life sciences that deals with the anatomy, physiology, biochemistry, or molecular biology of nerves and nervous tissue and esp. with their relation to behavior and learning — **neu·ro·sci·en·tist** \-ən-tist\ *n*

neu·ro·sis \nu̇-'rō-səs, nyu̇-\ *n, pl* **-ro·ses** \-ˌsēz\ : a mental and emotional disorder that is less serious than a psychosis, is not characterized by disturbance of the use of language, and is accompanied by various bodily and mental disturbances (as visceral symptoms, anxieties, or phobias)

neu·ro·sur·gery \ˌnu̇r-ō-'sər-jə-rē, ˌnyu̇r-\ *n* : surgery of nervous structures (as nerves, the brain, or the spinal cord) — **neu·ro·sur·geon** \-'sər-jən\ *n*

¹**neu·rot·ic** \nu̇-'rä-tik, nyu̇-\ *adj* : of, relating to, being, or affected with a neurosis — **neu·rot·i·cal·ly** \-ti-k(ə-)lē\ *adv*

²**neurotic** *n* : an emotionally unstable or neurotic person

neu·ro·trans·mit·ter \ˌnu̇r-ō-trans-'mi-tər, ˌnyu̇r-, -tranz-\ *n* : a substance (as acetylcholine) that transmits nerve impulses across a synapse

neut *abbr* neuter

¹**neu·ter** \'nu̇-tər, 'nyü-\ *adj* [ME *neutre*, fr. MF & L; MF *neutre*, fr. L *neuter*, lit., neither, fr. *ne-* not + *uter* which of two] **1** : of, relating to, or constituting the gender that includes most words or grammatical forms referring to things classed as neither masculine nor feminine **2** : lacking or having imperfectly developed sex organs

²**neuter** *n* **1** : a noun, pronoun, adjective, or inflectional form or class of the neuter gender; *also* : the neuter gender **2** : WORKER 2; *also* : a spayed or castrated animal

³**neuter** *vb* **1** : CASTRATE, SPAY **2** : to remove the force or effectiveness of

¹**neu·tral** \'nü-trəl, 'nyü-\ *n* **1** : one that is neutral **2** : a neutral color **3** : a position of disengagement (as of gears)

²**neutral** *adj* **1** : not favoring either side in a quarrel, contest, or war **2** : of or relating to a neutral state or power **3** : MIDDLING, INDIFFERENT **4** : having no hue : GRAY; *also* : not decided in color **5** : neither acid nor basic ⟨a ~ solution⟩ **6** : not electrically charged

neu·tral·ise *Brit var of* NEUTRALIZE

neu·tral·ism \'nü-trə-ˌli-zəm, 'nyü-\ *n* : a policy or the advocacy of neutrality esp. in international affairs

neu·tral·i·ty \nü-'tra-lə-tē, nyü-\ *n* : the quality or state of being neutral; *esp* : refusal to take part in a war between other powers

neu·tral·ize \'nü-trə-ˌlīz, 'nyü-\ *vb* **-ized; -iz·ing** : to make neutral; *esp* : COUNTERACT — **neu·tral·i·za·tion** \ˌnü-trə-lə-'zā-shən, ˌnyü-\ *n*

neu·tri·no \nü-'trē-nō, nyü-\ *n, pl* **-nos** : an uncharged elementary particle held to be massless or very light

neu·tron \'nü-ˌträn, 'nyü-\ *n* : an uncharged atomic particle that is nearly equal in mass to the proton

neutron bomb *n* : a nuclear bomb designed to produce lethal neutrons but less blast and fire damage than other nuclear bombs

neutron star *n* : a dense celestial object that results from the collapse of a large star

Nev *abbr* Nevada

nev·er \'ne-vər\ *adv* **1** : not ever **2** : not in any degree, way, or condition

nev·er·more \ˌne-vər-'mȯr\ *adv* : never again

nev·er–nev·er land \ˌne-vər-'ne-vər-\ *n* : an ideal or imaginary place

nev·er·the·less \ˌne-vər-thə-'les\ *adv* : in spite of that : HOWEVER

ne·vus \'nē-vəs\ *n, pl* **ne·vi** \-ˌvī\ : a usu. pigmented area on the skin : MOLE

¹**new** \'nü, 'nyü\ *adj* **1** : not old : RECENT, MODERN **2** : recently discovered, recognized, or learned about ⟨~ drugs⟩ **3** : UNFAMILIAR ⟨visit ~ places⟩ **4** : different from the former **5** : not accustomed ⟨~ to the work⟩ **6** : beginning as a repetition of a previous act or thing ⟨a ~ year⟩ **7** : REFRESHED, REGENERATED ⟨rest made a ~

man of him⟩ **8** : being in a position or place for the first time ⟨a ~ member⟩ **9** *cap* : having been in use after medieval times : MODERN ⟨*New* Latin⟩ ♦ **Synonyms** NOVEL, NEWFANGLED, FRESH — **new·ish** *adj* — **new·ness** *n*

²**new** *adv* : NEWLY ⟨*new*-mown hay⟩

¹**new age** *adj, often cap* N&A **1** : of, relating to, or being New Age **2** : CONTEMPORARY, MODERN

²**new age** *n* **1** *cap* : a group of late 20th century social attitudes adapted from a variety of ancient and modern beliefs relating to spirituality, right living, and health **2** : a soft soothing form of instrumental music

new·bie \'nü-bē, 'nyü-\ *n* : a newcomer esp. to cyberspace

new blood *n* : persons accepted into a group or organization and expected to provide fresh ideas and vitality

¹**new·born** \-ˌbȯrn\ *adj* **1** : recently born **2** : born anew ⟨~ hope⟩

²**newborn** *n, pl* **newborn** *or* **newborns** : a newborn individual

new·com·er \-ˌkə-mər\ *n* **1** : one recently arrived **2** : BEGINNER

New Deal *n* : the legislative and administrative program of President F. D. Roosevelt to promote economic recovery and social reform during the 1930s — **New Dealer** *n*

new·el \'nü-əl, 'nyü-\ *n* : a post about which the steps of a circular staircase wind; *also* : a post at the foot of a stairway or one at a landing

new·fan·gled \'nü-'faŋ-gəld, 'nyü-\ *adj* **1** : attracted to novelty **2** : of the newest style : NOVEL

new–fash·ioned \-'fa-shənd\ *adj* **1** : made in a new fashion or form **2** : UP-TO-DATE

new·found \-'faund\ *adj* : newly found

New Left *n* : a radical political movement originating in the 1960s

new·ly \'nü-lē, 'nyü-\ *adv* **1** : LATELY, RECENTLY ⟨a ~ married couple⟩ **2** : ANEW, AFRESH ⟨~ painted⟩

new·ly·wed \-ˌwed\ *n* : a person recently married

new moon *n* : the phase of the moon with its dark side toward the earth; *also* : the thin crescent moon seen for a few days after the new moon phase

news \'nüz, 'nyüz\ *n* **1** : a report of recent events : TIDINGS **2** : material reported in a newspaper or news periodical or on a newscast

news·boy \'nüz-ˌbȯi, 'nyüz-\ *n* : one who delivers or sells newspapers

news·cast \-ˌkast\ *n* : a radio or television broadcast of news — **news·cast·er** \-ˌkas-tər\ *n*

news·group \-ˌgrüp\ : an Internet bulletin devoted to a certain topic

news·let·ter \'nüz-ˌle-tər, 'nyüz-\ *n* : a small newspaper containing news or information of interest chiefly to a special group

news·mag·a·zine \-ˌma-gə-ˌzēn\ *n* : a usu. weekly magazine devoted chiefly to summarizing and analyzing news

news·man \-mən, -ˌman\ *n* : a person who gathers, reports, or comments on the news : REPORTER

news·pa·per \-ˌpā-pər\ *n* : a paper that is published at regular intervals and contains news, articles of opinion, features, and advertising

news·pa·per·man \-ˌpā-pər-ˌman\ *n* : a person who owns or is employed by a newspaper

news·print \-ˌprint\ *n* : paper made chiefly from wood pulp and used mostly for newspapers

news·reel \-ˌrēl\ *n* : a short motion picture portraying current events

news·stand \-ˌstand\ *n* : a place where newspapers and periodicals are sold

news·week·ly \-ˌwēk-lē\ *n* : a weekly newspaper or newsmagazine

news·wire \-ˌwī(-ə)r\ *n* : WIRE SERVICE

news·wom·an \-ˌwu̇-mən\ *n* : a woman who is a reporter

news·wor·thy \-ˌwər-thē\ *adj* : sufficiently interesting to the general public to warrant reporting

newsy \'nü-zē, 'nyü-\ *adj* **news·i·er; -est** : filled with news; *esp* : TALKATIVE

newt \'nüt, 'nyüt\ *n* [ME, alter. (from misdivision of *an ewte*) of *ewt, evete*, fr. OE *efete*] : any of various small chiefly aquatic salamanders

New Testament *n* : the second of the two chief divisions of the Christian Bible — see BIBLE table

new·ton \'nü-t³n, 'nyü-\ *n* : the unit of force in the metric system equal to the force required to impart an acceleration of one meter per second per second to a mass of one kilogram

new wave *n, often cap N&W* : the latest and esp. the most outrageous style — **new–wave** *adj*

New Year *n* **1** : NEW YEAR'S DAY; *also* : the first days of the year **2** : ROSH HASHANAH

New Year's Day *n* : January 1 observed as a legal holiday

¹next \'nekst\ *adj* : immediately preceding or following : NEAREST

²next *prep* : nearest or adjacent to

³next *adv* **1** : in the time, place, or order nearest or immediately succeeding **2** : on the first occasion to come

⁴next *n* : one that is next

nex·us \'nek-səs\ *n, pl* **nex·us·es** \-sə-səz\ *or* **nex·us** \-səs, -ˌsüs\ : CONNECTION, LINK

Nez Percé \'nez-'pərs\ *n* : a member of an American Indian people of Idaho, Washington, and Oregon; *also* : the language of the Nez Percé

NF *abbr* Newfoundland

NFC *abbr* National Football Conference

NFL *abbr* National Football League

Nfld *abbr* Newfoundland

NG *abbr* **1** National Guard **2** no good

ngul·trum \eŋ-'gůl-trəm\ *n* — see MONEY table

ngwee \eŋ-'gwē\ *n, pl* **ngwee** — see *kwacha* at MONEY table

NH *abbr* New Hampshire

NHL *abbr* National Hockey League

Ni *symbol* nickel

ni·a·cin \'nī-ə-sən\ *n* : an organic acid of the vitamin B complex found widely in plants and animals and used esp. against pellagra

nib \'nib\ *n* : POINT; *esp* : a pen point

¹nib·ble \'ni-bəl\ *vb* **nib·bled; nib·bling** : to bite gently or bit by bit

²nibble *n* : a small or cautious bite

ni·cad \'nī-ˌkad\ *n* : a rechargeable dry cell that has a nickel cathode and a cadmium anode

nice \'nīs\ *adj* **nic·er; nic·est** [ME, foolish, wanton, fr. AF, silly, simple, fr. L *nescius* ignorant, fr. *nescire* to not know] **1** : FASTIDIOUS, DISCRIMINATING **2** : marked by delicate discrimination or treatment **3** : PLEASING, AGREEABLE ⟨had a ∼ time⟩; *also* : well-executed ⟨a ∼ shot⟩ **4** : WELL-BRED ⟨∼ people⟩ **5** : VIRTUOUS, RESPECTABLE ♦ *Synonyms* CHOOSY, FINICKY, PARTICULAR, PERSNICKETY, PICKY — **nice·ly** *adv* — **nice·ness** *n*

nice–nel·ly \'nīs-'ne-lē\ *adj, often cap 2d N* **1** : marked by euphemism **2** : PRUDISH — **nice nelly** *n, often cap 2d N* — **nice–nel·ly·ism** \-ˌi-zəm\ *n, often cap 2d N*

nice·ty \'nī-sə-tē\ *n, pl* **-ties** **1** : a dainty, delicate, or elegant thing ⟨enjoy the *niceties* of life⟩ **2** : a fine point or distinction ⟨*niceties* of workmanship⟩ **3** : EXACTNESS, PRECISION, ACCURACY

niche \'nich\ *n* [F] **1** : a recess in a wall esp. for a statue **2** : a place, employment, or activity for which a person or thing is best fitted **3** : the living space or role of an organism in an ecological community esp. with regard to food consumption

¹nick \'nik\ *n* **1** : a small notch, groove, or chip **2** : the final critical moment ⟨in the ∼ of time⟩

²nick *vb* : NOTCH, CHIP

nick·el \'ni-kəl\ *n* **1** : a hard silver-white metallic chemical element capable of a high polish and used in alloys **2** : the U.S. 5-cent piece made of copper and nickel; *also* : the Canadian 5-cent piece

nick·el·ode·on \ˌni-kə-'lō-dē-ən\ *n* **1** : an early movie theater to which admission cost five cents **2** : JUKEBOX

nick·er \'ni-kər\ *vb* : NEIGH, WHINNY — **nicker** *n*

nick·name \'nik-ˌnām\ *n* [ME *nekename* additional name, alter. (from misdivision of *an ekename*) of *ekename*, fr. *eke* also + *name*] **1** : a usu. descriptive name given instead of or in addition to the one belonging to a person, place, or thing **2** : a familiar form of a proper name — **nickname** *vb*

nic·o·tine \'ni-kə-ˌtēn\ *n* : a poisonous and addictive substance in tobacco that is used as an insecticide

nic·o·tin·ic acid \ˌni-kə-'tē-nik-, -'ti-\ *n* : NIACIN

niece \'nēs\ *n* : a daughter of one's brother, sister, brother-in-law, or sister-in-law

nif·ty \'nif-tē\ *adj* **nif·ti·er; -est** : very good : very attractive

nig·gard \'ni-gərd\ *n* : a stingy person : MISER — **nig·gard·li·ness** \-lē-nəs\ *n* — **nig·gard·ly** *adj or adv*

nig·gling \'ni-gə-liŋ\ *adj* **1** : PETTY **2** : bothersome in a petty way ♦ *Synonyms* INCONSEQUENTIAL, MEASLY, PICAYUNE, PIDDLING, TRIFLING, TRIVIAL

¹nigh \'nī\ *adv* **1** : near in place, time, or relationship **2** : NEARLY, ALMOST

²nigh *adj* : CLOSE, NEAR

³nigh *prep* : NEAR

night \'nīt\ *n* **1** : the period between dusk and dawn **2** : the darkness of night **3** : a period of misery or unhappiness **4** : NIGHTFALL — **night** *adj*

night blindness *n* : reduced visual capacity in faint light (as at night)

night·cap \'nīt-ˌkap\ *n* **1** : a cloth cap worn with nightclothes **2** : a usu. alcoholic drink taken at bedtime

night·clothes \-ˌklōthz, -ˌklōz\ *n pl* : garments worn in bed

night·club \-ˌkləb\ *n* : a place of entertainment open at night usu. serving food and liquor and providing music for dancing

night crawl·er \-ˌkrȯ-lər\ *n* : EARTHWORM; *esp* : a large earthworm found on the soil surface at night

night·dress \'nīt-ˌdres\ *n* : NIGHTGOWN

night·fall \-ˌfȯl\ *n* : the coming of night

night·gown \-ˌgau̇n\ *n* : a loose garment for wear in bed

night·hawk \-ˌhȯk\ *n* : any of a genus of American birds related to and resembling the whip-poor-will

night·in·gale \'nī-t³n-ˌgāl, 'nī-tiŋ-\ *n* [ME, fr. OE *nihtegale*, fr. *niht* night + *galan* to sing] : any of several Old World thrushes noted for the sweet usu. nocturnal song of the male

night·life \'nīt-ˌlīf\ *n* : the activity of pleasure-seekers at night

night·ly \'nīt-lē\ *adj* **1** : happening, done, or produced by night or every night **2** : of or relating to the night or every night — **nightly** *adv*

night·mare \'nīt-ˌmer\ *n* **1** : a frightening dream **2** : a frightening or horrible experience — **nightmare** *adj* — **night·mar·ish** *adj*

night rider *n* : a member of a secret band who ride masked at night doing violence to punish or terrorize

night·shade \'nīt-ˌshād\ *n* : any of a large genus of herbs, shrubs, and trees that includes poisonous forms (as the belladonna), ornamentals (as the petunias), and important food plants (as the potato and eggplant)

night·shirt \-ˌshərt\ *n* : a nightgown resembling a shirt

night soil *n* : human feces used esp. for fertilizing the soil

night·stick \'nīt-ˌstik\ *n* : a police officer's club

night·time \-ˌtīm\ *n* : the time from dusk to dawn

night·walk·er \-ˌwȯ-kər\ *n* : a person who roves about at night esp. with criminal or immoral intent

ni·hil·ism \'nī-ə-ˌli-zəm, 'nē-hə-\ *n* **1** : a viewpoint that traditional values and beliefs are unfounded and that existence is senseless and useless **2** : ANARCHISM — **ni·hil·ist** \-list\ *n or adj* — **ni·hil·is·tic** \ˌnī-ə-'lis-tik, ˌnē-hə-\ *adj*

nil \'nil\ *n* : ZERO, NOTHING

nim·ble \'nim-bəl\ *adj* **nim·bler; nim·blest** [ME *nimel*, fr. OE *numol* holding much, fr. *niman* to take] **1** : quick and light in motion : AGILE ⟨a ∼ dancer⟩ **2** : quick in understanding and learning : CLEVER ⟨a ∼ mind⟩ ♦ *Synonyms* ACTIVE, BRISK, SPRIGHTLY, SPRY, ZIPPY — **nim·ble·ness** *n* — **nim·bly** \-blē\ *adv*

nim·bus \'nim-bəs\ *n, pl* **nim·bi** \-ˌbī, -bē\ *or* **nim·bus·es** **1** : a figure (as a disk) in an art work suggesting radiant light about the head of a divinity, saint, or sovereign **2** : a rain cloud; *also* : THUNDERHEAD

NIMBY \'nim-bē\ *n* [*not in my backyard*] : opposition to the placement of something undesirable (as a prison) in one's neighborhood

nim·rod \'nim-ˌräd\ *n* **1** : HUNTER **2** : IDIOT, JERK

nin·com·poop \'nin-kəm-ˌpüp\ *n* : FOOL, SIMPLETON

nine \'nīn\ *n* **1** : one more than eight **2** : the 9th in a set or series **3** : something having nine units; *esp* : a baseball team — **nine** *adj or pron* — **ninth** \'nīnth\ *adj or adv or n* — **to the nines** **1** : to perfection **2** : in an elaborate manner ⟨dressed *to the nines*⟩

nine days' wonder *n* : something that creates a short-lived sensation

nine·pins \'nīn-ˌpinz\ *n* : a bowling game using nine pins arranged usu. in a diamond-shaped configuration

nine·teen \'nīn-'tēn\ *n* : one more than 18 — **nineteen** *adj or pron* — **nine·teenth** \-'tēnth\ *adj or n*

nine·ty \'nīn-tē\ *n, pl* **nineties** : nine times 10 — **nine·ti·eth** \-tē-əth\ *adj or n* — **ninety** *adj or pron*

nin·ja \'nin-jə, -ˌ(ˌ)jä\ *n, pl* **ninja** *or* **ninjas** [Jp] : a person trained in ancient Japanese martial arts and employed esp. for espionage and assassinations

nin·ny \'ni-nē\ *n, pl* **ninnies** : FOOL

ni·o·bi·um \nī-'ō-bē-əm\ *n* : a gray metallic chemical element used in alloys

¹**nip** \'nip\ *vb* **nipped; nip·ping** **1** : to catch hold of and squeeze tightly between two surfaces, edges, or points **2** : ³CLIP **3** : to destroy the growth, progress, or fulfillment of ⟨*nipped* in the bud⟩ **4** : to injure or make numb with cold : CHILL **5** : SNATCH, STEAL

²**nip** *n* **1** : a sharp stinging cold **2** : a biting or pungent flavor **3** : PINCH, BITE **4** : a small portion : BIT

³**nip** *n* : a small quantity of liquor : SIP

⁴**nip** *vb* **nipped; nip·ping** : to take liquor in nips : TIPPLE

nip and tuck *adj or adv* : so close that the lead shifts rapidly from one contestant to another

nip·per \'ni-pər\ *n* **1** : one that nips **2** *pl* : PINCERS **3** : CHILD; *esp* : a small boy

nip·ple \'ni-pəl\ *n* : the protuberance of a mammary gland through which milk is drawn off : TEAT; *also* : something resembling a nipple

nip·py \'ni-pē\ *adj* **nip·pi·er; -est** **1** : PUNGENT, SHARP **2** : CHILLY

nir·va·na \nər-'vä-nə\ *n, often cap* [Skt *nirvāṇa*, lit., act of extinguishing, fr. *nis-* out + *vāti* it blows] **1** : the final freeing of a soul from all that enslaves it; *esp* : the supreme happiness that according to Buddhism comes when all passion, hatred, and delusion die out and the soul is released from the necessity of further purification **2** : OBLIVION; *also* : PARADISE

ni·sei \nē-'sā, 'nē-ˌsā\ *n, pl* **nisei** *often cap* : a son or daughter of immigrant Japanese parents who is born and educated in America

ni·si \'nī-ˌsī\ *adj* [L, unless, fr. *ne-* not + *si* if] : taking effect at a specified time unless previously modified or voided ⟨a divorce decree ∼⟩

nit \'nit\ *n* **1** : the egg of a parasitic insect (as a louse); *also* : the young insect **2** : a minor shortcoming

nite *var of* NIGHT

ni·ter \'nī-tər\ *n* : POTASSIUM NITRATE

nit–pick·ing \'nit-ˌpi-kiŋ\ *n* : minute and usu. unjustified criticism — **nit–pick·er** *n*

¹**ni·trate** \'nī-ˌtrāt, -trət\ *n* **1** : a salt or ester of nitric acid **2** : sodium nitrate or potassium nitrate used as a fertilizer

²**ni·trate** \-ˌtrāt\ *vb* **ni·trat·ed; ni·trat·ing** : to treat or combine with nitric acid or a nitrate — **ni·tra·tion** \nī-'trā-shən\ *n*

ni·tre *chiefly Brit var of* NITER

ni·tric acid \'nī-trik-\ *n* : a corrosive liquid acid used esp. in making dyes, explosives, and fertilizers

ni·tri·fi·ca·tion \ˌnī-trə-fə-'kā-shən\ *n* : the oxidation (as by bacteria) of ammonium salts to nitrites and then to nitrates — **ni·tri·fy·ing** \'nī-trə-ˌfī-iŋ\ *adj*

ni·trite \'nī-ˌtrīt\ *n* : a salt of nitrous acid

ni·tro \'nī-trō\ *n, pl* **nitros** : any of various nitrated products; *esp* : NITROGLYCERIN

ni·tro·gen \'nī-trə-jən\ *n* : a tasteless odorless gaseous chemical element constituting 78 percent of the atmosphere by volume — **ni·trog·e·nous** \nī-'trä-jə-nəs\ *adj*

nitrogen narcosis *n* : a state of euphoria and confusion caused by nitrogen forced into a diver's bloodstream from atmospheric air under pressure

ni·tro·glyc·er·in *or* **ni·tro·glyc·er·ine** \ˌnī-trə-'gli-sə-rən\ *n* : an oily explosive liquid used to make dynamite and in medicine to dilate blood vessels

ni·trous acid \'nī-trəs-\ *n* : an unstable nitrogen-containing acid known only in solution or in the form of its salts

nitrous oxide *n* : a colorless gas used esp. as an anesthetic in dentistry

nit·ty–grit·ty \'ni-tē-ˌgri-tē, ˌni-tē-'gri-tē\ *n* : what is essential and basic : specific practical details

nit·wit \'nit-ˌwit\ *n* : a scatterbrained or stupid person

¹**nix** \'niks\ *n* : NOTHING

²**nix** *vb* : VETO, REJECT

³**nix** *adv* : NO

NJ *abbr* New Jersey

NL *abbr* National League

NLRB *abbr* National Labor Relations Board

NM *abbr* **1** nautical mile **2** New Mexico

N Mex *abbr* New Mexico

NMI *abbr* no middle initial

NNE *abbr* north-northeast

NNW *abbr* north-northwest

¹**no** \'nō\ *adv* **1** — used to express the negative of an alternative ⟨shall we continue or ∼⟩ **2** : in no respect or degree ⟨he is ∼ better than the others⟩ **3** : not so ⟨∼, I'm not ready⟩ **4** — used with an adjective to imply a meaning opposite to the positive statement ⟨in ∼ uncertain terms⟩ **5** — used to introduce a more emphatic or explicit statement ⟨has the right, ∼, the duty to continue⟩ **6** — used as an interjection to express surprise or doubt ⟨∼—you don't say⟩ **7** — used in combination with a verb to form a compound adjective ⟨*no*-bake pie⟩ **8** : in negation ⟨shook his head ∼⟩

²**no** *adj* **1** : not any; *also* : hardly any **2** : not a ⟨she's ∼ expert⟩

³**no** \'nō\ *n, pl* **noes** *or* **nos** \'nōz\ **1** : REFUSAL, DENIAL ⟨got a ∼ in reply⟩ **2** : a negative vote or decision; *also, pl* : persons voting in the negative

⁴**no** *abbr* **1** north; northern **2** [L *numero*, abl. of *numerus*] number

¹**No** *var of* NOH

²**No** *symbol* nobelium

No·bel·ist \nō-'be-list\ *n* : a winner of a Nobel prize

no·bel·i·um \nō-'be-lē-əm\ *n* : a radioactive metallic chemical element produced artificially

No·bel prize \nō-'bel-, 'nō-ˌbel-\ *n* : any of various annual prizes (as in peace, literature, or medicine) established by the will of Alfred Nobel for the encouragement of persons who work for the interests of humanity

no·bil·i·ty \nō-'bi-lə-tē\ *n* **1** : the quality or state of being noble **2** : nobles considered as forming a class

¹**no·ble** \'nō-bəl\ *adj* **no·bler; no·blest** [ME, fr. AF, fr. L *nobilis* well known, noble, fr. *noscere* to come to know] **1** : ILLUSTRIOUS; *also* : FAMOUS, NOTABLE **2** : of high birth, rank, or station : ARISTOCRATIC **3** : EXCELLENT **4** : STATELY, IMPOSING ⟨a ∼ edifice⟩ **5** : of a superior nature ✦ *Synonyms* AUGUST, BARONIAL, GRAND, GRANDIOSE, MAGNIFICENT, MAJESTIC — **no·ble·ness** *n* — **no·bly** \-blē\ *adv*

²**no·ble** *n* : a person of noble rank or birth

noble gas *n* : any of a group of rare gases that include helium, neon, argon, krypton, xenon, and usu. radon and that exhibit great stability and extremely low reaction rates

no·ble·man \'nō-bəl-mən\ *n* : a member of the nobility : PEER

no·blesse oblige \nō-ˌbles-ə-'blēzh\ *n* [F, lit., nobility obligates] : the obligation of honorable, generous, and responsible behavior associated with high rank or birth

no·ble·wom·an \'nō-bəl-ˌwù-mən\ *n* : a woman of noble rank : PEERESS

¹**no·body** \'nō-ˌbä-dē, -bə-\ *pron* : no person

²**nobody** *n, pl* **no·bod·ies** : a person of no influence or importance

no–brain·er \'nō-'brā-nər\ *n* : something that requires a minimum of thought

noc·tur·nal \näk-'tər-nᵊl\ *adj* **1** : of, relating to, or occurring in the night **2** : active at night ⟨a ∼ bird⟩

noc·turne \'näk-ˌtərn\ *n* : a work of art dealing with night; *esp* : a dreamy pensive composition for the piano

noc·u·ous \'nä-kyə-wəs\ *adj* : HARMFUL — **noc·u·ous·ly** *adv*

nod \'näd\ *vb* **nod·ded; nod·ding** **1** : to bend the head downward or forward (as in bowing, going to sleep, or giving assent) **2** : to move up and down ⟨tulips *nodding* in the breeze⟩ **3** : to show by a nod of the head ⟨∼ agreement⟩ **4** : to make a slip or error in a moment of abstraction — **nod** *n*

nod·dle \'nä-dᵊl\ *n* : HEAD

nod·dy \'nä-dē\ *n, pl* **noddies** **1** : FOOL **2** : a stout-bodied tropical tern

node \'nōd\ *n* : a thickened, swollen, or differentiated area (as of tissue); *esp* : the part of a stem from which a leaf arises — **nod·al** \-ᵊl\ *adj*

nod·ule \'nä-jül\ *n* : a small lump or swelling — **nod·u·lar** \'nä-jə-lər\ *adj*

no·el \nō-'el\ *n* [F *noël* Christmas, carol, fr. OF *Nael* (*Deu*), *Noel* Christmas, fr. L *natalis* birthday] **1** : a Christmas carol **2** *cap* : the Christmas season

noes *pl of* NO

no–fault \'nō-'fȯlt\ *adj* **1** : of, relating to, or being a motor vehicle insurance plan under which someone involved in an accident is compensated usu. up to a stipulated limit for actual losses by that person's own insurance company regardless of who is responsible **2** : of, relating to, or being a divorce law under which neither party is held responsible for the breakup of the marriage

nog·gin \'nä-gən\ *n* **1** : a small mug or cup; *also* : a small quantity of drink **2** : a person's head

no–good \'nō-'gu̇d\ *adj* : having no worth, virtue, use, or chance of success — **no–good** \'nō-ˌgu̇d\ *n*

Noh \'nō\ *n, pl* **Noh** *also* **No** : classic Japanese dance-drama having a heroic theme, a chorus, and highly stylized action, costuming, and scenery

no–hit·ter \(ˌ)nō-'hi-tər\ *n* : a baseball game or part of a game in which a pitcher allows no base hits

no·how \'nō-ˌhau̇\ *adv* : in no manner

¹noise \'nȯiz\ *n* [ME, fr. AF, disturbance, noise, fr. L *nausea* nausea] **1** : loud, confused, or senseless shouting or outcry **2** : SOUND; *esp* : one that lacks agreeable musical quality or is noticeably unpleasant **3** : unwanted electronic signal or disturbance — **noise·less** *adj* — **noise·less·ly** *adv*

²noise *vb* **noised; nois·ing** : to spread by rumor or report ⟨the story was *noised* abroad⟩

noise·mak·er \'nȯiz-ˌmā-kər\ *n* : one that makes noise; *esp* : a device used to make noise at parties

noise pollution *n* : annoying or harmful noise in an environment

noi·some \'nȯi-səm\ *adj* **1** : HARMFUL, UNWHOLESOME **2** : offensive to the senses (as smell) : DISGUSTING ⟨~ habits⟩ ♦ *Synonyms* INSALUBRIOUS, NOXIOUS, SICKLY, UNHEALTHFUL, UNHEALTHY

noisy \'nȯi-zē\ *adj* **nois·i·er; -est** **1** : making loud noises **2** : full of noises : LOUD — **nois·i·ly** \-zə-lē\ *adv* — **nois·i·ness** \-zē-nəs\ *n*

nol·le pro·se·qui \ˌnä-lē-'prä-sə-ˌkwī\ *n* [L, to be unwilling to pursue] : an entry on the record of a legal action that the prosecutor or plaintiff will proceed no further in an action or suit or in some aspect of it

no·lo con·ten·de·re \ˌnō-lō-kən-'ten-də-rē\ *n* [L, I do not wish to contend] : a plea in a criminal prosecution that subjects the defendant to conviction but does not admit guilt or preclude denying the charges in another proceeding

nol–pros \'näl-'präs\ *vb* **nol–prossed; nol–pros·sing** : to discontinue by entering a nolle prosequi

nom *abbr* nominative

no·mad \'nō-ˌmad\ *n* **1** : a member of a people who have no fixed residence but move from place to place **2** : an individual who roams about aimlessly — **nomad** *adj* — **no·mad·ic** \nō-'ma-dik\ *adj*

no–man's–land \'nō-ˌmanz-ˌland\ *n* **1** : an area of unowned, unclaimed, or uninhabited land **2** : an unoccupied area between opposing troops

nom de guerre \ˌnäm-di-'ger\ *n, pl* **noms de guerre** *same or* ˌnämz-\ [F, lit., war name] : PSEUDONYM

nom de plume \-'plüm\ *n, pl* **noms de plume** *same or* ˌnämz-\ [F, pen name; prob. coined in E] : PEN NAME

no·men·cla·ture \'nō-mən-ˌklā-chər\ *n* **1** : NAME, DESIGNATION **2** : a system of terms used in a science or art

nom·i·nal \'nä-mə-nᵊl\ *adj* **1** : being something in name or form only ⟨~ head of a party⟩ **2** : TRIFLING ⟨a ~ price⟩ — **nom·i·nal·ly** *adv*

nom·i·nate \'nä-mə-ˌnāt\ *vb* **-nat·ed; -nat·ing** : to choose as a candidate for election, appointment, or honor ♦ *Synonyms* APPOINT, DESIGNATE, NAME, TAP — **nom·i·na·tion** \ˌnä-mə-'nā-shən\ *n*

nom·i·na·tive \'nä-mə-nə-tiv\ *adj* : of, relating to, or constituting a grammatical case marking typically the subject of a verb — **nominative** *n*

nom·i·nee \ˌnä-mə-'nē\ *n* : a person nominated for an office, duty, or position

non- \(')nän *or* ˌnän *before stressed syllables;* ˌnän *elsewhere*\ *prefix* **1** : not : reverse of : absence of **2** : having no importance

nonabrasive	noninterference
nonabsorbent	nonintoxicant
nonacademic	nonintoxicating
nonacceptance	noninvasive
nonacid	nonionizing
nonactivated	nonirritating
nonadaptive	nonlegal
nonaddictive	nonlethal
nonadhesive	nonlife
nonadjacent	nonlinear
nonadjustable	nonliterary
nonaggression	nonliving
nonalcoholic	nonlogical
nonappearance	nonmagnetic
nonaromatic	nonmalignant
nonathletic	nonmaterial
nonattendance	nonmember
nonbeliever	nonmembership
nonbelligerent	nonmigratory
nonbreakable	nonmilitary
noncancerous	nonmoral
noncandidate	nonmotile
noncellular	nonmoving
nonclerical	nonnegotiable
noncoital	nonobservance
noncombat	nonoccurrence
noncombative	nonofficial
noncombustible	nonoily
noncommercial	nonorthodox
noncommunist	nonparallel
noncompeting	nonparasitic
noncompetitive	nonparticipant
noncompliance	nonparticipating
noncomplying	nonpathogenic
nonconducting	nonpaying
nonconflicting	nonpayment
nonconformance	nonperformance
nonconforming	nonperishable
nonconstructive	nonphysical
noncontagious	nonpoisonous
noncontinuous	nonpolar
noncorroding	nonpolitical
noncorrosive	nonporous
noncritical	nonpregnant
noncrystalline	nonproductive
nondeductible	nonprofessional
nondelivery	nonprotein
nondemocratic	nonradioactive
nondenominational	nonrandom
nondepartmental	nonreactive
nondestructive	nonreciprocal
nondevelopment	nonrecognition
nondiscrimination	nonrecurrent
nondiscriminatory	nonrecurring
nondistinctive	nonrefillable
nondurable	nonreligious
noneconomic	nonrenewable
noneducational	nonresidential
nonelastic	nonrestricted
nonelection	nonreturnable
nonelective	nonreversible
nonelectric	nonrigid
nonelectrical	nonruminant
nonemotional	nonsalable
nonenforcement	nonscientific
nonethical	nonscientist
non-euclidean	nonseasonal
nonexclusive	nonsectarian
nonexempt	nonsegregated
nonexistence	nonselective
nonexistent	non-self-governing
nonexplosive	nonsexist
nonfarm	nonsexual
nonfatal	nonshrinkable
nonfattening	nonsinkable
nonfederated	nonsmoker
nonferrous	nonsmoking
nonfiction	nonsocial
nonfictional	nonspeaking
nonfilamentous	nonspecialist
nonfilterable	nonspecific
nonflammable	nonsteroidal
nonflowering	nonsuccess
nonfood	nonsurgical
nonfreezing	nontaxable
nonfulfillment	nonteaching
nonfunctional	nontechnical
nongraded	nontemporal
nonhereditary	nontenured
nonhomogeneous	nontheistic
nonhomologous	nonthreatening
nonhuman	nontoxic
nonidentical	nontraditional
nonimportation	nontransferable
nonindustrial	nontypical
noninfectious	nonuniform
noninflammable	nonvascular
nonintellectual	nonvenomous
nonintercourse	nonverbal

nonviable
nonvisual
nonvocal
nonvolatile
nonvoter

nonvoting
nonworker
nonworking
nonzero

non·age \'nä-nij, 'nō-\ *n* **1** : legal minority **2** : a period of youth **3** : IMMATURITY

no·na·ge·nar·i·an \ˌnō-nə-jə-'ner-ē-ən, ˌnä-\ *n* : a person whose age is in the nineties

non·aligned \ˌnän-ə-'līnd\ *adj* : not allied with other nations

no–name \'nō-ˌnäm\ *adj* : not having a readily recognizable name ⟨∼ brands⟩

non·book \'nän-ˌbůk\ *n* : a book of little literary merit that is often a compilation (as of pictures or speeches)

¹nonce \'näns\ *n* : the one, particular, or present occasion or purpose ⟨for the ∼⟩

²nonce *adj* : occurring, used, or made only once or for a special occasion ⟨a ∼ word⟩

non·cha·lant \ˌnän-shə-'länt\ *adj* [F, fr. OF, fr. prp. of *nonchaloir* to disregard, fr. *non-* not + *chaloir* to concern, fr. L *calēre* to be warm] : giving an effect of unconcern or indifference ◆ **Synonyms** COLLECTED, COMPOSED, COOL, IMPERTURBABLE, UNFLAPPABLE, UNRUFFLED — **non·cha·lance** \-'läns\ *n* — **non·cha·lant·ly** *adv*

non·com \'nän-ˌkäm\ *n* : NONCOMMISSIONED OFFICER

non·com·ba·tant \ˌnän-kəm-'ba-t⁹nt, nän-'käm-bə-tənt\ *n* : a member (as a chaplain) of the armed forces whose duties do not include fighting; *also* : CIVILIAN — **noncombatant** *adj*

non·com·mis·sioned officer \ˌnän-kə-'mi-shənd-\ *n* : a subordinate officer in the armed forces appointed from enlisted personnel

non·com·mit·tal \ˌnän-kə-'mi-t⁹l\ *adj* : indicating neither consent nor dissent ⟨a ∼ reply⟩

non com·pos men·tis \ˌnän-ˌkäm-pəs-'men-təs\ *adj* : not of sound mind

non·con·duc·tor \ˌnän-kən-'dək-tər\ *n* : a substance that is a very poor conductor of heat, electricity, or sound

non·con·form·ist \-kən-'fòr-mist\ *n* **1** *often cap* : a person who does not conform to an established church and esp. the Church of England **2** : a person who does not conform to a generally accepted pattern of thought or action ◆ **Synonyms** DISSENTER, DISSIDENT, HERETIC, SCHISMATIC, SECTARY, SEPARATIST — **non·con·for·mi·ty** \-'fòr-mə-tē\ *n*

non·co·op·er·a·tion \ˌnän-kō-ˌä-pə-'rā-shən\ *n* : failure or refusal to cooperate; *esp* : refusal through civil disobedience of a people to cooperate with the government of a country

non·cred·it \(ˌ)nän-'kre-dət\ *adj* : not offering credit toward a degree

non·cus·to·di·al \ˌnän-kə-'stō-dē-əl\ *adj* : of or being a parent who does not have legal custody of a child

non·dairy \'nän-ˌder-ē\ *adj* : containing no milk or milk products

non·de·script \ˌnän-di-'skript\ *adj* **1** : not belonging to any particular class or kind **2** : lacking distinctive qualities ⟨a ∼ building⟩

non·drink·er \-'driŋ-kər\ *n* : a person who abstains from alcohol

¹none \'nən\ *pron* **1** : not any ⟨∼ of them went⟩ **2** : not one ⟨∼ of the family⟩ **3** : not any such thing or person ⟨half a loaf is better than ∼⟩

²none *adj, archaic* : not any : NO

³none *adv* : by no means : not at all ⟨he got there ∼ too soon⟩

non·en·ti·ty \ˌnän-'en-tə-tē\ *n* **1** : something that does not exist or exists only in the imagination **2** : one of no consequence or significance ◆ **Synonyms** NOBODY, NOTHING, WHIPPERSNAPPER

nones \'nōnz\ *n sing or pl* : the 7th day of March, May, July, or October or the 5th day of any other month in the ancient Roman calendar

non·es·sen·tial \ˌnän-i-'sen-shəl\ *adj* **1** : not essential **2** : being a substance synthesized by the body in sufficient quantity to satisfy dietary needs

none·such \'nən-ˌsəch\ *n* : one without an equal — **none·such** *adj*

none·the·less \ˌnən-thə-'les\ *adv* : NEVERTHELESS

non·event \'nän-i-ˌvent\ *n* **1** : an event that fails to take place or to satisfy expectations **2** : a highly promoted event of little intrinsic interest

non·fat \-'fat\ *adj* : lacking fat solids : having fat solids removed ⟨∼ milk⟩

non·gono·coc·cal \ˌnän-ˌgä-nə-'kä-kəl\ *adj* : not caused by a gonococcus

non·he·ro \'nän-'hē-rō\ *n* : ANTIHERO

non–Hodg·kin's lymphoma \'nän-'häj-kənz-\ *n* : any of numerous malignant lymphomas not classified as Hodgkin's disease

non·in·ter·ven·tion \ˌnän-ˌin-tər-'ven-chən\ *n* : refusal or failure to intervene (as in the affairs of other countries)

non·is·sue \'nän-'i-shü\ *n* : an issue of little importance or concern

non·met·al \'nän-'me-t⁹l\ *n* : a chemical element (as carbon) that lacks the characteristics of a metal — **non·me·tal·lic** \ˌnän-mə-'ta-lik\ *adj*

non·neg·a·tive \-'ne-gə-tiv\ *adj* : not negative : being either positive or zero

non·nu·cle·ar \'nän-'nü-klē-ər\ *adj* **1** : not nuclear **2** : not having, using, or involving nuclear weapons

non·ob·jec·tive \ˌnän-əb-'jek-tiv\ *adj* **1** : not objective **2** : representing no natural or actual object, figure, or scene ⟨∼ art⟩

¹non·pa·reil \-pə-'rel\ *adj* : having no equal : PEERLESS

²nonpareil *n* **1** : an individual of unequaled excellence : PARAGON **2** : a small flat disk of chocolate covered with white sugar pellets

non·par·ti·san \'nän-'pär-tə-zən\ *adj* : not partisan; *esp* : not influenced by political party spirit or interests

non·per·son \-'pər-s⁹n\ *n* **1** : UNPERSON **2** : a person having no social or legal status

non·plus \'nän-'pləs\ *vb* **-plussed** *also* **-plused** \-'pləst\; **-plus·sing** *also* **-plus·ing** : PUZZLE, PERPLEX

non·pre·scrip·tion \ˌnän-pri-'skrip-shən\ *adj* : available for sale legally without a doctor's prescription

non·prof·it \'nän-'prä-fət\ *adj* : not conducted or maintained for the purpose of making a profit ⟨a ∼ organization⟩

non·pro·lif·er·a·tion \ˌnän-prə-ˌli-fə-'rā-shən\ *adj* : providing for the stoppage of proliferation (as of nuclear arms) ⟨a ∼ treaty⟩

non·read·er \'nän-ˌrē-dər\ *n* : one who does not read or has difficulty reading

non·rep·re·sen·ta·tion·al \ˌnän-ˌre-pri-ˌzen-'tā-shə-nəl\ *adj* : NONOBJECTIVE 2

non·res·i·dent \'nän-'re-zə-dənt\ *adj* : not living in a particular place — **non·res·i·dence** \-dəns\ *n* — **nonresident** *n*

non·re·sis·tance \ˌnän-ri-'zis-təns\ *n* : the principles or practice of passive submission to authority even when unjust or oppressive

non·re·stric·tive \-ri-'strik-tiv\ *adj* **1** : not serving or tending to restrict **2** : not limiting the reference of the word or phrase modified ⟨a ∼ clause⟩

non·sched·uled \'nän-'ske-jüld\ *adj* : licensed to carry passengers or freight by air without a regular schedule

non·sense \'nän-ˌsens, -səns\ *n* **1** : foolish or meaningless words or actions **2** : things of no importance or value — **non·sen·si·cal** \nän-'sen-si-kəl\ *adj* — **non·sen·si·cal·ly** \-k(ə-)lē\ *adv*

non se·qui·tur \nän-'se-kwə-tər\ *n* [L, it does not follow] : an inference that does not follow from the premises

non·skid \'nän-'skid\ *adj* : designed to prevent skidding

non·slip \-'slip\ *adj* : designed to prevent slipping

non·stan·dard \ˌnän-'stan-dərd\ *adj* **1** : not standard **2** : not conforming to the usage characteristic of educated native speakers of a language

non·start·er \'nän-'stär-tər\ *n* **1** : one that does not start **2** : one that is not productive or effective

non·stick \-'stik\ *adj* : allowing easy removal of cooked food particles

¹non·stop \-'stäp\ *adj* : done or made without a stop — **nonstop** *adv*

²nonstop *n* : a nonstop airplane flight

non·sup·port \ˌnän-sə-'pórt\ *n* : failure to support; *esp* : failure on the part of one under obligation to provide maintenance

non·threat·en·ing \-'thret-niŋ, -'thre-t⁹n-iŋ\ *adj* : not likely to cause danger or anxiety ⟨a ∼ illness⟩ ⟨a ∼ environment⟩

non–U \'nän-'yü\ *adj* : not characteristic of the upper classes

non·union \-'yü-nyən\ *adj* **1** : not belonging to a trade union ⟨~ carpenters⟩ **2** : not recognizing or favoring trade unions or their members ⟨~ employers⟩

non·us·er \-'yü-zər\ *n* : one who does not make use of something (as drugs)

non·vi·o·lence \'nän-'vī-ə-ləns\ *n* **1** : abstention from violence as a matter of principle **2** : avoidance of violence **3** : nonviolent political demonstrations — **non·vi·o·lent** \-lənt\ *adj*

non·white \,nän-'hwīt, -'wīt\ *n* : a person whose features and esp. skin color are different from those of peoples of northwestern Europe — **nonwhite** *adj*

non·wo·ven \'nän-'wō-vən\ *adj* : made of fibers held together by interlocking or bonding (as by chemical or thermal means) — **nonwoven** *n*

noo·dle \'nü-d°l\ *n* [G *Nudel*] : a food paste made usu. with egg and shaped typically in ribbon form

nook \'nük\ *n* **1** : an interior angle or corner formed usu. by two walls ⟨a chimney ~⟩ **2** : a sheltered or hidden place ⟨searched every ~ and cranny⟩ **3** : a usu. recessed section of a larger room ⟨a breakfast ~⟩

noon \'nün\ *n* : the middle of the day : 12 o'clock in the daytime — **noon** *adj*

noon·day \'nün-,dā\ *n* : NOON, MIDDAY

no one *pron* : NOBODY

noon·tide \'nün-,tīd\ *n* : NOON

noon·time \-,tīm\ *n* : NOON

noose \'nüs\ *n* : a loop with a slipknot that binds closer the more it is drawn

nope \'nōp\ *adv* : NO

nor \'nȯr\ *conj* : and not ⟨not for you ~ for me⟩ — used esp. to introduce and negate the second member and each later member of a series of items preceded by *neither* ⟨neither here ~ there⟩

Nor·dic \'nȯr-dik\ *adj* **1** : of or relating to the Germanic peoples of northern Europe and esp. of Scandinavia **2** : of or relating to competitive ski events involving cross-country racing, ski jumping, or biathlon — **Nordic** *n*

nor·epi·neph·rine \'nȯr-,e-pə-'ne-frən\ *n* : a nitrogen-containing neurotransmitter in parts of the sympathetic and central nervous systems

norm \'nȯrm\ *n* [L *norma,* lit., carpenter's square] **1** : an authoritative standard or model; *esp* : a set standard of development or achievement usu. derived from the average or median achievement of a large group **2** : a typical or widespread practice, procedure, or custom ✦ **Synonyms** AVERAGE, MEAN, MEDIAN, PAR

¹nor·mal \'nȯr-məl\ *adj* **1** : REGULAR, STANDARD, NATURAL **2** : of average intelligence; *also* : sound in mind and body — **nor·mal·cy** \-sē\ *n* — **nor·mal·i·ty** \nȯr-'ma-lə-tē\ *n* — **nor·mal·ly** *adv*

²normal *n* **1** : one that is normal **2** : the usual condition, level, or quantity

nor·mal·ise *Brit var of* NORMALIZE

nor·mal·ize \'nȯr-mə-,līz\ *vb* **-ized; -iz·ing** : to make or restore to normal — **nor·mal·i·za·tion** \,nȯr-mə-lə-'zā-shən\ *n*

Nor·man \'nȯr-mən\ *n* **1** : a native or inhabitant of Normandy **2** : one of the 10th century Scandinavian conquerors of Normandy **3** : one of the Norman-French conquerors of England in 1066 — **Norman** *adj*

nor·ma·tive \'nȯr-mə-tiv\ *adj* : of, relating to, or determining norms — **nor·ma·tive·ly** *adv* — **nor·ma·tive·ness** *n*

Norse \'nȯrs\ *n, pl* **Norse** **1** : NORWEGIAN; *also* : any of the western Scandinavian dialects or languages **2** *pl* : SCANDINAVIANS; *also* : NORWEGIANS

Norse·man \-mən\ *n* : any of the ancient Scandinavians

¹north \'nȯrth\ *adv* : to, toward, or in the north

²north *adj* **1** : situated toward or at the north **2** : coming from the north

³north *n* **1** : the direction to the left of one facing east **2** : the compass point directly opposite to south **3** *cap* : regions or countries north of a specified or implied point — **north·er·ly** \'nȯr-thər-lē\ *adv or adj* — **north·ern** \-thərn\ *adj* — **North·ern·er** \-thər-nər\ *n* — **north·ern·most** \-thərn-,mōst\ *adj* — **north·ward** \'nȯrth-wərd\ *adv or adj* — **north·wards** \-wərdz\ *adv*

north·east \nȯrth-'ēst\ *n* **1** : the general direction between north and east **2** : the compass point midway between north and east **3** *cap* : regions or countries northeast of a specified or implied point — **northeast** *adj or adv* — **north·east·er·ly** \-'thē-stər-lē\ *adv or adj* — **north·east·ern** \-stərn\ *adj*

north·east·er \-'ēs-tər\ *n* **1** : a strong northeast wind **2** : a storm with northeast winds

north·er \'nȯr-thər\ *n* **1** : a strong north wind **2** : a storm with north winds

northern lights *n pl* : AURORA BOREALIS

north pole *n, often cap N&P* : the northernmost point of the earth

North Star *n* : the star toward which the northern end of the earth's axis points

north·west \nȯrth-'west\ *n* **1** : the general direction between north and west **2** : the compass point midway between north and west **3** *cap* : regions or countries northwest of a specified or implied point — **northwest** *adj or adv* — **north·west·er·ly** \-'we-stər-lē\ *adv or adj* — **north·west·ern** \-'we-stərn\ *adj*

Norw *abbr* Norway; Norwegian

Nor·we·gian \nȯr-'wē-jən\ *n* **1** : a native or inhabitant of Norway **2** : the language of Norway — **Norwegian** *adj*

nos *abbr* numbers

¹nose \'nōz\ *n* **1** : the part of the face or head containing the nostrils and covering the front of the nasal cavity **2** : the sense of smell **3** : something (as a point, edge, or projecting front part) that resembles a nose ⟨the ~ of a plane⟩ — **nosed** \'nōzd\ *adj* — **on the nose** : on target : ACCURATELY — **under one's nose** : extremely near : in one's presence

²nose *vb* **nosed; nos·ing** **1** : to detect by or as if by smell : SCENT **2** : to push or move with the nose **3** : to touch or rub with the nose : NUZZLE **4** : PRY **5** : to move ahead slowly ⟨the ship *nosed* into her berth⟩

nose·bleed \'nōz-,blēd\ *n* : a bleeding from the nose

nose cone *n* : a protective cone constituting the forward end of an aerospace vehicle

nose·dive \'nōz-,dīv\ *n* **1** : a downward nose-first plunge (as of an airplane) **2** : a sudden extreme drop (as in prices)

nose·gay \'nōz-,gā\ *n* : a small bunch of flowers : POSY

nose out *vb* **1** : to discover often by prying **2** : to defeat by a narrow margin

nose·piece \-,pēs\ *n* **1** : a fitting at the lower end of a microscope tube to which the objectives are attached **2** : the bridge of a pair of eyeglasses

no–show \'nō-'shō\ *n* : a person who does not show up for an event as expected

nos·tal·gia \nä-'stal-jə\ *n* [NL, fr. Gk *nostos* return home + *algos* pain, grief] **1** : HOMESICKNESS **2** : a wistful yearning for something past or irrecoverable — **nos·tal·gic** \-jik\ *adj* — **nos·tal·gist** \-jist\ *n*

nos·tril \'näs-trəl\ *n* [ME *nosethirl,* fr. OE *nosthyrl,* fr. *nosu* nose + *thyrel* hole] **1** : either of the nares usu. with the adjoining nasal wall and passage **2** : either fleshy lateral wall of the nose

nos·trum \'näs-trəm\ *n* [L, neut. of *noster* our, ours, fr. *nos* we] : a questionable medicine or remedy

nosy *or* **nos·ey** \'nō-zē\ *adj* **nos·i·er; -est** : INQUISITIVE, PRYING

not \'nät\ *adv* **1** — used to make negative a group of words or a word ⟨the boys are ~ here⟩ **2** — used to stand for the negative of a preceding group of words ⟨sometimes hard to see and sometimes ~⟩

no·ta be·ne \,nō-tə-'bē-nē, -'be-\ [L, mark well] — used to call attention to something important

no·ta·bil·i·ty \,nō-tə-'bi-lə-tē\ *n, pl* **-ties** **1** : the quality or state of being notable **2** : NOTABLE

¹no·ta·ble \'nō-tə-bəl\ *adj* **1** : NOTEWORTHY, REMARKABLE ⟨a ~ achievement⟩ **2** : DISTINGUISHED, PROMINENT ⟨two ~ politicians made speeches⟩

²notable *n* : a person of note ✦ **Synonyms** BIGWIG, EMINENCE, NABOB, PERSONAGE, SOMEBODY, VIP

no·ta·bly \'nō-tə-blē\ *adv* **1** : in a notable manner **2** : ESPECIALLY, PARTICULARLY

no·tar·i·al \nō-'ter-ē-əl\ *adj* : of, relating to, or done by a notary public

no·ta·rize \'nō-tə-,rīz\ *vb* **-rized; -riz·ing** : to acknowledge or make legally authentic as a notary public

no·ta·ry public \\'nō-tə-rē-\\ *n, pl* **notaries public** *or* **notary publics** : a public official who attests or certifies writings (as deeds) to make them legally authentic

no·ta·tion \\nō-'tā-shən\\ *n* **1** : ANNOTATION, NOTE **2** : the act, process, or method of representing data by marks, signs, figures, or characters; *also* : a system of symbols (as letters, numerals, or musical notes) used in such notation

¹**notch** \\'näch\\ *n* **1** : a V-shaped hollow in an edge or surface **2** : a narrow pass between two mountains

²**notch** *vb* **1** : to cut or make notches in **2** : to score or record by or as if by cutting a series of notches ⟨~ed 20 points for the team⟩

notch·back \\'näch-ˌbak\\ *n* : an automobile with a trunk whose lid forms a distinct deck

¹**note** \\'nōt\\ *vb* **not·ed; not·ing 1** : to notice or observe with care; *also* : to record or preserve in writing **2** : to make special mention of : REMARK

²**note** *n* **1** : a musical sound **2** : a cry, call, or sound esp. of a bird **3** : a special tone in a person's words or voice ⟨a ~ of fear⟩ **4** : a character in music used to indicate duration of a tone by its shape and pitch by its position on the staff **5** : a characteristic feature : MOOD, QUALITY ⟨a ~ of optimism⟩ **6** : MEMORANDUM **7** : a brief and informal record; *also* : a written or printed comment or explanation **8** : a written promise to pay a debt **9** : a piece of paper money **10** : a short informal letter **11** : a formal diplomatic or official communication **12** : DISTINCTION, REPUTATION ⟨an artist of ~⟩ **13** : OBSERVATION, NOTICE, HEED ⟨take ~ of the time⟩

note·book \\'nōt-ˌbůk\\ *n* **1** : a book for notes or memoranda **2** : a portable microcomputer smaller than a laptop computer

not·ed \\'nō-təd\\ *adj* : well known by reputation : EMINENT, CELEBRATED

note·wor·thy \\'nōt-ˌwər-thē\\ *adj* : worthy of note : REMARKABLE

¹**noth·ing** \\'nə-thiŋ\\ *pron* **1** : no thing ⟨leaves ~ to the imagination⟩ **2** : no part **3** : one of no interest, value, or importance ⟨she's ~ to me⟩ **4** : a light playful remark ⟨sweet ~s⟩

²**nothing** *adv* : not at all : in no degree

³**nothing** *n* **1** : something that does not exist **2** : ZERO **3** : a person or thing of little or no value or importance

⁴**nothing** *adj* : of no account : WORTHLESS

noth·ing·ness \\'nə-thiŋ-nəs\\ *n* **1** : the quality or state of being nothing **2** : NONEXISTENCE; *also* : utter insignificance **3** : something insignificant or valueless

¹**no·tice** \\'nō-təs\\ *n* **1** : WARNING, ANNOUNCEMENT **2** : notification of the termination of an agreement or contract at a specified time **3** : ATTENTION, HEED ⟨bring the matter to my ~⟩ **4** : a written or printed announcement **5** : a short critical account or examination (as of a play) : REVIEW

²**notice** *vb* **no·ticed; no·tic·ing 1** : to make mention of : remark on : NOTE **2** : to take notice of : OBSERVE, MARK

no·tice·able \\'nō-tə-sə-bəl\\ *adj* **1** : worthy of notice **2** : likely to be noticed — **no·tice·ably** \\-blē\\ *adv*

no·ti·fy \\'nō-tə-ˌfī\\ *vb* **-fied; -fy·ing 1** : to give notice of : report the occurrence of **2** : to give notice to — **no·ti·fi·ca·tion** \\ˌnō-tə-fə-'kā-shən\\ *n*

no·tion \\'nō-shən\\ *n* **1** : IDEA, CONCEPTION ⟨have a ~ of what he means⟩ **2** : a belief held : OPINION, VIEW **3** : WHIM, FANCY ⟨a sudden ~ to go⟩ **4** *pl* : small useful articles (as pins, needles, or thread)

no·tion·al \\'nō-shə-nəl\\ *adj* **1** : existing in the mind only : IMAGINARY, UNREAL **2** : given to foolish or fanciful moods or ideas : WHIMSICAL

no·to·ri·ous \\nō-'tȯr-ē-əs\\ *adj* : generally known and talked of; *esp* : widely and unfavorably known — **no·to·ri·ety** \\ˌnō-tə-'rī-ə-tē\\ *n* — **no·to·ri·ous·ly** \\nō-'tȯr-ē-əs-lē\\ *adv*

¹**not·with·stand·ing** \\ˌnät-with-'stan-diŋ, -with-\\ *prep* : in spite of

²**notwithstanding** *adv* : NEVERTHELESS

³**notwithstanding** *conj* : ALTHOUGH

nou·gat \\'nü-gət\\ *n* [F, fr. Occitan, fr. Old Occitan, *nogat*, fr. *noga* nut, ultim. fr. L *nuc-, nux*] : a confection of nuts or fruit pieces in a sugar paste

nought *var of* NAUGHT

noun \\'naůn\\ *n* : a word that is the name of a subject of discourse (as a person or place)

nour·ish \\'nər-ish\\ *vb* : to promote the growth or development of

nour·ish·ing *adj* : giving nourishment

nour·ish·ment \\'nər-ish-mənt\\ *n* **1** : FOOD, NUTRIENT **2** : the action or process of nourishing

nou·veau riche \\ˌnü-ˌvō-'rēsh\\ *n, pl* **nou·veaux riches** *same*\\ [F] : a person newly rich : PARVENU

Nov *abbr* November

no·va \\'nō-və\\ *n, pl* **novas** *or* **no·vae** \\-(ˌ)vē, -ˌvī\\ [NL, fem. of L *novus* new] : a star that suddenly increases greatly in brightness and then within a few months or years grows dim again

¹**nov·el** \\'nä-vəl\\ *adj* **1** : having no precedent : NEW **2** : STRANGE, UNUSUAL

²**novel** *n* : a long invented prose narrative dealing with human experience through a connected sequence of events — **nov·el·ist** \\-və-list\\ *n*

nov·el·ette \\ˌnä-və-'let\\ *n* : a brief novel or long short story

nov·el·ize \\'nä-və-ˌlīz\\ *vb* **-ized; -iz·ing** : to convert into the form of a novel — **nov·el·i·za·tion** \\ˌnä-və-lə-'zā-shən\\ *n*

no·vel·la \\nō-'ve-lə\\ *n, pl* **novellas** *or* **no·vel·le** \\-'ve-lē\\ : NOVELETTE

nov·el·ty \\'nä-vəl-tē\\ *n, pl* **-ties 1** : something new or unusual **2** : NEWNESS **3** : a small manufactured article intended mainly for personal or household adornment — usu. used in pl.

No·vem·ber \\nō-'vem-bər\\ *n* [ME *Novembre*, fr. AF, fr. L *November* ninth month of the early Roman calendar, fr. *novem* nine] : the 11th month of the year

no·ve·na \\nō-'vē-nə\\ *n* : a Roman Catholic nine-day period of prayer

nov·ice \\'nä-vəs\\ *n* **1** : a new member of a religious order who is preparing to take the vows of religion **2** : one who is inexperienced or untrained

no·vi·tiate \\nō-'vi-shət\\ *n* **1** : the period or state of being a novice **2** : a house where novices are trained **3** : NOVICE

¹**now** \\'naů\\ *adv* **1** : at the present time or moment **2** : in the time immediately before the present **3** : IMMEDIATELY, FORTHWITH **4** — used with the sense of present time weakened or lost (as to express command, introduce an important point, or indicate a transition) ⟨~ hear this⟩ **5** : SOMETIMES ⟨~ one and ~ another⟩ **6** : under the present circumstances **7** : at the time referred to **8** : by this time

²**now** *conj* : in view of the fact ⟨~ that you're here, we'll start⟩

³**now** *n* : the present time or moment : PRESENT

⁴**now** *adj* **1** : of or relating to the present time ⟨the ~ president⟩ **2** : excitingly new ⟨~ clothes⟩; *also* : constantly aware of what is new ⟨~ people⟩

NOW *abbr* **1** National Organization for Women **2** negotiable order of withdrawal

now·a·days \\'naů-ə-ˌdāz\\ *adv* : at the present time

no·way \\'nō-ˌwā\\ *or* **no·ways** \\-ˌwāz\\ *adv* : NOWISE

no·where \\-ˌhwer\\ *adv* **1** : not anywhere **2** : not at all — usu. used with *near* ⟨~ near enough⟩ — **nowhere** *n*

no·wise \\'nō-ˌwīz\\ *adv* : in no way

nox·ious \\'näk-shəs\\ *adj* : harmful esp. to health or morals

noz·zle \\'nä-zəl\\ *n* : a short tube constricted in the middle or at one end and used (as on a hose) to speed up or direct a flow of fluid

np *abbr* **1** no pagination **2** no place (of publication)

Np *symbol* neptunium

NP *abbr* notary public

NR *abbr* not rated

NRA *abbr* National Rifle Association

NS *abbr* **1** not specified **2** Nova Scotia

NSA *abbr* National Security Agency

NSC *abbr* National Security Council

NSF *abbr* **1** National Science Foundation **2** not sufficient funds

NSW *abbr* New South Wales

NT *abbr* **1** New Testament **2** Northern Territory **3** Northwest Territories

nth \\'enth\\ *adj* **1** : numbered with an unspecified or indefinitely large ordinal number ⟨for the ~ time⟩ **2** : EXTREME, UTMOST ⟨to the ~ degree⟩

NTP *abbr* normal temperature and pressure

nt wt *or* **n wt** *abbr* net weight

nu \'nü, 'nyü\ *n* : the 13th letter of the Greek alphabet — N or ν

NU *abbr* name unknown

nu·ance \'nü-ˌäns, 'nyü-, nü-ˈäns, nyü-\ *n* [F] : a shade of difference : a delicate variation (as in tone or meaning)

nub \'nəb\ *n* 1 : KNOB, LUMP 2 : GIST, POINT ⟨the ∼ of the story⟩

nub·bin \'nə-bən\ *n* 1 : something (as an ear of Indian corn) that is small for its kind, stunted, undeveloped, or imperfect 2 : a small projecting bit

nu·bile \'nü-ˌbī(-ə)l, 'nyü-, -bəl\ *adj* 1 : of marriageable condition or age 2 : sexually attractive ⟨∼ young women⟩

nu·cle·ar \'nü-klē-ər, 'nyü-\ *adj* 1 : of, relating to, or constituting a nucleus 2 : of, relating to, or using the atomic nucleus or energy derived from it 3 : of, relating to, or being a weapon whose destructive power results from an uncontrolled nuclear reaction

nu·cle·ate \'nü-klē-ˌāt, 'nyü-\ *vb* **-at·ed; -at·ing** : to form, act as, or have a nucleus — **nu·cle·ation** \ˌnü-klē-ˈā-shən, ˌnyü-\ *n*

nu·cle·ic acid \nù-ˈklē-ik-, nyü-, -ˈklā-\ *n* : any of various complex organic acids (as DNA or RNA) found esp. in cell nuclei

nu·cle·o·tide \'nü-klē-ə-ˌtīd, 'nyü-\ *n* : any of several compounds that are the basic structural units of nucleic acids

nu·cle·us \'nü-klē-əs, 'nyü-\ *n, pl* **nu·clei** \-klē-ˌī\ *also* **cle·us·es** [NL, fr. L, kernel, dim. of *nuc-, nux* nut] 1 : a central mass or part about which matter gathers or is collected : CORE 2 : a cell part that is characteristic of all living things except viruses, bacteria, and certain algae, that is necessary for heredity and for making proteins, that contains the chromosomes with their genes, and that is enclosed in a membrane 3 : a mass of gray matter or group of cell bodies of neurons in the central nervous system 4 : the central part of an atom that comprises nearly all of the atomic mass 5 : a basic or essential part

¹**nude** \'nüd, 'nyüd\ *adj* **nud·er; nud·est** 1 : BARE, NAKED, UNCLOTHED 2 : featuring or catering to naked people ⟨a ∼ beach⟩ — **nu·di·ty** \'nü-də-tē, 'nyü-\ *n*

²**nude** *n* 1 : a nude human figure esp. as depicted in art 2 : the condition of being nude ⟨in the ∼⟩

nudge \'nəj\ *vb* **nudged; nudg·ing** : to touch or push gently (as with the elbow) usu. in order to seek attention — **nudge** *n*

nud·ism \'nü-ˌdi-zəm, 'nyü-\ *n* : the practice of going nude esp. in mixed groups at specially secluded places — **nud·ist** \-dist\ *n*

nu·ga·to·ry \-gə-ˌtȯr-ē\ *adj* 1 : INCONSEQUENTIAL, WORTHLESS 2 : having no force : INEFFECTUAL

nug·get \'nə-gət\ *n* 1 : a lump of precious metal (as gold) 2 : TIDBIT

nui·sance \'nü-s°ns, 'nyü-\ *n* : an annoying or troublesome person or thing

nuisance tax *n* : an excise tax collected in small amounts directly from the consumer

¹**nuke** \'nük, 'nyük\ *n* 1 : a nuclear weapon 2 : a nuclear power plant

²**nuke** *vb* **nuked; nuk·ing** 1 : to attack with nuclear weapons 2 : MICROWAVE

null \'nəl\ *adj* 1 : having no legal or binding force : INVALID, VOID 2 : amounting to nothing 3 : INSIGNIFICANT — **nul·li·ty** \'nə-lə-tē\ *n*

null and void *adj* : having no force, binding power, or validity

nul·li·fy \'nə-lə-ˌfī\ *vb* **-fied; -fy·ing** : to make null or valueless; *also* : ANNUL — **nul·li·fi·ca·tion** \ˌnə-lə-fə-ˈkā-shən\ *n*

num *abbr* numeral

Num *or* **Numb** *abbr* Numbers

numb \'nəm\ *adj* : lacking sensation or emotion : BENUMBED — **numb** *vb* — **numb·ly** *adv* — **numb·ness** *n*

¹**num·ber** \'nəm-bər\ *n* 1 : the total of individuals or units taken together 2 : an indefinite total ⟨a small ∼ of tickets remain unsold⟩ 3 : an ascertainable total ⟨the sands of the desert are without ∼⟩ 4 : a distinction of word form to denote reference to one or more than one 5 : a unit belonging to a mathematical system and subject to its laws; *also, pl* : ARITHMETIC 6 : a symbol used to represent a mathematical number; *also* : such a number used to identify or designate ⟨a phone ∼⟩ 7 : one in a

series of musical or theatrical performances 8 : an act of transforming or impairing ⟨tripped and did a ∼ on her knee⟩

²**number** *vb* 1 : COUNT, ENUMERATE 2 : to include with or be one of a group 3 : to restrict to a small or definite number 4 : to assign a number to 5 : to comprise in number : TOTAL

num·ber·less \-ləs\ *adj* : INNUMERABLE, COUNTLESS

Numbers *n* — see BIBLE table

numb·ing \'nə-miŋ\ *adj* : tending to make numb ⟨a ∼ lecture⟩ ⟨a ∼ realization⟩

numbskull *var of* NUMSKULL

nu·mer·a·cy \'nü-mə-rə-sē, 'nyü-\ *n* : the capacity for quantitative thought or expression

nu·mer·al \'nü-mə-rəl, 'nyü-\ *n* : a conventional symbol representing a number — **numeral** *adj*

nu·mer·ate \'nü-mə-ˌrāt, 'nyü-\ *vb* **-at·ed; -at·ing** : ENUMERATE

nu·mer·a·tor \-ˌrā-tər\ *n* : the part of a fraction above the line

nu·mer·ic \nù-ˈmer-ik, nyü-\ *adj* : NUMERICAL; *esp* : denoting a number or a system of numbers

nu·mer·i·cal \-ˈmer-i-kəl\ *adj* 1 : of or relating to numbers 2 : expressed in or involving numbers — **nu·mer·i·cal·ly** \-k(ə-)lē\ *adv*

nu·mer·ol·o·gy \ˌnü-mə-ˈrä-lə-jē, ˌnyü-\ *n* : the study of the occult significance of numbers — **nu·mer·ol·o·gist** \-jist\ *n*

nu·mer·ous \'nü-mə-rəs, 'nyü-\ *adj* : consisting of, including, or relating to a great number : MANY

nu·mis·mat·ics \ˌnü-məz-ˈma-tiks, ˌnyü-\ *n* : the study or collection of monetary objects — **nu·mis·mat·ic** \-tik\ *adj* — **nu·mis·ma·tist** \nü-ˈmiz-mə-tist, nyü-\ *n*

num·skull *also* **numb·skull** \'nəm-ˌskəl\ *n* : a stupid person : DUNCE

nun \'nən\ *n* : a woman belonging to a religious order; *esp* : one under solemn vows of poverty, chastity, and obedience

nun·cio \'nən-sē-ˌō, 'nùn-\ *n, pl* **-ci·os** [It, fr. L *nuntius* messenger] : a permanent high-ranking papal representative to a civil government

nun·nery \'nə-nə-rē\ *n, pl* **-ner·ies** : a convent of nuns

¹**nup·tial** \'nəp-shəl\ *adj* : of or relating to marriage or a wedding

²**nuptial** *n* : MARRIAGE, WEDDING — usu. used in pl.

¹**nurse** \'nərs\ *n* [ME *norice, nurse,* fr. AF *nurice,* fr. LL *nutricia,* fr. L, fem. of *nutricius* nourishing] 1 : a girl or woman employed to take care of children 2 : a person trained to care for sick people

²**nurse** *vb* **nursed; nurs·ing** 1 : SUCKLE 2 : to take charge of and watch over 3 : TEND ⟨∼ an invalid⟩ 4 : to treat with special care ⟨∼ a headache⟩ 5 : to hold in one's mind or consideration ⟨∼ a grudge⟩ 6 : to act or serve as a nurse

nurse·maid \'nərs-ˌmād\ *n* : NURSE 1

nurse–prac·ti·tion·er \-prak-ˈti-shə-nər\ *n* : a registered nurse who is qualified to assume some of the duties formerly assumed only by a physician

nurs·ery \'nər-sə-rē\ *n, pl* **-er·ies** 1 : a room for children 2 : a place where children are temporarily cared for in their parents' absence 3 : a place where young plants are grown usu. for transplanting

nurs·ery·man \-mən\ *n* : a man who keeps or works in a plant nursery

nursery school *n* : a school for children under kindergarten age

nursing home *n* : a private establishment providing care for persons (as the aged or the chronically ill) who are unable to care for themselves

nurs·ling \'nərs-liŋ\ *n* 1 : one that is solicitously cared for 2 : a nursing child

¹**nur·ture** \'nər-chər\ *n* 1 : TRAINING, UPBRINGING; *also* : the influences that modify the expression of an individual's heredity 2 : FOOD, NOURISHMENT

²**nurture** *vb* **nur·tured; nur·tur·ing** 1 : to care for : FEED, NOURISH 2 : EDUCATE, TRAIN 3 : FOSTER

nut \'nət\ *n* 1 : a dry fruit or seed with a hard shell and a firm inner kernel; *also* : its kernel 2 : a metal block with a hole through it that is fastened to a bolt or screw by means of a screw thread within the hole 3 : the ridge on the upper end of the fingerboard in a stringed musical in-

NUMBER TABLE

CARDINAL NUMBERS[1]			ORDINAL NUMBERS[4]	
NAME[2]	SYMBOL		NAME[5]	SYMBOL[6]
	Arabic	*Roman*[3]		
zero *or* naught *or* cipher	0			
one	1	I	first	1st
two	2	II	second	2d *or* 2nd
three	3	III	third	3d *or* 3rd
four	4	IV	fourth	4th
five	5	V	fifth	5th
six	6	VI	sixth	6th
seven	7	VII	seventh	7th
eight	8	VIII	eighth	8th
nine	9	IX	ninth	9th
ten	10	X	tenth	10th
eleven	11	XI	eleventh	11th
twelve	12	XII	twelfth	12th
thirteen	13	XIII	thirteenth	13th
fourteen	14	XIV	fourteenth	14th
fifteen	15	XV	fifteenth	15th
sixteen	16	XVI	sixteenth	16th
seventeen	17	XVII	seventeenth	17th
eighteen	18	XVIII	eighteenth	18th
nineteen	19	XIX	nineteenth	19th
twenty	20	XX	twentieth	20th
twenty-one	21	XXI	twenty-first	21st
twenty-two	22	XXII	twenty-second	22d *or* 22nd
twenty-three	23	XXIII	twenty-third	23d *or* 23rd
twenty-four	24	XXIV	twenty-fourth	24th
twenty-five	25	XXV	twenty-fifth	25th
twenty-six	26	XVI	twenty-sixth	26th
twenty-seven	27	XVII	twenty-seventh	27th
twenty-eight	28	XVIII	twenty-eighth	28th
twenty-nine	29	XXIX	twenty-ninth	29th
thirty	30	XXX	thirtieth	30th
thirty-one	31	XXXI	thirty-first	31st
thirty-two *etc*	32	XXXII	thirty-second *etc*	32d *or* 32nd
forty	40	XL	fortieth	40th
forty-one	41	XLI	forty-first	41st
forty-two *etc*	42	XLII	forty-second *etc*	42d *or* 42nd
fifty	50	L	fifty	50th
sixty	60	LX	sixty	60th
seventy	70	LXX	seventieth	70th
eighty	80	LXXX	eightieth	80th
ninety	90	XC	ninetieth	90th
one hundred	100	C	one hundredth	100th
one hundred and one	101	CI	one hundred and first	101st
one hundred and two *etc*	102	CII	one hundred and second *etc*	102d *or* 102nd
two hundred	200	CC	two hundredth	200th
three hundred	300	CCC	three hundredth	300th
four hundred	400	CD	four hundredth	400th
five hundred	500	D	five hundredth	500th
six hundred	600	DC	six hundredth	600th
seven hundred	700	DCC	seven hundredth	700th
eight hundred	800	DCCC	eight hundredth	800th
nine hundred	900	CM	nine hundredth	900th
one thousand	1,000	M	one thousandth	1,000th
two thousand *etc*	2,000	MM	two thousandth *etc*	2,000th
five thousand	5,000	$\overline{\text{V}}$	five thousandth	5,000th
ten thousand	10,000	$\overline{\text{X}}$	ten thousandth	10,000th
one hundred thousand	100,000	$\overline{\text{C}}$	hundred thousandth *or* one hundred thousandth	100,000th
one million	1,000,000	$\overline{\text{M}}$	millionth *or* one millionth	1,000,000th

[1] The cardinal numbers are used in simple counting or in answer to "how many?" The words for these numbers may be used as nouns (he counted to *twelve*), as pronouns (*twelve* were found), or as adjectives (*twelve* girls).

[2] In formal contexts the numbers one to one hundred and in less formal contexts the numbers one to nine are commonly written out in words, while larger numbers are given in numerals. In nearly all contexts a number occurring at the beginning of a sentence is usually written out. Except in very formal contexts numerals are invariably used for dates. Arabic numbers from 1,000 to 9,999 are often written without commas or spaces (1000, 9999). Year numbers are always written without commas (1783).

[3] The Roman numerals are written either in capitals or in lowercase letters.

[4] The ordinal numbers are used to show the order of succession in which such items as names, objects, and periods of time are considered (the *twelfth* month; the *fourth* row of seats; the *18th* century).

[5] Each of the terms for the ordinal numbers excepting *first* and *second* is used in designating one of a number of parts into which a whole may be divided (a *fourth*; a *sixth*; a *tenth*) and as the denominator in fractions designating the number of such parts constituting a certain portion of a whole *one fourth*; *three fifths*). When used as nouns the fractions are usually written as two words, although they are regularly hyphenated as adjectives (a *two-thirds* majority). When fractions are written in numerals, the cardinal symbols are used ($^1/_4$, $^3/_5$, $^5/_6$).

[6] The Arabic symbols for the cardinal numbers may be read as ordinals in certain contexts (January 1 = January first; 2 Samuel = Second Samuel). The Roman numerals are sometimes read as ordinals (Henry IV = Henry the Fourth); sometimes they are written with the ordinal suffixes (XIXth Dynasty).

strument over which the strings pass   **4** : a foolish, eccentric, or crazy person   **5** : ENTHUSIAST

nut·crack·er \'nət-ˌkra-kər\ *n* : an instrument for cracking nuts

nut·hatch \-ˌhach\ *n* : any of various small tree-climbing chiefly insect-eating birds

nuthatch

nut·meg \-ˌmeg, -ˌmāg\ *n* [ME *notemuge*, ultim. fr. Old Occitan *noz muscada*, lit., musky nut] : a spice made by grinding the nutlike aromatic seed of a tropical tree; *also* : the seed or tree

nu·tria \'nü-trē-ə, 'nyü-\ *n* [Sp]   **1** : the durable usu. light brown fur of a nutria   **2** : a large So. American aquatic rodent with webbed hind feet

¹nu·tri·ent \'nü-trē-ənt, 'nyü-\ *adj* : NOURISHING

²nutrient *n* : a nutritive substance or ingredient

nu·tri·ment \-trə-mənt\ *n* : NUTRIENT

nu·tri·tion \nú-'tri-shən, nyú-\ *n* : the act or process of nourishing; *esp* : the processes by which an individual takes in and utilizes food material — **nu·tri·tion·al** \-shə-nəl\ *adj* — **nu·tri·tion·al·ly** *adv* — **nu·tri·tion·ist** \-shə-nist\ *n* — **nu·tri·tive** \'nü-trə-tiv, 'nyü-\ *adj*

nu·tri·tious \-shəs\ *adj* : NOURISHING — **nu·tri·tious·ly** *adv*

nuts \'nəts\ *adj*   **1** : ENTHUSIASTIC, KEEN   **2** : CRAZY, DEMENTED

nut·shell \'nət-ˌshel\ *n* : the shell of a nut — **in a nutshell** : in a few words ⟨that's the story *in a nutshell*⟩

nut·ty \'nə-tē\ *adj* **nut·ti·er; -est**   **1** : containing or suggesting nuts ⟨a ∼ flavor⟩   **2** : mentally unbalanced

nuz·zle \'nə-zəl\ *vb* **nuz·zled; nuz·zling**   **1** : to root around, push, or touch with or as if with the nose   **2** : NESTLE, SNUGGLE

NV *abbr* Nevada

NW *abbr* northwest

NWT *abbr* Northwest Territories

NY *abbr* New York

NYC *abbr* New York City

ny·lon \'nī-ˌlän\ *n*   **1** : any of numerous strong tough elastic synthetic materials used esp. in textiles and plastics   **2** *pl* : stockings made of nylon

nymph \'nimf\ *n*   **1** : any of the lesser goddesses in ancient mythology represented as maidens living in the mountains, forests, meadows, and waters   **2** : GIRL   **3** : an immature insect resembling the adult but smaller, less differentiated, and usu. lacking developed wings

nym·pho·ma·nia \ˌnim-fə-'mā-nē-ə, -nyə\ *n* : excessive sexual desire by a female — **nym·pho·ma·ni·ac** \-nē-ˌak\ *n or adj*

NZ *abbr* New Zealand

¹o \'ō\ *n, pl* **o's** *or* **os** \'ōz\ *often cap*   **1** : the 15th letter of the English alphabet   **2** : ZERO

²o *abbr, often cap*   **1** ocean   **2** Ohio   **3** ohm

¹O *var of* OH

²O *symbol* oxygen

o/a *abbr* on or about

oaf \'ōf\ *n* : a stupid or awkward person — **oaf·ish** *adj*

oak \'ōk\ *n, pl* **oaks** *or* **oak** : any of a genus of trees or shrubs related to the beech and chestnut and bearing a rounded thin-shelled nut surrounded at the base by a hardened cup; *also* : the usu. tough hard durable wood of an oak — **oak·en** \'ō-kən\ *adj*

oa·kum \'ō-kəm\ *n* [ME *okum*, fr. OE *ācumba* flax fiber, from *a-* out + *-cumba* (akin to OE *camb* comb)] : loosely twisted hemp or jute fiber impregnated with tar and used esp. in caulking ships

oar \'ȯr\ *n* : a long pole with a broad blade at one end used for propelling or steering a boat

oar·lock \'ȯr-ˌläk\ *n* : a U-shaped device for holding an oar in place

oars·man \'ȯrz-mən\ *n* : one who rows esp. in a racing crew

OAS *abbr* Organization of American States

oa·sis \ō-'ā-səs\ *n, pl* **oa·ses** \-ˌsēz\ : a fertile or green area in an arid region

oat \'ōt\ *n* : a cereal grass widely grown for its edible seed; *also* : this seed — **oat·en** \'ō-t⁰n\ *adj*

oat·cake \'ōt-ˌkāk\ *n* : a thin flat oatmeal cake

oath \'ōth\ *n, pl* **oaths** \'ōthz, 'ōths\   **1** : a solemn appeal to God to witness to the truth of a statement or the sacredness of a promise   **2** : an irreverent or careless use of a sacred name

oat·meal \'ōt-ˌmēl\ *n*   **1** : ground or rolled oats   **2** : porridge made from ground or rolled oats

Ob *or* **Obad** *abbr* Obadiah

Oba·di·ah \ˌō-bə-'dī-ə\ *n* — see BIBLE table

ob·bli·ga·to \ˌä-blə-'gä-tō\ *n, pl* **-tos** *also* **-ti** \-'gä-tē\ [It] : an accompanying part usu. played by a solo instrument

ob·du·rate \'äb-də-rət, -dyə-\ *adj* : stubbornly resistant : UNYIELDING ◆ **Synonyms** INFLEXIBLE, ADAMANT, RIGID, UNCOMPROMISING — **ob·du·ra·cy** \-rə-sē\ *n*

obe·di·ent \ō-'bē-dē-ənt\ *adj* : submissive to the restraint or command of authority ◆ **Synonyms** DOCILE, TRACTABLE, AMENABLE, BIDDABLE — **obe·di·ence** \-əns\ *n* — **obe·di·ent·ly** *adv*

obei·sance \ō-'bē-səns, -'bā-\ *n*   **1** : a bow made to show respect or submission   **2** : DEFERENCE, HOMAGE ⟨makes ∼ to her mentors⟩

obe·lisk \'ä-bə-ˌlisk\ *n* [MF *obelisque*, fr. L *obeliscus*, fr. Gk *obeliskos*, fr. dim. of *obelos* spit, pointed pillar] : a 4-sided pillar that tapers toward the top and ends in a pyramid

obese \ō-'bēs\ *adj* [L *obesus*, fr. *ob-* against + *esus*, pp. of *edere* to eat] : having excessive body fat ◆ **Synonyms** CORPULENT, FLESHY, GROSS, OVERWEIGHT, PORTLY, STOUT — **obe·si·ty** \-'bē-sə-tē\ *n*

obey \ō-'bā\ *vb* **obeyed; obey·ing**   **1** : to follow the commands or guidance of : behave obediently   **2** : to comply with ⟨∼ orders⟩ ◆ **Synonyms** CONFORM, KEEP, MIND, OBSERVE

ob·fus·cate \'äb-fə-ˌskāt\ *vb* **-cat·ed; -cat·ing**   **1** : to make dark or obscure   **2** : CONFUSE — **ob·fus·ca·tion** \ˌäb-fəs-'kā-shən\ *n*

OB–GYN *abbr* obstetrician gynecologist; obstetrics gynecology

obi \'ō-bē\ *n* [Jp] : a broad sash worn esp. with a Japanese kimono

obit \ō-'bit, 'ō-bət\ *n* : OBITUARY

obi·ter dic·tum \ˌō-bə-tər-'dik-təm\ *n, pl* **obiter dic·ta** \-tə\ [LL, lit., something said in passing] : an incidental remark or observation

obit·u·ary \ə-'bi-chə-ˌwer-ē\ *n, pl* **-ar·ies** : a notice of a person's death usu. with a short biographical account

obj *abbr* object; objective

¹ob·ject \'äb-jikt\ *n*   **1** : something that may be seen or felt; *also* : something that may be perceived or examined mentally **2** : something that arouses an emotional response (as of affection or pity) **3** : AIM, PURPOSE ⟨the ∼ is to raise money⟩ **4** : a word or word group denoting that on or toward which the action of a verb is directed; *also* : a noun or noun equivalent in a prepositional phrase

²**ob·ject** \əb-ˈjekt\ *vb* **1** : to offer in opposition **2** : to oppose something; *also* : DISAPPROVE ✦ *Synonyms* PROTEST, REMONSTRATE, EXPOSTULATE — **ob·jec·tor** \-ˈjek-tər\ *n*

object code *n* : a computer program after translation from source code

ob·jec·ti·fy \əb-ˈjek-tə-ˌfī\ *vb* **-fied; -fy·ing** : to make objective

ob·jec·tion \əb-ˈjek-shən\ *n* **1** : the act of objecting **2** : a reason for or a feeling of disapproval

ob·jec·tion·able \əb-ˈjek-shə-nə-bəl\ *adj* : UNDESIRABLE, OFFENSIVE — **ob·jec·tion·ably** \-blē\ *adv*

¹**ob·jec·tive** \əb-ˈjek-tiv\ *adj* **1** : of or relating to an object or end **2** : existing outside and independent of the mind **3** : of, relating to, or constituting a grammatical case marking typically the object of a verb or preposition **4** : treating or dealing with facts without distortion by personal feelings or prejudices — **ob·jec·tive·ly** *adv* — **ob·jec·tive·ness** *n* — **ob·jec·tiv·i·ty** \ˌäb-ˌjek-ˈti-və-tē\ *n*

²**objective** *n* **1** : the lens (as in a microscope) nearest the object and forming an image of it **2** : an aim, goal, or end of action

ob·jet d'art \ˌȯb-ˌzhā-ˈdär\ *n, pl* **ob·jets d'art** *same*\ [F] **1** : an article of artistic worth **2** : CURIO ✦ *Synonyms* KNICKKNACK, BAUBLE, BIBELOT, GEWGAW, NOVELTY, TRINKET

ob·jet trou·vé \ˈȯb-ˌzhā-trü-ˈvā\ *n, pl* **objets trouvés** *same*\ [F, lit., found object] : a found natural or discarded object (as a piece of driftwood or an old bathtub) held to have aesthetic value

ob·jur·ga·tion \ˌäb-jər-ˈgā-shən\ *n* : a harsh rebuke — **ob·jur·gate** \ˈäb-jər-ˌgāt\ *vb*

obl *abbr* **1** oblique **2** oblong

ob·late \ä-ˈblāt\ *adj* : flattened or depressed at the poles ⟨an ∼ spheroid⟩

ob·la·tion \ə-ˈblā-shən\ *n* : a religious offering

ob·li·gate \ˈä-blə-ˌgāt\ *vb* **-gat·ed; -gat·ing** : to bind legally or morally

ob·li·ga·tion \ˌä-blə-ˈgā-shən\ *n* **1** : an act of obligating oneself to a course of action **2** : something (as a promise or a contract) that binds one to a course of action **3** : INDEBTEDNESS; *also* : LIABILITY **4** : DUTY — **oblig·a·to·ry** \ə-ˈbli-gə-ˌtȯr-ē\ *adj*

oblige \ə-ˈblīj\ *vb* **obliged; oblig·ing** [ME, fr. AF *obliger*, fr. L *obligare*, lit., to bind, fr. *ob-* toward + *ligare* to bind] **1** : FORCE, COMPEL ⟨the soldiers were *obliged* to retreat⟩ **2** : to bind by a favor; *also* : to do a favor for or do something as a favor

oblig·ing *adj* : willing to do favors — **oblig·ing·ly** *adv*

oblique \ō-ˈblēk\ *adj* **1** : neither perpendicular nor parallel : SLANTING **2** : not straightforward : INDIRECT — **oblique·ly** *adv* — **oblique·ness** *n* — **obliq·ui·ty** \-ˈbli-kwə-tē\ *n*

oblique case *n* : a grammatical case other than the nominative or vocative

oblit·er·ate \ə-ˈbli-tə-ˌrāt\ *vb* **-at·ed; -at·ing** [L *oblitterare*, fr. *ob* in the way of + *littera* letter] **1** : to remove from recognition or memory **2** : to make undecipherable by wiping out or covering over **3** : CANCEL — **oblit·er·a·tion** \-ˌbli-tə-ˈrā-shən\ *n*

obliv·i·on \ə-ˈbli-vē-ən\ *n* **1** : the condition of being oblivious **2** : the condition or state of being forgotten

obliv·i·ous \ə-ˈbli-ve-əs\ *adj* **1** : lacking memory or mindful attention **2** : UNAWARE ⟨∼ of the risks⟩ — **obliv·i·ous·ly** *adv* — **obliv·i·ous·ness** *n*

ob·long \ˈä-ˌblȯŋ\ *adj* : deviating from a square, circular, or spherical form by elongation in one dimension — **oblong** *n*

ob·lo·quy \ˈä-blə-kwē\ *n, pl* **-quies** **1** : strongly condemnatory utterance or language **2** : bad repute : DISGRACE ✦ *Synonyms* DISHONOR, SHAME, INFAMY, DISREPUTE, IGNOMINY

ob·nox·ious \äb-ˈnäk-shəs\ *adj* : REPUGNANT, OFFENSIVE — **ob·nox·ious·ly** *adv* — **ob·nox·ious·ness** *n*

oboe \ˈō-bō\ *n* [It, fr. F *hautbois*, fr. *haut* high + *bois* wood]

: a woodwind instrument with a slender conical tube and a double reed mouthpiece — **obo·ist** \ˈō-ˌbō-ist\ *n*

ob·scene \äb-ˈsēn\ *adj* **1** : REPULSIVE **2** : deeply offensive to morality or decency; *esp* : designed to incite to lust or depravity ✦ *Synonyms* GROSS, VULGAR, COARSE, CRUDE, INDECENT — **ob·scene·ly** *adv* — **ob·scen·i·ty** \-ˈse-nə-tē\ *n*

ob·scu·ran·tism \äb-ˈskyu̇r-ən-ˌti-zəm, ˌäb-skyu̇-ˈran-\ *n* **1** : opposition to the spread of **2** : deliberate vagueness or abstruseness — **ob·scu·ran·tist** \-tist\ *n or adj*

¹**ob·scure** \äb-ˈskyu̇r\ *adj* **1** : DIM, GLOOMY **2** : not readily understood : VAGUE **3** : REMOTE; *also* : HUMBLE ✦ *Synonyms* DARK, DUSKY, MURKY, TENEBROUS — **ob·scure·ly** *adv* — **ob·scu·ri·ty** \-ˈskyu̇r-ə-tē\ *n*

²**obscure** *vb* **ob·scured; ob·scur·ing** **1** : to make dark, dim, or indistinct **2** : to conceal or hide by or as if by covering

ob·se·qui·ous \əb-ˈsē-kwē-əs\ *adj* : humbly or excessively attentive (as to a person in authority) : FAWNING, SYCOPHANTIC ✦ *Synonyms* MENIAL, SERVILE, SLAVISH, SUBSERVIENT — **ob·se·qui·ous·ly** *adv* — **ob·se·qui·ous·ness** *n*

ob·se·quy \ˈäb-sə-kwē\ *n, pl* **-quies** : a funeral or burial rite — usu. used in pl.

ob·serv·able \əb-ˈzər-və-bəl\ *adj* **1** : NOTEWORTHY **2** : capable of being observed — **ob·serv·abil·i·ty** \-ˈbi-lə-tē\ *n*

ob·ser·vance \əb-ˈzər-vəns\ *n* **1** : a customary practice or ceremony **2** : an act or instance of following a custom, rule, or law **3** : OBSERVATION

ob·ser·vant \-vənt\ *adj* **1** : WATCHFUL ⟨∼ spectators⟩ **2** : KEEN, PERCEPTIVE **3** : MINDFUL ⟨∼ of the amenities⟩

¹**ob·ser·va·tion** \ˌäb-sər-ˈvā-shən, -zər-\ *n* **1** : an act or instance of observing **2** : the gathering of information (as for scientific studies) by noting facts or occurrences **3** : a conclusion drawn from observing; *also* : REMARK, STATEMENT **4** : the fact of being observed — **ob·ser·va·tion·al** \-shə-nəl\ *adj*

²**observation** *adj* : designed for use in viewing or in making observations

ob·ser·va·to·ry \əb-ˈzər-və-ˌtȯr-ē\ *n, pl* **-ries** : a place or institution equipped for observation of natural phenomena (as in astronomy)

ob·serve \əb-ˈzərv\ *vb* **ob·served; ob·serv·ing** **1** : to conform one's action or practice to **2** : CELEBRATE **3** : to make a scientific observation of **4** : to see or sense esp. through careful attention **5** : to come to realize esp. through consideration of noted facts **6** : REMARK — **ob·serv·er** *n*

ob·sess \əb-ˈses\ *vb* : to preoccupy intensely or abnormally

ob·ses·sion \äb-ˈse-shən\ *n* : a persistent disturbing preoccupation with an idea or feeling; *also* : an emotion or idea causing such a preoccupation — **ob·ses·sive** \-ˈse-siv\ *adj or n* — **ob·ses·sive·ly** *adv*

obsessive–compulsive *adj* : relating to, characterized by, or affected with recurring obsessions and compulsions esp. as symptoms of a neurotic state

ob·sid·i·an \əb-ˈsi-dē-ən\ *n* : a dark natural glass formed by the cooling of molten lava

ob·so·les·cent \ˌäb-sə-ˈle-sᵊnt\ *adj* : going out of use : becoming obsolete — **ob·so·les·cence** \-sᵊns\ *n*

ob·so·lete \ˌäb-sə-ˈlēt, ˈäb-sə-ˌlēt\ *adj* : no longer in use; *also* : OLD-FASHIONED ⟨an ∼ technology⟩ ✦ *Synonyms* EXTINCT, OUTWORN, PASSÉ, SUPERSEDED

ob·sta·cle \ˈäb-sti-kəl\ *n* : something that stands in the way or opposes

ob·stet·rics \əb-ˈste-triks\ *n sing or pl* : a branch of medicine that deals with birth and with its antecedents and sequels — **ob·stet·ric** \-trik\ *or* **ob·stet·ri·cal** \-tri-kəl\ *adj* — **ob·ste·tri·cian** \ˌäb-stə-ˈtri-shən\ *n*

ob·sti·nate \ˈäb-stə-nət\ *adj* : fixed and unyielding (as in an opinion or course) despite reason or persuasion : STUBBORN — **ob·sti·na·cy** \-nə-sē\ *n* — **ob·sti·nate·ly** *adv*

ob·strep·er·ous \əb-ˈstre-pə-rəs\ *adj* **1** : uncontrollably noisy **2** : stubbornly resistant to control : UNRULY — **ob·strep·er·ous·ness** *n*

ob·struct \əb-ˈstrəkt\ *vb* **1** : to block by an obstacle **2** : to impede the passage, action, or operation of **3** : to cut off from sight — **ob·struc·tive** \-ˈstrək-tiv\ *adj* — **ob·struc·tor** \-tər\ *n*

ob·struc·tion \əb-'strək-shən\ *n* 1 : an act of obstructing : the state of being obstructed 2 : something that obstructs : HINDRANCE

ob·struc·tion·ist \-shə-nist\ *n* : a person who hinders progress or business esp. in a legislative body — **ob·struc·tion·ism** \-shə-,ni-zəm\ *n*

ob·tain \əb-'tān\ *vb* 1 : to gain or attain usu. by planning or effort 2 : to be generally recognized or established ♦ **Synonyms** PROCURE, SECURE, WIN, EARN, ACQUIRE — **ob·tain·able** *adj*

ob·trude \əb-'trüd\ *vb* **ob·trud·ed; ob·trud·ing** 1 : to thrust out 2 : to thrust forward without warrant or request 3 : INTRUDE — **ob·tru·sion** \-'trü-zhən\ *n* — **ob·tru·sive** \-'trü-siv\ *adj* — **ob·tru·sive·ly** *adv* — **ob·tru·sive·ness** *n*

ob·tuse \äb-'tüs, -'tyüs\ *adj* **ob·tus·er; -est** 1 : exceeding 90 degrees but less than 180 degrees ⟨~ angle⟩ 2 : not pointed or acute : BLUNT 3 : not sharp or quick of wit — **ob·tuse·ly** *adv* — **ob·tuse·ness** *n*

obv *abbr* obverse

¹ob·verse \äb-'vərs, 'äb-,vərs\ *adj* 1 : facing the observer or opponent 2 : being a counterpart or complement — **ob·verse·ly** *adv*

²ob·verse \'äb-,vərs, äb-'vərs\ *n* 1 : the side (as of a coin) bearing the principal design and lettering 2 : a front or principal surface 3 : a counterpart having the opposite orientation or force

ob·vi·ate \'äb-vē-,āt\ *vb* **-at·ed; -at·ing** : to anticipate and prevent (as a situation) or make unnecessary (as an action) ♦ **Synonyms** PREVENT, AVERT, FORESTALL, FORFEND, PRECLUDE — **ob·vi·a·tion** \,äb-vē-'ā-shən\ *n*

ob·vi·ous \'äb-vē-əs\ *adj* [L *obvius*, fr. *obviam* in the way, fr. *ob* in the way of + *viam*, acc. of *via* way] : easily found, seen, or understood : PLAIN ♦ **Synonyms** EVIDENT, MANIFEST, PATENT, CLEAR — **ob·vi·ous·ly** *adv* — **ob·vi·ous·ness** *n*

OC *abbr* officer candidate

oc·a·ri·na \,ä-kə-'rē-nə\ *n* [It] : a wind instrument typically having an oval body with finger holes and a projecting mouthpiece

ocarina

occas *abbr* occasionally

¹oc·ca·sion \ə-'kā-zhən\ *n* 1 : a favorable opportunity 2 : a direct or indirect cause 3 : the time of an event 4 : EXIGENCY 5 *pl* : AFFAIRS, BUSINESS 6 : a special event : CELEBRATION

²occasion *vb* : BRING ABOUT, CAUSE

oc·ca·sion·al \ə-'kā-zhə-nəl\ *adj* 1 : happening or met with now and then ⟨~ visits⟩ 2 : used or designed for a special occasion ⟨~ verse⟩ ♦ **Synonyms** INFREQUENT, RARE, SPORADIC — **oc·ca·sion·al·ly** *adv*

oc·ci·den·tal \,äk-sə-'den-t°l\ *adj, often cap* [fr. *Occident* West, fr. ME, fr. AF, fr. L *occident-, occidens*, fr. prp. of *occidere* to fall, set (of the sun)] : WESTERN — **Occidental** *n*

Oc·ci·tan \'äk-sə-,tan\ *n* [F, fr. ML *occitanus*, fr. Old Occitan *oc* yes (contrasted with OF *oïl* yes)] : a Romance language spoken in southern France

oc·clude \ə-'klüd\ *vb* **oc·clud·ed; oc·clud·ing** 1 : OBSTRUCT ⟨an *occluded* artery⟩ 2 : to come together with opposing surfaces in contact — used of teeth — **oc·clu·sion** \-'klü-zhən\ *n* — **oc·clu·sive** \-'klü-siv\ *adj*

¹oc·cult \ə-'kəlt\ *adj* 1 : not revealed : SECRET 2 : ABSTRUSE, MYSTERIOUS 3 : of or relating to supernatural agencies, their effects, or knowledge of them — **oc·cult·ism** \-'kəl-,ti-zəm\ *n* — **oc·cult·ist** \-tist\ *n*

²occult *n* : occult matters — used with *the*

oc·cu·pan·cy \'ä-kyə-pən-sē\ *n, pl* **-cies** 1 : the act of occupying : the state of being occupied 2 : an occupied building or part of a building

oc·cu·pant \-pənt\ *n* : one who occupies something; *esp* : RESIDENT

oc·cu·pa·tion \,ä-kyə-'pā-shən\ *n* 1 : an activity in which one engages; *esp* : VOCATION 2 : the taking possession of property; *also* : the taking possession of an area by a foreign military force — **oc·cu·pa·tion·al** \-shə-nəl\ *adj* — **oc·cu·pa·tion·al·ly** *adv*

occupational therapy *n* : therapy by means of activity; *esp* : creative activity prescribed for its effect in promoting recovery or rehabilitation — **occupational therapist** *n*

oc·cu·py \'ä-kyə-,pī\ *vb* **-pied; -py·ing** 1 : to engage the attention or energies of 2 : to fill up (an extent in space or time) 3 : to take or hold possession of 4 : to reside in as owner or tenant — **oc·cu·pi·er** *n*

oc·cur \ə-'kər\ *vb* **oc·curred; oc·cur·ring** [L *occurrere*, fr. *ob-* in the way + *currere* to run] 1 : to be found or met with : APPEAR 2 : HAPPEN 3 : to come to mind

oc·cur·rence \ə-'kər-əns\ *n* 1 : something that takes place 2 : the action or process of occurring

ocean \'ō-shən\ *n* 1 : the whole body of salt water that covers nearly three fourths of the surface of the earth 2 : any of the large bodies of water into which the great ocean is divided — **oce·an·ic** \,ō-shē-'a-nik\ *adj*

ocean·ar·i·um \,ō-shə-'nar-ē-əm\ *n, pl* **-iums** *or* **-ia** \-ē-ə\ : a large marine aquarium

ocean·front \'ō-shən-,frənt\ *n* : a shore area on the ocean

ocean·go·ing \-,gō-iŋ\ *adj* : of, relating to, or suitable for travel on the ocean

ocean·og·ra·phy \,ō-shə-'nä-grə-fē\ *n* : a science dealing with the ocean and its phenomena — **ocean·og·ra·pher** \-fər\ *n* — **ocean·o·graph·ic** \-nə-'gra-fik\ *adj*

oce·lot \'ä-sə-,lät, 'ō-\ *n* : a medium-sized American wildcat ranging southward from Texas to northern Argentina and having a tawny yellow or gray coat with black markings

ocher *or* **ochre** \'ō-kər\ *n* : an earthy usu. red or yellow iron ore used as a pigment; *also* : the color esp. of yellow ocher

o'·clock \ə-'kläk\ *adv* : according to the clock

OCR *abbr* optical character reader; optical character recognition

OCS *abbr* officer candidate school

oct *abbr* octavo

Oct *abbr* October

oc·ta·gon \'äk-tə-,gän\ *n* : a polygon of eight angles and eight sides — **oc·tag·o·nal** \äk-'ta-gən-°l\ *adj*

oc·tane \'äk-,tān\ *n* : OCTANE NUMBER

octane number *n* : a number used to measure the antiknock properties of gasoline that increases as the likelihood of knocking decreases

oc·tave \'äk-tiv\ *n* 1 : a musical interval embracing eight degrees; *also* : a tone or note at this interval or the whole series of notes, tones, or keys within this interval 2 : a group of eight

oc·ta·vo \äk-'tā-vō, -'tä-\ *n, pl* **-vos** 1 : the size of a piece of paper cut eight from a sheet 2 : a book printed on octavo pages

oc·tet \äk-'tet\ *n* 1 : a musical composition for eight voices or eight instruments; *also* : the performers of such a composition 2 : a group or set of eight

Oc·to·ber \äk-'tō-bər\ *n* [ME *Octobre*, fr. OE *October*, fr. L, eighth month of the early Roman calendar, fr. *octo* eight] : the 10th month of the year

oc·to·ge·nar·i·an \,äk-tə-jə-'ner-ē-ən\ *n* : a person whose age is in the eighties

oc·to·pus \'äk-tə-pəs\ *n, pl* **-pus·es** *or* **-pi** \-,pī\ : any of various sea mollusks with eight long muscular arms furnished with suckers

oc·to·syl·lab·ic \,äk-tə-sə-'la-bik\ *adj* : composed of verses having eight syllables — **octosyllabic** *n*

¹oc·u·lar \'ä-kyə-lər\ *adj* 1 : VISUAL 2 : of or relating to the eye or the eyesight

²ocular *n* : EYEPIECE

oc·u·list \'ä-kyə-list\ *n* 1 : OPHTHALMOLOGIST 2 : OPTOMETRIST

¹OD \,ō-'dē\ *n* : an overdose of a drug and esp. a narcotic

²OD *vb* **OD'd** *or* **ODed; OD'ing; OD's** : to become ill or die from an OD

[3]OD *abbr* **1** doctor of optometry **2** [L *oculus dexter*] right eye **3** officer of the day **4** olive drab **5** overdraft **6** overdrawn

odd \\'äd\\ *adj* [ME *odde*, fr. ON *oddi* point of land, triangle, odd number] **1** : being only one of a pair or set ⟨an ~ shoe⟩ **2** : somewhat more than the number mentioned ⟨forty ~ years ago⟩ **3** : being an integer (as 1, 3, or 5) not divisible by two without leaving a remainder **4** : additional to what is usual ⟨~ jobs⟩ **5** : STRANGE ⟨an ~ way of behaving⟩ — **odd·ness** *n*

odd·ball \\'äd-ˌbȯl\\ *n* : one that is eccentric — **oddball** *adj*

odd·i·ty \\'ä-də-tē\\ *n, pl* **-ties** **1** : one that is odd **2** : the quality or state of being odd

odd·ly \\'äd-lē\\ *adv* **1** : in an odd manner **2** : as is odd

odd·ment \\'äd-mənt\\ *n* : something left over : REMNANT

odds \\'ädz\\ *n pl* **1** : a difference by which one thing is favored over another **2** : DISAGREEMENT — usu. used with *at* **3** : the ratio between the amount to be paid for a winning bet and the amount of the bet ⟨the horse went off at ~ of 6–1⟩

odds and ends *n pl* : miscellaneous things or matters

odds–on \\'ädz-ˌȯn, -ˌän\\ *adj* : having a better than even chance to win

ode \\'ōd\\ *n* : a lyric poem that expresses a noble feeling with dignity

odi·ous \\'ō-dē-əs\\ *adj* : arousing or deserving hatred or repugnance — **odi·ous·ly** *adv* — **odi·ous·ness** *n*

odi·um \\'ō-dē-əm\\ *n* **1** : merited loathing : HATRED **2** : DISGRACE

odom·e·ter \\ō-ˈdä-mə-tər\\ *n* [F *odomètre*, fr. Gk *hodometron*, fr. *hodos* way, road + *metron* measure] : an instrument for measuring distance traveled (as by a vehicle)

odor \\'ō-dər\\ *n* **1** : the quality of something that stimulates the sense of smell; *also* : a sensation resulting from such stimulation **2** : REPUTE, ESTIMATION — **odored** \\'ō-dərd\\ *adj* — **odor·less** *adj* — **odor·ous** *adj*

odor·if·er·ous \\ˌō-də-ˈri-fə-rəs\\ *adj* : having or yielding an odor

odour *chiefly Brit var of* ODOR

od·ys·sey \\'ä-də-sē\\ *n, pl* **-seys** [the *Odyssey*, epic poem attributed to Homer recounting the long wanderings of Odysseus] : a long wandering marked usu. by many changes of fortune

oe·cu·men·i·cal *esp Brit* ˌē-\\ *chiefly Brit var of* ECUMENICAL

OED *abbr* Oxford English Dictionary

oe·de·ma *chiefly Brit var of* EDEMA

oe·di·pal \\'e-də-pəl, 'ē-\\ *adj, often cap* : of, relating to, or resulting from the Oedipus complex

Oe·di·pus complex \\-pəs-\\ *n* : the positive sexual feelings of a child toward the parent of the opposite sex and hostile or jealous feelings toward the parent of the same sex that may be a source of adult personality disorder when unresolved

OEO *abbr* Office of Economic Opportunity

o'er \\'ȯr\\ *adv or prep* : OVER

OES *abbr* Order of the Eastern Star

oe·soph·a·gus *chiefly Brit var of* ESOPHAGUS

oeu·vre \\'ər-vrə, 'œvrᵊ\\ *n, pl* **oeuvres** *same*\\ : a substantial body of work constituting the lifework of a writer, an artist, or a composer

of \\'əv, 'äv\\ *prep* **1** : FROM ⟨a man ~ the West⟩ **2** : having as a significant background or character element ⟨a man ~ noble birth⟩ ⟨a woman ~ ability⟩ **3** : owing to ⟨died ~ flu⟩ **4** : BY ⟨the plays ~ Shakespeare⟩ **5** : having as component parts or material, contents, or members ⟨a house ~ brick⟩ ⟨a glass ~ water⟩ ⟨a pack ~ fools⟩ **6** : belonging to or included by ⟨the front ~ the house⟩ ⟨a time ~ life⟩ ⟨one ~ you⟩ ⟨the best ~ its kind⟩ ⟨the son ~ a doctor⟩ **7** : ABOUT ⟨tales ~ the West⟩ **8** : connected with : OVER ⟨the queen ~ England⟩ **9** : that is : signified as ⟨the city ~ Rome⟩ **10** — used to indicate apposition of the words it joins ⟨that fool ~ a husband⟩ **11** : as concerns : FOR ⟨love ~ nature⟩ **12** — used to indicate the application of an adjective ⟨fond ~ candy⟩ **13** : BEFORE ⟨quarter ~ ten⟩

OF *abbr* outfield

[1]off \\'ȯf\\ *adv* **1** : from a place or position ⟨drove ~ in a new car⟩; *also* : ASIDE ⟨turned ~ into a side road⟩ **2** : at a distance in time or space ⟨stood ~ a few yards⟩ ⟨several years ~⟩ **3** : so as to be unattached or removed ⟨the lid blew ~⟩ **4** : to a state of discontinuance, exhaustion, or completion ⟨shut the radio ~⟩ **5** : away from regular work ⟨took time ~ for lunch⟩

[2]off *prep* **1** : away from ⟨just ~ the highway⟩ ⟨take it ~ the table⟩ **2** : to seaward of ⟨two miles ~ the coast⟩ **3** : FROM ⟨borrowed a dollar ~ me⟩ **4** : at the expense of ⟨lives ~ his parents⟩ **5** : not now engaged in ⟨~ duty⟩ **6** : abstaining from ⟨~ liquor⟩ **7** : below the usual level of ⟨~ his game⟩

[3]off *adj* **1** : more removed or distant **2** : started on the way **3** : not operating **4** : not correct **5** : REMOTE, SLIGHT ⟨an ~ chance⟩ **6** : INFERIOR ⟨~ grade of oil⟩ **7** : provided for ⟨well ~⟩

[4]off *abbr* office; officer; official

of·fal \\'ȯ-fəl\\ *n* [ME, fr. *of* off + *fall* fall] : the waste or by-product of a process; *esp* : the viscera and trimmings of a butchered animal removed in dressing

off and on *adv* : INTERMITTENTLY ⟨rained *off and on*⟩

[1]off·beat \\'ȯf-ˌbēt\\ *n* : the unaccented part of a musical measure

[2]offbeat *adj* : ECCENTRIC, UNCONVENTIONAL ⟨an ~ style⟩

off–col·or \\'ȯf-ˈkə-lər\\ *or* **off–col·ored** \\-lərd\\ *adj* **1** : not having the right or standard color **2** : of doubtful propriety : verging on indecency ⟨~ stories⟩

of·fend \\ə-ˈfend\\ *vb* **1** : SIN, TRANSGRESS **2** : to cause discomfort or pain : HURT **3** : to cause dislike or vexation : ANNOY ✦ **Synonyms** AFFRONT, INSULT, OUTRAGE — **of·fend·er** *n*

of·fense *or* **of·fence** \\ə-ˈfens, *esp for 2 & 3* 'ä-ˌfens\\ *n* **1** : something that outrages the senses **2** : ATTACK, ASSAULT **3** : the offensive team or members of a team playing offensive positions **4** : DISPLEASURE **5** : SIN, MISDEED **6** : an infraction of law : CRIME

[1]of·fen·sive \\ə-ˈfen-siv *esp for 1 & 2* 'ä-ˌfen-\\ *adj* **1** : AGGRESSIVE **2** : of or relating to an attempt to score in a game; *also* : of or relating to a team in possession of the ball or puck **3** : OBNOXIOUS ⟨an ~ odor⟩ **4** : INSULTING ⟨~ remarks⟩ — **of·fen·sive·ly** *adv* — **of·fen·sive·ness** *n*

[2]offensive *n* : ATTACK

[1]of·fer \\'ȯ-fər\\ *vb* **of·fered; of·fer·ing** **1** : SACRIFICE **2** : to present for acceptance : TENDER; *also* : to propose as payment **3** : PROPOSE, SUGGEST; *also* : to declare one's readiness **4** : to try or begin to exert ⟨~ resistance⟩ **5** : to place on sale — **of·fer·ing** *n*

[2]offer *n* **1** : PROPOSAL **2** : BID **3** : TRY

of·fer·to·ry \\'ȯ-fər-ˌtȯr-ē\\ *n, pl* **-ries** : the presentation of offerings at a church service; *also* : the musical accompaniment during it

off–gas·sing \\'ȯf-ˌga-siŋ\\ *n* : the emission of esp. noxious gases (as from a building material)

off·hand \\'ȯf-ˈhand\\ *adv or adj* : without previous thought or preparation

off–hour \\-ˌau̇(-ə)r\\ *n* : a period of time other than a rush hour; *also* : a period of time other than business hours

of·fice \\'ȯ-fəs\\ *n* **1** : a special duty or position; *esp* : a position of authority in government ⟨run for ~⟩ **2** : a prescribed form or service of worship; *also* : RITE **3** : an assigned or assumed duty or role **4** : a place where a business is transacted or a service is supplied

of·fice·hold·er \\'ȯ-fəs-ˌhōl-dər\\ *n* : one holding a public office

of·fi·cer \\'ȯ-fə-sər\\ *n* **1** : one charged with the enforcement of law **2** : one who holds an office of trust or authority **3** : a person who holds a position of authority or command in the armed forces; *esp* : COMMISSIONED OFFICER

[1]of·fi·cial \\ə-ˈfi-shəl\\ *n* : OFFICER 2

[2]official *adj* **1** : of or relating to an office or to officers **2** : AUTHORIZED, AUTHORITATIVE ⟨~ statement⟩ **3** : befitting or characteristic of a person in office — **of·fi·cial·ly** *adv*

of·fi·cial·dom \\ə-ˈfi-shəl-dəm\\ *n* : officials as a class

of·fi·cial·ism \\ə-ˈfi-shə-ˌli-zəm\\ *n* : lack of flexibility and initiative combined with excessive adherence to regulations

of·fi·ci·ant \\ə-ˈfi-shē-ənt\\ *n* : one (as a priest) who officiates at a religious rite

of·fi·ci·ate \\ə-ˈfi-shē-ˌāt\\ *vb* **-at·ed; -at·ing** **1** : to perform a ceremony, function, or duty **2** : to act in an official capacity

of·fi·cious \ə-'fi-shəs\ adj : volunteering one's services where they are neither asked for nor needed — **of·fi·cious·ly** adv — **of·fi·cious·ness** n

off·ing \'o-fiŋ\ n : the near or foreseeable future

off–line \'of-'līn\ adj or adv : not connected to or controlled directly by a computer

off of prep : OFF

off·print \'of-,print\ n : a separately printed excerpt (as from a magazine)

off–road \-'rōd\ adj : of, relating to, or being a vehicle designed for use away from public roads — **off–road·er** \-'rō-dər\ n

off–sea·son \-,sē-z³n\ n : a time of suspended or reduced activity

¹off·set \-,set\ n 1 : a sharp bend (as in a pipe) by which one part is turned aside out of line 2 : a printing process in which an inked impression is first made on a rubber-blanketed cylinder and then transferred to the paper

²off·set vb **off·set; off·set·ting** 1 : to place over against : BALANCE 2 : to compensate for 3 : to form an offset in (∼ a wall)

off·shoot \'of-,shüt\ n 1 : a collateral or derived branch, descendant, or member 2 : a branch of a main stem (as of a plant)

¹off·shore \'of-'shōr\ adv 1 : at a distance from the shore 2 : outside the country : ABROAD

²off·shore \'of-,shōr\ adj 1 : moving away from the shore 2 : situated off the shore but within waters under a country's control

off·side \-'sīd\ adv or adj : illegally in advance of the ball or puck

off·spring \-,spriŋ\ n, pl **offspring** also **offsprings** : PROGENY, YOUNG

off·stage \'of-,stāj, -,stāj\ adv or adj 1 : off or away from the stage 2 : out of the public view ⟨deals made ∼⟩

off–the–record adj : given or made in confidence and not for publication

off–the–shelf adj : available as a stock item : not specially designed or made

off–the–wall adj : highly unusual : BIZARRE

off·track \'of-'trak\ adv or adj : away from a racetrack

off–white \'of-'hwīt\ n : a yellowish or grayish white color

off year n 1 : a year in which no major election is held 2 : a year of diminished activity or production

oft \'oft\ adv : OFTEN

of·ten \'o-fən\ adv : many times : FREQUENTLY

of·ten·times \-,tīmz\ or **oft·times** \'of-,tīmz, 'oft-\ adv : OFTEN

ogle \'ō-gəl\ vb **ogled; ogling** : to look at in a flirtatious way — **ogle** n — **ogler** n

ogre \'ō-gər\ n 1 : a monster of fairy tales and folklore that eats people 2 : a dreaded person or object

ogress \'ō-grəs\ n : a female ogre

oh also **O** \'ō\ interj 1 — used to express an emotion or in response to physical stimuli 2 — used in direct address

OH abbr Ohio

ohm \'ōm\ n : a unit of electrical resistance equal to the resistance of a circuit in which a potential difference of one volt produces a current of one ampere — **ohm·ic** \'ō-mik\ adj

ohm·me·ter \'ōm-,mē-tər\ n : an instrument for indicating resistance in ohms directly

¹oil \'oi(-ə)l\ n [ME oile, fr. AF, fr. L oleum olive oil, fr. Gk elaion, fr. elaia olive] 1 : any of numerous fatty or greasy liquid substances obtained from plants, animals, or minerals and used for fuel, food, medicines, and manufacturing 2 : PETROLEUM 3 : artists' colors made with oil; also : a painting in such colors — **oil·i·ness** \'oi-lē-nəs\ n — **oily** \'oi-lē\ adj

²oil vb : to put oil in or on — **oil·er** n

oil·cloth \'oi(-ə)l-,kloth\ n : cloth treated with oil or paint and used for table and shelf coverings

oil pan n : the lower section of a crankcase used as an oil reservoir

oil shale n : a rock (as shale) from which oil can be recovered

oil·skin \'oi(-ə)l-,skin\ n 1 : an oiled waterproof cloth 2 : an oilskin raincoat 3 pl : an oilskin coat and pants

oink \'oiŋk\ n : the natural noise of a hog — **oink** vb

oint·ment \'oint-mənt\ n : a salve for use on the skin

OJ abbr orange juice

Ojib·wa or **Ojib·way** or **Ojibwe** \ō-'jib-,wä\ n, pl **Ojibwa** or **Ojibwas** or **Ojibway** or **Ojibways** or **Ojibwe** or **Ojibwes** 1 : a member of an American Indian people of the region around Lake Superior and westward 2 : the Algonquian language of the Ojibwa people

OJT abbr on-the-job training

¹OK or **okay** \ō-'kā\ adv or adj : all right

²OK or **okay** vb **OK'd** or **okayed; OK·ing** or **okay·ing** : APPROVE, AUTHORIZE — **OK** or **okay** n

³OK abbr Oklahoma

Okla abbr Oklahoma

okra \'ō-krə\ n : a tall annual plant related to the mallows that has edible green pods; also : these pods

¹old \'ōld\ adj 1 : ANCIENT; also : of long standing 2 cap : belonging to an early period ⟨Old Irish⟩ 3 : having existed for a specified period of time 4 : of or relating to a past era 5 : advanced in years 6 : showing the effects of age or use 7 : no longer in use — **old·ish** \'ōl-dish\ adj

²old n : old or earlier time ⟨days of ∼⟩

old·en \'ōl-dən\ adj : of or relating to a bygone era

¹old–fash·ioned \'ōld-'fa-shənd\ adj 1 : OUT-OF-DATE, ANTIQUATED 2 : CONSERVATIVE

²old–fashioned n : a cocktail usu. made with whiskey, bitters, sugar, a twist of lemon peel, and water or soda water

old–growth \'ōld-'grōth\ adj : of, relating to, or being a forest with large old trees, numerous snags and woody debris, and a multilayered canopy

old guard n, often cap O&G : the conservative members of an organization

old hat adj 1 : OLD-FASHIONED 2 : STALE, TRITE

old·ie \'ōl-dē\ n : something old; esp : a popular song from the past

old–line \'ōld-'līn\ adj 1 : ORIGINAL, ESTABLISHED ⟨an ∼ business⟩ 2 : adhering to old policies or practices

old maid n 1 : SPINSTER 2 : a prim fussy person — **old–maid·ish** \'ōld-'mā-dish\ adj

old man n 1 : HUSBAND 2 : FATHER

old–school adj : adhering to traditional policies or practices

old·ster \'ōld-stər\ n : an old or elderly person

Old Testament n : the first of the two chief divisions of the Christian Bible — see BIBLE table

old–time \'ōld-'tīm\ adj 1 : of, relating to, or characteristic of an earlier period 2 : of long standing

old–tim·er \-'tī-mər\ n : VETERAN; also : OLDSTER

old–world \-'wərld\ adj : having old-fashioned charm

ole·ag·i·nous \,ō-lē-'a-jə-nəs\ adj : OILY

ole·an·der \'ō-lē-,an-dər\ n : a poisonous evergreen shrub often grown for its fragrant white to red flowers

oleo \'ō-lē-,ō\ n, pl **ole·os** : MARGARINE

oleo·mar·ga·rine \,ō-lē-ō-'mär-jə-rən\ n : MARGARINE

ol·fac·to·ry \äl-'fak-tə-rē, ōl-\ adj : of or relating to the sense of smell

oli·gar·chy \'ä-lə-,gär-kē, 'ō-\ n, pl **-chies** 1 : a government in which power is in the hands of a few 2 : a state having an oligarchy; also : the group holding power in such a state — **oli·garch** \-,gärk\ n — **oli·gar·chic** \,ä-lə-'gär-kik, ,ō-\ or **oli·gar·chi·cal** \-ki-kəl\ adj

Oli·go·cene \'ä-li-gō-,sēn, ə-'li-gə-,sēn\ adj : of, relating to, or being the epoch of the Tertiary between the Eocene and the Miocene — **Oligocene** n

olio \'ō-lē-,ō\ n, pl **oli·os** : HODGEPODGE, MEDLEY

ol·ive \'ä-liv\ n 1 : an Old World evergreen tree grown in warm regions for its fruit that is a food and the source of an edible oil (**olive oil**) 2 : a dull yellowish green color

olive drab n 1 : a grayish olive color 2 : an olive drab wool or cotton fabric; also : a uniform of this fabric

ol·iv·ine \'ä-lə-,vēn\ n : a usu. greenish mineral that is a complex silicate of magnesium and iron

Olym·pic Games \ō-'lim-pik-\ n pl : a modified revival of an ancient Greek festival consisting of international athletic contests that are held at separate winter and summer gatherings at four-year intervals

om \'ōm\ n : a mantra consisting of the sound "om" used in contemplating ultimate reality

Oma·ha \'ō-mə-,hä, -,hò\ n, pl **Omaha** or **Omahas** : a member of an American Indian people of northeastern Nebraska

om·buds·man \'äm-,bùdz-mən, äm-'bùdz-\ n, pl **-men** \-mən\ 1 : a government official appointed to investigate complaints made by individuals against abuses or capricious acts of public officials **2** : one that investigates reported complaints (as from students or consumers)

ome·ga \ō-'mā-gə\ *n* : the 24th and last letter of the Greek alphabet — Ω or ω

om·elet *or* **om·elette** \'äm-lət, 'ä-mə-\ *n* [F *omelette,* alter. of MF *amelette, alemette,* alter. of *alemelle* thin plate, ultim. fr. L *lamella,* dim. of *lamina*] : eggs beaten with milk or water, cooked without stirring until set, and folded over

omen \'ō-mən\ *n* : an event or phenomenon believed to be a sign or warning of a future occurrence

om·i·cron \'äm-ə-ˌkrän, 'ō-\ *n* : the 15th letter of the Greek alphabet — O or o

om·i·nous \'äm-ə-nəs\ *adj* : foretelling evil : THREATENING — **om·i·nous·ly** *adv* — **om·i·nous·ness** *n*

omis·si·ble \ō-'mi-sə-bəl\ *adj* : that may be omitted

omis·sion \ō-'mi-shən\ *n* **1** : something neglected or left undone **2** : the act of omitting : the state of being omitted

omit \ō-'mit\ *vb* **omit·ted**; **omit·ting** **1** : to leave out or leave unmentioned **2** : to leave undone : FAIL

¹om·ni·bus \'äm-ni-(ˌ)bəs\ *n* : BUS

²omnibus *adj* : of, relating to, or providing for many things at once ⟨an ~ bill⟩

om·nip·o·tent \äm-'ni-pə-tənt\ *adj* **1** *often cap* : ALMIGHTY 1 **2** : having unlimited authority or influence — **om·nip·o·tence** \-əns\ *n* — **om·nip·o·tent·ly** *adv*

om·ni·pres·ent \ˌäm-ni-'pre-zºnt\ *adj* : present in all places at all times — **om·ni·pres·ence** \-z°ns\ *n*

om·ni·scient \äm-'ni-shənt\ *adj* : having infinite awareness, understanding, and insight — **om·ni·science** \-shəns\ *n* — **om·ni·scient·ly** *adv*

om·ni·um-gath·er·um \ˌäm-nē-əm-'ga-thə-rəm\ *n, pl* **omnium-gatherums** : a miscellaneous collection

om·niv·o·rous \äm-'ni-və-rəs\ *adj* **1** : feeding on both animal and vegetable substances **2** : AVID ⟨an ~ reader⟩ — **om·ni·vore** \'äm-ni-ˌvȯr\ *n* — **om·niv·o·rous·ly** *adv*

¹on \'ȯn\ *prep* **1** : in or to a position over and in contact with ⟨jumped ~ his horse⟩ **2** : touching the surface of ⟨shadows ~ the wall⟩ **3** : AT, TO ⟨~ the right were the mountains⟩ **4** : IN, ABOARD ⟨went ~ the train⟩ **5** : during or at the time of ⟨came ~ Monday⟩ ⟨every hour ~ the hour⟩ **6** : through the agency of ⟨was cut ~ a tin can⟩ **7** : in a state or process of ⟨~ fire⟩ ⟨~ the wane⟩ **8** : connected with as a member or participant ⟨~ a committee⟩ ⟨~ tour⟩ **9** — used to indicate a basis, source, or standard of computation ⟨has it ~ good authority⟩ ⟨10 cents ~ the dollar⟩ **10** : with regard to ⟨a monopoly ~ wheat⟩ **11** : at or toward as an object ⟨crept up ~ her⟩ **12** : ABOUT, CONCERNING ⟨a book ~ minerals⟩

²on *adv* **1** : in or into a position of contact with or attachment to a surface **2** : FORWARD **3** : into operation

³on *adj* : being in operation or in progress

ON *abbr* Ontario

¹once \'wəns\ *adv* [ME *ones,* fr. genitive of *on* one] **1** : one time only **2** : at any one time ⟨didn't ~ thank me⟩ **3** : FORMERLY ⟨was ~ young⟩ **4** : by one degree of relationship ⟨first cousin ~ removed⟩

²once *n* : one single time — **at once 1** : at the same time **2** : IMMEDIATELY

³once *adj* : FORMER ⟨a ~ successful actor⟩

⁴once *conj* : AS SOON AS ⟨~ we're finished, we can leave⟩

once–over \'wəns-ˌō-vər\ *n* : a swift examination or survey

on·co·gene \'äŋ-kō-ˌjēn\ *n* : a gene having the potential to cause a normal cell to become cancerous

on·col·o·gy \än-'kä-lə-jē\ *n* : the study of tumors — **on·co·log·i·cal** \ˌäŋ-kə-'lä-ji-kəl\ *also* **on·co·log·ic** \-jik\ *adj* — **on·col·o·gist** \än-'kä-lə-jist\ *n*

on·com·ing \'ȯn-ˌkə-miŋ, 'än-\ *adj* : APPROACHING ⟨~ traffic⟩

¹one \'wən\ *adj* **1** : being a single unit or thing ⟨~ person went⟩ **2** : being one in particular ⟨early ~ morning⟩ **3** : being the same in kind or quality ⟨members of ~ race⟩; *also* : UNITED **4** : being not specified or fixed ⟨~ day soon⟩

²one *n* **1** : the number denoting a single unit **2** : the 1st in a set or series **3** : a single person or thing — **one·ness** \'wən-nəs\ *n*

³one *pron* **1** : a certain indefinitely indicated person or

thing ⟨saw ~ of his friends⟩ **2** : a person in general ⟨~ never knows⟩ **3** — used in place of a first-person pronoun

Onei·da \ō-'nī-də\ *n, pl* **Oneida** *or* **Oneidas** : a member of an American Indian people orig. of New York

one–man band *n* **1** : a musician who plays several instruments during a solo performance **2** : a person who alone undertakes or is responsible for several tasks

oner·ous \'ä-nə-rəs, 'ō-\ *adj* : imposing or constituting a burden : TROUBLESOME ♦ *Synonyms* OPPRESSIVE, EXACTING, BURDENSOME, WEIGHTY

one·self \(ˌ)wən-'self\ *also* **one's self** *pron* : one's own self — usu. used reflexively or for emphasis

one–sid·ed \'wən-'sī-dəd\ *adj* **1** : having or occurring on one side only; *also* : having one side prominent or more developed **2** : PARTIAL ⟨a ~ interpretation⟩

one·time \-ˌtīm\ *adj* : FORMER ⟨a ~ actor⟩

one–to–one \ˌwən-tə-'wən\ *adj* : pairing each element of a set uniquely with an element of another set

one up *adj* : being in a position of advantage ⟨was *one up* on the others⟩

one–way *adj* : moving, allowing movement, or functioning in only one direction ⟨~ streets⟩

on·go·ing \'ȯn-ˌgō-iŋ, 'än-\ *adj* : continuously moving forward

on·ion \'ən-yən\ *n* : the pungent edible bulb of a widely cultivated plant related to the lilies; *also* : this plant

on·ion·skin \-ˌskin\ *n* : a thin strong translucent paper of very light weight

on·line \'ȯn-'līn, 'än-\ *adj or adv* : connected to, served by, or available through a computer network (as the Internet); *also* : done while online ⟨~ shopping⟩ — **online** *adv*

on·look·er \'ȯn-ˌlu̇-kər, 'än-\ *n* : SPECTATOR

¹on·ly \'ōn-lē\ *adj* **1** : unquestionably the best **2** : SOLE ⟨the ~ one left⟩

²only *adv* **1** : MERELY, JUST ⟨~ $2⟩ **2** : SOLELY ⟨known ~ to me⟩ **3** : at the very least ⟨was ~ too true⟩ **4** : as a final result ⟨will ~ make you sick⟩

³only *conj* : except that

on·o·mato·poe·ia \ˌä-nə-ˌmä-tə-'pē-ə\ *n* [LL, fr. Gk *onomatopoiia,* fr. *onoma* name + *poiein* to make] **1** : formation of words in imitation of natural sounds (as *buzz* or *hiss*) **2** : the use of words whose sound suggests the sense — **on·o·mato·poe·ic** \-'pē-ik\ *or* **on·o·mato·po·et·ic** \-pō-'e-tik\ *adj* — **on·o·mato·poe·i·cal·ly** \-'pē-ə-k(ə-)lē\ *or* **on·o·mato·po·et·i·cal·ly** \-pō-'e-ti-k(ə-)lē\ *adv*

On·on·da·ga \ˌä-nən-'dȯ-gə, -'dä-, -'dä-\ *n, pl* **-ga** *or* **-gas** : a member of an American Indian people of New York and Canada

on·rush \'ȯn-ˌrəsh, 'än-\ *n* : a rushing onward — **on·rush·ing** *adj*

on–screen \'ȯn-'skrēn, 'än-\ *adv or adj* : on a computer or television screen

on·set \-ˌset\ *n* **1** : ATTACK **2** : BEGINNING ⟨the ~ of winter⟩

on·shore \-ˌshȯr\ *adj* **1** : moving toward the shore **2** : situated on or near the shore — **on·shore** \-'shȯr\ *adv*

on·slaught \'ȯn-ˌslȯt, 'än-\ *n* : a fierce attack; *also* : something resembling such an attack ⟨an ~ of questions⟩

Ont *abbr* Ontario

on·to \'ȯn-tü, 'än-\ *prep* : to a position or point on

onus \'ō-nəs\ *n* **1** : BURDEN **2** : OBLIGATION **3** : BLAME

¹on·ward \'ȯn-wərd, 'än-\ *also* **on·wards** \-wərdz\ *adv* : FORWARD ⟨kept moving ~⟩

²onward *adj* : directed or moving onward : FORWARD

on·yx \'ä-niks\ *n* [ME *oniche, onyx,* fr. AF & L; AF, fr. L *onyx,* fr. Gk, lit., claw, nail] : a translucent chalcedony in parallel layers of different colors

oo·dles \'ü-dºlz\ *n pl* : a great quantity

oo·lite \'ō-ə-ˌlīt\ *n* : a rock consisting of small round grains cemented together — **oo·lit·ic** \ˌō-ə-'li-tik\ *adj*

¹ooze \'üz\ *n* [ME *wose,* fr. OE *wāse* mire] **1** : a soft deposit (as of mud) on the bottom of a body of water **2** : soft wet ground : MUD — **oozy** \'ü-zē\ *adj*

²ooze *vb* **oozed**; **ooz·ing** **1** : to flow or leak out slowly or imperceptibly **2** : EXUDE ⟨~ confidence⟩

³ooze *n* : something that oozes

op *abbr* **1** operation; operative; operator **2** opportunity **3** opus

OP *abbr* **1** observation post **2** out of print

opac·i·ty \ō-'pa-sə-tē\ *n, pl* **-ties** **1** : obscurity of meaning 2 : mental dullness 3 : the quality or state of being opaque 4 : an opaque spot in a normally transparent structure

opal \'ō-pəl\ n : a mineral with iridescent colors that is used as a gem

opal·es·cent \ˌō-pə-'le-sᵊnt\ adj : IRIDESCENT — **opal·es·cence** \-sᵊns\ n

opaque \ō-'pāk\ adj 1 : blocking the passage of radiant energy and esp. light 2 : not easily understood; also : OBTUSE — **opaque·ly** adv — **opaque·ness** n

op art \'äp-\ n : OPTICAL ART — **op artist** n

op cit abbr [L opere citato] in the work cited

ope \'ōp\ vb **oped; op·ing** archaic : OPEN

OPEC abbr Organization of Petroleum Exporting Countries

op-ed \'äp-'ed\ n, often cap O&E : a page of special features usu. opposite the editorial page of a newspaper

¹**open** \'ō-pən\ adj **open·er; open·est** 1 : not shut or shut up ⟨an ∼ door⟩ 2 : not secret or hidden; also : FRANK 3 : not enclosed or covered ⟨an ∼ fire⟩; also : not protected 4 : free to be entered or used ⟨an ∼ tournament⟩ 5 : easy to get through or see ⟨∼ country⟩ 6 : spread out : EXTENDED 7 : not decided ⟨an ∼ question⟩ 8 : readily accessible and cooperative; also : GENEROUS 9 : having openings, interruptions, or spaces ⟨an ∼ mesh⟩; also : having components separated by a space in writing and printing ⟨the name Spanish moss is an ∼ compound⟩ 10 : ready to operate ⟨stores are ∼⟩ 11 : free from restraints or controls ⟨∼ season⟩ — **open·ly** adv — **open·ness** n

²**open** \'ō-pən\ vb **opened; open·ing** 1 : to change or move from a shut position; also : to make open by clearing away obstacles 2 : to make accessible 3 : to make openings in 4 : to make or become functional ⟨∼ a store⟩ 5 : REVEAL; also : ENLIGHTEN 6 : BEGIN ⟨∼ talks⟩ — **open·er** n

³**open** n 1 : OUTDOORS 2 : a contest or tournament open to all

open–air adj : OUTDOOR ⟨∼ theaters⟩

open arms n pl : an eager or warm welcome

open–faced \-'fāst\ also **open–face** \-'fās\ adj : served without a covering layer of bread ⟨an ∼ sandwich⟩

open–hand·ed \ˌō-pən-'han-dəd\ adj : GENEROUS — **open·hand·ed·ly** adv

open–heart adj : of, relating to, or performed on a heart temporarily relieved of circulatory function and laid open for repair of defects or damage

open–hearth adj : of, relating to, or being a process of making steel in a furnace that reflects the heat from the roof onto the material

opening n 1 : an act or instance of making or becoming open 2 : BEGINNING 3 : something that is open 4 : OCCASION; also : an opportunity for employment

open mike n : an event in which amateurs may perform

open–mind·ed \ˌō-pən-'mīn-dəd\ adj : free from rigidly fixed preconceptions — **open–mind·ed·ness** n

open sentence n : a statement (as in mathematics) containing at least one blank or unknown so that when the blank is filled or a quantity substituted for the unknown the statement becomes a complete statement that is either true or false

open shop n : an establishment having members and non-members of a labor union on the payroll

open·work \'ō-pən-ˌwərk\ n : work so made as to show openings through its substance ⟨a railing of wrought-iron ∼⟩ — **open–worked** \-ˌwərkt\ adj

¹**opera** pl of OPUS

²**op·era** \'ä-prə, -pə-rə\ n : a drama set to music — **op·er·at·ic** \ˌä-pə-'ra-tik\ adj

op·er·a·ble \'ä-pə-rə-bəl\ adj 1 : fit, possible, or desirable to use 2 : likely to result in a favorable outcome upon surgical treatment

opera glasses n pl : small binoculars for use in a theater

op·er·ate \'ä-pə-ˌrāt\ vb **-at·ed; -at·ing** 1 : to perform work : FUNCTION 2 : to produce an effect 3 : to put or keep in operation 4 : to perform or subject to an operation — **op·er·a·tor** \-ˌrā-tər\ n

operating system n : software that controls the operation of a computer

op·er·a·tion \ˌä-pə-'rā-shən\ n 1 : a doing or performing of a practical work 2 : an exertion of power or influence;

also : method or manner of functioning 3 : a surgical procedure 4 : a process of deriving one mathematical expression from others according to a rule 5 : a military action or mission 6 : a usu. small business — **op·er·a·tion·al** \-shə-nəl\ adj

¹**op·er·a·tive** \'ä-pə-rə-tiv, -ˌrā-\ adj 1 : producing an appropriate effect; also : most significant or essential 2 : OPERATING ⟨an ∼ force⟩ 3 : having to do with physical operations; also : WORKING ⟨an ∼ craftsman⟩ 4 : based on or consisting of an operation ⟨∼ dentistry⟩

²**operative** n 1 : OPERATOR; esp : a secret agent 2 : a person who works toward achieving the objectives of a larger interest

op·er·et·ta \ˌä-pə-'re-tə\ n [It, dim. of opera opera] : a light musical-dramatic work with a romantic plot, spoken dialogue, and dancing scenes

oph·thal·mic \äf-'thal-mik, äp-\ adj [Gk ophthalmikos, fr. ophthalmos eye] : of, relating to, or located near the eye

oph·thal·mol·o·gy \ˌäf-ˌthal-'mä-lə-jē, ˌäp-\ n : a branch of medicine dealing with the structure, functions, and diseases of the eye — **oph·thal·mol·o·gist** \-jist\ n

oph·thal·mo·scope \äf-'thal-mə-ˌskōp, äp-\ n : an instrument for use in viewing the interior of the eye and esp. the retina

opi·ate \'ō-pē-ət, -pē-ˌāt\ n : a preparation or derivative of opium; also : a narcotic or a substance with similar activity — **opiate** adj

opine \ō-'pīn\ vb **opined; opin·ing** : to express an opinion : STATE

opin·ion \ə-'pin-yən\ n 1 : JUDGMENT 2 : a belief stronger than impression and less strong than positive knowledge 3 : a formal statement by an expert after careful study

opin·ion·at·ed \ə-'pin-yə-ˌnā-təd\ adj : obstinately adhering to personal opinions

opi·um \'ō-pē-əm\ n [ME, fr. L, fr. Gk opion, fr. dim. of opos sap] : an addictive narcotic drug that is the dried latex of an Eurasian poppy

opos·sum \ə-'pä-səm\ n, pl **opossums** also **opossum** : an omnivorous tree-dwelling No. American marsupial that is active chiefly at night and has a pointed snout and a prehensile tail

opossum

opp abbr opposite

op·po·nent \ə-'pō-nənt\ n : one that opposes : ADVERSARY

op·por·tune \ˌä-pər-'tün, -'tyün\ adj [ME, fr. MF opportun, fr. L opportunus, fr. ob- toward + portus port, harbor] : SUITABLE ⟨an ∼ moment⟩ — **op·por·tune·ly** adv

op·por·tun·ism \ˌä-pər-'tü-ˌni-zəm, -'tyü-\ n : a taking advantage of opportunities or circumstances esp. with little regard for principles or ultimate consequences — **op·por·tun·ist** \-nist\ n — **op·por·tu·nis·tic** \-tü-'nis-tik, -tyü-\ adj

op·por·tu·ni·ty \ˌä-pər-'tü-nə-tē, -'tyü-\ n, pl **-ties** 1 : a favorable combination of circumstances, time, and place 2 : a chance for advancement

op·pose \ə-'pōz\ vb **op·posed; op·pos·ing** 1 : to place opposite or against something (as to provide resistance or contrast) 2 : to strive against : RESIST — **op·po·si·tion** \ˌä-pə-'zi-shən\ n

¹**op·po·site** \'ä-pə-zət\ adj 1 : set over against something that is at the other end or side 2 : OPPOSED, HOSTILE; also : CONTRARY 3 : contrarily turned or moving 4 : being the other of a matching or contrasting pair ⟨the ∼ sex⟩ — **op·po·site·ly** adv — **op·po·site·ness** n

²opposite *n* : one that is opposed or contrary

³opposite *adv* : on or to an opposite side

⁴opposite *prep* : across from and usu. facing ⟨the house ~ ours⟩

op·press \ə-'pres\ *vb* **1** : to crush by abuse of power or authority **2** : to weigh down : BURDEN ♦ *Synonyms* AGGRIEVE, WRONG, PERSECUTE — **op·pres·sive** \-'pre-siv\ *adj* — **op·pres·sive·ly** *adv* — **op·pres·sor** \-'pre-sər\ *n*

op·pres·sion \ə-'pre-shən\ *n* **1** : unjust or cruel exercise of power or authority **2** : DEPRESSION

op·pro·bri·ous \ə-'prō-brē-əs\ *adj* : expressing or deserving opprobrium — **op·pro·bri·ous·ly** *adv*

op·pro·bri·um \-brē-əm\ *n* **1** : something that brings disgrace **2** : public disgrace or ill fame

¹opt \'äpt\ *vb* : to make a choice; *esp* : to decide in favor of something

²opt *abbr* **1** optical; optician; optics **2** option; optional

op·tic \'äp-tik\ *adj* : of or relating to vision or the eye

op·ti·cal \'äp-ti-kəl\ *adj* **1** : relating to optics **2** : OPTIC **3** : of, relating to, or using light

optical art *n* : nonobjective art characterized by the use of geometric patterns often for an illusory effect

optical disk *n* : a disk on which information has been recorded digitally and which is read using a laser

optical fiber *n* : a single fiber-optic strand

op·ti·cian \äp-'ti-shən\ *n* **1** : a maker of or dealer in optical items and instruments **2** : a person who makes or orders eyeglasses and contact lenses to prescription and sells them

op·tics \'äp-tiks\ *n* : a science that deals with the nature and properties of light

op·ti·mal \'äp-tə-məl\ *adj* : most desirable or satisfactory — **op·ti·mal·ly** *adv*

op·ti·mism \'äp-tə-,mi-zəm\ *n* [F *optimisme*, fr. L *optimum*, n., best, fr. neut. of *optimus* best] **1** : a doctrine that this world is the best possible world **2** : an inclination to anticipate the best possible outcome of actions

op·ti·mize \'äp-tə-,mīz\ *vb* **-mized; -miz·ing** : to make as perfect, effective, or functional as possible — **op·ti·mi·za·tion** \,äp-tə-mə-'zā-shən\ *n*

op·ti·mum \'äp-tə-məm\ *n, pl* **-ma** \-mə\ *also* **-mums** [L] : the amount or degree of something most favorable to an end; *also* : greatest degree attained under implied or specified conditions

op·tion \'äp-shən\ *n* **1** : the power or right to choose **2** : a right to buy or sell something at a specified price during a specified period **3** : something offered for choice — **op·tion·al** \-shə-nəl\ *adj*

op·tom·e·try \äp-'tä-mə-trē\ *n* : the health-care profession concerned esp. with examining the eyes for defects of vision and with prescribing corrective lenses or eye exercises — **op·to·met·ric** \,äp-tə-'me-trik\ *adj* — **op·tom·e·trist** \äp-'tä-mə-trist\ *n*

opt out *vb* : to choose not to participate

op·u·lence \'ä-pyə-ləns\ *n* **1** : WEALTH **2** : ABUNDANCE

op·u·lent \'ä-pyə-lənt\ *adj* **1** : WEALTHY **2** : richly abundant — **op·u·lent·ly** *adv*

opus \'ō-pəs\ *n, pl* **opera** \'ō-pə-rə, 'ä-\ *also* **opus·es** \'ō-pə-səz\ : WORK; *esp* : a musical composition

or \'ȯr\ *conj* — used as a function word to indicate an alternative ⟨sink ~ swim⟩

OR *abbr* **1** operating room **2** Oregon

-or *n suffix* : one that does a (specified) thing ⟨calculat*or*⟩

or·a·cle \'ȯr-ə-kəl\ *n* **1** : one held to give divinely inspired answers or revelations **2** : an authoritative or wise utterance; *also* : a person of great authority or wisdom — **orac·u·lar** \ȯ-'ra-kyə-lər\ *adj*

¹oral \'ȯr-əl\ *adj* **1** : SPOKEN ⟨an ~ report⟩ **2** : of, given through, or involving the mouth ⟨an ~ vaccine⟩ **3** : of, relating to, or characterized by the first stage of psychosexual development in psychoanalytic theory in which libidinal gratification is derived from intake (as of food), by sucking, and later by biting **4** : relating to or characterized by personality traits of passive dependency and aggressiveness — **oral·ly** *adv*

²oral *n* : an oral examination — usu. used in pl.

oral sex *n* : oral stimulation of the genitals : CUNNILINGUS, FELLATIO

orang \ə-'raŋ\ *n* : ORANGUTAN

or·ange \'är-inj, 'ȯr-\ *n* **1** : a juicy citrus fruit with red-dish yellow rind; *also* : an evergreen tree with fragrant white flowers that bears this fruit **2** : a color between red and yellow — **or·ang·ey** *or* **or·angy** \'är-in-jē, 'ȯr-\ *adj*

or·ange·ade \,är-in-'jād, ,ȯr-\ *n* : a beverage of orange juice, sugar, and water

orange hawkweed *n* : a weedy herb related to the daisies with bright orange-red flower heads

or·ang·ery \'är-inj-rē, 'ȯr-\ *n, pl* **-ries** : a protected place (as a greenhouse) for raising oranges in cool climates

orang·utan \ə-'raŋ-ə-,taŋ, -,tan\ *n* [Bazaar Malay (Malay-based pidgin), fr. Malay *orang* man + *hutan* forest] : a large reddish brown tree-living anthropoid ape of Borneo and Sumatra

orate \ȯ-'rāt\ *vb* **orat·ed; orat·ing** : to speak in a declamatory manner

ora·tion \ə-'rā-shən\ *n* : an elaborate discourse delivered in a formal and dignified manner

or·a·tor \'ȯr-ə-tər\ *n* : one noted for skill and power as a public speaker

or·a·tor·i·cal \,ȯr-ə-'tȯr-i-kəl\ *adj* : of, relating to, or characteristic of an orator or oratory — **or·a·tor·i·cal·ly** \-'tȯr-i-k(ə-)lē\ *adv*

or·a·to·rio \,ȯr-ə-'tȯr-ē-,ō\ *n, pl* **-rios** : a lengthy choral work usu. on a scriptural subject

¹or·a·to·ry \'ȯr-ə-,tȯr-ē\ *n, pl* **-ries** : a private or institutional chapel

²oratory *n* : the art of speaking eloquently and effectively in public ♦ *Synonyms* RHETORIC, ELOCUTION

orb \'ȯrb\ *n* : a spherical body; *also* : EYE

¹or·bit \'ȯr-bət\ *n* [L *orbita*, lit., path, rut] **1** : a path described by one body in its revolution about another **2** : range or sphere of activity — **or·bit·al** \-bə-t²l\ *adj*

²orbit *vb* **1** : CIRCLE **2** : to send up and make revolve in an orbit ⟨~ a satellite⟩ — **or·bit·er** *n*

or·ca \'ȯr-kə\ *n* : KILLER WHALE

orch *abbr* orchestra

or·chard \'ȯr-chərd\ *n* [ME, fr. OE *ortgeard*, fr. *ort-* (fr. L *hortus* garden) + *geard* yard] : a place where fruit trees, sugar maples, or nut trees are grown; *also* : the trees of such a place — **or·chard·ist** \-chər-dist\ *n*

or·ches·tra \'ȯr-kə-strə\ *n* **1** : the front section of seats on the main floor of a theater **2** : a group of instrumentalists organized to perform ensemble music — **or·ches·tral** \ȯr-'kes-trəl\ *adj* — **or·ches·tral·ly** *adv*

or·ches·trate \'ȯr-kə-,strāt\ *vb* **-trat·ed; -trat·ing** **1** : to compose or arrange for an orchestra **2** : to arrange so as to achieve a desired effect — **or·ches·tra·tion** \,ȯr-kə-'strā-shən\ *n*

or·chid \'ȯr-kəd\ *n* : any of a large family of plants having often showy flowers with three petals of which the middle one is enlarged into a lip; *also* : a flower of an orchid

ord *abbr* **1** order **2** ordnance

or·dain \ȯr-'dān\ *vb* **1** : to admit to the ministry or priesthood by the ritual of a church **2** : DECREE, ENACT; *also* : DESTINE — **or·dain·ment** *n*

or·deal \ȯr-'dēl, 'ȯr-,dēl\ *n* : a severe trial or experience

¹or·der \'ȯr-dər\ *vb* **1** : ARRANGE, REGULATE **2** : COMMAND **3** : to place an order

²order *n* **1** : a group of people formally united; *also* : a badge or medal of such a group **2** : any of the several grades of the Christian ministry; *also, pl* : ORDINATION **3** : a rank, class, or special group of persons or things **4** : a category of biological classification ranking above the family and below the class **5** : ARRANGEMENT, SEQUENCE; *also* : the prevailing state of things **6** : a customary mode of procedure; *also* : the rule of law or proper authority **7** : a specific rule, regulation, or authoritative direction **8** : a style of building; *also* : an architectural column forming the unit of a style **9** : condition esp. with regard to repair **10** : a direction to pay money or to buy or sell goods; *also* : goods bought or sold — **in order** : APPROPRIATE, DESIRABLE ⟨apologies are *in order*⟩ — **in order to** : for the purpose of

¹or·der·ly \'ȯr-dər-lē\ *adj* **1** : arranged according to some order; *also* : NEAT, TIDY **2** : well behaved ⟨an ~ crowd⟩ ♦ *Synonyms* METHODICAL, SYSTEMATIC, REGULAR — **or·der·li·ness** *n*

²orderly *n, pl* **-lies** **1** : a soldier who attends a superior officer **2** : a hospital attendant who does general work

or·di·nal \'ȯrd-²n-əl\ *adj* : indicating order or rank (as sixth) in a series

ordinal number *n* : a number (as first, second, or third) that designates the place of an item in an ordered sequence — compare CARDINAL NUMBER

or·di·nance \'ȯr-də-nəns\ *n* : an authoritative decree or law; *esp* : a municipal regulation

or·di·nary \'ȯr-də-ˌner-ē\ *adj* 1 : to be expected : USUAL 2 : of common quality, rank, or ability ⟨∼ kids⟩; *also* : POOR, INFERIOR ⟨∼ wine⟩ ♦ *Synonyms* CUSTOMARY, ROUTINE, NORMAL, EVERYDAY — **or·di·nar·i·ly** \ˌȯr-də-ner-ə-lē\ *adv* — **or·di·nar·i·ness** \'ȯr-dən-ˌner-ē-nəs\ *n*

or·di·nate \'ȯr-də-nət, -ˌnāt\ *n* : the vertical coordinate of a point in a plane coordinate system obtained by measuring parallel to the y-axis

or·di·na·tion \ˌȯr-də-'nā-shən\ *n* : the act or ceremony by which a person is ordained

ord·nance \'ȯrd-nəns\ *n* 1 : military supplies 2 : CANNON, ARTILLERY

Or·do·vi·cian \ˌȯr-də-'vi-shən\ *adj* : of, relating to, or being the period of the Paleozoic era between the Cambrian and the Silurian — **Ordovician** *n*

or·dure \'ȯr-jər\ *n* : EXCREMENT

¹ore \'ȯr\ *n* : a naturally occurring mineral mined to obtain a substance that it contains

²ore \'ər-ə\ *n, pl* **ore** — see *krona, krone* at MONEY table

Ore *or* **Oreg** *abbr* Oregon

oreg·a·no \ə-'re-gə-ˌnō\ *n* : a bushy perennial mint used as a seasoning and a source of oil

org *abbr* organization; organized

or·gan \'ȯr-gən\ *n* 1 : a musical instrument having sets of pipes sounded by compressed air and controlled by keyboards; *also* : an electronic keyboard instrument that approximates the sounds of the pipe organ by electronic devices 2 : a differentiated animal or plant structure (as a heart or a leaf) made up of cells and tissues and performing some bodily function 3 : a group that performs a specialized function ⟨the various ∼s of government⟩ 4 : PERIODICAL

or·gan·dy *also* **or·gan·die** \'ȯr-gən-dē\ *n, pl* **-dies** [F *organdi*] : a fine transparent muslin with a stiff finish

or·gan·elle \ˌȯr-gə-'nel\ *n* : a specialized cell part that resembles an organ in having a special function

or·gan·ic \ȯr-'ga-nik\ *adj* 1 : of, relating to, or arising in a bodily organ 2 : of, relating to, or derived from living things 3 : of, relating to, or containing carbon compounds 4 : of or relating to a branch of chemistry dealing with carbon compounds 5 : involving, producing, or dealing in foods produced without the use of laboratory-made fertilizers, growth substances, antibiotics, or pesticides ⟨∼ farming⟩ 6 : ORGANIZED ⟨an ∼ whole⟩ — **or·gan·i·cal·ly** \-ni-k(ə-)lē\ *adv*

or·ga·ni·sa·tion, or·ga·nise *Brit var of* ORGANIZATION, ORGANIZE

or·gan·ism \'ȯr-gə-ˌni-zəm\ *n* : an individual living thing (as a person, animal, or plant) — **or·gan·is·mic** \ˌȯr-gə-'niz-mik\ *adj*

or·gan·ist \'ȯr-gə-nist\ *n* : a person who plays an organ

or·ga·ni·za·tion \ˌȯr-gə-nə-'zā-shən\ *n* 1 : the act or process of organizing or of being organized; *also* : the condition or manner of being organized 2 : ASSOCIATION, SOCIETY 3 : an administrative structure (as a business or a political party) — **or·ga·ni·za·tion·al** \-shə-nəl\ *adj*

or·ga·nize \'ȯr-gə-ˌnīz\ *vb* **-nized; -niz·ing** 1 : to develop an organic structure 2 : to form into a complete and functioning whole 3 : to set up an administrative structure for 4 : to arrange by systematic planning and united effort 5 : to join in a union; *also* : UNIONIZE ♦ *Synonyms* INSTITUTE, FOUND, ESTABLISH, CONSTITUTE — **or·ga·niz·er** *n*

or·gano·chlo·rine \ȯr-ˌga-nə-'klȯr-ˌēn\ *adj* : of, relating to, or being a chlorinated hydrocarbon pesticide (as DDT) — **organochlorine** *n*

or·gano·phos·phate \-'fäs-ˌfāt\ *n* : an organophosphorus pesticide — **organophosphate** *adj*

or·gano·phos·pho·rus \-'fäs-fə-rəs\ *also* **or·gano·phos·pho·rous** \-ˌfäs-'fȯr-əs\ *adj* : of, relating to, or being a phosphorus-containing organic pesticide (as malathion)

or·gan·za \ȯr-'gan-zə\ *n* : a sheer dress fabric resembling organdy and usu. made of silk, rayon, or nylon

or·gasm \'ȯr-ˌga-zəm\ *n* : the climax of sexual excitement — **or·gas·mic** \ȯr-'gaz-mik\ *adj*

or·gi·as·tic \ˌȯr-jē-'as-tik\ *adj* : of, relating to, or marked by orgies

or·gu·lous \'ȯr-gyə-ləs, -gə-\ *adj* : PROUD

or·gy \'ȯr-jē\ *n, pl* **orgies** : a gathering marked by unrestrained indulgence (as in sexual activity, alcohol, or drugs)

ori·el \'ȯr-ē-əl\ *n* : a window built out from a wall and usu. supported by a bracket

ori·ent \'ȯr-ē-ˌent\ *vb* 1 : to set in a definite position esp. in relation to the points of the compass 2 : to acquaint with an existing situation or environment 3 : to direct toward the interests of a particular group

Orient *n* : EAST 3; *esp* : the countries of eastern Asia

ori·en·tal \ˌȯr-ē-'en-tᵊl\ *adj, often cap* [fr. *Orient* East, fr. ME, fr. AF, fr. L *orient-, oriens,* fr. prp. of *oriri* to rise] : of or situated in Asia

ori·en·tate \'ȯr-ē-ən-ˌtāt\ *vb* **-tat·ed; -tat·ing** 1 : ORIENT 2 : to face east

ori·en·ta·tion \ˌȯr-ē-ən-'tā-shən\ *n* 1 : the act or state of being oriented 2 : a person's identity based on sexual tendencies

or·i·fice \'ȯr-ə-fəs\ *n* : OPENING, MOUTH

ori·flamme \'ȯr-ə-ˌflam\ *n* : a brightly colored banner used as a standard or ensign in battle

orig *abbr* original; originally

ori·ga·mi \ˌȯr-ə-'gä-mē\ *n* : the Japanese art or process of paper folding

or·i·gin \'ȯr-ə-jən\ *n* 1 : ANCESTRY 2 : rise, beginning, or derivation from a source; *also* : CAUSE 3 : the intersection of coordinate axes

¹orig·i·nal \ə-'ri-jə-nəl\ *n* : something from which a copy, reproduction, or translation is made : PROTOTYPE

²original *adj* 1 : FIRST, INITIAL 2 : not copied from something else : FRESH 3 : INVENTIVE — **orig·i·nal·i·ty** \-ˌri-jə-'na-lə-tē\ *n* — **orig·i·nal·ly** \-'ri-jə-nᵊl-ē\ *adv*

orig·i·nate \ə-'ri-jə-ˌnāt\ *vb* **-nat·ed; -nat·ing** 1 : to give rise to : INITIATE 2 : to come into existence : BEGIN — **orig·i·na·tor** \-ˌnā-tər\ *n*

ori·ole \'ȯr-ē-ˌōl\ *n* : any of various New World birds of which the males are usu. black and yellow or black and orange

or·i·son \'ȯr-ə-sən\ *n* : PRAYER

or·mo·lu \'ȯr-mə-ˌlü\ *n* : a golden or gilded brass used for decorative purposes

¹or·na·ment \'ȯr-nə-mənt\ *n* : something that lends grace or beauty — **or·na·men·tal** \ˌȯr-nə-'men-tᵊl\ *adj*

²or·na·ment \-ˌment\ *vb* : to provide with ornament : ADORN — **or·na·men·ta·tion** \ˌȯr-nə-mən-'tā-shən\ *n*

or·nate \ȯr-'nāt\ *adj* : elaborately decorated ⟨an ∼ mantel⟩ — **or·nate·ly** *adv* — **or·nate·ness** *n*

or·nery \'ȯr-nə-rē, 'ä-nə-\ *adj* : having an irritable disposition

or·ni·thol·o·gy \ˌȯr-nə-'thä-lə-jē\ *n, pl* **-gies** : a branch of zoology dealing with birds — **or·ni·tho·log·i·cal** \-thə-'lä-ji-kəl\ *adj* — **or·ni·thol·o·gist** \-'thä-lə-jist\ *n*

oro·tund \'ȯr-ə-ˌtənd\ *adj* 1 : SONOROUS ⟨an ∼ voice⟩ 2 : POMPOUS ⟨an ∼ speech⟩ — **oro·tun·di·ty** \ȯr-ə-'tən-di-tē\ *n*

or·phan \'ȯr-fən\ *n* : a child deprived by death of one or usu. both parents — **orphan** *vb*

or·phan·age \'ȯr-fə-nij\ *n* : an institution for the care of orphans

or·tho·don·tia \ˌȯr-thə-'dän-chə, -chē-ə\ *n* : ORTHODONTICS

or·tho·don·tics \ˌȯr-thə-'dän-tiks\ *n* : a branch of dentistry concerned with the correction of faults in the arrangement and placing of the teeth — **or·tho·don·tic** \-tik\ *adj* — **or·tho·don·tist** \-'dän-tist\ *n*

or·tho·dox \'ȯr-thə-ˌdäks\ *adj* [MF or LL; MF *orthodoxe,* fr. LL *orthodoxus,* fr. LGk *orthodoxos,* fr. Gk *orthos* right + *doxa* opinion] 1 : conforming to established doctrine esp. in religion 2 : CONVENTIONAL 3 *cap* : of or relating to a Christian church originating in the church of the Eastern Roman Empire — **or·tho·doxy** \-ˌdäk-sē\ *n*

or·thog·ra·phy \ȯr-'thä-grə-fē\ *n* : SPELLING — **or·tho·graph·ic** \ˌȯr-thə-'gra-fik\ *adj*

or·tho·pe·dics *also* **or·tho·pae·dics** \ˌȯr-thə-'pē-diks\ *n sing or pl* : a branch of medicine concerned with the correction or prevention of skeletal injuries or disorders — **or·tho·pe·dic** \-dik\ *also* **or·tho·pae·dic** *adj* — **or·tho·pe·dist** \-dist\ *n*

-ory *adj suffix* **1** : of, relating to, or characterized by ⟨anticipat*ory*⟩ **2** : serving for, producing, or maintaining ⟨illus*ory*⟩

Os *symbol* osmium

OS *abbr* **1** [L *oculus sinister*] left eye **2** ordinary seaman **3** out of stock

Osage \ō-ˈsāj\ *n, pl* **Osag·es** *or* **Osage** : a member of an American Indian people orig. of Missouri

os·cil·late \ˈä-sə-ˌlāt\ *vb* **-lat·ed; -lat·ing** **1** : to swing backward and forward like a pendulum **2** : to move or travel back and forth between two points **3** : VARY, FLUCTUATE — **os·cil·la·tion** \ˌä-sə-ˈlā-shən\ *n* — **os·cil·la·tor** \ˈä-sə-ˌlā-tər\ *n* — **os·cil·la·to·ry** \ˈä-sə-lə-ˌtōr-ē\ *adj*

os·cil·lo·scope \ä-ˈsi-lə-ˌskōp\ *n* : an instrument in which variations in current or voltage appear as a visible wave form on a fluorescent screen

os·cu·late \ˈäs-kyə-ˌlāt\ *vb* **-lat·ed; -lat·ing** : KISS — **os·cu·la·tion** \ˌäs-kyə-ˈlā-shən\ *n* — **os·cu·la·to·ry** \ˈäs-kyə-lə-ˌtōr-ē\ *adj*

Osee \ˈō-ˌzē, ō-ˈzā-ə\ *n* : HOSEA

OSHA \ˈō-shə\ *abbr* Occupational Safety and Health Administration

osier \ˈō-zhər\ *n* : any of various willows with pliable twigs used esp. in making baskets and furniture; *also* : a twig from an osier

os·mi·um \ˈäz-mē-əm\ *n* : a very heavy hard brittle metallic chemical element used esp. as a catalyst and in alloys

os·mo·sis \äz-ˈmō-səs, äs-\ *n* : movement of a solvent through a semipermeable membrane into a solution of higher concentration that tends to equalize the concentrations of the solutions on either side of the membrane — **os·mot·ic** \-ˈmä-tik\ *adj*

os·prey \ˈäs-prē, -ˌprā\ *n, pl* **ospreys** : a large dark brown and white fish-eating hawk

os·si·fy \ˈä-sə-ˌfī\ *vb* **-fied; -fy·ing** : to make or become hardened or set in one's ways — **os·si·fi·ca·tion** \ˌä-sə-fə-ˈkā-shən\ *n*

os·su·ary \ˈä-shə-ˌwer-ē, -syə-\ *n, pl* **-ar·ies** : a depository for the bones of the dead

os·ten·si·ble \ä-ˈsten-sə-bəl\ *adj* : shown outwardly : PROFESSED, APPARENT — **os·ten·si·bly** \-blē\ *adv*

os·ten·ta·tion \ˌäs-tən-ˈtā-shən\ *n* : pretentious or excessive display — **os·ten·ta·tious** \-shəs\ *adj* — **os·ten·ta·tious·ly** *adv*

os·te·o·ar·thri·tis \ˌäs-tē-ō-är-ˈthrī-təs\ *n* : arthritis marked by degeneration of the cartilage and bone of joints

os·teo·path \ˈäs-tē-ə-ˌpath\ *n* : a practitioner of osteopathy

os·te·op·a·thy \ˌäs-tē-ˈä-pə-thē\ *n* : a system of treating diseases emphasizing manipulation (as of joints) but not excluding other agencies (as the use of medicine and surgery) — **os·teo·path·ic** \ˌäs-tē-ə-ˈpa-thik\ *adj*

os·teo·po·ro·sis \ˌäs-tē-ō-pə-ˈrō-səs\ *n, pl* **-ro·ses** \-ˌsēz\ : a condition affecting esp. older women and characterized by fragile and porous bones

os·tra·cise *Brit var of* OSTRACIZE

os·tra·cize \ˈäs-trə-ˌsīz\ *vb* **-cized; -ciz·ing** [Gk *ostrakizein* to banish by voting with potsherds, fr. *ostrakon* shell, potsherd] : to exclude from a group by common consent — **os·tra·cism** \-ˌsi-zəm\ *n*

os·trich \ˈäs-trich, ˈós-\ *n* : a very large swift-footed flightless bird of Africa

Os·we·go tea \ä-ˈswē-gō-\ *n* : a No. American mint with showy scarlet flowers

OT *abbr* **1** occupational therapy **2** Old Testament **3** overtime

¹oth·er \ˈə-thər\ *adj* **1** : being the one left; *also* : being the ones distinct from those first mentioned **2** : ALTERNATE ⟨every ∼ day⟩ **3** : DIFFERENT **4** : ADDITIONAL **5** : recently past ⟨the ∼ night⟩

²other *pron* **1** : remaining one or ones **2** : a different or additional one ⟨something or ∼⟩

oth·er·wise \ˈə-thər-ˌwīz\ *adv* **1** : in a different way **2** : in different circumstances **3** : in other respects **4** : if not **5** : NOT — **otherwise** *adj*

oth·er·world \-ˌwərld\ *n* : a world beyond death or beyond present reality

oth·er·world·ly \ˌə-thər-ˈwərld-lē\ *adj* : not worldly : concerned with spiritual, intellectual, or imaginative matters

oti·ose \ˈō-shē-ˌōs, ˈō-tē-\ *adj* **1** : FUTILE **2** : IDLE **3** : USELESS ⟨∼ details⟩

oto·lar·yn·gol·o·gy \ˌō-tō-ˌla-rən-ˈgä-lə-jē\ *n* : a medical specialty concerned esp. with the ear, nose, and throat — **oto·lar·yn·gol·o·gist** \-jist\ *n*

oto·rhi·no·lar·yn·gol·o·gy \ˌō-tō-ˌrī-nō-ˌla-rən-ˈgä-lə-jē\ *n* : OTOLARYNGOLOGY — **oto·rhi·no·lar·yn·gol·o·gist** \-jist\ *n*

OTS *abbr* officers' training school

Ot·ta·wa \ˈä-tə-wə, -ˌwä, -ˌwó\ *n, pl* **Ottawas** *or* **Ottawa** : a member of an American Indian people of Michigan and southern Ontario

ot·ter \ˈä-tər\ *n, pl* **otters** *also* **otter** : any of various web-footed fish-eating mammals with dark brown fur that are related to the weasels; *also* : the fur

otter

ot·to·man \ˈä-tə-mən\ *n* : an upholstered seat or couch usu. without a back; *also* : an overstuffed footstool

ou·bli·ette \ˌü-blē-ˈet\ *n* [F, fr. MF, fr. *oublier* to forget, ultim. fr. L *oblivisci*] : a dungeon with an opening at the top

ought \ˈót\ *verbal auxiliary* — used to express moral obligation, advisability, natural expectation, or logical consequence

ou·gui·ya \ü-ˈgwē-ə, -ˈgē-\ *n, pl* **ouguiya** — see MONEY table

ounce \ˈauns\ *n* [ME, fr. AF *unce*, fr. L *uncia* twelfth part, ounce, fr. *unus* one] **1** : a unit of avoirdupois, troy, and apothecaries' weight — see WEIGHT table **2** : FLUID OUNCE

our \är, ˈau̇(-ə)r\ *adj* : of or relating to us or ourselves

ours \ˈau̇(-ə)z, ˈärz\ *pron* : that which belongs to us

our·selves \är-ˈselvz, au̇(-ə)r-\ *pron* : our own selves — used reflexively, for emphasis, or in absolute constructions ⟨we pleased ∼⟩ ⟨we'll do it ∼⟩ ⟨we were tourists ∼⟩

-ous *adj suffix* : full of : abounding in : having : possessing the qualities of ⟨clamor*ous*⟩ ⟨poison*ous*⟩

oust \ˈaust\ *vb* : to eject from or deprive of property or position : EXPEL ♦ **Synonyms** EVICT, DISMISS, BANISH, DEPORT

oust·er \ˈaus-tər\ *n* : EXPULSION

¹out \ˈaut\ *adv* **1** : in a direction away from the inside or center **2** : beyond control **3** : to extinction, exhaustion, or completion **4** : in or into the open **5** : so as to retire a batter or base runner; *also* : so as to be retired

²out *vb* : to become known ⟨the truth will ∼⟩

³out *prep* **1** : out through ⟨looked ∼ the window⟩ **2** : outward on or along ⟨drive ∼ the river road⟩

⁴out *adj* **1** : situated outside or at a distance **2** : not in : ABSENT; *also* : not being in power **3** : removed from play as a batter or base runner **4** : not being in vogue or fashion : not up-to-date **5** : attempting a particular activity ⟨won his first time ∼⟩

⁵out *n* **1** : one who is out of office **2** : the retiring of a batter or base runner

out·age \ˈau̇-tij\ *n* : a period or instance of interruption esp. of electricity

out–and–out *adj* : COMPLETE, THOROUGHGOING ⟨an ∼ fraud⟩

out·bid \ˌaut-ˈbid\ *vb* : to make a higher bid than

¹out·board \ˈaut-ˌbord\ *adj* **1** : situated outboard **2** : having or using an outboard motor

²outboard *adv* **1** : outside a ship's hull : away from the long axis of a ship **2** : in a position closer to the wing tip of an airplane

outboard motor *n* : a small internal combustion engine with propeller attached for mounting at the stern of a small boat

out·bound \ˈaut-ˌbau̇nd\ *adj* : outward bound ⟨∼ traffic⟩

out·break \-ˌbrāk\ *n* **1** : a sudden increase in activity, incidence, or numbers **2** : INSURRECTION, REVOLT

out·build·ing \-ˌbil-diŋ\ *n* : a building separate from but accessory to a main house

out·burst \-ˌbərst\ *n* : ERUPTION; *esp* : a violent expression of feeling

out·cast \-ˌkast\ *n* : one that is cast out by society

out·class \aut-ˈklas\ *vb* : SURPASS

out·come \ˈaut-ˌkəm\ *n* : a final consequence : RESULT

out·crop \-ˌkräp\ *n* : a coming out of bedrock to the surface of the ground; *also* : the part of a rock formation that thus appears — **outcrop** *vb*

out·cry \-ˌkrī\ *n* : a loud cry : CLAMOR

out·dat·ed \aut-ˈdā-təd\ *adj* : OUTMODED

out·dis·tance \-ˈdis-təns\ *vb* : to go far ahead of (as in a race) : OUTSTRIP

out·do \-ˈdü\ *vb* **-did** \-ˈdid\; **-done** \-ˈdən\; **-do·ing**; **-does** \-ˈdəz\ : to go beyond in action or performance

out·door \ˈaut-ˌdor, -ˈdor\ *also* **out·doors** \-ˌdorz, -ˈdorz\ *adj* **1** : of or relating to the outdoors **2** : performed outdoors **3** : not enclosed (as by a roof)

¹out·doors \ˈaut-ˌdorz, -ˈdorz\ *adv* : in or into the open air

²outdoors *n* **1** : the open air **2** : the world away from human habitation — **out·doorsy** \ˌaut-ˈdor-zē\ *adj*

out·draw \aut-ˈdro\ *vb* **-drew** \-ˈdrü\; **-drawn** \-ˈdron\; **-draw·ing** **1** : to attract a larger audience than **2** : to draw a handgun more quickly than

out·er \ˈau-tər\ *adj* **1** : EXTERNAL **2** : situated farther out; *also* : being away from a center

outer ear *n* : the outer visible portion of the ear that collects and directs sound waves toward the eardrum

out·er·most \-ˌmōst\ *adj* : farthest out

outer space *n* : SPACE 5

out·er·wear \ˈau-tər-ˌwer\ *n* **1** : clothing for outdoor wear **2** : outer clothing as opposed to underwear

out·face \aut-ˈfās\ *vb* **1** : to cause to waver or submit **2** : DEFY

out·field \ˈaut-ˌfēld\ *n* : the part of a baseball field beyond the infield and within the foul lines; *also* : players in the outfield — **out·field·er** \-ˌfēl-dər\ *n*

out·fight \aut-ˈfīt\ *vb* : to surpass in fighting : DEFEAT

¹out·fit \ˈaut-ˌfit\ *n* **1** : the equipment or apparel for a special purpose or occasion **2** : GROUP

²outfit *vb* **out·fit·ted**; **out·fit·ting** : EQUIP — **out·fit·ter** *n*

out·flank \aut-ˈflaŋk\ *vb* : to get around the flank of (an opposing force)

out·flow \ˈaut-ˌflō\ *n* **1** : a flowing out **2** : something that flows out

out·fox \aut-ˈfäks\ *vb* : OUTWIT

out·go \ˈaut-ˌgō\ *n, pl* **outgoes** : EXPENDITURES, OUTLAY

out·go·ing \-ˌgō-iŋ\ *adj* **1** : going out ⟨~ tide⟩ **2** : retiring from a place or position **3** : FRIENDLY

out·grow \aut-ˈgrō\ *vb* **-grew** \-ˈgrü\; **-grown** \-ˈgrōn\; **-grow·ing** **1** : to grow faster than **2** : to grow too large for

out·growth \ˈaut-ˌgrōth\ *n* : a product of growing out : OFFSHOOT; *also* : CONSEQUENCE, RESULT

out·guess \aut-ˈges\ *vb* : OUTWIT

out·gun \-ˈgən\ *vb* : to surpass in firepower

out·house \ˈaut-ˌhaus\ *n* : OUTBUILDING; *esp* : an outdoor toilet

out·ing \ˈau-tiŋ\ *n* : a brief stay or trip in the open

out·land·ish \aut-ˈlan-dish\ *adj* **1** : of foreign appearance or manner; *also* : BIZARRE **2** : remote from civilization — **out·land·ish·ly** *adv*

out·last \-ˈlast\ *vb* : to last longer than

¹out·law \ˈaut-ˌlo\ *n* **1** : a person excluded from the protection of the law **2** : a lawless person

²outlaw *vb* **1** : to deprive of the protection of the law **2** : to make illegal — **out·law·ry** \ˈaut-ˌlor-ē\ *n*

out·lay \ˈaut-ˌlā\ *n* **1** : the act of spending **2** : EXPENDITURE

out·let \ˈaut-ˌlet, -lət\ *n* **1** : EXIT, VENT **2** : a means of release (as for an emotion) **3** : a medium for usu. public expression : a media organization **4** : a market for a commodity **5** : a receptacle for the plug of an electrical device

¹out·line \ˈaut-ˌlīn\ *n* **1** : a line marking the outer limits of an object or figure **2** : a drawing in which only contours are marked **3** : SUMMARY, SYNOPSIS **4** : PLAN

²outline *vb* **1** : to draw the outline of **2** : to indicate the chief features or parts of

out·live \aut-ˈliv\ *vb* : to live longer than ◆ **Synonyms** OUTLAST, SURVIVE

out·look \ˈaut-ˌluk\ *n* **1** : a place offering a view; *also* : VIEW **2** : STANDPOINT **3** : the prospect for the future

out·ly·ing \-ˌlī-iŋ\ *adj* : distant from a center or main body

out·ma·neu·ver \ˌaut-mə-ˈnü-vər, -ˈnyü-\ *vb* : to defeat by more skillful maneuvering

out·mod·ed \aut-ˈmō-dəd\ *adj* **1** : no longer in style **2** : no longer acceptable or current

out·num·ber \-ˈnəm-bər\ *vb* : to exceed in number

out of *prep* **1** : out from within or behind ⟨walk *out of* the room⟩ ⟨look *out of* the window⟩ **2** : from a state of ⟨wake up *out of* a deep sleep⟩ **3** : beyond the limits of ⟨*out of* sight⟩ **4** : BECAUSE OF ⟨asked *out of* curiosity⟩ **5** : FROM, WITH ⟨built it *out of* scrap⟩ **6** : in or into a state of loss or not having ⟨cheated him *out of* $5000⟩ ⟨we're *out of* matches⟩ **7** : from among ⟨one *out of* four⟩ — **out of it** : SQUARE, OLD-FASHIONED

out–of–bounds *adv or adj* : outside the prescribed boundaries or limits

out–of–date *adj* : no longer in fashion or in use : OUTMODED

out–of–door *or* **out–of–doors** *adj* : OUTDOOR

out–of–the–way *adj* **1** : UNUSUAL **2** : being off the beaten track

out·pa·tient \ˈaut-ˌpā-shənt\ *n* : a patient who visits a hospital or clinic for diagnosis or treatment without staying overnight

out·per·form \ˌaut-pər-ˈform\ *vb* : to perform better than

out·play \aut-ˈplā\ *vb* : to play more skillfully than

out·point \-ˈpoint\ *vb* : to win more points than

out·post \ˈaut-ˌpōst\ *n* **1** : a security detachment dispatched by a main body of troops to protect it from enemy surprise; *also* : a military base established (as by treaty) in a foreign country **2** : an outlying or frontier settlement

out·pour·ing \-ˌpor-iŋ\ *n* : something that pours out or is poured out

out·pull \aut-ˈpul\ *vb* : OUTDRAW 1

¹out·put \ˈaut-ˌput\ *n* **1** : the amount produced (as by a machine or factory) : PRODUCTION **2** : the information produced by a computer

²output *vb* **out·put·ted** *or* **output**; **out·put·ting** : to produce as output

¹out·rage \ˈaut-ˌrāj\ *n* [ME, fr. AF *utrage, outrage* insult, excess, fr. *utre, outre* beyond, fr. L *ultra*] **1** : a violent or shameful act **2** : INJURY, INSULT **3** : the anger or resentment aroused by injury or insult

²outrage *vb* **out·raged**; **out·rag·ing** **1** : RAPE **2** : to subject to violent injury or gross insult **3** : to arouse to extreme resentment

out·ra·geous \aut-ˈrā-jəs\ *adj* : extremely offensive, insulting, or shameful : SHOCKING — **out·ra·geous·ly** *adv*

out·rank \-ˈraŋk\ *vb* : to rank higher than

ou·tré \ü-ˈtrā\ *adj* [F] : violating convention or propriety : BIZARRE

¹out·reach \aut-ˈrēch\ *vb* **1** : to surpass in reach **2** : to get the better of by trickery

²out·reach \ˈaut-ˌrēch\ *n* **1** : the act of reaching out **2** : the extent of reach **3** : the extending of services beyond usual limits

out·rid·er \-ˌrī-dər\ *n* : a mounted attendant

out·rig·ger \-ˌri-gər\ *n* **1** : a frame attached to the side of a boat to prevent capsizing **2** : a craft equipped with an outrigger

¹out·right \aut-ˈrīt\ *adv* **1** : COMPLETELY **2** : INSTANTANEOUSLY

²out·right \ˈaut-ˌrīt\ *adj* **1** : being exactly what is stated ⟨an ~ lie⟩ **2** : given or made without reservation or encumbrance ⟨an ~ sale⟩

out·run \aut-ˈrən\ *vb* **-ran** \-ˈran\; **-run**; **-run·ning** : to run faster than; *also* : EXCEED

out·sell \-ˈsel\ *vb* **-sold** \-ˈsōld\; **-sell·ing** : to exceed in sales

out·set \ˈaut-ˌset\ *n* : BEGINNING, START

out·shine \aut-ˈshīn\ *vb* **-shone** \-ˈshōn\ *or* **-shined**; **-shin·ing** **1** : to shine brighter than **2** : SURPASS

¹out·side \aut-ˈsīd, ˈaut-ˌsīd\ *n* **1** : a place or region beyond an enclosure or boundary **2** : EXTERIOR **3** : the utmost limit or extent

²outside *adj* **1** : OUTER **2** : coming from without ⟨~ in-

fluences⟩ **3** : being apart from one's regular duties ⟨∼ activities⟩ **4** : REMOTE ⟨an ∼ chance⟩
³outside *adv* : on or to the outside
⁴outside *prep* **1** : on or to the outside of **2** : beyond the limits of **3** : EXCEPT
outside of *prep* **1** : OUTSIDE **2** : BESIDES
out·sid·er \aut-'sī-dər\ *n* : a person who does not belong to a group
out·size \'aut-ˌsīz\ *also* **out·sized** \-ˌsīzd\ *adj* : unusually large : extravagant in size or degree
out·skirts \-ˌskərts\ *n pl* : the outlying parts (as of a city) : BORDERS
out·smart \aut-'smärt\ *vb* : OUTWIT
out·source \'aut-ˌsȯrs\ *vb* **-sourced; -sourcing** : to obtain (goods or services) from an outside supplier
out·spend \-'spend\ *vb* **1** : to exceed the limits of in spending ⟨∼s his income⟩ **2** : to spend more than
out·spo·ken \aut-'spō-kən\ *adj* : direct and open in speech or expression — **out·spo·ken·ly** *adv* — **out·spo·ken·ness** *n*
out·spread \-'spred\ *vb* **-spread; -spread·ing** : to spread out
out·stand·ing \-'stan-diŋ\ *adj* **1** : PROJECTING **2** : UNPAID; *also* : UNRESOLVED ⟨∼ warrants⟩ **3** : publicly issued and sold **4** : CONSPICUOUS; *also* : DISTINGUISHED — **out·stand·ing·ly** *adv*
out·stay \-'stā\ *vb* **1** : OVERSTAY **2** : to surpass in endurance
out·stretch \ˌaut-'strech\ *vb* : to stretch out : EXTEND
out·strip \-'strip\ *vb* **1** : to go faster than **2** : EXCEL, SURPASS
out·take \'aut-ˌtāk\ *n* : something taken out; *esp* : a take that is not used in an edited version of a film or videotape
out·vote \-'vōt\ *vb* : to defeat by a majority of votes
¹out·ward \'aut-wərd\ *adj* **1** : moving or directed toward the outside **2** : showing outwardly
²outward *or* **out·wards** \-wərdz\ *adv* : toward the outside
out·ward·ly \-wərd-lē\ *adv* : on the outside : EXTERNALLY
out·wear \aut-'wer\ *vb* **-wore** \-'wȯr\; **-worn** \-'wȯrn\; **-wear·ing** : to wear longer than : OUTLAST
out·weigh \-'wā\ *vb* : to exceed in weight, value, or importance
out·wit \-'wit\ *vb* : to get the better of by superior cleverness
¹out·work \-'wərk\ *vb* : to outdo in working
²out·work \'aut-ˌwərk\ *n* : a minor defensive position outside a fortified area
out·worn \aut-'wȯrn\ *adj* : OUTMODED
ou·zo \'ü-(ˌ)zō\ *n* : a colorless anise-flavored unsweetened Greek liqueur
ova *pl of* OVUM
oval \'ō-vəl\ *adj* [ML *ovalis*, fr. LL, of an egg, fr. L *ovum* egg] : egg-shaped; *also* : broadly elliptical — **oval** *n*
ova·ry \'ō-və-rē\ *n, pl* **-ries** **1** : one of the usu. paired female reproductive organs producing eggs and in vertebrates sex hormones **2** : the part of a flower in which seeds are produced — **ovar·i·an** \ō-'ver-ē-ən\ *adj*
ovate \'ō-ˌvāt\ *adj* : egg-shaped
ova·tion \ō-'vā-shən\ *n* [L *ovation-, ovatio*, fr. *ovare* to exult] : an enthusiastic popular tribute
ov·en \'ə-vən\ *n* : a chamber (as in a stove) for baking, heating, or drying
oven·bird \-ˌbərd\ *n* : a large olive-green American warbler that builds its dome-shaped nest on the ground
¹over \'ō-vər\ *adv* **1** : across a barrier or intervening space **2** : across the brim ⟨boil ∼⟩ **3** : so as to bring the underside up **4** : out of a vertical position **5** : beyond some quantity, limit, or norm **6** : ABOVE **7** : at an end **8** : THROUGH ⟨read it ∼⟩; *also* : THOROUGHLY **9** : AGAIN ⟨do it ∼⟩
²over *prep* **1** : above in position, authority, or scope ⟨towered ∼ her⟩ ⟨obeyed those ∼ him⟩ **2** : more than ⟨cost ∼ $100⟩ **3** : ON, UPON ⟨a cape ∼ her shoulders⟩ **4** : along the length of ⟨∼ the road⟩ **5** : through the medium of : ON ⟨spoke ∼ TV⟩ **6** : all through ⟨showed me ∼ the house⟩ **7** : on or to the other side or beyond ⟨jump ∼ a ditch⟩ **8** : DURING ⟨∼ the past 25 years⟩ **9** : on account of ⟨trouble ∼ money⟩
³over *adj* **1** : UPPER, HIGHER **2** : REMAINING **3** : ENDED
over- *prefix* **1** : so as to exceed or surpass **2** : excessive; excessively

overabundance
overabundant
overachiever
overactive
overaggressive
overambitious
overanxious
overbid
overbold
overbuild
overburden
overbuy
overcapacity
overcapitalize
overcareful
overcautious
overcompensation
overconfidence
overconfident
overconscientious
overcook
overcritical
overcrowd
overdecorated
overdependence
overdetermined
overdevelop
overdress
overeager
overeat
overeducated
overemphasis
overemphasize
overenthusiastic
overestimate
overexcite
overexcited
overexert
overexertion
overextend
overfatigued
overfeed
overfill
overgeneralization
overgeneralize

overgenerous
overgraze
overhasty
overheat
overindulge
overindulgence
overindulgent
overlarge
overlearn
overload
overlong
overmodest
overnice
overoptimism
overoptimistic
overpay
overpraise
overproduce
overproduction
overprotect
overprotective
overrate
overreact
overreaction
overrefinement
overrepresented
overripe
oversensitive
oversensitiveness
oversimple
oversimplification
oversimplify
overspecialization
overspecialize
overspend
overstimulation
overstock
oversubtle
oversupply
overtax
overtired
overtrain
overuse
overvalue
overzealous

over·act \ˌō-vər-'akt\ *vb* : to exaggerate in acting
¹over·age \ˌō-vər-'āj\ *adj* **1** : too old to be useful **2** : older than is normal for one's position, function, or grade
²over·age \'ō-və-rij\ *n* : SURPLUS
over·all \ˌō-vər-'ȯl\ *adj* : including everything ⟨∼ expenses⟩
over·alls \'ō-vər-ˌȯlz\ *n pl* : pants of strong material usu. with a piece extending up to cover the chest
over·arm \-ˌärm\ *adj* : done with the arm raised above the shoulder
over·awe \ˌō-vər-'ȯ\ *vb* : to restrain or subdue by awe
over·bal·ance \-'ba-ləns\ *vb* **1** : OUTWEIGH **2** : to cause to lose balance
over·bear·ing \-'ber-iŋ\ *adj* : ARROGANT, DOMINEERING
over·bite \'ō-vər-ˌbīt\ *n* : the projection of the upper front teeth over the lower
over·blown \-'blōn\ *adj* **1** : PORTLY **2** : INFLATED, PRETENTIOUS
over·board \'ō-vər-ˌbȯrd\ *adv* **1** : over the side of a ship into the water **2** : to extremes of enthusiasm
¹over·cast \'ō-vər-ˌkast\ *adj* : clouded over : GLOOMY
²overcast *n* ; *esp* : a covering of clouds
over·charge \ˌō-vər-'chärj\ *vb* **1** : to charge too much **2** : to fill or load too full — **over·charge** \'ō-vər-ˌchärj\ *n*
over·coat \'ō-vər-ˌkōt\ *n* : a warm coat worn over indoor clothing
over·come \ˌō-vər-'kəm\ *vb* **-came** \-'kām\; **-come; -coming** **1** : CONQUER **2** : to make helpless or exhausted
over·do \ˌō-vər-'dü\ *vb* **-did** \-'did\; **-done** \-'dən\; **-doing; -does** \-'dəz\ **1** : to do too much; *also* : to tire oneself **2** : EXAGGERATE **3** : to cook too long
over·dose \'ō-vər-ˌdōs\ *n* : too great a dose (as of medicine); *also* : a lethal or toxic amount (as of a drug) — **over·dose** \ˌō-vər-'dōs\ *vb*
over·draft \'ō-vər-ˌdraft\ *n* : an overdrawing of a bank account; *also* : the sum overdrawn
over·draw \ˌō-vər-'drȯ\ *vb* **-drew** \-'drü\; **-drawn** \-'drȯn\; **-draw·ing** **1** : to draw checks on a bank account for more than the balance **2** : EXAGGERATE
over·drive \'ō-vər-ˌdrīv\ *n* : an automotive transmission gear that transmits to the driveshaft a speed greater than the engine speed
over·dub \ˌō-vər-'dəb\ *vb* : to transfer (recorded sound)

onto an earlier recording for a combined effect — **over-dub** \'ō-vər-ˌdəb\ n

over·due \-'dü, -'dyü\ adj **1** : unpaid when due ⟨an ~ bill⟩; *also* : not appearing or presented on time ⟨an ~ train⟩ **2** : more than ready

over·ex·pose \ˌō-vər-ik-'spōz\ vb : to expose (as film) for more time than is needed — **over·ex·po·sure** \-'spō-zhər\ n

¹over·flow \-'flō\ vb **1** : INUNDATE; *also* : to pour forth in a flood **2** : to flow over the brim or top of

²over·flow \'ō-vər-ˌflō\ n **1** : FLOOD; *also* : SURPLUS **2** : an outlet for surplus liquid

over·fly \ˌō-vər-'flī\ vb **-flew** \-'flü\; **-flown** \-'flōn\; **-fly·ing** : to fly over in an aircraft or spacecraft — **over·flight** \'ō-vər-ˌflīt\ n

over·grow \ˌō-vər-'grō\ vb **-grew** \-'grü\; **-grown** \-'grōn\; **-grow·ing** **1** : to grow over so as to cover **2** : OUTGROW **3** : to grow excessively — **over·growth** \-ˌgrōth\ n

over·hand \'ō-vər-ˌhand\ adj : made with the hand brought down from above — **overhand** adv — **over·hand·ed** \-ˌhan-dəd\ adv or adj

¹over·hang \'ō-vər-ˌhaŋ, ˌō-vər-'haŋ\ vb **-hung** \-ˌhəŋ, -'həŋ\; **-hang·ing** **1** : to project over : jut out **2** : to hang over threateningly

²over·hang \'ō-vər-ˌhaŋ\ n : a part (as of a roof) that overhangs

over·haul \ˌō-vər-'hȯl\ vb **1** : to examine thoroughly and make necessary repairs and adjustments **2** : OVERTAKE

¹over·head \ˌō-vər-'hed\ adv : ALOFT

²over·head \'ō-vər-ˌhed\ adj : operating or lying above ⟨~ door⟩

³over·head \'ō-vər-ˌhed\ n : business expenses not chargeable to a particular part of the work

over·hear \ˌō-vər-'hir\ vb **-heard** \-'hərd\; **-hear·ing** : to hear without the speaker's knowledge or intention

over·joyed \ˌō-vər-'jȯid\ adj : filled with great joy

over·kill \'ō-vər-ˌkil\ n **1** : destructive capacity greatly exceeding that required for a target **2** : a large excess

over·land \'ō-vər-ˌland, -lənd\ adv or adj : by, on, or across land

over·lap \ˌō-vər-'lap\ vb **1** : to lap over **2** : to have something in common — **over·lap** \'ō-vər-ˌlap\ n

over·lay \ˌō-vər-'lā\ vb **-laid** \-'lād\; **-lay·ing** : to lay or spread over or across — **over·lay** \'ō-vər-ˌlā\ n

over·leap \ˌō-vər-'lēp\ vb **-leaped** or **-leapt** \-'lēpt, -'lept\; **-leap·ing** **1** : to leap over or across **2** : to defeat (oneself) by going too far

over·lie \ˌō-vər-'lī\ vb **-lay** \-'lā\; **-lain** \-'lān\; **-ly·ing** : to lie over or upon

¹over·look \ˌō-vər-'lu̇k\ vb **1** : INSPECT **2** : to look down on from above **3** : to fail to see **4** : IGNORE; *also* : EXCUSE **5** : SUPERINTEND

²over·look \'ō-vər-ˌlu̇k\ n : a place from which to look upon a scene below

over·lord \-ˌlȯrd\ n : a lord who has supremacy over other lords

over·ly \'ō-vər-lē\ adv : EXCESSIVELY

over·match \ˌō-vər-'mach\ vb : to be more than a match for : DEFEAT

over·much \-'məch\ adj or adv : too much

¹over·night \-'nīt\ adv **1** : on or during the night **2** : SUDDENLY ⟨became famous ~⟩

²overnight adj : of, lasting, or staying the night ⟨~ guests⟩

over·pass \'ō-vər-ˌpas\ n **1** : a crossing (as of two highways) at different levels by means of a bridge **2** : the upper level of an overpass

over·play \ˌō-vər-'plā\ vb **1** : EXAGGERATE; *also* : OVEREMPHASIZE **2** : to rely too much on the strength of

over·pop·u·la·tion \ˌō-vər-ˌpä-pyə-'lā-shən\ n : the condition of having a population so dense as to cause a decline in population or in living conditions — **over·pop·u·la·ted** \-ˌpä-pyə-ˌlā-təd\ adj

over·pow·er \-'pau̇(-ə)r\ vb : to overcome by superior force

over·price \ˌō-vər-'prīs\ vb : to price too high

over·print \-'print\ vb : to print over with something additional — **over·print** \'ō-vər-ˌprint\ n

over·qual·i·fied \-'kwä-lə-ˌfīd\ adj : having more education, training, or experience than a job calls for

over·reach \ˌō-vər-'rēch\ vb : to defeat (oneself) by too great an effort

over·ride \-'rīd\ vb **-rode** \-'rōd\; **-rid·den** \-'ri-d²n\; **-rid·ing** **1** : to ride over or across **2** : to prevail over; *also* : to set aside ⟨~ a veto⟩

over·rule \-'rül\ vb **1** : to prevail over **2** : to rule against **3** : to set aside

¹over·run \-'rən\ vb **-ran** \-'ran\; **-run; -run·ning** **1** : to defeat and occupy the positions of **2** : OVERSPREAD; *also* : INFEST **3** : to go beyond **4** : to flow over

²over·run \'ō-vər-ˌrən\ n **1** : an act or instance of overrunning; *esp* : an exceeding of estimated costs **2** : the amount by which something overruns

over·sea \ˌō-vər-'sē, 'ō-vər-ˌsē\ adj or adv : OVERSEAS

over·seas \ˌō-vər-'sēz, -ˌsēz\ adv or adj : beyond or across the sea : ABROAD

over·see \ˌō-vər-'sē\ vb **-saw** \-'sȯ\; **-seen** \-'sēn\; **-see·ing** **1** : OVERLOOK **2** : INSPECT; *also* : SUPERVISE — **over·seer** \'ō-vər-ˌsir\ n

over·sell \ˌō-vər-'sel\ vb **-sold; -sel·ling** : to sell too much to or too much of

over·sexed \ˌō-vər-'sekst\ adj : exhibiting excessive sexual drive or interest

over·shad·ow \-'sha-dō\ vb **1** : to cast a shadow over **2** : to exceed in importance

over·shoe \'ō-vər-ˌshü\ n : a protective outer shoe; *esp* : GALOSH

over·shoot \ˌō-vər-'shüt\ vb **-shot** \-'shät\; **-shoot·ing** **1** : to pass swiftly beyond **2** : to shoot over or beyond

over·sight \'ō-vər-ˌsīt\ n **1** : SUPERVISION **2** : an inadvertent omission or error

over·size \ˌō-vər-'sīz\ or **over·sized** \-'sīzd\ adj : of more than ordinary size

over·sleep \ˌō-vər-'slēp\ vb **-slept** \-'slept\; **-sleep·ing** : to sleep beyond the time for waking

over·spread \-'spred\ vb **-spread; -spread·ing** : to spread over or above

over·state \-'stāt\ vb : EXAGGERATE — **over·state·ment** n

over·stay \-'stā\ vb : to stay beyond the time or limits of

over·step \-'step\ vb : EXCEED

over·sub·scribe \-səb-'skrīb\ vb : to subscribe for more of than is available, asked for, or offered for sale

overt \ō-'vərt, 'ō-ˌvərt\ adj [ME, fr. AF, fr. pp. of *ovrir* to open] : not secret — **overt·ly** adv

over·take \ˌō-vər-'tāk\ vb **-took** \-'tu̇k\; **-tak·en** \-'tā-kən\; **-tak·ing** : to catch up with; *also* : to catch up with and pass by ⟨~ the lead runner⟩

over-the-counter adj : sold lawfully without a prescription ⟨~ drugs⟩

over-the-hill adj **1** : past one's prime **2** : advanced in age

over-the-top adj **1** : extremely flamboyant or outrageous ⟨an ~ performance⟩

over·throw \ˌō-vər-'thrō\ vb **-threw** \-'thrü\; **-thrown** \-'thrōn\; **-throw·ing** **1** : UPSET **2** : to bring down : DEFEAT ⟨~ a government⟩ **3** : to throw over or past — **over·throw** \'ō-vər-ˌthrō\ n

over·time \'ō-vər-ˌtīm\ n : time beyond a set limit; *esp* : working time in excess of a standard day or week — **overtime** adv

over·tone \-ˌtōn\ n **1** : one of the higher tones in a complex musical tone **2** : IMPLICATION, SUGGESTION

over·trick \'ō-vər-ˌtrik\ n : a card trick won in excess of the number bid

over·ture \'ō-vər-ˌchu̇r, -chər\ n [ME, lit., opening, fr. AF, fr. VL *opertura*, alter. of L *apertura*] **1** : an opening offer **2** : an orchestral introduction to a musical dramatic work

over·turn \ˌō-vər-'tərn\ vb **1** : to turn over : UPSET ⟨~ a vase⟩ **2** : INVALIDATE ⟨~ a court ruling⟩

over·view \'ō-vər-ˌvyü\ n : a general survey : SUMMARY

over·ween·ing \ˌō-vər-'wē-niŋ\ adj **1** : ARROGANT **2** : IMMODERATE

over·weight \'ō-vər-ˌwāt\ n **1** : weight above what is required or allowed **2** : bodily weight greater than normal — **overweight** adj

over·whelm \ˌō-vər-'hwelm\ vb **1** : OVERTHROW **2** : SUBMERGE **3** : to overcome completely

over·whelm·ing adj : EXTREME, GREAT ⟨~ joy⟩ — **over·whelm·ing·ly** adv

over·win·ter \-'win-tər\ vb : to survive or pass the winter

over·work \-'wərk\ vb **1** : to work or cause to work too hard or long **2** : to use too much — **overwork** n

over·wrought \ˌō-vər-ˈrȯt\ *adj* **1** : extremely excited **2** : elaborated to excess

ovi·duct \ˈō-və-ˌdəkt\ *n* : a tube that serves for the passage of eggs from an ovary

ovip·a·rous \ō-ˈvi-pə-rəs\ *adj* : reproducing by eggs that hatch outside the parent's body

ovoid \ˈō-ˌvȯid\ *or* **ovoi·dal** \ō-ˈvȯi-dᵊl\ *adj* : egg-shaped : OVAL

ovu·la·tion \ˌäv-yə-ˈlā-shən, ˌōv-\ *n* : the discharge of a mature egg from the ovary — **ovu·late** \ˈäv-yə-ˌlāt, ˈōv-\ *vb*

ovule \ˈä-vyül, ˈōv-\ *n* : any of the bodies in a plant ovary that after fertilization become seeds

ovum \ˈō-vəm\ *n, pl* **ova** \-və\ : EGG 2

ow \ˈaù\ *interj* — used esp. to express sudden pain

owe \ˈō\ *vb* **owed; ow·ing** **1** : to be under obligation to pay or render **2** : to be indebted to or for; *also* : to be in debt

owing to *prep* : BECAUSE OF

owl \ˈaù(-ə)l\ *n* : any of an order of chiefly nocturnal birds of prey with a large head and eyes and strong talons — **owl·ish** *adj* — **owl·ish·ly** *adv*

owl·et \ˈaù-lət\ *n* : a young or small owl

¹own \ˈōn\ *adj* : belonging to oneself — used as an intensive after a possessive adjective ⟨her ∼ car⟩

²own *vb* **1** : to have or hold as property **2** : to have power or mastery over **3** : ACKNOWLEDGE; *also* : CONFESS — **own·er** *n* — **own·er·ship** *n*

³own *pron* : one or ones belonging to oneself — **on one's own** : for or by oneself : left to one's own resources

ox \ˈäks\ *n, pl* **ox·en** \ˈäk-sən\ *also* **ox** : any of the large domestic bovine mammals kept for milk, draft, and meat; *esp* : an adult castrated male ox

ox·blood \ˈäks-ˌbləd\ *n* : a moderate reddish brown

ox·bow \-ˌbō\ *n* **1** : a U-shaped collar worn by a draft ox **2** : a U-shaped bend in a river — **oxbow** *adj*

ox·ford \ˈäks-fərd\ *n* : a low shoe laced or tied over the instep

ox·i·dant \ˈäk-sə-dənt\ *n* : OXIDIZING AGENT — **oxidant** *adj*

ox·i·da·tion \ˌäk-sə-ˈdā-shən\ *n* : the act or process of oxidizing; *also* : the condition of being oxidized — **ox·i·da·tive** \ˈäk-sə-ˌdā-tiv\ *adj*

ox·ide \ˈäk-ˌsīd\ *n* : a compound of oxygen with another element or group

ox·i·dize \ˈäk-sə-ˌdīz\ *vb* **-dized; -diz·ing** : to combine with oxygen ⟨iron rusts because it is *oxidized* by exposure to the air⟩ — **ox·i·diz·er** *n*

oxidizing agent *n* : a substance (as oxygen or nitric acid) that oxidizes by taking up electrons

ox·y·gen \ˈäk-si-jən\ *n* [F *oxygène*, fr. Gk *oxys* acidic, lit., sharp + *-genēs* giving rise to; so called because it was once thought to be an essential element of all acids] : a colorless odorless gaseous chemical element that is found in the air, is essential to life, and is involved in combustion

ox·y·gen·ate \ˈäk-si-jə-ˌnāt\ *vb* **-at·ed; -at·ing** : to impregnate, combine, or supply with oxygen — **ox·y·gen·a·tion** \ˌäk-si-jə-ˈnā-shən\ *n*

oxygen mask *n* : a device worn over the nose and mouth through which oxygen is supplied

oxygen tent *n* : a canopy which can be placed over a bedridden person and within which a flow of oxygen can be maintained

ox·y·mo·ron \ˌäk-sē-ˈmȯr-ˌän\ *n* : a combination of contradictory words (as *cruel kindness*) — **ox·y·mo·ron·ic** \-mə-ˈrä-nik\ *adj*

oys·ter \ˈȯi-stər\ *n* : any of various marine mollusks with an irregular 2-valved shell that include commercially important edible shellfish and pearl producers — **oys·ter·ing** *n* — **oys·ter·man** \-mən\ *n*

oz *abbr* [obs. It *onza* (now *oncia*)] ounce; ounces

ozone \ˈō-ˌzōn\ *n* **1** : a bluish gaseous reactive form of oxygen that is formed naturally in the atmosphere and is used for disinfecting, deodorizing, and bleaching **2** : pure and refreshing air

ozone layer *n* : an atmospheric layer at heights of about 25 miles (40 kilometers) with high ozone content which blocks most solar ultraviolet radiation

P

¹p \ˈpē\ *n, pl* **p's** *or* **ps** \ˈpēz\ *often cap* : the 16th letter of the English alphabet

²p *abbr, often cap* **1** page **2** participle **3** past **4** pawn **5** pence; penny **6** per **7** petite **8** pint **9** pressure **10** purl

P *symbol* phosphorus

pa \ˈpä, ˈpȯ\ *n* : FATHER

¹Pa *abbr* **1** pascal **2** Pennsylvania

²Pa *symbol* protactinium

¹PA \ˌ(ˌ)pē-ˈā\ *n* : PHYSICIAN'S ASSISTANT

²PA *abbr* **1** Pennsylvania **2** per annum **3** power of attorney **4** press agent **5** private account **6** professional association **7** public address **8** purchasing agent

pa·an·ga \pä-ˈäŋ-gə\ *n* — see MONEY table

pab·u·lum \ˈpa-byə-ləm\ *n* [L, food, fodder] : usu. soft digestible food

Pac *abbr* Pacific

PAC *abbr* political action committee

¹pace \ˈpās\ *n* **1** : rate of movement or progress (as in walking or working) **2** : a step in walking; *also* : a measure of length based on such a step **3** : GAIT; *esp* : a horse's gait in which the legs on the same side move together

²pace *vb* **paced; pac·ing** **1** : to go or cover at a pace or with slow steps **2** : to measure off by paces **3** : to set or regulate the pace of

³pace \ˈpä-sē; ˈpä-ˌkā, -ˌchä\ *prep* : contrary to the opinion of

pace·mak·er \ˈpās-ˌmā-kər\ *n* **1** : one that sets the pace for another **2** : a body part (as of the heart) that serves to establish and maintain a rhythmic activity **3** : an electrical device for stimulating or steadying the heartbeat

pac·er \ˈpā-sər\ *n* **1** : a horse that paces **2** : PACEMAKER

pachy·derm \ˈpa-ki-ˌdərm\ *n* [F *pachyderme*, fr. Gk *pachydermos* thick-skinned, fr. *pachys* thick + *derma* skin] : any of various thick-skinned hoofed mammals (as an elephant)

pach·ys·an·dra \ˌpa-ki-ˈsan-drə\ *n* : any of a genus of low perennial evergreen plants used as a ground cover

pa·cif·ic \pə-ˈsi-fik\ *adj* **1** : tending to lessen conflict **2** : CALM, PEACEFUL

pac·i·fi·er \ˈpa-sə-ˌfī(-ə)r\ *n* : one that pacifies; *esp* : a device for a baby to chew or suck on

pac·i·fism \ˈpa-sə-ˌfi-zəm\ *n* : opposition to war or violence as a means of settling disputes — **pac·i·fist** \-fist\ *n or adj* — **pac·i·fis·tic** \ˌpa-sə-ˈfis-tik\ *adj*

pac·i·fy \ˈpa-sə-ˌfī\ *vb* **-fied; -fy·ing** **1** : to allay anger or agitation in : SOOTHE **2** : SETTLE; *also* : SUBDUE — **pac·i·fi·ca·tion** \ˌpa-sə-fə-ˈkā-shən\ *n*

¹pack \ˈpak\ *n* **1** : a compact bundle; *also* : a flexible container for carrying a bundle esp. on the back **2** : a large amount : HEAP **3** : a set of playing cards **4** : a group or band of people or animals **5** : wet absorbent material for application to the body

²pack *vb* **1** : to stow goods in for transportation **2** : to fill in or surround so as to prevent passage of air, steam, or water **3** : to put into a protective container **4** : to load with a pack ⟨∼ a mule⟩ **5** : to crowd in **6** : to make into a pack **7** : to cause to go without ceremony ⟨∼ them off to school⟩ **8** : WEAR, CARRY ⟨∼ a gun⟩

³**pack** *vb* : to make up fraudulently so as to secure a desired result ⟨∼ a jury⟩

¹**pack·age** \'pa-kij\ *n* **1** : BUNDLE, PARCEL **2** : a group of related things offered as a whole

²**package** *vb* **pack·aged; pack·ag·ing** : to make into or enclose in a package

package deal *n* : an offer containing several items all or none of which must be accepted

package store *n* : a store that sells alcoholic beverages in sealed containers for consumption off the premises

pack·er \'pa-kər\ *n* : one that packs; *esp* : a wholesale food dealer

pack·et \'pa-kət\ *n* **1** : a small bundle or package **2** : a passenger boat carrying mail and cargo on a regular schedule

pack·horse \'pak-ˌhȯrs\ *n* : a horse used to carry goods or supplies

pack·ing \'pa-kiŋ\ *n* : material used to pack something

pack·ing·house \-ˌhaus\ *n* : an establishment for processing and packing food and esp. meat and its by-products

pack rat *n* **1** : a bushy-tailed rodent of western No. America that hoards food and miscellaneous objects; *also* : any of several rodents of similar habit **2** : a person who collects or saves many esp. unneeded items

pack·sad·dle \'pak-ˌsa-dᵊl\ *n* : a saddle for supporting loads on the back of an animal

pack·thread \-ˌthred\ *n* : strong thread for tying

pact \'pakt\ *n* : AGREEMENT, TREATY

¹**pad** \'pad\ *n* **1** : a cushioning part or thing : CUSHION **2** : the cushioned underside of the foot or toes of some mammals **3** : the floating leaf of a water plant **4** : a writing tablet **5** : LAUNCHPAD **6** : living quarters; *also* : BED

²**pad** *vb* **pad·ded; pad·ding** **1** : to furnish with a pad or padding **2** : to expand with needless or fraudulent matter

pad·ding *n* : the material with which something is padded

¹**pad·dle** \'pa-dᵊl\ *vb* **pad·dled; pad·dling** : to move the hands and feet about in shallow water

²**paddle** *n* **1** : an implement with a flat blade used in propelling and steering a small craft (as a canoe) **2** : an implement used for stirring, mixing, or beating **3** : a broad board on the outer rim of a waterwheel or a paddle wheel

³**paddle** *vb* **pad·dled; pad·dling** **1** : to move on or through water by or as if by using a paddle **2** : to beat or stir with a paddle

paddle wheel *n* : a wheel with paddles around its outer edge used to move a boat

paddle wheeler *n* : a steam-driven vessel propelled by a paddle wheel

paddle wheeler

pad·dock \'pa-dək\ *n* **1** : a usu. enclosed area for pasturing or exercising animals; *esp* : one where racehorses are saddled and paraded before a race **2** : an area at a racecourse where racing cars are parked

pad·dy \'pa-dē\ *n, pl* **paddies** : wet land where rice is grown

paddy wagon *n* : an enclosed motortruck for carrying prisoners

pad·lock \'pad-ˌläk\ *n* : a removable lock with a curved piece that snaps into a catch — **padlock** *vb*

pa·dre \'pä-drā\ *n* [Sp or It or Pg, lit., father, fr. L *pater*] **1** : PRIEST **2** : a military chaplain

pad thai \'päd-'tī\ *n, often cap T* : a Thai dish of rice noodles stir-fried with additional ingredients

pae·an \'pē-ən\ *n* : an exultant song of praise or thanksgiving

pae·di·at·ric, pae·di·a·tri·cian, pae·di·at·rics *chiefly Brit var of* PEDIATRIC, PEDIATRICIAN, PEDIATRICS

pa·el·la \pä-'e-lə; -'āl-yə, -'ä-yə\ *n* : a saffron-flavored dish of rice, meat, seafood, and vegetables

pa·gan \'pā-gən\ *n* [ME, fr. LL *paganus*, fr. L, civilian, country dweller, fr. *pagus* country district] : HEATHEN — **pagan** *adj* — **pa·gan·ism** \-gə-ˌni-zəm\ *n*

¹**page** \'pāj\ *n* : ATTENDANT; *esp* : one employed to deliver messages

²**page** *vb* **paged; pag·ing** **1** : to summon by repeatedly calling out the name of **2** : to send a message to via a pager

³**page** *n* **1** : a single leaf (as of a book); *also* : a single side of such a leaf **2** : the information at a single World Wide Web address

⁴**page** *vb* **paged; pag·ing** : to mark or number the pages of

pag·eant \'pa-jənt\ *n* [ME *pagyn, padgeant*, lit., scene of a play, fr. AF *pagine, pagent*, fr. ML *pagina*, perh. fr. L, page] : an elaborate spectacle, show, or procession esp. with tableaux or floats — **pag·eant·ry** \-jən-trē\ *n*

page·boy \'pāj-ˌbȯi\ *n* [¹*page*] : an often shoulder-length hairdo with the ends of the hair turned smoothly under

pag·er \'pā-jər\ *n* : one that pages; *esp* : a small radio receiver that alerts its user to incoming messages

pag·i·nate \'pa-jə-ˌnāt\ *vb* **-nat·ed; -nat·ing** : ⁴PAGE

pag·i·na·tion \ˌpa-jə-'nā-shən\ *n* **1** : the paging of written or printed matter **2** : the number and arrangement of pages (as of a book)

pa·go·da \pə-'gō-də\ *n* : a tower with roofs curving upward at the division of each of several stories

paid *past and past part of* PAY

pail \'pāl\ *n* : a usu. cylindrical vessel with a handle — **pail·ful** \-ˌful\ *n*

¹**pain** \'pān\ *n* **1** : PUNISHMENT, PENALTY **2** : suffering or distress of body or mind; *also* : a basic bodily sensation marked by discomfort (as throbbing or aching) **3** *pl* : great care **4** : one that irks or annoys — **pain·ful** \-fəl\ *adj* — **pain·ful·ly** *adv* — **pain·less** *adj* — **pain·less·ly** *adv*

²**pain** *vb* : to cause or experience pain

pain·kill·er \'pān-ˌki-lər\ *n* : something (as a drug) that relieves pain — **pain·kill·ing** *adj*

pains·tak·ing \-ˌstā-kiŋ\ *adj* : taking pains : showing care — **pains·taking** *n* — **pains·tak·ing·ly** *adv*

¹**paint** \'pānt\ *vb* **1** : to apply color, pigment, or paint to **2** : to produce or portray in lines or colors on a surface; *also* : to practice the art of painting **3** : to decorate with colors **4** : to use cosmetics **5** : to describe vividly **6** : SWAB — **paint·er** *n*

²**paint** *n* **1** : something produced by painting **2** : MAKEUP **3** : a mixture of a pigment and a liquid that forms a thin adherent coating when spread on a surface; *also* : the dry pigment used in making this mixture **4** : an applied coating of paint

paint·ball \'pānt-ˌbȯl\ *n* : a game in which two teams try to capture each other's flag using guns that shoot paint-filled pellets

paint·brush \'pānt-ˌbrəsh\ *n* : a brush for applying paint

painted lady *n* : a migratory butterfly with wings mottled in brown, orange, black, and white

painting *n* **1** : a work (as a picture) produced by painting **2** : the art or occupation of painting

¹**pair** \'per\ *n, pl* **pairs** *also* **pair** [ME *paire*, fr. AF, fr. L *paria* equal things, fr. neut. pl. of *par* equal] **1** : two things of a kind designed for use together **2** : something made up of two corresponding pieces ⟨a ∼ of pants⟩ **3** : a set of two people or animals

²**pair** *vb* **1** : to arrange in pairs **2** : to form a pair : MATCH **3** : to become associated with another

pai·sa \pī-'sä\ *n, pl* **paisa** *or* **pai·se** \-'sā\ — see *rupee, taka* at MONEY table

pais·ley \'pāz-lē\ *adj, often cap* : decorated with colorful curved abstract figures ⟨a ∼ shawl⟩

Pai·ute \'pī-ˌüt, -ˌyüt\ *n* : a member of an American Indian people orig. of Utah, Arizona, Nevada, and California

pa·ja·mas \pə-'jä-məz, -'ja-\ *n pl* : a loose suit for sleeping or lounging

pal \'pal\ *n* : a close friend

pal·ace \'pa-ləs\ *n* [ME *palais*, fr. AF, fr. L *palatium*, fr. *Palatium*, the Palatine Hill in Rome where the emperors' residences were built] **1** : the official residence of a chief of state **2** : MANSION

pal·a·din \'pa-lə-dən\ *n* **1** : a trusted military leader (as for a medieval prince) **2** : a leading champion of a cause

pa·laes·tra \pə-'les-trə\ *n, pl* **-trae** \-(,)trē\ : a school in ancient Greece or Rome for sports (as wrestling)

pa·lan·quin \,pa-lən-'kēn\ *n* : an enclosed couch for one person borne on the shoulders of men by means of poles

pal·at·able \'pa-lə-tə-bəl\ *adj* : agreeable to the taste ♦ **Synonyms** APPETIZING, SAVORY, TASTY, TOOTHSOME

pal·a·tal \'pa-lə-tᵊl\ *adj* **1** : of or relating to the palate **2** : pronounced with some part of the tongue near or touching the hard palate ⟨the \y\ in *yeast* and the \sh\ in *she* are ~ sounds⟩

pal·a·tal·ize \'pa-lə-tə-,līz\ *vb* **-ized; -iz·ing** : to pronounce as or change into a palatal sound — **pal·a·tal·i·za·tion** \,pa-lə-tə-lə-'zā-shən\ *n*

pal·ate \'pa-lət\ *n* **1** : the roof of the mouth separating the mouth from the nasal cavity **2** : TASTE

pa·la·tial \pə-'lā-shəl\ *adj* **1** : of, relating to, or being a palace **2** : MAGNIFICENT

pa·lat·i·nate \pə-'la-tə-nət\ *n* : the territory of a palatine

¹pal·a·tine \'pa-lə-,tīn\ *adj* **1** : possessing royal privileges; *also* : of or relating to a palatine or a palatinate **2** : of or relating to a palace : PALATIAL

²palatine *n* **1** : a feudal lord having sovereign power within his domains **2** : a high officer of an imperial palace

pa·la·ver \pə-'la-vər, -'lä-\ *n* [Pg *palavra* word, speech, fr. LL *parabola* parable, speech] **1** : a long parley **2** : idle talk — **palaver** *vb*

¹pale \'pāl\ *n* **1** : a stake or picket of a fence **2** : an enclosed place; *also* : a district or territory within certain bounds or under a particular jurisdiction **3** : LIMITS, BOUNDS ⟨conduct beyond the ~⟩

²pale *vb* **paled; pal·ing** : to enclose with or as if with pales : FENCE

³pale *adj* **pal·er; pal·est** **1** : deficient in color or intensity : WAN ⟨a ~ face⟩ **2** : lacking in brightness : DIM ⟨a ~ star⟩ **3** : not dark or intense in hue ⟨a ~ blue⟩ — **pale·ness** *n*

⁴pale *vb* **paled; pal·ing** : to make or become pale

pale ale *n* : a medium-colored very dry ale

pale·face \'pāl-,fās\ *n* : a white person

Pa·leo·cene \'pā-lē-ə-,sēn\ *adj* : of, relating to, or being the earliest epoch of the Tertiary — **Paleocene** *n*

pa·leo·con·ser·va·tive \,pā-lē-ō-kən-'sər-və-tiv\ *n* : a conservative espousing traditional principles and policies

pa·le·og·ra·phy \,pā-lē-'ä-grə-fē\ *n* [NL *palaeographia,* fr. Gk *palaios* ancient + *graphein* to write] : the study of ancient writings and inscriptions — **pa·le·og·ra·pher** *n*

Pa·leo·lith·ic \,pā-lē-ə-'li-thik\ *adj* : of or relating to the earliest period of the Stone Age characterized by rough or chipped stone implements

pa·le·on·tol·o·gy \,pā-lē-,än-'tä-lə-jē\ *n* : a science dealing with the life of past geologic periods as known from fossil remains — **pa·le·on·to·log·i·cal** \-,än-tə-'lä-ji-kəl\ *adj* — **pa·le·on·tol·o·gist** \-,än-'tä-lə-jist, -ən-\ *n*

Pa·leo·zo·ic \,pā-lē-ə-'zō-ik\ *adj* : of, relating to, or being the era of geologic history extending from about 570 million years ago to about 245 million years ago — **Paleozoic** *n*

pal·ette \'pa-lət\ *n* : a thin often oval board that a painter holds and mixes colors on; *also* : the colors on a palette

pal·frey \'pȯl-frē\ *n, pl* **palfreys** *archaic* : a saddle horse that is not a warhorse; *esp* : one suitable for a woman

pa·limp·sest \'pa-ləmp-,sest\ *n* [L *palimpsestus,* fr. Gk *palimpsēstos* scraped again] : writing material (as a parchment) used after the erasure of earlier writing

pal·in·drome \'pa-lən-,drōm\ *n* : a word, verse, or sentence (as "Able was I ere I saw Elba") or a number (as 1881) that reads the same backward or forward

pal·ing \'pā-liŋ\ *n* **1** : a fence of pales **2** : material for pales **3** : PALE, PICKET

pal·i·sade \,pa-lə-'sād\ *n* **1** : a high fence of stakes esp. for defense **2** : a line of steep cliffs

¹pall \'pȯl\ *vb* **1** : to lose in interest or attraction **2** : SATIATE, CLOY

²pall *n* **1** : a heavy cloth draped over a coffin **2** : something that produces a gloomy atmosphere

pal·la·di·um \pə-'lā-dē-əm\ *n* : a silver-white metallic chemical element used esp. as a catalyst and in alloys

pall·bear·er \'pȯl-,ber-ər\ *n* : a person who attends the coffin at a funeral

¹pal·let \'pa-lət\ *n* : a small, hard, or makeshift bed

²pallet *n* : a portable platform for transporting and storing materials

pal·li·ate \'pa-lē-,āt\ *vb* **-at·ed; -at·ing** **1** : to ease (as a disease) without curing **2** : to cover by excuses and apologies — **pal·li·a·tion** \,pa-lē-'ā-shən\ *n* — **pal·li·a·tive** \'pa-lē-,ā-tiv\ *adj or n*

pal·lid \'pa-ləd\ *adj* : PALE, WAN

pal·lor \'pa-lər\ *n* : PALENESS

¹palm \'päm, 'pälm\ *n* [ME, fr. OE, fr. L *palma* palm of the hand, palm tree; fr. the resemblance of the tree's leaves to the outstretched hand] **1** : any of a family of mostly tropical trees, shrubs, or vines usu. with a tall unbranched stem topped by a crown of large leaves **2** : a symbol of victory; *also* : VICTORY

²palm *n* : the underpart of the hand between the fingers and the wrist

³palm *vb* **1** : to conceal in or with the hand ⟨~ a card⟩ **2** : to impose by fraud

pal·mate \'pal-,māt, 'päl-\ *also* **pal·mat·ed** \-,mā-təd\ *adj* : resembling a hand with the fingers spread

pal·met·to \pal-'me-tō\ *n, pl* **-tos** *or* **-toes** : any of several usu. small palms with fan-shaped leaves

palm·ist·ry \'pä-mə-strē, 'päl-\ *n* : the practice of reading a person's character or future from the markings on the palms — **palm·ist** \'pä-mist, 'päl-\ *n*

Palm Sunday *n* : the Sunday preceding Easter and commemorating Christ's triumphal entry into Jerusalem

palm·top \'päm-,täp, 'pälm-\ *n* : a portable computer small enough to hold in the hand

palmy \'pä-mē, 'päl-\ *adj* **palm·i·er; -est** **1** : abounding in or bearing palms **2** : FLOURISHING, PROSPEROUS

pal·o·mi·no \,pa-lə-'mē-nō\ *n, pl* **-nos** [AmerSp, fr. Sp, like a dove, fr. L *palumbinus,* fr. *palumbes,* a species of dove] : a horse with a pale cream to golden coat and cream or white mane and tail

pal·pa·ble \'pal-pə-bəl\ *adj* **1** : capable of being touched or felt : TANGIBLE **2** : OBVIOUS, PLAIN ♦ **Synonyms** PERCEPTIBLE, SENSIBLE, APPRECIABLE, TANGIBLE, DETECTABLE — **pal·pa·bly** \-blē\ *adv*

pal·pate \'pal-,pāt\ *vb* **pal·pat·ed; pal·pat·ing** : to examine by touch esp. medically — **pal·pa·tion** \pal-'pā-shən\ *n*

pal·pi·tate \'pal-pə-,tāt\ *vb* **-tat·ed; -tat·ing** : to beat rapidly and strongly : THROB — **pal·pi·ta·tion** \,pal-pə-'tā-shən\ *n*

pal·sy \'pȯl-zē\ *n, pl* **palsies** **1** : PARALYSIS **2** : a condition marked by tremor — **pal·sied** \-zēd\ *adj*

pal·ter \'pȯl-tər\ *vb* **pal·tered; pal·ter·ing** **1** : to act insincerely : EQUIVOCATE **2** : HAGGLE

pal·try \'pȯl-trē\ *adj* **pal·tri·er; -est** **1** : TRASHY ⟨a ~ pamphlet⟩ **2** : MEAN, DESPICABLE ⟨a ~ trick⟩ **3** : TRIVIAL ⟨~ excuses⟩ **4** : MEAGER, MEASLY ⟨a ~ sum⟩

pam *abbr* pamphlet

pam·pas \'pam-pəz, 'päm-, -pəs\ *n pl* : wide grassy So. American plains

pam·per \'pam-pər\ *vb* : to treat with excessive attention : INDULGE ♦ **Synonyms** CODDLE, HUMOR, BABY, SPOIL

pam·phlet \'pam-flət\ *n* [ME *pamflet* unbound booklet, fr. *Pamphilus seu De Amore* Pamphilus or On Love, popular Latin love poem of the 12th cent.] : an unbound printed publication

pam·phle·teer \,pam-flə-'tir\ *n* : a writer of pamphlets attacking something or urging a cause

¹pan \'pan\ *n* **1** : a usu. broad, shallow, and open container for domestic use; *also* : something resembling such a container **2** : a basin or depression in land **3** : HARDPAN

²pan *vb* **panned; pan·ning** **1** : to wash earth or gravel in a pan in searching for gold **2** : to criticize severely

Pan *abbr* Panama

pan·a·cea \,pa-nə-'sē-ə\ *n* : a remedy for all ills or difficulties : CURE-ALL

pa·nache \pə-'nash, -'näsh\ *n* [MF *pennache,* ultim. fr. LL *pinnaculum* small wing] **1** : an ornamental tuft (as of feathers) esp. on a helmet **2** : dash or flamboyance in style and action

pan·a·ma \'pa-nə-,mä, -,mȯ\ *n, often cap* : a handmade hat braided from strips of the leaves from a tropical American tree

pan·a·tela \,pa-nə-'te-lə\ *n* : a long slender cigar with straight sides

pan·cake \'pan-ˌkāk\ *n* : a flat cake made of thin batter and fried on both sides

pan·chro·mat·ic \ˌpan-krō-'ma-tik\ *adj* : sensitive to all colors of visible light 〈~ film〉

pan·cre·as \'paŋ-krē-əs, 'pan-\ *n* : a large compound gland of vertebrates that produces insulin and discharges enzymes into the intestine — **pan·cre·at·ic** \ˌpaŋ-krē-'a-tik, ˌpan-\ *adj*

pan·da \'pan-də\ *n* **1** : a long-tailed reddish brown Himalayan mammal related to and resembling the racoon **2** : a large black-and-white mammal of China usu. classified with the bears

pan·dem·ic \pan-'de-mik\ *n* : a widespread outbreak of disease — **pandemic** *adj*

pan·de·mo·ni·um \ˌpan-də-'mō-nē-əm\ *n* : a wild uproar : TUMULT

¹pan·der \'pan-dər\ *vb* : to act as a pander

²pander *n* **1** : a go-between in love intrigues; *also* : PIMP **2** : a person who caters to or exploits others' desires or weaknesses

P & I *abbr* principal and interest

P & L *abbr* profit and loss

Pan·do·ra's box \pan-'dȯr-əz-\ *n* : a prolific source of troubles

pan·dow·dy \pan-'daù-dē\ *n, pl* **-dies** : a deep-dish apple dessert spiced, sweetened, and covered with a crust

pane \'pān\ *n* : a sheet of glass (as in a door or window)

pan·e·gyr·ic \ˌpa-nə-'jir-ik\ *n* : a eulogistic oration or writing — **pan·e·gyr·ist** \-'jir-ist\ *n*

¹pan·el \'pa-nᵊl\ *n* [ME, piece of cloth, jury list on a piece of parchment, fr. AF, fr. VL *pannellus, dim. of L pannus cloth, rag]* **1** : a list of persons appointed for special duty 〈a jury ~〉; *also* : a group of people taking part in a discussion or quiz program **2** : a section of something (as a wall or door) often sunk below the level of the frame; *also* : a flat piece of construction material **3** : a flat piece of wood on which a picture is painted **4** : a mount for controls or dials

²panel *vb* **-eled** *or* **-elled; -el·ing** *or* **-el·ling** : to decorate with panels

paneling *n* : decorative panels

pan·el·ist \'pa-nᵊl-ist\ *n* : a member of a discussion or quiz panel

panel truck *n* : a small motortruck with a fully enclosed body

pang \'paŋ\ *n* : a sudden sharp spasm (as of pain) or attack (as of remorse)

¹pan·han·dle \'pan-ˌhan-dᵊl\ *n* : a narrow projection of a larger territory (as a state) 〈the Texas ~〉

²panhandle *vb* **-dled; -dling** : to ask for money on the street — **pan·han·dler** *n*

¹pan·ic \'pa-nik\ *n* : a sudden overpowering fright; *also* : extreme anxiety 〈a ~ disorder〉 〈~ attacks〉 ♦ **Synonyms** TERROR, CONSTERNATION, DISMAY, ALARM, DREAD, FEAR — **pan·icky** \-ni-kē\ *adj*

²panic *vb* **pan·icked** \-nikt\; **pan·ick·ing** : to affect or be affected with panic

pan·i·cle \'pa-ni-kəl\ *n* : a branched flower cluster (as of a lilac) in which each branch from the main stem has one or more flowers

pan·jan·drum \pan-'jan-drəm\ *n, pl* **-drums** *also* **-dra** \-drə\ : a powerful personage or pretentious official

pan·nier *also* **pan·ier** \'pan-yər\ *n* : a large basket esp. for bearing on the back

pan·o·ply \'pa-nə-plē\ *n, pl* **-plies** **1** : a full suit of armor **2** : a protective covering **3** : an impressive array

pan·ora·ma \ˌpa-nə-'ra-mə, -'rä-\ *n* **1** : a picture unrolled before one's eyes **2** : a complete view in every direction — **pan·oram·ic** \-'ra-mik\ *adj*

pan out *vb* : TURN OUT; *esp* : SUCCEED

pan·sy \'pan-zē\ *n, pl* **pansies** [ME *pancy, pensee, fr. MF pensée, fr. pensée thought, fr. penser to think, fr. L pensare to ponder]* : a low-growing garden herb related to the violet; *also* : its showy flower

¹pant \'pant\ *vb* [ME, fr. AF *panteiser, fr. VL *phantasiare to have hallucinations, fr. Gk phantasioun, fr. phantasia appearance, imagination]* **1** : to breathe in a labored manner **2** : YEARN **3** : THROB

²pant *n* : a panting breath or sound

³pant *n* **1** : an outer garment covering each leg separately

and usu. extending from the waist to the ankle — usu. used in pl. **2** *pl* : PANTIE

pan·ta·loons \ˌpan-tə-'lünz\ *n pl* **1** : close-fitting pants of the 19th century usu. having straps passing under the instep **2** : loose-fitting usu. shorter than ankle-length trousers

pan·the·ism \'pan-thē-ˌi-zəm\ *n* : a doctrine that equates God with the forces and laws of the universe — **pan·the·ist** \-ist\ *n* — **pan·the·is·tic** \ˌpan-thē-'is-tik\ *adj*

pan·the·on \'pan-thē-ˌän, -ən\ *n* **1** : a temple dedicated to all the gods; *also* : the gods of a people **2** : a group of illustrious people

pan·ther \'pan-thər\ *n, pl* **panthers** *also* **panther** **1** : LEOPARD; *esp* : a black one **2** : COUGAR **3** : JAGUAR

pant·ie *or* **panty** \'pan-tē\ *n, pl* **pant·ies** : a woman's or child's short underpants — usu. used in pl.

pan·to·mime \'pan-tə-ˌmīm\ *n* **1** : a play in which the actors use no words **2** : expression of something by bodily or facial movements only — **pantomime** *vb* — **pan·to·mim·ic** \ˌpan-tə-'mi-mik\ *adj*

pan·try \'pan-trē\ *n, pl* **pantries** : a storage room for food or dishes

pant·suit \'pant-ˌsüt\ *n* : a woman's outfit consisting usu. of a long jacket and pants of the same material

panty hose *n pl* : a one-piece undergarment for women consisting of hosiery combined with a pantie

panty·waist \'pan-tē-ˌwāst\ *n* : SISSY

pap \'pap\ *n* : soft food for infants or invalids

pa·pa \'pä-pə\ *n* : FATHER

pa·pa·cy \'pā-pə-sē\ *n, pl* **-cies** **1** : the office of pope **2** : a succession of popes **3** : the term of a pope's reign **4** *cap* : the system of government of the Roman Catholic Church

pa·pa·in \pə-'pā-ən, -'pī-ən\ *n* : an enzyme in papaya juice used esp. as a meat tenderizer and in medicine

pa·pal \'pā-pəl\ *adj* : of or relating to the pope or to the Roman Catholic Church

papaw *var of* PAWPAW

pa·pa·ya \pə-'pī-ə\ *n* : a tropical American tree with large yellow black-seeded edible fruit; *also* : its fruit

pa·per \'pā-pər\ *n* [ME *papir, fr. AF, fr. L papyrus papyrus, paper, fr. Gk papyros papyrus]* **1** : a pliable substance made usu. of vegetable matter and used to write or print on, to wrap things in, or to cover walls; *also* : a single sheet of this substance **2** : a printed or written document **3** : NEWSPAPER **4** : WALLPAPER — **paper** *adj or vb* — **pa·pery** \'pā-pə-rē\ *adj*

pa·per·back \-ˌbak\ *n* : a paper-covered book

pa·per·board \-ˌbȯrd\ *n* : CARDBOARD

pa·per·hang·er \'pā-pər-ˌhaŋ-ər\ *n* : one that applies wallpaper — **pa·per·hang·ing** *n*

pa·per·weight \-ˌwāt\ *n* : an object used to hold down loose papers by its weight

pa·pier–mâ·ché \ˌpā-pər-mə-'shā, ˌpa-ˌpyā-mə-, -ma-\ *n* [F, lit., chewed paper] : a molding material of wastepaper and additives (as glue) — **papier–mâché** *adj*

pa·pil·la \pə-'pi-lə\ *n, pl* **-lae** \-(ˌ)lē, -ˌlī\ [L, nipple] : a small projecting bodily part (as one of the nubs on the surface of the tongue) that resembles a tiny nipple in form — **pap·il·lary** \'pa-pə-ˌler-ē, pə-'pi-lə-rē\ *adj*

pa·poose \pa-'püs, pə-\ *n* [Narragansett *papoòs]* : a young child of No. American Indian parents

pa·pri·ka \pə-'prē-kə, pa-\ *n* [Hung] : a mild red spice made from the fruit of various cultivated sweet peppers

Pap smear \'pap-\ *n* : a method for the early detection of cancer esp. of the uterine cervix

Pap test *n* : PAP SMEAR

pap·ule \'pa-pyül\ *n* : a small solid usu. conical elevation of the skin — **pap·u·lar** \-pyə-lər\ *adj*

pa·py·rus \pə-'pī-rəs\ *n, pl* **-ri** \-(ˌ)rē, -ˌrī\ *or* **-rus·es** **1** : a tall grassy sedge of the Nile valley **2** : paper made from papyrus pith

¹par \'pär\ *n* **1** : a stated value (as of a security) **2** : a common level : EQUALITY **3** : an accepted standard or normal condition **4** : the score standard set for each hole of a golf course — **par** *adj*

²par *abbr* **1** paragraph **2** parallel **3** parish

par·a·ble \'pa-rə-bəl\ *n* : a simple story told to illustrate a moral truth

pa·rab·o·la \pə-'ra-bə-lə\ *n* : a plane curve formed by a point moving so that its distance from a fixed point is equal to its distance from a fixed line — **par·a·bol·ic** \ˌpar-ə-ˈbä-lik\ *adj*

para·chute \ˈpa-rə-ˌshüt\ *n* [F, fr. *para*- (as in *parasol*) + *chute* fall] : a device for slowing the descent of a person or object through the air that consists of a usu. hemispherical canopy beneath which the person or object is suspended — **parachute** *vb* — **para·chut·ist** \-ˈshü-tist\ *n*

parachute pants *n pl* : baggy casual pants of lightweight fabric

¹**pa·rade** \pə-ˈrād\ *n* **1** : a pompous display : EXHIBITION **2** : MARCH, PROCESSION; *esp* : a ceremonial formation and march **3** : a place for strolling

²**parade** *vb* **pa·rad·ed; pa·rad·ing 1** : to march in a parade **2** : PROMENADE **3** : SHOW OFF ⟨*paraded* her knowledge⟩ **4** : MASQUERADE

par·a·digm \ˈpa-rə-ˌdīm, -ˌdim\ *n* **1** : MODEL, PATTERN **2** : a systematic inflection of a verb or noun showing a complete conjugation or declension — **par·a·dig·mat·ic** \ˌpa-rə-dig-ˈma-tik\ *adj*

par·a·dise \ˈpa-rə-ˌdīs, -ˌdīz\ *n* [ME *paradis*, fr. AF, fr. LL *paradisus*, fr. Gk *paradeisos*, lit., enclosed park, of Iranian origin] **1** : HEAVEN **2** : a place or state of bliss

par·a·di·si·a·cal \ˌpa-rə-də-ˈsī-ə-kəl\ *or* **par·a·dis·i·ac** \-ˈdi-zē-ˌak, -sē-\ *adj* : of, relating to, or resembling paradise

par·a·dox \ˈpa-rə-ˌdäks\ *n* : a statement that seems contrary to common sense and yet is perhaps true — **par·a·dox·i·cal** \ˌpa-rə-ˈdäk-si-kəl\ *adj* — **par·a·dox·i·cal·ly** \-k(ə-)lē\ *adv*

par·af·fin \ˈpa-rə-fən\ *n* : a waxy substance used esp. for making candles and sealing foods

para·glid·ing \ˈpa-rə-ˌglī-diŋ\ *n* : the sport of soaring from a slope or cliff using a modified parachute

par·a·gon \ˈpa-rə-ˌgän, -gən\ *n* : a model of perfection : PATTERN

¹**para·graph** \ˈpa-rə-ˌgraf\ *n* : a subdivision of a written composition that deals with one point or gives the words of one speaker; *also* : a character (as ¶) marking the beginning of a paragraph

²**paragraph** *vb* : to divide into paragraphs

par·a·keet \ˈpa-rə-ˌkēt\ *n* : any of numerous usu. small slender parrots with a long graduated tail

para·le·gal \ˌpa-rə-ˈlē-gəl\ *adj* : of, relating to, or being a paraprofessional who assists a lawyer — **paralegal** *n*

Par·a·li·pom·e·non \ˌpa-rə-lə-ˈpä-mə-ˌnän\ *n* : CHRONICLES

par·al·lax \ˈpa-rə-ˌlaks\ *n* : the difference in apparent direction of an object as seen from two different points

¹**par·al·lel** \ˈpa-rə-ˌlel\ *adj* [L *parallelus*, fr. Gk *parallēlos*, fr. *para* beside + *allēlōn* of one another, fr. *allos* . . . *allos* one . . . another, fr. *allos* other] **1** : lying or moving in the same direction but always the same distance apart **2** : similar in essential parts — **par·al·lel·ism** \-ˌle-ˌli-zəm\ *n*

²**parallel** *n* **1** : a parallel line, curve, or surface **2** : one of the imaginary circles on the earth's surface that parallel the equator and mark the latitude **3** : something essentially similar to another **4** : SIMILARITY, LIKENESS

³**parallel** *vb* **1** : COMPARE **2** : to correspond to **3** : to extend in a parallel direction with

par·al·lel·o·gram \ˌpa-rə-ˈle-lə-ˌgram\ *n* : a 4-sided geometric figure with opposite sides equal and parallel

par·a·lyse *Brit var of* PARALYZE

pa·ral·y·sis \pə-ˈra-lə-səs\ *n, pl* **-y·ses** \-ˌsēz\ : complete or partial loss of function esp. when involving the motion or sensation in a part of the body — **par·a·lyt·ic** \ˌpa-rə-ˈli-tik\ *adj or n*

par·a·lyze \ˈpa-rə-ˌlīz\ *vb* **-lyzed; -lyz·ing 1** : to affect with paralysis **2** : to make powerless or inactive — **par·a·lyz·ing·ly** *adv*

par·a·me·cium \ˌpa-rə-ˈmē-shəm, -shē-əm, -sē-əm\ *n, pl* **-cia** \-shə, -shē-ə, -sē-ə\ *also* **-ciums** : any of a genus of slipper-shaped protozoans that move by cilia

para·med·ic \ˌpa-rə-ˈme-dik\ *also* **para·med·i·cal** \-di-kəl\ *n* **1** : a person who assists a physician in a paramedical capacity **2** : a specially trained medical technician licensed to provide a wide range of emergency services before or during transportation to a hospital

para·med·i·cal \ˌpa-rə-ˈme-di-kəl\ *also* **para·med·ic** \-ˈme-dik\ *adj* : concerned with supplementing the work of trained medical professionals

pa·ram·e·ter \pə-ˈra-mə-tər\ *n* **1** : a quantity whose value characterizes a statistical population or a member of a

system (as a family of curves) **2** : a physical property whose value determines the characteristics or behavior of a system **3** : a characteristic element : FACTOR — **para·met·ric** \ˌpa-rə-ˈme-trik\ *adj*

para·mil·i·tary \ˌpa-rə-ˈmi-lə-ˌter-ē\ *adj* : formed on a military pattern esp. as an auxiliary military force

par·a·mount \ˈpa-rə-ˌmaunt\ *adj* : superior to all others : SUPREME ♦ **Synonyms** PREPONDERANT, PREDOMINANT, DOMINANT, CHIEF, SOVEREIGN

par·amour \ˈpa-rə-ˌmur\ *n* : an illicit lover

para·noia \ˌpa-rə-ˈnoi-ə\ *n* : a psychosis marked by delusions and irrational suspicion usu. without hallucinations — **par·a·noid** \ˈpa-rə-ˌnoid\ *adj or n*

para·nor·mal \ˌpa-rə-ˈnor-məl\ *adj* : not scientifically explainable : SUPERNATURAL

par·a·pet \ˈpa-rə-pət, -ˌpet\ *n* **1** : a protecting rampart **2** : a low wall or railing (as at the edge of a bridge)

parapet 1

par·a·pher·na·lia \ˌpa-rə-fə-ˈnāl-yə, -fər-\ *n sing or pl* **1** : personal belongings **2** : EQUIPMENT, APPARATUS

para·phrase \ˈpa-rə-ˌfrāz\ *n* : a restatement of a text giving the meaning in different words — **paraphrase** *vb*

para·ple·gia \ˌpa-rə-ˈplē-jə, -jē-ə\ *n* : paralysis of the lower trunk and legs — **para·ple·gic** \-jik\ *adj or n*

para·pro·fes·sion·al \-prə-ˈfe-shə-nəl\ *n* : a trained aide who assists a professional — **paraprofessional** *adj*

para·psy·chol·o·gy \ˌpa-rə-sī-ˈkä-lə-jē\ *n* : a field of study concerned with investigating paranormal psychological phenomena (as extrasensory perception) — **para·psy·chol·o·gist** \-jist\ *n*

par·a·site \ˈpa-rə-ˌsīt\ *n* [MF, fr. L *parasitus*, fr. Gk *parasitos*, fr. *para*- beside + *sitos* grain, food] **1** : a plant or animal living in, with, or on another organism usu. to its harm **2** : one depending on another and not making adequate return — **par·a·sit·ic** \ˌpa-rə-ˈsi-tik\ *adj* — **par·a·sit·ism** \ˈpa-rə-sə-ˌti-zəm, -ˌsī-ˌti-\ *n* — **par·a·sit·ize** \-sə-ˌtīz\ *vb*

par·a·si·tol·o·gy \ˌpa-rə-sə-ˈtä-lə-jē\ *n* : a branch of biology dealing with parasites and parasitism esp. among animals — **par·a·si·tol·o·gist** \-jist\ *n*

para·sol \ˈpa-rə-ˌsol\ *n* [F, fr. It *parasole*, fr. *parare* to shield + *sole* sun, fr. L *sol*] : a lightweight umbrella used as a shield against the sun

para·sym·pa·thet·ic nervous system \ˌpa-rə-ˌsim-pə-ˈthe-tik-\ *n* : the part of the autonomic nervous system that tends to induce secretion, to increase the tone and contractility of smooth muscle, and to slow heart rate

para·thi·on \ˌpa-rə-ˈthī-ən, -ˌän\ *n* : an extremely toxic insecticide

para·thy·roid \-ˈthī-ˌroid\ *n* : PARATHYROID GLAND — **parathyroid** *adj*

parathyroid gland *n* : any of usu. four small endocrine glands adjacent to or embedded in the thyroid gland that produce a hormone (**parathyroid hormone**) concerned with calcium and phosphorus metabolism

para·tran·sit \ˌpa-rə-ˈtran-sət, -zət\ *n* : transportation service that provides individualized rules without fixed routes or timetables

para·troop·er \ˈpa-rə-ˌtrü-pər\ *n* : a member of the paratroops

para·troops \-ˌtrüps\ *n pl* : troops trained to parachute from an airplane

para·ty·phoid \ˌpa-rə-ˈtī-ˌfoid\ *n* : a bacterial food poisoning resembling typhoid fever

par·boil \'pär-ˌbȯi(-ə)l\ *vb* : to boil briefly

¹par·cel \'pär-səl\ *n* 1 : a tract or plot of land 2 : COL-LECTION, LOT ⟨the story was a ~ of lies⟩ 3 : a wrapped bundle : PACKAGE

²parcel *vb* **-celed** *or* **-celled; -cel·ing** *or* **-cel·ling** : to divide into portions

parcel post *n* 1 : a mail service handling parcels 2 : packages handled by parcel post

parch \'pärch\ *vb* 1 : to toast under dry heat 2 : to shrivel with heat

parch·ment \'pärch-mənt\ *n* : the skin of an animal prepared for writing on; *also* : a writing on such material

pard \'pärd\ *n* : LEOPARD

¹par·don \'pär-dᵊn\ *n* : excuse of an offense without penalty; *esp* : an official release from legal punishment

²pardon *vb* : to free from penalty : EXCUSE, FORGIVE — **par·don·able** \'pär-dᵊn-ə-bəl\ *adj*

par·don·er \'pär-dᵊn-ər\ *n* 1 : a medieval preacher delegated to raise money for religious works by soliciting offerings and granting indulgences 2 : one that pardons

pare \'per\ *vb* **pared; par·ing** 1 : to trim off an outside part (as the skin or rind) of 2 : to reduce as if by paring ⟨~ expenses⟩ — **par·er** *n*

par·e·gor·ic \ˌper-ə-'gȯr-ik\ *n* : an alcoholic preparation of opium and camphor used esp. to relieve pain

par·ent \'per-ənt\ *n* 1 : one that begets or brings forth offspring : FATHER, MOTHER 2 : one who brings up and cares for another 3 : SOURCE, ORIGIN — **par·ent·age** \-ən-tij\ *n* — **pa·ren·tal** \pə-'ren-tᵊl\ *adj* — **par·ent·hood** *n*

pa·ren·the·sis \pə-'ren-thə-səs\ *n, pl* **-the·ses** \-ˌsēz\ 1 : a word, phrase, or sentence inserted in a passage to explain or modify the thought 2 : one of a pair of punctuation marks ( ) used esp. to enclose parenthetic matter — **par·en·thet·ic** \ˌper-ən-'the-tik\ *or* **par·en·thet·i·cal** \-ti-kəl\ *adj* — **par·en·thet·i·cal·ly** \-k(ə-)lē\ *adv*

pa·ren·the·size \pə-'ren-thə-ˌsīz\ *vb* **-sized; -siz·ing** : to make a parenthesis of

par·ent·ing \'per-ən-tiŋ\ *n* : the raising of a child by its parents

pa·re·sis \pə-'rē-səs, 'par-ə-\ *n, pl* **pa·re·ses** \-ˌsēz\ : a usu. incomplete paralysis; *also* : insanity caused by syphilitic alteration of the brain that leads to dementia and paralysis

par ex·cel·lence \ˌpär-ˌek-sə-'läⁿs\ *adj* [F, lit., by excellence] : being the best of a kind : PREEMINENT

par·fait \pär-'fā\ *n* [F, lit., something perfect] : a cold dessert made of layers of fruit, syrup, ice cream, and whipped cream

pa·ri·ah \pə-'rī-ə\ *n* : OUTCAST

pa·ri·etal \pə-'rī-ə-tᵊl\ *adj* 1 : of, relating to, or forming the walls of an anatomical structure 2 : of or relating to college living or its regulation

pari·mu·tu·el \ˌper-i-'myü-chə-wəl\ *n* : a betting system in which winners share the total stakes minus a percentage for the management

paring *n* : a pared-off piece

pa·ri pas·su \ˌpa-ri-'pa-sü\ *adv or adj* [L, with equal step] : at an equal rate or pace

par·ish \'per-ish\ *n* 1 : a church district in the care of one pastor; *also* : the residents of such an area 2 : a local church community 3 : a civil division of the state of Louisiana : COUNTY

pa·rish·io·ner \pə-'ri-shə-nər\ *n* : a member or resident of a parish

par·i·ty \'per-ə-tē\ *n, pl* **-ties** : EQUALITY, EQUIVALENCE

¹park \'pärk\ *n* 1 : a tract of ground kept as a game preserve or recreation area 2 : a place where vehicles (as automobiles) are parked 3 : an enclosed stadium used esp. for ball games

²park *vb* 1 : to leave a vehicle temporarily (as in a parking lot or garage) 2 : to set and leave temporarily

par·ka \'pär-kə\ *n* : a very warm jacket with a hood

Par·kin·son's disease \'pär-kən-sənz-\ *n* : a chronic progressive neurological disease chiefly of later life marked esp. by tremor and weakness of resting muscles and by a shuffling gait

Parkinson's Law *n* : an observation in office organization: work expands so as to fill the time available for its completion

park·way \'pärk-ˌwā\ *n* : a broad landscaped thoroughfare

par·lance \'pär-ləns\ *n* 1 : SPEECH 2 : manner of speaking ⟨military ~⟩

¹par·lay \'pär-ˌlā, -lē\ *vb* : to increase or change into something of much greater value

²parlay *n* : a series of bets in which the original stake plus its winnings are risked on successive wagers

par·ley \'pär-lē\ *n, pl* **parleys** : a conference usu. over matters in dispute : DISCUSSION — **parley** *vb*

par·lia·ment \'pär-lə-mənt\ *n* [ME, fr. AF *parlement*, fr. *parler* to speak, fr. ML *parabolare*, fr. LL *parabola* speech, parable] 1 : a formal governmental conference 2 *cap* : an assembly that constitutes the supreme legislative body of a country (as the United Kingdom) — **par·lia·men·ta·ry** \ˌpär-lə-'men-tə-rē\ *adj*

par·lia·men·tar·i·an \ˌpär-lə-ˌmen-'ter-ē-ən\ *n* 1 *often cap* : an adherent of the parliament during the English Civil War 2 : an expert in parliamentary procedure

par·lor \'pär-lər\ *n* 1 : a room for conversation or the reception of guests 2 : a place of business ⟨beauty ~⟩

par·lour \'pär-lər\ *chiefly Brit var of* PARLOR

par·lous \'pär-ləs\ *adj* : full of danger or risk : PRECARIOUS — **par·lous·ly** *adv*

Par·me·san \'pär-mə-ˌzän, -ˌzhän, -ˌzan\ *n* : a hard dry cheese with a sharp flavor

par·mi·gia·na \ˌpär-mi-'jä-nə, ˌpär-mi-'zhän\ *or* **par·mi·gia·no** \-'jä-(ˌ)nō\ *adj* : made or covered with Parmesan cheese ⟨veal ~⟩

pa·ro·chi·al \pə-'rō-kē-əl\ *adj* 1 : of or relating to a church parish 2 : limited in scope : NARROW, PROVINCIAL — **pa·ro·chi·al·ism** \-ə-ˌli-zəm\ *n*

parochial school *n* : a school maintained by a religious body

par·o·dy \'per-ə-dē\ *n, pl* **-dies** [L *parodia*, fr. Gk *parōidia*, fr. *para-* beside + *aidein* to sing] : a humorous or satirical imitation — **parody** *vb*

pa·role \pə-'rōl\ *n* : a conditional release of a prisoner whose sentence has not expired — **parole** *vb* — **pa·rol·ee** \-ˌrō-'lē, -'rō-ˌlē\ *n*

par·ox·ysm \'pa-rək-ˌsi-zəm, pə-'räk-\ *n* : a sudden sharp attack (as of pain or coughing) : CONVULSION — **par·ox·ys·mal** \ˌpa-rək-'siz-məl, pə-ˌräk-\ *adj*

par·quet \'pär-ˌkā, pär-'kā\ *n* [F] 1 : a flooring of parquetry 2 : the lower floor of a theater; *esp* : the forward part of the orchestra

par·que·try \'pär-kə-trē\ *n, pl* **-tries** : fine woodwork inlaid in patterns

par·ri·cide \'pa-rə-ˌsīd\ *n* 1 : one that murders a parent or a close relative 2 : the act of a parricide

par·rot \'per-ət\ *n* : any of numerous bright-colored tropical birds that have a stout hooked bill

parrot fever *n* : PSITTACOSIS

par·ry \'per-ē\ *vb* **par·ried; par·ry·ing** 1 : to ward off a weapon or blow 2 : to evade esp. by an adroit answer — **parry** *n*

parse \'pärs *also* 'pärz\ *vb* **parsed; pars·ing** : to give a grammatical description of a word or a group of words

par·sec \'pär-ˌsek\ *n* : a unit of measure for interstellar space equal to 3.26 light-years

par·si·mo·ny \'pär-sə-ˌmō-nē\ *n* : extreme or excessive frugality — **par·si·mo·ni·ous** \ˌpär-sə-'mō-nē-əs\ *adj* — **par·si·mo·ni·ous·ly** *adv*

pars·ley \'pär-slē\ *n* : a garden plant related to the carrot that has finely divided leaves used as a seasoning or garnish; *also* : the leaves

pars·nip \'pär-snəp\ *n* : a garden plant related to the carrot that has a long edible usu. whitish root which is cooked as a vegetable; *also* : the root

par·son \'pär-sᵊn\ *n* [ME *persone*, fr. AF, fr. ML *persona*, lit., person, fr. L] : MINISTER 2, PASTOR

par·son·age \'pär-sə-nij\ *n* : a house provided by a church for its pastor

¹part \'pärt\ *n* 1 : a division or portion of a whole 2 : the melody or score for a particular voice or instrument 3 : a spare piece for a machine 4 : DUTY, FUNCTION 5 : one of the sides in a dispute 6 : ROLE; *also* : an actor's lines in a play 7 *pl* : TALENTS, ABILITY ⟨a man of many ~s⟩ 8 : the line where one's hair divides (as in combing)

²part *vb* 1 : to take leave of someone 2 : to divide or break into parts : SEPARATE 3 : to go away : DEPART; *also* : DIE 4 : to give up possession ⟨~ed with her jewels⟩ 5 : APPORTION, SHARE

³**part** *abbr* **1** participial; participle **2** particular

par·take \pär-'tāk\ *vb* **-took** \-'tůk\; **-tak·en** \-'tā-kən\; **-tak·ing 1** : to have a share or part **2** : to take a portion (as of food) — **par·tak·er** *n*

par·terre \pär-'ter\ *n* [F, fr. MF, fr. *par terre* on the ground] **1** : an ornamental garden with paths between the flower beds **2** : the part of a theater floor behind the orchestra

par·the·no·gen·e·sis \pär-thə-nō-'je-nə-səs\ *n* [NL, fr. Gk *parthenos* virgin + L *genesis* genesis] : development of a new individual from an unfertilized usu. female sex cell — **par·the·no·ge·net·ic** \-jə-'ne-tik\ *adj*

par·tial \'pär-shəl\ *adj* **1** : not total or general : affecting a part only **2** : favoring one party over the other : BIASED **3** : markedly fond — used with *to* — **par·tial·i·ty** \pär-shē-'a-lə-tē\ *n* — **par·tial·ly** *adv*

par·tic·i·pate \pär-'ti-sə-ˌpāt\ *vb* **-pat·ed; -pat·ing 1** : to take part in something ⟨~ in a game⟩ **2** : SHARE — **par·tic·i·pant** \-pənt\ *adj or n* — **par·tic·i·pa·tion** \-ˌti-sə-'pā-shən\ *n* — **par·tic·i·pa·tor** \-'ti-sə-ˌpā-tər\ *n* — **par·tic·i·pa·to·ry** \-'ti-sə-pə-ˌtȯr-ē\ *adj*

par·ti·ci·ple \'pär-tə-ˌsi-pəl\ *n* : a word having the characteristics of both verb and adjective — **par·ti·cip·i·al** \pär-tə-'si-pē-əl\ *adj*

par·ti·cle \'pär-ti-kəl\ *n* **1** : a very small bit of matter **2** : a unit of speech (as an article, preposition, or conjunction) expressing some general aspect of meaning or some connective or limiting relation

par·ti·cle·board \-ˌbȯrd\ *n* : a board made of very small pieces of wood bonded together

par·ti–col·or \ˌpär-tē-'kə-lər\ *or* **par·ti–col·ored** \-lərd\ *adj* : showing different colors or tints; *esp* : having one main color broken by patches of one or more other colors

¹**par·tic·u·lar** \pər-'ti-kyə-lər\ *adj* **1** : of or relating to a specific person or thing ⟨the laws of a ~ state⟩ **2** : DISTINCTIVE, SPECIAL ⟨the ~ point of his talk⟩ **3** : SEPARATE, INDIVIDUAL ⟨each ~ hair⟩ **4** : attentive to details : PRECISE **5** : hard to please : EXACTING — **par·tic·u·lar·i·ty** \-ˌti-kyə-'lar-ə-tē\ *n* — **par·tic·u·lar·ly** *adv*

²**particular** *n* : an individual fact or detail

par·tic·u·lar·ise *Brit var of* PARTICULARIZE

par·tic·u·lar·ize \pər-'ti-kyə-lə-ˌrīz\ *vb* **-ized; -iz·ing 1** : to state in detail : SPECIFY **2** : to go into details

par·tic·u·late \pər-'ti-kyə-lət, pär-, -ˌlāt\ *adj* : relating to or existing as minute separate particles — **particulate** *n*

¹**part·ing** *n* : a place or point of separation or divergence

²**parting** *adj* : given, taken, or done at parting ⟨a ~ kiss⟩

par·ti·san *also* **par·ti·zan** \'pär-tə-zən, -sən\ *n* **1** : one that takes the part of another : ADHERENT **2** : GUERRILLA — **partisan** *adj* — **par·ti·san·ship** *n*

par·tite \'pär-ˌtīt\ *adj* : divided into a usu. specified number of parts

par·ti·tion \pär-'ti-shən\ *n* **1** : DIVISION **2** : something that divides or separates; *esp* : an interior dividing wall — **partition** *vb*

par·ti·tive \'pär-tə-tiv\ *adj* : of, relating to, or denoting a part

part·ly \'pärt-lē\ *adv* : in part : in some measure or degree

part·ner \'pärt-nər\ *n* **1** : ASSOCIATE, COLLEAGUE **2** : either of two persons who dance together **3** : one who plays on the same team with another **4** : SPOUSE **5** : one of two or more persons contractually associated as joint principals in a business — **part·ner·ship** *n*

part of speech : a class of words (as nouns or verbs) distinguished according to the kind of idea denoted and the function performed in a sentence

par·tridge \'pär-trij\ *n, pl* **partridge** *or* **par·tridg·es** : any of various stout-bodied Old World game birds

part–song \'pärt-ˌsȯŋ\ *n* : a song with two or more voice parts

part–time \-'tīm\ *adj or adv* : involving or working less than a full or regular schedule — **part–tim·er** \-ˌtī-mər\ *n*

par·tu·ri·tion \ˌpär-tə-'ri-shən, ˌpär-chə-, ˌpär-tyu̇-\ *n* : CHILDBIRTH

part·way \'pärt-ˌwā\ *adv* : to some extent : PARTLY

par·ty \'pär-tē\ *n, pl* **parties 1** : a person or group taking one side of a question; *esp* : a group of persons organized for the purpose of directing the policies of a government **2** : a person or group concerned in an action or affair : PARTICIPANT **3** : a group of persons detailed for a common task **4** : a social gathering

party animal *n* : a person known for frequent attendance at parties

par·ty·go·er \'pär-tē-ˌgō-ər\ *n* : a person who attends a party or who attends parties frequently

par·ve·nu \'pär-və-ˌnü, -ˌnyü\ *n* [F, fr. pp. of *parvenir* to arrive, fr. L *pervenire*, fr. *per* through + *venire* to come] : one who has recently or suddenly risen to wealth or power but has not yet secured the social position associated with it

pas \'pä\ *n, pl* **pas** *same or* 'päz\ : a dance step or combination of steps

pas·cal \pas-'kal\ *n* : a unit of pressure in the metric system equal to one newton per square meter

pas·chal \'pas-kəl\ *adj* : of, relating to, appropriate for, or used during Passover or Easter ceremonies

pa·sha \'pä-shə, 'pa-; pə-'shä\ *n* : a man (as formerly a governor in Turkey) of high rank

pash·mi·na \ˌpȯsh-'mē-nə\ *n* : a fine wool from the undercoat of domestic Himalayan goats; *also* : a shawl made from this wool

¹**pass** \'pas\ *vb* **1** : MOVE, PROCEED **2** : to go away; *also* : DIE **3** : to move past, beyond, or over **4** : to allow to elapse : SPEND **5** : to go or make way through **6** : to go or allow to go unchallenged **7** : to undergo transfer **8** : to render a legal judgment **9** : OCCUR **10** : to secure the approval of (as a legislature) **11** : to go or cause to go through an inspection, test, or course of study successfully **12** : to be regarded **13** : CIRCULATE ⟨~ a note⟩ **14** : VOID 2 **15** : to transfer the ball or puck to another player **16** : to decline to bid or bet on one's hand in a card game **17** : to give a base on balls to **18** : to let something go by without accepting ⟨~ed on his offer⟩ — **pass·er** *n*

²**pass** *n* : a gap in a mountain range

³**pass** *n* **1** : the act or an instance of passing **2** : REALIZATION, ACCOMPLISHMENT **3** : a state of affairs **4** : a written authorization to leave, enter, or move about freely **5** : a transfer of a ball or puck from one player to another **6** : BASE ON BALLS **7** : EFFORT, TRY **8** : a sexually inviting gesture or approach

⁴**pass** *abbr* **1** passenger **2** passive

pass·able \'pa-sə-bəl\ *adj* **1** : capable of being passed or traveled on **2** : just good enough : TOLERABLE — **pass·ably** \-blē\ *adv*

pas·sage \'pa-sij\ *n* **1** : a means (as a road or corridor) of passing **2** : the action or process of passing **3** : a voyage esp. by sea or air **4** : a right or permission to pass **5** : ENACTMENT **6** : a usu. brief portion or section (as of a book)

pas·sage·way \-ˌwā\ *n* : a way that allows passage

pass·book \'pas-ˌbůk\ *n* : BANKBOOK

pas·sé \pa-'sā\ *adj* **1** : past one's prime **2** : not up-to-date : OUTMODED

pas·sel \'pa-səl\ *n* : a large number

pas·sen·ger \'pa-sⁿn-jər\ *n* : a traveler in a public or private conveyance

pass·er·by \'pa-sər-ˌbī\ *n, pl* **pass·ers·by** : one who passes by

pas·ser·ine \'pa-sə-ˌrīn\ *adj* : of or relating to the large order of birds comprising singing birds that perch

pas·sim \'pa-səm\ *adv* [L, fr. *passus* scattered, fr. pp. of *pandere* to spread] : here and there : THROUGHOUT

pass·ing *n* : the act of one that passes or causes to pass; *esp* : DEATH

pas·sion \'pa-shən\ *n* **1** *often cap* : the sufferings of Christ between the night of the Last Supper and his death **2** : strong feeling; *also, pl* : the emotions as distinguished from reason **3** : RAGE, ANGER **4** : LOVE; *also* : an object of affection or enthusiasm **5** : sexual desire — **pas·sion·ate** \'pa-shə-nət\ *adj* — **pas·sion·ate·ly** *adv* — **pas·sion·less** *adj*

pas·sion·flow·er \'pa-shən-ˌflaů-(ə)r\ *n* [fr. the fancied resemblance of parts of the flower to the instruments of Christ's crucifixion] : any of a genus of chiefly tropical woody climbing vines or erect herbs with showy flowers and pulpy often edible berries (**passion fruit**)

pas·sive \'pa-siv\ *adj* **1** : not active : acted upon **2** : asserting that the grammatical subject is subjected to or affected by the action represented by the verb ⟨~ voice⟩ **3** : making use of the sun's heat usu. without the aid of mechanical devices **4** : SUBMISSIVE, PATIENT — **passive** *n* — **pas·sive·ly** *adv* — **pas·siv·i·ty** \pa-'si-və-tē\ *n*

pas·sive–ma·trix \-'mā-triks\ *adj* : of, relating to, or being on LCD in which pixels are controlled in groups

pass·key \'pas-ˌkē\ *n* : a key for opening two or more locks

pass out *vb* : to lose consciousness

Pass·over \'pas-ˌō-vər\ *n* [fr. the exemption of the Israelites from the slaughter of the firstborn in Egypt (Exod 12:23–27)] : a Jewish holiday celebrated in March or April in commemoration of the Hebrews' liberation from slavery in Egypt

pass·port \'pas-ˌpȯrt\ *n* : an official document issued by a country upon request to a citizen requesting protection during travel abroad

pass up *vb* : DECLINE, REJECT

pass·word \'pas-ˌwərd\ *n* 1 : a word or phrase that must be spoken by a person before being allowed to pass a guard 2 : a sequence of characters required for access to a computer system

¹past \'past\ *adj* 1 : AGO ⟨10 years ∼⟩ 2 : just gone or elapsed ⟨the ∼ month⟩ 3 : having existed or taken place in a period before the present : BYGONE 4 : of, relating to, or constituting a verb tense that expresses time gone by

²past *prep or adv* : BEYOND

³past *n* 1 : time gone by 2 : something that happened or was done in a former time 3 : the past tense; *also* : a verb form in it 4 : a secret past life

pas·ta \'päs-tə\ *n* [It] 1 : a paste in processed form (as macaroni) or in the form of fresh dough (as ravioli) 2 : a dish of cooked pasta

¹paste \'pāst\ *n* [ME, fr. AF, fr. LL *pasta* dough, paste] 1 : DOUGH 2 : a smooth food product made by evaporation or grinding ⟨tomato ∼⟩ 3 : a shaped dough (as spaghetti or ravioli) 4 : a preparation (as of flour and water) for sticking things together 5 : a brilliant glass used for artificial gems

²paste *vb* **past·ed; past·ing** : to cause to adhere by paste : STICK

paste·board \'pāst-ˌbȯrd\ *n* : CARDBOARD

¹pas·tel \pas-'tel\ *n* 1 : a paste made of powdered pigment; *also* : a crayon of such paste 2 : a drawing in pastel 3 : a pale or light color

²pastel *adj* 1 : of or relating to a pastel 2 : pale in color

pas·tern \'pas-tərn\ *n* : the part of a horse's foot extending from the fetlock to the top of the hoof

pas·teur·i·za·tion \ˌpas-chə-rə-'zā-shən, ˌpas-tə-\ *n* : partial sterilization of a substance (as milk) by heat or radiation — **pas·teur·ize** \'pas-chə-ˌrīz, 'pas-tə-\ *vb* — **pas·teur·iz·er** *n*

pas·tiche \pas-'tēsh\ *n* : a composition (as in literature or music) made up of selections from different works

pas·tille \pas-'tēl\ *n* : LOZENGE 2

pas·time \'pas-ˌtīm\ *n* : DIVERSION; *esp* : something that serves to make time pass agreeably

pas·tor \'pas-tər\ *n* [ME *pastour*, fr. AF, fr. L *pastor*, herdsman, fr. *pascere* to feed, pasture, nurture] : a minister or priest serving a local church or parish — **pas·tor·ate** \-tə-rət\ *n*

¹pas·to·ral \'pas-tə-rəl\ *adj* 1 : of or relating to shepherds or to rural life 2 : of or relating to spiritual guidance esp. of a congregation 3 : of or relating to the pastor of a church

²pastoral *n* : a literary work dealing with shepherds or rural life

pas·to·rale \ˌpas-tə-'räl, -'ral\ *n* [It] : a musical composition having a pastoral theme

past participle *n* : a participle that typically expresses completed action, that is one of the principal parts of the verb, and that is used in the formation of perfect tenses in the active voice and of all tenses in the passive voice

pas·tra·mi \pə-'strä-mē\ *n* [Yiddish *pastrame*] : a highly seasoned smoked beef prepared esp. from shoulder cuts

pas·try \'pā-strē\ *n, pl* **pastries** : sweet baked goods made of dough or with a crust made of enriched dough

pas·tur·age \'pas-chə-rij\ *n* : PASTURE

¹pas·ture \'pas-chər\ *n* 1 : plants (as grass) for the feeding esp. of grazing livestock 2 : land or a plot of land used for grazing

²pasture *vb* **pas·tured; pas·tur·ing** 1 : GRAZE 2 : to use as pasture

pasty \'pā-stē\ *adj* **past·i·er; -est** : resembling paste; *esp* : pallid and unhealthy in appearance

¹pat \'pat\ *n* 1 : a light tap esp. with the hand or a flat instrument; *also* : the sound made by it 2 : something (as butter) shaped into a small flat usu. square individual portion

²pat *adv* : in a pat manner : PERFECTLY

³pat *vb* **pat·ted; pat·ting** 1 : to strike lightly with a flat instrument 2 : to flatten, smooth, or put into place or shape with a pat 3 : to tap gently or lovingly with the hand

⁴pat *adj* 1 : exactly suited to the occasion : APT 2 : memorized exactly 3 : UNYIELDING ⟨stood ∼ on the issue⟩

PAT *abbr* point after touchdown

pa·ta·ca \pə-'tä-kə\ *n* — see MONEY table

¹patch \'pach\ *n* 1 : a piece used to cover a torn or worn place; *also* : one worn on a garment as an ornament or insignia 2 : a small area distinct from that about it 3 : a shield worn over the socket of an injured or missing eye

²patch *vb* 1 : to mend or cover with a patch 2 : to make of fragments 3 : to repair usu. in hasty fashion

patch·ou·li \'pa-chə-lē, pə-'chü-lē\ *n* : a heavy perfume made from the fragrant essential oil of an Asian mint; *also* : the plant itself

patch test *n* : a test for allergic sensitivity made by applying to the unbroken skin small pads soaked with the allergen to be tested

patch·work \'pach-ˌwərk\ *n* : something made of pieces of different materials, shapes, or colors

patchy \'pa-chē\ *adj* **patch·i·er; -est** : marked by or consisting of patches; *also* : irregular in appearance or quality — **patch·i·ness** \-chē-nəs\ *n*

pate \'pāt\ *n* : HEAD; *esp* : the crown of the head

pâ·té *also* **pate** \pä-'tā\ *n* [F] 1 : a meat or fish pie or patty 2 : a spread of finely chopped or pureed seasoned meat

pa·tel·la \pə-'te-lə\ *n, pl* **-lae** \-'te-(ˌ)lē, -ˌlī\ *or* **-las** [L] : KNEECAP — **pa·tel·lar** \-'te-lər\ *adj*

pat·en \'pa-tᵊn\ *n* 1 : PLATE; *esp* : one of precious metal for the eucharistic bread 2 : a thin disk

¹pa·tent \1 & 4 are 'pa-tᵊnt, Brit also 'pā-, 2 & 3 are 'pa-tᵊnt, 'pā-\ *adj* 1 : open to public inspection — used chiefly in the phrase *letters patent* 2 : free from obstruction 3 : EVIDENT, OBVIOUS 4 : protected by a patent ♦ **Synonyms** MANIFEST, DISTINCT, APPARENT, PALPABLE, PLAIN, CLEAR — **pat·ent·ly** *adv*

²pat·ent \'pa-tᵊnt, Brit also 'pā-\ *n* 1 : an official document conferring a right or privilege 2 : a document securing to an inventor for a term of years exclusive right to his or her invention 3 : something patented

³pat·ent *vb* : to secure by patent

pat·en·tee \ˌpa-tᵊn-'tē, Brit also ˌpā-\ *n* : one to whom a grant is made or a privilege secured by patent

pat·ent medicine \'pa-tᵊnt-\ *n* : a packaged nonprescription drug protected by a trademark; *also* : any proprietary drug

pa·ter·fa·mil·i·as \ˌpā-tər-fə-'mi-lē-əs\ *n, pl* **pa·tres·fa·mil·i·as** \ˌpā-ˌtrēz-\ [L] : the father of a family : the male head of a household

pa·ter·nal \pə-'tər-nᵊl\ *adj* 1 : FATHERLY 2 : related through or inherited or derived from a father — **pa·ter·nal·ly** *adv*

pa·ter·nal·ism \-nə-ˌli-zəm\ *n* : a system under which an authority treats those under its control paternally (as by regulating their conduct and supplying their needs)

¹pa·ter·ni·ty \pə-'tər-nə-tē\ *n* 1 : FATHERHOOD 2 : descent from a father

²paternity *adj* 1 : granted to a father ⟨∼ leave⟩ 2 : of or relating to the determination of paternity ⟨a ∼ suit⟩

¹path \'path, 'päth\ *n, pl* **paths** \'pathz, 'paths, 'päthz, 'päths\ 1 : a trodden way 2 : ROUTE, COURSE — **path·less** *adj*

²path *or* **pathol** *abbr* pathology

path·break·ing \'path-ˌbrā-kiŋ\ *adj* : TRAILBLAZING

pa·thet·ic \pə-'the-tik\ *adj* 1 : evoking tenderness, pity, or sorrow 2 : pitifully inadequate ⟨a ∼ performance⟩ ♦ **Synonyms** PITIFUL, PITEOUS, PITIABLE, POOR — **pa·thet·i·cal·ly** \-ti-k(ə-)lē\ *adv*

path·find·er \'path-ˌfīn-dər, 'päth-\ *n* : one that discovers a way; *esp* : one that explores untraveled regions to mark out a new route

patho·gen \'pa-thə-jən\ *n* : a specific agent (as a bacterium) causing disease — **patho·gen·ic** \ˌpa-thə-'je-nik\ *adj* — **patho·ge·nic·i·ty** \-jə-'ni-sə-tē\ *n*

pa·thog·ra·phy \pə-'thä-grə-fē\ *n* : biography focusing on a person's flaws and misfortunes

pa·thol·o·gy \pə-'thä-lə-jē\ *n, pl* **-gies** 1 : the study of the essential nature of disease 2 : the abnormality of structure and function characteristic of a disease 3 : deviation giving rise to social ills — **path·o·log·i·cal** \ˌpa-thə-'lä-ji-kəl\ *adj* — **pa·thol·o·gist** \pə-'thä-lə-jist\ *n*

pa·thos \'pā-ˌthäs, -ˌthȯs\ *n* : an element in experience or artistic representation evoking pity or compassion

path·way \'path-ˌwā, 'pàth-\ *n* : PATH

pa·tience \'pā-shəns\ *n* 1 : the capacity, habit, or fact of being patient 2 *chiefly Brit* : SOLITAIRE 2

¹**pa·tient** \'pā-shənt\ *adj* 1 : bearing pain or trials without complaint 2 : showing self-control : CALM 3 : STEADFAST, PERSEVERING — **pa·tient·ly** *adv*

²**patient** *n* : one under medical care

pa·ti·na \'pa-tə-nə, pə-'tē-\ *n, pl* **pa·ti·nas** \-nəz\ *or* **pa·ti·nae** \'pa-tə-ˌnē, -ˌnī\ 1 : a green film formed on copper and bronze by exposure to moist air 2 : a superficial covering or exterior

pa·tio \'pa-tē-ˌō, 'pä-\ *n, pl* **pa·ti·os** 1 : COURTYARD 2 : an often paved area near a dwelling used esp. for outdoor dining

pa·tois \'pa-ˌtwä\ *n, pl* **pa·tois** \-ˌtwäz\ [F] 1 : a dialect other than the standard dialect; *esp* : uneducated or provincial speech 2 : JARGON 2

pa·tri·arch \'pā-trē-ˌärk\ *n* 1 : a man revered as father or founder (as of a tribe) 2 : a venerable old man 3 : an ecclesiastical dignitary (as the bishop of an Eastern Orthodox see) — **pa·tri·ar·chal** \ˌpā-trē-'är-kəl\ *adj* — **pa·tri·arch·ate** \'pā-trē-ˌär-kət, -ˌkāt\ *n* — **pa·tri·ar·chy** \-ˌär-kē\ *n*

pa·tri·cian \pə-'tri-shən\ *n* : a person of high birth : ARISTOCRAT — **patrician** *adj*

pat·ri·cide \'pa-trə-ˌsīd\ *n* 1 : one who murders his or her own father 2 : the murder of one's own father

pat·ri·mo·ny \'pa-trə-ˌmō-nē\ *n* : something (as an estate) inherited or derived esp. from one's father : HERITAGE — **pat·ri·mo·ni·al** \ˌpa-trə-'mō-nē-əl\ *adj*

pa·tri·ot \'pā-trē-ət, -ˌät\ *n* [MF *patriote* compatriot, fr. LL *patriota*, fr. Gk *patriōtēs*, fr. *patria* lineage, fr. *patr-, patēr* father] : one who loves his or her country — **pa·tri·ot·ic** \ˌpā-trē-'ä-tik\ *adj* — **pa·tri·ot·i·cal·ly** \-ti-k(ə-)lē\ *adv* — **pa·tri·o·tism** \'pā-trē-ə-ˌti-zəm\ *n*

pa·tris·tic \pə-'tris-tik\ *adj* : of or relating to the church fathers or their writings

¹**pa·trol** \pə-'trōl\ *n* : the action of going the rounds (as of an area) for observation or the maintenance of security; *also* : a person or group performing such an action

²**patrol** *vb* **pa·trolled; pa·trol·ling** : to carry out a patrol

pa·trol·man \pə-'trōl-mən\ *n* : a police officer assigned to a beat

patrol wagon *n* : PADDY WAGON

pa·tron \'pā-trən\ *n* [ME, fr. AF, fr. ML & L; ML *patronus* patron saint, patron of a benefice, pattern, fr. L, defender, fr. *patr-, pater* father] 1 : a person chosen or named as special protector 2 : a wealthy or influential supporter ⟨~ of poets⟩; *also* : BENEFACTOR 3 : a regular client or customer ⟨diner ~s⟩

pa·tron·age \'pa-trə-nij, 'pā-\ *n* 1 : the support or influence of a patron 2 : the trade of customers 3 : control of appointment to government jobs

pa·tron·ess \'pā-trə-nəs\ *n* : a woman who is a patron

pa·tron·ise *Brit var of* PATRONIZE

pa·tron·ize \'pā-trə-ˌnīz, 'pa-\ *vb* **-ized; -iz·ing** 1 : to be a customer of 2 : to treat condescendingly, haughtily, or coolly

pat·ro·nym·ic \ˌpa-trə-'ni-mik\ *n* : a name derived from the name of one's father or a paternal ancestor usu. by the addition of an affix

pa·troon \pə-'trün\ *n* : the proprietor of a manorial estate esp. in New York under Dutch rule

pat·sy \'pat-sē\ *n, pl* **pat·sies** : a person who is easily duped or victimized

¹**pat·ter** \'pa-tər\ *vb* : to talk glibly or mechanically ◆ **Synonyms** CHATTER, PRATE, CHAT, PRATTLE, BABBLE

²**patter** *n* 1 : a specialized lingo 2 : extremely rapid talk ⟨a comedian's ~⟩

³**patter** *vb* : to strike, pat, or tap rapidly

⁴**patter** *n* : a quick succession of taps or pats ⟨the ~ of rain⟩

¹**pat·tern** \'pa-tərn\ *n* [ME *patron*, fr. AF, fr. ML *patronus*, fr. L, defender, fr. *patr-, pater* father] 1 : an ideal model 2 : something used as a model for making things ⟨a dressmaker's ~⟩ 3 : SAMPLE 4 : an artistic design 5 : CONFIGURATION 6 : a sample of a person's behaviors or characteristics ⟨a ~ of violence⟩

²**pattern** *vb* : to form according to a pattern

pat·ty *also* **pat·tie** \'pa-tē\ *n, pl* **patties** 1 : a little pie 2 : a small flat cake esp. of chopped food

pau·ci·ty \'pȯ-sə-tē\ *n* : smallness of number or quantity

paunch \'pȯnch\ *n* : a usu. large belly : POTBELLY — **paunchy** *adj*

pau·per \'pȯ-pər\ *n* : a person without means of support except from charity — **pau·per·ism** \-pə-ˌri-zəm\ *n* — **pau·per·ize** \-pə-ˌrīz\ *vb*

¹**pause** \'pȯz\ *n* 1 : a temporary stop; *also* : a period of inaction 2 : a brief suspension of the voice 3 : a sign ⌢ or above or below a musical note or rest to show it is to be prolonged 4 : a reason for pausing 5 : a function of an electronic device that pauses a recording

²**pause** *vb* **paused; paus·ing** : to stop, rest, or linger for a time

pave \'pāv\ *vb* **paved; pav·ing** : to cover (as a road) with hard material in order to smooth or firm the surface

pave·ment \'pāv-mənt\ *n* 1 : a paved surface 2 : the material with which something is paved

pa·vil·ion \pə-'vil-yən\ *n* [ME *pavilloun, pavillioun*, fr. AF, fr. L *papilion-, papilio* butterfly] 1 : a large tent 2 : a usu. open structure (as in a park) used for entertainment or shelter

pav·ing \'pā-viŋ\ *n* : PAVEMENT

¹**paw** \'pȯ\ *n* : the foot of a quadruped (as a dog or lion) having claws

²**paw** *vb* 1 : to touch or strike with a paw; *also* : to scrape with a hoof 2 : to feel or handle clumsily or rudely 3 : to flail about or grab for with the hands

pawl \'pȯl\ *n* : a pivoted tongue or sliding bolt designed to fall into notches on another machine part to permit motion in one direction only

¹**pawn** \'pȯn\ *n* [ME *pown*, fr. AF *peoun, paun*, fr. ML *pedon-, pedo* foot soldier, fr. LL, one with broad feet, fr. L *ped-, pes* foot] 1 : a chess piece of the least value 2 : one used for the purposes of another

²**pawn** *n* 1 : something deposited as security for a loan; *also* : HOSTAGE 2 : the state of being pledged

³**pawn** *vb* : to deposit as a pledge

pawn·bro·ker \'pȯn-ˌbrō-kər\ *n* : one who lends money on goods pledged

Paw·nee \pȯ-'nē\ *n, pl* **Pawnee** *or* **Pawnees** : a member of an American Indian people orig. of Kansas and Nebraska

pawn·shop \'pȯn-ˌshäp\ *n* : a pawnbroker's place of business

paw·paw *also* **pa·paw** 1 \pə-'pȯ\ : PAPAYA 2 \'pä-ˌpȯ, 'pȯ-\ : a No. American tree with green-skinned edible fruit; *also* : its fruit

¹**pay** \'pā\ *vb* **paid** \'pād\ *also in sense 7* **payed; pay·ing** [ME, fr. AF *paier*, fr. L *pacare* to pacify, fr. *pac-, pax* peace] 1 : to make due return to for goods or services 2 : to discharge indebtedness for : SETTLE ⟨~ a bill⟩ 3 : to give in forfeit ⟨~ the penalty⟩ 4 : REQUITE 5 : to give, offer, or make freely or as fitting ⟨~ attention⟩ 6 : to be profitable to : RETURN 7 : to make slack and allow to run out ⟨~ out a rope⟩ — **pay·able** *adj* — **pay·ee** \pā-'ē\ *n* — **pay·er** *n*

²**pay** *n* 1 : something paid; *esp* : WAGES 2 : the status of being paid by an employer : EMPLOY

³**pay** *adj* 1 : containing something valuable (as gold) ⟨~ dirt⟩ 2 : equipped to receive a fee for use ⟨~ telephone⟩ 3 : requiring payment

pay·back \'pā-ˌbak\ *n* 1 : a return on an investment equal to the original capital outlay 2 : something given in return, compensation, or retaliation

pay·check \'pā-ˌchek\ *n* 1 : a check in payment of wages or salary 2 : WAGES, SALARY

pay·load \-ˌlōd\ *n* : the load carried by a vehicle in addition to what is necessary for its operation; *also* : the weight of such a load

pay·mas·ter \-ˌmas-tər\ *n* : one who distributes the payroll

pay·ment \'pā-mənt\ *n* **1** : the act of paying **2** : something paid

pay-off \-ˌȯf\ *n* **1** : PROFIT, REWARD; *also* : RETRIBUTION **2** : the climax of an incident or enterprise ⟨the ∼ of a story⟩

pay–per–view *n* : a cable television service by which customers can order access to a single airing of a TV feature

pay·roll \-ˌrōl\ *n* : a list of persons entitled to receive pay; *also* : the money to pay those on such a list

payt *abbr* payment

pay up *vb* : to pay what is due; *also* : to pay in full

Pb *symbol* [L *plumbum*] lead

PBS *abbr* Public Broadcasting Service

PBX \ˌpē-(ˌ)bē-'eks\ *n* [*private branch exchange*] : a private telephone switchboard

¹PC \ˌpē-'sē\ *n, pl* **PCs** *or* **PC's** [*personal computer*] : MICROCOMPUTER

²PC *abbr* **1** Peace Corps **2** percent; percentage **3** politically correct **4** postcard **5** [L *post cibum*] after meals **6** professional corporation

PCB \ˌpē-ˌsē-'bē\ *n* : POLYCHLORINATED BIPHENYL

PCP \ˌpē-ˌsē-'pē\ *n* : PHENCYCLIDINE

pct *abbr* percent; percentage

pd *abbr* paid

Pd *symbol* palladium

PD *abbr* **1** per diem **2** police department **3** potential difference

PDA \ˌpē-ˌdē-'ā\ *n* [*personal digital assistant*] : a small microprocessor device for storing and organizing personal information

PDQ \ˌpē-ˌdē-'kyü\ *adv, often not cap* [abbr. of *pretty damned quick*] : IMMEDIATELY

PDT *abbr* Pacific daylight (saving) time

PE *abbr* **1** physical education **2** printer's error **3** professional engineer

pea \'pē\ *n, pl* **peas** *also* **pease** \'pēz\ **1** : the round edible protein-rich seed borne in the pod of a widely grown leguminous vine; *also* : this vine **2** : any of various plants resembling or related to the pea

peace \'pēs\ *n* **1** : a state of calm and quiet; *esp* : public security under law **2** : freedom from disturbing thoughts or emotions **3** : a state of concord (as between persons or governments); *also* : an agreement to end hostilities — **peace·able** \'pē-sə-bəl\ *adj* — **peace·ably** \-blē\ *adv* — **peace·ful** *adj* — **peace·ful·ly** *adv*

peace·keep·ing \'pēs-ˌkē-piŋ\ *n* : the preserving of peace; *esp* : international enforcement and supervision of a truce — **peace·keep·er** *n*

peace·mak·er \-ˌmā-kər\ *n* : one who settles an argument or stops a fight

peace·time \-ˌtīm\ *n* : a time when a nation is not at war

peach \'pēch\ *n* [ME *peche*, fr. AF *pesche, peche,*, fr. LL *persica*, fr. L (*malum*) *Persicum*, lit., Persian fruit] : a sweet juicy fuzzy-skinned fruit of a small usu. pink-flowered tree related to the cherry and plums; *also* : this tree — **peachy** *adj*

pea·cock \'pē-ˌkäk\ *n* [ME *pecok*, fr. *pe-* (fr. OE *pēa* peafowl, fr. L *pavo* peacock) + *cok* cock] : the male peafowl that can spread its long tail feathers to make a colorful display

pea·fowl \-ˌfau̇(-ə)l\ *n* : either of two large domesticated Asian pheasants

pea·hen \-ˌhen\ *n* : the female peafowl

¹peak \'pēk\ *n* **1** : a pointed or projecting part **2** : the top of a hill or mountain; *also* : MOUNTAIN **3** : the front projecting part of a cap **4** : the narrow part of a ship's bow or stern **5** : the highest level or greatest degree — **peak** *adj*

²peak *vb* : to bring to or reach a maximum

peak·ed \'pē-kəd\ *adj* : THIN, SICKLY

¹peal \'pēl\ *n* **1** : the loud ringing of bells **2** : a set of tuned bells **3** : a loud sound or succession of sounds

²peal *vb* : to give out peals : RESOUND

pea·nut \'pē-(ˌ)nət\ *n* **1** : an annual herb related to the pea but having pods that ripen underground; *also* : this pod or one of the edible seeds it bears **2** *pl* : a very small amount **3** : a pellet of polystyrene foam

pear \'per\ *n* : the fleshy fruit of a tree related to the apple; *also* : this tree

pearl \'pərl\ *n* **1** : a small hard often lustrous body formed within the shell of some mollusks and used as a gem **2** : one that is choice or precious ⟨∼s of wisdom⟩ **3** : a slightly bluish medium gray color — **pearly** \'pər-lē\ *adj*

peas·ant \'pe-zᵊnt\ *n* **1** : any of a class of small landowners or laborers tilling the soil **2** : a usu. uneducated person of low social status — **peas·ant·ry** \-z²n-trē\ *n*

pea·shoot·er \'pē-ˌshü-tər\ *n* : a toy blowgun for shooting peas

peat \'pēt\ *n* : a dark substance formed by partial decay of plants (as mosses) in water — **peaty** *adj*

peat moss *n* : SPHAGNUM

¹peb·ble \'pe-bəl\ *n* : a small usu. round stone — **peb·bly** \-b(ə-)lē\ *adj*

²pebble *vb* **peb·bled; peb·bling** : to produce a rough surface texture in ⟨∼ leather⟩

pec \'pek\ *n* : PECTORAL MUSCLE

pe·can \pi-'kän, -'kan; 'pē-ˌkan\ *n* : the smooth thin-shelled edible nut of a large American hickory; *also* : this tree

pec·ca·dil·lo \ˌpe-kə-'di-lō\ *n, pl* **-loes** *or* **-los** : a slight offense

pec·ca·ry \'pe-kə-rē\ *n, pl* **-ries** : any of several American chiefly tropical mammals resembling but smaller than the related pigs

pec·ca·vi \pe-'kä-ˌvē\ *n* [L, I have sinned, fr. *peccare* to sin] : an acknowledgment of sin

¹peck \'pek\ *n* — see WEIGHT table

²peck *vb* **1** : to strike or pierce with or as if with the bill **2** : to make (as a hole) by pecking **3** : to pick up with or as if with the bill

³peck *n* **1** : an impression made by pecking **2** : a quick sharp stroke

pecking order *also* **peck order** *n* : a basic pattern of social organization within a flock of poultry in which each bird pecks another lower in the scale without being pecked in return and submits to pecking by one of higher rank; *also* : a social hierarchy

pec·tin \'pek-tən\ *n* : any of various water-soluble plant substances that cause fruit jellies to set — **pec·tic** \-tik\ *adj*

pec·to·ral \'pek-tə-rəl\ *adj* : of or relating to the breast or chest

pectoral muscle *n* : either of two muscles on each side of the body which connect the front walls of the chest with the bones of the upper arm and shoulder

pe·cu·liar \pi-'kyül-yər\ *adj* [ME *peculier*, fr. L *peculiaris* of private property; special, fr. *peculium* private property, fr. *pecus* cattle] **1** : belonging exclusively to one person or group **2** : CHARACTERISTIC, DISTINCTIVE **3** : QUEER, ODD ♦ *Synonyms* IDIOSYNCRATIC, ECCENTRIC, SINGULAR, STRANGE, WEIRD — **pe·cu·liar·i·ty** \-ˌkyül-'ya-rə-tē, -ˌkyü-lē-'a-\ *n* — **pe·cu·liar·ly** *adv*

pe·cu·ni·ary \pi-'kyü-nē-ˌer-ē\ *adj* : of or relating to money : MONETARY

ped·a·gogue *also* **ped·a·gog** \'pe-də-ˌgäg\ *n* : TEACHER, SCHOOLMASTER

ped·a·go·gy \'pe-də-ˌgō-jē, -ˌgä-\ *n* : the art or profession of teaching; *esp* : EDUCATION 2 — **ped·a·gog·ic** \ˌpe-də-'gä-jik, -'gō-\ *or* **ped·a·gog·i·cal** \-ji-kəl\ *adj*

¹ped·al \'pe-dᵊl\ *n* : a lever worked by the foot

²pedal *adj* : of or relating to the foot

³pedal *vb* **ped·aled** *also* **ped·alled; ped·al·ing** *also* **ped·al·ling** **1** : to use or work a pedal (as of a piano or bicycle) **2** : to ride a bicycle

ped·ant \'pe-dᵊnt\ *n* **1** : a person who makes a show of knowledge **2** : a formal uninspired teacher — **pe·dan·tic** \pi-'dan-tik\ *adj* — **ped·ant·ry** \'pe-dᵊn-trē\ *n*

ped·dle \'pe-dᵊl\ *vb* **ped·dled; ped·dling** : to sell or offer for sale from place to place — **ped·dler** *also* **ped·lar** \'ped-lər\ *n*

ped·er·ast \'pe-də-ˌrast\ *n* [Gk *paiderastēs*, lit., lover of boys] : one who practices anal intercourse esp. with a boy — **ped·er·as·ty** \'pe-də-ˌras-tē\ *n*

ped·es·tal \'pe-dəs-tᵊl\ *n* **1** : the support or foot of something (as a column, statue, or vase) that is upright **2** : a position of high regard

¹pe·des·tri·an \pə-'des-trē-ən\ *adj* **1** : ORDINARY **2** : going on foot

²pedestrian *n* : WALKER

pe·di·at·rics \ˌpē-dē-'a-triks\ n : a branch of medicine dealing with the development, care, and diseases of children — **pe·di·at·ric** \-trik\ adj — **pe·di·a·tri·cian** \ˌpē-dē-ə-'tri-shən\ n

pedi·cab \'pe-di-ˌkab\ n : a pedal-driven tricycle with seats for a driver and two passengers

ped·i·cure \'pe-di-ˌkyu̇r\ n : care of the feet, toes, and nails; also : a single treatment of these parts — **ped·i·cur·ist** \-ˌkyu̇r-ist\ n

ped·i·gree \'pe-də-ˌgrē\ n [ME pedegru, fr. AF pé de grue, lit., crane's foot; fr. the shape made by the lines of a genealogical chart] 1 : a record of a line of ancestors 2 : an ancestral line — **ped·i·greed** \-ˌgrēd\ adj

ped·i·ment \'pe-də-mənt\ n : a low triangular gablelike decoration (as over a door or window) on a building

pe·dom·e·ter \pi-'dä-mə-tər\ n : an instrument that measures the distance one walks

pe·do·phile \'pe-də-ˌfī(-ə)l, 'pē-\ n : one affected with pedophilia

pe·do·phil·ia \ˌpe-də-'fi-lē-ə, ˌpē-\ n : sexual perversion in which children are the preferred sexual object

pe·dun·cle \'pē-ˌdəŋ-kəl\ n : a narrow supporting stalk

peek \'pēk\ vb 1 : to look furtively 2 : to peer from a place of concealment 3 : GLANCE — **peek** n

¹**peel** \'pēl\ vb [ME pelen, fr. AF peler, fr. L pilare to remove the hair from, fr. pilus hair] 1 : to strip the skin, bark, or rind from 2 : to strip off (as a coat); also : to come off 3 : to lose the skin, bark, or rind

²**peel** n : a skin or rind esp. of a fruit

peel·ing \'pē-liŋ\ n : a peeled-off piece or strip (as of skin or rind)

peen \'pēn\ n : the usu. hemispherical or wedge-shaped end of the head of a hammer opposite the face

¹**peep** \'pēp\ vb : to utter a feeble shrill sound or the slightest sound

²**peep** n : a feeble shrill sound

³**peep** vb 1 : to look slyly esp. through an aperture : PEEK 2 : to begin to emerge 3 : to look at : WATCH — **peep·er** n

⁴**peep** n 1 : a first faint appearance 2 : a brief or furtive look

peep·hole \'pēp-ˌhōl\ n : a hole to peep through

¹**peer** \'pir\ n 1 : one of equal standing with another : EQUAL 2 : NOBLE — **peer·age** \-ij\ n

²**peer** vb 1 : to look intently or curiously 2 : to come slightly into view

peer·ess \'pir-əs\ n : a woman who is a peer

peer·less \'pir-ləs\ adj : having no equal : MATCHLESS ✦ Synonyms SUPREME, UNEQUALED, UNPARALLELED, INCOMPARABLE

¹**peeve** \'pēv\ vb **peeved; peev·ing** : to make resentful : ANNOY

²**peeve** n 1 : a feeling or mood of resentment 2 : a particular grievance

pee·vish \'pē-vish\ adj : querulous in temperament : FRETFUL ✦ Synonyms IRRITABLE, PETULANT, HUFFY — **pee·vish·ly** adv — **pee·vish·ness** n

pee·wee \'pē-(ˌ)wē\ n 1 : one that is diminutive or tiny 2 : a level of sports usu. for young children — **peewee** adj

¹**peg** \'peg\ n 1 : a small pointed piece (as of wood) used to pin down or fasten things or to fit into holes 2 : a projecting piece used as a support or boundary marker 3 : SUPPORT, PRETEXT 4 : STEP, DEGREE 5 : THROW

²**peg** vb **pegged; peg·ging** 1 : to put a peg into : fasten, pin down, or attach with or as if with pegs 2 : to work hard and steadily : PLUG 3 : HUSTLE 4 : to mark by pegs 5 : to hold (as prices) at a set level or rate 6 : IDENTIFY ⟨was pegged as an intellectual⟩ 7 : THROW

PEI abbr Prince Edward Island

pei·gnoir \pān-'wär, pen-\ n [F, lit., garment worn while combing the hair, fr. MF, fr. peigner to comb the hair, fr. L pectinare, fr. pectin-, pecten comb] : NEGLIGEE

¹**pe·jo·ra·tive** \pi-'jȯr-ə-tiv\ n : a pejorative word or phrase

²**pejorative** adj : having negative connotations : DISPARAGING — **pe·jo·ra·tive·ly** adv

peke \'pēk\ n, often cap : PEKINGESE

Pe·king·ese or **Pe·kin·ese** \ˌpē-kə-'nēz, -'nēs; -kiŋ-'ēz, -'ēs\ n, pl **Pekingese** or **Pekinese** : any of a breed of Chinese origin of small short-legged long-haired dogs

pe·koe \'pē-(ˌ)kō\ n : a black tea made from young tea leaves

pel·age \'pe-lij\ n : the hairy covering of a mammal

pe·lag·ic \pə-'la-jik\ adj : OCEANIC

pelf \'pelf\ n : MONEY, RICHES

pel·i·can \'pe-li-kən\ n : any of a genus of large web-footed birds having a pouched lower bill used to scoop in fish

pel·la·gra \pə-'la-grə, -'lā-\ n : a disease caused by a diet with too little niacin and protein and marked by a skin rash, disease of the digestive system, and mental disturbances

pel·let \'pe-lət\ n 1 : a little ball (as of medicine) 2 : BULLET — **pel·let·al** \-lə-təl\ adj — **pel·let·ize** \-ˌtīz\ vb

pell—mell \ˌpel-'mel\ adv 1 : in mingled confusion ⟨papers strewn ∼ on the desk⟩ 2 : HEADLONG ⟨ran ∼ for the door⟩

pel·lu·cid \pə-'lü-səd\ adj : extremely clear : LIMPID, TRANSPARENT ⟨a ∼ stream⟩ ✦ Synonyms TRANSLUCENT, LUCID, LUCENT

pe·lo·ton \ˌpe-lə-'tän\ n : the main body of riders in a bicycle race

¹**pelt** \'pelt\ n : a skin esp. of a fur-bearing animal

²**pelt** vb : to strike with a succession of blows or missiles

pel·vis \'pel-vəs\ n, pl **pel·vis·es** \-və-səz\ or **pel·ves** \-ˌvēz\ : a basin-shaped part of the vertebrate skeleton consisting of the large bone of each hip and the nearby bones of the spine — **pel·vic** \-vik\ adj

pem·mi·can also **pem·i·can** \'pe-mi-kən\ n : dried meat pounded fine and mixed with melted fat

¹**pen** \'pen\ vb **penned; pen·ning** : to shut in or as if in a pen

²**pen** n 1 : a small enclosure for animals 2 : a small place of confinement or storage

³**pen** n 1 : an implement for writing or drawing with ink or a similar fluid 2 : a writing instrument regarded as a means of expression 3 : STYLUS 3

⁴**pen** vb **penned; pen·ning** : WRITE

⁵**pen** n : PENITENTIARY

⁶**pen** abbr peninsula

PEN abbr International Association of Poets, Playwrights, Editors, Essayists and Novelists

pe·nal \'pē-nᵊl\ adj : of or relating to punishment

pe·nal·ise Brit var of PENALIZE

pe·nal·ize \'pē-nə-ˌlīz, 'pe-\ vb **-ized; -iz·ing** : to put a penalty on

pen·al·ty \'pe-nᵊl-tē\ n, pl **-ties** 1 : punishment for crime or offense 2 : something forfeited when a person fails to do something agreed to 3 : disadvantage, loss, or hardship (as to a competitor) due to some action

pen·ance \'pe-nəns\ n 1 : an act performed to show sorrow or repentance for sin 2 : a sacrament (as in the Roman Catholic Church) consisting of confession, absolution, and a penance directed by the confessor

pence \'pens\ pl of PENNY

pen·chant \'pen-chənt\ n [F, fr. prp. of pencher to incline, fr. VL *pendicare, fr. L pendere to weigh] : a strong inclination : LIKING ✦ Synonyms LEANING, PROPENSITY, PREDILECTION, PREDISPOSITION

¹**pen·cil** \'pen-səl\ n : a writing or drawing tool consisting of or containing a slender cylinder of a solid marking substance

²**pencil** vb **-ciled** or **-cilled; -cil·ing** or **-cil·ling** 1 : to draw or write with a pencil 2 : to plan or designate tentatively ⟨∼ed in the appointment⟩

pen·dant also **pen·dent** \'pen-dənt\ n : a hanging ornament (as on a necklace)

pen·dent or **pen·dant** \'pen-dənt\ adj : SUSPENDED, OVERHANGING

Pekingese

¹**pend·ing** \'pen-diŋ\ *prep* **1** : DURING **2** : while awaiting ⟨∼ approval⟩

²**pending** *adj* **1** : not yet decided ⟨a ∼ application⟩ **2** : IMMINENT

pen·du·lous \'pen-jə-ləs, -də-\ *adj* : hanging loosely : DROOPING

pen·du·lum \-ləm\ *n* : a body that swings freely from a fixed point

pe·ne·plain *also* **pe·ne·plane** \'pē-ni-ˌplān\ *n* : a large almost flat land surface shaped by erosion

pen·e·trate \'pe-nə-ˌtrāt\ *vb* **-trat·ed; -trat·ing** **1** : to enter into : PIERCE **2** : PERMEATE **3** : to see into : UNDERSTAND **4** : to affect deeply — **pen·e·tra·ble** \-trə-bəl\ *adj* — **pen·e·tra·tion** \ˌpe-nə-'trā-shən\ *n* — **pen·e·tra·tive** \'pe-nə-ˌtrā-tiv\ *adj*

penetrating *adj* **1** : having the power of entering, piercing, or pervading ⟨a ∼ shriek⟩ ⟨a ∼ odor⟩ **2** : ACUTE, DISCERNING ⟨a ∼ look⟩

pen·guin \'peŋ-gwən, 'pen-\ *n* : any of various erect short-legged flightless seabirds of the southern hemisphere

pen·i·cil·lin \ˌpe-nə-'si-lən\ *n* : any of several antibiotics produced by molds or synthetically and used against various bacteria

pen·in·su·la \pə-'nin-sə-lə\ *n* [L *paeninsula*, fr. *paene* almost + *insula* island] : a long narrow portion of land extending out into the water — **pen·in·su·lar** \-lər\ *adj*

pe·nis \'pē-nəs\ *n, pl* **pe·nis·es** *also* **penes** \-ˌnēz\ : a male organ of copulation that in the human male also functions as the channel by which urine leaves the body

¹**pen·i·tent** \'pe-nə-tənt\ *adj* : feeling sorrow for sins or offenses : REPENTANT — **pen·i·tence** \-təns\ *n* — **pen·i·ten·tial** \ˌpe-nə-'ten-chəl\ *adj*

²**penitent** *n* : a penitent person

¹**pen·i·ten·tia·ry** \ˌpe-nə-'ten-chə-rē\ *n, pl* **-ries** : a state or federal prison

²**penitentiary** *adj* : of, relating to, or incurring confinement in a penitentiary

pen·knife \'pen-ˌnīf\ *n* : a small pocketknife

pen·light *also* **pen·lite** \-ˌlīt\ *n* : a small flashlight resembling a fountain pen in size or shape

pen·man \'pen-mən\ *n* **1** : COPYIST **2** : one skilled in penmanship **3** : AUTHOR

pen·man·ship \-ˌship\ *n* : the art or practice of writing with the pen

Penn *or* **Penna** *abbr* Pennsylvania

pen name *n* : an author's pseudonym

pen·nant \'pe-nənt\ *n* **1** : a tapering flag used esp. for signaling **2** : a flag symbolic of championship

pen·ne \'pe-nā\ *n* : short diagonally cut tubular pasta

pen·ni \'pe-nē\ *n, pl* **pen·nia** \-nē-ə\ *or* **pen·nis** \-nēz\ : a former monetary unit equal to ¹⁄₁₀₀ markka

pen·non \'pe-nən\ *n* **1** : a long narrow ribbonlike flag borne on a lance **2** : WING

Penn·syl·va·nian \ˌpen-səl-'vā-nyən\ *adj* **1** : of or relating to Pennsylvania or its people **2** : of, relating to, or being the period of the Paleozoic era between the Mississippian and the Permian — **Pennsylvanian** *n*

pen·ny \'pe-nē\ *n, pl* **pennies** \-nēz\ *or* **pence** \'pens\ **1** *pl usu* **pence** : a British monetary unit formerly equal to ¹⁄₁₂ shilling but now equal to ¹⁄₁₀₀ pound; *also* : a coin of this value — see *pound* at MONEY table **2** *pl* **pennies** : a cent of the U.S. or Canada **3** : a former monetary unit equal to ¹⁄₁₀₀ Irish pound — **pen·ni·less** \'pe-ni-ləs\ *adj*

pen·ny–pinch·ing \'pe-nē-ˌpin-chiŋ\ *n* : PARSIMONY — **pen·ny–pinch·er** *n* — **penny–pinching** *adj*

pen·ny–weight \-ˌwāt\ *n* — see WEIGHT table

pen·ny–wise \-ˌwīz\ *adj* : wise or prudent only in small matters

pe·nol·o·gy \pi-'nä-lə-jē\ *n* : a branch of criminology dealing with prisons and the treatment of offenders

¹**pen·sion** \'pen-chən\ *n* : a fixed sum paid regularly esp. to a person retired from service

²**pension** *vb* : to pay a pension to — **pen·sion·er** *n*

pen·sive \'pen-siv\ *adj* : musingly, dreamily, or sadly thoughtful ✦ *Synonyms* REFLECTIVE, SPECULATIVE, CONTEMPLATIVE, MEDITATIVE — **pen·sive·ly** *adv*

pen·stock \'pen-ˌstäk\ *n* **1** : a sluice or gate for regulating a flow **2** : a pipe for carrying water

pent \'pent\ *adj* : shut up : CONFINED

pen·ta·gon \'pen-tə-ˌgän\ *n* : a polygon of five angles and five sides — **pen·tag·o·nal** \pen-'ta-gə-nᵊl\ *adj*

pen·tam·e·ter \pen-'ta-mə-tər\ *n* : a line of verse containing five metrical feet

pen·tath·lon \pen-'tath-lən\ *n* : a composite athletic contest consisting of five events

Pen·te·cost \'pen-ti-ˌkȯst\ *n* : the 7th Sunday after Easter observed as a church festival commemorating the descent of the Holy Spirit on the apostles — **Pen·te·cos·tal** \ˌpen-ti-'käs-tᵊl\ *adj*

Pentecostal *n* : a member of a Christian religious body that stresses expressive worship, evangelism, and spiritual gifts — **Pen·te·cos·tal·ism** \ˌpen-ti-'käs-tə-ˌli-zəm\

pent·house \'pent-ˌhaús\ *n* [alter. of ME *pentis*, fr. AF *apentiz*, fr. *apent*, pp. of *apendre* to attach, hang against] **1** : a shed or sloping roof attached to a wall or building **2** : an apartment built on the roof of a building

pen·ul·ti·mate \pi-'nəl-tə-mət\ *adj* : next to the last ⟨∼ syllable⟩

pen·um·bra \pə-'nəm-brə\ *n, pl* **-brae** \-(ˌ)brē\ *or* **-bras** **1** : the partial shadow surrounding a complete shadow (as in an eclipse) **2** : something that covers or obscures ⟨a ∼ of secrecy⟩

pe·nu·ri·ous \pə-'nùr-ē-əs, -'nyùr-\ *adj* **1** : marked by penury **2** : MISERLY ✦ *Synonyms* STINGY, CLOSE, TIGHTFISTED, PARSIMONIOUS

pen·u·ry \'pe-nyə-rē\ *n* **1** : extreme poverty **2** : extreme frugality

pe·on \'pē-ˌän, -ən\ *n, pl* **peons** *or* **pe·o·nes** \pā-'ō-nēz\ **1** : a member of the landless laboring class in Spanish America **2** : one bound to service for payment of a debt — **pe·on·age** \-ə-nij\ *n*

pe·o·ny \'pē-ə-nē\ *n, pl* **-nies** : any of a genus of chiefly Eurasian plants with large often double red, pink, or white flowers; *also* : the flower

¹**peo·ple** \'pē-pəl\ *n, pl* **people** [ME *peple*, fr. AF *peple, peuple*, fr. L *populus*] **1** *pl* : human beings making up a group or linked by a common characteristic or interest **2** *pl* : human beings — often used in compounds instead of *persons* ⟨sales*people*⟩ or attributively ⟨∼ skills⟩ **3** *pl* : the mass of persons in a community : POPULACE; *also* : ELECTORATE ⟨the ∼'s choice⟩ **4** *pl* **peoples** : a body of persons (as a tribe, nation, or race) united by a common culture, sense of kinship, or political organization

²**people** *vb* **peo·pled; peo·pling** : to supply or fill with or as if with people

¹**pep** \'pep\ *n* : brisk energy or initiative — **pep·py** *adj*

²**pep** *vb* **pepped; pep·ping** : to put pep into : STIMULATE

¹**pep·per** \'pe-pər\ *n* **1** : either of two pungent condiments from the berry (**pep·per·corn** \-ˌkȯrn\) of an Indian climbing plant : BLACK PEPPER, WHITE PEPPER; *also* : this plant **2** : a plant related to the tomato and widely grown for its hot or mild sweet fruit; *also* : this fruit

²**pepper** *vb* **pep·pered; pep·per·ing** **1** : to shower with missiles or rapid blows **2** : to sprinkle or season with or as if with pepper **3** : to deliver something in rapid succession ⟨∼ed him with questions⟩

pep·per·mint \-ˌmint, -mənt\ *n* : a pungent aromatic mint; *also* : candy flavored with its oil

pep·per·o·ni \ˌpe-pə-'rō-nē\ *n* : a highly seasoned beef and pork sausage

pepper spray *n* : a temporarily disabling aerosol that causes irritation and blinding of the eyes and inflammation of the nose, throat, and skin

pep·pery \'pe-pə-rē\ *adj* **1** : having the qualities of pepper : PUNGENT, HOT **2** : having a hot temper **3** : FIERY

pep·sin \'pep-sən\ *n* : an enzyme of the stomach that promotes digestion by breaking down proteins; *also* : a preparation of this used medicinally

pep·tic \'pep-tik\ *adj* [L *pepticus*, fr. Gk *peptikos*, fr. *peptos* cooked, *peptein* to cook, digest] **1** : relating to or promoting digestion **2** : caused by digestive juices ⟨a ∼ ulcer⟩

pep·tide \'pep-ˌtīd\ *n* : any of various organic compounds composed of two or more amino acids bonded together

Pe·quot \'pē-ˌkwät\ *n* : a member of an American Indian people of eastern Connecticut

¹**per** \'pər\ *prep* **1** : by means of **2** : to or for each **3** : ACCORDING TO

²**per** *adv* : for each : APIECE

³**per** *abbr* **1** period **2** person

¹**per·ad·ven·ture** \'pər-əd-ˌven-chər\ *adv, archaic* : PERHAPS

²**per·ad·ven·ture** *n* **1** : DOUBT **2** : CHANCE 4

per·am·bu·late \pə-'ram-byə-ˌlāt\ *vb* **-lat·ed; -lat·ing** : to travel over esp. on foot — **per·am·bu·la·tion** \-ˌram-byə-'lā-shən\ *n*

per·am·bu·la·tor \pə-'ram-byə-ˌlā-tər\ *n, chiefly Brit* : a baby carriage

per an·num \(ˌ)pər-'a-nəm\ *adv* [ML] : in or for each year : ANNUALLY

per·cale \(ˌ)pər-'kāl, 'pər-ˌ; (ˌ)pər-'kal\ *n* : a fine woven cotton cloth

per cap·i·ta \(ˌ)pər-'ka-pə-tə\ *adv or adj* [ML, by heads] : by or for each person

per·ceive \pər-'sēv\ *vb* **per·ceived; per·ceiv·ing** **1** : to attain awareness : REALIZE **2** : to become aware of through the senses — **per·ceiv·able** *adj*

¹**per·cent** \pər-'sent\ *adv* [*per* + L *centum* hundred] : in each hundred

²**percent** *n, pl* **percent** *or* **percents** **1** : one part in a hundred : HUNDREDTH **2** : PERCENTAGE

per·cent·age \pər-'sen-tij\ *n* **1** : a part of a whole expressed in hundredths **2** : the result obtained by multiplying a number by a percent **3** : ADVANTAGE, PROFIT **4** : PROBABILITY; *also* : favorable odds

percentage point *n* : one hundredth of a whole ⟨rates rose one *percentage point* from 6.5 to 7.5 percent⟩

per·cen·tile \pər-'sen-ˌtī(-ə)l\ *n* : a value on a scale of one hundred indicating the standing of a score or grade in terms of the percentage of scores or grades falling with or below it

per·cept \'pər-ˌsept\ *n* : an impression of an object obtained by use of the senses

per·cep·ti·ble \pər-'sep-tə-bəl\ *adj* : capable of being perceived ⟨a barely ∼ light⟩ — **per·cep·ti·bly** \-blē\ *adv*

per·cep·tion \pər-'sep-shən\ *n* **1** : an act or result of perceiving **2** : awareness of one's environment through physical sensation **3** : ability to understand : INSIGHT, COMPREHENSION ♦ *Synonyms* PENETRATION, DISCERNMENT, DISCRIMINATION

per·cep·tive \pər-'sep-tiv\ *adj* : capable of or exhibiting keen perception : OBSERVANT — **per·cep·tive·ly** *adv*

per·cep·tu·al \pər-'sep-chə-wəl\ *adj* : of, relating to, or involving sensory stimulus as opposed to abstract concept — **per·cep·tu·al·ly** *adv*

¹**perch** \'pərch\ *n* **1** : a roost for a bird **2** : a high station or vantage point

²**perch** *vb* : ROOST

³**perch** *n, pl* **perch** *or* **perch·es** : either of two small freshwater bony fishes used for food; *also* : any of various fishes resembling or related to these

per·chance \pər-'chans\ *adv* : PERHAPS

per·cip·i·ent \pər-'si-pē-ənt\ *adj* : capable of or characterized by perception — **per·cip·i·ence** \-əns\ *n*

per·co·late \'pər-kə-ˌlāt\ *vb* **-lat·ed; -lat·ing** **1** : to trickle or filter through a permeable substance **2** : to filter hot water through to extract the essence ⟨∼ coffee⟩ — **per·co·la·tor** \-ˌlā-tər\ *n*

per con·tra \(ˌ)pər-'kän-trə\ *adv* [It, by the opposite side (of the ledger)] **1** : on the contrary **2** : by way of contrast

per·cus·sion \pər-'kə-shən\ *n* **1** : a sharp blow : IMPACT; *esp* : a blow upon a cap (**percussion cap**) designed to explode the charge in a firearm **2** : the beating or striking of a musical instrument; *also* : instruments sounded by striking, shaking, or scraping

per di·em \pər-'dē-əm, -'dī-\ *adv* [ML] : by the day — **per diem** *adj or n*

per·di·tion \pər-'di-shən\ *n* **1** : eternal damnation **2** : HELL

per·du·ra·ble \(ˌ)pər-'dùr-ə-bəl, -'dyùr-\ *adj* : very durable — **per·du·ra·bil·i·ty** \-ˌdùr-ə-'bi-lə-tē, -ˌdyùr-\ *n*

per·e·gri·na·tion \ˌper-ə-grə-'nā-shən\ *n* : a traveling about esp. on foot

per·e·grine falcon \'per-ə-grən, -ˌgrēn\ *n* : a swift nearly cosmopolitan falcon that often nests in cities and is often used in falconry

pe·remp·to·ry \pə-'remp-tə-rē\ *adj* **1** : barring a right of action or delay **2** : expressive of urgency or command : IMPERATIVE **3** : marked by arrogant self-assurance ♦ *Synonyms* IMPERIOUS, MASTERFUL, DOMINEERING, MAGISTERIAL — **pe·remp·to·ri·ly** \-tə-rə-lē\ *adv*

¹**pe·ren·ni·al** \pə-'re-nē-əl\ *adj* **1** : present at all seasons of the year ⟨∼ streams⟩ **2** : continuing to live from year to year ⟨∼ plants⟩ **3** : recurring regularly : PERMANENT ⟨∼ problems⟩ ♦ *Synonyms* LASTING, PERPETUAL, ENDURING, EVERLASTING — **pe·ren·ni·al·ly** *adv*

²**perennial** *n* : a perennial plant

perf *abbr* **1** perfect **2** perforated

¹**per·fect** \'pər-fikt\ *adj* **1** : being without fault or defect **2** : EXACT, PRECISE **3** : COMPLETE **4** : relating to or being a verb tense that expresses an action or state completed at the time of speaking or at a time spoken of — **per·fect·ly** *adv* — **per·fect·ness** *n*

²**per·fect** \pər-'fekt\ *vb* : to make perfect

³**per·fect** \'pər-fikt\ *n* : the perfect tense; *also* : a verb form in it

per·fect·ible \pər-'fek-tə-bəl, 'pər-fik-\ *adj* : capable of improvement or perfection — **per·fect·ibil·i·ty** \pər-ˌfek-tə-'bi-lə-tē, ˌpər-fik-\ *n*

per·fec·tion \pər-'fek-shən\ *n* **1** : the quality or state of being perfect **2** : the highest degree of excellence **3** : the act or process of perfecting

per·fec·tion·ist \-shə-nist\ *n* : a person who will not accept or be content with anything less than perfection

per·fec·to \pər-'fek-tō\ *n, pl* **-tos** : a cigar that is thick in the middle and tapers almost to a point at each end

per·fi·dy \'pər-fə-dē\ *n, pl* **-dies** [L *perfidia*, fr. *perfidus* faithless, fr. *per-* detrimental to + *fides* faith] : violation of faith or loyalty : TREACHERY — **per·fid·i·ous** \pər-'fi-dē-əs\ *adj* — **per·fid·i·ous·ly** *adv*

per·fo·rate \'pər-fə-ˌrāt\ *vb* **-rat·ed; -rat·ing** : to bore through : PIERCE; *esp* : to make a line of holes in to facilitate separation — **per·fo·ra·tion** \ˌpər-fə-'rā-shən\ *n*

per·force \pər-'fòrs\ *adv* : of necessity ⟨we attended ∼⟩

per·form \pər-'fòrm\ *vb* **1** : FULFILL **2** : CARRY OUT, DO **3** : FUNCTION **4** : to do in a set manner **5** : to give a performance — **per·form·er** *n*

per·for·mance \pər-'fòr-ˌməns\ *n* **1** : the act or process of performing **2** : DEED, FEAT **3** : a public presentation

¹**per·fume** \pər-'fyüm, 'pər-ˌfyüm\ *n* **1** : a usu. pleasant odor : FRAGRANCE **2** : a preparation used for scenting

²**per·fume** \pər-'fyüm, 'pər-ˌfyüm\ *vb* **per·fumed; per·fum·ing** : SCENT

per·fum·ery \ˌpər-'fyü-mə-rē\ *n, pl* **-er·ies** **1** : the art or process of making perfume **2** : PERFUMES **3** : an establishment where perfumes are made

per·func·to·ry \pər-'fəŋk-tə-rē\ *adj* : done merely as a duty — **per·func·to·ri·ly** *adv*

per·go·la \'pər-gə-lə\ *n* [It] : a structure consisting of posts supporting an open roof in the form of a trellis

perh *abbr* perhaps

per·haps \pər-'haps\ *adv* : possibly but not certainly

per·i·gee \'per-ə-ˌjē\ *n* [MF, fr. NL *perigeum*, fr. Gk *perigeion*, fr. *peri* around, near + *gē* earth] : the point at which an orbiting object is nearest the body (as the earth) being orbited

perigee: P perigee, A apogee

peri·he·lion \ˌper-ə-'hēl-yən\ *n, pl* **-he·lia** \-'hēl-yə\ : the point in the path of a celestial body (as a planet) that is nearest the sun

per·il \'per-əl\ *n* : DANGER; *also* : a source of danger : RISK — **per·il·ous** *adj* — **per·il·ous·ly** *adv*

pe·rim·e·ter \pə-'ri-mə-tər\ *n* **1** : the boundary of a closed plane figure; *also* : its length **2** : a line bounding or protecting an area

peri·na·tal \ˌper-ə-'nā-tᵊl\ *adj* : occurring in, concerned with, or being in the period around the time of birth ⟨∼ care⟩

¹**pe·ri·od** \'pir-ē-əd\ *n* [ultim. fr. Gk *periodos* circuit, period

of time, rhetorical period, fr. *peri* around + *hodos* way] **1** : SENTENCE; *also* : the full pause closing the utterance of a sentence **2** : END, STOP **3** : a punctuation mark . used esp. to mark the end of a declarative sentence or an abbreviation **4** : an extent of time; *esp* : one regarded as a stage or division in a process or development **5** : a portion of time in which a recurring phenomenon completes one cycle and is ready to begin again **6** : a single cyclic occurrence of menstruation

²period *adj* : of or relating to a particular historical period ⟨~ furniture⟩

pe·ri·od·ic \ˌpir-ē-ˈä-dik\ *adj* **1** : occurring at regular intervals of time **2** : happening repeatedly **3** : of or relating to a sentence that has no trailing elements following full grammatical statement of the essential idea

¹pe·ri·od·i·cal \ˌpir-ē-ˈä-di-kəl\ *adj* **1** : PERIODIC **2** : published at regular intervals **3** : of or relating to a periodical — **pe·ri·od·i·cal·ly** \-k(ə-)lē\ *adv*

²periodical *n* : a periodical publication

periodic table *n* : an arrangement of chemical elements based on their atomic structure and on their properties

peri·odon·tal \ˌper-ē-ō-ˈdän-tᵊl\ *adj* **1** : surrounding a tooth **2** : of or affecting periodontal tissues or regions

per·i·pa·tet·ic \ˌper-ə-pə-ˈte-tik\ *adj* : performed or performing while moving about : ITINERANT

pe·riph·er·al \pə-ˈri-fə-rəl\ *n* : a device connected to a computer to provide communication or auxiliary functions

peripheral nervous system *n* : the part of the nervous system that is outside the central nervous system and comprises the spinal nerves, the cranial nerves except the one supplying the retina, and the autonomic nervous system

pe·riph·ery \pə-ˈri-fə-rē\ *n, pl* **-er·ies 1** : the boundary of a rounded figure **2** : outward bounds : border area — **pe·riph·er·al** \-fə-rəl\ *adj*

pe·riph·ra·sis \pə-ˈri-frə-səs\ *n, pl* **-ra·ses** \-ˌsēz\ : CIRCUMLOCUTION

peri·scope \ˈper-ə-ˌskōp\ *n* : a tubular optical instrument enabling an observer to see an otherwise blocked field of view

per·ish \ˈper-ish\ *vb* : to become destroyed or ruined : cease to exist

per·ish·able \ˈper-i-shə-bəl\ *adj* : easily spoiled ⟨~ foods⟩ — **perishable** *n*

peri·stal·sis \ˌper-ə-ˈstȯl-səs, -ˈstal-\ *n, pl* **-stal·ses** : waves of contraction passing along the walls of a hollow muscular organ (as the intestine) and forcing its contents onward — **per·i·stal·tic** \-ˈstȯl-tik, -ˈstal-\ *adj*

peri·style \ˈper-ə-ˌstīl\ *n* : a row of columns surrounding a building or court

peri·to·ne·um \ˌper-ə-tə-ˈnē-əm\ *n, pl* **-ne·ums** *or* **-nea** : the smooth transparent serous membrane that lines the cavity of the abdomen — **peri·to·ne·al** \-ˈnē-əl\ *adj*

peri·to·ni·tis \ˌper-ə-tə-ˈnī-təs\ *n* : inflammation of the peritoneum

peri·wig \ˈper-i-ˌwig\ *n* : WIG

¹per·i·win·kle \ˈper-i-ˌwiŋ-kəl\ *n* : a usu. blue-flowered creeping plant cultivated as a ground cover

²periwinkle *n* : any of various small edible seashore snails

per·ju·ry \ˈpər-jə-rē\ *n* : the voluntary violation of an oath to tell the truth : lying under oath — **per·jure** \ˈpər-jər\ *vb* — **per·jur·er** *n*

¹perk \ˈpərk\ *vb* **1** : to thrust (as the head) up impudently or jauntily **2** : to regain vigor or spirit **3** : to make trim or brisk : FRESHEN — **perky** *adj*

²perk *vb* : PERCOLATE

³perk *n* : PERQUISITE — usu. used in pl.

per·lite \ˈpər-ˌlīt\ *n* : volcanic glass that when expanded by heat forms a lightweight material used esp. in concrete and plaster and for potting plants

¹perm \ˈpərm\ *n* : PERMANENT

²perm *vb* : to give (hair) a permanent

³perm *abbr* permanent

per·ma·frost \ˈpər-mə-ˌfrȯst\ *n* : a permanently frozen layer below the surface in frigid regions of a planet

¹per·ma·nent \ˈpər-mə-nənt\ *adj* : LASTING, STABLE — **per·ma·nence** \-nəns\ *n* — **per·ma·nen·cy** \-nən-sē\ *n* — **per·ma·nent·ly** *adv*

²permanent *n* : a long-lasting hair wave or straightening

permanent press *n* : the process of treating fabrics with chemicals (as resin) and heat for setting the shape and for aiding wrinkle resistance

per·me·able \ˈpər-mē-ə-bəl\ *adj* : having small openings that permit liquids or gases to seep through — **per·me·a·bil·i·ty** \ˌpər-mē-ə-ˈbi-lə-tē\ *n*

per·me·ate \ˈpər-mē-ˌāt\ *vb* **-at·ed; -at·ing 1** : PERVADE **2** : to seep through the pores of : PENETRATE — **per·me·ation** \ˌpər-mē-ˈā-shən\ *n*

Perm·ian \ˈpər-mē-ən\ *adj* : of, relating to, or being the latest period of the Paleozoic era — **Permian** *n*

per·mis·si·ble \pər-ˈmi-sə-bəl\ *adj* : that may be permitted : ALLOWABLE

per·mis·sion \pər-ˈmi-shən\ *n* : formal consent : AUTHORIZATION

per·mis·sive \pər-ˈmi-siv\ *adj* : granting permission; *esp* : INDULGENT — **per·mis·sive·ly** *adv* — **per·mis·sive·ness** *n*

¹per·mit \pər-ˈmit\ *vb* **per·mit·ted; per·mit·ting 1** : to consent to : ALLOW **2** : to make possible

²per·mit \ˈpər-ˌmit, pər-ˈmit\ *n* : a written permission : LICENSE

per·mu·ta·tion \ˌpər-myù-ˈtā-shən\ *n* **1** : a major or fundamental change **2** : the act or process of changing the order of an ordered set of objects ✦ *Synonyms* INNOVATION, MUTATION, VICISSITUDE

per·ni·cious \pər-ˈni-shəs\ *adj* [ME, fr. AF, fr. L *perniciosus*, fr. *pernicies* destruction, fr. *per-* through + *nec-, nex* violent death] : very destructive or injurious — **per·ni·cious·ly** *adv*

per·ora·tion \ˈper-ə-ˌrā-shən, ˈpər-\ *n* : the concluding part of a speech

¹per·ox·ide \pə-ˈräk-ˌsīd\ *n* : an oxide containing a large proportion of oxygen; *esp* : HYDROGEN PEROXIDE

²peroxide *vb* **-id·ed; -id·ing** : to bleach with hydrogen peroxide

perp *abbr* **1** perpendicular **2** perpetrator

per·pen·dic·u·lar \ˌpər-pən-ˈdi-kyə-lər\ *adj* **1** : standing at right angles to the plane of the horizon **2** : forming a right angle with each other or with a given line or plane — **perpendicular** *n* — **per·pen·dic·u·lar·i·ty** \-ˌdi-kyə-ˈla-rə-tē\ *n* — **per·pen·dic·u·lar·ly** *adv*

per·pe·trate \ˈpər-pə-ˌtrāt\ *vb* **-trat·ed; -trat·ing** : to carry out (as a crime) : COMMIT — **per·pe·tra·tion** \ˌpər-pə-ˈtrā-shən\ *n* — **per·pe·tra·tor** \ˈpər-pə-ˌtrā-tər\ *n*

per·pet·u·al \pər-ˈpe-chə-wəl\ *adj* **1** : continuing forever : EVERLASTING **2** : occurring continually : CONSTANT ⟨~ annoyance⟩ ✦ *Synonyms* CEASELESS, UNCEASING, CONTINUAL, CONTINUOUS, INCESSANT, UNREMITTING — **per·pet·u·al·ly** *adv*

per·pet·u·ate \pər-ˈpe-chə-ˌwāt\ *vb* **-at·ed; -at·ing** : to make perpetual : cause to last indefinitely — **per·pet·u·a·tion** \-ˌpe-chə-ˈwā-shən\ *n*

per·pe·tu·i·ty \ˌpər-pə-ˈtü-ə-tē, -ˈtyü-\ *n, pl* **-ties 1** : ETERNITY 1 **2** : the quality or state of being perpetual

per·plex \pər-ˈpleks\ *vb* : to disturb mentally; *esp* : CONFUSE — **per·plex·i·ty** \-ˈplek-sə-tē\ *n*

per·plexed \-ˈplekst\ *adj* **1** : filled with uncertainty : PUZZLED **2** : full of difficulty : COMPLICATED — **per·plexed·ly** \-ˈplek-səd-lē\ *adv*

per·qui·site \ˈpər-kwə-zət\ *n* : a privilege or profit beyond regular pay

pers *abbr* person; personal

¹per se \(ˌ)pər-ˈsā\ *adv* [L] : by, of, or in itself : as such

²per se *adj* : being such inherently, clearly, or as a matter of law

per·se·cute \ˈpər-si-ˌkyüt\ *vb* **-cut·ed; -cut·ing** : to pursue in such a way as to injure or afflict : HARASS; *esp* : to cause to suffer because of belief — **per·se·cu·tion** \ˌpər-si-ˈkyü-shən\ *n* — **per·se·cu·tor** \ˈpər-si-ˌkyü-tər\ *n*

per·se·vere \ˌpər-sə-ˈvir\ *vb* **-vered; -ver·ing** : to persist (as in an undertaking) in spite of difficulties — **per·se·ver·ance** \-ˈvir-əns\ *n*

Per·sian \ˈpər-zhən\ *n* **1** : a native or inhabitant of ancient Persia **2** : a member of one of the peoples of modern Iran **3** : the language of the Persians

Persian cat *n* : any of a breed of stocky round-headed domestic cats that have a long silky coat

Persian lamb *n* : a pelt with very silky tightly curled fur that is obtained from newborn lambs which are older than those yielding broadtail

per·si·flage \ˈpər-si-ˌfläzh, ˈper-\ *n* [F, fr. *persifler* to ban-

PERIODIC TABLE

This is the common long form of the table, with atomic numbers given along with the symbols. Roman numerals and letters heading the vertical columns indicate the groups. (There are differences of opinion regarding the letter designations, but those given here are probably the most generally used. International standards favor numbering the groups 1-18 from left to right using Arabic numerals, but the designations shown below remain quite common.) Horizontal rows represent the periods, with two very long periods and represented below the main table.

IA[1]	IIA[2]	IIIB	IVB	VB	VIB	VIIB	VIII			IB	IIB	IIIA	IVA	VA	VIA	VIIA[3]	VIIIA[4]
1 H																1 H	2 He
3 Li	4 Be											5 B	6 C	7 N	8 O	9 F	10 Ne
11 Na	12 Mg											13 Al	14 Si	15 P	16 S	17 Cl	18 Ar
19 K	20 Ca	21 Sc	22 Ti	23 V	24 Cr	25 Mn	26 Fe	27 Co	28 Ni	29 Cu	30 Zn	31 Ga	32 Ge	33 As	34 Se	35 Br	36 Kr
37 Rb	38 Sr	39 Y	40 Zr	41 Nb	42 Mo	43 Tc	44 Ru	45 Rh	46 Pd	47 Ag	48 Cd	49 In	50 Sn	51 Sb	52 Te	53 I	54 Xe
55 Cs	56 Ba	57 *La	72 Hf	73 Ta	74 W	75 Re	76 Os	77 Ir	78 Pt	79 Au	80 Hg	81 Tl	82 Pb	83 Bi	84 Po	85 At	86 Rn
87 Fr	88 Ra	89 #Ac	104 Rf	105 Db	106 Sg	107 Bh	108 Hs	109 Mt	110 Ds								

*LANTHANIDE SERIES	58 Ce	59 Pr	60 Nd	61 Pm	62 Sm	63 Eu	64 Gd	65 Tb	66 Dy	67 Ho	68 Er	69 Tm	70 Yb	71 Lu
#ACTINIDE SERIES	90 Th	91 Pa	92 U	93 Np	94 Pu	95 Am	96 Cm	97 Bk	98 Cf	99 Es	100 Fm	101 Md	102 No	103 Lr

[1]Group IA (excluding hydrogen) comprises the alkali metals.
[2]Group IIA comprises the alkaline earth metals.
[3]Group VIIA (excluding hydrogen) comprises the halogens.
[4]Group VIIIA (also called group Zero) comprises the noble gases.

ter, fr. *per-* thoroughly + *siffler* to whistle, hiss, boo, ultim. fr. L *sibilare*] : lightly jesting or mocking talk

per·sim·mon \pər-ˈsi-mən\ *n* : either of two trees related to the ebony; *also* : the edible usu. orange or red plumlike fruit of a persimmon

per·sist \pər-ˈsist, -ˈzist\ *vb* **1** : to go on resolutely or stubbornly in spite of difficulties **2** : to continue to exist — **per·sis·tence** \-ˈsis-təns, -ˈzis-\ *n* — **per·sis·ten·cy** \-tən-sē\ *n* — **per·sis·tent** \-tənt\ *adj* — **per·sis·tent·ly** *adv*

per·snick·e·ty \pər-ˈsni-kə-tē\ *adj* : fussy about small details

per·son \ˈpər-sən\ *n* [ME, fr. AF *persone*, fr. L *persona* actor's mask, character in a play, person, prob. fr. Etruscan *phersu* mask, fr. Gk *prosōpa*, pl. of *prosōpon* face, mask] **1** : a human being : INDIVIDUAL — used in combination esp. by those who prefer to avoid *man* in compounds applicable to both sexes ⟨chair*person*⟩ **2** : one of the three modes of being in the Godhead as understood by Trinitarians **3** : the body of a human being **4** : the individual personality of a human being : SELF **5** : reference of a segment of discourse to the speaker, to one spoken to, or to one spoken of esp. as indicated by certain pronouns

per·so·na \pər-ˈsō-nə\ *n, pl* **-nae** \-nē\ *or* **-nas** : the personality that a person projects in public

per·son·able \ˈpər-sə-nə-bəl\ *adj* : pleasant in person : ATTRACTIVE

per·son·age \ˈpər-sə-nij\ *n* : a person of rank, note, or distinction

¹per·son·al \ˈpər-sə-nəl\ *adj* **1** : of, relating to, or affecting a person : PRIVATE ⟨∼ correspondence⟩ **2** : done in person ⟨a ∼ inquiry⟩ **3** : relating to the person or body ⟨∼ injuries⟩ **4** : relating to an individual esp. in an offensive way ⟨resented such ∼ remarks⟩ **5** : of or relating to temporary or movable property as distinguished from real estate **6** : denoting grammatical person **7** : intended for use by one person

²personal *n* **1** : a short newspaper paragraph relating to a person or group or to personal matters **2** : a short personal or private communication in the classified ads section of a newspaper

personal computer *n* : a computer with a microprocessor designed for an individual user to run esp. commercial software

personal digital assistant *n* : PDA

per·son·al·ise *Brit var of* PERSONALIZE

per·son·al·i·ty \ˌpər-sə-ˈna-lə-tē\ *n, pl* **-ties** **1** : an offensively personal remark ⟨indulges in *personalities*⟩ **2** : the collection of emotional and behavioral traits that characterize a person **3** : distinction of personal and social traits **4** : a well-known person ⟨a TV ∼⟩ ♦ *Synonyms* INDIVIDUALITY, TEMPERAMENT, DISPOSITION, MAKEUP

per·son·al·ize \ˈpər-sə-nə-ˌlīz\ *vb* **-ized; -iz·ing** : to make personal or individual; *esp* : to mark as belonging to a particular person

per·son·al·ly \-nə-lē\ *adv* **1** : in person **2** : as a person **3** : as far as oneself is concerned ⟨∼, I don't want to go⟩

per·son·al·ty \ˈpər-sə-nəl-tē\ *n, pl* **-ties** : personal property

per·so·na non gra·ta \pər-ˈsō-nə-ˌnän-ˈgra-tə, -ˈgrä-\ *adj* [L] : being personally unacceptable or unwelcome

per·son·ate \ˈpər-sə-ˌnāt\ *vb* **-at·ed; -at·ing** : IMPERSONATE, REPRESENT

per·son·i·fy \pər-ˈsä-nə-ˌfī\ *vb* **-fied; -fy·ing** **1** : to think of or represent as a person **2** : to be the embodiment of : INCARNATE ⟨∼ the law⟩ — **per·son·i·fi·ca·tion** \-ˌsä-nə-fə-ˈkā-shən\ *n*

per·son·nel \ˌpər-sə-ˈnel\ *n* : a body of persons employed

per·spec·tive \pər-ˈspek-tiv\ *n* **1** : the science of painting and drawing so that objects represented have apparent depth and distance **2** : the aspect in which a subject or its parts are mentally viewed; *esp* : a view of things (as objects or events) in their true relationship or relative importance

per·spi·ca·cious \ˌpər-spə-ˈkā-shəs\ *adj* : having or showing keen understanding or discernment — **per·spi·cac·i·ty** \-ˈka-sə-tē\ *n*

per·spic·u·ous \pər-ˈspi-kyə-wəs\ *adj* : plain to the understanding — **per·spi·cu·i·ty** \ˌpər-spə-ˈkyü-ə-tē\ *n*

per·spire \pər-ˈspī(-ə)r\ *vb* **per·spired; per·spir·ing** : SWEAT — **per·spi·ra·tion** \ˌpər-spə-ˈrā-shən\ *n*

per·suade \pər-ˈswād\ *vb* **per·suad·ed; per·suad·ing** : to win over to a belief or course of action by argument or entreaty — **per·sua·sive** \-ˈswā-siv, -ziv\ *adj* — **per·sua·sive·ly** *adv* — **per·sua·sive·ness** *n*

per·sua·sion \pər-ˈswā-zhən\ *n* **1** : the act or process of persuading **2** : a system of religious beliefs; *also* : a group holding such beliefs

pert \ˈpərt\ *adj* [ME, evident, attractive, saucy, short for *apert* evident, fr. AF, fr. L *apertus* open, fr. pp. of *aperire* to open] **1** : saucily free and forward : IMPUDENT **2** : stylishly trim : JAUNTY **3** : LIVELY

per·tain \pər-ˈtān\ *vb* **1** : to belong to as a part, quality, or function ⟨duties ∼*ing* to the office⟩ **2** : to have reference : RELATE ⟨books ∼*ing* to birds⟩

per·ti·na·cious \ˌpər-tə-ˈnā-shəs\ *adj* **1** : holding resolutely to an opinion or purpose **2** : obstinately persistent ⟨a ∼ bill collector⟩ ♦ *Synonyms* DOGGED, MULISH, HEADSTRONG, PERVERSE — **per·ti·nac·i·ty** \-ˈna-sə-tē\ *n*

per·ti·nent \ˈpər-tə-nənt\ *adj* : relating to the matter under consideration ♦ *Synonyms* RELEVANT, GERMANE, APPLICABLE, APROPOS — **per·ti·nence** \-əns\ *n*

per·turb \pər-ˈtərb\ *vb* : to disturb greatly esp. in mind : UPSET — **per·tur·ba·tion** \ˌpər-tər-ˈbā-shən\ *n*

per·tus·sis \pər-ˈtə-səs\ *n* : WHOOPING COUGH

pe·ruke \pə-ˈrük\ *n* : WIG

pe·ruse \pə-ˈrüz\ *vb* **pe·rused; pe·rus·ing** : READ; *esp* : to read over attentively or leisurely — **pe·rus·al** \-ˈrü-zəl\ *n*

per·vade \pər-ˈvād\ *vb* **per·vad·ed; per·vad·ing** : to spread through every part of : PERMEATE, PENETRATE — **per·va·sive** \-ˈvā-siv, -ziv\ *adj*

per·verse \pər-ˈvərs\ *adj* **1** : turned away from what is right or good : CORRUPT **2** : obstinate in opposing what is reasonable or accepted **3** : marked by perversion — **per·verse·ly** *adv* — **per·verse·ness** *n* — **per·ver·si·ty** \-ˈvər-sə-tē\ *n*

per·ver·sion \pər-ˈvər-zhən\ *n* **1** : the action of perverting : the condition of being perverted **2** : a perverted form of something; *esp* : aberrant sexual behavior

¹per·vert \pər-ˈvərt\ *vb* **1** : to lead astray : CORRUPT ⟨∼ the young⟩ **2** : to divert to a wrong purpose : MISAPPLY ⟨∼ evidence⟩ ♦ *Synonyms* DEPRAVE, DEBASE, DEBAUCH, DEMORALIZE — **per·vert·er** *n*

²per·vert \ˈpər-ˌvərt\ *n* : one that is perverted; *esp* : one given to sexual perversion

pe·se·ta \pə-ˈsā-tə\ *n* : the former basic monetary unit of Spain

pe·se·wa \pə-ˈsā-wə\ *n* — see *cedi* at MONEY table

pes·ky \ˈpes-kē\ *adj* **pes·ki·er; -est** : causing annoyance : TROUBLESOME

pe·so \ˈpā-sō\ *n, pl* **pesos** — see MONEY table

pes·si·mism \ˈpe-sə-ˌmi-zəm\ *n* [F *pessimisme*, fr. L *pessimus* worst] : an inclination to take the least favorable view (as of events) or to expect the worst — **pes·si·mist** \-mist\ *n* — **pes·si·mis·tic** \ˌpe-sə-ˈmis-tik\ *adj*

pest \ˈpest\ *n* **1** : a destructive epidemic disease : PLAGUE **2** : a plant or animal detrimental to humans **3** : one that pesters : NUISANCE — **pesty** *adj*

pes·ter \ˈpes-tər\ *vb* : to harass with petty irritations : ANNOY

pes·ti·cide \ˈpes-tə-ˌsīd\ *n* : an agent used to destroy pests

pes·tif·er·ous \pes-ˈti-fə-rəs\ *adj* **1** : PESTILENT **2** : ANNOYING

pes·ti·lence \ˈpes-tə-ləns\ *n* : a destructive infectious swiftly spreading disease; *esp* : BUBONIC PLAGUE

pes·ti·lent \-lənt\ *adj* **1** : dangerous to life : DEADLY **2** : PERNICIOUS, HARMFUL **3** : TROUBLESOME **4** : INFECTIOUS, CONTAGIOUS

pes·ti·len·tial \ˌpes-tə-ˈlen-chəl\ *adj* **1** : causing or tending to cause pestilence : DEADLY **2** : morally harmful

pes·tle \ˈpes-əl, ˈpes-tᵊl\ *n* : an implement for grinding substances in a mortar — **pestle** *vb*

¹pet \ˈpet\ *n* **1** : FAVORITE, DARLING **2** : a domesticated animal kept for pleasure rather than utility

²pet *adj* **1** : kept or treated as a pet ⟨∼ dog⟩ **2** : expressing fondness ⟨∼ name⟩ **3** : particularly liked or favored

³pet *vb* **pet·ted; pet·ting** **1** : to stroke gently or lovingly **2** : to make a pet of : PAMPER **3** : to engage in amorous kissing and caressing

⁴pet *n* : a fit of peevishness, sulkiness, or anger — **pet·tish** *adj*

Pet abbr Peter

pet·al \'pe-t[ᵊ]l\ n : one of the modified leaves of a flower's corolla

pe·tard \pə-'tärd, -'tär\ n : a case containing an explosive to break down a door or gate or breach a wall

pe·ter \'pē-tər\ vb : to diminish gradually and come to an end ⟨his energy ~ed out⟩

Pe·ter \'pē-tər\ n — see BIBLE table

pet·i·ole \'pe-tē-ˌōl\ n : a slender stem that supports a leaf

pe·tite \pə-'tēt\ adj [F] : small and trim of figure ⟨a ~ woman⟩ — **petite** n

pe·tit four \ˌpe-tē-'fȯr\ n, pl **petits fours** or **petit fours** \-'fȯrz\ [F, lit., small oven] : a small cake cut from pound, or sponge cake and frosted

¹pe·ti·tion \pə-'ti-shən\ n : an earnest request : ENTREATY; esp : a formal written request made to an authority

²petition vb : to make a request to or for — **pe·ti·tion·er** n

pe·trel \'pe-trəl\ n : any of numerous seabirds that fly far from land

pe·tri dish \'pē-trē-\ n 1 : a small shallow dish used esp. for growing bacteria 2 : something fosterng development or innovation

pet·ri·fy \'pe-trə-ˌfī\ vb **-fied; -fy·ing** 1 : to convert (organic matter) into stone or stony material 2 : to make rigid or inactive (as from fear or awe) — **pet·ri·fac·tion** \ˌpe-trə-'fak-shən\ n

pet·ro·chem·i·cal \ˌpe-trō-'ke-mi-kəl\ n : a chemical isolated or derived from petroleum or natural gas — **pet·ro·chem·is·try** \-'ke-mə-strē\ n

pet·rol \'pe-trəl\ n, chiefly Brit : GASOLINE

pet·ro·la·tum \ˌpe-trə-'lā-təm\ n : PETROLEUM JELLY

pe·tro·leum \pə-'trō-lē-əm\ n [ML, fr. Gk petra rock + L oleum oil] : an oily flammable liquid obtained from wells drilled in the ground and refined into gasoline, fuel oils, and other products

petroleum jelly n : a tasteless, odorless, and oily or greasy substance from petroleum that is used esp. in ointments and dressings

¹pet·ti·coat \'pe-tē-ˌkōt\ n 1 : a skirt worn under a dress 2 : an outer skirt

²petticoat adj : of, relating to, or exercised by women : FEMALE

pet·ti·fog·ger \'pe-tē-ˌfȯ-gər, -ˌfä-\ n 1 : a lawyer whose methods are petty, underhanded, or disreputable 2 : one given to quibbling over trifles — **pet·ti·fog·ging** \-giŋ\ adj or n

pet·ty \'pe-tē\ adj **pet·ti·er; -est** [ME pety small, minor, alter. of petit, fr. AF, small] 1 : having secondary rank : MINOR ⟨~ prince⟩ 2 : of little importance : TRIFLING ⟨~ faults⟩ 3 : marked by narrowness or meanness — **pet·ti·ly** \'pe-tə-lē\ adv — **pet·ti·ness** \-tē-nəs\ n

petty officer n : a subordinate officer in the navy or coast guard appointed from among the enlisted men

petty officer first class n : a petty officer ranking below a chief petty officer

petty officer second class n : a petty officer ranking below a petty officer first class

petty officer third class n : a petty officer ranking below a petty officer second class

pet·u·lant \'pe-chə-lənt\ adj : marked by capricious ill humor ✦ Synonyms IRRITABLE, PEEVISH, FRETFUL, FRACTIOUS, QUERULOUS — **pet·u·lance** \-ləns\ n — **pet·u·lant·ly** adv

pe·tu·nia \pi-'tün-yə, -'tyün-\ n : any of a genus of tropical So. American herbs related to the potato and having bright funnel-shaped flowers

pew \'pyü\ n [ME pewe, fr. MF puie balustrade, fr. L podia, pl. of podium parapet, podium, fr. Gk podion base, dim. of pod-, pous foot] : any of the benches with backs fixed in rows in a church

pe·wee \'pē-(ˌ)wē\ n : any of various small American flycatchers

pew·ter \'pyü-tər\ n 1 : an alloy of tin used esp. for household utensils 2 : a bluish gray color — **pewter** adj — **pew·ter·er** n

pey·o·te \pā-'ō-tē\ also **pey·otl** \-'ō-t[ᵊ]l\ n 1 : a hallucinogenic drug derived from the peyote cactus and containing mescaline 2 : a small cactus of the southwestern U.S. and Mexico

pf abbr 1 pfennig 2 preferred

PFC or **Pfc** abbr private first class

pfd abbr preferred

pfen·nig \'fe-nig\ n, pl **pfennig** also **pfennigs** or **pfen·ni·ge** \'fe-ni-gə\ : a former monetary unit equal to ¹⁄₁₀₀ deutsche mark

pg abbr page

PG abbr postgraduate

PGA abbr Professional Golfers' Association

pH \(ˌ)pē-'āch\ n : a value used to express acidity and alkalinity; also : the condition represented by such a value

PH abbr 1 pinch hit 2 public health

pha·eton \'fā-ə-t[ᵊ]n\ n [F phaéton, fr. Gk Phaethōn, son of the sun god who persuaded his father to let him drive the chariot of the sun but who lost control of the horses with disastrous consequences] 1 : a light 4-wheeled horse-drawn vehicle 2 : an open automobile with two cross seats

phage \'fāj\ n : BACTERIOPHAGE

pha·lanx \'fā-ˌlaŋks\ n, pl **pha·lanx·es** or **pha·lan·ges** \fə-'lan-jēz\ 1 : a group or body (as of troops) in compact formation 2 pl **phalanges** : one of the digital bones of the hand or foot of a vertebrate

phal·a·rope \'fa-lə-ˌrōp\ n, pl **-ropes** also **-rope** : any of a genus of small shorebirds related to sandpipers

phal·lic \'fa-lik\ adj 1 : of, relating to, or resembling a phallus 2 : relating to or being the stage of psychosexual development in psychoanalytic theory during which children become interested in their own sexual organs

phal·lus \'fa-ləs\ n, pl **phal·li** \'fa-ˌlī\ or **phal·lus·es** : PENIS; also : a symbolic representation of the penis

Phan·er·o·zo·ic \ˌfa-nə-rə-'zō-ik\ adj : of, relating to, or being an eon of geologic history comprising the Paleozoic, Mesozoic, and Cenozoic

phan·tasm \'fan-ˌta-zəm\ n : a product of the imagination : ILLUSION — **phan·tas·mal** \ˌfan-'taz-məl\ adj

phan·tas·ma·go·ria \fan-ˌtaz-mə-'gȯr-ē-ə\ n : a constantly shifting complex succession of things seen or imagined; also : a scene that constantly changes or fluctuates

phantasy var of FANTASY

phan·tom \'fan-təm\ n 1 : something (as a specter) that is apparent to sense but has no substantial existence 2 : a mere show : SHADOW — **phantom** adj

pha·raoh \'fer-ō, 'fā-rō\ n, often cap : a ruler of ancient Egypt

phar·i·sa·ical \ˌfa-rə-'sā-ə-kəl\ adj : hypocritically self-righteous

phar·i·see \'fa-rə-ˌsē\ n 1 cap : a member of an ancient Jewish sect noted for strict observance of rites and ceremonies of the traditional law 2 : a self-righteous or hypocritical person — **phar·i·sa·ic** \ˌfa-rə-'sā-ik\ adj

pharm abbr pharmaceutical; pharmacist; pharmacy

phar·ma·ceu·ti·cal \ˌfär-mə-'sü-ti-kəl\ adj : of, relating to, or engaged in pharmacy or the manufacture and sale of medicinal drugs — **pharmaceutical** n

phar·ma·col·o·gy \ˌfär-mə-'kä-lə-jē\ n 1 : the science of drugs esp. as related to medicinal uses 2 : the reactions and properties of one or more drugs — **phar·ma·co·log·i·cal** \-kə-'lä-ji-kəl\ also **phar·ma·co·log·ic** \-kə-'lä-jik\ adj — **phar·ma·col·o·gist** \-'kä-lə-jist\ n

phar·ma·co·poe·ia also **phar·ma·co·pe·ia** \-kə-'pē-ə\ n 1 : a book describing drugs and medicinal preparations 2 : a stock of drugs

phar·ma·cy \'fär-mə-sē\ n, pl **-cies** 1 : the art, practice, or profession of preparing and dispensing medical drugs 2 : DRUGSTORE — **phar·ma·cist** \-sist\ n

phar·ynx \'fa-riŋks\ n, pl **pha·ryn·ges** \fə-'rin-jēz\ also **phar·ynx·es** : the muscular tubular passage extending from the back of the nasal cavity and mouth to the esophagus — **pha·ryn·ge·al** \fə-'rin-jəl, ˌfa-rən-'jē-əl\ adj

phase \'fāz\ n 1 : a particular appearance in a recurring series of changes ⟨~s of the moon⟩ 2 : a stage or interval in a process or cycle ⟨first ~ of an experiment⟩ 3 : an aspect or part under consideration — **pha·sic** \'fā-zik\ adj

phase down vb : to reduce the size or amount of by phases

phase in vb : to introduce in stages

phase-out \'fāz-ˌau̇t\ n : a gradual stopping of operations or production

phase out vb : to stop production or use of in stages

PhD abbr [L philosophiae doctor] doctor of philosophy

pheas·ant \'fe-z°nt\ *n, pl* **pheasant** *or* **pheasants** : any of numerous long-tailed brilliantly colored game birds related to the domestic chicken

pheasant

phen·cy·cli·dine \,fen-'sī-klə-,dēn\ *n* : a drug used esp. as a veterinary anesthetic and sometimes illicitly as a hallucinogenic drug

phe·no·bar·bi·tal \,fē-nō-'bär-bə-,tȯl\ *n* : a crystalline drug used as a hypnotic and sedative

phe·nol \'fē-,nȯl\ *n* : a corrosive poisonous acidic compound present in coal and wood tars and used in solution as a disinfectant

phe·nom·e·non \fi-'nä-mə-,nän, -nən\ *n, pl* **-na** \-nə\ *or* **-nons** [LL *phaenomenon,* fr. Gk *phainomenon,* fr. neut. of *phainomenos,* prp. of *phainesthai* to appear] **1** *pl* **-na** : an observable fact or event **2** : an outward sign of the working of a law of nature **3** *pl* **-nons** : an extraordinary person or thing : PRODIGY — **phe·nom·e·nal** \-'nä-mə-n°l\ *adj* — **phe·nom·e·non·al·ly** *adv*

pher·o·mone \'fer-ə-,mōn\ *n* : a chemical substance that is usu. produced by an animal and serves to stimulate a behavioral response in other individuals of the same species — **pher·o·mon·al** \,fer-ə-'mō-n°l\ *adj*

phi \'fī\ *n* : the 21st letter of the Greek alphabet — Φ or φ

phi·al \'fī(-ə)l\ *n* : VIAL

Phil *abbr* Philippians

phi·lan·der \fə-'lan-dər\ *vb* : to have casual or illicit sexual relations with many women — **phi·lan·der·er** *n*

phi·lan·thro·py \fə-'lan-thrə-pē\ *n, pl* **-pies** **1** : goodwill toward all people; *esp* : effort to promote human welfare **2** : a charitable act or gift; *also* : an organization that distributes or is supported by donated funds — **phil·an·throp·ic** \,fi-lən-'thrä-pik\ *adj* — **phil·an·throp·i·cal·ly** \-pi-k(ə-)lē\ *adv* — **phi·lan·thro·pist** \fə-'lan-thrə-pist\ *n*

phi·lat·e·ly \fə-'la-tə-lē\ *n* : the collection and study of postage and imprinted stamps — **phil·a·tel·ic** \,fi-lə-'te-lik\ *adj* — **phi·lat·e·list** \fə-'la-tə-list\ *n*

Phi·le·mon \fə-'lē-mən, fī-\ *n* — see BIBLE table

Phi·lip·pi·ans \fə-'li-pē-ənz\ *n* — see BIBLE table

phi·lip·pic \fə-'li-pik\ *n* : TIRADE

phi·lis·tine \'fi-lə-,stēn; fə-'lis-tən\ *n, often cap* [*Philistine,* inhabitant of ancient Philistia (Palestine)] : a person who is smugly insensitive or indifferent to intellectual or artistic values — **philistine** *adj, often cap*

Phil·lips \'fi-ləps\ *adj* : of, relating to, or being a screw having a head with a cross slot or its corresponding screwdriver

philo·den·dron \,fi-lə-'den-drən\ *n, pl* **-drons** *also* **-dra** \-drə\ [NL, fr. Gk, neut. of *philodendros* loving trees, fr. *philos* dear, friendly + *dendron* tree] : any of various plants of the arum family grown for their showy foliage

phi·lol·o·gy \fə-'lä-lə-jē\ *n* **1** : the study of literature and relevant fields **2** : LINGUISTICS; *esp* : historical and comparative linguistics — **phil·o·log·i·cal** \,fi-lə-'lä-ji-kəl\ *adj* — **phi·lol·o·gist** \fə-'lä-lə-jist\ *n*

philos *abbr* philosopher; philosophy

phi·los·o·pher \fə-'lä-sə-fər\ *n* **1** : a reflective thinker : SCHOLAR **2** : a student of or specialist in philosophy **3** : a person whose philosophical perspective makes it possible to meet trouble calmly

phi·los·o·phise *Brit var of* PHILOSOPHIZE

phi·los·o·phize \fə-'lä-sə-,fīz\ *vb* **-phized; -phiz·ing** **1** : to reason like a philosopher : THEORIZE **2** : to expound a philosophy esp. superficially

phi·los·o·phy \fə-'lä-sə-fē\ *n, pl* **-phies** **1** : sciences and liberal arts exclusive of medicine, law, and theology ⟨doc-

tor of ∼⟩ **2** : a critical study of fundamental beliefs and the grounds for them **3** : a system of philosophical concepts ⟨Aristotelian ∼⟩ **4** : a basic theory concerning a particular subject or sphere of activity **5** : the sum of the ideas and convictions of an individual or group ⟨her ∼ of life⟩ **6** : calmness of temper and judgment — **phil·o·soph·i·cal** \-fi·kəl\ *also* **phil·o·soph·ic** \,fi-lə-'sä-fik\ *adj* — **phil·o·soph·i·cal·ly** \-k(ə-)lē\ *adv*

phil·ter \'fil-tər\ *n* **1** : a magic potion **2** : a potion, drug, or charm held to arouse sexual passion

phil·tre *chiefly Brit var of* PHILTER

phle·bi·tis \fli-'bī-təs\ *n* : inflammation of a vein

phle·bot·o·my \fli-'bä-tə-mē\ *n, pl* **-mies** : the opening of a vein esp. for removing or releasing blood

phlegm \'flem\ *n* [ME *fleume,* fr. AF, fr. LL *phlegma,* fr. Gk, flame, inflammation, phlegm, fr. *phlegein* to burn] : thick mucus secreted in abnormal quantity esp. in the nose and throat

phleg·mat·ic \fleg-'ma-tik\ *adj* : having or showing a slow and stolid temperament ◆ **Synonyms** IMPASSIVE, APATHETIC, STOIC

phlo·em \'flō-,em\ *n* : a vascular plant tissue external to the xylem that carries dissolved food material and functions in support and storage

phlox \'fläks\ *n, pl* **phlox** *or* **phlox·es** : any of a genus of American herbs that have tall stalks with showy spreading terminal clusters of flowers

pho·bia \'fō-bē-ə\ *n* : an irrational persistent fear or dread — **pho·bic** \'fō-bik\ *adj*

phoe·be \'fē-(,)bē\ *n* : a flycatcher of the eastern U.S. that has a slight crest and is grayish brown above and yellowish white below

phoe·nix \'fē-niks\ *n* : a legendary bird held to live for centuries and then to burn itself to death and rise fresh and young from its ashes

¹phone \'fōn\ *n* **1** : TELEPHONE **2** : EARPHONE

²phone *vb* **phoned; phon·ing** : TELEPHONE

phone card *n* : a prepaid card used in paying for telephone calls

pho·neme \'fō-,nēm\ *n* : one of the elementary units of speech that distinguish one utterance from another — **pho·ne·mic** \fō-'nē-mik\ *adj*

pho·net·ics \fə-'ne-tiks\ *n* : the study and systematic classification of the sounds made in spoken utterance — **pho·net·ic** \-tik\ *adj* — **pho·ne·ti·cian** \,fō-nə-'ti-shən\ *n*

pho·nic \'fä-nik\ *adj* **1** : of, relating to, or producing sound **2** : of or relating to the sounds of speech or to phonics — **pho·ni·cal·ly** \-ni-k(ə-)lē\ *adv*

phon·ics \'fä-niks\ *n* : a method of teaching people to read and pronounce words by learning the phonetic value of letters, letter groups, and esp. syllables

pho·no·graph \'fō-nə-,graf\ *n* : an instrument for reproducing sounds by means of the vibration of a needle following a spiral groove on a revolving disc

pho·nol·o·gy \fə-'nä-lə-jē\ *n* : a study and description of the sound changes in a language — **pho·no·log·i·cal** \,fō-nə-'lä-ji-kəl\ *adj* — **pho·nol·o·gist** \fə-'nä-lə-jist\ *n*

pho·ny *also* **pho·ney** \'fō-nē\ *adj* **pho·ni·er; -est** : marked by empty pretension : FAKE — **phony** *n*

phos·phate \'fäs-,fāt\ *n* : a salt of a phosphoric acid — **phos·phat·ic** \fäs-'fa-tik\ *adj*

phos·phor \'fäs-fər\ *n* : a phosphorescent substance

phos·pho·res·cence \,fäs-fə-'re-s°ns\ *n* **1** : luminescence caused by the absorption of radiations (as light or electrons) and continuing after these radiations stop **2** : an enduring luminescence without sensible heat — **phos·pho·res·cent** \-s°nt\ *adj* — **phos·pho·res·cent·ly** *adv*

phosphoric acid \,fäs-'fȯr-ik-, -'fär-\ *n* : any of several oxygen-containing acids of phosphorus

phos·pho·rus *also* **phos·pho·rous** \'fäs-fə-rəs\ *n* [NL, fr. Gk *phōsphoros* light-bearing, fr. *phōs* light + *pherein* to carry, bring] : a nonmetallic chemical element that has characteristics similar to nitrogen and occurs widely esp. as phosphates — **phos·pho·ric** \fäs-'fȯr-ik, -'fär-\ *adj* — **phos·pho·rous** \'fäs-fə-rəs; fäs-'fȯr-əs\ *adj*

phot- *or* **photo-** *comb form* **1** : light ⟨*photography*⟩ **2** : photograph : photographic ⟨*photoengraving*⟩ **3** : photoelectric ⟨*photocell*⟩

pho·to \'fō-tō\ *n, pl* **photos** : PHOTOGRAPH — **photo** *vb or adj*

pho·to·cell \'fō-tə-,sel\ *n* : PHOTOELECTRIC CELL

pho·to·chem·i·cal \ˌfō-tō-ˈke-mi-kəl\ adj : of, relating to, or resulting from the chemical action of radiant energy

pho·to·com·pose \-kəm-ˈpōz\ vb : to compose reading matter for reproduction by means of characters photographed on film — **pho·to·com·po·si·tion** \-ˌkäm-pə-ˈzi-shən\ n

pho·to·copy \ˈfō-tə-ˌkä-pē\ n : a photographic reproduction of graphic matter — **photocopy** vb

pho·to·elec·tric \ˌfō-tō-i-ˈlek-trik\ adj : relating to an electrical effect due to the interaction of light with matter — **pho·to·elec·tri·cal·ly** \-tri-k(ə-)lē\ adv

photoelectric cell n : a device whose electrical properties are modified by the action of light

pho·to·en·grave \ˌfō-tō-in-ˈgrāv\ vb : to make a photoengraving of

pho·to·en·grav·ing n : a process by which an etched printing plate is made from a photograph or drawing; also : a print made from such a plate

photo finish n : a race finish so close that a photograph of the finish is used to determine the winner

pho·tog \fə-ˈtäg\ n : PHOTOGRAPHER

pho·to·gen·ic \ˌfō-tə-ˈje-nik\ adj : eminently suitable esp. aesthetically for being photographed

pho·to·graph \ˈfō-tə-ˌgraf\ n : a picture taken by photography — **photograph** vb — **pho·tog·ra·pher** \fə-ˈtä-grə-fər\ n

pho·tog·ra·phy \fə-ˈtä-grə-fē\ n : the art or process of producing images on a sensitive surface (as film or a CCD chip by the action of light — **pho·to·graph·ic** \ˌfō-tə-ˈgra-fik\ adj — **pho·to·graph·i·cal·ly** \-fi-k(ə-)lē\ adv

pho·to·gra·vure \ˌfō-tə-grə-ˈvyu̇r\ n : a process for making prints from an intaglio plate prepared by photographic methods

pho·to·li·thog·ra·phy \ˌfō-tō-li-ˈthä-grə-fē\ n : the process of photographically transferring a pattern to a surface for etching (as in making an integrated circuit)

pho·tom·e·ter \fō-ˈtä-mə-tər\ n : an instrument for measuring the intensity of light — **pho·to·met·ric** \ˌfō-tō-ˈme-trik\ adj — **pho·tom·e·try** \fō-ˈtä-mə-trē\ n

pho·to·mi·cro·graph \ˌfō-tə-ˈmī-krə-ˌgraf\ n : a photograph of a microscope image — **pho·to·mi·crog·ra·phy** \-mī-ˈkrä-grə-fē\ n

pho·ton \ˈfō-ˌtän\ n : a quantum of electromagnetic radiation

photo op n : a situation or event that lends itself to the taking of pictures which favor the individuals photographed

pho·to·play \ˈfō-tō-ˌplā\ n : MOTION PICTURE

pho·to·sen·si·tive \ˌfō-tə-ˈsen-sə-tiv\ adj : sensitive or sensitized to the action of radiant energy

pho·to·sphere \ˈfō-tə-ˌsfir\ n : the luminous surface of a star — **pho·to·spher·ic** \ˌfō-tə-ˈsfir-ik, -ˈsfer-\ adj

pho·to·syn·the·sis \ˌfō-tō-ˈsin-thə-səs\ n : the process by which chlorophyll-containing plants make carbohydrates from water and from carbon dioxide in the air in the presence of light — **pho·to·syn·the·size** \-ˌsīz\ vb — **pho·to·syn·thet·ic** \-sin-ˈthe-tik\ adj

phr abbr phrase

¹**phrase** \ˈfrāz\ n 1 : a brief expression 2 : a group of two or more grammatically related words that form a sense unit expressing a thought

²**phrase** vb phrased; phras·ing : to express in words

phrase·ol·o·gy \ˌfrā-zē-ˈä-lə-jē\ n, pl -gies : a manner of phrasing : STYLE

phras·ing n : style of expression

phre·net·ic archaic var of FRENETIC

phren·ic \ˈfre-nik\ adj : of or relating to the diaphragm ⟨~ nerves⟩

phre·nol·o·gy \fri-ˈnä-lə-jē\ n : the study of the conformation of the skull based on the belief that it indicates mental faculties and character traits

phy·lac·tery \fə-ˈlak-tə-rē\ n, pl -ter·ies 1 : one of two small square leather boxes containing slips inscribed with scripture passages and traditionally worn on the left arm and forehead by Jewish men during morning weekday prayers 2 : AMULET

phy·lum \ˈfī-ləm\ n, pl **phy·la** \-lə\ [NL, fr. Gk phylon tribe, race] : a major category in biological classification esp. of animals that ranks above the class and below the kingdom; also : a group (as of people) apparently of common origin

phys abbr 1 physical 2 physics

¹**phys·ic** \ˈfi-zik\ n 1 : the profession of medicine 2 : MEDICINE; esp : PURGATIVE

²**physic** vb phys·icked; phys·ick·ing : PURGE 2

¹**phys·i·cal** \ˈfi-zi-kəl\ adj 1 : of or relating to nature or the laws of nature 2 : material as opposed to mental or spiritual 3 : of, relating to, or produced by the forces and operations of physics 4 : of or relating to the body — **phys·i·cal·ly** \-k(ə-)lē\ adv

²**physical** n : PHYSICAL EXAMINATION

physical education n : instruction in the development and care of the body ranging from simple calisthenics to training in hygiene, gymnastics, and the performance and management of athletic games

physical examination n : an examination of the bodily functions and condition of an individual

phys·i·cal·ize \ˈfi-zə-kə-ˌlīz\ vb -ized; -iz·ing : to give physical form or expression to

physical science n : any of the sciences (as physics and astronomy) that deal primarily with nonliving materials — **physical scientist** n

physical therapy n : the treatment of disease by physical and mechanical means (as massage, exercise, water, or heat) — **physical therapist** n

phy·si·cian \fə-ˈzi-shən\ n : a doctor of medicine

physician's assistant n : a person certified to provide basic medical care usu. under a licensed physician's supervision

phys·i·cist \ˈfi-zə-sist\ n : a scientist who specializes in physics

phys·ics \ˈfi-ziks\ n [L physica, pl., natural sciences, fr. Gk physika, fr. physis growth, nature, fr. phyein to bring forth] 1 : the science of matter and energy and their interactions 2 : the physical properties and composition of something

phys·i·og·no·my \ˌfi-zē-ˈäg-nə-mē\ n, pl -mies : facial appearance esp. as a reflection of inner character

phys·i·og·ra·phy \ˌfi-zē-ˈä-grə-fē\ n : geography dealing with physical features of the earth — **phys·io·graph·ic** \ˌfi-zē-ō-ˈgra-fik\ adj

phys·i·ol·o·gy \ˌfi-zē-ˈä-lə-jē\ n 1 : a branch of biology dealing with the functions and functioning of living matter and organisms 2 : functional processes in an organism or any of its parts — **phys·i·o·log·i·cal** \-zē-ə-ˈlä-ji-kəl\ or **phys·i·o·log·ic** \-jik\ adj — **phys·i·o·log·i·cal·ly** \-ji-k(ə-)lē\ adv — **phys·i·ol·o·gist** \-zē-ˈä-lə-jist\ n

phys·io·ther·a·py \ˌfi-zē-ō-ˈther-ə-pē\ n : PHYSICAL THERAPY — **phys·io·ther·a·pist** \-pist\ n

phy·sique \fə-ˈzēk\ n : the build of a person's body : bodily constitution

phy·to·chem·i·cal \ˌfī-tō-ˈke-mi-kəl\ n : a chemical compound occurring naturally in plants

phy·to·plank·ton \ˈfī-tō-ˌplaŋk-tən\ n : plant life of the plankton

pi \ˈpī\ n, pl **pis** \ˈpīz\ 1 : the 16th letter of the Greek alphabet — Π or π 2 : the symbol π denoting the ratio of the circumference of a circle to its diameter; also : the ratio itself equal to approximately 3.1416

PI abbr private investigator

pi·a·nis·si·mo \ˌpē-ə-ˈni-sə-ˌmō\ adv or adj : very softly — used as a direction in music

pi·a·nist \pē-ˈa-nist, ˈpē-ə-\ n : a person who plays the piano

¹**pi·a·no** \pē-ˈä-nō\ adv or adj : SOFTLY — used as a direction in music

²**piano** \pē-ˈa-nō\ n, pl **pianos** [It, short for pianoforte, fr. gravicembalo col piano e forte, lit., harpsichord with soft and loud; fr. the fact that its tones could be varied in loudness] : a musical instrument having steel strings sounded by felt-covered hammers operated from a keyboard

pi·ano·forte \pē-ˌa-nō-ˈfȯr-ˌtā, -tē; pē-ˈa-nə-ˌfȯrt\ n : PIANO

pi·as·tre also **pi·as·ter** \pē-ˈas-tər\ n — see pound at MONEY table

pi·az·za \pē-ˈa-zə, esp for 1 -ˈat-sə\ n, pl **piazzas** or **pi·az·ze** \-ˈat-(ˌ)sā, -ˈät-\ [It, fr. L platea broad street] 1 : an open square esp. in an Italian town 2 : a long hall with an arched roof 3 dial : VERANDA, PORCH

pi·broch \ˈpē-ˌbräk\ n : a set of variations for the bagpipe

pic \ˈpik\ n, pl **pics** or **pix** \ˈpiks\ 1 : PHOTOGRAPH 2 : MOTION PICTURE

pi·ca \'pī-kə\ *n* : a typewriter type with 10 characters to the inch

pi·ca·resque \,pi-kə-'resk, ,pē-\ *adj* : of or relating to rogues ⟨~ fiction⟩

pic·a·yune \,pik-kē-'yün\ *adj* : of little value : TRIVIAL; *also* : PETTY

pic·ca·lil·li \,pi-kə-'li-lē\ *n* : a relish of chopped vegetables and spices

pic·co·lo \'pi-kə-,lō\ *n, pl* **-los** [It, short for *piccolo flauto* small flute] : a small shrill flute pitched an octave higher than the ordinary flute

pice \'pīs\ *n, pl* **pice** : PAISA

¹pick \'pik\ *vb* **1** : to pierce or break up with a pointed instrument **2** : to remove bit by bit; *also* : to remove covering matter from **3** : to gather by plucking ⟨~ apples⟩ **4** : CULL, SELECT **5** : ROB ⟨~ a pocket⟩ **6** : PROVOKE ⟨~ a quarrel⟩ **7** : to dig into or pull lightly at **8** : to pluck with fingers or a pick **9** : to loosen or pull apart with a sharp point ⟨~ wool⟩ **10** : to unlock with a wire **11** : to eat sparingly — **pick·er** *n* — **pick on** : to single out for criticism, teasing, or bullying

²pick *n* **1** : the act or privilege of choosing **2** : the best or choicest one **3** : the part of a crop gathered at one time

³pick *n* **1** : a heavy wooden-handled tool pointed at one or both ends **2** : a pointed implement used for picking **3** : a small thin piece (as of plastic) used to pluck the strings of a stringed instrument

pick·a·back \'pi-gē-,bak, 'pi-kə-\ *var of* PIGGYBACK

pick·ax \'pik-,aks\ *n* : ³PICK 1

pick·er·el \'pi-kə-rəl\ *n, pl* **pickerel** *or* **pickerels** : either of two bony fishes related to the pikes; *also* : WALLEYE 2

pickerel

pick·er·el·weed \-,wēd\ *n* : a No. American shallow-water herb that bears spikes of purplish blue flowers

¹pick·et \'pi-kət\ *n* **1** : a pointed stake (as for a fence) **2** : a detached body of soldiers on outpost duty; *also* : SENTINEL **3** : a person posted by a labor union where workers are on strike; *also* : a person posted for a protest

²picket *vb* **1** : to guard with pickets **2** : TETHER ⟨~ a horse⟩ **3** : to post pickets at ⟨~ a factory⟩ **4** : to serve as a picket

pick·ings \'pi-kiŋz, -kənz\ *n pl* **1** : gleanable or eatable fragments : SCRAPS **2** : yield for effort expended : RETURN

pick·le \'pi-kəl\ *n* **1** : a brine or vinegar solution for preserving foods; *also* : a food (as a cucumber) preserved in a pickle **2** : a difficult situation : PLIGHT — **pickle** *vb*

pick·lock \'pik-,läk\ *n* **1** : BURGLAR, THIEF **2** : a tool for picking locks

pick·pock·et \'pik-,pä-kət\ *n* : one who steals from pockets

¹pick·up \'pik-,əp\ *n* **1** : a hitchhiker who is given a ride **2** : a temporary chance acquaintance **3** : a picking up **4** : revival of business activity **5** : ACCELERATION **6** : the conversion of mechanical movements into electrical impulses in the reproduction of sound; *also* : a device for making such conversion **7** : a light truck having an enclosed cab and an open body with low sides and a tailgate **8** : a pickup game **9** : a player acquired from another team

²pickup *adj* : using or comprising local or available personnel ⟨a ~ game⟩

pick up *vb* **1** : to take hold of and lift **2** : IMPROVE **3** : to put in order

picky \'pi-kē\ *adj* **pick·i·er; -est** : FUSSY, FINICKY ⟨a ~ eater⟩

¹pic·nic \'pik-,nik\ *n* : an outing with food usu. provided by members of the group and eaten in the open

²picnic *vb* **pic·nicked; pic·nick·ing** : to go on a picnic : eat in picnic fashion

pi·cot \'pē-,kō\ *n* : one of a series of small loops forming an edging on ribbon or lace

pic·to·ri·al \pik-'tòr-ē-əl\ *adj* : of, relating to, or consisting of pictures

¹pic·ture \'pik-chər\ *n* **1** : a representation made by painting, drawing, or photography **2** : a vivid description in words **3** : IMAGE, COPY ⟨was the ~ of his father⟩ **4** : a transitory visual image (as on a TV screen) **5** : MOTION PICTURE **6** : SITUATION ⟨a bleak economic ~⟩

²picture *vb* **pic·tured; pic·tur·ing** **1** : to paint or draw a picture of **2** : to describe vividly in words **3** : to form a mental image of

pic·tur·esque \,pik-chə-'resk\ *adj* **1** : resembling a picture ⟨a ~ landscape⟩ **2** : CHARMING, QUAINT ⟨a ~ character⟩ **3** : GRAPHIC 3, VIVID ⟨a ~ account⟩ — **pic·tur·esque·ness** *n*

picture tube *n* : a cathode-ray tube on which the picture appears in a television

pid·dle \'pi-d⁹l\ *vb* **pid·dled; pid·dling** : to act or work idly : DAWDLE

pid·dling \'pi-d⁹l-ən, -iŋ\ *adj* : TRIVIAL, PALTRY ⟨spent a ~ sum⟩

pid·dly \'pid-lē\ *adj* : TRIVIAL, PIDDLING

pid·gin \'pi-jən\ *n* [fr. *pidgin English*, fr. Chinese Pidgin English *pidgin* business] : a simplified speech used for communication between people with different languages

pie \'pī\ *n* : a dish consisting of a pastry crust and a filling (as of fruit or meat)

¹pie·bald \'pī-,bóld\ *adj* : of different colors; *esp* : blotched with white and black ⟨a ~ horse⟩

²piebald *n* : a piebald animal

¹piece \'pēs\ *n* **1** : a part of a whole : FRAGMENT, PORTION **2** : one of a group, set, or mass ⟨~s of flatware⟩; *also* : of a single item ⟨a ~ of news⟩ **3** : a movable object used in a board game **4** : a length, weight, or size in which something is made or sold **5** : a product (as an essay) of creative work **6** : FIREARM **7** : COIN

²piece *vb* **pieced; piec·ing** **1** : to repair or complete by adding pieces : PATCH **2** : to join into a whole

pièce de ré·sis·tance \pē-,es-də-rā-,zē-'stäns\ *n, pl* **pièces de ré·sis·tance** *same*\ [F] **1** : the chief dish of a meal **2** : an outstanding item

piece·meal \'pēs-,mēl\ *adv or adj* : one piece at a time : GRADUALLY

piece·work \-,wərk\ *n* : work done and paid for by the piece — **piece·work·er** *n*

pie chart *n* : a circular chart that shows quantities or frequencies by parts of a circle shaped like pieces of pie

pied \'pīd\ *adj* : of two or more colors in blotches : VARIEGATED

pied-à-terre \pē-,ā-də-'ter\ *n, pl* **pieds-à-terre** *same*\ [F, lit., foot to the ground] : a temporary or second lodging

pier \'pir\ *n* **1** : a support for a bridge span **2** : a structure built out into the water for use as a landing place or a promenade or to protect or form a harbor **3** : an upright supporting part (as a pillar) of a building or structure

pierce \'pirs\ *vb* **pierced; pierc·ing** **1** : to enter or thrust into sharply or painfully : STAB **2** : to make a hole in or through : PERFORATE ⟨pierced ears⟩ **3** : to force or make a way into or through : PENETRATE **4** : to see through : DISCERN — **pierc·er** *n*

piercing *n* : a piece of jewelry attached to pierced flesh

pies *pl of* PI, *or of* PIE

pi·ety \'pī-ə-tē\ *n, pl* **pi·et·ies** **1** : fidelity to natural obligations (as to parents) **2** : dutifulness in religion : DEVOUTNESS **3** : a pious act

pif·fle \'pi-fəl\ *n* : trifling talk or action

pig \'pig\ *n* **1** : SWINE; *esp* : a young domesticated swine **2** : PORK **3** : a dirty, gluttonous, or repulsive person **4** : a crude casting of metal (as iron)

pi·geon \'pi-jən\ *n* : any of numerous stout-bodied short-legged birds with smooth thick plumage

¹pi·geon·hole \'pi-jən-,hōl\ *n* : a small open compartment (as in a desk) for keeping letters or documents

²pigeonhole *vb* **1** : to place in or as if in a pigeonhole : FILE **2** : to lay aside **3** : to assign to a usu. restrictive category

pi·geon–toed \-,tōd\ *adj* : having the toes and forefoot turned inward

pig·gish \'pi-gish\ *adj* **1** : GREEDY **2** : STUBBORN

pig·gy·back \'pi-gē-,bak\ *also* **pick·a·back** \'pi-gē-, 'pi-kə-\

adv or adj **1** : up on the back and shoulders **2** : on a railroad flatcar

pig·head·ed \'pig-'he-dəd\ *adj* : OBSTINATE, STUBBORN

pig latin *n, often cap L* : a jargon that is made by systematic alteration of English

pig·let \'pi-glət\ *n* : a small usu. young swine

pig·ment \'pig-mənt\ *n* **1** : coloring matter **2** : a powder mixed with a liquid to give color (as in paints) — **pig·ment·ed** \-mən-təd\ *adj*

pig·men·ta·tion \,pig-mən-'tā-shən\ *n* : coloration with or deposition of pigment; *esp* : an excessive deposition of bodily pigment

pigmy *var of* PYGMY

pig·nut \'pig-,nət\ *n* : the bitter nut of any of several hickory trees; *also* : any of these trees

pig·pen \-,pen\ *n* **1** : a pen for pigs **2** : a dirty place

pig·skin \-,skin\ *n* **1** : the skin of a swine or leather made of it **2** : FOOTBALL 2

pig·sty \-,stī\ *n* : PIGPEN

pig·tail \-,tāl\ *n* : a tight braid of hair

pi·ka \'pē-kə, 'pī-\ *n* : any of various small short-eared mammals related to the rabbits and occurring in rocky uplands of Asia and western No. America

¹pike \'pīk\ *n* : a sharp point or spike

²pike *n, pl* **pike** *or* **pikes** : a large slender long-snouted freshwater bony fish valued for food; *also* : any of various related fishes

³pike *n* : a long wooden shaft with a pointed steel head formerly used as a foot soldier's weapon

⁴pike *n* : TURNPIKE

pik·er \'pī-kər\ *n* **1** : one who does things in a small way or on a small scale **2** : TIGHTWAD, CHEAPSKATE

pike·staff \'pīk-,staf\ *n* : the staff of a foot soldier's pike

pi·laf *also* **pi·laff** \pi-'läf, 'pē-,läf\ *or* **pi·lau** \pi-'lō, -'lȯ, 'pē-lō, -,lȯ\ *n* : a dish made of seasoned rice often with meat

pi·las·ter \pi-'las-tər, 'pī-,las-tər\ *n* : an architectural support that looks like a rectangular column and projects slightly from a wall

pil·chard \'pil-chərd\ *n* : a small European marine fish related to the herrings and often packed as a sardine

¹pile \'pī(-ə)l\ *n* : a long slender column (as of wood or steel) driven into the ground to support a vertical load

²pile *n* **1** : a quantity of things heaped together **2** : PYRE **3** : a great number or quantity : LOT

³pile *vb* **piled; pil·ing** **1** : to lay in a pile : STACK **2** : to heap up : ACCUMULATE **3** : to press forward in a mass : CROWD

⁴pile *n* : a velvety surface of fine short hairs or threads (as on cloth) — **piled** \'pī(-ə)ld\ *adj* — **pile·less** *adj*

piles \'pī(-ə)lz\ *n pl* : HEMORRHOIDS

pil·fer \'pil-fər\ *vb* : to steal in small quantities

pil·grim \'pil-grəm\ *n* [ME, fr. AF *pelerin, pilegrin*, fr. LL *pelegrinus*, alter. of L *peregrinus* foreigner, fr. *peregrinus* foreign, fr. *peregri* abroad, fr. *per* through + *ager* land] **1** : one who journeys in foreign lands : WAYFARER **2** : one who travels to a shrine or holy place as an act of devotion **3** *cap* : one of the English settlers founding Plymouth colony in 1620

pil·grim·age \-grə-mij\ *n* : a journey of a pilgrim esp. to a shrine or holy place

pil·ing \'pī-liŋ\ *n* : a structure of piles

pill \'pil\ *n* **1** : a small rounded mass usu. of medicine that is swallowed whole **2** : a disagreeable or tiresome person **3** *often cap* : an oral contraceptive — usu. used with *the*

pil·lage \'pi-lij\ *vb* **pil·laged; pil·lag·ing** : to take booty : LOOT, PLUNDER — **pillage** *n* — **pil·lag·er** *n*

pil·lar \'pi-lər\ *n* **1** : a strong upright support (as for a roof) **2** : a column or shaft standing alone esp. as a monument **3** : an integral or upstanding member or part **4** : a fundamental tenet ⟨the five ∼s of Islam⟩ — **pil·lared** \-lərd\ *adj*

pill·box \'pil-,bäks\ *n* **1** : a shallow round box for pills **2** : a low concrete emplacement esp. for machine guns

pil·lion \'pil-yən\ *n* **1** : a pad or cushion placed behind a saddle for an extra rider **2** *chiefly Brit* : a motorcycle or bicycle saddle for a passenger

¹pil·lo·ry \'pi-lə-rē\ *n, pl* **-ries** : a wooden frame for public punishment having holes in which the head and hands can be locked

²pillory *vb* **-ried; -ry·ing** **1** : to set in a pillory **2** : to expose to public scorn

¹pil·low \'pi-lō\ *n* : a case filled with springy material (as feathers) and used to support the head of a resting person

²pillow *vb* : to rest or place on or as if on a pillow; *also* : to serve as a pillow for

pil·low·case \-,kās\ *n* : a removable covering for a pillow

¹pi·lot \'pī-lət\ *n* **1** : HELMSMAN, STEERSMAN **2** : a person qualified and licensed to take ships into and out of a port **3** : GUIDE, LEADER **4** : one that flies an aircraft or spacecraft **5** : a television show filmed or taped as a sample of a proposed series — **pi·lot·less** *adj*

²pilot *vb* : CONDUCT, GUIDE; *esp* : to act as pilot of

³pilot *adj* : serving as a guiding or activating device or as a testing or trial unit ⟨a ∼ light⟩ ⟨a ∼ factory⟩

pi·lot·house \'pī-lət-,hau̇s\ *n* : a shelter on the upper deck of a ship for the steering gear and the helmsman

pilot whale *n* : either of two mostly black medium-sized whales

pil·sner *also* **pil·sen·er** \'pilz-nər, 'pil-zə-\ *n* [G, lit., of Pilsen (Plzeň), city in the Czech Republic] **1** : a light beer with a strong flavor of hops **2** : a tall slender footed glass for beer

pi·men·to \pə-'men-tō\ *n, pl* **pimentos** *or* **pimento** [Sp *pimienta* allspice, pepper, fr. LL *pigmenta*, pl. of *pigmentum* plant juice, fr. L, pigment] **1** : ALLSPICE **2** : PIMIENTO

pi·mien·to \pə-'men-tō\ *n, pl* **-tos** : any of various mild red sweet pepper fruits used esp. to stuff olives and to make paprika

pimp \'pimp\ *n* : a man who solicits clients for a prostitute — **pimp** *vb*

pim·per·nel \'pim-pər-,nel, -nəl\ *n* : any of a genus of herbs related to the primroses

pim·ple \'pim-pəl\ *n* : a small inflamed swelling on the skin often containing pus — **pim·ply** \-p(ə-)lē\ *adj*

¹pin \'pin\ *n* **1** : a piece of wood or metal used esp. for fastening things together or as a support by which one thing may be suspended from another; *esp* : a small pointed piece of wire with a head used for fastening clothes or attaching papers **2** : an ornament or emblem fastened to clothing with a pin **3** : one of the pieces constituting the target (as in bowling); *also* : the staff of the flag marking a hole on a golf course **4** : LEG

²pin *vb* **pinned; pin·ning** **1** : to fasten, join, or secure with a pin **2** : to hold fast or immobile **3** : ATTACH, HANG ⟨*pinned* their hopes on one man⟩ **4** : to assign the blame for ⟨∼ a crime on someone⟩ **5** : to define clearly : ESTABLISH ⟨∼ down an idea⟩

PIN *abbr* personal identification number

pi·ña co·la·da \,pēn-yə-kō-'lä-də, ,pēn-ə-\ *n* [Sp, lit., strained pineapple] : a tall drink made of rum, cream of coconut, and pineapple juice mixed with ice

pin·afore \'pi-nə-,fȯr\ *n* : a sleeveless dress or apron fastened at the back

pin·ball machine \'pin-,bȯl-\ *n* : an amusement device in which a ball is maneuvered along a slanted surface among a series of targets for points

pince–nez \pa�207s-'nā\ *n, pl* **pince–nez** *same or* -'nāz\ [F, fr. *pincer* to pinch + *nez* nose] : eyeglasses clipped to the nose by a spring

pin·cer \'pin-sər\ *n* **1** *pl* : a gripping instrument with two handles and two grasping jaws **2** : a claw (as of a lobster) resembling pincers

¹pinch \'pinch\ *vb* [ME, fr. AF *pincher, pincer*, fr. VL *pinctiare, *punctiare*, fr. L *punctum* puncture] **1** : to squeeze between the finger and thumb or between the jaws of an instrument **2** : to compress painfully **3** : CONTRACT, SHRIVEL **4** : to be miserly; *also* : to subject to strict economy **5** : to confine or limit narrowly **6** : STEAL **7** : ARREST

²pinch *n* **1** : a critical point : EMERGENCY **2** : painful effect **3** : an act of pinching **4** : a very small quantity **5** : ARREST

³pinch *adj* : SUBSTITUTE ⟨a ∼ runner⟩

pinch–hit \,pinch-'hit\ *vb* **1** : to bat in the place of another player esp. when a hit is particularly needed **2** : to act or serve in place of another — **pinch hit** *n* — **pinch hitter** *n*

pin curl *n* : a curl made usu. by dampening a strand of hair, coiling it, and securing it by a hairpin or clip

pin·cush·ion \'pin-,ku̇-shən\ *n* : a cushion for pins not in use

¹pine \'pīn\ *n* : any of a genus of evergreen cone-bearing trees; *also* : the light durable resinous wood of a pine

²pine *vb* **pined; pin·ing** 1 : to lose vigor or health through distress 2 : to long for something intensely

pi·ne·al \'pī-nē-əl, pī-'nē-əl\ *n* : PINEAL GLAND — **pineal** *adj*

pineal gland *n* : a small usu. conical appendage of the brain of all vertebrates with a cranium that functions primarily as an endocrine organ

pine·ap·ple \'pīn-,a-pəl\ *n* : a tropical plant bearing a large edible juicy fruit; *also* : its fruit

pin·feath·er \'pin-,fe-thər\ *n* : a new feather just coming through the skin

ping \'piŋ\ *n* 1 : a sharp sound like that of a bullet striking 2 : engine knock

pin·hole \'pin-,hōl\ *n* : a small hole made by, for, or as if by a pin

¹pin·ion \'pin-yən\ *n* : the end section of a bird's wing; *also* : WING

²pinion *vb* : to restrain by binding the arms; *also* : SHACKLE

³pinion *n* : a gear with a small number of teeth designed to mesh with a larger wheel or rack

¹pink \'piŋk\ *n* 1 : any of a genus of plants with narrow leaves often grown for their showy flowers 2 : the highest degree : HEIGHT ⟨the ∼ of condition⟩

²pink *n* : a light tint of red

³pink *adj* 1 : of the color pink 2 : holding socialistic views — **pink·ish** *adj*

⁴pink *vb* 1 : to perforate in an ornamental pattern 2 : PIERCE, STAB 3 : to cut a saw-toothed edge on

pink·eye \'piŋk-,ī\ *n* : an acute contagious eye inflammation

pin·kie *or* **pin·ky** \'piŋ-kē\ *n, pl* **pinkies** : the smallest finger of the hand

pin·nace \'pi-nəs\ *n* 1 : a light sailing ship 2 : a ship's boat

pin·na·cle \'pi-ni-kəl\ *n* [ME *pinacle*, fr. AF, fr. LL *pinnaculum* small wing, gable, fr. L *pinna* wing, battlement] 1 : a turret ending in a small spire 2 : a lofty peak 3 : ACME

pin·nate \'pi-,nāt\ *adj* : resembling a feather esp. in having similar parts arranged on each side of an axis ⟨a ∼ leaf⟩ — **pin·nate·ly** *adv*

pi·noch·le \'pē-,nə-kəl\ *n* : a card game played with a 48-card deck

pi·ñon *or* **pin·yon** \'pin-,yōn, -,yän\ *n, pl* **pi·ñons** *or* **pin·yons** *or* **pi·ño·nes** \piṇ-'yō-nēz\ [AmerSp *piñón*] : any of various small pines of western No. America with edible seeds; *also* : the edible seed of a piñon

pin·point \'pin-,point\ *vb* : to locate, hit, or aim with great precision

pin·prick \-,prik\ *n* 1 : a small puncture made by or as if by a pin 2 : a petty irritation or annoyance

pins and needles *n pl* : a pricking tingling sensation in a limb growing numb or recovering from numbness — **on pins and needles** : in a nervous or jumpy state of anticipation

pin·stripe \'pin-,strīp\ *n* : a narrow stripe on a fabric; *also* : a suit with such stripes — **pin–striped** \-,strīpt\ *adj*

pint \'pīnt\ *n* — see WEIGHT table

pin·to \'pin-,tō\ *n, pl* **pintos** *also* **pintoes** : a spotted horse or pony

pinto bean *n* : a spotted seed produced by a kind of kidney bean and used for food

pin·up \'pin-,əp\ *adj* : suitable or designed for hanging on a wall; *also* : suited (as by beauty) to be the subject of a pinup photograph

pin·wheel \-,hwēl, -,wēl\ *n* 1 : a fireworks device in the form of a revolving wheel of colored fire 2 : a toy consisting of lightweight vanes that revolve at the end of a stick

pin·worm \-,wərm\ *n* : a nematode worm parasitic in the human intestine

pin·yin \'pin-'yin\ *n, often cap* : a system for writing Chinese ideograms by using Roman letters to represent the sounds

¹pi·o·neer \,pī-ə-'nir\ *n* 1 : one that originates or helps open up a new line of thought or activity 2 : an early settler in a territory

²pioneer *vb* 1 : to act as a pioneer 2 : to open or prepare for others to follow; *also* : SETTLE

pi·ous \'pī-əs\ *adj* 1 : marked by reverence for deity : DEVOUT 2 : excessively or affectedly religious 3 : SACRED, DEVOTIONAL 4 : showing loyal reverence for a person or thing : DUTIFUL 5 : marked by sham or hypocrisy — **pi·ous·ly** *adv*

¹pip \'pip\ *n* : one of the dots used on dice and dominoes to indicate numerical value

²pip *n* : a small fruit seed (as of an apple)

¹pipe \'pīp\ *n* 1 : a tubular musical instrument played by forcing air through it 2 : BAGPIPE 3 : a tube designed to conduct something (as water, steam, or oil) 4 : a device for smoking having a tube with a bowl at one end and a mouthpiece at the other 5 : a means of transmission (as of computer data)

²pipe *vb* **piped; pip·ing** 1 : to play on a pipe 2 : to speak in a high or shrill voice 3 : to convey by or as if by pipes — **pip·er** *n*

pipe down *vb* : to stop talking or making noise

pipe dream *n* : an illusory or fantastic hope

pipe·line \'pīp-,līn\ *n* 1 : a line of pipe with pumps, valves, and control devices for conveying fluids 2 : a channel for information 3 : PIPE 5

pi·pette *or* **pi·pet** \pī-'pet\ *n* : a device for measuring and transferring small volumes of liquid

pipe up *vb* : to speak loudly and distinctly; *also* : to express an opinion freely

pip·ing \'pī-piŋ\ *n* 1 : the music of pipes 2 : a narrow fold of material used to decorate edges or seams

piping hot *adj* : very hot

pip·pin \'pi-pən\ *n* : a crisp tart usu. yellowish apple

pip–squeak \'pip-,skwēk\ *n* : one that is small or insignificant

pi·quant \'pē-kənt\ *adj* 1 : pleasantly savory : PUNGENT 2 : engagingly provocative; *also* : having a lively charm — **pi·quan·cy** \-kən-sē\ *n*

¹pique \'pēk\ *n* [F] : a passing feeling of wounded vanity : RESENTMENT

²pique *vb* **piqued; piqu·ing** 1 : IRRITATE 1 2 : to arouse by a provocation or challenge : GOAD

pi·qué *or* **pi·que** \pi-'kā\ *n* : a durable ribbed clothing fabric

pi·quet \pi-'kā\ *n* : a 2-handed card game played with 32 cards

pi·ra·cy \'pī-rə-sē\ *n, pl* **-cies** 1 : robbery on the high seas; *also* : an act resembling such robbery 2 : the unauthorized use of another's production or invention

pi·ra·nha \pə-'rä-nə, -'rän-yə\ *n* [Pg, fr. Tupi (So. American Indian language) *pir{atildeac}ja*, fr. *pir´* fish + *{atildeac}ja* tooth] : any of various usu. small So. American fishes with sharp teeth that include some known to attack humans and large animals

pi·rate \'pī-rət\ *n* [ME, fr. MF or L; MF, fr. L *pirata*, fr. Gk *peiratēs*, fr. *peiran* to attempt, test] : one who commits piracy — **pirate** *vb* — **pi·rat·i·cal** \pə-'ra-ti-kəl, pī-\ *adj*

pir·ou·ette \,pir-ə-'wet\ *n* [F] : a rapid whirling about of the body; *esp* : a full turn on the toe or ball of one foot in ballet — **pirouette** *vb*

pis *pl of* PI

pis·ca·to·ri·al \,pis-kə-'tór-ē-əl\ *adj* : of or relating to fishing

Pi·sces \'pī-sēz\ *n* [ME, fr. L, lit., fishes] 1 : a zodiacal constellation between Aquarius and Aries usu. pictured as a fish 2 : the 12th sign of the zodiac in astrology; *also* : one born under this sign

pis·mire \'pis-,mī(-ə)r\ *n* : ANT

pi·so \'pē-(,)sō\ *n* : the peso of the Philippines

pis·ta·chio \pə-'sta-shē-,ō, -'stä-\ *n, pl* **-chios** : the greenish edible seed of a small Asian tree related to the sumacs; *also* : the tree

pis·til \'pist-²l\ *n* : the female reproductive organ in a flower — **pis·til·late** \'pis-tə-,lāt\ *adj*

pis·tol \'pist-²l\ *n* : a handgun whose chamber is integral with the barrel

pis·tol–whip \-,hwip\ *vb* [F] : to beat with a pistol

pis·ton \'pis-tən\ *n* : a sliding piece that receives and transmits motion and that usu. consists of a short cylinder inside a large cylinder

¹pit \'pit\ *n* 1 : a hole, shaft, or cavity in the ground 2 : an often sunken area designed for a particular use; *also* : an enclosed place (as for cockfights) 3 : HELL; *also, pl* : WORST ⟨it's the ∼s⟩ 4 : a natural hollow or indentation in a surface **5 :** a small indented mark or scar (as from disease or corrosion) **6 :** an area beside a racecourse where cars are fueled and repaired during a race

²**pit** *vb* **pit·ted; pit·ting 1 :** to form pits in or become marred with pits **2 :** to match for fighting

³**pit** *n* **:** the stony seed of some fruits (as the cherry, peach, and date)

⁴**pit** *vb* **pit·ted; pit·ting :** to remove the pit from

pi·ta \'pē-tə\ *n* [ModGk] **:** a thin flat bread

pit–a–pat \ˌpi-ti-'pat\ *n* **:** PITTER-PATTER — **pit–a–pat** *adv or adj*

pit bull *n* **:** a powerful compact short-haired dog developed for fighting

¹**pitch** \'pich\ *n* **1 :** a dark sticky substance left over esp. from distilling tar or petroleum **2 :** resin from various conifers — **pitchy** *adj*

²**pitch** *vb* **1 :** to erect and fix firmly in place ⟨∼ a tent⟩ **2 :** THROW, FLING **3 :** to deliver a baseball to a batter **4 :** to toss (as coins) toward a mark **5 :** to set at a particular level ⟨∼ the voice low⟩ **6 :** to fall headlong **7 :** to have the front end (as of a ship) alternately plunge and rise **8 :** to incline downward **:** SLOPE

³**pitch** *n* **1 :** the action or a manner of pitching **2 :** degree of slope ⟨∼ of a roof⟩ **3 :** the relative level of some quality or state ⟨a high ∼ of excitement⟩ **4 :** highness or lowness of sound; *also* **:** a standard frequency for tuning instruments **5 :** a presentation delivered to sell or promote something **6 :** the delivery of a baseball to a batter; *also* **:** the baseball delivered

pitch·blende \'pich-ˌblend\ *n* **:** a dark mineral that is the chief source of uranium

¹**pitch·er** \'pi-chər\ *n* **:** a container for liquids that usu. has a lip and a handle

²**pitcher** *n* **:** one that pitches esp. in a baseball game

pitcher plant *n* **:** any of various plants with leaves modified to resemble pitchers in which insects are trapped and digested

pitch·fork \'pich-ˌfôrk\ *n* **:** a long-handled fork used esp. in pitching hay

pitchfork

pitch in *vb* **1 :** to begin to work **2 :** to contribute to a common effort

pitch·man \'pich-mən\ *n* **:** SALESMAN; *esp* **:** one who sells merchandise on the streets or from a concession

pitch–per·fect \'pich-'pər-fikt\ *adj* **:** having just the right tone or style ⟨a ∼ translation⟩

pit·e·ous \'pi-tē-əs\ *adj* **:** arousing pity **:** PITIFUL — **pit·e·ous·ly** *adv*

pit·fall \'pit-ˌfôl\ *n* **1 :** TRAP, SNARE; *esp* **:** a covered pit used for capturing animals **2 :** a hidden danger or difficulty

pith \'pith\ *n* **1 :** loose spongy tissue esp. in the center of the stem of vascular plants **2 :** the essential part **:** CORE

pithy \'pi-thē\ *adj* **pith·i·er; -est 1 :** consisting of or filled with pith **2 :** having substance and point **:** CONCISE

piti·able \'pi-tē-ə-bəl\ *adj* **:** PITIFUL

piti·ful \'pi-ti-fəl\ *adj* **1 :** arousing or deserving pity ⟨a ∼ sight⟩ **2 :** lamentably inadequate **:** MEAGER — **piti·ful·ly** *adv*

piti·less \'pi-ti-ləs\ *adj* **:** devoid of pity **:** HARSH, CRUEL — **pit·i·less·ly** *adv*

pi·ton \'pē-ˌtän\ *n* [F] **:** a spike, wedge, or peg that can be driven into a rock or ice surface as a support

pit·tance \'pi-tᵊns\ *n* **:** a small portion, amount, or allowance

pit·ted \'pi-təd\ *adj* **:** marked with pits

pit·ter–pat·ter \'pi-tər-ˌpa-tər, 'pi-tē-\ *n* **:** a rapid succession of light taps or sounds — **pitter–patter** \ˌpi-tər-'pa-tər, ˌpi-tē-\ *adv or adj* — **pitter–patter** \same as adv\ *vb*

pi·tu·i·tary \pə-'tü-ə-ˌter-ē, -'tyü-\ *n, pl* **-itar·ies :** PITUITARY GLAND — **pituitary** *adj*

pituitary gland *n* **:** a small oval endocrine gland located at the base of the brain that produces various hormones that affect most basic bodily functions (as growth and reproduction)

pit viper *n* **:** any of various mostly New World venomous snakes with a sensory pit on each side of the head and hollow perforated fangs

¹**pity** \'pi-tē\ *n, pl* **pit·ies** [ME *pite*, fr. AF *pité*, fr. L *pietas* piety, pity, fr. *pius* pious] **1 :** sympathetic sorrow **:** COMPASSION **2 :** something to be regretted

²**pity** *vb* **pit·ied; pity·ing :** to feel pity for

¹**piv·ot** \'pi-vət\ *n* **:** a fixed pin on which something turns — **pivot** *adj*

²**pivot** *vb* **:** to turn on or as if on a pivot

piv·ot·al \'pi-və-tᵊl\ *adj* **1 :** of or relating to a pivot **2 :** vitally important **:** CRITICAL

pix *pl of* PIC

pix·el \'pik-səl, -ˌsel\ *n* **1 :** any of the small elements that together make up an image (as on a television screen) **2 :** any of the detecting elements of a charge-coupled device used as an optical sensor

pix·ie *also* **pixy** \'pik-sē\ *n, pl* **pix·ies :** FAIRY; *esp* **:** a mischievous sprite

piz·za \'pēt-sə\ *n* [It] **:** an open pie made of rolled bread dough spread with a spiced mixture (as of tomatoes, cheese, and ground meat) and baked

piz·zazz *or* **pi·zazz** \pə-'zaz\ *n* **1 :** GLAMOUR **2 :** VITALITY

piz·ze·ria \ˌpēt-sə-'rē-ə\ *n* **:** an establishment where pizzas are made and sold

piz·zi·ca·to \ˌpit-si-'kä-tō\ *adv or adj* [It] **:** by means of plucking instead of bowing — used as a direction in music

pj's \'pē-ˌjāz\ *n pl* **:** PAJAMAS

pk *abbr* **1** park **2** peak **3** peck **4** pike

pkg *abbr* package

pkt *abbr* **1** packet **2** pocket

pkwy *abbr* parkway

pl *abbr* **1** place **2** plate **3** plural

¹**plac·ard** \'pla-kərd, -ˌkärd\ *n* **:** a notice posted in a public place **:** POSTER

²**plac·ard** \-ˌkärd, -kərd\ *vb* **1 :** to cover with or as if with placards **2 :** to announce by or as if by posting

pla·cate \'plā-ˌkāt, 'pla-\ *vb* **pla·cat·ed; pla·cat·ing :** to soothe esp. by concessions **:** APPEASE — **pla·ca·ble** \'pla-kə-bəl, 'plā-\ *adj*

¹**place** \'plās\ *n* [ME, fr. AF, open space, fr. L *platea* broad street, fr. Gk *plateia (hodos)*, fr. fem. of *platys* broad, flat] **1 :** SPACE, ROOM **2 :** an indefinite region **:** AREA **3 :** a building or locality used for a special purpose **4 :** a center of population **5 :** a particular part of a surface **:** SPOT **6 :** relative position in a scale or sequence; *also* **:** position at the end of a competition ⟨last ∼⟩ **7 :** ACCOMMODATION; *esp* **:** SEAT **8 :** the position of a figure within a numeral ⟨12 is a two ∼ number⟩ **9 :** JOB; *esp* **:** public office **10 :** a public square **11 :** 2d place at the finish (as of a horse race) — **in place of :** INSTEAD OF — **out of place :** not in the proper location **:** INAPPROPRIATE

²**place** *vb* **placed; plac·ing 1 :** to put in a particular place **:** SET **2 :** to distribute in an orderly manner **:** ARRANGE **3 :** IDENTIFY **4 :** to give an order for ⟨∼ a bet⟩ **5 :** to earn a given spot in a competition; *esp* **:** to come in 2d

pla·ce·bo \plə-'sē-bō\ *n, pl* **-bos** [L, I shall please] **:** an inert medication used for its psychological effect or for purposes of comparison in an experiment

place·hold·er \'plās-ˌhōl-dər\ *n* **:** a symbol in a mathematical or logical expression that may be replaced by the name of any element of a set

place·kick \-ˌkik\ *n* **:** the kicking of a ball placed or held on the ground — **placekick** *vb* — **place·kick·er** *n*

place·ment \'plās-mənt\ *n* **:** an act or instance of placing

place–name \-ˌnām\ *n* **:** the name of a geographical locality

pla·cen·ta \plə-'sen-tə\ *n, pl* **-tas** *or* **-tae** \-(ˌ)tē\ [NL, fr. L, flat cake] **:** the organ in most mammals by which the fetus is joined to the maternal uterus and is nourished — **pla·cen·tal** \-'sen-tᵊl\ *adj or n*

plac·er \'pla-sər\ *n* **:** a deposit of sand or gravel containing particles of valuable mineral (as gold)

plac·id \'pla-səd\ *adj* **:** UNDISTURBED, PEACEFUL ♦ **Syno-**

nyms TRANQUIL, SERENE, CALM — **pla·cid·i·ty** \pla-'si-də-tē\ *n* — **plac·id·ly** *adv*

plack·et \'pla-kət\ *n* : a slit in a garment

pla·gia·rise *Brit var of* PLAGIARIZE

pla·gia·rize \'plā-jə-ˌrīz\ *vb* **-rized; -riz·ing** : to present the ideas or words of another as one's own — **pla·gia·rism** \-ˌri-zəm\ *n* — **pla·gia·rist** \-rist\ *n*

¹**plague** \'plāg\ *n* **1** : a disastrous evil or influx; *also* : NUISANCE **2** : PESTILENCE; *esp* : a destructive contagious bacterial disease (as bubonic plague)

²**plague** *vb* **plagued; plagu·ing** **1** : to afflict with or as if with disease or disaster **2** : TEASE, TORMENT, HARASS

plaid \'plad\ *n* [ScGael *plaide*] **1** : a rectangular length of tartan worn esp. over the left shoulder as part of the Scottish national costume **2** : a twilled woolen fabric with a tartan pattern **3** : a pattern of unevenly spaced repeated stripes crossing at right angles — **plaid** *adj*

¹**plain** \'plān\ *n* : an extensive area of level or rolling treeless country

²**plain** *adj* **1** : lacking ornament ⟨a ~ dress⟩ **2** : free of extraneous matter **3** : OPEN, UNOBSTRUCTED ⟨~ view⟩ **4** : EVIDENT, OBVIOUS **5** : easily understood : CLEAR **6** : CANDID, BLUNT **7** : SIMPLE, UNCOMPLICATED ⟨~ cooking⟩ **8** : lacking beauty or ugliness — **plain·ly** *adv* — **plain·ness** *n*

plain·clothes·man \'plān-ˈklōthz-mən, -ˈklōz-, -ˌman\ *n* : a police officer who wears civilian clothes instead of a uniform while on duty : DETECTIVE

plain·spo·ken \-ˈspō-kən\ *adj* : FRANK

plaint \'plānt\ *n* **1** : LAMENTATION, WAIL **2** : PROTEST, COMPLAINT

plain·tiff \'plān-təf\ *n* : the complaining party in a lawsuit

plain·tive \'plān-tiv\ *adj* : expressive of suffering or woe : MELANCHOLY ⟨a ~ sigh⟩ — **plain·tive·ly** *adv*

plait \'plāt, 'plat\ *n* **1** : PLEAT **2** : a braid esp. of hair or straw — **plait** *vb*

¹**plan** \'plan\ *n* **1** : a drawing or diagram showing the parts or details of something **2** : a method for accomplishing an objective; *also* : GOAL, AIM

²**plan** *vb* **planned; plan·ning** **1** : to form a plan of ⟨~ a new city⟩ **2** : INTEND ⟨planned to go⟩ — **plan·ner** *n*

¹**plane** \'plān\ *vb* **planed; plan·ing** : to smooth or level off with or as if with a plane — **plan·er** *n*

²**plane** *n* : PLANE TREE

³**plane** *n* : a tool for smoothing or shaping a wood surface

³**plane**

⁴**plane** *n* **1** : a level or flat surface **2** : a level of existence, consciousness, or development **3** : AIRPLANE

⁵**plane** *adj* **1** : FLAT, LEVEL **2** : dealing with flat surfaces or figures ⟨~ geometry⟩

plane·load \'plān-ˌlōd\ *n* : a load that fills an airplane

plan·et \'pla-nət\ *n* [ME *planete*, fr. AF, fr. LL *planeta*, fr. Gk *planēt-, planēs*, lit., wanderer, fr. *planasthai* to wander] : any of the large bodies in the solar system that revolve around the sun — **plan·e·tary** \-nə-ˌter-ē\ *adj*

plan·e·tar·i·um \ˌpla-nə-ˈter-ē-əm\ *n, pl* **-i·ums** *or* **-ia** \-ē-ə\ : a building or room housing a device to project images of celestial bodies

plan·e·tes·i·mal \ˌpla-nə-ˈtes-ə-məl\ *n* : any of numerous small solid celestial bodies which may have existed during the formation of the solar system

plan·e·toid \'pla-nə-ˌtȯid\ *n* : a body resembling a planet; *esp* : ASTEROID

plane tree *n* : any of a genus of trees (as a sycamore) with large lobed leaves and globe-shaped fruit

plan·gent \'plan-jənt\ *adj* **1** : having a loud reverberating sound ⟨a ~ roar⟩ **2** : having an expressive esp. plaintive quality ⟨~ lyrics⟩ — **plan·gen·cy** \-jən-sē\ *n*

¹**plank** \'plaŋk\ *n* **1** : a heavy thick board **2** : an article in the platform of a political party

²**plank** *vb* **1** : to cover with planks **2** : to set or lay down forcibly **3** : to cook and serve on a board

plank·ing \'plaŋ-kiŋ\ *n* : a quantity or covering of planks

plank·ton \'plaŋk-tən\ *n* [G, fr. Gk, neut. of *planktos* drifting] : the passively floating or weakly swimming animal and plant life of a body of water — **plank·ton·ic** \plaŋk-ˈtä-nik\ *adj*

¹**plant** \'plant\ *vb* **1** : to set in the ground to grow **2** : ESTABLISH, SETTLE **3** : to stock or provide with something **4** : to place firmly or forcibly **5** : to hide or arrange with intent to deceive

²**plant** *n* **1** : any of a kingdom of living things that usu. have no locomotor ability or obvious sense organs and have cellulose cell walls and usu. capacity for indefinite growth **2** : the land, buildings, and machinery used in carrying on a trade or business

¹**plan·tain** \'plan-tᵊn\ *n* [ME, fr. AF, fr. L *plantagin-, plantago*, fr. *planta* sole of the foot; fr. its broad leaves] : any of a genus of weedy herbs with spikes of tiny greenish flowers

²**plantain** *n* [Sp *plántano, plátano* plane tree, banana tree, fr. ML *plantanus* plane tree, alter. of L *platanus*] : a banana plant with starchy greenish fruit that is eaten cooked; *also* : its fruit

plan·tar \'plan-tər, -ˌtär\ *adj* : of or relating to the sole of the foot

plan·ta·tion \plan-ˈtā-shən\ *n* **1** : a large group of plants and esp. trees under cultivation **2** : an agricultural estate usu. worked by resident laborers

plant·er \'plan-tər\ *n* **1** : one that plants or sows; *esp* : an owner or operator of a plantation **2** : a container for plants

plant louse *n* : APHID

plaque \'plak\ *n* [F] **1** : an ornamental brooch **2** : a flat thin piece (as of metal) used for decoration; *also* : a commemorative tablet **3** : a bacteria-containing film on a tooth

plash \'plash\ *n* : SPLASH — **plash** *vb*

plas·ma \'plaz-mə\ *n* **1** : the fluid part of blood, lymph, or milk **2** : a gas composed of ionized particles **3** : a display (as a television screen) in which cells of plasma emit

PLANETS

NAME	SYMBOL	MEAN DISTANCE FROM THE SUN		PERIOD OF REVOLUTION IN DAYS OR YEARS	EQUATORIAL DIAMETER	
		million miles	million kilometers		miles	kilometers
Mercury	☿	35.99	57.91	87.97 d.	3,033	4,879
Venus	♀	67.25	108.21	224.70 d.	7,522	12,104
Earth	♁	92.98	149.60	365.26 d.	7,928	12,756
Mars	♂	141.67	227.94	686.99 d.	4,222	6,794
Jupiter	♃	483.78	778.41	11.86 y.	88,865	142,984
Saturn	♄	886.72	1,426.73	29.47 y.	74,914	120,536
Uranus	♅	1,784.32	2,870.97	84.02 y.	31,770	51,118
Neptune	♆	2,795.68	4,498.25	164.79 y.	30,782	49,528
Pluto	♇	3,670.84	5,906.38	247.92 y.	1,485	2,390

light upon receiving an electric current — **plas·mat·ic** \plaz-'ma-tik\ *adj*

¹plas·ter \'plas-tər\ *n* **1** : a dressing consisting of a backing spread with an often medicated substance that clings to the skin ⟨adhesive ~⟩ **2** : a paste that hardens as it dries and is used for coating walls and ceilings

²plaster *vb* : to cover with or as if with plaster — **plas·ter·er** *n*

plas·ter·board \'plas-tər-,bȯrd\ *n* : DRYWALL

plaster of par·is \-'pa-rəs\ *often cap 2d P* : a white powder made from gypsum and used as a quick-setting paste with water for casts and molds

¹plas·tic \'plas-tik\ *adj* [L *plasticus* of molding, fr. Gk *plastikos,* fr. *plassein* to mold, form] **1** : capable of being molded ⟨~ clay⟩ **2** : characterized by or using modeling ⟨~ arts⟩ **3** : made or consisting of a plastic ♦ **Synonyms** PLIABLE, PLIANT, DUCTILE, MALLEABLE, ADAPTABLE — **plas·tic·i·ty** \plas-'ti-sə-tē\ *n*

²plastic *n* : a plastic substance; *esp* : a synthetic or processed material that can be formed into rigid objects or into films or filaments

plastic surgery *n* : surgery to repair, restore, or improve lost, injured, defective, or misshapen body parts — **plastic surgeon** *n*

¹plat \'plat\ *n* **1** : a small plot of ground **2** : a plan of a piece of land with actual or proposed features (as lots)

²plat *vb* **plat·ted; plat·ting** : to make a plat of

¹plate \'plāt\ *n* **1** : a flat thin piece of material **2** : domestic hollowware made of or plated with gold, silver, or base metals **3** : DISH **4** : HOME PLATE **5** : the molded metal or plastic cast of a page of type to be printed from **6** : a sheet of glass or plastic coated with a chemical sensitive to light and used in photography **7** : the part of a denture that fits to the mouth; *also* : DENTURE **8** : something printed from an engraving **9** : a huge mobile segment of the earth's crust

²plate *vb* **plat·ed; plat·ing** **1** : to overlay with metal (as gold or silver) **2** : to make a printing plate of

pla·teau \pla-'tō\ *n, pl* **plateaus** *or* **pla·teaux** \-'tōz\ [F] : a large level area of high land

plate glass *n* : rolled, ground, and polished sheet glass

plate·let \'plāt-lət\ *n* : a minute flattened body; *esp.* : a minute colorless disklike body of mammalian blood that assists in blood clotting

plat·en \'pla-tᵊn\ *n* **1** : a flat plate; *esp* : one that exerts or receives pressure (as in a printing press) **2** : the roller of a typewriter or printer

plate tectonics *n* **1** : a theory in geology that the lithosphere is divided into plates at the boundaries of which much of earth's seismic activity occurs **2** : the process and dynamics of tectonic plate movement — **plate–tectonic** *adj*

plat·form \'plat-,fȯrm\ *n* **1** : a raised flooring or stage for speakers, performers, or workers **2** : a declaration of the principles on which a group of persons (as a political party) stands **3** : OPERATING SYSTEM

plat·ing \'plā-tiŋ\ *n* : a coating of metal plates or plate ⟨the ~ of a ship⟩

plat·i·num \'pla-tə-nəm\ *n* : a heavy grayish white metallic chemical element

plat·i·tude \'pla-tə-,tüd, -,tyüd\ *n* : a flat or trite remark — **plat·i·tu·di·nous** \-'tü-də-nəs, -'tyü-\ *adj*

pla·ton·ic love \plə-'tä-nik-, plā-\ *n, often cap P* : a close relationship between two persons without sexual desire

pla·toon \plə-'tün\ *n* [F *peloton* small detachment, lit., ball, fr. *pelote* little ball] **1** : a subdivision of a company-size military unit usu. consisting of two or more squads or sections **2** : a group of football players trained either for offense or for defense and sent into the game as a body

platoon sergeant *n* : a noncommissioned officer in the army ranking below a first sergeant

plat·ter \'pla-tər\ *n* **1** : a large serving plate **2** : a phonograph record

platy \'pla-tē\ *n, pl* **platy** *or* **plat·ys** *or* **plat·ies** : either of two small stocky usu. brilliantly colored bony-fishes often kept in tropical aquariums

platy·pus \'pla-ti-pəs\ *n, pl* **platy·pus·es** *also* **platy·pi** \-,pī\ [NL, fr. Gk *platypous* flat-footed, fr. *platys* broad, flat + *pous* foot] : a small aquatic egg-laying marsupial mammal of Australia with webbed feet and a fleshy bill like a duck's

plau·dit \'plȯ-dət\ *n* : an act of applause

plau·si·ble \'plȯ-zə-bəl\ *adj* [L *plausibilis* worthy of applause, fr. *plausus,* pp. of *plaudere* to applaud] : seemingly worthy of belief — **plau·si·bil·i·ty** \,plȯ-zə-'bi-lə-tē\ *n* — **plau·si·bly** \'plȯ-zə-blē\ *adv*

¹play \'plā\ *n* **1** : brisk handling of something (as a weapon) **2** : the course of a game; *also* : a particular act or maneuver in a game **3** : recreational activity; *esp* : the spontaneous activity of children **4** : JEST ⟨said in ~⟩ **5** : the act or an instance of punning **6** : GAMBLING **7** : OPERATION ⟨bring extra force into ~⟩ **8** : a brisk or light movement **9** : free motion (as of part of a machine) **10** : scope for action **11** : PUBLICITY **12** : an effort to arouse liking ⟨made a ~ for her⟩ **13** : a stage representation of a drama; *also* : a dramatic composition **14** : a function of an electronic device that causes a recording to play — **play·ful** \-fəl\ *adj* — **play·ful·ly** *adv* — **play·ful·ness** *n* — **in play** : in condition or position to be played

²play *vb* **1** : to engage in recreation : FROLIC **2** : to handle or behave lightly or absentmindedly **3** : to make a pun ⟨~ on words⟩ **4** : to take advantage ⟨~ on fears⟩ **5** : to move or operate in a brisk or irregular manner ⟨a flashlight ~ed over the wall⟩ **6** : to perform music ⟨~ on a violin⟩; *also* : to perform (music) on an instrument ⟨~ a waltz⟩ **7** : to perform music upon ⟨~ the piano⟩; *also* : to sound in performance ⟨the organ is ~ing⟩ **8** : to cause to emit sounds ⟨~ a radio⟩; *also* : to cause to reproduce recorded material ⟨~ a DVD⟩ **9** : to act in a dramatic medium; *also* : to act in the character of ⟨~ the hero⟩ **10** : GAMBLE **11** : to produce a specified impression in performance ⟨~s like a comedy⟩ **12** : to behave in a specified way ⟨~ safe⟩; *also* : COOPERATE ⟨~ along with him⟩ **13** : to deal with; *also* : EMPHASIZE ⟨~ up her good qualities⟩ **14** : to perform for amusement ⟨~ a trick⟩ **15** : WREAK **16** : to use as an esp. political strategy **17** : to contend with in a game; *also* : to fill (a certain position) on a team **18** : to make wagers on ⟨~ the races⟩ **19** : WIELD, PLY **20** : to keep in action — **play·er** *n*

play·act·ing \'plā-,ak-tiŋ\ *n* **1** : performance in theatrical productions **2** : insincere or artificial behavior

play·back \-,bak\ *n* : an act of reproducing recorded sound or pictures — **play back** *vb*

play·bill \-,bil\ *n* : a poster advertising the performance of a play

play·book \-,bu̇k\ *n* **1** : a notebook containing diagrammed football plays **2** : a stock of usual tactics or methods

play·boy \-,bȯi\ *n* : a man whose chief interest is the pursuit of pleasure

play·date \-,dāt\ *n* : a usu. prearranged play session for small children

play·go·er \-,gō-ər\ *n* : a person who frequently attends plays

play·ground \-,grau̇nd\ *n* : an area used for games and play esp. by children

play·house \-,hau̇s\ *n* **1** : THEATER **2** : a small house for children to play in

playing card *n* : any of a set of 24 to 78 cards marked to show its rank and suit and used to play a game of cards

play·let \'plā-lət\ *n* : a short play

play·mate \-,māt\ *n* : a companion in play

play·off \-,ȯf\ *n* : a contest or series of contests to break a tie or determine a championship

play out *vb* : DEVELOP, UNFOLD ⟨see how things *play out*⟩

play·pen \-,pen\ *n* : a portable enclosure in which a young child may play

play·suit \-,süt\ *n* : a sports and play outfit for women and children

play·thing \-,thiŋ\ *n* : TOY

play·wright \-,rīt\ *n* : a writer of plays

pla·za \'pla-zə, 'plä-\ *n* [Sp, fr. L *platea* broad street] **1** : a public square in a city or town **2** : a shopping center

PLC *abbr, Brit* public limited company

plea \'plē\ *n* **1** : a defendant's answer in law to a charge or indictment **2** : something alleged as an excuse **3** : ENTREATY, APPEAL

plead \'plēd\ *vb* **plead·ed** *or* **pled** \'pled\; **plead·ing** **1** : to argue before a court or authority ⟨~ a case⟩ **2** : to answer to a charge or indictment ⟨~ guilty⟩ **3** : to argue for or against something ⟨∼ for acquittal⟩ **4** : to appeal earnestly ⟨∼s for help⟩ **5** : to offer as a plea (as in defense) ⟨∼ed illness⟩ — **plead·er** n

pleas·ant \'ple-z°nt\ adj **1** : giving pleasure : AGREEABLE ⟨a ∼ experience⟩ **2** : marked by pleasing behavior or appearance ⟨a ∼ person⟩ — **pleas·ant·ly** adv — **pleas·ant·ness** n

pleas·ant·ry \-z°n-trē\ n, pl **-ries** : a pleasant and casual act or speech

¹please \'plēz\ vb **pleased; pleas·ing 1** : to give pleasure or satisfaction to **2** : LIKE ⟨do as you ∼⟩ **3** : to be the will or pleasure of ⟨may it ∼ his Majesty⟩

²please adv — used as a function word to express politeness or emphasis in a request ⟨∼ come in⟩

pleasing adj : giving pleasure — **pleas·ing·ly** adv

plea·sur·able \'ple-zhə-rə-bəl\ adj : PLEASANT, GRATIFYING — **plea·sur·ably** \-blē\ adv

plea·sure \'ple-zhər\ n **1** : DESIRE, INCLINATION ⟨await your ∼⟩ **2** : a state of gratification : ENJOYMENT **3** : a source of delight or joy

¹pleat \'plēt\ vb **1** : FOLD; esp : to arrange in pleats **2** : BRAID

²pleat n : a fold (as in cloth) made by doubling material over on itself

plebe \'plēb\ n : a freshman at a military or naval academy

¹ple·be·ian \pli-'bē-ən\ n **1** : a member of the Roman plebs **2** : one of the common people

²plebeian adj **1** : of or relating to plebeians **2** : COMMON, VULGAR

pleb·i·scite \'ple-bə-ˌsīt, -sət\ n : a vote of the people (as of a country) on a proposal submitted to them

plebs \'plebz\ n, pl **ple·bes** \'plē-bēz\ **1** : the general populace **2** : the common people of ancient Rome

plec·trum \'plek-trəm\ n, pl **plec·tra** \-trə\ or **plec·trums** [L] : ³PICK 3

¹pledge \'plej\ n [ME plegge security, fr. AF plege, fr. LL plebium, fr. *plebere to pledge, prob. of Gmc origin] **1** : something given as security for the performance of an act **2** : the state of being held as a security or guaranty **3** : TOAST 3 **4** : PROMISE, VOW

²pledge vb **pledged; pledg·ing 1** : to deposit as a pledge **2** : TOAST **3** : to bind by a pledge : PLIGHT **4** : PROMISE

Pleis·to·cene \'plī-stə-ˌsēn\ adj : of, relating to, or being the earlier epoch of the Quaternary — **Pleistocene** n

ple·na·ry \'plē-nə-rē, 'ple-\ adj **1** : FULL ⟨∼ power⟩ **2** : including all entitled to attend ⟨∼ session⟩

pleni·po·ten·tia·ry \ˌple-nə-pə-'ten-chə-rē, -'ten-chē-ˌer-ē\ n, pl **-ries** : a diplomatic agent having full authority — **plenipotentiary** adj

plen·i·tude \'ple-nə-ˌtüd, -ˌtyüd\ n **1** : COMPLETENESS **2** : ABUNDANCE

plen·te·ous \'plen-tē-əs\ adj **1** : FRUITFUL **2** : existing in plenty

plen·ti·ful \'plen-ti-fəl\ adj **1** : containing or yielding plenty **2** : ABUNDANT — **plen·ti·ful·ly** adv

plen·ty \'plen-tē\ n : a more than adequate number or amount

ple·num \'ple-nəm, 'plē-\ n, pl **-nums** or **-na** \-nə\ : a general assembly of all members esp. of a legislative body

pleth·o·ra \'ple-thə-rə\ n : an excessive quantity or fullness; also : PROFUSION

pleu·ri·sy \'plùr-ə-sē\ n : inflammation of the membrane that lines the chest and covers the lungs

plex·us \'plek-səs\ n, pl **plex·us·es** \-sə-səz\ : an interlacing network esp. of blood vessels or nerves

pli·able \'plī-ə-bəl\ adj **1** : FLEXIBLE **2** : yielding easily to others ♦ **Synonyms** PLASTIC, PLIANT, DUCTILE, MALLEABLE, ADAPTABLE — **pli·abil·i·ty** \ˌplī-ə-'bi-lə-tē\ n

pli·ant \'plī-ənt\ adj **1** : FLEXIBLE **2** : easily influenced : PLIABLE — **pli·an·cy** \-ən-sē\ n

pli·ers \'plī-ərz\ n pl : small pincers for bending or cutting wire or handling small objects

¹plight \'plīt\ vb : to put or give in pledge : ENGAGE

²plight n : an unfortunate, difficult, or precarious situation

plinth \'plinth\ n : the lowest part of the base of an architectural column

Plio·cene \'plī-ə-ˌsēn\ adj : of, relating to, or being the latest epoch of the Tertiary — **Pliocene** n

PLO abbr Palestine Liberation Organization

plod \'pläd\ vb **plod·ded; plod·ding 1** : to walk heavily or slowly : TRUDGE **2** : to work laboriously and monotonously : DRUDGE — **plod·der** n — **plod·ding·ly** adv

plonk var of PLUNK

plop \'pläp\ vb **plopped; plop·ping 1** : to fall or move with a sound like that of something dropping into water **2** : to set, drop, or throw heavily or hastily ⟨plopped down on the couch⟩ ⟨∼ down $20⟩ — **plop** n

¹plot \'plät\ n **1** : a small area of ground **2** : a ground plan (as of an area) **3** : the main story (as of a book or movie) **4** : a secret scheme : INTRIGUE

²plot vb **plot·ted; plot·ting 1** : to make a plot or plan of **2** : to mark on or as if on a chart **3** : to plan or contrive esp. secretly — **plot·ter** n

plo·ver \'plə-vər, 'plō-\ n, pl **plover** or **plovers** [ME, fr. AF, fr. VL *pluviarius, fr. L pluvia rain] : any of a family of shorebirds that differ from the sandpipers in having shorter stouter bills

¹plow or **plough** \'plaù\ n **1** : an implement used to cut, lift, turn over, and partly break up soil **2** : a device (as a snowplow) operating like a plow

²plow or **plough** vb **1** : to open, break up, or work with a plow **2** : to move through like a plow ⟨a ship ∼ing the waves⟩ **3** : to proceed laboriously — **plow·able** adj — **plow·er** n

plow·boy \'plaù-ˌbói\ n : a boy who leads the horse drawing a plow

plow·man \-mən, -ˌman\ n **1** : a man who guides a plow **2** : a farm laborer

plow·share \-ˌsher\ n : a part of a plow that cuts the earth

ploy \'plói\ n : a tactic intended to embarrass or frustrate an opponent

¹pluck \'plək\ vb **1** : to pull off or out : PICK; also : to pull something from **2** : to play (an instrument) by pulling the strings **3** : TUG, TWITCH

²pluck n **1** : an act or instance of plucking **2** : SPIRIT, COURAGE

plucky \'plə-kē\ adj **pluck·i·er; -est** : COURAGEOUS, SPIRITED

¹plug \'pləg\ n **1** : STOPPER; also : an obstructing mass **2** : a cake of tobacco **3** : a poor or worn-out horse **4** : SPARK PLUG **5** : a lure with several hooks used in fishing **6** : a device on the end of a cord for making an electrical connection **7** : a piece of favorable publicity

²plug vb **plugged; plug·ging 1** : to stop, make tight, or secure by inserting a plug **2** : HIT, SHOOT **3** : to publicize insistently **4** : PLOD, DRUDGE

plug and play n : a computer feature enabling the operating system to automatically detect and configure peripherals — **plug-and-play** adj

plugged–in \'pləgd-'in\ adj : technologically or socially informed and connected

plug–in \'pləg-ˌin\ n : a small piece of software that supplements a larger program

plum \'pləm\ n [ME, fr. OE plūme, modif. of L prunum plum, fr. Gk proumnon] **1** : a smooth-skinned juicy fruit borne by trees related to the peach and cherry; also : a tree bearing plums **2** : a raisin when used in desserts (as puddings) **3** : something excellent; esp : something desirable given in return for a favor

plum·age \'plü-mij\ n : the feathers of a bird — **plum·aged** \-mijd\ adj

¹plumb \'pləm\ n : a weight on the end of a line (**plumb line**) used esp. by builders to show vertical direction

²plumb adv **1** : VERTICALLY **2** : COMPLETELY **3** : EXACTLY; also : IMMEDIATELY

³plumb vb : to sound, adjust, or test with a plumb ⟨∼ the depth of a well⟩

⁴plumb adj **1** : VERTICAL **2** : COMPLETE

plumb·er \'plə-mər\ n : a worker who fits or repairs pipes and fixtures

plumb·ing \'plə-min\ n : a system of pipes in a building for supplying and carrying off water

plume \'plüm\ n : FEATHER; esp : a large, conspicuous, or showy feather — **plumed** \'plümd\ adj — **plumy** \'plü-mē\ adj

²plume vb **plumed; plum·ing 1** : to provide or deck with feathers **2** : to indulge (oneself) in pride

¹plum·met \'plə-mət\ n : PLUMB; also : PLUMB LINE

²plummet vb : to drop or plunge straight down

¹plump \'pləmp\ vb **1** : to drop or fall suddenly or heavily **2** : to favor something strongly ⟨∼ing for change⟩

²**plump** *n* : a sudden heavy fall or blow; *also* : the sound made by it

³**plump** *adv* **1** : straight down; *also* : straight ahead **2** : UNQUALIFIEDLY ⟨came out ∼ for free trade⟩

⁴**plump** *adj* : having a full rounded usu. pleasing form ♦ **Synonyms** FLESHY, STOUT, ROLY-POLY, ROTUND — **plump·ness** *n*

¹**plun·der** \'plən-dər\ *vb* : to take the goods of by force or wrongfully : PILLAGE — **plun·der·er** *n*

²**plunder** *n* : something taken by force or theft : LOOT

¹**plunge** \'plənj\ *vb* **plunged; plung·ing 1** : IMMERSE, SUBMERGE **2** : to enter or cause to enter a state or course of action suddenly or violently ⟨∼ into war⟩ **3** : to cast oneself into or as if into water **4** : to gamble heavily and recklessly **5** : to descend suddenly

²**plunge** *n* : a sudden dive, leap, or rush

plung·er \'plən-jər\ *n* **1** : one that plunges **2** : a sliding piece driven by or against fluid pressure : PISTON **3** : a rubber cup on a handle pushed against an opening to free a waste outlet of an obstruction

plunk \'pləŋk\ *or* **plonk** \'pläŋk, 'plȯŋk\ *vb* **1** : to make or cause to make a hollow metallic sound **2** : to drop heavily or suddenly — **plunk** *n*

plu·per·fect \(ˌ)plü-'pər-fikt\ *adj* [ME *pluperfyth*, modif. of LL *plusquamperfectus*, lit., more than perfect] : of, relating to, or constituting a verb tense that denotes an action or state as completed at or before a past time spoken of — **pluperfect** *n*

plu·ral \'plu̇r-əl\ *adj* [ME, fr. AF & L; AF *plurel*, fr. L *pluralis*, fr. *plur-*, *plus* more] : of, relating to, or constituting a word form used to denote more than one — **plural** *n*

plu·ral·i·ty \plu̇-'ra-lə-tē\ *n, pl* **-ties 1** : the state of being plural **2** : an excess of votes over those cast for an opposing candidate **3** : the greatest number of votes cast when not a majority

plu·ral·ize \'plu̇r-ə-ˌlīz\ *vb* **-ized; -iz·ing** : to make plural or express in the plural form — **plu·ral·i·za·tion** \ˌplu̇r-ə-lə-'zā-shən\ *n*

¹**plus** \'pləs\ *adj* [L, more] **1** : mathematically positive **2** : having or being in addition to what is anticipated **3** : falling high in a specified range ⟨a grade of B ∼⟩

²**plus** *n, pl* **plus·es** \'plə-səz\ *also* **plus·ses 1** : a sign + **(plus sign)** used in mathematics to indicate addition or a positive quantity **2** : an added quantity; *also* : a positive quality **3** : SURPLUS

³**plus** *prep* **1** : increased by : with the addition of ⟨3 ∼ 4⟩ **2** : BESIDES

⁴**plus** *conj* : AND ⟨soup ∼ salad and bread⟩

¹**plush** \'pləsh\ *n* : a fabric with a pile longer and less dense than velvet pile — **plushy** *adj*

²**plush** *adj* : notably luxurious — **plush·ly** *adv* — **plush·ness** *n*

plus/minus sign *n* : the sign ± used to indicate a quantity taking on both a positive value and its negative or to indicate a plus or minus quantity

plus or minus *adj* : indicating a quantity whose positive and negative values bracket a range of values ⟨*plus or minus 3 inches*⟩

Plu·to \'plü-tō\ *n* : the planet farthest from the sun — see PLANET table

plu·toc·ra·cy \plü-'tä-krə-sē\ *n, pl* **-cies 1** : government by the wealthy **2** : a controlling class of the wealthy — **plu·to·crat** \'plü-tə-ˌkrat\ *n* — **plu·to·crat·ic** \ˌplü-tə-'kra-tik\ *adj*

plu·to·ni·um \plü-'tō-nē-əm\ *n* : a radioactive chemical element formed by the decay of neptunium

plu·vi·al \'plü-vē-əl\ *adj* **1** : of or relating to rain **2** : characterized by abundant rain

¹**ply** \'plī\ *vb* **plied; ply·ing 1** : to use, practice, or work diligently ⟨∼ a trade⟩ **2** : to keep supplying something to ⟨plied them with liquor⟩ **3** : to go or travel regularly esp. by sea

²**ply** *n, pl* **plies** : one of the folds, thicknesses, or strands of which something (as plywood or yarn) is made

³**ply** *vb* **plied; ply·ing** : to twist together ⟨∼ yarns⟩

ply·wood \'plī-ˌwu̇d\ *n* : material made of thin sheets of wood glued and pressed together

pm *abbr* premium

Pm *symbol* promethium

PM *abbr* **1** paymaster **2** police magistrate **3** postmaster **4** post meridiem — often not cap. and often punctu-

ated **5** postmortem **6** prime minister **7** provost marshal

pmk *abbr* postmark

PMS \ˌpē-ˌem-'es\ *n* : PREMENSTRUAL SYNDROME

pmt *abbr* payment

pneu·mat·ic \nu̇-'ma-tik, nyu̇-\ *adj* **1** : of, relating to, or using air or wind **2** : moved by air pressure **3** : filled with compressed air — **pneu·mat·i·cal·ly** \-ti-k(ə-)lē\ *adv*

pneu·mo·coc·cus \ˌnü-mə-'kä-kəs, ˌnyü-\ *n, pl* **-coc·ci** \-'käk-ˌsī, -ˌsē; -'käk-ˌkī, -ˌkē\ : a bacterium that causes pneumonia — **pneu·mo·coc·cal** \-'kä-kəl\ *adj*

pneu·mo·co·ni·o·sis \ˌnü-mō-ˌkō-nē-'ō-səs, ˌnyü-\ *n* : a disease of the lungs caused by habitual inhalation of irritant mineral or metallic particles

pneu·mo·nia \nu̇-'mō-nyə, nyu̇-\ *n* : an inflammatory disease of the lungs

Po *symbol* polonium

PO *abbr* **1** petty officer **2** post office

¹**poach** \'pōch\ *vb* [ME *pocchen*, fr. MF *pocher*, fr. OF *poché* poached, lit., bagged, fr. *poche* bag, pouch, of Gmc origin] : to cook (as an egg or fish) in simmering liquid

²**poach** *vb* : to hunt or fish unlawfully — **poach·er** *n*

POB *abbr* post office box

po·bla·no \pō-'blä-nō\ *n, pl* **-nos** : a heart-shaped usu. mild chili pepper esp. when fresh and dark green

po'·boy \'pō-ˌbȯi\ *also* **poor boy** *n* : SUBMARINE 2

pock \'päk\ *n* : a small swelling on the skin (as in small-pox); *also* : a spot suggesting this

¹**pock·et** \'pä-kət\ *n* **1** : a small bag open at the top or side inserted in a garment **2** : supply of money : MEANS **3** : RECEPTACLE, CONTAINER **4** : a small isolated area or group **5** : a small body of ore — **pock·et·ful** *n*

²**pocket** *vb* **1** : to put in or as if in a pocket **2** : STEAL ⟨∼ed the profits⟩

³**pocket** *adj* **1** : small enough to fit in a pocket; *also* : SMALL, MINIATURE ⟨a ∼ park⟩ **2** : carried in or paid from one's own pocket

¹**pock·et·book** \-ˌbu̇k\ *n* **1** : PURSE; *also* : HANDBAG **2** : financial resources

²**pocketbook** *adj* : relating to money

pocket gopher *n* : GOPHER 2

pock·et·knife \'pä-kət-ˌnīf\ *n* : a knife with a folding blade to be carried in the pocket

pocket veto *n* : an indirect veto of a legislative bill by an executive through retention of the bill unsigned until after adjournment of the legislature

pock·mark \'päk-ˌmärk\ *n* : a pit or scar caused by small-pox or acne — **pock·marked** \-ˌmärkt\ *adj*

po·co \'pō-kō, ˌpȯ-\ *adv* [It, little, fr. L *paucus*] : SOME-WHAT — used to qualify a direction in music ⟨∼ allegro⟩

po·co a po·co \ˌpō-kō-ä-'pō-kō, ˌpȯ-kō-ä-'pȯ-\ *adv* : little by little : GRADUALLY — used as a direction in music

pod \'päd\ *n* **1** : a dry fruit (as of a pea) that splits open when ripe **2** : an external streamlined compartment (as for a jet engine) on an airplane **3** : a compartment (as for personnel, a power unit, or an instrument) on a ship or craft

POD *abbr* pay on delivery

po·di·a·try \pə-'dī-ə-trē, pō-\ *n* : the medical care and treatment of the human foot — **po·di·at·ric** \ˌpō-dē-'a-trik\ *adj* — **po·di·a·trist** \pə-'dī-ə-trist, pō-\ *n*

po·di·um \'pō-dē-əm\ *n, pl* **podiums** *or* **po·dia** \-dē-ə\ **1** : a dais esp. for an orchestral conductor **2** : LECTERN

POE *abbr* port of entry

po·em \'pō-əm\ *n* : a composition in verse

po·esy \'pō-ə-zē\ *n* : POETRY

po·et \'pō-ət\ *n* [ME, fr. AF *poete*, fr. L *poeta*, fr. Gk *poiētēs* maker, poet, fr. *poiein* to make] : a writer of poetry; *also* : a creative artist of great sensitivity

po·et·as·ter \'pō-ə-ˌtas-tər\ *n* : an inferior poet

po·et·ess \'pō-ə-təs\ *n* : a girl or woman who is a poet

poetic justice *n* : an outcome in which vice is punished and virtue rewarded usu. in a manner peculiarly or ironically appropriate

po·et·ry \'pō-ə-trē\ *n* **1** : metrical writing **2** : POEMS — **po·et·ic** \pō-'e-tik\ *or* **po·et·i·cal** \-ti-kəl\ *adj*

po·grom \'pō-grəm, pō-'gräm\ *n* [Yiddish, fr. Russ., lit., devastation] : an organized massacre of helpless people and esp. of Jews

poi \'pȯi\ *n, pl* **poi** *or* **pois** : a Hawaiian food of taro root cooked, pounded, and kneaded to a paste and often allowed to ferment

poi·gnant \\'pȯi-nyənt\\ *adj* **1** : painfully affecting the feelings ⟨∼ grief⟩ **2** : deeply moving ⟨∼ scene⟩ — **poi·gnan·cy** \\-nyən-sē\\ *n*

poin·ci·ana \\ˌpȯin-sē-'a-nə\\ *n* : any of several ornamental tropical leguminous trees or shrubs with bright orange or red flowers

poin·set·tia \\pȯin-'se-tē-ə\\ *n* : a showy tropical American spurge with usu. scarlet bracts that suggest petals and surround small yellow flowers

¹**point** \\'pȯint\\ *n* **1** : an individual detail; *also* : the most important essential **2** : PURPOSE ⟨no ∼ in continuing⟩ **3** : a geometric element that has position but no size **4** : a particular place : LOCALITY **5** : a particular stage or degree **6** : a sharp end : TIP **7** : a projecting piece of land **8** : a punctuation mark; *esp* : PERIOD **9** : DECIMAL POINT **10** : one of the divisions of the compass **11** : a unit of counting (as in a game score) — **point·less** *adj* — **pointy** \\'pȯin-tē\\ *adj* — **beside the point** : IRRELEVANT — **to the point** : RELEVANT, PERTINENT ⟨her remark was *to the point*⟩

²**point** *vb* **1** : to furnish with a point : SHARPEN **2** : PUNCTUATE **3** : to separate (a decimal fraction) from an integer by a decimal point — usu. used with *off* **4** : to indicate the position of esp. by extending a finger **5** : to direct attention to ⟨∼ out an error⟩ **6** : AIM, DIRECT **7** : to lie extended, aimed, or turned in a particular direction : FACE, LOOK

point–and–click *adj* : relating to or being a computer interface that allows the activation of a file by selection with a pointing device (as a mouse)

point–and–shoot *adj* : having or using preset or automatically adjusted controls ⟨a ∼ camera⟩

point–blank \\'pȯint-'blaŋk\\ *adj* **1** : so close to the target that a missile fired will travel in a straight line to the mark **2** : DIRECT, BLUNT ⟨a ∼ refusal⟩ — **point–blank** *adv*

point·ed \\'pȯin-təd\\ *adj* **1** : having a point **2** : being to the point : DIRECT **3** : aimed at a particular person or group; *also* : CONSPICUOUS, MARKED ⟨∼ indifference⟩ — **point·ed·ly** *adv*

point·er \\'pȯin-tər\\ *n* **1** : one that points out : INDICATOR **2** : a large short-haired hunting dog **3** : HINT, TIP ⟨gave me some ∼s on how to play⟩

poin·til·lism \\'pwan-tē-ˌyi-zəm, 'pȯin-tə-ˌli-zəm\\ *n* [F *pointillisme*, fr. *pointiller* to stipple, fr. *point* spot, point] : the theory or practice in painting of applying small strokes or dots of color to a surface so that from a distance they blend together — **poin·til·list** \\ˌpwan-tē-'yēst, 'pȯin-tə-list\\ *n or adj*

point man *n* : a principal spokesman or advocate

point of no return : a critical point at which turning back or reversal is not possible

point of view : a position from which something is considered or evaluated

point spread *n* : the number of points by which a favorite is expected to defeat an underdog

¹**poise** \\'pȯiz\\ *vb* **poised; pois·ing** : BALANCE

²**poise** *n* **1** : BALANCE **2** : self-possessed calmness; *also* : a particular way of carrying oneself

poi·sha \\'pȯi-shə\\ *n, pl* **poisha** : the paisa of Bangladesh

¹**poi·son** \\'pȯi-z°n\\ *n* [ME, fr. AF *poisun* drink, potion, poison, fr. L *potion-, potio* drink] : a substance that through its chemical action can injure or kill — **poi·son·ous** \\-z°n-əs\\ *adj*

²**poison** *vb* **1** : to injure or kill with poison **2** : to treat or taint with poison **3** : to affect destructively : CORRUPT ⟨∼ed her mind⟩ — **poi·son·er** *n*

poison hemlock *n* : a large branching poisonous herb with finely divided leaves and white flowers that is related to the carrot

poison ivy *n* **1** : a usu. climbing plant related to the sumacs that has leaves composed of three shiny leaflets and produces an irritating oil causing a usu. intensely itching skin rash; *also* : any of several related plants **2** : a skin rash caused by poison ivy

poison oak *n* : any of several shrubby plants closely related to poison ivy and having similar properties

poison sumac *n* : a No. American swamp shrub with pin-

nate leaves, greenish flowers, greenish white berries, and irritating properties

¹**poke** \\'pōk\\ *n, chiefly Southern & Midland* : BAG, SACK

²**poke** *vb* **poked; pok·ing** **1** : PROD; *also* : to stir up by prodding **2** : to make a prodding or jabbing movement esp. repeatedly **3** : HIT, PUNCH **4** : to thrust forward obtrusively **5** : RUMMAGE ⟨*poking* around the attic⟩ **6** : MEDDLE, PRY **7** : DAWDLE — **poke fun at** : RIDICULE, MOCK

³**poke** *n* : a quick thrust; *also* : PUNCH

¹**pok·er** \\'pō-kər\\ *n* : a metal rod for stirring a fire

²**po·ker** \\'pō-kər\\ *n* : any of several card games in which the player with the highest hand at the end of the betting wins

poke·weed \\'pōk-ˌwēd\\ *n* : a coarse American perennial herb with clusters of white flowers and dark purple juicy berries

poky *or* **pok·ey** \\'pō-kē\\ *adj* **pok·i·er; -est** **1** : small and cramped **2** : SHABBY, DULL **3** : annoyingly slow

pol \\'päl\\ *n* : POLITICIAN

po·lar \\'pō-lər\\ *adj* **1** : of or relating to a geographical pole **2** : of or relating to a pole (as of a magnet)

polar bear *n* : a large creamy-white bear that inhabits arctic regions

Po·lar·is \\pə-'ler-əs\\ *n* : NORTH STAR

po·lar·ise *Brit var of* POLARIZE

po·lar·i·ty \\pō-'ler-ə-tē\\ *n, pl* **-ties** : the condition of having poles and esp. magnetic or electrical poles

po·lar·i·za·tion \\ˌpō-lə-rə-'zā-shən\\ *n* **1** : the action of polarizing : the state of being polarized **2** : concentration about opposing extremes

po·lar·ize \\'pō-lə-ˌrīz\\ *vb* **-ized; -iz·ing** **1** : to cause (light waves) to vibrate in a definite way **2** : to give physical polarity to **3** : to break up into opposing groups

pol·der \\'pōl-dər, 'päl-\\ *n* [D] : a tract of low land reclaimed from the sea

¹**pole** \\'pōl\\ *n* : a long slender piece of wood or metal ⟨telephone ∼⟩

²**pole** *vb* **poled; pol·ing** : to impel or push with a pole

³**pole** *n* **1** : either end of an axis esp. of the earth **2** : either of the terminals of an electric device (as a battery or generator) **3** : one of two or more regions in a magnetized body at which the magnetism is concentrated — **pole·ward** \\'pōl-wərd\\ *adj or adv*

¹**pole·ax** \\'pōl-ˌaks\\ *n* : a battle-ax with a short handle

²**poleax** *vb* : to attack or fell with or as if with a poleax

pole·cat \\'pōl-ˌkat\\ *n, pl* **polecats** *or* **polecat** **1** : a European carnivorous mammal of which the ferret is considered a domesticated variety **2** : SKUNK

polecat 1

po·lem·ic \\pə-'le-mik\\ *n* : the art or practice of disputation — usu. used in pl. — **po·lem·i·cal** \\-mi-kəl\\ *also* **po·lem·ic** \\-mik\\ *adj* — **po·lem·i·cist** \\-sist\\ *n*

pole·star \\'pōl-ˌstär\\ *n* **1** : NORTH STAR **2** : a directing principle : GUIDE

pole vault *n* : a field contest in which each contestant uses a pole to vault for height over a crossbar — **pole–vault** *vb* — **pole–vault·er** *n*

¹**po·lice** \\pə-'lēs\\ *vb* **po·liced; po·lic·ing** **1** : to control, regulate, or keep in order esp. by use of police ⟨∼ a highway⟩ **2** : to make clean and put in order

²**police** *n, pl* **police** [F, government, fr. OF, fr. LL *politia*, fr. Gk *politeia*, fr. *politēs* citizen, fr. *polis* city, state] **1** : the department of government that keeps public order and safety and enforces the laws; *also* : the members of this department **2** : a private organization resembling a police force; *also* : its members **3** : military personnel detailed to clean and put in order

po·lice·man \\-mən\\ *n* : POLICE OFFICER

police officer *n* : a member of a police force

police state *n* : a state characterized by repressive, arbitrary, totalitarian rule by means of secret police

po·lice·wom·an \pə-'lēs-ˌwu̇-mən\ *n* : a woman who is a police officer

¹**pol·i·cy** \'pä-lə-sē\ *n, pl* **-cies** : a definite course or method of action selected to guide and determine present and future decisions

²**policy** *n, pl* **-cies** : a writing whereby a contract of insurance is made

pol·i·cy·hold·er \'pä-lə-sē-ˌhōl-dər\ *n* : one granted an insurance policy

po·lio \'pō-lē-ˌō\ *n* : POLIOMYELITIS — **polio** *adj*

po·lio·my·eli·tis \-ˌmī-ə-'lī-təs\ *n* : an acute virus disease marked by inflammation of the gray matter of the spinal cord leading usu. to paralysis

¹**pol·ish** \'pä-lish\ *vb* **1** : to make smooth and glossy usu. by rubbing **2** : to refine or improve in manners, condition, or style

²**polish** *n* **1** : a smooth glossy surface : LUSTER **2** : REFINEMENT, CULTURE **3** : the action or process of polishing **4** : a preparation used to produce a gloss

Pol·ish \'pō-lish\ *n* : the Slavic language of the Poles — **Polish** *adj*

polit *abbr* political; politician

po·lit·bu·ro \'pä-lət-ˌbyu̇r-ō, 'pō-, pə-'lit-\ *n* [Russ *politbyuro*] : the principal policy-making committee of a Communist party

po·lite \pə-'līt\ *adj* **po·lit·er; -est** **1** : REFINED, CULTIVATED ⟨~ society⟩ **2** : marked by correct social conduct : COURTEOUS; *also* : CONSIDERATE, TACTFUL — **po·lite·ly** *adv* — **po·lite·ness** *n*

po·li·tesse \ˌpä-li-'tes\ *n* [F] : formal politeness

pol·i·tic \'pä-lə-ˌtik\ *adj* **1** : wise in promoting a policy ⟨a ~ statesman⟩ **2** : shrewdly tactful ⟨a ~ move⟩

po·lit·i·cal \pə-'li-ti-kəl\ *adj* **1** : of or relating to government or politics **2** : involving or charged or concerned with acts against a government or a political system ⟨~ prisoners⟩ — **po·lit·i·cal·ly** \-k(ə-)lē\ *adv*

politically correct *adj* : conforming to a belief that language and practices which could offend sensibilities (as in matters of sex or race) should be eliminated — **political correctness** *n*

pol·i·ti·cian \ˌpä-lə-'ti-shən\ *n* : a person actively engaged in government or politics

pol·i·tick \'pä-lə-ˌtik\ *vb* : to engage in political discussion or activity

po·lit·i·co \pə-'li-ti-ˌkō\ *n, pl* **-cos** *also* **-coes** : POLITICIAN

pol·i·tics \'pä-lə-ˌtiks\ *n sing or pl* **1** : the art or science of government, of guiding or influencing governmental policy, or of winning and holding control over a government **2** : political affairs or business; *esp* : competition between groups or individuals for power and leadership **3** : political opinions

pol·i·ty \'pä-lə-tē\ *n, pl* **-ties** : a politically organized unit; *also* : the form or constitution of such a unit

pol·ka \'pōl-kə, 'pō-kə\ *n* [Czech, fr. *Polka* Polish woman, fem. of *Polák* Pole] : a lively couple dance of Bohemian origin; *also* : music for this dance — **polka** *vb*

pol·ka dot \'pō-kə-ˌdät\ *n* : a dot in a pattern of regularly distributed dots — **polka–dot** *or* **polka–dot·ted** \-ˌdä-təd\ *adj*

¹**poll** \'pōl\ *n* **1** : HEAD **2** : the casting and recording of votes; *also* : the total vote cast **3** : the place where votes are cast — usu. used in pl. **4** : a questioning of persons to obtain information or opinions to be analyzed

²**poll** *vb* **1** : to cut off or shorten a growth or part of : CLIP, SHEAR **2** : to receive and record the votes of **3** : to receive (as votes) in an election **4** : to question in a poll

pol·lack *or* **pol·lock** \'pä-lək\ *n, pl* **pollack** *or* **pollock** : an important No. Atlantic food fish that is related to the cods; *also* : a related food fish of the No. Pacific

pol·len \'pä-lən\ *n* [NL, fr. L, fine flour] : a mass of male spores of a seed plant usu. appearing as a yellow dust

pol·li·na·tion \ˌpä-lə-'nä-shən\ *n* : the carrying of pollen to the female part of a plant to fertilize the seed — **pol·li·nate** \'pä-lə-ˌnāt\ *vb* — **pol·li·na·tor** \-ˌnā-tər\ *n*

poll·ster \'pōl-stər\ *n* : one that conducts a poll or compiles data obtained by a poll

poll tax *n* : a tax of a fixed amount per person levied on adults and often linked to the right to vote

pol·lute \pə-'lüt\ *vb* **pol·lut·ed; pol·lut·ing** : to make impure; *esp* : to contaminate (an environment) esp. with man-made waste — **pol·lut·ant** \-'lüt-ᵊnt\ *n* — **pol·lut·er** *n* — **pol·lu·tion** \-'lü-shən\ *n*

pol·ly·wog *or* **pol·li·wog** \'pä-lē-ˌwäg\ *n* : TADPOLE

po·lo \'pō-lō\ *n* [Balti (Tibetan language of northern Kashmir), ball] : a game played by two teams on horseback using long-handled mallets to drive a wooden ball

po·lo·ni·um \pə-'lō-nē-əm\ *n* : a radioactive metallic chemical element

pol·ter·geist \'pōl-tər-ˌgīst\ *n* [G, fr. *poltern* to knock + *Geist* spirit] : a noisy usu. mischievous ghost held to be responsible for unexplained noises

pol·troon \päl-'trün\ *n* : COWARD

poly- *comb form* [Gk, fr. *polys* many] **1** : many : several ⟨*poly*syllabic⟩ **2** : polymeric ⟨*poly*ester⟩

poly·chlo·ri·nat·ed bi·phe·nyl \ˌpä-li-ˌklōr-ə-ˌnā-təd-ˌbī-'fen-ᵊl, -'fēn-\ *n* : any of several industrial compounds that are toxic environmental pollutants

poly·clin·ic \ˌpä-li-'kli-nik\ *n* : a clinic or hospital treating diseases of many sorts

poly·es·ter \'pä-lē-ˌes-tər\ *n* : a polymer composed of ester groups used esp. in making fibers or plastics; *also* : a product (as fabric) composed of polyester

poly·eth·yl·ene \ˌpä-lē-'e-thə-ˌlēn\ *n* : a lightweight plastic resistant to chemicals and moisture and used chiefly in packaging

po·lyg·a·my \pə-'li-gə-mē\ *n* : the practice of having more than one wife or husband at one time — **po·lyg·a·mist** \-mist\ *n* — **po·lyg·a·mous** \-məs\ *adj*

poly·glot \'pä-li-ˌglät\ *adj* **1** : speaking or writing several languages **2** : containing or made up of several languages — **polyglot** *n*

poly·gon \'pä-li-ˌgän\ *n* : a closed plane figure bounded by straight lines — **po·lyg·o·nal** \pə-'li-gə-nᵊl\ *adj*

poly·graph \'pä-li-ˌgraf\ *n* : an instrument (as a lie detector) for recording variations of several bodily functions (as blood pressure) simultaneously — **po·lyg·ra·pher** \pə-'li-grə-fər, 'pä-li-ˌgra-fər\ *n*

poly·he·dron \ˌpä-li-'hē-drən\ *n* : a solid formed by plane faces that are polygons — **poly·he·dral** \-drəl\ *adj*

poly·math \'pä-li-ˌmath\ *n* : a person of encyclopedic learning

poly·mer \'pä-lə-mər\ *n* : a chemical compound formed by union of small molecules and usu. consisting of repeating structural units — **poly·mer·ic** \ˌpä-lə-'mer-ik\ *adj*

po·lym·er·i·za·tion \pə-ˌli-mə-rə-'zā-shən\ *n* : a chemical reaction in which two or more small molecules combine to form polymers — **po·lym·er·ize** \pə-'li-mə-ˌrīz\ *vb*

Poly·ne·sian \ˌpä-lə-'nē-zhən\ *n* **1** : a member of any of the indigenous peoples of Polynesia **2** : a group of Austronesian languages spoken in Polynesia — **Polynesian** *adj*

poly·no·mi·al \ˌpä-lə-'nō-mē-əl\ *n* : an algebraic expression having one or more terms each of which consists of a constant multiplied by one or more variables raised to a nonnegative integral power — **polynomial** *adj*

pol·yp \'pä-ləp\ *n* **1** : an invertebrate animal (as a coral) that is a coelenterate having a hollow cylindrical body closed at one end **2** : a growth projecting from a mucous membrane (as of the colon or vocal cords)

po·lyph·o·ny \pə-'li-fə-nē\ *n* : music consisting of two or more melodically independent but harmonizing voice parts — **poly·phon·ic** \ˌpä-li-'fä-nik\ *adj*

poly·pro·pyl·ene \ˌpä-lē-'prō-pə-ˌlēn\ *n* : any of various polymer plastics or fibers

poly·sty·rene \ˌpä-li-'stī-ˌrēn\ *n* : a rigid transparent nonconducting thermoplastic used esp. in molded products and foams

poly·syl·lab·ic \-sə-'la-bik\ *adj* **1** : having more than three syllables **2** : characterized by polysyllabic words

poly·syl·la·ble \'pä-li-ˌsi-lə-bəl\ *n* : a polysyllabic word

poly·tech·nic \ˌpä-li-'tek-nik\ *adj* : of, relating to, or instructing in many technical arts or applied sciences

poly·the·ism \'pä-li-thē-ˌi-zəm\ *n* : belief in or worship of many gods — **poly·the·ist** \-ˌthē-ist\ *adj or n* — **poly·the·is·tic** \ˌpä-li-thē-'is-tik\ *adj*

poly·un·sat·u·rat·ed \ˌpä-lē-ˌən-'sa-chə-ˌrā-təd\ *adj* : having many double or triple bonds in a molecule — used esp. of an oil or fatty acid

poly·ure·thane \ˌpä-lē-ˈyu̇r-ə-ˌthān\ n : any of various polymers used esp. in foams and in resins (as for coatings)

poly·vi·nyl \ˌpä-li-ˈvī-nᵊl\ adj : of, relating to, or being a polymerized vinyl compound, resin, or plastic — often used in combination

pome·gran·ate \ˈpä-mə-ˌgra-nət\ n [ME poumgrenet, fr. AF pome garnette, lit., seedy fruit] : a many-seeded reddish fruit that has an edible crimson pulp and is borne by a tropical Asian tree; also : the tree

¹pom·mel \ˈpə-məl, ˈpä-\ n 1 : the knob on the hilt of a sword 2 : the knoblike bulge at the front and top of a saddlebow

²pom·mel \ˈpə-məl\ vb -meled or -melled; -mel·ing or -mel·ling : PUMMEL

pomp \ˈpämp\ n 1 : brilliant display : SPLENDOR 2 : OSTENTATION

pom·pa·dour \ˈpäm-pə-ˌdȯr\ n : a style of dressing the hair high over the forehead

pom·pa·no \ˈpäm-pə-ˌnō, ˈpəm-\ n, pl -no or -nos : a narrow silvery fish of coastal waters of the western Atlantic

pom–pom \ˈpäm-ˌpäm\ n 1 : an ornamental ball or tuft used on a cap or costume 2 : a fluffy ball flourished by cheerleaders

pom·pon \ˈpäm-ˌpän\ n 1 : POM-POM 2 : a chrysanthemum or dahlia with small rounded flower heads

pomp·ous \ˈpäm-pəs\ adj 1 : suggestive of pomp; esp : OSTENTATIOUS 2 : pretentiously dignified 3 : excessively elevated or ornate ♦ Synonyms ARROGANT, MAGISTERIAL, SELF-IMPORTANT — **pom·pos·i·ty** \päm-ˈpä-sə-tē\ n — **pomp·ous·ly** adv

pon·cho \ˈpän-chō\ n, pl ponchos [AmerSp, fr. Mapuche (American Indian language of Chile)] 1 : a blanket with a slit in the middle for the head so that it can be worn as a garment 2 : a waterproof garment resembling a poncho

pond \ˈpänd\ n : a small body of water

pon·der \ˈpän-dər\ vb pon·dered; pon·der·ing 1 : to weigh in the mind 2 : to consider carefully

pon·der·o·sa pine \ˈpän-də-ˌrō-sə-, -zə-\ n : a tall pine of western No. America with long needles; also : its strong reddish wood

pon·der·ous \ˈpän-də-rəs\ adj 1 : of very great weight 2 : UNWIELDY, CLUMSY ⟨a ∼ weapon⟩ 3 : oppressively dull ⟨a ∼ speech⟩ ♦ Synonyms CUMBROUS, CUMBERSOME, WEIGHTY

pone \ˈpōn\ n, Southern & Midland : an oval-shaped cornmeal cake; also : corn bread in the form of pones

pon·iard \ˈpän-yərd\ n : DAGGER

pon·tiff \ˈpän-təf\ n : POPE — **pon·tif·i·cal** \pän-ˈti-fi-kəl\ adj

¹pon·tif·i·cate \pän-ˈti-fi-kət, -fə-ˌkāt\ n : the state, office, or term of office of a pontiff

²pon·tif·i·cate \pän-ˈti-fə-ˌkāt\ vb -cat·ed; -cat·ing : to deliver dogmatic opinions

pon·toon \pän-ˈtün\ n 1 : a flat-bottomed boat 2 : a boat or float used in building a floating temporary bridge 3 : a float of a seaplane

po·ny \ˈpō-nē\ n, pl ponies : a small horse

po·ny·tail \-ˌtāl\ n : a style of arranging hair to resemble the tail of a pony

pooch \ˈpüch\ n : DOG

poo·dle \ˈpü-dᵊl\ n [G Pudel, short for Pudelhund, fr. pudeln to splash + Hund dog] : any of a breed of active intelligent dogs with a dense curly solid-colored coat

pooh–pooh \ˈpü-ˈpü\ also pooh \ˈpü\ vb 1 : to express contempt or impatience 2 : DERIDE, SCORN ⟨∼ed my idea⟩

¹pool \ˈpül\ n 1 : a small deep body of usu. fresh water 2 : a small body of standing liquid 3 : SWIMMING POOL

²pool vb : to form a pool

³pool n 1 : all the money bet on the result of a particular event 2 : any of several games of billiards played on a table having six pockets 3 : the amount contributed by the participants in a joint venture 4 : a combination between competing firms for mutual profit 5 : a readily available supply

⁴pool vb : to combine (as resources) in a common fund or effort

¹poop \ˈpüp\ n : an enclosed superstructure at the stern of a ship

²poop n, slang : INFORMATION

poop deck n : a partial deck above a ship's main afterdeck

poor \ˈpu̇r\ adj 1 : lacking material possessions ⟨∼ people⟩ 2 : less than adequate : MEAGER ⟨a ∼ crop⟩ 3 : arousing pity ⟨you ∼ thing⟩ 4 : inferior in quality or value 5 : UNPRODUCTIVE, BARREN ⟨∼ soil⟩ 6 : fairly unsatisfactory ⟨∼ prospects⟩; also : UNFAVORABLE ⟨∼ opinion⟩ — **poor·ly** adv

poor boy var of PO'BOY

poor·house \ˈpu̇r-ˌhau̇s\ n : a publicly supported home for needy or dependent persons

poor–mouth \-ˌmau̇th, -ˌmau̇th\ vb : to plead poverty as a defense or excuse

¹pop \ˈpäp\ vb popped; pop·ping 1 : to go, come, enter, or issue forth suddenly or quickly ⟨∼ into bed⟩ 2 : to put or thrust suddenly ⟨∼ questions⟩ 3 : to burst or cause to burst with a sharp sound; also : to make a sharp sound 4 : to protrude from the sockets 5 : SHOOT 6 : to hit a pop-up

²pop n 1 : a sharp explosive sound 2 : SHOT 3 : SODA POP

³pop n : FATHER

⁴pop adj 1 : POPULAR ⟨∼ music⟩ 2 : of or relating to pop music ⟨∼ singer⟩ 3 : of or relating to the popular culture disseminated through the mass media ⟨∼ psychology⟩ 4 : of, relating to, or imitating pop art ⟨∼ painter⟩

⁵pop n : pop music or culture; also : POP ART

⁶pop abbr population

pop art n, often cap P&A : art in which commonplace objects (as comic strips or soup cans) are used as subject matter — **pop artist** n

¹pop·corn \ˈpäp-ˌkȯrn\ n : an Indian corn whose kernels burst open into a white starchy mass when heated; also : the burst kernels

²popcorn adj : having widespread appeal but little artistic merit

pope \ˈpōp\ n, often cap : the head of the Roman Catholic Church

pop–eyed \ˈpäp-ˌīd\ adj : having eyes that bulge (as from disease)

pop fly n : POP-UP

pop·gun \ˈpäp-ˌgən\ n : a toy gun for shooting pellets with compressed air

pop·in·jay \ˈpä-pən-ˌjā\ n [ME papejay parrot, fr. MF papegai, papejai, fr. Ar babghā'] : a strutting supercilious person

pop·lar \ˈpä-plər\ n 1 : any of a genus of slender quick-growing trees (as a cottonwood) related to the willows 2 : the wood of a poplar

pop·lin \ˈpä-plən\ n : a strong plain-woven fabric with crosswise ribs

pop·over \ˈpäp-ˌō-vər\ n : a hollow muffin made from a thin batter rich in egg

pop·per \ˈpä-pər\ n : a utensil for popping corn

pop·py \ˈpä-pē\ n, pl poppies : any of a genus of herbs with showy flowers including one that yields opium

pop·py·cock \-ˌkäk\ n : empty talk or writing : NONSENSE

pop·u·lace \ˈpä-pyə-ləs\ n 1 : the common people 2 : POPULATION

pop·u·lar \ˈpä-pyə-lər\ adj 1 : of or relating to the general public ⟨∼ government⟩ 2 : suited to the tastes of the general public ⟨∼ style⟩ 3 : INEXPENSIVE ⟨∼ rates⟩ 4 : frequently encountered or widely accepted ⟨∼ notion⟩ 5 : commonly liked or approved ⟨a ∼ teacher⟩ — **pop·u·lar·i·ty** \ˌpä-pyə-ˈla-rə-tē\ n — **pop·u·lar·ize** \ˈpä-pyə-lə-ˌrīz\ vb — **pop·u·lar·ly** adv

pop·u·late \ˈpä-pyə-ˌlāt\ vb -lat·ed; -lat·ing 1 : to have a place in : INHABIT 2 : PEOPLE

pop·u·la·tion \ˌpä-pyə-ˈlā-shən\ n 1 : the people or number of people in an area 2 : the organisms inhabiting a particular locality 3 : a group of individuals or items from which samples are taken for statistical measurement

population explosion n : a pyramiding of numbers of a biological population; esp : the recent great increase in human numbers resulting from increased survival and exponential population growth

pop·u·list \ˈpä-pyə-list\ n : a believer in or advocate of the rights, wisdom, or virtues of the common people — **pop·u·lism** \-ˌli-zəm\ n

pop·u·lous \ˈpä-pyə-ləs\ adj 1 : densely populated; also : having a large population 2 : CROWDED — **pop·u·lous·ness** n

DICTIONARY

¹**pop–up** \'päp-ˌəp\ n : a short high fly in baseball

²**pop–up** adj : of, relating to, or having a component or device that pops up

por·ce·lain \'pȯr-sə-lən\ n : a fine-grained translucent ceramic ware

porch \'pȯrch\ n : a covered entrance usu. with a separate roof

por·cine \'pȯr-ˌsīn\ adj : of, relating to, or suggesting swine

por·ci·ni \pȯr-'chē-nē\ n, pl porcini [It] : a large edible brownish mushroom

por·ci·no \pȯr-'chē-nō\ n, pl -ni : PORCINI

por·cu·pine \'pȯr-kyə-ˌpīn\ n [ME porke despyne, fr. MF porc espin, fr. It porcospino, fr. L porcus pig + spina spine, prickle] : any of various mammals having stiff sharp spines mingled with their hair

¹**pore** \'pȯr\ vb pored; por·ing 1 : to read studiously or attentively ⟨∼ over a book⟩ 2 : PONDER, REFLECT

²**pore** n : a tiny hole or space (as in the skin or soil) — **pored** \'pȯrd\ adj

pork \'pȯrk\ n : the flesh of swine dressed for use as food

pork barrel n : government projects or appropriations yielding rich patronage benefits

pork·er \'pȯr-kər\ n : HOG; esp : a young pig suitable for use as fresh pork

por·nog·ra·phy \pȯr-'nä-grə-fē\ n : the depiction of erotic behavior intended to cause sexual excitement — **por·no·graph·ic** \ˌpȯr-nə-'gra-fik\ adj

po·rous \'pȯr-əs\ adj 1 : full of pores 2 : permeable to fluids : ABSORPTIVE — **po·ros·i·ty** \pə-'rä-sə-tē\ n

por·phy·ry \'pȯr-fə-rē\ n, pl -ries : a rock consisting of feldspar crystals embedded in a compact fine-grained base material — **por·phy·rit·ic** \ˌpȯr-fə-'ri-tik\ adj

por·poise \'pȯr-pəs\ n [ME porpoys, fr. AF porpeis, fr. ML porcopiscis, fr. L porcus pig + piscis fish] : any of a family of small gregarious blunt-snouted whales with spadelike teeth; also : DOLPHIN 1

porpoise

por·ridge \'pȯr-ij\ n : a soft food made by boiling meal of grains or legumes in milk or water

por·rin·ger \'pȯr-ən-jər\ n : a low one-handled metal bowl or cup

¹**port** \'pȯrt\ n 1 : HARBOR 2 : a city with a harbor 3 : AIRPORT

²**port** n 1 : an inlet or outlet (as in an engine) for a fluid 2 : PORTHOLE 3 : JACK 7

³**port** vb : to turn or put a helm to the left

⁴**port** n : the left side of a ship or airplane looking forward — **port** adj

⁵**port** n : a sweet fortified wine

portabella or **portabello** var of PORTOBELLO

por·ta·bil·i·ty \ˌpȯr-tə-'bil-ə-tē\ n, pl -ties 1 : the quality or state of being portable 2 : the ability to transfer benefits from one pension fund to another when a worker changes jobs

por·ta·ble \'pȯr-tə-bəl\ adj : capable of being carried — **portable** n

¹**por·tage** \'pȯr-tij, pȯr-'täzh\ n [ME, fr. AF, fr. porter to carry] : the carrying of boats and goods overland between navigable bodies of water; also : a route for such carrying

²**portage** vb por·taged; por·tag·ing : to carry gear over a portage

por·tal \'pȯr-t³l\ n : DOOR, ENTRANCE; esp : a grand or imposing one

portal–to–portal adj : of or relating to the time spent by a worker in traveling from the entrance to an employer's property to the worker's actual job site (as in a mine)

port·cul·lis \pȯrt-'kə-ləs\ n : a grating at the gateway of a castle or fortress that can be let down to stop entrance

porte co·chere \ˌpȯrt-kō-'sher\ n [F porte cochère, lit., coach door] : a roofed structure extending from the entrance of a building over an adjacent driveway and sheltering those getting in or out of vehicles

por·tend \pȯr-'tend\ vb 1 : to give a sign or warning of beforehand 2 : INDICATE, SIGNIFY ♦ Synonyms AUGUR, PROGNOSTICATE, FORETELL, PREDICT, FORECAST, PROPHESY

por·tent \'pȯr-ˌtent\ n 1 : something that foreshadows a coming event : OMEN 2 : MARVEL, PRODIGY

por·ten·tous \pȯr-'ten-təs\ adj 1 : of, relating to, or constituting a portent 2 : PRODIGIOUS 3 : self-consciously solemn : POMPOUS

¹**por·ter** \'pȯr-tər\ n, chiefly Brit : DOORKEEPER

²**porter** n 1 : a person who carries burdens; esp : one employed (as at a terminal) to carry baggage 2 : an attendant in a railroad car 3 : a dark heavy ale

por·ter·house \'pȯr-tər-ˌhaús\ n : a choice beefsteak with a large tenderloin

port·fo·lio \pȯrt-'fō-lē-ˌō\ n, pl -li·os 1 : a portable case for papers or drawings 2 : the office and functions of a minister of state 3 : the securities held by an investor

port·hole \'pȯrt-ˌhōl\ n : an opening (as a window) in the side of a ship or aircraft

por·ti·co \'pȯr-ti-ˌkō\ n, pl -coes or -cos [It] : a row of columns supporting a roof around or at the entrance of a building

¹**por·tion** \'pȯr-shən\ n 1 : one's part or share ⟨a ∼ of food⟩ 2 : DOWRY 3 : an individual's lot 4 : a part of a whole ⟨a ∼ of the sky⟩

²**portion** vb 1 : to divide into portions 2 : to allot to as a portion

port·land cement \'pȯrt-lənd-\ n : a cement made by calcining and grinding a mixture of clay and limestone

port·ly \'pȯrt-lē\ adj port·li·er; -est : somewhat stout

port·man·teau \pȯrt-'man-ˌtō\ n, pl -teaus or -teaux \-ˌtōz\ [MF portemanteau, fr. porter to carry + manteau mantle, fr. L mantellum] : a large traveling bag

por·to·bel·lo \pȯr-tə-'be-lō\ also **por·ta·bel·la** \-lə\ or **por·ta·bel·lo** \-lō\ n, pl -los also -las : a large dark mature mushroom noted for its meaty texture

port of call : an intermediate port where ships customarily stop for supplies, repairs, or transshipment of cargo

port of entry 1 : a place where foreign goods may be cleared through a customhouse 2 : a place where an alien may enter a country

por·trait \'pȯr-trət, -ˌtrāt\ n : a picture (as a painting or photograph) of a person usu. showing the face — **por·trait·ist** \-trə-tist\ n

por·trai·ture \'pȯr-trə-ˌchúr\ n : the practice or art of making portraits

por·tray \pȯr-'trā\ vb 1 : to make a picture of : DEPICT 2 : to describe in words 3 : to play the role of — **por·tray·al** n

Por·tu·guese \'pȯr-chə-ˌgēz, -ˌgēs; ˌpȯr-chə-'gēz, -'gēs\ n, pl Portuguese 1 : a native or inhabitant of Portugal 2 : the language of Portugal and Brazil — **Portuguese** adj

Portuguese man–of–war n : any of several large colonial marine invertebrate animals related to the jellyfishes and having a large sac by which the colony floats at the surface

por·tu·la·ca \ˌpȯr-chə-'la-kə\ n : any of a genus of succulent herbs cultivated for their showy flowers

pos abbr 1 position 2 positive

¹**pose** \'pōz\ vb posed; pos·ing 1 : to assume or cause to assume a posture usu. for artistic purposes 2 : to set forth : PROPOSE ⟨∼ a question⟩ 3 : to affect an attitude or character

²**pose** n 1 : a sustained posture; esp : one assumed by a model 2 : an attitude assumed for effect : PRETENSE

¹**pos·er** \'pō-zər\ n : a puzzling question

²**poser** n : a person who poses

po·seur \pō-'zər\ n [F, lit., poser] : an affected or insincere person

posh \'päsh\ adj : FASHIONABLE ⟨a ∼ restaurant⟩

pos·it \'pä-zət\ vb : to assume the existence of : POSTULATE

po·si·tion \pə-'zi-shən\ n 1 : an arranging in order 2 : the stand taken on a question 3 : the point or area occupied by something : SITUATION 4 : a certain arrangement of bodily parts ⟨exercise in a sitting ∼⟩ 5 : RANK,

STATUS **6** : EMPLOYMENT, JOB — **position** *vb* — **po·si·tion·al** \-'shə-nəl\ *adj*

¹pos·i·tive \'pä-zə-tiv\ *adj* **1** : expressed definitely ⟨her answer was a ∼ *no*⟩ **2** : CONFIDENT, CERTAIN ⟨∼ it was my book⟩ **3** : of, relating to, or constituting the degree of grammatical comparison that denotes no increase in quality, quantity, or relation **4** : not fictitious : REAL **5** : active and effective in function ⟨∼ leadership⟩ **6** : having the light and shade as existing in the original subject ⟨a ∼ photograph⟩ **7** : numerically greater than zero ⟨a ∼ number⟩ **8** : being, relating to, or charged with electricity of which the proton is the elementary unit **9** : AFFIRMATIVE ⟨a ∼ response⟩ **10** : FAVORABLE; *also* : marked by optimism — **pos·i·tive·ly** *adv* — **pos·i·tive·ness** *n*

²positive *n* **1** : the positive degree or a positive form in a language **2** : a positive photograph

pos·i·tron \'pä-zə-ˌträn\ *n* : a positively charged particle having the same mass and magnitude of charge as the electron

po·so·le *or* **po·zo·le** \pō-'sō-lā\ *n* : a thick Mexican soup made with pork, hominy, garlic, and chili

poss *abbr* possessive

pos·se \'pä-sē\ *n* [ML *posse comitatus*, lit., power or authority of the county] **1** : a body of persons organized to assist a sheriff in an emergency **2** : a body of attendants or followers

pos·sess \pə-'zes\ *vb* **1** : to have as property : OWN **2** : to have as an attribute, knowledge, or skill **3** : to enter into and control firmly ⟨∼*ed* by a devil⟩ — **pos·ses·sor** \-'ze-sər\ *n*

pos·ses·sion \-'ze-shən\ *n* **1** : control or occupancy of property **2** : OWNERSHIP **3** : something owned : PROPERTY **4** : domination by something (as an evil spirit, a passion, or an idea) **5** : SELF-CONTROL

pos·ses·sive \pə-'ze-siv\ *adj* **1** : of, relating to, or constituting a grammatical case denoting ownership **2** : showing the desire to possess ⟨a ∼ nature⟩ — **possessive** *n* — **pos·ses·sive·ness** *n*

pos·si·ble \'pä-sə-bəl\ *adj* **1** : being within the limits of ability, capacity, or realization **2** : being something that may or may not occur ⟨∼ dangers⟩ **3** : able or fitted to become ⟨a ∼ site for a bridge⟩ — **pos·si·bil·i·ty** \ˌpä-sə-'bi-lə-tē\ *n* — **pos·si·bly** \'pä-sə-blē\ *adv*

pos·sum \'pä-səm\ *n* : OPOSSUM

¹post \'pōst\ *n* **1** : an upright piece of timber or metal serving esp. as a support : PILLAR **2** : a pole or stake set up as a mark or indicator

²post *vb* **1** : to affix to a usual place (as a wall) for public notices **2** : to publish or announce by or as if by a public notice ⟨∼ grades⟩ **3** : to forbid (property) to trespassers by putting up a notice **4** : SCORE 4 **5** : to publish in an online forum

³post *n* **1** *obs* : COURIER **2** *chiefly Brit* : ¹MAIL; *also* : POST OFFICE **3** : something that is published online

⁴post *vb* **1** : to ride or travel with haste : HURRY **2** : MAIL ⟨∼ a letter⟩ **3** : to enter in a ledger **4** : INFORM ⟨kept him ∼*ed* on new developments⟩

⁵post *n* **1** : the place at which a soldier is stationed; *esp* : a sentry's beat or station **2** : a station or task to which a person is assigned **3** : the place at which a body of troops is stationed : CAMP **4** : OFFICE, POSITION **5** : a trading settlement or station

⁶post *vb* **1** : to station in a given place **2** : to put up (as bond)

post·age \'pōs-tij\ *n* : the fee for postal service; *also* : stamps representing this fee

post·al \'pōs-t³l\ *adj* : of or relating to the mails or the post office

postal card *n* : POSTCARD

postal service *n* : a government agency or department handling the transmission of mail

¹post·card \'pōst-ˌkärd\ *n* : a card on which a message may be written for mailing without an envelope

²postcard *adj* : PICTURESQUE

post chaise *n* : a 4-wheeled closed carriage for two to four persons

post·con·sum·er \ˌpōst-kən-'sü-mər\ *adj* **1** : discarded by a consumer **2** : having been used and recycled for reuse in another product

post·date \ˌpōst-'dāt\ *vb* : to date with a date later than that of execution ⟨∼ a check⟩

post·doc·tor·al \-'däk-tə-rəl\ *also* **post·doc·tor·ate** \-tə-rət\ *adj* : of, relating to, or engaged in advanced academic or professional work beyond a doctor's degree

post·er \'pō-stər\ *n* : a bill or placard for posting often in a public place

¹pos·te·ri·or \pō-'stir-ē-ər, pä-\ *adj* **1** : later in time **2** : situated behind

²pos·te·ri·or \pä-'stir-ē-ər, pō-\ *n* : the hinder bodily parts; *esp* : BUTTOCKS

pos·ter·i·ty \pä-'ster-ə-tē\ *n* **1** : the descendants from one ancestor **2** : all future generations

pos·tern \'pōs-tərn, 'päs-\ *n* **1** : a back door or gate **2** : a private or side entrance

post exchange *n* : a store at a military post that sells to military personnel and authorized civilians

post·grad \'pōst-ˌgrad\ *adj* : POSTGRADUATE

post·grad·u·ate \(ˌ)pōst-'gra-jə-wət\ *adj* : of or relating to studies beyond the bachelor's degree — **postgraduate** *n*

post·haste \'pōst-'hāst\ *adv* : with all possible speed

post·hole \-ˌhōl\ *n* : a hole for a post and esp. a fence post

post·hu·mous \'päs-chə-məs\ *adj* [L *posthumus*, alter. of *postumus* last-born, posthumous, fr. superl. of *posterus* coming after] **1** : born after the death of the father **2** : published after the death of the author — **post·hu·mous·ly** *adv*

post·hyp·not·ic \ˌpōst-hip-'nä-tik\ *adj* : of, relating to, or characteristic of the period following a hypnotic trance

pos·til·ion *or* **pos·til·lion** \pō-'stil-yən\ *n* : a rider on the left-hand horse of a pair drawing a coach

Post·im·pres·sion·ism \ˌpōst-im-'pre-shə-ˌni-zəm\ *n* : a late 19th century French theory or practice of art that stresses variously volume, picture structure, or expressionism

post·lude \'pōst-ˌlüd\ *n* : an organ solo played at the end of a church service

post·man \-mən, -ˌman\ *n* : MAILMAN

post·mark \-ˌmärk\ *n* : an official postal marking on a piece of mail; *esp* : the mark canceling the postage stamp — **postmark** *vb*

post·mas·ter \-ˌmas-tər\ *n* : a person who has charge of a post office

postmaster general *n, pl* **postmasters general** : an official in charge of a national postal service

post·men·o·paus·al \ˌpōst-ˌme-nə-'pȯ-zəl\ *adj* **1** : having undergone menopause **2** : occurring or administered after menopause

post me·ri·di·em \ˌpōst-mə-'ri-dē-əm\ *adj* [L] : being after noon

post·mis·tress \'pōst-ˌmis-trəs\ *n* : a woman in charge of a post office

post·mod·ern \ˌpōst-'mä-dərn\ *adj* : of, relating to, or being any of various movements in reaction to modernism

¹post·mor·tem \ˌpōst-'mȯr-təm\ *adj* [L *post mortem* after death] **1** : done, occurring, or collected after death **2** : following the event

²postmortem *n* **1** : AUTOPSY **2** : an analysis or discussion of an event after it is over

post·na·sal drip \'pōst-ˌnā-zəl-\ *n* : flow of mucous secretion from the posterior part of the nasal cavity onto the wall of the pharynx

post·na·tal \(ˌ)pōst-'nā-t³l\ *adj* : occurring or being after birth; *esp* : of or relating to a newborn infant

post office *n* **1** : POSTAL SERVICE **2** : a local branch of a post office department

post·op·er·a·tive \(ˌ)pōst-'ä-prə-tiv, -pə-ˌrā-\ *adj* : following or having undergone a surgical operation ⟨∼ care⟩

post·paid \'pōst-'pād\ *adj* : having the postage paid by the sender and not chargeable to the receiver

post·par·tum \(ˌ)pōst-'pär-təm\ *adj* [NL *post partum* after birth] : following parturition — **postpartum** *adv*

post·pone \post-'pōn\ *vb* **post·poned; post·pon·ing** : to put off to a later time — **post·pone·ment** *n*

post road *n* : a road over which mail is carried

post·script \'pōst-ˌskript\ *n* : a note added esp. to a completed letter

post time *n* : the designated time for the start of a horse race

post–traumatic *adj* : occurring after or as a result of trauma ⟨∼ stress⟩

pos·tu·lant \'päs-chə-lənt\ *n* : a probationary candidate for membership in a religious order

¹**pos·tu·late** \'päs-chə-ˌlāt\ *vb* **-lat·ed; -lat·ing** : to assume as true

²**pos·tu·late** \'päs-chə-lət, -ˌlāt\ *n* : a proposition taken for granted as true esp. as a basis for a chain of reasoning

¹**pos·ture** \'päs-chər\ *n* **1** : the position or bearing of the body or one of its parts **2** : STATE, CONDITION **3** : ATTITUDE ⟨a ∼ of arrogance⟩

²**posture** *vb* **pos·tured; pos·tur·ing** : to strike a pose esp. for effect

post–war \'pōst-'wȯr\ *adj* : occurring or existing after a war

po·sy \'pō-zē\ *n, pl* **posies 1** : a brief sentiment : MOTTO **2** : a bunch of flowers; *also* : FLOWER

¹**pot** \'pät\ *n* **1** : a rounded container used chiefly for domestic purposes **2** : the total of the bets at stake at one time **3** : RUIN ⟨go to ∼⟩ — **pot·ful** *n*

²**pot** *vb* **pot·ted; pot·ting 1** : to preserve or place in a pot **2** : SHOOT

³**pot** *n* : MARIJUANA

po·ta·ble \'pō-tə-bəl\ *adj* : suitable for drinking — **po·ta·bil·i·ty** \ˌpō-tə-'bi-lə-tē\ *n*

po·tage \pò-'täzh\ *n* : a thick soup

pot·ash \'pät-ˌash\ *n* [sing. of *pot ashes*] : potassium or any of its various compounds esp. as used in agriculture

po·tas·si·um \pə-'ta-sē-əm\ *n* : a silver-white soft metallic chemical element that occurs abundantly in nature

potassium bromide *n* : a crystalline salt used as a sedative and in photography

potassium carbonate *n* : a white salt used in making glass and soap

potassium nitrate *n* : a soluble salt used in making gunpowder, as a fertilizer, and in medicine

po·ta·tion \pō-'tā-shən\ *n* : a usu. alcoholic drink; *also* : the act of drinking

po·ta·to \pə-'tā-tō\ *n, pl* **-toes** : the edible starchy tuber of a plant related to the tomato; *also* : this plant

potato beetle *n* : COLORADO POTATO BEETLE

potato bug *n* : COLORADO POTATO BEETLE

potbellied pig *n* : any of an Asian breed of small pigs having a straight tail, potbelly, and black, white, or black and white coat

pot·bel·ly \'pät-ˌbe-lē\ *n* : a protruding abdomen — **pot·bel·lied** \-lēd\ *adj*

pot·boil·er \-ˌbòi-lər\ *n* : a usu. inferior work of art or literature produced chiefly for profit

po·tent \'pō-tᵊnt\ *adj* **1** : having authority or influence : POWERFUL **2** : chemically or medicinally effective **3** : able to copulate — used esp. of the male ♦ *Synonyms* FORCEFUL, FORCIBLE, MIGHTY, PUISSANT — **po·ten·cy** \-tᵊn-sē\ *n*

po·ten·tate \'pō-tᵊn-ˌtāt\ *n* : one who wields controlling power : RULER

¹**po·ten·tial** \pə-'ten-chəl\ *adj* : existing in possibility : capable of becoming actual ⟨a ∼ champion⟩ ♦ *Synonyms* DORMANT, LATENT, QUIESCENT — **po·ten·ti·al·i·ty** \pə-ˌten-chē-'a-lə-tē\ *n* — **po·ten·tial·ly** \-'ten-chə-lē\ *adv*

²**potential** *n* **1** : something that can develop or become actual ⟨a ∼ for violence⟩ **2** : the work required to move a unit positive charge from infinity to a point in question; *also* : POTENTIAL DIFFERENCE

potential difference *n* : the difference in potential between two points that represents the work involved in the transfer of a unit quantity of electricity from one point to the other

potential energy *n* : the energy an object has because of its position or nature or the arrangement of its parts

po·ten·ti·ate \pə-'ten-chē-ˌāt\ *vb* **-at·ed; -at·ing** : to make potent; *esp* : to augment the activity of (as a drug) synergistically — **po·ten·ti·a·tion** \-ˌten-chē-'ā-shən\ *n*

pot·head \'pät-ˌhed\ *n* : a person who frequently smokes marijuana

poth·er \'pä-thər\ *n* : a noisy disturbance; *also* : FUSS

pot·herb \'pät-ˌərb, -ˌhərb\ *n* : an herb whose leaves or stems are boiled for greens or used to season food

pot·hole \'pät-ˌhōl\ *n* : a large pit or hole (as in a road surface)

pot·hook \-ˌhùk\ *n* : an S-shaped hook for hanging pots and kettles over an open fire

po·tion \'pō-shən\ *n* : a mixture of liquids (as liquor or medicine)

pot·luck \'pät-ˈlək\ *n* : the regular meal available to a guest for whom no special preparations have been made

pot·pie \-ˈpī\ *n* : pastry-covered meat and vegetables cooked in a deep dish

pot·pour·ri \ˌpō-pú-'rē\ *n* [F *pot pourri*, lit., rotten pot] **1** : a mixture of flowers, herbs, and spices used for scent **2** : a miscellaneous collection

pot·sherd \'pät-ˌshərd\ *n* : a pottery fragment

pot·shot \-ˌshät\ *n* **1** : a shot taken from ambush or at a random or easy target **2** : a critical remark made in a random or sporadic manner

pot sticker *n* : a crescent-shaped dumpling that is steamed and fried

pot·tage \'pä-tij\ *n* : a thick soup of vegetables and often meat

¹**pot·ter** \'pä-tər\ *n* : one that makes pottery

²**potter** *vb* : PUTTER

pot·tery \'pä-tə-rē\ *n, pl* **-ter·ies 1** : a place where earthen pots and dishes are made **2** : the art of the potter **3** : dishes, pots, and vases made from clay

pot·ty–mouthed \'pä-tē-ˌmaùthd, -ˌmaùtht\ *adj* : given to the use of vulgar language

¹**pouch** \'paùch\ *n* [ME *pouche*, fr. AF, of Gmc origin; akin to OE *pocca* bag] **1** : a small bag (as for tobacco) carried on the person **2** : a bag for storing or transporting goods ⟨mail ∼⟩ ⟨diplomatic ∼⟩ **3** : an anatomical sac; *esp* : one for carrying the young on the abdomen of a female marsupial (as a kangaroo)

²**pouch** *vb* : to put or form into or as if into a pouch

poult \'pōlt\ *n* : a young fowl; *esp* : a young turkey

poul·ter·er \'pōl-tər-ər\ *n* : one that deals in poultry

poul·tice \'pōl-təs\ *n* : a soft usu. heated and medicated mass spread on cloth and applied to a sore or injury — **poultice** *vb*

poul·try \'pōl-trē\ *n* : domesticated birds kept for eggs or meat — **poul·try·man** \-mən\ *n*

pounce \'paùns\ *vb* **pounced; pounc·ing** : to spring or swoop upon and seize something

¹**pound** \'paùnd\ *n, pl* **pounds** *also* **pound 1** : a unit of avoirdupois, troy, and apothecaries' weight — see WEIGHT table **2** — see MONEY table **3** : the former basic monetary unit of Ireland

²**pound** *n* : a public enclosure where stray animals are kept

³**pound** *vb* **1** : to crush to a powder or pulp by beating **2** : to strike or beat heavily or repeatedly **3** : DRILL 1 **4** : to move or move along heavily

pound·age \'paùn-dij\ *n* : POUNDS; *also* : weight in pounds

pound cake *n* : a rich cake made with a large proportion of eggs and shortening

pound–fool·ish \'paùnd-'fü-lish\ *adj* : imprudent in dealing with large sums or large matters

pour \'pòr\ *vb* **1** : to flow or cause to flow in a stream or flood **2** : to rain hard **3** : to supply freely and copiously

pour·boire \pùr-'bwär\ *n* [F, fr. *pour boire* for drinking] : TIP, GRATUITY

pout \'paùt\ *vb* : to show displeasure by thrusting out the lips; *also* : to look sullen — **pout** *n*

pov·er·ty \'pä-vər-tē\ *n* [ME *poverte*, fr. AF *poverté*, fr. L *paupertat-, paupertas*, fr. *pauper* poor] **1** : lack of money or material possessions : WANT **2** : poor quality (as of soil)

poverty line *n* : a level of personal or family income below which one is classified as poor according to government standards

pov·er·ty–strick·en \'pä-vər-tē-ˌstri-kən\ *adj* : very poor : DESTITUTE

POW \ˌpē-(ˌ)ō-'də-bəl-(ˌ)yü\ *n* : PRISONER OF WAR

¹**pow·der** \'paù-dər\ *vb* **1** : to sprinkle or cover with or as if with powder **2** : to reduce to powder

²**powder** *n* [ME *poudre*, fr. AF *pudre, podre*, fr. L *pulver-, pulvis* dust] **1** : dry material made up of fine particles; *also* : a usu. medicinal or cosmetic preparation in this form **2** : a solid explosive (as gunpowder) — **pow·dery** *adj*

powder room *n* : a rest room for women

¹**pow·er** \'paù(-ə)r\ *n* **1** : the ability to act or produce an effect **2** : a position of ascendancy over others : AUTHORITY **3** : one that has control or authority; *esp* : a sovereign state **4** : physical might; *also* : mental or moral vigor **5** : the number of times as indicated by an exponent a num-

ber is to be multiplied by itself ⟨5 to the third ∼ is 125⟩; *also* : the product itself ⟨8 is a ∼ of 2⟩ **6** : force or energy used to do work; *also* : the time rate at which work is done or energy transferred **7** : MAGNIFICATION 2 — **pow·er·ful** \-fəl\ *adj* — **pow·er·ful·ly** *adv* — **pow·er·less** *adj*

²**power** *vb* : to supply with power and esp. motive power

³**power** *adj* **1** : operated mechanically or electrically rather than manually **2** : of, relating to, or utilizing strength

pow·er·boat \-ˌbōt\ *n* : MOTORBOAT

pow·er·house \ˈpau̇(-ə)r-ˌhau̇s\ *n* **1** : POWER PLANT 1 **2** : one having great drive, energy, or ability

power plant *n* **1** : a building in which electric power is generated **2** : an engine and related parts supplying the motive power of a self-propelled vehicle

pow·wow \ˈpau̇-ˌwau̇\ *n* **1** : a No. American Indian ceremony (as for victory in war) **2** : a meeting for discussion : CONFERENCE

pox \ˈpäks\ *n, pl* **pox** *or* **pox·es** : any of various diseases (as smallpox or syphilis) marked by a rash on the skin

pozole *var of* POSOLE

pp *abbr* **1** pages **2** pianissimo

PP *abbr* **1** parcel post **2** past participle **3** postpaid **4** prepaid

ppd *abbr* **1** postpaid **2** prepaid

PPO \ˌpē-ˌpē-ˈō\ *n, pl* **PPOs** [*preferred provider organization*] : a health-care organization that gives economic incentives to enrolled individuals who use certain health-care providers

PPS *abbr* [L *post postscriptum*] an additional postscript

ppt *abbr* precipitate

PQ *abbr* Province of Quebec

pr *abbr* **1** pair **2** price

Pr *symbol* praseodymium

¹**PR** *or* **p.r.** \ˈpē-ˈär\ *n* : PUBLIC RELATIONS

²**PR** *abbr* **1** payroll **2** public relations **3** Puerto Rico

prac·ti·ca·ble \ˈprak-ti-kə-bəl\ *adj* : capable of being put into practice, done, or accomplished — **prac·ti·ca·bil·i·ty** \ˌprak-ti-kə-ˈbi-lə-tē\ *n*

prac·ti·cal \ˈprak-ti-kəl\ *adj* **1** : of, relating to, or shown in practice ⟨∼ questions⟩ **2** : VIRTUAL ⟨∼ control⟩ **3** : capable of being put to use ⟨a ∼ knowledge of French⟩ **4** : inclined to action as opposed to speculation ⟨a ∼ person⟩ **5** : qualified by practice ⟨a good ∼ mechanic⟩ — **prac·ti·cal·i·ty** \ˌprak-ti-ˈka-lə-tē\ *n* — **prac·ti·cal·ly** \-k(ə-)lē\ *adv*

practical joke *n* : a prank intended to trick or embarrass someone or cause physical discomfort

practical nurse *n* : a professional nurse without all of the qualifications of a registered nurse; *esp* : LICENSED PRACTICAL NURSE

¹**prac·tice** *also* **prac·tise** \ˈprak-təs\ *vb* **prac·ticed** *also* **prac·tised; prac·tic·ing** *also* **prac·tis·ing 1** : CARRY OUT, APPLY ⟨∼ what you preach⟩ **2** : to perform or work at repeatedly so as to become proficient ⟨∼ tennis strokes⟩ **3** : to do or perform customarily ⟨∼ politeness⟩ **4** : to be professionally engaged in ⟨∼ law⟩

²**practice** *also* **practise** *n* **1** : actual performance or application **2** : customary action : HABIT **3** : systematic exercise for proficiency **4** : the exercise of a profession; *also* : a professional business

prac·ti·tion·er \prak-ˈti-shə-nər\ *n* : one who practices a profession

prae·tor \ˈprē-tər\ *n* : an ancient Roman magistrate ranking below a consul — **prae·to·ri·an** \prē-ˈtȯr-ē-ən\ *adj*

prag·mat·ic \prag-ˈma-tik\ *also* **prag·mat·i·cal** \-ti-kəl\ *adj* **1** : of or relating to practical affairs **2** : concerned with the practical consequences of actions or beliefs — **pragmatic** *n* — **prag·mat·i·cal·ly** \-ti-k(ə-)lē\ *adv*

prag·ma·tism \ˈprag-mə-ˌti-zəm\ *n* : a practical approach to problems and affairs

prai·rie \ˈprer-ē\ *n* [F, fr. OF *prairie*, fr. VL *prataria*, fr. L *pratum* meadow] : a broad tract of level or rolling grassland

prairie dog *n* : an American burrowing black-tailed rodent related to the squirrels and living in colonies

prairie schooner *n* : a covered wagon used by pioneers in cross-country travel

praise \ˈprāz\ *vb* **praised; prais·ing 1** : to express approval of : COMMEND **2** : to glorify (a divinity or a saint) esp. in song — **praise** *n*

praise·wor·thy \-ˌwər-thē\ *adj* : LAUDABLE ⟨a ∼ effort⟩

pra·line \ˈprä-ˌlēn, ˈprā-\ *n* [F] : a confection of nuts and sugar

pram \ˈpram\ *n, chiefly Brit* : PERAMBULATOR

prance \ˈprans\ *vb* **pranced; pranc·ing 1** : to spring from the hind legs ⟨a *prancing* horse⟩ **2** : SWAGGER; *also* : CAPER — **prance** *n* — **pranc·er** *n*

prank \ˈpraŋk\ *n* : a playful or mildly mischievous act : TRICK

prank·ster \ˈpraŋk-stər\ *n* : a person who plays pranks

pra·seo·dym·i·um \ˌprā-zē-ō-ˈdi-mē-əm\ *n* : a yellowish white metallic chemical element

prate \ˈprāt\ *vb* **prat·ed; prat·ing** : to talk long and idly : chatter foolishly

prat·fall \ˈprat-ˌfȯl\ *n* **1** : a fall on the buttocks **2** : a humiliating blunder

¹**prat·tle** \ˈpra-tᵊl\ *vb* **prat·tled; prat·tling** : PRATE, BABBLE

²**prattle** *n* : trifling or childish talk

prawn \ˈprȯn\ *n* : any of various edible shrimplike crustaceans; *also* : SHRIMP 1

pray \ˈprā\ *vb* **1** : ENTREAT, IMPLORE **2** : to ask earnestly for something **3** : to address God or a god esp. with supplication

prayer \ˈprer\ *n* **1** : a supplication or expression addressed to God or a god; *also* : a set order of words used in praying **2** : an earnest request or wish **3** : the act or practice of praying to God or a god **4** : a religious service consisting chiefly of prayers — often used in pl. **5** : something prayed for **6** : a slight chance

prayer book *n* : a book containing prayers and often directions for worship

prayer·ful \ˈprer-fəl\ *adj* **1** : DEVOUT **2** : EARNEST — **prayer·ful·ly** *adv*

praying mantis *n* : MANTIS

PRC *abbr* People's Republic of China

preach \ˈprēch\ *vb* **1** : to deliver a sermon **2** : to set forth in a sermon **3** : to advocate earnestly — **preach·er** *n* — **preach·ment** *n*

pre·ad·o·les·cence \ˌprē-ˌa-də-ˈle-sᵊns\ *n* : the period of human development just preceding adolescence — **pre·ad·o·les·cent** \-sᵊnt\ *adj or n*

pre·am·ble \ˈprē-ˌam-bəl\ *n* [ME, fr. MF *preambule*, fr. ML *preambulum*, fr. LL, neut. of *praeambulus* walking in front of, fr. L *prae* in front of + *ambulare* to walk] : an introductory part ⟨the ∼ to a constitution⟩

pre·ar·range \ˌprē-ə-ˈrānj\ *vb* : to arrange beforehand — **pre·ar·range·ment** *n*

pre·as·sign \ˌprē-ə-ˈsīn\ *vb* : to assign beforehand

Pre·cam·bri·an \ˈprē-ˈkam-brē-ən, -ˈkäm-\ *adj* : of, relating to, or being the era that is earliest in geologic history and is characterized esp. by the appearance of single-celled organisms — **Precambrian** *n*

pre·can·cel \ˌ(ˌ)prē-ˈkan-səl\ *vb* : to cancel (a postage stamp) in advance of use — **precancel** *n* — **pre·can·cel·la·tion** \ˌprē-ˌkan-sə-ˈlā-shən\ *n*

pre·can·cer·ous \ˌ(ˌ)prē-ˈkan-sə-rəs\ *adj* : likely to become cancerous

pre·car·i·ous \pri-ˈker-ē-əs\ *adj* : dependent on uncertain conditions : dangerously insecure : UNSTABLE ⟨a ∼ foothold⟩ ⟨∼ prosperity⟩ ♦ **Synonyms** DELICATE, SENSITIVE, TICKLISH, TOUCHY, TRICKY — **pre·car·i·ous·ly** *adv* — **pre·car·i·ous·ness** *n*

pre·cau·tion \pri-ˈkȯ-shən\ *n* : a measure taken beforehand to prevent harm or secure good — **pre·cau·tion·ary** \-shə-ˌner-ē\ *adj*

pre·cede \pri-ˈsēd\ *vb* **pre·ced·ed; pre·ced·ing** : to be, go, or come ahead or in front of (as in rank or time)

pre·ce·dence \ˈpre-sə-dəns, pri-ˈsēd-ᵊns\ *n* **1** : the act or fact of preceding **2** : consideration based on order of importance : PRIORITY

¹**pre·ce·dent** \pri-ˈsē-dᵊnt, ˈpre-sə-dənt\ *adj* : prior in time, order, or significance

²**prec·e·dent** \ˈpre-sə-dənt\ *n* : something said or done that may serve to authorize or justify further words or acts of the same or a similar kind

pre·ced·ing \pri-ˈsē-diŋ\ *adj* : that precedes ♦ **Synonyms** ANTECEDENT, FOREGOING, PRIOR, FORMER, ANTERIOR

pre·cen·tor \pri-ˈsen-tər\ *n* : a leader of the singing of a choir or congregation

pre·cept \ˈprē-ˌsept\ *n* : a command or principle intended as a general rule of action or conduct

pre·cep·tor \pri-'sep-tər, 'prē-,sep-\ *n* : TUTOR
pre·ces·sion \prē-'se-shən\ *n* : a slow gyration of the rotation axis of a spinning body (as the earth) — **pre·cess** \prē-'ses\ *vb* — **pre·ces·sion·al** \-'se-shə-nəl\ *adj*
pre·cinct \'prē-,siŋkt\ *n* **1** : an administrative subdivision (as of a city) : DISTRICT ⟨police ∼⟩ ⟨electoral ∼⟩ **2** : an enclosure bounded by the limits of a building or place — often used in pl. **3** *pl* : ENVIRONS
pre·ci·os·i·ty \,pre-shē-'ä-sə-tē\ *n, pl* **-ties** : fastidious refinement
pre·cious \'pre-shəs\ *adj* **1** : of great value ⟨∼ jewels⟩ **2** : greatly cherished : DEAR ⟨∼ memories⟩ **3** : AFFECTED ⟨∼ language⟩
prec·i·pice \'pre-sə-pəs\ *n* : a steep cliff
pre·cip·i·tan·cy \pri-'si-pə-tən-sē\ *n* : undue hastiness or suddenness
¹**pre·cip·i·tate** \pri-'si-pə-,tāt\ *vb* **-tat·ed; -tat·ing** [L *praecipitare,* fr. *praecipit-, praeceps* headlong, fr. *prae* in front of + *caput* head] **1** : to throw violently **2** : to throw down **3** : to cause to happen quickly or abruptly ⟨∼ a quarrel⟩ **4** : to cause to separate from solution or suspension **5** : to fall as rain, snow, or hail ✦ *Synonyms* SPEED, ACCELERATE, QUICKEN, HASTEN, HURRY
²**pre·cip·i·tate** \pri-'si-pə-tət, -,tāt\ *n* : the solid matter that separates from a solution or suspension
³**pre·cip·i·tate** \pri-'si-pə-tət\ *adj* **1** : showing extreme or unwise haste : RASH **2** : falling with steep descent; *also* : PRECIPITOUS — **pre·cip·i·tate·ly** *adv* — **pre·cip·i·tate·ness** *n*
pre·cip·i·ta·tion \pri-,si-pə-'tā-shən\ *n* **1** : rash haste **2** : the process of precipitating or forming a precipitate **3** : water that falls to earth esp. as rain or snow; *also* : the quantity of this water
pre·cip·i·tous \pri-'si-pə-təs\ *adj* **1** : PRECIPITATE **2** : having the character of a precipice : very steep ⟨a ∼ slope⟩; *also* : containing precipices ⟨∼ trails⟩ — **pre·cip·i·tous·ly** *adv*
pré·cis \prā-'sē\ *n, pl* **pré·cis** \-'sēz\ [F] : a concise summary of essentials
pre·cise \pri-'sīs\ *adj* **1** : exactly defined or stated : DEFINITE **2** : highly accurate : EXACT **3** : conforming strictly to a standard : SCRUPULOUS — **pre·cise·ly** *adv* — **pre·cise·ness** *n*
pre·ci·sion \pri-'si-zhən\ *n* : the quality or state of being precise
pre·clude \pri-'klüd\ *vb* **pre·clud·ed; pre·clud·ing** : to make impossible : BAR, PREVENT
pre·co·cious \pri-'kō-shəs\ *adj* [L *praecoc-, praecox,* lit., ripening early, fr. *prae-* ahead + *coquere* to cook] : early in development and esp. in mental development — **pre·co·cious·ly** *adv* — **pre·coc·i·ty** \pri-'kä-sə-tē\ *n*
pre·con·ceive \,prē-kən-'sēv\ *vb* : to form an opinion of beforehand — **pre·con·cep·tion** \-'sep-shən\ *n*
pre·con·di·tion \-'di-shən\ *vb* : to put in proper or desired condition or frame of mind in advance
pre·cook \,prē-'kùk\ *vb* : to cook partially or entirely before final cooking or reheating
pre·cur·sor \pri-'kər-sər\ *n* : one that precedes and indicates the approach of another : FORERUNNER
pred *abbr* predicate
pre·da·ceous *or* **pre·da·cious** \pri-'dā-shəs\ *adj* : living by preying on others : PREDATORY
pre·date \'prē-'dāt\ *vb* : ANTEDATE
pre·da·tion \pri-'dā-shən\ *n* **1** : the act of preying or plundering **2** : a mode of life in which food is primarily obtained by killing and consuming animals
pred·a·tor \'pre-də-tər\ *n* : an animal that lives by predation
pred·a·to·ry \'pre-də-,tòr-ē\ *adj* **1** : of or relating to plunder ⟨∼ warfare⟩ **2** : disposed to exploit others **3** : preying upon other animals
pre·dawn \(')prē-'dòn\ *adj* : of or relating to the time just before dawn
pre·de·cease \,prē-di-'sēs\ *vb* **-ceased; -ceas·ing** : to die before another person
pre·de·ces·sor \'pre-də-,se-sər, 'prē-\ *n* : a previous holder of a position to which another has succeeded
pre·des·ig·nate \(,)prē-'de-zig-,nāt\ *vb* : to designate beforehand
pre·des·ti·na·tion \,prē-,des-tə-'nā-shən\ *n* : the act of foreordaining to an earthly lot or eternal destiny by divine decree; *also* : the state of being so foreordained — **pre·des·ti·nate** \prē-'des-tə-,nāt\ *vb*
pre·des·tine \prē-'des-tən\ *vb* : to settle beforehand : FOREORDAIN
pre·de·ter·mine \,prē-di-'tər-mən\ *vb* : to determine beforehand
pred·i·ca·ble \'pre-di-kə-bəl\ *adj* : capable of being predicated or affirmed
pre·dic·a·ment \pri-'di-kə-mənt\ *n* : a difficult or trying situation ✦ *Synonyms* DILEMMA, PICKLE, QUAGMIRE, JAM
¹**pred·i·cate** \'pre-di-kət\ *n* : the part of a sentence or clause that expresses what is said of the subject
²**pred·i·cate** \'pre-də-,kāt\ *vb* **-cat·ed; -cat·ing** **1** : AFFIRM **2** : to assert to be a quality or attribute **3** : FOUND, BASE — usu. used with *on* — **pred·i·ca·tion** \,pre-də-'kā-shən\ *n*
pre·dict \pri-'dikt\ *vb* : to declare in advance — **pre·dict·abil·i·ty** \-,dik-tə-'bi-lə-tē\ *n* — **pre·dict·able** \-'dik-tə-bəl\ *adj* — **pre·dict·ably** \-blē\ *adv* — **pre·dic·tion** \-'dik-shən\ *n*
pre·di·gest \,prē-dī-'jest\ *vb* : to simplify for easy use; *also* : to subject to artificial or natural partial digestion
pre·di·lec·tion \,pre-də-'lek-shən, ,prē-\ *n* : an established preference for something
pre·dis·pose \,prē-di-'spōz\ *vb* : to incline in advance : make susceptible — **pre·dis·po·si·tion** \,prē-,dis-pə-'zi-shən\ *n*
pre·dom·i·nant \pri-'dä-mə-nənt\ *adj* : greater in importance, strength, influence, or authority — **pre·dom·i·nance** \-nəns\ *n*
pre·dom·i·nant·ly \-nənt-lē\ *adv* : for the most part : MAINLY
pre·dom·i·nate \pri-'dä-mə-,nāt\ *vb* : to be superior esp. in power or numbers : PREVAIL
pre·dom·i·nate·ly \pri-'dä-mə-nət-lē\ *adv* : PREDOMINANTLY
pree·mie \'prē-mē\ *n* : a premature baby
pre·em·i·nent \prē-'e-mə-nənt\ *adj* : having highest rank : OUTSTANDING — **pre·em·i·nence** \-nəns\ *n* — **pre·em·i·nent·ly** *adv*
pre·empt \prē-'empt\ *vb* **1** : to settle upon (public land) with the right to purchase before others; *also* : to take by such right **2** : to seize upon before someone else can **3** : to take the place of ✦ *Synonyms* USURP, CONFISCATE, APPROPRIATE, EXPROPRIATE — **pre·emp·tion** \-'emp-shən\ *n*
pre·emp·tive \prē-'emp-tiv\ *adj* : marked by the seizing of the initiative : initiated by oneself ⟨∼ attack⟩
preen \'prēn\ *vb* [ME *prenen,* alter. of *proynen, prunen,* fr. AF *puroindre, proindre,* fr. *pur-* thoroughly + *oindre* to anoint, rub, fr. L *unguere*] **1** : to groom with the bill — used of a bird **2** : to dress or smooth up : PRIMP **3** : to pride (oneself) for achievement
pre·ex·ist \,prē-ig-'zist\ *vb* : to exist before — **pre·ex·is·tence** \-'zis-təns\ *n* — **pre·ex·is·tent** \-tənt\ *adj*
pref *abbr* **1** preface **2** preference **3** preferred **4** prefix
¹**pre·fab** \(,)prē-'fab, 'prē-,fab\ *adj* : produced by prefabrication
²**pre·fab** *n* : a prefabricated structure
pre·fab·ri·cate \(,)prē-'fa-brə-,kāt\ *vb* : to manufacture the parts of (a structure) beforehand for later assembly — **pre·fab·ri·ca·tion** \,prē-,fa-bri-'kā-shən\ *n*
¹**pref·ace** \'pre-fəs\ *n* : the introductory remarks of a speaker or writer — **pref·a·to·ry** \'pre-fə-,tòr-ē\ *adj*
²**preface** *vb* **pref·aced; pref·ac·ing** : to introduce with a preface
pre·fect \'prē-,fekt\ *n* **1** : a high official; *esp* : a chief officer or magistrate **2** : a student monitor
pre·fec·ture \'prē-,fek-chər\ *n* : the office, term, or residence of a prefect
pre·fer \pri-'fər\ *vb* **pre·ferred; pre·fer·ring** **1** : PROMOTE **2** : to like better **3** : to bring (as a charge) against a person — **pref·er·a·ble** \'pre-fə-rə-bəl\ *adj* — **pref·er·a·bly** \-blē\ *adv*
pref·er·ence \'pre-frəns, -fə-rəns\ *n* **1** : a special liking for one thing over another **2** : CHOICE, SELECTION — **pref·er·en·tial** \,pre-fə-'ren-chəl\ *adj*
pref·er·ment \pri-'fər-mənt\ *n* : PROMOTION, ADVANCEMENT

preferred provider organization *n* : PPO

pre·fig·ure \prē-ˈfi-gyər\ *vb* **1** : FORESHADOW **2** : to imagine beforehand

¹pre·fix \ˈprē-ˌfiks, prē-ˈfiks\ *vb* : to place before ⟨∼ a title to a name⟩

²pre·fix \ˈprē-ˌfiks\ *n* : an affix occurring at the beginning of a word

pre·flight \ˌprē-ˈflīt\ *adj* : preparing for or preliminary to flight

pre·form \(ˌ)prē-ˈfȯrm, ˈprē-ˌfȯrm\ *vb* : to form or shape beforehand

preg·na·ble \ˈpreg-nə-bəl\ *adj* : vulnerable to capture ⟨a ∼ fort⟩

preg·nant \ˈpreg-nənt\ *adj* **1** : containing unborn offspring within the body **2** : rich in significance : MEANINGFUL — **preg·nan·cy** \-nən-sē\ *n*

pre·heat \ˌprē-ˈhēt\ *vb* : to heat beforehand; *esp* : to heat (an oven) to a designated temperature before using

pre·hen·sile \prē-ˈhen-səl, -ˌsī(-ə)l\ *adj* : adapted for grasping esp. by wrapping around ⟨a monkey with a ∼ tail⟩

pre·his·tor·ic \ˌprē-his-ˈtȯr-ik\ *also* **pre·his·tor·i·cal** \-i-kəl\ *adj* : of, relating to, or existing in the period before written history began

pre·judge \(ˌ)prē-ˈjəj\ *vb* : to judge before full hearing or examination

¹prej·u·dice \ˈpre-jə-dəs\ *n* **1** : DAMAGE; *esp* : detriment to one's rights or claims **2** : an opinion made without adequate basis — **prej·u·di·cial** \ˌpre-jə-ˈdi-shəl\ *adj*

²prejudice *vb* **-diced; -dic·ing 1** : to damage by a judgment or action esp. at law **2** : to cause to have prejudice

pre·kin·der·gar·ten \(ˈ)prē-ˈkin-dər-ˌgär-tᵊn\ *n* **1** : NURSERY SCHOOL **2** : a class or program preceding kindergarten

prel·ate \ˈpre-lət\ *n* : an ecclesiastic (as a bishop) of high rank — **prel·a·cy** \-lə-sē\ *n*

pre·launch \ˈprē-ˈlȯnch\ *adj* : preparing for or preliminary to launch

pre·lim \ˈprē-ˌlim, pri-ˈlim\ *n or adj* : PRELIMINARY

¹pre·lim·i·nary \pri-ˈli-mə-ˌner-ē\ *n, pl* **-nar·ies** : something that precedes or introduces the main business or event

²preliminary *adj* : preceding the main discourse or business

pre·lude \ˈprel-ˌyüd; ˈpre-ˌlüd, ˈprā-\ *n* **1** : an introductory performance or event **2** : a musical section or movement introducing the main theme; *also* : an organ solo played at the beginning of a church service

pre·mar·i·tal \(ˌ)prē-ˈmer-ə-tᵊl\ *adj* : existing or occurring before marriage

pre·ma·ture \ˌprē-mə-ˈtu̇r, -ˈtyu̇r, -ˈchu̇r\ *adj* : happening, coming, born, or done before the usual or proper time — **pre·ma·ture·ly** *adv*

¹pre·med \ˈprē-ˌmed\ *n* : a premedical student or course of study

²premed *adj* : PREMEDICAL

pre·med·i·cal \(ˌ)prē-ˈme-di-kəl\ *adj* : preceding and preparing for the professional study of medicine

pre·med·i·tate \pri-ˈme-də-ˌtāt\ *vb* : to consider and plan beforehand — **pre·med·i·ta·tion** \-ˌme-də-ˈtā-shən\ *n*

pre·men·o·paus·al \(ˌ)prē-ˌme-nə-ˈpȯ-zəl\ *adj* : of, relating to, or being in the period preceding menopause

pre·men·stru·al \(ˌ)prē-ˈmen-strə-wəl\ *adj* : of, relating to, or occurring in the period just before before menstruation

premenstrual syndrome *n* : a varying group of symptoms manifested by some women prior to menstruation

premie *var of* PREEMIE

¹pre·mier \pri-ˈmir, -ˈmyir, ˈprē-mē-ər\ *adj* [ME *primer, primier,* fr. AF, first, chief, fr. L *primarius* of the first rank] : first in rank or importance : CHIEF; *also* : first in time : EARLIEST

²premier *n* : PRIME MINISTER — **pre·mier·ship** *n*

¹pre·miere \pri-ˈmyer, -ˈmir\ *n* : a first performance

²premiere *also* **pre·mier** *same as* ¹PREMIERE\ *vb* **pre·miered; pre·mier·ing** : to give or receive a first public performance

¹prem·ise \ˈpre-məs\ *n* **1** : a statement of fact or a supposition made or implied as a basis of argument **2** *pl* : a piece of land with the structures on it; *also* : the place of business of an enterprise

²premise *vb* **prem·ised; prem·is·ing** : to base on certain assumptions

pre·mi·um \ˈprē-mē-əm\ *n* [L *praemium* booty, profit, reward, fr. *prae* before + *emere* to take, buy] **1** : REWARD,

PRIZE **2** : a sum over and above the stated value **3** : something paid over and above a fixed wage or price **4** : something given with a purchase **5** : the sum paid for a contract of insurance **6** : an unusually high value

pre·mix \ˌprē-ˈmiks\ *vb* : to mix before use

pre·mo·lar \(ˌ)prē-ˈmō-lər\ *adj* : situated in front of or preceding the molar teeth; *esp* : being or relating to those teeth of a mammal in front of the true molars and behind the canines — **premolar** *n*

pre·mo·ni·tion \ˌprē-mə-ˈni-shən, ˌpre-\ *n* **1** : previous warning **2** : PRESENTIMENT — **pre·mon·i·to·ry** \pri-ˈmä-nə-ˌtȯr-ē\ *adj*

pre·na·tal \ˈprē-ˈnā-tᵊl\ *adj* : occurring, existing, or taking place before birth

pre·nup·tial \ˈprē-ˈnəp-shəl\ *adj* : made or occurring before marriage

prenuptial agreement *n* : an agreement between a man and woman before marrying in which they give up future rights to each other's property in the event of divorce or death

pre·oc·cu·pa·tion \ˌprē-ˌä-kyə-ˈpā-shən\ *n* : complete absorption of the mind or interests; *also* : something that causes such absorption

pre·oc·cu·pied \prē-ˈä-kyə-ˌpīd\ *adj* **1** : lost in thought; *also* : absorbed in some preoccupation **2** : already occupied ♦ *Synonyms* ABSTRACTED, ABSENT, ABSENTMINDED

pre·oc·cu·py \-ˌpī\ *vb* **1** : to occupy the attention of beforehand **2** : to take possession of before another

pre·op·er·a·tive \(ˌ)prē-ˈä-prə-tiv, -pə-ˌrā-\ *adj* : occurring before a surgical operation

pre·or·dain \ˌprē-ȯr-ˈdān\ *vb* : FOREORDAIN

pre—owned \(ˌ)prē-ˈōnd\ *adj* : SECONDHAND ⟨∼ vehicles⟩

prep *abbr* **1** preparatory **2** preposition

pre·pack·age \(ˌ)prē-ˈpa-kij\ *vb* : to package (as food) before offering for sale to the customer

preparatory school *n* **1** : a usu. private school preparing students primarily for college **2** *Brit* : a private elementary school preparing students primarily for British public schools

pre·pare \pri-ˈper\ *vb* **pre·pared; pre·par·ing 1** : to make or get ready ⟨∼ dinner⟩ ⟨∼ a student for college⟩ **2** : to get ready beforehand **3** : to put together : COMPOUND ⟨∼ a prescription⟩ — **prep·a·ra·tion** \ˌpre-pə-ˈrā-shən\ *n* — **pre·pa·ra·to·ry** \pri-ˈper-ə-ˌtȯr-ē\ *adj*

pre·pared·ness \pri-ˈper-əd-nəs\ *n* : a state of adequate preparation

pre·pay \(ˌ)prē-ˈpā\ *vb* **-paid** \-ˈpād\; **-pay·ing** : to pay or pay the charge on in advance

pre·pon·der·ant \pri-ˈpän-də-rənt\ *adj* : having greater weight, force, influence, or frequency — **pre·pon·der·ance** \-rəns\ *n* — **pre·pon·der·ant·ly** *adv*

pre·pon·der·ate \pri-ˈpän-də-ˌrāt\ *vb* **-at·ed; -at·ing** [L *praeponderare,* fr. *prae-* ahead + *ponder-, pondus* weight] : to exceed in weight, force, influence, or frequency : PREDOMINATE

prep·o·si·tion \ˌpre-pə-ˈzi-shən\ *n* : a word that combines with a noun or pronoun to form a phrase — **prep·o·si·tion·al** \-ˈzi-shə-nəl\ *adj*

pre·pos·sess \ˌprē-pə-ˈzes\ *vb* **1** : to cause to be preoccupied **2** : to influence beforehand esp. favorably

pre·pos·sess·ing *adj* : tending to create a favorable impression ⟨a ∼ manner⟩

pre·pos·ses·sion \-ˈze-shən\ *n* **1** : PREJUDICE **2** : an exclusive concern with one idea or object

pre·pos·ter·ous \pri-ˈpäs-tə-rəs\ *adj* : contrary to nature or reason : ABSURD

prep·py *or* **prep·pie** \ˈpre-pē\ *n, pl* **preppies 1** : a student at or a graduate of a preparatory school **2** : a person deemed to dress or behave like a preppy

pre·puce \ˈprē-ˌpyüs\ *n* : FORESKIN

pre·quel \ˈprē-kwəl\ *n* : a literary or dramatic work whose story precedes that of an earlier work

pre·re·cord·ed \(ˌ)prē-ri-ˈkȯr-dəd\ *adj* : recorded for later broadcast or play

pre·req·ui·site \ˌprē-ˈre-kwə-zət\ *n* : something required beforehand or for the end in view — **prerequisite** *adj*

pre·rog·a·tive \pri-ˈrä-gə-tiv\ *n* : an exclusive or special right, power, or privilege

pres *abbr* **1** present **2** president

¹pres·age \ˈpre-sij\ *n* [ME, fr. L *praesagium,* fr. *praesagus* having a foreboding, fr. *prae* before + *sagus* prophetic] **1** : something that foreshadows a future event : OMEN **2** : FOREBODING

²**pres·age** \'pre-sij, pri-'sāj\ *vb* **pre·saged; pre·sag·ing 1** : to give an omen or warning of : FORESHADOW **2** : FORETELL, PREDICT

pres·by·o·pia \₁prez-bē-'ō-pē-ə\ *n* : a visual condition in which loss of elasticity of the lens of the eye causes defective accommodation and inability to focus sharply for near vision — **pres·by·op·ic** \-'ō-pik, -'ä-\ *adj or n*

pres·by·ter \'prez-bə-tər\ *n* [LL, elder, priest, fr. Gk *presbyteros*, compar. of *presbys* elder, old man] **1** : PRIEST, MINISTER **2** : an elder in a Presbyterian church

¹**Pres·by·te·ri·an** \₁prez-bə-'tir-ē-ən\ *n* : a member of a Presbyterian church

²**Presbyterian** *adj* **1** *often not cap* : characterized by a graded system of representative ecclesiastical bodies (as presbyteries) exercising legislative and judicial powers **2** : of or relating to a group of Protestant Christian bodies that are presbyterian in government — **Pres·by·te·ri·an·ism** \-ə-₁ni-zəm\ *n*

pres·by·tery \'prez-bə-₁ter-ē\ *n, pl* **-ter·ies 1** : the part of a church reserved for the officiating clergy **2** : a ruling body in Presbyterian churches consisting of the ministers and representative elders of a district

¹**pre·school** \'prē-₁skül\ *adj* : of or relating to the period in a child's life from infancy to the age of five or six — **pre·school·er** \-₁skü-lər\ *n*

²**preschool** *n* : NURSERY SCHOOL

pre·science \'pre-shəns, 'prē-\ *n* : foreknowledge of events; *also* : FORESIGHT — **pre·scient** \-shənt, -shē-ənt\ *adj*

pre·scribe \pri-'skrīb\ *vb* **pre·scribed; pre·scrib·ing 1** : to lay down as a guide or rule of action **2** : to direct the use of (as a medicine) as a remedy

pre·scrip·tion \pri-'skrip-shən\ *n* **1** : the action of prescribing rules or directions **2** : a written direction for the preparation and use of a medicine; *also* : a medicine prescribed

pre·scrip·tive \pri-'skrip-tiv\ *adj* **1** : serving to prescribe ⟨~ rules⟩ **2** : acquired by, based on, or determined by prescription or by custom

pres·ence \'pre-z²ns\ *n* **1** : the fact or condition of being present **2** : the space immediately around a person **3** : one that is present **4** : the bearing of a person; *esp* : stately bearing

¹**pres·ent** \'pre-z²nt\ *n* : something presented : GIFT

²**pre·sent** \pri-'zent\ *vb* **1** : to bring into the presence or acquaintance of : INTRODUCE **2** : to bring before the public ⟨~ a play⟩ **3** : to make a gift to **4** : to give formally **5** : to lay (as a charge) before a court for inquiry **6** : to aim or direct (as a weapon) so as to face in a particular direction — **pre·sent·able** *adj* — **pre·sen·ta·tion** \₁prē-₁zen-'tā-shən, ₁pre-z²n-\ *n* — **pre·sent·ment** \pri-'zent-mənt\ *n*

³**pres·ent** \'pre-z²nt\ *adj* **1** : now existing or in progress ⟨~ conditions⟩ **2** : being in view or at hand ⟨~ at the meeting⟩ **3** : under consideration ⟨the ~ problem⟩ **4** : of, relating to, or constituting a verb tense that expresses present time or the time of speaking

⁴**pres·ent** \'pre-z²nt\ *n* **1** *pl* : the present legal document **2** : the present tense; *also* : a verb form in it **3** : the present time

pres·ent–day \'pre-z²nt-'dā\ *adj* : now existing or occurring : CURRENT

pre·sen·ti·ment \pri-'zen-tə-mənt\ *n* : a feeling that something is about to happen : PREMONITION

pres·ent·ly \'pre-z²nt-lē\ *adv* **1** : SOON ⟨~ they arrived⟩ **2** : NOW ⟨~ busy⟩

present participle *n* : a participle that typically expresses present action and that in English is formed with the suffix *-ing* and is used in the formation of the progressive tenses

¹**pre·serve** \pri-'zərv\ *vb* **pre·served; pre·serv·ing 1** : to keep safe : GUARD, PROTECT **2** : to keep from decaying; *esp* : to process food (as by canning or pickling) to prevent spoilage **3** : MAINTAIN ⟨~ silence⟩ — **pres·er·va·tion** \₁pre-zər-'vā-shən\ *n* — **pre·ser·va·tive** \pri-'zər-və-tiv\ *adj or n* — **pre·serv·er** *n*

²**preserve** *n* **1** : preserved fruit — often used in pl. **2** : an area for the protection of natural resources (as animals)

pre·set \'prē-₁set\ *vb* **-set; -set·ting** : to set beforehand — **preset** *n*

pre·shrink \prē-'shriŋk\ *vb* **-shrank** \-'shraŋk\; **-shrunk** \-'shrəŋk\ : to shrink (as a fabric) before making into a garment

pre·side \pri-'zīd\ *vb* **pre·sid·ed; pre·sid·ing** [L *praesidēre* to guard, preside over, fr. *prae* in front of + *sedēre* to sit] **1** : to exercise guidance or control **2** : to occupy the place of authority; *esp* : to act as chairman

pres·i·dent \'pre-zə-dənt\ *n* **1** : one chosen to preside ⟨~ of the assembly⟩ **2** : the chief officer of an organization (as a corporation or society) **3** : an elected official serving as both chief of state and chief political executive; *also* : a chief of state often with only minimal political powers — **pres·i·den·cy** \-dən-sē\ *n* — **pres·i·den·tial** \₁pre-zə-'den-chəl\ *adj*

pre·si·dio \pri-'sē-dē-₁ō, -'si-\ *n, pl* **-di·os** [Sp] : a military post or fortified settlement in an area currently or orig. under Spanish control

pre·sid·i·um \pri-'si-dē-əm\ *n, pl* **-ia** \-dē-ə\ *or* **-iums** [Russ *prezidium*, fr. L *praesidium* garrison] : a permanent executive committee that acts for a larger body in a Communist country

¹**pre·soak** \₍₁₎prē-'sōk\ *vb* : to soak beforehand

²**pre·soak** \'prē-₁sōk\ *n* **1** : an instance of presoaking **2** : a preparation used in presoaking clothes

pre·sort \₍₁₎prē-'sȯrt\ *vb* : to sort (mail) by zip code usu. before delivery to a post office

¹**press** \'pres\ *n* **1** : a crowded condition : THRONG **2** : a machine for exerting pressure **3** : CLOSET, CUPBOARD **4** : PRESSURE **5** : the properly creased condition of a freshly pressed garment **6** : PRINTING PRESS; *also* : the act or the process of printing **7** : a printing or publishing establishment **8** : the media (as newspapers and magazines) of public news and comment; *also* : persons (as reporters) employed in these media **9** : comment in newspapers and periodicals

²**press** *vb* **1** : to bear down upon : push steadily against **2** : ASSAIL, COMPEL **3** : to squeeze out the juice or contents of ⟨~ grapes⟩ **4** : to squeeze to a desired density, shape, or smoothness; *esp* : IRON **5** : to try hard to persuade : URGE **6** : to follow through : PROSECUTE **7** : CROWD **8** : to force one's way **9** : to require haste or speed in action — **press·er** *n*

press agent *n* : an agent employed to establish and maintain good public relations through publicity

press·ing *adj* : URGENT ⟨a ~ need⟩

press·man \'pres-mən, -₁man\ *n* : the operator of a press and esp. a printing press

press·room \-₁rüm, -₁rum\ *n* **1** : a room in a printing plant containing the printing presses **2** : a room for the use of reporters

¹**pres·sure** \'pre-shər\ *n* **1** : the burden of physical or mental distress **2** : the action of pressing; *esp* : the application of force to something by something else in direct contact with it **3** : the force exerted over a surface divided by its area **4** : the stress or urgency of matters demanding attention

²**pressure** *vb* **pres·sured; pres·sur·ing** : to apply pressure to

pressure group *n* : a group that seeks to influence governmental policy but not to elect candidates to office

pressure suit *n* : an inflatable suit for high-altitude flight or spaceflight to protect the body from low pressure

pres·sur·ise *Brit var of* PRESSURIZE

pres·sur·ize \'pre-shə-₁rīz\ *vb* **-ized; -iz·ing 1** : to maintain higher pressure within than without; *esp* : to maintain normal atmospheric pressure within (as an airplane cabin) during high-altitude flight or spaceflight **2** : to apply pressure to **3** : to design to withstand pressure — **pres·sur·i·za·tion** \₁pre-shə-rə-'zā-shən\ *n*

pres·ti·dig·i·ta·tion \₁pres-tə-₁di-jə-'tā-shən\ *n* : SLEIGHT OF HAND

pres·tige \pres-'tēzh, -'tēj\ *n* [F, fr. MF, conjuror's trick, illusion, fr. LL *praestigium*, fr. L *praestigiae*, pl., conjuror's tricks, fr. *praestringere* to graze, blunt, constrict, fr. *prae-* in front of + *stringere* to bind tight] : standing or estimation in the eyes of people : REPUTATION ♦ **Synonyms** INFLUENCE, AUTHORITY, WEIGHT, CACHET — **pres·ti·gious** \-'ti-jəs, -'tē\ *adj*

¹pres·to \'pres-tō\ *interj* [It, quick, quickly] — used to indicate the sudden appearance or occurrence of something

²presto *adv or adj* **1** : suddenly as if by magic : IMMEDIATELY **2** : at a rapid tempo — used as a direction in music

pre·stress \(ˌ)prē-'stres\ *vb* : to introduce internal stresses into (as a structural beam) to counteract later load stresses

pre·sum·ably \pri-'zü-mə-blē\ *adv* : by reasonable assumption

pre·sume \pri-'züm\ *vb* **pre·sumed; pre·sum·ing 1** : to take upon oneself without leave or warrant : DARE **2** : to take for granted : ASSUME **3** : to act or behave with undue boldness — **pre·sum·able** \-'zü-mə-bəl\ *adj*

pre·sump·tion \pri-'zəmp-shən\ *n* **1** : presumptuous attitude or conduct : AUDACITY **2** : an attitude or belief dictated by probability; *also* : the grounds lending probability to a belief — **pre·sump·tive** \-tiv\ *adj*

pre·sump·tu·ous \pri-'zəmp-chə-wəs\ *adj* : overstepping due bounds : taking liberties — **pre·sump·tu·ous·ly** *adv*

pre·sup·pose \ˌprē-sə-'pōz\ *vb* **1** : to suppose beforehand **2** : to require beforehand as a necessary condition — **pre·sup·po·si·tion** \(ˌ)prē-ˌsə-pə-'zi-shən\ *n*

pre·teen \'prē-ˌtēn\ *n* : a boy or girl not yet 13 years old — **preteen** *adj*

pre·tend \pri-'tend\ *vb* **1** : PROFESS ⟨doesn't ~ to be scientific⟩ **2** : FEIGN ⟨~ to be angry⟩ **3** : to lay claim ⟨~ to a throne⟩ — **pre·tend·er** *n*

pre·tense *or* **pre·tence** \'prē-ˌtens, pri-'tens\ *n* **1** : CLAIM; *esp* : one not supported by fact **2** : mere display : SHOW **3** : an attempt to attain a certain condition ⟨made a ~ at discipline⟩ **4** : false show : PRETEXT — **pre·ten·sion** \pri-'ten-chən\ *n*

pre·ten·tious \pri-'ten-chəs\ *adj* **1** : making or possessing usu. unjustified claims (as to excellence) ⟨a ~ literary style⟩ **2** : making demands on one's ability or means : AMBITIOUS ⟨too ~ an undertaking⟩ — **pre·ten·tious·ly** *adv* — **pre·ten·tious·ness** *n*

pret·er·it *or* **pret·er·ite** \'pre-tə-rət\ *n* : a verb form expressing action in the past

pre·term \(ˌ)prē-'tərm, 'prē-ˌ\ *adj* : of, relating to, being, or brought forth by premature birth ⟨a ~ infant⟩

pre·ter·nat·u·ral \ˌprē-tər-'na-chə-rəl\ *adj* **1** : exceeding what is natural **2** : inexplicable by ordinary means — **pre·ter·nat·u·ral·ly** *adv*

pre·text \'prē-ˌtekst\ *n* : a purpose stated or assumed to cloak the real intention or state of affairs

pret·ti·fy \'pri-ti-ˌfī\ *vb* **-fied; -fy·ing** : to make pretty — **pret·ti·fi·ca·tion** \ˌpri-ti-fə-'kā-shən\ *n*

¹pret·ty \'pri-tē\ *adj* **pret·ti·er; -est** [ME *praty, prety,* fr. OE *prættig* tricky, fr. *prætt* trick] **1** : pleasing by delicacy or grace : having conventionally accepted elements of beauty ⟨~ flowers⟩ **2** : MISERABLE, TERRIBLE ⟨a ~ state of affairs⟩ **3** : moderately large ⟨a ~ profit⟩ **4** : PLEASANT — usu. used in negative constructions ⟨the truth was not so ~⟩ ✦ **Synonyms** COMELY, FAIR, BEAUTIFUL, ATTRACTIVE, LOVELY — **pret·ti·ly** \-tə-lē\ *adv* — **pret·ti·ness** \-tē-nəs\ *n*

²pretty *adv* : in some degree : MODERATELY; *also* : QUITE, MAINLY

³pretty *vb* **pret·tied; pret·ty·ing** : to make pretty — usu. used with *up*

pretty boy *n* : a man who is notably good-looking

pret·zel \'pret-səl\ *n* [G *Brezel,* ultim. fr. L *brachiatus* having branches like arms, fr. *brachium* arm] : a brittle or chewy glazed usu. salted slender bread often shaped like a loose knot

prev *abbr* previous; previously

pre·vail \pri-'vāl\ *vb* **1** : to win mastery : TRIUMPH **2** : to be or become effective : SUCCEED **3** : to urge successfully ⟨~ed upon her to sing⟩ **4** : to be frequent : PREDOMINATE — **pre·vail·ing·ly** *adv*

prev·a·lent \'pre-və-lənt\ *adj* : generally or widely existent : WIDESPREAD — **prev·a·lence** \-ləns\ *n*

pre·var·i·cate \pri-'ver-ə-ˌkāt\ *vb* **-cat·ed; -cat·ing** [L *praevaricari* to act in collusion, lit., to straddle, fr. *prae* in front of + *varicare* to straddle, fr. *varus* bowlegged] : to deviate from the truth : EQUIVOCATE — **pre·var·i·ca·tion** \-ˌver-ə-'kā-shən\ *n* — **pre·var·i·ca·tor** \-'ver-ə-ˌkā-tər\ *n*

pre·vent \pri-'vent\ *vb* **1** : to keep from happening or existing ⟨steps to ~ war⟩ **2** : to hold back : HINDER, STOP

⟨~ us from going⟩ — **pre·vent·able** *also* **pre·vent·ible** \-'ven-tə-bəl\ *adj* — **pre·ven·tion** \-'ven-chən\ *n* — **pre·ven·tive** \-'ven-tiv\ *adj or n* — **pre·ven·ta·tive** \-'ven-tə-tiv\ *adj or n*

pre·ver·bal \ˌprē-'vər-bəl\ *adj* : having not yet acquired the faculty of speech

¹pre·view \'prē-ˌvyü\ *vb* : to see or discuss beforehand; *esp* : to view or show in advance of public presentation

²preview *n* **1** : FORETASTE **2** : an advance showing or viewing **3** *also* **pre·vue** \-ˌvyü\ : a showing of snatches from a motion picture advertised for future appearance

pre·vi·ous \'prē-vē-əs\ *adj* : going before : EARLIER, FORMER ✦ **Synonyms** FOREGOING, PRIOR, PRECEDING, ANTECEDENT — **pre·vi·ous·ly** *adv*

pre·vi·sion \prē-'vi-zhən\ *n* **1** : FORESIGHT, PRESCIENCE **2** : FORECAST, PREDICTION

pre·war \'prē-'wȯr\ *adj* : occurring or existing before a war

¹prey \'prā\ *n, pl* **prey** *also* **preys 1** : an animal taken for food by a predator; *also* : VICTIM **2** : the act or habit of preying

²prey *vb* **1** : to raid for booty **2** : to seize and devour prey **3** : to have a harmful or wearing effect

prf *abbr* proof

¹price \'prīs\ *n* **1** *archaic* : VALUE **2** : the amount of money paid or asked for the sale of a specified thing; *also* : the cost at which something is obtained

²price *vb* **priced; pric·ing 1** : to set a price on **2** : to ask the price of **3** : to drive by raising prices ⟨*priced* themselves out of the market⟩

price–fix·ing \'prīs-ˌfik-siŋ\ *n* : the setting of prices artificially (as by producers or government)

price·less \-ləs\ *adj* : having a value beyond any price : INVALUABLE ✦ **Synonyms** PRECIOUS, COSTLY, EXPENSIVE

price support *n* : artificial maintenance of prices of a commodity at a level usu. fixed through government action

price war *n* : a period of commercial competition in which prices are repeatedly cut by the competitors

pric·ey *also* **pricy** \'prī-sē\ *adj* **pric·i·er; -est** : EXPENSIVE

¹prick \'prik\ *n* **1** : a mark or small wound made by a pointed instrument **2** : something sharp or pointed **3** : an instance of pricking; *also* : a sensation of being pricked

²prick *vb* **1** : to pierce slightly with a sharp point; *also* : to have or cause a pricking sensation **2** : to affect with anguish or remorse ⟨~s his conscience⟩ **3** : to outline with punctures ⟨~ out a pattern⟩ **4** : to stand or cause to stand erect ⟨the dog's ears ~ed up at the sound⟩ ✦ **Synonyms** PUNCH, PUNCTURE, PERFORATE, BORE, DRILL

prick·er \'pri-kər\ *n* : BRIAR; *also* : THORN

¹prick·le \'pri-kəl\ *n* **1** : a small sharp process (as on a plant) **2** : a slight stinging pain — **prick·ly** \'pri-klē\ *adj*

²prickle *vb* **prick·led; prick·ling 1** : to prick lightly **2** : TINGLE

prickly heat *n* : a red cutaneous eruption with intense itching and tingling caused by inflammation around the ducts of the sweat glands

prickly pear *n* : any of numerous cacti with usu. yellow flowers and prickly flat or rounded joints; *also* : the sweet pulpy pear-shaped edible fruit of various prickly pears

¹pride \'prīd\ *n* **1** : CONCEIT **2** : justifiable self-respect **3** : elation over an act or possession **4** : haughty behavior : DISDAIN **5** : ostentatious display — **pride·ful** *adj*

²pride *vb* **prid·ed; prid·ing** : to indulge (as oneself) in pride

priest \'prēst\ *n* [ME *preist,* fr. OE *prēost,* ultim. fr. LL *presbyter* elder, priest, fr. Gk *presbyteros,* fr. compar. of *presbys* old man, elder] : a person having authority to perform the sacred rites of a religion; *esp* : a member of the Anglican, Eastern, or Roman Catholic clergy ranking below a bishop and above a deacon — **priest·hood** *n* — **priest·li·ness** *n* — **priest·ly** *adj*

priest·ess \'prēs-təs\ *n* : a woman authorized to perform the sacred rites of a religion

prig \'prig\ *n* : one who irritates by rigid or pointed observance of proprieties — **prig·gish** \'pri-gish\ *adj* — **prig·gish·ly** *adv*

¹prim \'prim\ *adj* **prim·mer; prim·mest** : stiffly formal and precise — **prim·ly** *adv* — **prim·ness** *n*

²prim *abbr* **1** primary **2** primitive

pri·ma·cy \'prī-mə-sē\ *n* **1** : the state of being first (as in rank) **2** : the office, rank, or character of an ecclesiastical primate

pri·ma don·na \ˌpri-mə-ˈdä-nə\ *n, pl* **prima donnas** [It, lit., first lady] **1** : a principal female singer (as in an opera company) **2** : a vain undisciplined usu. uncooperative person

pri·ma fa·cie \ˈprī-mə-ˈfā-shə, -sē, -shē\ *adj or adv* [L, at first view] **1** : based on immediate impression : APPARENT **2** : SELF-EVIDENT

pri·mal \ˈprī-məl\ *adj* **1** : ORIGINAL, PRIMITIVE **2** : first in importance

pri·mar·i·ly \prī-ˈmer-ə-lē\ *adv* **1** : FUNDAMENTALLY **2** : ORIGINALLY

¹**pri·ma·ry** \ˈprī-ˌmer-ē, -mə-rē\ *adj* **1** : first in order of time or development; *also* : PREPARATORY **2** : of first rank or importance; *also* : FUNDAMENTAL **3** : not derived from or dependent on something else ⟨∼ sources⟩

²**primary** *n, pl* **-ries** : a preliminary election in which voters nominate or express a preference among candidates usu. of their own party

primary care *n* : health care provided by a medical professional with whom a patient has initial contact

primary color *n* : any of a set of colors from which all other colors may be derived

primary school *n* **1** : a school usu. including grades 1–3 and sometimes kindergarten **2** : ELEMENTARY SCHOOL

pri·mate \ˈprī-ˌmāt *or esp for 1* -mət\ *n* **1** *often cap* : the highest-ranking bishop of a province or nation **2** : any of an order of mammals including humans, apes, and monkeys

¹**prime** \ˈprīm\ *n* **1** : the earliest stage of something; *esp* : SPRINGTIME **2** : the most active, thriving, or successful stage or period (as of one's life) **3** : the best individual; *also* : the best part of something **4** : any integer other than 0, +1, or −1 that is not divisible without remainder by any integer except +1, −1, and plus or minus itself; *esp* : any such integer that is positive

²**prime** *adj* **1** : standing first (as in time, rank, significance, or quality) ⟨∼ requisite⟩ **2** : of, relating to, or being a number that is prime

³**prime** *vb* **primed; prim·ing 1** : FILL, LOAD **2** : to lay a preparatory coating upon (as in painting) **3** : to put in working condition **4** : to instruct beforehand : COACH

prime meridian *n* : the meridian of 0° longitude which runs through Greenwich, England, and from which other longitudes are reckoned east and west

prime minister *n* **1** : the chief minister of a ruler or state **2** : the chief executive of a parliamentary government

¹**prim·er** \ˈpri-mər\ *n* [ME, layperson's prayer book, fr. AF, fr. ML *primarium*, fr. LL, neut. of *primarius* primary] **1** : a small book for teaching children to read **2** : a small introductory book on a subject **3** : a short informative piece of writing

²**prim·er** \ˈprī-mər\ *n* **1** : one that primes **2** : a device for igniting an explosive **3** : material for priming a surface

prime rate *n* : an interest rate announced by a bank to be the lowest available to its most credit-worthy customers

prime time *n* **1** : the time period when the television or radio audience is largest; *also* : television shows aired in prime time **2** : the choicest or busiest time

pri·me·val \prī-ˈmē-vəl\ *adj* : of or relating to the earliest ages : PRIMITIVE

¹**prim·i·tive** \ˈpri-mə-tiv\ *adj* **1** : ORIGINAL, PRIMARY **2** : of, relating to, or characteristic of an early stage of development or evolution **3** : ELEMENTAL, NATURAL **4** : of, relating to, or produced by a tribal people or culture **5** : SELF-TAUGHT; *also* : produced by a self-taught artist — **prim·i·tive·ly** *adv* — **prim·i·tive·ness** *n* — **prim·i·tiv·i·ty** \ˌpri-mə-ˈti-və-tē\ *n*

²**primitive** *n* **1** : something primitive **2** : a primitive artist **3** : a member of a primitive people

prim·i·tiv·ism \ˈpri-mə-ti-ˌvi-zəm\ *n* **1** : primitive practices or procedures; *also* : a primitive quality or state **2** : belief in the superiority of a simple way of life close to nature **3** : the style of art of primitive peoples or primitive artists

pri·mo·gen·i·tor \ˌprī-mō-ˈje-nə-tər\ *n* : ANCESTOR, FOREFATHER

pri·mo·gen·i·ture \-ˈje-nə-ˌchùr\ *n* **1** : the state of being the firstborn of a family **2** : an exclusive right of inheritance belonging to the eldest son

pri·mor·di·al \prī-ˈmòr-dē-əl\ *adj* : first created or developed : existing in its original state : PRIMEVAL

primp \ˈprimp\ *vb* : to dress in a careful or finicky manner

prim·rose \ˈprim-ˌrōz\ *n* : any of a genus of perennial herbs with large leaves arranged at the base of the stem and clusters of showy flowers

prin *abbr* **1** principal **2** principle

prince \ˈprins\ *n* [ME, fr. AF, fr. L *princeps* leader, initiator, fr. *primus* first + *capere* to take] **1** : MONARCH, KING **2** : a male member of a royal family; *esp* : a son of the monarch **3** : a person of high standing (as in a class) — **prince·dom** \-dəm\ *n* — **prince·ly** *adj*

prince·ling \-liŋ\ *n* : a petty prince

prin·cess \ˈprin-səs, -ˌses\ *n* **1** : a female member of a royal family **2** : the consort of a prince

¹**prin·ci·pal** \ˈprin-sə-pəl\ *adj* : most important — **prin·ci·pal·ly** *adv*

²**principal** *n* **1** : a leading person (as in a play) **2** : the chief officer of an educational institution **3** : the person from whom an agent's authority derives **4** : a capital sum earning interest or used as a fund

prin·ci·pal·i·ty \ˌprin-sə-ˈpa-lə-tē\ *n, pl* **-ties** : the position, territory, or jurisdiction of a prince

principal parts *n pl* : the inflected forms of a verb

prin·ci·ple \ˈprin-sə-pəl\ *n* **1** : a general or fundamental law, doctrine, or assumption **2** : a rule or code of conduct; *also* : devotion to such a code **3** : the laws or facts of nature underlying the working of an artificial device **4** : a primary source : ORIGIN; *also* : an underlying faculty or endowment **5** : the active part (as of a drug)

prin·ci·pled \-pəld\ *adj* : exhibiting, based on, or characterized by principle ⟨high-*principled*⟩

prink \ˈpriŋk\ *vb* : PRIMP

¹**print** \ˈprint\ *n* [ME *prente*, fr. AF, fr. *preint, prient*, pp. of *priendre* to press, fr. L. *premere*] **1** : a mark made by pressure **2** : something stamped with an impression **3** : printed state or form **4** : printed matter **5** : a copy made by printing **6** : cloth with a pattern applied by printing

²**print** *vb* **1** : to stamp (as a mark) in or on something **2** : to produce impressions of (as from type) **3** : to write in letters like those of printer's type **4** : to make (a positive picture) from a photographic negative

print·able \ˈprin-tə-bəl\ *adj* **1** : capable of being printed or of being printed from **2** : worthy or fit to be published

print·er \ˈprin-tər\ *n* : one that prints; *esp* : a device that produces printout

print·ing *n* **1** : reproduction in printed form **2** : the art, practice, or business of a printer **3** : IMPRESSION 5

printing press *n* : a machine that produces printed copies

print·out \ˈprint-ˌaùt\ *n* : a printed output produced by a computer — **print out** *vb*

¹**pri·or** \ˈpr(ī)-ər\ *n* : the superior ranking next to the abbot or abbess of a religious house

²**prior** *adj* **1** : earlier in time or order **2** : taking precedence logically or in importance — **pri·or·i·ty** \prī-ˈòr-ə-tē\ *n*

pri·or·ess \ˈprī-ə-rəs\ *n* : a nun corresponding in rank to a prior

pri·or·i·tize \prī-ˈòr-ə-ˌtīz, ˈprī-ə-rə-ˌtīz\ *vb* **-tized; -tiz·ing** : to list or rate in order of priority

prior to *prep* : in advance of : BEFORE

pri·o·ry \ˈprī-ə-rē\ *n, pl* **-ries** : a religious house under a prior or prioress

prise *chiefly Brit var of* ⁵PRIZE

prism \ˈpri-zəm\ *n* [LL *prisma*, fr. Gk, lit., something sawed, fr. *priein* to saw] **1** : a solid whose sides are parallelograms and whose bases are parallel and alike in shape and size **2** : a usu. 3-sided transparent object that refracts light so that it breaks up into rainbow colors — **pris·mat·ic** \priz-ˈma-tik\ *adj*

pris·on \ˈpri-zⁿn\ *n* : a place or state of confinement esp. for criminals

pris·on·er \ˈpri-zⁿn-ər\ *n* : a person deprived of liberty; *esp* : one on trial or in prison

prisoner of war : a person captured in war

pris·sy \ˈpri-sē\ *adj* **pris·si·er; -est** : being overly prim and precise : PRIGGISH — **pris·si·ness** \-sē-nəs\ *n*

pris·tine \ˈpris-ˌtēn, pri-ˈstēn\ *adj* **1** : PRIMITIVE **2** : having the purity of its original state : UNSPOILED

prith·ee \'pri-ᵗẖē\ *interj, archaic* — used to express a wish or request

pri·va·cy \'prī-və-sē\ *n, pl* **-cies** 1 : the quality or state of being apart from others 2 : SECRECY

¹**pri·vate** \'prī-vət\ *adj* 1 : belonging to or intended for a particular individual or group ⟨∼ property⟩ 2 : restricted to the individual : PERSONAL ⟨∼ opinion⟩ 3 : carried on by the individual independently ⟨∼ study⟩ 4 : not holding public office ⟨a ∼ citizen⟩ 5 : withdrawn from company or observation ⟨a ∼ place⟩ 6 : not known publicly ⟨∼ dealings⟩ — **pri·vate·ly** *adv*

²**private** *n* : an enlisted man of the lowest rank in the marine corps or of one of the two lowest ranks in the army — **in private** : not openly or in public

pri·va·teer \ˌprī-və-'tir\ *n* : an armed private ship licensed to attack enemy shipping; *also* : a sailor on such a ship

private first class *n* : an enlisted man ranking next below a corporal in the army and next below a lance corporal in the marine corps

pri·va·tion \prī-'vā-shən\ *n* 1 : DEPRIVATION 1 2 : the state of being deprived; *esp* : lack of what is needed for existence

priv·et \'pri-vət\ *n* : a nearly evergreen shrub related to the olive and widely used for hedges

privet: branch and hedge

¹**priv·i·lege** \'priv-lij, 'pri-və-\ *n* [ME, fr. AF, fr. L *privilegium* law for or against a private person, fr. *privus* private + *leg-, lex* law] : a right or immunity granted as an advantage or favor esp. to some and not others

²**privilege** *vb* **-leged; -leg·ing** 1 : to grant a privilege to 2 : to accord a higher value to : FAVOR

privileged *adj* 1 : having or enjoying one or more privileges ⟨∼ classes⟩ 2 : not subject to disclosure in a court of law ⟨a ∼ communication⟩

¹**privy** \'pri-vē\ *adj* 1 : PERSONAL, PRIVATE 2 : SECRET 3 : admitted as one sharing in a secret ⟨∼ to the conspiracy⟩ — **priv·i·ly** \'pri-və-lē\ *adv*

²**privy** *n, pl* **priv·ies** : TOILET; *esp* : OUTHOUSE

¹**prize** \'prīz\ *n* 1 : something offered or striven for in competition or in contests of chance 2 : something exceptionally desirable

²**prize** *adj* 1 : awarded or worthy of a prize ⟨a ∼ essay⟩; *also* : awarded as a prize ⟨a ∼ medal⟩ 2 : OUTSTANDING

³**prize** *vb* **prized; priz·ing** : to value highly : ESTEEM ⟨a *prized* possession⟩

⁴**prize** *n* : property (as a ship) lawfully captured in time of war

⁵**prize** *vb* **prized; priz·ing** : PRY

prize·fight \'prīz-ˌfīt\ *n* : a professional boxing match — **prize·fight·er** *n* — **prize·fight·ing** *n*

prize·win·ner \-ˌwi-nər\ *n* : a winner of a prize — **prize·win·ning** *adj*

¹**pro** \'prō\ *n, pl* **pros** : a favorable argument, person, or position

²**pro** *adv* : in favor : FOR

³**pro** *n or adj* : PROFESSIONAL

PRO *abbr* public relations officer

pro·ac·tive \prō-'ak-tiv\ *adj* : acting in anticipation of future problems or needs — **pro·ac·tive·ly** *adv*

pro–am \'prō-'am\ *adj* : involving professionals competing alongside or against amateurs ⟨a ∼ tournament⟩ — **pro–am** *n*

prob *abbr* 1 probable; probably 2 problem

prob·a·bil·i·ty \ˌprä-bə-'bi-lə-tē\ *n, pl* **-ties** 1 : the quality or state of being probable 2 : something probable 3 : a measure of how often a particular event will occur if something (as tossing a coin) is done repeatedly which results in any of a number of possible events

prob·a·ble \'prä-bə-bəl\ *adj* 1 : apparently or presumably true ⟨a ∼ hypothesis⟩ 2 : likely to be or become true or real ⟨a ∼ result⟩ — **prob·a·bly** \-bə-blē\ *adv*

¹**pro·bate** \'prō-ˌbāt\ *n* : the judicial determination of the validity of a will

²**pro·bate** *vb* **pro·bat·ed; pro·bat·ing** : to establish (a will) by probate as genuine and valid

pro·ba·tion \prō-'bā-shən\ *n* 1 : subjection of an individual to a period of testing and trial to ascertain fitness (as for a job) 2 : the action of giving a convicted offender freedom during good behavior under the supervision of a probation officer — **pro·ba·tion·ary** \-shə-ˌner-ē\ *adj*

pro·ba·tion·er \-shə-nər\ *n* 1 : a person (as a newly admitted student nurse) whose fitness is being tested during a trial period 2 : a convicted offender on probation

pro·ba·tive \'prō-bə-tiv\ *adj* 1 : serving to test or try 2 : serving to prove

¹**probe** \'prōb\ *n* 1 : a slender instrument for examining a cavity (as a wound) 2 : an information-gathering device sent into outer space 3 : a penetrating investigation ◆ *Synonyms* INQUIRY, INQUEST, RESEARCH, INQUISITION

²**probe** *vb* **probed; prob·ing** 1 : to examine with a probe 2 : to investigate thoroughly

pro·bi·ty \'prō-bə-tē\ *n* : UPRIGHTNESS, HONESTY

prob·lem \'prä-bləm\ *n* 1 : a question raised for consideration or solution 2 : an intricate unsettled question 3 : a source of perplexity or vexation — **problem** *adj*

prob·lem·at·ic \ˌprä-blə-'ma-tik\ *also* **prob·lem·at·i·cal** \-ti-kəl\ *adj* 1 : difficult to solve or decide : PUZZLING 2 : DUBIOUS, QUESTIONABLE

pro·bos·cis \prə-'bä-səs, -'bäs-kəs\ *n, pl* **-bos·cis·es** *also* **-bos·ci·des** \-'bä-sə-ˌdēz\ [L, fr. Gk *proboskis*, fr. *pro-* before + *boskein* to feed] : a long flexible snout (as the trunk of an elephant)

proc *abbr* proceedings

pro·caine \'prō-ˌkān\ *n* : a drug used esp. as a local anesthetic

pro·ce·dure \prə-'sē-jər\ *n* 1 : a particular way of doing something ⟨democratic ∼⟩ 2 : a series of steps followed in a regular order ⟨a surgical ∼⟩ — **pro·ce·dur·al** \-'sē-jə-rəl\ *adj*

pro·ceed \prō-'sēd\ *vb* 1 : to come forth : ISSUE 2 : to go on in an orderly way; *also* : CONTINUE 3 : to begin and carry on an action 4 : to take legal action 5 : to go forward : ADVANCE

pro·ceed·ing *n* 1 : PROCEDURE 2 *pl* : DOINGS 3 *pl* : legal action 4 : TRANSACTION 5 *pl* : an official record of things said or done

pro·ceeds \'prō-ˌsēdz\ *n pl* : the total amount or the profit arising from a business deal : RETURN

¹**pro·cess** \'prä-ˌses, 'prō-\ *n, pl* **pro·cess·es** \-ˌse-səz, -sə-səz, -sə-ˌsēz\ 1 : PROGRESS, ADVANCE 2 : something going on : PROCEEDING 3 : a natural phenomenon marked by gradual changes that lead toward a particular result ⟨the ∼ of growth⟩ 4 : a series of actions or operations directed toward a particular result ⟨a manufacturing ∼⟩ 5 : legal action 6 : a mandate issued by a court; *esp* : SUMMONS 7 : a projecting part of an organism or organic structure

²**process** *vb* : to subject to a special process

pro·ces·sion \prə-'se-shən\ *n* : a group of individuals moving along in an orderly often ceremonial way

pro·ces·sion·al \-'se-shə-nəl\ *n* 1 : music for a procession 2 : a ceremonial procession

pro·ces·sor \'prä-ˌse-sər, 'prō-\ *n* 1 : one that processes 2 : CPU

pro–choice \ˌprō-'chois\ *adj* : favoring the legalization of abortion

pro·claim \prō-'klām\ *vb* : to make known publicly : DECLARE

proc·la·ma·tion \ˌprä-klə-'mā-shən\ *n* : an official public announcement

pro·cliv·i·ty \prō-'kli-və-tē\ *n, pl* **-ties** : an inherent inclination esp. toward something objectionable

pro·con·sul \-'kän-səl\ *n* 1 : a governor or military commander of an ancient Roman province 2 : an administrator in a modern colony or occupied area — **pro·con·su·lar** \-sə-lər\ *adj*

pro·cras·ti·nate \prə-'kras-tə-ˌnāt, prō-\ *vb* **-nat·ed; -nat·ing** [L *procrastinare*, fr. *pro-* forward + *crastinus* of tomorrow, fr. *cras* tomorrow] : to put off usu. habitually doing something that should be done ♦ *Synonyms* DAWDLE, DELAY — **pro·cras·ti·na·tion** \-ˌkras-tə-'nā-shən\ *n* — **pro·cras·ti·na·tor** \-'kras-tə-ˌnā-tər\ *n*

pro·cre·ate \'prō-krē-ˌāt\ *vb* **-at·ed; -at·ing** : to beget or bring forth offspring ♦ *Synonyms* REPRODUCE, BREED, GENERATE, PROPAGATE — **pro·cre·ation** \ˌprō-krē-'ā-shən\ *n* — **pro·cre·ative** \'prō-krē-ˌā-tiv\ *adj* — **pro·cre·ator** \-ˌā-tər\ *n*

pro·crus·te·an \prə-'krəs-tē-ən\ *adj, often cap* [fr. *Procrustes*, villain of Greek mythology who made victims fit his bed by stretching them or cutting off their legs] : marked by arbitrary often ruthless disregard of individual differences or special circumstances

proc·tor \'präk-tər\ *n* : one appointed to supervise students (as at an examination) — **proctor** *vb* — **proc·to·ri·al** \präk-'tȯr-ē-əl\ *adj*

proc·u·ra·tor \'prä-kyə-ˌrā-tər\ *n* : a Roman provincial administrator

pro·cure \prə-'kyu̇r\ *vb* **pro·cured; pro·cur·ing** **1** : to get possession of : OBTAIN **2** : to make women available for promiscuous sexual intercourse **3** : ACHIEVE ♦ *Synonyms* SECURE, ACQUIRE, GAIN, WIN, EARN — **pro·cur·able** \-'kyu̇r-ə-bəl\ *adj* — **pro·cure·ment** *n* — **pro·cur·er** *n*

¹prod \'präd\ *vb* **prod·ded; prod·ding** **1** : to thrust a pointed instrument into : GOAD **2** : INCITE, STIR — **prod** *n*

²prod *abbr* product; production

prod·i·gal \'prä-di-gəl\ *adj* **1** : recklessly extravagant; *also* : LUXURIANT **2** : WASTEFUL, LAVISH ♦ *Synonyms* PROFUSE, LUSH, OPULENT — **prodigal** *n* — **prod·i·gal·i·ty** \ˌprä-də-'ga-lə-tē\ *n*

pro·di·gious \prə-'di-jəs\ *adj* **1** : exciting wonder **2** : extraordinary in size or degree : ENORMOUS ♦ *Synonyms* MONSTROUS, TREMENDOUS, STUPENDOUS, MONUMENTAL — **pro·di·gious·ly** *adv*

prod·i·gy \'prä-də-jē\ *n, pl* **-gies** **1** : something extraordinary : WONDER **2** : a highly talented child

¹pro·duce \prə-'düs, -'dyüs\ *vb* **pro·duced; pro·duc·ing** **1** : to present to view : EXHIBIT **2** : to give birth or rise to : YIELD **3** : EXTEND, PROLONG **4** : to give being or form to : BRING ABOUT, MAKE; *esp* : MANUFACTURE **5** : to sponsor or oversee the making of **6** : to cause to accrue ⟨~ a profit⟩ — **pro·duc·er** *n*

²pro·duce \'prä-(ˌ)düs, 'prō- *also* -(ˌ)dyüs\ *n* : PRODUCT 2; *also* : agricultural products and esp. fresh fruits and vegetables

prod·uct \'prä-(ˌ)dəkt\ *n* **1** : the number resulting from multiplication **2** : something produced

pro·duc·tion \prə-'dək-shən\ *n* **1** : something produced : PRODUCT **2** : the act or process of producing — **pro·duc·tive** \-'dək-tiv\ *adj* — **pro·duc·tive·ness** *n* — **pro·duc·tiv·i·ty** \(ˌ)prō-ˌdək-'ti-və-tē, ˌprä-(ˌ)dək-\ *n*

product placement *n* : the inclusion of a product in a television program or film as a means of advertising

pro·em \'prō-ˌem\ *n* **1** : preliminary comment : PREFACE **2** : PRELUDE

¹prof \'präf\ *n* : PROFESSOR

²prof *abbr* professional

¹pro·fane \prō-'fān\ *vb* **pro·faned; pro·fan·ing** **1** : to treat (something sacred) with irreverence or contempt **2** : to debase by an unworthy use — **prof·a·na·tion** \ˌprä-fə-'nā-shən\ *n*

²profane *adj* [ME *prophane*, fr. MF, fr. L *profanus*, fr. *pro-* before + *fanum* temple] **1** : not concerned with religion : SECULAR **2** : not holy because unconsecrated, impure, or defiled **3** : serving to debase what is holy : IRREVERENT **4** : OBSCENE, VULGAR — **pro·fane·ly** *adv* — **pro·fane·ness** *n*

pro·fan·i·ty \prō-'fa-nə-tē\ *n, pl* **-ties** **1** : the quality or state of being profane **2** : the use of profane language **3** : profane language

pro·fess \prə-'fes\ *vb* **1** : to declare or admit openly : AFFIRM **2** : to declare in words only : PRETEND **3** : to confess one's faith in **4** : to practice or claim to be versed in (a calling or occupation) — **pro·fess·ed·ly** \-'fe-səd-lē\ *adv*

pro·fes·sion \prə-'fe-shən\ *n* **1** : an open declaration or avowal of a belief or opinion **2** : a calling requiring specialized knowledge and often long academic preparation **3** : the whole body of persons engaged in a calling

¹pro·fes·sion·al \prə-'fe-shə-nəl\ *adj* **1** : of, relating to, or characteristic of a profession **2** : engaged in one of the professions **3** : participating for gain in an activity often engaged in by amateurs — **pro·fes·sion·al·ly** *adv*

²professional *n* : one that engages in an activity professionally

pro·fes·sion·al·ism \-nə-ˌli-zəm\ *n* **1** : the conduct, aims, or qualities that characterize or mark a profession or a professional person **2** : the following of a profession (as athletics) for gain or livelihood

pro·fes·sion·al·ize \-nə-ˌlīz\ *vb* **-ized; -iz·ing** : to give a professional nature to

pro·fes·sor \prə-'fe-sər\ *n* : a teacher at a university or college; *esp* : a faculty member of the highest academic rank — **pro·fes·so·ri·al** \ˌprō-fə-'sȯr-ē-əl, ˌprä-\ *adj* — **pro·fes·sor·ship** *n*

prof·fer \'prä-fər\ *vb* **prof·fered; prof·fer·ing** : to present for acceptance : OFFER — **proffer** *n*

pro·fi·cient \prə-'fi-shənt\ *adj* : well advanced in an art, occupation, or branch of knowledge ♦ *Synonyms* ADEPT, SKILLFUL, EXPERT, MASTERFUL, MASTERLY — **pro·fi·cien·cy** \-shən-sē\ *n* — **proficient** *n* — **pro·fi·cient·ly** *adv*

¹pro·file \'prō-ˌfī(-ə)l\ *n* [It *profilo*, fr. *profilare* to draw in outline, fr. *pro-* forward (fr. L) + *filare* to spin, fr. LL, fr. L *filum* thread] **1** : a representation of something in outline; *esp* : a human head seen in side view **2** : a concise biographical sketch **3** : degree or level of public exposure ⟨keep a low ~⟩

²profile *vb* **pro·filed; pro·fil·ing** : to write or draw a profile of

profiling *n* : the act of suspecting or targeting a person solely on the basis of observed characteristics or behavior ⟨racial ~⟩

¹prof·it \'prä-fət\ *n* **1** : a valuable return : GAIN **2** : the excess of the selling price of goods over their cost — **prof·it·less** *adj*

²profit *vb* **1** : to be of use : BENEFIT **2** : to derive benefit : GAIN — **prof·it·able** \'prä-fə-tə-bəl\ *adj* — **prof·it·ably** \-blē\ *adv*

prof·i·teer \ˌprä-fə-'tir\ *n* : one who makes what is considered an unreasonable profit — **profiteer** *vb*

prof·li·gate \'prä-fli-gət, -flə-ˌgāt\ *adj* **1** : completely given up to dissipation and licentiousness **2** : wildly extravagant — **prof·li·ga·cy** \-gə-sē\ *n* — **profligate** *n* — **prof·li·gate·ly** *adv*

pro for·ma \(ˌ)prō-'fȯr-mə\ *adj* : done or existing as a matter of form

pro·found \prə-'fau̇nd, prō-\ *adj* **1** : marked by intellectual depth or insight ⟨a ~ thought⟩ **2** : coming from or reaching to a depth ⟨a ~ sigh⟩ **3** : deeply felt : INTENSE ⟨~ sympathy⟩ — **pro·found·ly** *adv* — **pro·fun·di·ty** \-'fən-də-tē\ *n*

pro·fuse \prə-'fyüs, prō-\ *adj* : pouring forth liberally : ABUNDANT ⟨~ bleeding⟩ ♦ *Synonyms* LAVISH, PRODIGAL, LUXURIANT, EXUBERANT — **pro·fuse·ly** *adv* — **pro·fu·sion** \-'fyü-zhən\ *n*

prog *abbr* program

pro·gen·i·tor \prō-'je-nə-tər\ *n* **1** : a direct ancestor : FOREFATHER **2** : ORIGINATOR, PRECURSOR

prog·e·ny \'prä-jə-nē\ *n, pl* **-nies** : OFFSPRING, CHILDREN, DESCENDANTS

pro·ges·ter·one \prō-'jes-tə-ˌrōn\ *n* : a female hormone that causes the uterus to undergo changes so as to provide a suitable environment for a fertilized egg

prog·na·thous \'präg-nə-thəs\ *adj* : having the lower jaw projecting beyond the upper part of the face

prog·no·sis \präg-'nō-səs\ *n, pl* **-no·ses** \-ˌsēz\ **1** : the prospect of recovery from disease **2** : FORECAST

¹prog·nos·tic \präg-'näs-tik\ *n* **1** : PORTENT **2** : PROPHECY

²prognostic *adj* : of, relating to, or serving as ground for prognostication or a prognosis

prog·nos·ti·cate \präg-'näs-tə-ˌkāt\ *vb* **-cat·ed; -cat·ing** : to foretell from signs or symptoms — **prog·nos·ti·ca·tion** \-ˌnäs-tə-'kā-shən\ *n* — **prog·nos·ti·ca·tor** \-'näs-tə-ˌkā-tər\ *n*

¹pro·gram \'prō-ˌgram, -grəm\ *n* [F *programme* agenda, public notice, fr. Gk *programma*, fr. *prographein* to write in advance, fr. *pro-* before + *graphein* to write] **1** : a brief outline of the order to be pursued or the subjects included (as in a public entertainment); *also* : PERFORMANCE **2** : a plan of procedure esp. toward a goal **3** : coded instructions for a computer — **pro·gram·mat·ic** \ˌprō-grə-'ma-tik\ *adj*

²program *also* **programme** *vb* **-grammed** *or* **-gramed**; **-gram·ming** *or* **-gram·ing** **1** : to arrange or furnish a program of or for **2** : to enter in a program **3** : to provide (as a computer) with a program — **pro·gram·ma·bil·i·ty** \(ˌ)prō-ˌgra-mə-'bi-lə-tē\ *n* — **pro·gram·ma·ble** \'prō-ˌgra-mə-bəl\ *adj* — **pro·gram·mer** *also* **pro·gram·er** \'prō-ˌgra-mər, -grə-\ *n*

programme *chiefly Brit var of* PROGRAM

programmed instruction *n* : instruction through information given in small steps with each requiring a correct response by the learner before going on to the next step

pro·gram·ming *also* **pro·gram·ing** *n* **1** : the planning, scheduling, or performing of a program **2** : the process of instructing or learning by means of an instruction program **3** : the process of preparing an instruction program

¹prog·ress \'prä-grəs, -ˌgres\ *n* **1** : a forward movement : ADVANCE **2** : a gradual betterment

²pro·gress \prə-'gres\ *vb* **1** : to move forward : PROCEED **2** : to develop to a more advanced stage : IMPROVE

pro·gres·sion \prə-'gre-shən\ *n* **1** : an act of progressing : ADVANCE **2** : a continuous and connected series

¹pro·gres·sive \prə-'gre-siv\ *adj* **1** : of, relating to, or characterized by progress ⟨a ~ city⟩ **2** : moving forward or onward : ADVANCING **3** : increasing in extent or severity ⟨a ~ disease⟩ **4** *often cap* : of or relating to political Progressives **5** : of, relating to, or constituting a verb form that expresses action in progress at the time of speaking or a time spoken of — **pro·gres·sive·ly** *adv*

²progressive *n* **1** : one that is progressive **2** : a person believing in moderate political change and social improvement by government action; *esp, cap* : a member of a Progressive Party in the U.S.

pro·hib·it \prō-'hi-bət\ *vb* **1** : to forbid by authority **2** : to prevent from doing something

pro·hi·bi·tion \ˌprō-ə-'bi-shən\ *n* **1** : the act of prohibiting **2** : the forbidding by law of the sale or manufacture of alcoholic beverages — **pro·hi·bi·tion·ist** \-'bi-shə-nist\ *n* — **pro·hib·i·tive** \prō-'hi-bə-tiv\ *adj* — **pro·hib·i·tive·ly** *adv* — **pro·hib·i·to·ry** \-'hi-bə-ˌtōr-ē\ *adj*

¹proj·ect \'prä-ˌjekt, -jikt\ *n* **1** : a specific plan or design : SCHEME **2** : a planned undertaking ⟨a research ~⟩

²pro·ject \prə-'jekt\ *vb* **1** : to devise in the mind : DESIGN **2** : to throw forward **3** : PROTRUDE **4** : to cause (light or shadow) to fall into space or (an image) to fall on a surface ⟨~ a beam of light⟩ **5** : to attribute (a thought, feeling, or personal characteristic) to a person, group, or object **6** : to display outwardly — **pro·jec·tion** \-'jek-shən\ *n*

pro·jec·tile \prə-'jek-t²l, -'jek-ˌtī(-ə)l\ *n* **1** : a body hurled or projected by external force; *esp* : a missile for a firearm **2** : a self-propelling weapon

pro·jec·tion·ist \prə-'jek-shə-nist\ *n* : one that operates a motion-picture projector or television equipment

pro·jec·tor \-'jek-tər\ *n* : one that projects; *esp* : a device for projecting pictures on a screen

pro·lapse \prō-'laps, 'prō-ˌ\ *n* : the falling down or slipping of a body part from its usual position

pro·le·gom·e·non \ˌprō-li-'gä-mə-ˌnän, -nən\ *n, pl* **-e·na** \-nə\ : prefatory remarks

pro·le·tar·i·an \ˌprō-lə-'ter-ē-ən\ *n* [L *proletarius* belonging to the lowest class of citizens, fr. *proles* progeny, fr. *pro-* forth + *-oles* (akin to *alere* to nourish)] : a member of the proletariat — **proletarian** *adj*

pro·le·tar·i·at \-ē-ət\ *n* : the laboring class; *esp* : industrial workers who sell their labor to live

pro–life \(ˌ)prō-'līf\ *n* : ANTIABORTION

pro·lif·er·ate \prə-'li-fə-ˌrāt\ *vb* **-at·ed; -at·ing** : to grow or increase by rapid production of new units (as cells, offspring, or nuclear weapons) — **pro·lif·er·a·tion** \-ˌli-fə-'rā-shən\ *n*

pro·lif·ic \prə-'li-fik\ *adj* **1** : producing young or fruit

abundantly **2** : marked by abundant inventiveness or productivity ⟨a ~ writer⟩ — **pro·lif·i·cal·ly** \-fi-k(ə-)lē\ *adv*

pro·lix \prō-'liks, 'prō-ˌliks\ *adj* : VERBOSE ✦ **Synonyms** WORDY, DIFFUSE, REDUNDANT — **pro·lix·i·ty** \prō-'lik-sə-tē\ *n*

pro·logue *also* **pro·log** \'prō-ˌlóg, -ˌläg\ *n* : PREFACE ⟨~ of a play⟩

pro·long \prə-'lóŋ\ *vb* **1** : to lengthen in time : CONTINUE ⟨~ a meeting⟩ **2** : to lengthen in extent or range ✦ **Synonyms** PROTRACT, EXTEND, ELONGATE, STRETCH — **pro·lon·ga·tion** \ˌprō-ˌlóŋ-'gā-shən\ *n*

prom \'präm\ *n* : a formal dance given by a high school or college class

¹prom·e·nade \ˌprä-mə-'nād, -'näd\ *vb* **-nad·ed; -nad·ing** **1** : to take a promenade **2** : to walk about in or on

²promenade *n* [F, fr. *promener* to take for a walk, fr. MF, alter. of OF *pourmener*, fr. *pour-* completely (fr. L *pro-*) + *mener* to lead, fr. LL *minare* to drive, fr. L *minari* to threaten] **1** : a place for strolling **2** : a leisurely walk for pleasure or display **3** : an opening grand march at a formal ball

pro·me·thi·um \prə-'mē-thē-əm\ *n* : a metallic chemical element obtained from uranium or neodymium

prom·i·nence \'prä-mə-nəns\ *n* **1** : something prominent **2** : the quality, state, or fact of being prominent or conspicuous **3** : a mass of cloudlike gas that arises from the sun's chromosphere

prom·i·nent \-nənt\ *adj* **1** : jutting out : PROJECTING **2** : readily noticeable : CONSPICUOUS **3** : DISTINGUISHED, EMINENT ✦ **Synonyms** REMARKABLE, OUTSTANDING, STRIKING, SALIENT — **prom·i·nent·ly** *adv*

pro·mis·cu·ous \prə-'mis-kyə-wəs\ *adj* **1** : consisting of various sorts and kinds : MIXED **2** : not restricted to one class or person **3** : having a number of sexual partners ✦ **Synonyms** MISCELLANEOUS, ASSORTED, HETEROGENEOUS, MOTLEY, VARIED — **pro·mis·cu·i·ty** \ˌprä-mis-'kyü-ə-tē, ˌprō-ˌmis-\ *n* — **pro·mis·cu·ous·ly** *adv* — **pro·mis·cu·ous·ness** *n*

¹prom·ise \'prä-məs\ *n* **1** : a pledge to do or not to do something specified **2** : ground for expectation of success or improvement **3** : something promised

²promise *vb* **prom·ised; prom·is·ing** **1** : to engage to do, bring about, or provide ⟨~ help⟩ **2** : to suggest beforehand ⟨dark clouds ~ rain⟩ **3** : to give ground for expectation ⟨it ~s to be a good game⟩

promising *adj* : likely to succeed or yield good results ⟨a ~ new medicine⟩ — **prom·is·ing·ly** *adv*

prom·is·so·ry \'prä-mə-ˌsór-ē\ *adj* : containing a promise

prom·on·to·ry \'prä-mən-ˌtór-ē\ *n, pl* **-ries** : a point of land jutting into the sea : HEADLAND

pro·mote \prə-'mōt\ *vb* **pro·mot·ed; pro·mot·ing** **1** : to advance in station, rank, or honor **2** : to contribute to the growth or prosperity of : FURTHER **3** : LAUNCH — **pro·mo·tion** \-'mō-shən\ *n* — **pro·mo·tion·al** \-shə-nəl\ *adj*

pro·mot·er \-'mō-tər\ *n* : one that promotes; *esp* : one that assumes the financial responsibilities of a sports event ⟨a boxing ~⟩

¹prompt \'prämpt\ *vb* **1** : INCITE **2** : to assist (one acting or reciting) by suggesting the next words **3** : INSPIRE, URGE — **prompt·er** *n*

²prompt *adj* **1** : being ready and quick to act; *also* : PUNCTUAL **2** : performed readily or immediately ⟨~ service⟩ — **prompt·ly** *adv* — **prompt·ness** *n*

prompt·book \-ˌbúk\ *n* : a copy of a play with directions for performance used by a theater prompter

promp·ti·tude \'prämp-tə-ˌtüd, -ˌtyüd\ *n* : the quality or habit of being prompt : PROMPTNESS

pro·mul·gate \'prä-məl-ˌgāt; prō-'məl-\ *vb* **-gat·ed; -gat·ing** : to make known or put into force by open declaration — **prom·ul·ga·tion** \ˌprä-məl-'gā-shən, ˌprō-(ˌ)məl-\ *n*

pron *abbr* **1** pronoun **2** pronounced **3** pronunciation

prone \'prōn\ *adj* **1** : having a tendency or inclination : DISPOSED **2** : lying face downward; *also* : lying flat or prostrate ✦ **Synonyms** SUBJECT, EXPOSED, OPEN, LIABLE, SUSCEPTIBLE — **prone·ness** *n*

prong \'próŋ\ *n* : one of the sharp points of a fork : TINE; *also* : a slender projecting part (as of an antler) — **pronged** \'próŋd\ *adj*

prong·horn \'pròŋ-ˌhòrn\ *n, pl* **pronghorn** *or* **pronghorns** : a swift horned ruminant mammal chiefly of grasslands of western No. America that resembles an antelope

pro·noun \'prō-ˌnaùn\ *n* : a word used as a substitute for a noun

pro·nounce \prə-'naùns\ *vb* **pro·nounced; pro·nounc·ing 1** : to utter officially or as an opinion ⟨∼ sentence⟩ **2** : to employ the organs of speech in order to produce ⟨∼ a word⟩; *esp* : to say or speak correctly ⟨she can't ∼ his name⟩ — **pro·nounce·able** *adj* — **pro·nun·ci·a·tion** \-ˌnən-sē-'ā-shən\ *n*

pro·nounced *adj* : strongly marked : DECIDED ⟨a ∼ dislike⟩

pro·nounce·ment \prə-'naùns-mənt\ *n* : a formal declaration of opinion; *also* : ANNOUNCEMENT

pron·to \'prän-ˌtō\ *adv* [Sp, fr. L *promptus* prompt] : QUICKLY

pro·nu·clear \'prō-'nü-klē-ər, -'nyü-\ *adj* : supporting the use of nuclear-powered electric generating stations

pro·nun·ci·a·men·to \prō-ˌnən-sē-ə-'men-tō\ *n, pl* **-tos** *or* **-toes** : PROCLAMATION, MANIFESTO

¹**proof** \'prüf\ *n* [ME *prof, prove,* alter. of *preve,* fr. AF *preove,* fr. LL *proba,* fr. L *probare* to test, prove, fr. *probus* good, honest] **1** : the evidence that compels acceptance by the mind of a truth or fact **2** : a process or operation that establishes validity or truth : TEST **3** : a trial impression (as from type) **4** : a trial print from a photographic negative **5** : alcoholic content (as of a beverage) indicated by a number that is twice the percent by volume of alcohol present ⟨whiskey of 90 ∼ is 45% alcohol⟩

²**proof** *adj* **1** : successful in resisting or repelling ⟨∼ against tampering⟩ ⟨water*proof*⟩ **2** : of standard strength or quality or alcoholic content

proof·read \-ˌrēd\ *vb* : to read and mark corrections in — **proof·read·er** *n*

¹**prop** \'präp\ *n* : something that props

²**prop** *vb* **propped; prop·ping 1** : to support by placing something under or against **2** : SUSTAIN, STRENGTHEN

³**prop** *n* : PROPERTY 4

⁴**prop** *n* : PROPELLER

⁵**prop** *abbr* **1** property **2** proposition **3** proprietor

pro·pa·gan·da \ˌprä-pə-'gan-də, ˌprō-\ *n* [NL, fr. *Congregatio de propaganda fide* Congregation for propagating the faith, organization established by Pope Gregory XV] : the spreading of ideas or information to further or damage a cause; *also* : ideas or allegations spread for such a purpose — **pro·pa·gan·dist** \-dist\ *n*

pro·pa·gan·dize \-ˌdīz\ *vb* **-dized; -diz·ing** : to subject to or carry on propaganda

prop·a·gate \'prä-pə-ˌgāt\ *vb* **-gat·ed; -gat·ing 1** : to reproduce or cause to reproduce biologically : MULTIPLY **2** : to cause to spread — **prop·a·ga·tion** \ˌprä-pə-'gā-shən\ *n*

pro·pane \'prō-ˌpān\ *n* : a heavy flammable gas found in petroleum and natural gas and used esp. as a fuel

pro·pel \prə-'pel\ *vb* **pro·pelled; pro·pel·ling** : to drive forward or onward ✦ *Synonyms* PUSH, SHOVE, THRUST

pro·pel·lant *also* **pro·pel·lent** \-'pe-lənt\ *n* : something (as a fuel) that propels — **propellant** *also* **propellent** *adj*

pro·pel·ler \prə-'pe-lər\ *n* : a device consisting of a hub fitted with blades that is used to propel a vehicle (as a motorboat or an airplane)

pro·pen·si·ty \prə-'pen-sə-tē\ *n, pl* **-ties** : an often intense natural inclination or preference

¹**prop·er** \'prä-pər\ *adj* **1** : referring to one individual only ⟨∼ noun⟩ **2** : belonging characteristically to a species or individual : PECULIAR **3** : very satisfactory : EXCELLENT **4** : strictly limited to a specified thing ⟨the city ∼⟩ **5** : CORRECT ⟨the ∼ way to proceed⟩ **6** : strictly decorous : GENTEEL **7** : marked by suitability or rightness ⟨∼ punishment⟩ ✦ *Synonyms* MEET, APPROPRIATE, FITTING, SEEMLY — **prop·er·ly** *adv*

²**proper** *n* : the parts of the Mass that vary according to the liturgical calendar

prop·er·tied \'prä-pər-tēd\ *adj* : owning property and esp. much property

prop·er·ty \'prä-pər-tē\ *n, pl* **-ties 1** : a quality peculiar to an individual or thing **2** : something owned; *esp* : a piece of real estate **3** : OWNERSHIP **4** : an article or object

used in a play or motion picture other than painted scenery and actor's costumes

proph·e·cy *also* **proph·e·sy** \'prä-fə-sē\ *n, pl* **-cies** *also* **-sies 1** : an inspired utterance of a prophet **2** : PREDICTION

proph·e·sy \-ˌsī\ *vb* **-sied; -sy·ing 1** : to speak or utter by divine inspiration **2** : PREDICT — **proph·e·si·er** *n*

proph·et \'prä-fət\ *n* [ME *prophete,* fr. AF, fr. L *propheta,* fr. Gk *prophētēs,* fr. *pro* for + *phanai* to speak] **1** : one who utters divinely inspired revelations **2** : one who foretells future events

proph·et·ess \'prä-fə-təs\ *n* : a woman who is a prophet

pro·phet·ic \prə-'fe-tik\ *or* **pro·phet·i·cal** \-ti-kəl\ *adj* : of, relating to, or characteristic of a prophet or prophecy — **pro·phet·i·cal·ly** \-ti-k(ə-)lē\ *adv*

Proph·ets \'prä-fəts\ *n pl* — see BIBLE table

¹**pro·phy·lac·tic** \ˌprō-fə-'lak-tik, ˌprä-\ *adj* **1** : preventing or guarding from the spread or occurrence of disease or infection **2** : PREVENTIVE

²**prophylactic** *n* : something prophylactic; *esp* : a device (as a condom) for preventing venereal infection or conception

pro·phy·lax·is \-'lak-səs\ *n, pl* **-lax·es** \-'lak-ˌsēz\ : measures designed to preserve health and prevent the spread of disease

pro·pin·qui·ty \prə-'piŋ-kwə-tē\ *n* **1** : KINSHIP **2** : nearness in place or time : PROXIMITY

pro·pi·ti·ate \prō-'pi-shē-ˌāt\ *vb* **-at·ed; -at·ing** : to gain or regain the favor of : APPEASE — **pro·pi·ti·a·tion** \-ˌpi-shē-'ā-shən\ *n* — **pro·pi·tia·to·ry** \-'pi-shē-ə-ˌtòr-ē\ *adj*

pro·pi·tious \prə-'pi-shəs\ *adj* **1** : favorably disposed ⟨∼ deities⟩ **2** : being of good omen ⟨∼ circumstances⟩

prop·man \'präp-ˌman\ *n* : one who is in charge of stage properties

pro·po·nent \prə-'pō-nənt\ *n* : one who argues in favor of something

¹**pro·por·tion** \prə-'pòr-shən\ *n* **1** : BALANCE, SYMMETRY **2** : SHARE, QUOTA **3** : the relation of one part to another or to the whole with respect to magnitude, quantity, or degree : RATIO **4** : SIZE, DEGREE — **in proportion** : PROPORTIONAL

²**proportion** *vb* **-tioned; -tion·ing 1** : to adjust (a part or thing) in size relative to other parts or things **2** : to make the parts of harmonious

pro·por·tion·al \prə-'pòr-shə-nəl\ *adj* : corresponding in size, degree, or intensity; *also* : having the same or a constant ratio — **pro·por·tion·al·ly** *adv*

pro·por·tion·ate \prə-'pòr-shə-nət\ *adj* : PROPORTIONAL — **pro·por·tion·ate·ly** *adv*

pro·pose \prə-'pōz\ *vb* **pro·posed; pro·pos·ing 1** : PLAN, INTEND ⟨∼s to buy a house⟩ **2** : to make an offer of marriage **3** : to offer for consideration : SUGGEST ⟨∼ a policy⟩ — **pro·pos·al** \-'pō-zəl\ *n* — **pro·pos·er** *n*

¹**prop·o·si·tion** \ˌprä-pə-'zi-shən\ *n* **1** : something proposed for consideration : PROPOSAL **2** : a request for sexual intercourse **3** : a statement of something to be discussed, proved, or explained **4** : SITUATION, AFFAIR ⟨a tough ∼⟩ — **prop·o·si·tion·al** \-'zi-shə-nəl\ *adj*

²**proposition** *vb* **-tioned; -tion·ing** : to make a proposal to; *esp* : to suggest sexual intercourse to

pro·pound \prə-'paùnd\ *vb* : to set forth for consideration ⟨∼ a doctrine⟩

pro·pri·e·tary \prə-'prī-ə-ˌter-ē\ *adj* **1** : of, relating to, or characteristic of a proprietor ⟨∼ rights⟩ **2** : made and sold by one with the sole right to do so ⟨∼ medicines⟩ ⟨∼ software⟩

pro·pri·e·tor \prə-'prī-ə-tər\ *n* : OWNER — **pro·pri·e·tor·ship** *n*

pro·pri·e·tress \-'prī-ə-trəs\ *n* : a woman who is a proprietor

pro·pri·e·ty \prə-'prī-ə-tē\ *n, pl* **-ties 1** : the standard of what is socially acceptable in conduct or speech **2** *pl* : the customs of polite society

props \'präps\ *n sing or pl* **1** *slang* : DUE 1 ⟨gave him his ∼⟩ **2** *slang* : RESPECT 2 ⟨earned the ∼ of his peers⟩ **3** *slang* : ACKNOWLEDGMENT ⟨deserves ∼ for the effort⟩

pro·pul·sion \prə-'pəl-shən\ *n* **1** : the action or process of propelling **2** : something that propels — **pro·pul·sive** \-siv\ *adj*

pro ra·ta \(ˌ)prō-'rä-tə, -'rä-\ *adv* : in proportion to the share of each : PROPORTIONATELY

pro·rate \(ˌ)prō-ˈrāt\ vb **pro·rat·ed; pro·rat·ing** : to divide, distribute, or assess proportionately

pro·rogue \prə-ˈrōg\ vb **pro·rogued; pro·rogu·ing** : to suspend or end a session of (a legislative body) — **pro·ro·ga·tion** \ˌprō-rō-ˈgā-shən\ n

pros pl of PRO

pro·sa·ic \prō-ˈzā-ik\ adj : lacking imagination or excitement : DULL

pro·sce·ni·um \prō-ˈsē-nē-əm\ n **1** : the part of a stage in front of the curtain **2** : the wall containing the arch that frames the stage

pro·scribe \prō-ˈskrīb\ vb **pro·scribed; pro·scrib·ing 1** : OUTLAW **2** : to condemn or forbid as harmful — **pro·scrip·tion** \-ˈskrip-shən\ n

prose \ˈprōz\ n [ME, fr. AF, fr. L prosa, fr. fem. of prorsus, prosus, straightforward, being in prose, alter. of proversus, pp. of provertere to turn forward] : the ordinary language people use in speaking or writing

pros·e·cute \ˈprä-si-ˌkyüt\ vb **-cut·ed; -cut·ing 1** : to follow to the end ⟨~ an investigation⟩ **2** : to seek legal punishment of ⟨~ a forger⟩ — **pros·e·cu·tion** \ˌprä-si-ˈkyü-shən\ n — **pros·e·cu·tor** \ˈprä-si-ˌkyü-tər\ n — **pros·e·cu·to·ri·al** \ˌprä-si-kyü-ˈtȯr-ē-əl\ adj

¹pros·e·lyte \ˈprä-sə-ˌlīt\ n : a new convert to a religion, belief, or party — **pros·e·ly·tism** \-ˌlī-ˌti-zəm\ n

²proselyte vb **-lyt·ed; -lyt·ing** : PROSELYTIZE

pros·e·ly·tise Brit var of PROSELYTIZE

pros·e·ly·tize \ˈprä-sə-lə-ˌtīz\ vb **-tized; -tiz·ing 1** : to induce someone to convert to one's faith **2** : to recruit someone to join one's party, institution, or cause

pros·o·dy \ˈprä-sə-dē, -zə-\ n, pl **-dies** : the study of versification and esp. of metrical structure — **pro·sod·ic** \prə-ˈsä-dik\ adj

¹pros·pect \ˈprä-ˌspekt\ n **1** : an extensive view; also : OUTLOOK **2** : the act of looking forward **3** : a mental vision of something to come **4** : something that is awaited or expected : POSSIBILITY **5** : a potential buyer or customer; also : a likely candidate (as for a job) — **pro·spec·tive** \prə-ˈspek-tiv, ˈprä-ˌspek-\ adj — **pro·spec·tive·ly** adv

²pros·pect \ˈprä-ˌspekt\ vb : to explore esp. for mineral deposits — **pros·pec·tor** \-ˌspek-tər, prä-ˈspek-\ n

pros·pec·tus \prə-ˈspek-təs\ n : a preliminary statement that describes an enterprise and is distributed to prospective buyers or participants

pros·per \ˈprä-spər\ vb **pros·pered; pros·per·ing** : SUCCEED; esp : to achieve economic success

pros·per·i·ty \prä-ˈsper-ə-tē\ n : thriving condition : SUCCESS; esp : economic well-being

pros·per·ous \ˈprä-spə-rəs\ adj **1** : FAVORABLE ⟨~ winds⟩ **2** : marked by success or economic well-being ⟨a ~ business⟩

pros·ta·glan·din \ˌprä-stə-ˈglan-dən\ n : any of various oxygenated unsaturated fatty acids of animals that perform a variety of hormonelike actions

pros·tate \ˈprä-ˌstāt\ n [NL prostata, fr. Gk prostatēs, fr. proïstanai to put in front] : PROSTATE GLAND — **pros·tat·ic** \prä-ˈsta-tik\ adj

prostate gland n : a glandular body about the base of the male urethra that produces a secretion which is a major part of the fluid ejaculated during an orgasm

pros·ta·ti·tis \ˌprä-stə-ˈtī-təs\ n : inflammation of the prostate gland

pros·the·sis \präs-ˈthē-səs, ˈpräs-thə-\ n, pl **-the·ses** \-ˌsēz\ : an artificial replacement for a missing body part — **pros·thet·ic** \präs-ˈthe-tik\ adj

pros·thet·ics \-ˈthe-tiks\ n pl : the surgical or dental specialty concerned with the design, construction, and fitting of prostheses

¹pros·ti·tute \ˈprä-stə-ˌtüt, -ˌtyüt\ vb **-tut·ed; -tut·ing 1** : to offer indiscriminately for sexual activity esp. for money **2** : to devote to corrupt or unworthy purposes — **pros·ti·tu·tion** \ˌprä-stə-ˈtü-shən, -ˈtyü-\ n

²prostitute n : one who engages in sexual activities for money

¹pros·trate \ˈprä-ˌstrāt\ adj **1** : stretched out with face on the ground in adoration or submission **2** : lying flat **3** : completely overcome ⟨~ with a cold⟩

²prostrate vb **pros·trat·ed; pros·trat·ing 1** : to throw or put into a prostrate position **2** : to reduce to a weak or powerless condition — **pros·tra·tion** \prä-ˈstrā-shən\ n

prosy \ˈprō-zē\ adj **pros·i·er; -est 1** : PROSAIC, ORDINARY **2** : TEDIOUS

Prot abbr Protestant

prot·ac·tin·i·um \ˌprō-tak-ˈti-nē-əm\ n : a metallic radioactive chemical element of relatively short life

pro·tag·o·nist \prō-ˈta-gə-nist\ n **1** : the principal character in a drama or story **2** : a leader or supporter of a cause

pro·te·an \ˈprō-tē-ən\ adj : able to assume different shapes or roles

pro·tect \prə-ˈtekt\ vb : to shield from injury : GUARD

pro·tec·tion \prə-ˈtek-shən\ n **1** : the act of protecting : the state of being protected **2** : one that protects ⟨wear a helmet as a ~⟩ **3** : the supervision or support of one that is smaller and weaker **4** : the freeing of producers from foreign competition in their home market by high duties on foreign competitive goods — **pro·tec·tive** \-ˈtek-tiv\ adj

pro·tec·tion·ist \-shə-nist\ n : an advocate of government economic protection for domestic producers through restrictions on foreign competitors — **pro·tec·tion·ism** \-shə-ˌni-zəm\ n

pro·tec·tor \prə-ˈtek-tər\ n **1** : one that protects : GUARDIAN **2** : a device used to prevent injury : GUARD **3** : REGENT 1

pro·tec·tor·ate \-tə-rat\ n **1** : government by a protector **2** : the relationship of superior authority assumed by one state over a dependent one; also : the dependent political unit in such a relationship

pro·té·gé \ˈprō-tə-ˌzhā\ n [F] : one who is protected, trained, or guided by an influential person

pro·tein \ˈprō-ˌtēn\ n [F protéine, fr. LGk prōteios primary, fr. Gk prōtos first] : any of various complex nitrogen-containing substances that consist of chains of amino acids, are present in all living cells, and are an essential part of the human diet

pro tem \prō-ˈtem\ adv : PRO TEMPORE

pro tem·po·re \prō-ˈtem-pə-rē\ adv [L] : for the time being

Pro·te·ro·zo·ic \ˌprä-tə-rə-ˈzō-ik, ˌprō-\ adj : of, relating to, or being the eon of geologic history between the Archean and the Phanerozoic — **Proterozoic** n

¹pro·test \ˈprō-ˌtest\ n **1** : the act of protesting; esp : an organized public demonstration of disapproval **2** : a complaint or objection against an idea, an act, or a course of action

²pro·test \prō-ˈtest\ vb **1** : to assert positively : make solemn declaration of ⟨~s his innocence⟩ **2** : to object strongly : make a protest against ⟨~ a ruling⟩ — **pro·tes·ta·tion** \ˌprä-təs-ˈtā-shən\ n — **pro·test·er** or **pro·tes·tor** \-tər\ n

Prot·es·tant \ˈprä-təs-tənt, 3 also prə-ˈtes-\ n **1** : a member or adherent of one of the Christian churches deriving from the Reformation **2** : a Christian not of a Catholic or Orthodox church **3** not cap : one who makes a protest — **Prot·es·tant·ism** \ˈprä-təs-tən-ˌti-zəm\ n

pro·tha·la·mi·on \ˌprō-thə-ˈlā-mē-ən\ or **pro·tha·la·mi·um** \-mē-əm\ n, pl **-mia** \-mē-ə\ : a song in celebration of a marriage

pro·to·col \ˈprō-tə-ˌkȯl\ n [MF prothocole, fr. ML protocollum, fr. LGk prōtokollon first sheet of a papyrus roll bearing data of manufacture, fr. Gk prōtos first + kollan to glue together, fr. kolla glue] **1** : an original draft or record **2** : a preliminary memorandum of diplomatic negotiation **3** : a code of diplomatic or military etiquette **4** : a set of conventions for formatting data in an electronic communications system

pro·ton \ˈprō-ˌtän\ n [Gk prōton, neut. of prōtos first] : a positively charged atomic particle present in all atomic nuclei — **pro·ton·ic** \-ˈtä-nik\ adj

pro·to·plasm \ˈprō-tə-ˌpla-zəm\ n : the complex colloidal largely protein substance of living plant and animal cells — **pro·to·plas·mic** \ˌprō-tə-ˈplaz-mik\ adj

pro·to·type \ˈprō-tə-ˌtīp\ n : an original model : ARCHETYPE

pro·to·zo·an \ˌprō-tə-ˈzō-ən\ n : any of a phylum or subkingdom of unicellular lower invertebrate animals that include some pathogenic parasites of humans and domestic animals — **protozoan** adj

pro·tract \prō-ˈtrakt\ vb : to prolong in time or space
♦ **Synonyms** EXTEND, LENGTHEN, ELONGATE, STRETCH

pro·trac·tor \-'trak-tər\ *n* : an instrument for drawing and measuring angles

protractor

pro·trude \prō-'trüd\ *vb* **pro·trud·ed; pro·trud·ing** : to stick out or cause to stick out : jut out — **pro·tru·sion** \-'trü-zhən\ *n*

pro·tu·ber·ance \prō-'tü-bə-rəns, -'tyü-\ *n* : something that protrudes

pro·tu·ber·ant \-rənt\ *adj* : extending beyond the surrounding surface in a bulge

proud \'praùd\ *adj* **1** : having or showing excessive self-esteem : HAUGHTY **2** : highly pleased : EXULTANT **3** : having proper self-respect ⟨too ∼ to beg⟩ **4** : GLORIOUS ⟨a ∼ occasion⟩ **5** : SPIRITED ⟨a ∼ steed⟩ ◆ **Synonyms** ARROGANT, INSOLENT, OVERBEARING, DISDAINFUL — **proud·ly** *adv*

prov *abbr* **1** province; provincial **2** provisional

Prov *abbr* Proverbs

prove \'prüv\ *vb* **proved; proved** *or* **prov·en** \'prü-vən\; **prov·ing 1** : to test by experiment or by a standard **2** : to establish the truth of by argument or evidence **3** : to show to be correct, valid, or genuine **4** : to turn out esp. after trial or test ⟨the car *proved* to be a good choice⟩ — **prov·able** \'prü-və-bəl\ *adj*

prov·e·nance \'prä-və-nəns\ *n* : ORIGIN, SOURCE

Pro·ven·çal \ˌprō-vän-'säl, ˌprä-vən-\ **1** : a native or inhabitant of Provence **2** : OCCITAN — **Provençal** *adj*

prov·en·der \'prä-vən-dər\ *n* **1** : dry food for domestic animals : FEED **2** : FOOD, VICTUALS

pro·ve·nience \prə-'vē-nyəns\ *n* : ORIGIN, SOURCE

prov·erb \'prä-ˌvərb\ *n* : a pithy popular saying : ADAGE

pro·ver·bi·al \prə-'vər-bē-əl\ *adj* **1** : of, relating to, or resembling a proverb **2** : commonly spoken of

Proverbs *n* — see BIBLE table

pro·vide \prə-'vīd\ *vb* **pro·vid·ed; pro·vid·ing** [ME, fr. L *providēre*, lit., to see ahead, fr. *pro-* forward + *vidēre* to see] **1** : to take measures beforehand ⟨∼ against inflation⟩ **2** : to make a proviso or stipulation **3** : to supply what is needed ⟨∼ for a family⟩ **4** : EQUIP **5** : to supply for use : YIELD — **pro·vid·er** *n*

pro·vid·ed *conj* : on condition that : IF

prov·i·dence \'prä-və-dəns\ *n* **1** *often cap* : divine guidance or care **2** *cap* : GOD **3** : the quality or state of being provident

prov·i·dent \-dənt\ *adj* **1** : making provision for the future : PRUDENT **2** : FRUGAL — **prov·i·dent·ly** *adv*

prov·i·den·tial \ˌprä-və-'den-chəl\ *adj* **1** : of, relating to, or determined by Providence **2** : OPPORTUNE, LUCKY

providing *conj* : PROVIDED

prov·ince \'prä-vəns\ *n* **1** : an administrative district or division of a country **2** *pl* : all of a country except the metropolises **3** : proper business or scope : SPHERE

pro·vin·cial \prə-'vin-chəl\ *adj* **1** : of or relating to a province **2** : limited in outlook : NARROW ⟨∼ ideas⟩ — **pro·vin·cial·ism** \-chə-ˌli-zəm\ *n*

proving ground *n* : a place for scientific experimentation or testing

¹pro·vi·sion \prə-'vi-zhən\ *n* **1** : the act or process of providing; *also* : a measure taken beforehand **2** : a stock of needed supplies; *esp* : a stock of food — usu. used in pl. **3** : PROVISO

²provision *vb* : to supply with provisions

pro·vi·sion·al \-'vi-zhə-nəl\ *adj* : provided for a temporary need : CONDITIONAL — **pro·vi·sion·al·ly** *adv*

pro·vi·so \prə-'vī-zō\ *n, pl* **-sos** *also* **-soes** [ME, fr. ML *proviso quod* provided that] : an article or clause that introduces a condition : STIPULATION

pro·vo·ca·teur \prō-ˌvä-kə-'tər\ *n* : one who provokes

prov·o·ca·tion \ˌprä-və-'kā-shən\ *n* **1** : the act of provoking **2** : something that provokes

pro·voc·a·tive \prə-'vä-kə-tiv\ *adj* : serving to provoke or excite

pro·voke \prə-'vōk\ *vb* **pro·voked; pro·vok·ing 1** : to incite to anger : INCENSE **2** : to call forth : EVOKE ⟨a remark that *provoked* laughter⟩ **3** : to stir up on purpose ⟨∼ an argument⟩ ◆ **Synonyms** IRRITATE, EXASPERATE, AGGRAVATE, INFLAME, RILE, PIQUE — **pro·vok·er** *n*

pro·vo·lo·ne \ˌprō-və-'lō-nē\ *n* : a usu. firm pliant often smoked Italian cheese

pro·vost \'prō-ˌvōst, 'prä-vəst\ *n* : a high official : DIGNITARY; *esp* : a high-ranking university administrative officer

pro·vost mar·shal \ˌprō-ˌvō-'mär-shəl\ *n* : an officer who supervises the military police of a command

prow \'praù\ *n* : the bow of a ship

prow·ess \'praù-əs\ *n* **1** : military valor and skill **2** : extraordinary ability

prowl \'praù(-ə)l\ *vb* : to roam about stealthily — **prowl** *n* — **prowl·er** *n*

prox·i·mal \'präk-sə-məl\ *adj* **1** : next to or nearest the point of attachment or origin; *esp* : located toward the center of the body **2** : of, relating to, or being the mesial and distal surfaces of a tooth — **prox·i·mal·ly** *adv*

prox·i·mate \'präk-sə-mət\ *adj* **1** : DIRECT ⟨the ∼ cause⟩ **2** : very near

prox·im·i·ty \präk-'si-mə-tē\ *n* : NEARNESS

prox·i·mo \'präk-sə-ˌmō\ *adj* [L *proximo mense* in the next month] : of or occurring in the next month after the present

proxy \'präk-sē\ *n, pl* **prox·ies** [ME *proxi, procucie,* alter. of *procuracie,* fr. AF, fr. ML *procuratia,* alter. of L *procuratio* appointment of another as an agent, fr. *procurare* to take care of] : the authority or power to act for another; *also* : a document giving such authorization — **proxy** *adj*

prude \'prüd\ *n* : a person who shows or affects extreme modesty — **prud·ery** \'prü-də-rē\ *n* — **prud·ish** *adj* — **prud·ish·ly** *adv*

pru·dent \'prü-d²nt\ *adj* **1** : shrewd in the management of practical affairs **2** : CAUTIOUS, DISCREET **3** : PROVIDENT, FRUGAL ◆ **Synonyms** JUDICIOUS, FORESIGHTED, SENSIBLE, SANE — **pru·dence** \-²ns\ *n* — **pru·den·tial** \prü-'den-chəl\ *adj* — **pru·dent·ly** *adv*

¹prune \'prün\ *n* : a dried plum

²prune *vb* **pruned; prun·ing** : to cut off unwanted parts (as of a tree)

pru·ri·ent \'prùr-ē-ənt\ *adj* : LASCIVIOUS; *also* : exciting to lasciviousness — **pru·ri·ence** \-ē-əns\ *n*

¹pry \'prī\ *vb* **pried; pry·ing** : to look closely or inquisitively; *esp* : SNOOP

²pry *vb* **pried; pry·ing 1** : to raise, move, or pull apart with a pry or lever **2** : to detach or open with difficulty

³pry *n* : a tool for prying

Ps *or* **Psa** *abbr* Psalms

PS *abbr* **1** [L *postscriptum*] postscript **2** public school

PSA *abbr* public service announcement

psalm \'säm, 'sälm\ *n, often cap* [ME, fr. OE *psealm,* fr. LL *psalmus,* fr. Gk *psalmos,* lit., twanging of a harp, fr. *psallein* to pluck, play a stringed instrument] : a sacred song or poem; *esp* : one of the hymns collected in the Book of Psalms — **psalm·ist** *n*

psalm·o·dy \'sä-mə-dē, 'säl-\ *n* : the singing of psalms in worship

Psalms *n* — see BIBLE table

Psal·ter \'sȯl-tər\ *n* : the Book of Psalms; *also* : a collection of the Psalms arranged for devotional use

pseud *abbr* pseudonym; pseudonymous

pseu·do \'sü-dō\ *adj* : SPURIOUS, SHAM

pseu·do·nym \'sü-də-ˌnim\ *n* : a fictitious name — **pseu·don·y·mous** \sü-'dä-nə-məs\ *adj*

pseu·do·sci·ence \ˌsü-dō-'sī-əns\ *n* : a system of theories, assumptions, and methods erroneously regarded as scientific — **pseu·do·sci·en·tif·ic** \-ˌsī-ən-'ti-fik\ *adj*

PSG *abbr* platoon sergeant

¹psi \'sī, 'psī\ *n* : the 23d letter of the Greek alphabet — Ψ or ψ

²psi *abbr* pounds per square inch

psit·ta·co·sis \ˌsi-tə-'kō-səs\ *n* : an infectious disease of birds marked by diarrhea and wasting and transmissible to humans

pso·ri·a·sis \sə-'rī-ə-səs\ *n* : a chronic skin disease characterized by red patches covered with white scales

PST *abbr* Pacific standard time

¹psych *or* **psyche** \'sīk\ *vb* **psyched; psych·ing** 1 : OUTWIT, OUTGUESS; *also* : to analyze beforehand 2 : INTIMIDATE; *also* : to prepare oneself psychologically ⟨get *psyched* up for the game⟩

²psych *abbr* psychology

psy·che \'sī-kē\ *n* : SOUL, PERSONALITY; *also* : MIND

psy·che·del·ic \ˌsī-kə-'de-lik\ *adj* 1 : of, relating to, or causing abnormal psychic effects ⟨~ drugs⟩ 2 : relating to the taking of psychedelic drugs ⟨~ experience⟩ 3 : imitating, suggestive of, or reproducing the effects of psychedelic drugs ⟨~ art⟩ ⟨~ colors⟩ — **psychedelic** *n* — **psy·che·del·i·cal·ly** \-li-k(ə-)lē\ *adv*

psy·chi·a·try \sə-'kī-ə-trē, sī-\ *n* [prob. fr. F *psychiatrie*, fr. *psychiatre* psychiatrist, fr. Gk *psychē* breath, soul + *iatros* physician] : a branch of medicine dealing with mental, emotional, and behavioral disorders — **psy·chi·at·ric** \ˌsī-kē-'a-trik\ *adj* — **psy·chi·a·trist** \sə-'kī-ə-trist, sī-\ *n*

¹psy·chic \'sī-kik\ *also* **psy·chi·cal** \-ki-kəl\ *adj* 1 : of or relating to the psyche 2 : lying outside the sphere of physical science 3 : sensitive to nonphysical or supernatural forces — **psy·chi·cal·ly** \-k(ə-)lē\ *adv*

²psychic *n* : a person apparently sensitive to nonphysical forces; *also* : MEDIUM 6

psy·cho \'sī-kō\ *n, pl* **psychos** : a mentally disturbed person — **psycho** *adj*

psy·cho·ac·tive \ˌsī-kō-'ak-tiv\ *adj* : affecting the mind or behavior

psy·cho·anal·y·sis \ˌsī-kō-ə-'na-lə-səs\ *n* : a method of dealing with psychic disorders by having the patient talk freely about personal experiences and esp. about early childhood and dreams — **psy·cho·an·a·lyst** \-'a-nə-list\ *n* — **psy·cho·an·a·lyt·ic** \-ˌa-nə-'li-tik\ *adj* — **psy·cho·an·a·lyze** \-'a-nə-ˌlīz\ *vb*

psy·cho·bab·ble \'sī-kō-ˌba-bəl\ *n* : psychological jargon esp. when used in a trite or simplistic manner

psy·cho·dra·ma \ˌsī-kə-'drä-mə, -'dra-\ *n* 1 : an extemporized dramatization designed to afford catharsis for one or more of the participants from whose life the plot is taken 2 : a dramatic event or story with psychological overtones

psy·cho·gen·ic \-'je-nik\ *adj* : originating in the mind or in mental or emotional conflict

psy·cho·graph·ics \ˌsī-kə-'gra-fiks\ *n sing or pl* : market research or statistics classifying population groups according to psychological variables

psychol *abbr* psychologist; psychology

psy·chol·o·gy \sī-'kä-lə-jē\ *n, pl* **-gies** 1 : the science of mind and behavior 2 : the mental and behavioral characteristics of an individual or group — **psy·cho·log·i·cal** \ˌsī-kə-'lä-ji-kəl\ *adj* — **psy·cho·log·i·cal·ly** \-ji-k(ə-)lē\ *adv* — **psy·chol·o·gist** \sī-'kä-lə-jist\ *n*

psy·cho·path \'sī-kō-ˌpath\ *n* : a mentally ill or unstable person; *esp* : a person who engages in antisocial behavior and exhibits a pervasive disregard for the rights, feelings, and safety of others — **psy·cho·path·ic** \ˌsī-kə-'pa-thik\ *adj*

psy·cho·sex·u·al \ˌsī-kō-'sek-shə-wəl\ *adj* 1 : of or relating to the mental, emotional, and behavioral aspects of sexual development 2 : of or relating to the physiological psychology of sex

psy·cho·sis \sī-'kō-səs\ *n, pl* **-cho·ses** \-ˌsēz\ : a serious mental illness (as schizophrenia) marked by loss of or greatly lessened ability to test whether what one is thinking and feeling about the real world is really true

psy·cho·so·cial \ˌsī-kō-'sō-shəl\ *adj* 1 : involving both psychological and social aspects 2 : relating social conditions to mental health

psy·cho·so·mat·ic \ˌsī-kō-sə-'ma-tik\ *adj* : of, relating to, involving, or concerned with bodily symptoms caused by mental or emotional disturbance

psy·cho·ther·a·py \ˌsī-kō-'ther-ə-pē\ *n* : treatment of mental or emotional disorder or of related bodily ills by psychological means — **psy·cho·ther·a·pist** \-pist\ *n*

psy·chot·ic \sī-'kä-tik\ *adj* : of or relating to psychosis ⟨~ behavior⟩ ⟨a ~ patient⟩ — **psychotic** *n*

psy·cho·tro·pic \ˌsī-kə-'trō-pik\ *adj* : acting on the mind ⟨~ drugs⟩

pt *abbr* 1 part 2 payment 3 pint 4 point 5 port

Pt *symbol* platinum

PT *abbr* 1 Pacific time 2 part-time 3 physical therapy 4 physical training

PTA *abbr* Parent-Teacher Association

ptar·mi·gan \'tär-mi-gən\ *n, pl* **-gan** *or* **-gans** : any of various grouses of northern regions with completely feathered feet

PT boat \(ˌ)pē-'tē-\ *n* [*patrol torpedo*] : a small fast patrol craft usu. armed with torpedos

pte *abbr, Brit* private

ptg *abbr* printing

PTO *abbr* 1 Parent-Teacher Organization 2 please turn over

pto·maine \'tō-ˌmān\ *n* : any of various chemical substances formed by bacteria in decaying matter (as meat) and including a few poisonous ones

Pu *symbol* plutonium

¹pub \'pəb\ *n* 1 *chiefly Brit* : PUBLIC HOUSE 2 : TAVERN

²pub *abbr* 1 public 2 publication 3 published; publisher; publishing

pu·ber·ty \'pyü-bər-tē\ *n* : the condition of being or period of becoming first capable of reproducing sexually — **pu·ber·tal** \-bər-t³l\ *adj*

pu·bes \'pyü-bēz\ *n, pl* **pubes** [NL, fr. L, manhood, body hair, pubic region] 1 : the hair that appears upon the lower middle region of the abdomen at puberty 2 : the pubic region

pu·bes·cence \pyü-'be-s³ns\ *n* 1 : the quality or state of being pubescent 2 : a pubescent covering or surface

pu·bes·cent \-s³nt\ *adj* 1 : arriving at or having reached puberty 2 : covered with fine soft short hairs

pu·bic \'pyü-bik\ *adj* : of, relating to, or situated near the pubes or the pubis

pu·bis \'pyü-bəs\ *n, pl* **pu·bes** \-bēz\ : the ventral and anterior of the three principal bones composing either half of the pelvis

publ *abbr* 1 publication 2 published; publisher

¹pub·lic \'pə-blik\ *adj* 1 : exposed to general view ⟨the story became ~⟩ 2 : of, relating to, or affecting the people as a whole ⟨~ opinion⟩ 3 : CIVIC, GOVERNMENTAL ⟨~ expenditures⟩ 4 : of, relating to, or serving the community ⟨~ officials⟩ 5 : not private : SOCIAL ⟨~ morality⟩ 6 : open to all ⟨~ library⟩ 7 : well known : PROMINENT ⟨~ figures⟩ 8 : supported by public funds and private contributions rather than by income from commercials — **pub·lic·ly** *adv*

²public *n* 1 : the people as a whole : POPULACE 2 : a group of people having common interests

pub·li·can \'pə-bli-kən\ *n* 1 : a Jewish tax collector for the ancient Romans 2 *chiefly Brit* : the licensee of a pub

pub·li·ca·tion \ˌpə-blə-'kā-shən\ *n* 1 : the act or process of publishing 2 : a published work

public house *n* 1 : INN 2 *chiefly Brit* : a licensed saloon or bar

pub·li·cise *Brit var of* PUBLICIZE

pub·li·cist \'pə-blə-sist\ *n* : one that publicizes; *esp* : PRESS AGENT

pub·lic·i·ty \(ˌ)pə-'bli-sə-tē\ *n* 1 : information with news value issued to gain public attention or support 2 : public attention or acclaim

pub·li·cize \'pə-blə-ˌsīz\ *vb* **-cized; -ciz·ing** : to bring to public attention : ADVERTISE

pub·lic-key \'pə-blik-'kē\ *n* : the publicly shared element of a code usable only to encode messages

public relations *n sing or pl* : the business of fostering public goodwill toward a person, firm, or institution; *also* : the degree of goodwill and understanding achieved

public school *n* 1 : an endowed secondary boarding school in Great Britain offering a classical curriculum and preparation for the universities or public service 2 : a free tax-supported school controlled by a local governmental authority

public–spirited *adj* : motivated by devotion to the general or national welfare

public works *n pl* : works (as schools or highways) constructed with public funds for public use

pub·lish \'pə-blish\ *vb* 1 : to make generally known : announce publicly 2 : to produce or release literature, information, musical scores or sometimes recordings, or art for sale to the public — **pub·lish·er** *n*

¹**puck** \'pək\ n : a mischievous sprite — **puck·ish** adj — **puck·ish·ly** adv

²**pucker** n : a disk used in ice hockey

¹**puck·er** \'pə-kər\ vb : to contract into folds or wrinkles

²**pucker** n : FOLD, WRINKLE

pud·ding \'pu̇-diŋ\ n : a soft, spongy, or thick creamy dessert

pud·dle \'pə-dᵊl\ n : a very small pool of usu. dirty or muddy water

pu·den·dum \pyu̇-'den-dəm\ n, pl **-da** \-də\ [NL, fr. L pudēre to be ashamed] : the human external genital organs esp. of a woman

pudgy \'pə-jē\ adj **pudg·i·er; -est** : being short and plump : CHUBBY

pueb·lo \'pwe-blō, pu̇-'e-\ n, pl **-los** [Sp, village, lit., people, fr. L populus] **1** : an American Indian village of Arizona or New Mexico that consists of flat-roofed stone or adobe houses joined in groups sometimes several stories high **2** cap : a member of a group of American Indian peoples of the southwestern U.S.

pu·er·ile \'pyu̇-ə-rəl\ adj : CHILDISH, SILLY ⟨~ remarks⟩ — **pu·er·il·i·ty** \ˌpyu̇-ə-'ri-lə-tē\ n

pu·er·per·al \pyu̇-'ər-pə-rəl\ adj : of, relating to, or occurring during childbirth or the period immediately following ⟨~ infection⟩ ⟨~ depression⟩

puerperal fever n : an abnormal condition that results from infection of the placental site following childbirth or abortion

¹**puff** \'pəf\ vb **1** : to blow in short gusts **2** : PANT **3** : to emit small whiffs or clouds **4** : BLUSTER, BRAG **5** : INFLATE, SWELL **6** : to make proud or conceited **7** : to praise extravagantly

²**puff** n **1** : a short discharge (as of air or smoke); also : a slight explosive sound accompanying it **2** : a light fluffy pastry **3** : a slight swelling **4** : a fluffy mass; also : a small pad for applying cosmetic powder **5** : a laudatory notice or review — **puffy** adj

³**puff** adj : of, relating to, or designed for promotion or flattery ⟨~ articles on the new TV series⟩

puff·ball \'pəf-ˌbȯl\ n : any of various globe-shaped and often edible fungi

puf·fin \'pə-fən\ n : any of several seabirds having a short neck and a deep grooved parti-colored bill

¹**pug** \'pəg\ n **1** : any of a breed of small stocky short-haired dogs with a wrinkled face **2** : a close coil of hair

²**pug** n : ¹BOXER

pu·gi·lism \'pyü-jə-ˌli-zəm\ n : BOXING — **pu·gi·list** \-list\ n — **pu·gi·lis·tic** \ˌpyü-jə-'lis-tik\ adj

pug·na·cious \ˌpəg-'nā-shəs\ adj : having a quarrelsome or combative nature ♦ **Synonyms** BELLIGERENT, BELLICOSE, CONTENTIOUS, TRUCULENT — **pug·nac·i·ty** \-'na-sə-tē\ n

puis·sance \'pwi-səns, 'pyü-ə-\ n : POWER, STRENGTH — **puis·sant** \-sənt\ adj

puke \'pyük\ vb **puked; puk·ing** : VOMIT — **puke** n

puk·ka \'pə-kə\ adj [Hindi pakkā cooked, ripe, solid, fr. Skt pakva] : GENUINE, AUTHENTIC; also : FIRST-CLASS, COMPLETE

pul \'pül\ n, pl **puls** \'pülz\ or **pul** — see afghani at MONEY table

pu·la \'pü-lə, 'pyü-\ n, pl **pula** — see MONEY table

pul·chri·tude \'pəl-krə-ˌtüd, -ˌtyüd\ n : BEAUTY — **pul·chri·tu·di·nous** \ˌpəl-krə-'tüd-ᵊn-əs, -'tyü-\ adj

pule \'pyül\ vb **puled; pul·ing** : WHINE, WHIMPER

¹**pull** \'pu̇l\ vb **1** : to exert force so as to draw (something) toward the force; also : MOVE ⟨~ out of a driveway⟩ **2** : PLUCK; also : EXTRACT ⟨~ a tooth⟩ **3** : STRETCH, STRAIN ⟨~ a tendon⟩ **4** : to draw apart : TEAR **5** : to make (as a proof) by printing **6** : REMOVE ⟨~ed the pitcher in the third inning⟩ **7** : DRAW ⟨~ a gun⟩ **8** : to carry out esp. with daring ⟨~ a robbery⟩ **9** : PERPETRATE, COMMIT **10** : ATTRACT **11** : to express strong sympathy — **pull·er** n

²**pull** n **1** : the act or an instance of pulling **2** : the effort expended in moving **3** : ADVANTAGE ⟨had the ~ of a respected family name⟩; esp : special influence **4** : a device for pulling something or for operating by pulling **5** : a force that attracts or compels **6** : an injury from abnormal straining or stretching ⟨a muscle ~⟩

pull·back \'pu̇l-ˌbak\ n : an orderly withdrawal of troops

pull–down adj : appearing below a selected item (as a menu title) on a computer display ⟨a ~ menu⟩

pul·let \'pu̇-lət\ n : a young hen esp. of the domestic chicken when less than a year old

pul·ley \'pu̇-lē\ n, pl **pulleys** : a wheel used to transmit power by means of a belt, rope, or chain; esp : one with a grooved rim that forms part of a tackle for hoisting or for changing the direction of a force

Pull·man \'pu̇l-mən\ n : a railroad passenger car with comfortable furnishings esp. for night travel

pull off vb : to accomplish successfully

pull·out \'pu̇l-ˌau̇t\ n : PULLBACK

pull·over \'pu̇l-ˌō-vər\ adj : put on by being pulled over the head ⟨~ sweater⟩ — **pull·over** n

pull–up \'pu̇l-ˌəp\ n : CHIN-UP

pull up vb : to bring or come to an often abrupt halt : STOP

pul·mo·nary \'pu̇l-mə-ˌner-ē, 'pəl-\ adj : of, relating to, or carried on by the lungs ⟨the ~ circulation⟩

pulp \'pəlp\ n **1** : the soft juicy or fleshy part of a fruit or vegetable **2** : a soft moist mass **3** : the soft sensitive tissue that fills the central cavity of a tooth **4** : a material (as from wood) used in making paper **5** : a magazine using cheap paper and often dealing with sensational material — **pulpy** adj

pul·pit \'pu̇l-ˌpit\ n : a raised platform or high reading desk used in preaching or conducting a worship service

pulp·wood \'pəlp-ˌwu̇d\ n : wood used in making pulp for paper

pul·sar \'pəl-ˌsär\ n : a celestial source of pulsating electromagnetic radiation (as radio waves)

pul·sate \'pəl-ˌsāt\ vb **pul·sat·ed; pul·sat·ing** : to expand and contract rhythmically : BEAT — **pul·sa·tion** \ˌpəl-'sā-shən\ n

pulse \'pəls\ n **1** : the regular throbbing in the arteries caused by the contractions of the heart **2** : rhythmical beating, vibrating, or sounding **3** : a brief change in electrical current or voltage — **pulse** vb

pul·ver·ise Brit var of PULVERIZE

pul·ver·ize \'pəl-və-ˌrīz\ vb **-ized; -iz·ing 1** : to reduce (as by crushing or grinding) or be reduced to very small particles **2** : DEMOLISH

pu·ma \'pü-mə, 'pyü-\ n, pl **pumas** also **puma** [Sp, fr. Quechua] : COUGAR

pum·ice \'pə-məs\ n : a light porous volcanic glass used esp. for smoothing and polishing

pum·mel \'pə-məl\ vb **-meled** also **-melled; -mel·ing** also **-mel·ling** : POUND, BEAT

¹**pump** \'pəmp\ n : a device for raising, transferring, or compressing fluids esp. by suction or pressure

²**pump** vb **1** : to raise (as water) with a pump **2** : to draw fluid from with a pump; also : to fill by means of a pump ⟨~ up a tire⟩ **3** : to force or propel in the manner of a pump — **pump·er** n

³**pump** n : a low shoe that grips the foot chiefly at the toe and heel

pumped \'pəmpt\ adj : filled with energetic excitement and enthusiasm

pum·per·nick·el \'pəm-pər-ˌni-kəl\ n : a dark rye bread

pump·kin \'pəm-kən, 'pəŋ-kən\ n : the large usu. orange fruit of a vine of the gourd family that is widely used as food; also : this vine

pun \'pən\ n : the humorous use of a word in a way that suggests two or more interpretations — **pun** vb

¹**punch** \'pənch\ n : a tool for piercing, stamping, cutting, or forming

²**punch** vb **1** : PROD, POKE; also : DRIVE, HERD ⟨~ing cattle⟩ **2** : to strike with the fist **3** : to emboss, perforate, or make with a punch **4** : to operate, produce, or enter (as data) by or as if by punching — **punch·er** n

³**punch** n **1** : a quick blow with or as if with the fist **2** : effective energy or forcefulness

⁴**punch** n [perh. fr. Hindi pāc five, fr. Skt pañca; fr. the number of ingredients] : a drink usu. composed of wine or alcoholic liquor and nonalcoholic beverages; also : a drink composed of nonalcoholic beverages

punch card n : a card with holes punched in particular positions to represent data

punch–drunk \'pənch-ˌdrəŋk\ adj **1** : suffering from brain injury resulting from repeated head blows received in boxing **2** : DAZED, CONFUSED

pun·cheon \'pən-chən\ n : a large cask

punch line *n* : the sentence or phrase in a joke that makes the point

punch list *n* : a list of tasks to be completed at the end of a project

punchy \'pən-chē\ *adj* **punch·i·er; -est** **1** : having punch : FORCEFUL **2** : DAZED, CONFUSED **3** : VIVID, VIBRANT ⟨~ graphics⟩

punc·til·io \,pəŋk-'ti-lē-,ō\ *n, pl* **-i·os** **1** : a nice detail of conduct in a ceremony or in observance of a code **2** : careful observance of forms (as in social conduct)

punc·til·i·ous \,pəŋk-'ti-lē-əs\ *adj* : marked by precise accordance with codes or conventions ♦ **Synonyms** METICULOUS, SCRUPULOUS, CAREFUL, PUNCTUAL

punc·tu·al \'pəŋk-chə-wəl\ *adj* : being on time : PROMPT — **punc·tu·al·i·ty** \,pəŋk-chə-'wa-lə-tē\ *n* — **punc·tu·al·ly** *adv*

punc·tu·ate \'pəŋk-chə-,wāt\ *vb* **-at·ed; -at·ing** **1** : to mark or divide (written matter) with punctuation marks **2** : to break into at intervals **3** : EMPHASIZE

punc·tu·a·tion \,pəŋk-chə-'wā-shən\ *n* : the act, practice, or system of inserting standardized marks in written matter to clarify the meaning and separate structural units

¹punc·ture \'pəŋk-chər\ *n* **1** : an act of puncturing **2** : a small hole or wound made by puncturing

²puncture *vb* **punc·tured; punc·tur·ing** **1** : to make a hole in : PIERCE **2** : to make useless as if by a puncture

pun·dit \'pən-dət\ *n* [Hindi *paṇḍit,* fr. Skt *paṇḍita,* fr. *paṇḍita* learned] **1** : a learned person : TEACHER **2** : AUTHORITY, CRITIC

pun·dit·oc·ra·cy \,pən-dət-'ä-krə-sē\ *n, pl* **-cies** : a group of powerful and influential political commentators

pun·gent \'pən-jənt\ *adj* **1** : having a sharp incisive quality : CAUSTIC ⟨a ~ editorial⟩ **2** : causing a sharp, intense, or irritating sensation (as of taste or smell); *esp* : ACRID ⟨a ~ odor⟩ — **pun·gen·cy** \-jən-sē\ *n* — **pun·gent·ly** *adv*

pun·ish \'pə-nish\ *vb* **1** : to impose a penalty on for a fault or crime ⟨~ an offender⟩ **2** : to inflict a penalty for ⟨~ treason with death⟩ **3** : to inflict injury on : HURT ♦ **Synonyms** CHASTISE, CASTIGATE, CHASTEN, DISCIPLINE, CORRECT — **pun·ish·able** *adj*

pun·ish·ment *n* **1** : retributive suffering, pain, or loss : PENALTY **2** : rough treatment

pu·ni·tive \'pyü-nə-tiv\ *adj* : inflicting, involving, or aiming at punishment

¹punk \'pəŋk\ *n* **1** : a young inexperienced person **2** : a petty hoodlum

²punk *adj* : very poor : INFERIOR

³punk *n* : dry crumbly wood useful for tinder; *also* : a substance made from fungi for use as tinder

pun·ster \'pən-stər\ *n* : one who is given to punning

¹punt \'pənt\ *n* : a long narrow flat-bottomed boat with square ends

¹punt

²punt *vb* : to propel (as a punt) with a pole

³punt *vb* : to kick a football or soccer ball dropped from the hands before it touches the ground

⁴punt *n* : the act or an instance of punting a ball

pu·ny \'pyü-nē\ *adj* **pu·ni·er; -est** [AF *puisné* younger, weakly, lit., born afterward, fr. *puis* afterward (fr. L *post*) + *né* born, fr. L *natus*] : slight in power, size, or importance : WEAK

pup \'pəp\ *n* : a young dog; *also* : one of the young of some other animals

pu·pa \'pyü-pə\ *n, pl* **pu·pae** \-(,)pē\ *or* **pupas** [NL, fr. L *pupa* doll] : a form of some insects (as a bee, moth, or beetle) between the larva and the adult that usu. has a protective covering (as a cocoon) — **pu·pal** \-pəl\ *adj*

¹pu·pil \'pyü-pəl\ *n* **1** : a child or young person in school or in the charge of a tutor **2** : DISCIPLE

²pupil *n* : the dark central opening of the iris of the eye

pup·pet \'pə-pət\ *n* [ME *popet* youth, doll, fr. MF *poupette,* ultim. fr. L *pupa* doll] **1** : a small figure of a person or animal moved by hand or by strings or wires **2** : DOLL **3** : one whose acts are controlled by an outside force or influence

pup·pe·teer \,pə-pə-'tir\ *n* : one who manipulates puppets

pup·py \'pə-pē\ *n, pl* **puppies** : a young domestic dog

pu·pu \'pü-,pü\ *n* : an Asian dish consisting of a variety of foods

pur·blind \'pər-,blīnd\ *adj* **1** : partly blind **2** : lacking in insight : OBTUSE

¹pur·chase \'pər-chəs\ *vb* **pur·chased; pur·chas·ing** : to obtain by paying money or its equivalent : BUY — **pur·chas·able** \-chə-sə-bəl\ *adj* — **pur·chas·er** *n*

²purchase *n* **1** : an act or instance of purchasing **2** : something purchased **3** : a secure hold or grasp; *also* : advantageous leverage

pur·dah \'pər-də\ *n* : seclusion of women from public observation among Muslims and some Hindus esp. in India; *also* : a state of seclusion

pure \'pyúr\ *adj* **pur·er; pur·est** **1** : unmixed with any other matter : free from taint ⟨~ gold⟩ ⟨~ water⟩ **2** : SHEER, ABSOLUTE ⟨~ nonsense⟩ **3** : ABSTRACT, THEORETICAL ⟨~ mathematics⟩ **4** : free from what vitiates, weakens, or pollutes ⟨speaks a ~ French⟩ **5** : free from moral fault : INNOCENT **6** : CHASTE, CONTINENT — **pure·ly** *adv*

pure–blood·ed \-,blə-dəd\ *or* **pure–blood** \-,bləd\ *adj* : FULL-BLOODED — **pure·blood** *n*

pure·bred \-'bred\ *adj* : bred from members of a recognized breed, strain, or kind without crossbreeding over many generations — **pure·bred** \-,bred\ *n*

¹pu·ree \pyú-'rā, -'rē\ *n* [F *purée,* fr. MF, fr. fem. of *puré,* pp. of *purer* to purify, strain, fr. L *purare* to purify] : a paste or thick liquid suspension usu. made from finely ground cooked food; *also* : a thick soup made of pureed vegetables

²puree *vb* **pu·reed; pu·ree·ing** : to make a puree of

pur·ga·tion \,pər-'gā-shən\ *n* : the act or result of purging

¹pur·ga·tive \'pər-gə-tiv\ *adj* : purging or tending to purge

²purgative *n* : a strong laxative : CATHARTIC

pur·ga·to·ry \'pər-gə-,tór-ē\ *n, pl* **-ries** **1** : an intermediate state after death for expiatory purification **2** : a place or state of temporary punishment — **pur·ga·tor·i·al** \,pər-gə-'tór-ē-əl\ *adj*

¹purge \'pərj\ *vb* **purged; purg·ing** **1** : to cleanse or purify esp. from sin **2** : to have or cause strong and usu. repeated emptying of the bowels **3** : to get rid of ⟨the leaders had been *purged*⟩

²purge *n* **1** : something that purges; *esp* : PURGATIVE **2** : an act or result of purging; *esp* : a ridding of persons regarded as treacherous or disloyal

pu·ri·fy \'pyúr-ə-,fī\ *vb* **-fied; -fy·ing** : to make or become pure — **pu·ri·fi·ca·tion** \,pyúr-ə-fə-'kā-shən\ *n* — **pu·ri·fi·ca·to·ry** \pyü-'ri-fi-kə-,tór-ē\ *adj* — **pu·ri·fi·er** *n*

Pu·rim \'púr-(,)im\ *n* : a Jewish holiday celebrated in February or March in commemoration of the deliverance of the Jews from the massacre plotted by Haman

pu·rine \'pyúr-,ēn\ *n* : any of a group of bases including several (as adenine or guanine) that are constituents of DNA or RNA

pur·ism \'pyúr-,i-zəm\ *n* : rigid adherence to or insistence on purity or nicety esp. in use of words — **pur·ist** \-ist\ *n* — **pu·ris·tic** \pyú-'ris-tik\ *adj*

pu·ri·tan \'pyúr-ə-tən\ *n* **1** *cap* : a member of a 16th and 17th century Protestant group in England and New England opposing the ceremonies and government of the Church of England **2** : one who practices or preaches a stricter or professedly purer moral code than that which prevails — **pu·ri·tan·i·cal** \,pyúr-ə-'ta-ni-kəl\ *adj* — **pu·ri·tan·i·cal·ly** *adv*

pu·ri·ty \'pyúr-ə-tē\ *n* : the quality or state of being pure

¹purl \'pərl\ *n* : a stitch in knitting

²purl *vb* : to knit in purl stitch

³purl *n* : a gentle murmur or movement (as of purling water)

⁴purl *vb* **1** : EDDY, SWIRL **2** : to make a soft murmuring sound

pur·lieu \'pər-lü, 'pərl-yü\ *n* **1** : an outlying district : SUBURB **2** *pl* : ENVIRONS

pur·loin \(,)pər-'lȯin, 'pər-,lȯin\ *vb* : STEAL, FILCH

¹pur·ple \'pər-pəl\ *adj* **pur·pler; pur·plest** **1** : of the color purple **2** : highly rhetorical ⟨a ∼ passage⟩ **3** : PROFANE ⟨∼ language⟩ — **pur·plish** *adj*

²purple *n* **1** : a bluish red color **2** : a purple robe emblematic esp. of regal rank or authority

¹pur·port \'pər-,pȯrt\ *n* [ME, fr. AF, content, tenor, fr. *purporter* to carry, mean, purport, fr. *pur-* thoroughly + *porter* to carry] : meaning conveyed or implied; *also* : GIST

²pur·port \(,)pər-'pȯrt\ *vb* : to convey or profess outwardly as the meaning or intention : CLAIM — **pur·port·ed·ly** \-'pȯr-təd-lē\ *adv*

¹pur·pose \'pər-pəs\ *n* **1** : an object or result aimed at : INTENTION **2** : RESOLUTION, DETERMINATION — **pur·pose·ful** \-fəl\ *adj* — **pur·pose·ful·ly** *adv* — **pur·pose·less** *adj* — **pur·pose·ly** *adv*

²purpose *vb* **pur·posed; pur·pos·ing** : to propose as an aim to oneself

purr \'pər\ *n* : a low murmur typical of a contented cat — **purr** *vb*

¹purse \'pərs\ *n* **1** : a receptacle (as a pouch) to carry money and often other small objects in **2** : RESOURCES **3** : a sum of money offered as a prize or present

²purse *vb* **pursed; purs·ing** : PUCKER

purs·er \'pər-sər\ *n* : an official on a ship who keeps accounts and attends to the comfort of passengers

purs·lane \'pər-slən, -,slān\ *n* : a fleshy-leaved weedy trailing plant with tiny yellow flowers that is sometimes used in salads

pur·su·ance \pər-'sü-əns\ *n* : the act of carrying out or into effect

pur·su·ant to \-'sü-ənt-\ *prep* : in carrying out : ACCORDING TO

pur·sue \pər-'sü\ *vb* **pur·sued; pur·su·ing** **1** : to follow in order to overtake or overcome : CHASE **2** : to seek to accomplish ⟨∼ a goal⟩ **3** : to proceed along ⟨∼ a course⟩ **4** : to engage in ⟨∼ a career⟩ — **pur·su·er** *n*

pur·suit \pər-'süt\ *n* **1** : the act of pursuing **2** : OCCUPATION, BUSINESS

pu·ru·lent \'pyu̇r-ə-lənt, -yə-\ *adj* : containing or accompanied by pus ⟨a ∼ discharge⟩ — **pu·ru·lence** \-ləns\ *n*

pur·vey \(,)pər-'vā\ *vb* **pur·veyed; pur·vey·ing** : to supply (as provisions) usu. as a business — **pur·vey·ance** \-əns\ *n* — **pur·vey·or** \-ər\ *n*

pur·view \'pər-,vyü\ *n* **1** : the range or limit esp. of authority, responsibility, or intention **2** : range of vision, understanding, or cognizance

pus \'pəs\ *n* : thick yellowish white fluid matter (as in a boil) formed at a place of inflammation and infection (as an abscess) and containing germs, white blood cells, and tissue debris

¹push \'pu̇sh\ *vb* [ME *possen, pusshen*, prob. fr. OF *pousser* to exert pressure, fr. L *pulsare*, fr. *pellere* to drive, strike] **1** : to press against with force in order to drive or impel **2** : to thrust forward, downward, or outward **3** : to urge on : press forward **4** : to cause to increase ⟨∼ prices to record levels⟩ **5** : to urge or press the advancement, adoption, or practice of; *esp* : to make aggressive efforts to sell **6** : to engage in the illicit sale of narcotics

²push *n* **1** : a vigorous effort : DRIVE **2** : an act of pushing : SHOVE **3** : vigorous enterprise : ENERGY

push–button *adj* **1** : operated or done by means of push buttons **2** : using or dependent on complex and more or less automatic mechanisms ⟨∼ warfare⟩

push button *n* : a small button or knob that when pushed operates something esp. by closing an electric circuit

push·cart \'pu̇sh-,kärt\ *n* : a cart or barrow pushed by hand

push·er \'pu̇-shər\ *n* : one that pushes; *esp* : one that pushes illegal drugs

push·over \-,ō-vər\ *n* **1** : something easily accomplished **2** : an opponent easy to defeat **3** : SUCKER

push–up \-,əp\ *n* : a conditioning exercise performed in a prone position by raising and lowering the body with the straightening and bending of the arms while keeping the back straight and supporting the body on the hands and toes

pushy \'pu̇-shē\ *adj* **push·i·er; -est** : aggressive often to an objectionable degree

pu·sil·lan·i·mous \,pyü-sə-'la-nə-məs\ *adj* [LL *pusillanimis*, fr. L *pusillus* very small (dim. of *pusus* boy) + *animus* spirit] : contemptibly timid : COWARDLY — **pu·sil·la·nim·i·ty** \,pyü-sə-lə-'ni-mə-tē\ *n*

¹puss \'pu̇s\ *n* : CAT

²puss *n, slang* : FACE

¹pussy \'pu̇-sē\ *n, pl* **puss·ies** : CAT

²pus·sy \'pə-sē\ *adj* **pus·si·er; -est** : full of or resembling pus

pussy·cat \'pu̇-sē-,kat\ *n* : CAT

pussy·foot \-,fu̇t\ *vb* **1** : to tread or move warily or stealthily **2** : to refrain from committing oneself

pussy willow \'pu̇-sē-\ *n* : a willow having large silky catkins

pus·tule \'pəs-chül\ *n* : a pus-filled pimple

put \'pu̇t\ *vb* **put; put·ting** **1** : to bring into a specified position : PLACE ⟨∼ the book on the table⟩ **2** : SEND, THRUST **3** : to throw with an upward pushing motion ⟨∼ the shot⟩ **4** : to bring into a specified state ⟨∼ the plan into effect⟩ **5** : SUBJECT ⟨∼ traitors to death⟩ **6** : IMPOSE **7** : to set before one for decision ⟨∼ the question⟩ **8** : EXPRESS, STATE ⟨∼ my feelings into words⟩ **9** : TRANSLATE, ADAPT **10** : APPLY, ASSIGN ⟨∼ them to work⟩ **11** : ESTIMATE ⟨∼ the number at 20⟩ **12** : ATTACH, ATTRIBUTE ⟨∼ a high value on it⟩ **13** : to take a specified course ⟨the ship ∼ out to sea⟩

pu·ta·tive \'pyü-tə-tiv\ *adj* **1** : commonly accepted **2** : assumed to exist or to have existed

put–down \'pu̇t-,dau̇n\ *n* : a belittling remark

put in *vb* **1** : to come in with : INTERPOSE ⟨*put in* a good word for me⟩ **2** : to spend time at some occupation or job ⟨*put in* eight hours at the office⟩

put off *vb* : POSTPONE, DELAY ⟨*put off* my visit⟩

¹put–on \'pu̇t-,ȯn, -,än\ *adj* : PRETENDED, ASSUMED

²put–on *n* **1** : a deliberate act of misleading someone **2** : PARODY, SPOOF

put·out \'pu̇t-,au̇t\ *n* : the retiring of a base runner or batter in baseball

put out *vb* **1** : EXTINGUISH **2** : ANNOY; *also* : INCONVENIENCE **3** : to cause to be out (as in baseball)

pu·tre·fy \'pyü-trə-,fī\ *vb* **-fied; -fy·ing** : to make or become putrid : ROT — **pu·tre·fac·tion** \,pyü-trə-'fak-shən\ *n* — **pu·tre·fac·tive** \-tiv\ *adj*

pu·tres·cent \pyü-'tre-s³nt\ *adj* : becoming putrid : ROTTING — **pu·tres·cence** \-s³ns\ *n*

pu·trid \'pyü-trəd\ *adj* **1** : ROTTEN, DECAYED ⟨∼ meat⟩ **2** : VILE, CORRUPT — **pu·trid·i·ty** \pyü-'tri-də-tē\ *n*

putsch \'pu̇ch\ *n* [G] : a secretly plotted and suddenly executed attempt to overthrow a government

putt \'pət\ *n* : a golf stroke made on the green to cause the ball to roll into the hole — **putt** *vb*

put·ta·nes·ca \,pu̇-tä-'nes-kä\ *adj* : served with or being a pungent tomato sauce

put·tee \,pə-'tē, 'pə-tē\ *n* [Hindi *paṭṭī* strip of cloth] **1** : a cloth strip wrapped around the lower leg **2** : a leather legging

¹put·ter \'pu̇-tər\ *n* : one that puts

²putt·er \'pə-tər\ *n* **1** : a golf club used in putting **2** : one that putts

³put·ter \'pə-tər\ *vb* **1** : to move or act aimlessly or idly **2** : TINKER

put·ty \'pə-tē\ *n, pl* **putties** [F *potée* potter's glaze, lit., potful, fr. OF, fr. *pot* pot] **1** : a doughlike cement used esp. to fasten glass in sashes **2** : one who is easily manipulated — **putty** *vb*

put up *vb* **1** : SHEATHE **2** : to prepare so as to preserve for later use **3** : to offer for public sale ⟨*put* the house *up* for auction⟩ **4** : ACCOMMODATE, LODGE ⟨*put* us *up* for the night⟩ **5** : BUILD **6** : to engage in ⟨*put up* a struggle⟩ **7** : CONTRIBUTE, PAY — **put up with** : TOLERATE **2**

¹puz·zle \'pə-zəl\ *vb* **puz·zled; puz·zling** **1** : to bewilder mentally : PERPLEX **2** : to solve with difficulty or ingenuity ⟨∼ out a riddle⟩ **3** : to be in a quandary ⟨∼ over what to do⟩ **4** : to attempt a solution of a puzzle ⟨∼ over a person's words⟩ ♦ *Synonyms* MYSTIFY, BEWILDER, NONPLUS, CONFOUND — **puz·zle·ment** *n* — **puz·zler** *n*

²puzzle *n* **1** : something that puzzles **2** : a question, problem, or contrivance designed for testing ingenuity

PVC *abbr* polyvinyl chloride

pvt *abbr* private

PW *abbr* prisoner of war

pwt *abbr* pennyweight

PX *abbr* post exchange

pya \pē-'ä\ *n* — see *kyat* at MONEY table

pyg·my *also* **pig·my** \'pig-mē\ *n, pl* **pygmies** *also* **pigmies** [ME *pigmei*, fr. L *pygmaeus* of a pygmy, dwarfish, fr. Gk *pygmaios*, fr. *pygmē* fist, measure of length] **1** *cap* : any of a small people of equatorial Africa **2** : an unusually small person; *also* : an insignificant or unimpressive person — **pygmy** *adj*

py·ja·mas \pə-'jä-məz\ *chiefly Brit var of* PAJAMAS

py·lon \'pī-,län, -lən\ *n* **1** : a usu. massive gateway; *esp* : an Egyptian one flanked by flat-topped pyramids **2** : a tower that supports wires over a long span **3** : a post or tower marking the course in an airplane race

py·or·rhea \,pī-ə-'rē-ə\ *n* : an inflammation with pus of the sockets of the teeth

¹pyr·a·mid \'pir-ə-,mid\ *n* **1** : a massive structure with a square base and four triangular faces meeting at a point **2** : a geometrical solid having a polygon for its base and three or more triangles for its sides that meet at a point to form the top — **py·ra·mi·dal** \pə-'ra-mə-d³l, ,pir-ə-'mid-\ *adj*

²pyramid *vb* **1** : to build up in the form of a pyramid : heap up **2** : to increase rapidly on a broadening base

pyramid scheme *n* : a usu. illegal operation in which participants pay to join and profit from payments made by subsequent participants

pyre \'pī(-ə)r\ *n* : a combustible heap for burning a dead body as a funeral rite

py·re·thrum \pī-'rē-thrəm\ *n* : an insecticide made from the dried heads of any of several Old World chrysanthemums

py·rim·i·dine \pī-'ri-mə-,dēn\ *n* : any of a group of bases including several (as cytosine, thymine, or uracil) that are constituents of DNA or RNA

py·rite \'pī-,rīt\ *n* : a mineral containing sulfur and iron that is brass-yellow in color

py·rol·y·sis \pī-'rä-lə-səs\ *n* : chemical change caused by the action of heat

py·ro·ma·nia \,pī-rō-'mā-nē-ə\ *n* : an irresistible impulse to start fires — **py·ro·ma·ni·ac** \-nē-,ak\ *n*

py·ro·tech·nics \,pī-rə-'tek-niks\ *n pl* **1** : a display of fireworks **2** : a spectacular display (as of extreme virtuosity) — **py·ro·tech·nic** \-nik\ *also* **py·ro·tech·ni·cal** \-ni-kəl\ *adj*

Pyr·rhic \'pir-ik\ *adj* : achieved at excessive cost ⟨a ∼ victory⟩; *also* : costly to the point of outweighing expected benefits

Py·thag·o·re·an theorem \pī-,tha-gə-'rē-ən-\ *n* : a theorem in geometry: the square of the length of the hypotenuse of a right triangle equals the sum of the squares of the lengths of the other two sides

py·thon \'pī-,thän, -thən\ *n* [L, monstrous serpent killed by the god Apollo, fr. Gk *Pythōn*] : a large snake (as a boa) that squeezes and suffocates its prey; *esp* : any of the large Old World snakes that include the largest snakes living at the present time

pyx \'piks\ *n* : a small case used to carry the Eucharist to the sick

¹q \'kyü\ *n, pl* **q's** *or* **qs** \'kyüz\ *often cap* : the 17th letter of the English alphabet

²q *abbr, often cap* **1** quart **2** quarto **3** queen **4** query **5** question

QB *abbr* quarterback

QED *abbr* [L *quod erat demonstrandum*] which was to be demonstrated

qin·tar \kin-'tär\ *n, pl* **qin·dar·ka** \kin-'där-kə\ — see *lek* at MONEY table

qi·vi·ut \'kē-vē-,üt\ *n* [Inuit] : the wool of the undercoat of the musk ox

Qld *abbr* Queensland

QM *abbr* quartermaster

QMC *abbr* quartermaster corps

QMG *abbr* quartermaster general

qq v *abbr* [L *quae vide*] which (*pl*) see

qr *abbr* quarter

Q rating *n* [*q*uotient] : a scale measuring popularity based on dividing an assessment of familiarity or recognition by an assessment of favorable opinion; *also* : position on such a scale

qt *abbr* **1** quantity **2** quart

q.t. \,kyü-'tē\ *n, often cap Q&T* : QUIET — usu. used in the phrase *on the q.t.*

qto *abbr* quarto

qty *abbr* quantity

qu *or* **ques** *abbr* question

¹quack \'kwak\ *vb* : to make the characteristic cry of a duck

²quack *n* : a sound made by quacking

³quack *n* **1** : CHARLATAN **2** : a pretender to medical skill ◆ *Synonyms* FAKER, IMPOSTOR, MOUNTEBANK — **quack** *adj* — **quack·ery** \'kwa-kə-rē\ *n* — **quack·ish** *adj*

¹quad \'kwäd\ *n* : QUADRANGLE

²quad *n* **1** : QUADRUPLET **2** : a ski lift that accommodates four people

³quad *abbr* quadrant

quad·ran·gle \'kwä-,draŋ-gəl\ *n* **1** : QUADRILATERAL **2** : a 4-sided courtyard or enclosure — **quad·ran·gu·lar** \kwä-'draŋ-gyə-lər\ *adj*

quad·rant \'kwä-drənt\ *n* **1** : one quarter of a circle : an arc of 90° **2** : any of the four quarters into which something is divided by two lines intersecting each other at right angles

qua·drat·ic \kwä-'dra-tik\ *adj* : having or being a term in which the variable (as *x*) is squared but containing no term in which the variable is raised to a higher power than a square ⟨a ∼ equation⟩ — **quadratic** *n*

qua·dren·ni·al \kwä-'dre-nē-əl\ *adj* **1** : consisting of or lasting for four years **2** : occurring every four years

qua·dren·ni·um \-nē-əm\ *n, pl* **-ni·ums** *or* **-nia** \-nē-ə\ : a period of four years

quad·ri·ceps \'kwä-drə-,seps\ *n* : a muscle of the front of the thigh that is divided into four parts

¹quad·ri·lat·er·al \,kwä-drə-'la-tə-rəl\ *n* : a polygon of four sides

quadrilaterals

²quadrilateral *adj* : having four sides

qua·drille \kwä-'dril, kə-\ *n* : a square dance made up of five or six figures in various rhythms

quad·ri·par·tite \,kwä-drə-'pär-,tīt\ *adj* **1** : consisting of four parts **2** : shared by four parties or persons

quad·ri·ple·gia \,kwä-drə-'plē-jə, -jē-ə\ *n* : paralysis of both arms and both legs —**quad·ri·ple·gic** \-jik\ *adj or n*

qua·driv·i·um \kwä-'dri-vē-əm\ *n* : the four liberal arts of arithmetic, music, geometry, and astronomy in a medieval university

quad·ru·ped \'kwä-drə-ˌped\ *n* : an animal having four feet — **qua·dru·pe·dal** \kwä-'drü-pə-dᵊl, ˌkwä-drə-'pe-\ *adj*

¹**qua·dru·ple** \kwä-'drü-pəl, -'drə-; 'kwä-drə-\ *vb* **qua·dru·pled; qua·dru·pling** : to make or become four times as great or as many

²**quadruple** *adj* : FOURFOLD

qua·dru·plet \kwä-'drə-plət, -'drü-; 'kwä-drə-\ *n* **1** : a combination of four of a kind **2** : one of four offspring born at one birth

¹**qua·dru·pli·cate** \kwä-'drü-pli-kət\ *adj* **1** : repeated four times **2** : FOURTH

²**qua·dru·pli·cate** \-plə-ˌkāt\ *vb* **-cat·ed; -cat·ing** **1** : QUADRUPLE **2** : to prepare in quadruplicate — **qua·dru·pli·ca·tion** \-ˌdrü-plə-'kā-shən\ *n*

³**qua·dru·pli·cate** \-'drü-pli-kət\ *n* **1** : four copies all alike 〈typed in ⁓〉 **2** : one of four like things

quaff \'kwäf, 'kwaf\ *vb* : to drink deeply or repeatedly — **quaff** *n*

quag·mire \'kwag-ˌmī(-ə)r, 'kwäg-\ *n* **1** : soft miry land that yields under the foot **2** : PREDICAMENT

qua·hog \'kō-ˌhȯg, 'kwȯ-, 'kwō-, -ˌhäg\ *n* [modif. of Narragansett *poquaûhock*] : a round thick-shelled edible clam of the U.S.

quai \'kā\ *n* : QUAY

¹**quail** \'kwāl\ *n, pl* **quail** *or* **quails** [ME *quaile*, fr. AF, fr. ML *quaccula*, of imit. origin] : any of numerous small short-winged plump game birds (as a bobwhite) related to the domestic chicken

²**quail** *vb* [ME, to grow feeble, fr. MD *quelen*] : to lose heart : COWER ♦ **Synonyms** RECOIL, SHRINK, FLINCH, WINCE, BLANCH

quaint \'kwānt\ *adj* : unusual or different in character or appearance; *esp* : pleasingly old-fashioned or unfamiliar ♦ **Synonyms** ODD, QUEER, CURIOUS, STRANGE — **quaint·ly** *adv* — **quaint·ness** *n*

¹**quake** \'kwāk\ *vb* **quaked; quak·ing** **1** : to shake usu. from shock or instability **2** : to tremble usu. from cold or fear

²**quake** *n* : a shaking or trembling; *esp* : EARTHQUAKE

Quak·er \'kwā-kər\ *n* : FRIEND 5

qual *abbr* quality

qual·i·fi·ca·tion \ˌkwä-lə-fə-'kā-shən\ *n* **1** : LIMITATION, MODIFICATION 〈her statement stands without ⁓〉 **2** : a special skill that fits a person for some work or position **3** : REQUIREMENT 〈a ⁓ for membership〉

qual·i·fied \'kwä-lə-ˌfīd\ *adj* **1** : fitted for a given purpose or job **2** : limited in some way 〈⁓ approval〉

qual·i·fi·er \'kwä-lə-ˌfī(-ə)r\ *n* **1** : one that satisfies requirements **2** : a word or word group that limits the meaning of another word or word group

qual·i·fy \'kwä-lə-ˌfī\ *vb* **-fied; -fy·ing** **1** : to reduce from a general to a particular form : MODIFY **2** : to make less harsh **3** : to limit the meaning of (as a noun) **4** : to fit by skill or training for some purpose **5** : to give or have a legal right to do something **6** : to demonstrate the necessary ability 〈⁓ for the finals〉 ♦ **Synonyms** MODERATE, TEMPER

qual·i·ta·tive \'kwä-lə-ˌtā-tiv\ *adj* : of, relating to, or involving quality — **qual·i·ta·tive·ly** *adv*

¹**qual·i·ty** \'kwä-lə-tē\ *n, pl* **-ties** **1** : peculiar and essential character : NATURE **2** : degree of excellence **3** : high social status **4** : a distinguishing attribute

²**quality** *adj* : being of high quality

qualm \'kwäm, 'kwälm\ *n* **1** : a sudden attack (as of nausea) **2** : a sudden feeling of doubt, fear, or uneasiness esp. in not following one's conscience or better judgment

qualm·ish \'kwä-mish, 'kwäl-\ *adj* **1** : feeling qualms : NAUSEATED **2** : overly scrupulous : SQUEAMISH **3** : of, relating to, or producing qualms

quan·da·ry \'kwän-drē\ *n, pl* **-ries** : a state of perplexity or doubt

quan·ti·fy \'kwän-tə-ˌfī\ *vb* **-fied; -fy·ing** : to determine, express, or measure the quantity of — **quan·ti·fi·able** \ˌkwän-tə-'fī-ə-bəl\ *adj*

quan·ti·ta·tive \'kwän-tə-ˌtā-tiv\ *adj* : of, relating to, or involving quantity — **quan·ti·ta·tive·ly** *adv*

quan·ti·ty \'kwän-tə-tē\ *n, pl* **-ties** **1** : AMOUNT, NUMBER **2** : a considerable amount

quan·tize \'kwän-ˌtīz\ *vb* **quan·tized; quan·tiz·ing** : to subdivide (as energy) into small units

¹**quan·tum** \'kwän-təm\ *n, pl* **quan·ta** \-tə\ [L, neut. of *quantus* how much] **1** : QUANTITY, AMOUNT **2** : an elemental unit of energy

²**quantum** *adj* **1** : LARGE, SIGNIFICANT **2** : relating to or employing the principles of quantum mechanics

quantum mechanics *n sing or pl* : a theory of matter based on the concept of possession of wave properties by elementary particles — **quantum mechanical** *adj* — **quantum mechanically** *adv*

quantum theory *n* **1** : a theory in physics based on the idea that radiant energy (as light) is composed of small separate packets of energy **2** : QUANTUM MECHANICS

quar *abbr* quarterly

quar·an·tine \'kwȯr-ən-ˌtēn\ *n* [modif. of It *quarantena*, lit., period of forty days, fr. *quaranta* forty, fr. L *quadraginta*] **1** : a period during which a ship suspected of carrying contagious disease is forbidden contact with the shore **2** : a restraint on the movements of persons or goods to prevent the spread of pests or disease **3** : a place or period of quarantine **4** : a state of enforced isolation — **quarantine** *vb*

quark \'kwȯrk, 'kwärk\ *n* : a hypothetical elementary particle that carries a fractional charge and is held to be a constituent of heavier particles (as protons and neutrons)

¹**quar·rel** \'kwȯr-əl\ *n* **1** : a ground of dispute **2** : a verbal clash : CONFLICT — **quar·rel·some** \-səm\ *adj*

²**quarrel** *vb* **-reled** *or* **-relled; -rel·ing** *or* **-rel·ling** **1** : to find fault **2** : to dispute angrily : WRANGLE

¹**quar·ry** \'kwȯr-ē\ *n, pl* **quarries** [ME *querre* entrails of game given to the hounds, fr. AF *cureie, quereie*, fr. *quir, cuir* skin, hide (on which the entrails were placed), fr. L *corium*] **1** : game hunted with hawks **2** : PREY

²**quarry** *n, pl* **quarries** [ME *quarey*, alter. of *quarrere*, fr. AF, fr. VL *quadraria*, fr. LL *quadrus* hewn (lit., squared) stone, fr. L *quadrum* square] : an open excavation usu. for obtaining building stone or limestone — **quarry** *vb*

quart \'kwȯrt\ *n* — see WEIGHT table

¹**quar·ter** \'kwȯr-tər\ *n* **1** : one of four equal parts **2** : a fourth of a dollar; *also* : a coin of this value **3** : a district of a city **4** *pl* : LODGINGS 〈moved into new ⁓s〉 **5** : MERCY, CLEMENCY 〈gave no ⁓〉 **6** : a fourth part of the moon's period

²**quarter** *vb* **1** : to divide into four equal parts **2** : to provide with shelter

¹**quar·ter·back** \-ˌbak\ *n* : a football player who calls the signals and directs the offensive play for the team

²**quarterback** *vb* **1** : to direct the offensive play of a football team **2** : LEAD, BOSS

quar·ter·deck \-ˌdek\ *n* : the stern area of a ship's upper deck

quarter horse *n* : any of a breed of compact muscular saddle horses characterized by great endurance and by high speed for short distances

¹**quar·ter·ly** \'kwȯr-tər-lē\ *adv* : at 3-month intervals

²**quarterly** *adj* : occurring, issued, or payable at 3-month intervals

³**quarterly** *n, pl* **-lies** : a periodical published four times a year

quar·ter·mas·ter \-ˌmas-tər\ *n* **1** : a petty officer who attends to a ship's helm, binnacle, and signals **2** : an army officer who provides clothing and subsistence for troops

quar·ter·staff \-ˌstaf\ *n, pl* **-staves** \-ˌstavz, -ˌstāvz\ : a long stout staff formerly used as a weapon

quar·tet *also* **quar·tette** \kwȯr-'tet\ *n* **1** : a musical composition for four instruments or voices **2** : a group of four and esp. of four musicians

quar·to \'kwȯr-tō\ *n, pl* **quartos** **1** : the size of a piece of paper cut four from a sheet **2** : a book printed on quarto pages

quartz \'kwȯrts\ *n* : a common often transparent crystalline mineral that is a form of silica

quartz·ite \'kwȯrt-ˌsīt\ *n* : a compact granular rock composed of quartz and derived from sandstone

qua·sar \'kwā-ˌzär, -ˌsär\ *n* : any of a class of extremely distant starlike celestial objects

¹**quash** \'kwäsh, 'kwȯsh\ *vb* : to suppress or extinguish summarily and completely : QUELL

²**quash** *vb* : to nullify by judicial action

qua·si \'kwä-ˌzī, -ˌsī; 'kwä-zē, -sē\ *adj* : being in some sense or degree ⟨a ~ corporation⟩

quasi- *comb form* [L, as if, as it were, approximately, fr. *quam* as + *si* if] : in some sense or degree ⟨*quasi*-histori-cal⟩

qua·si–gov·ern·men·tal \-gə-vərn-'men-t°l\ *adj* : supported by the government but managed privately

Qua·ter·na·ry \'kwä-tər-ˌner-ē, kwə-'tər-nə-rē\ *adj* : of, relating to, or being the geologic period from the end of the Tertiary to the present — **Quaternary** *n*

qua·train \'kwä-ˌtrān\ *n* : a unit of four lines of verse

qua·tre·foil \'ka-tər-ˌfói(-ə)l, 'ka-trə-\ *n* : a stylized figure often of a flower with four petals

qua·ver \'kwā-vər\ *vb* 1 : TREMBLE, SHAKE 2 : TRILL 3 : to speak in tremulous tones ♦ *Synonyms* SHUDDER, QUAKE, TWITTER, QUIVER, SHIVER — **quaver** *n*

quay \'kē, 'kwā, 'kā\ *n* : WHARF

Que *abbr* Quebec

quean \'kwēn\ *n* : PROSTITUTE

quea·sy \'kwē-zē\ *adj* **quea·si·er; -est** : NAUSEATED — **quea·si·ly** \-zə-lē\ *adv* — **quea·si·ness** \-zē-nəs\ *n*

Que·chua \'ke-chə-wə, 'kech-wə\ *n* : a family of languages spoken in Peru and adjacent countries of the So. American Andes

queen \'kwēn\ *n* [ME *quene*, fr. OE *cwēn* woman, wife, queen] 1 : the wife or widow of a king 2 : a female monarch 3 : a woman notable for rank, power, or attractiveness 4 : the most powerful piece in the game of chess 5 : a playing card bearing the figure of a queen 6 : a fertile female of a social insect (as a bee or termite) — **queen·ly** *adj*

Queen Anne's lace \-'anz-\ *n* : a widely naturalized Eurasian herb from which the cultivated carrot originated

queen consort *n, pl* **queens consort** : the wife of a reigning king

queen mother *n* : a dowager queen who is mother of the reigning sovereign

queen–size *adj* : having dimensions of approximately 60 inches by 80 inches ⟨a ~ bed⟩; *also* : of a size that fits a queen-size bed

¹queer \'kwir\ *adj* 1 : COUNTERFEIT ⟨~ money⟩ 2 : differing from the usual or normal : PECULIAR, STRANGE 3 *often disparaging* : HOMOSEXUAL; *also, sometimes offensive* : of, relating to, or used by homosexuals ♦ *Synonyms* WEIRD, BIZARRE, ECCENTRIC, CURIOUS — **queer** *n* — **queer·ly** *adv* — **queer·ness** *n*

²queer *vb* : to spoil the effect of : DISRUPT ⟨~ed our plans⟩

queer theory *n* : an approach to literary and cultural study that rejects traditional categories of gender and sexuality

quell \'kwel\ *vb* 1 : to put an end to by force ⟨~ a riot⟩ 2 : CALM, PACIFY ⟨~ fears⟩

quench \'kwench\ *vb* 1 : PUT OUT, EXTINGUISH 2 : SUBDUE 3 : SLAKE, SATISFY ⟨~ed his thirst⟩ — **quench·able** *adj* — **quench·er** *n* — **quench·less** *adj*

quer·u·lous \'kwer-ə-ləs, -yə-\ *adj* 1 : constantly complaining 2 : FRETFUL, WHINING ⟨a ~ voice⟩ ♦ *Synonyms* PETULANT, PETTISH, IRRITABLE, PEEVISH, HUFFY — **quer·u·lous·ly** *adv* — **quer·u·lous·ness** *n*

que·ry \'kwir-ē, 'kwer-\ *n, pl* **queries** : QUESTION — **query** *vb*

que·sa·dil·la \ˌkā-sə-'dē-ə\ *n* : a tortilla filled with a savory mixture, folded, and usu. fried

quest \'kwest\ *n* : SEARCH ⟨in ~ of game⟩ — **quest** *vb*

¹ques·tion \'kwes-chən\ *n* 1 : an interrogative expression 2 : a subject for debate; *also* : a proposition to be voted on 3 : INQUIRY 4 : DISPUTE ⟨true beyond ~⟩

²question *vb* 1 : to ask questions 2 : DOUBT, DISPUTE ⟨~ed the verdict⟩ 3 : to subject to analysis : EXAMINE ♦ *Synonyms* INTERROGATE, QUIZ, QUERY — **question·er** *n*

ques·tion·able \'kwes-chə-nə-bəl\ *adj* 1 : not certain or exact : DOUBTFUL 2 : not believed to be true, sound, or moral ♦ *Synonyms* DUBIOUS, PROBLEMATICAL, MOOT, DEBATABLE — **ques·tion·ably** \-blē\ *adv*

question mark *n* : a punctuation mark ? used esp. at the end of a sentence to indicate a direct question

ques·tion·naire \ˌkwes-chə-'ner\ *n* : a set of questions for obtaining information

quet·zal \ket-'säl, -'sal\ *n, pl* **quetzals** *or* **quet·za·les** \-'sä-

läs, -'sa-\ 1 : a Central American bird with brilliant plumage 2 *pl* **quetzales** — see MONEY table

¹queue \'kyü\ *n* [F, lit., tail, fr. OF *cue, coe*, fr. L *cauda, coda*] 1 : a braid of hair usu. worn hanging at the back of the head 2 : a waiting line (as of persons)

²queue *vb* **queued; queu·ing** *or* **queue·ing** : to line up in a queue

quib·ble \'kwi-bəl\ *n* 1 : an evasion of or shifting from the point at issue 2 : a minor objection or criticism — **quibble** *vb* — **quib·bler** *n*

¹quick \'kwik\ *adj* 1 : LIVING 2 : RAPID, SPEEDY ⟨~ steps⟩ 3 : prompt to understand, think, or perceive : ALERT 4 : easily aroused ⟨a ~ temper⟩ 5 : turning or bending sharply ⟨a ~ turn in the road⟩ ♦ *Synonyms* FLEET, FAST, HASTY, EXPEDITIOUS — **quick** *adv* — **quick·ly** *adv* — **quick·ness** *n*

²quick *n* 1 : a sensitive area of living flesh 2 : a vital part : HEART

quick bread *n* : a bread made with a leavening agent that permits immediate baking of the dough or batter

quick·en \'kwi-kən\ *vb* 1 : to come to life : REVIVE 2 : AROUSE, STIMULATE ⟨curiosity ~ed my interest⟩ 3 : to increase in speed : HASTEN 4 : to show vitality (as by growing or moving) ♦ *Synonyms* ANIMATE, ENLIVEN, LIVEN, VIVIFY

quick–freeze \'kwik-'frēz\ *vb* **-froze** \-'frōz\; **-fro·zen** \-'frō-z°n\; **-freez·ing** : to freeze (food) for preservation so rapidly that the natural juices and flavor are not lost

quick·ie \'kwi-kē\ *n* : something hurriedly done or made

quick·lime \'kwik-ˌlīm\ *n* : ¹LIME

quick·sand \-ˌsand\ *n* : a deep mass of loose sand mixed with water

quick·sil·ver \-ˌsil-vər\ *n* : MERCURY 1

quick·step \-ˌstep\ *n* : a spirited march tune or dance

quick–wit·ted \'kwik-'wi-təd\ *adj* : mentally alert ♦ *Synonyms* CLEVER, BRIGHT, SMART, INTELLIGENT

quid \'kwid\ *n* : a lump of something chewable ⟨a ~ of tobacco⟩

quid pro quo \ˌkwid-ˌprō-'kwō\ *n* [NL, something for something] : something given or received for something else

qui·es·cent \kwī-'e-s°nt\ *adj* : being at rest : QUIET ♦ *Synonyms* LATENT, DORMANT, POTENTIAL — **qui·es·cence** \-s°ns\ *n*

¹qui·et \'kwī-ət\ *n* : REPOSE

²quiet *adj* 1 : marked by little motion or activity : CALM 2 : GENTLE, MILD ⟨a ~ disposition⟩ 3 : enjoyed in peace and relaxation ⟨a ~ cup of tea⟩ 4 : free from noise or uproar 5 : not showy : MODEST ⟨~ clothes⟩ 6 : SECLUDED ⟨a ~ nook⟩ — **quiet** *adv* — **qui·et·ly** *adv* — **qui·et·ness** *n*

³quiet *vb* 1 : CALM, PACIFY 2 : to become quiet — usu. used with *down*

qui·etude \'kwī-ə-ˌtüd, -ˌtyüd\ *n* : QUIETNESS, REPOSE

qui·etus \kwī-'ē-təs\ *n* [ME *quietus est*, fr. ML, he is quit, formula of discharge from obligation] 1 : final settlement (as of a debt) 2 : DEATH

quill \'kwil\ *n* 1 : a large stiff feather; *also* : the hollow tubular part of a feather 2 : one of the hollow sharp spines of a hedgehog or porcupine 3 : a pen made from a feather

¹quilt \'kwilt\ *n* : a padded bed coverlet

²quilt *vb* 1 : to fill, pad, or line like a quilt 2 : to stitch or sew in layers with padding in between 3 : to make quilts

quince \'kwins\ *n* : a hard yellow applelike fruit; *also* : a tree related to the roses that bears this fruit

qui·nine \'kwī-ˌnīn\ *n* : a bitter white drug obtained from cinchona bark and used esp. in treating malaria

qui·noa \'kēn-ˌwä, kē-'nō-ə\ *n* [Sp, fr. Quechua *kinua*] : the starchy seeds of an annual herb related to spinach which are used as food and ground into flour; *also* : this herb

quint \'kwint\ *n* : QUINTUPLET

quin·tal \'kwin-t°l, 'kan-\ *n* : HUNDREDWEIGHT

quin·tes·sence \kwin-'te-s°ns\ *n* 1 : the purest essence of something 2 : the most typical example — **quin·tes·sen·tial** \ˌkwin-tə-'sen-chəl\ *adj* — **quin·tes·sen·tial·ly** *adv*

quin·tet \kwin-'tet\ *n* 1 : a musical composition for five instruments or voices 2 : a group of five and esp. of five musicians

¹quin·tu·ple \kwin-'tü-pəl, -'tyü-, -'tə-\ *adj* 1 : having five units or members **2** : being five times as great or as many — **quintuple** *n*

²**quintuple** *vb* **quin·tu·pled; quin·tu·pling** : to make or become five times as great or as many

quin·tu·plet \kwin-'tə-plət, -'tü-, -'tyü-\ *n* **1** : a group of five of a kind **2** : one of five offspring born at one birth

¹**quin·tu·pli·cate** \kwin-'tü-pli-kət, -'tyü-\ *adj* **1** : repeated five times **2** : FIFTH ⟨file the ∼ copy⟩

²**quintuplicate** *n* **1** : one of five like things **2** : five copies all alike ⟨typed in ∼⟩

³**quin·tu·pli·cate** \-plə-ˌkāt\ *vb* **-cat·ed; -cat·ing 1** : QUINTUPLE **2** : to provide in quintuplicate

¹**quip** \'kwip\ *n* : a clever remark : GIBE

²**quip** *vb* **quipped; quip·ping 1** : to make quips : GIBE **2** : to jest or gibe at

quire \'kwī(-ə)r\ *n* : a set of 24 or sometimes 25 sheets of paper of the same size and quality

quirk \'kwərk\ *n* : a peculiarity of action or behavior — **quirky** *adj*

quirt \'kwərt\ *n* : a riding whip with a short handle and a rawhide lash

quis·ling \'kwiz-liŋ\ *n* [Vidkun *Quisling* †1945 Norw. politician who collaborated with the Nazis] : one who helps the invaders of one's own country

quit \'kwit\ *vb* **quit** *also* **quit·ted; quit·ting 1** : CONDUCT, BEHAVE ⟨∼ themselves well⟩ **2** : to depart from : LEAVE; *also* : to bring to an end **3** : to give up for good ⟨∼ smoking⟩ ⟨∼ my job⟩ ♦ *Synonyms* ACQUIT, COMPORT, DEPORT, DEMEAN — **quit·ter** *n*

quite \'kwīt\ *adv* **1** : COMPLETELY, WHOLLY ⟨not ∼ finished⟩ **2** : to an extreme : POSITIVELY **3** : to a considerable extent : RATHER

quits \'kwits\ *adj* : even or equal with another

quit·tance \'kwi-tᵊns\ *n* : REQUITAL

¹**quiv·er** \'kwi-vər\ *n* : a case for carrying arrows

¹**quiver**

²**quiver** *vb* **quiv·ered; quiv·er·ing** : to shake with a slight trembling motion ♦ *Synonyms* SHIVER, SHUDDER, QUAVER, QUAKE, TREMBLE — **quiv·er·ing·ly** *adv*

³**quiver** *n* : the act or action of quivering : TREMOR

qui vive \kē-'vēv\ *n* [F *qui-vive*, fr. *qui vive?* long live who?, challenge of a French sentry] : ALERT ⟨on the *qui vive* for prowlers⟩

quix·ot·ic \kwik-'sä-tik\ *adj* [fr. Don *Quixote*, hero of the novel *Don Quixote de la Mancha* by Cervantes] : foolishly impractical esp. in the pursuit of ideals — **quix·ot·i·cal·ly** \-ti-kə-lē\ *adv*

¹**quiz** \'kwiz\ *n*, *pl* **quiz·zes 1** : an eccentric person **2** : PRACTICAL JOKE **3** : a short oral or written test

²**quiz** *vb* **quizzed; quiz·zing 1** : MOCK **2** : to look at inquisitively **3** : to question closely ♦ *Synonyms* ASK, INTERROGATE, QUERY

quiz·zi·cal \'kwi-zi-kəl\ *adj* **1** : comically quaint **2** : mildly teasing or mocking **3** : expressive of puzzlement, curiosity, or disbelief

quoit \'kwät, 'kwóit, 'kóit\ *n* **1** : a flattened ring of iron or circle of rope used in a throwing game **2** *pl* : a game in which quoits are thrown at an upright pin in an attempt to ring the pin

quon·dam \'kwän-dəm, -ˌdam\ *adj* [L, at one time, formerly, fr. *quom, cum* when] : FORMER ⟨a ∼ friend⟩

quo·rum \'kwór-əm\ *n* : the number of members required to be present for business to be legally transacted

quot *abbr* quotation

quo·ta \'kwō-tə\ *n* : a proportional part esp. when assigned : SHARE

quot·able \'kwō-tə-bəl\ *adj* : fit for or worth quoting — **quot·abil·i·ty** \-'bi-lə-tē\ *n*

quo·ta·tion \kwō-'tā-shən\ *n* **1** : the act or process of quoting **2** : the price currently bid or offered for something **3** : something that is quoted

quotation mark *n* : one of a pair of punctuation marks " " or ' ' used esp. to indicate the beginning and end of a quotation in which exact phraseology is directly cited

quote \'kwōt\ *vb* **quot·ed; quot·ing** [ML *quotare* to mark the number of, number references, fr. L *quotus* of what number or quantity, fr. *quot* how many, (as) many as] **1** : to speak or write a passage from another usu. with acknowledgment; *also* : to repeat a passage in substantiation or illustration **2** : to state the market price of a commodity, stock, or bond **3** : to inform a hearer or reader that matter following is quoted — **quote** *n*

quoth \'kwōth\ *vb past* [ME, past of *quethen* to say, fr. OE *cwethan*] *archaic* : SAID — usu. used in the 1st and 3d persons with the subject following

quo·tid·i·an \kwō-'ti-dē-ən\ *adj* **1** : DAILY **2** : COMMONPLACE, ORDINARY ⟨∼ concerns⟩

quo·tient \'kwō-shənt\ *n* : the number obtained by dividing one number by another

qv *abbr* [L *quod vide*] which see

qy *abbr* query

R

¹**r** \'är\ *n*, *pl* **r's** *or* **rs** \'ärz\ *often cap* : the 18th letter of the English alphabet

²**r** *abbr*, *often cap* **1** rabbi **2** radius **3** rare **4** Republican **5** rerun **6** resistance **7** right **8** river **9** roentgen **10** rook **11** run

Ra *symbol* radium

RA *abbr* **1** regular army **2** Royal Academy

¹**rab·bet** \'ra-bət\ *n* : a groove in the edge or face of a surface (as a board) esp. to receive another piece

²**rabbet** *vb* : to cut a rabbet in; *also* : to join by means of a rabbet

rab·bi \'ra-ˌbī\ *n* [ME, fr. OE, fr. LL, fr. Gk *rhabbi*, fr. Heb *rabbī* my master, fr. *rabh* master + *-ī* my] **1** : MASTER, TEACHER — used by Jews as a term of address **2** : a Jew trained and ordained for professional religious leadership — **rab·bin·ic** \rə-'bi-nik\ *or* **rab·bin·i·cal** \-ni-kəl\ *adj*

rab·bin·ate \'ra-bə-nət, -ˌnāt\ *n* **1** : the office of a rabbi **2** : the whole body of rabbis

rab·bit \'ra-bət\ *n*, *pl* **rabbit** *or* **rabbits** : any of various long-eared short-tailed burrowing mammals distinguished from the related hares by being blind, furless, and helpless at birth; *also* : the pelt of a rabbit

rabbit ears *n pl* : an indoor V-shaped television antenna

rab·ble \'ra-bəl\ *n* **1** : MOB 2 **2** : the lowest class of people

rab·ble-rous·er \'ra-bəl-ˌraù-zər\ *n* : one that stirs up (as to hatred or violence) the masses of the people

ra·bid \'ra-bəd\ *adj* **1** : VIOLENT, FURIOUS **2** : being fanatical or extreme **3** : affected with rabies — **ra·bid·ly** *adv*

ra·bies \'rā-bēz\ *n*, *pl* **rabies** [NL, fr. L, madness] : an acute deadly virus disease of the nervous system transmitted by the bite of an affected animal

rac·coon \ra-'kün\ *n*, *pl* **raccoon** *or* **raccoons** : a gray No. American chiefly tree-dwelling mammal with a black mask, a bushy ringed tail, and nocturnal habits; *also* : its pelt

¹race \ˈrās\ *n* **1** : a strong current of running water; *also* : its channel **2** : an onward course (as of time or life) **3** : a contest of speed **4** : a contest for a desired end (as election to office)

²race *vb* **raced; rac·ing 1** : to run in a race **2** : to run swiftly : RUSH **3** : to engage in a race with **4** : to drive or ride at high speed — **rac·er** *n*

³race *n* **1** : a family, tribe, people, or nation of the same stock **2** : a group of individuals within a biological species able to breed together **3** : a category of humankind that shares certain distinctive physical traits — **ra·cial** \ˈrā-shəl\ *adj* — **ra·cial·ly** *adv*

race·course \ˈrās-ˌkȯrs\ *n* : a course for racing

race·horse \-ˌhȯrs\ *n* : a horse bred or kept for racing

ra·ceme \rā-ˈsēm\ *n* [L *racemus* bunch of grapes] : a flower cluster with flowers borne along a stem and blooming from the base toward the tip — **rac·e·mose** \ˈra-sə-ˌmōs\ *adj*

race·track \ˈrās-ˌtrak\ *n* : a usu. oval course on which races are run

race·way \-ˌwā\ *n* **1** : a channel for a current of water **2** : RACECOURSE

ra·cial·ism \ˈrā-shə-ˌli-zəm\ *n* : a theory that race determines human traits and capacities; *also* : RACISM — **ra·cial·ist** \-list\ *n* — **ra·cial·is·tic** \ˌrā-shə-ˈlis-tik\ *adj*

ra·cial·ize \ˈrā-shə-ˌlīz\ *vb* **-ized; -iz·ing** : to give a racial character to

racing form *n* : a paper giving data about racehorses for use by bettors

rac·ism \ˈrā-ˌsi-zəm\ *n* : a belief that some races are by nature superior to others; *also* : discrimination based on such belief — **rac·ist** \-sist\ *n*

¹rack \ˈrak\ *n* **1** : an instrument of torture on which a body is stretched **2** : a framework on or in which something may be placed (as for display or storage) **3** : a bar with teeth on one side to mesh with a pinion or worm gear

rack 3: with pinion gear

²rack *vb* **1** : to torture on or as if on a rack **2** : to stretch or strain by force **3** : TORMENT **4** : to place on or in a rack

¹rack·et *or* **rac·quet** \ˈra-kət\ *n* [MF *raquette*, ultim. fr. ML *rasceta* wrist, carpus, fr. Ar *rusgh* wrist] : a light bat made of netting stretched in an oval open frame having a handle and used for striking a ball or shuttlecock

²racket *n* **1** : confused noise : DIN **2** : a fraudulent or dishonest scheme or activity

³racket *vb* : to make a racket

rack·e·teer \ˌra-kə-ˈtir\ *n* : a person who obtains money by an illegal enterprise usu. involving intimidation — **rack·e·teer·ing** *n*

rack up *vb* : ACHIEVE, GAIN ⟨*racked up* their 10th victory⟩

ra·con·teur \ˌra-ˌkän-ˈtər\ *n* : one good at telling anecdotes

rac·quet·ball \ˈra-kət-ˌbȯl\ *n* : a game similar to handball that is played on a 4-walled court with a short-handled racket

racy \ˈrā-sē\ *adj* **rac·i·er; -est 1** : full of zest **2** : PUNGENT, SPICY **3** : RISQUÉ, SUGGESTIVE ⟨~ jokes⟩ — **rac·i·ly** \ˈrā-sə-lē\ *adv* — **rac·i·ness** \-sē-nəs\ *n*

rad *abbr* **1** radical **2** radio **3** radius

ra·dar \ˈrā-ˌdär\ *n* [*radio detecting and ranging*] : a device that emits radio waves for detecting and locating an object by the reflection of the radio waves and that may use this reflection to determine the object's direction and speed

radar gun *n* : a handheld device that uses radar to measure the speed of a moving object

ra·dar·scope \ˈrā-ˌdär-ˌskōp\ *n* : a visual display for a radar receiver

¹ra·di·al \ˈrā-dē-əl\ *adj* : arranged or having parts arranged like rays around a common center ⟨the ~ form of a starfish⟩ — **ra·di·al·ly** *adv*

²radial *n* : a pneumatic tire with cords laid perpendicular to the center line

radial engine *n* : an internal combustion engine with cylinders arranged radially like the spokes of a wheel

ra·di·an \ˈrā-dē-ən\ *n* : a unit of measure for angles that is equal to approximately 57.3 degrees

ra·di·ant \ˈrā-dē-ənt\ *adj* **1** : SHINING, GLOWING **2** : beaming with happiness **3** : transmitted by radiation ◆ *Synonyms* BRILLIANT, BRIGHT, LUMINOUS, LUSTROUS — **ra·di·ance** \-əns\ *n* — **ra·di·ant·ly** *adv*

radiant energy *n* : energy traveling as electromagnetic waves

ra·di·ate \ˈrā-dē-ˌāt\ *vb* **-at·ed; -at·ing 1** : to send out rays : SHINE, GLOW **2** : to issue in or as if in rays ⟨light ~s⟩ **3** : to spread around as from a center

ra·di·a·tion \ˌrā-dē-ˈā-shən\ *n* **1** : the action or process of radiating **2** : the process of emitting radiant energy in the form of waves or particles; *also* : something (as an X-ray beam) that is radiated

radiation sickness *n* : sickness that results from exposure to radiation and is commonly marked by fatigue, nausea, vomiting, loss of teeth and hair, and in more severe cases by damage to blood-forming tissue

radiation therapy *n* : RADIOTHERAPY

ra·di·a·tor \ˈrā-dē-ˌā-tər\ *n* : any of various devices (as a set of pipes or tubes) for transferring heat from a fluid within to an area or object outside

¹rad·i·cal \ˈra-di-kəl\ *adj* [ME, fr. LL *radicalis*, fr. L *radic-, radix* root] **1** : FUNDAMENTAL, EXTREME, THOROUGHGOING **2** : of or relating to radicals in politics — **rad·i·cal·ism** \-kə-ˌli-zəm\ *n* — **rad·i·cal·ly** *adv*

²radical *n* **1** : a person who favors rapid and sweeping changes in laws and methods of government **2** FREE RADICAL; *also* : a group of atoms considered as a unit in certain reactions or as a subunit of a larger molecule **3** : a mathematical expression indicating a root by means of a radical sign; *also* : RADICAL SIGN

rad·i·cal·ise *Brit var of* RADICALIZE

rad·i·cal·ize \-kə-ˌlīz\ *vb* **-ized; -iz·ing** : to make radical esp. in politics — **rad·i·cal·i·za·tion** \ˌra-di-kə-lə-ˈzā-shən\ *n*

radical sign *n* : the sign √ placed before a mathematical expression to indicate that its root is to be taken

ra·dic·chio \ra-ˈdi-kē-ō\ *n, pl* **-chios** : a chicory with reddish variegated leaves

radii *pl of* RADIUS

¹ra·dio \ˈrā-dē-ˌō\ *n, pl* **ra·di·os 1** : the wireless transmission or reception of signals using electromagnetic waves **2** : a radio receiving set **3** : the radio broadcasting industry — **radio** *adj*

²radio *vb* : to communicate or send a message to by radio

ra·dio·ac·tiv·i·ty \ˌrā-dē-ō-ˌak-ˈti-və-tē\ *n* : the property that some elements or isotopes have of spontaneously emitting energetic particles by the disintegration of their atomic nuclei — **ra·dio·ac·tive** \-ˈak-tiv\ *adj*

radio astronomy *n* : astronomy dealing with radio waves received from outside the earth's atmosphere

ra·dio·car·bon \ˌrā-dē-ō-ˈkär-bən\ *n* : CARBON 14

radio frequency *n* : an electromagnetic wave frequency intermediate between audio frequencies and infrared frequencies used esp. for communication and radar signals

ra·dio·gram \ˈrā-dē-ō-ˌgram\ *n* : a message transmitted by radio

ra·dio·graph \-ˌgraf\ *n* : a photograph made by some form of radiation other than light; *esp* : an X-ray photograph — **radiograph** *vb* — **ra·dio·graph·ic** \ˌrā-dē-ō-ˈgra-fik\ *adj* — **ra·dio·graph·i·cal·ly** \-fi-k(ə-)lē\ *adv* — **ra·di·og·ra·phy** \ˌrā-dē-ˈä-grə-fē\ *n*

ra·dio·iso·tope \ˌrā-dē-ō-ˈī-sə-ˌtōp\ *n* : a radioactive isotope

ra·di·ol·o·gy \ˌrā-dē-ˈä-lə-jē\ *n* : the use of radiant energy (as X-rays and radium radiations) in medicine — **ra·di·ol·o·gist** \-jist\ *n*

ra·dio·man \ˈrā-dē-ō-ˌman\ *n* : a radio operator or technician

ra·di·om·e·ter \ˌrā-dē-ˈä-mə-tər\ *n* : an instrument for measuring the intensity of radiant energy — **ra·dio·met·ric** \ˌrā-dē-ō-ˈme-trik\ *adj* — **ra·di·om·e·try** \-mə-trē\ *n*

ra·dio·phone \ˈrā-dē-ə-ˌfōn\ *n* : RADIOTELEPHONE

ra·dio·sonde \'rā-dē-ō-ˌsänd\ *n* : a small radio transmitter carried aloft (as by balloon) and used to transmit meteorological data

ra·dio·tele·phone \ˌrā-dē-ō-'te-lə-ˌfōn\ *n* : a telephone that uses radio waves wholly or partly instead of connecting wires — **ra·dio·te·le·pho·ny** \-tə-'le-fə-nē, -'te-lə-ˌfō-nē\ *n*

radio telescope *n* : a radio receiver-antenna combination used for observation in radio astronomy

ra·dio·ther·a·py \ˌrā-dē-ō-'ther-ə-pē\ *n* : the treatment of disease by means of radiation (as X-rays) — **ra·dio·ther·a·pist** \-pist\ *n*

rad·ish \'ra-dish\ *n* [ME, alter. of OE *rædic*, fr. L *radic-, radix* root, radish] : a pungent fleshy root usu. eaten raw; *also* : a plant related to the mustards that produces this root

ra·di·um \'rā-dē-əm\ *n* [NL, fr. L *radius* ray] : a very radioactive metallic chemical element that is used in the treatment of cancer

ra·di·us \'rā-dē-əs\ *n, pl* **ra·dii** \-ē-ˌī\ *also* **ra·di·us·es** 1 : a straight line extending from the center of a circle or a sphere to the circumference or surface; *also* : the length of a radius 2 : the bone on the thumb side of the human forearm 3 : a circular area defined by the length of its radius ♦ **Synonyms** RANGE, REACH, SCOPE, COMPASS

RADM *abbr* rear admiral

ra·don \'rā-ˌdän\ *n* : a heavy radioactive gaseous chemical element

RAF *abbr* Royal Air Force

raf·fia \'ra-fē-ə\ *n* : fiber used esp. for making baskets and hats that is obtained from the stalks of the leaves of a tropical African palm (**raffia palm**)

raff·ish \'ra-fish\ *adj* : jaunty or sporty esp. in a flashy or vulgar manner — **raff·ish·ly** *adv* — **raff·ish·ness** *n*

¹**raf·fle** \'ra-fəl\ *vb* **raf·fled; raf·fling** : to dispose of by a raffle

²**raffle** *n* : a lottery in which the prize is won by one of a number of persons buying chances

¹**raft** \'raft\ *n* 1 : a number of logs or timbers fastened together to form a float 2 : a flat structure for support or transportation on water

²**raft** *vb* 1 : to travel or transport by raft 2 : to make into a raft

³**raft** *n* : a large amount or number

raf·ter \'raf-tər\ *n* : any of the parallel beams that support a roof

¹**rag** \'rag\ *n* 1 : a waste piece of cloth 2 : a sleazy newspaper

²**rag** *n* : a composition in ragtime

ra·ga \'rä-gə\ *n* 1 : a traditional melodic pattern or mode in Indian music 2 : an improvisation based on a raga

rag·a·muf·fin \'ra-gə-ˌmə-fən\ *n* [ME *Ragamuffyn*, name for a ragged, oafish person] : a ragged dirty person; *esp* : a poorly clothed often dirty child

¹**rage** \'rāj\ *n* 1 : violent and uncontrolled anger 2 : VOGUE, FASHION

²**rage** *vb* **raged; rag·ing** 1 : to be furiously angry : RAVE 2 : to continue out of control ⟨the fire *raged*⟩

rag·ged \'ra-gəd\ *adj* 1 : TORN, TATTERED ⟨a ~ dress⟩; *also* : wearing tattered clothes 2 : done in an uneven way ⟨a ~ performance⟩ — **rag·ged·ly** *adv* — **rag·ged·ness** *n*

rag·lan \'ra-glən\ *n* : an overcoat with sleeves (**raglan sleeves**) sewn in with seams slanting from neck to underarm

ra·gout \ra-'gü\ *n* [F *ragoût*, fr. *ragoûter* to revive the taste, fr. MF *ragouster*, fr. *re-* + *a-* to (fr. L *ad-*) + *goust* taste, fr. L *gustus*] : a highly seasoned meat stew with vegetables

rag·pick·er \'rag-ˌpi-kər\ *n* : one who collects rags and refuse for a living

rag·time \-ˌtīm\ *n* : music in which there is more or less continuous syncopation in the melody

rag·top \'rag-ˌtäp\ *n* : CONVERTIBLE

rag·weed \-ˌwēd\ *n* : any of several chiefly No. American weedy composite herbs with allergenic pollen

¹**raid** \'rād\ *n* : a sudden usu. surprise attack or invasion : FORAY

²**raid** *vb* : to make a raid on — **raid·er** *n*

¹**rail** \'rāl\ *n* [ME *raile*, fr. AF *raille, reille* bar, rule, fr. L *regula* straightedge, rule, fr. *regere* to keep straight, direct] 1 : a bar extending from one support to another as a guard or barrier 2 : a bar of steel forming a track for wheeled vehicles 3 : RAILROAD

²**rail** *vb* : to provide with a railing

³**rail** *n, pl* **rail** *or* **rails** : any of numerous small wading birds often hunted as game birds

⁴**rail** *vb* [ME, fr. MF *railler* to mock, prob. fr. OF *reillier* to growl, mutter, fr. VL **ragulare* to bray, fr. LL *ragere* to neigh] : to complain angrily : SCOLD, REVILE — **rail·er** *n*

rail·ing \'rā-liŋ\ *n* : a barrier of rails

rail·lery \'rā-lə-rē\ *n, pl* **-ler·ies** : good-natured ridicule : BANTER

¹**rail·road** \'rāl-ˌrōd\ *n* : a permanent road with rails fixed to ties providing a track for cars; *also* : such a road and its assets constituting a property

²**railroad** *vb* 1 : to put through (as a law) too hastily 2 : to convict hastily or with insufficient or improper evidence 3 : to send by rail 4 : to work on a railroad — **rail·road·er** *n* — **rail·road·ing** *n*

rail·way \-ˌwā\ *n* : RAILROAD

rai·ment \'rā-mənt\ *n* : CLOTHING

¹**rain** \'rān\ *n* 1 : water falling in drops from the clouds 2 : a shower of objects ⟨a ~ of bullets⟩ — **rainy** *adj*

²**rain** *vb* 1 : to send down rain 2 : to fall as or like rain 3 : to pour down

¹**rain·bow** \-ˌbō\ *n* : an arc or circle of colors formed by the refraction and reflection of the sun's rays in rain, spray, or mist

²**rainbow** *adj* 1 : having many colors 2 : of, relating to, or made up of people of different races or cultural backgrounds

rainbow trout *n* : a large stout-bodied fish of western No. America closely related to the salmons of the Pacific and usu. having red or pink stripes with black dots along its sides

rain check *n* 1 : a ticket stub good for a later performance when the scheduled one is rained out 2 : an assurance of a deferred extension of an offer

rain·coat \'rān-ˌkōt\ *n* : a waterproof or water-repellent coat

rain date *n* : an alternative date for an event postponed due to rain

rain·drop \-ˌdräp\ *n* : a drop of rain

rain·fall \-ˌfȯl\ *n* 1 : amount of precipitation measured by depth 2 : a fall of rain

rain forest *n* : a tropical woodland having an annual rainfall of at least 100 inches (254 centimeters) and marked by lofty broad-leaved evergreen trees forming a continuous canopy

rain·mak·ing \'rān-ˌmā-kiŋ\ *n* : the action or process of producing or attempting to produce rain by artificial means — **rain·mak·er** *n*

rain out *vb* : to interrupt or prevent by rain

rain·storm \'rān-ˌstȯrm\ *n* : a storm of or with rain

rain·wa·ter \-ˌwȯ-tər, -ˌwä-\ *n* : water fallen as rain

¹**raise** \'rāz\ *vb* **raised; rais·ing** 1 : to cause or help to rise : LIFT ⟨~ a window⟩ 2 : AWAKEN, AROUSE ⟨enough to ~ the dead⟩ 3 : BUILD, ERECT ⟨~ a monument⟩ 4 : PROMOTE ⟨was *raised* to captain⟩ 5 : END ⟨~ a siege⟩ 6 : COLLECT ⟨~ money⟩ 7 : BREED, GROW ⟨~ cattle⟩ ⟨~ corn⟩; *also* : BRING UP ⟨~ a family⟩ 8 : PROVOKE ⟨~ a laugh⟩ 9 : to bring to notice ⟨~ an objection⟩ 10 : INCREASE ⟨~ prices⟩; *also* : to bet more than 11 : to make light and spongy ⟨~ dough⟩ 12 : to multiply a quantity by itself a specified number of times ⟨~ 2 to the third power⟩ 13 : to cause to form ⟨~ a blister⟩ ♦ **Synonyms** LIFT, HOIST, BOOST, ELEVATE — **rais·er** *n* — **raise the bar** : to set a higher standard

²**raise** *n* : an increase in amount (as of a bid or bet); *also* : an increase in pay

rai·sin \'rā-zᵊn\ *n* [ME, fr. AF, grape, raisin, fr. L *racemus* cluster of grapes or berries] : a grape dried for food

rai·son d'être \ˌrā-ˌzōⁿ-'detrᵊ\ *n, pl* **rai·sons d'être** \-ˌzōⁿz-\ : reason or justification for existence

ra·ja *or* **ra·jah** \'rä-jə\ *n* [Hindi *rājā*, fr. Skt *rājan* king] : an Indian prince

¹**rake** \'rāk\ *n* : a long-handled garden tool having a crossbar with prongs

²**rake** *vb* **raked; rak·ing** 1 : to gather, loosen, or smooth with or as if with a rake 2 : to sweep the length of (as a trench or ship) with gunfire

³**rake** *n* : inclination from either perpendicular or horizontal : SLANT

⁴**rake** *n* : a dissolute man : LIBERTINE

rake–off \'rāk-ˌȯf\ *n* : a percentage or cut taken

¹rak·ish \'rā-kish\ *adj* : DISSOLUTE — **rak·ish·ly** *adv* — **rak·ish·ness** *n*

²rakish *adj* **1** : having a trim appearance indicative of speed ⟨a ∼ sloop⟩ **2** : JAUNTY, SPORTY ⟨∼ clothes⟩ — **rak·ish·ly** *adv* — **rak·ish·ness** *n*

¹ral·ly \'ra-lē\ *vb* **ral·lied; ral·ly·ing 1** : to bring together for a common purpose; *also* : to bring back to order ⟨a leader ∼ing his forces⟩ **2** : to arouse to activity or from depression or weakness **3** : to make a comeback ♦ *Synonyms* STIR, ROUSE, AWAKEN, WAKEN, KINDLE

²rally *n, pl* **rallies 1** : an act of rallying **2** : a mass meeting to arouse enthusiasm **3** : a competitive automobile event run over public roads

³rally *vb* **ral·lied; ral·ly·ing** : BANTER

rallying cry *n* : WAR CRY 2

¹ram \'ram\ *n* **1** : a male sheep **2** : BATTERING RAM

²ram *vb* **rammed; ram·ming 1** : to force or drive in or through **2** : CRAM, CROWD **3** : to strike against violently

RAM \'ram\ *n* : a computer memory that provides the main internal storage for programs and data

¹ram·ble \'ram-bəl\ *vb* **ram·bled; ram·bling** : to go about aimlessly : ROAM, WANDER

²ramble *n* : a leisurely excursion; *esp* : an aimless walk

ram·bler \'ram-blər\ *n* **1** : a person who rambles **2** : any of various climbing roses with large clusters of small often double flowers

ram·bunc·tious \ram-'bəŋk-shəs\ *adj* : UNRULY

ra·mie \'rā-mē, 'ra-\ *n* : a strong lustrous bast fiber from an Asian nettle

ram·i·fi·ca·tion \ˌra-mə-fə-'kā-shən\ *n* **1** : the act or process of branching **2** : CONSEQUENCE, OUTGROWTH ⟨the ∼s of the decision⟩

ram·i·fy \'ra-mə-ˌfī\ *vb* **-fied; -fy·ing** : to branch out

ramp \'ramp\ *n* : a sloping passage or roadway connecting different levels

¹ram·page \'ram-ˌpāj, (ˌ)ram-'pāj\ *vb* **ram·paged; ram·pag·ing** : to rush about wildly

²ram·page \'ram-ˌpāj\ *n* : a course of violent or riotous action or behavior — **ram·pa·geous** \ram-'pā-jəs\ *adj*

ram·pant \'ram-pənt\ *adj* : unchecked in growth or spread : RIFE ⟨fear was ∼ in the town⟩ — **ram·pan·cy** \-pən-sē\ *n* — **ram·pant·ly** *adv*

ram·part \'ram-ˌpärt\ *n* **1** : a protective barrier **2** : a broad embankment raised as a fortification

¹ram·rod \'ram-ˌräd\ *n* **1** : a rod used to ram a charge into a muzzle-loading gun **2** : a cleaning rod for small arms **3** : BOSS, OVERSEER

²ramrod *adj* : marked by rigidity or severity

³ramrod *vb* : to direct, supervise, and control

ram·shack·le \'ram-ˌsha-kəl\ *adj* : RICKETY, TUMBLE-DOWN

ran *past of* RUN

¹ranch \'ranch\ *n* [MexSp *rancho* small ranch, fr. Sp, camp, hut & Sp dial., small farm, fr. Old Spanish *ranchear* (*se*) to take up quarters, fr. MF (*se*) *ranger* to take up a position, fr. *ranger* to set in a row] **1** : an establishment for the raising and grazing of livestock (as cattle, sheep, or horses) **2** : a large farm devoted to a specialty **3** : RANCH HOUSE 2

²ranch *vb* : to live or work on a ranch — **ranch·er** *n*

ranch house *n* **1** : the main house on a ranch **2** : a one-story house typically with a low-pitched roof

ran·cho \'ran-chō, 'rän-\ *n, pl* **ranchos** : RANCH 1

ran·cid \'ran-səd\ *adj* **1** : having a rank smell or taste **2** : OFFENSIVE 3 — **ran·cid·i·ty** \ran-'si-də-tē\ *n*

ran·cor \'raŋ-kər\ *n* : bitter deep-seated ill will ♦ *Synonyms* ANTAGONISM, ANIMOSITY, ANTIPATHY, ENMITY, HOSTILITY — **ran·cor·ous** *adj*

ran·cour *Brit var of* RANCOR

rand \'rand, 'ränd, 'ränt\ *n, pl* **rand** — see MONEY table

R & B *abbr* rhythm and blues

R & D *abbr* research and development

ran·dom \'ran-dəm\ *adj* : CHANCE, HAPHAZARD — **ran·dom·ly** *adv* — **ran·dom·ness** *n*

random–access *adj* : allowing access to stored data in any order the user desires

random–access memory *n* : RAM

ran·dom·ize \'ran-də-ˌmīz\ *vb* **-ized; -iz·ing** : to select, assign, or arrange in a random way — **ran·dom·i·za·tion** \ˌran-də-mə-'zā-shən\ *n*

R & R *abbr* rest and recreation; rest and recuperation

rang *past of* RING

¹range \'rānj\ *n* **1** : a series of things in a row **2** : a cooking stove having an oven and a flat top with burners **3** : open land where animals (as livestock) may roam and graze **4** : the region throughout which an organism occurs **5** : the act of ranging about **6** : the distance a weapon will shoot or is to be shot **7** : a place where shooting is practiced **8** : the space or extent included, covered, or used : SCOPE **9** : a variation within limits ♦ *Synonyms* REACH, COMPASS, RADIUS, CIRCLE

²range *vb* **ranged; rang·ing** [ME, fr. AF *renger*, fr. *renc*, *reng* line, place, row, of Gmc origin] **1** : to set in a row or in proper order **2** : to set in place among others of the same kind **3** : to roam over or through : EXPLORE **4** : to roam at large or freely **5** : to correspond in direction or line **6** : to vary within limits **7** : to find the range of an object by instrument (as radar)

rang·er \'rān-jər\ *n* **1** : FOREST RANGER **2** : a member of a body of troops who range over a region **3** : an expert in close-range fighting and raiding tactics

rangy \'rān-jē\ *adj* **rang·i·er; -est** : being long-limbed and slender — **rang·i·ness** \'rān-jē-nəs\ *n*

ra·ni *or* **ra·nee** \rä-'nē, 'rä-ˌnē\ *n* : a raja's wife

¹rank \'raŋk\ *adj* **1** : strong and vigorous and usu. coarse in growth **2** : unpleasantly strong-smelling — **rank·ly** *adv* — **rank·ness** *n*

²rank *n* **1** : ROW ⟨∼s of houses⟩ **2** : a line of soldiers ranged side by side **3** *pl* : the body of enlisted personnel ⟨rose from the ∼s⟩ **4** : position in a group **5** : superior position **6** : a grade of official standing (as in an army) **7** : an orderly arrangement **8** : CLASS, DIVISION — usu. used in pl.

³rank *vb* **1** : to arrange in lines or in regular formation **2** : RATE **3** : to rate above (as in official standing) **4** : to take or have a relative position

rank and file *n* : the general membership of a body as contrasted with its leaders

rank·ing \'raŋ-kiŋ\ *adj* **1** : having a high position : of the highest rank **2** : being next to the chairman in seniority

ran·kle \'raŋ-kəl\ *vb* **ran·kled; ran·kling** [ME *ranclen* to fester, fr. AF *rancler*, fr. OF *draoncler*, *raoncler*, fr. *draoncle*, *raoncle* festering sore, fr. ML *dracunculus*, fr. L, dim. of *draco* serpent] : to cause anger, irritation, or bitterness

ran·sack \'ran-ˌsak\ *vb* : to search thoroughly; *esp* : to search through and rob

¹ran·som \'ran-səm\ *n* [ME *ransoun*, fr. OF *rançun*, fr. L *redemption-*, *redemptio* act of buying back, fr. *redimere* to buy back, redeem] **1** : something paid or demanded for the freedom of a captive **2** : the act of ransoming

²ransom *vb* : to free from captivity or punishment by paying a price — **ran·som·er** *n*

rant \'rant\ *vb* **1** : to talk loudly and wildly **2** : to scold violently — **rant·er** *n* — **rant·ing·ly** *adv*

¹rap \'rap\ *n* **1** : a sharp blow **2** : a sharp rebuke **3** : a negative often undeserved reputation ⟨a bum ∼⟩ **4** : responsibility for or consequences of an action ⟨take the ∼⟩

²rap *vb* **rapped; rap·ping 1** : to strike sharply : KNOCK **2** : to utter sharply **3** : to criticize sharply

³rap *vb* **rapped; rap·ping 1** : to talk freely and frankly **2** : to perform rap music — **rap·per** *n*

⁴rap *n* **1** : TALK, CONVERSATION **2** : a rhythmic chanting of usu. rhymed couplets to a musical accompaniment; *also* : a piece so performed

ra·pa·cious \rə-'pā-shəs\ *adj* **1** : excessively greedy or covetous **2** : living on prey **3** : RAVENOUS 2 ⟨a ∼ appetite⟩ — **ra·pa·cious·ly** *adv* — **ra·pa·cious·ness** *n* — **ra·pac·i·ty** \-'pa-sə-tē\ *n*

¹rape \'rāp\ *n* : an Old World herb related to the mustards that is grown as a forage crop and for its seeds (**rapeseed** \-ˌsēd\)

²rape *vb* **raped; rap·ing** : to commit rape on — **rap·er** *n* — **rap·ist** \'rā-pist\ *n*

³rape *n* **1** : a carrying away by force **2** : unlawful sexual activity and usu. sexual intercourse carried out forcibly or under threat of injury

¹rap·id \'ra-pəd\ *adj* [L *rapidus* strong-flowing, rapid, fr. *rapere* to seize, carry away] : very fast : SWIFT ♦ *Synonyms* FLEET, QUICK, SPEEDY — **ra·pid·i·ty** \rə-'pi-də-tē\ *n* — **rap·id·ly** *adv*

²**rapid** *n* : a place in a stream where the current flows very fast usu. over obstructions — usu. used in pl.

rapid eye movement *n* : rapid conjugate movement of the eyes associated with REM sleep

rapid transit *n* : fast passenger transportation (as by subway) in cities

¹**ra·pi·er** \'rā-pē-ər\ *n* : a straight 2-edged sword with a narrow pointed blade

rapier

²**rapier** *adj* : extremely sharp or keen ⟨~ wit⟩

rap·ine \'ra-pən, -pīn\ *n* : PILLAGE, PLUNDER

rap·pel \ra-'pel, ra-\ *vb* **-pelled; -pel·ling** : to descend (as from a cliff) by sliding down a rope

rap·pen \'rä-pən\ *n, pl* **rappen** : the centime of Switzerland

rap·port \ra-'pȯr\ *n* : RELATION; *esp* : relation characterized by harmony

rap·proche·ment \ˌra-ˌprȯsh-'mäⁿ, ra-'prȯsh-ˌmäⁿ\ *n* : the establishment of or a state of having cordial relations

rap·scal·lion \rap-'skal-yən\ *n* : RASCAL, SCAMP

rapt \'rapt\ *adj* **1** : carried away with emotion **2** : ABSORBED, ENGROSSED ⟨listened with ~ attention⟩ — **rapt·ly** \'rapt-lē\ *adv* — **rapt·ness** *n*

rap·tor \'rap-tər, -ˌtȯr\ *n* **1** : BIRD OF PREY **2** : a usu. small-to-medium-sized predatory dinosaur

rap·ture \'rap-chər\ *n* : spiritual or emotional ecstasy — **rap·tur·ous** \-chə-rəs\ *adj* — **rap·tur·ous·ly** *adv*

rapture of the deep : NITROGEN NARCOSIS

ra·ra avis \ˌrer-ə-'ā-vəs, ˌrär-ə-'ä-wəs\ *n, pl* **ra·ra avis·es** \-'ā-və-səz\ *or* **ra·rae aves** \ˌrär-ˌī-'ä-ˌwās\ [L, rare bird] : a rare person or thing : RARITY

¹**rare** \'rar\ *adj* **rar·er; rar·est** **1** : not thick or dense : THIN ⟨~ air⟩ **2** : unusually fine : EXCELLENT, SPLENDID **3** : seldom met with — **rare·ly** *adv* — **rare·ness** *n* — **rar·i·ty** \'rar-ə-tē\ *n*

²**rare** *adj* **rar·er; rar·est** : cooked so that the inside is still red ⟨~ beef⟩

rare·bit \'rer-bət\ *n* : WELSH RABBIT

rar·efac·tion \ˌrer-ə-'fak-shən\ *n* **1** : the action or process of rarefying **2** : the state of being rarefied

rar·e·fy *also* **rar·i·fy** \'rer-ə-ˌfī\ *vb* **-fied; -fy·ing** : to make or become rare, thin, or less dense

rar·ing \'rer-ən, -iŋ\ *adj* : full of enthusiasm or eagerness ⟨~ to go⟩

ras·cal \'ras-kəl\ *n* [ME *rascaile* foot soldiers, commoners, worthless person, fr. AF *rascaille*, fr. OF dial. **rasquer* to scrape, clean off, ultim. fr. L *radere* to scrape, shave] **1** : a mean or dishonest person **2** : a mischievous person — **ras·cal·i·ty** \ras-'ka-lə-tē\ *n* — **ras·cal·ly** \'ras-kə-lē\ *adj*

¹**rash** \'rash\ *adj* : having or showing little regard for consequences : too hasty in decision, action, or speech : RECKLESS ♦ *Synonyms* DARING, FOOLHARDY, ADVENTUROUS, VENTURESOME — **rash·ly** *adv* — **rash·ness** *n*

²**rash** *n* : an eruption on the body

rash·er \'ra-shər\ *n* : a thin slice of bacon or ham broiled or fried; *also* : a portion consisting of several such slices

¹**rasp** \'rasp\ *vb* **1** : to rub with or as if with a rough file **2** : to grate harshly on (as one's nerves) **3** : to speak in a grating tone

²**rasp** *n* : a coarse file with cutting points instead of ridges

rasp·ber·ry \'raz-ˌber-ē, -bə-rē\ *n* **1** : any of various edible usu. black or red berries produced by some brambles; *also* : such a bramble **2** : a sound of contempt made by protruding the tongue through the lips and expelling air forcibly

¹**rat** \'rat\ *n* **1** : any of numerous rodents larger than the related mice **2** : a contemptible person; *esp* : one that betrays friends or associates

²**rat** *vb* **rat·ted; rat·ting** **1** : to betray or inform on one's associates **2** : to hunt or catch rats

rat cheese *n* : CHEDDAR

ratch·et \'ra-chət\ *n* : a device that consists of a bar or wheel having slanted teeth into which a pawl drops so as to allow motion in only one direction

ratchet

¹**rate** \'rāt\ *vb* **rat·ed; rat·ing** : to scold violently

²**rate** *n* **1** : quantity, amount, or degree measured by some standard **2** : an amount (as of payment) measured by its relation to some other amount (as of time) **3** : a charge, payment, or price fixed according to a ratio, scale, or standard ⟨tax ~⟩ **4** : RANK, CLASS

³**rate** *vb* **rat·ed; rat·ing** **1** : ESTIMATE **2** : CONSIDER, REGARD ⟨*rated* as a good pianist⟩ **3** : to settle the relative rank or class of **4** : to be classed : RANK **5** : to have a right to : DESERVE **6** : to be of consequence — **rat·er** *n*

rath·er \'ra-thər, 'rä-, 'rə-\ *adv* [ME, fr. OE *hrathor*, compar. of *hrathe* quickly] **1** : more properly **2** : PREFERABLY ⟨I'd ~ not go⟩ **3** : more correctly speaking **4** : to the contrary : INSTEAD **5** : SOMEWHAT ⟨~ warm⟩

rather than *prep* : INSTEAD OF

raths·kel·ler \'rät-ˌske-lər, 'rat-\ *n* [obs. G (now *Ratskeller*), city-hall basement restaurant, fr. *Rat* council + *Keller* cellar] : a usu. basement tavern or restaurant

rat·i·fy \'ra-tə-ˌfī\ *vb* **-fied; -fy·ing** : to approve and accept formally — **rat·i·fi·ca·tion** \ˌra-tə-fə-'kā-shən\ *n*

rat·ing \'rā-tiŋ\ *n* **1** : a classification according to grade : RANK **2** *Brit* : a naval enlisted man **3** : an estimate of the credit standing and business responsibility of a person or firm

ra·tio \'rā-shō, -shē-ō\ *n, pl* **ra·tios** **1** : the indicated quotient of two numbers or mathematical expressions **2** : the relationship in number, quantity, or degree between two or more things

ra·ti·o·ci·na·tion \ˌra-tē-ˌō-sə-'nā-shən, -ˌä-\ *n* : exact thinking : REASONING — **ra·ti·o·ci·nate** \-'ō-sə-ˌnāt, -'ä-\ *vb* — **ra·ti·o·ci·na·tive** \-'ō-sə-ˌnā-tiv, -'ä-\ *adj* — **ra·ti·o·ci·na·tor** \-'ō-sə-ˌnā-tər, -'ä-sə-\ *n*

¹**ra·tion** \'ra-shən, 'rä-\ *n* **1** : a food allowance for one day **2** : FOOD, PROVISIONS, DIET — usu. used in pl. **3** : SHARE, ALLOTMENT

²**ration** *vb* **1** : to supply with or allot as rations **2** : to use or allot sparingly ♦ *Synonyms* APPORTION, PORTION, PRORATE, PARCEL

¹**ra·tio·nal** \'ra-shə-nəl\ *adj* **1** : having reason or understanding **2** : of or relating to reason **3** : relating to, consisting of, or being one or more rational numbers — **ra·tio·nal·ly** *adv*

²**rational** *n* : RATIONAL NUMBER

ra·tio·nale \ˌra-shə-'nal\ *n* **1** : an explanation of principles controlling belief or practice **2** : an underlying reason

ra·tio·nal·ise *Brit var of* RATIONALIZE

ra·tio·nal·ism \'ra-shə-nə-ˌli-zəm\ *n* : the practice of guiding one's actions and opinions solely by what seems reasonable — **ra·tio·nal·ist** \-list\ *n* — **rationalist** *or* **ra·tio·nal·is·tic** \ˌra-shə-nə-'lis-tik\ *adj* — **ra·tio·nal·is·ti·cal·ly** \-ti-k(ə-)lē\ *adv*

ra·tio·nal·i·ty \ˌra-shə-'na-lə-tē\ *n, pl* **-ties** : the quality or state of being rational

ra·tio·nal·ize \'ra-shə-nə-ˌlīz\ *vb* **-ized; -iz·ing** **1** : to make (something irrational) appear rational or reasonable **2** : to provide a natural explanation of (as a myth) **3** : to justify (as one's behavior or weaknesses) esp. to oneself **4** : to find plausible but untrue reasons for conduct — **ra·tio·nal·i·za·tion** \ˌra-shə-nə-lə-'zā-shən\ *n*

rational number *n* : a number that can be expressed as an integer or the quotient of an integer divided by a nonzero integer

rat race *n* : strenuous, tiresome, and usu. competitive activity or rush

rat·tan \ra-ˈtan, rə-\ *n* : a cane or switch made from one of the long stems of an Asian climbing palm; *also* : this palm

rat·ter \ˈra-tər\ *n* : a rat-catching dog or cat

¹rat·tle \ˈra-tᵊl\ *vb* **rat·tled; rat·tling** **1** : to make or cause to make a series of clattering sounds **2** : to move with a clattering sound **3** : to say or do in a brisk lively fashion ⟨~ off the answers⟩ **4** : CONFUSE, UPSET ⟨~ a witness⟩

²rattle *n* **1** : a toy that produces a rattle when shaken **2** : a series of clattering and knocking sounds **3** : a rattling organ at the end of a rattlesnake's tail

rat·tler \ˈrat-lər\ *n* : RATTLESNAKE

rat·tle·snake \ˈra-tᵊl-ˌsnāk\ *n* : any of various American pit vipers with a rattle at the end of the tail

rat·tle·trap \ˈra-tᵊl-ˌtrap\ *n* : something (as an old car) rickety and full of rattles

rat·tling \ˈrat-liŋ\ *adj* **1** : LIVELY, BRISK ⟨moved at a ~ pace⟩ **2** : FIRST-RATE, SPLENDID

rat·trap \ˈrat-ˌtrap\ *n* **1** : a trap for rats **2** : a dilapidated building

rat·ty \ˈra-tē\ *adj* **rat·ti·er; -est** **1** : infested with rats **2** : of, relating to, or suggestive of rats **3** : SHABBY ⟨a ~ old coat⟩

rau·cous \ˈrȯ-kəs\ *adj* **1** : HARSH, HOARSE, STRIDENT ⟨~ voices⟩ **2** : boisterously disorderly — **rau·cous·ly** *adv* — **rau·cous·ness** *n*

raun·chy \ˈrȯn-chē, ˈrän-\ *adj* **raun·chi·er; -est** **1** : SLOVENLY, DIRTY **2** : OBSCENE, SMUTTY ⟨~ jokes⟩ — **raun·chi·ness** \-chē-nəs\ *n*

¹rav·age \ˈra-vij\ *n* [F] : an act or result of ravaging : DEVASTATION

²ravage *vb* **rav·aged; rav·ag·ing** : to lay waste : DEVASTATE — **rav·ag·er** *n*

¹rave \ˈrāv\ *vb* **raved; rav·ing** **1** : to talk wildly in or as if in delirium : STORM, RAGE **2** : to talk with extreme enthusiasm — **rav·er** *n*

²rave *n* **1** : an act or instance of raving **2** : an extravagantly favorable criticism

¹rav·el \ˈra-vəl\ *vb* **-eled** *or* **-elled; -el·ing** *or* **-el·ling** **1** : UNRAVEL, UNTWIST **2** : TANGLE, CONFUSE

²ravel *n* **1** : something tangled **2** : something raveled out; *esp* : a loose thread

¹ra·ven \ˈrā-vən\ *n* : a large black bird related to the crow

²raven *adj* : black and glossy like a raven's feathers

³rav·en \ˈra-vən\ *vb* **1** : to devour greedily **2** : DESPOIL, PLUNDER **3** : PREY

rav·en·ous \ˈra-və-nəs\ *adj* **1** : RAPACIOUS, VORACIOUS ⟨~ wolves⟩ **2** : eager for food : very hungry — **rav·en·ous·ly** *adv* — **rav·en·ous·ness** *n*

ra·vine \rə-ˈvēn\ *n* : a small narrow steep-sided valley larger than a gully

rav·i·o·li \ˌra-vē-ˈō-lē\ *n, pl* **ravioli** *also* **raviolis** [It, fr. It dial., pl. of *raviolo*, lit., little turnip, dim. of *rava* turnip, fr. L *rapa*] : small cases of dough with a savory filling (as of meat or cheese)

rav·ish \ˈra-vish\ *vb* **1** : to seize and take away by violence **2** : to overcome with emotion and esp. with joy or delight **3** : RAPE — **rav·ish·er** *n* — **rav·ish·ment** *n*

¹raw \ˈrȯ\ *adj* **raw·er** \ˈrȯ-ər\; **raw·est** \ˈrȯ-əst\ **1** : not cooked **2** : changed little from the original form : not processed ⟨~ materials⟩ **3** : having the surface abraded or irritated ⟨a ~ sore⟩ **4** : not trained or experienced ⟨~ recruits⟩ **5** : VULGAR, COARSE ⟨~ language⟩ **6** : disagreeably cold and damp ⟨a ~ day⟩ **7** : UNFAIR ⟨~ deal⟩ — **raw·ness** *n*

²raw *n* : a raw place or state — **in the raw** : NAKED

raw·boned \ˈrȯ-ˌbōnd\ *adj* : LEAN, GAUNT; *also* : having a heavy frame that seems to have little flesh

raw·hide \ˈrȯ-ˌhīd\ *n* : the untanned skin of cattle; *also* : a whip made of this

¹ray \ˈrā\ *n* : any of an order of large flat cartilaginous fishes that have the eyes on the upper surface and the hind end of the body slender and taillike

²ray *n* [ME, fr. AF *rai*, fr. L *radius* rod, ray] **1** : any of the lines of light that appear to radiate from a bright object **2** : a thin beam of radiant energy (as light) **3** : light from a beam **4** : a thin line like a beam of light **5** : an animal or plant structure resembling a ray **6** : a tiny bit : PARTICLE ⟨a ~ of hope⟩

ray·on \ˈrā-ˌän\ *n* : a fiber made from cellulose; *also* : a yarn, thread, or fabric made from such fibers

raze \ˈrāz\ *vb* **razed; raz·ing** **1** : to scrape, cut, or shave off **2** : to destroy to the ground : DEMOLISH

ra·zor \ˈrā-zər\ *n* : a sharp cutting instrument used to shave off hair

ra·zor–backed \ˈrā-zər-ˌbakt\ *or* **ra·zor·back** \-ˌbak\ *adj* : having a sharp narrow back ⟨a ~ horse⟩

razor clam *n* : any of a family of marine bivalve mollusks having a long narrow curved thin shell

razor wire *n* : coiled wire fitted with sharp edges and used as an obstacle or barrier

¹razz \ˈraz\ *n* : RASPBERRY 2

²razz *vb* : RIDICULE, TEASE ⟨fans ~ed visiting players⟩

Rb *symbol* rubidium

RBC *abbr* red blood cells

RBI \ˌär-(ˌ)bē-ˈī, ˈri-bē\ *n, pl* **RBIs** *or* **RBI** [*run batted in*] : a run in baseball that is driven in by a batter

RC *abbr* **1** Red Cross **2** Roman Catholic

RCAF *abbr* Royal Canadian Air Force

RCMP *abbr* Royal Canadian Mounted Police

RCN *abbr* Royal Canadian Navy

rct *abbr* recruit

rd *abbr* **1** road **2** rod **3** round

RD *abbr* rural delivery

-rd *symbol* — used after the figure 3 to indicate the ordinal number third

RDA *abbr* recommended daily allowance; recommended dietary allowance

re \ˈrā, ˈrē\ *prep* : with regard to

Re *symbol* rhenium

re- \ˌrē, ˌrē, ˈrē\ *prefix* **1** : again : for a second time **2** : anew : in a new or different form **3** : back : backward

reabsorb	reattempt
reacquire	reauthorization
reactivate	reauthorize
reactivation	reawaken
readdress	rebaptism
readjust	rebaptize
readjustment	rebid
readmission	rebind
readmit	reboil
reaffirm	rebroadcast
reaffirmation	reburial
realign	rebury
realignment	recalculate
reallocate	recalculation
reallocation	rechannel
reanalysis	recharge
reanalyze	rechargeable
reanimate	recharter
reanimation	recheck
reannex	rechristen
reannexation	reclassification
reappear	reclassify
reappearance	recoin
reapplication	recolonization
reapply	recolonize
reappoint	recolor
reappointment	recombine
reapportion	recommence
reapportionment	recommission
reappraisal	recommit
reappraise	recompile
rearm	recompose
rearmament	recomputation
rearouse	recompute
rearrange	reconceive
rearrangement	reconcentrate
rearrest	reconception
reascend	recondensation
reassemble	recondense
reassembly	reconfirm
reassert	reconfirmation
reassess	reconnect
reassessment	reconquer
reassign	reconquest
reassignment	reconsecrate
reassume	reconsecration
reattach	recontact
reattachment	recontaminate
reattain	recontamination

reconvene
reconvert
recook
recopy
recross
recrystallize
recut
redecorate
redecoration
rededicate
rededication
redefine
redefinition
redeposit
redesign
redetermination
redetermine
redevelop
redevelopment
redirect
rediscount
rediscover
rediscovery
redissolve
redistill
redistillation
redraft
redraw
reecho
reedit
reelect
reelection
reemerge
reemergence
reemphasis
reemphasize
reemploy
reemployment
reenact
reenactment
reenergize
reenlist
reenlistment
reenter
reequip
reestablish
reestablishment
reevaluate
reevaluation
reexamination
reexamine
reexport
refashion
refight
refigure
refinish
refit
refix
refloat
refold
reforge
reformulate
reformulation
refortify
refound
refreeze
refuel
refurnish
regain
regather
regild
regive
regrade
regrind
regrow
regrowth
rehandle
rehear
reheat
rehouse
reimpose

reimposition
reincorporate
reinsert
reinsertion
reintegrate
reinterpret
reinterpretation
reintroduce
reintroduction
reinvention
reinvest
reinvestment
reinvigorate
reinvigoration
reissue
rejudge
rekindle
reknit
relaunch
relearn
relight
reline
reload
remanufacture
remap
remarriage
remarry
rematch
remelt
remigration
remold
rename
renegotiate
renegotiation
renominate
renomination
renumber
reoccupy
reoccur
reopen
reorder
reorganization
reorganize
reorient
reorientation
repack
repaint
repass
repeople
rephotograph
rephrase
replant
repopulate
reprice
reprocess
reprogram
republication
republish
repurchase
reradiate
reread
rereading
rerecord
reroute
reschedule
rescore
rescreen
reseal
reseed
resell
reset
resettle
resettlement
resew
reshow
resocialization
resow
respell
restaff
restart
restate

restatement
restock
restrengthen
restructure
restudy
restuff
restyle
resubmit
resummon
resupply
resurface
resurvey
resynthesis
resynthesize
retaste
retell
retest
retool
retrain

retransmission
retransmit
retrial
reunification
reunify
reunite
reusable
reuse
revaluate
revaluation
revalue
revisit
rewarm
rewash
reweave
rewed
reweigh
rewire
rezone

¹**reach** \'rēch\ *vb* **1** : to stretch out **2** : to touch or attempt to touch or seize **3** : to extend to **4** : to communicate with **5** : to arrive at ♦ *Synonyms* GAIN, REALIZE, ACHIEVE, ATTAIN — **reach·able** *adj* — **reach·er** *n*

²**reach** *n* **1** : an unbroken stretch of a river **2** : the act of reaching **3** : a reachable distance; *also* : ability to reach **4** : a range of knowledge or comprehension

re·act \rē-'akt\ *vb* **1** : to exert a return or counteracting influence **2** : to have or show a reaction **3** : to act in opposition to a force or influence **4** : to move or tend in a reverse direction **5** : to undergo chemical reaction

re·ac·tant \rē-'ak-tənt\ *n* : a chemically reacting substance

re·ac·tion \rē-'ak-shən\ *n* **1** : the act or process of reacting **2** : a counter tendency; *esp* : a tendency toward a former esp. outmoded political or social order or policy **3** : bodily, mental, or emotional response to a stimulus **4** : chemical change **5** : a process involving change in atomic nuclei

re·ac·tion·ary \rē-'ak-shə-ner-ē\ *adj* : relating to, marked by, or favoring esp. political reaction — **reactionary** *n*

re·ac·tive \rē-'ak-tiv\ *adj* : reacting or tending to react

re·ac·tor \rē-'ak-tər\ *n* **1** : one that reacts **2** : a device for the controlled release of nuclear energy

¹**read** \'rēd\ *vb* **read** \'red\; **read·ing** [ME *reden* to advise, interpret, read, fr. OE *rǣdan*] **1** : to understand language by interpreting written symbols for speech sounds **2** : to utter aloud written or printed words **3** : to learn by observing ⟨~ nature's signs⟩ **4** : to study by a course of reading ⟨~s law⟩ **5** : to discover the meaning of ⟨~ the clues⟩ **6** : to recognize or interpret as if by reading **7** : to attribute (a meaning) to something ⟨~ guilt in his manner⟩ **8** : INDICATE ⟨thermometer ~s 10°⟩ **9** : to consist in phrasing or meaning ⟨the two versions ~ differently⟩ — **read·abil·i·ty** \rē-də-'bi-lə-tē\ *n* — **read·able** \'rē-də-bəl\ *adj* — **read·ably** \-blē\ *adv* — **read·er** *n*

²**read** \'red\ *adj* : informed by reading ⟨widely ~⟩

read·er·ship \'rē-dər-ship\ *n* : the mass or a particular group of readers

read·ing *n* **1** : something read or for reading **2** : a particular version **3** : data indicated by an instrument ⟨thermometer ~⟩ **4** : a particular interpretation (as of a law) **5** : a particular performance (as of a musical work) **6** : an indication of a certain state of affairs

read—only memory *n* : ROM

read·out \'rēd-aut\ *n* **1** : the process of removing information from an automatic device (as a computer) and displaying it in an understandable form; *also* : the information removed from such a device **2** : an electronic device that presents information in visual form

read out *vb* **1** : to read aloud **2** : to expel from an organization

¹**ready** \'re-dē\ *adj* **read·i·er; -est 1** : prepared for use or action **2** : likely to do something indicated; *also* : willingly disposed : INCLINED **3** : spontaneously prompt ⟨her ~ wit⟩ **4** : immediately available ⟨~ cash⟩ — **read·i·ly** \'re-də-lē\ *adv* — **read·i·ness** \-dē-nəs\ *n* — **at the ready** : ready for immediate use

²**ready** *vb* **read·ied; ready·ing** : to make ready : PREPARE

ready—made \re-dē-'mād\ *adj* : already made up for general sale : not specially made — **ready—made** *n*

ready room *n* : a room in which pilots are briefed and await orders

re·agent \rē-ˈā-jənt\ *n* : a substance that takes part in or brings about a particular chemical reaction

¹**re·al** \ˈrēl\ *adj* [ME, real, relating to things (in law), fr. AF, fr. ML & LL; ML *realis* relating to things (in law), fr. LL, real, fr. L *res* thing, fact] **1** : of or relating to fixed or immovable things (as land) ⟨∼ property⟩ **2** : not artificial : GENUINE; *also* : not imaginary — **re·al·ness** *n* — **for real 1** : in earnest **2** : GENUINE ⟨the threat was *for real*⟩

²**real** *adv* : VERY ⟨had a ∼ good time⟩

³**re·al** \rā-ˈäl\ *n* — see MONEY table

real estate *n* : property in buildings and land

re·al·ism \ˈrē-ə-ˌli-zəm\ *n* **1** : the disposition to face facts and to deal with them practically **2** : true and faithful portrayal of nature and of people in art or literature — **re·al·ist** \-list\ *adj or n* — **re·al·is·tic** \ˌrē-ə-ˈlis-tik\ *adj* — **re·al·is·ti·cal·ly** \-ti-k(ə-)lē\ *adv*

re·al·i·ty \rē-ˈa-lə-tē\ *n, pl* **-ties 1** : the quality or state of being real **2** : something real **3** : the totality of real things and events

re·al·ize \ˈrē-ə-ˌlīz\ *vb* **-ized; -iz·ing 1** : to make actual : ACCOMPLISH **2** : to convert into money ⟨∼ assets⟩ **3** : OBTAIN, GAIN ⟨∼ a profit⟩ **4** : to be aware of : UNDERSTAND — **re·al·iz·able** *adj* — **re·al·i·za·tion** \ˌrē-ə-lə-ˈzā-shən\ *n*

re·al·ly \ˈrē-lē, ˈri-\ *adv* : in truth : in fact : ACTUALLY

realm \ˈrelm\ *n* **1** : KINGDOM **2** : SPHERE, DOMAIN ⟨within the ∼ of possibility⟩

real number *n* : a number that has no imaginary part ⟨the set of all *real numbers* comprises the rationals and the irrationals⟩

re·al·po·li·tik \rā-ˈäl-ˌpō-li-ˌtēk\ *n, often cap* [G] : politics based on practical and material factors rather than on theoretical or ethical objectives

real time *n* : the actual time during which something takes place — **real–time** *adj*

re·al·ty \ˈrēl-tē\ *n* : REAL ESTATE

¹**ream** \ˈrēm\ *n* [ME *reme*, fr. AF, ultim. fr. Ar *rizmah*, lit., bundle] : a quantity of paper that is variously 480, 500, or 516 sheets

²**ream** *vb* : to enlarge, shape, or clear with a reamer

ream·er \ˈrē-mər\ *n* : a tool with cutting edges that is used to enlarge or shape a hole

reap \ˈrēp\ *vb* **1** : to cut or clear with a scythe, sickle, or machine **2** : to gather by or as if by cutting : HARVEST ⟨∼ a reward⟩ — **reap·er** *n*

¹**rear** \ˈrir\ *vb* **1** : to erect by building **2** : to set or raise upright **3** : to breed and raise for use or market ⟨∼ livestock⟩ **4** : BRING UP, FOSTER **5** : to lift or rise up; *esp* : to rise on the hind legs

²**rear** *n* **1** : the unit (as of an army) or area farthest from the enemy **2** : BACK; *also* : the position at the back of something

³**rear** *adj* : being at the back

rear admiral *n* : a commissioned officer in the navy or coast guard ranking next below a vice admiral

¹**rear·ward** \ˈrir-wərd\ *adj* **1** : being at or toward the rear **2** : directed toward the rear ⟨a ∼ glance⟩

²**rear·ward** *also* **rear·wards** \-wərdz\ *adv* : at or toward the rear ⟨looking ∼⟩

reas *abbr* reasonable

¹**rea·son** \ˈrē-zᵊn\ *n* [ME *resoun*, fr. AF *raisun*, fr. L *ration-, ratio* reason, computation] **1** : a statement offered in explanation or justification **2** : GROUND, CAUSE **3** : the power to think : INTELLECT **4** : a sane or sound mind **5** : due exercise of the faculty of logical thought

²**reason** *vb* **1** : to talk with another to cause a change of mind **2** : to use the faculty of reason : THINK **3** : to discover or formulate by the use of reason — **rea·son·er** *n* — **rea·son·ing** *n*

rea·son·able \ˈrē-zᵊn-ə-bəl\ *adj* **1** : being within the bounds of reason : not extreme **2** : INEXPENSIVE **3** : able to reason : RATIONAL — **rea·son·able·ness** *n* — **rea·son·ably** \-blē\ *adv*

re·as·sure \ˌrē-ə-ˈshúr\ *vb* **1** : to assure again **2** : to restore confidence to : free from fear — **re·as·sur·ance** \-ˈshúr-əns\ *n* — **re·as·sur·ing·ly** *adv*

¹**re·bate** \ˈrē-ˌbāt\ *vb* **re·bat·ed; re·bat·ing** : to make or give a rebate

²**rebate** *n* : a return of part of a payment ♦ *Synonyms* DEDUCTION, ABATEMENT, DISCOUNT

¹**reb·el** \ˈre-bəl\ *adj* [ME, fr. AF fr. L *rebellis*, fr. *re-* + *bellum* war] : of or relating to rebels

²**rebel** *n* : one that rebels against authority

³**re·bel** \ri-ˈbel\ *vb* **re·belled; re·bel·ling 1** : to resist the authority of one's government **2** : to act in or show disobedience **3** : to feel or exhibit anger or revulsion

re·bel·lion \ri-ˈbel-yən\ *n* : resistance to authority; *esp* : defiance against a government through uprising or revolt

re·bel·lious \-yəs\ *adj* **1** : given to or engaged in rebellion **2** : inclined to resist authority — **re·bel·lious·ly** *adv* — **re·bel·lious·ness** *n*

re·birth \ˌrē-ˈbərth\ *n* **1** : a new or second birth **2** : RENAISSANCE, REVIVAL

re·born \-ˈbórn\ *adj* : born again : REGENERATED, REVIVED

¹**re·bound** \ˌrē-ˈbaúnd, ˈrē-ˌbaúnd\ *vb* **1** : to spring back on or as if on impact with another body **2** : to recover from a setback or frustration

²**re·bound** \ˈrē-ˌbaúnd\ *n* **1** : the action of rebounding **2** : a rebounding ball **3** : a reaction to setback or frustration

re·buff \ri-ˈbəf\ *vb* : to reject or criticize sharply : SNUB — **rebuff** *n*

re·build \(ˌ)rē-ˈbild\ *vb* **-built** \-ˈbilt\; **-build·ing 1** : REPAIR, RECONSTRUCT; *also* : REMODEL **2** : to build again

¹**re·buke** \ri-ˈbyük\ *vb* **re·buked; re·buk·ing** : to reprimand sharply : REPROVE

²**rebuke** *n* : a sharp reprimand

re·bus \ˈrē-bəs\ *n* [L, by things, abl. pl. of *res* thing] : a representation of syllables or words by means of pictures; *also* : a riddle composed of such pictures

rebus

re·but \ri-ˈbət\ *vb* **re·but·ted; re·but·ting** : to refute esp. formally (as in debate) by evidence and arguments ♦ *Synonyms* DISPROVE, CONTROVERT, CONFUTE — **re·but·ter** *n*

re·but·tal \ri-ˈbə-tᵊl\ *n* : the act of rebutting

rec *abbr* **1** receipt **2** record; recording **3** recreation

re·cal·ci·trant \ri-ˈkal-sə-trənt\ *adj* [LL *recalcitrant-, recalcitrans*, prp. of *recalcitrare* to be stubbornly disobedient, fr. L, to kick back, fr. *re-* back, again + *calcitrare* to kick, fr. *calc-, calx* heel] **1** : stubbornly resisting authority **2** : resistant to handling or treatment ♦ *Synonyms* REFRACTORY, HEADSTRONG, WILLFUL, UNRULY, UNGOVERNABLE — **re·cal·ci·trance** \-trəns\ *n*

¹**re·call** \ri-ˈkól\ *vb* **1** : REVOKE, CANCEL **2** : to call back **3** : REMEMBER, RECOLLECT ⟨∼ed their last meeting⟩

²**re·call** \ri-ˈkól, ˈrē-ˌkól\ *n* **1** : a summons to return **2** : the procedure of removing an official by popular vote **3** : remembrance of things learned or experienced **4** : the act of revoking **5** : a call by a manufacturer for the return of a product that may be defective or contaminated

re·cant \ri-ˈkant\ *vb* : to take back (something one has said) publicly : make an open confession of error — **re·can·ta·tion** \ˌrē-ˌkan-ˈtā-shən\ *n*

¹**re·cap** \ˈrē-ˌkap, rē-ˈkap\ *vb* **re·capped; re·cap·ping** : RECAPITULATE — **re·cap** \ˈrē-ˌkap\ *n*

²**recap** *vb* **re·capped; re·cap·ping** : RETREAD — **re·cap** \ˈrē-ˌkap\ *n*

re·ca·pit·u·late \ˌrē-kə-ˈpi-chə-ˌlāt\ *vb* **-lat·ed; -lat·ing** : to restate briefly : SUMMARIZE — **re·ca·pit·u·la·tion** \-ˌpi-chə-ˈlā-shən\ *n*

re·cap·ture \(ˌ)rē-ˈkap-chər\ *vb* **1** : to capture again **2** : to experience again ⟨∼ happy times⟩

re·cast \(ˌ)rē-ˈkast\ *vb* **1** : to cast again **2** : REVISE, REMODEL ⟨∼ a sentence⟩

recd *abbr* received

re·cede \ri-ˈsēd\ *vb* **re·ced·ed; re·ced·ing 1** : to move back or away ⟨a *receding* hairline⟩ **2** : to slant backward **3** : DIMINISH, CONTRACT ⟨a *receding* deficit⟩

¹re•ceipt \ri-'sēt\ *n* **1** : RECIPE **2** : the act of receiving **3** : something received — usu. used in pl. **4** : a written acknowledgment of something received

²receipt *vb* **1** : to give a receipt for **2** : to mark as paid

re•ceiv•able \ri-'sē-və-bəl\ *adj* **1** : capable of being received; *esp* : acceptable as legal ⟨∼ certificates⟩ **2** : subject to call for payment ⟨notes ∼⟩

re•ceive \ri-'sēv\ *vb* re•ceived; re•ceiv•ing **1** : to take in or accept (as something sent or paid) : come into possession of : GET **2** : CONTAIN, HOLD **3** : to permit to enter : GREET, WELCOME **4** : to be at home to visitors **5** : to accept as true or authoritative **6** : to be the subject of : UNDERGO, EXPERIENCE ⟨∼ a shock⟩ **7** : to change incoming radio waves into sounds or pictures

re•ceiv•er \ri-'sē-vər\ *n* **1** : one that receives **2** : a person legally appointed to receive and have charge of property or money involved in a lawsuit **3** : a device for converting electromagnetic waves or signals into audio or visual form ⟨telephone ∼⟩

re•ceiv•er•ship \-,ship\ *n* **1** : the office or function of a receiver **2** : the condition of being in the hands of a receiver

re•cen•cy \'rē-s°n-sē\ *n* : RECENTNESS

re•cent \'rē-s°nt\ *adj* **1** : of the present time or time just past ⟨∼ history⟩ **2** : having lately come into existence : NEW, FRESH **3** *cap* : HOLOCENE — re•cent•ly *adv* — re•cent•ness *n*

re•cep•ta•cle \ri-'sep-ti-kəl\ *n* **1** : something used to receive and hold something else : CONTAINER **2** : the enlarged end of a flower stalk upon which the parts of the flower grow **3** : an electrical fitting containing the live parts of a circuit

re•cep•tion \ri-'sep-shən\ *n* **1** : the act of receiving **2** : a social gathering at which guests are formally welcomed

re•cep•tion•ist \ri-'sep-shə-nist\ *n* : a person employed to greet callers

re•cep•tive \ri-'sep-tiv\ *adj* : able or inclined to receive; *esp* : open and responsive to ideas, impressions, or suggestions — re•cep•tive•ly *adv* — re•cep•tive•ness *n* — re•cep•tiv•i•ty \,rē-,sep-'ti-və-tē\ *n*

re•cep•tor \ri-'sep-tər\ *n* **1** : one that receives stimuli : SENSE ORGAN **2** : a chemical group or molecule in the outer cell membrane or in the cell interior that has an affinity for a specific chemical group, molecule, or virus

¹re•cess \'rē-,ses, ri-'ses\ *n* **1** : a secret or secluded place **2** : an indentation in a line or surface (as an alcove in a room) **3** : a suspension of business or procedure for rest or relaxation

²recess *vb* **1** : to put into a recess **2** : to make a recess in **3** : to interrupt for a recess **4** : to take a recess

re•ces•sion \ri-'se-shən\ *n* **1** : the act of receding : WITHDRAWAL **2** : a departing procession (as at the end of a church service) **3** : a period of reduced economic activity

re•ces•sion•al \ri-'se-shə-nəl\ *n* **1** : a hymn or musical piece at the conclusion of a service or program **2** : RECESSION 2

¹re•ces•sive \ri-'se-siv\ *adj* **1** : tending to recede **2** : producing or being a bodily characteristic that is masked or not expressed when a contrasting dominant gene or trait is present ⟨∼ genes⟩ ⟨∼ traits⟩

²recessive *n* : a recessive characteristic or gene; *also* : an individual that has one or more recessive characteristics

re•cher•ché \rə-,sher-'shā, -'sher-,shā\ *adj* [F] **1** : CHOICE, RARE **2** : excessively refined

re•cid•i•vism \ri-'si-də-,vi-zəm\ *n* : a tendency to relapse into a previous condition; *esp* : relapse into criminal behavior — re•cid•i•vist \-vist\ *n*

rec•i•pe \'re-sə-(,)pē\ *n* [L, take, imperative of *recipere* to take, receive, fr. *re-* back + *capere* to take] **1** : a set of instructions for making something from various ingredients **2** : a method of procedure : FORMULA

re•cip•i•ent \ri-'si-pē-ənt\ *n* : one that receives

¹re•cip•ro•cal \ri-'si-prə-kəl\ *adj* **1** : inversely related **2** : MUTUAL, SHARED **3** : serving to reciprocate **4** : mutually corresponding — re•cip•ro•cal•ly *adv*

²reciprocal *n* **1** : something in a reciprocal relationship to another **2** : one of a pair of numbers (as ⅔ and 3⁄2) whose product is one

re•cip•ro•cate \-,kāt\ *vb* -cat•ed; -cat•ing **1** : to move backward and forward alternately **2** : to give and take mutually **3** : to make a return for something done or given — re•cip•ro•ca•tion \-,si-prə-'kā-shən\ *n*

rec•i•proc•i•ty \,re-sə-'prä-sə-tē\ *n, pl* -ties **1** : the quality or state of being reciprocal **2** : mutual exchange of privileges (as trade advantages between countries)

re•cit•al \ri-'sī-t°l\ *n* **1** : an act or instance of reciting : ACCOUNT **2** : a public reading or recitation ⟨a poetry ∼⟩ **3** : a concert given by a musician, dancer, or dance troupe **4** : a public exhibition of skill given by music or dance pupils — re•cit•al•ist \-t°l-ist\ *n*

rec•i•ta•tion \,re-sə-'tā-shən\ *n* **1** : RECITING, RECITAL **2** : delivery before an audience usu. of something memorized **3** : a classroom exercise in which pupils answer questions on a lesson they have studied

re•cite \ri-'sīt\ *vb* re•cit•ed; re•cit•ing **1** : to repeat verbatim (as something memorized) **2** : to recount in some detail : RELATE **3** : to reply to a teacher's questions on a lesson — re•cit•er *n*

reck•less \'re-kləs\ *adj* : lacking caution ⟨a ∼ driver⟩
♦ **Synonyms** HASTY, BRASH, HOTHEADED, THOUGHTLESS — reck•less•ly *adv* — reck•less•ness *n*

reck•on \'re-kən\ *vb* **1** : COUNT, CALCULATE, COMPUTE **2** : CONSIDER, REGARD **3** *chiefly dial* : THINK, SUPPOSE, GUESS

reck•on•ing *n* **1** : an act or instance of reckoning **2** : a settling of accounts ⟨day of ∼⟩

re•claim \ri-'klām\ *vb* **1** : to recall from wrong conduct : REFORM **2** : to change from an undesirable to a desired condition ⟨∼ marshy land⟩ **3** : to obtain from a waste product or by-product ⟨∼ed plastic⟩ **4** : to demand or obtain the return of — re•claim•able *adj* — rec•la•ma•tion \,re-klə-'mā-shən\ *n*

re•cline \ri-'klīn\ *vb* re•clined; re•clin•ing **1** : to lean or incline backward **2** : to lie down : REST

re•clin•er \ri-'klī-nər\ *n* : a chair with an adjustable back and footrest

re•cluse \'re-,klüs, ri-'klüs\ *n* : a person who leads a secluded or solitary life : HERMIT — re•clu•sive \ri-'klü-siv\ *adj*

rec•og•nise *chiefly Brit var of* RECOGNIZE

rec•og•ni•tion \,re-kəg-'ni-shən\ *n* **1** : the act of recognizing : the state of being recognized : ACKNOWLEDGMENT **2** : special notice or attention

re•cog•ni•zance \ri-'käg-nə-zəns\ *n* : a promise recorded before a court or magistrate to do something (as to appear in court or to keep the peace) usu. under penalty of a money forfeiture

rec•og•nize \'re-kəg-,nīz\ *vb* -nized; -niz•ing **1** : to acknowledge (as a speaker in a meeting) as one entitled to be heard at the time **2** : to acknowledge the existence or the independence of (a country or government) **3** : to take notice of **4** : to acknowledge with appreciation **5** : to acknowledge acquaintance with **6** : to identify as previously known **7** : to perceive clearly : REALIZE — rec•og•niz•able \'re-kəg-,nī-zə-bəl\ *adj* — rec•og•niz•ably \-blē\ *adv*

¹re•coil \ri-'kȯi(-ə)l\ *vb* [ME *reculen, recoilen,* fr. AF *reculer, reculier,* fr. *re-* back + *cul* backside, fr. L *culus*] **1** : to draw back : RETREAT **2** : to spring back to or as if to a starting point ♦ **Synonyms** SHRINK, FLINCH, WINCE, QUAIL, BLENCH

²re•coil \'rē-,kȯi(-ə)l, ri-'kȯil\ *n* : the action of recoiling (as by a gun or spring)

re•coil•less \-,kȯi(-ə)l-ləs, -'kȯi(-ə)l-\ *adj* : venting expanding propellant gas before recoil is produced ⟨∼ gun⟩

rec•ol•lect \,re-kə-'lekt\ *vb* : to recall to mind : REMEMBER
♦ **Synonyms** RECALL, REMIND, REMINISCE, BETHINK

rec•ol•lec•tion \,re-kə-'lek-shən\ *n* **1** : the act or power of recollecting **2** : something recollected

re•com•bi•nant \(,)rē-'käm-bə-nənt\ *adj* **1** : relating to genetic recombination **2** : containing or produced by recombinant DNA ⟨∼ vaccines⟩

recombinant DNA *n* : genetically engineered DNA prepared in vitro by joining together DNA usu. from more than one species of organism

re•com•bi•na•tion \,rē-,käm-bə-'nā-shən\ *n* : the formation of new combinations of genes

rec•om•mend \,re-kə-'mend\ *vb* **1** : to present as deserving of acceptance or trial **2** : to give in charge : COMMIT

3 : to make acceptable **4** : ADVISE, COUNSEL — **rec·om·mend·able** \-'men-də-bəl\ adj

rec·om·men·da·tion \,re-kə-mən-'dā-shən\ n **1** : the act of recommending **2** : something recommended **3** : something that recommends

¹rec·om·pense \'re-kəm-,pens\ vb **-pensed; -pens·ing 1** : to give compensation to : pay for **2** : to return in kind : REQUITE ✦ *Synonyms* REIMBURSE, INDEMNIFY, REPAY, COMPENSATE

²recompense n : COMPENSATION

rec·on·cile \'re-kən-,sī(-ə)l\ vb **-ciled; -cil·ing 1** : to cause to be friendly or harmonious again **2** : ADJUST, SETTLE ⟨~ differences⟩ **3** : to bring to submission or acceptance ✦ *Synonyms* CONFORM, ACCOMMODATE, HARMONIZE, COORDINATE — **rec·on·cil·able** adj — **rec·on·cile·ment** n — **rec·on·cil·er** n

rec·on·cil·i·a·tion \,re-kən-,si-lē-'ā-shən\ n **1** : the action of reconciling **2** : the Roman Catholic sacrament of penance

re·con·dite \'re-kən-,dīt\ adj **1** : hard to understand : PROFOUND, ABSTRUSE **2** : little known : OBSCURE

re·con·di·tion \,rē-kən-'di-shən\ vb **1** : to restore to good condition (as by replacing parts) **2** : to condition anew

re·con·nais·sance \ri-'kä-nə-zəns, -səns\ n [F, lit., recognition] : a preliminary survey of an area; esp : an exploratory military survey of enemy territory

re·con·noi·ter or **re·con·noi·tre** \,rē-kə-'nói-tər, ,re-\ vb **-noi·tered** or **-noi·tred; -noi·ter·ing** or **-noi·tring** : to make a reconnaissance of : engage in reconnaissance

re·con·sid·er \,rē-kən-'si-dər\ vb : to consider again with a view to changing or reversing — **re·con·sid·er·a·tion** \-,si-də-'rā-shən\ n

re·con·sti·tute \rē-'kän-stə-,tüt, -,tyüt\ vb : to restore to a former condition by adding water ⟨~ powdered milk⟩

re·con·struct \,rē-kən-'strəkt\ vb : to construct again : REBUILD

re·con·struc·tion \,rē-kən-'strək-shən\ n **1** : the action of reconstructing : the state of being reconstructed **2** often cap : the reorganization and reestablishment of the seceded states in the Union after the American Civil War **3** : something reconstructed

¹re·cord \ri-'kórd\ vb [ME, lit., to recall, fr. AF recorder, fr. L recordari, fr. re- back, again + cord-, cors heart] **1** : to set down in writing **2** : to register permanently **3** : INDICATE, READ **4** : to give evidence of **5** : to cause (as sound or visual images) to be registered (as on a disc or a magnetic tape) in a form that permits reproduction

²rec·ord \'re-kərd\ n **1** : the act of being recorded **2** : a written account of proceedings **3** : known facts about a person; also : a collection of items of information (as in a database) treated as a unit **4** : an attested top performance **5** : something on which sound or visual images have been recorded

³re·cord \ri-'kórd\ n : a function of an electronic device that causes it to record

re·cord·er \ri-'kór-dər\ n **1** : a judge in some city courts **2** : one who records transactions officially **3** : a recording device **4** : a wind instrument with a whistle mouthpiece and eight fingerholes

re·cord·ing n : RECORD 5

re·cord·ist \ri-'kór-dist\ n : one who records sound esp. on film

¹re·count \ri-'kaunt\ vb : to relate in detail : TELL ✦ *Synonyms* RECITE, REHEARSE, NARRATE, DESCRIBE, STATE, REPORT

²re·count \'rē-,kaunt, (,)rē-'kaunt\ vb : to count again

³re·count \'rē-,kaunt, (,)rē-'kaunt\ n : a second or fresh count

re·coup \ri-'küp\ vb : to get an equivalent or compensation for : make up for something lost

re·course \'rē-,kórs, ri-'kórs\ n **1** : a turning to someone or something for assistance or protection **2** : a source of aid : RESORT

re·cov·er \ri-'kə-vər\ vb **1** : to get back again : REGAIN, RETRIEVE **2** : to regain normal health, poise, or status **3** : to make up for : RECOUP ⟨~ed all his losses⟩ **4** : RECLAIM ⟨~ land from the sea⟩ **5** : to obtain a legal judgment in one's favor — **re·cov·er·able** adj — **re·cov·ery** \-'kə-və-rē\ n

re–cov·er \,rē-'kə-vər\ vb : to cover again

recovering adj : being in the process of overcoming a shortcoming or problem ⟨a ~ alcoholic⟩

re·cov·ery \ri-'kə-və-rē\ n **1** : an act or instance of recovering; esp : an economic upturn **2** : the process of combating a disorder or problem

¹re·cre·ant \'re-krē-ənt\ adj [ME, fr. AF, fr. prp. of (se) recreire to give up, yield, fr. ML (se) recredere to resign oneself (to a judgment), fr. L re- back +credere to believe] **1** : COWARDLY **2** : UNFAITHFUL

²recreant n **1** : COWARD **2** : DESERTER

rec·re·ate \'re-krē-,āt\ vb **-at·ed; -at·ing 1** : to give new life or freshness to **2** : to take recreation — **rec·re·ative** \-,ā-tiv\ adj

re–cre·ate \,rē-krē-'āt\ vb : to create again — **re·cre·ation** \-'ā-shən\ n — **re·cre·ative** \-'ā-tiv\ adj

rec·re·ation \,re-krē-'ā-shən\ n : a refreshing of strength or spirits after work; also : a means of refreshment ✦ *Synonyms* DIVERSION, ENTERTAINMENT, AMUSEMENT — **rec·re·ation·al** \-shə-nəl\ adj

recreational vehicle n : a vehicle designed for recreational use (as camping)

re·crim·i·na·tion \ri-,kri-mə-'nā-shən\ n : a retaliatory accusation — **re·crim·i·nate** \-'kri-mə-,nāt\ vb — **re·crim·i·na·tory** \-'kri-mə-nə-,tór-ē\ adj

re·cru·des·cence \,rē-krü-'de-sᵊns\ n : a renewal or breaking out again esp. of something unhealthful or dangerous

¹re·cruit \ri-'krüt\ vb **1** : to form or strengthen with new members ⟨~ an army⟩ **2** : to enlist as a member of an armed service **3** : to secure the services of **4** : to seek to enroll **5** : to restore or increase in health or vigor ⟨resting to ~ his strength⟩ — **re·cruit·er** n — **re·cruit·ment** n

²recruit n [F recrute, recrue fresh growth, new levy of soldiers, fr. MF, fr. recroistre to grow up again, fr. L recrescere] : a newcomer to an activity or field; esp : a newly enlisted member of the armed forces

rec·tal \'rek-tᵊl\ adj : of or relating to the rectum — **rec·tal·ly** adv

rect·an·gle \'rek-,taŋ-gəl\ n : a 4-sided figure with four right angles; esp : one with adjacent sides of unequal length — **rect·an·gu·lar** \rek-'taŋ-gyə-lər\ adj

rec·ti·fi·er \'rek-tə-,fī(-ə)r\ n : one that rectifies; esp : a device for converting alternating current into direct current

rec·ti·fy \'rek-tə-,fī\ vb **-fied; -fy·ing** : to make or set right : CORRECT ✦ *Synonyms* EMEND, AMEND, MEND, RIGHT — **rec·ti·fi·ca·tion** \,rek-tə-fə-'kā-shən\ n

rec·ti·lin·ear \,rek-tə-'li-nē-ər\ adj **1** : moving in a straight line ⟨~ motion⟩ **2** : characterized by straight lines

rec·ti·tude \'rek-tə-,tüd, -,tyüd\ n **1** : moral integrity **2** : correctness of procedure ✦ *Synonyms* VIRTUE, GOODNESS, MORALITY, PROBITY

rec·to \'rek-tō\ n, pl **rectos** : a right-hand page

rec·tor \'rek-tər\ n **1** : a priest or minister in charge of a parish **2** : the head of a university or school — **rec·to·ri·al** \rek-'tór-ē-əl\ adj

rec·to·ry \'rek-tə-rē\ n, pl **-ries** : the residence of a rector or a parish priest

rec·tum \'rek-təm\ n, pl **rectums** or **rec·ta** \-tə\ [ME, fr. ML, fr. rectum intestinum, lit., straight intestine] : the last part of the intestine joining the colon and anus

re·cum·bent \ri-'kəm-bənt\ adj : lying down : RECLINING

re·cu·per·ate \ri-'kü-pə-,rāt, -'kyü-\ vb **-at·ed; -at·ing** : to get back (as health or strength) : RECOVER — **re·cu·per·a·tion** \-,kü-pə-'rā-shən, -,kyü-\ n — **re·cu·per·a·tive** \-'kü-pə-,rā-tiv, -'kyü-\ adj

re·cur \ri-'kər\ vb **re·curred; re·cur·ring 1** : to go or come back in thought or discussion **2** : to occur or appear again esp. after an interval : occur time after time ⟨recurring headaches⟩ — **re·cur·rence** \-'kər-əns\ n — **re·cur·rent** \-ənt\ adj

re·cy·cle \rē-'sī-kəl\ vb **1** : to pass again through a cycle of changes or treatment **2** : to process (as liquid body waste, glass, or cans) in order to regain materials for human use — **re·cy·cla·bil·i·ty** \-,sī-klə-'bil-ə-tē\ n — **re·cy·cla·ble** \-k(ə)lə-bəl\ adj — **recycle** n

¹red \'red\ adj **red·der; red·dest 1** : of the color red **2** : endorsing radical social or political change esp. by force **3** often cap : of or relating to the former U.S.S.R. or its allies — **red·ly** adv — **red·ness** n

²red n **1** : the color of blood or of the ruby **2** : a revolutionary in politics **3** *cap* : COMMUNIST **4** : the condition of showing a loss ⟨in the ∼⟩

re·dact \ri-'dakt\ *vb* **1** : to put in writing : FRAME **2** : EDIT — **re·dac·tor** \-'dak-tər\ *n*

re·dac·tion \-'dak-shən\ *n* **1** : an act or instance of redacting **2** : EDITION

red alga *n* : any of a group of reddish usu. marine algae

red blood cell *n* : any of the hemoglobin-containing cells that carry oxygen from the lungs to the tissues and are responsible for the red color of vertebrate blood

red·breast \'red-ˌbrest\ *n* : ROBIN

red–carpet *adj* : marked by ceremonial courtesy

red cedar *n* : an American juniper with scalelike leaves and fragrant close-grained red wood; *also* : its wood

red clover *n* : a European clover that has globe-shaped heads of reddish flowers and is widely cultivated for hay and forage

red·coat \'red-ˌkōt\ *n* : a British soldier esp. during the Revolutionary War

red·den \'re-dᵊn\ *vb* : to make or become red or reddish : FLUSH, BLUSH

red·dish \'re-dish\ *adj* : tinged with red — **red·dish·ness** *n*

red dwarf *n* : a star with lower temperature and less mass than the sun

re·deem \ri-'dēm\ *vb* [ME *redemen*, fr. AF *rdemer*, modif. of L *redimere*, fr. *re-*, *red-* back, again + *emere* to take, buy] **1** : to recover (property) by discharging an obligation **2** : to ransom, free, or rescue by paying a price **3** : to free from the consequences of sin **4** : to remove the obligation of by payment ⟨the government ∼s savings bonds⟩; *also* : to convert into something of value **5** : to make good (a promise) by performing : FULFILL **6** : to atone for — **re·deem·able** *adj* — **re·deem·er** *n*

re·demp·tion \ri-'demp-shən\ *n* : the act of redeeming : the state of being redeemed — **re·demp·tive** \-tiv\ *adj* — **re·demp·to·ry** \-tə-rē\ *adj*

re·de·ploy \ˌrē-di-'ploi\ *vb* **1** : to transfer from one area or activity to another **2** : to relocate men or equipment — **re·de·ploy·ment** *n*

red–eye \'red-ˌī\ *n* **1** : cheap whiskey **2** : a late night or overnight flight

red·fish \'red-ˌfish\ *n* : any of various reddish marine fishes of the Atlantic including some used for food

red fox *n* : a fox with orange-red to reddish brown fur

red giant *n* : a very large star with a relatively low surface temperature

red–hand·ed \'red-'han-dəd\ *adv or adj* : in the act of committing a misdeed

red·head \-ˌhed\ *n* : a person having red hair — **red·head·ed** \-ˌhe-dəd\ *adj*

red herring *n* : a diversion intended to distract attention from the real issue

red–hot \'red-'hät\ *adj* **1** : extremely hot; *esp* : glowing with heat **2** : EXCITED, FURIOUS **3** : very new ⟨∼ news⟩

re·dial \'rē-ˌdī(-ə)l\ *n* : a telephone function that automatically repeats the dialing of the last number called — **redial** *vb*

re·dis·trib·ute \ˌrē-də-'stri-byüt\ *vb* **1** : to alter the distribution of **2** : to spread to other areas — **re·dis·tri·bu·tion** \(ˌ)rē-ˌdis-trə-'byü-shən\ *n*

re·dis·trict \ˌrē-'dis-(ˌ)trikt\ *vb* : to organize into new territorial and esp. political divisions

red–let·ter \'red-ˌle-tər\ *adj* : of special significance : MEMORABLE

red–light *adj* : having many houses of prostitution ⟨a ∼district⟩

re·do \(ˌ)rē-'dü\ *vb* : to do over or again; *esp* : REDECORATE

red oak *n* : any of various No. American oaks with leaves usu. having spiny-tipped lobes and acorns that take two years to mature; *also* : the wood of a red oak

red·o·lent \'re-də-lənt\ *adj* **1** : FRAGRANT, AROMATIC **2** : having a specified fragrance ⟨a room ∼ of cooked cabbage⟩ **3** : REMINISCENT, SUGGESTIVE — **red·o·lence** \-ləns\ *n* — **red·o·lent·ly** *adv*

re·dou·ble \(ˌ)rē-'də-bəl\ *vb* : to make twice as great in size or amount; *also* : INTENSIFY

re·doubt \ri-'daút\ *n* [F *redoute*, fr. It *ridotto*, fr. ML *reductus* secret place, fr. L, withdrawn, fr. *reducere* to lead

back, fr. *re-* back + *ducere* to lead] : a small usu. temporary fortification

re·doubt·able \ri-'daú-tə-bəl\ *adj* [ME *redoutable*, fr. AF, fr. *reduter* to dread, fr. *re-* back, again + *duter* to doubt] : arousing dread or fear : FORMIDABLE

re·dound \ri-'daúnd\ *vb* **1** : to have an effect **2** : to become added or transferred : ACCRUE

red pepper *n* **1** : CAYENNE PEPPER **2** : a mature red hot pepper or sweet pepper

¹re·dress \ri-'dres\ *vb* **1** : to set right : REMEDY **2** : COMPENSATE **3** : to remove the cause of (a grievance) **4** : AVENGE

²re·dress *n* **1** : relief from distress **2** : means or possibility of seeking a remedy **3** : compensation for loss or injury **4** : an act or instance of redressing

red·shift \'red-'shift\ *n* : displacement of the spectrum of a heavenly body toward longer wavelength; *also* : a measure of this displacement

red snapper *n* : any of various reddish fishes including several food fishes

red spider *n* : SPIDER MITE

red squirrel *n* : a common No. American squirrel with the upper parts chiefly red

red–tailed hawk \'red-ˌtāld-\ *n* : a rodent-eating No. American hawk with a rather short tyically reddish tail

red tape *n* [fr. the red tape formerly used to bind legal documents in England] : official routine or procedure marked by excessive complexity which results in delay or inaction

red tide *n* : seawater discolored by the presence of large numbers of dinoflagellates which produce a toxin that renders infected shellfish poisonous

re·duce \ri-'düs, -'dyüs\ *vb* **re·duced; re·duc·ing 1** : LESSEN **2** : to bring to a specified state or condition ⟨*reduced* them to tears⟩ **3** : to put in a lower rank or grade **4** : CONQUER ⟨∼ a fort⟩ **5** : to bring into a certain order or classification **6** : to correct (as a fracture) by restoration of displaced parts **7** : to lessen one's weight ✦ ***Synonyms*** DECREASE, DIMINISH, ABATE, DWINDLE, RECEDE — **re·duc·er** *n* — **re·duc·ible** \-'dü-sə-bəl, -'dyü-\ *adj*

re·duc·tion \ri-'dək-shən\ *n* **1** : the act of reducing : the state of being reduced **2** : something made by reducing **3** : the amount taken off in reducing something

re·dun·dan·cy \ri-'dən-dən-sē\ *n, pl* **-cies 1** : the quality or state of being redundant : SUPERFLUITY **2** : something redundant or in excess **3** : the use of surplus words

re·dun·dant \-dənt\ *adj* **1** : exceeding what is needed or normal : SUPERFLUOUS; *esp* : using more words than necessary **2** : marked by repetition — **re·dun·dant·ly** *adv*

red–winged blackbird \'red-ˌwiŋd-\ *n* : a No. American blackbird of which the adult male is black with a patch of bright scarlet on the wings

red·wood \'red-ˌwúd\ *n* : a tall coniferous timber tree esp. of coastal California; *also* : its durable wood

reed \'rēd\ *n* **1** : any of various tall slender grasses of wet areas; *also* : a stem or growth of reed **2** : a musical instrument made from the hollow stem of a reed **3** : an elastic tongue of cane, wood, or metal by which tones are produced in organ pipes and certain other wind instruments — **reedy** *adj*

re·ed·u·cate \(ˌ)rē-'e-jə-ˌkāt\ *vb* : to train again; *esp* : to rehabilitate through education — **re·ed·u·ca·tion** *n*

¹reef \'rēf\ *n* **1** : a part of a sail taken in or let out in regulating the sail's size **2** : reduction in sail area by reefing

²reef *vb* : to reduce the area of a sail by rolling or folding part of it

³reef *n* : a ridge of rocks, sand or coral at or near the surface of the water

reef·er \'rē-fər\ *n* : a marijuana cigarette

¹reek \'rēk\ *n* : a strong or disagreeable fume or odor

²reek *vb* **1** : to give off or become permeated with a strong or offensive odor **2** : to give a strong impression of some constituent quality ⟨an excuse that ∼ed of falsehood⟩ — **reek·er** *n* — **reeky** \'rē-kē\ *adj*

¹reel \'rēl\ *n* : a revolvable device on which something flexible (as film or tape) is wound; *also* : a quantity of something wound on such a device

²reel *vb* **1** : to wind on or as if on a reel **2** : to pull or draw (as a fish) by reeling a line — **reel·able** *adj* — **reel·er** *n*

³**reel** vb **1** : WHIRL; also : to be giddy **2** : to waver or fall back (as from a blow) **3** : to walk or move unsteadily

⁴**reel** n : a reeling motion

⁵**reel** n : a lively Scottish dance or its music

reel off vb **1** : to tell or recite rapidly and easily ⟨*reeled off* the right answers⟩ **2** : to achieve usu. consecutively ⟨*reeled off* six straight wins⟩

re·en·try \rē-'en-trē\ n **1** : a second or new entry **2** : the action of reentering the earth's atmosphere from space

reeve \'rēv\ vb **rove** \'rōv\ or **reeved**; **reev·ing** : to pass (as a rope) through a hole in a block or cleat

¹**ref** \'ref\ n : REFEREE 2

²**ref** abbr **1** reference **2** referred **3** reformed **4** refunding

re·fec·tion \ri-'fek-shən\ n **1** : refreshment esp. after hunger or fatigue **2** : food and drink together : REPAST

re·fec·to·ry \ri-'fek-tə-rē\ n, pl **-ries** : a dining hall (as in a monastery or college)

re·fer \ri-'fər\ vb **re·ferred**; **re·fer·ring** [ME referren, fr. AF referer, referir, fr. L referre to bring back, report, refer, fr. re- back + ferre to carry] **1** : to assign to a certain source, cause, or relationship **2** : to direct or send to some person or place (as for information or help) **3** : to submit to someone else for consideration or action **4** : to have recourse (as for information or aid) **5** : to have connection : RELATE **6** : to direct attention : speak of : MENTION, ALLUDE ◆ *Synonyms* RECUR, REPAIR, RESORT, APPLY, GO, TURN — **re·fer·able** \'re-fə-rə-bəl, ri-'fər-ə-\ adj

¹**ref·er·ee** \,re-fə-'rē\ n **1** : a person to whom an issue esp. in law is referred for investigation or settlement **2** : an umpire in certain games

²**referee** vb **-eed**; **-ee·ing** : to act as referee

ref·er·ence \'re-frəns, -fə-rəns\ n **1** : the act of referring **2** : RELATION, RESPECT **3** : ALLUSION, MENTION **4** : something that refers a reader to another passage or book **5** : consultation esp. for obtaining information ⟨books for ∼⟩ **6** : a person of whom inquiries as to character or ability can be made **7** : a written recommendation of a person for employment

ref·er·en·dum \,re-fə-'ren-dəm\ n, pl **-da** \-də\ or **-dums** : the submitting of legislative measures to the voters for approval or rejection; also : a vote on a measure so submitted

ref·er·ent \'re-frənt, -fə-rənt\ n : one that refers or is referred to; esp : the thing a word stands for — **referent** adj

re·fer·ral \ri-'fər-əl\ n **1** : the act or an instance of referring **2** : one that is referred

¹**re·fill** \,rē-'fil\ vb : to fill again : REPLENISH — **re·fill·able** adj

²**re·fill** \'rē-,fil\ n : a new or fresh supply of something

re·fi·nance \,rē-fə-'nans, (,)rē-'fī-nans\ vb : to renew or reorganize the financing of

re·fine \ri-'fīn\ vb **re·fined**; **re·fin·ing** **1** : to free from impurities or waste matter **2** : IMPROVE, PERFECT **3** : to free or become free of what is coarse or uncouth **4** : to make improvements by introducing subtle changes — **re·fin·er** n

re·fined \ri-'fīnd\ adj **1** : freed from impurities **2** : CULTURED, CULTIVATED **3** : SUBTLE

re·fine·ment \ri-'fīn-mənt\ n **1** : the action of refining **2** : the quality or state of being refined **3** : a refined feature or method; also : something intended to improve or perfect

re·fin·ery \ri-'fī-nə-rē\ n, pl **-er·ies** : a building and equipment for refining metals, oil, or sugar

re·flect \ri-'flekt\ vb [ME, fr. L reflectere to bend back, fr. re- back + flectere to bend] **1** : to bend or cast back (as light, heat, or sound) **2** : to give back a likeness or image of as a mirror does **3** : to bring as a result ⟨∼ed credit on him⟩ **4** : to make apparent : SHOW ⟨figures that ∼ economic growth⟩ **5** : to cast reproach or blame ⟨their bad conduct ∼ed on their training⟩ **6** : PONDER, MEDITATE — **re·flec·tion** \-'flek-shən\ n — **re·flec·tive** \-tiv\ adj — **re·flec·tiv·i·ty** \(,)rē-,flek-'ti-və-tē\ n

re·flec·tor \ri-'flek-tər\ n : one that reflects; esp : a polished surface for reflecting radiation (as light)

¹**re·flex** \'rē-,fleks\ n **1** : an automatic and usu. inborn response to a stimulus not involving higher mental centers **2** pl : the power of acting or responding with enough speed ⟨an athlete with great ∼es⟩

²**reflex** adj **1** : bent or directed back **2** : of, relating to, or produced by a reflex ⟨a ∼ action⟩ — **re·flex·ly** adv

¹**re·flex·ive** \ri-'flek-siv\ adj : of or relating to an action directed back upon the doer or the grammatical subject ⟨a ∼ verb⟩ ⟨the ∼ pronoun himself⟩ — **re·flex·ive·ly** adv — **re·flex·ive·ness** n

²**reflexive** n : a reflexive verb or pronoun

re·flex·ol·o·gy \,rē-,flek-'sä-lə-jē\ n : massage in which pressure is applied to specific points on the hands or feet

re·flux \'rē-,fləks\ n : a flowing back

re·fo·cus \(,)rē-'fō-kəs\ vb **1** : to focus again **2** : to change the emphasis or direction of ⟨∼ed her life⟩

re·for·es·ta·tion \,rē-,fòr-ə-'stā-shən\ n : the action of renewing forest cover by planting seeds or young trees — **re·for·est** \rē-'fòr-əst\ vb

¹**re·form** \ri-'fòrm\ vb **1** : to make better or improve by removal of faults **2** : to correct or improve one's own character or habits ◆ *Synonyms* CORRECT, RECTIFY, EMEND, REMEDY, REDRESS, REVISE — **re·form·able** adj — **re·for·ma·tive** \-'fòr-mə-tiv\ adj

²**reform** n : improvement or correction of what is corrupt or defective

re–form \,rē-'fòrm\ vb : to form again

ref·or·ma·tion \,re-fər-'mā-shən\ n **1** : the act of reforming : the state of being reformed **2** cap : a 16th century religious movement marked by the establishment of the Protestant churches

¹**re·for·ma·to·ry** \ri-'fòr-mə-,tòr-ē\ adj : aiming at or tending toward reformation : REFORMATIVE

²**reformatory** n, pl **-ries** : a penal institution for reforming esp. young or first offenders

re·form·er \ri-'fòr-mər\ n **1** : one that works for or urges reform **2** cap : a leader of the Protestant Reformation

refr abbr refraction

re·fract \ri-'frakt\ vb [L refractus, pp. of refringere to break open, break up, fr. re- back + frangere to break] : to subject to refraction

re·frac·tion \ri-'frak-shən\ n : the bending of a ray (as of light) when it passes obliquely from one medium into another in which its speed is different — **re·frac·tive** \-tiv\ adj

refractive index n : the ratio of the speed of radiation in one medium to that in another medium

re·frac·to·ry \ri-'frak-tə-rē\ adj **1** : OBSTINATE, STUBBORN, UNMANAGEABLE **2** : capable of enduring high temperature ⟨∼ bricks⟩ ◆ *Synonyms* RECALCITRANT, INTRACTABLE, UNGOVERNABLE, UNRULY, HEADSTRONG, WILLFUL — **re·frac·to·ri·ness** \ri-'frak-tə-rē-nəs\ n — **re·frac·to·ry** n

¹**re·frain** \ri-'frān\ vb : to hold oneself back : FORBEAR — **re·frain·ment** n

²**refrain** n : a phrase or verse recurring regularly in a poem or song

re·fresh \ri-'fresh\ vb **1** : to make or become fresh or fresher **2** : to revive by or as if by renewal of supplies ⟨∼ one's memory⟩ **3** : to freshen up **4** : to supply or take refreshment **5** : to update or renew esp. by sending a new signal ⟨∼ the Web page⟩ ◆ *Synonyms* RESTORE, REJUVENATE, RENOVATE, REFURBISH — **re·fresh·er** n — **re·fresh·ing·ly** adv

re·fresh·ment \-mənt\ n **1** : the act of refreshing : the state of being refreshed **2** : something that refreshes **3** pl : a light meal; also : assorted light foods

re·fried beans \'rē-,frīd-\ n pl : beans cooked with seasonings, fried, then mashed and fried again

refrig abbr refrigerating; refrigeration

re·frig·er·ate \ri-'fri-jə-,rāt\ vb **-at·ed**; **-at·ing** : to make cool; esp : to chill or freeze (food) for preservation — **re·frig·er·ant** \-jə-rənt\ adj or n — **re·frig·er·a·tion** \-,fri-jə-'rā-shən\ n — **re·frig·er·a·tor** \'fri-jə-,rā-tər\ n

ref·uge \'re-,fyüj\ n **1** : shelter or protection from danger or distress **2** : a place that provides protection

ref·u·gee \,re-fyù-'jē\ n : one who flees for safety esp. to a foreign country

re·ful·gence \ri-'fùl-jəns, -'fəl-\ n : a radiant or resplendent quality or state — **re·ful·gent** \-jənt\ adj

¹**re·fund** \ri-'fənd, 'rē-,fənd\ vb : to give or put back (money) : REPAY — **re·fund·able** adj

²**re·fund** \'rē-,fənd\ n **1** : the act of refunding **2** : a sum refunded

re·fur·bish \ri-'fər-bish\ *vb* : to brighten or freshen up : RENOVATE

¹re·fuse \ri-'fyüz\ *vb* **re·fused; re·fus·ing 1** : to decline to accept : REJECT **2** : to decline to do, give, or grant : DENY — **re·fus·al** \-'fyü-zəl\ *n*

²ref·use \'re-ˌfyüs, -ˌfyüz\ *n* : rejected or worthless matter : RUBBISH, TRASH

re·fute \ri-'fyüt\ *vb* **re·fut·ed; re·fut·ing** [L *refutare* to check, suppress, refute] : to prove to be false by argument or evidence — **ref·u·ta·tion** \ˌre-fyu̇-'tā-shən\ *n* — **re·fut·er** *n*

¹reg \'reg\ *n* : REGULATION

²reg *abbr* **1** region **2** register; registered; registration **3** regular

re·gal \'rē-gəl\ *adj* **1** : of, relating to, or befitting a king : ROYAL **2** : STATELY, SPLENDID — **re·gal·ly** *adv*

re·gale \ri-'gāl\ *vb* **re·galed; re·gal·ing 1** : to entertain richly or agreeably **2** : to give pleasure or amusement to ⟨*regaled* us with stories⟩ ◆ *Synonyms* GRATIFY, DELIGHT, PLEASE, REJOICE, GLADDEN

re·ga·lia \ri-'gāl-yə\ *n pl* **1** : the emblems, symbols, or paraphernalia of royalty (as the crown and scepter) **2** : the insignia of an office or order **3** : special costume : FINERY

¹re·gard \ri-'gärd\ *n* **1** : CONSIDERATION, HEED; *also* : CARE, CONCERN **2** : GAZE, GLANCE, LOOK **3** : RESPECT, ESTEEM ⟨held in high ∼⟩ **4** *pl* : friendly greetings implying respect and esteem **5** : an aspect to be considered : PARTICULAR — **re·gard·ful** *adj* — **re·gard·less** *adj*

²regard *vb* **1** : to think of : CONSIDER **2** : to pay attention to **3** : to show respect for : HEED ⟨∼s his elders⟩ **4** : to hold in high esteem : care for **5** : to look at : gaze upon ⟨∼ed the landscape⟩ **6** *archaic* : to relate to

re·gard·ing *prep* : CONCERNING

regardless of \ri-'gärd-ləs-\ *prep* : in spite of

re·gat·ta \ri-'gä-tə, -'ga-\ *n* : a boat race or a series of boat races

re·gen·cy \'rē-jən-sē\ *n, pl* **-cies 1** : the office or government of a regent or body of regents **2** : a body of regents **3** : the period during which a regent governs

re·gen·er·a·cy \ri-'je-nə-rə-sē\ *n* : the state of being regenerated

¹re·gen·er·ate \ri-'je-nə-rət\ *adj* **1** : formed or created again **2** : spiritually reborn or converted

²re·gen·er·ate \ri-'je-nə-ˌrāt\ *vb* **1** : to subject to spiritual renewal **2** : to reform completely **3** : to replace (a body part) by a new growth of tissue **4** : to give new life to : REVIVE — **re·gen·er·a·tion** \-ˌje-nə-'rā-shən\ *n* — **re·gen·er·a·tive** \-'je-nə-ˌrā-tiv\ *adj* — **re·gen·er·a·tor** \-ˌrā-tər\ *n*

re·gent \'rē-jənt\ *n* **1** : a person who rules during the childhood, absence, or incapacity of the sovereign **2** : a member of a governing board (as of a state university) — **regent** *adj*

reg·gae \'re-ˌgā\ *n* : popular music of Jamaican origin that combines native styles with elements of rock and soul music

reg·i·cide \'re-jə-ˌsīd\ *n* **1** : one who murders a king **2** : murder of a king

re·gime *also* **ré·gime** \rā-'zhēm, ri-\ *n* **1** : REGIMEN **2** : a form or system of government **3** : a government in power; *also* : a period of rule

reg·i·men \'re-jə-mən\ *n* [ME, fr. ML, position of authority, direction, set of rules, fr. L, steering, control, fr. *regere* to direct] **1** : a systematic course of treatment or training ⟨a strict dietary ∼⟩ **2** : GOVERNMENT

¹reg·i·ment \'re-jə-mənt\ *n* : a military unit consisting usu. of a number of battalions — **reg·i·men·tal** \ˌre-jə-'men-təl\ *adj*

²reg·i·ment \'re-jə-ˌment\ *vb* : to organize rigidly esp. for regulation or central control; *also* : to subject to order or uniformity — **reg·i·men·ta·tion** \ˌre-jə-mən-'tā-shən\ *n*

reg·i·men·tals \ˌre-jə-'men-təlz\ *n pl* **1** : a regimental uniform **2** : military dress

re·gion \'rē-jən\ *n* [ME, fr. AF *regiun*, fr. L *region-, regio*, line, direction, area, fr. *regere* to rule] : an often indefinitely defined part or area

re·gion·al \'rē-jə-nəl\ *adj* **1** : affecting a particular region : LOCALIZED **2** : of, relating to, characteristic of, or serving a region — **re·gion·al·ly** *adv*

¹reg·is·ter \'re-jə-stər\ *n* **1** : a record of items or details; *also* : a book or system for keeping such a record **2** : the range of a voice or instrument **3** : a device to regulate ventilation or heating **4** : an automatic device recording a number or quantity **5** : CASH REGISTER

²register *vb* **-tered; -ter·ing 1** : to enter in a register (as in a list of guests) **2** : to record automatically **3** : to secure special care for (mail matter) by paying additional postage **4** : to convey an impression of : EXPRESS **5** : to make or adjust so as to correspond exactly

registered nurse *n* : a graduate trained nurse who has been licensed to practice by a state authority after passing qualifying examinations

reg·is·trant \'re-jə-strənt\ *n* : one that registers or is registered

reg·is·trar \-ˌsträr\ *n* : an official recorder or keeper of records (as at an educational institution)

reg·is·tra·tion \ˌre-jə-'strā-shən\ *n* **1** : the act of registering **2** : an entry in a register **3** : the number of persons registered : ENROLLMENT **4** : a document certifying an act of registering

reg·is·try \'re-jə-strē\ *n, pl* **-tries 1** : ENROLLMENT, REGISTRATION **2** : a place of registration **3** : an official record book or an entry in one

reg·nant \'reg-nənt\ *adj* **1** : REIGNING **2** : DOMINANT **3** : of common or widespread occurrence

¹re·gress \'rē-ˌgres\ *n* **1** : an act or the privilege of going or coming back **2** : RETROGRESSION

²re·gress \ri-'gres\ *vb* : to go or cause to go back or to a lower level — **re·gres·sive** *adj* — **re·gres·sor** \-'gre-sər\ *n*

re·gres·sion \ri-'gre-shən\ *n* : the act or an instance of regressing; *esp* : reversion to an earlier mental or behavioral level

¹re·gret \ri-'gret\ *vb* **re·gret·ted; re·gret·ting 1** : to mourn the loss or death of **2** : to be very sorry for **3** : to experience regret — **re·gret·ta·ble** \-'gre-tə-bəl\ *adj* — **re·gret·ter** *n*

²regret *n* **1** : sorrow caused by something beyond one's power to remedy **2** : an expression of sorrow **3** *pl* : a note politely declining an invitation — **re·gret·ful** \-fəl\ *adj* — **re·gret·ful·ly** *adv*

re·gret·ta·bly \-'gre-tə-blē\ *adv* **1** : to a regrettable extent **2** : it is to be regretted

re·group \(ˌ)rē-'grüp\ *vb* : to form into a new grouping

regt *abbr* regiment

¹reg·u·lar \'re-gyə-lər\ *adj* [ME *reguler*, fr. AF, fr. LL *regularis* regular, fr. L, of a bar, fr. *regula* rule, straightedge, fr. *regere* to keep straight, direct] **1** : belonging to a religious order **2** : made, built, or arranged according to a rule, standard, or type; *also* : even or symmetrical in form or structure **3** : ORDERLY, METHODICAL ⟨∼ habits⟩; *also* : not varying : STEADY ⟨a ∼ pace⟩ **4** : made, selected, or conducted according to rule or custom **5** : properly qualified ⟨not a ∼ lawyer⟩ **6** : conforming to the normal or usual manner or inflection **7** : of, relating to, or constituting the permanent standing military force of a state — **reg·u·lar·i·ty** \ˌre-gyə-'la-rə-tē\ *n* — **reg·u·lar·ize** \'re-gyə-lə-ˌrīz\ *vb* — **reg·u·lar·ly** *adv*

²regular *n* **1** : one that is regular (as in attendance) **2** : a member of the regular clergy **3** : a soldier in a regular army **4** : a player on an athletic team who is usu. in the starting lineup

reg·u·late \'re-gyə-ˌlāt\ *vb* **-lat·ed; -lat·ing 1** : to govern or direct according to rule : CONTROL **2** : to bring under the control of law or authority **3** : to put in good order **4** : to fix or adjust the time, amount, degree, or rate of — **reg·u·la·tive** \-ˌlā-tiv\ *adj* — **reg·u·la·tor** \-ˌlā-tər\ *n* — **reg·u·la·to·ry** \-lə-ˌtȯr-ē\ *adj*

reg·u·la·tion \ˌre-gyə-'lā-shən\ *n* **1** : the act of regulating : the state of being regulated **2** : a rule dealing with details of procedure **3** : an order issued by an executive authority of a government and having the force of law

re·gur·gi·tate \rē-'gər-jə-ˌtāt\ *vb* **-tat·ed; -tat·ing** [ML *regurgitare*, fr. L *re-* re- + LL *gurgitare* to engulf, fr. L *gurgit-, gurges* whirlpool] : to throw or be thrown back, up, or out ⟨∼ food⟩ — **re·gur·gi·ta·tion** \-ˌgər-jə-'tā-shən\ *n*

re·hab \'rē-ˌhab\ *n* **1** : REHABILITATION **2** : a rehabilitated building — **rehab** *vb*

re·ha·bil·i·tate \ˌrē-hə-'bi-lə-ˌtāt, ˌrē-ə-\ *vb* **-tat·ed; -tat·ing 1** : to restore to a former capacity, rank, or right

: REINSTATE **2** : to restore to good condition or health — **re·ha·bil·i·ta·tion** \-,bi-lə-'tā-shən\ *n* — **re·ha·bil·i·ta·tive** \-,tā-tiv\ *adj*

re·hash \,rē-'hash\ *vb* : to present again in another form without real change or improvement — **rehash** *n*

re·hear·ing \,rē-'hir-iŋ\ *n* : a second or new hearing by the same tribunal

re·hears·al \ri-'hər-səl\ *n* **1** : something told again : RECITAL **2** : a private performance or practice session preparatory to a public appearance

re·hearse \ri-'hərs\ *vb* **re·hearsed; re·hears·ing** **1** : to say again : REPEAT **2** : to recount in order : ENUMERATE; *also* : RELATE 1 **3** : to give a rehearsal of **4** : to train by rehearsal **5** : to engage in a rehearsal — **re·hears·er** *n*

¹reign \'rān\ *n* **1** : the authority or rule of a sovereign **2** : the time during which a sovereign rules

²reign *vb* **1** : to rule as a sovereign **2** : to be predominant or prevalent

re·im·burse \,rē-əm-'bərs\ *vb* **-bursed; -burs·ing** [*re-* re- + obs. E *imburse* to put in the pocket, pay, fr. ML *imbursare* to put into a purse, fr. L *in-* + ML *bursa* purse, fr. LL, hide of an ox, fr. Gk *byrsa*] : to pay back : make restitution : REPAY ✦ **Synonyms** INDEMNIFY, RECOMPENSE, REQUITE, COMPENSATE — **re·im·burs·able** *adj* — **re·im·burse·ment** *n*

¹rein \'rān\ *n* **1** : a strap fastened to a bit by which a rider or driver controls an animal **2** : a restraining influence : CHECK **3** : controlling or guiding power **4** : complete freedom — usu. used in the phrase *give rein to*

²rein *vb* : to check or direct by reins

re·in·car·na·tion \,rē-(,)in-(,)kär-'nā-shən\ *n* : rebirth of the soul in a new body — **re·in·car·nate** \,rē-in-'kär-,nāt\ *vb*

rein·deer \'rān-,dir\ *n* [ME *reindere,* fr. ON *hreinn* reindeer + ME *deer* animal, deer] : CARIBOU — used esp. for one of the Old World

reindeer moss *n* : a gray, erect, tufted, and much-branched edible lichen of northern regions that is an important food of reindeer

re·in·fec·tion \,rē-in-'fek-shən\ *n* : infection following another infection of the same type

re·in·force \,rē-ən-'fōrs\ *vb* **1** : to strengthen with additional forces ⟨∼ our troops⟩ **2** : to strengthen with new force, aid, material, or support — **re·in·force·ment** *n* — **re·in·forc·er** *n*

re·in·scribe \,rē-ən-'skrīb\ *vb* : to reestablish or rename in a new and esp. stronger form or context

re·in·state \,rē-in-'stāt\ *vb* **-stat·ed; -stat·ing** : to restore to a former position, condition, or capacity — **re·in·state·ment** *n*

re·in·vent \,rē-in-'vent\ *vb* **1** : to make as if for the first time something already invented ⟨∼ the wheel⟩ **2** : to remake completely

re·it·er·ate \rē-'i-tə-,rāt\ *vb* **-at·ed; -at·ing** : to state or do over again or repeatedly — **re·it·er·a·tion** \-,i-tə-'rā-shən\ *n*

¹re·ject \ri-'jekt\ *vb* **1** : to refuse to accept, consider, use, or submit to **2** : to refuse to hear, receive, or admit : REPEL **3** : to rebuff or withhold love from **4** : to throw out esp. as useless or unsatisfactory **5** : to subject (a transplanted tissue) to an attack by immune system components of the recipient organism — **re·jec·tion** \-'jek-shən\ *n*

²re·ject \'rē-jekt\ *n* : a rejected person or thing

re·joice \ri-'jóis\ *vb* **re·joiced; re·joic·ing** **1** : to give joy to : GLADDEN **2** : to feel joy or great delight — **re·joic·er** *n*

re·join \(,)rē-'jóin *for 1,* ri- *for 2*\ *vb* **1** : to join again **2** : to say in answer (as to a plaintiff's plea in court) : REPLY

re·join·der \ri-'join-dər\ *n* : REPLY; *esp* : an answer to a reply

re·ju·ve·nate \ri-'jü-və-,nāt\ *vb* **-nat·ed; -nat·ing** : to make young or youthful again : give new vigor to ✦ **Synonyms** RENEW, REFRESH, RENOVATE, RESTORE — **re·ju·ve·na·tion** \-,jü-və-'nā-shən\ *n*

rel *abbr* **1** relating; relative **2** religion; religious

¹re·lapse \ri-'laps, 'rē-,laps\ *n* [ME, fr. ML *relapsus,* fr. L *relabi* to slide back] **1** : the act or process of backsliding or worsening **2** : a recurrence of illness after a period of improvement

²re·lapse \ri-'laps\ *vb* **re·lapsed; re·laps·ing** : to slip or fall back into a former worse state (as of illness)

re·late \ri-'lāt\ *vb* **re·lat·ed; re·lat·ing** **1** : to give an account of : TELL, NARRATE **2** : to show or establish logical or causal connection between **3** : to have relationship or connection **4** : to have or establish relationship ⟨the way a child ∼s to a teacher⟩ **5** : to respond favorably — **re·lat·able** *adj* — **re·lat·er** *or* **re·la·tor** \-'lā-tər\ *n*

re·lat·ed *adj* **1** : connected by some understood relationship **2** : connected through membership in the same family — **re·lat·ed·ness** *n*

re·la·tion \ri-'lā-shən\ *n* **1** : NARRATION, ACCOUNT **2** : CONNECTION, RELATIONSHIP **3** : connection by blood or marriage : KINSHIP; *also* : RELATIVE **4** : REFERENCE, RESPECT ⟨in ∼ to⟩ **5** : the state of being mutually interested or involved (as in social or commercial matters) **6** *pl* : DEALINGS, AFFAIRS ⟨foreign ∼s⟩ **7** *pl* : SEXUAL INTERCOURSE — **re·la·tion·al** \-shə-nəl\ *adj*

re·la·tion·ship \-,ship\ *n* : the state of being related or interrelated

¹rel·a·tive \'re-lə-tiv\ *n* **1** : a word referring grammatically to an antecedent **2** : a thing having a relation to or a dependence upon another thing **3** : a person connected with another by blood or marriage

²relative *adj* **1** : introducing a subordinate clause qualifying an expressed or implied antecedent ⟨∼ pronoun⟩; *also* : introduced by such a connective ⟨∼ clause⟩ **2** : PERTINENT, RELEVANT ⟨matters ∼ to world peace⟩ **3** : not absolute or independent : COMPARATIVE **4** : expressed as the ratio of the specified quantity to the total magnitude or to the mean of all quantities involved ✦ **Synonyms** DEPENDENT, CONTINGENT, CONDITIONAL — **rel·a·tive·ly** *adv* — **rel·a·tive·ness** *n*

relative humidity *n* : the ratio of the amount of water vapor actually present in the air to the greatest amount possible at the same temperature

rel·a·tiv·is·tic \,re-lə-ti-'vis-tik\ *adj* **1** : of, relating to, or characterized by relativity **2** : moving at a velocity that is a significant fraction of the speed of light so that effects predicted by the theory of relativity become evident ⟨a ∼ electron⟩ — **rel·a·tiv·is·ti·cal·ly** \-ti-k(ə-)lē\ *adv*

rel·a·tiv·i·ty \,re-lə-'ti-və-tē\ *n, pl* **-ties** **1** : the quality or state of being relative **2** : a theory in physics that considers mass and energy to be equivalent and that predicts changes in mass, dimension, and time which are related to speed but are noticeable esp. at speeds approaching that of light; *also* : an extension of the theory to include gravitation and related acceleration phenomena

re·lax \ri-'laks\ *vb* **1** : to make or become less firm, tense, or rigid **2** : to make less severe or strict **3** : to seek rest or recreation — **re·lax·er** *n*

¹re·lax·ant \ri-'lak-sənt\ *adj* : of, relating to, or producing relaxation

²relaxant *n* : a relaxing agent; *esp* : a drug that induces muscular relaxation

re·lax·ation \,rē-,lak-'sā-shən\ *n* **1** : the act of relaxing or state of being relaxed : a lessening of tension **2** : DIVERSION, RECREATION

¹re·lay \'rē-,lā\ *n* [ME, set of fresh hounds, fr. *relayen* to release fresh hounds, take a fresh horse, fr. MF *relaier,* fr. *re-* again + *laier* to let go, leave] **1** : a fresh supply (as of horses or men) arranged beforehand to relieve others **2** : a race between teams in which each team member covers a specified part of a course **3** : an electromagnetic device in which the opening or closing of one circuit activates another device (as a switch in another circuit) **4** : the act of passing along by stages

²re·lay \'rē-,lā, ri-'lā\ *vb* **re·layed; re·lay·ing** **1** : to place in or provide with relays **2** : to pass along by relays **3** : to control or operate by a relay

³re·lay \(,)rē-'lā\ *vb* **-laid** \-'lād\; **-lay·ing** : to lay again

¹re·lease \ri-'lēs\ *vb* **re·leased; re·leas·ing** **1** : to set free from confinement or restraint; *also* : DISMISS ⟨released from her job⟩ **2** : to relieve from something that oppresses, confines, or burdens **3** : RELINQUISH ⟨∼ a claim⟩ **4** : to permit publication, performance, exhibition, or sale of; *also* : to make available to the public ✦ **Synonyms** EMANCIPATE, DISCHARGE, FREE, LIBERATE

²release *n* **1** : relief or deliverance from sorrow, suffering, or trouble **2** : discharge from an obligation or responsibility   **3** : an act of setting free : the state of being freed **4** : a document effecting a legal release   **5** : a releasing for performance or publication; *also* : the matter released (as to the press)   **6** : a device for holding or releasing a mechanism as required

rel·e·gate \'re-lə-ˌgāt\ *vb* **-gat·ed; -gat·ing**   **1** : to send into exile : BANISH   **2** : to remove or dismiss to some less prominent position   **3** : to assign to a particular class or sphere   **4** : to submit to someone or something for appropriate action : DELEGATE   ✦ **Synonyms** COMMIT, ENTRUST, CONSIGN, COMMEND — **rel·e·ga·tion** \ˌre-lə-'gā-shən\ *n*

re·lent \ri-'lent\ *vb*   **1** : to become less stern, severe, or harsh   **2** : SLACKEN

re·lent·less \-ləs\ *adj* : showing or promising no abatement of severity, intensity, or pace ⟨∼ pressure⟩ — **re·lent·less·ly** *adv* — **re·lent·less·ness** *n*

rel·e·vance \'re-lə-vəns\ *n* : relation to the matter at hand; *also* : practical and esp. social applicability

rel·e·van·cy \-vən-sē\ *n* : RELEVANCE

rel·e·vant \'re-lə-vənt\ *adj* : bearing on the matter at hand : PERTINENT   ✦ **Synonyms** GERMANE, MATERIAL, APPLICABLE, APROPOS — **rel·e·vant·ly** *adv*

re·li·able \ri-'lī-ə-bəl\ *adj* : fit to be trusted or relied on : DEPENDABLE, TRUSTWORTHY — **re·li·abil·i·ty** \-ˌlī-ə-'bi-lə-tē\ *n* — **re·li·able·ness** *n* — **re·li·ably** \-'lī-ə-blē\ *adv*

re·li·ance \ri-'lī-əns\ *n*   **1** : the act of relying   **2** : the state of being reliant   **3** : one relied on

re·li·ant \ri-'lī-ənt\ *adj* : having reliance on someone or something : DEPENDENT

rel·ic \'re-lik\ *n*   **1** : an object venerated because of its association with a saint or martyr   **2** : SOUVENIR, MEMENTO   **3** *pl* : REMAINS, RUINS   **4** : a remaining trace : VESTIGE

rel·ict \'re-likt\ *n* : WIDOW

re·lief \ri-'lēf\ *n*   **1** : removal or lightening of something oppressive, painful, or distressing   **2** : WELFARE 2   **3** : military assistance to an endangered post or force   **4** : release from a post or from performance of a duty; *also* : one that takes the place of another on duty   **5** : legal remedy or redress   **6** : projection of figures or ornaments from the background (as in sculpture)   **7** : the state of being distinguished by contrast   **8** : the elevations of a land surface

relief pitcher *n* : a baseball pitcher who takes over for another during a game

re·lieve \ri-'lēv\ *vb* **re·lieved; re·liev·ing**   **1** : to free partly or wholly from a burden or from distress   **2** : to bring about the removal or alleviation of : MITIGATE   **3** : to release from a post or duty; *also* : to take the place of   **4** : to break the monotony of   **5** : to discharge the bladder or bowels of (oneself)   ✦ **Synonyms** ALLEVIATE, LIGHTEN, ASSUAGE, ALLAY — **re·liev·er** *n*

relig *abbr* religion

re·li·gion \ri-'li-jən\ *n*   **1** : the service and worship of God or the supernatural   **2** : devotion to a religious faith   **3** : a personal set or institutionalized system of religious beliefs, attitudes, and practices   **4** : a cause, principle, or belief held to with faith and ardor — **re·li·gion·ist** *n*

¹re·li·gious \ri-'li-jəs\ *adj*   **1** : relating or devoted to an acknowledged ultimate reality or deity   **2** : of or relating to religious beliefs or observances   **3** : scrupulously and conscientiously faithful   **4** : FERVENT, ZEALOUS — **re·li·gious·ly** *adv*

²religious *n, pl* **religious** : a member of a religious order under monastic vows

re·lin·quish \ri-'liŋ-kwish, -'lin-\ *vb*   **1** : to withdraw or retreat from : ABANDON, QUIT   **2** : GIVE UP ⟨∼ a title⟩   **3** : to let go of : RELEASE   ✦ **Synonyms** YIELD, LEAVE, RESIGN, SURRENDER, CEDE, WAIVE — **re·lin·quish·ment** *n*

rel·i·quary \'re-lə-ˌkwer-ē\ *n, pl* **-quar·ies** : a container for religious relics

¹rel·ish \'re-lish\ *n* [ME *reles* taste, fr. OF, something left behind, release, fr. *relessier* to relax, release, fr. L *relaxare*]   **1** : characteristic flavor : SAVOR   **2** : keen enjoyment or delight in something : GUSTO   **3** : APPETITE, INCLINATION ⟨has no ∼ for sports⟩   **4** : a highly seasoned sauce (as of pickles) eaten with other food to add flavor

²relish *vb*   **1** : to add relish to   **2** : to take pleasure in : ENJOY   **3** : to eat with pleasure — **rel·ish·able** *adj*

re·live \(ˌ)rē-'liv\ *vb* : to live again or over again; *esp* : to experience again in the imagination

re·lo·cate \(ˌ)rē-'lō-ˌkāt, ˌrē-lō-'kāt\ *vb*   **1** : to locate again   **2** : to move to a new location — **re·lo·ca·tion** \ˌrē-lō-'kā-shən\ *n*

re·luc·tant \ri-'lək-tənt\ *adj* : feeling or showing aversion, hesitation or unwillingness ⟨∼ to get involved⟩   ✦ **Synonyms** DISINCLINED, INDISPOSED, HESITANT, LOATH, AVERSE — **re·luc·tance** \-təns\ *n* — **re·luc·tant·ly** *adv*

re·ly \ri-'lī\ *vb* **re·lied; re·ly·ing** [ME *relien* to rally, fr. AF *relier* to retie, gather, rally, fr. L *religare* to tie out of the way, fr. *re-* back + *ligare* to tie] : to place faith or confidence : DEPEND

REM \'rem\ *n* : RAPID EYE MOVEMENT

re·main \ri-'mān\ *vb*   **1** : to be left after others have been removed, subtracted, or destroyed   **2** : to be something yet to be shown, done, or treated ⟨it ∼s to be seen⟩   **3** : to stay after others have gone   **4** : to continue unchanged

re·main·der \ri-'mān-dər\ *n*   **1** : that which is left over : a remaining group, part, or trace   **2** : the number left after a subtraction   **3** : the number that is left over from the dividend after division and that is less than the divisor   **4** : a book sold at a reduced price by the publisher after sales have slowed   ✦ **Synonyms** LEAVINGS, REST, BALANCE, REMNANT, RESIDUE

re·mains \-'mānz\ *n pl*   **1** : a remaining part or trace ⟨the ∼ of a meal⟩   **2** : a dead body

¹re·make \(ˌ)rē-'māk\ *vb* **-made** \-'mād\; **-mak·ing** : to make anew or in a different form

²re·make \'rē-ˌmāk\ *n* : one that is remade; *esp* : a new version of a motion picture

re·mand \ri-'mand\ *vb* : to order back; *esp* : to return to custody pending trial or for further detention

¹re·mark \ri-'märk\ *n*   **1** : the act of remarking : OBSERVATION, NOTICE   **2** : a passing observation or comment

²remark *vb*   **1** : to take notice of : OBSERVE   **2** : to express as an observation or comment : SAY

re·mark·able \ri-'mär-kə-bəl\ *adj* : worthy of being or likely to be noticed : UNUSUAL, EXTRAORDINARY, NOTEWORTHY — **re·mark·able·ness** *n*

re·mark·ably \ri-'mär-kə-blē\ *adv*   **1** : in a remarkable manner   **2** : as is remarkable ⟨∼, no one was hurt⟩

re·me·di·able \ri-'mē-dē-ə-bəl\ *adj* : capable of being remedied

re·me·di·al \ri-'mē-dē-əl\ *adj* : intended to remedy or improve

¹rem·e·dy \'re-mə-dē\ *n, pl* **-dies** [ME *remedie*, fr. AF, fr. L *remedium*, fr. *re-* back, again + *mederi* to heal]   **1** : a medicine or treatment that cures or relieves a disease or condition   **2** : something that corrects or counteracts an evil or compensates for a loss

²remedy *vb* **-died; -dy·ing** : to provide or serve as a remedy for

re·mem·ber \ri-'mem-bər\ *vb* **-bered; -ber·ing**   **1** : to bring to mind or think of again : RECOLLECT   **2** : to keep from forgetting : keep in mind   **3** : to convey greetings from   **4** : COMMEMORATE

re·mem·brance \-brəns\ *n*   **1** : an act of remembering : RECOLLECTION   **2** : the ability to remember : MEMORY   **3** : the period over which one's memory extends   **4** : a memory of a person, thing, or event   **5** : something that serves to bring to mind : REMINDER   **6** : a greeting or gift recalling or expressing friendship or affection

re·mind \ri-'mīnd\ *vb* : to put in mind of something ; cause to remember — **re·mind·er** *n*

rem·i·nisce \ˌre-mə-'nis\ *vb* **-nisced; -nisc·ing** : to indulge in reminiscence

rem·i·nis·cence \-'ni-sᵊns\ *n*   **1** : a recalling or telling of a past experience   **2** : an account of a memorable experience

rem·i·nis·cent \-sᵊnt\ *adj*   **1** : of or relating to reminiscence   **2** : marked by or given to reminiscence   **3** : serving to remind : SUGGESTIVE — **rem·i·nis·cent·ly** *adv*

re·miss \ri-'mis\ *adj*   **1** : negligent or careless in the performance of work or duty   **2** : showing neglect or inattention   ✦ **Synonyms** LAX, NEGLECTFUL, DELINQUENT, DERELICT — **re·miss·ness** *n*

re·mis·sion \ri-'mi-shən\ *n*   **1** : the act or process of remitting   **2** : a state or period during which something is remitted

re·mit \ri-'mit\ *vb* **re·mit·ted; re·mit·ting 1** : FORGIVE, PARDON ⟨~ sins⟩ **2** : to give or gain relief from (as pain) **3** : to refer for consideration, report, or decision **4** : to refrain from exacting or enforcing (as a penalty) **5** : to send (money) in payment of a bill

re·mit·tal \ri-'mi-t°l\ *n* : REMISSION

re·mit·tance \ri-'mi-t°ns\ *n* **1** : a sum of money remitted **2** : transmittal of money (as to a distant place)

rem·nant \'rem-nənt\ *n* **1** : a usu. small part or trace remaining **2** : an unsold or unused end of a fabric that is sold by the yard

re·mod·el \ˌrē-'mä-d°l\ *vb* : to alter the structure of : MAKE OVER

re·mon·strance \ri-'män-strəns\ *n* : an act or instance of remonstrating

re·mon·strant \-strənt\ *adj* : vigorously objecting or opposing — **remonstrant** *n* — **re·mon·strant·ly** *adv*

re·mon·strate \ri-'män-ˌstrāt\ *vb* **-strat·ed; -strat·ing** : to plead in opposition to something : speak in protest or reproof ✦ **Synonyms** EXPOSTULATE, OBJECT, PROTEST — **re·mon·stra·tion** \ri-ˌmän-'strā-shən, ˌre-mən-\ *n* — **re·mon·stra·tor** \ri-'män-ˌstrā-tər\ *n*

rem·o·ra \'re-mə-rə\ *n* : any of a family of marine bony fishes with sucking organs on the head by which they cling esp. to other fishes

remora: on a shark

re·morse \ri-'mȯrs\ *n* [ME, fr. AF *remors,* fr. ML *remorsus,* fr. LL, act of biting again, fr. L *remordēre* to bite again, fr. *re-* again + *mordēre* to bite] : a gnawing distress arising from a sense of guilt for past wrongs ✦ **Synonyms** PENITENCE, REPENTANCE, CONTRITION — **re·morse·ful** *adj*

re·morse·less \-ləs\ *adj* **1** : MERCILESS **2** : PERSISTENT, RELENTLESS

¹re·mote \ri-'mōt\ *adj* **re·mot·er; -est 1** : far off in place or time : not near **2** : not closely related : DISTANT **3** : located out of the way : SECLUDED **4** : acting, acted on, or controlled indirectly or from a distance **5** : small in degree : SLIGHT ⟨a ~ chance⟩ **6** : distant in manner — **re·mote·ly** *adv* — **re·mote·ness** *n*

²remote *n* **1** : a radio or television program or a portion of a program originating outside the studio **2** : REMOTE CONTROL 2

remote control *n* **1** : control (as by radio signal) of operation from a point at some distance removed **2** : a device or mechanism for controlling something from a distance

¹re·mount \ˌrē-'maunt\ *vb* **1** : to mount again **2** : to furnish remounts to

²re·mount \'rē-ˌmaunt\ *n* : a fresh horse to replace one no longer available

¹re·move \ri-'müv\ *vb* **re·moved; re·mov·ing 1** : to move from one place to another : TRANSFER **2** : to move by lifting or taking off or away **3** : DISMISS, DISCHARGE **4** : to get rid of : ELIMINATE ⟨~ a fire hazard⟩ **5** : to change one's residence or location **6** : to go away : DEPART **7** : to be capable of being removed — **re·mov·able** *adj* — **re·mov·al** \-'mü-vəl\ *n* — **re·mov·er** *n*

²remove *n* **1** : a transfer from one location to another : MOVE **2** : a degree or stage of separation

REM sleep *n* : a state of sleep that recurs cyclically several times during normal sleep and is associated with rapid eye movements and dreaming

re·mu·ner·ate \ri-'myü-nə-ˌrāt\ *vb* **-at·ed; -at·ing** : to pay an equivalent for or to : RECOMPENSE — **re·mu·ner·a·tor** \-ˌrā-tər\ *n*

re·mu·ner·a·tion \ri-ˌmyü-nə-'rā-shən\ *n* : COMPENSATION, PAYMENT

re·mu·ner·a·tive \ri-'myü-nə-rə-tiv, -ˌrā-\ *adj* : serving to remunerate : GAINFUL

re·nais·sance \ˌre-nə-'säns, -'zäns\ *n* **1** *cap* : the cultural revival and beginnings of modern science in Europe in the 14th-17th centuries; *also* : the period of the Renaissance **2** *often cap* : a movement or period of vigorous artistic and intellectual activity **3** : REBIRTH, REVIVAL

re·nal \'rē-n°l\ *adj* : of, relating to, or located in or near the kidneys

re·na·scence \ri-'na-s°ns, -'nā-\ *n, often cap* : RENAISSANCE

rend \'rend\ *vb* **rent** \'rent\; **rend·ing 1** : to remove by violence : WREST **2** : to tear forcibly apart : SPLIT

ren·der \'ren-dər\ *vb* **1** : to extract (as lard) by heating **2** : to give to another; *also* : YIELD **3** : to give in return **4** : to do (a service) for another ⟨~ aid⟩ **5** : to cause to be or become : MAKE **6** : to reproduce or represent by artistic or verbal means **7** : TRANSLATE ⟨~ into English⟩

¹ren·dez·vous \'rän-di-ˌvü, -dā-\ *n, pl* **ren·dez·vous** \-ˌvüz\ [MF, fr. *rendez vous* present yourselves] **1** : a place appointed for a meeting; *also* : a meeting at an appointed place **2** : a place of popular resort **3** : the process of bringing two spacecraft together

²rendezvous *vb* **-voused** \-ˌvüd\; **-vous·ing** \-ˌvü-iŋ\; **-vouses** \-ˌvüz\ : to come or bring together at a rendezvous

ren·di·tion \ren-'di-shən\ *n* : an act or a result of rendering ⟨first ~ of the work into English⟩

ren·e·gade \'re-ni-ˌgād\ *n* [Sp *renegado,* fr. ML *renegatus,* fr. pp. of *renegare* to deny, fr. L *re-* re- + *negare* to deny] : a deserter from one faith, cause, principle, or party for another

re·nege \ri-'neg\ *vb* **re·neged; re·neg·ing 1** : to go back on a promise or commitment **2** : to fail to follow suit when able in a card game in violation of the rules — **re·neg·er** *n*

re·new \ri-'nü, -'nyü\ *vb* **1** : to make or become new, fresh, or strong again **2** : to restore to existence : RECREATE, REVIVE **3** : to make or do again : REPEAT ⟨~ a complaint⟩ **4** : to begin again : RESUME ⟨~ed his efforts⟩ **5** : REPLACE ⟨~ the lining of a coat⟩ **6** : to grant or obtain an extension of or on ⟨~ a lease⟩ ⟨~ a subscription⟩ — **re·new·er** *n*

re·new·able \ri-'nü-ə-bəl, -'nyü-\ *adj* **1** : capable of being renewed **2** : capable of being replaced by natural ecological cycles or sound management procedures ⟨~ resources⟩

re·new·al \ri-'nü-əl, -'nyü-\ *n* **1** : the act of renewing : the state of being renewed **2** : something renewed

ren·net \'re-nət\ *n* **1** : the contents of the stomach of an unweaned animal (as a calf) or the lining membrane of the stomach used for curdling milk **2** : rennin or a substitute used to curdle milk

ren·nin \'re-nən\ *n* : a stomach enzyme that coagulates casein and is used commercially to curdle milk in the making of cheese

re·nounce \ri-'nauns\ *vb* **re·nounced; re·nounc·ing 1** : to give up, refuse, or resign usu. by formal declaration **2** : to refuse further to follow, obey, or recognize : REPUDIATE — **re·nounce·ment** *n*

ren·o·vate \'re-nə-ˌvāt\ *vb* **-vat·ed; -vat·ing 1** : to make like new again : put in good condition : REPAIR **2** : to restore to vigor or activity — **ren·o·va·tion** \ˌre-nə-'vā-shən\ *n* — **ren·o·va·tor** \'re-nə-ˌvā-tər\ *n*

re·nown \ri-'naun\ *n* : a state of being widely acclaimed and honored : FAME, CELEBRITY ✦ **Synonyms** HONOR, GLORY, REPUTATION, REPUTE — **re·nowned** \-'naund\ *adj*

¹rent \'rent\ *n* **1** : money or the amount of money paid or due at intervals for the use of another's property **2** : property rented or for rent

²rent *vb* **1** : to give possession and use of in return for rent **2** : to take and hold under an agreement to pay rent **3** : to be for rent ⟨~s for $100 a month⟩ — **rent·er** *n*

³rent *n* **1** : a tear made by or as if by rending **2** : a split in a party or organized group : SCHISM

¹rent·al \'ren-təl\ *n* **1** : an amount paid or collected as rent **2** : something that is rented **3** : an act of renting

²**rental** *adj* : of or relating to rent

re·nun·ci·a·tion \ri-ˌnən-sē-ˈā-shən\ *n* : the act of renouncing : REPUDIATION

¹**rep** \ˈrep\ *n* : REPRESENTATIVE ⟨sales ∼s⟩

²**rep** *abbr* **1** repair **2** repeat **3** report; reporter **4** republic

Rep *abbr* Republican

re·pack·age \(ˌ)rē-ˈpa-kij\ *vb* : to package again or anew; *esp* : to put into a more attractive form

¹**re·pair** \ri-ˈper\ *vb* [ME, fr. AF *repairer* to go back, return, fr. LL *repatriare* to go home again, fr. L *re-* back + *patria* native country] : to make one's way : GO ⟨∼ed to the drawing room⟩

²**repair** *vb* [ME, fr. AF *reparer*, fr. L *reparare*, fr. *re-* back + *parare* to prepare] **1** : to restore to good condition : FIX **2** : to restore to a healthy state **3** : REMEDY ⟨∼ a wrong⟩ — **re·pair·er** *n* — **re·pair·man** \-ˌman\ *n*

³**repair** *n* **1** : a result of repairing **3** : an act of repairing **3** : condition with respect to need of repairing ⟨in bad ∼⟩

rep·a·ra·tion \ˌre-pə-ˈrā-shən\ *n* **1** : the act of making amends for a wrong **2** : amends made for a wrong; *esp* : money paid by a defeated nation in compensation for damages caused during hostilities — usu. used in pl.
✦ *Synonyms* REDRESS, RESTITUTION, INDEMNITY

re·par·a·tive \ri-ˈpa-rə-tiv\ *adj* **1** : of, relating to, or effecting repairs **2** : serving to make amends

rep·ar·tee \ˌre-pər-ˈtē\ *n* **1** : a witty reply **2** : a succession of clever replies; *also* : skill in making such replies

re·past \ri-ˈpast, ˈrē-ˌpast\ *n* : a supply of food and drink served as a meal

re·pa·tri·ate \rē-ˈpā-trē-ˌāt\ *vb* **-at·ed; -at·ing** : to send or bring back to the country of origin or citizenship ⟨∼ prisoners of war⟩ — **re·pa·tri·ate** \-trē-ət, -trē-ˌāt\ *n* — **re·pa·tri·a·tion** \-ˌpā-trē-ˈā-shən\ *n*

re·pay \rē-ˈpā\ *vb* **-paid** \-ˈpād\; **-pay·ing** **1** : to pay back : REFUND **2** : to give or do in return or requital **3** : to make a return payment to : RECOMPENSE, REQUITE
✦ *Synonyms* REMUNERATE, COMPENSATE, REIMBURSE, INDEMNIFY — **re·pay·able** *adj* — **re·pay·ment** *n*

re·peal \ri-ˈpēl\ *vb* [ME *repelen*, fr. AF *repeler*, fr. *re-* back + *apeler* to appeal, call] : to annul by authoritative and esp. legislative action — **repeal** *n* — **re·peal·er** *n*

¹**re·peat** \ri-ˈpēt\ *vb* **1** : to say again **2** : to do again **3** : to say over from memory — **re·peat·able** *adj* — **re·peat·er** *n*

²**re·peat** \ri-ˈpēt, ˈrē-ˌpēt\ *n* **1** : the act of repeating **2** : something repeated or to be repeated (as a radio or television program)

³**re·peat** \ri-ˈpēt\ *adj* : of, relating to, or being one that repeats an offense, achievement, or action

re·peat·ed \ri-ˈpē-təd\ *adj* : done or recurring again and again : FREQUENT — **re·peat·ed·ly** *adv*

re·pel \ri-ˈpel\ *vb* **re·pelled; re·pel·ling** **1** : to drive away : REPULSE **2** : to fight against : RESIST **3** : to turn away : REJECT **4** : to cause aversion in : DISGUST

¹**re·pel·lent** *also* **re·pel·lant** \ri-ˈpe-lənt\ *adj* **1** : tending to drive away ⟨a mosquito-*repellent* spray⟩ **2** : causing disgust

²**repellent** *also* **repellant** *n* : something that repels; *esp* : a substance that repels insects

re·pent \ri-ˈpent\ *vb* **1** : to turn from sin and resolve to reform one's life **2** : to feel sorry for (something done) : REGRET — **re·pen·tance** \ri-ˈpen-t°ns\ *n* — **re·pen·tant** \-t°nt\ *adj*

re·per·cus·sion \ˌrē-pər-ˈkə-shən, ˌre-\ *n* **1** : REVERBERATION **2** : a reciprocal action or effect **3** : a widespread, indirect, or unforeseen effect of something done or said

rep·er·toire \ˈre-pər-ˌtwär\ *n* [F] **1** : a list of plays, operas, pieces, or parts which a company or performer is prepared to present **2** : a list of the skills or devices possessed by a person or needed in a person's occupation

rep·er·to·ry \ˈre-pər-ˌtȯr-ē\ *n, pl* **-ries** **1** : REPOSITORY **2** : REPERTOIRE **3** : a company that presents its repertoire in the course of one season at one theater

rep·e·ti·tion \ˌre-pə-ˈti-shən\ *n* **1** : the act or an instance of repeating **2** : the fact of being repeated

rep·e·ti·tious \-ˈti-shəs\ *adj* : marked by repetition; *esp* : tediously repeating — **rep·e·ti·tious·ly** *adv* — **rep·e·ti·tious·ness** *n*

re·pet·i·tive \ri-ˈpe-tə-tiv\ *adj* : REPETITIOUS — **re·pet·i·tive·ly** *adv* — **re·pet·i·tive·ness** *n*

re·pine \ri-ˈpīn\ *vb* **re·pined; re·pin·ing** **1** : to feel or express discontent or dejection **2** : to long for something

repl *abbr* replace; replacement

re·place \ri-ˈplās\ *vb* **1** : to restore to a former place or position **2** : to take the place of : SUPPLANT **3** : to put something new in the place of — **re·place·able** *adj* — **re·plac·er** *n*

re·place·ment \ri-ˈplās-mənt\ *n* **1** : the act of replacing : the state of being replaced **2** : one that replaces another esp. in a job or function

¹**re·play** \(ˌ)rē-ˈplā\ *vb* : to play again or over

²**re·play** \ˈrē-ˌplā\ *n* **1** : an act or instance of replaying **2** : the playing of a tape (as a videotape)

re·plen·ish \ri-ˈple-nish\ *vb* : to fill or build up again : stock or supply anew — **re·plen·ish·ment** *n*

re·plete \ri-ˈplēt\ *adj* **1** : fully provided ⟨a kit ∼ with instructions⟩ **2** : FULL; *esp* : full of food — **re·plete·ness** *n* — **re·ple·tion** \ri-ˈplē-shən\ *n*

rep·li·ca \ˈre-pli-kə\ *n* [It, repetition, fr. *replicare* to repeat, fr. LL, fr. L, to fold back, fr. *re-* back + *plicare* to fold] **1** : an exact reproduction (as of a painting) executed by the original artist **2** : a copy exact in all details : DUPLICATE

¹**rep·li·cate** \ˈre-plə-ˌkāt\ *vb* **-cat·ed; -cat·ing** : DUPLICATE, REPEAT

²**rep·li·cate** \-pli-kət\ *n* : one of several identical experiments or procedures

rep·li·ca·tion \ˌre-plə-ˈkā-shən\ *n* **1** : ANSWER, REPLY **2** : precise copying or reproduction; *also* : an act or process of this ⟨∼ of DNA⟩

¹**re·ply** \ri-ˈplī\ *vb* **re·plied; re·ply·ing** : to say or do in answer : RESPOND

²**reply** *n, pl* **replies** : ANSWER, RESPONSE

repo \ˈrē-ˌpō\ *adj* : of, relating to, or being in the business of repossessing property (as a car)

¹**re·port** \ri-ˈpȯrt\ *n* [ME, fr. AF, fr. *reporter* to bring back, report, fr. L *reportare*, fr. *re-* back + *portare* to carry] **1** : common talk : RUMOR **2** : FAME, REPUTATION ⟨a person of good ∼⟩ **3** : a usu. detailed account or statement **4** : an explosive noise

²**report** *vb* **1** : to give an account of : RELATE, TELL **2** : to serve as carrier of (a message) **3** : to prepare or present (as an account of an event) for a newspaper or a broadcast **4** : to make a charge of misconduct against **5** : to present oneself (as for work) **6** : to make known to the authorities ⟨∼ a fire⟩ **7** : to return or present (as a matter referred to a committee) with conclusions and recommendations **8** : to work as a subordinate ⟨∼s to the vice president⟩ — **re·port·able** *adj*

re·port·age \ri-ˈpȯr-tij, *esp for 2* ˌre-pər-ˈtäzh, ˌre-ˌpȯr-\ *n* [F] **1** : the act or process of reporting news **2** : writing intended to give an account of observed or documented events

report card *n* : a periodic report on a student's grades

re·port·ed·ly \ri-ˈpȯr-təd-lē\ *adv* : according to report

re·port·er \ri-ˈpȯr-tər\ *n* : one that reports; *esp* : a person who gathers and reports news for a news medium — **re·por·to·ri·al** \ˌre-pər-ˈtȯr-ē-əl\ *adj*

¹**re·pose** \ri-ˈpōz\ *vb* **re·posed; re·pos·ing** **1** : to lay at rest **2** : to lie at rest **3** : to lie dead **4** : to take a rest **5** : to rest for support : LIE

²**repose** *n* **1** : a state of resting (as after exertion); *esp* : SLEEP **2** : eternal or heavenly rest **3** : CALM, PEACE ⟨the ∼ of the bayous⟩ **4** : cessation or absence of activity, movement, or animation **5** : composure of manner : POISE — **re·pose·ful** *adj*

³**repose** *vb* **re·posed; re·pos·ing** **1** : to place (as trust) in someone or something **2** : to place for control, management, or use

re·pos·i·to·ry \ri-ˈpä-zə-ˌtȯr-ē\ *n, pl* **-ries** **1** : a place where something is deposited or stored **2** : a person to whom something is entrusted

re·pos·sess \ˌrē-pə-ˈzes\ *vb* **1** : to regain possession of **2** : to take possession of in default of the payment of installments due — **re·pos·ses·sion** \-ˈze-shən\ *n*

rep·re·hend \ˌre-pri-ˈhend\ *vb* : to express disapproval of : CENSURE ✦ *Synonyms* CRITICIZE, CONDEMN, DENOUNCE, BLAME, PAN — **rep·re·hen·sion** \-ˈhen-chən\ *n*

rep·re·hen·si·ble \-ˈhen-sə-bəl\ *adj* : deserving blame or censure : CULPABLE — **rep·re·hen·si·bly** \-blē\ *adv*

rep·re·sent \ˌre-pri-'zent\ *vb* **1** : to present a picture or a likeness of : PORTRAY, DEPICT **2** : to serve as a sign or symbol of **3** : to act the role of **4** : to stand in the place of : act or speak for; *also* : to manage the legal and business affairs of **5** : to be a member or example of : TYPIFY **6** : to serve as an elected representative of **7** : to describe as having a specified quality or character **8** : to state with the purpose of affecting judgment or action

rep·re·sen·ta·tion \ˌre-pri-ˌzen-'tā-shən\ *n* **1** : the act of representing **2** : one (as a picture or image) that represents something else **3** : the state of being represented in a legislative body; *also* : the body of persons representing a constituency **4** : a usu. formal statement made to effect a change

¹rep·re·sen·ta·tive \ˌre-pri-'zen-tə-tiv\ *adj* **1** : serving to represent **2** : standing or acting for another **3** : founded on the principle of representation : carried on by elected representatives ⟨∼ government⟩ — **rep·re·sen·ta·tive·ly** *adv* — **rep·re·sen·ta·tive·ness** *n*

²representative *n* **1** : one that represents another; *esp* : one representing a district in a legislative body usu. as a member of a lower house **2** : a typical example of a group, class, or quality

re·press \ri-'pres\ *vb* **1** : CURB, SUBDUE **2** : RESTRAIN, SUPPRESS **3** : to exclude from consciousness — **re·pres·sion** \-'pre-shən\ *n* — **re·pres·sive** \-'pre-siv\ *adj*

¹re·prieve \ri-'prēv\ *vb* **re·prieved; re·priev·ing 1** : to delay the punishment or execution of **2** : to give temporary relief to

²reprieve *n* **1** : the act of reprieving : the state of being reprieved **2** : a formal temporary suspension of a sentence esp. of death **3** : a temporary respite

¹rep·ri·mand \'re-prə-ˌmand\ *n* : a severe or formal reproof

²reprimand *vb* : to reprove severely or formally

¹re·print \(ˌ)rē-'print\ *vb* : to print again

²re·print \'rē-ˌprint\ *n* : a reproduction of printed matter

re·pri·sal \ri-'prī-zəl\ *n* : an act in retaliation for something done by another

re·prise \ri-'prēz\ *n* : a recurrence, renewal, or resumption of an action; *also* : a musical repetition

¹re·proach \ri-'prōch\ *n* **1** : an expression of disapproval **2** : DISGRACE, DISCREDIT **3** : the act of reproaching : REBUKE **4** : a cause or occasion of blame or disgrace — **re·proach·ful** \-fəl\ *adj* — **re·proach·ful·ly** *adv* — **re·proach·ful·ness** *n*

²reproach *vb* **1** : CENSURE, REBUKE **2** : to cast discredit on ◆ *Synonyms* CHIDE, ADMONISH, REPROVE, REPRIMAND — **re·proach·able** *adj*

rep·ro·bate \'re-prə-ˌbāt\ *n* **1** : a person foreordained to damnation **2** : a thoroughly bad person : SCOUNDREL — **reprobate** *adj*

rep·ro·ba·tion \ˌre-prə-'bā-shən\ *n* : strong disapproval : CONDEMNATION

re·pro·duce \ˌrē-prə-'düs, -'dyüs\ *vb* **1** : to produce again or anew **2** : to produce offspring — **re·pro·duc·ible** \-'dü-sə-bəl, -'dyü-\ *adj* — **re·pro·duc·tion** \-'dək-shən\ *n* — **re·pro·duc·tive** \-'dək-tiv\ *adj*

re·proof \ri-'prüf\ *n* : blame or censure for a fault

re·prove \ri-'prüv\ *vb* **re·proved; re·prov·ing 1** : to administer a rebuke to **2** : to express disapproval of ◆ *Synonyms* REPRIMAND, ADMONISH, REPROACH, CHIDE — **re·prov·er** *n*

rept *abbr* report

rep·tile \'rep-tī(-ə)l, -t²l\ *n* [ME *reptil*, fr. MF or LL; MF *reptile*, fr. LL *reptile*, fr. L *repere* to crawl] : any of a large class of air-breathing scaly vertebrates including snakes, lizards, alligators, turtles, and extinct related forms (as dinosaurs) — **rep·til·i·an** \rep-'ti-lē-ən\ *adj or n*

re·pub·lic \ri-'pə-blik\ *n* [F *république*, fr. MF *republique*, fr. L *respublica*, fr. *res* thing, wealth + *publica*, fem. of *publicus* public] **1** : a government having a chief of state who is not a monarch and is usu. a president; *also* : a nation or other political unit having such a government **2** : a government in which supreme power is held by the citizens entitled to vote and is exercised by elected officers and representatives governing according to law; *also* : a nation or other political unit having such a form of government **3** : a constituent political and territorial unit of the former nations of Czechoslovakia, the U.S.S.R., or Yugoslavia

¹re·pub·li·can \-bli-kən\ *n* **1** : one that favors or supports a republican form of government **2** *cap* : a member of a republican party and esp. of the Republican party of the U.S.

²republican *adj* **1** : of, relating to, or resembling a republic **2** : favoring or supporting a republic **3** *cap* : of, relating to, or constituting one of the two major political parties in the U.S. evolving in the mid-19th century — **re·pub·li·can·ism** *n, often cap*

re·pu·di·ate \ri-'pyü-dē-ˌāt\ *vb* **-at·ed; -at·ing** [L *repudiare* to cast off, divorce, fr. *repudium* rejection of a prospective spouse, divorce] **1** : to cast off : DISOWN **2** : to refuse to have anything to do with : refuse to acknowledge, accept, or pay ⟨∼ a charge⟩ ⟨∼ a debt⟩ ◆ *Synonyms* SPURN, REJECT, DECLINE — **re·pu·di·a·tion** \-ˌpyü-dē-'ā-shən\ *n* — **re·pu·di·a·tor** \-'pyü-dē-ˌā-tər\ *n*

re·pug·nance \ri-'pəg-nəns\ *n* **1** : the quality or fact of being contradictory or inconsistent **2** : strong dislike, distaste, or antagonism

re·pug·nant \-nənt\ *adj* **1** : marked by repugnance **2** : contrary to a person's tastes or principles : exciting distaste or aversion ◆ *Synonyms* REPELLENT, ABHORRENT, DISTASTEFUL, OBNOXIOUS, REVOLTING, LOATHSOME — **re·pug·nant·ly** *adv*

¹re·pulse \ri-'pəls\ *vb* **re·pulsed; re·puls·ing 1** : to drive or beat back : REPEL **2** : to repel by discourtesy or denial : REBUFF **3** : to cause a feeling of repulsion in : DISGUST

²repulse *n* **1** : REBUFF, REJECTION **2** : the action of repelling an attacker : the fact of being repelled

re·pul·sion \ri-'pəl-shən\ *n* **1** : the action of repulsing : the state of being repulsed **2** : the force with which bodies, particles, or like forces repel one another **3** : a feeling of aversion

re·pul·sive \-siv\ *adj* **1** : serving or tending to repel or reject **2** : arousing aversion or disgust ◆ *Synonyms* REPUGNANT, REVOLTING, LOATHSOME, NOISOME — **re·pul·sive·ly** *adv* — **re·pul·sive·ness** *n*

re·pur·pose \(ˌ)rē-'pər-pəs\ *vb* : to give a new purpose or use to

rep·u·ta·ble \'re-pyə-tə-bəl\ *adj* : having a good reputation : ESTIMABLE — **rep·u·ta·bly** \-blē\ *adv*

rep·u·ta·tion \ˌre-pyü-'tā-shən\ *n* **1** : overall quality or character as seen or judged by people in general **2** : place in public esteem or regard

¹re·pute \ri-'pyüt\ *vb* **re·put·ed; re·put·ing** : BELIEVE, CONSIDER ⟨*reputed* to be a millionaire⟩

²repute *n* **1** : REPUTATION ⟨knew her by ∼⟩ **2** : the state of being favorably known or spoken of

re·put·ed \ri-'pyü-təd\ *adj* **1** : REPUTABLE **2** : according to reputation : SUPPOSED — **re·put·ed·ly** *adv*

req *abbr* **1** request **2** require; required **3** requisition

¹re·quest \ri-'kwest\ *n* **1** : an act or instance of asking for something **2** : a thing asked for **3** : the condition of being asked for ⟨available on ∼⟩

²request *vb* **1** : to make a request to or of **2** : to ask for — **re·quest·er** *or* **re·quest·or** *n*

re·qui·em \'re-kwē-əm, 'rā-\ *n* [ME, fr. L (first word of the requiem mass), acc. of *requies* rest, fr. *quies* quiet, rest] **1** : a mass for a dead person; *also* : a musical setting for this **2** : a musical service or hymn in honor of the dead

re·quire \ri-'kwī(-ə)r\ *vb* **re·quired; re·quir·ing 1** : to demand as necessary or essential **2** : COMMAND, ORDER ⟨the law ∼s that everyone pay the tax⟩

re·quire·ment \-mənt\ *n* **1** : something (as a condition or quality) required ⟨entrance ∼s⟩ **2** : NECESSITY ⟨production was sufficient to satisfy military ∼s⟩

req·ui·site \'re-kwə-zət\ *adj* : REQUIRED, NECESSARY — **requisite** *n*

req·ui·si·tion \ˌre-kwə-'zi-shən\ *n* **1** : formal application or demand (as for supplies) **2** : the state of being in demand or use — **requisition** *vb*

re·quite \ri-'kwīt\ *vb* **re·quit·ed; re·quit·ing 1** : to make return for : REPAY **2** : to make retaliation for : AVENGE **3** : to make return to — **re·quit·al** \-'kwī-t²l\ *n*

rere·dos \'rer-ə-ˌdäs\ *n* : a usu. ornamental wood or stone screen or partition wall behind an altar

re·run \'rē-ˌrən, (ˌ)rē-'rən\ *n* : the act or an instance of running again or anew; *esp* : a showing of a motion picture or television program after its first run — **re·run** \(ˌ)rē-'rən\ *vb*

res *abbr* **1** research **2** reservation; reserve **3** reservoir **4** residence; resident **5** resolution

re·sale \'rē-ˌsāl, (ˌ)rē-ˈsāl\ *n* : the act of selling again usu. to a new party — **re·sal·able** \(ˌ)rē-ˈsā-lə-bəl\ *adj*

re·scind \ri-ˈsind\ *vb* : REPEAL, CANCEL, ANNUL — **re·scis·sion** \-ˈsi-zhən\ *n*

re·script \'rē-ˌskript\ *n* : an official or authoritative order or decree

res·cue \'res-kyü\ *vb* **res·cued; res·cu·ing** [ME *rescouen, rescuen,* fr. AF *rescure,* fr. *re-* back, again + *escure* to shake off, fr. L *excutere*] : to free from danger, harm, or confinement — **rescue** *n* — **res·cu·er** *n*

re·search \ri-ˈsərch, 'rē-ˌsərch\ *n* **1** : careful or diligent search **2** : studious inquiry or examination aimed at the discovery and interpretation of new knowledge **3** : the collecting of information about a particular subject — **research** *vb* — **re·search·er** *n*

re·sec·tion \ri-ˈsek-shən\ *n* : the surgical removal of part of an organ or structure

re·sem·blance \ri-ˈzem-bləns\ *n* : the quality or state of resembling

re·sem·ble \ri-ˈzem-bəl\ *vb* **-bled; -bling** : to be like or similar to

re·sent \ri-ˈzent\ *vb* : to feel or exhibit annoyance or indignation at — **re·sent·ful** \-fəl\ *adj* — **re·sent·ful·ly** *adv* — **re·sent·ment** *n*

re·ser·pine \ri-ˈsər-ˌpēn, -pən\ *n* : a drug used in treating high blood pressure and nervous tension

res·er·va·tion \ˌre-zər-ˈvā-shən\ *n* **1** : an act of reserving **2** : something (as a room in a hotel) arranged for in advance **3** : something reserved; *esp* : a tract of public land set aside for special use **4** : a limiting condition

¹re·serve \ri-ˈzərv\ *vb* **re·served; re·serv·ing 1** : to store for future or special use **2** : to hold back for oneself **3** : to set aside or arrange to have set aside or held for special use

²reserve *n* **1** : something reserved : STOCK, STORE **2** : a military force withheld from action for later use — usu. used in pl. **3** : the military forces of a country not part of the regular services; *also* : RESERVIST **4** : a tract set apart : RESERVATION **5** : an act of reserving **6** : restraint or caution in one's words or bearing **7** : money or its equivalent kept in hand or set apart to meet liabilities

re·served \ri-ˈzərvd\ *adj* **1** : restrained in words and actions **2** : set aside for future or special use — **re·serv·ed·ly** \-ˈzər-vəd-lē\ *adv* — **re·serv·ed·ness** \-vəd-nəs\ *n*

re·serv·ist \ri-ˈzər-vist\ *n* : a member of a military reserve

res·er·voir \'re-zə-ˌvwär, -zər-, -ˌvwȯr\ *n* [F] : a place where something is kept in store; *esp* : an artificial lake where water is collected and kept for use

re·shuf·fle \rē-ˈshə-fəl\ *vb* **1** : to shuffle again **2** : to reorganize usu. by redistribution of existing elements — **reshuffle** *n*

re·side \ri-ˈzīd\ *vb* **re·sid·ed; re·sid·ing 1** : to make one's home : DWELL **2** : to be present as a quality or vested as a right

res·i·dence \'re-zə-dəns\ *n* **1** : the act or fact of residing in a place as a dweller or in discharge of a duty or an obligation **2** : the place where one actually lives **3** : a building used as a home : DWELLING **4** : the period of living in a place

res·i·den·cy \'re-zə-dən-sē\ *n, pl* **-cies 1** : the residence of or the territory under a diplomatic resident **2** : a period of advanced training in a medical specialty

¹res·i·dent \-dənt\ *adj* **1** : RESIDING **2** : being in residence **3** : not migratory

²resident *n* **1** : one who resides in a place **2** : a diplomatic representative with governing powers (as in a protectorate) **3** : a physician serving a residency

res·i·den·tial \ˌre-zə-ˈden-chəl\ *adj* **1** : used as a residence or by residents **2** : occupied by or restricted to residences — **res·i·den·tial·ly** *adv*

¹re·sid·u·al \ri-ˈzi-jə-wəl\ *n* **1** : a residual product or substance **2** : a payment (as to an actor or writer) for each rerun after an initial showing (as of a taped TV show)

²residual *adj* : being a residue or remainder

re·sid·u·ary \ri-ˈzi-jə-ˌwer-ē\ *adj* : of, relating to, or constituting a residue esp. of an estate

res·i·due \'re-zə-ˌdü, -ˌdyü\ *n* : a part remaining after another part has been taken away : REMAINDER

re·sid·u·um \ri-ˈzi-jə-wəm\ *n, pl* **re·sid·ua** \-jə-wə\ [L] **1** : something remaining or residual after certain deductions are made **2** : a residual product

re·sign \ri-ˈzīn\ *vb* [ME, fr. AF *resigner,* fr. L *resignare,* lit., to unseal, cancel, fr. *signare* to sign, seal] **1** : to give up deliberately (as one's position) esp. by a formal act **2** : to give (oneself) over (as to grief or despair) without resistance — **re·sign·ed·ly** \-ˈzī-nəd-lē\ *adv*

re–sign \(ˌ)rē-ˈsīn\ *vb* : to sign again

res·ig·na·tion \ˌre-zig-ˈnā-shən\ *n* **1** : an act or instance of resigning; *also* : a formal notification of such an act **2** : the quality or state of being resigned

re·sil·ience \ri-ˈzil-yəns\ *n* **1** : the ability of a body to regain its original size and shape after being compressed, bent, or stretched **2** : an ability to recover from or adjust easily to change or misfortune

re·sil·ien·cy \-yən-sē\ *n* : RESILIENCE

re·sil·ient \-yənt\ *adj* : marked by resilience

res·in \'re-zᵊn\ *n* : any of various substances obtained from the gum or sap of some trees and used esp. in varnishes, plastics, and medicine; *also* : a comparable synthetic product — **res·in·ous** *adj*

¹re·sist \ri-ˈzist\ *vb* **1** : to fight against : OPPOSE ⟨~ aggression⟩ **2** : to withstand the force or effect of ⟨~ed temptation⟩ ⟨~ disease⟩ ♦ **Synonyms** COMBAT, REPEL — **re·sist·ible** \-ˈzis-tə-bəl\ *adj* — **re·sist·less** *adj*

²resist *n* : something (as a coating) that resists or prevents a particular action

re·sis·tance \ri-ˈzis-təns\ *n* **1** : the act or an instance of resisting : OPPOSITION **2** : the power or capacity to resist; *esp* : the inherent ability of an organism to resist harmful influences (as disease or infection) **3** : the opposition offered by a body to the passage through it of a steady electric current

re·sis·tant \-tənt\ *adj* : giving, capable of, or exhibiting resistance

re·sis·tor \ri-ˈzis-tər\ *n* : a device used to provide resistance to the flow of an electric current in a circuit

res·o·lute \'re-zə-ˌlüt\ *adj* : firmly determined in purpose : RESOLVED ⟨a ~ leader⟩ ♦ **Synonyms** STEADFAST, STAUNCH, FAITHFUL, TRUE, LOYAL — **res·o·lute·ly** *adv* — **res·o·lute·ness** *n*

res·o·lu·tion \ˌre-zə-ˈlü-shən\ *n* **1** : the act or process of resolving **2** : the action of solving; *also* : SOLUTION **3** : the quality of being resolute : FIRMNESS, DETERMINATION **4** : a formal statement expressing the opinion, will, or intent of a body of persons **5** : a measure of the sharpness of an image or of the fineness with which a device can produce or record such an image

¹re·solve \ri-ˈzälv\ *vb* **re·solved; re·solv·ing 1** : to break up into constituent parts : ANALYZE **2** : to distinguish between or make visible adjacent parts of **3** : to find an answer to : SOLVE ⟨~ a dispute⟩ **4** : DETERMINE, DECIDE **5** : to make or pass a formal resolution — **re·solv·able** *adj*

²resolve *n* **1** : fixity of purpose **2** : something resolved

res·o·nance \'re-zə-nəns\ *n* **1** : the quality or state of being resonant **2** : a reinforcement of sound in a vibrating body caused by waves from another body vibrating at nearly the same rate

res·o·nant \-nənt\ *adj* **1** : continuing to sound : RESOUNDING **2** : relating to or exhibiting resonance **3** : intensified and enriched by or as if by resonance — **res·o·nant·ly** *adv*

res·o·nate \-ˌnāt\ *vb* **-nat·ed; -nat·ing 1** : to produce or exhibit resonance **2** : REVERBERATE, RESOUND **3** : to relate harmoniously ⟨~ with voters⟩

res·o·na·tor \-ˌnā-tər\ *n* : something that resounds or exhibits resonance

re·sorp·tion \rē-ˈsȯrp-shən, -ˈzȯrp-\ *n* : the action or process of breaking down and assimilating something (as a tooth or an embryo)

¹re·sort \ri-ˈzȯrt\ *n* [ME, return, source of aid, fr. AF, fr. *resortir* to rebound, resort, fr. *sortir* to go out, leave] **1** : one looked to for help : REFUGE **2** : RECOURSE **3** : frequent or general visiting ⟨place of ~⟩ **4** : a frequently visited place : HAUNT **5** : a place providing recreation esp. to vacationers

²resort *vb* **1** : to go often or habitually **2** : to have recourse ⟨~ed to violence⟩

re·sound \ri-ˈzau̇nd\ *vb* **1** : to become filled with sound : REVERBERATE, RING **2** : to sound loudly

re·sound·ing *adj* **1** : RESONATING, RESONANT **2** : impressively sonorous ⟨~ name⟩ **3** : EMPHATIC, UNEQUIVOCAL ⟨a ~ success⟩ — **re·sound·ing·ly** *adv*

re·source \'rē-ˌsȯrs, ri-'sȯrs\ *n* [F *ressource*, fr. OF *ressourse* relief, resource, fr. *resourdre* to relieve, lit., to rise again, fr. L *resurgere*, fr. *re-* again + *surgere* to rise] **1** : a source of supply or support — usu. used in pl. **2** : a natural feature or phenomenon that enhances the quality of human life **3** *pl* : available funds **4** : a possibility of relief or recovery **5** : a means of spending leisure time **6** : ability to meet and handle situations — **re·source·ful** \ri-'sȯrs-fəl\ *adj* — **re·source·ful·ness** *n*

¹re·spect \ri-'spekt\ *n* **1** : relation to something usu. specified : REGARD ⟨in ~ to⟩ **2** : high or special regard : ESTEEM **3** *pl* : an expression of respect or deference **4** : DETAIL, PARTICULAR — **re·spect·ful** \-fəl\ *adj* — **re·spect·ful·ly** *adv* — **re·spect·ful·ness** *n*

²respect *vb* **1** : to consider deserving of high regard : ESTEEM **2** : to refrain from interfering with ⟨~ another's privacy⟩ **3** : to have reference to : CONCERN — **re·spect·er** *n*

re·spect·able \ri-'spek-tə-bəl\ *adj* **1** : worthy of respect : ESTIMABLE **2** : decent or correct in conduct : PROPER **3** : fair in size, quantity, or quality ⟨a ~ score⟩ : MODERATE, TOLERABLE **4** : fit to be seen : PRESENTABLE — **re·spect·a·bil·i·ty** \-ˌspek-tə-'bi-lə-tē\ *n* — **re·spect·ably** \-'spek-tə-blē\ *adv*

re·spect·ing *prep* : with regard to

re·spec·tive \-tiv\ *adj* : PARTICULAR, SEPARATE ⟨returned to their ~ homes⟩

re·spec·tive·ly \-lē\ *adv* **1** : as relating to each **2** : each in the order given

res·pi·ra·tion \ˌres-pə-'rā-shən\ *n* **1** : an act or the process of breathing **2** : the physical and chemical processes (as breathing and oxidation) by which a living thing obtains oxygen and eliminates waste gases (as carbon dioxide) — **re·spi·ra·to·ry** \'res-pə-rə-ˌtȯr-ē, ri-'spī-rə-\ *adj* — **re·spire** \ri-'spī(-ə)r\ *vb*

res·pi·ra·tor \'res-pə-ˌrā-tər\ *n* **1** : a device covering the mouth and nose esp. to prevent inhaling harmful vapors **2** : a device for artificial respiration

re·spite \'res-pət\ *n* [ME *respit*, fr. AF, fr. ML *respectus*, fr. L, act of looking back] **1** : a temporary delay **2** : an interval of rest or relief

re·splen·dent \ri-'splen-dənt\ *adj* : shining brilliantly : gloriously bright : SPLENDID — **re·splen·dence** \-dəns\ *n* — **re·splen·dent·ly** *adv*

re·spond \ri-'spänd\ *vb* **1** : ANSWER, REPLY **2** : REACT ⟨~ed to a call for help⟩ **3** : to show favorable reaction ⟨~ to medication⟩ — **re·spond·er** *n*

re·spon·dent \ri-'spän-dənt\ *n* : one who responds; *esp* : one who answers in various legal proceedings — **respondent** *adj*

re·sponse \ri-'späns\ *n* **1** : an act of responding **2** : something constituting a reply or a reaction

re·spon·si·bil·i·ty \ri-ˌspän-sə-'bi-lə-tē\ *n, pl* **-ties** **1** : the quality or state of being responsible **2** : something for which one is responsible

re·spon·si·ble \ri-'spän-sə-bəl\ *adj* **1** : liable to be called upon to answer for one's acts or decisions : ANSWERABLE **2** : able to fulfill one's obligations : RELIABLE, TRUSTWORTHY **3** : able to choose for oneself between right and wrong **4** : involving accountability or important duties ⟨~ position⟩ — **re·spon·si·ble·ness** *n* — **re·spon·si·bly** \-blē\ *adv*

re·spon·sive \-siv\ *adj* **1** : RESPONDING **2** : quick to respond : SENSITIVE **3** : using responses ⟨~ readings⟩ — **re·spon·sive·ly** *adv* — **re·spon·sive·ness** *n*

¹rest \'rest\ *n* **1** : REPOSE, SLEEP **2** : freedom from work or activity **3** : a state of motionlessness or inactivity **4** : a place of shelter or lodging **5** : a silence in music equivalent in duration to a note of the same value; *also* : a character indicating this **6** : something used as a support — **rest·ful** \-fəl\ *adj* — **rest·ful·ly** *adv*

¹rest 5: symbols for five kinds

²rest *vb* **1** : to get rest by lying down; *esp* : SLEEP **2** : to cease from action or motion **3** : to give rest to : set at rest **4** : to sit or lie fixed or supported **5** : to place on or against a support **6** : to remain based or founded **7** : to cause to be firmly fixed : GROUND **8** : to remain for action : DEPEND

³rest *n* : something left over

res·tau·rant \'res-trənt, -tə-ˌränt\ *n* [F, fr. prp. of *restaurer* to restore, fr. L *restaurare*] : a public eating place

res·tau·ra·teur \ˌres-tə-rə-'tər\ *also* **res·tau·ran·teur** \-ˌrän-\ *n* : the operator or proprietor of a restaurant

rest home *n* : an establishment that gives care for the aged or convalescent

res·ti·tu·tion \ˌres-tə-'tü-shən, -'tyü-\ *n* : the act of restoring : the state of being restored; *esp* : restoration of something to its rightful owner ◆ *Synonyms* AMENDS, REDRESS, REPARATION, INDEMNITY, COMPENSATION

res·tive \'res-tiv\ *adj* [ME *restyf*, fr. AF *restif*, fr. *rester* to stop, resist, remain, fr. L *restare*, fr. *re-* back + *stare* to stand] **1** : BALKY **2** : UNEASY, FIDGETY ◆ *Synonyms* RESTLESS, IMPATIENT, NERVOUS — **res·tive·ly** *adv* — **res·tive·ness** *n*

rest·less \'rest-ləs\ *adj* **1** : lacking or denying rest ⟨a ~ night⟩ **2** : never resting or settled : always moving ⟨the ~ sea⟩ **3** : marked by or showing unrest esp. of mind ⟨~ pacing back and forth⟩ ◆ *Synonyms* RESTIVE, IMPATIENT, NERVOUS, FIDGETY — **rest·less·ly** *adv* — **rest·less·ness** *n*

re·stor·able \ri-'stȯr-ə-bəl\ *adj* : fit for restoring or reclaiming

res·to·ra·tion \ˌres-tə-'rā-shən\ *n* **1** : an act of restoring : the state of being restored **2** : something (as a building) that has been restored

re·stor·ative \ri-'stȯr-ə-tiv\ *n* : something that restores esp. to consciousness or health — **restorative** *adj*

re·store \ri-'stȯr\ *vb* **re·stored; re·stor·ing** **1** : to give back : RETURN **2** : to put back into use or service **3** : to put or bring back into a former or original state **4** : to put again in possession of something — **re·stor·er** *n*

re·strain \ri-'strān\ *vb* **1** : to prevent from doing something **2** : to limit, restrict, or keep under control : CURB **3** : to place under restraint or arrest — **re·strain·able** *adj* — **re·strain·er** *n*

re·strained \ri-'strānd\ *adj* : marked by restraint : DISCIPLINED — **re·strain·ed·ly** \-'strā-nəd-lē\ *adv*

restraining order *n* : a legal order directing one person to stay away from another

re·straint \ri-'strānt\ *n* **1** : an act of restraining : the state of being restrained **2** : a restraining force, agency, or device **3** : deprivation or limitation of liberty : CONFINEMENT **4** : control over one's feelings : RESERVE

re·strict \ri-'strikt\ *vb* **1** : to confine within bounds : LIMIT **2** : to place under restriction as to use — **re·stric·tive** *adj* — **re·stric·tive·ly** *adv*

re·stric·tion \ri-'strik-shən\ *n* **1** : something (as a law or rule) that restricts **2** : an act of restricting : the state of being restricted

rest room *n* : a room or suite of rooms that includes sinks and toilets

¹re·sult \ri-'zəlt\ *vb* [ME, fr. ML *resultare*, fr. L, to rebound, fr. *re-* re- + *saltare* to leap] : to come about as an effect or consequence ⟨an injury ~ing from a fall⟩ — **re·sul·tant** \-'zəl-tᵊnt\ *adj or n*

²result *n* **1** : something that results : EFFECT, CONSEQUENCE **2** : beneficial or discernible effect **3** : something obtained by calculation or investigation

re·sume \ri-'züm\ *vb* **re·sumed; re·sum·ing** **1** : to take or assume again **2** : to return to or begin again after interruption **3** : to take back to oneself — **re·sump·tion** \-'zəmp-shən\ *n*

ré·su·mé *or* **re·su·me** *or* **re·su·mé** \'re-zə-ˌmā, ˌre-zə-'mā\ *n* [F *résumé*] **1** : SUMMARY; *esp* : a short account of one's career and qualifications usu. prepared by a job applicant **2** : a set of accomplishments ⟨a musical ~⟩

re·sur·gence \ri-'sər-jəns\ *n* : a rising again into life, activity, or prominence — **re·sur·gent** \-jənt\ *adj*

res·ur·rect \ˌre-zə-'rekt\ *vb* **1** : to raise from the dead **2** : to bring to attention or use again

res·ur·rec·tion \ˌre-zə-'rek-shən\ *n* **1** *cap* : the rising of Christ from the dead **2** *often cap* : the rising to life of all human dead before the final judgment **3** : REVIVAL

re·sus·ci·tate \ri-'sə-sə-ˌtāt\ vb -**tat·ed**; -**tat·ing** : to revive from apparent death or unconsciousness; also : REVITALIZE — **re·sus·ci·ta·tion** \ri-ˌsə-sə-'tā-shən, ˌrē-\ n — **re·sus·ci·ta·tor** \ri-'sə-sə-ˌtā-tər\ n

ret abbr retired

¹**re·tail** \'rē-ˌtāl, esp for 2 also ri-'tāl\ vb **1** : to sell in small quantities directly to the ultimate consumer **2** : to tell in detail or to one person after another — **re·tail·er** n

²**re·tail** \'rē-ˌtāl\ n : the sale of goods in small amounts to ultimate consumers — **retail** adj or adv

re·tain \ri-'tān\ vb **1** : to hold in possession or use **2** : to engage (as a lawyer) by paying a fee in advance **3** : to keep in a fixed place or position ✦ **Synonyms** DETAIN, WITHHOLD, RESERVE

¹**re·tain·er** \ri-'tā-nər\ n **1** : one that retains **2** : a servant in a wealthy household; also : EMPLOYEE **3** : a device that holds something (as teeth) in place

²**retainer** n : a fee paid to secure services (as of a lawyer)

¹**re·take** \(ˌ)rē-'tāk\ vb -**took** \-'tuk\; -**tak·en** \-'tā-kən\; -**tak·ing** **1** : to take or seize again **2** : to photograph again

²**re·take** \'rē-ˌtāk\ n : a second photographing of a motion= picture scene

re·tal·i·ate \ri-'ta-lē-ˌāt\ vb -**at·ed**; -**at·ing** : to return like for like; esp : to get revenge — **re·tal·i·a·tion** \-ˌta-lē-'ā-shən\ n — **re·tal·ia·to·ry** \-'tal-yə-ˌtòr-ē\ adj

re·tard \ri-'tärd\ vb : to hold back : delay the progress of ✦ **Synonyms** SLOW, SLACKEN, DETAIN — **re·tar·da·tion** \ˌrē-ˌtär-'dā-shən, ri-\ n — **re·tard·er** n

re·tar·dant \ri-'tär-dᵊnt\ adj : serving or tending to retard — **retardant** n

re·tard·ed adj, sometimes offensive : slow or limited in intellectual, emotional, or academic progress

retch \'rech\ vb : to try to vomit; also : VOMIT

re·ten·tion \ri-'ten-chən\ n **1** : the act of retaining : the state of being retained **2** : the power of retaining esp. in the mind : RETENTIVENESS

re·ten·tive \-'ten-tiv\ adj : having the power of retaining; esp : retaining knowledge easily — **re·ten·tive·ness** n

re·think \(ˌ)rē-'think\ vb -**thought** \-'thot\; -**think·ing** : to think about again : RECONSIDER

ret·i·cent \'re-tə-sənt\ adj **1** : tending not to talk or give out information **2** : RELUCTANT ✦ **Synonyms** RESERVED, TACITURN, CLOSEMOUTHED — **ret·i·cence** \-səns\ n — **ret·i·cent·ly** adv

ret·i·na \'re-tə-nə\ n, pl **retinas** or **ret·i·nae** \-ˌnē\ : the sensory membrane lining the eye that receives the image formed by the lens — **ret·i·nal** \'re-tə-nəl\ adj

ret·i·nue \'re-tə-ˌnü, -ˌnyü\ n : the body of attendants or followers of a distinguished person

re·tire \ri-'tī(-ə)r\ vb -**tired**; -**tir·ing** **1** : RETREAT **2** : to withdraw esp. for privacy **3** : to withdraw from one's occupation or position : conclude one's career **4** : to withdraw from use or service **5** : to go to bed **6** : to cause to be out in baseball — **re·tire·ment** n

re·tired \ri-'tī(-ə)rd\ adj **1** : SECLUDED, QUIET **2** : withdrawn from active duty or from one's career

re·tir·ee \ri-ˌtī-'rē\ n : a person who has retired from a career

re·tir·ing adj : SHY, RESERVED

re·tool \(ˌ)rē-'tül\ vb **1** : to reequip with tools **2** : to modify with usu. minor improvements ⟨~ed the team for next year⟩

¹**re·tort** \ri-'tòrt\ vb [L retortus, pp. of retorquēre, lit., to twist back, hurl back, fr. re- back + torquēre to twist] **1** : to say in reply : answer back usu. sharply **2** : to answer (an argument) by a counter argument **3** : RETALIATE

²**retort** n : a quick, witty, or cutting reply

³**re·tort** \ri-'tòrt, 'rē-ˌtòrt\ n [MF retorte, fr. ML retorta, fr. L, fem. of retortus, pp. of retorquēre to twist back; fr. its shape] : a vessel in which substances are distilled or broken up by heat

re·touch \(ˌ)rē-'təch\ vb : TOUCH UP; esp : to change (as a photographic negative) in order to produce a more desirable appearance

re·trace \(ˌ)rē-'trās\ vb : to go over again or in a reverse direction ⟨retraced his steps⟩

re·tract \ri-'trakt\ vb **1** : to draw back or in **2** : to withdraw (as a charge or promise) : DISAVOW — **re·tract·able** adj — **re·trac·tion** \-'trak-shən\ n

re·trac·tile \ri-'trak-tᵊl, -'trak-ˌtī(-ə)l\ adj : capable of being drawn back or in ⟨~ claws⟩

¹**re·tread** \(ˌ)rē-'tred\ vb **re·tread·ed**; **re·tread·ing** : to put a new tread on (a worn tire)

²**re·tread** \'rē-ˌtred\ n **1** : a retreaded tire **2** : one pressed into service again; also : REMAKE

¹**re·treat** \ri-'trēt\ n **1** : an act of withdrawing esp. from something dangerous, difficult, or disagreeable **2** : a military signal for withdrawal; also : a military flag-lowering ceremony **3** : a place of privacy or safety : REFUGE **4** : a group withdrawal for prayer, meditation, or study

²**retreat** vb **1** : to make a retreat : WITHDRAW **2** : to slope backward

re·trench \ri-'trench\ vb [obs. F retrencher (now retrancher), fr. MF retrenchier, fr. re- + trenchier to cut] **1** : to cut down or pare away : REDUCE, CURTAIL **2** : to cut down expenses : ECONOMIZE — **re·trench·ment** n

ret·ri·bu·tion \ˌre-trə-'byü-shən\ n : something administered or exacted in recompense; esp : PUNISHMENT ✦ **Synonyms** REPRISAL, VENGEANCE, REVENGE, RETALIATION — **re·trib·u·tive** \ri-'tri-byə-tiv\ adj — **re·trib·u·to·ry** \-byə-ˌtòr-ē\ adj

re·trieve \ri-'trēv\ vb **re·trieved**; **re·triev·ing** **1** : to search about for and bring in (killed or wounded game) **2** : RECOVER, RESTORE — **re·triev·able** adj — **re·triev·al** \-'trē-vəl\ n

re·triev·er \ri-'trē-vər\ n : one that retrieves; esp : a dog of any of several breeds used esp. for retrieving game

ret·ro \'re-ˌtrō\ adj : relating to or being the styles and fashions of the past ⟨~ clothing⟩

ret·ro·ac·tive \ˌre-trō-'ak-tiv\ adj : made effective as of a date prior to enactment ⟨a ~ pay raise⟩ — **ret·ro·ac·tive·ly** adv

ret·ro·fit \'re-trō-ˌfit, ˌre-trō-'fit\ vb **1** : to furnish (as an aircraft) with newly available equipment **2** : to adapt to a new purpose or need : MODIFY — **ret·ro·fit** \'re-trō-ˌfit\ n

¹**ret·ro·grade** \'re-trə-ˌgrād\ adj **1** : moving or tending backward **2** : tending toward or resulting in a worse condition

²**retrograde** vb **1** : RETREAT **2** : DETERIORATE, DEGENERATE

ret·ro·gres·sion \ˌre-trə-'gre-shən\ n : return to a former and less complex level of development or organization — **ret·ro·gress** \ˌre-trə-'gres\ vb — **ret·ro·gres·sive** \ˌre-trə-'gre-siv\ adj

ret·ro·rock·et \'re-trō-ˌrä-kət\ n : an auxiliary rocket engine (as on a spacecraft) used to slow forward motion

ret·ro·spect \'re-trə-ˌspekt\ n : a review of past events — **ret·ro·spec·tion** \ˌre-trə-'spek-shən\ n

ret·ro·spec·tive \ˌre-trə-'spek-tiv\ n **1** : a comprehensive examination of an artist's work over many years **2** : REVIEW 4 ⟨a war ~⟩ — **retrospective** adj — **ret·ro·spec·tive·ly** adv

ret·ro·vi·rus \'re-trō-ˌvī-rəs\ n : any of a group of RNA= containing viruses (as HIV) that make DNA using RNA instead of the reverse — **re·tro·vi·ral** \-rəl\ adj

¹**re·turn** \ri-'tərn\ vb **1** : to go or come back **2** : to pass, give, or send back to an earlier possessor **3** : to put back to or in a former place or state **4** : REPLY, ANSWER **5** : to report esp. officially **6** : to elect to office **7** : to bring in (as profit) : YIELD **8** : to give or perform in return ⟨~ a favor⟩ — **re·turn·er** n

²**return** n **1** : an act of coming or going back to or from a former place or state **2** : RECURRENCE **3** : a report of the results of balloting **4** : a formal statement of taxable income **5** : the profit from labor, investment, or business : YIELD **6** : the act of returning something **7** : something that returns or is returned; also : a means for conveying something (as water) back to its starting point **8** : something given in repayment or reciprocation; also : ANSWER, RETORT **9** : an answering play — **return** adj

¹**re·turn·able** \ri-'tər-nə-bəl\ adj : capable of being returned (as for reuse); also : permitted to be returned

²**returnable** n : a returnable beverage container

re·turn·ee \ri-ˌtər-'nē\ n : one who returns

re·union \rē-'yün-yən\ n **1** : an act of reuniting : the state of being reunited **2** : a meeting of persons after separation

¹**rev** \'rev\ n : a revolution of a motor

²**rev** vb **revved**; **rev·ving** **1** : to increase the revolutions per minute of (a motor) **2** : STIMULATE, EXCITE

³**rev** abbr **1** revenue **2** reverse **3** review; reviewed **4** revised; revision **5** revolution

Rev *abbr* **1** Revelation **2** Reverend

re·vamp \(ˌ)rē-ˈvamp\ *vb* : RECONSTRUCT, REVISE; *also* : RENOVATE

re·vanche \rə-ˈväⁿsh\ *n* [F] : REVENGE; *esp* : a usu. political policy designed to recover lost territory or status

re·veal \ri-ˈvēl\ *vb* **1** : to make known **2** : to show plainly : open up to view

rev·eil·le \ˈre-və-lē\ *n* [modif. of F *réveillez,* imper. pl. of *réveiller* to awaken, fr. MF *eveiller* to awaken, fr. (assumed) VL *exvigilare,* fr. L *vigilare* to keep watch, stay awake] : a military signal sounded at about sunrise

¹rev·el \ˈre-vəl\ *vb* **-eled** *or* **-elled; -el·ing** *or* **-el·ling 1** : to take part in a revel **2** : to take great pleasure or satisfaction ⟨∼ed in the quiet⟩ — **rev·el·er** *or* **rev·el·ler** *n* — **rev·el·ry** \-vəl-rē\ *n*

²revel *n* : a usu. wild party or celebration

rev·e·la·tion \ˌre-və-ˈlā-shən\ *n* **1** : an act of revealing **2** : something revealed; *esp* : an enlightening or astonishing disclosure

Revelation *n* — see BIBLE table

¹re·venge \ri-ˈvenj\ *vb* **re·venged; re·veng·ing** : to inflict harm or injury in return for (a wrong) : AVENGE — **re·veng·er** *n*

²revenge *n* **1** : a desire for revenge **2** : an act or instance of retaliation to get even **3** : an opportunity for getting satisfaction ♦ **Synonyms** VENGEANCE, RETRIBUTION, REPRISAL — **re·venge·ful** *adj*

rev·e·nue \ˈre-və-ˌnü, -ˌnyü\ *n* [ME, return, revenue, fr. AF, fr. *revenir* to return, fr. L *revenire,* fr. *re-* back + *venire* to come] **1** : investment income **2** : money collected by a government (as through taxes)

rev·e·nu·er \ˈre-və-ˌnü-ər, -ˌnyü-\ *n* : a revenue officer or boat

re·verb \ri-ˈvərb, ˈrē-ˌvərb\ *n* : an electronically produced echo effect in recorded music; *also* : a device for producing reverb

re·ver·ber·ate \ri-ˈvər-bə-ˌrāt\ *vb* **-at·ed; -at·ing 1** : REFLECT ⟨∼ light or heat⟩ **2** : to resound in or as if in a series of echoes — **re·ver·ber·a·tion** \-ˌvər-bə-ˈrā-shən\ *n*

re·vere \ri-ˈvir\ *vb* **re·vered; re·ver·ing** : to show honor and devotion to : VENERATE ⟨a teacher *revered* by students⟩ ♦ **Synonyms** REVERENCE, WORSHIP, ADORE

¹rev·er·ence \ˈre-vrəns, -və-rəns\ *n* **1** : honor or respect felt or shown **2** : a gesture (as a bow or curtsy) of respect

²reverence *vb* **-enced; -enc·ing** : to regard or treat with reverence

¹rev·er·end \ˈre-vrənd, -və-rənd\ *adj* **1** : worthy of reverence : REVERED **2** : being a member of the clergy — used as a title

²reverend *n* : a member of the clergy

rev·er·ent \ˈre-vrənt, -və-rənt\ *adj* : expressing reverence — **rev·er·ent·ly** *adv*

rev·er·en·tial \ˌre-və-ˈren-chəl\ *adj* : REVERENT

rev·er·ie *also* **rev·ery** \ˈre-və-rē\ *n, pl* **-er·ies** [F *rêverie,* fr. MF, delirium, fr. *resver, rever* to wander, be delirious] **1** : DAYDREAM **2** : the state of being lost in thought

re·ver·sal \ri-ˈvər-səl\ *n* : an act or process of reversing

¹re·verse \ri-ˈvərs\ *adj* **1** : opposite to a previous or normal condition ⟨in ∼ order⟩ **2** : acting or working in a manner opposite the usual **3** : bringing about reverse movement ⟨∼ gear⟩ — **re·verse·ly** *adv*

²reverse *vb* **re·versed; re·vers·ing 1** : to turn upside down or completely about in position or direction **2** : to set aside or change (as a legal decision) **3** : to change to the contrary ⟨∼ a policy⟩ **4** : to go or cause to go in the opposite direction **5** : to put (as a car) in reverse — **re·vers·ible** \-ˈvər-sə-bəl\ *adj*

³reverse *n* **1** : something contrary to something else : OPPOSITE **2** : an act or instance of reversing; *esp* : a change for the worse **3** : the back side of something (as a coin or card) **4** : a gear that reverses something

reverse engineer *vb* : to disassemble or analyze in detail in order to discover concepts involved in manufacture — **reverse engineering** *n*

re·ver·sion \ri-ˈvər-zhən\ *n* **1** : the right of succession or future possession (as to a title or property) **2** : return toward some former or ancestral condition; *also* : a product of this — **re·ver·sion·ary** \-zhə-ˌner-ē\ *adj*

re·vert \ri-ˈvərt\ *vb* **1** : to come or go back ⟨∼ed to savagery⟩ **2** : to return to a proprietor or his or her heirs **3** : to return to an ancestral type

¹re·view \ri-ˈvyü\ *n* **1** : an act of revising **2** : a formal military inspection **3** : a general survey **4** : INSPECTION, EXAMINATION; *esp* : REEXAMINATION **5** : a critical evaluation (as of a book) **6** : a magazine devoted to reviews and essays **7** : a renewed study of previously studied material **8** : REVUE

²re·view \ri-ˈvyü, *1 also* ˈrē-\ *vb* **1** : to examine or study again; *esp* : to reexamine judicially **2** : to hold a review of ⟨∼ troops⟩ **3** : to write a critical examination of ⟨∼ a novel⟩ **4** : to look back over ⟨∼ed her accomplishments⟩ **5** : to study material again

re·view·er \ri-ˈvyü-ər\ *n* : one that reviews; *esp* : a writer of critical reviews

re·vile \ri-ˈvī(-ə)l\ *vb* **re·viled; re·vil·ing** : to abuse verbally : rail at ♦ **Synonyms** VITUPERATE, BERATE, RATE, UPBRAID, SCOLD — **re·vile·ment** *n* — **re·vil·er** *n*

re·vise \ri-ˈvīz\ *vb* **re·vised; re·vis·ing 1** : to look over something written in order to correct or improve ⟨∼ an essay⟩ **2** : to make a new version of ⟨∼ an almanac⟩ — **re·vis·able** *adj* — **re·vise** *n* — **re·vis·er** *or* **re·vi·sor** \-ˈvī-zər\ *n* — **re·vi·sion** \-ˈvi-zhən\ *n*

re·vi·tal·ise *Brit var of* REVITALIZE

re·vi·tal·ize \ˌrē-ˈvīt-ə-ˌlīz\ *vb* **-ized; -iz·ing** : to give new life or vigor to ⟨∼ the shopping district⟩ — **re·vi·tal·i·za·tion** \(ˌ)rē-ˌvī-tə-lə-ˈzā-shən\ *n*

re·viv·al \ri-ˈvī-vəl\ *n* **1** : an act of reviving : the state of being revived **2** : a new publication or presentation (as of a book or play) **3** : an evangelistic meeting or series of meetings

re·vive \ri-ˈvīv\ *vb* **re·vived; re·viv·ing 1** : to bring back to life, consciousness, or activity : make or become fresh or strong again **2** : to bring back into use — **re·viv·er** *n*

re·viv·i·fy \rē-ˈvi-və-ˌfī\ *vb* : REVIVE — **re·viv·i·fi·ca·tion** \-ˌvi-və-fə-ˈkā-shən\ *n*

re·vo·ca·ble \ˈre-və-kə-bəl *also* ri-ˈvō-kə-bəl\ *adj* : capable of being revoked

re·vo·ca·tion \ˌre-və-ˈkā-shən\ *n* : an act or instance of revoking

re·voke \ri-ˈvōk\ *vb* **re·voked; re·vok·ing 1** : to annul by recalling or taking back : REPEAL, RESCIND ⟨∼ a license⟩ **2** : RENEGE — **re·vok·er** *n*

¹re·volt \ri-ˈvōlt\ *vb* [MF *revolter,* fr. It *rivoltare* to overthrow, fr. VL *revolvitare,* fr. L *revolvere* to revolve, roll back] **1** : to throw off allegiance to a ruler or government : REBEL **2** : to experience disgust or shock **3** : to turn or cause to turn away with disgust or abhorrence — **re·volt·er** *n*

²revolt *n* : REBELLION, INSURRECTION

re·volt·ing *adj* : extremely offensive ⟨a ∼ odor⟩ — **re·volt·ing·ly** *adv*

rev·o·lu·tion \ˌre-və-ˈlü-shən\ *n* **1** : the action by a heavenly body of going round in an orbit **2** : ROTATION **3** : a sudden, radical, or complete change; *esp* : the overthrow or renunciation of one ruler or government and substitution of another by the governed

¹rev·o·lu·tion·ary \-shə-ˌner-ē\ *adj* **1** : of or relating to revolution **2** : tending to or promoting revolution **3** : constituting or bringing about a major change

²revolutionary *n, pl* **-ar·ies** : one who takes part in a revolution or who advocates revolutionary doctrines

rev·o·lu·tion·ise *Brit var of* REVOLUTIONIZE

rev·o·lu·tion·ist \ˌre-və-ˈlü-shə-nist\ *n* : REVOLUTIONARY — **revolutionist** *adj*

rev·o·lu·tion·ize \-ˌnīz\ *vb* **-ized; -iz·ing** : to change fundamentally or completely ⟨∼ an industry⟩ — **rev·o·lu·tion·iz·er** *n*

re·volve \ri-ˈvälv\ *vb* **re·volved; re·volv·ing 1** : to turn over in the mind : reflect upon : PONDER **2** : to move in an orbit; *also* : ROTATE **3** : to have a specified focus ⟨the debate *revolved* around taxes⟩ — **re·volv·able** *adj*

re·volv·er \ri-ˈväl-vər\ *n* : a pistol with a revolving cylinder of several chambers

re·vue \ri-ˈvyü\ *n* : a theatrical production consisting typically of brief often satirical sketches and songs

re·vul·sion \ri-ˈvəl-shən\ *n* **1** : a strong sudden reaction or change of feeling **2** : a feeling of complete distaste or repugnance

revved *past and past part of* REV

revving *pres part of* REV

¹re·ward \ri-'word\ *vb* **1** : to give a reward to or for **2** : RECOMPENSE

²reward *n* **1** : something given in return for good or evil done or received or for some service or attainment **2** : a stimulus that is administered to an organism after a response and that increases the probability of occurrence of the response ✦ **Synonyms** PREMIUM, PRIZE, AWARD

¹re·wind \(,)rē-'wīnd\ *vb* **-wound; -wind·ing** **1** : to wind again **2** : to reverse the winding of (as film)

²re·wind \'rē-,wīnd\ *n* **1** : something that rewinds **2** : an act of rewinding **3** : a function of an electronic device that reverses a recording to a previous portion

re·work \(,)rē-'wərk\ *vb* **1** : REVISE **2** : to reprocess for further use

¹re·write \(,)rē-'rīt\ *vb* **-wrote; -writ·ten; -writ·ing** : to make a revision of : REVISE

²re·write \'rē-,rīt\ *n* : an instance or a piece of rewriting

RF *abbr* radio frequency

RFD *abbr* rural free delivery

Rh *symbol* rhodium

RH *abbr* right hand

rhap·so·dy \'rap-sə-dē\ *n, pl* **-dies** [L *rhapsodia* portion of an epic poem adapted for recitation, fr. Gk *rhapsōidia* recitation of selections from epic poetry, ultim. fr. *rhaptein* to sew, stitch together + *aidein* to sing] **1** : an expression of extravagant praise or ecstasy **2** : a musical of irregular form — **rhap·sod·ic** \rap-'sä-dik\ *adj* — **rhap·sod·i·cal·ly** \-di-k(ə-)lē\ *adv* — **rhap·so·dize** \'rap-sə-,dīz\ *vb*

rhea \'rē-ə\ *n* : either of two large flightless 3-toed So. American birds that resemble but are smaller than the African ostrich

rhe·ni·um \'rē-nē-əm\ *n* : a rare heavy metallic chemical element

rheo·stat \'rē-ə-,stat\ *n* : a resistor for regulating an electric current by means of variable resistances — **rheo·stat·ic** \,rē-ə-'sta-tik\ *adj*

rhe·sus monkey \'rē-səs-\ *n* : a pale brown Asian monkey often used in medical research

rhet·o·ric \'re-tə-rik\ *n* [ME *rethorik*, fr. AF *rethorique*, fr. L *rhetorica*, fr. Gk *rhētorikē*, lit., art of oratory, fr. *rhētōr* public speaker, fr. *eirein* to speak] : the art of speaking or writing effectively — **rhet·o·ri·cian** \,re-tə-'ri-shən\ *n*

rhe·tor·i·cal \ri-'tór-i-kəl\ *adj* **1** : of or relating to rhetoric **2** : asked merely for effect with no answer expected ⟨a ~ question⟩

rheum \'rüm\ *n* : a watery discharge from the mucous membranes esp. of the eyes or nose — **rheumy** *adj*

rheu·mat·ic fever \ru̇-'ma-tik-\ *n* : an acute disease chiefly of children and young adults that is characterized by fever, by inflammation and pain in and around the joints, and by inflammation of the membranes surrounding the heart and the heart valves

rheu·ma·tism \'rü-mə-,ti-zəm, 'ru̇-\ *n* **1** : any of various conditions marked by stiffness, pain, or swelling in muscles or joints **2** : RHEUMATOID ARTHRITIS — **rheu·mat·ic** \ru̇-'ma-tik\ *adj*

rheu·ma·toid arthritis \-,tȯid-\ *n* : a usu. chronic progressive autoimmune disease characterized by inflammation and swelling of joint structures

rheu·ma·tol·o·gy \,rü-mə-'tä-lə-jē, ,ru̇-\ *n* : a medical science dealing with rheumatic diseases — **rheu·ma·tol·o·gist** \-jist\ *n*

Rh factor \,är-'āch-\ *n* [*rh*esus monkey (in which it was first detected)] : any of one or more inherited substances in red blood cells that may cause dangerous reactions in some infants or in transfusions

rhine·stone \'rīn-,stōn\ *n* : a colorless imitation stone of high luster made of glass, paste, or gem quartz

rhi·no \'rī-nō\ *n, pl* **rhinos** *also* **rhino** : RHINOCEROS

rhi·noc·er·os \rī-'nä-sə-rəs\ *n, pl* **-noc·er·os·es** *also* **-noc·er·os** *or* **-noc·eri** \-'nä-sə-,rī\ [ME *rinoceros*, fr. AF, fr. L *rhinoceros*, fr. Gk *rhinokerōs*, fr. *rhin-, rhis* nose + *keras* horn] : any of a family of large thick-skinned mammals of Africa and Asia with one or two upright horns of keratin on the snout and three toes on each foot

rhi·zome \'rī-,zōm\ *n* : a fleshy, rootlike, and usu. horizontal underground plant stem that forms shoots above and roots below — **rhi·zom·a·tous** \rī-'zä-mə-təs\ *adj*

Rh–neg·a·tive \,är-'āch-'ne-gə-tiv\ *adj* : lacking Rh factors in the red blood cells

rho \'rō\ *n* : the 17th letter of the Greek alphabet — P or ρ

rho·di·um \'rō-dē-əm\ *n* : a rare hard ductile metallic chemical element

rho·do·den·dron \,rō-də-'den-drən\ *n* : any of a genus of shrubs or trees of the heath family with clusters of large bright flowers

rhom·boid \'räm-,bȯid\ *n* : a parallelogram with unequal adjacent sides and angles that are not right angles — **rhomboid** *or* **rhom·boi·dal** \räm-'bȯi-d°l\ *adj*

rhom·bus \'räm-bəs\ *n, pl* **rhom·bus·es** *or* **rhom·bi** \-,bī\ : a parallelogram having all four sides equal

Rh–pos·i·tive \,är-,āch-'pä-zə-tiv\ *adj* : containing one or more Rh factors in the red blood cells

rhu·barb \'rü-,bärb\ *n* [ME *rubarbe*, fr. AF *reubarbe*, fr. ML *reubarbarum*, alter. of *rha barbarum*, lit., barbarian rhubarb] : a garden plant related to the buckwheat having leaves with thick juicy edible pink and red stems

¹rhyme *also* **rime** \'rīm\ *n* **1** : a composition in verse that rhymes; *also* : POETRY **2** : correspondence in terminal sounds (as of two lines of verse)

²rhyme *also* **rime** *vb* **rhymed** *also* **rimed; rhym·ing** *also* **rim·ing** **1** : to make rhymes; *also* : to write poetry **2** : to have rhymes : be in rhyme

rhythm \'ri-thəm\ *n* **1** : regular rise and fall in the flow of sound in speech **2** : a movement or activity in which some action or element recurs regularly — **rhyth·mic** \'rith-mik\ *or* **rhyth·mi·cal** \-mi-kəl\ *adj* — **rhyth·mi·cal·ly** \-k(ə-)lē\ *adv*

rhythm and blues *n* : popular music based on blues and black folk music

rhythm method *n* : birth control by refraining from sexual intercourse during the time when ovulation is most likely to occur

RI *abbr* Rhode Island

ri·al \rē-'ȯl, -'äl\ *n* — see MONEY table

¹rib \'rib\ *n* **1** : any of the series of curved bones of the chest of most vertebrates that are joined to the backbone in pairs and help to support the body wall and protect the organs inside **2** : something resembling a rib in shape or function **3** : an elongated ridge (as in fabric)

²rib *vb* **ribbed; rib·bing** **1** : to furnish or strengthen with ribs **2** : to knit so as to form ridges

³rib *vb* **ribbed; rib·bing** : to poke fun at : TEASE — **rib·ber** *n*

rib·ald \'ri-bəld\ *adj* : coarse or indecent esp. in language ⟨~ jokes⟩ — **rib·ald·ry** \-bəl-drē\ *n*

rib·and \'ri-bənd\ *n* : RIBBON

rib·bon \'ri-bən\ *n* **1** : a narrow fabric typically of silk or velvet used for trimming and for badges **2** : a strip of inked cloth (as in a typewriter) **3** : TATTER, SHRED ⟨torn to ~s⟩

ri·bo·fla·vin \,rī-bə-'flā-vən, 'rī-bə-,flā-vən\ *n* : a growth-promoting vitamin of the vitamin B complex occurring esp. in milk and liver

ri·bo·nu·cle·ic acid \,rī-bō-nu̇-,klē-ik-, -nyu̇-, -,klā-\ *n* : RNA

ri·bose \'rī-,bōs\ *n* : a sugar with five carbon atoms and five oxygen atoms in each molecule that is part of RNA

ri·bo·some \'rī-bə-,sōm\ *n* : any of the RNA-rich cytoplasmic granules in a cell that are sites of protein synthesis — **ri·bo·som·al** \,rī-bə-'sō-məl\ *adj*

rice \'rīs\ *n* : the starchy seeds of an annual grass that are cooked and used for food; *also* : this widely cultivated grass of warm wet areas

rich \'rich\ *adj* **1** : possessing or controlling great wealth : WEALTHY **2** : COSTLY, VALUABLE **3** : deep and pleasing in color or tone **4** : ABUNDANT **5** : containing much sugar, fat, or seasoning; *also* : high in combustible content **6** : FRUITFUL, FERTILE — **rich·ly** *adv* — **rich·ness** *n*

rhinoceros

rich·es \'ri-chəz\ *n pl* [ME, sing. or pl., fr. *richesse* wealth, fr. AF *richesce*, fr. *riche* rich] : things that make one rich : WEALTH

Rich·ter scale \'rik-tər-\ *n* : a scale for expressing the magnitude of a seismic disturbance (as an earthquake) in terms of the energy dissipated in it

rick \'rik\ *n* : a large stack (as of hay) in the open air

rick·ets \'ri-kəts\ *n* : a childhood deficiency disease marked esp. by soft deformed bones and caused by lack of vitamin D

rick·ett·sia \ri-'ket-sē-ə\ *n, pl* **-si·as** or **-si·ae** \-sē-ˌē\ : any of a group of usu. rod-shaped bacteria that cause various diseases (as typhus)

rick·ety \'ri-kə-tē\ *adj* **1** : affected with rickets **2** : SHAKY; *also* : in unsound physical condition ⟨~ stairs⟩

rick·shaw *also* **rick·sha** \'rik-ˌshȯ\ *n* : a small covered 2-wheeled carriage pulled by one person and used orig. in Japan

rickshaw

¹ric·o·chet \'ri-kə-ˌshā, *Brit also* -ˌshet\ *n* [F] : a bouncing off at an angle (as of a bullet off a wall); *also* : an object that ricochets

²ricochet *vb* **-cheted** \-ˌshād\ *also* **-chet·ted** \-ˌshe-təd\; **-chet·ing** \-ˌshā-iŋ\ *or* **-chet·ting** \-ˌshe-tiŋ\ : to bounce or skip with or as if with a glancing rebound

ri·cot·ta \ri-'kä-tə, -'kȯ-\ *n* : a white unripened whey cheese of Italy that resembles cottage cheese

rid \'rid\ *vb* **rid** *also* **rid·ded**; **rid·ding** : to make free : CLEAR, RELIEVE — **rid·dance** \'ri-dᵊns\ *n*

rid·den \'ri-dᵊn\ *adj* **1** : harassed, oppressed, or obsessed by ⟨debt-*ridden*⟩ **2** : excessively full of or supplied with ⟨slum-*ridden*⟩

¹rid·dle \'ri-dᵊl\ *n* : a puzzling question to be solved or answered by guessing

²riddle *vb* **rid·dled**; **rid·dling** **1** : EXPLAIN, SOLVE **2** : to speak in riddles

³riddle *n* : a coarse sieve

⁴riddle *vb* **rid·dled**; **rid·dling** **1** : to sift with a riddle **2** : to pierce with many holes **3** : PERMEATE

¹ride \'rīd\ *vb* **rode** \'rōd\; **rid·den** \'ri-dᵊn\; **rid·ing** **1** : to go on an animal's back or in a conveyance (as a boat, car, or airplane); *also* : to sit on and control so as to be carried along ⟨~ a bicycle⟩ **2** : to float or move on water ⟨~ at anchor⟩; *also* : to move like a floating object **3** : to bear along : CARRY ⟨*rode* her on their shoulders⟩ **4** : to travel over a surface ⟨the car ~s well⟩ **5** : to proceed over on horseback **6** : to torment by nagging or teasing

²ride *n* **1** : an act of riding; *esp* : a trip on horseback or by vehicle **2** : a way (as a road or path) suitable for riding **3** : a mechanical device (as a merry-go-round) for riding on **4** : a means of transportation

rid·er \'rī-dər\ *n* **1** : one that rides **2** : an addition to a document often attached on a separate piece of paper **3** : a clause dealing with an unrelated matter attached to a legislative bill during passage — **rid·er·less** *adj*

¹ridge \'rij\ *n* [ME *rigge*, fr. OE *hrycg*] **1** : an elevated body part or structure **2** : a range of hills **3** : a raised line or strip **4** : the line made where two sloping surfaces (as of a roof) meet — **ridgy** *adj*

²ridge *vb* **ridged**; **ridg·ing** **1** : to form into a ridge **2** : to extend in ridges

rid·i·cule \'ri-də-ˌkyül\ *n* : the act of ridiculing : DERISION, MOCKERY

²ridicule *vb* **-culed**; **-cul·ing** : to laugh at or make fun of mockingly or contemptuously ⟨was *ridiculed* by his peers⟩ ♦ **Synonyms** DERIDE, TAUNT, TWIT, MOCK

ri·dic·u·lous \rə-'di-kyə-ləs\ *adj* : arousing or deserving ridicule : ABSURD, PREPOSTEROUS ♦ **Synonyms** LAUGHABLE, LUDICROUS, FARCICAL, RISIBLE — **ri·dic·u·lous·ly** *adv* — **ri·dic·u·lous·ness** *n*

rid·ley \'rid-lē\ *n* : either of two relatively small sea turtles

ri·el \rē-'el\ *n* — see MONEY table

Ries·ling \'rēz-liŋ, 'rēs-\ *n* : a sweet to very dry white wine made from a single variety of grape orig. grown in Germany

RIF *abbr* reduction in force

rife \'rīf\ *adj* : WIDESPREAD, PREVALENT, ABOUNDING — **rife** *adv* — **rife·ly** *adv*

¹riff \'rif\ *n* : a repeated phrase in jazz typically supporting a solo improvisation; *also* : a piece based on such a phrase **2** : a usu. witty or improvised remark or outpouring **3** : a distinct variation : TAKE — **riff** *vb*

riff·raff \'rif-ˌraf\ *n* [ME *riffe raffe*, fr. *rif and raf* every single one, fr. AF *rif et raf* altogether] **1** : RABBLE **2** : REFUSE, RUBBISH

¹ri·fle \'rī-fəl\ *vb* **ri·fled**; **ri·fling** : to ransack esp. with the intent to steal — **ri·fler** *n*

²rifle *vb* **ri·fled**; **ri·fling** : to cut spiral grooves into the bore of ⟨*rifled* pipe⟩ — **rifling** *n*

³rifle *n* **1** : a shoulder weapon with a rifled bore **2** *pl* : soldiers armed with rifles — **ri·fle·man** \-fəl-mən\ *n*

rift \'rift\ *n* **1** : CLEFT, FISSURE **2** : FAULT 6 **3** : ESTRANGEMENT, SEPARATION ⟨a ~ between spouses⟩ — **rift** *vb*

¹rig \'rig\ *vb* **rigged**; **rig·ging** **1** : to fit out (as a ship) with rigging **2** : CLOTHE, DRESS **3** : EQUIP **4** : to set up esp. as a makeshift ⟨~ up a shelter⟩

²rig *n* **1** : the distinctive shape, number, and arrangement of sails and masts of a ship **2** : a carriage with its horse **3** : CLOTHING, DRESS **4** : EQUIPMENT

³rig *vb* **rigged**; **rig·ging** **1** : to manipulate or control esp. by deceptive or dishonest means **2** : to fix in advance for a desired result — **rig·ger** *n*

rig·ging \'ri-giŋ, -gən\ *n* **1** : the ropes and chains that hold and move masts, sails, and spars of a ship **2** : a network (as in theater scenery) used for support and manipulation

¹right \'rīt\ *adj* **1** : RIGHTEOUS, UPRIGHT **2** : JUST, PROPER **3** : conforming to truth or fact : CORRECT **4** : APPROPRIATE, SUITABLE **5** : STRAIGHT ⟨a ~ line⟩ **6** : GENUINE, REAL **7** : of, relating to, or being the side of the body which is away from the side on which the heart is mostly located **8** : located nearer to the right hand; *esp* : being on the right when facing in the same direction as the observer **9** : made to be placed or worn outward ⟨~ side of a rug⟩ **10** : NORMAL, SOUND ⟨not in her ~ mind⟩ ♦ **Synonyms** CORRECT, ACCURATE, EXACT, PRECISE, NICE — **right·ness** *n*

²right *n* **1** : qualities that constitute what is correct, just, proper, or honorable **2** : something (as a power or privilege) to which one has a just or lawful claim **3** : just action or decision : the cause of justice **4** : the side or part that is on or toward the right side **5** *cap* : political conservatives **6** *often cap* : a conservative position — **right·ward** \-wərd\ *adj or adv*

³right *adv* **1** : according to what is right ⟨live ~⟩ **2** : EXACTLY, PRECISELY ⟨~ here and now⟩ **3** : DIRECTLY ⟨went ~ home⟩ **4** : according to fact or truth ⟨guess ~⟩ **5** : all the way : COMPLETELY ⟨~ to the end⟩ **6** : IMMEDIATELY ⟨~ after lunch⟩ **7** : QUITE, VERY ⟨~ nice weather⟩ **8** : on or to the right ⟨looked ~ and left⟩

⁴right *vb* **1** : to relieve from wrong **2** : to adjust or restore to a proper state or position **3** : to bring or restore to an upright position **4** : to become upright — **right·er** *n*

right angle *n* : an angle whose measure is 90° : an angle whose sides are perpendicular to each other — **right–angled** \'rīt-'aŋ-gəld\ *or* **right–an·gle** \-gəl\ *adj*

right circular cone *n* : CONE 2

right·eous \'rī-chəs\ *adj* : acting or being in accordance with what is just, honorable, and free from guilt or wrong : UPRIGHT ♦ **Synonyms** VIRTUOUS, NOBLE, MORAL, ETHICAL — **right·eous·ly** *adv* — **right·eous·ness** *n*

right·ful \'rīt-fəl\ *adj* **1** : JUST; *also* : FITTING **2** : having or held by a legally just claim — **right·ful·ly** *adv* — **right·ful·ness** *n*

right–hand \'rīt-ˌhand\ *adj* **1** : situated on the right **2** : RIGHT-HANDED **3** : chiefly relied on ⟨his ~ man⟩

right–hand·ed \-'han-dəd\ *adj* **1** : using the right hand habitually or better than the left **2** : designed for or done with the right hand **3** : CLOCKWISE ⟨a ~ twist⟩ — **right–handed** *adv* — **right–hand·ed·ly** *adv* — **right–hand·ed·ness** *n*

right·ly \'rīt-lē\ *adv* **1** : FAIRLY, JUSTLY **2** : PROPERLY **3** : CORRECTLY, EXACTLY

right–of–way *n, pl* **rights–of–way** **1** : a legal right of passage over another person's ground **2** : the area over which a right-of-way exists **3** : the land on which a public road is built **4** : the land occupied by a railroad **5** : the land used by a public utility **6** : the right of traffic to take precedence over other traffic

right on *interj* — used to express agreement or give encouragement

right–to–life *adj* : ANTIABORTION — **right–to–lifer** *n*

right triangle *n* : a triangle having one right angle

right whale *n* : any of a family of large baleen whales having a very large head on a stocky body

rig·id \'ri-jəd\ *adj* **1** : lacking flexibility **2** : strictly observed ✦ **Synonyms** SEVERE, STERN, RIGOROUS, STRINGENT — **ri·gid·i·ty** \rə-'ji-də-tē\ *n* — **rig·id·ly** *adv*

rig·ma·role \'ri-gə-mə-ˌrōl\ *n* [alter. of obs. *ragman roll* long list, catalog] **1** : confused or senseless talk **2** : a complex and ritualistic procedure

rig·or \'ri-gər\ *n* **1** : the quality of being inflexible or unyielding : STRICTNESS **2** : HARSHNESS, SEVERITY **3** : a tremor caused by a chill **4** : strict precision : EXACTNESS — **rig·or·ous** *adj* — **rig·or·ous·ly** *adv*

rig·or mor·tis \ˌri-gər-'mȯr-təs\ *n* [NL, stiffness of death] : temporary rigidity of muscles occurring after death

rig·our *chiefly Brit var of* RIGOR

rile \'rī(-ə)l\ *vb* **riled; ril·ing** **1** : to make angry **2** : ROIL 1

rill \'ril\ *n* : a very small brook

¹rim \'rim\ *n* **1** : the outer part of a wheel **2** : an outer edge esp. of something curved : BORDER, MARGIN

²rim *vb* **rimmed; rim·ming** **1** : to serve as a rim for : BORDER **2** : to run around the rim of

¹rime \'rīm\ *n* : FROST **2** — **rimy** \'rī-mē\ *adj*

²rime *var of* RHYME

rind \'rīnd\ *n* : a usu. hard or tough outer layer ⟨lemon ~⟩

¹ring \'riŋ\ *n* **1** : a circular band worn as an ornament or token or used for holding or fastening ⟨wedding ~⟩ ⟨key ~⟩ **2** : something circular in shape ⟨smoke ~⟩ **3** : a place for contest or display ⟨boxing ~⟩; *also* : PRIZEFIGHTING **4** : ANNUAL RING **5** : a group of people who work together for selfish or dishonest purposes — **ringed** *adj* — **ring·like** \'riŋ-ˌlīk\ *adj*

²ring *vb* **ringed; ring·ing** \'riŋ-iŋ\ **1** : ENCIRCLE **2** : to throw a ring over (a mark) in a game (as quoits) **3** : to move in a ring or spirally

³ring *vb* **rang** \'raŋ\; **rung** \'rəŋ\; **ring·ing** \'riŋ-iŋ\ **1** : to sound resonantly when struck; *also* : to feel as if filled with such sound **2** : to cause to make a clear metallic sound by striking **3** : to announce or call by or as if by striking a bell ⟨~ an alarm⟩ **4** : to repeat loudly and persistently **5** : to summon esp. by a bell ⟨~ for the butler⟩ — **ring a bell** : to arouse a response ⟨that name *rings a bell*⟩

⁴ring *n* **1** : a set of bells **2** : the clear resonant sound of vibrating metal **3** : resonant tone : SONORITY **4** : a sound or character expressive of a particular quality **5** : an act or instance of ringing; *esp* : a telephone call

¹ring·er \'riŋ-ər\ *n* **1** : one that sounds by ringing **2** : one that enters a competition under false representations **3** : one that closely resembles another

²ringer *n* : one that encircles or puts a ring around

ring finger *n* : the third finger of the left hand counting the index finger as the first

ring·git \'riŋ-git\ *n* — see MONEY table

ring·lead·er \'riŋ-ˌlē-dər\ *n* : a leader esp. of a group of troublemakers

ring·let \-lət\ *n* : a long curl

ring·mas·ter \-ˌmas-tər\ *n* : one in charge of performances in a circus ring

ring up *vb* **1** : to total and record esp. by means of a cash register **2** : ACHIEVE ⟨*rang up* many triumphs⟩

ring·worm \'riŋ-ˌwərm\ *n* : any of several contagious skin diseases caused by fungi and marked by ring-shaped discolored patches

rink \'riŋk\ *n* : a level extent of ice marked off for skating or various games; *also* : a similar surface (as of wood) marked off or enclosed for a sport or game ⟨roller-skating ~⟩

¹rinse \'rins\ *vb* **rinsed; rins·ing** [ME *rincen*, AF *rincer*, alter. of OF *recincier*, fr. VL **recentiare*, fr. L *recent-*, *recens* fresh, recent] **1** : to wash lightly or in water only **2** : to cleanse (as of soap) with clear water **3** : to treat (hair) with a rinse — **rins·er** *n*

²rinse *n* **1** : an act of rinsing **2** : a liquid used for rinsing **3** : a solution that temporarily tints hair

ri·ot \'rī-ət\ *n* **1** *archaic* : disorderly behavior **2** : disturbance of the public peace; *esp* : a violent public disorder **3** : random or disorderly profusion ⟨a ~ of color⟩ **4** : one that is wildly amusing ⟨the comedy is a ~⟩ — **riot** *vb* — **ri·ot·er** *n* — **ri·ot·ous** *adj*

¹rip \'rip\ *vb* **ripped; rip·ping** **1** : to cut or tear open **2** : to saw or split (wood) with the grain **3** : CRITICIZE, DISPARAGE — **rip·per** *n*

²rip *n* : a rent made by ripping

RIP *abbr* [L *requiescat in pace*] may he rest in peace, may she rest in peace; [L *requiescant in pace*] may they rest in peace

ri·par·i·an \rə-'per-ē-ən\ *adj* : of or relating to the bank of a stream, river, or lake ⟨~ trees⟩

rip cord *n* : a cord that is pulled to release a parachute out of its container

ripe \'rīp\ *adj* **rip·er; rip·est** **1** : fully grown and developed : MATURE ⟨~ fruit⟩ **2** : fully prepared : READY ⟨slaves ~ for a revolt⟩ — **ripe·ly** *adv* — **ripe·ness** *n*

rip·en \'rī-pən\ *vb* **rip·ened; rip·en·ing** **1** : to grow or make ripe **2** : to bring to completeness or perfection; *also* : to age or cure (cheese) to develop characteristic flavor, odor, body, texture, and color

rip–off \'rip-ˌȯf\ *n* **1** : an act of stealing : THEFT **2** : a cheap imitation — **rip off** *vb*

ri·poste \ri-'pōst\ *n* [F, modif. of It *risposta*, lit., answer] **1** : a fencer's return thrust after a parry **2** : a retaliatory maneuver or response; *esp* : a quick retort — **riposte** *vb*

ripped \'ript\ *adj* : having high muscle definition

rip·ple \'ri-pəl\ *vb* **rip·pled; rip·pling** **1** : to become lightly ruffled on the surface **2** : to make a sound like that of rippling water — **ripple** *n*

rip·saw \'rip-ˌsȯ\ *n* : a coarse-toothed saw used to cut wood in the direction of the grain

rip·stop \-ˌstäp\ *adj* : being a fabric woven in such a way that small tears do not spread ⟨~ nylon⟩ — **ripstop** *n*

¹rise \'rīz\ *vb* **rose** \'rōz\; **ris·en** \'riz-ᵊn\; **ris·ing** **1** : to get up from sitting, kneeling, or lying **2** : to get up from sleep or from one's bed **3** : to return from death **4** : to take up arms **5** : to end a session : ADJOURN **6** : to appear above the horizon **7** : to move upward : ASCEND **8** : to extend above other objects **9** : to attain a higher level or rank **10** : to increase in quantity, intensity, or pitch **11** : to come into being : HAPPEN, BEGIN, ORIGINATE

²rise *n* **1** : a spot higher than surrounding ground **2** : an upward slope **3** : an act of rising : a state of being risen **4** : BEGINNING, ORIGIN **5** : the elevation of one point above another **6** : an increase in amount, number, or volume **7** : an angry reaction

ris·er \'rī-zər\ *n* **1** : one that rises **2** : the upright part between stair treads

ris·i·bil·i·ty \ˌri-zə-'bi-lə-tē\ *n, pl* **-ties** : the ability or inclination to laugh — often used in pl.

ris·i·ble \'ri-zə-bəl\ *adj* **1** : able or inclined to laugh **2** : arousing laughter; *esp* : amusingly ridiculous

¹risk \'risk\ *n* **1** : exposure to possible loss or injury : DANGER, PERIL **2** : the chance that an investment will lose value — **risk·i·ness** \'ris-kē-nəs\ *n* — **risky** *adj*

²risk *vb* **1** : to expose to danger ⟨~ed his life⟩ **2** : to incur the danger of

ri·sot·to \ri-'sȯ-tō, -'zȯ-\ *n, pl* **-tos** : rice cooked usu. in meat or seafood stock and seasoned

ris·qué \ris-'kā\ *adj* [F] : verging on impropriety or indecency ⟨~ jokes⟩

ri·tard \ri-'tärd\ *adv or adj* : with a gradual slackening in tempo — used as a direction in music

rite \'rīt\ *n* **1** : a set form for conducting a ceremony **2** : the liturgy of a church **3** : a ceremonial act or action

rit·u·al \'ri-chə-wəl\ *n* **1** : the established form esp. for a religious ceremony **2** : a system of rites **3** : a ceremonial act or action **4** : an act or series of acts regularly repeated in a precise manner — **ritual** *adj* — **rit·u·al·ism** \-wə-ˌli-zəm\ *n* — **rit·u·al·is·tic** \ˌri-chə-wə-'lis-tik\ *adj* — **rit·u·al·is·ti·cal·ly** \-ti-k(ə-)lē\ *adv* — **rit·u·al·ly** *adv*
ritzy \'rit-sē\ *adj* **ritz·i·er; -est** : showily elegant : POSH
riv *abbr* river
¹ri·val \'rī-vəl\ *n* [MF or L; MF, fr. L *rivalis* one using the same stream as another, rival in love, fr. *rivalis* of a stream, fr. *rivus* stream] **1** : one of two or more trying to get what only one can have **2** : one striving for competitive advantage **3** : one that equals another esp. in desired qualities : MATCH, PEER
²rival *adj* : COMPETING
³rival *vb* **-valed** *or* **-valled; -val·ing** *or* **-val·ling** **1** : to be in competition with **2** : to try to equal or excel **3** : to have qualities that approach or equal another's
ri·val·ry \'rī-vəl-rē\ *n, pl* **-ries** : COMPETITION
rive \'rīv\ *vb* **rived** \'rīvd\; **riv·en** \'ri-vən\ *also* **rived; riv·ing** **1** : SPLIT, REND **2** : SHATTER ⟨nations *riven* by war⟩
riv·er \'ri-vər\ *n* **1** : a natural stream larger than a brook **2** : a large stream or flow
riv·er·bank \-ˌbaŋk\ *n* : the bank of a river
riv·er·bed \-ˌbed\ *n* : the channel occupied by a river
riv·er·boat \-ˌbōt\ *n* : a boat for use on a river
riv·er·front \-ˌfrənt\ *n* : the land or area along a river
riv·er·side \-ˌsīd\ *n* : the side or bank of a river
¹riv·et \'ri-vət\ *n* : a metal bolt with a head at one end used to join parts by being put through holes in them and then being flattened on the plain end to make another head
²rivet *vb* : to fasten with or as if with a rivet — **riv·et·er** *n*
riv·u·let \'ri-vyə-lət, -və-\ *n* : a small stream
ri·yal *also* **ri·al** \rē-'äl, -'al\ *n* — see MONEY table
rm *abbr* room
Rn *symbol* radon
¹RN \ˌär-'en\ *n* : REGISTERED NURSE
²RN *abbr* Royal Navy
RNA \ˌär-(ˌ)en-'ā\ *n* : any of various nucleic acids (as messenger RNA) that are found esp. in the cytoplasm of cells, have ribose as the 5-carbon sugar, and are associated with the control of cellular chemical activities
rnd *abbr* round
¹roach \'rōch\ *n, pl* **roach** *also* **roach·es** : any of various bony fishes related to the carp; *also* : any of several sunfishes
²roach *n* **1** : COCKROACH **2** : the butt of a marijuana cigarette
road \'rōd\ *n* [ME *rode*, fr. OE *rād* ride, journey] **1** : ROADSTEAD — often used in pl. **2** : an open way for vehicles, persons, and animals : HIGHWAY **3** : a way to a conclusion or end ⟨the ∼ to success⟩ **4** : a series of scheduled visits (as games or performances) in several locations or the travel necessary to make these visits ⟨the team is on the ∼⟩
road·bed \'rōd-ˌbed\ *n* **1** : the foundation of a road or railroad **2** : the part of the surface of a road on which vehicles travel
road·block \-ˌbläk\ *n* **1** : a barricade on the road ⟨a police ∼⟩ **2** : an obstruction to progress
road·ie \'rō-dē\ *n* : a person who works for traveling entertainers
road·kill \'rōd-ˌkil\ *n* **1** : the remains of an animal that has been killed on a road by a motor vehicle **2** : one that falls victim to intense competition ⟨political ∼⟩
road·run·ner \-ˌrə-nər\ *n* : a largely terrestrial bird of the southwestern U.S. and Mexico that is a speedy runner
road·side \'rōd-ˌsīd\ *n* : the strip of land along a road — **roadside** *adj*
road·stead \-ˌsted\ *n* : an anchorage for ships usu. less sheltered than a harbor
road·ster \'rōd-stər\ *n* **1** : a driving horse **2** : an open automobile that seats two often with a storage compartment or rumble seat in the rear
road·way \-ˌwā\ *n* : ROAD; *esp* : ROADBED
road·work \-ˌwərk\ *n* **1** : work done in constructing or repairing roads **2** : conditioning for an athletic contest (as a boxing match) consisting mainly of long runs
roam \'rōm\ *vb* **1** : WANDER, ROVE **2** : to range or wander over or about **3** : to use a cell phone outside one's local calling area

¹roan \'rōn\ *adj* : of dark color (as black, red, or brown) sprinkled with white ⟨a ∼ horse⟩
²roan *n* : an animal (as a horse) with a roan coat; *also* : its color
¹roar \'rȯr\ *vb* **1** : to utter a full loud prolonged sound **2** : to make a loud confused sound (as of wind or waves) — **roar·er** *n*
²roar *n* : a sound of roaring
¹roast \'rōst\ *vb* **1** : to cook by exposure to dry heat or an open flame **2** : to criticize severely or kiddingly
²roast *n* **1** : a piece of meat suitable for roasting **2** : an outing at which food is roasted ⟨corn ∼⟩ **3** : severe criticism or kidding
³roast *adj* : ROASTED
roast·er \'rō-stər\ *n* **1** : one that roasts **2** : a device for roasting **3** : something (as a young chicken) fit for roasting
rob \'räb\ *vb* **robbed; rob·bing** **1** : to steal from **2** : to deprive of something due or expected **3** : to commit robbery — **rob·ber** *n*
robber fly *n* : any of a family of predaceous flies resembling bumblebees
rob·bery \'rä-bə-rē\ *n, pl* **-ber·ies** : the act or practice of robbing; *esp* : theft of something from a person by use of violence or threat
¹robe \'rōb\ *n* **1** : a long flowing outer garment; *esp* : one used for ceremonial occasions **2** : a wrap or covering for the lower body (as for sitting outdoors)
²robe *vb* **robed; rob·ing** **1** : to clothe with or as if with a robe **2** : DRESS
rob·in \'rä-bən\ *n* **1** : a small chiefly European thrush with a somewhat orange face and breast **2** : a large No. American thrush with a grayish back, a streaked throat, and a chiefly dull reddish breast
ro·bot \'rō-ˌbät, -bət\ *n* [Czech, fr. *robota* compulsory labor] **1** : a machine that looks and acts like a human being **2** : an efficient but insensitive person **3** : a device that automatically performs esp. repetitive tasks **4** : something guided by automatic controls — **ro·bot·ic** \rō-'bä-tik\ *adj*
ro·bot·ics \rō-'bä-tiks\ *n* : technology dealing with the design, construction, and operation of robots
ro·bust \rō-'bəst, 'rō-(ˌ)bəst\ *adj* [L *robustus* oaken, strong, fr. *robur* oak, strength] **1** : strong and vigorously healthy **2** : capable of performing without failure under a wide range of conditions ⟨∼ software⟩ — **ro·bust·ly** *adv* — **ro·bust·ness** *n*
ROC *abbr* Republic of China (Taiwan)
¹rock \'räk\ *vb* **1** : to move back and forth in or as if in a cradle **2** : to sway or cause to sway back and forth **3** : to arouse to excitement (as with rock music) ⟨∼ed the crowd⟩ **4** *slang* : to be extremely enjoyable or effective ⟨this car ∼s⟩
²rock *n* **1** : a rocking movement **2** : popular music usu. played on electric instruments and characterized by a strong beat and much repetition
³rock *n* **1** : a mass of stony material; *also* : broken pieces of stone **2** : solid mineral deposits **3** : something like a rock in firmness **4** : GEM; *esp* : DIAMOND — **rock** *adj* — **rock·like** *adj* — **rocky** *adj* — **on the rocks** **1** : in a state of ruin ⟨a marriage *on the rocks*⟩ **2** : on ice cubes ⟨bourbon *on the rocks*⟩
rock and roll *n* : ²ROCK 2

roadrunner

rock·bound \'räk-ˌbau̇nd\ *adj* : fringed or covered with rocks

rock·er \'rä-kər\ *n* **1** : one of the curved pieces on which something (as a chair or cradle) rocks **2** : a chair that rocks on rockers **3** : a device that works with a rocking motion **4** : a rock performer, song, or enthusiast

¹rock·et \'rä-kət\ *n* [It *rocchetta*, lit., small distaff] **1** : a firework that is propelled through the air by the discharge of gases produced by a burning substance **2** : a jet engine that operates on the same principle as a firework rocket but carries the oxygen needed for burning its fuel **3** : a rocket-propelled bomb or missile

²rocket *vb* **1** : to convey by means of a rocket **2** : to rise abruptly and rapidly

rock·et·ry \'rä-kə-trē\ *n* : the study or use of rockets

rocket ship *n* : a rocket-propelled spacecraft

rock·fall \'räk-ˌfȯl\ *n* : a mass of falling or fallen rocks

rock·fish \-ˌfish\ *n* : any of various bony fishes that live among rocks or on rocky bottoms

rock salt *n* : common salt in rocklike masses or large crystals

Rocky Mountain sheep *n* : BIGHORN

ro·co·co \rə-'kō-kō\ *adj* [F, irreg. fr. *rocaille* style of ornament, lit., stone debris] : of or relating to an artistic style esp. of the 18th century marked by fanciful curved forms and elaborate ornamentation — **rococo** *n*

rod \'räd\ *n* **1** : a straight slender stick **2** : a stick or bundle of twigs used in punishing a person; *also* : PUNISHMENT **3** : a staff borne to show rank **4** — see WEIGHT table **5** : any of the rod-shaped receptor cells of the retina that are sensitive to faint light **6** *slang* : HANDGUN

rode *past of* RIDE

ro·dent \'rō-dᵊnt\ *n* [ultim. fr. L *rodent-, rodens*, prp. of *rodere* to gnaw] : any of an order of relatively small mammals (as mice, squirrels, and beavers) with sharp front teeth used for gnawing

ro·deo \'rō-dē-ˌō, rə-'dā-ō\ *n, pl* **ro·de·os** [Sp, fr. *rodear* to surround, fr. *rueda* wheel, fr. L *rota*] **1** : ROUNDUP 1 **2** : a public performance featuring cowboy skills (as riding and roping)

¹roe \'rō\ *n, pl* **roe** *or* **roes** : DOE

²roe *n* : the eggs of a fish esp. while bound together in a mass

roe·buck \'rō-ˌbək\ *n, pl* **roebuck** *or* **roebucks** : a male roe deer

roe deer *n* : either of two small nimble European or Asian deers

roent·gen \'rent-gən, 'rənt-, -jən\ *n* : the international unit of measurement for X-rays and gamma rays

rog·er \'rä-jər\ *interj* — used esp. in radio and signaling to indicate that a message has been received and understood

¹rogue \'rōg\ *n* **1** : a dishonest person : SCOUNDREL **2** : a mischievous person : SCAMP — **rogu·ery** \'rō-gə-rē\ *n* — **rogu·ish** *adj* — **rogu·ish·ly** *adv* — **rogu·ish·ness** *n*

²rogue *adj* **1** : CORRUPT, DISHONEST ⟨∼ cops⟩ **2** : of or being a nation whose leaders defy international law or norms

roil \'rȯi(-ə)l, *for 2 also* 'rī(-ə)l\ *vb* **1** : to make cloudy or muddy by stirring up **2** : RILE 1 — **roily** \'rȯi-lē\ *adj*

rois·ter \'rȯi-stər\ *vb* **rois·tered; rois·ter·ing** : to engage in noisy revelry : CAROUSE — **rois·ter·er** *n* — **rois·ter·ous** \-stə-rəs\ *adj*

ROK *abbr* Republic of Korea (South Korea)

role *also* **rôle** \'rōl\ *n* **1** : an assigned or assumed character; *also* : a part played (as by an actor) **2** : FUNCTION

role model *n* : a person whose behavior in a particular role is imitated by others

¹roll \'rōl\ *n* [ME *rolle* scroll, fr. AF, fr. ML *rolla*, alter. of *rotula*, fr. L, dim. of *rota* wheel] **1** : a document containing an official record **2** : an official list of names **3** : something (as a bun) that is rolled up or rounded as if rolled **4** : something that rolls : ROLLER

²roll *vb* **1** : to move by turning over and over ⟨∼ dice⟩ ⟨∼ed her eyes⟩ **2** : to press with a roller ⟨∼ dough⟩ **3** : to move on wheels **4** : to sound with a full reverberating tone **5** : to make a continuous beating sound (as on a drum) **6** : to utter with a trill **7** : to move onward as if by completing a revolution ⟨years ∼ed by⟩ **8** : to flow or seem to flow in a continuous stream or with a rising and falling motion ⟨the river ∼ed on⟩ **9** : to swing or sway from side to side **10** : to shape or become shaped in rounded form ⟨∼ up the paper⟩ **11** : to move by or as if by turning a crank ⟨∼ down the window⟩

³roll *n* **1** : a sound produced by rapid strokes on a drum **2** : a heavy reverberating sound **3** : a rolling movement or action **4** : a swaying movement (as of a ship) **5** : a somersault made in contact with the ground

roll·back \'rōl-ˌbak\ *n* : the act or an instance of rolling back

roll back *vb* **1** : to reduce (as a commodity price) on a national scale **2** : to cause to withdraw : push back

roll bar *n* : an overhead metal bar on an automobile designed to protect riders in case the automobile overturns

roll call *n* : the act or an instance of calling off a list of names (as of soldiers); *also* : a time for a roll call

roll·er \'rō-lər\ *n* **1** : a revolving cylinder used for moving, pressing, shaping, applying, or smoothing something **2** : a rod on which something is rolled up **3** : a long heavy ocean wave

roll·er coast·er \'rō-lər-ˌkō-stər\ *n* : an amusement ride consisting of an elevated railway having sharp curves and steep slopes

roller skate *n* : a skate with wheels instead of a runner — **roller–skate** *vb* — **roller skater** *n*

rol·lick \'rä-lik\ *vb* : ROMP, FROLIC

rol·lick·ing *adj* : full of fun and good spirits ⟨a ∼ good time⟩

roly–poly \ˌrō-lē-'pō-lē\ *adj* : ROTUND

Rom *abbr* **1** Roman **2** Romance **3** Romania; Romanian **4** Romans

ROM \'räm\ *n* : a computer memory that contains special-purpose information (as a program) which cannot be altered

ro·maine \rō-'mān\ *n* [F, lit., Roman] : a garden lettuce with a tall loose head of long crisp leaves

¹Ro·man \'rō-mən\ *n* **1** : a native or resident of Rome **2** *not cap* : roman letters or type

²Roman *adj* **1** : of or relating to Rome or the Romans and esp. the ancient Romans **2** *not cap* : relating to type in which the letters are upright **3** : of or relating to the Roman Catholic Church

Roman candle *n* : a cylindrical firework that discharges balls of fire

Roman Catholic *adj* : of, relating to, or being a Christian church led by the pope and having a liturgy centered in the Mass — **Roman Catholicism** *n*

¹ro·mance \rō-'mans, 'rō-ˌmans\ *n* [ME *romauns*, fr. AF *romanz* French, something written in French, tale in verse, fr. ML *Romanice* in a vernacular language, ultim. fr. L *Romanus* Roman] **1** : a medieval tale of knightly adventure **2** : a prose narrative dealing with heroic or mysterious events set in a remote time or place **3** : a love story **4** : a romantic attachment or episode between lovers — **ro·manc·er** *n*

²romance *vb* **ro·manced; ro·manc·ing 1** : to exaggerate or invent detail or incident **2** : to have romantic fancies **3** : to carry on a romantic episode with

Ro·mance \rō-'mans, 'rō-ˌmans\ *adj* : of or relating to any of several languages developed from Latin

Ro·ma·nian \ru̇-'mā-nē-ən, rō-, -nyən\ *also* **Ru·ma·nian** \ru̇-\ *n* **1** : a native or inhabitant of Romania **2** : the language of the Romanians

Roman numeral *n* : a numeral in a system of notation that is based on the ancient Roman system

Ro·ma·no \rō-'mä-nō\ *n* : a hard Italian cheese that is sharper than Parmesan

Ro·mans \'rō-mənz\ *n* — see BIBLE table

¹ro·man·tic \rō-'man-tik\ *adj* **1** : IMAGINARY **2** : VISIONARY **3** : having an imaginative or emotional appeal **4** : of, relating to, or having the characteristics of romanticism — **ro·man·ti·cal·ly** \-ti-k(ə-)lē\ *adv*

²romantic *n* : a romantic person; *esp* : a romantic writer, composer, or artist

ro·man·ti·cism \rō-'man-tə-ˌsi-zəm\ *n, often cap* : a literary movement (as in early 19th century England) marked esp. by emphasis on the imagination and the emotions and by the use of autobiographical material — **ro·man·ti·cist** \-sist\ *n, often cap*

ro·man·ti·cize \-'man-tə-ˌsīz\ *vb* **-cized; -ciz·ing 1** : to make romantic **2** : to have romantic ideas

romp \'rämp\ *vb* **1** : to play actively and noisily **2** : to win a contest easily — **romp** *n*

romp·er \\'räm-pər\ *n* **1** : one that romps **2** : a jumpsuit usu. for infants — usu. used in pl.

rood \\'rüd\ *n* : CROSS, CRUCIFIX

¹roof \\'rüf, 'rüf\ *n, pl* **roofs** \\'rüfs, 'rüfs; 'rüvz, 'rüvz\ **1** : the upper covering part of a building **2** : something suggesting a roof of a building — **roofed** \\'rüft, 'rüft\ *adj* — **roof·ing** *n* — **roof·less** *adj* — **through the roof** : to an extremely high level ⟨prices went *through the roof*⟩

²roof *vb* : to cover with a roof

roof·top \\-ˌtäp\ *n* : a roof esp. of a house

¹rook \\'rùk\ *n* : a common Old World bird resembling the related crow

²rook *vb* : CHEAT, SWINDLE

³rook *n* : a chess piece that can move parallel to the sides of the board across any number of unoccupied squares

rook·ery \\'rù-kə-rē\ *n, pl* **-er·ies** : a breeding ground or haunt of gregarious birds or mammals; *also* : a colony of such birds or mammals

rook·ie \\'rù-kē\ *n* : BEGINNER, RECRUIT; *esp* : a first-year player in a professional sport

¹room \\'rüm, 'rùm\ *n* **1** : an extent of space occupied by or sufficient or available for something **2** : a partitioned part of a building : CHAMBER; *also* : the people in a room **3** : OPPORTUNITY, CHANCE ⟨∼ to develop his talents⟩ — **room·ful** *n* — **roomy** *adj*

²room *vb* : to occupy or share lodgings : LODGE — **room·er** *n*

room·ette \\rü-'met, rù-\ *n* : a small private room on a railroad sleeping car

room·mate \\'rüm-ˌmāt, 'rùm-\ *n* : one of two or more persons sharing the same room or dwelling

¹roost \\'rüst\ *n* : a support on which or a place where birds perch

²roost *vb* : to settle on or as if on a roost

roost·er \\'rüs-tər, 'rùs-\ *n* : an adult male domestic chicken : COCK

¹root \\'rüt, 'rùt\ *n* **1** : the leafless usu. underground part of a seed plant that functions in absorption, aeration, and storage or as a means of anchorage; *also* : an underground plant part esp. when fleshy and edible **2** : something (as the basal part of a tooth or hair) resembling a root **3** : SOURCE, ORIGIN; *esp* : ANCESTRY — usu. used in pl. **4** : the essential core : HEART ⟨get to the ∼ of the matter⟩ **5** : a number that when taken as a factor an indicated number of times gives a specified number **6** : the lower part — **root·less** *adj* — **root·like** *adj*

²root *vb* **1** : to form roots **2** : to fix or become fixed by or as if by roots : ESTABLISH **3** : UPROOT

³root *vb* **1** : to turn up or dig with the snout ⟨pigs ∼ing⟩ **2** : to poke or dig around (as in search of something)

⁴root \\'rüt\ *vb* **1** : to applaud or encourage noisily : CHEER **2** : to wish success or lend support to — **root·er** *n*

root beer *n* : a sweetened carbonated beverage flavored with extracts of roots and herbs

root canal *n* : a dental operation to save a tooth by removing the pulp in the root of the tooth and filling the cavity with a protective substance

root·let \\'rüt-lət, 'rùt-\ *n* : a small root

root·stock \\-ˌstäk\ *n* : an underground part of a plant that resembles a rhizome

¹rope \\'rōp\ *n* **1** : a large strong cord made of strands of fiber **2** : a hangman's noose **3** : a thick string (as of pearls) made by twisting or braiding

²rope *vb* **roped; rop·ing** **1** : to bind, tie, or fasten together with a rope **2** : to separate or divide by means of a rope **3** : LASSO

Ror·schach test \\'ror-ˌshäk-\ *n* : a psychological test in which a subject interprets ink-blot designs in terms that reveal emotional and intellectual factors

ro·sa·ry \\'rō-zə-rē\ *n, pl* **-ries** **1** *often cap* : a Roman Catholic devotion consisting of meditation on sacred mysteries during recitation of Hail Marys **2** : a string of beads used in praying

¹rose *past of* RISE

²rose \\'rōz\ *n* **1** : any of a genus of usu. prickly often climbing shrubs with divided leaves and bright often fragrant flowers; *also* : one of these flowers **2** : something resembling a rose in form **3** : a moderate purplish red color — **rose** *adj*

ro·sé \\rō-'zā\ *n* [F] : a light pink wine

ro·se·ate \\'rō-zē-ət, -zē-ˌāt\ *adj* **1** : resembling a rose esp. in color **2** : OPTIMISTIC ⟨a ∼ view of the future⟩

rose·bud \\'rōz-ˌbəd\ *n* : the flower of a rose when it is at most partly open

rose·bush \\-ˌbùsh\ *n* : a shrubby rose

rose·mary \\'rōz-ˌmer-ē\ *n, pl* **-mar·ies** [ME *rosmarine*, fr. AF *rosmarin*, fr. L *rosmarinus*, fr. *ros* dew + *marinus* of the sea, fr. *mare* sea] : a fragrant shrubby Mediterranean mint; *also* : its leaves used as a seasoning

ro·sette \\rō-'zet\ *n* [F] **1** : a usu. small badge or ornament of ribbon gathered in the shape of a rose **2** : a circular ornament filled with representations of leaves

rose wa·ter \\'rōz-ˌwò-tər, -ˌwä-\ *n* : a watery solution of the fragrant constituents of the rose used as a perfume

rose·wood \\-ˌwùd\ *n* : any of various tropical trees with dark red wood streaked with black; *also* : this wood

Rosh Ha·sha·nah \\ˌräsh-hə-'shä-nə, ˌrōsh-, -'shò-\ *n* [Heb *rōsh hashshānāh*, lit., beginning of the year] : the Jewish New Year observed as a religious holiday in September or October

ros·in \\'rä-zᵊn\ *n* : a brittle resin obtained esp. from pine trees and used esp. in varnishes and on violin bows

ros·ter \\'räs-tər\ *n* **1** : a list of personnel; *also* : the persons listed on a roster **2** : an itemized list

ros·trum \\'räs-trəm\ *n, pl* **rostrums** *or* **ros·tra** \\-trə\ [L *Rostra*, pl., a platform for speakers in the Roman Forum decorated with the beaks of captured ships, fr. pl. of *rostrum* beak, ship's beak, fr. *rodere* to gnaw] : a stage or platform for public speaking

rosy \\'rō-zē\ *adj* **ros·i·er; -est** **1** : of the color rose **2** : HOPEFUL, PROMISING ⟨a ∼ outlook⟩ — **ros·i·ly** \\'rō-zə-lē\ *adv* — **ros·i·ness** \\-zē-nəs\ *n*

¹rot \\'rät\ *vb* **rot·ted; rot·ting** : to undergo decomposition : DECAY

²rot *n* **1** : DECAY **2** : any of various diseases of plants or animals in which tissue breaks down **3** : NONSENSE

¹ro·ta·ry \\'rō-tə-rē\ *adj* **1** : turning on an axis like a wheel **2** : having a rotating part ⟨a ∼ telephone⟩

²rotary *n, pl* **-ries** **1** : a rotary machine **2** : a one-way circular road junction

ro·tate \\'rō-ˌtāt\ *vb* **ro·tat·ed; ro·tat·ing** **1** : to turn or cause to turn about an axis or a center : REVOLVE **2** : to alternate in a series ♦ **Synonyms** TURN, CIRCLE, SPIN, WHIRL, TWIRL — **ro·ta·tion** \\rō-'tā-shən\ *n* — **ro·ta·tor** \\'rō-ˌtā-tər\ *n* — **ro·ta·to·ry** \\'rō-tə-ˌtòr-ē\ *adj*

ROTC *abbr* Reserve Officers' Training Corps

rote \\'rōt\ *n* **1** : repetition from memory often without attention to meaning ⟨learn by ∼⟩ **2** : mechanical or unthinking routine or repetition — **rote** *adj*

ro·tis·ser·ie \\rō-'ti-sə-rē\ *n* [F] **1** : a restaurant specializing in broiled and barbecued meats **2** : an appliance fitted with a spit on which food is rotated before or over a source of heat

ro·to·gra·vure \\ˌrō-tə-grə-'vyùr\ *n* : PHOTOGRAVURE

ro·tor \\'rō-tər\ *n* **1** : a part that rotates; *esp* : the rotating part of an electrical machine **2** : a system of rotating horizontal blades for supporting a helicopter

ro·to·till·er \\'rō-tō-ˌti-lər\ *n* : an engine-powered machine with rotating blades used to lift and turn over soil

rot·ten \\'rä-tᵊn\ *adj* **1** : having rotted **2** : CORRUPT **3** : extremely unpleasant or inferior — **rot·ten·ness** *n*

rot·ten·stone \\'rä-tᵊn-ˌstōn\ *n* : a decomposed siliceous limestone used for polishing

rott·wei·ler \\'rät-ˌwī-lər\ *n, often cap* : any of a breed of tall powerful black-and-tan short-haired dogs

ro·tund \\rō-'tənd\ *adj* : rounded out ♦ **Synonyms** PLUMP, CHUBBY, PORTLY, STOUT — **ro·tun·di·ty** \\-'tən-də-tē\ *n*

ro·tun·da \\rō-'tən-də\ *n* **1** : a round building; *esp* : one covered by a dome **2** : a large round room

rouble *var of* RUBLE

roué \\rü-'ā\ *n* [F, lit., broken on the wheel, fr. pp. of *rouer* to break on the wheel, fr. ML *rotare*, fr. L, to rotate; fr. the feeling that such a person deserves this punishment] : a man devoted to a life of sensual pleasure : RAKE

rouge \\'rüzh, 'rüj\ *n* [F, lit., red] : a cosmetic used to give a red color to cheeks and lips — **rouge** *vb*

¹rough \\'rəf\ *adj* **rough·er; rough·est** **1** : uneven in surface : not smooth **2** : SHAGGY **3** : not calm : TURBULENT, TEMPESTUOUS **4** : marked by harshness or violence **5** : DIFFICULT, TRYING **6** : coarse or rugged in character or appearance **7** : marked by lack of refinement **8** : CRUDE, UNFINISHED **9** : done or made hastily or tentatively — **rough·ly** adv — **rough·ness** n

²rough n **1** : uneven ground covered with high grass esp. along a golf fairway **2** : a crude, unfinished, or preliminary state; also : something in such a state **3** : ROWDY, TOUGH

³rough vb **1** : ROUGHEN **2** : MANHANDLE **3** : to make or shape roughly esp. in a preliminary way — **rough·er** n

rough·age \'rə-fij\ n : FIBER 2; also : food containing much indigestible material acting as fiber

rough–and–ready \ˌrə-fən-'re-dē\ adj : rude or unpolished in nature, method, or manner but effective in action or use ⟨a ~ solution⟩

rough–and–tum·ble \-'təm-bəl\ n : rough unrestrained fighting or struggling — **rough–and–tumble** adj

rough·en \'rə-fən\ vb **rough·ened**; **rough·en·ing** : to make or become rough

rough–hewn \'rəf-'hyün\ adj **1** : being rough and unfinished ⟨~ beams⟩ **2** : lacking smooth manners or social grace — **rough–hew** \-'hyü\ vb

rough·house \'rəf-ˌhaus\ vb **rough·housed**; **rough·hous·ing** : to participate in rough noisy behavior — **rough·house** n

rough·neck \'rəf-ˌnek\ n **1** : ROWDY, TOUGH **2** : a worker on a crew drilling oil wells

rough·shod \'rəf-ˌshäd\ adv : in a roughly forceful manner ⟨rode ~ over the opposition⟩

rou·lette \rü-'let\ n [F, lit., small wheel] **1** : a gambling game in which a whirling wheel is used **2** : a wheel or disk with teeth around the outside

¹round \'raund\ adj **1** : having every part of the surface or circumference the same distance from the center **2** : CYLINDRICAL **3** : COMPLETE, FULL **4** : approximately correct; esp : exact only to a specific decimal or place ⟨~ numbers⟩ **5** : liberal or ample in size or amount **6** : BLUNT, OUTSPOKEN **7** : moving in or forming a circle **8** : having curves rather than angles — **round·ish** adj — **round·ness** n

²round prep or adv : AROUND

³round n **1** : something round (as a circle, globe, or ring) **2** : a curved or rounded part (as a rung of a ladder) **3** : an indirect path or course; also : a regularly covered route (as of a security guard) **4** : a series or cycle of recurring actions or events **5** : one shot fired by a soldier or a gun; also : ammunition for one shot **6** : a period of time or a unit of play in a game or contest **7** : a cut of meat (as beef) esp. between the rump and the lower leg — **in the round** **1** : FREESTANDING **2** : with a center stage surrounded by an audience ⟨theater in the round⟩

⁴round vb **1** : to make or become round **2** : to go or pass around or part way around **3** : COMPLETE, FINISH **4** : to become plump or shapely **5** : to express as a round number — often used with off **6** : to follow a winding course : BEND

¹round·about \'raun-də-ˌbaut\ adj : INDIRECT, CIRCUITOUS

²roundabout n, Brit : MERRY-GO-ROUND

roun·de·lay \'raun-də-ˌlā\ n **1** : a simple song with a refrain **2** : a poem with a recurring refrain

round·house \'raund-ˌhaus\ n **1** : a circular building for housing and repairing locomotives **2** : a blow with the hand made with a wide swing — **roundhouse** adj

round·ly \'raund-lē\ adv **1** : in a complete manner; also : WIDELY **2** : in a blunt way **3** : with vigor

round–rob·in \'round-ˌrä-bən\ n : a tournament in which each contestant meets every other contestant in turn

round–shoul·dered \-ˌshōl-dərd\ adj : having the shoulders stooping or rounded

round–trip n : a trip to a place and back

round·up \'raund-ˌəp\ n **1** : the gathering together of cattle on the range by riding around them and driving them in; also : the ranch hands and horses engaged in a roundup **2** : a gathering in of scattered persons or things **3** : SUMMARY ⟨news ~⟩ — **round up** vb

round·worm \-ˌwərm\ n : NEMATODE

rouse \'rauz\ vb **roused**; **rous·ing** **1** : to excite to activity : stir up **2** : to wake from sleep — **rous·er** n

roust·about \'raus-tə-ˌbaut\ n **1** : one who does heavy unskilled labor (as on a dock or in an oil field) **2** : a laborer at a circus **3** : a person with no established home or occupation

¹rout \'raut\ n **1** : MOB 1, 2 **2** : DISTURBANCE **3** : a fashionable gathering

²rout vb **1** : RUMMAGE **2** : to gouge out **3** : to expel by force

³rout n **1** : a state of wild confusion or disorderly retreat **2** : a disastrous defeat

⁴rout vb **1** : to put to flight **2** : to defeat decisively

¹route \'rüt, 'raut\ n [ME, fr. AF rute, fr. VL *rupta (via), lit., broken way] **1** : a traveled way **2** : CHANNEL **3** : a line of travel

²route vb **rout·ed**; **rout·ing** : to send by a selected route : DIRECT

route·man \-mən, -ˌman\ n : a person who sells and makes deliveries on an assigned route

rout·er \'rau-tər\ n : a machine with a revolving spindle and cutter for shaping a surface (as of wood)

rou·tine \rü-'tēn\ n [F, fr. MF, fr. route traveled way] **1** : a regular course of procedure **2** : an often repeated speech or formula **3** : a part fully worked out ⟨a comedy ~⟩ **4** : a set of computer instructions that will perform a certain task — **routine** adj — **rou·tine·ly** adv — **rou·tin·ize** \-ˈtē-ˌnīz\ vb

¹rove \'rōv\ vb **roved**; **rov·ing** : to wander over or through — **rov·er** n

²rove past and past part of REEVE

¹row \'rō\ vb **1** : to propel a boat with oars **2** : to transport in a rowboat **3** : to pull an oar in a crew — **row·er** \'rō-ər\ n

²row n : an act or instance of rowing

³row n **1** : a number of objects in an orderly sequence **2** : WAY, STREET

⁴row \'rau\ n : a noisy quarrel

⁵row \'rau\ vb : to engage in a row

row·boat \'rō-ˌbōt\ n : a small boat designed to be rowed

row·dy \'rau-dē\ adj **row·di·er; -est** : coarse or boisterous in behavior : ROUGH — **row·di·ness** \'rau-dē-nəs\ n — **rowdy** n — **row·dy·ish** adj — **row·dy·ism** n

row·el \'rau-(ə)l\ n : a small pointed wheel on a rider's spur — **rowel** vb

¹roy·al \'rói-(ə)l\ adj [ME roial, fr. AF real, roial, fr. L regalis, fr. reg-, rex king] **1** : of or relating to a sovereign : REGAL **2** : fit for a king or queen ⟨a ~ welcome⟩ — **roy·al·ly** adv

²royal n : a person of royal blood

royal flush n : a straight flush having an ace as the highest card

roy·al·ist \'rói-ə-list\ n : an adherent of a king or of monarchical government

roy·al·ty \'rói-əl-tē\ n, pl **-ties** **1** : the state of being royal **2** : royal persons **3** : a share of a product or profit (as of a mine or oil well) claimed by the owner for allowing another person to use the property **4** : a payment made to an author or composer for each copy of a work sold or to an inventor for each article sold under a patent

RP abbr **1** relief pitcher **2** Republic of the Philippines

rpm abbr revolutions per minute

rps abbr revolutions per second

rpt abbr **1** repeat **2** report

RR abbr **1** railroad **2** rural route

RS abbr **1** recording secretary **2** revised statutes **3** Royal Society

RSV abbr Revised Standard Version

RSVP abbr [F répondez s'il vous plaît] please reply

rt abbr **1** right **2** route

RT abbr round-trip

rte abbr route

Ru symbol ruthenium

¹rub \'rəb\ vb **rubbed**; **rub·bing** **1** : to use pressure and friction on a body or object **2** : to fret or chafe with friction **3** : to scour, polish, erase, or smear by pressure and friction

²rub n **1** : DIFFICULTY, OBSTRUCTION **2** : something grating to the feelings

¹rub·ber \'rə-bər\ n **1** : one that rubs **2** : ERASER **3** : a flexible waterproof elastic substance made from the milky juice of various tropical plants or made synthetically; also : something made of this material **4** : CONDOM — **rubber** adj — **rub·ber·ize** \'rə-bə-ˌrīz\ vb — **rub·bery** adj

²rubber n **1** : a contest that consists of an odd number of games and is won by the side that takes a majority **2** : an extra game played to decide a tie

¹**rub·ber·neck** \-ˌnek\ *n* **1** : an idly or overly inquisitive person **2** : a person on a guided tour

²**rubberneck** *vb* : to look about, stare, or listen with excessive curiosity ⟨~ing drivers⟩ — **rub·ber·neck·er** *n*

rub·bish \ˈrə-bish\ *n* **1** : useless waste or rejected matter : TRASH **2** : something worthless or nonsensical

rub·ble \ˈrə-bəl\ *n* : broken fragments esp. of a destroyed building

ru·bel·la \rü-ˈbe-lə\ *n* : GERMAN MEASLES

ru·bi·cund \ˈrü-bi-ˌkənd\ *adj* : RED, RUDDY

ru·bid·i·um \rü-ˈbi-dē-əm\ *n* : a soft silvery metallic chemical element

ru·ble *also* **rou·ble** \ˈrü-bəl\ *n* — see MONEY table

ru·bric \ˈrü-brik\ *n* [ME *rubrike* red ocher, heading in red letters of part of a book, fr. AF, fr. L *rubrica*, fr. *ruber* red] **1** : HEADING, TITLE; *also* : CLASS, CATEGORY **2** : a rule esp. for the conduct of a religious service

ru·by \ˈrü-bē\ *n, pl* **rubies** : a clear red precious stone — **ruby** *adj*

ru·by–throat·ed hummingbird \ˈrü-bē-ˌthrōt-əd-\ *n* : a bright green and whitish hummingbird of eastern No. America with a red throat in the male

ruck·us \ˈrə-kəs\ *n* : ROW, DISTURBANCE

rud·der \ˈrə-dər\ *n* : a movable flat piece attached at the rear of a ship or aircraft for steering

rud·dy \ˈrə-dē\ *adj* **rud·di·er; -est** : REDDISH; *esp* : of a healthy reddish complexion — **rud·di·ness** \ˈrə-dē-nəs\ *n*

rude \ˈrüd\ *adj* **rud·er; rud·est** **1** : roughly made : CRUDE **2** : UNDEVELOPED, PRIMITIVE **3** : IMPOLITE **4** : UNSKILLED — **rude·ly** *adv* — **rude·ness** *n*

ru·di·ment \ˈrü-də-mənt\ *n* **1** : an elementary principle or basic skill — usu. used in pl. ⟨the ~s of mathematics⟩ **2** : something not fully developed — usu. used in pl. ⟨the ~s of a plan⟩ — **ru·di·men·ta·ry** \ˌrü-də-ˈmen-tə-rē\ *adj*

¹**rue** \ˈrü\ *n* : REGRET, SORROW — **rue·ful** \-fəl\ *adj* — **rue·ful·ly** *adv* — **rue·ful·ness** *n*

²**rue** *vb* **rued; ru·ing** : to feel regret, remorse, or penitence for

³**rue** *n* : a European strong-scented woody herb with bitter-tasting leaves

ruff \ˈrəf\ *n* **1** : a large round pleated collar worn about 1600 **2** : a fringe of long hair or feathers around the neck of an animal — **ruffed** \ˈrəft\ *adj*

ruf·fi·an \ˈrə-fē-ən\ *n* : a brutal person — **ruf·fi·an·ly** *adj*

¹**ruf·fle** \ˈrə-fəl\ *vb* **ruf·fled; ruf·fling** **1** : to roughen the surface of **2** : IRRITATE, VEX **3** : to erect (as hair or feathers) in or like a ruff **4** : to flip through (as pages) **5** : to draw into or provide with plaits or folds

²**ruffle** *n* **1** : a strip of fabric gathered or pleated on one edge **2** : RUFF 2 **3** : RIPPLE — **ruf·fly** \ˈrə-fə-lē, -flē\ *adj*

ru·fi·yaa \ˈrü-fē-ˌyä\ *n, pl* **rufiyaa** — see MONEY table

RU–486 \ˌär-ˌyü-ˌfȯr-ˌā-tē-ˈsiks\ *n* : a drug taken orally to induce abortion esp. early in pregnancy

rug \ˈrəg\ *n* **1** : a covering for the legs, lap, and feet **2** : a piece of heavy fabric usu. with a nap or pile used as a floor covering

rug·by \ˈrəg-bē\ *n, often cap* [*Rugby* School, Rugby, England, where it was first played] : a football game in which play is continuous and interference and forward passing are not permitted

rug·ged \ˈrə-gəd\ *adj* **1** : having a rough uneven surface **2** : TURBULENT, STORMY **3** : HARSH, STERN **4** : ROBUST, STURDY — **rug·ged·ize** \ˈrə-gə-ˌdīz\ *vb* — **rug·ged·ly** *adv* — **rug·ged·ness** *n*

¹**ru·in** \ˈrü-ən\ *n* **1** : complete collapse or destruction **2** : the remains of something destroyed — usu. used in pl. **3** : a cause of destruction **4** : the action of destroying

²**ruin** *vb* **1** : DESTROY **2** : to damage beyond repair **3** : BANKRUPT

ru·in·ation \ˌrü-ə-ˈnā-shən\ *n* : RUIN, DESTRUCTION

ru·in·ous \ˈrü-ə-nəs\ *adj* **1** : RUINED, DILAPIDATED **2** : causing ruin — **ru·in·ous·ly** *adv*

¹**rule** \ˈrül\ *n* [ME *reule*, fr. AF, fr. L *regula* straightedge, rule, fr. *regere* to keep straight, direct] **1** : a guide or principle for governing action : REGULATION **2** : the usual way of doing something **3** : the exercise of authority or control : GOVERNMENT **4** : RULER 2

²**rule** *vb* **ruled; rul·ing** **1** : CONTROL; *also* : GOVERN **2** : to be supreme or outstanding in **3** : to give or state as a considered decision **4** : to mark on paper with or as if with a ruler **5** *slang* : to be extremely cool or popular

rul·er \ˈrü-lər\ *n* **1** : SOVEREIGN **2** : a straight strip of material (as wood or metal) marked off in units and used for measuring or as a straightedge

rum \ˈrəm\ *n* **1** : an alcoholic liquor made from sugar-cane products (as molasses) **2** : alcoholic liquor

Ru·ma·nian *var of* ROMANIAN

rum·ba \ˈrəm-bə, ˈrùm-\ *n* : a dance of Cuban origin marked by strong rhythmic movements

¹**rum·ble** \ˈrəm-bəl\ *vb* **rum·bled; rum·bling** : to make a low heavy rolling sound; *also* : to move along with such a sound — **rum·bler** *n*

²**rumble** *n* **1** : a low heavy rolling sound **2** : a street fight esp. among gangs

rumble seat *n* : a folding seat in the back of an automobile that is not covered by the top

rum·bling \ˈrəm-bliŋ\ *n* **1** : RUMBLE **2** : widespread talk or complaints — usu. used in pl.

ru·men \ˈrü-mən\ *n, pl* **ru·mi·na** \-mə-nə\ *or* **rumens** : the large first compartment of the stomach of a ruminant (as a cow)

¹**ru·mi·nant** \ˈrü-mə-nənt\ *n* : a ruminant mammal

²**ruminant** *adj* **1** : chewing the cud; *also* : of or relating to a group of hoofed mammals (as cattle, deer, and camels) that chew the cud and have a complex 3- or 4-chambered stomach **2** : MEDITATIVE

ru·mi·nate \ˈrü-mə-ˌnāt\ *vb* **-nat·ed; -nat·ing** [L *ruminari* to chew the cud, muse upon, fr. *rumin-, rumen* first stomach chamber of a ruminant] **1** : MEDITATE, MUSE **2** : to chew the cud — **ru·mi·na·tion** \ˌrü-mə-ˈnā-shən\ *n*

¹**rum·mage** \ˈrə-mij\ *vb* **rum·maged; rum·mag·ing** : to search thoroughly — **rum·mag·er** *n*

²**rummage** *n* **1** : a miscellaneous collection **2** : an act of rummaging

rum·my \ˈrə-mē\ *n* : any of several card games for two or more players

ru·mor \ˈrü-mər\ *n* **1** : common talk **2** : a statement or report current but not authenticated — **rumor** *vb*

ru·mour *chiefly Brit var of* RUMOR

rump \ˈrəmp\ *n* **1** : the rear part of an animal; *also* : a cut of meat (as beef) behind the upper sirloin **2** : a small or inferior remnant (as of a group)

rum·ple \ˈrəm-pəl\ *vb* **rum·pled; rum·pling** : TOUSLE, MUSS, WRINKLE — **rumple** *n* — **rum·ply** \ˈrəm-pə-lē\ *adj*

rum·pus \ˈrəm-pəs\ *n* : DISTURBANCE, RUCKUS

rumpus room *n* : a room usu. in the basement of a home that is used for games, parties, and recreation

¹**run** \ˈrən\ *vb* **ran** \ˈran\; **run; run·ning** **1** : to go faster than a walk **2** : to take to flight : FLEE **3** : to go without restraint ⟨let chickens ~ loose⟩ **4** : to go rapidly or hurriedly : HASTEN, RUSH **5** : to make a quick or casual trip or visit **6** : to contend in a race; *esp* : to enter an election ⟨~ for mayor⟩ **7** : to put forward as a candidate for office **8** : to move on or as if on wheels : pass or slide freely **9** : to go back and forth : PLY **10** : to move in large numbers esp. to a spawning ground ⟨shad are *running*⟩ **11** : FUNCTION, OPERATE ⟨~s on gasoline⟩ ⟨software that ~s on her computer⟩ **12** : to continue in force ⟨two years to ~⟩ **13** : to flow rapidly or under pressure : MELT, FUSE, DISSOLVE; *also* : DISCHARGE 7 ⟨my nose is *running*⟩ **14** : to tend to produce or to recur ⟨family ~s to blonds⟩ ⟨stubbornness ~s in the family⟩ **15** : to take a certain direction **16** : to be worded or written **17** : to be current ⟨rumors *running* wild⟩ **18** : to cause to produce a flow ⟨*ran* the faucet⟩ **19** : TRACE ⟨~ down a rumor⟩ **20** : to perform or bring about by running **21** : to cause to pass ⟨~ a wire from the antenna⟩ **22** : to cause to collide **23** : SMUGGLE **24** : MANAGE, CONDUCT, OPERATE ⟨~ a business⟩ **25** : INCUR ⟨~ a risk⟩ **26** : to permit to accumulate before settling ⟨~ up a bill⟩ **27** : PRINT, PUBLISH ⟨~ a news story⟩

²**run** *n* **1** : an act or the action of running **2** : a migration of fish; *also* : the migrating fish **3** : a score in baseball **4** : BROOK, CREEK **5** : a continuous series esp. of similar things **6** : persistent heavy demands from depositors, creditors, or customers **7** : the quantity of work turned out in a continuous operation; *also* : a period of operation (as of a machine or plant) **8** : the usual or normal kind ⟨the ordinary ~ of students⟩ **9** : the distance covered in continuous travel or sailing **10** : a regular course or trip **11** : freedom of movement in a place or area ⟨has the ~ of the house⟩ **12** : an enclosure for animals **13** : an in-

clined course (as for skiing) **14** : a lengthwise ravel (as in a stocking) — **run·less** *adj*
run·about \'rə-nə-ˌbaut\ *n* : a light wagon, automobile, or motorboat
run·a·gate \'rə-nə-ˌgāt\ *n* **1** : VAGABOND **2** : FUGITIVE
run·around \'rə-nə-ˌraund\ *n* : evasive or delaying action esp. in response to a request
¹**run·away** \'rə-nə-ˌwā\ *n* **1** : one that runs away : FUGITIVE **2** : the act of running away out of control; *also* : something (as a horse) that is running out of control
²**runaway** *adj* **1** : FUGITIVE **2** : won by a long lead; *also* : extremely successful **3** : subject to uncontrolled changes ⟨∼ inflation⟩ **4** : operating out of control ⟨a ∼ locomotive⟩
run–down \'rən-ˌdaun\ *n* : an item-by-item report or review : SUMMARY
run–down \'rən-'daun\ *adj* **1** : EXHAUSTED, WORN-OUT ⟨that ∼ feeling⟩ **2** : being in poor repair ⟨a ∼ farm⟩
run down *vb* **1** : to collide with and knock down **2** : to chase until exhausted or captured **3** : to find by search **4** : DISPARAGE **5** : to cease to operate for lack of motive power **6** : to decline in physical condition
rune \'rün\ *n* **1** : any of the characters of any of several alphabets formerly used by the Germanic peoples **2** : MYSTERY, MAGIC **3** : a poem esp. in Finnish or Old Norse — **ru·nic** \'rü-nik\ *adj*

ᚢᚾᚦᚨᚱᛉ

rune 1

¹**rung** *past part of* RING
²**rung** \'rəŋ\ *n* **1** : a rounded crosspiece between the legs of a chair **2** : one of the crosspieces of a ladder
run–in \'rən-ˌin\ *n* **1** : ALTERCATION, QUARREL **2** : something run in
run in *vb* **1** : to insert as additional matter **2** : to arrest esp. for a minor offense **3** : to pay a casual visit
run·nel \'rə-nᵊl\ *n* : BROOK, STREAMLET
run·ner \'rə-nər\ *n* **1** : one that runs **2** : BASE RUNNER **3** : BALLCARRIER **4** : a thin piece or part on which something (as a sled or an ice skate) slides **5** : the support of a drawer or a sliding door **6** : a horizontal branch from the base of a plant that produces new plants **7** : a plant producing runners **8** : a long narrow carpet **9** : a narrow decorative cloth cover for a table or dresser top
run·ner–up \'rə-nər-ˌəp\ *n*, *pl* **runners–up** *also* **runner–ups** : the competitor in a contest who finishes second
¹**run·ning** *adj* **1** : FLOWING **2** : FLUID, RUNNY **3** : CONTINUOUS, INCESSANT **4** : measured in a straight line ⟨cost per ∼ foot⟩ **5** : of or relating to an act of running **6** : made or trained for running ⟨∼ horse⟩ ⟨∼ shoes⟩
²**running** *adv* : in succession
running light *n* : any of the lights carried by a vehicle (as a ship) at night
run·ny \'rə-nē\ *adj* : having a tendency to run ⟨a ∼ dough⟩ ⟨a ∼ nose⟩
run·off \'rən-ˌof\ *n* : a final contest (as an election) to decide a previous indecisive contest
run–of–the–mill *adj* : not outstanding : AVERAGE
run on *vb* **1** : to talk at length **2** : to continue (matter in type) without a break or a new paragraph **3** : to place or add (as an entry in a dictionary) at the end of a paragraphed item — **run–on** \'rən-ˌon, -ˌän\ *n*
run out *vb* : to use up or exhaust a supply ⟨*ran out* of gas⟩
runt \'rənt\ *n* : an unusually small person or animal : DWARF — **runty** *adj*
run·way \'rən-ˌwā\ *n* **1** : a beaten path made by animals; *also* : a passage for animals **2** : a paved strip of ground for the landing and takeoff of aircraft **3** : a narrow plat-

form from a stage into an auditorium **4** : a support (as a track) on which something runs
ru·pee \rü-'pē, 'rü-ˌpē\ *n* — see MONEY table
ru·pi·ah \rü-'pē-ə\ *n*, *pl* **rupiah** *or* **rupiahs** — see MONEY table
¹**rup·ture** \'rəp-chər\ *n* : a breaking or tearing apart; *also* : HERNIA
²**rupture** *vb* **rup·tured; rup·tur·ing** : to cause or undergo rupture
ru·ral \'rur-əl\ *adj* : of or relating to the country, country people, or agriculture
ruse \'rüs, 'rüz\ *n* : a wily subterfuge : TRICK, ARTIFICE
¹**rush** \'rəsh\ *n* : any of various often tufted and hollow-stemmed grasslike marsh plants — **rushy** *adj*
²**rush** *vb* [ME *russhen*, fr. AF *reuser, ruser, russher* to drive back, repulse, fr. L *recusare* to oppose] **1** : to move forward or act with too great haste or eagerness or without preparation **2** : to perform in a short time or at high speed **3** : ATTACK, CHARGE **4** : to advance a football by running — **rush·er** *n*
³**rush** *n* **1** : a violent forward motion **2** : unusual demand or activity **3** : a crowding of people to one place **4** : a running play in football **5** : a sudden feeling of pleasure
⁴**rush** *adj* : requiring or marked by special speed or urgency ⟨∼ orders⟩
rush hour *n* : a time when the amount of traffic or business is at a peak
rusk \'rəsk\ *n* : a sweet or plain bread baked, sliced, and baked again until dry and crisp
rus·set \'rə-sət\ *n* **1** : a coarse reddish brown cloth **2** : a reddish brown **3** : a baking potato — **russet** *adj*
Rus·sian \'rə-shən\ *n* **1** : a native or inhabitant of Russia **2** : a Slavic language of the Russian people — **Russian** *adj*
rust \'rəst\ *n* **1** : a reddish coating formed on iron when it is exposed to esp. moist air **2** : any of numerous plant diseases characterized by usu. reddish spots; *also* : a fungus causing rust **3** : a strong reddish brown — **rust** *vb* — **rusty** *adj*
¹**rus·tic** \'rəs-tik\ *adj* : of, relating to, or suitable for the country or country people — **rus·ti·cal·ly** \-ti-k(ə-)lē\ *adv* — **rus·tic·i·ty** \ˌrəs-'ti-sə-tē\ *n*
²**rustic** *n* : a rustic person
rus·ti·cate \'rəs-ti-ˌkāt\ *vb* **-cat·ed; -cat·ing** : to go into or reside in the country — **rus·ti·ca·tion** \ˌrəs-ti-'kā-shən\ *n*
¹**rus·tle** \'rə-səl\ *vb* **rus·tled; rus·tling** **1** : to make or cause a rustle **2** : to cause to rustle ⟨∼ a newspaper⟩ **3** : to act or move with energy or speed; *also* : to procure in this way **4** : to forage food **5** : to steal cattle from the range — **rus·tler** *n*
²**rustle** *n* : a quick series of small sounds ⟨∼ of leaves⟩
¹**rut** \'rət\ *n* : state or period of sexual excitement esp. in male deer — **rut** *vb*
²**rut** *n* **1** : a track worn by wheels or by habitual passage of something **2** : a usual or fixed routine
ru·ta·ba·ga \ˌrü-tə-'bā-gə, ˌrü-\ *n* : a turnip with a large yellowish root
Ruth \'rüth\ *n* — see BIBLE table
ru·the·ni·um \rü-'thē-nē-əm\ *n* : a rare hard metallic chemical element
ruth·er·ford·ium \ˌrə-thər-'for-dē-əm\ *n* : an artificially produced radioactive chemical element
ruth·less \'rüth-ləs\ *adj* [fr. *ruth* compassion, pity, fr. ME *ruthe*, fr. *ruen* to rue, fr. OE *hrēowan*] : having no pity : MERCILESS, CRUEL ⟨a ∼ tyrant⟩ — **ruth·less·ly** *adv* — **ruth·less·ness** *n*
¹**RV** \ˌär-'vē\ *n* : RECREATIONAL VEHICLE
²**RV** *abbr* Revised Version
R–value \'är-ˌval-yü\ *n* : a measure of resistance to the flow of heat through a substance (as insulation)
RW *abbr* **1** right worshipful **2** right worthy
rwy *or* **ry** *abbr* railway
-ry *n suffix* : -ERY ⟨bigot*ry*⟩
rye \'rī\ *n* **1** : a hardy annual grass grown for grain or as a cover crop; *also* : its seed **2** : a whiskey distilled from a rye mash

¹s \'es\ *n, pl* **s's** *or* **ss** \'e-səz\ *often cap* : the 19th letter of the English alphabet

²s *abbr, often cap* **1** saint **2** second **3** senate **4** series **5** shilling **6** singular **7** small **8** son **9** south; southern

¹-s \s *after sounds* f, k, k̲, p, t, th; əz *after sounds* ch, j, s, sh, z, zh; z *after other sounds*\ *n pl suffix* — used to form the plural of most nouns that do not end in s, z, sh, or ch or y following a consonant ⟨heads⟩ ⟨books⟩ ⟨boys⟩ ⟨beliefs⟩, to form the plural of proper nouns that end in y following a consonant ⟨Marys⟩, and with or without a preceding apostrophe to form the plural of abbreviations, numbers, letters, and symbols used as nouns ⟨MCs⟩ ⟨4s⟩ ⟨#s⟩ ⟨B's⟩

²-s *adv suffix* — used to form adverbs denoting usual or repeated action or state ⟨works nights⟩

³-s *vb suffix* — used to form the third person singular present of most verbs that do not end in s, z, sh, or ch or y following a consonant ⟨falls⟩ ⟨takes⟩ ⟨plays⟩

S *symbol* sulfur

SA *abbr* **1** Salvation Army **2** seaman apprentice **3** sex appeal **4** [L *sine anno* without year] without date **5** South Africa **6** South America **7** subject to approval

Saami *var of* SAMI

Sab·bath \'sa-bəth\ *n* [ME *sabat,* fr. AF & OE, fr. L *sabbatum,* fr. Gk *sabbaton,* fr. Heb *shabbāth,* lit., rest] **1** : the 7th day of the week observed as a day of worship by Jews and some Christians **2** : Sunday observed among Christians as a day of worship

sab·bat·i·cal \sə-'ba-ti-kəl\ *n* : a leave often with pay granted (as to a college professor) usu. every 7th year for rest, travel, or research

sa·ber *or* **sa·bre** \'sā-bər\ *n* [F *sabre*] : a cavalry sword with a curved blade and thick back

saber

saber saw *n* : a portable electric saw with a pointed reciprocating blade; *esp* : JIGSAW

sa·ble \'sā-bəl\ *n, pl* **sables** **1** : the color black **2** *pl* : mourning garments **3** : a dark brown mammal chiefly of northern Asia related to the weasels; *also* : its fur or pelt

¹sab·o·tage \'sa-bə-,täzh\ *n* [F] **1** : deliberate destruction of an employer's property or hindering of production by workers **2** : destructive or hampering action by enemy agents or sympathizers in time of war

²sabotage *vb* **-taged; -tag·ing** : to practice sabotage on : WRECK

sab·o·teur \,sa-bə-'tər\ *n* : a person who practices sabotage

sac \'sak\ *n* : a pouch in an animal or plant often containing a fluid

SAC *abbr* Strategic Air Command

sac·cha·rin \'sa-kə-rən\ *n* : a white crystalline compound used as an artificial calorie-free sweetener

sac·cha·rine \'sa-kə-rən\ *adj* : nauseatingly sweet ⟨∼ poetry⟩

sac·er·do·tal \,sa-sər-'dō-t°l, -kər-\ *adj* : PRIESTLY

sac·er·do·tal·ism \-t°-,li-zəm\ *n* : a religious belief emphasizing the powers of priests as essential mediators between God and man

sa·chem \'sā-chəm\ *n* [Narragansett *sâchim*] : a No. American Indian chief

sa·chet \sa-'shā\ *n* [MF, fr. OF, dim. of *sac* bag] : a small bag filled with perfumed powder for scenting clothes

¹sack \'sak\ *n* **1** : a usu. rectangular-shaped bag (as of paper or burlap) **2** : a loose jacket or short coat

²sack *vb* : DISMISS, FIRE

³sack *n* [modif. of MF *sec* dry, fr. L *siccus*] : a white wine popular in England in the 16th and 17th centuries

⁴sack *vb* : to plunder a captured town

sack·cloth \-,klóth\ *n* : a rough garment worn as a sign of penitence

sac·ra·ment \'sa-krə-mənt\ *n* **1** : a formal religious act or rite; *esp* : one (as baptism or the Eucharist) held to have been instituted by Christ **2** : the elements of the Eucharist — **sac·ra·men·tal** \,sa-krə-'men-t°l\ *adj*

sa·cred \'sā-krəd\ *adj* **1** : set apart for the service or worship of deity **2** : devoted exclusively to one service or use **3** : worthy of veneration or reverence **4** : of or relating to religion : RELIGIOUS ✦ *Synonyms* BLESSED, DIVINE, HALLOWED, HOLY, SANCTIFIED — **sa·cred·ly** *adv* — **sa·cred·ness** *n*

sacred cow *n* : one that is often unreasonably immune from criticism

¹sac·ri·fice \'sa-krə-,fīs\ *n* **1** : the offering of something precious to deity **2** : something offered in sacrifice **3** : LOSS, DEPRIVATION **4** : a bunt allowing a base runner to advance while the batter is put out; *also* : a fly ball allowing a runner to score after the catch — **sac·ri·fi·cial** \,sa-krə-'fi-shəl\ *adj* — **sac·ri·fi·cial·ly** *adv*

²sac·ri·fice *vb* **-ficed; -fic·ing** **1** : to offer up or kill as a sacrifice **2** : to accept the loss or destruction of for an end, cause, or ideal **3** : to make a sacrifice in baseball

sac·ri·lege \'sa-krə-lij\ *n* [ME, fr. AF, fr. L *sacrilegium,* fr. *sacrilegus* one who robs sacred property fr. *sacr-, sacer* sacred + *legere* to gather, steal] **1** : violation of something consecrated to God **2** : gross irreverence toward a hallowed person, place, or thing — **sac·ri·le·gious** \,sa-krə-'li-jəs, -'lē-\ *adj* — **sac·ri·le·gious·ly** *adv*

sac·ris·tan \'sa-krə-stən\ *n* **1** : a church officer in charge of the sacristy **2** : SEXTON

sac·ris·ty \'sa-krə-stē\ *n, pl* **-ties** : VESTRY

sac·ro·il·i·ac \,sa-krō-'i-lē-,ak\ *n* : the joint between the upper part of the hipbone and the sacrum

sac·ro·sanct \'sa-krō-,saŋkt\ *adj* : SACRED, INVIOLABLE

sa·crum \'sa-krəm, 'sā-\ *n, pl* **sa·cra** \'sa-krə, 'sā-\ : the part of the vertebral column that is directly connected with or forms a part of the pelvis and in humans consists of five fused vertebrae

sad \'sad\ *adj* **sad·der; sad·dest** **1** : GRIEVING, MOURNFUL, DOWNCAST **2** : causing sorrow **3** : DULL, SOMBER — **sad·ly** *adv* — **sad·ness** *n*

sad·den \'sa-d°n\ *vb* : to make sad

¹sad·dle \'sa-d°l\ *n* : a usu. padded leather-covered seat (as for a rider on horseback)

²saddle *vb* **sad·dled; sad·dling** **1** : to put a saddle on **2** : OPPRESS, BURDEN

sad·dle·bow \'sa-d°l-,bō\ *n* : the arch in the front of a saddle

saddle horse *n* : a horse suited for or trained for riding

Sad·du·cee \'sa-jə-,sē, -dyə-\ *n* : a member of an ancient Jewish sect consisting of a ruling class of priests and rejecting certain doctrines — **Sad·du·ce·an** \,sa-jə-'sē-ən, ,sa-dyə-\ *adj*

sad·iron \'sa-,dī-ərn\ *n* : a flatiron with a removable handle

sa·dism \'sā-,di-zəm, 'sa-\ *n* : a sexual perversion in which gratification is obtained by inflicting physical or mental pain on others — **sa·dist** \'sā-dist, 'sa-\ *n* — **sa·dis·tic** \sə-'dis-tik\ *adj* — **sa·dis·ti·cal·ly** \-ti-k(ə-)lē\ *adv*

sa·do·mas·och·ism \,sā-(,)dō-'ma-sə-,ki-zəm, ,sa-, -'ma-zə-\ *n* : the derivation of pleasure from the infliction of physical or mental pain either on others or on oneself — **sa·do·mas·och·is·tic** \-,ma-sə-'kis-tik, -,ma-zə-\ *adj*

SAE *abbr* **1** self-addressed envelope **2** Society of Automotive Engineers **3** stamped addressed envelope

sa·fa·ri \sə-'fär-ē\ *n* [Swahili, trip, fr. Ar *safarī* of a trip] **1** : a hunting expedition esp. in eastern Africa **2** : JOURNEY, TRIP

¹**safe** \'sāf\ *adj* **saf·er; saf·est 1** : free from harm or risk **2** : affording safety; *also* : secure from danger or loss **3** : RELIABLE — **safe·ly** *adv*

²**safe** *n* : a container for keeping articles (as valuables) safe

safe–con·duct \-'kän-(ˌ)dəkt\ *n* : a pass permitting a person to go through enemy lines

¹**safe·guard** \-ˌgärd\ *n* : a measure or device for preventing accident

²**safeguard** *vb* : to provide a safeguard for : PROTECT

safe·keep·ing \'sāf-'kē-piŋ\ *n* : a keeping or being kept in safety

safer sex *n* : SAFE SEX

safe sex *n* : sexual activity and esp. sexual intercourse in which various measures (as the use of latex condoms) are taken to avoid disease (as AIDS) transmitted by sexual contact

safe·ty \'sāf-tē\ *n, pl* **safeties 1** : freedom from danger : SECURITY **2** : a protective device **3** : a football play in which the ball is downed by the offensive team behind its own goal line **4** : a defensive football back in the deepest position — **safety** *adj*

safety glass *n* : shatter-resistant material formed of two sheets of glass with a sheet of clear plastic between them

safety match *n* : a match that ignites only when struck on a special surface

saf·flow·er \'sa-ˌflaú(-ə)r\ *n* : a widely grown Old World herb related to the daisies that has large orange or red flower heads yielding a dyestuff and seeds rich in edible oil

saf·fron \'sa-frən\ *n* : a deep orange powder from the flower of a crocus used to color and flavor foods

sag \'sag\ *vb* **sagged; sag·ging 1** : to droop or settle from or as if from pressure **2** : to lose firmness or vigor — **sag** *n*

sa·ga \'sä-gə\ *n* [ON] : a narrative of heroic deeds; *esp* : one recorded in Iceland in the 12th and 13th centuries

sa·ga·cious \sə-'gā-shəs\ *adj* : of keen mind : SHREWD — **sa·gac·i·ty** \-'ga-sə-tē\ *n*

sag·a·more \'sa-gə-ˌmór\ *n* : a subordinate No. American Indian chief

¹**sage** \'sāj\ *adj* [ME, fr. AF, fr. VL *sapius, fr. L *sapere* to taste, have good taste, be wise] : WISE, PRUDENT — **sage·ly** *adv*

²**sage** *n* : one who is distinguished for wisdom

³**sage** *n* [ME, fr. AF *sage, salge, fr. L *salvia, fr. *salvus* healthy; fr. its use as a medicinal herb] **1** : a perennial mint with aromatic leaves used in flavoring; *also* : its leaves **2** : SAGEBRUSH **3** : a light grayish green

sage·brush \'sāj-ˌbrəsh\ *n* : any of several low shrubby No. American composite plants; *esp* : one of the western U.S. with a sagelike odor

Sag·it·tar·i·us \ˌsa-jə-'ter-ē-əs\ *n* [L, lit., archer] **1** : a zodiacal constellation between Scorpio and Capricorn usu. pictured as a centaur archer **2** : the 9th sign of the zodiac in astrology; *also* : one born under this sign

sa·go \'sā-gō\ *n, pl* **sagos** : a dry granulated starch esp. from the pith of various tropical palms (**sago palm**)

sa·gua·ro \sə-'wär-ə, -'gwär-, -ō\ *n, pl* **-ros** [MexSp] : a tall columnar usu. sparsely-branched cactus of dry areas of the southwestern U.S. and Mexico that may attain a height of up to 50 feet (16 meters)

said *past and past part of* SAY

¹**sail** \'sāl\ *n* **1** : a piece of fabric by means of which the wind is used to propel a ship **2** : a sailing ship **3** : something resembling a sail **4** : a trip on a sailboat

²**sail** *vb* **1** : to travel on a sailing ship **2** : to pass over in a ship **3** : to manage or direct the course of a ship **4** : to move with ease, grace, or nonchalance

sail·board \'sāl-ˌbórd\ *n* : a modified surfboard having a mast and sailed by a standing person

sail·boat \-ˌbōt\ *n* : a boat propelled primarily by sail

sail·cloth \-ˌklóth\ *n* : a heavy canvas used for sails, tents, or upholstery

sail·fish \-ˌfish\ *n* : any of a genus of large marine bony fishes with a large dorsal fin that are related to marlins

sail·ing *n* : the sport of handling or riding in a sailboat

sail·or \'sā-lər\ *n* : one that sails; *esp* : a member of a ship's crew

sail·plane \'sāl-ˌplān\ *n* : a glider designed to rise in an upward air current

saint \'sānt, *before a name* (ˌ)sānt *or* sənt\ *n* **1** : one offi-cially recognized as preeminent for holiness **2** : one of the spirits of the departed in heaven **3** : a holy or godly person — **saint·ed** \-'sān-təd\ *adj* — **saint·hood** \-ˌhúd\ *n*

Saint Ber·nard \-bər-'närd\ *n* : any of a Swiss alpine breed of tall powerful working dogs used esp. formerly in aiding lost travelers

Saint–John's–wort \'sānt-'jänz-ˌwərt, -ˌwórt\ *n* **1** : any of a genus of herbs and shrubs with showy yellow flowers **2** : the dried aerial parts of a Saint-John's-wort used esp. in herbal remedies

saint·ly \'sānt-lē\ *adj* : relating to, resembling, or befitting a saint — **saint·li·ness** \-lē-nəs\ *n*

Saint Val·en·tine's Day \-'va-lən-ˌtīnz-\ *n* : VALENTINE'S DAY

¹**sake** \'sāk\ *n* **1** : END, PURPOSE **2** : personal or social welfare, safety, or well-being

²**sa·ke** *or* **sa·ki** \'sä-kē\ *n* : a Japanese alcoholic beverage of fermented rice

sa·laam \sə-'läm\ *n* [Ar *salām*, lit., peace] **1** : a salutation or ceremonial greeting in the East **2** : an obeisance performed by bowing very low and placing the right palm on the forehead — **salaam** *vb*

sa·la·cious \sə-'lā-shəs\ *adj* **1** : arousing sexual desire or imagination **2** : LUSTFUL — **sa·la·cious·ly** *adv* — **sa·la·cious·ness** *n*

sal·ad \'sa-ləd\ *n* : a cold dish (as of lettuce, vegetables, fish, eggs, or fruit) served with dressing

sal·a·man·der \'sa-lə-ˌman-dər\ *n* : any of numerous amphibians that look like lizards but have scaleless usu. smooth moist skin

sa·la·mi \sə-'lä-mē\ *n* [It] : a highly seasoned sausage of pork and beef

sal·a·ry \'sa-lə-rē\ *n, pl* **-ries** [ME *salarie, fr. AF, fr. L *salarium* pension, salary, fr. neut. of *salarius* of salt, fr. *sal* salt] : payment made at regular intervals for services

sale \'sāl\ *n* **1** : transfer of ownership of property from one person to another in return for money **2** : ready market : DEMAND **3** : AUCTION **4** : a selling of goods at bargain prices — **sal·able** *or* **sale·able** \'sā-lə-bəl\ *adj*

sales·girl \'sālz-ˌgərl\ *n* : SALESWOMAN

sales·man \-mən\ *n* : a person who sells in a store or to outside customers — **sales·man·ship** *n*

sales·per·son \-ˌpər-sən\ *n* : a salesman or saleswoman

sales·wom·an \-ˌwú-mən\ *n* : a woman who sells merchandise

sal·i·cyl·ic acid \ˌsa-lə-'si-lik-\ *n* : a crystalline organic acid used in making aspirin and other medicinal preparations (as skin lotions)

¹**sa·lient** \'sāl-yənt, 'sā-lē-ənt\ *adj* : jutting forward beyond a line; *also* : PROMINENT ◆ **Synonyms** CONSPICUOUS, STRIKING, NOTICEABLE

²**salient** *n* : a projecting part in a line of defense

¹**sa·line** \'sā-ˌlēn, -ˌlīn\ *adj* : consisting of or containing salt : SALTY — **sa·lin·i·ty** \sā-'li-nə-tē, sə-\ *n*

²**saline** *n* **1** : a metallic salt esp. with a purgative action **2** : a saline solution

sa·li·va \sə-'lī-və\ *n* : a liquid secreted into the mouth that helps digestion — **sal·i·vary** \'sa-lə-ˌver-ē\ *adj*

sal·i·vate \'sa-lə-ˌvāt\ *vb* **-vat·ed; -vat·ing** : to produce saliva esp. in excess — **sal·i·va·tion** \ˌsa-lə-'vā-shən\ *n*

sal·low \'sa-lō\ *adj* : of a yellowish sickly color ⟨a ∼ face⟩

sal·ly \'sa-lē\ *n, pl* **sallies 1** : a rushing attack on besiegers by troops of a besieged place **2** : a witty remark or retort **3** : a brief excursion — **sally** *vb*

salm·on \'sa-mən\ *n, pl* **salmon** *also* **salmons 1** : any of several bony fishes with pinkish flesh that are used for food and are related to the trouts **2** : a strong yellowish pink color

sal·mo·nel·la \ˌsal-mə-'ne-lə\ *n, pl* **-nel·lae** \-'ne-(ˌ)lē, -ˌlī\ *or* **-nellas** *or* **-nella** : any of a genus of rod-shaped bacteria that cause various illnesses (as food poisoning)

sa·lon \sə-'län, 'sa-ˌlän, sa-'lōⁿ\ *n* [F] : an elegant drawing room; *also* : a fashionable shop ⟨beauty ∼⟩

sa·loon \sə-'lün\ *n* **1** : a large public cabin on a ship **2** : a place where liquors are sold and drunk : BARROOM **3** *Brit* : SEDAN 2

sal·sa \'sól-sə, 'säl-\ *n* : a spicy sauce of tomatoes, onions, and hot peppers

¹**salt** \'sólt\ *n* **1** : a white crystalline substance that consists of sodium and chlorine and is used in seasoning foods **2**

: a saltlike cathartic substance (as Epsom salts) **3** : a compound formed usu. by action of an acid on metal **4** : SAILOR — **salt·i·ness** \'sȯl-tē-nəs\ n — **salty** \'sȯl-tē\ adj

²**salt** vb : to preserve, season, or feed with salt

³**salt** adj : preserved or treated with salt; also : SALTY

SALT abbr Strategic Arms Limitation Talks

salt away vb : to lay away safely : SAVE

salt-box \'sȯlt-ˌbäks\ n : a frame dwelling with two stories in front and one behind and a long sloping roof

salt·cel·lar \-ˌse-lər\ n : a small container for holding salt at the table

sal·tine \sȯl-'tēn\ n : a thin crisp cracker sprinkled with salt

salt lick n : LICK 5

salt·pe·ter \'sȯlt-'pē-tər\ n [ME salt petre, alter. of salpetre, fr. ML sal petrae, lit., salt of the rock] **1** : POTASSIUM NITRATE **2** : SODIUM NITRATE

salt·wa·ter \-ˌwȯ-tər, -ˌwä-\ adj : of, relating to, or living in salt water

sa·lu·bri·ous \sə-'lü-brē-əs\ adj : favorable to health ⟨a ∼ climate⟩

sal·u·tary \'sal-yə-ˌter-ē\ adj : health-giving; also : BENEFICIAL ⟨∼ effects⟩

sal·u·ta·tion \ˌsal-yə-'tā-shən\ n : an expression of greeting, goodwill, or courtesy usu. by word or gesture

sa·lu·ta·to·ri·an \sə-ˌlü-tə-'tȯr-ē-ən\ n : the student having the 2d highest rank in a graduating class who delivers the salutatory address

sa·lu·ta·to·ry \sə-'lü-tə-ˌtȯr-ē\ adj : relating to or being the welcoming oration delivered at an academic commencement

¹**sa·lute** \sə-'lüt\ vb **sa·lut·ed; sa·lut·ing 1** : GREET **2** : to honor by special ceremonies **3** : to show respect to (a superior officer) by a formal position of hand, rifle, or sword

²**salute** n **1** : GREETING **2** : the formal position assumed in saluting a superior

¹**sal·vage** \'sal-vij\ n **1** : money paid for saving a ship, its cargo, or passengers when the ship is wrecked or in danger **2** : the saving of a ship **3** : the saving of possessions in danger of being lost **4** : things saved from loss or destruction (as by a wreck or fire)

²**salvage** vb **sal·vaged; sal·vag·ing** : to rescue from destruction

sal·va·tion \sal-'vā-shən\ n **1** : the saving of a person from sin or its consequences esp. in the life after death **2** : the saving from danger, difficulty, or evil **3** : something that saves

¹**salve** \'sav, 'säv\ n **1** : a medicinal substance applied to the skin **2** : a soothing influence

²**salve** vb **salved; salv·ing** : EASE, SOOTHE

sal·ver \'sal-vər\ n [F salve, fr. Sp salva sampling of food to detect poison, tray, fr. salvar to save, sample food to detect poison, fr. LL salvare to save, fr. L salvus safe] : a small serving tray

sal·vo \'sal-vō\ n, pl **salvos** or **salvoes** : a simultaneous discharge of guns

Sam or **Saml** abbr Samuel

SAM \'sam, ˌes-ˌā-'em\ n [surface-to-air missile] : a guided missile for use against aircraft by ground units

Sa·mar·i·tan \sə-'mer-ə-tən\ n **1** : a native or inhabitant of Samaria **2** : a person who is generous in helping those in distress

sa·mar·i·um \sə-'mer-ē-əm\ n : a silvery-white lustrous rare metallic chemical element

¹**same** \'sām\ adj **1** : being the one referred to : not different **2** : SIMILAR — **same·ness** n

²**same** pron : the same one or ones

³**same** adv : in the same manner

Sa·mi also **Saa·mi** \'sä-mē\ n, pl **Sami** or **Samis** also **Saami** or **Saamis** : a member of a people of northern Scandinavia, Finland, and the Kola Peninsula of Russia

Sa·mo·an \sə-'mō-ən\ n : a native or inhabitant of Samoa — **Samoan** adj

sa·mo·sa \sə-'mō-sə\ n : a small triangular pastry filled with spiced meat or vegetables and fried

sam·o·var \'sa-mə-ˌvär\ n [Russ, fr. samo- self + varit' to boil] : an urn with a spigot at the base used esp. in Russia to boil water for tea

sam·pan \'sam-ˌpan\ n : a flat-bottomed skiff of eastern Asia usu. propelled by two short oars

¹**sam·ple** \'sam-pəl\ n : a representative piece, item, or set of individuals that shows the quality or nature of the whole from which it was taken : EXAMPLE, SPECIMEN

²**sample** vb **sam·pled; sam·pling** : to judge the quality of by a sample

sam·pler \'sam-plər\ n : a piece of needlework; esp : one testing skill in embroidering

Sam·u·el \'sam-yə-wəl\ n — see BIBLE table

sam·u·rai \'sa-mə-ˌrī, 'sam-yə-\ n, pl **samurai** : a military retainer of a Japanese feudal lord who adhered to strict principles of honor and duty

san·a·to·ri·um \ˌsa-nə-'tȯr-ē-əm\ n, pl **-ri·ums** or **-ria** \-ē-ə\ **1** : a health resort **2** : an establishment for the care esp. of convalescents or the chronically ill

sanc·ti·fy \'saŋk-tə-ˌfī\ vb **-fied; -fy·ing 1** : to make holy : CONSECRATE **2** : to free from sin — **sanc·ti·fi·ca·tion** \ˌsaŋk-tə-fə-'kā-shən\ n

sanc·ti·mo·nious \ˌsaŋk-tə-'mō-nē-əs\ adj : hypocritically pious — **sanc·ti·mo·nious·ly** adv

¹**sanc·tion** \'saŋk-shən\ n **1** : authoritative approval **2** : a measure (as a threat or fine) designed to enforce a law or standard ⟨economic ∼s⟩

²**sanction** vb : to give approval to : RATIFY ♦ **Synonyms** ENDORSE, ACCREDIT, CERTIFY, APPROVE

sanc·ti·ty \'saŋk-tə-tē\ n, pl **-ties 1** : GODLINESS **2** : SACREDNESS

sanc·tu·ary \'saŋk-chə-ˌwer-ē\ n, pl **-ar·ies 1** : a consecrated place (as the part of a church in which the altar is placed) **2** : a place of refuge ⟨bird ∼⟩

sanc·tum \'saŋk-təm\ n, pl **sanctums** also **sanc·ta** \-tə\ : a private office or study : DEN ⟨an editor's ∼⟩

¹**sand** \'sand\ n : loose particles of hard broken rock — **sandy** adj

²**sand** vb **1** : to cover or fill with sand **2** : to scour, smooth, or polish with an abrasive (as sandpaper) — **sand·er** n

san·dal \'san-dᵊl\ n : a shoe consisting of a sole strapped to the foot; also : a low or open slipper or rubber overshoe

san·dal·wood \-ˌwu̇d\ n : the fragrant yellowish heartwood of a parasitic tree of southern Asia that is much used in ornamental carving and cabinetwork; also : the tree

sand·bag \'sand-ˌbag\ n : a bag filled with sand and used in fortifications, as ballast, or as a weapon

sand·bank \-ˌbaŋk\ n : a deposit of sand (as in a bar or shoal)

sand·bar \-ˌbär\ n : a ridge of sand formed in water by tides or currents

sand·blast \-ˌblast\ vb : to treat with a stream of sand blown (as for cleaning stone) by compressed air — **sand·blast·er** n

sand dollar n : any of numerous flat circular sea urchins living chiefly on sandy bottoms in shallow water

S & H abbr shipping and handling

sand·hog \'sand-ˌhȯg, -ˌhäg\ n : a laborer who builds underwater tunnels

sand·lot \-ˌlät\ n : a vacant lot esp. when used for the unorganized sports of children — **sand·lot** adj — **sand·lot·ter** n

sand·man \-ˌman\ n : the genie of folklore who makes children sleepy

sand·pa·per \-ˌpā-pər\ n : paper with abrasive (as sand) glued on one side used in smoothing and polishing surfaces — **sandpaper** vb

sand·pip·er \-ˌpī-pər\ n : any of various shorebirds with a soft-tipped bill longer than that of the related plovers

sand·stone \-ˌstōn\ n : rock made of sand united by a natural cement

sand·storm \-ˌstȯrm\ n : a windstorm that drives clouds of sand

sand trap n : a hazard on a golf course consisting of a hollow containing sand

¹**sand·wich** \'sand-(ˌ)wich\ n [after John Montagu, 4th Earl of Sandwich †1792 Eng. diplomat] **1** : two or more slices of bread with a layer (as of meat or cheese) spread between them **2** : something resembling a sandwich

²**sandwich** vb : to squeeze or crowd in

sane \'sān\ adj **san·er; san·est** : mentally sound and healthy; also : SENSIBLE, RATIONAL — **sane·ly** adv

sang past of SING

sang·froid \'sän-'frwä\ n [F sang-froid, lit., cold blood]

: self-possession or an imperturbable state esp. under strain

san·gui·nary \'saŋ-gwə-,ner-ē\ *adj* : BLOODY ⟨~ battle⟩

san·guine \'saŋ-gwən\ *adj* **1** : RUDDY **2** : CHEERFUL, HOPEFUL

sanit *abbr* sanitary; sanitation

san·i·tar·i·an \,sa-nə-'ter-ē-ən\ *n* : a specialist in sanitation and public health

san·i·tar·i·um \,sa-nə-'ter-ē-əm\ *n, pl* **-i·ums** *or* **-ia** \-ē-ə\ : SANATORIUM

san·i·tary \'sa-nə-,ter-ē\ *adj* **1** : of or relating to health : HYGIENIC **2** : free from filth or infective matter

sanitary napkin *n* : a disposable absorbent pad used to absorb uterine flow (as during menstruation)

san·i·ta·tion \,sa-nə-'tā-shən\ *n* : the act or process of making sanitary; *also* : protection of health by maintenance of sanitary conditions

san·i·tize \'sa-nə-,tīz\ *vb* **-tized; -tiz·ing 1** : to make sanitary **2** : to make more acceptable by removing unpleasant features

san·i·ty \'sa-nə-tē\ *n* : soundness of mind

sank *past of* SINK

sans \'sanz\ *prep* : WITHOUT

San·skrit \'san-,skrit\ *n* : an ancient language that is the classical language of India and of Hinduism — **Sanskrit** *adj*

San·ta Ana \,san-tə-'a-nə\ *n* [*Santa Ana* Mountains in southern Calif.] : a hot dry wind from the north, northeast, or east in southern California

san·tims \'sän-,tims\ *n, pl* **san·ti·mi** \-ti-mē\ — see *lats* at MONEY table

¹sap \'sap\ *n* **1** : a vital fluid; *esp* : a watery fluid that circulates through a vascular plant **2** : a foolish gullible person — **sap·less** *adj*

²sap *vb* **sapped; sap·ping 1** : UNDERMINE **2** : to weaken gradually

sap·id \'sa-pəd\ *adj* : FLAVORFUL

sa·pi·ent \'sā-pē-ənt, 'sa-\ *adj* : WISE, DISCERNING — **sa·pi·ence** \-əns\ *n*

sap·ling \'sa-pliŋ\ *n* : a young tree

sap·phire \'sa-,fī(-ə)r\ *n* : a hard transparent usu. rich blue gem

sap·py \'sa-pē\ *adj* **sap·pi·er; -est 1** : full of sap **2** : overly sentimental **3** : SILLY, FOOLISH

sap·ro·phyte \'sa-prə-,fīt\ *n* : a living thing and esp. a plant living on dead or decaying organic matter — **sap·ro·phyt·ic** \,sa-prə-'fi-tik\ *adj*

sap·suck·er \'sap-,sə-kər\ *n* : any of a genus of No. American woodpeckers

sap·wood \-,wu̇d\ *n* : the younger active and usu. lighter and softer outer layer of wood (as of a tree trunk)

sar·casm \'sär-,ka-zəm\ *n* **1** : a cutting or contemptuous remark **2** : ironic criticism or reproach — **sar·cas·tic** \sär-'kas-tik\ *adj* — **sar·cas·ti·cal·ly** \-ti-k(ə-)lē\ *adv*

sar·co·ma \sär-'kō-mə\ *n, pl* **-mas** *also* **-ma·ta** \-mə-tə\ : a malignant tumor esp. of connective tissue, bone, cartilage, or striated muscle

sar·coph·a·gus \sär-'kä-fə-gəs\ *n, pl* **-gi** \-,gī, -,jī\ *also* **-gus·es** [L *sarcophagus* (*lapis*) limestone used for coffins, fr. Gk (*lithos*) *sarkophagos*, lit., flesh-eating stone, fr. *sark-, sarx* flesh + *phagein* to eat] : a large stone coffin

sar·dine \sär-'dēn\ *n, pl* **sardines** *also* **sardine** : a young or small fish preserved for use as food

sar·don·ic \sär-'dä-nik\ *adj* : disdainfully or skeptically humorous : derisively mocking ✦ **Synonyms** IRONIC, SATIRIC, SARCASTIC — **sar·don·i·cal·ly** \-ni-k(ə-)lē\ *adv*

sa·ri *also* **sa·ree** \'sär-ē\ *n* [Hindi *sāṛī*] : a garment worn by women in southern Asia that consists of a long cloth draped around the body and head or shoulder

sa·rin \'sär-ən, zä-'rēn\ *n* : an extremely toxic chemical weapon used as a lethal nerve gas

sa·rong \sə-'rȯŋ, -'räŋ\ *n* : a loose garment wrapped around the body and worn by men and women of the Malay Archipelago and the Pacific islands

sar·sa·pa·ril·la \,sas-pə-'ri-lə, ,särs-\ *n* **1** : the dried roots of a tropical American smilax used esp. for flavoring; *also* : the plant **2** : a sweetened carbonated beverage flavored with sassafras and an oil from a birch

sar·to·ri·al \sär-'tȯr-ē-əl\ *adj* : of or relating to a tailor or tailored clothes — **sar·to·ri·al·ly** *adv*

SASE *abbr* self-addressed stamped envelope

¹sash \'sash\ *n* : a broad band worn around the waist or over the shoulder

²sash *n, pl* **sash** *also* **sash·es** : a frame for panes of glass in a door or window; *also* : the movable part of a window

sa·shay \sa-'shā\ *vb* **1** : WALK, GLIDE, GO **2** : to strut or move about in an ostentatious manner **3** : to proceed in a diagonal or sideways manner

Sask *abbr* Saskatchewan

Sas·quatch \'sas-,kwach, -,kwäch\ *n* [Halkomelem (American Indian language of British Columbia) *sésq̓əc*] : a large hairy humanlike creature reported to exist in the northwestern U.S. and western Canada

sas·sa·fras \'sa-sə-,fras\ *n* [Sp *sasafrás*] : an aromatic No. American tree related to the laurel; *also* : its carcinogenic dried root bark

sassy \'sa-sē\ *adj* **sass·i·er; -est** : SAUCY

¹sat *past and past part of* SIT

²sat *abbr* **1** satellite **2** saturated

Sat *abbr* Saturday

Sa·tan \'sā-t³n\ *n* : DEVIL

sa·tang \sə-'täŋ\ *n, pl* **satang** *or* **satangs** — see *baht* at MONEY table

sa·tan·ic \sə-'ta-nik, sā-\ *adj* **1** : of or characteristic of Satan **2** : extremely malicious or wicked — **sa·tan·i·cal·ly** \-ni-k(ə-)lē\ *adv*

satch·el \'sa-chəl\ *n* : SUITCASE

sate \'sāt\ *vb* **sat·ed; sat·ing** : to satisfy to the full; *also* : SURFEIT, GLUT

sa·teen \sa-'tēn, sə-\ *n* : a cotton cloth finished to resemble satin

sat·el·lite \'sa-tə-,līt\ *n* [MF, fr. L *satelles* attendant] **1** : an obsequious follower of a distinguished person : TOADY **2** : a celestial body that orbits a larger body **3** : a manufactured object that orbits a celestial body

satellite dish *n* : a microwave dish for receiving usu. television transmissions from an orbiting satellite

sa·ti·ate \'sā-shē-,āt\ *vb* **-at·ed; -at·ing** : to satisfy fully or to excess

sa·ti·ety \sə-'tī-ə-tē\ *n* : fullness to the point of excess

sat·in \'sa-t³n\ *n* : a fabric (as of silk) with a glossy surface — **sat·iny** *adj*

sat·in·wood \'sa-t³n-,wu̇d\ *n* : a hard yellowish brown wood of satiny luster; *also* : a tree yielding this wood

sat·ire \'sa-,tī(-ə)r\ *n* : biting wit, irony, or sarcasm used to expose vice or folly; *also* : a literary work having these qualities — **sa·tir·ic** \sə-'tir-ik\ *or* **sa·tir·i·cal** \-i-kəl\ *adj* — **sa·tir·i·cal·ly** *adv* — **sat·i·rist** \'sa-tə-rist\ *n* — **sat·i·rize** \-tə-,rīz\ *vb*

sat·is·fac·tion \,sa-təs-'fak-shən\ *n* **1** : payment through penance of punishment incurred by sin **2** : CONTENTMENT, GRATIFICATION **3** : reparation for an insult **4** : settlement of a claim

sat·is·fac·to·ry \-'fak-tə-rē\ *adj* : giving satisfaction : ADEQUATE — **sat·is·fac·to·ri·ly** \-tə-rə-lē\ *adv*

sat·is·fy \'sa-təs-,fī\ *vb* **-fied; -fy·ing 1** : to answer or discharge (a claim) in full **2** : to make happy : GRATIFY **3** : to pay what is due to **4** : CONVINCE **5** : to meet the requirements of — **sat·is·fy·ing·ly** *adv*

sa·trap \'sā-,trap, 'sa-\ *n* [ME, fr. L *satrapes*, fr. Gk *satrapēs*, fr. OPers *khshathrapāvan*, lit., protector of the dominion] : a petty prince : a subordinate ruler

sat·u·rate \'sa-chə-,rāt\ *vb* **-rat·ed; -rat·ing 1** : to soak thoroughly **2** : to treat or charge with something to the point where no more can be absorbed, dissolved, or retained — **sat·u·ra·ble** \'sa-chə-rə-bəl\ *adj* — **sat·u·ra·tion** \,sa-chə-'rā-shən\ *n*

saturated *adj* **1** : full of moisture **2** : having no double or triple bonds between carbon atoms ⟨~ fats⟩

Sat·ur·day \'sa-tər-dē, -,dā\ *n* : the 7th day of the week

Saturday night special *n* : a cheap easily concealed handgun

Sat·urn \'sa-tərn\ *n* : the planet 6th in order from the sun — see PLANET table

sat·ur·nine \'sa-tər-,nīn\ *adj* : SULLEN, SARDONIC

sa·tyr \'sā-tər\ *n* **1** *often cap* : a woodland deity in Greek mythology having certain characteristics of a horse or goat **2** : a lecherous man

¹sauce \'sȯs, 3 *usu* 'sas\ *n* **1** : a fluid dressing or topping for food **2** : stewed fruit **3** : IMPUDENCE

²sauce \'sȯs, 2 *usu* 'sas\ *vb* **sauced; sauc·ing 1** : to put sauce on; *also* : to add zest to **2** : to be impudent to

sauce·pan \'sȯs-ˌpan\ *n* : a small deep cooking pan with a handle

sau·cer \'sȯ-sər\ *n* : a rounded shallow dish for use under a cup

saucy \'sa-sē, 'sȯ-\ *adj* **sauc·i·er; -est** : IMPUDENT, PERT — **sauc·i·ly** \-sə-lē\ *adv* — **sauc·i·ness** \-sē-nəs\ *n*

Sau·di \'saü-dē, 'sȯ-; sä-'ü-dē\ *n* : SAUDI ARABIAN — **Saudi** *adj*

Saudi Arabian *n* : a native or inhabitant of Saudi Arabia — **Saudi Arabian** *adj*

sau·er·kraut \'saü-(-ə)r-ˌkraüt\ *n* [G, fr. *sauer* sour + *Kraut* greens] : finely cut cabbage fermented in brine

Sauk \'sȯk\ *or* **Sac** \'sak, 'sȯk\ *n, pl* **Sauk** *or* **Sauks** *or* **Sac** *or* **Sacs** : a member of an American Indian people formerly living in what is now Wisconsin

sau·na \'sȯ-nə, 'saü-nə\ *n* **1** : a Finnish steam bath in which the steam is provided by water thrown on hot stones **2** : a dry heat bath; *also* : a room or cabinet used for such a bath

saun·ter \'sȯn-tər, 'sän-\ *vb* : STROLL

sau·ro·pod \'sȯr-ə-ˌpäd\ *n* : any of a suborder of plant-eating dinosaurs (as a brontosaurus) with a long neck and tail and a small head — **sauropod** *adj*

sau·sage \'sȯ-sij\ *n* [ME *sausige*, fr. AF *sauseche*, fr. LL *salsicia*, fr. L *salsus* salted] : minced and highly seasoned meat (as pork) usu. enclosed in a tubular casing

S Aust *abbr* South Australia

sau·té \sȯ-'tā, sō-\ *vb* **sau·téed** *or* **sau·téd; sau·té·ing** [F] : to fry lightly in a little fat — **sauté** *n*

sau·terne \sō-'tərn, sȯ-\ *n, often cap* : a usu. semisweet American white wine

¹sav·age \'sa-vij\ *adj* [ME, fr. AF *salvage, savage*, LL *salvaticus*, alter. of L *silvaticus* of the woods, wild, fr. *silva* forest] **1** : WILD, UNTAMED **2** : UNCIVILIZED, BARBAROUS **3** : CRUEL, FIERCE — **sav·age·ly** *adv* — **sav·age·ness** *n* — **sav·age·ry** \-rē\ *n*

²savage *n* **1** : a member of a primitive human society **2** : a rude, unmannerly, or brutal person

sa·van·na *or* **sa·van·nah** \sə-'va-nə\ *n* [Sp *zavana*] : grassland containing scattered trees

sa·vant \sa-'vänt, sə-, 'sa-vənt\ *n* : a learned person : SCHOLAR

¹save \'sāv\ *vb* **saved; sav·ing** **1** : to redeem from sin **2** : to rescue from danger **3** : to preserve or guard from destruction or loss; *also* : to store (data) in a computer or on a storage device **4** : to put aside as a store or reserve — **sav·er** *n*

²save *n* : a play that prevents an opponent from scoring or winning

³save *prep* : EXCEPT

⁴save *conj* : BUT

savings and loan association *n* : a cooperative association that holds savings of members in the form of dividend-bearing shares and that invests chiefly in mortgage loans

savings bank *n* : a bank that holds funds of individual depositors in interest-bearing accounts and makes long-term investments (as mortgage loans)

savings bond *n* : a registered U.S. bond issued in denominations of $50 to $10,000

sav·ior *or* **sav·iour** \'sāv-yər\ *n* **1** : one who saves **2** *cap* : Jesus Christ

sa·voir faire \ˌsav-ˌwär-'fer\ *n* [F *savoir-faire*, lit., knowing how to do] : sureness in social behavior

¹sa·vor *also* **sa·vour** \'sā-vər\ *n* **1** : the taste and odor of something **2** : a special flavor or quality — **sa·vory** *adj*

²savor *also* **savour** *vb* **1** : to have a specified taste, smell, or quality **2** : to taste with pleasure

sa·vo·ry \'sā-və-rē\ *n, pl* **-ries** : either of two aromatic mints used in cooking

¹sav·vy \'sa-vē\ *vb* **sav·vied; sav·vy·ing** : UNDERSTAND, COMPREHEND

²savvy *n* : practical know-how ⟨political ∼⟩ — **savvy** *adj*

¹saw *past of* SEE

²saw \'sȯ\ *n* : a cutting tool with a blade having a line of teeth along its edge

³saw *vb* **sawed** \'sȯd\; **sawed** *or* **sawn** \'sȯn\; **saw·ing** : to cut or shape with or as if with a saw

⁴saw *n* : a common saying : MAXIM

saw·dust \'sȯ-(ˌ)dəst\ *n* : fine particles made by a saw in cutting

saw·fly \-ˌflī\ *n* : any of numerous insects belonging to the same order as bees and wasps and including many whose larvae are plant-feeding pests

saw·horse \-ˌhȯrs\ *n* : a rack on which wood is rested while being sawed by hand

saw·mill \-ˌmil\ *n* : a mill for sawing logs

saw palmetto *n* **1** : any of several shrubby palms with spiny-toothed petioles **2** : the fruit of a saw palmetto used esp. in herbal remedies

saw·yer \'sȯ-yər\ *n* : a person who saws timber

sax \'saks\ *n* : SAXOPHONE

sax·i·frage \'sak-sə-frij, -ˌfräj\ *n* [ME, fr. AF, fr. LL *saxifraga*, fr. L, fem. of *saxifragus*, breaking rocks] : any of a genus of plants with showy flowers and usu. with leaves growing in tufts close to the ground

sax·o·phone \'sak-sə-ˌfōn\ *n* : a musical instrument having a conical metal tube with a reed mouthpiece and finger keys — **sax·o·phon·ist** \-ˌfō-nist\ *n*

¹say \'sā\ *vb* **said** \'sed\; **say·ing; says** \'sez\ **1** : to express in words ⟨∼ what you mean⟩ **2** : to state as opinion or belief **3** : PRONOUNCE; *also* : RECITE, REPEAT ⟨∼ your prayers⟩ **4** : INDICATE ⟨the clock ∼s noon⟩

²say *n, pl* **says** \'sāz\ **1** : an expression of opinion **2** : power of decision

say·ing *n* : a commonly repeated statement

say–so \'sā-(ˌ)sō\ *n* : an esp. authoritative assertion or decision; *also* : the right to decide

sb *abbr* substantive

Sb *symbol* [L *stibium*] antimony

SB *abbr* [NL *scientiae baccalaureus*] bachelor of science

SBA *abbr* Small Business Administration

sc *abbr* **1** scene **2** science

Sc *symbol* scandium

SC *abbr* **1** South Carolina **2** supreme court

¹scab \'skab\ *n* **1** : scabies of domestic animals **2** : a crust of hardened blood forming over a wound **3** : a worker who replaces a striker or works under conditions not authorized by a union **4** : any of various bacterial or fungus plant diseases marked by crusted spots on stems or leaves — **scab·by** *adj*

²scab *vb* **scabbed; scab·bing** **1** : to become covered with a scab **2** : to work as a scab

scab·bard \'ska-bərd\ *n* : a sheath for the blade of a weapon (as a sword)

sca·bies \'skā-bēz\ *n* [L] : contagious itch or mange caused by mites living as parasites under the skin

sca·brous \'ska-brəs, 'skā-\ *adj* **1** : DIFFICULT, KNOTTY **2** : rough to the touch : SCALY, SCURFY ⟨a ∼ leaf⟩ **3** : dealing with suggestive, indecent, or scandalous themes; *also* : SQUALID

scad \'skad\ *n* : a large number or quantity — usu. used in pl.

scaf·fold \'ska-fəld, -ˌfōld\ *n* **1** : a raised platform for workers to sit or stand on **2** : a platform on which a criminal is executed (as by hanging)

scaf·fold·ing *n* : a system of scaffolds; *also* : materials for scaffolds

scal·a·wag *or* **scal·ly·wag** \'ska-li-ˌwag\ *n* : RASCAL

¹scald \'skȯld\ *vb* **1** : to burn with or as if with hot liquid or steam **2** : to heat to just below the boiling point

²scald *n* : a burn caused by scalding

¹scale \'skāl\ *n* **1** : either pan of a balance **2** : BALANCE — usu. used in pl. **3** : a weighing instrument

²scale *vb* **scaled; scal·ing** : WEIGH

³scale *n* **1** : one of the small thin plates that cover the body esp. of a fish or reptile **2** : a thin plate or flake **3** : a thin coating, layer, or incrustation **4** : SCALE INSECT — **scaled** \'skāld\ *adj* — **scale·less** \'skāl-ləs\ *adj* — **scaly** *adj*

⁴scale *vb* **scaled; scal·ing** : to strip of scales

⁵scale *n* [ME, fr. LL *scala* ladder, staircase, fr. L *scalae*, pl., stairs, rungs, ladder] **1** : something divided into regular spaces as a help in drawing or measuring **2** : a graduated series **3** : the size of a sample (as a model) in proportion to the size of the actual thing **4** : a standard of estimation or judgment **5** : a series of musical tones going up or down in pitch according to a specified scheme

⁶scale *vb* **scaled; scal·ing** **1** : to climb by or as if by a ladder **2** : to arrange in a graded series

scale insect *n* : any of numerous small insects with wingless scale-covered females that are related to aphids and feed on and are often pests of plants

scale·pan \'skāl-ˌpan\ *n* : ¹SCALE 1

scal·lion \'skal-yən\ *n* [ultim. fr. L *ascalonia (caepa)* onion of Ascalon (seaport in Palestine)] : an onion without an enlarged bulb

¹**scal·lop** \'skä-ləp, 'ska-\ *n* **1** : any of numerous marine bivalve mollusks with radially ridged shells; *also* : a large edible muscle of this mollusk **2** : one of a continuous series of rounded projections forming an edge

²**scallop** *vb* **1** : to bake in a casserole ⟨∼ed potatoes⟩ **2** : to shape, cut, or finish in scallops ⟨∼ed edges⟩

¹**scalp** \'skalp\ *n* : the part of the skin and flesh of the head usu. covered with hair

²**scalp** *vb* **1** : to remove the scalp from **2** : to resell at greatly increased prices ⟨∼ tickets⟩ — **scalp·er** *n*

scal·pel \'skal-pəl\ *n* : a small straight knife with a thin blade used esp. in surgery

scam \'skam\ *n* : a fraudulent or deceptive act or operation

scamp \'skamp\ *n* : RASCAL

scam·per \'skam-pər\ *vb* : to run nimbly and playfully — **scamper** *n*

scam·pi \'skam-pē\ *n, pl* **scampi** [It] : a usu. large shrimp; *also* : large shrimp prepared with a garlic-flavored sauce

¹**scan** \'skan\ *vb* **scanned**; **scan·ning** **1** : to read (verses) so as to show metrical structure **2** : to examine closely **3** : to input or examine systematically in order to obtain data esp. for display or storage **4** : to make a scan of (as the human body) — **scan·ner** *n*

²**scan** *n* **1** : the act or process of scanning **2** : a picture of the distribution of radioactive material in something; *also* : an image of a bodily part produced (as by computer) by combining radiographic data obtained from several angles or sections

Scand *abbr* Scandinavia

scan·dal \'skan-dᵊl\ *n* [ME, fr. LL *scandalum* stumbling block, offense, fr. Gk *skandalon*] **1** : DISGRACE, DISHONOR **2** : malicious gossip : SLANDER — **scan·dal·ize** *vb* — **scan·dal·ous** *adj* — **scan·dal·ous·ly** *adv*

scan·dal·mon·ger \-ˌmən-gər, -ˌmäŋ-\ *n* : a person who circulates scandal

Scan·di·na·vian \ˌskan-də-'nā-vē-ən\ *n* : a native or inhabitant of Scandinavia — **Scandinavian** *adj*

scan·di·um \'skan-dē-əm\ *n* : a silvery-white metallic chemical element

scan·ner \'ska-nər\ *n* **1** : a radio receiver that sequentially scans a range of frequencies for a signal **2** : a device that scans an image or document esp. for use or storage on a computer

¹**scant** \'skant\ *adj* **1** : barely sufficient **2** : having scarcely enough ♦ *Synonyms* SCANTY, SKIMPY, MEAGER, SPARSE, EXIGUOUS

²**scant** *vb* **1** : SKIMP **2** : STINT

scant·ling \'skant-liŋ\ *n* : a small piece of lumber (as an upright in a house)

scanty \'skan-tē\ *adj* **scant·i·er; -est** : barely sufficient : SCANT — **scant·i·ly** \'skan-tə-lē\ *adv* — **scant·i·ness** \-tē-nəs\ *n*

scape·goat \'skāp-ˌgōt\ *n* : one that bears the blame for others

scape·grace \-ˌgrās\ *n* [*scape* (escape)] : an incorrigible rascal

scap·u·la \'ska-pyə-lə\ *n, pl* **-lae** \-ˌlē\ *or* **-las** [L] : SHOULDER BLADE

scap·u·lar \-lər\ *n* : a pair of small cloth squares worn on the breast and back under the clothing esp. for religious purposes

scar \'skär\ *n* : a mark left after injured tissue has healed — **scar** *vb*

scar·ab \'ska-rəb\ *n* [MF *scarabee,* fr. L *scarabaeus*] : any of a family of large stout beetles; *also* : an ornament (as a gem) representing such a beetle

scarce \'skers\ *adj* **scarc·er; scarc·est** **1** : deficient in quantity or number : not plentiful **2** : intentionally absent ⟨made himself ∼ at inspection time⟩ — **scar·ci·ty** \'sker-sə-tē\ *n*

scarce·ly \-lē\ *adv* **1** : BARELY **2** : almost not **3** : very probably not

¹**scare** \'sker\ *vb* **scared; scar·ing** : FRIGHTEN, STARTLE

²**scare** *n* : FRIGHT — **scary** *adj*

scare·crow \'sker-ˌkrō\ *n* : a crude figure set up to scare birds away from crops

¹**scarf** \'skärf\ *n, pl* **scarves** \'skärvz\ *or* **scarfs** **1** : a broad band (as of cloth) worn about the shoulders, around the neck, over the head, or about the waist **2** : a long narrow cloth cover for a table or dresser top

²**scarf** *vb* [alter. of earlier *scoff* eat greedily] : to eat greedily

scar·i·fy \'sker-ə-ˌfī\ *vb* **-fied; -fy·ing** **1** : to make scratches or small cuts in ⟨∼ skin for vaccination⟩ ⟨∼ seeds to help them germinate⟩ **2** : to lacerate the feelings of **3** : to break up and loosen the surface of (as a road) — **scar·i·fi·ca·tion** \ˌskar-ə-fə-'kā-shən\ *n*

scar·let \'skär-lət\ *n* : a bright red color — **scarlet** *adj*

scarlet fever *n* : an acute contagious disease marked by fever, sore throat, and red rash and caused by certain streptococci

scarp \'skärp\ *n* : a line of cliffs produced by faulting or erosion

scath·ing \'skā-thiŋ\ *adj* : bitterly severe ⟨a ∼ condemnation⟩

scat·o·log·i·cal \ˌska-tə-'lä-ji-kəl\ *adj* : concerned with obscene matters

scat·ter \'ska-tər\ *vb* **1** : to distribute or strew about irregularly **2** : DISPERSE

scat·ter·brain \'ska-tər-ˌbrān\ *n* : a silly careless person — **scat·ter·brained** \-ˌbrānd\ *adj*

scav·enge \'ska-vənj\ *vb* **scav·enged; scav·eng·ing** : to work or function as a scavenger

scav·en·ger \'ska-vən-jər\ *n* [alter. of earlier *scavager,* fr. AF *scawageour* collector of scavage (duty imposed on nonresident street merchants), fr. *skawage* scavage, fr. MF dial. (Flanders) *escauver* to inspect, fr. MD *scouwen*] : a person or animal that collects, eats, or disposes of refuse or waste

sce·nar·io \sə-'ner-ē-ˌō\ *n, pl* **-i·os** : the plot or outline of a dramatic work; *also* : an account of a possible action

scene \'sēn\ *n* [MF, stage, fr. L *scena, scaena* stage, scene, prob. fr. Etruscan, fr. Gk *skēnē* temporary shelter, tent, building forming the background for a dramatic performance, stage] **1** : a division of one act of a play **2** : a single situation or sequence in a play or motion picture **3** : a stage setting **4** : VIEW, PROSPECT **5** : the place of an occurrence or action **6** : a display of strong feeling and esp. anger **7** : a sphere of activity ⟨the fashion ∼⟩ — **sce·nic** \'sē-nik\ *adj*

scen·ery \'sē-nə-rē\ *n, pl* **-er·ies** **1** : the painted scenes or hangings and accessories used on a theater stage **2** : a picturesque view or landscape

¹**scent** \'sent\ *n* **1** : ODOR, SMELL **2** : sense of smell **3** : course of pursuit : TRACK **4** : PERFUME 2 — **scent·ed** \'sen-təd\ *adj* — **scent·less** *adj*

²**scent** *vb* **1** : SMELL **2** : to imbue or fill with odor

scep·ter \'sep-tər\ *n* : a staff borne by a sovereign as an emblem of authority

sceptic *var of* SKEPTIC

scep·tre *Brit var of* SCEPTER

sch *abbr* school

¹**sched·ule** \'ske-jül, *esp Brit* 'she-dyül\ *n* **1** : a list of items or details **2** : TIMETABLE

²**schedule** *vb* **sched·uled; sched·ul·ing** **1** : to appoint, assign, or designate for a fixed time **2** : to make a schedule of; *also* : to enter on a schedule

sche·ma \'skē-mə\ *n, pl* **sche·ma·ta** \-mə-tə\ *also* **sche·mas** : a diagrammatic presentation or plan : OUTLINE

sche·mat·ic \ski-'ma-tik\ *adj* : of or relating to a scheme or diagram : DIAGRAMMATIC — **schematic** *n* — **sche·mat·i·cal·ly** \-ti-k(ə-)lē\ *adv*

¹**scheme** \'skēm\ *n* **1** : a plan for doing something; *esp* : a crafty plot **2** : a systematic design ⟨a color ∼⟩

²**scheme** *vb* **schemed; schem·ing** : to form a plot : INTRIGUE — **schem·er** *n*

schil·ling \'shi-liŋ\ *n* — see MONEY table

schism \'si-zəm, 'ski-\ *n* **1** : DIVISION, SPLIT; *also* : DISCORD, DISSENSION **2** : a formal division in or separation from a religious body

schis·mat·ic \siz-'ma-tik, ski-\ *n* : one who creates or takes part in schism — **schismatic** *adj*

schist \'shist\ *n* : a metamorphic crystalline rock

schizo·phre·nia \ˌskit-sə-'frē-nē-ə\ *n* [NL, fr. Gk *schizein* to split + *phrēn* diaphragm, mind] : a psychotic mental illness that is characterized by a distorted view of the real world, by a greatly reduced ability to carry out one's daily tasks, and by abnormal ways of thinking, feeling, perceiving, and behaving — **schiz·oid** \'skit-ˌsȯid\ *adj or n* — **schizo·phren·ic** \ˌskit-sə-'fre-nik\ *adj or n*

schle·miel *also* **shle·miel** \shlə-'mēl\ *n* : an unlucky bungler : CHUMP

schlep *or* **schlepp** \'shlep\ *vb* [Yiddish *shlepn*] **1** : DRAG, HAUL **2** : to move slowly or awkwardly

schlock \'shläk\ *or* **schlocky** \'shlä-kē\ *adj* : of low quality or value — **schlock** *n*

schlub *also* **shlub** \'shləb\ *n* [Yiddish *zhlob, zhlub* yokel, boor] *slang* : a stupid, ineffectual, or unattractive person

schmaltz *also* **schmalz** \'shmȯlts, 'shmälts\ *n* [Yiddish *shmalts*, lit., rendered fat] : sentimental or florid music or art — **schmaltzy** *adj*

schmooze *or* **shmooze** \'shmüz\ *vb* : to chat informally esp. to gain favor — **schmooze** *n*

schnapps \'shnaps\ *n, pl* **schnapps** : a liquor (as gin) of high alcoholic content

schnau·zer \'shnaů-zər, 'shnaůt-sər\ *n* [G, fr. *Schnauze* snout] : a dog of any of three breeds that are characterized by a wiry coat, long head, pointed ears, heavy eyebrows, and long hair on the muzzle

schol·ar \'skä-lər\ *n* **1** : STUDENT, PUPIL **2** : a learned person : SAVANT — **schol·ar·ly** *adj*

schol·ar·ship \-ˌship\ *n* **1** : the qualities or learning of a scholar **2** : money awarded to a student to help pay for further education

scho·las·tic \skə-'las-tik\ *adj* : of or relating to schools, scholars, or scholarship

¹school \'skül\ *n* **1** : an institution for teaching and learning; *also* : the pupils in attendance **2** : a body of persons of like opinions or beliefs ⟨the radical ∼⟩

²school *vb* : TEACH, TRAIN, DRILL

³school *n* : a large number of one kind of water animal swimming and feeding together

school·boy \-ˌbȯi\ *n* : a boy attending school

school·fel·low \-ˌfe-lō\ *n* : SCHOOLMATE

school·girl \-ˌgərl\ *n* : a girl attending school

school·house \-ˌhaůs\ *n* : a building used as a school

school·marm \-ˌmärm\ *or* **school·ma'am** \-ˌmäm, -ˌmam\ *n* **1** : a woman who is a schoolteacher **2** : a person who exhibits characteristics popularly attributed to schoolteachers

school·mas·ter \-ˌmas-tər\ *n* : a man who is a schoolteacher

school·mate \-ˌmāt\ *n* : a school companion

school·mis·tress \-ˌmis-trəs\ *n* : a woman who is a schoolteacher

school·room \-ˌrüm, -ˌrům\ *n* : CLASSROOM

school·teach·er \-ˌtē-chər\ *n* : one who teaches in a school

schoo·ner \'skü-nər\ *n* : a fore-and-aft rigged sailing ship

schtick *var of* SHTICK

schuss \'shůs, 'shüs\ *vb* [G *Schuss*, n., lit., shot] : to ski down a slope at high speed — **schuss** *n*

sci *abbr* science; scientific

sci·at·i·ca \sī-'a-ti-kə\ *n* : pain in the region of the hips or along the course of the nerve at the back of the thigh

sci·ence \'sī-əns\ *n* [ME, fr. AF, fr. L *scientia*, fr. *scient-, sciens* having knowledge, fr. prp. of *scire* to know] **1** : an area of knowledge that is an object of study; *esp* : NATURAL SCIENCE **2** : knowledge covering general truths or the operation of general laws especially as obtained and tested through the scientific method — **sci·en·tif·ic** \ˌsī-ən-'ti-fik\ *adj* — **sci·en·tif·i·cal·ly** \-fi-k(ə-)lē\ *adv* — **sci·en·tist** \'sī-ən-tist\ *n*

science fiction *n* : fiction dealing principally with the impact of actual or imagined science on society or individuals

scientific method *n* : the rules and methods for the pursuit of knowledge involving the finding and stating of a problem, the collection of facts through observation and experiment, and the making and testing of ideas that need to be proven right or wrong

scim·i·tar \'si-mə-tər\ *n* : a curved sword used chiefly by Arabs and Turks

scin·til·la \sin-'ti-lə\ *n* : SPARK, TRACE

scin·til·late \'sin-tə-ˌlāt\ *vb* **-lat·ed; -lat·ing** : SPARKLE, GLEAM — **scin·til·la·tion** \ˌsin-tə-'lā-shən\ *n*

sci·on \'sī-ən\ *n* **1** : a shoot of a plant joined to a stock in grafting **2** : DESCENDANT

scis·sors \'si-zərz\ *n pl* : a cutting instrument like shears but usu. smaller

scissors kick *n* : a swimming kick in which the legs move like scissors

sclero·der·ma \ˌskler-ə-'dər-mə\ *n* : a chronic disease characterized by the usu. progressive hardening and thickening of the skin

scle·ro·sis \sklə-'rō-səs\ *n* : abnormal hardening of tissue (as of an artery); *also* : a disease characterized by this — **scle·rot·ic** \-'rä-tik\ *adj*

scoff \'skäf\ *vb* : MOCK, JEER — **scoff·er** *n*

scoff·law \-ˌlȯ\ *n* : a contemptuous law violator

¹scold \'skōld\ *n* : a person who scolds

²scold *vb* : to censure severely or angrily

sconce \'skäns\ *n* : a candlestick or an electric light fixture fastened to a wall

scone \'skōn, 'skän\ *n* : a biscuit (as of oatmeal) baked on a griddle

¹scoop \'sküp\ *n* **1** : a large shovel; *also* : a utensil with a shovellike or rounded end **2** : the amount contained by a scoop **3** : an act of scooping **4** : information of immediate interest

²scoop *vb* **1** : to take out or up or empty with or as if with a scoop **2** : to make hollow **3** : to report a news item in advance of

scoot \'sküt\ *vb* : to move swiftly

scoot·er \'skü-tər\ *n* **1** : a child's vehicle consisting of a narrow board mounted between two wheels tandem with an upright steering handle attached to the front wheel **2** : MOTOR SCOOTER

¹scope \'skōp\ *n* [It *scopo* purpose, goal, fr. Gk *skopos*] **1** : space or opportunity for action or thought **2** : extent covered : RANGE

²scope *n* : an instrument (as a microscope or telescope) for viewing

scorch \'skȯrch\ *vb* : to burn the surface of; *also* : to dry or shrivel with heat ⟨∼ed lawns⟩

¹score \'skȯr\ *n, pl* **scores** *or pl* **score** : TWENTY **2** : CUT, SCRATCH, SLASH **3** : a record of points made (as in a game) **4** : DEBT **5** : REASON, GROUND **6** : the music of a composition or arrangement with different parts indicated **7** : success in obtaining something (as drugs) esp. illegally

²score *vb* **scored; scor·ing** **1** : RECORD **2** : to keep score in a game **3** : to mark with lines, grooves, scratches, or notches **4** : to gain or tally in or as if in a game ⟨*scored* a point⟩ **5** : to assign a grade or score to ⟨∼ the tests⟩ **6** : to compose a score for **7** : SUCCEED **8** : ACQUIRE ⟨*scored* tickets to the game⟩ — **score·less** *adj* — **scor·er** *n*

¹scorn \'skȯrn\ *n* : an emotion involving both anger and disgust : CONTEMPT — **scorn·ful** \-fəl\ *adj* — **scorn·ful·ly** *adv*

²scorn *vb* : to hold in contempt : DISDAIN — **scorn·er** *n*

Scor·pio \'skȯr-pē-ˌō\ *n* [L, lit., scorpion] **1** : a zodiacal constellation between Libra and Sagittarius usu. pictured as a scorpion **2** : the 8th sign of the zodiac in astrology; *also* : one born under this sign

scor·pi·on \'skȯr-pē-ən\ *n* : any of an order of arthropods related to the spiders that have a poisonous stinger at the tip of a long jointed tail

¹Scot \'skät\ *n* : a native or inhabitant of Scotland

²Scot *abbr* Scotland; Scottish

Scotch \'skäch\ *n* **1** : SCOTS **2** **Scotch** *pl* : the people of Scotland **3** : a whiskey distilled in Scotland esp. from malted barley — **Scotch** *adj* — **Scotch·man** \-mən\ *n* — **Scotch·wom·an** \-ˌwů-mən\ *n*

Scotch bonnet *n* : a small roundish very hot chili pepper esp. of the Caribbean

Scotch pine *n* : a pine that is naturalized in the U.S. from northern Europe and Asia and is a valuable timber tree

Scotch terrier *n* : SCOTTISH TERRIER

scot–free \'skät-'frē\ *adj* : free from obligation, harm, or penalty

Scots \'skäts\ *n* : the English language of Scotland

Scots·man \'skäts-mən\ *n* : SCOT

Scots·wom·an \-ˌwů-mən\ *n* : a woman who is a Scot

Scot·tie \'skä-tē\ *n* : SCOTTISH TERRIER

Scot·tish \'skä-tish\ *adj* : of, relating to, or characteristic of Scotland, Scots, or the Scots

Scottish terrier *n* : any of an old Scottish breed of terrier with short legs, a long head with small erect ears, a broad deep chest, and a thick rough coat

scoun·drel \'skaun-drəl\ *n* : a disreputable person : VILLAIN

¹**scour** \'skaů(-ə)r\ *vb* **1** : to rub (as with a gritty substance) in order to clean **2** : to cleanse by or as if by rubbing

²**scour** *vb* **1** : to move rapidly through : RUSH **2** : to examine thoroughly

¹**scourge** \'skərj\ *n* **1** : LASH, WHIP **2** : PUNISHMENT; *also* : a cause of affliction (as a plague)

²**scourge** *vb* **scourged; scourg·ing 1** : LASH, FLOG **2** : to punish severely

¹**scout** \'skaůt\ *vb* [ME, fr. AF *escuter* to listen, fr. L *auscultare*] **1** : to look around : RECONNOITER **2** : to inspect or observe to get information

²**scout** *n* **1** : a person sent out to get information; *also* : a soldier, airplane, or ship sent out to reconnoiter **2** : BOY SCOUT **3** : GIRL SCOUT — **scout·mas·ter** \-,mas-tər\ *n*

³**scout** *vb* : SCORN, SCOFF

scow \'skaů\ *n* : a large flat-bottomed boat with square ends

scowl \'skaů(-ə)l\ *vb* : to make a frowning expression of displeasure — **scowl** *n*

SCPO *abbr* senior chief petty officer

scrab·ble \'skra-bəl\ *vb* **scrab·bled; scrab·bling 1** : SCRAPE, SCRATCH **2** : CLAMBER, SCRAMBLE **3** : to work hard and long **4** : SCRIBBLE — **scrabble** *n* — **scrab·bler** *n*

scrag·gly \'skra-glē\ *adj* : IRREGULAR; *also* : RAGGED, UNKEMPT ⟨a ∼ beard⟩

scram \'skram\ *vb* **scrammed; scram·ming** : to go away at once

scram·ble \'skram-bəl\ *vb* **scram·bled; scram·bling 1** : to clamber clumsily around **2** : to struggle for or as if for possession of something **3** : to spread irregularly **4** : to mix together **5** : to cook (eggs) by stirring during frying — **scramble** *n*

¹**scrap** \'skrap\ *n* **1** : FRAGMENT, PIECE **2** : discarded material : REFUSE

²**scrap** *vb* **scrapped; scrap·ping 1** : to make into scrap ⟨∼ a battleship⟩ **2** : to get rid of as useless ⟨*scrapped* the plans⟩

³**scrap** *n* : FIGHT

⁴**scrap** *vb* **scrapped; scrap·ping** : FIGHT, QUARREL — **scrap·per** *n*

scrap·book \'skrap-,bůk\ *n* : a blank book in which mementos are kept

¹**scrape** \'skrāp\ *vb* **scraped; scrap·ing 1** : to remove by drawing a knife over; *also* : to clean or smooth by rubbing off the covering **2** : to damage or injure the surface of by contact with something rough **3** : to draw across a surface with a grating sound **4** : to get together (money) by strict economy **5** : to get along with difficulty ⟨barely *scraping* by on her income⟩ — **scrap·er** *n*

²**scrape** *n* **1** : the act or the effect of scraping **2** : a bow accompanied by a drawing back of the foot **3** : an unpleasant predicament

scra·pie \'skrā-pē\ *n* : a usu. fatal degenerative disease of the brain esp. of sheep that is related to mad cow disease

¹**scrap·py** \'skra-pē\ *adj* **scrap·pi·er; -est** : DISCONNECTED, FRAGMENTARY

²**scrappy** *adj* **scrap·pi·er; -est 1** : QUARRELSOME **2** : having an aggressive and determined spirit ⟨a ∼ competitor⟩

¹**scratch** \'skrach\ *vb* **1** : to scrape, dig, or rub with or as if with claws or nails ⟨a dog ∼*ing* at the door⟩ ⟨∼*ed* my arm⟩ **2** : SCRAPE **3** ⟨∼*ed* his nails across the blackboard⟩ **3** : SCRAPE **4** **4** : to cancel or erase by or as if by drawing a line through **5** : to withdraw from a contest — **scratchy** *adj* — **scratch one's head** : to become confused or perplexed

²**scratch** *n* **1** : a mark or injury made by or as if by scratching; *also* : a sound so made **2** : the starting line in a race — **from scratch** : with no steps completed or ingredients prepared ahead of time ⟨built from ∼⟩

³**scratch** *adj* **1** : made or done by chance ⟨a ∼ hit⟩ **2** : made as or used for a trial attempt ⟨∼ paper⟩

¹**scrawl** \'skról\ *vb* : to write hastily and carelessly — **scrawl** *n*

scraw·ny \'skró-nē\ *adj* **scraw·ni·er; -est** : very thin : SKINNY

¹**scream** \'skrēm\ *vb* : to cry out loudly and shrilly

²**scream** *n* : a loud shrill cry

scream·ing \'skrē-miŋ\ *adj* : so striking as to attract notice as if by screaming ⟨∼ headlines⟩

screech \'skrēch\ *vb* : SHRIEK — **screech** *n* — **screechy** \'skrē-chē\ *adj*

screech·ing \'skrē-chiŋ\ *adj* : ABRUPT ⟨came to a ∼ halt⟩

¹**screen** \'skrēn\ *n* **1** : a device or partition used to hide, restrain, protect, or decorate ⟨a window ∼⟩; *also* : something that shelters, protects, or conceals **2** : a sieve or perforated material for separating finer from coarser parts (as of sand) **3** : a surface on which an image is made to appear (as in television); *also* : the information displayed on a computer screen at one time **4** : the motion-picture industry

²**screen** *vb* **1** : to shield with or as if with a screen **2** : to separate with a screen; *also* : to select or categorize methodically ⟨∼ contestants⟩ **3** : to present (as a motion picture) on the screen

screen·ing \'skrē-niŋ\ *n* **1** : metal or plastic mesh (as for window screens) **2** : a showing of a motion picture

screen saver *n* : a computer program that displays something (as images) on the screen of a computer that is on but not in use

¹**screw** \'skrü\ *n* [ME, fr. MF *escroe* female screw, nut, fr. ML *scrofa*, fr. L, sow] **1** : a machine consisting of a solid cylinder with a spiral groove around it and a corresponding hollow cylinder into which it fits **2** : a naillike metal piece with a spiral groove and a head with a slot that is inserted into material by rotating and is used to fasten pieces of solid material together **3** : PROPELLER

²**screw** *vb* **1** : to fasten or close by means of a screw **2** : to operate or adjust by means of a screw **3** : to move or cause to move spirally; *also* : to close or set in position by such an action

screw·ball \'skrü-,ból\ *n* **1** : a baseball pitch breaking in a direction opposite to a curve **2** : a whimsical, eccentric, or crazy person

screw·driv·er \-,drī-vər\ *n* **1** : a tool for turning screws **2** : a drink made of vodka and orange juice

screw·worm \'skrü-,wərm\ *n* : an American blowfly of warm regions whose larva matures in wounds or sores of mammals and may cause disease or death; *esp* : its larva

screwy \'skrü-ē\ *adj* **screw·i·er; -est 1** : crazily absurd, eccentric, or unusual **2** : CRAZY, INSANE

scrib·ble \'skri-bəl\ *vb* **scrib·bled; scrib·bling** : to write hastily or carelessly — **scribble** *n* — **scrib·bler** *n*

scribe \'skrīb\ *n* **1** : a scholar of Jewish law in New Testament times **2** : a person whose business is the copying of writing **3** : JOURNALIST

scrim \'skrim\ *n* : a light loosely woven cotton or linen cloth

scrim·mage \'skri-mij\ *n* : the play between two football teams beginning with the snap of the ball; *also* : practice play between two teams — **scrimmage** *vb*

scrimp \'skrimp\ *vb* : to economize greatly ⟨∼ and save⟩

scrim·shaw \'skrim-,shó\ *n* : carved or engraved articles made orig. by American whalers usu. from baleen or whale ivory — **scrimshaw** *vb*

scrip \'skrip\ *n* **1** : a certificate showing its holder is entitled to something (as stock or land) **2** : paper money issued for temporary use in an emergency

¹**script** \'skript\ *n* **1** : written matter (as lines for a play or broadcast) **2** : HANDWRITING

²**script** *abbr* scripture

scrip·ture \'skrip-chər\ *n* **1** *cap* : the books of the Bible — often used in pl. **2** : the sacred writings of a religion — **scrip·tur·al** \'skrip-chə-rəl\ *adj* — **scrip·tur·al·ly** *adv*

scriv·en·er \'skri-və-nər\ *n* : SCRIBE, COPYIST, WRITER

scrod \'skräd\ *n* [prob. fr. Brit. dial. (Cornwall) *scrawed*, pp. of *scraw, scrawl* to split, salt, and dry (young fish)] : a young fish (as a cod or haddock); *esp* : one split and boned for cooking

scrof·u·la \'skró-fyə-lə\ *n* : tuberculosis of lymph nodes esp. in the neck

¹**scroll** \'skrōl\ *n* : a roll of paper or parchment for writing

a document; *also* : a spiral or coiled ornamental form suggesting a loosely or partly rolled scroll

²**scroll** *vb* : to move or cause to move text or graphics up, down, or across a display screen

scroll saw *n* 1 : FRETSAW 2 : a machine saw with a narrow vertically reciprocating blade for cutting curved lines or openwork

scro·tum \'skrō-təm\ *n, pl* **scro·ta** \-tə\ *or* **scrotums** [L] : a pouch that in most male mammals contains the testes

scrounge \'skrau̇nj\ *vb* **scrounged; scroung·ing** : to collect by or as if by foraging

¹**scrub** \'skrəb\ *n* 1 : a thick growth of stunted trees or shrubs; *also* : an area of land covered with scrub 2 : an inferior domestic animal 3 : a person of insignificant size or standing 4 : a player not on the first team — **scrub** *adj* — **scrub·by** *adj*

²**scrub** *vb* **scrubbed; scrub·bing** 1 : to clean or wash by rubbing ⟨∼ clothes⟩ ⟨∼ out a spot⟩ 2 : CANCEL

³**scrub** *n* 1 : an act or instance of scrubbing ⟨gave the clothes a good ∼⟩ 2 *pl* : loose-fitting clothing worn by hospital staff ⟨surgical ∼s⟩

scrub·ber \'skrə-bər\ *n* : one that scrubs; *esp* : an apparatus for removing impurities esp. from gases

scruff \'skrəf\ *n* : the loose skin of the back of the neck : NAPE

scruffy \'skrə-fē\ *adj* **scruff·i·er; -est** : UNKEMPT, SLOVENLY

scrump·tious \'skrəmp-shəs\ *adj* : DELIGHTFUL, EXCELLENT; *esp* : DELICIOUS — **scrump·tious·ly** *adv*

scrunch·ie *or* **scrunchy** \'skrən-chē, 'skrun-\ *n* : a fabric-covered elastic for the hair

¹**scru·ple** \'skrü-pəl\ *n* [ME *scrupil, scriple,* fr. AF *scruble,* fr. L *scrupulus,* dim. of *scrupus* source of uneasiness, lit., sharp stone] 1 : a point of conscience or honor 2 : hesitation due to ethical considerations

²**scruple** *vb* **scru·pled; scru·pling** : to be reluctant on grounds of conscience : HESITATE

scru·pu·lous \'skrü-pyə-ləs\ *adj* 1 : having moral integrity 2 : PAINSTAKING — **scru·pu·lous·ly** *adv* — **scru·pu·lous·ness** *n*

scru·ti·nise *Brit var of* SCRUTINIZE

scru·ti·nize \'skrü-tə-ˌnīz\ *vb* **-nized; -niz·ing** : to examine closely

scru·ti·ny \'skrü-tə-nē\ *n, pl* **-nies** [L *scrutinium,* fr. *scrutari* to search, examine, prob. fr. *scruta* trash] : a careful looking over ♦ **Synonyms** INSPECTION, EXAMINATION, ANALYSIS

scu·ba \'skü-bə\ *n* [*self-contained underwater breathing apparatus*] : an apparatus for breathing while swimming underwater

scuba diver *n* : one who swims underwater with the aid of scuba gear

¹**scud** \'skəd\ *vb* **scud·ded; scud·ding** : to move speedily

²**scud** *n* : light clouds driven by the wind

¹**scuff** \'skəf\ *vb* 1 : to scrape the feet while walking : SHUFFLE 2 : to scratch or become scratched or worn away

²**scuff** *n* 1 : a mark or injury caused by scuffing 2 : a flat-soled slipper without heel strap

scuf·fle \'skə-fəl\ *vb* **scuf·fled; scuf·fling** 1 : to struggle confusedly at close quarters 2 : to shuffle one's feet — **scuffle** *n*

¹**scull** \'skəl\ *n* 1 : an oar for use in sculling; *also* : one of a pair of short oars for a single oarsman 2 : a racing shell propelled by one or two persons using sculls

²**scull** *vb* : to propel (a boat) by an oar over the stern

scul·lery \'skə-lə-rē\ *n, pl* **-ler·ies** [ME *squilerie, sculerie* department of household in charge of dishes, fr. AF *esquilerie,* fr. *escuele* bowl, fr. L *scutella* drinking bowl] : a small room near the kitchen used for cleaning dishes, cooking utensils, and vegetables

scul·lion \'skəl-yən\ *n* : a kitchen helper

sculpt \'skəlpt\ *vb* : CARVE, SCULPTURE

sculp·tor \'skəlp-tər\ *n* : a person who produces works of sculpture

¹**sculp·ture** \'skəlp-chər\ *n* : the act, process, or art of carving or molding material (as stone, wood, or plastic); *also* : work produced this way — **sculp·tur·al** \'skəlp-chə-rəl\ *adj*

²**sculpture** *vb* **sculp·tured; sculp·tur·ing** : to form or alter as or as if a work of sculpture

scum \'skəm\ *n* 1 : a slimy or filmy covering on the surface of a liquid 2 : waste matter 3 : RABBLE

scup·per \'skə-pər\ *n* [ME *skopper-,* perh. fr. AF **escopoir,* fr. *escopir* to spit out] : an opening in the side of a ship through which water on deck is drained overboard

scurf \'skərf\ *n* : thin dry scales of skin (as dandruff); *also* : a scaly deposit or covering — **scurfy** \'skər-fē\ *adj*

scur·ri·lous \'skər-ə-ləs\ *adj* : coarsely jesting : OBSCENE, VULGAR

scur·ry \'skər-ē\ *vb* **scur·ried; scur·ry·ing** : SCAMPER

¹**scur·vy** \'skər-vē\ *n* : a disease caused by a lack of vitamin C and characterized by spongy gums, loosened teeth, and bleeding under the skin

²**scurvy** *adj* : MEAN, CONTEMPTIBLE — **scur·vi·ly** \'skər-və-lē\ *adv*

scutch·eon \'skə-chən\ *n* : ESCUTCHEON

¹**scut·tle** \'skə-t³l\ *n* : a pail for carrying coal

¹**scuttle**

²**scuttle** *n* : a small opening with a lid esp. in the deck, side, or bottom of a ship

³**scuttle** *vb* **scut·tled; scut·tling** : to cut a hole in the deck, side, or bottom of (a ship) in order to sink

⁴**scuttle** *vb* **scut·tled; scut·tling** : SCURRY, SCAMPER

scut·tle·butt \'skə-t³l-ˌbət\ *n* : GOSSIP

scythe \'sīth\ *n* : an implement for mowing (as grass or grain) by hand — **scythe** *vb*

SD *abbr* 1 South Dakota 2 special delivery

S Dak *abbr* South Dakota

SDI *abbr* Strategic Defense Initiative

Se *symbol* selenium

SE *abbr* southeast

sea \'sē\ *n* 1 : a large body of salt water 2 : OCEAN 3 : rough water; *also* : a large wave 4 : something likened to the sea esp. in vastness — **sea** *adj* — **at sea** : LOST, BEWILDERED

sea anemone *n* : any of numerous coelenterate polyps whose form, bright and varied colors, and cluster of tentacles superficially resemble a flower

sea·bird \'sē-ˌbərd\ *n* : a bird (as a gull) frequenting the open ocean

sea·board \-ˌbȯrd\ *n* : SEACOAST; *also* : the land bordering a coast

sea·borg·i·um \sē-'bȯr-gē-əm\ *n* : a short-lived radioactive chemical element produced artificially

sea·coast \-ˌkōst\ *n* : the shore of the sea

sea·far·er \-ˌfer-ər\ *n* : SEAMAN 1

sea·far·ing \-ˌfer-iŋ\ *n* : the use of the sea for travel or transportation — **seafaring** *adj*

sea·food \-ˌfüd\ *n* : edible marine fish and shellfish

sea·go·ing \-ˌgō-iŋ\ *adj* : OCEANGOING

sea·gull \'sē-ˌgəl\ *n* : GULL

sea horse *n* : any of a genus of small marine fishes with the head and forepart of the body sharply flexed like the head and neck of a horse

¹**seal** \'sēl\ *n, pl* **seals** *also* **seal** [ME *sele,* fr. OE *seolh*] 1 : any of numerous large carnivorous sea mammals occurring chiefly in cold regions and having limbs adapted for swimming 2 : the pelt of a seal

²**seal** *vb* : to hunt seals

³**seal** *n* [ME *sele, seel,* fr. AF *seal, sel,* fr. L *sigillum,* fr. dim. of *signum* sign, seal] 1 : GUARANTEE, PLEDGE 2 : a device having a raised design that can be stamped on clay or wax; *also* : the impression made by stamping with such a device 3 : something that seals or closes up ⟨safety ∼⟩

⁴**seal** *vb* 1 : to affix a seal to; *also* : AUTHENTICATE 2 : to fasten with or as if with a seal to prevent tampering 3 : to close or make secure against access, leakage, or passage 4 : to determine irrevocably ⟨∼ed his fate⟩

sea–lane \'sē-ˌlān\ *n* : an established sea route

seal·ant \'sē-lənt\ *n* : a sealing agent

seal·er \'sē-lər\ *n* : a coat applied to prevent subsequent coats of paint or varnish from sinking in

sea level *n* : the level of the surface of the sea esp. at its mean midway between mean high and low water

sea·lift \'sē-ˌlift\ *n* : transport of military personnel and equipment by ship

sea lion *n* : any of several large Pacific seals with small external ears

seal·skin \'sēl-ˌskin\ *n* **1** : ¹SEAL 2 **2** : a garment of sealskin

¹seam \'sēm\ *n* **1** : the line of junction of two edges and esp. of edges of fabric sewn together **2** : a layer of mineral matter **3** : WRINKLE

²seam *vb* **1** : to join by or as if by sewing **2** : WRINKLE, FURROW

sea·man \'sē-mən\ *n* **1** : one who assists in the handling of ships : MARINER **2** : an enlisted man in the navy ranking next below a petty officer third class

seaman apprentice *n* : an enlisted man in the navy ranking next below a seaman

seaman recruit *n* : an enlisted man of the lowest rank in the navy

sea·man·ship \'sē-mən-ˌship\ *n* : the art or skill of handling a ship

seam·less \'sēm-ləs\ *adj* : having no flaws or interruptions ⟨a ∼ transition⟩ — **seam·less·ly** *adv*

sea·mount \'sē-ˌmaunt\ *n* : an underwater mountain

seam·stress \'sēm-strəs\ *n* : a woman who does sewing

seamy \'sē-mē\ *adj* **seam·i·er; -est 1** : UNPLEASANT **2** : DEGRADED, SORDID ⟨the ∼ part of town⟩

sé·ance \'sā-ˌäns\ *n* [F] : a meeting to receive communications from spirits

sea·plane \'sē-ˌplān\ *n* : an airplane that can take off from and land on water

sea·port \-ˌpȯrt\ *n* : a port for oceangoing ships

sear \'sir\ *vb* **1** : WITHER **2** : to cook, burn, or scorch esp. on the surface; *also* : BRAND — **sear** *n*

¹search \'sərch\ *vb* [ME *cerchen,* fr. AF *cercher* to travel about, investigate, search, fr. LL *circare* to go about, fr. L *circum* round about] **1** : to look through in trying to find something **2** : SEEK **3** : PROBE — **search·er** *n*

²search *n* : the act of searching

search engine *n* : computer software or a Web site used to search data (as text or other Web sites) for specified information

search·light \-ˌlīt\ *n* : an apparatus for projecting a powerful beam of light; *also* : the light projected

sear·ing \'sir-iŋ\ *adj* : very sharp, harsh or intense ⟨∼ pain⟩ ⟨a ∼ review⟩

sea scallop *n* : a large scallop of the Atlantic coast of No. America that is harvested for food

sea·scape \'sē-ˌskāp\ *n* **1** : a view of the sea **2** : a picture representing a scene at or of the sea

sea·shell \'sē-ˌshel\ *n* : the shell of a marine animal and esp. a mollusk

sea·shore \-ˌshȯr\ *n* : the shore of a sea

sea·sick \-ˌsik\ *adj* : nauseated by or as if by the motion of a ship — **sea·sick·ness** *n*

sea·side \'sē-ˌsīd\ *n* : SEASHORE

¹sea·son \'sē-zən\ *n* [ME *sesoun,* fr. AF *seison* natural season, appropriate time, fr. L *sation-, satio* action of sowing, fr. *serere* to sow] **1** : one of the divisions of the year (as spring or summer) **2** : a period of the year associated with a particular activity, event, or holiday ⟨the Easter ∼⟩ ⟨hunting ∼⟩ — **sea·son·al** \-zə-nəl\ *adj* — **sea·son·al·ly** *adv*

²season *vb* **1** : to make pleasant to the taste by use of salt, pepper, or spices **2** : to make (as by aging or drying) suitable for use **3** : to accustom or habituate to something (as hardship) ✦ *Synonyms* HARDEN, INURE, ACCLIMATE, TOUGHEN — **sea·son·er** *n*

sea·son·able \'sē-zə-nə-bəl\ *adj* : occurring at a good or proper time ✦ *Synonyms* TIMELY, PROPITIOUS, OPPORTUNE — **sea·son·ably** \-blē\ *adv*

seasonal affective disorder *n* : depression that recurs as the days grow shorter during the fall and winter

sea·son·ing *n* : something that seasons : CONDIMENT

¹seat \'sēt\ *n* **1** : a chair, bench, or stool for sitting on **2** : a place which serves as a capital or center

²seat *vb* **1** : to place in or on a seat **2** : to provide seats for

seat belt *n* : straps designed to hold a person in a seat

SEATO \'sē-ˌtō\ *abbr* Southeast Asia Treaty Organization

seat–of–the–pants *adj* : employing or based on personal experience, judgment, and effort rather than technological aids ⟨∼ navigation⟩

sea turtle *n* : any of two families of marine turtles that have the feet modified into paddles

sea urchin *n* : any of numerous spiny marine echinoderms having thin brittle globular shells

sea·wall \'sē-ˌwȯl\ *n* : an embankment to protect the shore from erosion

¹sea·ward \'sē-wərd\ *n* : the direction or side away from land and toward the open sea

²seaward *also* **sea·wards** \-wərdz\ *adv* : toward the sea

³seaward *adj* **1** : directed or situated toward the sea **2** : coming from the sea

sea·wa·ter \'sē-ˌwȯ-tər, -ˌwä-\ *n* : water in or from the sea

sea·way \-ˌwā\ *n* : an inland waterway that admits ocean shipping

sea·weed \-ˌwēd\ *n* : a marine alga (as a kelp); *also* : a mass of marine algae

sea·wor·thy \-ˌwər-thē\ *adj* : fit for a sea voyage ⟨a ∼ ship⟩

se·ba·ceous \si-'bā-shəs\ *adj* : of, relating to, or secreting fatty material

sec *abbr* **1** second; secondary **2** secretary **3** section **4** [L *secundum*] according to

SEC *abbr* Securities and Exchange Commission

se·cede \si-'sēd\ *vb* **se·ced·ed; se·ced·ing** : to withdraw from an organized body and esp. from a political body

se·ces·sion \si-'se-shən\ *n* : the act of seceding — **se·ces·sion·ist** *n*

se·clude \si-'klüd\ *vb* **se·clud·ed; se·clud·ing** : to keep or shut away from others

se·clu·sion \si-'klü-zhən\ *n* : the act of secluding : the state of being secluded — **se·clu·sive** \-siv\ *adj*

¹sec·ond \'se-kənd\ *adj* [ME, fr. AF *secund,* fr. L *secundus* second, following, favorable, fr. *sequi* to follow] **1** : being number two in a countable series **2** : next after the first **3** : ALTERNATE ⟨every ∼ year⟩ — **second** *or* **sec·ond·ly** *adv*

²second *n* **1** : one that is second **2** : one who assists another (as in a duel) **3** : an inferior or flawed article (as of) **4** : the second forward gear in a motor vehicle

³second *n* [ME *secounde,* fr. ML *secunda,* fr. L, fem. of *secundus* second; fr. its being the second division of a unit into 60 parts, as a minute is the first] **1** : the 60th part of a minute of time or angular measure **2** : an instant of time

⁴second *vb* **1** : to encourage or give support to **2** : to act as a second to **3** : to support (a motion) by adding one's voice to that of a proposer

¹sec·ond·ary \'se-kən-ˌder-ē\ *adj* **1** : second in rank, value, or occurrence : LESSER **2** : belonging to a second or later stage of development **3** : coming after the primary or elementary ⟨∼ schools⟩ ✦ *Synonyms* SUBORDINATE, COLLATERAL, DEPENDENT

²secondary *n, pl* **-ar·ies** : the defensive backfield of a football team

secondary sex characteristic *n* : a physical characteristic that appears in members of one sex at puberty or in seasonal breeders at breeding season and is not directly concerned with reproduction

second fiddle *n* : one that plays a supporting or subservient role

sec·ond–guess \ˌse-kənd-'ges\ *vb* **1** : to think out other strategies or explanations for after the event **2** : to seek to anticipate or predict

sec·ond·hand \-'hand\ *adj* **1** : not original **2** : not new : USED ⟨∼ clothes⟩ **3** : dealing in used goods

secondhand smoke *n* : tobacco smoke that is exhaled by smokers or is given off by burning tobacco and is inhaled by persons nearby

second lieutenant *n* : a commissioned officer (as in the army) ranking next below a first lieutenant

sec·ond–rate \ˌse-kənd-'rāt\ *adj* : INFERIOR

sec·ond–string \'se-kənd-'striŋ\ *adj* : being a substitute (as on a team)

se·cre·cy \'sē-krə-sē\ *n, pl* **-cies 1** : the habit or practice of being secretive **2** : the condition of being hidden or concealed

¹**se·cret** \'sē-krət\ *adj* **1** : HIDDEN, CONCEALED ⟨a ∼ staircase⟩ **2** : COVERT, STEALTHY; *also* : engaged in detecting or spying ⟨a ∼ agent⟩ **3** : kept from general knowledge — **se·cret·ly** *adv*

²**secret** *n* **1** : MYSTERY **2** : something kept from the knowledge of others

sec·re·tar·i·at \,se-krə-'ter-ē-ət\ *n* **1** : the office of a secretary **2** : the secretarial staff in an office **3** : the administrative department of a governmental organization ⟨the UN ∼⟩

sec·re·tary \'se-krə-,ter-ē\ *n, pl* **-tar·ies** **1** : a person employed to handle records, correspondence, and routine work for another person **2** : an officer of a corporation or business who is in charge of correspondence and records **3** : an official at the head of a department of government **4** : a writing desk — **sec·re·tari·al** \,se-krə-'ter-ē-əl\ *adj* — **sec·re·tary·ship** \'se-krə-,ter-ē-,ship\ *n*

¹**se·crete** \si-'krēt\ *vb* **se·cret·ed; se·cret·ing** : to form and give off (a secretion)

²**se·crete** \si-'krēt, 'sē-krət\ *vb* **se·cret·ed; se·cret·ing** : HIDE, CONCEAL

se·cre·tion \si-'krē-shən\ *n* **1** : the process of secreting something **2** : a product of glandular activity; *esp* : one (as a hormone) useful in the organism **3** : the act of hiding something — **se·cre·to·ry** \'sē-krə-,tȯr-ē\ *adj*

se·cre·tive \'sē-krə-tiv, si-'krē-\ *adj* : tending to keep secrets or to act secretly — **se·cre·tive·ly** *adv* — **se·cre·tive·ness** *n*

¹**sect** \'sekt\ *n* **1** : a dissenting religious body **2** : a religious denomination **3** : a group adhering to a distinctive doctrine or to a leader

²**sect** *abbr* section; sectional

¹**sec·tar·i·an** \sek-'ter-ē-ən\ *adj* **1** : of or relating to a sect or sectarian **2** : limited in character or scope — **sec·tar·i·an·ism** *n*

²**sectarian** *n* **1** : an adherent of a sect **2** : a narrow or bigoted person

sec·ta·ry \'sek-tə-rē\ *n, pl* **-ries** : a member of a sect

¹**sec·tion** \'sek-shən\ *n* **1** : a part cut off or separated **2** : a distinct part **3** : the appearance that a thing has or would have if cut straight through

²**section** *vb* **1** : to separate or become separated into sections **2** : to represent in sections

sec·tion·al \'sek-shə-nəl\ *adj* **1** : of, relating to, or characteristic of a section **2** : local or regional rather than general in character **3** : divided into sections — **sec·tion·al·ism** *n*

sec·tor \'sek-tər\ *n* **1** : a part of a circle between two radii **2** : an area assigned to a military leader to defend **3** : a subdivision of society

sec·u·lar \'se-kyə-lər\ *adj* **1** : not sacred or ecclesiastical **2** : not bound by monastic vows ⟨a ∼ priest⟩

sec·u·lar·ise *Brit var of* SECULARIZE

sec·u·lar·ism \'se-kyə-lə-,ri-zəm\ *n* : indifference to or exclusion of religion — **sec·u·lar·ist** \-rist\ *n* — **secularist** *also* **sec·u·lar·is·tic** \,se-kyə-lə-'ris-tik\ *adj*

sec·u·lar·ize \'se-kyə-lə-,rīz\ *vb* **-ized; -iz·ing** **1** : to make secular **2** : to transfer from ecclesiastical to civil or lay use, possession, or control — **sec·u·lar·i·za·tion** \,se-kyə-lə-rə-'zā-shən\ *n* — **sec·u·lar·iz·er** \'se-kyə-lə-,rī-zər\ *n*

¹**se·cure** \si-'kyu̇r\ *adj* **se·cur·er; -est** [L *securus* safe, secure, fr. *se* without + *cura* care] **1** : easy in mind : free from fear **2** : free from danger or risk of loss : SAFE **3** : CERTAIN, SURE — **se·cure·ly** *adv*

²**secure** *vb* **se·cured; se·cur·ing** **1** : to make safe : GUARD **2** : to assure payment of by giving a pledge or collateral **3** : to fasten safely ⟨∼ a door⟩ **4** : GET, ACQUIRE

se·cu·ri·ty \si-'kyu̇r-ə-tē\ *n, pl* **-ties** **1** : SAFETY **2** : freedom from worry **3** : something given as pledge of payment ⟨a ∼ deposit⟩ **4** *pl* : bond or stock certificates **5** : PROTECTION

secy *abbr* secretary

se·dan \si-'dan\ *n* **1** : a covered chair borne on poles by two men **2** : an automobile seating four or more people and usu. having a permanent top

¹**se·date** \si-'dāt\ *adj* : quiet and dignified in behavior ♦ *Synonyms* STAID, SOBER, SERIOUS, SOLEMN — **se·date·ly** *adv*

²**sedate** *vb* **se·dat·ed; se·dat·ing** : to dose with sedatives — **se·da·tion** \si-'dā-shən\ *n*

¹**sed·a·tive** \'se-də-tiv\ *adj* : serving or tending to relieve tension

²**sedative** *n* : a sedative drug

sed·en·tary \'se-dᵊn-,ter-ē\ *adj* : characterized by or requiring much sitting

sedge \'sej\ *n* : any of a family of plants esp. of marshy areas that differ from the related grasses esp. in having solid stems — **sedgy** \'se-jē\ *adj*

sed·i·ment \'se-də-mənt\ *n* **1** : the material that settles to the bottom of a liquid **2** : material (as stones and sand) deposited by water, wind, or a glacier — **sed·i·men·ta·ry** \,se-də-'men-tə-rē\ *adj* — **sed·i·men·ta·tion** \-mən-'tā-shən, -,men-\ *n*

se·di·tion \si-'di-shən\ *n* : the causing of discontent, insurrection, or resistance against a government — **se·di·tious** \-shəs\ *adj*

se·duce \si-'düs, -'dyüs\ *vb* **se·duced; se·duc·ing** **1** : to persuade to disobedience or disloyalty **2** : to lead astray **3** : to entice to sexual intercourse ♦ *Synonyms* TEMPT, ENTICE, INVEIGLE, LURE — **se·duc·er** *n* — **se·duc·tion** \-'dək-shən\ *n* — **se·duc·tive** \-tiv\ *adj*

sed·u·lous \'se-jə-ləs\ *adj* [L *sedulus*, fr. *sedulo* sincerely, diligently, fr. *se* without + *dolus* guile] : DILIGENT, PAINSTAKING

¹**see** \'sē\ *vb* **saw** \'sȯ\; **seen** \'sēn\; **see·ing** **1** : to perceive by the eye; *also* : to have the power of sight **2** : EXPERIENCE **3** : UNDERSTAND **4** : to make sure ⟨∼ that order is kept⟩ **5** : to meet with **6** : to keep company with esp. in dating **7** : ACCOMPANY, ESCORT ⟨∼ the guests to the door⟩ ♦ *Synonyms* BEHOLD, DESCRY, ESPY, VIEW, OBSERVE, NOTE, DISCERN — **see red** : to become very angry — **see the light** : to realize an obscured truth

²**see** *n* : the authority or jurisdiction of a bishop

¹**seed** \'sēd\ *n, pl* **seed** *or* **seeds** **1** : the grains of plants used for sowing **2** : a ripened ovule of a flowering plant that may develop into a new plant; *also* : a plant structure (as a spore or small dry fruit) capable of producing a new plant **3** : DESCENDANTS **4** : SOURCE, ORIGIN **5** : a competitor seeded in a tournament — **seed·less** *adj* — **go to seed** *or* **run to seed** **1** : to develop seed **2** : DECAY, DETERIORATE

²**seed** *vb* **1** : SOW, PLANT ⟨∼ land with grass⟩ **2** : to bear or shed seeds **3** : to remove seeds from **4** : to rank or schedule (contestants) in a tournament — **seed·er** *n*

seed·bed \-,bed\ *n* : soil or a bed of soil prepared for planting seed

seed·ling \'sēd-liŋ\ *n* **1** : a young plant grown from seed **2** : a young tree before it becomes a sapling

seed·time \'sēd-,tīm\ *n* : the season for sowing

seedy \'sē-dē\ *adj* **seed·i·er; -est** **1** : containing or full of seeds **2** : SHABBY

seek \'sēk\ *vb* **sought** \'sȯt\; **seek·ing** **1** : to search for **2** : to try to reach or obtain **3** : ATTEMPT — **seek·er** *n*

seem \'sēm\ *vb* **1** : to appear to the observation or understanding **2** : to give the impression of being : APPEAR

seem·ing *adj* : outwardly apparent — **seem·ing·ly** *adv*

seem·ly \'sēm-lē\ *adj* **seem·li·er; -est** **1** : conventionally proper **2** : FIT

seep \'sēp\ *vb* : to flow or pass slowly through fine pores or cracks — **seep·age** \'sē-pij\ *n*

seer \'sir\ *n* : a person who foresees or predicts events : PROPHET

seer·suck·er \'sir-,sə-kər\ *n* [Hindi *śīrśakar*, fr. Pers *shīr-o-shakar*, lit., milk and sugar] : a light fabric of linen, cotton, or rayon usu. striped and slightly puckered

see·saw \'sē-,sȯ\ *n* **1** : a contest in which each side assumes then relinquishes the lead **2** : a children's sport of riding up and down on the ends of a plank supported in the middle; *also* : the plank so used — **seesaw** *vb*

seethe \'sēth\ *vb* **seethed; seeth·ing** [archaic *seethe* boil] : to become violently agitated ⟨∼ with jealousy⟩

seg·ment \'seg-mənt\ *n* **1** : a part cut off from a geometrical figure (as a circle) by one or more points, lines, or planes **2** : a division of a thing : SECTION — **seg·men·tal** \seg-'men-tᵊl\ *adj* — **seg·men·ta·tion** \,seg-mən-'tā-shən\ *n* — **seg·ment·ed** \'seg-,men-təd\ *adj*

seg·re·gate \'se-gri-,gāt\ *vb* **-gat·ed; -gat·ing** [L *segregare*, fr. *se-* apart + *greg-, grex* herd, flock] : to cut off from oth-

ers; *esp* : to separate esp. by races or ethnic groups —
seg·re·ga·tion \,se-gri-'gā-shən\ *n*

seg·re·ga·tion·ist \,se-gri-'gā-shə-nist\ *n* : one who believes in or practices the segregation of races

sei·gneur \sān-'yər\ *n, often cap* [MF, fr. ML *senior*, fr. L, adj., elder] : a feudal lord

¹**seine** \'sān\ *n* : a large weighted fishing net

²**seine** *vb* **seined; sein·ing** : to fish or catch with a seine —
sein·er *n*

seis·mic \'sīz-mik, 'sīs-\ *adj* : of, relating to, resembling, or caused by an earthquake — **seis·mi·cal·ly** \-mi-k(ə-)lē\ *adv* — **seis·mic·i·ty** \sīz-'mi-sə-tē, sīs-\ *n*

seis·mo·gram \'sīz-mə-,gram, 'sīs-\ *n* : the record of an earth tremor made by a seismograph

seis·mo·graph \-,graf\ *n* : an apparatus to measure and record seismic vibrations — **seis·mo·graph·ic** \,sīz-mə-'gra-fik, ,sīs-\ *adj* — **seis·mog·ra·phy** \sīz-'mä-grə-fē, sīs-\ *n*

seis·mol·o·gy \sīz-'mä-lə-jē, sīs-\ *n* : a science that deals with earthquakes — **seis·mo·log·i·cal** \,sīz-mə-'lä-ji-kəl, ,sīs-\ *adj* — **seis·mol·o·gist** \sīz-'mä-lə-jist, sīs-\ *n*

seis·mom·e·ter \sīz-'mä-mə-tər, sīs-\ *n* : a seismograph measuring the actual movement of the ground

seize \'sēz\ *vb* **seized; seiz·ing** **1** : to lay hold of or take possession of by force **2** : ARREST **3** : UNDERSTAND **4** : to attack or overwhelm physically : AFFLICT ♦ **Synonyms** TAKE, GRASP, CLUTCH, SNATCH, GRAB

sei·zure \'sē-zhər\ *n* **1** : the act of seizing : the state of being seized **2** : a sudden attack (as of disease)

sel *abbr* select; selected; selection

sel·dom \'sel-dəm\ *adv* : not often : RARELY

¹**se·lect** \sə-'lekt\ *adj* **1** : CHOSEN, PICKED; *also* : CHOICE **2** : judicious or restrictive in choice : DISCRIMINATING

²**select** *vb* : to choose from a number or group : pick out

se·lec·tion \sə-'lek-shən\ *n* **1** : the act or process of selecting **2** : something selected : CHOICE **3** : a natural or artificial process that tends to favor the survival and reproduction of individuals with certain traits but not those with others

se·lec·tive \sə-'lek-tiv\ *adj* : of or relating to selection : selecting or tending to select ⟨∼ shoppers⟩

selective service *n* : a system for calling men up for military service : DRAFT

se·lect·man \si-'lekt-,man, -mən\ *n* : one of a board of officials elected in towns of most New England states to administer town affairs

se·le·ni·um \sə-'lē-nē-əm\ *n* : a photosensitive chemical element

self \'self\ *n, pl* **selves** \'selvz\ **1** : the essential person distinct from all other persons in identity **2** : a particular side of a person's character **3** : personal interest : SELFISHNESS

self- *comb form* **1** : oneself : itself **2** : of oneself or itself **3** : by oneself or itself; *also* : automatic **4** : to, for, or toward oneself

self-abasement	self-confident
self-absorbed	self-congratulation
self-absorption	self-congratulatory
self-acceptance	self-constituted
self-accusation	self-contempt
self-acting	self-contradiction
self-addressed	self-contradictory
self-adjusting	self-control
self-administer	self-correcting
self-advancement	self-created
self-aggrandizement	self-criticism
self-aggrandizing	self-cultivation
self-analysis	self-deceit
self-anointed	self-deception
self-appointed	self-defeating
self-appraisal	self-definition
self-asserting	self-delusion
self-assertion	self-denial
self-assertive	self-denying
self-assurance	self-deprecating
self-assured	self-deprecation
self-awareness	self-depreciation
self-betrayal	self-described
self-cleaning	self-despair
self-closing	self-destruct
self-complacent	self-destruction
self-conceit	self-destructive
self-concern	self-determination
self-condemned	self-directed
self-confessed	self-discipline
self-confidence	self-distrust

self-doubt	self-portrait
self-educated	self-possessed
self-employed	self-possession
self-employment	self-preservation
self-enhancement	self-proclaimed
self-esteem	self-professed
self-examination	self-promotion
self-explaining	self-propelled
self-explanatory	self-propelling
self-expression	self-protection
self-forgetful	self-realization
self-giving	self-referential
self-governing	self-regard
self-government	self-reliance
self-hate	self-reliant
self-hypnosis	self-renewing
self-identity	self-reproach
self-image	self-respect
self-importance	self-respecting
self-important	self-restraint
self-imposed	self-revelation
self-improvement	self-rule
self-incrimination	self-sacrifice
self-induced	self-sacrificing
self-indulgence	self-satisfaction
self-indulgent	self-satisfied
self-inflicted	self-service
self-instruction	self-serving
self-interest	self-starting
self-knowledge	self-styled
self-limiting	self-sufficiency
self-love	self-sufficient
self-lubricating	self-supporting
self-luminous	self-sustaining
self-operating	self-taught
self-perception	self-torment
self-perpetuating	self-winding
self-pity	self-worth

self–cen·tered \'self-'sen-tərd\ *adj* : concerned only with one's own self — **self–cen·tered·ness** *n*

self–com·posed \,self-kəm-'pōzd\ *adj* : having control over one's emotions

self–con·scious \'self-'kän-chəs\ *adj* : uncomfortably conscious of oneself as an object of observation by others — **self–con·scious·ly** *adv* — **self–con·scious·ness** *n*

self–con·tained \,self-kən-'tānd\ *adj* **1** : complete in itself **2** : showing self-control; *also* : reserved in manner

self–de·fense \'self-di-'fens\ *n* **1** : a plea of justification for the use of force or for homicide **2** : the act of defending oneself, one's property, or a close relative

self–ef·fac·ing \-ə-'fā-siŋ\ *adj* : RETIRING, SHY

self–ev·i·dent \'self-'e-və-dənt\ *adj* : evident without proof or reasoning

self–fer·til·i·za·tion \,self-,fər-tə-lə-'zā-shən\ *n* : fertilization of a plant or animal by its own pollen or sperm

self–ful·fill·ing \,self-fül-'fi-liŋ\ *adj* : becoming real or true by virtue of having been predicted or expected ⟨a ∼ prophecy⟩

self–help \'self-'help\ *n* : the process of bettering oneself or coping with one's problems without the aid of others — **self–help** *adj*

self·ish \'sel-fish\ *adj* : concerned with one's own welfare excessively or without regard for others — **self·ish·ly** *adv* — **self·ish·ness** *n*

self·less \'self-ləs\ *adj* : UNSELFISH — **self·less·ness** *n*

self–made \'self-'mād\ *adj* : having achieved success or prominance by one's own efforts ⟨a ∼ man⟩

self–pol·li·na·tion \,self-,pä-lə-'nā-shən\ *n* : pollination of a flower by its own pollen or sometimes by pollen from another flower on the same plant

self–reg·u·lat·ing \'self-'re-gyə-,lā-tiŋ\ *adj* : AUTOMATIC

self–righ·teous \-'rī-chəs\ *adj* : strongly convinced of one's own righteousness — **self–righ·teous·ly** *adv*

self·same \'self-,sām\ *adj* : precisely the same : IDENTICAL

self–seal·ing \'self-'sē-liŋ\ *adj* : capable of sealing itself (as after puncture)

self–seek·ing \'self-'sē-kiŋ\ *adj* : seeking only to further one's own interests — **self–seeking** *n*

self–start·er \-'stär-tər\ *n* : a person who has initiative

self–will \'self-'wil\ *n* : OBSTINACY

sell \'sel\ *vb* **sold** \'sōld\; **sell·ing** **1** : to transfer (property) in return for money or something else of value **2** : to deal in as a business **3** : to be sold ⟨cars are ∼*ing* well⟩ — **sell·er** *n*

sell out *vb* **1** : to dispose of entirely by sale; *esp* : to sell one's business **2** : BETRAY — **sell·out** \'sel-,aut\ *n*

selt·zer \'selt-sər\ *n* [modif. of G *Selterser (Wasser)* water of Selters, fr. Nieder *Selters,* Germany] : artificially carbonated water

sel·vage *or* **sel·vedge** \'sel-vij\ *n* : the edge of a woven fabric so formed as to prevent raveling

selves *pl of* SELF

sem *abbr* **1** semicolon **2** seminar **3** seminary

se·man·tic \si-'man-tik\ *also* **se·man·ti·cal** \-ti-kəl\ *adj* : of or relating to meaning in language

se·man·tics \si-'man-tiks\ *n sing or pl* : the study of meanings in language

sema·phore \'se-mə-ˌfȯr\ *n* **1** : a visual signaling apparatus with movable arms **2** : signaling by hand-held flags

sem·blance \'sem-bləns\ *n* **1** : outward appearance **2** : IMAGE, LIKENESS

se·men \'sē-mən\ *n* [NL, fr. L, seed] : a sticky whitish fluid of the male reproductive tract that contains the sperm

se·mes·ter \sə-'mes-tər\ *n* [G, fr. L *semestris* half-yearly, fr. *sex* six + *mensis* month] **1** : half a year **2** : one of the two terms into which many colleges divide the school year

semi- \'se-mi, -ˌmī\ *prefix* **1** : precisely half of **2** : half in quantity or value; *also* : half of or occurring halfway through a specified period **3** : partly : incompletely **4** : partial : incomplete **5** : having some of the characteristics of

semiannual	semiofficial
semiarid	semipermanent
semicentennial	semipolitical
semicircle	semiprecious
semicircular	semiprivate
semicivilized	semiprofessional
semiclassical	semireligious
semiconscious	semiretired
semidarkness	semiskilled
semidivine	semisoft
semiformal	semisolid
semigloss	semisweet
semi–independent	semitransparent
semiliquid	semiweekly
semiliterate	semiyearly
semimonthly	

semi \'se-ˌmī\ *n, pl* **sem·is** : SEMITRAILER

semi·au·to·mat·ic \ˌse-mē-ˌȯ-tə-'ma-tik\ *adj, of a firearm* : able to fire repeatedly but requiring release and another press of the trigger for each successive shot

semi·co·lon \'se-mi-ˌkō-lən\ *n* : a punctuation mark; used esp. to separate major sentence elements

semi·con·duc·tor \ˌse-mi-kən-'dək-tər\ *n* : a substance whose electrical conductivity is between that of a conductor and an insulator — **semi·con·duct·ing** *adj*

¹semi·fi·nal \ˌse-mi-'fī-nᵊl\ *adj* : being next to the last in an elimination tournament

²semi·fi·nal \'se-mi-ˌfī-nᵊl\ *n* : a semifinal round or match — **semi·fi·nal·ist** \-ist\ *n*

semi·lu·nar \-'lü-nər\ *adj* : LUNATE

sem·i·nal \'se-mə-nᵊl\ *adj* **1** : of, relating to, or consisting of seed or semen **2** : containing or contributing the seeds of later development : CREATIVE, ORIGINAL — **sem·i·nal·ly** *adv*

sem·i·nar \'se-mə-ˌnär\ *n* **1** : a course of study pursued by a group of advanced students doing original research under a professor **2** : CONFERENCE

sem·i·nary \'se-mə-ˌner-ē\ *n, pl* **-nar·ies** [ME, seedbed, nursery, fr. L *seminarium,* fr. *semen* seed] : an educational institution; *esp* : one that gives theological training — **sem·i·nar·i·an** \ˌse-mə-'ner-ē-ən\ *n*

Sem·i·nole \'se-mə-ˌnōl\ *n, pl* **Semi·noles** *or* **Seminole** : a member of an American Indian people of Florida

semi·per·me·able \ˌse-mi-'pər-mē-ə-bəl\ *adj* : partially but not freely or wholly permeable; *esp* : permeable to some usu. small molecules but not to other usu. larger particles ⟨a ∼ membrane⟩ — **semi·per·me·abil·i·ty** \-ˌpər-mē-ə-'bi-lə-tē\ *n*

Sem·ite \'se-ˌmīt\ *n* : a member of any of a group of peoples (as the Hebrews or Arabs) of southwestern Asia — **Se·mit·ic** \sə-'mi-tik\ *adj*

semi·trail·er \'se-mi-ˌtrā-lər, -ˌmī-\ *n* : a freight trailer that when attached is supported at its forward end by the truck tractor; *also* : a semitrailer with attached tractor

sem·o·li·na \ˌse-mə-'lē-nə\ *n* : the purified hard grains produced from the milling of wheat and used esp. for pasta

sempstress *var of* SEAMSTRESS

¹sen \'sen\ *n, pl* **sen** — see *yen* at MONEY table

²sen *n, pl* **sen** — see *dollar, ringgit, rupiah* at MONEY table

³sen *n, pl* **sen** — see *riel* at MONEY table

⁴sen *abbr* **1** senate; senator **2** senior

sen·ate \'se-nət\ *n* : the second of two chambers of a legislature

sen·a·tor \'se-nə-tər\ *n* : a member of a senate — **sen·a·to·ri·al** \ˌse-nə-'tȯr-ē-əl\ *adj*

send \'send\ *vb* **sent** \'sent\; **send·ing** **1** : to cause to go **2** : EMIT **3** : to propel or drive esp. with force **4** : to put or bring into a certain condition ⟨*sent* them into a rage⟩ **5** : to convey or transmit by an agent — **send·er** *n*

send–off \'send-ˌȯf\ *n* : a demonstration of goodwill and enthusiasm at the start of a new venture (as a trip)

send–up \'send-ˌəp\ *n* : PARODY, TAKEOFF

se·ne \'sā-(ˌ)nā\ *n, pl* **sene** — see *tala* at MONEY table

Sen·e·ca \'se-ni-kə\ *n, pl* **Seneca** *or* **Senecas** : a member of an American Indian people of western New York

Sen·e·ga·lese \ˌse-ni-gə-'lēz, -'lēs\ *n, pl* **Senegalese** : a native or inhabitant of Senegal — **Senegalese** *adj*

se·nes·cence \si-'ne-sᵊns\ *n* : the state of being old; *also* : the process of becoming old — **se·nes·cent** \-ᵊnt\ *adj*

se·nile \'sē-ˌnī(-ə)l, 'se-\ *adj* : OLD, AGED; *esp* : exhibiting a loss of cognitive abilities associated with old age — **se·nil·i·ty** \si-'ni-lə-tē\ *n*

¹se·nior \'sē-nyər\ *n* **1** : a person older or of higher rank than another **2** : a member of the graduating class of a high school or college

²senior *adj* [ME, fr. L, older, elder, compar. of *senex* old] **1** : ELDER **2** : more advanced in dignity or rank **3** : belonging to the final year of a school or college course

senior chief petty officer *n* : a petty officer in the navy or coast guard ranking next below a master chief petty officer

senior citizen *n* : an elderly person; *esp* : one who has retired

senior high school *n* : a school usu. including grades 10 to 12

se·nior·i·ty \sēn-'yȯr-ə-tē\ *n* **1** : the quality or state of being senior **2** : a privileged status owing to length of continuous service

senior master sergeant *n* : a noncommissioned officer in the air force ranking next below a chief master sergeant

sen·i·ti \'se-nə-tē\ *n, pl* **seniti** — see *pa'anga* at MONEY table

sen·na \'se-nə\ *n* **1** : CASSIA 2; *esp* : one used medicinally **2** : the dried leaflets or pods of a cassia used as a purgative

sen·sa·tion \sen-'sā-shən\ *n* **1** : awareness (as of noise or heat) or a mental process (as seeing or hearing) due to stimulation of a sense organ; *also* : an indefinite bodily feeling **2** : a condition of excitement; *also* : the thing that causes this condition

sen·sa·tion·al \-shə-nəl\ *adj* **1** : of or relating to sensation or the senses **2** : arousing an intense and usu. superficial interest or emotional reaction — **sen·sa·tion·al·ly** *adv*

sen·sa·tion·al·ise *Brit var of* SENSATIONALIZE

sen·sa·tion·al·ism \-nə-ˌli-zəm\ *n* : the use or effect of sensational subject matter or treatment — **sen·sa·tion·al·ist** \-nə-list\ *adj or n* — **sen·sa·tion·al·is·tic** \-ˌsā-shə-nə-'lis-tik\ *adj*

sen·sa·tion·al·ize \-nə-ˌlīz\ *vb* **-ized; -iz·ing** : to present in a sensational manner

¹sense \'sens\ *n* **1** : semantic content : MEANING **2** : the faculty of perceiving by means of sense organs; *also* : a bodily function or mechanism (as sight, hearing, or smell) involving the action and effect of a stimulus on a sense organ **3** : SENSATION, AWARENESS **4** : INTELLIGENCE, JUDGMENT **5** : OPINION ⟨the ∼ of the meeting⟩ — **sense·less** *adj* — **sense·less·ly** *adv* — **sense·less·ness** *n*

²sense *vb* **sensed; sens·ing** **1** : to be or become aware of ⟨∼ danger⟩; *also* : to perceive by the senses **2** : to detect (as radiation) automatically

sense organ *n* : a bodily structure (as an eye or ear) that receives stimuli (as heat or light) which excite neurons to send information to the brain

sen·si·bil·i·ty \ˌsen-sə-'bi-lə-tē\ *n, pl* **-ties** : delicacy of feeling : SENSITIVITY

sen·si·ble \'sen-sə-bəl\ *adj* **1** : capable of being perceived by the senses or the mind; *also* : capable of receiving sense impressions **2** : AWARE, CONSCIOUS **3** : REASONABLE, RATIONAL — **sen·si·bly** \-blē\ *adv*

sen·si·tive \'sen-sə-tiv\ *adj* **1** : subject to excitation by or responsive to stimuli **2** : having power of feeling **3** : of such a nature as to be easily affected **4** : TOUCHY ⟨a ~ issue⟩ — **sen·si·tive·ly** *adv* — **sen·si·tive·ness** *n* — **sen·si·tiv·i·ty** \ˌsen-sə-'ti-və-tē\ *n*

sensitive plant *n* : any of several mimosas with leaves that fold or droop when touched

sen·si·tize \'sen-sə-ˌtīz\ *vb* **-tized; -tiz·ing** : to make or become sensitive or hypersensitive — **sen·si·ti·za·tion** \ˌsen-sə-tə-'zā-shən\ *n*

sen·sor \'sen-ˌsȯr, -sər\ *n* : a device that responds to a physical stimulus

sen·so·ry \'sen-sə-rē\ *adj* **1** : of or relating to sensation or the senses **2** : AFFERENT

sen·su·al \'sen-shə-wəl\ *adj* **1** : relating to gratification of the senses **2** : devoted to the pleasures of the senses — **sen·su·al·ist** *n* — **sen·su·al·i·ty** \ˌsen-shə-'wa-lə-tē\ *n* — **sen·su·al·ly** *adv*

sen·su·ous \'sen-shə-wəs\ *adj* **1** : relating to the senses or to things that can be perceived by the senses **2** : VOLUPTUOUS — **sen·su·ous·ly** *adv* — **sen·su·ous·ness** *n*

¹sent *past and past part of* SEND

²sent \'sent\ *n, pl* **sen·ti** \'sen-tē\ — see *kroon* at MONEY table

sen·te \'sen-tē\ *n, pl* **li·cen·te** *or* **li·sen·te** \li-'sen-tē\ — see *loti* at MONEY table

¹sen·tence \'sen-t³ns, -t³nz\ *n* [ME, fr. AF, fr. L *sententia*, lit., feeling, opinion, fr. *sentire* to feel] **1** : the punishment set by a court **2** : a grammatically self-contained speech unit that expresses an assertion, a question, a command, a wish, or an exclamation

²sentence *vb* **sen·tenced; sen·tenc·ing** : to impose a sentence on

sen·ten·tious \sen-'ten-chəs\ *adj* : using wise sayings or proverbs; *also* : using pompous language — **sen·ten·tious·ly** *adv* — **sen·ten·tious·ness** *n*

sen·tient \'sen-chənt, -chē-ənt\ *adj* : capable of feeling : having perception

sen·ti·ment \'sen-tə-mənt\ *n* **1** : FEELING; *also* : thought and judgment influenced by feeling : emotional attitude **2** : OPINION, NOTION

sen·ti·men·tal \ˌsen-tə-'men-t³l\ *adj* **1** : influenced by tender feelings **2** : affecting the emotions ◆ *Synonyms* BATHETIC, MAUDLIN, MAWKISH, MUSHY — **sen·ti·men·tal·ism** *n* — **sen·ti·men·tal·i·ty** \-ˌmen-'ta-lə-tē, -mən-\ *n* — **sen·ti·men·tal·ly** *adv*

sen·ti·men·tal·ise *Brit var of* SENTIMENTALIZE

sen·ti·men·tal·ize \-'men-tə-ˌlīz\ *vb* **-ized; -iz·ing** **1** : to indulge in sentiment **2** : to look upon or imbue with sentiment — **sen·ti·men·tal·i·za·tion** \-ˌmen-tə-lə-'zā-shən\ *n*

sen·ti·mo \sen-'tē-(ˌ)mō\ *n, pl* **-mos** — see *peso* at MONEY table

sen·ti·nel \'sen-t³n-əl\ *n* [MF *sentinelle*, fr. It *sentinella*, fr. *sentina* vigilance, fr. *sentire* to perceive, fr. L] : SENTRY

sen·try \'sen-trē\ *n, pl* **sentries** : a guard at a point of passage

sep *abbr* separate, separated

Sep *abbr* September

SEP *abbr* simplified employee pension

se·pal \'sē-pəl, 'se-\ *n* : one of the modified leaves comprising a flower calyx

sep·a·ra·ble \'se-pə-rə-bəl\ *adj* : capable of being separated — **sep·a·ra·bil·i·ty** \ˌse-pə-rə-'bi-lə-tē\ *n*

¹sep·a·rate \'se-pə-ˌrāt\ *vb* **-rat·ed; -rat·ing** **1** : to set or keep apart : DISCONNECT, SEVER **2** : to keep apart by something intervening **3** : to cease to be together : PART

²sep·a·rate \'se-prət, -pə-rət\ *adj* **1** : not connected **2** : divided from each other **3** : SINGLE, PARTICULAR ⟨the ~ pieces of the puzzle⟩ — **sep·a·rate·ly** *adv*

³sep·a·rate \'se-prət, -pə-rət\ *n* : an article of dress designed to be worn interchangeably with others to form various combinations

sep·a·ra·tion \ˌse-pə-'rā-shən\ *n* **1** : the act or process of separating : the state of being separated **2** : a point, line, means, or area of division **3** : a formal separating of a married couple by agreement but without divorce

sep·a·rat·ist \'se-prə-tist, 'se-pə-ˌrā-\ *n* : an advocate of separation (as from a political body) — **sep·a·rat·ism** \'se-prə-ˌti-zəm\ *n*

sep·a·ra·tive \'se-pə-ˌrā-tiv, 'se-prə-tiv\ *adj* : tending toward, causing, or expressing separation

sep·a·ra·tor \'se-pə-ˌrā-tər\ *n* : one that separates; *esp* : a device for separating cream from milk

se·pia \'sē-pē-ə\ *n* : a brownish gray to dark brown color

sep·sis \'sep-səs\ *n, pl* **sep·ses** \'sep-ˌsēz\ : a toxic condition due to spread of bacteria or their toxic products in the body

Sept *abbr* September

Sep·tem·ber \sep-'tem-bər\ *n* [ME *Septembre*, fr. AF & OE, both fr. L *September* (seventh month), fr. *septem* seven] : the 9th month of the year having 30 days

sep·tic \'sep-tik\ *adj* **1** : PUTREFACTIVE **2** : relating to or involving sepsis **3** : of, relating to, or used for sewage treatment and disposal

sep·ti·ce·mia \ˌsep-tə-'sē-mē-ə\ *n* : BLOOD POISONING

septic tank *n* : a tank in which sewage is disintegrated by bacteria

septic tank

sep·tu·a·ge·nar·i·an \sep-ˌtü-ə-jə-'ner-ē-ən, -ˌtyü-\ *n* : a person whose age is in the seventies — **septuagenarian** *adj*

Sep·tu·a·gint \sep-'tü-ə-jənt, -'tyü-\ *n* : a Greek version of the Old Testament prepared in the 3d and 2d centuries B.C. by Jewish scholars

sep·tum \'sep-təm\ *n, pl* **sep·ta** \-tə\ : a dividing wall or membrane esp. between bodily spaces or masses of soft tissue

se·pul·chral \sə-'pəl-krəl\ *adj* **1** : relating to burial or the grave **2** : GLOOMY

¹sep·ul·chre *or* **sep·ul·cher** \'se-pəl-kər\ *n* : a burial vault : TOMB

²sepulchre *or* **sepulcher** *vb* **-chred** *or* **-chered; -chring** *or* **-cher·ing** : BURY, ENTOMB

sep·ul·ture \'se-pəl-ˌchür\ *n* **1** : BURIAL **2** : SEPULCHRE

se·quel \'sē-kwəl\ *n* **1** : logical consequence **2** : a literary or cinematic work continuing a story begun in a preceding one

¹se·quence \'sē-kwəns\ *n* **1** : SERIES **2** : chronological order of events **3** : RESULT, SEQUEL ◆ *Synonyms* SUCCESSION, CHAIN, PROGRESSION, TRAIN — **se·quen·tial** \si-'kwen-chəl\ *adj* — **se·quen·tial·ly** *adv*

²sequence *vb* **se·quenced; se·quenc·ing** **1** : to arrange in a sequence **2** : to determine the sequence of chemical constituents in ⟨~ DNA⟩

se·quent \'sē-kwənt\ *adj* **1** : SUCCEEDING, CONSECUTIVE **2** : RESULTANT

se·ques·ter \si-'kwes-tər\ *vb* : to set apart : SEGREGATE ⟨~ a jury⟩

se·ques·trate \'sē-kwəs-ˌtrāt, si-'kwes-\ *vb* **-trat·ed; -trat·ing** : SEQUESTER — **se·ques·tra·tion** \ˌsē-kwəs-'trā-shən, ˌse-\ *n*

se·quin \'sē-kwən\ *n* **1** : an old gold coin of Turkey and Italy **2** : a small metal or plastic plate used for ornamentation esp. on clothing — **se·quined** *or* **se·quinned** \-kwənd\ *adj*

se·quoia \si-'kwȯi-ə\ *n* : either of two huge California coniferous trees

ser *abbr* **1** serial **2** series **3** service

sera *pl of* SERUM

se·ra·glio \sə-'ral-yō\ *n, pl* **-glios** [It *serraglio*] : HAREM

se·ra·pe \sə-'rä-pē\ *n* : a colorful woolen shawl worn over the shoulders esp. by Mexican men

ser·aph \'ser-əf\ *n, pl* **ser·a·phim** \-ə-ˌfim, -ˌfēm\ *or* **ser·aphs** : one of the 6-winged angels standing in the presence of God

ser·a·phim \'ser-ə-ˌfim, -ˌfēm\ *n pl* **1** : the highest order of angels **2** *sing, pl* **seraphim** : SERAPH — **se·raph·ic** \sə-'ra-fik\ *adj*

Ser·bi·an \'sər-bē-ən\ n **1** : SERB **2** : a south Slavic language spoken by the Serbian people — **Serbian** adj

Ser·bo–Cro·a·tian \ˌsər-(ˌ)bō-krō-'ā-shən\ n : the Serbian and Croatian languages together with the Slavic speech of Bosnia, Herzegovina, and Montenegro taken as a single language with regional variants

sere \'sir\ adj : DRY, WITHERED

¹ser·e·nade \ˌser-ə-'nād\ n [F, fr. It serenata, fr. sereno clear, calm (of weather) fr. L serenus] : music sung or played as a compliment esp. outdoors at night for a woman being courted

²serenade vb **-nad·ed; -nad·ing** : to entertain with or perform a serenade

ser·en·dip·i·ty \ˌser-ən-'di-pə-tē\ n [fr. its possession by the heroes of the Persian fairy tale *The Three Princes of Serendip*] : the gift of finding valuable or agreeable things not sought for — **ser·en·dip·i·tous** \-təs\ adj — **ser·en·dip·i·tous·ly** adv

se·rene \sə-'rēn\ adj **1** : CLEAR ⟨~ skies⟩ **2** : QUIET, CALM ◆ *Synonyms* TRANQUIL, PEACEFUL, PLACID — **se·rene·ly** adv — **se·ren·i·ty** \sə-'re-nə-tē\ n

serf \'sərf\ n : a member of a servile class bound to the land and subject to the will of the landowner — **serf·dom** \-dəm\ n

serge \'sərj\ n : a twilled woolen cloth

ser·geant \'sär-jənt\ n [ME, servant, attendant, sergeant, fr. AF sergant, serjant, fr. L servient-, serviens, prp. of servire to serve] **1** : a noncommissioned officer (as in the army) ranking next below a staff sergeant **2** : an officer in a police force

sergeant at arms : an officer of an organization who preserves order and executes commands

sergeant first class n : a noncommissioned officer in the army ranking next below a master sergeant

sergeant major n, pl **sergeants major** or **sergeant majors** **1** : a noncommissioned officer in the army or marine corps serving as chief administrative assistant in a headquarters **2** : a noncommissioned officer in the marine corps ranking above a first sergeant

¹se·ri·al \'sir-ē-əl\ adj **1** : appearing in parts that follow regularly ⟨a ~ story⟩ **2** : performing a series of similar acts over a period of time ⟨a ~ killer⟩; also : occurring in such a series — **se·ri·al·ly** adv

²serial n : a serial story or other writing — **se·ri·al·ist** \-ə-list\ n

se·ries \'sir-ēz\ n, pl **series** : a number of things or events arranged in order and connected by being alike in some way ◆ *Synonyms* SUCCESSION, PROGRESSION, SEQUENCE, CHAIN, TRAIN, STRING

seri·graph \'ser-ə-ˌgraf\ n : an original silk-screen print — **se·rig·ra·pher** \sə-'ri-grə-fər\ n — **se·rig·ra·phy** \-fē\ n

se·ri·ous \'sir-ē-əs\ adj **1** : thoughtful or subdued in appearance or manner : SOBER **2** : requiring much thought or work **3** : EARNEST, DEVOTED **4** : DANGEROUS, HARMFUL **5** : excessive or impressive in quantity or degree ⟨making ~ money⟩ ◆ *Synonyms* GRAVE, SEDATE, STAID — **se·ri·ous·ly** adv — **se·ri·ous·ness** n

ser·mon \'sər-mən\ n [ME, fr. AF sermun, fr. ML sermon-, sermo, fr. L, speech, conversation, fr. serere to link together] **1** : a religious discourse esp. as part of a worship service **2** : a lecture on conduct or duty

ser·mon·ize \'sər-mə-ˌnīz\ vb **-ized; -iz·ing 1** : to compose or deliver a sermon **2** : to preach to or on at length

se·rol·o·gy \sə-'rä-lə-jē\ n : a science dealing with serums and esp. their reactions and properties — **se·ro·log·i·cal** \ˌsir-ə-'lä-ji-kəl\ or **se·ro·log·ic** \-jik\ adj — **se·ro·log·i·cal·ly** \-ji-k(ə-)lē\ adv

se·ro·to·nin \ˌsir-ə-'tō-nən, ˌser-\ n : a neurotransmitter that is a powerful vasoconstrictor

se·rous \'sir-əs\ adj : of, relating to, resembling, or producing serum; esp : of thin watery constitution

ser·pent \'sər-pənt\ n : SNAKE

¹ser·pen·tine \'sər-pən-ˌtēn, -ˌtīn\ adj **1** : SLY, CRAFTY **2** : WINDING, TURNING

²serpentine \-ˌtēn\ n : a dull-green mineral having a mottled appearance

ser·rate \'ser-ˌāt\ adj : having a saw-toothed edge ⟨a ~ leaf⟩

ser·ried \'ser-ēd\ adj : crowded together

se·rum \'sir-əm\ n, pl **serums** or **se·ra** \-ə\ [L, whey, wheylike fluid] : the clear yellowish antibody-containing fluid that can be separated from blood when it clots; also : a preparation of animal serum containing specific antibodies and used to prevent or cure disease

serv abbr service

ser·vant \'sər-vənt\ n : one that serves others; esp : a person employed for domestic or personal work

¹serve \'sərv\ vb **served; serv·ing 1** : to work as a servant **2** : to render obedience and worship to (God) **3** : to comply with the commands or demands of **4** : to work through or perform a term of service (as in the army) **5** : PUT IN ⟨served five years in jail⟩ **6** : to be of use : ANSWER ⟨pine boughs served for a bed⟩ **7** : BENEFIT **8** : to prove adequate or satisfactory for ⟨a pie that ~s eight people⟩ **9** : to make ready and pass out ⟨~ drinks⟩ **10** : to furnish or supply with something ⟨one power company serving the whole state⟩ **11** : to wait on ⟨~ a customer⟩ **12** : to treat or act toward in a specified way **13** : to put the ball in play (as in tennis)

²serve n : the act of serving a ball (as in tennis)

serv·er \'sər-vər\ n **1** : one that serves **2** : a computer in a network that is used to provide services (as access to files) to other computers in the network

¹ser·vice \'sər-vəs\ n **1** : the occupation of a servant **2** : HELP, BENEFIT **3** : a meeting for worship; also : a form followed in worship or in a ceremony ⟨burial ~⟩ **4** : the act, fact, or means of serving **5** : performance of official or professional duties **6** : SERVE **7** : a set of dishes or silverware **8** : a branch of public employment; also : the persons in it ⟨civil ~⟩ **9** : military or naval duty

²service vb **ser·viced; ser·vic·ing** : to do maintenance or repair work on or for

ser·vice·able \'sər-və-sə-bəl\ adj : prepared for service : USEFUL, USABLE

ser·vice·man \'sər-vəs-ˌman, -mən\ n **1** : a man who is a member of the armed forces **2** : a man employed to repair or maintain equipment

service mark n : a mark or device used to identify a service (as transportation or insurance) offered to customers

service station n : GAS STATION

ser·vice·wom·an \'sər-vəs-ˌwu̇-mən\ n : a woman who is a member of the armed forces

ser·vile \'sər-vəl, -ˌvī(-ə)l\ adj **1** : befitting a slave or servant **2** : behaving like a slave : SUBMISSIVE — **ser·vile·ly** adv — **ser·vil·i·ty** \ˌsər-'vi-lə-tē\ n

serv·ing \'sər-viŋ\ n : HELPING

ser·vi·tor \'sər-və-tər\ n : a male servant

ser·vi·tude \'sər-və-ˌtüd, -ˌtyüd\ n : SLAVERY, BONDAGE

ser·vo \'sər-vō\ n, pl **servos 1** : SERVOMOTOR **2** : SERVOMECHANISM

ser·vo·mech·a·nism \'sər-vō-ˌme-kə-ˌni-zəm\ n : a device for automatically correcting the performance of a mechanism

ser·vo·mo·tor \-ˌmō-tər\ n : a mechanism that supplements a primary control

ses·a·me \'se-sə-mē\ n : a widely cultivated annual herb of warm regions; also : its seeds that yield an edible oil (**sesame oil**) and are used in flavoring

ses·qui·cen·ten·ni·al \ˌses-kwi-sen-'te-nē-əl\ n [L sesqui- one and a half, half again] : a 150th anniversary or its celebration — **sesquicentennial** adj

ses·qui·pe·da·lian \ˌses-kwə-pə-'dāl-yən\ adj **1** : having many syllables : LONG **2** : using long words

ses·sile \'se-sī(-ə)l, -səl\ adj : permanently attached and not free to move about

ses·sion \'se-shən\ n **1** : a meeting or series of meetings of a body (as a court or legislature) for the transaction of business **2** : a meeting or period devoted to a particular activity

¹set \'set\ vb **set; set·ting 1** : to cause to sit **2** : PLACE **3** : ARRANGE, ADJUST **4** : to cause to be or do **5** : SETTLE, DECREE **6** : to fix in a frame **7** : to fix at a certain amount **8** : WAGER, STAKE **9** : to make or become fast or rigid **10** : to adapt (as words) to something (as music) **11** : to become fixed or firm or solid **12** : to be suitable : FIT **13** : BROOD **14** : to have a certain direction **15** : to pass below the horizon **16** : to defeat in bridge — **set about** : to begin to do — **set forth** : to begin a trip — **set off** **1** : to start out on a course or a trip **2** : to cause to explode — **set out** : to begin a trip or undertaking — **set sail** : to begin a voyage — **set upon** : to attack usu. with violence

²**set** *n* **1** : a setting or a being set **2** : DIRECTION, COURSE; *also* : TENDENCY **3** : FORM, BUILD **4** : the fit of something (as a coat) **5** : an artificial setting for the scene of a play or motion picture **6** : a group of tennis games in which one side wins at least six **7** : a group of persons or things of the same kind or having a common characteristic usu. classed together **8** : a collection of things and esp. of mathematical elements (as numbers or points) **9** : an electronic apparatus ⟨a television ∼⟩

³**set** *adj* **1** : DELIBERATE, INTENT **2** : fixed by authority or custom **3** : RIGID **4** : PERSISTENT

set·back \'set-ˌbak\ *n* : a temporary defeat : REVERSE

set back *vb* **1** : HINDER, DELAY; *also* : REVERSE **2** : COST

set piece **1** : a composition (as in literature or music) executed in fixed or ideal form often with brilliant effect **2** : a scene, depiction, speech, or event obviously designed to have an imposing effect

set·screw \'set-ˌskrü\ *n* : a screw screwed through one part tightly upon or into another part to prevent relative movement

set·tee \se-'tē\ *n* : a bench or sofa with a back and arms

set·ter \'se-tər\ *n* : a large long-coated hunting dog

set·ting \'se-tiŋ\ *n* **1** : the frame in which a gem is set **2** : the time, place, and circumstances in which something occurs or develops; *also* : SCENERY **3** : music written for a text (as of a poem) **4** : the eggs that a fowl sits on for hatching at one time

set·tle \'se-t°l\ *vb* **set·tled; set·tling** [ME *settlen* to seat, bring to rest, come to rest, fr. OE *setlan*, fr. *setl* seat] **1** : to place so as to stay **2** : to establish in residence; *also* : COLONIZE **3** : to make compact **4** : QUIET, CALM **5** : to establish or secure permanently **6** : to direct one's efforts **7** : to fix by agreement **8** : to give legally **9** : ADJUST, ARRANGE **10** : DECIDE, DETERMINE **11** : to make a final disposition of ⟨∼ an account⟩ **12** : to come to rest **13** : to reach an agreement on **14** : to sink gradually to a lower level **15** : to become clear by depositing sediment — **set·tler** *n*

set·tle·ment \'se-t°l-mənt\ *n* **1** : the act or process of settling **2** : BESTOWAL ⟨a marriage ∼⟩ **3** : payment or adjustment of an account **4** : COLONY **5** : a small village **6** : an institution providing various community services esp. to large city populations **7** : adjustment of doubts and differences

set–to \'set-ˌtü\ *n, pl* **set–tos** : FIGHT

set·up \'set-ˌəp\ *n* **1** : the manner or act of arranging **2** : glass, ice, and nonalcoholic beverage for mixing served to patrons who supply their own liquor **3** : something (as a plot) that has been constructed or contrived; *also* : FRAME-UP

set up *vb* **1** : to place in position; *also* : ASSEMBLE **2** : CAUSE **3** : FOUND, ESTABLISH **4** : FRAME **5**

sev·en \'se-vən\ *n* **1** : one more than six **2** : the 7th in a set or series **3** : something having seven units — **seven** *adj or pron* — **sev·enth** \-vənth\ *adj or adv or n*

sev·en·teen \ˌse-vən-'tēn\ *n* : one more than 16 — **seventeen** *adj or pron* — **sev·en·teenth** \-'tēnth\ *adj or n*

seventeen–year locust *n* : a cicada of the U.S. that has in the North a life of 17 years and in the South of 13 years of which most is spent underground as a nymph and only a few weeks as a winged adult

sev·en·ty \'se-vən-tē\ *n, pl* **-ties** : seven times 10 — **sev·en·ti·eth** \-tē-əth\ *adj or n* — **seventy** *adj or pron*

sev·er \'se-vər\ *vb* **sev·ered; sev·er·ing** : DIVIDE; *esp* : to separate by or as if by cutting — **sev·er·ance** \'sev-rəns, 'se-və-\ *n*

sev·er·al \'sev-rəl, 'se-və-\ *adj* [ME, fr. AF, fr. ML *separalis*, fr. L *separ* separate, fr. *separare* to separate] **1** : INDIVIDUAL, DISTINCT ⟨federal union of the ∼ states⟩ **2** : consisting of an indefinite number but yet not very many — **sev·er·al·ly** *adv*

severance pay *n* : extra pay given an employee on termination of employment

se·vere \sə-'vir\ *adj* **se·ver·er; -est** **1** : marked by strictness or sternness : AUSTERE **2** : strict in discipline **3** : causing distress and esp. physical discomfort or pain ⟨∼ weather⟩ ⟨a ∼ wound⟩ **4** : hard to endure ⟨∼ trials⟩ **5** : SERIOUS ⟨∼ depression⟩ ♦ *Synonyms* STERN, ASCETIC, ASTRINGENT — **se·vere·ly** *adv* — **se·ver·i·ty** \-'ver-ə-tē\ *n*

sew \'sō\ *vb* **sewed; sewn** \'sōn\ *or* **sewed; sew·ing** **1** : to unite or fasten by stitches **2** : to engage in sewing

sew·age \'sü-ij\ *n* : waste materials carried off by sewers

¹**sew·er** \'sō-ər\ *n* : one that sews

²**sew·er** \'sü-ər\ *n* : an artificial pipe or channel to carry off waste matter

sew·er·age \'sü-ə-rij\ *n* **1** : a system of sewers **2** : SEWAGE

sew·ing *n* **1** : the activity of one who sews **2** : material that has been or is to be sewed

sex \'seks\ *n* **1** : either of the two major forms that occur in many living things and are designated male or female according to their role in reproduction; *also* : the qualities by which these sexes are differentiated and which directly or indirectly function in reproduction involving two parents **2** : sexual activity or behavior; *also* : SEXUAL INTERCOURSE — **sexed** \'sekst\ *adj* — **sex·less** *adj*

sex·a·ge·nar·i·an \ˌsek-sə-jə-'ner-ē-ən\ *n* : a person whose age is in the sixties — **sexagenarian** *adj*

sex appeal : personal appeal or physical attractiveness esp. for members of the opposite sex

sex cell *n* : an egg cell or sperm cell

sex chromosome *n* : one of usu. a pair of chromosomes that are usu. similar in one sex but different in the other sex and are concerned with the inheritance of sex

sex hormone *n* : a steroid hormone (as estrogen or testosterone) that is produced esp. by the gonads or adrenal cortex an chiefly affects the growth or function of the reproductive organs

sex·ism \'sek-ˌsi-zəm\ *n* : prejudice or discrimination based on sex; *esp* : discrimination against women — **sex·ist** \'sek-sist\ *adj or n*

sex·ol·o·gy \sek-'sä-lə-jē\ *n* : the study of sex or of the interactions of the sexes — **sex·ol·o·gist** \-jist\ *n*

sex·pot \'seks-ˌpät\ *n* : a conspicuously sexy woman

sex symbol *n* : a usu. renowned person (as an entertainer) noted and admired for conspicuous attractiveness

sex·tant \'sek-stənt\ *n* [NL *sextant-, sextans* sixth part of a circle, fr. L, sixth part, fr. *sextus* sixth] : a navigational instrument for determining latitude

sex·tet \sek-'stet\ *n* **1** : a musical composition for six voices or instruments; *also* : the performers of such a composition **2** : a group or set of six

sex·ton \'sek-stən\ *n* : one who takes care of church property

sex·u·al \'sek-shə-wəl\ *adj* : of, relating to, or involving sex or the sexes ⟨a ∼ spore⟩ ⟨∼ relations⟩ — **sex·u·al·i·ty** \ˌsek-shə-'wa-lə-tē\ *n* — **sex·u·al·ly** \'sek-shə-wə-lē\ *adv*

sexual intercourse *n* **1** : intercourse between a male and a female in which the penis is inserted into the vagina **2** : intercourse between individuals involving genital contact other than insertion of the penis into the vagina

sexually transmitted disease *n* : a disease (as syphilis, gonorrhea, AIDS, or the genital form of herpes simplex) that is caused by a microorganism or virus usu. or often transmitted by direct sexual contact

sexual relations *n pl* : SEXUAL INTERCOURSE

sexy \'sek-sē\ *adj* **sex·i·er; -est** : sexually suggestive or stimulating : EROTIC — **sex·i·ly** \-sə-lē\ *adv* — **sex·i·ness** \-sē-nəs\ *n*

SF *abbr* **1** sacrifice fly **2** science fiction **3** square feet

SFC *abbr* sergeant first class

Sg *symbol* seaborgium

SG *abbr* **1** sergeant **2** solicitor general **3** surgeon general

sgd *abbr* signed

Sgt *abbr* sergeant

Sgt Maj *abbr* sergeant major

sh *abbr* share

shab·by \'sha-bē\ *adj* **shab·bi·er; -est** **1** : dressed in worn clothes **2** : threadbare and faded from wear **3** : DESPICABLE, MEAN; *also* : UNFAIR ⟨∼ treatment⟩ — **shab·bi·ly** \'sha-bə-lē\ *adv* — **shab·bi·ness** \-bē-nəs\ *n*

shack \'shak\ *n* : HUT, SHANTY

¹**shack·le** \'sha-kəl\ *n* **1** : something (as a manacle or fetter) that confines the legs or arms **2** : a check on free action made as if by fetters **3** : a device for making something fast or secure

²**shackle** *vb* **shack·led; shack·ling** : to bind or fasten with shackles

shad \'shad\ *n, pl* **shad** : any of several sea fishes related to the herrings that swim up rivers to spawn and include some important food fishes

¹shade \'shād\ *n* **1** : partial obscurity **2** : space sheltered from the light esp. of the sun **3** : PHANTOM **4** : something that shelters from or intercepts light or heat; *also, pl* : SUNGLASSES **5** : a dark color or a variety of a color **6** : a small difference

²shade *vb* **shad·ed**; **shad·ing** **1** : to shelter from light and heat **2** : DARKEN, OBSCURE **3** : to mark with degrees of light or color **4** : to show slight differences esp. in color or meaning

shad·ing *n* : the color and lines representing darkness or shadow in a drawing or painting

¹shad·ow \'sha-dō\ *n* **1** : partial darkness in a space from which light rays are cut off **2** : SHELTER **3** : shade cast upon a surface by something intercepting rays from a light ⟨the ∼ of a tree⟩ **4** : PHANTOM **5** : a shaded portion of a picture **6** : a small portion or degree : TRACE ⟨a ∼ of doubt⟩ **7** : a source of gloom or unhappiness — **shad·owy** *adj*

²shadow *vb* **1** : to cast a shadow on **2** : to represent faintly or vaguely **3** : to follow and watch closely : TRAIL

shad·ow·box \'sha-dō-ˌbäks\ *vb* : to box with an imaginary opponent esp. for training

shady \'shā-dē\ *adj* **shad·i·er**; **-est** **1** : affording shade **2** : of questionable honesty or reputation

¹shaft \'shaft\ *n, pl* **shafts** **1** : the long handle of a spear or lance **2** : SPEAR, LANCE **3** *or pl* **shaves** \'shavz\ : POLE; *esp* : one of two poles between which a horse is hitched to pull a vehicle **4** : something (as a column) long and slender **5** : a bar to support a rotating piece or to transmit power by rotation **6** : an inclined opening in the ground (as for finding or mining ore) **7** : a vertical opening (as for an elevator) through the floors of a building **8** : harsh or unfair treatment — usu. used with *the*

²shaft *vb* **1** : to fit with a shaft **2** : to treat unfairly or harshly

shag \'shag\ *n* : a shaggy tangled mass or covering (as of wool) : long coarse or matted fiber, nap, or pile

shag·gy \'sha-gē\ *adj* **shag·gi·er**; **-est** **1** : rough with or as if with long hair or wool **2** : tangled or rough in surface

shah \'shä, 'shò\ *n, often cap* : a sovereign of Iran

Shak *abbr* Shakespeare

¹shake \'shāk\ *vb* **shook** \'shùk\; **shak·en** \'shā-kən\; **shak·ing** **1** : to move or cause to move jerkily or irregularly **2** : BRANDISH, WAVE ⟨*shaking* his fist⟩ **3** : to disturb emotionally ⟨*shaken* by her death⟩ **4** : WEAKEN ⟨*shook* his faith⟩ **5** : to bring or come into a certain position, condition, or arrangement by or as if by moving jerkily **6** : to clasp (hands) in greeting or as a sign of goodwill or agreement ♦ *Synonyms* TREMBLE, QUAKE, QUAVER, SHIVER, QUIVER — **shak·able** *or* **shake·able** \'shā-kə-bəl\ *adj*

²shake *n* **1** : the act or a result of shaking **2** : DEAL, TREATMENT ⟨a fair ∼⟩

shake·down \'shāk-ˌdaùn\ *n* **1** : an improvised bed **2** : EXTORTION **3** : a process or period of adjustment **4** : a test (as of a new ship or airplane) under operating conditions

shake down *vb* **1** : to take up temporary quarters **2** : to occupy a makeshift bed **3** : to become accustomed esp. to new surroundings or duties **4** : to settle down **5** : to give a shakedown test to **6** : to obtain money from in a deceitful or illegal manner **7** : to bring about a reduction of

shak·er \'shā-kər\ *n* **1** : one that shakes ⟨pepper ∼⟩ **2** *cap* : a member of a religious sect founded in England in 1747

Shake·spear·ean *or* **Shake·spear·ian** \shāk-'spir-ē-ən\ *adj* : of, relating to, or having the characteristics of Shakespeare or his writings

shake–up \'shāk-ˌəp\ *n* : an extensive often drastic reorganization

shaky \'shā-kē\ *adj* **shak·i·er**; **-est** : UNSOUND, WEAK — **shak·i·ly** \'shā-kə-lē\ *adv* — **shak·i·ness** \-kē-nəs\ *n*

shale \'shāl\ *n* : a finely layered rock formed from clay, mud, or silt

shall \shəl, 'shal\ *vb, past* **should** \shəd, 'shùd\ *pres sing & pl* **shall** — used as an auxiliary to express a command, what seems inevitable or likely in the future, simple futurity, or determination

shal·lop \'sha-ləp\ *n* : a light open boat

shal·lot \shə-'lät, 'sha-lət\ *n* [modif. of F *échalote*] **1** : a small clustered bulb that is used in seasoning and is produced by a perennial herb belonging to a subspecies of the onion; *also* : this herb **2** : GREEN ONION

¹shal·low \'sha-lō\ *adj* **1** : not deep **2** : not intellectually profound

²shallow *n* : a shallow place in a body of water — usu. used in pl.

¹sham \'sham\ *n* **1** : an ornamental covering for a pillow **2** : COUNTERFEIT, IMITATION **3** : a person who shams

²sham *vb* **shammed**; **sham·ming** : FEIGN, PRETEND — **sham·mer** *n*

³sham *adj* : not genuine : FALSE, FEIGNED

sha·man \'shä-mən, 'shā-\ *n* [ultim. fr. Evenki (a language of Siberia) *šamān*] : a priest or priestess who uses magic to cure the sick, to divine the hidden, and to control events

sham·ble \'sham-bəl\ *vb* **sham·bled**; **sham·bling** : to shuffle along — **sham·ble** *n*

sham·bles \'sham-bəlz\ *n* **1** : a scene of great slaughter **2** : a scene or state of great destruction or disorder; *also* : MESS

¹shame \'shām\ *n* **1** : a painful sense of having done something wrong, improper, or immodest **2** : DISGRACE, DISHONOR **3** : a cause of feeling shame **4** : something to be regretted ⟨it's a ∼ you'll miss the party⟩ — **shame·ful** \-fəl\ *adj* — **shame·ful·ly** *adv* — **shame·less** *adj* — **shame·less·ly** *adv*

²shame *vb* **shamed**; **sham·ing** **1** : DISGRACE **2** : to make ashamed

shame·faced \'shām-ˌfāst\ *adj* : ASHAMED, ABASHED — **shame·faced·ly** \-ˌfā-səd-lē, -ˌfāst-lē\ *adv*

¹sham·poo \sham-'pü\ *vb* [Hindi *cāpo*, imper. of *cāpnā* to press, shampoo] : to wash (as the hair) with soap and water or with a special preparation; *also* : to clean (as a rug) similarly

²shampoo *n, pl* **shampoos** **1** : the act or an instance of shampooing **2** : a preparation for use in shampooing

sham·rock \'sham-ˌräk\ *n* [Ir *seamróg*, dim. of *seamar* clover] : a plant of folk legend with leaves composed of three leaflets that is associated with St. Patrick and Ireland

shang·hai \shaŋ-'hī\ *vb* **shang·haied**; **shang·hai·ing** [*Shanghai*, China] : to force aboard a ship for service as a sailor; *also* : to trick or force into an undesirable position

Shan·gri–la \ˌshaŋ-gri-'lä\ *n* [*Shangri-La*, imaginary land depicted in the novel *Lost Horizon* (1933) by James Hilton] : a remote idyllic hideaway

shank \'shaŋk\ *n* **1** : the part of the leg between the knee and the human ankle or a corresponding part of a quadruped **2** : a cut of meat from the leg **3** : the narrow part of the sole of a shoe beneath the instep **4** : the part of a tool or instrument (as a key or anchor) connecting the functioning part with a part by which it is held or moved

shan·tung \ˌshan-'təŋ\ *n* : a fabric in plain weave having a slightly irregular surface

shan·ty \'shan-tē\ *n, pl* **shanties** [prob. fr. CanF *chantier* lumber camp, hut, fr. F, builder's yard, ways, support for barrels, fr. OF, support, fr. L *cantherius* rafter, trellis] : a small roughly built shelter or dwelling

¹shape \'shāp\ *vb* **shaped**; **shap·ing** **1** : to form esp. in a particular shape **2** : DESIGN **3** : ADAPT, ADJUST **4** : REGULATE ♦ *Synonyms* MAKE, FASHION, FABRICATE, MANUFACTURE, FRAME, MOLD

²shape *n* **1** : APPEARANCE **2** : surface configuration : FORM **3** : bodily contour apart from the head and face : FIGURE **4** : PHANTOM **5** : CONDITION — **shaped** *adj*

shape·less \'shā-pləs\ *adj* **1** : having no definite shape **2** : not shapely — **shape·less·ly** *adv* — **shape·less·ness** *n*

shape·ly \'shā-plē\ *adj* **shape·li·er**; **-est** : having a pleasing shape — **shape·li·ness** *n*

shape–shift·er \'shāp-ˌshif-tər\ *n* : one that seems able to change form or identity at will

shard \'shärd\ *also* **sherd** \'shərd\ *n* : a broken piece : FRAGMENT

¹share \'sher\ *n* : PLOWSHARE

²share *n* **1** : a portion belonging to one person or group **2** : any of the equal interests into which the capital stock of a corporation is divided

³share *vb* **shared**; **shar·ing** **1** : APPORTION **2** : to use or enjoy with others **3** : PARTICIPATE — **shar·er** *n*

share·crop·per \-ˌkrä-pər\ *n* : a farmer who works anoth-

er's land in return for a share of the crop — **share·crop**
vb

share·hold·er \-ₕhōl-dər\ *n* : STOCKHOLDER

share·ware \'sher-ₕwer\ *n* : software available for usu. limited trial use at little or no cost but that can be upgraded for a fee

¹**shark** \'shärk\ *n* : any of various active, usu. predatory, and mostly large marine cartilaginous fishes

¹shark

²**shark** *n* : a greedy crafty person

shark·skin \-ₛskin\ *n*   **1** : the hide of a shark or leather made from it   **2** : a fabric woven from strands of many fine threads and having a sleek appearance and silky feel

¹**sharp** \'shärp\ *adj*   **1** : having a thin cutting edge or fine point : not dull or blunt   **2** : COLD, NIPPING ⟨a ~ wind⟩   **3** : keen in intellect, perception, or attention   **4** : BRISK, ENERGETIC   **5** : IRRITABLE ⟨a ~ temper⟩   **6** : causing intense distress ⟨a ~ pain⟩   **7** : HARSH, CUTTING ⟨a ~ rebuke⟩   **8** : affecting the senses as if cutting or piercing ⟨a ~ sound⟩ ⟨a ~ smell⟩   **9** : not smooth or rounded ⟨~ features⟩   **10** : involving an abrupt or extreme change ⟨a ~ turn⟩   **11** : CLEAR, DISTINCT ⟨mountains in ~ relief⟩; *also* : easy to perceive ⟨a ~ contrast⟩   **12** : higher than the true pitch; *also* : raised by a half step   **13** : STYLISH ⟨a ~ dresser⟩ ♦ *Synonyms* KEEN, ACUTE, QUICK-WITTED, PENETRATIVE — **sharp·ly** *adv* — **sharp·ness** *n*

²**sharp** *adv*   **1** : in a sharp manner   **2** : EXACTLY, PRECISELY ⟨left at 8 ~⟩

³**sharp** *n*   **1** : a sharp edge or point   **2** : a character ♯ which indicates that a specified note is to be raised by a half step; *also* : the resulting note   **3** : SHARPER

⁴**sharp** *vb* : to raise in pitch by a half step

shar–pei \ₛshä-'pā, ₛshär-\ *n, pl* **shar–peis** *often cap S&P* [Chin (Guangdong dial.) *sà* sand + *péi* fur] : any of a Chinese breed of dogs that have loose wrinkled skin esp. when young

sharp·en \'shär-pən\ *vb* : to make or become sharp — **sharp·en·er** *n*

sharp·er \'shär-pər\ *n* : SWINDLER; *esp* : a cheating gambler

sharp·ie *or* **sharpy** \'shär-pē\ *n, pl* **sharp·ies**   **1** : SHARPER   **2** : a person who is exceptionally keen or alert

sharp·shoot·er \'shärp-ₛshü-tər\ *n* : a proficient marksman — **sharp·shoot·ing** *n*

shat·ter \'sha-tər\ *vb* : to dash or burst into fragments — **shat·ter·proof** \'sha-tər-ₚprüf\ *adj*

¹**shave** \'shāv\ *vb* **shaved**; **shaved** *or* **shav·en** \'shā-vən\; **shav·ing**   **1** : to slice in thin pieces   **2** : to make bare or smooth by cutting the hair from   **3** : to cut or pare off by the sliding movement of a razor   **4** : to skim along or near the surface of

²**shave** *n*   **1** : any of various tools for cutting thin slices   **2** : an act or process of shaving

shav·er \'shā-vər\ *n*   **1** : an electric razor   **2** : BOY, YOUNGSTER

shaves *pl of* SHAFT

shaving *n*   **1** : the act of one that shaves   **2** : something shaved off

shawl \'shȯl\ *n* : a square or oblong piece of fabric used esp. by women as a loose covering for the head or shoulders

Shaw·nee \shȯ-'nē, shä-\ *n, pl* **Shawnee** *or* **Shawnees** : a member of an American Indian people orig. of the central Ohio valley; *also* : their language

shd *abbr* should

she \'shē\ *pron* : that female one ⟨who is ~⟩; *also* : that one regarded as feminine ⟨~'s a fine ship⟩

sheaf \'shēf\ *n, pl* **sheaves** \'shēvz\   **1** : a bundle of stalks and ears of grain   **2** : a group of things bound together

¹**shear** \'shir\ *vb* **sheared**; **sheared** *or* **shorn** \'shȯrn\; **shear·ing**   **1** : to cut the hair or wool from : CLIP, TRIM   **2** : to deprive by or as if by cutting   **3** : to cut or break sharply

²**shear** *n*   **1** : any of various cutting tools that consist of two blades fastened together so that the edges slide one by the other — usu. used in pl.   **2** *chiefly Brit* : the act, an instance, or the result of shearing   **3** : an action or stress caused by applied forces that causes two parts of a body to slide on each other

shear·wa·ter \'shir-ₛwȯ-tər, -ₓwä-\ *n* : any of several seabirds related to the petrels that often skim along waves in flight

sheath \'shēth\ *n, pl* **sheaths** \'shēthz, 'shēths\   **1** : a case for a blade (as of a knife); *also* : an anatomical covering suggesting such a case   **2** : a close-fitting dress usu. worn without a belt

sheathe \'shēth\ *also* **sheath** \'shēth\ *vb* **sheathed**; **sheath·ing**   **1** : to put into a sheath   **2** : to cover with something that guards or protects

sheath·ing \'shē-thiŋ, -thiŋ\ *n* : material used to sheathe something; *esp* : the first covering of boards or of waterproof material on the outside wall of a frame house or on a timber roof

sheave \'shiv, 'shēv\ *n* : a grooved wheel or pulley (as on a pulley block)

she-bang \shi-'baŋ\ *n* : everything involved in what is under consideration ⟨sold the whole ~⟩

¹**shed** \'shed\ *vb* **shed**; **shed·ding**   **1** : to cause to flow from a cut or wound ⟨~ blood⟩   **2** : to pour down in drops ⟨~ tears⟩   **3** : to give out (as light) : DIFFUSE   **4** : to throw off (as a natural covering) : DISCARD ⟨~ skin⟩

²**shed** *n* : a slight structure built for shelter or storage

sheen \'shēn\ *n* : a subdued luster

sheep \'shēp\ *n, pl* **sheep**   **1** : any of various cud-chewing mammals that are stockier than the related goats and lack a beard in the male; *esp* : one raised for meat or for its wool or skin   **2** : a timid or defenseless person   **3** : SHEEPSKIN

sheep·dog \'shēp-ₓdȯg\ *n* : a dog used to tend, drive, or guard sheep

sheep·fold \'shēp-ₓfōld\ *n* : a pen or shelter for sheep

sheep·herd·er \-ₓhər-dər\ *n* : a worker in charge of sheep esp. on open range — **sheep·herd·ing** *n*

sheep·ish \'shē-pish\ *adj* : BASHFUL, TIMID; *esp* : embarrassed by consciousness of a fault — **sheep·ish·ly** *adv*

sheep·skin \'shēp-ₓskin\ *n*   **1** : the hide of a sheep or leather prepared from it; *also* : PARCHMENT   **2** : DIPLOMA

¹**sheer** \'shir\ *vb* : to turn from a course

²**sheer** *adj*   **1** : very thin or transparent   **2** : UNQUALIFIED ⟨~ folly⟩   **3** : very steep ♦ *Synonyms* PURE, SIMPLE, ABSOLUTE, UNADULTERATED, UNMITIGATED — **sheer** *adv*

¹**sheet** \'shēt\ *n*   **1** : a broad piece of cloth (as for a bed); *also* : SAIL 1   **2** : a single piece of paper   **3** : a broad flat surface ⟨a ~ of ice⟩   **4** : something broad and long and relatively thin

²**sheet** *n* : a rope used to trim a sail

sheet·ing \'shē-tiŋ\ *n* : material in the form of sheets or suitable for forming into sheets

sheikh *or* **sheik** \'shēk, 'shāk\ *n* : an Arab chief — **sheikh·dom** *or* **sheik·dom** \-dəm\ *n*

shek·el \'she-kəl\ *n* — see MONEY table

shelf \'shelf\ *n, pl* **shelves** \'shelvz\   **1** : a thin flat usu. long and narrow structure fastened horizontally (as on a wall) above the floor to hold things   **2** : something (as a sandbar) that suggests a shelf

shelf life *n* : the period of storage time during which a material will remain useful

¹**shell** \'shel\ *n*   **1** : a hard or tough often thin outer covering of an animal (as a beetle, turtle, or mollusk) or of an egg or a seed or fruit (as a nut); *also* : something that resembles a shell ⟨a pastry ~⟩   **2** : a light narrow racing boat propelled by oarsmen   **3** : a case holding an explosive and designed to be fired from a cannon; *also* : a case holding the charge of powder and shot or bullet for small arms   **4** : a plain usu. sleeveless blouse or sweater — **shelled** \'sheld\ *adj* — **shelly** \'she-lē\ *adj*

²**shell** *vb*   **1** : to remove from a shell or husk   **2** : BOMBARD — **shell·er** *n*

¹**shel·lac** \shə-'lak\ *n*   **1** : a purified lac   **2** : lac dissolved in alcohol and used as a wood filler or finish

²**shellac** *vb* **shel·lacked; shel·lack·ing** **1** : to coat or treat with shellac **2** : to defeat decisively

shellacking *n* : a sound drubbing

shell bean *n* : a bean grown esp. for its edible seeds; *also* : its edible seed

shell·fish \-ˌfish\ *n* : an invertebrate water animal (as an oyster or lobster) with a shell

shell out *vb* : PAY

shell shock *n* : COMBAT FATIGUE — **shell–shocked** \'shel-ˌshäkt\ *adj*

¹**shel·ter** \'shel-tər\ *n* : something that gives protection : REFUGE

²**shelter** *vb* **shel·tered; shel·ter·ing** : to give protection or refuge to

shelve \'shelv\ *vb* **shelved; shelv·ing** **1** : to slope gradually **2** : to store on shelves **3** : to dismiss from service or use **4** : to put aside : DEFER ⟨∼ a proposal⟩

shelv·ing \'shel-viŋ\ *n* : material for shelves; *also* : SHELVES

she·nan·i·gan \shə-'na-ni-gən\ *n* **1** : an underhand trick **2** : questionable conduct — usu. used in pl. **3** : high-spirited or mischievous activity — usu. used in pl.

¹**shep·herd** \'she-pərd\ *n* **1** : one who tends sheep **2** : GERMAN SHEPHERD

²**shepherd** *vb* : to tend as or in the manner of a shepherd

shep·herd·ess \'she-pər-dəs\ *n* : a woman who tends sheep

shepherd's pie *n* : a meat pie with a mashed potato crust

sheqel *n, pl* **sheqalim** *var of* SHEKEL

sher·bet \'shər-bət\ *n* [Turk *şerbet,* fr. Pers *sharbat,* fr. Ar *sharba* drink] **1** : a drink of sweetened diluted fruit juice **2** *also* **sher·bert** \-bərt\ : a frozen dessert of fruit juices, sugar, milk or water, and egg whites or gelatin

sherd *var of* SHARD

sher·iff \'sher-əf\ *n* [ME *shirreve,* fr. OE *scīrgerēfa,* lit., shire reeve (local official)] : a county officer charged with the execution of the law and the preservation of order

sher·ry \'sher-ē\ *n, pl* **sherries** [alter. of earlier *sherris* (taken as pl.), fr. *Xeres* (now *Jerez*), Spain] : a fortified wine with a nutty flavor

Shet·land pony \'shet-lənd-\ *n* : any of a breed of small stocky hardy ponies

shew \'shō\ *Brit var of* SHOW

shi·at·su *also* **shi·at·zu** \shē-'ät-sü\ *n* : a form of acupressure originating in Japan

shib·bo·leth \'shi-bə-ləth\ *n* [Heb *shibbōleth* stream; fr. the use of this word as a test to distinguish the men of Gilead from members of the tribe of Ephraim (Judges 12:5, 6)] **1** : CATCHPHRASE **2** : language that is a criterion for distinguishing members of a group

¹**shield** \'shēld\ *n* **1** : a broad piece of defensive armor carried on the arm **2** : something that protects or hides **3** : a police officer's badge

²**shield** *vb* : to protect or hide with a shield ✦ *Synonyms* PROTECT, GUARD, SAFEGUARD

shier *comparative of* SHY

shiest *superlative of* SHY

¹**shift** \'shift\ *vb* **1** : EXCHANGE, REPLACE **2** : to change place, position, or direction : MOVE; *also* : to change gears **3** : GET BY, MANAGE

²**shift** *n* **1** : SCHEME, TRICK **2** : a woman's slip or loose-fitting dress **3** : a change in direction, emphasis, or attitude **4** : a group working together alternating with other groups **5** : TRANSFER **6** : GEARSHIFT

shift·less \'shift-ləs\ *adj* : LAZY, INEFFICIENT — **shift·less·ness** *n*

shifty \'shif-tē\ *adj* **shift·i·er; -est** **1** : TRICKY; *also* : ELUSIVE **2** : indicative of a tricky nature ⟨∼ eyes⟩

shih tzu \'shēd-'zü, 'shēt-'sü\ *n, pl* **shih tzus** *also* **shih tzu** *often cap S&T* [Chin (Beijing) *shīzi* (*gǒu,*) fr. *shīzi* lion + *gǒu* dog] : any of a breed of small short-legged dogs of Chinese origin that have a short muzzle and a long dense coat

shii·ta·ke \shē-'tä-kē\ *n* [Jp] : a dark Asian mushroom widely cultivated for its edible cap

shill \'shil\ *n* : one who acts as a decoy (as for a pitchman) — **shill** *vb*

shil·le·lagh *also* **shil·la·lah** \shə-'lā-lē\ *n* [*Shillelagh,* town in Ireland] : CUDGEL, CLUB

shil·ling \'shi-liŋ\ *n* : a former basic monetary unit of Austria

shil·ly–shal·ly \'shi-lē-ˌsha-lē\ *vb* **shilly–shall·ied; shilly–shally·ing** **1** : to show hesitation or lack of decisiveness **2** : to waste time

shim \'shim\ *n* : a thin often tapered piece of wood, metal, or stone used (as in leveling) to fill in space

shim·mer \'shi-mər\ *vb* : to shine waveringly or tremulously : GLIMMER ✦ *Synonyms* FLASH, GLEAM, GLINT, SPARKLE, GLITTER — **shimmer** *n* — **shim·mery** *adj*

shim·my \'shi-mē\ *n, pl* **shimmies** : an abnormal vibration esp. in the front wheels of a motor vehicle — **shimmy** *vb*

¹**shin** \'shin\ *n* : the front part of the leg below the knee

²**shin** *vb* **shinned; shin·ning** : to climb (as a pole) by gripping alternately with arms or hands and legs

shin·bone \'shin-ˌbōn\ *n* : TIBIA

¹**shine** \'shīn\ *vb* **shone** \'shōn\ *or* **shined; shin·ing** **1** : to give or cause to give light **2** : GLEAM, GLITTER **3** : to be eminent, conspicuous, or distinguished ⟨gave her a chance to ∼⟩ **4** : POLISH ⟨∼ your shoes⟩

²**shine** *n* **1** : BRIGHTNESS, RADIANCE **2** : LUSTER, BRILLIANCE **3** : fair weather : SUNSHINE ⟨rain or ∼⟩ **4** : LIKING, FANCY ⟨took a ∼ to them⟩ **5** : a polish given to shoes

shin·er \'shī-nər\ *n* **1** : a silvery fish; *esp* : any of numerous small freshwater American fishes related to the carp **2** : BLACK EYE

¹**shin·gle** \'shiŋ-gəl\ *n* **1** : a small thin piece of building material used in overlapping rows for covering a roof or outside wall **2** : a small sign

²**shingle** *vb* **shin·gled; shin·gling** : to cover with shingles

³**shingle** *n* : a beach strewn with gravel; *also* : coarse gravel (as on a beach)

shin·gles \'shiŋ-gəlz\ *n* : an acute inflammation of the spinal and cranial nerves caused by reactivation of the chicken pox virus and associated with eruptions and pain along the course of the affected nerves

shin·ny \'shi-nē\ *vb* **shin·nied; shin·ny·ing** : SHIN

shin splints *n sing or pl* : a condition marked by pain and sometimes tenderness and swelling in the shin caused by repeated small injuries to muscles and associated tissue esp. from running

Shin·to \'shin-ˌtō\ *n* : the indigenous religion of Japan consisting esp. in reverence of the spirits of natural forces and imperial ancestors — **Shin·to·ism** *n* — **Shin·to·ist** *n or adj*

shiny \'shī-nē\ *adj* **shin·i·er; -est** : BRIGHT, RADIANT; *also* : POLISHED

¹**ship** \'ship\ *n* **1** : a large oceangoing boat **2** : a ship's officers and crew **3** : AIRSHIP, AIRCRAFT, SPACECRAFT

²**ship** *vb* **shipped; ship·ping** **1** : to put or receive on board a ship for transportation **2** : to have transported by a carrier **3** : to take or draw into a boat ⟨∼ oars⟩ ⟨∼ water⟩ **4** : to engage to serve on a ship — **ship·per** *n*

-ship \ˌship\ *n suffix* **1** : state : condition : quality ⟨friend*ship*⟩ **2** : office : dignity : profession ⟨lord*ship*⟩ ⟨clerk*ship*⟩ **3** : art : skill ⟨horseman*ship*⟩ **4** : something showing, exhibiting, or embodying a quality or state ⟨town*ship*⟩ **5** : one entitled to a (specified) rank, title, or appellation ⟨his Lord*ship*⟩ **6** : the body of persons engaged in a specified activity ⟨reader*ship*⟩

ship·board \'ship-ˌbórd\ *n* : SHIP

ship·build·er \-ˌbil-dər\ *n* : one who designs or builds ships

ship·fit·ter \-ˌfi-tər\ *n* **1** : one who constructs ships **2** : a naval enlisted man who works as a plumber

ship·mate \-ˌmāt\ *n* : a fellow sailor

ship·ment \-mənt\ *n* : the process of shipping; *also* : the goods shipped

shipping *n* **1** : SHIPS; *esp* : ships in one port or belonging to one country **2** : transportation of goods

ship·shape \'ship-ˌshāp\ *adj* : TRIM, TIDY ⟨kept the garage ∼⟩

ship·worm \-ˌwərm\ *n* : any of various wormlike marine clams that have a shell used for burrowing in wood and damage wooden ships and wharves

¹**ship·wreck** \-ˌrek\ *n* **1** : a wrecked ship **2** : destruction or loss of a ship **3** : total loss or failure : RUIN

²**shipwreck** *vb* : to cause or meet disaster at sea through destruction or foundering

ship·wright \'ship-ˌrīt\ *n* : a carpenter skilled in ship construction and repair

ship·yard \-ˌyärd\ *n* : a place where ships are built or repaired

shire \'shī-(-ə)r, *in place-name compounds* ˌshir, shər\ *n* : a county in Great Britain

shirk \'shərk\ *vb* : to avoid performing (duty or work) — **shirk·er** *n*

shirr \'shər\ *vb* **1** : to make shirring in **2** : to bake (eggs removed from the shell) until set

shirr·ing \'shər-iŋ\ *n* : a decorative gathering in cloth made by drawing up parallel lines of stitches

shirt \'shərt\ *n* **1** : a loose cloth garment usu. having a collar, sleeves, a front opening, and a tail long enough to be tucked inside pants or a skirt **2** : UNDERSHIRT — **shirt·less** *adj*

shirt·ing \'shər-tiŋ\ *n* : cloth suitable for making shirts

shish ke·bab \'shish-kə-ˌbäb\ *n* [Turk *şiş kebabı*, fr. *şiş* spit + *kebap* roast meat] : kebab cooked on skewers

shiv \'shiv\ *n, slang* : KNIFE

¹shiv·er \'shi-vər\ *vb* : TREMBLE, QUIVER ♦ *Synonyms* SHUDDER, QUAVER, SHAKE, QUAKE

²shiver *n* : an instance of shivering — **shiv·ery** *adj*

shlemiel *var of* SCHLEMIEL

shlub *var of* SCHLUB

shmooze *var of* SCHMOOZE

Sho·ah \'shō-ə, -ˌä\ *n* : HOLOCAUST 2

¹shoal \'shōl\ *n* **1** : SHALLOW **2** : a sandbank or bar creating a shallow

²shoal *n* : a large group (as of fish)

shoat \'shōt\ *n* : a weaned young pig

¹shock \'shäk\ *n* : a pile of sheaves of grain or cornstalks set up in a field

²shock *n* [MF *choc*, fr. *choquer* to strike against] **1** : a sharp impact or violent shake or jar **2** : a sudden violent mental or emotional disturbance **3** : a state of bodily collapse that is often marked by a drop in blood pressure and volume and that is caused esp. by crushing wounds, blood loss, or burns **4** : the effect of a charge of electricity passing through the body **5** : SHOCK ABSORBER — **shock·proof** \-ˌprüf\ *adj*

³shock *vb* **1** : to strike with surprise, horror, or disgust **2** : to subject to the action of an electrical discharge

⁴shock *n* : a thick bushy mass (as of hair)

shock absorber *n* : any of several devices for absorbing the energy of sudden shocks in machinery

shock·er \'shä-kər\ *n* : one that shocks; *esp* : a sensational work of fiction or drama

shock·ing \'shä-kiŋ\ *adj* : extremely startling and offensive — **shock·ing·ly** *adv*

shock therapy *n* : the treatment of mental disorder by induction of coma or convulsions by drugs or electricity

shock wave *n* : a wave formed by the sudden violent compression of the medium through which it travels

¹shod·dy \'shä-dē\ *n* **1** : wool reclaimed from old rags; *also* : a fabric made from it **2** : inferior or imitation material

²shoddy *adj* **shod·di·er; -est** **1** : made of shoddy **2** : poorly done or made — **shod·di·ly** \'shä-də-lē\ *adv* — **shod·di·ness** \-dē-nəs\ *n*

¹shoe \'shü\ *n* **1** : a covering for the human foot **2** : HORSESHOE **3** : the part of a brake that presses on the wheel

²shoe *vb* **shod** \'shäd\ *also* **shoed** \'shüd\; **shoe·ing** : to put a shoe or shoes on

shoe·horn \-ˌhȯrn\ *n* : a curved implement (as of horn or plastic) used in putting on a shoe

shoe·lace \'shü-ˌlās\ *n* : a lace or string for fastening a shoe

shoe·mak·er \-ˌmā-kər\ *n* : one who makes or repairs shoes

shoe·string \-ˌstriŋ\ *n* **1** : SHOELACE **2** : a small sum of money

sho·gun \'shō-gən\ *n* [Jp *shōgun* general] : any of a line of military governors ruling Japan until the revolution of 1867–68 — **sho·gun·ate** \'shō-gə-nət, -ˌnāt\ *n*

shone *past and past part of* SHINE

shook *past of* SHAKE

shook–up \(ˌ)shůk-'əp\ *adj* : nervously upset : AGITATED

¹shoot \'shüt\ *vb* **shot** \'shät\; **shoot·ing** **1** : to drive (as an arrow or bullet) forward quickly or forcibly **2** : to hit, kill, or wound with a missile **3** : to cause a missile to be driven forth or forth from ⟨~ a gun⟩ **4** : to send forth (as a ray of light) **5** : to thrust forward or out **6** : to pass rapidly along ⟨~ the rapids⟩ **7** : PHOTOGRAPH,

FILM **8** : to move swiftly : DART **9** : to grow by or as if by sending out shoots; *also* : MATURE, DEVELOP — **shoot·er** *n*

²shoot *n* **1** : a plant stem with its leaves and branches esp. when not yet mature **2** : an act of shooting **3** : a shooting match

shooting iron *n* : FIREARM

shooting star *n* : METEOR 2

shoot up *vb* : to inject a narcotic into a vein

¹shop \'shäp\ *n* [ME *shoppe*, fr. OE *sceoppa* booth] **1** : a place where things are made or worked on : FACTORY, MILL **2** : a retail store ⟨dress ~⟩

²shop *vb* **shopped; shop·ping** : to visit stores for purchasing or examining goods — **shop·per** *n*

shop·keep·er \'shäp-ˌkē-pər\ *n* : a retail merchant

shop·lift \-ˌlift\ *vb* : to steal goods on display from a store — **shop·lift·er** *n*

shop·talk \-ˌtȯk\ *n* : talk about one's business or special interests

shop·worn \-ˌwȯrn\ *adj* : soiled or frayed from much handling in a store

¹shore \'shȯr\ *n* : land along the edge of a body of water — **shore·less** *adj*

²shore *vb* **shored; shor·ing** : to give support to : BRACE

³shore *n* : ¹PROP

shore·bird \-ˌbərd\ *n* : any of a suborder of birds (as the plovers and sandpipers) found mostly along the seashore

shore patrol *n* : a branch of a navy that exercises guard and police functions

shor·ing \'shȯr-iŋ\ *n* : a group of things that shore something up

shorn *past part of* SHEAR

¹short \'shȯrt\ *adj* **1** : not long or tall **2** : not great in distance **3** : brief in time **4** : not coming up to standard or to an expected amount **5** : CURT, ABRUPT **6** : insufficiently supplied ⟨~ of cash⟩ **7** : made with shortening : FLAKY **8** : consisting of or relating to a sale of securities or commodities that the seller does not possess or has not contracted for at the time of the sale ⟨~ sale⟩ — **short·ness** *n*

²short *adv* **1** : ABRUPTLY, CURTLY **2** : at some point before a goal aimed at

³short *n* **1** : something shorter than normal or standard **2** *pl* : drawers or pants of less than knee length **3** : SHORT CIRCUIT

⁴short *vb* : SHORT-CIRCUIT

short·age \'shȯr-tij\ *n* : LACK, DEFICIT

short·cake \'shȯrt-ˌkāk\ *n* : a dessert consisting of short biscuit spread with sweetened fruit

short·change \-'chānj\ *vb* : to cheat esp. by giving less than the correct amount of change

short circuit *n* : a connection made between points in an electric circuit where current is not intended to flow — **short–circuit** *vb*

short·com·ing \'shȯrt-ˌkə-miŋ\ *n* : FAULT 1, FLAW

short·cut \-ˌkət\ *n* **1** : a route more direct than that usu. taken **2** : a quicker way of doing something

short·en \'shȯr-tᵊn\ *vb* : to make or become short ♦ *Synonyms* CURTAIL, ABBREVIATE, ABRIDGE, RETRENCH

short·en·ing \'shȯr-tᵊn-iŋ\ *n* : a substance (as lard or butter) that makes pastry tender and flaky

short·hand \'shȯrt-ˌhand\ *n* : a method of writing rapidly by using symbols and abbreviations for letters, words, or phrases : STENOGRAPHY

short·hand·ed \ˌshȯrt-'han-dəd\ *adj* : short of the needed number of people

short·horn \'shȯrt-ˌhȯrn\ *n, often cap* : any of a breed of red, roan, or white cattle of English origin

short hundredweight *n* — see WEIGHT table

short–lived \'shȯrt-'livd, -'līvd\ *adj* : of short life or duration

short·ly \'shȯrt-lē\ *adv* **1** : in a few words **2** : in a short time : SOON

short–or·der \'shȯrt-ˌȯr-dər\ *adj* : preparing or serving food that can be quickly cooked

short shrift *n* **1** : a brief respite from death **2** : little consideration

short·sight·ed \'shȯrt-'sī-təd\ *adj* **1** : lacking foresight **2** : NEARSIGHTED — **short·sight·ed·ness** *n*

short·stop \-ˌstäp\ *n* : a baseball player defending the area between second and third base

short story *n* : a short work of fiction usu. dealing with a few characters and a single event

short–tem·pered \ˌshȯrt-ˈtem-pərd\ *adj* : having a quick temper

short–term \ˈshȯrt-ˌtərm\ *adj* **1** : occurring over or involving a relatively short period of time **2** : of or relating to a financial transaction based on a term usu. of less than a year

short ton *n* — see WEIGHT table

short·wave \ˈshȯrt-ˌwāv\ *n* : a radio wave with a wavelength between 10 and 100 meters

Sho·sho·ne *or* **Sho·sho·ni** \shə-ˈshō-nē\ *n, pl* **Shoshones** *or* **Shoshoni** : a member of an American Indian people orig. ranging through California, Idaho, Nevada, Utah, and Wyoming

¹shot \ˈshät\ *n* **1** : an act of shooting **2** : a stroke or throw in some games **3** : something that is shot : MISSILE, PROJECTILE; *esp* : small pellets forming a charge for a shotgun **4** : a metal sphere that is thrown for distance in the shot put **5** : RANGE, REACH **6** : MARKSMAN **7** : a single photographic exposure **8** : a single sequence of a motion picture or a television program made by one camera **9** : an injection (as of medicine) into the body **10** : a small serving of undiluted liquor or other beverage

²shot *past and past part of* SHOOT

shot·gun \ˈshät-ˌgən\ *n* : a gun with a smooth bore used to fire shot at short range

shot put *n* : a field event in which a shot is heaved for distance

should \ˈshu̇d, shəd\ *past of* SHALL — used as an auxiliary to express condition, obligation or propriety, probability, or futurity from a point of view in the past

¹shoul·der \ˈshōl-dər\ *n* **1** : the part of the body of a person or animal where the arm or foreleg joins the body **2** : either edge of a roadway **3** : a rounded or sloping part (as of a bottle) where the neck joins the body

²shoulder *vb* **1** : to push or thrust with the shoulder **2** : to bear on the shoulder **3** : to take the responsibility of

shoulder belt *n* : an automobile safety belt worn across the torso and over the shoulder

shoulder blade *n* : a flat triangular bone at the back of each shoulder

shout \ˈshau̇t\ *vb* : to utter a sudden loud cry — **shout** *n*

shove \ˈshəv\ *vb* **shoved; shov·ing** : to push along, aside, or away — **shove** *n*

¹shov·el \ˈshə-vəl\ *n* **1** : a broad long-handled scoop used to lift and throw material **2** : the amount a shovel will hold — **shov·el·ful** \ˈshə-vəl-ˌfu̇l\ *n*

²shovel *vb* **-eled** *or* **-elled; -el·ing** *or* **-el·ling** **1** : to take up and throw with a shovel **2** : to dig or clean out with a shovel

¹show \ˈshō\ *vb* **showed** \ˈshōd\; **shown** \ˈshōn\ *or* **showed; show·ing** **1** : to cause or permit to be seen : EXHIBIT ⟨~ anger⟩ **2** : CONFER, BESTOW ⟨~ mercy⟩ **3** : REVEAL, DISCLOSE ⟨~ed courage in battle⟩ **4** : INSTRUCT ⟨~ me how⟩ **5** : PROVE ⟨~s he was guilty⟩ **6** : APPEAR **7** : to be noticeable **8** : to be third in a horse race

²show *n* **1** : a demonstrative display **2** : outward appearance ⟨a ~ of resistance⟩ **3** : SPECTACLE **4** : a theatrical presentation **5** : a radio or television program **6** : third place in a horse race

¹show·case \ˈshō-ˌkās\ *n* : a cabinet for displaying items (as in a store)

²showcase *vb* **show·cased; show·cas·ing** : EXHIBIT

show·down \ˈshō-ˌdau̇n\ *n* : a decisive confrontation or contest; *esp* : the showing of poker hands to determine the winner of a pot

¹show·er \ˈshau̇(-ə)r\ *n* **1** : a brief fall of rain **2** : a party given by friends who bring gifts **3** : a bath in which water is showered on the person; *also* : a facility (as a stall) for such a bath — **show·ery** *adj*

²shower *vb* **1** : to rain or fall in a shower **2** : to bathe in a shower

show·man \ˈshō-mən\ *n* : a notably spectacular, dramatic, or effective performer — **show·man·ship** *n*

show–off \ˈshō-ˌȯf\ *n* : one that seeks to attract attention by conspicuous behavior

show off *vb* **1** : to display proudly **2** : to act as a show-off

show·piece \ˈshō-ˌpēs\ *n* : an outstanding example used for exhibition

show·place \-ˌplās\ *n* : an estate or building that is a showpiece

show up *vb* : ARRIVE

showy \ˈshō-ē\ *adj* **show·i·er; -est** : superficially impressive or striking ⟨a ~ orchid⟩ — **show·i·ly** \ˈshō-ə-lē\ *adv* — **show·i·ness** \-ē-nəs\ *n*

shpt *abbr* shipment

shrap·nel \ˈshrap-nəl\ *n, pl* **shrapnel** [Henry *Shrapnel* †1842 Eng. artillery officer] : bomb, mine, or shell fragments

¹shred \ˈshred\ *n* : a narrow strip cut or torn off : a small fragment

²shred *vb* **shred·ded; shred·ding** : to cut or tear into shreds

shrew \ˈshrü\ *n* **1** : any of a family of very small mammals with short velvety fur that are related to the moles **2** : a scolding woman

shrewd \ˈshrüd\ *adj* : CLEVER, ASTUTE — **shrewd·ly** *adv* — **shrewd·ness** *n*

shrew·ish \ˈshrü-ish\ *adj* : having an irritable disposition : ILL-TEMPERED — **shrew·ish·ly** *adv* — **shrew·ish·ness** *n*

shriek \ˈshrēk\ *n* : a shrill cry : SCREAM, YELL — **shriek** *vb*

shrift \ˈshrift\ *n, archaic* : the act of shriving : CONFESSION

shrike \ˈshrīk\ *n* : any of numerous usu. largely grayish or brownish birds that often impale their usu. insect prey upon thorns before devouring it

¹shrill \ˈshril\ *vb* : to make a high-pitched piercing sound

²shrill *adj* : high-pitched : PIERCING ⟨~ whistle⟩ — **shril·ly** *adv*

shrimp \ˈshrimp\ *n, pl* **shrimps** *or* **shrimp** **1** : any of various small marine crustaceans related to the lobsters **2** : a small or puny person

shrimp 1

shrine \ˈshrīn\ *n* [ME, receptacle for the relics of a saint, fr. OE *scrīn*, fr. L *scrinium* case, chest] **1** : the tomb of a saint; *also* : a place where devotion is paid to a saint or deity **2** : a place or object hallowed by its associations

¹shrink \ˈshriŋk\ *vb* **shrank** \ˈshraŋk\ *or* **shrunk** \ˈshrəŋk\; **shrunk** *or* **shrunk·en** \ˈshrəŋ-kən\; **shrink·ing** **1** : to draw back or away **2** : to become smaller or more compact **3** : to lessen in value ◆ *Synonyms* CONTRACT, CONSTRICT, COMPRESS, CONDENSE — **shrink·able** *adj*

²shrink *n* : a clinical psychiatrist or psychologist

shrink·age \ˈshriŋ-kij\ *n* **1** : the act of shrinking **2** : the amount lost by shrinkage

shrive \ˈshrīv\ *vb* **shrived** *or* **shrove** \ˈshrōv\; **shriv·en** \ˈshri-vən\ *or* **shrived** [ME, fr. OE *scrīfan* to prescribe, allot, shrive, fr. L *scribere* to write] : to administer the sacrament of reconciliation to

shriv·el \ˈshri-vəl\ *vb* **-eled** *or* **-elled; -el·ing** *or* **-el·ling** : to shrink and draw into wrinkles : DWINDLE

¹shroud \ˈshrau̇d\ *n* **1** : something that covers or screens **2** : a cloth placed over a dead body **3** : any of the ropes leading from the masthead of a ship to the side to support the mast

²shroud *vb* : to veil or screen from view

shrub \ˈshrəb\ *n* : a low usu. several-stemmed woody plant — **shrub·by** *adj*

shrub·bery \ˈshrə-bə-rē\ *n, pl* **-ber·ies** : a planting or growth of shrubs

shrug \ˈshrəg\ *vb* **shrugged; shrug·ging** : to hunch (the shoulders) up to express aloofness, indifference, or uncertainty — **shrug** *n*

shrug off *vb* **1** : to brush aside : MINIMIZE **2** : to shake off **3** : to remove (a garment) by wriggling out

shtick *also* **schtick** *or* **shtik** \ˈshtik\ *n* [Yiddish *shtik* pranks, lit., piece] **1** : a usu. comic or repetitious performance or routine **2** : one's special trait, interest, or activity

¹shuck \'shək\ *n* : SHELL, HUSK

²shuck *vb* : to strip of shucks

shud·der \'shə-dər\ *vb* : TREMBLE, QUAKE — **shudder** *n*

shuf·fle \'shə-fəl\ *vb* **shuf·fled; shuf·fling 1** : to mix in a disorderly mass **2** : to rearrange the order of (cards in a pack) by mixing two parts of the pack together **3** : to shift from place to place **4** : to move with a sliding or dragging gait **5** : to dance in a slow lagging manner — **shuffle** *n*

shuf·fle·board \'shə-fəl-ˌbȯrd\ *n* : a game in which players use long-handled cues to shove disks into scoring areas marked on a smooth surface

shun \'shən\ *vb* **shunned; shun·ning** : to avoid deliberately or habitually ◆ *Synonyms* EVADE, ELUDE, ESCAPE, DUCK

¹shunt \'shənt\ *vb* [ME, to turn away] : to turn off to one side; *esp* : to switch (a train) from one track to another

²shunt *n* **1** : a method or device for turning or thrusting aside **2** : a conductor joining two points in an electrical circuit forming an alternate path through which a portion of the current may pass

shut \'shət\ *vb* **shut; shut·ting 1** : CLOSE **2** : to forbid entrance into **3** : to lock up **4** : to fold together ⟨~ a penknife⟩ **5** : to cease or suspend activity ⟨~ down an assembly line⟩

shut·down \-ˌdaün\ *n* : a temporary cessation of activity (as in a factory)

shut–in \'shət-ˌin\ *n* : a person confined to home, a room, or bed because of illness or incapacity

shut·out \'shət-ˌaüt\ *n* : a game or contest in which one side fails to score

shut out *vb* **1** : EXCLUDE **2** : to prevent (an opponent) from scoring in a game or contest

shut·ter \'shə-tər\ *n* **1** : a movable cover for a door or window : BLIND **2** : the part of a camera that opens and closes to allow light to enter

shut·ter·bug \'shə-tər-ˌbəg\ *n* : a photography enthusiast

¹shut·tle \'shə-tᵊl\ *n* **1** : an instrument used in weaving for passing the horizontal threads between the vertical threads **2** : a vehicle traveling back and forth over a short route ⟨a ~ bus⟩ **3** : SPACE SHUTTLE

²shuttle *vb* **shut·tled; shut·tling** : to move back and forth frequently

shut·tle·cock \'shə-tᵊl-ˌkäk\ *n* : a light conical object (as of cork or plastic) used in badminton

shut up *vb* : to cease or cause to cease talking

¹shy \'shī\ *adj* **shi·er** *or* **shy·er** \'shī-ər\; **shi·est** *or* **shy·est** \'shī-əst\ **1** : easily frightened : TIMID **2** : WARY **3** : BASHFUL **4** : DEFICIENT, LACKING — **shy·ly** *adv* — **shy·ness** *n*

²shy *vb* **shied; shy·ing 1** : to show a dislike : RECOIL **2** : to start suddenly aside through fright ⟨the horse *shied*⟩

shy·ster \'shīs-tər\ *n* : an unscrupulous lawyer or politician

Si *symbol* silicon

SI *abbr* [F *Système International d'Unités*] International System of Units

Si·a·mese \ˌsī-ə-ˈmēz, -ˈmēs\ *n, pl* **Sia·mese** : THAI — **Siamese** *adj*

Siamese cat *n* : any of a breed of slender blue-eyed short= haired domestic cats of Asian origin

Siamese twin *n* [fr. Chang †1874 and Eng †1874 twins born in Siam with bodies united] : one of a pair of twins with bodies joined together at birth

Siberian husky *n* : any of a breed of thick-coated compact dogs orig. developed in Siberia to pull sleds

¹sib·i·lant \'si-bə-lənt\ *adj* : having, containing, or producing the sound of or a sound resembling that of the *s* or the *sh* in *sash* — **sib·i·lant·ly** *adv*

²sibilant *n* : a sibilant speech sound (as English \s\, \z\, \sh\, \zh\, \ch (=tsh)\, or \j (=dzh)\)

sib·ling \'si-bliŋ\ *n* : a brother or sister considered irrespective of sex; *also* : one of two or more offspring having one common parent

sib·yl \'si-bəl\ *n, often cap* : PROPHETESS — **sib·yl·line** \-bə-ˌlīn, -ˌlēn\ *adj*

sic \'sik, 'sēk\ *adv* : intentionally so written — used after a printed word or passage to indicate that it exactly reproduces an original ⟨said he seed [~] it all⟩

sick \'sik\ *adj* **1** : not in good health : ILL; *also* : of, relating to, or intended for use in sickness ⟨~ pay⟩ **2** : NAUSEATED **3** : DISGUSTED **4** : PINING **5** : mentally or emotionally unsound **6** : MACABRE, SADISTIC ⟨~ jokes⟩ — **sick·ly** *adj*

sick·bed \'sik-ˌbed\ *n* : a bed on which one lies sick

sick·en \'si-kən\ *vb* : to make or become sick — **sick·en·ing·ly** *adv*

sick·le \'si-kəl\ *n* : a cutting tool consisting of a curved metal blade with a short handle

sickle–cell anemia *n* : an inherited anemia in which red blood cells tend to become crescent-shaped and clog small blood vessels and which occurs esp. in individuals of African, Mediterranean, or southwest Asian ancestry

sick·ness \'sik-nəs\ *n* **1** : ill health; *also* : a specific disease **2** : NAUSEA

side \'sīd\ *n* **1** : the right or left part of the trunk of a body **2** : a place away from a central point or line **3** : a border of an object; *esp* : one of the longer borders as contrasted with an end **4** : an outer surface of an object **5** : a position regarded as opposite to another **6** : a body of contestants — **side** *adj* — **on the side** : in addition to the main portion

side·arm \-ˌärm\ *adj* : made with a sideways sweep of the arm ⟨a ~ pitch⟩ — **sidearm** *adv*

side arm *n* : a weapon worn at the side or in the belt

side·bar \'sīd-ˌbär\ *n* : a short news story accompanying a major story and presenting related information

side·board \-ˌbȯrd\ *n* : a piece of dining-room furniture for holding articles of table service

side·burns \-ˌbərnz\ *n pl* : whiskers on the side of the face in front of the ears

side by side *adv* **1** : beside one another **2** : in the same place, time, or circumstance — **side–by–side** *adj*

side·car \-ˌkär\ *n* : a one-wheeled passenger car attached to the side of a motorcycle

side effect *n* : a secondary and usu. adverse effect (as of a drug)

side·kick \'sīd-ˌkik\ *n* : PAL, PARTNER

side·line \'sīd-ˌlīn\ *n* **1** : an activity pursued in addition to one's regular occupation **2** : the space immediately outside the lines of an athletic field or court **3** : a sphere of little or no participation — usu. used in pl.

¹side·long \'sīd-ˌlȯŋ\ *adv* : in the direction of or along the side : OBLIQUELY

²sidelong *adj* : directed to one side ⟨~ look⟩

side·man \'sīd-ˌman\ *n* : a member of a jazz or swing orchestra

side·piece \-ˌpēs\ *n* : a piece forming or contained in the side of something

si·de·re·al \sī-ˈdir-ē-əl, sə-\ *adj* [L *sidereus*, fr. *sider-, sidus* star, constellation] **1** : of or relating to the stars **2** : measured by the apparent motion of the stars

side·sad·dle \'sīd-ˌsa-dᵊl\ *n* : a saddle for women on which the rider sits with both legs on the same side of the horse — **sidesaddle** *adv*

side·show \'sīd-ˌshō\ *n* **1** : a minor show offered in addition to a main exhibition (as of a circus) **2** : an incidental diversion

side·step \-ˌstep\ *vb* **1** : to step aside **2** : AVOID, EVADE

side·stroke \-ˌstrōk\ *n* : a swimming stroke which is executed on the side and in which the arms are swept backward and downward and the legs do a scissors kick

side·swipe \-ˌswīp\ *vb* : to strike with a glancing blow along the side — **sideswipe** *n*

¹side·track \-ˌtrak\ *n* : SIDING 1

²sidetrack *vb* **1** : to switch from a main railroad line to a siding **2** : to turn aside from a purpose

side·walk \'sīd-ˌwȯk\ *n* : a paved walk at the side of a road or street

side·wall \-ˌwȯl\ *n* **1** : a wall forming the side of something **2** : the side of an automobile tire

side·ways \-ˌwāz\ *adv or adj* **1** : from the side **2** : with one side to the front **3** : to, toward, or at one side

side·wind·er \-ˌwīn-dər\ *n* : a small pale-colored desert rattlesnake of the southwestern U.S.

sid·ing \'sī-diŋ\ *n* **1** : a short railroad track connected with the main track **2** : material (as boards) covering the outside of frame buildings

si·dle \'sī-dᵊl\ *vb* **si·dled; si·dling** : to move sideways or with one side foremost

SIDS *abbr* sudden infant death syndrome

siege \'sēj\ *n* **1** : the placing of an army around or before a fortified place to force its surrender **2** : a persistent attack (as of illness)

sie·mens \'sē-mənz, 'zē-\ *n* : a unit of conductance equivalent to one ampere per volt

si·er·ra \sē-'er-ə\ *n* [Sp, lit., saw, fr. L *serra*] : a range of mountains esp. with jagged peaks

si·es·ta \sē-'es-tə\ *n* [Sp, fr. L *sexta (hora)* noon, lit., sixth hour] : a midday rest or nap

sieve \'siv\ *n* : a utensil with meshes or holes to separate finer particles from coarser or solids from liquids

sift \'sift\ *vb* **1** : to pass through a sieve **2** : to separate with or as if with a sieve **3** : to examine carefully **4** : to scatter by or as if by passing through a sieve — **sift·er** *n*

sig *abbr* signature

SIG *abbr* special interest group

sigh \'sī\ *vb* **1** : to let out a deep audible breath (as in weariness or sorrow) **2** : GRIEVE, YEARN — **sigh** *n*

¹sight \'sīt\ *n* **1** : something seen or worth seeing **2** : the process or power of seeing; *esp* : the sense of which the eye is the receptor and by which qualities of appearance (as position, shape, and color) are perceived **3** : INSPECTION **4** : a device (as a small bead on a gun barrel) that aids the eye in aiming **5** : VIEW, GLIMPSE **6** : the range of vision — **sight·less** *adj*

²sight *vb* **1** : to get sight of **2** : to aim by means of a sight

sight·ed \'sī-təd\ *adj* : having sight

sight·ly \-lē\ *adj* : pleasing to the sight

sight·see·ing \'sīt-,sē-iŋ\ *adj* : engaged in or used for seeing sights of interest — **sight·seer** \-,sē-ər\ *n*

sig·ma \'sig-mə\ *n* : the 18th letter of the Greek alphabet — Σ or σ or ς

¹sign \'sīn\ *n* **1** : a gesture expressing a command, wish, or thought **2** : SYMBOL **3** : a notice publicly displayed for advertising purposes or for giving direction or warning **4** : OMEN, PORTENT **5** : TRACE, VESTIGE

²sign *vb* **1** : to mark with a sign **2** : to represent by a sign **3** : to make a sign or signal **4** : to write one's name in token of assent or obligation **5** : to assign legally **6** : to use sign language — **sign·er** *n*

¹sig·nal \'sig-nəl\ *n* **1** : a sign agreed on as the start of some joint action **2** : a sign giving warning or notice of something **3** : the message, sound, or image transmitted in electronic communication (as radio)

²signal *vb* **-naled** *or* **-nalled; -nal·ing** *or* **-nal·ling** **1** : to notify by a signal **2** : to communicate by signals

³signal *adj* : DISTINGUISHED ⟨a ~ honor⟩ — **sig·nal·ly** *adv*

sig·nal·ize \'sig-nə-,līz\ *vb* **-ized; -iz·ing** : to point out or make conspicuous — **sig·nal·i·za·tion** \,sig-nə-lə-'zā-shən\ *n*

sig·nal·man \'sig-nəl-mən, -,man\ *n* : a person who signals or works with signals

sig·na·to·ry \'sig-nə-,tòr-ē\ *n, pl* **-ries** : a person or government that signs jointly with others — **signatory** *adj*

sig·na·ture \'sig-nə-,chùr\ *n* **1** : the name of a person written by himself or herself **2** : the sign placed after the clef to indicate the key or the meter of a piece of music

sign·board \'sīn-,bòrd\ *n* : a board bearing a sign or notice

sig·net \'sig-nət\ *n* : a small intaglio seal (as in a ring)

sig·nif·i·cance \sig-'ni-fi-kəns\ *n* **1** : something signified : MEANING **2** : SUGGESTIVENESS **3** : CONSEQUENCE, IMPORTANCE

sig·nif·i·cant \-kənt\ *adj* **1** : having meaning; *esp* : having a hidden or special meaning **2** : having or likely to have considerable influence or effect : IMPORTANT — **sig·nif·i·cant·ly** *adv*

sig·ni·fy \'sig-nə-,fī\ *vb* **-fied; -fy·ing** **1** : to show by a sign **2** : MEAN, IMPORT **3** : to have significance — **sig·ni·fi·ca·tion** \,sig-nə-fə-'kā-shən\ *n*

sign in *vb* : to make a record of arrival (as by signing a register)

sign language *n* : a formal system of hand gestures used for communication (as by the deaf)

sign off *vb* : to announce the end (as of a program or broadcast)

sign of the cross : a gesture of the hand forming a cross (as to invoke divine blessing)

sign on *vb* **1** : ENLIST **2** : to announce the start of broadcasting for the day

sign out *vb* : to make a record of departure (as by signing a register)

sign·post \'sīn-,pōst\ *n* : a post bearing a sign

sign up *vb* : to sign one's name in order to obtain, do, or join something

Sikh \'sēk\ *n* : an adherent of a religion of India marked by rejection of caste — **Sikh·ism** *n*

si·lage \'sī-lij\ *n* : fodder fermented (as in a silo) to produce a rich moist animal feed

¹si·lence \'sī-ləns\ *n* **1** : the state of being silent **2** : STILLNESS **3** : SECRECY

²silence *vb* **si·lenced; si·lenc·ing** **1** : to reduce to silence : STILL **2** : to cause to cease hostile firing or criticism

si·lenc·er \'sī-lən-sər\ *n* : a device for muffling the noise of a gunshot

si·lent \'sī-lənt\ *adj* **1** : not speaking : MUTE; *also* : TACITURN **2** : STILL, QUIET **3** : performed or borne without utterance ♦ **Synonyms** RETICENT, RESERVED, CLOSEMOUTHED, CLOSE — **si·lent·ly** *adv*

¹sil·hou·ette \,si-lə-'wet\ *n* [F] **1** : a representation of the outlines of an object filled in with black or some other uniform color **2** : OUTLINE ⟨~ of a ship⟩

²silhouette *vb* **-ett·ed; -ett·ing** : to represent by a silhouette; *also* : to show against a light background

sil·i·ca \'si-li-kə\ *n* : a mineral that consists of silicon and oxygen

sil·i·cate \'si-lə-,kāt, 'si-li-kət\ *n* : a chemical salt that consists of a metal combined with silicon and oxygen

si·li·ceous *also* **si·li·cious** \sə-'li-shəs\ *adj* : of, relating to, or containing silica or a silicate

sil·i·con \'si-li-kən, 'si-lə-,kän\ *n* : a nonmetallic chemical element that occurs in combination as the most abundant element next to oxygen in the earth's crust and is used esp. in alloys and semiconductors

sil·i·cone \'si-lə-,kōn\ *n* : an organic silicon compound used esp. for lubricants and varnishes

sil·i·co·sis \,si-lə-'kō-səs\ *n* : a lung disease caused by prolonged inhaling of silica dusts

silk \'silk\ *n* **1** : a fine strong lustrous protein fiber produced by various insect larvae usu. for their cocoons; *esp* : one from moth larvae (**silk·worms** \-,wərmz\) used for cloth **2** : thread or cloth made from silk — **silk·en** \'sil-kən\ *adj* — **silky** *adj*

silk screen *n* : a stencil process in which coloring matter is forced through the meshes of a prepared silk or organdy screen; *also* : a print made by this process — **silk–screen** *vb*

sill \'sil\ *n* : a heavy crosspiece (as of wood or stone) that forms the bottom member of a window frame or a doorway; *also* : a horizontal supporting piece at the base of a structure

sil·ly \'si-lē\ *adj* **sil·li·er; -est** [ME *sely, silly* happy, innocent, pitiable, feeble, fr. OE *sǣlig*, fr. *sǣl* happiness] : FOOLISH, ABSURD, STUPID — **sil·li·ness** *n*

si·lo \'sī-lō\ *n, pl* **silos** [Sp] **1** : a trench, pit, or esp. a tall cylinder for making and storing silage **2** : an underground structure for housing a guided missile

¹silt \'silt\ *n* **1** : fine earth; *esp* : particles of such soil floating in rivers, ponds, or lakes **2** : a deposit (as by a river) of silt — **silty** *adj*

²silt *vb* : to obstruct or cover with silt — **silt·ation** \sil-'tā-shən\ *n*

Si·lu·ri·an \sī-'lùr-ē-ən\ *adj* : of, relating to, or being the period of the Paleozoic era between the Ordovician and the Devonian marked by the appearance of the first land plants — **Silurian** *n*

¹sil·ver \'sil-vər\ *n* **1** : a white ductile metallic chemical element that takes a high polish and is a better conductor of heat and electricity than any other substance **2** : coin made of silver **3** : FLATWARE **4** : a grayish white color — **sil·very** *adj*

²silver *adj* **1** : relating to, made of, or coated with silver **2** : SILVERY

³silver *vb* **sil·vered; sil·ver·ing** : to coat with or as if with silver — **sil·ver·er** *n*

silver bromide *n* : a light-sensitive compound used esp. in photography

sil·ver·fish \'sil-vər-,fish\ *n* : any of various small wingless insects found in houses and sometimes injurious esp. to sized paper and starched clothes

silver iodide *n* : a light-sensitive compound used in photography, rainmaking, and medicine

silver maple *n* : a No. American maple with deeply cut leaves that are green above and silvery white below

silver nitrate *n* : a soluble compound used in photography and as an antiseptic

sil·ver·ware \'sil-vər-ˌwer\ *n* : FLATWARE

sim *abbr* simulation; simulator

sim·i·an \'si-mē-ən\ *n* : MONKEY, APE — **simian** *adj*

simian immunodeficiency virus *n* : SIV

sim·i·lar \'si-mə-lər\ *adj* : marked by correspondence or resemblance ♦ **Synonyms** ALIKE, AKIN, COMPARABLE, PARALLEL — **sim·i·lar·i·ty** \ˌsi-mə-ˈler-ə-tē\ *n* — **sim·i·lar·ly** *adv*

sim·i·le \'si-mə-(ˌ)lē\ *n* [ME, fr. L, likeness, comparison, fr. neut. of *similis* like, similar] : a figure of speech in which two dissimilar things are compared by the use of *like* or *as* (as in "cheeks like roses")

si·mil·i·tude \sə-ˈmi-lə-ˌtüd, -ˌtyüd\ *n* : LIKENESS, RESEMBLANCE

sim·mer \'si-mər\ *vb* **sim·mered; sim·mer·ing** 1 : to stew at or just below the boiling point 2 : to be on the point of bursting out with violence or emotional disturbance — **simmer** *n*

simmer down *vb* : to become calm or peaceful

si·mo·nize \'sī-mə-ˌnīz\ *vb* **-nized; -niz·ing** : to polish with or as if with wax

si·mo·ny \'sī-mə-nē, 'si-\ *n* [ME *symonie*, fr. AF *simonie*, fr. LL *simonia*, fr. *Simon* Magus sorcerer of Samaria in Acts 8:9–24] : the buying or selling of a church office

sim·pa·ti·co \sim-ˈpä-ti-ˌkō, -ˈpa-\ *adj* : CONGENIAL, LIKABLE

sim·per \'sim-pər\ *vb* : to smile in a silly manner — **simper** *n*

sim·ple \'sim-pəl\ *adj* **sim·pler** \-pə-lər\; **sim·plest** \-pə-ləst\ [ME, fr. AF, plain, uncomplicated, artless, fr. L *simplus, simplex*, lit., single; L *simplus* fr. *sim-* one + *-plus* multiplied by; L *simplex* fr. *sim-* + *-plex* -fold] 1 : free from dishonesty or vanity : INNOCENT 2 : free from ostentation 3 : of humble origin or modest position 4 : STUPID 5 : not complex : PLAIN ⟨a ~ melody⟩ ⟨~ directions⟩ 6 : lacking education, experience, or intelligence 7 : developing from a single ovary ⟨a ~ fruit⟩ ♦ **Synonyms** EASY, FACILE, LIGHT, EFFORTLESS — **simple·ness** *n* — **sim·ply** *adv*

simple interest *n* : interest paid or computed on the original principal only of a loan or on the amount of an account

sim·ple·ton \'sim-pəl-tən\ *n* : FOOL

sim·plic·i·ty \sim-ˈpli-sə-tē\ *n, pl* **-ties** 1 : lack of complication : CLEARNESS 2 : CANDOR, ARTLESSNESS 3 : plainness in manners or way of life 4 : SILLINESS, FOLLY

sim·pli·fy \'sim-plə-ˌfī\ *vb* **-fied; -fy·ing** : to make less complex — **sim·pli·fi·ca·tion** \ˌsim-plə-fə-ˈkā-shən\ *n*

sim·plis·tic \sim-ˈplis-tik\ *adj* : excessively simple : tending to overlook complexities ⟨a ~ solution⟩

sim·u·late \'sim-yə-ˌlāt\ *vb* **-lat·ed; -lat·ing** : to give or create the effect or appearance of : IMITATE; *also* : to make a simulation of — **sim·u·la·tor** \'sim-yə-ˌlā-tər\ *n*

sim·u·la·tion \ˌsim-yə-ˈlā-shən\ *n* 1 : the act or process of simulating 2 : an object that is not genuine 3 : the imitation by one system or process of the way in which another system or process works

si·mul·ta·ne·ous \ˌsī-məl-ˈtā-nē-əs, ˌsi-\ *adj* : occurring or operating at the same time — **si·mul·ta·ne·ous·ly** *adv* — **si·mul·ta·ne·ous·ness** *n*

¹sin \'sin\ *n* 1 : an offense esp. against God 2 : FAULT 3 : a weakened state of human nature in which the self is estranged from God — **sin·less** *adj*

²sin *vb* **sinned; sin·ning** : to commit a sin — **sin·ner** *n*

³sin *abbr* sine

¹since \'sins\ *adv* 1 : from a past time until now 2 : backward in time : AGO 3 : after a time in the past

²since *conj* 1 : from the time when 2 : seeing that : BECAUSE

³since *prep* 1 : in the period after ⟨changes made ~ the war⟩ 2 : continuously from ⟨has been here ~ 1980⟩

sin·cere \sin-ˈsir\ *adj* **sin·cer·er; sin·cer·est** 1 : free from hypocrisy : HONEST 2 : GENUINE, REAL — **sin·cere·ly** *adv* — **sin·cer·i·ty** \-ˈser-ə-tē\ *n*

sine \'sīn\ *n* [ML *sinus*, fr. L, curve] : the trigonometric function that is the ratio between the side opposite an acute angle in a right triangle and the hypotenuse

si·ne·cure \'sī-ni-ˌkyur, 'si-\ *n* : a paying job that requires little or no work

si·ne die \ˌsī-ni-ˈdī-ˌē, ˌsi-nā-ˈdē-ˌā\ *adv* [L, without day] : INDEFINITELY ⟨the meeting adjourned *sine die*⟩

si·ne qua non \ˌsi-ni-ˌkwä-ˈnän, -ˈnōn\ *n, pl* **sine qua nons** *also* **sine qui·bus non** \-ˌkwi-(ˌ)bùs-\ [LL, without which not] : something indispensable or essential

sin·ew \'sin-yü\ *n* 1 : TENDON 2 : physical strength — **sin·ewy** *adj*

sin·ful \'sin-fəl\ *adj* : marked by or full of sin : WICKED — **sin·ful·ly** *adv* — **sin·ful·ness** *n*

¹sing \'siŋ\ *vb* **sang** \'saŋ\ *or* **sung** \'səŋ\; **sung; sing·ing** 1 : to produce musical tones with the voice; *also* : to utter with musical tones 2 : to make a prolonged shrill sound ⟨locusts ~ing⟩ 3 : to produce harmonious sustained sounds ⟨birds ~ing⟩ 4 : CHANT, INTONE 5 : to write poetry; *also* : to celebrate in song or verse 6 : to give information or evidence — **sing·er** *n*

²sing *abbr* singular

singe \'sinj\ *vb* **singed; singe·ing** : to scorch lightly the outside of; *esp* : to remove the hair or down from usu. by passing over a flame

¹sin·gle \'siŋ-gəl\ *adj* 1 : UNMARRIED 2 : being alone : being the only one 3 : having only one feature or part 4 : made for one person ♦ **Synonyms** SOLE, UNIQUE, LONE, SOLITARY, SEPARATE, PARTICULAR — **sin·gle·ness** *n* — **sin·gly** *adv*

²single *n* 1 : a separate person or thing; *also* : an unmarried person 2 : a hit in baseball that enables the batter to reach first base 3 *pl* : a tennis match with one player on each side

³single *vb* **sin·gled; sin·gling** 1 : to select (one) from a group 2 : to hit a single

single bond *n* : a chemical bond in which one pair of electrons is shared by two atoms in a molecule

single–lens reflex *n* : a camera having a single lens that forms an image which is reflected to the viewfinder or recorded on film

sin·gle–mind·ed \ˌsiŋ-gəl-ˈmīn-dəd\ *adj* : having one driving purpose or resolve — **sin·gle–mind·ed·ly** *adv* — **sin·gle–mind·ed·ness** *n*

sing·song \'siŋ-ˌsòŋ\ *n* 1 : verse with marked and regular rhythm and rhyme 2 : a voice delivery marked by monotonous rhythm — **sing·songy** \-ˌsòŋ-ē\ *adj*

sin·gu·lar \'siŋ-gyə-lər\ *adj* 1 : of, relating to, or constituting a word form denoting one person, thing, or instance 2 : OUTSTANDING, EXCEPTIONAL 3 : of unusual quality 4 : ODD, PECULIAR — **singular** *n* — **sin·gu·lar·i·ty** \ˌsiŋ-gyə-ˈler-ə-tē\ *n* — **sin·gu·lar·ly** *adv*

sin·is·ter \'si-nəs-tər\ *adj* [ME *sinistre*, fr. AF *senestre* on the left, fr. L *sinister* on the left side, inauspicious] 1 : singularly evil or productive of evil 2 : accompanied by or leading to disaster ♦ **Synonyms** BALEFUL, MALIGN, MALEFIC, MALEFICENT — **sin·is·ter·ly** *adv*

¹sink \'siŋk\ *vb* **sank** \'saŋk\ *or* **sunk** \'səŋk\; **sunk; sink·ing** 1 : SUBMERGE 2 : to descend lower and lower 3 : to grow less in volume or height 4 : to slope downward 5 : to penetrate downward 6 : to fail in health or strength 7 : LAPSE, DEGENERATE 8 : to cause (a ship) to descend to the bottom 9 : to make (a hole or shaft) by digging, boring, or cutting 10 : INVEST — **sink·able** *adj*

²sink *n* 1 : DRAIN, SEWER 2 : a basin connected with a drain 3 : an extensive depression in the land surface

sink·er \'siŋ-kər\ *n* : a weight for sinking a fishing line or net

sink·hole \'siŋk-ˌhōl\ *n* : a hollow place in which drainage collects

si·nol·o·gy \sī-ˈnä-lə-jē\ *n, often cap* : the study of the Chinese and esp. their language, history, and culture — **si·no·log·i·cal** \ˌsī-nə-ˈlä-ji-kəl\ *adj, often cap* — **si·nol·o·gist** \sī-ˈnä-lə-jist\ *n, often cap*

sin tax *n* : a tax on substances or activities considered sinful or harmful

sin·u·ous \'sin-yə-wəs\ *adj* : bending in and out : WINDING — **sin·u·os·i·ty** \ˌsin-yə-ˈwä-sə-tē\ *n* — **sin·u·ous·ly** *adv*

si·nus \'sī-nəs\ *n* [ME, fr. ML, fr. L, curve, hollow] 1 : any of several cavities of the skull usu. connecting with the nostrils **2** : a space forming a channel (as for the passage of blood)

si·nus·itis \ˌsī-nə-ˈsī-təs\ *n* : inflammation of a sinus of the skull

Sioux \ˈsü\ *n, pl* **Sioux** *same or* ˈsüz\ [AmerF, short for *Nadouessioux*, fr. Ojibwa *naʼtoweʼssiw-*, prob. fr. Algonquian **aʼtowe-* speak another language] **:** DAKOTA

sip \ˈsip\ *vb* **sipped; sip·ping** : to drink in small quantities — **sip** *n*

¹**si·phon** *also* **sy·phon** \ˈsī-fən\ *n* **1** : a bent tube through which a liquid can be transferred by means of air pressure up and over the edge of one container and into another container placed at a lower level **2** *usu* **sy·phon** : a bottle that ejects soda water through a tube when a valve is opened

²**siphon** *also* **sypon** *vb* **si·phoned** *also* **sy·phoned; si·phon·ing** *also* **sy·phon·ing** : to draw off by means of a siphon

sir \ˈsər\ *n* [ME *sir, sire*, fr. AF, lord, feudal superior, fr. VL **seior*, alter. of L *senior*, compar. of *senex* old, old man] **1** : a man of rank or position — used as a title before the given name of a knight or baronet **2** — used as a usu. respectful form of address

Si·rach \ˈsī-rak, sə-ˈräk\ *n* — see BIBLE table

¹**sire** \ˈsī(-ə)r\ *n* **1** : FATHER; *also, archaic* : FOREFATHER **2** *archaic* : LORD — used as a form of address and a title **3** : the male parent of an animal (as a horse or dog)

²**sire** *vb* **sired; sir·ing** : BEGET

si·ren \ˈsī-rən\ *n* **1** : a seductive or alluring woman **2** : an electrically operated device for producing a loud shrill warning signal — **siren** *adj*

sir·loin \ˈsər-ˌlȯin\ *n* [alter. of earlier *surloin*, modif. of MF *surlonge*, fr. *sur* over (fr. L *super*) + *longe* loin] : a cut of beef taken from the part in front of the round

sirup *var of* SYRUP

si·sal \ˈsī-səl, -zəl\ *n* : a strong cordage fiber from an agave; *also* : this agave

sis·sy \ˈsi-sē\ *n, pl* **sissies** : an effeminate boy or man; *also* : a timid or cowardly person

sis·ter \ˈsis-tər\ *n* **1** : a female having one or both parents in common with another individual **2** : a member of a religious order of women : NUN **3** *chiefly Brit* : NURSE **4 a** : a girl or woman regarded as a comrade **b** : a girl or woman who shares with another a common national or racial origin — **sis·ter·ly** *adj*

sis·ter·hood \-ˌhu̇d\ *n* **1** : the state of being a sister **2** : a community or society of sisters **3** : the solidarity of women based on shared conditions

sis·ter–in–law \ˈsis-tə-rən-ˌlȯ\ *n, pl* **sisters–in–law** : the sister of one's spouse; *also* : the wife of one's brother

sit \ˈsit\ *vb* **sat** \ˈsat\; **sit·ting 1** : to rest upon the buttocks or haunches **2** : ROOST, PERCH **3** : to occupy a seat **4** : to hold a session **5** : to cover eggs for hatching : BROOD **6** : to pose for a portrait **7** : to remain quiet or inactive **8** : FIT **9** : to cause (oneself) to be seated **10** : to place in position **11** : to keep one's seat on ⟨∼ a horse⟩ **12** : BABYSIT — **sit·ter** *n*

si·tar \si-ˈtär\ *n* [Hindi & Urdu *sitār*] : an Indian lute with a long neck and a varying number of strings

sit·com \ˈsit-ˌkäm\ *n* : SITUATION COMEDY

site \ˈsīt\ *n* **1** : LOCATION **2** : WEB SITE

sit–in \ˈsit-ˌin\ *n* : an act of sitting in the seats or on the floor of an establishment as a means of organized protest

sit·u·at·ed \ˈsi-chə-ˌwā-təd\ *adj* : LOCATED, PLACED

sit·u·a·tion \ˌsi-chə-ˈwā-shən\ *n* **1** : LOCATION, SITE **2** : JOB **3** : CONDITION, CIRCUMSTANCES — **sit·u·a·tion·al** \-shə-nəl\ *adj*

situation comedy *n* : a radio or television comedy series that involves a continuing cast of characters in a succession of episodes

sit–up \ˈsit-ˌəp\ *n* : an exercise performed from a supine position by raising the torso to a sitting position and returning to the original position without lifting the feet

SIV \ˌes-ˌī-ˈvē\ *n* [simian *i*mmunodeficiency *v*irus] : a retrovirus related to HIV that causes a disease in monkeys similar to AIDS

six \ˈsiks\ *n* **1** : one more than five **2** : the 6th in a set or series **3** : something having six units — **six** *adj or pron* — **sixth** \ˈsiksth\ *adj or adv or n*

six–gun \ˈsiks-ˌgən\ *n* : a 6-chambered revolver

six–pack \-ˌpak\ *n* : six bottles or cans (as of beer) pack-

aged and purchased together; *also* : the contents of a six-pack

six·pence \-pəns, US also -ˌpens\ *n* : the sum of six pence; *also* : an English silver coin of this value

six–shoot·er \ˈsiks-ˌshü-tər\ *n* : SIX-GUN

six·teen \ˌsiks-ˈtēn\ *n* : one more than 15 — **sixteen** *adj or pron* — **six·teenth** \-ˈtēnth\ *adj or n*

six·ty \ˈsiks-tē\ *n, pl* **sixties** : six times 10 — **six·ti·eth** \ˈsiks-tē-əth\ *adj or n* — **sixty** *adj or pron*

siz·able *or* **size·able** \ˈsī-zə-bəl\ *adj* : quite large — **siz·ably** \-blē\ *adv*

¹**size** \ˈsīz\ *n* [ME *sise* assize, judgment, quantity, fr. AF, short for *assise* assize] : physical extent or bulk : DIMENSIONS; *also* : considerable proportions — **sized** \ˈsīzd\ *adj*

²**size** *vb* **sized; siz·ing 1** : to grade or classify according to size **2** : to form a judgment of ⟨∼ up the situation⟩

³**size** *n* : a gluey material used for filling the pores in paper, plaster, or textiles — **siz·ing** *n*

⁴**size** *vb* **sized; siz·ing** : to cover, stiffen, or glaze with size

siz·zle \ˈsi-zəl\ *vb* **siz·zled; siz·zling** : to fry or shrivel up with a hissing sound — **sizzle** *n*

SJ *abbr* Society of Jesus

SK *abbr* Saskatchewan

ska \ˈskä\ *n* : popular music of Jamaican origin combining traditional Caribbean rhythms and jazz

¹**skate** \ˈskāt\ *n, pl* **skates** *also* **skate** : any of a family of rays with thick broad winglike fins

²**skate** *n* **1** : a metal frame and runner attached to a shoe and used for gliding over ice **2** : ROLLER SKATE; *esp* : IN-LINE SKATE — **skate** *vb* — **skat·er** *n*

skate·board \ˈskāt-ˌbȯrd\ *n* : a short board mounted on small wheels — **skateboard** *vb* — **skate·board·er** *n*

skeet \ˈskēt\ *n* : trapshooting in which clay targets are thrown in such a way that their angle of flight simulates that of a flushed game bird

skein \ˈskān\ *n* : a loosely twisted quantity of yarn or thread wound on a reel

skel·e·ton \ˈske-lə-tᵊn\ *n* **1** : a usu. bony supporting framework of an animal body **2** : a bare minimum **3** : FRAMEWORK — **skel·e·tal** \-lə-tᵊl\ *adj*

skep·tic \ˈskep-tik\ *n* **1** : one who believes in skepticism **2** : a person disposed to skepticism esp. regarding religion — **skep·ti·cal** \-ti-kəl\ *adj* — **skep·ti·cal·ly** \-k(ə-)lē\ *adv*

skep·ti·cism \ˈskep-tə-ˌsi-zəm\ *n* **1** : a doubting state of mind **2** : a doctrine that certainty of knowledge cannot be attained **3** : doubt concerning religion

sketch \ˈskech\ *n* [D *schets*, fr. It *schizzo*, lit., splash] **1** : a rough drawing or outline **2** : a short or light literary composition (as a story or essay); *also* : a short comedy piece — **sketch** *vb* — **sketchy** *adj*

¹**skew** \ˈskyü\ *vb* : TWIST, SWERVE

²**skew** *n* : SLANT

skew·er \ˈskyü-ər\ *n* : a long pin for holding small pieces of meat and vegetables for broiling — **skewer** *vb*

¹**ski** \ˈskē\ *n, pl* **skis** [Norw, fr. ON *skīth* stick of wood, ski] : one of a pair of long strips (as of wood, metal, or plastic) curving upward in front that are used for gliding over snow or water

²**ski** *vb* **skied** \ˈskēd\; **ski·ing** : to glide on skis — **ski·able** \ˈskē-ə-bəl\ *adj* — **ski·er** *n*

¹**skid** \ˈskid\ *n* **1** : a plank for supporting something above the ground **2** : a device placed under a wheel to prevent turning **3** : a timber or rail over or on which something is slid or rolled **4** : the act of skidding **5** : a runner on the landing gear of an aircraft **6** : ²PALLET

²**skid** *vb* **skid·ded; skid·ding 1** : to slide without rotating ⟨a *skidding* wheel⟩ **2** : to slide sideways on the road ⟨the car *skidded* on ice⟩ **3** : SLIDE, SLIP

skid row *n* : a district of cheap saloons frequented by vagrants and alcoholics

skiff \ˈskif\ *n* : a small boat

ski jump *n* : a jump made by a person wearing skis; *also* : a course or track prepared for such jumping — **ski jump** *vb* — **ski jumper** *n*

skil·ful *chiefly Brit var of* SKILLFUL

ski lift *n* : a mechanical device (as a chairlift) for carrying skiers up a long slope

skill \ˈskil\ *n* **1** : ability to use one's knowledge effectively in doing something **2** : developed or acquired ability

◆ *Synonyms* ART, CRAFT, CUNNING, DEXTERITY, EXPERTISE, KNOW-HOW — **skilled** \ˈskild\ *adj*

skil·let \'ski-lət\ *n* : a frying pan

skill·ful \'skil-fəl\ *adj* **1** : having or displaying skill : EXPERT **2** : accomplished with skill — **skill·ful·ly** *adv* — **skill·ful·ness** *n*

¹skim \'skim\ *vb* **skimmed; skim·ming 1** : to take off from the top of a liquid; *also* : to remove (scum or cream) from ⟨∼ milk⟩ **2** : to read rapidly and superficially **3** : to pass swiftly over — **skim·mer** *n*

²skim *adj* : having the cream removed

skimp \'skimp\ *vb* : to give insufficient attention, effort, or funds; *also* : to save by skimping

skimpy \'skim-pē\ *adj* **skimp·i·er; -est** : deficient in supply or execution — **skimp·i·ly** \-pə-lē\ *adv*

¹skin \'skin\ *n* **1** : the outer limiting layer of an animal body; *also* : the usu. thin tough tissue of which this is made **2** : an outer or surface layer (as a rind or peel) — **skin·less** *adj* — **skinned** *adj*

²skin *vb* **skinned; skin·ning** : to free from skin : remove the skin of

³skin *adj* : devoted to showing nudes ⟨∼ magazines⟩

skin diving *n* : the sport of swimming under water with a face mask and flippers and esp. without a portable breathing device — **skin–dive** *vb* — **skin diver** *n*

skin·flint \'skin-,flint\ *n* : a very stingy person

skin graft *n* : a piece of skin surgically removed from one area to replace skin in another area — **skin grafting** *n*

skin·head \'skin-,hed\ *n* : a person whose hair is cut very short

¹skin·ny \'ski-nē\ *adj* **skin·ni·er; -est 1** : resembling skin **2** : very thin

²skinny *n* : inside information

skin·ny–dip \'ski-nē-,dip\ *vb* : to swim in the nude — **skin·ny–dip·per** \-,di-pər\ *n*

skin·tight \'skin-'tīt\ *adj* : closely fitted to the figure ⟨∼ pants⟩

¹skip \'skip\ *vb* **skipped; skip·ping 1** : to move with leaps and bounds **2** : to leap lightly over **3** : to pass from point to point (as in reading) disregarding what is in between **4** : to pass over without notice or mention

²skip *n* : a light bouncing step; *also* : a gait of alternate hops and steps

skip·jack \'skip-,jak\ *n* : a small sailboat with vertical sides and a bottom similar to a flat V

skip·per \'ski-pər\ *n* [ME, fr. MD *schipper,* fr. *schip* ship] : the master of a ship; *also* : the manager of a baseball team — **skipper** *vb*

skir·mish \'skər-mish\ *n* : a minor engagement in war; *also* : a minor dispute or contest — **skirmish** *vb*

¹skirt \'skərt\ *n* : a free-hanging garment or part of a garment extending from the waist down

²skirt *vb* **1** : to pass around the outer edge of **2** : BORDER **3** : EVADE

skit \'skit\ *n* : a brief dramatic sketch

ski tow *n* : SKI LIFT

skit·ter \'ski-tər\ *vb* : to glide or skip lightly or quickly : skim along a surface

skit·tish \'ski-tish\ *adj* **1** : CAPRICIOUS **2** : easily frightened ⟨a ∼ horse⟩; *also* : WARY

ski·wear \'skē-,wer\ *n* : clothing suitable for wear while skiing

skosh \'skōsh\ *n* [Jp *sukoshi*] : a small amount : BIT

skul·dug·gery *or* **skull·dug·gery** \,skəl-'də-gə-rē\ *n, pl* **-ger·ies** : underhanded or unscrupulous behavior

skulk \'skəlk\ *vb* : to move furtively : SNEAK, LURK — **skulk·er** *n*

skull \'skəl\ *n* : the skeleton of the head of a vertebrate that protects the brain and supports the jaws

skull and crossbones *n, pl* **skulls and crossbones** : a depiction of a human skull over crossbones usu. indicating a danger

skull·cap \'skəl-,kap\ *n* : a close-fitting brimless cap

¹skunk \'skəŋk\ *n, pl* **skunks** *also* **skunk 1** : any of various black-and-white New World mammals related to the weasels that can forcibly eject an ill-smelling fluid when startled **2** : a contemptible person

²skunk *vb* : to defeat decisively; *esp* : to prevent entirely from scoring in a game

skunk cabbage *n* : either of two No. American perennial herbs related to the arums that occur in shaded wet to swampy areas and have a fetid odor suggestive of a skunk

sky \'skī\ *n, pl* **skies** [ME, sky, cloud, fr. ON *skȳ* cloud] **1** : the upper air **2** : HEAVEN — **sky·ey** \'skī-ē\ *adj*

sky·cap \-,kap\ *n* : a person employed to carry luggage at an airport

sky·div·ing \-,dī-viŋ\ *n* : the sport of jumping from an airplane and executing various body maneuvers before opening a parachute — **skydiver** *n*

sky·jack \-,jak\ *vb* : to commandeer an airplane in flight by threat of violence — **sky·jack·er** *n* — **sky·jack·ing** *n*

¹sky·lark \-,lärk\ *n* : a European lark noted for singing during flight

²skylark *vb* : FROLIC, SPORT

sky·light \-,līt\ *n* : a window in a roof or ceiling — **sky·light·ed** \-,lī-təd\ *adj*

sky·line \-,līn\ *n* **1** : HORIZON **2** : an outline (as of buildings) against the sky

¹sky·rock·et \-,rä-kət\ *n* : ROCKET 1

²skyrocket *vb* : ROCKET 2

sky·scrap·er \-,skrā-pər\ *n* : a very tall building

sky·surf·ing \-,sər-fiŋ\ *n* : skydiving with a short modified surfboard attached to the feet — **sky·surf·er** \-fər\ *n*

sky·walk \-,wȯk\ *n* : an aerial walkway connecting two buildings

sky·ward \-wərd\ *adv* : toward the sky

sky·writ·ing \-,rī-tiŋ\ *n* : writing in the sky formed by smoke emitted from an airplane — **sky·writ·er** *n*

sl *abbr* **1** slightly **2** slip **3** slow

slab \'slab\ *n* : a thick flat piece or slice

¹slack \'slak\ *adj* **1** : CARELESS, NEGLIGENT **2** : SLUGGISH, LISTLESS **3** : not taut : LOOSE **4** : not busy or active ♦ *Synonyms* LAX, REMISS, NEGLECTFUL, DELINQUENT, DERELICT — **slack·ly** *adv* — **slack·ness** *n*

²slack *vb* **1** : to make or become slack : LOOSEN, RELAX **2** : SLAKE 2

³slack *n* **1** : cessation of movement or flow : LETUP **2** : a part that hangs loose without strain ⟨∼ of a rope⟩ **3** : pants esp. for casual wear — usu. used in pl.

slack·en \'sla-kən\ *vb* : to make or become slack

slack·er \'sla-kər\ *n* **1** : one that shirks work or evades military duty **2** : a young person perceived to be disaffected, apathetic, cynical, or lacking ambition

slag \'slag\ *n* : the waste left after the melting of ores and the separation of metal from them

slain *past part of* SLAY

slake \'slāk, *for 2 also* 'slak\ *vb* **slaked; slak·ing 1** : to relieve or satisfy with or as if with refreshing drink ⟨∼ thirst⟩ **2** : to cause (lime) to crumble by mixture with water

sla·lom \'slä-ləm\ *n* [Norw *slalam,* lit., sloping track] : skiing in a zigzag course between obstacles

¹slam \'slam\ *n* : the winning of every trick or of all tricks but one in bridge

²slam *n* **1** : a heavy jarring impact : BANG **2** : harsh criticism **3** : a poetry competition

³slam *vb* **slammed; slam·ming 1** : to shut violently and noisily **2** : to throw or strike with a loud impact **3** : to criticize harshly

slam·mer \'sla-mər\ *n* : JAIL, PRISON

¹slan·der \'slan-dər\ *vb* : to utter slander against : DEFAME — **slan·der·er** *n*

²slander *n* [ME *sclaundre, slaundre,* fr. AF *esclandre,* alter. of *escandle,* fr. LL *scandalum* stumbling block, offense] : a false report maliciously uttered and tending to injure the reputation of a person — **slan·der·ous** *adj*

slang \'slaŋ\ *n* : an informal nonstandard vocabulary composed typically of invented words, arbitrarily changed words, and extravagant figures of speech — **slangy** *adj*

skunk 1

¹**slant** \'slant\ *n* **1** : a sloping direction, line, or plane **2** : a particular or personal viewpoint — **slant** *adj* — **slant-wise** \-ˌwīz\ *adv or adj*

²**slant** *vb* **1** : SLOPE **2** : to interpret or present in accordance with a special viewpoint or bias ♦ *Synonyms* INCLINE, LEAN, LIST, TILT, HEEL — **slant-ing-ly** *adv*

slap \'slap\ *vb* **slapped; slap-ping 1** : to strike sharply with the open hand **2** : REBUFF, INSULT — **slap** *n*

slap-stick \-ˌstik\ *n* : comedy stressing horseplay

¹**slash** \'slash\ *vb* **1** : to cut with sweeping strokes **2** : to cut slits in (a garment) **3** : to reduce sharply — **slash-er** \'sla-shər\ *n*

²**slash** *n* **1** : GASH : an ornamental slit in a garment **3** : a mark / used to denote "or" (as in *and/or*), "and or" (as in *straggler/deserter*), or "per" (as in *feet/second*)

slat \'slat\ *n* : a thin narrow flat strip

¹**slate** \'slāt\ *n* **1** : a dense fine-grained rock that splits into thin layers **2** : a roofing tile or a writing tablet made from this rock **3** : a written or unwritten record ⟨start with a clean ∼⟩ **4** : a list of candidates for election

²**slate** *vb* **slat-ed; slat-ing 1** : to cover with slate **2** : to designate for action or appointment

slath-er \'sla-thər\ *vb* : to spread with or on thickly or lavishly

slat-tern \'sla-tərn\ *n* : a slovenly woman — **slat-tern-ly** *adj*

¹**slaugh-ter** \'slȯ-tər\ *n* **1** : the butchering of livestock for market **2** : great destruction of lives esp. in battle

²**slaughter** *vb* **1** : to kill (animals) for food : BUTCHER **2** : to kill in large numbers or in a bloody way : MASSACRE

slaugh-ter-house \-ˌhaus\ *n* : an establishment where animals are butchered

Slav \'släv, 'slav\ *n* : a person speaking a Slavic language

¹**slave** \'slāv\ *n* [ME *sclave*, fr. AF or ML; AF *esclave*, fr. ML *sclavus*, fr. *Sclavus* Slav; fr. the enslavement of Slavs in central Europe in the Middle Ages] **1** : a person held in servitude as property **2** : a device (as the printer of a computer) that is directly responsive to another — **slave** *adj*

²**slave** *vb* **slaved; slav-ing** : to work like a slave : DRUDGE

¹**sla-ver** \'sla-vər, 'slā-\ *n* : SLOBBER — **slaver** *vb*

²**slav-er** \'slā-vər\ *n* : a ship or a person engaged in transporting slaves

slav-ery \'slāv-rē, 'slā-və-\ *n* **1** : wearisome drudgery **2** : the condition of being a slave **3** : the practice of owning slaves ♦ *Synonyms* SERVITUDE, BONDAGE, ENSLAVEMENT

¹**Slav-ic** \'slä-vik, 'slä-\ *n* : a branch of the Indo-European language family including various languages (as Russian or Polish) of eastern Europe

²**Slavic** *adj* : of or relating to the Slavs or their languages

slav-ish \'slā-vish\ *adj* **1** : SERVILE **2** : obeying or imitating with no freedom of judgment or choice — **slav-ish-ly** *adv*

slaw \'slȯ\ *n* : COLESLAW

slay \'slā\ *vb* **slew** \'slü\; **slain** \'slān\; **slay-ing** : KILL — **slay-er** *n*

SLBM *abbr* submarine-launched ballistic missile

sleaze \'slēz\ *n* : a sleazy quality, appearance, or behavior

slea-zy \'slē-zē\ *adj* **slea-zi-er; -est 1** : FLIMSY, SHODDY **2** : marked by low character or quality

¹**sled** \'sled\ *n* : a vehicle usu. on runners adapted esp. for sliding on snow

²**sled** *vb* **sled-ded; sled-ding** : to ride or carry on a sled

¹**sledge** \'slej\ *n* : SLEDGEHAMMER

²**sledge** *n* : a strong heavy sled

sledge-ham-mer \'slej-ˌha-mər\ *n* : a large heavy hammer wielded with both hands — **sledgehammer** *adj or vb*

¹**sleek** \'slēk\ *vb* **1** : to make smooth or glossy **2** : to gloss over

²**sleek** *adj* **1** : having a smooth well-groomed look **2** : trim and graceful in design ⟨a ∼ car⟩

¹**sleep** \'slēp\ *n* **1** : the natural periodic suspension of consciousness during which bodily powers are restored **2** : a state (as death or coma) suggesting sleep — **sleep-less** *adj* — **sleep-less-ness** *n*

²**sleep** *vb* **slept** \'slept\; **sleep-ing 1** : to rest or be in a state of sleep; *also* : to spend in sleep **2** : to have sexual intercourse — usu. used with *with* **3** : to provide sleeping space for

sleep-er \'slē-pər\ *n* **1** : one that sleeps **2** : a horizontal beam to support something on or near ground level **3**

: SLEEPING CAR **4** : someone or something unpromising or unnoticed that suddenly attains prominence or value

sleeping bag *n* : a warmly lined bag for sleeping esp. outdoors

sleeping car *n* : a railroad car with berths for sleeping

sleeping pill *n* : a drug in tablet or capsule form taken to induce sleep

sleeping sickness *n* : a serious disease of tropical Africa that is marked by fever, lethargy, confusion, and sleep disturbances and is caused by protozoans transmitted by the tsetse fly

sleep-over \'slēp-ˌō-vər\ *n* : an overnight stay (as at another's home)

sleep-walk-er \'slēp-ˌwȯ-kər\ *n* : one that walks while or as if while asleep — **sleep-walk** \-ˌwȯk\ *vb*

sleepy \'slē-pē\ *adj* **sleep-i-er; -est 1** : ready for sleep **2** : quietly inactive — **sleep-i-ly** \'slē-pə-lē\ *adv* — **sleep-i-ness** \-pē-nəs\ *n*

sleet \'slēt\ *n* : frozen or partly frozen rain — **sleet** *vb* — **sleety** *adj*

sleeve \'slēv\ *n* **1** : a part of a garment covering an arm **2** : a tubular part designed to fit over another part — **sleeved** *adj* — **sleeve-less** *adj*

¹**sleigh** \'slā\ *n* : an open usu. horse-drawn vehicle on runners for use on snow or ice

²**sleigh** *vb* : to drive or travel in a sleigh

sleight \'slīt\ *n* **1** : TRICK **2** : DEXTERITY

sleight of hand : a trick requiring skillful manual manipulation

slen-der \'slen-dər\ *adj* **1** : SLIM, THIN **2** : WEAK, SLIGHT **3** : MEAGER, INADEQUATE

slen-der-ize \-də-ˌrīz\ *vb* **-ized; -iz-ing** : to make slender

sleuth \'slüth\ *n* [short for *sleuthhound* bloodhound, fr. ME (Sc) *sleuth hund*, fr. ME *sleuth, sloith, sloth* track of an animal or person, fr. ON *slōth*] : DETECTIVE

¹**slew** \'slü\ *past of* SLAY

²**slew** *vb* : TURN, VEER, SKID

¹**slice** \'slīs\ *vb* **sliced; slic-ing 1** : to cut a slice from; *also* : to cut into slices **2** : to hit (a ball) so that a slice results

²**slice** *n* **1** : a thin flat piece cut from something **2** : a flight of a ball (as in golf) that curves in the direction of the dominant hand of the player hitting it

¹**slick** \'slik\ *vb* : to make smooth or sleek

²**slick** *adj* **1** : very smooth : SLIPPERY **2** : CLEVER, SMART ⟨a ∼ salesperson⟩

³**slick** *n* **1** : a smooth patch of water covered with a film of oil **2** : a popular magazine printed on coated paper

slick-er \'sli-kər\ *n* **1** : a long loose raincoat **2** : a sly tricky person **3** : a city dweller esp. of natty appearance or sophisticated mannerisms

¹**slide** \'slīd\ *vb* **slid** \'slid\; **slid-ing** \'slī-diŋ\ **1** : to move smoothly along a surface **2** : to fall by a loss of support **3** : to pass unobtrusively **4** : to move or pass smoothly; *also* : to pass unnoticed ⟨let it ∼ by⟩ **5** : to fall or dive toward a base in baseball

²**slide** *n* **1** : an act or instance of sliding **2** : something (as a cover or fastener) that operates by sliding **3** : a fall of a mass of earth or snow down a hillside **4** : a surface on which something slides **5** : a glass plate on which a specimen is mounted for examination under a microscope **6** : a small transparent photograph that can be projected on a screen

slid-er \'slī-dər\ *n* **1** : one that slides **2** : a baseball pitch that looks like a fastball but curves slightly

slide rule *n* : a manual device for calculation consisting of a ruler and a movable middle piece graduated with logarithmic scales

slier *comparative of* SLY

sliest *superlative of* SLY

¹**slight** \'slīt\ *adj* **1** : SLENDER; *also* : FRAIL **2** : UNIMPORTANT : small of its kind or in amount ⟨a ∼ odor⟩ — **slight-ly** *adv*

²**slight** *vb* **1** : to treat as unimportant **2** : to ignore discourteously **3** : to perform or attend to carelessly

³**slight** *n* : a humiliating discourtesy

¹**slim** \'slim\ *adj* **slim-mer; slim-mest** [D, bad, inferior, fr. MD, *slimp* crooked, bad] **1** : SLENDER, SLIGHT, THIN **2** : SMALL, SLIGHT ⟨a ∼ chance⟩

²**slim** *vb* **slimmed; slim-ming** : to make or become slender

slime \'slīm\ *n* **1** : sticky mud **2** : a slippery substance (as on the skin of a slug or catfish) — **slimy** *adj*

¹**sling** \'sliŋ\ *vb* **slung** \'sləŋ\; **sling·ing** **1** : to throw forcibly : FLING **2** : to hurl with or as if with a sling

²**sling** *n* **1** : a short strap with strings attached for hurling stones or shot **2** : something (as a rope or chain) used to hoist, lower, support, or carry; *esp* : a bandage hanging from the neck to support an arm or hand

sling·shot \'sliŋ-ˌshät\ *n* : a forked stick with elastic bands for shooting small stones or shot

slink \'sliŋk\ *vb* **slunk** \'sləŋk\ *also* **slinked** \'sliŋkt\; **slink·ing** **1** : to move stealthily or furtively **2** : to move sinuously — **slinky** *adj*

¹**slip** \'slip\ *vb* **slipped**; **slip·ping** **1** : to escape quietly or secretly **2** : to slide along or cause to slide along smoothly **3** : to make a mistake **4** : to pass unnoticed or undone **5** : to fall off from a standard or level

²**slip** *n* **1** : a ramp for repairing ships **2** : a ship's berth between two piers **3** : secret or hurried departure, escape, or evasion **4** : BLUNDER **5** : a sudden mishap **6** : a woman's one-piece garment worn under a dress **7** : PILLOWCASE

³**slip** *n* **1** : a shoot or twig from a plant for planting or grafting **2** : a long narrow strip; *esp* : one of paper used for a record ⟨deposit ∼⟩

⁴**slip** *vb* **slipped**; **slip·ping** : to take slips from (a plant)

slip·knot \'slip-ˌnät\ *n* : a knot that slips along the rope around which it is made

slipped disk *n* : a protrusion of one of the disks of cartilage between vertebrae with pressure on spinal nerves resulting esp. in low back pain

slip·per \'sli-pər\ *n* : a light low shoe that may be easily slipped on and off

slip·pery \'sli-pə-rē\ *adj* **slip·per·i·er; -est** **1** : icy, wet, smooth, or greasy enough to cause one to fall or lose one's hold **2** : not to be trusted : TRICKY — **slip·per·i·ness** *n*

slip·shod \'slip-'shäd\ *adj* : SLOVENLY, CARELESS ⟨∼ work⟩

slip·stream \'slip-ˌstrēm\ *n* : a stream (as of air) driven aft by a propeller

slip-up \'slip-ˌəp\ *n* **1** : MISTAKE **2** : ACCIDENT

¹**slit** \'slit\ *vb* **slit**; **slit·ting** **1** : SLASH **2** : to cut off or away

²**slit** *n* : a long narrow cut or opening

slith·er \'sli-thər\ *vb* : to slip or glide along like a snake — **slith·ery** *adj*

sliv·er \'sli-vər\ *n* : SPLINTER

slob \'släb\ *n* : a slovenly or boorish person

slob·ber \'slä-bər\ *vb* **slob·bered; slob·ber·ing** : to dribble saliva — **slobber** *n*

sloe \'slō\ *n* : the fruit of the blackthorn

slog \'släg\ *vb* **slogged; slog·ging** **1** : to hit hard : BEAT **2** : to work hard and steadily

slo·gan \'slō-gən\ *n* [alter. of earlier *slogorn*, fr. ScGael *sluagh-ghairm*, fr. *sluagh* army, host + *gairm* cry] : a word or phrase expressing the spirit or aim of a party, group, or cause

slo–mo \'slō-ˌmō\ *n* : SLOW MOTION — **slo–mo** *adj*

sloop \'slüp\ *n* [D *sloep*] : a single-masted sailboat with a jib and a fore-and-aft mainsail

¹**slop** \'släp\ *n* **1** : thin tasteless drink or liquid food — usu. used in pl. **2** : food waste for animal feed : SWILL **3** : excreted body waste — usu. used in pl.

²**slop** *vb* **slopped; slop·ping** **1** : SPILL **2** : to feed with slop ⟨∼ hogs⟩

¹**slope** \'slōp\ *vb* **sloped; slop·ing** : SLANT, INCLINE

²**slope** *n* **1** : upward or downward slant or degree of slant **2** : ground that forms an incline **3** : the part of a landmass draining into a particular ocean

slop·py \'slä-pē\ *adj* **slop·pi·er; -est** **1** : MUDDY, SLUSHY **2** : SLOVENLY, MESSY

sloppy joe \-ˈjō\ *n* : ground beef cooked in a thick spicy sauce and usu. served on a bun

slosh \'släsh\ *vb* **1** : to flounder through or splash about in or with water, mud, or slush **2** : to move with a splashing motion

slot \'slät\ *n* **1** : a long narrow opening or groove **2** : a position in a sequence

slot car *n* : an electric toy racing car that runs on a grooved track

sloth \'slöth\ *n, pl* **sloths** \'slöths, 'slö<u>th</u>z\ **1** : LAZINESS, INDOLENCE **2** : any of several slow-moving plant-eating arboreal mammals of So. and Central America — **slothful** *adj*

slot machine *n* **1** : a machine whose operation is begun by dropping a coin into a slot **2** : a coin-operated gambling machine that pays off according to the matching of symbols on wheels spun by a handle

¹**slouch** \'slau̇ch\ *n* **1** : a lazy or incompetent person **2** : a loose or drooping gait or posture

²**slouch** *vb* : to walk, stand, or sit with a slouch : SLUMP

¹**slough** \'slü, 2 *usu* 'slau̇\ *n* **1** : a wet and marshy or muddy place (as a swamp) **2** : a discouraged state of mind

²**slough** \'sləf\ *also* **sluff** *n* : something that has been or may be shed or cast off

³**slough** \'sləf\ *also* **sluff** *vb* : to cast off

Slo·vak \'slō-ˌväk, -ˌvak\ *n* **1** : a member of a Slavic people of Slovakia **2** : the language of the Slovaks — **Slovak** *adj* — **Slo·va·ki·an** \slō-'vä-kē-ən, -'va-\ *adj or n*

slov·en \'slə-vən\ *n* [ME *sloveyn* slut, rascal, perh. fr. MD *slof* negligent] : an untidy person

Slo·vene \'slō-ˌvēn\ *n* **1** : a member of a Slavic people living largely in Slovenia **2** : the language of the Slovenes — **Slovene** *adj* — **Slo·ve·nian** \slō-'vē-nē-ən\ *adj or n*

slov·en·ly \'slə-vən-lē\ *adj* **1** : untidy in dress or person **2** : lazily or carelessly done : SLIPSHOD

¹**slow** \'slō\ *adj* **1** : SLUGGISH; *also* : dull in mind : STUPID **2** : moving, flowing, or proceeding at less than the usual speed **3** : taking more than the usual time **4** : registering behind the correct time **5** : not lively : BORING ◆ **Synonyms** DILATORY, LAGGARD, DELIBERATE, LEISURELY — **slow** *adv* — **slow·ly** *adv* — **slow·ness** *n*

²**slow** *vb* **1** : to make slow : hold back **2** : to go slower

slow motion *n* : motion-picture action photographed so as to appear much slower than normal — **slow–motion** *adj*

SLR *abbr* single-lens reflex

sludge \'sləj\ *n* : a slushy mass : OOZE; *esp* : solid matter produced by sewage treatment processes

slue *var of* ²SLEW

¹**slug** \'sləg\ *n* **1** : a small mass of metal; *esp* : BULLET **2** : a metal disk for use (as in a slot machine) in place of a coin **3** : any of numerous wormlike mollusks related to the snails **4** : a quantity of liquor drunk

²**slug** *vb* **slugged; slug·ging** : to strike forcibly and heavily — **slug·ger** *n*

slug·gard \'slə-gərd\ *n* : a lazy person

slug·gish \'slə-gish\ *adj* **1** : SLOTHFUL, LAZY **2** : slow in movement or flow **3** : STAGNANT, DULL — **slug·gish·ly** *adv* — **slug·gish·ness** *n*

¹**sluice** \'slüs\ *n* [ME *sluse, scluse*, fr. AF *escluse*, fr. LL *exclusa*, fr. L, fem. of *exclusus*, pp. of *excludere* to shut out, exclude] **1** : an artificial passage for water with a gate for controlling the flow; *also* : the gate so used **2** : a channel that carries off surplus water **3** : an inclined trough or flume for washing ore or floating logs

²**sluice** *vb* **sluiced; sluic·ing** **1** : to draw off through a sluice **2** : to wash with running water : FLUSH

¹**slum** \'sləm\ *n* : a thickly populated area marked by poverty and dirty or deteriorated houses — **slum·my** \'slə-mē\ *adj*

²**slum** *vb* **slummed; slum·ming** : to visit slums esp. out of curiosity; *also* : to go somewhere or do something that might be considered beneath one's station

¹**slum·ber** \'sləm-bər\ *vb* **slum·bered; slum·ber·ing** **1** : DOZE; *also* : SLEEP **2** : to be in a sluggish or torpid state

²**slumber** *n* : SLEEP

slum·ber·ous \'sləm-bə-rəs\ *or* **slum·brous** \-brəs\ *adj* **1** : SLUMBERING, SLEEPY **2** : PEACEFUL, INACTIVE

slum·lord \'sləm-ˌlord\ *n* : a landlord who receives unusually large profits from substandard properties

slump \'sləmp\ *vb* **1** : to sink down suddenly : COLLAPSE **2** : SLOUCH **3** : to decline sharply — **slump** *n*

slung *past and past part of* SLING

slunk *past and past part of* SLINK

¹**slur** \'slər\ *n* : a slighting remark : ASPERSION — **slur** *vb*

²**slur** *vb* **slurred; slur·ring** **1** : to slide or slip over without due mention or emphasis **2** : to perform two or more successive notes of different pitch in a smooth or connected way

³**slur** *n* : a curved line connecting notes to be slurred; *also* : a group of slurred notes

slurp \'slərp\ *vb* : to eat or drink noisily — **slurp** *n*

slur·ry \'slər-ē\ *n, pl* **slur·ries** : a watery mixture of insoluble matter

slush \'sləsh\ *n* **1** : partly melted or watery snow **2** : soft mud — **slushy** *adj*

slush fund *n* : an unregulated fund often for illicit purposes

slut \'slət\ *n* **1** : a slovenly woman **2** : a promiscuous woman — **slut·tish** *adj*

sly \'slī\ *adj* **sly·er** *also* **sli·er** \'slī-ər\; **sly·est** *also* **sli·est** \'slī-əst\ **1** : CRAFTY, CUNNING **2** : SECRETIVE, FURTIVE **3** : ROGUISH ◆ *Synonyms* TRICKY, WILY, ARTFUL, FOXY, GUILEFUL — **sly·ly** *also* **sli·ly** *adv* — **slyness** *n*

sm *abbr* small

Sm *symbol* samarium

SM *abbr* **1** master of science **2** sergeant major **3** service mark **4** stage manager

SMA *abbr* sergeant major of the army

¹**smack** \'smak\ *n* : characteristic flavor; *also* : a slight trace

²**smack** *vb* **1** : to have a taste **2** : to have a trace or suggestion ⟨∼s of treason⟩

³**smack** *vb* **1** : to move (the lips) so as to make a sharp noise **2** : to kiss or slap with a loud noise

⁴**smack** *n* **1** : a sharp noise made by the lips **2** : a loud kiss or slap

⁵**smack** *adv* : squarely and sharply

⁶**smack** *n* : a sailing ship used in fishing

⁷**smack** *n, slang* : HEROIN

SMaj *abbr* sergeant major

¹**small** \'smȯl\ *adj* **1** : little in size or amount **2** : operating on a limited scale **3** : little or close to zero (as in number or value) **4** : made up of little things **5** : TRIFLING, UNIMPORTANT **6** : MEAN, PETTY ◆ *Synonyms* DIMINUTIVE, PETITE, WEE, TINY, MINUTE — **small·ish** *adj* — **small·ness** *n*

²**small** *n* : a small part or product ⟨the ∼ of the back⟩

small·pox \'smȯl-ˌpäks\ *n* : a contagious virus disease of humans formerly common but now eradicated

small talk *n* : light or casual conversation

small–time \'smȯl-'tīm\ *adj* : insignificant in performance and standing : MINOR — **small–tim·er** *n*

smarmy \'smär-mē\ *adj* **smarm·i·er; -est** : marked by a smug, ingratiating, or false earnestness

¹**smart** \'smärt\ *adj* **1** : making one smart ⟨a ∼ blow⟩ **2** : mentally quick : BRIGHT **3** : WITTY, CLEVER **4** : STYLISH **5** : being a guided missile **6** : containing a microprocessor for limited computing capability ⟨∼ terminal⟩ ◆ *Synonyms* KNOWING, QUICK-WITTED, INTELLIGENT, BRAINY, SHARP — **smart·ly** *adv* — **smart·ness** *n*

²**smart** *vb* **1** : to cause or feel a stinging pain **2** : to feel or endure distress — **smart** *n*

smart al·eck \'smärt-ˌa-lik\ *n* : a person given to obnoxious cleverness

smart card *n* : a small plastic card that has a built-in microprocessor to store and handle data

smart·en \'smär-t°n\ *vb* : to make smart or smarter — usu. used with *up*

¹**smash** \'smash\ *n* **1** : a smashing blow **2** : a hard, overhand stroke in tennis **3** : the act or sound of smashing **4** : collision of vehicles : CRASH **5** : COLLAPSE, RUIN; *esp* : BANKRUPTCY **6** : a striking success : HIT — **smash** *adj*

²**smash** *vb* **1** : to break or be broken into pieces **2** : to move forward with force and shattering effect **3** : to destroy utterly : WRECK

smat·ter·ing \'sma-tə-riŋ\ *n* **1** : superficial knowledge **2** : a small scattered number or amount

¹**smear** \'smir\ *n* **1** : a spot left by an oily or sticky substance **2** : material smeared on a surface (as of a microscope slide)

²**smear** *vb* **1** : to overspread esp. with something oily or sticky **2** : SMUDGE, SOIL **3** : to injure by slander or insults

¹**smell** \'smel\ *vb* **smelled** \'smeld\ *or* **smelt** \'smelt\; **smell·ing** **1** : to perceive the odor of by sense organs of the nose; *also* : to detect or seek with or as if with these organs **2** : to have or give off an odor

²**smell** *n* **1** : ODOR, SCENT **2** : the process or power of perceiving odor; *also* : the sense by which one perceives odor **3** : an act of smelling — **smelly** *adj*

smelling salts *n pl* : an aromatic preparation used as a stimulant and restorative (as to relieve faintness)

¹**smelt** \'smelt\ *n, pl* **smelts** *or* **smelt** : any of a family of small food fishes of coastal or fresh waters that are related to the trouts and salmons

²**smelt** *vb* : to melt or fuse (ore) in order to separate the metal; *also* : REFINE

smelt·er \'smel-tər\ *n* **1** : one that smelts **2** : an establishment for smelting

smid·gen *also* **smid·geon** *or* **smid·gin** \'smi-jən\ *n* : a small amount : BIT

smi·lax \'smī-ˌlaks\ *n* **1** : any of various mostly climbing and prickly plants related to the lilies **2** : an ornamental plant related to the asparagus

¹**smile** \'smī(-ə)l\ *vb* **smiled; smil·ing** **1** : to look with a smile **2** : to be favorable **3** : to express by a smile

²**smile** *n* : a change of facial expression to express amusement, pleasure, or affection — **smile·less** \'smī(-ə)l-ləs\ *adj*

smil·ey \'smī-lē\ *adj* : exhibiting a smile : frequently smiling

smirch \'smərch\ *vb* **1** : to make dirty or stained **2** : to bring disgrace on — **smirch** *n*

smirk \'smərk\ *vb* : to smile in an affected or smug manner : SIMPER — **smirk** *n*

smite \'smīt\ *vb* **smote** \'smōt\; **smit·ten** \'smi-t°n\ *or* **smote; smit·ing** \'smī-tiŋ\ **1** : to strike heavily; *also* : to kill by striking **2** : to affect as if by a heavy blow

smith \'smith\ *n* : a worker in metals; *esp* : BLACKSMITH

smith·er·eens \ˌsmi-thə-'rēnz\ *n pl* [perh. fr. Ir *smidiríní*] : FRAGMENTS, BITS

smithy \'smi-thē\ *n, pl* **smith·ies** **1** : a smith's workshop **2** : BLACKSMITH

¹**smock** \'smäk\ *n* : a loose garment worn over other clothes as a protection

²**smock** *vb* : to gather (cloth) in regularly spaced tucks — **smock·ing** *n*

smog \'smäg, 'smȯg\ *n* [blend of *smoke* and *fog*] : a thick haze caused by the action of sunlight on air polluted by smoke and automobile exhaust fumes — **smog·gy** *adj*

¹**smoke** \'smōk\ *n* **1** : the gas from burning material (as coal, wood, or tobacco) in which are suspended particles of soot **2** : a mass or column of smoke **3** : something (as a cigarette) to smoke; *also* : the act of smoking — **smoke·less** *adj* — **smoky** *adj*

²**smoke** *vb* **smoked; smok·ing** **1** : to emit smoke **2** : to inhale and exhale the fumes of burning tobacco; *also* : to use in smoking ⟨∼ a pipe⟩ **3** : to stupefy or drive away by smoke **4** : to discolor with smoke **5** : to cure (as meat) with smoke — **smok·er** *n*

smoke detector *n* : an alarm that sounds automatically when it detects smoke

smoke jumper *n* : a forest firefighter who parachutes to locations otherwise difficult to reach

smoke screen *n* **1** : a screen of smoke to hinder enemy observation **2** : something designed to obscure, confuse, or mislead

smoke·stack \'smōk-ˌstak\ *n* : a pipe or funnel through which smoke and gases are discharged

smol·der *or* **smoul·der** \'smōl-dər\ *vb* **smol·dered** *or* **smoul·dered; smol·der·ing** *or* **smoul·der·ing** **1** : to burn and smoke without flame **2** : to burn inwardly — **smolder** *n*

smooch \'smüch\ *vb* : KISS, PET — **smooch** *n*

¹**smooth** \'smüth\ *adj* **1** : not rough or uneven **2** : not jarring or jolting **3** : BLAND, MILD **4** : fluent in speech and agreeable in manner — **smooth·ly** *adv* — **smooth·ness** *n*

²**smooth** *vb* **1** : to make smooth **2** : to free from trouble or difficulty

smooth muscle *n* : muscle with no cross striations that is typical of visceral organs (as the stomach and bladder) and is not under voluntary control

smoothy *or* **smooth·ie** \'smü-thē\ *n, pl* **smooth·ies** **1** : an artfully suave person **2** *smoothie* : a creamy beverage of fruit blended with juice, milk, or yogurt

s'more \'smȯr\ *n* : a dessert of marshmallow and pieces of chocolate sandwiched between graham crackers

smor·gas·bord \'smȯr-gəs-ˌbȯrd\ *n* [Sw *smörgasbord*, fr. *smörgas* open sandwich + *bord* table] : a luncheon or supper buffet consisting of many foods

smote *past and past part of* SMITE

¹**smoth·er** \'smə-thər\ *n* **1** : thick stifling smoke **2** : a dense cloud (as of fog or dust) **3** : a confused multitude of things

: SOAKED, DRENCHED **3** : heavy or doughy from being improperly cooked ⟨∼ biscuits⟩

so·di·um \'sō-dē-əm\ *n* : a soft waxy silver white metallic chemical element occurring in nature in combined form (as in salt)

sodium bicarbonate *n* : a white weakly alkaline salt used esp. in baking powders, fire extinguishers, and medicine

sodium carbonate *n* : a carbonate of sodium used esp. in washing and bleaching textiles

sodium chloride *n* : SALT 1

sodium fluoride *n* : a salt used chiefly in tiny amounts (as in fluoridation) to prevent tooth decay

sodium hydroxide *n* : a white brittle caustic substance used in making soap and rayon and in bleaching

sodium nitrate *n* : a crystalline salt used as a fertilizer and in curing meat

sodium thiosulfate *n* : a hygroscopic crystalline salt used as a photographic fixing agent

sod·omy \'sä-də-mē\ *n* : anal or oral sexual intercourse with a member of the same or opposite sex; *also* : sexual intercourse with an animal — **sod·om·ize** \'sä-də-ˌmīz\ *vb*

so·ev·er \sō-'e-vər\ *adv* **1** : in any degree or manner ⟨how bad ∼⟩ **2** : at all : of any kind ⟨any help ∼⟩

so·fa \'sō-fə\ *n* [earlier, raised carpeted floor, fr. It *sofa,* fr. Turk *sofa,* fr. Ar *suffa* carpet, divan] : a couch usu. with upholstered back and arms

soft \'soft\ *adj* **1** : not hard or rough : NONVIOLENT **2** : RESTFUL, GENTLE, SOOTHING **3** : emotionally susceptible **4** : not prepared to endure hardship **5** : not containing certain salts that prevent lathering ⟨∼ water⟩ **6** : occurring at such a speed as to avoid destructive impact ⟨∼ landing of a spacecraft on the moon⟩ **7** : BIODEGRADABLE ⟨a ∼ pesticide⟩ **8** : not alcoholic ⟨∼ drinks⟩ **9** : less detrimental than a hard narcotic ⟨∼ drugs⟩ — **soft·ly** *adv* — **soft·ness** *n*

soft·ball \'soft-ˌbol\ *n* : a game similar to baseball played with a ball larger and softer than a baseball; *also* : the ball used in this game

soft·bound \-ˌbaund\ *adj* : not bound in hard covers ⟨∼ books⟩

soft coal *n* : BITUMINOUS COAL

soft·en \'so-fən\ *vb* : to make or become soft — **soft·en·er** *n*

soft palate *n* : the fold at the back of the hard palate that partially separates the mouth from the pharynx

soft·ware \'soft-ˌwer\ *n* : the entire set of programs, procedures, and related documentation associated with a system; *esp* : computer programs

soft·wood \-ˌwud\ *n* **1** : the wood of a coniferous tree as compared to that of a broad-leaved deciduous tree **2** : a tree yielding softwood — **softwood** *adj*

sog·gy \'sä-gē\ *adj* **sog·gi·er; -est** : heavy with water or moisture — **sog·gi·ly** \'sä-gə-lē\ *adv* — **sog·gi·ness** \-gē-nəs\ *n*

soi·gné *or* **soi·gnée** \swän-'yā\ *adj* : elegantly maintained; *esp* : WELL-GROOMED

¹soil \'soi(-ə)l\ *vb* **1** : CORRUPT, POLLUTE **2** : to make or become dirty **3** : STAIN, DISGRACE ⟨∼ed his reputation⟩

²soil *n* **1** : STAIN, DEFILEMENT **2** : EXCREMENT, WASTE

³soil *n* **1** : firm land : EARTH **2** : the upper layer of earth in which plants grow **3** : COUNTRY, REGION

soi·ree *or* **soi·rée** \swä-'rā\ *n* [F *soirée* evening period, evening party, fr. MF, fr. *soir* evening, fr. L *sero* at a late hour] : an evening party

so·journ \'sō-jərn, sō-'jərn\ *vb* : to dwell in a place temporarily — **so·journ** *n* — **so·journ·er** *n*

¹sol \'säl, 'sōl\ *n* — see MONEY table

²sol *n* : a fluid colloidal system

³sol *abbr* **1** solicitor **2** soluble **3** solution

Sol \'säl\ *n* : SUN

¹sol·ace \'sä-ləs\ *n* : COMFORT

²solace *vb* **so·laced; so·lac·ing** : to give solace to : CONSOLE

so·lar \'sō-lər\ *adj* **1** : of, derived from, or relating to the sun **2** : measured by the earth's course in relation to the sun ⟨the ∼ year⟩ **3** : operated by or using the sun's light or heat ⟨∼ energy⟩

solar cell *n* : a photoelectric cell used as a power source

solar collector *n* : a device for the absorption of solar radiation for the heating of water or buildings or the production of electricity

solar flare *n* : a sudden temporary outburst of energy from a small area of the sun's surface

so·lar·i·um \sō-'ler-ē-əm\ *n, pl* **-ia** \-ē-ə\ *also* **-iums** : a room exposed to the sun; *esp* : a room (as in a hospital) for exposure of the body to sunshine

solar mass *n* : a unit of mass equal to the mass of the sun or about 2×10^{30} kilograms

solar plexus *n* : the general area of the stomach below the sternum

solar system *n* : the sun together with the group of celestial bodies that revolve around it

solar wind *n* : plasma continuously ejected from the sun's surface

sold *past and past part of* SELL

sol·der \'sä-dər, 'so-\ *n* : a metallic alloy used when melted to mend or join metallic surfaces — **solder** *vb*

soldering iron *n* : a metal device for applying heat in soldering

¹sol·dier \'sōl-jər\ *n* [ME *soudeour,* fr. AF, mercenary, fr. *soude* shilling's worth, wage, fr. *sou, soud* shilling, fr. LL *solidus* a Roman coin, fr. L, solid] : a person in military service; *esp* : an enlisted man or woman — **sol·dier·ly** *adj or adv*

²soldier *vb* **sol·diered; sol·dier·ing** **1** : to serve as a soldier **2** : to pretend to work while actually doing nothing

soldier of fortune *n* : ADVENTURER 2

sol·diery \'sōl-jə-rē\ *n* : a body of soldiers

¹sole \'sōl\ *n* : any of various flatfishes including some used for food

²sole *n* **1** : the undersurface of the foot **2** : the bottom of a shoe

³sole *vb* **soled; sol·ing** : to furnish (a shoe) with a sole

⁴sole *adj* : SINGLE, ONLY ⟨the ∼ survivor⟩ — **sole·ly** \'sōl-lē\ *adv*

so·le·cism \'sä-lə-ˌsi-zəm, 'sō-\ *n* **1** : a mistake in grammar **2** : a breach of etiquette

sol·emn \'sä-ləm\ *adj* **1** : marked by or observed with full religious ceremony ⟨a ∼ oath⟩ **2** : FORMAL, CEREMONIOUS **3** : highly serious : GRAVE ⟨a ∼ gathering⟩ **4** : SOMBER, GLOOMY ⟨a ∼ city⟩ — **so·lem·ni·ty** \sə-'lem-nə-tē\ *n* — **sol·emn·ly** \'sä-ləm-lē\ *adv*

sol·em·nize \'sä-ləm-ˌnīz\ *vb* **-nized; -niz·ing** **1** : to observe or honor with solemnity **2** : to celebrate (a marriage) with religious rites — **sol·em·ni·za·tion** \ˌsä-ləm-nə-'zā-shən\ *n*

so·le·noid \'sō-lə-ˌnoid, 'sä-\ *n* : a coil of wire usu. in cylindrical form that when carrying a current acts like a magnet

so·lic·it \sə-'li-sət\ *vb* **1** : ENTREAT, BEG **2** : to approach with a request or plea **3** : TEMPT, LURE **4** : to try to obtain by request ⟨∼ donations⟩ — **so·lic·i·ta·tion** \-ˌli-sə-'tā-shən\ *n*

so·lic·i·tor \sə-'li-sə-tər\ *n* **1** : one that solicits **2** : LAWYER; *esp* : a legal official of a city or state

so·lic·i·tous \sə-'li-sə-təs\ *adj* **1** : WORRIED, CONCERNED **2** : EAGER, WILLING ♦ *Synonyms* AVID, IMPATIENT, KEEN, ANXIOUS — **so·lic·i·tous·ly** *adv*

so·lic·i·tude \sə-'li-sə-ˌtüd, -ˌtyüd\ *n* : CONCERN, ANXIETY

¹sol·id \'sä-ləd\ *adj* **1** : not hollow; *also* : written as one word without a hyphen ⟨a ∼ compound⟩ **2** : having, involving, or dealing with three dimensions or with solids ⟨∼ geometry⟩ **3** : not loose or spongy : COMPACT ⟨a ∼ mass of rock⟩; *also* : neither gaseous nor liquid : HARD, RIGID ⟨∼ ice⟩ **4** : of good substantial quality or kind ⟨∼ comfort⟩ **5** : thoroughly dependable : RELIABLE ⟨a ∼ citizen⟩; *also* : serious in purpose or character ⟨∼ reading⟩ **6** : UNANIMOUS, UNITED ⟨∼ for pay increases⟩ **7** : of one substance or character — **solid** *adv* — **so·lid·i·ty** \sə-'li-də-tē\ *n* — **sol·id·ly** *adv* — **sol·id·ness** *n*

²solid *n* **1** : a geometrical figure (as a cube or sphere) having three dimensions **2** : a solid substance

sol·i·dar·i·ty \ˌsä-lə-'der-ə-tē\ *n* : unity based on shared interests, objectives, or standards

so·lid·i·fy \sə-'li-də-ˌfī\ *vb* **-fied; -fy·ing** : to make or become solid — **so·lid·i·fi·ca·tion** \-ˌli-də-fə-'kā-shən\ *n*

solid–state *adj* **1** : relating to the structure and properties of solid material **2** : using semiconductor devices rather than vacuum tubes

so·lil·o·quize \sə-'li-lə-ˌkwīz\ *vb* **-quized; -quiz·ing** : to talk to oneself : utter a soliloquy

so·lil·o·quy \sə-'li-lə-kwē\ *n, pl* **-quies** [LL *soliloquium,* fr.

L *solus* alone + *loqui* to speak] **1** : the act of talking to oneself **2** : a dramatic monologue that represents unspoken reflections by a character

sol·i·taire \'sä-lə-ˌter\ *n* **1** : a single gem (as a diamond) set alone **2** : a card game for one person

sol·i·tary \'sä-lə-ˌter-ē\ *adj* **1** : being or living apart from others **2** : LONELY, SECLUDED **3** : SOLE, ONLY

sol·i·tude \'sä-lə-ˌtüd, -ˌtyüd\ *n* **1** : the state of being alone : SECLUSION **2** : a lonely place

soln *abbr* solution

¹so·lo \'sō-lō\ *n, pl* **solos** [It, fr. *solo* alone, fr. L *solus*] **1** : a piece of music for a single voice or instrument with or without accompaniment **2** : an action in which there is only one performer — **solo** *adj or vb* — **so·lo·ist** *n*

²solo *adv* : without a companion : ALONE

so·lon \'sō-lən\ *n* **1** : a wise and skillful lawgiver **2** : a member of a legislative body

sol·stice \'säl-stəs, 'sōl-\ *n* [ME, fr. L *solstitium*, fr. *sol* sun + *-stit-*, *-stes* standing] : the time of the year when the sun is farthest north of the equator (**summer solstice**) about June 22 or farthest south (**winter solstice**) about Dec. 22 — **sol·sti·tial** \säl-'sti-shəl, sōl-\ *adj*

sol·u·ble \'säl-yə-bəl\ *adj* **1** : capable of being dissolved in or as if in a liquid **2** : capable of being solved or explained — **sol·u·bil·i·ty** \ˌsäl-yə-'bi-lə-tē\ *n*

sol·ute \'säl-ˌyüt\ *n* : a dissolved substance

so·lu·tion \sə-'lü-shən\ *n* **1** : an action or process of solving a problem; *also* : an answer to a problem **2** : an act or the process by which one substance is homogeneously mixed with another usu. liquid substance; *also* : a mixture thus formed

solve \'sälv\ *vb* **solved; solv·ing** : to find the answer to or a solution for — **solv·able** *adj*

sol·ven·cy \'säl-vən-sē\ *n* : the condition of being solvent

¹sol·vent \-vənt\ *adj* **1** : able or sufficient to pay all legal debts **2** : dissolving or able to dissolve

²solvent *n* : a usu. liquid substance capable of dissolving or dispersing one or more other substances

som \'sōm\ *n, pl* **som** — see MONEY table

so·mat·ic \sō-'ma-tik\ *adj* : of, relating to, or affecting the body in contrast to the mind or the sex cells and their precursors

som·ber *or* **som·bre** \'säm-bər\ *adj* **1** : DARK, GLOOMY **2** : GRAVE, MELANCHOLY — **som·ber·ly** *adv*

som·bre·ro \səm-'brer-ō\ *n, pl* **-ros** [Sp, fr. *sombra* shade] : a broad-brimmed felt hat worn esp. in the Southwest and in Mexico

¹some \'səm\ *adj* **1** : one unspecified ⟨~ man called⟩ **2** : an unspecified or indefinite number of ⟨~ berries are ripe⟩ **3** : at least a few or a little ⟨~ years ago⟩

²some *pron* : a certain number or amount ⟨~ of the berries are ripe⟩ ⟨~ of it is missing⟩

¹-some \səm\ *adj suffix* : characterized by a (specified) thing, quality, state, or action ⟨awesome⟩ ⟨burdensome⟩

²-some *n suffix* : a group of (so many) members and esp. persons ⟨foursome⟩

¹some·body \'səm-ˌbä-dē, -bə-\ *pron* : some person

²somebody *n* : a person of importance

some·day \'səm-ˌdā\ *adv* : at some future time

some·how \-ˌhau̇\ *adv* : by some means

some·one \-ˌ(ˌ)wən\ *pron* : some person

som·er·sault *also* **sum·mer·sault** \'sə-mər-ˌsȯlt\ *n* [MF *sombresaut* leap, ultim. fr. L *super* over + *saltus* leap, fr. *salire* to jump] : a leap or roll in which a person turns heels over head — **somersault** *vb*

som·er·set \-ˌset\ *n or vb* : SOMERSAULT

some·thing \'səm-thiŋ\ *pron* : some undetermined or unspecified thing

some·time \-ˌtīm\ *adv* **1** : at a future time **2** : at an unknown or unnamed time

some·times \-ˌtīmz\ *adv* : OCCASIONALLY

¹some·what \-ˌhwät, -ˌhwət\ *pron* : SOMETHING

²somewhat *adv* : in some degree

some·where \-ˌhwer\ *adv* : in, at, or to an unknown or unnamed place

som·nam·bu·lism \säm-'nam-byə-ˌli-zəm\ *n* : performance of motor acts (as walking) during sleep; *also* : an abnormal condition of sleep characterized by this — **som·nam·bu·list** \-list\ *n*

som·no·lent \'säm-nə-lənt\ *adj* : SLEEPY, DROWSY — **som·no·lence** \-ləns\ *n*

so·mo·ni \ˌsō-mō-'nē\ *n* — see MONEY table

son \'sən\ *n* **1** : a male offspring or descendant **2** *cap* : Jesus Christ **3** : a person deriving from a particular source (as a country, race, or school)

so·nar \'sō-ˌnär\ *n* [*sound navigation ranging*] : a method or device for detecting and locating submerged objects (as submarines) by sound waves

so·na·ta \sə-'nä-tə\ *n* [It] : an instrumental composition with three or four movements differing in rhythm and mood but related in key

son·a·ti·na \ˌsä-nə-'tē-nə\ *n* [It, dim. of *sonata*] : a short usu. simplified sonata

song \'sȯŋ\ *n* **1** : vocal music; *also* : a short composition of words and music **2** : poetic composition **3** : a distinctive or characteristic sound (as of a bird) **4** : a small amount ⟨sold for a ~⟩

song·bird \'sȯŋ-ˌbərd\ *n* : a bird that utters a series of musical tones

Song of Sol·o·mon \-'sä-lə-mən\ — see BIBLE table

Song of Songs — see BIBLE table

song·ster \'sȯŋ-stər\ *n* : one that sings

song·stress \-strəs\ *n* : a girl or woman who is a singer

son·ic \'sä-nik\ *adj* : of or relating to sound waves or the speed of sound

sonic boom *n* : an explosive sound produced by an aircraft traveling at supersonic speed

son–in–law \'sən-ən-ˌlȯ\ *n, pl* **sons–in–law** : the husband of one's daughter

son·net \'sä-nət\ *n* : a poem of 14 lines usu. in iambic pentameter with a definite rhyme scheme

son of a gun *n* : an offensive or disagreeable person

so·no·rous \sə-'nȯr-əs, 'sä-nə-rəs\ *adj* **1** : giving out sound when struck **2** : loud, deep, or rich in sound : RESONANT **3** : high-sounding : IMPRESSIVE — **so·nor·i·ty** \sə-'nȯr-ə-tē\ *n*

soon \'sün\ *adv* **1** : before long **2** : PROMPTLY, QUICKLY **3** *archaic* : EARLY **4** : WILLINGLY, READILY

soot \'su̇t, 'sət, 'süt\ *n* : a fine black powder consisting chiefly of carbon that is formed when something burns and that colors smoke — **sooty** *adj*

sooth \'süth\ *n, archaic* : TRUTH

soothe \'süth\ *vb* **soothed; sooth·ing** **1** : to please by flattery or attention **2** : RELIEVE, ALLEVIATE ⟨~ a burn⟩ **3** : to calm down : COMFORT ⟨~ a child⟩ — **sooth·er** *n* — **sooth·ing·ly** *adv*

sooth·say·er \'süth-ˌsā-ər\ *n* : one who foretells events — **sooth·say·ing** *n*

¹sop \'säp\ *n* : a conciliatory bribe, gift, or concession

²sop *vb* **sopped; sop·ping** **1** : to steep or dip in or as if in a liquid **2** : to wet thoroughly : SOAK; *also* : to mop up (a liquid)

SOP *abbr* standard operating procedure; standing operating procedure

soph *abbr* sophomore

soph·ism \'sä-ˌfi-zəm\ *n* **1** : an argument correct in form but embodying a subtle fallacy **2** : SOPHISTRY

soph·ist \'sä-fist\ *n* : PHILOSOPHER; *esp* : a captious or fallacious reasoner

so·phis·tic \sä-'fis-tik, sə-\ *or* **so·phis·ti·cal** \-ti-kəl\ *adj* : of or characteristic of sophists or sophistry ♦ **Synonyms** FALLACIOUS, ILLOGICAL, UNREASONABLE, SPECIOUS

so·phis·ti·cat·ed \sə-'fis-tə-ˌkā-təd\ *adj* **1** : COMPLEX ⟨~ instruments⟩ **2** : made worldly-wise by wide experience **3** : intellectually appealing ⟨a ~ novel⟩ — **so·phis·ti·ca·tion** \-ˌfis-tə-'kā-shən\ *n*

soph·ist·ry \'sä-fə-strē\ *n* : subtly deceptive reasoning or argument

soph·o·more \'säf-ˌmȯr, 'sä-fə-\ *n* : a student in the second year of high school or college

soph·o·mor·ic \ˌsäf-'mȯr-ik, ˌsä-fə-\ *adj* **1** : being overconfident of knowledge but poorly informed and immature ⟨~ reasoning⟩ **2** : of, relating to, or characteristic of a sophomore ⟨~ humor⟩

So·pho·ni·as \ˌsä-fə-'nī-əs, ˌsō-\ *n* : ZEPHANIAH

sop·o·rif·ic \ˌsä-pə-'ri-fik\ *adj* **1** : causing sleep or drowsiness **2** : LETHARGIC

so·pra·no \sə-'pra-nō, -'prä-\ *n, pl* **-nos** [It, fr. *sopra* above, fr. L *supra*] **1** : the highest singing voice; *also* : a singer with this voice **2** : the highest part in a 4-part chorus — **soprano** *adj*

sor·bet \sȯr-'bā\ n : a usu. fruit-flavored ice served for dessert or between courses as a palate refresher

sor·cery \'sȯr-sə-rē\ n [ME *sorcerie*, fr. AF, fr. *sorcer* sorcerer, fr. ML *sortiarius*, fr. L *sort-*, *sors* chance, lot] : the use of magic : WITCHCRAFT — **sor·cer·er** \-rər\ n — **sor·cer·ess** \-rəs\ n

sor·did \'sȯr-dəd\ adj **1** : marked by baseness or grossness : VILE **2** : DIRTY, SQUALID — **sor·did·ly** adv — **sor·did·ness** n

¹sore \'sȯr\ adj **sor·er; sor·est 1** : causing pain or distress ⟨a ~ bruise⟩ **2** : painfully sensitive ⟨~ muscles⟩ **3** : SEVERE, INTENSE **4** : IRRITATED, ANGRY — **sore·ly** adv — **sore·ness** n

²sore n **1** : a sore spot on the body; *esp* : one (as an ulcer) with the tissues broken and usu. infected **2** : a source of pain or vexation

sore·head \'sȯr-,hed\ n : a person easily angered or discontented

sore throat n : painful throat due to inflammation of the fauces and pharynx

sor·ghum \'sȯr-gəm\ n : a tall variable Old World tropical grass grown widely for its edible seed, for forage, or for its sweet juice which yields a syrup

so·ror·i·ty \sə-'rȯr-ə-tē\ n, *pl* **-ties** [ML *sororitas* sisterhood, fr. L *soror* sister] : a club or organization usu. of female students for social purposes

¹sor·rel \'sȯr-əl\ n : a brownish orange to light brown color; *also* : a sorrel-colored animal (as a horse)

²sorrel n : any of various herbs having a sour juice

sor·row \'sär-ō\ n **1** : deep distress, sadness, or regret; *also* : resultant unhappy or unpleasant state **2** : a cause of grief or sadness **3** : a display of grief or sadness — **sorrow** vb — **sor·row·ful** \-fəl\ adj — **sor·row·ful·ly** \-f(ə-)lē\ adv

sor·ry \'sär-ē\ adj **sor·ri·er; -est 1** : feeling sorrow, regret, or penitence ⟨~ for yelling at her⟩ **2** : MOURNFUL, SAD **3** : causing sorrow, pity, or scorn : PITIFUL ⟨a ~ lot of ragamuffins⟩

¹sort \'sȯrt\ n **1** : a group of persons or things that have similar characteristics : CLASS **2** : QUALITY, NATURE **3** : an instance of sorting — **all sorts of** : many different — **out of sorts 1** : somewhat ill **2** : GROUCHY, IRRITABLE

²sort vb **1** : to put in a certain place according to kind, class, or nature **2** : to be in accord : AGREE **3** : SEARCH ⟨~ through this mess⟩ — **sort·er** n

sor·tie \'sȯr-tē, sȯr-'tē\ n **1** : a sudden issuing of troops from a defensive position against the enemy **2** : one mission or attack by one airplane

sort of adv : to a moderate degree

SOS \,es-(,)ō-'es\ n : a call or request for help or rescue

so–so \'sō-'sō\ adv or adj : PASSABLY

sot \'sät\ n : a habitual drunkard — **sot·tish** adj — **sot·tish·ly** adv

souf·flé \sü-'flā\ n [F, fr. *soufflé*, pp. of *souffler* to blow, puff up, fr. OF *sufler*, fr. L *sufflare*, fr. *sub-* up + *flare* to blow] : a spongy dish made light in baking by stiffly beaten egg whites

sough \'saù, 'səf\ vb : to make a moaning or sighing sound — **sough** n

sought *past and past part of* SEEK

¹soul \'sōl\ n **1** : the immaterial essence of an individual life **2** : the spiritual principle embodied in human beings or the universe **3** : an active or essential part **4** : the moral and emotional nature of human beings **5** : spiritual or moral force **6** : PERSON ⟨a kindly ~⟩ **7** : a strong, positive feeling (as of intense sensitivity and emotional fervor) conveyed esp. by black American performers; *also* : NEGRITUDE **8** : SOUL MUSIC — **souled** \'sōld\ adj — **soul·less** \'sōl-ləs\ adj

²soul adj **1** : of, relating to, or characteristic of black Americans or their culture ⟨~ food⟩ **2** : designed for or controlled by blacks ⟨~ radio stations⟩

soul brother n : a black male

soul·ful \'sōl-fəl\ adj : full of or expressing deep feeling ⟨a ~ ballad⟩ — **soul·ful·ly** adv

soul music n : music that is closely related to rhythm and blues and characterized by intensity of feeling

¹sound \'saùnd\ adj **1** : not diseased or sickly **2** : free from flaw or defect ⟨a ~ structure⟩ **3** : FIRM, STRONG **4** : free from error or fallacy : RIGHT ⟨~ logic⟩ **5** : LEGAL, VALID **6** : THOROUGH **7** : UNDISTURBED ⟨~ sleep⟩ **8** : showing good judgment — **sound·ly** adv — **sound·ness** n

²sound n **1** : the sensation of hearing; *also* : mechanical energy transmitted by longitudinal pressure waves (**sound waves**) (as in air) that is the stimulus to hearing **2** : something heard : NOISE, TONE; *also* : hearing distance : EARSHOT **3** : a musical style — **sound·less** adj — **sound·less·ly** adv — **sound·proof** \-,prüf\ adj or vb

³sound vb **1** : to make or cause to make a sound **2** : to order or proclaim by a sound ⟨~ the alarm⟩ **3** : to convey a certain impression : SEEM ⟨that ~s like fun⟩ **4** : to examine the condition of by causing to give out sounds — **sound·able** \'saùn-də-bəl\ adj

⁴sound n : a long passage of water wider than a strait often connecting two larger bodies of water

⁵sound vb **1** : to measure the depth of (water) esp. by a weighted line dropped from the surface : FATHOM **2** : PROBE **3** : to dive down suddenly ⟨the hooked fish ~ed⟩ — **sound·ing** n

sound bite n : a brief recorded statement broadcast esp. on a news program — **sound–bite** adj

sound card n : a circuit board in a computer system designed to produce or reproduce sound

sound·er \'saùn-dər\ n : one that sounds; *esp* : a device for making soundings

sound·stage \'saùnd-,stāj\ n : the part of a motion-picture studio in which a production is filmed

sound·track \'saùn(d)-,trak\ n : music recorded to accompany a film or videotape

soup \'süp\ n **1** : a liquid food with stock as its base and often containing pieces of solid food **2** : something having the consistency of soup **3** : an unfortunate predicament ⟨in the ~⟩

soup·çon \süp-'sōⁿ\ n [F, lit., suspicion] : a little bit : ¹TRACE 2

soup up vb : to increase the power of — **souped–up** \'süpt-'əp\ adj

soupy \'sü-pē\ adj **soup·i·er; -est 1** : having the consistency of soup **2** : densely foggy or cloudy

¹sour \'saù(-ə)r\ adj **1** : having an acid or tart taste ⟨~ as vinegar⟩ **2** : SPOILED, PUTRID ⟨a ~ odor⟩ **3** : UNPLEASANT, DISAGREEABLE ⟨~ disposition⟩ — **sour·ish** adj — **sour·ly** adv — **sour·ness** n

²sour vb : to become or make sour

source \'sȯrs\ n **1** : ORIGIN, BEGINNING **2** : a supplier of information **3** : the beginning of a stream of water

source code n : a computer program in its original programming language and before translation (as by a compiler)

¹souse \'saùs\ vb **soused; sous·ing 1** : PICKLE **2** : to plunge into a liquid **3** : DRENCH **4** : to make drunk

²souse n **1** : something (as pigs' feet) steeped in pickle **2** : a soaking in liquid **3** : DRUNKARD

¹south \'saùth\ adv : to or toward the south; *also* : into a state of decline

²south adj **1** : situated toward or at the south **2** : coming from the south

³south n **1** : the direction to the right of one facing east **2** : the compass point directly opposite to north **3** cap : regions or countries south of a specified or implied point; *esp* : the southeastern part of the U.S. — **south·er·ly** \'sə-thər-lē\ adj or adv — **south·ern** \'sə-thərn\ adj — **South·ern·er** n — **south·ern·most** \-,mōst\ adj — **south·ward** \'saùth-wərd\ adv or adj — **south·wards** \-wərdz\ adv

south·east \saù-'thēst, *naut* saù-'ēst\ n **1** : the general direction between south and east **2** : the compass point midway between south and east **3** cap : regions or countries southeast of a specified or implied point — **southeast** adv or adj — **south·east·er·ly** adv or adj — **south·east·ern** \-'ēs-tərn\ adj

south·paw \'saùth-,pȯ\ n : a left-handed person; *esp* : a left-handed baseball pitcher — **southpaw** adj

south pole n, *often cap S&P* : the southernmost point of the earth

south·west \saùth-'west, *naut* saù-'west\ n **1** : the general direction between south and west **2** : the compass point midway between south and west **3** cap : regions or countries southwest of a specified or implied point — **southwest** adj or adv — **south·west·er·ly** adv or adj — **south·west·ern** \-'wes-tərn\ adj

DICTIONARY

sou·ve·nir \ˌsü-və-ˈnir\ *n* [F] : something serving as a reminder

sou'·west·er \saů-ˈwes-tər\ *n* : a long waterproof coat worn at sea in stormy weather; *also* : a waterproof hat

¹sov·er·eign \ˈsä-vrən, -və-rən\ *n* 1 : one possessing the supreme power and authority in a state 2 : a gold coin of the United Kingdom

²sovereign *adj* 1 : EXCELLENT, FINE 2 : supreme in power or authority 3 : CHIEF, HIGHEST 4 : having independent authority ◆ *Synonyms* DOMINANT, PREDOMINANT, PARAMOUNT, PREPONDERANT

sov·er·eign·ty \-tē\ *n, pl* **-ties** 1 : supremacy in rule or power 2 : power to govern without external control 3 : the supreme political power in a state

so·vi·et \ˈsō-vē-ˌet, ˈsä-, -ət\ *n* 1 : an elected governmental council in a Communist country 2 *pl, cap* : the people and esp. the leaders of the U.S.S.R. — **soviet** *adj, often cap* — **so·vi·et·ize** *vb, often cap*

¹sow \ˈsaů\ *n* : an adult female swine

²sow \ˈsō\ *vb* **sowed; sown** \ˈsōn\ *or* **sowed; sow·ing** 1 : to plant seed for growing esp. by scattering 2 : to strew with seed 3 : to scatter abroad — **sow·er** \ˈsō-ər\ *n*

sow bug \ˈsaů-\ *n* : WOOD LOUSE

sox *pl of* SOCK

soy \ˈsȯi\ *n* : a sauce made from soybeans fermented in brine

soy·bean \ˈsȯi-ˌbēn\ *n* : an Asian legume widely grown for forage and for its edible seeds that yield a valuable oil (**soybean oil**); *also* : its seed

sp *abbr* 1 special 2 species 3 specimen 4 spelling 5 spirit

Sp *abbr* Spain

SP *abbr* 1 shore patrol; shore patrolman 2 shore police 3 specialist

spa \ˈspä\ *n* [*Spa*, watering place in Belgium] 1 : a mineral spring; *also* : a resort with mineral springs 2 : a health and fitness facility 3 : a hot tub with a whirlpool device

¹space \ˈspās\ *n* 1 : a period of time 2 : some small measurable distance, area, or volume 3 : the limitless area in which all things exist and move 4 : an empty place 5 : the region beyond the earth's atmosphere 6 : a definite place (as a seat on a train or ship) 7 : the distance from others that a person needs for comfort

²space *vb* **spaced; spac·ing** : to place at intervals — **spac·er** *n*

space–age \ˈspās-ˌāj\ *adj* : of or relating to the age of space exploration

space·craft \-ˌkraft\ *n* : a vehicle for travel beyond the earth's atmosphere

space·flight \-ˌflīt\ *n* : flight beyond the earth's atmosphere

space heater *n* : a usu. portable device for heating a relatively small area

space·man \ˈspās-ˌman, -mən\ *n* : one who travels outside the earth's atmosphere

space out *vb* : to become distracted or inattentive

space·ship \-ˌship\ *n* : a vehicle used for space travel

space shuttle *n* : a reusable spacecraft designed to transport people and cargo between earth and space

space station *n* : a large artificial satellite serving as a base (as for scientific observation)

space suit *n* : a suit equipped to make life in space possible for its wearer

space walk *n* : a period of activity outside a spacecraft by an astronaut in space — **space·walk** \ˈspās-ˌwȯk\ *vb* — **space·walk·er** *n*

spa·cious \ˈspā-shəs\ *adj* : very large in extent : ROOMY ◆ *Synonyms* COMMODIOUS, CAPACIOUS, AMPLE — **spa·cious·ly** *adv* — **spa·cious·ness** *n*

¹spade \ˈspād\ *n* : a shovel with a blade for digging — **spade·ful** *n*

²spade *vb* **spad·ed; spad·ing** : to dig with a spade — **spad·er** *n*

³spade *n* : any of a suit of playing cards marked with a black figure resembling an inverted heart with a short stem at the bottom

spa·dix \ˈspā-diks\ *n, pl* **spa·di·ces** \ˈspā-də-ˌsēz\ : a floral spike with a fleshy or succulent axis usu. enclosed in a spathe

spa·ghet·ti \spə-ˈge-tē\ *n* [It, fr. pl. of *spaghetto*, dim. of *spago* cord, string] : pasta made in thin solid strings

spam \ˈspam\ *n* : unsolicited usu. commercial e-mail sent to a large number of addresses — **spam** *vb*

¹span \ˈspan\ *n* 1 : an English unit of length equal to nine inches (about 23 centimeters) 2 : a limited portion of time 3 : the spread (as of an arch) from one support to another

²span *vb* **spanned; span·ning** 1 : MEASURE 2 : to extend across

³span *n* : a pair of animals (as mules) driven together

Span *abbr* Spanish

span·dex \ˈspan-ˌdeks\ *n* : any of various elastic synthetic textile fibers

span·gle \ˈspaŋ-gəl\ *n* : a small disk of shining metal or plastic used esp. on a dress for ornament — **spangle** *vb*

Span·glish \ˈspaŋ-glish\ *n* : Spanish with many English words included; *also* : a combination of Spanish and English

Span·iard \ˈspan-yərd\ *n* : a native or inhabitant of Spain

span·iel \ˈspan-yəl\ *n* [ME *spaynel, spaniell*, fr. AF *espainnel*, alter. of *espaignol*, Spaniard] : a dog of any of several breeds of mostly small and short-legged dogs usu. with long wavy hair and large drooping ears

Span·ish \ˈspa-nish\ *n* 1 : the chief language of Spain and of the countries colonized by the Spanish 2 **Spanish** *pl* : the people of Spain — **Spanish** *adj*

Spanish American *n* : a resident of the U.S. whose native language is Spanish; *also* : a native or inhabitant of one of the countries of America in which Spanish is the national language — **Spanish–American** *adj*

Spanish fly *n* : a toxic preparation of dried green European beetles that causes the skin to blister and is thought to be an aphrodisiac

Spanish moss *n* : a plant related to the pineapple that grows in pendent tufts of grayish green filaments on trees from the southern U.S. to Argentina

Spanish onion *n* : a large mild-flavored onion

spank \ˈspaŋk\ *vb* : to hit on the buttocks with the open hand — **spank** *n*

spank·ing \ˈspaŋ-kiŋ\ *adj* : BRISK, LIVELY 〈∼ breeze〉 — **spanking** *adv*

¹spar \ˈspär\ *n* : a rounded wood or metal piece (as a mast, yard, boom, or gaff) for supporting sail rigging

²spar *vb* **sparred; spar·ring** : to box for practice without serious hitting; *also* : SKIRMISH, WRANGLE

¹spare \ˈsper\ *vb* **spared; spar·ing** 1 : to refrain from punishing or injuring : show mercy to 2 : to exempt from something 3 : to get along without 4 : to use frugally or rarely

²spare *adj* **spar·er; spar·est** 1 : held in reserve 2 : SUPERFLUOUS 3 : not liberal or profuse 4 : LEAN, THIN 5 : SCANTY ◆ *Synonyms* MEAGER, SPARSE, SKIMPY, EXIGUOUS, SCANT — **spare·ness** *n*

³spare *n* 1 : a duplicate kept in reserve; *esp* : a spare tire 2 : the knocking down of all the bowling pins with the first two balls

sparing *adj* : SAVING, FRUGAL ◆ *Synonyms* THRIFTY, ECONOMICAL, PROVIDENT — **spar·ing·ly** *adv*

¹spark \ˈspärk\ *n* 1 : a small particle of a burning substance or a hot glowing particle struck from a mass (as by steel on flint) 2 : a short bright flash of electricity between two points 3 : SPARKLE 4 : a particle capable of being kindled or developed : GERM

²spark *vb* 1 : to emit or produce sparks 2 : to stir to activity : INCITE

³spark *vb* : WOO, COURT

¹spar·kle \ˈspär-kəl\ *vb* **spar·kled; spar·kling** 1 : FLASH, GLEAM 2 : to perform brilliantly 3 : EFFERVESCE — **spar·kler** *n*

²sparkle *n* 1 : GLEAM 2 : ANIMATION

spark plug *n* : a device that produces a spark to ignite the fuel mixture in an engine cylinder

spark plug

spar·row \'spa-rō\ *n* : any of several small dull-colored singing birds

sparse \'spärs\ *adj* **spars·er; spars·est** : thinly scattered : SCANTY ◆ *Synonyms* MEAGER, SPARE, SKIMPY, EXIGUOUS, SCANT — **sparse·ly** *adv* — **sparse·ness** *n*

¹Spar·tan \'spär-t³n\ *n* **1** : a native or inhabitant of ancient Sparta **2** : a person of great courage and self-discipline

²Spartan *adj* **1** : of or relating to Sparta or Spartans **2** *often not cap* : marked by simplicity, frugality, or avoidance of luxury and comfort ⟨a ~ room⟩

spasm \'spa-zəm\ *n* **1** : an involuntary and abnormal muscular contraction **2** : a sudden, violent, and temporary effort, emotion, or sensation — **spas·mod·ic** \spaz-'mä-dik\ *adj* — **spas·mod·i·cal·ly** \-di-k(ə-)lē\ *adv*

spas·tic \'spas-tik\ *adj* : of, relating to, marked by, or affected with muscular spasm ⟨~ paralysis⟩ — **spastic** *n*

¹spat \'spat\ *past and past part of* SPIT

²spat *n, pl* **spat** *or* **spats** : a young bivalve mollusk (as an oyster)

³spat *n* : a gaiter covering instep and ankle

⁴spat *n* : a brief petty quarrel : DISPUTE

⁵spat *vb* **spat·ted; spat·ting** : to quarrel briefly

spate \'spāt\ *n* : a sudden outburst

spathe \'spāth\ *n* : a sheathing bract or pair of bracts enclosing an inflorescence (as of the calla lily) and esp. a spadix on the same axis

spa·tial \'spā-shəl\ *adj* : of or relating to space or to the facility to perceive objects in space — **spa·tial·ly** *adv*

spat·ter \'spa-tər\ *vb* **1** : to splash with drops of liquid **2** : to sprinkle around — **spatter** *n*

spat·u·la \'spa-chə-lə\ *n* : a flexible knifelike implement for scooping, spreading, or mixing soft substances

spav·in \'spa-vən\ *n* : a bony enlargement of the hock of a horse — **spav·ined** \-vənd\ *adj*

¹spawn \'spȯn\ *vb* [ME, fr. AF *espandre* to spread out, shed, scatter, spawn, fr. L *expandere*, fr. *ex-* out + *pandere* to spread] **1** : to produce eggs or offspring esp. in large numbers **2** : GENERATE ⟨~ed much protest⟩ — **spawn·er** *n*

²spawn *n* **1** : the eggs of water animals (as fishes or oysters) that lay many small eggs **2** : offspring esp. when produced in great numbers

spay \'spā\ *vb* **spayed; spay·ing** : to remove the ovaries of (a female animal)

SPCA *abbr* Society for the Prevention of Cruelty to Animals

SPCC *abbr* Society for the Prevention of Cruelty to Children

speak \'spēk\ *vb* **spoke** \'spōk\; **spo·ken** \'spō-kən\; **speak·ing** **1** : to utter words **2** : to express orally **3** : to mention in speech or writing **4** : to address an audience **5** : to use or be able to use (a language) in talking — **to speak of** : worthy of mention ⟨no progress *to speak of*⟩

speak·easy \'spēk-ₑē-zē\ *n, pl* **-eas·ies** : an illicit drinking place

speak·er \'spē-kər\ *n* **1** : one that speaks **2** : the presiding officer of a deliberative assembly **3** : LOUDSPEAKER

¹spear \'spir\ *n* **1** : a long-shafted weapon with a sharp point for thrusting or throwing **2** : a sharp-pointed instrument with barbs used in spearing fish — **spear·man** \-mən\ *n*

²spear *vb* : to strike or pierce with or as if with a spear — **spear·er** *n*

³spear *n* : a usu. young blade, shoot, or sprout (as of asparagus)

spear·head \-ₕhed\ *n* : a leading force, element, or influence — **spearhead** *vb*

spear·mint \-ₘmint\ *n* : a common highly aromatic garden mint

¹spec *abbr* **1** special **2** specifically

²spec \'spek\ *n* : SPECIFICATION 2 — usu. used in pl.

spe·cial \'spe-shəl\ *adj* **1** : UNCOMMON, NOTEWORTHY **2** : particularly favored **3** : INDIVIDUAL, UNIQUE **4** : EXTRA, ADDITIONAL **5** : confined to or designed for a definite field of action, purpose, or occasion — **special** *n*

special delivery *n* : delivery of mail by messenger for an extra fee

special effects *n pl* : visual or sound effects introduced into a motion picture, video recording, or taped television production

Special Forces *n pl* : a branch of the army composed of soldiers specially trained in guerrilla warfare

spe·cial·ise *Brit var of* SPECIALIZE

spe·cial·ist \'spe-shə-list\ *n* **1** : a person who specializes in a particular branch of learning or activity **2** : any of four enlisted ranks in the army corresponding to the grades of corporal through sergeant first class

spe·cial·ize \'spe-shə-ₗlīz\ *vb* **-ized; -iz·ing** : to concentrate one's efforts in a special activity or field; *also* : to change in an adaptive manner — **spe·cial·i·za·tion** \ₛspe-shə-lə-'zā-shən\ *n*

spe·cial·ly \'spe-shə-lē\ *adv* **1** : in a special manner **2** : for a special purpose : in particular

spe·cial·ty \'spe-shəl-tē\ *n, pl* **-ties** **1** : a particular quality or detail **2** : a product of a special kind or of special excellence **3** : a skill or discipline in which one specializes

spe·cie \'spē-shē, -sē\ *n* : money in coin

spe·cies \'spē-shēz, -sēz\ *n, pl* **spe·cies** [ME, fr. L, appearance, kind, species, fr. *specere* to look] **1** : SORT, KIND **2** : a category of biological classification ranking just below the genus or subgenus and comprising closely related organisms potentially able to breed with one another

specif *abbr* specific; specifically

¹spe·cif·ic \spi-'si-fik\ *adj* **1** : having a unique effect or influence or reacting in only one way or with only one thing ⟨~ antibodies⟩ ⟨~ enzymes⟩ **2** : DEFINITE, EXACT ⟨a ~ agreement⟩ **3** : of, relating to, or constituting a species — **spe·cif·i·cal·ly** \-fi-k(ə-)lē\ *adv* — **spec·i·fic·i·ty** \ₛspe-sə-'fi-sə-tē\ *n*

²specific *n* : something specific : DETAIL, PARTICULAR — usu. used in pl.

spec·i·fi·ca·tion \ₛspe-sə-fə-'kā-shən\ *n* **1** : the act or process of specifying **2** : a description of work to be done and materials to be used (as in building) — usu. used in pl.

specific gravity *n* : the ratio of the density of a substance to the density of some substance (as water) taken as a standard when both densities are obtained by weighing in air

spec·i·fy \'spe-sə-ₗfī\ *vb* **-fied; -fy·ing** : to mention or name explicitly

spec·i·men \'spe-sə-mən\ *n* : an item or part typical of a group or whole

spe·cious \'spē-shəs\ *adj* : seeming to be genuine, correct, or beautiful but not really so ⟨~ reasoning⟩

speck \'spek\ *n* **1** : a small spot or blemish **2** : a small particle — **speck** *vb*

speck·le \'spe-kəl\ *n* : a little speck — **speckle** *vb*

specs \'speks\ *n pl* : GLASSES

spec·ta·cle \'spek-ti-kəl\ *n* **1** : an unusual or impressive public display **2** *pl* : GLASSES — **spec·ta·cled** \-kəld\ *adj*

spec·tac·u·lar \spek-'ta-kyə-lər\ *adj* : exciting to see : SENSATIONAL

spec·ta·tor \'spek-ₜtā-tər\ *n* : a person who looks on (as at a sports event) ◆ *Synonyms* OBSERVER, WITNESS, BYSTANDER, ONLOOKER, EYEWITNESS

spec·ter *or* **spec·tre** \'spek-tər\ *n* : a visible disembodied spirit : GHOST

spec·tral \'spek-trəl\ *adj* **1** : of, relating to, or resembling a specter **2** : of, relating to, or made by a spectrum

spec·tro·gram \'spek-trə-ₗgram\ *n* : a photograph, image, or diagram of a spectrum

spec·tro·graph \-ₗgraf\ *n* : an instrument for dispersing radiation into a spectrum and recording or mapping the spectrum — **spec·tro·graph·ic** \ₛspek-trə-'gra-fik\ *adj* — **spec·tro·graph·i·cal·ly** \-fi-k(ə-)lē\ *adv*

spec·trom·e·ter \spek-'trä-mə-tər\ *n* : an instrument for measuring spectra — **spec·tro·met·ric** \ₛspek-trə-'me-trik\ *adj* — **spec·trom·e·try** \spek-'trä-mə-trē\ *n*

spec·tro·scope \'spek-trə-ₗskōp\ *n* : an instrument that produces spectra esp. of visible electromagnetic radiation — **spec·tro·scop·ic** \ₛspek-trə-'skä-pik\ *adj* — **spec·tro·scop·i·cal·ly** \-pi-k(ə-)lē\ *adv* — **spec·tros·co·pist** \spek-'träs-kə-pist\ *n* — **spec·tros·co·py** \-pē\ *n*

spec·trum \'spek-trəm\ *n, pl* **spec·tra** \-trə\ *or* **spectrums** [NL, fr. L, appearance, fr. *specere* to look] **1** : a series of colors formed when a beam of white light is dispersed (as by a prism) so that its parts are arranged in the order of their wavelengths **2** : a series of radiations arranged in regular order **3** : a continuous sequence or range ⟨a wide ∼ of political opinions⟩

spec·u·late \'spe-kyə-ˌlāt\ vb **-lat·ed; -lat·ing** [L speculari to spy out, examine, fr. specula lookout post, fr. specere to look, look at] **1** : to think or wonder about a subject **2** : to take a business risk in hope of gain ✦ **Synonyms** REASON, THINK, DELIBERATE, COGITATE — **spec·u·la·tion** \ˌspe-kyə-ˈlā-shən\ n — **spec·u·la·tive** \'spe-kyə-ˌlā-tiv\ adj — **spec·u·la·tive·ly** adv — **spec·u·la·tor** \-ˌlā-tər\ n

speech \'spēch\ n **1** : the act of speaking **2** : TALK, CONVERSATION **3** : a public talk or lecture **4** : LANGUAGE, DIALECT **5** : an individual manner of speaking **6** : the power of speaking — **speech·less** adj

¹speed \'spēd\ n **1** archaic : SUCCESS **2** : SWIFTNESS, RAPIDITY **3** : rate of motion or performance **4** : a transmission gear (as of a bicycle) **5** : METHAMPHETAMINE; also : a related drug ✦ **Synonyms** HASTE, HURRY, DISPATCH, CELERITY — **speed·i·ly** \'spē-də-lē\ adv — **speedy** adj

²speed vb **sped** \'sped\ or **speed·ed; speed·ing** **1** archaic : PROSPER; also : GET ALONG, FARE **2** : to go fast; esp : to go at an excessive or illegal speed **3** : to cause to go faster — **speed·er** n

speed·boat \-ˌbōt\ n : a fast motorboat

speed bump n : a low raised ridge across a roadway (as in a parking lot) to limit vehicle speed

speed of light : a fundamental physical constant that is the speed of electromagnetic radiation propagation in a vacuum and has the value of 299,792,458 meters per second

speed·om·e·ter \spi-'dä-mə-tər\ n : an instrument for indicating speed

speed·up \'spēd-ˌəp\ n : ACCELERATION

speed·way \-ˌwā\ n : a racecourse for motor vehicles

speed·well \'spēd-ˌwel\ n : VERONICA

¹spell \'spel\ vb **spelled** \'speld, 'spelt\; **spell·ing** [ME, to signify, read by spelling out, fr. AF espeleir, of Gmc origin] **1** : to name, write, or print in order the letters of a word **2** : MEAN ⟨another drought may ∼ famine⟩

²spell n [ME, talk, tale, fr. OE] **1** : a magic formula : INCANTATION **2** : a controlling influence

³spell n **1** : one's turn at work or duty **2** : a stretch of a specified kind of weather **3** : a period of bodily or mental distress or disorder : ATTACK

⁴spell vb **spelled** \'speld\; **spell·ing** : to take the place of for a time in work or duty : RELIEVE

spell·bind·er \-ˌbīn-dər\ n : a speaker of compelling eloquence; also : one that compels attention

spell·bound \-ˌbau̇nd\ adj : held by or as if by a spell : FASCINATED

spell–check·er \'spel-ˌche-kər\ n : a computer program that identifies possible misspellings in a block of text — **spell–check** \-ˌchek\ vb

spell·er \'spe-lər\ n **1** : one who spells words **2** : a book with exercises for teaching spelling

spelt \'spelt\ chiefly Brit past and past part of ¹SPELL

spe·lunk·er \spi-'lən-kər, 'spē-ˌlən-kər\ n [L spelunca cave, fr. Gk spēlynx] : one who makes a hobby of exploring caves — **spe·lunk·ing** n

spend \'spend\ vb **spent** \'spent\; **spend·ing** **1** : to pay out : EXPEND **2** : WEAR OUT, EXHAUST; also : to consume wastefully **3** : to cause or permit to elapse : PASS — **spend·er** n

spend·thrift \'spend-ˌthrift\ n : one who spends wastefully or recklessly

spent \'spent\ adj : drained of energy

sperm \'spərm\ n, pl **sperm** or **sperms** **1** : SEMEN **2** : a male gamete

sper·ma·to·zo·on \(ˌ)spər-ˌma-tə-'zō-ˌän, -'zō-ən\ n, pl **-zoa** \-'zō-ə\ : a motile male gamete of an animal usu. with a rounded or elongated head and a long posterior flagellum

sperm cell n : SPERM 2

sper·mi·cide \'spər-mə-ˌsīd\ n : a preparation or substance used to kill sperm — **sper·mi·cid·al** \ˌspər-mə-'sī-dəl\ adj

sperm whale n : a large whale with a massive square-shaped head containing a fluid-filled cavity

spew \'spyü\ vb : VOMIT

SPF abbr sun protection factor

sp gr abbr specific gravity

sphag·num \'sfag-nəm\ n : any of a genus of atypical mosses that grow in wet acid areas where their remains become compacted with other plant debris to form peat; also : a mass of these mosses

sphere \'sfir\ n [ME spere globe, celestial sphere, fr. AF espere, fr. L sphaera, fr. Gk sphaira, lit., ball] **1** : a globe-shaped body : BALL **2** : a celestial body **3** : a solid figure so shaped that every point on its surface is an equal distance from the center **4** : range of action or influence — **spher·i·cal** \'sfir-i-kəl, 'sfer-\ adj — **spher·i·cal·ly** \-i-k(ə-)lē\ adv

spher·oid \'sfir-ˌȯid, 'sfer-\ n : a figure similar to a sphere but not perfectly round — **sphe·roi·dal** \sfir-'ȯi-dəl\ adj

sphinc·ter \'sfiŋk-tər\ n : a muscular ring that closes a bodily opening

sphinx \'sfiŋks\ n, pl **sphinx·es** or **sphin·ges** \'sfin-ˌjēz\ **1** : a winged monster in Greek mythology having a woman's head and a lion's body and noted for killing anyone unable to answer its riddle **2** : an enigmatic or mysterious person **3** : an ancient Egyptian image having the body of a lion and the head of a man, ram, or hawk

spice \'spīs\ n **1** : any of various aromatic plant products (as pepper or nutmeg) used to season or flavor foods **2** : something that adds interest and relish — **spice** vb — **spicy** adj

spick–and–span or **spic–and–span** \ˌspik-ənd-'span\ adj : quite new; also : spotlessly clean

spic·ule \'spi-kyül\ n : a slender pointed body esp. of calcium or silica ⟨sponge ∼s⟩

spi·der \'spī-dər\ n **1** : any of an order of arachnids that have a 2-part body, eight legs, and two or more pairs of abdominal organs for spinning threads of silk used esp. in making webs for catching prey **2** : a cast-iron frying pan — **spi·dery** adj

spider mite n : any of various small web-spinning mites that feed on and are pests of plants

spider plant n : a houseplant of the lily family having long green leaves usu. striped with white and producing tufts of small plants on long hanging stems

spi·der·web \'spī-dər-ˌweb\ n : the web spun by a spider

spiel \'spēl\ vb : to talk in a fast, smooth, and usu. colorful manner — **spiel** n

spig·ot \'spi-gət, -kət\ n : FAUCET

¹spike \'spīk\ n **1** : a very large nail **2** : any of various pointed projections (as on the sole of a shoe to prevent slipping) — **spiky** adj

²spike vb **spiked; spik·ing** **1** : to fasten with spikes **2** : to put an end to : QUASH ⟨∼ a rumor⟩ **3** : to pierce with or impale on a spike **4** : to add alcoholic liquor to (a drink)

³spike n **1** : an ear of grain **2** : a long cluster of usu. stemless flowers

¹spill \'spil\ vb **spilled** \'spild, 'spilt\ also **spilt** \'spilt\; **spill·ing** **1** : to cause or allow to fall, flow, or run out esp. unintentionally **2** : to cause (blood) to be lost by wounding **3** : to run out or over with resulting loss or waste **4** : to let out : DIVULGE — **spill·able** adj

²spill n **1** : an act of spilling; also : a fall from a horse or vehicle or an erect position **2** : something spilled

spill·way \-ˌwā\ n : a passage for surplus water to run over or around an obstruction (as a dam)

¹spin \'spin\ vb **spun** \'spən\; **spin·ning** **1** : to draw out (fiber) and twist into thread; also : to form (thread) by such means **2** : to form thread by extruding a sticky quickly hardening fluid; also : to construct from such thread ⟨spiders ∼ their webs⟩ **3** : to produce slowly and by degrees ⟨∼ a story⟩ **4** : TWIRL **5** : WHIRL, REEL ⟨my head is spinning⟩ **6** : to move rapidly along **7** : to present (as information) with a particular spin — **spin·ner** n

²spin n **1** : a rapid rotating motion **2** : an excursion in a wheeled vehicle **3** : a particular point of view, emphasis, or interpretation

spi·na bi·fi·da \ˌspī-nə-'bi-fə-də\ n : a birth defect in which the spinal column has a fissure

sperm whale

spin·ach \'spi-nich\ *n* : a dark green herb grown for its edible leaves

spi·nal \'spī-n°l\ *adj* : of or relating to the backbone or spinal cord — **spi·nal·ly** *adv*

spinal column *n* : BACKBONE 1

spinal cord *n* : the thick cord of nervous tissue that extends from the brain along the back in the cavity of the backbone and carries nerve impulses to and from the brain

spinal nerve *n* : any of the paired nerves which arise from the spinal cord and pass to various parts of the body and of which there are normally 31 pairs in human beings

spin control *n* : the act or practice of attempting to manipulate the way an event is interpreted

spin·dle \'spin-d°l\ *n* **1** : a round tapering stick or rod by which fibers are twisted in spinning **2** : a turned part of a piece of furniture ⟨the ~s of a chair⟩ **3** : a slender pin or rod which turns or on which something else turns

spin·dling \'spind-lin\ *adj* : SPINDLY

spin·dly \'spind-lē\ *adj* : being long or tall and thin and usu. weak

spin·drift \'spin-ˌdrift\ *n* : spray blown from waves

spine \'spīn\ *n* **1** : BACKBONE **2** : a stiff sharp process esp. on a plant or animal **3** : the part of a book where the pages are attached — **spiny** *adj*

spi·nel \spə-'nel\ *n* : a hard crystalline mineral of variable color used as a gem

spine·less \'spīn-ləs\ *adj* **1** : having no spines, thorns, or prickles **2** : lacking a backbone **3** : lacking courage or determination

spin·et \'spi-nət\ *n* **1** : an early harpsichord having a single keyboard and only one string for each note **2** : a small upright piano

spin·na·ker \'spi-ni-kər\ *n* : a large triangular sail set on a long light pole

spinning jen·ny \-'je-nē\ *n* : an early multiple-spindle machine for spinning wool or cotton

spinning wheel *n* : a small machine for spinning thread or yarn in which a large wheel drives a single spindle

spin—off \'spin-ˌȯf\ *n* **1** : a usu. useful by-product **2** : something (as a TV show) derived from an earlier work — **spin off** *vb*

spin·ster \'spin-stər\ *n* : an unmarried woman past the common age for marrying — **spin·ster·hood** \-ˌhu̇d\ *n*

spiny lobster *n* : any of several edible crustaceans differing from the related lobsters in lacking the large front claws and in having a spiny carapace

¹spi·ral \'spī-rəl\ *adj* : winding or coiling around a center or axis and usu. getting closer to or farther away from it — **spi·ral·ly** *adv*

²spiral *n* **1** : something that has a spiral form; *also* : a single turn in a spiral object **2** : a continuously spreading and accelerating increase or decrease

³spiral *vb* **-raled** *or* **-ralled; -ral·ing** *or* **-ral·ling** **1** : to move and esp. to rise or fall in a spiral course **2** : to form into a spiral

spi·rant \'spī-rənt\ *n* : a consonant (as \f\, \s\, \sh\) uttered with decided friction of the breath against some part of the oral passage — **spirant** *adj*

spire \'spī(-ə)r\ *n* **1** : a slender tapering stalk (as of grass) **2** : a pointed tip (as of an antler) **3** : STEEPLE — **spiry** *adj*

spi·rea *or* **spi·raea** \spī-'rē-ə\ *n* : any of a genus of shrubs related to the roses with dense clusters of small usu. white or pink flowers

¹spir·it \'spir-ət\ *n* [ME, fr. AF or L; AF, fr. L *spiritus,* lit., breath, fr. *spirare* to blow, breathe] **1** : a life-giving force; *also* : the animating principle : SOUL **2** *cap* : HOLY SPIRIT **3** : SPECTER, GHOST **4** : PERSON ⟨a bold ~⟩ **5** : DISPOSITION, MOOD ⟨in good ~s⟩ **6** : VIVACITY, ARDOR **7** : essential or real meaning : INTENT **8** : distilled alcoholic liquor **9** : LOYALTY ⟨school ~⟩ — **spir·it·less** *adj*

²spirit *vb* : to carry off secretly or mysteriously

spir·it·ed \'spir-ə-təd\ *adj* : full of energy, animation, or courage

¹spir·i·tu·al \'spir-i-chəl, -chə-wəl\ *adj* **1** : of, relating to, consisting of, or affecting the spirit : INCORPOREAL **2** : of or relating to sacred matters **3** : ecclesiastical rather than lay or temporal — **spir·i·tu·al·i·ty** \ˌspir-i-chə-'wa-lə-tē\ *n* — **spir·i·tu·al·ize** \'spir-i-chə-ˌlīz, -chə-wə-\ *vb* — **spir·i·tu·al·ly** *adv*

²spiritual *n* : a religious song originating among blacks of the southern U.S.

spir·i·tu·al·ism \'spir-i-chə-ˌli-zəm, -chə-wə-\ *n* : a belief that spirits of the dead communicate with the living usu. through a medium — **spir·i·tu·al·ist** \-list\ *n, often cap* — **spir·i·tu·al·is·tic** \ˌspir-i-chə-'lis-tik, -chə-wə-\ *adj*

spir·i·tu·ous \'spir-i-chəs, -chə-wəs; 'spir-ə-təs\ *adj* : containing alcohol

spi·ro·chete *also* **spi·ro·chaete** \'spī-rə-ˌkēt\ *n* : any of an order of spirally undulating bacteria including those causing syphilis and Lyme disease

spirt *var of* SPURT

¹spit \'spit\ *n* **1** : a thin pointed rod for holding meat over a fire **2** : a point of land that runs out into the water

²spit *vb* **spit·ted; spit·ting** : to pierce with or as if with a spit

³spit *vb* **spit** *or* **spat** \'spat\; **spit·ting** **1** : to eject (saliva) from the mouth **2** : to express by or as if by spitting **3** : to rain or snow lightly

⁴spit *n* **1** : SALIVA **2** : perfect likeness ⟨~ and image of his father⟩

spit·ball \'spit-ˌbȯl\ *n* **1** : paper chewed and rolled into a ball to be thrown as a missile **2** : a baseball pitch delivered after the ball has been moistened with saliva or sweat

¹spite \'spīt\ *n* : ill will with a wish to annoy, anger, or frustrate : petty malice ♦ *Synonyms* MALIGNITY, SPLEEN, GRUDGE, MALEVOLENCE — **spite·ful** \-fəl\ *adj* — **spite·ful·ly** *adv* — **spite·ful·ness** *n* — **in spite of** : in defiance or contempt of : NOTWITHSTANDING

²spite *vb* **spit·ed; spit·ing** : to treat maliciously : ANNOY, OFFEND

spit·tle \'spi-t°l\ *n* : SALIVA

spit·tle·bug \-ˌbəg\ *n* : any of a family of leaping insects with froth-secreting larvae that are related to aphids

spit·toon \spi-'tün\ *n* : a receptacle for spit

splash \'splash\ *vb* **1** : to dash a liquid about **2** : to scatter a liquid on : SPATTER **3** : to fall or strike with a splashing noise ♦ *Synonyms* SPRINKLE, BESPATTER, DOUSE, SPLATTER — **splash** *n*

splash·down \'splash-ˌdau̇n\ *n* : the landing of a manned spacecraft in the ocean — **splash down** *vb*

splashy \'spla-shē\ *adj* **splash·i·er; -est** : conspicuously showy : OSTENTATIOUS

¹splat·ter \'spla-tər\ *vb* : SPATTER — **splatter** *n*

²splatter *adj* : extremely gory or violent ⟨a ~ movie⟩

¹splay \'splā\ *vb* : to spread outward or apart — **splay** *n*

²splay *adj* **1** : spread out : turned outward **2** : AWKWARD, CLUMSY

spleen \'splēn\ *n* **1** : a vascular organ located near the stomach in most vertebrates that is concerned esp. with the filtration and storage of blood, destruction of red blood cells, and production of lymphocytes **2** : SPITE, MALICE ♦ *Synonyms* MALIGNITY, GRUDGE, MALEVOLENCE, ILL WILL, SPITEFULNESS

splen·did \'splen-dəd\ *adj* [L *splendidus,* fr. *splendēre* to shine] **1** : SHINING, BRILLIANT **2** : SHOWY, GORGEOUS **3** : ILLUSTRIOUS **4** : EXCELLENT ⟨a ~ opportunity⟩ ♦ *Synonyms* RESPLENDENT, GLORIOUS, SUBLIME, SUPERB — **splen·did·ly** *adv*

splen·dor \'splen-dər\ *n* **1** : BRILLIANCE ⟨the ~ of the sun⟩ **2** : POMP, MAGNIFICENCE

splen·dour \'splen-dər\ *chiefly Brit var of* SPLENDOR

sple·net·ic \spli-'ne-tik\ *adj* : marked by bad temper or spite

splen·ic \'sple-nik\ *adj* : of, relating to, or located in the spleen

splice \'splīs\ *vb* **spliced; splic·ing** **1** : to unite (as two ropes) by weaving the strands together **2** : to unite (as two lengths of film) by connecting the ends together — **splice** *n*

splint \'splint\ *n* **1** : a thin strip of wood interwoven with others to make something (as a basket) **2** : material or a device used to protect and keep in place an injured body part (as a broken arm)

¹splin·ter \'splin-tər\ *n* : a thin piece of something split off lengthwise : SLIVER

²splinter *vb* : to split into splinters

split \'split\ *vb* **split; split·ting** **1** : to divide lengthwise or along a grain or seam **2** : to burst or break in pieces **3** : to divide into parts or sections **4** : LEAVE ⟨~ the party⟩ ♦ *Synonyms* REND, CLEAVE, RIP, TEAR — **split** *n*

split-lev·el \'split-'le-vəl\ *n* : a house divided so that the floor in one part is about halfway between two floors in the other

split personality *n* : SCHIZOPHRENIA; *also* : MULTIPLE PERSONALITY DISORDER

split–second \'split-'se-kənd\ *adj* 1 : occurring in a very brief time 2 : extremely precise ⟨∼ timing⟩

split·ting *adj* : causing a piercing sensation ⟨a ∼ headache⟩

splotch \'spläch\ *n* : BLOTCH

splurge \'splərj\ *vb* splurged; splurg·ing : to spend more than usual esp. on oneself — **splurge** *n*

splut·ter \'splə-tər\ *n* : SPUTTER — **splutter** *vb*

¹spoil \'spói(-ə)l\ *n* : PLUNDER ⟨∼s of war⟩

²spoil *vb* spoiled \'spói(-ə)ld, 'spói(-ə)lt\ *or* spoilt \'spói(-ə)lt\; spoil·ing 1 : ROB, PILLAGE 2 : to damage seriously : RUIN 3 : to impair the quality or effect of 4 : to damage the disposition of by pampering; *also* : INDULGE, CODDLE 5 : DECAY, ROT 6 : to have an eager desire ⟨∼ing for a fight⟩ ♦ *Synonyms* INJURE, HARM, HURT, MAR — **spoil·age** \'spói-lij\ *n*

spoil·er \'spói-lər\ *n* 1 : one that spoils 2 : a device (as on an airplane or automobile) used to disrupt airflow and decrease lift

spoil·sport \'spói(-ə)l-ˌspórt\ *n* : one who spoils the fun of others

¹spoke \'spōk\ *past & archaic past part of* SPEAK

²spoke *n* : any of the rods extending from the hub of a wheel to the rim

spo·ken \'spō-kən\ *past part of* SPEAK

spokes·man \'spōks-mən\ *n* : a person who speaks as the representative of another or others

spokes·mod·el \-ˌmä-dᵊl\ *n* : a model who is a spokesman or spokeswoman

spokes·per·son \-ˌpər-sən\ *n* : SPOKESMAN

spokes·wom·an \-ˌwú-mən\ *n* : a woman who speaks as the representative of another or others

spo·li·a·tion \ˌspō-lē-'ā-shən\ *n* : the act of plundering : the state of being plundered

¹sponge \'spənj\ *n* 1 : an elastic porous water-absorbing mass of fibers that forms the skeleton of various primitive sea animals; *also* : any of a phylum of chiefly marine sea animals that are the source of natural sponges 2 : a spongelike or porous mass or material — **spongy** \'spən-jē\ *adj*

²sponge *vb* sponged; spong·ing 1 : to bathe or wipe with a sponge 2 : to live at another's expense 3 : to gather sponges — **spong·er** *n*

sponge cake *n* : a light cake made without shortening

sponge rubber *n* : a cellular rubber resembling natural sponge

spon·sor \'spän-sər\ *n* [LL, fr. L, guarantor, surety, fr. *spondēre* to promise] 1 : one who takes the responsibility for some other person or thing : SURETY 2 : GODPARENT 3 : a business firm that pays the cost of a radio or television program usu. in return for advertising time during its course — **sponsor** *vb* — **spon·sor·ship** *n*

spon·ta·ne·ous \spän-'tä-nē-əs\ *adj* [LL *spontaneus*, fr. L *sponte* of one's free will, voluntarily] 1 : done or produced freely or naturally 2 : acting or taking place without external force or cause ♦ *Synonyms* IMPULSIVE, INSTINCTIVE, AUTOMATIC, UNPREMEDITATED — **spon·ta·ne·ity** \ˌspän-tə-'nē-ə-tē, -'nā-\ *n* — **spon·ta·ne·ous·ly** *adv*

spontaneous combustion *n* : a bursting into flame of material through heat produced within itself by chemical action (as oxidation)

spoof \'spüf\ *vb* 1 : DECEIVE, HOAX 2 : to make good-natured fun of — **spoof** *n*

¹spook \'spük\ *n* 1 : GHOST, APPARITION 2 : SPY 2 — **spooky** *adj*

²spook *vb* : FRIGHTEN

¹spool \'spül\ *n* : a cylinder on which flexible material (as thread) is wound

²spool *vb* 1 : to wind on a spool 2 : to regulate data flow by means of a spooler

spool·er \'spü-lər\ *n* : a computer program or routine for regulating data flow

spoon \'spün\ *n* [ME, fr. OE *spōn* splinter, chip] 1 : an eating or cooking implement consisting of a small shallow bowl with a handle 2 : a metal piece used on a fishing line as a lure — **spoon** *vb* — **spoon·ful** *n*

spoon·bill \'spün-ˌbil\ *n* : any of several wading birds related to the ibises that have a bill with a broad flat tip

spoon–feed \-ˌfēd\ *vb* -fed \-ˌfed\; -feed·ing : to feed by means of a spoon

spoor \'spúr, 'spór\ *n, pl* spoor *or* spoors : a track, a trail, a scent, or droppings esp. of a wild animal

spo·rad·ic \spə-'ra-dik\ *adj* : occurring now and then ⟨∼ outbreaks of disease⟩ ♦ *Synonyms* OCCASIONAL, RARE, SCARCE, INFREQUENT, UNCOMMON — **spo·rad·i·cal·ly** \-di-k(ə-)lē\ *adv*

spore \'spór\ *n* : a primitive usu. one-celled often environmentally resistant dormant or reproductive body produced by plants, fungi, and some microorganisms

¹sport \'spórt\ *vb* [ME, to divert, amuse, short for *disporten*, fr. AF *desporter*, to carry away, comfort, entertain, fr. *des-* (fr. L *dis-* apart) + *porter* to carry, fr. L *portare*] 1 : to amuse oneself : FROLIC 2 : SHOW OFF 1 ⟨∼ing new shoes⟩ — **sport·ive** *adj*

²sport *n* 1 : a source of diversion : PASTIME 2 : physical activity engaged in for pleasure 3 : JEST 4 : MOCKERY ⟨make ∼ of his efforts⟩ 5 : BUTT, LAUGHINGSTOCK 6 : one who accepts results cheerfully whether favorable or not 7 : an individual exhibiting marked deviation from its normal type esp. as a result of mutation ♦ *Synonyms* PLAY, FROLIC, FUN, RECREATION — **sporty** *adj*

³sport *or* sports *adj* : of, relating to, or suitable for sport or casual wear ⟨∼ coats⟩

sport fish *n* : a fish noted for the sport it affords anglers

sports·cast \'spórts-ˌkast\ *n* : a broadcast dealing with sports events — **sports·cast·er** \-ˌkas-tər\ *n*

sports·man \'spórts-mən\ *n* 1 : a person who engages in sports (as in hunting or fishing) 2 : one who plays fairly and wins or loses gracefully — **sports·man·like** \-ˌlīk\ *adj* — **sports·man·ship** *n*

sports medicine *n* : a field of medicine dealing with the prevention and treatment of sports-related injuries

sports·wom·an \-ˌwú-mən\ *n* : a woman who engages in sports

sports·writ·er \-ˌrī-tər\ *n* : one who writes about sports esp. for a newspaper — **sports·writ·ing** *n*

sport–util·ity vehicle \'spórt-yü-'ti-lə-tē\ *n* : SUV

¹spot \'spät\ *n* 1 : STAIN, BLEMISH 2 : a small part different (as in color) from the main part 3 : LOCATION, SITE — **spot·less** *adj* — **spot·less·ly** *adv* — **on the spot** 1 : at the place of action 2 : in difficulty or danger

²spot *vb* spot·ted; spot·ting 1 : to mark or disfigure with spots 2 : to pick out : RECOGNIZE, IDENTIFY

³spot *adj* 1 : being, done, or originating on the spot ⟨a ∼ broadcast⟩ 2 : paid upon delivery 3 : made at random or at a few key points ⟨a ∼ check⟩

spot–check \'spät-ˌchek\ *vb* : to make a spot check of

spot·light \-ˌlīt\ *n* 1 : a circle of brilliant light projected upon a particular area, person, or object (as on a stage); *also* : the device that produces this light 2 : public notice — **spotlight** *vb*

spot–on \'spät-'än\ *adj* : exactly correct ⟨a ∼ forecast⟩

spotted owl *n* : a rare large dark brown dark-eyed owl of humid old growth forests and thickly wooded canyons from British Columbia to southern California and central Mexico

spot·ter \'spä-tər\ *n* 1 : one that keeps watch : OBSERVER 2 : one that removes spots

spot·ty \'spä-tē\ *adj* spot·ti·er; -est : uneven in quality; *also* : sparsely distributed ⟨∼ attendance⟩

spou·sal \'spaú-zəl, -səl\ *n* : MARRIAGE 2, WEDDING — usu. used in pl.

spouse \'spaús\ *n* : one's husband or wife — **spou·sal** \'spaú-zəl, -səl\ *adj*

¹spout \'spaút\ *vb* 1 : to eject or issue forth forcibly and freely ⟨wells ∼ing oil⟩ 2 : to speak pompously

²spout *n* 1 : a pipe or hole through which liquid spouts 2 : a jet of liquid; *esp* : WATERSPOUT 2

spp *abbr, pl* species

¹sprain \'sprān\ *n* : a sudden or severe twisting of a joint with stretching or tearing of ligaments; *also* : a sprained condition

²sprain *vb* : to subject to sprain

sprat \'sprat\ *n* : a small European fish related to the herring; *also* : SARDINE

sprawl \'sprói\ *vb* 1 : to lie or sit with limbs spread out awkwardly 2 : to spread out irregularly — **sprawl** *n*

¹**spray** \'sprā\ n : a usu. flowering branch; *also* : a decorative arrangement of flowers and foliage

²**spray** n   1 : liquid flying in small drops like water blown from a wave   2 : a jet of fine vapor (as from an atomizer)   3 : an instrument (as an atomizer) for scattering fine liquid

³**spray** vb   1 : to discharge spray on or into   2 : to scatter or let fall in a spray — **spray·er** n

spray can n : a pressurized container from which aerosols are sprayed

spray gun n : a device for spraying liquids (as paint or insecticide)

¹**spread** \'spred\ vb **spread; spread·ing**   1 : to scatter over a surface   2 : to flatten out : open out   3 : to distribute over a period of time or among many persons   4 : to cover something with ⟨~ rugs on the floor⟩   5 : to prepare for a meal ⟨~ a table⟩   6 : to pass on from person to person   7 : to stretch, force, or push apart — **spread·er** n

²**spread** n   1 : the act or process of spreading   2 : EXPANSE, EXTENT   3 : a prominent display in a periodical   4 : a food to be spread on bread or crackers   5 : a cloth cover for a bed   6 : distance between two points : GAP

spread·sheet \'spred-ˌshēt\ n : an accounting program for a computer

spree \'sprē\ n : an unrestrained outburst ⟨buying ~⟩; *also* : a drinking bout

sprig \'sprig\ n : a small shoot or twig

spright·ly \'sprīt-lē\ adj **spright·li·er; -est** : LIVELY, SPIRITED ⟨a ~ musical⟩ ♦ **Synonyms** ANIMATED, VIVACIOUS, GAY — **spright·li·ness** n

¹**spring** \'spriŋ\ vb **sprang** \'spraŋ\ or **sprung** \'sprəŋ\; **sprung; spring·ing**   1 : to move suddenly upward or forward   2 : to grow quickly ⟨weeds *sprang* up overnight⟩   3 : to come from by birth or descent   4 : to move quickly by elastic force   5 : WARP   6 : to develop (a leak) through the seams   7 : to cause to close suddenly ⟨~ a trap⟩   8 : to make known suddenly ⟨~ a surprise⟩   9 : to make lame : STRAIN

²**spring** n   1 : a source of supply; *esp* : an issuing of water from the ground   2 : SOURCE, ORIGIN; *also* : MOTIVE   3 : the season between winter and summer   4 : an elastic body or device that recovers its original shape when it is released after being distorted   5 : the act or an instance of leaping up or forward   6 : RESILIENCE — **springy** adj

spring·board \'spriŋ-ˌbȯrd\ n : a springy board used in jumping or vaulting or for diving

spring fever n : a lazy or restless feeling often associated with the onset of spring

spring tide n : a tide of greater-than-average range that occurs at each new moon and full moon

spring·time \'spriŋ-ˌtīm\ n : the season of spring

¹**sprin·kle** \'spriŋ-kəl\ vb **sprin·kled; sprin·kling** : to scatter in small drops or particles — **sprin·kler** n

²**sprinkle** n : a light rainfall

sprin·kling n : SMATTERING

¹**sprint** \'sprint\ vb : to run at top speed esp. for a short distance — **sprint·er** n

²**sprint** n   1 : a short run at top speed   2 : a short-distance race

sprite \'sprīt\ n   1 : GHOST, SPIRIT   2 : ELF, FAIRY

spritz vb : SPRAY

sprock·et \'sprä-kət\ n : a toothed wheel whose teeth engage the links of a chain

sprocket

¹**sprout** \'spraůt\ vb : to send out new growth ⟨~ing seeds⟩

²**sprout** n : a usu. young and growing plant shoot (as from a seed)

¹**spruce** \'sprüs\ vb **spruced; spruc·ing** : to make or become spruce

²**spruce** adj **spruc·er; spruc·est** : neat and smart in appearance ♦ **Synonyms** STYLISH, FASHIONABLE, MODISH, DAPPER, NATTY

³**spruce** n, pl **spruc·es** also **spruce** : any of a genus of evergreen pyramid-shaped trees related to the pines and having soft light wood; *also* : the wood of a spruce

sprung *past and past part of* SPRING

spry \'sprī\ adj **spri·er** or **spry·er** \'sprī-ər\; **spri·est** or **spry·est** \'sprī-əst\ : NIMBLE, ACTIVE ⟨a ~ 75-year-old⟩ ♦ **Synonyms** AGILE, BRISK, LIVELY, SPRIGHTLY

spud \'spəd\ n   1 : a sharp narrow spade   2 : POTATO

spume \'spyüm\ n : frothy matter on liquids : FOAM — **spumy** \'spyü-mē\ adj

spu·mo·ni also **spu·mo·ne** \spů-'mō-nē\ n [It *spumone*, fr. *spuma* foam] : ice cream in layers of different colors, flavors, and textures often with candied fruits and nuts

spun *past and past part of* SPIN

spun glass n : FIBERGLASS

spunk \'spəŋk\ n [fr. *spunk* tinder, fr. ScGael *spong* sponge, tinder, fr. Middle Irish *spongc*, fr. L *spongia* sponge] : PLUCK, COURAGE — **spunky** adj

¹**spur** \'spər\ n   1 : a pointed device fastened to a rider's boot and used to urge on a horse   2 : something that urges to action   3 : a stiff sharp spine (as on the leg of a cock); *also* : a hollow projecting appendage of a flower (as a columbine)   4 : a ridge extending sideways from a mountain   5 : a branch of railroad track extending from the main line ♦ **Synonyms** GOAD, MOTIVE, IMPULSE, INCENTIVE, INDUCEMENT — **spurred** \'spərd\ adj — **on the spur of the moment** : on hasty impulse

²**spur** vb **spurred; spur·ring**   1 : to urge a horse on with spurs   2 : INCITE

spurge \'spərj\ n : any of a family of herbs and woody plants with a bitter milky juice

spu·ri·ous \'spyůr-ē-əs\ adj [LL *spurius* false, fr. L, *spurius*, n., son of an unknown father] : not genuine : FALSE ⟨~ eminence⟩

spurn \'spərn\ vb   1 : to kick away or trample on   2 : to reject with disdain

¹**spurt** \'spərt\ vb : to gush out : SPOUT

²**spurt** n : a sudden gushing or spouting

³**spurt** n   1 : a sudden brief burst of effort, speed, or development   2 : a sharp increase of activity ⟨~ in sales⟩

⁴**spurt** vb : to make a spurt

sput·ter \'spə-tər\ vb   1 : to spit small scattered particles : SPLUTTER   2 : to utter words hastily or explosively in excitement or confusion   3 : to make small popping sounds — **sputter** n

spu·tum \'spyü-təm\ n, pl **spu·ta** \-tə\ [L] : material (as phlegm) that is spit out or coughed up esp. during illness

¹**spy** \'spī\ vb **spied; spy·ing**   1 : to watch or search for information secretly : act as a spy   2 : to get a momentary or quick glimpse of : SEE

²**spy** n, pl **spies**   1 : one who secretly watches others   2 : a secret agent who tries to get information for one country in the territory of an enemy

spy·glass \'spī-ˌglas\ n : a small telescope

sq abbr   1 squadron   2 square

squab \'skwäb\ n, pl **squabs** or **squab** : a young bird and esp. a pigeon

squab·ble \'skwä-bəl\ n : a noisy altercation : WRANGLE ♦ **Synonyms** QUARREL, SPAT, ROW, TIFF — **squabble** vb

squad \'skwäd\ n   1 : a small organized group of military personnel   2 : a small group engaged in a common effort

squad car n : a police car connected by two-way radio with headquarters

squad·ron \'skwä-drən\ n : any of several units of military organization

squal·id \'skwä-ləd\ adj   1 : filthy or degraded through neglect or poverty   2 : SORDID, DEBASED ⟨a ~ political ploy⟩ ♦ **Synonyms** NASTY, FOUL, DIRTY, GRUBBY

squall \'skwȯl\ n : a sudden violent gust of wind often with rain or snow — **squally** adj

squa·lor \'skwä-lər\ n : the quality or state of being squalid

squa·mous cell \'skwä-məs-\ n : a scalelike cell of the outer layers of the skin from which a type of carcinoma arises

squan·der \'skwän-dər\ vb : to spend wastefully or foolishly

¹**square** \'skwer\ n   1 : an instrument used to lay out or

test right angles **2** : a rectangle with all four sides equal **3** : something square **4** : the product of a number multiplied by itself **5** : an area bounded by four streets **6** : an open area in a city where streets meet **7** : a highly conventional person

²square *adj* **squar·er; squar·est 1** : having four equal sides and four right angles **2** : forming a right angle ⟨cut a ∼ corner⟩ **3** : multiplied by itself : SQUARED ⟨x^2 is the symbol for x ∼⟩ **4** : being a unit of square measure equal to a square each side of which measures one unit ⟨a ∼ foot⟩ **5** : being of a specified length in each of two dimensions ⟨an area 10 feet ∼⟩ **6** : exactly adjusted **7** : JUST, FAIR ⟨a ∼ deal⟩ **8** : leaving no balance ⟨make accounts ∼⟩ **9** : SUBSTANTIAL ⟨a ∼ meal⟩ **10** : highly conservative or conventional — **square·ly** *adv*

³square *vb* **squared; squar·ing 1** : to form with four equal sides and right angles or with flat surfaces ⟨∼ a timber⟩ **2** : to multiply (a number) by itself **3** : CONFORM, AGREE **4** : BALANCE, SETTLE ⟨∼ an account⟩

square dance *n* : a dance for four couples arranged to form a square

square measure *n* : a unit or system of units for measuring area — see METRIC SYSTEM table, WEIGHT table

square–rigged \'skwer-'rigd\ *adj* : having the chief sails extended on yards that are fastened to the masts horizontally and at their center

square–rig·ger \-ˌri-gər\ *n* : a square-rigged craft

square root *n* : either of the two numbers whose squares are equal to a given number ⟨the *square root* of 9 is +3 or –3⟩

¹squash \'skwäsh, 'skwȯsh\ *vb* **1** : to beat or press into a pulp or flat mass **2** : QUASH, SUPPRESS ⟨∼ a revolt⟩

²squash *n* **1** : the impact of something soft and heavy; *also* : the sound of such impact **2** : a crushed mass **3** : a game played on a 4-wall court with a racket and rubber ball

³squash *n, pl* **squash·es** *or* **squash** : any of various fruits of plants of the gourd family that are used esp. as vegetables; *also* : a plant and esp. a vine bearing squashes

squash racquets *n* : SQUASH 3

¹squat \'skwät\ *vb* **squat·ted; squat·ting** [ME *squatten* to crush, crouch in hiding, fr. MF (dial. of Picardy) *esquatir, escuater,* fr. OF *es- ex- + quatir* to hide, fr. VL *coactire* to squeeze, alter. of L *coactare* to compel, fr. *cogere* to compel] **1** : to sit down upon the hams or heels **2** : to settle on land without right or title; *also* : to settle on public land with a view to acquiring title — **squat·ter** *n*

²squat *adj* **squat·ter; squat·test** : low to the ground; *also* : short and thick in stature ♦ *Synonyms* THICKSET, STOCKY, HEAVYSET, STUBBY

³squat *n* : the act or posture of squatting

squawk \'skwȯk\ *n* : a harsh loud cry; *also* : a noisy protest — **squawk** *vb*

squeak \'skwēk\ *vb* **1** : to utter or speak in a weak shrill tone **2** : to make a thin high-pitched sound — **squeak** *n* — **squeaky** *adj*

¹squeal \'skwēl\ *vb* **1** : to make a shrill sound or cry **2** : to betray a secret or turn informer **3** : COMPLAIN, PROTEST

²squeal *n* : a shrill sharp cry or noise

squea·mish \'skwē-mish\ *adj* **1** : easily nauseated; *also* : NAUSEATED **2** : easily disgusted ♦ *Synonyms* FUSSY, NICE, DAINTY, FASTIDIOUS, PERSNICKETY — **squea·mish·ness** *n*

squee·gee \'skwē-jē\ *n* : a blade set crosswise on a handle and used for spreading or wiping liquid on, across, or off a surface — **squeegee** *vb*

¹squeeze \'skwēz\ *vb* **squeezed; squeez·ing 1** : to exert pressure on the opposite sides or parts of **2** : to obtain by pressure ⟨∼ juice from a lemon⟩ **3** : to force, thrust, or cause to pass by pressure — **squeez·er** *n*

²squeeze *n* **1** : an act of squeezing **2** : a quantity squeezed out

squeeze bottle *n* : a flexible plastic bottle that dispenses its contents when it is squeezed

squelch \'skwelch\ *vb* **1** : to suppress completely : CRUSH ⟨∼ resistance⟩ **2** : to move in soft mud — **squelch** *n*

squib \'skwib\ *n* : a brief witty writing or speech

squid \'skwid\ *n, pl* **squid** *or* **squids** : any of an order of long-bodied sea mollusks having eight short arms and two longer tentacles and usu. a slender internal shell

squint \'skwint\ *vb* **1** : to look or aim obliquely **2** : to look or peer with the eyes partly closed **3** : to be cross-eyed — **squint** *n or adj*

¹squire \'skwī(-ə)r\ *n* [ME *squier,* fr. AF *esquier,* fr. LL *scutarius,* fr. L *scutum* shield] **1** : an armor-bearer of a knight **2** : a man gallantly devoted to a lady **3** : a member of the British gentry ranking below a knight and above a gentleman; *also* : a prominent landowner **4** : a local magistrate

²squire *vb* **squired; squir·ing** : to attend as a squire or escort

squirm \'skwərm\ *vb* : to twist about like a worm : WRIGGLE

¹squir·rel \'skwər-əl\ *n, pl* **squirrels** *also* **squirrel** [ME *squirel,* fr. AF *escurel, esquirel,* fr. VL **scuriolus,* dim. of **scurius,* alter. of L *sciurus,* fr. Gk *skiouros,* prob. fr. *skia* shadow + *oura* tail] : any of various rodents usu. with a long bushy tail and strong hind legs; *also* : the fur of a squirrel

²squirrel *vb* **-reled** *or* **-relled; -rel·ing** *or* **-rel·ling** : to store up for future use

¹squirt \'skwərt\ *vb* : to eject liquid in a thin spurt

²squirt *n* **1** : an instrument (as a syringe) for squirting **2** : a small forcible jet of liquid

¹Sr *abbr* **1** senior **2** sister

²Sr *symbol* strontium

SR *abbr* seaman recruit

¹SRO \ˌes-(ˌ)är-'ō\ *n* [*single-room occupancy*] : a house or apartment building in which low-income tenants live in single rooms

²SRO *abbr* standing room only

SS *abbr* **1** saints **2** Social Security **3** steamship **4** sworn statement

SSA *abbr* Social Security Administration

SSE *abbr* south-southeast

SSG *or* **SSgt** *abbr* staff sergeant

SSI *abbr* supplemental security income

SSM *abbr* staff sergeant major

SSN *abbr* Social Security Number

ssp *abbr* subspecies

SSR *abbr* Soviet Socialist Republic

SSS *abbr* Selective Service System

SST \ˌes-(ˌ)es-'tē\ *n* [*supersonic transport*] : a supersonic passenger airplane

SSW *abbr* south-southwest

st *abbr* **1** stanza **2** state **3** stitch **4** stone **5** street

St *abbr* saint

ST *abbr* **1** short ton **2** standard time

¹-st — see -EST

²-st *symbol* — used after the figure 1 to indicate the ordinal number first

sta *abbr* station; stationary

¹stab \'stab\ *n* **1** : a wound produced by a pointed weapon **2** : a quick thrust **3** : a brief attempt

²stab *vb* **stabbed; stab·bing** : to pierce or wound with or as if with a pointed weapon; *also* : THRUST, DRIVE

sta·bile \'stā-ˌbēl\ *n* : an abstract sculpture or construction similar to a mobile but made to be stationary

sta·bi·lize \'stā-bə-ˌlīz\ *vb* **-lized; -liz·ing 1** : to make stable **2** : to hold steady ⟨∼ prices⟩ — **sta·bi·li·za·tion** \ˌstā-bə-lə-'zā-shən\ *n* — **sta·bi·liz·er** \'stā-bə-ˌlī-zər\ *n*

¹sta·ble \'stā-bəl\ *n* : a building in which domestic animals are sheltered and fed — **sta·ble·man** \-mən, -ˌman\ *n*

²stable *vb* **sta·bled; sta·bling** : to put or keep in a stable

³stable *adj* **sta·bler; sta·blest 1** : firmly established; *also* : mentally and emotionally healthy **2** : steady in purpose : CONSTANT **3** : DURABLE, ENDURING ⟨∼ civilizations⟩ **4** : resistant to chemical or physical change ♦ *Synonyms* LASTING, PERMANENT, PERPETUAL, PERDURABLE — **sta·bil·i·ty** \stə-'bi-lə-tē\ *n*

stac·ca·to \stə-'kä-tō\ *adj or adv* [It] : cut short so as not to sound connected ⟨∼ notes⟩

¹stack \'stak\ *n* **1** : a large pile (as of hay or grain) **2** : an orderly pile (as of poker chips) **3** : a large quantity **4** : a vertical pipe : SMOKESTACK **5** : a rack with shelves for storing books

²stack *vb* **1** : to pile up **2** : to arrange (cards) secretly for cheating

stack up *vb* : MEASURE UP ⟨how do they *stack up* against the competition?⟩

sta·di·um \'stā-dē-əm\ *n, pl* **-dia** \-dē-ə\ *or* **-di·ums** : a structure with tiers of seats for spectators built around a field for sports events

¹staff \'staf\ *n, pl* **staffs** \'stafs, 'stavz\ *or* **staves** \'stavz, 'stāvz\ **1** : a pole, stick, rod, or bar used for supporting, for measuring, or as a symbol of authority; *also* : CLUB, CUDGEL **2** : something that sustains ⟨bread is the ∼ of life⟩ **3** : the five horizontal lines on which music is written **4** : a body of assistants to an executive **5** : a group of officers holding no command but having duties concerned with planning and managing

staff 3

²staff *vb* : to supply with a staff or with workers

staff·er \'sta-fər\ *n* : a member of a staff (as of a newspaper)

staff sergeant *n* : a noncommissioned officer ranking in the army next below a sergeant first class, in the air force next below a technical sergeant, and in the marine corps next below a gunnery sergeant

¹stag \'stag\ *n, pl* **stags** *or* **stag** : an adult male of various large deer

²stag *adj* : restricted to or intended for men ⟨a ∼ party⟩ ⟨∼ movies⟩

³stag *adv* : unaccompanied by a date

¹stage \'stāj\ *n* [ME, fr. AF *estage* abode, story of a building, stage, fr. VL *staticum,* fr. L *stare* to stand] **1** : a raised platform on which an orator may speak or a play may be presented **2** : the acting profession : THEATER **3** : the scene of a notable action or event **4** : a station or resting place on a traveled road **5** : STAGECOACH **6** : a degree of advance in an undertaking, process, or development **7** : a propulsion unit in a rocket — **stagy** \'stā-jē\ *adj*

²stage *vb* **staged; stag·ing** : to produce or perform on or as if on a stage — **stage·able** *adj*

stage·coach \'stāj-ˌkōch\ *n* : a horse-drawn coach that runs regularly between stations

stage manager *n* : one who supervises the physical aspects of a stage production

stag·fla·tion \ˌstag-'flā-shən\ *n* : inflation with stagnant economic activity and high unemployment

¹stag·ger \'sta-gər\ *vb* **1** : to reel from side to side : TOTTER **2** : to begin to doubt : WAVER **3** : to cause to reel or waver **4** : to arrange in overlapping or alternating positions or times ⟨∼ working hours⟩ **5** : ASTONISH — **stag·ger·ing·ly** *adv*

²stagger *n* **1** *sing or pl* : an abnormal condition of domestic animals associated with damage to the central nervous system and marked by lack of coordination and a reeling unsteady gait **2** : a reeling or unsteady gait or stance

stag·ing \'stā-jin\ *n* **1** : SCAFFOLDING **2** : the assembling of troops and matériel in transit in a particular place

staging post *n* : STOPOVER 2

stag·nant \'stag-nənt\ *adj* **1** : not flowing : MOTIONLESS ⟨∼ water in a pond⟩ **2** : DULL, INACTIVE ⟨∼ business⟩

stag·nate \'stag-ˌnāt\ *vb* **stag·nat·ed; stag·nat·ing** : to be or become stagnant — **stag·na·tion** \stag-'nā-shən\ *n*

staid \'stād\ *adj* : SOBER, SEDATE ♦ **Synonyms** GRAVE, SERIOUS, EARNEST

¹stain \'stān\ *vb* **1** : DISCOLOR, SOIL **2** : TAINT, CORRUPT **3** : DISGRACE **4** : to color (as wood, paper, or cloth) by processes affecting the material itself

²stain *n* **1** : a small soiled or discolored area **2** : a taint of guilt : STIGMA **3** : a preparation (as a dye or pigment) used in staining — **stain·less** *adj*

stainless steel *n* : steel alloyed with chromium that is highly resistant to stain, rust, and corrosion

stair \'ster\ *n* **1** : a series of steps or flights of steps for passing from one level to another — often used in pl. **2** : one step of a stairway

stair·case \-ˌkās\ *n* : a flight of steps with their supporting framework, casing, and balusters

stair·way \-ˌwā\ *n* : one or more flights of stairs with connecting landings

stair·well \-ˌwel\ *n* : a vertical shaft in which stairs are located

¹stake \'stāk\ *n* **1** : a pointed piece of material (as of wood) driven into the ground as a marker or a support **2** : a post to which a person is bound for death by burning; *also* : execution by burning at the stake **3** : something that is staked for gain or loss **4** : the prize in a contest

²stake *vb* **staked; stak·ing** **1** : to mark the limits of by or as if by stakes **2** : to tie to a stake **3** : to support or secure with stakes **4** : BET, WAGER

stake·out \'stāk-ˌaut\ *n* : a surveillance by police (as of a suspected criminal)

sta·lac·tite \stə-'lak-ˌtīt\ *n* [NL *stalactites,* fr. Gk *stalaktos* dripping, fr. *stalassein* to let drip] : an icicle-shaped deposit hanging from the roof or sides of a cavern

sta·lag·mite \stə-'lag-ˌmīt\ *n* [NL *stalagmites,* fr. Gk *stalagma* drop or *stalagmos* dripping, fr. *stalassein* to let drip] : a deposit resembling an inverted stalactite rising from the floor of a cavern

stale \'stāl\ *adj* **stal·er; stal·est** **1** : having lost good taste and quality from age ⟨∼ bread⟩ **2** : used or heard so often as to be dull ⟨∼ news⟩ **3** : not as strong or effective as before ⟨∼ from lack of practice⟩ — **stale·ness** *n*

stale·mate \'stāl-ˌmāt\ *n* : a drawn contest : DEADLOCK — **stalemate** *vb*

¹stalk \'stok\ *n* : a plant stem; *also* : any slender usu. upright supporting or connecting part — **stalked** \'stokt\ *adj*

²stalk *vb* **1** : to pursue (game) stealthily **2** : to walk stiffly or haughtily

¹stall \'stol\ *n* **1** : a compartment in a stable or barn for one animal **2** : a booth or counter where articles may be displayed for sale **3** : a seat in a church choir; *also* : a church pew **4** *chiefly Brit* : a front orchestra seat in a theater

²stall *vb* : to bring or come to a standstill unintentionally ⟨∼ an engine⟩

³stall *n* : the condition of an airfoil or aircraft in which lift is lost and the airfoil or aircraft tends to drop

⁴stall *n* [alter. of *stale* lure] : a ruse to deceive or delay

⁵stall *vb* : to hold off, divert, or delay by evasion or deception

stal·lion \'stal-yən\ *n* : a male horse

stal·wart \'stol-wərt\ *adj* : STOUT, STRONG; *also* : BRAVE, VALIANT

sta·men \'stā-mən\ *n* : an organ of a flower that produces pollen

stam·i·na \'sta-mə-nə\ *n* [L, pl. of *stamen* warp, thread of life spun by the Fates] : VIGOR, ENDURANCE

sta·mi·nate \'stā-mə-nət, 'sta-mə-, -ˌnāt\ *adj* **1** : having or producing stamens **2** : having stamens but no pistils

stam·mer \'sta-mər\ *vb* : to hesitate or stumble in speaking — **stammer** *n* — **stam·mer·er** *n*

¹stamp \'stamp; *for 2 also* 'stämp *or* 'stomp\ *vb* **1** : to pound or crush with a heavy instrument **2** : to strike or beat with the bottom of the foot **3** : IMPRESS, IMPRINT ⟨∼ "paid" on the bill⟩ **4** : to cut out or indent with a stamp or die **5** : to attach a postage stamp to

²stamp *n* **1** : a device or instrument for stamping **2** : the mark made by stamping; *also* : a distinctive mark or quality **3** : the act of stamping **4** : a stamped or printed paper affixed to show that a charge has been paid ⟨postage ∼⟩ ⟨tax ∼⟩

¹stam·pede \stam-'pēd\ *n* : a wild headlong rush or flight esp. of frightened animals

²stampede *vb* **stam·ped·ed; stam·ped·ing** **1** : to flee or cause to flee in panic **2** : to act or cause to act together suddenly and heedlessly

stance \'stans\ *n* : a way of standing

¹stanch \'stonch, 'stänch, 'stanch\ *or* **staunch** \'stonch, 'stänch\ *vb* : to check the flowing of (as blood); *also* : to cease flowing or bleeding

²stanch *var of* ²STAUNCH

stan·chion \'stan-chən\ *n* : an upright bar, post, or support

¹stand \'stand\ *vb* **stood** \'stud\; **stand·ing** **1** : to take or be at rest in an upright or firm position **2** : to assume a specified position **3** : to remain stationary or unchanged **4** : to be steadfast **5** : to act in resistance ⟨∼ against a foe⟩ **6** : to maintain a relative position or rank **7** : to gather slowly and remain ⟨tears *stood* in her eyes⟩ **8** : to set upright **9** : ENDURE, TOLERATE ⟨I won't ∼ for that⟩ **10** : to submit to ⟨∼ trial⟩ — **stand pat** : to oppose or resist change

²**stand** *n* **1** : an act of standing, staying, or resisting **2** : a stop made to give a performance **3** : POSITION, VIEWPOINT **4** : a place taken by a witness to testify in court **5** *pl* : tiered seats for spectators **6** : a raised platform (as for speakers) **7** : a structure for a small retail business **8** : a structure for supporting or holding something upright ⟨music ∼⟩ **9** : a group of plants growing in a continuous area

stand–alone \'stan-də-ˌlōn\ *adj* : SELF-CONTAINED; *esp* : capable of operation independent of a computer system

¹**stan·dard** \'stan-dərd\ *n* **1** : a figure adopted as an emblem by a people **2** : the personal flag of a ruler; *also* : FLAG **3** : something set up as a rule for measuring or as a model to be followed **4** : an upright support ⟨lamp ∼⟩

²**standard** *adj* **1** : used as or meeting a standard established by law or custom **2** : regularly and widely used ⟨a ∼ practice⟩ **3** : well established by usage in speech or writing

stan·dard–bear·er \-ˌber-ər\ *n* : the leader of a cause

standard deviation *n* : a measure of dispersion in a set of data

stan·dard·ise *Brit var of* STANDARDIZE

stan·dard–is·sue \'stan-dərd-'i-shü\ *adj* : STANDARD, TYPICAL ⟨a ∼ blue suit⟩

stan·dard·ize \'stan-dər-ˌdīz\ *vb* **-ized; -iz·ing** : to make standard or uniform — **stan·dard·i·za·tion** \ˌstan-dər-də-'zā-shən\ *n*

standard of living : the necessities, comforts, and luxuries that a person or group is accustomed to

standard time *n* : the time established by law or by general usage over a region or country

¹**stand·by** \'stand-ˌbī\ *n, pl* **stand-bys** \-ˌbīz\ **1** : one that can be relied on **2** : a substitute in reserve — **on standby** : ready or available for immediate action or use

²**standby** *adj* **1** : ready for use **2** : relating to airline travel in which the passenger must wait for an available unreserved seat — **standby** *adv*

stand–in \'stan-ˌdin\ *n* **1** : someone employed to occupy an actor's place while lights and camera are readied **2** : SUBSTITUTE

¹**stand·ing** \'stan-diŋ\ *adj* **1** : ERECT ⟨∼ timber⟩ **2** : not flowing : STAGNANT **3** : remaining at the same level or amount for an indefinite period ⟨∼ offer⟩ **4** : PERMANENT ⟨a ∼ army⟩ **5** : done from a standing position ⟨a ∼ jump⟩

²**standing** *n* **1** : length of service; *also* : relative position in society or in a profession : RANK **2** : DURATION ⟨a custom of long ∼⟩

stand·off \'stan-ˌdȯf\ *n* : TIE, DRAW

stand·off·ish \stan-'dȯ-fish\ *adj* : somewhat cold and reserved

stand·out \'stan-ˌdaut\ *n* : something conspicuously excellent

stand·pipe \'stand-ˌpīp\ *n* : a high vertical pipe or reservoir for water used to produce a uniform pressure

stand·point \-ˌpȯint\ *n* : a position from which objects or principles are judged

stand·still \-ˌstil\ *n* : a state of rest

stand–up \'stan-ˌdəp\ *adj* : done or performing in a standing position ⟨a ∼ comic⟩ ⟨∼ comedy⟩

stank *past of* STINK

stan·za \'stan-zə\ *n* [It] : a group of lines forming a division of a poem

sta·pes \'stā-ˌpēz\ *n, pl* **stapes** *or* **sta·pe·des** \'stā-pə-ˌdēz\ : the innermost bone of the middle ear of mammals

staph \'staf\ *n* : STAPHYLOCOCCUS

staph·y·lo·coc·cus \ˌsta-fə-lō-'kä-kəs\ *n, pl* **-coc·ci** \-'kä-ˌkī, -'käk-ˌsī\ : any of a genus of spherical bacteria including some pathogens of skin and mucous membranes — **staph·y·lo·coc·cal** \-'kä-kəl\ *adj*

¹**sta·ple** \'stā-pəl\ *n* : a U-shaped piece of metal or wire with sharp points to be driven into a surface or through thin layers (as paper) for attaching or holding together — **staple** *vb* — **sta·pler** *n*

²**staple** *n* **1** : a chief commodity or product **2** : a chief part of something ⟨a ∼ of their diet⟩ **3** : unmanufactured or raw material **4** : a textile fiber suitable for spinning into yarn

³**staple** *adj* **1** : regularly produced in large quantities **2** : PRINCIPAL, MAIN ⟨the ∼ crop⟩

¹**star** \'stär\ *n* **1** : a celestial body that appears as a fixed point of light; *esp* : such a body that is gaseous, self-luminous, and of great mass **2** : a planet or configuration of planets that is held in astrology to influence one's fortune — usu. used in pl. **3** *obs* : DESTINY **4** : a conventional figure representing a star; *esp* : ASTERISK **5** : an actor or actress playing the leading role **6** : a brilliant performer — **star·dom** \'stär-dəm\ *n* — **star·less** *adj* — **star·like** *adj* — **star·ry** *adj*

²**star** *vb* **starred; star·ring** **1** : to adorn with stars **2** : to mark with an asterisk **3** : to play the leading role

star anise *n* : the small brown star-shaped fruit of an Asian tree used as a spice esp. in Chinese cooking

star·board \'stär-bərd\ *n* [ME *sterbord*, fr. OE *stēorbord*, fr. *stēor-* steering oar + *bord* ship's side] : the right side of a ship or airplane looking forward — **starboard** *adj*

star·burst \'stär-bərst\ *n* : a pattern that resembles diverging rays of light

¹**starch** \'stärch\ *vb* : to stiffen with or as if with starch

²**starch** *n* : a complex carbohydrate that is stored in plants, is an important foodstuff, and is used in adhesives and sizes, in laundering, and in pharmacy — **starchy** *adj*

stare \'ster\ *vb* **stared; star·ing** : to look fixedly with wide-open eyes — **stare** *n* — **star·er** *n*

star·fish \'stär-ˌfish\ *n* : any of a class of echinoderms that have usu. five arms arranged around a central disk and feed largely on mollusks

star fruit *n* : CARAMBOLA 1

¹**stark** \'stärk\ *adj* **1** : rigid as if in death; *also* : STRICT **2** *archaic* : STRONG, ROBUST **3** : SHEER, UTTER ⟨∼ nonsense⟩ **4** : BARREN, DESOLATE ⟨∼ landscape⟩; *also* : UNADORNED ⟨∼ realism⟩ **5** : sharply delineated — **stark·ly** *adv*

²**stark** *adv* : WHOLLY, ABSOLUTELY ⟨∼ naked⟩

star·light \'stär-ˌlīt\ *n* : the light given by the stars

star·ling \'stär-liŋ\ *n* : a dark brown or in summer glossy greenish black European bird related to the crows that is naturalized nearly worldwide and often considered a pest

¹**start** \'stärt\ *vb* **1** : to give an involuntary twitch or jerk (as from surprise) **2** : BEGIN, COMMENCE **3** : to set going ⟨∼ an engine⟩ **4** : to enter or cause to enter a game or contest; *also* : to be in the starting lineup — **start·er** *n*

²**start** *n* **1** : a sudden involuntary motion : LEAP **2** : a spasmodic and brief effort or action **3** : BEGINNING; *also* : the place of beginning

start·er \'stär-tər\ *adj* : being an item acquired with the expectation that a more elaborate one will be acquired in the future ⟨a ∼ home⟩

star·tle \'stär-tᵊl\ *vb* **star·tled; star·tling** : to frighten or surprise suddenly : cause to start

star·tling *adj* : causing sudden fear, surprise, or anxiety — **star·tling·ly** *adv*

starve \'stärv\ *vb* **starved; starv·ing** [ME *sterven* to die, fr. OE *steorfan*] **1** : to die or cause to die from hunger **2** : to suffer extreme hunger or deprivation ⟨*starving* for affection⟩ **3** : to subdue by famine — **star·va·tion** \stär-'vā-shən\ *n*

starve·ling \'stärv-liŋ\ *n* : one that is thin from lack of nourishment

stash \'stash\ *vb* : to store in a secret place for future use — **stash** *n*

sta·sis \'stā-səs, 'sta-\ *n, pl* **sta·ses** \'stā-ˌsēz, 'sta-\ **1** : a stoppage or slowing of the normal flow of a bodily fluid (as blood) **2** : a state of static balance : STAGNATION

¹**stat** \'stat\ *adv* [L *statim*] : without delay : IMMEDIATELY

²**stat** *abbr* statute

¹**state** \'stāt\ *n* [ME *stat*, fr. AF & L; AF *estat*, fr. L *status*, fr. *stare* to stand] **1** : mode or condition of being ⟨the four ∼s of matter⟩ **2** : condition of mind **3** : social position **4** : a body of people occupying a territory and organized under one government; *also* : the government of such a body of people **5** : one of the constituent units of a nation having a federal government — **state·hood** \-ˌhud\ *n*

²**state** *vb* **stat·ed; stat·ing** **1** : to set by regulation or authority **2** : to express in words

state·craft \'stāt-,kraft\ *n* : the art of conducting state affairs

state·house \-,haùs\ *n* : the building in which a state legislature meets

state·ly \'stāt-lē\ *adj* **state·li·er; -est** 1 : having lofty dignity : HAUGHTY 2 : IMPRESSIVE, MAJESTIC ⟨~ homes⟩ ◆ *Synonyms* MAGNIFICENT, IMPOSING, AUGUST — **state·li·ness** *n*

state·ment \'stāt-mənt\ *n* 1 : the act or result of presenting in words 2 : a summary of a financial account

state·room \'stāt-,rüm, -,rùm\ *n* : a private room on a ship or railroad car

state·side \'stāt-,sīd\ *adj* : of or relating to the U.S. as regarded from outside its continental limits — **stateside** *adv*

states·man \'stāts-mən\ *n* : a person engaged in fixing the policies and conducting the affairs of a government; *esp* : one wise and skilled in such matters — **states·man·like** *adj* — **states·man·ship** *n*

¹**stat·ic** \'sta-tik\ *adj* 1 : acting by mere weight without motion ⟨~ pressure⟩ 2 : relating to bodies at rest or forces in equilibrium 3 : showing little change 4 : not moving : not active 5 : of or relating to stationary charges of electricity 6 : of, relating to, or caused by radio static

²**static** *n* : noise produced in a radio or television receiver by atmospheric or other electrical disturbances

stat·in \'sta-tᵊn\ *n* : any of a group of drugs that inhibit the synthesis of cholesterol

¹**sta·tion** \'stā-shən\ *n* 1 : the place where a person or thing stands or is assigned to remain 2 : a regular stopping place on a transportation route : DEPOT 3 : a place where a fleet is assigned for duty 4 : a stock farm or ranch esp. in Australia or New Zealand 5 : social standing 6 : a complete assemblage of radio or television equipment for sending or receiving

²**station** *vb* : to assign to a station

sta·tion·ary \'stā-shə-,ner-ē\ *adj* 1 : fixed in a station, course, or mode 2 : unchanging in condition ⟨a ~ population⟩

stationary front *n* : the boundary between two air masses neither of which is advancing

station break *n* : a pause in a radio or television broadcast to announce the identity of the network or station

sta·tio·ner \'stā-shə-nər\ *n* : one that sells stationery

sta·tio·nery \'stā-shə-,ner-ē\ *n* : materials (as paper, pens, or ink) for writing; *esp* : letter paper with envelopes

station wagon *n* : an automobile having a long interior, one or more folding or removable rear seats, and usu. a door at the rear

sta·tis·tic \stə-'tis-tik\ *n* 1 : a single term or datum in a collection of statistics 2 : a quantity (as the mean) that is computed from a sample

sta·tis·tics \-tiks\ *n sing or pl* [G *Statistik* study of political facts and figures, fr. NL *statisticus* of politics, fr. L *status* state] : a branch of mathematics dealing with the collection, analysis, and interpretation of masses of numerical data; *also* : a collection of such numerical data — **sta·tis·ti·cal** \-ti-kəl\ *adj* — **sta·tis·ti·cal·ly** \-ti-k(ə-)lē\ *adv* — **stat·is·ti·cian** \,sta-tə-'sti-shən\ *n*

stat·u·ary \'sta-chə-,wer-ē\ *n, pl* **-ar·ies** 1 : the art of making statues 2 : STATUES

stat·ue \'sta-chü\ *n* : a likeness (as of a person or animal) sculptured, modeled, or cast in a solid substance

stat·u·esque \,sta-chə-'wesk\ *adj* : tall and shapely

stat·u·ette \,sta-chə-'wet\ *n* : a small statue

stat·ure \'sta-chər\ *n* 1 : natural height (as of a person) 2 : quality or status gained (as by achievement)

sta·tus \'stā-təs, 'sta-\ *n* 1 : the condition of a person in the eyes of others or of the law 2 : state or condition with respect to circumstances

sta·tus quo \-'kwō\ *n* [L, state in which] : the existing state of affairs

stat·ute \'sta-chüt\ *n* : a law enacted by a legislative body

stat·u·to·ry \'sta-chə-,tór-ē\ *adj* : imposed by statute : LAWFUL

statutory rape *n* : sexual intercourse with a person who is below the statutory age of consent

¹**staunch** *var of* ¹STANCH

²**staunch** \'stónch, 'stänch\ *adj* 1 : WATERTIGHT ⟨a ~ ship⟩ 2 : FIRM, STRONG; *also* : STEADFAST, LOYAL

◆ *Synonyms* RESOLUTE, CONSTANT, TRUE, FAITHFUL — **staunch·ly** *adv*

¹**stave** \'stāv\ *n* 1 : CUDGEL, STAFF 2 : any of several narrow strips of wood placed edge to edge to make something (as a barrel) 3 : STANZA

²**stave** *vb* **staved** *or* **stove** \'stōv\; **stav·ing** 1 : to break in the staves of; *also* : to break a hole in 2 : to drive or thrust away

staves *pl of* STAFF

¹**stay** \'stā\ *n* 1 : a strong rope or wire used to support a mast 2 : ¹GUY

²**stay** *vb* **stayed** \'stād\ *also* **staid** \'stād\; **stay·ing** 1 : PAUSE, WAIT 2 : REMAIN 3 : to stand firm 4 : LIVE, DWELL 5 : DELAY, POSTPONE 6 : to last out (as a race) 7 : STOP, CHECK 8 : to satisfy (as hunger) for a time ◆ *Synonyms* REMAIN, ABIDE, LINGER, TARRY

³**stay** *n* 1 : STOP, HALT 2 : a residence or sojourn in a place

⁴**stay** *n* 1 : PROP, SUPPORT 2 : CORSET — usu. used in pl.

⁵**stay** *vb* : to hold up : PROP

staying power *n* : STAMINA

stbd *abbr* starboard

std *abbr* standard

STD \,es-(,)tē-'dē\ *n* : SEXUALLY TRANSMITTED DISEASE

Ste *abbr* [F *sainte*] saint (female)

stead \'sted\ *n* 1 : ADVANTAGE ⟨stood him in good ~⟩ 2 : the place or function ordinarily occupied or carried out by another ⟨acted in her brother's ~⟩

stead·fast \'sted-,fast\ *adj* 1 : firmly fixed in place 2 : not subject to change 3 : firm in belief, determination, or adherence : LOYAL ◆ *Synonyms* RESOLUTE, TRUE, FAITHFUL, STAUNCH — **stead·fast·ly** *adv* — **stead·fast·ness** *n*

¹**steady** \'ste-dē\ *adj* **steadi·er; -est** 1 : direct or sure in movement; *also* : CALM 2 : FIRM, FIXED ⟨held the pole ~⟩ 3 : STABLE ⟨~ prices⟩ 4 : not easily disturbed 5 : RELIABLE ⟨~ friends⟩ 6 : temperate in character or demeanor ◆ *Synonyms* UNIFORM, EVEN — **steadi·ly** \-də-lē\ *adv* — **steadi·ness** \-dē-nəs\ *n* — **steady** *adv*

²**steady** *vb* **stead·ied; steady·ing** : to make or become steady

steak \'stāk\ *n* : a slice of meat and esp. beef; *also* : a slice of a large fish

¹**steal** \'stēl\ *vb* **stole** \'stōl\; **sto·len** \'stō-lən\; **steal·ing** 1 : to take and carry away without right or permission 2 : to come or go secretly or gradually 3 : to get for oneself slyly or by skill and daring ⟨~ a kiss⟩ ⟨~ the ball in basketball⟩ 4 : to gain or attempt to gain a base in baseball by running without the aid of a hit or an error ◆ *Synonyms* PILFER, FILCH, PURLOIN, SWIPE

²**steal** *n* 1 : an act of stealing 2 : BARGAIN

¹**stealth** \'stelth\ *n* 1 : secret or unobtrusive procedure 2 : an aircraft design intended to produce a weak radar return

²**stealth** *adj* : STEALTHY ⟨a ~ campaign⟩

stealthy \'stel-thē\ *adj* **stealth·i·er; -est** : done by stealth : FURTIVE, SLY ◆ *Synonyms* SECRET, COVERT, CLANDESTINE, SURREPTITIOUS, UNDERHANDED — **stealth·i·ly** \'stel-thə-lē\ *adv*

¹**steam** \'stēm\ *n* 1 : the vapor into which water is changed when heated to the boiling point 2 : water vapor when compressed so that it supplies heat and power 3 : POWER, FORCE, ENERGY — **steamy** *adj*

²**steam** *vb* 1 : to pass off as vapor 2 : to emit vapor 3 : to move by or as if by the agency of steam — **steam·er** *n*

steam·boat \'stēm-,bōt\ *n* : a boat driven by steam

steam engine *n* : a reciprocating engine having a piston driven by steam

steam·fit·ter \'stēm-,fi-tər\ *n* : a worker who puts in or repairs equipment (as steam pipes) for heating, ventilating, or refrigerating systems

steam·roll·er \-,rō-lər\ *n* : a machine for compacting roads or pavements — **steam·roll·er** *also* **steam·roll** \-,rōl\ *vb*

steam·ship \-,ship\ *n* : a ship driven by steam

steed \'stēd\ *n* : HORSE

¹**steel** \'stēl\ *n* 1 : iron treated with intense heat and mixed with carbon to make it hard and tough 2 : an article made of steel 3 : a quality (as hardness of mind) that suggests steel — **steel** *adj* — **steely** *adj*

²**steel** *vb* : to fill with courage or determination

steel wool *n* : long fine steel shavings used esp. for cleaning and polishing

¹**steep** \'stēp\ *adj* **1** : having a very sharp slope : PRECIPITOUS **2** : too high ⟨∼ prices⟩ — **steep·ly** *adv* — **steep·ness** *n*

²**steep** *n* : a steep slope

³**steep** *vb* **1** : to soak in a liquid; *esp* : to extract the essence of by soaking ⟨∼ tea⟩ **2** : SATURATE ⟨∼ed in learning⟩

stee·ple \'stē-pəl\ *n* : a tall tapering structure built on top of a church tower; *also* : a church tower

stee·ple·chase \-ˌchās\ *n* [fr. the use of church steeples as landmarks to guide the riders] : a horse race across country; *also* : a race over a course obstructed by hurdles

¹**steer** \'stir\ *n* : a male bovine animal castrated before sexual maturity and usu. raised for beef

²**steer** *vb* **1** : to direct the course of (as by a rudder or wheel) **2** : GUIDE, CONTROL **3** : to pursue a course of action **4** : to be subject to guidance or direction — **steers·man** \'stirz-mən\ *n*

steer·age \'stir-ij\ *n* **1** : DIRECTION, GUIDANCE **2** : a section in a passenger ship for passengers paying the lowest fares

stego·sau·rus \ˌste-gə-'sȯr-əs\ *n* : any of a genus of plant-eating armored dinosaurs with a series of bony plates along the backbone

stein \'stīn\ *n* : an earthenware mug

stel·lar \'ste-lər\ *adj* : of or relating to stars : resembling a star

¹**stem** \'stem\ *n* **1** : the main stalk of a plant; *also* : a plant part that supports another part (as a leaf or fruit) **2** : the bow of a ship **3** : a line of ancestry : STOCK **4** : that part of an inflected word which remains unchanged throughout a given inflection **5** : something resembling the stem of a plant — **stem·less** *adj* — **stemmed** \'stemd\ *adj*

²**stem** *vb* **stemmed**; **stem·ming** : to have a specified source : DERIVE

³**stem** *vb* **stemmed**; **stem·ming** : to make headway against ⟨∼ the tide⟩

⁴**stem** *vb* **stemmed**; **stem·ming** : to stop or check by or as if by damming

stem cell *n* : an undifferentiated cell that may give rise to many different types of cell

stench \'stench\ *n* : STINK

sten·cil \'sten-səl\ *n* [prob. ultim. fr. ME *stanseld* brightly ornamented, fr. AF *estencelé* spangled, pp. of *estenceler* to sparkle, fr. *estencele* spark, fr. VL *stincilla*, alter. of L *scintilla*] : an impervious material (as metal or paper) perforated with lettering or a design through which a substance (as ink or paint) is applied to a surface to be printed — **stencil** *vb*

ste·nog·ra·phy \stə-'nä-grə-fē\ *n* : the art or process of writing in shorthand — **ste·nog·ra·pher** \-fər\ *n* — **steno·graph·ic** \ˌste-nə-'gra-fik\ *adj*

ste·no·sis \stə-'nō-səs\ *n, pl* **-no·ses** \-ˌsēz\ : a narrowing of a bodily passage or orifice

stent \'stent\ *n* : a short narrow tube inserted into an anatomical vessel esp. to keep a passage open

sten·to·ri·an \sten-'tȯr-ē-ən\ *adj* : extremely loud ⟨∼ tones⟩

¹**step** \'step\ *n* **1** : a rest for the foot in ascending or descending : STAIR **2** : an advance made by raising one foot and putting it down elsewhere **3** : manner of walking **4** : a small space or distance **5** : a degree, rank, or plane in a series **6** : a sequential measure leading to a result

²**step** *vb* **stepped**; **step·ping** **1** : to advance or recede by steps **2** : to go on foot : WALK **3** : to move along briskly **4** : to press down with the foot **5** : to measure by steps **6** : to construct or arrange in or as if in steps

step aerobics *n sing or pl* : aerobics that involves repeatedly stepping on and off a raised platform

step aside *vb* : STEP DOWN

step·broth·er \'step-ˌbrə-thər\ *n* : the son of one's stepparent by a former marriage

step·child \-ˌchī(-ə)ld\ *n* : a child of one's husband or wife by a former marriage

step·daugh·ter \-ˌdȯ-tər\ *n* : a daughter of one's wife or husband by a former marriage

step down *vb* **1** : to give up a position : RETIRE, RESIGN **2** : to lower (a voltage) by means of a transformer

step·fa·ther \-ˌfä-thər\ *n* : the husband of one's mother when distinct from one's natural or legal father

step·lad·der \'step-ˌla-dər\ *n* : a light portable set of steps in a hinged frame

step·moth·er \-ˌmə-thər\ *n* : the wife of one's father when distinct from one's natural or legal mother

step·par·ent \-ˌper-ənt\ *n* : a person who is a stepfather or stepmother

steppe \'step\ *n* [Russ *step'*] : dry level grass-covered treeless land in regions of wide temperature range esp. in southeastern Europe and Asia

step·sis·ter \'step-ˌsis-tər\ *n* : the daughter of one's stepparent by a former marriage

step·son \-ˌsən\ *n* : a son of one's wife or husband by a former marriage

step up *vb* **1** : to increase (a voltage) by means of a transformer **2** : INCREASE, ACCELERATE **3** : to come forward — **step–up** \'step-ˌəp\ *n*

ster *abbr* sterling

ste·reo \'ster-ē-ˌō, 'stir-\ *n, pl* **ste·re·os** **1** : stereophonic reproduction **2** : a stereophonic sound system — **stereo** *adj*

ste·reo·phon·ic \ˌster-ē-ə-'fä-nik, ˌstir-\ *adj* : of or relating to sound reproduction designed to create the effect of listening to the original — **ste·reo·phon·i·cal·ly** \-'fä-ni-k(ə-)lē\ *adv*

ster·e·o·scope \'ster-ē-ə-ˌskōp, 'stir-\ *n* [Gk *stereos* solid + *-skopion* means for viewing] : an optical instrument that blends two slightly different pictures of the same subject to give the effect of depth

stereoscope

ste·reo·scop·ic \ˌster-ē-ə-'skä-pik, ˌstir-\ *adj* **1** : of or relating to the stereoscope **2** : characterized by the seeing of objects in three dimensions ⟨∼ vision⟩ — **ste·reo·scop·i·cal·ly** \-'skä-pi-k(ə-)lē\ *adv* — **ste·re·os·co·py** \ˌster-ē-'äs-kə-pē, ˌstir-\ *n*

ste·reo·type \'ster-ē-ə-ˌtīp, 'stir-\ *n* **1** : a metal printing plate cast from a mold made from set type **2** : something agreeing with a pattern; *esp* : an idea that many people have about a thing or a group and that may often be untrue or only partly true — **stereotype** *vb* — **ste·reo·typ·i·cal** \ˌster-ē-ə-'ti-pi-kəl\ *adj* — **ste·reo·typ·i·cal·ly** \-pi-k(ə-)lē\ *adv*

ste·reo·typed \-ˌtīpt\ *adj* : lacking originality or individuality ♦ *Synonyms* TRITE, CLICHÉD, COMMONPLACE, HACKNEYED, STALE, THREADBARE

ster·ile \'ster-əl\ *adj* **1** : unable to bear fruit, crops, or offspring **2** : free from living things and esp. germs — **ste·ril·i·ty** \stə-'ri-lə-tē\ *n*

ster·il·ize \'ster-ə-ˌlīz\ *vb* **-ized**; **-iz·ing** : to make sterile; *esp* : to free from germs — **ster·il·i·za·tion** \ˌster-ə-lə-'zā-shən\ *n* — **ster·il·iz·er** \'ster-ə-ˌlī-zər\ *n*

¹**ster·ling** \'stər-liŋ\ *n* **1** : British money **2** : sterling silver

²**sterling** *adj* **1** : of, relating to, or calculated in terms of British sterling **2** : having a fixed standard of purity represented by an alloy of 925 parts of silver with 75 parts of copper **3** : made of sterling silver **4** : EXCELLENT ⟨a ∼ record of achievement⟩

¹**stern** \'stərn\ *adj* **1** : SEVERE, AUSTERE ⟨∼ taskmasters⟩ **2** : STOUT, STURDY ⟨∼ resolve⟩ — **stern·ly** *adv* — **stern·ness** *n*

²**stern** *n* : the rear end of a boat

ster·num \'stər-nəm\ *n, pl* **sternums** *or* **ster·na** \-nə\ : a long flat bone or cartilage at the center front of the chest connecting the ribs of the two sides

ste·roid \'stir-,oid, 'ster-\ *n* : any of various compounds including numerous hormones (as anabolic steroids) and sugar derivatives — **steroid** *or* **ste·roi·dal** \stə-'roi-d°l\ *adj*

stetho·scope \'ste-thə-,skōp\ *n* : an instrument used to detect and listen to sounds produced in the body

ste·ve·dore \'stē-və-,dòr\ *n* [Sp *estibador,* fr. *estibar* to pack, fr. L *stipare* to press together] : one who works at loading and unloading ships

¹stew \'stü, 'styü\ *n* 1 : a dish of stewed meat and vegetables served in gravy 2 : a state of agitation, worry, or resentment

²stew *vb* 1 : to boil slowly : SIMMER 2 : to be in a state of agitation, worry, or resentment

stew·ard \'stü-ərd, 'styü-\ *n* [ME, fr. OE *stīweard,* fr. *stī, stig* hall, sty + *weard* ward] 1 : one employed on a large estate to manage domestic concerns 2 : one who supervises the provision and distribution of food (as on a ship); *also* : an employee on a ship or airplane who serves passengers 3 : one actively concerned with the direction of the affairs of an organization — **stew·ard·ship** *n*

stew·ard·ess \'stü-ər-dəs, 'styü-\ *n* : a woman who is a steward esp. on an airplane

stg *abbr* sterling

¹stick \'stik\ *n* 1 : a cut or broken branch or twig; *also* : a long slender piece of wood 2 : ROD, STAFF 3 : something resembling a stick 4 : a dull uninteresting person 5 *pl* : remote usu. rural areas

²stick *vb* **stuck** \'stək\; **stick·ing** 1 : STAB, PRICK 2 : IMPALE 3 : ATTACH, FASTEN 4 : to thrust or project in some direction or manner 5 : to be unable to proceed or move freely 6 : to hold fast by or as if by gluing : ADHERE 7 : to hold to something firmly or closely : CLING 8 : to become jammed or blocked

stick·er \'sti-kər\ *n* : one that sticks (as a bur) or causes sticking (as glue); *esp* : an adhesive label

sticker shock *n* : astonishment and dismay on being informed of a product's unexpectedly high price

stick insect *n* : any of various usu. wingless insects with a long round body resembling a stick

stick·ler \'sti-klər, -kə-lər\ *n* : one who insists on exactness or completeness

stick shift *n* : a manually operated automobile gearshift usu. mounted on the floor

stick–to–it·ive·ness \stik-'tü-ə-tiv-nəs\ *n* : dogged perseverance : TENACITY

stick up *vb* : to rob at gunpoint — **stick·up** \'stik-,əp\ *n*

sticky \'sti-kē\ *adj* **stick·i·er; -est** 1 : ADHESIVE 2 : VISCOUS, GLUEY 3 : tending to stick ⟨∼ valve⟩ 4 : DIFFICULT

¹stiff \'stif\ *adj* 1 : not pliant : RIGID 2 : not limber ⟨∼ joints⟩; *also* : TENSE, TAUT 3 : not flowing or working easily ⟨∼ paste⟩ 4 : not natural and easy : FORMAL 5 : STRONG, FORCEFUL ⟨∼ breeze⟩ 6 : HARSH, SEVERE ⟨a ∼ penalty⟩ ♦ *Synonyms* INFLEXIBLE, INELASTIC — **stiff·ly** *adv* — **stiff·ness** *n*

²stiff *vb* : to refuse to pay or tip

stiff–arm \'stif-,ärm\ *vb* : to treat with disdain or neglect ⟨∼ed her advice⟩

stiff·en \'sti-fən\ *vb* : to make or become stiff — **stiff·en·er** *n*

stiff–necked \'stif-'nekt\ *adj* : STUBBORN, HAUGHTY

sti·fle \'stī-fəl\ *vb* **sti·fled; sti·fling** 1 : to kill by depriving of or die from lack of oxygen or air : SMOTHER 2 : to keep in check by effort : SUPPRESS ⟨∼ a sneeze⟩ — **sti·fling·ly** *adv*

stig·ma \'stig-mə\ *n, pl* **stig·ma·ta** \stig-'mä-tə, 'stig-mə-tə\ *or* **stigmas** [L] 1 : a mark of disgrace or discredit 2 *stigmata pl* : bodily marks resembling the wounds of the crucified Jesus 3 : the upper part of the pistil of a flower that receives the pollen in fertilization — **stig·mat·ic** \stig-'ma-tik\ *adj*

stig·ma·tize \'stig-mə-,tīz\ *vb* **-tized; -tiz·ing** 1 : to mark with a stigma 2 : to characterize as disgraceful

stile \'stī(-ə)l\ *n* : steps used for crossing a fence or wall

sti·let·to \stə-'le-tō\ *n, pl* **-tos** *or* **-toes** [It, dim. of *stilo* stylus, dagger] : a slender dagger

¹still \'stil\ *adj* 1 : MOTIONLESS 2 : making no sound : SILENT — **still·ness** *n*

²still *vb* : to make or become still

³still *adv* 1 : without motion ⟨sit ∼⟩ 2 : up to and during

this or that time 3 : in spite of that : NEVERTHELESS 4 : EVEN ⟨ran ∼ faster⟩ 5 : YET ⟨has ∼ to be recognized⟩

⁴still *n* 1 : STILLNESS, SILENCE 2 : a static photograph esp. from a motion picture

⁵still *n* 1 : DISTILLERY 2 : apparatus used in distillation

still·birth \'stil-,bərth\ *n* : the birth of a dead fetus

still·born \-'bòrn\ *adj* : born dead

still life *n, pl* **still lifes** : a picture of inanimate objects

stilt \'stilt\ *n* : one of a pair of poles for walking with each having a step or loop for the foot to elevate the wearer above the ground; *also* : a polelike support of a structure above ground or water level

stilt·ed \'stil-təd\ *adj* : not easy and natural ⟨∼ language⟩

Stil·ton \'stil-t°n\ *n* : a blue cheese of English origin

stim·u·lant \'sti-myə-lənt\ *n* 1 : an agent (as a drug) that temporarily increases the activity of an organism or any of its parts 2 : STIMULUS 3 : an alcoholic beverage — **stimulant** *adj*

stim·u·late \-,lāt\ *vb* **-lat·ed; -lat·ing** : to make active or more active : ANIMATE, AROUSE ♦ *Synonyms* EXCITE, PROVOKE, MOTIVATE, QUICKEN — **stim·u·la·tion** \,sti-myə-'lā-shən\ *n* — **stim·u·la·tive** \'sti-myə-,lā-tiv\ *adj* — **stim·u·la·tor** \-,lā-tər\ *n* — **stim·u·la·to·ry** \-lə-,tòr-ē\ *adj*

stim·u·lus \'sti-myə-ləs\ *n, pl* **-li** \-,lī\ [L] 1 : something that moves to activity 2 : an agent that directly influences the activity of a living organism or one of its parts

¹sting \'stiŋ\ *vb* **stung** \'stəŋ\; **sting·ing** 1 : to prick painfully esp. with a sharp or poisonous process 2 : to cause to suffer acutely — **sting·er** *n*

²sting *n* 1 : an act of stinging; *also* : a resultant wound, sore, or pain 2 : a pointed often venom-bearing organ (as of a bee) : STINGER 3 : an elaborate confidence game; *esp* : one worked by undercover police to trap criminals

sting·ray \'stiŋ-,rā\ *n* : any of numerous rays with sharp stinging spines on a whiplike tail

stin·gy \'stin-jē\ *adj* **stin·gi·er; -est** : not generous : giving or spending as little as possible — **stin·gi·ness** *n*

stink \'stiŋk\ *vb* **stank** \'staŋk\ *or* **stunk** \'stəŋk\; **stunk; stink·ing** : to give forth a strong and offensive smell; *also* : to be extremely bad in quality or repute — **stink** *n* — **stink·er** *n*

stink·bug \'stiŋk-,bəg\ *n* : any of various true bugs that emit a disagreeable odor

¹stint \'stint\ *vb* 1 : to be sparing or frugal 2 : to cut short in amount

²stint *n* 1 : an assigned amount of work 2 : RESTRAINT, LIMITATION 3 : a period of time spent at a particular activity

sti·pend \'stī-,pend, -pənd\ *n* [ME, alter. of *stipendy,* fr. L *stipendium,* fr. *stips* gift + *pendere* to weigh, pay] : a fixed sum of money paid periodically for services or to defray expenses

stip·ple \'sti-pəl\ *vb* **stip·pled; stip·pling** 1 : to engrave by means of dots and light strokes 2 : to apply (as paint or ink) with small short touches — **stipple** *n*

stip·u·late \'sti-pyə-,lāt\ *vb* **-lat·ed; -lat·ing** : to make an agreement; *esp* : to make a special demand for something as a condition in an agreement — **stip·u·la·tion** \,sti-pyə-'lā-shən\ *n*

¹stir \'stər\ *vb* **stirred; stir·ring** 1 : to move slightly 2 : AROUSE, EXCITE 3 : to mix, dissolve, or make by continued circular movement ⟨∼ eggs into cake batter⟩ 4 : to move to activity (as by pushing, beating, or prodding)

²stir *n* 1 : a state of agitation or activity 2 : an act of stirring

stir–fry \'stər-,frī\ *vb* : to fry quickly over high heat while stirring continuously — **stir–fry** *n*

¹stir·ring \'stər-iŋ\ *adj* 1 : ACTIVE, BUSTLING 2 : ROUSING, INSPIRING ⟨a ∼ speech⟩

²stirring *n* : a beginning of activity ⟨the first ∼s of revolution⟩

stir·rup \'stər-əp\ *n* [ME *stirop,* fr. OE *stigrāp,* lit., mounting rope] 1 : a light frame hung from a saddle to support the rider's foot 2 : STAPES

¹stitch \'stich\ *n* 1 : a sudden sharp pain esp. in the side 2 : one of the series of loops formed by or over a needle in sewing

²stitch *vb* 1 : to fasten or join with stitches 2 : to decorate with stitches 3 : SEW

stk *abbr* stock

stoat \'stōt\ *n, pl* **stoats** *also* **stoat** : the common Old and New World ermine esp. in its brown summer coat

¹stock \'stäk\ *n* **1** *archaic* : a block of wood **2** : a stupid person **3** : a wooden part of a thing serving as its support, frame, or handle **4** *pl* : a device for publicly punishing offenders consisting of a wooden frame with holes in which the feet and hands can be locked **5** : the original from which others derive; *also* : a group having a common origin : FAMILY **6** : LIVESTOCK **7** : a supply of goods **8** : the ownership element in a corporation divided to give the owners an interest and usu. voting power **9** : a company of actors playing at a particular theater and presenting a series of plays **10** : liquid in which meat, fish, or vegetables have been simmered that is used as a basis for soup, gravy, or sauce

²stock *vb* : to provide with stock

³stock *adj* : kept regularly for sale or use; *also* : commonly used : STANDARD

stock·ade \stä-'kād\ *n* [Sp *estacada*, fr. *estaca* stake, pale, of Gmc origin] : an enclosure (as of posts and stakes) for defense or confinement

stock·bro·ker \-ˌbrō-kər\ *n* : one who executes orders to buy and sell securities

stock car *n* : a racing car that is similar to a regular car

stock exchange *n* : a place where the buying and selling of securities is conducted

stock·hold·er \'stäk-ˌhōl-dər\ *n* : one who owns corporate stock

stock·i·nette *or* **stock·i·net** \ˌstä-kə-'net\ *n* : an elastic knitted fabric used esp. for infants' wear and bandages

stock·ing \'stä-kiŋ\ *n* : a close-fitting knitted covering for the foot and leg

stock market *n* **1** : STOCK EXCHANGE **2** : a market for stocks

stock·pile \'stäk-ˌpī(-ə)l\ *n* : a reserve supply esp. of something essential — **stockpile** *vb*

stocky \'stä-kē\ *adj* **stock·i·er; -est** : being short and relatively thick : STURDY ✦ *Synonyms* THICKSET, SQUAT, HEAVYSET, STUBBY

stock·yard \'stäk-ˌyärd\ *n* : a yard for stock; *esp* : one for livestock about to be slaughtered or shipped

stodgy \'stä-jē\ *adj* **stodg·i·er; -est** **1** : thick in texture : HEAVY ⟨∼ bread⟩ **2** : not interesting : DULL ⟨a ∼ accountant⟩ **3** : extremely old-fashioned

¹sto·ic \'stō-ik\ *n* [ME, fr. L *stoicus*, fr. Gk *stōïkos*, lit., of the portico, fr. *Stoa (Poikilē)* the Painted Portico, portico at Athens where the philosopher Zeno taught] : one who suffers without complaining

²stoic *or* **sto·i·cal** \-i-kəl\ *adj* : not affected by passion or feeling; *esp* : showing indifference to pain ✦ *Synonyms* IMPASSIVE, PHLEGMATIC, APATHETIC, STOLID — **sto·i·cal·ly** \-i-k(ə-)lē\ *adv* — **sto·icism** \'stō-ə-ˌsi-zəm\ *n*

stoke \'stōk\ *vb* **stoked; stok·ing** **1** : to stir up a fire **2** : to tend and supply fuel to a furnace — **stok·er** *n*

STOL *abbr* short takeoff and landing

¹stole *past of* STEAL

²stole \'stōl\ *n* **1** : a long narrow band worn round the neck by some members of the clergy **2** : a long wide scarf or similar covering worn by women

stolen *past part of* STEAL

stol·id \'stä-ləd\ *adj* : not easily aroused or excited : showing little or no emotion ✦ *Synonyms* PHLEGMATIC, APATHETIC, IMPASSIVE, STOIC — **sto·lid·i·ty** \stä-'li-də-tē\ *n* — **stol·id·ly** *adv*

sto·lon \'stō-lən, -ˌlän\ *n* : RUNNER 6

¹stom·ach \'stə-mək\ *n* **1** : a saclike digestive organ of a vertebrate into which food goes from the mouth by way of the throat and which opens below into the intestine **2** : a cavity in an invertebrate animal that is analogous to a stomach **3** : ABDOMEN **4** : desire for food caused by hunger : APPETITE **5** : INCLINATION, DESIRE ⟨had no ∼ for an argument⟩

²stomach *vb* : to bear without open resentment : put up with

stom·ach·ache \-ˌāk\ *n* : pain in or in the region of the stomach

stom·ach·er \'stə-mi-kər, -chər\ *n* : the front of a bodice often appearing between the laces of an outer garment (as in 16th century costume)

stomp \'stämp, 'stȯmp\ *vb* : STAMP — **stomp** *n*

¹stone \'stōn\ *n* **1** : hardened earth or mineral matter : ROCK **2** : a small piece of rock **3** : a precious stone : GEM **4** : CALCULUS 3 **5** : a hard stony seed (as of a date) or one (as of a plum) with a stony covering **6** *pl usu* **stone** : a British unit of weight equal to 14 pounds — **stony** *also* **ston·ey** \'stō-nē\ *adj*

²stone *vb* **stoned; ston·ing** **1** : to pelt or kill with stones **2** : to remove the stones of (a fruit)

Stone Age *n* : the first known period of prehistoric human culture characterized by the use of stone tools

stoned \'stōnd\ *adj* **1** : DRUNK **2** : being under the influence of a drug

stone·wall \'stōn-ˌwȯl\ *vb* : to refuse to comply or cooperate with

stone·washed \'stōn-ˌwȯsht, -ˌwäsht\ *adj* : having been washed with stones during manufacture to create a softer fabric ⟨∼ jeans⟩

stood *past and past part of* STAND

stooge \'stüj\ *n* **1** : a person who plays a subordinate or compliant role to a principal **2** : STRAIGHT MAN

stool \'stül\ *n* **1** : a seat usu. without back or arms **2** : FOOTSTOOL **3** : a seat used while urinating or defecating **4** : a discharge of fecal matter

stool pigeon *n* : DECOY, INFORMER

¹stoop \'stüp\ *vb* **1** : to bend forward and downward **2** : CONDESCEND **3** : to lower oneself morally

²stoop *n* **1** : an act of bending forward **2** : a bent position of head and shoulders

³stoop *n* [D *stoep*] : a porch, platform, or entrance stairway at a house door

¹stop \'stäp\ *vb* **stopped; stop·ping** **1** : to close (an opening) by filling or covering closely **2** : BLOCK, HALT **3** : to cease to go on **4** : to bring activity or operation to an end **5** : STAY, TARRY ✦ *Synonyms* QUIT, DISCONTINUE, DESIST, CEASE

²stop *n* **1** : END, CESSATION **2** : a set of organ pipes of one tone quality; *also* : a control knob for such a set **3** : OBSTRUCTION **4** : PLUG, STOPPER **5** : an act of stopping : CHECK **6** : a delay in a journey : STAY **7** : a place for stopping **8** *chiefly Brit* : any of several punctuation marks **9** : a function of an electronic device that stops a recording

stop·ac·tion \'stäp-ˌak-shən\ *n* : STOP-MOTION

stop·gap \'stäp-ˌgap\ *n* : something that serves as a temporary expedient

stop·light \-ˌlīt\ *n* : TRAFFIC LIGHT

stop·mo·tion \'stäp-'mō-shən\ *n* : a filming technique in which successive positions of objects are photographed to produce the appearance of movement

stop·over \'stäp-ˌō-vər\ *n* **1** : a stop at an intermediate point in one's journey **2** : a stopping place on a journey

stop·page \'stä-pij\ *n* : the act of stopping : the state of being stopped

stop·per \'stä-pər\ *n* : something (as a cork) for sealing an opening

stop·watch \'stäp-ˌwäch\ *n* : a watch that can be started or stopped at will for exact timing

stor·age \'stȯr-ij\ *n* **1** : space for storing; *also* : cost of storing **2** : MEMORY 6 **3** : the act of storing; *esp* : the safekeeping of goods (as in a warehouse)

storage battery *n* : a group of connected rechargeable electrochemical cells used to provide electric current

¹store \'stȯr\ *vb* **stored; stor·ing** **1** : to place or leave in a safe location for preservation or future use **2** : to provide esp. for a future need

²store *n* **1** : something accumulated and kept for future use **2** : a large or ample quantity **3** : STOREHOUSE **4** : a retail business establishment

store·house \-ˌhau̇s\ *n* : a building for storing goods or supplies; *also* : an abundant source or supply

store·keep·er \-ˌkē-pər\ *n* : one who operates a retail store

store·room \-ˌrüm, -ˌru̇m\ *n* : a room for storing goods or supplies

sto·ried \'stȯr-ēd\ *adj* : celebrated in story or history

stork \'stȯrk\ *n* : any of various large stout-billed Old World wading birds related to the herons and ibises

¹storm \'stȯrm\ *n* **1** : a heavy fall of rain, snow, or hail with high wind **2** : a violent outbreak or disturbance **3** : a mass attack on a defended position — **storm·i·ly** \'stȯr-mə-lē\ *adv* — **storm·i·ness** \-mē-nəs\ *n* — **stormy** *adj*

²storm *vb* **1** : to blow with violence; *also* : to rain, snow, or hail heavily **2** : to make a mass attack against **3** : to be violently angry : RAGE **4** : to rush along furiously

¹sto·ry \'stȯr-ē\ *n, pl* **stories** **1** : NARRATIVE, ACCOUNT **2** : REPORT, STATEMENT **3** : ANECDOTE **4** : SHORT STORY **5** : LIE, FALSEHOOD **6** : a news article or broadcast ✦ *Synonyms* UNTRUTH, TALE, CANARD

²story *also* **sto·rey** \'stȯr-ē\ *n, pl* **stories** *also* **storeys** : a floor of a building or the space between two adjacent floor levels

sto·ry·tell·er \-ˌte-lər\ *n* : a teller of stories

sto·tin \stō-'tēn\ *n, pl* **sto·ti·nov** \stō-'tē-ˌnȯv\ — see *tolar* at MONEY table

sto·tin·ka \stō-'tiŋ-kə\ *n, pl* **-tin·ki** \-kē\ — see *lev* at MONEY table

¹stout \'staȯt\ *adj* **1** : BRAVE **2** : FIRM ⟨a ~ refusal⟩ **3** : STURDY **4** : STAUNCH, ENDURING ⟨~ loyalty⟩ **5** : SOLID **6** : FORCEFUL, VIOLENT ⟨a ~ attack⟩ ⟨a ~ wind⟩ **7** : BULKY, THICKSET ✦ *Synonyms* FLESHY, FAT, PORTLY, CORPULENT, OBESE, PLUMP — **stout·ly** *adv* — **stout·ness** *n*

²stout *n* : a dark heavy ale

¹stove \'stōv\ *n* : an apparatus that burns fuel or uses electricity to provide heat (as for cooking or heating)

²stove *past and past part of* STAVE

stow \'stō\ *vb* **1** : HIDE, STORE **2** : to pack in a compact mass

stow·away \'stō-ə-ˌwā\ *n* : one who hides on a vehicle to ride free

STP *abbr* standard temperature and pressure

strad·dle \'stra-dᵊl\ *vb* **strad·dled; strad·dling** **1** : to stand, sit, or walk with legs spread apart **2** : to favor or seem to favor two apparently opposite sides — **straddle** *n*

strafe \'strāf\ *vb* **strafed; straf·ing** [G *Gott strafe England* may God punish England, propaganda slogan during World War I] : to fire upon with machine guns from a low-flying airplane

strag·gle \'stra-gəl\ *vb* **strag·gled; strag·gling** **1** : to wander from the direct course : ROVE, STRAY **2** : to become separated from others of the same kind — **strag·gler** *n* — **strag·gly** \'stra-g(ə-)lē\ *adj*

¹straight \'strāt\ *adj* **1** : free from curves, bends, angles, or irregularities **2** : not wandering from the main point or proper course ⟨~ thinking⟩ **3** : HONEST ⟨a ~ answer⟩ **4** : having the elements in correct order **5** : UNMIXED, UNDILUTED ⟨~ whiskey⟩ **6** : CONVENTIONAL, SQUARE **7** : HETEROSEXUAL

²straight *adv* : in a straight manner

³straight *n* **1** : a straight line, course, or arrangement **2** : the part of a racetrack between the last turn and the finish **3** : a sequence of five cards in a poker hand

straight–arm \'strāt-ˌärm\ *n* : an act of warding off a person with the arm fully extended — **straight–arm** *vb*

straight·away \'strā-tə-ˌwā\ *n* : a straight stretch (as at a racetrack)

straight·edge \'strāt-ˌej\ *n* : a piece of material with a straight edge for testing straight lines and surfaces or for cutting along or drawing straight lines

straight·en \'strā-tᵊn\ *vb* : to make or become straight

straight flush *n* : a poker hand containing five cards of the same suit in sequence

straight·for·ward \strāt-'fȯr-wərd\ *adj* **1** : FRANK, CANDID, HONEST ⟨a ~ account⟩ **2** : proceeding in a straight course or manner

straight man *n* : an entertainer who feeds lines to a comedian who replies with usu. humorous quips

straight shooter *n* : a thoroughly upright straightforward person

straight·way \'strāt-'wā, -ˌwā\ *adv* : IMMEDIATELY ⟨get ~ to work⟩

¹strain \'strān\ *n* [ME *streen* progeny, lineage, fr. OE *strēon* gain, acquisition] **1** : LINEAGE, ANCESTRY **2** : a group (as of people or plants) of presumed common ancestry **3** : an inherited or inherent character or quality ⟨a ~ of madness in the family⟩ **4** : STREAK, TRACE ⟨a ~ of fanaticism⟩ **5** : MELODY **6** : the general style or tone

²strain *vb* [ME, fr. AF *estreindre*, fr. L *stringere* to bind or draw tight, press together] **1** : to draw taut **2** : to exert to the utmost **3** : to strive violently **4** : to injure by improper or excessive use **5** : to filter or remove by filtering **6** : to stretch beyond a proper limit — **strain·er** *n*

³strain *n* **1** : excessive tension or exertion (as of body or mind) **2** : bodily injury from excessive tension, effort, or use; *esp* : one in which muscles or ligaments are unduly stretched usu. from a wrench or twist **3** : deformation of a material body under the action of applied forces

¹strait \'strāt\ *adj* [ME, fr. AF *estreit*, fr. L *strictus* strait, strict, fr. pp. of *stringere*] **1** *archaic* : STRICT **2** *archaic* : NARROW **3** *archaic* : CONSTRICTED **4** : DIFFICULT, STRAITENED

²strait *n* **1** : a narrow channel connecting two bodies of water **2** *pl* : DISTRESS

strait·en \'strā-tᵊn\ *vb* **1** : to hem in : CONFINE **2** : to make distressing or difficult

strait·jack·et *also* **straight·jack·et** \'strāt-ˌja-kət\ *n* : a cover or garment of strong material (as canvas) used to bind the body and esp. the arms closely in restraining a violent prisoner or patient — **straitjacket** *vb*

strait·laced *or* **straight·laced** \-'lāst\ *adj* : strict in manners, morals, or opinion

¹strand \'strand\ *n* : SHORE, BEACH

²strand *vb* **1** : to run, drift, or drive upon the shore ⟨a ~ed ship⟩ **2** : to place or leave in a helpless position

³strand *n* **1** : one of the fibers twisted or plaited together into a cord, rope, or cable; *also* : a cord, rope, or cable made up of such fibers **2** : a twisted or plaited ropelike mass ⟨a ~ of pearls⟩ — **strand·ed** \'stran-dəd\ *adj*

¹strange \'strānj\ *adj* **strang·er; strang·est** [ME, fr. AF *estrange*, fr. L *extraneus*, lit., external, fr. *extra* outside] **1** : of external origin, kind, or character **2** : NEW, UNFAMILIAR ⟨moved to a ~ neighborhood⟩ **3** : DISTANT 6 **4** : UNACCUSTOMED, INEXPERIENCED ⟨she was ~ to his ways⟩ ✦ *Synonyms* SINGULAR, PECULIAR, ECCENTRIC, ERRATIC, ODD, QUEER, QUAINT, CURIOUS — **strange·ly** *adv* — **strange·ness** *n*

²strange *n* : a quark with a charge of $-\frac{1}{3}$ and a measured energy of approximately 150 million electron volts

strang·er \'strān-jər\ *n* **1** : FOREIGNER **2** : INTRUDER **3** : a person with whom one is unacquainted

stran·gle \'straŋ-gəl\ *vb* **stran·gled; stran·gling** **1** : to choke to death : THROTTLE **2** : STIFLE, SUPPRESS ⟨repression ~s free speech⟩ — **stran·gler** *n*

strangler fig *n* : any of several figs that begin life atop a host tree and then send down roots that surround it

stran·gu·late \'straŋ-gyə-ˌlāt\ *vb* **-lat·ed; -lat·ing** **1** : STRANGLE, CONSTRICT **2** : to become so constricted as to stop circulation

stran·gu·la·tion \ˌstraŋ-gyə-'lā-shən\ *n* : the act or process of strangling or strangulating; *also* : the state of being strangled or strangulated

¹strap \'strap\ *n* : a narrow strip of flexible material used esp. for fastening, holding together, or wrapping

²strap *vb* **strapped; strap·ping** **1** : to secure with a strap **2** : BIND, CONSTRICT **3** : to flog with a strap **4** : STROP

strap·less \-ləs\ *adj* : having no straps; *esp* : having no shoulder straps

¹strapping *adj* : LARGE, STRONG, HUSKY

²strapping *n* : material for a strap

strat·a·gem \'stra-tə-jəm, -ˌjem\ *n* **1** : a trick to deceive or outwit the enemy; *also* : a deceptive scheme **2** : skill in deception

strat·e·gy \'stra-tə-jē\ *n, pl* **-gies** [Gk *stratēgia* generalship, fr. *stratēgos* general, fr. *stratos* camp, army + *agein* to lead] **1** : the science and art of military command aimed at meeting the enemy under conditions advantageous to one's own force **2** : a careful plan or method esp. for achieving an end — **stra·te·gic** \strə-'tē-jik\ *adj* — **strat·e·gist** \'stra-tə-jist\ *n*

strat·i·fy \'stra-tə-ˌfī\ *vb* **-fied; -fy·ing** : to form or arrange in layers — **strat·i·fi·ca·tion** \ˌstra-tə-fə-'kā-shən\ *n*

stra·tig·ra·phy \strə-'ti-grə-fē\ *n* : geology that deals with rock strata — **strati·graph·ic** \ˌstra-tə-'gra-fik\ *adj*

strato·sphere \'stra-tə-ˌsfir\ *n* : the part of the earth's atmosphere between about 7 miles (11 kilometers) and 31 miles (50 kilometers) above the earth — **strato·spher·ic** \ˌstra-tə-'sfir-ik, -'sfer-\ *adj*

stra·tum \'strā-təm, 'stra-\ *n, pl* **stra·ta** \'strā-tə, 'stra-\ [NL, fr. L, spread, bed, fr. neut. of *stratus*, pp. of *sternere* to spread out] **1** : a bed, layer, or sheetlike mass (as of one kind of rock lying between layers of other kinds of rock) **2** : a level of culture; *also* : a group of people representing one stage in cultural development

¹straw \'strȯ\ *n* **1** : stalks of grain after threshing; *also* : a single coarse dry stem (as of a grass) **2** : a thing of small worth **3** : TRIFLE **3** : a tube (as of paper or plastic) for sucking up a beverage

²straw *adj* **1** : made of straw **2** : having no real force or validity ⟨a ~ vote⟩

straw·ber·ry \'strȯ‚ber-ē, -bə-rē\ *n* : an edible juicy usu. red pulpy fruit of any of several low herbs with white flowers and long slender runners; *also* : one of these herbs

straw boss *n* : a foreman of a small group of workers

straw·flow·er \'strȯ‚flaȯ(-ə)r\ *n* : any of several plants whose flowers can be dried with little loss of form or color

¹stray \'strā\ *n* **1** : a domestic animal wandering at large or lost **2** : WAIF

²stray *vb* **1** : to wander or roam without purpose **2** : DEVIATE

³stray *adj* **1** : having strayed : separated from the group or the main body **2** : occurring at random ⟨~ remarks⟩

¹streak \'strēk\ *n* **1** : a line or mark of a different color or texture from its background **2** : a narrow band of light; *also* : a lightning bolt **3** : a slight admixture : TRACE **4** : a brief run (as of luck); *also* : an unbroken series

²streak *vb* **1** : to form streaks in or on **2** : to move very swiftly

¹stream \'strēm\ *n* **1** : a body of water (as a river) flowing on the earth; *also* : any body of flowing fluid (as water or gas) **2** : a continuous procession ⟨a ~ of traffic⟩

²stream *vb* **1** : to flow in or as if in a stream **2** : to pour out streams of liquid **3** : to trail out in length **4** : to move forward in a steady stream

stream·bed \'strēm‚bed\ *n* : the channel occupied by a stream

stream·er \'strē-mər\ *n* **1** : a long narrow ribbonlike flag **2** : a long ribbon on a dress or hat **3** : a newspaper headline that runs across the entire sheet **4** *pl* : AURORA

stream·ing \'strē-miŋ\ *adj* : relating to or being the transfer of data (as music) in a continuous stream esp. for immediate processing or playback

stream·let \'strēm-lət\ *n* : a small stream

stream·lined \-‚līnd\ *adj* **1** : made with contours to reduce resistance to motion through water or air **2** : SIMPLIFIED **3** : MODERNIZED — **stream·line** *vb*

street \'strēt\ *n* [ME *strete*, fr. OE *strǣt*, fr. LL *strata* paved road, fr. L, fem. of *stratus*, pp. of *sternere* to spread out] **1** : a thoroughfare esp. in a city, town, or village **2** : the occupants of the houses on a street

street·car \-‚kär\ *n* : a passenger vehicle running on rails on city streets

streetcar

street fighter *n* : a tough belligerent person

street hockey *n* : a game resembling ice hockey played on a hard surface with hockey sticks and a small ball

street railway *n* : a company operating streetcars or buses

street·walk·er \'strēt-‚wȯ-kər\ *n* : PROSTITUTE

strength \'streŋth\ *n* **1** : the quality of being strong : ability to do or endure : POWER **2** : TOUGHNESS, SOLIDITY **3** : power to resist attack **4** : INTENSITY **5** : force as measured in numbers ⟨the ~ of an army⟩

strength·en \'streŋ-thən\ *vb* : to make or become stronger — **strength·en·er** *n*

stren·u·ous \'stren-yə-wəs\ *adj* **1** : VIGOROUS, ENERGETIC **2** : requiring energy or stamina — **stren·u·ous·ly** *adv*

strep \'strep\ *n* : STREPTOCOCCUS

strep throat *n* : an inflammatory sore throat caused by streptococci and marked by fever, prostration, and toxemia

strep·to·coc·cus \‚strep-tə-'kä-kəs\ *n, pl* **-coc·ci** \-'kä-‚kī, -'käk-‚sī, -'kä-‚kē, -'käk-‚sē\ : any of various spherical bacteria that usu. grow in chains and include some causing serious diseases — **strep·to·coc·cal** \-kəl\ *adj*

strep·to·my·cin \-'mī-sᵊn\ *n* : an antibiotic produced by soil bacteria and used esp. in treating tuberculosis

¹stress \'stres\ *n* **1** : PRESSURE, STRAIN; *esp* : a force that tends to distort a body **2** : a factor that induces bodily or mental tension; *also* : a state induced by such a stress **3** : EMPHASIS **4** : relative prominence of sound **5** : ACCENT; *also* : any syllable carrying the accent — **stress·ful** \'stres-fəl\ *adj*

²stress *vb* **1** : to put pressure or strain on **2** : to put emphasis on : ACCENT

¹stretch \'strech\ *vb* **1** : to spread or reach out : EXTEND ⟨~ed out her arm⟩ **2** : to draw out in length or breadth : EXPAND **3** : to make tense : STRAIN **4** : EXAGGERATE **5** : to become extended without breaking ⟨rubber ~es easily⟩ — **stretchy** \'stre-chē\ *adj*

²stretch *n* **1** : an act of extending or drawing out beyond ordinary or normal limits **2** : a continuous extent in length, area, or time **3** : the extent to which something may be stretched **4** : either of the straight sides of a racecourse

³stretch *adj* : easily stretched ⟨~ pants⟩

¹stretch·er \'stre-chər\ *n* **1** : one that stretches **2** : a device for carrying a sick, injured, or dead person

²stretcher *vb* : to carry or transport on a stretcher

stretch marks *n pl* : striae on the skin (as of the abdomen) due to excessive stretching and rupture of elastic fibers (as from pregnancy)

strew \'strü\ *vb* **strewed; strewed** *or* **strewn** \'strün\; **strew·ing** **1** : to spread by scattering **2** : to cover by or as if by scattering something over or on **3** : DISSEMINATE

stria \'strī-ə\ *n, pl* **stri·ae** \'strī-‚ē\ **1** : STRIATION 3 **2** : a stripe or line (as in the skin)

stri·at·ed muscle \'strī-‚ā-təd-\ *n* : muscle tissue made up of long thin cells with many nuclei and alternate light and dark stripes that includes esp. the muscle of the heart and muscle that moves the vertebrate skeleton and is mostly under voluntary control

stri·a·tion \strī-'ā-shən\ *n* **1** : the state of being marked with stripes or lines **2** : arrangement of striations or striae **3** : a minute groove, scratch, or channel esp. when one of a parallel series

strick·en \'stri-kən\ *adj* **1** : afflicted by or as if by disease, misfortune, or sorrow **2** : WOUNDED

strict \'strikt\ *adj* **1** : allowing no evasion or escape : RIGOROUS ⟨~ discipline⟩ **2** : ACCURATE, PRECISE ⟨the ~ sense of the word⟩ ✦ **Synonyms** STRINGENT, RIGID — **strict·ly** *adv* — **strict·ness** *n*

stric·ture \'strik-chər\ *n* **1** : an abnormal narrowing of a bodily passage; *also* : the narrowed part **2** : hostile criticism : a critical remark

¹stride \'strīd\ *vb* **strode** \'strōd\; **strid·den** \'stri-dᵊn\; **strid·ing** : to walk or run with long regular steps — **strid·er** *n*

²stride *n* **1** : a long step **2** : a stage of progress **3** : manner of striding : GAIT

stri·dent \'strī-dᵊnt\ *adj* : harsh sounding : GRATING, SHRILL

strife \'strīf\ *n* : CONFLICT, FIGHT, STRUGGLE ✦ **Synonyms** DISCORD, CONTENTION, DISSENSION

¹strike \'strīk\ *vb* **struck** \'strək\; **struck** *also* **strick·en** \'stri-kən\; **strik·ing** **1** : to take a course : GO ⟨**struck** off through the brush⟩ **2** : to touch or hit sharply; *also* : to deliver a blow **3** : to produce by or as if by a blow ⟨**struck** terror in the foe⟩ **4** : to lower (as a flag or sail) **5** : to collide with; *also* : to injure or destroy by collision **6** : DELETE, CANCEL **7** : to produce by impressing ⟨**struck** a medal⟩; *also* : COIN ⟨~ a new cent⟩ **8** : to cause to sound ⟨~ a bell⟩ **9** : to afflict suddenly : lay low ⟨**stricken** with a high fever⟩ **10** : to appear to; *also* : to appear to as remarkable : IMPRESS **11** : to reach by reckoning ⟨~ an average⟩ **12** : to stop work in order to obtain a change in conditions of employment **13** : to cause (a match) to ignite by rubbing **14** : to come upon ⟨~ gold⟩ **15** : TAKE ON, ASSUME ⟨~ a pose⟩ — **strik·er** *n*

²**strike** *n* **1** : an act or instance of striking **2** : a sudden discovery of rich ore or oil deposits **3** : a pitched baseball that is swung at but not hit **4** : the knocking down of all the bowling pins with the 1st ball **5** : a military attack

strike·break·er \-ˌbrā-kər\ *n* : a person hired to replace a striking worker

strike·out \-ˌaut\ *n* : an out in baseball as a result of a batter's being charged with three strikes

strike out *vb* **1** : to enter upon a course of action **2** : to start out vigorously **3** : to make an out in baseball by a strikeout

strike–slip \ˈstrīk-ˌslip\ *n* : a fault about which movement is predominantly horizontal

strike up *vb* **1** : to begin or cause to begin to sing or play **2** : BEGIN ⟨~ a conversation⟩

strike zone *n* : the area over home plate through which a pitched baseball must pass to be called a strike

striking *adj* : attracting attention : very noticeable ✦ *Synonyms* ARRESTING, SALIENT, CONSPICUOUS, OUTSTANDING, REMARKABLE, PROMINENT — **strik·ing·ly** *adv*

¹**string** \ˈstriŋ\ *n* **1** : a line usu. composed of twisted threads **2** : a series of things arranged as if strung on a cord **3** : a plant fiber (as a leaf vein) **4** *pl* : the stringed instruments of an orchestra ✦ *Synonyms* SUCCESSION, PROGRESSION, SEQUENCE, CHAIN, TRAIN

²**string** *vb* **strung** \ˈstrəŋ\; **string·ing** **1** : to provide with strings ⟨~ a racket⟩ **2** : to make tense **3** : to thread on or as if on a string ⟨~ pearls⟩ **4** : to hang, tie, or fasten by a string **5** : to take the strings out of ⟨~ beans⟩ **6** : to extend like a string

string bean *n* : a bean of one of the older varieties of kidney bean that have stringy fibers on the lines of separation of the pods; *also* : SNAP BEAN

string bikini *n* : a scanty bikini

string cheese *n* : cheese that can be pulled apart in narrow strips

stringed \ˈstriŋd\ *adj* **1** : having strings ⟨~ instruments⟩ **2** : produced by strings

strin·gen·cy \ˈstrin-jən-sē\ *n* **1** : STRICTNESS, SEVERITY **2** : SCARCITY ⟨~ of money⟩ — **strin·gent** \-jənt\ *adj*

string·er \ˈstriŋ-ər\ *n* **1** : a long horizontal member in a framed structure or a bridge **2** : a news correspondent paid by the amount of copy

stringy \ˈstriŋ-ē\ *adj* **string·i·er; -est** **1** : resembling string esp. in tough, fibrous, or disordered quality ⟨~ meat⟩ ⟨~ hair⟩ **2** : lean and sinewy in build

¹**strip** \ˈstrip\ *vb* **stripped** \ˈstript\ *also* **stript; strip·ping** **1** : to take the covering or clothing from **2** : to take off one's clothes **3** : to pull or tear off **4** : to make bare or clear (as by cutting or grazing) **5** : PLUNDER, PILLAGE ✦ *Synonyms* DIVEST, DENUDE, DEPRIVE, DISMANTLE — **strip·per** *n*

²**strip** *n* **1** : a long narrow flat piece **2** : AIRSTRIP

¹**stripe** \ˈstrīp\ *vb* **striped** \ˈstrīpt\; **strip·ing** : to make stripes on

²**stripe** *n* **1** : a line or long narrow division having a different color from the background **2** : a strip of braid (as on a sleeve) indicating military rank or length of service **3** : TYPE, CHARACTER — **striped** \ˈstrīpt, ˈstrī-pəd\ *adj*

striped bass *n* : a large black-striped marine bony fish that occurs along the Atlantic and Pacific coasts of the U.S. and is an excellent food and sport fish

strip·ling \ˈstri-pliŋ\ *n* : YOUTH, LAD

strip mall *n* : a long building or group of buildings housing several retail stores or service establishments

strip mine *n* : a mine that is worked from the earth's surface by the stripping of the topsoil — **strip–mine** *vb*

strip·tease \ˈstrip-ˌtēz\ *n* : a burlesque act in which a performer removes clothing piece by piece — **strip·teas·er** *n*

strive \ˈstrīv\ *vb* **strove** \ˈstrōv\ *also* **strived** \ˈstrīvd\; **striv·en** \ˈstri-vən\ *or* **strived; striv·ing** **1** : to make effort : labor hard **2** : to struggle in opposition : CONTEND ✦ *Synonyms* ENDEAVOR, ATTEMPT, TRY, ASSAY

strobe \ˈstrōb\ *n* **1** : STROBOSCOPE **2** : a device for high-speed intermittent illumination (as in photography)

stro·bo·scope \ˈstrō-bə-ˌskōp\ *n* : an instrument for studying rapid motion by means of a rapidly flashing light

strode *past of* STRIDE

¹**stroke** \ˈstrōk\ *vb* **stroked; strok·ing** **1** : to rub gently **2** : to flatter in a manner designed to persuade

²**stroke** *n* **1** : the act of striking : BLOW, KNOCK **2** : a sud-

den action or process producing an impact ⟨~ of lightning⟩; *also* : an unexpected result **3** : sudden weakening or loss of consciousness or the power to move or feel caused by rupture or obstruction (as by a clot) of a blood vessel of the brain **4** : one of a series of movements against air or water to get through or over it ⟨the ~ of a bird's wing⟩ **5** : a rower who sets the pace for a crew **6** : a vigorous effort **7** : the sound of striking (as of a clock) **8** : a single movement with or as if with a tool or implement (as a pen)

stroll \ˈstrōl\ *vb* : to walk in a leisurely or idle manner — **stroll** *n* — **stroll·er** *n*

strong \ˈstrȯŋ\ *adj* **stron·ger** \ˈstrȯŋ-gər\; **stron·gest** \ˈstrȯŋ-gəst\ **1** : POWERFUL, VIGOROUS **2** : HEALTHY, ROBUST **3** : of a specified number ⟨an army 10 thousand ~⟩ **4** : not mild or weak **5** : VIOLENT ⟨~ wind⟩ **6** : ZEALOUS ⟨a ~ supporter⟩ **7** : not easily broken **8** : FIRM, SOLID ⟨~ beliefs⟩ ✦ *Synonyms* STOUT, STURDY, STALWART, TOUGH — **strong·ly** *adv*

strong–arm \ˈstrȯŋ-ˌärm\ *adj* : having or using undue force ⟨~ operatives⟩

strong force *n* : the physical force responsible for binding together nucleons in the atomic nucleus

strong·hold \-ˌhōld\ *n* : a fortified place : FORTRESS

strong·man \-ˌman\ *n* : one who leads or controls by force of will and character or by military strength

stron·tium \ˈsträn-chē-əm, ˈsträn-tē-əm\ *n* : a soft malleable metallic chemical element

¹**strop** \ˈsträp\ *n* : STRAP; *esp* : one for sharpening a razor

²**strop** *vb* **stropped; strop·ping** : to sharpen a razor on a strop

stro·phe \ˈstrō-fē\ *n* [Gk *strophē*, lit., act of turning] : a division of a poem — **stroph·ic** \ˈsträ-fik\ *adj*

strove *past of* STRIVE

struck *past and past part of* STRIKE

¹**struc·ture** \ˈstrək-chər\ *n* [ME, fr. L *structura*, fr. *structus*, pp. of *struere* to heap up, build] **1** : the action of building : CONSTRUCTION **2** : something built (as a house or a dam); *also* : something made up of interdependent parts in a definite pattern of organization **3** : arrangement or relationship of elements (as particles, parts, or organs) in a substance, body, or system — **struc·tur·al** *adj*

²**structure** *vb* **struc·tured; struc·tur·ing** : to make into a structure

stru·del \ˈstrü-dᵊl, ˈshtrü-\ *n* [G, lit., whirlpool] : a pastry made of a thin sheet of dough rolled up with filling and baked ⟨apple ~⟩

¹**strug·gle** \ˈstrə-gəl\ *vb* **strug·gled; strug·gling** **1** : to make strenuous efforts against opposition : STRIVE **2** : to proceed with difficulty or with great effort ✦ *Synonyms* ENDEAVOR, ATTEMPT, TRY, ASSAY

²**struggle** *n* **1** : CONTEST, STRIFE **2** : a violent effort or exertion

strum \ˈstrəm\ *vb* **strummed; strum·ming** : to play on a stringed instrument by brushing the strings with the fingers ⟨~ a guitar⟩

strum·pet \ˈstrəm-pət\ *n* : PROSTITUTE

strung \ˈstrəŋ\ *past and past part of* STRING

¹**strut** \ˈstrət\ *vb* **strut·ted; strut·ting** : to walk with an affectedly proud gait

²**strut** *n* **1** : a bar or rod for resisting lengthwise pressure **2** : a haughty or pompous gait

strych·nine \ˈstrik-ˌnīn, -nən, -ˌnēn\ *n* : a bitter poisonous plant alkaloid used as a poison (as for rats) and medicinally as a stimulant of the central nervous system

¹**stub** \ˈstəb\ *n* **1** : STUMP 2 **2** : a short blunt end **3** : a small part of each leaf (as of a checkbook) kept as a memorandum of the items on the detached part

²**stub** *vb* **stubbed; stub·bing** : to strike (as one's toe) against something

stub·ble \ˈstə-bəl\ *n* **1** : the cut stem ends of herbs and esp. grasses left in the soil after harvest **2** : a rough surface or growth resembling stubble — **stub·bly** \-b(ə-)lē\ *adj*

stub·born \ˈstə-bərn\ *adj* **1** : FIRM, DETERMINED **2** : done or continued in a willful, unreasonable, or persistent manner **3** : not easily controlled or remedied ⟨a ~ cold⟩ — **stub·born·ly** *adv* — **stub·born·ness** *n*

stub·by \ˈstə-bē\ *adj* : short, blunt, and thick like a stub

stuc·co \ˈstə-kō\ *n, pl* **stuccos** *or* **stuccoes** [It] : plaster for coating exterior walls — **stuc·coed** \ˈstə-kōd\ *adj*

stuck *past and past part of* STICK

stuck–up \'stək-'əp\ *adj* : CONCEITED

¹stud \'stəd\ *n* : a male animal and esp. a horse (**stud·horse** \-ˌhȯrs\) kept for breeding

²stud *n* **1** : one of the smaller uprights in a building to which the wall materials are fastened **2** : a removable device like a button used as a fastener or ornament ⟨shirt ∼*s*⟩ **3** : a projecting nail, pin, or rod

³stud *vb* **stud·ded**; **stud·ding 1** : to supply with or adorn with studs **2** : DOT ⟨the sky was *studded* with stars⟩

⁴stud *abbr* student

stud·book \'stəd-ˌbu̇k\ *n* : an official record of the pedigree of purebred animals (as horses or dogs)

studding *n* : the studs in a building or wall

stu·dent \'stü-dᵊnt, 'styü-\ *n* : SCHOLAR, PUPIL; *esp* : one who attends a school

stud·ied \'stə-dēd\ *adj* : INTENTIONAL ⟨a ∼ insult⟩ ✦ **Synonyms** DELIBERATE, CONSIDERED, PREMEDITATED, DESIGNED

stu·dio \'stü-dē-ˌō, 'styü-\ *n, pl* **-dios 1** : a place where an artist works; *also* : a place for the study of an art **2** : a place where motion pictures are made **3** : a place equipped for the transmission of radio or television programs

stu·di·ous \'stü-dē-əs, 'styü-\ *adj* : devoted to study — **stu·di·ous·ly** *adv*

¹study \'stə-dē\ *n, pl* **stud·ies 1** : the use of the mind to gain knowledge **2** : the act or process of learning about something **3** : careful examination **4** : INTENT, PURPOSE **5** : a branch of learning **6** : a room esp. for reading and writing

²study *vb* **stud·ied**; **study·ing 1** : to engage in study or the study of **2** : to consider attentively or in detail ✦ **Synonyms** CONSIDER, CONTEMPLATE, WEIGH

¹stuff \'stəf\ *n* [ME, fr. AF *estuffes* goods, fr. *estuffer* to fill in (with rubble), furnish, equip, of Gmc origin] **1** : personal property **2** : raw material **3** : a finished textile fabric; *esp* : a worsted fabric **4** : writing, talk, or ideas of little or transitory worth **5** : an unspecified material substance or aggregate of matter **6** : fundamental material **7** : special knowledge or capability

²stuff *vb* **1** : to fill by packing things in : CRAM **2** : to eat greedily : GORGE **3** : to prepare (as meat) by filling with a stuffing **4** : to fill (as a cushion) with a soft material **5** : to stop up : PLUG

stuffed shirt \'stəft-\ *n* : a smug, conceited, and usu. pompous and inflexibly conservative person

stuff·ing *n* : material used to fill tightly; *esp* : a mixture of bread crumbs and spices used to stuff food

stuffy \'stə-fē\ *adj* **stuff·i·er**; **-est 1** : STODGY **2** : lacking fresh air : CLOSE; *also* : blocked up ⟨a ∼ nose⟩

stul·ti·fy \'stəl-tə-ˌfī\ *vb* **-fied**; **-fy·ing 1** : to cause to appear foolish or stupid **2** : to impair, invalidate, or make ineffective **3** : to have a dulling effect on — **stul·ti·fi·ca·tion** \ˌstəl-tə-fə-'kā-shən\ *n*

stum·ble \'stəm-bəl\ *vb* **stum·bled**; **stum·bling 1** : to blunder morally **2** : to trip in walking or running **3** : to walk unsteadily; *also* : to speak or act in a blundering or clumsy manner **4** : to happen by chance — **stumble** *n*

stumbling block *n* : an obstacle to belief, understanding, or progress

¹stump \'stəmp\ *n* **1** : the base of a bodily part (as a leg or tooth) left after the rest is removed **2** : the part of a plant and esp. a tree remaining with the root after the trunk is cut off **3** : a place or occasion for political public speaking — **stumpy** *adj*

²stump *vb* **1** : BAFFLE, PERPLEX **2** : to clear (land) of stumps **3** : to tour (a region) making political speeches **4** : to walk clumsily and heavily

stun \'stən\ *vb* **stunned**; **stun·ning 1** : to make senseless or dizzy by or as if by a blow **2** : BEWILDER, STUPEFY ⟨*stunned* by the news⟩

stung *past and past part of* STING

stunk *past and past part of* STINK

stun·ning *adj* **1** : causing astonishment or disbelief **2** : strikingly beautiful — **stun·ning·ly** *adv*

¹stunt \'stənt\ *vb* : to hinder the normal growth or progress of

²stunt *n* : an unusual or spectacular feat

stu·pe·fy \'stü-pə-ˌfī, 'styü-\ *vb* **-fied**; **-fy·ing 1** : to make stupid, groggy, or insensible **2** : ASTONISH — **stu·pe·fac·tion** \ˌstü-pə-'fak-shən, ˌstyü-\ *n*

stu·pen·dous \stu̇-'pen-dəs, styü-\ *adj* : causing astonishment esp. because of great size or height ✦ **Synonyms** TREMENDOUS, PRODIGIOUS, MONUMENTAL, MONSTROUS — **stu·pen·dous·ly** *adv*

stu·pid \'stü-pəd, 'styü-\ *adj* [MF *stupide*, fr. L *stupidus*, fr. *stupēre* to be numb, be astonished] **1** : very dull in mind **2** : showing or resulting from dullness of mind — **stu·pid·i·ty** \stu̇-'pi-də-tē, styü-\ *n* — **stu·pid·ly** *adv*

stu·por \'stü-pər, 'styü-\ *n* **1** : a condition of greatly dulled or completely suspended sense or feeling **2** : a state of extreme apathy or torpor often following stress or shock — **stu·por·ous** *adj*

stur·dy \'stər-dē\ *adj* **stur·di·er**; **-est** [ME, brave, stubborn, fr. AF *esturdi* stunned, fr. pp. of *esturdir* to stun, fr. VL *exturdire, fr. L *ex-* + VL *turdus simpleton, fr. L *turdus* thrush] **1** : STRONG, ROBUST **2** : RESOLUTE, UNYIELDING ✦ **Synonyms** STOUT, STALWART, TOUGH, TENACIOUS — **stur·di·ly** \-də-lē\ *adv* — **stur·di·ness** \-dē-nəs\ *n*

stur·geon \'stər-jən\ *n* : any of a family of large bony fishes including some whose roe are made into caviar

stut·ter \'stə-tər\ *vb* : to speak with involuntary disruption or blocking of sounds — **stutter** *n* — **stut·ter·er** *n*

stutter step *n* : a move made by a runner (as in football) done to fake a defender out of position

¹sty \'stī\ *n, pl* **sties** : PIGPEN

²sty *or* **stye** *n, pl* **sties** *or* **styes** : an inflamed swelling of a skin gland on the edge of an eyelid

¹style \'stī(-ə)l\ *n* **1** : mode of address : TITLE **2** : a way of speaking or writing; *esp* : one characteristic of an individual, period, school, or nation ⟨ornate ∼⟩ **3** : manner or method of acting, making, or performing; *also* : a distinctive or characteristic manner **4** : a slender pointed instrument or process; *esp* : STYLUS **5** : a fashionable manner or mode **6** : overall excellence, skill, or grace in performance, manner, or appearance **7** : the custom followed in spelling, capitalization, punctuation, and typography — **sty·lis·tic** \stī-'lis-tik\ *adj*

²style *vb* **styled**; **styl·ing 1** : NAME, DESIGNATE **2** : to make or design in accord with a prevailing mode

styling *n* : the way in which something is styled

styl·ise *Brit var of* STYLIZE

styl·ish \'stī-lish\ *adj* : conforming to current fashion ✦ **Synonyms** MODISH, SMART, CHIC — **styl·ish·ly** *adv* — **styl·ish·ness** *n*

styl·ist \'stī-list\ *n* **1** : one (as a writer) noted for a distinctive style **2** : a developer or designer of styles

styl·ize \'stī-ˌlīz, 'stī-ə-\ *vb* **styl·ized**; **styl·iz·ing** : to conform to a style; *esp* : to represent or design according to a pattern or style rather than according to nature or tradition — **styl·i·za·tion** \ˌstī-lə-'zā-shən\ *n*

sty·lus \'stī-ləs\ *n, pl* **sty·li** \'stī-ˌlī\ *also* **sty·lus·es** \'stī-lə-səz\ [L *stylus, stilus* spike, stylus] **1** : a pointed implement used by the ancients for writing on wax **2** : a phonograph needle **3** : a pen-shaped pointing device for entering data into a computer

sty·mie \'stī-mē\ *vb* **sty·mied**; **sty·mie·ing** : BLOCK, FRUSTRATE ⟨managed to ∼ opposition⟩

styp·tic \'stip-tik\ *adj* : tending to check bleeding — **styptic** *n*

suave \'swäv\ *adj* [F, fr. MF, pleasant, sweet, fr. L *suavis*] : persuasively pleasing : smoothly agreeable ✦ **Synonyms** URBANE, SMOOTH, BLAND — **suave·ly** *adv* — **suav·i·ty** \'swä-və-tē\ *n*

¹sub \'səb\ *n* : SUBSTITUTE — **sub** *vb*

²sub *n* : SUBMARINE

³sub *abbr* **1** subtract **2** suburb

sub- \'səb\ *prefix* **1** : under : beneath **2** : subordinate : secondary **3** : subordinate portion of : subdivision of **4** : with repetition of a process described in a simple verb so as to form, stress, or deal with subordinate parts or relations **5** : somewhat **6** : falling nearly in the category of : bordering on

subacute	subatmospheric
subagency	subaverage
subagent	subbasement
subaqueous	subcategory
subarctic	subcellular
subarea	subchapter

subclass
subclassify
subcommittee
subcontract
subcontractor
subculture
subcutaneous
subdiscipline
subentry
subfamily
subfield
subfreezing
subgenre
subgenus
subgroup
subhead
subheading
subhuman
subkingdom
sublethal
subliterate
subminimal
subminimum
suboptimal
suborder
subparagraph

subparallel
subphylum
subplot
subpopulation
subproblem
subprofessional
subprogram
subregion
subroutine
subsection
subsense
subsoil
substage
substation
subsystem
subteen
subthreshold
subtopic
subtotal
subtreasury
subtype
subunit
subvariety
subvisible
subzero

sub·al·pine \ˌsəb-ˈal-ˌpīn\ *adj* **1** : of or relating to the region about the foot and lower slopes of the Alps **2** : of, relating to, or inhabiting high upland slopes esp. just below the timberline

sub·al·tern \sə-ˈbȯl-tərn\ *n* : SUBORDINATE; *esp* : a junior officer (as in the British army)

sub·as·sem·bly \ˌsəb-ə-ˈsem-blē\ *n* : an assembled unit to be incorporated with other units in a finished product

sub·atom·ic \ˌsəb-ə-ˈtä-mik\ *adj* : of or relating to the inside of the atom or to particles smaller than atoms

sub·clin·i·cal \ˌsəb-ˈkli-nə-kəl\ *adj* : not detectable by the usual clinical tests ⟨a ∼ infection⟩

sub·com·pact \ˈsəb-ˈkäm-ˌpakt\ *n* : an automobile smaller than a compact

¹sub·con·scious \ˌsəb-ˈkän-chəs, ˈsəb-\ *adj* : existing in the mind without entering conscious awareness — **sub·con·scious·ly** *adv* — **sub·con·scious·ness** *n*

²subconscious *n* : mental activities just below the threshold of consciousness

sub·con·ti·nent \ˌsəb-ˈkän-tə-nənt\ *n* : a major subdivision of a continent — **sub·con·ti·nen·tal** \ˌsəb-ˌkän-tə-ˈnen-tᵊl\ *adj*

sub·di·vide \ˌsəb-də-ˈvīd, ˈsəb-də-ˌvīd\ *vb* : to divide the parts of into more parts; *esp* : to divide (a tract of land) into building lots — **sub·di·vi·sion** \-ˈvi-zhən, -ˌvi-\ *n*

sub·duc·tion \səb-ˈdək-shən\ *n* : the descent of the edge of one crustal plate beneath the edge of an adjacent plate

sub·due \səb-ˈdü, -ˈdyü\ *vb* **sub·dued; sub·du·ing** **1** : to bring into subjection : VANQUISH **2** : to bring under control : CURB **3** : to reduce the intensity of

subj *abbr* **1** subject **2** subjunctive

¹sub·ject \ˈsəb-jikt\ *n* [ME *suget, subget,* fr. AF, fr. L *subjectus* one under authority & *subjectum* subject of a proposition, fr. *subicere* to subject, lit., to throw under, fr. *sub-* under + *jacere* to throw] **1** : a person under the authority of another **2** : a person subject to a sovereign **3** : an individual that is studied or experimented on **4** : the person or thing discussed or treated : TOPIC, THEME **5** : a word or word group denoting that of which something is predicated

²subject *adj* **1** : being under the power or rule of another **2** : LIABLE, EXPOSED ⟨∼ to floods⟩ **3** : dependent on some act or condition ⟨appointment ∼ to senate approval⟩ **♦ Synonyms** SUBORDINATE, SECONDARY, TRIBUTARY, COLLATERAL, DEPENDENT

³sub·ject \səb-ˈjekt\ *vb* **1** : to bring under control : CONQUER **2** : to make liable **3** : to cause to undergo or endure — **sub·jec·tion** \-ˈjek-shən\ *n*

sub·jec·tive \ˌ(ˌ)səb-ˈjek-tiv\ *adj* : of, relating to, or constituting a subject **2** : of, relating to, or arising within one's self or mind in contrast to what is outside : PERSONAL ⟨∼ judgments⟩ ⟨a ∼ sensation⟩ — **sub·jec·tive·ly** *adv* — **sub·jec·tiv·i·ty** \-ˌjek-ˈti-və-tē\ *n*

subject matter *n* : matter presented for consideration, discussion, or study

sub·join \(ˌ)səb-ˈjȯin\ *vb* : APPEND ⟨∼ed a statement of expenses to her report⟩

sub ju·di·ce \(ˌ)süb-ˈyü-di-ˌkā, ˌsəb-ˈjü-də-(ˌ)sē\ *adv* [L] : before a judge or court : not yet legally decided

sub·ju·gate \ˈsəb-ji-ˌgāt\ *vb* **-gat·ed; -gat·ing** : CONQUER, SUBDUE; *also* : ENSLAVE **♦ Synonyms** REDUCE, OVERCOME, OVERTHROW, VANQUISH, DEFEAT, BEAT — **sub·ju·ga·tion** \ˌsəb-ji-ˈgā-shən\ *n*

sub·junc·tive \səb-ˈjəŋk-tiv\ *adj* : of, relating to, or constituting a verb form that represents an act or state as contingent or possible or viewed emotionally (as with desire) ⟨the ∼ mood⟩ — **subjunctive** *n*

sub·lease \ˈsəb-ˈlēs, -ˌlēs\ *n* : a lease by a lessee of part or all of leased premises to another person with the original lessee retaining some right under the original lease — **sublease** *vb*

¹sub·let \ˈsəb-ˈlet\ *vb* **-let; -let·ting** : to let all or a part of (a leased property) to another; *also* : to rent (a property) from a lessee

²sublet \-ˌlet\ *n* : property and esp. housing obtained by or available through a sublease

sub·li·mate \ˈsə-blə-ˌmāt\ *vb* **-mat·ed; -mat·ing** **1** : SUBLIME **2** : to direct the expression of (as a desire or impulse) from a primitive to a more socially and culturally acceptable form — **sub·li·ma·tion** \ˌsə-blə-ˈmā-shən\ *n*

¹sub·lime \sə-ˈblīm\ *vb* **sub·limed; sub·lim·ing** : to pass or cause to pass directly from the solid to the vapor state

²sublime *adj* **1** : EXALTED, NOBLE **2** : having awe-inspiring beauty or grandeur **♦ Synonyms** GLORIOUS, SPLENDID, SUPERB, RESPLENDENT, GORGEOUS — **sub·lime·ly** *adv* — **sub·lim·i·ty** \-ˈbli-mə-tē\ *n*

sub·lim·i·nal \(ˌ)səb-ˈli-mə-nᵊl, ˈsəb-\ *adj* [*sub-* + L *limin-, limen* threshold] **1** : inadequate to produce a sensation or mental awareness ⟨∼ stimuli⟩ **2** : existing or functioning below the threshold of consciousness ⟨the ∼ mind⟩ ⟨∼ advertising⟩

sub·ma·chine gun \ˌsəb-mə-ˈshēn-ˌgən\ *n* : an automatic firearm fired from the shoulder or hip

¹sub·ma·rine \ˈsəb-mə-ˌrēn, ˌsəb-mə-ˈrēn\ *adj* : UNDERWATER; *esp* : UNDERSEA

²submarine *n* **1** : a naval vessel designed to operate underwater **2** : a large sandwich made from a long split roll with any of a variety of fillings

sub·merge \səb-ˈmərj\ *vb* **sub·merged; sub·merg·ing** **1** : to put or plunge under the surface of water **2** : INUNDATE — **sub·mer·gence** \-ˈmər-jəns\ *n*

sub·merse \səb-ˈmərs\ *vb* **sub·mersed; sub·mers·ing** : SUBMERGE — **sub·mer·sion** \-ˈmər-zhən\ *n*

¹sub·mers·ible \səb-ˈmər-sə-bəl\ *adj* : capable of being submerged

²submersible *n* : something that is submersible; *esp* : a small underwater craft used for deep-sea research

sub·mi·cro·scop·ic \ˌsəb-ˌmī-krə-ˈskä-pik\ *adj* : too small to be seen in an ordinary light microscope

sub·min·ia·ture \ˌsəb-ˈmi-nē-ə-ˌchu̇r, ˈsəb-, -ˈmi-ni-ˌchu̇r, -chər\ *adj* : very small

sub·mit \səb-ˈmit\ *vb* **sub·mit·ted; sub·mit·ting** **1** : to commit to the discretion or decision of another or of others **2** : YIELD, SURRENDER **3** : to put forward as an opinion — **sub·mis·sion** \-ˈmi-shən\ *n* — **sub·mis·sive** \-ˈmi-siv\ *adj*

sub·nor·mal \ˌsəb-ˈnȯr-məl\ *adj* : falling below what is normal; *also* : having less of something and esp. intelligence than is normal — **sub·nor·mal·i·ty** \ˌsəb-nȯr-ˈma-lə-tē\ *n*

sub·or·bit·al \ˌsəb-ˈȯr-bə-tᵊl, ˈsəb-\ *adj* : being or involving less than one orbit

¹sub·or·di·nate \sə-ˈbȯr-də-nət\ *adj* **1** : of lower class or rank ⟨a ∼ officer⟩ **2** : INFERIOR **3** : submissive to authority **4** : subordinated to other elements in a sentence : DEPENDENT ⟨∼ clause⟩ **♦ Synonyms** SECONDARY, SUBJECT, TRIBUTARY, COLLATERAL

²subordinate *n* : one that is subordinate

³sub·or·di·nate \sə-ˈbȯr-də-ˌnāt\ *vb* **-nat·ed; -nat·ing** **1** : SUBDUE **2** : to place in a lower rank or class — **sub·or·di·na·tion** \-ˌbȯr-də-ˈnā-shən\ *n*

sub·orn \sə-ˈbȯrn\ *vb* **1** : to induce secretly to do an unlawful thing **2** : to induce to commit perjury — **sub·or·na·tion** \ˌsə-ˌbȯr-ˈnā-shən\ *n*

¹sub·poe·na \sə-ˈpē-nə\ *n* [ME *suppena,* fr. L *sub poena* under penalty] : a writ commanding the person named in it to attend court under penalty for failure to do so

²**subpoena** *vb* **-naed; -na·ing** : to summon with a subpoena

sub–Sa·ha·ran \ˌsəb-sə-ˈher-ən\ *adj* : of, relating to, or being the part of Africa south of the Sahara

sub·scribe \səb-ˈskrīb\ *vb* **sub·scribed; sub·scrib·ing** **1** : to sign one's name to a document **2** : to give consent by or as if by signing one's name **3** : to promise to contribute by signing one's name with the amount promised **4** : to place an order by signing **5** : to receive a periodical or service regularly on order **6** : FAVOR, APPROVE ◆ *Synonyms* AGREE, ACQUIESCE, ASSENT, ACCEDE — **sub·scrib·er** *n*

sub·script \ˈsəb-ˌskript\ *n* : a symbol (as a letter or number) immediately below or below and to the right or left of another written character — **subscript** *adj*

sub·scrip·tion \səb-ˈskrip-shən\ *n* **1** : the act of subscribing : SIGNATURE **2** : a purchase by signed order

sub·se·quent \ˈsəb-si-kwənt, -sə-ˌkwent\ *adj* : following after : SUCCEEDING ⟨∼ events⟩ — **sub·se·quent·ly** *adv*

sub·ser·vi·ence \səb-ˈsər-vē-əns\ *n* **1** : a subordinate place or condition **2** : SERVILITY — **sub·ser·vi·en·cy** \-ən-sē\ *n* — **sub·ser·vi·ent** \-ənt\ *adj*

sub·set \ˈsəb-ˌset\ *n* : a set each of whose elements is an element of an inclusive set

sub·side \səb-ˈsīd\ *vb* **sub·sid·ed; sub·sid·ing** [L *subsidere*, fr. *sub-* under + *sidere* to sit down, sink] **1** : to settle to the bottom of a liquid **2** : to tend downward : DESCEND **3** : SINK, SUBMERGE ⟨*subsided* into a chair⟩ **4** : to become quiet and tranquil ◆ *Synonyms* ABATE, WANE, MODERATE, SLACKEN — **sub·sid·ence** \səb-ˈsīd⁰ns, ˈsəb-sə-dəns\ *n*

¹**sub·sid·iary** \səb-ˈsi-dē-ˌer-ē\ *adj* **1** : furnishing aid or support **2** : of secondary importance **3** : of or relating to a subsidy ◆ *Synonyms* AUXILIARY, CONTRIBUTORY, SUBSERVIENT, ACCESSORY

²**subsidiary** *n, pl* **-iar·ies** : one that is subsidiary; *esp* : a company controlled by another

sub·si·dise *Brit var of* SUBSIDIZE

sub·si·dize \ˈsəb-sə-ˌdīz\ *vb* **-dized; -diz·ing** : to aid or furnish with a subsidy

sub·si·dy \ˈsəb-sə-dē\ *n, pl* **-dies** [ME, *subsidie*, fr. AF, fr. L *subsidium* reserve troops, support, assistance, fr. *sub-* near + *sedēre* to sit] : a gift of public money to a private person or company or to another government

sub·sist \səb-ˈsist\ *vb* **1** : EXIST, PERSIST **2** : to have the means (as food and clothing) of maintaining life; *esp* : to nourish oneself

sub·sis·tence \səb-ˈsis-təns\ *n* **1** : EXISTENCE **2** : means of subsisting : the minimum (as of food and clothing) necessary to support life

sub·son·ic \ˌsəb-ˈsä-nik, ˈsəb-\ *adj* : being or relating to a speed less than that of sound; *also* : moving at such a speed

sub·species \ˈsəb-ˌspē-shēz, -sēz\ *n* : a subdivision of a species; *esp* : a category in biological classification ranking just below a species that designates a geographic population genetically distinct from other such populations and potentially able to breed with them where its range overlaps theirs

sub·stance \ˈsəb-stəns\ *n* **1** : essential nature : ESSENCE ⟨divine ∼⟩; *also* : the fundamental or essential part or quality ⟨the ∼ of the speech⟩ **2** : physical material from which something is made or which has discrete existence; *also* : matter of particular or definite chemical constitution **3** : something (as drugs or alcohol) deemed harmful and usu. subject to legal restriction ⟨∼ abuse⟩ **4** : material possessions : PROPERTY, WEALTH

sub·stan·dard \ˌsəb-ˈstan-dərd\ *adj* : falling short of a standard or norm

sub·stan·tial \səb-ˈstan-chəl\ *adj* **1** : existing as or in substance : MATERIAL; *also* : not illusory : REAL **2** : IMPORTANT, ESSENTIAL ⟨a ∼ difference in the stories⟩ **3** : NOURISHING, SATISFYING ⟨∼ meal⟩ **4** : having means : WELL-TO-DO **5** : CONSIDERABLE ⟨∼ profit⟩ **6** : STRONG, FIRM — **sub·stan·tial·ly** *adv*

sub·stan·ti·ate \səb-ˈstan-chē-ˌāt\ *vb* **-at·ed; -at·ing** **1** : to give substance or body to **2** : VERIFY, PROVE ⟨∼ a charge⟩ — **sub·stan·ti·a·tion** \-ˌstan-chē-ˈā-shən\ *n*

sub·stan·tive \ˈsəb-stən-tiv\ *n* : NOUN; *also* : a word or phrase used as a noun

¹**sub·sti·tute** \ˈsəb-stə-ˌtüt, -ˌtyüt\ *n* : a person or thing replacing another — **substitute** *adj*

²**substitute** *vb* **-tut·ed; -tut·ing** **1** : to put or use in the place of another **2** : to serve as a substitute — **sub·sti·tu·tion** \ˌsəb-stə-ˈtü-shən, -ˈtyü-\ *n*

sub·strate \ˈsəb-ˌstrāt\ *n* **1** : the base on which a plant or animal lives **2** : a substance acted upon (as by an enzyme)

sub·stra·tum \ˈsəb-ˌstrā-təm, -ˌstra-\ *n, pl* **-stra·ta** \-tə\ : the layer or structure (as subsoil) lying underneath

sub·struc·ture \ˈsəb-ˌstrək-chər\ *n* : FOUNDATION, GROUNDWORK

sub·sume \səb-ˈsüm\ *vb* **sub·sumed; sub·sum·ing** : to include or place within something larger or more comprehensive

sub·sur·face \ˈsəb-ˌsər-fəs\ *n* : earth material near the surface of the ground — **subsurface** *adj*

sub·ter·fuge \ˈsəb-tər-ˌfyüj\ *n* : a trick or device used in order to conceal, escape, or evade ◆ *Synonyms* FRAUD, DECEPTION, TRICKERY

sub·ter·ra·nean \ˌsəb-tə-ˈrā-nē-ən\ *adj* **1** : lying or being underground **2** : SECRET, HIDDEN ⟨a ∼ network of criminals⟩

sub·tile \ˈsə-t⁰l\ *adj* **sub·til·er** \ˈsə-t⁰l-ər\; **sub·til·est** \ˈsə-t⁰l-əst\ : SUBTLE ⟨a ∼ aroma⟩

sub·ti·tle \ˈsəb-ˌtī-t⁰l\ *n* **1** : a secondary or explanatory title (as of a book) **2** : printed matter projected on a motion-picture screen during or between the scenes

sub·tle \ˈsə-t⁰l\ *adj* **sub·tler** \ˈsə-t⁰l-ər\; **sub·tlest** \ˈsə-t⁰l-əst\ **1** : hardly noticeable ⟨∼ differences⟩ **2** : SHREWD, PERCEPTIVE ⟨a ∼ mind⟩ **3** : CLEVER, SLY ⟨a ∼ rogue⟩ — **sub·tle·ty** \-tē\ *n* — **sub·tly** \ˈsə-t⁰l-ē\ *adv*

sub·tract \səb-ˈtrakt\ *vb* : to take away (as one part or number) from another; *also* : to perform the operation of deducting one number from another — **sub·trac·tion** \-ˈtrak-shən\ *n*

sub·tra·hend \ˈsəb-trə-ˌhend\ *n* : a number that is to be subtracted from another

sub·trop·i·cal \ˌsəb-ˈträ-pi-kəl, ˈsəb-\ *also* **sub·trop·ic** \-pik\ *adj* : of, relating to, or being regions bordering on the tropical zone ⟨a ∼ environment⟩ — **sub·trop·ics** \-piks\ *n pl*

sub·urb \ˈsə-ˌbərb\ *n* **1** : an outlying part of a city; *also* : a small community adjacent to a city **2** *pl* : a residential area adjacent to a city — **sub·ur·ban** \sə-ˈbər-bən\ *adj or n* — **sub·ur·ban·ite** \sə-ˈbər-bə-ˌnīt\ *n*

sub·ur·bia \sə-ˈbər-bē-ə\ *n* **1** : SUBURBS **2** : suburban people or customs

sub·ven·tion \səb-ˈven-chən\ *n* : SUBSIDY, ENDOWMENT

sub·vert \səb-ˈvərt\ *vb* **1** : OVERTHROW, RUIN **2** : CORRUPT — **sub·ver·sion** \-ˈvər-zhən\ *n* — **sub·ver·sive** \-ˈvər-siv\ *adj*

sub·way \ˈsəb-ˌwā\ *n* : an underground way; *esp* : an underground electric railway

sub·woof·er \ˈsəb-ˈwu̇-fər\ *n* : a loudspeaker responsive only to the lowest acoustic frequencies

suc·ceed \sək-ˈsēd\ *vb* **1** : to follow next in order or next after another; *esp* : to inherit sovereignty, rank, title, or property **2** : to attain a desired object or end : be successful

suc·cess \sək-ˈses\ *n* **1** : favorable or desired outcome **2** : the gaining of wealth and fame **3** : one that succeeds — **suc·cess·ful** \-fəl\ *adj* — **suc·cess·ful·ly** *adv*

suc·ces·sion \sək-ˈse-shən\ *n* **1** : the order, act, or right of succeeding to a property, title, or throne **2** : the act or process of following in order **3** : a series of persons or things that follow one after another ◆ *Synonyms* PROGRESSION, SEQUENCE, CHAIN, TRAIN, STRING

suc·ces·sive \sək-ˈse-siv\ *adj* : following in order : CONSECUTIVE — **suc·ces·sive·ly** *adv*

suc·ces·sor \sək-ˈse-sər\ *n* : one that succeeds (as to a throne, title, estate, or office)

suc·cinct \(ˌ)sək-ˈsiŋkt, sə-ˈsiŋkt\ *adj* : BRIEF, CONCISE ⟨a ∼ description⟩ ◆ *Synonyms* TERSE, LACONIC, SUMMARY, CURT, SHORT — **suc·cinct·ly** *adv* — **suc·cinct·ness** *n*

suc·cor \ˈsə-kər\ *n* [ME *socour, sucurs* (taken as pl.), fr. AF *sucur, sucors*, fr. ML *succursus*, fr. L *succurrere* to run to the rescue, bring aid] : AID, HELP, RELIEF — **succor** *vb*

suc·co·tash \ˈsə-kə-ˌtash\ *n* [Narragansett *msíckquatash* boiled corn kernels] : beans and corn kernels cooked together

suc·cour *chiefly Brit var of* SUCCOR

¹**suc·cu·lent** \ˈsə-kyə-lənt\ *adj* : full of juice : JUICY; *also* : having fleshy tissues that conserve moisture ⟨∼ plants⟩ — **suc·cu·lence** \-ləns\ *n*

²**suc·cu·lent** *n* : a succulent plant (as a cactus or an aloe)

suc·cumb \sə-'kəm\ *vb* **1** : to yield to superior strength or force or overpowering appeal or desire **2** : DIE ✦ **Synonyms** SUBMIT, CAPITULATE, RELENT, DEFER

¹**such** \'səch, 'sich\ *adj* **1** : of this or that kind **2** : having a quality just specified or to be specified

²**such** *pron* **1** : such a one or ones ⟨he's a star, and acted as ∼⟩ **2** : that or those similar or related thereto ⟨boards and nails and ∼⟩

³**such** *adv* : to that degree : so

such·like \'səch-‚līk\ *adj* : SIMILAR

¹**suck** \'sək\ *vb* **1** : to draw in liquid and esp. mother's milk with the mouth **2** : to draw liquid from by action of the mouth ⟨∼ an orange⟩ **3** : to take in or up or remove by or as if by suction **4** *slang* : to be objectionable

²**suck** *n* **1** : a sucking movement or force **2** : the act of sucking

suck·er \'sə-kər\ *n* **1** : one that sucks **2** : a part of an animal's body used for sucking or for clinging **3** : any of numerous freshwater fishes with thick soft lips for sucking in food **4** : a shoot from the roots or lower part of a plant **5** : a person easily deceived **6** — used as a generalized term of reference ⟨see if you can get that ∼ working again⟩

suck·le \'sə-kəl\ *vb* **suck·led; suck·ling** : to give or draw milk from the breast or udder; *also* : NURTURE

suck·ling \'sə-kliŋ\ *n* : a young unweaned mammal

suck–up \'sək-‚əp\ *n* : a person who seeks to gain favor by flattery ⟨a ∼ to the teacher⟩

su·cre \'sü-(‚)krā\ *n* — see MONEY table

su·crose \'sü-‚krōs, -‚krōz\ *n* : a sweet sugar obtained commercially esp. from sugarcane or sugar beets

suc·tion \'sək-shən\ *n* **1** : the act of sucking **2** : the act or process of drawing something (as liquid or dust) into a space (as in a vacuum cleaner or a pump) by partially exhausting the air in the space — **suc·tion·al** \-shə-nəl\ *adj*

suction cup *n* : a cup-shaped device in which a partial vacuum is produced when applied to a surface

sud·den \'sə-d²n\ *adj* [ME *sodain*, fr. AF *sudain*, fr. L *subitaneus*, fr. *subitus* sudden, fr. pp. of *subire* to come up] **1** : happening or coming unexpectedly ⟨∼ shower⟩; *also* : changing angle or character all at once ⟨∼ turn⟩ ⟨∼ descent⟩ **2** : HASTY, RASH ⟨∼ decision⟩ **3** : made or brought about in a short time ⟨∼ cure⟩ ✦ **Synonyms** PRECIPITATE, HEADLONG, IMPETUOUS — **sud·den·ly** *adv* — **sud·den·ness** *n*

sudden infant death syndrome *n* : death due to unknown causes of an apparently healthy infant usu. before one year of age and esp. during sleep

suds \'sədz\ *n pl* : soapy water esp. when frothy — **sudsy** \'səd-zē\ *adj*

sue \'sü\ *vb* **sued; su·ing** [ME *sewen, siuen* to follow, strive for, petition, fr. AF *sivre, siure,* fr. VL **sequere,* fr. L *sequi* to follow] **1** : PETITION, SOLICIT **2** : to seek justice or right by bringing legal action

suede *also* **suède** \'swād\ *n* [F *gants de Suède* Swedish gloves] **1** : leather with a napped surface **2** : a fabric with a suedelike nap

su·et \'sü-ət\ *n* : the hard fat from beef and mutton that yields tallow

suff *abbr* **1** sufficient **2** suffix

suf·fer \'sə-fər\ *vb* **suf·fered; suf·fer·ing** **1** : to feel or endure pain **2** : EXPERIENCE, UNDERGO ⟨∼ a defeat⟩ **3** : to bear loss, damage, or injury **4** : ALLOW, PERMIT ✦ **Synonyms** ENDURE, ABIDE, TOLERATE, STAND, BROOK, STOMACH — **suf·fer·able** \'sə-fə-rə-bəl\ *adj* — **suf·fer·er** *n*

suf·fer·ance \'sə-frəns, -fə-rəns\ *n* **1** : consent or approval implied by lack of interference or resistance **2** : ENDURANCE, PATIENCE

suf·fer·ing \'sə-friŋ, -fə-riŋ\ *n* : PAIN, MISERY, HARDSHIP

suf·fice \sə-'fīs\ *vb* **suf·ficed; suf·fic·ing** **1** : to satisfy a need : be sufficient **2** : to be capable or competent

suf·fi·cien·cy \sə-'fi-shən-sē\ *n* **1** : a sufficient quantity to meet one's needs **2** : ADEQUACY

suf·fi·cient \sə-'fi-shənt\ *adj* : adequate to accomplish a purpose or meet a need — **suf·fi·cient·ly** *adv*

¹**suf·fix** \'sə-‚fiks\ *n* : an affix occurring at the end of a word

²**suf·fix** \'sə-fiks, (‚)sə-'fiks\ *vb* : to attach as a suffix — **suf·fix·ation** \‚sə-‚fik-'sā-shən\ *n*

suf·fo·cate \'sə-fə-‚kāt\ *vb* **-cat·ed; -cat·ing** : STIFLE,

SMOTHER, CHOKE — **suf·fo·cat·ing·ly** *adv* — **suf·fo·ca·tion** \‚sə-fə-'kā-shən\ *n*

suf·fra·gan \'sə-fri-gən\ *n* : an assistant bishop; *esp* : one not having the right of succession — **suffragan** *adj*

suf·frage \'sə-frij\ *n* [L *suffragium*] **1** : VOTE **2** : the right to vote : FRANCHISE

suf·frag·ette \‚sə-fri-'jet\ *n* : a woman who advocates suffrage for women

suf·frag·ist \'sə-fri-jist\ *n* : one who advocates extension of the suffrage esp. to women

suf·fuse \sə-'fyüz\ *vb* **suf·fused; suf·fus·ing** : to spread over or through in the manner of a fluid or light ✦ **Synonyms** INFUSE, IMBUE, INGRAIN, STEEP — **suf·fu·sion** \-'fyü-zhən\ *n*

¹**sug·ar** \'shu̇-gər\ *n* **1** : a sweet substance that is colorless or white when pure and is chiefly sucrose from sugarcane or sugar beets **2** : a water-soluble compound (as glucose) similar to sucrose — **sug·ary** *adj*

²**sugar** *vb* **sug·ared; sug·ar·ing** **1** : to mix, cover, or sprinkle with sugar **2** : SWEETEN ⟨∼ advice with flattery⟩ **3** : to form sugar ⟨a syrup that ∼s⟩ **4** : GRANULATE

sugar beet *n* : a large beet with a white root from which sugar is made

sug·ar·cane \'shu̇-gər-‚kān\ *n* : a tall grass widely grown in warm regions for the sugar in its stalks

sugar daddy *n* **1** : a well-to-do usu. older man who supports or spends lavishly on a mistress or girlfriend **2** : a generous benefactor of a cause

sugar maple *n* : a maple with a sweet sap; *esp* : one of eastern No. America with sap that is the chief source of maple syrup and maple sugar

sugar pea *n* : SNOW PEA

sug·ar·plum \'shu̇-gər-‚pləm\ *n* : a small ball of candy

sug·gest \səg-'jest, sə-\ *vb* **1** : to put (as a thought, plan, or desire) into a person's mind **2** : to remind or evoke by association of ideas ✦ **Synonyms** IMPLY, HINT, INTIMATE, INSINUATE, CONNOTE

sug·gest·ible \səg-'jes-tə-bəl, sə-\ *adj* : easily influenced by suggestion

sug·ges·tion \-'jes-chən\ *n* **1** : an act or instance of suggesting; *also* : something suggested **2** : a slight indication

sug·ges·tive \-'jes-tiv\ *adj* : tending to suggest something; *esp* : suggesting something improper or indecent — **sug·ges·tive·ly** *adv* — **sug·ges·tive·ness** *n*

¹**sui·cide** \'sü-ə-‚sīd\ *n* **1** : the act of killing oneself purposely **2** : one that commits or attempts suicide — **sui·cid·al** \‚sü-ə-'sī-d²l\ *adj*

²**suicide** *adj* : being or performing a deliberate act resulting in the voluntary death of the person who does it ⟨a ∼ mission⟩ ⟨a ∼ bomber⟩

sui ge·ne·ris \‚sü-‚ī-'je-nə-rəs; ‚sü-ē-\ *adj* [L, of its own kind] : being in a class by itself : UNIQUE

¹**suit** \'süt\ *n* **1** : an action in court to recover a right or claim **2** : an act of suing or entreating; *esp* : COURTSHIP **3** : a number of things used together ⟨∼ of clothes⟩ **4** : all the playing cards in a pack bearing the same symbol

²**suit** *vb* **1** : to be appropriate or fitting **2** : to be becoming to **3** : to meet the needs or desires of : PLEASE

suit·able \'sü-tə-bəl\ *adj* : FITTING, PROPER, APPROPRIATE ⟨∼ dress⟩ ✦ **Synonyms** FIT, MEET, APT, HAPPY — **suit·abil·i·ty** \‚sü-tə-'bi-lə-tē\ *n* — **suit·able·ness** \'sü-tə-bəl-nəs\ *n* — **suit·ably** \-tə-blē\ *adv*

suit·case \'süt-‚kās\ *n* : a portable case designed to hold a traveler's clothing and personal articles

suite \'swēt, *for 4 also* 'süt\ *n* **1** : RETINUE **2** : a group of rooms occupied as a unit **3** : a modern instrumental composition in several movements of different character; *also* : a long orchestral concert arrangement in suite form of material drawn from a longer work **4** : a set of matched furniture for a room

suit·ing \'sü-tiŋ\ *n* : fabric for suits of clothes

suit·or \'sü-tər\ *n* **1** : one who sues or petitions **2** : one who courts a woman or seeks to marry her

su·ki·ya·ki \skē-'yä-kē, ‚su̇-kē-'yä-\ *n* : thin slices of meat, tofu, and vegetables cooked in soy sauce and sugar

sul·fa drug \'səl-fə-\ *n* : any of various synthetic organic bacteria-inhibiting drugs

sul·fate \'səl-‚fāt\ *n* : a salt or ester of sulfuric acid

sul·fide \'səl-‚fīd\ *n* : a compound of sulfur

sul·fur *also* **sul·phur** \'səl-fər\ *n* : a nonmetallic chemical element used esp. in the chemical and paper industries and in vulcanizing rubber

sulfur di·ox·ide \-dī-'äk-sīd\ *n* : a heavy pungent toxic gas that is used esp. in bleaching, as a preservative, and as a refrigerant, and is a major air pollutant

sul·fu·ric \ˌsəl-'fyūr-ik\ *adj* : of, relating to, or containing sulfur

sulfuric acid *or* **sul·phu·ric acid** \ˌsəl-'fyūr-ik-\ *n* : a heavy corrosive oily strong acid

sul·fu·rous *also* **sul·phu·rous** \'səl-fə-rəs, -fyə-, *also esp for 1* ˌsəl-'fyūr-əs\ *adj* 1 : of, relating to, or containing sulfur 2 : of or relating to brimstone or the fire of hell : INFERNAL 3 : FIERY, INFLAMED ⟨∼ sermons⟩

¹sulk \'səlk\ *vb* : to be or become moodily silent or irritable

²sulk *n* : a sulky mood or spell

¹sulky \'səl-kē\ *adj* **sulk·i·er; -est** : inclined to sulk : MOROSE, MOODY ♦ *Synonyms* SURLY, GLUM, SULLEN, GLOOMY — **sulk·i·ly** \'səl-kə-lē\ *adv* — **sulk·i·ness** \-kē-nəs\ *n*

²sulky *n, pl* **sulkies** : a light 2-wheeled horse-drawn vehicle with a seat for the driver and usu. no body

sul·len \'sə-lən\ *adj* 1 : gloomily silent : MOROSE 2 : DISMAL, GLOOMY ⟨a ∼ sky⟩ ♦ *Synonyms* GLUM, SURLY, DOUR, SATURNINE — **sul·len·ly** *adv* — **sul·len·ness** *n*

sul·ly \'sə-lē\ *vb* **sul·lied; sul·ly·ing** : SOIL, SMIRCH, DEFILE

sul·tan \'səl-tᵊn\ *n* : a sovereign esp. of a Muslim state — **sul·tan·ate** \-ˌāt\ *n*

sul·ta·na \ˌsəl-'ta-nə\ *n* 1 : a female member of a sultan's family 2 : a pale seedless grape; *also* : a raisin of this grape

sul·try \'səl-trē\ *adj* **sul·tri·er; -est** [obs. E *sulter* to swelter, alter. of E *swelter*] : very hot and moist : SWELTERING; *also* : exciting sexual desire

¹sum \'səm\ *n* [ME *summe*, fr. AF *sume, somme*, fr. L *summa*, fr. fem. of *summus* highest] 1 : a quantity of money 2 : the whole amount 3 : GIST ⟨the ∼ of an argument⟩ 4 : the result obtained by adding numbers 5 : a problem in arithmetic

²sum *vb* **summed; sum·ming** : to find the sum of by adding or counting

su·mac *also* **su·mach** \'sü-ˌmak, 'shü-\ *n* : any of a genus of trees, shrubs, and woody vines having spikes or loose clusters of red or whitish berries

sum·ma·rise *Brit var of* SUMMARIZE

sum·ma·rize \'sə-mə-ˌrīz\ *vb* **-rized; -riz·ing** : to tell in a summary

¹sum·ma·ry \'sə-mə-rē\ *adj* 1 : covering the main points briefly : CONCISE 2 : done without delay or formality ⟨∼ punishment⟩ ♦ *Synonyms* TERSE, SUCCINCT, LACONIC — **sum·mar·i·ly** \(ˌ)sə-'mer-ə-lē, 'sə-mə-rə-lē\ *adv*

²summary *n, pl* **-ries** : a concise statement of the main points

sum·ma·tion \(ˌ)sə-'mā-shən\ *n* : a summing up; *esp* : a speech in court summing up the arguments in a case

sum·mer \'sə-mər\ *n* : the season of the year in a region in which the sun shines most directly : the warmest period of the year — **sum·mery** *adj*

sum·mer·house \'sə-mər-ˌhaūs\ *n* : a covered structure in a garden or park to provide a shady retreat

summersault *var of* SOMERSAULT

summer squash *n* : any of various squashes (as zucchini) used as a vegetable while immature

sum·mit \'sə-mət\ *n* 1 : the highest point 2 : a conference of highest-level officials ⟨an economic ∼⟩

sum·mon \'sə-mən\ *vb* [ME *somnen, somonen*, fr. AF *somondre*, fr. VL *summonere*, alter. of L *summonēre* to remind secretly] 1 : to call to a meeting : CONVOKE 2 : to send for; *also* : to order to appear in court 3 : to evoke esp. by an act of the will ⟨∼ up courage⟩ — **sum·mon·er** *n*

sum·mons \'sə-mənz\ *n, pl* **sum·mons·es** 1 : an authoritative call to appear at a designated place or to attend to a duty 2 : a warning or citation to appear in court at a specified time to answer charges

sump·tu·ous \'səmp-shə-wəs, -chə-\ *adj* : LAVISH, LUXURIOUS ⟨a ∼ banquet⟩ ⟨a ∼ residence⟩

sum up *vb* : SUMMARIZE

¹sun \'sən\ *n* 1 : the shining celestial body around which the earth and other planets revolve and from which they receive light and heat 2 : a celestial body like the sun 3 : SUNSHINE — **sun·less** *adj* — **sun·ny** *adj*

²sun *vb* **sunned; sun·ning** 1 : to expose to or as if to the rays of the sun 2 : to sun oneself

Sun *abbr* Sunday

sun·bath \'sən-ˌbath, -ˌbäth\ *n* : an exposure to sunlight or a sunlamp — **sun·bathe** \-ˌbāth\ *vb*

sun·beam \-ˌbēm\ *n* : a ray of sunlight

sun·block \'sən-ˌbläk\ *n* : a preparation used on the skin to prevent sunburn (as by blocking ultraviolet radiation)

sun·bon·net \-ˌbä-nət\ *n* : a bonnet with a wide brim to shield the face and neck from the sun

¹sun·burn \-ˌbərn\ *vb* **-burned** \-ˌbərnd\ *or* **-burnt** \-ˌbərnt\; **-burn·ing** : to cause or become affected with sunburn

²sunburn *n* : a skin inflammation caused by overexposure to ultraviolet radiation esp. from sunshine

sun·dae \'sən-(ˌ)dā, -dē\ *n* : ice cream served with topping

Sun·day \'sən-ˌdā, -dē\ *n* : the 1st day of the week : the Christian Sabbath

sun·der \'sən-dər\ *vb* : to force apart ♦ *Synonyms* SEVER, PART, DISJOIN, DISUNITE

sun·di·al \'sən-ˌdī(-ə)l\ *n* : a device for showing the time of day from the shadow cast on a plate by an object with a straight edge

sundial

sun·down \-ˌdaūn\ *n* : SUNSET 2

sun·dries \'sən-drēz\ *n pl* : various small articles or items

sun·dry \'sən-drē\ *adj* : SEVERAL, DIVERS, VARIOUS ⟨for ∼ reasons⟩

sun·fish \'sən-ˌfish\ *n* 1 : a large marine fish with a deep flattened body 2 : any of numerous often brightly colored No. American freshwater fishes related to the perches and usu. having the body flattened from side to side

sun·flow·er \-ˌflaū(-ə)r\ *n* : any of a genus of tall New World plants related to the daisies and often grown for the oil-rich seeds of their yellow-petaled dark-centered flower heads

sung *past and past part of* SING

sun·glasses \'sən-ˌgla-səz\ *n pl* : glasses to protect the eyes from the sun

sunk *past and past part of* SINK

sunk·en \'səŋ-kən\ *adj* 1 : SUBMERGED ⟨∼ ships⟩ 2 : fallen in : HOLLOW ⟨∼ cheeks⟩ 3 : lying in a depression ⟨∼ garden⟩; *also* : constructed below the general floor level ⟨a ∼ living room⟩

sun·lamp \'sən-ˌlamp\ *n* : an electric lamp designed to emit radiation of wavelengths from ultraviolet to infrared

sun·light \-ˌlīt\ *n* : SUNSHINE

sun·lit \-ˌlit\ *adj* : lighted by or as if by the sun

sun protection factor *n* : a number that is the factor by which the time required for unprotected skin to become sunburned is increased when a sunscreen is used

sun·rise \-ˌrīz\ *n* 1 : the apparent rising of the sun above the horizon 2 : the time at which the sun rises

sun·roof \-ˌrüf, -ˌrūf\ *n* : a panel in an automobile roof that can be opened

sun·screen \-ˌskrēn\ *n* : a preparation on the skin to prevent sunburn (as by absorbing ultraviolet radiation)

sun·set \-ˌset\ *n* 1 : the apparent descent of the sun below the horizon 2 : the time at which the sun sets

sun·shade \'sən-ˌshād\ *n* : something (as a parasol or awning) used as a protection from the sun's rays

sun·shine \-ˌshīn\ *n* : the direct light of the sun — **sun·shiny** *adj*

sun·spot \-ˌspät\ *n* : any of the dark spots that appear at times on the sun's surface

sun·stroke \-ˌstrōk\ *n* : heatstroke caused by direct exposure to the sun

sun·tan \-ˌtan\ *n* : a browning of the skin from exposure to the sun's rays

sun·up \-ˌəp\ *n* : SUNRISE 2

¹**sup** \ˈsəp\ *vb* **supped; sup·ping** : to take or drink in swallows or gulps

²**sup** *n* : a mouthful esp. of liquor or broth; *also* : a small quantity of liquid

³**sup** *vb* **supped; sup·ping** 1 : to eat the evening meal 2 : to make one's supper ⟨*supped* on roast beef⟩

⁴**sup** *abbr* 1 superior 2 supplement; supplementary 3 supply 4 supra

¹**su·per** \ˈsü-pər\ *adj* 1 : very fine : EXCELLENT 2 : EXTREME, EXCESSIVE ⟨~ secrecy⟩

²**super** *n* : SUPERINTENDENT

super- \ˌsü-pər\ *prefix* 1 : over and above : higher in quantity, quality, or degree than : more than 2 : in addition 3 : extra 3 : exceeding a norm 4 : in excessive degree or intensity 5 : surpassing all or most others of its kind 6 : situated above, on, or at the top of 7 : next above or higher 8 : more inclusive than 9 : superior in status or position

superabsorbent	superpatriotism
superachiever	superpremium
superagency	superrich
superblock	supersalesman
superbomb	supersecret
supercity	supersize
superclean	supersized
superexpensive	supersmart
superfast	supersophisticated
superfine	superspy
superheat	superstar
superheavy	superstate
superhero	superstore
superhuman	superstratum
superhumanly	superstrength
superindividual	superstrong
superliner	supersubtle
superman	supersystem
supernormal	supertanker
superpatriot	superthin
superpatriotic	superwoman

su·per·abun·dant \ˌsü-pər-ə-ˈbən-dənt\ *adj* : more than ample — **su·per·abun·dance** \-dəns\ *n*

su·per·an·nu·ate \ˌsü-pər-ˈan-yə-ˌwāt\ *vb* **-at·ed; -at·ing** 1 : to make out-of-date 2 : to retire and pension because of age or infirmity — **su·per·an·nu·at·ed** *adj*

su·perb \sù-ˈpərb\ *adj* [L *superbus* excellent, proud, fr. *super* above] : marked to the highest degree by excellence, brilliance, or competence ♦ *Synonyms* RESPLENDENT, GLORIOUS, GORGEOUS, SUBLIME — **su·perb·ly** *adv*

su·per·charg·er \ˈsü-pər-ˌchär-jər\ *n* : a device for increasing the amount of air supplied to an internal combustion engine

su·per·cil·ious \ˌsü-pər-ˈsi-lē-əs\ *adj* [L *superciliosus*, fr. *supercilium* eyebrow, haughtiness] : haughtily contemptuous ♦ *Synonyms* DISDAINFUL, OVERBEARING, ARROGANT, LORDLY, SUPERIOR

su·per·com·pu·ter \ˈsü-pər-kəm-ˌpyü-tər\ *n* : a large very fast mainframe

su·per·con·duc·tiv·i·ty \ˌsü-pər-ˌkän-ˌdək-ˈti-və-tē\ *n* : a complete disappearance of electrical resistance in a substance esp. at very low temperatures — **su·per·con·duc·tive** \-kən-ˈdək-tiv\ *adj* — **su·per·con·duc·tor** \-ˈdək-tər\ *n*

su·per·con·ti·nent \ˈsü-pər-ˌkän-tə-nənt\ *n* : a former large continent from which other continents are held to have broken off and drifted away

su·per·ego \ˌsü-pər-ˈē-gō\ *n* : the one of the three divisions of the psyche in psychoanalytic theory that functions to reward and punish through a system of moral attitudes, conscience, and a sense of guilt

su·per·fi·cial \ˌsü-pər-ˈfi-shəl\ *adj* 1 : of or relating to the surface or appearance only 2 : not thorough : SHALLOW — **su·per·fi·ci·al·i·ty** \-ˌfi-shē-ˈa-lə-tē\ *n* — **su·per·fi·cial·ly** *adv*

su·per·flu·ous \sù-ˈpər-flə-wəs\ *adj* : exceeding what is sufficient or necessary : SURPLUS ♦ *Synonyms* EXTRA, SPARE, SUPERNUMERARY — **su·per·flu·i·ty** \ˌsü-pər-ˈflü-ə-tē\ *n*

su·per·high·way \ˌsü-pər-ˈhī-ˌwā\ *n* : a broad highway designed for high-speed traffic

su·per·im·pose \-im-ˈpōz\ *vb* : to lay (one thing) over or above something else

su·per·in·tend \ˌsü-pə-rin-ˈtend\ *vb* : to have or exercise the charge and oversight of : DIRECT — **su·per·in·ten·dence** \-ˈten-dəns\ *n* — **su·per·in·ten·den·cy** \-dən-sē\ *n* — **su·per·in·ten·dent** \-dənt\ *n*

¹**su·pe·ri·or** \sù-ˈpir-ē-ər\ *adj* 1 : situated higher up, over, or near the top; *also* : higher in rank or numbers 2 : of greater value or importance 3 : courageously indifferent (as to pain or misfortune) 4 : better than most others of its kind 5 : ARROGANT, HAUGHTY — **su·pe·ri·or·i·ty** \-ˌpir-ē-ˈòr-ə-tē\ *n*

²**superior** *n* 1 : one who is above another in rank, office, or station; *esp* : the head of a religious house or order 2 : one higher in quality or merit

¹**su·per·la·tive** \sù-ˈpər-lə-tiv\ *adj* 1 : of, relating to, or constituting the degree of grammatical comparison that denotes an extreme or unsurpassed level or extent 2 : surpassing others : SUPREME ♦ *Synonyms* PEERLESS, INCOMPARABLE, SUPERB — **su·per·la·tive·ly** *adv*

²**superlative** *n* 1 : the superlative degree or a superlative form in a language 2 : the utmost degree : ACME

su·per·mar·ket \ˈsü-pər-ˌmär-kət\ *n* : a self-service retail market selling foods and household merchandise

su·per·mod·el \ˈsü-pər-ˌmä-dᵊl\ *n* : a famous and successful fashion model

su·per·mom \ˈsü-pər-ˌmäm\ *n* : an exemplary mother; *also* : a woman who performs the duties of housekeeping and raising children while also having a full-time job

su·per·nal \sù-ˈpər-nəl\ *adj* 1 : being or coming from on high 2 : of heavenly or spiritual character

su·per·nat·u·ral \ˌsü-pər-ˈna-chə-rəl\ *adj* : of or relating to phenomena beyond or outside of nature; *esp* : relating to or attributed to a divinity, ghost, or devil — **su·per·nat·u·ral·ly** *adv*

su·per·no·va \ˌsü-pər-ˈnō-və\ *n* : the explosion of a very large star

¹**su·per·nu·mer·ary** \-ˈnü-mə-ˌrer-ē, -ˈnyü-\ *adj* : exceeding the usual or required number : EXTRA ♦ *Synonyms* SURPLUS, SUPERFLUOUS, SPARE

²**supernumerary** *n, pl* **-ar·ies** : an extra person or thing; *esp* : an actor hired for a nonspeaking part

su·per·pose \ˌsü-pər-ˈpōz\ *vb* **-posed; -pos·ing** : SUPERIMPOSE — **su·per·po·si·tion** \-pə-ˈzi-shən\ *n*

su·per·pow·er \ˈsü-pər-ˌpaù-(ə)r\ *n* 1 : excessive or superior power 2 : one of a few politically and militarily dominant nations

su·per·sat·u·rat·ed \-ˈsa-chə-ˌrā-təd\ *adj* : containing an amount of a substance greater than that required for saturation

su·per·scribe \ˈsü-pər-ˌskrīb, ˌsü-pər-ˈskrīb\ *vb* **-scribed; -scrib·ing** : to write on the top or outside : ADDRESS — **su·per·scrip·tion** \ˌsü-pər-ˈskrip-shən\ *n*

su·per·script \ˈsü-pər-ˌskript\ *n* : a symbol (as a numeral or letter) written immediately above or above and to one side of another character

su·per·sede \ˌsü-pər-ˈsēd\ *vb* **-sed·ed; -sed·ing** [ME (Sc) *superceden* to defer, fr. MF *superceder*, fr. L *supersedēre* to be superior to, refrain from, fr. *super-* above + *sedēre* to sit] : to take the place of : REPLACE

su·per·son·ic \-ˈsä-nik\ *adj* 1 : ULTRASONIC 2 : being or relating to speeds from one to five times the speed of sound; *also* : capable of moving at such a speed ⟨a ~ airplane⟩

su·per·sti·tion \ˌsü-pər-ˈsti-shən\ *n* 1 : beliefs or practices resulting from ignorance, fear of the unknown, or trust in magic or chance 2 : an unreasoning fear of nature, the unknown, or God resulting from superstition — **su·per·sti·tious** \-shəs\ *adj*

su·per·struc·ture \ˈsü-pər-ˌstrək-chər\ *n* : something built on a base or as a vertical extension

su·per·ti·tle \ˈsü-pər-ˌtī-tᵊl\ *n* : a translation of foreign-language dialogue displayed above a screen or performance

su·per·vene \ˌsü-pər-ˈvēn\ *vb* **-vened; -ven·ing** : to occur as something additional or unexpected

su·per·vise \ˈsü-pər-ˌvīz\ *vb* **-vised; -vis·ing** : OVERSEE, SUPERINTEND — **su·per·vi·sion** \ˌsü-pər-ˈvi-zhən\ *n* — **su·per·vi·sor** \ˈsü-pər-ˌvī-zər\ *n* — **su·per·vi·so·ry** \ˌsü-pər-ˈvī-zə-rē\ *adj*

su·pine \su̇-'pīn\ adj 1 : lying on the back or with the face upward 2 : LETHARGIC, SLUGGISH; also : ABJECT ✦ *Synonyms* INACTIVE, INERT, PASSIVE, IDLE

supp or **suppl** abbr supplement; supplementary

sup·per \'sə-pər\ n : the evening meal esp. when dinner is taken at midday — **sup·per·time** \-,tīm\ n

sup·plant \sə-'plant\ vb 1 : to take the place of (another) esp. by force or trickery 2 : REPLACE

sup·ple \'sə-pəl\ adj **sup·pler; sup·plest** 1 : COMPLIANT, ADAPTABLE ⟨a ~ soprano⟩ 2 : capable of bending without breaking or creasing : LIMBER ✦ *Synonyms* RESILIENT, ELASTIC, FLEXIBLE

¹sup·ple·ment \'sə-plə-mənt\ n 1 : something that supplies a want or makes an addition 2 : DIETARY SUPPLEMENT 3 : a continuation (as of a book) containing corrections or additional material — **sup·ple·men·tal** \,sə-plə-'men-t³l\ adj — **sup·ple·men·ta·ry** \-'men-tə-rē\ adj

²sup·ple·ment \'sə-plə-,ment\ vb : to fill up the deficiencies of : add to — **sup·ple·men·ta·tion** \,sə-plə-,men-'tā-shən, -mən-\ n

sup·pli·ant \'sə-plē-ənt\ n : one who supplicates : PETITIONER, PLEADER

sup·pli·cant \'sə-pli-kənt\ n : SUPPLIANT

sup·pli·cate \'sə-plə-,kāt\ vb **-cat·ed; -cat·ing** 1 : to make a humble entreaty; esp : to pray to God 2 : to ask earnestly and humbly : BESEECH ✦ *Synonyms* IMPLORE, BEG, ENTREAT, PLEAD — **sup·pli·ca·tion** \,sə-plə-'kā-shən\ n

¹sup·ply \sə-'plī\ vb **sup·plied; sup·ply·ing** [ME supplien, to complete, compensate for, fr. MF soupplier fr. L supplēre to fill up, supplement, supply, fr. sub- under, up to + plēre to fill] 1 : to add as a supplement 2 : to satisfy the needs of 3 : FURNISH, PROVIDE — **sup·pli·er** n

²supply n, pl **supplies** 1 : the quantity or amount (as of a commodity) needed or available; also : PROVISIONS, STORES — usu. used in pl. 2 : the act or process of filling a want or need : PROVISION 3 : the quantities of goods or services offered for sale at a particular time or at one price

sup·ply–side \sə-'plī-,sīd\ adj : of, relating to, or being an economic theory that recommends the reduction of tax rates to expand economic activity

¹sup·port \sə-'pȯrt\ vb 1 : BEAR, TOLERATE 2 : to take sides with : BACK, ASSIST 3 : to provide with food, clothing, and shelter 4 : to hold up or serve as a foundation for ✦ *Synonyms* UPHOLD, ADVOCATE, CHAMPION — **sup·port·able** adj — **sup·port·er** n — **sup·port·ive** \-'pȯr-tiv\ adj

²support n 1 : the act of supporting : the state of being supported 2 : one that supports : PROP, BASE

support group n : a group of people with common experiences and concerns who provide emotional and moral support for one another

sup·pose \sə-'pōz\ vb **sup·posed; sup·pos·ing** 1 : to assume to be true (as for the sake of argument) 2 : EXPECT ⟨I am supposed to go⟩ 3 : to think probable — **sup·pos·al** n

sup·posed \sə-'pōzd, -'pō-zəd\ adj : BELIEVED; also : mistakenly believed — **sup·pos·ed·ly** \-'pō-zəd-lē, -'pōzd-lē\ adv

sup·pos·ing conj : if by way of hypothesis : on the assumption that ⟨~ I did agree with you⟩

sup·po·si·tion \,sə-pə-'zi-shən\ n 1 : something that is supposed : HYPOTHESIS 2 : the act of supposing

sup·pos·i·to·ry \sə-'pä-zə-,tȯr-ē\ n, pl **-ries** [ME suppositorie, fr. AF, fr. ML suppositorium, fr. LL, neut. of suppositorius placed beneath] : a small easily melted mass of usu. medicated material for insertion (as into the rectum)

sup·press \sə-'pres\ vb 1 : to put down by authority or force : SUBDUE ⟨~ a revolt⟩ 2 : to keep from being known; also : to stop the publication or circulation of 3 : to hold back : REPRESS ⟨~ anger⟩ ⟨~ a cough⟩ — **sup·press·ible** \-'pre-sə-bəl\ adj — **sup·pres·sion** \-'pre-shən\ n — **sup·pres·sor** \-'pre-sər\ n

sup·pres·sant \sə-'pre-s³nt\ n : an agent (as a drug) suppressing rather than eliminating something ⟨a cough ~⟩

sup·pu·rate \'sə-pyə-,rāt\ vb **-rat·ed; -rat·ing** : to form or give off pus — **sup·pu·ra·tion** \,sə-pyə-'rā-shən\ n

su·pra \'sü-prə, -,prä\ adv : earlier in this writing : ABOVE

su·pra·na·tion·al \,sü-prə-'na-shə-nəl, -,prä-\ adj : going beyond national boundaries, authority, or interests ⟨~ organizations⟩

su·prem·a·cist \su̇-'pre-mə-sist\ n : an advocate of group supremacy

su·prem·a·cy \su̇-'pre-mə-sē\ n, pl **-cies** : supreme rank, power, or authority

su·preme \su̇-'prēm\ adj [L supremus, superl. of superus upper, fr. super over, above] 1 : highest in rank or authority 2 : highest in degree or quality ⟨~ among poets⟩ 3 : ULTIMATE ⟨the ~ sacrifice⟩ ✦ *Synonyms* SUPERLATIVE, SURPASSING, PEERLESS, INCOMPARABLE — **su·preme·ly** adv — **su·preme·ness** n

Supreme Being n : GOD 1

supt abbr superintendent

sur·cease \'sər-,sēs\ n : CESSATION, RESPITE

¹sur·charge \'sər-,chärj\ vb 1 : to fill to excess : OVERLOAD 2 : to apply a surcharge to (postage stamps)

²surcharge n 1 : an extra fee or cost 2 : an excessive load or burden 3 : something officially printed on a postage stamp esp. to change its value

sur·cin·gle \'sər-,siŋ-gəl\ n : a band put around a horse's body to make something (as a saddle) fast

¹sure \'shu̇r\ adj **sur·er; sur·est** [ME, seur, sure, fr. AF seur, fr. L securus secure] 1 : firmly established 2 : TRUSTWORTHY, RELIABLE ⟨a ~ friend⟩ 3 : CONFIDENT ⟨I'm ~ I'm right⟩ 4 : not to be disputed : UNDOUBTED 5 : bound to happen 6 : careful to remember or attend to something ⟨be ~ to lock the door⟩ ✦ *Synonyms* CERTAIN, COCKSURE, POSITIVE — **sure·ness** n

²sure adv : SURELY

sure·fire \'shu̇r-'fī(-ə)r\ adj : certain to get results : DEPENDABLE

sure·ly \'shu̇r-lē\ adv 1 : in a sure manner 2 : without doubt 3 : INDEED, REALLY ⟨~, you don't believe that⟩

sure·ty \'shu̇r-ə-tē\ n, pl **-ties** 1 : SURENESS, CERTAINTY 2 : something that makes sure : GUARANTEE 3 : one who is a guarantor for another person

¹surf \'sərf\ n : waves that break upon the shore; also : the sound or foam of breaking waves

²surf vb 1 : to ride the surf (as on a surfboard) 2 : to scan the offerings of (as television or the Internet) for something of interest — **surf·er** n — **surf·ing** n

¹sur·face \'sər-fəs\ n 1 : the outside of an object or body 2 : outward aspect or appearance — **surface** adj

²surface vb **sur·faced; sur·fac·ing** 1 : to give a surface to : make smooth 2 : to rise to the surface

surf·board \'sərf-,bȯrd\ n : a buoyant board used in surfing

¹sur·feit \'sər-fət\ n 1 : EXCESS, SUPERABUNDANCE 2 : excessive indulgence (as in food or drink) 3 : disgust caused by excess

²surfeit vb : to feed, supply, or indulge to the point of surfeit : CLOY

surg abbr surgeon; surgery; surgical

¹surge \'sərj\ vb **surged; surg·ing** 1 : to rise and fall actively : TOSS 2 : to move in waves 3 : to rise suddenly to an excessive or abnormal value

²surge n 1 : a sweeping onward like a wave of the sea ⟨a ~ of emotion⟩ 2 : a large billow 3 : a transient sudden increase of current or voltage in an electrical circuit

sur·geon \'sər-jən\ n : a physician who specializes in surgery

sur·gery \'sər-jə-rē\ n, pl **-ger·ies** [ME surgerie, fr. AF cirurgerie, surgerie, fr. L chirurgia, fr. Gk cheirourgia, fr. cheirourgos surgeon, fr. cheirourgos doing by hand, fr. cheir hand + ergon work] 1 : a branch of medicine concerned with the correction of physical defects, the repair of injuries, and the treatment of disease esp. by operations 2 : a room or area where surgery is performed 3 : the work done by a surgeon

sur·gi·cal \'sər-ji-kəl\ adj : of, relating to, or associated with surgeons or surgery — **sur·gi·cal·ly** \-k(ə-)lē\ adv

sur·ly \'sər-lē\ adj **sur·li·er; -est** [alter. of ME serreli lordly, imperious, prob. fr. sire, ser sire] : having a rude unfriendly disposition ✦ *Synonyms* MOROSE, GLUM, SULLEN, SULKY, GLOOMY — **sur·li·ness** \-lē-nəs\ n

sur·mise \sər-'mīz\ vb **sur·mised; sur·mis·ing** : to form a notion of from scanty evidence ✦ *Synonyms* CONJECTURE, PRESUME, SUPPOSE — **surmise** n

sur·mount \sər-'mau̇nt\ vb 1 : to prevail over : OVERCOME 2 : to get to or lie at the top of

sur·name \'sər-ˌnām\ *n* **1** : NICKNAME **2** : the name borne in common by members of a family

sur·pass \sər-'pas\ *vb* **1** : to be superior to in quality, degree, or performance : EXCEL **2** : to go beyond the reach or powers of ✦ *Synonyms* TRANSCEND, OUTDO, OUTSTRIP, EXCEED — **sur·pass·ing·ly** *adv*

sur·plice \'sər-pləs\ *n* : a loose white outer vestment usu. of knee length

sur·plus \'sər-(ˌ)pləs\ *n* **1** : quantity left over : EXCESS **2** : the excess of assets over liabilities ✦ *Synonyms* SUPERFLUITY, OVERABUNDANCE, SURFEIT

¹sur·prise \sər-'prīz\ *n* **1** : an attack made without warning **2** : a taking unawares **3** : something that surprises **4** : AMAZEMENT, ASTONISHMENT

²surprise *vb* **sur·prised; sur·pris·ing 1** : to come upon and attack unexpectedly **2** : to take unawares **3** : AMAZE ⟨his conduct *surprised* me⟩ **4** : to cause astonishment or surprise ⟨her success didn't ∼⟩ ✦ *Synonyms* ASTONISH, ASTOUND, DUMBFOUND — **sur·pris·ing** *adj*

sur·pris·ing·ly \-'prī-ziŋ-lē\ *adv* **1** : in a surprising manner or degree **2** : it is surprising that ⟨∼, voter turnout was high⟩

sur·re·al \sə-'rē-əl, -'rēl\ *adj* **1** : having the intense irrational reality of a dream **2** : of or relating to surrealism — **sur·re·al·ly** *adv*

sur·re·al·ism \sə-'rē-ə-ˌli-zəm\ *n* : art, literature, or theater characterized by fantastic or incongruous imagery or effects produced by unnatural juxtapositions and combinations — **sur·re·al·ist** \-list\ *n or adj* — **sur·re·al·is·tic** \sə-ˌrē-ə-'lis-tik\ *adj* — **sur·re·al·is·ti·cal·ly** \-ti-k(ə-)lē\ *adv*

¹sur·ren·der \sə-'ren-dər\ *vb* **1** : to yield to the power of another : give up under compulsion **2** : RELINQUISH

²surrender *n* : the act of giving up or yielding oneself or the possession of something to another

sur·rep·ti·tious \ˌsər-əp-'ti-shəs\ *adj* : done, made, or acquired by stealth : CLANDESTINE ✦ *Synonyms* UNDERHAND, COVERT, FURTIVE — **sur·rep·ti·tious·ly** *adv*

sur·rey \'sər-ē\ *n, pl* **surreys** : a 2-seated horse-drawn carriage

surrey

sur·ro·ga·cy \'sər-ə-gə-sē\ *n* : SURROGATE MOTHERHOOD

sur·ro·gate \'sər-ə-ˌgāt, -gət\ *n* **1** : DEPUTY, SUBSTITUTE **2** : a law officer in some states with authority in the probate of wills, the settlement of estates, and the appointment of guardians **3** : SURROGATE MOTHER

surrogate mother *n* : a woman who becomes pregnant (as by surgical implantation of a fertilized egg) in order to carry the fetus for another woman — **surrogate motherhood** *n*

sur·round \sə-'raúnd\ *vb* **1** : to enclose on all sides : ENCIRCLE **2** : to enclose so as to cut off retreat or escape

sur·round·ings \sə-'raún-diŋz\ *n pl* : conditions by which one is surrounded

surround sound *n* : sound reproduction that uses three or more transmission channels

sur·tax \'sər-ˌtaks\ *n* : an additional tax over and above a normal tax

sur·tout \(ˌ)sər-'tü\ *n* [F, fr. *sur* over + *tout* all] : a man's long close-fitting overcoat

surv *abbr* survey; surveying; surveyor

sur·veil·lance \sər-'vā-ləns\ *n* [F] : close watch; *also* : SUPERVISION

¹sur·vey \sər-'vā\ *vb* **sur·veyed; sur·vey·ing** [ME, fr. AF *surveer* to look over, fr. *sur-* over + *veer* to see, fr. L *vidēre*] **1** : to look over and examine closely **2** : to find and represent the contours, measurements, and position

of a part of the earth's surface (as a tract of land) **3** : to view or study something as a whole ✦ *Synonyms* SCRUTINIZE, EXAMINE, INSPECT, STUDY — **sur·vey·or** \-ər\ *n*

²sur·vey \'sər-ˌvā\ *n, pl* **surveys** : the act or an instance of surveying; *also* : something that is surveyed

sur·viv·al·ism \sər-'vī-və-ˌli-zəm\ *n* : an attitude, policy, or practice based on the primacy of survival as a value — **sur·viv·al·ist** \-və-list\ *n or adj*

sur·vive \sər-'vīv\ *vb* **sur·vived; sur·viv·ing 1** : to remain alive or existent **2** : OUTLIVE, OUTLAST — **sur·viv·al** *n* — **sur·vi·vor** \-'vī-vər\ *n*

sus·cep·ti·ble \sə-'sep-tə-bəl\ *adj* **1** : of such a nature as to permit ⟨words ∼ of being misunderstood⟩ **2** : having little resistance to a stimulus or agency ⟨∼ to colds⟩ **3** : IMPRESSIONABLE, RESPONSIVE ⟨a ∼ mind⟩ ✦ *Synonyms* SENSITIVE, SUBJECT, EXPOSED, PRONE, LIABLE, OPEN — **sus·cep·ti·bil·i·ty** \-ˌsep-tə-'bi-lə-tē\ *n*

su·shi \'sü-shē\ *n* [Jp] : cold rice formed into various shapes and garnished esp. with bits of raw fish or seafood

¹sus·pect \'səs-ˌpekt, sə-'spekt\ *adj* : regarded with suspicion; *also* : QUESTIONABLE

²sus·pect \'səs-ˌpekt\ *n* : one who is suspected (as of a crime)

³sus·pect \sə-'spekt\ *vb* **1** : to have doubts of : MISTRUST **2** : to imagine to be guilty without proof **3** : SURMISE

sus·pend \sə-'spend\ *vb* **1** : to bar temporarily from a privilege, office, or function **2** : to stop temporarily : make inactive for a time **3** : to withhold (judgment) for a time **4** : HANG; *esp* : to hang so as to be free except at one point **5** : to put or hold in suspension **6** : to keep from falling or sinking by some invisible support

sus·pend·er \sə-'spen-dər\ *n* : one of two supporting straps which pass over the shoulders and to which the pants are fastened

sus·pense \sə-'spens\ *n* **1** : SUSPENSION **2** : mental uncertainty : ANXIETY **3** : excitement as to an outcome — **sus·pense·ful** *adj*

sus·pen·sion \sə-'spen-chən\ *n* **1** : the act of suspending : the state or period of being suspended **2** : the state of a substance when its particles are mixed with but undissolved in a fluid or solid; *also* : a substance in this state **3** : something suspended **4** : the system of devices supporting the upper part of a vehicle on the axles

sus·pen·so·ry \sə-'spen-sə-rē\ *adj* **1** : SUSPENDED; *also* : fitted or serving to suspend something **2** : temporarily leaving undetermined

sus·pi·cion \sə-'spi-shən\ *n* **1** : the act or an instance of suspecting something wrong without proof **2** : TRACE, SOUPÇON ⟨a ∼ of garlic⟩ ✦ *Synonyms* MISTRUST, UNCERTAINTY, DOUBT, SKEPTICISM

sus·pi·cious \sə-'spi-shəs\ *adj* **1** : open to or arousing suspicion **2** : inclined to suspect **3** : showing suspicion — **sus·pi·cious·ly** *adv*

sus·tain \sə-'stān\ *vb* **1** : to provide with nourishment **2** : to keep going : PROLONG ⟨∼ed effort⟩ **3** : to hold up : PROP **4** : to hold up under : ENDURE **5** : SUFFER ⟨∼ a broken arm⟩ **6** : to support as true, legal, or valid **7** : PROVE, CORROBORATE — **sus·tain·able** \səs-'tā-nə-bəl\ *adj*

sus·te·nance \'səs-tə-nəns\ *n* **1** : FOOD, NOURISHMENT **2** : a supplying with the necessities of life **3** : something that sustains or supports

su·ture \'sü-chər\ *n* **1** : material or a stitch for sewing a wound together **2** : a seam or line along which two things or parts are joined by or as if by sewing

SUV \ˌes-ˌyü-'vē\ *n* [*s*port-*u*tility *v*ehicle] : a vehicle similar to a station wagon but built on a light-truck chassis

su·zer·ain \'sü-zə-rən, -ˌrān\ *n* [F] **1** : a feudal lord **2** : a nation that has political control over the foreign relations of another nation — **su·zer·ain·ty** \-tē\ *n*

svc *or* **svce** *abbr* service

svelte \'sfelt\ *adj* **svelt·er; svelt·est** [F, fr. It *svelto*, fr. pp. of *svellere* to pluck out, modif. of L *evellere*, fr. *e-* out + *vellere* to pluck] : SLENDER, LITHE

svgs *abbr* savings

SW *abbr* **1** shortwave **2** southwest

¹swab \'swäb\ *n* **1** : MOP **2** : a wad of absorbent material esp. for applying medicine or for cleaning; *also* : a sample taken with a swab **3** : SAILOR

²swab *vb* **swabbed; swab·bing** : to use a swab on : MOP

swad·dle \'swä-dᵊl\ *vb* **swad·dled; swad·dling 1** : to bind (an infant) in bands of cloth **2** : to wrap up : SWATHE

swaddling clothes *n pl* : bands of cloth wrapped around an infant

swag \'swag\ *n* : stolen goods : LOOT

swag·ger \'swa-gər\ *vb* **1** : to walk with a conceited swing or strut **2** : BOAST, BRAG — **swagger** *n*

Swa·hi·li \swä-'hē-lē\ *n* : a language that is a trade and governmental language over much of eastern Africa and the Congo region

swain \'swān\ *n* [ME *swein* boy, servant, fr. ON *sveinn*] **1** : RUSTIC; *esp* : SHEPHERD **2** : ADMIRER, SUITOR

SWAK *abbr* sealed with a kiss

¹**swal·low** \'swä-lō\ *n* : any of numerous small long-winged migratory birds that often have a deeply forked tail

²**swallow** *vb* **1** : to take into the stomach through the throat **2** : to envelop or take in as if by swallowing **3** : to accept or believe without question, protest, or anger

³**swallow** *n* **1** : an act of swallowing **2** : an amount that can be swallowed at one time

swal·low·tail \'swä-lō-ˌtāl\ *n* **1** : a deeply forked and tapering tail like that of a swallow **2** : TAILCOAT **3** : any of various large butterflies with the border of each hind wing usu. drawn out into a process resembling a tail — **swal·low–tailed** \-ˌtāld\ *adj*

swam *past of* SWIM

swa·mi \'swä-mē\ *n* [Hindi *svāmī*, fr. Skt *svāmin* owner, lord] : a Hindu ascetic or religious teacher

¹**swamp** \'swämp\ *n* : a spongy wetland — **swamp** *adj* — **swampy** *adj*

²**swamp** *vb* **1** : to fill or become filled with or as if with water **2** : OVERWHELM 3

swamp·land \-ˌland\ *n* : SWAMP

swan \'swän\ *n, pl* **swans** *also* **swan** : any of various heavy-bodied long-necked mostly pure white swimming birds related to the geese

¹**swank** \'swaŋk\ *or* **swanky** \'swaŋ-kē\ *adj* **swank·er** *or* **swank·i·er; -est** : showily smart and dashing; *also* : fashionably elegant

²**swank** *n* **1** : PRETENTIOUSNESS **2** : ELEGANCE

swans·down \'swänz-ˌdaun\ *n* **1** : the very soft down of a swan used esp. for trimming **2** : a soft thick cotton flannel

swan song *n* : a farewell appearance, act, or pronouncement

swap \'swäp\ *vb* **swapped; swap·ping** : TRADE, EXCHANGE — **swap** *n*

sward \'swörd\ *n* : the grassy surface of land

¹**swarm** \'swörm\ *n* **1** : a great number of honeybees leaving together from a hive with a queen to start a new colony; *also* : a hive of bees **2** : a large crowd

²**swarm** *vb* **1** : to form in a swarm and depart from a hive **2** : to throng together : gather in great numbers

swart \'swört\ *adj* : SWARTHY

swar·thy \'swör-_t͟hē, -t͟hē\ *adj* **swar·thi·er; -est** : dark in color or complexion : dark-skinned

swash \'swäsh\ *vb* : to move about with a splashing sound — **swash** *n*

swash·buck·ler \-ˌbə-klər\ *n* : a swaggering or daring soldier or adventurer — **swash·buck·ling** *adj*

swas·ti·ka \'swäs-ti-kə\ *n* [Skt *svastika*, fr. *svasti* well-being, fr. *su-* well + *as-* to be] : a symbol or ornament in the form of a cross with the ends of the arms bent at right angles

swat \'swät\ *vb* **swat·ted; swat·ting** : to hit sharply ⟨~ a fly⟩ ⟨~ a ball⟩ — **swat** *n* — **swat·ter** *n*

SWAT *abbr* Special Weapons and Tactics

swatch \'swäch\ *n* : a sample piece (as of fabric) or a collection of samples

swath \'swäth, 'swȯth\ *or* **swathe** \'swäth, 'swȯth, 'swäth\ *n* [ME, fr. OE *swæth* footstep, trace] **1** : a row of cut grass or grain **2** : the sweep of a scythe or mowing machine or the path cut in mowing

swathe \'swäth, 'swȯth, 'swäth\ *vb* **swathed; swath·ing** : to bind or wrap with or as if with a bandage

¹**sway** \'swā\ *n* **1** : a gentle swinging from side to side **2** : controlling influence or power : DOMINION

²**sway** *vb* **1** : to swing gently from side to side **2** : RULE, GOVERN **3** : to cause to swing from side to side **4** : BEND, SWERVE; *also* : INFLUENCE ♦ *Synonyms* OSCILLATE, FLUCTUATE, VIBRATE, WAVER

sway·backed \'swā-ˌbakt\ *also* **sway·back** \-ˌbak\ *adj* : having an abnormally sagging back ⟨a ~ mare⟩ — **swayback** *n*

swear \'swer\ *vb* **swore** \'swȯr\; **sworn** \'swȯrn\; **swear·ing** **1** : to make a solemn statement or promise under oath **2** : to assert or promise emphatically or earnestly **3** : to administer an oath to **4** : to bind by or as if by an oath **5** : to use profane or obscene language — **swear·er** *n*

swear in *vb* : to induct into office by administration of an oath

sweat \'swet\ *vb* **sweat** *or* **sweat·ed; sweat·ing** **1** : to excrete salty moisture from glands of the skin : PERSPIRE **2** : to form drops of moisture on the surface **3** : to work so that one sweats : TOIL **4** : to cause to sweat **5** : to draw out or get rid of by or as if by sweating **6** : to make a person overwork — **sweat** *n* — **sweaty** *adj*

sweat·er \'swe-tər\ *n* **1** : one that sweats **2** : a knitted or crocheted jacket or pullover

sweat·shirt \'swet-ˌshərt\ *n* : a loose collarless pullover or jacket usu. of heavy cotton jersey

sweat·shop \'swet-ˌshäp\ *n* : a shop or factory in which workers are employed for long hours at low wages and under unhealthy conditions

Swed *abbr* Sweden

swede \'swēd\ *n* **1** *cap* : a native or inhabitant of Sweden **2** *chiefly Brit* : RUTABAGA

Swed·ish \'swē-dish\ *n* **1** : the language of Sweden **2** **Swedish** *pl* : the people of Sweden — **Swedish** *adj*

¹**sweep** \'swēp\ *vb* **swept** \'swept\; **sweep·ing** **1** : to remove or clean by or as if by brushing **2** : to destroy completely; *also* : to remove or take with a single swift movement **3** : to remove from sight or consideration **4** : to move over with speed and force ⟨the tide *swept* over the shore⟩ **5** : to win an overwhelming victory in; *also* : to win all the games or contests of **6** : to move or extend in a wide curve — **sweep·er** *n*

²**sweep** *n* **1** : something (as a long oar) that operates with a sweeping motion **2** : a clearing off or away **3** : a winning of all the contests or prizes in a competition **4** : a sweeping movement **5** : CURVE, BEND **6** : RANGE, SCOPE

sweeping *adj* : EXTENSIVE ⟨~ reforms⟩; *also* : indiscriminately inclusive ⟨~ generalities⟩

sweep·ings \'swē-piŋz\ *n pl* : things collected by sweeping

sweep–sec·ond hand \'swēp-ˌse-kənd-\ *n* : a hand marking seconds on a timepiece

sweep·stakes \'swēp-ˌstāks\ *also* **sweep·stake** \-ˌstāk\ *n, pl* **sweepstakes** **1** : a race or contest in which the entire prize may go to the winner **2** : any of various lotteries

¹**sweet** \'swēt\ *adj* **1** : being or causing the one of the four basic taste sensations that is caused esp. by table sugar and is identified esp. by the taste buds at the front of the tongue; *also* : pleasing to the taste **2** : AGREEABLE ⟨how ~ it is⟩ **3** : pleasing to a sense other than taste ⟨a ~ smell⟩ ⟨~ music⟩ **4** : not stale or spoiled : WHOLESOME ⟨~ milk⟩ **5** : not salted ⟨~ butter⟩ — **sweet·ish** *adj* — **sweet·ly** *adv* — **sweet·ness** *n*

²**sweet** *n* **1** : something sweet : CANDY **2** : DARLING

sweet·bread \'swēt-ˌbred\ *n* : the pancreas or thymus of an animal (as a calf or lamb) used for food

sweet·bri·ar *or* **sweet·bri·er** \-ˌbrī-ər\ *n* : a thorny Old World rose with fragrant white to deep pink flowers

sweet clover *n* : any of a genus of erect legumes widely grown for soil improvement or hay

sweet corn *n* : an Indian corn with wrinkled translucent kernels that are rich in sugar

sweet·en \'swē-tᵊn\ *vb* **sweet·ened; sweet·en·ing** : to make sweet — **sweet·en·er** *n* — **sweet·en·ing** *n*

sweet·heart \'swēt-ˌhärt\ *n* : one who is loved

sweet·meat \-ˌmēt\ *n* : CANDY 1

sweet pea *n* : a garden plant of the legume family with climbing stems and fragrant flowers of many colors; *also* : its flower

sweet pepper *n* : any of various large mild thick-walled fruits of a pepper; *also* : a plant bearing sweet peppers

sweet potato *n* : a tropical vine related to the morning glory; *also* : its large sweet edible root

sweet–talk \'swēt-ˌtȯk\ *vb* : FLATTER, COAX — **sweet talk** *n*

sweet tooth *n* : a craving or fondness for sweet food

sweet wil·liam \swēt-'wil-yəm\ *n, often cap W* : a widely cultivated Old World pink with small white to deep red or purple flowers often showily spotted, banded, or mottled

¹**swell** \'swel\ *vb* **swelled; swelled** *or* **swol·len** \'swō-lən\ **swell·ing 1** : to grow big or make bigger **2** : to expand or distend abnormally or excessively ⟨a *swollen* joint⟩; *also* : BULGE **3** : to fill or be filled with emotion (as pride) ◆ **Synonyms** EXPAND, AMPLIFY, DISTEND, INFLATE, DILATE — **swell·ing** *n*

²**swell** *n* **1** : a long crestless wave or series of waves in the open sea **2** : the condition of being protuberant **3** : a person dressed in the height of fashion; *also* : a person of high social position

³**swell** *adj* **1** : STYLISH; *also* : socially prominent **2** : EXCELLENT

swelled head *n* : an exaggerated opinion of oneself : SELF-CONCEIT

swel·ter \'swel-tər\ *vb* [ME *sweltren*, fr. *swelten* to die, be overcome by heat, fr. OE *sweltan* to die] **1** : to be faint or oppressed with the heat **2** : to become exceedingly hot — **swel·ter·ing** \-tə-riŋ\ *adj*

swept *past and past part of* SWEEP

swerve \'swərv\ *vb* **swerved; swerv·ing** : to move abruptly aside from a straight line or course — **swerve** *n*

¹**swift** \'swift\ *adj* **1** : moving or capable of moving with great speed **2** : occurring suddenly **3** : READY, ALERT — **swift·ly** *adv* — **swift·ness** *n*

²**swift** *n* : any of numerous small insect-eating birds with long narrow wings

swig \'swig\ *vb* **swigged; swig·ging** : to drink in long drafts — **swig** *n*

¹**swill** \'swil\ *vb* **1** : to swallow greedily : GUZZLE **2** : to feed (as hogs) on swill

²**swill** *n* **1** : food for animals composed of edible refuse mixed with liquid **2** : GARBAGE

¹**swim** \'swim\ *vb* **swam** \'swam\; **swum** \'swəm\; **swim·ming 1** : to propel oneself along in water by natural means (as by hands and legs, by tail, or by fins) **2** : to glide smoothly along **3** : FLOAT **4** : to be covered with or as if with a liquid **5** : to be dizzy ⟨his head *swam*⟩ **6** : to cross or go over by swimming — **swim·mer** *n*

²**swim** *n* **1** : an act of swimming **2** : the main current of activity ⟨in the ∼⟩

swim·ming *n* : the action, art, or sport of swimming and diving

swimming pool *n* : a tank (as of concrete or plastic) designed for swimming

swim·suit \'swim-,süt\ *n* : a suit for swimming or bathing

swim·wear \'swim-,wer\ *n* : clothing for wear while swimming or bathing

swin·dle \'swin-dᵊl\ *vb* **swin·dled; swin·dling** [fr. *swindler*, fr. G *Schwindler* giddy person, fr. *schwindeln* to be dizzy] : CHEAT, DEFRAUD — **swindle** *n* — **swin·dler** *n*

swine \'swīn\ *n, pl* **swine 1** : any of a family of stout short-legged hoofed mammals with bristly skin and a long flexible snout; *esp* : one widely raised as a meat animal **2** : a contemptible person — **swin·ish** *adj*

¹**swing** \'swiŋ\ *vb* **swung** \'swəŋ\; **swing·ing 1** : to move or cause to move rapidly in an arc **2** : to sway or cause to sway back and forth **3** : to hang so as to move freely back and forth or in a curve **4** : to be executed by hanging **5** : to move or turn on a hinge or pivot **6** : to manage or handle successfully **7** : to march or walk with free swaying movements **8** : to have a steady pulsing rhythm; *also* : to play swing music **9** : to be lively and up-to-date; *also* : to engage freely in sex ◆ **Synonyms** WIELD, MANIPULATE, PLY, MANEUVER — **swing·er** *n* — **swing·ing** *adj*

²**swing** *n* **1** : the act of swinging **2** : a swinging blow, movement, or rhythm **3** : the distance through which something swings : FLUCTUATION **4** : progression of an activity or process ⟨in full ∼⟩ **5** : a seat suspended by a rope or chain for swinging back and forth for pleasure **6** : jazz music played esp. by a large band and marked by a steady lively rhythm, simple harmony, and a basic melody often submerged in improvisation

³**swing** *adj* **1** : of or relating to musical swing **2** : that may swing decisively either way (as on an issue) ⟨∼ voters⟩

¹**swipe** \'swīp\ *n* : a strong sweeping blow

²**swipe** *vb* **swiped; swip·ing 1** : to strike or wipe with a

sweeping motion **2** : PILFER, SNATCH **3** : to slide (a card having a magnetic code) through a reading device

swirl \'swərl\ *vb* : to move or cause to move with a whirling motion — **swirl** *n* — **swirly** \'swər-lē\ *adj*

swish \'swish\ *n* **1** : a prolonged hissing sound **2** : a light sweeping or brushing sound — **swish** *vb*

Swiss \'swis\ *n* **1** *pl* **Swiss** : a native or inhabitant of Switzerland **2** : a hard cheese with large holes — **Swiss** *adj*

Swiss chard *n* : a beet having large leaves and succulent stalks often cooked as a vegetable

¹**switch** \'swich\ *n* **1** : a slender flexible whip, rod, or twig **2** : a blow with a switch **3** : a shift from one thing to another; *also* : change from the usual **4** : a device for adjusting the rails of a track so that a locomotive or train may be turned from one track to another; *also* : a railroad siding **5** : a device for making, breaking, or changing the connections in an electrical circuit **6** : a heavy strand of hair often used in addition to a person's own hair for some coiffures

²**switch** *vb* **1** : to punish or urge on with a switch **2** : WHISK ⟨a cow ∼ing her tail⟩ **3** : to shift or turn by operating a switch **4** : CHANGE, EXCHANGE

switch·back \'swich-,bak\ *n* : a zigzag road, trail, or section of railroad tracks for climbing a steep hill

switch·blade \-,blād\ *n* : a pocket-knife with a spring-operated blade

switch·board \-,bōrd\ *n* : a panel for controlling the operation of a number of electric circuits; *esp* : one used to make and break telephone connections

switch–hit·ter \-'hi-tər\ *n* : a baseball player who bats either right-handed or left-handed — **switch–hit** \-'hit\ *vb*

switch·man \'swich-mən\ *n* : one who attends a railroad switch

Switz *abbr* Switzerland

¹**swiv·el** \'swi-vəl\ *n* : a device joining two parts so that one or both can turn freely

²**swivel** *vb* **-eled** *or* **-elled; -el·ing** *or* **-el·ling** : to swing or turn on or as if on a swivel

swiv·et \'swi-vət\ *n* : an agitated state

swiz·zle stick \'swi-zəl-\ *n* : a stick used to stir mixed drinks

swollen *past part of* SWELL

swoon \'swün\ *vb* : FAINT — **swoon** *n*

swoop \'swüp\ *vb* : to move with a sweep ⟨the eagle ∼ed down on its prey⟩ — **swoop** *n*

swoopy \'swü-pē\ *adj* : having lines that extend in a wide curve ⟨a ∼ silhouette⟩

swop *chiefly Brit var of* SWAP

sword \'sȯrd\ *n* **1** : a weapon with a long blade for cutting or thrusting **2** : the use of force

sword·fish \-,fish\ *n* : a very large ocean fish used for food that has the upper jaw prolonged into a long swordlike beak

swordfish

sword·play \-,plā\ *n* : the art or skill of wielding a sword

swords·man \'sȯrdz-mən\ *n* : one skilled in swordplay; *esp* : FENCER

sword·tail \'sȯrd-,tāl\ *n* : a small brightly marked Central American fish often kept in aquariums

swore *past of* SWEAR

sworn *past part of* SWEAR

swum *past part of* SWIM

swung *past and past part of* SWING

syb·a·rite \'si-bə-,rīt\ *n* : a lover of luxury : VOLUPTUARY — **syb·a·rit·ic** \,si-bə-'ri-tik\ *adj*

syc·a·more \'si-kə-,mȯr\ *n* : a large spreading tree chiefly of the eastern and central U.S. that has light brown flaky bark and small round fruits hanging on long stalks

sy·co·phant \'si-kə-fənt\ *n* : a servile flatterer — **sy·co·phan·cy** \'si-kə-fən-sē\ *n* — **sy·co·phan·tic** \,si-kə-'fan-tik\ *adj*

syl *or* **syll** *abbr* syllable

syl·lab·i·ca·tion \sə-ˌla-bə-ˈkā-shən\ *n* : the division of words into syllables

syl·lab·i·fy \sə-ˈla-bə-ˌfī\ *vb* **-fied; -fy·ing** : to form or divide into syllables — **syl·lab·i·fi·ca·tion** \-ˌla-bə-fə-ˈkā-shən\ *n*

syl·la·ble \ˈsi-lə-bəl\ *n* [ME, fr. AF *sillabe, silable,* fr. L *syllaba,* fr. Gk *syllabē,* fr. *syllambanein* to gather together, fr. *syn-* with + *lambanein* to take] : a unit of spoken language consisting of an uninterrupted utterance and forming either a whole word (as *cat*) or a commonly recognized division of a word (as *syl* in *syl-la-ble*); *also* : one or more letters representing such a unit — **syl·lab·ic** \sə-ˈla-bik\ *adj*

syl·la·bus \ˈsi-lə-bəs\ *n, pl* **-bi** \-ˌbī\ *or* **-bus·es** : a summary containing the heads or main topics of a speech, book, or course of study

syl·lo·gism \ˈsi-lə-ˌji-zəm\ *n* : a logical scheme of a formal argument consisting of a major and a minor premise and a conclusion which must logically be true if the premises are true — **syl·lo·gis·tic** \ˌsi-lə-ˈjis-tik\ *adj*

sylph \ˈsilf\ *n* **1** : an imaginary being inhabiting the air **2** : a slender graceful woman

syl·van \ˈsil-vən\ *adj* **1** : living or located in a wooded area; *also* : of, relating to, or characteristic of forest **2** : abounding in woods or trees

sym *abbr* **1** symbol **2** symmetrical

sym·bi·o·sis \ˌsim-ˌbī-ˈō-səs, -bē-\ *n, pl* **-o·ses** \-ˌsēz\ : the living together in close association of two dissimilar organisms esp. when mutually beneficial — **sym·bi·ot·ic** \-ˈä-tik\ *adj*

sym·bol \ˈsim-bəl\ *n* **1** : something that stands for something else; *esp* : something concrete that represents or suggests another thing that cannot in itself be pictured ⟨the lion is a ∼ of bravery⟩ **2** : a letter, character, or sign used in writing or printing to represent operations, quantities, elements, sounds, or other ideas — **sym·bol·ic** \sim-ˈbä-lik\ *also* **sym·bol·i·cal** \-li-kəl\ *adj* — **sym·bol·i·cal·ly** \-k(ə-)lē\ *adv*

sym·bol·ise *Brit var of* SYMBOLIZE

sym·bol·ism \ˈsim-bə-ˌli-zəm\ *n* : representation of abstract or intangible things by means of symbols

sym·bol·ize \ˈsim-bə-ˌlīz\ *vb* **-ized; -iz·ing** **1** : to serve as a symbol of **2** : to represent by symbols — **sym·bol·i·za·tion** \ˌsim-bə-lə-ˈzā-shən\ *n*

sym·me·try \ˈsi-mə-trē\ *n, pl* **-tries** **1** : an arrangement marked by regularity and balanced proportions **2** : correspondence in size, shape, and position of parts that are on opposite sides of a dividing line or center — **sym·met·ri·cal** \sə-ˈme-tri-kəl\ *or* **sym·met·ric** \sə-ˈme-trik\ *adj* — **sym·met·ri·cal·ly** \-k(ə-)lē\ *adv*

sympathetic nervous system *n* : the part of the autonomic nervous system that is concerned esp. with the body's repsonse to stress and that tends to decrease the tone and contractility of smooth muscle and increase blood pressure and the activity of the heart

sym·pa·thise *chiefly Brit var of* SYMPATHIZE

sym·pa·thize \ˈsim-pə-ˌthīz\ *vb* **-thized; -thiz·ing** : to feel or show sympathy — **sym·pa·thiz·er** *n*

sym·pa·thy \ˈsim-pə-thē\ *n, pl* **-thies** **1** : a relationship between persons or things wherein whatever affects one similarly affects the other **2** : harmony of interests and aims **3** : FAVOR, SUPPORT **4** : the capacity for entering into and sharing the feelings or interests of another; *also* : COMPASSION, PITY **5** : an expression of sorrow for another's loss, grief, or misfortune — **sym·pa·thet·ic** \ˌsim-pə-ˈthe-tik\ *adj* — **sym·pa·thet·i·cal·ly** \-ti-k(ə-)lē\ *adv*

sym·pho·ny \ˈsim-fə-nē\ *n, pl* **-nies** **1** : harmony of sounds **2** : a large and complex composition for a full orchestra **3** : a large orchestra of a kind that plays symphonies — **sym·phon·ic** \sim-ˈfä-nik\ *adj*

sym·po·sium \sim-ˈpō-zē-əm\ *n, pl* **-sia** \-zē-ə\ *or* **-siums** : a conference at which a particular topic is discussed by various speakers; *also* : a collection of opinions about a subject

symp·tom \ˈsimp-təm\ *n* [LL *symptoma,* fr. Gk *symptōma* happening, attribute, symptom, fr. *sympiptein* to happen, fr. *syn-* with + *piptein* to fall] **1** : something that indicates the presence of disease or abnormality; *esp* : something (as a headache) that can be sensed only by the individual affected **2** : SIGN, INDICATION ⟨∼s of inner turmoil⟩ — **symp·tom·at·ic** \ˌsimp-tə-ˈma-tik\ *adj*

syn *abbr* synonym; synonymous; synonymy

syn·a·gogue *also* **syn·a·gog** \ˈsi-nə-ˌgäg\ *n* [ME *synagoge,* fr. AF, fr. LL *synagoga,* fr. Gk *synagōgē* assembly, synagogue, fr. *synagein* to bring together] **1** : a Jewish congregation **2** : the house of worship of a Jewish congregation

syn·apse \ˈsi-ˌnaps, sə-ˈnaps\ *n* : the point at which a nervous impulse passes from one neuron to another — **syn·ap·tic** \sə-ˈnap-tik\ *adj*

¹sync *also* **synch** \ˈsiŋk\ *vb* **synced** *also* **synched** \ˈsiŋkt\; **sync·ing** *also* **synch·ing** \ˈsiŋ-kiŋ\ : SYNCHRONIZE

²sync *also* **synch** *n* : SYNCHRONIZATION, SYNCHRONISM — **sync** *adj*

syn·chro·ni·sa·tion, syn·chro·nise *Brit var of* SYNCHRONIZATION, SYNCHRONIZE

syn·chro·nize \ˈsiŋ-krə-ˌnīz, ˈsin-\ *vb* **-nized; -niz·ing** **1** : to occur or cause to occur at the same instant **2** : to represent, arrange, or tabulate according to dates or time **3** : to cause to agree in time **4** : to make synchronous in operation — **syn·chro·nism** \-ˌni-zəm\ *n* — **syn·chro·ni·za·tion** \ˌsiŋ-krə-nə-ˈzā-shən, ˌsin-\ *n* — **syn·chro·niz·er** *n*

syn·chro·nous \ˈsiŋ-krə-nəs, ˈsin-\ *adj* **1** : happening at the same time : CONCURRENT **2** : working, moving, or occurring together at the same rate and at the proper time

syn·co·pa·tion \ˌsiŋ-kə-ˈpā-shən, ˌsin-\ *n* : a shifting of the regular musical accent : occurrence of accented notes on the weak beat — **syn·co·pate** \ˈsiŋ-kə-ˌpāt, ˈsin-\ *vb*

syn·co·pe \ˈsiŋ-kə-(ˌ)pē, ˈsin-\ *n* : the loss of one or more sounds or letters in the interior of a word (as in *fo'c's'le* for *forecastle*)

¹syn·di·cate \ˈsin-di-kət\ *n* **1** : a group of persons who combine to carry out a financial or industrial undertaking **2** : a loose association of racketeers **3** : a business concern that sells materials for publication in many newspapers and periodicals at the same time

²syn·di·cate \-də-ˌkāt\ *vb* **-cat·ed; -cat·ing** **1** : to combine into or manage as a syndicate **2** : to publish through a syndicate — **syn·di·ca·tion** \ˌsin-də-ˈkā-shən\ *n*

syn·drome \ˈsin-ˌdrōm\ *n* : a group of signs and symptoms that occur together and characterize a particular abnormality or condition

syn·er·gism \ˈsin-ər-ˌji-zəm\ *n* : interaction of discrete agencies (as industrial firms), agents (as drugs), or conditions such that the total effect is greater than the sum of the individual effects — **syn·er·gist** \-jist\ *n* — **syn·er·gis·tic** \ˌsin-ər-ˈjis-tik\ *adj* — **syn·er·gis·ti·cal·ly** \-ti-k(ə-)lē\ *adv*

syn·er·gy \ˈsi-nər-je\ *n, pl* **-gies** : SYNERGISM

syn·fuel \ˈsin-ˌfyül\ *n* [*synthetic*] : a fuel derived esp. from a fossil fuel

syn·od \ˈsi-nəd\ *n* : COUNCIL, ASSEMBLY; *esp* : a religious governing body — **syn·od·al** \-nə-dᵊl, -ˌnä-dᵊl\ *adj* — **syn·od·ic** \sə-ˈnä-dik\ *or* **syn·od·i·cal** \-di-kəl\ *adj*

syn·onym \ˈsi-nə-ˌnim\ *n* : one of two or more words in the same language which have the same or very nearly the same meaning — **syn·on·y·mous** \sə-ˈnä-nə-məs\ *adj* — **syn·on·y·mous·ly** *adv* — **syn·on·y·my** \-mē\ *n*

syn·op·sis \sə-ˈnäp-səs\ *n, pl* **-op·ses** \-ˌsēz\ : a condensed statement or outline (as of a treatise) : ABSTRACT

syn·op·tic \sə-ˈnäp-tik\ *also* **syn·op·ti·cal** \-ti-kəl\ *adj* : characterized by or affording a comprehensive view

syn·tax \ˈsin-ˌtaks\ *n* : the way in which words are put together to form phrases, clauses, or sentences — **syn·tac·tic** \sin-ˈtak-tik\ *or* **syn·tac·ti·cal** \-ti-kəl\ *adj*

syn·the·sis \ˈsin-thə-səs\ *n, pl* **-the·ses** \-ˌsēz\ : the combination of parts or elements into a whole; *esp* : the production of a substance by union of chemically simpler substances — **syn·the·size** \-ˌsīz\ *vb* — **syn·the·siz·er** *n*

syn·thet·ic \sin-ˈthe-tik\ *adj* : produced artificially esp. by chemical means; *also* : not genuine — **synthetic** *n* — **syn·thet·i·cal·ly** \-ti-k(ə-)lē\ *adv*

syph·i·lis \ˈsi-fə-ləs\ *n* [NL, fr. *Syphilus,* hero of the poem *Syphilis sive Morbus Gallicus (Syphilis or the French disease)* (1530) by Girolamo Fracastoro †1553 Ital. physician] : an infectious usu. venereal disease caused by a spirochete — **syph·i·lit·ic** \ˌsi-fə-ˈli-tik\ *adj or n*

syphon *var of* SIPHON

Sy·rah \sē-ˈrä\ *n* : a red wine

¹sy·ringe \sə-ˈrinj\ *n* : a device used esp. for injecting liquids into or withdrawing them from the body

²**syringe** *vb* **sy·ringed; sy·ring·ing** : to flush or cleanse with or as if with a syringe

syr·up \'sər-əp, 'sir-əp\ *n* **1** : a thick sticky solution of sugar and water often flavored or medicated **2** : the concentrated juice of a fruit or plant — **syr·upy** *adj*

syst *abbr* system

sys·tem \'sis-təm\ *n* **1** : a group of units so combined as to form a whole and to operate in unison **2** : the body as a functioning whole; *also* : a group of bodily organs (as the nervous system) that together carry on some vital function **3** : a definite scheme or method of procedure or classification **4** : regular method or order — **sys·tem·at·ic** \,sis-tə-'ma-tik\ — **sys·tem·at·i·cal·ly** \-ti-k(ə-)lē\ *adv*

sys·tem·a·tise *Brit var of* SYSTEMATIZE

sys·tem·a·tize \'sis-tə-mə-,tīz\ *vb* **-tized; -tiz·ing** : to make into a system : arrange methodically

¹**sys·tem·ic** \sis-'te-mik\ *adj* **1** : of, relating to, or affecting the whole body ⟨∼ disease⟩ **2** : of, relating to, or being a pesticide that when absorbed into the sap or bloodstream makes the entire plant or animal toxic to a pest (as an insect or fungus)

²**systemic** *n* : a systemic pesticide

systemic lupus erythematosus *n* : a systemic disease esp. of women characterized by fever, skin rash, and arthritis, often by anemia, by small hemorrhages of the skin and mucous membranes, and in serious cases by involvement of internal organs

sys·tem·ize \'sis-tə-,mīz\ *vb* **-ized; -iz·ing** : SYSTEMATIZE

systems analyst *n* : a person who studies a procedure or business to determine its goals or purposes and to discover the best ways to accomplish them — **systems analysis** *n*

sys·to·le \'sis-tə-(,)lē\ *n* : a rhythmically recurrent contraction of the heart — **sys·tol·ic** \sis-'tä-lik\ *adj*

¹**t** \'tē\ *n, pl* **t's** *or* **ts** \'tēz\ *often cap* : the 20th letter of the English alphabet

²**t** *abbr, often cap* **1** tablespoon **2** teaspoon **3** temperature **4** ton **5** transitive **6** troy **7** true

T *abbr* **1** toddler **2** T-shirt

Ta *symbol* tantalum

TA *abbr* teaching assistant

¹**tab** \'tab\ *n* **1** : a short projecting flap, loop, or tag; *also* : a small insert or addition **2** : close surveillance : WATCH ⟨keep ∼s on him⟩ **3** : BILL, CHECK **4** : a key on a keyboard esp. for putting data in columns

²**tab** *vb* **tabbed; tab·bing** : DESIGNATE

tab·by \'ta-bē\ *n, pl* **tabbies** : a usu. striped or mottled domestic cat; *also* : a female domestic cat

tab·er·na·cle \'ta-bər-,na-kəl\ *n* [ME, fr. AF, fr. LL *tabernaculum*, fr. L, tent, fr. *taberna* hut] **1** *often cap* : a tent sanctuary used by the Israelites during the Exodus **2** : a receptacle for the consecrated elements of the Eucharist **3** : a house of worship

¹**ta·ble** \'tā-bəl\ *n* **1** : TABLET **1** **2** : a piece of furniture consisting of a smooth flat top fixed on legs **3** : a supply of food : BOARD, FARE **4** : a group of people assembled at or as if at a table **5** : an orderly arrangement of data usu. in rows and columns **6** : a short list ⟨∼ of contents⟩ — **ta·ble·top** \-,täp\ *n*

²**table** *vb* **ta·bled; ta·bling** **1** *Brit* : to place on the agenda **2** : to remove (a parliamentary motion) from consideration indefinitely

tab·leau \'ta-,blō\ *n, pl* **tab·leaux** \-,blōz\ *also* **tableaus** [F] : a scene or event usu. presented on a stage by silent and motionless costumed participants

ta·ble·cloth \'tā-bəl-,klôth\ *n* : a covering spread over a dining table before the table is set

ta·ble d'hôte \,tä-bəl-'dōt\ *n* [F, lit., host's table] : a complete meal of several courses offered at a fixed price

ta·ble·land \'tā-bəl-,land\ *n* : PLATEAU

ta·ble·spoon \-,spün\ *n* **1** : a large spoon used esp. for serving **2** : a unit of measure equal to ½ fluid ounce (15 milliliters)

ta·ble·spoon·ful \-,fül\ *n, pl* **-spoonfuls** \-,fülz\ *also* **-spoons·ful** \-,spünz-fül\ : TABLESPOON **2**

tab·let \'ta-blət\ *n* **1** : a flat slab suited for or bearing an inscription **2** : a collection of sheets of paper glued together at one edge **3** : a compressed or molded block of material; *esp* : a usu. disk-shaped medicated mass

table tennis *n* : a game resembling tennis played on a tabletop with wooden paddles and a small hollow plastic ball

ta·ble·ware \'tā-bəl-,wer\ *n* : utensils (as of china or silver) for table use

¹**tab·loid** \'ta-,blòid\ *adj* : condensed into small scope

²**tabloid** *n* : a newspaper marked by small pages, condensation of the news, and usu. many photographs

¹**ta·boo** *also* **ta·bu** \tə-'bü, ta-\ *adj* [Tongan (a Polynesian language) *tabu*] : prohibited by a taboo

²**taboo** *also* **tabu** *n, pl* **taboos** *also* **tabus** **1** : a prohibition against touching, saying, or doing something for fear of immediate harm from a supernatural force **2** : a prohibition imposed by social custom

ta·bor *also* **ta·bour** \'tā-bər\ *n* : a small drum used to accompany a pipe or fife played by the same person

tab·u·lar \'ta-byə-lər\ *adj* **1** : having a flat surface **2** : arranged in a table; *esp* : set up in rows and columns **3** : computed by means of a table

tab·u·late \-,lāt\ *vb* **-lat·ed; -lat·ing** : to put into tabular form — **tab·u·la·tion** \,ta-byə-'lā-shən\ *n* — **tab·u·la·tor** \'ta-byə-,lā-tər\ *n*

TAC \'tak\ *abbr* Tactical Air Command

tach \'tak\ *n* : TACHOMETER

ta·chom·e·ter \ta-'kä-mə-tər, tə-\ *n* [ultim. fr. Gk *tachos* speed] : a device to indicate speed of rotation

tachy·car·dia \,ta-ki-'kär-dē-ə\ *n* : relatively rapid heart action

tachy·on \'ta-kē-,än\ *n* : a hypothetical particle held to travel faster than light

tac·it \'ta-sət\ *adj* [F or L; F *tacite*, fr. L *tacitus* silent, fr. *tacēre* to be silent] **1** : expressed without words or speech **2** : implied or indicated but not actually expressed ⟨∼ consent⟩ — **tac·it·ly** *adv* — **tac·it·ness** *n*

tac·i·turn \'ta-sə-,tərn\ *adj* : disinclined to talk ♦ **Synonyms** UNCOMMUNICATIVE, RESERVED, RETICENT, CLOSEMOUTHED — **tac·i·tur·ni·ty** \,ta-sə-'tər-nə-tē\ *n*

¹**tack** \'tak\ *vb* **1** : to fasten with tacks; *also* : to add on **2** : to change the direction of (a sailing ship) from one tack to another **3** : to follow a zigzag course

²**tack** *n* **1** : a small sharp nail with a broad flat head **2** : the direction toward the wind that a ship is sailing ⟨starboard ∼⟩; *also* : the run of a ship on one tack **3** : a change of course from one tack to another **4** : a zigzag course **5** : a course of action

³**tack** *n* : gear for harnessing a horse

¹**tack·le** \'ta-kəl, *naut often* 'tā-\ *n* **1** : GEAR, APPARATUS, EQUIPMENT **2** : the rigging of a ship **3** : an arrangement of ropes and pulleys for hoisting or pulling heavy objects **4** : the act or an instance of tackling; *also* : a football lineman playing between guard and end

²**tackle** *vb* **tack·led; tack·ling** **1** : to attach and secure with or as if with tackle **2** : to seize, grapple with, or throw down with the intention of subduing or stopping **3** : to set about dealing with ⟨∼ a problem⟩ — **tack·ler** *n*

¹**tacky** \'ta-kē\ *adj* **tack·i·er; -est** : sticky to the touch

²**tacky** *adj* **tack·i·er; -est** **1** : SHABBY, SEEDY **2** : marked by lack of style or good taste; *also* : cheaply showy ⟨a ∼ publicity stunt⟩ ⟨a ∼ outfit⟩

ta·co \'tä-kō\ *n, pl* **tacos** \-kōz\ [MexSp] : a usu. fried tortilla rolled up with or folded over a filling

tact \'takt\ *n* [F, sense of touch, fr. L *tactus*, fr. *tangere* to touch] : a keen sense of what to do or say to keep good relations with others — **tact·ful** \-fəl\ *adj* — **tact·ful·ly** *adv* — **tact·less** *adj* — **tact·less·ly** *adv*

tac·tic \'tak-tik\ *n* : a planned action for accomplishing an end

tac·tics \'tak-tiks\ *n sing or pl* **1** : the science of maneuvering forces in combat **2** : the skill of using available means to accomplish an end — **tac·ti·cal** \-ti-kəl\ *adj* — **tac·ti·cian** \tak-'ti-shən\ *n*

tac·tile \'takt-ᵊl, 'tak-ˌtī(-ə)l\ *adj* : of, relating to, or perceptible through the sense of touch

tad·pole \'tad-ˌpōl\ *n* [ME *taddepol*, fr. *tode* toad + *polle* head] : an aquatic larva of a frog or toad that has a tail and gills

tadpole: in stages

tae kwon do \'tī-'kwän-'dō\ *n* : a Korean martial art of self-defense

taf·fe·ta \'ta-fə-tə\ *n* : a crisp lustrous fabric (as of silk or rayon)

taff·rail \'taf-ˌrāl, -rəl\ *n* : the rail around a ship's stern

taf·fy \'ta-fē\ *n, pl* **taffies** : a candy usu. of molasses or brown sugar stretched until porous and light-colored

¹tag \'tag\ *n* **1** : a metal or plastic binding on an end of a shoelace **2** : a piece of hanging or attached material **3** : a hackneyed quotation or saying **4** : a descriptive or identifying epithet

²tag *vb* **tagged; tag·ging 1** : to provide or mark with or as if with a tag; *esp* : IDENTIFY **2** : to attach as an addition **3** : to follow closely and persistently ⟨∼s along everywhere we go⟩ **4** : to hold responsible for something

³tag *n* : a game in which one player chases others and tries to touch one of them

⁴tag *vb* **tagged; tag·ging 1** : to touch in or as if in a game of tag **2** : SELECT

TAG *abbr* the adjutant general

tag sale *n* : GARAGE SALE

Ta·hi·tian \tə-'hē-shən\ *n* **1** : a native or inhabitant of Tahiti **2** : the Polynesian language of the Tahitians — **Tahitian** *adj*

tai·ga \'tī-gə\ *n* [Russ *taĭga*] : a moist coniferous subarctic forest extending south from the tundra

¹tail \'tāl\ *n* **1** : the rear end or a process extending from the rear end of an animal **2** : something resembling an animal's tail **3** *pl* : full evening dress for men **4** : the back, last, lower, or inferior part of something; *esp* : the reverse of a coin — usu. used in pl. ⟨∼s, I win⟩ **5** : one who follows or keeps watch on someone — **tailed** \'tāld\ *adj* — **tail·less** \'tāl-ləs\ *adj*

²tail *vb* : FOLLOW; *esp* : to follow for the purpose of surveillance

tail·coat \-'kōt\ *n* : a coat with tails; *esp* : a man's full-dress coat with two long tapering skirts at the back

¹tail·gate \-ˌgāt\ *n* : a board or gate at the back end of a vehicle that can be let down (as for loading)

²tailgate *vb* **tail·gat·ed; tail·gat·ing 1** : to drive dangerously close behind another vehicle **2** : to hold a tailgate picnic

³tailgate *adj* : relating to or being a picnic set up on a tailgate

tail·light \-ˌlīt\ *n* : a usu. red warning light mounted at the rear of a vehicle

¹tai·lor \'tā-lər\ *n* [ME *taillour*, fr. AF *taillur*, fr. *tailler* to cut, fr. LL *taliare*, fr. L *talea* twig, cutting] : a person whose occupation is making or altering garments

²tailor *vb* **1** : to make or fashion as the work of a tailor **2** : to make or adapt to suit a special purpose

tail·pipe \'tāl-ˌpīp\ *n* : an outlet by which engine exhaust gases are expelled from a vehicle (as an automobile)

tail·spin \'tāl-ˌspin\ *n* : a rapid descent or downward spiral

tail·wind \'tāl-ˌwind\ *n* : a wind blowing in the same general direction as a course of movement (as of an aircraft)

¹taint \'tānt\ *vb* **1** : CORRUPT, CONTAMINATE **2** : to affect or become affected with something bad (as putrefaction)

²taint *n* : a contaminating mark or influence

ta·ka \'tä-kə\ *n* — see MONEY table

¹take \'tāk\ *vb* **took** \'tůk\; **tak·en** \'tā-kən\; **tak·ing** [ME, fr. OE *tacan*, fr. ON *taka*] **1** : to get into one's hands or possession : GRASP, SEIZE **2** : CAPTURE; *also* : DEFEAT **3** : to obtain or secure for use **4** : to catch or attack through the effect of a sudden force or influence ⟨*taken* ill⟩ **5** : CAPTIVATE, DELIGHT **6** : to bring into a relation ⟨∼ a wife⟩ **7** : REMOVE, SUBTRACT ⟨∼ three from eight⟩ **8** : to pick out : CHOOSE **9** : ASSUME, UNDERTAKE **10** : RECEIVE, ACCEPT **11** : to use for transportation ⟨∼ a bus⟩ **12** : to become impregnated with : ABSORB ⟨∼s a dye⟩ **13** : to receive into one's body (as by swallowing) ⟨∼ a pill⟩ **14** : ENDURE, UNDERGO ⟨∼ a cut in pay⟩ **15** : to lead, carry, or cause to go along to another place **16** : NEED, REQUIRE ⟨∼s a size nine shoe⟩ **17** : to obtain as the result of a special procedure ⟨∼ a snapshot⟩ **18** : to undertake and do, make, or perform ⟨∼ a walk⟩ **19** : to take effect : ACT, OPERATE ♦ **Synonyms** GRAB, CLUTCH, SNATCH, SEIZE, NAB, GRAPPLE — **tak·er** *n* — **take advantage of 1** : to profit by **2** : EXPLOIT — **take after** : RESEMBLE — **take care** : to be careful — **take care of** : to attend to — **take effect** : to become operative — **take exception** : OBJECT — **take for** : to suppose to be; *esp* : to mistake for — **take place** : HAPPEN — **take to 1** : to go to **2** : to apply or devote oneself to **3** : to conceive a liking for

²take *n* **1** : the number or quantity taken; *also* : PROCEEDS, RECEIPTS **2** : an act or the action of taking **3** : a television or movie scene filmed or taped at one time; *also* : a sound recording made at one time **4** : a distinct or personal point of view

take·off \'tāk-ˌof\ *n* **1** : IMITATION; *esp* : PARODY **2** : an act or instance of taking off

take off *vb* **1** : REMOVE **2** : DEDUCT **3** : to set out : go away **4** : to begin flight

take on *vb* **1** : to begin to perform or deal with; *also* : to contend with as an opponent **2** : ENGAGE, HIRE **3** : to assume or acquire as or as if one's own **4** : to make an unusual show of one's feelings esp. of grief or anger

take over *vb* : to assume control or possession of or responsibility for — **take·over** \'tāk-ˌō-vər\ *n*

take up *vb* **1** : PICK UP **2** : to begin to occupy (land) **3** : to absorb or incorporate into itself ⟨plants *taking up* nutrients⟩ **4** : to begin to engage in ⟨*took up* jogging⟩ **5** : to make tighter or shorter ⟨*take up* the slack⟩

tak·ings \'tā-kiŋz\ *n pl, chiefly Brit* : receipts esp. of money

ta·la \'tä-lə\ *n, pl* **tala** — see MONEY table

talc \'talk\ *n* : a soft mineral with a soapy feel used esp. in making a soothing powder (**tal·cum powder** \'tal-kəm-\) for the skin

tale \'tāl\ *n* **1** : a relation of a series of events **2** : a report of a confidential matter **3** : idle talk; *esp* : harmful gossip **4** : a usu. imaginative narrative **5** : FALSEHOOD **6** : COUNT, TALLY

tal·ent \'ta-lənt\ *n* **1** : an ancient unit of weight and value **2** : the natural endowments of a person **3** : a special often creative or artistic aptitude **4** : mental power : ABILITY **5** : a person of talent ♦ **Synonyms** GENIUS, GIFT, FACULTY, APTITUDE, KNACK — **tal·ent·ed** *adj*

ta·ler \'tä-lər\ *n* : any of numerous silver coins issued by German states from the 15th to the 19th centuries

tales·man \'tālz-mən\ *n* : a person summoned for jury duty

tal·is·man \'ta-ləs-mən, -ləz-\ *n, pl* **-mans** [F *talisman* or Sp *talismán* or It *talismano*, fr. Ar *ṭilsam*, fr. MGk *telesma*, fr. Gk, consecration, fr. *telein* to initiate into the mysteries, complete, fr. *telos* end] : an object thought to act as a charm

¹talk \'tök\ *vb* **1** : to express in speech : utter words : SPEAK **2** : DISCUSS ⟨∼ business⟩ **3** : to influence or cause by talking ⟨∼ed him into going⟩ **4** : to use (a language) for communicating **5** : CONVERSE **6** : to reveal confidential information; *also* : GOSSIP **7** : to give a talk

: LECTURE — **talk·er** *n* — **talk back** : to answer impertinently

²**talk** *n* **1** : the act of talking **2** : a way of speaking **3** : a formal discussion **4** : REPORT, RUMOR **5** : the topic of comment or gossip ⟨the ∼ of the town⟩ **6** : an informal address or lecture

talk·ative \ˈtȯ-kə-tiv\ *adj* : given to talking ✦ **Synonyms** LOQUACIOUS, CHATTY, GABBY, GARRULOUS — **talk·ative·ly** *adv* — **talk·ative·ness** *n*

talk·ing–to \ˈtȯ-kiŋ-ˌtü\ *n* : REPRIMAND, REPROOF

talk radio *n* : radio programming consisting of call-in shows

tall \ˈtȯl\ *adj* **1** : high in stature; *also* : of a specified height ⟨six feet ∼⟩ **2** : LARGE, FORMIDABLE ⟨a ∼ order⟩ **3** : UNBELIEVABLE, IMPROBABLE ⟨a ∼ story⟩ — **tall·ness** *n*

tal·low \ˈta-lō\ *n* : a hard white fat rendered usu. from cattle or sheep tissues and used esp. in candles

¹**tal·ly** \ˈta-lē\ *n, pl* **tallies** **1** : a device for visibly recording or accounting esp. business transactions **2** : a recorded account **3** : a corresponding part; *also* : CORRESPONDENCE

²**tally** *vb* **tal·lied; tal·ly·ing** **1** : to mark on or as if on a tally **2** : to make a count of : RECKON; *also* : SCORE **3** : CORRESPOND, MATCH ✦ **Synonyms** SQUARE, ACCORD, HARMONIZE, CONFORM, JIBE

tal·ly·ho \ˌta-lē-ˈhō\ *n, pl* **-hos** : a call of a huntsman at sight of the fox

Tal·mud \ˈtäl-ˌmu̇d, ˈtal-məd\ *n* [Late Heb *talmūdh,* lit., instruction] : the authoritative body of Jewish tradition — **Tal·mu·dic** \tal-ˈmü-dik, -ˈmyü-, -ˈmə-; täl-ˈmu̇-\ *adj* — **Tal·mud·ist** \ˈtäl-mu̇-dist, ˈtal-mə-\ *n*

tal·on \ˈta-lən\ *n* : the claw of an animal and esp. of a bird of prey

ta·lus \ˈtā-ləs, ˈta-\ *n* : rock debris at the base of a cliff

tam \ˈtam\ *n* : TAM-O'-SHANTER

ta·ma·le \tə-ˈmä-lē\ *n* [MexSp *tamales,* pl. of *tamal* tamale, fr. Nahuatl *tamalli* steamed cornmeal dough] : ground meat seasoned with chili, rolled in cornmeal dough, wrapped in corn husks, and steamed

tam·a·rack \ˈta-mə-ˌrak\ *n* : a larch of northern No. America; *also* : its hard resinous wood

tam·a·rin \ˈta-mə-rən\ *n* : any of several small So. American monkeys related to the marmosets

tam·a·rind \ˈta-mə-rənd, -ˌrind\ *n* [Sp & Pg *tamarindo,* fr. Ar *tamr hindī,* lit., Indian date] : a tropical tree of the legume family with hard yellowish wood and feathery leaves; *also* : its acid fruit

tam·ba·la \täm-ˈbä-lə\ *n, pl* **-la** *or* **-las** — see *kwacha* at MONEY table

tam·bou·rine \ˌtam-bə-ˈrēn\ *n* : a small shallow drum with loose disks at the sides played by shaking or striking with the hand

¹**tame** \ˈtām\ *adj* **tam·er; tam·est** **1** : reduced from a state of native wildness esp. so as to be useful to humans : DOMESTICATED **2** : made docile : SUBDUED **3** : lacking spirit or interest : INSIPID ✦ **Synonyms** SUBMISSIVE, DOMESTIC, DOMESTICATED — **tame·ly** *adv* — **tame·ness** *n*

²**tame** *vb* **tamed; tam·ing** **1** : to make or become tame; *also* : to subject (land) to cultivation **2** : HUMBLE, SUBDUE — **tam·able** *or* **tame·able** \ˈtā-mə-bəl\ *adj* — **tame·less** *adj* — **tam·er** *n*

tam–o'–shan·ter \ˈta-mə-ˌshan-tər\ *n* [fr. poem *Tam o' Shanter* (1790) by Robert Burns †1796 Scot. poet] : a Scottish woolen cap with a wide flat circular crown and usu. a pom-pom in the center

ta·mox·i·fen \tə-ˈmäk-sə-ˌfen\ *n* : a drug used esp. to treat breast cancer

tamp \ˈtamp\ *vb* : to drive down or in by a series of light blows

tam·per \ˈtam-pər\ *vb* **1** : to carry on underhand negotiations (as by bribery) ⟨∼ with a witness⟩ **2** : to interfere so as to weaken or change for the worse ⟨∼ with a document⟩ **3** : to try foolish or dangerous experiments

tam·pon \ˈtam-ˌpän\ *n* [F, lit., plug] : a plug (as of cotton) introduced into a body cavity usu. to absorb secretions (as from menstruation) or to arrest bleeding

¹**tan** \ˈtan\ *vb* **tanned; tan·ning** **1** : to change (hide) into leather esp. by soaking in a liquid containing tannin **2** : to make or become brown (as by exposure to the sun) **3** : WHIP, THRASH

²**tan** *n* **1** : a brown skin color induced by sun or weather **2** : a light yellowish brown color

³**tan** *abbr* tangent

tan·a·ger \ˈta-ni-jər\ *n* : any of numerous American birds that are often brightly colored

tan·bark \ˈtan-ˌbärk\ *n* : bark (as of oak or sumac) that is rich in tannin and used in tanning

¹**tan·dem** \ˈtan-dəm\ *n* [L, at last, at length (taken to mean "lengthwise"), fr. *tam* so] **1** : a 2-seated carriage with horses hitched tandem; *also* : its team **2** : a bicycle for two persons sitting one behind the other — **in tandem** : in a tandem arrangement

²**tandem** *adv* : one behind another

³**tandem** *adj* **1** : consisting of things arranged one behind the other **2** : working in conjunction with each other

tang \ˈtaŋ\ *n* **1** : a part in a tool that connects the blade with the handle **2** : a sharp distinctive flavor; *also* : a pungent odor — **tangy** *adj*

¹**tan·gent** \ˈtan-jənt\ *adj* [L *tangent-, tangens,* prp. of *tangere* to touch] : TOUCHING; *esp* : touching a circle or sphere at only one point

²**tangent** *n* **1** : the trigonometric function that is the ratio between the side opposite and the side adjacent to an acute angle in a right triangle **2** : a tangent line, curve, or surface **3** : an abrupt change of course

tan·gen·tial \tan-ˈjen-chəl\ *adj* **1** : TANGENT **2** : touching lightly : INCIDENTAL ⟨∼ involvement⟩ — **tan·gen·tial·ly** *adv*

tan·ger·ine \ˈtan-jə-ˌrēn, ˌtan-jə-ˈrēn\ *n* : a deep orange loose-skinned citrus fruit; *also* : a tree that bears tangerines

¹**tan·gi·ble** \ˈtan-jə-bəl\ *adj* **1** : perceptible esp. by the sense of touch : PALPABLE **2** : substantially real : MATERIAL ⟨∼ rewards⟩ **3** : capable of being appraised ⟨∼ assets⟩ ✦ **Synonyms** APPRECIABLE, PERCEPTIBLE, SENSIBLE, DISCERNIBLE — **tan·gi·bil·i·ty** \ˌtan-jə-ˈbi-lə-tē\ *n*

²**tangible** *n* : something tangible; *esp* : a tangible asset

¹**tan·gle** \ˈtaŋ-gəl\ *vb* **tan·gled; tan·gling** **1** : to involve so as to hamper or embarrass; *also* : ENTRAP **2** : to unite or knit together in intricate confusion : ENTANGLE

²**tangle** *n* **1** : a tangled twisted mass **2** : a confusedly complicated state : MUDDLE

tan·go \ˈtaŋ-gō\ *n, pl* **tangos** : a dance of Latin-American origin — **tango** *vb*

tank \ˈtaŋk\ *n* **1** : a large artificial receptacle for liquids **2** : a heavily armed and armored combat vehicle that moves on tracks — **tank·ful** *n*

tan·kard \ˈtaŋ-kərd\ *n* : a tall one-handled drinking vessel

tank·er \ˈtaŋ-kər\ *n* : a vehicle equipped for transporting a liquid

tank top *n* : a sleeveless collarless pullover shirt with shoulder straps

tank town *n* : a small town

tan·ner \ˈta-nər\ *n* : one that tans hides

tan·nery \ˈta-nə-rē\ *n, pl* **-ner·ies** : a place where tanning is carried on

tan·nic acid \ˈta-nik-\ *n* : TANNIN

tan·nin \ˈta-nən\ *n* : any of various plant substances used esp. in tanning and dyeing, in inks, and as astringents

tan·sy \ˈtan-zē\ *n, pl* **tansies** : a common weedy herb related to the daisies with an aromatic odor and bitter-tasting finely divided leaves

tan·ta·lise *Brit var of* TANTALIZE

tan·ta·lize \ˈtan-tə-ˌlīz\ *vb* **-lized; -liz·ing** [fr. *Tantalus,* king of Greek myth punished in Hades by having to stand up to his chin in water that receded as he bent to drink] : to tease or torment by presenting something desirable but keeping it out of reach — **tan·ta·liz·er** *n* — **tan·ta·liz·ing·ly** *adv*

tan·ta·lum \ˈtan-tə-ləm\ *n* : a gray-white ductile metallic chemical element

tan·ta·mount \ˈtan-tə-ˌmau̇nt\ *adj* : equivalent in value or meaning ⟨a relationship ∼ to marriage⟩

tan·trum \ˈtan-trəm\ *n* : a fit of bad temper

Tao·ism \ˈtau̇-ˌi-zəm, ˈdau̇-\ *n* : a Chinese mystical philosophy; *also* : a religion developed from Taoist philosophy and Buddhism — **Tao·ist** \-ist\ *adj or n*

¹**tap** \ˈtap\ *n* **1** : FAUCET, COCK **2** : liquor drawn through a tap **3** : the removing of fluid from a container or cavity by tapping **4** : a tool for forming an internal screw

thread **5** : a point in an electric circuit where a connection may be made

²tap *vb* **tapped; tap·ping 1** : to release or cause to flow by piercing or by drawing a plug from a container or cavity **2** : to pierce so as to let out or draw off a fluid **3** : to draw from ⟨~ resources⟩ **4** : to cut in on (as a telephone signal) to get information **5** : to form an internal screw thread in by means of a tap **6** : to connect (as a gas or water main) with a local supply — **tap·per** *n*

³tap *vb* **tapped; tap·ping 1** : to rap lightly **2** : to bring about by repeated light blows **3** : SELECT; *esp* : to elect to membership

⁴tap *n* **1** : a light blow or stroke; *also* : its sound **2** : a small metal plate for the sole or heel of a shoe

ta·pa \'tä-pə, 'ta-\ *n* [Sp, lit., cover, lid] : an hors d'oeuvre served with drinks esp. in Spanish bars — usu. used in pl.

¹tape \'tāp\ *n* **1** : a narrow flexible band or strip (as of woven fabric) **2** : MAGNETIC TAPE; *also* : CASSETTE

²tape *vb* **taped; tap·ing 1** : to fasten or support with tape **2** : to record on magnetic tape

tape deck *n* : a device used to play back cassette tapes that usu. has to be connected to an audio system

tape measure *n* : a tape marked off in units (as inches) for measuring

¹ta·per \'tā-pər\ *n* **1** : a slender wax candle; *also* : a long waxed wick **2** : a gradual lessening of thickness or width in a long object

²taper *vb* **ta·pered; ta·per·ing 1** : to make or become gradually smaller toward one end **2** : to diminish gradually

tape—re·cord \ˌtāp-ri-'kȯrd\ *vb* : to make a recording of on magnetic tape — **tape recorder** *n* — **tape recording** *n*

tap·es·try \'ta-pə-strē\ *n, pl* **-tries** : a heavy reversible textile that has designs or pictures woven into it and is used esp. as a wall hanging

tape·worm \'tāp-ˌwərm\ *n* : any of a class of long flat segmented worms parasitic esp. in vertebrate intestines

tap·i·o·ca \ˌta-pē-'ō-kə\ *n* : a usu. granular preparation of cassava starch used esp. in puddings; *also* : a dish (as pudding) that contains tapioca

ta·pir \'tā-pər\ *n, pl* **tapirs** *also* **tapir** [Pg *tapir, tapira,* fr. Tupinambà (American Indian language of Brazil) *tapiʔira*] : any of a genus of large herbivorous hoofed mammals of tropical America and southeastern Asia

tap·pet \'ta-pət\ *n* : a lever or projection moved by some other piece (as a cam) or intended to move something else

tap·room \'tap-ˌrüm, -ˌrům\ *n* : BARROOM

tap·root \-ˌrüt, -ˌrůt\ *n* : a large main root growing straight down and giving off small side roots

taps \'taps\ *n sing or pl* : the last bugle call at night blown as a signal that lights are to be put out; *also* : a similar call blown at military funerals and memorial services

tap·ster \'tap-stər\ *n* : BARTENDER

¹tar \'tär\ *n* **1** : a thick dark sticky liquid distilled from organic material (as wood or coal) **2** : SAILOR, SEAMAN

²tar *vb* **tarred; tar·ring** : to cover or smear with or as if with tar

tar·an·tel·la \ˌtä-rən-'te-lə\ *n* : a lively folk dance of southern Italy in 6/8 time

ta·ran·tu·la \tə-'ran-chə-lə, -tə-lə\ *n, pl* **tarantulas** *also* **ta·ran·tu·lae** \-'ran-chə-ˌlē, -tə-ˌlē\ : any of a family of large hairy American spiders with a sharp bite that is not very poisonous to human beings

tar·dy \'tär-dē\ *adj* **tar·di·er; -est 1** : moving slowly : SLUGGISH **2** : LATE ◆ *Synonyms* BEHINDHAND, OVERDUE, BELATED — **tar·di·ly** \-də-lē\ *adv* — **tar·di·ness** \-dē-nəs\ *n*

¹tare \'ter\ *n* : a weed of grain fields

²tare *n* : a deduction from the gross weight of a substance and its container made in allowance for the weight of the container — **tare** *vb*

¹tar·get \'tär-gət\ *n* [ME, fr. MF *targette,* dim. of *targe* light shield, of Gmc origin] **1** : a mark to shoot at **2** : an object of ridicule or criticism **3** : a goal to be achieved

²target *vb* : to make a target of

tar·iff \'ta-rəf\ *n* [It *tariffa,* fr. Ar *taʿrīf* notification] **1** : a schedule of duties imposed by a government esp. on imported goods; *also* : a duty or rate of duty imposed in such a schedule **2** : a schedule of rates or charges

tar·mac \'tär-ˌmak\ *n* : a surface paved with crushed stone covered with tar

tarn \'tärn\ *n* : a small mountain lake

tar·nish \'tär-nish\ *vb* : to make or become dull or discolored — **tarnish** *n*

ta·ro \'tär-ō, 'ter-\ *n, pl* **taros** : a large-leaved tropical plant related to the arums that is grown for its edible starchy corms; *also* : its corms

tar·ot \'ter-ō, 'ta-rō\ *n* : one of a set of usu. 78 playing cards used esp. for fortune-telling

tar·pau·lin \tär-'pȯ-lən, 'tär-pə-\ *n* : a piece of material (as durable plastic) used for protecting exposed objects

tar·pon \'tär-pən\ *n, pl* **tarpon** *or* **tarpons** : a large silvery bony fish often caught for sport in the warm coastal waters of the Atlantic esp. off Florida

tar·ra·gon \'ter-ə-gän\ *n* [MF *targon,* ultim. fr. Ar *ṭarkhūn*] : a small widely cultivated perennial wormwood with aromatic leaves used as a seasoning; *also* : its leaves

¹tar·ry \'ta-rē\ *vb* **tar·ried; tar·ry·ing 1** : to be tardy : DELAY; *esp* : to be slow in leaving **2** : to stay in or at a place : SOJOURN ◆ *Synonyms* REMAIN, WAIT, LINGER, ABIDE

²tar·ry \'tär-ē\ *adj* : of, resembling, or smeared with tar

tar sand *n* : sand or sandstone that is naturally soaked with the heavy sticky portions of petroleum

tar·sus \'tär-səs\ *n, pl* **tar·si** \-ˌsī\ [NL] : the part of a vertebrate foot between the metatarsus and the leg; *also* : the small bones that support this part — **tar·sal** \-səl\ *adj or n*

¹tart \'tärt\ *adj* **1** : agreeably sharp to the taste : PUNGENT **2** : BITING, CAUSTIC — **tart·ly** *adv* — **tart·ness** *n*

²tart *n* **1** : a small pie or pastry shell containing jelly, custard, or fruit **2** : PROSTITUTE

tar·tan \'tärt-ᵊn\ *n* : a plaid textile design of Scottish origin usu. distinctively patterned to designate a particular clan

tartan

tar·tar \'tär-tər\ *n* **1** : a substance in the juice of grapes deposited (as in wine casks) as a reddish crust or sediment **2** : a crust on the teeth formed from plaque hardened by calcium salts

tar·tar sauce *or* **tar·tare sauce** \'tär-tər-\ *n* : mayonnaise with chopped pickles, olives, or capers

¹task \'task\ *n* [ME *taske,* fr. MF dial. *tasque,* fr. ML *tasca* tax or service imposed by a feudal superior, fr. *taxare* to tax] : a piece of assigned work ◆ *Synonyms* JOB, DUTY, CHORE, STINT, ASSIGNMENT

²task *vb* : to oppress with great labor

task force *n* : a temporary grouping to accomplish a particular objective

task·mas·ter \'task-ˌmas-tər\ *n* : one that imposes a task or burdens another with labor

¹tas·sel \'ta-səl, 'tä-\ *n* **1** : a hanging ornament made of a bunch of cords of even length fastened at one end **2** : something suggesting a tassel; *esp* : a male flower cluster of Indian corn

²tassel *vb* **-seled** *or* **-selled; -sel·ing** *or* **-sel·ling** : to adorn with or put forth tassels

¹taste \'tāst\ *vb* **tast·ed; tast·ing 1** : EXPERIENCE, UNDERGO **2** : to try or determine the flavor of by taking a bit into the mouth **3** : to eat or drink esp. in small quantities : SAMPLE **4** : to have a specific flavor

²taste *n* **1** : a small amount tasted **2** : BIT; *esp* : a sample of experience **3** : the special sense that perceives and identifies sweet, sour, bitter, or salty qualities and is mediated by taste buds on the tongue **4** : a quality perceptible to the sense of taste; *also* : the sensation obtained from a substance in the mouth : FLAVOR **5** : individual preference **6** : critical judgment, discernment, or appreciation; *also* : aesthetic quality ◆ *Synonyms* TANG, RELISH, FLAVOR, SAVOR — **taste·ful** \-fəl\ *adj* — **taste·ful·ly** *adv* — **taste·less** *adj* — **taste·less·ly** *adv* — **tast·er** *n*

taste bud *n* : a sense organ mediating the sensation of taste

tasty \'tā-stē\ *adj* **tast·i·er; -est** : pleasing to the taste : SAVORY ◆ **Synonyms** PALATABLE, APPETIZING, TOOTHSOME, FLAVORSOME — **tast·i·ness** \'tā-stē-nəs\ *n*

tat \'tat\ *vb* **tat·ted; tat·ting** : to work at or make by tatting

¹tat·ter \'ta-tər\ *vb* : to make or become ragged

²tatter *n* **1** : a part torn and left hanging **2** *pl* : tattered clothing

tat·ter·de·ma·lion \,ta-tər-di-'māl-yən\ *n* : one that is ragged or disreputable

tat·ter·sall \'ta-tər-,sȯl, -səl\ *n* : a pattern of colored lines forming squares on solid background; *also* : a fabric in a tattersall pattern

tat·ting \'ta-tiŋ\ *n* : a delicate handmade lace formed usu. by looping and knotting with a single thread and a small shuttle; *also* : the act or process of making such lace

tat·tle \'tat-ᵊl\ *vb* **tat·tled; tat·tling 1** : CHATTER, PRATE **2** : to tell secrets; *also* : to inform against another — **tat·tler** *n*

tat·tle·tale \'tat-ᵊl-,tāl\ *n* : one that tattles : INFORMER

¹tat·too \ta-'tü\ *n, pl* **tattoos** [alter. of earlier *taptoo*, fr. D *taptoe*, fr. the phrase *tap toe!* taps shut!] **1** : a call sounded before taps as notice to go to quarters **2** : a rapid rhythmic rapping

²tattoo *vb* : to mark (the skin) with tattoos

³tattoo *n, pl* **tattoos** [Tahitian *tatau*] : an indelible figure fixed upon the body esp. by insertion of pigment under the skin

tau \'taù, 'tȯ\ *n* : the 19th letter of the Greek alphabet — T or τ

taught *past and past part of* TEACH

¹taunt \'tȯnt\ *n* : a sarcastic challenge or insult

²taunt *vb* : to reproach or challenge in a mocking manner : jeer at ◆ **Synonyms** MOCK, DERIDE, RIDICULE, TWIT — **taunt·er** *n*

taupe \'tōp\ *n* : a brownish gray

Tau·rus \'tȯr-əs\ *n* [L, lit., bull] **1** : a zodiacal constellation between Aries and Gemini usu. pictured as a bull **2** : the 2d sign of the zodiac in astrology; *also* : one born under this sign

taut \'tȯt\ *adj* **1** : tightly drawn : not slack **2** : extremely nervous : TENSE **3** : TRIM, TIDY ⟨a ∼ ship⟩ — **taut·ly** *adv* — **taut·ness** *n*

tau·tol·o·gy \tȯ-'tä-lə-jē\ *n, pl* **-gies** : needless repetition of an idea, statement, or word; *also* : an instance of such repetition — **tau·to·log·i·cal** \,tȯt-ə-'lä-ji-kəl\ *adj* — **tau·to·log·i·cal·ly** \-ji-k(ə-)lē\ *adv* — **tau·tol·o·gous** \tȯ-'tä-lə-gəs\ *adj* — **tau·tol·o·gous·ly** *adv*

tav·ern \'ta-vərn\ *n* [ME *taverne*, fr. AF, fr. L *taberna* hut, shop] **1** : an establishment where alcoholic liquors are sold to be drunk on the premises **2** : INN

taw \'tȯ\ *n* **1** : a marble used as a shooter **2** : the line from which players shoot at marbles

taw·dry \'tȯ-drē\ *adj* **taw·dri·er; -est** [*tawdry lace* a tie of lace for the neck, fr. *St. Audrey* (St. Etheldreda) †679 queen of Northumbria] : cheap and gaudy in appearance and quality ◆ **Synonyms** GARISH, FLASHY, CHINTZY, MERETRICIOUS — **taw·dri·ly** *adv*

taw·ny \'tȯ-nē\ *adj* **taw·ni·er; -est** : of a brownish orange color

¹tax \'taks\ *vb* **1** : to levy a tax on **2** : CHARGE, ACCUSE **3** : to put under pressure — **tax·able** \'tak-sə-bəl\ *adj* — **tax·a·tion** \tak-'sā-shən\ *n*

²tax *n* **1** : a charge usu. of money imposed by authority on persons or property for public purposes **2** : a heavy charge : STRAIN

¹taxi \'tak-sē\ *n, pl* **tax·is** \-sēz\ *also* **tax·ies** : TAXICAB; *also* : a similarly operated boat or aircraft

²taxi *vb* **tax·ied; taxi·ing** *or* **taxy·ing; tax·is** *or* **tax·ies 1** : to move along the ground or on the water under an aircraft's own power when starting or after a landing **2** : to go by taxicab

taxi·cab \'tak-sē-,kab\ *n* : an automobile that carries passengers for a fare usu. based on the distance traveled

taxi·der·my \'tak-sə-,dər-mē\ *n* : the skill or occupation of preparing, stuffing, and mounting skins of animals — **taxi·der·mist** \-mist\ *n*

tax·on \'tak-,sän\ *n, pl* **taxa** \-sə\; *also* **taxons** : a taxonomic group or entity

tax·on·o·my \tak-'sä-nə-mē\ *n* : classification esp. of animals or plants according to natural relationships — **tax·o·nom·ic** \,tak-sə-'nä-mik\ *adj* — **tax·on·o·mist** \tak-'sä-nə-mist\ *n*

tax·pay·er \'taks-,pā-ər\ *n* : one who pays or is liable for a tax — **tax·pay·ing** *adj*

Tay–Sachs disease \'tā-'saks-\ *n* : a hereditary disorder caused by the absence of an enzyme needed to break down fatty material, marked by buildup of lipids in nervous tissue, and causing death in childhood

tb *abbr* tablespoon; tablespoonful

Tb *symbol* terbium

TB \,tē-'bē\ *n* : TUBERCULOSIS

TBA *abbr, often not cap* to be announced

T–bar \'tē-,bär\ *n* : a ski lift with a series of T-shaped bars

tbs *or* **tbsp** *abbr* tablespoon; tablespoonful

Tc *symbol* technetium

TC *abbr* teachers college

T cell *n* : any of several lymphocytes (as a helper T cell) specialized esp. for activity in and control of immunity and the immune response

TCP/IP \,tē-(,)sē-'pē-,ī-'pē\ *n* [*transmission control protocol/Internet protocol*] : a set of communications protocols used over networks and esp. the Internet

TD *abbr* **1** touchdown **2** Treasury Department

TDD *abbr* telecommunications device for the deaf

TDY *abbr* temporary duty

Te *symbol* tellurium

tea \'tē\ *n* [Chin (dialect of Fujian province) *dé*] **1** : the cured leaves and leaf buds of a shrub grown chiefly in China, Japan, India, and Sri Lanka; *also* : this shrub **2** : a drink made by steeping tea in boiling water **3** : refreshments usu. including tea served in late afternoon; *also* : a reception at which tea is served

teach \'tēch\ *vb* **taught** \'tȯt\; **teach·ing 1** : to cause to know something : act as a teacher **2** : to show how ⟨∼ a child to swim⟩ **3** : to make to know the disagreeable consequences of an action **4** : to guide the studies of **5** : to impart the knowledge of ⟨∼ algebra⟩ — **teach·able** *adj* — **teach·er** *n*

teach·ing *n* **1** : the act, practice, or profession of a teacher **2** : something taught; *esp* : DOCTRINE

tea·cup \'tē-,kəp\ *n* : a small cup used with a saucer for hot beverages

teak \'tēk\ *n* : the hard durable yellowish brown wood of a tall tropical Asian timber tree related to the vervains; *also* : this tree

tea·ket·tle \'tē-,ket-ᵊl\ *n* : a covered kettle with a handle and spout for boiling water

teal \'tēl\ *n, pl* **teal** *or* **teals 1** : any of various small short-necked wild ducks **2** : a dark greenish blue color

¹team \'tēm\ *n* [ME *teme*, fr. OE *tēam* offspring, lineage, group of draft animals] **1** : two or more draft animals harnessed to the same vehicle or implement **2** : a number of persons associated in work or activity; *esp* : a group on one side in a match

²team *adj* : of or performed by a team; *also* : marked by devotion to teamwork ⟨a ∼ player⟩

³team *vb* **1** : to haul with or drive a team **2** : to form a team : join forces

team·mate \-,māt\ *n* : a fellow member of a team

team·ster \'tēm-stər\ *n* : one who drives a team or truck

team·work \-,wərk\ *n* : the work or activity of a number of persons acting in close association as members of a unit

tea·pot \'tē-,pät\ *n* : a vessel with a spout for brewing and serving tea

¹tear \'tir\ *n* : a drop of the salty liquid that moistens the eye and inner side of the eyelids; *also, pl* : an act of weeping or grieving — **tear·ful** \-fəl\ *adj* — **tear·ful·ly** *adv* — **teary** \'tir-ē\ *adj*

²tear \'tir\ *vb* : to fill with or shed tears ⟨eyes ∼ing in the wind⟩

³tear \'ter\ *vb* **tore** \'tȯr\; **torn** \'tȯrn\; **tear·ing 1** : to separate parts of or pull apart by force : REND **2** : LACERATE **3** : to disrupt by the pull of contrary forces **4** : to remove by force : WRENCH **5** : to move or act with violence, haste, or force ◆ **Synonyms** RIP, SPLIT, CLEAVE, REND

⁴tear \'ter\ *n* **1** : the act of tearing **2** : a hole or flaw made by tearing : RENT

tear gas \'tir-\ *n* : a substance that on dispersion in the atmosphere blinds the eyes with tears — **tear gas** *vb*

tear·jerk·er \'tir-ˌjər-kər\ *n* : an extravagantly pathetic story, song, play, movie, or broadcast

¹**tease** \'tēz\ *vb* **teased; teas·ing** 1 : to disentangle and lay parallel by combing or carding ⟨~ wool⟩ 2 : to scratch the surface of (cloth) so as to raise a nap 3 : to annoy persistently esp. in fun by goading, coaxing, or tantalizing 4 : to comb (hair) by taking a strand and pushing the short hairs toward the scalp with the comb ♦ *Synonyms* HARASS, WORRY, PESTER, ANNOY

²**tease** *n* 1 : the act of teasing or state of being teased 2 : one that teases

tea·sel \'tē-zəl\ *n* : a prickly herb or its flower head covered with stiff hooked bracts and used to raise the nap on cloth; *also* : an artificial device used for this purpose

tea·spoon \'tē-ˌspün\ *n* 1 : a small spoon suitable for stirring beverages 2 : a unit of measure equal to ⅙ fluid ounce (5 milliliters)

tea·spoon·ful \-ˌfül\ *n, pl* **-spoonfuls** *also* **-spoons·ful** \-ˌspünz-ˌfül\ : TEASPOON 2

teat \'tit, 'tēt\ *n* : the protuberance through which milk is drawn from an udder or breast

tech *abbr* 1 technical; technically; technician 2 technological; technology

tech·ne·tium \tek-'nē-shē-əm\ *n* : a radioactive metallic chemical element

tech·nic \'tek-nik, tek-'nēk\ *n* : TECHNIQUE 1

tech·ni·cal \'tek-ni-kəl\ *adj* [Gk *technikos* of art, skillful, fr. *technē* art, craft, skill] 1 : having special knowledge esp. of a mechanical or scientific subject ⟨~ experts⟩ 2 : of or relating to a particular and esp. a practical or scientific subject ⟨~ training⟩ 3 : according to a strict interpretation of the rules 4 : of or relating to technique — **tech·ni·cal·ly** \-k(ə-)lē\ *adv*

tech·ni·cal·i·ty \ˌtek-nə-'ka-lə-tē\ *n, pl* **-ties** 1 : a detail meaningful only to a specialist 2 : the quality or state of being technical

technical sergeant *n* : a noncommissioned officer in the air force ranking next below a master sergeant

tech·ni·cian \tek-'ni-shən\ *n* : a person who has acquired the technique of a specialized skill or subject

tech·nique \tek-'nēk\ *n* [F] 1 : the manner in which technical details are treated or basic physical movements are used 2 : technical methods

tech·no \'tek-nō\ *n* : dance music featuring a fast beat and electronically created sounds usu. without vocals

tech·noc·ra·cy \tek-'nä-krə-sē\ *n* : management of society by technical experts — **tech·no·crat** \'tek-nə-ˌkrat\ *n* — **tech·no·crat·ic** \ˌtek-nə-'kra-tik\ *adj*

tech·nol·o·gy \tek-'nä-lə-jē\ *n, pl* **-gies** : ENGINEERING; *also* : a manner of accomplishing a task using technical methods or knowledge — **tech·no·log·i·cal** \ˌtek-nə-'lä-ji-kəl\ *adj*

tec·ton·ics \tek-'tä-niks\ *n sing or pl* 1 : geological structural features 2 : geology dealing esp. with the faulting and folding of a planet or moon — **tec·ton·ic** \-nik\ *adj*

ted·dy bear \'te-dē-ˌber\ *n* [*Teddy* Roosevelt; fr. a cartoon depicting the president sparing the life of a bear cub while hunting] : a stuffed toy bear

te·dious \'tē-dē-əs\ *adj* : tiresome because of length or dullness ♦ *Synonyms* BORING, TIRING, IRKSOME — **te·dious·ly** *adv* — **te·dious·ness** *n*

te·di·um \'tē-dē-əm\ *n* : TEDIOUSNESS; *also* : BOREDOM

¹**tee** \'tē\ *n* : a small mound or peg on which a golf ball is placed to be hit at the beginning of play on a hole; *also* : the area from which the ball is hit to begin play

²**tee** *vb* **teed; tee·ing** : to place (a ball) on a tee

teem \'tēm\ *vb* : to become filled to overflowing : ABOUND ♦ *Synonyms* SWARM, CRAWL, FLOW

teen *adj* : TEENAGE

teen·age \'tēn-ˌnāj\ *or* **teen·aged** \-ˌnājd\ *adj* : of, being, or relating to people in their teens — **teen·ag·er** \-ˌnā-jər\ *n*

teens \'tēnz\ *n pl* : the numbers 13 to 19 inclusive; *esp* : the years 13 to 19 in a person's life

tee·ny \'tē-nē\ *adj* **tee·ni·er; -est** : TINY

teepee *var of* TEPEE

tee shirt *var of* T-SHIRT

tee·ter \'tē-tər\ *vb* 1 : to move unsteadily 2 : SEESAW — **teeter** *n*

teeth *pl of* TOOTH

teethe \'tēth\ *vb* **teethed; teeth·ing** : to experience the rising of one's teeth through the gums : to grow teeth

teething *n* : growth of the first set of teeth through the gums with its accompanying phenomena

tee·to·tal·er *or* **tee·to·tal·ler** \'tē-'tō-t³l-ər\ *n* : a person who practices complete abstinence from alcoholic drinks — **tee·to·tal** \'tē-'tō-t³l, -ˌtō-\ *adj* — **tee·to·tal·ism** \-³l-ˌi-zəm\ *n*

TEFL *abbr* teaching English as a foreign language

Te·ja·no \tā-'hä-(ˌ)nō\ *n, pl* **-nos** [Mex Sp, fr. *Tejas* Texas] : a Texan of Hispanic descent

tek·tite \'tek-ˌtīt\ *n* : a glassy body of probably meteoric origin

tel *abbr* 1 telegram 2 telegraph 3 telephone

tele·cast \'te-li-ˌkast\ *vb* **-cast** *also* **-cast·ed; -cast·ing** : to broadcast by television — **telecast** *n* — **tele·cast·er** *n*

tel·e·com \'te-li-ˌkäm\ *n* : TELECOMMUNICATION; *also* : the telecommunications industry

tele·com·mu·ni·ca·tion \ˌte-li-kə-ˌmyü-nə-'kā-shən\ *n* : communication at a distance (as by telephone or radio)

tele·com·mute \'te-li-kə-ˌmyüt\ *vb* : to work at home by the use of an electronic linkup with a central office

tele·con·fer·ence \'te-li-ˌkän-fə-rəns\ *n* : a conference among people remote from one another held using telecommunications — **tele·con·fer·enc·ing** *n*

teleg *abbr* telegraphy

tele·gen·ic \ˌte-lə-'je-nik, -'jē-\ *adj* : markedly attractive to television viewers

tele·gram \'te-lə-ˌgram\ *n* : a message sent by telegraph

¹**tele·graph** \-ˌgraf\ *n* : an electric apparatus or system for sending messages by a code over wires — **tele·graph·ic** \ˌte-lə-'gra-fik\ *adj*

²**telegraph** *vb* : to send or communicate by or as if by telegraph — **te·leg·ra·pher** \tə-'le-grə-fər\ *n*

te·leg·ra·phy \tə-'le-grə-fē\ *n* : the use or operation of a telegraph apparatus or system

tele·mar·ket·ing \ˌte-lə-'mär-kə-tiŋ\ *n* : the marketing of goods or services by telephone — **tele·mar·ket·er** \-tər\ *n*

tele·med·i·cine \ˌte-lə-'me-də-sən\ *n* : the practice of medicine using two-way voice and visual communication

te·lem·e·try \tə-'le-mə-trē\ *n* : the transmission esp. by radio of measurements made by automatic instruments to a distant station — **tele·me·ter** \'te-lə-ˌmē-tər\ *n*

te·lep·a·thy \tə-'le-pə-thē\ *n* : apparent communication from one mind to another by extrasensory means — **tele·path·ic** \ˌte-lə-'pa-thik\ *adj* — **tele·path·i·cal·ly** \-thi-k(ə-)lē\ *adv*

¹**tele·phone** \'te-lə-ˌfōn\ *n* : an instrument for sending and receiving sounds over long distances by electricity

²**telephone** *vb* **-phoned; -phon·ing** 1 : to send or communicate by telephone 2 : to speak to (a person) by telephone — **tele·phon·er** *n*

te·le·pho·ny \tə-'le-fə-nē, 'te-lə-ˌfō-\ *n* : use or operation of an apparatus for transmission of sounds as electrical signals between distant points — **tel·e·phon·ic** \ˌte-lə-'fä-nik\ *adj*

tele·pho·to \ˌte-lə-'fō-tō\ *adj* : being a camera lens giving a large image of a distant object — **tele·pho·tog·ra·phy** \-fə-'tä-grə-fē\ *n*

tele·play \'te-li-ˌplā\ *n* : a story prepared for television production

tele·print·er \'te-lə-ˌprin-tər\ *n* : TELETYPEWRITER

tele·prompt·er \'te-lə-ˌprämp-tər\ *n* : a device for displaying prepared text to a speaker or performer

¹**tele·scope** \'te-lə-ˌskōp\ *n* 1 : a cylindrical instrument equipped with lenses or mirrors for viewing distant objects 2 : RADIO TELESCOPE

²**telescope** *vb* **-scoped; -scop·ing** 1 : to slide or pass or cause to slide or pass one within another like the sections of a collapsible hand telescope 2 : COMPRESS, CONDENSE

tele·scop·ic \ˌte-lə-'skä-pik\ *adj* 1 : of or relating to a telescope 2 : seen only by a telescope 3 : able to discern objects at a distance 4 : having parts that telescope — **tele·scop·i·cal·ly** \-pi-k(ə-)lē\ *adv*

tele·text \'te-lə-ˌtekst\ *n* : a system for broadcasting text over a television signal and displaying it on a decoder-equipped television

tele·thon \'te-lə-ˌthän\ *n* : a long television program usu. to solicit funds for a charity

tele·type·writ·er \ˌte-lə-'tīp-ˌrī-tər\ *n* : a printing device resembling a typewriter used to send and receive signals over telephone lines

tele·vise \'te-lə-ˌvīz\ *vb* **-vised; -vis·ing** : to broadcast by television

tele·vi·sion \'te-lə-ˌvi-zhən\ *n* [F *télévision*, fr. Gk *tēle* far, at a distance + F *vision* vision] : a system for transmitting images and sound by converting them into electrical or radio waves which are converted back into images and sound by a receiver; *also* : a television receiving set

tell \'tel\ *vb* **told** \'tōld\; **tell·ing 1** : COUNT, ENUMERATE **2** : to relate in detail : NARRATE ⟨*told* us what happened⟩ **3** : SAY, UTTER **4** : to make known : REVEAL **5** : to report to : INFORM ⟨*told* me her name⟩ **6** : ORDER, DIRECT **7** : to find out by observing ⟨can ∼ the difference⟩ **8** : to have a marked effect **9** : to serve as evidence ✦ *Synonyms* DISCLOSE, DISCOVER, BETRAY

tell·er \'te-lər\ *n* **1** : one that relates : NARRATOR **2** : one that counts **3** : a bank employee handling money received or paid out

tell·ing \'te-liŋ\ *adj* : producing a marked effect : EFFECTIVE ⟨∼ evidence⟩ ✦ *Synonyms* COGENT, CONVINCING, SOUND

tell off *vb* : REPRIMAND, SCOLD

tell·tale \'tel-ˌtāl\ *n* **1** : INFORMER, TATTLETALE **2** : something that serves to disclose : INDICATION — **telltale** *adj*

tel·lu·ri·um \tə-'lur-ē-əm\ *n* : a chemical element used esp. in alloys

tel·net \'tel-ˌnet\ *n* : a telecommunications protocol for accessing and using a remote computer via a local computer — **telnet** *vb*

tem·blor \'tem-blər\ *n* [Sp., lit., trembling] : EARTHQUAKE

te·mer·i·ty \tə-'mer-ə-tē\ *n, pl* **-ties** : rash or presumptuous daring : BOLDNESS ✦ *Synonyms* AUDACITY, EFFRONTERY, GALL, NERVE, CHEEK

¹temp \'temp\ *n* **1** : TEMPERATURE **2** : a temporary worker

²temp *abbr* temporary

¹tem·per \'tem-pər\ *vb* **1** : to dilute or soften by the addition of something else ⟨∼ justice with mercy⟩ **2** : to bring (as steel) to a desired hardness by reheating and cooling **3** : to toughen (glass) by gradual heating and cooling **4** : TOUGHEN **5** : TUNE

²temper *n* **1** : characteristic tone : TENDENCY **2** : the hardness or toughness of a substance ⟨the ∼ of a knife blade⟩ **3** : a characteristic frame of mind : DISPOSITION **4** : calmness of mind : COMPOSURE **5** : state of feeling or frame of mind at a particular time **6** : heat of mind or emotion ✦ *Synonyms* TEMPERAMENT, CHARACTER, PERSONALITY, MAKEUP — **tem·pered** \'tem-pərd\ *adj*

tem·pera \'tem-pə-rə\ *n* [It] : a painting process using an albuminous or colloidal medium as a vehicle; *also* : a painting done in tempera

tem·per·a·ment \'tem-prə-mənt, -pər-mənt\ *n* **1** : characteristic or habitual inclination or mode of emotional response : DISPOSITION ⟨nervous ∼⟩ **2** : excessive sensitiveness or irritability ✦ *Synonyms* CHARACTER, PERSONALITY, NATURE, MAKEUP — **tem·per·a·men·tal** \ˌtem-prə-'ment-ᵊl, -pər-'ment-\ *adj*

tem·per·ance \'tem-prəns, -pə-rəns\ *n* : habitual moderation in the indulgence of the appetites or passions; *esp* : moderation in or abstinence from the use of alcoholic beverages

tem·per·ate \'tem-prət, -pə-rət\ *adj* **1** : not extreme or excessive : MILD **2** : moderate in indulgence of appetite or desire **3** : moderate in the use of alcoholic beverages **4** : having a moderate climate ✦ *Synonyms* SOBER, CONTINENT, ABSTEMIOUS

temperate zone *n, often cap T&Z* : the region between the Tropic of Cancer and the arctic circle or between the Tropic of Capricorn and the antarctic circle

tem·per·a·ture \'tem-pər-ˌchu̇r, -prə-ˌchu̇r, -chər\ *n* **1** : degree of hotness or coldness of something (as air, water, or the body) as shown by a thermometer **2** : FEVER 1

tem·pest \'tem-pəst\ *n* [ME *tempeste*, fr. AF, ultim. fr. L *tempestas* season, weather, storm, fr. *tempus* time] : a violent storm

tempest in a teapot : a great commotion over an unimportant matter

tem·pes·tu·ous \tem-'pes-chə-wəs\ *adj* : of, involving, or resembling a tempest : STORMY — **tem·pes·tu·ous·ly** *adv* — **tem·pes·tu·ous·ness** *n*

tem·plate \'tem-plət\ *n* : a gauge, mold, or pattern that functions as a guide to the form or structure of something being made

¹tem·ple \'tem-pəl\ *n* **1** : a building reserved for religious practice **2** : a place devoted to a special or exalted purpose ⟨a ∼ of cuisine⟩

²temple *n* : the flattened space on each side of the forehead esp. of humans

tem·po \'tem-pō\ *n, pl* **tem·pi** \-(ˌ)pē\ *or* **tempos** [It, lit., time] **1** : the rate of speed of a musical piece or passage **2** : rate of motion or activity : PACE

¹tem·po·ral \'tem-pə-rəl\ *adj* **1** : of, relating to, or limited by time ⟨∼ and spatial bounds⟩ **2** : of or relating to earthly life or secular concerns ⟨∼ power⟩

²temporal *adj* : of or relating to the temples or the sides of the skull

¹tem·po·rary \'tem-pə-ˌrer-ē\ *adj* : lasting for a time only : TRANSITORY ✦ *Synonyms* TRANSIENT, EPHEMERAL, MOMENTARY, IMPERMANENT — **tem·po·rar·i·ly** \ˌtem-pə-'rer-ə-lē\ *adv*

²temporary *n, pl* **-rar·ies** : one serving for a limited time

tem·po·rise *Brit var of* TEMPORIZE

tem·po·rize \'tem-pə-ˌrīz\ *vb* **-rized; -riz·ing 1** : to adapt one's actions to the time or the dominant opinion : COMPROMISE **2** : to draw out matters so as to gain time — **tem·po·riz·er** *n*

tempt \'tempt\ *vb* **1** : to entice to do wrong by promise of pleasure or gain **2** : PROVOKE ⟨∼ fate⟩ **3** : to risk the dangers of **4** : to induce to do something : INCITE ✦ *Synonyms* INVEIGLE, DECOY, SEDUCE, LURE — **tempt·er** *n* — **tempt·ing·ly** *adv*

temp·ta·tion \temp-'tā-shən\ *n* **1** : the act of tempting : the state of being tempted **2** : something that tempts

tempt·ress \'temp-trəs\ *n* : a woman who tempts

ten \'ten\ *n* **1** : one more than nine **2** : the 10th in a set or series **3** : something having 10 units — **ten** *adj or pron* — **tenth** \'tenth\ *adj or adv or n*

ten·a·ble \'te-nə-bəl\ *adj* : capable of being held, maintained, or defended — **ten·a·bil·i·ty** \ˌte-nə-'bi-lə-tē\ *n*

te·na·cious \tə-'nā-shəs\ *adj* **1** : not easily pulled apart : COHESIVE, TOUGH ⟨a ∼ metal⟩ **2** : holding fast ⟨∼ of his rights⟩ **3** : RETENTIVE ⟨a ∼ memory⟩ — **te·na·cious·ly** *adv* — **te·nac·i·ty** \tə-'na-sə-tē\ *n*

ten·an·cy \'te-nən-sē\ *n, pl* **-cies** : the temporary possession or occupancy of something (as a house) that belongs to another; *also* : the period of a tenant's occupancy

ten·ant \'te-nənt\ *n* **1** : one who rents or leases (as a house) from a landlord **2** : DWELLER, OCCUPANT — **tenant** *vb* — **ten·ant·less** *adj*

tenant farmer *n* : a farmer who works land owned by another and pays rent either in cash or in shares of produce

ten·ant·ry \'te-nən-trē\ *n, pl* **-ries** : the body of tenants esp. on an estate

Ten Commandments *n pl* : the commandments of God given to Moses on Mount Sinai

¹tend \'tend\ *vb* **1** : to apply oneself ⟨∼ to your affairs⟩ **2** : to take care of ⟨∼ a plant⟩ **3** : to manage the operations of ⟨∼ a machine⟩

²tend *vb* **1** : to move or develop one's course in a particular direction **2** : to show an inclination or tendency

ten·den·cy \'ten-dən-sē\ *n, pl* **-cies 1** : DRIFT, TREND **2** : a proneness to or readiness for a particular kind of thought or action : PROPENSITY ✦ *Synonyms* BENT, LEANING, DISPOSITION, INCLINATION

ten·den·tious \ten-'den-chəs\ *adj* : marked by a tendency in favor of a particular point of view : BIASED — **ten·den·tious·ly** *adv* — **ten·den·tious·ness** *n*

¹ten·der \'ten-dər\ *adj* [ME, fr. AF *tendre*, fr. L *tener*] **1** : having a soft texture : easily broken, chewed, or cut **2** : physically weak : DELICATE; *also* : IMMATURE **3** : expressing or responsive to love or sympathy : LOVING, COMPASSIONATE **4** : SENSITIVE, TOUCHY ⟨a ∼ ego⟩ ✦ *Synonyms* SYMPATHETIC, WARM, WARMHEARTED — **ten·der·ly** *adv* — **ten·der·ness** *n*

²tender *n* [AF *tendre*, fr. *tendre*, v., to stretch, hold out, offer, fr. L *tendere* to stretch, direct] **1** : an offer or proposal made for acceptance; *esp* : an offer of a bid for a contract **2** : something (as money) that may be offered in payment

³tender *vb* : to present for acceptance

⁴tend·er \'ten-dər\ *n* **1** : one that tends or takes care **2** : a boat carrying passengers and freight to a larger ship   **3** : a car attached to a steam locomotive for carrying fuel and water

⁵tender *n* [prob. short for *tenderloin*] : a strip of meat (as chicken) often breaded

ten·der·foot \'ten-dər-ˌfut\ *n, pl* **-feet** \-ˌfēt\ *also* **-foots** \-ˌfuts\   **1** : one not hardened to frontier or rough outdoor life   **2** : an inexperienced beginner

ten·der·heart·ed \ˌten-dər-'här-təd\ *adj* : easily moved to love, pity, or sorrow

ten·der·ize \'ten-də-ˌrīz\ *vb* **-ized; -iz·ing** : to make (meat) tender — **ten·der·iz·er** \'ten-də-ˌrī-zər\ *n*

ten·der·loin \'ten-dər-ˌloin\ *n*   **1** : a tender strip of beef or pork from near the backbone   **2** : a district of a city largely devoted to vice

ten·di·ni·tis *or* **ten·don·itis** \ˌten-də-'nī-təs\ *n* : inflammation of a tendon

ten·don \'ten-dən\ *n* : a tough cord of dense white fibrous tissue uniting a muscle with another part (as a bone) — **ten·di·nous** \-də-nəs\ *adj*

ten·dril \'ten-drəl\ *n* : a slender coiling organ by which some climbing plants attach themselves to a support

ten·e·brous \'te-nə-brəs\ *adj* : shut off from the light : GLOOMY, OBSCURE

ten·e·ment \'te-nə-mənt\ *n*   **1** : a house used as a dwelling   **2** : a building divided into apartments for rent to families; *esp* : one meeting only minimum standards of safety and comfort   **3** : APARTMENT, FLAT

te·net \'te-nət\ *n* [L, he holds, fr. *tenēre* to hold] : one of the principles or doctrines held in common by members of a group (as a church or profession) ♦ *Synonyms* DOCTRINE, DOGMA, BELIEF

ten·fold \'ten-ˌfōld, -'fōld\ *adj* : being 10 times as great or as many — **ten·fold** \-'fōld\ *adv*

ten–gallon hat *n* : a wide-brimmed hat with a large soft crown

Tenn *abbr* Tennessee

ten·nis \'te-nəs\ *n* : a game played with a ball and racket on a court divided by a net

ten·on \'te-nən\ *n* : a projecting part in a piece of material (as wood) for insertion into a mortise to make a joint

ten·or \'te-nər\ *n*   **1** : the general drift of something spoken or written   **2** : the highest natural adult male voice; *also* : a singer having this voice   **3** : a continuing in a course, movement, or activity ⟨the ∼ of my life⟩

tenpenny nail *n* : a nail three inches (about 7.6 centimeters) long

ten·pin \'ten-ˌpin\ *n* : a bottle-shaped bowling pin set in groups of 10 and bowled at in a game (**tenpins**)

¹tense \'tens\ *n* [ME *tens* time, tense, fr. AF, fr. L *tempus*] : distinction of form of a verb to indicate the time of the action or state

²tense *adj* **tens·er; tens·est** [L *tensus,* fr. pp. of *tendere* to stretch]   **1** : stretched tight : TAUT   **2** : feeling or showing nervous tension ⟨a ∼ smile⟩ ♦ *Synonyms* STIFF, RIGID, INFLEXIBLE — **tense·ly** *adv* — **tense·ness** *n* — **ten·si·ty** \'ten-sə-tē\ *n*

³tense *vb* **tensed; tens·ing** : to make or become tense

ten·sile \'ten-səl, -ˌsī(-ə)l\ *adj* : of or relating to tension ⟨∼ strength⟩

ten·sion \'ten-chən\ *n*   **1** : the act of straining or stretching; *also* : the condition of being strained or stretched   **2** : a state of mental unrest often with signs of bodily stress   **3** : a state of latent hostility or opposition

ten–speed \'ten-ˌspēd\ *n* : a bicycle with a derailleur having 10 possible combinations of gears

¹tent \'tent\ *n*   **1** : a collapsible shelter of material stretched and supported by poles   **2** : a canopy placed over the head and shoulders to retain vapors or oxygen given for medical reasons

²tent *vb*   **1** : to lodge in tents   **2** : to cover with or as if with a tent

ten·ta·cle \'ten-ti-kəl\ *n* : any of various long flexible projections about the head or mouth (as of an insect, mollusk, or fish) — **ten·ta·cled** \-kəld\ *adj* — **ten·tac·u·lar** \ten-'ta-kyə-lər\ *adj*

ten·ta·tive \'ten-tə-tiv\ *adj*   **1** : not fully worked out or developed ⟨∼ plans⟩   **2** : HESITANT, UNCERTAIN ⟨a ∼ smile⟩ — **ten·ta·tive·ly** *adv* — **ten·ta·tive·ness** *n*

ten·u·ous \'ten-yə-wəs\ *adj*   **1** : not dense : RARE ⟨a ∼ fluid⟩   **2** : not thick : SLENDER ⟨a ∼ rope⟩   **3** : having lit-

tle substance : FLIMSY, WEAK ⟨∼ influences⟩   **4** : lacking stability : SHAKY ⟨∼ reasoning⟩ — **te·nu·i·ty** \te-'nü-ə-tē, tə-, -'nyü-\ *n* — **ten·u·ous·ly** *adv* — **ten·u·ous·ness** *n*

ten·ure \'ten-yər\ *n* : the act, right, manner, or period of holding something (as a landed property, an office, or a position)

ten·ured \'ten-yərd\ *adj* : having tenure ⟨∼ faculty members⟩

te·o·sin·te \ˌtā-ō-'sin-tē\ *n* : a tall annual grass of Mexico that is closely related to Indian corn

te·pee *or* **tee·pee** \'tē-(ˌ)pē\ *n* [Dakota *t-ípi,* fr. *t-i-* to dwell] : an American Indian conical tent usu. of skins

tep·id \'te-pəd\ *adj*   **1** : moderately warm : LUKEWARM   **2** : HALFHEARTED

te·qui·la \tə-'kē-lə, tā-\ *n* : a Mexican liquor distilled from an agave's sap

ter *abbr*   **1** terrace   **2** territory

tera·byte \'ter-ə-ˌbīt\ *n* [*tera-* trillion (10^{12}), fr. Gk *terat-, teras* monster] : 1024 gigabytes; *also* : one trillion bytes

ter·bi·um \'tər-bē-əm\ *n* : a metallic chemical element

ter·cen·te·na·ry \ˌtər-ˌsen-'te-nə-rē, tər-'sen-tə-ˌner-ē\ *n, pl* **-ries** : a 300th anniversary or its celebration — **tercentenary** *adj*

ter·cen·ten·ni·al \ˌtər-ˌsen-'te-nē-əl\ *adj or n* : TERCENTENARY

te·re·do \tə-'rē-dō, -'rā-\ *n, pl* **-dos** [L] : SHIPWORM

ter·i·ya·ki \ˌter-ē-'yä-kē\ *n* [Jp] : a Japanese dish of meat or fish soaked in a soy marinade and cooked

¹term \'tərm\ *n*   **1** : END, TERMINATION   **2** : DURATION; *esp* : a period of time fixed esp. by law or custom   **3** : a mathematical expression connected with another by a plus or minus sign; *also* : an element (as a numerator) of a fraction or proportion   **4** : a word or expression that has a precise meaning in some uses or is limited to a particular subject or field   **5** *pl* : PROVISIONS, CONDITIONS ⟨∼s of a contract⟩   **6** *pl* : mutual relationship ⟨on good ∼s⟩   **7** : AGREEMENT, CONCORD   **8** : a state of acceptance ⟨come to ∼s with his grief⟩

²term *vb* : to apply a term to : CALL

ter·ma·gant \'tər-mə-gənt\ *n* : an overbearing or nagging woman : SHREW

¹ter·mi·nal \'tər-mə-nᵊl\ *adj*   **1** : of, relating to, or forming an end, limit, or terminus   **2** : FATAL 2 ⟨∼ cancer⟩; *also* : being in or relating to the final stages of a fatal disease ⟨a ∼ patient⟩ ♦ *Synonyms* FINAL, CONCLUDING, LAST, LATEST — **ter·mi·nal·ly** *adv*

²terminal *n*   **1** : EXTREMITY, END   **2** : a device at the end of a wire or on electrical equipment for making a connection   **3** : either end of a transportation line (as a railroad) with its offices and freight and passenger stations; *also* : a freight or passenger station   **4** : a device (as in a computer system) for data entry and display

ter·mi·nate \'tər-mə-ˌnāt\ *vb* **-nat·ed; -nat·ing** : to bring or come to an end ♦ *Synonyms* CONCLUDE, FINISH, COMPLETE — **ter·mi·na·ble** \-nə-bəl\ *adj* — **ter·mi·na·tion** \ˌtər-mə-'nā-shən\ *n* — **ter·mi·na·tor** \'tər-mə-ˌnā-tər\ *n*

ter·mi·nol·o·gy \ˌtər-mə-'nä-lə-jē\ *n, pl* **-gies** : the technical or special terms used in a business, art, science, or special subject

ter·mi·nus \'tər-mə-nəs\ *n, pl* **-ni** \-ˌnī\ *or* **-nus·es** [L]   **1** : final goal : END   **2** : either end of a transportation line or travel route; *also* : the station or city at such a place

ter·mite \'tər-ˌmīt\ *n* : any of numerous pale soft-bodied social insects that feed on wood

tern \'tərn\ *n* : any of various chiefly marine birds with narrow wings and often a forked tail

ter·na·ry \'tər-nə-rē\ *adj*   **1** : of, relating to, or proceeding by threes   **2** : having three elements or parts

terr *abbr* territory

¹ter·race \'ter-əs\ *n*   **1** : a flat roof or open platform   **2** : a level area next to a building   **3** : an embankment with level top   **4** : a bank or ridge on a slope to conserve moisture and soil   **5** : a row of houses on raised land; *also* : a street with such a row of houses   **6** : a strip of park in the middle of a street

²terrace *vb* **ter·raced; ter·rac·ing** : to form into a terrace or supply with terraces

ter·ra–cot·ta \ˌter-ə-'kä-tə\ *n* [It *terra cotta,* lit., baked earth] : a reddish brown earthenware

terra fir·ma \-'fər-mə\ *n* [NL] : solid ground

ter·rain \tə-'rān\ *n* : the surface features of an area of land ⟨a rough ∼⟩

ter·ra in·cog·ni·ta \'ter-ə-,in-'käg-'nē-tə\ *n, pl* **ter·rae in·cog·ni·tae** \'ter-,ī-,in-,käg-'nē-tī\ [L] : an unexplored area or field of knowledge

ter·ra·pin \'ter-ə-pən\ *n* : any of various turtles of fresh or brackish water

terrapin

ter·rar·i·um \tə-'rer-ē-əm\ *n, pl* **-ia** \-ē-ə\ *or* **-i·ums** : a usu. transparent enclosure for keeping or raising plants or small animals indoors

ter·res·tri·al \tə-'res-trē-əl\ *adj* **1** : of or relating to the earth or its inhabitants **2** : living or growing on land ⟨∼ plants⟩ **♦ Synonyms** MUNDANE, EARTHLY, WORLDLY

ter·ri·ble \'ter-ə-bəl\ *adj* **1** : exciting terror : FEARFUL, DREADFUL ⟨∼ weapons⟩ **2** : hard to bear : DISTRESSING ⟨a ∼ situation⟩ **3** : extreme in degree : INTENSE ⟨∼ heat⟩ **4** : of very poor quality : AWFUL ⟨a ∼ play⟩ **♦ Synonyms** FRIGHTFUL, HORRIBLE, SHOCKING, APPALLING — **ter·ri·bly** \-blē\ *adv*

ter·ri·er \'ter-ē-ər\ *n* [ME *terryer, terrer*, fr. AF (*chen*) *terrer*, lit., earth dog, fr. *terre* earth, fr. L *terra*] : any of various usu. small energetic dogs orig. used by hunters to drive small game animals from their holes

ter·rif·ic \tə-'ri-fik\ *adj* **1** : exciting terror **2** : EXTRAORDINARY, ASTOUNDING ⟨∼ speed⟩ **3** : MAGNIFICENT ⟨makes ∼ chili⟩

ter·ri·fy \'ter-ə-,fī\ *vb* **-fied; -fy·ing** : to fill with terror : FRIGHTEN **♦ Synonyms** SCARE, TERRORIZE, STARTLE, ALARM — **ter·ri·fy·ing·ly** *adv*

ter·ri·to·ri·al·i·ty \,terə,tòrē'alətē\ *n* : persistent attachment to a specific territory

ter·ri·to·ry \'ter-ə-,tòr-ē\ *n, pl* **-ries** **1** : a geographic area belonging to or under the jurisdiction of a governmental authority **2** : a part of the U.S. not included within any state but organized with a separate legislature **3** : REGION, DISTRICT; *also* : a region in which one feels at home **4** : a field of knowledge or interest **5** : an assigned area **6** : an area occupied and defended by one or a group of animals — **ter·ri·to·ri·al** \,ter-ə-'tòr-ē-əl\ *adj* —
go with the territory *or* **come with the territory** : to accompany a situation naturally

ter·ror \'ter-ər\ *n* **1** : a state of intense fear : FRIGHT **2** : one that inspires fear **3** : violent or destructive acts committed to intimidate a people or government **♦ Synonyms** PANIC, CONSTERNATION, DREAD, ALARM, DISMAY, HORROR, TREPIDATION

ter·ror·ism \'ter-ər-,i-zəm\ *n* : the systematic use of terror esp. as a means of coercion — **ter·ror·ist** \-ist\ *adj or n*

ter·ror·ize \'ter-ər-,īz\ *vb* **-ized; -iz·ing** **1** : to fill with terror : SCARE **2** : to coerce by threat or violence **♦ Synonyms** TERRIFY, FRIGHTEN, ALARM, STARTLE

ter·ry \'ter-ē\ *n, pl* **terries** : an absorbent fabric with a loose pile of uncut loops

terse \'tərs\ *adj* **ters·er; ters·est** [L *tersus* clean, neat, fr. pp. of *tergēre* to wipe off] : effectively brief : CONCISE — **terse·ly** *adv* — **terse·ness** *n*

ter·tia·ry \'tər-shē-,er-ē\ *adj* **1** : of third rank, importance, or value **2** *cap* : of, relating to, or being the earlier period of the Cenozoic era **3** : occurring in or being the third stage

Tertiary *n* : the Tertiary period

TESL *abbr* teaching English as a second language

TESOL *abbr* Teachers of English to Speakers of Other Languages

¹**test** \'test\ *n* [ME, vessel in which metals were assayed, potsherd, fr. AF, pot, fr. L *testum* earthen vessel] **1** : a critical examination or evaluation : TRIAL **2** : a means or result of testing

²**test** *vb* **1** : to put to test : TRY, EXAMINE **2** : to undergo or score on tests

³**test** *adj* : relating to or used in testing ⟨a ∼ group⟩

tes·ta·ment \'tes-tə-mənt\ *n* **1** *cap* : either of two main divisions of the Bible **2** : EVIDENCE, WITNESS **3** : CREED **4** : the legal instructions for the disposition of one's property after death : WILL — **tes·ta·men·ta·ry** \,tes-tə-'men-tə-rē\ *adj*

tes·tate \'tes-,tāt, -tət\ *adj* : having left a valid will

tes·ta·tor \'tes-,tā-tər, tes-'tā-\ *n* : a person who dies leaving a valid will

tes·ta·trix \tes-'tā-triks\ *n* : a woman who is a testator

¹**tes·ter** \'tes-tər, 'tes-\ *n* : a canopy over a bed, pulpit, or altar

²**test·er** \'tes-tər\ *n* : one that tests

tes·ti·cle \'tes-ti-kəl\ *n* : TESTIS; *esp* : one of a mammal usu. with its enclosing structures — **tes·tic·u·lar** *adj*

tes·ti·fy \'tes-tə-,fī\ *vb* **-fied; -fy·ing** **1** : to make a statement based on personal knowledge or belief : bear witness **2** : to serve as evidence or proof

tes·ti·mo·ni·al \,tes-tə-'mō-nē-əl\ *n* **1** : a statement testifying to benefits received; *also* : a character reference **2** : an expression of appreciation : TRIBUTE — **testimonial** *adj*

tes·ti·mo·ny \'tes-tə-,mō-nē\ *n, pl* **-nies** **1** : evidence based on observation or knowledge **2** : an outward sign : SYMBOL **3** : a solemn declaration made by a witness under oath esp. in a court **♦ Synonyms** EVIDENCE, CONFIRMATION, PROOF, TESTAMENT

tes·tis \'tes-təs\ *n, pl* **tes·tes** \'tes-,tēz\ [L, witness, testis] : a typically paired male reproductive gland that produces sperm and testosterone and that in most mammals is contained within the scrotum at sexual maturity

tes·tos·ter·one \te-'stäs-tə-,rōn\ *n* : a male sex hormone causing development of the male reproductive system and secondary sex characteristics

test–tube *adj* **1** : IN VITRO ⟨∼ experiments⟩ **2** : produced by in vitro fertilization ⟨∼ babies⟩

test tube *n* : a glass tube closed at one end and used esp. in chemistry and biology

tes·ty \'tes-tē\ *adj* **tes·ti·er; -est** [ME *testif*, fr. AF, headstrong, fr. *teste* head, fr. LL *testa* skull, fr. L, shell] : easily annoyed; *also* : marked by ill humor

tet·a·nus \'te-tə-nəs\ *n* : an infectious disease caused by bacterial poisons and marked by muscle stiffness and spasms esp. of the jaws — **tet·a·nal** \-əl\ *adj*

tetchy \'te-chē\ *adj* **tetchi·er; -est** : irritably or peevishly sensitive

¹**tête–à–tête** \'tāt-ə-,tāt\ *n* [F, lit., head to head] : a private conversation between two persons

²**tête–à–tête** \,tāt-ə-'tāt\ *adv* : in private

³**tête–à–tête** \'tāt-ə-,tāt\ *adj* : being face-to-face : PRIVATE

¹**teth·er** \'te-thər\ *n* **1** : something (as a rope) by which an animal is fastened **2** : the limit of one's strength or resources

²**tether** *vb* : to fasten or restrain by or as if by a tether

tet·ra·eth·yl lead \,te-trə-'e-thəl-\ *n* : a heavy oily poisonous liquid used esp. formerly as an antiknock agent in gasoline

tet·ra·he·dron \-'hē-drən\ *n, pl* **-drons** *or* **-dra** \-drə\ : a polyhedron that has four faces — **tet·ra·he·dral** \-drəl\ *adj*

tet·ra·hy·dro·can·nab·i·nol \-,hī-drə-kə-'na-bə-,nòl, -,nōl\ *n* : THC

te·tram·e·ter \te-'tra-mə-tər\ *n* : a line of verse consisting of four metrical feet

Teu·ton·ic \tü-'tä-nik, tyü-\ *adj* : GERMANIC

Tex *abbr* Texas

Tex–Mex \'teks-'meks\ *adj* : characteristic of Mexican-American culture and esp. that of southern Texas

text \'tekst\ *n* **1** : the actual words of an author's work **2** : the main body of printed or written matter on a page **3** : a scriptural passage chosen as the subject esp. of a sermon **4** : THEME, TOPIC **5** : TEXTBOOK — **tex·tu·al** \'teks-chə-wəl\ *adj*

text·book \'tekst-,bùk\ *n* : a book used in the study of a subject

tex·tile \'tek-,stī(-ə)l, 'teks-t³l\ *n* : CLOTH; *esp* : a woven or knit cloth

tex·ture \'teks-chər\ *n* **1** : the visual or tactile surface characteristics and appearance of something ⟨a coarse

~⟩ **2** : essential part **3** : basic scheme or structure : FABRIC **4** : overall structure — **tex·tur·al** \-chə-rəl\ *adj*

TGIF *abbr* thank God it's Friday

¹**Th** *abbr* Thursday

²**Th** *symbol* thorium

¹**-th** — see ¹-ETH

²**-th** *or* **-eth** *adj suffix* — used in forming ordinal numbers ⟨hundred*th*⟩

³**-th** *n suffix* **1** : act or process **2** : state or condition ⟨dear*th*⟩

Thai \'tī\ *n, pl* **Thai** *or* **Thais 1** : a native or inhabitant of Thailand **2** : the official language of Thailand — **Thai** *adj*

thal·a·mus \'tha-lə-məs\ *n, pl* **-mi** \-ˌmī\ [NL] : a subdivision of the brain that serves as a relay station to and from the cerebral cortex and functions in arousal and the integration of sensory information — **tha·lam·ic** \thə-'la-mik\ *adj*

thal·as·se·mia \ˌtha-lə-'sē-mē-ə\ *n* : any of a group of inherited disorders of hemoglobin synthesis

tha·las·so·ther·a·py \thə-ˌla-sō-'ther-ə-pē\ *n* [Gk *thalassa* sea] : the use of seawater or sea products (as seaweed) for the benefit of health or beauty

thal·li·um \'tha-lē-əm\ *n* : a poisonous metallic chemical element

¹**than** \'thən, 'than\ *conj* **1** — used after a comparative adjective or adverb to introduce the second part of a comparison expressing inequality ⟨older ~ I am⟩ **2** — used after *other* or a word of similar meaning to express a difference of kind, manner, or identity ⟨adults other ~ parents⟩

²**than** *prep* : in comparison with ⟨older ~ me⟩

thane \'thān\ *n* **1** : a free retainer of an Anglo-Saxon lord **2** : a Scottish feudal lord

thank \'thaŋk\ *vb* : to express gratitude to ⟨~ed them for the present⟩

thank·ful \'thaŋk-fəl\ *adj* **1** : conscious of benefit received **2** : expressive of thanks **3** : GLAD — **thank·ful·ness** *n*

thank·ful·ly \-fə-lē\ *adv* **1** : in a thankful manner **2** : as makes one thankful

thank·less \'thaŋ-kləs\ *adj* **1** : UNAPPRECIATED **2** : UNGRATEFUL

thanks \'thaŋks\ *n pl* : an expression of gratitude

thanks·giv·ing \thaŋks-'gi-viŋ\ *n* **1** : the act of giving thanks **2** : a prayer expressing gratitude **3** *cap* : the 4th Thursday in November observed as a legal holiday for giving thanks for divine goodness

¹**that** \'that, thət\ *pron, pl* **those** \'thōz\ **1** : the one indicated, mentioned, or understood ⟨~ is my house⟩ **2** : the one farther away or first mentioned ⟨this is an elm, ~'s a maple⟩ **3** : what has been indicated or mentioned ⟨after ~, we left⟩ **4** : the one or ones : IT, THEY ⟨*those* who wish to leave may do so⟩

²**that** \thət, 'that\ *conj* **1** : the following, namely ⟨he said ~ he would⟩; *also* : which is, namely ⟨there's a chance ~ it may fail⟩ **2** : to this end or purpose ⟨shouted ~ all might hear⟩ **3** : as to result in the following, namely ⟨so heavy ~ it can't be moved⟩ **4** : for this reason, namely : BECAUSE ⟨we're glad ~ you came⟩

³**that** *adj, pl* **those 1** : being the one mentioned, indicated, or understood ⟨~ boy⟩ ⟨*those* people⟩ **2** : being the one farther away or less immediately under discussion ⟨this chair or ~ one⟩

⁴**that** \thət, 'that\ *pron* **1** : WHO, WHOM, WHICH ⟨the man ~ saw you⟩ ⟨the man ~ you saw⟩ ⟨the money ~ was spent⟩ **2** : in, on, or at which ⟨the way ~ he drives⟩ ⟨the day ~ it rained⟩

⁵**that** \'that\ *adv* : to such an extent or degree ⟨I like it, but not ~ much⟩

¹**thatch** \'thach\ *vb* : to cover with or as if with thatch — **thatch·er** *n*

²**thatch** *n* **1** : plant material (as straw) for use as roofing **2** : a mat of grass clippings accumulated next to the soil on a lawn **3** : a covering of or as if of thatch ⟨a ~ of white hair⟩

thaw \'thȯ\ *vb* **1** : to melt or cause to melt **2** : to become so warm as to melt ice or snow **3** : to abandon aloofness or hostility — **thaw** *n*

THC \ˌtē-(ˌ)āch-'sē\ *n* [*tetra*hydrocannabinol] : a physio-

logically active chemical from hemp plant resin that is the chief intoxicant in marijuana

¹**the** \thə, *before vowel sounds usu* thē\ *definite article* **1** : that in particular **2** — used before adjectives functioning as nouns ⟨a word to ~ wise⟩

²**the** *adv* **1** : to what extent ⟨~ sooner, the better⟩ **2** : to that extent ⟨the sooner, ~ better⟩

theat *abbr* theater; theatrical

the·ater *or* **the·atre** \'thē-ə-tər\ *n* [ME *theatre*, fr. MF, fr. L *theatrum*, fr. Gk *theatron*, fr. *theasthai* to view, fr. *thea* act of seeing] **1** : a building or area for dramatic performances; *also* : a building or area for showing motion pictures **2** : a place of enactment of significant events ⟨~ of war⟩ **3** : a place (as a lecture room) resembling a theater **4** : dramatic literature or performance

theater–in–the–round *n* : a theater with the stage in the center of the auditorium

the·at·ri·cal \thē-'a-tri-kəl\ *also* **the·at·ric** \-trik\ *adj* **1** : of or relating to the theater **2** : marked by artificiality of emotion : HISTRIONIC **3** : marked by extravagant display : SHOWY

the·at·ri·cals \-kəlz\ *n pl* : the performance of plays

the·at·rics \thē-'a-triks\ *n pl* **1** : THEATRICALS **2** : staged or contrived effects

the·be \'thā-bā\ *n, pl* **thebe** — see *pula* at MONEY table

thee \'thē\ *pron, archaic objective case of* THOU

theft \'theft\ *n* : the act of stealing

thegn \'thān\ *n* : THANE 1

their \thər, 'ther\ *adj* : of or relating to them or themselves

theirs \'therz\ *pron* : their one : their ones

the·ism \'thē-ˌi-zəm\ *n* : belief in the existence of a god or gods — **the·ist** \-ist\ *n or adj* — **the·is·tic** \thē-'is-tik\ *adj*

them \thəm, 'them\ *pron, objective case of* THEY

theme \'thēm\ *n* **1** : a subject or topic of discourse or of artistic representation **2** : a written exercise : COMPOSITION **3** : a melodic subject of a musical composition or movement — **the·mat·ic** \thi-'ma-tik\ *adj*

them·selves \thəm-'selvz, them-\ *pron pl* : THEY, THEM — used reflexively, for emphasis, or in absolute constructions ⟨they govern ~⟩ ⟨they ~ came⟩ ⟨~ busy, they sent me⟩

¹**then** \'then\ *adv* **1** : at that time **2** : soon after that : NEXT **3** : in addition : BESIDES **4** : in that case **5** : CONSEQUENTLY

²**then** *n* : that time ⟨since ~⟩

³**then** *adj* : existing or acting at that time ⟨the ~ attorney general⟩

thence \'thens, 'thens\ *adv* **1** : from that place **2** *archaic* : THENCEFORTH **3** : from that fact : THEREFROM

thence·forth \-ˌfȯrth\ *adv* : from that time forward : THEREAFTER

thence·for·ward \thens-'fȯr-wərd, thens-\ *also* **thence·for·wards** \-wərdz\ *adv* : onward from that place or time

the·oc·ra·cy \thē-'ä-krə-sē\ *n, pl* **-cies 1** : government by officials regarded as divinely inspired **2** : a state governed by a theocracy — **the·o·crat·ic** \ˌthē-ə-'kra-tik\ *adj*

theol *abbr* theological; theology

the·ol·o·gy \thē-'ä-lə-jē\ *n, pl* **-gies 1** : the study of religious faith, practice, and experience; *esp* : the study of God and of God's relation to the world **2** : a theory or system of theology — **the·o·lo·gian** \ˌthē-ə-'lō-jən\ *n* — **the·o·log·i·cal** \-'lä-ji-kəl\ *adj*

the·o·rem \'thē-ə-rəm, 'thir-əm\ *n* **1** : a statement esp. in mathematics that has been or is to be proved **2** : an idea accepted or proposed as a demonstrable truth : PROPOSITION

the·o·ret·i·cal \ˌthē-ə-'re-ti-kəl\ *also* **the·o·ret·ic** \-tik\ *adj* **1** : relating to or having the character of theory **2** : existing only in theory : HYPOTHETICAL — **the·o·ret·i·cal·ly** \-ti-k(ə-)lē\ *adv*

the·o·rise *Brit var of* THEORIZE

the·o·rize \'thē-ə-ˌrīz\ *vb* **-rized; -riz·ing** : to form a theory : SPECULATE — **the·o·rist** \-rist\ *n*

the·o·ry \'thē-ə-rē, 'thir-ē\ *n, pl* **-ries 1** : abstract thought **2** : the general principles of a subject **3** : a plausible or scientifically acceptable general principle offered to explain observed facts **4** : HYPOTHESIS, CONJECTURE

theory of games : GAME THEORY

the·os·o·phy \thē-'ä-sə-fē\ *n* : belief about God and the world held to be based on mystical insight — **theo·soph·i·cal** \ˌthē-ə-'sä-fi-kəl\ *adj* — **the·os·o·phist** \thē-'ä-sə-fist\ *n*

ther·a·peu·tic \ˌther-ə-'pyü-tik\ *adj* [Gk *therapeutikos*, fr. *therapeuein* to attend, treat, fr. *theraps* attendant] : of, relating to, or dealing with healing and esp. with remedies for diseases — **ther·a·peu·ti·cal·ly** \-ti-k(ə-)lē\ *adv*

ther·a·peu·tics \ˌther-ə-'pyü-tiks\ *n* : a branch of medical or dental science dealing with the use of remedies

ther·a·py \'ther-ə-pē\ *n, pl* **-pies** : treatment of bodily, mental, or behavioral disorders — **ther·a·pist** \-pist\ *n*

¹**there** \'ther\ *adv* **1** : in or at that place — often used interjectionally **2** : to or into that place : THITHER **3** : in that matter or respect

²**there** \ther, thər\ *pron* — used as a function word to introduce a sentence or clause ⟨∼'s a pen here⟩

³**there** \'ther\ *n* **1** : that place ⟨get away from ∼⟩ **2** : that point ⟨you take it from ∼⟩

there·abouts \ˌthr-ə-'bauts, 'ther-ə-ˌbauts\ *or* **there·about** \-'baut, -ˌbaut\ *adv* **1** : near that place or time **2** : near that number, degree, or quantity

there·af·ter \thr-'af-tər\ *adv* : after that : AFTERWARD

there·at \-'at\ *adv* **1** : at that place **2** : at that occurrence : on that account

there·by \ther-'bī, 'ther-ˌbī\ *adv* **1** : by that : by that means **2** : connected with or with reference to that

there·for \ther-'fȯr\ *adv* : for or in return for that

there·fore \'ther-ˌfȯr\ *adv* : for that reason : CONSEQUENTLY

there·from \ther-'frəm\ *adv* : from that or it

there·in \ther-'in\ *adv* **1** : in or into that place, time, or thing **2** : in that respect

there·of \-'əv, -'äv\ *adv* **1** : of that or it **2** : from that : THEREFROM

there·on \-'ȯn, -'än\ *adv* **1** : on that **2** *archaic* : THEREUPON **3**

there·to \ther-'tü\ *adv* : to that

there·un·to \ther-'ən-(ˌ)tü, ˌther-ən-'tü\ *adv, archaic* : THERETO

there·upon \'ther-ə-ˌpȯn, -ˌpän; ˌther-ə-'pȯn, -'pän\ *adv* **1** : on that matter **2** : THEREFORE **3** : immediately after that : at once

there·with \ther-'with -'with\ *adv* **1** : with that **2** *archaic* : THEREUPON, FORTHWITH

there·with·al \'ther-wi-ˌthȯl, -ˌthȯl\ *adv* **1** *archaic* : BESIDES **2** : THEREWITH

therm *abbr* thermometer

ther·mal \'thər-məl\ *adj* **1** : of, relating to, or caused by heat **2** : designed to prevent the loss of body heat ⟨∼ underwear⟩ — **ther·mal·ly** *adv*

thermal pollution *n* : the discharge of heated liquid (as waste water from a factory) into natural waters at a temperature harmful to the environment

therm·is·tor \'thər-ˌmis-tər\ *n* : an electrical resistor whose resistance varies sharply with temperature

ther·mo·cline \'thər-mə-ˌklīn\ *n* : the region in a thermally stratified body of water that separates warmer surface water from cold deep water

ther·mo·cou·ple \'thər-mə-ˌkə-pəl\ *n* : a device for measuring temperature by measuring the temperature-dependent potential difference created at the junction of two dissimilar metals

ther·mo·dy·nam·ics \ˌthər-mə-dī-'na-miks\ *n* : physics that deals with the mechanical action or relations of heat — **ther·mo·dy·nam·ic** \-mik\ *adj* — **ther·mo·dy·nam·i·cal·ly** \-mi-k(ə-)lē\ *adv*

ther·mom·e·ter \thər-'mä-mə-tər\ *n* [F *thermomètre*, fr. Gk *thermē* heat + *metron* measure] : an instrument for measuring temperature typically by the rise or fall of a liquid (as mercury) in a thin glass tube — **ther·mo·met·ric** \ˌthər-mə-'me-trik\ *adj* — **ther·mo·met·ri·cal·ly** \-tri-k(ə-)lē\ *adv*

ther·mo·nu·cle·ar \ˌthər-mō-'nü-klē-ər, -'nyü-\ *adj* **1** : of or relating to changes in the nucleus of atoms of low atomic weight (as hydrogen) that require a very high temperature (as in the hydrogen bomb) **2** : utilizing or relating to a thermonuclear bomb ⟨∼ war⟩

ther·mo·plas·tic \ˌthər-mə-'plas-tik\ *adj* : capable of softening when heated and of hardening again when cooled ⟨∼ resins⟩ — **thermoplastic** *n*

ther·mos \'thər-məs\ *n* : a cylindrical container with a

vacuum between an inner and an outer wall used to keep liquids hot or cold

ther·mo·sphere \'thər-mə-ˌsfir\ *n* : the part of the earth's atmosphere that lies above the mesosphere and that is characterized by steadily increasing temperature with height

ther·mo·stat \'thər-mə-ˌstat\ *n* : a device that automatically controls temperature — **ther·mo·stat·ic** \ˌthər-mə-'sta-tik\ *adj* — **ther·mo·stat·i·cal·ly** \-ti-k(ə-)lē\ *adv*

the·sau·rus \thi-'sȯr-əs\ *n, pl* **-sau·ri** \-'sȯr-ˌī\ *or* **-sau·rus·es** \-'sȯr-ə-səz\ [NL, fr. L, treasure, collection, fr. Gk *thēsauros*] : a book of words and their synonyms — **the·sau·ral** \-'sȯr-əl\ *adj*

these *pl of* THIS

the·sis \'thē-səs\ *n, pl* **the·ses** \'thē-ˌsēz\ **1** : a proposition that a person advances and offers to maintain by argument **2** : an essay embodying results of original research; *esp* : one written for an academic degree

¹**thes·pi·an** \'thes-pē-ən\ *adj, often cap* [fr. *Thespis*, 6th cent. B.C. Greek poet and reputed originator of tragedy] : relating to the drama : DRAMATIC

²**thespian** *n* : ACTOR

Thess *abbr* Thessalonians

Thes·sa·lo·nians \ˌthe-sə-'lō-nyənz, -nē-ənz\ *n* — see BIBLE table

the·ta \'thā-tə\ *n* : the 8th letter of the Greek alphabet — Θ or θ

thew \'thü, 'thyü\ *n* : MUSCLE, SINEW — usu. used in pl.

they \'thā\ *pron* **1** : those individuals under discussion : the ones previously mentioned or referred to **2** : unspecified persons : PEOPLE

thi·a·mine \'thī-ə-mən, -ˌmēn\ *also* **thi·a·min** \-mən\ *n* : a vitamin of the vitamin B complex essential to normal metabolism and nerve function

¹**thick** \'thik\ *adj* **1** : having relatively great depth or extent from one surface to its opposite ⟨a ∼ plank⟩; *also* : heavily built : THICKSET **2** : densely massed : CROWDED; *also* : FREQUENT, NUMEROUS **3** : dense or viscous in consistency ⟨∼ syrup⟩ **4** : marked by haze, fog, or mist ⟨∼ weather⟩ **5** : measuring in thickness ⟨one meter ∼⟩ **6** : imperfectly articulated : INDISTINCT ⟨∼ speech⟩ **7** : STUPID, OBTUSE **8** : associated on close terms : INTIMATE **9** : EXCESSIVE ♦ *Synonyms* COMPACT, CLOSE, TIGHT — **thick·ly** *adv*

²**thick** *n* **1** : the most crowded or active part **2** : the part of greatest thickness

thick and thin *n* : every difficulty and obstacle ⟨was loyal through *thick and thin*⟩

thick·en \'thi-kən\ *vb* : to make or become thick — **thick·en·er** *n*

thick·et \'thi-kət\ *n* : a dense growth of bushes or small trees

thick·ness \-nəs\ *n* **1** : the smallest of three dimensions ⟨length, width, and ∼⟩ **2** : the quality or state of being thick **3** : LAYER, SHEET ⟨a single ∼ of canvas⟩

thick·set \'thik-'set\ *adj* **1** : closely placed or planted **2** : having a thick body : BURLY

thick-skinned \-'skind\ *adj* **1** : having a thick skin **2** : not easily bothered by criticism or insult

thief \'thēf\ *n, pl* **thieves** \'thēvz\ : one that steals esp. secretly

thieve \'thēv\ *vb* **thieved; thiev·ing** : STEAL, ROB ♦ *Synonyms* FILCH, PILFER, PURLOIN, SWIPE

thiev·ery \'thē-və-rē\ *n, pl* **-er·ies** : the act of stealing : THEFT

thigh \'thī\ *n* : the part of the vertebrate hind or lower limb between the knee and the hip

thigh·bone \'thī-ˌbōn\ *n* : FEMUR

thim·ble \'thim-bəl\ *n* : a cap or guard worn on the finger to push the needle in sewing — **thim·ble·ful** *n*

¹**thin** \'thin\ *adj* **thin·ner; thin·nest** **1** : having little extent from one surface through to its opposite : not thick : SLENDER **2** : not closely set or placed : SPARSE ⟨∼ hair⟩ **3** : not dense or not dense enough : more fluid or rarefied than normal ⟨∼ air⟩ ⟨∼ syrup⟩ **4** : lacking substance, fullness, or strength ⟨∼ broth⟩ **5** : FLIMSY ⟨a ∼ excuse⟩ — **thin·ly** *adv* — **thin·ness** *n*

²**thin** *vb* **thinned; thin·ning** : to make or become thin

thine \'thīn\ *pron, archaic* : one or the ones belonging to thee

thing \'thiŋ\ *n* **1** : a matter of concern : AFFAIR ⟨∼s to do⟩ **2** *pl* : state of affairs ⟨∼s are improving⟩ **3** : EVENT, CIRCUMSTANCE ⟨the crime was a terrible ∼⟩ **4** : DEED, ACT ⟨expected great ∼s of him⟩ **5** : a distinct entity : OBJECT **6** : an inanimate object distinguished from a living being **7** *pl* : POSSESSIONS, EFFECTS **8** : an article of clothing **9** : DETAIL, POINT ⟨checks every little ∼⟩ **10** : IDEA, NOTION ⟨says the first ∼ he thinks of⟩ **11** : something one likes to do : SPECIALTY ⟨doing her ∼⟩

think \'think\ *vb* **thought** \'thȯt\; **think•ing 1** : to form or have in the mind **2** : to have as an opinion : BELIEVE **3** : to reflect on : PONDER **4** : to call to mind : REMEMBER **5** : REASON **6** : to form a mental picture of : IMAGINE **7** : to devise by thinking ⟨*thought* up a plan to escape⟩ ♦ **Synonyms** CONCEIVE, FANCY, REALIZE, ENVISAGE — **think•er** *n*

think tank *n* : an institute, corporation, or group organized for interdisciplinary research (as in technological or social problems)

thin•ner \'thi-nər\ *n* : a volatile liquid (as turpentine) used to thin paint

thin–skinned \'thin-'skind\ *adj* **1** : having a thin skin or rind **2** : extremely sensitive to criticism or insult

¹**third** \'thərd\ *adj* : next after the second — **third** *or* **third•ly** *adv*

²**third** *n* **1** : one of three equal parts of something **2** : one that is number three in a countable series **3** : the 3d forward gear in an automotive vehicle

third degree *n* : the subjection of a prisoner to mental or physical torture to force a confession

third dimension *n* **1** : thickness, depth, or apparent thickness or depth that confers solidity on an object **2** : a quality that confers reality — **third–dimensional** *adj*

third world *n, often cap T&W* : the aggregate of the underdeveloped nations of the world

¹**thirst** \'thərst\ *n* **1** : a feeling of dryness in the mouth and throat associated with a desire to drink; *also* : a bodily condition producing this **2** : an ardent desire : CRAVING ⟨a ∼ for knowledge⟩ — **thirsty** *adj*

²**thirst** *vb* **1** : to need drink : suffer thirst **2** : to have a strong desire : CRAVE

thir•teen \,thər-'tēn\ *n* : one more than 12 — **thirteen** *adj or pron* — **thir•teenth** \-'tēnth\ *adj or n*

thir•ty \'thər-tē\ *n, pl* **thirties** : three times 10 — **thir•ti•eth** \-tē-əth\ *adj or n* — **thirty** *adj or pron*

¹**this** \'this\ *pron, pl* **these** \'thēz\ **1** : the one close or closest in time or space ⟨∼ is your book⟩ **2** : what is in the present or under immediate observation or discussion ⟨∼ is a mess⟩; *also* : what is happening or being done now ⟨after ∼ we'll leave⟩

²**this** *adj, pl* **these 1** : being the one near, present, just mentioned, or more immediately under observation ⟨∼ book⟩ **2** : constituting the immediate past or future ⟨friends all *these* years⟩

³**this** *adv* : to such an extent or degree ⟨didn't expect to wait ∼ long⟩

this•tle \'thi-səl\ *n* : any of various tall prickly composite plants with often showy heads of tightly packed tubular flowers

this•tle•down \-,daủn\ *n* : the down from the ripe flower head of a thistle

¹**thith•er** \'thi-thər\ *adv* : to that place

²**thither** *adj* : being on the farther side

thith•er•ward \-wərd\ *adv* : toward that place : THITHER

thong \'thȯŋ\ *n* **1** : a strip esp. of leather or hide **2** : a sandal held on the foot by a thong between the toes **3** : a narrow strip of swimwear or underwear that passes between the thighs

tho•rax \'thȯr-,aks\ *n, pl* **tho•rax•es** *or* **tho•ra•ces** \'thȯr-ə-,sēz\ **1** : the part of the body of a mammal between the neck and the abdomen; *also* : its cavity containing the heart and lungs **2** : the middle of the three main divisions of the body of an insect — **tho•rac•ic** \thə-'ra-sik\ *adj*

tho•ri•um \'thȯr-ē-əm\ *n* : a radioactive metallic chemical element

thorn \'thȯrn\ *n* **1** : a woody plant bearing sharp processes **2** : a sharp rigid plant process that is usu. a modified leafless branch **3** : something that causes distress — **thorny** *adj*

thor•ough \'thər-ō\ *adj* **1** : COMPLETE, EXHAUSTIVE ⟨a ∼ search⟩ **2** : very careful : PAINSTAKING ⟨a ∼ schol-

ar⟩ **3** : having full mastery — **thor•ough•ly** *adv* — **thor•ough•ness** *n*

¹**thor•ough•bred** \'thər-ə-,bred\ *adj* **1** : bred from the best blood through a long line **2** *cap* : of or relating to the Thoroughbred breed of horses **3** : marked by high-spirited grace

²**thoroughbred** *n* **1** *cap* : any of an English breed of light speedy horses kept chiefly for racing **2** : one (as a pedigreed animal) of excellent quality

thor•ough•fare \-,far\ *n* : a public road or street

thor•ough•go•ing \,thər-ə-'gō-iŋ\ *adj* : marked by thoroughness or zeal

thorp \'thȯrp\ *n, archaic* : VILLAGE

those *pl of* THAT

¹**thou** \'thaủ\ *pron, archaic* : the person addressed

²**thou** \'thaủ\ *n, pl* **thou** : a thousand of something (as dollars)

¹**though** \'thō\ *conj* **1** : despite the fact that ⟨∼ the odds are hopeless, they fight on⟩ **2** : granting that ⟨∼ it may look bad, still, all is not lost⟩

²**though** *adv* : HOWEVER, NEVERTHELESS ⟨not for long, ∼⟩

¹**thought** \'thȯt\ *past and past part of* THINK

²**thought** *n* **1** : the process of thinking **2** : serious consideration : REGARD **3** : reasoning power **4** : the power to imagine : CONCEPTION **5** : IDEA, NOTION **6** : OPINION, BELIEF ⟨spoke his ∼s freely⟩

thought•ful \'thȯt-fəl\ *adj* **1** : absorbed in thought **2** : marked by careful thinking ⟨a ∼ essay⟩ **3** : considerate of others ⟨a ∼ host⟩ — **thought•ful•ly** *adv* — **thought•ful•ness** *n*

thought•less \-ləs\ *adj* **1** : insufficiently alert : CARELESS ⟨a ∼ worker⟩ **2** : RECKLESS ⟨a ∼ act⟩ **3** : lacking concern for others : INCONSIDERATE ⟨∼ remarks⟩ — **thought•less•ly** *adv* — **thought•less•ness** *n*

thou•sand \'thaủz-ᵊnd\ *n, pl* **thousands** *or* **thousand** : 10 times 100 — **thousand** *adj* — **thou•sandth** \-ᵊnth\ *adj or n*

thousands place *n* : the place four to the left of the decimal point in an Arabic number

thrall \'thrȯl\ *n* **1** : SLAVE, BONDMAN **2** : a state of servitude — **thrall•dom** *or* **thral•dom** \'thrȯl-dəm\ *n*

¹**thrash** \'thrash\ *vb* **1** : THRESH 1 **2** : BEAT, WHIP; *also* : DEFEAT **3** : to move about violently **4** : to go over again and again ⟨∼ over the matter⟩; *also* : to hammer out ⟨∼ out a plan⟩

²**thrash** *n* : rock music that is extremely fast and loud

¹**thrash•er** \'thra-shər\ *n* : one that thrashes or threshes

²**thrasher** *n* : any of various long-tailed American songbirds related to the mockingbird

¹**thread** \'thred\ *n* **1** : a thin continuous strand of spun and twisted textile fibers **2** : something resembling a textile thread **3** : the ridge or groove that winds around a screw **4** : a line of reasoning or train of thought **5** : a continuing element **6** : a tenuous or feeble support

²**thread** *vb* **1** : to pass a thread through the eye of (a needle) **2** : to pass (as film) through something **3** : to make one's way through or between **4** : to put together on a thread ⟨∼ beads⟩ **5** : to form a screw thread on or in

thread•bare \-,ber\ *adj* **1** : having the nap worn off so that the thread shows : SHABBY **2** : TRITE

thready \'thre-dē\ *adj* **1** : consisting of or bearing fibers of filaments ⟨a ∼ bark⟩ **2** : lacking in fullness, body, or vigor ⟨a ∼ voice⟩

threat \'thret\ *n* **1** : an expression of intent to do harm **2** : one that threatens

threat•en \'thre-tᵊn\ *vb* **1** : to utter threats against **2** : to give signs or warning of : PORTEND **3** : to hang over as a threat : MENACE **4** : to cause to feel insecure or anxious — **threat•en•ing•ly** *adv*

threat•ened \-tᵊnd\ *adj* : having an uncertain chance of continued survival; *esp* : likely to become an endangered species

three \'thrē\ *n* **1** : one more than two **2** : the 3d in a set or series **3** : something having three units — **three** *adj or pron*

3–D \'thrē-'dē\ *n* : a three-dimensional form or picture

three–dimensional *adj* **1** : relating to or having three dimensions **2** : giving the illusion of varying distances ⟨a ∼ picture⟩

three•fold \'thrē-,fōld, -'fōld\ *adj* **1** : having three parts

: TRIPLE **2** : being three times as great or as many —
three·fold \-'fōld\ adv
three·pence \'thre-pəns, 'thri-, 'thrə-, US also 'thrē-pens\
n **1** pl **threepence** or **three·penc·es** : a coin worth
three pennies **2** : the sum of three British pennies
three·score \'thrē-'skȯr\ adj : being three times twenty
: SIXTY
three·some \'thrē-səm\ n : a group of three persons or
things
thren·o·dy \'thre-nə-dē\ n, pl **-dies** : a song of lamentation
: ELEGY
thresh \'thresh, 'thrash\ vb **1** : to separate (as grain from
straw) mechanically **2** : THRASH — **thresh·er** n
thresh·old \'thresh-ˌhōld\ n **1** : the sill of a door **2** : a
point or place of beginning or entering : OUTSET **3** : a
point at which a physiological or psychological effect begins to be produced
threw past of THROW
thrice \'thrīs\ adv **1** : three times **2** : in a threefold manner or degree
thrift \'thrift\ n [ME, fr. ON, prosperity, fr. thrīfask to
thrive] : careful management esp. of money : FRUGALITY
— **thrift·i·ly** \'thrif-tə-lē\ adv — **thrift·less** adj — **thrifty**
adj
thrill \'thril\ vb [ME thirlen, thrillen to pierce, fr. OE thyr-
lian, fr. thyrel hole, fr. thurh through] **1** : to have or
cause to have sudden sharp feeling of excitement; also
: TINGLE, SHIVER **2** : TREMBLE, VIBRATE — **thrill** n —
thrill·er n — **thrill·ing·ly** adv
thrips \'thrips\ n, pl **thrips** : any of an order of minute
sucking insects including many plant-feeding pests
thrive \'thrīv\ vb **thrived** or **throve** \'thrōv\; **thrived** also
thriv·en \'thri-vən\; **thriv·ing** **1** : to grow luxuriantly
: FLOURISH **2** : to gain in wealth or possessions : PROSPER
throat \'thrōt\ n : the part of the neck in front of the spinal
column; also : the passage through it to the stomach and
lungs — **throat·ed** adj
throaty \'thrō-tē\ adj **throat·i·er; -est** **1** : uttered or produced from low in the throat ⟨a ~ voice⟩ **2** : heavy,
thick, or deep as if from the throat ⟨~ notes of a horn⟩
— **throat·i·ly** \-tə-lē\ adv — **throat·i·ness** \-tē-nəs\ n
¹throb \'thräb\ vb **throbbed; throb·bing** : to pulsate or
pound esp. with abnormal force or rapidity : BEAT, VI-
BRATE
²throb n : BEAT, PULSE
throe \'thrō\ n **1** : PANG, SPASM ⟨death ~s⟩ **2** pl : a
hard or painful struggle
throm·bo·lyt·ic \ˌthräm-bə-'li-tik\ adj : destroying or
breaking up a thrombus — **thrombolytic** n
throm·bo·sis \thräm-'bō-səs\ n, pl **-bo·ses** \-ˌsēz\ : the
formation or presence of a clot in a blood vessel —
throm·bot·ic \-'bä-tik\ adj
throm·bus \'thräm-bəs\ n, pl **throm·bi** \-ˌbī\ [NL, fr. Gk
thrombos lump, clot] : a clot of blood formed within a
blood vessel and remaining attached to its place of origin
throne \'thrōn\ n **1** : the chair of state of a sovereign or
high dignitary **2** : royal power : SOVEREIGNTY
¹throng \'thrȯŋ\ n **1** : MULTITUDE **2** : a crowding together of many persons
²throng vb **thronged; throng·ing** : CROWD
¹throt·tle \'thrä-t³l\ vb **throt·tled; throt·tling** [ME throtlen,
fr. throte throat] **1** : CHOKE, STRANGLE **2** : SUPPRESS
⟨policies that ~ creativity⟩ **3** : to reduce the speed of
(an engine) by closing the throttle — **throt·tler** n
²throttle n : a valve regulating the flow of steam or fuel to
an engine; also : the lever controlling this valve
¹through \'thrü\ prep **1** : into at one side and out at the
other side of ⟨go ~ the door⟩ **2** : by way of ⟨entered ~
a skylight⟩ **3** : in the midst of ⟨a path ~ the trees⟩ **4** : by
means of ⟨succeeded ~ hard work⟩ **5** : over the whole of
⟨rumors swept ~ the office⟩ **6** : during the whole of ⟨~
the night⟩ **7** : to and including ⟨Monday ~ Friday⟩
²through adv **1** : from one end or side to the other **2**
: from beginning to end : to completion ⟨see it ~⟩ **3** : to
the core : THOROUGHLY ⟨he was wet ~⟩ **4** : into the
open : OUT ⟨break ~⟩
³through adj **1** : permitting free passage ⟨a ~ street⟩ **2**
: going from point of origin to destination without change
or transfer ⟨a ~ train⟩ **3** : coming from or going to
points outside a local area ⟨~ traffic⟩ **4** : FINISHED ⟨~
with the job⟩

¹through·out \thrü-'aut\ adv **1** : EVERYWHERE **2** : from
beginning to end
²throughout prep **1** : in or to every part of **2** : during the
whole period of
through·put \'thrü-ˌput\ n : OUTPUT, PRODUCTION ⟨the
~ of a computer⟩
throve past of THRIVE
¹throw \'thrō\ vb **threw** \'thrü\; **thrown** \'thrōn\; **throw·ing**
[ME, to cause to twist, throw, fr. OE thrāwan to cause to
twist] **1** : to propel through the air esp. with a forward
motion of the hand and arm ⟨~ a ball⟩ **2** : to cause to
fall or fall off **3** : to put suddenly in a certain position or
condition ⟨~ into panic⟩ **4** : to put on or take off hastily ⟨~ on a coat⟩ **5** : to lose intentionally ⟨~ a game⟩ **6**
: to move (a lever) so as to connect or disconnect parts of
something (as a clutch) **7** : to put (an automobile) into a
different gear **8** : to act as host for ⟨~ a party⟩ ♦ **Synonyms** TOSS, FLING, PITCH, SLING — **throw·er** n
²throw n **1** : an act of throwing, hurling, or flinging; also
: CAST **2** : the distance a missile may be thrown **3** : a
light coverlet **4** : a woman's scarf or light wrap
¹throw·away \'thrō-ə-ˌwā\ n : something that is or is designed to be thrown away esp. after one use
²throwaway adj : overly wasteful ⟨a ~ society⟩
throw·back \-ˌbak\ n : reversion to an earlier type or
phase; also : an instance or product of this
throw up vb **1** : to build hurriedly **2** : VOMIT
thrum \'thrəm\ vb **thrummed; thrum·ming** : to play or
pluck a stringed instrument idly : STRUM
thrush \'thrəsh\ n : any of numerous small or medium-
sized songbirds that are mostly of a plain color often with
spotted underparts
¹thrust \'thrəst\ vb **thrust; thrust·ing** **1** : to push or drive
with force : SHOVE **2** : STAB, PIERCE **3** : INTERJECT **4**
: to press the acceptance of upon someone
²thrust n **1** : a lunge with a pointed weapon **2** : ATTACK
3 : the pressure of one part of a construction against another (as of an arch against an abutment) **4** : the force
produced by a propeller or jet or rocket engine that
drives a vehicle (as an aircraft) forward **5** : a violent
push : SHOVE **6** : prominent or essential element
thrust·er also **thrust·or** \'thrəs-tər\ n : one that thrusts; esp
: a rocket engine
thru·way \'thrü-ˌwā\ n : EXPRESSWAY
¹thud \'thəd\ n **1** : ⁴BLOW **2** : a dull sound
²thud vb **thud·ded; thud·ding** : to move or strike so as to
make a thud
thug \'thəg\ n [Hindi & Urdu thag, lit., thief] : a brutal ruffian or assassin — **thug·gish** adj
thu·li·um \'thü-lē-əm, 'thyü-\ n : a rare metallic chemical
element
¹thumb \'thəm\ n **1** : the short thick first digit of the
human hand or a corresponding digit of a lower animal
2 : the part of a glove or mitten that covers the thumb
²thumb vb **1** : to leaf through (pages) with the thumb **2**
: to wear or soil with the thumb by frequent handling **3**
: to request or obtain (a ride) in a passing automobile by
signaling with the thumb
¹thumb·nail \'thəm-ˌnāl\ n : the nail of the thumb
²thumbnail adj : BRIEF, CONCISE ⟨a ~ description⟩ ⟨a ~
picture⟩
thumb·print \-ˌprint\ n : an impression made by the thumb
thumb·screw \-ˌskrü\ n **1** : a device of torture for squeezing the thumb **2** : a screw with a head that may be
turned by the thumb and forefinger
thumb·tack \-ˌtak\ n : a tack with a broad flat head for
pressing with one's thumb into a board or wall
¹thump \'thəmp\ vb **1** : to strike with or as if with something thick or heavy so as to cause a dull sound **2**
: POUND
²thump n : a blow with or as if with something blunt or
heavy; also : the sound made by such a blow
¹thun·der \'thən-dər\ n **1** : the sound following a flash of
lightning; also : a noise like such a sound **2** : a loud utterance or threat
²thunder vb **1** : to produce thunder **2** : ROAR, SHOUT
thun·der·bolt \-ˌbōlt\ n : a flash of lightning with its accompanying thunder
thun·der·clap \-ˌklap\ n : a crash of thunder
thun·der·cloud \-ˌklaud\ n : a cloud charged with electricity and producing lightning and thunder

thun·der·head \-ˌhed\ *n* : a large cumulus or cumulonimbus cloud often appearing before a thunderstorm

thun·der·ous \'thən-də-rəs\ *adj* : producing thunder; *also* : making a noise like thunder — **thun·der·ous·ly** *adv*

thun·der·show·er \'thən-dər-ˌshau̇(-ə)r\ *n* : a shower accompanied by thunder and lightning

thun·der·storm \-ˌstȯrm\ *n* : a storm accompanied by thunder and lightning

thun·der·struck \-ˌstrək\ *adj* : stunned as if struck by a thunderbolt

Thurs *or* **Thu** *abbr* Thursday

Thurs·day \'thərz-ˌdā, -dē\ *n* [ME, fr. OE *thursdæg*, fr. ON *thōrsdagr,* lit., day of Thor (Norse god)] : the 5th day of the week

thus \'thəs\ *adv* **1** : in this or that manner **2** : to this degree or extent : SO **3** : because of this or that : HENCE

¹thwack \'thwak\ *vb* : to strike with or as if with something flat or heavy

²thwack *n* : a heavy blow : WHACK

¹thwart \'thwȯrt\ *vb* **1** : FOIL, BAFFLE **2** : BLOCK, DEFEAT
◆ *Synonyms* BALK, OUTWIT, FRUSTRATE

²thwart \'thwȯrt, *naut often* 'thȯrt\ *adv* : ATHWART

³thwart *adj* : situated or placed across something else

⁴thwart *n* : a seat extending across a boat

thy \'thī\ *adj, archaic* : of, relating to, or done by or to thee or thyself

thyme \'tīm, 'thīm\ *n* [ME, fr. AF *time*, fr. L *thymum*, fr. Gk *thymon*, prob. fr. *thyein* to make a burnt offering, sacrifice] : a garden mint with small aromatic leaves used esp. in seasoning; *also* : its leaves so used

thy·mine \'thī-ˌmēn\ *n* : a pyrimidine base that is one of the four bases coding genetic information in the molecular chain of DNA

thy·mus \'thī-məs\ *n, pl* **thy·mus·es** : a glandular organ of the neck region that is composed largely of lymphoid tissue, functions esp. in the development of the immune system, and tends to atrophy in the adult

thy·ris·tor \thī-ˈris-tər\ *n* : a semiconductor device that acts as a switch, rectifier, or voltage regulator

thy·roid \'thī-ˌrȯid\ *adj* [NL *thyroides*, fr. Gk *thyreoeidēs* shield-shaped, thyroid, fr. *thyreos* shield shaped like a door, fr. *thyra* door] : a large 2-lobed endocrine gland that lies at the base of the neck and produces several iodine-containing hormones that affect growth, development, and metabolism — **thyroid** *also* **thy·roi·dal** \thī-ˈrȯi-dᵊl\ *adj*

thy·rox·ine *or* **thy·rox·in** \thī-ˈräk-ˌsēn, -sən\ *n* : an iodine-containing hormone that is produced by the thyroid gland, increases metabolic rate, and is used to treat thyroid disorders

thy·self \thī-ˈself\ *pron, archaic* : YOURSELF

Ti *symbol* titanium

ti·ara \tē-ˈer-ə, -ˈär-\ *n* **1** : a 3-tiered crown worn by the pope **2** : a decorative headband or semicircle for formal wear by women

Ti·bet·an \tə-ˈbet-ᵊn\ *n* **1** : the language of the Tibetan people **2** : a native or inhabitant of Tibet — **Tibetan** *adj*

tib·ia \'ti-bē-ə\ *n, pl* **-i·ae** \-bē-ˌē\ *also* **-i·as** [L] : the inner of the two bones of the vertebrate hind or lower limb between the knee and the ankle

tic \'tik\ *n* : a local and habitual twitching of muscles esp. of the face

ti·cal \ti-ˈkäl, 'ti-kəl\ *n, pl* **ticals** *or* **tical** : BAHT

¹tick \'tik\ *n* : any of a large group of small bloodsucking arachnids

²tick *n* : the fabric case of a mattress or pillow; *also* : a mattress consisting of a tick and its filling

³tick *n* **1** : a light rhythmic audible tap or beat **2** : a small mark used to draw attention to or check something

⁴tick *vb* **1** : to make the sound of a tick or series of ticks **2** : to mark, count, or announce by or as if by ticking beats **3** : to mark or check with a tick **4** : to function as an operating mechanism : RUN

⁵tick *n, chiefly Brit* : CREDIT; *also* : a credit account

tick·er \'ti-kər\ *n* **1** : something (as a watch) that ticks **2** : a telegraph instrument that prints information (as stock prices) on paper tape **3** *slang* : HEART

ticker tape *n* : the paper ribbon on which a telegraphic ticker prints

¹tick·et \'ti-kət\ *n* [MF *etiquet, estiquette* notice attached to something, fr. MF dial. *estiquier* to attach, fr. MD *steken* to stick] **1** : CERTIFICATE, LICENSE, PERMIT; *esp* : a certificate or token showing that a fare or admission fee has been paid **2** : TAG, LABEL **3** : SLATE 4 **4** : a summons issued to a traffic offender

²ticket *vb* **1** : to attach a ticket to **2** : to furnish or serve with a ticket

tick·ing \'ti-kiŋ\ *n* : a strong fabric used in upholstering and as a mattress covering

tick·le \'ti-kəl\ *vb* **tick·led; tick·ling** **1** : to excite or stir up agreeably : PLEASE, AMUSE **2** : to have a tingling sensation **3** : to touch (as a body part) lightly so as to cause uneasiness, laughter, or spasmodic movements — **tickle** *n* — **tick·ler** *n*

tick·lish \-kə-lish\ *adj* **1** : OVERSENSITIVE, TOUCHY **2** : UNSTABLE ⟨a ~ foothold⟩ **3** : requiring delicate handling ⟨~ subject⟩ **4** : sensitive to tickling — **tick·lish·ly** *adv* — **tick·lish·ness** *n*

tidal wave *n* **1** : an unusually high sea wave that sometimes follows an earthquake **2** : an unusual rise of water alongshore due to strong winds

tid·bit \'tid-ˌbit\ *n* : a choice morsel

¹tide \'tīd\ *n* [ME, time, fr. OE *tīd*] **1** : the alternate rising and falling of the surface of the ocean **2** : something that fluctuates like the tides of the sea — **tid·al** \'tī-dᵊl\ *adj*

²tide *vb* **tid·ed; tid·ing** : to carry through or help along as if by the tide ⟨a loan to ~ us over⟩

tide·land \'tīd-ˌland, -lənd\ *n* **1** : land overflowed during flood tide **2** : land under the ocean within a nation's territorial waters — often used in pl.

tide·wa·ter \-ˌwȯ-tər, -ˌwä-\ *n* **1** : water overflowing land at flood tide **2** : low-lying coastal land

tid·ings \'tī-diŋz\ *n pl* : NEWS, MESSAGE

¹ti·dy \'tī-dē\ *adj* **ti·di·er; -est** **1** : well ordered and cared for : NEAT **2** : LARGE, SUBSTANTIAL ⟨a ~ sum⟩ — **ti·di·ness** \'tī-dē-nəs\ *n*

²tidy *vb* **ti·died; ti·dy·ing** **1** : to put in order **2** : to make things tidy

³tidy *n, pl* **tidies** : a decorated covering used to protect the back or arms of a chair from wear or soil

¹tie \'tī\ *n* **1** : a line, ribbon, or cord used for fastening, uniting, or closing **2** : a structural element (as a beam or rod) holding two pieces together **3** : one of the cross supports to which railroad rails are fastened **4** : a connecting link : BOND ⟨family ~s⟩ **5** : an equality in number (as of votes or scores); *also* : an undecided or deadlocked contest **6** : NECKTIE

²tie *vb* **tied; ty·ing** *or* **tie·ing** **1** : to fasten, attach, or close by means of a tie **2** : to bring together firmly : UNITE **3** : to form a knot or bow in ⟨~ a scarf⟩ **4** : to restrain from freedom of action : CONSTRAIN **5** : to make or have an equal score with

tie·back \'tī-ˌbak\ *n* : a decorative strip for draping a curtain to the side of a window

tie–dye·ing \'tī-ˌdī-iŋ\ *n* : a method of producing patterns in textiles by tying parts of the fabric so that they will not absorb the dye — **tie–dyed** \-ˌdīd\ *adj*

tie–in \'tī-ˌin\ *n* : CONNECTION

tier \'tir\ *n* : ROW, LAYER; *esp* : one of two or more rows arranged one above another — **tiered** \'tird\ *adj*

tie–rod \'tī-ˌräd\ *n* : a rod used as a connecting member or brace

tie–up \-ˌəp\ *n* **1** : a slowing or stopping of traffic or business **2** : CONNECTION

tiff \'tif\ *n* : a petty quarrel — **tiff** *vb*

Tif·fa·ny \'ti-fə-nē\ *adj* : made of pieces of stained glass ⟨a ~ lamp⟩

ti·ger \'tī-gər\ *n* : a very large tawny black-striped Asian cat — **ti·ger·ish** *adj*

tiger

¹**tight** \'tīt\ *adj* **1** : so close in structure as to prevent passage of a liquid or gas **2** : strongly fixed or held : SECURE **3** : TAUT **4** : fitting usu. too closely ⟨~ shoes⟩ **5** : set close together : COMPACT ⟨a ~ formation⟩ **6** : DIFFICULT, TRYING ⟨get in a ~ spot⟩ **7** : STINGY, MISERLY **8** : evenly contested : CLOSE **9** : INTOXICATED **10** : low in supply : hard to get ⟨money is ~⟩ — **tight·ly** *adv* — **tight·ness** *n*

²**tight** *adv* **1** : TIGHTLY, FIRMLY **2** : SOUNDLY ⟨sleep ~⟩

tight·en \'tī-t⁰n\ *vb* : to make or become tight

tight-fist·ed \'tīt-'fis-təd\ *adj* : STINGY

tight·rope \-,rōp\ *n* : a taut rope or wire for acrobats to perform on

tights \'tīts\ *n pl* : skintight garments covering the body esp. below the waist; *also, Brit* : PANTY HOSE

tight·wad \'tīt-,wäd\ *n* : a stingy person

ti·gress \'tī-grəs\ *n* : a female tiger

ti·la·pia \tə-'lä-pē-ə, -'lä-\ *n, pl* **tilapia** *also* **ti·la·pi·as** : any of numerous chiefly African freshwater fishes widely raised for food

til·de \'til-də\ *n* [Sp, fr. ML *titulus* tittle] : a mark ˜ placed esp. over the letter *n* (as in Spanish *señor* sir) to denote the sound \nʸ\ or over vowels (as in Portuguese *irmã* sister) to indicate nasal quality

¹**tile** \'tī(-ə)l\ *n* **1** : a flat or curved piece of fired clay, stone, or concrete used for roofs, floors, or walls; *also* : a pipe of earthenware or concrete used for a drain **2** : a thin piece (as of linoleum) used for covering walls or floors — **til·ing** \'tī-liŋ\ *n*

²**tile** *vb* **tiled; til·ing** : to cover with tiles — **til·er** *n*

¹**till** \'til\ *prep or conj* : UNTIL

²**till** *vb* : to work by plowing, sowing, and raising crops : CULTIVATE — **till·able** *adj*

³**till** *n* : DRAWER; *esp* : a money drawer in a store or bank

till·age \'ti-lij\ *n* **1** : the work of tilling land **2** : cultivated land

¹**til·ler** \'ti-lər\ *n* [OE *telgor, telgra* twig, shoot] : a sprout or stalk esp. from the base or lower part of a plant

²**till·er** \'ti-lər\ *n* : one that tills

³**til·ler** \'ti-lər\ *n* [ME *tiler* stock of a crossbow, tiller, fr. AF *teiler* stock of a crossbow] : a lever used for turning a boat's rudder from side to side

¹**tilt** \'tilt\ *n* **1** : a contest in which two combatants charging usu. with lances try to unhorse each other : JOUST; *also* : a tournament of tilts **2** : a verbal contest : DISPUTE **3** : a sloping surface : SLANT

²**tilt** *vb* **1** : to move or shift so as to incline : TIP **2** : to engage in or as if in combat with lances : JOUST, ATTACK

tilth \'tilth\ *n* **1** : TILLAGE 2 **2** : the state of a soil esp. in relation to the suitability of its particle size and structure for growing crops

Tim *abbr* Timothy

tim·ber \'tim-bər\ *n* [ME, fr. OE, building, wood] **1** : growing trees or their wood — often used interjectionally to warn of a falling tree **2** : wood for use in making something **3** : a usu. large squared or dressed piece of wood

tim·bered \'tim-bərd\ *adj* : having walls framed by exposed timbers

tim·ber·land \'tim-bər-,land\ *n* : wooded land

tim·ber·line \'tim-bər-,līn\ *n* : the upper limit of tree growth in mountains or high latitudes

timber rattlesnake *n* : a widely distributed rattlesnake of the eastern U.S.

timber wolf *n* : GRAY WOLF

tim·bre *also* **tim·ber** \'tam-bər, 'tim-\ *n* [F, fr. MF, bell struck by a hammer, fr. OF, drum, fr. MGk *tymbanon* kettledrum, fr. Gk *tympanon*] : the distinctive quality given to a sound by its overtones

tim·brel \'tim-brəl\ *n* : a small hand drum or tambourine

¹**time** \'tīm\ *n* **1** : a period during which an action, process, or condition exists or continues ⟨gone a long ~⟩ **2** : LEISURE ⟨found ~ to read⟩ **3** : a point or period when something occurs : OCCASION ⟨the last ~ we met⟩ **4** : a set or customary moment or hour for something to occur ⟨arrived on ~⟩ **5** : AGE, ERA **6** : state of affairs : CONDITIONS ⟨hard ~s⟩ **7** : a rate of speed : TEMPO **8** : a moment, hour, day, or year as indicated by a clock or calendar ⟨what ~ is it⟩ **9** : a system of reckoning time ⟨solar ~⟩ **10** : one of a series of recurring instances; *also, pl* : added or accumulated quantities or examples ⟨five ~s greater⟩ **11** : a person's experience during a particular period ⟨had a good ~⟩ **12** : the hours or days of one's work; *also* : an hourly pay rate ⟨straight ~⟩ **13** : TIME-OUT 1

²**time** *vb* **timed; tim·ing** **1** : to arrange or set the time of : SCHEDULE ⟨~s his calls conveniently⟩ **2** : to set the tempo or duration of ⟨~ a performance⟩ **3** : to cause to keep time with **4** : to determine or record the time, duration, or rate of ⟨~ a sprinter⟩ — **tim·er** *n*

time bomb *n* **1** : a bomb so made as to explode at a predetermined time **2** : something with a potentially dangerous delayed reaction

time clock *n* : a clock that records the time workers arrive and depart

time frame *n* : a period of time esp. with respect to some action or project

time-hon·ored \'tīm-,ä-nərd\ *adj* : honored because of age or long usage

time·keep·er \-,kē-pər\ *n* **1** : a clerk who keeps records of the time worked by employees **2** : one appointed to mark and announce the time in an athletic game or contest

time·less \-ləs\ *adj* **1** : ETERNAL **2** : not limited or affected by time ⟨~ works of art⟩ — **time·less·ly** *adv* — **time·less·ness** *n*

time·ly \-lē\ *adj* **time·li·er; -est** **1** : coming early or at the right time ⟨a ~ decision⟩ ⟨~ payment⟩ **2** : appropriate to the time ⟨a ~ book⟩ — **time·li·ness** *n*

time–out \'tīm-'aút\ *n* **1** : a brief suspension of activity esp. in an athletic game **2** : a quiet period used esp. as a disciplinary measure for a child

time·piece \-,pēs\ *n* : a device (as a clock) to show the passage of time

times \'tīmz\ *prep* : multiplied by ⟨2 ~ 2 is 4⟩

time–shar·ing \'tīm-,sher-iŋ\ *n* **1** : simultaneous use of a computer by many users **2** *or* **time–share** \-,sher\ : joint ownership or rental of a vacation lodging by several persons with each taking turns using the place

times sign *n* : the symbol × used to indicate multiplication

time·ta·ble \'tīm-,tā-bəl\ *n* **1** : a table of the departure and arrival times (as of trains) **2** : a schedule showing a planned order or sequence

time warp *n* : an anomaly, discontinuity, or suspension held to occur in the progress of time

time·worn \-,wórn\ *adj* **1** : worn by time **2** : HACKNEYED, STALE ⟨a ~ joke⟩

tim·id \'ti-məd\ *adj* : lacking in courage or self-confidence : FEARFUL — **ti·mid·i·ty** \tə-'mi-də-tē\ *n* — **tim·id·ly** *adv*

tim·o·rous \'ti-mə-rəs\ *adj* : of a timid disposition : AFRAID — **tim·o·rous·ly** *adv* — **tim·o·rous·ness** *n*

tim·o·thy \'ti-mə-thē\ *n* : a perennial grass with long cylindrical spikes widely grown for hay in the U.S.

Tim·o·thy \'ti-mə-thē\ *n* — see BIBLE table

tim·pa·ni \'tim-pə-nē\ *n sing or pl* [It] : a set of kettledrums played by one performer in an orchestra — **tim·pa·nist** \-nist\ *n*

¹**tin** \'tin\ *n* **1** : a soft white crystalline metallic chemical element malleable at ordinary temperatures that is used esp. in solders and alloys **2** : a container (as a can) made of metal (as tinplate)

²**tin** *vb* **tinned; tin·ning** **1** : to cover or plate with tin **2** : to pack in tins

TIN *abbr* taxpayer identification number

tinct \'tiŋkt\ *n* : TINCTURE, TINGE

¹**tinc·ture** \'tiŋk-chər\ *n* **1** *archaic* : a substance that colors **2** : a slight admixture : TRACE **3** : an alcoholic solution of a medicinal substance ♦ **Synonyms** TOUCH, SUGGESTION, SUSPICION, TINGE

²**tincture** *vb* **tinc·tured; tinc·tur·ing** **1** : COLOR, TINGE **2** : AFFECT

tin·der \'tin-dər\ *n* **1** : a very flammable substance used as kindling **2** : something serving to incite or inflame

tin·der·box \'tin-dər-,bäks\ *n* **1** : a metal box for holding tinder and usu. flint and steel for striking a spark **2** : a highly flammable object or place

tine \'tīn\ *n* : a slender pointed part (as of a fork or an antler) : PRONG

tin·foil \'tin-,fói(-ə)l\ *n* : a thin metal sheeting usu. of aluminum or tin-lead alloy

¹**tinge** \'tinj\ *vb* **tinged; tinge·ing** *or* **ting·ing** **1** : to color slightly : TINT **2** : to affect or modify esp. with a slight odor or taste

²**tinge** *n* : a slight coloring, flavor, or quality : TRACE
♦ **Synonyms** TOUCH, SUGGESTION, SUSPICION, TINC-
TURE, SOUPÇON

tin·gle \'tiŋ-gəl\ *vb* **tin·gled; tin·gling** 1 : to feel a prickling or thrilling sensation 2 : TINKLE — **tingle** *n*

¹**tin·ker** \'tiŋ-kər\ *n* 1 : a usu. itinerant mender of household utensils 2 : an unskillful mender : BUNGLER

²**tinker** *vb* : to repair or adjust something in an unskillful or
experimental manner — **tin·ker·er** *n*

¹**tin·kle** \'tiŋ-kəl\ *vb* **tin·kled; tin·kling** : to make or cause
to make a tinkle

²**tinkle** *n* : a series of short high ringing or clinking sounds

tin·ni·tus \'ti-nə-təs, tə-'nī-təs\ *n* : a sensation of noise (as
ringing or roaring) in the ears

tin·ny \'ti-nē\ *adj* **tin·ni·er; -est** 1 : abounding in or yielding tin 2 : resembling tin; *also* : LIGHT, CHEAP 3 : thin in
tone ⟨a ~ voice⟩ — **tin·ni·ly** \-nə-lē\ *adv* — **tin·ni·ness**
\-nē-nəs\ *n*

tin·plate \'tin-'plāt\ *n* : thin sheet iron or steel coated with
tin — **tin-plate** *vb*

tin·sel \'tin-səl\ *n* [ME *tyneseyle* cloth interwoven with
metallic thread, prob. fr. AF *tencelé*, pp. of *tenceler, estenceler* to sparkle] 1 : threads, strips, or sheets of metal,
paper, or plastic used to produce a glittering appearance
2 : something superficially attractive but of little worth

tin·smith \'tin-ˌsmith\ *n* : one that works with sheet metal
(as tinplate)

¹**tint** \'tint\ *n* 1 : a slight or pale coloration : HUE 2 : any
of various shades of a color

²**tint** *vb* : to impart a tint to : COLOR

tin·tin·nab·u·la·tion \ˌtin-tə-ˌna-byə-'lā-shən\ *n* 1 : the
ringing of bells 2 : a tingling sound as if of bells

tin·ware \'tin-ˌwer\ *n* : articles and esp. utensils made of
tinplate

ti·ny \'tī-nē\ *adj* **ti·ni·er; -est** : very small : MINUTE ♦ **Synonyms** MINIATURE, DIMINUTIVE, WEE, LILLIPUTIAN

¹**tip** \'tip\ *vb* **tipped; tip·ping** 1 : OVERTURN, UPSET 2
: LEAN, SLANT; *also* : to raise and tilt forward ⟨*tipped* his
hat⟩

²**tip** *n* : the act or an instance of tipping

³**tip** *vb* **tipped; tip·ping** 1 : to furnish with a tip 2 : to
cover or adorn the tip of

⁴**tip** *n* 1 : the usu. pointed end of something 2 : a small
piece or part serving as an end, cap, or point

⁵**tip** *n* : a light touch or blow

⁶**tip** *vb* **tipped; tip·ping** : to strike lightly : TAP

⁷**tip** *n* : a piece of advice or expert or confidential information : HINT

⁸**tip** *vb* **tipped; tip·ping** : to impart a piece of information
about or to

⁹**tip** *vb* **tipped; tip·ping** : to give a gratuity to — **tip·per** *n*

¹⁰**tip** *n* : a gift or small sum given for a service performed or
anticipated

tip-off \'tip-ˌof\ *n* : WARNING, TIP

tip·pet \'ti-pət\ *n* : a long scarf or shoulder cape

tip·ple \'ti-pəl\ *vb* **tip·pled; tip·pling** : to drink intoxicating liquor esp. habitually or excessively — **tipple** *n* — **tippler** *n*

tip·ster \'tip-stər\ *n* : a person who gives or sells tips esp.
for gambling

tip·sy \'tip-sē\ *adj* **tip·si·er; -est** : unsteady or foolish from
the effects of alcohol — **tip·si·ly** \-sə-lē\ *adv* — **tip·si-
ness** \-sē-nəs\ *n*

¹**tip·toe** \'tip-ˌtō\ *n* : the position of being balanced on the
balls of the feet and toes with the heels raised; *also* : the
ends of the toes

²**tiptoe** *adv or adj* : on or as if on tiptoe

³**tiptoe** *vb* **tip·toed; tip·toe·ing** : to walk or proceed on or
as if on tiptoe ⟨~ around the issue⟩

¹**tip-top** \'tip-'täp\ *n* : the highest point

²**tip-top** *adj* : EXCELLENT, FIRST-RATE

ti·rade \'tī-ˌrād\ *n* [F, shot, tirade, fr. MF, fr. It *tirata*, fr.
tirare to draw, shoot] : a prolonged speech of abuse or
condemnation

tir·a·mi·su \ˌtir-ə-'mē-sü, -mē-'sü\ *n* [It *tiramisù*] : a dessert
made with ladyfingers, mascarpone, and espresso

¹**tire** \'tī(-ə)r\ *vb* **tired; tir·ing** 1 : to make or become weary
: FATIGUE 2 : to wear out the patience of : BORE

²**tire** *n* 1 : a metal hoop that forms the tread of a wheel 2
: a rubber cushion usu. containing compressed air that
encircles a wheel (as of a bike)

tired *adj* 1 : WEARY, FATIGUED 2 : HACKNEYED —
tired·ness *n*

tire·less \'tī(-ə)r-ləs\ *adj* : not tiring : UNTIRING, INDE-
FATIGABLE — **tire·less·ly** *adv* — **tire·less·ness** *n*

tire·some \-səm\ *adj* : tending to bore : WEARISOME, TE-
DIOUS — **tire·some·ly** *adv* — **tire·some·ness** *n*

ti·ro *chiefly Brit var of* TYRO

tis·sue \'ti-shü\ *n* [ME *tysshewe, tyssew*, a rich fabric, fr.
AF, fr. *tistre* to weave, fr. L *texere*] 1 : a fine lightweight
often sheer fabric 2 : NETWORK, WEB ⟨a ~ of lies⟩ 3 : a
soft absorbent paper 4 : a mass or layer of cells forming
a basic structural material of an animal or plant

¹**tit** \'tit\ *n* : TEAT

²**tit** *n* : any of various small plump Old World songbirds related to the titmice

Tit *abbr* Titus

ti·tan \'tī-tᵊn\ *n* 1 *cap* : one of a family of giants overthrown by the gods in Greek mythology 2 : one gigantic
in size or power

ti·tan·ic \tī-'ta-nik\ *adj* : enormous in size, force, or power
♦ **Synonyms** IMMENSE, GIGANTIC, GIANT, COLOSSAL,
MAMMOTH

ti·ta·ni·um \tī-'tā-nē-əm\ *n* : a gray light strong metallic
chemical element used esp. in alloys

titbit *var of* TIDBIT

tithe \'tīth\ *n* [ME, fr. OE *teogotha* tenth] : a 10th part paid
or given esp. for the support of a church — **tithe** *vb* —
tith·er *n*

tit·il·late \'ti-tᵊl-ˌāt\ *vb* **-lat·ed; -lat·ing** 1 : to excite pleasurably 2 : TICKLE 3 — **tit·il·la·tion** \ˌti-tᵊl-'ā-shən\ *n*

tit·i·vate *or* **tit·ti·vate** \'ti-tə-ˌvāt\ *vb* **-vat·ed; -vat·ing** : to
dress up : spruce up — **tit·i·va·tion** \ˌti-tə-'vā-shən\ *n*

ti·tle \'tī-tᵊl\ *n* 1 : CLAIM, RIGHT; *esp* : a legal right to the
ownership of property 2 : the distinguishing name of a
written, filmed, or musical production or a work of art 3
: an appellation of honor, rank, or office 4 : CHAMPI-
ONSHIP ♦ **Synonyms** DESIGNATION, DENOMINATION,
APPELLATION

ti·tled \'tī-tᵊld\ *adj* : having a title esp. of nobility

title page *n* : a page of a book bearing the title and usu.
the names of the author and publisher

tit·mouse \'tit-ˌmaùs\ *n, pl* **tit·mice** \-ˌmīs\ : any of several
small long-tailed No. American songbirds related to the
chickadees

ti·tra·tion \tī-'trā-shən\ *n* : a process of finding the concentration of a solution (as of an acid) by adding small
portions of a second solution of known concentration (as
of a base) to a fixed amount of the first until an expected
change (as in color) occurs

tit·ter \'ti-tər\ *vb* : to laugh in an affected or in a nervous
or half-suppressed manner : GIGGLE — **titter** *n*

tit·tle \'ti-tᵊl\ *n* : a tiny part

tit·tle-tat·tle \'ti-tᵊl-ˌta-tᵊl\ *n* : idle talk : GOSSIP —
tittle-tattle *vb*

tit·u·lar \'ti-chə-lər\ *adj* 1 : existing in title only : NOMINAL
⟨~ ruler⟩ 2 : of, relating to, or bearing a title ⟨~ role⟩

Ti·tus \'tī-təs\ *n* — see BIBLE table

tiz·zy \'ti-zē\ *n, pl* **tizzies** : a highly excited and distracted
state of mind

tk *abbr* 1 tank 2 truck

TKO \ˌtē-ˌkā-'ō\ *n* [*technical knockout*] : the termination
of a boxing match when a boxer is declared unable to
continue the fight

tkt *abbr* ticket

Tl *symbol* thallium

TLC *abbr* tender loving care

T lymphocyte *n* : T CELL

Tm *symbol* thulium

TM *abbr* trademark

T-man \'tē-ˌman\ *n* : a special agent of the U.S. Treasury
Department

tn *abbr* 1 ton 2 town

TN *abbr* Tennessee

tng *abbr* training

tnpk *abbr* turnpike

TNT \ˌtē-(ˌ)en-'tē\ *n* : a flammable toxic compound used as
a high explosive and in chemical synthesis

¹**to** \tə, ˌtü\ *prep* 1 : in the direction of and reaching ⟨drove
~ town⟩ 2 : in the direction of : TOWARD 3 : ON,
AGAINST ⟨apply salve ~ a burn⟩ 4 : as far as ⟨can pay
up ~ a dollar⟩ 5 : so as to become or bring about ⟨beat-

en ~ death⟩ ⟨broken ~ pieces⟩ **6** : BEFORE ⟨it's five minutes ~ six⟩ **7** : UNTIL ⟨from May ~ December⟩ **8** : fitting or being a part of : FOR ⟨key ~ the lock⟩ **9** : with the accompaniment of ⟨sing ~ the music⟩ **10** : in relation or comparison with ⟨similar ~ that one⟩ ⟨won 10 ~ 6⟩ **11** : in accordance with ⟨add salt ~ taste⟩ **12** : within the range of ⟨~ my knowledge⟩ **13** : contained, occurring, or included in ⟨two pints ~ a quart⟩ **14** : as regards ⟨agreeable ~ everyone⟩ **15** : affecting as the receiver or beneficiary ⟨whispered ~ her⟩ ⟨gave it ~ me⟩ **16** : for no one except ⟨a room ~ myself⟩ **17** : into the action of ⟨we got ~ talking⟩ **18** — used for marking the following verb as an infinitive ⟨wants ~ go⟩ and often used by itself at the end of a clause in place of an infinitive suggested by the preceding context ⟨goes to town whenever he wants ~⟩ ⟨can leave if you'd like ~⟩

²to \'tü\ *adv* **1** : in a direction toward ⟨run ~ and fro⟩ **2** : into contact esp. with the frame of a door ⟨the door slammed ~⟩ **3** : to the matter in hand ⟨fell ~ and ate heartily⟩ **4** : to a state of consciousness or awareness ⟨came ~ hours after the accident⟩

TO *abbr* turn over

toad \'tōd\ *n* : any of numerous tailless leaping amphibians differing typically from the related frogs in having a shorter stockier build, rough dry warty skin, and less aquatic habits

toad·stool \-ˌstül\ *n* : MUSHROOM; *esp* : one that is poisonous or inedible

toady \'tō-dē\ *n, pl* **toad·ies** : a person who flatters in the hope of gaining favors : SYCOPHANT — **toady** *vb*

to–and–fro \ˌtü-ən-'frō\ *adj* : forward and backward — **to–and–fro** *n*

¹toast \'tōst\ *vb* **1** : to warm thoroughly **2** : to make (as bread) crisp, hot, and brown by heat **3** : to become toasted

²toast *n* **1** : sliced toasted bread **2** : someone or something in whose honor persons drink **3** : an act of drinking in honor of a toast

³toast *vb* : to propose or drink to as a toast

toast·er \'tō-stər\ *n* : an electrical appliance for toasting

toaster oven *n* : a portable electrical appliance that bakes, broils, and toasts

toast·mas·ter \'tōst-ˌmas-tər\ *n* : a person who presides at a banquet and introduces the after-dinner speakers

toast·mis·tress \-ˌmis-trəs\ *n* : a woman who acts as toastmaster

toasty \'tō-stē\ *adj* **toast·i·er; -est** : pleasantly warm

Tob *abbr* Tobit

to·bac·co \tə-'ba-kō\ *n, pl* **-cos** [Sp *tabaco*] **1** : a tall broad-leaved herb related to the potato; *also* : its leaves prepared for smoking or chewing or as snuff **2** : manufactured tobacco products; *also* : smoking as a practice

to·bac·co·nist \tə-'ba-kə-nist\ *n* : a dealer in tobacco

To·bi·as \tō-'bī-əs\ *n* : TOBIT

To·bit \'tō-bət\ *n* — see BIBLE table

¹to·bog·gan \tə-'bä-gən\ *n* : a long flat-bottomed light sled made of thin boards curved up at one end

toboggan

²toboggan *vb* **1** : to coast on or as if on a toboggan **2** : to decline suddenly (as in value) — **to·bog·gan·er** *n*

toc·sin \'täk-sən\ *n* **1** : an alarm bell **2** : a warning signal

¹to·day \tə-'dā\ *adv* **1** : on or for this day **2** : at the present time

²today *n* : the present day, time, or age

tod·dle \'täd-əl\ *vb* **tod·dled; tod·dling** : to walk with short tottering steps in the manner of a young child — **toddle** *n* — **tod·dler** *n*

tod·dy \'tä-dē\ *n, pl* **toddies** [Hindi & Urdu *tāṛī* juice of a palm, fr. *tāṛ* a palm, fr. Skt *tāla*] : a drink made of liquor, sugar, spices, and hot water

to–do \tə-'dü\ *n, pl* **to–dos** \-'düz\ : BUSTLE, STIR, FUSS

¹toe \'tō\ *n* **1** : one of the jointed parts of the front end of the vertebrate foot **2** : the front part of a foot or hoof

²toe *vb* **toed; toe·ing** : to touch, reach, or drive with the toes

toea \'tȯi-ə\ *n* — see *kina* at MONEY table

toe·hold \'tō-ˌhōld\ *n* **1** : a place of support for the toes **2** : a slight footing

toe·nail \'tō-ˌnāl\ *n* : a nail of a toe

tof·fee *or* **tof·fy** \'tȯ-fē, 'tä-\ *n, pl* **toffees** *or* **toffies** : candy of brittle but tender texture made by boiling sugar and butter together

to·fu \'tō-(ˌ)fü\ *n* [Jp *tōfu*] : a soft white food product made from soybeans

tog \'täg, 'tȯg\ *vb* **togged; tog·ging** : to put togs on : DRESS

to·ga \'tō-gə\ *n* : the loose outer garment worn in public by citizens of ancient Rome — **to·gaed** \-gəd\ *adj*

¹to·geth·er \tə-'ge-thər\ *adv* **1** : in or into one place or group **2** : in or into contact or association ⟨mix ~⟩ **3** : at one time : SIMULTANEOUSLY ⟨talk and work ~⟩ **4** : in succession ⟨for days ~⟩ **5** : in or into harmony or coherence ⟨get ~ on a plan⟩ **6** : as a group : JOINTLY — **to·geth·er·ness** *n*

²together *adj* : composed in mind or manner

together with *prep* : in addition to : in association with

tog·gery \'tä-gə-rē, 'tȯ-\ *n* : CLOTHING

tog·gle \'tä-gəl\ *vb* : to switch between two options esp. of an electronic device

toggle switch *n* : an electric switch operated by pushing a projecting lever through a small arc

togs \'tägz, 'tȯgz\ *n pl* : CLOTHING; *esp* : clothes for a specified use ⟨riding ~⟩

¹toil \'tȯi(-ə)l\ *n* **1** : laborious effort **2** : long fatiguing labor : DRUDGERY — **toil·ful** \-fəl\ *adj* — **toil·some** *adj*

²toil *vb* [ME, to argue, struggle, fr. AF *toiller* to make dirty, fight, wrangle, fr. L *tudiculare* to crush, grind, fr. *tudicula* machine for crushing olives, dim. of *tudes* hammer] **1** : to work hard and long **2** : to proceed with great effort : PLOD — **toil·er** *n*

³toil *n* [ME *toile* cloth, net, fr. OF *teile*, fr. L *tela* cloth on a loom] : NET, TRAP — usu. used in pl. ⟨caught in the ~s of the law⟩

toi·let \'tȯi-lət\ *n* **1** : the act or process of dressing and grooming oneself **2** : BATHROOM **3** : a fixture for use in urinating and defecating; *esp* : one consisting essentially of a water-flushed bowl and seat — **toilet** *vb*

toi·let·ry \'tȯi-lə-trē\ *n, pl* **-ries** : an article or preparation used in cleaning or grooming oneself — usu. used in pl.

toi·lette \twä-'let\ *n* **1** : TOILET 1 **2** : formal attire; *also* : a particular costume

toilet training *n* : the process of training a child to control bladder and bowel movements and to use the toilet — **toilet train** *vb*

toil·worn \'tȯi(-ə)l-ˌwȯrn\ *adj* : showing the effects of toil

To·kay \tō-'kā\ *n* : naturally sweet wine from Hungary

toke \'tōk\ *n, slang* : a puff on a marijuana cigarette or pipe

¹to·ken \'tō-kən\ *n* **1** : an outward sign **2** : SYMBOL, EMBLEM **3** : SOUVENIR, KEEPSAKE **4** : a small part representing the whole **5** : a piece resembling a coin issued as money or for use by a particular group on specified terms

²token *adj* **1** : done or given as a token esp. in partial fulfillment of an obligation **2** : representing only a symbolic effort : MINIMAL, PERFUNCTORY

to·ken·ism \'tō-kə-ˌni-zəm\ *n* : the policy or practice of making only a symbolic effort (as to desegregate)

told *past and past part of* TELL

tole \'tōl\ *n* : sheet metal and esp. tinplate for use in domestic and ornamental wares

tol·er·a·ble \'tä-lə-rə-bəl\ *adj* **1** : capable of being borne or endured **2** : moderately good : PASSABLE — **tol·er·a·bly** \-blē\ *adv*

tol·er·ance \'tä-lə-rəns\ *n* **1** : the act or practice of tolerating; *esp* : sympathy or indulgence for beliefs or practices differing from one's own **2** : the allowable deviation from a standard (as of size) **3** : the body's capacity to become less responsive over time to something (as a drug used repeatedly) — **tol·er·ant** *adj* — **tol·er·ant·ly** *adv*

tol·er·ate \'tä-lə-ˌrāt\ *vb* **-at·ed; -at·ing** **1** : to exhibit physiological tolerance for (as a drug) **2** : to allow to be or to be done without hindrance ♦ *Synonyms* ABIDE, BEAR, SUFFER, STAND, BROOK — **tol·er·a·tion** \ˌtä-lə-ˈrā-shən\ *n*

¹toll \'tōl\ *n* **1** : a tax paid for a privilege (as for passing over a bridge) **2** : a charge for a service (as for a long-distance telephone call) **3** : the cost in life, health, loss, or suffering

²toll *vb* **1** : to cause the slow regular sounding of (a bell) esp. by pulling a rope **2** : to give signal of : SOUND **3** : to sound with slow measured strokes **4** : to announce by tolling

³toll *n* : the sound of a tolling bell

toll·booth \'tōl-ˌbüth\ *n* : a booth where tolls are paid

toll·gate \-ˌgāt\ *n* : a point where vehicles stop to pay a toll

toll·house \-ˌhaus\ *n* : a house or booth where tolls are paid

tol·u·ene \'täl-yə-ˌwēn\ *n* : a liquid hydrocarbon used esp. as a solvent

tom \'täm\ *n* : the male of various animals (as a cat or turkey)

¹tom·a·hawk \'tä-mə-ˌhök\ *n* : a light ax used as a missile and as a hand weapon esp. by No. American Indians

²tomahawk *vb* : to strike or kill with a tomahawk

to·ma·til·lo \ˌtō-mə-'tē-(ˌ)yō\ *n, pl* **-los** : a small round usu. pale green edible fruit of a Mexican herb related to the tomato; *also* : this herb

to·ma·to \tə-'mā-tō, -'mä-\ *n, pl* **-toes** [alter. of earlier *tomate,* fr. Sp, fr. Nahuatl *tomatl*] : a usu. large, rounded, and red or yellow pulpy edible berry of a widely grown tropical herb related to the potato; *also* : this herb

tomb \'tüm\ *n* **1** : a place of burial : GRAVE **2** : a house, chamber, or vault for the dead — **tomb** *vb*

tom·boy \'täm-ˌböi\ *n* : a girl who behaves in a manner usu. considered boyish — **tom·boy·ish** *adj*

tomb·stone \'tüm-ˌstōn\ *n* : a stone marking a grave

tom·cat \'täm-ˌkat\ *n* : a male domestic cat

Tom Col·lins \'täm-'kä-lənz\ *n* : a tall iced drink with a base of gin

tome \'tōm\ *n* : BOOK; *esp* : a large or weighty one

tom·fool·ery \täm-'fü-lə-rē\ *n* : playful or foolish behavior

tom·my gun \'tä-mē-ˌgən\ *n* : SUBMACHINE GUN — **tommy–gun** *vb*

to·mog·ra·phy \tō-'mä-grə-fē\ *n* : a method of producing a three-dimensional image of the internal structures of a solid object (as the human body or the earth) — **to·mo·graph·ic** \ˌtō-mə-'gra-fik\ *adj*

to·mor·row \tə-'mär-ō\ *adv* : on or for the day after today — **tomorrow** *n*

tom–tom \'täm-ˌtäm\ *n* : a small-headed drum beaten with the hands

ton \'tən\ *n, pl* **tons** *also* **ton** **1** — see WEIGHT table **2** : a unit equal to the volume of a long ton weight of seawater used in reckoning the displacement of ships and equal to 35 cubic feet

to·nal·i·ty \tō-'na-lə-tē\ *n, pl* **-ties** : tonal quality

¹tone \'tōn\ *n* [ME, fr. L *tonus* tension, tone, fr. Gk *tonos,* lit., act of stretching; fr. the dependence of the pitch of a musical string on its tension] **1** : vocal or musical sound; *esp* : sound quality **2** : a sound of definite pitch **3** : WHOLE STEP **4** : accent or inflection expressive of an emotion **5** : the pitch of a word often used to express differences of meaning **6** : style or manner of expression **7** : color quality; *also* : SHADE, TINT **8** : the effect in painting of light and shade together with color **9** : healthy and vigorous condition of a living body or bodily part; *also* : the state of partial contraction characteristic of normal muscle **10** : general character, quality, or trend ♦ *Synonyms* ATMOSPHERE, FEELING, MOOD, VEIN — **ton·al** \'tōn-ᵊl\ *adj*

²tone *vb* **toned; ton·ing** **1** : to give a particular intonation or inflection to **2** : to impart tone to **3** : SOFTEN, MELLOW **4** : to harmonize in color : BLEND

tone·arm *n* : the movable part of a record player that carries the pickup and the needle

toney *var of* TONY

tong \'täŋ, 'töŋ\ *n* : a Chinese secret society in the U.S.

tongs \'täŋz, 'töŋz\ *n pl* : a grasping device consisting of two pieces joined at one end by a pivot or hinged like scissors — **tong** *vb*

¹tongue \'təŋ\ *n* **1** : a fleshy movable process of the floor of the mouth used in tasting and in taking and swallowing food and in humans as a speech organ **2** : the flesh of a tongue (as of the ox) used as food **3** : the power of communication **4** : LANGUAGE 1 **5** : manner or quality of utterance; *also* : intended meaning **6** : ecstatic usu. unintelligible utterance accompanying religious excitation — usu. used in pl. **7** : something resembling an animal's tongue esp. in being elongated and fastened at one end only — **tongued** \'təŋd\ *adj* — **tongue·less** *adj*

²tongue *vb* **tongued; tongu·ing** **1** : to touch or lick with the tongue **2** : to articulate notes on a wind instrument

tongue–in–cheek *adj* : characterized by insincerity, irony, or whimsical exaggeration — **tongue in cheek** *adv*

tongue–lash \'təŋ-ˌlash\ *vb* : CHIDE, REPROVE — **tongue–lash·ing** \-iŋ\ *n*

tongue–tied \-ˌtīd\ *adj* : unable or disinclined to speak clearly or freely (as from shyness or a tongue impairment)

tongue twister *n* : an utterance that is difficult to articulate because of a succession of similar consonants

¹ton·ic \'tä-nik\ *adj* **1** : of, relating to, or producing a healthy physical or mental condition : INVIGORATING **2** : relating to or based on the 1st tone of a scale — **to·nic·i·ty** \tō-'ni-sə-tē\ *n*

²tonic *n* **1** : the 1st degree of a musical scale **2** : something that invigorates, restores, or refreshes

tonic water *n* : a carbonated beverage flavored with a bit of quinine, lemon, and lime

¹to·night \tə-'nīt\ *adv* : on this present night or the coming night

²tonight *n* : the present or the coming night

ton·nage \'tə-nij\ *n* **1** : a duty on ships based on tons carried **2** : ships in terms of the number of tons registered or carried **3** : total weight in tons shipped, carried, or mined

ton·sil \'tän-səl\ *n* : either of a pair of oval masses of lymphoid tissue that lie one on each side of the throat at the back of the mouth

ton·sil·lec·to·my \ˌtän-sə-'lek-tə-mē\ *n, pl* **-mies** : the surgical removal of the tonsils

ton·sil·li·tis \-'lī-təs\ *n* : inflammation of the tonsils

ton·so·ri·al \tän-'sör-ē-əl\ *adj* : of or relating to a barber or a barber's work

ton·sure \'tän-chər\ *n* [ME, fr. AF, ML *tonsura,* fr. L, act of shearing, fr. *tonsus,* pp. of *tondēre* to shear] **1** : the rite of admission to the clerical state by the clipping or shaving of the head **2** : the shaven crown or patch worn by clerics (as monks) — **tonsure** *vb*

tony *also* **ton·ey** \'tō-nē\ *adj* **ton·i·er; -est** : marked by an aristocratic manner or style

too \'tü\ *adv* **1** : in addition : ALSO **2** : EXCESSIVELY **3** : to such a degree as to be regrettable **4** : VERY ⟨didn't seem ~ interested⟩

took *past of* TAKE

¹tool \'tül\ *n* **1** : a hand instrument that aids in accomplishing a task **2** : the cutting or shaping part in a machine; *also* : a machine for shaping metal in any way **3** : something used in doing a job ⟨a scholar's books are his ~s⟩; *also* : a means to an end **4** : a person used by another : DUPE **5** *pl* : natural ability

²tool *vb* **1** : to shape, form, or finish with a tool; *esp* : to letter or decorate (as a book cover) by means of hand tools **2** : to equip a plant or industry with machines and tools for production **3** : DRIVE, RIDE ⟨~ing along at 60 miles per hour⟩

tool bar *n* : a strip of icons on a computer display providing quick access to the pictured functions

¹toot \'tüt\ *vb* **1** : to sound or cause to sound in short blasts **2** : to blow an instrument (as a horn) — **toot·er** *n*

²toot *n* : a short blast (as on a horn)

tooth \'tüth\ *n, pl* **teeth** \'tēth\ **1** : one of the hard bony structures borne esp. on the jaws of vertebrates and used for seizing and chewing food and as weapons; *also* : a hard sharp structure esp. around the mouth of an invertebrate **2** : something resembling an animal's tooth **3** : any of the projections on the edge of a wheel that fits into corresponding projections on another wheel **4** *pl*

: effective means of enforcement — **toothed** \'tütht\ *adj*
— **tooth·less** *adj*

tooth·ache \'tüth-ˌāk\ *n* : pain in or about a tooth

tooth·brush \-ˌbrəsh\ *n* : a brush for cleaning the teeth

tooth·paste \-ˌpāst\ *n* : a paste for cleaning the teeth

tooth·pick \-ˌpik\ *n* : a pointed instrument for removing food particles caught between the teeth

tooth powder *n* : a powder for cleaning the teeth

tooth·some \'tüth-səm\ *adj* **1** : AGREEABLE, ATTRACTIVE **2** : pleasing to the taste : DELICIOUS ♦ *Synonyms* PALATABLE, APPETIZING, SAVORY, TASTY

toothy \'tü-thē\ *adj* **tooth·i·er; -est** : having or showing prominent teeth

¹**top** \'täp\ *n* **1** : the highest part, point, or level of something **2** : the part of a plant with edible roots lying above the ground ⟨beet ∼s⟩ **3** : the upper end, edge, or surface ⟨the ∼ of a page⟩ **4** : an upper piece, lid, or covering **5** : the highest degree, pitch, or rank **6** : a quark with a charge of +⅔ and a measured energy of approximately 175 billion electron volts

²**top** *vb* **topped; top·ping 1** : to remove or trim the top of : PRUNE ⟨∼ a tree⟩ **2** : to cover with a top or on the top : CROWN, CAP **3** : to be superior to : EXCEL, SURPASS **4** : to go over the top of **5** : to strike (a ball) above the center **6** : to make an end or conclusion ⟨∼ off a meal with coffee⟩

³**top** *adj* **1** : of, relating to, or being at the top : HIGHEST **2** : CHIEF

⁴**top** *n* : a toy that has a tapering point on which it is made to spin

to·paz \'tō-ˌpaz\ *n* : a hard silicate of aluminum; *esp* : a yellow transparent topaz used as a gem

top·coat \'täp-ˌkōt\ *n* **1** : a lightweight overcoat **2** : a protective coating (as of paint)

top dollar *n* : the highest amount being paid for a commodity or service

top–dress \-ˌdres\ *vb* : to apply material to (as land) without working it in; *esp* : to scatter fertilizer over

top·dress·ing \-ˌdre-siŋ\ *n* : a material used to top-dress soil

top–end \'täp-ˈend\ *adj* : TOPFLIGHT

top·flight \'täp-ˈflīt\ *adj* : of, relating to, or being the highest level of excellence or rank — **top flight** *n*

top hat *n* : a tall-crowned hat usu. of beaver or silk

top–heavy \'täp-ˌhe-vē\ *adj* : having the top part too heavy for the lower part

to·pi·ary \'tō-pē-ˌer-ē\ *n, pl* **-ar·ies** : the art of training and trimming trees or shrubs with decorative shapes — **topiary** *adj*

top·ic \'tä-pik\ *n* **1** : a heading in an outlined argument **2** : the subject of a discourse or a section of it : THEME

top·i·cal \-pi-kəl\ *adj* **1** : of, relating to, or arranged by topics ⟨a ∼ outline⟩ **2** : relating to current or local events **3** : designed to be applied to or to work on a part (as of the body) — **top·i·cal·ly** \-k(ə-)lē\ *adv*

top·knot \'täp-ˌnät\ *n* **1** : an ornament (as a knot of ribbons) forming a headdress **2** : a crest of feathers or tuft of hair on the top of the head

top·less \-ləs\ *adj* **1** : wearing no clothing on the upper body **2** : featuring topless waitresses or entertainers

top·mast \'täp-ˌmast, -məst\ *n* : the 2d mast above a ship's deck

top·most \'täp-ˌmōst\ *adj* : highest of all : UPPERMOST

top–notch \-ˈnäch\ *adj* : of the highest quality : FIRST-RATE

top–of–the–line *adj* : being or belonging to the highest or most expensive class

to·pog·ra·phy \tə-ˈpä-grə-fē\ *n* **1** : the art of showing in detail on a map or chart the physical features of a place or region **2** : the outline of the form of a place showing its relief and the position of features (as rivers, roads, or cities) — **to·pog·ra·pher** \-fər\ *n* — **top·o·graph·ic** \ˌtä-pə-ˈgra-fik\ *or* **top·o·graph·i·cal** \-fi-kəl\ *adj*

topping *n* : a food served on top of another to make it look or taste better

top·ple \'tä-pəl\ *vb* **top·pled; top·pling 1** : to fall from or as if from being top-heavy **2** : to push over : OVERTURN; *also* : OVERTHROW

¹**tops** \'täps\ *adj* : topmost in quality or importance ⟨∼ in his field⟩

²**tops** *adv* : at the very most

top·sail \'täp-ˌsāl, -səl\ *also* **top·s'l** \-səl\ *n* : the sail next above the lowest sail on a mast in a square-rigged ship

top secret *adj* : demanding complete secrecy among those concerned

top·side \'täp-ˈsīd\ *adv or adj* **1** : to or on the top or surface **2** : on deck

top·sides \-ˈsīdz\ *n pl* : the top portion of the outer surface of a ship on each side above the waterline

top·soil \'täp-ˌsȯi(-ə)l\ *n* : surface soil usu. including the organic layer in which plants have most of their roots

top·sy–tur·vy \ˌtäp-sē-ˈtər-vē\ *adv* **1** : in utter confusion **2** : UPSIDE DOWN — **topsy–turvy** *adj*

toque \'tōk\ *n* : a woman's small hat without a brim

tor \'tȯr\ *n* : a high craggy hill

To·rah \'tȯr-ə\ *n* **1** : a scroll of the first five books of the Old Testament used in a synagogue; *also* : these five books **2** : the body of divine knowledge and law found in the Jewish scriptures and tradition

¹**torch** \'tȯrch\ *n* **1** : a flaming light made of something that burns brightly and usu. carried in the hand **2** : something that resembles a torch in giving light, heat, or guidance **3** : a portable burner for producing a hot flame **4** *chiefly Brit* : FLASHLIGHT

²**torch** *vb* : to set fire to

torch·bear·er \'tȯrch-ˌber-ər\ *n* **1** : a person who carries a torch **2** : one in the forefront (as of a political campaign)

torch·light \-ˌlīt\ *n* : light given by torches

torch song *n* : a popular sentimental song of unrequited love

tore *past of* TEAR

to·re·ador \'tȯr-ē-ə-ˌdȯr\ *n* : BULLFIGHTER

to·re·ro \tə-ˈrer-ō\ *n, pl* **-ros** [Sp] : BULLFIGHTER

¹**tor·ment** \'tȯr-ˌment\ *n* **1** : extreme pain or anguish of body or mind **2** : a source of vexation or pain

²**tor·ment** \tȯr-ˈment\ *vb* **1** : to cause severe suffering of body or mind to **2** : DISTORT, TWIST ♦ *Synonyms* RACK, AFFLICT, TRY, TORTURE — **tor·men·tor** \-ˈmen-tər\ *n*

torn *past part of* TEAR

tor·na·do \tȯr-ˈnā-dō\ *n, pl* **-does** *or* **-dos** [modif of Sp *tronada* thunderstorm, fr. *tronar* to thunder, fr. L *tonare*] : a violent destructive whirling wind accompanied by a funnel-shaped cloud that moves over a narrow path

¹**tor·pe·do** \tȯr-ˈpē-dō\ *n, pl* **-does** : a thin cylindrical self=propelled underwater weapon

²**torpedo** *vb* **tor·pe·doed; tor·pe·do·ing** : to hit or destroy with or as if with a torpedo

torpedo boat *n* : a small very fast boat for firing torpedoes

tor·pid \'tȯr-pəd\ *adj* **1** : having lost motion or the power of exertion : DORMANT **2** : SLUGGISH **3** : lacking vigor — **tor·pid·i·ty** \tȯr-ˈpi-də-tē\ *n*

tor·por \'tȯr-pər\ *n* **1** : DULLNESS, APATHY **2** : extreme sluggishness : STAGNATION ♦ *Synonyms* STUPOR, LETHARGY, LANGUOR, LASSITUDE

¹**torque** \'tȯrk\ *n* : a force that produces or tends to produce rotation or torsion

²**torque** *vb* **torqued; torqu·ing** : to impart torque to : cause to twist (as about an axis)

tor·rent \'tȯr-ənt\ *n* [F, fr. L *torrent-, torrens*, fr. *torrent-, torrens* burning, seething, rushing, fr. prp. of *torrēre* to parch, burn] **1** : a tumultuous outburst **2** : a rushing stream (as of water)

tor·ren·tial \tȯ-ˈren-chəl\ *adj* : relating to or resembling a torrent ⟨∼ rains⟩

tor·rid \'tȯr-əd\ *adj* **1** : parched with heat esp. of the sun : HOT **2** : ARDENT

torrid zone *n* : the region of the earth between the Tropic of Cancer and the Tropic of Capricorn

tor·sion \'tȯr-shən\ *n* **1** : a wrenching by which one part of a body is under pressure to turn about a longitudinal axis while the other part is held fast or is under pressure to turn in the opposite direction **2** : a twisting of a bodily organ or part on its own axis — **tor·sion·al** \'tȯr-shə-nəl\ *adj* — **tor·sion·al·ly** *adv*

tor·so \'tȯr-sō\ *n, pl* **torsos** *or* **tor·si** \'tȯr-ˌsē\ [It, lit., stalk] : the trunk of the human body

tort \'tȯrt\ *n* : a wrongful act which does not involve a breach of contract and for which the injured party can recover damages in a civil action

tor·ti·lla \tȯr-ˈtē-ə\ *n* : a round thin cake of unleavened cornmeal or wheat flour bread

tor·toise \'tȯr-təs\ *n* : TURTLE; *esp* : any of a family of land turtles

tor·toise·shell \-,shel\ *n* : the mottled horny substance of the shell of some turtles used in inlaying and in making various ornamental articles — **tortoiseshell** *adj*

tor·to·ni \tȯr-'tō-nē\ *n* : rich ice cream often made with minced almonds and chopped cherries and flavored with rum

tor·tu·ous \'tȯr-chə-wəs\ *adj* **1** : marked by twists or turns : WINDING **2** : DEVIOUS, TRICKY

¹**tor·ture** \'tȯr-chər\ *n* **1** : anguish of body or mind **2** : the infliction of severe pain esp. to punish or coerce — **tor·tur·ous** \'tȯrch-rəs, 'tȯr-chə-\ *adj*

²**torture** *vb* **tor·tured; tor·tur·ing** **1** : to cause intense suffering to : TORMENT **2** : to punish or coerce by inflicting severe pain **3** : TWIST, DISTORT ♦ *Synonyms* RACK, HARROW, AFFLICT, TRY — **tor·tur·er** *n*

To·ry \'tȯr-ē\ *n, pl* **Tories** **1** : a member of a chiefly 18th century British party upholding the established church and the traditional political structure **2** : an American supporter of the British during the American Revolution **3** *often not cap* : an extreme conservative — **Tory** *adj*

¹**toss** \'tȯs, 'täs\ *vb* **1** : to fling to and fro or up and down **2** : to throw with a quick light motion; *also* : BANDY **3** : to fling or lift with a sudden motion ⟨~ed her head angrily⟩ **4** : to move restlessly or turbulently ⟨~es on the waves⟩ **5** : to twist and turn repeatedly **6** : FLOUNCE **7** : to accomplish readily ⟨~ off an article⟩ **8** : to decide an issue by flipping a coin

²**toss** *n* : an act or instance of tossing; *esp* : TOSS-UP 1

toss–up \-,əp\ *n* **1** : a deciding by flipping a coin **2** : an even chance **3** : something that offers no clear basis for choice

¹**tot** \'tät\ *n* **1** : a small child **2** : a small drink of alcoholic liquor : SHOT

²**tot** *vb* **tot·ted; tot·ting** : to add up

³**tot** *abbr* total

¹**to·tal** \'tō-t⁰l\ *adj* **1** : making up a whole : ENTIRE ⟨~ amount⟩ **2** : COMPLETE, UTTER ⟨a ~ failure⟩ ⟨a ~ stranger⟩ **3** : involving a complete and unified effort esp. to achieve a desired effect — **to·tal·ly** *adv*

²**total** *n* **1** : SUM 4 **2** : the entire amount ♦ *Synonyms* AGGREGATE, WHOLE, GROSS, TOTALITY

³**total** *vb* **to·taled** *or* **to·talled; to·tal·ing** *or* **to·tal·ling** **1** : to add up : COMPUTE **2** : to amount to : NUMBER **3** : to make a total wreck of (a car)

to·tal·i·tar·i·an \tō-,ta-lə-'ter-ē-ən\ *adj* : of, relating to, or advocating a political regime based on subordination of the individual to the state and strict control of all aspects of life esp. by coercive measures — **totalitarian** *n* — **to·tal·i·tar·i·an·ism** \-ē-ə-,ni-zəm\ *n*

to·tal·i·ty \tō-'ta-lə-tē\ *n, pl* **-ties** **1** : an aggregate amount : SUM, WHOLE **2** : ENTIRETY, WHOLENESS

to·tal·iza·tor *or* **to·tal·isa·tor** \'tō-t⁰l-ə-,zā-tər\ *n* : a machine for registering and indicating the number of bets and the odds on a horse or dog race

¹**tote** \'tōt\ *vb* **tot·ed; tot·ing** : CARRY

²**tote** *vb* **tot·ed; tot·ing** : ADD, TOTAL — usu. used with *up*

to·tem \'tō-təm\ *n* [Ojibwa *oto·te·man* his totem] : an object (as an animal or plant) serving as the emblem of a family or clan and often as a reminder of its ancestry; *also* : something usu. carved or painted to represent such an object

totem pole *n* : a pole that is carved with a series of totems and is erected before the houses of some northwest American Indians

tot·ter \'tä-tər\ *vb* **1** : to tremble or rock as if about to fall : SWAY **2** : to move unsteadily : STAGGER

tou·can \'tü-,kan\ *n* [F, fr. Pg *tucano*, fr. Tupinambá (American Indian language of Brazil) *tukána*] : any of a family of chiefly fruit-eating birds of tropical America with brilliant coloring and a very large bill

¹**touch** \'təch\ *vb* **1** : to bring a bodily part (as the hand) into contact with so as to feel **2** : to be or cause to be in contact **3** : to strike or push lightly esp. with the hand or foot **4** : DISTURB, HARM **5** : to make use of ⟨never ~es alcohol⟩ **6** : to induce to give or lend **7** : to get to : REACH **8** : to refer to in passing : MENTION **9** : to affect the interest of : CONCERN **10** : to leave a mark on; *also* : BLEMISH **11** : to move to sympathetic feeling **12** : to come close : VERGE **13** : to have a bearing : RELATE

14 : to make a usu. brief or incidental stop in port ♦ *Synonyms* AFFECT, INFLUENCE, IMPRESS, STRIKE, SWAY

²**touch** *n* **1** : a light stroke or tap **2** : the act or fact of touching or being touched **3** : the sense by which pressure or traction on the skin or mucous membrane is perceived; *also* : a particular sensation conveyed by this sense **4** : mental or moral sensitiveness : TACT **5** : a small quantity : HINT ⟨a ~ of spring in the air⟩ **6** : a manner of striking or touching esp. the keys of a keyboard instrument **7** : an improving detail ⟨add a few ~es to the painting⟩ **8** : distinctive manner or skill ⟨the ~ of a master⟩ **9** : the state of being in contact ⟨keep in ~⟩ ♦ *Synonyms* SUGGESTION, SUSPICION, TINCTURE, TINGE

touch·down \'təch-,daun\ *n* : the act of scoring six points in American football by being lawfully in possession of the ball on, above, or behind an opponent's goal line

tou·ché \tü-'shā\ *interj* [F] — used to acknowledge a hit in fencing or the success of an argument, an accusation, or a witty point

touch football *n* : football in which touching is substituted for tackling

touch·ing \'tə-chiŋ\ *adj* : capable of stirring emotions ♦ *Synonyms* MOVING, IMPRESSIVE, POIGNANT, AFFECTING

touch off *vb* **1** : to describe with precision **2** : to start by or as if by touching with fire

touch·stone \'təch-,stōn\ *n* : a test or criterion of genuineness or quality ♦ *Synonyms* STANDARD, GAUGE, BENCHMARK, YARDSTICK

touch–tone \'təch-'tōn\ *adj* : of, relating to, or being a telephone having push buttons that produce tones corresponding to numbers

touch up *vb* : to improve or perfect by small additional strokes or alterations — **touch–up** \'təch-,əp\ *n*

touchy \'tə-chē\ *adj* **touch·i·er; -est** **1** : easily offended : PEEVISH **2** : calling for tact in treatment ⟨a ~ subject⟩ ♦ *Synonyms* IRASCIBLE, CRANKY, CROSS, TETCHY, TESTY

¹**tough** \'təf\ *adj* **1** : strong or firm in texture but flexible and not brittle **2** : not easily chewed **3** : characterized by severity and determination ⟨a ~ policy⟩ **4** : capable of enduring strain or hardship : ROBUST **5** : hard to influence : STUBBORN **6** : difficult to accomplish, resolve, or cope with ⟨a ~ problem⟩ **7** : ROWDYISH ♦ *Synonyms* TENACIOUS, STOUT, STURDY, STALWART — **tough·ly** *adv* — **tough·ness** *n*

²**tough** *n* : a tough person : ROWDY

tough·en \'tə-fən\ *vb* **tough·ened; tough·en·ing** : to make or become tough

tou·pee \tü-'pā\ *n* [F *toupet* forelock] : a small wig for a bald spot

¹**tour** \'tur, *1 is also* 'taù-(ə)r\ *n* **1** : one's turn : SHIFT **2** : a journey in which one returns to the starting point

²**tour** *vb* : to make a tour

tour de force \,tur-də-'fȯrs\ *n, pl* **tours de force** \same\ [F] : a feat or display of strength, skill, or ingenuity

Tou·rette's syndrome \tu-'rets-\ *n* : a familial neurological disorder marked by recurrent involuntary tics and vocal sounds

tour·ism \'tur-,i-zəm\ *n* **1** : the practice of traveling for recreation **2** : promotion of touring **3** : accommodation of tourists — **tour·ist** \-ist\ *n*

tourist class *n* : economy accommodations (as on a ship)

tour·ma·line \'tur-mə-lən, -,lēn\ *n* : a mineral that when transparent is valued as a gem

tour·na·ment \'tur-nə-mənt, 'tər-\ *n* **1** : a medieval sport in which mounted armored knights contended with blunted lances or swords **2** : a championship series of games or athletic contests

tour·ney \-nē\ *n, pl* **tourneys** : TOURNAMENT

tour·ni·quet \'tur-ni-kət, 'tər-\ *n* : a device (as a tight bandage) to check bleeding or blood flow

tou·sle \'tau-zəl\ *vb* **tou·sled; tou·sling** : to disorder by rough handling : DISHEVEL, MUSS

tout \'taut, *2 is also* 'tüt\ *vb* **1** : to give a tip or solicit bets on a racehorse **2** : to praise or publicize loudly — **tout** *n*

¹**tow** \'tō\ *vb* : to draw or pull along behind

²**tow** *n* **1** : an act of towing or condition of being towed **2** : something (as a barge) that is towed

³**tow** *n* : short or broken fiber (as of flax or hemp) used esp. for yarn, twine, or stuffing

to·ward \'tȯrd, 'tō-ərd, tə-'wȯrd\ *or* **to·wards** \'tȯrdz, 'tō-ərdz, tə-'wȯrdz\ *prep* **1** : in the direction of ⟨heading ∼ the river⟩ **2** : along a course leading to ⟨efforts ∼ reconciliation⟩ **3** : in regard to ⟨tolerance ∼ minorities⟩ **4** : so as to face ⟨turn the chair ∼ the window⟩ **5** : close upon ⟨it was getting along ∼ sundown⟩ **6** : for part payment of ⟨here's $100 ∼ your tuition⟩

tow·boat \'tō-ˌbōt\ *n* : TUGBOAT

tow·el \'taú(-ə)l\ *n* : an absorbent cloth or paper for wiping or drying

tow·el·ing *or* **tow·el·ling** *n* : a cotton or linen fabric for making towels

¹**tow·er** \'taú(-ə)r\ *n* **1** : a tall structure either isolated or built upon a larger structure ⟨an observation ∼⟩ **2** : a towering citadel **3** : a personal computer case that stands in an upright position — **tow·ered** *adj*

²**tower** *vb* : to reach or rise to a great height

tow·er·ing \'taú(-ə)r-iŋ\ *adj* **1** : LOFTY ⟨∼ pines⟩ **2** : reaching high intensity ⟨a ∼ rage⟩ **3** : EXCESSIVE ⟨∼ ambition⟩

tow·head \'tō-ˌhed\ *n* : a person having whitish blond hair — **tow·head·ed** \-ˌhe-dəd\ *adj*

to·whee \'tō-ˌhē, 'tō-(ˌ)ē, tō-'hē\ *n* : a common finch of eastern No. America having the male black, white, and reddish; *also* : any of several closely related finches

to wit *adv* : NAMELY

town \'taún\ *n* **1** : a compactly settled area usu. larger than a village but smaller than a city **2** : CITY **3** : the inhabitants of a town **4** : a New England territorial and political unit usu. containing both rural and urban areas; *also* : a New England community in which matters of local government are decided by a general assembly (**town meeting**) of qualified voters

town house *n* **1** : the city residence of a person having a country home **2** : a single-family house of two or sometimes three stories connected to another house by a common wall

town·ie *or* **towny** \'taú-nē\ *n, pl* **townies** : a permanent resident of a town as distinguished from a member of another group

towns·folk \'taúnz-ˌfōk\ *n pl* : TOWNSPEOPLE

town·ship \'taún-ˌship\ *n* **1** : TOWN **2** : a unit of local government in some states **3** : an unorganized subdivision of a county **4** : a division of territory in surveys of U.S. public land containing 36 square miles **5** : an area in the Republic of South Africa segregated for occupation by persons of non-European descent

towns·man \'taúnz-mən\ *n* **1** : a native or resident of a town or city **2** : a fellow citizen of a town

towns·peo·ple \-ˌpē-pəl\ *n pl* **1** : the inhabitants of a town or city **2** : town-bred persons

towns·wom·an \-ˌwú-mən\ *n* **1** : a woman who is a native or resident of a town or city **2** : a woman who is a fellow citizen of a town

tow·path \'tō-ˌpath, -ˌpäth\ *n* : a path (as along a canal) traveled esp. by draft animals towing boats

tow truck *n* : a truck equipped for towing vehicles

tox·emia \täk-'sē-mē-ə\ *n* : a bodily disorder associated with the presence of toxic substances in the blood

tox·ic \'täk-sik\ *adj* [LL *toxicus*, fr. L *toxicum* poison, fr. Gk *toxikon* arrow poison, fr. neut. of *toxikos* of a bow, fr. *toxon* bow, arrow] : of, relating to, or caused by poison or a toxin : POISONOUS — **tox·ic·i·ty** \täk-'si-sə-tē\ *n*

tox·i·col·o·gy \ˌtäk-si-'kä-lə-jē\ *n* : a science that deals with poisons and esp. with problems of their use and control — **tox·i·co·log·i·cal** \-kə-'lä-ji-kəl\ *also* **tox·i·co·log·ic** \-kə-'lä-jik\ *adj* — **tox·i·col·o·gist** \-'kä-lə-jist\ *n*

toxic shock syndrome *n* : an acute disease associated with the presence of a bacterium that is characterized by fever, diarrhea, nausea, diffuse erythema, and shock and occurs esp. in menstruating females using tampons

tox·in \'täk-sən\ *n* : a poisonous substance produced by metabolic activities of a living organism that is usu. unstable, very toxic when introduced into the tissues, and usu. capable of inducing antibodies

¹**toy** \'tȯi\ *n* **1** : something trifling **2** : a small ornament : BAUBLE **3** : something for a child to play with

²**toy** *vb* **1** : to deal with something lightly : TRIFLE **2** : FLIRT **3** : to amuse oneself as if with a plaything

³**toy** *adj* **1** : DIMINUTIVE ⟨a ∼ dog⟩ **2** : designed for use as a toy

tp *abbr* **1** title page **2** township

tpk *or* **tpke** *abbr* turnpike

tr *abbr* **1** translated; translation; translator **2** transpose **3** troop

¹**trace** \'trās\ *n* **1** : a mark (as a footprint or track) left by something that has passed **2** : a minute or barely detectable amount

²**trace** *vb* **traced; trac·ing** **1** : to mark out : SKETCH **2** : to form (as letters) carefully **3** : to copy (a drawing) by marking lines on transparent paper laid over the drawing to be copied **4** : to follow the trail of : track down **5** : to study out and follow the development of — **trace·able** *adj*

³**trace** *n* : either of two lines of a harness for fastening a draft animal to a vehicle

trac·er \'trā-sər\ *n* **1** : one that traces **2** : ammunition containing a chemical to mark the flight of projectiles by a trail of smoke or light

trac·ery \'trā-sə-rē\ *n, pl* **-er·ies** : ornamental work having a design with branching or interlacing lines

tracery

tra·chea \'trā-kē-ə\ *n, pl* **-che·ae** \-kē-ˌē\ *also* **-che·as** *or* **-chea** : the main tube by which air passes from the larynx to the lungs of vertebrates — **tra·che·al** \-kē-əl\ *adj*

tra·che·ot·o·my \ˌtrā-kē-'ä-tə-mē\ *n, pl* **-mies** : the surgical operation of cutting into the trachea esp. through the skin

trac·ing *n* **1** : the act of one that traces **2** : something that is traced **3** : a graphic record made by an instrument for measuring vibrations or pulsations

¹**track** \'trak\ *n* **1** : a mark left in passing **2** : PATH, ROUTE, TRAIL **3** : a course laid out for racing; *also* : track-and-field sports **4** : one of a series of paths along which material (as music) is recorded (as on a compact disc or magnetic tape) **5** : the course along which something moves; *esp* : a way made by two parallel lines of metal rails **6** : awareness of a fact or progression ⟨lost ∼ of time⟩ **7** : either of two endless metal belts on which a vehicle (as a bulldozer) travels

²**track** *vb* **1** : to follow the tracks or traces of : TRAIL **2** : to observe the moving path of (as a missile) **3** : to make tracks on **4** : to carry (as mud) on the feet and deposit — **track·er** *n*

track·age \'tra-kij\ *n* : lines of railway track

track–and–field *adj* : of or relating to athletic contests held on a running track or on the adjacent field

¹**tract** \'trakt\ *n* **1** : an area without precise boundaries ⟨huge ∼s of land⟩ **2** : a defined area of land **3** : a system of body parts or organs that act together to perform some function ⟨the digestive ∼⟩

²**tract** *n* : a pamphlet of political or religious propaganda

trac·ta·ble \'trak-tə-bəl\ *adj* : easily controlled : DOCILE ◆ **Synonyms** AMENABLE, OBEDIENT, BIDDABLE

tract house *n* : any of many similar houses built on a tract of land

trac·tion \'trak-shən\ *n* **1** : the act of drawing : the state of being drawn **2** : the drawing of a vehicle by motive power; *also* : the particular form of motive power used **3** : the adhesive friction of a body on a surface on which it moves **4** : a pulling force applied to a skeletal structure (as a broken bone) by means of a special device; *also* : a state of tension created by such a pulling force ⟨a leg in ∼⟩ — **trac·tion·al** \-shə-nəl\ *adj* — **trac·tive** \'trak-tiv\ *adj*

trac·tor \'trak-tər\ *n* 1 : an automotive vehicle used esp. for drawing farm equipment 2 : a truck for hauling a trailer

¹**trade** \'trād\ *n* 1 : one's regular business or work : OCCUPATION 2 : an occupation requiring manual or mechanical skill 3 : the persons engaged in a business or industry 4 : the business of buying and selling or bartering commodities 5 : an act of trading : TRANSACTION

²**trade** *vb* **trad·ed; trad·ing** 1 : to give in exchange for another commodity : BARTER 2 : to engage in the exchange, purchase, or sale of goods 3 : to deal regularly as a customer — **trade on** : EXPLOIT ⟨*trades on* his family name⟩

trade–in \'trād-ₔin\ *n* : an item of merchandise traded in
trade in *vb* : to turn in as part payment for a purchase

¹**trade·mark** \'trād-ₔmärk\ *n* : a device (as a word or mark) that points distinctly to the origin or ownership of merchandise to which it is applied and that is legally reserved for the exclusive use of the owner; *also* : something that identifies a person or thing

²**trademark** *vb* : to secure the trademark rights for

trade name *n* : a name that is given by a manufacturer or merchant to a product to distinguish it as made or sold by him and that may be used and protected as a trademark

trad·er \'trā-dər\ *n* 1 : a person whose business is buying or selling 2 : a ship engaged in trade

trades·man \'trādz-mən\ *n* 1 : one who runs a retail store : SHOPKEEPER 2 : CRAFTSMAN

trades·peo·ple \-ₔpē-pəl\ *n pl* : people engaged in trade

trade union *n* : LABOR UNION

trade wind *n* : a wind blowing almost constantly in one direction

trading stamp *n* : a printed stamp given as a premium to a retail customer that when accumulated may be redeemed for merchandise

tra·di·tion \trə-'di-shən\ *n* 1 : an inherited, established, or customary pattern of thought or action 2 : the handing down of beliefs and customs by word of mouth or by example without written instruction; *also* : a belief or custom thus handed down — **tra·di·tion·al** \-'di-shə-nəl\ *adj* — **tra·di·tion·al·ly** *adv*

tra·duce \trə-'düs, -'dyüs\ *vb* **tra·duced; tra·duc·ing** : to lower the reputation of : DEFAME, SLANDER ◆ **Synonyms** MALIGN, LIBEL, CALUMNIATE — **tra·duc·er** *n*

¹**traf·fic** \'tra-fik\ *n* 1 : the business of bartering or buying and selling 2 : communication or dealings between individuals or groups 3 : the movement (as of vehicles) along a route; *also* : the vehicles, people, ships, or planes moving along a route 4 : the passengers or cargo carried by a transportation system

²**traffic** *vb* **traf·ficked; traf·fick·ing** 1 : to carry on business dealings 2 : DEAL, TRADE — **traf·fick·er** *n*

traffic circle *n* : ROTARY 2

traffic light *n* : a visual signal (as a system of lights) for controlling traffic

tra·ge·di·an \trə-'jē-dē-ən\ *n* 1 : a writer of tragedies 2 : an actor who plays tragic roles

tra·ge·di·enne \trə-ₔjē-dē-'en\ *n* [F] : an actress who plays tragic roles

trag·e·dy \'tra-jə-dē\ *n, pl* **-dies** [ME *tragedie,* fr. MF, fr. L *tragoedia,* fr. Gk *tragōidia,* fr. *tragos* goat + *aeidein* to sing] 1 : a serious drama with a sorrowful or disastrous conclusion 2 : a disastrous event : CALAMITY; *also* : MISFORTUNE 3 : tragic quality or element ⟨the ~ of life⟩

trag·ic \'tra-jik\ *also* **trag·i·cal** \-ji-kəl\ *adj* 1 : of, relating to, or expressive of tragedy 2 : appropriate to tragedy 3 : LAMENTABLE, UNFORTUNATE — **trag·i·cal·ly** \-ji-k(ə-)lē\ *adv*

¹**trail** \'trāl\ *vb* 1 : to hang down so as to drag along or sweep the ground 2 : to draw or drag along behind 3 : to extend over a surface in a straggling manner 4 : to lag behind 5 : to follow the track of : PURSUE 6 : DWINDLE ⟨her voice ~ed off⟩

²**trail** *n* 1 : something that trails or is trailed ⟨a ~ of smoke⟩ 2 : a trace or mark left by something that has passed or been drawn along : SCENT, TRACK ⟨a ~ of blood⟩ 3 : a beaten path; *also* : a marked path through woods

trail bike *n* : a small motorcycle for off-road use

trail·blaz·er \-ₔblā-zər\ *n* : PATHFINDER, PIONEER — **trail·blaz·ing** *adj or n*

trail·er \'trā-lər\ *n* 1 : one that trails; *esp* : a creeping plant (as an ivy) 2 : a vehicle that is hauled by another (as a tractor) 3 : a vehicle equipped to serve wherever parked as a dwelling or place of business 4 : PREVIEW 2

trailer park *n* : a site equipped to accommodate mobile homes

trailing arbutus *n* : a creeping spring-flowering plant of the heath family with fragrant pink or white flowers

¹**train** \'trān\ *n* [ME, fr. AF, fr. *trainer* to draw, drag] 1 : a part of a gown that trails behind the wearer 2 : RETINUE 3 : a moving file of persons, vehicles, or animals 4 : a connected series ⟨a ~ of thought⟩ 5 : AFTERMATH 6 : a connected line of railroad cars usu. hauled by a locomotive ◆ **Synonyms** SUCCESSION, SEQUENCE, PROCESSION, CHAIN

²**train** *vb* [ME, to trail, drag, train, fr. AF *trainer*] 1 : to cause to grow as desired ⟨~ a vine on a trellis⟩ 2 : to form by instruction, discipline, or drill 3 : to make or become prepared (as by exercise) for a test of skill 4 : to aim or point at an object ⟨~ guns on a fort⟩ ◆ **Synonyms** DISCIPLINE, SCHOOL, EDUCATE, INSTRUCT — **train·er** *n*

train·ee \trā-'nē\ *n* : one who is being trained esp. for a job

train·ing \'trā-niŋ\ *n* 1 : the act, process, or method of one who trains 2 : the skill, knowledge, or experience gained by one who trains

train·man \-mən\ *n* : a member of a train crew

traipse \'trāps\ *vb* **traipsed; traips·ing** : TRAMP, WALK ⟨~ the countryside⟩

trait \'trāt\ *n* 1 : a distinguishing quality (as of personality) 2 : an inherited characteristic

trai·tor \'trā-tər\ *n* [ME *traytour,* fr. AF *traitre,* fr. L *traditor,* fr. *tradere* to hand over, deliver, betray, fr. *trans-* across + *dare* to give] 1 : one who betrays another's trust or is false to an obligation 2 : one who commits treason — **trai·tor·ous** *adj*

tra·jec·to·ry \trə-'jek-tə-rē\ *n, pl* **-ries** : the curve that a body (as a planet in its orbit) describes in space

tram \'tram\ *n* 1 : a boxlike car running on rails (as in a mine) 2 *chiefly Brit* : STREETCAR 3 : an overhead cable car

¹**tram·mel** \'tra-məl\ *n* [ME *tramayle,* a kind of net, fr. OF *tramail,* fr. LL *tremaculum,* fr. L *tres* three + *macula* mesh, spot] : something impeding activity, progress, or freedom — usu. used in pl.

²**trammel** *vb* **-meled** *or* **-melled; -mel·ing** *or* **-mel·ling** 1 : to catch and hold in or as if in a net 2 : HAMPER ◆ **Synonyms** CLOG, FETTER, SHACKLE, HOBBLE

¹**tramp** \'tramp, *1 & 3 are also* 'trämp, 'trȯmp\ *vb* 1 : to walk, tread, or step heavily 2 : to walk about or through; *also* : HIKE 3 : to tread on forcibly and repeatedly

²**tramp** \'tramp, *5 is also* 'trämp, 'trȯmp\ *n* 1 : a begging or thieving vagrant 2 : a foot traveler 3 : an immoral woman; *esp* : PROSTITUTE 4 : a walking trip : HIKE 5 : the succession of sounds made by the beating of feet on a road 6 : a ship that does not follow a regular course but takes cargo to any port — **trampy** \'tram-pē\ *adj*

tram·ple \'tram-pəl\ *vb* **tram·pled; tram·pling** 1 : to tread heavily so as to bruise, crush, or injure 2 : to inflict injury or destruction 3 : to press down or crush by or as if by treading — **trample** *n* — **tram·pler** *n*

tram·po·line \ₔtram-pə-'lēn, 'tram-pə-ₔlēn\ *n* [It *trampolino* springboard] : a resilient sheet or web (as of nylon) supported by springs in a metal frame and used as a springboard in tumbling — **tram·po·lin·ist** \-'lē-nist, -ₔlē-\ *n*

trampoline

trance \'trans\ *n* [ME, fr. AF *transe,* death, coma, rapture, fr. *transir* to depart, die, fr. L *transire* to cross, pass by, fr. *trans-* across + *ire* to go] 1 : STUPOR, DAZE 2 : a sleeplike state of altered consciousness (as of deep hypnosis) **3** : a state of very deep absorption — **trance·like** \-ˌlīk\ adj

tran·quil \ˈtraŋ-kwəl, ˈtran-\ adj : free from agitation or disturbance : QUIET ◆ **Synonyms** SERENE, PLACID, PEACEFUL — **tran·quil·li·ty** or **tran·quil·i·ty** \tran-ˈkwi-lə-tē, traŋ-\ n — **tran·quil·ly** adv

tran·quil·ize also **tran·quil·lize** \ˈtraŋ-kwə-ˌlīz, ˈtran-\ vb **-ized** also **-lized; -iz·ing** also **-liz·ing** : to make or become tranquil; esp : to relieve of mental tension and anxiety by means of drugs

tran·quil·iz·er also **tran·quil·liz·er** \-ˌlī-zər\ n : a drug used to relieve mental disturbance (as tension and anxiety)

trans abbr **1** transaction **2** transitive **3** translated; translation; translator **4** transmission **5** transportation **6** transverse

trans·act \tran-ˈzakt, -ˈsakt\ vb : CARRY OUT, PERFORM; also : CONDUCT

trans·ac·tion \-ˈzak-shən, -ˈsak-\ n **1** : something transacted; esp : a business deal **2** : an act or process of transacting **3** pl : the records of the proceedings of a society or organization — **trans·ac·tion·al** \-shnəl, -shə-nᵊl\ adj

trans·at·lan·tic \ˌtrans-ət-ˈlan-tik, ˌtranz-\ adj : crossing or extending across or situated beyond the Atlantic Ocean ⟨a ~ flight⟩

trans·ax·le \trans-ˈak-səl\ n : a unit combining the transmission and differential gear of a front-wheel-drive automobile

trans·ceiv·er \tran-ˈsē-vər\ n : a radio transmitter-receiver that uses many of the same components for both transmission and reception

tran·scend \tran-ˈsend\ vb **1** : to rise above the limits of **2** : SURPASS ◆ **Synonyms** EXCEED, OUTDO, OUTSHINE, OUTSTRIP

tran·scen·dent \-ˈsen-dənt\ adj **1** : exceeding usual limits : SURPASSING **2** : transcending material existence ◆ **Synonyms** SUPERLATIVE, SUPREME, PEERLESS, INCOMPARABLE

tran·scen·den·tal \ˌtran-ˌsen-ˈden-tᵊl, -sən-\ adj **1** : TRANSCENDENT 2 **2** : of, relating to, or characteristic of transcendentalism; also : ABSTRUSE

tran·scen·den·tal·ism \-tə-ˌli-zəm\ n : a philosophy holding that ultimate reality is unknowable or asserting the primacy of the spiritual over the material and empirical — **tran·scen·den·tal·ist** \-tə-list\ adj or n

trans·con·ti·nen·tal \ˌtrans-ˌkän-tə-ˈnent-ᵊl\ adj : extending or going across a continent ⟨a ~ railroad⟩

tran·scribe \trans-ˈkrīb\ vb **tran·scribed; tran·scrib·ing** **1** : to write a copy of **2** : to make a copy of (dictated or recorded matter) in longhand or on a typewriter **3** : to represent (speech sounds) by means of phonetic symbols; also : to make a musical transcription of

tran·script \ˈtran-ˌskript\ n **1** : a written, printed, or typed copy **2** : an official copy esp. of a student's educational record

tran·scrip·tion \tran-ˈskrip-shən\ n **1** : an act or process of transcribing **2** : COPY, TRANSCRIPT **3** : an arrangement of a musical composition for some instrument or voice other than the original **4** : the process of constructing a messenger RNA molecule using a DNA molecule as a template

tran·scrip·tion·ist \-shə-nist\ n : one that transcribes; esp : a typist who transcribes medical reports

trans·der·mal \trans-ˈdər-məl, ˈtranz-\ adj : relating to, being, or supplying a medication in a form for absorption through the skin ⟨~ nicotine patch⟩

trans·duc·er \trans-ˈdü-sər, tranz-, -ˈdyü-\ n : a device that is actuated by power from one system and supplies power usu. in another form to a second system

tran·sept \ˈtran-ˌsept\ n : the part of a cruciform church that crosses at right angles to the greatest length; also : either of the projecting ends

trans fat \ˈtran(t)s-, ˈtranz-\ n : a fat containing unsaturated fatty acids (**trans-fatty acids**) that have been linked to an increase in blood cholesterol

¹trans·fer \trans-ˈfər, ˈtrans-ˌfər\ vb **trans·ferred; trans·fer·ring** **1** : to pass or cause to pass from one person, place, or situation to another : MOVE, TRANSMIT **2** : to make over the possession of : CONVEY **3** : to print or copy from one surface to another by contact **4** : to change from one vehicle or transportation line to another — **trans·fer·able** \trans-ˈfər-ə-bəl\ adj — **trans·fer·al** \- əl\ n

²trans·fer \ˈtrans-ˌfər\ n **1** : conveyance of right, title, or interest in property from one person to another **2** : an act or process of transferring **3** : one that transfers or is transferred **4** : a ticket entitling a passenger to continue a trip on another route

trans·fer·ence \trans-ˈfər-əns\ n : an act, process, or instance of transferring

trans·fig·ure \trans-ˈfi-gyər\ vb **-ured; -ur·ing** **1** : to change the form or appearance of **2** : EXALT, GLORIFY — **trans·fig·u·ra·tion** \ˌtrans-ˌfi-gyə-ˈrā-shən, -gə-\ n

trans·fix \trans-ˈfiks\ vb **1** : to pierce through with or as if with a pointed weapon **2** : to hold motionless by or as if by piercing ⟨stood ~ed by her gaze⟩

trans·form \trans-ˈförm\ vb : to change in structure, appearance, or character ◆ **Synonyms** TRANSMUTE, TRANSFIGURE, TRANSMOGRIFY — **trans·for·ma·tion** \ˌtrans-fər-ˈmā-shən\ n — **trans·for·ma·tive** \trans-ˈför-mə-tiv\ adj

trans·form·er \trans-ˈför-mər\ n : one that transforms; esp : a device for converting variations of current in one circuit into variations of voltage and current in another circuit

trans·fuse \trans-ˈfyüz\ vb **trans·fused; trans·fus·ing** **1** : to cause to pass from one to another **2** : to diffuse into or through **3** : to transfer (as blood) into a vein or an artery of a person or animal — **trans·fu·sion** \-ˈfyü-zhən\ n

trans·gen·der \tranz-ˈjen-dər\ adj : having physical or behavioral characteristics transcending traditional gender boundaries

trans·gen·ic \tran(t)s-ˈje-nik\ adj : being or used to produce an organism or cell with genes introduced from another species of organism ⟨~ crops⟩

trans·gress \trans-ˈgres, tranz-\ vb [ME, fr. MF transgresser, fr. L transgressus, pp. of transgredi to step beyond or across, fr. trans- across + gradi to step] **1** : to go beyond the limits set by ⟨~ the divine law⟩ **2** : to go beyond : EXCEED **3** : SIN — **trans·gres·sion** \-ˈgre-shən\ n — **trans·gres·sor** \-ˈgre-sər\ n

¹tran·sient \ˈtran-shənt; -sē-ənt, -shē-, -zē-\ adj **1** : not lasting long : SHORT-LIVED ⟨~ optimism⟩ **2** : passing through a place with only a brief stay ⟨~visitors⟩ ◆ **Synonyms** TRANSITORY, PASSING, MOMENTARY, FLEETING — **tran·sient·ly** adv

²transient n : one that is transient; esp : a transient guest

tran·sis·tor \tran-ˈzis-tər, -ˈsis-\ n [transfer + resistor; fr. its transferring an electrical signal across a resistor] **1** : a small electronic semiconductor device used in electronic equipment **2** : a radio having transistors

tran·sis·tor·ized \-tə-ˌrīzd\ adj : having or using transistors

tran·sit \ˈtran-sət, -zət\ n **1** : a passing through, across, or over : PASSAGE **2** : conveyance of persons or things from one place to another **3** : usu. local transportation esp. of people by public conveyance **4** : a surveyor's instrument for measuring angles

tran·si·tion \tran-ˈsi-shən, -ˈzi-\ n : passage from one state, place, stage, or subject to another : CHANGE — **tran·si·tion·al** \-ˈsi-shə-nəl, ˈzi-\ adj

tran·si·tive \ˈtran-sə-tiv, -zə-\ adj **1** : having or containing an object required to complete the meaning **2** : TRANSITIONAL — **tran·si·tive·ly** adv — **tran·si·tive·ness** n — **tran·si·tiv·i·ty** \ˌtran-sə-ˈti-və-tē, -zə-\ n

tran·si·to·ry \ˈtran-sə-ˌtȯr-ē, -zə-\ adj : of brief duration : SHORT-LIVED, TEMPORARY ◆ **Synonyms** TRANSIENT, PASSING, MOMENTARY, FLEETING

transl abbr translated; translation

trans·late \trans-ˈlāt, tranz-\ vb **trans·lat·ed; trans·lat·ing** **1** : to change from one place, state, or form to another **2** : to convey to heaven without death **3** : to turn into one's own or another language — **trans·lat·able** adj — **trans·la·tor** \-ˈlā-tər\ n

trans·la·tion \tran(t)s-ˈlā-shən, tranz-\ n **1** : an act, process, or instance of translating **2** : the process of forming a protein molecule from information in messenger RNA — **trans·la·tion·al** \-shnəl, -shə-nᵊl\ adj

trans·lit·er·ate \trans-ˈli-tə-ˌrāt, tranz-\ vb **-at·ed; -at·ing** : to represent or spell in the characters of another alphabet — **trans·lit·er·a·tion** \ˌtrans-ˌli-tə-ˈrā-shən, ˌtranz-\ n

trans·lu·cent \trans-ˈlü-sᵊnt, tranz-\ adj : not transparent but clear enough to allow light to pass through — **trans·lu·cence** \-sᵊns\ n — **trans·lu·cen·cy** \-sᵊn-sē\ n — **trans·lu·cent·ly** adv

trans·mi·grate \-'mī-ˌgrāt\ *vb* : to pass at death from one body or being to another — **trans·mi·gra·tion** \ˌtrans-mī-'grā-shən, ˌtranz-\ *n* — **trans·mi·gra·to·ry** \trans-'mī-grə-ˌtȯr-ē\ *adj*

trans·mis·sion \-'mi-shən\ *n* 1 : an act or process of transmitting 2 : the passage of radio waves between transmitting stations and receiving stations 3 : the gears by which power is transmitted from the engine of an automobile to the axle that propels the vehicle 4 : something transmitted

trans·mit \-'mit\ *vb* **trans·mit·ted; trans·mit·ting** 1 : to transfer from one person or place to another : FORWARD 2 : to pass on by or as if by inheritance 3 : to cause or allow to spread abroad or to another ⟨∼ a disease⟩ 4 : to cause (as light, electricity, or force) to pass through space or a medium 5 : to send out (radio or television signals) ✦ *Synonyms* CONVEY, COMMUNICATE, IMPART — **trans·mis·si·ble** \-'mi-sə-bəl\ *adj* — **trans·mit·ta·ble** \-'mi-tə-bəl\ *adj* — **trans·mit·tal** \-'mit-ᵊl\ *n*

trans·mit·ter \-'mi-tər\ *n* : one that transmits; *esp* : an apparatus for transmitting telegraph, radio, or television signals

trans·mog·ri·fy \trans-'mä-grə-ˌfī, tranz-\ *vb* **-fied; -fy·ing** : to change or alter often with grotesque or humorous effect — **trans·mog·ri·fi·ca·tion** \-ˌmä-grə-fə-'kā-shən\ *n*

trans·mute \-'myüt\ *vb* **trans·muted; trans·mut·ing** : to change or alter in form, appearance, or nature ✦ *Synonyms* TRANSFORM, CONVERT, TRANSFIGURE, METAMORPHOSE — **trans·mu·ta·tion** \ˌtrans-myü-'tā-shən, ˌtranz-\ *n*

trans·na·tion·al \-'na-shə-nəl\ *adj* : extending beyond national boundaries

trans·oce·an·ic \ˌtrans-ˌō-shē-'a-nik, ˌtranz-\ *adj* 1 : lying or dwelling beyond the ocean 2 : crossing or extending across the ocean

tran·som \'tran-səm\ *n* 1 : a piece (as a crossbar in the frame of a window or door) that lies crosswise in a structure 2 : a window above an opening (as a door) built on and often hinged to a horizontal crossbar

tran·son·ic *also* **trans–son·ic** \tran-'sä-nik\ *adj* : being or relating to speeds near that of sound in air or about 741 miles (1185 kilometers) per hour

trans·pa·cif·ic \ˌtrans-pə-'si-fik\ *adj* : crossing, extending across, or situated beyond the Pacific Ocean

trans·par·ent \trans-'per-ənt\ *adj* 1 : clear enough to be seen through 2 : SHEER, DIAPHANOUS ⟨a ∼ fabric⟩ 3 : readily understood : CLEAR; *also* : easily detected ⟨a ∼ lie⟩ ✦ *Synonyms* LUCID, TRANSLUCENT, LUCENT — **trans·par·en·cy** \-ən-sē\ *n* — **trans·par·ent·ly** *adv*

tran·spire \trans-'pī(-ə)r\ *vb* **trans·pired; trans·pir·ing** [MF *transpirer*, fr. ML *transpirare*, fr. *trans-* across + *spirare* to breathe] 1 : to pass or give off (as water vapor) through pores or a membrane 2 : to become known 3 : to take place : HAPPEN — **tran·spi·ra·tion** \ˌtrans-pə-'rā-shən\ *n*

¹**trans·plant** \trans-'plant\ *vb* 1 : to dig up and plant elsewhere 2 : to remove from one place and settle or introduce elsewhere : TRANSPORT 3 : to transfer (an organ or tissue) from one part or individual to another — **trans·plan·ta·tion** \ˌtrans-ˌplan-'tā-shən\ *n*

²**trans·plant** \'trans-ˌplant\ *n* 1 : a person or thing transplanted 2 : the act or process of transplanting

trans·po·lar \trans-'pō-lər\ *adj* : going or extending across either of the polar regions

transponder \tran-'spän-dər\ *n* [*trans*mitter + re*sponder*] : a radio or radar set that upon receiving a certain signal emits a radio signal and that is used to locate and identify objects and in satellites to relay communications signals

¹**trans·port** \trans-'pȯrt\ *vb* 1 : to convey from one place to another : CARRY 2 : to carry away by strong emotion : ENRAPTURE 3 : to send to a penal colony overseas ✦ *Synonyms* BEAR, FERRY — **trans·por·ta·tion** \ˌtrans-pər-'tā-shən\ *n* — **trans·port·er** *n*

²**trans·port** \'trans-ˌpȯrt\ *n* 1 : an act of transporting 2 : strong or intensely pleasurable emotion ⟨∼s of joy⟩ 3 : a ship used in transporting troops or supplies; *also* : a vehicle (as a truck or plane) used to transport persons or goods

trans·pose \trans-'pōz\ *vb* **trans·posed; trans·pos·ing** 1 : to change the position or sequence of ⟨∼ the letters

in a word⟩ 2 : to write or perform (a musical composition) in a different key — **trans·po·si·tion** \ˌtrans-pə-'zi-shən\ *n*

trans·sex·u·al \(ˌ)trans-'sek-shə-wəl\ *n* : a person who psychologically identifies with the opposite sex and may seek to live as a member of this sex esp. by undergoing surgery to modify the external sex organs

trans·ship \tran-'ship, trans-\ *vb* : to transfer for further transportation from one ship or conveyance to another — **trans·ship·ment** *n*

tran·sub·stan·ti·a·tion \ˌtran-səb-ˌstan-chē-'ā-shən\ *n* : the change in the eucharistic elements from the substance of bread and wine to the substance of the body of Christ with only the appearances of bread and wine remaining

trans·verse \trans-'vərs, tranz-\ *adj* : lying across : set crosswise — **transverse** \'trans-ˌvərs, 'tranz-\ *n* — **trans·verse·ly** *adv*

trans·ves·tite \trans-'ves-ˌtīt, tranz-\ *n* : a person and esp. a male who adopts the dress and often the behavior of the opposite sex — **transvestite** *adj* — **trans·ves·tism** \-ˌti-zəm\ *n*

¹**trap** \'trap\ *n* 1 : a device for catching animals 2 : something by which one is caught unawares; *also* : a situation from which escape is difficult or impossible 3 : a machine for throwing clay pigeons into the air; *also* : SAND TRAP 4 : a light one-horse carriage on springs 5 : a device to allow some one thing to pass through while keeping other things out ⟨a ∼ in a drainpipe⟩ 6 *pl* : a group of percussion instruments (as in a dance orchestra)

²**trap** *vb* **trapped; trap·ping** 1 : to catch in or as if in a trap; *also* : CONFINE 2 : to provide or set (a place) with traps 3 : to set traps for animals esp. as a business ✦ *Synonyms* SNARE, ENTRAP, ENSNARE, BAG, LURE, DECOY — **trap·per** *n*

trap·door \'trap-'dȯr\ *n* : a lifting or sliding door covering an opening in a floor or roof

tra·peze \tra-'pēz\ *n* : a gymnastic apparatus consisting of a horizontal bar suspended by two parallel ropes

trap·e·zoid \'tra-pə-ˌzȯid\ *n* [NL *trapezoïdes*, fr. Gk *trapezoeidēs* trapezoidal, fr. *trapeza* table, fr. *trapeza* + *peza* foot] : a 4-sided polygon with exactly two sides parallel — **trap·e·zoi·dal** \ˌtra-pə-'zȯid-ᵊl\ *adj*

trap·pings \'tra-piŋz\ *n pl* 1 : CAPARISON 1 2 : outward decoration or dress; *also* : outward sign ⟨∼ of success⟩

traps \'traps\ *n pl* : personal belongings : LUGGAGE

trap·shoot·ing \'trap-ˌshü-tiŋ\ *n* : shooting at clay pigeons sprung from a trap into the air away from the shooter

¹**trash** \'trash\ *n* 1 : something of little worth : RUBBISH 2 : empty or disparaging talk 3 : a worthless person; *also* : such persons as a group : RIFFRAFF — **trashy** *adj*

²**trash** *vb* 1 : to dispose of : DISCARD ⟨∼ed the plans⟩ 2 : VANDALIZE, DESTROY 3 : ATTACK 4 : SPOIL, RUIN 5 : to criticize or disparage harshly

trau·ma \'traů-mə, 'trȯ-\ *n, pl* **traumas** *also* **trau·ma·ta** \-mə-tə\ [Gk, wound] : a bodily or mental injury usu. caused by an external agent; *also* : a cause of trauma — **trau·mat·ic** \trə-'ma-tik, trȯ-, traů-\ *adj*

trau·ma·tize \-ˌtīz\ *vb* **-tized; -tiz·ing** : to inflict trauma upon

¹**tra·vail** \trə-'vāl, 'tra-ˌvāl\ *n* 1 : painful work or exertion : TOIL 2 : AGONY, TORMENT 3 : CHILDBIRTH, LABOR

²**travail** *vb* : to labor hard : TOIL

¹**trav·el** \'tra-vəl\ *vb* **-eled** *or* **-elled; -el·ing** *or* **-el·ling** [ME *travailen* to torment, labor, journey, fr. AF *travailler* strive, fr. VL *trepaliare* to torture, fr. LL *trepalium* instrument of torture] 1 : to go on or as if on a trip or tour : JOURNEY 2 : to move as if by traveling ⟨news ∼s fast⟩ 3 : ASSOCIATE 4 : to go from place to place as a sales representative 5 : to move from point to point ⟨light waves ∼ very fast⟩ 6 : to journey over or through ⟨∼ing the highways⟩ 7 : to take excessive steps while holding a basketball — **trav·el·er** *or* **trav·el·ler** *n*

²**travel** *n* 1 : the act of traveling : PASSAGE 2 : JOURNEY, TRIP — often used in pl. 3 : the number traveling : TRAFFIC 4 : the motion of a piece of machinery and esp. when to and fro

traveler's check *n* : a check paid for in advance that is signed when bought and signed again when cashed

traveling bag *n* : SUITCASE

trav·el·ogue *or* **trav·el·og** \'tra-və-ˌlȯg, -ˌläg\ *n* : a usu. illustrated lecture on travel

¹**tra·verse** \'tra-vərs\ *n* : something that crosses or lies across

²**tra·verse** \trə-'vərs, tra-'vərs *or* 'tra-vərs\ *vb* **tra·versed; tra·vers·ing** **1** : to go or travel across or over **2** : to move or pass along or through **3** : to extend over **4** : SWIVEL

³**tra·verse** \'tra-vərs\ *adj* : TRANSVERSE

trav·er·tine \'tra-vər-ˌtēn, -tən\ *n* : a crystalline mineral formed by deposition from spring waters

¹**trav·es·ty** \'tra-və-stē\ *vb* **-tied; -ty·ing** : to make a travesty of

²**travesty** *n, pl* **-ties** [obs. E *travesty* disguised, parodied, fr. F *travesti*, pp. of *travestir* to disguise, fr. It *travestire*, fr. *tra-* across (fr. L *trans-*) + *vestire* to dress] : an imitation that makes crude fun of something; *also* : an inferior imitation

¹**trawl** \'trȯl\ *vb* : to fish or catch with a trawl — **trawl·er** *n*

²**trawl** *n* **1** : a large conical net dragged along the sea bottom in fishing **2** : a long heavy fishing line equipped with many hooks in series

tray \'trā\ *n* : an open receptacle with flat bottom and low rim for holding, carrying, or exhibiting articles

treach·er·ous \'tre-chə-rəs\ *adj* **1** : characterized by treachery **2** : UNTRUSTWORTHY, UNRELIABLE **3** : providing insecure footing or support ⟨a ∼ slope⟩ ♦ *Synonyms* TRAITOROUS, FAITHLESS, FALSE, DISLOYAL — **treach·er·ous·ly** *adv*

treach·ery \'tre-chə-rē\ *n, pl* **-er·ies** : violation of allegiance or trust

trea·cle \'trē-kəl\ *n* [ME *triacle* a medicinal compound, fr. AF, fr. L *theriaca*, fr. Gk *thēriakē* antidote against a poisonous bite, fr. *thērion* wild animal] *chiefly Brit* : MOLASSES — **trea·cly** \-k(ə-)lē\ *adj*

¹**tread** \'tred\ *vb* **trod** \'träd\; **trod·den** \'trä-dᵊn\ *or* **trod; tread·ing** **1** : to step or walk on or over **2** : to move on foot : WALK; *also* : DANCE **3** : to beat or press with the feet — **tread water** : to stay afloat and upright in water by sustaining a walking motion

²**tread** *n* **1** : a mark made by or as if by treading **2** : the manner or sound of stepping **3** : the part of a wheel that makes contact with a road **4** : the horizontal part of a step

trea·dle \'tre-dᵊl\ *n* : a lever device pressed by the foot to drive a machine — **treadle** *vb*

tread·mill \'tred-ˌmil\ *n* **1** : a mill worked by persons who tread on steps around the edge of a wheel or by animals that walk on an endless belt **2** : a device with an endless belt on which a person walks or runs in place **3** : a wearisome routine

treas *abbr* treasurer; treasury

trea·son \'trē-zᵊn\ *n* : the offense of attempting to overthrow the government of one's country or of assisting its enemies in war — **trea·son·able** \-zᵊn-ə-bəl\ *adj* — **trea·son·ous** \-ᵊn-əs\ *adj*

¹**trea·sure** \'tre-zhər, 'trā-\ *n* [ME *tresor*, fr. AF, fr. L *thesaurus*, fr. Gk *thēsauros*] **1** : wealth stored up or held in reserve **2** : something of great value

²**treasure** *vb* **trea·sured; trea·sur·ing** **1** : HOARD **2** : to keep as precious : CHERISH ♦ *Synonyms* PRIZE, VALUE, APPRECIATE, ESTEEM

trea·sur·er \'tre-zhə-rər, 'trā-\ *n* : an officer of a club, business, or government who has charge of money taken in and paid out

treasure trove \-ˌtrōv\ *n* **1** : treasure of unknown ownership found buried or hidden **2** : a valuable discovery

trea·sury \'tre-zhə-rē, 'trā-\ *n, pl* **-sur·ies** **1** : a place in which stores of wealth are kept **2** : the place where collected funds are stored and paid out **3** *cap* : a governmental department in charge of finances

¹**treat** \'trēt\ *vb* **1** : NEGOTIATE **2** : to deal with esp. in writing; *also* : HANDLE **3** : to pay for the food or entertainment of **4** : to behave or act toward ⟨∼ them well⟩ **5** : to regard in a specified manner ⟨∼ as inferiors⟩ **6** : to give medical or surgical care to **7** : to subject to some action ⟨∼ soil with lime⟩

²**treat** *n* **1** : an entertainment given free to those invited; *also* : food, drink, or entertainment provided at another's expense **2** : a source of joy or amusement

trea·tise \'trē-təs\ *n* : a systematic written exposition or argument

treat·ment \'trēt-mənt\ *n* : the act or manner or an instance of treating someone or something; *also* : a substance or method used in treating

trea·ty \'trē-tē\ *n, pl* **treaties** : an agreement made by negotiation or diplomacy esp. between two or more states or governments

¹**tre·ble** \'tre-bəl\ *n* **1** : the highest of the four voice parts in vocal music : SOPRANO **2** : a high-pitched or shrill voice or sound **3** : the upper half of the musical pitch range

²**treble** *adj* **1** : triple in number or amount **2** : relating to or having the range of a musical treble **3** : high-pitched : SHRILL — **tre·bly** *adv*

³**treble** *vb* **tre·bled; tre·bling** : to make or become three times the size, amount, or number

¹**tree** \'trē\ *n* **1** : a woody perennial plant usu. with a single main stem and a head of branches and leaves at the top **2** : a piece of wood adapted to a particular use ⟨a shoe ∼⟩ **3** : something resembling a tree ⟨a genealogical ∼⟩ — **tree·less** *adj*

²**tree** *vb* **treed; tree·ing** : to drive to or up a tree ⟨∼ a raccoon⟩

tree farm *n* : an area of forest land managed to ensure continuous commercial production

tree frog *n* : any of numerous usu. tree-dwelling amphibians with adhesive disks on the toes

tree line *n* : TIMBERLINE

tree of heaven *n* : a Chinese ailanthus widely grown as an ornamental tree

tree surgery *n* : operative treatment of diseased trees esp. for control of decay — **tree surgeon** *n*

tre·foil \'trē-ˌfȯi(-ə)l, 'tre-\ *n* **1** : an herb (as a clover) with leaves that have three leaflets **2** : a decorative design with three leaflike parts

¹**trek** \'trek\ *vb* **trekked; trek·king** **1** *chiefly southern Africa* : to travel or migrate by ox wagon **2** : to make one's way arduously

²**trek** *n* **1** *chiefly southern Africa* : a migration esp. of settlers by ox wagon **2** : a slow or difficult journey

¹**trel·lis** \'tre-ləs\ *n* [ME *trelis*, fr. AF *treleis*, fr. OF *treille* arbor, fr. L *trichila* summerhouse] : a frame of latticework used esp. to support climbing plants

²**trellis** *vb* : to provide with a trellis; *esp* : to train (as a vine) on a trellis

trem·a·tode \'tre-mə-ˌtōd\ *n* : any of a class of parasitic worms

¹**trem·ble** \'trem-bəl\ *vb* **trem·bled; trem·bling** **1** : to shake involuntarily (as with fear or cold) : SHIVER **2** : to move, sound, pass, or come to pass as if shaken or tremulous **3** : to be affected with fear or doubt

²**tremble** *n* : a spell of shaking or quivering

tre·men·dous \tri-'men-dəs\ *adj* **1** : causing dread, awe, or terror : TERRIFYING **2** : unusually large, powerful, great, or excellent ♦ *Synonyms* STUPENDOUS, MONUMENTAL, MONSTROUS — **tre·men·dous·ly** *adv*

trem·o·lo \'tre-mə-ˌlō\ *n, pl* **-los** [It] : a rapid fluttering of a tone or alternating tones

trem·or \'tre-mər\ *n* **1** : a trembling or shaking esp. from weakness, emotional stress, or disease **2** : a quivering motion of the earth (as during an earthquake)

trem·u·lous \'trem-yə-ləs\ *adj* **1** : marked by trembling or tremors : QUIVERING **2** : TIMOROUS, TIMID — **trem·u·lous·ly** *adv*

¹**trench** \'trench\ *n* [ME *trenche* track cut through a wood, fr. AF, act of cutting, fr. *trencher* to cut, prob. fr. VL **trinicare* to cut in three, fr. L *trini* three each] **1** : a long narrow cut in the ground : DITCH; *esp* : a ditch protected by banks of earth and used to shelter soldiers **2** *pl* : a place or situation likened to warfare conducted from trenches **3** : a long narrow steep-sided depression in the ocean floor

²**trench** *vb* **1** : to cut or dig trenches in **2** : to protect (troops) with trenches **3** : to come close : VERGE

tren·chant \'tren-chənt\ *adj* **1** : vigorously effective; *also* : CAUSTIC **2** : sharply perceptive : KEEN **3** : CLEAR-CUT, DISTINCT

tren·cher \'tren-chər\ *n* : a wooden platter for serving food

tren·cher·man \'tren-chər-mən\ *n* : a hearty eater

trench foot *n* : a painful foot disorder resembling frostbite and resulting from exposure to cold and wet

trench mouth *n* : a progressive painful bacterial infection of the mouth and adjacent parts marked by ulceration, bleeding gums, and foul breath

¹**trend** \'trend\ *vb* **1** : to have or take a general direction : TEND **2** : to show a tendency : INCLINE

²**trend** *n* **1** : a general direction taken (as by a stream or mountain range) **2** : a prevailing tendency : DRIFT **3** : a current style or preference : VOGUE

trendy \'tren-dē\ *adj* **trend·i·er; -est** : very fashionable; *also* : marked by superficial or faddish appeal or taste

trep·i·da·tion \ˌtre-pə-'dā-shən\ *n* : nervous agitation : APPREHENSION ✦ *Synonyms* HORROR, TERROR, PANIC, CONSTERNATION, DREAD, FRIGHT, DISMAY

¹**tres·pass** \'tres-pəs, -ˌpas\ *n* **1** : SIN, OFFENSE **2** : unlawful entry on someone else's land ✦ *Synonyms* TRANSGRESSION, VIOLATION, INFRACTION, INFRINGEMENT

²**trespass** *vb* **1** : to commit an offense : ERR, SIN **2** : INTRUDE, ENCROACH; *esp* : to enter unlawfully upon the land of another — **tres·pass·er** *n*

tress \'tres\ *n* : a long lock of hair — usu. used in pl.

tres·tle *also* **tres·sel** \'tre-səl\ *n* **1** : a supporting framework consisting usu. of a horizontal piece with spreading legs at each end **2** : a braced framework of timbers, piles, or steel for carrying a road or railroad over a depression

T. rex \'tē-'reks\ *n* : TYRANNOSAUR

trey \'trā\ *n, pl* **treys** : a card or the side of a die with three spots

tri·ad \'trī-ˌad, -əd\ *n* : a union or group of three usu. closely related persons or things

tri·age \trē-'äzh, 'trē-ˌäzh\ *n* [F, sorting] : the sorting of and allocation of treatment to patients and esp. battle or disaster victims according to a system of priorities designed to maximize the number of survivors

tri·al \'trī-əl\ *n* **1** : the action or process of trying or putting to the proof : TEST **2** : the hearing and judgment of a matter in issue before a competent tribunal **3** : a source of vexation or annoyance **4** : an experiment to test quality, value, or usefulness **5** : EFFORT, ATTEMPT ✦ *Synonyms* CROSS, ORDEAL, TRIBULATION, AFFLICTION — **trial** *adj*

tri·an·gle \'trī-ˌaŋ-gəl\ *n* **1** : a polygon that has three sides **2** : something shaped like a triangle — **tri·an·gu·lar** \trī-'aŋ-gyə-lər\ *adj* — **tri·an·gu·lar·ly** *adv*

triangle 1: three kinds

tri·an·gu·la·tion \(ˌ)trī-ˌaŋ-gyə-'lā-shən\ *n* : a method using trigonometry to find the location of a point using bearings from two fixed points a known distance apart — **tri·an·gu·late** \trī-'aŋ-gyə-ˌlāt\ *vb*

Tri·as·sic \trī-'a-sik\ *adj* : of, relating to, or being the earliest period of the Mesozoic era marked by the first appearance of the dinosaurs — **Triassic** *n*

tri·ath·lon \trī-'ath-lən, -ˌlän\ *n* : an athletic contest consisting of three phases (as swimming, bicycling, and running)

trib *abbr* tributary

tribe \'trīb\ *n* **1** : a social group comprising numerous families, clans, or generations **2** : a group of persons having a common character, occupation, or interest **3** : a group of related plants or animals ⟨the cat ∼⟩ — **trib·al** \'trī-bəl\ *adj*

tribes·man \'trībz-mən\ *n* : a member of a tribe

trib·u·la·tion \ˌtri-byə-'lā-shən\ *n* [ME *tribulacion*, fr. AF, fr. L *tribulatio*, fr. *tribulare* to press, oppress, fr. *tribulum* drag used in threshing] : distress or suffering resulting from oppression or persecution; *also* : a trying experience ✦ *Synonyms* TRIAL, AFFLICTION, CROSS, ORDEAL

tri·bu·nal \trī-'byün-ᵊl, tri-\ *n* **1** : the seat of a judge **2** : a court of justice **3** : something that decides or determines ⟨the ∼ of public opinion⟩

tri·bune \'tri-ˌbyün, tri-'byün\ *n* **1** : an official in ancient Rome with the function of protecting the interests of ple-

beian citizens from the patricians **2** : a defender of the people

¹**trib·u·tary** \'tri-byə-ˌter-ē\ *adj* **1** : paying tribute : SUBJECT **2** : flowing into a larger stream or a lake ✦ *Synonyms* SUBORDINATE, SECONDARY, DEPENDENT

²**tributary** *n, pl* **-tar·ies** **1** : a ruler or state that pays tribute **2** : a tributary stream

trib·ute \'tri-(ˌ)byüt, -byət\ *n* **1** : a payment by one ruler or nation to another as an act of submission or price of protection **2** : a usu. excessive tax, rental, or levy exacted by a sovereign or superior **3** : a gift or service showing respect, gratitude, or affection; *also* : PRAISE ✦ *Synonyms* EULOGY, CITATION, ENCOMIUM, PANEGYRIC

trice \'trīs\ *n* : INSTANT, MOMENT

tri·ceps \'trī-ˌseps\ *n, pl* **triceps** : a large muscle along the back of the upper arm that is attached at its upper end by three main parts and acts to extend the forearm at the elbow joint

tri·cer·a·tops \(ˌ)trī-'ser-ə-ˌtäps\ *n, pl* **-tops** *also* **-tops·es** [NL, fr. Gk *tri*- three + *kerat-, keras* horn + *ōps* face] : any of a genus of large plant-eating Cretaceous dinosaurs with three horns, a bony crest on the neck, and hoofed toes

tri·chi·na \tri-'kī-nə\ *n, pl* **-nae** \-(ˌ)nē\ *also* **-nas** : a small slender nematode worm that in the larval state is parasitic in the striated muscles of flesh-eating mammals (as humans)

trich·i·no·sis \ˌtri-kə-'nō-səs\ *n* : infestation with or disease caused by trichinae and marked esp. by muscular pain, fever, and swelling

¹**trick** \'trik\ *n* **1** : a crafty procedure meant to deceive **2** : a mischievous action : PRANK **3** : a childish action **4** : a deceptive or ingenious feat designed to puzzle or amuse **5** : PECULIARITY, MANNERISM **6** : a quick or artful way of getting a result : KNACK ⟨∼s of the trade⟩ **7** : the cards played in one round of a card game **8** : a tour of duty : SHIFT ✦ *Synonyms* RUSE, MANEUVER, ARTIFICE, WILE, FEINT

²**trick** *vb* **1** : to deceive by cunning or artifice : CHEAT **2** : to dress ornately

trick·ery \'tri-kə-rē\ *n* : deception by tricks and stratagems

trick·le \'tri-kəl\ *vb* **trick·led; trick·ling** **1** : to run or fall in drops **2** : to flow in a thin gentle stream — **trickle** *n*

trick·ster \'trik-stər\ *n* : one who tricks or cheats

tricky \'tri-kē\ *adj* **trick·i·er; -est** **1** : inclined to trickery **2** : requiring skill or caution ⟨a ∼ situation to handle⟩ **3** : UNRELIABLE ⟨a ∼ lock⟩

tri·col·or \'trī-ˌkə-lər\ *n* : a flag of three colors ⟨the French ∼⟩

tri·cy·cle \'trī-(ˌ)si-kəl\ *n* : a 3-wheeled vehicle usu. propelled by pedals

tri·dent \'trī-dᵊnt\ *n* [L *trident-, tridens*, fr. *tri*- three + *dent-, dens* tooth] : a 3-pronged spear

tried \'trīd\ *adj* **1** : found trustworthy through testing **2** : subjected to trials

tri·en·ni·al \trī-'e-nē-əl\ *adj* **1** : occurring or being done every three years **2** : lasting for three years — **triennial** *n*

¹**tri·fle** \'trī-fəl\ *n* **1** : something of little value or importance **2** : a dessert of cake soaked with liqueur and served with toppings (as fruit or cream)

²**trifle** *vb* **tri·fled; tri·fling** **1** : to talk in a jesting or mocking manner **2** : to treat someone or something as unimportant **3** : DALLY, FLIRT **4** : to handle idly : TOY — **tri·fler** *n*

tri·fling \'trī-fliŋ\ *adj* **1** : FRIVOLOUS **2** : TRIVIAL, INSIGNIFICANT ✦ *Synonyms* PETTY, PALTRY, MEASLY, INCONSEQUENTIAL

tri·fo·cals \trī-'fō-kəlz\ *n pl* : eyeglasses with lenses having one part for close focus, one for intermediate focus, and one for distant focus

tri·fo·li·ate \trī-'fō-lē-ət\ *adj* : having three leaves or leaflets

¹**trig** \'trig\ *adj* : stylishly trim : SMART

²**trig** *n* : TRIGONOMETRY

¹**trig·ger** \'tri-gər\ *n* [alter. of earlier *tricker*, fr. D *trekker*, fr. MD *trecker* one that pulls, fr. *trecken* to pull] : a movable lever that activates a device when it is squeezed; *esp* : the part of a firearm lock moved by the finger to fire a gun — **trigger** *adj* — **trig·gered** *adj*

²**trigger** *vb* **1** : to fire by pulling a trigger **2** : to initiate, actuate, or set off as if by a trigger ⟨remarks that ∼ed a fight⟩

tri·glyc·er·ide \trī-'gli-sə-ˌrīd\ *n* : any of a group of lipids that are formed from glycerol and fatty acids and are widespread in animal tissue

trig·o·nom·e·try \ˌtri-gə-'nä-mə-trē\ *n* : the branch of mathematics dealing with the properties of triangles and esp. with finding unknown angles or sides given the size or length of some angles or sides — **trig·o·no·met·ric** \-nə-'me-trik\ *also* **trig·o·no·met·ri·cal** \-tri-kəl\ *adj*

trike \'trīk\ *n* : TRICYCLE

¹trill \'tril\ *n* **1** : the alternation of two musical tones a scale degree apart **2** : WARBLE **3** : the rapid vibration of one speech organ against another (as of the tip of the tongue against the teeth)

²trill *vb* : to utter as or with a trill

tril·lion \'tril-yən\ *n* **1** : a thousand billions **2** *Brit* : a million billions — **trillion** *adj* — **tril·lionth** \-yənth\ *adj or n*

tril·li·um \'tri-lē-əm\ *n* : any of a genus of spring-blooming herbs that are related to the lilies and have an erect stem bearing a whorl of three leaves and a solitary flower

tril·o·gy \'tri-lə-jē\ *n, pl* **-gies** : a series of three dramas or literary or musical compositions that are closely related and develop one theme

¹trim \'trim\ *vb* **trimmed; trim·ming** [OE *trymian, trymman* to strengthen, arrange, fr. *trum* strong, firm] **1** : to put ornaments on : ADORN **2** : to defeat esp. resoundingly **3** : to make trim, neat, regular, or less bulky by or as if by cutting ⟨~ a beard⟩ ⟨~ a budget⟩ **4** : to cause (a boat) to assume a desired position in the water by arrangement of the load; *also* : to adjust (as a submarine or airplane) esp. for horizontal motion **5** : to adjust (a sail) to a desired position **6** : to change one's views for safety or expediency — **trim·ly** *adv* — **trim·mer** *n* — **trim·ness** *n*

²trim *adj* **trim·mer; trim·mest** : showing neatness, good order, or compactness ⟨a ~ figure⟩ ♦ *Synonyms* TIDY, TRIG, SMART, SPRUCE, SHIPSHAPE

³trim *n* **1** : good condition : FITNESS **2** : material used for ornament or trimming; *esp* : the woodwork in the finish of a house esp. around doors and windows **3** : the position of a ship or boat esp. with reference to the horizontal; *also* : the relation between the plane of a sail and the direction of a ship **4** : the position of an airplane at which it will continue in level flight with no adjustments to the controls **5** : something that is trimmed off

tri·ma·ran \'trī-mə-ˌran, ˌtrī-mə-'ran\ *n* : a sailboat with three hulls

tri·mes·ter \trī-'mes-tər, 'trī-ˌmes-tər\ *n* **1** : a period of three or about three months (as in pregnancy) **2** : one of three terms into which an academic year is sometimes divided

trim·e·ter \'tri-mə-tər\ *n* : a line of verse consisting of three metrical feet

trim·ming \'tri-miŋ\ *n* **1** : DEFEAT **2** : the action of one that trims **3** : something that trims, ornaments, or completes

tri·month·ly \trī-'mənth-lē\ *adj* : occurring every three months

trine \'trīn\ *adj* : THREEFOLD, TRIPLE

Trin·i·da·di·an \ˌtri-nə-'dā-dē-ən, -'da-\ *n* : a native or inhabitant of the island of Trinidad — **Trinidadian** *adj*

Trin·i·tar·i·an \ˌtri-nə-'ter-ē-ən\ *n* : a believer in the doctrine of the Trinity — **Trin·i·tar·i·an·ism** \-ē-ə-ˌni-zəm\ *n*

Trin·i·ty \'tri-nə-tē\ *n* **1** : the unity of Father, Son, and Holy Spirit as three persons in one Godhead **2** *not cap* : TRIAD

trin·ket \'triŋ-kət\ *n* **1** : a small ornament (as a jewel or ring) **2** : TRIFLE 1

trio \'trē-ō\ *n, pl* **tri·os** **1** : a musical composition for three voices or three instruments **2** : the performers of a trio **3** : a group or set of three

¹trip \'trip\ *vb* **tripped; trip·ping** **1** : to move with light quick steps **2** : to catch the foot against something so as to stumble or cause to stumble **3** : to make a mistake : SLIP; *also* : to detect in a misstep : EXPOSE **4** : to release (as a spring or switch) by moving a catch; *also* : ACTIVATE ⟨~ an alarm⟩ **5** : to get high on a usu. hallucinatory drug

²trip *n* **1** : JOURNEY, VOYAGE **2** : a quick light step **3** : a false step : STUMBLE; *also* : ERROR **4** : the action of tripping mechanically; *also* : a device for tripping **5** : an intense experience; *esp* : one triggered by a hallucinatory drug **6** : absorption in an attitude or state of mind ⟨an ego ~⟩

tri·par·tite \trī-'pär-ˌtīt\ *adj* **1** : divided into three parts **2** : having three corresponding parts or copies **3** : made between three parties ⟨a ~ treaty⟩

tripe \'trīp\ *n* **1** : stomach tissue esp. of a ruminant (as an ox) used as food **2** : something poor, worthless, or offensive : TRASH

¹tri·ple \'tri-pəl\ *vb* **tri·pled; tri·pling** **1** : to make or become three times as great or as many **2** : to hit a triple

²triple *n* **1** : a triple quantity **2** : a group of three **3** : a hit in baseball that lets the batter reach third base

³triple *adj* **1** : being three times as great or as many **2** : having three units or members **3** : repeated three times

triple bond *n* : a chemical bond in which three pairs of electrons are shared by two atoms in a molecule

triple point *n* : the condition of temperature and pressure under which the gaseous, liquid, and solid forms of a substance can exist in equilibrium

trip·let \'tri-plət\ *n* **1** : a unit of three lines of verse **2** : a group of three of a kind **3** : one of three offspring born at one birth

tri·plex \'tri-ˌpleks, 'trī-\ *adj* : THREEFOLD, TRIPLE

¹trip·li·cate \'tri-pli-kət\ *adj* : made in three identical copies

²trip·li·cate \-plə-ˌkāt\ *vb* **-cat·ed; -cat·ing** **1** : TRIPLE **2** : to provide three copies of ⟨~ a document⟩

³trip·li·cate \-pli-kət\ *n* : three copies all alike — used with *in* ⟨typed in ~⟩

tri·ply \'tri-plē, 'trī-pə-lē\ *adv* : in a triple degree, amount, or manner

tri·pod \'trī-ˌpäd\ *n* : something (as a caldron, stool, or camera stand) that rests on three legs — **tripod** *or* **tri·po·dal** \'trī-pəd-ᵊl, 'trī-ˌpäd-\ *adj*

trip·tych \'trip-tik\ *n* : a picture or carving in three panels side by side

tri·reme \'trī-ˌrēm\ *n* : an ancient galley having three banks of oars

tri·sect \'trī-ˌsekt, trī-'sekt\ *vb* : to divide into three usu. equal parts — **tri·sec·tion** \'trī-ˌsek-shən\ *n*

trite \'trīt\ *adj* **trit·er; trit·est** [L *tritus*, fr. pp. of *terere* to rub, wear away] : used so commonly that the novelty is worn off : STALE ♦ *Synonyms* HACKNEYED, STEREOTYPED, COMMONPLACE, CLICHÉD

tri·ti·um \'tri-tē-əm, 'tri-shē-\ *n* : a radioactive form of hydrogen with one proton and two neutrons in its nucleus and three times the mass of ordinary hydrogen

tri·ton \'trī-tᵊn\ *n* : any of various large marine gastropod mollusks with a heavy elongated conical shell; *also* : the shell of a triton

trit·u·rate \'tri-chə-ˌrāt\ *vb* **-rat·ed; -rat·ing** : to rub or grind to a fine powder

¹tri·umph \'trī-əmf\ *n* **1** : the joy or exultation of victory or success **2** : VICTORY, CONQUEST — **tri·um·phal** \trī-'əm-fəl\ *adj*

²triumph *vb* **1** : to obtain victory : PREVAIL **2** : to celebrate victory or success exultantly — **tri·um·phant** \trī-'əm-fənt\ *adj* — **tri·um·phant·ly** *adv*

tri·um·vir \trī-'əm-vər\ *n, pl* **-virs** *also* **-vi·ri** \-və-ˌrī\ : a member of a triumvirate

tri·um·vi·rate \-və-rət\ *n* : a ruling body of three persons

tri·une \'trī-ˌün, -ˌyün\ *adj* : being three in one ⟨the ~ God⟩

triv·et \'tri-vət\ *n* **1** : a 3-legged stand : TRIPOD **2** : a usu. metal stand with short feet for use under a hot dish

triv·ia \'tri-vē-ə\ *n sing or pl* : unimportant matters : obscure facts or details ⟨movie ~⟩

triv·i·al \'tri-vē-əl\ *adj* [L *trivialis* found everywhere, commonplace, fr. *trivium* crossroads, fr. *tri-* three + *via* way] : of little importance — **triv·i·al·i·ty** \ˌtri-vē-'a-lə-tē\ *n*

triv·i·um \'tri-vē-əm\ *n, pl* **triv·ia** \-vē-ə\ : the three liberal arts of grammar, rhetoric, and logic in a medieval university

tri·week·ly \trī-'wē-klē\ *adj* **1** : occurring or appearing three times a week **2** : occurring or appearing every three weeks — **triweekly** *adv*

tro·che \'trō-kē\ *n* : LOZENGE 2

tro·chee \'trō-(ˌ)kē\ *n* : a metrical foot of one accented syllable followed by one unaccented syllable — **tro·cha·ic** \trō-'kā-ik\ *adj*

trod *past and past part of* TREAD

trodden *past part of* TREAD

troi·ka \'tròi-kə\ *n* [Russ *troĭka*, fr. *troe* three] : a group of three; *esp* : an administrative or ruling body of three

¹troll \\'trōl\ *vb* **1** : to sing the parts of (a song) in succession **2** : to fish by trailing a lure or baited hook from a moving boat **3** : to sing or play jovially

²troll *n* : a lure used in trolling; *also* : the line with its lure

³troll *n* : a dwarf or giant in Scandinavian folklore inhabiting caves or hills

trol·ley *also* **trol·ly** \\'trä-lē\ *n, pl* **trolleys** *also* **trollies 1** : a device (as a grooved wheel on the end of a pole) to carry current from a wire to an electrically driven vehicle **2** : a streetcar powered electrically by overhead wires **3** : a wheeled carriage running on an overhead rail or track

trol·ley·bus \\'trä-lē-ˌbəs\ *n* : a bus powered electrically by overhead wires

trolley car *n* : TROLLEY 2

trol·lop \\'trä-ləp\ *n* : a disreputable woman; *esp* : one who engages in sex promiscuously

trom·bone \\'träm-ˌbōn, 'träm-ˌbōn\ *n* [It, fr. *tromba* trumpet] : a brass wind instrument that consists of a long metal tube with two turns and a flaring end and that usu. has a movable slide to vary the pitch — **trom·bon·ist** \-'bō-nist, -ˌbō-\ *n*

tromp \\'trämp, 'trömp\ *vb* **1** : TRAMP, MARCH **2** : to stamp with the foot **3** : to defeat decisively

trompe l'oeil \\(ˌ)trömp-'lə-ē, trönp-'lœi\ *n* [F *trompe-l'oeil*, lit., deceives the eye] : a style of painting in which objects are depicted with photographic detail

¹troop \\'trüp\ *n* **1** : a cavalry unit corresponding to an infantry company **2** *pl* : armed forces : SOLDIERS **3** : a collection of people, animals, or things **4** : a unit of Girl Scouts or Boy Scouts under an adult leader

²troop *vb* : to move or gather in crowds

troop·er \\'trü-pər\ *n* **1** : an enlisted cavalryman; *also* : a cavalry horse **2** : a mounted or a state police officer

troop·ship \\'trüp-ˌship\ *n* : a ship or aircraft for carrying troops

trope \\'trōp\ *n* : a word or expression used in a figurative sense

tro·phic \\'trō-fik\ *adj* : of or relating to nutrition

tro·phy \\'trō-fē\ *n, pl* **trophies** : something gained or given in conquest or victory esp. when preserved or mounted as a memorial

trop·ic \\'trä-pik\ *n* [ME *tropik*, fr. L *tropicus* of the solstice, fr. Gk *tropikos*, fr. *tropē* turn] **1** : either of the two parallels of latitude approximately 23½ degrees north (**Tropic of Can·cer**) or south (**Tropic of Cap·ri·corn**) of the equator where the sun is directly overhead when it reaches its most northerly or southerly point in the sky **2** *pl, often cap* : the region lying between the tropics — **trop·i·cal** \-pi-kəl\ *or* **tropic** *adj*

tro·pism \\'trō-ˌpi-zəm\ *n* : an automatic movement by an organism in response to a source of stimulation; *also* : a reflex reaction involving this

tro·po·sphere \\'trō-pə-ˌsfir, 'trä-\ *n* : the part of the atmosphere between the earth's surface and the stratosphere in which most weather changes occur — **tro·po·spher·ic** \ˌtrō-pə-'sfir-ik, ˌträ-, -'sfer-\ *adj*

¹trot \\'trät\ *n* **1** : a moderately fast gait of a 4-footed animal (as a horse) in which the legs move in diagonal pairs **2** : a human jogging gait between a walk and a run

²trot *vb* **trot·ted; trot·ting 1** : to ride, drive, or go at a trot **2** : to proceed briskly : HURRY — **trot·ter** *n*

troth \\'träth, 'trōth, 'trôth\ *n* **1** : pledged faithfulness **2** : one's pledged word; *also* : BETROTHAL

trou·ba·dour \\'trü-bə-ˌdôr\ *n* [F, fr. Old Occitan *trobador*, fr. *trobar* to compose] : any of a class of poet-musicians flourishing esp. in southern France and northern Italy during the 11th, 12th, and 13th centuries

¹trou·ble \\'trə-bəl\ *vb* **trou·bled; trou·bling 1** : to agitate mentally or spiritually : DISTURB, WORRY **2** : to produce physical disorder in : AFFLICT **3** : to put to inconvenience **4** : RUFFLE ⟨~ the waters⟩ **5** : to make an effort ✦ *Synonyms* DISTRESS, AIL, UPSET — **trou·ble·some** *adj* — **trou·ble·some·ly** *adv* — **trou·blous** \-bə-ləs\ *adj*

²trouble *n* **1** : the quality or state of being troubled esp. mentally **2** : an instance of distress or annoyance **3** : DISEASE, AILMENT ⟨heart ~⟩ **4** : EXERTION, PAINS ⟨took the ~ to phone⟩ **5** : a cause of disturbance or distress

trou·ble·mak·er \-ˌmā-kər\ *n* : a person who causes trouble

trou·ble·shoot·er \-ˌshü-tər\ *n* **1** : a worker employed to locate trouble and make repairs in equipment **2** : an expert in resolving disputes or problems — **trou·ble·shoot** *vb*

trough \\'trôf, 'trôth\ *n, pl* **troughs** \\'trôfs, 'trôvz; 'trôths, 'trôthz\ **1** : a long shallow open boxlike container esp. for water or feed for livestock **2** : a gutter along the eaves of a house **3** : a long channel or depression (as between waves or hills) **4** : an elongated area of low barometric pressure

trounce \\'traůns\ *vb* **trounced; trounc·ing 1** : to thrash or punish severely **2** : to defeat decisively

troupe \\'trüp\ *n* : COMPANY; *esp* : a group of performers on the stage — **troup·er** *n*

trou·sers \\'traů-zərz\ *n pl* [alter. of earlier *trouse*, fr. Sc Gael *triubhas*] : PANTS — **trouser** *adj*

trous·seau \\'trü-sō, trü-'sō\ *n, pl* **trous·seaux** \-sōz, -'sōz\ *or* **trous·seaus** [F] : the personal outfit of a bride

trout \\'traůt\ *n, pl* **trout** *also* **trouts** [ME, fr. OE *trūht*, fr. LL *tructa*, a fish with sharp teeth, fr. Gk *trōktēs*, lit., gnawer] : any of various mostly freshwater food and game fishes usu. smaller than the related salmons

trout

trow \\'trō\ *vb, archaic* : THINK, SUPPOSE

trow·el \\'traů-(-ə)l\ *n* **1** : a hand tool used for spreading, shaping, or smoothing loose or plastic material (as mortar or plaster) **2** : a scoop-shaped tool used in gardening — **trowel** *vb*

troy \\'trói\ *adj* : expressed in troy weight ⟨~ ounce⟩

troy weight *n* : a system of weights based on a pound of 12 ounces and an ounce of 480 grains (31 grams) — see WEIGHT table

tru·ant \\'trü-ənt\ *n* [ME, vagabond, idler, fr. AF, of Celt origin] : a student who stays out of school without permission — **tru·an·cy** \-ən-sē\ *n* — **truant** *adj*

truce \\'trüs\ *n* **1** : ARMISTICE **2** : a respite esp. from something unpleasant

¹truck \\'trək\ *vb* **1** : EXCHANGE, BARTER **2** : to have dealings : TRAFFIC

²truck *n* **1** : BARTER **2** : DEALINGS **3** : small goods or merchandise; *esp* : vegetables grown for market

³truck *n* **1** : a wheeled vehicle (as a strong heavy automobile) designed for carrying heavy articles or hauling a trailer **2** : a swiveling frame with springs and one or more pairs of wheels used to carry and guide one end of a locomotive or railroad car

⁴truck *vb* **1** : to transport on a truck **2** : to be employed in driving a truck — **truck·er** *n*

truck farm *n* : a farm growing vegetables for market — **truck farmer** *n*

truck·le \\'trə-kəl\ *vb* **truck·led; truck·ling** : to yield slavishly to the will of another : SUBMIT ✦ *Synonyms* FAWN, TOADY, CRINGE, COWER

truc·u·lent \\'trə-kyə-lənt\ *adj* **1** : feeling or showing ferocity : SAVAGE **2** : aggressively self-assertive : BELLIGERENT — **truc·u·lence** \-ləns\ *n* — **truc·u·len·cy** \-lən-sē\ *n* — **truc·u·lent·ly** *adv*

trudge \\'trəj\ *vb* **trudged; trudg·ing** : to walk or march steadily and usu. laboriously

¹true \\'trü\ *adj* **tru·er; tru·est 1** : STEADFAST, LOYAL **2** : agreeing with facts or reality ⟨a ~ description⟩ **3** : CONSISTENT ⟨~ to expectations⟩ **4** : properly so called ⟨~ love⟩ **5** : RIGHTFUL ⟨~ and lawful king⟩ **6** : conformable to a standard or pattern; *also* : placed or formed accurately ✦ *Synonyms* CONSTANT, STAUNCH, RESOLUTE, STEADFAST

²**true** *adv* **1** : TRUTHFULLY **2** : ACCURATELY ⟨the bullet flew straight and ∼⟩; *also* : without variation from type ⟨breed ∼⟩

³**true** *n* **1** : TRUTH, REALITY — usu. used with *the* **2** : the state of being accurate (as in alignment) ⟨out of ∼⟩

⁴**true** *vb* **trued; true·ing** *also* **tru·ing** : to bring or restore to a desired precision

true–blue *adj* : marked by unswerving loyalty

true bug *n* : BUG 2

true–heart·ed \'trü-'här-təd\ *adj* : FAITHFUL, LOYAL ⟨a ∼ soldier⟩

truf·fle \'trə-fəl, 'trü-\ *n* **1** : the dark or light edible spore-bearing organ of any of several European fungi that grow underground; *also* : one of these fungi **2** : a candy made of chocolate, butter, and sugar shaped into balls and coated with cocoa

tru·ism \'trü-ˌi-zəm\ *n* : an undoubted or self-evident truth ✦ *Synonyms* COMMONPLACE, PLATITUDE, CLICHÉ

tru·ly \'trü-lē\ *adv* **1** : in all sincerity **2** : in agreement with fact **3** : ACCURATELY **4** : in a proper or suitable manner

¹**trump** \'trəmp\ *n* : TRUMPET

²**trump** *n* : a card of a designated suit any of whose cards will win over a card that is not of this suit; *also* : the suit itself — often used in pl.

³**trump** *vb* : to take with a trump

trumped–up \'trəmpt-'əp\ *adj* : fraudulently concocted : SPURIOUS

trum·pery \'trəm-pə-rē\ *n* **1** : NONSENSE **2** : trivial articles : JUNK

¹**trum·pet** \'trəm-pət\ *n* **1** : a wind instrument consisting of a long curved metal tube flaring at one end and with a cup-shaped mouthpiece at the other **2** : something that resembles a trumpet or its tonal quality **3** : a funnel-shaped instrument for collecting, directing, or intensifying sound

²**trumpet** *vb* **1** : to blow a trumpet **2** : to proclaim on or as if on a trumpet ⟨∼ the news⟩ — **trum·pet·er** *n*

¹**trun·cate** \'trəŋ-ˌkāt, 'trən-\ *adj* : having the end square or blunt

²**truncate** *vb* **trun·cat·ed; trun·cat·ing** : to shorten by or as if by cutting : LOP — **trun·ca·tion** \ˌtrəŋ-'kā-shən\ *n*

trun·cheon \'trən-chən\ *n* : a police officer's billy club

trun·dle \'trən-dᵊl\ *vb* **trun·dled; trun·dling** : to roll along : WHEEL

trundle bed *n* : a low bed that can be stored under a higher bed

trunk \'trəŋk\ *n* **1** : the main stem of a tree **2** : the body of a person or animal apart from the head and limbs **3** : the main or central part of something **4** : a box or chest used to hold usu. clothes or personal effects (as of a traveler); *also* : the enclosed luggage space in the rear of an automobile **5** : the long muscular nose of an elephant **6** *pl* : men's shorts worn chiefly for sports ⟨swimming ∼s⟩ **7** : a usu. major channel or passage

trunk line *n* : a transportation system handling long-distance through traffic

¹**truss** \'trəs\ *vb* **1** : to secure tightly : BIND **2** : to arrange for cooking by binding close the wings or legs of (a fowl) **3** : to support, strengthen, or stiffen by or as if by a truss

²**truss** *n* **1** : a collection of structural parts (as beams) forming a rigid framework (as in bridge or building construction) **2** : a device worn to reduce a hernia by pressure

¹**trust** \'trəst\ *n* **1** : assured reliance on the character, strength, or truth of someone or something **2** : a basis of reliance, faith, or hope **3** : confident hope **4** : financial credit **5** : a property interest held by one person for the benefit of another **6** : a combination of firms formed by a legal agreement; *esp* : one that reduces competition **7** : something entrusted to one to be cared for in the interest of another **8** : CARE, CUSTODY ✦ *Synonyms* CONFIDENCE, DEPENDENCE, FAITH, RELIANCE

²**trust** *vb* **1** : to place confidence : DEPEND **2** : to be confident : HOPE **3** : ENTRUST **4** : to permit to stay or go or to do something without fear or misgiving **5** : to rely on or on the truth of : BELIEVE **6** : to extend credit to

trust·ee \ˌtrəs-'tē\ *n* **1** : a person to whom property is legally committed in trust **2** : a country charged with the supervision of a trust territory

trust·ee·ship \ˌtrəs-'tē-ˌship\ *n* **1** : the office or function of a trustee **2** : supervisory control by one or more nations over a trust territory

trust·ful \'trəst-fəl\ *adj* : full of trust : CONFIDING — **trust·ful·ly** *adv* — **trust·ful·ness** *n*

trust territory *n* : a non-self-governing territory placed under a supervisory authority by the Trusteeship Council of the United Nations

trust·wor·thy \-ˌwər-ˈthē\ *adj* : worthy of confidence : DEPENDABLE ✦ *Synonyms* TRUSTY, TRIED, RELIABLE — **trust·wor·thi·ness** *n*

¹**trusty** \'trəs-tē\ *adj* **trust·i·er; -est** : TRUSTWORTHY, DEPENDABLE ⟨a ∼ friend⟩

²**trusty** \'trəs-tē, ˌtrəs-'tē\ *n, pl* **trust·ies** : a trusted person; *esp* : a convict considered trustworthy and allowed special privileges

truth \'trüth\ *n, pl* **truths** \'trüthz, 'trüths\ **1** : TRUTHFULNESS, HONESTY **2** : the real state of things : FACT **3** : the body of real events or facts : ACTUALITY **4** : a true or accepted statement or proposition ⟨the ∼s of science⟩ **5** : agreement with fact or reality : CORRECTNESS ✦ *Synonyms* VERACITY, VERITY

truth·ful \'trüth-fəl\ *adj* : telling or disposed to tell the truth — **truth·ful·ly** *adv* — **truth·ful·ness** *n*

truth serum *n* : a drug held to induce a subject under questioning to talk freely

¹**try** \'trī\ *vb* **tried; try·ing** [ME *trien*, fr. AF *trier* to select, sort, examine, prob. fr. LL *tritare* to grind] **1** : to examine or investigate judicially **2** : to conduct the trial of **3** : to put to test or trial **4** : to subject to strain, affliction, or annoyance **5** : to extract or clarify (as lard) by melting **6** : to make an effort to do something : ATTEMPT, ENDEAVOR ✦ *Synonyms* ESSAY, ASSAY, STRIVE, STRUGGLE

²**try** *n, pl* **tries** : an experimental trial

try·ing *adj* : severely straining the powers of endurance

try on *vb* : to put on (a garment) to test the fit and looks

try out *vb* : to participate in competition esp. for a position on an athletic team or a part in a play — **try·out** \'trī-ˌaut\ *n*

tryp·to·phan \'trip-tə-ˌfan\ *n* : a crystalline essential amino acid that is widely distributed in proteins

tryst \'trist\ *n* **1** : an agreement (as between lovers) to meet **2** : an appointed meeting or meeting place — **tryst** *vb* — **tryst·er** *n*

tsar *var of* CZAR

tsarina *var of* CZARINA

tset·se fly \'tset-sē-, 'tset-, 'tet-, 'tēt-, 'set-, 'sēt-\ *n* : any of several sub-Saharan African dipteran flies including the vector of sleeping sickness

TSgt *abbr* technical sergeant

T–shirt \'tē-ˌshərt\ *n* : a collarless short-sleeved or sleeveless cotton undershirt; *also* : an outer shirt of similar design — **T–shirt·ed** \-ˌshər-təd\ *adj*

tsk *a click; often read as* 'tisk\ *interj* — used to express disapproval

tsp *abbr* teaspoon; teaspoonful

T square *n* : a ruler with a crosspiece at one end for making parallel lines

tsu·na·mi \su̇-'nä-mē, tsu̇-\ *n* [Jp] : a tidal wave caused esp. by an underwater earthquake or volcanic eruption

TT *abbr* Trust Territories

TTY *abbr* teletypewriter

Tu *abbr* Tuesday

tub \'təb\ *n* **1** : a wide low bucketlike vessel **2** : BATHTUB; *also* : the amount that a tub will hold

tu·ba \'tü-bə, 'tyü-\ *n* : a large low-pitched brass wind instrument

tub·al \'tü-bəl, 'tyü-\ *adj* : of, relating to, or involving a tube and esp. a fallopian tube ⟨∼ infection⟩

tube \'tüb, 'tyüb\ *n* **1** : any of various usu. cylindrical structures or devices; *esp* : one to convey fluids **2** : a slender hollow anatomical part (as a fallopian tube) functioning as a channel in a plant or animal body : DUCT **3** : a soft round container from which a paste is squeezed **4** : a tunnel for vehicular or rail travel **5** : INNER TUBE **6** : ELECTRON TUBE **7** : TELEVISION — **tubed** \'tübd, 'tyübd\ *adj* — **tube·less** *adj* — **tube·like** \'tüb-ˌlīk, 'tyüb-\ *adj*

tu·ber \'tü-bər, 'tyü-\ *n* : a short fleshy usu. underground stem (as of a potato plant) bearing minute scalelike leaves each with a bud at its base

tu·ber·cle \'tü-bər-kəl, 'tyü-\ *n* **1** : a small knobby prominence or outgrowth esp. on an animal or plant **2** : a small abnormal lump in an organ or on the skin; *esp* : one caused by tuberculosis

tubercle bacillus *n* : a bacterium that is the cause of tuberculosis

tu·ber·cu·lar \tů-'bər-kyə-lər, tyů-\ *adj* **1** : TUBERCULOUS **2** : of, resembling, or being a tubercle

tu·ber·cu·lin \tů-'bər-kyə-lən, tyů-\ *n* : a sterile liquid extracted from the tubercle bacillus and used in the diagnosis of tuberculosis esp. in children and cattle

tu·ber·cu·lo·sis \tů-,bər-kyə-'lō-səs, tyů-\ *n, pl* **-lo·ses** \-,sēz\ : a communicable bacterial disease that affects esp. the lungs and is typically marked by fever, cough, difficulty in breathing, and formation of tubercles — **tu·ber·cu·lous** \-'bər-kyə-ləs\ *adj*

tube·rose \'tüb-,rōz, 'tyüb-\ *n* : a bulbous herb related to the agaves and often grown for its spike of fragrant waxy= white flowers

tu·ber·ous \'tü-bə-rəs, 'tyü-\ *adj* : of, resembling, or being a tuber

tub·ing \'tü-biŋ, 'tyü-\ *n* **1** : material in the form of a tube; *also* : a length of tube **2** : a series or system of tubes

tu·bu·lar \'tü-byə-lər, 'tyü-\ *adj* : having the form of or consisting of a tube; *also* : made with tubes

tu·bule \'tü-byül, 'tyü-\ *n* : a small tube

¹**tuck** \'tək\ *vb* **1** : to pull up into a fold ⟨~ed up her skirt⟩ **2** : to make tucks in **3** : to put into a snug often concealing place ⟨~ a book under the arm⟩ **4** : to secure in place by pushing the edges under ⟨~ in a blanket⟩ **5** : to cover by tucking in bedclothes

²**tuck** *n* **1** : a fold stitched into cloth to shorten, decorate, or control fullness **2** : a cosmetic surgical operation for the removal of excess skin or fat ⟨a tummy ~⟩

tuck·er \'tə-kər\ *vb* **tuck·ered; tuck·er·ing** : EXHAUST, FATIGUE ⟨was ~ed out after a long day's work⟩

Tues *or* **Tue** *abbr* Tuesday

Tues·day \'tüz-dē, 'tyüz-, -dā\ *n* : the 3d day of the week

tu·fa \'tü-fə, 'tyü-\ *n* : a porous rock (as travertine) formed as a deposit from springs or streams

tuff \'təf\ *n* : a rock composed of volcanic detritus

¹**tuft** \'təft\ *n* **1** : a small cluster of long flexible outgrowths (as hairs); *also* : a bunch of soft fluffy threads cut off short and used as ornament **2** : CLUMP, CLUSTER — **tuft·ed** *adj*

²**tuft** *vb* **1** : to provide or adorn with a tuft **2** : to make (as a mattress) firm by stitching at intervals and sewing on tufts — **tuft·er** *n*

¹**tug** \'təg\ *vb* **tugged; tug·ging** **1** : to pull hard **2** : to struggle in opposition : CONTEND **3** : to move by pulling hard : HAUL **4** : to tow with a tugboat

²**tug** *n* **1** : a harness trace **2** : an act of tugging : PULL **3** : a straining effort **4** : a struggle between opposing people or forces **5** : TUGBOAT

tug·boat \-,bōt\ *n* : a strongly built boat used for towing or pushing

tug–of–war \,təg-əv-'wȯr\ *n, pl* **tugs–of–war** **1** : a struggle for supremacy **2** : an athletic contest in which two teams pull against each other at opposite ends of a rope

tu·grik *or* **tu·ghrik** \'tü-grik\ *n* — see MONEY table

tu·ition \tù-'i-shən, tyù-\ *n* : money paid for instruction ⟨college ~⟩

tu·la·re·mia \,tü-lə-'rē-mē-ə, ,tyü-\ *n* : an infectious bacterial disease esp. of wild rabbits, rodents, humans, and some domestic animals that in humans is marked by symptoms (as fever) similar to those of influenza

tu·lip \'tü-ləp, 'tyü-\ *n* [NL *tulipa,* fr. Turk *tülbent* turban] : any of a genus of Eurasian bulbous herbs related to the lilies and grown for their large showy erect cup-shaped flowers; *also* : a flower or bulb of a tulip

tulip tree *n* : a tall No. American timber tree that is related to the magnolias and has greenish tulip-shaped flowers and soft white wood

tulle \'tül\ *n* : a sheer often stiffened silk, rayon, or nylon net ⟨a veil of ~⟩

¹**tum·ble** \'təm-bəl\ *vb* **tum·bled; tum·bling** [ME, fr. *tumben* to dance, fr. OE *tumbian*] **1** : to fall or cause to fall suddenly and helplessly **2** : to fall into ruin **3** : to perform gymnastic feats of rolling and turning **4** : to roll over and over : TOSS **5** : to issue forth hurriedly and confusedly **6** : to come to understand **7** : to throw together in a confused mass

²**tumble** *n* **1** : a disorderly state **2** : an act or instance of tumbling

tum·ble·down \'təm-bəl-'daůn\ *adj* : DILAPIDATED, RAMSHACKLE

tum·bler \'təm-blər\ *n* **1** : one that tumbles; *esp* : ACROBAT **2** : a drinking glass without foot or stem **3** : a movable obstruction in a lock that must be adjusted to a particular position (as by a key) before the bolt can be thrown

tum·ble·weed \'təm-bəl-,wēd\ *n* : a plant that breaks away from its roots in autumn and is driven about by the wind

tum·brel *or* **tum·bril** \'təm-brəl\ *n* **1** : CART **2** : a vehicle carrying condemned persons (as during the French Revolution) to a place of execution

tu·mid \'tü-məd, 'tyü-\ *adj* **1** : SWOLLEN, DISTENDED **2** : BOMBASTIC, TURGID

tum·my \'tə-mē\ *n, pl* **tummies** : BELLY, ABDOMEN, STOMACH

tu·mor \'tü-mər, 'tyü-\ *n* : an abnormal and functionless new growth of tissue that arises from uncontrolled cellular proliferation — **tu·mor·ous** *adj*

tu·mour *chiefly Brit var of* TUMOR

tu·mult \'tü-,məlt, 'tyü-\ *n* **1** : UPROAR **2** : violent agitation of mind or feelings

tu·mul·tu·ous \tù-'məl-chə-wəs, tyù-, -chəs\ *adj* **1** : marked by tumult **2** : tending to incite a tumult **3** : marked by violent upheaval

tun \'tən\ *n* : a large cask

tu·na \'tü-nə, 'tyü-\ *n, pl* **tuna** *or* **tunas** : any of several mostly large marine fishes related to the mackerels and caught for food and sport; *also* : the flesh of a tuna

tun·able \'tü-nə-bəl, 'tyü-\ *adj* : capable of being tuned — **tun·abil·i·ty** \,tü-nə-'bi-lə-tē, ,tyü-\ *n*

tun·dra \'tən-drə\ *n* [Russ] : a treeless plain of arctic and subarctic regions

¹**tune** \'tün, 'tyün\ *n* **1** : a succession of pleasing musical tones : MELODY **2** : correct musical pitch **3** : harmonious relationship : AGREEMENT ⟨in ~ with the times⟩ **4** : general attitude ⟨changed his ~⟩ **5** : AMOUNT, EXTENT ⟨in debt to the ~ of millions⟩

²**tune** *vb* **tuned; tun·ing** **1** : to adjust in musical pitch **2** : to bring or come into harmony : ATTUNE **3** : to put in good working order **4** : to adjust a radio or television receiver so as to receive a broadcast **5** : to adjust the frequency of the output of (a device) to a chosen frequency — **tun·er** *n*

tune·ful \-fəl\ *adj* : MELODIOUS, MUSICAL ⟨a ~ ballad⟩ — **tune·ful·ly** *adv* — **tune·ful·ness** *n*

tune·less \-ləs\ *adj* **1** : UNMELODIOUS **2** : not producing music — **tune·less·ly** *adv*

tune–up \'tün-,əp, 'tyün-\ *n* : an adjustment to ensure efficient functioning ⟨an engine ~⟩

tung·sten \'təŋ-stən\ *n* [Sw, fr. *tung* heavy + *sten* stone] : a gray-white hard heavy ductile metallic chemical element used esp. in carbide materials, electrical components, and alloys

tu·nic \'tü-nik, 'tyü-\ *n* **1** : a usu. knee-length belted garment worn by ancient Greeks and Romans **2** : a hip= length or longer blouse or jacket

tuning fork *n* : a 2-pronged metal implement that gives a fixed tone when struck and is useful for tuning musical instruments

¹**tun·nel** \'tə-nᵊl\ *n* : an enclosed passage (as a tube or conduit); *esp* : one underground (as in a mine)

²**tunnel** *vb* **-neled** *or* **-nelled; -nel·ing** *or* **-nel·ling** : to make a tunnel through or under — **tun·nel·er** \'tən-lər, 'tə-nᵊl-ər\ *n*

tun·ny \'tə-nē\ *n, pl* **tunnies** *also* **tunny** : TUNA

tuque \'tük, 'tyük\ *n* [CanF] : a warm knitted cone-shaped cap

tur·ban \'tər-bən\ *n* **1** : a headdress worn esp. by Muslims and made of a cap around which is wound a long cloth **2** : a headdress resembling a turban; *esp* : a woman's close= fitting hat without a brim

tur·bid \'tər-bəd\ *adj* [L *turbidus* confused, turbid, fr. *turba* confusion, crowd] **1** : cloudy or discolored by suspended particles ⟨a ~ stream⟩ **2** : CONFUSED, MUDDLED — **tur·bid·i·ty** \,tər-'bi-də-tē\ *n*

tur·bine \'tər-bən, -,bīn\ *n* [F, fr. L *turbin-, turbo* top, whirlwind, whirl] : an engine whose central driveshaft is fitted with curved vanes spun by the pressure of water, steam, or gas

tur·bo·fan \'tər-bō-ˌfan\ *n* : a jet engine having a fan driven by a turbine for supplying air for combustion

tur·bo·jet \-ˌjet\ *n* : an airplane powered by a jet engine **(turbojet engine)** having a turbine-driven air compressor supplying compressed air to the combustion chamber

tur·bo·prop \-ˌpräp\ *n* : an airplane powered by a jet engine **(turboprop engine)** having a turbine-driven propeller

tur·bot \'tər-bət\ *n, pl* **turbot** *also* **turbots** : a European flatfish that is a popular food fish; *also* : any of several similar flatfishes

tur·bu·lence \'tər-byə-ləns\ *n* : the quality or state of being turbulent

tur·bu·lent \-lənt\ *adj* **1** : causing violence or disturbance **2** : marked by agitation or tumult : TEMPESTUOUS ⟨a ~ marriage⟩ — **tur·bu·lent·ly** *adv*

tu·reen \tə-'rēn, tyu̇-\ *n* [F *terrine*, fr. MF, fr. fem. of *terrin* of earth] : a deep bowl from which foods (as soup) are served at table

¹**turf** \'tərf\ *n, pl* **turfs** \'tərfs\ *also* **turves** \'tərvz\ **1** : the upper layer of soil bound by grass and roots into a close mat; *also* : a piece of this **2** : an artificial substitute for turf (as on a playing field) **3** : a piece of peat dried for fuel **4** : a track or course for horse racing; *also* : horse racing as a sport or business

²**turf** *vb* : to cover with turf

tur·gid \'tər-jəd\ *adj* **1** : being in a swollen state **2** : excessively embellished in style or language : BOMBASTIC — **tur·gid·i·ty** \ˌtər-'ji-də-tē\ *n*

tur·key \'tər-kē\ *n, pl* **turkeys** [*Turkey*, country in western Asia and southeastern Europe; fr. confusion with the guinea fowl, supposed to be imported from Turkish territory] : a large No. American bird related to the domestic chicken and widely raised for food

turkey buzzard *n* : TURKEY VULTURE

turkey vulture *n* : an American vulture with a red head and whitish bill

Turk·ish \'tər-kish\ *n* : the language of Turkey — **Turkish** *adj*

tur·mer·ic \'tər-mə-rik\ *n* : a spice or dyestuff obtained from the large aromatic deep-yellow rhizome of an Indian perennial herb related to the ginger; *also* : this herb

tur·moil \'tər-ˌmȯi(-ə)l\ *n* : an extremely confused or agitated condition

¹**turn** \'tərn\ *vb* **1** : to move or cause to move around an axis or center : ROTATE, REVOLVE ⟨~ a wheel⟩ **2** : to effect a desired end by turning something ⟨~ the oven on⟩ **3** : WRENCH ⟨~ an ankle⟩ **4** : to change or cause to change position by moving through an arc of a circle ⟨~ed her chair to the fire⟩ **5** : to cause to move around a center so as to show another side of ⟨~ a page⟩ **6** : to revolve mentally : PONDER **7** : to become dizzy : REEL **8** : to reverse the sides or surfaces of ⟨~ a pancake⟩ **9** : UPSET, DISORDER ⟨things were ~ed topsy-turvy⟩ **10** : to set in another esp. contrary direction **11** : to change one's course or direction **12** : to go around ⟨~ a corner⟩ **13** : BECOME ⟨my hair ~ed gray⟩ ⟨~ed twenty-one⟩ **14** : to direct toward or away from something; *also* : DEVOTE, APPLY **15** : to have recourse **16** : to become or make hostile **17** : to cause to become of a specified nature or appearance ⟨~s the leaves yellow⟩ **18** : to make or become spoiled : SOUR **19** : to pass from one state to another ⟨water ~s to ice⟩ **20** : CONVERT, TRANSFORM **21** : TRANSLATE, PARAPHRASE **22** : to give a rounded form to; *esp* : to shape by means of a lathe **23** : to gain by passing in trade ⟨~ a quick profit⟩ — **turn·able** \'tər-nə-bəl\ *adj* — **turn color 1** : BLUSH **2** : to become pale — **turn loose** : to set free

²**turn** *n* **1** : a turning about a center or axis : REVOLUTION, ROTATION **2** : the action or an act of giving or taking a different direction ⟨make a left ~⟩ **3** : a change of course or tendency ⟨a ~ for the better⟩ **4** : a place at which something turns : BEND, CURVE **5** : a short walk or trip round about ⟨take a ~ around the block⟩ **6** : an act affecting another ⟨did him a good ~⟩ **7** : a place, time, or opportunity accorded in a scheduled order ⟨waited his ~ in line⟩ **8** : a period of duty : SHIFT **9** : a short act esp. in a variety show **10** : a special purpose or requirement ⟨the job serves his ~⟩ **11** : a skillful fashioning ⟨neat ~ of phrase⟩ **12** : a single round (as of rope passed around an object) **13** : natural or special apti-

tude **14** : a usu. sudden and brief disorder of body or spirits; *esp* : a spell of nervous shock or faintness

turn·about \'tərn-ə-ˌbȧut\ *n* **1** : a reversal of direction, trend, or policy **2** : RETALIATION

turn·buck·le \'tərn-ˌbə-kəl\ *n* : a link with a screw thread at one or both ends for tightening a rod or stay

turnbuckles

turn·coat \-ˌkōt\ *n* : one who switches to an opposing side or party : TRAITOR

turn down *vb* : to decline to accept : REJECT — **turn·down** \'tərn-ˌdȧun\ *n*

turn·er \'tər-nər\ *n* **1** : one that turns or is used for turning **2** : one that forms articles with a lathe

turn·ery \'tər-nə-rē\ *n, pl* **-er·ies** : the work, products, or shop of a turner

turn in *vb* **1** : to deliver up **2** : to inform on **3** : to acquit oneself of ⟨*turn* in a good job⟩ **4** : to go to bed

turn·ing \'tər-niŋ\ *n* **1** : the act or course of one that turns **2** : a place of a change of direction

tur·nip \'tər-nəp\ *n* **1** : a garden herb related to the cabbage with a thick edible usu. white root **2** : RUTABAGA **3** : the root of a turnip

turn·key \'tərn-ˌkē\ *n, pl* **turnkeys** : one who has charge of a prison's keys

turn·off \'tərn-ˌȯf\ *n* : a place for turning off esp. from an expressway

turn off *vb* **1** : to deviate from a straight course or a main road **2** : to stop the functioning or flow of **3** : to cause to lose interest; *also* : to evoke a negative feeling in

turn on *vb* **1** : to cause to flow, function, or operate **2** : to get high or cause to get high as a result of using a drug (as marijuana) **3** : EXCITE, STIMULATE

turn·out \'tərn-ˌȧut\ *n* **1** : an act of turning out **2** : the number of people who participate or attend an event **3** : a widened place in a highway for vehicles to pass or park **4** : manner of dress **5** : net yield : OUTPUT

turn out *vb* **1** : EXPEL, EVICT **2** : PRODUCE **3** : to cause to stop functioning by turning a switch **4** : to come forth and assemble **5** : to get out of bed **6** : to prove to be in the end

¹**turn·over** \'tərn-ˌō-vər\ *n* **1** : UPSET **2** : SHIFT, REVERSAL **3** : a filled pastry made by turning half of the crust over the other half **4** : the volume of business done **5** : movement (as of goods or people) into, through, and out of a place **6** : the number of persons hired within a period to replace those leaving or dropped **7** : an instance of a team's losing possession of the ball esp. through error

²**turnover** *adj* : capable of being turned over

turn over *vb* : TRANSFER ⟨*turn* the job *over* to her⟩

turn·pike \'tərn-ˌpīk\ *n* [ME *turnepike* revolving frame bearing spikes and serving as a barrier, fr. *turnen* to turn + *pike*] **1** : TOLLGATE; *also* : an expressway on which tolls are charged **2** : a main road

turn·stile \-ˌstī(-ə)l\ *n* : a post with arms pivoted on the top set in a passageway so that persons can pass through only on foot one by one

turn·ta·ble \-ˌtā-bəl\ *n* : a circular platform that revolves (as for turning a locomotive or a phonograph record)

turn to *vb* : to apply oneself to work

turn up *vb* **1** : to come to light or bring to light : DISCOVER, APPEAR **2** : to raise or increase by or as if by turning a control **3** : to arrive at an appointed time or place **4** : to happen unexpectedly

tur·pen·tine \'tər-pən-ˌtīn\ *n* **1** : a mixture of oil and resin obtained from various cone-bearing trees (as pines) **2**

: an oil distilled from turpentine or pine wood and used as a solvent and paint thinner

tur·pi·tude \'tər-pə-ˌtüd, -ˌtyüd\ *n* : inherent baseness : DEPRAVITY

tur·quoise *also* **tur·quois** \'tər-ˌkȯiz, -ˌkwȯiz\ *n* [ME *turkeys*, fr. AF *turkeise*, fr. fem. of *turkeis* Turkish, fr. *Turc* Turk] 1 : a blue, bluish green, or greenish gray mineral that is valued as a gem 2 : a light greenish blue color

tur·ret \'tər-ət\ *n* 1 : a little ornamental tower often at a corner of a building 2 : a low usu. revolving structure (as on a tank or warship) in which one or more guns are mounted — **tur·ret·ed** \'tər-ə-təd\ *adj*

¹tur·tle \'tər-t³l\ *n, archaic* : TURTLEDOVE

²turtle *n, pl* **turtles** *also* **turtle** : any of an order of horny-beaked land, freshwater, or sea reptiles with the trunk enclosed in a bony shell

tur·tle·dove \'tər-t³l-ˌdəv\ *n* : any of several small pigeons noted for plaintive cooing

tur·tle·neck \-ˌnek\ *n* : a high close-fitting turnover collar (as on a sweater); *also* : a sweater or shirt with a turtleneck — **tur·tle·necked** \-ˌnekt\ *adj*

turves *pl of* TURF

Tus·ca·ro·ra \ˌtəs-kə-ˈrȯr-ə\ *n, pl* **Tuscarora** *or* **Tuscaroras** : a member of an American Indian people of No. Carolina and later of New York and Ontario

tusk \'təsk\ *n* : a long enlarged protruding tooth (as of an elephant, walrus, or boar) used esp. to dig up food or as a weapon — **tusked** \'təskt\ *adj*

tusk·er \'təs-kər\ *n* : an animal with tusks; *esp* : a male elephant with two normally developed tusks

¹tus·sle \'tə-səl\ *n* 1 : a physical struggle : SCUFFLE 2 : an intense argument, controversy, or struggle

²tussle *vb* **tus·sled; tus·sling** : to struggle roughly

tus·sock \'tə-sək\ *n* : a dense tuft esp. of grass or sedge; *also* : a hummock in a marsh or bog bound together by roots — **tus·socky** *adj*

tu·te·lage \'tü-t³l-ij, 'tyü-\ *n* 1 : an act of guarding or protecting 2 : the state of being under a guardian or tutor 3 : instruction esp. of an individual

tu·te·lary \'tü-tə-ˌler-ē, 'tyü-\ *adj* : acting as a guardian ⟨~ deity⟩

¹tu·tor \'tü-tər, 'tyü-\ *n* 1 : a person charged with the instruction and guidance of another 2 : a private teacher

²tutor *vb* 1 : to have the guardianship of 2 : to teach or guide individually : COACH ⟨~ed her in Latin⟩ 3 : to receive instruction esp. privately

tu·to·ri·al \tü-ˈtȯr-ē-əl, tyü-\ *n* : a class conducted by a tutor for one student or a small number of students

tut·ti \'tü-tē, 'tu̇-, -ˌtē\ *adj or adv* [It, pl. of *tutto* all] : with all voices and instruments playing together — used as a direction in music

tut·ti-frut·ti \ˌtü-ti-ˈfrü-tē, ˌtu̇-\ *n* [It, lit., all fruits] : a confection or ice cream containing chopped usu. candied fruits

tu·tu \'tü-(ˌ)tü\ *n* [F] : a short projecting skirt worn by a ballerina

tux·e·do \ˌtək-ˈsē-dō\ *n, pl* **-dos** *or* **-does** [*Tuxedo* Park, N.Y.] 1 : a usu. black or blackish blue jacket 2 : a semiformal evening suit for men

TV \'tē-ˈvē\ *n* : TELEVISION

TVA *abbr* Tennessee Valley Authority

TV dinner *n* : a frozen packaged dinner that needs only heating before serving

twad·dle \'twä-d³l\ *n* : silly idle talk : DRIVEL — **twaddle** *vb*

twain \'twān\ *n* 1 : TWO 2 : PAIR

¹twang \'twaŋ\ *n* 1 : a harsh quick ringing sound like that of a plucked bowstring 2 : nasal speech or resonance 3 : the characteristic speech of a region

²twang *vb* **twanged; twang·ing** 1 : to sound or cause to sound with a twang 2 : to speak with a nasal twang

tweak \'twēk\ *vb* 1 : to pinch and pull with a sudden jerk and twitch 2 : to make small adjustments to — **tweak** *n*

tweed \'twēd\ *n* 1 : a rough woolen fabric made usu. in twill weaves 2 *pl* : tweed clothing; *esp* : a tweed suit

tweedy \'twē-dē\ *adj* **tweed·i·er; -est** 1 : of or resembling tweed 2 : given to wearing tweeds 3 : suggestive of the outdoors in taste or habits

tween \'twēn\ *prep* : BETWEEN

tweet \'twēt\ *n* : a chirping note — **tweet** *vb*

tweet·er \'twē-tər\ *n* : a small loudspeaker that reproduces sounds of high pitch

twee·zers \'twē-zərz\ *n pl* [obs. E *tweeze* n., case for small implements, short for obs. E *etweese*, fr. pl. of obs. E *etwee*, fr. F *étui*] : a small pincerlike implement usu. held between the thumb and index finger and used for grasping something

twelve \'twelv\ *n* 1 : one more than 11 2 : the 12th in a set or series 3 : something having 12 units — **twelfth** \'twelfth\ *adj or n* — **twelve** *adj or pron*

twelve·month \-ˌmənth\ *n* : YEAR

12-step \'twelv-ˌstep\ *adj* : of, relating to, or being a program designed esp. to help someone overcome a problem (as an addiction) by following 12 tenets

twen·ty \'twen-tē\ *n, pl* **twenties** : two times 10 — **twen·ti·eth** \-tē-əth\ *adj or n* — **twenty** *adj or pron*

twenty-twenty *or* **20/20** \ˌtwen-tē-'twen-tē\ *adj* : characterized by a visual capacity for seeing detail that is normal for the human eye ⟨~ vision⟩

twice \'twīs\ *adv* 1 : on two occasions 2 : two times ⟨~ two is four⟩

¹twid·dle \'twi-d³l\ *vb* **twid·dled; twid·dling** 1 : to be busy with trifles; *also* : to play idly with something 2 : to rotate lightly or idly

²twiddle *n* : TURN, TWIST

twig \'twig\ *n* : a small branch — **twig·gy** *adj*

twi·light \'twī-ˌlīt\ *n* 1 : the light from the sky between full night and sunrise or between sunset and full night 2 : a state of imperfect clarity 3 : a period of decline

twilight zone *n* 1 : an area just beyond ordinary legal or ethical limits 2 : TWILIGHT 2 3 : a world of fantasy or unreality

twill \'twil\ *n* [ME *twyll*, fr. OE *twilic* having a double thread, part trans. of L *bilic-, bilix*, fr. *bi-* two + *licium* thread] 1 : a fabric with a twill weave 2 : a textile weave that gives an appearance of diagonal lines

twilled \'twild\ *adj* : made with a twill weave

twin \'twin\ *n* 1 : either of two offspring produced at a birth 2 : one of two persons or things closely related to or resembling each other

²twin *vb* **twinned; twin·ning** 1 : to be coupled with another 2 : to bring forth twins

³twin *adj* 1 : born with one other or as a pair at one birth ⟨~ brother⟩ ⟨~ girls⟩ 2 : made up of two similar or related members or parts ⟨~ city⟩

¹twine \'twīn\ *n* 1 : a strong thread of two or three strands twisted together 2 : an act of entwining or interlacing — **twiny** *adj*

²twine *vb* **twined; twin·ing** 1 : to twist together; *also* : to form by twisting 2 : INTERLACE, WEAVE 3 : to coil about a support 4 : to stretch or move in a sinuous manner — **twin·er** *n*

¹twinge \'twinj\ *vb* **twinged; twing·ing** *or* **twinge·ing** : to affect with or feel a sharp sudden pain

²twinge *n* : a sudden sharp stab (as of pain or distress)

¹twin·kle \'twiŋ-kəl\ *vb* **twin·kled; twin·kling** 1 : to shine or cause to shine with a flickering or sparkling light 2 : to appear bright with merriment 3 : to flutter or flit rapidly — **twin·kler** *n*

²twinkle *n* 1 : a wink of the eyelids; *also* : the duration of a wink 2 : an intermittent radiance 3 : a rapid flashing motion — **twin·kly** \'twiŋ-klē\ *adj*

twin·kling \'twiŋ-kliŋ\ *n* : the time required for a wink : INSTANT

¹twirl \'twərl\ *vb* : to turn or cause to turn rapidly ⟨~ a baton⟩ ◆ **Synonyms** REVOLVE, ROTATE, CIRCLE, SPIN, SWIRL, PIROUETTE — **twirl·er** *n*

²twirl *n* 1 : an act of twirling 2 : COIL, WHORL — **twirly** \'twər-lē\ *adj*

¹twist \'twist\ *vb* 1 : to unite by winding one thread or strand round another 2 : WREATHE, TWINE 3 : to turn so as to hurt : SPRAIN ⟨~ed my ankle⟩ 4 : to twirl into spiral shape 5 : to subject (as a shaft) to torsion 6 : to turn from the true form or meaning 7 : to pull off or break by torsion 8 : to follow a winding course 9 : to turn around

²twist *n* 1 : something formed by twisting or winding 2 : an act of twisting : the state of being twisted 3 : a spiral turn or curve; *also* : SPIN 4 : a turning aside 5 : ECCENTRICITY 6 : a distortion of meaning 7 : an unexpected turn or development 8 : DEVICE, TRICK 9 : a variant approach or method

twist·er \'twis-tər\ n **1** : one that twists; *esp* : a ball with a forward and spinning motion **2** : TORNADO; *also* : WATERSPOUT 2

¹twit \'twit\ n : FOOL

²twit vb **twit·ted; twit·ting** : to ridicule as a fault; *also* : TAUNT ◆ *Synonyms* DERIDE, MOCK, RAZZ

¹twitch \'twich\ vb **1** : to move or pull with a sudden motion : JERK **2** : to move jerkily : QUIVER **3** : to have a twitch

²twitch n **1** : an act or movement of twitching **2** : a brief spasmodic contraction of muscle fibers

¹twit·ter \'twi-tər\ vb **1** : to make a succession of chirping noises **2** : to talk in a chattering fashion **3** : to tremble with agitation : FLUTTER

²twitter n **1** : a slight agitation of the nerves **2** : a small tremulous intermittent noise (as made by a swallow) **3** : a light chattering

twixt \'twikst\ prep : BETWEEN ⟨∼ the two extremes⟩

two \'tü\ n, pl **twos** **1** : one more than one **2** : the second in a set or series **3** : something having two units — **two** adj or pron

two cents n **1** or **two cents' worth** : an opinion offered on a topic under discussion **2** : a sum or object of very small value

two–faced \'tü-'fāst\ adj **1** : DOUBLE-DEALING, FALSE **2** : having two faces

two·fold \'tü-ˌfōld, -'fōld\ adj **1** : having two units or members **2** : being twice as much or as many — **twofold** \-'fōld\ adv

2,4–D \ˌtü-ˌfȯr-'dē\ n : an irritant compound used esp. as a weed killer

2,4,5–T \-ˌfīv-'tē\ n : an irritant compound used esp. as an herbicide and defoliant

two·pence \'tə-pəns, US also 'tü-ˌpens\ n : the sum of two pence

two·pen·ny \'tə-pə-nē, US also 'tü-ˌpe-nē\ adj : of the value of or costing twopence

two–ply \'tü-'plī\ adj **1** : woven as a double cloth **2** : consisting of two strands or thicknesses

two·some \'tü-səm\ n **1** : a group of two persons or things : COUPLE **2** : a golf match between two players

two–step \'tü-ˌstep\ n : a ballroom dance performed with a sliding step in march or polka time; *also* : a piece of music for this dance — **two–step** vb

two–time \'tü-ˌtīm\ vb : to betray (a spouse or lover) by secret lovemaking with another — **two–tim·er** n

two–way adj : involving two elements or allowing movement or use in two directions or manners

2WD abbr two-wheel drive

twp abbr township

TWX abbr teletypewriter exchange

TX abbr Texas

ty·coon \tī-'kün\ n [Jp *taikun* feudal lord] **1** : a masterful leader (as in politics) **2** : a powerful businessman or industrialist

tyin \'tēn\ n, pl **tyin** — see *tenge* at MONEY table

tying pres part of TIE

ty·iyn \tē-'en\ n, pl **tyiyn** — see *som* at MONEY table

tyke \'tīk\ n : a small child

tym·pan·ic membrane \tim-'pa-nik-\ n : EARDRUM

tym·pa·num \'tim-pə-nəm\ n, pl **-na** \-nə\ also **-nums** : EARDRUM; *also* : MIDDLE EAR — **tym·pan·ic** \tim-'pa-nik\ adj

¹type \'tīp\ n [ME, fr. LL *typus*, fr. L & Gk; L *typus* image, fr. Gk *typos* blow, impression, model, fr. *typtein* to strike, beat] **1** : a person, thing, or event that foreshadows another to come : TOKEN, SYMBOL **2** : MODEL, EXAMPLE **3** : a distinctive stamp, mark, or sign : EMBLEM **4** : rectangular blocks usu. of metal each having a face so shaped as to produce a character when printed **5** : the letters or characters printed from or as if from type **6** : general character or form common to a number of individuals and setting them off as a distinguishable class ⟨horses of draft ∼⟩ **7** : a class, kind, or group set apart by common characteristics ⟨a seedless ∼ of orange⟩; *also* : something distinguishable as a variety ⟨reactions of this ∼⟩ ◆ *Synonyms* SORT, NATURE, CHARACTER, DESCRIPTION

²type vb **typed; typ·ing** **1** : to represent beforehand as a type **2** : to produce a copy of; *also* : REPRESENT, TYPIFY **3** : to write with a typewriter or computer keyboard **4** : to identify as belonging to a type : TYPECAST

type A adj : relating to, having, or being a personality marked esp. by impatience and aggressiveness

type·cast \-ˌkast\ vb **-cast; -cast·ing** **1** : to cast (an actor) in a part calling for characteristics possessed by the actor **2** : to cast repeatedly in the same type of role

type·face \-ˌfās\ n : all type of a single design

type 1 diabetes \'tīp-'wən-\ n : a form of diabetes mellitus usu. developing before adulthood and marked by severe insulin deficiency

type·script \'tīp-ˌskript\ n : typewritten matter

type·set \-ˌset\ vb **-set; -set·ting** : to set in type : COMPOSE — **type·set·ter** n

type 2 diabetes \-'tü-\ n : a form of diabetes mellitus developing esp. in adults and usu. in obese individuals and marked by excess sugar in the blood

type·write \-ˌrīt\ vb **-wrote** \-ˌrōt\; **-writ·ten** \-ˌri-tᵊn\ : TYPE 3

type·writ·er \-ˌrī-tər\ n **1** : a machine for writing in characters similar to those produced by printers' type by means of types striking a ribbon to transfer ink or carbon impressions onto paper **2** : TYPIST

type·writ·ing \-ˌrī-tiŋ\ n : the use of a typewriter ⟨teach ∼⟩; *also* : writing produced with a typewriter

¹ty·phoid \'tī-ˌfȯid, tī-'fȯid\ adj : of, relating to, or being a communicable bacterial disease (**typhoid fever**) marked by fever, diarrhea, prostration, and intestinal inflammation

²typhoid n : TYPHOID FEVER

ty·phoon \tī-'fün\ n : a hurricane occurring esp. in the region of the Philippines or the China sea

ty·phus \'tī-fəs\ n : a severe infectious disease transmitted esp. by body lice, caused by a rickettsia, and marked by high fever, stupor and delirium, intense headache, and a dark red rash

typ·i·cal \'ti-pi-kəl\ adj **1** : being or having the nature of a type **2** : exhibiting the essential characteristics of a group **3** : conforming to a type — **typ·i·cal·i·ty** \ˌti-pə-'ka-lə-tē\ n — **typ·i·cal·ness** n

typ·i·cal·ly \-pi-k(ə-)lē\ adv **1** : in a typical manner **2** : in typical circumstances

typ·i·fy \'ti-pə-ˌfī\ vb **-fied; -fy·ing** **1** : to represent by an image, form, model, or resemblance **2** : to embody the essential or common characteristics of

typ·ist \'tī-pist\ n : a person who types esp. as a job

ty·po \'tī-pō\ n, pl **typos** : an error (as of spelling) in typed or typeset material

ty·pog·ra·pher \tī-'pä-grə-fər\ n : one who designs or arranges printing

ty·pog·ra·phy \tī-'pä-grə-fē\ n : the art of printing with type; *also* : the style, arrangement, or appearance of printed matter — **ty·po·graph·ic** \ˌtī-pə-'gra-fik\ or **ty·po·graph·i·cal** \-fi-kəl\ adj — **ty·po·graph·i·cal·ly** adv

ty·ran·ni·cal \tə-'ra-ni-kəl, tī-\ also **ty·ran·nic** \-nik\ adj : of or relating to a tyrant : DESPOTIC ◆ *Synonyms* ARBITRARY, ABSOLUTE, AUTOCRATIC — **ty·ran·ni·cal·ly** \-ni-k(ə-)lē\ adv

tyr·an·nise *Brit var of* TYRANNIZE

tyr·an·nize \'tir-ə-ˌnīz\ vb **-nized; -niz·ing** : to act as a tyrant : rule with unjust severity — **tyr·an·niz·er** n

ty·ran·no·saur \tə-'ra-nə-ˌsȯr\ n : a massive American flesh-eating dinosaur of the Cretaceous that had small forelegs and walked on its hind legs

ty·ran·no·sau·rus \tə-ˌra-nə-'sȯr-əs\ n : TYRANNOSAUR

tyr·an·nous \'tir-ə-nəs\ adj : unjustly severe — **tyr·an·nous·ly** adv

tyr·an·ny \'tir-ə-nē\ n, pl **-nies** **1** : oppressive power **2** : the rule or authority of a tyrant : government in which absolute power is vested in a single ruler **3** : a tyrannical act

ty·rant \'tī-rənt\ n **1** : an absolute ruler : DESPOT **2** : a ruler who governs oppressively or brutally **3** : one who uses authority or power harshly

tyre *chiefly Brit var of* ²TIRE

ty·ro \'tī-rō\ n, pl **tyros** [ML, fr. L *tiro* young soldier, tyro] : a beginner in learning : NOVICE

tzar, tzarist *var of* CZAR, CZARIST

¹u \'yü\ *n, pl* **u's** *or* **us** \'yüz\ *often cap* : the 21st letter of the English alphabet
²u *abbr, often cap* unit
¹U \'yü\ *adj* : characteristic of the upper classes
²U *abbr* **1** [abbr. of *Union of Orthodox Hebrew Congregations*] kosher certification — often enclosed in a circle **2** university **3** unsatisfactory
³U *symbol* uranium
UAE *abbr* United Arab Emirates
UAR *abbr* United Arab Republic
UAW *abbr* United Automobile Workers
ubiq·ui·tous \yü-'bi-kwə-təs\ *adj* : existing or being everywhere at the same time : OMNIPRESENT — **ubiq·ui·tous·ly** *adv* — **ubiq·ui·ty** \-kwə-tē\ *n*
U–boat \'yü-,bōt\ *n* [trans. of G *U-boot*, short for *Unterseeboot*, lit., undersea boat] : a German submarine
UC *abbr* uppercase
ud·der \'ə-dər\ *n* : an organ (as of a cow) consisting of two or more milk glands enclosed in a large hanging sac and each provided with a nipple
UFO \,yü-(,)ef-'ō\ *n, pl* **UFO's** *or* **UFOs** \-'ōz\ : an unidentified flying object; *esp* : FLYING SAUCER
ug·ly \'ə-glē\ *adj* **ug·li·er; -est** [ME, fr. ON *uggligr*, fr. *uggr* fear] **1** : FRIGHTFUL, DIRE **2** : offensive to the sight : HIDEOUS **3** : offensive or unpleasant to any sense **4** : morally objectionable : REPULSIVE **5** : likely to cause inconvenience or discomfort **6** : SURLY, QUARRELSOME ⟨an ~ disposition⟩ — **ug·li·ness** \-glē-nəs\ *n*
UHF *abbr* ultrahigh frequency
UK *abbr* United Kingdom
ukase \yü-'kās, -'kāz\ *n* [F & Russ; F, fr. Russ *ukaz*, fr. *ukazat'* to show, order] : an edict esp. of a Russian emperor or government
uku·le·le *also* **uke·le·le** \,yü-kə-'lā-lē\ *n* [Hawaiian *'ukulele*, fr. *'uku* flea + *lele* jumping] : a small usu. 4-stringed guitar popularized in Hawaii
ul·cer \'əl-sər\ *n* **1** : an open eroded sore of skin or mucous membrane often discharging pus **2** : something that festers and corrupts like an open sore — **ul·cer·ous** *adj*
ul·cer·ate \'əl-sə-,rāt\ *vb* **-at·ed; -at·ing** : to become affected with an ulcer — **ul·cer·a·tive** \'əl-sə-,rā-tiv\ *adj*
ul·cer·a·tion \,əl-sə-'rā-shən\ *n* **1** : the process of forming or state of having an ulcer **2** : ULCER 1
ul·na \'əl-nə\ *n* : the bone on the little-finger side of the human forearm; *also* : a corresponding bone of the forelimb of vertebrates above fishes
ul·ster \'əl-stər\ *n* : a long loose overcoat
ult *abbr* **1** ultimate **2** ultimo
ul·te·ri·or \,əl-'tir-ē-ər\ *adj* **1** : lying farther away : more remote **2** : situated beyond or on the farther side **3** : going beyond what is openly said or shown : HIDDEN ⟨~ motives⟩
¹ul·ti·mate \'əl-tə-mət\ *adj* **1** : most remote in space or time : FARTHEST **2** : last in a progression : FINAL **3** : the best or most extreme of its kind **4** : arrived at as the last resort **5** : FUNDAMENTAL, ABSOLUTE, SUPREME ⟨~ reality⟩ **6** : incapable of further analysis or division : ELEMENTAL **7** : MAXIMUM ♦ *Synonyms* CONCLUDING, EVENTUAL, LATEST, TERMINAL — **ul·ti·mate·ly** *adv*
²ultimate *n* : something ultimate
ul·ti·ma·tum \,əl-tə-'mā-təm, -'mä-\ *n, pl* **-tums** *or* **-ta** \-tə\ : a final condition or demand whose rejection will bring about a resort to forceful action
ul·ti·mo \'əl-tə-,mō\ *adj* [L *ultimo mense* in the last month] : of or occurring in the month preceding the present
¹ul·tra \'əl-trə\ *adj* : going beyond others or beyond due limits : EXTREME
²ultra *n* : EXTREMIST
ul·tra·con·ser·va·tive \-kən-'sər-və-tiv\ *adj* : extremely conservative
ul·tra·high frequency \-'hī-\ *n* : a radio frequency between 300 and 3000 megahertz

¹ul·tra·light \'əl-trə-,līt\ *adj* : extremely light esp. in weight
²ultralight *n* : a very light recreational aircraft typically carrying only one person
ul·tra·ma·rine \,əl-trə-mə-'rēn\ *n* **1** : a deep blue pigment **2** : a very bright deep blue color
ul·tra·mi·cro·scop·ic \-,mī-krə-'skä-pik\ *adj* : too small to be seen with an ordinary microscope
ul·tra·mod·ern \-'mä-dərn\ *adj* : extremely or excessively modern in idea, style, or tendency
ul·tra·mon·tane \-'män-,tān, -,män-'tān\ *adj* **1** : of or relating to countries or peoples beyond the mountains (as the Alps) **2** : favoring greater or absolute supremacy of papal over national or diocesan authority in the Roman Catholic Church — **ultramontane** *n, often cap* — **ul·tra·mon·tan·ism** \-'män-tə-,ni-zəm\ *n*
ul·tra·pure \-'pyur\ *adj* : of the utmost purity
ul·tra·short \-'short\ *adj* **1** : having a wavelength below 10 meters **2** : very short in duration
ul·tra·son·ic \,əl-trə-'sä-nik\ *adj* : having a frequency too high to be heard by the human ear — **ul·tra·son·i·cal·ly** \-ni-k(ə-)lē\ *adv*
ul·tra·son·ics \-'sä-niks\ *n sing or pl* **1** : ultrasonic vibrations **2** : the science of ultrasonic phenomena
ul·tra·sound \-,saund\ *n* **1** : ultrasonic vibrations **2** : the diagnostic or therapeutic use of ultrasound and esp. a technique involving the formation of a two-dimensional image of internal body structures **3** : a diagnostic examination using ultrasound
ul·tra·vi·o·let \-'vī-ə-lət\ *adj* : having a wavelength shorter than those of visible light and longer than those of X-rays ⟨~ radiation⟩; *also* : producing or employing ultraviolet radiation — **ultraviolet** *n*
ul·tra vi·res \'əl-trə-'vī-rēz\ *adv or adj* [NL, lit., beyond power] : beyond the scope of legal power or authority
ul·u·late \'əl-yə-,lāt\ *vb* **-lat·ed; -lat·ing** : HOWL, WAIL
uma·mi \ü-'mä-mē\ *n* [Jp, flavor] : a meaty or savory taste sensation produced esp. by monosodium glutamate
um·bel \'əm-bəl\ *n* : a flat-topped or rounded flower cluster in which the individual flower stalks all arise near one point on the main stem
um·ber \'əm-bər\ *n* : a brown earthy substance valued as a pigment either in its raw state or burnt — **umber** *adj*
umbilical cord *n* : a cord containing blood vessels that connects the navel of a fetus with the placenta of its mother
um·bi·li·cus \,əm-'bi-li-kəs, ,əm-bə-'lī-\ *n, pl* **um·bi·li·ci** \,əm-'bi-lə-,kī; ,əm-bə-'lī-,kī, -,sī\ *or* **um·bi·li·cus·es** : NAVEL — **um·bil·i·cal** \,əm-'bi-li-kəl\ *adj*
um·bra \'əm-brə\ *n, pl* **umbras** *or* **um·brae** \-(,)brē, -,brī\ **1** : SHADE, SHADOW **2** : the conical part of the shadow of a celestial body from which the sun's light is completely blocked
um·brage \'əm-brij\ *n* **1** : SHADE; *also* : FOLIAGE **2** : RESENTMENT, OFFENSE ⟨take ~ at a remark⟩
um·brel·la \,əm-'bre-lə\ *n* **1** : a collapsible shade for protection against weather consisting of fabric stretched over hinged ribs radiating from a center pole **2** : something that provides protection **3** : something that covers a range of elements
umi·ak \'ü-mē-,ak\ *n* : an open Eskimo boat made of a wooden frame covered with skins
ump \'əmp\ *n* : UMPIRE
um·pire \'əm-,pī(-ə)r\ *n* [ME *oumpere*, alter. of *noumpere* (the phrase *a noumpere* being understood as *an oumpere*), fr. AF *nounpier* single, odd, fr. *non* not + *per* equal, fr. L *par*] **1** : one having authority to decide finally a controversy or question between parties **2** : an official in a sport who rules on plays — **umpire** *vb*
ump·teen \'əmp-,tēn\ *adj* : very many : indefinitely numerous — **ump·teenth** \-,tēnth\ *adj*
UN *abbr* United Nations

un- \ˌən, ˈən\ *prefix* **1** : not : IN-, NON- **2** : opposite of : contrary to

unabashed
unabated
unabsorbed
unabsorbent
unacademic
unaccented
unacceptable
unacclimatized
unaccommodating
unaccredited
unacknowledged
unacquainted
unadapted
unadjusted
unadorned
unadventurous
unadvertised
unaesthetic
unaffiliated
unafraid
unaggressive
unaided
unalike
unaltered
unambiguous
unambiguously
unambitious
unanchored
unannounced
unanswerable
unanswered
unanticipated
unapologetic
unapparent
unappealing
unappeased
unappetizing
unappreciated
unappreciative
unapproachable
unappropriated
unapproved
unarguable
unarguably
unarmored
unartistic
unashamed
unasked
unassertive
unassisted
unathletic
unattainable
unattended
unattested
unattractive
unauthentic
unauthorized
unavailable
unavowed
unawakened
unbaked
unbaptized
unbeloved
unbleached
unblemished
unblinking
unbound
unbranched
unbranded
unbreakable
unbridgeable
unbruised
unbrushed
unbudging
unburied
unburned
uncanceled
uncanonical
uncap
uncapitalized
uncared{ndash}for
uncataloged
uncaught
uncensored
uncensured
unchallenged
unchangeable
unchanged
unchanging
unchaperoned
uncharacteristic
unchaste
unchastely

unchasteness
unchastity
unchecked
unchivalrous
unchristened
unclad
unclaimed
unclassified
uncleaned
unclear
uncleared
unclouded
uncluttered
uncoated
uncollected
uncolored
uncombed
uncombined
uncomely
uncomic
uncommercial
uncompensated
uncomplaining
uncompleted
uncomplicated
uncomplimentary
uncompounded
uncomprehending
unconcealed
unconfined
unconfirmed
unconformable
uncongenial
unconnected
unconquered
unconsecrated
unconsidered
unconsolidated
unconstrained
unconsumed
unconsummated
uncontaminated
uncontested
uncontrolled
uncontroversial
unconverted
unconvincing
uncooked
uncooperative
uncoordinated
uncorrected
uncorroborated
uncountable
uncreative
uncredited
uncropped
uncrowded
uncrowned
uncrystallized
uncultivated
uncultured
uncured
uncurious
uncurtained
uncustomary
undamaged
undamped
undated
undecided
undecipherable
undeclared
undecorated
undefeated
undefended
undefiled
undefinable
undefined
undemanding
undemocratic
undenominational
undependable
undeserved
undeserving
undesired
undetected
undetermined
undeterred
undeveloped
undifferentiated
undigested
undignified
undiluted
undiminished

undimmed
undiplomatic
undirected
undisciplined
undisclosed
undiscovered
undiscriminating
undisguised
undismayed
undisputed
undissolved
undistinguished
undistributed
undisturbed
undivided
undogmatic
undomesticated
undone
undoubled
undramatic
undraped
undreamed
undressed
undrinkable
undulled
undutiful
undyed
uneager
uneatable
uneaten
uneconomic
uneconomical
unedifying
unedited
uneducated
unembarrassed
unemotional
unemphatic
unenclosed
unencumbered
unendurable
unenforceable
unenforced
unenlightened
unenterprising
unenthusiastic
unenviable
unequipped
unessential
unethical
unexamined
unexcelled
unexceptional
unexcited
unexciting
unexpired
unexplained
unexploded
unexplored
unexposed
unexpressed
unexpurgated
unfading
unfaltering
unfashionable
unfashionably
unfathomable
unfavorable
unfavorably
unfeasible
unfeminine
unfenced
unfermented
unfertilized
unfilled
unfiltered
unfitted
unflagging
unflattering
unflavored
unfocused
unfolded
unforced
unforeseeable
unforeseen
unforgivable
unforgiving
unformulated
unfortified
unframed
unfree
unfulfilled
unfunded
unfunny
unfurnished

unfussy
ungentle
ungentlemanly
ungerminated
unglamorous
unglazed
ungoverned
ungraceful
ungracefully
ungraded
ungrammatical
unground
ungrudging
unguided
unhackneyed
unhampered
unhardened
unharmed
unharvested
unhatched
unhealed
unhealthful
unheated
unheeded
unhelpful
unheralded
unheroic
unhesitating
unhindered
unhistorical
unhonored
unhoused
unhurried
unhurt
unhygienic
unidentifiable
unidentified
unidiomatic
unimaginable
unimaginative
unimpaired
unimpassioned
unimpeded
unimportant
unimposing
unimpressed
unimpressive
unimproved
unincorporated
uninfected
uninfluenced
uninformative
uninformed
uninhabitable
uninhabited
uninitiated
uninjured
uninspired
uninstructed
uninstructive
uninsured
unintelligent
unintelligible
unintelligibly
unintended
unintentional
unintentionally
uninteresting
uninterrupted
uninvited
uninviting
unjointed
unjustifiable
unjustified
unkept
unknowable
unknowledgeable
unlabeled
unladylike
unlamented
unleavened
unlicensed
unlighted
unlikable
unlimited
unlined
unlit
unliterary
unlivable
unlovable
unloved
unloving
unmade
unmalicious
unmanageable

unmanned
unmapped
unmarked
unmarketable
unmarred
unmarried
unmasculine
unmatched
unmeant
unmeasurable
unmeasured
unmelodious
unmentioned
unmerited
unmilitary
unmilled
unmixed
unmodified
unmolested
unmotivated
unmounted
unmovable
unmoved
unmusical
unnameable
unnamed
unnecessary
unneeded
unnewsworthy
unnoticeable
unnoticed
unobjectionable
unobservant
unobserved
unobstructed
unobtainable
unofficial
unofficially
unopened
unopposed
unoriginal
unorthodox
unorthodoxy
unostentatious
unowned
unpaged
unpaid
unpainted
unpaired
unpalatable
unpardonable
unpasteurized
unpatriotic
unpaved
unpeeled
unperceived
unperceptive
unperformed
unpersuaded
unpersuasive
unperturbed
unplanned
unplanted
unpleasing
unplowed
unpoetic
unpolished
unpolitical
unpolluted
unposed
unpractical
unpredictability
unpredictable
unprejudiced
unpremeditated
unprepared
unpreparedness
unprepossessing
unpressed
unpretending
unpretty
unprivileged
unprocessed
unproductive
unprofessed
unprofessional
unprogrammed
unprogressive
unpromising
unprompted
unpronounceable
unpropitious
unproven
unprovided
unprovoked

unpublished
unpunished
unquenchable
unquestioned
unraised
unrated
unratified
unreachable
unreadable
unready
unrealistic
unrealized
unrecognizable
unrecognized
unrecorded
unrecoverable
unredeemable
unrefined
unreflecting
unreflective
unregistered
unregulated
unrehearsed
unrelated
unreliable
unrelieved
unremarkable
unremembered
unremovable
unrepentant
unreported
unrepresentative
unrepresented
unrepressed
unresistant
unresisting
unresolved
unresponsive
unresponsiveness
unrestful
unrestricted
unreturnable
unrewarding
unrhymed
unrhythmic
unripened
unromantic
unromantically
unsafe
unsaid
unsalable
unsalted
unsanctioned
unsanitary
unsatisfactory
unsatisfied
unscented
unscheduled
unscholarly
unsealed
unseasoned
unseaworthy
unsegmented
unself–conscious
unself–consciously
unsensational
unsentimental
unserious
unserviceable
unsexual
unshaded
unshakable
unshaken
unshapely
unshaven
unshorn
unsifted
unsigned
unsinkable
unsmiling
unsociable
unsoiled
unsold
unsoldierly
unsolicited
unsolvable
unsolved
unsorted
unspecified
unspectacular
unspent
unspiritual
unspoiled
unspoken
unsportsmanlike

unstained
unstated
unsterile
unstructured
unstylish
unsubdued
unsubstantiated
unsubtle
unsuccessful
unsuccessfully
unsuitable
unsuited
unsullied
unsupervised
unsupportable
unsupported
unsure
unsurpassed
unsurprising
unsurprisingly
unsuspected
unsuspecting
unsuspicious
unsweetened
unsymmetrical
unsympathetic
unsystematic
untactful
untainted
untalented
untamed
untanned
untapped
untarnished
untaxed
unteachable
untenable
untenanted
untended
untested
unthrifty
untidy
untilled

untraceable
untraditional
untrained
untrammeled
untranslatable
untranslated
untraveled
untraversed
untreated
untrimmed
untrod
untrodden
untroubled
untrustworthy
untruthful
untypical
unusable
unvaried
unvarying
unventilated
unverifiable
unverified
unversed
unvisited
unwanted
unwarranted
unwary
unwashed
unwavering
unweaned
unwearable
unwearied
unweathered
unwed
unwelcome
unwilling
unwillingly
unwillingness
unwomanly
unworkable
unworn
unworried
unwounded
unwoven

un·able \ˌən-ˈā-bəl\ *adj* **1** : not able **2** : UNQUALIFIED, INCOMPETENT

un·abridged \ˌən-ə-ˈbrijd\ *adj* **1** : not abridged ⟨an ∼ edition of Shakespeare⟩ **2** : complete of its class : not based on one larger ⟨an ∼ dictionary⟩

un·ac·com·pa·nied \ˌən-ə-ˈkəm-pə-nēd\ *adj* : not accompanied; *esp* : being without instrumental accompaniment

un·ac·count·able \ˌən-ə-ˈkauṅ-tə-bəl\ *adj* **1** : not to be accounted for : INEXPLICABLE **2** : not responsible — **un·ac·count·ably** \-blē\ *adv*

un·ac·count·ed \-ˈkauṅ-təd\ *adj* : not accounted ⟨the loss was ∼ for⟩

un·ac·cus·tomed \ˌən-ə-ˈkəs-təmd\ *adj* **1** : not customary : not usual or common **2** : not accustomed or habituated ⟨∼ to noise⟩

un·adul·ter·at·ed \ˌən-ə-ˈdəl-tə-ˌrā-təd\ *adj* : PURE, UNMIXED ✦ *Synonyms* ABSOLUTE, SHEER, SIMPLE, UNALLOYED, UNDILUTED, UNMITIGATED

un·af·fect·ed \ˌən-ə-ˈfek-təd\ *adj* **1** : not influenced or changed mentally, physically, or chemically **2** : free from affectation : NATURAL, GENUINE — **un·af·fect·ed·ly** *adv*

un·alien·able \-ˈāl-yə-nə-bəl, -ˈā-lē-ə-\ *adj* : INALIENABLE

un·aligned \ˌən-ə-ˈlīnd\ *adj* : not associated with any one of competing international blocs ⟨∼ nations⟩

un·al·loyed \ˌən-ə-ˈlȯid\ *adj* : UNMIXED, UNQUALIFIED, PURE ⟨∼ happiness⟩

un·al·ter·able \ˌən-ˈȯl-tə-rə-bəl\ *adj* : not capable of being altered or changed — **un·al·ter·ably** \-blē\ *adv*

un–Amer·i·can \ˌən-ə-ˈmer-ə-kən\ *adj* : not characteristic of or consistent with American customs or principles

unan·i·mous \yu̇-ˈna-nə-məs\ *adj* [L *unanimus*, fr. *unus* one + *animus* mind] **1** : being of one mind : AGREEING **2** : formed with or indicating the agreement of all — **una·nim·i·ty** \ˌyü-nə-ˈni-mə-tē\ *n* — **unan·i·mous·ly** *adv*

un·arm \ˌən-ˈärm\ *vb* : DISARM

un·armed \-ˈärmd\ *adj* : not armed or armored ⟨∼ civilians⟩

un·as·sail·able \ˌən-ə-ˈsā-lə-bəl\ *adj* : not liable to doubt, attack, or question ⟨an ∼ argument⟩

un·as·sum·ing \ˌən-ə-ˈsü-miŋ\ *adj* : MODEST ⟨an ∼ librarian⟩ ⟨an ∼ manner⟩ ⟨an ∼ neighborhood⟩ ✦ *Synonyms* HUMBLE, LOWLY, MEEK un·at·tached \ˌən-ə-ˈtacht\ *adj* 1 : not married or engaged 2 : not joined or united

un·avail·ing \ˌən-ə-ˈvā-liŋ\ *adj* : being of no avail — un·avail·ing·ly *adv*

un·avoid·able \ˌən-ə-ˈvȯi-də-bəl\ *adj* : not avoidable : INEVITABLE ✦ *Synonyms* CERTAIN, INELUCTABLE, INESCAPABLE, NECESSARY — un·avoid·ably \-blē\ *adv*

¹un·aware \ˌən-ə-ˈwer\ *adv* : UNAWARES

²unaware *adj* : not aware : IGNORANT — un·aware·ness *n*

un·awares \-ˈwerz\ *adv* 1 : without knowing : UNINTENTIONALLY 2 : without warning : by surprise ⟨taken ∼⟩

un·bal·anced \ˌən-ˈba-lənst\ *adj* 1 : not in a state of balance 2 : mentally disordered 3 : not adjusted so as to make credits equal to debits

un·bar \-ˈbär\ *vb* : UNBOLT, OPEN

un·bear·able \ˌən-ˈber-ə-bəl\ *adj* : greater than can be borne ⟨∼ pain⟩ ✦ *Synonyms* INSUFFERABLE, INSUPPORTABLE, INTOLERABLE, UNENDURABLE, UNSUPPORTABLE — un·bear·ably \-blē\ *adv*

un·beat·able \-ˈbē-tə-bəl\ *adj* : not capable of being defeated ✦ *Synonyms* INDOMITABLE, INVINCIBLE, INVULNERABLE, UNCONQUERABLE

un·beat·en \-ˈbē-tᵊn\ *adj* 1 : not pounded, beaten, or whipped 2 : UNTRODDEN 3 : UNDEFEATED

un·be·com·ing \ˌən-bi-ˈkə-miŋ\ *adj* : not becoming : UNSUITABLE, IMPROPER ✦ *Synonyms* INDECOROUS, INDECENT, INDELICATE, UNSEEMLY — un·be·com·ing·ly *adv*

un·be·knownst \ˌən-bi-ˈnōnst\ *also* un·be·known \-ˈnōn\ *adj* : happening or existing without one's knowledge

un·be·lief \ˌən-bə-ˈlēf\ *n* : the withholding or absence of belief : DOUBT — un·be·liev·ing \-ˈlē-viŋ\ *adj*

un·be·liev·able \-ˈlē-və-bəl\ *adj* : too improbable for belief; *also* : of such a superlative degree as to be hard to believe ⟨an ∼ catch for a touchdown⟩ ✦ *Synonyms* INCONCEIVABLE, UNIMAGINABLE, UNTHINKABLE — un·be·liev·ably \-blē\ *adv*

un·be·liev·er \-ˈlē-vər\ *n* 1 : INFIDEL 2 : DOUBTER

un·bend \-ˈbend\ *vb* -bent \-ˈbent\; -bend·ing 1 : to free from being bent : make or become straight 2 : UNTIE 3 : to make or become less stiff or more affable : RELAX

un·bend·ing *adj* : formal and distant in manner : INFLEXIBLE

un·bi·ased \ˌən-ˈbī-əst\ *adj* : free from bias; *esp* : UNPREJUDICED ⟨an ∼ opinion⟩ ✦ *Synonyms* DISINTERESTED, DISPASSIONATE, IMPARTIAL, NONDISCRIMINATORY, NONPARTISAN, OBJECTIVE, UNCOLORED

un·bid·den \-ˈbi-dᵊn\ *also* un·bid \-ˈbid\ *adj* : not bidden : UNASKED

un·bind \-ˈbīnd\ *vb* -bound \-ˈbau̇nd\; -bind·ing 1 : to remove bindings from : UNTIE 2 : RELEASE

un·blessed *also* un·blest \ˌən-ˈblest\ *adj* 1 : not blessed 2 : EVIL

un·block \-ˈbläk\ *vb* : to free from being blocked

un·blush·ing \-ˈblə-shiŋ\ *adj* 1 : not blushing 2 : SHAMELESS ⟨∼ greed⟩ — un·blush·ing·ly *adv*

un·bod·ied \-ˈbä-dēd\ *adj* 1 : having no body; *also* : DISEMBODIED 2 : FORMLESS

un·bolt \ˌən-ˈbōlt\ *vb* : to open or unfasten by withdrawing a bolt

un·bolt·ed \-ˈbōl-təd\ *adj* : not fastened by bolts

un·born \-ˈbȯrn\ *adj* : not yet born

un·bos·om \-ˈbu̇-zəm, -ˈbü-\ *vb* 1 : DISCLOSE, REVEAL 2 : to disclose the thoughts or feelings of oneself

un·bound·ed \-ˈbau̇n-dəd\ *adj* : having no bounds or limits ⟨∼ enthusiasm⟩ ✦ *Synonyms* BOUNDLESS, ENDLESS, IMMEASURABLE, LIMITLESS, MEASURELESS, UNLIMITED

un·bowed \ˌən-ˈbau̇d\ *adj* 1 : not bowed down 2 : UNSUBDUED

un·bri·dled \-ˈbrī-dᵊld\ *adj* 1 : UNRESTRAINED ⟨∼ enthusiasm⟩ 2 : not confined by a bridle

un·bro·ken \-ˈbrō-kən\ *adj* 1 : not damaged 2 : not subdued or tamed 3 : not interrupted : CONTINUOUS

un·buck·le \-ˈbə-kəl\ *vb* : to loose the buckle of : UNFASTEN ⟨∼ a belt⟩

un·bur·den \-ˈbər-dᵊn\ *vb* 1 : to free or relieve from a burden 2 : to relieve oneself of (as cares or worries)

un·but·ton \-ˈbə-tᵊn\ *vb* : to unfasten the buttons of ⟨∼ your coat⟩

un·called-for \ˌən-ˈkȯld-ˌfȯr\ *adj* : not called for, needed, or wanted

un·can·ny \-ˈka-nē\ *adj* 1 : GHOSTLY, MYSTERIOUS, EERIE 2 : suggesting superhuman or supernatural powers ✦ *Synonyms* SPOOKY, UNEARTHLY, WEIRD — un·can·ni·ly \-ˈka-nə-lē\ *adv*

un·ceas·ing \-ˈsē-siŋ\ *adj* : never ceasing ✦ *Synonyms* CEASELESS, CONTINUOUS, ENDLESS, INTERMINABLE, UNENDING, UNREMITTING — un·ceas·ing·ly *adv*

un·cer·e·mo·ni·ous \ˌən-ˌser-ə-ˈmō-nē-əs\ *adj* : acting without or lacking ordinary courtesy : ABRUPT — un·cer·e·mo·ni·ous·ly *adv*

un·cer·tain \ˌən-ˈsər-tᵊn\ *adj* 1 : not determined or fixed ⟨an ∼ quantity⟩ 2 : subject to chance or change : not dependable ⟨∼ weather⟩ 3 : not definitely known 4 : not sure ⟨∼ of the truth⟩ — un·cer·tain·ly *adv*

un·cer·tain·ty \-tᵊn-tē\ *n* 1 : lack of certainty : DOUBT 2 : something that is uncertain ✦ *Synonyms* CONCERN, DOUBT, DUBIETY, INCERTITUDE, SKEPTICISM, SUSPICION

un·chain \ˌən-ˈchān\ *vb* : to free by or as if by removing a chain

un·charged \ˌən-ˈchärjd\ *adj* : having no electrical charge

un·char·i·ta·ble \-ˈcha-rə-tə-bəl\ *adj* : not charitable; *esp* : severe in judging others — un·char·i·ta·ble·ness *n* — un·char·i·ta·bly \-blē\ *adv*

un·chart·ed \-ˈchär-təd\ *adj* 1 : not recorded on a map, chart, or plan 2 : UNKNOWN ⟨discussion moving into ∼ territory⟩

un·chris·tian \-ˈkris-chən\ *adj* 1 : not of the Christian faith 2 : contrary to the Christian spirit

un·churched \-ˈchərcht\ *adj* : not belonging to or connected with a church

un·cial \ˈən-shəl, -chəl; ˈən-sē-əl\ *adj* : relating to or written in a form of script with rounded letters used esp. in early Greek and Latin manuscripts — uncial *n*

un·cir·cu·lat·ed \ˌən-ˈsər-kyə-ˌlā-təd\ *adj* : issued for use as money but kept out of circulation

un·cir·cum·cised \ˌən-ˈsər-kəm-ˌsīzd\ *adj* 1 : not circumcised 2 : HEATHEN

un·civ·il \ˌən-ˈsi-vəl\ *adj* 1 : not civilized : BARBAROUS 2 : DISCOURTEOUS, ILL-MANNERED, IMPOLITE ⟨∼ remarks⟩

un·civ·i·lized \-ˈsi-və-ˌlīzd\ *adj* 1 : not civilized : BARBAROUS 2 : remote from civilization : WILD

un·clasp \-ˈklasp\ *vb* : to open by or as if by loosing the clasp

un·cle \ˈən-kəl\ *n* [ME, fr. AF, fr. L *avunculus* mother's brother] 1 : the brother of one's father or mother 2 : the husband of one's aunt

un·clean \ˌən-ˈklēn\ *adj* 1 : morally or spiritually impure 2 : prohibited by ritual law for use or contact 3 : DIRTY, SOILED — un·clean·li·ness \-ˈlē-nəs\ *n* — un·clean·ly *adj* — un·clean·ness *n*

un·clench \-ˈklench\ *vb* : to open from a clenched position : RELAX

Uncle Tom \-ˈtäm\ *n* [fr. *Uncle Tom,* faithful slave in Harriet Beecher Stowe's novel *Uncle Tom's Cabin* (1851-52)] : a black who is eager to win the approval of whites

un·cloak \ˌən-ˈklōk\ *vb* 1 : to remove a cloak or cover from 2 : UNMASK, REVEAL ⟨∼ an impostor⟩

un·clog \-ˈkläg\ *vb* : to remove an obstruction from

un·close \-ˈklōz\ *vb* : OPEN — un·closed \-ˈklōzd\ *adj*

un·clothe \-ˈklōth\ *vb* : to strip of clothes or a covering — un·clothed \-ˈklōthd\ *adj*

un·coil \ˌən-ˈkȯi(-ə)l\ *vb* : to release or become released from a coiled state

undercarriage 2

un·com·fort·able \ˌən-ˈkəmf-tə-bəl, -ˈkəm-fər-tə-\ *adj* 1 : causing discomfort 2 : feeling discomfort — un·com·fort·ably \-blē\ *adv*

un·com·mit·ted \ˌən-kə-ˈmi-təd\ *adj* : not committed; *esp* : not pledged to a particular belief, allegiance, or program ⟨∼ voters⟩

un·com·mon \ˌən-ˈkä-mən\ *adj* **1** : not ordinarily encountered : UNUSUAL, RARE **2** : REMARKABLE, EXCEPTIONAL ⟨a soldier of ∼ courage⟩ ♦ *Synonyms* EXTRAORDINARY, PHENOMENAL, SINGULAR, UNIQUE — **un·com·mon·ly** *adv*

un·com·mu·ni·ca·tive \ˌən-kə-ˈmyü-nə-ˌkā-tiv, -ni-kə-\ *adj* : not inclined to talk or impart information : RESERVED ♦ *Synonyms* CLOSEMOUTHED, RETICENT, SILENT, TACITURN

un·com·pro·mis·ing \ˌən-ˈkäm-prə-ˌmī-ziŋ\ *adj* : not making or accepting a compromise : UNYIELDING ♦ *Synonyms* ADAMANT, INFLEXIBLE, OBDURATE, RIGID, UNBENDING

un·con·cern \ˌən-kən-ˈsərn\ *n* : lack of care or interest : INDIFFERENCE **2** : freedom from excessive concern

un·con·cerned \-ˈsərnd\ *adj* **1** : not having any part or interest **2** : not anxious or upset : free of worry ♦ *Synonyms* ALOOF, DETACHED, INCURIOUS, REMOTE, UNCURIOUS, UNINTERESTED — **un·con·cern·ed·ly** \-ˈsər-nəd-lē\ *adv*

un·con·di·tion·al \ˌən-kən-ˈdi-shə-nəl\ *adj* : not limited in any way ⟨∼ surrender⟩ — **un·con·di·tion·al·ly** *adv*

un·con·di·tioned \-ˈdi-shənd\ *adj* **1** : not subject to conditions **2** : not acquired or learned : NATURAL ⟨∼ responses⟩ **3** : producing an unconditioned response ⟨∼ stimuli⟩

un·con·quer·able \ˌən-ˈkäŋ-kə-rə-bəl\ *adj* : incapable of being conquered or overcome : INDOMITABLE

un·con·scio·na·ble \-ˈkän-shə-nə-bəl\ *adj* **1** : not guided or controlled by conscience **2** : not in accordance with what is right or just ⟨∼ sales practices⟩ ♦ *Synonyms* UNREASONABLE, UNDUE, UNJUSTIFIABLE, UNWARRANTABLE, UNWARRANTED — **un·con·scio·na·bly** \-blē\ *adv*

¹un·con·scious \ˌən-ˈkän-chəs, -shəs\ *adj* **1** : not knowing or perceiving : not aware **2** : not done consciously or on purpose **3** : having lost consciousness **4** : of or relating to the unconscious — **un·con·scious·ly** *adv* — **un·con·scious·ness** *n*

²unconscious *n* : the part of one's mental life of which one is not ordinarily aware but which is often a powerful force in influencing behavior

un·con·sti·tu·tion·al \ˌən-ˌkän-stə-ˈtü-shə-nəl, -ˈtyü-\ *adj* : not according to or consistent with the constitution of a state or society — **un·con·sti·tu·tion·al·i·ty** \-ˌtü-shə-ˈna-lə-tē, -ˌtyü-\ *n* — **un·con·sti·tu·tion·al·ly** \-ˈtü-shə-nə-lē, -ˈtyü-\ *adv*

un·con·trol·la·ble \ˌən-kən-ˈtrō-lə-bəl\ *adj* : incapable of being controlled : UNGOVERNABLE — **un·con·trol·la·bly** \-blē\ *adv*

un·con·ven·tion·al \-ˈven-chə-nəl\ *adj* : not conventional : being out of the ordinary — **un·con·ven·tion·al·i·ty** \-ˌven-chə-ˈna-lə-tē\ *n* — **un·con·ven·tion·al·ly** \-ˈven-chə-nə-lē\ *adv*

un·cork \ˌən-ˈkȯrk\ *vb* **1** : to draw a cork from **2** : to release from a sealed or pent-up state; *also* : to let go

un·count·ed \-ˈkaun-təd\ *adj* **1** : not counted **2** : INNUMERABLE

un·cou·ple \-ˈkə-pəl\ *vb* : DISCONNECT ⟨∼ railroad cars⟩

un·couth \-ˈküth\ *adj* [ME, unfamiliar, fr. OE *uncūth*, fr. *un-* + *cūth* known] **1** : strange, awkward, and clumsy in shape or appearance **2** : vulgar in conduct or speech : RUDE ♦ *Synonyms* DISCOURTEOUS, ILL-MANNERED, IMPOLITE, UNGRACIOUS, UNMANNERED, UNMANNERLY

un·cov·er \-ˈkə-vər\ *vb* **1** : to make known : DISCLOSE, REVEAL **2** : to expose to view by removing some covering **3** : to take the cover from **4** : to remove the hat from; *also* : to take off the hat as a token of respect — **un·covered** *adj*

un·crit·i·cal \ˌən-ˈkri-ti-kəl\ *adj* **1** : not critical : lacking in discrimination **2** : showing lack or improper use of critical standards or procedures — **un·crit·i·cal·ly** \-k(ə-)lē\ *adv*

un·cross \-ˈkrȯs\ *vb* : to change from a crossed position ⟨∼ed his legs⟩

unc·tion \ˈəŋk-shən\ *n* **1** : the act of anointing as a rite of consecration or healing **2** : exaggerated or insincere earnestness of language or manner

unc·tu·ous \ˈəŋk-chə-wəs\ *adj* [ME, fr. MF or ML; MF *unctueus*, fr. ML *unctuosus*, fr. L *unctus* act of anointing, fr. *unguere* to anoint] **1** : FATTY, OILY **2** : insincerely smooth in speech and manner — **unc·tu·ous·ly** *adv*

un·curl \ˌən-ˈkərl\ *vb* : to make or become straightened out from a curled or coiled position

un·cut \ˌən-ˈkət\ *adj* **1** : not cut down or into **2** : not shaped by cutting ⟨an ∼ diamond⟩ **3** : not having the folds of the leaves slit ⟨an ∼ book⟩ **4** : not abridged or curtailed ⟨the ∼ version of the film⟩ **5** : not diluted ⟨∼ heroin⟩

un·daunt·ed \-ˈdȯn-təd\ *adj* : not daunted : not discouraged or dismayed ♦ *Synonyms* BOLD, BRAVE, DAUNTLESS, FEARLESS, INTREPID, VALIANT — **un·daunt·ed·ly** *adv*

un·de·ceive \ˌən-di-ˈsēv\ *vb* : to free from deception, illusion, or error

un·de·mon·stra·tive \ˌən-di-ˈmän-strə-tiv\ *adj* : restrained in expression of feeling : RESERVED

un·de·ni·able \ˌən-di-ˈnī-ə-bəl\ *adj* **1** : plainly true : INCONTESTABLE **2** : unquestionably excellent or genuine ♦ *Synonyms* INCONTROVERTIBLE, INDISPUTABLE, INDUBITABLE, UNQUESTIONABLE — **un·de·ni·ably** \-blē\ *adv*

¹un·der \ˈən-dər\ *adv* **1** : in or into a position below or beneath something **2** : below some quantity, level, or limit ⟨$10 or ∼⟩ **3** : in or into a condition of subjection, subordination, or unconsciousness ⟨the ether put him ∼⟩

²un·der \ˌən-dər, ˈən-\ *prep* **1** : lower than and overhung, surmounted, or sheltered by ⟨∼ a tree⟩ **2** : subject to the authority or guidance of ⟨served ∼ him⟩ ⟨was ∼ contract⟩ **3** : subject to the action or effect of ⟨∼ the influence of alcohol⟩ **4** : within the division or grouping of ⟨items ∼ this heading⟩ **5** : less or lower than (as in size, amount, or rank) ⟨earns ∼ $5000⟩

³under \ˈən-dər\ *adj* **1** : lying below, beneath, or on the ventral side **2** : facing or protruding downward **3** : SUBORDINATE **4** : lower than usual, proper, or desired in amount, quality, or degree

un·der·achiev·er \ˌən-dər-ə-ˈchē-vər\ *n* : one (as a student) who performs below an expected level of proficiency

un·der·act \-ˈakt\ *vb* : to perform feebly or with restraint

un·der·ac·tive \-ˈak-tiv\ *adj* : characterized by abnormally low activity ⟨an ∼ thyroid gland⟩ — **un·der·ac·tiv·i·ty** \-ˌak-ˈti-və-tē\ *n*

un·der·age \-ˈāj\ *adj* : of less than mature or legal age

un·der·arm \-ˈärm\ *adj* **1** : UNDERHAND 2 ⟨an ∼ throw⟩ **2** : placed under or on the underside of the arms ⟨∼ seams⟩ — **underarm** *adv or n*

un·der·bel·ly \ˈən-dər-ˌbe-lē\ *n* **1** : a vulnerable area **2** : the underside of a body or mass

un·der·bid \ˌən-dər-ˈbid\ *vb* **-bid; -bid·ding** **1** : to bid less than another **2** : to bid too low

un·der·body \ˈən-dər-ˌbä-dē\ *n* : the lower parts of the body of a vehicle

un·der·bred \ˌən-dər-ˈbred\ *adj* : marked by lack of good breeding

un·der·brush \ˈən-dər-ˌbrəsh\ *n* : shrubs, bushes, or small trees growing beneath large trees

un·der·car·riage \-ˌka-rij\ *n* **1** : a supporting framework or underside (as of an automobile) **2** : the landing gear of an airplane

un·der·charge \ˌən-dər-ˈchärj\ *vb* : to charge (as a person) too little — **undercharge** \ˈən-dər-ˌchärj\ *n*

un·der·class \ˈən-dər-ˌklas\ *n* : LOWER CLASS

un·der·class·man \ˌən-dər-ˈklas-mən\ *n* : a member of the freshman or sophomore class

un·der·clothes \ˈən-dər-ˌklōthz\ *n pl* : UNDERWEAR

un·der·cloth·ing \-ˌklō-thiŋ\ *n* : UNDERWEAR

un·der·coat \-ˌkōt\ *n* **1** : a coat worn under another **2** : a growth of short hair or fur partly concealed by the longer and usu. coarser hairs of a mammal **3** : a coat of paint under another

un·der·coat·ing \-ˌkō-tiŋ\ *n* : a special waterproof coating applied to the underside of a vehicle

un·der·cov·er \ˌən-dər-ˈkə-vər\ *adj* : acting or executed in secret; *esp* : employed or engaged in secret investigation ⟨an ∼ agent⟩

un·der·croft \ˈən-dər-ˌkrȯft\ *n* [ME, fr. *under* + *crofte* crypt, fr. MD, fr. ML *crupta*, fr. L *crypta*] : a vaulted chamber under a church

un·der·cur·rent \-ˌkər-ənt\ *n* **1** : a current below the surface **2** : a hidden tendency of feeling or opinion ⟨an ∼ of dread⟩

un·der·cut \ˌən-dər-'kət\ vb **-cut; -cut·ting 1 :** to cut away the underpart of **2 :** to offer to sell or to work at a lower rate than **3 :** to strike (the ball) obliquely downward so as to give a backward spin or elevation to the shot — **un·der·cut** \'ən-dər-ˌkət\ n

un·der·de·vel·oped \ˌən-dər-di-'ve-ləpt\ adj **1 :** not normally or adequately developed ⟨∼ muscles⟩ **2 :** having a relatively low level of economic development ⟨the ∼ nations⟩

un·der·dog \'ən-dər-ˌdȯg\ n **:** the loser or predicted loser in a struggle

un·der·done \ˌən-dər-'dən\ adj **:** not thoroughly done or cooked : RARE

un·der·draw·ers \'ən-dər-ˌdrȯrz, -ˌdrȯ-ərz\ n pl **:** UNDERPANTS

un·der·draw·ing \'ən-dər-ˌdrȯ-iŋ\ n **:** a preliminary sketch made prior to painting

un·der·em·pha·size \ˌən-dər-'em-fə-ˌsīz\ vb **:** to emphasize inadequately — **un·der·em·pha·sis** \-səs\ n

un·der·em·ployed \-im-'plȯid\ adj **:** having less than full-time or adequate employment

un·der·es·ti·mate \-'es-tə-ˌmāt\ vb **:** to set too low a value on

un·der·ex·pose \-ik-'spōz\ vb **:** to expose (a photographic plate or film) for less time than is needed — **un·der·ex·po·sure** \-'spō-zhər\ n

un·der·feed \ˌən-dər-'fēd\ vb **-fed** \-'fed\; **-feed·ing :** to feed with too little food

un·der·foot \-'fut\ adv **1 :** under the feet ⟨flowers trampled ∼⟩ **2 :** close about one's feet : in the way

un·der·fur \'ən-dər-ˌfər\ n **:** an undercoat of fur esp. when thick and soft

un·der·gar·ment \-ˌgär-mənt\ n **:** a garment to be worn under another

un·der·gird \ˌən-dər-'gərd\ vb **:** to brace up : STRENGTHEN

un·der·go \ˌən-dər-'gō\ vb **-went** \-'went\; **-gone** \-'gȯn, -'gän\; **-go·ing 1 :** to submit to : ENDURE **2 :** to go through ⟨∼ a change⟩

un·der·grad \'ən-dər-ˌgrad\ n **:** UNDERGRADUATE

un·der·grad·u·ate \ˌən-dər-'gra-jə-wət, -jə-ˌwāt\ n **:** a student at a university or college who has not received a first degree

¹**un·der·ground** \ˌən-dər-'graund\ adv **1 :** beneath the surface of the earth **2 :** in or into hiding or secret operation

²**un·der·ground** \'ən-dər-ˌgraund\ n **1 :** a space under the surface of the ground; esp : SUBWAY **2 :** a secret political movement or group; esp : an organized body working in secret to overthrow a government or an occupying power **3 :** an avant-garde group or movement that operates outside the establishment

³**underground** \'ən-dər-ˌgraund\ adj **1 :** being, growing, operating, or located below the surface of the ground ⟨∼ stems⟩ **2 :** conducted by secret means **3 :** produced or published by the underground ⟨∼ publications⟩; also : of or relating to the avant-garde underground

un·der·growth \'ən-dər-ˌgrōth\ n **:** low growth (as of herbs and shrubs) on the floor of a forest

¹**un·der·hand** \'ən-dər-ˌhand\ adv **1 :** in an underhanded or secret manner **2 :** with an underhand motion

²**underhand** adj **1 :** UNDERHANDED **2 :** made with the hand kept below the level of the shoulder ⟨an ∼ pitch⟩

¹**un·der·hand·ed** \ˌən-dər-'han-dəd\ adv **:** UNDERHAND

²**underhanded** adj **:** marked by secrecy and deception — **un·der·hand·ed·ly** adv — **un·der·hand·ed·ness** n

un·der·lie \-'lī\ vb **-lay** \-'lā\; **-lain** \-'lān\; **-ly·ing** \-'lī-iŋ\ **1 :** to lie or be situated under **2 :** to be at the basis of : form the foundation of : SUPPORT

un·der·line \'ən-dər-ˌlīn\ vb **1 :** to draw a line under **2 :** EMPHASIZE, STRESS — **underline** n

un·der·ling \ˌən-dər-liŋ\ n **:** SUBORDINATE, INFERIOR

un·der·lip \ˌən-dər-'lip\ n **:** the lower lip

un·der·ly·ing \ˌən-dər-'lī-iŋ\ adj **1 :** lying under or below **2 :** FUNDAMENTAL, BASIC ⟨∼ principles⟩

un·der·mine \-'mīn\ vb **1 :** to excavate beneath **2 :** to weaken or wear away secretly or gradually

un·der·most \'ən-dər-ˌmōst\ adj **:** lowest in relative position — **undermost** adv

¹**un·der·neath** \ˌən-dər-'nēth\ prep **1 :** directly under **2 :** under subjection to

²**underneath** adv **1 :** below a surface or object : BENEATH **2 :** on the lower side

un·der·nour·ished \ˌən-dər-'nər-isht\ adj **:** supplied with insufficient nourishment — **un·der·nour·ish·ment** \-'nər-ish-mənt\ n

un·der·pants \'ən-dər-ˌpants\ n pl **:** a usu. short undergarment for the lower trunk : DRAWERS

un·der·part \-ˌpärt\ n **:** a part lying on the lower side (as of a bird or mammal)

un·der·pass \-ˌpas\ n **:** a crossing of a highway and another way (as a road) at different levels; also : the lower level

un·der·pay \ˌən-dər-'pā\ vb **:** to pay less than what is normal or required

un·der·pin·ning \'ən-dər-ˌpi-niŋ\ n **:** the material and construction (as a foundation) used for support of a structure — **un·der·pin** \ˌən-dər-'pin\ vb

un·der·play \ˌən-dər-'plā\ vb **:** to treat or handle with restraint; esp : to play a role with subdued force

un·der·pop·u·lat·ed \ˌən-dər-'pä-pyə-ˌlā-təd\ adj **:** having a lower than normal or desirable density of population

un·der·priv·i·leged \-'priv-lijd, -'pri-və-lijd\ adj **:** having fewer esp. economic and social privileges than others

un·der·pro·duc·tion \ˌən-dər-prə-'dək-shən\ n **:** the production of less than enough to satisfy the demand or of less than the usual supply

un·der·rate \-'rāt\ vb **:** to rate or value too low

un·der·rep·re·sent·ed \-ˌre-pri-'zen-təd\ adj **:** inadequately represented

un·der·score \'ən-dər-ˌskȯr\ vb **1 :** to draw a line under : UNDERLINE **2 :** EMPHASIZE — **underscore** n

¹**un·der·sea** \ˌən-dər-'sē\ adj **:** being, carried on, or used beneath the surface of the sea

²**undersea** or **un·der·seas** \-'sēz\ adv **:** beneath the surface of the sea

un·der·sec·re·tary \ˌən-dər-'se-krə-ˌter-ē\ n **:** a secretary immediately subordinate to a principal secretary ⟨∼ of state⟩

un·der·sell \-'sel\ vb **-sold** \-'sōld\; **-sell·ing :** to sell articles cheaper than

un·der·sexed \-'sekst\ adj **:** deficient in sexual desire

un·der·shirt \'ən-dər-ˌshərt\ n **:** a collarless undergarment with or without sleeves

un·der·shoot \ˌən-dər-'shüt\ vb **-shot** \-'shät\; **-shoot·ing 1 :** to shoot short of or below (a target) **2 :** to fall short of (a runway) in landing an airplane

un·der·shorts \'ən-dər-ˌshȯrts\ n pl **:** underpants for men or boys

un·der·shot \'ən-dər-ˌshät\ adj **1 :** moved by water passing beneath ⟨an ∼ waterwheel⟩ **2 :** having the lower front teeth projecting beyond the upper when the mouth is closed

un·der·side \'ən-dər-ˌsīd, ˌən-dər-'sīd\ n **:** the side or surface lying underneath

un·der·signed \'ən-dər-ˌsīnd\ n, pl **undersigned :** one whose name is signed at the end of a document

un·der·sized \ˌən-dər-'sīzd\ also **un·der·size** \-'sīz\ adj **:** of a size less than is common, proper, or normal

un·der·skirt \'ən-dər-ˌskərt\ n **:** a skirt worn under an outer skirt; esp : PETTICOAT

un·der·staffed \ˌən-dər-'staft\ adj **:** inadequately staffed

un·der·stand \ˌən-dər-'stand\ vb **-stood** \-'stud\; **-stand·ing 1 :** to grasp the meaning of : COMPREHEND **2 :** to have thorough or technical acquaintance with or expertness in ⟨∼ finance⟩ **3 :** to have reason to believe ⟨I ∼ you are leaving tomorrow⟩ **4 :** INTERPRET ⟨we ∼ this to be a refusal⟩ **5 :** to have a sympathetic attitude **6 :** to accept as settled ⟨it is understood that he will pay the expenses⟩ — **un·der·stand·able** \-'stan-də-bəl\ adj

un·der·stand·ably \-blē\ adv **:** as can be easily understood

¹**un·der·stand·ing** \ˌən-dər-'stan-diŋ\ n **1 :** knowledge and ability to judge : INTELLIGENCE ⟨a person of ∼⟩ **2 :** agreement of opinion or feeling **3 :** a mutual agreement informally or tacitly entered into

²**understanding** adj **:** endowed with understanding : TOLERANT, SYMPATHETIC

un·der·state \ˌən-dər-'stāt\ vb **1 :** to represent as less than is the case **2 :** to state with restraint esp. for effect — **un·der·state·ment** n

un·der·stood \ˌən-dər-'stud\ adj **1 :** agreed upon **2 :** IMPLICIT

un·der·sto·ry \'ən-dər-ˌstȯr-ē\ n **:** the vegetative layer between the top layer of a forest and the ground cover

un·der·study \'ən-dər-ˌstə-dē\ n **:** one who is prepared to act another's part or take over another's duties — **under-study** \'ən-dər-ˌstə-dē, ˌən-dər-'stə-dē\ *vb*

un·der·sur·face \'ən-dər-ˌsər-fəs\ *n* : UNDERSIDE

un·der·take \ˌən-dər-'tāk\ *vb* **-took** \-'túk\; **-tak·en** \-'tā-kən\; **-tak·ing** 1 : to take upon oneself : set about ⟨~ a task⟩ 2 : to put oneself under obligation 3 : GUARANTEE, PROMISE

un·der·tak·er \'ən-dər-ˌtā-kər\ *n* : one whose business is to prepare the dead for burial and to arrange and manage funerals

un·der·tak·ing \'ən-dər-ˌtā-kiŋ, ˌən-dər-'tā-kiŋ; 2 is 'ən-dər-ˌtā-kiŋ only\ *n* 1 : the act of one who undertakes or engages in any project 2 : the business of an undertaker 3 : something undertaken 4 : PROMISE, GUARANTEE

under-the-counter *adj* : UNLAWFUL, ILLICIT ⟨~ sale of drugs⟩

un·der·tone \'ən-dər-ˌtōn\ *n* 1 : a low or subdued tone or utterance 2 : a subdued color (as seen through and modifying another color)

un·der·tow \-ˌtō\ *n* : the current beneath the surface that flows seaward when waves are breaking upon the shore

un·der·val·ue \ˌən-dər-'val-yü\ *vb* 1 : to value or estimate below the real worth 2 : to esteem lightly

un·der·wa·ter \ˌən-dər-'wȯ-tər, -'wä-\ *adj* : lying, growing, worn, or operating below the surface of the water — **un·der·wa·ter** *adv*

under way \-'wā\ *adv* 1 : into motion from a standstill 2 : in progress

un·der·wear \'ən-dər-ˌwer\ *n* : clothing or a garment worn next to the skin and under other clothing

un·der·weight \ˌən-dər-'wāt\ *adj* : weighing below what is normal, average, or necessary — **underweight** *n*

un·der·wire \'ən-dər-ˌwī(-ə)r\ *n* : a wire running through the bottom of a brassiere to aid in support

un·der·world \'ən-dər-ˌwərld\ *n* 1 : the place of departed souls : HADES 2 : the side of the world opposite to one 3 : the world of organized crime

un·der·write \'ən-dər-ˌrīt, ˌən-dər-'rīt\ *vb* **-wrote** \-ˌrōt, -'rōt\; **-writ·ten** \-ˌri-t°n, -'ri-t°n\; **-writ·ing** 1 : to write under or at the end of something else 2 : to set one's name to an insurance policy and thereby become answerable for a designated loss or damage 3 : to subscribe to : agree to 4 : to guarantee financial support of — **un·der·writ·er** *n*

un·de·sign·ing \ˌən-di-'zī-niŋ\ *adj* : having no artful, ulterior, or fraudulent purpose : SINCERE

un·de·sir·able \-'zī-rə-bəl\ *adj* : not desirable — **undesirable** *n*

un·de·vi·at·ing \ˌən-'dē-vē-ˌā-tiŋ\ *adj* : keeping a true course

un·dies \'ən-dēz\ *n pl* : UNDERWEAR; *esp* : women's underwear

un·do \ˌən-'dü\ *vb* **-did** \-'did\; **-done** \-'dən\; **-do·ing** 1 : to make or become unfastened or loosened : OPEN 2 : to make null or as if not done : REVERSE 3 : to bring to ruin; *also* : UPSET

un·doc·u·ment·ed \ˌən-'dä-kyə-ˌmen-təd\ *adj* 1 : not supported by documentary evidence 2 : lacking documents required for legal immigration

un·do·ing *n* : a cause of ruin

un·doubt·ed \-'daú-təd\ *adj* : not doubted or called into question : CERTAIN — **un·doubt·ed·ly** *adv*

¹un·dress \ˌən-'dres\ *vb* : to remove the clothes or covering of : STRIP, DISROBE

²undress *n* 1 : informal dress; *esp* : a loose robe or dressing gown 2 : ordinary dress 3 : NUDITY

un·due \-'dü, -'dyü\ *adj* 1 : not due 2 : exceeding or violating propriety or fitness : EXCESSIVE ⟨~ force⟩

un·du·lant \'ən-jə-lənt, 'ən-də-, -dyə-\ *adj* : rising and falling in waves

undulant fever *n* : a human disease caused by bacteria from infected domestic animals or their products and marked by intermittent fever, chills, headache, weakness, and weight loss

un·du·late \-ˌlāt\ *vb* **-lat·ed**; **-lat·ing** [LL *undula* small wave, fr. L *unda* wave] 1 : to have a wavelike motion or appearance 2 : to rise and fall in pitch or volume

un·du·la·tion \ˌən-jə-'lā-shən, ˌən-də-, -dyə-\ *n* 1 : wavy or wavelike motion 2 : pulsation of sound 3 : a wavy appearance or outline — **un·du·la·to·ry** \'ən-jə-lə-ˌtȯr-ē, 'ən-də-, -dyə-\ *adj*

un·du·ly \ˌən-'dü-lē, 'ən-, -'dyü-\ *adv* : in an undue manner : EXCESSIVELY

un·dy·ing \-'dī-iŋ\ *adj* : not dying : IMMORTAL, PERPETUAL

un·earned \-'ərnd\ *adj* : not earned by labor, service, or skill ⟨~ income⟩

un·earth \ˌən-'ərth\ *vb* 1 : to dig up out of or as if out of the earth ⟨~ buried treasure⟩ 2 : to bring to light : DISCOVER ⟨~ a secret⟩

un·earth·ly \-lē\ *adj* 1 : not of or belonging to the earth 2 : SUPERNATURAL, WEIRD; *also* : ABSURD

un·easy \ˌən-'ē-zē\ *adj* 1 : AWKWARD, EMBARRASSED ⟨~ among strangers⟩ 2 : disturbed by pain or worry; *also* : RESTLESS 3 : UNSTABLE ⟨an ~ truce⟩ — **un·eas·i·ly** \-'ē-zə-lē\ *adv* — **un·eas·i·ness** \-'ē-zē-nəs\ *n*

un·em·ployed \ˌən-im-'plȯid\ *adj* : not being used; *also* : having no job

un·em·ploy·ment \-'plȯi-mənt\ *n* 1 : lack of employment 2 : money paid at regular intervals (as by a government agency) to an unemployed person

un·end·ing \ˌən-'en-diŋ\ *adj* : having no ending : ENDLESS

un·equal \ˌən-'ē-kwəl\ *adj* 1 : not alike (as in size, amount, number, or value) 2 : not uniform : VARIABLE 3 : badly balanced or matched 4 : INADEQUATE, INSUFFICIENT ⟨~ to the task⟩ — **un·equal·ly** *adv*

un·equaled *or* **un·equalled** \-kwəld\ *adj* : not equaled : UNPARALLELED ⟨an artist of ~ talent⟩

un·equiv·o·cal \ˌən-i-'kwi-və-kəl\ *adj* : leaving no doubt : CLEAR — **un·equiv·o·cal·ly** *adv*

un·err·ing \ˌən-'er-iŋ, -'ər-\ *adj* : making no errors : CERTAIN, UNFAILING ⟨~ accuracy⟩ — **un·err·ing·ly** *adv*

UNES·CO \yù-'nes-kō\ *abbr* United Nations Educational, Scientific, and Cultural Organization

un·even \ˌən-'ē-vən\ *adj* 1 : ODD 3 2 : not even : not level or smooth : RUGGED, RAGGED 3 : IRREGULAR; *also* : varying in quality — **un·even·ly** *adv* — **un·even·ness** *n*

un·event·ful \ˌən-i-'vent-fəl\ *adj* : lacking interesting or noteworthy incidents — **un·event·ful·ly** *adv*

un·evolved \ˌən-i-'välvd\ *adj* 1 : not fully developed ⟨an ~ wine⟩ 2 : lacking cultural refinement

un·ex·am·pled \ˌən-ig-'zam-pəld\ *adj* : UNPRECEDENTED, UNPARALLELED ⟨fought with ~ passion⟩

un·ex·cep·tion·able \ˌən-ik-'sep-shə-nə-bəl\ *adj* : not open to exception or objection : beyond reproach

un·ex·pect·ed \ˌən-ik-'spek-təd\ *adj* : not expected : UNFORESEEN — **un·ex·pect·ed·ly** *adv*

un·fail·ing \ˌən-'fā-liŋ\ *adj* 1 : not failing, flagging, or waning : CONSTANT 2 : INEXHAUSTIBLE ⟨a subject of ~ interest⟩ 3 : INFALLIBLE, SURE ⟨an ~ test⟩ — **un·fail·ing·ly** *adv*

un·fair \-'fer\ *adj* 1 : marked by injustice, partiality, or deception : UNJUST 2 : not equitable in business dealings — **un·fair·ly** *adv* — **un·fair·ness** *n*

un·faith·ful \ˌən-'fāth-fəl\ *adj* 1 : not observant of vows, allegiance, or duty : DISLOYAL 2 : INACCURATE, UNTRUSTWORTHY ⟨an ~ copy of a document⟩ — **un·faith·ful·ly** *adv* — **un·faith·ful·ness** *n*

un·fa·mil·iar \ˌən-fə-'mil-yər\ *adj* 1 : not well-known : STRANGE ⟨an ~ place⟩ 2 : not well acquainted ⟨~ with the subject⟩ — **un·fa·mil·iar·i·ty** \-ˌmi-lē-'er-, -'yer-\ *n*

un·fas·ten \ˌən-'fa-s°n\ *vb* : to make or become loose : UNDO, DETACH

un·feel·ing \-'fē-liŋ\ *adj* 1 : lacking feeling : INSENSATE 2 : HARDHEARTED, CRUEL — **un·feel·ing·ly** *adv*

un·feigned \-'fānd\ *adj* : not feigned : not hypocritical : GENUINE

un·fet·ter \-'fe-tər\ *vb* 1 : to free from fetters 2 : LIBERATE

un·fil·ial \ˌən-'fi-lē-əl, -'fil-yəl\ *adj* : not observing the obligations of a child to a parent : UNDUTIFUL

un·fin·ished \ˌən-'fi-nisht\ *adj* 1 : not brought to an end 2 : being in a rough or unpolished state

¹un·fit \-'fit\ *adj* : not fit or suitable; *esp* : physically or mentally unsound — **un·fit·ness** *n*

²unfit *vb* : to make unfit : DISQUALIFY

un·fix \-'fiks\ *vb* 1 : to loosen from a fastening : DETACH 2 : UNSETTLE

un·flap·pa·ble \-'fla-pə-bəl\ *adj* : not easily upset or panicked — **un·flap·pa·bly** *adv*

un·fledged \ˌən-'flejd\ *adj* : not feathered or ready for flight; *also* : IMMATURE, CALLOW

un·flinch·ing \-'flin-chiŋ\ *adj* : not flinching or shrinking : STEADFAST — **un·flinch·ing·ly** *adv*

un·fold \-'fōld\ *vb* **1** : to open the folds of : open up **2** : to lay open to view : DISCLOSE **3** : BLOSSOM, DEVELOP

un·for·get·ta·ble \,ən-fər-'ge-tə-bəl\ *adj* : incapable of being forgotten — **un·for·get·ta·bly** \-blē\ *adv*

un·formed \-'fòrmd\ *adj* : not regularly formed or ordered : UNDEVELOPED

un·for·tu·nate \-'fòr-chə-nət\ *adj* **1** : not fortunate : UNLUCKY **2** : attended with misfortune **3** : UNSUITABLE ⟨an ∼ choice of words⟩ — **unfortunate** *n*

un·for·tu·nate·ly \-nət-lē\ *adv* **1** : in an unfortunate manner **2** : it is unfortunate

un·found·ed \,ən-'faùn-dəd\ *adj* : lacking a sound basis : GROUNDLESS

un·freeze \-'frēz\ *vb* **-froze** \-'frōz\; **-fro·zen** \-'frō-z°n\; **-freez·ing** **1** : to cause to thaw **2** : to remove from a freeze ⟨∼ prices⟩

un·fre·quent·ed \,ən-frē-'kwen-təd; ,ən-'frē-kwən-\ *adj* : seldom visited or traveled over

un·friend·ly \,ən-'frend-lē\ *adj* **1** : not friendly or kind : HOSTILE **2** : UNFAVORABLE ⟨∼ to new business⟩ — **un·friend·li·ness** \-lē-nəs\ *n*

un·frock \-'fräk\ *vb* : DEFROCK

un·fruit·ful \-'früt-fəl\ *adj* **1** : not producing fruit or offspring : BARREN **2** : yielding no valuable result : UNPROFITABLE — **un·fruit·ful·ness** *n*

un·furl \-'fərl\ *vb* : to loose from a furled state : UNFOLD

un·gain·ly \-'gān-lē\ *adj* [*un*- + obs. *gainly* proper, becoming, fr. *gain* direct, handy, fr. ME *geyn*, fr. OE *gēn*, fr. ON *gegn* against] : CLUMSY, AWKWARD — **un·gain·li·ness** \-lē-nəs\ *n*

un·gen·er·ous \,ən-'je-nə-rəs\ *adj* : not generous or liberal : STINGY

un·glued \,ən-'glüd\ *adj* : UPSET, DISORDERED

un·god·ly \,ən-'gäd-lē, -'gòd-\ *adj* **1** : IMPIOUS, IRRELIGIOUS **2** : SINFUL, WICKED **3** : OUTRAGEOUS ⟨an ∼ hour⟩ — **un·god·li·ness** \-lē-nəs\ *n*

un·gov·ern·able \-'gə-vər-nə-bəl\ *adj* : not capable of being governed, guided, or restrained : UNRULY

un·gra·cious \-'grā-shəs\ *adj* **1** : not courteous : RUDE **2** : not pleasing : DISAGREEABLE ⟨an ∼ task⟩

un·grate·ful \,ən-'grāt-fəl\ *adj* **1** : not thankful for favors **2** : DISAGREEABLE; *also* : THANKLESS — **un·grate·ful·ly** *adv* — **un·grate·ful·ness** *n*

un·guard·ed \-'gär-dəd\ *adj* **1** : UNPROTECTED **2** : DIRECT, INCAUTIOUS ⟨∼ remarks⟩

un·guent \'əŋ-gwənt, 'ən-\ *n* : a soothing or healing salve : OINTMENT

¹**un·gu·late** \'əŋ-gyə-lət, 'ən-, -,lāt\ *adj* [LL *ungulatus*, fr. L *ungula* hoof, fr. *unguis* nail, hoof] : having hoofs

²**ungulate** *n* : a hoofed mammal (as a cow, horse, or rhinoceros)

un·hal·lowed \,ən-'ha-lōd\ *adj* **1** : not consecrated : UNHOLY **2** : IMPIOUS, PROFANE **3** : contrary to accepted standards : IMMORAL

un·hand \,ən-'hand\ *vb* : to remove the hand from : let go

un·hand·some \-'han-səm\ *adj* **1** : not beautiful or handsome : HOMELY **2** : UNBECOMING **3** : DISCOURTEOUS, RUDE

un·handy \-'han-dē\ *adj* : INCONVENIENT; *also* : AWKWARD

un·hap·py \-'ha-pē\ *adj* **1** : UNLUCKY, UNFORTUNATE ⟨an ∼ coincidence⟩ **2** : SAD, MISERABLE **3** : INAPPROPRIATE ⟨an ∼ choice⟩ — **un·hap·pi·ly** \-'ha-pə-lē\ *adv* — **un·hap·pi·ness** \-pē-nəs\ *n*

un·har·ness \-'här-nəs\ *vb* : to remove the harness from (as a horse)

un·healthy \-'hel-thē\ *adj* **1** : not conducive to health : UNWHOLESOME **2** : SICKLY, DISEASED

un·heard \-'hərd\ *adj* **1** : not heard **2** : not granted a hearing

unheard–of *adj* : previously unknown; *esp* : UNPRECEDENTED ⟨moving at ∼ speeds⟩

un·hinge \,ən-'hinj\ *vb* **1** : to make unstable esp. mentally **2** : to take from the hinges

un·hitch \-'hich\ *vb* : UNFASTEN, LOOSE

un·ho·ly \-'hō-lē\ *adj* **1** : not holy : PROFANE, WICKED **2** : very unpleasant ⟨an ∼ mess⟩ — **un·ho·li·ness** \-lē-nəs\ *n*

un·hook \-'hùk\ *vb* : to loose from a hook

un·horse \-'hòrs\ *vb* : to dislodge from or as if from a horse

uni·cam·er·al \,yü-ni-'ka-mə-rəl\ *adj* : having a single legislative house or chamber

UNI·CEF \'yü-nə-,sef\ *abbr* [*U*nited *N*ations *I*nternational *C*hildren's *E*mergency *F*und, its former name] United Nations Children's Fund

uni·cel·lu·lar \,yü-ni-'sel-yə-lər\ *adj* : having or consisting of a single cell

uni·corn \'yü-nə-,kòrn\ *n* [ME *unicorne*, fr. AF, fr. LL *unicornis*, fr. L, having one horn, fr. *unus* one + *cornu* horn] : a mythical animal with one horn in the middle of the forehead

uni·cy·cle \'yü-ni-,sī-kəl\ *n* : a vehicle that has a single wheel and is usu. propelled by pedals

uni·di·rec·tion·al \,yü-ni-də-'rek-shə-nəl, -dī-\ *adj* : having, moving in, or responsive in a single direction

uni·fi·ca·tion \,yü-nə-fə-'kā-shən\ *n* : the act, process, or result of unifying : the state of being unified

¹**uni·form** \'yü-nə-,fòrm\ *adj* **1** : not varying ⟨∼ procedures⟩ **2** : of the same form with others — **uni·form·ly** *adv*

²**uniform** *vb* : to clothe with a uniform

³**uniform** *n* : distinctive dress worn by members of a particular group (as an army or a police force)

uni·for·mi·ty \,yü-nə-'fòr-mə-tē\ *n, pl* **-ties** : the state of being uniform

uni·fy \'yü-nə-,fī\ *vb* **-fied; -fy·ing** : to make into a coherent whole : UNITE

uni·lat·er·al \,yü-nə-'la-tə-rəl\ *adj* : of, having, affecting, or done by one side only — **uni·lat·er·al·ly** *adv*

un·im·peach·able \,ən-im-'pē-chə-bəl\ *adj* : not liable to accusation : IRREPROACHABLE ⟨an ∼ reputation⟩

un·in·hib·it·ed \,ən-in-'hi-bə-təd\ *adj* : free from inhibition; *also* : boisterously informal — **un·in·hib·it·ed·ly** *adv*

un·in·stall \,ən-in-'stòl\ *vb* : to remove (software) from a computer system

un·in·tel·li·gent \-'te-lə-jənt\ *adj* : lacking intelligence

un·in·tel·li·gi·ble \-jə-bəl\ *adj* : not intelligible : OBSCURE — **un·in·tel·li·gi·bly** \-blē\ *adv*

un·in·ter·est·ed \,ən-'in-trəs-təd, -tə-rəs-, -tə-,res-\ *adj* : not interested : not having the mind or feelings engaged or aroused

un·in·ter·rupt·ed \,ən-,in-tə-'rəp-təd\ *adj* : not interrupted : CONTINUOUS

union \'yün-yən\ *n* **1** : an act or instance of uniting two or more things into one : the state of being so united : COMBINATION, JUNCTION **2** : a uniting in marriage **3** : something formed by a combining of parts or members; *esp* : a confederation of independent individuals (as nations or persons) for some common purpose **4** : an organization of workers (as a labor union or a trade union) formed to advance its members' interests esp. in respect to wages and working conditions **5** : a device emblematic of union used on or as a national flag; *also* : the upper inner corner of a flag **6** : a device for connecting parts (as of a machine); *esp* : a coupling for pipes

unionise *Brit var of* UNIONIZE

union·ism \'yün-yə-,ni-zəm\ *n* **1** : the principle or policy of forming or adhering to a union; *esp, cap* : adherence to the policy of a firm federal union before or during the U.S. Civil War **2** : the principles or system of trade unions — **union·ist** *n*

union·ize \'yün-yə-,nīz\ *vb* **-ized; -iz·ing** : to form into or cause to join a labor union — **union·i·za·tion** \,yün-yə-nə-'zā-shən\ *n*

union jack *n* **1** : a flag consisting of the part of a national flag that signifies union **2** *cap U&J* : the national flag of the United Kingdom

unique \yù-'nēk\ *adj* **1** : being the only one of its kind : SINGLE, SOLE **2** : very unusual : NOTABLE — **unique·ly** *adv* — **unique·ness** *n*

uni·sex \'yü-nə-,seks\ *adj* : not distinguishable as male or female; *also* : suitable or designed for both males and females — **unisex** *n*

uni·sex·u·al \,yü-nə-'sek-shə-wəl\ *adj* **1** : having only male or only female sex organs **2** : UNISEX

uni·son \'yü-nə-sən, -zən\ *n* [ME *unisoun*, fr. MF *unisson*, fr. ML *unisonus* having the same sound, fr. L *unus* one + *sonus* sound] **1** : sameness or identity in musical pitch **2** : the condition of being tuned or sounded at the same pitch or in octaves ⟨sing in ∼⟩ **3** : harmonious agreement or union : ACCORD

unit \'yü-nət\ *n* **1** : the smallest whole number greater than zero : ONE **2** : a definite amount or quantity used as a standard of measurement **3** : a single thing, person, or group that is a constituent of a whole; *also* : a part of a military establishment that has a prescribed organization — **unit** *adj*

Uni·tar·i·an \ˌyü-nə-'ter-ē-ən\ *n* : a member of a religious denomination stressing individual freedom of belief — **Uni·tar·i·an·ism** *n*

uni·tary \'yü-nə-ˌter-ē\ *adj* **1** : of or relating to a unit **2** : not divided — **uni·tar·i·ly** \ˌyü-nə-'ter-ə-lē\ *adv*

unite \yu̇-'nīt\ *vb* **unit·ed; unit·ing** **1** : to put or join together so as to make one : COMBINE, COALESCE **2** : to join by a legal or moral bond; *also* : to join in interest or fellowship **3** : AMALGAMATE, CONSOLIDATE **4** : to act in concert

unit·ed \yu̇-'nī-təd\ *adj* **1** : made one : COMBINED **2** : relating to or produced by joint action **3** : being in agreement : HARMONIOUS

unit·ize \'yü-nə-ˌtīz\ *vb* **-ized; -iz·ing** **1** : to form or convert into a unit **2** : to divide into units

uni·ty \'yü-nə-tē\ *n, pl* **-ties** **1** : the quality or state of being or being made one : ONENESS **2** : a definite quantity or combination of quantities taken as one or for which 1 is made to stand in calculation **3** : CONCORD, ACCORD, HARMONY **4** : continuity without change ⟨~ of purpose⟩ **5** : reference of all the parts of a literary or artistic composition to a single main idea **6** : totality of related parts ♦ **Synonyms** SOLIDARITY, UNION, INTEGRITY

univ *abbr* **1** universal **2** university

uni·valve \'yü-ni-ˌvalv\ *n* : a mollusk having a shell with only one piece; *esp* : GASTROPOD — **univalve** *adj*

uni·ver·sal \ˌyü-nə-'vər-səl\ *adj* **1** : including, covering, or affecting the whole without limit or exception : available or applying to everyone ⟨~ privileges⟩ ⟨a ~ rule⟩ **2** : present or occurring everywhere **3** : used or for use among all ⟨a ~ language⟩ **4** : adaptable for various purposes ⟨a ~ remote control⟩ — **uni·ver·sal·ly** *adv*

uni·ver·sal·i·ty \-ˌvər-'sa-lə-tē\ *n* : the quality or state of being universal

uni·ver·sal·ize \-'vər-sə-ˌlīz\ *vb* **-ized; -iz·ing** : to make universal : GENERALIZE — **uni·ver·sal·i·za·tion** \-ˌvər-sə-lə-'zā-shən\ *n*

universal joint *n* : a shaft coupling for transmitting rotation from one shaft to another not in a straight line with it

universal joint

Universal Product Code *n* : a combination of a bar code and numbers by which a scanner can identify a product and usu. assign a price

uni·verse \'yü-nə-ˌvərs\ *n* [ME, fr. L *universum,* fr. neut. of *universus* entire, whole, fr. *unus* one + *versus* turned toward, fr. pp. of *vertere* to turn] : the whole body of things observed or assumed : COSMOS

uni·ver·si·ty \ˌyü-nə-'vər-sə-tē\ *n, pl* **-ties** : an institution of higher learning authorized to confer degrees in various special fields (as theology, law, and medicine) as well as in the arts and sciences generally

un·just \ˌən-'jəst\ *adj* : characterized by injustice — **un·just·ly** *adv*

un·kempt \-'kempt\ *adj* **1** : lacking order or neatness; *also* : ROUGH, UNPOLISHED **2** : not combed : DISHEVELED

un·kind \-'kīnd\ *adj* : not kind or sympathetic ⟨an ~ remark⟩ — **un·kind·ly** *adv* — **un·kind·ness** *n*

un·kind·ly \-'kīnd-lē\ *adj* : UNKIND — **un·kind·li·ness** *n*

un·know·ing \ˌən-'nō-iŋ\ *adj* : not knowing — **un·know·ing·ly** *adv*

un·known \-'nōn\ *adj* : not known or not well-known — **unknown** *n*

un·lace \ˌən-'lās\ *vb* : to loose by undoing a lace

un·lade \-'lād\ *vb* **-lad·ed; -laded** *or* **-lad·en** \-'lā-d°n\; **-lad·ing** : to take the load or cargo from : UNLOAD

un·latch \-'lach\ *vb* **1** : to open or loose by lifting the latch **2** : to become loosed or opened

un·law·ful \ˌən-'lȯ-fəl\ *adj* **1** : not lawful : ILLEGAL **2** : ILLEGITIMATE — **un·law·ful·ly** *adv*

un·lead·ed \-'le-dəd\ *adj* : not treated or mixed with lead or lead compounds

un·learn \-'lərn\ *vb* : to put out of one's knowledge or memory; *also* : to discard the habit of

un·learned \-'lər-nəd *for 1;* -'lərnd *for 2*\ *adj* **1** : UNEDUCATED, ILLITERATE **2** : not gained by study or training

un·leash \-'lēsh\ *vb* : to free from or as if from a leash : let loose

un·less \ən-'les, 'ən-ˌles\ *conj* : except on condition that ⟨won't go ~ you do⟩

un·let·tered \ˌən-'le-tərd\ *adj* : not educated : ILLITERATE

¹**un·like** \-'līk\ *adj* **1** : not like : DISSIMILAR, DIFFERENT **2** : UNEQUAL — **un·like·ness** *n*

²**unlike** *prep* **1** : different from ⟨she's quite ~ her sister⟩ **2** : unusual for ⟨it's ~ you to be late⟩ **3** : differently from ⟨behaves ~ his brother⟩

un·like·li·hood \ˌən-'līk-klē-ˌhu̇d\ *n* : IMPROBABILITY

un·like·ly \-'līk-klē\ *adj* **1** : not likely : IMPROBABLE **2** : likely to fail

un·lim·ber \ˌən-'lim-bər\ *vb* : to get ready for action

un·list·ed \ˌən-'lis-təd\ *adj* **1** : not appearing on a list; *esp* : not appearing in a telephone book **2** : not listed on a stock exchange

un·load \-'lōd\ *vb* **1** : to take away or off : REMOVE ⟨~ cargo from a hold⟩; *also* : to get rid of **2** : to take a load from ⟨~ the ship⟩; *also* : to relieve or set free : UNBURDEN ⟨~ one's mind of worries⟩ **3** : to draw the charge from ⟨~ed the gun⟩ **4** : to sell in volume

un·lock \-'läk\ *vb* **1** : to open or unfasten through release of a lock **2** : RELEASE ⟨~ a flood of emotions⟩ **3** : DISCLOSE, REVEAL ⟨~ nature's secrets⟩

un·looked–for \-'lu̇kt-ˌfȯr\ *adj* : UNEXPECTED

un·loose \ˌən-'lüs\ *vb* : to relax the strain of : set free; *also* : UNTIE

un·loos·en \-'lü-s°n\ *vb* : UNLOOSE

un·love·ly \-'ləv-lē\ *adj* : having no charm or appeal : not amiable

un·luck·i·ly \-'lə-kə-lē\ *adv* : UNFORTUNATELY

un·lucky \-'lə-kē\ *adj* **1** : UNFORTUNATE, ILL-FATED **2** : likely to bring misfortune : INAUSPICIOUS **3** : REGRETTABLE

un·man \ˌən-'man\ *vb* **1** : to deprive of manly courage **2** : CASTRATE

un·man·ly \-'man-lē\ *adj* : not manly : COWARDLY; *also* : EFFEMINATE

un·man·ner·ly \-'ma-nər-lē\ *adj* : RUDE, IMPOLITE — **unmannerly** *adv*

un·mask \ˌən-'mask\ *vb* **1** : to strip of a mask or a disguise : EXPOSE **2** : to remove one's mask

un·mean·ing \-'mē-niŋ\ *adj* : having no meaning : SENSELESS

un·me·di·at·ed \ˌən-'mē-dē-ˌā-təd\ *adj* : not mediated : not communicated or transformed by an intervening agency

un·meet \-'mēt\ *adj* : not meet or fit : UNSUITABLE, IMPROPER

un·men·tion·able \-'men-chə-nə-bəl\ *adj* : not fit or proper to be talked about ⟨an ~ topic⟩

un·mer·ci·ful \-'mər-si-fəl\ *adj* : not merciful : CRUEL, MERCILESS — **un·mer·ci·ful·ly** *adv*

un·mind·ful \-'mīnd-fəl\ *adj* : not mindful : CARELESS, UNAWARE

un·mis·tak·able \ˌən-mə-'stā-kə-bəl\ *adj* : not capable of being mistaken or misunderstood : CLEAR, OBVIOUS — **un·mis·tak·ably** \-blē\ *adv*

un·mit·i·gat·ed \ˌən-'mi-tə-ˌgā-təd\ *adj* **1** : not softened or lessened **2** : ABSOLUTE, DOWNRIGHT ⟨an ~ liar⟩

un·moor \-'mu̇r\ *vb* : to loose from or as if from moorings

un·mor·al \-'mȯr-əl\ *adj* : having no moral perception or quality : AMORAL — **un·mo·ral·i·ty** \ˌən-mə-'ra-lə-tē\ *n*

un·muz·zle \-'mə-zəl\ *vb* : to remove a muzzle from

un·nat·u·ral \ˌən-'na-chə-rəl\ *adj* : contrary to or acting contrary to nature or natural instincts; *also* : ABNORMAL — **un·nat·u·ral·ly** *adv* — **un·nat·u·ral·ness** *n*

un·nec·es·sar·i·ly \ˌən-ˌne-sə-ˈser-ə-lē\ adv **1** : not by necessity **2** : to an unnecessary degree ⟨~ harsh⟩

un·nerve \ˌən-ˈnərv\ vb : to deprive of courage, strength, or steadiness; also : UPSET

un·num·bered \ˌən-ˈnəm-bərd\ adj : not numbered or counted : INNUMERABLE

un·ob·tru·sive \ˌən-əb-ˈtrü-siv\ adj : not obtrusive or forward : not bold : INCONSPICUOUS — **un·ob·tru·sive·ly** adv

un·oc·cu·pied \ˌən-ˈä-kyə-ˌpīd\ adj **1** : not busy : UNEMPLOYED **2** : not occupied : EMPTY, VACANT

un·or·ga·nized \-ˈȯr-gə-ˌnīzd\ adj **1** : not formed or brought into an integrated or ordered whole **2** : not organized into unions ⟨~ labor⟩

un·pack \ˌən-ˈpak\ vb **1** : to separate and remove things packed **2** : to open and remove the contents of

un·par·al·leled \ˌən-ˈpa-rə-ˌleld\ adj : having no parallel; esp : having no equal or match

un·par·lia·men·ta·ry \ˌən-ˌpär-lə-ˈmen-tə-rē\ adj : contrary to parliamentary practice

un·peg \ˌən-ˈpeg\ vb **1** : to remove a peg from **2** : to unfasten by or as if by removing a peg

un·per·son \ˈən-ˌpər-sⁿn, -ˈpər-\ n : a person who usu. for political or ideological reasons is removed from recognition or consideration

un·pile \ˌən-ˈp(-ə)l\ vb : to take or disentangle from a pile

un·pin \-ˈpin\ vb : to remove a pin from : UNFASTEN

un·pleas·ant \-ˈple-zⁿnt\ adj : not pleasant : DISAGREEABLE — **un·pleas·ant·ly** adv — **un·pleas·ant·ness** n

un·plug \ˌən-ˈpləg\ vb **1** : UNCLOG **2** : to remove (a plug) from a receptacle; also : to disconnect from an electric circuit by removing a plug

un·plumbed \-ˈpləmd\ adj **1** : not tested or measured with a plumb line **2** : not thoroughly explored

un·pop·u·lar \ˌən-ˈpä-pyə-lər\ adj : not popular : looked upon or received unfavorably — **un·pop·u·lar·i·ty** \ˌən-ˌpä-pyə-ˈla-rə-tē\ n

un·prec·e·dent·ed \ˌən-ˈpre-sə-ˌden-təd\ adj : having no precedent : NOVEL

un·pre·ten·tious \ˌən-pri-ˈten-chəs\ adj : not pretentious : MODEST

un·prin·ci·pled \ˌən-ˈprin-sə-pəld\ adj : lacking sound or honorable principles : UNSCRUPULOUS

un·print·able \-ˈprin-tə-bəl\ adj : unfit or too offensive to be printed ⟨~ remarks⟩

un·prof·it·able \ˌən-ˈprä-fə-tə-bəl\ adj : not profitable : USELESS, VAIN

un·pro·tect·ed \ˌən-prə-ˈtek-təd\ adj **1** : lacking protection **2** : performed without measures to prevent pregnancy or sexually transmitted disease ⟨~ sex⟩

un·qual·i·fied \ˌən-ˈkwä-lə-ˌfīd\ adj **1** : not having requisite qualifications **2** : not modified or restricted by reservations : COMPLETE — **un·qual·i·fied·ly** \-ˌfī-əd-lē\ adv

un·ques·tion·able \-ˈkwes-chə-nə-bəl\ adj : not questionable : INDISPUTABLE — **un·ques·tion·ably** \-blē\ adv

un·ques·tion·ing \-chə-niŋ\ adj : not questioning : accepting without examination or hesitation — **un·ques·tion·ing·ly** adv

un·qui·et \-ˈkwī-ət\ adj **1** : not quiet : AGITATED, DISTURBED **2** : physically, emotionally, or mentally restless : UNEASY

un·quote \ˈən-ˌkwōt\ n — used orally to indicate the end of a direct quotation

un·rav·el \ˌən-ˈra-vəl\ vb **1** : to separate the threads of **2** : SOLVE ⟨~ a mystery⟩ **3** : to become unraveled

un·read \-ˈred\ adj **1** : not read; also : left unexamined **2** : lacking the benefits or the experience of reading

un·re·al \-ˈrēl\ adj : lacking in reality, substance, or genuineness — **un·re·al·i·ty** \-ˌpər-rē-ˈa-lə-tē\ n

un·rea·son·able \-ˈrē-zⁿn-ə-bəl\ adj **1** : not governed by or acting according to reason; also : not conformable to reason : ABSURD **2** : exceeding the bounds of reason or moderation — **un·rea·son·able·ness** n — **un·rea·son·ably** adv

un·rea·soned \-ˈrē-zⁿnd\ adj : not based on reason or reasoning ⟨~ fears⟩

un·rea·son·ing \-ˈrē-zⁿn-iŋ\ adj : not using or showing the use of reason as a guide or control

un·re·con·struct·ed \ˌən-ˌrē-kən-ˈstrək-təd\ adj : not reconciled to some political, economic, or social change; esp

: holding stubbornly to a particular belief, view, place, or style

un·reel \ˌən-ˈrēl\ vb **1** : to unwind from or as if from a reel **2** : to perform successfully

un·re·gen·er·ate \ˌən-ri-ˈje-nə-rət\ adj : not regenerated or reformed

un·re·lent·ing \-ˈlen-tiŋ\ adj **1** : not yielding in determination : STERN ⟨~ leader⟩ **2** : not letting up or weakening in vigor or pace : CONSTANT — **un·re·lent·ing·ly** adv

un·re·mit·ting \-ˈmi-tiŋ\ adj : CONSTANT, INCESSANT ⟨~ pain⟩ — **un·re·mit·ting·ly** adv

un·re·quit·ed \ˌən-ri-ˈkwī-təd\ adj : not requited : not reciprocated or returned in kind ⟨~ love⟩

un·re·served \-ˈzərvd\ adj **1** : not limited or partial ⟨~ enthusiasm⟩ **2** : not cautious or reticent : FRANK, OPEN **3** : not set aside for special use — **un·re·serv·ed·ly** \-ˈzər-vəd-lē\ adv

un·rest \ˌən-ˈrest\ n : a disturbed or uneasy state : TURMOIL

un·re·strained \ˌən-ri-ˈstrānd\ adj **1** : IMMODERATE, UNCONTROLLED ⟨~ anger⟩ **2** : SPONTANEOUS

un·re·straint \-ri-ˈstrānt\ n : lack of restraint

un·rid·dle \ˌən-ˈri-dⁿl\ vb : to find the explanation of : SOLVE

un·righ·teous \-ˈrī-chəs\ adj **1** : SINFUL, WICKED **2** : UNJUST — **un·righ·teous·ness** n

un·ripe \-ˈrīp\ adj : not ripe : IMMATURE

un·ri·valed or **un·ri·valled** \ˌən-ˈrī-vəld\ adj : having no rival : SUPREME

un·robe \-ˈrōb\ vb : DISROBE, UNDRESS

un·roll \-ˈrōl\ vb **1** : to unwind a roll of : open out **2** : DISPLAY, DISCLOSE **3** : to become unrolled or spread out

un·roof \-ˈrüf, -ˈru̇f\ vb : to strip off the roof or covering of

un·ruf·fled \ˌən-ˈrə-fəld\ adj **1** : not agitated or upset **2** : not ruffled : SMOOTH ⟨~ water⟩

un·ruly \-ˈrü-lē\ adj [ME unreuly, fr. un- + reuly disciplined, fr. reule rule, fr. AF, fr. L regula straightedge, rule, fr. regere to direct] : not submissive to rule or restraint : TURBULENT ⟨~ passions⟩ — **un·rul·i·ness** \-ˈrü-lē-nəs\ n

un·sad·dle \ˌən-ˈsa-dⁿl\ vb **1** : to remove the saddle from a horse **2** : UNHORSE

un·sat·u·rat·ed \-ˈsa-chə-ˌrā-təd\ adj **1** : capable of absorbing or dissolving more of something **2** : containing double or triple bonds between carbon atoms ⟨~ fat⟩ — **un·sat·u·rate** \-rət\ n

un·saved \ˌən-ˈsāvd\ adj : not saved; esp : not rescued from eternal punishment

un·sa·vory \-ˈsā-və-rē\ adj **1** : TASTELESS **2** : unpleasant to taste or smell **3** : morally offensive ⟨~ characters⟩

un·say \-ˈsā\ vb **-said** \-ˈsed\; **-say·ing** : to take back (something said) : RETRACT, WITHDRAW

un·scathed \-ˈskāt͟hd\ adj : wholly unharmed : not injured

un·schooled \-ˈskül̩d\ adj : not schooled : UNTAUGHT, UNTRAINED

un·sci·en·tif·ic \ˌən-ˌsī-ən-ˈti-fik\ adj : not scientific : not in accord with the principles and methods of science

un·scram·ble \ˌən-ˈskram-bəl\ vb **1** : RESOLVE, CLARIFY **2** : to restore (as a radio message) to intelligible form

un·screw \-ˈskrü\ vb **1** : to draw the screws from **2** : to loosen by turning

un·scru·pu·lous \-ˈskrü-pyə-ləs\ adj : not scrupulous : UNPRINCIPLED — **un·scru·pu·lous·ly** adv — **un·scru·pu·lous·ness** n

un·seal \-ˈsēl\ vb : to break or remove the seal of : OPEN

un·search·able \-ˈsər-chə-bəl\ adj : not capable of being searched or explored ⟨~ forests⟩

un·sea·son·able \-ˈsē-zⁿn-ə-bəl\ adj : not seasonable : happening or coming at the wrong time : UNTIMELY — **un·sea·son·ably** \-blē\ adv

un·seat \-ˈsēt\ vb **1** : to throw from one's seat esp. on horseback **2** : to remove from political office

un·seem·ly \-ˈsēm-lē\ adj : not according with established standards of good form or taste; also : not suitable — **un·seem·li·ness** n

un·seen \ˌən-ˈsēn\ adj : not seen : INVISIBLE ⟨~ dangers⟩

un·seg·re·gat·ed \-ˈse-gri-ˌgā-təd\ adj : not segregated; esp : free from racial segregation

un·self·ish \-ˈsel-fish\ adj : not selfish : GENEROUS — **un·self·ish·ly** adv — **un·self·ish·ness** n

un·set·tle \ˌən-ˈse-tⁿl\ vb : to move or loosen from a settled position : DISPLACE, DISTURB

un·set·tled \-'se-t³ld\ *adj* **1** : not settled : not fixed (as in position or character) **2** : not calm : DISTURBED **3** : not decided in mind : UNRESOLVED **4** : not paid ⟨~ accounts⟩ **5** : not occupied by settlers

un·shack·le \-'sha-kəl\ *vb* : to free from shackles

un·shaped \-'shāpt\ *adj* : not shaped; *esp* : not being in finished, final, or perfect form ⟨~ ideas⟩ ⟨~ timber⟩

un·sheathe \ˌən-'shēth\ *vb* : to draw from or as if from a sheath

un·ship \-'ship\ *vb* **1** : to remove from a ship **2** : to remove or become removed from position ⟨~ an oar⟩

un·shod \ˌən-'shäd\ *adj* : not wearing or provided with shoes

un·sight·ly \ˌən-'sīt-lē\ *adj* : unpleasant to the sight : UGLY ⟨an ~ mess⟩

un·skilled \-'skild\ *adj* **1** : not skilled; *esp* : not skilled in a specified branch of work **2** : not requiring skill

un·skill·ful \-'skil-fəl\ *adj* : lacking in skill or proficiency — **un·skill·ful·ly** *adv*

un·sling \-'sliŋ\ *vb* -**slung** \-'sləŋ\; -**sling·ing** : to remove from being slung

un·snap \-'snap\ *vb* : to loosen or free by or as if by undoing a snap

un·snarl \-'snärl\ *vb* : to remove snarls from : UNTANGLE

un·so·phis·ti·cat·ed \ˌən-sə-'fis-tə-ˌkā-təd\ *adj* **1** : not worldly-wise : lacking sophistication **2** : SIMPLE

un·sought \ˌən-'sȯt\ *adj* : not sought : not searched for or asked for : not obtained by effort ⟨~ honors⟩

un·sound \-'saund\ *adj* **1** : not healthy or whole; *also* : not mentally normal ⟨of ~ mind⟩ **2** : not valid **3** : not firmly made or fixed ⟨structurally ~⟩ — **un·sound·ly** *adv* — **un·sound·ness** *n*

un·spar·ing \-'sper-iŋ\ *adj* **1** : HARD, RUTHLESS ⟨~ criticism⟩ **2** : not frugal : LIBERAL, PROFUSE ⟨~ generosity⟩

un·speak·able \-'spē-kə-bəl\ *adj* **1** : impossible to express in words **2** : extremely bad ⟨~ offenses⟩ — **un·speak·ably** \-blē\ *adv*

un·spool \ˌən-'spül\ *vb* **1** : to unwind from a spool **2** : to present artfully ⟨~ a new film⟩

un·spot·ted \-'spä-təd\ *adj* : not spotted or stained; *esp* : free from moral stain

un·sprung \-'sprəŋ\ *adj* : not sprung; *esp* : not equipped with springs

un·sta·ble \-'stā-bəl\ *adj* **1** : not stable **2** : FICKLE, VACILLATING; *also* : lacking effective emotional control **3** : readily changing (as by decomposing) in chemical or physical composition or in biological activity ⟨an ~ atomic nucleus⟩

un·steady \ˌən-'ste-dē\ *adj* : not steady : UNSTABLE — **un·stead·i·ly** \-'ste-də-lē\ *adv* — **un·stead·i·ness** \-'ste-dē-nəs\ *n*

un·stint·ing \-'stin-tiŋ\ *adj* **1** : not restricting or holding back **2** : giving or being given freely or generously ⟨~ praise⟩

un·stop \-'stäp\ *vb* **1** : UNCLOG **2** : to remove a stopper from

un·stop·pa·ble \ˌən-'stä-pə-bəl\ *adj* : incapable of being stopped

un·strap \-'strap\ *vb* : to remove or loose a strap from

un·stressed \ˌən-'strest\ *adj* : not stressed; *esp* : not bearing a stress or accent ⟨~ syllables⟩

un·strung \-'strəŋ\ *adj* **1** : having the strings loose or detached **2** : made weak, disordered, or unstable

un·stud·ied \-'stə-dēd\ *adj* **1** : not acquired by study **2** : NATURAL, UNFORCED ⟨moved with ~ grace⟩

un·sub·stan·tial \ˌən-səb-'stan-chəl\ *adj* : INSUBSTANTIAL

un·sung \ˌən-'səŋ\ *adj* **1** : not sung **2** : not celebrated in song or verse ⟨~ heroes⟩

un·swerv·ing \ˌən-'swər-viŋ\ *adj* **1** : not swerving or turning aside **2** : STEADY

un·tan·gle \-'taŋ-gəl\ *vb* **1** : DISENTANGLE **2** : to straighten out : RESOLVE ⟨~ a problem⟩

un·taught \-'tȯt\ *adj* **1** : not instructed or taught : IGNORANT **2** : NATURAL, SPONTANEOUS ⟨~ kindness⟩

un·think·able \-'thiŋ-kə-bəl\ *adj* : not to be thought of or considered as possible ⟨~ cruelty⟩

un·think·ing \ˌən-'thiŋ-kiŋ\ *adj* : not thinking; *esp* : THOUGHTLESS, HEEDLESS — **un·think·ing·ly** *adv*

un·thought \ˌən-'thȯt\ *adj* : not anticipated : UNEXPECTED — often used with *of* ⟨*unthought*-of development⟩

un·tie \-'tī\ *vb* -**tied**; -**ty·ing** *or* -**tie·ing** **1** : to free from

something that ties, fastens, or restrains : UNBIND **2** : DISENTANGLE, RESOLVE **3** : to become loosened or unbound

un·til \ˌən-'til\ *prep* : up to the time of ⟨worked ~ 5 o'-clock⟩

²**until** *conj* **1** : up to the time that ⟨wait ~ he calls⟩ **2** : to the point or degree that ⟨ran ~ she was breathless⟩

¹**un·time·ly** \ˌən-'tīm-lē\ *adv* : at an inopportune time : UNSEASONABLY; *also* : PREMATURELY

²**untimely** *adj* : PREMATURE ⟨~ death⟩; *also* : INOPPORTUNE, UNSEASONABLE

un·tir·ing \ˌən-'tī-riŋ\ *adj* : not becoming tired : INDEFATIGABLE ⟨an ~ worker⟩ — **un·tir·ing·ly** *adv*

un·to \'ən-ˌtü\ *prep* : TO

un·told \ˌən-'tōld\ *adj* **1** : too great or numerous to count **2** : not told : not revealed

¹**un·touch·able** \ˌən-'tə-chə-bəl\ *adj* : forbidden to the touch

²**untouchable** *n* : a member of the lowest social class in India having in traditional Hindu belief the quality of defiling by contact a member of a higher caste

un·touched \ˌən-'təcht\ *adj* **1** : not subjected to touching **2** : not described or dealt with **3** : not tasted **4** : being in a primeval state or condition **5** : UNAFFECTED ⟨~ by scandals⟩

un·to·ward \ˌən-'tord, -'tō-ərd; ˌən-tə-'word\ *adj* **1** : difficult to manage : STUBBORN, WILLFUL ⟨an ~ child⟩ **2** : INCONVENIENT, TROUBLESOME ⟨an ~ encounter⟩

un·tried \ˌən-'trīd\ *adj* : not tested or proved by experience or trial; *also* : not tried in court

un·true \-'trü\ *adj* **1** : not faithful : DISLOYAL **2** : not according with a standard of correctness **3** : FALSE

un·truth \ˌən-'trüth, 'ən-ˌtrüth\ *n* **1** : lack of truthfulness **2** : FALSEHOOD

un·tune \-'tün, -'tyün\ *vb* **1** : to put out of tune **2** : DISARRANGE, DISCOMPOSE

un·tu·tored \-'tü-tərd, -'tyü-\ *adj* : UNTAUGHT, UNLEARNED, IGNORANT

un·twine \-'twīn\ *vb* : UNWIND, DISENTANGLE

un·twist \ˌən-'twist\ *vb* **1** : to separate the twisted parts of : UNTWINE **2** : to become untwined

un·used \-'yüst, -'yüzd *for 1*; -'yüzd *for 2*\ *adj* **1** : UNACCUSTOMED ⟨~ to such treatment⟩ **2** : not used

un·usu·al \-'yü-zhə-wəl\ *adj* : not usual : UNCOMMON, RARE — **un·usu·al·ly** *adv*

un·ut·ter·able \ˌən-'ə-tə-rə-bəl\ *adj* : being beyond the powers of description : INEXPRESSIBLE ⟨~ shame⟩ — **un·ut·ter·ably** \-blē\ *adv*

un·var·nished \-'vär-nisht\ *adj* **1** : not varnished **2** : not embellished : PLAIN ⟨the ~ truth⟩

un·veil \ˌən-'vāl\ *vb* **1** : to remove a veil or covering from : DISCLOSE **2** : to remove a veil : reveal oneself

un·voiced \-'vȯist\ *adj* **1** : not verbally expressed : UNSPOKEN **2** : VOICELESS 2

un·war·rant·able \-'wȯr-ən-tə-bəl\ *adj* : not justifiable : INEXCUSABLE — **un·war·rant·ably** \-blē\ *adv*

un·weave \-'wēv\ *vb* -**wove** \-'wōv\; -**wo·ven** \-'wō-vən\; -**weav·ing** : DISENTANGLE, RAVEL

un·well \ˌən-'wel\ *adj* : SICK, AILING

un·whole·some \-'hōl-səm\ *adj* **1** : harmful to physical, mental, or moral well-being ⟨~ food⟩ **2** : CORRUPT, UNSOUND ⟨~ deals⟩; *also* : offensive to the senses : LOATHSOME ⟨an ~ stench⟩

un·wieldy \ˌən-'wēl-dē\ *adj* : not easily managed, handled, or used (as because of bulk, weight, or complexity) : AWKWARD ⟨an ~ tool⟩

un·wind \-'wīnd\ *vb* -**wound** \-'waund\; -**wind·ing** **1** : to undo something that is wound : loose from coils **2** : to become unwound : be capable of being unwound **3** : RELAX

un·wise \ˌən-'wīz\ *adj* : not wise : FOOLISH — **un·wise·ly** *adv*

un·wit·ting \-'wi-tiŋ\ *adj* **1** : not knowing : UNAWARE **2** : not intended : INADVERTENT ⟨~ mistake⟩ — **un·wit·ting·ly** *adv*

un·wont·ed \-'wȯn-təd, -'wōn-\ *adj* **1** : RARE, UNUSUAL **2** : not accustomed by experience — **un·wont·ed·ly** *adv*

un·world·ly \-'wərld-lē\ *adj* **1** : not of this world; *esp* : SPIRITUAL **2** : NAIVE **3** : not swayed by worldly considerations — **un·world·li·ness** \-lē-nəs\ *n*

un·wor·thy \ˌən-'wər-thē\ *adj* **1** : BASE, DISHONORABLE **2** : not meritorious : not worthy : UNDESERVING **3** : not deserved : UNMERITED ⟨~ treatment⟩ — **un·wor·thi·ly** \-thə-lē\ *adv* — **un·wor·thi·ness** \-thē-nəs\ *n*

un·wrap \-'rap\ *vb* : to remove the wrapping from : DIS-CLOSE

un·writ·ten \-'ri-t³n\ *adj* **1** : not in writing : ORAL, TRADI-TIONAL ⟨an ~ law⟩ **2** : containing no writing : BLANK

un·yield·ing \ˌən-'yēl-diŋ\ *adj* **1** : characterized by lack of softness or flexibility **2** : characterized by firmness or obduracy

un·yoke \-'yōk\ *vb* : to remove a yoke from; *also* : SEPA-RATE, DISCONNECT

un·zip \-'zip\ *vb* : to zip open : open by means of a zipper

¹up \'əp\ *adv* **1** : in or to a higher position or level; *esp* : away from the center of the earth **2** : from beneath a surface (as ground or water) **3** : from below the hori-zon **4** : in or into an upright position; *esp* : out of bed **5** : with greater intensity ⟨speak ~⟩ **6** : to or at a greater rate or amount ⟨prices went ~⟩ **7** : in or into a better or more advanced state or a state of greater intensity or ac-tivity ⟨stir ~ a fire⟩ **8** : into existence, evidence, or knowledge ⟨the missing book turned ~⟩ **9** : into con-sideration ⟨brought the matter ~⟩ **10** : to or at bat **11** : into possession or custody ⟨gave himself ~⟩ **12** : EN-TIRELY, COMPLETELY ⟨eat it ~⟩ **13** — used for empha-sis ⟨clean ~ a room⟩ **14** : ASIDE, BY ⟨lay ~ supplies⟩ **15** : so as to arrive or approach ⟨ran ~ the path⟩ **16** : in a direction opposite to down **17** : in or into parts ⟨tear ~ paper⟩ **18** : to a stop ⟨pull ~ at the curb⟩ **19** : for each side ⟨the score was 15 ~⟩

²up *adj* **1** : risen above the horizon ⟨the sun is ~⟩ **2** : being out of bed ⟨~ by 6 o'clock⟩ **3** : relatively high ⟨prices are ~⟩ **4** : RAISED, LIFTED ⟨windows are ~⟩ **5** : BUILT, CONSTRUCTED ⟨the house is ~⟩ **6** : grown above a surface ⟨the corn is ~⟩ **7** : moving, inclining, or directed upward **8** : marked by agitation, excitement, or activity **9** : READY; *esp* : highly prepared **10** : going on : taking place ⟨find out what is ~⟩ **11** : EXPIRED, ENDED ⟨the time is ~⟩ **12** : extensively aware or in-formed ⟨~ on the news⟩ **13** : being ahead or in advance of an opponent ⟨one hole ~ in a match⟩ **14** : presented for or being under consideration ⟨~ for promotion⟩ **15** : charged before a court ⟨~ for robbery⟩

³up *prep* **1** : to, toward, or at a higher point of ⟨~ a lad-der⟩ **2** : to or toward the source of ⟨~ the river⟩ **3** : to or toward the northern part of ⟨~ the coast⟩ **4** : to or toward the interior of ⟨traveling ~ the country⟩ **5** : ALONG ⟨walk ~ the street⟩

⁴up *n* **1** : an upward course or slope **2** : a period or state of prosperity or success ⟨he had his ~s and downs⟩ **3** : a quark with a charge of +⅔ that is one of the constituents of the proton and neutron

⁵up *vb* **upped** \'əpt\ *or in 2* **up**; **upped**; **up·ping**; **ups** *or in 2* **up** **1** : to rise from a lying or sitting position **2** : to act abruptly or surprisingly ⟨she *upped* and left home⟩ **3** : to move or cause to move upward ⟨*upped* the prices⟩

Upa·ni·shad \ü-'pän-i-ˌshäd\ *n* : one of a set of Vedic philosophical treatises

¹up·beat \'əp-ˌbēt\ *n* : an unaccented beat in a musical measure; *esp* : the last beat of the measure

²upbeat *adj* : OPTIMISTIC, CHEERFUL

up·braid \ˌəp-'brād\ *vb* : to criticize, reproach, or scold se-verely

up·bring·ing \'əp-ˌbriŋ-iŋ\ *n* : the process of bringing up and training

UPC *abbr* Universal Product Code

up·chuck \'əp-ˌchək\ *vb* : VOMIT

up·com·ing \'əp-ˌkə-miŋ\ *adj* : FORTHCOMING, AP-PROACHING ⟨the ~ election⟩

up·coun·try \'əp-ˌkən-trē\ *adj* : of or relating to the interi-or of a country or a region — **up·country** \'əp-'kən-\ *adv*

up·date \ˌəp-'dāt\ *vb* : to bring up to date — **update** \'əp-ˌdāt\ *n*

up·draft \'əp-ˌdraft, -ˌdräft\ *n* : an upward movement of gas (as air)

up·end \ˌəp-'end\ *vb* : to set, stand, or rise on end; *also* : OVERTURN

up–front \'əp-ˌfrənt, ˌəp-'frənt\ *adj* **1** : HONEST, CANDID ⟨an ~ answer⟩ **2** : ADVANCE ⟨~ payment⟩

up front *adv* : in advance ⟨paid *up front*⟩

¹up·grade \'əp-ˌgrād\ *n* **1** : an upward grade or slope **2** : INCREASE, RISE

²up·grade \'əp-ˌgrād, ˌəp-'grād\ *vb* **1** : to raise to a higher grade or position; *esp* : to advance to a job requiring a higher level of skill **2** : to improve or replace (as soft-ware or a device) for increased usefulness

up·growth \'əp-ˌgrōth\ *n* : the process of growing upward : DEVELOPMENT; *also* : a product or result of this

up·heav·al \ˌəp-'hē-vəl\ *n* **1** : the action or an instance of uplifting esp. of part of the earth's crust **2** : a violent ag-itation or change

¹up·hill \'əp-'hil\ *adv* : upward on a hill or incline; *also* : against difficulties

²up·hill \-ˌhil\ *adj* **1** : situated on elevated ground **2** : AS-CENDING **3** : DIFFICULT, LABORIOUS ⟨an ~ struggle⟩

up·hold \ˌəp-'hōld\ *vb* **-held** \-'held\; **-hold·ing** **1** : to give support to **2** : to support against an opponent **3** : to keep elevated — **up·hold·er** *n*

up·hol·ster \ˌəp-'hōl-stər\ *vb* : to furnish with or as if with upholstery — **up·hol·ster·er** *n*

up·hol·stery \-stə-rē\ *n, pl* **-ster·ies** [ME *upholdester* up-holsterer, fr. *upholden* to uphold, fr. *up* + *holden* to hold] : materials (as fabrics, padding, and springs) used to make a soft covering esp. for a seat

UPI *abbr* United Press International

up·keep \'əp-ˌkēp\ *n* : the act or cost of keeping up or maintaining; *also* : the state of being maintained

up·land \'əp-lənd, -ˌland\ *n* : high land esp. at some dis-tance from the sea — **upland** *adj*

¹up·lift \ˌəp-'lift\ *vb* **1** : to lift or raise up : ELEVATE **2** : to improve the condition of esp. morally, socially, or intel-lectually

²up·lift \'əp-ˌlift\ *n* **1** : a lifting up; *esp* : an upheaval of the earth's surface **2** : moral or social improvement ⟨spiritu-al ~⟩; *also* : a movement to make such improvement

up·mar·ket \ˌəp-'mär-kət\ *adj* : appealing to wealthy con-sumers

up·most \'əp-ˌmōst\ *adj* : UPPERMOST

up·on \ə-'pȯn, -'pän\ *prep* : ON

¹up·per \'ə-pər\ *adj* **1** : higher in physical position, rank, or order ⟨~ management⟩ **2** : constituting the smaller and more restricted branch of a bicameral legislature **3** *cap* : being a later part or formation of a specific geolog-ical period **4** : being toward the interior ⟨the ~ Ama-zon⟩ **5** : NORTHERN ⟨~ Minnesota⟩

²upper *n* : one that is upper; *esp* : the parts of a shoe or boot above the sole

up·per·case \ˌə-pər-'kās\ *adj* : CAPITAL 1 — **uppercase** *n*

upper class *n* : a social class occupying a position above the middle class and having the highest status in a society — **upper–class** *adj*

up·per·class·man \ˌə-pər-'klas-mən\ *n* : a junior or senior in a college or high school

upper crust *n* : the highest social class or group; *esp* : the highest circle of the upper class

up·per·cut \'ə-pər-ˌkət\ *n* : a short swinging punch deliv-ered (as in boxing) in an upward direction usu. with a bent arm

upper hand *n* : MASTERY, ADVANTAGE

up·per·most \'ə-pər-ˌmōst\ *adv* : in or into the highest or most prominent position — **uppermost** *adj*

up·pish \'ə-pish\ *adj* : UPPITY

up·pi·ty \'ə-pə-tē\ *adj* : ARROGANT, PRESUMPTUOUS

up·raise \ˌəp-'rāz\ *vb* : to lift up : ELEVATE

¹up·right \'əp-ˌrīt\ *adj* **1** : PERPENDICULAR, VERTICAL **2** : erect in carriage or posture **3** : morally correct : JUST — **upright** *adv* — **up·right·ly** *adv* — **up·right·ness** *n*

²upright *n* **1** : the state of being upright : a vertical posi-tion **2** : something that stands upright

upright piano *n* : a piano whose strings run vertically

upright piano

up·ris·ing \ˈəp-ˌrī-ziŋ\ *n* : INSURRECTION, REVOLT, REBELLION

up·riv·er \ˈəp-ˈri-vər\ *adv or adj* : toward or at a point nearer the source of a river

up·roar \ˈəp-ˌrȯr\ *n* [D *oproer*, fr. MD, fr. *op* up + *roer* motion] : a state of commotion, excitement, or violent disturbance

up·roar·i·ous \ˌəp-ˈrȯr-ē-əs\ *adj* 1 : marked by uproar 2 : extremely funny — **up·roar·i·ous·ly** *adv*

up·root \ˌəp-ˈrüt, -ˈrut\ *vb* 1 : to remove by or as if by pulling up by the roots 2 : DISPLACE 1 ⟨families were ∼ed⟩

¹up·set \ˌəp-ˈset\ *vb* **-set; -set·ting** 1 : to force or be forced out of the usual upright, level, or proper position 2 : to disturb emotionally : WORRY; *also* : to make somewhat ill 3 : UNSETTLE, DISARRANGE 4 : to defeat unexpectedly

²up·set \ˈəp-ˌset\ *n* 1 : an upsetting or being upset; *esp* : a minor illness 2 : a derangement of plans or ideas 3 : an unexpected defeat

³up·set \(ˌ)əp-ˈset\ *adj* : emotionally disturbed or agitated

up·shot \ˈəp-ˌshät\ *n* : the final result

¹up·side \ˈəp-ˌsīd\ *n* 1 : the upper side 2 : a positive aspect 3 : PROMISE ⟨rookies with much ∼⟩

²up·side \ˌəp-ˈsīd\ *prep* : up on or against the side of ⟨knocked him ∼ the head⟩

up·side down \ˌəp-ˌsīd-ˈdaun\ *adv* 1 : with the upper and the lower parts reversed in position 2 : in or into confusion or disorder — **upside–down** *adj*

up·si·lon \ˈüp-sə-ˌlän, ˈyüp-, ˈəp-\ *n* : the 20th letter of the Greek alphabet — Y or υ

¹up·stage \ˈəp-ˈstāj\ *adv or adj* : toward or at the rear of a theatrical stage

²up·stage \ˌəp-ˈstāj\ *vb* : to draw attention away from (as an actor)

¹up·stairs \ˌəp-ˈsterz\ *adv* 1 : up the stairs : to or on a higher floor 2 : to or at a higher position

²up·stairs \ˈəp-ˈsterz\ *adj* : situated above the stairs esp. on an upper floor ⟨∼ bedroom⟩

³up·stairs \ˈəp-ˈsterz, ˈəp-ˌsterz\ *n sing or pl* : the part of a building above the ground floor

up·stand·ing \ˌəp-ˈstan-diŋ, ˈəp-\ *adj* 1 : ERECT 2 : STRAIGHTFORWARD, HONEST

¹up·start \ˌəp-ˈstärt\ *vb* : to jump up suddenly

²up·start \ˈəp-ˌstärt\ *n* : one that has risen suddenly; *esp* : one that claims more personal importance than is warranted — **up·start** \-ˈstärt\ *adj*

up·state \ˈəp-ˈstāt\ *adj* : of, relating to, or characteristic of a part of a state away from a large city and esp. to the north — **upstate** *adv* — **upstate** *n*

up·stream \ˈəp-ˈstrēm\ *adv* : at or toward the source of a stream — **upstream** *adj*

up·stroke \ˈəp-ˌstrōk\ *n* : an upward stroke (as of a pen)

up·surge \-ˌsərj\ *n* : a rapid or sudden rise ⟨an ∼ in interest⟩

up·swept \ˈəp-ˌswept\ *adj* : swept upward ⟨∼ hairdo⟩

up·swing \ˈəp-ˌswiŋ\ *n* : an upward swing; *esp* : a marked increase or rise (as in activity)

up·take \ˈəp-ˌtāk\ *n* 1 : UNDERSTANDING, COMPREHENSION ⟨quick on the ∼⟩ 2 : an act or instance of absorbing and incorporating esp. into a living organism, tissue, or cell

up·thrust \ˈəp-ˌthrəst\ *n* : an upward thrust (as of the earth's crust) — **upthrust** *vb*

up·tight \ˈəp-ˈtīt\ *adj* 1 : TENSE, NERVOUS, UNEASY; *also* : ANGRY, INDIGNANT 2 : rigidly conventional

up–to–date *adj* 1 : extending up to the present time 2 : abreast of the times : MODERN — **up–to–date·ness** *n*

up·town \ˈəp-ˌtaun\ *n* : the upper part of a town or city; *esp* : the residential district — **up·town** \ˈəp-ˈtaun\ *adj or adv*

¹up·turn \ˈəp-ˌtərn, ˌəp-ˈtərn\ *vb* 1 : to turn (as earth) up or over 2 : to turn or direct upward

²up·turn \ˈəp-ˌtərn\ *n* : an upward turn esp. toward better conditions or higher prices

¹up·ward \ˈəp-wərd\ *or* **up·wards** \-wərdz\ *adv* 1 : in a direction from lower to higher 2 : toward a higher or better condition 3 : toward a greater amount or higher number, degree, or rate

²upward *adj* : directed or moving toward or situated in a higher place or level : ASCENDING — **up·ward·ly** *adv*

upwards of *also* **upward of** *adv* : more than : in excess of ⟨they cost *upwards of* $25 each⟩

up·well \ˌəp-ˈwel\ *vb* : to move or flow upward

up·well·ing \-ˈwe-liŋ\ *n* : a rising or an appearance of rising to the surface and flowing outward; *esp* : the movement of deep cold usu. nutrient-rich ocean water to the surface

up·wind \ˈəp-ˈwind\ *adv or adj* : in the direction from which the wind is blowing

ura·cil \ˈyur-ə-ˌsil\ *n* : a pyrimidine base that is one of the four bases coding genetic information in the molecular chain of RNA

ura·ni·um \yu-ˈrā-nē-əm\ *n* : a silvery heavy radioactive metallic chemical element used as a source of atomic energy

Ura·nus \ˈyur-ə-nəs, yu-ˈrā-\ *n* [LL, the sky personified as a god, fr. Gk *Ouranos*, fr. *ouranos* sky, heaven] : the planet 7th in order from the sun — see PLANET table

ur·ban \ˈər-bən\ *adj* : of, relating to, characteristic of, or constituting a city

ur·bane \ˌər-ˈbān\ *adj* [L *urbanus* urban, urbane, fr. *urbs* city] : very polite and polished in manner : SUAVE

ur·ban·ite \ˈər-bə-ˌnīt\ *n* : a person who lives in a city

ur·ban·i·ty \ˌər-ˈba-nə-tē\ *n, pl* **-ties** : the quality or state of being urbane

ur·ban·ize \ˈər-bə-ˌnīz\ *vb* **-ized; -iz·ing** : to cause to take on urban characteristics — **ur·ban·i·za·tion** \ˌər-bə-nə-ˈzā-shən\ *n*

ur·chin \ˈər-chən\ *n* [ME, hedgehog, fr. AF *heriçun*, *hirechoun*, ultim. fr. L *ericius*] : a pert or mischievous youngster

Ur·du \ˈur-dü, ˈər-\ *n* [Hindi & Urdu *urdū*, fr. Pers *zabān-e-urdū-e-muallā* language of the Exalted Comp (the imperial bazaar in Delhi)] : an Indo-Aryan language that is the official language of Pakistan and that is widely used by Muslims in urban areas of India

urea \yu-ˈrē-ə\ *n* : a soluble nitrogenous compound that is the chief solid constituent of mammalian urine

ure·mia \yu-ˈrē-mē-ə\ *n* : accumulation in the blood of materials normally passed off in the urine resulting in a poisoned condition — **ure·mic** \-mik\ *adj*

ure·ter \ˈyur-ə-tər\ *n* : a duct that carries the urine from a kidney to the bladder

ure·thra \yu-ˈrē-thrə\ *n, pl* **-thras** *or* **-thrae** \-(ˌ)thrē\ : the canal that in most mammals carries off the urine from the bladder and in the male also serves to carry semen from the body — **ure·thral** \-thrəl\ *adj*

ure·thri·tis \ˌyur-i-ˈthrī-təs\ *n* : inflammation of the urethra

¹urge \ˈərj\ *vb* **urged; urg·ing** 1 : to present, advocate, or demand earnestly 2 : to try to persuade or sway ⟨∼ a guest to stay⟩ 3 : to serve as a motive or reason for 4 : to impress or impel to some course or activity ⟨the dog *urged* the sheep onward⟩

²urge *n* 1 : the act or process of urging 2 : a force or impulse that urges or drives

ur·gent \ˈər-jənt\ *adj* 1 : calling for immediate attention : PRESSING 2 : urging insistently — **ur·gen·cy** \-jən-sē\ *n* — **ur·gent·ly** *adv*

uric \ˈyur-ik\ *adj* : of, relating to, or found in urine

uric acid *n* : a nearly insoluble acid that is the chief nitrogenous excretory product of birds but is present in only small amounts in mammalian urine

uri·nal \ˈyur-ə-nᵊl\ *n* 1 : a receptacle for urine 2 : a place for urinating

uri·nal·y·sis \ˌyur-ə-ˈna-lə-səs\ *n* : chemical analysis of urine

uri·nary \ˈyur-ə-ˌner-ē\ *adj* 1 : relating to, occurring in, or being organs for the formation and discharge of urine 2 : of, relating to, or for urine

urinary bladder *n* : a membranous sac in many vertebrates that serves for the temporary retention of urine and discharges by the urethra

uri·nate \ˈyur-ə-ˌnāt\ *vb* **-nat·ed; -nat·ing** : to release or give off urine — **uri·na·tion** \ˌyur-ə-ˈnā-shən\ *n*

urine \ˈyur-ən\ *n* : a waste material from the kidneys that is usu. a yellowish watery liquid in mammals but is semisolid in birds and reptiles

URL \ˌyü-(ˌ)är-ˈel, ˈər(-ə)l\ *n* [*uniform (or universal) resource locator*] : a series of usu. alphanumeric characters that specifies the storage location of a resource on the Internet

urn \\'ərn\\ *n* **1** : a vessel that typically has the form of a vase on a pedestal and often is used to hold the ashes of the dead **2** : a closed vessel usu. with a spout for serving a hot beverage

uro·gen·i·tal \\,yùr-ō-'je-nə-t³l\\ *adj* : of, relating to, or being the excretory and reproductive organs or functions

urol·o·gy \\yù-'rä-lə-jē\\ *n* : a branch of medical science dealing with the urinary or urogenital tract and its disorders — **uro·log·i·cal** \\,yùr-ə-'lä-ji-kəl\\ *also* **uro·log·ic** \\-jik\\ *adj* — **urol·o·gist** \\yù-'rä-lə-jist\\ *n*

Ur·sa Ma·jor \\,ər-sə-'mā-jər\\ *n* [L, lit., greater bear] : the northern constellation that contains the stars which form the Big Dipper

Ursa Mi·nor \\-'mī-nər\\ *n* [L, lit., lesser bear] : the constellation including the north pole of the heavens and the stars that form the Little Dipper with the North Star at the tip of the handle

ur·sine \\'ər-,sīn\\ *adj* : of, relating to, or resembling a bear

ur·ti·car·ia \\,ər-tə-'ker-ē-ə\\ *n* [NL, fr. L *urtica* nettle] : HIVES

us \\'əs\\ *pron, objective case of* WE

US *abbr* United States

USA *abbr* **1** United States Army **2** United States of America

us·able *also* **use·able** \\'yü-zə-bəl\\ *adj* : suitable or fit for use — **us·abil·i·ty** \\,yü-zə-'bi-lə-tē\\ *n*

USAF *abbr* United States Air Force

us·age \\'yü-sij, -zij\\ *n* **1** : habitual or customary practice or procedure **2** : the way in which words and phrases are actually used **3** : the action or mode of using **4** : manner of treating

USB \\,yü-(,)es-'bē\\ *n* [*universal serial bus*] : a standardized computer interface for attaching peripherals

USCG *abbr* United States Coast Guard

USDA *abbr* United States Department of Agriculture

¹use \\'yüs\\ *n* **1** : the act or practice of using or employing something : EMPLOYMENT, APPLICATION **2** : the fact or state of being used **3** : the way of using **4** : USAGE, CUSTOM **5** : the privilege or benefit of using something **6** : the ability or power to use something (as a limb) **7** : the legal enjoyment of property that consists in its employment, occupation, or exercise; *also* : the benefit or profit esp. from property held in trust **8** : USEFULNESS, UTILITY; *also* : the end served : OBJECT, FUNCTION **9** : something useful or beneficial ⟨it's no ~ arguing⟩ **10** : the occasion or need to employ ⟨he had no more ~ for it⟩ **11** : ESTEEM, LIKING ⟨had no ~ for modern art⟩

²use \\'yüz\\ *vb* **used** \\'yüzd\\; *"used to" usu* 'yüs-tə\\; **us·ing** **1** : to put into action or service : EMPLOY **2** : to consume or take (as drugs) regularly **3** : UTILIZE ⟨~ tact⟩; *also* : MANIPULATE ⟨*used* his friends to get ahead⟩ **4** : to expend or consume by putting to use **5** : to behave toward : TREAT ⟨*used* the horse cruelly⟩ **6** : to benefit from ⟨house could ~ a coat of paint⟩ **7** — used in the past with *to* to indicate a former practice, fact, or state ⟨we *used* to work harder⟩ — **us·er** *n*

used \\'yüzd\\ *adj* **1** : having been used by another : SECONDHAND ⟨~ cars⟩ **2** : ACCUSTOMED, HABITUATED ⟨~ to the heat⟩

use·ful \\'yüs-fəl\\ *adj* : capable of being put to use : ADVANTAGEOUS; *esp* : serviceable for a beneficial end — **use·ful·ly** *adv* — **use·ful·ness** *n*

use·less \\-ləs\\ *adj* : having or being of no use : WORTHLESS, INEFFECTUAL — **use·less·ly** *adv* — **use·less·ness** *n*

USES *abbr* United States Employment Service

use up *vb* : to consume completely

¹ush·er \\'ə-shər\\ *n* [ME *ussher*, fr. AF *ussier, usscher*, fr. VL *ustiarius* doorkeeper, fr. L *ostium, ustium* door, mouth of a river] **1** : an officer who walks before a person of rank **2** : one who escorts people to their seats (as in a church or theater)

²usher *vb* **1** : to conduct to a place **2** : to precede as an usher, forerunner, or harbinger **3** : INAUGURATE, INTRODUCE ⟨~ in a new era⟩

ush·er·ette \\,ə-shə-'ret\\ *n* : a girl or woman who is an usher (as in a theater)

USIA *abbr* United States Information Agency

USMC *abbr* United States Marine Corps

USN *abbr* United States Navy

USO *abbr* United Service Organizations

USP *abbr* United States Pharmacopeia

USPS *abbr* United States Postal Service

USS *abbr* United States ship

USSR *abbr* Union of Soviet Socialist Republics

usu *abbr* usual; usually

usu·al \\'yü-zhə-wəl\\ *adj* **1** : accordant with usage, custom, or habit : NORMAL **2** : commonly or ordinarily used **3** : ORDINARY ✦ *Synonyms* CUSTOMARY, HABITUAL, ACCUSTOMED, ROUTINE — **usu·al·ly** \\'yü-zhə-wə-lē, 'yü-zhə-lē\\ *adv*

usu·fruct \\'yü-zə-,frəkt\\ *n* [L *ususfructus*, fr. *usus et fructus* use and enjoyment] : the legal right to use and enjoy the benefits and profits of something belonging to another

usu·rer \\'yü-zhər-ər\\ *n* : one that lends money esp. at an exorbitant rate

usu·ri·ous \\yù-'zhùr-ē-əs\\ *adj* : practicing, involving, or constituting usury ⟨a ~ rate of interest⟩

usurp \\yù-'sərp, -'zərp\\ *vb* [ME, fr. AF *usorper*, fr. L *usurpare*, to take possession of without legal claim, fr. *usu* (abl. of *usus* use) + *rapere* to seize] : to seize and hold by force or without right ⟨~ a throne⟩ — **usur·pa·tion** \\,yü-sər-'pā-shən, -zər-\\ *n* — **usurp·er** \\yù-'sər-pər, -'zər-\\ *n*

usu·ry \\'yü-zhə-rē\\ *n, pl* **-ries** **1** : the lending of money with an interest charge for its use **2** : an excessive rate or amount of interest charged; *esp* : interest above an established legal rate

UT *abbr* Utah

Ute \\'yüt\\ *n, pl* **Ute** *or* **Utes** : a member of an American Indian people orig. ranging through Utah, Colorado, Arizona, and New Mexico

uten·sil \\yù-'ten-səl\\ *n* [ME, vessels for domestic use, fr. MF *utensile*, fr. L *utensilia*, fr. neut. pl. of *utensilis* useful, fr. *uti* to use] **1** : an instrument or vessel used in a household and esp. a kitchen **2** : a useful tool

uter·us \\'yü-tə-rəs\\ *n, pl* **uter·us·es** *or* **uteri** \\'yü-tə-,rī\\ : the muscular organ of a female mammal in which the young develop before birth — **uter·ine** \\-,rīn, -rən\\ *adj*

utile \\'yüt-³l, 'yü-,tī(-ə)l\\ *adj* : USEFUL

uti·lise *Brit var of* UTILIZE

¹util·i·tar·i·an \\yù-,ti-lə-'ter-ē-ən\\ *n* : a person who believes in utilitarianism

²utilitarian *adj* **1** : of or relating to utilitarianism **2** : of or relating to utility : aiming at usefulness rather than beauty; *also* : serving a useful purpose

util·i·tar·i·an·ism \\yù-,ti-lə-'ter-ē-ə-,ni-zəm\\ *n* : a theory that the greatest good for the greatest number should be the main consideration in making a choice of actions

¹util·i·ty \\yù-'ti-lə-tē\\ *n, pl* **-ties** **1** : USEFULNESS **2** : something useful or designed for use **3** : a business organization performing a public service and subject to special governmental regulation **4** : a public service or a commodity (as electricity or water) provided by a public utility; *also* : equipment to provide such or a similar service

²utility *adj* **1** : capable of serving esp. as a substitute in various uses or positions ⟨a ~ outfielder⟩ ⟨a ~ cord⟩ **2** : being of a usable but poor quality ⟨~ beef⟩

utility knife *n* : a knife designed for general use; *esp* : one with a retractable blade

uti·lize \\'yü-tə-,līz\\ *vb* **-lized; -liz·ing** : to make use of : turn to profitable account or use — **uti·li·za·tion** \\,yü-tə-lə-'zā-shən\\ *n*

ut·most \\'ət-,mōst\\ *adj* **1** : situated at the farthest or most distant point : EXTREME **2** : of the greatest or highest degree, quantity, number, or amount — **utmost** *n*

uto·pia \\yù-'tō-pē-ə\\ *n* [*Utopia*, imaginary island described in Sir Thomas More's *Utopia*, fr. Gk *ou* not, no + *topos* place] **1** *often cap* : a place of ideal perfection esp. in laws, government, and social conditions **2** : an impractical scheme for social improvement

¹uto·pi·an \\-pē-ən\\ *adj, often cap* **1** : of, relating to, or resembling a utopia **2** : proposing ideal social and political schemes that are impractical **3** : VISIONARY

²utopian *n* **1** : a believer in the perfectibility of human society **2** : one who proposes or advocates utopian schemes

¹ut·ter \\'ə-tər\\ *adj* [ME, remote, fr. OE *ūtera* outer, compar. adj. fr. *ūt* out, adv.] : ABSOLUTE, TOTAL ⟨~ ruin⟩ — **ut·ter·ly** *adv*

²utter *vb* [ME *uttren*, fr. *utter* outside, adv., fr. OE *ūtor*, compar. of *ūt* out] **1** : to send forth as a sound : express in usu. spoken words : PRONOUNCE, SPEAK **2** : to put (as currency) into circulation — **ut·ter·er** *n*

ut·ter·ance \'ə-tə-rəns\ *n* **1** : something uttered; *esp* : an oral or written statement **2** : the action of uttering with the voice : SPEECH **3** : power, style, or manner of speaking

ut·ter·most \'ə-tər-ˌmōst\ *adj* : EXTREME, UTMOST ⟨the ~ parts of the earth⟩ — **uttermost** *n*

U–turn \'yü-ˌtərn\ *n* : a turn resembling the letter U; *esp* : a 180-degree turn made by a vehicle in a road

UV *abbr* ultraviolet

uvu·la \'yü-vyə-lə\ *n, pl* **-las** *or* **-lae** \-ˌlē, -ˌlī\ : the fleshy lobe hanging at the back of the roof of the mouth — **uvu·lar** \-lər\ *adj*

UW *abbr* underwriter

ux·o·ri·ous \ˌək-'sòr-ē-əs, ˌəg-'zòr-\ *adj* : excessively devoted or submissive to a wife

¹v \'vē\ *n, pl* **v's** *or* **vs** \'vēz\ *often cap* **1** : the 22d letter of the English alphabet **2** : five in Roman numerals

²v *abbr, often cap* **1** vector **2** velocity **3** verb **4** verse **5** versus **6** very **7** victory **8** vide **9** voice **10** voltage **11** volume **12** vowel

V *symbol* **1** vanadium **2** volt

Va *abbr* Virginia

VA *abbr* **1** Veterans Administration **2** vice admiral **3** Virginia

va·can·cy \'vā-kən-sē\ *n, pl* **-cies** **1** : a vacating esp. of an office, position, or piece of property **2** : a vacant office, position, or tenancy; *also* : the period during which it stands vacant **3** : empty space : VOID **4** : the state of being vacant

va·cant \'vā-kənt\ *adj* **1** : not occupied ⟨~ seat⟩ ⟨~ room⟩ **2** : EMPTY ⟨~ space⟩ **3** : free from business or care ⟨a few ~ hours⟩ **4** : devoid of thought, reflection, or expression ⟨a ~ smile⟩ — **va·cant·ly** *adv*

va·cate \'vā-ˌkāt\ *vb* **va·cat·ed; va·cat·ing** **1** : to make void : ANNUL **2** : to make vacant (as an office or house); *also* : to give up the occupancy of

¹va·ca·tion \vā-'kā-shən, və-\ *n* : a period of rest from work : HOLIDAY

²vacation *vb* : to take or spend a vacation — **va·ca·tion·er** *n*

va·ca·tion·ist \-shə-nist\ *n* : a person taking a vacation

va·ca·tion·land \-shən-ˌland\ *n* : an area with recreational attractions and facilities for vacationists

vac·ci·nate \'vak-sə-ˌnāt\ *vb* **-nat·ed; -nat·ing** : to administer a vaccine to usu. by injection

vac·ci·na·tion \ˌvak-sə-'nā-shən\ *n* **1** : the act of vaccinating **2** : the scar left by vaccinating

vac·cine \vak-'sēn, 'vak-ˌsēn\ *n* [F *vaccin,* fr. *vaccine* cowpox, fr. NL *vaccina* (in *variolae vaccinae* cowpox), fr. L, fem. of *vaccinus* of or from cows, fr. *vacca* cow] : a preparation of material (as of killed or weakened viruses or bacteria) used in vaccinating to produce or increase immunity to a disease

vac·cin·ia \vak-'si-nē-ə\ *n* : COWPOX

vac·il·late \'va-sə-ˌlāt\ *vb* **-lat·ed; -lat·ing** **1** : SWAY, TOTTER; *also* : FLUCTUATE **2** : to incline first to one course or opinion and then to another : WAVER — **vac·il·la·tion** \ˌva-sə-'lā-shən\ *n*

va·cu·ity \va-'kyü-ə-tē\ *n, pl* **-ities** **1** : an empty space **2** : the state, fact, or quality of being vacuous **3** : something that is vacuous

vac·u·ole \'va-kyə-ˌwōl\ *n* : a usu. fluid-filled cavity esp. in the cytoplasm of an individual cell — **vac·u·o·lar** \ˌva-kyə-'wō-lər, -ˌlär\ *adj*

vac·u·ous \'va-kyə-wəs\ *adj* **1** : EMPTY, VACANT, BLANK **2** : DULL, STUPID, INANE ⟨~ movies⟩ — **vac·u·ous·ly** *adv* — **vac·u·ous·ness** *n*

¹vac·u·um \'va-(ˌ)kyüm, -kyəm\ *n, pl* **vacuums** *or* **vac·ua** \-kyə-wə\ [L, fr. neut. of *vacuus* empty] **1** : a space entirely empty of matter **2** : a space from which most of the air has been removed (as by a pump) **3** : VOID, GAP **4** : VACUUM CLEANER — **vacuum** *adj*

²vacuum *vb* : to use a vacuum device (as a vacuum cleaner) on ⟨~ the den⟩

vacuum bottle *n* : THERMOS

vacuum cleaner *n* : a household appliance for cleaning (as floors or rugs) by suction

vacuum–packed *adj* : having much of the air removed before being hermetically sealed ⟨~ fish⟩

vacuum tube *n* : an electron tube from which most of the air has been removed

va·de me·cum \ˌvā-dē-'mē-kəm, ˌvä-dē-'mā-\ *n, pl* **vade mecums** [L, go with me] : something (as a handbook or manual) regularly carried about

VADM *abbr* vice admiral

¹vag·a·bond \'va-gə-ˌbänd\ *adj* **1** : WANDERING, HOMELESS **2** : of, characteristic of, or leading the life of a vagrant or tramp **3** : leading an unsettled or irresponsible life

²vagabond *n* : one leading a vagabond life; *esp* : VAGRANT, TRAMP

va·gar·i·ous \vā-'ger-ē-əs\ *adj* : marked by vagaries : CAPRICIOUS ⟨~ leadership⟩ — **va·gar·i·ous·ly** *adv*

va·ga·ry \'vā-gə-rē, və-'ger-ē\ *n, pl* **-ries** : an odd or eccentric idea or action : WHIM, CAPRICE

va·gi·na \və-'jī-nə\ *n, pl* **-nae** \-(ˌ)nē\ *or* **-nas** [L, lit., sheath] : a canal that leads from the uterus to the external opening of the female sex organs — **vag·i·nal** \'va-jə-nᵊl\ *adj* — **vag·i·nal·ly** \-nᵊl-ē\ *adv*

vag·i·ni·tis \ˌva-jə-'nī-təs\ *n* : inflammation of the vagina

va·gran·cy \'vā-grən-sē\ *n, pl* **-cies** **1** : the quality or state of being vagrant; *also* : a vagrant act or notion **2** : the offense of being a vagrant

¹va·grant \'vā-grənt\ *n* : a person who has no job and wanders from place to place

²vagrant *adj* **1** : of, relating to, or characteristic of a vagrant **2** : following no fixed course : RANDOM, CAPRICIOUS ⟨~ thoughts⟩ — **va·grant·ly** *adv*

vague \'vāg\ *adj* **vagu·er; vagu·est** [MF, fr. L *vagus,* lit., wandering] **1** : not clear, definite, or distinct ⟨a ~ plan⟩ ⟨~ silhouettes⟩ **2** : not clearly felt or analyzed ⟨a ~ unrest⟩ ◆ **Synonyms** OBSCURE, DARK, ENIGMATIC, AMBIGUOUS, EQUIVOCAL — **vague·ly** *adv* — **vague·ness** *n*

vain \'vān\ *adj* [ME, fr. AF, empty, futile, fr. L *vanus*] **1** : of no real value : IDLE, WORTHLESS **2** : FUTILE, UNSUCCESSFUL **3** : proud of one's looks or abilities ◆ **Synonyms** CONCEITED, NARCISSISTIC, VAINGLORIOUS — **vain·ly** *adv* — **in vain** **1** : without success ⟨her efforts were *in vain*⟩ **2** : in a blasphemous manner ⟨took the Lord's name *in vain*⟩

vain·glo·ri·ous \ˌvān-'glòr-ē-əs\ *adj* : marked by vainglory : BOASTFUL

vain·glo·ry \'vān-ˌglòr-ē\ *n* **1** : excessive or ostentatious pride esp. in one's own achievements **2** : vain display : VANITY

val *abbr* value; valued

va·lance \'va-ləns, 'vā-\ *n* **1** : drapery hanging from an edge (as of an altar, table, or bed) **2** : a drapery or a decorative frame across the top of a window

vale \'vāl\ *n* : VALLEY, DALE

vale·dic·tion \ˌva-lə-'dik-shən\ *n* [L *valedicere* to say farewell, fr. *vale* farewell + *dicere* to say] : an act or utterance of leave-taking : FAREWELL

vale·dic·to·ri·an \-ˌdik-'tòr-ē-ən\ *n* : the student usu. of the highest rank in a graduating class who delivers the valedictory address at commencement

vale·dic·to·ry \-'dik-tə-rē\ *adj* : bidding farewell : delivered as a valediction ⟨a ~ address⟩ — **valedictory** *n*

va·lence \'vā-ləns\ *n* [LL *valentia* power, capacity, fr. L *valēre* to be strong] : the combining power of an atom as shown by the number of its electrons that are lost, gained, or shared in the formation of chemical bonds

Va·len·ci·ennes \və-ˌlen-sē-'en, ˌva-lən-sē-, -'enz\ *n* : a fine handmade lace

val·en·tine \'va-lən-ˌtīn\ *n* : a sweetheart chosen or complimented on Valentine's Day; *also* : a gift or greeting given on this day

Valentine's Day *also* **Valentine Day** *n* : February 14 observed in honor of St. Valentine and as a time for exchanging valentines

¹**va·let** \'va-lət, -(ˌ)lā; va-'lā\ *n* **1** : a male servant who takes care of a man's clothes and performs personal services **2** : an attendant in a hotel or restaurant who performs personal services (as parking cars) for customers

²**valet** *vb* : to serve as a valet

val·e·tu·di·nar·i·an \ˌva-lə-ˌtü-də-'ner-ē-ən, -ˌtyü-\ *n* : a person of a weak or sickly constitution; *esp* : one whose chief concern is his or her ill health — **val·e·tu·di·nar·i·an·ism** \-ē-ə-ˌni-zəm\ *n*

val·iant \'val-yənt\ *adj* : having or showing valor : BRAVE, HEROIC ✦ **Synonyms** VALOROUS, DOUGHTY, COURAGEOUS, BOLD, AUDACIOUS, DAUNTLESS, UNDAUNTED, INTREPID — **val·iant·ly** *adv*

val·id \'va-ləd\ *adj* **1** : having legal force ⟨a ~ contract⟩ **2** : founded on truth or fact : capable of being justified or defended : SOUND ⟨a ~ argument⟩ ⟨~ reasons⟩ — **va·lid·i·ty** \və-'li-də-tē\ *n* — **val·id·ly** *adv*

val·i·date \'va-lə-ˌdāt\ *vb* **-dat·ed; -dat·ing** **1** : to make legally valid **2** : to confirm the validity of **3** : VERIFY — **val·i·da·tion** \ˌva-lə-'dā-shən\ *n*

va·lise \və-'lēs\ *n* [F] : SUITCASE

val·ley \'va-lē\ *n, pl* **valleys** : a long depression between ranges of hills or mountains

val·or \'va-lər\ *n* [ME *valour*, worth, worthiness, bravery, fr. AF fr. ML *valor*, fr. L *valēre* to be strong] : personal bravery ✦ **Synonyms** HEROISM, PROWESS, GALLANTRY — **val·or·ous** \'va-lə-rəs\ *adj*

val·o·ri·za·tion \ˌva-lə-rə-'zā-shən\ *n* : the support of commodity prices by any of various forms of government subsidy — **val·o·rize** \'va-lə-ˌrīz\ *vb*

val·our *chiefly Brit var of* VALOR

¹**valu·able** \'val-yə-bəl, -yə-wə-bəl\ *adj* **1** : having money value **2** : having great money value **3** : of great use or service ✦ **Synonyms** INVALUABLE, PRICELESS, COSTLY, EXPENSIVE, DEAR, PRECIOUS

²**valuable** *n* : a usu. personal possession of considerable value ⟨their ~s were stolen⟩

val·u·ate \'val-yə-ˌwāt\ *vb* **-at·ed; -at·ing** : to place a value on : APPRAISE — **val·u·a·tor** \-ˌwā-tər\ *n*

val·u·a·tion \ˌval-yə-'wā-shən\ *n* **1** : the act or process of valuing; *esp* : appraisal of property **2** : the estimated or determined market value of a thing

¹**val·ue** \'val-yü\ *n* **1** : a fair return or equivalent in money, goods, or services for something exchanged **2** : the monetary worth of a thing; *also* : relative worth, utility, or importance ⟨nothing of ~ to say⟩ **3** : an assigned or computed numerical quantity ⟨the ~ of x in an equation⟩ **4** : relative lightness or darkness of a color : LUMINOSITY **5** : the relative length of a tone or note **6** : something (as a principle or ideal) intrinsically valuable or desirable ⟨human rather than material ~s⟩ — **val·ue·less** *adj*

²**value** *vb* **val·ued; valu·ing** **1** : to estimate the monetary worth of : APPRAISE **2** : to rate in usefulness, importance, or general worth **3** : to consider or rate highly : PRIZE, ESTEEM ⟨*valued* your opinions⟩ — **val·u·er** *n*

val·ue–add·ed tax *n* : an incremental excise tax that is levied on the value added at each stage of the processing of a raw material or the production and distribution of a commodity

valve \'valv\ *n* **1** : a structure (as in a vein) that temporarily closes a passage or that permits movement in one direction only **2** : a device by which the flow of a fluid material may be regulated by a movable part; *also* : the movable part of such a device **3** : a device in a brass wind instrument for quickly varying the tube length in order to change the fundamental tone by some definite interval **4** : one of the separate usu. hinged pieces of

which the shell of some animals and esp. bivalve mollusks consists **5** : one of the pieces into which a ripe seed capsule or pod separates — **valved** \'valvd\ *adj* — **valve·less** *adj*

val·vu·lar \'val-vyə-lər\ *adj* : of, relating to, or affecting a valve esp. of the heart ⟨~ heart disease⟩

va·moose \va-'müs, va-\ *vb* **va·moosed; va·moos·ing** [Sp *vamos* let us go] : to leave or go away quickly

¹**vamp** *n* **1** : the part of a boot or shoe upper covering esp. the front part of the foot **2** : a short introductory musical passage often repeated

²**vamp** \'vamp\ *vb* **1** : to provide with a new vamp **2** : to patch up with a new part **3** : INVENT, IMPROVISE ⟨~ up an excuse⟩

³**vamp** *n* : a woman who uses her charm or wiles to seduce and exploit men

⁴**vamp** *vb* : to practice seductive wiles on : to act like a vamp

vam·pire \'vam-ˌpī(-ə)r\ *n* [F, fr. G *Vampir*, fr. Serbian *vampir*] **1** : a night-wandering bloodsucking ghost **2** : a person who preys on other people; *esp* : a woman who exploits and ruins her lover **3** : VAMPIRE BAT

vampire bat *n* : any of various bats of Central and South America that feed on the blood of animals; *also* : any of several other bats that do not feed on blood but are sometimes reputed to do so

¹**van** \'van\ *n* : VANGUARD

²**van** *n* : a usu. enclosed wagon or motortruck for moving goods or animals; *also* : a versatile enclosed box-like motor vehicle

va·na·di·um \və-'nā-dē-əm\ *n* : a soft grayish ductile metallic chemical element used esp. to form alloys

Van Al·len belt \van-'a-lən-\ *n* : a belt of intense radiation in the magnetosphere composed of charged particles trapped by earth's magnetic field

van·co·my·cin \ˌvan-kə-'mī-sᵊn\ *n* : an antibiotic used esp. against staphylococci

van·dal \'van-dᵊl\ *n* **1** *cap* : a member of a Germanic people who sacked Rome in A.D. 455 **2** : a person who willfully mars or destroys property

van·dal·ise *Brit var of* VANDALIZE

van·dal·ism \'van-də-ˌli-zəm\ *n* : willful or malicious destruction or defacement of public or private property

van·dal·ize \-ˌlīz\ *vb* **-ized; -iz·ing** : to subject to vandalism : DAMAGE

Van·dyke \van-'dīk\ *n* : a trim pointed beard

vane \'vān\ *n* [ME, fr. OE *fana* banner] **1** : a movable device attached to a high object for showing wind direction **2** : a thin flat or curved object that is rotated about an axis by a flow of fluid or that rotates to cause a fluid to flow or that redirects a flow of fluid ⟨the ~s of a windmill⟩ **3** : a feather fastened near the back end of an arrow for stability in flight

van·guard \'van-ˌgärd\ *n* **1** : the troops moving at the front of an army **2** : the forefront of an action or movement

va·nil·la \və-'ni-lə\ *n* [NL, genus name, fr. Sp *vainilla* vanilla (plant and fruit), dim. of *vaina* sheath, fr. L *vagina*] : a flavoring extract made synthetically or obtained from the long beanlike pods (**vanilla beans**) of a tropical American climbing orchid; *also* : this orchid

van·ish \'va-nish\ *vb* : to pass from sight or existence : disappear completely — **van·ish·er** *n*

van·i·ty \'va-nə-tē\ *n, pl* **-ties** **1** : something that is vain, empty, or useless **2** : the quality or fact of being useless or futile : FUTILITY **3** : undue pride in oneself or one's appearance : CONCEIT **4** : a small case for cosmetics : COMPACT

vanity plate *n* : an automobile license plate bearing distinctive letters or numbers designated by the owner

van·quish \'vaŋ-kwish, 'van-\ *vb* **1** : to overcome in battle or in a contest **2** : to gain mastery over (as an emotion)

van·tage \'van-tij\ *n* **1** : superiority in a contest **2** : a position giving a strategic advantage or a commanding perspective

va·pid \'va-pəd, 'vā-\ *adj* : lacking spirit, liveliness, or zest : FLAT, INSIPID ⟨~ gossip⟩ — **va·pid·i·ty** \va-'pi-də-tē\ *n* — **vap·id·ly** *adv* — **vap·id·ness** *n*

va·por \'vā-pər\ *n* **1** : fine separated particles (as fog or smoke) floating in the air and clouding it **2** : a substance in the gaseous state; *esp* : one that is liquid under ordinary conditions **3** : something insubstantial or fleeting **4** *pl* : a depressed or hysterical nervous condition

va·por·ing \'vā-pə-riŋ\ *n* : an idle, boastful, or high-flown expression or speech — usu. used in pl.

va·por·ise *Brit var of* VAPORIZE

va·por·ize \'vā-pə-ˌrīz\ *vb* **-ized; -iz·ing** **1** : to convert into vapor **2** : to destroy as if by converting to vapor ⟨*vaporized* enemy tanks⟩ — **va·por·i·za·tion** \ˌvā-pə-rə-'zā-shən\ *n*

va·por·iz·er \-ˌrī-zər\ *n* : a device that vaporizes something (as a medicated liquid)

vapor lock *n* : an interruption of flow of a fluid (as fuel in an engine) caused by the formation of vapor in the feeding system

va·por·ous \'vā-pə-rəs\ *adj* **1** : full of vapors : FOGGY, MISTY **2** : UNSUBSTANTIAL, VAGUE ⟨∼ speculations⟩ — **va·por·ous·ly** *adv* — **va·por·ous·ness** *n*

va·pory \'vā-pə-rē\ *adj* : MISTY

va·pour *chiefly Brit var of* VAPOR

va·que·ro \vä-'ker-ō\ *n, pl* **-ros** [Sp, fr. *vaca* cow, fr. L *vacca*] : a ranch hand : COWBOY

var *abbr* **1** variable **2** variant; variation **3** variety **4** various

¹var·i·able \'ver-ē-ə-bəl\ *adj* **1** : able or apt to vary : CHANGEABLE **2** : FICKLE **3** : not true to type : ABERRANT ⟨a ∼ wheat⟩ — **var·i·abil·i·ty** \ˌver-ē-ə-'bi-lə-tē, ˌvar-\ *n* — **var·i·ably** \-blē\ *adv*

²variable *n* **1** : a quantity that may take on any of a set of values; *also* : a mathematical symbol representing a variable **2** : something that is variable

var·i·ance \'ver-ē-əns\ *n* **1** : variation or a degree of variation : DEVIATION **2** : DISAGREEMENT, DISPUTE **3** : a license to do something contrary to the usual rule ⟨a zoning ∼⟩ **4** : the square of the standard deviation ✦ *Synonyms* DISCORD, CONTENTION, DISSENSION, STRIFE, CONFLICT

¹var·i·ant \'ver-ē-ənt\ *adj* **1** : differing from others of its kind or class **2** : varying usu. slightly from the standard or type

²variant *n* **1** : one that exhibits variation from a type or norm **2** : one of two or more different spellings or pronunciations of a word

var·i·a·tion \ˌver-ē-'ā-shən\ *n* **1** : the act, process, or an instance of varying : a change in form, position, or condition : MODIFICATION, ALTERATION **2** : extent of change or difference **3** : divergence in the characteristics of an organism from those typical or usual for its group; *also* : one exhibiting such variation **4** : repetition of a musical theme with modifications in rhythm, tune, harmony, or key

vari·col·ored \'ver-i-ˌkə-lərd\ *adj* : having various colors : VARIEGATED

var·i·cose \'va-rə-ˌkōs\ *adj* : abnormally swollen and dilated ⟨∼ veins⟩ — **var·i·cos·i·ty** \ˌva-rə-'kä-sə-tē\ *n*

var·ied \'ver-ēd\ *adj* **1** : having many forms or types : DIVERSE **2** : VARIEGATED — **var·ied·ly** *adv*

var·ie·gat·ed \'ver-ē-ə-ˌgā-təd\ *adj* **1** : having patches, stripes, or marks of different colors ⟨∼ flowers⟩ **2** : VARIED **1** — **var·ie·gate** \-ˌgāt\ *vb* — **var·ie·ga·tion** \ˌver-ē-ə-'gā-shən\ *n*

¹va·ri·etal \və-'rī-ə-tᵊl\ *adj* : of or relating to a variety; *esp* : of, relating to, or producing a varietal

²varietal *n* : a wine bearing the name of the principal grape from which it is made

va·ri·ety \və-'rī-ə-tē\ *n, pl* **-et·ies** **1** : the state of being varied or various : DIVERSITY **2** : a collection of different things : ASSORTMENT **3** : something varying from others of the same general kind **4** : any of various groups of plants or animals within a species distinguished by characteristics insufficient to separate species : SUBSPECIES **5** : entertainment such as is given in a stage presentation comprising a series of performances (as songs, dances, or acrobatic acts)

var·i·o·rum \ˌver-ē-'ōr-əm\ *n* : an edition or text of a work containing notes by various persons or variant readings of the text

var·i·ous \'ver-ē-əs\ *adj* **1** : VARICOLORED **2** : of differing kinds : MULTIFARIOUS **3** : UNLIKE ⟨animals as ∼ as the jaguar and the sloth⟩ **4** : having a number of different aspects **5** : NUMEROUS, MANY **6** : INDIVIDUAL, SEP-

ARATE ✦ *Synonyms* DIVERGENT, DISPARATE, DIFFERENT, DISSIMILAR, DIVERSE, UNALIKE — **var·i·ous·ly** *adv*

var·let \'vär-lət\ *n* **1** : ATTENDANT **2** : SCOUNDREL, KNAVE

var·mint \'vär-mənt\ *n* [alter. of *vermin*] **1** : an animal considered a pest; *esp* : one classed as vermin and unprotected by game law **2** : a contemptible person : RASCAL

¹var·nish \'vär-nish\ *n* **1** : a liquid preparation that is applied to a surface and dries into a hard glossy coating; *also* : the glaze of this coating **2** : something suggesting varnish by its gloss **3** : outside show : deceptive or superficial appearance

²varnish *vb* **1** : to cover with varnish **2** : to cover or conceal with something that gives a fair appearance : GLOSS

var·si·ty \'vär-sə-tē\ *n, pl* **-ties** [by shortening & alter. fr. *university*] **1** *Brit* : UNIVERSITY **2** : the principal team representing a college, school, or club

vary \'ver-ē\ *vb* **var·ied; vary·ing** **1** : ALTER, CHANGE **2** : to make or be of different kinds : introduce or have variety : DIVERSIFY, DIFFER **3** : DEVIATE, SWERVE **4** : to change in bodily structure or function away from what is usual for members of a group

vas·cu·lar \'vas-kyə-lər\ *adj* [NL *vascularis*, fr. L *vasculum* small vessel, dim. of *vas* vase, vessel] : of or relating to a channel or system of channels for the conveyance of a body fluid (as blood or sap); *also* : supplied with or containing such vessels and esp. blood vessels ⟨the ∼ system⟩

vascular plant *n* : a plant having a specialized system for carrying fluids that includes xylem and phloem

vas def·er·ens \ˌvas-'de-fə-rənz\ *n, pl* **va·sa def·er·en·tia** \ˌvā-zə-ˌde-fə-'ren-shē-ə\ : a sperm-carrying duct of the testis

vase \'vās, 'vāz\ *n* : a usu. round vessel of greater depth than width used chiefly for ornament or for flowers

va·sec·to·my \və-'sek-tə-mē, vā-'zek-\ *n, pl* **-mies** : surgical excision of all or part of the vas deferens usu. to induce sterility

va·so·con·stric·tion \ˌvā-zō-kən-'strik-shən\ *n* : narrowing of the interior diameter of blood vessels

va·so·con·stric·tor \-tər\ *n* : an agent (as a nerve fiber or a drug) that initiates or induces vasoconstriction

vas·sal \'va-səl\ *n* **1** : a person under the protection of a feudal lord to whom he owes homage and loyalty : a feudal tenant **2** : one occupying a dependent or subordinate position — **vassal** *adj*

vas·sal·age \-sə-lij\ *n* **1** : the state of being a vassal **2** : the homage and loyalty due from a vassal **3** : SERVITUDE, SUBJECTION

¹vast \'vast\ *adj* : very great in size, amount, degree, intensity, or esp. extent ⟨∼ plains⟩ ⟨∼ knowledge⟩ ✦ *Synonyms* ENORMOUS, HUGE, GIGANTIC, COLOSSAL, MAMMOTH — **vast·ly** *adv* — **vast·ness** *n*

²vast *n* : a great expanse : IMMENSITY

vasty \'vas-tē\ *adj* : VAST, IMMENSE

vat \'vat\ *n* : a large vessel (as a tub or barrel) esp. for holding liquids in manufacturing processes

VAT *abbr* value-added tax

vat·ic \'va-tik\ *adj* : PROPHETIC, ORACULAR

Vat·i·can \'va-ti-kən\ *n* **1** : the papal headquarters in Rome **2** : the papal government

va·tu \'vä-ˌtü\ *n, pl* **vatu** — see MONEY table

vaude·ville \'vȯd-vəl, 'väd-, 'vȯd-, -ˌvil\ *n* [F, fr. MF, satirical song, alter. of *vaudevire*, fr. *vau-de-Vire* valley of Vire, town in northwest France where such songs were composed] : a stage entertainment consisting of unrelated acts (as of acrobats, comedians, dancers, or singers)

¹vault \'vȯlt\ *n* **1** : an arched masonry structure usu. forming a ceiling or roof; *also* : something (as the sky) resembling a vault **2** : a room or space covered by a vault esp. when underground **3** : a room or compartment for the safekeeping of valuables **4** : a burial chamber; *also* : a usu. metal or concrete case in which a casket is enclosed at burial — **vaulty** *adj*

²vault *vb* : to form or cover with a vault

³vault *vb* : to leap vigorously esp. by aid of the hands or a pole — **vault·er** *n*

⁴vault *n* : an act of vaulting : LEAP

vault·ed \'vȯl-təd\ *adj* **1** : built in the form of a vault : ARCHED **2** : covered with a vault

vault·ing \-tiŋ\ *adj* : reaching for the heights ⟨∼ ambition⟩

vaunt \'vȯnt\ *vb* [ME, fr. AF *vanter*, fr. LL *vanitare*, ultim. fr. L *vanus* vain] : BRAG, BOAST — **vaunt** *n*

vaunt·ed \'vȯn-təd\ *adj* : much praised or boasted of

vb *abbr* verb; verbal

V–chip \'vē-ˌchip\ *n* : a computer chip in a television set used to block based on content the viewing of certain programs

VCR \ˌvē-(ˌ)sē-'är\ *n* [*videocassette recorder*] : a device that records and plays back videotapes

VD *abbr* venereal disease

VDT *abbr* video display terminal

veal \'vēl\ *n* : the flesh of a young calf

vec·tor \'vek-tər\ *n* 1 : a quantity that has magnitude and direction 2 : an organism (as a fly or tick) that transmits a pathogen

Ve·da \'vā-də\ *n* [Skt, lit., knowledge] : any of a class of Hindu sacred writings — **Ve·dic** \'vā-dik\ *adj*

Ve·dan·ta \vā-'dän-tə, və-, -'dan-\ *n* : an orthodox Hindu philosophy based on the Upanishads

vee·jay \'vē-ˌjā\ *n* : an announcer of a program featuring music videos

veep \'vēp\ *n* : VICE PRESIDENT

veer \'vir\ *vb* : to shift from one direction or course to another ◆ *Synonyms* TURN, AVERT, DEFLECT, DIVERT — **veer** *n*

veg·an \'vē-gən, 'vā-; 've-jən, -ˌjan\ *n* : a strict vegetarian who consumes no animal food or dairy products — **veg·an·ism** \'vē-gə-ˌni-zəm, 'vā-, 've-\ *n*

¹**veg·e·ta·ble** \'vej-tə-bəl, 've-jə-\ *adj* [ME, fr. ML *vegetabilis* vegetative, fr. *vegetare* to grow, fr. L, to animate, fr. *vegetus* lively, fr. *vegēre* to enliven] 1 : of, relating to, or growing like plants ⟨the ∼ kingdom⟩ 2 : made from, obtained from, or containing plants or plant products ⟨∼ oils⟩ 3 : suggesting that of a plant (as in inertness) ⟨a ∼ existence⟩

²**vegetable** *n* 1 : PLANT 1 2 : a usu. herbaceous plant grown for an edible part that is usu. eaten as part of a meal; *also* : such an edible part

veg·e·tal \'ve-jə-tᵊl\ *adj* 1 : VEGETABLE 2 : VEGETATIVE

veg·e·tar·i·an \ˌve-jə-'ter-ē-ən\ *n* : one that believes in or practices living on a diet of vegetables, fruits, grains, nuts, and sometimes animal products (as milk and cheese) — **vegetarian** *adj* — **veg·e·tar·i·an·ism** \-ē-ə-ˌni-zəm\ *n*

veg·e·tate \'ve-jə-ˌtāt\ *vb* **-tat·ed; -tat·ing** : to live or grow in the manner of a plant; *esp* : to lead a dull inert life

veg·e·ta·tion \ˌve-jə-'tā-shən\ *n* 1 : the act or process of vegetating; *also* : inert existence 2 : plant life or cover (as of an area) — **veg·e·ta·tion·al** \-shə-nəl\ *adj*

veg·e·ta·tive \'ve-jə-ˌtā-tiv\ *adj* 1 : of or relating to nutrition and growth esp. as contrasted with reproduction 2 : of, relating to, or composed of vegetation 3 : VEGETABLE 3

veg out \'vej-\ *vb* **vegged out; vegging out** [short for *vegetate*] : to spend time idly or passively

ve·he·ment \'vē-ə-mənt\ *adj* 1 : marked by great force or energy 2 : marked by strong feeling or expression : PASSIONATE, FERVID — **ve·he·mence** \-məns\ *n* — **ve·he·ment·ly** *adv*

ve·hi·cle \'vē-ə-kəl, 'vē-ˌhi-\ *n* 1 : a medium by which a thing is applied or administered ⟨linseed oil is a ∼ for pigments⟩ 2 : a medium through or by means of which something is conveyed or expressed 3 : a means of transporting persons or goods ◆ *Synonyms* INSTRUMENT, AGENT, AGENCY, ORGAN, CHANNEL — **ve·hic·u·lar** \vē-'hi-kyə-lər\ *adj*

¹**veil** \'vāl\ *n* 1 : a piece of often sheer or diaphanous material used to screen or curtain something or to cover the head or face 2 : the life of a nun ⟨take the ∼⟩ 3 : something that hides or obscures like a veil ⟨a ∼ of secrecy⟩

²**veil** *vb* : to cover with or as if with a veil : wear a veil

¹**vein** \'vān\ *n* 1 : a fissure in rock filled with mineral matter; *also* : a bed of useful mineral matter 2 : any of the tubular branching vessels that carry blood from the capillaries toward the heart 3 : any of the bundles of vascular vessels forming the framework of a leaf 4 : any of the thickened ribs that stiffen the wings of an insect 5 : something (as a wavy variegation in marble) suggesting veins 6 : a distinctive style of expression 7 : a distinctive

element or quality : STRAIN 8 : MOOD, HUMOR — **veined** \'vānd\ *adj*

²**vein** *vb* : to pattern with or as if with veins — **vein·ing** *n*

vel *abbr* velocity

ve·lar \'vē-lər\ *adj* : of or relating to a velum and esp. that of the soft palate

veld *or* **veldt** \'velt, 'felt\ *n* [Afrikaans *veld*, fr. D, field] : an open grassland esp. in southern Africa usu. with scattered shrubs or trees

vel·lum \'ve-ləm\ *n* [ME *velym*, fr. AF *velim, veeslin*, fr. **veelin*, adj., of a calf, fr. *veel* calf] 1 : a fine-grained lambskin, kidskin, or calfskin prepared for writing on or for binding books 2 : a strong cream-colored paper — **vellum** *adj*

ve·loc·i·pede \və-'lä-sə-ˌpēd\ *n* : an early bicycle

ve·loc·i·rap·tor \və-'lä-sə-ˌrap-tər\ *n* : any of a genus of agile flesh-eating bipedal dinosaurs of the Cretaceous having a sickle-shaped claw on each foot

ve·loc·i·ty \və-'lä-sə-tē\ *n, pl* **-ties** : quickness of motion : SPEED ⟨the ∼ of light⟩

ve·lour *or* **ve·lours** \və-'lu̇r\ *n, pl* **velours** \-'lu̇rz\ : any of various textile fabrics with pile like that of velvet

ve·lum \'vē-ləm\ *n, pl* **ve·la** \-lə\ : a membranous body part (as the soft palate) resembling a veil

vel·vet \'vel-vət\ *n* [ME *veluet, velvet*, fr. AF, fr. *velu* shaggy, ultim. fr. L *villus* shaggy hair] 1 : a fabric having a short soft dense warp pile 2 : something resembling or suggesting velvet (as in softness or luster) 3 : the soft skin covering the growing antlers of deer — **velvet** *adj* — **velvety** *adj*

vel·ve·teen \ˌvel-və-'tēn\ *n* 1 : a fabric woven usu. of cotton in imitation of velvet 2 *pl* : clothes made of velveteen

Ven *abbr* venerable

ve·nal \'vē-nᵊl\ *adj* : capable of being bought or bribed : MERCENARY, CORRUPT — **ve·nal·i·ty** \vi-'na-lə-tē\ *n* — **ve·nal·ly** \'vē-nᵊl-ē\ *adv*

ve·na·tion \ve-'nā-shən, vē-\ *n* : an arrangement or system of veins ⟨the ∼ of the hand⟩ ⟨leaf ∼⟩

vend \'vend\ *vb* : SELL; *esp* : to sell as a hawker or peddler — **vend·ible** *adj*

vend·ee \ven-'dē\ *n* : one to whom a thing is sold : BUYER

ven·det·ta \ven-'de-tə\ *n* : a feud marked by acts of revenge

vending machine *n* : a coin-operated machine for selling merchandise

ven·dor \'ven-dər, *for 1 also* ven-'dȯr\ *n* 1 : one that vends : SELLER 2 : VENDING MACHINE

¹**ve·neer** \və-'nir\ *n* [G *Furnier*, fr. *furnieren* to veneer, fr. F *fournir* to furnish] 1 : a thin usu. superficial layer of material ⟨brick ∼⟩; *esp* : a thin layer of fine wood glued over a cheaper wood 2 : superficial display : GLOSS

²**veneer** *vb* : to overlay with a veneer

ven·er·a·ble \'ve-nə-rə-bəl\ *adj* 1 : deserving to be venerated — often used as a religious title 2 : made sacred by association

ven·er·ate \'ve-nə-ˌrāt\ *vb* **-at·ed; -at·ing** : to regard with reverential respect ◆ *Synonyms* ADORE, REVERE, REVERENCE, WORSHIP — **ven·er·a·tion** \ˌve-nə-'rā-shən\ *n*

ve·ne·re·al \və-'nir-ē-əl\ *adj* : of or relating to sexual intercourse or to diseases transmitted by it ⟨a ∼ infection⟩

venereal disease *n* : a contagious disease (as gonorrhea or syphilis) usu. acquired by having sexual intercourse with someone who already has it

ve·ne·tian blind \və-'nē-shən-\ *n* : a blind having thin horizontal parallel slats that can be adjusted to admit a desired amount of light

ven·geance \'ven-jəns\ *n* : punishment inflicted in retaliation for an injury or offense : REVENGE

venge·ful \'venj-fəl\ *adj* : filled with a desire for revenge : VINDICTIVE — **venge·ful·ly** *adv*

ve·nial \'vē-nē-əl\ *adj* : capable of being forgiven : EXCUSABLE ⟨∼ sin⟩

ve·ni·re \və-'nī-rē\ *n* : a panel from which a jury is drawn

ve·ni·re fa·ci·as \-'fā-shē-əs\ *n* [ME, fr. ML, you should cause to come] : a writ summoning persons to appear in court to serve as jurors

ve·ni·re·man \və-'nī-rē-mən, -'nir-ē-\ *n* : a member of a venire

ven·i·son \'ven-ə-sən, -zən\ *n, pl* **venisons** *also* **venison** [ME, fr. AF *veneisun* game, venison, fr. L *venatio*, fr. *venari* to hunt, pursue] : the edible flesh of a deer

ven·om \'ve-nəm\ *n* [ME *venim,* fr. AF, ultim. fr. L *venenum* magic charm, drug, poison] **1** : poisonous material secreted by some animals (as snakes, spiders, or bees) and transmitted usu. by biting or stinging **2** : ILL WILL, MALEVOLENCE

ven·om·ous \'ve-nə-məs\ *adj* **1** : full of venom : POISONOUS **2** : SPITEFUL, MALEVOLENT **3** : secreting and using venom ⟨~ snakes⟩ — **ven·om·ous·ly** *adv*

ve·nous \'vē-nəs\ *adj* **1** : of, relating to, or full of veins **2** : being purplish red oxygen-deficient blood rich in carbon dioxide that is present in most veins

¹vent \'vent\ *vb* **1** : to provide with a vent **2** : to serve as a vent for **3** : EXPEL, DISCHARGE **4** : to relieve oneself by vigorous or emotional expression

²vent *n* **1** : an opportunity or way of escape or passage : OUTLET **2** : an opening for the escape of a gas or liquid or for the relief of pressure

³vent *n* : a slit in a garment esp. in the lower part of a seam (as of a jacket or skirt)

ven·ti·late \'ven-tə-ˌlāt\ *vb* **-lat·ed; -lat·ing** **1** : to discuss freely and openly ⟨~ a question⟩ **2** : to give vent to ⟨~ one's grievances⟩ **3** : to cause fresh air to circulate through (as a room or mine) so as to replace foul air **4** : to provide with a vent or outlet ♦ *Synonyms* EXPRESS, VENT, AIR, UTTER, VOICE, BROACH — **ven·ti·la·tor** \-ˌlā-tər\ *n*

ven·ti·la·tion \ˌven-tə-ˈlā-shən\ *n* **1** : the act or process of ventilating **2** : circulation of air (as in a room) **3** : a system or means of providing fresh air

ven·tral \'ven-trəl\ *adj* **1** : of or relating to the belly : ABDOMINAL **2** : of, relating to, or located on or near the surface of the body that in humans is the front but in most other animals is the lower surface — **ven·tral·ly** *adv*

ven·tri·cle \'ven-tri-kəl\ *n* **1** : a chamber of the heart that receives blood from the atrium of the same side and pumps it into the arteries **2** : any of the communicating cavities of the brain that are continuous with the central canal of the spinal cord — **ven·tric·u·lar** \ven-ˈtri-kyə-lər\ *adj*

ven·tril·o·quism \ven-ˈtri-lə-ˌkwi-zəm\ *n* [LL *ventriloquus* ventriloquist, fr. L *venter* belly + *loqui* to speak; fr. the belief that the voice is produced from the ventriloquist's stomach] : the production of the voice in such a manner that the sound appears to come from a source other than the speaker — **ven·tril·o·quist** \-kwist\ *n*

ven·tril·o·quy \-kwē\ *n* : VENTRILOQUISM

¹ven·ture \'ven-chər\ *vb* **ven·tured; ven·tur·ing** **1** : to expose to hazard : RISK **2** : to undertake the risks of : BRAVE **3** : to offer at the risk of rebuff, rejection, or censure ⟨~ an opinion⟩ **4** : to proceed despite danger : DARE

²venture *n* **1** : an undertaking involving chance or risk; *esp* : a speculative business enterprise **2** : something risked in a speculative venture : STAKE

ven·ture·some \'ven-chər-səm\ *adj* **1** : involving risk : DANGEROUS, HAZARDOUS **2** : inclined to venture : BOLD, DARING ♦ *Synonyms* ADVENTUROUS, VENTUROUS, RASH, RECKLESS, FOOLHARDY — **ven·ture·some·ly** *adv* — **ven·ture·some·ness** *n*

ven·tur·ous \'ven-chə-rəs\ *adj* : VENTURESOME — **ven·tur·ous·ly** *adv* — **ven·tur·ous·ness** *n*

ven·ue \'ven-yü\ *n* [AF, alter. of *vinné, visné,* lit., neighborhood, neighbors, ultim. fr. L *vicinitas* vicinity] **1** : the place from which the jury is taken and where the trial is held **2** : the place in which the alleged events from which a legal action arises took place **3** : a place where events are held ⟨music ~s⟩

Ve·nus \'vē-nəs\ *n* : the planet 2d in order from the sun — see PLANET table

Ve·nu·sian \vi-ˈnü-zhən, -ˈnyü-\ *adj* : of or relating to the planet Venus

Venus fly·trap *or* **Ve·nus's–fly·trap** \'vē-nə-səz-ˈflī-ˌtrap\ *n* : an insect-eating plant of the Carolina coast that has the leaf tip modified into an insect trap

ve·ra·cious \və-ˈrā-shəs\ *adj* **1** : TRUTHFUL, HONEST **2** : TRUE, ACCURATE ⟨~ details⟩ — **ve·ra·cious·ly** *adv*

ve·rac·i·ty \və-ˈra-sə-tē\ *n, pl* **-ties** **1** : devotion to truth : TRUTHFULNESS **2** : conformity with fact : ACCURACY **3** : something true

ve·ran·da *or* **ve·ran·dah** \və-ˈran-də\ *n* : a long open usu. roofed porch

veranda

verb \'vərb\ *n* : a word that is the grammatical center of a predicate and expresses an act, occurrence, or mode of being

¹ver·bal \'vər-bəl\ *adj* **1** : of, relating to, or consisting of words; *esp* : having to do with words rather than with the ideas to be conveyed **2** : expressed in usu. spoken words : not written : ORAL ⟨a ~ contract⟩ **3** : of, relating to, or formed from a verb **4** : LITERAL, VERBATIM — **ver·bal·ly** *adv*

²verbal *n* : a word that combines characteristics of a verb with those of a noun or adjective

verbal auxiliary *n* : an auxiliary verb

ver·bal·ize \'vər-bə-ˌlīz\ *vb* **-ized; -iz·ing** **1** : to speak or write in wordy or empty fashion **2** : to express something in words : describe verbally **3** : to convert into a verb — **ver·bal·i·za·tion** \ˌvər-bə-lə-ˈzā-shən\ *n*

verbal noun *n* : a noun derived directly from a verb or verb stem and in some uses having the sense and constructions of a verb

ver·ba·tim \(ˌ)vər-ˈbā-təm\ *adv or adj* : in the same words : word for word

ver·be·na \(ˌ)vər-ˈbē-nə\ *n* : VERVAIN; *esp* : any of several garden vervains of hybrid origin with showy spikes of bright often fragrant flowers

ver·biage \'vər-bē-ij, -bij\ *n* **1** : superfluity of words usu. of little or obscure content **2** : DICTION, WORDING

ver·bose \(ˌ)vər-ˈbōs\ *adj* : using more words than are needed : WORDY ♦ *Synonyms* PROLIX, DIFFUSE, REDUNDANT, WINDY — **ver·bos·i·ty** \-ˈbä-sə-tē\ *n*

ver·bo·ten \vər-ˈbō-tᵊn, fər-\ *adj* [G] : forbidden usu. by dictate

ver·dant \'vər-dᵊnt\ *adj* : green with growing plants — **ver·dant·ly** *adv*

ver·dict \'vər-(ˌ)dikt\ *n* [ME *verdit, verdict,* fr. AF *veirdit,* fr. *veir* true (fr. L *verus*) + *dit* saying, dictum, fr. L *dictum,* fr. *dicere* to say] **1** : the finding or decision of a jury **2** : DECISION, JUDGMENT

ver·di·gris \'vər-də-ˌgrēs, -ˌgris\ *n* : a green or bluish deposit that forms on copper, brass, or bronze surfaces

ver·dure \'vər-jər\ *n* : the greenness of growing vegetation; *also* : such vegetation

¹verge \'vərj\ *n* [[ME, rod, measuring rod, margin, fr. AF, rod, area of jurisdiction, fr. L *virga* twig, rod, line] **1** : a staff carried as an emblem of authority or office **2** : something that borders or bounds : EDGE, MARGIN **3** : BRINK, THRESHOLD ⟨on the ~ of collapse⟩

²verge *vb* **verged; verg·ing** **1** : to be contiguous **2** : to be on the verge

³verge *vb* **verged; verg·ing** **1** : to move or extend in some direction or toward some condition : INCLINE **2** : to be in transition or change

verg·er \'vər-jər\ *n* **1** *chiefly Brit* : an attendant who carries a verge (as before a bishop) **2** : SEXTON

ve·rid·i·cal \və-ˈri-di-kəl\ *adj* **1** : TRUTHFUL **2** : not illusory : GENUINE

ver·i·fy \'ver-ə-ˌfī\ *vb* **-fied; -fy·ing** **1** : to confirm in law by oath **2** : to establish the truth, accuracy, or reality of ⟨~ the claim⟩ ♦ *Synonyms* AUTHENTICATE, CORROBORATE, SUBSTANTIATE, VALIDATE — **ver·i·fi·able** *adj* — **ver·i·fi·ca·tion** \ˌver-ə-fə-ˈkā-shən\ *n*

ver·i·ly \'ver-ə-lē\ *adv* **1** : in very truth : CERTAINLY **2** : TRULY, CONFIDENTLY

veri·si·mil·i·tude \ˌver-ə-sə-ˈmi-lə-ˌtüd, -ˌtyüd\ *n* : the quality or state of appearing to be true or real

DICTIONARY

ver·i·ta·ble \'ver-ə-tə-bəl\ *adj* : ACTUAL, GENUINE, TRUE — **ver·i·ta·bly** *adv*

ver·i·ty \'ver-ə-tē\ *n, pl* **-ties** 1 : the quality or state of being true or real : TRUTH, REALITY 2 : something (as a statement) that is true 3 : HONESTY, VERACITY

ver·meil *n* [MF] 1 \'vər-məl, -,māl\ : VERMILION 2 \ver-'mā\ : gilded silver

ver·mi·cel·li \,vər-mə-'che-lē, -'se-\ *n* [It, fr. pl. of *vermicello*, dim. of *verme* worm] : a pasta made in thinner strings than spaghetti

ver·mic·u·lite \vər-'mi-kyə-,līt\ *n* : any of various lightweight water-absorbent minerals derived from mica

ver·mi·form appendix \'vər-mə-,form-\ *n* : APPENDIX 2

ver·mil·ion *also* **ver·mil·lion** \vər-'mil-yən\ *n* : a bright reddish orange color; *also* : any of various red pigments

ver·min \'vər-mən\ *n, pl* **vermin** 1 : small common harmful or objectionable animals (as lice or mice) that are difficult to get rid of 2 : birds and mammals that prey on game — **ver·min·ous** *adj*

ver·mouth \vər-'müth\ *n* [F *vermout*, fr. G *Wermut* wormwood] : a dry or sweet wine flavored with herbs and often used in mixed drinks

¹**ver·nac·u·lar** \vər-'na-kyə-lər\ *adj* [L *vernaculus* native, fr. *verna* slave born in the master's house, native] 1 : of, relating to, or being a language or dialect native to a region or country rather than a literary, cultured, or foreign language 2 : of, relating to, or being the normal spoken form of a language 3 : applied to a plant or animal in common speech as distinguished from biological nomenclature ⟨∼ names⟩

²**vernacular** *n* 1 : a vernacular language 2 : the mode of expression of a group or class 3 : a vernacular name of a plant or animal

ver·nal \'vər-n³l\ *adj* : of, relating to, or occurring in the spring

ver·ni·er \'vər-nē-ər\ *n* : a short scale made to slide along the divisions of a graduated instrument to indicate parts of divisions

ve·ron·i·ca \və-'rä-ni-kə\ *n* : any of a genus of herbs related to the snapdragons that have small usu. bluish flowers

ver·sa·tile \'vər-sə-t³l\ *adj* : turning with ease from one thing or position to another; *esp* : having many aptitudes — **ver·sa·til·i·ty** \,vər-sə-'ti-lə-tē\ *n*

¹**verse** \'vərs\ *n* 1 : a line of poetry; *also* : STANZA 2 : metrical writing distinguished from poetry esp. by its lower level of intensity 3 : POETRY 4 : POEM 5 : one of the short divisions of a chapter in the Bible

²**verse** *vb* **versed; vers·ing** : to familiarize by experience, study, or practice ⟨*well versed* in the theater⟩

ver·si·cle \'vər-si-kəl\ *n* : a verse or sentence said or sung by a leader in public worship and followed by a response from the people

ver·si·fi·ca·tion \,vər-sə-fə-'kā-shən\ *n* 1 : the making of verses 2 : metrical structure

ver·si·fy \'vər-sə-,fī\ *vb* **-fied; -fy·ing** 1 : to write verse 2 : to turn into verse — **ver·si·fi·er** \-,fī-ər\ *n*

ver·sion \'vər-zhən\ *n* 1 : TRANSLATION; *esp* : a translation of the Bible 2 : an account or description from a particular point of view esp. as contrasted with another 3 : a form or variant of a type or original

vers li·bre \,ver-'lēbr³\ *n, pl* **vers li·bres** *same*\ [F] : FREE VERSE

ver·so \'vər-sō\ *n, pl* **versos** : a left-hand page

ver·sus \'vər-səs\ *prep* 1 : AGAINST ⟨the champion ∼ the challenger⟩ 2 : in contrast or as an alternative to ⟨free trade ∼ protection⟩

vert *abbr* vertical

ver·te·bra \'vər-tə-brə\ *n, pl* **-brae** \-,brā, -(,)brē\ *or* **-bras** [L] : one of the segments of bone or cartilage making up the backbone

ver·te·bral \(,)vər-'tē-brəl, 'vər-tə-\ *adj* : of, relating to, or made up of vertebrae : SPINAL

vertebral column *n* : BACKBONE 1

¹**ver·te·brate** \'vər-tə-brət, -,brāt\ *adj* 1 : having a backbone 2 : of or relating to the vertebrates

²**vertebrate** *n* : any of a large group of animals (as mammals, birds, reptiles, amphibians, or fishes) that have a backbone or in some primitive forms (as a lamprey) a flexible rod of cells and that have a tubular nervous system arranged along the back and divided into a brain and spinal cord

ver·tex \'vər-,teks\ *n, pl* **ver·ti·ces** \'vər-tə-,sēz\ *also* **ver·tex·es** [ME, top of the head, fr. L *vertex, vortex* whirl, whirlpool, top of the head, summit, fr. *vertere* to turn] 1 : the point opposite to and farthest from the base of a geometrical figure 2 : the point where the sides of an angle or three or more edges of a polyhedron (as a cube) meet 3 : the highest point : TOP, SUMMIT

ver·ti·cal \'vər-ti-kəl\ *adj* 1 : of, relating to, or located at the vertex : directly overhead 2 : rising perpendicularly from a level surface : UPRIGHT — **vertical** *n* — **ver·ti·cal·i·ty** \,vər-tə-'ka-lə-tē\ *n* — **ver·ti·cal·ly** \-k(ə-)lē\ *adv*

ver·tig·i·nous \(,)vər-'ti-jə-nəs\ *adj* : marked by, affected with, or tending to cause dizziness

ver·ti·go \'vər-ti-,gō\ *n, pl* **-goes** *or* **-gos** : DIZZINESS, GIDDINESS

vertu *var of* VIRTU

ver·vain \'vər-,vān\ *n* : any of a genus of chiefly American herbs or low woody plants with often showy heads or spikes of tubular flowers

verve \'vərv\ *n* : liveliness of imagination; *also* : VIVACITY

¹**very** \'ver-ē\ *adj* [ME *verray, verry*, fr. AF *verai*, ultim. fr. L *verax* truthful, fr. *verus* true] 1 : EXACT, PRECISE ⟨the ∼ heart of the city⟩ 2 : exactly suitable ⟨the ∼ tool for the job⟩ 3 : ABSOLUTE, UTTER ⟨the *veriest* nonsense⟩ 4 : used as an intensive esp. to emphasize identity ⟨before my ∼ eyes⟩ 5 : MERE, BARE ⟨the ∼ idea scared him⟩ 6 : SELFSAME, IDENTICAL ⟨the ∼ man I saw⟩

²**very** *adv* 1 : in actual fact : TRULY 2 : to a high degree : EXTREMELY

very high frequency *n* : a radio frequency of between 30 and 300 megahertz

ves·i·cant \'ve-si-kənt\ *n* : an agent that causes blistering — **vesicant** *adj*

ves·i·cle \'ve-si-kəl\ *n* : a membranous and usu. fluid-filled cavity in a plant or animal; *also* : BLISTER — **ve·sic·u·lar** \və-'si-kyə-lər\ *adj*

¹**ves·per** \'ves-pər\ *n* 1 *cap archaic* : EVENING STAR 2 : a vesper bell 3 *archaic* : EVENING, EVENTIDE

²**vesper** *adj* : of or relating to vespers or the evening

ves·pers \-pərz\ *n pl, often cap* : a late afternoon or evening worship service

ves·sel \'ve-səl\ *n* 1 : a container (as a barrel, bottle, bowl, or cup) for holding something 2 : a person held to be the recipient of a quality (as grace) 3 : a craft bigger than a rowboat 4 : a tube in which a body fluid (as blood or sap) is contained and circulated

¹**vest** \'vest\ *vb* 1 : to place or give into the possession or discretion of some person or authority 2 : to grant or endow with a particular authority, right, or property 3 : to become legally vested 4 : to clothe with or as if with a garment; *esp* : to garb in ecclesiastical vestments

²**vest** *n* 1 : a sleeveless garment for the upper body usu. worn over a shirt 2 *chiefly Brit* : a man's sleeveless undershirt 3 : a front piece of a dress resembling the front of a vest

¹**ves·tal** \'ves-t³l\ *adj* : CHASTE

²**vestal** *n* : VESTAL VIRGIN

vestal virgin *n* 1 : a virgin consecrated to the Roman goddess Vesta and to the service of watching the sacred fire perpetually kept burning on her altar 2 : a chaste woman

vest·ed \'ves-təd\ *adj* : fully and unconditionally guaranteed as a legal right, benefit, or privilege

vested interest *n* : an interest (as in an existing political, economic, or social arrangement) to which the holder has a strong commitment; *also* : one (as a corporation) having a vested interest

ves·ti·bule \'ves-tə-,byül\ *n* 1 : a passage or room between the outer door and the interior of a building 2 : any of various bodily cavities forming or suggesting an entrance to some other cavity or space — **ves·tib·u·lar** \ve-'sti-byə-lər\ *adj*

ves·tige \'ves-tij\ *n* [F, fr. L *vestigium* footprint, track, vestige] : a trace or visible sign left by something lost or vanished; *also* : a minute remaining amount — **ves·ti·gial** \ve-'sti-jē-əl, -jəl\ *adj* — **ves·ti·gial·ly** *adv*

vest·ing \'ves-tin\ *n* : the conveying to an employee of inalienable rights to share in a pension fund; *also* : the right so conveyed

vest·ment \'vest-mənt\ *n* 1 : an outer garment; *esp* : a ceremonial or official robe **2** *pl* : CLOTHING, GARB **3** : a garment or insignia worn by a cleric when officiating or assisting at a religious service

vest–pocket *adj* : very small ⟨a ∼ park⟩

ves·try \'ves-trē\ *n, pl* **vestries** **1** : a room in a church for vestments, altar linens, and sacred vessels **2** : a room used for church meetings and classes **3** : a body administering the temporal affairs of an Episcopal parish

ves·try·man \-mən\ *n* : a member of a vestry

ves·ture \'ves-chər\ *n* **1** : a covering garment **2** : CLOTHING, APPAREL

¹vet \'vet\ *n* : VETERINARIAN

²vet *adj or n* : VETERAN

³vet *vb* : to evaluate for appraisal or acceptance ⟨∼ a manuscript⟩

vetch \'vech\ *n* : any of a genus of twining leguminous herbs including some grown for fodder and green manure

vet·er·an \'ve-trən, -tə-rən\ *n* [L *veteranus*, fr. *veteranus* old, of long experience, fr. *veter-*, *vetus* old] **1** : an old soldier of long service **2** : a former member of the armed forces **3** : a person of long experience usu. in an occupation or skill — **veteran** *adj*

Veterans Day *n* : November 11 observed as a legal holiday in commemoration of the end of hostilities in 1918 and 1945

vet·er·i·nar·i·an \,ve-trə-'ner-ē-ən, ,ve-tə-rə-\ *n* : one qualified and authorized to practice veterinary medicine

¹vet·er·i·nary \'ve-trə-,ner-ē, 've-tə-rə-\ *adj* : of, relating to, or being the medical care of animals and esp. domestic animals

²veterinary *n, pl* **-nar·ies** : VETERINARIAN

¹ve·to \'vē-tō\ *n, pl* **vetoes** [L, I forbid] **1** : an authoritative prohibition **2** : a power of one part of a government to forbid the carrying out of projects attempted by another part; *esp* : a power vested in a chief executive to prevent the carrying out of measures adopted by a legislature **3** : the exercise of the power of veto

²veto *vb* **1** : FORBID, PROHIBIT **2** : to refuse assent to (a legislative bill) so as to prevent enactment or cause reconsideration — **ve·to·er** *n*

vex \'veks\ *vb* **vexed** *also* **vext; vex·ing** **1** : to bring trouble, distress, or agitation to **2** : to annoy continually with little irritations

vex·a·tion \vek-'sā-shən\ *n* **1** : the act of vexing **2** : the quality or state of being vexed : IRRITATION **3** : a cause of trouble or annoyance

vex·a·tious \-shəs\ *adj* **1** : causing vexation : ANNOYING **2** : full of distress or annoyance : TROUBLED — **vex·a·tious·ly** *adv* — **vex·a·tious·ness** *n*

vexed \'vekst\ *adj* : fully debated or discussed ⟨a ∼ question⟩

VF *abbr* **1** video frequency **2** visual field

VFD *abbr* volunteer fire department

VFW *abbr* Veterans of Foreign Wars

VG *abbr* **1** very good **2** vicar-general

VHF *abbr* very high frequency

VI *abbr* Virgin Islands

via \'vī-ə, 'vē-ə\ *prep* **1** : by way of **2** : by means of

vi·a·ble \'vī-ə-bəl\ *adj* **1** : capable of living; *esp* : sufficiently developed as to be capable of surviving outside the mother's womb ⟨a ∼ fetus⟩ **2** : capable of growing and developing ⟨∼ seeds⟩ **3** : capable of being put into practice : WORKABLE **4** : having a reasonable chance of succeeding ⟨a ∼ candidate⟩ — **vi·a·bil·i·ty** \,vī-ə-'bi-lə-tē\ *n* — **vi·a·bly** \'vī-ə-blē\ *adv*

via·duct \'vī-ə-,dəkt\ *n* : a long elevated roadway usu. consisting of a series of short spans supported on arches, piers, or columns

vi·al \'vī-əl\ *n* : a small vessel for liquids

vi·and \'vī-ənd\ *n* : an article of food

vi·at·i·cum \vī-'a-ti-kəm, vē-\ *n, pl* **-cums** *or* **-ca** \-kə\ **1** : the Christian Eucharist given to a person in danger of death **2** : an allowance esp. in money for traveling needs and expenses

vibes \'vībz\ *n pl* **1** : VIBRAPHONE **2** : VIBRATIONS

vi·brant \'vī-brənt\ *adj* **1** : VIBRATING, PULSATING **2** : pulsating with vigor or activity ⟨a ∼ personality⟩ **3** : readily set in vibration : RESPONSIVE **4** : sounding from vibration **5** : BRIGHT ⟨∼ colors⟩ — **vi·bran·cy** \-brən-sē\ *n*

vi·bra·phone \'vī-brə-,fōn\ *n* : a percussion instrument like the xylophone but with metal bars and motor-driven resonators

vi·brate \'vī-,brāt\ *vb* **vi·brat·ed; vi·brat·ing** **1** : OSCILLATE **2** : to set in vibration **3** : to be in vibration **4** : WAVER, FLUCTUATE **5** : to respond sympathetically : THRILL

vi·bra·tion \vī-'brā-shən\ *n* **1** : a rapid to-and-fro motion of the particles of an elastic body or medium (as a stretched cord) that produces sound **2** : an act of vibrating : a state of being vibrated : OSCILLATION **3** : a trembling motion **4** : VACILLATION **5** : a feeling or impression that someone or something gives off — usu. used in pl. ⟨good ∼s⟩ — **vi·bra·tion·al** \-shə-nəl\ *adj*

vi·bra·to \vi-'brä-tō\ *n, pl* **-tos** [It] : a slightly tremulous effect imparted to vocal or instrumental music

vi·bra·tor \'vī-,brā-tər\ *n* : one that vibrates or causes vibration; *esp* : a vibrating electrical device used in massage or for sexual stimulation

vi·bra·to·ry \'vī-brə-,tōr-ē\ *adj* : consisting of, capable of, or causing vibration

vi·bur·num \vī-'bər-nəm\ *n* : any of a genus of widely distributed shrubs or small trees related to the honeysuckle and bearing small usu. white flowers in broad clusters

vic *abbr* vicinity

Vic *abbr* Victoria

vic·ar \'vi-kər\ *n* **1** : an administrative deputy **2** : a minister in charge of a church who serves under the authority of another minister — **vi·car·i·ate** \vī-'ker-ē-ət\ *n*

vic·ar·age \'vi-kə-rij\ *n* : a vicar's home

vicar–general *n, pl* **vicars–general** : an administrative deputy (as of a Roman Catholic or Anglican bishop)

vi·car·i·ous \vī-'ker-ē-əs\ *adj* [L *vicarius*, fr. *vicis* change, alternation, stead] **1** : acting for another **2** : done or suffered by one person on behalf of another or others ⟨a ∼ sacrifice⟩ **3** : sharing in someone else's experience through the use of the imagination or sympathetic feelings — **vi·car·i·ous·ly** *adv* — **vi·car·i·ous·ness** *n*

¹vice \'vīs\ *n* **1** : DEPRAVITY, WICKEDNESS **2** : a moral fault or failing **3** : a habitual usu. trivial fault **4** : an undesirable behavior pattern in a domestic animal

²vice *chiefly Brit var of* VISE

³vi·ce \'vī-sē\ *prep* : in the place of; *also* : rather than

vice admiral *n* : a commissioned officer in the navy or coast guard ranking above a rear admiral

vice·ge·rent \'vīs-'jir-ənt\ *n* : an administrative deputy of a king or magistrate — **vice·ge·ren·cy** \-ən-sē\ *n*

vi·cen·ni·al \vī-'se-nē-əl\ *adj* : occurring once every 20 years

vice presidency *n* : the office of vice president

vice president *n* **1** : an officer ranking next to a president and usu. empowered to act for the president during an absence or disability **2** : any of several of a president's deputies

vice·re·gal \'vīs-'rē-gəl\ *adj* : of or relating to a viceroy

vice·roy \'vīs-,rói\ *n* : the governor of a country or province who rules as representative of the sovereign — **vice·roy·al·ty** \-əl-tē\ *n*

vice ver·sa \,vī-si-'vər-sə, 'vīs-'vər-\ *adv* : with the order reversed

vi·chys·soise \,vi-shē-'swäz, ,vē-\ *n* [F] : a soup made esp. from leeks or onions and potatoes, cream, and chicken stock and usu. served cold

vic·i·nage \'vi-sə-nij\ *n* : a neighboring or surrounding district : VICINITY

vi·cin·i·ty \və-'si-nə-tē\ *n, pl* **-ties** [MF *vicinité*, fr. L *vicinitas*, fr. *vicinus* neighboring, fr. *vicus* row of houses, village] **1** : NEARNESS, PROXIMITY **2** : a surrounding area : NEIGHBORHOOD

vi·cious \'vi-shəs\ *adj* **1** : having the quality of vice : WICKED, DEPRAVED **2** : DEFECTIVE, FAULTY; *also* : INVALID **3** : IMPURE, FOUL **4** : having a savage disposition; *also* : marked by violence or ferocity **5** : MALICIOUS, SPITEFUL ⟨∼ gossip⟩ **6** : worsened by internal causes that augment each other ⟨∼ wage-price spiral⟩ — **vi·cious·ly** *adv* — **vi·cious·ness** *n*

vi·cis·si·tude \və-'si-sə-,tüd, vī-, -,tyüd\ *n* : an irregular, unexpected, or surprising change

vic·tim \'vik-təm\ *n* **1** : a living being offered as a sacrifice in a religious rite **2** : an individual injured or killed (as by disease or accident) **3** : a person cheated, fooled, or injured ⟨a ∼ of circumstances⟩

vic·tim·ise Brit var of VICTIMIZE
vic·tim·ize \'vik-tə-ˌmīz\ vb **-ized; -iz·ing** : to make a victim of — **vic·tim·i·za·tion** \ˌvik-tə-mə-'zā-shən\ n — **vic·tim·iz·er** \'vik-tə-ˌmī-zər\ n
vic·tim·less \'vik-təm-ləs\ adj : having no victim ⟨considered gambling to be a ~ crime⟩
vic·tor \'vik-tər\ n : WINNER, CONQUEROR
vic·to·ria \vik-'tȯr-ē-ə\ n : a low 4-wheeled carriage with a folding top and a raised driver's seat in front

victoria

¹Vic·to·ri·an \vik-'tȯr-ē-ən\ adj **1** : of or relating to the reign of Queen Victoria of England or the art, letters, or tastes of her time **2** : typical of the standards, attitudes, or conduct of the age of Victoria esp. when considered prudish or narrow
²Victorian n **1** : a person and esp. an author of the Victorian period **2** : a typically large ornate house built during Queen Victoria's reign
vic·to·ri·ous \vik-'tȯr-ē-əs\ adj **1** : having won a victory **2** : of, relating to, or characteristic of victory ⟨~ exuberance⟩ — **vic·to·ri·ous·ly** adv
vic·to·ry \'vik-tə-rē\ n, pl **-ries 1** : the overcoming of an enemy or an antagonist **2** : achievement of mastery or success in a struggle or endeavor
¹vict·ual \'vi-t²l\ n [ME vitaille, victuayle, fr. AF, fr. LL victualia, pl., provisions, food, fr. neut. pl. of victualis of nourishment, fr. L victus nourishment, way of living, fr. vivere to live] **1** : food fit for human consumption **2** pl : food supplies
²victual vb **-ualed** or **-ualled; -ual·ing** or **-ual·ling 1** : to supply with food **2** : to store up provisions
vict·ual·ler or **vict·ual·er** \'vi-t²l-ər\ n : one that supplies provisions (as to an army or a ship)
vi·cu·ña or **vi·cu·na** \vi-'kün-yə, vī-; vī-'kü-nə, -'kyü-\ n **1** : a So. American wild mammal related to the llama and alpaca; also : its wool **2** : a soft fabric woven from the wool of the vicuña; also : a sheep's wool imitation of this
vi·de \'vī-dē, 'vē-ˌdā\ vb imper [L] : SEE — used to direct a reader to another item
vi·de·li·cet \və-'de-lə-ˌset, vī-; vi-'dā-li-ˌket\ adv [ME, fr. L, fr. vidēre to see + licet it is permitted] : that is to say : NAMELY
¹vid·eo \'vi-dē-ˌō\ n **1** : TELEVISION **2** : VIDEOTAPE; also : a recording similar to a videotape but stored in digital form **3** : a videotaped performance ⟨music ~s⟩
²video adj **1** : relating to or used in transmission or reception of the television image **2** : relating to or being images on a television screen or computer display ⟨a ~ terminal⟩
video camera n : a camera that records visual images and usu. sound; esp : CAMCORDER
vid·eo·cas·sette \ˌvi-dē-ō-kə-'set\ n **1** : a case containing videotape for use with a VCR **2** : a recording (as of a movie) on a videocassette
videocassette recorder n : VCR
vid·eo·disc or **vid·eo·disk** \'vi-dē-ō-ˌdisk\ n **1** : OPTICAL DISK **2** : a recording (as of a movie) on a videodisc
video game n : an electronic game played on a video screen
vid·e·o·gen·ic \ˌvi-dē-ō-'je-nik\ adj : TELEGENIC
vid·eo·phone \'vid-ē-ə-ˌfōn\ n : a telephone for transmitting both audio and video signals
¹vid·eo·tape \'vid-ē-ō-ˌtāp\ n : a recording of visual images and sound made on magnetic tape; also : the magnetic tape used for such a recording
²videotape vb : to make a videotape of
videotape recorder n : a device for recording and playing back videotapes
vie \'vī\ vb **vied; vy·ing** \'vī-iŋ\ : to compete for superiority : CONTEND — **vi·er** \'vī-ər\ n

Viet·cong \vē-'et-'käŋ, ˌvē-ət-, -'kȯŋ\ n, pl **Vietcong** : a guerrilla member of the Vietnamese communist movement
¹view \'vyü\ n **1** : the act of seeing or examining : INSPECTION; also : SURVEY **2** : a way of looking at or regarding something **3** : ESTIMATE, JUDGMENT ⟨stated his ~s⟩ **4** : a sight (as of a landscape) regarded for its pictorial quality **5** : extent or range of vision ⟨within ~⟩ **6** : OBJECT, PURPOSE ⟨done with a ~ to promotion⟩ **7** : a picture of a scene
²view vb **1** : to look at attentively : EXAMINE **2** : SEE, WATCH ⟨~ a film⟩ **3** : to examine mentally : CONSIDER — **view·er** n
view·er·ship \'vyü-ər-ˌship\ n : a television audience esp. with respect to size or makeup
view·find·er \'vyü-ˌfīn-dər\ n : a device on a camera for showing the view to be included in the picture
view·point \-ˌpȯint\ n : POINT OF VIEW, STANDPOINT
vi·ges·i·mal \vī-'je-sə-məl\ adj : based on the number 20
vig·il \'vi-jəl\ n **1** : a religious observance formerly held on the night before a religious feast **2** : the day before a religious feast observed as a day of spiritual preparation **3** : evening or nocturnal devotions or prayers — usu. used in pl. **4** : an act or a time of keeping awake when sleep is customary; esp : WATCH 1
vigilance committee n : a committee of vigilantes
vig·i·lant \'vi-jə-lənt\ adj : alertly watchful esp. to avoid danger — **vig·i·lance** \-ləns\ n — **vig·i·lant·ly** adv
vig·i·lan·te \ˌvi-jə-'lan-tē\ n : a member of a volunteer committee organized to suppress and punish crime summarily (as when the processes of law are viewed as inadequate); also : a self-appointed doer of justice — **vig·i·lan·tism** \-'lan-ˌti-zəm\ n
¹vi·gnette \vin-'yet\ n [F, fr. MF vignete, fr. dim. of vigne vine] **1** : a small decorative design **2** : a picture (as an engraving or a photograph) that shades off gradually into the surrounding ground **3** : a short descriptive literary sketch
²vignette vb **vi·gnett·ed; vi·gnett·ing 1** : to finish (as a photograph) like a vignette **2** : to describe briefly
vig·or \'vi-gər\ n **1** : active strength or energy of body or mind **2** : INTENSITY, FORCE ⟨the ~ of their quarrel⟩
vig·or·ous \'vi-gə-rəs\ adj **1** : having vigor : ROBUST **2** : done with force and energy — **vig·or·ous·ly** adv — **vig·or·ous·ness** n
vig·our chiefly Brit var of VIGOR
Vi·king \'vī-kiŋ\ n [ON víkingr] : any of the pirate Norsemen who raided or invaded the coasts of Europe in the 8th to 10th centuries
vile \'vī(-ə)l\ adj **vil·er; vil·est 1** : morally despicable **2** : physically repulsive : FOUL **3** : of little worth **4** : DEGRADING, IGNOMINIOUS **5** : utterly bad or contemptible ⟨~ weather⟩ — **vile·ly** \'vī(-ə)l-lē\ adv — **vile·ness** n
vil·i·fy \'vi-lə-ˌfī\ vb **-fied; -fy·ing** : to blacken the character of with abusive language : DEFAME ♦ **Synonyms** MALIGN, CALUMNIATE, SLANDER, LIBEL, TRADUCE — **vil·i·fi·ca·tion** \ˌvi-lə-fə-'kā-shən\ n — **vil·i·fi·er** \'vi-lə-ˌfī-ər\ n
vil·la \'vi-lə\ n **1** : a country estate **2** : the rural or suburban residence of a wealthy person
vil·lage \'vi-lij\ n [ME, fr. AF vilage, fr. vile manorial estate, farmstead, fr. L villa] **1** : a settlement usu. larger than a hamlet and smaller than a town **2** : an incorporated minor municipality **3** : the people of a village
vil·lag·er \'vi-li-jər\ n : an inhabitant of a village
vil·lain \'vi-lən\ n **1** : VILLEIN **2** : an evil person : SCOUNDREL
vil·lain·ess \-lə-nəs\ n : a woman who is a villain
vil·lain·ous \-lə-nəs\ adj **1** : befitting a villain : WICKED, EVIL **2** : highly objectionable : DETESTABLE ♦ **Synonyms** VICIOUS, INIQUITOUS, NEFARIOUS, INFAMOUS, CORRUPT, DEGENERATE — **vil·lain·ous·ly** adv — **vil·lain·ous·ness** n
vil·lainy \-lə-nē\ n, pl **-lain·ies 1** : villainous conduct; also : a villainous act **2** : villainous character or nature
vil·lein \'vi-lən, -ˌlān\ n **1** : a free villager of Anglo-Saxon times **2** : an unfree peasant having the status of a slave to a feudal lord
vil·len·age \'vil-ə-nij\ n **1** : the holding of land at the will of a feudal lord **2** : the status of a villein
vil·lous \'vi-ləs\ adj : covered with fine hairs or villi
vil·lus \'vi-ləs\ n, pl **vil·li** \-ˌlī, -(ˌ)lē\ : a slender usu. vascu-

lar process; *esp* : one of the tiny projections of the mucous membrane of the small intestine that function in the absorption of food

vim \'vim\ *n* : robust energy and enthusiasm : VITALITY

VIN *abbr* vehicle identification number

vin·ai·grette \ˌvi-ni-ˈgret\ *n* [F] : a sauce made typically of oil, vinegar, and seasonings

vin·ci·ble \'vin-sə-bəl\ *adj* : capable of being overcome or subdued

vin·di·cate \'vin-də-ˌkāt\ *vb* **-cat·ed; -cat·ing** 1 : AVENGE 2 : EXONERATE, ABSOLVE 3 : CONFIRM, SUBSTANTIATE 4 : to provide defense for : JUSTIFY 5 : to maintain a right to : ASSERT — **vin·di·ca·tor** \-ˌkā-tər\ *n*

vin·di·ca·tion \ˌvin-də-ˈkā-shən\ *n* : the act of vindicating or the state of being vindicated; *esp* : justification against denial or censure : DEFENSE

vin·dic·tive \vin-ˈdik-tiv\ *adj* 1 : disposed to revenge 2 : intended for or involving revenge 3 : VICIOUS, SPITEFUL — **vin·dic·tive·ly** *adv* — **vin·dic·tive·ness** *n*

vine \'vīn\ *n* [ME, fr. AF *vigne*, fr. L *vinea* vine, vineyard, fr. fem. of *vineus* of wine, fr. *vinum* wine] 1 : GRAPE 2 2 : a plant whose stem requires support and which climbs (as by tendrils) or trails along the ground; *also* : the stem of such a plant

vin·e·gar \'vi-ni-gər\ *n* [ME *vinegre*, fr. AF *vin egre*, lit., sour wine] : a sour liquid obtained by fermentation (as of cider, wine, or malt) and used to flavor or preserve foods

vin·e·gary \-gə-rē\ *adj* 1 : resembling vinegar : SOUR 2 : disagreeable in manner or disposition : CRABBED

vine·yard \'vin-yərd\ *n* 1 : a field of grapevines esp. to produce grapes for wine production 2 : a sphere of activity : field of endeavor

vi·nous \'vī-nəs\ *adj* 1 : of, relating to, or made with wine ⟨~ medications⟩ 2 : showing the effects of the use of wine ⟨~ bloodshot eyes⟩

¹vin·tage \'vin-tij\ *n* 1 : a season's yield of grapes or wine 2 : WINE; *esp* : a usu. superior wine which comes from a single year 3 : the act or period of gathering grapes or making wine 4 : a period of origin ⟨clothes of 1890 ~⟩

²vintage *adj* 1 : of, relating to, or produced in a particular vintage 2 : of old, recognized, and enduring interest, importance, or quality : CLASSIC ⟨~ cars⟩ 3 : of the best and most characteristic — used with a proper noun

vint·ner \'vint-nər\ *n* : a dealer in wines

vi·nyl \'vī-nᵊl\ *n* 1 : a chemical derived from ethylene by the removal of one hydrogen atom 2 : a polymer of a vinyl compound or a product (as a textile fiber) made from one

vinyl chloride *n* : a flammable gaseous carcinogenic compound used esp. to make vinyl resins

vi·ol \'vī-əl\ *n* : a bowed stringed instrument chiefly of the 16th and 17th centuries having a fretted neck and usu. six strings

¹vi·o·la \vī-ˈō-lə, ˈvī-ə-lə\ *n* : VIOLET 1; *esp* : any of various hybrid garden plants with white, yellow, purple, or variously colored flowers that resemble but are smaller than those of the related pansies

²vi·o·la \vē-ˈō-lə\ *n* : an instrument of the violin family slightly larger and tuned lower than a violin — **vi·o·list** \-list\ *n*

vi·o·la·ble \'vī-ə-lə-bəl\ *adj* : capable of being violated

vi·o·late \'vī-ə-ˌlāt\ *vb* **-lat·ed; -lat·ing** 1 : BREAK, DISREGARD ⟨~ a law⟩ ⟨~ a frontier⟩ 2 : RAPE 3 : PROFANE, DESECRATE 4 : INTERRUPT, DISTURB ⟨violated his privacy⟩ — **vi·o·la·tor** \-ˌlā-tər\ *n*

vi·o·la·tion \ˌvī-ə-ˈlā-shən\ *n* : an act or instance of violating : the state of being violated ♦ *Synonyms* BREACH, INFRACTION, TRESPASS, INFRINGEMENT, TRANSGRESSION

vi·o·lence \'vī-ləns, 'vī-ə-\ *n* 1 : exertion of physical force so as to injure or abuse 2 : injury by or as if by infringement or profanation 3 : intense or furious often destructive action or force 4 : vehement feeling or expression : INTENSITY 5 : jarring quality : DISCORDANCE ♦ *Synonyms* COMPULSION, COERCION, DURESS, CONSTRAINT

vi·o·lent \-lənt\ *adj* 1 : marked by extreme force or sudden intense activity 2 : caused by or showing strong feeling ⟨~ words⟩ 3 : EXTREME, INTENSE ⟨~ pain⟩ ⟨~ colors⟩ 4 : emotionally agitated to the point of loss of self-control 5 : caused by force : not natural ⟨~ death⟩ — **vi·o·lent·ly** *adv*

vi·o·let \'vī-ə-lət\ *n* 1 : any of a genus of herbs or small shrubs usu. with heart-shaped leaves and both aerial and underground flowers; *esp* : one with small usu. solid-colored flowers 2 : a reddish blue color

vi·o·lin \ˌvī-ə-ˈlin\ *n* : a bowed stringed instrument with four strings that has a shallow body, a fingerboard without frets, and a curved bridge — **vi·o·lin·ist** \-ˈli-nist\ *n*

vi·o·lon·cel·lo \ˌvī-ə-lən-ˈche-lō\ *n* [It] : CELLO — **vi·o·lon·cel·list** \-list\ *n*

VIP \ˌvē-ˌī-ˈpē\ *n, pl* **VIPs** \-ˈpēz\ [*v*ery *i*mportant *p*erson] : a person of great influence or prestige; *esp* : a high official with special privileges

vi·per \'vī-pər\ *n* 1 : a common stout-bodied Eurasian venomous snake having a bite only rarely fatal to humans; *also* : any snake (as a pit viper) of the same family as the viper 2 : any venomous or reputedly venomous snake 3 : a vicious or treacherous person — **vi·per·ine** \-pə-ˌrīn\ *adj*

vi·ra·go \və-ˈrä-gō, -ˈrä-\ *n, pl* **-goes** *or* **-gos** [ME, fr. L, strong or heroic woman, fr. *vir* man] 1 : a loud overbearing woman 2 : a woman of great strength and courage

vi·ral \'vī-rəl\ *adj* : of, relating to, or caused by a virus ⟨a ~ infection⟩ — **vi·ral·ly** *adv*

vir·eo \'vir-ē-ˌō\ *n, pl* **-e·os** [L, a small bird, fr. *virēre* to be green] : any of various small insect-eating American songbirds mostly olive green and grayish in color

¹vir·gin \'vər-jən\ *n* 1 : an unmarried woman devoted to religion 2 : an unmarried girl or woman 3 *cap* : the mother of Jesus 4 : a person who has not had sexual intercourse

²virgin *adj* 1 : free from stain : PURE, SPOTLESS 2 : CHASTE 3 : befitting a virgin : MODEST 4 : FRESH, UNSPOILED; *esp* : not altered by human activity ⟨~ forest⟩ 5 : INITIAL, FIRST

¹vir·gin·al \'vər-jə-nᵊl\ *adj* : of, relating to, or characteristic of a virgin or virginity — **vir·gin·al·ly** *adv*

²virginal *n* : a small rectangular spinet without legs popular in the 16th and 17th centuries

Vir·gin·ia creeper \vər-ˈjin-yə-\ *n* : a No. American vine related to the grapes that has leaves with five leaflets and bluish-black berries

Virginia reel *n* : an American country-dance

vir·gin·i·ty \vər-ˈji-nə-tē\ *n, pl* **-ties** 1 : the quality or state of being virgin; *esp* : MAIDENHOOD 2 : the unmarried life : CELIBACY

Vir·go \'vər-ˌgō\ *n* [L, lit., virgin] 1 : a zodiacal constellation between Leo and Libra usu. pictured as a young woman 2 : the 6th sign of the zodiac in astrology; *also* : one born under this sign

vir·gule \'vər-gyül\ *n* : ²SLASH 3

vir·i·des·cent \ˌvir-ə-ˈde-sᵊnt\ *adj* : slightly green : GREENISH

vir·ile \'vir-əl\ *adj* 1 : having the nature, powers, or qualities of a man 2 : MASCULINE, MALE 3 : MASTERFUL, FORCEFUL — **vi·ril·i·ty** \və-ˈri-lə-tē\ *n*

vir·i·on \'vī-rē-ˌän, 'vir-ē-\ *n* : a complete virus particle consisting of an RNA or DNA core with a protein coat

vi·rol·o·gy \vī-ˈrä-lə-jē\ *n* : a branch of science that deals with viruses and viral diseases — **vi·rol·o·gist** \-jist\ *n*

vir·tu \vər-ˈtü, ˌvir-\ *or* **ver·tu** \vər-, ˌver-\ *n* [It *virtù*, lit., virtue] 1 : a love of or taste for objects of art 2 : objects of art (as curios and antiques)

vir·tu·al \'vər-chə-wəl\ *adj* 1 : being in essence or in effect though not formally recognized or admitted ⟨a ~ dictator⟩ 2 : being on or simulated on a computer or computer network

vir·tu·al·ly \'vər-chə-wə-lē\ *adv* 1 : almost entirely : NEARLY 2 : for all practical purposes ⟨~ unknown⟩

virtual reality *n* : an artificial environment that is experienced through sensory stimuli (as sights and sounds) provided by an interactive computer program; *also* : the technology used to create or access a virtual reality

vir·tue \'vər-chü\ *n* [ME *vertu*, fr. AF, fr. L *virtus* strength, manliness, virtue, fr. *vir* man] 1 : conformity to a standard of right : MORALITY 2 : a particular moral excellence 3 : manly strength or courage : VALOR 4 : a commendable quality : MERIT 5 : active power to accomplish a given effect : POTENCY, EFFICACY 6 : chastity esp. in a woman

vir·tu·os·i·ty \ˌvər-chə-ˈwä-sə-tē\ *n, pl* **-ties** : great technical skill in the practice of a fine art

vir·tu·o·so \ˌvər-chə-'wō-sō, -zō\ *n, pl* **-sos** *or* **-si** \-sē, -zē\ [It] **1** : one skilled in or having a taste for the fine arts **2** : one who excels in the technique of an art; *esp* : a highly skilled musical performer ♦ *Synonyms* EXPERT, ADEPT, ARTIST, DOYEN, MASTER — **virtuoso** *adj*

vir·tu·ous \'vər-chə-wəs\ *adj* **1** : having or showing virtue and esp. moral virtue **2** : CHASTE — **vir·tu·ous·ly** *adv*

vir·u·lent \'vir-ə-lənt, 'vir-yə-\ *adj* **1** : highly infectious ⟨a ~ germ⟩; *also* : marked by a rapid, severe, and often deadly course ⟨a ~ disease⟩ **2** : extremely poisonous or venomous : NOXIOUS **3** : full of malice : MALIGNANT — **vir·u·lence** \-ləns\ *n* — **vir·u·lent·ly** *adv*

vi·rus \'vī-rəs\ *n, pl* **vi·rus·es** [L, venom, poisonous emanation] **1** : any of a large group of submicroscopic infectious agents that have an outside coat of protein around a core of RNA or DNA, that can grow and multiply only in living cells, and that cause important diseases in human beings, lower animals, and plants; *also* : a disease caused by a virus **2** : something (as a corrupting influence) that poisons the mind or spirit **3** : a computer program that is usu. hidden within another program and that reproduces itself and inserts the copies into other programs and usu. performs a malicious action (as destroying data)

vis *abbr* **1** visibility **2** visual

¹vi·sa \'vē-zə, -sə\ *n* [F] **1** : an endorsement by the proper authorities on a passport to show that it has been examined and the bearer may proceed **2** : a signature by a superior official signifying approval of a document

²visa *vb* **vi·saed** \-zəd, -səd\; **vi·sa·ing** \-zə-iŋ, -sə-\ : to give a visa to (a passport)

vis·age \'vi-zij\ *n* : the face or countenance of a person or sometimes an animal; *also* : LOOK, APPEARANCE

¹vis-à-vis \ˌvēz-ə-'vē, ˌvēs-\ *prep* [F, lit., face-to-face] **1** : face-to-face with : OPPOSITE **2** : in relation to **3** : as compared with

²vis-à-vis *n, pl* **vis-à-vis** *same or* -'vēz\ **1** : one that is face-to-face with another **2** : ESCORT **3** : COUNTERPART **4** : TÊTE-À-TÊTE

³vis-à-vis *adv* : in company : TOGETHER

viscera *pl of* VISCUS

vis·cer·al \'vi-sə-rəl\ *adj* **1** : felt in or as if in the viscera **2** : not intellectual : INSTINCTIVE **3** : of or relating to the viscera — **vis·cer·al·ly** *adv*

vis·cid \'vi-səd\ *adj* : VISCOUS — **vis·cid·i·ty** \vi-'si-də-tē\ *n*

vis·cos·i·ty \vis-'kä-sə-tē\ *n, pl* **-ties** : the quality of being viscous; *esp* : the property of resistance to flow in a fluid

vis·count \'vī-ˌkaunt\ *n* : a member of the British peerage ranking below an earl and above a baron

vis·count·ess \-ˌkaun-təs\ *n* **1** : the wife or widow of a viscount **2** : a woman who holds the rank of viscount in her own right

vis·cous \'vis-kəs\ *adj* [ME *viscouse,* fr. AF *viscos,* fr. LL *viscosus* full of birdlime, viscous, fr. L *viscum* mistletoe, birdlime] **1** : having the sticky consistency of glue **2** : having or characterized by viscosity

vis·cus \'vis-kəs\ *n, pl* **vis·cera** \'vi-sə-rə\ : an internal organ of the body; *esp* : one (as the heart or liver) located in the cavity of the trunk

vise \'vīs\ *n* [ME *vys, vice* screw, fr. AF *vyz,* fr. L *vitis* vine] : a tool with two jaws for holding work that typically close by a screw or lever

vise

vis·i·bil·i·ty \ˌvi-zə-'bi-lə-tē\ *n, pl* **-ties** **1** : the quality, condition, or degree of being visible **2** : the degree of clearness of the atmosphere

vis·i·ble \'vi-zə-bəl\ *adj* : capable of being seen ⟨~ stars⟩;

also : MANIFEST, APPARENT ⟨has no ~ means of support⟩ — **vis·i·bly** \-blē\ *adv*

¹vi·sion \'vi-zhən\ *n* **1** : something seen otherwise than by ordinary sight (as in a dream or trance) **2** : a vivid picture created by the imagination **3** : the act or power of imagination **4** : unusual wisdom in foreseeing what is going to happen **5** : the act or power of seeing : SIGHT **6** : something seen; *esp* : a lovely sight

²vision *vb* : IMAGINE, ENVISION

¹vi·sion·ary \'vi-zhə-ˌner-ē\ *adj* **1** : of the nature of a vision : ILLUSORY, UNREAL **2** : not practical : UTOPIAN **3** : seeing or likely to see visions : given to dreaming or imagining ♦ *Synonyms* IMAGINARY, FANTASTIC, CHIMERICAL, QUIXOTIC

²visionary *n, pl* **-ar·ies** **1** : one whose ideas or projects are impractical : DREAMER **2** : one who sees visions

¹vis·it \'vi-zət\ *vb* **1** : to go to see in order to comfort or help **2** : to call on either as an act of courtesy or friendship **3** : to dwell with for a time as a guest **4** : to come to or upon as a reward, affliction, or punishment **5** : INFLICT ⟨~ed his wrath upon them⟩ **6** : to make a visit or regular or frequent visits **7** : CHAT, CONVERSE ⟨enjoys ~ing with the neighbors⟩ — **vis·it·able** *adj*

²visit *n* **1** : a short stay : CALL **2** : a brief residence as a guest **3** : a journey to and stay at a place **4** : a formal or professional call (as by a doctor)

vis·i·tant \'vi-zə-tənt\ *n* : VISITOR

vis·i·ta·tion \ˌvi-zə-'tā-shən\ *n* **1** : VISIT; *esp* : an official visit **2** : a special dispensation of divine favor or wrath; *also* : a severe trial

visiting nurse *n* : a nurse employed to visit sick persons or perform public health services in a community

vis·i·tor \'vi-zə-tər\ *n* : one that visits

vi·sor \'vī-zər\ *n* **1** : the front piece of a helmet; *esp* : a movable upper piece **2** : VIZARD **3** : a projecting part (as on a cap) to shade the eyes — **vi·sored** \-zərd\ *adj*

vis·ta \'vis-tə\ *n* **1** : a distant view through or along an avenue or opening **2** : an extensive mental view over a series of years or events

VISTA *abbr* Volunteers in Service to America

¹vi·su·al \'vi-zhə-wəl\ *adj* **1** : of, relating to, or used in vision ⟨~ organs⟩ **2** : perceived by vision ⟨a ~ impression⟩ **3** : VISIBLE ⟨~ objects⟩ **4** : done by sight only ⟨~ navigation⟩ **5** : of or relating to instruction by means of sight ⟨~ aids⟩ — **vi·su·al·ly** *adv*

²visual *n* : something (as a graphic) that appeals to the sight and is used for illustration, demonstration, or promotion — usu. used in pl.

vi·su·al·ize \'vi-zhə-wə-ˌlīz\ *vb* **-ized; -iz·ing** : to make visible; *esp* : to form a mental image of — **vi·su·al·i·za·tion** \ˌvi-zhə-wə-lə-'zā-shən\ *n* — **vi·su·al·iz·er** *n*

vi·ta \'vē-tə, 'vī-\ *n, pl* **vi·tae** \'vē-ˌtī, 'vī-tē\ [L, lit., life] : a brief autobiographical sketch

vi·tal \'vī-t²l\ *adj* **1** : concerned with or necessary to the maintenance of life **2** : full of life and vigor : ANIMATED **3** : of, relating to, or characteristic of life or living beings **4** : FATAL, MORTAL ⟨~ wound⟩ **5** : FUNDAMENTAL, INDISPENSABLE — **vi·tal·ly** *adv*

vi·tal·i·ty \vī-'ta-lə-tē\ *n, pl* **-ties** **1** : the property distinguishing the living from the nonliving **2** : mental and physical vigor **3** : enduring quality **4** : ANIMATION, LIVELINESS

vi·tal·ize \'vī-tə-ˌlīz\ *vb* **-ized; -iz·ing** : to impart life or vigor to : ANIMATE — **vi·tal·i·za·tion** \ˌvī-tə-lə-'zā-shən\ *n*

vi·tals \'vī-t²lz\ *n pl* **1** : vital organs (as the heart and brain) **2** : essential parts

vital signs *n pl* : the pulse rate, respiratory rate, body temperature, and often blood pressure of a person

vital statistics *n pl* : statistics dealing with births, deaths, marriages, health, and disease

vi·ta·min \'vī-tə-mən\ *n* : any of various organic substances that are essential in tiny amounts to the nutrition of most animals and some plants and are mostly obtained from foods

vitamin A *n* : any of several vitamins (as from egg yolk or fish-liver oils) required esp. for good vision

vitamin B *n* **1** : VITAMIN B COMPLEX **2** *or* **vitamin B₁** : THIAMINE

vitamin B complex *n* : a group of vitamins that are found widely in foods and are essential for normal function of certain enzymes and for growth

vitamin B₆ \-'bē-'siks\ *n* : any of several compounds that are considered essential to vertebrate nutrition

vitamin B₁₂ \-'bē-'twelv\ *n* : a complex cobalt-containing compound that occurs esp. in liver and is essential to normal blood formation, neural function, and growth; *also* : any of several compounds of similar action

vitamin C *n* : a vitamin found esp. in fruits and vegetables that is needed by the body to prevent scurvy

vitamin D *n* : any or all of several vitamins that are needed for normal bone and tooth structure and are found esp. in fish-liver oils, egg yolk, and milk or are produced by the body in response to ultraviolet light

vitamin E *n* : any of various oily fat-soluble liquid vitamins whose absence in the body is associated with such ailments as infertility, the breakdown of muscles, and vascular problems and which are found esp. in leaves and in seed germ oils

vitamin K *n* : any of several vitamins needed for blood to clot properly

vi·ti·ate \'vi-shē-,āt\ *vb* **-at·ed; -at·ing** **1** : CONTAMINATE, POLLUTE; *also* : DEBASE, PERVERT **2** : to make legally ineffective : INVALIDATE ⟨~ a contract⟩ — **vi·ti·a·tion** \,vi-shē-'ā-shən\ *n* — **vi·ti·a·tor** \'vi-shē-,ā-tər\ *n*

vi·ti·cul·ture \'vi-tə-,kəl-chər\ *n* : the growing of grapes — **vi·ti·cul·tur·al** \,vi-tə-'kəl-chə-rəl\ *adj* — **vi·ti·cul·tur·ist** \-rist\ *n*

vit·re·ous \'vi-trē-əs\ *adj* **1** : of, relating to, or resembling glass : GLASSY ⟨~ rocks⟩ **2** : of, relating to, or being the clear colorless transparent jelly (**vitreous humor**) behind the lens in the eyeball

vit·ri·ol \'vi-trē-əl\ *n* : something resembling acid in being caustic, corrosive, or biting — **vit·ri·ol·ic** \,vi-trē-'ä-lik\ *adj*

vit·tles \'vi-t³lz\ *n pl* : VICTUALS

vi·tu·per·ate \vī-'tü-pə-,rāt, və-, -'tyü-\ *vb* **-at·ed; -at·ing** : to abuse in words : SCOLD ✦ *Synonyms* REVILE, BERATE, RATE, UPBRAID, RAIL, LASH — **vi·tu·per·a·tive** \-'tü-pə-rə-tiv, -'tyü-, -,rā-\ *adj* — **vi·tu·per·a·tive·ly** *adv*

vi·tu·per·a·tion \(,)vī-tü-pə-'rā-shən, və-, -'tyü-\ *n* : lengthy harsh criticism or abuse

vi·va \'vē-və\ *interj* [It & Sp, long live] — used to express goodwill or approval

vi·va·ce \vē-'vä-chä\ *adv or adj* [It] : in a brisk spirited manner — used as a direction in music

vi·va·cious \və-'vā-shəs, vī-\ *adj* : lively in temper, conduct, or spirit : SPRIGHTLY — **vi·va·cious·ly** *adv* — **vi·va·cious·ness** *n*

vi·vac·i·ty \-'va-sə-tē\ *n* : the quality or state of being vivacious

vi·va vo·ce \,vī-və-'vō-sē, ,vē-və-'vō-,chā\ *adj* [ML, with the living voice] : expressed or conducted by word of mouth : ORAL — **viva voce** *adv*

viv·id \'vi-vəd\ *adj* **1** : BRILLIANT, INTENSE ⟨a ~ red⟩ **2** : having the appearance of vigorous life **3** : producing a strong impression on the senses; *esp* : producing distinct mental pictures ⟨a ~ description⟩ — **viv·id·ly** *adv* — **viv·id·ness** *n*

viv·i·fy \'vi-və-,fī\ *vb* **-fied; -fy·ing** **1** : to put life into : ANIMATE **2** : to make vivid — **viv·i·fi·ca·tion** \,vi-və-fə-'kā-shən\ *n* — **viv·i·fi·er** *n*

vi·vip·a·rous \vī-'vi-pə-rəs, və-\ *adj* : producing living young from within the body rather than from eggs — **vi·vi·par·i·ty** \,vī-və-'pa-rə-tē, ,vi-\ *n*

viv·i·sec·tion \,vi-və-'sek-shən, 'vi-və-,sek-\ *n* : the cutting of or operation on a living animal; *also* : animal experimentation esp. if causing distress to the subject

vix·en \'vik-sən\ *n* **1** : an ill-tempered scolding woman **2** : a female fox

viz *abbr* videlicet

viz·ard \'vi-zərd\ *n* : a mask for disguise or protection

vi·zier \və-'zir\ *n* : a high executive officer of many Muslim countries

VJ *abbr* veejay

VOA *abbr* Voice of America

voc *abbr* **1** vocational **2** vocative

vocab *abbr* vocabulary

vo·ca·ble \'vō-kə-bəl\ *n* : TERM, NAME; *esp* : a word as such without regard to its meaning

vo·cab·u·lary \vō-'ka-byə-,ler-ē\ *n, pl* **-lar·ies** **1** : a list or collection of words usu. alphabetically arranged and defined or explained : LEXICON **2** : a stock of words in a language used by a class or individual or in relation to a subject

vocabulary entry *n* : a word (as the noun *book*), hyphened or open compound (as the verb *cross-refer* or the noun *boric acid*), word element (as the affix *-an*), abbreviation (as *agt*), verbalized symbol (as *Na*), or term (as *master of ceremonies*) entered alphabetically in a dictionary for the purpose of definition or identification or expressly included as an inflected form (as the noun *mice* or the verb *saw*) or as a derived form (as the noun *godlessness* or the adverb *globally*) or related phrase (as *in spite of*) run at its base word and usu. set in a type (as boldface) readily distinguishable from that of the lightface running text which defines, explains, or identifies the entry

¹**vo·cal** \'vō-kəl\ *adj* **1** : uttered by the voice : ORAL **2** : relating to, composed or arranged for, or sung by the human voice ⟨~ music⟩ **3** : given to expressing oneself freely or insistently : OUTSPOKEN **4** : of or relating to the voice

²**vocal** *n* **1** : a vocal sound **2** : a vocal composition or its performance

vocal cords *n pl* : either of two pairs of elastic folds of mucous membrane that project into the cavity of the larynx and function in the production of vocal sounds

vo·cal·ic \vō-'ka-lik\ *adj* : of, relating to, or functioning as a vowel

vo·cal·ise *Brit var of* VOCALIZE

vo·cal·ist \'vō-kə-list\ *n* : SINGER

vo·cal·ize \-,līz\ *vb* **-ized; -iz·ing** **1** : to give vocal expression to : UTTER; *esp* : SING **2** : to make voiced rather than voiceless — **vo·cal·iz·er** *n*

vo·ca·tion \vō-'kā-shən\ *n* **1** : a summons or strong inclination to a particular state or course of action ⟨religious ~⟩ **2** : regular employment : OCCUPATION, PROFESSION — **vo·ca·tion·al** \-shə-nəl\ *adj*

vo·ca·tion·al·ism \-shə-nə-,li-zəm\ *n* : emphasis on vocational training in education

voc·a·tive \'vä-kə-tiv\ *adj* : of, relating to, or constituting a grammatical case marking the one addressed — **vocative** *n*

vo·cif·er·ate \vō-'si-fə-,rāt\ *vb* **-at·ed; -at·ing** [L *vociferari*, fr. *voc-, vox* voice + *ferre* to bear] : to cry out loudly : CLAMOR, SHOUT — **vo·cif·er·a·tion** \-,si-fə-'rā-shən\ *n*

vo·cif·er·ous \vō-'si-fə-rəs\ *adj* : making or given to loud outcry — **vo·cif·er·ous·ly** *adv* — **vo·cif·er·ous·ness** *n*

vod·ka \'väd-kə\ *n* [Russ, fr. *voda* water] : a colorless liquor distilled from a mash (as of rye or wheat)

vogue \'vōg\ *n* [MF, action of rowing, course, fashion, fr. *voguer* to sail, fr. OF, fr. OIt *vogare* to row] **1** : popular acceptance or favor : POPULARITY **2** : a period of popularity **3** : one that is in fashion at a particular time ✦ *Synonyms* MODE, FAD, RAGE, CRAZE, TREND, FASHION

vogu·ish \'vō-gish\ *adj* **1** : FASHIONABLE, SMART **2** : suddenly or temporarily popular

¹**voice** \'vȯis\ *n* **1** : sound produced through the mouth by vertebrates and esp. by human beings (as in speaking or singing) **2** : musical sound produced by the vocal cords : the power to produce such sound; *also* : one of the melodic parts in a vocal or instrumental composition **3** : the vocal organs as a means of tone production ⟨train the ~⟩ **4** : sound produced by vibration of the vocal cords as heard in vowels and some consonants **5** : the power of speaking **6** : a sound suggesting a voice ⟨the ~ of the sea⟩ **7** : an instrument or medium of expression **8** : a choice, opinion, or wish openly expressed; *also* : right of expression **9** : distinction of form of a verb to indicate the relation of the subject to the action expressed by the verb

²**voice** *vb* **voiced; voic·ing** : to give voice or expression to : UTTER ⟨~ a complaint⟩ ✦ *Synonyms* EXPRESS, VENT, AIR, VENTILATE

voice box *n* : LARYNX

voiced \'vȯist\ *adj* **1** : having a voice ⟨soft-*voiced*⟩ **2** : uttered with voice ⟨a ~ consonant⟩ — **voiced·ness** \'vȯist-nəs, 'vȯi-səd-nəs\ *n*

voice·less \'vȯis-ləs\ *adj* **1** : having no voice **2** : not pronounced with voice — **voice·less·ly** *adv* — **voice·less·ness** *n*

voice mail *n* : an electronic communication system in which spoken messages are recorded for later playback to the intended recipient; *also* : such a message

voice—over *n* : the voice in a film or television program of a person who is heard but not seen or not seen talking

voice·print \'vȯis-ˌprint\ *n* : an individually distinctive pattern of voice characteristics that is spectrographically produced

¹**void** \'vȯid\ *adj* **1** : UNOCCUPIED, VACANT ⟨a ∼ bishopric⟩ **2** : containing nothing : EMPTY **3** : LACKING, DEVOID ⟨proposals ∼ of sense⟩ **4** : VAIN, USELESS **5** : of no legal force or effect : NULL

²**void** *n* **1** : empty space : EMPTINESS, VACUUM **2** : a feeling of want or hollowness

³**void** *vb* **1** : to make or leave empty; *also* : VACATE, LEAVE **2** : DISCHARGE, EMIT ⟨∼ urine⟩ **3** : to render void : ANNUL, NULLIFY ⟨∼ a contract⟩ — **void·able** *adj* — **void·er** *n*

voi·là \vwä-'lä\ *interj* [F] — used to call attention or to express satisfaction or approval

voile \'vȯi(-ə)l\ *n* : a sheer fabric used for women's clothing and curtains

vol *abbr* **1** volume **2** volunteer

vol·a·tile \'vä-lə-t⁹l\ *adj* **1** : readily becoming a vapor at a relatively low temperature ⟨a ∼ liquid⟩ **2** : tending to erupt into violence **3** : likely to change suddenly — **vol·a·til·i·ty** \ˌvä-lə-'ti-lə-tē\ *n* — **vol·a·til·ize** \'vä-lə-tə-ˌlīz\ *vb*

vol·ca·nic \väl-'ka-nik\ *adj* **1** : of, relating to, or produced by a volcano **2** : explosively violent ⟨∼ emotions⟩

vol·ca·nism \'väl-kə-ˌni-zəm\ *n* : volcanic action or activity

vol·ca·no \väl-'kā-nō\ *n, pl* **-noes** *or* **-nos** [It or Sp; It *vulcano*, fr. Sp *vulcán*, ultim fr. L *Volcanus*, Roman god of fire and metalworking] : an opening in the crust of the earth, a planet, or a moon from which molten rock and steam issue; *also* : a hill or mountain composed of the ejected material

vol·ca·nol·o·gy \ˌväl-kə-'nä-lə-jē\ *n* : a branch of geology that deals with volcanic phenomena — **vol·ca·nol·o·gist** \-kə-'nä-lə-jist\ *n*

vole \'vōl\ *n* : any of various small rodents that are closely related to the lemmings and muskrats

vole

vo·li·tion \vō-'li-shən\ *n* **1** : the act or the power of making a choice or decision : WILL **2** : a choice or decision made — **vo·li·tion·al** \-'li-shə-nəl\ *adj*

¹**vol·ley** \'vä-lē\ *n, pl* **volleys** **1** : a flight of missiles (as arrows) **2** : simultaneous discharge of a number of missile weapons **3** : an act of volleying **4** : a burst of many things at once ⟨a ∼ of angry letters⟩

²**volley** *vb* **vol·leyed; vol·ley·ing** **1** : to discharge or become discharged in or as if in a volley **2** : to hit an object of play (as a ball) in the air before it touches the ground

vol·ley·ball \-ˌbȯl\ *n* : a game played by volleying an inflated ball over a net; *also* : the ball used in this game

volt \'vōlt\ *n* : the meter-kilogram-second unit of electrical potential difference and electromotive force equal to the difference in potential between two points in a wire carrying a constant current of one ampere when the power dissipated between the points is equal to one watt

volt·age \'vōl-tij\ *n* : potential difference measured in volts

vol·ta·ic \väl-'tā-ik, vōl-\ *adj* : of, relating to, or producing direct electric current by chemical action

volte–face \ˌvȯlt-'fäs, ˌvȯl-tə-\ *n* : a reversal in policy : ABOUT-FACE

volt·me·ter \'vōlt-ˌmē-tər\ *n* : an instrument for measuring in volts the difference in potential between different points of an electrical circuit

vol·u·ble \'väl-yə-bəl\ *adj* : fluent and smooth in speech

: GLIB ✦ *Synonyms* GARRULOUS, LOQUACIOUS, TALKATIVE — **vol·u·bil·i·ty** \ˌväl-yə-'bi-lə-tē\ *n* — **vol·u·bly** \'väl-yə-blē\ *adv*

vol·ume \'väl-yəm, -(ˌ)yüm\ *n* [ME, fr. AF, fr. L *volumen* roll, scroll, fr. *volvere* to roll] **1** : a series of printed sheets bound typically in book form; *also* : an arbitrary number of issues of a periodical **2** : space occupied as measured by cubic units ⟨the ∼ of a cylinder⟩ **3** : sufficient matter to fill a book ⟨her glance spoke ∼s⟩ **4** : AMOUNT ⟨increasing ∼ of business⟩ **5** : the degree of loudness of a sound ✦ *Synonyms* BODY, BULK, MASS

vo·lu·mi·nous \və-'lü-mə-nəs\ *adj* : having or marked by great volume or bulk : LARGE — **vo·lu·mi·nous·ly** *adv* — **vo·lu·mi·nous·ness** *n*

¹**vol·un·tary** \'vä-lən-ˌter-ē\ *adj* **1** : done, made, or given freely and without compulsion ⟨a ∼ sacrifice⟩ **2** : done on purpose : INTENTIONAL ⟨∼ manslaughter⟩ **3** : of, relating to, or regulated by the will ⟨∼ behavior⟩ **4** : having power of free choice **5** : provided or supported by voluntary action ⟨a ∼ organization⟩ ✦ *Synonyms* DELIBERATE, WILLFUL, WILLING, WITTING — **vol·un·tar·i·ly** \ˌvä-lən-'ter-ə-lē\ *adv*

²**voluntary** *n, pl* **-tar·ies** : an organ solo played in a religious service

voluntary muscle *n* : muscle (as most striated muscle) under voluntary control

¹**vol·un·teer** \ˌvä-lən-'tir\ *n* **1** : a person who voluntarily undertakes a service or duty **2** : a plant growing spontaneously esp. from seeds lost from a previous crop

²**volunteer** *vb* **1** : to offer or give voluntarily **2** : to offer oneself as a volunteer

vo·lup·tu·ary \və-'ləp-chə-ˌwer-ē\ *n, pl* **-ar·ies** : a person whose chief interest in life is the indulgence of sensual appetites

vo·lup·tu·ous \-chə-wəs\ *adj* **1** : giving sensual gratification **2** : given to or spent in enjoyment of luxury or pleasure ✦ *Synonyms* LUXURIOUS, EPICUREAN, SENSUOUS — **vo·lup·tu·ous·ly** *adv* — **vo·lup·tu·ous·ness** *n*

vo·lute \və-'lüt\ *n* : a spiral or scroll-shaped decoration

¹**vom·it** \'vä-mət\ *n* : an act or instance of throwing up the contents of the stomach through the mouth; *also* : the matter thrown up

²**vomit** *vb* **1** : to throw up the contents of the stomach through the mouth **2** : to belch forth : GUSH

voo·doo \'vü-dü\ *n, pl* **voodoos** **1** : a religion that is derived from African polytheism and is practiced chiefly in Haiti **2** : a person who deals in spells and necromancy; *also* : ¹SPELL 1 **3** : a charm used in voodoo — **voodoo** *adj*

voo·doo·ism \-ˌi-zəm\ *n* **1** : VOODOO 1 **2** : the practice of witchcraft

vo·ra·cious \vȯ-'rā-shəs, və-\ *adj* **1** : having a huge appetite : RAVENOUS **2** : very eager ⟨a ∼ reader⟩ ✦ *Synonyms* GLUTTONOUS, RAVENING, RAPACIOUS — **vo·ra·cious·ly** *adv* — **vo·ra·cious·ness** *n* — **vo·rac·i·ty** \-'ra-sə-tē\ *n*

vor·tex \'vȯr-ˌteks\ *n, pl* **vor·ti·ces** \'vȯr-tə-ˌsēz\ *also* **vor·tex·es** \'vȯr-ˌtek-səz\ : WHIRLPOOL; *also* : something resembling a whirlpool

vo·ta·ry \'vō-tə-rē\ *n, pl* **-ries** **1** : ENTHUSIAST, DEVOTEE; *also* : a devoted adherent or admirer **2** : a devout or zealous worshiper

¹**vote** \'vōt\ *n* [ME (Sc), fr. L *votum* vow, wish, fr. *vovēre* to vow] **1** : a choice or opinion of a person or body of persons expressed usu. by a ballot, spoken word, or raised hand; *also* : the ballot, word, or gesture used to express a choice or opinion **2** : the decision reached by voting **3** : the right of suffrage **4** : a group of voters with some common characteristics ⟨the big city ∼⟩ — **vote·less** *adj*

²**vote** *vb* **vot·ed; vot·ing** **1** : to cast a vote **2** : to elect, decide, pass, defeat, grant, or make legal by a vote **3** : to declare by general agreement **4** : to offer as a suggestion : PROPOSE **5** : to cause to vote esp. in a given way — **vot·er** *n*

vo·tive \'vō-tiv\ *adj* : consisting of or expressing a vow, wish, or desire

vou *abbr* voucher

vouch \'vau̇ch\ *vb* **1** : PROVE, SUBSTANTIATE **2** : to verify by examining documentary evidence **3** : to give a guarantee **4** : to supply supporting evidence or testimony; *also* : to give personal assurance

vouch·er \'vaù-chər\ *n* **1** : an act of vouching **2** : one that vouches for another **3** : a documentary record of a business transaction **4** : a written affidavit or authorization **5** : a form indicating a credit against future purchases or expenditures

vouch·safe \vaùch-'sāf\ *vb* **vouch·safed; vouch·saf·ing** : to grant or give as or as if a privilege or a special favor

¹**vow** \'vaù\ *n* : a solemn promise or statement; *esp* : one by which a person is bound to an act, service, or condition ⟨marriage ∼s⟩

²**vow** *vb* **1** : to make a vow or as a vow **2** : to bind or commit by a vow — **vow·er** *n*

vow·el \'vaù(-ə)l\ *n* **1** : a speech sound produced without obstruction or friction in the mouth **2** : a letter representing such a sound

vox po·pu·li \'väks-'pä-pyə-ˌlī\ *n* [L, voice of the people] : popular sentiment

¹**voy·age** \'vói-ij\ *n* [ME, *viage, veyage*, fr. AF *veiage*, fr. LL *viaticum*, fr. L, traveling money, fr. neut. of *viaticus* of a journey, fr. *via* way] : a journey esp. by water from one place or country to another

²**voyage** *vb* **voy·aged; voy·ag·ing** : to take or make a voyage — **voy·ag·er** *n*

voya·geur \ˌvói-ə-'zhər, ˌvwä-yä-\ *n* [CanF] : a person employed by a fur company to transport goods to and from remote stations esp. in the Canadian Northwest

voy·eur \vwä-'yər, vói-'ər\ *n* **1** : one who obtains sexual pleasure from viewing esp. covertly the nudity or sexual activity of others **2** : an observer of the sordid — **voy·eur·ism** \-ˌi-zəm\ *n* — **voy·eur·is·tic** \ˌvwä-(ˌ)yər-'is-tik, ˌvói-ər-\ *adj*

VP *abbr* **1** verb phrase **2** vice president

vs *abbr* **1** verse **2** versus

vss *abbr* **1** verses **2** versions

V/STOL *abbr* vertical or short takeoff and landing

Vt *or* **VT** *abbr* Vermont

VTOL *abbr* vertical takeoff and landing

VTR *abbr* videotape recorder

vul·ca·nize \'vəl-kə-ˌnīz\ *vb* **-nized; -niz·ing** : to treat rubber or rubberlike material chemically to give useful properties (as elasticity and strength)

Vulg *abbr* Vulgate

vul·gar \'vəl-gər\ *adj* [ME, fr. L *vulgaris* of the mob, vulgar, fr. *vulgus* mob, common people] **1** : VERNACULAR ⟨the ∼ tongue⟩ **2** : of or relating to the common people : GENERAL, COMMON **3** : lacking cultivation or refinement : BOORISH; *also* : offensive to good taste or refined feelings ✦ *Synonyms* GROSS, OBSCENE, RIBALD, DIRTY, INDECENT, PROFANE — **vul·gar·ly** *adv*

vul·gar·i·an \ˌvəl-'ger-ē-ən\ *n* : a vulgar person

vul·gar·ism \'vəl-gə-ˌri-zəm\ *n* **1** : VULGARITY **2** : a word or expression originated or used chiefly by illiterate persons **3** : a coarse expression : OBSCENITY

vul·gar·i·ty \ˌvəl-'ga-rə-tē\ *n, pl* **-ties** **1** : something vulgar **2** : the quality or state of being vulgar

vul·gar·ize \'vəl-gə-ˌrīz\ *vb* **-ized; -iz·ing** : to make vulgar — **vul·gar·i·za·tion** \ˌvəl-gə-rə-'zā-shən\ *n* — **vul·gar·iz·er** \'vəl-gə-ˌrī-zər\ *n*

Vul·gate \'vəl-ˌgāt\ *n* [ML *vulgata*, fr. LL *vulgata editio* edition in general circulation] : a Latin version of the Bible used by the Roman Catholic Church

vul·ner·a·ble \'vəl-nə-rə-bəl\ *adj* **1** : capable of being wounded : susceptible to wounds **2** : open to attack **3** : liable to increased penalties in contract bridge — **vul·ner·a·bil·i·ty** \ˌvəl-nə-rə-'bi-lə-tē\ *n* — **vul·ner·a·bly** \'vəl-nə-rə-blē\ *adv*

vul·pine \'vəl-ˌpīn\ *adj* : of, relating to, or resembling a fox esp. in cunning ⟨∼ charms⟩

vul·ture \'vəl-chər\ *n* **1** : any of various large birds (as a turkey vulture) related to the hawks, eagles, and falcons but having weaker claws and the head usu. naked and living chiefly on carrion **2** : a rapacious person

vul·va \'vəl-və\ *n, pl* **vul·vae** \-ˌvē\ [ME, fr. ML, fr. L *volva, vulva* womb, female genitals] : the external parts of the female genital organs — **vul·val** \'vəl-vəl\ *or* **vul·var** \-vər, -ˌvär\ *adj*

vv *abbr* **1** verses **2** vice versa

VX \'vē-'eks\ *n* : an extremely toxic chemical weapon

vying *pres part of* VIE

¹**w** \'də-bəl-(ˌ)yü\ *n, pl* **w's** *or* **ws** *often cap* : the 23d letter of the English alphabet

²**w** *abbr, often cap* **1** water **2** watt **3** week **4** weight **5** west; western **6** wide; width **7** wife **8** with

W *symbol* [G *Wolfram*] tungsten

WA *abbr* **1** Washington **2** Western Australia

wacky \'wa-kē\ *adj* **wack·i·er; -est** : ECCENTRIC, CRAZY

¹**wad** \'wäd\ *n* **1** : a little mass, bundle, or tuft ⟨∼s of clay⟩ **2** : a soft mass of usu. light fibrous material **3** : a pliable plug (as of felt) used to retain a powder charge (as in a cartridge) **4** : a considerable amount (as of money) **5** : a roll of paper money

²**wad** *vb* **wad·ded; wad·ding** **1** : to push a wad into ⟨∼ a gun⟩ **2** : to form into a wad **3** : to hold in by a wad ⟨∼ a bullet in a gun⟩ **4** : to stuff or line with a wad : PAD

wad·ding \'wä-diŋ\ *n* **1** : WADS; *also* : material for making wads **2** : a soft mass or sheet of short loose fibers used for stuffing or padding

wad·dle \'wä-d²l\ *vb* **wad·dled; wad·dling** : to walk with short steps swaying from side to side like a duck — **wad·dle** *n*

wade \'wād\ *vb* **wad·ed; wad·ing** **1** : to step in or through a medium (as water) more resistant than air **2** : to move or go with difficulty or labor and often with determination ⟨∼ through a dull book⟩ — **wad·able** *or* **wade·able** \'wā-də-bəl\ *adj* — **wade** *n*

wad·er \'wā-dər\ *n* **1** : one that wades **2** : SHOREBIRD; *also* : WADING BIRD **3** *pl* : a waterproof garment consisting of pants with attached boots for wading

wa·di \'wä-dē\ *n* [Ar *wādī*] : a streambed of southwest Asia and northern Africa that is dry except in the rainy season

wading bird *n* : any of an order of long-legged birds (as sandpipers, cranes, or herons) that wade in water in search of food

wa·fer \'wā-fər\ *n* **1** : a thin crisp cake or cracker **2** : a thin round piece of unleavened bread used in the Eucharist **3** : something (as a piece of candy) that resembles a wafer

¹**waf·fle** \'wä-fəl\ *n* : a soft but crisped cake of batter cooked in a special hinged metal utensil (**waffle iron**)

²**waffle** *vb* **waf·fled; waf·fling** \-f(ə)liŋ\ : to speak or write in a vague or evasive manner

¹**waft** \'wäft, 'waft\ *vb* : to cause to move or go lightly by or as if by the impulse of wind or waves

²**waft** *n* **1** : a slight breeze : PUFF **2** : the act of waving

¹**wag** \'wag\ *vb* **wagged; wag·ging** **1** : to sway or swing shortly from side to side or to-and-fro ⟨the dog *wagged* his tail⟩ **2** : to move in chatter or gossip ⟨scandal caused tongues to ∼⟩

²**wag** *n* : an act of wagging : a wagging movement

³**wag** *n* : WIT, JOKER

¹**wage** \'wāj\ *n* **1** : payment for labor or services usu. according to contract **2** *pl* : RECOMPENSE, REWARD

²**wage** *vb* **waged; wag·ing** **1** : to engage in : CARRY ON ⟨∼ a war⟩ **2** : to be in process of being waged

¹**wa·ger** \'wā-jər\ *n* **1** : BET, STAKE **2** : something on which bets are laid : GAMBLE

²**wager** *vb* : BET — **wa·ger·er** *n*

wag·gery \'wa-gə-rē\ *n, pl* **-ger·ies** **1** : mischievous merriment : PLEASANTRY **2** : JEST, TRICK
wag·gish \'wa-gish\ *adj* **1** : resembling or characteristic of a wag : MISCHIEVOUS **2** : SPORTIVE, HUMOROUS
wag·gle \'wa-gəl\ *vb* **wag·gled; wag·gling** : to move backward and forward or from side to side : WAG — **waggle** *n*
wag·gon *chiefly Brit var of* WAGON
wag·on \'wa-gən\ *n* **1** : a 4-wheeled vehicle; *esp* : one drawn by animals and used for freight or merchandise **2** : PADDY WAGON **3** : a child's 4-wheeled cart **4** : STATION WAGON

wagon 1

wag·on·er \'wa-gə-nər\ *n* : the driver of a wagon
wag·on·ette \ˌwa-gə-'net\ *n* : a light wagon with two facing seats along the sides behind a cross seat in front
wa·gon-lit \vä-gōⁿ-'lē\ *n, pl* **wagons-lits** *or* **wagon-lits** *same or* -'lēz\ [F, fr. *wagon* railroad car + *lit* bed] : a railroad sleeping car
wagon train *n* : a column of wagons traveling together
wag·tail \'wag-ˌtāl\ *n* : any of various slender-bodied mostly Old World birds with a long tail that jerks up and down
wa·hi·ne \wä-'hē-nē, -ˌnä\ *n* **1** : a Polynesian woman **2** : a female surfer
wa·hoo \'wä-ˌhü\ *n, pl* **wahoos** : a large vigorous food and sport fish related to the mackerel and found in warm seas
waif \'wāf\ *n* **1** : something found without an owner and esp. by chance **2** : a stray person or animal; *esp* : a homeless child
wail \'wāl\ *vb* **1** : LAMENT, WEEP **2** : to make a sound suggestive of a mournful cry **3** : COMPLAIN — **wail** *n*
wail·ful \-fəl\ *adj* : SORROWFUL, MOURNFUL ✦ *Synonyms* MELANCHOLY, DOLEFUL, LUGUBRIOUS, LAMENTABLE, PLAINTIVE, WOEFUL — **wail·ful·ly** *adv*
wain \'wān\ *n* : a usu. large heavy farm wagon
wain·scot \'wān-skət, -ˌskōt, -ˌskät\ *n* **1** : a usu. paneled wooden lining of an interior wall of a room **2** : the lower part of an interior wall when finished differently from the rest — **wainscot** *vb*
wain·scot·ing *or* **wain·scot·ting** \-ˌskō-tiŋ, -ˌskä-, -skə-\ *n* : material for a wainscot; *also* : WAINSCOT
waist \'wāst\ *n* **1** : the narrowed part of the body between the chest and hips **2** : a part resembling the human waist esp. in narrowness or central position ⟨the ∼ of a ship⟩ **3** : a garment or part of a garment (as a blouse or bodice) for the upper part of the body
waist·band \-ˌband\ *n* : a band (as on pants or a skirt) that fits around the waist
waist·coat \'wes-kət, 'wāst-ˌkōt\ *n, chiefly Brit* : VEST 1
waist·line \'wāst-ˌlīn\ *n* **1** : a line around the waist at its narrowest part; *also* : the length of this **2** : the line at which the bodice and skirt of a dress meet
¹wait \'wāt\ *vb* **1** : to remain inactive in readiness or expectation : AWAIT ⟨∼ for orders⟩ **2** : to delay serving (a meal) **3** : to act as attendant or servant ⟨∼ on customers⟩ **4** : to attend as a waiter : SERVE ⟨∼ tables⟩ ⟨∼ at a banquet⟩ **5** : to be ready
²wait *n* **1** : a position of concealment usu. with intent to attack or surprise ⟨lie in ∼⟩ **2** : an act or period of waiting
wait·er \'wā-tər\ *n* **1** : one that waits on another; *esp* : a person who waits tables **2** : TRAY
waiting game *n* : a strategy in which one or more participants withhold action in the hope of an opportunity for more effective action later
waiting room *n* : a room (as at a doctor's office) for the use of persons who are waiting
wait·per·son \'wāt-ˌpər-sən\ *n* : a waiter or waitress
wait·ress \'wā-trəs\ *n* : a woman who waits tables
waive \'wāv\ *vb* **waived; waiv·ing** [ME *weiven* to decline, reject, give up, fr. AF *waiver, gaiver,* fr. *waif* lost, stray] **1** : to give up claim to ⟨*waived* his right to a trial⟩ **2** : POSTPONE

waiv·er \'wā-vər\ *n* : the act of waiving right, claim, or privilege; *also* : a document containing a declaration of such an act
¹wake \'wāk\ *vb* **woke** \'wōk\ *also* **waked** \'wākt\; **wo·ken** \'wō-kən\ *also* **waked** *or* **woke; wak·ing** **1** : to be or remain awake; *esp* : to keep watch (as over a corpse) **2** : AWAKE, AWAKEN ⟨the baby *woke* up early⟩
²wake *n* **1** : the state of being awake **2** : a watch held over the body of a dead person prior to burial
³wake *n* : the track left by a ship in the water; *also* : a track left behind
wake·board \'wāk-ˌbȯrd\ *n* : a short board with foot bindings on which a rider is towed by a motorboat across its wake — **wake·board·er** *n* — **wake·board·ing** *n*
wake·ful \'wāk-fəl\ *adj* : not sleeping or able to sleep : SLEEPLESS, ALERT — **wake·ful·ness** *n*
wak·en \'wā-kən\ *vb* : WAKE
wake–rob·in \'wāk-ˌrä-bən\ *n* : TRILLIUM
wak·ing \'wā-kiŋ\ *adj* : passed in a conscious or alert state ⟨every ∼ hour⟩
wale \'wāl\ *n* : a ridge esp. on cloth; *also* : the texture esp. of a fabric
¹walk \'wȯk\ *vb* [partly fr. ME *walken,* fr. OE *wealcan* to roll, toss and partly fr. ME *walkien,* fr. OE *wealcian* to roll up, muffle up] **1** : to move or cause to move on foot usu. at a natural unhurried gait ⟨∼ to town⟩ ⟨∼ a horse⟩ **2** : to pass over, through, or along by walking ⟨∼ the streets⟩ **3** : to perform or accomplish by walking ⟨∼ guard⟩ **4** : to follow a course of action or way of life ⟨∼ humbly in the sight of God⟩ **5** : WALK OUT **6** : to receive a base on balls; *also* : to give a base on balls to — **walk·er** *n*
²walk *n* **1** : a going on foot ⟨go for a ∼⟩ **2** : a place, path, or course for walking **3** : distance to be walked ⟨a quarter-mile ∼ from here⟩ **4** : manner of living : CONDUCT, BEHAVIOR **5** : social or economic status ⟨various ∼s of life⟩ **6** : manner of walking : GAIT; *esp* : a slow 4-beat gait of a horse **7** : BASE ON BALLS
walk·away \'wȯ-kə-ˌwā\ *n* : an easily won contest
walk·ie–talk·ie \ˌwȯ-kē-'tȯ-kē\ *n* : a small portable radio transmitting and receiving set
¹walk–in \'wȯk-ˌin\ *adj* : large enough to be walked into ⟨a ∼ refrigerator⟩
²walk–in *n* **1** : an easy election victory **2** : one that walks in
walking papers *n pl* : DISMISSAL, DISCHARGE
walking stick *n* **1** : a stick used in walking **2** : STICK INSECT; *esp* : one of the U.S. and Canada
walk–on \'wȯk-ˌȯn, -ˌän\ *n* : a small part in a dramatic production
walk·out \-ˌau̇t\ *n* **1** : a labor strike **2** : the action of leaving a meeting or organization as an expression of disapproval
walk out *vb* **1** : to leave suddenly often as an expression of disapproval **2** : to go on strike
walk·over \-ˌō-vər\ *n* : a one-sided contest : an easy victory
walk–up \'wȯk-ˌəp\ *n* : a building or apartment house without an elevator — **walk–up** *adj*
walk·way \-ˌwā\ *n* : a passage for walking
¹wall \'wȯl\ *n* [ME, fr. OE *weall,* fr. L *vallum* rampart, fr. *vallus* stake, palisade] **1** : a structure (as of stone or brick) intended for defense or security or for enclosing something **2** : one of the upright enclosing parts of a building or room **3** : the inside surface of a cavity or container ⟨the ∼ of a boiler⟩ **4** : something like a wall in appearance, function, or effect ⟨a tariff ∼⟩ — **walled** \'wȯld\ *adj*
²wall *vb* **1** : to provide, separate, or surround with or as if with a wall ⟨∼ in a garden⟩ **2** : to close (an opening) with or as if with a wall ⟨∼ up a door⟩
wal·la·by \'wä-lə-bē\ *n, pl* **wallabies** *also* **wallaby** : any of various small or medium-sized kangaroos
wall·board \'wȯl-ˌbȯrd\ *n* : a structural material (as of wood pulp or plaster) made in large sheets and used for sheathing interior walls and ceilings
wal·let \'wä-lət\ *n* **1** : a bag or sack for carrying things on a journey **2** : a pocketbook with compartments (as for personal papers and usu. unfolded money) : BILLFOLD
wall·eye \'wȯl-ˌī\ *n* **1** : an eye with a whitish iris or an opaque white cornea **2** : a large vigorous No. American

food and sport fish related to the perches — **wall·eyed** \-ˌlīd\ *adj*

wall·flow·er \ˈwȯl-ˌflau̇(-ə)r\ *n* **1** : any of several Old World herbs related to the mustards; *esp* : one with showy fragrant flowers **2** : a person who usu. from shyness or unpopularity remains alone (as at a dance)

Wal·loon \wä-ˈlün\ *n* : a member of a people of southern and southeastern Belgium and adjacent parts of France — **Walloon** *adj*

¹**wal·lop** \ˈwä-ləp\ *vb* **1** : to beat soundly : TROUNCE **2** : to hit hard ♦ **Synonyms** BATTER, BEAT, LAMBASTE, POUND, PUMMEL, THRASH

²**wallop** *n* **1** : a powerful blow or impact **2** : the ability to hit hard **3** : emotional, sensory, or psychological force : IMPACT ⟨a story with a ∼⟩

wal·lop·ing \ˈwä-lə-piŋ\ *adj* **1** : LARGE, WHOPPING **2** : exceptionally fine or impressive

¹**wal·low** \ˈwä-lō\ *vb* **1** : to roll oneself about sluggishly in or as if in deep mud ⟨hogs ∼ing in the mire⟩ **2** : to indulge oneself excessively ⟨∼ in luxury⟩ **3** : to become or remain helpless ⟨∼ in ignorance⟩ ♦ **Synonyms** BASK, INDULGE, LUXURIATE, REVEL, WELTER

²**wallow** *n* : a muddy or dust-filled area where animals wallow

wall·pa·per \ˈwȯl-ˌpā-pər\ *n* : decorative paper for the walls of a room — **wallpaper** *vb*

wall-to-wall *adj* **1** : covering the entire floor ⟨*wall-to-wall* carpeting⟩ **2** : covering or filling one entire space or time ⟨crowds of *wall-to-wall* people⟩

wal·nut \ˈwȯl-ˌnət\ *n* [ME *walnot*, fr. OE *wealhhnutu*, lit., foreign nut, fr. *Wealh* Welshman, foreigner + *hnutu* nut] **1** : a nut with a furrowed usu. rough shell and an adherent husk from any of a genus of trees related to the hickories; *esp* : the large edible nut of a Eurasian tree **2** : a tree that bears walnuts **3** : the usu. reddish to dark brown wood of a walnut used esp. in cabinetwork and veneers

wal·rus \ˈwȯl-rəs, ˈwäl-\ *n, pl* **walrus** *or* **wal·rus·es** : a large mammal of arctic waters that is related to the seals and has long ivory tusks

walrus

¹**waltz** \ˈwȯlts\ *n* [G *Walzer*, fr. *walzen* to roll, dance] **1** : a gliding dance done to music having three beats to the measure **2** : music for or suitable for waltzing

²**waltz** *vb* **1** : to dance a waltz **2** : to move or advance easily, successfully, or conspicuously ⟨he ∼ed off with the championship⟩ — **waltz·er** *n*

wam·ble \ˈwäm-bəl\ *vb* **wam·bled; wam·bling** : to progress unsteadily or with a lurching shambling gait

Wam·pa·no·ag \ˌwäm-pə-ˈnō-(ˌ)ag; ˌwȯm-\ *n, pl* **Wampanoag** *or* **Wampanoags** [Narragansett, lit., easterners] : a member of an American Indian people of parts of Rhode Island and Massachusetts

wam·pum \ˈwäm-pəm\ *n* [short for *wampumpeag*, fr. Massachuset (an Algonquian Indian language) *wampompeag*, fr. *wampan* white + *api* string + *-ag*, pl. suffix] **1** : beads made of shells strung in strands, belts, or sashes and used by No. American Indians as money and ornaments **2** *slang* : MONEY

wan \ˈwän\ *adj* **wan·ner; wan·nest** **1** : SICKLY, PALLID; *also* : FEEBLE **2** : DIM, FAINT **3** : LANGUID ⟨a ∼ smile⟩ ♦ **Synonyms** ASHEN, BLANCHED, DOUGHY, LIVID, PALE, WAXEN — **wan·ly** *adv* — **wan·ness** *n*

wand \ˈwänd\ *n* **1** : a slender staff carried in a procession **2** : the staff of a fairy, diviner, or magician

wan·der \ˈwän-dər\ *vb* **1** : to move about aimlessly or without a fixed course or goal : RAMBLE **2** : to go astray in conduct or thought; *esp* : to become delirious ♦ **Synonyms** GAD, GALLIVANT, MEANDER, RANGE, ROAM, ROVE — **wan·der·er** *n*

wandering Jew *n* : either of two trailing or creeping plants cultivated for their showy and often white-striped foliage

wan·der·lust \ˈwän-dər-ˌləst\ *n* : strong longing for or impulse toward wandering

¹**wane** \ˈwän\ *vb* **waned; wan·ing** **1** : to grow gradually smaller or less ⟨the full moon ∼s to new⟩ ⟨his strength *waned*⟩ **2** : to lose power, prosperity, or influence **3** : to draw near an end ⟨summer is *waning*⟩ ♦ **Synonyms** ABATE, EBB, MODERATE, RELENT, SLACKEN, SUBSIDE

²**wane** *n* : a waning (as in size or power); *also* : a period in which something is waning

wan·gle \ˈwaŋ-gəl\ *vb* **wan·gled; wan·gling** **1** : to obtain by sly or devious means; *also* : to use trickery or questionable means to achieve an end **2** : MANIPULATE; *also* : FINAGLE

wan·na–be *also* **wan·na·bee** \ˈwä-nə-ˌbē\ *n* : a person who wants or aspires to be someone or something else or who tries to look or act like someone else

¹**want** \ˈwȯnt, ˈwänt\ *vb* **1** : to fail to possess : LACK ⟨they ∼ the necessities of life⟩ **2** : to feel or suffer the need of **3** : NEED, REQUIRE ⟨the house ∼s painting⟩ **4** : to desire earnestly : WISH

²**want** *n* **1** : a lack of a required or usual amount : SHORTAGE **2** : dire need : DESTITUTION **3** : something wanted : DESIRE **4** : personal defect : FAULT

¹**want·ing** \ˈwȯn-tiŋ, ˈwän-\ *adj* **1** : not present or in evidence : ABSENT **2** : falling below standards or expectations **3** : lacking in ability or capacity : DEFICIENT ⟨∼ in common sense⟩

²**wanting** *prep* **1** : LESS, MINUS ⟨a month ∼ two days⟩ **2** : WITHOUT ⟨a book ∼ a cover⟩

¹**wan·ton** \ˈwȯn-tᵊn, ˈwän-\ *adj* [ME, undisciplined, fr. *wan*-deficient, wrong + *towen*, pp. of *teen* to draw, train, discipline] **1** : UNCHASTE, LEWD, LUSTFUL; *also* : SENSUAL **2** : having no regard for justice or for other persons' feelings, rights, or safety : MERCILESS, INHUMANE ⟨∼ cruelty⟩ **3** : having no just cause ⟨a ∼ attack⟩ — **wan·ton·ly** *adv* — **wan·ton·ness** *n*

²**wanton** *n* : a wanton individual; *esp* : a lewd or immoral person

³**wanton** *vb* **1** : to be wanton : act wantonly **2** : to pass or waste wantonly

wa·pi·ti \ˈwä-pə-tē\ *n, pl* **wapiti** *or* **wapitis** : ELK 2

¹**war** \ˈwȯr\ *n* **1** : a state or period of usu. open and declared armed fighting between states or nations **2** : the art or science of warfare **3** : a state of hostility, conflict, or antagonism **4** : a struggle between opposing forces or for a particular end ⟨∼ against disease⟩ — **war·less** \-ləs\ *adj*

²**war** *vb* **warred; war·ring** : to engage in warfare : be in conflict

³**war** *abbr* warrant

¹**war·ble** \ˈwȯr-bəl\ *n* **1** : a melodious succession of low pleasing sounds **2** : a musical trill

²**warble** *vb* **war·bled; war·bling** **1** : to sing or utter in a trilling manner or with variations **2** : to express by or as if by warbling

³**warble** *n* : a swelling under the skin esp. of the back of cattle, horses, and wild mammals caused by the maggot of a fly (**warble fly**); *also* : its maggot

war·bler \ˈwȯr-blər\ *n* **1** : SONGSTER **2** : any of various small slender-billed chiefly Old World songbirds related to the thrushes and noted for their singing **3** : any of numerous small bright-colored insect-eating American birds with a usu. weak and unmusical song

war·bon·net \ˈwȯr-ˌbä-nət\ *n* : a feathered American Indian ceremonial headdress

war crime *n* : a crime (as genocide) committed during or in connection with war

war cry *n* **1** : a cry used by fighters in war **2** : a slogan used esp. to rally people to a cause

¹**ward** \ˈwȯrd\ *n* **1** : a guarding or being under guard or guardianship; *esp* : CUSTODY **2** : a body of guards **3** : a division of a prison **4** : a division in a hospital **5** : a division of a city for electoral or administrative purposes **6** : a person (as a child) under the protection of a guardian or a law court **7** : a person or body of persons under the protection or tutelage of a government **8** : a means of defense : PROTECTION

²**ward** *vb* : to turn aside : DEFLECT — usu. used with *off* ⟨∼ off a blow⟩

¹**-ward** *also* **-wards** *adj suffix* **1** : that moves, tends, faces,

or is directed toward ⟨wind*ward*⟩ **2** : that occurs or is situated in the direction of ⟨sea*ward*⟩

²**ward** *or* **-wards** *adv suffix* **1** : in a (specified) direction ⟨up*wards*⟩ ⟨after*ward*⟩ **2** : toward a (specified) point, position, or area ⟨sky*ward*⟩

war dance *n* : a dance performed (as by American Indians) before going to war or in celebration of victory

war·den \'wȯr-d°n\ *n* **1** : GUARDIAN, KEEPER **2** : the governor of a town, district, or fortress **3** : an official charged with special supervisory or enforcement duties ⟨game ∼⟩ ⟨air raid ∼⟩ **4** : an official in charge of the operation of a prison **5** : one of two ranking lay officers of an Episcopal parish **6** : any of various British college officials

ward·er \'wȯr-dər\ *n* : WATCHMAN, WARDEN

ward heel·er \-ˌhē-lər\ *n* : a local worker for a political boss

ward·robe \'wȯr-ˌdrōb\ *n* [ME *warderobe*, fr. AF **warderobe, garderobe*, fr. *warder, garder* to guard + *robe* robe] **1** : a room or closet where clothes are kept; *also* : CLOTHESPRESS **2** : a collection of wearing apparel ⟨his summer ∼⟩

ward·room \-ˌdrüm, -ˌdru̇m\ *n* : the dining area for officers aboard a warship

ward·ship \'wȯrd-ˌship\ *n* **1** : GUARDIANSHIP **2** : the state of being under care of a guardian

ware \'wer\ *n* **1** : manufactured articles or products of art or craft : GOODS ⟨glass*ware*⟩ **2** : an article of merchandise ⟨a peddler hawking his ∼s⟩ **3** : items (as dishes) of fired clay : POTTERY

ware·house \-ˌhau̇s\ *n* : a place for the storage of merchandise or commodities : STOREHOUSE — **warehouse** *vb* — **ware·house·man** \-mən\ *n* — **ware·hous·er** \-ˌhau̇-zər, -sər\ *n*

ware·room \'wer-ˌrüm, -ˌru̇m\ *n* : a room in which goods are exhibited for sale

war·fare \'wȯr-ˌfer\ *n* **1** : military operations between enemies : WAR; *also* : an activity undertaken by one country to weaken or destroy another ⟨economic ∼⟩ **2** : STRUGGLE, CONFLICT

war·fa·rin \'wȯr-fə-rən\ *n* : an anticoagulant compound used as a rodent poison and in medicine

war·head \'wȯr-ˌhed\ *n* : the section of a missile containing the charge

war·horse \-ˌhȯrs\ *n* **1** : a horse for use in war **2** : a veteran soldier or public person (as a politician) **3** : a musical composition that is often performed

war·like \-ˌlīk\ *adj* **1** : fond of war ⟨∼ peoples⟩ **2** : of, relating to, or useful in war : MILITARY, MARTIAL ⟨∼ supplies⟩ **3** : befitting or characteristic of war or of soldiers ⟨∼ attitudes⟩

war·lock \-ˌläk\ *n* [ME *warloghe*, fr. OE *wǣrloga* one that breaks faith, the Devil, fr. *wǣr* faith, troth + *-loga* (fr. *lēogan* to lie)] : SORCERER, WIZARD

war·lord \-ˌlȯrd\ *n* **1** : a high military leader **2** : a military commander exercising local civil power by force ⟨former Chinese ∼s⟩

¹**warm** \'wȯrm\ *adj* **1** : having or giving out heat to a moderate or adequate degree ⟨∼ milk⟩ ⟨a ∼ stove⟩ **2** : serving to retain heat ⟨∼ clothes⟩ **3** : feeling or inducing sensations of heat ⟨∼ from exercise⟩ ⟨a ∼ climb⟩ **4** : showing or marked by strong feeling : ARDENT ⟨∼ support⟩ **5** : marked by tense excitement or hot anger ⟨a ∼ campaign⟩ **6** : giving a pleasant impression of warmth, cheerfulness, or friendliness ⟨∼ colors⟩ ⟨a ∼ tone of voice⟩ **7** : marked by or tending toward injury, distress, or pain ⟨made things ∼ for the enemy⟩ **8** : newly made : FRESH ⟨a ∼ scent⟩ **9** : near to a goal ⟨getting ∼ in a search⟩ — **warm·ly** *adv*

²**warm** *vb* **1** : to make or become warm **2** : to give a feeling of warmth or vitality to **3** : to experience feelings of affection or pleasure ⟨she ∼ed to her guest⟩ **4** : to reheat for eating ⟨∼ed over the roast⟩ **5** : to make ready for operation or performance by preliminary exercise or operation ⟨∼ up the motor⟩ **6** : to become increasingly ardent, interested, or competent ⟨the speaker ∼ed to his topic⟩ — **warm·er** *n*

warm–blood·ed \-'blə-dəd\ *adj* : able to maintain a relatively high and constant body temperature relatively independent of that of the surroundings

warmed–over \'wȯrmd-'ō-vər\ *adj* **1** : REHEATED ⟨∼ cabbage⟩ **2** : not fresh or new ⟨∼ ideas⟩

warm front *n* : an advancing edge of a warm air mass

warm·heart·ed \'wȯrm-'här-təd\ *adj* : marked by warmth of feeling : CORDIAL — **warm·heart·ed·ness** *n*

warming pan *n* : a long-handled covered pan filled with live coals and formerly used to warm a bed

war·mon·ger \'wȯr-ˌmən-gər, -ˌmäŋ-\ *n* : one who urges or attempts to stir up war — **war·mon·ger·ing** \-g(ə-)riŋ\ *n*

warmth \'wȯrmth\ *n* **1** : the quality or state of being warm **2** : ZEAL, ARDOR, FERVOR

warm up *vb* : to engage in exercise or practice esp. before entering a game or contest — **warm–up** \'wȯrm-ˌəp\ *n*

warn \'wȯrn\ *vb* **1** : to put on guard : CAUTION; *also* : ADMONISH, COUNSEL **2** : to notify esp. in advance : INFORM **3** : to order to go or keep away

¹**warn·ing** \'wȯr-niŋ\ *n* **1** : the act of warning : the state of being warned **2** : something that warns or serves to warn ⟨a tornado ∼⟩

²**warning** *adj* : serving as an alarm, signal, summons, or admonition ⟨a ∼ bell⟩ — **warn·ing·ly** *adv*

¹**warp** \'wȯrp\ *n* **1** : the lengthwise threads on a loom or in a woven fabric **2** : a twist out of a true plane or straight line ⟨a ∼ in a board⟩

²**warp** *vb* [ME, fr. OE *weorpan* to throw] **1** : to turn or twist out of shape; *also* : to become so twisted **2** : to lead astray : PERVERT; *also* : FALSIFY, DISTORT

war paint *n* : paint put on the face and body by American Indians as a sign of going to war

war·path \'wȯr-ˌpath, -ˌpäth\ *n* : the course taken by a party of American Indians going on a hostile expedition — **on the warpath** : ready to fight or argue

war·plane \-ˌplān\ *n* : a military airplane; *esp* : one armed for combat

warp speed *n* : the highest possible speed

¹**war·rant** \'wȯr-ənt, 'wär-\ *n* **1** : AUTHORIZATION; *also* : JUSTIFICATION, GROUND **2** : evidence (as a document) of authorization; *esp* : a legal writ authorizing an officer to take action (as in making an arrest, seizure, or search) **3** : a certificate of appointment issued to an officer of lower rank than a commissioned officer

²**warrant** *vb* **1** : to guarantee security or immunity to : SECURE **2** : to declare or maintain positively ⟨I ∼ this is so⟩ **3** : to assure (a person) of the truth of what is said **4** : to guarantee to be as it appears or as it is represented ⟨∼ goods as of the first quality⟩ **5** : SANCTION, AUTHORIZE **6** : to give proof of : ATTEST; *also* : GUARANTEE **7** : JUSTIFY ⟨his need ∼s the expenditure⟩

warrant officer *n* **1** : an officer in the armed forces ranking next below a commissioned officer **2** : a commissioned officer ranking below an ensign in the navy or coast guard and below a second lieutenant in the marine corps

war·ran·ty \'wȯr-ən-tē, 'wär-\ *n, pl* **-ties** : an expressed or implied statement that some situation or thing is as it appears to be or is represented to be; *esp* : a usu. written guarantee of the integrity of a product and of the maker's responsibility for the repair or replacement of defective parts

war·ren \'wȯr-ən, 'wär-\ *n* **1** : an area where rabbits breed; *also* : a structure where rabbits are bred or kept **2** : a crowded tenement or district

war·rior \'wȯr-yər; 'wȯr-ē-ər, 'wär-\ *n* : a man engaged or experienced in warfare

war·ship \'wȯr-ˌship\ *n* : a naval vessel

wart \'wȯrt\ *n* **1** : a small usu. horny projecting growth on the skin; *esp* : one caused by a virus **2** : a protuberance resembling a wart (as on a plant) — **warty** *adj*

wart·hog \'wȯrt-ˌhȯg, -ˌhäg\ *n* : a wild African hog that has large tusks and in the male two pairs of rough warty protuberances below the eyes

warthog

war·time \'wȯr-ˌtīm\ *n* : a period during which a war is in progress

wary \'wer-ē\ *adj* **war·i·er; -est** : very cautious; *esp* : careful in guarding against danger or deception — **war·i·ly** \'wer-ə-lē\ *adv* — **war·i·ness** \'wer-ē-nəs\ *n*

was *past 1st & 3d sing of* BE

wa·sa·bi \'wä-sə-bē; wä-'sä-\ *n* [Jp] : a condiment prepared from the ground greenish root of an Asian herb and similar in flavor and use to horseradish; *also* : the herb or its root

¹wash \'wȯsh, 'wäsh\ *vb* **1** : to clean with water and usu. soap or detergent ⟨∼ clothes⟩ ⟨∼ your hands⟩ **2** : to wet thoroughly : DRENCH **3** : to flow along the border of ⟨waves ∼ the shore⟩ **4** : to pour or flow in a stream or current **5** : to move or remove by or as if by the action of water **6** : to cover or daub lightly with a liquid (as whitewash) **7** : to run water over (as gravel or ore) in order to separate valuable matter from refuse ⟨∼ sand for gold⟩ **8** : to undergo laundering ⟨a dress that doesn't ∼ well⟩ **9** : to stand a test ⟨that story will not ∼⟩ **10** : to be worn away by water

²wash *n* **1** : the act or process or an instance of washing or being washed **2** : articles to be washed or being washed **3** : a thin coat of paint (as watercolor) **4** : the flow or action of a mass of water (as a wave) **5** : worthless esp. liquid waste : REFUSE, SWILL **6** : erosion by waves (as of the sea) **7** : a disturbance in a fluid (as water or the air) caused by the passage of a wing or propeller **8** *West* : the dry bed of a stream

³wash *adj* : WASHABLE

Wash *abbr* Washington

wash·able \'wȯ-shə-bəl, 'wä-\ *adj* : capable of being washed without damage — **wash·abil·i·ty** \ˌwȯ-shə-'bi-lə-tē, ˌwä-\ *n*

wash–and–wear *adj* : of, relating to, or being a fabric or garment that needs little or no ironing after washing

wash·ba·sin \'wȯsh-ˌbā-sᵊn, 'wäsh-\ *n* : WASHBOWL

wash·board \-ˌbȯrd\ *n* : a grooved board to scrub clothes on

wash·bowl \-ˌbōl\ *n* : a large bowl for water for washing hands and face

wash·cloth \-ˌklȯth\ *n* : a cloth used for washing one's face and body

washed–out \'wȯsht-'aút, 'wäsht-\ *adj* **1** : faded in color **2** : EXHAUSTED ⟨felt ∼ after working all night⟩

washed–up \-'əp\ *adj* : no longer successful, popular, skillful, or needed

wash·er \'wȯ-shər, 'wä-\ *n* **1** : a ring or perforated plate used around a bolt or screw to ensure tightness or relieve friction **2** : one that washes; *esp* : a machine for washing

wash·er·wom·an \-ˌwu̇-mən\ *n* : a woman whose occupation is washing clothes

wash·ing \'wȯ-shiŋ, 'wä-\ *n* **1** : material obtained by washing **2** : articles washed or to be washed

washing soda *n* : SODIUM CARBONATE

Wash·ing·ton's Birthday \'wȯ-shiŋ-tənz-, 'wä-\ *n* : the 3d Monday in February observed as a legal holiday

wash·out \'wȯsh-ˌaút, 'wäsh-\ *n* **1** : the washing away of earth (as from a road); *also* : a place where earth is washed away **2** : a complete failure

wash·room \-ˌrüm, -ˌru̇m\ *n* : BATHROOM

wash·stand \-ˌstand\ *n* **1** : a stand holding articles needed for washing face and hands **2** : LAVATORY 1

wash·tub \-ˌtəb\ *n* : a tub for washing or soaking clothes

wash·wom·an \'wȯsh-ˌwu̇-mən, 'wäsh-\ *n* : WASHERWOMAN

washy \'wȯ-shē, 'wä-\ *adj* **wash·i·er; -est** **1** : WEAK, WATERY **2** : PALLID **3** : lacking in vigor, individuality, or definiteness

wasp \'wäsp, 'wȯsp\ *n* : any of numerous social or solitary winged insects related to the bees and ants with biting mouthparts and in females and workers an often formidable sting

WASP *or* **Wasp** *n* [white Anglo-Saxon Protestant] : an American of northern European and esp. British ancestry and of Protestant background

wasp·ish \'wäs-pish, 'wȯs-\ *adj* **1** : SNAPPISH, IRRITABLE **2** : resembling a wasp in form; *esp* : slightly built ♦ **Synonyms** FRACTIOUS, FRETFUL, HUFFY, PEEVISH, PETULANT, QUERULOUS

wasp waist *n* : a very slender waist

¹was·sail \'wä-səl, wä-'säl\ *n* [ME wæs hæil, washayl, fr. ON ves heill be well] **1** : an early English toast to someone's health **2** : a hot drink made with wine, beer, or cider, spices, sugar, and usu. baked apples and traditionally served at Christmas **3** : riotous drinking : REVELRY

²wassail *vb* **1** : CAROUSE **2** : to drink to the health of — **was·sail·er** *n*

Was·ser·mann test \'wä-sər-mən-, 'vä-\ *n* : a blood test for the detection of syphilis

wast·age \'wā-stij\ *n* : WASTE 3

¹waste \'wāst\ *n* **1** : a sparsely settled or barren region : DESERT; *also* : uncultivated land **2** : the act or an instance of wasting : the state of being wasted **3** : gradual loss or decrease by use, wear, or decay **4** : material left over, rejected, or thrown away; *also* : an unwanted by-product of a manufacturing or chemical process **5** : refuse (as garbage) that accumulates about habitations **6** : material (as feces) produced but not used by a living organism — **waste·ful** \-fəl\ *adj* — **waste·ful·ly** *adv* — **waste·ful·ness** *n*

²waste *vb* **wast·ed; wast·ing** **1** : DEVASTATE **2** : to wear away or diminish gradually : CONSUME **3** : to spend or use carelessly or uselessly : SQUANDER **4** : to lose or cause to lose weight, strength, or energy ⟨wasting away from fever⟩ **5** : to become diminished in bulk or substance : DWINDLE ♦ **Synonyms** DEPREDATE, DESOLATE, DESPOIL, RAVAGE, SPOIL, STRIP — **wast·er** *n*

³waste *adj* **1** : being wild and uninhabited : BARREN, DESOLATE; *also* : UNCULTIVATED **2** : being in a ruined condition **3** : discarded as worthless after being used ⟨∼ water⟩ **4** : excreted from or stored in inert form in a living organism as a by-product of vital activity ⟨∼ matter from birds⟩

waste·bas·ket \'wāst-ˌbas-kət\ *n* : a receptacle for refuse

waste·land \-ˌland, -lənd\ *n* : land that is barren or unfit for cultivation

waste·pa·per \-'pā-pər\ *n* : paper thrown away as used, not needed, or not fit for use

wast·rel \'wā-strəl\ *n* : a person who wastes resources : SPENDTHRIFT

¹watch \'wäch, 'wȯch\ *vb* **1** : to be or stay awake intentionally : keep vigil ⟨∼ed by the patient's bedside⟩ ⟨∼ and pray⟩ **2** : to be on the lookout for danger : be on one's guard **3** : to keep guard ⟨∼ outside the door⟩ **4** : OBSERVE ⟨∼ a game⟩ **5** : to keep in view so as to prevent harm or warn of danger ⟨∼ a brush fire carefully⟩ **6** : to keep oneself informed about ⟨∼ his progress⟩ **7** : to lie in wait for esp. so as to take advantage of ⟨∼ed her opportunity⟩ — **watch·er** *n*

²watch *n* **1** : the act of keeping awake to guard, protect, or attend; *also* : a state of alert and continuous attention **2** : a public weather alert ⟨a winter storm ∼⟩ **3** : close observation **4** : LOOKOUT, WATCHMAN, GUARD **5** : a period during which a part of a ship's crew is on duty; *also* : the part of a crew on duty during a watch **6** : a portable timepiece carried on the person

watch·band \'wäch-ˌband, 'wȯch-\ *n* : the bracelet or strap of a wristwatch

watch·dog \-ˌdȯg\ *n* **1** : a dog kept to guard property **2** : one that guards or protects

watch·ful \-fəl\ *adj* : steadily attentive and alert esp. to danger : VIGILANT — **watch·ful·ly** *adv* — **watch·ful·ness** *n*

watch·mak·er \-ˌmā-kər\ *n* : a person who makes or repairs watches — **watch·mak·ing** \-ˌmā-kiŋ\ *n*

watch·man \-mən\ *n* : a person assigned to watch : GUARD

watch night *n* : a devotional service lasting until after midnight esp. on New Year's Eve

watch·tow·er \'wäch-ˌtaú(-ə)r, 'wȯch-\ *n* : a tower for a lookout

watch·word \-ˌwərd\ *n* **1** : a secret word used as a signal or sign of recognition **2** : a word or motto used as a slogan or rallying cry

¹wa·ter \'wȯ-tər, 'wä-\ *n* **1** : the liquid that descends as rain and forms rivers, lakes, and seas **2** : a natural mineral water — usu. used in pl. **3** *pl* : the water occupying or flowing in a particular bed; *also* : a band of seawater bordering on and under the control of a country **4** : any of various liquids containing or resembling water; *esp* : a watery fluid (as tears, urine, or sap) formed or circulating in a living organism **5** : a specified degree of thoroughness or completeness ⟨a scoundrel of the first ∼⟩

²water *vb* **1** : to supply with or get or take water ⟨~ horses⟩ ⟨the ship ~ed at each port⟩ **2** : to treat (as cloth) so as to give a lustrous appearance in wavy lines **3** : to dilute by or as if by adding water to **4** : to form or secrete water or watery matter ⟨her eyes ~ed⟩ ⟨my mouth ~ed⟩

water bed *n* : a bed whose mattress is a watertight bag filled with water

wa·ter·borne \-ˌbȯrn\ *adj* : supported, carried, or transmitted by water

water buffalo *n* : a common oxlike often domesticated Asian bovine

water chestnut *n* : a whitish crunchy vegetable used esp. in Chinese cooking that is the peeled tuber of a widely cultivated Asian sedge; *also* : the tuber or the sedge itself

water closet *n* : a compartment or room with a toilet bowl : BATHROOM; *also* : a toilet bowl along with its accessories

wa·ter·col·or \ˈwȯ-tər-ˌkə-lər, ˈwä-\ *n* **1** : a paint whose liquid part is water **2** : the art of painting with watercolors **3** : a picture made with watercolors

wa·ter·course \-ˌkȯrs\ *n* : a stream of water; *also* : the bed of a stream

wa·ter·craft \-ˌkraft\ *n* : a craft for water transport : SHIP, BOAT

wa·ter·cress \-ˌkres\ *n* : an aquatic perennial Eurasian cress that is naturalized in the U.S. and has edible leaves used esp. in salads

wa·ter·fall \-ˌfȯl\ *n* : a very steep descent of the water of a stream

wa·ter·fowl \ˈwȯ-tər-ˌfau̇(-ə)l, ˈwä-\ *n, pl* **-fowl** *also* **-fowls** : a bird that frequents water; *esp* : a swimming bird (as a duck) hunted as game

wa·ter·front \-ˌfrənt\ *n* : land or a section of a town fronting or abutting on a body of water

water gap *n* : a pass in a mountain ridge through which a stream runs

water glass *n* : a drinking glass

water hyacinth *n* : a showy floating aquatic plant of tropical America that often clogs waterways (as in the southern U.S.)

watering hole *n* : a place (as a bar) where people gather socially

watering place *n* : a resort that features mineral springs or bathing

water lily *n* : any of various aquatic plants with floating roundish leaves and showy solitary flowers

wa·ter·line \ˈwȯ-tər-ˌlīn, ˈwä-\ *n* : a line that marks the level of the surface of water on something (as a ship or the shore)

wa·ter·logged \-ˌlȯgd, -ˌlägd\ *adj* : so filled or soaked with water as to be heavy or unmanageable ⟨a ~ boat⟩

wa·ter·loo \ˌwȯ-tər-ˈlü, ˌwä-\ *n, pl* **-loos** [*Waterloo*, Belgium, scene of Napoleon's defeat in 1815] : a decisive or final defeat or setback

¹wa·ter·mark \ˈwȯ-tər-ˌmärk, ˈwä-\ *n* **1** : a mark indicating height to which water has risen **2** : a marking in paper visible when the paper is held up to the light

²watermark *vb* : to mark (paper) with a watermark

wa·ter·mel·on \-ˌme-lən\ *n* : a large roundish or oblong fruit with sweet juicy usu. red pulp; *also* : a widely grown African vine related to the squashes that produces watermelons

water moccasin *n* : a venomous pit viper chiefly of the southeastern U.S. that is related to the copperhead

water ou·zel \-ˈü-zəl\ *n* : DIPPER 1

water park *n* : an amusement park with a pool and wetted slides

water pill *n* : DIURETIC

water pipe *n* : a pipe for smoking that has a long flexible tube whereby the smoke is cooled by passing through water

water pistol *n* : a toy pistol for squirting a jet of liquid

water polo *n* : a team game played in a swimming pool with a ball resembling a soccer ball

wa·ter·pow·er \ˈwȯ-tər-ˌpau̇(-ə)r, ˈwä-\ *n* : the power of moving water used to run machinery

¹wa·ter·proof \ˈwȯ-tər-ˌprüf, ˈwä-\ *adj* : not letting water through; *esp* : covered or treated with a material to prevent permeation by water — **wa·ter·proof·ing** *n*

²waterproof *n* **1** : a waterproof fabric **2** *chiefly Brit* : RAINCOAT

³waterproof *vb* : to make waterproof

wa·ter–re·pel·lent \ˌwȯ-tər-ri-ˈpe-lənt, ˌwä-\ *adj* : treated with a finish that is resistant to water penetration

wa·ter–re·sis·tant \-ri-ˈzis-tənt\ *adj* : WATER-REPELLENT

wa·ter·shed \ˈwȯ-tər-ˌshed, ˈwä-\ *n* **1** : a dividing ridge between two drainage areas **2** : the region or area drained by a particular body of water

wa·ter·side \-ˌsīd\ *n* : the land bordering a body of water

water ski *n* : a ski used on water when the wearer is towed — **wa·ter–ski** *vb* — **wa·ter–ski·er** \-ˌskē-ər\ *n*

water snake *n* : any of various snakes found in or near freshwater and feeding largely on aquatic animals

wa·ter·spout \ˈwȯ-tər-ˌspau̇t, ˈwä-\ *n* **1** : a pipe for carrying water from a roof **2** : a funnel-shaped cloud extending from a cloud down to a spray torn up by whirling winds from an ocean or lake

water strider *n* : any of various long-legged bugs that move about swiftly on the surface of water

water table *n* : the upper limit of the portion of the ground wholly saturated with water

wa·ter·tight \ˌwȯ-tər-ˈtīt, ˌwä-\ *adj* **1** : constructed so as to keep water out **2** : allowing no possibility for doubt or uncertainty ⟨a ~ case against the accused⟩

wa·ter·way \ˈwȯ-tər-ˌwā, ˈwä-\ *n* : a navigable body of water

wa·ter·wheel \-ˌhwēl, -ˌwēl\ *n* : a wheel made to turn by water flowing against it

water wings *n pl* : an air-filled device to give support to a person's body esp. when learning to swim

wa·ter·works \ˈwȯ-tər-ˌwərks, ˈwä-\ *n pl* : a system for supplying water (as to a city)

wa·tery \ˈwȯ-tə-rē, ˈwä-\ *adj* **1** : containing, full of, or giving out water ⟨~ clouds⟩ **2** : being like water : THIN, WEAK ⟨~ lemonade⟩; *also* : being soft and soggy ⟨~ turnips⟩

WATS \ˈwäts\ *abbr* Wide-Area Telecommunications Service

watt \ˈwät\ *n* [James *Watt* †1819 Scottish engineer and inventor] : the metric unit of power equal to the work done at the rate of one joule per second or to the power produced by a current of one ampere across a potential difference of one volt

watt·age \ˈwä-tij\ *n* : amount of power expressed in watts

wat·tle \ˈwä-tᵊl\ *n* **1** : a framework of rods with flexible branches or reeds interlaced used esp. formerly in building; *also* : material for this framework **2** : a naked fleshy process hanging usu. from the head or neck (as of a bird) — **wat·tled** \-tᵊld\ *adj*

W Aust *abbr* Western Australia

¹wave \ˈwāv\ *vb* **waved**; **wav·ing** **1** : FLUTTER ⟨flags *waving* in the breeze⟩ **2** : to motion with the hands or with something held in them in signal or salute **3** : to become moved or brandished to-and-fro; *also* : BRANDISH, FLOURISH ⟨~ a sword⟩ **4** : to move before the wind with a wavelike motion ⟨fields of *waving* grain⟩ **5** : to curve up and down like a wave : UNDULATE

²wave *n* **1** : a moving ridge or swell on the surface of water **2** : a wavelike formation or shape ⟨a ~ in the hair⟩ **3** : the action or process of making wavy or curly **4** : a waving motion; *esp* : a signal made by waving something **5** : FLOW, GUSH ⟨a ~ of anger swept over her⟩ **6** : a peak of activity ⟨a ~ of selling⟩ **7** : a disturbance that transfers energy progressively from point to point in a medium ⟨light travels in ~s⟩ ⟨a sound ~⟩ **8** : a period of hot or cold weather — **wave·like** *adj*

wave·length \ˈwāv-ˌleŋth\ *n* **1** : the distance in the line of advance of a wave from any one point (as a crest) to the next corresponding point **2** : a line of thought that reveals a common understanding

wave·let \-lət\ *n* : a little wave : RIPPLE

wa·ver \ˈwā-vər\ *vb* **1** : to fluctuate in opinion, allegiance, or direction **2** : REEL, TOTTER; *also* : QUIVER, FLICKER ⟨~*ing* flames⟩ **3** : FALTER **4** : to give an unsteady sound : QUAVER ♦ *Synonyms* FALTER, HESITATE, SHILLY-SHALLY, VACILLATE — **waver** *n* — **wa·ver·er** *n* — **wa·ver·ing·ly** *adv*

wavy \ˈwā-vē\ *adj* **wav·i·er**; **-est** : having waves : moving in waves

¹wax \ˈwaks\ *n* **1** : a yellowish plastic substance secreted by bees for constructing the honeycomb **2** : any of various substances like beeswax

²wax *vb* : to treat or rub with wax — **wax·er** *n*

³wax *vb* **1** : to increase in size, numbers, strength, volume, or duration **2** : to increase in apparent size ⟨the moon ~es toward the full⟩ **3** : to take on a quality or state : BECOME ⟨~ed indignant⟩ ⟨the party ~ed merry⟩

wax bean *n* : a kidney bean with pods that turn creamy yellow to bright yellow when mature enough to use as snap beans

wax·en \'wak-sən\ *adj* **1** : made of or covered with wax **2** : resembling wax (as in color or consistency)

wax museum *n* : a place where wax effigies are exhibited

wax myrtle *n* : any of a genus of shrubs or trees with aromatic leaves; *esp* : an evergreen shrub or small tree of the eastern U.S. that produces small hard berries with a thick coating of bluish-white wax used for candles

wax·wing \'waks-ˌwiŋ\ *n* : any of a genus of chiefly brown to gray singing birds with a showy crest and red waxy material on the tips of some wing feathers

wax·work \-ˌwərk\ *n* **1** : an effigy usu. of a person in wax **2** *pl* : an exhibition of wax figures

waxy \'wak-sē\ *adj* **wax·i·er; -est** **1** : made of or full of wax **2** : WAXEN 2

way \'wā\ *n* **1** : a thoroughfare for travel or passage : ROAD, PATH, STREET **2** : ROUTE ⟨knew the ~ home⟩ **3** : a course of action ⟨chose the easy ~⟩; *also* : opportunity, capability, or fact of doing as one pleases ⟨always had your own ~⟩ **4** : a possible course : POSSIBILITY ⟨no two ~s about it⟩ **5** : METHOD, MODE ⟨this ~ of thinking⟩ ⟨a new ~ of painting⟩ **6** : FEATURE, RESPECT ⟨a good worker in many ~s⟩ **7** : the usual or characteristic state of affairs ⟨as is the ~ with old people⟩; *also* : individual characteristic or peculiarity ⟨used to her ~s⟩ **8** : DISTANCE ⟨a short ~ from here⟩ ⟨a long ~ from success⟩ **9** : progress along a course ⟨working my ~ through college⟩ **10** : something having direction : LOCALITY ⟨out our ~⟩ **11** : STATE, CONDITION ⟨the ~ things are⟩ **12** *pl* : an inclined structure upon which a ship is built or is supported in launching **13** : CATEGORY, KIND ⟨get what you need in the ~ of supplies⟩ **14** : motion or speed of a boat through the water — **by the way** : by way of interjection or digression — **by way of 1** : for the purpose of ⟨*by way of* illustration⟩ **2** : by the route through : VIA — **out of the way 1** : WRONG, IMPROPER **2** : SECLUDED, REMOTE

way·bill \'wā-ˌbil\ *n* : a paper that accompanies a freight shipment and gives details of goods, route, and charges

way·far·er \'wā-ˌfer-ər\ *n* : a traveler esp. on foot — **way·far·ing** \-ˌfer-iŋ\ *adj*

way·lay \'wā-ˌlā\ *vb* **-laid** \-ˌlād\; **-lay·ing** : to lie in wait for or attack from ambush

way–out \'wā-ˈaut\ *adj* : FAR-OUT

-ways *adv suffix* : in (such) a way, course, direction, or manner ⟨side*ways*⟩

ways and means *n pl* : methods and resources esp. for raising revenues needed by a state; *also* : a legislative committee concerned with this function

way·side \'wā-ˌsīd\ *n* : the side of or land adjacent to a road or path

way station *n* : an intermediate station on a line of travel (as a railroad)

way·ward \'wā-wərd\ *adj* [ME, short for *awayward* turned away, fr. *away*, adv. + *-ward* directed toward] **1** : following one's own capricious or wanton inclinations ⟨~ children⟩ **2** : UNPREDICTABLE, IRREGULAR ⟨a ~ act⟩

WBC *abbr* white blood cells

WC *abbr* **1** water closet **2** without charge

WCTU *abbr* Women's Christian Temperance Union

we \'wē\ *pron* **1** — used of a group that includes the speaker or writer **2** — used for the singular *I* by a monarch, editor, or writer

weak \'wēk\ *adj* **1** : lacking strength or vigor : FEEBLE **2** : not able to sustain or resist much weight, pressure, or strain **3** : deficient in vigor of mind or character; *also* : resulting from or indicative of such deficiency ⟨a ~ policy⟩ ⟨a ~ will⟩ **4** : not supported by truth or logic ⟨a ~ argument⟩ **5** : lacking skill or proficiency; *also* : indicative of a lack of skill or aptitude **6** : lacking vigor of expression or effect **7** : of less than usual strength ⟨~ tea⟩ **8** : not having or exerting authority ⟨~ government⟩; *also* : INEFFECTIVE, IMPOTENT ⟨~ measures to control crime⟩ **9** : of, relating to, or consti-

tuting a verb or verb conjugation that forms the past tense and past participle by adding *-ed* or *-d* or *-t* — **weak·ly** *adv*

weak·en \'wē-kən\ *vb* : to make or become weak ✦ **Synonyms** ENFEEBLE, DEBILITATE, UNDERMINE, SAP, CRIPPLE, DISABLE

weak·fish \'wēk-ˌfish\ *n* [obs. D *weekvis*, fr. D *week* soft + *vis* fish] : a common marine fish of the Atlantic coast of the U.S. caught for food and sport; *also* : any of several related food fishes

weak force *n* : the physical force responsible for particle decay processes in radioactivity

weak–kneed \'wēk-ˈnēd\ *adj* : lacking willpower or resolution

weak·ling \'wē-kliŋ\ *n* : a person who is physically, mentally, or morally weak

weak·ly \'wē-klē\ *adj* : FEEBLE, WEAK

weak·ness \'wēk-nəs\ *n* **1** : the quality or state of being weak; *also* : an instance or period of being weak ⟨in a moment of ~ he agreed to go⟩ **2** : FAULT, DEFECT **3** : an object of special desire or fondness ⟨chocolate is her ~⟩

¹weal \'wēl\ *n* : WELL-BEING, PROSPERITY

²weal *n* : WELT

weald \'wēld\ *n* [The *Weald,* wooded district in England, fr. ME *Weeld,* fr. OE *weald* forest] **1** : FOREST **2** : WOLD

wealth \'welth\ *n* [ME *welthe* welfare, prosperity, fr. *wele* weal] **1** : abundance of possessions or resources : AFFLUENCE, RICHES **2** : abundant supply : PROFUSION ⟨a ~ of detail⟩ **3** : all property that has a money or an exchange value; *also* : all objects or resources that have economic value ✦ **Synonyms** FORTUNE, PROPERTY, SUBSTANCE, WORTH

wealthy \'wel-thē\ *adj* **wealth·i·er; -est** : having wealth : RICH

wean \'wēn\ *vb* **1** : to accustom (a young mammal) to take food by means other than nursing **2** : to free from a source of dependence; *also* : to free from a usu. unwholesome habit or interest

weap·on \'we-pən\ *n* **1** : something (as a gun, knife, or club) used to injure, defeat, or destroy **2** : a means of contending against another — **weap·on·less** \-ləs\ *adj*

weap·on·ry \-rē\ *n* : WEAPONS

¹wear \'wear\ *vb* **wore** \'wōr\; **worn** \'wȯrn\; **wear·ing** **1** : to use as an article of clothing or adornment ⟨~ a coat⟩ ⟨~s earrings⟩; *also* : to carry on the person ⟨~ a gun⟩ **2** : EXHIBIT, PRESENT ⟨~ a smile⟩ **3** : to impair, diminish, or decay by use or by scraping or rubbing ⟨clothes *worn* to shreds⟩; *also* : to produce gradually by friction, rubbing, or wearing away ⟨~ a hole in the rug⟩ **4** : to exhaust or lessen the strength of : WEARY, FATIGUE ⟨*worn* by care and toil⟩ **5** : to endure use : last under use or the passage of time ⟨this cloth ~s well⟩ **6** : to diminish or fail with the passage of time ⟨the day ~s on⟩ ⟨the effect of the drug *wore* off⟩ **7** : to grow or become by attrition, use, or age ⟨the coin was *worn* thin⟩ — **wear·able** \'wer-ə-bəl\ *adj* — **wear·er** *n*

²wear *n* **1** : the act of wearing : the state of being worn ⟨clothes for everyday ~⟩ **2** : clothing usu. of a particular kind or for a special occasion or use ⟨children's ~⟩ **3** : wearing or lasting quality ⟨the coat still has lots of ~ in it⟩ **4** : the result of wearing or use : impairment due to use ⟨the suit shows ~⟩

wear and tear *n* : the loss, injury, or stress to which something is subjected in the course of use; *esp* : normal depreciation

wear down *vb* : to weary and overcome by persistent resistance or pressure

wea·ri·some \'wir-ē-səm\ *adj* : causing weariness : TIRESOME — **wea·ri·some·ly** *adv* — **wea·ri·some·ness** *n*

wear out *vb* **1** : TIRE **2** : to make or become useless by wear

¹wea·ry \'wir-ē\ *adj* **wea·ri·er; -est** **1** : worn out in strength, energy, or freshness **2** : expressing or characteristic of weariness ⟨a ~ sigh⟩ **3** : having one's patience, tolerance, or pleasure exhausted ⟨~ of war⟩ — **wea·ri·ly** \'wir-ə-lē\ *adv* — **wea·ri·ness** \-ē-nəs\ *n*

²weary *vb* **wea·ried; wea·ry·ing** : to become or make weary : TIRE

¹wea·sel \'wē-zəl\ *n, pl* **weasels** : any of various small slender flesh-eating mammals related to the minks — **wea·sel·ly** *also* **wea·sely** \'wēz-lē, 'wē-zə-lē\ *adj*

²**weasel** *vb* **wea·seled; wea·sel·ing 1 :** to use weasel words **:** EQUIVOCATE **2 :** to escape from or evade a situation or obligation — often used with *out*

weasel word *n* [fr. the weasel's reputed habit of sucking the contents out of an egg while leaving the shell intact] **:** a word used to avoid a direct or forthright statement or position

¹**weath·er** \'we-thər\ *n* **1 :** the state of the atmosphere with respect to heat or cold, wetness or dryness, calm or storm, clearness or cloudiness **2 :** a particular and esp. a disagreeable atmospheric state **:** RAIN, STORM

²**weather** *vb* **1 :** to expose to or endure the action of weather; *also* **:** to alter (as in color or texture) by such exposure **2 :** to bear up against successfully ⟨∼ a storm⟩ ⟨∼ troubles⟩

³**weather** *adj* **:** WINDWARD

weath·er–beat·en \'we-thər-,bē-t°n\ *adj* **:** worn or damaged by exposure to the weather; *also* **:** toughened or tanned by the weather ⟨∼ face⟩

weath·er·cock \-,käk\ *n* **:** a weather vane shaped like a rooster

weath·er·ing \'we-thə-riŋ\ *n* **:** the action of the weather in altering the color, texture, composition, or form of exposed objects; *also* **:** alteration thus effected

weath·er·ize \'we-thə-,rīz\ *vb* **-ized; -iz·ing :** to make (as a house) better protected against winter weather (as by adding insulation)

weath·er·man \-,man\ *n* **:** one who reports and forecasts the weather **:** METEOROLOGIST

weath·er·per·son \-,pər-sən\ *n* **:** a person who reports and forecasts the weather **:** METEOROLOGIST

weath·er·proof \'we-thər-,prüf\ *adj* **:** able to withstand exposure to weather — **weatherproof** *vb*

weath·er·strip·ping \'we-thər-,stri-piŋ\ *n* **:** material used to seal a door or window at the edges — **weath·er·strip** *vb* — **weather strip** *n*

weather vane *n* **:** VANE 1

weath·er·worn \'we-thər-,wȯrn\ *adj* **:** worn by exposure to the weather

¹**weave** \'wēv\ *vb* **wove** \'wōv\ *or* **weaved; wo·ven** \'wō-vən\ *or* **weaved; weav·ing 1 :** to form by interlacing strands of material; *esp* **:** to make on a loom by interlacing warp and filling threads ⟨∼ cloth⟩ **2 :** to interlace (as threads) into a fabric and esp. cloth **3 :** SPIN 2 **4 :** to make as if by weaving together parts **5 :** to insert as a part **:** work in **6 :** to move in a winding or zigzag course esp. to avoid obstacles ⟨we *wove* our way through the crowd⟩ — **weav·er** *n*

²**weave** *n* **:** something woven; *also* **:** a pattern or method of weaving ⟨a loose ∼⟩

¹**web** \'web\ *n* **1 :** a fabric on a loom or coming from a loom **2 :** COBWEB; *also* **:** SNARE, ENTANGLEMENT ⟨caught in a ∼ of deceit⟩ **3 :** an animal or plant membrane; *esp* **:** one uniting the toes (as in many birds) **4 :** NETWORK ⟨a ∼ of highways⟩ **5 :** the series of barbs on each side of the shaft of a feather **6 :** WORLD WIDE WEB — **webbed** \'webd\ *adj*

²**web** *vb* **webbed; web·bing 1 :** to make a web **2 :** to cover or provide with webs or a network **3 :** ENTANGLE, ENSNARE

web·bing \'we-biŋ\ *n* **:** a strong closely woven tape designed for bearing weight and used esp. for straps, harness, or upholstery

web·cam \'web-,kam\ *n* **:** a camera used in transmitting live images over the World Wide Web

web·cast \'web-,kast\ *n* **:** a transmission of sound and images via the World Wide Web — **webcast** *vb*

web–foot·ed \'web-'fu̇-təd\ *adj* **:** having webbed feet

web·mas·ter \'web-,mas-tər\ *n, often cap* **:** a person responsible for the creation or maintenance of a Web site

Web site *n* **:** a group of World Wide Web pages made available online (as by an individual or business)

wed \'wed\ *vb* **wed·ded** *also* **wed; wed·ding 1 :** to take, give, enter into, or join in marriage **:** MARRY **2 :** to unite firmly

Wed *abbr* Wednesday

wed·ding \'we-diŋ\ *n* **1 :** a marriage ceremony usu. with accompanying festivities **:** NUPTIALS **2 :** a joining in

---

close association **3 :** a wedding anniversary or its celebration

¹**wedge** \'wej\ *n* **1 :** a piece of wood or metal that tapers to a thin edge and is used to split logs or rocks or to raise heavy weights **2 :** something (as an action or policy) that serves to open up a way for a breach, change, or intrusion **3 :** a wedge-shaped object or part ⟨a ∼ of pie⟩

²**wedge** *vb* **wedged; wedg·ing 1 :** to hold firm by or as if by driving in a wedge **2 :** to force (something) into a narrow space

wed·lock \'wed-,läk\ *n* [ME *wedlok,* fr. OE *wedlāc* marriage bond, fr. *wedd* pledge + *-lāc,* suffix denoting activity] **:** the state of being married **:** MARRIAGE, MATRIMONY

Wednes·day \'wenz-(,)dā-dē\ *n* [ME, fr. OE *wōdensdæg,* lit., day of Woden (supreme god of the pagan Anglo-Saxons)] **:** the 4th day of the week

wee \'wē\ *adj* [ME (Sc) *wei,* fr. *we,* n., little bit, fr. OE *wǣge* weight] **1 :** very small **:** TINY **2 :** very early ⟨∼ hours of the morning⟩

¹**weed** \'wēd\ *n* **1 :** a plant that tends to grow thickly where it is not wanted and to choke out more desirable plants **2 :** MARIJUANA

²**weed** *vb* **1 :** to clear of or remove weeds or something harmful, inferior, or superfluous ⟨∼ a garden⟩ **2 :** to get rid of ⟨∼ out the troublemakers⟩ — **weed·er** *n*

³**weed** *n* **:** mourning clothes — usu. used in pl. ⟨widow's ∼s⟩

weedy \'wē-dē\ *adj* **1 :** full of weeds **2 :** resembling a weed esp. in vigor of growth or spread **3 :** noticeably lean and scrawny **:** LANKY

week \'wēk\ *n* **1 :** seven successive days; *esp* **:** a calendar period of seven days beginning with Sunday and ending with Saturday **2 :** the working or school days of the calendar week

week·day \'wēk-,dā\ *n* **:** a day of the week except Sunday or sometimes except Saturday and Sunday

¹**week·end** \-,end\ *n* **:** the period between the close of one working or business or school week and the beginning of the next

²**weekend** *vb* **:** to spend the weekend

¹**week·ly** \'wē-klē\ *adj* **1 :** occurring, appearing, or done every week **2 :** computed in terms of one week ⟨∼ rental rates⟩ — **weekly** *adv*

²**weekly** *n, pl* **weeklies :** a weekly publication

ween \'wēn\ *vb, archaic* **:** SUPPOSE 3

wee·ny \'wē-nē\ *also* **ween·sy** \'wēn-sē\ *adj* **:** exceptionally small

weep \'wēp\ *vb* **wept** \'wept\; **weep·ing 1 :** to express emotion and esp. sorrow by shedding tears **:** BEWAIL, CRY **2 :** to give off fluid slowly **:** OOZE — **weep·er** *n*

weeping *adj* **1 :** TEARFUL ⟨∼ gratitude⟩ **2 :** having slender drooping branches

weeping willow *n* **:** a willow with slender drooping branches

weepy \'wē-pē\ *adj* **:** inclined to weep

wee·vil \'wē-vəl\ *n* **:** any of a large group of beetles having a long head usu. curved into a snout and including many whose larvae are destructive plant-feeding pests — **wee·vily** *or* **wee·vil·ly** \'wē-və-lē\ *adj*

weft \'weft\ *n* **1 :** a filling thread or yarn in weaving **2 :** WEB, FABRIC; *also* **:** something woven

¹**weigh** \'wā\ *vb* [ME *weyen,* fr. OE *wegan* to move, carry, weigh] **1 :** to find the heaviness of **2 :** to have weight or a specified weight **3 :** to consider carefully **:** PONDER **4 :** to merit consideration as important **:** COUNT ⟨evidence ∼*ing* against him⟩ **5 :** to raise before sailing ⟨∼ anchor⟩ **6 :** to press down with or as if with a heavy weight

²**weigh** *n* [alter. of *way*] **:** WAY — used in the phrase *under weigh*

¹**weight** \'wāt\ *n* **1 :** the amount that something weighs; *also* **:** the standard amount that something should weigh **2 :** a quantity or object weighing a usu. specified amount **3 :** a unit (as a pound or kilogram) of weight or mass; *also* **:** a system of such units **4 :** a heavy object for holding or pressing something down; *also* **:** a heavy object for throwing or lifting in an athletic contest **5 :** a mental or emotional burden **6 :** IMPORTANCE; *also* **:** INFLUENCE ⟨threw his ∼ around⟩ **7 :** overpowering force **8 :** relative thickness (as of a textile) ⟨summer-*weight* clothes⟩ **♦ Synonyms** SIGNIFICANCE, MOMENT, CONSEQUENCE, IMPORT, AUTHORITY, PRESTIGE, CREDIT ☞ the U.S. WEIGHTS AND MEASURES table is on page 566

U.S. WEIGHTS AND MEASURES

LENGTH

UNIT (SYMBOL)	U.S. EQUIVALENT	METRIC EQUIVALENT
mile (mi)	5280 feet, 1760 yards	1.609 kilometers
rod (rd)	5.50 yards, 16.5 feet	5.029 meters
yard (yd)	3 feet, 36 inches	0.9144 meter
foot (ft *or* ')	12 inches	30.48 centimeters
inch (in *or* ")	0.083 foot, 0.028 yard	2.54 centimeters

AREA

UNIT (SYMBOL)	U.S. EQUIVALENT	METRIC EQUIVALENT
square mile (sq mi *or* mi²)	640 acres	2.590 square kilometers
acre (ac)	4840 square yards, 43,560 square feet	4047 square meters,
square rod (sq rd *or* rd²)	30.25 square yards	25.293 square meters
square yard (sq yd *or* yd²)	9 square feet	0.836 square meter
square foot (sq ft *or* ft²)	144 square inches	0.093 square meter
square inch (sq in *or* in²)	0.0069 square foot	6.452 square centimeter

VOLUME

UNIT (SYMBOL)	U.S. EQUIVALENT	METRIC EQUIVALENT
cubic yard (cu yd *or* yd³)	27 cubic feet	0.765 cubic meter
cubic foot (cu ft *or* ft³)	1728 cubic inches	0.028 cubic meter
cubic inch (cu in *or* in³)	0.00058 cubic foot	16.387 cubic centimeter

WEIGHT——AVOIRDUPOIS

UNIT (SYMBOL)	U.S. EQUIVALENT	METRIC EQUIVALENT
ton		
short ton	2000 pounds	0.907 metric ton
long ton	2240 pounds	1.016 metric tons
hundredweight (cwt)		
short hundredweight	100 pounds	45.359 kilograms
long hundredweight	112 pounds	50.802 kilograms
pound (lb *also* #)	16 ounces	0.454 kilogram
ounce (oz)	16 drams, 437.5 grains	28.350 grams
dram (dr)	27.344 grains	1.772 grams
grain (gr)	0.037 dram	0.0648 gram

CAPACITY

UNIT (SYMBOL)	U.S. EQUIVALENT	METRIC EQUIVALENT
	LIQUID MEASURE	
gallon (gal)	4 quarts	3.785 liters
quart (qt)	2 pints	0.946 liter
pint (pt)	4 gills	473.176 milliliters
gill (gi)	4 fluid ounces	118.294 milliliters
fluid ounce (fl oz *or* f℥)	8 fluid drams	29.573 milliliters
fluid dram (fl dr *or* f℈)	60 minims	3.697 milliliters
minim (min *or* ♏)	⅟₆₀ fluid dram	0.061610 milliliter
	DRY MEASURE	
bushel (bu)	4 pecks	35.239 liters
peck (pk)	8 quarts	8.810 liters
quart (qt)	2 pints	1.101 liters
pint (pt)	½ quart	0.551 liter

²**weight** *vb* **1** : to oppress with a burden ⟨~ed down with cares⟩ **2** : to load with or as if with a weight

weight·less \'wāt-ləs\ *adj* : having little weight : lacking apparent gravitational pull — **weight·less·ly** *adv* — **weight·less·ness** *n*

weighty \'wā-tē\ *adj* **weight·i·er; -est 1** : of much importance or consequence : MOMENTOUS, SERIOUS ⟨~ problems⟩ **2** : SOLEMN ⟨a ~ manner⟩ **3** : HEAVY **4** : POWERFUL, TELLING ⟨~ arguments⟩

weiner *var of* WIENER

weir \'wer, 'wir\ *n* **1** : a fence set in a waterway for catching fish **2** : a dam in a stream to raise the water level or divert its flow

weird \'wird\ *adj* [ME *wird, werd* fate, destiny, fr. OE *wyrd*] **1** : MAGICAL **2** : ODD, UNUSUAL ♦ **Synonyms** EERIE, UNCANNY, SPOOKY — **weird·ly** *adv* — **weird·ness** *n*

weirdo \'wir-(ˌ)dō\ *n, pl* **weird·os** : a person who is extraordinarily strange or eccentric

Welch *var of* WELSH

¹**wel·come** \'wel-kəm\ *vb* **wel·comed; wel·com·ing 1** : to greet cordially or courteously **2** : to accept, meet, or face with pleasure ⟨he ~s criticism⟩

²**welcome** *adj* **1** : received gladly into one's presence ⟨a ~ visitor⟩ **2** : giving pleasure : PLEASING ⟨~ news⟩ **3** : willingly permitted or admitted ⟨all are ~ to use the books⟩ **4** — used in the phrase "You're welcome" as a reply to an expression of thanks

³**welcome** *n* **1** : a cordial greeting or reception **2** : the state of being welcome ⟨overstayed their ~⟩

¹**weld** \'weld\ *vb* **1** : to unite (metal or plastic parts) either by heating and allowing the parts to flow together or by hammering or pressing together **2** : to unite closely or intimately ⟨~ed together in friendship⟩ — **weld·er** *n*

²**weld** *n* **1** : a welded joint **2** : union by welding

wel·fare \'wel-ˌfer\ *n* **1** : the state of doing well esp. in respect to happiness, well-being, or prosperity **2** : aid in the form of money or necessities for those in need; *also* : the agency through which the aid is given

welfare state *n* : a nation or state that assumes primary responsibility for the individual and social welfare of its citizens

wel·kin \'wel-kən\ *n* : SKY; *also* : AIR

¹**well** \'wel\ *n* **1** : a spring with its pool : FOUNTAIN; *also* : a source of supply ⟨a ~ of information⟩ **2** : a hole sunk in the earth to obtain a natural deposit (as of water, oil, or gas) **3** : an open space (as for a staircase) extending vertically through floors of a structure **4** : something suggesting a well

²**well** *vb* : to rise up and flow out

³**well** *adv* **bet·ter** \'be-tər\; **best** \'best\ **1** : in a good or proper manner : RIGHTLY; *also* : EXCELLENTLY, SKILLFULLY **2** : SATISFACTORILY, FORTUNATELY ⟨the party turned out ~⟩ **3** : ABUNDANTLY ⟨eat ~⟩ **4** : with reason or courtesy : PROPERLY ⟨I cannot ~ refuse⟩ **5** : COMPLETELY, FULLY, QUITE ⟨~ worth the price⟩ ⟨*well*-hidden⟩ **6** : INTIMATELY, CLOSELY ⟨I know him ~⟩ **7** : CONSIDERABLY, FAR ⟨~ over a million⟩ **8** : without trouble or difficulty ⟨we could ~ have gone⟩ **9** : EXACTLY, DEFINITELY ⟨remember it ~⟩

⁴**well** *adj* **1** : PROSPEROUS; *also* : being in satisfactory condition or circumstances **2** : SATISFACTORY, PLEASING ⟨all is ~⟩ **3** : ADVISABLE, DESIRABLE ⟨it is not ~ to anger him⟩ **4** : free or recovered from ill health : HEALTHY **5** : FORTUNATE ⟨it is ~ that this has happened⟩

well–ad·just·ed \ˌwel-ə-'jəs-təd\ *adj* : WELL-BALANCED 2

well–ad·vised \-əd-'vīzd\ *adj* **1** : PRUDENT ⟨~ restraint⟩ **2** : resulting from, based on, or showing careful deliberation or wise counsel ⟨~ plans⟩

well–ap·point·ed \-ə-'pȯin-təd\ *adj* : properly fitted out ⟨a ~ house⟩

well–bal·anced \'wel-'ba-lənst\ *adj* **1** : nicely or evenly balanced or arranged **2** : emotionally or psychologically untroubled

well–be·ing \-'bē-iŋ\ *n* : the state of being happy, healthy, or prosperous

well–born \-'bȯrn\ *adj* : born of noble or wealthy lineage

well–bred \-'bred\ *adj* : having or indicating good breeding : REFINED

well–de·fined \-di-'fīnd\ *adj* : having clearly distinguishable limits or boundaries

well–dis·posed \-di-'spōzd\ *adj* : disposed to be friendly, favorable, or sympathetic

well–done \'wel-'dən\ *adj* **1** : rightly or properly performed **2** : cooked thoroughly

well–en·dowed \'wel-in-'daůd\ *adj* **1** : having plenty of money or property **2** : having large breasts

well–fa·vored \-'fā-vərd\ *adj* : GOOD-LOOKING, HANDSOME ⟨a ~ face⟩

well–fixed \-'fikst\ *adj* : WELL-HEELED

well–found·ed \-'faůn-dəd\ *adj* : based on good reasons

well–groomed \-'grümd, -'grůmd\ *adj* : neatly dressed or cared for

well–ground·ed \-'graůn-dəd\ *adj* **1** : having a firm foundation **2** : WELL-FOUNDED

well–head \-ˌhed\ *n* **1** : the source of a spring or a stream **2** : principal source **3** : the top of or a structure built over a well

well–heeled \-'hēld\ *adj* : financially well-off

well–known \-'nōn\ *adj* : fully or widely known

well–mean·ing \-'mē-niŋ\ *adj* : having or based on good intentions

well·ness \-nəs\ *n* : good health esp. as an actively sought goal ⟨~ clinics⟩ ⟨lifestyles that promote ~⟩

well–nigh \-'nī\ *adv* : ALMOST, NEARLY ⟨~ impossible⟩

well–off \-'ȯf\ *adj* : being in good condition or circumstances; *esp* : WELL-TO-DO

well–or·dered \-'ȯr-dərd\ *adj* : having an orderly procedure or arrangement

well–placed \-'plāst\ *adj* : appropriately or advantageously directed or positioned

well–read \-'red\ *adj* : well informed through reading

well–round·ed \-'raůn-dəd\ *adj* **1** : broadly trained, educated, and experienced **2** : COMPREHENSIVE ⟨a ~ program of activities⟩

well–spo·ken \'wel-'spō-kən\ *adj* **1** : speaking well and esp. courteously **2** : spoken with propriety ⟨~ words⟩

well·spring \-ˌspriŋ\ *n* : a source of continuous supply

well–timed \-'tīmd\ *adj* : TIMELY ⟨a ~ announcement⟩

well–to–do \ˌwel-tə-'dü\ *adj* : having more than adequate financial resources : PROSPEROUS

well–turned \'wel-'tərnd\ *adj* **1** : pleasingly shaped ⟨a ~ ankle⟩ **2** : pleasingly expressed ⟨a ~ phrase⟩

well–wish·er \'wel-ˌwi-shər\ *n* : an admiring supporter or fan — **well–wish·ing** *adj or n*

welsh \'welsh, 'welch\ *vb* **1** : to avoid payment **2** : to break one's word ⟨~ed on his promises⟩

Welsh \'welsh\ *also* **Welch** \'welch\ *n* [ME *walisch, welisch,* adj., Welsh, fr. OE *wælisc* foreign, British, Welsh, fr. *Wealh* foreigner, Briton, Welshman] **1 Welsh** *pl* : the people of Wales **2** : the Celtic language of Wales — **Welsh** *adj* — **Welsh·man** \-mən\ *n*

Welsh cor·gi \-'kȯr-gē\ *n* [W *corgi,* fr. *cor* dwarf + *ci* dog] : a short-legged long-backed dog with foxy head of either of two breeds of Welsh origin

Welsh rabbit *n* : melted often seasoned cheese served over toast or crackers

Welsh rare·bit \-'rer-bət\ *n* : WELSH RABBIT

¹**welt** \'welt\ *n* **1** : the narrow strip of leather between a shoe upper and sole to which other parts are stitched **2** : a doubled edge, strip, insert, or seam for ornament or reinforcement **3** : a ridge or lump raised on the skin usu. by a blow; *also* : a heavy blow

²**welt** *vb* **1** : to furnish with a welt **2** : to hit hard

¹**wel·ter** \'wel-tər\ *vb* **1** : WRITHE, TOSS; *also* : WALLOW **2** : to rise and fall or toss about in or with waves **3** : to become deeply sunk, soaked, or involved **4** : to be in turmoil

²**welter** *n* **1** : TURMOIL **2** : a chaotic mass or jumble

wel·ter·weight \'wel-tər-ˌwāt\ *n* : a boxer weighing more than 135 but not over 147 pounds

wen \'wen\ *n* : an abnormal growth or a cyst protruding from a surface esp. of the skin

wench \'wench\ *n* [ME *wenche,* short for *wenchel* child, fr. OE *wencel*] **1** : a young woman **2** : a female servant

wend \'wend\ *vb* : to direct one's course : proceed on (one's way)

went *past of* GO

wept *past and past part of* WEEP

were *past 2d sing, past pl, or past subjunctive of* BE

were·wolf \'wer-ˌwůlf, 'wir-, 'wər-\ *n, pl* **were·wolves** \-ˌwůlvz\ [ME, fr. OE *werwulf,* fr. *wer* man + *wulf* wolf] : a person transformed into a wolf or capable of assuming a wolf's form

wes·kit \'wes-kət\ *n* : VEST 1

¹**west** \'west\ *adv* : to or toward the west

²**west** *adj* **1** : situated toward or at the west **2** : coming from the west

³**west** *n* **1** : the general direction of sunset **2** : the compass point directly opposite to east **3** *cap* : regions or countries west of a specified or implied point **4** *cap* : Europe and the Americas — **west·er·ly** \'wes-tər-lē\ *adv or adj* — **west·ward** *adv or adj* — **west·wards** *adv*

¹**west·ern** \'wes-tərn\ *adj* **1** : lying toward or coming from the west **2** *cap* : of, relating to, or characteristic of a region conventionally designated West **3** *cap* : of or relating to the Roman Catholic or Protestant segment of Christianity — **West·ern·er** *n*

²**western** *n, often cap* : a novel, story, film, or radio or television show about life in the western U.S. during the latter half of the 19th century

west·ern·ize \'wes-tər-ˌnīz\ *vb* **-ized; -iz·ing** : to give western characteristics to — **west·ern·i·za·tion** \ˌwes-tər-nə-ˈzā-shən\ *n*

West Nile virus \-ˈnī(-ə)l-\ *n* [*West Nile* province of Uganda] : a virus that is transmitted to humans by mosquitoes and causes an illness marked by fever, headache, muscle ache, and sometimes encephalitis or meningitis; *also* : this illness

¹**wet** \'wet\ *adj* **wet·ter; wet·test 1** : consisting of or covered or soaked with liquid (as water) **2** : RAINY ⟨~ days⟩ **3** : not dry ⟨~ paint⟩ **4** : permitting or advocating the manufacture and sale of alcoholic beverages ⟨a ~ town⟩ ⟨a ~ candidate⟩ ♦ *Synonyms* DAMP, DANK, MOIST, HUMID — **wet·ly** *adv* — **wet·ness** *n*

²**wet** *n* **1** : WATER; *also* : WETNESS, MOISTURE **2** : rainy weather : RAIN **3** : an advocate of a wet liquor policy

³**wet** *vb* **wet** *or* **wet·ted; wet·ting** : to make or become wet

wet blanket *n* : one that quenches or dampens enthusiasm or pleasure

weth·er \'we-thər\ *n* : a castrated male sheep or goat

wet·land \'wet-ˌland, -lənd\ *n* : land or areas (as swamps) containing much soil moisture — usu. used in pl.

wet nurse *n* : a woman who cares for and suckles children not her own

wet suit *n* : a rubber suit for swimmers that acts to retain body heat by keeping a layer of water against the body as insulation

wh *abbr* **1** which **2** white

¹**whack** \'hwak\ *vb* **1** : to strike with a smart or resounding blow **2** : to cut with or as if with a whack

²**whack** *n* **1** : a smart or resounding blow; *also* : the sound of such a blow **2** : PORTION, SHARE ⟨must each pay our ~⟩ **3** : CONDITION, STATE ⟨the machine is out of ~⟩ **4** : an opportunity or attempt to do something : CHANCE **5** : a single action or occasion ⟨made three pies at a ~⟩

¹**whale** \'hwāl\ *n, pl* **whales 1** *or pl* **whale** : CETACEAN; *esp* : one (as a sperm whale or killer whale) of large size **2** : a person or thing impressive in size or quality ⟨a ~ of a story⟩

²**whale** *vb* **whaled; whal·ing** : to fish or hunt for whales

³**whale** *vb* **whaled; whal·ing 1** : THRASH **2** : to strike or hit vigorously

whale·boat \-ˌbōt\ *n* : a long narrow rowboat originally used by whalers

whale·bone \-ˌbōn\ *n* : BALEEN

whal·er \'hwā-lər\ *n* **1** : a person or ship that hunts whales **2** : WHALEBOAT

whale shark *n* : a shark of warm waters that is the largest known fish

wham·my \'hwa-mē\ *n, pl* **wham·mies** : JINX, HEX

wharf \'hwȯrf\ *n, pl* **wharves** \'hwȯrvz\ *also* **wharfs** : a structure alongside which ships lie to load and unload

¹**what** \'hwät, 'hwȯt\ *pron* **1** — used to inquire about the identity or nature of a being, an object, or some matter or situation ⟨~ is he, a salesman⟩ ⟨~'s that⟩ ⟨~ happened⟩ **2** : that which ⟨I know ~ you want⟩ **3** : WHATEVER 1 ⟨take ~ you want⟩

²**what** *adv* **1** : in what respect : HOW ⟨~ does he care⟩ **2** — used with *with* to introduce a prepositional phrase that expresses cause ⟨kept busy ~ with school and work⟩

³**what** *adj* **1** — used to inquire about the identity or nature of a person, object, or matter ⟨~ books do you read⟩ **2** : how remarkable or surprising ⟨~ an idea⟩ **3** : WHATEVER

¹**what·ev·er** \hwät-ˈe-vər, hwət-\ *pron* **1** : anything or everything that ⟨does ~ he wants to⟩ **2** : no matter what ⟨~ you do, don't cheat⟩ **3** : WHAT 1 — used as an intensive ⟨~ do you mean⟩

²**whatever** *adj* : of any kind at all ⟨no food ~⟩

³**whatever** *adv* : in any case : whatever the case may be — often used to suggest the unimportance of an issue or choice ⟨see a movie, watch TV,—~⟩

¹**what·not** \'hwät-ˌnät, 'hwət-\ *pron* : any of various other things that might also be mentioned ⟨needles, pins, and ~⟩

²**whatnot** *n* : a light open set of shelves for small ornaments

what·so·ev·er \ˌhwät-sō-ˈe-vər, ˌhwət-\ *pron or adj* : WHATEVER

wheal \'hwēl\ *n* : a rapidly formed flat slightly raised itching or burning patch on the skin; *also* : WELT

wheat \'hwēt\ *n* : a cereal grain that yields a fine white flour used chiefly in breads, baked goods, and pastas; *also* : any of several widely grown grasses yielding wheat — **wheat·en** *adj*

wheat germ *n* : the vitamin-rich wheat embryo separated in milling

whee·dle \'hwē-dᵊl\ *vb* **whee·dled; whee·dling 1** : to entice by flattery **2** : to gain or get by wheedling

¹**wheel** \'hwēl\ *n* **1** : a disk or circular frame that turns on a central axis **2** : a device whose main part is a wheel **3** : something resembling a wheel in shape or motion **4** : a curving or circular movement **5** : machinery that imparts motion : moving power ⟨the ~s of government⟩ **6** : a person of importance **7** *pl, slang* : AUTOMOBILE — **wheeled** \'hwēld\ *adj* — **wheel·less** *adj*

²**wheel** *vb* **1** : ROTATE, REVOLVE **2** : to change direction as if turning on a pivot **3** : to convey or move on wheels or in a vehicle

wheel·bar·row \-ˌber-ō\ *n* : a vehicle with handles and usu. one wheel for carrying small loads

wheel·base \-ˌbās\ *n* : the distance in inches between the front and rear axles of an automotive vehicle

wheel·chair \-ˌcher\ *n* : a chair mounted on wheels esp. for the use of disabled persons

wheel·er \'hwē-lər\ *n* **1** : one that wheels **2** : WHEELHORSE **3** : something that has wheels — used in combination ⟨a side-*wheeler*⟩

wheel·er–deal·er \ˌhwē-lər-ˈdē-lər\ *n* : a shrewd operator esp. in business or politics

wheel·horse \'hwēl-ˌhȯrs\ *n* **1** : a horse in a position nearest the front wheels of a wagon **2** : a steady and effective worker esp. in a political body

wheel·house \-ˌhaus\ *n* : PILOTHOUSE

wheel–thrown \'hwēl-ˌthrōn\ *adj* : made on a potter's wheel

wheel·wright \-ˌrīt\ *n* : a maker and repairer of wheels and wheeled vehicles

¹**wheeze** \'hwēz\ *vb* **wheezed; wheez·ing** : to breathe with difficulty usu. with a whistling sound

²**wheeze** *n* **1** : a sound of wheezing **2** : an often repeated and well-known joke **3** : a trite saying

wheezy \'hwē-zē\ *adj* **wheez·i·er; -est 1** : inclined to wheeze **2** : having a wheezing sound — **wheez·i·ly** \-zə-lē\ *adv* — **wheez·i·ness** \-zē-nəs\ *n*

whelk \'hwelk\ *n* : a large sea snail; *esp* : one much used as food in Europe

whelk

whelm \'hwelm\ *vb* : to overcome or engulf completely : OVERWHELM

¹whelp \\'hwelp\ *n* : any of the young of various carnivorous mammals (as a dog)
²whelp *vb* : to give birth to (whelps); *also* : bring forth young
¹when \\'hwen\ *adv* **1** : at what time ⟨~ will you return⟩ **2** : at or during which time ⟨a time ~ things were better⟩
²when *conj* **1** : at or during the time that ⟨leave ~ I do⟩ **2** : every time that ⟨they all clapped ~ he sang⟩ **3** : in the event that : IF ⟨disqualified ~ you cheat⟩ **4** : ALTHOUGH ⟨quit politics ~ he might have had a great career in it⟩
³when *pron* : what or which time ⟨since ~ have you been the boss⟩
⁴when *n* : the time of a happening
whence \\'hwens\ *adv or conj* : from what place, source, or cause
when·ev·er \hwe-'ne-vər, hwə-\ *conj or adv* : at whatever time
when·so·ev·er \\'hwen-sō-₁e-vər\ *conj* : at any or every time that
¹where \\'hwer\ *adv* **1** : at, in, or to what place ⟨~ is it⟩ ⟨~ will we go⟩ **2** : at, in, or to what situation, position, direction, circumstances, or respect ⟨~ does this road lead⟩
²where *conj* **1** : at, in, or to what place ⟨knows ~ the house is⟩ **2** : at, in, or to what situation, position, direction, circumstances, or respect ⟨shows ~ the road leads⟩ **3** : WHEREVER ⟨goes ~ she likes⟩ **4** : at, in, or to which place ⟨the town ~ we live⟩ **5** : at, in, or to the place at, in, or to which ⟨stay ~ you are⟩ **6** : in a case, situation, or respect in which ⟨outstanding ~ endurance is called for⟩
³where *n* : PLACE, LOCATION ⟨the ~ and how of the accident⟩
¹where·abouts \-ə-₁baùts\ *also* **where·about** \-₁baút\ *adv* : about where : near what place ⟨~ does he live⟩
²whereabouts *n sing or pl* : the place where a person or thing is ⟨his present ~ are unknown⟩
where·as \hwer-'az\ *conj* **1** : while on the contrary; *also* : ALTHOUGH **2** : in view of the fact that : SINCE
where·at \-'at\ *conj* **1** : at or toward which **2** : in consequence of which : WHEREUPON
where·by \-'bī\ *conj* : by, through, or in accordance with which ⟨the means ~ we achieved our goals⟩
¹where·fore \\'hwer-₁fòr\ *adv* **1** : for what reason or purpose : WHY **2** : THEREFORE
²wherefore *n* : an answer or statement giving an explanation : REASON
¹where·in \hwer-'in\ *adv* : in what : in what respect ⟨~ was I wrong⟩
²wherein *conj* **1** : in which : WHERE ⟨the city ~ we live⟩ **2** : during which **3** : in what way : HOW ⟨showed me ~ I was wrong⟩
where·of \-'əv, -'äv\ *conj* **1** : of what ⟨knows ~ he speaks⟩ **2** : of which or whom ⟨books ~ the best are lost⟩
where·on \-'òn, -'än\ *conj* : on which ⟨the base ~ it rests⟩
where·so·ev·er \\'hwer-sō-₁e-vər\ *conj* : WHEREVER
where·to \\'hwer-₁tü\ *conj* : to which
where·up·on \\'hwer-ə-₁pòn, -₁pän\ *conj* **1** : on which **2** : closely following and in consequence of which
¹wher·ev·er \hwer-'e-vər\ *adv* : where in the world ⟨~ did he get that tie⟩
²wherever *conj* **1** : at, in, or to whatever place ⟨thrives ~ he goes⟩ **2** : in any circumstance in which
where·with \\'hwer-₁with, -₁with\ *conj* : with or by means of which ⟨lack the tools ~ to repair the damage⟩
where·with·al \\'hwer-wi-₁thòl, -₁thòl\ *n* : MEANS, RESOURCES; *esp* : MONEY
wher·ry \\'hwer-ē\ *n, pl* **wherries** : a long light rowboat sharp at both ends
whet \\'hwet\ *vb* **whet·ted**; **whet·ting** **1** : to sharpen by rubbing on or with something abrasive (as a whetstone) **2** : to make keen : STIMULATE ⟨~ the appetite⟩
wheth·er \\'hwe-thər\ *conj* **1** : if it is or was true that ⟨ask ~ he is going⟩ **2** : if it is or was better ⟨uncertain ~ to go or stay⟩ **3** : whichever is or was the case, namely that ⟨~ we succeed or fail, we must try⟩ **4** : EITHER ⟨turned out well ~ by accident or design⟩
whet·stone \\'hwet-₁stōn\ *n* : a stone for sharpening blades
whey \\'hwā\ *n* : the watery part of milk that separates after the milk sours and thickens

¹which \\'hwich\ *adj* **1** : being what one or ones out of a group ⟨~ shirt should I wear⟩ **2** : WHICHEVER
²which *pron* **1** : which one or ones ⟨~ is yours⟩ ⟨~ are his⟩ ⟨it's in May or June, I'm not sure ~⟩ **2** : WHICHEVER ⟨we have all kinds; take ~ you like⟩ **3** — used to introduce a relative clause and to serve as a substitute therein for the noun modified by the clause ⟨the money ~ is coming to me⟩
¹which·ev·er \hwich-'e-vər\ *adj* : no matter which ⟨~ way you go⟩
²whichever *pron* : whatever one or ones
which·so·ev·er \₁hwich-sō-'e-vər\ *pron or adj, archaic* : WHICHEVER
whick·er \\'hwi-kər\ *vb* : NEIGH, WHINNY — **whicker** *n*
¹whiff \\'hwif\ *n* **1** : a quick puff or slight gust (as of air) **2** : an inhalation of odor, gas, or smoke **3** : a slight trace ⟨a ~ of scandal⟩ **4** : STRIKEOUT
²whiff *vb* **1** : to expel, puff out, or blow away in or as if in whiffs **2** : to inhale an odor **3** : STRIKE OUT 3
Whig \\'hwig\ *n* [short for *Whiggamore*, member of a Scottish group that marched to Edinburgh in 1648 to oppose the court party] **1** : a member or supporter of a British political group of the late 17th through early 19th centuries seeking to limit royal authority and increase parliamentary power **2** : an American favoring independence from Great Britain during the American Revolution **3** : a member or supporter of an American political party formed about 1834 to oppose the Democrats
¹while \\'hwī(-ə)l\ *n* **1** : a period of time ⟨stay a ~⟩ **2** : the time and effort used : TROUBLE ⟨worth your ~⟩
²while *conj* **1** : during the time that ⟨she called ~ you were out⟩ **2** : AS LONG AS ⟨~ there's life there's hope⟩ **3** : ALTHOUGH ⟨~ he's respected, he's not liked⟩
³while *vb* **whiled**; **whil·ing** : to cause to pass esp. pleasantly ⟨~ away an hour⟩
¹whi·lom \\'hwī-ləm\ *adv* [ME, lit., at times, fr. OE *hwīlum*, dat. pl. of *hwīl* time, while] *archaic* : FORMERLY
²whilom *adj* : FORMER ⟨his ~ friends⟩
whilst \\'hwīlst\ *conj, chiefly Brit* : WHILE
whim \\'hwim\ *n* : a sudden wish, desire, or change of mind
whim·per \\'hwim-pər\ *vb* : to make a low whining plaintive or broken sound — **whimper** *n*
whim·si·cal \\'hwim-zi-kəl\ *adj* **1** : full of whims : CAPRICIOUS **2** : resulting from or characterized by whim or caprice : ERRATIC — **whim·si·cal·i·ty** \₁hwim-zə-'ka-lə-tē\ *n* — **whim·si·cal·ly** \\'hwim-zi-k(ə-)lē\ *adv*
whim·sy *also* **whim·sey** \\'hwim-zē\ *n, pl* **whimsies** *also* **whimseys** **1** : WHIM, CAPRICE **2** : a fanciful or fantastic device, object, or creation esp. in writing or art
whine \\'hwīn\ *vb* **whined**; **whin·ing** [ME, fr. OE *hwīnan* to whiz] **1** : to utter a usu. high-pitched plaintive or distressed cry; *also* : to make a sound similar to such a cry **2** : to complain with or as if with a whine — **whine** *n* — **whin·er** *n* — **whiny** *also* **whin·ey** \\'hwī-nē\ *adj*
¹whin·ny \\'hwi-nē\ *vb* **whin·nied**; **whin·ny·ing** : to neigh usu. in a low or gentle manner
²whinny *n, pl* **whinnies** : NEIGH
¹whip \\'hwip\ *vb* **whipped**; **whip·ping** **1** : to move, snatch, or jerk quickly or forcefully ⟨~ out a gun⟩ **2** : to strike with a slender lithe implement (as a lash) esp. as a punishment; *also* : SPANK **3** : to drive or urge on by or as if by using a whip **4** : to bind or wrap (as a rope or rod) with cord in order to protect and strengthen; *also* : to wind or wrap around something **5** : DEFEAT **6** : to stir up : INCITE ⟨~ up enthusiasm⟩ **7** : to produce in a hurry ⟨~ up a meal⟩ **8** : to beat (as eggs or cream) into a froth **9** : to proceed nimbly or briskly; *also* : to flap about forcefully ⟨flags *whipping* in the wind⟩ — **whip·per** *n* — **whip into shape** : to bring forcefully to a desired state or condition
²whip *n* **1** : a flexible instrument used for whipping **2** : a stroke or cut with or as if with a whip **3** : a dessert made by whipping a portion of the ingredients ⟨prune ~⟩ **4** : a person who handles a whip **5** : a member of a legislative body appointed by a party to enforce party discipline **6** : a whipping or thrashing motion
whip·cord \-₁kòrd\ *n* **1** : a thin tough braided cord **2** : a strong cloth with fine diagonal cords or ribs
whip hand *n* : positive control : ADVANTAGE
whip·lash \\'hwip-₁lash\ *n* **1** : the lash of a whip **2** : injury resulting from a sudden sharp movement of the neck and

head (as of a person in a vehicle that is struck from the rear)

whip·per·snap·per \'hwi-pər-ˌsna-pər\ *n* : a small, insignificant, or presumptuous person

whip·pet \'hwi-pət\ *n* : any of a breed of small swift slender dogs that are used for racing

whipping boy *n* : SCAPEGOAT

whip-poor-will \'hwi-pər-ˌwil\ *n* : an American insect-eating bird with dull variegated plumage whose call at nightfall and just before dawn is suggestive of its name

whip·saw \'hwip-ˌsȯ\ *vb* : to beset with two or more adverse conditions or situations at once

¹**whir** *also* **whirr** \'hwər\ *vb* **whirred; whir·ring** : to move, fly, or revolve with a whir

²**whir** *also* **whirr** *n* : a continuous fluttering or vibratory sound made by something in rapid motion

¹**whirl** \'hwərl\ *vb* **1** : to move or drive in a circle or curve esp. with force or speed **2** : to turn or cause to turn rapidly in circles **3** : to turn abruptly : WHEEL **4** : to move or go quickly **5** : to become dizzy or giddy : REEL

²**whirl** *n* **1** : a rapid rotating or circling movement; *also* : something whirling **2** : COMMOTION, BUSTLE ⟨the social ∼⟩ **3** : a state of mental confusion **4** : TRY ⟨gave it a ∼⟩

whirl·i·gig \'hwər-li-ˌgig\ *n* [ME *whirlegigg*, fr. *whirlen* to whirl + *gigg* top] **1** : a child's toy having a whirling motion **2** : something that continuously whirls or changes

whirl·pool \'hwərl-ˌpül\ *n* : water moving rapidly in a circle so as to produce a depression in the center into which floating objects may be drawn

whirl·wind \-ˌwind\ *n* **1** : a small whirling windstorm **2** : a confused rush **3** : a violent or destructive force

whirly·bird \'hwər-lē-ˌbərd\ *n* : HELICOPTER

¹**whish** \'hwish\ *vb* : to move with a whish or swishing sound

²**whish** *n* : a rushing sound : SWISH

¹**whisk** \'hwisk\ *n* **1** : a quick light sweeping or brushing motion **2** : a usu. wire kitchen implement for beating food by hand **3** : WHISK BROOM

²**whisk** *vb* **1** : to move nimbly and quickly **2** : to move or convey briskly ⟨∼ed the children off to bed⟩ **3** : to beat or whip lightly ⟨∼ eggs⟩ **4** : to brush or wipe off lightly ⟨∼ a coat⟩

whisk broom *n* : a small broom with a short handle used esp. as a clothes brush

whis·ker \'hwis-kər\ *n* **1** : one hair of the beard **2** *pl* : the part of the beard that grows on the sides of the face or on the chin **3** : one of the long bristles or hairs growing near the mouth of an animal (as a cat or mouse) — **whis·kered** \-kərd\ *adj*

whis·key *or* **whis·ky** \'hwis-kē\ *n, pl* **whiskeys** *or* **whiskies** [Ir *uisce beatha* & ScGael *uisge beatha*, lit., water of life] : a liquor distilled from fermented wort (as that obtained from rye, corn, or barley mash)

¹**whis·per** \'hwis-pər\ *vb* **1** : to speak very low or under the breath; *also* : to tell or utter by whispering ⟨∼ a secret⟩ **2** : to make a low rustling sound — **whis·per·er** \-pər-ər\ *n*

²**whisper** *n* **1** : something communicated by or as if by whispering : HINT, RUMOR **2** : an act or instance of whispering

whist \'hwist\ *n* : a card game played by four players in two partnerships with a deck of 52 cards

¹**whis·tle** \'hwi-səl\ *n* **1** : a device by which a shrill sound is produced ⟨steam ∼⟩ ⟨tin ∼⟩ **2** : a shrill clear sound made by forcing breath out or air in through the puckered lips **3** : the sound or signal produced by a whistle or as if by whistling **4** : the shrill clear note of an animal (as a bird)

²**whistle** *vb* **whis·tled; whis·tling** **1** : to utter a shrill clear sound by blowing or drawing air through the puckered lips **2** : to utter a shrill note or call resembling a whistle **3** : to make a shrill clear sound esp. by rapid movements ⟨the wind *whistled*⟩ **4** : to blow or sound a whistle **5** : to signal or call by a whistle **6** : to produce, utter, or express by whistling ⟨∼ a tune⟩ — **whis·tler** *n*

whis·tle-blow·er \'hwi-səl-ˌblō-ər\ *n* : INFORMER

whis·tle-stop \-ˌstäp\ *n* : a brief personal appearance by a political candidate orig. on the rear platform of a touring train

whit \'hwit\ *n* [prob. alter. of ME *wiht, wight* creature, thing, fr. OE *wiht*] : the smallest part or particle : BIT

¹**white** \'hwīt\ *adj* **whit·er; whit·est** **1** : free from color **2** : of the color of new snow or milk; *esp* : of the color white **3** : light or pallid in color ⟨lips ∼ with fear⟩ **4** : SILVERY; *also* : made of silver **5** : of, relating to, or being a member of a group or race characterized by light-colored skin **6** : free from spot or blemish : PURE, INNOCENT **7** : BLANK 2 ⟨∼ space in printed matter⟩ **8** : not intended to cause harm ⟨a ∼ lie⟩ **9** : wearing white ⟨∼ friars⟩ **10** : marked by snow ⟨∼ Christmas⟩ **11** : consisting of a wide range of frequencies ⟨∼ light⟩ — **white·ness** \-nəs\ *n* — **whit·ish** \'hwī-tish\ *adj*

²**white** *n* **1** : the color of maximal lightness that characterizes objects which both reflect and transmit light : the opposite of black **2** : a white or light-colored part or thing ⟨the ∼ of an egg⟩; *also, pl* : white garments **3** : the light-colored pieces in a 2-player board game; *also* : the person by whom these are played **4** : one that is or approaches the color white **5** : a person of a light-skinned race

white ant *n* : TERMITE

white blood cell *n* : any of the colorless blood cells (as lymphocytes) that do not contain hemoglobin but do have a nucleus

white-bread \'hwīt-ˈbred\ *adj* : being, typical of, or having qualities (as blandness) associated with the white middle class

white-cap \'hwīt-ˌkap\ *n* : a wave crest breaking into white foam

white chocolate *n* : a whitish confection chiefly of cocoa butter, milk, and sugar

white-col·lar \'hwīt-ˈkä-lər\ *adj* : of, relating to, or constituting the class of salaried workers whose duties do not require the wearing of work clothes or protective clothing

white dwarf *n* : a small very dense whitish star of low luminosity

white elephant *n* **1** : an Indian elephant of a pale color that is sometimes venerated in India, Sri Lanka, Thailand, and Myanmar **2** : something requiring much care and expense and giving little profit or enjoyment

white feather *n* [fr. the superstition that a white feather in the plumage of a gamecock is a mark of a poor fighter] : a mark or symbol of cowardice

white-fish \'hwīt-ˌfish\ *n* : any of various freshwater food fishes related to the salmons and trouts

white flag *n* : a flag of pure white used to signify truce or surrender

white gold *n* : a pale alloy of gold resembling platinum in appearance

white goods *n pl* : white fabrics or articles (as sheets or towels) typically made of cotton or linen

White·hall \'hwīt-ˌhȯl\ *n* : the British government

white hat *n* **1** : an admirable and honorable person **2** : a mark or symbol of goodness

white·head \-ˌhed\ *n* : a small whitish lump in the skin due to retention of secretion in an oil gland duct

white heat *n* : a temperature higher than red heat at which a body becomes brightly incandescent

white-hot *adj* **1** : being at or radiating white heat **2** : FERVID ⟨∼ enthusiasm⟩

White House \-ˌhaus\ *n* **1** : a residence of the president of the U.S. **2** : the executive department of the U.S. government

white lead *n* : a heavy white poisonous carbonate of lead used esp. formerly as a pigment in exterior paints

white matter *n* : whitish nerve tissue esp. of the brain and spinal cord that consists largely of neuron processes enclosed in a fatty material and that typically lies under the cortical gray matter

whit·en \'hwī-tᵊn\ *vb* : to make or become white ♦ **Synonyms** BLANCH, BLEACH — **whit·en·er** *n*

white oak *n* : any of various oaks with acorns that take one year to mature; *also* : its hard durable wood

white pepper *n* : a spice that consists of the berry of a pepper plant ground after removal of its black husk

white pine *n* : a tall-growing pine of eastern No. America with needles in clusters of five; *also* : its wood

white sale *n* : a sale on white goods

white shark *n* : GREAT WHITE SHARK

white slave *n* : a woman or girl held unwillingly for purposes of prostitution — **white slavery** *n*

white·tail \'hwīt-ˌtāl\ *n* : WHITE-TAILED DEER

white-tailed deer *n* : a No. American deer with a rather long tail white on the underside and the males of which have forward-arching antlers

white–tie \-ˈtī\ *adj* : characterized by or requiring formal evening clothes consisting of usu. white tie and tailcoat for men and a formal gown for women

white·wall \ˈhwīt-ˌwȯl\ *n* : an automobile tire having a white band on the sidewall

¹white·wash \-ˌwȯsh, -ˌwäsh\ *vb* **1** : to whiten with whitewash **2** : to clear of a charge of wrongdoing by offering excuses, hiding facts, or conducting a perfunctory investigation **3** : SHUT OUT 2

²whitewash *n* **1** : a liquid mixture (as of lime and water) for whitening a surface **2** : a clearing of wrongdoing by whitewashing

white water *n* : frothy water (as in breakers, rapids, or falls)

white·wood \-ˌwu̇d\ *n* : any of various trees and esp. a tulip tree having light-colored wood; *also* : such wood

¹whith·er \ˈhwi-t͟hər\ *adv* **1** : to what place **2** : to what situation, position, degree, or end ⟨~ will this drive him⟩

²whither *conj* **1** : to the place at, in, or to which; *also* : to which place **2** : to whatever place

whith·er·so·ev·er \ˌhwi-t͟hər-sō-ˈe-vər\ *conj* : to whatever place

¹whit·ing \ˈhwī-tiŋ\ *n, pl* **whiting** *also* **whit·ings** : any of several usu. light or silvery food fishes (as a hake) found mostly near seacoasts

²whiting *n* : calcium carbonate in powdered form used esp. as a pigment and in putty

whit·low \ˈhwit-ˌlō\ *n* : a deep inflammation of a finger or toe with pus formation

Whit·sun·day \ˈhwit-ˈsən-dē, -sən-ˌdā\ *n* [ME *Whitsonday,* fr. OE *hwīta sunnandæg,* lit., white Sunday; prob. fr. the custom of wearing white robes by those newly baptized at this season] : PENTECOST

whit·tle \ˈhwi-tᵊl\ *vb* **whit·tled; whit·tling** **1** : to pare or cut off chips from the surface of (wood) with a knife; *also* : to cut or shape by such paring **2** : to reduce as if by paring down ⟨~ down expenses⟩

¹whiz *or* **whizz** \ˈhwiz\ *vb* **whizzed; whiz·zing** : to hum, whir, or hiss like a speeding object (as an arrow or ball) passing through air

²whiz *or* **whizz** *n, pl* **whiz·zes** : a hissing, buzzing, or whizzing sound

³whiz *n, pl* **whiz·zes** : WIZARD 2

who \ˈhü\ *pron* **1** : what or which person or persons ⟨~ did it⟩ ⟨~ is he⟩ ⟨~ are they⟩ **2** : the person or persons that ⟨knows ~ did it⟩ **3** — used to introduce a relative clause and to serve as a substitute therein for the substantive modified by the clause ⟨the person ~ lives there is rich⟩

WHO *abbr* World Health Organization

whoa \ˈwō, ˈhwō, ˈhō\ *vb imper* **1** — a command to an animal to stand still **2** : cease or slow a course of action or a line of thought

who·dun·it *also* **who·dun·nit** \hü-ˈdə-nət\ *n* : a detective or mystery story

who·ev·er \hü-ˈe-vər\ *pron* : whatever person : no matter who

¹whole \ˈhōl\ *adj* [ME *hool* healthy, unhurt, entire, fr. OE *hāl*] **1** : being in healthy or sound condition : free from defect or damage **2** : having all its proper parts or elements ⟨~ milk⟩ **3** : constituting the total sum of : ENTIRE ⟨owns the ~ island⟩ **4** : each or all of the ⟨the ~ family⟩ **5** : not scattered or divided : CONCENTRATED ⟨gave me his ~ attention⟩ **6** : seemingly complete or total ⟨the ~ idea is to help, not hinder⟩ ♦ *Synonyms* PERFECT, INTACT, SOUND — **whole·ness** *n*

²whole *n* **1** : a complete amount or sum **2** : something whole or entire — **on the whole 1** : in view of all the circumstances or conditions **2** : in general

³whole *adv* : COMPLETELY, WHOLLY, ENTIRELY ⟨a ~ new term⟩

whole food *n* : a food eaten in its natural state with little or no artificial additives

whole·heart·ed \ˈhōl-ˈhär-təd\ *adj* : undivided in purpose, enthusiasm, will, or commitment

whole hog *adv* : to the fullest extent : COMPLETELY ⟨accepted the proposals *whole hog*⟩

whole note *n* : a musical note equal to one measure of four beats

whole number *n* : any of the set of nonnegative integers; *also* : INTEGER

¹whole·sale \ˈhōl-ˌsāl\ *n* : the sale of goods in quantity usu. for resale by a retail merchant

²wholesale *adj* **1** : performed on a large scale without discrimination ⟨~ slaughter⟩ **2** : of, relating to, or engaged in wholesaling — **wholesale** *adv*

³wholesale *vb* **whole·saled; whole·sal·ing** : to sell at wholesale — **whole·sal·er** *n*

whole·some \ˈhōl-səm\ *adj* **1** : promoting mental, spiritual, or bodily health or well-being ⟨a ~ environment⟩ **2** : sound in body, mind, or morals : HEALTHY **3** : PRUDENT ⟨~ respect for the law⟩ — **whole·some·ness** *n*

whole step *n* : a musical interval comprising two half steps (as C–D or F♯–G♯)

whole wheat *adj* : made of ground entire wheat kernels

whol·ly \ˈhōl-lē\ *adv* **1** : COMPLETELY, TOTALLY **2** : SOLELY, EXCLUSIVELY

whom \ˈhüm\ *pron, objective case of* WHO

whom·ev·er \hü-ˈme-vər\ *pron, objective case of* WHOEVER

whom·so·ev·er \ˌhüm-sō-ˈe-vər\ *pron, objective case of* WHOSOEVER

¹whoop \ˈhwu̇p, ˈhwu̇p, ˈhu̇p, ˈhu̇p\ *vb* **1** : to shout or call loudly and vigorously **2** : to make the characteristic whoop of whooping cough **3** : to go or pass with a loud noise **4** : to utter or express with a whoop; *also* : to urge, drive, or cheer with a whoop

²whoop *n* **1** : a whooping sound or utterance : SHOUT, HOOT **2** : a crowing intake of breath after a fit of coughing in whooping cough

¹whoop·ee \ˈhwu̇-(ˌ)pē, ˈhwü-\ *interj* — used to express exuberance

²whoopee *n* **1** : boisterous fun **2** : sexual play — usu. used with *make*

whooping cough *n* : an infectious bacterial disease esp. of children marked by convulsive coughing fits often followed by a shrill gasping intake of breath

whooping crane *n* : a large white nearly extinct No. American crane noted for its loud whooping call

whoop·la \ˈhwu̇p-ˌlä, ˈhwu̇p-\ *n* **1** : HOOPLA **2** : boisterous merrymaking

whop·per \ˈhwä-pər\ *n* **1** : something unusually large or extreme of its kind; *esp* : a monstrous lie

whop·ping \ˈhwä-piŋ\ *adj* : extremely large ⟨a ~ increase⟩

whore \ˈhȯr\ *n* : PROSTITUTE

whorl \ˈhwȯrl, ˈhwərl\ *n* **1** : a group of parts (as leaves or petals) encircling an axis and esp. a plant stem **2** : something that whirls or coils around a center : COIL, SPIRAL **3** : one of the turns of a snail shell

whorled \ˈhwȯrld, ˈhwərld\ *adj* : having or arranged in whorls

¹whose \ˈhüz\ *adj* : of or relating to whom or which esp. as possessor or possessors, agent or agents, or object or objects of an action ⟨asked ~ bag it was⟩

²whose *pron* : whose one or ones ⟨~ is this car⟩ ⟨~ are those books⟩

who·so \ˈhü-ˌsō\ *pron* : WHOEVER

who·so·ev·er \ˌhü-sō-ˈe-vər\ *pron* : WHOEVER

whs *or* **whse** *abbr* warehouse

whsle *abbr* wholesale

¹why \ˈhwī\ *adv* : for what reason, cause, or purpose ⟨~ did you do it?⟩

²why *conj* **1** : the cause, reason, or purpose for which ⟨that is ~ you did it⟩ **2** : for which : on account of which ⟨knows the reason ~ you did it⟩

³why *n, pl* **whys** : REASON, CAUSE ⟨the ~s of racial prejudice⟩

⁴why \ˈwī, ˈhwī\ *interj* — used to express surprise, hesitation, approval, disapproval, or impatience ⟨~, here's what I was looking for⟩

WI *abbr* **1** West Indies **2** Wisconsin

WIA *abbr* wounded in action

Wic·ca \ˈwi-kə\ *n* [prob. fr. OE *wicca* wizard] : a religion that affirms the existence of supernatural power (as magic) and of deities who inhere in nature and that ritually observes seasonal and life cycles

wick \ˈwik\ *n* : a loosely bound bundle of soft fibers that draws up oil, tallow, or wax to be burned in a candle, oil lamp, or stove

wick·ed \ˈwi-kəd\ *adj* **1** : morally bad : EVIL, SINFUL **2**

DICTIONARY

: FIERCE, VICIOUS **3** : ROGUISH ⟨a ∼ glance⟩ **4** : RE-PUGNANT, VILE ⟨a ∼ odor⟩ **5** : HARMFUL, DANGEROUS ⟨a ∼ attack⟩ **6** : impressively excellent ⟨throws a ∼ fastball⟩ — **wick·ed·ly** *adv* — **wick·ed·ness** *n*

wick·er \'wi-kər\ *n* **1** : a small pliant branch (as an osier or a withe) **2** : WICKERWORK — **wicker** *adj*

wick·er·work \-ˌwərk\ *n* : work made of osiers, twigs, or rods : BASKETRY

wick·et \'wi-kət\ *n* **1** : a small gate or door; *esp* : one forming a part of or placed near a larger one **2** : a window-like opening usu. with a grille or grate (as at a ticket office) **3** : a set of three upright rods topped by two crosspieces bowled at in cricket **4** : an arch or hoop in croquet

wick·i·up \'wi-kē-ˌəp\ *n* : a hut used by nomadic Indians of the western and southwestern U.S. with a usu. oval base and a rough frame covered with reed mats, grass, or brushwood

wid *abbr* widow, widower

¹**wide** \'wīd\ *adj* **wider; wid·est** **1** : covering a vast area **2** : measured across or at right angles to the length **3** : not narrow : BROAD; *also* : ROOMY **4** : opened to full width ⟨eyes ∼ with wonder⟩ **5** : not limited : EXTENSIVE ⟨∼ experience⟩ **6** : far from the goal, mark, or truth ⟨was ∼ of the truth⟩ — **wide·ly** *adv*

²**wide** *adv* **wid·er; wid·est** **1** : over a great distance or extent : WIDELY ⟨searched far and ∼⟩ **2** : over a specified distance, area, or extent **3** : so as to leave a wide space between ⟨∼ apart⟩ **4** : so as to clear by a considerable distance ⟨ran ∼ around left end⟩ **5** : COMPLETELY, FULLY ⟨opened her eyes ∼⟩

wide area network *n* : a computer network (as the Internet) over a large area (as a country or the globe) for sharing resources or exchanging data

wide–awake \ˌwīd-ə-'wāk\ *adj* : fully awake; *also* : KNOWING, ALERT

wide–body \'wīd-ˌbä-dē\ *n* : a large jet aircraft having a wide cabin

wide–eyed \'wīd-'īd\ *adj* **1** : having the eyes wide open esp. with wonder or astonishment **2** : NAIVE

wide·mouthed \-'maûthd, -'maûtht\ *adj* **1** : having one's mouth opened wide (as in awe) **2** : having a wide mouth ⟨∼ jars⟩

wid·en \'wī-d³n\ *vb* : to increase in width, scope, or extent

wide·spread \'wīd-'spred\ *adj* **1** : widely scattered or prevalent **2** : widely extended or spread out ⟨∼ wings⟩

widgeon *var of* WIGEON

¹**wid·ow** \'wi-dō\ *n* : a woman who has lost her husband by death and has not married again — **wid·ow·hood** *n*

²**widow** *vb* : to cause to become a widow or widower

wid·ow·er \'wi-də-wər\ *n* : a man who has lost his wife by death and has not married again

width \'width\ *n* **1** : a distance from side to side : the measurement taken at right angles to the length : BREADTH **2** : largeness of extent or scope; *also* : FULLNESS **3** : a measured and cut piece of material ⟨a ∼ of calico⟩

wield \'wēld\ *vb* **1** : to use or handle esp. effectively ⟨∼ a broom⟩ **2** : to exert authority by means of : EMPLOY ⟨∼ influence⟩ — **wield·er** *n*

wie·ner *also* **wei·ner** \'wē-nər\ *n* [short for *wienerwurst*, fr. G, lit., Vienna sausage] : FRANKFURTER

wife \'wīf\ *n, pl* **wives** \'wīvz\ **1** *dial* : WOMAN **2** : a woman acting in a specified capacity — used in combination ⟨fish*wife*⟩ **3** : a female partner in a marriage — **wife·hood** *n* — **wife·less** *adj* — **wife·ly** *adj*

wig \'wig\ *n* [short for *periwig*, modif. of MF *perruque*, fr. It *parrucca, perrucca* hair, wig] : a manufactured covering of natural or synthetic hair for the head; *also* : TOUPEE

wi·geon *or* **wid·geon** \'wi-jən\ *n, pl* **wigeon** *or* **wigeons** *or* **widgeon** *or* **widgeons** : any of several medium-sized freshwater ducks

wig·gle \'wi-gəl\ *vb* **wig·gled; wig·gling** **1** : to move to and fro with quick jerky or shaking movements : JIGGLE **2** : WRIGGLE — **wiggle** *n*

wig·gler \'wi-glər, -gə-lər\ *n* **1** : a larva or pupa of a mosquito **2** : one that wiggles

wig·gly \'wi-glē, -gə-lē\ *adj* **1** : tending to wiggle ⟨a ∼ worm⟩ **2** : WAVY ⟨∼ lines⟩

wight \'wīt\ *n* : a living being : CREATURE

wig·let \'wi-glət\ *n* : a small wig used esp. to enhance a hairstyle

¹**wig·wag** \'wig-ˌwag\ *vb* **1** : to signal by or as if by a flag or light waved according to a code **2** : to make or cause to make a signal (as with the hand or arm)

²**wigwag** *n* : the art or practice of wigwagging

wig·wam \'wig-ˌwäm\ *n* : a hut of the Indians of the eastern U.S. having typically an arched framework of poles overlaid with bark, rush mats, or hides

wigwam

¹**wild** \'wī(-ə)ld\ *adj* **1** : living in a state of nature and not ordinarily tamed ⟨∼ ducks⟩ **2** : growing or produced without human aid or care ⟨∼ honey⟩ ⟨∼ plants⟩ **3** : WASTE, DESOLATE ⟨∼ country⟩ **4** : UNCONTROLLED, UNRESTRAINED, UNRULY ⟨∼ passions⟩ ⟨a ∼ young stallion⟩ **5** : TURBULENT, STORMY ⟨a ∼ night⟩ **6** : EXTRAVAGANT, FANTASTIC, CRAZY ⟨∼ ideas⟩ **7** : indicative of strong passion, desire, or emotion ⟨a ∼ stare⟩ **8** : UNCIVILIZED, SAVAGE **9** : deviating from the natural or expected course : ERRATIC ⟨a ∼ throw⟩ **10** : able to represent any playing card designated by the holder ⟨deuces ∼⟩ — **wild·ly** *adv* — **wild·ness** *n*

²**wild** *adv* **1** : WILDLY **2** : without regulation or control ⟨running ∼⟩

³**wild** *n* **1** : WILDERNESS **2** : a natural or undomesticated state or existence

wild boar *n* : an Old World wild hog from which most domestic swine have been derived

wild card *n* **1** : an unknown or unpredictable factor **2** : one picked to fill a leftover play-off or tournament position **3** *usu* **wild-card** : a symbol (as ? or *) used in a keyword search to represent the presence of unspecified characters

wild carrot *n* : QUEEN ANNE'S LACE

¹**wild·cat** \'wī(-ə)ld-ˌkat\ *n, pl* **wildcats** **1** : any of various small or medium-sized cats (as a lynx or ocelot) **2** : a quick-tempered hard-fighting person

²**wildcat** *adj* **1** : not sound or safe ⟨∼ schemes⟩ **2** : initiated by a group of workers without formal union approval ⟨∼ strike⟩

³**wildcat** *vb* **wild·cat·ted; wild·cat·ting** : to drill an oil or gas well in a region not known to be productive

wil·de·beest \'wil-də-ˌbēst\ *n, pl* **wildebeests** *also* **wildebeest** [Afrikaans *wildebees*, fr. *wilde* wild + *bees* ox] : either of two large African antelopes with an oxlike head and horns and a horselike mane and tail

wil·der·ness \'wil-dər-nəs\ *n* [ME, fr. *wildern* wild, fr. OE *wilddēoren* of wild beasts] : an uncultivated and uninhabited region

wild·fire \'wī(-ə)ld-ˌfī(-ə)r\ *n* : an uncontrollable fire — **like wildfire** : very rapidly

wild·flow·er \-ˌflaù(-ə)r\ *n* : the flower of a wild or uncultivated plant or the plant bearing it

wild·fowl \-ˌfaù(-ə)l\ *n* : a bird and esp. a waterfowl hunted as game

wild–goose chase *n* : the pursuit of something unattainable

wild·life \'wī(-ə)ld-ˌlīf\ *n* : nonhuman living things and esp. wild animals living in their natural environment

wild oat *n* **1** : any of several Old World wild grasses **2** *pl* : offenses and indiscretions attributed to youthful exuberance — usu. used in the phrase *sow one's wild oats*

wild rice *n* : a No. American aquatic grass; *also* : its edible seed

wild type *n* : a gene or trait that is typical of a natural population of organisms in contrast to that of mutant forms; *also* : an organism with such a gene or trait

wild·wood \'wī(-ə)ld-ˌwùd\ *n* : a wood unaltered or unfrequented by humans

¹**wile** \'wī(-ə)l\ *n* **1** : a trick or stratagem intended to ensnare or deceive; *also* : a playful trick **2** : TRICKERY, GUILE

²**wile** *vb* **wiled; wil·ing** : LURE, ENTICE

¹**will** \'wil\ *vb, past* **would** \'wud\ *pres sing & pl* **will** **1** : WISH, DESIRE ⟨call it what you ∼⟩ **2** — used as an auxiliary verb to express (1) desire, willingness, or in negative constructions refusal ⟨∼ you have another⟩ ⟨he *won't* do it⟩, (2) customary or habitual action ⟨∼ get angry over nothing⟩, (3) simple futurity ⟨tomorrow we ∼ go shopping⟩, (4) capability or sufficiency ⟨the back seat ∼ hold three⟩, (5) determination or willfulness ⟨I ∼ go despite them⟩, (6) probability ⟨that ∼ be the mailman⟩, (7) inevitability ⟨accidents ∼ happen⟩, or (8) a command ⟨you ∼ do as I say⟩

²**will** *n* **1** : wish or desire often combined with determination ⟨the ∼ to win⟩ **2** : something desired; *esp* : a choice or determination of one having authority or power **3** : the act, process, or experience of willing : VOLITION **4** : the mental powers manifested as wishing, choosing, desiring, or intending **5** : a disposition to act according to principles or ends **6** : power of controlling one's own actions or emotions ⟨a leader of iron ∼⟩ **7** : a legal document in which a person declares to whom his or her possessions are to go after death

³**will** *vb* **1** : to dispose of by or as if by a will : BEQUEATH **2** : to determine by an act of choice; *also* : DECREE, ORDAIN **3** : INTEND, PURPOSE; *also* : CHOOSE

will·ful *or* **wil·ful** \'wil-fəl\ *adj* **1** : governed by will without regard to reason : OBSTINATE **2** : INTENTIONAL ⟨∼ murder⟩ — **will·ful·ly** *adv*

wil·lies \'wi-lēz\ *n pl* : a fit of nervousness : JITTERS — used with *the*

will·ing \'wi-liŋ\ *adj* **1** : inclined or favorably disposed in mind : READY ⟨∼ to go⟩ **2** : prompt to act or respond ⟨∼ workers⟩ **3** : done, borne, or accepted voluntarily or without reluctance **4** : of or relating to the will : VOLITIONAL — **will·ing·ly** *adv* — **will·ing·ness** *n*

wil·li·waw \'wi-lē-ˌwò\ *n* : a sudden violent gust of cold land air common along mountainous coasts of high latitudes

will–o'–the–wisp \ˌwil-ə-thə-'wisp\ *n* **1** : a light that appears at night over marshy grounds **2** : a misleading or elusive goal or hope

wil·low \'wi-lō\ *n* **1** : any of a genus of quick-growing shrubs and trees with tough pliable shoots **2** : an object made of willow wood

wil·low·ware \-ˌwer\ *n* : dinnerware that is usu. blue and white and that is decorated with a story-telling design featuring a large willow tree by a little bridge

wil·lowy \'wi-lə-wē\ *adj* : PLIANT; *also* : gracefully tall and slender

will·pow·er \'wil-ˌpaù-(ə)r\ *n* : energetic determination : RESOLUTENESS

wil·ly–nil·ly \ˌwi-lē-'ni-lē\ *adv or adj* [alter. of *will I nill I or will ye nill ye or will he nill he*; *nill* fr. archaic *nill* to be unwilling, fr. ME *nilen*, fr. OE *nyllan*, fr. *ne* not + *wyllan* to wish] : without regard for one's choice : by compulsion ⟨they rushed us along ∼⟩

¹**wilt** \'wilt\ *vb* **1** : to lose or cause to lose freshness and become limp esp. from lack of water : DROOP **2** : to grow weak or faint : LANGUISH

²**wilt** *n* : any of various plant disorders marked by wilting and often shriveling

wily \'wī-lē\ *adj* **wil·i·er; -est** : full of guile : TRICKY — **wil·i·ness** \-lē-nəs\ *n*

wimp \'wimp\ *n* : a weak, cowardly, or ineffectual person — **wimpy** \'wim-pē\ *adj*

¹**wim·ple** \'wim-pəl\ *n* : a cloth covering worn over the head and around the neck and chin by women esp. in the late medieval period and by some nuns

²**wimple** *vb* **wim·pled; wim·pling** **1** : to cover with or as if with a wimple **2** : to ripple or cause to ripple

¹**win** \'win\ *vb* **won** \'wən\; **win·ning** [ME *winnen*, fr. OE *winnan* to struggle] **1** : to get possession of esp. by effort : GAIN; *also* : to obtain by work : EARN **2** : to gain in or as if in battle or contest; *also* : to be the victor in ⟨won the war⟩ **3** : to solicit and gain the favor of; *esp* : to induce to accept oneself in marriage

²**win** *n* : VICTORY; *esp* : 1st place at the finish (as of a horse race)

wince \'wins\ *vb* **winced; winc·ing** : to shrink back involuntarily (as from pain) : FLINCH — **wince** *n*

winch \'winch\ *n* : a machine that has a drum on which is wound a rope or cable for hauling or hoisting — **winch** *vb*

¹**wind** \'wind\ *n* **1** : a movement of the air **2** : a prevailing force or influence : TENDENCY, TREND **3** : BREATH ⟨he had the ∼ knocked out of him⟩ **4** : gas produced in the stomach or intestines **5** : something insubstantial; *esp* : idle words **6** : air carrying a scent (as of game) **7** : INTIMATION ⟨they got ∼ of our plans⟩ **8** : WIND INSTRUMENTS; *also, pl* : players of wind instruments

²**wind** *vb* **1** : to get a scent of ⟨the dogs ∼ed the game⟩ **2** : to cause to be out of breath ⟨he was ∼ed from the climb⟩ **3** : to allow (as a horse) to rest so as to recover breath

³**wind** \'wind, 'wind\ *vb* **wind·ed** \'win-dəd, 'win-\ *or* **wound** \'waund\; **wind·ing** : to sound by blowing ⟨∼ a horn⟩

⁴**wind** \'wind\ *vb* **wound** \'waund\ *also* **wind·ed; wind·ing** **1** : ENTANGLE, INVOLVE **2** : to introduce stealthily : INSINUATE **3** : to encircle or cover with something pliable : WRAP, COIL, TWINE ⟨∼ a bobbin⟩ **4** : to hoist or haul by a rope or chain and a winch **5** : to tighten the spring of; *also* : CRANK **6** : to raise to a high level (as of excitement) **7** : to cause to move in a curving line or path **8** : to have a curving course or shape ⟨a river ∼ing through the valley⟩ **9** : to move or lie so as to encircle

⁵**wind** \'wind\ *n* : COIL, TURN

wind·age \'win-dij\ *n* : the influence of the wind in deflecting the course of a projectile through the air; *also* : the amount of such deflection

wind·bag \'wind-ˌbag\ *n* : an overly talkative person

wind·blown \-ˌblōn\ *adj* : blown by the wind; *also* : having the appearance of being blown by the wind

wind·break \-ˌbrāk\ *n* : a growth of trees or shrubs serving to break the force of the wind; *also* : a shelter from the wind

wind·burned \-ˌbərnd\ *adj* : irritated and inflamed by exposure to the wind — **wind·burn** \-ˌbərn\ *n*

wind·chill \-ˌchil\ *n* : a still-air temperature that would have the same cooling effect on exposed human skin as a given combination of temperature and wind speed

windchill factor *n* : WINDCHILL

wind down *vb* **1** : to draw toward an end **2** : RELAX, UNWIND

wind·er \'win-dər\ *n* : one that winds

wind·fall \'wind-ˌfòl\ *n* **1** : something (as a tree or fruit) blown down by the wind **2** : an unexpected or sudden gift, gain, or advantage

wind·flow·er \-ˌflaù-(ə)r\ *n* : ANEMONE

¹**wind·ing** \'win-diŋ\ *n* : material (as wire) wound or coiled about an object

²**winding** *adj* **1** : having a pronounced curve or spiral ⟨∼ stairs⟩ **2** : having a course that winds ⟨a ∼ road⟩

wind·ing–sheet \-ˌshēt\ *n* : SHROUD

wind instrument *n* : a musical instrument (as a flute or horn) sounded by wind and esp. by the breath

wind·jam·mer \'wind-ˌja-mər\ *n* : a sailing ship; *also* : one of its crew

wind·lass \'wind-ləs\ *n* [ME *wyndlas*, alter. of *wyndase*, fr. OF *guindas, windas*, fr. ON *vindāss*, fr. *vinda* to wind + *āss* pole] : a winch used esp. on ships for hoisting or hauling

wind·mill \'wind-ˌmil\ *n* : a mill or machine worked by the wind turning sails or vanes that radiate from a central shaft

win·dow \'win-dō\ *n* [ME *windowe*, fr. ON *vindauga*, fr. *vindr* wind + *auga* eye] **1** : an opening in the wall of a building to let in light and air; *also* : the framework with fittings that closes such an opening **2** : WINDOWPANE **3** : an opening resembling or suggesting that of a window in a building **4** : an interval of time during which certain conditions or an opportunity exists **5** : a rectangular box appearing on a computer screen on which information (as files or program output) is displayed — **win·dow·less** *adj*

window box *n* : a box for growing plants in or by a window

window dressing *n* **1** : display of merchandise in a store window **2** : a showing made to create a deceptively favorable impression

win·dow·pane \'win-dō-ˌpān\ *n* : a pane in a window
win·dow–shop \-ˌshäp\ *vb* : to look at the displays in store windows without going inside the stores to make purchases — **win·dow–shop·per** *n*
win·dow·sill \-ˌsil\ *n* : the horizontal member at the bottom of a window
wind·pipe \'wind-ˌpīp\ *n* : TRACHEA
wind·proof \-'prüf\ *adj* : impervious to wind ⟨a ∼ jacket⟩
wind·row \'wind-ˌrō\ *n* **1** : hay raked up into a row to dry **2** : a row of something (as dry leaves) swept up by or as if by the wind
wind shear *n* : a radical shift in wind speed and direction that occurs over a very short distance
wind·shield \'wind-ˌshēld\ *n* : a transparent screen (as of glass) in front of the occupants of a vehicle
wind sock *n* : an open-ended truncated cloth cone mounted in an elevated position to indicate wind direction
wind·storm \-ˌstorm\ *n* : a storm with high wind and little or no rain
wind·surf·ing \-ˌsər-fiŋ\ *n* : the sport or activity of riding a sailboard — **wind·surf** \-ˌsərf\ *vb* — **wind·surf·er** *n*
wind·swept \'wind-ˌswept\ *adj* : swept by or as if by wind ⟨∼ plains⟩
wind tunnel *n* : an enclosed passage through which air is blown to investigate air flow around an object
wind·up \'wīn-ˌdəp\ *n* **1** : CONCLUSION, FINISH **2** : a series of regular and distinctive motions made by a pitcher preliminary to delivering a pitch
wind up *vb* **1** : to bring up or come to a conclusion : END **2** : to put in order for the purpose of bringing to an end **3** : to arrive in a place, situation, or condition at the end or as a result of a course of action ⟨*wound up* as paupers⟩ **4** : to make a pitching windup
¹**wind·ward** \'win-dwərd\ *n* : the side or direction from which the wind is blowing
²**windward** *adj* : being in or facing the direction from which the wind is blowing
windy \'win-dē\ *adj* **wind·i·er; -est** **1** : having wind : exposed to winds ⟨a ∼ day⟩ ⟨a ∼ prairie⟩ **2** : STORMY **3** : FLATULENT **4** : indulging in or characterized by useless talk : VERBOSE
¹**wine** \'wīn\ *n* [ME *win*, fr. OE *wīn*, ultim. fr. L *vinum*] **1** : fermented grape juice used as a beverage **2** : the usu. fermented juice of a plant product (as fruit) used as a beverage ⟨rice ∼⟩
²**wine** *vb* **wined; win·ing** : to treat to or drink wine
wine cellar *n* : a room for storing wines; *also* : a stock of wines
wine·grow·er \-ˌgrō-ər\ *n* : one that cultivates a vineyard and makes wine
wine·press \-ˌpres\ *n* : a vat in which juice is pressed from grapes
win·ery \'wī-nə-rē, 'wīn-rē\ *n, pl* **-eries** : a wine-making establishment
¹**wing** \'wiŋ\ *n* **1** : one of the movable feathered or membranous paired appendages by means of which a bird, bat, or insect flies **2** : something suggesting a wing; *esp* : an airfoil that develops the lift which supports an aircraft in flight **3** : a plant or animal appendage or part likened to a wing **4** : a turned-back or extended edge on an article of clothing **5** : a means of flight or rapid progress **6** : the act or manner of flying : FLIGHT **7** *pl* : the area at the side of the stage out of sight **8** : one of the positions or players on either side of a center position or line **9** : either of two opposing groups within an organization : FACTION **10** : a unit in military aviation consisting of two or more squadrons — **wing·less** *adj* — **wing·like** \-ˌlīk\ *adj* — **on the wing** : in flight : FLYING — **under one's wing** : in one's charge or care
²**wing** *vb* **1** : to fit with wings; *also* : to enable to fly easily **2** : to pass through in flight : FLY ⟨∼ the air⟩ ⟨swallows ∼*ing* southward⟩ **3** : to let fly : DISPATCH **4** : to wound in the wing ⟨∼ a bird⟩; *also* : to wound without killing **5** : to perform without preparation : IMPROVISE ⟨∼*ing* it⟩
wing·ding \'wiŋ-ˌdiŋ\ *n* : a wild, lively, or lavish party
winged \'wiŋd, 'wiŋ-əd, *in compounds* 'wiŋd\ *adj* **1** : having wings esp. of a specified character **2** : soaring with or as if with wings : ELEVATED **3** : SWIFT, RAPID
wing nut *n* : a nut with winglike extensions that can be gripped with the thumb and finger

wing·span \'wiŋ-ˌspan\ *n* : the distance between the tips of a pair of wings
wing·spread \-ˌspred\ *n* : the spread of the wings; *esp* : the distance between the tips of the fully extended wings of a winged animal
¹**wink** \'wiŋk\ *vb* **1** : to close and open one eye quickly as a signal or hint **2** : to close and open the eyes quickly : BLINK **3** : to avoid seeing or noticing something ⟨∼ at a traffic violation⟩ **4** : TWINKLE, FLICKER — **wink·er** \'wiŋ-kər\ *n*
²**wink** *n* **1** : a brief period of sleep : NAP **2** : an act of winking; *esp* : a hint or sign given by winking **3** : INSTANT ⟨dries in a ∼⟩
win·ner \'wi-nər\ *n* : one that wins
¹**win·ning** \'wi-niŋ\ *n* **1** : VICTORY **2** : something won; *esp* : money won at gambling ⟨large ∼*s*⟩
²**winning** *adj* **1** : successful esp. in competition **2** : ATTRACTIVE, CHARMING
win·now \'wi-nō\ *vb* **1** : to remove (as chaff) by a current of air; *also* : to free (as grain) from waste in this manner **2** : to sort or separate as if by winnowing
wino \'wī-nō\ *n, pl* **win·os** : one who is addicted to drinking wine
win·some \'win-səm\ *adj* [ME *winsum*, fr. OE *wynsum*, fr. *wynn* joy] **1** : generally pleasing and engaging **2** : CHEERFUL, GAY — **win·some·ly** *adv* — **win·some·ness** *n*
¹**win·ter** \'win-tər\ *n* : the season of the year in any region in which the noonday sun shines most obliquely : the coldest period of the year
²**winter** *vb* **1** : to pass the winter ⟨∼*ed* in Florida⟩ **2** : to feed or find food during the winter ⟨∼*ed* on hay⟩
³**winter** *adj* : sown in autumn for harvesting in the following spring or summer ⟨∼ wheat⟩
win·ter·green \'win-tər-ˌgrēn\ *n* **1** : a low evergreen plant of the heath family with white bell-shaped flowers and spicy red berries **2** : an aromatic oil or its flavor from the wintergreen
win·ter·ize \'win-tə-ˌrīz\ *vb* **-ized; -iz·ing** : to make ready for winter
win·ter·kill \'win-tər-ˌkil\ *vb* : to kill or die by exposure to winter weather
winter squash *n* : any of various hard-shelled squashes that keep well in storage
win·ter·tide \-ˌtīd\ *n* : WINTER
win·ter·time \-ˌtīm\ *n* : WINTER
win·try \'win-trē\ *also* **win·tery** \'win-tə-rē\ *adj* **win·tri·er; -est** **1** : of, relating to, or characteristic of winter ⟨∼ weather⟩ **2** : CHILLING, CHEERLESS ⟨a ∼ welcome⟩
¹**wipe** \'wīp\ *vb* **wiped; wip·ing** **1** : to clean or dry by rubbing ⟨∼ dishes⟩ **2** : to remove by or as if by rubbing away tears⟩ **3** : to erase completely : OBLITERATE **4** : to pass or draw over a surface ⟨*wiped* his hand across his face⟩ — **wip·er** *n*
²**wipe** *n* **1** : an act or instance of wiping; *also* : BLOW, STRIKE, SWIPE **2** : something used for wiping
wipe out *vb* : to destroy completely
¹**wire** \'wī(-ə)r\ *n* **1** : metal in the form of a thread or slender rod; *also* : a thread or rod of metal **2** : hidden or secret influences controlling the action of a person or organization — usu. used in pl. ⟨pull ∼*s*⟩ **3** : a line of wire for conducting electric current **4** : a telegraph or telephone wire or system **5** : TELEGRAM, CABLEGRAM **6** : the finish line of a race
²**wire** *vb* **wired; wir·ing** **1** : to provide or equip with wire ⟨∼ a house⟩ **2** : to bind, string, or mount with wire **3** : to send or send word to by telegraph
wired *adj* **1** : furnished with wires **2** : connected to the Internet **3** : feverishly excited
wire·hair \'wī(-ə)r-ˌher\ *n* : a wirehaired dog or cat
wire·haired \-'herd\ *adj* : having a stiff wiry outer coat of hair
¹**wire·less** \-ləs\ *adj* **1** : having no wire or wires **2** : RADIO **3** : of or relating to data communications using radio waves
²**wireless** *n* **1** : telecommunication involving signals transmitted by radio waves; *also* : the technology used in radio telecommunication **2** *chiefly Brit* : RADIO
wire·pull·er \-ˌpu̇-lər\ *n* : one who uses secret or underhanded means to influence the acts of a person or organization — **wire–pull·ing** *n*

wire service *n* : a news agency that sends out syndicated news copy to subscribers by wire or satellite

wire·tap \-ˌtap\ *n* : the act or an instance of tapping a telephone or telegraph wire to get information; *also* : an electrical connection used for such tapping — **wiretap** *vb* — **wire·tap·per** \-ˌta-pər\ *n*

wire·worm \-ˌwərm\ *n* : any of various slender hard-coated beetle larvae esp. destructive to plant roots

wir·ing \ˈwī-(ə)r-iŋ\ *n* : a system of wires

wiry \ˈwī-(ə)r-ē\ *adj* **wir·i·er** \ˈwī-rē-ər\; **-est 1** : made of or resembling wire **2** : slender yet strong and sinewy — **wir·i·ness** \ˈwī-rē-nəs\ *n*

Wis *or* **Wisc** *abbr* Wisconsin

Wisd *abbr* Wisdom

wis·dom \ˈwiz-dəm\ *n* [ME, fr. OE *wīsdōm*, fr. *wīs* wise] **1** : accumulated philosophic or scientific learning : KNOWLEDGE; *also* : INSIGHT **2** : good sense : JUDGMENT **3** : a wise attitude or course of action

Wisdom *n* — see BIBLE table

Wisdom of Sol·o·mon \-ˈsä-lə-mən\ — see BIBLE table

wisdom tooth *n* : the last tooth of the full set on each side of the upper and lower jaws of humans

¹wise \ˈwīz\ *n* : WAY, MANNER, FASHION ⟨in no ∼⟩ ⟨in this ∼⟩

²wise *adj* **wis·er; wis·est 1** : having wisdom : SAGE **2** : having or showing good sense or good judgment **3** : aware of what is going on : KNOWING ⟨got ∼ to his secrets⟩; *also* : CRAFTY, SHREWD **4** : possessing inside information **5** : INSOLENT, FRESH ⟨a ∼ retort⟩ — **wise·ly** *adv*

-wise \-ˌwīz\ *adv comb form* : in the manner or direction of ⟨slant*wise*⟩

wise·acre \ˈwīz-ˌā-kər\ *n* [MD *wijssegger* soothsayer] : SMART ALECK

¹wise·crack \ˈwīz-ˌkrak\ *n* : a clever, smart, or flippant remark

²wisecrack *vb* : to make a wisecrack

wise guy *n* : SMART ALECK

¹wish \ˈwish\ *vb* **1** : to have a desire : long for ⟨∼ you were here⟩ ⟨∼ for a puppy⟩ **2** : to form or express a wish concerning ⟨∼ed him a happy birthday⟩ **3** : BID ⟨he ∼ed me good morning⟩ **4** : to request by expressing a desire ⟨I ∼ you to go now⟩

²wish *n* **1** : an act or instance of wishing or desire : WANT; *also* : GOAL **2** : an expressed will or desire

wish·bone \-ˌbōn\ *n* : a forked bone in front of the breastbone in most birds

wish·ful \ˈwish-fəl\ *adj* **1** : expressive of a wish; *also* : having a wish **2** : according with wishes rather than fact ⟨∼ thinking⟩

wishy–washy \ˈwi-shē-ˌwȯ-shē, -ˌwä-\ *adj* : WEAK, INSIPID; *also* : morally feeble

wisp \ˈwisp\ *n* **1** : a small handful (as of hay or straw) **2** : a thin strand, strip, or fragment ⟨a ∼ of hair⟩; *also* : a thready streak ⟨a ∼ of smoke⟩ **3** : something frail, slight, or fleeting ⟨a ∼ of a smile⟩ — **wispy** *adj*

wis·te·ria \wis-ˈtir-ē-ə\ *also* **wis·tar·ia** \-ˈtir-ē-ə *also* -ˈter-\ *n* : any of a genus of chiefly Asian mostly woody vines related to the peas and widely grown for their long showy clusters of blue, white, purple, or rose flowers

wist·ful \ˈwist-fəl\ *adj* : feeling or showing a timid desire — **wist·ful·ly** *adv* — **wist·ful·ness** *n*

wit \ˈwit\ *n* **1** : reasoning power : INTELLIGENCE **2** : mental soundness : SANITY — usu. used in pl. **3** : RESOURCEFULNESS, INGENUITY; *esp* : quickness and cleverness in handling words and ideas **4** : a talent for making clever remarks; *also* : a person noted for making witty remarks — **wit·ted** \ˈwi-təd\ *adj* — **at one's wit's end** : at a loss for a means of solving a problem

¹witch \ˈwich\ *n* **1** : a person believed to have magic power; *esp* : SORCERESS **2** : an ugly old woman : HAG **3** : a charming or alluring girl or woman

²witch *vb* : BEWITCH

witch·craft \ˈwich-ˌkraft\ *n* : the power or practices of a witch : SORCERY

witch doctor *n* : a person in a primitive society who uses magic to treat sickness and to fight off evil spirits

witch·ery \ˈwi-chə-rē\ *n, pl* **-er·ies 1** : SORCERY **2** : FASCINATION, CHARM

witch–grass \ˈwich-ˌgras\ *n* : any of several grasses that are weeds in cultivated areas

witch ha·zel \ˈwich-ˌhā-zəl\ *n* **1** : a shrub of eastern No. America bearing small yellow flowers in the fall **2** : a soothing alcoholic lotion made from witch hazel bark

witch–hunt \ˈwich-ˌhənt\ *n* **1** : a searching out and persecution of persons accused of witchcraft **2** : the searching out and deliberate harassment esp. of political opponents

witch·ing \ˈwi-chiŋ\ *adj* : of, relating to, or suitable for sorcery or supernatural occurrences

with \ˈwith, ˈwith\ *prep* **1** : AGAINST ⟨a fight ∼ his brother⟩ **2** : FROM ⟨parting ∼ friends⟩ **3** : in mutual relation to ⟨talk ∼ a friend⟩ **4** : in the company of ⟨went there ∼ her⟩ **5** : AS REGARDS, TOWARD ⟨is patient ∼ children⟩ **6** : compared to ⟨on equal terms ∼ another⟩ **7** : in support of ⟨I'm ∼ you all the way⟩ **8** : in the presence of : CONTAINING ⟨tea ∼ sugar⟩ **9** : in the opinion of : as judged by ⟨their arguments had weight ∼ her⟩ **10** : BECAUSE OF, THROUGH ⟨pale ∼ anger⟩; *also* : by means of ⟨hit him ∼ a club⟩ **11** : in a manner indicating ⟨work ∼ a will⟩ **12** : GIVEN, GRANTED ⟨∼ your permission I'll leave⟩ **13** : HAVING ⟨came ∼ good news⟩ ⟨stood there ∼ his mouth open⟩ **14** : characterized by ⟨boys ∼ good morals⟩ **15** : at the time of : right after ⟨∼ that we left⟩ **16** : DESPITE ⟨∼ all her cleverness, she failed⟩ **17** : in the direction of ⟨swim ∼ the tide⟩

with·al \wi-ˈthȯl, -ˈthȯl\ *adv* **1** : together with this : BESIDES **2** : on the other hand : NEVERTHELESS

with·draw \with-ˈdrȯ, with-\ *vb* **-drew** \-ˈdrü\; **-drawn** \-ˈdrȯn\; **-draw·ing** \-ˈdrȯ-iŋ\ **1** : to take back or away : REMOVE **2** : to call back (as from consideration); *also* : RETRACT **3** : to go away : RETREAT, LEAVE **4** : to terminate one's participation in or use of something

with·draw·al \-ˈdrȯ-əl\ *n* **1** : an act or instance of withdrawing **2** : the discontinuance of the use or administration of a drug and esp. an addicting drug; *also* : the period following such discontinuance marked by often painful physiological and psychological symptoms **3** : a pathological retreat from the real world (as in some schizophrenic states)

with·drawn \with-ˈdrȯn\ *adj* **1** : ISOLATED, SECLUDED **2** : socially detached and unresponsive

withe \ˈwith\ *n* : a slender flexible twig or branch

with·er \ˈwi-thər\ *vb* **1** : to shrivel from or as if from loss of bodily moisture and esp. sap **2** : to lose or cause to lose vitality, force, or freshness ⟨their enthusiasm ∼ed⟩ **3** : to cause to feel shriveled ⟨∼ed him with a glance⟩

with·ers \ˈwi-thərz\ *n pl* : the ridge between the shoulder bones of a horse; *also* : the corresponding part in other 4-footed animals

with·hold \with-ˈhōld, with-\ *vb* **-held** \-ˈheld\; **-hold·ing 1** : to hold back : RESTRAIN; *also* : RETAIN **2** : to refrain from granting, giving, or allowing ⟨∼ permission⟩ ⟨∼ names⟩

withholding tax *n* : a tax on income withheld at the source

¹with·in \wi-ˈthin, -ˈthin\ *adv* **1** : in or into the interior : INSIDE **2** : inside oneself : INWARDLY

²within *prep* **1** : inside the limits or influence of ⟨∼ call⟩ **2** : in the limits or compass of ⟨∼ a mile⟩ **3** : in or to the inner part of ⟨∼ the room⟩

with–it \ˈwi-thət, -thət\ *adj* : socially or culturally up-to-date

¹with·out \wi-ˈthaut, -ˈthaut\ *prep* **1** : OUTSIDE **2** : LACKING ⟨∼ hope⟩; *also* : not accompanied by or showing ⟨spoke ∼ thinking⟩

²without *adv* **1** : on the outside : EXTERNALLY **2** : with something lacking or absent ⟨has learned to do ∼⟩

with·stand \with-ˈstand, with-\ *vb* **-stood** \-ˈstud\; **-stand·ing** : to stand against : RESIST; *esp* : to oppose (as an attack) successfully

wit·less \ˈwit-ləs\ *adj* : lacking wit or understanding : FOOLISH — **wit·less·ly** *adv* — **wit·less·ness** *n*

¹wit·ness \ˈwit-nəs\ *n* [ME *witnesse*, fr. OE *witnes* knowledge, testimony, witness, fr. *wit* mind, intelligence] **1** : TESTIMONY ⟨bear ∼ to the fact⟩ **2** : one that gives evidence; *esp* : one who testifies in a cause or before a court **3** : one present at a transaction so as to be able to testify that it has taken place **4** : one who has personal knowledge or experience of something **5** : something serving as evidence or proof : SIGN

²witness *vb* **1** : to bear witness : TESTIFY **2** : to act as legal witness of **3** : to furnish proof of : BETOKEN **4** : to be a witness of **5** : to be the scene of ⟨this region has ~ed many wars⟩

wit·ti·cism \'wi-tə-ˌsi-zəm\ *n* : a witty saying or phrase

wit·ting \'wi-tiŋ\ *adj* : done knowingly : INTENTIONAL — **wit·ting·ly** *adv*

wit·ty \'wi-tē\ *adj* **wit·ti·er; -est** : marked by or full of wit : AMUSING ⟨a ~ writer⟩ ⟨a ~ remark⟩ ♦ *Synonyms* HUMOROUS, FACETIOUS, JOCULAR, JOCOSE — **wit·ti·ly** \-tə-lē\ *adv* — **wit·ti·ness** \-tē-nəs\ *n*

wive \'wīv\ *vb* **wived; wiv·ing** : to take a wife

wives *pl of* WIFE

wiz·ard \'wi-zərd\ *n* [ME *wysard* wise man, fr. *wys* wise] **1** : MAGICIAN, SORCERER **2** : a very clever or skillful person ⟨a ~ at chess⟩

wiz·ard·ry \'wi-zər-drē\ *n, pl* **-ries** **1** : magic skill : SORCERY **2** : great skill or cleverness in an activity

wiz·en \'wi-zᵊn, 'wē-\ *vb* : to become or cause to become dry, shrunken, or wrinkled ⟨a face ~ed by age⟩

wk *abbr* **1** week **2** work

WL *abbr* wavelength

wmk *abbr* watermark

WNW *abbr* west-northwest

WO *abbr* warrant officer

w/o *abbr* without

woad \'wōd\ *n* : a European herb related to the mustards; *also* : a blue dyestuff made from its leaves

wob·ble \'wä-bəl\ *vb* **wob·bled; wob·bling** **1** : to move or cause to move with an irregular rocking or side-to-side motion **2** : TREMBLE, QUAVER **3** : WAVER, VACILLATE — **wobble** *n* — **wob·bly** \-bə-lē\ *adj*

woe \'wō\ *n* **1** : deep suffering from misfortune, affliction, or grief **2** : TROUBLE, MISFORTUNE ⟨economic ~s⟩

woe·be·gone \'wō-bi-ˌgȯn\ *adj* : exhibiting woe, sorrow, or misery; *also* : being in a sorry condition

woe·ful *also* **wo·ful** \'wō-fəl\ *adj* **1** : full of woe : AFFLICTED **2** : involving, bringing, or relating to woe ⟨~ stories⟩ **3** : DEPLORABLE ⟨~ test scores⟩ — **woe·ful·ly** *adv*

wok \'wäk\ *n* [Chin (Guangzhou & Hong Kong dial.) *wohk*] : a bowl-shaped cooking utensil used esp. in stir-frying

woke *past and past part of* WAKE

woken *past part of* WAKE

wold \'wōld\ *n* : an upland plain or stretch of rolling land without woods

¹wolf \'wu̇lf\ *n, pl* **wolves** \'wu̇lvz\ **1** : any of several large erect-eared bushy-tailed doglike predatory mammals that live and hunt in packs; *esp* : GRAY WOLF **2** : a fierce or destructive person — **wolf·ish** *adj* — **wolf in sheep's clothing** : one who hides a hostile intention with a friendly manner

²wolf *vb* : to eat greedily : DEVOUR

wolf·hound \-ˌhau̇nd\ *n* : any of several large dogs orig. used in hunting wolves

wol·fram \'wu̇l-frəm\ *n* : TUNGSTEN

wol·ver·ine \ˌwu̇l-və-'rēn\ *n, pl* **wolverines** *also* **wolverine** : a dark shaggy-coated flesh-eating mammal of northern forests and associated tundra that is related to the weasels

wom·an \'wu̇-mən\ *n, pl* **wom·en** \'wi-mən\ [ME, fr. OE *wīfman*, fr. *wīf* woman, wife + *man* human being, man] **1** : an adult female person **2** : WOMANKIND **3** : feminine nature : WOMANLINESS **4** : a female servant or attendant

wom·an·hood \'wu̇-mən-ˌhu̇d\ *n* **1** : the state of being a woman : the distinguishing qualities of a woman or of womankind **2** : WOMEN, WOMANKIND

wom·an·ish \'wu̇-mə-nish\ *adj* **1** : associated with or characteristic of women rather than men **2** : suggestive of a weak character : EFFEMINATE

wom·an·ize \'wu̇-mə-ˌnīz\ *vb* : to pursue casual sexual relationships with numerous women — **wom·an·iz·er** *n*

wom·an·kind \'wu̇-mən-ˌkīnd\ *n* : the females of the human race : WOMEN

wom·an·like \-ˌlīk\ *adj* : WOMANLY

wom·an·ly \-lē\ *adj* : having qualities characteristic of a woman — **wom·an·li·ness** \-lē-nəs\ *n*

woman suffrage *n* : possession and exercise of suffrage by women

womb \'wüm\ *n* **1** : UTERUS **2** : a place where something is generated

wom·bat \'wäm-ˌbat\ *n* : any of several stocky burrowing Australian marsupials that resemble small bears

wom·en·folk \'wi-mən-ˌfōk\ *also* **wom·en·folks** \-ˌfōks\ *n pl* : WOMEN

¹won \'wən\ *past and past part of* WIN

²won \'wȯn\ *n, pl* **won** — see MONEY table

¹won·der \'wən-dər\ *n* **1** : a cause of astonishment or surprise : MARVEL; *also* : MIRACLE **2** : the quality of exciting wonder ⟨the charm and ~ of the scene⟩ **3** : a feeling (as of awed astonishment or uncertainty) aroused by something extraordinary or affecting

²wonder *vb* **1** : to feel surprise or amazement **2** : to feel curiosity or doubt ⟨~ about the future⟩

wonder drug *n* : MIRACLE DRUG

won·der·ful \'wən-dər-fəl\ *adj* **1** : exciting wonder : MARVELOUS, ASTONISHING **2** : unusually good : ADMIRABLE ⟨did a ~ job⟩ — **won·der·ful·ly** \-f(ə-)lē\ *adv* — **won·der·ful·ness** *n*

won·der·land \-ˌland, -lənd\ *n* **1** : an imaginary place of delicate beauty or magical charm **2** : a place that excites admiration or wonder ⟨a scenic ~⟩

won·der·ment \-mənt\ *n* **1** : ASTONISHMENT, SURPRISE **2** : a cause of or occasion for wonder **3** : curiosity about something

won·drous \'wən-drəs\ *adj* : WONDERFUL, MARVELOUS ⟨a ~ feat⟩ — **won·drous·ly** *adv* — **won·drous·ness** *n*

wonk \'wäŋk, 'wȯŋk\ *n* : one who works in a specialized usu. intellectual field ⟨computer ~s⟩

¹wont \'wȯnt, 'wōnt\ *adj* [ME *woned, wont*, fr. pp. of *wonen* to dwell, be used to, fr. OE *wunian*] **1** : ACCUSTOMED, USED ⟨as we are ~ to do⟩ **2** : INCLINED, APT

²wont *n* : CUSTOM, USAGE, HABIT ⟨according to her ~⟩

won't \'wōnt\ : will not

wont·ed \'wȯn-təd, 'wōn-\ *adj* : ACCUSTOMED, CUSTOMARY ⟨his ~ courtesy⟩

woo \'wü\ *vb* **1** : to try to gain the love of : COURT **2** : SOLICIT, ENTREAT **3** : to try to gain or bring about ⟨~ public favor⟩ — **woo·er** *n*

¹wood \'wu̇d\ *n* **1** : a dense growth of trees usu. larger than a grove and smaller than a forest — often used in pl. **2** : a hard fibrous substance that is basically xylem and forms the bulk of trees and shrubs beneath the bark; *also* : this material fit or prepared for some use (as burning or building) **3** : something made of wood

²wood *adj* **1** : WOODEN **2** : suitable for holding, cutting, or working with wood **3** *or* **woods** \'wu̇dz\ : living or growing in woods

³wood *vb* **1** : to supply or load with wood esp. for fuel **2** : to cover with a growth of trees

wood alcohol *n* : METHANOL

wood·bine \'wu̇d-ˌbīn\ *n* : any of several honeysuckles; *also* : VIRGINIA CREEPER

wood·block \-ˌbläk\ *n* : WOODCUT

wood·chop·per \-ˌchä-pər\ *n* : one engaged esp. in chopping down trees

wood·chuck \-ˌchək\ *n* : a thickset grizzled marmot of Alaska, Canada, and the northeastern U.S.

wood·cock \'wu̇d-ˌkäk\ *n, pl* **woodcocks** : a brown eastern No. American game bird with a short neck and long bill that is related to the snipe; *also* : a related and similar Old World bird

wood·craft \-ˌkraft\ *n* **1** : skill and practice in matters relating to the woods and esp. in how to take care of oneself in them **2** : skill in shaping or constructing articles from wood

wood·cut \-ˌkət\ *n* **1** : a relief printing surface engraved on a block of wood **2** : a print from a woodcut

wood·cut·ter \-ˌkə-tər\ *n* : a person who cuts wood

wood duck *n* : a showy crested American duck of which the male has iridescent multicolored plumage

wood·ed \'wu̇-dəd\ *adj* : covered with woods or trees ⟨~ slopes⟩

wood·en \'wu̇-dᵊn\ *adj* **1** : made of wood **2** : lacking flexibility : awkwardly stiff — **wood·en·ly** *adv* — **wood·en·ness** *n*

wood·en·ware \'wu̇-dᵊn-ˌwer\ *n* : articles made of wood for domestic use

wood·land \'wu̇d-lənd, -ˌland\ *n* : land covered with trees : FOREST — **woodland** *adj*

wood·lot \'wu̇d-ˌlät\ *n* : a restricted area of woodland usu. privately kept to meet fuel and timber needs

wood louse *n* : any of various small flat crustaceans that live esp. in ground litter and under stones and bark

wood·man \'wu̇d-mən\ *n* : WOODSMAN

wood·note \-ˌnōt\ *n* : verbal expression that is natural and artless

wood nymph *n* : a nymph living in the woods

wood·peck·er \'wu̇d-ˌpe-kər\ *n* : any of numerous usu. brightly marked climbing birds with stiff spiny tail feathers and a chisellike bill used to drill into trees for insects

wood·pile \-ˌpī(-ə)l\ *n* : a pile of wood and esp. firewood

wood rat *n* : PACK RAT

wood·shed \-ˌshed\ *n* : a shed for storing wood and esp. firewood

woods·man \'wu̇dz-mən\ *n* : a person who frequents or works in the woods; *esp* : one skilled in woodcraft

woodsy \'wu̇d-zē\ *adj* **woods·i·er; -est** : relating to or suggestive of woods ⟨a ～ odor⟩

wood·wind \'wu̇d-ˌwind\ *n* : one of a group of wind instruments including flutes, clarinets, oboes, bassoons, and sometimes saxophones

wood·work \-ˌwərk\ *n* : work made of wood; *esp* : interior fittings (as moldings or stairways) of wood

woody \'wu̇-dē\ *adj* **wood·i·er; -est 1** : abounding or overgrown with woods ⟨a ～ trail⟩ **2** : of or containing wood or wood fibers ⟨～ plants⟩ **3** : characteristic or suggestive of wood — **wood·i·ness** \'wu̇-dē-nəs\ *n*

woof \'wu̇f\ *n* [alter. of ME *oof*, fr. OE *ōwef*, fr. ō- (fr. *on* on) + *wefan* to weave] **1** : WEFT 1 **2** : a woven fabric; *also* : its texture

woof·er \'wu̇-fər\ *n* : a loudspeaker that reproduces sounds of low pitch

wool \'wu̇l\ *n* **1** : the soft wavy or curly hair of some mammals and esp. the domestic sheep; *also* : something (as a textile or garment) made of wool **2** : material that resembles a mass of wool — **wooled** \'wu̇ld\ *adj*

¹wool·en *or* **wool·len** \'wu̇-lən\ *adj* **1** : made of wool **2** : of or relating to the manufacture or sale of woolen products ⟨～ mills⟩

²woolen *or* **woollen** *n* **1** : a fabric made of wool **2** : garments of woolen fabric — usu. used in pl.

wool·gath·er·ing \-ˌga-thə-riŋ\ *n* : idle daydreaming

¹wool·ly *also* **wooly** \'wu̇-lē\ *adj* **wool·li·er; -est 1** : of, relating to, or bearing wool **2** : consisting of or resembling wool **3** : mentally confused ⟨～ thinking⟩ **4** : marked by a lack of order or restraint ⟨the wild and ～ West⟩

²wool·ly *also* **wool·ie** *or* **wooly** \'wu̇-lē\ *n, pl* **wool·lies** : a garment made from wool; *esp* : underclothing of knitted wool — usu. used in pl.

woolly adel·gid \-ə-ˈdel-jəd\ *n* : either of two aphids accidentally introduced into No. America where they are serious pests of firs and hemlocks

woolly bear *n* : any of numerous very hairy moth caterpillars

woolly mammoth *n* : a heavy-coated mammoth formerly inhabiting colder parts of the northern hemisphere

woo·zy \'wü-zē\ *adj* **woo·zi·er; -est 1** : BEFUDDLED **2** : somewhat dizzy, nauseated, or weak **3** : somewhat indistinct or unfocused : FUZZY — **woo·zi·ness** \'wü-zē-nəs\ *n*

¹word \'wərd\ *n* **1** : something that is said; *esp* : a brief remark **2** : a speech sound or series of speech sounds that communicates a meaning; *also* : a graphic representation of such a sound or series of sounds **3** : ORDER, COMMAND **4** *often cap* : the 2d person of the Trinity; *also* : GOSPEL **5** : NEWS, INFORMATION **6** : PROMISE **7** *pl* : QUARREL, DISPUTE **8** : a verbal signal : PASSWORD — **word·less** *adj*

²word *vb* : to express in words : PHRASE

word·age \'wər-dij\ *n* **1** : WORDS **2** : number of words **3** : WORDING

word·book \'wərd-ˌbu̇k\ *n* : VOCABULARY, DICTIONARY

word·ing \'wər-diŋ\ *n* : verbal expression : PHRASEOLOGY

word of mouth : oral communication

word·play \'wərd-ˌplā\ *n* : playful use of words

word processing *n* : the production of typewritten documents with automated and usu. computerized text-editing equipment — **word process** *vb*

word processor *n* : a keyboard-operated terminal for use in word processing; *also* : software to perform word processing

wordy \'wər-dē\ *adj* **word·i·er; -est** : using many words : VERBOSE ◆ *Synonyms* PROLIX, DIFFUSE, REDUNDANT — **word·i·ness** \-dē-nəs\ *n*

wore *past of* WEAR

¹work \'wərk\ *n* **1** : TOIL, LABOR; *also* : EMPLOYMENT ⟨out of ～⟩ **2** : TASK, JOB ⟨have ～ to do⟩ **3** : the energy used when a force is applied over a given distance **4** : DEED, ACHIEVEMENT **5** : a fortified structure **6** *pl* : engineering structures **7** *pl* : a place where industrial labor is done : PLANT, FACTORY **8** *pl* : the moving parts of a mechanism **9** : something produced by mental effort or physical labor; *esp* : an artistic production (as a book or needlework) **10** : WORKMANSHIP ⟨careless ～⟩ **11** : material in the process of manufacture **12** *pl* : everything possessed, available, or belonging ⟨the whole ～s went overboard⟩; *also* : drastic treatment ⟨gave him the ～s⟩ ◆ *Synonyms* OCCUPATION, EMPLOYMENT, BUSINESS, PURSUIT, CALLING — **in the works** : in process of preparation

²work *adj* **1** : used for work ⟨～ elephants⟩ **2** : suitable or styled for wear while working ⟨～ clothes⟩

³work *vb* **worked** \'wərkt\ *or* **wrought** \'rȯt\; **work·ing 1** : to bring to pass : EFFECT **2** : to fashion or create a useful or desired product through labor or exertion **3** : to prepare for use (as by kneading) **4** : to bring into a desired form by a manufacturing process ⟨～ cold steel⟩ **5** : to set or keep in operation : OPERATE ⟨a pump ～ed by hand⟩ **6** : to solve by reasoning or calculation ⟨～ out a problem⟩ **7** : to cause to toil or labor ⟨～ed the men hard⟩; *also* : to make use of ⟨～ a mine⟩ **8** : to pay for with labor or service ⟨～ off a debt⟩ **9** : to bring or get into some position or condition by stages ⟨the stream ～ed itself clear⟩ ⟨the knot ～ed loose⟩ **10** : CONTRIVE, ARRANGE ⟨～ it so you can leave early⟩ **11** : to practice trickery or cajolery on ⟨～ed the management for a free ticket⟩ **12** : EXCITE, PROVOKE ⟨～ed himself into a rage⟩ **13** : to exert oneself physically or mentally; *esp* : to perform work regularly for wages **14** : to function according to plan or design **15** : to produce a desired effect : SUCCEED ⟨the plan ～ed⟩ **16** : to make way slowly and with difficulty ⟨he ～ed forward through the crowd⟩ **17** : to permit of being worked ⟨this wood ～s easily⟩ **18** : to be in restless motion; *also* : FERMENT 1 — **work on 1** : AFFECT **2** : to try to influence or persuade — **work upon** : to have effect upon : operate on : INFLUENCE

work·able \'wər-kə-bəl\ *adj* **1** : capable of being worked ⟨～ clay⟩ **2** : PRACTICABLE, FEASIBLE — **work·able·ness** *n*

work·a·day \'wər-kə-ˌdā\ *adj* **1** : relating to or suited for working days **2** : PROSAIC, ORDINARY ⟨～ chores⟩

work·a·hol·ic \ˌwər-kə-ˈhȯ-lik, -ˈhä-\ *n* : a compulsive worker

work·bench \-ˌbench\ *n* : a bench on which work esp. of mechanics, machinists, and carpenters is performed

work·book \-ˌbu̇k\ *n* **1** : a worker's manual **2** : a student's book of problems to be answered directly on the pages

work·day \'wərk-ˌdā\ *n* **1** : a day on which work is done as distinguished from a day off **2** : the period of time in a day when work is performed

work·er \'wər-kər\ *n* **1** : one that works; *esp* : a person who works for wages **2** : any of the sexually undeveloped individuals of a colony of social insects (as bees, ants, or termites) that perform the work of the community

workers' compensation *n* : a system of insurance that reimburses an employer for damages paid to an employee who was injured while working

work ethic *n* : belief in work as a moral good

work farm *n* : a farm on which persons guilty of minor law violations are confined

work·horse \'wərk-ˌhȯrs\ *n* **1** : a horse used for hard work **2** : a person who does most of the work of a group task **3** : something that is useful, durable, or dependable

work·house \-ˌhau̇s\ *n* **1** *Brit* : POORHOUSE **2** : a house of correction for persons guilty of minor law violations

¹work·ing \'wər-kiŋ\ *n* **1** : manner of functioning — usu. used in pl. **2** *pl* : an excavation made in mining or tunneling

²working *adj* **1** : engaged in work ⟨a ～ journalist⟩ **2** : adequate to allow work to be done ⟨a ～ majority⟩ ⟨a ～ knowledge of French⟩ **3** : adopted or assumed to help further work or activity ⟨a ～ draft⟩ **4** : spent at work ⟨～ life⟩

work·ing·man \'wər-kiŋ-ˌman\ *n* : WORKER 1

work·man \\'wərk-mən\ *n* **1** : WORKER 1 **2** : ARTISAN, CRAFTSMAN

work·man·like \\-,līk\ *adj* : worthy of a good workman : SKILLFUL

work·man·ship \\-,ship\ *n* : the art or skill of a workman : CRAFTSMANSHIP; *also* : the quality of a piece of work ⟨a vase of exquisite ∼⟩

work·out \\'wərk-,aút\ *n* **1** : a practice or exercise to test or improve one's fitness, ability, or performance **2** : a test or trial to determine ability or capacity or suitability

work out *vb* **1** : to bring about esp. by resolving difficulties **2** : DEVELOP, ELABORATE **3** : to prove effective, practicable, or suitable ⟨our plan didn't *work out*⟩ **4** : to amount to a total or calculated figure — used with *at* **5** : to engage in a workout

work·place \\'wərk-,plās\ *n* : a place (as an office) where work is done

work·room \\'wərk-,rüm, -,rùm\ *n* : a room used for work

work·shop \\-,shäp\ *n* **1** : a shop where manufacturing or handicrafts are carried on **2** : a seminar emphasizing exchange of ideas and practical methods

work·sta·tion \\-,stā-shən\ *n* : an area with equipment for the performance of a specialized task; *also* : a personal computer usu. connected to a computer network

world \\'wərld\ *n* [ME, fr. OE *woruld* human existence, this world, age, fr. a prehistoric compound whose first constituent is represented by OE *wer* man and whose second constituent is akin to OE *eald* old] **1** : the earth with its inhabitants and all things upon it **2** : people in general : MANKIND **3** : human affairs ⟨withdraw from the ∼⟩ **4** : UNIVERSE, CREATION **5** : a state of existence : scene of life and action ⟨the ∼ of the future⟩ **6** : a distinctive class of persons or their sphere of interest ⟨the musical ∼⟩ **7** : a part or section of the earth or its inhabitants by itself **8** : a great number or quantity ⟨a ∼ of troubles⟩ **9** : a celestial body

world–beat·er \\-,bē-tər\ *n* : one that excels all others of its kind : CHAMPION

world-class *adj* : of the highest caliber in the world ⟨a ∼ athlete⟩

world·ling \\-liŋ\ *n* : a person absorbed in the concerns of the present world

world·ly \\-lē\ *adj* **1** : of, relating to, or devoted to this world and its pursuits rather than to religion or spiritual affairs **2** : WORLDLY-WISE, SOPHISTICATED — **world·li·ness** \\-lē-nəs\ *n*

world·ly–wise \\-,wīz\ *adj* : possessing a practical and often shrewd understanding of human affairs

world·wide \\'wərld-'wīd\ *adj* : extended throughout the entire world — **worldwide** *adv*

World Wide Web *n* : a part of the Internet usu. accessed through a browser and containing files connected by hyperlinks

¹worm \\'wərm\ *n* **1** : any of various small long usu. naked and soft-bodied round or flat invertebrate animals (as an earthworm, nematode, tapeworm, or maggot) **2** : a human being who is an object of contempt, loathing, or pity : WRETCH **3** : something that inwardly torments or devours worms **4** *pl* : infestation with or disease caused by parasitic worms **5** : a spiral or wormlike thing (as the thread of a screw) — **worm·like** \\-,līk\ *adj* — **wormy** *adj*

²worm *vb* **1** : to move or cause to move or proceed slowly and deviously **2** : to insinuate or introduce (oneself) by devious or subtle means **3** : to obtain or extract by artful or insidious pleading, asking, or persuading ⟨∼*ed* the truth out of him⟩ **4** : to treat (an animal) with a drug to destroy or expel parasitic worms

worm–eat·en \\'wərm-,ē-t³n\ *adj* : eaten or burrowed by worms

worm gear *n* : a mechanical linkage consisting of a short rotating screw whose threads mesh with the teeth of a gear wheel

worm·hole \\'wərm-,hōl\ *n* : a hole or passage burrowed by a worm

worm·wood \\-,wùd\ *n* **1** : any of a genus of aromatic woody plants (as a sagebrush); *esp* : one of Europe used in absinthe **2** : something bitter or grievous : BITTERNESS

worn *past part of* WEAR

worn–out \\'wōrn-'aút\ *adj* : exhausted or used up by or as if by wear

wor·ri·some \\'wər-ē-səm\ *adj* **1** : causing distress or worry ⟨∼ news⟩ **2** : inclined to worry or fret ⟨a ∼ mother⟩

¹wor·ry \\'wər-ē\ *vb* **wor·ried; wor·ry·ing 1** : to shake and mangle with the teeth ⟨a terrier ∼*ing* a rat⟩ **2** : to make anxious or upset ⟨her poor health *worries* me⟩ **3** : to feel or express great care or anxiety : FRET ⟨∼*ing* about his health⟩ — **wor·ri·er** *n*

²worry *n, pl* **worries 1** : ANXIETY **2** : a cause of anxiety : TROUBLE

wor·ry·wart \\'wər-ē-,wòrt\ *n* : one who is inclined to worry unduly

¹worse \\'wərs\ *adj, comparative of* BAD, *or of* ILL **1** : bad or evil in a greater degree : less good **2** : more unfavorable, unpleasant, or painful; *also* : SICKER

²worse *n* **1** : one that is worse **2** : a greater degree of ill or badness ⟨a turn for the ∼⟩

³worse *adv, comparative of* BAD, *or of* ILL : in a worse manner : to a worse extent or degree

wors·en \\'wər-s³n\ *vb* : to make or become worse ⟨the rash ∼*ed*⟩

¹wor·ship \\'wər-shəp\ *n* [ME *worshipe* worthiness, respect, reverence paid to a divine being, fr. OE *weorthscipe* worthiness, respect, fr. *weorth* worthy, worth + -*scipe* -ship, suffix denoting quality or condition] **1** *chiefly Brit* : a person of importance — used as a title for officials **2** : reverence toward a divine being or supernatural power; *also* : the expression of such reverence **3** : extravagant respect or admiration or devotion ⟨∼ of the dollar⟩

²worship *vb* **-shipped; -shiped; -shipp·ing** *or* **-ship·ing 1** : to honor or reverence as a divine being or supernatural power **2** : IDOLIZE ⟨∼*s* his brother⟩ **3** : to perform or take part in worship — **wor·ship·er** *or* **wor·ship·per** *n*

wor·ship·ful \\'wər-shəp-fəl\ *adj* **1** *archaic* : NOTABLE, DISTINGUISHED **2** *chiefly Brit* — used as a title for various persons or groups of rank or distinction **3** : VENERATING, WORSHIPING

¹worst \\'wərst\ *adj, superlative of* BAD, *or of* ILL **1** : most bad, evil, ill, or corrupt ⟨the ∼ criminals⟩ **2** : most unfavorable, unpleasant, or painful ⟨the ∼ scenario⟩; *also* : most unsuitable, faulty, or unattractive **3** : least skillful or efficient ⟨her ∼ students⟩

²worst *adv, superlative of* ILL, *or of* BAD, *or* BADLY **1** : to the extreme degree of badness or inferiority ⟨the ∼ dressed person⟩ : in the worst manner **2** : MOST ⟨those who need help ∼⟩

³worst *n* : one that is worst

⁴worst *vb* : DEFEAT

wor·sted \\'wùs-təd, 'wər-stəd\ *n* [ME, fr. *Worsted* (now *Worstead*), England] : a smooth compact yarn from long wool fibers; *also* : a fabric made from such yarn

wort \\'wərt, 'wòrt\ *n* : a sweet liquid drained from mash and fermented to form beer and whiskey

¹worth \\'wərth\ *n* **1** : monetary value; *also* : the equivalent of a specified amount or figure ⟨$5 ∼ of gas⟩ **2** : the value of something measured by its qualities **3** : MERIT, EXCELLENCE

²worth *prep* **1** : equal in value to; *also* : having possessions or income equal to **2** : deserving of ⟨well ∼ the effort⟩

worth·less \\'wərth-ləs\ *adj* **1** : lacking worth : VALUELESS; *also* : USELESS **2** : LOW, DESPICABLE — **worth·less·ness** *n*

worth·while \\'wərth-'hwī(-ə)l\ *adj* : being worth the time or effort spent

¹wor·thy \\'wər-thē\ *adj* **wor·thi·er; -est 1** : having worth or value : ESTIMABLE ⟨a ∼ cause⟩ **2** : HONORABLE, MERITORIOUS ⟨my ∼ opponent⟩ **3** : having sufficient

worm gear

worth ⟨~ of the honor⟩ — **wor·thi·ly** \'wər-thə-lē\ *adv* — **wor·thi·ness** \-thē-nəs\ *n*

²**worthy** *n, pl* **worthies** : a worthy person

would \'wud\ *past of* WILL   **1** *archaic* : wish for : WANT   **2** : strongly desire : WISH ⟨I ~ I were young again⟩   **3** — used as an auxiliary to express (1) preference ⟨~ rather run than fight⟩, (2) wish, desire, or intent ⟨those who ~ forbid gambling⟩, (3) habitual action ⟨we ~ meet often for lunch⟩, (4) a contingency or possibility ⟨if he were coming, he ~ be here by now⟩, (5) probability ⟨~ have won if he hadn't tripped⟩, or (6) a request ⟨~ you help us⟩   **4** : COULD   **5** : SHOULD

would–be \'wud-'bē\ *adj* : desiring or pretending to be ⟨a ~ artist⟩

¹**wound** \'wünd\ *n*   **1** : an injury involving cutting or breaking of bodily tissue (as by violence, accident, or surgery)   **2** : an injury or hurt to feelings or reputation

²**wound** *vb* : to inflict a wound to or in

³**wound** \'waund\ *past and past part of* WIND

wove *past of* WEAVE

woven *past part of* WEAVE

¹**wow** \'waú\ *n* : a striking success : HIT

²**wow** *vb* : to arouse enthusiastic approval ⟨~ed the critics⟩

WP *abbr*   word processing; word processor

WPM *abbr*   words per minute

wpn *abbr*   weapon

wrack \'rak\ *n* [ME, fr. OE *wræc* misery, punishment, something driven by the sea] : violent or total destruction

wraith \'rāth\ *n, pl* **wraiths** \'rāths, 'rāthz\   **1** : GHOST, SPECTER   **2** : an insubstantial appearance : SHADOW

¹**wran·gle** \'raŋ-gəl\ *vb* **wran·gled; wran·gling**   **1** : to quarrel angrily or peevishly : BICKER   **2** : ARGUE   **3** : to obtain by persistent arguing   **4** : to herd and care for (livestock) on the range — **wran·gler** *n*

²**wrangle** *n* : an angry, noisy, or prolonged dispute; *also* : CONTROVERSY

¹**wrap** \'rap\ *vb* **wrapped; wrap·ping**   **1** : to cover esp. by winding or folding   **2** : to envelop and secure for transportation or storage   **3** : to enclose wholly : ENFOLD   **4** : to coil, fold, draw, or twine about something   **5** : SURROUND, ENVELOP ⟨*wrapped* in mystery⟩   **6** : INVOLVE, ENGROSS ⟨*wrapped* up in a hobby⟩   **7** : to complete filming or recording

²**wrap** *n*   **1** : WRAPPER, WRAPPING   **2** : an article of clothing that may be wrapped around a person   **3** *pl* : SECRECY ⟨kept under ~s⟩   **4** : completion of filming or recording

wrap·around \'ra-pə-,raund\ *n* : a garment (as a dress) adjusted to the figure by wrapping around

wrap·per \'ra-pər\ *n*   **1** : that in which something is wrapped   **2** : one that wraps   **3** : an article of clothing worn wrapped around the body

wrap·ping \'ra-piŋ\ *n* : something used to wrap an object : WRAPPER

wrap–up \'rap-,əp\ *n* : SUMMARY

wrap up *vb*   **1** : SUMMARIZE, SUM UP   **2** : to bring to a usu. successful conclusion

wrasse \'ras\ *n* : any of a large family of usu. brightly colored marine fishes including many food fishes

wrath \'rath\ *n*   **1** : violent anger : RAGE   **2** : divine punishment ✦ **Synonyms** INDIGNATION, IRE, FURY, ANGER

wrath·ful \-fəl\ *adj*   **1** : filled with wrath : very angry   **2** : showing, marked by, or arising from anger — **wrath·ful·ly** *adv* — **wrath·ful·ness** *n*

wreak \'rēk\ *vb* [ME *wreken*, fr. OE *wrecan* to drive, punish, avenge]   **1** : to exact as a punishment : INFLICT ⟨~ vengeance on an enemy⟩   **2** : to give free scope or rein to ⟨~ed his wrath⟩   **3** : BRING ABOUT, CAUSE ⟨~ havoc⟩

wreath \'rēth\ *n, pl* **wreaths** \'rēthz, 'rēths\ : a circular band of flowers or leaves usu. for decoration; *also* : something having a circular or coiling form ⟨a ~ of smoke⟩

wreathe \'rēth\ *vb* **wreathed; wreath·ing**   **1** : to shape or take on the shape of a wreath   **2** : to crown, decorate, or cover with or as if with a wreath ⟨a face *wreathed* in smiles⟩

¹**wreck** \'rek\ *n*   **1** : something (as goods) cast up on the land by the sea after a shipwreck   **2** : SHIPWRECK   **3** : a destructive crash ⟨a car ~⟩   **4** : the action of breaking up or destroying something   **5** : broken remains (as of a vehicle after a crash)   **6** : something disabled or in a state of ruin; *also* : an individual broken in health or strength, or spirits ⟨he's a nervous ~⟩

²**wreck** *vb*   **1** : SHIPWRECK   **2** : to ruin or damage by breaking up : involve in disaster or ruin

wreck·age \'re-kij\ *n*   **1** : the act of wrecking : the state of being wrecked : RUIN   **2** : the remains of a wreck

wreck·er \'re-kər\ *n*   **1** : one that searches for or works upon the wrecks of ships   **2** : TOW TRUCK   **3** : one that wrecks; *esp* : one whose work is the demolition of buildings

wren \'ren\ *n* : any of a family of small mostly brown singing birds with short wings and often a tail that points upward

¹**wrench** \'rench\ *vb*   **1** : to move with a violent twist   **2** : to pull, strain, or tighten with violent twisting or force   **3** : to injure or disable by a violent twisting or straining ⟨~ed her back⟩   **4** : to snatch forcibly : WREST

²**wrench** *n*   **1** : a forcible twisting; *also* : an injury (as to one's ankle) by twisting   **2** : a tool for holding, twisting, or turning (as nuts or bolts)

¹**wrest** \'rest\ *vb*   **1** : to pull or move by a forcible twisting movement   **2** : to gain with difficulty by or as if by force or violence ⟨~ control of the government from the dictator⟩

²**wrest** *n* : a forcible twist : WRENCH

¹**wres·tle** \'re-səl, 'ra-\ *vb* **wres·tled; wres·tling**   **1** : to grapple with and try to throw down an opponent   **2** : to compete against in wrestling   **3** : to struggle for control (as of something difficult) ⟨~ with a problem⟩ — **wres·tler** \'res-lər, 'ras-\ *n*

²**wrestle** *n* : the action or an instance of wrestling : STRUGGLE

wres·tling \'res-liŋ\ *n* : the sport in which two opponents wrestle each other

wretch \'rech\ *n* [ME *wrecche*, fr. OE *wrecca* outcast, exile]   **1** : a miserable unhappy person   **2** : a base, despicable, or vile person

wretch·ed \'re-chəd\ *adj*   **1** : deeply afflicted, dejected, or distressed : MISERABLE   **2** : WOEFUL, GRIEVOUS ⟨a ~ accident⟩   **3** : DESPICABLE ⟨a ~ trick⟩   **4** : poor in quality or ability : INFERIOR ⟨~ workmanship⟩ — **wretch·ed·ly** *adv* — **wretch·ed·ness** *n*

wrig·gle \'ri-gəl\ *vb* **wrig·gled; wrig·gling**   **1** : to twist or move to and fro like a worm : SQUIRM ⟨*wriggled* in his chair⟩ ⟨~ your toes⟩; *also* : to move along by twisting and turning ⟨a snake *wriggled* along the path⟩   **2** : to extricate oneself as if by wriggling ⟨~ out of difficulty⟩ — **wriggle** *n*

wrig·gler *n*   **1** : one that wriggles   **2** : WIGGLER 1

wring \'riŋ\ *vb* **wrung** \'rəŋ\; **wring·ing** \'riŋ-iŋ\   **1** : to squeeze or twist esp. so as to make dry or to extract moisture or liquid ⟨~ wet clothes⟩   **2** : to get by or as if by twisting or pressing ⟨~ the truth out of him⟩   **3** : to twist so as to strain or sprain : CONTORT ⟨~ his neck⟩   **4** : to twist together as a sign of anguish ⟨*wrung* her hands⟩   **5** : to affect painfully as if by wringing : TORMENT ⟨her plight *wrung* my heart⟩

wring·er \'riŋ-ər\ *n* : one that wrings; *esp* : a device for squeezing out liquid or moisture ⟨clothes ~⟩

¹**wrin·kle** \'riŋ-kəl\ *n*   **1** : a crease or small fold on a smooth surface (as in the skin or in cloth)   **2** : a clever or new method, trick, or idea — **wrin·kly** \-k(ə-)lē\ *adj*

²**wrinkle** *vb* **wrin·kled; wrin·kling** : to develop or cause to develop wrinkles

wrist \'rist\ *n* : the joint or region between the hand and the arm; *also* : a corresponding part in a lower animal

wrist·band \-,band\ *n* : a band or the part of a sleeve encircling the wrist

wrist·let \-lət\ *n* : WRISTBAND; *esp* : a close-fitting knitted band attached to the top of a glove or the end of a sleeve

wrist·watch \-,wäch\ *n* : a small watch attached to a bracelet or strap to fasten about the wrist

writ \'rit\ *n*   **1** : something written   **2** : a written legal order signed by a court officer

writ·able \'rī-tə-bəl\ *adj* : being an electronic storage medium on which it is possible to introduce new data ⟨a ~ DVD⟩

write \'rīt\ *vb* **wrote** \'rōt\; **writ·ten** \'ri-t°n\ *also* **writ** \'rit\; **writ·ing** \'rī-tiŋ\ [ME, fr. OE *wrītan* to scratch, draw, inscribe]   **1** : to form characters, letters, or words on a surface ⟨learn to read and ~⟩   **2** : to form the letters or the words of ⟨~ your name⟩ ⟨~ a check⟩   **3** : to put down on paper : express in writing   **4** : to make up and set down for others to read ⟨∼ a book⟩ ⟨∼ music⟩ **5** : to write a letter to **6** : to communicate by letter : CORRESPOND

write–in \'rīt-,in\ n : a vote cast by writing in the name of a candidate; *also* : a candidate whose name is written in

write in vb : to insert (a name not listed on a ballot) in an appropriate space; *also* : to cast (a vote) in this manner

write off vb : to eliminate (an asset) from a bookkeeping record : enter as a loss or expense

writ•er \'rī-tər\ n : one that writes esp. as a business or occupation : AUTHOR

writer's cramp n : a painful spasmodic contraction of muscles of the hand or fingers brought on by excessive writing

write–up \'rīt-,əp\ n : a written account (as in a newspaper); *esp* : a flattering article

writhe \'rīth\ vb **writhed; with•ing** **1** : to twist and turn this way and that ⟨∼ in pain⟩ **2** : to suffer with shame or confusion

writing n **1** : the act of one that writes; *also* : HANDWRITING **2** : something that is written or printed **3** : a style or form of composition **4** : the occupation of a writer

Writings \'rī-tiŋz\ n pl : the third part of the Jewish scriptures

wrnt abbr warrant

¹**wrong** \'rȯŋ\ n **1** : an injurious, unfair, or unjust act **2** : a violation of the legal rights of another person **3** : something that is wrong : wrong principles, practices, or conduct ⟨know right from ∼⟩ **4** : the state, position, or fact of being wrong

²**wrong** adj **wrong•er** \'rȯŋ-ər\; **wrong•est** \'rȯŋ-əst\ **1** : SINFUL, IMMORAL **2** : not right according to a standard or code : IMPROPER **3** : INCORRECT ⟨a ∼ solution⟩ **4** : UNSATISFACTORY **5** : UNSUITABLE, INAPPROPRIATE **6** : constituting a surface that is considered the back, bottom, inside, or reverse of something ⟨iron only on the ∼ side of the fabric⟩ ✦ **Synonyms** FALSE, ERRONEOUS, INCORRECT, INACCURATE, UNTRUE — **wrong•ly** adv

³**wrong** adv **1** : INCORRECTLY **2** : in a wrong direction, manner, or relation

⁴**wrong** vb **wronged; wrong•ing** \'rȯŋ-iŋ\ **1** : to do wrong to : INJURE, HARM **2** : to treat unjustly : DISHONOR, MALIGN ✦ **Synonyms** OPPRESS, PERSECUTE, AGGRIEVE

wrong•do•er \'rȯŋ-,dü-ər\ n : a person who does wrong and esp. moral wrong — **wrong•do•ing** \-,dü-iŋ\ n

wrong•ful \'rȯŋ-fəl\ adj **1** : WRONG, UNJUST **2** : UNLAWFUL — **wrong•ful•ly** adv — **wrong•ful•ness** n

wrong•head•ed \-'he-dəd\ adj : stubborn in clinging to wrong opinion or principles — **wrong•head•ed•ly** adv — **wrong•head•ed•ness** n

wrote past of WRITE

wroth \'rȯth, 'rōth\ adj : filled with wrath : ANGRY

wrought \'rȯt\ adj [ME, fr. pp. of *worken* to work] **1** : FASHIONED, FORMED ⟨carefully ∼ essays⟩ **2** : ORNAMENTED **3** : beaten into shape by tools : HAMMERED ⟨∼ metals⟩ **4** : deeply stirred : EXCITED ⟨gets easily ∼ up⟩

wrung past and past part of WRING

wry \'rī\ adj **wry•er** \'rī-ər\; **wry•est** \'rī-əst\ **1** : having a bent or twisted shape ⟨a ∼ smile⟩; *also* : turned abnormally to one side : CONTORTED ⟨a ∼ neck⟩ **2** : cleverly and often ironically humorous — **wry•ly** adv — **wryness** n

wry–neck \'rī-,nek\ n **1** : either of two Old World woodpeckers that differ from typical woodpeckers in having a peculiar manner of twisting the head and neck **2** : an abnormal twisting of the neck and head to one side caused by muscle spasms

WSW abbr west-southwest

wt abbr weight

wurst \'wərst, 'wu̇rst\ n : SAUSAGE

wuss \'wu̇s\ n : WIMP — **wussy** \'wu̇-sē\ adj

WV or **W Va** abbr West Virginia

WW abbr World War

w/w abbr wall-to-wall

WY or **Wyo** abbr Wyoming

WYS•I•WYG \'wi-zē-,wig\ adj [*what you see is what you get*] : of, relating to, or being a computer display that shows a document exactly as it will appear when printed out

¹**x** \'eks\ n, pl **x's** or **xs** \'ek-səz\ often cap **1** : the 24th letter of the English alphabet **2** : ten in Roman numerals **3** : an unknown quantity

²**x** vb **x-ed** also **x'd** or **xed** \'ekst\; **x-ing** or **x'ing** \'ek-siŋ\ : to cancel or obliterate with a series of x's — usu. used with *out*

³**x** abbr **1** ex **2** experimental **3** extra

⁴**x** symbol **1** times ⟨3 x 2 is 6⟩ **2** by ⟨a 3 x 5 index card⟩ **3** often cap power of magnification

Xan•a•du \'za-nə-,dü, -,dyü\ n [fr. *Xanadu*, locality in *Kubla Khan* (1798), poem by Eng. poet Samuel Taylor Coleridge †1834] : an idyllic, exotic, or luxurious place

Xan•thip•pe \zan-'thi-pē, -'ti-\ or **Xan•tip•pe** \-'ti-pē\ n [Gk *Xanthippē*, shrewish wife of Socrates] : an ill-tempered woman

x–ax•is \'eks-,ak-səs\ n : the axis of a graph or of a system of coordinates in a plane parallel to which abscissas are measured

X–C abbr cross-country

X chromosome n : a sex chromosome that usu. occurs paired in each female cell and single in each male cell in organisms (as humans) in which the male normally has two unlike sex chromosomes

Xe symbol xenon

xe•non \'zē-,nän, 'ze-\ n [Gk, neut. of *xenos* strange] : a heavy gaseous chemical element occurring in minute quantities in air

xe•no•pho•bia \,ze-nə-'fō-bē-ə, ,zē-\ n : fear and hatred of strangers or foreigners or of what is strange or foreign —

xe•no•phobe \'ze-nə-,fōb, 'zē-\ n — **xe•no•pho•bic** \,zenə-'fō-bik, ,zē-\ adj

xe•ric \'zir-ik, 'zer-\ adj : characterized by or requiring only a small amount of moisture ⟨a ∼ habitat⟩

xeri•scape \'zir-ə-,skāp, 'zer-\ n, often cap : a landscaping method utilizing water-conserving techniques

xe•rog•ra•phy \zə-'rä-grə-fē\ n : a process for copying printed matter by the action of light on an electrically charged surface in which the latent image is developed with a powder — **xe•ro•graph•ic** \,zir-ə-'gra-fik\ adj

xe•ro•phyte \'zir-ə-,fīt\ n : a plant adapted for growth with a limited water supply — **xe•ro•phyt•ic** \,zir-ə-'fitik\ adj

xi \'zī, 'ksī\ n : the 14th letter of the Greek alphabet — Ξ or ξ

XL abbr **1** extra large **2** extra long

Xmas \'kris-məs also 'eks-məs\ n [X (symbol for *Christ*, fr. the Gk letter chi (X), initial of *Christos* Christ) + *-mas* (in *Christmas*)] : CHRISTMAS

XML \,eks-(,)em-'el\ n : a markup language that indicates the structural type of data

XO abbr executive officer

x–ra•di•a•tion \,eks-,rā-dē-'ā-shən\ n, often cap **1** : exposure to X-rays **2** : radiation consisting of X-rays

x–ray \'eks-,rā\ vb, often cap : to examine, treat, or photograph with X-rays

X–ray \'eks-,rā\ n **1** : a radiation with an extremely short wavelength of less than 100 angstroms that is able to penetrate through various thicknesses of solids and to act on

photographic film **2** : a photograph taken with X-rays —
X–ray *adj*
XS *abbr* extra small
xu \ˈsü\ *n, pl* **xu** — see *dong* at MONEY table
xy·lem \ˈzī-ləm, -ˌlem\ *n* : a woody tissue of vascular plants
that transports water and dissolved materials upward,
functions in support and storage, and lies central to the
phloem
xy·lo·phone \ˈzī-lə-ˌfōn\ *n* [Gk *xylon* wood + *phōnē* voice,
sound] : a musical instrument consisting of a series of
wooden bars graduated in length to produce the musical
scale, supported on belts of straw or felt, and sounded by
striking with two small wooden hammers — **xy·lo·phon·
ist** \-ˌfō-nist\ *n*

xylophone

Y

¹**y** \ˈwī\ *n, pl* **y's** *or* **ys** \ˈwīz\ *often cap* : the 25th letter of the
English alphabet
²**y** *abbr* **1** yard **2** year
¹**Y** \ˈwī\ *n* : YMCA, YWCA
²**Y** *symbol* yttrium
¹**-y** *also* **-ey** \ē\ *adj suffix* **1** : characterized by : full of
⟨dirt*y*⟩ ⟨clay*ey*⟩ **2** : having the character of : composed
of ⟨ic*y*⟩ **3** : like : like that of ⟨home*y*⟩ ⟨wintr*y*⟩ ⟨stag*y*⟩
4 : tending or inclined to ⟨sleep*y*⟩ ⟨chatt*y*⟩ **5** : giving occasion for (specified) action ⟨tear*y*⟩ **6** : performing
(specified) action ⟨curl*y*⟩
²**-y** \ē\ *n suffix, pl* **-ies** **1** : state : condition : quality ⟨beg-
gar*y*⟩ **2** : activity, place of business, or goods dealt with
⟨laundr*y*⟩ **3** : whole body or group ⟨soldier*y*⟩
³**-y** *n suffix, pl* **-ies** : instance of a (specified) action ⟨en-
treat*y*⟩ ⟨inquir*y*⟩
YA *abbr* young adult
¹**yacht** \ˈyät\ *n* [obs. D *jaght*, fr. Middle Low German *jacht*,
short for *jachtschip*, lit., hunting ship] : a usu. large recreational watercraft
²**yacht** *vb* : to race or cruise in a yacht
yacht·ing \ˈyä-tiŋ\ *n* : the sport of racing or cruising in a
yacht
yachts·man \ˈyäts-mən\ *n* : a person who owns or sails a
yacht
ya·hoo \ˈyä-hü, ˈyä-\ *n, pl* **yahoos** [fr. *Yahoo*, one of a race
of brutes having the form of men in Jonathan Swift's *Gul-
liver's Travels*] : a boorish, crass, or stupid person
Yah·weh \ˈyä-ˌwä\ *also* **Yah·veh** \-ˌvä\ *n* : GOD 1 — used
esp. by the Hebrews
¹**yak** \ˈyak\ *n, pl* **yaks** *also* **yak** : a large long-haired wild or
domesticated ox of Tibet and adjacent Asian uplands
²**yak** *also* **yack** \ˈyak\ *n* : persistent or voluble talk — **yak**
also **yack** *vb*
yam \ˈyam\ *n* **1** : the edible starchy root of various twining plants used as a staple food in tropical areas; *also* : a
plant that produces yams **2** : a usu. deep orange sweet
potato
yam·mer \ˈya-mər\ *vb* [ME *yameren*, alter. of *yomeren* to
murmur, be sad, fr. OE *gēomrian*] **1** : WHIMPER **2**
: CHATTER — **yammer** *n*
¹**yank** \ˈyaŋk\ *vb* : to pull with a quick vigorous movement
²**yank** *n* : a strong sudden pull : JERK
Yank \ˈyaŋk\ *n* : YANKEE
Yan·kee \ˈyaŋ-kē\ *n* **1** : a native or inhabitant of New
England; *also* : a native or inhabitant of the northern
U.S. **2** : AMERICAN 2
yan·qui \ˈyäŋ-kē\ *n, often cap* [Sp] : a citizen of the U.S. as
distinguished from a Latin American
¹**yap** \ˈyap\ *vb* **yapped**; **yap·ping** **1** : BARK, YELP **2** : GAB
²**yap** *n* **1** : a quick sharp bark **2** : CHATTER
¹**yard** \ˈyärd\ *n* [ME, fr. OE *geard* enclosure, yard] **1** : a
small enclosed area open to the sky and adjacent to a
building **2** : the grounds of a building **3** : the grounds
surrounding a house usu. covered with grass **4** : an enclosure for livestock **5** : an area set aside for a particular

business or activity **6** : a system of railroad tracks for
storing cars and making up trains
²**yard** *n* [ME *yarde*, fr. OE *gierd* twig, measure, yard] **1** —
see WEIGHT table **2** : a long spar tapered toward the ends
that supports and spreads the head of a sail — **the whole
nine yards** : all of a set of circumstances, conditions, or
details
yard·age \ˈyär-dij\ *n* : an aggregate number of yards; *also*
: the length, extent, or volume of something as measured
in yards
yard·arm \ˈyärd-ˌärm\ *n* : either end of the yard of a
square-rigged ship
yard·man \-mən, -ˌman\ *n* : a person employed in or about
a yard
yard·mas·ter \-ˌmas-tər\ *n* : the person in charge of a railroad yard
yard·stick \-ˌstik\ *n* **1** : a graduated measuring stick three
feet long **2** : a standard for making a critical judgment
: CRITERION ◆ *Synonyms* GAUGE, TOUCHSTONE,
BENCHMARK, MEASURE
yar·mul·ke \ˈyä-mə-kə, ˈyär-, -məl-\ *n* [Yiddish *yarmlke*] : a
skullcap worn esp. by Jewish males in the synagogue and
the home
yarn \ˈyärn\ *n* **1** : a continuous often plied strand composed of fibers or filaments and used in weaving and knitting to form cloth **2** : STORY; *esp* : a tall tale
yar·row \ˈya-rō\ *n* : a strong-scented herb related to the
daisies that has white or pink flowers in flat clusters
yaw \ˈyo\ *vb* : to deviate erratically from a course ⟨the ship
~ed in the heavy seas⟩ — **yaw** *n*
yawl \ˈyol\ *n* : a 2-masted sailboat with the shorter mast aft
of the rudder
¹**yawn** \ˈyon\ *vb* : to open wide; *esp* : to open the mouth
wide and take a deep breath usu. as an involuntary reaction to fatigue or boredom — **yawn·er** *n*
²**yawn** *n* : the act of yawning
yawp *or* **yaup** \ˈyop\ *vb* **1** : to make a raucous noise
: SQUAWK **2** : CLAMOR, COMPLAIN — **yawp·er** *n*
yaws \ˈyoz\ *n pl* : a contagious tropical disease caused by
a spirochete closely resembling the causative agent of
syphilis and marked by skin lesions
y–ax·is \ˈwī-ˌak-səs\ *n* : the axis of a graph or of a system
of coordinates in a plane parallel to which the ordinates
are measured
Yb *symbol* ytterbium
YB *abbr* yearbook
Y chromosome *n* : a sex chromosome that is characteristic of male cells in organisms (as humans) in which the
male typically has two unlike sex chromosomes
yd *abbr* yard
¹**ye** \ˈyē\ *pron* : YOU 1
²**ye** \yē, yə, *originally same as* THE\ *definite article, archaic*
: THE — used by early printers to represent the manuscript word *þe* (*the*)
¹**yea** \ˈyā\ *adv* **1** : YES — used in oral voting **2** : INDEED,
TRULY

²yea *n* : an affirmative vote; *also* : a person casting such a vote

yeah \'yeə, 'yaə\ *adv* : YES

year \'yir\ *n* **1** : the period of about 365¼ solar days required for one revolution of the earth around the sun; *also* : the time in which a planet completes a revolution about the sun **2** : a cycle of 365 or 366 days beginning with January 1; *also* : a calendar year specified usu. by a number **3** *pl* : a time of special significance ⟨their glory ∼s⟩ **4** *pl* : AGE ⟨advanced in ∼s⟩ **5** : a period of time other than a calendar year ⟨the school ∼⟩

year·book \-ˌbu̇k\ *n* **1** : a book published annually esp. as a report **2** : a school publication recording the history and activities of a graduating class

year·ling \'yir-liŋ, 'yər-lən\ *n* **1** : one that is a year old **2** : a racehorse between January of the year after the year in which it was born and the next January

year·long \'yir-ˈlȯŋ\ *adj* : lasting through a year

¹year·ly \'yir-lē\ *adj* : ANNUAL

²yearly *adv* : every year

yearn \'yərn\ *vb* **1** : to feel a longing or craving **2** : to feel tenderness or compassion ♦ *Synonyms* LONG, PINE, HANKER, HUNGER, THIRST

yearn·ing *n* : a tender or urgent longing

year–round \'yir-ˈrau̇nd\ *adj* : effective, employed, or operating for the full year : not seasonal ⟨a ∼ resort⟩

yeast \'yēst\ *n* **1** : a surface froth or a sediment in sugary liquids (as fruit juices) that consists largely of cells of a tiny fungus and is used in making alcoholic liquors and as a leaven in baking **2** : a commercial product containing yeast fungi in a moist or dry medium **3** : a minute one-celled fungus present and functionally active in yeast that reproduces by budding; *also* : any of several similar fungi **4** *archaic* : the foam of waves : SPUME **5** : something that causes ferment or activity

yeast infection *n* : infection of the vagina with an excess growth of a normally present fungus that resembles a yeast

yeasty \'yē-stē\ *adj* **yeast·i·er; -est** **1** : of, relating to, or resembling yeast **2** : UNSETTLED **3** : full of vitality; *also* : FRIVOLOUS

yegg \'yeg\ *n* : one that breaks open safes to steal; *also* : ROBBER

¹yell \'yel\ *vb* : to utter a loud cry or scream : SHOUT — **yell·er** *n*

²yell *n* **1** : SHOUT **2** : a cheer used esp. to encourage an athletic team (as at a college)

¹yel·low \'ye-lō\ *adj* **1** : of the color yellow **2** : having a yellow complexion or skin **3** : SENSATIONAL ⟨∼ journalism⟩ **4** : COWARDLY — **yel·low·ish** \'ye-lə-wish\ *adj*

²yellow *n* **1** : a color between green and orange in the spectrum : the color of ripe lemons or sunflowers **2** : something yellow; *esp* : the yolk of an egg **3** *pl* : any of several plant diseases marked by stunted growth and yellowing of foliage

³yellow *vb* : to make or turn yellow

yellow birch *n* : a No. American birch with thin lustrous gray or yellow bark; *also* : its strong hard wood

yellow fever *n* : an acute infectious viral disease marked by prostration, jaundice, fever, and often hemorrhage and transmitted by a mosquito

yellow jack *n* : YELLOW FEVER

yellow jacket *n* : any of various small social wasps having the body barred with bright yellow

yel·low·tail \'ye-lō-ˌtāl\ *n* : any of various fishes with a yellow or yellowish tail including several valuable food fishes

yelp \'yelp\ *vb* [ME, to boast, cry out, fr. OE *gielpan* to boast, exult] : to utter a sharp quick shrill cry — **yelp** *n*

Ye·me·ni \'ye-mə-nē\ *n* : YEMENITE — **Yemeni** *adj*

Ye·men·ite \'ye-mə-ˌnīt\ *n* : a native or inhabitant of Yemen — **Yemenite** *adj*

¹yen \'yen\ *n, pl* **yen** — see MONEY table

²yen *n* [obs. E argot *yen-yen* craving for opium, fr. Chin (Guangdong dial.) *yīn-yáhn,* fr. *yīn* opium + *yáhn* craving] : a strong desire : LONGING

yeo·man \'yō-mən\ *n* **1** : an attendant or officer in a royal or noble household **2** : a naval petty officer who performs clerical duties **3** : a person who owns and cultivates a small farm; *esp* : one of a class of English freeholders below the gentry — **yeo·man·ly** \-lē\ *adj*

yeo·man·ry \-rē\ *n* : the body of yeomen and esp. of small landed proprietors

-yer — see -ER

¹yes \'yes\ *adv* — used as a function word esp. to express assent or agreement or to introduce a more emphatic or explicit phrase

²yes *n* : an affirmative reply

ye·shi·va *also* **ye·shi·vah** \yə-'shē-və\ *n, pl* **yeshivas** *or* **ye·shi·voth** \-ˌshē-'vōt, -'vōth\ : a Jewish school esp. for religious instruction

yes–man \'yes-ˌman\ *n* : a person who endorses uncritically every opinion or proposal of a superior

¹yes·ter·day \'yes-tər-dē, -ˌdā\ *adv* **1** : on the day preceding today **2** : only a short time ago

²yesterday *n* **1** : the day last past **2** : time not long past

yes·ter·year \'yes-tər-ˌyir\ *n* **1** : last year **2** : the recent past

¹yet \'yet\ *adv* **1** : in addition : BESIDES; *also* : EVEN 6 **2** : up to now; *also* : STILL **3** : so soon as now ⟨not time to go ∼⟩ **4** : EVENTUALLY **5** : NEVERTHELESS, HOWEVER

²yet *conj* : but nevertheless : BUT

ye·ti \'ye-tē, 'yā-\ *n* : ABOMINABLE SNOWMAN

yew \'yü\ *n* **1** : any of a genus of evergreen trees and shrubs with dark stiff poisonous needles and fleshy fruits **2** : the wood of a yew; *esp* : that of an Old World yew

Yid·dish \'yi-dish\ *n* [Yiddish *yidish,* short for *yidish daytsh,* lit., Jewish German] : a language derived from medieval German and spoken by Jews esp. of eastern European origin — **Yiddish** *adj*

¹yield \'yēld\ *vb* **1** : to give as fitting, owed, or required **2** : GIVE UP; *esp* : to give up possession of on claim or demand **3** : to bear as a natural product **4** : PRODUCE, SUPPLY **5** : to bring in : RETURN **6** : to give way (as to force or influence) **7** : to give place ♦ *Synonyms* RELINQUISH, CEDE, WAIVE, SURRENDER

²yield *n* : something yielded; *esp* : the amount or quantity produced or returned

yield·ing \'yēl-diŋ\ *adj* **1** : not rigid or stiff : FLEXIBLE **2** : SUBMISSIVE, COMPLIANT

yikes \'yīks\ *interj* — used to express fear or astonishment

yip \'yip\ *vb* **yipped; yip·ping** : YAP

YK *abbr* Yukon Territory

YMCA \ˌwī-ˌem-(ˌ)sē-'ā\ *n* : Young Men's Christian Association

YMHA \ˌwī-ˌem-ˌāch-'ā\ *n* : Young Men's Hebrew Association

yo \'yō\ *interj* — used to call attention, indicate attentiveness, or express affirmation

YOB *abbr* year of birth

yo·del \'yō-dᵊl\ *vb* **yo·deled** *or* **yo·delled; yo·del·ing** *or* **yo·del·ling** : to sing by suddenly changing from chest voice to falsetto and back; *also* : to shout or call in this manner — **yodel** *n* — **yo·del·er** *n*

yo·ga \'yō-gə\ *n* [Skt, lit., yoking, fr. *yunakti* he yokes] **1** *cap* : a Hindu theistic philosophy teaching the suppression of all activity of body, mind, and will in order that the self may realize its distinction from them and attain liberation **2** : a system of exercises for attaining bodily or mental control and well-being — **yo·gic** \-gik\ *adj, often cap*

yo·gi \'yō-gē\ *also* **yo·gin** \-gən, -ˌgin\ *n* **1** : a person who practices yoga **2** *cap* : an adherent of Yoga philosophy

yo·gurt *also* **yo·ghurt** \'yō-gərt\ *n* [Turk *yoğurt*] : a soured slightly acid often flavored semisolid food made of milk and milk solids to which cultures of bacteria have been added

¹yoke \'yōk\ *n, pl* **yokes** **1** : a wooden bar or frame by which two draft animals (as oxen) are coupled at the heads or necks for working together; *also* : a frame fitted to a person's shoulders to carry a load in two equal portions **2** : a clamp that embraces two parts to hold or unite them in position **3** *pl usu* yoke : two animals yoked together **4** : SERVITUDE, BONDAGE **5** : TIE, LINK ⟨the ∼ of matrimony⟩ **6** : a fitted or shaped piece esp. at the shoulder of a garment ♦ *Synonyms* COUPLE, PAIR, BRACE

²yoke *vb* **yoked; yok·ing** **1** : to put a yoke on : couple with a yoke **2** : to attach a draft animal to ⟨∼ a plow⟩ **3** : JOIN; *esp* : MARRY

yo·kel \'yō-kəl\ *n* : a naive or gullible country person

yolk \'yōk\ *n* 1 : the yellow rounded inner mass of the egg of a bird or reptile 2 : the stored food material of an egg that supplies nutrients (as proteins and cholesterol) to the developing embryo — **yolked** \'yōkt\ *adj*

Yom Kip·pur \,yōm-ki-'púr, ,yäm-, -'ki-pər\ *n* [Heb *yōm kippūr*, lit., day of atonement] : a Jewish holiday observed in September or October with fasting and prayer as a day of atonement

¹**yon** \'yän\ *adj* : YONDER

²**yon** *adv* 1 : YONDER 2 : THITHER ⟨ran hither and ∼⟩

¹**yon·der** \'yän-dər\ *adv* : at or to that place

²**yonder** *adj* 1 : more distant ⟨the ∼ side of the river⟩ 2 : being at a distance within view ⟨∼ hills⟩

yore \'yòr\ *n* [ME, fr. *yore*, adv., long ago, fr. OE *geāra*, fr. *gēar* year] : time long past ⟨in days of ∼⟩

York·ie \'yòr-kē\ *n* : YORKSHIRE TERRIER

York·shire terrier \'yòrk-,shir-, -shər-\ *n* : any of a breed of compact toy terriers with long straight silky hair

you \'yü\ *pron* 1 : the person or persons addressed ⟨∼ are a nice person⟩ ⟨∼ are nice people⟩ 2 : ONE 2 ⟨∼ turn this knob to open it⟩

¹**young** \'yəŋ\ *adj* **young·er** \'yəŋ-gər\; **young·est** \'yəŋ-gəst\ 1 : being in the first or an early stage of life, growth, or development 2 : having little experience 3 : recently come into being 4 : YOUTHFUL 5 *cap* : belonging to or representing a new or revived usu. political group or movement — **young·ish** \'yəŋ-ish\ *adj*

²**young** *n, pl* **young** : young persons; *also* : young animals

young·ling \'yəŋ-liŋ\ *n* : one that is young — **youngling** *adj*

young·ster \-stər\ *n* 1 : a young person 2 : CHILD

your \'yùr, 'yòr, yər\ *adj* : of or relating to you or yourself

yours \'yùrz, 'yòrz\ *pron* : one or the ones belonging to you

your·self \yər-'self\ *pron, pl* **yourselves** \-'selvz\ : YOU — used reflexively, for emphasis, or in absolute constructions ⟨you'll hurt ∼⟩ ⟨do it ∼⟩

youth \'yüth\ *n, pl* **youths** \'yüthz, 'yüths\ 1 : the period of life between childhood and maturity 2 : a young man; *also* : young persons 3 : YOUTHFULNESS

youth·ful \'yüth-fəl\ *adj* 1 : of, relating to, or appropriate to youth 2 : being young and not yet mature 3 : FRESH, VIGOROUS — **youth·ful·ly** *adv* — **youth·ful·ness** *n*

youth hostel *n* : HOSTEL 2

yowl \'yaù(-ə)l\ *vb* : to utter a loud long mournful cry : WAIL — **yowl** *n*

yo–yo \'yō-(,)yō\ *n, pl* **yo–yos** [prob. fr. Ilocano (a Philippine language) *yóyo*] : a thick grooved double disk with a string attached to its center that is made to fall and rise to the hand by unwinding and rewinding on the string — **yo–yo** *vb*

yr *abbr* 1 year 2 your

yrbk *abbr* yearbook

YT *abbr* Yukon Territory

yt·ter·bi·um \i-'tər-bē-əm\ *n* : a rare metallic chemical element

yt·tri·um \'i-trē-əm\ *n* : a rare metallic chemical element

yu·an \'yü-ən, yü-'än\ *n, pl* **yuan** 1 — see MONEY table 2 : the dollar of the Republic of China (Taiwan)

yuc·ca \'yə-kə\ *n* : any of a genus of plants related to the agaves that grow esp. in warm dry regions and bear large clusters of white cup-shaped flowers atop a long stiff stalk

yuck *also* **yuk** \'yək\ *interj* — used to express rejection or disgust

yule \'yül\ *n, often cap* : CHRISTMAS

Yule log *n* : a large log formerly put on the hearth on Christmas Eve as the foundation of the fire

yule·tide \'yül-,tīd\ *n, often cap* : CHRISTMASTIDE

yum·my \'yə-mē\ *adj* **yum·mi·er; -est** : highly attractive or pleasing

yup·pie \'yə-pē\ *n* [prob. fr. *y*oung *u*rban *p*rofessional + *-ie* (as in hipp*ie*)] : a young college-educated adult employed in a well-paying profession and living and working in or near a large city — **yup·pie·dom** \-dəm\ *n*

yurt \'yùrt\ *n* : a light round tent of skins or felt stretched over a lattice framework used by pastoral peoples of inner Asia

yurt

YWCA \,wī-,də-bəl-yü-(,)sē-'ā\ *n* : Young Women's Christian Association

YWHA \-,āch-'ā\ *n* : Young Women's Hebrew Association

Z

¹**z** \'zē\ *n, pl* **z's** *or* **zs** \'zēz\ *often cap* : the 26th letter of the English alphabet

²**z** *abbr* 1 zero 2 zone

Z *symbol* atomic number

Zach *abbr* Zacharias

Zach·a·ri·as \,za-kə-'rī-əs\ *n* : ZECHARIAH

¹**za·ny** \'zā-nē\ *n, pl* **zanies** [It *zanni*, a traditional masked clown, fr. It dial. *Zanni*, nickname for It *Giovanni* John] 1 : CLOWN, BUFFOON 2 : a silly or foolish person

²**zany** *adj* **za·ni·er; -est** 1 : characteristic of a zany 2 : CRAZY, FOOLISH ⟨a ∼ movie⟩ — **za·ni·ly** \'zā-nə-lē\ *adv* — **za·ni·ness** \'zā-nē-nəs\ *n*

zap \'zap\ *vb* **zapped; zap·ping** 1 : DESTROY, KILL 2 : to irradiate esp. with microwaves

zeal \'zēl\ *n* : eager and ardent interest in the pursuit of something : FERVOR ♦ *Synonyms* ENTHUSIASM, PASSION, ARDOR

zeal·ot \'ze-lət\ *n* : a zealous person; *esp* : a fanatical partisan ⟨a religious ∼⟩ ♦ *Synonyms* ENTHUSIAST, BIGOT

zeal·ous \'ze-ləs\ *adj* : filled with, characterized by, or due to zeal — **zeal·ous·ly** *adv* — **zeal·ous·ness** *n*

ze·bra \'zē-brə\ *n, pl* **zebras** *also* **zebra** : any of several African mammals related to the horse but conspicuously striped with black or dark brown and white or buff

zebra

zebra mussel *n* : a freshwater Eurasian mollusk introduced into U.S. waterways where it colonizes and clogs water intake pipes

ze·bu \'zē-bü, -byü\ *n* : any of various breeds of domestic oxen developed in India that have a large fleshy hump over the shoulders, a dewlap, drooping ears, and marked resistance to heat and to insect attack

Zech *abbr* Zechariah

Zech·a·ri·ah \,ze-kə-'rī-ə\ *n* — see BIBLE table

zed \'zed\ *n, chiefly Brit* : the letter z

zeit·geist \'tsīt-,gīst, 'zīt-\ *n* [G, fr. *Zeit* time + *Geist* spirit] : the general intellectual, moral, and cultural state of an era

Zen \'zen\ *n* : a Japanese Buddhist sect that teaches self-discipline, meditation, and attainment of enlightenment through direct intuitive insight

ze·na·na \zə-'nä-nə\ *n* : HAREM

ze·nith \'zē-nəth\ *n* **1** : the point in the heavens directly overhead **2** : the highest point : ACME ⟨the ~ of her career⟩ ◆ **Synonyms** CULMINATION, PINNACLE, APEX

ze·o·lite \'zē-ə-,līt\ *n* : any of various feldsparlike silicates used esp. as water softeners

Zeph *abbr* Zephaniah

Zeph·a·ni·ah \,ze-fə-'nī-ə\ *n* — see BIBLE table

zeph·yr \'ze-fər\ *n* : a breeze from the west; *also* : a gentle breeze

zep·pe·lin \'ze-plən, -pə-lən\ *n* [Count Ferdinand von *Zeppelin* †1917 Ger. airship manufacturer] : a cylindrical rigid blimplike airship

¹ze·ro \'zē-rō, 'zir-ō\ *n, pl* **zeros** *also* **zeroes** [ultim. fr. Ar *ṣifr*] **1** : the numerical symbol 0 **2** : the number represented by the symbol 0 **3** : the point at which the graduated degrees or measurements on a scale (as of a thermometer) begin **4** : the lowest point

²zero *adj* **1** : of, relating to, or being a zero **2** : having no magnitude or quantity **3** : ABSENT, LACKING; *esp* : having no modified inflectional form

³zero *vb* : to adjust the sights of a firearm to hit the point aimed at — usu. used with *in*

zero hour *n* : the time at which an event (as a military operation) is scheduled to begin

zest \'zest\ *n* **1** : a quality of enhancing enjoyment : PIQUANCY **2** : keen enjoyment : GUSTO — **zest·ful** \-fəl\ *adj* — **zest·ful·ly** *adv* — **zest·ful·ness** *n* — **zesty** \'zes-tē\ *adj*

ze·ta \'zā-tə, 'zē-\ *n* : the 6th letter of the Greek alphabet — Z or ζ

zi·do·vu·dine \zi-'dō-vyü-,dēn\ *n* : AZT

¹zig·zag \'zig-,zag\ *n* : one of a series of short sharp turns, angles, or alterations in a course; *also* : something marked by such a series

²zigzag *adv* : in or by a zigzag path

³zigzag *adj* : having short sharp turns or angles

⁴zigzag *vb* **zig·zagged; zig·zag·ging** : to form into or proceed along a zigzag

zil·lion \'zil-yən\ *n* : a large indeterminate number

zinc \'zink\ *n* : a bluish-white metallic chemical element that is commonly found in minerals and is used esp. in alloys and as a protective coating for iron and steel

zinc oxide *n* : a white solid used esp. as a pigment, in compounding rubber, and in ointments and sunblocks

zine \'zēn\ *n* : a noncommercial publication usu. devoted to specialized subject matter

zin·fan·del \'zin-fən-,del\ *n, often cap* : a dry red table wine made chiefly in California

zing \'zin\ *n* **1** : a shrill humming noise **2** : VITALITY **4** — **zing** *vb*

zing·er \'zin-ər\ *n* : a pointed witty remark or retort

zin·nia \'zi-nē-ə, 'zēn-yə\ *n* : any of a genus of tropical American herbs or low shrubs related to the daisies and widely grown for their showy long-lasting flowers

Zi·on \'zī-ən\ *n* **1** : the Jewish people **2** : the Jewish homeland as a symbol of Judaism or of Jewish national aspiration **3** : HEAVEN **4** : UTOPIA

Zi·on·ism \'zī-ə-,ni-zəm\ *n* : an international movement orig. for the establishment of a Jewish national or religious community in Palestine and later for the support of modern Israel — **Zi·on·ist** \-nist\ *adj or n*

¹zip \'zip\ *vb* **zipped; zip·ping** : to move, act, or function with speed or vigor

²zip *n* **1** : a sudden sharp hissing sound **2** : ENERGY, VIM

³zip *n* : NOTHING, ZERO ⟨the score was 27 to ~⟩

⁴zip *vb* **zipped; zip·ping** : to close or open with a zipper

zip code *n, often cap Z&I&P* [*z*one *i*mprovement *p*lan] : a number that identifies each postal delivery area in the U.S.

zip·per \'zi-pər\ *n* : a fastener consisting of two rows of metal or plastic teeth on strips of tape and a sliding piece that closes an opening by drawing the teeth together

zip·py \'zi-pē\ *adj* **zip·pi·er; -est** **1** : very speedy ⟨a ~ car⟩ **2** : strikingly appealing ⟨~ clothes⟩

zir·con \'zər-,kän\ *n* : a zirconium-containing mineral transparent varieties of which are used as gems

zir·co·ni·um \,zər-'kō-nē-əm\ *n* : a gray corrosion-resistant metallic chemical element used esp. in alloys and ceramics

zit \'zit\ *n* : PIMPLE

zith·er \'zi-thər, -thər\ *n* : a musical instrument having 30 to 40 strings played with plectrum and fingers

zi·ti \'zē-tē\ *n, pl* **ziti** [It] : medium-size tubular pasta

zlo·ty \'zlò-tē\ *n, pl* **zlo·tys** \-tēz\ *or* **zloty** — see MONEY table

Zn *symbol* zinc

zo·di·ac \'zō-dē-,ak\ *n* [ME, fr. AF, fr. L *zodiacus*, fr. Gk *zōidiakos*, fr. *zōidion* carved figure, sign of the zodiac, fr. dim. of *zōion* living being, figure] **1** : an imaginary belt in the heavens that encompasses the paths of most of the planets and that is divided into 12 constellations or signs **2** : a figure representing the signs of the zodiac and their symbols — **zo·di·a·cal** \zō-'dī-ə-kəl\ *adj*

zom·bie *also* **zom·bi** \'zäm-bē\ *n* : a person who is believed to have died and been brought back to life without speech or free will

zon·al \'zō-nᵊl\ *adj* : of, relating to, or having the form of a zone — **zon·al·ly** *adv*

¹zone \'zōn\ *n* [ME, fr. AF, fr. L *zona* belt, zone, fr. Gk *zōnē*] **1** : any of five great divisions of the earth's surface made according to latitude and temperature including the torrid zone, two temperate zones, and two frigid zones **2** : something that forms an encircling band ⟨a ~ of tissue⟩ **3** : a region or area set off as distinct from surrounding parts ⟨business ~⟩ ⟨postal ~⟩

²zone *vb* **zoned; zon·ing** **1** : ENCIRCLE **2** : to arrange in or mark off into zones; *esp* : to divide (as a city) into sections reserved for different purposes

zonked \'zäŋkt\ *adj* : being or acting as if under the influence of alcohol or a drug : HIGH

zoo \'zü\ *n, pl* **zoos** : a park where wild animals are kept for exhibition

zoo·ge·og·ra·phy \,zō-ə-jē-'ä-grə-fē\ *n* : a branch of biogeography concerned with the geographical distribution of animals — **zoo·ge·og·ra·pher** \-fər\ *n* — **zoo·geo·graph·ic** \-,jē-ə-'gra-fik\ *also* **zoo·geo·graph·i·cal** \-fi-kəl\ *adj*

zoo·keep·er \'zü-,kē-pər\ *n* : a person who cares for animals in a zoo

zool *abbr* zoological; zoology

zoological garden *n* : ZOO

zo·ol·o·gy \zō-'ä-lə-jē\ *n* : a branch of biology that deals with the classification and the properties and vital phenomena of animals — **zo·o·log·i·cal** \,zō-ə-'lä-ji-kəl\ *adj* — **zo·ol·o·gist** \zō-'ä-lə-jist\ *n*

zoom \'züm\ *vb* **1** : to move with a loud hum or buzz **2** : to gain altitude quickly **3** : to focus a camera or microscope using a special lens that permits the apparent distance of the object to be varied — **zoom** *n*

zoom lens *n* : a camera lens in which the image size can be varied continuously while the image remains in focus

zoo·mor·phic \,zō-ə-'mòr-fik\ *adj* **1** : having the form of an animal **2** : of, relating to, or being the representation of a deity in the form or with the attributes of an animal

zoo·plank·ton \,zō-ə-'plaŋk-tən, -,tän\ *n* : plankton composed of animals

zoo·spore \'zō-ə-,spòr\ *n* : a motile spore

zoot suit \'züt-\ *n* : a flashy suit of extreme cut typically consisting of a thigh-length jacket with wide padded shoulders and pants that are wide at the top and narrow at the bottom — **zoot·suit·er** \-,sü-tər\ *n*

Zo·ro·as·tri·an·ism \,zòr-ə-'was-trē-ə-,ni-zəm\ *n* : a religion founded by the Persian prophet Zoroaster — **Zo·ro·as·tri·an** \-trē-ən\ *adj or n*

zounds \'zaůndz\ *interj* [euphemism for *God's wounds*] — used as a mild oath

zoy·sia \ˈzȯi-shə, -zhə, -sē-ə, -zē-ə\ *n* : any of a genus of creeping perennial grasses having fine wiry leaves and including some used as lawn grasses

ZPG *abbr* zero population growth

Zr *symbol* zirconium

zuc·chet·to \zü-ˈke-tō, tsü-\ *n, pl* **-tos** [It] : a small round skullcap worn by Roman Catholic ecclesiastics

zuc·chi·ni \zu̇-ˈkē-nē\ *n, pl* **-ni** *or* **-nis** [It] : a smooth cylindrical usu. dark green summer squash; *also* : a plant that bears zucchini

Zu·lu \ˈzü-ˌlü\ *n, pl* **Zulu** *or* **Zulus** : a member of a Bantu-speaking people of South Africa; *also* : the Bantu language of the Zulus

Zu·ni \ˈzü-nē\ *or* **Zu·ñi** \-nyē\ *n, pl* **Zuni** *or* **Zunis** *or* **Zuñi** *or* **Zuñis** : a member of an American Indian people of western New Mexico; *also* : the language of the Zuni people

zwie·back \ˈswē-ˌbak, ˈswī-, ˈzwē-, ˈzwī-, -ˌbäk\ *n* [G, lit., twice baked, fr. *zwie-* twice + *backen* to bake] : a usu. sweetened bread that is baked and then sliced and toasted until dry and crisp

Zwing·li·an \ˈzwiŋ-glē-ən, ˈswiŋ-, -lē-; ˈtsfiŋ-lē-\ *adj* : of or relating to the Swiss religious reformer Ulrich Zwingli or his teachings — **Zwinglian** *n*

zy·de·co \ˈzī-də-ˌkō\ *n* : popular music of southern Louisiana that combines tunes of French origin with elements of Caribbean music and the blues

zy·gote \ˈzī-ˌgōt\ *n* : a cell formed by the union of two sexual cells; *also* : the developing individual produced from such a cell — **zy·got·ic** \zī-ˈgä-tik\ *adj*

DICTIONARY

Foreign Words & Phrases

Biographical Names

Geographical Names

Handbook of Style

Basic English Grammar

English Word Roots

Irregular English Verbs

Confused and Misused Words

DICTIONARY

FOREIGN WORDS & PHRASES

These words and phrases occur frequently enough in English context to be included in a general English dictionary, but they merit a special section because they have not become a part of the English vocabulary.

---

ab·eunt stu·dia in mo·res \'ä-be-ˌu̇nt-ˈstü-dē-ˌä-in-ˈmō-ˌräs\ [L] : practices zealously pursued pass into habits

à bien·tôt \ä-byaⁿ-tō\ [F] : so long

ab in·cu·na·bu·lis \ˌäb-ˌiŋ-kü-ˈnä-bü-ˌlēs\ [L] : from the cradle : from infancy

à bon chat, bon rat \ä-bōⁿ-ˈshä bōⁿ-ˈrä\ [F] : to a good cat, a good rat : retaliation in kind

à bouche ou·verte \ä-bü-shü-vert\ [F] : with open mouth : eagerly : uncritically

ab ovo us·que ad ma·la \äb-ˈō-vō-ˌu̇s-kwe-ˌäd-ˈmä-lä\ [L] : from egg to apples : from soup to nuts : from beginning to end

à bras ou·verts \ä-brä-zü-ver\ [F] : with open arms : cordially

ab·sit in·vi·dia \'äb-ˌsit-in-ˈwi-dē-ˌä\ [L] : let there be no envy or ill will

ab uno dis·ce om·nes \äb-ˈü-nō-ˌdis-ke-ˈóm-ˌnäs\ [L] : from one learn to know all

ab ur·be con·di·ta \äb-ˈu̇r-be-ˈkón-di-ˌtä\ [L] : from the founding of the city (Rome, founded 753 B.C.) — used by the Romans in reckoning dates

ab·usus non tol·lit usum \'ä-ˌbü-su̇s-ˌnōn-ˌtó-lit-ˈü-su̇m\ [L] : abuse does not take away use, i.e., is not an argument against proper use

à compte \ä-ˈkōⁿt\ [F] : on account

à coup sûr \ä-kü-sœr\ [F] : with sure stroke : surely

acte gra·tuit \äk-tə-grä-twᵉ̄\ [F] : gratuitous impulsive act

ad ar·bi·tri·um \ˌad-är-ˈbi-trē- u̇m\ [L] : at will : arbitrarily

ad as·tra per as·pe·ra \ˌad-ˈas-trə-ˌpər-ˈas-pə-rə\ [L] : to the stars by hard ways — motto of Kansas

ad ex·tre·mum \ˌäd-ek-ˈsträ-ˌmu̇m, ˌad-ik-ˈstrē-məm\ [L] : to the extreme : at last

ad ka·len·das Grae·cas \ˌäd-kä-ˈlen-däs-ˈgrī-ˌkäs\ [L] : at the Greek calends : never (since the Greeks had no calends)

ad ma·jo·rem Dei glo·ri·am \äd-mä-ˈyór-em-ˈde-ē-ˈglór-ē-ˌäm\ [L] : to the greater glory of God — motto of the Society of Jesus

ad pa·tres \äd-ˈpä-ˌträs\ [L] : (gathered) to his fathers : deceased

ad re·fe·ren·dum \ˌäd-ˌre-fe-ˈren-du̇m\ [L] : for reference : for further consideration by one having the authority to make a final decision

à droite \ä-drwät\ [F] : to or on the right hand

ad un·guem \äd-ˈu̇ŋ-ˌgwem\ [L] : to the fingernail : to a nicety : exactly (from the use of the fingernail to test the smoothness of marble)

ad utrum·que pa·ra·tus \ˌäd-ù-ˈtru̇m-kwe-pä-ˈrä-tu̇s\ [L] : prepared for either (event)

ad vi·vum \äd-ˈwē-ˌwu̇m\ [L] : to the life

ae·gri som·nia \ˌī-grē-ˈsóm-nē-ˌä\ [L] : a sick man's dreams

ae·quam ser·va·re men·tem \ˌī-kwäm-ser-ˌwä-rä-ˈmen-ˌtem\ [L] : to preserve a calm mind

ae·quo ani·mo \ˌī-kwō-ˈä-ni-ˌmō\ [L] : with even mind : calmly

ae·re per·en·ni·us \ˌī-rä-pe-ˈre-nē-ˌu̇s\ [L] : more lasting than bronze

à gauche \ä-gōsh\ [F] : to or on the left hand

age quod agis \ˈä-ge-ˌkwòd-ˈä-ˌgis\ [L] : do what you are doing : to the business at hand

à grands frais \ä-gräⁿ-fre\ [F] : at great expense

à huis clos \ä-wᵉ̄-klō\ [F] : with closed doors : behind closed doors

aide—toi, le ciel t'ai·dera \ed-twä lə-ˈsyel-te-drä\ [F] : help yourself (and) heaven will help you

aî·né \e-nä\ [F] : elder : senior (masc.)

aî·née \e-nä\ [F] : elder : senior (fem.)

à l'aban·don \ä-lä-bäⁿ-dōⁿ\ [F] : carelessly : in disorder

à la belle étoile \ä-lä-bel-ä-twäl\ [F] : under the beautiful star : in the open air at night

à la bonne heure \ä-lä-bò-nœr\ [F] : at a good time : well and good : all right

à la fran·çaise \ä-lä-fräⁿ-sez\ [F] : in the French manner

à l'amé·ri·caine \ä-lä-mä-rē-ken\ [F] : in the American manner : of the American kind

à l'an·glaise \ä-läⁿ-glez\ [F] : in the English manner

à la page \ä-lä-päzh\ [F] : at the page : up-to-the-minute

à la russe \ä-lä-rœs\ [F] : in the Russian manner

alea jac·ta est \'ä-lē-ˌä-ˌyäk-tä-ˈest\ [L] : the die is cast

à l'im·pro·viste \ä-laⁿ-prò-vēst\ [F] : unexpectedly

ali·quan·do bo·nus dor·mi·tat Ho·me·rus \ˌä-li-ˌkwän-dō-ˌbò-nùs-dòr-ˌmē-ˌtät-hō-ˈmer-ùs\ [L] : sometimes (even) good Homer nods

alis vo·lat pro·pri·is \'ä-ˌlēs-ˌwò-ˌlät-ˈprō-prē-ˌēs\ [L] : she flies with her own wings — motto of Oregon

al—ki \'al-ˌkī, -kē\ [Chinook Jargon] : by and by — motto of Washington

alo·ha oe \ä-ˌlō-hä-ˈòi, -ˈō-ē\ [Hawaiian] : love to you : greetings : farewell

al·ter idem \ˌòl-tər-ˈī-ˌdem, ˌäl-ter-ˈē-\ [L] : second self

à mer·veille \ä-mer-vä\ [F] : marvelously : wonderfully

ami·cus hu·ma·ni ge·ne·ris \ä-ˌmē-kùs-hü-ˌmä-nē-ˈge-ne-ris\ [L] : friend of the human race

ami·cus us·que ad aras \-ˌùs-kwe-ˌäd-ˈär-ˌäs\ [L] : a friend as far as to the altars, i.e., except in what is contrary to one's religion; *also* : a friend to the last extremity

ami de cour \ä-ˌmē-də-ˈkùr\ [F] : court friend : insincere friend

amor pa·tri·ae \'ä-ˌmòr-ˈpä-trē-ˌī\ [L] : love of one's country

amor vin·cit om·nia \'ä-ˌmòr-ˌwiŋ-kit-ˈòm-nē-ä\ [L] : love conquers all things

an·cienne no·blesse \äⁿ-syen-nó-bles\ [F] : old-time nobility : the French nobility before the Revolution of 1789

an·guis in her·ba \ˌäŋ-gwis-in-ˈher-ˌbä\ [L] : snake in the grass

ani·mal bi·pes im·plu·me \'ä-ni-ˌmäl-ˌbi-ˌpäs-im-ˈplü-me\ [L] : two-legged animal without feathers (i.e., the human race)

ani·mis opi·bus·que pa·ra·ti \'ä-ni-ˌmēs-ˌò-pi-ˈbùs-kwe-pä-ˈrä-tē\ [L] : prepared in mind and resources — one of the mottoes of South Carolina

an·no ae·ta·tis su·ae \'ä-nō-ī-ˌtä-tis-ˈsü-ˌī\ [L] : in the (specified) year of his (or her) age

an·no mun·di \ˌä-nō-ˈmùn-dē\ [L] : in the year of the world — used in reckoning dates from the supposed period of the creation of the world, esp. as fixed by James Ussher at 4004 B.C., or by the Jews at 3761 B.C.

an·no ur·bis con·di·tae \ˌä-nō-ˌùr-bis-ˈkón-di-ˌtī\ [L] : in the year of the founded city : in the year that the city was founded (Rome, founded 753 B.C.)

an·nu·it coep·tis \ˌä-nü-ˌit-ˈkóip-ˌtēs\ [L] : He (God) has approved our beginnings — motto on the reverse of the Great Seal of the United States

à peu près \ä-pœ-pre\ [F] : nearly : approximately

à pied \ä-pyä\ [F] : on foot

à point \ä-pwaⁿ\ [F] : at the right time

après moi le dé·luge \ä-pre-mwä-lə-dä-lüezh\ *or* **après nous le déluge** \ä-pre-nü-\ [F] : after me the deluge — attributed to Louis XV

à pro·pos de bottes \ä-prə-pō-də-bót\ [F] : apropos of boots — used to change the subject

à pro·pos de rien \-ryaⁿ\ [F] : apropos of nothing

aqua et ig·ni in·ter·dic·tus \ˌä-kwä-et-ˈig-nē-ˌin-ter-ˈdik-tùs\ [L] : forbidden to be furnished with water and fire : outlawed

Ar·ca·des am·bo \\'är-kä-ˌdes-'äm-bō\\ [L] : both Arcadians : two persons of like occupations or tastes; *also* : two rascals

ar·rec·tis au·ri·bus \\ä-'rek-ˌtēs-'aù-ri-ˌbús\\ [L] : with ears pricked up : attentively

ar·ri·ve·der·ci \\ˌär-ē-vä-'der-chē\\ [It] : till we meet again : farewell

ars lon·ga, vi·ta bre·vis \\ärs-'lȯŋ-ˌgä ˌwē-ˌtä-'bre-wis\\ : art is long, life is short : human life span limits all that might be accomplished

as·sa·laam alai·kum \\əs-sə-'läm-ə-'lī-kùm\\ [Ar *as-salāmu 'alaykum*] : peace to you — used as a traditional greeting among Muslims

a ter·go \\ä-'ter-(ˌ)gō\\ [L] : from behind

à tort et à tra·vers \\ä-tȯr-ä-ä-trä-ver\\ [F] : wrong and crosswise : at random : without rhyme or reason

au bout de son la·tin \\ō-büd-sȯⁿ-lä-taⁿ, -bü-də-\\ [F] : at the end of one's Latin : at the end of one's mental resources

au con·traire \\ō-kōⁿ-trer\\ [F] : on the contrary

au·de·mus ju·ra nos·tra de·fen·de·re \\aù-'dä-mùs-ˌyùr-ä-'nō-strä-dä-'fen-de-rä\\ [L] : we dare defend our rights — motto of Alabama

au·den·tes for·tu·na ju·vat \\aù-'den-ˌtäs-fȯr-ˌtü-nä-'yù-ˌwät\\ [L] : fortune favors the bold

au·di al·te·ram par·tem \\'aù-ˌdē-ˌäl-te-ˌräm-'pär-ˌtem\\ [L] : hear the other side

au fait \\ō-fet, -fe\\ [F] : to the point : fully competent : fully informed : socially correct

au fond \\ō-fōⁿ\\ [F] : at bottom : fundamentally

au grand sé·rieux \\ō-grän-sä-ryœ\\ [F] : in all seriousness

au mieux \\ō-myœ\\ [F] : on the best terms : on intimate terms

au pays des aveugles les borgnes sont rois \\ō-pā-ē-dä-zä-vœgl°-lā-bȯrnʸ-ə-sōⁿ-rwä\\ [F] : in the country of the blind the one-eyed men are kings

au·rea me·di·o·cri·tas \\'aù-rē-ä-ˌme-dē-'ȯ-kri-ˌtäs\\ : the golden mean

au reste \\ō-rest\\ [F] : for the rest : besides

au sé·rieux \\ō-sä-ryœ\\ [F] : seriously

aus·si·tôt dit, aus·si·tôt fait \\ō-sē-tō-dē ō-sē-tō-fe\\ [F] : no sooner said than done

aut Cae·sar aut ni·hil \\aùt-'kī-sär-ˌaùt-'ni-ˌhil\\ [L] : either a Caesar or nothing

au·tres temps, au·tres mœurs \\ō-trə-täⁿ ō-trə-mœrs\\ [F] : other times, other customs

aut vin·ce·re aut mo·ri \\aùt-'wiŋ-ke-rä-ˌaùt-'mȯ-ˌrē\\ [L] : either to conquer or to die

aux armes \\ō-zärm\\ [F] : to arms

avant la lettre \\ä-väⁿ-lä-letrᵉ\\ [F] : before the letter : before a (specified) name or entity existed

ave at·que va·le \\'ä-ˌwä-ˌät-kwe-'wä-ˌlä\\ [L] : hail and farewell

à vo·tre san·té \\ä-vȯt-säⁿ-tā, -vȯ-trə-\\ [F] : to your health — used as a toast

ax·is mun·di \\'ak-səs-'mùn-dē\\ [L] : turning point of the world : line through the earth's center around which the universe revolves

bel·la fi·gu·ra \\'bel-lə-fē-'gü-rä\\ [It] : fine appearance or impression

belle laide \\bel-led\\ [F] : beautiful ugly woman : woman who is attractive though not conventionally beautiful

bel·lum om·ni·um con·tra om·nes \\'be-lùm-'ȯm-nē-ùm-ˌkȯn-trä-'ȯm-ˌnäs\\ [L] : war of all against all

bien en·ten·du \\byaⁿ-näⁿ-täⁿ-dœ\\ [F] : well understood : of course

bien—pen·sant \\byaⁿ-päⁿ-säⁿ\\ [F] : right-minded : one who holds orthodox views

bien·sé·ance \\byaⁿ-sā-äⁿs\\ [F] : propriety

bis dat qui ci·to dat \\'bis-ˌdät-kwē-'ki-tō-ˌdät\\ [L] : he gives twice who gives promptly

bon ap·pé·tit \\bȯ-nä-pā-tē\\ [F] : good appetite : enjoy your meal

bon gré, mal gré \\'bōⁿ-ˌgrā 'mäl-ˌgrā\\ [F] : whether with good grace or bad : willy-nilly

bon·jour \\bōⁿ-zhür\\ [F] : good day : good morning

bonne foi \\bȯn-fwä\\ [F] : good faith

bon·soir \\bōⁿ-swär\\ [F] : good evening

bru·tum ful·men \\ˌbrü-tùm-'fúl-men\\ [L] : insensible thunderbolt : a futile threat or display of force

ca·dit quae·stio \\ˌkä-dit-'kwī-stē-ˌō\\ [L] : the question drops : the argument collapses

carte d'iden·ti·té \\kärt-dē-däⁿ-tē-tä\\ [F] : identity card

cau·sa si·ne qua non \\'kaù-ˌsä-ˌsi-nä-kwä-'nōn\\ [L] : an indispensable cause or condition

ça va sans dire \\sä-vä-säⁿ-dir\\ [F] : it goes without saying

ca·ve ca·nem \\ˌkä-wä-'kä-ˌnem\\ [L] : beware the dog

ce·dant ar·ma to·gae \\'kā-ˌdänt-ˌär-mə-'tō-ˌgī\\ [L] : let arms yield to the toga : let military power give way to civil power — motto of Wyoming

ce n'est que le pre·mier pas qui coûte \\snek-lə-prə-myä-pä-kē-küt\\ [F] : it is only the first step that costs

c'est-à—dire \\se-tä-dir\\ [F] : that is to say : namely

c'est au·tre chose \\se-tōt-shōz, -tō-trə-\\ [F] : that's a different thing

c'est la guerre \\se-lä-ger\\ [F] : that's war : it cannot be helped

c'est la vie \\se-lä-vē\\ [F] : that's life : that's how things happen

c'est plus qu'un crime, c'est une faute \\se-plœ-kœⁿ-krĕm se-tœn-fōt\\ [F] : it is worse than a crime, it is a blunder

ce·te·ra de·sunt \\ˌkä-te-ˌrä-'dä-ˌsùnt\\ [L] : the rest is missing

cha·cun à son goût \\shä-kœⁿ-nä-sōⁿ-gü\\ [F] : everyone to his taste

châ·teau en Es·pagne \\shä-tō-äⁿ-nes-pänʸ\\ [F] : castle in Spain : a visionary project

cher·chez la femme \\sher-shä-lä-fäm\\ [F] : look for the woman

che sa·rà, sa·rà \\kä-sä-ˌrä sä-'rä\\ [It] : what will be, will be

che·val de ba·taille \\shə-väl-də-bä-täʸ\\ [F] : warhorse : argument constantly relied on : favorite subject

co·gi·to, er·go sum \\'kō-gi-ˌtō ˌer-gō-'sùm\\ [L] : I think, therefore I exist

co·mé·die hu·maine \\kȯ-mä-dē-œ-men\\ [F] : human comedy : the whole variety of human life

comme ci, comme ça \\kȯm-sē kȯm-sä\\ [F] : so-so

com·pa·gnon de voy·age \\kōⁿ-pä-nʸōⁿ-də-vwä-yäzh\\ [F] : traveling companion

compte ren·du \\kōⁿt-räⁿ-dœ\\ [F] : report (as of proceedings in an investigation)

con·cor·dia dis·cors \\kȯn-'kȯr-dē-ä-'dis-ˌkȯrs\\ [L] : discordant harmony

con·fes·sio fi·dei \\kȯn-'fe-sē-ō-'fi-dē-ˌē\\ [L] : confession of faith

cor·rup·tio op·ti·mi pes·si·ma \\kȯ-'rúp-tē-ˌō-'äp-ti-ˌmē-'pe-si-ˌmä\\ [L] : the corruption of the best is the worst of all

coup de maî·tre \\küd-metrᵊ, kü-də-\\ [F] : masterstroke

coup d'es·sai \\kü-dä-se\\ [F] : experiment : trial

coûte que coûte \\küt-kə-küt\\ [F] : cost what it may

cre·do quia ab·sur·dum est \\krä-dō-'kwē-ä-äp-ˌsùr-dùm-'est\\ [L] : I believe it because it is absurd

cres·cit eun·do \\ˌkres-kit-'eùn-dō\\ [L] : it grows as it goes — motto of New Mexico

crise de nerfs *or* **crise des nerfs** \\krēz-də-ner\\ [F] : crisis of nerves : nervous collapse : hysterical fit

crux cri·ti·co·rum \\'krúks-ˌkri-ti-'kōr-ùm\\ [L] : crux of critics

cu·jus re·gio, ej·us re·li·gio \\'kü-yùs-'re-gē-ˌō ˌe-yùs-re-'li-gē-ˌō\\ [L] : whose region, his or her religion : subjects are to accept the religion of their ruler

cum gra·no sa·lis \\kùm-ˌgrä-nō-'sä-lis\\ [L] : with a grain of salt

cur·sus ho·no·rum \\'kùr-sùs-hȯ-'nȯr-ùm\\ [L] : course of honors : succession of offices of increasing importance

cus·tos mo·rum \\ˌkùs-tōs-'mȯr-ùm\\ [L] : guardian of manners or morals : censor

d'ac·cord \\dä-kȯr\\ [F] : in accord : agreed

dame d'hon·neur \\däm-dȯ-nœr\\ [F] : lady-in-waiting

dam·nant quod non in·tel·li·gunt \\'däm-ˌnänt-ˌkwȯd-ˌnȯn-in-'te-li-ˌgùnt\\ [L] : they condemn what they do not understand

de bonne grâce \\də-bȯn-gräs\\ [F] : with good grace : willingly

de gus·ti·bus non est dis·pu·tan·dum \\dä-'gús-tə-ˌbús-ˌnȯn-ˌest-ˌdis-pù-'tän-ˌdùm\\ [L] : there is no disputing about tastes

Dei gra·tia \\ˌde-ˌē-'grä-tē-ˌä\\ [L] : by the grace of God

de in·te·gro \\dä-'in-te-ˌgrō\\ [L] : anew : afresh

de·len·da est Car·tha·go \\dā-'len-dä-ˌest-kär-'tä-gō\\ [L] : Carthage must be destroyed

de·li·ne·a·vit \dā-ˌlē-nā-ˈä-wit\ [L] : he (or she) drew it

de mal en pis \də-mä-läⁿ-pē\ [F] : from bad to worse

de mi·ni·mis non cu·rat lex \dā-ˈmi-ni-ˌmēs-ˌnōn-ˌkü-ˌrät-ˈleks\ [L] : the law takes no account of trifles

de mor·tu·is nil ni·si bo·num \dā-ˈmòr-tù-ˌēs-ˌnēl-ˌni-sē-ˈbò-ˌnùm\ [L] : of the dead (say) nothing but good

de nos jours \də-nō-zhür\ [F] : of our time : contemporary — used postpositively esp. after a proper name

Deo fa·ven·te \ˌdā-ō-fä-ˈven-tä\ [L] : with God's favor

Deo gra·ti·as \ˌdā-ō-ˈgrä-tē-ˌäs\ [L] : thanks (be) to God

de pro·fun·dis \ˌdā-prō-ˈfun-dēs\ [L] : out of the depths

der Geist der stets ver·neint \dər-ˈgīst-dər-ˌshtäts-fer-ˈnīnt\ [G] : the spirit that ever denies — applied originally to Mephistopheles

de·si·pe·re in lo·co \dā-ˈsi-pe-rā-in-ˈlō-kō\ [L] : to indulge in trifling at the proper time

de te fa·bu·la nar·ra·tur \ˌdā-ˌtā-ˈfä-bù-lä-nä-ˈrä-ˌtùr\ [L] : the story applies to you

De·us ab·scon·di·tus \ˌdā-ùs-ˌäp-ˈskòn-di-ˌtùs\ [L] : hidden God : God unknowable by the human mind

De·us vult \ˌdā-ùs-ˈwùlt\ [L] : God wills it — rallying cry of the First Crusade

di·es fau·stus \ˌdē-ˌäs-ˈfaù-stùs\ [L] : lucky day

dies in·fau·stus \-ˈin-ˌfaù-stùs\ [L] : unlucky day

dies irae \-ˈē-ˌrī, -ˌrā\ [L] : day of wrath — used of the Judgment Day

Dieu et mon droit \dyœ-ā-mòⁿ-drwä\ [F] : God and my right — motto on the British royal arms

Dieu vous garde \dyœ-vü-gärd\ [F] : God keep you

di·ri·go \ˈdē-ri-ˌgō\ [L] : I direct — motto of Maine

dis ali·ter vi·sum \ˌdēs-ˌä-li-ter-ˈwē-ˌsùm\ [L] : the Gods decreed otherwise

di·tat De·us \ˌdē-ˌtät-ˈdā-ˌùs\ [L] : God enriches — motto of Arizona

di·vi·de et im·pe·ra \ˈdē-wi-ˌde-ˌet-ˈim-pe-ˌrä\ [L] : divide and rule

do·cen·do dis·ci·mus \dò-ˌken-dō-ˈdis-ki-ˌmùs\ [L] : we learn by teaching

Do·mi·ne, di·ri·ge nos \ˈdò-mi-ne ˈdē-ri-ˌge-ˈnōs\ [L] : Lord, direct us — motto of the City of London

Do·mi·nus vo·bis·cum \ˌdò-mi-ˌnùs-wō-ˈbēs-ˌkùm\ [L] : the Lord be with you

dul·ce et de·co·rum est pro pa·tria mo·ri \ˌdùl-ke-et-de-ˈkòr-ùm-ˌest-prō-ˌpä-trē-ˌä-ˈmó-ˌrē\ [L] : it is sweet and seemly to die for one's country

dum spi·ro, spe·ro \ˌdùm-ˈspē-rō ˈspā-rō\ [L] : while I breathe, I hope — one of the mottoes of South Carolina

dum vi·vi·mus vi·va·mus \ˌdùm-ˈwē-wē-ˌmùs-wē-ˈwä-mùs\ [L] : while we live, let us live

d'un cer·tain âge \dœⁿ-ser-te-näzh\ [F] : of a certain age : no longer young

dux fe·mi·na fac·ti \ˌdùks-ˌfā-mi-nä-ˈfäk-ˌtē\ [L] : a woman was leader of the exploit

ec·ce sig·num \ˌe-ke-ˈsig-ˌnùm\ [L] : behold the sign : look at the proof

e con·tra·rio \ˌā-kòn-ˈträr-ē-ˌō\ [L] : on the contrary

écra·sez l'in·fâme \ā-krä-zā-laⁿ-ˈfäm\ [F] : crush the infamous thing

eheu fu·ga·ces la·bun·tur an·ni \ˌā-ˌheù-fù-ˈgä-ˌkäs-lä-ˈbùn-ˌtùr-ˈä-ˌnē\ [L] : alas! the fleeting years glide on

ein' fes·te Burg ist un·ser Gott \īn-ˌfes-tə-ˈbùrk-ist-ˌùn-zər-ˈgòt\ [G] : a mighty fortress is our God

em·bar·ras de choix \äⁿ-bä-rä-də-shwä\ *or* **embarras du choix** \-dœ-shwä\ [F] : embarrassing variety of choice

em·bar·ras de ri·chesses *or* **embarras de ri·chesse** \äⁿ-bä-räd-rē-shes, -rä-də-\ [F] : embarrassing surplus of riches : confusing abundance

en ami \äⁿ-nä-mē\ [F] : as a friend

en ef·fet \äⁿ-nä-fe\ [F] : in fact : indeed

en fa·mille \äⁿ-fä-mē\ [F] : in or with one's family : at home : informally

en·fant ché·ri \äⁿ-fäⁿ-shä-rē\ [F] : loved or pampered child : one that is highly favored

en·fant gâ·té \äⁿ-fäⁿ-gä-tä\ [F] : spoiled child

en·fants per·dus \äⁿ-fäⁿ-per-dœ\ [F] : lost children : soldiers sent to a dangerous post

en·fin \äⁿ-faⁿ\ [F] : in conclusion : in a word

en gar·çon \äⁿ-gär-sōⁿ\ [F] : as or like a bachelor

en garde \äⁿ-gärd\ [F] : on guard

en pan·tou·fles \äⁿ-päⁿ-tüflᵊ\ [F] : in slippers : at ease : informally

en plein air \äⁿ-ple-ner\ [F] : in the open air

en plein jour \äⁿ-plaⁿ-zhür\ [F] : in broad day

en règle \äⁿ-reglᵊ\ [F] : in order : in due form

en re·tard \äⁿr-(ə)tär\ [F] : behind time : late

en re·traite \äⁿr-(ə-)tret\ [F] : in retreat : in retirement

en re·vanche \äⁿr-(ə-)väⁿsh\ [F] : in return : in compensation

en se·condes noces \äⁿs-gōⁿd-nòs, äⁿ-sə-\ [F] : in a second marriage

en·se pe·tit pla·ci·dam sub li·ber·ta·te qui·e·tem \ˌen-se-ˌpe-tit-ˈplä-ki-ˌdäm-sùb-ˌlē-ber-ˌtä-te-kwē-ˈä-ˌtem\ : with the sword she seeks calm repose under liberty : by the sword we seek peace, but peace only under liberty — motto of Massachusetts

eo ip·so \ā-ō-ˈip-(ˌ)sō\ [L] : by that itself : by that fact alone

épa·ter le bour·geois \ā-pä-tä-lə-bür-zhwä\ *or* **épater les bour·geois** \-lä-bür-\ [F] : to shock the middle classes

e plu·ri·bus unum \ˌē-ˌplùr-ə-bəs-ˈ(y)ü-nəm, ˌā-ˌplùr-i-bùs-ˈü-nùm\ [L] : one out of many — used on the Great Seal of the U.S. and on several U.S. coins

ep·pur si muo·ve \äp-ˌpür-sē-ˈmwò-vä\ [It] : and yet it does move — attributed to Galileo after recanting his assertion of the earth's motion

Erin go bragh \ˌer-ən-gə-ˈbrò, -gō-ˈbrä\ [Ir *go brách* or *go bráth*, lit., till doomsday] : Ireland forever

er·ra·re hu·ma·num est \e-ˈrär-ä-hü-ˌmä-nùm-ˈest\ [L] : to err is human

es·prit de l'es·ca·lier \es-prēd-les-kä-lyä\ *or* **es·prit d'es·ca·lier** \-prē-des-\ [F] : wit of the staircase : repartee thought of only too late

es·se quam vi·de·ri \ˈe-sä-ˌkwäm-wi-ˈdä-rē\ [L] : to be rather than to seem — motto of North Carolina

est mo·dus in re·bus \est-ˈmò-ˌdùs-in-ˈrä-ˌbùs\ [L] : there is a proper measure in things, i.e., the golden mean should always be observed

es·to per·pe·tua \ˈes-ˌtō-per-ˈpe-tù-ˌä\ [L] : may she endure forever — motto of Idaho

et hoc ge·nus om·ne \et-ˌhòk-ˌge-nùs-ˈóm-ne\ *or* **et id genus omne** \et-ˌid-\ [L] : and everything of this kind

et in Ar·ca·dia ego \ˌet-in-är-ˌkä-dē-ä-ˈe-gō\ [L] : I too (lived) in Arcadia

et sic de si·mi·li·bus \et-ˌsēk-dä-si-ˈmi-li-ˌbùs\ [L] : and so of like things

et tu Bru·te \et-ˈtü-ˈbrü-te\ [L] : thou too, Brutus — exclamation attributed to Julius Caesar on seeing his friend Brutus among his assassins

eu·re·ka \yù-ˈrē-kä\ [Gk] : I have found it — motto of California

Ewig–Weib·li·che \ˌā-vik-ˈvīp-li-kə\ [G] : eternal feminine

ex·al·té \eg-zäl-tä\ [F] : emotionally excited or elated : fanatic

ex ani·mo \eks-ˈä-ni-ˌmō\ [L] : from the heart : sincerely

ex·cel·si·or \ik-ˈsel-sē-ər, eks-ˈkel-sē-ˌór\ [L] : still higher — motto of New York

ex·cep·tio pro·bat re·gu·lam de re·bus non ex·cep·tis \eks-ˈkep-tē-ˌō-ˌprō-bät-ˈrä-gù-ˌläm-dä-ˈrä-ˌbùs-ˌnōn-eks-ˈkep-ˌtēs\ [L] : an exception establishes the rule as to things not excepted

ex·cep·tis ex·ci·pi·en·dis \eks-ˈkep-ˌtēs-eks-ˌki-pē-ˈen-ˌdēs\ [L] : with the proper or necessary exceptions

ex·i·tus ac·ta pro·bat \ˈek-si-ˌtùs-ˌäk-tä-ˈprò-ˌbät\ [L] : the outcome justifies the deed

ex li·bris \eks-ˈlē-bris\ [L] : from the books of — used on bookplates

ex me·ro mo·tu \eks-ˌmer-ō-ˈmō-tü\ [L] : out of mere impulse : of one's own accord

ex ne·ces·si·ta·te rei \ˌeks-ne-ˌke-si-ˈtä-te-ˈrā(-ˌē)\ [L] : from the necessity of the case

ex ni·hi·lo ni·hil fit \eks-ˈni-hi-ˌlō-ˌni-ˌhil-ˈfit\ [L] : from nothing nothing is produced

ex pe·de Her·cu·lem \eks-ˌpe-de-ˈher-kù-ˌlem\ [L] : from the foot (we may judge of the size of) Hercules : from a part we may judge of the whole

ex·per·to cre·de \eks-ˌper-tō-ˈkrä-de\ *or* **experto cre·di·te** \-ˈkrä-di-ˌte\ [L] : believe one who has had experience

ex un·gue le·o·nem \eks-ˈùn-gwe-le-ˈō-ˌnem\ [L] : from the claw (we may judge of) the lion : from a part we may judge of the whole

ex vi ter·mi·ni \eks-ˌwē-ˈter-mə-ˌnē\ [L] : from the force of the term

fa·ci·le prin·ceps \ˌfä-ki-le-'priŋ-ˌkeps\ [L] : easily first

fa·ci·lis de·scen·sus Aver·no \'fä-ki-ˌlis-dā-ˌskän-ˌsüs-ä-'wer-nō\ *or* **facilis descensus Aver·ni** \-(ˌ)nē\ [L] : the descent to Avernus is easy : the road to evil is easy

fa·çon de par·ler \fä-sōⁿ-də-pär-lä\ [F] : manner of speaking : figurative or conventional expression

faire suivre \fer-swˀēvrˀ\ [F] : have forwarded : please forward

fas est et ab ho·ste do·ce·ri \fäs-ˌest-et-äb-'hȯ-ste-dȯ-'kā-(ˌ)rē\ [L] : it is right to learn even from an enemy

Fa·ta vi·am in·ve·ni·ent \ˌfä-tä-'wē-ˌäm-in-'we-nē-ˌent\ [L] : the Fates will find a way

fat·ti mas·chii, pa·ro·le fe·mi·ne \ˌfät-tē-'mäs-ˌkē pä-ˌrō-lā-'fā-mē-ˌnä\ [It] : deeds are males, words are females : deeds are more effective than words — motto of Maryland, where it is generally interpreted as meaning "manly deeds, womanly words"

faux bon·homme \fō-bȯ-nȯm\ [F] : pretended good fellow

faux–naïf \fō-nä-ēf\ [F] : spuriously or affectedly childlike : artfully simple

fe·lix cul·pa \'fā-liks-'kȯl-pä\ [L] : fortunate fault — used esp. of original sin in relation to the consequent coming of Christ

femme de cham·bre \fäm-də-shäⁿbrˀ\ [F] : chambermaid : lady's maid

fe·sti·na len·te \fe-ˌstē-nä-'len-ˌtä\ [L] : make haste slowly

feux d'ar·ti·fice \fœ-där-tē-fēs\ [F] : fireworks : display of wit

fi·at ex·pe·ri·men·tum in cor·po·re vi·li \'fē-ˌät-ek-ˌsper-ē-'men-ˌtüm-in-ˌkȯr-pȯ-re-'wē-lē\ [L] : let experiment be made on a worthless body

fi·at ju·sti·tia, ru·at cae·lum \ˌfē-ˌät-yu̇s-'ti-tē-ä ˌrü-ˌät-'kī-ˌlu̇m\ [L] : let justice be done though the heavens fall

fi·at lux \'fē-ˌät-'lu̇ks\ [L] : let there be light

Fi·dei De·fen·sor \ˌfi-de-ˌē-dā-'fän-ˌsȯr\ [L] : Defender of the Faith — a title of the sovereigns of England

fille de cham·bre \fē-də-shäⁿbrˀ\ [F] : lady's maid

fille d'hon·neur \fē-dȯ-nœr\ [F] : maid of honor

fi·nem re·spi·ce \ˌfē-ˌnem-'rä-spi-ke\ [L] : consider the end

fi·nis co·ro·nat opus \ˌfē-nis-kȯ-ˌrō-ˌnät-'ō-ˌpu̇s\ [L] : the end crowns the work

flo·re·at \'flō-re-ˌät\ [L] : may (he, she, or it) flourish — usu. followed by a name

fluc·tu·at nec mer·gi·tur \'flu̇k-tu̇-ˌät-ˌnek-'mer-gi-ˌtu̇r\ [L] : it is tossed by the waves but does not sink — motto of Paris

fo·lie de gran·deur *or* **fo·lie des gran·deurs** \fȯ-lē-də-gräⁿ-dœr\ [F] : delusion of greatness : megalomania

force de frappe \ˌfȯrs-də-fräp\ [F] : a force equipped to deal a retaliatory blow

fors·an et haec olim me·mi·nis·se ju·va·bit \ˌfȯr-ˌsän-et-'hīk-ˌȯ-lim-ˌme-mi-'ni-se-yu̇-'wä-bit\ [L] : perhaps this too will be a pleasure to look back on one day

for·tes for·tu·na ju·vat \'fȯr-ˌtās-fȯr-ˌtü-nä-'yu̇-ˌwät\ [L] : fortune favors the brave

fron·ti nul·la fi·des \'frȯn-ˌtē-ˌnu̇-lä-'fi-ˌdäs\ [L] : no reliance can be placed on appearance

fu·it Ili·um \'fu̇-it-'i-lē-u̇m\ [L] : Troy has been (i.e., is no more)

fu·ror lo·quen·di \ˌfu̇r-ˌȯr-lȯ-'kwen-(ˌ)dē\ [L] : rage for speaking

furor po·e·ti·cus \-pȯ-'ā-ti-ku̇s\ [L] : poetic frenzy

furor scri·ben·di \-skrē-'ben-(ˌ)dē\ [L] : rage for writing

Gal·li·ce \'gä-li-ˌke\ [L] : in French : after the French manner

gar·çon d'hon·neur \gär-sōⁿ-dȯ-nœr\ [F] : bridegroom's attendant

garde du corps \gärd-dœ-kȯr\ [F] : bodyguard

gar·dez la foi \gär-dā-lä-fwä\ [F] : keep faith

gau·de·a·mus igi·tur \ˌgau̇-dē-'ä-mu̇s-'i-gi-ˌtu̇r\ [L] : let us then be merry

gens d'é·glise \zhäⁿ-dā-glēz\ [F] : church people : clergy

gens de guerre \zhäⁿ-də-ger\ [F] : military people : soldiery

gens du monde \zhäⁿ-dœ-mōⁿd\ [F] : people of the world : fashionable people

gno·thi se·au·ton \'gnō-thē-ˌse-au̇-'tȯn\ [Gk] : know thyself

goût de ter·roir \gü-də-te-rwär\ [F] : taste of the earth

grand monde \gräⁿ-mōⁿd\ [F] : great world : high society

gros·so mo·do \ˌgrȯs-(ˌ)sō-'mō-(ˌ)dȯ\ [It] : roughly

guerre à ou·trance \ger-ä-ü-träⁿs\ [F] : war to the uttermost

gu·ten Tag \ˌgü-tən-'täk\ [G] : good day

has·ta la vis·ta \ˌäs-tə-lä-'vēs-tə\ [Sp] : good-bye

haute vul·ga·ri·sa·tion \ōt-vœl-gä-rē-zä-syōⁿ\ [F] : high popularization : effective presentation of a difficult subject to a general audience

haut goût \ō-gü\ [F] : high flavor : slight taint of decay

hic et nunc \'hēk-et-'nu̇ŋk\ [L] : here and now

hic et ubi·que \ˌhēk-et-u̇-'bē-kwe\ [L] : here and everywhere

hic ja·cet \hik-'jā-sət, hēk-'yä-ket\ [L] : here lies — used preceding a name on a tombstone

hinc il·lae la·cri·mae \ˌhiŋk-ˌi-ˌlī-'lä-kri-ˌmī\ [L] : hence those tears

hoc age \ˌhōk-'ä-ge\ [L] : do this : apply yourself to what you are about

homme d'af·faires \ȯm-dä-fer\ [F] : man of business : business agent

homme d'es·prit \ȯm-des-prē\ [F] : man of wit

homme moyen sen·suel \ȯm-mwä-yaⁿ-säⁿ-swˀel\ [F] : the average nonintellectual man

ho·mo sum: hu·ma·ni nil a me ali·e·num pu·to \'hȯ-mō-ˌsu̇m hü-ˌmä-nē-'nēl-ä-ˌmā-ˌä-lē-'ä-nu̇m-'pu̇-tō\ [L] : I am a human being: I regard nothing of human concern as foreign to my interests

ho·ni soit qui mal y pense \ȯ-nē-swä-kē-mäl-ē-päⁿs\ [F] : shamed be he who thinks evil of it — motto of the Order of the Garter

hors com·merce \ȯr-kȯ-mers\ [F] : outside the trade : not offered through regular commercial channels

hu·ma·num est er·ra·re \hü-ˌmä-nu̇m-ˌest-e-'rär-ä\ [L] : to err is human

ich dien \iḵ-'dēn\ [G] : I serve — motto of the Prince of Wales

ici on parle fran·çais \ē-sē-ōⁿ-pärl-fräⁿ-se\ [F] : French is spoken here

idées re·çues \ē-dār-(ə-)sœ\ [F] : received ideas : conventional opinions

id est \id-'est\ [L] : that is

ig·no·ran·tia ju·ris ne·mi·nem ex·cu·sat \ˌig-nȯ-ˌrän-tē-ä-'yu̇r-is-'nä-mi-ˌnem-eks-'kü-ˌsät\ [L] : ignorance of the law excuses no one

ig·no·tum per ig·no·ti·us \ig-'nō-tu̇m-ˌper-ig-'nō-tē-ˌu̇s\ [L] : (explaining) the unknown by means of the more unknown

il faut cul·ti·ver no·tre jar·din \ēl-fō-kœl-tē-vä-nȯt-zhär-daⁿ, -nȯ-trə-zhär-\ [F] : we must cultivate our garden : we must tend to our own affairs

in ae·ter·num \in-ī-'ter-ˌnu̇m\ [L] : forever

in du·bio \in-'du̇-bē-ˌō\ [L] : in doubt : undetermined

in fu·tu·ro \ˌin-fu̇-'tu̇r-ō\ [L] : in the future

in hoc sig·no vin·ces \in-hōk-'sig-nō-'wiŋ-ˌkās\ [L] : by this sign (the Cross) you will conquer

in li·mi·ne \in-'lē-mi-ˌne\ [L] : on the threshold : at the beginning

in om·nia pa·ra·tus \in-'ȯm-nē-ä-pä-'rä-ˌtu̇s\ [L] : ready for all things

in par·ti·bus in·fi·de·li·um \in-'pär-ti-ˌbu̇s-ˌin-fi-'dā-lē-ˌu̇m\ [L] : in the regions of the infidels — used of a titular bishop having no diocesan jurisdiction, usu. in non-Christian countries

in prae·sen·ti \ˌin-prī-'sen-ˌtē\ [L] : at the present time

in sae·cu·la sae·cu·lo·rum \in-'sī-ku̇-ˌlä-ˌsī-ku̇-'lȯr- u̇m, -'sā-ku̇-ˌlä-ˌsā-\ [L] : for ages of ages : forever and ever

in·shal·lah \ˌin-shä-'lä\ [Ar *in shā' Allāh*] : if Allah wills : God willing

in sta·tu quo an·te bel·lum \in-'stä-ˌtü-kwō-ˌän-te-'be-lu̇m\ [L] : in the same state as before the war

in·te·ger vi·tae sce·le·ris·que pu·rus \ˌin-te-ger-'wē-ˌtī-ˌske-le-'ris-kwe-'pü-ru̇s\ [L] : upright of life and free from wickedness

in·ter nos \ˌin-ter-'nōs\ [L] : between ourselves

in·tra mu·ros \ˌin-trä-'mü-ˌrōs\ [L] : within the walls

in utrum·que pa·ra·tus \in-ü-'tru̇m-kwe-pä-'rä-ˌtu̇s\ [L] : prepared for either (event)

in·ve·nit \in-'wā-nit\ [L] : he or she devised it

in vi·no ve·ri·tas \in-wē-nō-'wā-ri-ˌtäs\ [L] : there is truth in wine

in·vi·ta Mi·ner·va \in-ˌwē-ˌtä-mi-'ner-ˌwä\ [L] : Minerva being unwilling : without natural talent or inspiration

ip·sis·si·ma ver·ba \ip-ˌsi-si-ˌmä-'wer-ˌbä\ [L] : the very words

ira fu·ror bre·vis est \ˌē-rä-'fúr-ˌór-'bre-wis-ˌest\ : anger is a brief madness

j'ac·cuse \zhä-kuez\ [F] : I accuse : bitter denunciation

jac·ta alea est \'yäk-ˌtä-ˌä-lē-ˌä-'est\ [L] : the die is cast

j'adoube \zhä-düb\ [F] : I adjust — used in chess when touching a piece without intending to move it

ja·nu·is clau·sis \ˌyä-nú-ˌēs-'klaú-ˌsēs\ [L] : behind closed doors

je main·tien·drai \zhə-manᵀ-tyaⁿ-drā\ [F] : I will maintain — motto of the Netherlands

jeu de mots \zhœd-mō, zhœ-də-\ [F] : play on words : pun

Jo·an·nes est no·men eius \yō-'ä-näs-est-ˌnō-men-'ä-yús\ [L] : John is his name — motto of Puerto Rico

jo·lie laide \zhó-lē-led\ [F] : good-looking ugly woman : woman who is attractive though not conventionally pretty

jour·nal in·time \zhür-näl-aⁿ-tēm\ [F] : intimate journal : private diary

jus di·vi·num \ˌyüs-di-'wē-ˌnúm\ [L] : divine law

jus·ti·tia om·ni·bus \yús-ˌti-tē-ˌä-'óm-ni-ˌbús\ [L] : justice for all — motto of the District of Columbia

j'y suis, j'y reste \zhē-swᵞē zhē-rest\ : here I am, here I remain

Kin·der, Kir·che, Küche \'kin-dər 'kir-k̲ə 'kue-k̲ə\ [G] : children, church, kitchen

la belle dame sans mer·ci \lä-bel-däm-säⁿ-mer-sē\ [F] : the beautiful lady without mercy

la·bo·ra·re est ora·re \'lä-bō-ˌrär-ä-ˌest-'ō-ˌrär-ä\ [L] : to work is to pray

labor om·nia vin·cit \'lä-ˌbór-ˌóm-nē-ˌä-'wiŋ-kit\ [L] : labor conquers all things — motto of Oklahoma

la·cri·mae re·rum \ˌlä-kri-ˌmī-'rä-ˌrúm\ [L] : tears for things : pity for misfortune; *also* : tears in things : tragedy of life

lais·sez-al·ler *or* **lais·ser-al·ler** \le-sä-ä-lā\ [F] : letting go : lack of restraint

lap·sus ca·la·mi \ˌläp-sús-'kä-lä-ˌmē\ [L] : slip of the pen

lap·sus lin·guae \ˌ-'liŋ-ˌgwī\ [L] : slip of the tongue

la reine le veut \lä-ren-lə-vœ\ [F] : the queen wills it

la·scia·te ogni spe·ran·za, voi ch'en·tra·te \läsh-'shä-tä-ˌō-nᵞē-spä-'rän-tsä ˌvō-ē-kän-'trä-tä\ [It] : abandon all hope, ye who enter

lau·da·tor tem·po·ris ac·ti \laú-'dä-ˌtór-ˌtem-pó-ris-'äk-ˌtē\ [L] : one who praises past times

laus Deo \laús-'dä-ō\ [L] : praise (be) to God

Le·bens·welt \'lā-bəns-ˌvelt\ [G] : life world : world of lived experience

le cœur a ses rai·sons que la rai·son ne con·naît point \lə-kœr-ä-sā-re-zōⁿk-lä-re-zōⁿn-kó-ne-pwaⁿ\ [F] : the heart has its reasons that reason knows nothing of

le roi est mort, vive le roi \lə-rwä-e-mór vēv-lə-rwä\ [F] : the king is dead, long live the king

le roi le veut \lə-rwä-lə-vœ\ [F] : the king wills it

le roi s'avi·se·ra \lə-rwä-sä-vēz-rä\ [F] : the king will consider

le style, c'est l'homme \lə-stēl se-lóm\ [F] : the style is the man

l'état, c'est moi \lä-tä se-mwä\ [F] : the state, it is I

l'étoile du nord \lā-twäl-due-nór\ [F] : the star of the north — motto of Minnesota

Lie·der·kranz \'lē-dər-ˌkränts\ [G] : wreath of songs : German singing society

lit·tera scrip·ta ma·net \ˌli-te-ˌrä-ˌskrip-tä-'mä-net\ [L] : the written letter abides

lo·cus in quo \ˌlō-kús-in-'kwō\ [L] : place in which

l'union fait la force \lue-nyōⁿ-fe-lä-fórs\ [F] : union makes strength — motto of Belgium

lu·sus na·tu·rae \ˌlü-sús-nä-'túr-ē, -'túr-ˌī\ [L] : freak of nature

ma foi \mä-fwä\ [F] : my faith! : indeed

mag·na est ve·ri·tas et prae·va·le·bit \ˌmäg-nä-ˌest-'wä-ri-ˌtäs-et-ˌprī-wä-'lä-bit\ [L] : truth is mighty and will prevail

mag·ni no·mi·nis um·bra \ˌmäg-nē-ˌnō-mi-nis-'úm-brä\ [L] : the shadow of a great name

ma·ha·lo \'mä-hä-lō\ [Hawaiian] : thank you

ma·lade ima·gi·naire \mä-läd-ē-mä-zhē-ner\ [F] : imaginary invalid : hypochondriac

mal de siècle \mäl-də-syeklᵃ\ [F] : illness from worldly concerns : world-weariness

ma·lis avi·bus \ˌmä-ˌlēs-'ä-wi-ˌbús\ [L] : under evil auspices

man spricht Deutsch \män-shprikt-'dóich\ [G] : German spoken

ma·riage de con·ve·nance \mä-ryäzh-də-kōⁿv-näⁿs\ [F] : marriage of convenience

ma·ri com·plai·sant \mä-rē-kōⁿ-ple-zäⁿ\ [F] : complaisant husband : cuckold who accepts his wife's infidelity

mau·vaise honte \mó-vez-ōⁿt\ [F] : bad shame : bashfulness

mau·vais quart d'heure \mó-ve-kär-dœr\ [F] : bad quarter hour : an uncomfortable though brief experience

me·dio tu·tis·si·mus ibis \'me-dē-ˌō-tü-ˌti-si-mús-'ē-bis\ [L] : you will go most safely by the middle course

me ju·di·ce \mā-'yü-di-ke\ [L] : I being judge : in my judgment

mens sa·na in cor·po·re sa·no \ˌmäns-'sä-nä-in-ˌkór-pó-re-'sä-nō\ [L] : a sound mind in a sound body

me·um et tu·um \ˌmē-əm-ˌet-'tü-əm, ˌme-úm-ˌet-'tü-úm\ [L] : mine and thine : distinction of private property

mi·ra·bi·le vi·su \mi-ˌrä-bi-lä-'wē-sü\ [L] : wonderful to behold

mi·ra·bi·lia \ˌmir-ə-'bi-lē-ˌä\ [L] : wonders : miracles

mœurs \mœr(s)\ [F] : mores : attitudes, customs, and manners of a society

mo·le ru·it sua \'mō-le-'rú-it-ˌsú-ä\ [L] : it collapses from its own bigness

monde \mōⁿd\ [F] : world : fashionable world : society

mon·ta·ni sem·per li·be·ri \mòn-'tä-nē-ˌsem-per-'lē-be-ˌrē\ [L] : mountaineers are always free — motto of West Virginia

mo·nu·men·tum ae·re per·en·ni·us \ˌmó-nú-'men-túm-ˌī-re-pe-'re-nē-ùs\ [L] : a monument more lasting than bronze — used of an immortal work of art or literature

mo·re suo \ˌmór-ä-'sü-ō\ [L] : in his (or her) own manner

mo·ri·tu·ri te sa·lu·ta·mus \ˌmór-i-'túr-ē-ˌtä-sä-lú-'tä-mús\ *or* **morituri te sa·lu·tant** \-'sä-lú-ˌtänt\ [L] : we (or those) who are about to die salute thee

mul·tum in par·vo \ˌmúl-túm-in-'pär-vō, -'pär-wō\ [L] : much in little

mu·ta·to no·mi·ne de te fa·bu·la nar·ra·tur \mü-ˌtä-tō-'nō-mi-ne-ˌdä-ˌtä-'fä-bú-lä-nä-'rä-ˌtùr\ [L] : with the name changed the story applies to you

my·ster·i·um tre·men·dum \mi-'ster-ē-ˌùm-tre-'men-dùm\ [L] : overwhelming mystery

na·tu·ram ex·pel·las fur·ca, ta·men us·que re·cur·ret \nä-'tü-ˌräm-ek-ˌspe-läs-'fúr-ˌkä-ˌtä-men-'ús-kwe-re-'kúr-et\ [L] : you may drive nature out with a pitchfork, but she will keep coming back

na·tu·ra non fa·cit sal·tum \nä-'tü-rä-ˌnōn-ˌfä-kit-'säl-ˌtúm\ [L] : nature makes no leap

ne ce·de ma·lis \nä-ˌkä-de-'mä-ˌlēs\ [L] : yield not to misfortunes

ne·mo me im·pu·ne la·ces·sit \'nä-mō-'mä-im-ˌpü-nä-lä-'ke-sit\ [L] : no one attacks me with impunity — motto of Scotland and of the Order of the Thistle

ne quid ni·mis \ˌnä-ˌkwid-'ni-mis\ [L] : not anything in excess

n'est–ce pas? \nes-pä\ [F] : isn't it so?

nicht wahr? \nikt-'vär\ [G] : not true? : isn't it so?

nil ad·mi·ra·ri \ˌnēl-ˌäd-mi-'rär-ē\ [L] : to be excited by nothing : equanimity

nil de·spe·ran·dum \ˌnēl-ˌdä-spä-'rän-dùm\ [L] : never despair

nil si·ne nu·mi·ne \ˌnēl-ˌsi-nä-'nü-mi-ne\ [L] : nothing without the divine will — motto of Colorado

n'im·porte \naⁿ-pórt\ [F] : it's no matter

no·lens vo·lens \ˌnō-ˌlenz-'vō-ˌlenz\ [L] : unwilling (or) willing : willy-nilly

non om·nia pos·su·mus om·nes \nōn-'óm-nē-ä-ˌpó-sù-mùs-'óm-ˌnäs\ [L] : we can't all (do) all things

non om·nis mo·ri·ar \nōn-'óm-nis-'mór-ē-ˌär\ [L] : I shall not wholly die

non sans droict \nōⁿ-säⁿ-drwä\ [OF] : not without right — motto on Shakespeare's coat of arms

non sum qua·lis eram \ˌnōn-ˌsùm-ˌkwä-lis-'er-ˌäm\ [L] : I am not what I used to be

nos·ce te ip·sum \ˌnȯs-ke-ˌtā-'ip-ˌsu̇m\ [L] : know thyself

nos·tal·gie de la boue \nȯs-tȧl-zhēd-lȧ-bü, -zhē-də-\ [F] : yearning for the mud : attraction to what is unworthy, crude, or degrading

nous avons chan·gé tout ce·la \nü-zä-vōⁿ-shäⁿ-zhä-tü-sə-lä\ [F] : we have changed all that

nous ver·rons ce que nous ver·rons \nü-ve-rōⁿs-kə-nü-ve-rōⁿ, -rōⁿ-sə-kə-\ [F] : we shall see what we shall see

no·vus ho·mo \ˌnȯ-wu̇s-'hȯ-mō\ [L] : new man : man newly ennobled : upstart

novus or·do se·clo·rum \-'ȯr-ˌdō-sä-'klȯr-u̇m\ [L] : a new cycle of the ages — motto on the reverse of the Great Seal of the United States

nu·gae \'nü-ˌgī\ [L] : trifles

nuit blanche \nwʸē-bläⁿsh\ [F] : white night : a sleepless night

nyet \'nyet\ [Russ] : no

ob·iit \'ȯ-bē-ˌit\ [L] : he or she died

ob·scu·rum per ob·scu·ri·us \ȯb-'skyu̇r-u̇m-ˌper-ȯb-'skyu̇r-ē-u̇s\ [L] : (explaining) the obscure by means of the more obscure

ode·rint dum me·tu·ant \'ō-de-ˌrint-ˌdu̇m-me-tu̇-ˌänt\ [L] : let them hate, so long as they fear

odi et amo \'ō-ˌdē-et-'ä-(ˌ)mō\ [L] : I hate and I love

omer·tà \ȯ-'mer-tä\ [It] : conspiracy of silence

om·ne ig·no·tum pro mag·ni·fi·co \ˌȯm-ne-ig-'nȯ-ˌtu̇m-prō-mäg-'ni-fi-ˌkō\ [L] : everything unknown (is taken) as grand : the unknown tends to be exaggerated in importance or difficulty

om·nia mu·tan·tur, nos et mu·ta·mur in il·lis \ˌȯm-nē-ä-mü-'tän-ˌtu̇r ˌnȯs-et-mü-tä-mu̇r-in-'i-ˌlēs\ [L] : all things are changing, and we are changing with them

om·nia vin·cit amor \'ȯm-nē-ä-'wiŋ-kit-'ä-ˌmȯr\ [L] : love conquers all

onus pro·ban·di \ˌō-nu̇s-prō-'ban-ˌdī, -dē\ [L] : burden of proof

ora pro no·bis \ˌō-rä-prō-'nō-ˌbēs\ [L] : pray for us

ore ro·tun·do \ˌȯr-ē-rō-'tən-dō\ [L] : with round mouth : eloquently

oro y pla·ta \ˌȯr-ō-ē-'plä-tä\ [Sp] : gold and silver — motto of Montana

o tem·po·ra! o mo·res! \ō-'tem-pȯ-rä ō-'mō-ˌräs\ [L] : oh the times! oh the manners!

oti·um cum dig·ni·ta·te \'ō-tē-ˌu̇m-ku̇m-ˌdig-ni-'tä-te\ [L] : leisure with dignity

où sont les neiges d'an·tan? \ü-sōⁿ-lä-nezh-däⁿ-täⁿ\ [F] : where are the snows of yesteryear?

outre-mer \ütrᵉ-mer\ [F] : overseas : distant lands

pal·li·da Mors \ˌpa-li-dä-'mȯrz\ [L] : pale Death

pa·nem et cir·cen·ses \'pä-ˌnem-et-kir-'kän-ˌsäs\ [L] : bread and circuses : provision of the means of life and recreation by government to appease discontent

pan·ta rhei \ˌpän-tä-'rā\ [Gk] : all things are in flux

par avance \pär-ä-väⁿs\ [F] : in advance : by anticipation

par avion \pär-ä-vyōⁿ\ [F] : by airplane — used on airmail

par ex·em·ple \pär-äg-zäⁿplᵉ\ [F] : for example

pars pro to·to \'pärs-(ˌ)prō-'tō-(ˌ)tō\ [L] : part (taken) for the whole

par·tu·ri·unt mon·tes, nas·ce·tur ri·di·cu·lus mus \pär-'tu̇r-ē-ˌu̇nt-'mȯn-ˌtäs näs-'kä-ˌtu̇r-ri-ˌdi-ku̇-lu̇s-'mu̇s\ [L] : the mountains are in labor, and a ridiculous mouse will be brought forth

pa·ter pa·tri·ae \'pä-ˌter-'pä-trē-ˌī\ [L] : father of his country

pau·cis ver·bis \ˌpau̇-kēs-'wer-ˌbēs\ [L] : in a few words

pax vo·bis·cum \ˌpäks-vō-'bēs-ˌku̇m\ [L] : peace (be) with you

peine forte et dure \pen-fȯr-tä-du̇r\ [F] : strong and hard punishment : torture

per an·gus·ta ad au·gus·ta \per-'än-ˌgu̇s-tä-äd-'au̇-ˌgu̇s-tä\ [L] : through difficulties to honors

per·fide Al·bion \per-fēd-äl-byōⁿ\ [F] : perfidious Albion (England)

peu à peu \pœ-ä-pœ\ [F] : little by little

peu de chose \pœd-shōz, pœ-də-\ [F] : a trifle

pièce d'oc·ca·sion \pyes-dȯ-kä-zyōⁿ\ [F] : piece for a special occasion

pinx·it \'piŋk-sit\ [L] : he or she painted it

place aux dames \pläs-ō-däm\ [F] : (make) room for the ladies

ple·no ju·re \ˌplä-nō-'yu̇r-e\ [L] : with full right

plus ça change, plus c'est la même chose \plœ-sä-shäⁿzh plœ-se-lä-mem-shōz\ [F] : the more that changes, the more it's the same thing — often shortened to *plus ça change*

plus roy·a·liste que le roi \plœ-rwä-yä-lēst-kəl-rwä\ [F] : more royalist than the king

po·cas pa·la·bras \ˌpō-käs-pä-'lä-vräs\ [Sp] : few words

po·eta nas·ci·tur, non fit \pȯ-ˌä-tä-'näs-ki-ˌtu̇r nōn-'fit\ [L] : a poet is born, not made

po·ète mau·dit \pȯ-et-mō-dē\ [F] : accursed poet : a writer dogged by misfortune and lack of recognition

pol·li·ce ver·so \ˌpȯ-li-ke-'wer-sō\ [L] : with thumb turned : with a gesture or expression of condemnation

post hoc, er·go prop·ter hoc \ˌpȯst-ˌhȯk ˌer-gō-'prȯp-ter-ˌhȯk\ [L] : after this, therefore on account of it (a fallacy of argument)

post ob·itum \ˌpȯst-'ȯ-bi-ˌtu̇m\ [L] : after death

pour ac·quit \pür-ä-kē\ [F] : received payment

pour en·cou·ra·ger les autres \pür-äⁿ-kü-rä-zhä-lä-zōtrᵃ\ [F] : in order to encourage the others — said ironically of an action (as an execution) carried out in order to compel others to obey

pour le mé·rite \pür-lə-mä-rēt\ [F] : for merit

pri·mum non no·ce·re \ˌprē-mu̇m-ˌnōn-nȯ-'kä-rä\ [L] : the first thing (is) to do no harm

pro aris et fo·cis \ˌprō-ˌä-ˌrēs-et-'fȯ-ˌkēs\ [L] : for altars and firesides

pro bo·no pu·bli·co \ˌprō-ˌbȯ-nō-'pü-bli-ˌkō\ [L] : for the public good

pro hac vi·ce \ˌprō-ˌhäk-'wi-ke\ [L] : for this occasion

pro pa·tria \ˌprō-'pä-trē-ˌä\ [L] : for one's country

pro re·ge, le·ge, et gre·ge \ˌprō-'rä-ˌge 'lä-ˌge et-'gre-ˌge\ [L] : for the king, the law, and the people

pro re na·ta \ˌprō-ˌrä-'nä-tä\ [L] : for an occasion that has arisen : as needed — used in medical prescriptions

quand même \käⁿ-mem\ [F] : even so : all the same

quan·tum mu·ta·tus ab il·lo \ˌkwän-tu̇m-mü-'tä-tu̇s-äb-'i-lō\ [L] : how changed from what he once was

quan·tum suf·fi·cit \ˌkwän-təm-'sə-fə-ˌkit\ [L] : as much as suffices : a sufficient quantity — used chiefly in medical prescriptions

¿quién sa·be? \kyän-'sä-vä\ [Sp] : who knows?

qui fa·cit per ali·um fa·cit per se \kwē-'fä-kit-ˌper-'ä-lē-ˌu̇m-ˌfä-kit-ˌper-'sä\ [L] : he who does (something) through another does it through himself

quis cus·to·di·et ip·sos cus·to·des? \ˌkwis-ku̇s-'tō-dē-ˌet-ˌip-ˌsōs-ku̇s-'tō-ˌdäs\ [L] : who will keep the keepers themselves?

qui s'ex·cuse s'ac·cuse \kē-'sek-ˌskuez-'sä-ˌkuez\ [F] : he who excuses himself accuses himself

quis se·pa·ra·bit? \ˌkwis-ˌsä-pə-'rä-bit\ [L] : who shall separate (us)? — motto of the Order of St. Patrick

qui trans·tu·lit sus·ti·net \kwē-'träns-tù-ˌlit-'su̇s-ti-ˌnet\ [L] : He who transplanted sustains (us) — motto of Connecticut

qui va là? \kē-vä-lä\ [F] : who goes there?

quo·ad hoc \ˌkwȯ-ˌäd-'hȯk\ [L] : as far as this : to this extent

quod erat de·mon·stran·dum \ˌkwȯd-'er-ˌät-ˌde-mən-'stran-dəm, -ˌdä-ˌmȯn-'strän-ˌdu̇m\ [L] : which was to be proved

quod erat fa·ci·en·dum \-ˌfä-kē-'en-ˌdu̇m\ [L] : which was to be done

quod sem·per, quod ubi·que, quod ab om·ni·bus \kwȯd-'sem-ˌper kwȯd-'ù-bi-ˌkwä ˌkwȯd-äb-'ȯm-ni-ˌbùs, -ˌkwȯd-ù-'bē-(ˌ)kwä-\ [L] : what (has been held) always, everywhere, by everybody

quod vi·de \kwȯd-'wi-ˌde\ [L] : which see

quo·rum pars mag·na fui \'kwȯr-ùm-ˌpärs-ˌmäg-nä-'fù-ē\ [L] : in which I played a great part

quos de·us vult per·de·re pri·us de·men·tat \kwōs-'dä-ùs-ˌwùlt-'per-de-ˌrä-ˌpri-ùs-dä-'men-ˌtät\ [L] : those whom a god wishes to destroy he first drives mad

quot ho·mi·nes, tot sen·ten·ti·ae \kwȯt-'hȯ-mi-ˌnäs ˌtȯt-sen-'ten-tē-ˌī\ [L] : there are as many opinions as there are men

quo va·dis? \kwō-'wä-dis, -'vä-dəs\ [L] : whither are you going?

rai·son d'état \re-zōⁿ-dä-tä\ [F] : reason of state

re·cu·ler pour mieux sau·ter \rə-kue-lä-pür-myœ-sō-tä\ [F] : to draw back in order to make a better jump

reg·nat po·pu·lus \,reg-,nät-'pȯ-pu̇-,lu̇s\ [L] : the people rule — motto of Arkansas

re in·fec·ta \,rä-in-'fek-,tä\ [L] : the business being unfinished : without accomplishing one's purpose

re·li·gio lo·ci \re-'li-gē-,ō-'lȯ-,kē\ [L] : religious sanctity of a place

rem acu te·ti·gis·ti \rem-'ä-,kü-,te-ti-'gis-tē\ [L] : you have touched the point with a needle : you have hit the nail on the head

ré·pon·dez s'il vous plaît \rä-pōⁿ-dā-sēl-vü-ple\ [F] : reply, if you please

re·qui·es·cat in pa·ce \,re-kwē-'es-,kät-in-'pä-,ke, ,rä-kwē-'es-,kät-in-'pä-,chā\ [L] : may he or she rest in peace — used on tombstones

re·spi·ce fi·nem \,rā-spi-,ke-'fē-,nem\ [L] : look to the end : consider the outcome

re·sur·gam \re-'su̇r-,gäm\ [L] : I shall rise again

re·te·nue \rət-nœ\ [F] : self-restraint : reserve

re·ve·nons à nos mou·tons \rəv-nōⁿ-ä-nō-mü-tōⁿ\ [F] : let us return to our sheep : let us get back to the subject

ruse de guerre \rᵫz-də-ger\ [F] : war stratagem

rus in ur·be \rüs-in-'u̇r-,be\ [L] : country in the city

sae·va in·dig·na·tio \,sī-wä-,in-dig-'nä-tē-,ō\ [L] : fierce indignation

sal At·ti·cum \sal-'ȧ-ti-kəm\ [L] : Attic salt : wit

salle à man·ger \säl-ä-mäⁿ-zhā\ [F] : dining room

sa·lon des re·fu·sés \sä-lōⁿ-dār-(ə-)fᵫ-zā\ [F] : salon of the refused : exhibition of art that has been rejected by an official body

sa·lus po·pu·li su·pre·ma lex es·to \,sä-,lüs-'pȯ-pu̇-,lē-su̇-,prā-mä-,leks-'es-tō\ [L] : let the welfare of the people be the supreme law — motto of Missouri

sanc·ta sim·pli·ci·tas \,sȧngk-tä-sim-'pli-ki-,täs\ [L] : holy simplicity — often used ironically in reference to another's naïveté

sans doute \säⁿ-düt\ [F] : without doubt : probably

sans gêne \säⁿ-zhen\ [F] : without embarrassment or constraint

sans peur et sans re·proche \säⁿ-pœr-ā-säⁿ-rə-'prȯsh\ [F] : without fear and without reproach

sans sou·ci \säⁿ-sü-sē\ [F] : without worry

sa·yo·na·ra \,sī-ə-'när-ə, ,sä-yə-\ [Jp] : good-bye

sculp·sit \'skəlp-sət, 'sku̇lp-sit\ [L] : he or she carved it

scu·to bo·nae vo·lun·ta·tis tu·ae co·ro·nas·ti nos \'skü-,tō-'bȯ-,nī-,vȯ-,lùn-,tä-tis-'tù-,ī-'kȯr-ȯ-,näs-tē-'nōs\ [L] : Thou hast crowned us with the shield of Thy good will — a motto on the Great Seal of Maryland

se·cun·dum ar·tem \se-,kùn-dùm-'är-,tem\ [L] : according to the art : according to the accepted practice of a profession or trade

secundum na·tu·ram \-nä-'tü-,räm\ [L] : according to nature : naturally

se de·fen·den·do \'sā-,dā-,fen-'den-dō\ [L] : in self-defense

se ha·bla es·pa·ñol \sā-,äv-lä-,äs-pä-'nʸȯl\ [Sp] : Spanish spoken

sem·per ea·dem \,sem-,per-'e-ä-,dem\ [L] : always the same (fem.) — motto of Queen Elizabeth I

sem·per fi·de·lis \,sem-pər-fə-'dä-ləs\ [L] : always faithful — motto of the U.S. Marine Corps

sem·per idem \,sem-,per-'ē-,dem\ [L] : always the same (masc.)

sem·per pa·ra·tus \,sem-pər-pə-'rä-təs\ [L] : always prepared — motto of the U.S. Coast Guard

se non è ve·ro, è ben tro·va·to \sā-,nōn-e-'vä-rō e-,ben-trō-'vä-tō\ [It] : even if it is not true, it is well conceived

sha·lom alei·chem \shȯ-ləm-ə-'lä-kəm, shō-, -kəm\ [Heb *shālōm 'alēkhem*] : peace to you — used as a traditional Jewish greeting

sic itur ad as·tra \sēk-'i-,tu̇r-,ȧd-'äs-trə\ [L] : thus one goes to the stars : such is the way to immortality

sic sem·per ty·ran·nis \,sik-,sem-pər-tə-'ra-nəs\ [L] : thus ever to tyrants — motto of Virginia

sic trans·it glo·ria mun·di \sēk-'trän-sit-,glȯr-ē-ä-'mu̇n-dē\ [L] : so passes away the glory of the world

si jeu·nesse sa·vait, si vieil·lesse pou·vait! \sē-'zhœ-nes-'sä-ve sē-'vye-yes-'pü-ve\ [F] : if youth only knew, if age only could!

si·lent le·ges in·ter ar·ma \,si-,lent-'lā-,gās-,in-ter-'är-mä\ [L] : the laws are silent in the midst of arms (i.e., in time of war)

s'il vous plaît \sēl-vü-ple\ [F] : if you please

si·mi·lia si·mi·li·bus cu·ran·tur \si-'mi-lē-ä-si-'mi-li-bu̇s-ku̇-'rän-tu̇r\ [L] : like is cured by like

si·mi·lis si·mi·li gau·det \'si-mi-lis-'si-mi-lē-'gau̇-,det\ [L] : like takes pleasure in like

si mo·nu·men·tum re·qui·ris, cir·cum·spi·ce \,sē-,mȯ-nú-,men-tùm-re-'kwē-ris kir-'kúm-spi-ke\ [L] : if you seek his monument, look around — epitaph of Sir Christopher Wren in St. Paul's, London, of which he was architect

sim·pliste \saⁿ-plēst\ [F] : simplistic : overly simple or naïve

si quae·ris pen·in·su·lam amoe·nam, cir·cum·spi·ce \sē-'kwī-ris-pā-'nin-sə-,läm-ä-'mȯi-,näm kir-'kúm-spi-ke\ [L] : if you seek a beautiful peninsula, look around — motto of Michigan

sis·te vi·a·tor \,sis-te-wē-'ä-,tȯr\ [L] : stop, traveler — used on Roman roadside tombs

si vis pa·cem, pa·ra bel·lum \sē-'wēs-'pä-,kem 'pä-rä-'be-,lu̇m\ [L] : if you wish peace, prepare for war

sol·vi·tur am·bu·lan·do \'sȯl-wi-,tu̇r-,äm-bu̇-'län-dō\ [L] : it is solved by walking : the problem is solved by a practical experiment

spo·lia opi·ma \,spȯ-lē-ä-ō-'pē-mä\ [L] : rich spoils : the arms taken by the victorious from the vanquished general

sta·tus quo an·te bel·lum \'stä-tu̇s-,kwō-,än-te-'be-lu̇m\ [L] : the state existing before the war

sua·vi·ter in mo·do, for·ti·ter in re \'swä-wi-,ter-in-'mȯ-dō 'fȯr-ti-,ter-in-'rä\ [L] : gently in manner, strongly in deed

sub ver·bo \su̇b-'wer-bō, ,sǝb-'vǝr-bō\ *or* **sub vo·ce** \su̇b-'wō-ke, ,sǝb-'vō-sē\ [L] : under the word — introducing a cross-reference in a dictionary or index

sunt la·cri·mae re·rum \su̇nt-,lä-kri-,mī-'rä-rùm\ [L] : there are tears for things : tears attend trials

suo ju·re \,sù-ō-'yu̇r-e\ [L] : in his or her own right

suo lo·co \-'lȯ-kō\ [L] : in its proper place

suo Mar·te \-'mär-te\ [L] : by one's own exertions

su·um cui·que \,sù-u̇m-'kwi-kwe\ [L] : to each his own

tant mieux \täⁿ-myœ\ [F] : so much the better

tant pis \-pē\ [F] : so much the worse : too bad

tem·po·ra mu·tan·tur, nos et mu·ta·mur in il·lis \,tem-pȯ-rä-mü-'tän-,tu̇r ,nȯs-,et-mü-,tä-mùr-in-'i-,lēs\ [L] : the times are changing, and we are changing with them

tem·pus edax re·rum \'tem-pu̇s-,e-,däks-'rä-rùm\ [L] : time, that devours all things

tem·pus fu·git \,tem-pǝs-'fyü-jǝt, ,tem-pu̇s-'fü-git\ [L] : time flies

ti·meo Da·na·os et do·na fe·ren·tes \,ti-mē-,ō-'dä-nä-,ōs-,et-,dō-nä-fe-'ren-,täs\ [L] : I fear the Greeks even when they bring gifts

to·ti·dem ver·bis \,tȯ-ti-,dem-'wer-,bēs\ [L] : in so many words

to·tis vi·ri·bus \,tō-,tēs-'wē-ri-,bùs\ [L] : with all one's might

to·to cae·lo \,tō-tō-'kī-lō\ *or* **toto coe·lo** \-'kȯi-lō\ [L] : by the whole extent of the heavens : diametrically

tou·jours per·drix \tü-zhu̇r-per-drē\ [F] : always partridge : too much of a good thing

tour d'ho·ri·zon \tùr-dȯ-rē-zōⁿ\ [F] : circuit of the horizon : general survey

tous frais faits \tü-fre-fe\ [F] : all expenses defrayed

tout à fait \tü-tä-fe\ [F] : altogether : quite

tout au con·traire \tü-tō-kōⁿ-trer\ [F] : quite the contrary

tout à vous \tü-tä-vü\ [F] : wholly yours : at your service

tout bien ou rien \tü-'byaⁿ-nü-'ryaⁿ\ [F] : everything well (done) or nothing (attempted)

tout com·pren·dre c'est tout par·don·ner \'tü-kōⁿ-präⁿ-drǝ-se-'tü-pär-dȯ-nā\ [F] : to understand all is to forgive all

tout court \tü-kür\ [F] : quite short : and nothing else : simply : just; *also* : brusquely

tout de même \tüt-mem\ [F] : all the same : nevertheless

tout de suite \tüt-swʸēt\ [F] : immediately; *also* : all at once : consecutively

tout en·sem·ble \tü-täⁿ-säⁿblᵊ\ [F] : all together : general effect

tout est per·du fors l'hon·neur \tü-te-per-dᵫ-fȯr-lȯ-nœr\ *or* **tout est perdu hors l'honneur** \-dᵫ-ȯr-\ [F] : all is lost save honor

tout le monde \tü-lǝ-mōⁿd\ [F] : all the world : everybody

tra·hi·son des clercs \trä-ē-zȯⁿ-dā-klerk\ [F] : treason of the intellectuals

tranche de vie \träⁿsh-də-'vē\ [F] : slice of life

trist·esse \trē-stes\ [F] : melancholy

tru·di·tur di·es die \'trü-di-ˌtùr-'di-ˌäs-'di-ˌā\ [L] : day is pushed forth by day : one day hurries on another

tu·e·bor \tü-'ā-ˌbȯr\ [L] : I will defend — a motto on the Great Seal of Michigan

ua mau ke ea o ka ai·na i ka po·no \ˌu̇-ä-'mä-u̇-kā-'ā-ä-ō-kä-'ä-ē-nä-ˌē-kä-'pō-nō\ [Hawaiian] : the life of the land is perpetuated in righteousness — motto of Hawaii

über al·les \ˌu̇e-ber-'ä-les\ [G] : above everything else

Über·mensch \'u̇e-bər-ˌmench\ [G] : superman

ul·ti·ma ra·tio re·gum \'ùl-ti-mä-ˌrä-tē-ō-'rā-gùm\ [L] : the final argument of kings, i.e., war

und so wei·ter \ˌu̇nt-zō-'vī-tər\ [G] : and so on

uno ani·mo \ˌü-nō-'ä-ni-ˌmō\ [L] : with one mind : unanimously

ur·bi et or·bi \ˌu̇r-bē-ˌet-'ȯr-bē\ [L] : to the city (Rome) and the world : to everyone

uti·le dul·ci \ˌü-ti-le-'dùl-ˌkē\ [L] : the useful with the agreeable

ut in·fra \ùt-'in-frä\ [L] : as below

ut su·pra \ùt-'sü-prä\ [L] : as above

va·de re·tro me, Sa·ta·na \ˌwä-de-'rä-trō-ˌmā 'sä-tä-ˌnä\ [L] : get thee behind me, Satan

vae vic·tis \wī-'wik-ˌtēs\ [L] : woe to the vanquished

va·ria lec·tio \ˌwär-ē-ä-'lek-tē-ˌō\ *pl* **va·ri·ae lec·ti·o·nes** \'wär-ē-ˌī-ˌlek-tē-'ō-ˌnäs\ [L] : variant reading

va·ri·um et mu·ta·bi·le sem·per fe·mi·na \ˌwär-ē-ùm-ˌet-ˌmü-'tä-bi-le-ˌsem-per-'fä-mi-nä\ [L] : woman is ever a fickle and changeable thing

ve·di Na·po·li e poi mo·ri \ˌvä-dē-'nä-pō-lē-ä-ˌpȯ-ē-'mȯ-rē\ [It] : see Naples and then die

ve·ni, vi·di, vi·ci \ˌwā-nē ˌwē-dē 'wē-kē, ˌvā-nē ˌvē-dē 'vē-chē\ [L] : I came, I saw, I conquered

ven·tre à terre \väⁿ-trä-ter\ [F] : belly to the ground : at very great speed

ver·ba·tim ac lit·te·ra·tim \wer-'bä-tim-ˌäk-ˌli-te-'rä-tim\ [L] : word for word and letter for letter

ver·bum sat sa·pi·en·ti est \ˌwer-bùm-'sät-ˌsä-pē-'en-tē-ˌest\ [L] : a word to the wise is sufficient

via cru·cis \wē-ä-'krü-sis\ [L] : Way of the Cross : path of suffering

vieux jeu \vyœ-zhœ\ [F] : old game : old hat

vin·cit om·nia ve·ri·tas \ˌwiŋ-kit-'ȯm-nē-ä-'wā-ri-ˌtäs\ [L] : truth conquers all things

vin·cu·lum ma·tri·mo·nii \ˌwiŋ-kù-lùm-ˌmä-tri-'mō-nē-ˌē\ [L] : bond of marriage

vin du pays \vaⁿ-dœ-pä-ē\ *or* **vin de pays** \vaⁿ-də-\ [F] : wine of the locality

vir·gi·ni·bus pu·e·ris·que \wir-'gi-ni-bùs-ˌpù-e-'rēs-kwe\ [L] : for girls and boys

vir·go in·tac·ta \'vir-gō-in-'täk-tä\ [L] : untouched virgin

vir·tu·te et ar·mis \wir-'tü-te-ˌet-'är-mēs\ [L] : by valor and arms — motto of Mississippi

vis me·di·ca·trix na·tu·rae \'wēs-ˌme-di-'kä-triks-nä-'tü-ˌrī\ [L] : the healing power of nature

vive la dif·fé·rence \vēv-lä-dē-fä-räⁿs\ [F] : long live the difference (between the sexes)

vive la reine \vēv-lä-ren\ [F] : long live the queen

vive le roi \vēv-lə-rwä\ [F] : long live the king

vix·e·re for·tes an·te Aga·mem·no·na \wik-ˌsä-re-'fȯr-ˌtäs-ˌän-te-ˌä-gä-'mem-nȯ-ˌnä\ [L] : brave men lived before Agamemnon

vogue la ga·lère \vȯg-lä-gä-ler\ [F] : let the galley be kept rowing : keep on, whatever may happen

voi·là tout \vwä-lä-tü\ [F] : that's all

vox et prae·te·rea ni·hil \'wȯks-et-prī-'ter-e-ä-'ni-ˌhil\ [L] : voice and nothing more

vox po·pu·li vox Dei \wȯks-'pȯ-pù-ˌlē-wȯks-'dā-ē\ [L] : the voice of the people is the voice of God

Wan·der·jahr \'vän-dər-ˌyär\ [G] : year of wandering

wie geht's? \vē-'gāts\ [G] : how goes it? : how is it going? — used as a greeting

wun·der·bar \'vùn-dər-ˌbär\ [G] : wonderful

BIOGRAPHICAL NAMES

This section gives basic information on many notable figures from contemporary culture, history, legend, mythology, and biblical tradition. Figures from the Bible, myth, and legend are clearly identified as such.

In cases where individuals have alternate names, they are entered under the name by which they are best known. Names are generally alphabetized by the main element of the surname, without regard for connectives such as *da, de, van,* or *von* (as **Gama** . . . Vasco da). Names appearing in the entry in italics are original names, maiden names, or nicknames.

The first dates given in the entry are birth/death dates; other dates refer to terms in office, reigns, achievements, or honors. Abbreviations used here are listed in the front section Abbreviations in This Work.

Aar·on \'er-ən\ brother of Moses and 1st high priest of the Hebrews in the Bible

Aaron Hank 1934–   *Henry Louis Aaron* Amer. baseball player

Abel \'ā-bəl\ son of Adam and Eve and brother of Cain in the Bible

Abra·ham \'ā-brə-ˌham\ patriarch and founder of the Hebrew people in the Bible; also revered by Muslims

Achil·les \ə-'ki-lēz\ hero of the Trojan War in Greek mythology

Ad·am \'a-dəm\ the 1st man in biblical tradition

Ad·ams \'a-dəmz\ Abigail 1744–1818 née *Smith* Amer. writer; wife of John Adams

Adams Ansel Easton 1902–1984 Amer. photographer

Adams John 1735–1826 2d pres. of the U.S. (1797–1801)

Adams John Quin·cy \'kwin-zē, -sē\ 1767–1848 6th pres. of the U.S. (1825–29); son of John and Abigail Adams

Adams Samuel 1722–1803 patriot in the Amer. Revolution

Ad·dams \'a-dəmz\ Jane 1860–1935 Amer. social worker; Nobel Prize winner (1931)

Ado·nis \ə-'dä-nəs, -'dō-\ youth in Greek mythology loved by Aphrodite

Ae·ne·as \i-'nē-əs\ Trojan hero in Greek and Roman mythology

Ae·o·lus \'ē-ə-ləs\ god of the winds in Greek mythology

Aes·chy·lus \'es-kə-ləs, 'ēs-\ 525–456 B.C. Greek dramatist

Aes·cu·la·pi·us \ˌes-k(y)ə-'lā-pē-əs\ god of medicine in Roman mythology — compare ASCLEPIUS

Ae·sop \'ē-ˌsäp, -səp\ legendary Greek writer of fables

Ag·a·mem·non \ˌa-gə-'mem-ˌnän, -nən\ leader of the Greeks during the Trojan War in Greek mythology

Ag·nes \'ag-nəs\ Saint *died* 304 A.D. Christian martyr

Ahab \'ā-ˌhab\ king of Israel in the 9th cent. B.C. and husband of Jezebel

Ajax \'ā-ˌjaks\ hero in Greek mythology who kills himself because the armor of Achilles is awarded to Odysseus during the Trojan War

Alad·din \ə-'la-dᵊn\ youth in the *Arabian Nights' Entertainments* who acquires a magic lamp

Al·bright \'ȯl-ˌbrīt\ Madeleine 1937–   née *Korbel* Amer. (Czech-born) diplomat; U.S. secretary of state (1997–2001)

Al·cott \'ȯl-kət, 'al-, -ˌkät\ Louisa May 1832–1888 Amer. author

Al·ex·an·der \ˌa-lig-'zan-dər, ˌe-\ name of eight popes: esp. 1431–1503 (pope 1492–1503)

Alexander the Great 356–323 B.C. *Alexander III* king of Macedonia (336–323)

Al·fred \'al-frəd, -fərd\ 849–899 *Alfred the Great* king of the West Saxons (871–899)

Ali \ä-'lē\ Muhammed 1942–   orig. *Cassius Clay* Amer. boxer

Ali Ba·ba \ˌa-lē-'bä-bə, ˌä-lē-\ woodcutter in the *Arabian Nights' Entertainments* who enters the cave of the Forty Thieves by using the password *Sesame*

Al·len \'a-lən\ Ethan 1738–1789 Amer. Revolutionary soldier

Amerigo Vespucci — see VESPUCCI

Am·herst \'a-(ˌ)mərst\ Jeffery 1717–1797 Baron *Amherst* Brit. general in America

Amund·sen \'ä-mən-sən\ Roald 1872–1928 Norwegian explorer

An·a·ni·as \ˌa-nə-'nī-əs\ early Christian in the Bible struck dead for lying

An·der·sen \'an-dər-sən\ Hans Christian 1805–1875 Danish writer of fairy tales

An·der·son \'an-dər-sən\ Marian 1897–1993 Amer. contralto

An·ge·lou \'an-jə-(ˌ)lō, *commonly* -ˌlü\ Maya 1928– orig. *Marguerite Johnson* Amer. author

Anne \'an\ 1665–1714 queen of Great Britain (1702–14)

An·tho·ny \'an(t)-thə-nē\ Susan Brownell 1820–1906 Amer. suffragist

An·tig·o·ne \an-'ti-gə-(ˌ)nē\ daughter of Oedipus and Jocasta in Greek mythology

An·to·ny \'an-tə-nē\ Mark *ca* 82–30 B.C. *Marc Anthony; Marcus An·to·ni·us* \an-'tō-nē-əs\ Roman general and triumvir (43–30)

Aph·ro·di·te \ˌa-frə-'dī-tē\ goddess of love and beauty in Greek mythology — compare VENUS

Apol·lo \ə-'pä-(ˌ)lō\ god of sunlight, prophecy, music, and poetry in Greek and Roman mythology

Ap·ple·seed \'ap-əl-ˌsēd\ Johnny 1774–1845 orig. *John Chapman* Amer. pioneer

Aqui·nas \ə-'kwī-nəs\ Saint Thomas 1224/25–1274 Ital. theologian

Ar·chi·me·des \ˌär-kə-'mē-dēz\ *ca* 287–212 B.C. Greek mathematician and inventor

Ares \'a-(ˌ)rēz, 'er-(ˌ)ēz\ god of war in Greek mythology — compare MARS

Ar·is·toph·a·nes \ˌa-rə-'stä-fə-ˌnēz\ *ca* 450–*ca* 388 B.C. Greek playwright

Ar·is·tot·le \'a-rə-ˌstä-tᵊl\ 384–322 B.C. Greek philosopher

Arm·strong \'ärm-ˌstrȯŋ\ Lance 1971–   Amer. cyclist

Armstrong Louis 1901–1971 *Satch·mo* \'sach-ˌmō\ Amer. jazz musician

Armstrong Neil Alden 1930–   Amer. astronaut; 1st man on the moon (1969)

Ar·nold \'är-nᵊld\ Benedict 1741–1801 Amer. Revolutionary general and traitor

Ar·te·mis \'är-tə-məs\ goddess of the moon, wild animals, and hunting in Greek mythology — compare DIANA

Ar·thur \'är-thər\ legendary king of the Britons whose story is based on traditions of a 6th-century military leader — **Ar·thu·ri·an** \är-'thùr-ē-ən, -'thyùr-\ *adj*

Arthur Chester Alan 1829–1886 21st pres. of the U.S. (1881–85)

As·cle·pi·us \ə-'sklē-pē-əs\ god of medicine in Greek mythology — compare AESCULAPIUS

As·tor \'as-tər\ John Jacob 1763–1848 Amer. (Ger.-born) fur trader and capitalist

Athe·na \ə-'thē-nə *or* Athe·ne \-nē\ goddess of wisdom in Greek mythology — compare MINERVA

At·las \'at-ləs\ Titan in Greek mythology forced to bear the heavens on his shoulders

At·ti·la \'a-tə-lə, ə-'ti-lə\ 406?–453 A.D. king of the Huns

At·tucks \'a-təks\ Crispus 1723?–1770 Amer. patriot

Au·du·bon \'ȯ-də-bən, -ˌbän\ John James 1785–1851 Amer. (Haitian-born) artist and naturalist

Au·gus·tine \'ò-gə-ˌstēn; ò-'gəs-tən, ə-\ Saint 354–430 A.D. church father; bishop of Hippo (396–430)

Au·gus·tus \ò-'gəs-təs, ə-\ *or* Caesar Augustus *or* Oc·ta·vi·an \äk-'tā-vē-ən\ 63 B.C., –14 A.D., 1st Roman emperor (27 B.C.,–14 A.D.)

Au·ro·ra \ə-'ròr-ə, ò-\ goddess of the dawn in Roman mythology — compare EOS

Aus·ten \'òs-tən, 'äs-\ Jane 1775–1817 Eng. author

Bac·chus \'ba-kəs, 'bä-\ — see DIONYSUS

Bach \'bäk̲, 'bäk\ Johann Sebastian 1685–1750 Ger. composer

Ba·con \'bā-kən\ Francis 1561–1626 Eng. philosopher and author

Ba·den-Pow·ell \'bā-dᵊn-'pō-əl\ Robert Stephenson Smyth 1857–1941 Baron *Baden-Powell* Brit. general and founder of Boy Scout movement

Baf·fin \'ba-fən\ William *ca* 1584–1622 Eng. navigator

Bal·boa \bal-'bō-ə\ Vasco Núñez de 1475–1519 Span. explorer

Bal·ti·more \'bòl-tə-ˌmòr, -mər\ Lord — see George CALVERT

Bal·zac \'bòl-ˌzak, 'bal-\ Honoré de 1799–1850 French author

Ba·rab·bas \bə-'ra-bəs\ prisoner in the Bible released in preference to Jesus at the demand of the multitude

Bar·num \'bär-nəm\ P. T. 1810–1891 *Phineas Taylor Barnum* Amer. showman

Bar·rie \'ba-rē\ Sir James Matthew 1860–1937 Scot. author

Bar·thol·di \bär-'täl-dē, -'tòl-, -'thäl-, -'thòl-\ Frédéric⁼ Auguste 1834–1904 French sculptor of the Statue of Liberty

Bar·ton \'bär-tᵊn\ Clara 1821–1912 founder of American Red Cross

Beau·re·gard \'bòr-ə-ˌgärd\ Pierre Gustave Toutant 1818–1893 Amer. Confederate general

Beck·et \'be-kət\ Saint Thomas *ca* 1118–1170 *Thomas à Becket* archbishop of Canterbury (1162–70)

Beck·ett \'be-kət\ Samuel 1906–1989 Irish playwright in France; Nobel Prize winner (1969)

Bee·tho·ven \'bā-ˌtō-vən\ Ludwig van 1770–1827 Ger. composer

Bell \'bel\ Alexander Graham 1847–1922 Amer. (Scot.-born) inventor of the telephone

Bel·low \'be-(ˌ)lō\ Saul 1915– Amer. (Canad.-born) author

Ben·e·dict \'be-nə-ˌdikt\ name of 15 popes: esp. XIV 1675–1758 (pope 1740–58); XV 1854–1922 (pope 1914–22)

Be·nét \bə-'nā\ Stephen Vincent 1898–1943 Amer. author

Ben·ja·min \'ben-jə-mən\ youngest son of Jacob and ancestor of one of the 12 tribes of Israel in the Bible

Ben·ton \'ben-tᵊn\ Thomas Hart 1889–1975 Amer. painter

Be·o·wulf \'bā-ə-ˌwùlf\ legendary warrior and hero of the Old Eng. poem *Beowulf*

Be·ring \'ber-iŋ, 'bir-\ Vitus 1681–1741 Danish navigator and explorer for Russia

Ber·lin \(ˌ)bər-'lin\ Irving 1888–1989 Amer. (Russ.-born) composer

Ber·ni·ni \ber-'nē-nē\ Gian Lorenzo 1598–1680 Ital. sculptor, architect, and painter

Bes·se·mer \'be-sə-mər\ Sir Henry 1813–1898 Eng. engineer and inventor

Be·thune \bə-'thün, -'thyün\ Mary 1875–1955 née *McLeod* Amer. educator

Bi·zet \bē-'zā\ Georges 1838–1875 French composer

Black Hawk \'blak-ˌhòk\ 1767–1838 Amer. Indian chief

Black·well \'blak-ˌwel, -wəl\ Elizabeth 1821–1910 Amer. (Eng.-born) physician

Blair \'bler\ Tony 1953– *Anthony Charles Lynton Blair* Brit. prime minister (1997–)

Blake \'blāk\ William 1757–1827 Eng. poet and artist

Bloom·er \'blü-mər\ Amelia 1818–1894 née *Jenks* Amer. social reformer

Boc·cac·cio \bō-'kä-ch(ē-ˌ)ō\ Giovanni 1313–1375 Ital. author

Bohr \'bòr\ Niels 1885–1962 Danish physicist; Nobel Prize winner (1922)

Bo·leyn \bù-'lin, -'lēn\ Anne 1507?–1536 2d wife of Henry VIII and mother of Elizabeth I of England

Bo·lí·var \bə-'lē-ˌvär; 'bä-lə-ˌvär, -vər\ Si·món \sē-ˌmōn, ˌsī-mən\ 1783–1830 South Amer. liberator

Bon·i·face \'bä-nə-fəs, -ˌfäs\ name of 9 popes: esp. VIII *ca* 1235 (or 1240)–1303 (pope 1294–1303)

Boone \'bün\ Daniel 1734–1820 Amer. pioneer

Booth \'büth\ John Wilkes 1838–1865 Amer. actor; assassin of Abraham Lincoln

Bo·re·as \'bòr-ē-əs\ god of the north wind in Greek mythology

Bot·ti·cel·li \ˌbä-tə-'che-lē\ Sandro 1445–1510 Ital. painter

Bow·ie \'bü-ē, 'bō-\ Jim 1796–1836 *James Bowie* Amer. popular hero of the Texas revolution

Boyle \'bòi(-ə)l\ Robert 1627–1691 Eng. physicist and chemist

Brad·bury \'brad-ˌber-ē, -b(ə-)rē\ Ray Douglas 1920– Amer. author

Brad·dock \'bra-dək\ Edward 1695–1755 Brit. general in America

Brad·ford \'brad-fərd\ William 1590–1657 Pilgrim leader

Brad·street \'brad-ˌstrēt\ Anne *ca* 1612–1672 Amer. poet

Bra·dy \'brā-dē\ Mathew B. 1823?–1896 Amer. photographer

Brahe \'brä; 'brä-hē, -hə\ Tycho 1546–1601 Danish astronomer

Brah·ma \'brä-mə\ creator god of the Hindu sacred triad — compare SHIVA; VISHNU

Brahms \'brämz\ Johannes 1833–1897 Ger. composer

Braille \'brāl, 'brī\ Louis 1809–1852 French blind teacher of the blind

Brant \'brant\ Joseph 1742–1807 *Thayendanegea* Mohawk Indian chief

Brant Mary 1736?–1796 *Molly Brant* Mohawk Indian leader; sister of Joseph Brant

Braun \'braùn\ Wernher von 1912–1977 Amer. (Ger.⁼born) rocket engineer

Brezh·nev \'brezh-ˌnef\ Leonid Ilich 1906–1982 Soviet leader of the Communist Party (1964–82); pres. of the U.S.S.R. (1960–64; 1977–82)

Bron·të \'brän-tē, -(ˌ)tā\ family of Eng. writers: Charlotte 1816–1855 and her sisters Emily 1818–1848 and Anne 1820–1849

Brooks \'brùks\ Gwendolyn Elizabeth 1917–2000 Amer. poet

Brown \'braùn\ John 1800–1859 Amer. abolitionist

Brow·ning \'braù-niŋ\ Elizabeth Barrett 1806–1861 Eng. poet

Browning Robert 1812–1889 Eng. poet; husband of the preceding

Bru·tus \'brü-təs\ Marcus Junius 85–42 B.C. Roman politician; one of Julius Caesar's assassins

Bry·an \'brī-ən\ William Jennings 1860–1925 Amer. lawyer and politician

Bu·chan·an \byü-'ka-nən, bə-\ James 1791–1868 15th pres. of the U.S. (1857–61)

Buck \'bək\ Pearl S. 1892–1973 née *Sydenstricker* Amer. author; Nobel Prize winner (1938)

Bud·dha \'bü-də, 'bù-\ *ca* 563–*ca* 483 B.C. orig. *Siddhartha Gautama* Indian founder of Buddhism

Buffalo Bill — see W. F. CODY

Bun·yan \'bən-yən\ John 1628–1688 Eng. preacher and author

Bunyan Paul — see PAUL BUNYAN

Bur·bank \'bər-ˌbaŋk\ Luther 1849–1926 Amer. horticulturist

Bur·goyne \(ˌ)bər-'gòin, 'bər-ˌ\ John 1722–1792 Brit. general in America

Burns \'bərnz\ Robert 1759–1796 Scot. poet

Burn·side \'bərn-ˌsīd\ Ambrose Everett 1824–1881 Amer. general

Burr \'bər\ Aaron 1756–1836 vice pres. of the U.S. (1801–5)

Bush \'bùsh\ George (Herbert Walker) 1924– 41st pres. of the U.S. (1989–93)

Bush George W. 1946– *George Walker Bush* 43rd pres. of the U.S. (2001–); son of the preceding

By·ron \'bī-rən\ Lord 1788–1824 *George Gordon Byron*, 6th Baron *Byron* Eng. poet

Cab·ot \'ka-bət\ John *ca* 1450–*ca* 1499 orig. *Giovanni Cabo·to* \kä-'bō-tō\ Ital. navigator; explorer for England

Cabot Sebastian 1476?–1557 Eng. navigator; son of J. Cabot

Ca·bri·ni \kə-'brē-nē\ Saint Frances Xavier 1850–1917 *Mother Cabrini* 1st Amer. (Ital.-born) saint (1946)

Cae·sar \'sē-zər\ (Gaius) Julius 100?–44 B.C. Roman general, political leader, and writer

Cain \'kān\ son of Adam and Eve and brother of Abel in the Bible

Calamity Jane \kə-'la-mə-tē-\ 1852?–1903 *Martha Jane Burk* \'bərk\ née *Can·nary* \'ka-nə-rē\ Amer. frontier figure

Cal·houn \kal-'hün\ John Caldwell 1782–1850 vice pres. of the U.S. (1825–32)

Ca·lig·u·la \kə-'li-gyə-lə\ 12–41 A.D. Roman emperor (37–41)

Cal·li·ope \kə-'lī-ə-(ˌ)pē\ muse of heroic poetry in Greek mythology

Cal·vert \'kal-vərt\ George 1580?–1632 Baron *Baltimore* Eng. colonist in America

Cal·vin \'kal-vən\ John 1509–1564 *Jean Calvin* or *Cau·vin* \kō-'va\ᴺ French theologian and reformer

Ca·mus \kä-'mᵫ\ Albert 1913–1960 French author; Nobel Prize winner (1957)

Ca·nute \kə-'nüt, -'nyüt\ *died* 1035 *Canute the Great* Danish king of England (1016–35); of Denmark (1018–35); of Norway (1028–35)

Car·ne·gie \kär-'ne-gē, 'kär-nə-gē\ Andrew 1835–1919 Amer. (Scot.-born) industrialist and philanthropist

Car·roll \'ka-rəl\ Lewis 1832–1898 pseud. of *Charles Lutwidge Dodgson* Eng. author and mathematician

Car·son \'kär-sᵊn\ Kit 1809–1868 *Christopher Carson* Amer. frontiersman and guide

Carson Rachel Louise 1907–1964 Amer. scientist and writer

Car·ter \'kär-tər\ Jimmy 1924–　　orig. *James Earl Carter, Jr.* 39th pres. of the U.S. (1977–81); Nobel Prize winner (2002)

Car·tier \kär-'tyā, 'kär-tē-ˌā\ Jacques 1491–1557 French explorer

Ca·ru·so \kə-'rü-(ˌ)sō, -(ˌ)zō\ En·ri·co \en-'rē-kō\ 1873–1921 Ital. tenor

Car·ver \'kär-vər\ George Washington 1861?–1943 Amer. agricultural chemist and agronomist

Ca·sa·no·va \ˌka-zə-'nō-və, ˌka-sə-\ Giovanni Giacomo 1725–1798 Ital. adventurer

Cas·san·dra \kə-'san-drə, -'sän-\ daughter of Priam in Greek mythology who is endowed with the gift of prophecy but fated never to be believed

Cas·satt \kə-'sat\ Mary 1845–1926 Amer. painter

Cas·tro \'käs-(ˌ)trō\ **(Ruz)** \'rüs\ Fidel 1926–　　Cuban premier (1959–　　)

Cath·er \'ka-thər\ Willa 1873–1947 Amer. author

Cath·er·ine \'ka-th(ə-)rən\ name of 1st, 5th, and 6th wives of Henry VIII of England: Catherine of Aragon 1485–1536; Catherine Howard 1520?–1542; Catherine Parr 1512–1548

Catherine I 1684–1727 wife of Peter the Great; empress of Russia (1725–27)

Catherine II 1729–1796 *Catherine the Great* empress of Russia (1762–96)

Catherine de Mé·di·cis \-də-ˌmā-dē-'sēs, -'me-də-(ˌ)chē\ 1519–1589 Ital. *Ca·te·ri·na de' Me·di·ci* \ˌkä-tā-'rē-nä-dā-'me-dē-(ˌ)chē\ queen consort of Henry II of France (1547–59) and regent of France (1560–74)

Cav·en·dish \'ka-vən-(ˌ)dish\ Henry 1731–1810 Eng. scientist

Ce·ci·lia \sə-'sēl-yə, -'sil-\ Saint *fl.* 3d cent. A.D. Christian martyr; patron saint of music

Ce·res \'sir-(ˌ)ēz\ goddess of agriculture in Roman mythology — compare DEMETER

Cer·van·tes \sər-'van-ˌtēz, -'vän-ˌtās\ Miguel de 1547–1616 Span. author

Cé·zanne \sā-'zan\ Paul 1839–1906 French painter

Cha·gall \shə-'gäl, -'gal\ Marc 1887–1985 Russ. painter in France

Cham·plain \ˌsham-'plān, shä\ᴺ-'pla\ᴺ Samuel de 1567–1635 French explorer in America

Chap·lin \'cha-plən\ Charlie 1889–1977 Sir *Charles Spencer Chaplin* Brit. actor and producer

Chapman \'chap-mən\ John — see Johnny APPLESEED

Char·le·magne \'shär-lə-ˌmān\ 742–814 A.D. *Charles the Great* or *Charles I* Frankish king (768–814); emperor of the West (800–814)

Charles \'chär(-ə)lz\ name of 10 kings of France: esp. **II** 823–877 A.D. *Charles the Bald* (r. 840–77); Holy Roman emperor (875–77); **IV** 1294–1328 *Charles the Fair* (r. 1322–28); **V** 1337–1380 *Charles the Wise* (r. 1364–80); **VI** 1368–1422 *Charles the Mad* or *the Beloved* (r. 1380–1422); **VII** 1403–1461 *Charles the Well-Served* or *the Victorious* (r. 1422–61); **IX** 1550–1574 (r. 1560–74); **X** 1757–1836 (r. 1824–30)

Charles name of 2 kings of Great Britain: 1600–1649 (r. 1625–49); 1630–1685 (r. 1660–85); son of Charles I

Charles V 1500–1558 Holy Roman emperor (1519–56); king of Spain as *Charles I* (1516–56)

Charles Edward Stuart — see Charles Edward STUART

Charles Mar·tel \-mär-'tel\ *ca* 688–741 A.D. Frankish ruler (719–41); grandfather of Charlemagne

Cha·ryb·dis \kə-'rib-dəs\ whirlpool off the coast of Sicily personified in Greek mythology as a female monster

Chau·cer \'chȯ-sər\ Geoffrey *ca* 1342–1400 Eng. poet

Che·khov \'che-ˌkȯf, -ˌkȯv\ Anton Pavlovich 1860–1904 Russ. author

Che·ney \'chē-nē, *commonly* 'chā-\ Richard Bruce 1941–　　vice pres. of the U.S. (2001–　　)

Cheops — see KHUFU

Ches·ter·ton \'ches-tər-tən\ G. K. 1874–1936 *Gilbert Keith Chesterton* Eng. author

Cho·pin \'shō-ˌpan, -ˌpa\ᴺ Frédéric François 1810–1849 Polish composer

Chou En–lai *or* **Zhou Enlai** \'jō-'en-'lī\ 1898–1976 Chinese Communist politician; premier (1949–76)

Chré·tien \krā-'tya\ᴺ Jean 1934–　　Canad. prime minister (1993–2003)

Christ Jesus — see JESUS

Chris·tie \'kris-tē\ Dame Agatha 1890–1976 née *Miller* Eng. author

Chur·chill \'chər-ˌchil, 'chərch-ˌhil\ Sir Winston Leonard Spencer 1874–1965 Brit. prime minister (1940–45; 1951–55) Nobel Prize winner (1953)

Clark \'klärk\ George Rogers 1752–1818 Amer. soldier and frontiersman

Clark William 1770–1838 Amer. explorer (with Meriwether Lewis)

Clay \'klā\ Henry 1777–1852 Amer. politician and orator

Clem·ens \'kle-mənz\ Samuel Langhorne — see Mark TWAIN

Cle·o·pa·tra \ˌklē-ə-'pa-trə, -'pä-\ 69–30 B.C. queen of Egypt (51–30)

Cleve·land \'klēv-lənd\ (Stephen) Grover 1837–1908 22nd and 24th pres. of the U.S. (1885–89; 1893–97)

Clin·ton \'klin-tᵊn\ William Jefferson 1946–　　*Bill Clinton* 42nd pres. of the U.S. (1993–2001)

Cly·tem·nes·tra \ˌklī-təm-'nes-trə\ wife of Agamemnon in Greek mythology

Cobb \'käb\ Ty 1886–1961 *Tyrus Raymond Cobb* Amer. baseball player

Co·chise \kō-'chēs\ 1812?–1874 Apache Indian chief

Co·dy \'kō-dē\ William Frederick 1846–1917 *Buffalo Bill* Amer. hunter, guide, and showman

Co·han \'kō-ˌhan\ George Michael 1878–1942 Amer. composer

Cole·ridge \'kōl-rij, 'kō-lə-rij\ Samuel Taylor 1772–1834 Eng. poet

Co·lette \kȯ-'let\ 1873–1954 orig. *Sidonie-Gabrielle Colette* French author

Co·lum·bus \kə-'ləm-bəs\ Christopher 1451–1506 Ital. navigator and explorer for Spain

Con·fu·cius \kən-'fyü-shəs\ 551–479 B.C. Chinese philosopher

Con·rad \'kän-ˌrad\ Joseph 1857–1924 Brit. (Polish-born) author

Con·sta·ble \'kən(t)-stə-bəl, 'kän(t)-\ John 1776–1837 Eng. painter

Con·stan·tine I \'kän(t)-stən-ˌtēn, -ˌtīn\ *after* 280–337 A.D. *Constantine the Great* Roman emperor (306–37)

Cook \'kuk\ Captain James 1728–1779 Eng. navigator

Coo·lidge \'kü-lij\ (John) Calvin 1872–1933 30th pres. of the U.S. (1923–29)

Coo·per \'kü-pər, 'ku-\ James Fenimore 1789–1851 Amer. author

Co·per·ni·cus \kō-'pər-ni-kəs\ Nicolaus 1473–1543 Polish astronomer

Cop·land \'kō-plənd\ Aaron 1900–1990 Amer. composer

Cop·ley \'kä-plē\ John Singleton 1738–1815 Amer. painter

Corn·plan·ter \'kȯrn-ˌplan-tər\ *ca* 1732–1836 *John O'Bail* Seneca Indian leader of partly European ancestry

Corn·wal·lis \kȯrn-'wä-ləs\ Charles 1738–1805 1st Marquess *Cornwallis* Brit. general in America

Co·ro·na·do \ˌkȯr-ə-'nä-(ˌ)dō, ˌkär-\ Francisco Vásquez de *ca* 1510–1554 Span. explorer of southwestern U.S.

Cor·tés \kȯr-'tez, ˌkȯr-ˌ\ Hernán *or* Hernando 1485–1547 Span. conqueror of Mexico

Cous·teau \kü-'stō\ Jacques-Yves 1910–1997 French marine explorer

Crane \'krān\ Stephen 1871–1900 Amer. author

Crazy Horse \'krā-zē-ˌhȯrs\ 1842?–1877 *Ta-sunko-witko* Sioux Indian chief

Crock·ett \'krä-kət\ *Davy* 1786–1836 *David Crockett* Amer. frontiersman

Crom·well \'kräm-ˌwel, 'krəm-, -wəl\ Oliver 1599–1658 Eng. general; lord protector of England (1653–58)

Cro·nus \'krō-nəs, 'krä-\ Titan in Greek mythology overthrown by his son Zeus

Cum·mings \'kə-miɴz\ Edward Estlin 1894–1962 known as *e. e. cummings* Amer. poet

Cu·pid \'kyü-pəd\ god of love in Roman mythology — compare EROS

Cu·rie \kyu̇-'rē, 'kyu̇r-(ˌ)ē\ Marie 1867–1934 née *Sklo·dow·ska* \sklə-'dȯf-skə\ French (Polish-born) chemist; Nobel Prize winner (1903, 1911)

Curie Pierre 1859–1906 French chemist; husband of M. Curie; Nobel Prize winner (1903)

Cus·ter \'kəs-tər\ George Armstrong 1839–1876 Amer. general

Cy·ra·no de Ber·ge·rac \'sir-ə-ˌnō-də-'ber-zhə-ˌrak\ Savinien 1619–1655 French playwright

Cy·rus II \'sī-rəs\ *ca* 585–*ca* 529 B.C. *Cyrus the Great* king of Persia (*ca* 550–529)

Dae·da·lus \'de-də-ləs, 'dē-\ builder in Greek mythology of the Cretan labyrinth and inventor of wings by which he and his son Icarus escape imprisonment

Dahl \'däl\ Roald 1916–1990 Brit. writer

Da·lí \'dä-lē, *by himself* dä-'lē\ Salvador 1904–1989 Span. painter

Dal·ton \'dȯl-tᵊn\ John 1766–1844 Eng. chemist and physicist

Da·na \'dā-nə\ Richard Henry 1815–1882 Amer. author

Dan·iel \'dan-yəl\ prophet in the Bible who is held captive in Babylon and delivered from a den of lions

Dan·te \'dän-(ˌ)tā, 'dan-, -(ˌ)tē\ 1265–1321 *Dante Ali·ghie·ri* \ˌa-lə-'gyer-ē\ Ital. poet

Dare \'der\ Virginia 1587–? 1st child born in America of Eng. parents

Da·ri·us I \də-'rī-əs\ 550–486 B.C. *Darius the Great* king of Persia (522–486)

Dar·row \'da-(ˌ)rō\ Clarence Seward 1857–1938 Amer. lawyer

Dar·win \'där-wən\ Charles Robert 1809–1882 Eng. naturalist

Da·vid \'dā-vəd\ a youth in the Bible who slays Goliath and succeeds Saul as king of Israel

Da·vis \'dā-vəs\ Jefferson 1808–1889 pres. of the Confederate States of America (1861–65)

Dawes \'dȯz\ William 1745–1799 Amer. patriot

Debs \'debz\ Eugene Victor 1855–1926 Amer. socialist and labor organizer

De·bus·sy \ˌde-byü-'sē, ˌdā-\ Claude 1862–1918 French composer

De·ca·tur \di-'kā-tər\ Stephen 1779–1820 Amer. naval officer

De·foe \di-'fō\ Daniel 1660–1731 Eng. author

De·gas \də-'gä\ Edgar 1834–1917 French painter

de Gaulle \di-'gōl, -'gȯl\ Charles 1890–1970 French general; pres. of Fifth Republic (1958–69)

De·li·lah \di-'lī-lə\ mistress and betrayer of Samson in the Bible

De·me·ter \di-'mē-tər\ goddess of agriculture in Greek mythology — compare CERES

de Mille \də-'mil\ Agnes 1905–1993 Amer. dancer and choreographer

De·mos·the·nes \di-'mäs-thə-ˌnēz\ 384–322 B.C. Athenian orator and statesman

Demp·sey \'dem(p)-sē\ Jack 1895–1983 orig. *William Harrison Dempsey* Amer. boxer

Des·cartes \dā-'kärt\ René 1596–1650 French mathematician and philosopher

de So·to \thä-'sō-(ˌ)tō, di-\ Hernando *ca* 1496–1542 Span. explorer

Dew·ey \'dü-ē, 'dyü-\ George 1837–1917 Amer. admiral

Dewey John 1859–1952 Amer. philosopher and educator

Dewey Melvil 1851–1931 Amer. librarian

Di·ana \dī-'a-nə\ ancient Ital. goddess of the forest and of childbirth who was identified with Artemis by the Romans

Dick·ens \'di-kənz\ Charles 1812–1870 pseud. *Boz* \'bäz, 'bȯz\ Eng. author

Dick·in·son \'di-kən-sən\ Emily Elizabeth 1830–1886 Amer. poet

Di·do \'dī-(ˌ)dō\ legendary queen of Carthage who falls in love with Aeneas and kills herself when he leaves her

Di·Mag·gio \də-'mä-zhē-(ˌ)ō, -'ma-jē-(ˌ)ō\ Joe 1914–1999 *Joseph Paul DiMaggio* Amer. baseball player

Di·o·ny·sus \ˌdī-ə-'nī-səs, -'nē-\ god of wine and ecstasy in classical mythology

Dis·ney \'diz-nē\ Walt 1901–1966 *Walter Elias Disney* Amer. film producer and cartoonist

Dis·rae·li \diz-'rā-lē\ Benjamin 1804–1881 Earl of *Beaconsfield* Brit. prime minister (1868; 1874–80)

Dix \'diks\ Dorothea Lynde 1802–1887 Amer. social reformer

Dodg·son \'däd-sən, 'däj-\ Charles Lutwidge — see Lewis CARROLL

Donne \'dən\ John 1572–1631 Eng. poet and clergyman

Don Qui·xote \ˌdän-kē-'(h)ō-tē, ˌdän-\ hero of Cervantes' *Don Quixote*

Dos·to·yev·sky \ˌdäs-tə-'yef-skē, -'yev-\ Fyodor Mikhaylovich 1821–1881 Russ. novelist

Doug·las \'də-gləs\ Stephen Arnold 1813–1861 Amer. politician

Doug·lass \'də-gləs\ Frederick 1817–1895 Amer. abolitionist

Doyle \'dȯi(-ə)l\ Sir Arthur Conan 1859–1930 Brit. physician and author

Drake \'drāk\ Sir Francis *ca* 1540–1596 Eng. navigator, explorer, and admiral

Drei·ser \'drī-sər, -zər\ Theodore 1871–1945 Amer. author

Du·Bois \dü-'bȯis, dyü-\ William Edward Burghardt 1868–1963 Amer. educator and writer

Du·mas \dü-'mä, dyü-\ Alexandre 1802–1870 *Dumas père* \'per\ French author

Dumas Alexandre 1824–1895 *Dumas fils* \'fēs\ French author

Dun·can \'dəɴ-kən\ Isadora 1877–1927 Amer. dancer

Dü·rer \'du̇r-ər, 'dyu̇r-, 'du̇er-\ Albrecht 1471–1528 Ger. painter and engraver

Ea·kins \'ā-kənz\ Thomas 1844–1916 Amer. artist

Ear·hart \'er-ˌhärt, 'ir-\ Amelia 1897–1937 Amer. aviator

Earp \'ərp\ Wyatt 1848–1929 Amer. frontiersman and lawman

Ed·dy \'e-dē\ Mary Baker 1821–1910 Amer. founder of Christian Science

Ed·i·son \'e-də-sən\ Thomas Alva 1847–1931 Amer. inventor

Ed·ward \'ed-wərd\ name of 8 post-Norman kings of England: **I** 1239–1307 *Edward Longshanks* (r. 1272–1307); **II** 1284–1327 (r. 1307–27); **III** 1312–1377 (r. 1327–77); **IV** 1442–1483 (r. 1461–70; 1471–83); **V** 1470–1483 (r. 1483); **VI** 1537–1553 (r. 1547–53); son of Henry VIII and Jane Seymour; **VII** 1841–1910 (r. 1901–10); son of Queen Victoria; **VIII** 1894–1972 (r. 1936; abdicated) *Duke of Windsor*; son of George V

Ein·stein \'īn-ˌstīn\ Albert 1879–1955 Amer. (Ger.-born) physicist; Nobel Prize winner (1921)

Ei·sen·how·er \'ī-z°n-ˌhau̇(-ə)r\ Dwight David 1890–1969 Amer. general; 34th pres. of the U.S. (1953–61)

Elec·tra \i-'lek-trə\ sister of Orestes in Greek mythology who aids him in avenging their father's murder

Eli·jah \i-'lī-jə\ Hebrew prophet of the 9th cent. B.C.

El·i·on \'e-lē-ən\ Gertrude Belle 1918–1999 Amer. pharmacologist; Nobel Prize winner (1988)

El·iot \'e-lē-ət, 'el-yət\ George 1819–1880 pseud. of *Mary Ann Evans* Eng. author

Eliot T. S. 1888–1965 *Thomas Stearns Eliot* Brit. (Amer.-born) poet; Nobel Prize winner (1948)

Eliz·a·beth I \i-'li-zə-bəth\ 1533–1603 queen of England (1558–1603); daughter of Henry VIII and Anne Boleyn

Elizabeth II 1926– queen of the United Kingdom (1952–); daughter of George VI

El·ling·ton \'e-liŋ-tən\ Duke 1899–1974 *Edward Kennedy Ellington* Amer. bandleader and composer

Em·er·son \'e-mər-sən\ Ralph Waldo 1803–1882 Amer. essayist and poet

En·dym·i·on \en-'di-mē-ən\ beautiful youth in Greek mythology loved by the goddess of the moon

Eos \'ē-,äs\ goddess of the dawn in Greek mythology — compare AURORA

Ep·i·cu·rus \,e-pi-'kyūr-əs\ 341–270 B.C. Greek philosopher

Er·ik the Red \'er-ik\ *fl.* 10th cent. orig. *Erik Thorvaldson* Norwegian explorer; father of Leif Eriksson

Eriksson Leif — see LEIF ERIKSSON

Eros \'er-,äs, 'ir-\ god of love in Greek mythology — compare CUPID

Esau \'ē-(,)sȯ\ son of Isaac and Rebekah and elder twin brother of Jacob in the Bible

Es·ther \'es-tər\ Hebrew woman in the Bible who as the queen of Persia delivers her people from destruction

Eu·clid \'yü-kləd\ *fl.* ca 300 B.C. Greek mathematician

Eu·rip·i·des \yū-'ri-pə-,dēz\ ca 484–406 B.C. Greek playwright

Eu·ro·pa \yū-'rō-pə\ princess in Greek mythology who was carried off by Zeus disguised as a white bull

Eu·ryd·i·ce \yū-'ri-də-(,)sē\ wife of Orpheus in Greek mythology

Eve \'ēv\ the 1st woman in biblical tradition; wife of Adam

Eze·kiel \i-'zē-kyəl, -kē-əl\ Hebrew prophet of the 6th cent. B.C.

Fahr·en·heit \'fa-rən-,hīt, 'fär-ən-\ Daniel Gabriel 1686–1736 Ger. physicist

Far·a·day \'fa-rə-,dā, -dē\ Michael 1791–1867 Eng. chemist and physicist

Far·ra·gut \'fa-rə-gət\ David Glasgow 1801–1870 Amer. admiral

Faulk·ner \'fȯk-nər\ William 1897–1962 Amer. author; Nobel Prize winner (1949)

Faust \'faůst\ *or* **Fau·stus** \'faů-stəs, 'fȯ-\ magician in Ger. legend who sells his soul to the devil for knowledge and power

Fawkes \'fȯks\ Guy 1570–1606 Eng. conspirator

Fer·di·nand \'fər-də-,nand\ **V** of Castile *or* **II** of Aragon 1452–1516 *Ferdinand the Catholic* king of Castile (1474–1504), of Aragon (1479–1516), of Naples (1504–16); husband of Isabella I

Fer·mi \'fer-(,)mē\ Enrico 1901–1954 Amer. (Ital.-born) physicist; Nobel Prize winner (1938)

Field·ing \'fēl-diŋ\ Henry 1707–1754 Eng. author

Fill·more \'fil-,mȯr\ Millard 1800–1874 13th pres. of the U.S. (1850–53)

Fitz·ger·ald \fits-'jer-əld\ Ella 1917–1996 Amer. singer

Fitzgerald F. Scott 1896–1940 *Francis Scott Key Fitzgerald* Amer. author

Flem·ing \'fle-miŋ\ Sir Alexander 1881–1955 Brit. bacteriologist; Nobel Prize winner (1945)

Flo·ra \'flȯr-ə\ goddess of flowers in Roman mythology

Flying Dutchman legendary Dutch mariner condemned to sail the seas until Judgment Day

Ford \'fȯrd\ Gerald Rudolph 1913– 38th pres. of the U.S. (1974–77)

Ford Henry 1863–1947 Amer. automobile manufacturer

Fos·sey \'fȯ-sē, 'fä-\ Dian 1932–1985 Amer. zoologist

Fos·ter \'fȯs-tər, 'fäs-\ Stephen Collins 1826–1864 Amer. songwriter

Fran·cis of As·si·si \'fran(t)-səs-əv-ə-'si-sē, -'sē-\ Saint 1181/1182–1226 Ital. friar; founder of Franciscan order

Fran·co \'fräŋ-(,)kō, 'fraŋ-\ Francisco 1892–1975 Span. general, dictator, and head of Span. state (1936–75)

Frank \'fraŋk, 'fräŋk\ Anne 1929–1945 Ger.-born diarist during the Holocaust

Frank·lin \'fraŋ-klən\ Benjamin 1706–1790 Amer. patriot, author, and inventor

Fred·er·ick I \'fre-d(ə-)rik\ ca 1123–1190 *Frederick Barbarossa* Holy Roman emperor (1152–90)

Frederick II 1712–1786 *Frederick the Great* king of Prussia (1740–86)

Fré·mont \'frē-,mänt\ John Charles 1813–1890 Amer. general and explorer

French \'french\ Daniel Chester 1850–1931 Amer. sculptor

Freud \'frȯid\ Sigmund 1856–1939 Austrian neurologist; founder of psychoanalysis

Frig·ga \'fri-gə\ wife of Odin and goddess of married love and the hearth in Norse mythology

Frost \'frȯst\ Robert Lee 1874–1963 Amer. poet

Ful·ler \'fů-lər\ (Richard) Buckminster 1895–1983 Amer. engineer and architect

Fuller (Sarah) Margaret 1810–1850 Amer. author and reformer

Ful·ton \'fůl-tᵊn\ Robert 1765–1815 Amer. inventor

Ga·bri·el \'gā-brē-əl\ archangel named in Hebrew tradition — compare MICHAEL; RAPHAEL; URIEL

Ga·ga·rin \gə-'gär-ən\ Yury Alekseyevich 1934–1968 Russ. astronaut; 1st man in space (1961)

Gage \'gāj\ Thomas 1721–1787 Brit. general in America

Gal·a·had \'ga-lə-,had\ knight of the Round Table in medieval legend who finds the Holy Grail

Gal·a·tea \,ga-lə-'tē-ə\ female figure sculpted by Pygmalion in Greek mythology and given life by Aphrodite in answer to the sculptor's prayer

Ga·len \'gā-lən\ 129–ca 216 A.D. Greek physician and writer

Ga·li·leo \,ga-lə-'lē-(,)ō, -'lā-\ 1564–1642 *Galileo Galilei* Ital. astronomer and physicist

Gall \'gȯl\ 1840?–1894 Sioux Indian leader

Ga·ma \'ga-mə, 'gä-\ Vasco da ca 1460–1524 Portuguese navigator and explorer

Gan·dhi \'gän-dē, 'gan-\ Indira 1917–1984 Indian prime minister (1966–77; 1980–84); daughter of Jawaharlal Nehru

Gandhi Mohandas Karamchand 1869–1948 *Ma·hat·ma* \mə-'hät-mə, -'hat-\ Indian leader

Gar·field \'gär-,fēld\ James Abram 1831–1881 20th pres. of the U.S. (1881)

Gar·i·bal·di \,ga-rə-'bȯl-dē\ Giuseppe 1807–1882 Ital. patriot

Gar·ri·son \'ga-rə-sən\ William Lloyd 1805–1879 Amer. abolitionist

Gates \'gāts\ Bill 1955– *William Henry Gates III* Amer. computer software manufacturer

Gau·guin \gō-'gaⁿ\ Paul 1848–1903 French painter

Gau·ta·ma Buddha \'gaů-tə-mə, -'gō-\ — see BUDDHA

Geh·rig \'ger-ig\ Lou 1903–1941 *Henry Louis Gehrig* Amer. baseball player

Gei·sel \'gī-zəl\ Theodor Seuss 1904–1991 pseud. *Dr. Seuss* Amer. author and illustrator

Gen·ghis Khan \,jeŋ-gəs-'kän, ,geŋ-\ ca 1162–1227 Mongol conqueror

George \'jȯrj\ name of 6 kings of Great Britain: **I** 1660–1727 (r. 1714–27); **II** 1683–1760 (r. 1727–60); **III** 1738–1820 (r. 1760–1820); **IV** 1762–1830 (r. 1820–30); **V** 1865–1936 (r. 1910–36); **VI** 1895–1952 (r. 1936–52); father of Elizabeth II

Ge·ron·i·mo \jə-'rä-nə-,mō\ 1829–1909 Apache Indian leader

Gersh·win \'gər-shwən\ George 1898–1937 Amer. composer

Gid·e·on \'gi-dē-ən\ Hebrew hero in the Bible

Gil·bert \'gil-bərt\ Sir William Schwenck 1836–1911 Eng. librettist and poet; collaborator with Sir Arthur Sullivan

Gins·burg \'ginz-,bərg\ Ruth Bader 1933– Amer. jurist

Glad·stone \'glad-,stōn, *chiefly Brit* -stən\ William Ewart 1809–1898 Brit. prime minister (1868–74; 1880–85; 1886; 1892–94)

Glenn \'glen\ John Herschel 1921– Amer. astronaut and politician; 1st Amer. to orbit the earth (1962)

Go·di·va \gə-'dī-və\ an Eng. gentlewoman who in legend rode naked through Coventry to save citizens from a tax

Goe·thals \'gō-thəlz\ George Washington 1858–1928 Amer. engineer who directed the building of the Panama Canal

Goe·the \'gə(r)-tə, 'gœ-tə\ Johann Wolfgang von 1749–1832 Ger. author

Gogh, van \van-'gō, -'gäk\ Vincent Willem 1853–1890 Dutch painter

Gol·ding \'gōl-diŋ\ William Gerald 1911–1993 Eng. author; Nobel Prize winner (1983)

Go·li·ath \gə-'lī-əth\ Philistine giant who is killed by David in the Bible

Gom·pers \'gäm-pərz\ Samuel 1850–1924 Amer. (Brit.-born) labor leader

Goo·dall \'gù-(,)dól, -(,)däl\ Jane 1934–   Brit. zoologist

Good·year \'gùd-,yir\ Charles 1800–1860 Amer. inventor

Gor·ba·chev \,gór-bə-'chóf, -'chef\ Mikhail Sergeyevich 1931–   Soviet leader of Communist party (1985–91); pres. of U.S.S.R. (1990–91); Nobel Prize winner (1990)

Gore \'gór\ Albert, Jr. 1948–   vice pres. of the U.S. (1993–2001)

Gor·gas \'gór-gəs\ William Crawford 1854–1920 Amer. army surgeon

Gra·ham \'grā-əm, 'gra(-ə)m\ Martha 1893–1991 Amer. dancer and choreographer

Grant \'grant\ Ulysses S. 1822–1885 orig. *Hiram Ulysses Grant* Amer. general; 18th pres. of the U.S. (1869–77)

Gre·co, El \el-'gre-(,)kō\ 1541–1614 *Doménikos Theotokópoulos* Span. (Cretan-born) painter

Gree·ley \'grē-lē\ Horace 1811–1872 Amer. journalist and politician

Greene \'grēn\ (Henry) Graham 1904–1991 Brit. author

Greene Nathanael 1742–1786 Amer. Revolutionary general

Greg·o·ry \'gre-g(ə-)rē\ name of 16 popes: esp. Saint *ca* 540–604 A.D. *Gregory the Great* (pope 590–604); Saint *ca* 1020–1085 (pope 1073–85); 1502–1585 (pope 1572–85)

Grey \'grā\ Lady Jane 1537–1554 queen of England for 9 days (1553)

Grey Zane 1872–1939 Amer. author

Grieg \'grēg\ Edward Hagerup 1843–1907 Norwegian composer

Grimm \'grim\ Jacob 1785–1863 and his brother Wilhelm 1786–1859 Ger. philologists and folklorists

Guin·e·vere \'gwi-nə-,vir\ legendary wife of King Arthur and lover of Lancelot

Gu·ten·berg \'gü-t°n-,bərg\ Johannes *ca* 1400–1468 Ger. inventor of printing method from movable type

Ha·des \'hā-(,)dēz\ — see PLUTO

Ha·dri·an \'hā-drē-ən\ 76–138 A.D. Roman emperor (117–138)

Ha·gar \'hā-,gär, -gər\ mistress of Abraham and mother of Ishmael in the Bible

Hai·le Se·las·sie \'hī-lē-sə-'la-sē, -'lä-\ 1892–1975 emperor of Ethiopia (1930–36; 1941–74)

Hale \'hāl\ Edward Everett 1822–1909 Amer. minister and author

Hale Nathan 1755–1776 Amer. Revolutionary hero

Hal·ley \'ha-lē\ Edmond *or* Edmund 1656–1742 Eng. astronomer and mathematician

Hal·sey \'hól-sē, -zē\ William Frederick 1882–1959 Amer. admiral

Ham·il·ton \'ha-məl-tən\ Alexander 1755–1804 Amer. political leader

Ham·mu·ra·bi \,ha-mə-'rä-bē\ *died ca* 1750 B.C. king of Babylon (*ca* 1792–50)

Han·cock \'han-,käk\ John 1737–1793 Amer. Revolutionary patriot

Han·del \'han-d°l\ George Frideric 1685–1759 Brit. (Ger.-born) composer

Han·dy \'han-dē\ W. C. 1873–1958 *William Christopher Handy* Amer. blues musician and composer

Han·ni·bal \'ha-nə-bəl\ 247–183? B.C. Carthaginian general

Har·ding \'här-diŋ\ Warren Gamaliel 1865–1923 29th pres. of the U.S. (1921–23)

Har·dy \'här-dē\ Thomas 1840–1928 Eng. author

Har·ri·son \'ha-rə-sən\ Benjamin 1833–1901 23rd pres. of the U.S. (1889–93); grandson of W. H. Harrison

Harrison William Henry 1773–1841 Amer. general; 9th pres. of the U.S. (1841)

Harte \'härt\ Bret 1836–1902 orig. *Francis Brett Harte* Amer. author

Har·vey \'här-vē\ William 1578–1657 Eng. physician and anatomist

Haw·thorne \'hó-,thórn\ Nathaniel 1804–1864 Amer. author

Haydn \'hī-d°n\ Franz Joseph 1732–1809 Austrian composer

Hayes \'hāz\ Rutherford Birchard 1822–1893 19th pres. of the U.S. (1877–81)

Hearst \'hərst\ William Randolph 1863–1951 Amer. newspaper publisher

Hec·tor \'hek-tər\ son of Priam and Hecuba; Trojan hero slain by Achilles in Greek mythology

Hec·u·ba \'he-kyə-bə\ wife of Priam in Greek mythology

Hel·en of Troy \,he-lən-əv-'tròi\ wife of Menelaus whose abduction by Paris in Greek mythology causes the Trojan War

He·li·os \'hē-lē-əs, -(,)ös\ god of the sun in Greek mythology — compare SOL

Hem·ing·way \'he-miŋ-,wā\ Ernest Miller 1899–1961 Amer. author; Nobel Prize winner (1954)

Hen·ry \'hen-rē\ name of 8 kings of England: **I** 1068–1135 (r. 1100–35); **II** 1133–1189 (r. 1154–89); **III** 1207–1272 (r. 1216–72); **IV** 1366–1413 (r. 1399–1413); **V** 1387–1422 (r. 1413–22); **VI** 1421–1471 (r. 1422–61; 1470–71); **VII** 1457–1509 (r. 1485–1509); **VIII** 1491–1547 (r. 1509–47)

Henry name of 4 kings of France: **I** *ca* 1008–1060 (r. 1031–60); **II** 1519–1559 (r. 1547–59); **III** 1551–1589 (r. 1574–89); **IV** 1553–1610 *Henry of Navarre* (r. 1589–1610)

Henry O. 1862–1910 pseud. of *William Sydney Porter* Amer. author

Henry Patrick 1736–1799 Amer. patriot and orator

Hen·son \'hen(t)-sən\ Matthew Alexander 1866–1955 Amer. arctic explorer

He·phaes·tus \hi-'fes-təs, -'fēs-\ god of fire and of metalworking in Greek mythology — compare VULCAN

He·ra \'hir-ə, 'he-rə, 'her-ə\ sister and wife of Zeus and goddess of women and marriage in Greek mythology — compare JUNO

Her·cu·les \'hər-kyə-,lēz\ *or* **Her·a·cles** \'her-ə-,klēz-, 'he-rə-\ hero in Greek mythology noted for his strength

Her·maph·ro·di·tus \(,)hər-,ma-frə-'dī-təs\ son of Hermes and Aphrodite who in Greek mythology is joined with a nymph into one body

Her·mes \'hər-(,)mēz\ god of commerce, eloquence, invention, travel, and theft who serves as herald and messenger of the other gods in Greek mythology — compare MERCURY

Her·od \'her-əd\ 73–4 B.C. *Herod the Great* Roman king of Judea (37–4)

Herod An·ti·pas \'an-tə-pəs, -,pas\ 21 B.C.–39 A.D., Roman governor of Galilee (4 B.C., –39 A.D.); son of Herod the Great

Hes·se \'he-sə\ Hermann 1877–1962 Ger. author; Nobel Prize winner (1946)

Hey·er·dahl \'hā-ər-,däl\ Thor 1914–2002 Norwegian explorer and author

Hi·a·wa·tha \,hī-ə-'wò-thə, ,hē-ə-, -'wä-\ legendary Iroquois Indian chief

Hick·ok \'hi-,käk\ Wild Bill 1837–1876 orig. *James Butler Hickok* Amer. frontiersman and U.S. marshal

Hil·ton \'hil-t°n\ James 1900–1954 Eng. novelist

Hip·poc·ra·tes \hi-'pä-krə-,tēz\ *ca* 460–*ca* 377 B.C. Greek physician

Hi·ro·hi·to \,hir-ō-'hē-(,)tō\ 1901–1989 emperor of Japan (1926–89)

Hit·ler \'hit-lər\ Adolf 1889–1945 Ger. (Austrian-born) chancellor and dictator (1933–45)

Hodg·kin \'häj-kin\ Dorothy Mary 1910–1994 née *Crowfoot* Brit. physicist; Nobel Prize winner (1964)

Holmes \'hōmz, 'hōlmz\ Oliver Wendell 1809–1894 Amer. physician and author

Holmes Oliver Wendell, Jr. 1841–1935 Amer. jurist; son of the preceding

Ho·mer \'hō-mər\ *fl.* 9th *or* 8th cent. B.C. Greek epic poet

Homer Winslow 1836–1910 Amer. painter

Hooke \'hùk\ Robert 1635–1703 Eng. scientist

Hook·er \'hù-kər\ Thomas 1586?–1647 Eng. colonist; a founder of Connecticut

Hoo·ver \'hü-vər\ Herbert Clark 1874–1964 31st pres. of the U.S. (1929–33)

Hoover John Edgar 1895–1972 Amer. director of the Federal Bureau of Investigation (1924–72)

Hop·per \'hä-pər\ Grace 1906–1992 née *Murray* Amer. admiral, mathematician, and computer scientist

Hou·di·ni \hü-'dē-nē\ Harry 1874–1926 orig. *Erik Weisz* Amer. magician

Hous·ton \'hyü-stən, 'yü-\ Sam 1793–1863 *Samuel Houston* Amer. politician; pres. of the Republic of Texas (1836–38; 1841–44)

Howe \'haú\ Elias 1819–1867 Amer. inventor

Howe Julia 1819–1910 née *Ward* Amer. suffragist and reformer

Hud·son \'həd-sən\ Henry *ca* 1565–1611 Eng. explorer

Hughes \'hyüz\ (James) Langston 1902–1967 Amer. author

Hugo \'hyü-(,)gō, 'yü-\ Victor 1802–1885 French author

Hus·sein I \hü-'sān\ 1935–1999 king of Jordan (1952–99)

Hutch·in·son \'hə-chə(n)-sən\ Anne 1591–1643 née *Marbury* Eng. colonist and religious leader in America

Hutchinson Thomas 1711–1780 Amer. colonial administrator

Hux·ley \'həks-lē\ Aldous Leonard 1894–1963 Eng. author

Hy·men \'hī-mən\ god of marriage in Greek mythology

Ib·sen \'ib-sən, 'ip-\ Henrik 1828–1906 Norwegian playwright

Ic·a·rus \'i-kə-rəs\ son of Daedalus who in Greek mythology falls into the sea when the wax of his artificial wings melts as he flies too near the sun

Ig·na·tius \ig-'nā-sh(ē-)əs\ Saint 1491–1556 *Ignatius of Loyola* Span. priest; founder of Society of Jesus (Jesuits)

In·no·cent \'i-nə-sənt\ name of 13 popes: esp. **II** *died* 1143 (pope 1130–43); **III** 1160/61–1216 (pope 1198–1216); **IV** *died* 1254 (pope 1243–54); **XI** 1611–1689 (pope 1676–89)

Ir·ving \'ər-vin\ Washington 1783–1859 Amer. author

Isaac \'ī-zik, -zək\ son of Abraham and father of Jacob in the Bible

Is·a·bel·la I \,i-zə-'be-lə\ 1451–1504 queen of Castile (1474–1504) and of Aragon (1479–1504); wife of Ferdinand V

Isa·iah \ī-'zā-ə, *chiefly Brit* -'zī-\ Hebrew prophet of the 8th cent. B.C.

Ish·ma·el \'ish-(,)mā-əl, -mē-\ outcast son of Abraham and Hagar in the Bible

Ives \'īvz\ Charles Edward 1874–1954 Amer. composer

Jack·son \'jak-sən\ Andrew 1767–1845 Amer. general; 7th pres. of the U.S. (1829–37)

Jackson Thomas Jonathan 1824–1863 *Stonewall Jackson* Amer. Confederate general

Ja·cob \'jā-kəb\ son of Isaac and Rebekah and younger twin brother of Esau in the Bible

James \'jāmz\ one of the 12 apostles in the Bible

James *the Less* one of the 12 apostles in the Bible

James name of 2 kings of Great Britain: **I** 1566–1625 (r. 1603–25); king of Scotland as *James VI* (r. 1567–1625); **II** 1633–1701 (r. 1685–88)

James Henry 1843–1916 Brit. (Amer.-born) author

Ja·nus \'jā-nəs\ god of gates and doors and of all beginnings in Roman mythology and that is pictured with two opposite faces

Ja·son \'jā-sⁿ\ hero in Greek mythology noted for his successful quest of the Golden Fleece

Jay \'jā\ John 1745–1829 Amer. jurist and statesman; 1st chief justice of the U.S. Supreme Court (1789–95)

Jef·fer·son \'je-fər-sən\ Thomas 1743–1826 3d pres. of the U.S. (1801–09)

Jem·i·son \'je-mə-sən\ Mae 1956–   Amer. astronaut and physician

Jer·e·mi·ah \,jer-ə-'mī-ə\ Hebrew prophet of the 7th–6th cent. B.C.

Je·sus \'jē-zəs, -zəz\ *or* **Jesus Christ** *ca* 6 B.C.–*ca* 30 A.D. source of the Christian religion and Savior in the Christian faith

Jez·e·bel \'je-zə-,bel\ queen of Israel and wife of Ahab who is noted for her wickedness in the Bible

Joan of Arc \,jōn-əv-'ärk\ Saint *ca* 1412–1431 *the Maid of Orléans* French national heroine

Job \'jōb\ man in the Bible who has many sufferings but keeps his faith

Jo·cas·ta \jō-'kas-tə\ queen of Thebes in Greek mythology who unknowingly marries her son Oedipus

John \'jän\ one of the 12 apostles believed to be the author of the 4th Gospel, three Epistles, and the Book of Revelation

John name of 21 popes: esp. **XXIII** 1881–1963 (pope 1958–63)

John 1167–1216 *John Lackland* king of England (1199–1216)

John·son \'jän(t)-sən\ Andrew 1808–1875 17th pres. of the U.S. (1865–69)

Johnson Lyndon Baines 1908–1973 36th pres. of the U.S. (1963–69)

Johnson Samuel 1709–1784 *Dr. Johnson* Eng. lexicographer and author

John the Baptist Saint, 1st cent. A.D. prophet and baptizer of Jesus in the Bible

Jol·liet *or* **Jo·liet** \zhól-'yā\ Louis 1645–1700 French-Canad. explorer

Jo·nah \'jō-nə\ Hebrew prophet who in the Bible spends three days in the belly of a great fish

Jones \'jōnz\ John Paul 1747–1792 Amer. (Scot.-born) naval officer

Jop·lin \'jä-plən\ Scott 1868–1917 Amer. pianist and composer

Jor·dan \'jór-dⁿ\ Michael 1963–   Amer. basketball player

Jo·seph \'jō-zəf\ son of Jacob in the Bible who rises to high office in Egypt after being sold into slavery by his brothers

Joseph Chief *ca* 1840–1904 Nez Percé Indian chief

Joseph Saint, husband of Mary, the mother of Jesus, in the Bible

Josh·ua \'jä-sh(ə-)wə\ Hebrew leader in the Bible who succeeds Moses during the settlement of the Israelites in Canaan

Joyce \'jóis\ James Augustine 1882–1941 Irish author

Juan Car·los \'(h)wän-'kär-,lōs\ 1938–   king of Spain (1975–   )

Ju·dah \'jü-də\ son of Jacob and ancestor of one of the 12 tribes of Israel in the Bible

Ju·das \'jü-dəs\ *or* **Judas Is·car·i·ot** \-is-'ka-rē-ət\ one of the 12 apostles and the betrayer of Jesus in the Bible

Jung \'yùn\ Carl Gustav 1875–1961 Swiss psychologist

Ju·no \'jü-(,)nō\ queen of heaven, wife of Jupiter, and goddess of light, birth, women, and marriage in Roman mythology — compare HERA

Ju·pi·ter \'jü-pə-tər\ chief god and god of light, of the sky and weather, and of the state in Roman mythology — compare ZEUS

Kalb \'kälp, 'kalb\ Johann 1721–1780 Baron *de Kalb* \di-'kalb\ Ger. general in Amer. Revolutionary army

Ka·me·ha·me·ha I \kə-,mā-ə-'mā-(,)hä\ 1758?–1819 orig. *Pai·ea* Hawaiian king (1795–1819)

Keats \'kēts\ John 1795–1821 Eng. poet

Kel·ler \'ke-lər\ Helen Adams 1880–1968 Amer. deaf and blind lecturer and author

Kel·vin \'kel-vən\ 1st Baron 1824–1907 *William Thomson* Brit. mathematician and physicist

Ken·ne·dy \'ke-nə-dē\ John Fitzgerald 1917–1963 35th pres. of the U.S. (1961–63)

Kennedy Robert Francis 1925–1968 attorney general of the U.S. (1961–64); brother of the preceding

Ke·o·kuk \'kē-ə-,kək\ 1780?–1848 Amer. Indian chief

Key \'kē\ Francis Scott 1779–1843 Amer. lawyer; author of "The Star-Spangled Banner"

Khayyám Omar — see OMAR KHAYYÁM

Khru·shchev \krüsh-'chóf, -'chóv\ Nikita Sergeyevich 1894–1971 premier of U.S.S.R. (1958–64)

Khu·fu \'kü-(,)fü\ *or Greek* **Che·ops** \'kē-,äps\ *fl.* 25th cent. B.C. king of Egypt and pyramid builder

Kidd \'kid\ William *ca* 1645–1701 *Captain Kidd* Scot. pirate

Kier·ke·gaard \'kir-kə-,gär(d), -,gór\ Søren 1813–1855 Danish philosopher

King \'kin\ Billie Jean 1943–   Amer. tennis player

King Martin Luther, Jr. 1929–1968 Amer. minister and civil rights leader; Nobel Prize winner (1964)

Kip·ling \'kip-lin\ Rudyard 1865–1936 Eng. author; Nobel Prize winner (1907)

Kis·sin·ger \'ki-sⁿ-jər\ Henry Alfred 1923–   Amer. (Ger.-born) government official; U.S. secretary of state (1973–77); Nobel Prize winner (1973)

Knox \'näks\ John *ca* 1514–1572 Scot. religious reformer

Koch \'kók, 'kók, 'kōk, 'kōk\ Robert 1843–1910 Ger. bacteriologist; Nobel Prize winner (1905)

Koś·ciusz·ko \,kösh-'chüsh-(,)kō, ,kä-sē-'əs-,kō\ Tadeusz 1746–1817 Polish patriot and general in Amer. Revolutionary army

Krish·na \'krish-nə, 'krēsh-\ god worshipped in later Hinduism

Ku·blai Khan \'kü-,blə-'kän, -,blī-\ 1215–1294 Mongol leader; grandson of Genghis Khan

La·fa·yette \,lä-fē-'et, ,la-\ Marquis de 1757–1834 French general in Amer. Revolutionary army

La·ius \'lā-əs, 'lī-əs\ king of Thebes who in Greek mythology is killed by his son Oedipus

Lan·ce·lot \'lan(t)-sə-ˌlät, 'län(t)-, -s(ə-)lət\ legendary knight of the Round Table and lover of Queen Guinevere

Lange \'laŋ\ Dorothea 1895–1965 Amer. photographer

Lao–tzu \'laúd-'zə\ *fl.* 6th cent. B.C. Chinese philosopher

La Salle \lə-'sal\ Sieur de 1643–1687 *René-Robert Cavelier* French explorer

La·voi·sier \ləv-'wä-zē-ˌā\ Antoine-Laurent 1743–1794 French chemist

Law·rence \'lôr-ən(t)s, 'lär-\ D. H. 1885–1930 *David Herbert Lawrence* Eng. author

Lawrence Thomas Edward 1888–1935 *Lawrence of Arabia* Brit. soldier and author

Laz·a·rus \'laz-rəs, 'la-zə-\ brother of Mary and Martha who in the Bible is raised by Jesus from the dead

Lazarus beggar in the biblical parable of the rich man and the beggar

Le·da \'lē-də\ Spartan princess in Greek mythology who is courted by Zeus in the form of a swan

Lee \'lē\ Ann 1736–1784 Eng. mystic; founder of Shaker society in the U.S.

Lee Henry 1756–1818 *Light-Horse Harry* Amer. general

Lee Robert Edward 1807–1870 Amer. Confederate general; son of the preceding

Leeu·wen·hoek \'lā-vən-ˌhúk\ Antonie van 1632–1723 Dutch naturalist

Leif Er·iks·son *or* **Er·ics·son** \ˌlāv-'er-ik-sən, ˌlēf-\ *fl.* 1000 Norwegian explorer; son of Erik the Red

Le·nin \'le-nən\ 1870–1924 orig. *Vladimir Ilyich Ul·ya·nov* \ül-'yän-əf, -ˌóf, -ˌóv\ Russ. Communist leader

Leo \'lē-(ˌ)ō\ name of 13 popes: esp. **I** Saint *died* 461 A.D. *Leo the Great* (pope 440–61); **III** Saint *died* 816 (pope 795–816); **XIII** 1810–1903 (pope 1878–1903)

Le·o·nar·do da Vin·ci \ˌlē-ə-'när-(ˌ)dō-də-'vin-chē, ˌlā-, -'vēn-\ 1452–1519 Ital. painter, sculptor, architect, and engineer

Lew·is \'lü-əs\ C. S. 1898–1963 *Clive Staples Lewis* Brit. author

Lewis John Llewellyn 1880–1969 Amer. labor leader

Lewis Meriwether 1774–1809 Amer. explorer (with William Clark)

Lewis Sinclair 1885–1951 Amer. author; Nobel Prize winner (1930)

Lin·coln \'liŋ-kən\ Abraham 1809–1865 16th pres. of the U.S. (1861–65)

Lind·bergh \'lin(d)-ˌbərg\ Charles Augustus 1902–1974 Amer. aviator

Lin·nae·us \lə-'nē-əs, -'nā-\ Carolus 1707–1778 *Carl von Linné* Swedish botanist

Lis·ter \'lis-tər\ Joseph 1827–1912 Eng. surgeon and medical scientist

Liszt \'list\ Franz 1811–1886 Hungarian pianist and composer

Liv·ing·stone \'li-viŋ-stən\ David 1813–1873 Scot. missionary in Africa

Lon·don \'lən-dən\ Jack 1876–1916 *John Griffith London* Amer. author

Long·fel·low \'lóŋ-ˌfe-(ˌ)lō\ Henry Wadsworth 1807–1882 Amer. poet

Lou·is \'lü-ē, lü-ē\ name of 18 kings of France: esp. **IX** Saint 1214–1270 (r. 1226–70); **XI** 1423–1483 (r. 1461–83); **XII** 1462–1515 (r. 1498–1515); **XIII** 1601–1643 (r. 1610–43); **XIV** 1638–1715 (r. 1643–1715); **XV** 1710–1774 (r. 1715–74); **XVI** 1754–1793 (r. 1774–92; guillotined); **XVII** 1785–1795 (r. in name 1793–95); **XVIII** 1755–1824 (r. 1814–15; 1815–24)

Lou·is \'lü-əs\ Joe 1914–1981 orig. *Joseph Louis Barrow* Amer. boxer

Low \'lō\ Juliette 1860–1927 née *Gordon* Amer. founder of the Girl Scouts

Low·ell \'lō-əl\ Amy 1874–1925 Amer. poet

Lowell James Russell 1819–1891 Amer. author

Luke \'lük\ physician and companion of the apostle Paul believed to be the author of the 3d Gospel and the Book of Acts

Lu·ther \'lü-thər\ Martin 1483–1546 Ger. Reformation leader

Ly·on \'lī-ən\ Mary 1797–1849 Amer. educator

Mac·Ar·thur \mə-'kär-thər\ Douglas 1880–1964 Amer. general

Ma·cy \'mā-sē\ Anne Sullivan 1866–1936 née *Sullivan* Amer. educator; teacher of Helen Keller

Mad·i·son \'ma-də-sən\ James 1751–1836 4th pres. of the U.S. (1809–17)

Ma·gel·lan \mə-'je-lən, *chiefly Brit* -'ge-\ Ferdinand *ca* 1480–1521 Portuguese navigator and explorer

Mal·colm X \'mal-kəm-'eks\ 1925–1965 Amer. civil rights leader

Man·dela \man-'de-lə\ Nelson Rolihlahla 1918– pres. of South Africa (1994–99); Nobel Prize winner (1993)

Ma·net \ma-'nā, mä-\ Édouard 1832–1883 French painter

Mann \'man\ Horace 1796–1859 Amer. educator

Mao Tse-tung *or* **Mao Zedong** \'maú-(ˌ)(d)zə-'dùŋ, -(ˌ)tsə-\ 1893–1976 Chinese Communist leader of People's Republic of China (1949–76)

Mar·co·ni \mär-'kō-nē\ Guglielmo 1874–1937 Ital. physicist and inventor; Nobel Prize winner (1909)

Marco Polo — see POLO

Ma·rie An·toi·nette \ˌan-twə-'net, -tə-\ 1755–1793 wife of Louis XVI of France

Mar·i·on \'mer-ē-ən\ Francis 1732?–1795 *the Swamp Fox* Amer. commander in Revolution

Mark \'märk\ evangelist believed to be the author of the 2d Gospel

Mark Antony — see ANTONY

Mar·quette \mär-'ket\ Jacques 1637–1675 *Père Marquette* French-born Jesuit missionary and explorer in America

Mars \'märz\ god of war in Roman mythology — compare ARES

Mar·shall \'mär-shəl\ George Catlett 1880–1959 Amer. general and diplomat; Nobel Prize winner (1953)

Marshall John 1755–1835 Amer. jurist; chief justice of the U.S. Supreme Court (1801–35)

Mar·tha \'mär-thə\ sister of Lazarus and Mary and friend of Jesus in the Bible

Mar·tin \'mär-tᵊn, mär-'taⁿ\ Saint 316–397 *Martin of Tours* \-'túr\ patron saint of France

Mar·tin \'mär-tᵊn\ Paul (Edgar Phillipe) 1938– Canad. prime minister (2003–)

Marx \'märks\ Karl 1818–1883 Ger. political philosopher and socialist

Mary \'mer-ē, 'ma-rē, 'mā-rē\ *Saint Mary*; *Virgin Mary* mother of Jesus

Mary sister of Lazarus and Martha in the Bible

Mary I 1516–1558 *Mary Tudor*; *Bloody Mary* queen of England (1553–58)

Mary II 1662–1694 joint Brit. sovereign with William III (1689–94)

Mary Mag·da·lene \'mag-də-lən, -ˌlēn\ woman in the Bible who sees the risen Christ

Mary, Queen of Scots 1542–1587 *Mary Stuart* queen of Scotland (1542–67)

Mas·sa·soit \ˌma-sə-'sóit\ *died* 1661 Amer. Indian chief

Math·er \'ma-thər, -thər\ Cotton 1663–1728 Amer. religious leader and author

Mather Increase 1639–1723 Amer. minister and author; father of Cotton Mather

Ma·tisse \ma-'tēs, mə-\ Henri 1869–1954 French painter

Mat·thew \'ma-(ˌ)thyü\ apostle believed to be the author of the 1st Gospel

Mau·pas·sant \ˌmō-pə-'säⁿ\ Guy de 1850–1893 French author

Mays \'māz\ Willie Howard 1931– Amer. baseball player

Mc·Au·liffe \mə-'kól-əf\ Christa 1948–1986 Amer. teacher; 1st private citizen in space (1986)

Mc·Car·thy \mə-'kär-thē\ Joseph Raymond 1908–1957 Amer. politician

Mc·Clel·lan \mə-'kle-lən\ George Brinton 1826–1885 Amer. general

Mc·Clin·tock \mə-'klin-tək\ Barbara 1902–1992 Amer. botanist; Nobel Prize winner (1983)

Mc·Cor·mick \mə-'kór-mik\ Cyrus Hall 1809–1884 Amer. inventor

Mc·Kin·ley \mə-'kin-lē\ William 1843–1901 25th pres. of the U.S. (1897–1901)

Mead \'mēd\ Margaret 1901–1978 Amer. anthropologist

Meade \'mēd\ George Gordon 1815–1872 Amer. Civil War general

Mea·ny \'mē-nē\ George 1894–1980 Amer. labor leader

Me·dea \mə-'dē-ə\ woman with magic powers in Greek

mythology who helps Jason to win the Golden Fleece and who kills her children when he leaves her

Medici Catherine de' — see CATHERINE DE MÉDICIS

Me·di·ci \'me-də-chē\ Lorenzo de' 1449–1492 *Lorenzo the Magnificent* Florentine statesman, ruler, and patron of the arts

Me·du·sa \mi-'dü-sə, -'dyü-, -zə\ Gorgon in Greek mythology slain by Perseus

Me·ir \mā-'ir\ Golda 1898–1978 prime minister of Israel (1969–74)

Mel·ville \'mel-,vil\ Herman 1819–1891 Amer. author

Men·del \'men-dᵊl\ Gregor Johann 1822–1884 Austrian botanist

Men·dels·sohn (–Bar·thol·dy) \'men-dᵊl-sən(-bär-'tȯl-dē, -'thȯl-)\ Felix 1809–1847 Ger. composer

Men·e·la·us \,me-nə-'lā-əs\ king of Sparta, brother of Agamemnon, and husband of Helen of Troy in Greek mythology

Meph·is·toph·e·les \,me-fə-'stä-fə-,lēz\ chief devil in the Faust legend

Mer·ca·tor \(,)mər-'kā-tər\ Gerardus 1512–1594 orig. *Gerhard Kremer* Flemish cartographer

Mer·cu·ry \'mər-kyə-rē, -k(ə-)rē\ god of commerce, eloquence, travel, and theft who serves as messenger of the other gods in Roman mythology — compare HERMES

Mer·lin \'mər-lən\ prophet and magician in the legend of King Arthur

Met·a·com \'me-tə-,käm\ *or* **King Philip** ca 1638–1676 *Met·a·com·et* \,me-tə-'käm-ət\ Amer. Indian chief; son of Massasoit

Mi·chael \'mī-kəl\ archangel named in Hebrew tradition — compare GABRIEL; RAPHAEL; URIEL

Mi·chel·an·ge·lo \,mī-kə-'lan-jə-,lō, ,mi-, ,mē-kə-'län-\ 1475–1564 Ital. sculptor, painter, architect, and poet

Mi·das \'mī-dəs\ legendary king having the power to turn everything he touched into gold

Mil·lay \mi-'lā\ Edna St. Vincent 1892–1950 Amer. poet

Mil·ler \'mi-lər\ Arthur 1915–   Amer. playwright

Milne \'mil(n)\ A. A. 1882–1956 *Alan Alexander Milne* Eng. author

Mil·ton \'mil-tᵊn\ John 1608–1674 Eng. poet

Mi·ner·va \mə-'nər-və\ goddess of wisdom in Roman mythology — compare ATHENA

Mi·no·taur \'mi-nə-,tȯr, 'mī-\ monster in Greek mythology shaped half like a man and half like a bull

Min·u·it \'min-yə-wət\ Peter *ca* 1580–1638 Dutch colonial administrator in America

Mitch·ell \'mi-chəl\ Maria 1818–1889 Amer. astronomer

Mo·lière \mōl-'yer, 'mōl-,\ 1622–1673 orig. *Jean-Baptiste Poquelin* French actor and playwright

Mo·net \mō-'nā\ Claude 1840–1926 French painter

Mon·roe \mən-'rō\ James 1758–1831 5th pres. of the U.S. (1817–25)

Mont·calm \mänt-'kälm-, -'käm-\ Marquis de 1712–1759 *Louis-Joseph de Montcalm-Grozon* French field marshal in Canada

Mon·tes·so·ri \,män-tə-'sȯr-ē\ Maria 1870–1952 Ital. educator

Mon·te·zu·ma II \,män-tə-'zü-mə\ 1466–1520 last Aztec emperor of Mexico (1502–20)

Moore \'mȯr, 'mu̇r\ Marianne 1887–1972 Amer. poet

More \'mȯr\ Sir Thomas 1478–1535 *Saint Thomas More* Eng. public official and author

Mor·gan \'mȯr-gən\ J. P. 1837–1913 *John Pierpont Morgan* Amer. financier

Mor·ri·son \'mȯr-ə-sən, 'mär-\ Toni 1931–   orig. *Chloe Anthony Wofford* Amer. author; Nobel Prize winner (1993)

Morse \'mȯrs\ Samuel Finley Breese 1791–1872 Amer. artist and inventor

Mo·ses \'mō-zəz\ Hebrew prophet and lawgiver in the Bible

Moses Grandma 1860–1961 *Anna Mary Moses* née *Robertson* Amer. painter

Mott \'mät\ Lucretia 1793–1880 Amer. reformer

Mo·zart \'mōt-,särt\ Wolfgang Amadeus 1756–1791 Austrian composer

Mu·ham·mad \mō-'ha-məd, -'hä-\ *ca* 570–632 A.D. Arab prophet and founder of Islam

Mus·so·li·ni \,mü-sə-'lē-nē, ,mu̇-\ Be·ni·to \bə-'nēt-ō\ 1883–1945 *Il Du·ce* \ēl-'dü-chā\ Ital. fascist premier (1922–43)

Na·bo·kov \nə-'bȯ-kəf\ Vladimir 1899–1977 Amer. (Russ.⸗ born) author

Na·po·leon I \nə-'pōl-yən, -'pō-lē-ən\ *or* **Napoleon Bo·na·parte** \'bō-nə-,pärt\ 1769–1821 French general and emperor of the French (1804–15)

Nar·cis·sus \när-'si-səs\ beautiful youth in Greek mythology who pines away for love of his own reflection and is then turned into the narcissus flower

Nash \'nash\ Ogden 1902–1971 Amer. poet

Na·tion \'nā-shən\ Car·ry \'kar-ē\ Amelia 1846–1911 née *Moore* Amer. temperance agitator

Nav·ra·ti·lo·va \,nav-rə-tə-'lō-və\ Martina 1956– Amer. (Czech-born) tennis player

Neb·u·cha·drez·zar II \,ne-byə-kə-'dre-zər, -bə-\ *or* **Neb·u·chad·nez·zar** \-kəd-'ne-\ *ca* 630–*ca* 561 B.C. Chaldean king of Babylon (605–562)

Neh·ru \'ner-(,)ü, 'nā-(,)rü\ Ja·wa·har·lal \jə-'wä-hər-,läl\ 1889–1964 1st prime minister of Republic of India (1947–64)

Nel·son \'nel-sən\ Horatio 1758–1805 Viscount *Nelson* Brit. admiral

Nem·e·sis \'ne-mə-səs\ goddess of reward and punishment in Greek mythology

Nep·tune \'nep-,tün, -,tyün\ god of the sea in Roman mythology — compare POSEIDON

Ne·ro \'nē-(,)rō, 'nir-(,)ō\ 37–68 A.D. Roman emperor (54–68)

Nev·el·son \'ne-vəl-sən\ Louise 1900?–1988 Amer. sculptor

New·ton \'nü-tᵊn, 'nyü-\ Sir Isaac 1642–1727 Eng. mathematician and physicist

Nich·o·las \'ni-k(ə-)ləs\ Saint *fl.* 4th cent. A.D. Christian bishop

Nicholas I 1796–1855 czar of Russia (1825–55)

Nicholas II 1868–1918 last czar of Russia (1894–1917)

Nietz·sche \'nē-chə, -chē\ Friedrich Wilhelm 1844–1900 Ger. philosopher

Night·in·gale \'nī-tᵊn-,gāl, -tiŋ-\ Florence 1820–1910 *Lady of the Lamp* Eng. nurse and philanthropist

Ni·ke \'nī-kē\ goddess of victory in Greek mythology

Ni·o·be \'nī-ə-bē\ bereaved mother in Greek mythology who while weeping for her slain children is turned into a stone from which her tears continue to flow

Nix·on \'nik-sən\ Richard Milhous 1913–1994 37th pres. of the U.S. (1969–74)

No·ah \'nō-ə\ biblical builder of the ark in which he, his family, and living creatures of every kind survive the biblical Flood

No·bel \nō-'bel\ Alfred Bernhard 1833–1896 Swedish manufacturer, inventor, and philanthropist

Nor·man \'nȯr-mən\ Jessye 1945–   Amer. soprano

Oak·ley \'ōk-lē\ Annie 1860–1926 orig. *Phoebe Anne Oakley Moses* Amer. sharpshooter

Oce·anus \ō-'sē-ə-nəs\ Titan who rules over a great river encircling the earth in Greek mythology

O'·Con·nor \ō-'kä-nər\ (Mary) Flannery 1925–1964 Amer. author

O'Connor Sandra Day 1930–   Amer. jurist

Odin \'ō-dᵊn\ *or* **Wo·den** \'wō-dᵊn\ chief god, god of war, and patron of heroes in Norse mythology

Odys·seus \ō-'di-sē-əs, -'dis-yəs, -'di-shəs, -'di-,shüs\ *or* **Ulys·ses** \yu̇-'li-(,)sēz\ king of Ithaca and hero in Greek mythology

Oe·di·pus \'e-də-pəs, 'ē-\ son of Laius and Jocasta who in Greek mythology kills his father and marries his mother not knowing their identity

Ogle·thorpe \'ō-gəl-,thȯrp\ James Edward 1696–1785 Eng. general and founder of Georgia

O'·Keeffe \ō-'kēf\ Georgia 1887–1986 Amer. painter

Olaf V \'ō-ləf, -,läf, -laf\ 'ü-,läf\ 1903–1991 king of Norway (1957–91)

Omar Khay·yám \,ō-,mär-,kī-'yäm, ,ō-mər-, -'yam\ 1048–1131 Persian poet and astronomer

O'·Neill \ō-'nēl\ Eugene Gladstone 1888–1953 Amer. playwright; Nobel Prize winner (1936)

Or·pheus \'ȯr-,fyüs, -fē-əs\ poet and musician in Greek mythology

Or·well \'ȯr-,wel, -wəl\ George 1903–1950 pseud. of *Eric Arthur Blair* Eng. author

Osce·o·la \,ä-sē-'ō-lə, ,ō-\ *ca* 1804–1838 Seminole Indian chief

Otis \ 'ō-təs\ James 1725–1783 Amer. Revolutionary patriot

Ov·id \'ä-vəd\ 43 B.C., –17 A.D.? Roman poet

Ow·en \'ō-ən\ Robert 1771–1858 Welsh social reformer

Ow·ens \'ō-ənz\ Jesse 1913–1980 orig. *James Cleveland Owens* Amer. track-and-field athlete

Paine \'pān\ Thomas 1737–1809 Amer. (Eng.-born) political philosopher and author

Pan \'pan\ god of pastures, flocks, and shepherds in Greek mythology who is usu. represented as having the legs, ears, and horns of a goat

Pan·do·ra \pan-'dȯr-ə\ woman in Greek mythology who out of curiosity opens a box and lets loose all of the evils that trouble humans

Pank·hurst \'paŋk-ˌhərst\ Emmeline 1858–1928 née *Goulden* Eng. suffragist

Par·is \'pa-rəs\ son of Priam whose abduction of Helen of Troy in Greek mythology leads to the Trojan War

Park·man \'pärk-mən\ Francis 1823–1893 Amer. historian

Parks \'pärks\ Rosa 1913–   née *McCauley* Amer. civil rights activist

Pas·cal \pa-'skal, päs-'käl\ Blaise 1623–1662 French mathematician and philosopher

Pas·ter·nak \'pas-tər-ˌnak\ Boris Leonidovich 1890–1960 Russ. author; Nobel Prize winner (1958)

Pas·teur \pas-'tər\ Louis 1822–1895 French chemist and microbiologist

Pat·rick \pa-'trik\ Saint *fl.* 5th cent. A.D. apostle and patron saint of Ireland

Pat·ton \'pa-tⁿn\ George Smith 1885–1945 Amer. general

Paul \'pȯl\ Saint *died ca* 67 A.D. Christian missionary and author of several New Testament epistles

Paul name of 6 popes: esp. III 1468–1549 (pope 1534–49); V 1552–1621 (pope 1605–21); VI 1897–1978 (pope 1963–78)

Paul Bun·yan \'bən-yən\ giant lumberjack in Amer. folklore

Pau·ling \'pȯ-liŋ\ Linus Carl 1901–1994 Amer. chemist; Nobel Prize winner (1954, 1962)

Pav·lov \'päv-ˌlȯf, 'pav-, -ˌlȯv\ Ivan Petrovich 1849–1936 Russ. physiologist; Nobel Prize winner (1904)

Pa·vlo·va \'pav-lə-və, pav-'lō-\ Anna 1881–1931 Russ. ballerina

Pea·ry \'pir-ē\ Robert Edwin 1856–1920 Amer. arctic explorer

Pe·cos Bill \ˌpā-kəs-'bil\ cowboy in Amer. folklore known for his extraordinary feats

Peg·a·sus \'pe-gə-səs\ winged horse in Greek mythology

Penn \'pen\ William 1644–1718 Eng. Quaker leader and founder of Pennsylvania

Per·i·cles \'per-ə-ˌklēz\ *ca* 495–429 B.C. Athenian political leader

Per·ry \'per-ē\ Matthew Calbraith 1794–1858 Amer. commodore

Perry Oliver Hazard 1785–1819 Amer. naval officer; brother of the preceding

Per·seph·o·ne \pər-'se-fə-nē\ daughter of Zeus and Demeter who in Greek mythology is abducted by Pluto to rule with him over the underworld

Per·shing \'pər-shiŋ, -zhiŋ\ John Joseph 1860–1948 Amer. general

Pe·ter \'pē-tər\ Saint *died ca* 64 A.D. orig. *Si·mon* \'sī-mən-\ one of the 12 apostles in the Bible

Peter I 1672–1725 *Peter the Great* czar of Russia (1682–1725)

Phil·ip \'fi-ləp\ Saint, one of the 12 apostles in the Bible

Philip King — see METACOM

Philip name of 6 kings of France: esp. II *or* Philip Augustus 1165–1223 (r. 1179–1223); IV 1268–1314 *Philip the Fair* (r. 1285–1314); VI 1293–1350 (r. 1328–50)

Philip name of 5 kings of Spain: esp. II 1527–1598 (r. 1556–98); V 1683–1746 (r. 1700–46)

Philip II 382–336 B.C. king of Macedon (359–336); father of Alexander the Great

Pi·cas·so \pi-'kä-(ˌ)sō, -'ka-\ Pablo 1881–1973 Span. painter and sculptor in France

Pic·card \pi-'kär, -'kärd\ Auguste 1884–1962 and his son Jacques 1922–   Swiss scientists and developers of the bathyscaphe

Pick·ett \'pi-kət\ George Edward 1825–1875 Amer. Confederate general

Pierce \'pirs\ Franklin 1804–1869 14th pres. of the U.S. (1853–57)

Pi·late \'pī-lət\ Pon·tius \'pän-chəs, 'pən-chəs\ *died after* 36 A.D. Roman governor of Judea (26–36)

Pinkerton \'piŋ-kər-tⁿn\ Allan 1819–1884 Amer. (Scot.-born) detective

Pis·sar·ro \pə-'sär-(ˌ)ō\ Camille 1830–1903 French (West Indian-born) painter

Pitt \'pit\ William 1759–1806 *the Younger Pitt* Eng. prime minister (1783–1801; 1804–6)

Pi·us \'pī-əs\ name of 12 popes: esp. VII 1742–1823 (pope 1800–23); IX 1792–1878 (pope 1846–78); X Saint 1835–1914 (pope 1903–14); XI 1857–1939 (pope 1922–39); XII 1876–1958 (pope 1939–58)

Pi·zar·ro \pə-'zär-(ˌ)ō\ Francisco *ca* 1475–1541 Span. conqueror of Peru

Pla·to \'plā-(ˌ)tō\ *ca* 428–348 (*or* 347) B.C. Greek philosopher

Plu·to \'plü-(ˌ)tō\ god of the underworld in Greek mythology

Po·ca·hon·tas \ˌpō-kə-'hän-təs\ *ca* 1595–1617 Amer. Indian friend of the colonists at Jamestown; daughter of Powhatan

Poe \'pō\ Edgar Allan 1809–1849 Amer. author

Polk \'pōk\ James Knox 1795–1849 11th pres. of the U.S. (1845–49)

Po·lo \'pō-(ˌ)lō\ Marco *ca* 1254–1324 Venetian merchant and traveler

Poly·phe·mus \ˌpä-lə-'fē-məs\ a one-eyed creature in Greek mythology that is blinded by Odysseus

Ponce de Le·ón \ˌpän(t)-sə-ˌdā-lē-'ōn, ˌpänts-də-, -'lē-ən\ Juan 1460–1521 Span. explorer

Pon·ti·ac \'pän-tē-ˌak\ *ca* 1720–1769 Ottawa Indian chief

Por·ter \'pȯr-tər\ Cole Albert 1891–1964 Amer. composer

Porter Katherine Anne 1890–1980 Amer. author

Porter William Sydney — see O. HENRY

Po·sei·don \pə-'sī-dⁿn\ god of the sea in Greek mythology — compare NEPTUNE

Pot·ter \'pä-tər\ (Helen) Beatrix 1866–1943 Brit. author and illustrator

Pound \'paùnd\ Ezra Loomis 1885–1972 Amer. poet

Pound·mak·er \'paùnd-ˌmā-kər\ 1826–1886 Cree Indian chief

Pow·ell \'paù(-ə)l\ Colin Luther 1937–   Amer. general; U.S. secretary of state (2001–   )

Pow·ha·tan \ˌpaù-ə-'tan, paù-'ha-tⁿn\ 1550?–1618 Amer. Indian chief of a confederacy of Algonquian-speaking tribes; father of Pocahontas

Pres·ley \'pres-lē, 'prez-\ Elvis Aaron 1935–1977 Amer. popular singer

Pri·am \'prī-əm, -ˌam\ king of Troy during the Trojan War in Greek mythology

Price \'prīs\ (Mary) Leontyne 1927–   Amer. soprano

Pro·me·theus \prə-'mē-thē-əs, -ˌthyüs\ Titan in Greek mythology who is punished by Zeus for stealing fire from heaven and giving it to humans

Pro·teus \'prō-tyüs, -tē-əs\ sea god in Greek mythology who is capable of assuming different forms

Ptol·e·my \'tä-lə-mē\ *fl.* 2d cent. A.D. Greco-Egyptian astronomer, geographer, and mathematician in Alexandria

Puc·ci·ni \pü-'chē-nē\ Giacomo 1858–1924 Ital. composer

Pu·las·ki \pə-'las-kē, pyü-\ Kazimierz 1747–1779 Polish soldier in Amer. Revolutionary army

Pu·lit·zer \'pü-lət-sər (*family's pron*), 'pyü-\ Joseph 1847–1911 Amer. (Hungarian-born) journalist

Pu·tin \'pü-tin\ Vladimir Vladimirovich 1952–   pres. of Russia (2000–   )

Pyg·ma·lion \pig-'māl-yən, -'mā-lē-ən\ sculptor in Greek mythology who creates Galatea

Py·thag·o·ras \pə-'tha-gə-rəs, pī-\ *ca* 580–*ca* 500 B.C. Greek philosopher and mathematician

Ra \'rä\ god of the sun and chief deity of ancient Egypt

Ra·leigh *or* Ra·legh \'rȯ-lē, 'rä- *also* 'ra-\ Sir Walter 1554?–1618 Eng. navigator and writer

Ram·ses \'ram-ˌsēz\ *or* Ram·e·ses \'ra-mə-ˌsēz\ name of 12 kings of Egypt: esp. II (r. 1279–1213 B.C.,); III (r. 1187–1156 B.C.)

Ran·dolph \'ran-ˌdälf\ Asa Philip 1889–1979 Amer. labor and civil rights leader

Ra·pha·el \'ra-fē-əl, 'rä-, -ˌel\ archangel named in Hebrew tradition — compare GABRIEL; MICHAEL; URIEL

Ra·pha·el \'ra-fē-əl, 'rā-, 'rä-\ 1483–1520 orig. *Raffaello Sanzio* or *Santi* Ital. painter

Ras·pu·tin \ra-'spyü-t⁸n, -'spü-, -'spù-\ Grigory Yefimovich 1872–1916 Russ. mystic

Rea·gan \'rā-gən\ Ronald Wilson 1911–2004 40th pres. of the U.S. (1981–89)

Re·bek·ah \ri-'be-kə\ wife of Isaac and mother of Jacob in the Bible

Red Cloud \'red-ˌklaùd\ 1822–1909 Sioux Indian chief

Red Jack·et \'red-ˌja-kət\ 1758?–1830 *Sa·go·ye·wa·tha* \säˌgoi-(y)ə-'wä-thə\ Seneca Indian chief

Reed \'rēd\ Walter 1851–1902 Amer. army surgeon

Rem·brandt \'rem-ˌbrant *also* -ˌbränt\ 1606–1669 *Rembrandt (Harmenszoon) van Rijn* Dutch painter

Rem·ing·ton \'re-miŋ-tən\ Frederic 1861–1909 Amer. painter and sculptor

Re·mus \'rē-məs\ son of Mars who in Roman mythology is killed by his twin brother Romulus

Re·noir \'ren-ˌwär, rən-'\ (Pierre-) Auguste 1841–1919 French painter

Re·vere \ri-'vir\ Paul 1735–1818 Amer. patriot and silversmith

Rich·ard \'ri-chərd\ name of 3 kings of England: **I** 1157–1199 *Richard the Lion-Hearted* (r. 1189–99); **II** 1367–1400 (r. 1377–99); **III** 1452–1485 (r. 1483–85)

Ride \'rīd\ Sally Kristen 1951– Amer. astronaut; 1st Amer. woman in space (1983)

Rob·in Good·fel·low \'rä-bən-'gùd-ˌfe-(ˌ)lō\ mischievous elf in Eng. folklore

Robin Hood \ˌhùd\ legendary Eng. outlaw who gave to the poor what he stole from the rich

Rob·in·son \'rä-bən-sən\ Edwin Arlington 1869–1935 Amer. poet

Robinson Jackie 1919–1972 *Jack Roosevelt Robinson* Amer. baseball player

Rob·in·son Cru·soe \'rä-bə(n)-sən-'krü-(ˌ)sō\ shipwrecked sailor in Daniel Defoe's *Robinson Crusoe* who lives for many years on a desert island

Ro·cham·beau \ˌrō-ˌsham-'bō\ Comte de 1725–1807 French general in Amer. Revolution

Rocke·fel·ler \'rä-ki-ˌfe-lər\ John Davison 1839–1937 and his son John Davison, Jr. 1874–1960 Amer. oil magnates and philanthropists

Ro·ma·nov \rō-'mä-nəf, 'rō-mə-ˌnäf\ Michael 1596–1645 1st czar (1613–45) of Russ. Romanov dynasty (1613–1917)

Rom·u·lus \'räm-yə-ləs\ son of Mars in Roman mythology who is the twin brother of Remus and the founder of Rome

Rönt·gen *or* **Roent·gen** \'rent-gən, 'rənt-, -jən\ Wilhelm Conrad 1845–1923 Ger. physicist; Nobel Prize winner (1901)

Roo·se·velt \'rō-zə-vəlt, -ˌvelt\ (Anna) Eleanor 1884–1962 Amer. lecturer and writer; wife of F. D. Roosevelt

Roosevelt Franklin Delano 1882–1945 32nd pres. of the U.S. (1933–45)

Roosevelt Theodore 1858–1919 26th pres. of the U.S. (1901–09); Nobel Prize winner (1906)

Ross \'rós\ Betsy 1752–1836 née *Griscom* reputed maker of 1st Amer. flag

Ros·si·ni \rò-'sē-nē, rə-\ Gioacchino Antonio 1792–1868 Ital. composer

Row·ling \'rō-liŋ\ J. K. 1965– *Joanne Kathleen Rowling* Brit. author

Ru·bens \'rü-bənz\ Peter Paul 1577–1640 Flemish painter

Ru·dolph \'rü-ˌdólf, -ˌdälf\ Wilma Glodean 1940–1994 Amer. athlete

Rus·sell \'rə-səl\ Bertrand Arthur William 1872–1970 3d Earl *Russell* Eng. mathematician and philosopher; Nobel Prize winner (1950)

Ruth \'rüth\ woman in the Bible who was one of the ancestors of King David

Ruth Babe 1895–1948 *George Herman Ruth* Amer. baseball player

Ruth·er·ford \'rə-thə(r)-fərd, -thə(r)-\ Ernest 1871–1937 Baron *Rutherford* Brit. physicist; Nobel Prize winner (1908)

Sa·bin \'sā-bin\ Albert Bruce 1906–1993 Amer. (Polish=born) physician and microbiologist

Sac·a·ga·wea \ˌsa-kə-jə-'wē-ə\ 1786?–1812 Shoshone Indian guide to Lewis and Clark

Sa·dat \sə-'dat, -'dät\ Anwar el- 1918–1981 pres. of Egypt (1970–81); Nobel Prize winner (1978)

Sa·gan \'sā-gən\ Carl Edward 1934–1996 Amer. astronomer and science writer

Saint Nicholas — see Saint NICHOLAS; SANTA CLAUS

Sal·in·ger \'sa-lən-jər\ J. D. 1919– *Jerome David Salinger* Amer. author

Salk \'só(l)k\ Jonas Edward 1914–1995 Amer. physician and medical researcher

Sa·lo·me \sə-'lō-mē, 'sa-lə-(ˌ)mā\ niece of Herod Antipas who in the Bible is given the head of John the Baptist as a reward for her dancing

Sa·mo·set \'sa-mə-ˌset, sə-'mä-sət\ *died ca* 1653 Amer. Indian leader

Sam·son \'sam(p)-sən\ powerful Hebrew hero in the Bible who fights against the Philistines but is betrayed by Delilah

Sam·u·el \'sam-yə-wəl, -yəl\ Hebrew judge in the Bible who appoints Saul and then David king

Sand·burg \'san(d)-ˌbərg\ Carl 1878–1967 Amer. author

Sang·er \'saŋ-ər\ Margaret 1883–1966 née *Higgins* Amer. birth-control activist

San·ta Claus \'san-tə-ˌklóz\ plump white-bearded and red-suited old man in modern folklore who delivers presents to good children at Christmastime

Sap·pho \'sa-(ˌ)fō\ *fl. ca* 610–*ca* 580 B.C. Greek poet

Sa·rah \'ser-ə, 'sā-rə\ wife of Abraham and mother of Isaac in the Bible

Sar·gent \'sär-jənt\ John Singer 1856–1925 Amer. painter

Sar·tre \'särtr⁹\ Jean-Paul 1905–1980 French philosopher and author

Sat·urn \'sa-tərn\ god of agriculture in Roman mythology

Saul \'sól, 'säl\ 1st king of Israel in the Bible

Saul *or* **Saul of Tarsus** the apostle Paul in the Bible

Sche·her·a·zade \shə-ˌher-ə-'zäd\ fictional wife of a sultan and narrator of the tales in the *Arabian Nights' Entertainments*

Schin·dler \'shind-lər\ Oskar 1908–1974 Ger. humanitarian during the Holocaust

Schu·bert \'shü-bərt, -ˌbert\ Franz Peter 1797–1828 Austrian composer

Schu·mann \'shü-ˌmän, -mən\ Clara 1819–1896 née *Wieck* \'vēk\ Ger. pianist; wife of R. Schumann

Schumann Robert Alexander 1810–1856 Ger. composer

Schweit·zer \'shwīt-sər, 'shvīt-, 'swīt-\ Albert 1875–1965 French theologian, philosopher, physician, and music scholar; Nobel Prize winner (1952)

Scott \'skät\ Dred \'dred\ 1795?–1858 Amer. slave

Scott Robert Falcon 1868–1912 Brit. polar explorer

Scott Sir Walter 1771–1832 Scot. author

Scott Winfield 1786–1866 Amer. general

Scyl·la \'si-lə\ nymph in Greek mythology who is changed into a monster and inhabits a cave opposite the whirlpool Charybdis off the coast of Sicily

Se·at·tle \sē-'a-t⁹l\ 1786?–1866 Amer. Indian chief

Se·le·ne \sə-'lē-nē\ goddess of the moon in classical mythology

Se·quoy·ah *or* **Se·quoia** \si-'kwòi-ə\ *ca* 1760–1843 *George Guess* Cherokee Indian scholar

Ser·ra \'ser-ə\ Junípero 1713–1784 Span. missionary in Mexico and California

Se·ton \'sē-t⁹n\ Saint Elizabeth Ann 1774–1821 *Mother Seton* née *Bayley* Amer. religious leader

Seu·rat \sə-'rä\ Georges 1859–1891 French painter

Sew·ard \'sü-ərd, 'sùrd\ William Henry 1801–1872 Amer. politician; U.S. secretary of state (1861–69)

Shack·le·ton \'sha-kəl-tən\ Sir Ernest Henry 1874–1922 Brit. polar explorer

Shake·speare \'shāk-ˌspir\ William 1564–1616 Eng. playwright and poet

Shaw \'shó\ George Bernard 1856–1950 Brit. playwright; Nobel Prize winner (1925)

Shaw Robert Gould 1837–1863 Amer. soldier

Shel·ley \'she-lē\ Mary Wollstonecraft 1797–1851 née *Godwin* Eng. author; wife of P. B. Shelley

Shelley Percy Bysshe \'bish\ 1792–1822 Eng. poet

Shep·ard \'she-pərd\ Alan Bartlett, Jr. 1923–1998 Amer. astronaut; 1st Amer. in space (1961)

Sher·i·dan \'sher-ə-dən\ Philip Henry 1831–1888 Amer. general

DICTIONARY

Sher·lock Holmes \\'shər-ˌläk-'hōmz, -'hōlmz\\ detective in stories by Sir Arthur Conan Doyle

Sher·man \\'shər-mən\\ John 1823–1900 Amer. statesman; brother of W. T. Sherman

Sherman William Tecumseh 1820–1891 Amer. general

Shi·va \\'shi-və, 'shē-\\ *or* **Si·va** \\'si-və, 'shi-, 'sē-, 'shē-\\ god of destruction and regeneration in the Hindu sacred triad — compare BRAHMA; VISHNU

Sieg·fried \\'sig-ˌfrēd, 'sēg-\\ hero in Germanic legend who kills a dragon guarding a gold hoard

Si·mon \\'sī-mən\\ *or* **Simon the Zealot** one of the 12 apostles in the Bible

Si·na·tra \\sə-'nä-trə\\ Frank 1915–1998 *Francis Albert Sinatra* Amer. singer and actor

Sind·bad the Sailor \\'sin-ˌbad\\ citizen of Baghdad whose adventures are narrated in the *Arabian Nights' Entertainments*

Sis·y·phus \\'si-sə-fəs\\ king of Corinth who in Greek mythology is condemned to roll a heavy stone up a hill in Hades only to have it roll down again as it nears the top

Sit·ting Bull \\ˌsi-tiŋ-'bùl\\ *ca* 1831–1890 Sioux Indian chief

Siva — see SHIVA

Smith \\'smith\\ Bessie 1894?–1937 Amer. blues singer

Smith John *ca* 1580–1631 Eng. colonist in America

Smith Joseph 1805–1844 Amer. founder of the Mormon Church

Soc·ra·tes \\'sä-krə-ˌtēz\\ *ca* 470–399 B.C. Greek philosopher

Sol \\'säl\\ god of the sun in Roman mythology — see HELIOS

Sol·o·mon \\'sä-lə-mən\\ 10th-century B.C. king of Israel noted for his wisdom

Soph·o·cles \\'sä-fə-ˌklēz\\ *ca* 496–406 B.C. Greek playwright

Sou·sa \\'sü-zə, 'sü-sə\\ John Philip 1854–1932 Amer. bandmaster and composer

Spar·ta·cus \\'spär-tə-kəs\\ *died* 71 B.C. Roman slave and gladiator

Sphinx \\'sfiŋ(k)s\\ monster in Greek mythology having a lion's body, wings, and the head and bust of a woman

Spiel·berg \\'spēl-ˌbərg\\ Steven 1947– Amer. filmmaker

Squan·to \\'skwän-tō\\ *died* 1622 Amer. Indian friend of the Pilgrims

Sta·lin \\'stä-lən, 'sta-, -ˌlēn\\ Joseph 1879–1953 Soviet Communist party leader (1922–53), premier (1941–53), and dictator

Stan·dish \\'stan-dish\\ Myles *or* Miles 1584?–1656 Amer. colonist

Stan·ley \\'stan-lē\\ Sir Henry Morton 1841–1904 Brit. explorer in Africa

Stan·ton \\'stan-tᵊn\\ Elizabeth Cady 1815–1902 Amer. suffragist

Stein \\'stīn\\ Gertrude 1874–1946 Amer. author

Stein·beck \\'stīn-ˌbek\\ John Ernst 1902–1968 Amer. author; Nobel Prize winner (1962)

Steu·ben \\'stü-bən, 'styü-, 'shtȯi-\\ Friedrich Wilhelm von 1730–1794 Prussian-born general in Amer. Revolution

Ste·ven·son \\'stē-vən-sən\\ Adlai Ewing 1900–1965 Amer. politician

Stevenson Robert Louis 1850–1894 Scot. author

Sto·ker \\'stō-kər\\ Bram 1847–1912 *Abraham Stoker* Irish author

Stowe \\'stō\\ Harriet Beecher 1811–1896 Amer. author

Stra·di·va·ri \\ˌstra-də-'vär-ē, -'ver-\\ Antonio 1644?–1737 Ital. violin maker

Strauss \\'shtraùs, 'straùs\\ Johann 1804–1849 and his sons Johann, Jr. 1825–1899 and Josef 1827–1870 Austrian composers

Strauss Richard 1864–1949 Ger. composer

Stra·vin·sky \\strə-'vin(t)-skē\\ Igor 1882–1971 Amer. (Russ.-born) composer

Stu·art \\'stü-ərt, 'styü-; 'st(y)ùrt\\ Charles Edward 1720–1788 *the Young Pretender; Bonnie Prince Charlie* claimant to the Brit. throne

Stuart Gilbert Charles 1755–1828 Amer. painter

Stuart Jeb 1833–1864 *James Ewell Brown Stuart* Amer. Confederate general

Stuy·ve·sant \\'stī-və-sənt\\ Peter *ca* 1610–1672 Dutch colonial administrator in America

Sul·li·van \\'sə-lə-vən\\ Sir Arthur Seymour 1842–1900 Eng. composer; collaborator with Sir William Gilbert

Sullivan Louis Henri 1856–1924 Amer. architect

Sum·ner \\'səm-nər\\ Charles 1811–1874 Amer. politician

Sun Yat–sen \\'sùn-'yät-'sen\\ 1866–1925 Chinese statesman

Sut·ter \\'sə-tər, 'sü-\\ John Augustus 1803–1880 Amer. (Ger.-born) pioneer in California

Swift \\'swift\\ Jonathan 1667–1745 Eng. (Irish-born) author

Synge \\'siŋ\\ John Millington 1871–1909 Irish playwright

Taft \\'taft\\ William Howard 1857–1930 27th pres. of the U.S. (1909–13); chief justice of the U.S. Supreme Court (1921–30)

Ta·gore \\tə-'gȯr\\ Ra·bin·dra·nath \\rə-'bin-drə-ˌnät\\ 1861–1941 Indian poet; Nobel Prize winner (1913)

Tall·chief \\'tȯl-ˌchēf\\ Maria 1925– Amer. dancer

Tan \\'tan\\ Amy 1952– Amer. author

Ta·ney \\'tȯ-nē\\ Roger Brooke 1777–1864 Amer. jurist; chief justice of the U.S. Supreme Court (1836–64)

Tan·ta·lus \\'tan-tə-ləs\\ king in Greek mythology who is condemned to stand up to his chin in a pool of water in Hades and beneath fruit-laden boughs only to have the water or fruit go out of reach at each attempt to drink or eat

Tay·lor \\'tā-lər\\ Zachary 1784–1850 Amer. general; 12th pres. of the U.S. (1849–50)

Tchai·kov·sky \\chī-'kȯf-skē, chə-, -'kȯv-\\ Pyotr Ilich 1840–1893 Russ. composer

Te·cum·seh \\tə-'kəm(p)-sə, -sē\\ 1768–1813 Shawnee Indian chief

Tek·a·kwitha \\ˌte-kə-'kwi-thə\\ Kateri 1656–1680 *Lily of the Mohawks* beatified Mohawk Indian religious

Ten·ny·son \\'te-nə-sən\\ Alfred 1809–1892 Baron *Tennyson* known as *Alfred, Lord Tennyson* Eng. poet

Te·re·sa \\tə-'rā-zə, -'rē-sə\\ Mother 1910–1997 beatified Albanian religious in India; Nobel Prize winner (1979)

Teresa vi·la \\'ä-vi-lə\\ Saint 1515–1582 Span. nun and mystic

Tes·la \\'tes-lə\\ Nikola 1856–1943 Amer. (Croatian-born) electrical engineer and inventor

Thatch·er \\'tha-chər\\ Margaret Hilda 1925– Baroness *Thatcher of Kesteven* née *Roberts* Brit. prime minister (1979–90)

The·seus \\'thē-ˌsüs, -sē-əs\\ hero in Greek mythology who kills the Minotaur and conquers the Amazons

Thom·as \\'tä-məs\\ apostle in the Bible who demanded proof of Jesus' resurrection

Thomas à Becket — see Saint Thomas BECKET

Thomas Aquinas Saint — see AQUINAS

Thor \\'thȯr\\ god of thunder, weather, and crops in Norse mythology

Tho·reau \\thə-'rō, thȯ-\\ Henry David 1817–1862 Amer. author

Thorpe \\'thȯrp\\ Jim 1888–1953 *James Francis Thorpe* Amer. athlete

Thur·ber \\'thər-bər\\ James Grover 1894–1961 Amer. author

Ti·be·ri·us \\tī-'bir-ē-əs\\ 42 B.C.–37 A.D. Roman emperor (14–37)

Tocque·ville \\'tōk-ˌvil, 'tȯk-, 'täk-, -ˌvēl, -vəl\\ Alexis de 1805–1859 French politician and author

Tol·kien \\'tȯl-ˌkēn\\ J. R. R. 1892–1973 *John Ronald Reuel Tolkien* Brit. author

Tol·stoy \\tȯl-'stȯi, tȯl-', täl-', 'tȯl-ˌ, 'tȯl-ˌ, 'täl-ˌ\\ Leo 1828–1910 Count *Lev Nikolayevich Tolstoy* Russ. author

Tou·louse–Lau·trec \\tü-ˌlüz-lō-'trek\\ Henri de 1864–1901 French painter

Tri·ton \\'trī-tᵊn\\ sea god in Greek mythology who is half man and half fish

Trots·ky \\'trät-skē\\ Leon 1879–1940 orig. *Lev Davidovich Bronstein* Russ. Communist leader

Tru·deau \\'trü-(ˌ)dō, trü-'\\ Pierre Elliott 1919–2000 Canad. prime minister (1968–79, 1980–84)

Tru·man \\'trü-mən\\ Harry S. 1884–1972 33rd pres. of the U.S. (1945–53)

Truth \\'trüth\\ Sojourner 1797?–1883 Amer. abolitionist

Tub·man \\'təb-mən\\ Harriet *ca* 1820–1913 Amer. abolitionist

Tut·ankh·a·men \\ˌtü-ˌtaŋ-'kä-mən, -ˌtäŋ-\\ originally *Tut·ankh·a·ten* \\-'kä-tᵊn\\ *ca* 1370–1352 B.C., king of Egypt (1361–1352 B.C.)

Twain \'klē-mənz\ Mark 1835–1910 pseud. of *Samuel Langhorne Clem·ens* \'klem-ənz\ Amer. author

Tweed \'twēd\ William Marcy 1823–1878 *Boss Tweed* Amer. politician

Ty·ler \'tī-lər\ John 1790–1862 10th pres. of the U.S. (1841–45)

Ulysses — see ODYSSEUS

Ura·nus \'yùr-ə-nəs, yù-'rā-\ the sky personified as a god and father of the Titans in Greek mythology

Ur·ban \'ər-bən\ name of eight popes: esp. **II** *ca* 1035–1099 (pope 1088–99)

Uri·el \'yùr-ē-əl\ archangel named in Hebrew tradition — compare GABRIEL; MICHAEL; RAPHAEL

Val·en·tine \'va-lən-ˌtīn\ Saint, 3d cent. Christian martyr

Van Bu·ren \van-'byùr-ən, vən-\ Martin 1782–1862 8th pres. of the U.S. (1837–41)

Van Dyck *or* **Van·dyke** \van-'dīk, vən-\ Sir Anthony 1599–1641 Flemish painter

van Gogh Vincent — see GOGH, VAN

Ve·láz·quez \və-'las-kəs, -'läs-, -kwiz, -(ˌ)käs\ Diego 1599–1660 Span. painter

Ve·nus \'vē-nəs\ goddess of love and beauty in Roman mythology — compare APHRODITE

Ver·di \'ver-dē\ Giuseppe 1813–1901 Ital. composer

Ver·meer \vər-'mer, -'mir\ Jan *or* Johannes 1632–1675 Dutch painter

Verne \'vərn, 'vern\ Jules \'jülz\ 1828–1905 French author

Ves·puc·ci \ve-'spü-chē, -'spyü-\ Ame·ri·go \ə-'mer-i-ˌgō\ 1454–1512 Latin *Amer·i·cus Ves·pu·cius* \ə-'mer-ə-kəs-ˌves-'pyü-sh(ē-)əs\ Ital. navigator for Spain and namesake of America

Vic·to·ria \vik-'tòr-ē-ə\ 1819–1901 *Alexandrina Victoria* queen of the United Kingdom (1837–1901)

Vinci, da Leonardo — see LEONARDO DA VINCI

Vir·gil *also* **Ver·gil** \'vər-jəl\ 70–19 B.C. Roman poet

Vish·nu \'vish-(ˌ)nü\ god of preservation in the Hindu sacred triad — compare BRAHMA; SHIVA

Vol·ta \'vōl-tə, väl-, vòl-\ Alessandro 1745–1827 Ital. physicist

Vol·taire \vōl-'tar, väl-, vòl-, -'ter\ 1694–1778 orig. *François-Marie Arouet* French author

Vul·can \'vəl-kən\ god of fire and metalworking in Roman mythology — compare HEPHAESTUS

Wag·ner \'väg-nər\ Ri·chard \'ri-ˌkärt, -ˌkärt\ 1813–1883 Ger. composer

Walk·er \'wò-kər\ Alice Malsenior 1944–   Amer. writer

Wal·len·berg \'wä-lən-ˌbərg\ Raoul 1912–1947? Swedish diplomat and hero of the Holocaust

War·ren \'wòr-ən, 'wär-\ Earl 1891–1974 Amer. jurist; chief justice of the U.S. Supreme Court (1953–69)

Wash·ing·ton \'wò-shiŋ-tən, 'wä-\ Booker Tal·ia·ferro \'tä-lə-vər\ 1856–1915 Amer. educator

Washington George 1732–1799 Amer. general; 1st pres. of the U.S. (1789–97)

Watt \'wät\ James 1736–1819 Scot. inventor

Wayne \'wān\ Anthony 1745–1796 *Mad Anthony* Amer. general

Web·ster \'web-stər\ Daniel 1782–1852 Amer. politician

Webster Noah 1758–1843 Amer. lexicographer

Wel·ling·ton \'we-liŋ-tən\ Duke of 1769–1852 *Arthur Wellesley; the Iron Duke* Brit. general and statesman

Wells \'welz\ H. G. 1866–1946 *Herbert George Wells* Eng. author and historian

Wel·ty \'wel-tē\ Eudora 1909–2001 Amer. author

Wes·ley \'wes-lē, 'wez-\ John 1703–1791 Eng. founder of Methodism

Wes·ting·house \'wes-tiŋ-ˌhaùs\ George 1846–1914 Amer. inventor and industrialist

Whar·ton \'hwòr-t³n, 'wòr-\ Edith 1862–1937 née *Jones* Amer. author

Whis·tler \'hwis-lər, 'wis-\ James (Abbott) McNeill 1834–1903 Amer. artist

Whit·man \'hwit-mən, 'wit-\ Walt 1819–1892 Amer. poet

Whit·ney \'hwit-nē, 'wit-\ Eli 1765–1825 Amer. inventor

Whit·ti·er \'hwi-tē-ər, 'wit-\ John Greenleaf 1807–1892 Amer. poet

Wie·sel \vē-'zel, wē-\ Elie 1928–   Amer. (Romanian-born) author; Nobel Prize winner (1986)

Wilde \'wī(-ə)ld\ Oscar 1854–1900 Irish author

Wil·der \'wī(-ə)l-dər\ Thornton Niven 1897–1975 Amer. author

Wil·liam \'wil-yəm\ name of 4 kings of England: **I** *ca* 1028–1087 *William the Conqueror* (r. 1066–87); **II** *ca* 1056–1100 *William Rufus* \'rü-fəs\ (r. 1087–1100); **III** 1650–1702 (r. 1689–1702); **IV** 1765–1837 (r. 1830–37)

Wil·liam Tell \ˌwil-yəm-'tel\ legendary Swiss patriot commanded to shoot an apple off his son's head

Wil·liams \'wil-yəmz\ Roger 1603?–1683 Eng. colonist

Williams Ted 1918–2002 *Theodore Samuel Williams* Amer. baseball player

Williams Tennessee 1911–1983 orig. *Thomas Lanier Williams* Amer. playwright

Williams Venus 1980–   and her sister Serena 1981–   Amer. tennis players

Wil·son \'wil-sən\ (Thomas) Woodrow 1856–1924 28th pres. of the U.S. (1913–21); Nobel Prize winner (1919)

Win·throp \'win(t)-thrəp\ John 1588–1649 1st governor of Massachusetts Bay Colony

Woden — see ODIN

Woll·stone·craft \'wùl-stən-ˌkraft\ Mary 1759–1797 Eng. feminist and writer

Woods \'wùdz\ Tiger 1975–   *Eldrick Woods* Amer. golfer

Woolf \'wùlf\ Virginia 1882–1941 Eng. author

Words·worth \'wərdz-(ˌ)wərth\ William 1770–1850 Eng. poet

Wo·vo·ka \wō-'vō-kə\ 1858?–1932 *Jack Wilson* Paiute Indian mystic

Wren \'ren\ Sir Christopher 1632–1723 Eng. architect

Wright \'rīt\ Frank Lloyd 1867–1959 Amer. architect

Wright Orville 1871–1948 and his brother Wilbur 1867–1912 Amer. pioneers in aviation

Wright Richard 1908–1960 Amer. author

Wy·eth \'wī-əth\ Andrew Newell 1917–   Amer. painter

Yeats \'yāts\ William Butler 1865–1939 Irish author

Yel·tsin \'yelt-sən, 'yel-sin\ Boris Nikolayevich 1931–   pres. of Russia (1990–99)

York \'yòrk\ Alvin Cullum 1887–1964 Amer. hero in World War I

Young \'yəŋ\ Brig·ham \'brig-əm\ 1801–1877 Amer. Mormon leader

Za·har·i·as \zə-'ha-rē-əs\ Babe Didrikson 1914–1956 *Mildred Ella Zaharias* née *Didrikson* Amer. athlete

Zech·a·ri·ah \ˌze-kə-'rī-ə\ Hebrew prophet of the 6th cent. B.C.

Zeng·er \'zeŋ-gər, -ər\ John Peter 1697–1746 Amer. (Ger.-born) journalist and printer

Zeph·y·rus \'ze-fə-rəs\ god of the west wind in Greek mythology

Zeus \'züs\ chief god and ruler of the sky and weather in Greek mythology — compare JUPITER

DICTIONARY

GEOGRAPHICAL NAMES

This section gives basic information about the world's countries, regions, cities, and major physical features. The latest population figures are given for nations, cities, and some regions. For many of these entries, derived nouns and adjectives are also listed (as **Iceland** . . . **Icelander** . . . *n*). Other derived words not shown here have been separately entered in the main A-Z section, because of the presence of additional senses (as **Chinese**).

Abbreviations used here are listed in the front section Abbreviations in This Work. The capital letters N, E, S, and W, used singly or in combination and without a period, indicate direction. For example, "N India" means "northern India." Where direction is a part of the name, the word is spelled out.

The symbol ✳ denotes a capital. Sizes are given in conventional U.S. units, with metric equivalents following.

Ab·er·deen \ˌa-bər-'dēn\ city NE Scotland; *pop* 211,080 — **Ab·er·do·ni·an** \ˌa-bər-'dō-nē-ən\ *adj or n*

Ab·i·djan \ˌä-bē-'jän, ˌa-bi-\ city, seat of government of Ivory Coast; *pop* 1,934,342

Abilene \'a-bə-ˌlēn\ city NW *cen* Texas; *pop* 115,930

Abu Dha·bi \ˌä-bü-'dä-bē, -'thä-\ city, ✳ of United Arab Emirates; *pop* 347,000

Abu·ja \ä-'bü-jä\ city *cen* Nigeria; its ✳; *pop* 423,391

Ab·ys·sin·ia \ˌa-bə-'si-nē-ə, -nyə\ — see ETHIOPIA — **Ab·ys·sin·i·an** \-nē-ən, -nyən\ *adj or n*

Aca·dia \ə-'kā-dē-ə\ *or French* **Aca·die** \ä-kä-'dē\ NOVA SCOTIA — an early name — **Aca·di·an** \-ē-ən\ *adj or n*

Aca·pul·co \ˌä-kä-'pül-(ˌ)kō, ˌa-\ city & port S Mexico on the Pacific; *pop* 687,292

Ac·cra \'ä-krə, 'a-; ə-'krä\ city & port, ✳ of Ghana; *pop* 867,459

Acon·ca·gua \ˌä-kōn-'kä-gwä\ mountain 22,834 ft. (6960 m.) W Argentina; highest in the Andes & in Western Hemisphere

Ad·dis Aba·ba \'ä-dis-'ä-bä-bä, ˌa-dəs-'a-bə-bə\ city, ✳ of Ethiopia; *pop* 2,646,000

Ad·e·laide \'a-də-ˌlād\ city S Australia, ✳ of South Australia; *pop* 917,000

Aden \'ä-dᵊn, 'ā-\ city & port S Yemen; *pop* 240,370

Aden, Gulf of arm of Indian Ocean between Yemen (Arabia) & Somalia (Africa)

Adirondack \ˌa-də-'rän-ˌdak\ mountains NE New York; highest Mount Marcy 5344 ft. (1629 m.)

Admiralty \'ad-m(ə-)rəl-tē\ **1** island SE Alaska **2** islands W Pacific N of New Guinea; part of Papua New Guinea

Adri·at·ic Sea \ˌā-drē-'a-tik, ˌa-\ arm of Mediterranean between Italy & Balkan Peninsula

Ae·ge·an Sea \i-'jē-ən\ arm of Mediterranean between Asia Minor & Greece

Af·ghan·i·stan \af-'ga-nə-ˌstan, -'ga-nə-ˌstän\ country W Asia E of Iran; ✳, Kabul; *pop* (est.) 28,717,000

Af·ri·ca \'a-fri-kə\ continent S of the Mediterranean

Aga·na \ä-'gä-nyä\ town, ✳ of Guam; *pop* 1139

Agra \'ä-grə, 'ə-\ city N India SSE of Delhi; *pop* 1,259,979

Aguas·ca·lien·tes \ˌä-gwäs-ˌkäl-'yen-ˌtäs\ city *cen* Mexico NE of Guadalajara; metropolitan area *pop* 637,303

Agul·has, Cape \ə-'gə-ləs\ cape Republic of South Africa; most southerly point of Africa, at 34° 52′ S latitude

Ahaggar \ə-'hä-gər, ˌä-hə-'gär\ mountains S Algeria in W *cen* Sahara

Ah·mad·abad \'ä-mə-də-ˌbäd, -ˌbad\ city W India N of Bombay; *pop* 3,515,361

Ak·ron \'a-krən\ city NE Ohio; *pop* 217,074

Al·a·bama \ˌa-lə-'ba-mə\ state SE U.S.; ✳, Montgomery; *pop* 4,447,100 — **Al·a·bam·i·an** \-'ba-mē-ən\ *or* **Al·a·bam·an** \-'ba-mən\ *adj or n*

Alas·ka \ə-'las-kə\ **1** peninsula SW Alaska SW of Cook Inlet **2** state of U.S. in NW North America; ✳, Juneau; *pop* 626,932 **3** mountain range S Alaska extending from Alaska Peninsula to Yukon boundary — **Alas·kan** \-kən\ *adj or n*

Alaska, Gulf of inlet of Pacific off S Alaska between Alaska Peninsula on W & Alexander Archipelago on E

Al·ba·nia \al-'bā-nē-ə, -nyə\ country S Europe in Balkan Peninsula on Adriatic; ✳, Tirane; *pop* 3,069,275

Al·ba·ny \'ȯl-bə-nē\ city, ✳ of New York; *pop* 95,658

Albemarle Sound \'al-bə-ˌmärl\ inlet of the Atlantic in NE North Carolina

Albert, Lake \'al-bərt\ lake E Africa between Uganda & Democratic Republic of the Congo in course of the Nile

Al·ber·ta \al-'bər-tə\ province W Canada; ✳, Edmonton; *pop* 2,974,807 — **Al·ber·tan** \-'bər-tᵊn\ *adj or n*

Al·bu·quer·que \'al-bə-ˌkər-kē\ city *cen* New Mexico; *pop* 448,607

Al·ca·traz \'al-kə-ˌtraz\ island California in San Francisco Bay

Al·da·bra \äl-'dä-brə\ island NW Indian Ocean N of Madagascar; belongs to Seychelles

Al·der·ney \'ȯl-dər-nē\ — see CHANNEL

Alep·po \ə-'le-(ˌ)pō\ city N Syria; *pop* 1,445,000

Aleu·tian \ə-'lü-shən\ islands SW Alaska extending 1700 mi. (2735 km.) W from Alaska Peninsula

Al·ex·an·der \ˌal-ig-'zan-dər, ˌel-\ archipelago SE Alaska

Al·ex·an·dria \ˌa-lig-'zan-drē-ə, -e-\ **1** city N Virginia S of District of Columbia; *pop* 128,283 **2** city N Egypt on the Mediterranean; *pop* 3,170,000 — **Al·ex·an·dri·an** \-drē-ən\ *adj or n*

Al·ge·ria \al-'jir-ē-ə\ country NW Africa on Mediterranean; ✳, Algiers; *pop* 22,971,000 — **Al·ge·ri·an** \-ē-ən\ *adj or n*

Al·giers \al-'jirz\ city, ✳ of Algeria; *pop* 1,365,400 — **Al·ge·rine** \ˌal-jə-'rēn\ *adj or n*

Al·lah·abad \'ä-lä-hä-ˌbäd, 'a-lə-hə-ˌbad\ city N India on the Ganges; *pop* 990,298

Al·le·ghe·ny \ˌa-lə-'gā-nē\ **1** river 325 mi. (523 km.) long W Pennsylvania & SW New York **2** mountains of Appalachian system E U.S. in Pennsylvania, Maryland, Virginia, & West Virginia

Al·len·town \'a-lən-ˌtaun\ city E Pennsylvania; *pop* 106,632

Al·maty \əl-'mä-tē\ *or* **Al·ma-Ata** \əl-'mä-ə-'tä; ˌal-mə-'ä-tə, -ə-'tä\ city, former ✳ of Kazakhstan; *pop* 1,156,200

Alps \'alps\ mountain system *cen* Europe — see MONT BLANC

Al·tai *or* **Al·tay** \al-'tī\ mountain system *cen* Asia between Mongolia & W China & between Kazakhstan & Russia

Ama·ga·sa·ki \ˌä-mä-gä-'sä-kē\ city Japan in W *cen* Honshu; *pop* 466,187

Am·a·ril·lo \ˌa-mə-'ri-(ˌ)lō, -lə\ city NW Texas; *pop* 173,627

Am·a·zon \'a-mə-ˌzän, -zən\ river 3900 mi. (6436 km.) long N South America flowing from Peruvian Andes into Atlantic in N Brazil

Amer·i·ca \ə-'mer-ə-kə, -'me-rə-\ **1** either continent (**North America** *or* **South America**) of Western Hemisphere **2** *or* the **Amer·i·cas** \-kəz\ lands of Western Hemisphere including North, Central, & South America & West Indies **3** UNITED STATES OF AMERICA — **American** *adj or n*

American Falls — see NIAGARA FALLS

American Samoa or **Eastern Samoa** islands SW cen Pacific; U.S. territory; ✱, Pago Pago (on Tutuila Island); pop 57,291

Am·man \ä-ˈmän, a-, -ˈman\ city, ✱ of Jordan; pop 627,505

Am·ster·dam \ˈam(p)-stər-ˌdam, ˈam(p)-stər-ˈdam\ city, official ✱ of the Netherlands; pop 735,526

Amur \ä-ˈmu̇r\ river 1780 mi. (2784 km.) long E Asia flowing into the Pacific & forming part of boundary between China & Russia

An·a·heim \ˈa-nə-ˌhīm\ city SW California E of Long Beach; pop 328,014

An·a·to·lia \ˌa-nə-ˈtō-lē-ə, -ˈtōl-yə\ — see ASIA MINOR — **An·a·to·li·an** \-ˈtō-lē-ən, -ˈtōl-yən\ adj or n

An·chor·age \ˈaŋ-k(ə-)rij\ city S cen Alaska; pop 260,283

An·da·man \ˈan-də-mən, -ˌman\ **1** islands India in Bay of Bengal S of Myanmar & N of Nicobar Islands **2** sea, arm of Bay of Bengal S of Myanmar — **An·da·man·ese** \ˌan-də-mə-ˈnēz, -ˈnēs\ adj or n

An·des \ˈan-(ˌ)dēz\ mountain system W South America extending from Panama to Tierra del Fuego — see ACONCAGUA \ˌä-kəŋ-ˈkä-gwə\ — **An·de·an** \ˈan-(ˌ)dē-ən, an-ˈ\ adj — **An·dine** \ˈan-ˌdēn, -ˌdīn\ adj

An·dor·ra \an-ˈdȯr-ə, -ˈdär-ə\ country SW Europe in E Pyrenees between France & Spain; ✱, Andorra la Vella; pop 57,110 — **An·dor·ran** \-ən\ adj or n

Andorra la Vel·la \lä-ˈvel-yä\ town, ✱ of Andorra; pop 21,513

An·dros \ˈan-drəs\ island, largest of Bahamas

An·gel Falls \ˈān-jəl\ waterfall 3212 ft. (979 m.) SE Venezuela; world's highest waterfall

Ang·kor \ˈaŋ-ˌkȯr\ ruins of ancient city NW Cambodia

An·gle·sey \ˈaŋ-gəl-sē\ island NW Wales

An·go·la \aŋ-ˈgō-lə, an-\ country SW Africa S of mouth of Congo River; ✱, Luanda; pop 10,609,000 — **An·go·lan** \-lən\ adj or n

An·i·ak·chak Crater \ˌa-nē-ˈak-ˌchak\ volcanic crater SW Alaska on Alaska Peninsula; 6 mi. (10 km.) in diameter

An·ka·ra \ˈaŋ-kə-rə, ˈäŋ-\ city, ✱ of Turkey in N cen Anatolia; pop 2,559,471

An·nap·o·lis \ə-ˈna-pə-lis\ city, ✱ of Maryland; pop 35,838

Ann Ar·bor \(ˌ)an-ˈär-bər\ city SE Michigan; pop 114,024

An·shan \ˈän-ˈshän\ city NE China; pop 1,203,986

An·ta·nan·a·ri·vo \ˌän-tä-ˌnä-nä-ˈrē-(ˌ)vō\ city, ✱ of Madagascar; pop 958,929

Ant·arc·ti·ca \ˌant-ˈärk-ti-kə, -ˈär-ti-\ body of land around the South Pole; plateau covered by great ice cap

An·ti·gua \an-ˈtē-gə, -gwə\ island West Indies in the Leewards; with Barbuda forms independent **Antigua and Barbuda**; ✱, Saint John's; pop 83,000

An·til·les \an-ˈti-lēz\ the West Indies except for the Bahamas — see GREATER ANTILLES; LESSER ANTILLES — **An·til·le·an** \-lē-ən\ adj

An·trim \ˈan-trəm\ district E Northern Ireland; pop 44,322

Ant·werp \ˈant-ˌwərp, ˈan-ˌtwərp\ city N Belgium; pop 448,709

Aomen — see MACAO

Aorangi — see COOK, MOUNT

Ap·en·nines \ˈa-pə-ˌnīnz\ mountain chain Italy extending length of the peninsula; highest peak Monte Corno (NE of Rome) 9560 ft. (2897 m.) — **Ap·en·nine** \ˈa-pə-ˌnīnz\ adj

Apia \ä-ˈpē-ä\ town, ✱ of Samoa; pop 38,000

Apo, Mount \ä-(ˌ)pō\ volcano Philippines in SE Mindanao 9692 ft. (2954 m.); highest peak in the Philippines

Ap·pa·la·chia \ˌa-pə-ˈlā-chə, -ˈla-chə, -ˈlā-shə\ region E U.S. including Appalachian Mountains from S cen New York to cen Alabama

Ap·pa·la·chian Mountains \ˌa-pə-ˈlā-ch(ē-)ən, -sh(ē-)ən\ mountain system E North America extending from S Quebec to cen Alabama — see MITCHELL, MOUNT

Aqa·ba, Gulf of \ˈä-kä-bə\ arm of Red Sea E of Sinai Peninsula

Aquid·neck \ə-ˈkwid-ˌnek\ or **Rhode** island SE Rhode Island in Narragansett Bay

Ara·bia \ə-ˈrā-bē-ə\ peninsula of SW Asia including Saudi Arabia, Yemen, Oman, & Persian Gulf States

Ara·bi·an \ə-ˈrā-bē-ən\ **1** desert E Egypt between the Nile & Red Sea **2** sea NW section of Indian Ocean between Arabia & India

Ara·fu·ra \ˌä-rä-ˈfü-rä\ sea between N Australia & W New Guinea

Ar·al Sea \ˈa-rəl\ formerly **Lake Aral** lake W Asia between Kazakhstan & Uzbekistan

Ar·a·rat \ˈa-rə-ˌrat\ mountain 16,946 ft. (5165 m.) E Turkey near border of Iran

Arc·tic \ˈärk-tik, ˈär-tik\ **1** ocean N of Arctic Circle **2** Arctic regions **3** archipelago N Canada in Nunavut & Northwest Territories

Ar·da·bil or **Ar·de·bil** \ˌär-də-ˈbēl\ city NW Iran; pop 281,973

Ards \ˈärdz\ district E Northern Ireland; pop 64,026

Are·ci·bo \ˌä-rä-ˈsē-(ˌ)bō\ city & port N Puerto Rico; pop 100,131

Ar·gen·ti·na \ˌär-jən-ˈtē-nə\ country S South America between the Andes & the Atlantic; ✱, Buenos Aires; pop 33,070,000 — **Ar·gen·tine** \ˈär-jən-ˌtīn, -ˌtēn\ adj or n — **Ar·gen·tin·ean** or **Ar·gen·tin·i·an** \ˌär-jən-ˈti-nē-ən\ adj or n

Ar·gos \ˈär-ˌgós, -gəs\ ancient Greek city-state S Greece

Ar·i·zo·na \ˌa-rə-ˈzō-nə\ state SW U.S.; ✱, Phoenix; pop 5,130,632 — **Ar·i·zo·nan** \-nən\ or **Ar·i·zo·nian** \-nē-ən, -nyən\ adj or n

Ar·kan·sas \ˈär-kən-ˌsȯ\ **1** river 1450 mi. (2334 km.) long SW cen U.S. flowing SE into the Mississippi **2** state S cen U.S.; ✱, Little Rock; pop 2,673,400 — **Ar·kan·san** \är-ˈkan-zən\ adj or n

Ar·ling·ton \ˈär-liŋ-tən\ city N Texas; pop 332,969

Ar·magh \är-ˈmä, ˈär-\ **1** district N Northern Ireland; pop 51,331 **2** town cen Armagh district; pop 14,265

Ar·me·nia \är-ˈmē-nē-ə, -nyə\ **1** region W Asia in mountainous area SE of Black Sea & SW of Caspian Sea divided between Iran, Turkey, & Armenia (country) **2** country E Europe; ✱, Yerevan; pop 3,426,000

Arn·hem Land \ˈär-nəm\ region N Australia on N coast of Northern Territory

Ar·no \ˈär-(ˌ)nō\ river 150 mi. (241 km.) long cen Italy flowing through Florence

Aru·ba \ə-ˈrü-bə\ island Netherlands Antilles off coast of NW Venezuela; pop 69,000

Ar·va·da \är-ˈva-də\ city N cen Colorado NW of Denver; pop 102,153

Ash·ga·bat \ˈäsh-gə-ˌbät\ or **Ashkh·a·bad** \ˈash-kə-ˌbad, -ˌbäd\ city, ✱ of Turkmenistan; pop 412,200

Asia \ˈā-zhə, -shə\ continent of Eastern Hemisphere N of the Equator — see EURASIA

Asia Mi·nor \-ˈmī-nər\ or **An·a·to·lia** \ˌa-nə-ˈtō-lē-ə, -ˈtōl-yə\ peninsula in modern Turkey between Black Sea on N & the Mediterranean on S

As·ma·ra \az-ˈmä-rə, -ˈma-rə\ city, ✱ of Eritrea; pop 342,706

As·syr·ia \ə-ˈsir-ē-ə\ ancient empire W Asia extending along the middle Tigris & over foothills to the E — **As·syr·i·an** \-ən\ adj or n

As·ta·na \ä-stä-ˈnä\ city, ✱ of Kazakhstan; pop 319,318

Asun·ción \ä-sün-ˈsyȯn\ city, ✱ of Paraguay; pop 502,426

As·wân \a-ˈswän, ä-\ city S Egypt on the Nile near site of **Aswân High Dam**; pop 191,461

Ata·ca·ma \ˌä-tä-ˈkä-mä\ desert N Chile

Atchaf·a·laya \(ə-)ˌcha-fə-ˈlī-ə\ river 225 mi. (362 km.) long S Louisiana flowing S into Gulf of Mexico

Ath·a·bas·ca or **Ath·a·bas·ka** \ˌa-thə-ˈbas-kə, -ˌä-\ river 765 mi. (1231 km.) long NE Alberta flowing into **Lake Athabasca** on Alberta–Saskatchewan border

Ath·ens \ˈa-thənz\ **1** city NE Georgia; pop 101,489 **2** city, ✱ of Greece; pop 748,110 — **Athe·nian** \ə-ˈthē-nē-ən, -nyən\ adj or n

At·lan·ta \ət-ˈlan-tə, at-\ city, ✱ of Georgia; pop 416,474

At·lan·tic \ət-ˈlan-tik, at-\ ocean separating North America & South America from Europe & Africa; often divided into **North Atlantic** and **South Atlantic** — **Atlantic** adj

At·las \ˈat-ləs\ mountains NW Africa extending from SW Morocco to N Tunisia

At·ti·ca \ˈa-ti-kə\ ancient state E Greece; chief city Athens — **At·tic** \ˈat-ik\ adj

Auck·land \ˈȯ-klənd\ city N New Zealand on NW North Island; urban area pop 1,074,510

Au·gus·ta \ȯ-'gəs-tə, ə-\ **1** city E Georgia; *pop* 199,775 **2** city, ✳ of Maine; *pop* 18,560

Au·ro·ra \ə-'rȯr-ə, ȯ-\ **1** city NE *cen* Colorado; *pop* 276,393 **2** city NE Illinois; *pop* 142,990

Auschwitz — see OSWIECIM

Aus·tin \'ȯs-tən, 'äs-\ city, ✳ of Texas; *pop* 656,562

Aus·tral·asia \ȯs-trə-'lā-zhə, äs-, -'lā-shə\ Australia, Tasmania, New Zealand, & Melanesia — **Aus·tral·asian** \-zhən, -shən\ *adj or n*

Aus·tra·lia \ȯ-'strāl-yə, ä-, ə-\ **1** continent of Eastern Hemisphere SE of Asia **2** country including continent of Australia & island of Tasmania; ✳, Canberra; *pop* 17,562,000 — **Aus·tra·lian** \-yən\ *adj or n*

Australian Alps mountain range SE Australia in E Victoria & SE New South Wales; part of Great Dividing Range

Australian Capital Territory district SE Australia including two areas, one containing Canberra (✳ of Australia) & the other on Jervis Bay (inlet of the South Pacific); surrounded by New South Wales

Aus·tria \'ȯs-trē-ə, 'äs-\ country *cen* Europe; ✳, Vienna; *pop* 7,812,100 — **Aus·tri·an** \-ən\ *adj or n*

Aus·tria–Hun·ga·ry \-'həŋ-gə-rē\ country 1867–1918 *cen* Europe including Bohemia, Moravia, Transylvania, Galicia, and what are now Austria, Hungary, Slovenia, Crotia, & part of NE Italy — **Aus·tro–Hun·gar·i·an** \'ȯs-(,)trō-,həŋ-'ger-ē-ən, 'äs-\ *adj or n*

Aus·tro·ne·sia \ȯs-trə-'nē-zhə, äs-, -'nē-shə\ **1** islands of the South Pacific **2** area extending from Madagascar through Malay Peninsula & Malay Archipelago to Hawaii & Easter Island — **Aus·tro·ne·sian** \-zhən, -shən\ *adj or n*

Avon \'ā-vən, 'a-\ river 96 mi. (154 km.) long *cen* England flowing WSW into the Severn

Ayers Rock \'erz\ outcrop *cen* Australia in SW Northern Territory

Ayles·bury \'ālz-b(ə-)rē\ town SE *cen* England; *pop* 41,288

Ayr \'er\ *or* **Ayr·shire** \-,shir, -shər\ former county SW Scotland

Azer·bai·jan \,a-zər-'bī-'jän, ,ä-\ country SE Europe bordering on Caspian Sea; ✳, Baku; *pop* 7,029,000 — **Azer·bai·ja·ni** \,a-zər-,bī-'jä-nē, ,ä-\ *adj or n*

Azores \'ā-,zȯrz, ə-\ islands Portugal in North Atlantic lying 800 mi. (1287 km.) W of Portuguese coast; *pop* 241,763 — **Azor·e·an** *or* **Azor·i·an** \ā-'zȯr-ē-ən, ə-\ *adj or n*

Bab·y·lon \'ba-bə-lən, -,län\ ancient city, ✳ of Babylonia; site 55 mi. (89 km.) S of Baghdad near the Euphrates — **Bab·y·lo·nian** \,ba-bə-'lō-nyən, -nē-ən\ *adj or n*

Bab·y·lo·nia \,ba-bə-'lō-nyə, -nē-ə\ ancient country W Asia in valley of lower Euphrates and Tigris rivers

Bac·tria \'bak-trē-ə\ ancient country W Asia in present NE Afghanistan — **Bac·tri·an** \'bak-trē-ən\ *adj or n*

Bad·lands barren region SW South Dakota & NW Nebraska

Baf·fin \'ba-fən\ **1** bay of the Atlantic between W Greenland & E Baffin Island **2** island NE Canada in Arctic Archipelago N of Hudson Strait

Bagh·dad \'bag-,dad, ,bäg-'däd\ city, ✳ of Iraq on the Tigris; *pop* (est.) 5,949,000

Ba·guio \,bä-gē-'ō\ city, former summer ✳ of the Philippines in NW *cen* Luzon; *pop* 183,000

Ba·ha·mas \bə-'hä-məz\ islands in N Atlantic SE of Florida; ✳, Nassau; *pop* 303,611 — **Ba·ha·mi·an** \bə-'hā-mē-ən, -'hä-\ *or* **Ba·ha·man** \-'hä-mən, -'häm-ən\ *adj or n*

Bahia — see SALVADOR

Bah·rain \bä-'rān\ islands in Persian Gulf off coast of Arabia; country; ✳, Manama; *pop* 485,600 — **Bah·raini** \-'rā-nē\ *adj or n*

Bai·kal, Lake *or* **Lake Bay·kal** \bī-'käl, -'kal\ lake Russia, in mountains N of Mongolia

Ba·ja California \'bä-(,)hä\ peninsula NW Mexico W of Gulf of California

Bakersfield \'bā-kərz-,fēld\ city S California; *pop* 247,057

Ba·ku \bä-'kü\ city, ✳ of Azerbaijan on W coast of Caspian Sea; *pop* 1,150,000

Bal·a·ton \'ba-lə-,tän, 'bȯ-lȯ-,tōn\ lake W Hungary

Bal·boa Heights \(,)bal-'bō-ə\ town Panama; formerly the center of administration for Canal Zone

Bal·e·ar·ic Islands \,ba-lē-'a-rik\ islands E Spain in the W Mediterranean

Ba·li \'bä-lē, 'ba-\ island Indonesia off E end of Java; *pop* 2,777,811 — **Ba·li·nese** \,bäl-i-nēz, ,bal-, -'nēs\ *adj or n*

Bal·kan \'bȯl-kən\ **1** mountains N Bulgaria extending from Serbia border to Black Sea; highest 7793 ft. (2375 m.) **2** peninsula SE Europe between Adriatic & Ionian seas on the W & Aegean & Black seas on the E

Bal·kans \'bȯl-kənz\ *or* **Balkan States** countries occupying the Balkan Peninsula: Slovenia, Croatia, Bosnia and Herzegovina, independent Macedonia, Serbia and Montenegro, Romania, Bulgaria, Albania, Greece, Turkey (in Europe)

Bal·ly·me·na \,ba-lē-'mē-nə\ district NE *cen* Northern Ireland; *pop* 56,032

Bal·ly·mon·ey \,ba-lē-'mə-nē\ district N *cen* Northern Ireland; *pop* 23,984

Bal·tic Sea \'bȯl-tik\ arm of the Atlantic N Europe E of Scandinavian Peninsula

Bal·ti·more \'bȯl-tə-,mȯr, -mər\ city N *cen* Maryland; *pop* 651,154

Ba·ma·ko \'bä-mä-,kō\ city, ✳ of Mali on the Niger; *pop* 745,787

Ban·bridge \ban-'brij\ district SE *cen* Northern Ireland; *pop* 33,102

Ban·dar Se·ri Be·ga·wan \,bən-dər-,ser-ē-bə-'gä-wän\ town, ✳ of Brunei; *pop* 27,285

Ban·dung \'bän-,duŋ\ city Indonesia in W Java SE of Jakarta; *pop* 2,057,442

Ban·ga·lore \'baŋ-gə-,lȯr\ city S India W of Madras; *pop* 4,292,223

Bang·kok \'baŋ-,käk, baŋ-'\ city, ✳ of Thailand; *pop* 6,320,200

Ban·gla·desh \,bäŋ-glə-'desh, ,baŋ-, ,bəŋ-, -'däsh\ country S Asia E of India; ✳, Dhaka; *pop* 115,075,000 — see EAST PAKISTAN — **Ban·gla·deshi** \-'de-shē, -'dä-\ *adj or n*

Ban·gor \'baŋ-,gȯr, 'ban-,gȯr\ town E Northern Ireland; *pop* 46,585

Ban·gui \bäŋ-'gē\ city, ✳ of Central African Republic; *pop* 300,723

Ban·jul \'bän-,jül\ *formerly* **Bath·urst** \'bath-(,)ərst\ city & port, ✳ of Gambia; *pop* 44,188

Bao·tou *or* **Pao–t'ou** \'bau̇-'tō\ city N China; *pop* 983,508

Bar·ba·dos \bär-'bā-(,)dōs, -dəs, -(,)dōz\ island West Indies in Lesser Antilles E of Windward Islands; country, ✳, Bridgetown; *pop* 250,010 — **Bar·ba·di·an** \-'bā-dē-ən\ *adj or n*

Bar·bu·da \bär-'bü-də\ island West Indies; part of independent Antigua and Barbuda

Bar·ce·lo·na \,bär-sə-'lō-nə\ city NE Spain on the Mediterranean; chief city of Catalonia; *pop* 1,503,884

Bar·king and Dag·en·ham \'bär-kiŋ-ən(d)-'da-gə-nəm\ borough of E Greater London, England; *pop* 139,900

Bar·na·ul \,bär-nə-'ül\ city S Russia; *pop* 606,000

Bar·net \'bär-nət\ borough of N Greater London, England; *pop* 283,000

Bar·ran·qui·lla \,bär-än-'kē-yä\ city N Colombia; *pop* 1,018,800

Barren Grounds treeless plains N Canada W of Hudson Bay

Bar·row, Point \'ba-(,)rō\ most northerly point of Alaska & of U.S. at about 71°25' N latitude

Ba·si·lan \bä-'sē-,län\ island S Philippines

Bas·il·don \'ba-zəl-dən\ town SE England; *pop* 157,500

Bass \'bas\ strait separating Tasmania & continent of Australia

Basse·terre \bas-'ter, bäs-\ seaport Saint Kitts, ✳ of Saint Kitts-Nevis; *pop* 14,725

Basutoland — see LESOTHO

Bathurst — see BANJUL

Bat·on Rouge \,ba-t²n-'rüzh\ city, ✳ of Louisiana; *pop* 227,818

Ba·var·ia \bə-'ver-ē-ə\ *or German* **Bay·ern** \'bī-ərn\ state SE Germany bordering on Czech Republic & Austria; *pop* 11,448,800 — **Ba·var·i·an** \bə-'ver-ē-ən, -'var-\ *adj or n*

Ba·ya·mon \,bī-ä-'mōn\ city NE *cen* Puerto Rico; *pop* 224,004

Beau·fort \'bō-fərt\ sea consisting of part of Arctic Ocean NE of Alaska & NW of Canada

Beau·mont \'bō-,mänt, bō-'\ city SE Texas; *pop* 113,866

Bech·u·a·na·land \,bech-'wä-nə-,land, ,be-chə-\ **1** region S Africa N of Orange River **2** — see BOTSWANA — **Bech·u·a·na** \,bech-'wä-nə, ,be-chə-\ *adj or n*

Bed·ford·shire \'bed-fərd-,shir, -shər\ *or* **Bedford** county SE England

Bedloe's — see LIBERTY

Bei·jing \'bā-'jiŋ\ *or* **Pe·king** \'pē-'kiŋ, 'pā-\ city, ✳ of China; *pop* 10,819,407

Bei·rut \bā-'rüt\ city, ✳ of Lebanon; urban area *pop* 1,100,000

Be·la·rus \,bē-lə-'rüs, ,bye-lə-\ country *cen* Europe; ✳, Minsk; *pop* 9,899,000 — **Be·la·ru·si·an** \-'rü-sē-ən, -'rə-shən\ *or* **Be·la·rus·sian** \-'rə-shən\ *adj or n*

Belau — see PALAU

Be·lém \be-'lem\ city N Brazil; *pop* 1,280,614

Bel·fast \'bel-,fast, bel-'\ city, ✳ of Northern Ireland; *pop* 295,100

Bel·gium \'bel-jəm\ *or French* **Bel·gique** \bel-'zhēk\ *or Flemish* **Bel·gië** \'bel-kē-ə\ country W Europe; ✳, Brussels; *pop* 10,309,725 — **Bel·gian** \'bel-jən\ *adj or n*

Bel·grade \'bel-,grād, -,gräd, -,grad, bel-'\ *or* **Beo·grad** \bā-'ȯ-,gräd\ city, ✳ of Serbia and Montenegro on the Danube; *pop* 1,553,854

Be·lize \bə-'lēz\ *formerly* **British Honduras** country Central America on the Caribbean; ✳, Belmopan; *pop* 241,000 — **Be·liz·ean** *adj or n*

Belize City seaport E Belize; *pop* 45,158

Belle·vue \'bel-,vyü\ city W Washington E of Seattle; *pop* 109,569

Bel·mo·pan \,bel-mō-'pän\ city, ✳ of Belize; *pop* 6500

Be·lo Ho·ri·zon·te \'bā-lō-,ȯr-ē-'zȯn-tē\ city E Brazil N of Rio de Janeiro; *pop* 2,238,526

Be·lo·rus·sia \,be-lō-'rə-shə, ,bye-lō-\ *or* **Bye·lo·rus·sia** \bē-,e-lō-, ,bye-lō-\ former republic of U.S.S.R.; became independent Belarus in 1991 — **Belo·rus·sian** \,be-lō-'rə-shən, ,bye-\ *adj or n*

Ben·gal \ben-'gȯl, beŋ-, -'gäl\ region S Asia including delta of Ganges & Brahmaputra rivers; divided between Bangladesh & India — **Ben·gal·ese** \,beŋ-gə-'lēz, ,ben-, -'lēs\ *adj or n*

Bengal, Bay of arm of Indian Ocean between India & Myanmar

Be·nin \bə-'nēn, -'nin; 'be-nin\ *formerly* **Da·ho·mey** \də-'hō-mē\ country W Africa on Gulf of Guinea; ✳, Porto-Novo; *pop* 5,074,000 — **Ben·i·nese** \bə-,ni-'nēz, -,nē-, -'nēs; ,be-ni-'nēz, -'nēs\ *adj or n*

Ben Nev·is \ben-'ne-vəs\ mountain 4406 ft. (1343 m.) W Scotland in the Grampians; highest in Great Britain

Beograd — see BELGRADE

Ber·gen \'bər-gən, 'ber-\ city & port SW Norway; *pop* 209,375

Be·ring \'bir-iŋ, 'ber-\ **1** sea, arm of the North Pacific between Alaska & NE Siberia **2** strait at narrowest point 53 mi. (85 km.) wide between North America (Alaska) and Asia (Russia)

Berke·ley \'bər-klē\ city W California on San Francisco Bay N of Oakland; *pop* 102,743

Berk·shire \'bərk-,shir, -shər\ hills W Massachusetts; highest point Mount Greylock 3491 ft. (1064 m.)

Ber·lin \(,)bər-'lin\ city, ✳ of Germany; divided 1945–90 into **East Berlin** (✳ of East Germany) & **West Berlin** (city of West Germany lying within East Germany); *pop* 3,392,900 — **Ber·lin·er** \(,)bər-'li-nər\ *n*

Ber·mu·da \(,)bər-'myü-də\ islands W Atlantic ESE of Cape Hatteras; a British colony; ✳, Hamilton; *pop* 62,059 — **Ber·mu·dan** \-dᵊn\ *or* **Ber·mu·di·an** \-dē-ən\ *adj or n*

Bern \'bərn, 'bern\ city, ✳ of Switzerland; *pop* 122,469 — **Ber·nese** \(,)bər-'nēz, -'nēs\ *adj or n*

Bes·sa·ra·bia \,be-sə-'rā-bē-ə\ region SE Europe now chiefly in Moldova — **Bes·sa·ra·bi·an** \-bē-ən\ *adj or n*

Beth·le·hem \'beth-li-,hem, -lē-həm, -lē-əm\ town of ancient Palestine in Judea; the present-day town is SW of Jerusalem in the West Bank; *pop* 34,180

Bev·er·ly Hills \'be-vər-lē\ city SW California within Los Angeles; *pop* 33,784

Bex·ley \'bek-slē\ borough of E Greater London, England; *pop* 211,200

Bho·pal \bō-'päl\ city N *cen* India; *pop* 1,433,875

Bhu·tan \bü-'tän, -'tan\ country S Asia in the Himalayas on NE border of India; ✳, Thimphu; *pop* 1,546,000 — **Bhu·ta·nese** \,bü-tə-'nēz, -'nēs\ *adj or n*

Bi·ki·ni \bi-'kē-nē\ atoll W Pacific in Marshall Islands

Bil·lings \'bi-liŋz\ city S *cen* Montana; largest in state; *pop* 89,847

Bi·loxi \bə-'lək-sē, -'läk-\ city & port SE Mississippi on Gulf of Mexico; *pop* 50,644

Bi·o·ko \bē-'ō-(,)kō\ *formerly* **Fer·nan·do Pó·o** \fer-'nän-(,)dō-'pō\ island portion of Equatorial Guinea in Gulf of Guinea

Bir·ken·head \'bər-kən-,hed, ,bər-kən-\ borough NW England on the Mersey opposite Liverpool; *pop* 123,907

Bir·ming·ham \'bər-miŋ-,ham\ **1** city N *cen* Alabama; *pop* 242,820 **2** city W *cen* England; *pop* 934,900

Bis·cay, Bay of \'bis-,kā, -kē\ inlet of the Atlantic between W coast of France & N coast of Spain

Bish·kek \bish-'kek\ *formerly* **1926–91 Frun·ze** \'frün-zi\ city, ✳ of Kyrgyzstan; *pop* 641,400

Bis·marck \'biz-,märk\ **1** city, ✳ of North Dakota; *pop* 55,532 **2** archipelago W Pacific N of E end of New Guinea

Bis·sau \bi-'saủ\ city, ✳ of Guinea-Bissau; *pop* 125,000

Bi·thyn·ia \bə-'thi-nē-ə\ ancient country NW Asia Minor bordering on Sea of Marmara and Black Sea — **Bi·thyn·i·an** \-nē-ən\ *adj or n*

Bit·ter·root \'bi-tə(r)-,rüt, -,rút\ range of the Rockies along Idaho–Montana boundary

Black·burn \'blak-(,)bərn\ town NW England; *pop* 132,800

Black Forest forested mountain region Germany along E bank of the upper Rhine

Black Hills mountains W South Dakota & NE Wyoming

Black·pool \'blak-,pül\ town NW England on Irish Sea; *pop* 144,500

Black Sea sea between Europe & Asia connected with Aegean Sea through the Bosporus, Sea of Marmara, & Dardanelles

Blanc, Mont — see MONT BLANC

Blan·tyre \'blan-,tī(-ə)r\ city S Malawi; *pop* 554,578

Bloem·fon·tein \'blüm-fən-,tān, -,fän-\ city Republic of South Africa, judicial ✳ of the country; *pop* 149,836

Blue Ridge E range of the Appalachians E U.S. extending from S Pennsylvania to N Georgia

Bodh Gaya \'bōd-'gī-ä\ village NE India; one of the holiest sites of Buddhism

Boe·o·tia \bē-'ō-sh(ē-)ə\ ancient state E *cen* Greece NW of Attica; chief ancient city, Thebes — **Boe·o·tian** \bē-'ō-shən\ *adj or n*

Bo·go·tá \,bō-gō-'tä, -'tȯ, 'bō-gə-,\ city, ✳ of Colombia; *pop* 4,921,300

Bo Hai *or* **Po Hai** \'bō-'hī\ *or* **Gulf of Chih·li** \'chē-'lē, 'jir-\ arm of Yellow Sea NE China

Bo·he·mia \bō-'hē-mē-ə\ region W Czech Republic; chief city, Prague

Bo·hol \bō-'hȯl\ island S *cen* Philippines

Boi·se \'bȯi-sē, -zē\ city, ✳ of Idaho; *pop* 185,787

Bo·liv·ia \bə-'li-vē-ə\ country W *cen* South America; administrative ✳, La Paz; constitutional ✳, Sucre; *pop* 8,274,325 — **Bo·liv·i·an** \-vē-ən\ *adj or n*

Bo·lo·gna \bō-'lō-nyä\ city N Italy; *pop* 379,964

Bol·ton \'bōl-tᵊn\ town NW England; *pop* 253,300

Bom·bay \bäm-'bā\ *or* **Mum·bai** \'məm-,bī\ city & port W India; *pop* 11,914,398

Bonn \'bän, 'bȯn\ city Germany on the Rhine SSE of Cologne, formerly (1949–99) ✳ of West Germany; *pop* 296,244

Boo·thia \'bü-thē-ə\ peninsula N Canada W of Baffin Island; its N tip is most northerly point in mainland North America

Bor·ders \'bȯr-dərz\ former administrative region SE Scotland

Bor·neo \'bȯr-nē-,ō\ island Malay Archipelago SW of the Philippines; divided between Brunei, Indonesia, and Malaysia

Bos·nia \'bäz-nē-ə, 'bȯz\ region S Europe; with Herzegovina forms independent **Bosnia and Her·ze·go·vi·na**

\ˌhert-sə-gō-ˈvē-nə, ˌhert-, -ˈgō-və-nə\; *, Sarajevo; *pop* 4,422,000 — **Bos·ni·an** \-nē-ən\ *adj or n*

Bos·po·rus \ˈbäs-p(ə-)rəs\ strait 18 mi. (29 km.) long between Turkey in Europe & Turkey in Asia connecting Sea of Marmara & Black Sea

Bos·ton \ˈbȯs-tən\ city, * of Massachusetts; *pop* 589,141 — **Bos·to·nian** \bȯ-ˈstō-nē-ən, -nyən\ *adj or n*

Bot·a·ny Bay \ˈbä-tə-nē\ inlet of South Pacific SE Australia in New South Wales S of Sydney

Both·nia, Gulf of \ˈbäth-nē-ə\ arm of Baltic Sea between Sweden & Finland

Bo·tswa·na \bät-ˈswä-nə\ *formerly* **Bech·u·a·na·land** \ˌbech-ˈwä-nə-land\ country S Africa; *, Gaborone; *pop* 1,611,021

Boul·der \ˈbōl-dər\ city N *cen* Colorado; *pop* 94,673

Boulder Dam — see HOOVER DAM

Bourne·mouth \ˈbȯrn-məth, ˈburn-\ town S England on English Channel; *pop* 154,400

Brad·ford \ˈbrad-fərd\ city N England; *pop* 280,691

Brah·ma·pu·tra \ˌbrä-mə-ˈpü-trə\ river about 1800 mi. (2900 km.) long S Asia flowing from the Himalayas in Tibet to Ganges Delta

Bra·sí·lia \brə-ˈzil-yə\ city, * of Brazil; *pop* 2,051,146

Bra·ti·sla·va \ˌbra-tə-ˈslä-və, ˌbrä\ city on the Danube; * of Slovakia; *pop* 428,672

Bra·zil \brə-ˈzil\ country E & *cen* South America; *, Brasília; *pop* 169,799,170 — **Bra·zil·ian** \brə-ˈzil-yən\ *adj or n*

Braz·za·ville \ˈbra-zə-ˌvil, ˈbrä-zə-ˌvēl\ city, * of Republic of the Congo on W bank of lower Congo River; *pop* 937,579

Bre·men \ˈbre-mən, ˈbrā-\ city & port NW Germany; *pop* 552,746

Bren·ner \ˈbre-nər\ pass 4495 ft. (1370 m.) high in the Alps between Austria & Italy

Brent \ˈbrent\ borough of W Greater London, England; *pop* 226,100

Bret·on, Cape \kāp-ˈbre-tᵊn, kə-ˈbre-, -ˈbri-\ cape Canada; most easterly point of Cape Breton Island & of Nova Scotia

Bridge·port \ˈbrij-ˌpȯrt\ city SW Connecticut on Long Island Sound; *pop* 139,529

Bridge·town \ˈbrij-ˌtaun\ city, * of Barbados; *pop* 5996

Brigh·ton \ˈbrī-tᵊn\ town S England on English Channel; *pop* 133,400

Bris·bane \ˈbriz-bən, -ˌbān\ city & port E Australia, * of Queensland; *pop* 751,115

Bris·tol \ˈbris-tᵊl\ **1** city & port SW England; *pop* 370,330 **2** channel between S Wales & SW England

Brit·ain \ˈbri-tᵊn\ **1** the island of Great Britain **2** UNITED KINGDOM

British Columbia province W Canada on Pacific coast; *, Victoria; *pop* 3,907,738

British Commonwealth — see COMMONWEALTH, THE

British Empire former empire consisting of Great Britain & the British dominions & dependencies

British Guiana — see GUYANA

British Honduras — see BELIZE

British India the part of India formerly under direct British administration

British Indian Ocean Territory British colony in Indian Ocean consisting of Chagos Archipelago

British Isles island group W Europe consisting of Great Britain, Ireland, & nearby islands

British Virgin Islands E islands of Virgin Islands; a British possession; *pop* 14,786

British West Indies islands of the West Indies including Jamaica, Trinidad and Tobago, & the Bahama & Cayman islands, Windward Islands, Leeward Islands, & British Virgin Islands

Brit·ta·ny \ˈbri-tə-nē\ region NW France SW of Normandy

Brom·ley \ˈbräm-lē\ borough of SE Greater London, England; *pop* 281,700

Bronx \ˈbräŋks\ *or* **The Bronx** borough of New York City NE of Manhattan; *pop* 1,332,650

Brook·lyn \ˈbruk-lən\ borough of New York City at SW end of Long Island; *pop* 2,465,326

Brooks Range \ˈbruks\ mountains N Alaska

Browns·ville \ˈbraunz-ˌvil, -vəl\ city S Texas on the Rio Grande; *pop* 139,722

Bru·nei \brü-ˈnī, ˈbrü-ˌnī\ country NE Borneo; *, Bandar Seri Begawan; *pop* 332,844 — **Bru·nei·an** \brü-ˈnī-ən\ *adj or n*

Brus·sels \ˈbrə-səlz\ city, * of Belgium; *pop* 136,730

Bu·cha·rest \ˈbü-kə-ˌrest, ˈbyü\ city, * of Romania; *pop* 1,921,751

Buck·ing·ham·shire \ˈbə-kiŋ-əm-ˌshir\ *or* **Buckingham** county SE *cen* England

Bu·da·pest \ˈbü-də-ˌpest\ city, * of Hungary; *pop* 2,008,546

Bue·nos Ai·res \ˌbwā-nəs-ˈa-rēz, *Sp* ˌbwā-nōs-ˈī-rās\ city, * of Argentina; *pop* 2,960,976

Buf·fa·lo \ˈbə-fə-ˌlō\ city W New York on Lake Erie; *pop* 292,648

Bu·jum·bu·ra \ˌbü-jəm-ˈbur-ə\ city, * of Burundi; *pop* 236,334

Bu·ko·vi·na \ˌbü-kō-ˈvē-nə\ region E *cen* Europe in foothills of E Carpathians

Bul·gar·ia \ˌbəl-ˈger-ē-ə, bul-\ country SE Europe on Black Sea; *, Sofia; *pop* 8,466,000 — **Bul·gar·i·an** \ˌbəl-ˈger-ē-ən, bul-\ *adj or n*

Bull Run \ˈbul-ˈrən\ stream NE Virginia

Bun·ker Hill \ˈbəŋ-kər\ height in Boston, Massachusetts

Bur·bank \ˈbər-ˌbaŋk\ city SW California; *pop* 100,316

Bur·gun·dy \ˈbər-gən-dē\ region E France — **Bur·gun·di·an** \(ˌ)bər-ˈgən-dē-ən\ *adj or n*

Bur·ki·na Fa·so \bur-ˈkē-nə-ˈfä-sō, bər-\ *formerly* **Upper Vol·ta** \ˈvōl-tə, ˈvȯl-\ country W Africa N of Ivory Coast, Ghana, & Togo; *, Ouagadougou; *pop* 9,780,000

Bur·ling·ton \ˈbər-liŋ-tən\ city NW Vermont; largest in state; *pop* 38,889

Bur·ma \ˈbər-mə\ — see MYANMAR — **Bur·mese** \ˌbər-ˈmēz, -ˈmēs\ *adj or n*

Bu·run·di \bu-ˈrün-dē, -ˈrun-\ country E *cen* Africa; *, Bujumbura; *pop* 5,665,000 — **Bu·run·di·an** \-dē-ən\ *adj or n*

Busan — see PUSAN

Bute \ˈbyüt\ island SW Scotland in Firth of Clyde

Butte \ˈbyüt\ city SW Montana; county *pop* 34,606

Byelorussia — see BELORUSSIA

By·zan·tine Empire \ˈbi-zᵊn-ˌtēn, ˈbī-, -ˌtīn; bə-ˈzan-ˌtēn, -tīn, bī-\ empire of SE & S Europe and W Asia from 4th to 15th century

By·zan·ti·um \bə-ˈzan-sh(ē-)əm, -ˈzant-ē-əm\ ancient city on site of modern Istanbul

Caer·nar·von \kär-ˈnär-vən, kə(r)-\ town & seaport NW Wales; *pop* 9506

Ca·guas \ˈkä-ˌgwäs\ town E *cen* Puerto Rico; *pop* 140,502

Cai·ro \ˈkī-(ˌ)rō\ city, * of Egypt; *pop* 6,633,000 — **Cai·rene** \kī-ˈrēn\ *adj or n*

Ca·la·bria \kə-ˈlä-brē-ə, -ˈlä-\ district of ancient Italy consisting of area forming heel of Italian Peninsula — **Ca·la·bri·an** \kə-ˈlä-brē-ən, -ˈlä-\ *adj or n*

Cal·cut·ta \kal-ˈkə-tə\ *or* **Kol·ka·ta** \kōl-ˈkä-tä\ city E India on Hugli River; *pop* 4,580,544 — **Cal·cut·tan** \-ˈkə-tᵊn\ *adj or n*

Cal·e·do·nia \ˌka-lə-ˈdō-nyə, -nē-ə\ — see SCOTLAND — **Cal·e·do·nian** \-nyən, -nē-ən\ *adj or n*

Cal·ga·ry \ˈkal-gə-rē\ city SW Alberta, Canada; *pop* 878,866

Ca·li \ˈkä-lē\ city W Colombia; *pop* 1,624,400

Cal·i·for·nia \ˌka-lə-ˈfȯr-nyə\ state SW U.S.; *, Sacramento; *pop* 33,871,648 — **Cal·i·for·nian** \-nyən\ *adj or n*

California, Gulf of arm of the Pacific NW Mexico

Cal·va·ry \ˈkal-v(ə-)rē\ place outside ancient Jerusalem where Jesus was crucified

Cambay, Gulf of — see KHAMBHAT (Gulf of)

Cam·bo·dia \kam-ˈbō-dē-ə\ *or* **Kam·pu·chea** \ˌkam-pu-ˈchē-ə\ country SE Asia in S Indochina; *, Phnom Penh; *pop* 11,437,656 — **Cam·bo·di·an** \kam-ˈbō-dē-ən\ *adj or n*

Cam·bria \ˈkam-brē-ə\ WALES — an old name

Cam·bridge \ˈkām-brij\ **1** city E Massachusetts W of Boston; *pop* 101,355 **2** city E England; *pop* 92,772

Cam·bridge·shire \ˈkām-brij-ˌshir, -shər\ *or* **Cambridge** county E England

Cam·den \ˈkam-dən\ borough of N Greater London, England; *pop* 170,500

Cam·er·oon *or French* **Cam·er·oun** \ˌka-mə-ˈrün\ country W Africa; ✻, Yaoundé; *pop* 13,103,000 — **Cam·er·oo·nian** \-ˈrü-nē-ən, -rü-nyən\ *adj or n*

Ca·mi·guin \ˌkä-mē-ˈgēn\ island Philippines, off N coast of Mindanao

Ca·naan \ˈkā-nən\ ancient region SW Asia; approximately the area later called Palestine — **Ca·naan·ite** \ˈkā-nə-ˌnīt\ *adj or n*

Can·a·da \ˈka-nə-də\ country N North America; ✻, Ottawa; *pop* 27,296,859 — **Ca·na·di·an** \kə-ˈnā-dē-ən\ *adj or n*

Canadian Falls — see NIAGARA FALLS

Canadian Shield *or* **Lau·ren·tian Plateau** \lȯ-ˈren(t)-shən\ plateau region E Canada & NE U.S. extending from Mackenzie River basin E to Davis Strait & S to S Quebec, S *cen* Ontario, NE Minnesota, N Wisconsin, NW Michigan, and NE New York including the Adirondacks

Canal Zone *or* **Panama Canal Zone** strip of territory Panama leased to U.S. (until 1979) for Panama Canal

Ca·nary \kə-ˈner-ē\ islands Spain in the Atlantic off NW coast of Africa; *pop* 1,493,784

Ca·nav·er·al, Cape \kə-ˈnav-rəl, -ˈna-və-\ *or 1963–73* **Cape Ken·ne·dy** \-ˈken-ə-dē\ cape E Florida in the Atlantic on **Canaveral Peninsula** E of Indian River

Can·ber·ra \ˈkan-b(ə-)rə, -ˌber-ə\ city, ✻ of Australia in Australian Capital Territory; *pop* 348,600

Cannes \ˈkan, ˈkän\ port SE France; *pop* 69,363

Can·ter·bury \ˈkan-tə(r)-ˌber-ē, -b(ə-)rē\ city SE England; *pop* 34,404

Canton — see GUANGZHOU

Cape Bret·on Island \kāp-ˈbre-tᵊn, kə-ˈbre-, -ˈbri-\ island NE Nova Scotia

Cape Coral city SW Florida; *pop* 102,286

Cape Horn — see HORN, CAPE

Cape of Good Hope — see GOOD HOPE, CAPE OF

Cape Province *or* **Cape of Good Hope** *or before 1910* **Cape Colony** former province S Republic of South Africa

Cape Town \ˈkāp-ˌtau̇n\ city, legislative ✻ of Republic of South Africa and formerly ✻ of Cape Province; *pop* 776,617

Cape Verde \ˈvərd\ islands in the North Atlantic off W Africa; country; ✻, Praia; *pop* 350,000 — **Cape Verd·ean** \ˈvər-dē-ən\ *adj or n*

Cape York Peninsula \ˈyȯrk\ peninsula NE Australia in N Queensland

Ca·pri \kä-ˈprē, kə-; ˈkä-(ˌ)prē, ˈka-\ island Italy S of Bay of Naples; *pop* 7270

Ca·ra·cas \kä-ˈrä-käs\ city, ✻ of Venezuela; *pop* 1,824,892

Car·diff \ˈkär-dif\ city, ✻ of Wales; *pop* 272,600

Ca·rib·be·an Sea \ˌka-rə-ˈbē-ən, kə-ˈri-bē-\ arm of the Atlantic; on N & E are the West Indies, on S is South America, & on W is Central America — **Caribbean** *adj*

Car·lisle \kär-ˈlī(-ə)l, kər-, ˈkär-ˌ\ city NW England; *pop* 99,800

Carls·bad Caverns \ˈkär(-ə)lz-ˌbad\ series of caves SE New Mexico

Car·mar·then \kär-ˈmär-thən, kə(r)-\ port S Wales; *pop* 54,800

Car·o·li·na \ˌka-rə-ˈlī-nə\ English colony on E coast of North America founded 1663 & divided 1729 into North Carolina & South Carolina (the **Carolinas**) — **Car·o·lin·i·an** \ˌka-rə-ˈli-nē-ən, -nyən\ *adj or n*

Ca·ro·li·na \ˌkä-rō-ˈlē-nä\ city NE Puerto Rico; *pop* 186,076

Car·o·line \ˈka-rə-ˌlīn, -lən\ islands W Pacific E of S Philippines; comprising Palau & the Federated States of Micronesia

Car·pa·thi·an \kär-ˈpā-thē-ən\ mountains E *cen* Europe along boundary between Slovakia & Poland & in N & *cen* Romania; highest Gerlachovksky 8711 ft. (2655 m.)

Car·pen·tar·ia, Gulf of \ˌkär-pən-ˈter-ē-ə\ inlet of Arafura Sea N of Australia

Car·rick·fer·gus \ˌka-rik-ˈfər-gəs\ district E Northern Ireland; *pop* 32,439

Car·roll·ton \ˈka-rəl-tən\ city N Texas; *pop* 109,576

Car·son City \ˈkär-sᵊn\ city, ✻ of Nevada; *pop* 52,457

Car·thage \ˈkär-thij\ ancient city N Africa NE of modern Tunis; ✻ of an empire that once included much of NW

Africa, E Spain, & Sicily — **Car·tha·gin·ian** \ˌkär-thə-ˈji-nyən, -nē-ən\ *adj or n*

Ca·sa·blan·ca \ˌka-sə-ˈblaŋ-kə, ˌkä-sə-ˈbläŋ-, -zə-\ city W Morocco on the Atlantic; *pop* 3,102,000

Cas·cade Range \(ˌ)kas-ˈkād\ mountains NW U.S. in Washington, Oregon, & N California — see RAINIER, MOUNT

Cas·per \ˈkas-pər\ city *cen* Wyoming; *pop* 49,644

Cas·pi·an Sea \ˈkas-pē-ən\ salt lake between Europe and Asia about 90 ft. (27 m.) below sea level

Cas·tile \ka-ˈstēl\ *or in full* **Cas·ti·lla** \kä-ˈstēl-yä, -ˈstē-yä\ region & ancient kingdom *cen* N Spain

Cast·le·reagh \ˈka-səl-(ˌ)rā\ district E Northern Ireland; *pop* 60,649

Cas·tries \ˈkas-ˌtrēz, -ˌtrēs\ seaport, ✻ of Saint Lucia; *pop* 1814

Cat·a·lo·nia \ˌka-tə-ˈlō-nyə, -nē-ə\ region NE Spain bordering on France & the Mediterranean; chief city, Barcelona; *pop* 6,059,494 — **Cat·a·lo·nian** \-ˈlō-nyən, -nē-ən\ *adj or n*

Ca·thay \ka-ˈthā\ an old name for China

Cats·kill \ˈkat-ˌskil\ mountains in Appalachian system SE New York W of the Hudson

Cau·ca·sus \ˈkȯ-kə-səs\ mountain system SE Europe between Black & Caspian seas in Russia, Georgia, Azerbaijan, & Armenia

Cay·enne \kī-ˈen, kā-\ city, ✻ of French Guiana; *pop* 37,917

Cay·man \(ˌ)kā-ˈman, *attributively* ˈkā-mən\ islands West Indies NW of Jamaica; a British colony; *pop* 23,881

Ce·bu \sä-ˈbü\ island E *cen* Philippines

Ce·dar Rapids \ˈsē-dər\ city E Iowa; *pop* 120,758

Cel·tic Sea \ˈkel-tik, ˈsel-\ inlet of the Atlantic in British Isles SE of Ireland, SW of Wales, & W of SW England

Central African Republic country N *cen* Africa; ✻, Bangui; *pop* 2,998,000

Central America narrow portion of North America from S border of Mexico to South America — **Central American** *adj or n*

Central Valley valley of Sacramento & San Joaquin rivers in California between Sierra Nevada & Coast Ranges

Cey·lon \si-ˈlän, sā-\ **1** island in Indian Ocean off S India **2** — see SRI LANKA — **Cey·lon·ese** \ˌsā-lə-ˈnēz, ˌse-, ˌse-, -ˈnēs\ *adj or n*

Chad \ˈchad\ country N *cen* Africa; ✻, N'Djamena; *pop* 5,200,000 — **Chad·ian** \ˈcha-dē-ən\ *adj or n*

Chad, Lake shallow lake N *cen* Africa at junction of boundaries of Chad, Niger, & Nigeria

Cha·gos Archipelago \ˈchä-gəs\ island group *cen* Indian Ocean; forms British Indian Ocean Territory — see DIEGO GARCIA

Chal·dea \kal-ˈdē-ə\ ancient region SW Asia on Euphrates River & Persian Gulf — **Chal·de·an** \-ˈdē-ən\ *adj or n* — **Chal·dee** \ˈkal-ˌdē\ *n*

Cham·pagne \sham-ˈpān\ region NE France

Cham·plain, Lake \sham-ˈplān\ lake between New York & Vermont extending N into Quebec

Chan·di·garh \ˈchən-dē-gər\ city N India N of Delhi; *pop* 510,565

Chan·dler \ˈchan(d)-lər\ city SW *cen* Arizona; *pop* 176,581

Chang \ˈchäŋ\ *or* **Yang·tze** \ˈyaŋ-ˈsē, ˈyaŋ(k)t-ˈsē; ˈyäŋ-ˈtsə\ river 3434 mi. (5525 km.) long *cen* China flowing into East China Sea

Chang·chun \ˈchäŋ-ˈchün\ city NE China; *pop* 1,679,270

Chang·sha \ˈchäŋ-ˈshä\ city SE *cen* China; *pop* 1,113,312

Channel islands in English Channel including Jersey, Guernsey, & Alderney & belonging to United Kingdom; *pop* 135,694

Charles \ˈchär(-ə)lz\ river 47 mi. (76 km.) long E Massachusetts flowing into Boston harbor

Charles, Cape cape E Virginia N of entrance to Chesapeake Bay

Charles·ton \ˈchär(-ə)l-stən\ **1** seaport SE South Carolina; *pop* 96,650 **2** city, ✻ of West Virginia; *pop* 53,421

Char·lotte \ˈshär-lət\ city S North Carolina; *pop* 540,828

Charlotte Ama·lie \ə-ˈmäl-yə, ˈa-mə-lē\ city, ✻ of Virgin Islands of the U.S.; on island of Saint Thomas; *pop* 12,331

Char·lottes·ville \ˈshär-ləts-ˌvil, -vəl\ city *cen* Virginia; *pop* 45,049

Char·lotte·town \\'shär-lət-ˌtaún\ city, * of Prince Edward Island, Canada; *pop* 32,245

Chat·ta·noo·ga \ˌcha-tə-'nü-gə\ city SE Tennessee; *pop* 155,554

Chech·nya \chech-'nyä, 'chech-nyə\ republic of SE Russia in Europe; *, Grozny

Chelms·ford \\'chemz-fərd\ town SE England; *pop* 150,000

Che·lya·binsk \chel-'yä-bən(t)sk\ city W Russia; *pop* 1,143,000

Cheng–chou — see ZHENGZHOU

Cheng·du *or* **Ch'eng·tu** \'chəŋ-'dü\ city SW *cen* China; *pop* 1,713,255

Chennai — see MADRAS

Cher·no·byl \chər-'nō-bəl, (ˌ)cher-\ site N Ukraine of town abandoned after 1986 nuclear accident

Ches·a·peake \'che-sə-ˌpēk, 'ches-ˌpēk\ city SE Virginia; *pop* 199,184

Chesapeake Bay inlet of the Atlantic in Virginia & Maryland

Chesh·ire \'che-shər, -ˌshir\ *or* **Ches·ter** \'ches-tər\ county W England bordering on Wales

Chester \'ches-tər\ city NW England; *pop* 58,436

Chev·i·ot \'chē-vē-ət, 'che-\ hills along English–Scottish border

Chey·enne \shī-'an, -'en\ city, * of Wyoming; *pop* 53,011

Chi·ba \'chē-bä\ city E Japan in Honshu on Tokyo Bay E of Tokyo; *pop* 887,164

Chi·ca·go \shə-'kä-(ˌ)gō, -'kó-, -gə\ city & port NE Illinois on Lake Michigan; *pop* 2,896,016 — **Chi·ca·go·an** \-'kä-gō-ən, -'kó-\ *n*

Chi·chén It·zá \chē-ˌchen-ēt-'sä, -'ēt-sə\ ruined Mayan city SE Mexico in Yucatán Peninsula

Chich·es·ter \'chi-chəs-tər\ city S England; *pop* 24,189

Ch'i–ch'i–ha–erh — see QIQIHAR

Chihli, Gulf of — see BO HAI

Chi·le \'chi-lē, 'chē-(ˌ)lä\ country SW South America; *, Santiago; *pop* 15,116,435 — **Chil·ean** \'chi-lē-ən, chə-'lā-ən\ *adj or n*

Chim·bo·ra·zo \ˌchēm-bō-'rä-(ˌ)zō\ mountain 20,561 ft. (6267 m.) W *cen* Ecuador

Chi·na \'chī-nə\ **1** country E Asia; *, Beijing; *pop* 1,179,467,000 — see TAIWAN **2** sea section of the W Pacific; divided at Taiwan strait into East China & South China seas

Chin–chou *or* **Chinchow** — see JINZHOU

Chi·si·nau \ˌkē-shē-'naú\ *or* **Ki·shi·nev** \ˌki-shi-'nyóf; 'ki-shə-ˌnef, -ˌnev\ city *cen* Moldova; its *; *pop* 665,000

Chit·ta·gong \'chi-tə-ˌgäŋ, -ˌgóŋ\ city SE Bangladesh on Bay of Bengal; *pop* 1,566,070

Chong·qing *or* **Ch'ung–ch'ing** \'chúŋ-'chiŋ\ *or* **Chung·king** \'chùŋ-'kiŋ\ city SW *cen* China; *pop* 2,266,772

Christ·church \'krīs(t)-ˌchərch\ city New Zealand on E coast of South Island; urban area *pop* 334,107

Christ·mas \'kris-məs\ island E Indian Ocean SW of Java; governed by Australia; *pop* 1000

Chu·la Vis·ta \ˌchü-lə-'vis-tə\ city SW California S of San Diego; *pop* 173,556

Chuuk \'chúk\ *or* **Truk** \'trək, 'trúk\ islands *cen* Carolines, part of Federated States of Micronesia

Cin·cin·na·ti \ˌsin(t)-sə-'na-tē, -'na-tə\ city SW Ohio; *pop* 331,285

Ci·u·dad Juá·rez \syü-'thäth-'hwär-es, 'wäs-; ˌsē-ü-'dad-\ city Mexico on Texas border; urban area *pop* 1,011,786

Ciudad Trujillo — see SANTO DOMINGO

Clarks·ville \'klärks-ˌvil, -vəl\ city N Tennessee NW of Nashville; *pop* 103,455

Clear·wa·ter \'klir-ˌwó-tər, -ˌwä-\ city W Florida NW of St. Petersburg; *pop* 108,787

Cleve·land \'klēv-lənd\ city & port NE Ohio on Lake Erie; *pop* 478,403

Clyde \'klīd\ river 106 mi. (171 km.) long SW Scotland flowing into **Firth of Clyde** (estuary)

Coast Mountains mountain range W British Columbia, Canada; the N continuation of Cascade Range

Coast Ranges chain of mountain ranges W North America extending along Pacific coast W of Sierra Nevada & Cascade Range & through Vancouver Island into S Alaska to Kenai Peninsula & Kodiak Island

Cod, Cape \-'käd\ peninsula SE Massachusetts

Coim·ba·tore \ˌkóim-bə-'tór\ city S India; *pop* 816,321

Cole·raine \kōl-'rān, 'kōl-ˌ\ **1** district N Northern Ireland; *pop* 51,062 **2** port in Coleraine district

Co·logne \kə-'lōn\ city W Germany on the Rhine; *pop* 956,690

Co·lom·bia \kə-'ləm-bē-ə\ country NW South America; *, Bogotá; *pop* 26,525,670 — **Co·lom·bi·an** \-bē-ən\ *adj or n*

Co·lom·bo \kə-'ləm-(ˌ)bō\ city, * of Sri Lanka; *pop* 615,000

Col·o·ra·do \ˌkä-lə-'ra-(ˌ)dō\ **1** river 1450 mi. (2334 km.) long SW U.S. & NW Mexico flowing from N Colorado into Gulf of California **2** desert SE California **3** plateau region SW U.S. W of Rocky Mountains **4** state W U.S.; *, Denver; *pop* 4,301,261 — **Col·o·rad·an** \-'ra-dᵊn, -'rä-\ *or* **Co·lo·ra·do·an** \-'ra-dō-ən, -'rä-\ *adj or n*

Colorado Springs city *cen* Colorado E of Pikes Peak; *pop* 360,890

Co·lum·bia \kə-'ləm-bē-ə\ **1** river 1214 mi. (1953 km.) long SW Canada & NW U.S. flowing S & W from SE British Columbia into the Pacific **2** plateau in Columbia River basin in E Washington, E Oregon, & SW Idaho **3** city, * of South Carolina; *pop* 116,278

Co·lum·bus \kə-'ləm-bəs\ **1** city W Georgia; *pop* 186,291 **2** city, * of Ohio; *pop* 711,470

Com·mon·wealth, the \'käm-ən-ˌwel(t)th\ *or* **Commonwealth of Nations** *formerly* **British Commonwealth** the United Kingdom & most of the countries formerly dependent on it

Com·o·ros \'kä-mə-ˌrōz\ islands off SE Africa NW of Madagascar; country (except for Mayotte Island); *, Moroni; *pop* 519,527

Con·a·kry \'kä-nə-krē\ city, * of Guinea; *pop* 581,000

Con·cord \'kän-ˌkórd, 'kän-\ **1** city W California; *pop* 121,780 **2** town E Massachusetts NW of Boston; *pop* 16,993 **3** city, * of New Hampshire; *pop* 40,687

Con·go \'käŋ-(ˌ)gō\ **1** *or* **Zaire** \zä-'ir\ river over 2700 mi. (4344 km.) long W Africa flowing into the Atlantic **2** *officially* **Democratic Republic of the Congo** *formerly* **1971–97 Zaire** country *cen* Africa consisting of most of Congo River basin E of lower Congo River; *, Kinshasa; *pop* 43,775,000 **3** *or officially* **Republic of the Congo** country W *cen* Africa W of lower Congo River; *, Brazzaville; *pop* 2,775,000 — **Con·go·lese** \ˌkäŋ-gə-'lēz, -'lēs\ *adj or n*

Con·nacht \'kä-ˌnót\ province W Ireland; *pop* 422,909

Con·nect·i·cut \kə-'ne-ti-kət\ **1** river 407 mi. (655 km.) long NE U.S. flowing S from N New Hampshire into Long Island Sound **2** state NE U.S.; *, Hartford; *pop* 3,405,565

Constantinople — see ISTANBUL

Continental Divide line of highest points of land separating the waters flowing W from those flowing N or E and extending SSE from NW Canada across W U.S. through Mexico & Central America to South America where it joins the Andes Mountains

Cook \'kúk\ **1** inlet of the Pacific S Alaska W of Kenai Peninsula **2** islands South Pacific SW of Society Islands belonging to New Zealand; *pop* 17,614 **3** strait New Zealand between North Island & South Island

Cook, Mount *formerly* **Ao·rangi** \aú-'räŋ-ē\ mountain 12,349 ft. (3764 m.) New Zealand in W *cen* South Island in Southern Alps; highest in New Zealand

Cooks·town \'kúks-ˌtaún\ district *cen* Northern Ireland; *pop* 30,808

Co·pen·ha·gen \ˌkō-pən-'hā-gən, -'hä-\ city, * of Denmark; *pop* 501,285

Cor·al Sea \'kór-əl, 'kär-\ arm of the W Pacific NE of Australia

Coral Springs city SE Florida; *pop* 117,549

Cór·do·ba \'kór-də-bə, 'kór-thō-ˌvä\ city N *cen* Argentina; *pop* 1,179,067

Cor·inth \'kór-ən(t)th, 'kär-\ **1** region of ancient Greece **2** ancient city; site SW of present city of Corinth — **Co·rin·thi·an** \kə-'rint(h)-thē-ən\ *adj or n*

Corinth, Gulf of inlet of Ionian Sea *cen* Greece N of the Peloponnese

Cork \'kórk\ city S Ireland; *pop* 123,062

Corn·wall \'kórn-ˌwól, -wəl\ *or since 1974* **Cornwall and Isles of Scilly** \'si-lē\ county SW England

Co·ro·na \kə-'rō-nə\ city SW California E of Los Angeles; *pop* 124,966

Cor·pus Chris·ti \ˌkȯr-pəs-'kris-tē\ city & port S Texas; *pop* 277,454

Cor·reg·i·dor \kə-'re-gə-ˌdȯr\ island Philippines at entrance to Manila Bay

Cor·si·ca \'kȯr-si-kə\ island France in the Mediterranean N of Sardinia; *pop* 260,149 — **Cor·si·can** \'kȯr-si-kən\ *adj or n*

Cos·ta Me·sa \'mā-sə\ city SW California; *pop* 108,724

Costa Ri·ca \'rē-kə\ country Central America between Nicaragua & Panama; ✳, San José; *pop* 4,075,863 — **Cos·ta Ri·can** \-kən\ *adj or n*

Côte d'Ivoire — see IVORY COAST

Cots·wold \'kät-ˌswōld, -swəld\ hills SW *cen* England

Cov·en·try \'kə-vən-trē\ city *cen* England; *pop* 292,500

Craig·av·on \krā-'ga-vən\ district *cen* Northern Ireland; *pop* 74,494

Cra·ter \'krā-tər\ lake 1932 ft. (589 m.) deep SW Oregon in Cascade Range

Crete \'krēt\ island Greece in E Mediterranean; *pop* 536,980 — **Cre·tan** \'krē-t°n\ *adj or n*

Cri·mea \krī-'mē-ə, krə-\ peninsula SE Europe in S Ukraine, extending into Black Sea — **Cri·me·an** \krī-'mē-ən, krə-\ *adj*

Cro·atia \krō-'ā-sh(ē-)ə\ country SE Europe; ✳, Zagreb; *pop* 4,437,460 — **Croat** \'krō-ˌat\ *n*

Croy·don \'krȯi-d°n\ borough of S Greater London, England; *pop* 299,600

Cu·ba \'kyü-bə, 'kü-vä\ island in the West Indies; country; ✳, Havana; *pop* 10,892,000 — **Cu·ban** \'kyü-bən\ *adj or n*

Cum·ber·land \'kəm-bər-lənd\ river 687 mi. (1106 km.) long S Kentucky & N Tennessee

Cumberland Gap pass through Cumberland Plateau NE Tennessee

Cumberland Plateau mountain region E U.S.; part of S Appalachian Mountains extending from S West Virginia to NE Alabama

Cum·bria \'kəm-brē-ə\ county NW England; *pop* 486,900

Cum·bri·an \'kəm-brē-ən\ mountains NW England chiefly in Cumbria county

Cu·par \'kü-pər\ town E Scotland; *pop* 6642

Cu·ri·ti·ba \ˌkur-ə-'tē-bə\ city S Brazil SW of São Paulo; *pop* 1,587,315

Cush \'kəsh, 'kush\ ancient country NE Africa in upper Nile valley S of Egypt — **Cush·ite** \'kə-ˌshīt, 'kü-\ *n* — **Cush·it·ic** \kə-'shi-tik, kü-\ *adj*

Cuz·co \'küs-(ˌ)kō\ city S *cen* Peru; *pop* 316,804

Cymru — see WALES

Cy·prus \'sī-prəs\ island E Mediterranean S of Turkey; country; ✳, Nicosia; *pop* 793,100 — **Cyp·ri·ot** \'si-prē-ət, -ˌät\ *or* **Cyp·ri·ote** \-ˌōt, -ət\ *adj or n*

Cy·re·na·ica \ˌsir-ə-'nā-ə-kə, ˌsī-rə-\ ancient region N Africa on coast W of Egypt — **Cy·re·na·i·can** \-'nā-ə-kən\ *adj or n*

Czecho·slo·va·kia \ˌche-kə-slō-'vä-kē-ə, -slə-, -'va-\ former country *cen* Europe divided into the independent states of the Czech Republic & Slovakia — **Czecho·slo·vak** \'slō-ˌväk, -ˌvak\ *adj or n* — **Czecho·slo·va·ki·an** \-slō-'vä-kē-ən, -slə-, -'va-\ *adj or n*

Czech Republic country *cen* Europe; ✳, Prague; *pop* 10,332,000

Daegu — see TAEGU

Daejeon — see TAEJON

Dahomey — see BENIN

Dairen — see DALIAN

Da·kar \'da-ˌkär, dä-'kär\ city, ✳ of Senegal; *pop* 1,729,823

Da·ko·ta \də-'kō-tə\ **1** *or* **James** river 710 mi. (1143 km.) long North Dakota & South Dakota flowing S into the Missouri **2** territory 1861–89 NW U.S. divided 1889 into states of North Dakota & South Dakota (the **Dakotas** \-təz\ )

Da·lian \'dä-'lyen\ *or* **Ta–lien** \'dä-'lyen\ *or* **Lü·da** *or* **Lü–ta** \'lü-'dä\ *or* **Dai·ren** \'dī-'ren\ city NE China; *pop* 1,723,302

Dal·las \'da-ləs, -lis\ city NE Texas; *pop* 1,188,580

Dal·ma·tia \dal-'mā-sh(ē-)ə\ region W Balkan Peninsula on the Adriatic — **Dal·ma·tian** \-shən\ *adj or n*

Da·ly City \'dā-lē\ city W California S of San Francisco; *pop* 103,621

Da·mas·cus \də-'mas-kəs\ city, ✳ of Syria; *pop* 1,451,000

Dan·ube \'dan-(ˌ)yüb\ river 1771 mi. (2850 km.) long S Europe flowing from SW Germany into Black Sea — **Da·nu·bi·an** \də-'nü-bē-əs, da-, -'nyü-\ *adj*

Dar·da·nelles \ˌdär-də-'nelz\ *or* **Hel·les·pont** \'he-lə-ˌspänt\ strait NW Turkey connecting Sea of Marmara & the Aegean

Dar es Sa·laam \ˌdär-ˌe(s)-sə-'läm\ city, ✳ of Tanzania; *pop* 1,360,850

Dar·ling \'där-liŋ\ river about 1700 mi. (2735 km.) long SE Australia in Queensland & New South Wales flowing SW into the Murray

Dar·win \'där-wən\ city Australia, ✳ of Northern Territory; *pop* 70,071

Da·vao \'dä-ˌvaù, dä-'vaù\ city S Philippines in E Mindanao on Davao Gulf; *pop* 850,000

Dav·en·port \'da-vən-ˌpȯrt\ city E Iowa; *pop* 98,359

Da·vis \'dä-vəs\ strait between SW Greenland & E Baffin Island connecting Baffin Bay & the Atlantic

Day·ton \'dā-t°n\ city SW Ohio; *pop* 166,169

Dead Sea salt lake between Israel & Jordan; 1312 ft. (400 m.) below sea level

Death Valley dry valley E California & S Nevada containing lowest point in U.S. (282 ft. or 86 m. below sea level)

Dec·can \'de-kən, -ˌkan\ plateau region S India

Del·a·ware \'de-lə-ˌwer, -wər\ **1** river 296 mi. (476 km.) long E U.S. flowing S from S New York into Delaware Bay **2** state E U.S.; ✳, Dover; *pop* 783,600 — **Del·a·war·ean** *or* **Del·a·war·ian** \ˌde-lə-'wer-ē-ən\ *adj or n*

Delaware Bay inlet of the Atlantic between SW New Jersey & E Delaware

Del·hi \'de-lē\ city N India; *pop* 9,817,439 — see NEW DELHI

De·los \'dē-ˌläs\ island Greece — **De·lian** \'dē-lē-ən, 'dēl-yən\ *adj or n*

Del·phi \'del-ˌfī\ ancient town *cen* Greece on S slope of Mt. Parnassus

Democratic Republic of the Congo — see CONGO 2

Denali — see MCKINLEY, MOUNT

Den·mark \'den-ˌmärk\ country N Europe occupying most of Jutland & neighboring islands; ✳, Copenhagen; *pop* 5,383,507

Den·ver \'den-vər\ city, ✳ of Colorado; *pop* 554,636

Der·by \'där-bē\ city N *cen* England; *pop* 214,000

Der·by·shire \'där-bē-ˌshir, -shər\ *or* **Derby** county N *cen* England

Der·ry \'der-ē\ *or* **Lon·don·der·ry** \ˌlən-dən-'der-ē\ city & port NW Northern Ireland; *pop* 62,697

Des Moines \di-'mȯin\ city, ✳ of Iowa; *pop* 198,682

De·troit \di-'trȯit\ **1** river 31 mi. (50 km.) long between SE Michigan & Ontario connecting Lake Saint Clair & Lake Erie **2** city SE Michigan; *pop* 951,270

Dev·on \'de-vən\ *or* **De·von·shire** \'de-vən-ˌshir, -shər\ county SW England

Dha·ka \'dä-kə\ city, ✳ of Bangladesh; *pop* 3,637,892

Die·go Gar·cia \dē-ˌā-gō-ˌgär-'sē-ə\ island in Indian Ocean; chief island of Chagos Archipelago

Dili *or* **Dilli** \'di-lē\ city & port N Timor, ✳ of East Timor

Di·nar·ic Alps \də-'na-rik\ range of the E Alps in W Slovenia, W Croatia, Bosnia and Herzegovina, & Montenegro

District of Co·lum·bia \kə-'ləm-bē-ə\ federal district E U.S. coextensive with city of Washington; *pop* 572,059

Djakarta — see JAKARTA

Dji·bou·ti \jə-'bü-tē\ **1** country E Africa on Gulf of Aden; *pop* 510,000 **2** city, its ✳; *pop* 300,000

Dni·pro·pe·trovs'k *or* **Dne·pro·pe·trovsk** \də-ˌnye-prə-pə-'trȯfsk\ city E *cen* Ukraine; *pop* 1,189,000

Dodge City \'däj\ city S Kansas on Arkansas River; *pop* 25,176

Do·do·ma \dō-'dō-(ˌ)mä\ city NE *cen* Tanzania designated as future national ✳; *pop* 203,833

Do·ha \'dō-(ˌ)hä\ city & port, ✳ of Qatar on Persian Gulf; *pop* 217,294

Dom·i·ni·ca \ˌdä-mə-'nē-kə\ island West Indies in the Leeward Islands; country; ✳, Roseau; *pop* 71,242

Do·min·i·can Republic \də-'mi-ni-kən\ country West Indies in E Hispaniola; ✳, Santo Domingo; *pop* 8,533,744 — **Dominican** *adj or n*

Don \'dän\ river 1224 mi. (1969 km.) long SW Russia

Do·nets'k \də-'nyetsk\ city E Ukraine; *pop* 1,121,000
Dor·ches·ter \'dòr-chəs-tər, -ˌches-\ town S England; *pop* 14,049
Dor·set \'dòr-sət\ *or* **Dor·set·shire** \-ˌshir, -shər\ county S England on English Channel
Dort·mund \'dòrt-ˌmùnt, -mənd\ city W Germany in the Ruhr; *pop* 601,007
Dou·a·la \dü-'ä-lä\ seaport W Cameroon; *pop* 810,000
Dou·ro \'dòr-(ˌ)ü\ *or Spanish* **Due·ro** \'dwe(ə)r-ō\ river 556 mi. (895 km.) long N Spain & N Portugal flowing into the Atlantic
Do·ver \'dō-vər\ city, ✳ of Delaware; *pop* 32,135
Dover, Strait of channel between SE England & N France; the most easterly section of English Channel
Down \'daùn\ district SE Northern Ireland; *pop* 57,511
Downey \'daù-nē\ city SW California SE of Los Angeles; *pop* 107,323
Down·pat·rick \daùn-'pa-trik\ town E Northern Ireland; *pop* 8245
Dra·kens·berg \'drä-kənz-ˌbərg\ mountain range E Republic of South Africa & Lesotho; highest peak Thabana Ntlenyana 11,425 ft. (3482 m.)
Dres·den \'drez-dən\ city E Germany; *pop* 485,132
Dub·lin \'də-blən\ city, ✳ of Ireland; *pop* 495,781
Dud·ley \'dəd-lē\ town W *cen* England; *pop* 300,000
Duis·burg \'dü-əs-ˌbərg, 'düz-ˌ, 'dyüz-\ city W Germany at junction of Rhine & Ruhr rivers; *pop* 537,441
Du·luth \də-'lüth\ city & port NE Minnesota; *pop* 86,918
Dum·fries \ˌdəm-'frēs, -'frēz\ burgh S Scotland; *pop* 32,084
Dumfries and Gal·lo·way \'ga-lə-ˌwā\ administrative subdivision of S Scotland
Dun·dee \ˌdən-'dē\ city E Scotland; *pop* 172,860
Dun·gan·non \ˌdən-'ga-nən\ district W Northern Ireland; *pop* 45,322
Dur·ban \'dər-bən\ city and seaport E Republic of South Africa; *pop* 736,852
Dur·ham \'dər-əm, 'də-rəm, 'dùr-əm\ city N *cen* North Carolina; *pop* 187,035
Du·shan·be \dü-'sham-bə, dyü-, -'shäm-, 'dyü-ˌ; ˌdyü-shäm-'bä\ city, ✳ of Tajikistan; *pop* 595,000
Düs·sel·dorf \'dü-səl-ˌdòrf, 'dyü-, 'dùe-\ city W Germany on the Rhine; *pop* 577,561
Ea·ling \'ē-liŋ\ borough of W Greater London, England; *pop* 263,300
East An·glia \'aŋ-glē-ə\ region E England; *pop* 1,366,300
East China Sea — see CHINA
Eas·ter \'ē-stər\ island Chile SE Pacific about 2000 mi. (3200 km.) W of Chilean coast
Eastern Cape province SE Republic of South Africa; *pop* 6,504,000
Eastern Ghats \'gäts, 'gòts, 'gəts\ chain of low mountains SE India along coast
Eastern Hemisphere the half of the earth E of the Atlantic Ocean including Europe, Asia, Australia, and Africa
Eastern Roman Empire the Byzantine Empire from 395 to 474
Eastern Samoa — see AMERICAN SAMOA
East Germany — see GERMANY
East Indies the Malay Archipelago — **East Indian** *adj or n*
East London city S Republic of South Africa; *pop* 119,727
East Pakistan the former E division of Pakistan consisting of E portion of Bengal; now Bangladesh
East River strait SE New York connecting upper New York Bay & Long Island Sound and separating Manhattan & Long Island
East Sea — see JAPAN, SEA OF
East Sus·sex \'sə-siks\ county SE England; *pop* 670,600
East Timor country SE Asia on E Timor; ✳, Dili; *pop* 747,750
Ebro \'ā-(ˌ)brō\ river 565 mi. (909 km.) long NE Spain flowing into the Mediterranean
Ec·ua·dor \'e-kwə-ˌdòr, ˌe-kwä-'thòr\ country W South America; ✳, Quito; *pop* 12,156,608 — **Ec·ua·dor·an** \ˌe-kwə-'dòr-ən\ *or* **Ec·ua·dor·ean** *or* **Ec·ua·dor·ian** \-ē-ən\ *adj or n*
Ed·in·burgh \'e-dᵊn-ˌbər-ə\ city, ✳ of Scotland; *pop* 434,520

Ed·mon·ton \'ed-mən-tən\ city, ✳ of Alberta, Canada; *pop* 666,104
Edom \'ē-dəm\ ancient country SW Asia S of Judaea & Dead Sea — **Edom·ite** \'ēd-ə-ˌmīt\ *n*
Egypt \'ē-jipt\ country NE Africa & Sinai Peninsula of SW Asia bordering on Mediterranean & Red seas; ✳, Cairo; *pop* 67,313,000
Eire — see IRELAND
Elam \'ē-ləm\ ancient country SW Asia at head of Persian Gulf E of Babylonia — **Elam·ite** \'ē-lə-ˌmīt\ *n*
Elbe \'el-bə, 'elb\ river 720 mi. (1159 km.) long N Czech Republic & NE Germany flowing NW into North Sea
El·bert, Mount \'el-bərt\ mountain 14,433 ft. (4399 m.) W *cen* Colorado; highest in Colorado & the Rocky Mountains
El·brus, Mount \el-'brüz, -'brüs\ mountain 18,510 ft. (5642 m.) Russia; highest in the Caucasus & in Europe
El·burz \el-'bùrz\ mountains N Iran
Eliz·a·beth \i-'li-zə-bəth\ city NE New Jersey; *pop* 120,568
Elles·mere \'elz-ˌmir\ island N Canada in Nunavut
Ellice — see TUVALU
El·lis Island \'e-ləs\ island SE New York S of Manhattan; served as immigration station 1892–1954
El Mon·te \el-'män-tē\ city SW California E of Los Angeles; *pop* 115,965
El Paso \el-'pa-(ˌ)sō\ city W Texas on Rio Grande; *pop* 563,662
El Sal·va·dor \el-'sal-və-ˌdòr, -ˌsal-və-'; ˌel-ˌsäl-vä-'thòr\ country Central America bordering on the Pacific; ✳, San Salvador; *pop* 5,517,000
Ely, Isle of \'ē-lē\ area of high ground amid marshes in East Anglia, England
En·field \'en-ˌfēld\ borough of N Greater London, England; *pop* 248,900
En·gland \'iŋ-glənd, 'iŋ-lənd\ country S Great Britain; a division of United Kingdom; ✳, London; *pop* 49,138,831
English Channel arm of the Atlantic between S England & N France
En·nis·kil·len \ˌe-nə-'ski-lən\ town SW Northern Ireland in Fermanagh district
Ephra·im \'ē-frē-əm\ **1** hilly region N Jordan E of Jordan River **2** — see ISRAEL — **Ephra·im·ite** \'ē-frē-ə-ˌmīt\ *n*
Equatorial Guinea *formerly* **Spanish Guinea** country W Africa including Mbini & Bioko; ✳, Malabo; *pop* 376,000
Erie \'ir-ē\ **1** city & port NW Pennsylvania; *pop* 103,717 **2** canal New York between Hudson River at Albany & Lake Erie at Buffalo; now superseded by New York State Barge Canal
Erie, Lake lake E *cen* North America in U.S. & Canada; one of the Great Lakes
Er·in \'er-ən\ poetic name of Ireland
Er·i·trea \ˌer-ə-'trē-ə, -'trā-\ country NE Africa; ✳, Asmara; *pop* 3,317,611 — **Er·i·tre·an** \-ən\ *adj or n*
Es·con·di·do \ˌes-kən-'dē-(ˌ)dō\ city SW California N of San Diego; *pop* 133,559
Es·fa·han \ˌes-fə-'hän, -'han\ *or* **Is·fa·han** \ˌis-\ city W *cen* Iran; *pop* 986,753
Española — see HISPANIOLA
Es·sen \'e-sᵊn\ city W Germany in the Ruhr; *pop* 626,989
Es·sex \'e-siks\ county SE England on North Sea
Es·to·nia \e-'stō-nē-ə, -nyə\ country E Europe on Baltic Sea; ✳, Tallinn; *pop* 1,361,242 — **Es·to·nian** \e-'stō-nē-ən, -nyən\ *adj or n*
Ethi·o·pia \ˌē-thē-'ō-pē-ə\ *formerly* **Ab·ys·sin·ia** \ˌa-bə-'si-nē-ə, -nyə\ country E Africa; ✳, Addis Ababa; *pop* 67,220,000 — **Ethi·o·pi·an** \-pē-ən\ *adj or n*
Et·na, Mount \'et-nə\ volcano 10,902 ft. (3323 m.) Italy in NE Sicily
Eto·bi·coke \e-'tō-bi-ˌkō\ former city Canada in SE Ontario; now part of Toronto
Etru·ria \i-'trùr-ē-ə\ ancient country *cen* peninsula of Italy
Eu·gene \yü-'jēn\ city W Oregon; *pop* 137,893
Eu·phra·tes \yù-'frā-(ˌ)tēz\ river 1700 mi. (2736 km.) long SW Asia flowing from E Turkey & uniting with the Tigris to form the Shatt al Arab
Eur·asia \yu-'rā-zhə, -shə\ landmass consisting of Europe & Asia — **Eur·asian** \-zhən, -shən\ *adj or n*
Eu·rope \'yùr-əp\ continent of the Eastern Hemisphere between Asia & the Atlantic; *pop* 498,000,000

European Union economic, scientific, & political organization consisting of Belgium, France, Italy, Luxembourg, Netherlands, Germany, Denmark, Greece, Ireland, United Kingdom, Spain, Portugal, Austria, Finland, & Sweden

Ev·ans·ville \'ev-ənz-ˌvil\ city SW Indiana; *pop* 121,582

Ev·er·est, Mount \'ev-rəst, 'e-və-\ mountain 29,035 ft. (8850 m.) S Asia in the Himalayas on border between Nepal & Tibet; highest in the world

Ev·er·glades \'e-vər-ˌglādz\ swamp region S Florida now partly drained

Ex·e·ter \'ek-sə-tər\ city SW England; *pop* 101,100

Faer·oe *or* **Far·oe** \'fer-(ˌ)ō\ islands NE Atlantic NW of the Shetlands belonging to Denmark; *pop* 47,653 — **Faeroese** \ˌfar-ə-'wēz, ˌfer-, -'wēs\ *adj or n*

Fair·banks \'fer-ˌbaŋks\ city E *cen* Alaska; *pop* 30,224

Fair·field \'fer-ˌfēld\ municipality SE Australia in E New South Wales; *pop* 175,099

Fai·sa·la·bad \ˌfī-ˌsä-lə-'bäd, -ˌsa-lə-'bad\ *formerly* **Ly·all·pur** \lē-ˌäl-'pu̇r\ city NE Pakistan W of Lahore; *pop* 2,008,861

Falk·land Islands \'fȯ-klənd, 'fȯl-\ *or Spanish* **Is·las Mal·vi·nas** \ˌēs-läs-mäl-'vē-näs\ island group SW Atlantic E of S end of Argentina; a British colony; ✱, Stanley; *pop* 2100

Far East the countries of E Asia & the Malay Archipelago — usually thought to consist of the Asian countries bordering on the Pacific but sometimes including also India, Sri Lanka, Bangladesh, Tibet, & Myanmar — **Far Eastern** *adj*

Far·go \'fär-(ˌ)gō\ city E North Dakota; largest in state; *pop* 90,599

Faroe — see FAEROE

Fay·ette·ville \'fā-ət-ˌvil, -vəl\ city SE *cen* North Carolina; *pop* 121,015

Fear, Cape \'fir\ cape SE North Carolina at mouth of Cape Fear River

Fer·man·agh \fər-'ma-nə\ district SW Northern Ireland; *pop* 54,062

Fernando Póo — see BIOKO

Fez \'fez\ city N *cen* Morocco; *pop* 774,574

Fife \'fīf\ administrative subdivision of E Scotland

Fi·ji \'fē-(ˌ)jē\ islands SW Pacific; country; ✱, Suva; *pop* 775,077 — **Fi·ji·an** \'fē-(ˌ)jē-ən, fi-\ *adj or n*

Fin·land \'fin-lənd\ country NE Europe; ✱, Helsinki; *pop* 5,058,000 — **Fin·land·er** *n*

Flan·ders \'flan-dərz\ **1** region W Belgium & N France on North Sea **2** semiautonomous region W Belgium; *pop* 5,972,781

Flat·tery, Cape \'fla-tə-rē\ cape NW Washington at entrance to Strait of Juan de Fuca

Flint \'flint\ city SE Michigan; *pop* 124,943

Flor·ence \'flȯr-ən(t)s, 'flär-\ *or Italian* **Fi·ren·ze** \fē-'rent-sä\ city *cen* Italy; *pop* 374,501 — **Flor·en·tine** \'flȯr-ən-ˌtēn, 'flär-, -ˌtīn\ *adj or n*

Flor·i·da \'flȯr-ə-də, 'flär-\ state SE U.S.; ✱, Tallahassee; *pop* 15,982,378 — **Flo·rid·i·an** \flə-'ri-dē-ən\ *or* **Flor·i·dan** \'flȯr-ə-dən, 'flär-\ *adj or n*

Florida, Straits of channel between Florida Keys on NW & Cuba & Bahamas on S & E connecting Gulf of Mexico & the Atlantic

Florida Keys chain of islands off S tip of Florida

Foochow — see FUZHOU

For·a·ker, Mount \'fȯr-i-kər, 'fär-\ mountain 17,400 ft. (5304 m.) S *cen* Alaska in Alaska Range

For·mo·sa \fȯr-'mō-sə, fər-, -zə\ — see TAIWAN — **For·mo·san** \fȯr-'mō-sᵊn, fər-, -zᵊn\ *adj or n*

For·ta·le·za \ˌfȯr-tə-'lā-zə\ city & port NE Brazil on the Atlantic; *pop* 2,141,402

Fort Col·lins \'kä-lənz\ city N Colorado; *pop* 118,652

Fort–de–France \ˌfȯr-də-'fräⁿs\ city West Indies, ✱ of Martinique on W coast; *pop* 93,598

Forth \'fȯrth\ river 116 mi. (187 km.) long S *cen* Scotland flowing E into North Sea through **Firth of Forth**

Fort Knox \'näks\ military reservation N *cen* Kentucky SSW of Louisville; location of U.S. Gold Bullion Depository

Fort Lau·der·dale \'lȯ-dər-ˌdāl\ city SE Florida; *pop* 152,397

Fort Wayne \'wān\ city NE Indiana; *pop* 205,727

Fort Worth \'wərth\ city NE Texas; *pop* 534,694

Fox \'fäks\ islands SW Alaska in the E Aleutians

Foxe Basin \'fäks\ inlet of the Atlantic N Canada in E Nunavut W of Baffin Island

France \'fran(t)s, 'fräⁿs\ country W Europe between the English Channel & the Mediterranean; ✱, Paris; *pop* 58,520,688

Frank·fort \'fraŋk-fərt\ city, ✱ of Kentucky; *pop* 27,741

Frank·furt \'fraŋk-fərt, 'fräŋk-ˌfu̇rt\ *or in full* **Frankfurt am Main** \(ˌ)äm-'mīn\ city W Germany on Main River; *pop* 654,679

Frank·lin \'fraŋ-klən\ former district N Canada in Northwest Territories including Arctic Archipelago & Boothia & Melville peninsulas

Fra·ser \'frā-zər, -zhər\ river 850 mi. (1368 km.) long Canada in S *cen* British Columbia flowing into the Pacific

Fred·er·ic·ton \'fre-drik-tən, 'fre-də-rik-\ city, ✱ of New Brunswick, Canada; *pop* 47,560

Free State *formerly* **Or·ange Free State** \'ȯr-inj, 'är-, -ˌənj\ province E *cen* Republic of South Africa; *pop* 2,767,000

Free·town \'frē-ˌtau̇n\ city, ✱ of Sierra Leone; *pop* 178,600

Fre·mont \'frē-ˌmänt\ city W California; *pop* 203,413

French Guiana country N South America on the Atlantic; an overseas division of France; ✱, Cayenne; *pop* 128,000

French INDOCHINA — see INDOCHINA

Fres·no \'frez-(ˌ)nō\ city S *cen* California SE of San Francisco; *pop* 427,652

Frunze — see BISHKEK

Fu·ji, Mount \'fü-jē\ *or* **Fu·ji·ya·ma** \ˌfü-jē-'yä-mä\ mountain 12,388 ft. (3776 m.) Japan in S *cen* Honshu; highest in Japan

Fu·ku·o·ka \ˌfü-kü-'ō-kä\ city Japan in N Kyushu; *pop* 1,341,470

Ful·ler·ton \'fu̇-lər-tən\ city SW California; *pop* 126,003

Fu·na·fu·ti \ˌfü-nä-'fü-tē\ city, ✱ of Tuvalu; *pop* 1328

Fun·dy, Bay of \'fən-dē\ inlet of the Atlantic SE Canada between New Brunswick & Nova Scotia

Fu·shun \'fü-'shu̇n\ city NE China E of Shenyang; *pop* 1,202,388

Fu·zhou \'fü-'jō\ *or* **Foo·chow** \'fü-'jō, -'chau̇\ city & port SE China; *pop* 874,809

Ga·bon \gä-'bōⁿ\ country W Africa on the Equator; ✱, Libreville; *pop* 1,014,976 — **Gab·o·nese** \ˌga-bə-'nēz, -'nēs\ *adj or n*

Ga·bo·rone \ˌgä-bō-'rō-(ˌ)nä, ˌkä-\ city, ✱ of Botswana; *pop* 133,468

Gads·den Purchase \'gadz-dən\ area of land S of Gila River in present Arizona & New Mexico purchased 1853 by the U.S. from Mexico

Ga·la·pa·gos Islands \gə-'lä-pə-gəs, -'la-, -ˌgōs\ island group Ecuador in the Pacific 600 mi. (965 km.) W of South America; *pop* 9785

Ga·la·tia \gə-'lā-sh(ē-)ə\ ancient country *cen* Asia Minor in region around modern Ankara, Turkey — **Ga·la·tian** \-shən\ *adj or n*

Ga·li·cia \gə-'li-sh(ē-)ə\ **1** region E *cen* Europe now divided between Poland & Ukraine **2** region NW Spain on the Atlantic — **Ga·li·cian** \-'li-shən\ *adj or n*

Gal·i·lee \'ga-lə-ˌlē\ hilly region N Israel — **Gal·i·le·an** \ˌga-lə-'lē-ən\ *adj or n*

Galilee, Sea of *or modern* **Lake Ti·be·ri·as** \tī-'bir-ē-əs\ lake N Israel on Syrian border; crossed by Jordan River

Gal·lo·way \'ga-lə-ˌwā\ former administrative district of SW Scotland — see DUMFRIES AND GALLOWAY

Gam·bia \'gam-bē-ə, 'gäm-\ country W Africa; ✱, Banjul; *pop* 687,817 — **Gam·bi·an** \-bē-ən\ *adj or n*

Gan·ges \'gan-ˌjēz\ river 1550 mi. (2494 km.) long N India flowing from the Himalayas SE & E to unite with the Brahmaputra and empty into Bay of Bengal through a vast delta — **Gan·get·ic** \gan-'je-tik\ *adj*

Garden Grove city SW California; *pop* 165,196

Gar·land \'gär-lənd\ city NE Texas NNE of Dallas; *pop* 215,768

Ga·ronne \gə-'rän, gä-'rȯn\ river 355 mi. (571 km.) long SE France flowing NW

Gary \'ger-ē\ city NW Indiana on Lake Michigan; *pop* 102,746

Gas·co·ny \'gas-kə-nē\ region SW France — **Gas·con** \'gas-kən\ *adj or n*

Gas·pé \ga-'spā, 'ga-,\ peninsula SE Quebec E of mouth of the Saint Lawrence — **Gas·pe·sian** \ga-'spē-zhən\ *adj or n*

Gaul \'gol\ *or Latin* **Gal·lia** \'ga-lē-ə\ ancient country W Europe chiefly consisting of region occupied by modern France & Belgium

Gau·teng \'gaù-,teŋ\ province *cen* NE Republic of South Africa; *pop* 6,864,000

Ga·za Strip \'gä-zə, 'ga-\ district NE Sinai Peninsula on the Mediterranean

Ge·ne·va \jə-'nē-və\ city SW Switzerland on Lake Geneva; *pop* 175,998 — **Ge·ne·van** \-vən\ *adj or n* — **Gen·e·vese** \,je-nə-'vēz, -'vēs\ *adj or n*

Geneva, Lake lake on border between SW Switzerland & E France

Gen·oa \'je-nō-ə\ *or Italian* **Ge·no·va** \'je-nō-(,)vä\ city & port NW Italy; *pop* 632,366 — **Gen·o·ese** \,je-nō-'ēz, -'ēs\ *or* **Gen·o·vese** \-nə-'vēz, -'vēs\ *adj or n*

George·town \'jorj-,taùn\ 1 a W section of Washington, District of Columbia 2 city & port, ✳ of Guyana; *pop* 162,000

Geor·gia \'jor-jə\ 1 state SE U.S.; ✳, Atlanta; *pop* 8,186,453 2 *or* **Republic of Georgia** country SE Europe on Black Sea S of Caucasus Mountains; ✳, Tbilisi; *pop* 5,493,000 — **Geor·gian** \'jor-jən\ *adj or n*

Georgia, Strait of channel Canada & U.S. between Vancouver Island & main part of British Columbia NW of Puget Sound

Georgian Bay inlet of Lake Huron in S Ontario

Ger·man·town \'jər-mən-,taùn\ a NW section of Philadelphia, Pennsylvania

Ger·ma·ny \'jər-mə-nē\ country *cen* Europe bordering on North & Baltic seas; ✳, Berlin; divided 1946–90 into two independent states: the **Federal Republic of Germany** (West Germany; ✳, Bonn) & the **German Democratic Republic** (East Germany; ✳, East Berlin); *pop* 82,440,000

Get·tys·burg \'ge-tēz-,bərg\ town S Pennsylvania; *pop* 7490

Gha·na \'gä-nə, 'ga-\ *formerly* **Gold Coast** country W Africa on Gulf of Guinea; ✳, Accra; *pop* 15,636,000 — **Gha·na·ian** \gä-'nā-ən, ga-, -'nī-ən\ *or* **Gha·ni·an** \'gä-nē-ən, 'ga-, -nyən\ *adj or n*

Ghats \'gots\ two mountain chains S India consisting of **Eastern Ghats** & **Western Ghats**

Ghent \'gent\ city NW *cen* Belgium; *pop* 226,220

Gi·bral·tar \jə-'brol-tər\ British colony on S coast of Spain including Rock of Gibraltar; *pop* 29,760

Gibraltar, Rock of cape on S coast of Spain in Gibraltar at E end of Strait of Gibraltar; highest point 1396 ft. (426 m.)

Gibraltar, Strait of passage between Spain & Africa connecting the Atlantic & the Mediterranean

Gi·la \'hē-lə\ river 630 mi. (1014 km.) long SW New Mexico and S Arizona flowing W into the Colorado

Gil·bert \'gil-bərt\ town SW *cen* Arizona; *pop* 109,697

Gilbert and El·ice Islands \'e-lis\ island group W Pacific; divided into Kiribati and Tuvalu

Gil·e·ad \'gi-lē-əd\ mountain region of NE ancient Palestine E of Jordan River; now in NW Jordan — **Gil·e·ad·ite** \-lē-ə-,dīt\ *n*

Gi·za \'gē-zə\ city N Egypt on the Nile SW of Cairo; *pop* 2,096,000

Gla·cier Bay \'glā-shər\ inlet SE Alaska at S end of Saint Elias Range

Glas·gow \'glas-(,)kō, 'glas-(,)gō, 'glaz-(,)gō\ city S *cen* Scotland on the Clyde; *pop* 681,470 — **Glas·we·gian** \gla-'swē-jən, glaz-\ *adj or n*

Glen·dale \'glen-,dāl\ 1 city *cen* Arizona NW of Phoenix; *pop* 218,812 2 city S California NE of Los Angeles; *pop* 194,973

Glouces·ter \'gläs-tər, 'glos\ town SW *cen* England; *pop* 91,800

Glouces·ter·shire \'gläs-tər-,shir, -shər, 'glos-\ *or* **Gloucester** county SW *cen* England

Goa \'gō-ə\ district W India on Malabar coast

Goat Island island W New York in Niagara River — see NIAGARA FALLS

Go·bi \'gō-(,)bē\ desert E *cen* Asia in Mongolia & N China

Godt·hab — see NUUK

Godwin Austen — see K2

Go·lan Heights \'gō-,län, -lən\ hilly region NE of Sea of Galilee

Gol·con·da \gäl-'kän-də\ ruined city *cen* India W of Hyderabad

Gold Coast 1 — see GHANA 2 coast region W Africa on N shore of Gulf of Guinea E of Ivory Coast

Golden Gate strait W California connecting San Francisco Bay with Pacific Ocean

Good Hope, Cape of \,gùd-'hōp\ cape S Republic of South Africa on SW coast of Western Cape province

Gorki — see NIZHNIY NOVGOROD

Gö·te·borg \,yœ-tə-'bor-ē\ city & port SW Sweden; *pop* 474,921

Gram·pi·an \'gram-pē-ən\ hills N *cen* Scotland

Grand Banks shallow area in the W North Atlantic SE of Newfoundland

Grand Canyon gorge of Colorado River NW Arizona

Grand Canyon of the Snake HELLS CANYON

Grande, Rio — see RIO GRANDE

Grand Prairie city NE *cen* Texas W of Dallas; *pop* 127,427

Grand Rapids city SW Michigan; *pop* 197,800

Graz \'gräts\ city S Austria; *pop* 226,244

Great Australian Bight wide bay on S coast of Australia

Great Barrier Reef coral reef Australia off NE coast of Queensland

Great Basin region W U.S. between Sierra Nevada & Wasatch Range including most of Nevada & parts of California, Idaho, Utah, Wyoming, & Oregon; has no drainage to ocean

Great Bear lake Canada in Northwest Territories draining through Great Bear River into Mackenzie River

Great Brit·ain \'bri-t°n\ 1 island W Europe NW of France consisting of England, Scotland, & Wales; *pop* 53,917,000 2 UNITED KINGDOM

Great Dividing Range mountain system E Australia & Tasmania extending S from Cape York Peninsula — see KOSCIUSKO, MOUNT

Greater Antilles group of islands of the West Indies including Cuba, Hispaniola, Jamaica, & Puerto Rico — see LESSER ANTILLES

Greater London metropolitan county SE England consisting of City of London & 32 surrounding boroughs

Greater Manchester metropolitan county NW England including city of Manchester

Great Lakes chain of five lakes (Superior, Michigan, Huron, Erie, & Ontario) *cen* North America in U.S. & Canada

Great Plains elevated plains region W *cen* U.S. & W Canada E of the Rockies; extending from W Texas to NE British Columbia & NW Alberta

Great Rift Valley basin SW Asia & E Africa extending with several breaks from valley of the Jordan S to *cen* Mozambique

Great Salt Lake lake N Utah having salty waters & no outlet

Great Slave Lake lake NW Canada in S Northwest Territories drained by Mackenzie River

Great Smoky mountains between W North Caroiina & E Tennessee; highest Clingmans Dome 6643 ft. (2025 m.)

Greece \'grēs\ country S Europe at S end of Balkan Peninsula; ✳, Athens; *pop* 10,964,020

Green \'grēn\ 1 mountains E North America in the Appalachians extending from S Quebec S through Vermont into W Massachusetts 2 river 730 mi. (1175 km.) long W U.S. flowing from W Wyoming S into the Colorado in SE Utah

Green Bay 1 inlet of NW Lake Michigan 120 mi. (193 km.) long in NW Michigan & NE Wisconsin 2 city NE Wisconsin on Green Bay; *pop* 102,313

Green·land \'grēn-lənd, -,land\ island in the North Atlantic off NE North America belonging to Denmark; ✳, Nuuk; *pop* 55,171

Greens·boro \'grēnz-,bər-ō\ city N *cen* North Carolina; *pop* 223,891

Green·wich \'gre-nich, 'grēn-,wich, 'grin-,wich\ borough of SE Greater London, England; *pop* 200,800

Green·wich Village \'gre-nich\ section of New York City in Manhattan on lower W side

Gre·na·da \grə-'nā-də\ island West Indies in S Windward

Islands; independent country; ✲, Saint George's; *pop* 102,632

Gren·a·dines, the \\,gre-nə-'dēnz, 'gre-nə-,\\ islands West Indies in *cen* Windward Islands; N islands part of Saint Vincent and the Grenadines; S islands dependency of Grenada

Groz·ny \\'gróz-nē, 'gräz-\\ city S Russia in Europe; ✲ of Chechnya; *pop* 388,000

Gua·da·la·ja·ra \\,gwä-də-lə-'här-ə, ,gwä-<u>th</u>ä-lä-'hä-rä\\ city W *cen* Mexico; *pop* 2,987,194

Gua·dal·ca·nal \\,gwä-dᵊl-kə-'nal, ,gwä-də-kə-\\ island W Pacific in the SE Solomons; *pop* 23,922

Gua·dal·qui·vir \\,gwä-dᵊl-ki-'vir, -'kwi-vər\\ river 408 mi. (656 km.) long S Spain flowing into the Atlantic

Gua·de·loupe \\,gwä-də-,lüp\\ two islands separated by a narrow channel in West Indies in *cen* Leeward Islands; an overseas division of France; *pop* 418,000

Gua·lla·ti·ri \\,gwä-yə-'tir-ē, ,gwī-ə-\\ volcano 19,882 ft. (6060 m.) high N Chile

Guam \\'gwäm\\ island W Pacific in S Marianas belonging to U.S.; ✲, Agana; *pop* 154,805 — **Gua·ma·ni·an** \\gwä-'mä-nē-ən\\ *adj or n*

Gua·na·ba·ra Bay \\,gwä-nä-'bär-ə\\ inlet of the Atlantic SE Brazil on which city of Rio de Janeiro is located

Guang·dong \\'gwäŋ-'dùŋ\\ *or* **Kwang·tung** \\'gwäŋ-'dùŋ, 'kwäŋ-, -'tùŋ\\ province SE China bordering on South China Sea & Gulf of Tonkin; ✲, Guangzhou; *pop* 62,829,236

Guang·zhou \\'gwäŋ-'jō\\ *or* **Can·ton** \\'kan-,tän, kan-'\\ city & port SE China; *pop* 2,914,281

Guan·tá·na·mo Bay \\gwän-'tä-nä-,mō\\ inlet of the Caribbean in SE Cuba; site of U.S. naval station

Gua·te·ma·la \\,gwä-tə-'mä-lə, -tä-'mä-lä\\ **1** country Central America; *pop* 9,713,000 **2** *or* **Guatemala City** city, its ✲; *pop* 1,132,730 — **Gua·te·ma·lan** \\-'mä-lən\\ *adj or n*

Gua·ya·quil \\,gwī-ə-'kēl, -'kil\\ city & port W Ecuador; *pop* 1,508,444

Guay·na·bo \\gwī-'nä-(,)bō, -(,)vō\\ city NE *cen* Puerto Rico; *pop* 100,053

Guern·sey \\'gərn-zē\\ — see CHANNEL

Gui·a·na \\gē-'a-nə, -'ä-nə; gī-'a-nə\\ region N South America on the Atlantic; includes Guyana, French Guiana, Suriname, & nearby parts of Brazil & Venezuela — **Gui·a·nan** \\-nən\\ *adj or n*

Guin·ea \\'gi-nē\\ **1** region W Africa on the Atlantic extending along coast from Gambia to Angola **2** country W Africa N of Sierra Leone & Liberia; ✲, Conakry; *pop* 7,300,000 — **Guin·ean** \\'gi-nē-ən\\ *adj or n*

Guinea, Gulf of arm of the Atlantic W *cen* Africa

Guin·ea–Bis·sau \\,gi-nē-bi-'saù\\ country W Africa; ✲, Bissau; *pop* 1,036,000

Gui·yang \\'gwä-'yäŋ\\ *or* **Kuei–yang** \\'gwā-'yäŋ\\ city S China; *pop* 1,018,619

Gulf States states of U.S. bordering on Gulf of Mexico: Florida, Alabama, Mississippi, Louisiana, and Texas

Gulf Stream warm current of the Atlantic Ocean flowing from Gulf of Mexico NE along coast of U.S. to Nantucket Island and from there eastward

Guy·ana \\gī-'an-ə\\ *formerly* **British Guiana** country N South America on the Atlantic; ✲, Georgetown; *pop* 755,000 — **Guy·a·nese** \\,gī-ə-'nēz, -'nēs\\ *adj or n*

Gwangju — see KWANGJU

Gwent \\'gwent\\ former county SE Wales

Gwyn·edd \\'gwi-ne<u>th</u>\\ former county NW Wales

Hack·ney \\'hak-nē\\ borough of N Greater London, England; *pop* 164,200

Hague, The \\<u>th</u>ə-'hāg\\ city SW Netherlands; a national ✲; *pop* 457,726

Hai·kou \\'hī-'kō\\ city & port SE China; *pop* 280,153

Hai·phong \\'hī-'fòŋ, -'fäŋ\\ city & port N Vietnam; *pop* 1,726,900

Hai·ti \\'hā-tē\\ country West Indies in W Hispaniola; ✲, Port-au-Prince; *pop* 6,902,000 — **Hai·tian** \\'hā-shən\\ *adj or n*

Ha·le·a·ka·la Crater \\,hä-lā-,ä-kä-'lä\\ crater over 2500 ft. (762 m.) deep Hawaii in E Maui

Hal·i·fax \\'ha-lə-,faks\\ municipality & port, ✲ of Nova Scotia, Canada; *pop* 359,111

Ham·burg \\'ham-,bərg; 'häm-,bùrg, -,bùrk\\ city N Ger-

many on the Elbe; *pop* 1,668,800 — **Ham·burg·er** \\-,bər-gər, -,bùr-\\ *n*

Ham·hung \\'häm-,hùŋ\\ city E *cen* North Korea; *pop* 701,000

Ham·il·ton \\'ha-məl-tən\\ **1** town, ✲ of Bermuda; *pop* 969 **2** city & port, S Ontario, Canada on Lake Ontario; *pop* 490,268

Ham·mer·smith and Ful·ham \\'ha-mər-,smith-ənd-'fù-ləm\\ borough of SW Greater London, England; *pop* 136,500

Hamp·shire \\'hamp-,shir, -shər\\ county S England on English Channel

Hamp·ton \\'hamp-tən\\ city SE Virginia; *pop* 146,437

Hampton Roads channel SE Virginia through which James River flows into Chesapeake Bay

Hang·zhou \\'häŋ-'jō\\ *or* **Hang–chow** \\'haŋ-'chaù, 'häŋ-'jō\\ *or* **Hang–chou** \\'jō\\ city E China; *pop* 1,099,660

Han·ni·bal \\'ha-nə-bəl\\ city NE Missouri on the Mississippi River; *pop* 17,757

Han·no·ver *or* **Han·o·ver** \\'ha-,nō-vər, -nə-vər, *G* hä-'nō-fər\\ city N *cen* Germany; *pop* 517,746

Ha·noi \\ha-'nòi, hə-, hä-\\ city, ✲ of Vietnam; *pop* 2,931,400

Ha·ra·re \\hə-'rä-(,)rā\\ *formerly* **Salis·bury** \\'sólz-,ber-ē, -b(ə-)rē\\ city, ✲ of Zimbabwe; *pop* 1,184,169

Har·bin \\'här-bən, här-'bin\\ *or* **Ha–erh–pin** \\'hä-'ər-'bin\\ city NE China; *pop* 2,443,398

Har·in·gey \\'ha-riŋ-,gā\\ borough of N Greater London, England; *pop* 187,300

Har·lem \\'här-ləm\\ section of New York City in N Manhattan

Har·ris·burg \\'ha-rəs-,bərg\\ city, ✲ of Pennsylvania; *pop* 48,950

Har·row \\'ha-(,)rō\\ borough of NW Greater London, England; *pop* 194,300

Hart·ford \\'härt-fərd\\ city, ✲ of Connecticut; *pop* 121,578

Hat·ter·as, Cape \\'ha-tə-rəs\\ cape North Carolina on **Hatteras Island**

Ha·va·na \\hə-'va-nə\\ city, ✲ of Cuba; *pop* 2,096,054

Hav·ant \\'ha-vənt\\ town S England; *pop* 117,400

Ha·ver·ing \\'hāv-riŋ, 'ha-və-riŋ\\ borough of NE Greater London, England; *pop* 224,400

Ha·waii \\hə-'wä-yē, -'wä-,ē\\ **1** *or* **Ha·wai·ian Islands** *formerly* **Sand·wich Islands** \\,san-(d)wich-\\ group of islands *cen* Pacific belonging to U.S. **2** island, largest of the group **3** state of U.S., ✲, Honolulu; *pop* 1,211,537

Hay·ward \\'hā-wərd\\ city W California SE of Oakland; *pop* 140,030

Heb·ri·des \\'he-brə-,dēz\\ islands W Scotland in the North Atlantic consisting of **Outer Hebrides** (to W) and **Inner Hebrides** (to E); *pop* 30,660 — **Heb·ri·de·an** \\,he-brə-'dē-ən\\ *adj or n*

Hel·e·na \\'he-lə-nə\\ city, ✲ of Montana; *pop* 25,780

Hellespont — see DARDANELLES

Hells Canyon \\'helz\\ canyon of Snake River on Idaho–Oregon boundary

Hel·sin·ki \\'hel-,siŋ-kē, hel-'\\ city, ✲ of Finland; *pop* 559,718

Hen·der·son \\'hen-dər-sən\\ city S Nevada; *pop* 175,381

Hen·ry, Cape \\'hen-rē\\ cape E Virginia S of entrance to Chesapeake Bay

Her·e·ford and Wor·ces·ter \\'her-ə-fərd-ᵊn-'wùs-tər\\ former county W England bordering on Wales

Hert·ford·shire \\'här-fərd-,shir, 'härt-, -shər\\ *or* **Hertford** county SE England

Her·ze·go·vi·na \\,hert-sə-gō-'vē-nə, ,hərt-, -'gō-və-nə\\ *or Serb* **Her·ce·go·vi·na** \\'kert-sə-gō-vē-nə\\ region S Europe S of Bosnia & NW of Montenegro; part of Bosnia and Herzegovina — **Her·ze·go·vi·nian** \\,hert-sə-gō-'vē-nē-ən, ,hərt-, -nyən\\ *n*

Hi·a·le·ah \\,hī-ə-'lē-ə\\ city SE Florida; *pop* 226,419

Hi·ber·nia \\hī-'bər-nē-ə\\ — see IRELAND — **Hi·ber·ni·an** \\-ən\\ *adj or n*

Hi·ga·shi·ōsa·ka \\hē-,gä-shē-'ō-sä-kä\\ city Japan in S Honshu E of Osaka; *pop* 515,094

High·land \\'hī-lənd\\ administrative subdivision of NW Scotland

High·lands \\'hī-lənd\\ the mountainous N part of Scotland lying N & W of the Lowlands

High Plains the Great Plains esp. from Nebraska southward

Hil·ling·don \'hi-liŋ-dən\ borough of W Greater London, England; *pop* 225,800

Hi·ma·la·yas, the \ˌhi-mə-'lā-əz\ *or* **the Himalaya** mountain system S Asia on border between India & Tibet and in Kashmir, Nepal, & Bhutan — see EVEREST, MOUNT — **Hi·ma·la·yan** \ˌhim-ə-'lā-ən, hə-'mäl-(ə-)yən\ *adj*

Hin·du Kush \ˌhin-(ˌ)dü-'kush, -'kəsh\ mountain range *cen* Asia SW of the Pamirs on border of Kashmir and in Afghanistan

Hin·du·stan \ˌhin-(ˌ)dü-'stan, -də-, -'stän\ **1** a name for N India **2** the subcontinent of India **3** the country of India

Hi·ro·shi·ma \ˌhir-ə-'shē-mə, hə-'rō-shə-mə\ city Japan in SW Honshu on Inland Sea; *pop* 1,126,239

His·pan·io·la \ˌhis-pə-'nyō-lə\ *or Spanish* **Es·pa·ño·la** \ˌes-ˌpä-'nyō-lä\ island West Indies in Greater Antilles; divided between Haiti on W & Dominican Republic on E

Ho·bart \'hō-bərt\ city Australia, ✳ of Tasmania; *pop* 47,106

Ho Chi Minh City \'hō-ˌchē-'min\ *formerly* **Sai·gon** \sī-'gän, 'sī-ˌ\ city S Vietnam; *pop* 5,479,000

Hoh·hot \'hō-'hōt\ *or* **Hu·he·hot** \'hü-(ˌ)hä-'hōt\ city N China, ✳ of Inner Mongolia; *pop* 652,534

Hok·kai·do \hō-'kī-(ˌ)dō\ island N Japan N of Honshu; *pop* 5,683,062

Hol·land \'hä-lənd\ **1** county of Holy Roman Empire bordering on North Sea & consisting of area now forming part of W Netherlands **2** — see NETHERLANDS — **Hol·land·er** \-lən-dər\ *n*

Hol·ly·wood \'hä-lē-ˌwud\ **1** section of Los Angeles, California, NW of downtown district **2** city SE Florida; *pop* 139,357

Holy Roman Empire empire consisting mainly of German & Italian territories & existing from 9th or 10th century to 1806

Hon·du·ras \hän-'dur-əs, -'dyur-; ón-'dü-räs\ country Central America; ✳, Tegucigalpa; *pop* 4,604,800 — **Hon·du·ran** \-ən\ *adj or n*

Hong Kong \'häŋ-ˌkäŋ, -'käŋ\ *or Chinese* **Xiang·gang** \'shyäŋ-ˌgäŋ\ special administrative region China on SE coast including Hong Kong Island & Jiulong Peninsula; chief city Victoria; *pop* 6,843,000

Ho·ni·a·ra \ˌhō-nē-'är-ə\ town, ✳ of Solomon Islands; *pop* 35,288

Ho·no·lu·lu \ˌhä-nə-'lü-(ˌ)lü, ˌhō-nə-\ city, ✳ of Hawaii on Oahu; *pop* 371,657

Hon·shu \'hän-(ˌ)shü, 'hòn-\ island Japan; largest of the four chief islands; *pop* 102,324,961

Hood, Mount \'hud\ mountain 11,235 ft. (3424 m.) NW Oregon in Cascade Range

Hoo·ver Dam \'hü-vər\ *or* **Boul·der Dam** \'bōl-dər\ dam 726 ft. (221 m.) high in Colorado River between Arizona & Nevada — see MEAD, LAKE

Hormuz, Strait of \'(h)òr-ˌməz, (h)òr-'müz\ strait connecting Persian Gulf & Gulf of Oman

Horn, Cape \'hòrn\ cape S Chile on an island in Tierra del Fuego; the most southerly point of South America at 56° S latitude

Horn of Africa the easternmost projection of Africa; variously used to refer to Somalia, SE or all of Ethiopia, & sometimes Djibouti

Horseshoe Falls — see NIAGARA FALLS

Houns·low \'haunz-(ˌ)lō\ borough of SW Greater London, England; *pop* 193,400

Hous·ton \'hyüs-tən, 'yüs-\ city SE Texas; *pop* 1,953,631

How·rah \'hau-rə\ city E India on Hugli River opposite Calcutta; *pop* 1,008,704

Hsi–an — see XI'AN

Huang *or* **Hwang** \'hwäŋ\ *or* **Yellow** river about 3000 mi. (4828 km.) long N China flowing into Bo Hai

Hud·ders·field \'hə-dərz-ˌfēld\ town N England NE of Manchester; *pop* 123,888

Hud·son \'həd-sən\ **1** river 306 mi. (492 km.) long E New York flowing S **2** bay, inlet of the Atlantic in N Canada **3** strait NE Canada connecting Hudson Bay & the Atlantic

Hu·gli *or* **Hoo·ghly** \'hü-glē\ river 120 mi. (193 km.) long E India flowing S into Bay of Bengal

Huhehot — see HOHHOT

Hull \'həl\ *or* **Kings·ton upon Hull** \'kiŋ-stən\ city & port N England; *pop* 242,200

Hun·ga·ry \'həŋ-gə-rē\ country *cen* Europe; ✳, Budapest; *pop* 10,142,000

Hunt·ing·ton Beach \'hən-tiŋ-tən\ city SW California; *pop* 189,594

Hunts·ville \'hənts-ˌvil, -vəl\ city N Alabama; *pop* 158,216

Hu·ron, Lake \'hyur-ˌän, 'yur-\ lake E *cen* North America in U.S. & Canada; one of the Great Lakes

Hy·der·abad \'hī-d(ə-)rə-ˌbad, -ˌbäd\ **1** city S *cen* India; *pop* 3,449,878 **2** city SE Pakistan on the Indus; *pop* 1,166,894

Iba·dan \i-'bä-dªn, -'ba-\ city SW Nigeria; *pop* 1,263,000

Ibe·ri·an \ī-'bir-ē-ə\ peninsula SW Europe occupied by Spain & Portugal

Ice·land \'īs-lənd, 'īs-ˌland\ island SE of Greenland between Arctic & Atlantic oceans; country; ✳, Reykjavik; *pop* 282,849 — **Ice·land·er** \'īs-ˌlan-dər, 'īs-lən-\ *n*

Ida·ho \'ī-də-ˌhō\ state NW U.S.; ✳, Boise; *pop* 1,293,953 — **Ida·ho·an** \ˌī-də-'hō-ən\ *adj or n*

Igua·çú *or* **Igua·zú** \ˌē-gwə-'sü\ river 745 mi. (1199 km.) long S Brazil flowing W

IJs·sel *or* **Ijs·sel** \'ī-səl, 'ā-\ river 70 mi. (113 km.) long E Netherlands flowing out of Rhine N into IJsselmeer

IJs·sel·meer \'ī-səl-ˌmer, 'ā-\ *or* **Lake Ijs·sel** freshwater lake N Netherlands separated from North Sea by a dike; part of former Zuider Zee (inlet of North Sea)

Ilium — see TROY

Il·li·nois \ˌi-lə-'nói\ state N *cen* U.S.; ✳, Springfield; *pop* 12,419,293 — **Il·li·nois·an** \ˌi-lə-'nói-ən\ *adj or n*

Il·lyr·ia \i-'lir-ē-ə\ ancient country S Europe and Balkan Peninsula on the Adriatic — **Il·lyr·i·an** \-ē-ən\ *adj or n*

Im·pe·ri·al Valley \im-'pir-ē-əl\ valley SE corner of California & partly in NE Baja California, Mexico

In·chon \'in-ˌchən\ city South Korea on Yellow Sea; *pop* 2,466,338

In·de·pen·dence \ˌin-də-'pen-dən(t)s\ city W Missouri E of Kansas City; *pop* 113,288

In·dia \'in-dē-ə\ **1** subcontinent S Asia S of the Himalayas between Bay of Bengal & Arabian Sea **2** country consisting of major portion of the subcontinent; ✳, New Delhi; *pop* 896,567,000 **3** *or* **Indian Empire** before 1947 those parts of the subcontinent of India under British rule or protection

In·di·an \'in-dē-ən\ ocean E of Africa, S of Asia, W of Australia, & N of Antarctica

In·di·ana \ˌin-dē-'a-nə\ state E *cen* U.S.; ✳, Indianapolis; *pop* 6,080,485 — **In·di·an·an** \-'a-nən\ *or* **In·di·an·i·an** \-'a-nē-ən\ *adj or n*

In·di·a·nap·o·lis \ˌin-dē-ə-'na-pə-lis\ city, ✳ of Indiana; *pop* 791,926

Indian River lagoon 165 mi. (266 km.) long E Florida between main part of the state & coastal islands

Indian Territory former territory S U.S. in present state of Oklahoma

In·dies \'in-(ˌ)dēz\ **1** EAST INDIES **2** WEST INDIES

In·do·chi·na \ˌin-(ˌ)dō-'chī-nə\ **1** peninsula SE Asia including Myanmar, Malay Peninsula, Thailand, Cambodia, Laos, & Vietnam **2** *or* **French Indochina** former country SE Asia consisting of area now forming Cambodia, Laos, & Vietnam — **In·do–Chi·nese** \-chī-'nēz, -'nēs\ *adj or n*

In·do·ne·sia \ˌin-də-'nē-zhə, -shə\ country SE Asia in Malay Archipelago consisting of Sumatra, Java, S & E Borneo, Sulawesi, W New Guinea, & many smaller islands; ✳, Jakarta; *pop* 187,468,250 — **In·do·ne·sian** \-zhən, -shən\ *adj or n*

In·dore \in-'dór\ city W *cen* India; *pop* 1,597,441

In·dus \'in-dəs\ river 1800 mi. (2897 km.) long S Asia flowing from Tibet NW & SSW through Pakistan into Arabian Sea

In·gle·wood \'iŋ-gəl-ˌwud\ city SW California; *pop* 112,580

In·land Sea \'in-ˌland, -lənd\ inlet of the Pacific in SW Japan between Honshu on N and Shikoku and Kyushu on S

Inner Hebrides — see HEBRIDES

Inner Mon·go·lia \män-'gōl-yə, mäŋ-, -'gō-lē-ə\ region N China; *pop* 21,456,798

Inside Passage protected shipping route between Puget Sound, Washington, & Skagway, Alaska

In·ver·ness \ˌin-vər-'nes\ town NW Scotland; *pop* 63,090

Io·ni·an \ī-'ō-nē-ən\ sea, arm of the Mediterranean between SE Italy & W Greece

Io·wa \'ī-ə-wə\ state N *cen* U.S.; ✳, Des Moines; *pop* 2,926,324 — **Io·wan** \-wən\ *adj or n*

Ips·wich \'ip-(ˌ)swich\ town SE England; *pop* 115,500

Iqa·lu·it \ē-'ka-lü-ət\ town Canada, ✳ of Nunavut on Baffin Island; *pop* 5236

Iran \i-'rän, -'ran\ *formerly* **Per·sia** \'pər-zhə\ country SW Asia; ✳, Tehran; *pop* 59,570,000 — **Irani** \-'rä-nē, -'ra-\ *adj or n* — **Ira·nian** \i-'rä-nē-ən, -'ran-ē-, -'rān-ē-\ *adj or n*

Iraq \i-'räk, -'rak\ country SW Asia in Mesopotamia; ✳, Baghdad; *pop* (est.) 24,683,000 — **Iraqi** \-'räk-ē, -'rak-\ *adj or n*

Ire·land \'ī(-ə)r-lənd\ **1** *or Latin* **Hi·ber·nia** \hī-'bər-nē-ə\ island W Europe in the North Atlantic; one of the British Isles **2** *or* **Eire** \'er-ə\ country occupying major portion of the Ireland (island); ✳, Dublin; *pop* 3,917,203

Irian Jaya — see WEST PAPUA

Irish Sea arm of the North Atlantic between Great Britain & Ireland

Ir·kutsk \ir-'kütsk, ˌər-\ city S Russia near Lake Baikal; *pop* 639,000

Ir·ra·wad·dy \ˌir-ə-'wä-dē\ river 1300 mi. (2092 km.) long Myanmar flowing S into Bay of Bengal

Ir·tysh \ir-'tish, ˌər-\ river over 2600 mi. (4180 km.) long *cen* Asia flowing NW & N from Altay Mountains in China, through Kazakhstan, & into W *cen* Russia

Ir·vine \'ər-ˌvīn\ city SW California; *pop* 143,072

Ir·ving \'ər-viŋ\ city NE Texas NW of Dallas; *pop* 191,615

Isfahan — see ESFAHAN

Is·lam·abad \is-'lä-mə-ˌbäd, iz-, -'la-mə-ˌbad\ city, ✳ of Pakistan; *pop* 529,180

Islas Malvinas — see FALKLAND ISLANDS

Isle of Man — see MAN, ISLE OF

Isle of Wight \'wīt\ island England in English Channel

Isle Roy·ale \ˌī(-ə)l-'rȯi(-ə)l\ island Michigan in Lake Superior

Isles of Scilly 1 — see CORNWALL AND ISLES OF SCILLY **2** — see SCILLY

Is·ling·ton \'iz-liŋ-tən\ borough of N Greater London, England; *pop* 155,200

Ispahan — see ESFAHAN

Is·ra·el \'iz-rē(-ə)l, -(ˌ)rā(-ə)l\ **1** kingdom in ancient Palestine consisting of lands occupied by the Hebrew people **2** *or* **Ephra·im** \'ē-frē-əm\ the N part of the Hebrew kingdom after about 933 B.C. **3** country SW Asia; ✳, Jerusalem; *pop* 4,037,620 — **Is·rae·li** \iz-'rā-lē\ *adj or n*

Is·tan·bul \ˌis-tən-'bül, -ˌtan-, -ˌtän-, -'bül, ˌis-tən-ˌ, *or with* m *for* n\ *formerly* **Con·stan·ti·no·ple** \ˌkän-ˌstan-tə-'nō-pəl\ city NW Turkey on the Bosporus & Sea of Marmara; *pop* 6,620,241

Is·tria \'is-trē-ə\ peninsula in Croatia & Slovenia extending into the N Adriatic — **Is·tri·an** \-trē-ən\ *adj or n*

It·a·ly \'i-tə-lē\ country S Europe including a boot-shaped peninsula & the islands of Sicily & Sardinia; ✳, Rome; *pop* 57,844,017

Itas·ca, Lake \ī-'tas-kə\ lake NW *cen* Minnesota; source of the Mississippi

Ivory Coast *or* **Côte d'Ivoire** \ˌkōt-dē-'vwär\ country W Africa on Gulf of Guinea; official ✳, Yamoussoukro; seat of government, Abidjan; *pop* 13,459,000 — **Ivor·i·an** \(ˌ)ī-'vȯr-ē-ən\ *adj or n* — **Ivory Coast·er** \'kō-stər\ *n*

Iwo Ji·ma \ˌē-(ˌ)wō-'jē-mə\ island Japan in W Pacific SSE of Tokyo

Izhevsk \'ē-ˌzhefsk\ *or 1985–87* **Usti·nov** \'üs-ti-ˌnȯf, -ˌnȯv\ city W Russia; *pop* 651,000

Iz·mir \iz-'mir\ *formerly* **Smyr·na** \'smər-nə\ city W Turkey; *pop* 1,757,414

Jack·son \'jak-sən\ city, ✳ of Mississippi; *pop* 184,256

Jack·son·ville \'jak-sən-ˌvil\ city NE Florida; *pop* 735,617

Jai·pur \'jī-ˌpu̇r\ city NW India; *pop* 2,324,319

Ja·kar·ta *formerly* **Dja·kar·ta** \jə-'kär-tə\ city, ✳ of Indonesia in NW Java; *pop* 6,503,449

Ja·mai·ca \jə-'mā-kə\ island West Indies in Greater Antilles; country; ✳, Kingston; *pop* 2,599,334 — **Ja·mai·can** \-kən\ *adj or n*

James \'jāmz\ **1** — see DAKOTA **2** river 340 mi. (547 km.) long Virginia flowing E into Chesapeake Bay

James Bay the S extension of Hudson Bay between NE Ontario & W Quebec

James·town \'jāmz-ˌtau̇n\ ruined village E Virginia on James River; first permanent English settlement in America (1607)

Jam·shed·pur \'jäm-ˌshed-ˌpu̇r\ city E India; *pop* 570,349

Ja·pan \jə-'pan, ja-\ country E Asia consisting of Honshu, Hokkaido, Kyushu, Shikoku, & other islands in the W Pacific; ✳, Tokyo; *pop* 126,925,843

Japan, Sea of *or* **East Sea** arm of the Pacific between Japan & main part of Asia

Ja·va \'jä-və, 'ja-\ island Indonesia SW of Borneo; chief city, Jakarta; *pop* 107,581,306 — **Ja·va·nese** \ˌja-və-'nēz, ˌjä-, -'nēs\ *n*

Jef·fer·son City \'je-fər-sən\ city, ✳ of Missouri; *pop* 39,636

Jer·sey \'jər-zē\ — see CHANNEL

Jersey City city NE New Jersey on Hudson River; *pop* 240,055

Je·ru·sa·lem \jə-'rü-s(ə-)ləm, -'rü-z(ə-)ləm\ city NW of Dead Sea, ✳ of Israel; *pop* 544,200

Jid·da *or* **Jid·dah** \'ji-də\ *or* **Jed·da** *or* **Jed·dah** \'je-də\ city W Saudi Arabia on Red Sea; *pop* 561,104

Ji·lin \'jē-'lin\ *or* **Ki·rin** \'kē-'rin\ city NE China; *pop* 1,036,858

Ji·nan *or* **Tsi·nan** \'jē-'nän\ city E China; *pop* 1,500,000

Jin·zhou *or* **Chin–chou** *or* **Chin–chow** \'jin-'jō\ city NE China; *pop* 400,000

Jiu·long \'jü-'lȯŋ\ *or* **Kow·loon** \'kau̇-'lün\ **1** peninsula SE China in Hong Kong opposite Hong Kong Island **2** city on Jiulong Peninsula; *pop* 1,975,265

Jo·han·nes·burg \jō-'hä-nəs-ˌbərg, -'ha-\ city NE Republic of South Africa; *pop* 654,232

Jo·li·et \ˌjō-lē-'et\ city NE Illinois; *pop* 106,221

Jor·dan \'jȯr-dᵊn\ **1** river 200 mi. (322 km.) long Israel & Jordan flowing S from Syria into Dead Sea **2** country SW Asia in NW Arabia; ✳, Amman; *pop* 5,182,000 — **Jor·da·ni·an** \jȯr-'dā-nē-ən\ *adj or n*

Juan de Fu·ca, Strait of \ˌwän-də-'fyü-kə, ˌhwän-\ strait 100 mi. (161 km.) long between Vancouver Island, British Columbia, & Olympic Peninsula, Washington

Ju·daea *or* **Ju·dea** \jü-'dē-ə, -'dā-\ region of ancient Palestine forming its S division under Persian, Greek, & Roman rule — **Ju·dean** \-ən\ *adj or n*

Ju·neau \'jü-(ˌ)nō, jü-'\ city, ✳ of Alaska; *pop* 30,711

Ju·ra \'ju̇r-ə\ mountain range extending along boundary between France & Switzerland N of Lake of Geneva

Jut·land \'jət-lənd\ **1** peninsula N Europe extending into North Sea and consisting of main part of Denmark & N portion of Germany **2** the main part of Denmark

Ka·bul \'kä-bəl, -ˌbül; kə-'bül\ city, ✳ of Afghanistan; *pop* (est.) 2,272,000

Ka Lae \kä-'lä-ā\ *or* **South Cape** *or* **South Point** most southerly point of Hawaii & of U.S.

Kal·a·ha·ri \ˌka-lə-'här-ē, ˌkä-\ desert region S Africa N of Orange River in S Botswana & NW Republic of South Africa

Kalgan — see ZHANGJIAKOU

Ka·li·man·tan \ˌka-lə-'man-ˌtan, ˌkä-lē-'män-ˌtän\ **1** BORNEO — its Indonesian name **2** the S & E portion of Borneo belonging to Indonesia

Ka·li·nin·grad \kə-'lē-nən-ˌgrad, -nyən-, -ˌgrät\ *formerly* **Kö·nigs·berg** \'kā-nigz-ˌbərg\ city & port W Russia; *pop* 424,000

Kam·chat·ka \kam-'chat-kə, -'chät-\ peninsula 750 mi. (1207 km.) long E Russia

Kam·pa·la \käm-'pä-lä, kam-\ city, ✳ of Uganda; *pop* 773,463

Kampuchea — see CAMBODIA

Kan·da·har \'kən-də-ˌhär\ city SE Afghanistan; *pop* (est.) 359,700

Ka·no \'kä-(ˌ)nō\ city N *cen* Nigeria; *pop* 594,800

Kan·pur \'kän-ˌpu̇r\ city N India on the Ganges; *pop* 2,532,138

Kan·sas \'kan-zəs\ state W *cen* U.S.; ✳, Topeka; *pop* 2,688,418 — **Kan·san** \'kan-zən\ *adj or n*

Kansas City 1 city NE Kansas bordering on Kansas City, Missouri; *pop* 146,866 **2** city W Missouri; *pop* 441,545

Kao–hsiung \'kau̇-'shyu̇ŋ, 'gau̇-\ city & port SW Taiwan; *pop* 1,405,860

Ka·ra·chi \kə-'rä-chē\ city S Pakistan on Arabian Sea; *pop* 9,339,023

Ka·ra·gan·da \ˌkär-ə-'gän-də\ *or* **Qa·ra·ghan·dy** \-dē\ city *cen* Kazakhstan *pop* 608,600

Kar·a·ko·ram Pass \ˌkär-ə-'kȯr-əm\ mountain pass NE Kashmir in **Karakoram Range** (system connecting the Himalayas with the Pamirs)

Ka·re·lia \kə-'rē-lē-ə, -'rēl-yə\ region NE Europe in Finland & Russia; *pop* 800,000 — **Ka·re·lian** \kə-'rē-lē-ən, -'rēl-yən\ *adj or n*

Ka·roo *or* **Kar·roo** \kə-'rü\ plateau region W Republic of South Africa W of Drakensberg Mountains

Kash·mir \'kash-ˌmir, 'kazh-, kash-', kazh-'\ disputed territory N subcontinent of India; claimed by India & Pakistan — **Kash·miri** \kash-'mi(ə)r-ē, kazh-\ *adj or n*

Ka·thi·a·war \ˌkä-tē-ə-'wär\ peninsula W India N of Gulf of Cambay

Kath·man·du *or* **Kat·man·du** \ˌkat-ˌman-'dü, ˌkät-ˌmän-\ city, ✳ of Nepal; metropolitan area *pop* 671,846

Kat·mai, Mount \'kat-ˌmī\ volcano 6715 ft. (2047 m.) S Alaska on Alaska Peninsula

Kat·te·gat \'ka-ti-ˌgat\ arm of North Sea between Sweden & E coast of Jutland Peninsula of Denmark

Kau·ai \kä-'wä-ē\ island Hawaii NW of Oahu

Kau·nas \'kau̇-nəs, -ˌnäs\ city *cen* Lithuania; *pop* 378,943

Ka·wa·sa·ki \ˌkä-wä-'sä-kē\ city Japan in E Honshu S of Tokyo; *pop* 1,249,905

Ka·zakh·stan *or* **Ka·zak·stan** \ˌkä-(ˌ)zak-'stan\ country NW *cen* Asia; ✳, Astana; *pop* 17,186,000 — **Ka·zakh** *also* **Ka·zak** \kə-'zak, -'zäk\ *n*

Ka·zan \kə-'zan\ city W Russia; *pop* 1,098,000

Kee·wa·tin \kē-'wä-tᵊn, -'wä-\ former district N Canada in E Northwest Territories NW of Hudson Bay; area now part of Nunavut

Ke·me·ro·vo \'kye-mə-rə-və\ city S *cen* Russia; *pop* 521,000

Ke·nai \'kē-ˌnī\ peninsula S Alaska E of Cook Inlet

Kennedy, Cape — see CANAVERAL, CAPE

Ken·sing·ton and Chel·sea \'ken-ziŋ-tən-ənd-'chel-sē, 'ken(t)-siŋ-\ borough of W Greater London, England; *pop* 127,600

Kent \'kent\ county SE England — **Kent·ish** \'ken-tish\ *adj*

Ken·tucky \kən-'tə-kē\ state E *cen* U.S.; ✳, Frankfort; *pop* 4,041,769 — **Ken·tuck·i·an** \-kē-ən\ *adj or n*

Ken·ya \'ke-nyə, 'kē-\ **1** mountain 17,058 ft. (5199 m.) *cen* Kenya **2** country E Africa S of Ethiopia; ✳, Nairobi; *pop* 28,662,239 — **Ken·yan** \-nyən\ *adj or n*

Key West \'west\ city SW Florida on Key West (island); *pop* 25,478

Kha·ba·rovsk \kə-'bär-əfsk, ˌkə-\ city SE Russia; *pop* 615,000

Kham·bhat, Gulf of \'kəm-bət\ *or* **Gulf of Cam·bay** \kam-'bā\ inlet of Arabian Sea in India N of Bombay

Khar·kiv \'kär-kəf, -\ *or* **Khar·kov** \'kär-ˌkȯf, 'kär-, -ˌkȯv, -kəf\ city NE Ukraine; *pop* 1,623,000

Khar·toum \kär-'tüm\ city, ✳ of Sudan; *pop* 1,950,000

Khy·ber \'kī-bər\ pass 33 mi. (53 km.) long on border between Afghanistan & Pakistan

Ki·bo \'kē-(ˌ)bō\ mountain peak 19,340 ft. (5895 m.) NE Tanzania; highest peak of Kilimanjaro & highest point in Africa

Kiel \'kēl\ — SEE NORD-OSTSEE

Ki·ev \'kē-ˌef, -ˌev, -if\ *or Ukrainian* **Kyiv** \'kyē-ü\ city, ✳ of Ukraine; *pop* 2,587,000

Ki·ga·li \kē-'gä-lē\ city, ✳ of Rwanda; *pop* 232,733

Ki·lau·ea \ˌkē-ˌlä-'wä-ä\ volcanic crater Hawaii on Hawaii Island on E slope of Mauna Loa

Kil·i·man·ja·ro \ˌki-lə-mən-'jä-(ˌ)rō, -'ja-(ˌ)rō\ mountain NE Tanzania; highest in Africa — see KIBO

Kil·lar·ney, Lakes of \ki-'lär-nē\ three lakes SW Ireland

Kings·ton \'kiŋ-stən\ city & port, ✳ of Jamaica; *pop* 103,771

Kingston upon Hull — see HULL

Kingston upon Thames borough of SW Greater London, England; *pop* 130,600

Kings·town \'kiŋz-ˌtau̇n\ seaport, ✳ of Saint Vincent and the Grenadines; *pop* 15,670

Kin·sha·sa \kin-'shä-sə\ city, ✳ of Democratic Republic of the Congo; *pop* 3,804,000

Ki·ri·bati \'kir-ə-ˌbas\ island group W Pacific; country; ✳, Tarawa; *pop* 78,600

Kirin — see JILIN

Kirk·wall \'kər-ˌkwȯl\ town and port N Scotland, ✳ of Orkney Islands; *pop* 5947

Kishinev — see CHIŞINĂU

Ki·ta·kyu·shu \kē-ˌtä-'kyü-(ˌ)shü\ city Japan in N Kyushu; *pop* 1,011,471

Kitch·e·ner \'kich-nər, 'ki-chə-\ city SE Ontario, Canada; *pop* 190,399

Kit·ty Hawk \'kit-ē-ˌhȯk\ town E North Carolina; *pop* 2991

Klon·dike \'klän-ˌdīk\ region NW Canada in *cen* Yukon Territory in valley of Klondike River

Knox·ville \'näks-ˌvil, -vəl\ city E Tennessee; *pop* 173,890

Ko·be \'kō-bē, -ˌbā\ city Japan in S Honshu; *pop* 1,493,398

Ko·di·ak \'kō-dē-ˌak\ island S Alaska E of Alaska Peninsula

Ko·la \'kō-lə\ peninsula NW Russia

Ko·rea \kə-'rē-ə\ peninsula E Asia between Yellow Sea & Sea of Japan (East Sea); divided 1948 into independent countries of North Korea & South Korea — **Ko·re·an** \kə-'rē-ən\ *adj or n*

Ko·ror \'kȯr-ˌȯr\ town, ✳ of Palau; *pop* 13,303

Kos·ci·us·ko, Mount \ˌkä-zē-'əs-(ˌ)kō, ˌkä-sē-\ mountain 7310 ft. (2228 m.) SE Australia in SE New South Wales; highest in Great Dividing Range & in Australia

Ko·so·vo \'kȯ-sə-ˌvō, 'kä-\ autonomous province S Serbia and Montenegro; *pop* (est.) 2,092,000

Kowloon — see JIULONG

Krak·a·tau \ˌkra-kə-'tau̇\ *or* **Krak·a·toa** \-'tō-ə\ island & volcano Indonesia between Sumatra & Java

Kra·kow \'krä-ˌkau̇, 'kra-, 'krä-, -(ˌ)kō, *Pol* 'krä-ˌküf\ city S Poland; *pop* 748,356

Kras·no·dar \ˌkräs-nə-'där\ city SW Russia; *pop* 635,000

Kras·no·yarsk \ˌkräs-nə-'yärsk\ city S *cen* Russia; *pop* 925,000

Kry·vyy Rih \kri-'vē-'rik\ *or* **Kri·voy Rog** \ˌkri-ˌvȯi-'rȯg, -'rȯk\ city SE *cen* Ukraine; *pop* 724,000

K2 \ˌkä-'tü\ *or* **God·win Aus·ten** \gä-dwən-'ȯs-tən, ˌgȯ-, -'äs-\ mountain 28,250 ft. (8611 m.) N Kashmir in Karakoram Range; second highest in the world

Kua·la Lum·pur \ˌkwä-lə-'lùm-ˌpùr, -'ləm-, -ˌlùm-'\ city, ✳ of Malaysia; *pop* 1,145,075

Kuei–yang — see GUIYANG

Kun·lun \'kün-'lün\ mountain system W China extending E from the Pamirs; highest peak Ulugh Muztagh 25,340 ft. (7724 m.)

Kun·ming \'kùn-'miŋ\ city S China; *pop* 1,127,411

Kur·di·stan \ˌkùr-də-'stan, ˌkər-, -'stän; 'kər-də-\ region SW Asia chiefly in E Turkey, NW Iran, & N Iraq — **Kurd** \'kùrd, 'kərd\ *n* — **Kurd·ish** \'kùr-dish, 'kər-\ *adj*

Ku·ril *or* **Ku·rile** \'kùr-ˌēl; 'kùr-; kyù-'rēl, kú-\ islands Russia in W Pacific between Kamchatka Peninsula & Hokkaido Island

Ku·wait \kú-'wät\ **1** country SW Asia in Arabia at head of Persian Gulf; *pop* 1,355,827 **2** city, its ✳; *pop* 181,774 — **Ku·waiti** \-'wä-tē\ *adj or n*

Kuybyshev — see SAMARA

Kuz·netsk Basin \kúz-'netsk\ *or* **Kuz·bas** *or* **Kuz·bass** \'kúz-ˌbas\ basin S *cen* Russia

Kwa·ja·lein \'kwä-jə-lən, -ˌlän\ island W Pacific in Marshall Islands

Kwang·ju *or* **Gwang·ju** \'gwäŋ-(ˌ)jü\ city SW South Korea; *pop* 1,350,948

Kwa·Zu·lu–Na·tal \kwä-'zü-(ˌ)lü-nə-'täl\ province E Republic of South Africa; *pop* 8,553,000

Kyo·to \kē-'ōt-ō\ city Japan in W *cen* Honshu; *pop* 1,467,785

Kyr·gyz·stan \kir-gi-'stan, -'stän\ country W *cen* Asia; ✳, Bishkek; *pop* 4,526,000

Kyu·shu \\'kyü-(ˌ)shü\ island Japan S of W end of Honshu; *pop* 13,445,561

Lab·ra·dor \\'la-brə-ˌdȯr\ **1** peninsula E Canada between Hudson Bay & the Atlantic divided between the provinces of Quebec & Newfoundland and Labrador **2** the part of the peninsula belonging to the province of Newfoundland and Labrador — **Lab·ra·dor·ean** *or* **Lab·ra·dor·ian** \ˌla-brə-'dȯr-ē-ən\ *adj or n*

Lac·ca·dive \\'la-kə-ˌdēv, -ˌdīv, -div\ islands India in Arabian Sea N of Maldive Islands

La·co·nia \lə-'kō-nē-ə, -nyə\ ancient country S Greece in SE Peloponnese; ✳, Sparta — **La·co·nian** \-nē-ən, -nyən\ *adj or n*

La·fay·ette \ˌla-fē-'et, ˌlä-\ city S Louisiana; *pop* 110,257

La·gos \\'lä-ˌgäs, -ˌgōs\ city, former ✳ (1960–91) of Nigeria; *pop* 1,340,000

La·hore \lə-'hȯr\ city E Pakistan; *pop* 5,143,495

Lake District region NW England containing many lakes & mountains

Lake·hurst \\'lāk-(ˌ)hərst\ borough E New Jersey; *pop* 2522

Lake·wood \\'lāk-ˌwu̇d\ city *cen* Colorado; *pop* 144,126

Lam·beth \\'lam-bəth, -ˌbeth\ borough of S Greater London, England; *pop* 220,100

La·nai \lə-'nī, lä-\ island Hawaii W of Maui

Lan·ca·shire \\'laŋ-kə-ˌshir, -shər\ *or* **Lan·cas·ter** \\'laŋ-kəs-tər\ county NW England — **Lan·cas·tri·an** \laŋ-'kas-trē-ən, lan-\ *adj or n*

Lan·cas·ter \\'laŋ-kəs-tər, 'lan-ˌkas-tər\ city NW England; *pop* 125,600

Land's End \\'landz-'end\ cape SW England; most westerly point of England

Lan·sing \\'lan-siŋ\ city, ✳ of Michigan; *pop* 119,128

Lan·zhou *or* **Lan–chou** \\'län-'jō\ city W China; *pop* 1,194,640

Laos \\'lau̇s, 'lä-(ˌ)ōs, 'lä-ˌäs\ country SE Asia in Indochina NE of Thailand; ✳, Vientiane; *pop* 4,533,000 — **Lao·tian** \lā-'ō-shən, 'lau̇-shən\ *adj or n*

La Paz \lä-'päz, -'päs\ city, administrative ✳ of Bolivia; *pop* 711,036

Lap·land \\'lap-ˌland, -lənd\ region N Europe above the Arctic Circle in N Norway, N Sweden, N Finland, & Kola Peninsula of Russia — **Lap·land·er** \-ˌlan-dər, -lən-\ *n*

La·re·do \lə-'rā-(ˌ)dō\ city S Texas on the Rio Grande; *pop* 176,576

Larne \\'lärn\ district NE Northern Ireland; *pop* 29,181

Las·sen Peak \\'la-sᵊn\ volcano 10,457 ft. (3187 m.) N California at S end of Cascade Range

Las Ve·gas \läs-'vā-gəs\ city SE Nevada; *pop* 478,434

Latin America **1** Spanish America and Brazil **2** all of the Americas S of the U.S. — **Latin–American** *adj* — **Latin American** *n*

Latin Quarter section of Paris, France S of the Seine

Lat·via \\'lat-vē-ə\ country E Europe on Baltic Sea; ✳, Riga; *pop* 2,345,768

Lau·ren·tian Mountains \lȯ-'ren(t)-shən\ hills E Canada in S Quebec N of the Saint Lawrence on S edge of Canadian Shield

Laurentian Plateau — see CANADIAN SHIELD

La·val \lə-'val\ city S Quebec NW of Montreal; *pop* 343,005

Law·rence \\'lȯr-ən(t)s, 'lär-\ city NE corner of Massachusetts; *pop* 72,043

League of Nations political organization established at the end of World War I; replaced by United Nations 1946

Leb·a·non \\'le-bə-nən\ **1** mountains Lebanon (country) running parallel to coast **2** country SW Asia on the Mediterranean; ✳, Beirut; *pop* 2,909,000 — **Leb·a·nese** \ˌle-bə-'nēz, -'nēs\ *adj or n*

Leeds \\'lēdz\ city N England; *pop* 674,400

Lee·ward Islands \\'lē-wərd, 'lü-ərd\ **1** islands Hawaii extending WNW from main islands of the group **2** islands South Pacific in W Society Islands **3** islands West Indies in N Lesser Antilles extending from Virgin Islands (on N) to Dominica (on S)

Le Ha·vre \lə-'hävrᵊ, -'häv\ city N France on English Channel; *pop* 190,924

Leh·man Caves \\'lē-mən\ limestone caverns E Nevada

Leices·ter \\'les-tər\ city *cen* England ENE of Birmingham; *pop* 270,600

Leices·ter·shire \\'les-tər-ˌshir, -shər\ *or* **Leicester** county *cen* England

Lein·ster \\'len(t)-stər\ province E Ireland; *pop* 2,105,579

Leip·zig \\'līp-sig, -sik\ city E Germany; *pop* 503,191

Le·na \\'lē-nə, 'lā-\ river about 2700 mi. (4345 km.) long E Russia, flowing NE & N from mountains W of Lake Baikal into Arctic Ocean

Leningrad — see SAINT PETERSBURG

Le·ón \lā-'ōn\ city *cen* Mexico; metropolitan area *pop* 1,174,180

Ler·wick \\'lər-(ˌ)wik, 'ler-\ town and port N Scotland in the Shetlands; *pop* 7223

Le·so·tho \lə-'sō-(ˌ)tō, -'sü-(ˌ)tü\ *formerly* **Ba·su·to·land** \bə-'sü-tō-ˌland\ country S Africa surrounded by Republic of South Africa; ✳, Maseru; *pop* 1,903,000

Lesser Antilles islands in the West Indies including Virgin Islands, Leeward Islands, & Windward Islands, Barbados, Trinidad, Tobago, & islands in the S Caribbean N of Venezuela — see GREATER ANTILLES

Le·vant \lə-'vant\ the countries bordering on the E Mediterranean — **Lev·an·tine** \\'lev-ən-ˌtīn, -ˌtēn, lə-'van-\ *adj or n*

Lew·es \\'lü-əs\ town S England

Lew·i·sham \\'lü-ə-shəm\ borough of SE Greater London, England; *pop* 215,300

Lewis with Har·ris \\'lü-əs-with-'ha-rəs, -with-\ island NW Scotland in Outer Hebrides

Lex·ing·ton \\'lek-siŋ-tən\ **1** city NE *cen* Kentucky; county *pop* 260,512 **2** town NE Massachusetts; *pop* 30,355

Ley·te \\'lā-tē\ island Philippines S of Samar

Lha·sa \\'lä-sə, 'la-\ city SW China, ✳ of Tibet; *pop* 106,885

Li·be·ria \lī-'bir-ē-ə\ country W Africa on the North Atlantic; ✳, Monrovia; *pop* 2,101,628 — **Li·be·ri·an** \-ē-ən\ *adj or n*

Lib·er·ty \\'li-bər-tē\ *formerly* **Bed·loe's** \\'bed-ˌlōz\ island SE New York; site of the Statue of Liberty

Li·bre·ville \\'lē-brə-ˌvil, -ˌvēl\ city, ✳ of Gabon; *pop* 419,596

Lib·ya \\'li-bē-ə\ country N Africa on the Mediterranean W of Egypt; ✳, Tripoli; *pop* 4,573,000 — **Lib·y·an** \\'li-bē-ən\ *adj or n*

Libyan desert N Africa W of the Nile in Libya, Egypt, & Sudan

Liech·ten·stein \\'lik-tən-ˌstīn, 'lik-tən-ˌshtīn\ country W Europe between Austria & Switzerland; ✳, Vaduz; *pop* 33,525 — **Liech·ten·stein·er** \-ˌstī-nər, -ˌshtī-\ *n*

Lif·fey \\'li-fē\ river 50 mi. (80 km.) long E Ireland

Li·gu·ria \lə-'gyu̇r-ē-ə\ region NW on Ligurian Sea — **Li·gu·ri·an** \-ē-ən\ *adj or n*

Ligurian Sea arm of the Mediterranean N of Corsica

Li·lon·gwe \li-'lȯŋ-(ˌ)gwā\ city, ✳ of Malawi; *pop* 498,185

Li·ma \\'lī-mə\ city, ✳ of Peru; *pop* 5,825,900

Lim·a·vady \ˌli-mə-'va-dē\ district NW Northern Ireland; *pop* 29,201

Lim·po·po \lim-'pō-(ˌ)pō\ river 1000 mi. (1609 km.) long Africa flowing from Republic of South Africa into Indian Ocean in Mozambique

Lin·coln \\'liŋ-kən\ **1** city, ✳ of Nebraska; *pop* 225,581 **2** city E England; *pop* 81,900

Lin·coln·shire \\'liŋ-kən-ˌshir, -shər\ *or* **Lincoln** county E England

Line \\'līn\ islands Kiribati S of Hawaii; *pop* 4782

Lis·bon \\'liz-bən\ *or Portuguese* **Lis·boa** \lēzh-'vō-ə\ city, ✳ of Portugal; *pop* 564,657

Lis·burn \\'liz-(ˌ)bərn\ district E Northern Ireland; *pop* 99,162

Lith·u·a·nia \ˌli-thə-'wā-nē-ə, ˌli-thyə-, -nyə\ country E Europe; ✳, Vilnius; *pop* 3,483,972

Lit·tle Rock \\'li-tᵊl-ˌräk\ city, ✳ of Arkansas; *pop* 183,133

Liv·er·pool \\'li-vər-ˌpül\ city NW England; *pop* 448,300

Li·vo·nia \lə-'vō-nē-ə, -nyə\ city SE Michigan; *pop* 100,545

Lju·blja·na \lē-ˌü-blē-'ä-nə\ city, ✳ of Slovenia; *pop* 323,291

Lla·no Es·ta·ca·do \ˌlä-(ˌ)nō-ˌes-tə-'kä-(ˌ)dō, ˌlä-, 'yä-\ *or* **Staked Plain** \\'stāk(t)-\ plateau region SE New Mexico & NW Texas

Lo·bam·ba \lō-'bäm-bə\ town, legislative ✳ of Swaziland; *pop* (est.) 10,000

Lodz \\'lüj, 'lädz\\ city *cen* Poland WSW of Warsaw; *pop* 851,690

Lo·fo·ten \\'lō-ˌfōt-ᵊn\\ islands NW Norway

Lo·gan, Mount \\'lō-gən\\ mountain 19,524 ft. (5951 m.) NW Canada in Saint Elias Range; highest in Canada & second highest in North America

Loire \\lə-'wär, 'lwär\\ river 634 mi. (1020 km.) long *cen* France flowing NW & W into Bay of Biscay

Lo·mé \\lō-'mā\\ city, ✶ of Togo; *pop* 229,400

Lo·mond, Loch \\'lō-mənd\\ lake S *cen* Scotland

Lon·don \\'lən-dən\\ **1** city SE Ontario, Canada; *pop* 336,539 **2** city, ✶ of England & of United Kingdom on the Thames; consists of City of London & Greater London metropolitan county; *pop* 6,377,900 — **Lon·don·er** \\-də-nər\\ *n*

Londonderry — see DERRY

Long Beach city SW California S of Los Angeles; *pop* 461,522

Long Island island 118 mi. (190 km.) long SE New York S of Connecticut

Long Island Sound inlet of the Atlantic between Connecticut & Long Island, New York

Lon·gueuil \\lȯŋ-'gāl\\ city Canada in S Quebec E of Montreal; *pop* 128,016

Lor·raine \\lə-'rān, lȯ-\\ region NE France

Los An·ge·les \\lȯs-'an-jə-ləs\\ city SW California; *pop* 3,694,820

Lou·ise, Lake \\lü-'ēz\\ lake SW Alberta, Canada

Lou·i·si·ana \\lü-ˌē-zē-'a-nə, ˌlü-ə-zē-, ˌlü-zē-\\ state S U.S.; ✶, Baton Rouge; *pop* 4,468,976 — **Lou·i·si·an·ian** \\-'a-nē-ən, -'a-nyən\\ *or* **Lou·i·si·an·an** \\-'a-nən\\ *adj or n*

Louisiana Purchase area W *cen* U.S. between Rocky Mountains & the Mississippi purchased 1803 from France

Lou·is·ville \\'lü-i-ˌvil, -vəl\\ city N Kentucky on the Ohio River; *pop* 256,231

Low Countries region W Europe consisting of modern Belgium, Luxembourg, & the Netherlands

Lowell \\'lō-əl\\ city NE Massachusetts NW of Boston; *pop* 105,167

Lower 48 the continental states of the U.S. excluding Alaska

Low·lands \\'lō-ləndz, -ˌlandz\\ the *cen* & E part of Scotland

Lu·an·da \\lü-'än-də\\ city, ✶ of Angola; *pop* 1,544,400

Lub·bock \\'lə-bək\\ city NW Texas; *pop* 199,564

Lu·bum·ba·shi \\ˌlü-büm-'bä-shē\\ city SE Democratic Republic of the Congo; *pop* (est.) 1,138,000

Luck·now \\'lək-ˌnaú\\ city N India ESE of Delhi; *pop* 2,207,340

Lüda *or* **Lü·ta** — see DALIAN

Lu·ray Caverns \\'lü-ˌrā, lü-'\\ series of caves N Virginia

Lu·sa·ka \\lü-'sä-kä\\ city, ✶ of Zambia; *pop* 982,362

Lü·shun \\'lü-'shün, 'lᵫ-\\ *or* **Port Ar·thur** \\-'är-thər\\ seaport NE China; part of greater Dalian

Lu·ton \\'lü-tᵊn\\ town SE *cen* England; *pop* 167,300

Lux·em·bourg *or* **Lux·em·burg** \\'lək-səm-ˌbərg, 'lük-səm-ˌbúrk\\ **1** country W Europe bordered by Belgium, France, & Germany; *pop* 392,000 **2** city, its ✶; *pop* 75,377 — **Lux·em·bourg·er** \\-ˌbər-gər, -ˌbúr-\\ *n* — **Lux·em·bourg·ian** \\ˌlək-səm-'bər-gē-ən, ˌlük-səm-'búr-\\ *adj*

Lu·zon \\lü-'zän\\ island N Philippines; *pop* 23,900,796

L'viv \\lə-'vē-ü, -'vēf\\ *or* **L'vov** \\lə-'vȯf, -'vȯv\\ *or Polish* **Lwów** \\lə-'vüf, -'vüv\\ city W Ukraine; *pop* 802,000

Lyallpur — see FAISALABAD

Lyd·ia \\'li-dē-ə\\ ancient country W Asia Minor on the Aegean — **Lyd·i·an** \\-ē-ən\\ *adj or n*

Lyon \\'lyōⁿ\\ *or* **Lyons** \\lē-'ōⁿ, 'lī-ənz\\ city SE *cen* France; *pop* 445,274

Ma·cao *or Portuguese* **Ma·cau** \\mə-'kaú\\ *or Chinese* **Ao·men** \\'aú-'mən\\ **1** special administrative region on coast of SE China W of Hong Kong; *pop* 488,000 **2** city, its ✶; *pop* 161,252 — **Mac·a·nese** \\ˌmä-kə-'nēz, -'nēs\\ *n*

Mac·e·do·nia \\ˌmas-ə-'dō-nē-ə, -nyə\\ region S Europe in Balkan Peninsula in NE Greece, the former Yugoslav section & now independent country of Macedonia, & SW Bulgaria including territory of ancient kingdom of Macedonia (**Mac·e·don** \\'mas-ə-dən, -ə-ˌdän\\ ) **2** country S *cen* Balkan Peninsula; ✶, Skopje; a former republic of Yugoslavia; *pop* 2,038,059 — **Mac·e·do·nian** \\ˌmas-ə-'dō-nyən, -nē-ən\\ *adj or n*

Mac·gil·li·cud·dy's Reeks \\mə-'gi-lə-ˌkə-dēz-'rēks\\ mountains SW Ireland; highest Carrantuohill 3414 ft. (1041 m.)

Ma·chu Pic·chu \\ˌmä-(ˌ)chü-'pē-(ˌ)chü, -'pēk-\\ site SE Peru of ancient Inca city

Mac·ken·zie \\mə-'ken-zē\\ river 1120 mi. (1802 km.) long NW Canada flowing from Great Slave Lake NW into Beaufort Sea

Mack·i·nac, Straits of \\'ma-kə-ˌnȯ, -ˌnak\\ channel N Michigan connecting Lake Huron & Lake Michigan

Ma·con \\'mā-kən\\ city *cen* Georgia; *pop* 97,255

Mad·a·gas·car \\ˌma-də-'gas-kər, -kär\\ *formerly* **Mal·a·gasy Re·public** \\ˌma-lə-'ga-sē\\ island country W Indian Ocean off SE Africa; ✶, Antananarivo; *pop* 16,694,272 — **Mad·a·gas·can** \\ˌma-də-'gas-kən\\ *adj or n*

Ma·dei·ra \\mə-'dir-ə, -'der-ə\\ **1** river 2013 mi. (3239 km.) long W Brazil flowing NE into the Amazon **2** islands Portugal in the North Atlantic N of the Canary Islands; *pop* 245,011 **3** island; chief of the Madeira group — **Ma·dei·ran** \\-'dir-ən, -'der-\\ *adj or n*

Ma·di·nat ash Sha'b \\mə-'dē-ˌnə-tash-'shab\\ city S Yemen

Mad·i·son \\'ma-də-sən\\ city, ✶ of Wisconsin; *pop* 208,054

Ma·dras \\mə-'dras, -'dräs\\ *or* **Chen·nai** \\'che-ˌnī\\ city SE India; *pop* 4,216,268

Ma·drid \\mə-'drid\\ city, ✶ of Spain; *pop* 2,938,723

Ma·du·rai \\ˌmä-də-'rī\\ city S India; *pop* 922,913

Mag·da·len Islands \\'mag-də-lən\\ *or F* **Îles de la Ma·de·leine** \\ˌēl-də-lä-mäd-'len, -mä-də-'len\\ islands Canada in Gulf of Saint Lawrence between Newfoundland & Prince Edward Island

Ma·gel·lan, Strait of \\mə-'je-lən, *chiefly Brit* -'ge-\\ strait at S end of South America between mainland & Tierra del Fuego

Magh·er·a·felt \\'mär-ə-ˌfelt, 'ma-kə-rə-ˌfelt\\ district *cen* Northern Ireland; *pop* 35,874

Maid·stone \\'mād-stən, -ˌstōn\\ town SE England; *pop* 133,200

Main \\'mīn, 'män\\ river 325 mi. (523 km.) long S *cen* Germany flowing W into the Rhine

Maine \\'mān\\ state NE U.S.; ✶, Augusta; *pop* 1,274,923 — **Main·er** \\'mā-nər\\ *n*

Ma·jor·ca \\mə-'jȯr-kə, mə-, -'yȯr-\\ *or Spanish* **Ma·llor·ca** \\mä-'yȯr-kä\\ island Spain in W Mediterranean — **Ma·jor·can** \\-'jȯr-kən, -'yȯr\\ *adj or n*

Ma·ju·ro \\mə-'jùr-(ˌ)ō\\ atoll, ✶ of Marshall Islands; *pop* (est.) 20,000

Mal·a·bar Coast \\'ma-lə-ˌbär\\ region SW India on Arabian Sea

Ma·la·bo \\mä-'lä-(ˌ)bō\\ city, ✶ of Equatorial Guinea; *pop* 37,237

Ma·lac·ca, Strait of \\mə-'la-kə, -'lä-\\ channel between S Malay Peninsula & island of Sumatra

Ma·la·wi \\mə-'lä-wē\\ *formerly* **Ny·asa·land** \\nī-'a-sə-ˌland, nē-\\ country SE Africa on Lake Nyasa; ✶, Lilongwe; *pop* 10,475,257 — **Ma·la·wi·an** \\-ən\\ *adj or n*

Ma·lay \\mə-'lā, 'mā-(ˌ)lā\\ **1** archipelago SE Asia including Sumatra, Java, Borneo, Sulawesi, Moluccas, & Timor; usu. thought to include the Philippines & sometimes New Guinea **2** peninsula SE Asia divided between Thailand & Malaysia (country)

Ma·laya \\mə-'lā-ə, mä-\\ **1** the Malay Peninsula **2** former country SE Asia on Malay Peninsula; now part of Malaysia

Ma·lay·sia \\mə-'lā-zh(ē-)ə, -sh(ē-)ə\\ **1** the Malay Archipelago **2** the Malay Peninsula & Malay Archipelago **3** country SE Asia; ✶, Kuala Lumpur; *pop* 19,077,000 — **Ma·lay·sian** \\mə-'lā-zhən, -shən\\ *adj or n*

Mal·dives \\'mȯl-ˌdēvz, -ˌdīvz\\ islands in Indian Ocean SW of Sri Lanka; country; ✶, Male Atoll; *pop* 270,101 — **Mal·div·i·an** \\mȯl-'di-vē-ən, mal-\\ *adj or n*

Ma·le \\'mä-lē\\ atoll, ✶ of Maldives; *pop* (est.) 63,000

Ma·li \\'mä-lē, 'ma-\\ country W Africa; ✶, Bamako; *pop* 8,646,000 — **Ma·li·an** \\-lē-ən\\ *adj or n*

Mal·ta \\'mȯl-tə\\ islands in the Mediterranean S of Sicily; country since 1964; ✶, Valletta; *pop* 397,296 — **Mal·tese** \\mȯl-'tēz, -'tēs\\ *adj or n*

Malvinas, Islas — see FALKLAND ISLANDS

Mam·moth Cave \\'ma-məth\ limestone caverns SW *cen* Kentucky

Man, Isle of \\'man\ island British Isles in Irish Sea; has own legislature & laws; *pop* 60,496

Ma·na·gua \mä-'nä-gwä\ city, ✳ of Nicaragua; *pop* 552,900

Ma·na·ma \mə-'na-mə\ city, ✳ of Bahrain; *pop* 136,999

Man·ches·ter \'man-ˌches-tər, -chəs-tər\ **1** city S *cen* New Hampshire; *pop* 107,006 **2** city NW England; *pop* 406,900

Man·chu·ria \man-'chu̇r-ē-ə\ region NE China S of the Amur — **Man·chu·ri·an** \-ē-ən\ *adj or n*

Man·hat·tan \man-'ha-tᵊn, mən-\ **1** island SE New York in New York City **2** borough of New York City consisting chiefly of Manhattan Island; *pop* 1,537,195

Ma·nila \mə-'ni-lə\ city, ✳ of Philippines in W Luzon; *pop* 1,587,000

Man·i·to·ba \ˌma-nə-'tō-bə\ province *cen* Canada; ✳, Winnipeg; *pop* 1,150,034 — **Man·i·to·ban** \-bən\ *adj or n*

Man·i·tou·lin \ˌma-nə-'tü-lən\ island 80 mi. (129 km.) long S Ontario in Lake Huron

Ma·pu·to \mä-'pü-(ˌ)tō, -(ˌ)tü\ city, ✳ of Mozambique; *pop* 966,800

Mar·a·cai·bo \ˌma-rə-'kī-(ˌ)bō, ˌmär-ä-\ city NW Venezuela; *pop* 1,207,513

Maracaibo, Lake extension of a gulf of the Caribbean NW Venezuela

Mar·a·thon \'ma-rə-ˌthän\ plain E Greece NE of Athens

Mar·i·ana \ˌmer-ē-'a-nə\ islands W Pacific N of Caroline Islands; comprise Commonwealth of Northern Mariana Islands & Guam

Mariana Trench ocean trench W Pacific extending from SE of Guam to NW of Mariana Islands; deepest in world

Ma·rin·du·que \ˌma-rən-'dü-(ˌ)kā, ˌmär-ēn-\ island *cen* Philippines; *pop* 173,715

Maritime Provinces the Canadian provinces of New Brunswick, Nova Scotia, & Prince Edward Island & sometimes thought to include Newfoundland and Labrador

Ma·ri·u·pol \ˌma-rē-'ü-ˌpȯl, -pəl\ *or 1949–89* **Zhda·nov** \zhə-'dä-nəf\ city E Ukraine; *pop* 417,000

Mar·ma·ra, Sea of \'mär-mə-rə\ sea NW Turkey connected with Black Sea by the Bosporus & with Aegean Sea by the Dardanelles

Marne \'märn\ river 325 mi. (523 km.) long NE France flowing W into the Seine

Mar·que·sas \mär-'kā-zəz, -zəs, -səz, -səs\ islands South Pacific; belonging to France; *pop* 7358 — **Mar·que·san** \-zən, -sən\ *adj or n*

Mar·ra·kech \ˌma-rə-'kesh, 'ma-rə-ˌ, mə-'rä-kish\ city *cen* Morocco; *pop* 439,728

Mar·seille \mär-'sā\ *or* **Mar·seilles** \mär-'sā, -'sālz\ city SE France; *pop* 797,491

Mar·shall Islands \'mär-shəl\ islands W Pacific E of the Carolines; republic, in association with U.S.; ✳, Majuro; *pop* 70,822

Mar·tha's Vineyard \'mär-thəz\ island SE Massachusetts off SW coast of Cape Cod WNW of Nantucket

Mar·ti·nique \ˌmär-tə-'nēk\ island West Indies in the Windward Islands; an overseas division of France; ✳, Fort-de-France; *pop* 377,000

Mary·land \'mer-ə-lənd\ state E U.S.; ✳, Annapolis; *pop* 5,296,486 — **Mary·land·er** \-lən-dər, -ˌlan-\ *n*

Mas·ba·te \mäz-'bä-tē, mäs-\ island *cen* Philippines

Mas·e·ru \'ma-sə-ˌrü, -zə-\ city, ✳ of Lesotho; *pop* 71,500

Mash·had \mə-'shad\ city NE Iran; *pop* 1,463,508

Ma·son–Dix·on Line \'mā-sᵊn-'dik-sən\ boundary between Maryland & Pennsylvania; often considered the boundary between N & S states

Mas·qat \'məs-ˌkät\ *or* **Mus·cat** \-ˌkät, -ˌkat, -kət\ town E Arabia, ✳ of Oman; *pop* 100,000

Mas·sa·chu·setts \ˌma-sə-'chü-səts, -zəts\ state NE U.S.; ✳, Boston; *pop* 6,349,097

Mat·a·be·le·land \ˌma-tə-'bē-lē-ˌland, ˌmä-tä-'bä-lä-\ region SW Zimbabwe

Mat·lock \'mat-ˌläk\ town N England; *pop* 20,610

Mat·ter·horn \'ma-tər-ˌhȯrn, 'mä-\ mountain 14,691 ft. (4478 m.) on border between Switzerland & Italy

Maui \'maủ-ē\ island Hawaii NW of Hawaii Island

Mau·na Kea \ˌmaủ-nä-'kā-ä, ˌmȯ-\ extinct volcano 13,796 ft. (4205 m.) Hawaii in N *cen* Hawaii Island

Mau·na Loa \-'lō-ə\ volcano 13,680 ft. (4170 m.) Hawaii in S *cen* Hawaii Island

Mau·re·ta·nia *or* **Mau·ri·ta·nia** \ˌmȯr-ə-'tā-nē-ə, ˌmär-, -nyə\ ancient country NW Africa in modern Morocco & W Algeria — **Mau·re·ta·ni·an** *or* **Mau·ri·ta·ni·an** \-nē-ən, -nyən\ *adj or n*

Mauritania country NW Africa on the Atlantic N of Senegal River; ✳, Nouakchott; *pop* 2,171,000 — **Mauritanian** *adj or n*

Mau·ri·tius \mȯ-'ri-sh(ē-)əs\ island in Indian Ocean E of Madagascar; country; ✳, Port Louis; *pop* 1,210,196 — **Mau·ri·tian** \-'ri-shən\ *adj or n*

May, Cape \'mā\ cape S New Jersey at entrance to Delaware Bay

Ma·yon, Mount \mä-'yȯn\ volcano 8077 ft. (2462 m.) Philippines in SE Luzon

Ma·yotte \mä-'yät, -'yȯt\ island Comoros group; French dependency; *pop* 90,000 — see COMOROS

Ma·za·ma, Mount \mə-'zäm-ə\ prehistoric mountain SW Oregon the collapse of whose top formed Crater Lake

Mba·bane \ˌəm-bä-'bä-nä\ city, ✳ of Swaziland; *pop* 57,992

Mbi·ni \em-'bē-nē\ *formerly* **Río Mu·ni** \ˌrē-ō-'mü-nē\ mainland portion of Equatorial Guinea

Mc·Al·len \mə-'ka-lən\ city S Texas; *pop* 106,414

Mc·Kin·ley, Mount \mə-'kin-lē\ *or* **De·na·li** \də-'nä-lē\ mountain 20,320 ft. (6194 m.) S *cen* Alaska in Alaska Range; highest in U.S. & North America

Mead, Lake \'mēd\ reservoir NW Arizona & SE Nevada formed by Hoover Dam in Colorado River

Mec·ca \'me-kə\ city W Saudi Arabia containing the Great Mosque of Islam; *pop* 366,801

Me·dan \mā-'dän\ city Indonesia, in N Sumatra; *pop* 1,730,752

Me·de·llín \ˌme-də-'lēn, ˌmā-thā-'yēn\ city NW Colombia; *pop* 1,581,400

Me·di·na \mə-'dī-nə\ city W Saudi Arabia; *pop* 608,295

Med·i·ter·ra·nean \ˌme-də-tə-'rā-nē-ən, -nyən\ sea 2300 mi. (3700 km.) long between Europe & Africa connecting with the Atlantic through Strait of Gibraltar

Me·kong \'mā-'kȯŋ, -'käŋ; 'mā-ˌ\ river 2600 mi. (4184 km.) long SE Asia flowing from E Tibet S & SE into South China Sea in S Vietnam

Mel·a·ne·sia \ˌme-lə-'nē-zhə, -shə\ islands of the Pacific NE of Australia & S of Micronesia including Bismarck, the Solomons, Vanuatu, New Caledonia, & the Fijis

Mel·bourne \'mel-bərn\ city SE Australia, ✳ of Victoria; metropolitan area *pop* 2,761,995

Melos — see MÍLOS

Mel·ville \'mel-ˌvil\ **1** island N Canada, split between Northwest Territories & Nunavut **2** peninsula Canada in Nunavut

Mem·phis \'mem(p)-fəs\ **1** city SW Tennessee; *pop* 650,100 **2** ancient city N Egypt S of modern Cairo

Mem·phre·ma·gog, Lake \ˌmem(p)-fri-'mā-ˌgäg\ lake on border between Canada (Quebec) & United States (Vermont)

Men·do·ci·no, Cape \ˌmen-də-'sē-(ˌ)nō\ cape NW California

Mer·cia \'mər-sh(ē-)ə\ ancient Anglo-Saxon kingdom *cen* England — **Mer·cian** \'mər-shən\ *adj or n*

Mer·sey \'mər-zē\ river 70 mi. (113 km.) long NW England flowing NW & W into Irish Sea

Mer·sey·side \'mər-zē-ˌsīd\ metropolitan county NW England; includes Liverpool

Mer·ton \'mər-tᵊn\ borough of SW Greater London, England; *pop* 161,800

Me·sa \'mā-sə\ city S *cen* Arizona; *pop* 396,375

Me·sa·bi Range \mə-'sä-bē\ region NE Minnesota that contains iron ore

Mes·o·po·ta·mia \ˌme-s(ə-)pə-'tā-mē-ə, -myə\ **1** region SW Asia between Euphrates & Tigris rivers **2** the entire Tigris–Euphrates valley — **Mes·o·po·ta·mian** \-mē-ən, -myən\ *adj or n*

Mes·quite \mə-'skēt, me-\ city NE Texas E of Dallas; *pop* 124,523

Meuse \'myüz, 'mə(r)z, 'mœz\ river 580 mi. (933 km.)

long W Europe flowing from NE France into North Sea in the Netherlands

Mex·i·co \'mek-si-ˌkō\ **1** country S North America; *pop* 89,995,000 **2** *or* **Mexico City** city, its ✳; metropolitan area *pop* 16,674,160 — **Mex·i·can** \'mek-si-kən\ *adj or n*

Mexico, Gulf of inlet of the Atlantic SE North America

Mi·ami \mī-'a-mē\ city & port SE Florida; *pop* 362,470

Miami Beach city SE Florida; *pop* 87,933

Mich·i·gan \'mi-shi-gən\ state N *cen* U.S.; ✳, Lansing; *pop* 9,938,444 — **Mich·i·gan·der** \ˌmi-shi-'gan-dər\ *n* — **Mich·i·ga·ni·an** \ˌmi-shə-'gä-nē-ən, -'ga-\ *n* — **Mich·i·gan·ite** \'mi-shi-gə-ˌnīt\ *n*

Michigan, Lake lake N *cen* U.S.; one of the Great Lakes

Mi·cro·ne·sia \ˌmī-krə-'nē-zhə, -shə\ islands of the W Pacific E of the Philippines & N of Melanesia including Caroline, Kiribati, Mariana, & Marshall groups — **Mi·cro·ne·sian** \-zhən, -shən\ *adj or n*

Micronesia, Federated States of islands W Pacific in the Carolines; country in association with U.S.; ✳, Palikir; *pop* 134,597

Middle East the countries of SW Asia & N Africa— usually thought to include the countries extending from Libya on the W to Afghanistan on the E — **Middle Eastern** *adj*

Mid·dles·brough \'mi-dᵊlz-brə\ town N England; *pop* 141,100

Middle West — see MIDWEST

Mid Gla·mor·gan \'mid-glə-'mȯr-gən\ former county SE Wales

Mid·i·an \'mi-dē-ən\ ancient region NW Arabia E of Gulf of Aqaba — **Mid·i·an·ite** \-ē-ə-ˌnīt\ *n*

Mid·lands \'mid-ləndz\ the *cen* counties of England

Mid·way \'mid-ˌwā\ islands *cen* Pacific 1300 mi. (2092 km.) WNW of Honolulu belonging to U.S.

Mid·west \ˌmid-'west\ *or* **Middle West** region N *cen* U.S. including area around Great Lakes & in upper Mississippi valley from Ohio on the E to North Dakota, South Dakota, Nebraska, & Kansas on the W — **Mid·west·ern** \ˌmid-'wes-tərn\ *or* **Middle Western** *adj* — **Mid·west·ern·er** \ˌmid-'wes-tə(r)-nər\ *or* **Middle Westerner** *n*

Mi·lan \mə-'lan, -'län\ *or Italian* **Mi·la·no** \mē-'lä-(ˌ)nō\ city NW Italy; *pop* 1,449,403 — **Mil·a·nese** \ˌmi-lə-'nēz, -'nēs\ *adj or n*

Mí·los *or* **Me·los** \'mē-ˌlȯs\ island Greece

Mil·wau·kee \mil-'wȯ-kē\ city SE Wisconsin on Lake Michigan; *pop* 596,974

Mi·nas Basin \'mī-nəs\ bay *cen* Nova Scotia; NE extension of Bay of Fundy

Min·da·nao \ˌmin-də-'nä-ō, -'naú\ island S Philippines; *pop* 13,966,000

Min·do·ro \min-'dȯr-(ˌ)ō\ island *cen* Philippines; *pop* 473,940

Min·ne·ap·o·lis \ˌmi-nē-'a-pə-lis\ city SE Minnesota; *pop* 382,618

Min·ne·so·ta \ˌmi-nə-'sō-tə\ state N *cen* U.S.; ✳, Saint Paul; *pop* 4,919,479 — **Min·ne·so·tan** \-'sō-tᵊn\ *adj or n*

Mi·nor·ca \mə-'nȯr-kə\ island Spain in W Mediterranean — **Mi·nor·can** \mə-'nȯr-kən\ *adj or n*

Minsk \'min(t)sk\ city, ✳ of Belarus; *pop* 1,589,000

Mis·sis·sau·ga \ˌmi-sə-'sȯ-gə\ city Canada in S Ontario; *pop* 612,925

Mis·sis·sip·pi \ˌmi-sə-'si-pē\ **1** river 2340 mi. (3765 km.) long U.S. flowing into Gulf of Mexico — see ITASCA, LAKE **2** state S U.S.; ✳, Jackson; *pop* 2,844,658

Mis·sou·ri \mə-'zúr-ē\ **1** river 2466 mi. (3968 km.) long W U.S. flowing from SW Montana to the Mississippi in E Missouri (state) **2** state *cen* U.S.; ✳, Jefferson City; *pop* 5,595,211 — **Mis·sou·ri·an** \-'zúr-ē-ən\ *adj or n*

Mitch·ell, Mount \'mi-chəl\ mountain 6684 ft. (2037 m.) W North Carolina in the Appalachians; highest in U.S. E of the Mississippi

Mo·bile \mō-'bēl, 'mō-ˌbēl\ city SW Alabama on **Mobile Bay** (inlet of Gulf of Mexico); *pop* 198,915

Mo·des·to \mə-'des-(ˌ)tō\ city *cen* California; *pop* 188,856

Mog·a·di·shu \ˌmä-gə-'di-(ˌ)shü, ˌmō-, -'dē-\ *or* **Mog·a·di·scio** \-(ˌ)shō\ city, ✳ of Somalia; *pop* 349,245

Mo·hawk \'mō-ˌhȯk\ river E *cen* New York flowing into the Hudson

Mo·hen·jo Da·ro \mō-'hen-(ˌ)jō-'där-(ˌ)ō\ prehistoric city in valley of the Indus NE of modern Karachi, Pakistan

Mo·ja·ve *or* **Mo·ha·ve** \mə-'hä-vē, mō-\ desert S California SE of S end of Sierra Nevada

Mol·da·via \mäl-'dā-vē-ə, -vyə\ region E Europe in NE Romania & Moldova — **Mol·da·vian** \-vē-ən, -vyən\ *adj or n*

Mol·do·va \mäl-'dō-və, mȯl-\ country E Europe in E Moldavia region; ✳, Chisinau; *pop* 4,362,000 — **Mol·do·van** \-vən\ *adj or n*

Mo·lo·kai \ˌmä-lə-'kī, ˌmō-lō-'kä-ē\ island Hawaii ESE of Oahu

Mo·luc·cas \mə-'lə-kəz\ islands Indonesia E of Sulawesi; *pop* 1,857,790 — **Mo·luc·ca** \mə-'lə-kə\ *adj* — **Mo·luc·can** \-kən\ *adj or n*

Mom·ba·sa city & port S Kenya; *pop* 665,018

Mo·na·co \'mä-nə-ˌkō\ country W Europe on Mediterranean coast of France; ✳, Monaco; *pop* 30,500 — **Mo·na·can** \'mä-nə-kən, mə-'nä-kən\ *adj or n* — **Mon·e·gasque** \ˌmä-ni-'gask\ *n*

Mon·go·lia \män-'gōl-yə, mäŋ-, -'gō-lē-ə\ **1** region E Asia E of Altay Mountains; includes Gobi Desert **2** country E Asia consisting of major portion of Mongolia region; ✳, Ulaanbaatar; *pop* 2,182,000

Mo·non·ga·he·la \mə-ˌnäŋ-gə-'hē-lə, -ˌnäŋ-gə-, -'hā-lə\ river N West Virginia & SW Pennsylvania

Mon·ro·via \(ˌ)mən-'rō-vē-ə\ city, ✳ of Liberia; *pop* 243,243

Mon·ta·na \män-'ta-nə\ state NW U.S.; ✳, Helena; *pop* 902,195 — **Mon·tan·an** \-nən\ *adj or n*

Mont Blanc \ˌmōⁿ-'bläⁿ\ mountain 15,771 ft. (4807 m.) SE France on Italian border; highest in the Alps

Mon·te·go Bay \män-'tē-(ˌ)gō\ city & port NW Jamaica on **Montego Bay** (inlet of the Caribbean); *pop* 83,446

Mon·te·ne·gro \ˌmän-tə-'nē-(ˌ)grō, -'nä-, -'ne-\ republic of S Serbia and Montenegro on the Adriatic Sea; *pop* 616,327

Mon·ter·rey \ˌmän-tə-'rā\ city NE Mexico; metropolitan area *pop* 3,022,268

Mon·te·vi·deo \ˌmän-tə-və-'dā-(ˌ)ō, -'vi-dē-ˌō; ˌmȯn-tā-vē-'thā-ō\ city, ✳ of Uruguay; *pop* 1,260,753

Mont·gom·ery \(ˌ)mən(t)-'gə-mə-rē, män(t)-, -'gä-; -'gəm-rē, -'gäm-\ city, ✳ of Alabama; *pop* 201,568

Mont·pe·lier \mänt-'pēl-yər, -'pil-\ city, ✳ of Vermont; *pop* 8035

Mon·tre·al \ˌmän-trē-'ȯl, ˌmən-\ city S Quebec, Canada on **Montreal Island** in the Saint Lawrence; *pop* 1,039,534

Mont·ser·rat \ˌmän(t)-sə-'rat\ island British West Indies in the Leeward Islands; *pop* 12,100

Mo·ra·via \mə-'rā-vē-ə\ region E Czech Republic — **Mo·ra·vi·an** \mə-'rā-vē-ən\ *adj or n*

Mo·rea \mə-'rē-ə\ PELOPONNESE — an old name — **Mo·re·an** \-'rē-ən\ *adj or n*

Mo·re·no Valley \mə-'rē-(ˌ)nō\ city S California; *pop* 142,381

Mo·roc·co \mə-'rä-(ˌ)kō\ country NW Africa; ✳, Rabat; *pop* 29,631,000 — **Mo·roc·can** \-kən\ *adj or n*

Mo·ro·ni \mȯ-'rō-nē\ city, ✳ of Comoros; *pop* 23,432

Mos·cow \'mäs-(ˌ)kō, -ˌkaú\ *or Russian* **Mos·kva** \mäsk-'vä\ city, ✳ of Russia; *pop* 8,769,000

Mo·selle \mō-'zel\ river about 340 mi. (545 km.) long E France & W Germany

Moyle \'mȯi(-ə)l\ district N Northern Ireland; *pop* 14,617

Mo·zam·bique \ˌmō-zəm-'bēk\ **1** channel SE Africa between Mozambique (country) & Madagascar **2** country SE Africa; ✳, Maputo; *pop* 16,099,246 — **Mo·zam·bi·can** \ˌmō-zəm-'bē-kən\ *adj or n*

Mpu·ma·lan·ga \əm-ˌpü-mä-'läŋ-gä\ province NE Republic of South Africa; *pop* 2,911,000

Mukden — see SHENYANG

Mul·tan \múl-'tän\ city NE Pakistan SW of Lahore; *pop* 1,197,384

Mumbai — see BOMBAY

Mu·nich \'myü-nik\ *or German* **Mün·chen** \'mυen-kən\ city S Germany in Bavaria; *pop* 1,229,052

Mun·ster \'mən(t)-stər\ province S Ireland; *pop* 1,100,614

Mur·cia \'mər-sh(ē-)ə\ region & ancient kingdom SE Spain — **Mur·cian** \-shən\ *adj or n*

Mur·ray \'mər-ē, 'mə-rē\ river 1609 mi. (2589 km.) long SE Australia flowing W from E Victoria into Indian Ocean in South Australia

Mur·rum·bidg·ee \ˌmər-əm-ˈbi-jē, ˌmə-rəm-\ river almost 1000 mi. (1609 km.) long SE Australia in New South Wales flowing W into the Murray

Muscat — see MASQAT

Myan·mar \ˈmyän-ˌmär\ or **Bur·ma** \ˈbər-mə\ country SE Asia; ✳, Yangon; pop 45,573,000

My·ce·nae \mī-ˈsē-(ˌ)nē\ ancient city S Greece in NE Peloponnese

Myr·tle Beach \ˈmər-tᵊl\ city E South Carolina on the Atlantic; pop 22,759

My·sore \mī-ˈsȯr\ city S India; pop 742,261

Nab·a·taea or **Nab·a·tea** \ˌna-bə-ˈtē-ə\ ancient Arab kingdom SE of Palestine — **Nab·a·tae·an** or **Nab·a·te·an** \-ˈtē-ən\ adj or n

Na·goya \nə-ˈgȯi-ə, ˈnä-gȯ-(ˌ)yä\ city Japan in S cen Honshu; pop 2,171,557

Nag·pur \ˈnäg-ˌpu̇r\ city E cen India; pop 2,051,320

Nai·ro·bi \nī-ˈrō-bē\ city, ✳ of Kenya; pop 2,083,509

Na·mib·ia \nə-ˈmi-bē-ə\ formerly **South–West Africa** country SW Africa on the Atlantic; ✳, Windhoek; pop 1,511,600 — **Na·mib·ian** \-bē-ən, -byən\ adj or n

Nan·chang \ˈnän-ˈchäŋ\ city SE China; pop 1,086,124

Nan·jing \ˈnän-ˈjiŋ\ or **Nan·king** \ˈnan-ˈkiŋ, ˈnän-\ city E China; pop 2,090,204

Nan·tuck·et \nan-ˈtə-kət\ island SE Massachusetts S of Cape Cod; pop 6012

Na·per·ville \ˈnā-pər-ˌvil\ city NE Illinois W of Chicago; pop 128,358

Na·ples \ˈnā-pəlz\ or Italian **Na·po·li** \ˈnä-pō-lē\ ancient **Ne·ap·o·lis** \nē-ˈa-pə-ləs\ city S Italy on Bay of Naples; pop 1,000,470 — **Ne·a·pol·i·tan** \ˌnē-ə-ˈpäl-ə-tən\ adj or n

Nar·ra·gan·sett Bay \ˌna-rə-ˈgan(t)-sət\ inlet of the Atlantic SE Rhode Island

Nash·ville \ˈnash-ˌvil, -vəl\ city, ✳ of Tennessee; pop 569,891

Nas·sau \ˈna-ˌsȯ\ city, ✳ of Bahamas on New Providence Island; pop 172,196

Na·tal \nə-ˈtal, -ˈtäl\ former province E Republic of South Africa

Na·u·ru \nä-ˈü-(ˌ)rü\ island W Pacific S of the Equator; country; ✳, Yaren; pop 10,000 — **Na·u·ru·an** \-ˈü-rə-wən\ adj or n

Naz·a·reth \ˈna-zə-rəth\ town of ancient Palestine in cen Galilee; now a city of N Israel; pop 49,800

N'Dja·me·na \ən-jä-ˈmä-nä, -ˈmē-\ city, ✳ of Chad; pop 687,800

Neagh, Lough \ˌläk-ˈnä\ lake Northern Ireland; largest in British Isles

Near East the countries of NE Africa & SW Asia — **Near Eastern** adj

Ne·bras·ka \nə-ˈbras-kə\ state cen U.S.; ✳, Lincoln; pop 1,711,263 — **Ne·bras·kan** \-kən\ adj or n

Neg·ev \ˈne-ˌgev\ desert region S Israel

Ne·gro \ˈnā-(ˌ)grō, ˈne-\ river 1400 mi. (2253 km.) long in E Colombia & N Brazil flowing into the Amazon

Ne·gros \ˈnā-(ˌ)grōs, ˈne-\ island cen Philippines

Ne·pal \nə-ˈpȯl, nä-\ country Asia on NE border of India in the Himalayas; ✳, Kathmandu; pop 23,151,423 — **Nep·a·lese** \ˌne-pə-ˈlēz, -ˈlēs\ adj or n — **Ne·pali** \nə-ˈpȯl-ē, -ˈpäl-, -ˈpal-\ adj or n

Ness, Loch \ˈnes\ lake NW Scotland

Neth·er·lands \ˈne-thər-ləndz\ **1** or Dutch **Ne·der·land** \ˈnād-ər-ˌlänt\ also **Holland** country NW Europe on North Sea; ✳, Amsterdam; seat of the government, The Hague; pop 15,009,000 **2** LOW COUNTRIES — an historical usage — **Neth·er·land** \ˈne-thər-lənd\ adj — **Neth·er·land·er** \-ˌlan-dər, -lən-\ n — **Neth·er·land·ish** \-ˌlan-dish, -lən-\ adj

Netherlands Antilles islands of the West Indies belonging to the Netherlands; ✳, Willemstad; pop 190,566

Ne·va \ˈnē-və, ˈnä-, nye-ˈvä\ river 40 mi. (64 km.) long W Russia; flows through Saint Petersburg

Ne·vada \nə-ˈva-də\ state W U.S.; ✳, Carson City; pop 1,998,257 — **Ne·vad·an** \-ˈva-dᵊn, -ˈvä-\ or **Ne·vad·i·an** \-ˈva-dē-ən, -ˈvä-\ adj or n

Ne·vis \ˈnē-vəs\ island West Indies in the Leeward Islands — see SAINT KITTS

New Amsterdam town founded 1625 on island of Man-

hattan by the Dutch; renamed New York 1664 by the British

New·ark \ˈnü-ərk, ˈnyü-\ city NE New Jersey; pop 273,546

New Britain island W Pacific in Bismarck group; pop 263,500

New Bruns·wick \-ˈbrənz-(ˌ)wik\ province SE Canada; ✳, Fredericton; pop 757,077

New Caledonia island SW Pacific SW of Vanuatu; an overseas department of France; ✳, Nouméa; pop 183,100

New·cas·tle \ˈnü-ˌka-səl, ˈnyü-\ city SE Australia in E New South Wales; metropolitan area pop 262,331

Newcastle or **Newcastle upon Tyne** \ˈtīn\ city N England; pop 263,000

New Delhi city, ✳ of India S of Delhi; pop 294,783

New England section of NE U.S. consisting of states of Maine, New Hampshire, Vermont, Massachusetts, Rhode Island, & Connecticut — **New En·gland·er** \ˈiŋ-glən-dər\ n

New·found·land \ˈnü-fən(d)-lənd, ˈnyü-, -ˌland; ˌnü-fən(d)-ˈland, ˌnyü-\ island Canada in the Atlantic — **New·found·land·er** \-lən-dər, -ˌlan-\ n

Newfoundland and Labrador province E Canada consisting of Newfoundland Island and Labrador; ✳, Saint John's; pop 533,761

New France the possessions of France in North America before 1763

New Guinea 1 island W Pacific N of E Australia; divided between West Papua, Indonesia & independent Papua New Guinea **2** the NE portion of the island of New Guinea together with some nearby islands; now part of Papua New Guinea — **New Guinean** adj or n

New·ham \ˈnü-əm, ˈnyü-\ borough of E Greater London, England; pop 200,200

New Hamp·shire \ˈhamp-shər, -ˌshir\ state NE U.S.; ✳, Concord; pop 1,235,786 — **New Hamp·shire·man** \-mən\ n — **New Hamp·shir·ite** \-ˌīt\ n

New Ha·ven \ˈhā-vən\ city S Connecticut; pop 123,626

New Hebrides — see VANUATU

New Jersey state E U.S.; ✳, Trenton; pop 8,414,350 — **New Jer·sey·an** \-ən\ n — **New Jer·sey·ite** \-ˌīt\ n

New Mex·i·co \ˈmek-si-ˌkō\ state SW U.S.; ✳, Santa Fe; pop 1,819,046 — **New Mex·i·can** \-si-kən\ adj or n

New Neth·er·land \ˈne-thər-lənd\ former Dutch colony (1613–64) North America along Hudson & lower Delaware rivers

New Or·leans \ˈȯr-lē-ənz, ˈȯr-lənz, ˈȯrl-yənz, (ˌ)ȯr-ˈlēnz\ city SE Louisiana; pop 484,674

New·port \ˈnü-ˌpȯrt, ˈnyü-, -ˌpȯrt\ **1** town S England in Isle of Wight; pop 23,570 **2** city SE Wales; pop 129,900

Newport News \ˈnü-ˌpȯrt-ˈnüz, ˈnyü-ˌpȯrt-ˈnyüz, -pərt-\ city SE Virginia; pop 180,150

New Providence island NW cen Bahamas; chief town, Nassau; pop 210,832

New·ry \ˈnü-rē, ˈnyü-\ urban district S Northern Ireland

New South Wales state SE Australia; ✳, Sydney; pop 5,732,032

New Spain former Spanish possessions in North America, Central America, West Indies, & the Philippines

New Sweden former Swedish colony (1638–55) North America on W bank of Delaware River

New·town·ab·bey \ˌnü-tᵊn-ˈa-bē, ˌnyü-\ district E Northern Ireland; pop 73,832

Newtown Saint Bos·wells \ˈnü-ˌtau̇n-sənt-ˈbäz-wəlz, ˈnyü-, -ˌsänt-\ village S Scotland

New World the Western Hemisphere including North America and South America

New York 1 state NE U.S.; ✳, Albany; pop 18,976,457 **2** or **New York City** city SE New York (state); pop 8,008,278 — **New York·er** \ˈyȯr-kər\ n

New York State Barge Canal — see ERIE

New Zea·land \ˈzē-lənd\ country SW Pacific ESE of Australia; ✳, Wellington; pop 3,737,277 — **New Zea·land·er** \-lən-dər\ n

Ni·ag·a·ra Falls \(ˌ)nī-ˈa-g(ə-)rə\ falls New York & Ontario in **Niagara River** (flowing N from Lake Erie into Lake Ontario); divided by Goat Island into Horseshoe Falls, or Canadian Falls (158 ft. or 48 m. high) & American Falls (167 ft. or 51 m. high)

Nia·mey \nē-'ä-(ˌ)mā, nyä-'mā\ city, ✱ of Niger; *pop* 392,165

Ni·caea \nī-'sē-ə *or* **Nice** \'nīs\ ancient city W Bithynia; site at modern village in NW Turkey — **Ni·cae·an** \nī-'sē-ən\ *adj or n* — **Ni·cene** \'nī-ˌsēn, nī-'sēn\ *adj*

Ni·ca·ra·gua \ˌnī-kə-'rä-gwə, ˌnē-kä-'rä-gwä\ **1** lake about 100 mi. (160 km.) long S Nicaragua **2** country Central America; ✱, Managua; *pop* 4,265,000 — **Ni·ca·ra·guan** \-'rä-gwən-'rä-gwən\ *adj or n*

Nice \'nēs\ city & port SE France on the Mediterranean; *pop* 345,892

Nic·o·bar \'ni-kə-ˌbär\ islands India in Bay of Bengal S of the Andamans; *pop* 14,563

Nic·o·sia \ˌni-kə-'sē-ə\ city, ✱ of Cyprus; *pop* 206,200

Ni·ger \'nī-jər, nē-'zher\ **1** river 2600 mi. (4184 km.) long W Africa flowing into Gulf of Guinea **2** country W Africa N of Nigeria; ✱, Niamey; *pop* 8,516,000 — **Ni·ger·ien** \ˌnī-jir-ē-'en, nē-'zher-ē-ən\ *adj or n* — **Ni·ger·ois** \nē-zhər-'wä, -zher-\ *n*

Ni·ge·ria \nī-'jir-ē-ə\ country W Africa on Gulf of Guinea; ✱, Abuja; *pop* 88,514,501 — **Ni·ge·ri·an** \-ē-ən\ *adj or n*

Nii·hau \'nē-ˌhaú\ island Hawaii WSW of Kauai

Nile \'nī(-ə)l\ river 4160 mi. (6693 km.) long E Africa flowing from Lake Victoria in Uganda N into the Mediterranean in Egypt

Nil·gi·ri \'nil-gə-rē\ hills S India

Nin·e·veh \'ni-nə-və\ ancient city, ✱ of Assyria; ruins in Iraq on the Tigris

Nip·i·gon, Lake \'ni-pə-ˌgän\ lake Canada in W Ontario N of Lake Superior

Nizh·niy Nov·go·rod \'nizh-nē-'näv-gə-ˌräd, -'nóv-gə-rət\ *formerly 1932–89* **Gor·ki** \'gór-kē\ city W Russia; *pop* 1,433,000

Nord–Ost·see \'nórt-'óst-zä\ *or* **Kiel** \'kēl\ canal 61 mi. (98 km.) long N Germany across base of Jutland Peninsula connecting Baltic Sea & North Sea

Nor·folk \'nór-fək\ city & port SE Virginia; *pop* 234,403

Nor·man·dy \'nór-mən-dē\ region NW France NE of Brittany

North **1** river estuary of the Hudson between NE New Jersey & SE New York **2** sea, arm of the Atlantic E of Great Britain **3** island N New Zealand; *pop* 2,829,798

North·al·ler·ton \nór-'tha-lər-tən\ town N England; *pop* 9556

North America continent of Western Hemisphere NW of South America & N of the Equator — **North American** *adj or n*

North·amp·ton \nór-'tham(p)-tən, nórth-'ham(p)-\ town *cen* England; *pop* 145,421

North·amp·ton·shire \-ˌshir, -shər\ *or* **Northampton** county *cen* England

North Cape cape New Zealand at N end of North Island

North Car·o·li·na \ˌker(-ə)-'lī-nə, ˌka-rə-\ state E U.S.; ✱, Raleigh; *pop* 8,049,313 — **North Car·o·lin·ian** \-'li-nē-ən, -'li-nyən\ *adj or n*

North Da·ko·ta \də-'kō-tə\ state N U.S.; ✱, Bismarck; *pop* 642,200 — **North Da·ko·tan** \-'kō-tᵊn\ *adj or n*

North Down district E Northern Ireland; *pop* 70,308

Northern Cape province W Republic of South Africa; *pop* 749,000

Northern Cook islands S *cen* Pacific N of Cook Islands

Northern Hemisphere the half of the earth that lies N of the Equator

Northern Ireland region N Ireland comprising 26 districts of Ulster; a division of United Kingdom; ✱, Belfast; *pop* 1,685,267

Northern Mar·i·ana Islands \ˌmer-ē-'a-nə\ islands W Pacific; commonwealth in association with U.S.; ✱ on Saipan; *pop* 69,221

Northern Rhodesia — see ZAMBIA

Northern Territory territory N & *cen* Australia; ✱, Darwin; *pop* 169,300

North Korea *or* **Democratic People's Republic of Korea** country N half of Korean Peninsula in E Asia; ✱, Pyongyang; *pop* 22,646,000

North Las Vegas city SE Nevada; *pop* 115,448

North Slope region N Alaska between Brooks Range & Arctic Ocean

North·um·ber·land \nór-'thəm-bər-lənd\ county N England

North·um·bria \nór-'thəm-brē-ə\ ancient country Great Britain in what is now N England and S Scotland — **North·um·bri·an** \-brē-ən\ *adj or n*

North Vietnam — see VIETNAM

North West province N Republic of South Africa; *pop* 3,349,000

Northwest Passage sea passage between the Atlantic and the Pacific along the N coast of North America

Northwest Territories territory NW Canada consisting of the area of the mainland north of 60° between Yukon Territory & Nunavut; ✱, Yellowknife; *pop* 40,860

North York former city Canada in SE Ontario; now part of Toronto

North Yorkshire county N England

Nor·walk \'nór-ˌwók\ city SW California SE of Los Angeles; *pop* 103,298

Nor·way \'nór-ˌwä\ country N Europe in Scandinavia; ✱, Oslo; *pop* 4,552,200

Nor·wich \'nór-(ˌ)wich\ city E England; *pop* 120,700

Not·ting·ham \'nä-tiŋ-əm\ city N *cen* England; *pop* 261,500

Not·ting·ham·shire \'nä-tiŋ-əm-ˌshir, -shər\ *or* **Nottingham** county N *cen* England

Nouak·chott \nú-'äk-ˌshät\ city, ✱ of Mauritania; *pop* 393,325

Nou·méa \nü-'mā-ə\ city, ✱ of New Caledonia; *pop* 65,110

Nova Sco·tia \nō-və-'skō-shə\ province SE Canada; ✱, Halifax; *pop* 942,691 — **Nova Sco·tian** \-shən\ *adj or n*

No·vo·kuz·netsk \ˌnō-(ˌ)vō-kúz-'netsk, ˌnó-və-küz-'nyetsk\ city S Russia in Asia; *pop* 600,000

No·vo·si·birsk \ˌnō-(ˌ)vō-sə-'birsk, ˌnō-və-\ city S Russia in Asia; *pop* 1,442,000

Nu·bia \'nü-bē-ə, 'nyü-\ region NE Africa in Nile valley in S Egypt & N Sudan — **Nu·bi·an** \'nü-bē-ən, 'nyü-\ *adj or n*

Nu·ku·a·lo·fa \ˌnü-kü-ä-'lō-fä\ seaport, ✱ of Tonga; *pop* 22,400

Nu·mid·ia \nú-'mi-dē-ə, nyü-\ ancient country N Africa E of Mauretania in modern Algeria — **Nu·mid·i·an** \-dē-ən\ *adj or n*

Nu·na·vut \'nü-nə-ˌvüt\ semiautonomous territory NE Canada; ✱, Iqaluit; *pop* 28,159

Nu·rem·berg \'nùr-əm-ˌbərg, 'nyùr-\ *or German* **Nürnberg** \'nuern-ˌberk\ city S Germany; *pop* 497,496

Nuuk \'nük\ *or* **Godt·háb** \'gót-ˌhóp\ town, ✱ of Greenland on SW coast; *pop* 12,181

Ny·asa, Lake \nī-'as-ə, nē-\ lake SE Africa in Malawi, Mozambique, & Tanzania

Nyasaland — see MALAWI

Oa·hu \ō-'ä-(ˌ)hü\ island Hawaii; site of Honolulu

Oak·land \'ō-klənd\ city W California on San Francisco Bay E of San Francisco; *pop* 399,484

Ob' \'äb, 'ób\ river over 2250 mi. (3620 km.) long W Russia in Asia flowing NW & N into Arctic Ocean

Oce·a·nia \ˌō-shē-'a-nē-ə, -'ä-\ lands of the *cen* & S Pacific: Micronesia, Melanesia, Polynesia including New Zealand, & sometimes Australia & Malay Archipelago

Ocean·side \'ō-shən-ˌsīd\ city SW California NNW of San Diego; *pop* 161,029

Oder \'ō-dər\ *or* **Odra** \'ō-drə\ river about 565 mi. (909 km.) long *cen* Europe flowing from Silesia NW into Baltic Sea; forms part of boundary between Poland & Germany

Odes·sa \ō-'de-sə\ city & port S Ukraine on Black Sea; *pop* 1,101,000

Ohio \ō-'hī-(ˌ)ō, ə-, -ə\ **1** river about 981 mi. (1578 km.) long E U.S. flowing from W Pennsylvania into the Mississippi **2** state E *cen* U.S.; ✱, Columbus; *pop* 11,353,140 — **Ohio·an** \-'hī-ō-ən\ *adj or n*

Oka·ya·ma \ˌō-kä-'yä-mä\ city Japan in W Honshu on Inland Sea; *pop* 626,642

Okee·cho·bee, Lake \ˌō-kə-'chō-bē\ lake S *cen* Florida

Oke·fe·no·kee \ˌō-kə-fə-'nō-kē, ˌō-kē-\ swamp SE Georgia & NE Florida

Okhotsk, Sea of \ō-'kätsk, ə-'kótsk\ inlet of the North Pacific E Russia in Asia

Oki·na·wa \ˌō-kə-'nä-wə, -'naú-ə\ **1** islands Japan in *cen*

Ryukyus **2** island, chief of group — **Oki·na·wan** \-'nä-wən, -'naü-ən\ *adj or n*

Okla·ho·ma \ˌō-klə-'hō-mə\ state S *cen* U.S.; ✳, Oklahoma City; *pop* 3,450,654 — **Okla·ho·man** \-mən\ *adj or n*

Oklahoma City city, ✳ of Oklahoma; *pop* 506,132

Old·ham \'ōl-dəm\ city NW England; *pop* 211,400

Old Point Comfort cape SE Virginia N of entrance to Hampton Roads

Ol·du·vai Gorge \'ōl-də-ˌvī\ canyon N Tanzania SE of Serengeti Plain; site of fossil beds

Old World the half of the earth to the E of the Atlantic Ocean including Europe, Asia, and Africa & esp. the continent of Europe

Olym·pia \ə-'lim-pē-ə, ō-\ **1** city, ✳ of Washington; *pop* 42,514 **2** plain S Greece in NW Peloponnese

Olym·pic \-pik\ mountains NW Washington on Olympic Peninsula; highest Mt. Olympus 7965 ft. (2428 m.)

Olym·pus \ə-'lim-pəs, ō-\ mountains NE Greece

Omagh \'ō-mə, -(ˌ)mä\ **1** district W Northern Ireland; *pop* 45,343 **2** town in Omagh district; *pop* 17,280

Oma·ha \'ō-mə, -(ˌ)mä\ **1** beach NW France in Normandy **2** city E Nebraska on Missouri River; *pop* 390,007

Oman \ō-'män, -'man\ country SW Asia in SE Arabia; ✳, Masqat; *pop* 2,477,687 — **Omani** \ō-'mä-nē, -'ma-\ *adj or n*

Oman, Gulf of arm of Arabian Sea between Oman & SE Iran

Omsk \'ȯm(p)sk, 'äm(p)sk\ city SW Russia in Asia; *pop* 1,169,000

On·tar·io \än-'ter-ē-ˌō\ **1** city SW California; *pop* 158,007 **2** province E Canada; ✳, Toronto; *pop* 11,874,436 — **On·tar·i·an** \-ē-ən\ *adj or n*

Ontario, Lake lake E *cen* North America in U.S. & Canada; one of the Great Lakes

Oran \ȯ-'rän\ city & port NW Algeria; *pop* 628,558

Or·ange \'är-inj, 'är-(ə)nj, 'ȯr-inj, 'ȯr-(ə)nj\ **1** city SW California; *pop* 128,821 **2** river 1300 mi. (2092 km.) long S Africa flowing W from Drakensberg Mountains into the Atlantic

Orange Free State — see FREE STATE

Or·e·gon \'ȯr-i-gən, 'är-\ state NW U.S.; ✳, Salem; *pop* 3,421,399 — **Or·e·go·nian** \ˌȯr-i-'gō-nē-ən, ˌär-, -nyən\ *adj or n*

Oregon Trail pioneer route to the NW about 2000 mi. (3220 km.) long from Missouri to Washington

Ori·no·co \ˌȯr-ē-'nō-(ˌ)kō\ river 1336 mi. (2150 km.) long Venezuela flowing into the Atlantic

Ork·ney \'ȯrk-nē\ islands N Scotland; *pop* 19,570

Or·lan·do \ȯr-'lan-(ˌ)dō\ city *cen* Florida; *pop* 185,951

Osa·ka \ō-'sä-kä, 'ō-sä-ˌkä\ city Japan in S Honshu; *pop* 2,598,774

Osh·a·wa \'ä-shə-wə, -ˌwä, -ˌwȯ\ city SE Ontario, Canada on Lake Ontario ENE of Toronto; *pop* 139,051

Os·lo \'äz-(ˌ)lō, 'äs-\ city, ✳ of Norway; *pop* 507,831

Oś·wię·cim \ˌȯsh-'fyen-chēm\ *or German* **Ausch·witz** \'aüsh-ˌvits\ town S Poland W of Krakow; *pop* 45,282

Ot·ta·wa \'ä-tə-wə, -ˌwä, -ˌwȯ\ **1** river 696 mi. (1120 km.) E Canada in SE Ontario & S Quebec flowing E into the Saint Lawrence **2** city, ✳ of Canada in SE Ontario on Ottawa River; *pop* 774,072

Ot·to·man Empire \'ä-tə-mən\ former Turkish sultanate in SE Europe, W Asia, & N Africa

Oua·ga·dou·gou \ˌwä-gä-'dü-(ˌ)gü\ city, ✳ of Burkina Faso; *pop* 366,000

Outer Hebrides — see HEBRIDES

Over·land Park \'ō-vər-lənd\ city NE Kansas; *pop* 149,080

Ox·ford \'äks-fərd\ city *cen* England; *pop* 109,000

Ox·ford·shire \'äks-fərd-ˌshir, -shər\ *or* Oxford county *cen* England

Ox·nard \'äks-ˌnärd\ city SW California; *pop* 170,358

Ozark Plateau \'ō-ˌzärk\ *or* **Ozark Mountains** eroded plateau N Arkansas, S Missouri, & NE Oklahoma with E extension into S Illinois

Pa·cif·ic \pə-'si-fik\ ocean extending from Arctic Circle to the Equator (**North Pacific**) and from the Equator to the Antarctic regions (**South Pacific**) & from W North America & W South America to E Asia & Australia — **Pacific** *adj*

Pacific Islands, Trust Territory of the grouping of islands in W Pacific formerly under U.S. administration: the Carolines & the Marshalls

Pacific Rim the countries bordering on or located in the Pacific Ocean — used esp. of Asian countries on the Pacific

Pa·dang \'pä-ˌdäŋ\ city Indonesia in W Sumatra; *pop* 631,543

Pa·dre \'pä-drē, -drä\ island 113 mi. (182 km.) long S Texas in Gulf of Mexico

Pa·go Pa·go \ˌpä-(ˌ)gō-'pä-(ˌ)gō, ˌpäŋ-(ˌ)ō-'päŋ-(ˌ)ō\ town, ✳ of American Samoa on Tutuila Island; *pop* 4278

Painted Desert region N *cen* Arizona

Pak·i·stan \'pa-ki-ˌstan, ˌpä-ki-'stän\ country S Asia NW of India; ✳, Islamabad; *pop* 131,434,000 — see EAST PAKISTAN — **Pak·i·stani** \ˌpa-ki-'sta-nē, ˌpä-ki-'stä-\ *adj or n*

Pa·lau \pə-'laü\ *or* **Be·lau** \bə-\ island group W Pacific in the W Carolines in association with U.S.; country; ✳, Koror; *pop* 17,225 — **Pa·lau·an** \pə-'laü-ən\ *n*

Pa·la·wan \pə-'lä-wən, -ˌwän\ island W Philippines between South China & Sulu seas; *pop* 528,287

Pa·lem·bang \ˌpä-ləm-'bäŋ\ city Indonesia in SE Sumatra; *pop* 1,141,036

Pa·ler·mo \pə-'ler-(ˌ)mō, pä-'ler-\ city Italy, ✳ of Sicily; *pop* 679,290

Pal·es·tine \'pa-lə-ˌstīn\ **1** ancient region SW Asia bordering on E coast of the Mediterranean and extending E of Jordan River **2** region bordering on the Mediterranean on W and Dead Sea on E; now approximately coextensive with Israel & the West Bank — **Pal·es·tin·ian** \ˌpa-lə-'sti-nē-ən, -nyən\ *adj or n*

Pa·li·kir \ˌpä-lē-'kir\ town, ✳ of Federated States of Micronesia on Pohnpei Island; *pop* 6227

Pal·i·sades \ˌpa-lə-'sādz\ line of high cliffs 15 mi. (24 km.) long on W bank of the Hudson in SE New York & NE New Jersey

Palm·dale \'päm-ˌdāl, 'pälm-\ city SW California NE of Los Angeles; *pop* 116,670

Pa·mirs \pə-'mirz\ elevated mountainous region *cen* Asia in E Tajikistan & on borders of China, India, Pakistan, & Afghanistan; many peaks over 20,000 ft. (6096 m.)

Pam·li·co Sound \'pam-li-ˌkō\ inlet of the North Atlantic E North Carolina between main part of the state & offshore islands

Pam·pa \'pam-pə\ city NW Texas; *pop* 17,887

Pan·a·ma \'pan-ə-ˌmä, -ˌmȯ, ˌpan-ə-'mä, -'mȯ\ **1** country S Central America; *pop* 2,839,177 **2** *or* **Panama City** city, its ✳ on the Pacific; *pop* 411,549 **3** canal 40 mi. (64 km.) long Panama connecting Atlantic & Pacific oceans — **Pan·a·ma·ni·an** \ˌpan-ə-'mä-nē-ən\ *adj or n*

Panama, Isthmus of *formerly* **Isthmus of Dar·i·en** \ˌder-ē-'en\ strip of land *cen* Panama connecting North America & South America

Panama Canal Zone — see CANAL ZONE

Pa·nay \pə-'nī\ island *cen* Philippines

Pan·gaea \pan-'jē-ə\ hypothetical land area believed to have once connected the landmasses of the Southern Hemisphere with those of the Northern Hemisphere

Pan·mun·jom *or* **Pan·mun·jeom** \ˌpän-ˌmùn-'jəm\ village on North Korea–South Korea border

Pao–t'ou — see BAOTOU

Pap·ua, Territory of \'pa-pyü-wə, 'pä-pù-wə\ former British territory consisting of SE New Guinea & offshore islands; now part of Papua New Guinea

Papua New Guinea country SW Pacific combining former territories of Papua & New Guinea; ✳, Port Moresby; *pop* 5,190,736

Par·a·guay \'pa-rə-ˌgwī, -ˌgwä\ **1** river 1584 mi. (2549 km.) long *cen* South America flowing from Brazil S into the Paraná in Paraguay **2** country *cen* South America; ✳, Asunción; *pop* 4,643,000 — **Par·a·guay·an** \ˌpa-rə-'gwī-ən, -'gwä-\ *adj or n*

Par·a·mar·i·bo \ˌpa-rə-'ma-rə-ˌbō\ city, ✳ of Suriname; *pop* 200,000

Pa·ra·ná \ˌpär-ə-'nä\ river about 2500 mi. (4022 km.) long *cen* South America flowing S from Brazil into Argentina

Pa·ri·cu·tin \pä-ˌrē-kü-'tēn\ **1** former village Mexico **2** volcano on site of former village of Paricutin

Par·is \'pa-rəs\ city, ✳ of France; *pop* 2,125,851 — **Pa·ri·sian** \pə-'ri-zhən, -'rē-\ *adj or n*

Par·nas·sus \pär-'na-səs\ mountain *cen* Greece

Par·os \'pär-ˌós\ island Greece — **Par·i·an** \'par-ē-ən, 'per-\ *adj*

Par·ra·mat·ta \ˌpa-rə-'ma-tə\ city SE Australia in New South Wales NW of Sydney; *pop* 132,798

Par·thia \'pär-thē-ə\ ancient country SW Asia in NE modern Iran — **Par·thi·an** \-thē-ən\ *adj or n*

Pas·a·de·na \ˌpa-sə-'dē-nə\ **1** city SW California E of Glendale; *pop* 133,936 **2** city SE Texas; *pop* 141,674

Pat·a·go·nia \ˌpa-tə-'gō-nyə, -nē-ə\ region South America S of about 40° S latitude in S Argentina & S tip of Chile; sometimes thought to include Tierra del Fuego — **Pat·a·go·nian** \-nyən, -nē-ən\ *adj or n*

Pat·er·son \'pa-tər-sən\ city NE New Jersey; *pop* 149,222

Pat·mos \'pat-məs\ island Greece SSW of Samos

Pat·na \'pət-nə\ city NE India on the Ganges; *pop* 1,376,950

Pearl Harbor inlet Hawaii on S coast of Oahu W of Honolulu

Peking — see BEIJING

Pe·li·on \'pē-lē-ən\ mountain 5089 ft. (1551 m.) NE Greece

Pel·o·pon·nese \'pe-lə-pə-ˌnēz, -ˌnēs\ *or* **Pel·o·pon·ni·sos** \ˌpe-lə-pə-'nē-səs\ peninsula forming S part of mainland of Greece

Pem·broke Pines \'pem-ˌbrōk\ city SE Florida; *pop* 137,427

Pen·nine Chain \'pe-ˌnīn\ mountains N England; highest Cross Fell 2930 ft. (893 m.)

Penn·syl·va·nia \ˌpen(t)-səl-'vā-nyə, -nē-ə\ state E U.S.; ✳, Harrisburg; *pop* 12,281,054

Pe·o·ria \pē-'òr-ē-ə\ **1** town SW *cen* Arizona; *pop* 108,364 **2** city N *cen* Illinois; *pop* 112,936

Per·ga·mum \'pər-gə-məm\ *or* **Per·ga·mus** \-məs\ ancient Greek kingdom including most of Asia Minor

Perm \'pərm, 'perm\ city E Russia in Europe; *pop* 1,099,000

Pernambuco — see RECIFE

Persia — see IRAN

Per·sian Gulf \'pər-zhən\ arm of Arabian Sea between Iran & Arabia

Perth \'pərth\ city, ✳ of Western Australia; *pop* 80,517

Pe·ru \pə-'rü, pā-\ country W South America; ✳, Lima; *pop* 22,916,000 — **Pe·ru·vi·an** \-'rü-vē-ən\ *adj or n*

Pe·tra \'pē-trə, 'pe-\ ancient city NW Arabia; site in SW Jordan

Petrograd — see SAINT PETERSBURG

Phil·a·del·phia \ˌfi-lə-'del-fyə, -fē-ə\ city SE Pennsylvania; *pop* 1,517,550 — **Phil·a·del·phian** \-fyən, -fē-ən\ *adj or n*

Phil·ip·pines \ˌfi-lə-ˌpēnz, 'fi-lə-ˌpēnz\ island group approximately 500 mi. (805 km.) off SE coast of Asia; country; ✳, Manila; *pop* 64,954,000 — **Phil·ip·pine** \ˌfi-lə-ˌpēn, 'fi-lə-ˌ\ *adj*

Phnom Penh \(pə-)'näm-ˌpen, (pə-)'nóm-\ city, ✳ of Cambodia; *pop* 800,000

Phoe·ni·cia \fi-'ni-sh(ē-)ə, -'nē-\ ancient country SW Asia on the Mediterranean in modern Syria & Lebanon

Phoe·nix \'fē-niks\ city, ✳ of Arizona; *pop* 1,321,045

Phry·gia \'fri-j(ē-)ə\ ancient country W *cen* Asia Minor

Pic·ar·dy \'pi-kər-dē\ *or F* **Pi·car·die** \pē-kär-'dē\ region & former province N France bordering on English Channel N of Normandy — **Pi·card** \'pi-ˌkärd, -kərd\ *adj or n*

Pied·mont \'pēd-ˌmänt\ plateau region E U.S. E of the Appalachians between SE New York & NE Alabama

Pierre \'pir\ city, ✳ of South Dakota; *pop* 13,876

Pie·ter·mar·itz·burg \ˌpē-tər-'ma-rəts-ˌbərg\ city E Republic of South Africa; *pop* 128,598

Pigs, Bay of \'pigz\ *or* **Ba·hía de Co·chi·nos** \bä-'ē-ä-thä-kō-'chē-nōs\ bay W Cuba on S coast

Pikes Peak \'pīks\ mountain 14,110 ft. (4301 m.) E *cen* Colorado in a range of the Rockies

Pin·dus \'pin-dəs\ mountains W Greece; highest point 8136 ft. (2480 m.)

Pi·sa \'pē-zə, *It* -sä\ city W *cen* Italy W of Florence; *pop* 91,977

Pit·cairn \'pit-ˌkern\ island South Pacific; a British colony; *pop* less than 100

Pitts·burgh \'pits-ˌbərg\ city SW Pennsylvania; *pop* 334,563

Plac·id, Lake \'pla-səd\ lake NE New York

Pla·no \'plā-(ˌ)nō\ city NE Texas N of Dallas; *pop* 222,030

Plov·div \'plòv-ˌdif, -ˌdiv\ city S Bulgaria; *pop* 379,083

Plym·outh \'pli-məth\ **1** town SE Massachusetts; *pop* 51,701 **2** city & port SW England; *pop* 238,800

Po \'pō\ river 405 mi. (652 km.) N Italy flowing into the Adriatic

Po Hai — see BO HAI

Pohn·pei \'pón-ˌpā\ *or* **Po·na·pe** \'pō-nə-ˌpā\ island W Pacific in the E Carolines; part of Federated States of Micronesia

Po·land \'pō-lənd\ country *cen* Europe on Baltic Sea; ✳, Warsaw; *pop* 38,038,400 — **Pole** *n*

Pol·y·ne·sia \ˌpä-lə-'nē-zhə, -shə\ islands of the *cen* & S Pacific including Hawaii, the Line, Tonga, Cook, & Samoa islands, & often New Zealand among others

Pom·er·a·nia \ˌpä-mə-'rā-nē-ə, -nyə\ region N Europe on Baltic Sea; formerly in Germany, now mostly in Poland

Po·mo·na \pə-'mō-nə\ city SW California E of Los Angeles; *pop* 149,473

Pom·peii \päm-'pā, -'pā-ˌē\ ancient city S Italy SE of Naples destroyed 79 A.D. by eruption of Vesuvius — **Pom·pe·ian** \-'pā-ən\ *adj or n*

Pon·ce \'pón(t)-(ˌ)sā\ city S Puerto Rico; *pop* 186,475

Pon·do·land \'pän-(ˌ)dō-ˌland\ region S Republic of South Africa

Pon·ta Del·ga·da \ˌpón-tə-del-'gä-də\ city & port Portugal, largest in the Azores; *pop* 65,854

Pont·char·train, Lake \'pänt-shər-ˌträn, ˌpänt-shər-'\ lake SE Louisiana E of the Mississippi & N of New Orleans

Pon·tus \'pän-təs\ ancient country NE Asia Minor — **Pon·tic** \'pänt-ik\ *adj or n*

Poole \'pül\ town S England on English Channel; *pop* 130,900

Po·po·ca·te·petl \ˌpō-pə-'ka-tə-ˌpe-t°l, -ˌka-tə-'\ volcano 17,887 ft. (5452 m.) SE *cen* Mexico

Port Arthur — see LÜSHUN

Port–au–Prince \ˌpòrt-ō-'prin(t)s, ˌpòr-(t)ō-'praⁿs\ city, ✳ of Haiti; *pop* 752,600

Port Jack·son \'jak-sən\ inlet of South Pacific SE Australia in New South Wales; harbor of Sydney

Port·land \'pòrt-lənd\ **1** city SW Maine; largest in state; *pop* 64,249 **2** city NW Oregon; *pop* 529,121

Port Lou·is \'lü-əs, 'lü-ē\ city, ✳ of Mauritius; *pop* 146,876

Port Mores·by \'mòrz-bē\ city, ✳ of Papua New Guinea; *pop* 254,158

Por·to \'pòr-(ˌ)tü\ city & port NW Portugal; *pop* 310,600

Por·to Ale·gre \'pòr-(ˌ)tü-ä-'lā-grē\ city & port S Brazil; *pop* 1,360,590

Port of Spain city NW Trinidad, ✳ of Trinidad and Tobago; *pop* 49,031

Por·to–No·vo \ˌpòr-tō-'nō-(ˌ)vō\ city, ✳ of Benin; *pop* 192,000

Port Phil·lip Bay \'fi-ləp\ inlet of South Pacific SE Australia in Victoria; harbor of Melbourne

Port Said \sä-'ēd, 'sīd\ city & port NE Egypt on the Mediterranean at N end of the Suez Canal; *pop* 262,760

Ports·mouth \'pòrts-məth\ **1** city SE Virginia; *pop* 100,565 **2** city S England; *pop* 174,400

Por·tu·gal \'pòr-chi-gəl, 'pür-tü-'gäl\ country SW Europe; ✳, Lisbon; *pop* 10,356,117

Portuguese India former Portuguese possession on W coast of India; became part of India 1962

Port–Vi·la \pòrt-'vē-lə\ *or* **Vila**, city, ✳ of Vanuatu; *pop* 18,905

Po·to·mac \pə-'tō-mək, -mik\ river 287 mi. (462 km.) long flowing from West Virginia into Chesapeake Bay and forming boundary between Maryland & Virginia

Pough·keep·sie \pə-'kip-sē, pō-\ city & river port SE New York on the Hudson; *pop* 29,871

Po·wys \'pō-əs\ administrative subdivision E *cen* Wales

Prague \'präg\ *or Czech* **Pra·ha** \'prä-(ˌ)hä\ city, ✳ of Czech Republic; *pop* 1,162,179

Praia \'prī-ə\ town, ✳ of Cape Verde; *pop* 61,797

Prairie Provinces the Canadian provinces of Alberta, Manitoba, & Saskatchewan

Pres·ton \'pres-tən\ town NW England; *pop* 126,200

Pre·to·ria \pri-'tȯr-ē-ə\ city Republic of South Africa, administrative ✳ of the country; *pop* 303,684

Prib·i·lof \'pri-bə-ˌlȯf\ islands Alaska in Bering Sea

Prince Ed·ward Island \'ed-wərd\ island SE Canada in Gulf of Saint Lawrence; a province; ✳, Charlottetown; *pop* 138,514

Prince Ru·pert's Land \'rü-pərts\ historical region N & W Canada consisting of drainage basin of Hudson Bay

Prince·ton \'prin(t)-stən\ borough W *cen* New Jersey; *pop* 14,203

Prín·ci·pe \'prin(t)-si-pē\ island W Africa in Gulf of Guinea — see SÃO TOMÉ AND PRÍNCIPE

Pro·vence \prə-'vän(t)s, prō-'väⁿs\ region SE France on the Mediterranean

Prov·i·dence \'prä-və-dən(t)s, -ˌden(t)s\ city, ✳ of Rhode Island; *pop* 173,618

Pro·vo \'prō-(ˌ)vō\ city N *cen* Utah; *pop* 105,166

Prud·hoe Bay \'prü-(ˌ)dō, 'prə-\ inlet of Beaufort Sea N Alaska

Prus·sia \'prə-shə\ former kingdom, & later, state Germany — **Prus·sian** \'prə-shən\ *adj or n*

Pueb·lo \'pwe-ˌblō\ city SE *cen* Colorado SSE of Colorado Springs; *pop* 102,121

Puer·to Ri·co \ˌpȯr-tə-'rē-(ˌ)kō, ˌpwer-tō-\ island West Indies E of Hispaniola; a self-governing commonwealth associated with U.S.; ✳, San Juan; *pop* 3,808,610 — **Puer·to Ri·can** \'rē-kən\ *adj or n*

Pu·get Sound \'pyü-jət\ arm of the North Pacific W Washington

Pu·ne \'pü-nə\ city W India, ESE of Bombay; *pop* 2,540,069

Pun·jab \ˌpən-'jäb, -'jab, 'pən-\ region in Pakistan & NW India in valley of the Indus

Pu·san \'pü-ˌsän, 'bü-\ *or* **Bu·san** \'bü-\ city SE South Korea; *pop* 3,655,437

Pyong·yang \'pyȯŋ-'yaŋ, 'pyəŋ-, -'yäŋ\ city, ✳ of North Korea; *pop* 2,355,000

Pyr·e·nees \'pir-ə-ˌnēz\ mountains on French–Spanish border extending from Bay of Biscay to the Mediterranean; highest Pico de Aneto 11,168 ft. (3404 m.)

Qaraghandy — see KARAGANDA

Qa·tar \'kä-tər, 'gä-, 'gə-; kə-'tär\ country E Arabia on peninsula extending into Persian Gulf; ✳, Doha; *pop* 539,000 — **Qa·tari** \kə-'tär-ē, gə-\ *adj or n*

Qing·dao \'chiŋ-'dau̇\ *or* **Tsing·tao** \'chiŋ-'dau̇, '(t)siŋ-'dau̇\ city & port E China; *pop* 1,459,195

Qi·qi·har \'chē-'chē-'här\ *or* **Ch'i-ch'i-ha-erh** \'chē-'chē-'hä-'ər\ city NE China; *pop* 1,500,000

Que·bec \kwi-'bek, ki-\ *or French* **Qué·bec** \kā-'bek\ **1** province E Canada; *pop* 7,410,504 **2** city, its ✳, on the Saint Lawrence; *pop* 169,076

Queens \'kwēnz\ borough of New York City on Long Island E of Brooklyn; *pop* 2,229,379

Queens·land \'kwēnz-ˌland, -lənd\ state NE Australia; ✳, Brisbane; *pop* 3,116,200 — **Queens·land·er** \-ˌlan-dər, -ˌlən-\ *n*

Que·zon City \'kā-ˌsȯn\ city Philippines in Luzon; formerly ✳ of the country; *pop* 1,632,000

Qui·to \'kē-(ˌ)tō\ city, ✳ of Ecuador; *pop* 1,100,847

Ra·bat \rə-'bät\ city, ✳ of Morocco; *pop* 668,000

Rai·nier, Mount \rə-'nir, rā-\ mountain 14,410 ft. (4392 m.) W *cen* Washington; highest in Cascade Range

Raj·pu·ta·na \ˌräj-pə-'tä-nə\ *or* **Ra·ja·sthan** \'räj-ə-ˌstän\ region NW India S of Punjab

Ra·leigh \'rȯ-lē, 'rä-lē\ city, ✳ of North Carolina; *pop* 276,093

Ran·cho Cu·ca·mon·ga \'ran-(ˌ)chō-ˌkü-kə-'məŋ-gə, 'rän-, -'mäŋ-\ city SW California; *pop* 127,743

Rand — see WITWATERSRAND

Rand·wick \'ran-(ˌ)dwik\ municipality SE Australia in E New South Wales; *pop* 115,349

Rangoon — see YANGON

Ra·wal·pin·di \ˌrä-wəl-'pin-dē, ˌraul-'\ city NE Pakistan NNW of Lahore; *pop* 1,409,768

Read·ing \'re-diŋ\ town S England; *pop* 122,600

Re·ci·fe \ri-'sē-fē\ *formerly* **Per·nam·bu·co** \ˌpər-nəm-'bü-(ˌ)kō, -'byü-\ city NE Brazil; *pop* 1,422,905

Red \'red\ **1** river 1018 mi. (1638 km.) long flowing E on Oklahoma–Texas boundary and into the Atchafalaya & the Mississippi in Louisiana **2** sea between Arabia & NE Africa

Red·bridge \'red-(ˌ)brij\ borough of NE Greater London, England; *pop* 220,600

Re·gi·na \ri-'jī-nə\ city, ✳ of Saskatchewan, Canada; *pop* 178,225

Re·no \'rē-(ˌ)nō\ city NW Nevada; *pop* 180,480

Republic of the Congo — see CONGO 3

Ré·union \rē-'yü-nyən, ˌrā-ᵫ-'nyōⁿ\ island W Indian Ocean; an overseas division of France; ✳, Saint-Denis; *pop* 634,000

Reyk·ja·vik \'rā-kyə-ˌvik, -ˌvēk\ city, ✳ of Iceland; *pop* 112,490

Rhine \'rīn\ river 820 mi. (1320 km.) long W Europe flowing from SE Switzerland to North Sea in the Netherlands — **Rhen·ish** \'re-nish, 'rē-\ *adj*

Rhine·land \'rīn-ˌland, -lənd\ *or German* **Rhein·land** \'rīn-ˌlänt\ the part of Germany W of the Rhine — **Rhine·land·er** \'rīn-ˌlan-dər, -lən-\ *n*

Rhode Is·land \rōd-'ī-lənd\ **1** *or officially* **Rhode Island and Providence Plantations** state NE U.S.; ✳, Providence; *pop* 1,048,319 **2** — see AQUIDNECK — **Rhode Is·land·er** \-lən-dər\ *n*

Rhodes \'rōdz\ island Greece in the SE Aegean

Rho·de·sia \rō-'dē-zh(ē-)ə\ — see ZIMBABWE — **Rho·de·sian** \-zh(ē-)ən\ *adj or n*

Rhone *or French* **Rhône** \'rōn\ river 505 mi. (813 km.) long Switzerland & SE France

Rich·mond \'rich-mənd\ **1** — see STATEN ISLAND **2** city, ✳ of Virginia; *pop* 197,790

Richmond upon Thames borough of SW Greater London, England; *pop* 154,600

Ri·ga \'rē-gə\ city, ✳ of Latvia; *pop* 747,157

Rio de Ja·nei·ro \'rē-(ˌ)ō-dā-zhə-'ner-(ˌ)ō, -dē-\ city SE Brazil on Guanabara Bay; *pop* 5,857,904

Rio Grande \ˌrē-(ˌ)ō-'grand, -'gran-dē\ *or Mexican* **Rio Bra·vo** \ˌrē-(ˌ)ō-'brä-(ˌ)vō\ river 1885 mi. (3034 km.) long SW U.S. forming part of U.S.–Mexico boundary and flowing into Gulf of Mexico

Río Muni — see MBINI

Riv·er·side \'ri-vər-ˌsīd\ city S California; *pop* 255,166

Riv·i·era \ˌri-vē-'er-ə\ coast region SE France & NW Italy

Ri·yadh \rē-'yäd\ city, ✳ of Saudi Arabia; *pop* 4,700,000

Ro·a·noke \'rō-(ə-)ˌnōk\ city W Virginia; *pop* 94,911

Roanoke Island island North Carolina S of entrance to Albemarle Sound

Rob·son, Mount \'räb-sən\ mountain 12,972 ft. (3954 m.) W Canada in E British Columbia; highest in the Canadian Rockies

Roch·es·ter \'rä-chəs-tər, -ˌches-tər\ city W New York; *pop* 219,773

Rock·ford \'räk-fərd\ city N Illinois; *pop* 150,115

Rocky Mountains *or* **Rock·ies** \'rä-kēz\ mountains W North America extending SE from N Alaska to *cen* New Mexico

Roman Empire the empire of ancient Rome

Ro·ma·nia \rú-'mä-nē-ə, rō-, -nyə\ *or* **Ru·ma·nia** \rú-\ country SE Europe on Black Sea; ✳, Bucharest; *pop* 21,698,181

Rom·blon \räm-'blōn\ island group *cen* Philippines

Rome \'rōm\ *or Italian* **Ro·ma** \'rō-mä\ city, ✳ of Italy; *pop* 2,655,970

Ro·sa·rio \rō-'zär-ē-ˌō, -'sär-\ city E *cen* Argentina on the Paraná; *pop* 591,428

Ro·seau \rō-'zō\ seaport, ✳ of Dominica; *pop* 14,847

Ros·tov–on–Don \rə-'stȯf-ˌän-'dän, -'stȯv-, -ȯn-\ city S Russia in Europe; *pop* 1,027,000

Ros·well \'räz-ˌwel, -wəl\ city SE New Mexico; *pop* 45,293

Ro·ta \'rō-tə\ island W Pacific in the Marianas

Rot·ter·dam \'rä-tər-ˌdam, -ˌdäm\ city & port SW Netherlands; *pop* 598,660

Ru·an·da–Urun·di \rü-ˌän-dä-ü-'rün-dē\ former trust territory E *cen* Africa bordering on Lake Tanganyika; now divided into Burundi & Rwanda

Rudolf, Lake — see TURKANA, LAKE

Ruhr \'rur\ **1** river 146 mi. (235 km.) long W Germany flowing NW & W to the Rhine **2** industrial district W Germany E of the Rhine in valley of Ruhr River

Rumania — see ROMANIA

Rupert's Land PRINCE RUPERT'S LAND
Rush·more, Mount \'rəsh-ˌmȯr\ mountain 5600 ft. (1707 m.) W South Dakota in Black Hills
Rus·sia \'rə-shə\ **1** former empire largely having the same boundaries as U.S.S.R. **2** UNION OF SOVIET SOCIALIST REPUBLICS **3** country E Europe & N Asia; ✳, Moscow; *pop* 148,000,000
Ru·the·nia \rü-'thē-nyə, -nē-ə\ region W Ukraine W of the N Carpathians — **Ru·the·nian** \-'thē-nyən, -nē-ən\ *adj or n*
Ru·wen·zo·ri \ˌrü-ən-'zȯr-ē\ mountain group E *cen* Africa between Uganda & Democratic Republic of the Congo; highest Mount Margherita 16,763 ft. (5109 m.)
Rwan·da *formerly* **Ru·an·da** \rü-'än-dä\ country E *cen* Africa; ✳, Kigali; *pop* 7,584,000 — **Rwan·dan** \-dən\ *adj or n*
Ryu·kyu \rē-'yü-(ˌ)kyü, -(ˌ)kü\ islands Japan extending in an arc from S Japan, to N tip of Taiwan; *pop* 1,222,458 — **Ryu·kyu·an** \-ˌkyü-ən, -ˌkü-\ *adj or n*
Saar \'sär, 'zär\ **1** river about 150 mi. (241 km.) long Europe flowing from E France to W Germany **2** or **Saar·land** \'sär-ˌland, 'zär-\ region W Europe in valley of Saar River between France & Germany
Sac·ra·men·to \ˌsa-krə-'men-(ˌ)tō\ **1** river 382 mi. (615 km.) long N California flowing S into Suisun Bay **2** city, ✳ of California; *pop* 407,018
Sag·ue·nay \'sa-gə-ˌnā, ˌsa-gə-'\ river 105 mi. (169 km.) long Canada in S Quebec flowing E into the Saint Lawrence
Sa·ha·ra \sə-'her-ə, -'här-\ desert region N Africa extending from Atlantic coast to Red Sea — **Sa·ha·ran** \-ən\ *adj*
Sa·hel \'sa-hil, sə-'hil\ the S fringe of the Sahara
Saigon — see HO CHI MINH CITY
Saint Al·bans \'ȯl-bənz\ city SE England; *pop* 122,400
Saint Cath·a·rines \'ka-th(ə-)rənz\ city Canada in SE Ontario; *pop* 129,170
Saint Christopher — see SAINT KITTS
Saint Clair, Lake \'kler\ lake SE Michigan & SE Ontario connected by **Saint Clair River** (40 mi. or 64 km. long) with Lake Huron & draining by Detroit River into Lake Erie
Saint Croix \sānt-'krȯi, sənt-\ **1** river 129 mi. (208 km.) long Canada & U.S. on border between New Brunswick & Maine **2** island West Indies; largest of Virgin Islands of the U.S.; *pop* 50,139
Saint Eli·as, Mount \i-'lī-əs\ mountain 18,008 ft. (5489 m.) on Alaska–Canada boundary in **Saint Elias Range**
Saint George's \'jȯr-jəz\ town, ✳ of Grenada; *pop* 29,400
Saint George's Channel channel British Isles between SW Wales & Ireland
Saint Gott·hard \sānt-'gä-tərd, sənt-, 'gät-hərd\ pass S *cen* Switzerland in Saint Gotthard Range of the Alps
Saint He·le·na \ˌsānt-ə-'lē-nə, ˌsānt-hə-'lē-\ island South Atlantic; a British colony; *pop* 5644
Saint Hel·ens, Mount \sānt-'he-lənz, sənt-\ volcano S Washington
Saint John \sānt-'jän, sənt-\ city & port Canada in New Brunswick; *pop* 69,661
Saint John's \sānt-'jänz, sənt-\ **1** city, ✳ of Antigua and Barbuda; *pop* 22,342 **2** city, ✳ of Newfoundland and Labrador, Canada; *pop* 99,182
Saint Kitts \'kits\ or **Saint Chris·to·pher** \'kris-tə-fər\ island West Indies in the Leeward Islands; with Nevis forms independent **Saint Kitts–Nevis**; ✳, Basseterre (on Saint Kitts); *pop* 41,800
Saint Law·rence \sānt-'lȯr-ən(t)s, sənt-, -'lär-\ **1** river 760 mi. (1223 km.) long E Canada in Ontario & Quebec bordering on U.S. in New York and flowing from Lake Ontario NE into the **Gulf of Saint Lawrence** (inlet of the Atlantic) **2** seaway Canada & U.S. in and along the Saint Lawrence between Lake Ontario & Montreal
Saint Lou·is \sānt-'lü-əs, sənt-\ city E Missouri on the Mississippi; *pop* 348,189
Saint Lu·cia \sānt-'lü-shə, sənt-\ island West Indies in the Windwards S of Martinique; country; ✳, Castries; *pop* 157,775
Saint Mo·ritz \ˌsānt-mə-'rits, ˌsaⁿ-mə-\ or G **Sankt Mo·ritz** \ˌzäŋkt-mə-'rits\ town E Switzerland; *pop* 5900
Saint Paul \'pȯl\ city, ✳ of Minnesota; *pop* 287,151

Saint Pe·ters·burg \'pē-tərz-ˌbərg\ **1** city W Florida; *pop* 248,232 **2** *formerly 1914–24* **Pet·ro·grad** \'pe-trə-ˌgrad, -ˌgrät\ *or 1924–91* **Le·nin·grad** \'le-nən-ˌgrad, -ˌgrät\ city W Russia in Europe; *pop* 4,952,000
Saint Thom·as \'tä-məs\ island West Indies, one of Virgin Islands of the U.S.; chief town, Charlotte Amalie
Saint Vin·cent \sānt-'vin(t)-sənt, sənt-\ island West Indies in the *cen* Windward Islands; with N Grenadines forms independent **Saint Vincent and the Grenadines**; ✳, Kingstown (on Saint Vincent); *pop* 109,000
Sai·pan \sī-'pan, -'pän, 'sī-ˌ\ island W Pacific in S *cen* Marianas; *pop* 38,896
Sa·kai \(ˌ)sä-'kī\ city Japan in S Honshu; *pop* 792,018
Sa·kha·lin \'sa-kə-ˌlēn, -lən; ˌsä-kä-'lēn\ island SE Russia in W Pacific N of Hokkaido, Japan
Sal·a·mis \'sa-lə-məs\ ancient city Cyprus on E coast
Sa·lem \'sā-ləm\ city, ✳ of Oregon; *pop* 136,924
Sa·li·nas \sə-'lē-nəs\ city W California; *pop* 151,060
Salisbury — see HARARE
Salisbury Plain plateau S England; site of Stonehenge
Salop — see SHROPSHIRE
Salt Lake City city, ✳ of Utah; *pop* 181,743
Sal·ton Sea \'sȯl-tᵊn\ saline lake about 235 ft. (72 m.) below sea level SE California; formed by diversion of water from Colorado River
Sal·va·dor \'sal-və-ˌdȯr, ˌsal-və-'\ or **Ba·hia** \bä-'ē-ə\ city NE Brazil on the Atlantic; *pop* 2,443,107 — **Sal·va·dor·an** \ˌsal-və-'dȯr-ən\ or **Sal·va·dor·ean** or **Sal·va·dor·ian** \-ē-ən\ *adj or n*
Sal·ween \'sal-ˌwēn\ river about 1500 mi. (2415 km.) long SE Asia flowing from Tibet S into Bay of Bengal in Myanmar
Sa·mar \'sä-ˌmär\ island *cen* Philippines
Sa·ma·ra \sə-'mär-ə\ or *1935–91* **Kuy·by·shev** \'kwē-bə-ˌshef, 'kü-ē-bə-, -ˌshev\ city W Russia, on the Volga; *pop* 1,239,000
Sa·mar·ia \sə-'mer-ē-ə\ district of ancient Palestine W of the Jordan between Galilee & Judaea
Sam·ar·qand or **Sam·ar·kand** \'sa-mər-ˌkand\ city E Uzbekistan; *pop* 370,500
Sam·ni·um \'sam-nē-əm\ ancient country S *cen* Italy — **Sam·nite** \'sam-ˌnīt\ *adj or n*
Sa·moa \sə-'mō-ə\ **1** islands SW *cen* Pacific N of Tonga; divided at longitude 171° W into American Samoa (or Eastern Samoa) & independent Samoa **2** *formerly* **Western Samoa** islands Samoa W of 171° W; country; ✳ Apia; *pop* 156,349 — **Sa·mo·an** \sə-'mō-ən\ *adj or n*
Sa·mos \'sā-ˌmäs, 'sä-ˌmȯs\ island Greece in the Aegean off coast of Turkey
San·aa or **Sana** \sa-'nä, 'sa-ˌnä\ city SW Arabia, ✳ of Yemen; *pop* 125,093
San An·dre·as Fault \ˌsan-an-'drā-əs\ zone of faults in California extending from N coast toward head of Gulf of California
San An·to·nio \ˌsan-ən-'tō-nē-ˌō\ city S Texas; *pop* 1,144,646
San Ber·nar·di·no \ˌsan-ˌbər-nə(r)-'dē-(ˌ)nō\ city S California; *pop* 185,401
San Di·ego \ˌsan-dē-'ā-(ˌ)gō\ coastal city SW California; *pop* 1,223,400
San·i·bel Island \'sa-nə-bəl, -ˌbel\ island SW Florida
Sand·wich \'san(d)-(ˌ)wich\ town SE England; *pop* 4227
Sandwich Islands — see HAWAII
San Fran·cis·co \ˌsan-frən-'sis-(ˌ)kō\ city W California on San Francisco Bay & Pacific Ocean; *pop* 776,733
San Joa·quin \ˌsan-wä-'kēn, -wȯ-\ river 350 mi. (563 km.) long *cen* California flowing NW into the Sacramento
San Jo·se \ˌsan-(h)ō-'zā\ city W California SE of San Francisco; *pop* 894,943
San Jo·sé \ˌsän-hō-'sä, ˌsan-(h)ō-'zā\ city, ✳ of Costa Rica; *pop* 330,529
San Juan \san-'wän, ˌsän-'hwän\ city, ✳ of Puerto Rico; *pop* 434,374
San Ma·ri·no \ˌsan-mə-'rē-(ˌ)nō\ **1** small country S Europe surrounded by Italy ENE of Florence near Adriatic Sea; *pop* 24,000 **2** town, its ✳; *pop* 2300 — **Sam·mar·i·nese** \ˌsa(m)-ˌma-rə-'nēz, -'nēs\ *n* — **San Mar·i·nese** \ˌsan-ˌma-\ *adj or n*

San Pe·dro Su·la \san-'pā-(ˌ)thrō-'sü-lä\ city NW Honduras; *pop* 300,400

San Sal·va·dor \san-'sal-və-ˌdòr, ˌsän-'säl-vä-ˌthòr\ **1** island *cen* Bahamas **2** city, ✳ of El Salvador; *pop* 349,333

San·ta Ana \ˌsan-tə-'a-nə, ˌsän-tä-'ä-nä\ city SW California ESE of Long Beach; *pop* 337,977

San·ta Bar·ba·ra \'bär-b(ə-)rə\ *or* **Channel** islands California off SW coast in the North Pacific

Santa Clara \'kler-ə\ city W California NW of San Jose; *pop* 102,361

Santa Cla·ri·ta \klə-'rē-tə\ city S California N of Los Angeles; *pop* 151,088

San·ta Fe \ˌsan-tə-'fā\ city, ✳ of New Mexico; *pop* 62,203

Santa Fe Trail pioneer route to the SW U.S. about 1200 mi. (1930 km.) long used esp. 1821–80 from vicinity of Kansas City, Missouri, to Santa Fe, New Mexico

Santa Rosa \ˌsan-tə-'rō-zə\ city W California N of San Francisco; *pop* 147,595

San·ti·a·go \ˌsan-tē-'ä-(ˌ)gō, ˌsän-\ city, ✳ of Chile; *pop* 200,792

San·to Do·min·go \ˌsan-tə-də-'miṇ-(ˌ)gō\ *formerly* **Tru·ji·llo** \trü-'hē-(ˌ)yō\ city, ✳ of Dominican Republic; metropolitan area *pop* 2,677,056

São Pau·lo \saúⁿ-'paú-(ˌ)lü, -(ˌ)lō\ city SE Brazil; *pop* 10,434,252

São To·mé \ˌsaúⁿ-tə-'mā\ town, ✳ of São Tomé and Príncipe; *pop* 43,420

São Tomé and Príncipe country W Africa; ✳ São Tomé; *pop* 128,000

Sap·po·ro \'sä-pō-ˌrō; sä-'pòr-(ˌ)ō\ city Japan on W Hokkaido; *pop* 1,822,368

Sa·ra·je·vo \ˌsa-rə-'yä-(ˌ)vō, ˌsär-ə-\ city SE *cen* Bosnia and Herzegovina, its ✳; *pop* (est.) 602,500

Sa·ra·tov \sə-'rä-təf\ city W Russia, on the Volga; *pop* 909,000

Sar·din·ia \sär-'di-nē-ə, -'di-nyə\ island Italy in the Mediterranean S of Corsica; *pop* 1,648,044 — **Sar·din·ian** \sär-'di-nē-ən, -'din-yən\ *adj or n*

Sar·gas·so Sea \sär-'ga-(ˌ)sō\ area of nearly still water in the North Atlantic lying chiefly between 20° & 35° N latitude & 30° & 70° W longitude

Sas·katch·e·wan \sə-'ska-chə-wən, sa-, -ˌwän\ province W Canada; ✳, Regina; *pop* 1,015,783

Sas·ka·toon \ˌsas-kə-'tün\ city *cen* Saskatchewan, Canada; *pop* 196,811

Sau·di Ara·bia \'saú-dē, 'sò-dē, sä-'ü-dē\ country SW Asia occupying largest part of Arabian Peninsula; ✳, Riyadh; *pop* 20,800,000 — **Saudi** *adj or n* — **Saudi Arabian** *adj or n*

Sault Sainte Ma·rie Canals \'sü-(ˌ)sänt-mə-'rē\ *or* **Soo Canals** \ˌsü\ three ship canals, two in U.S. (Michigan) & one in Canada (Ontario), at rapids in river connecting Lake Superior & Lake Huron

Sa·vaii \sə-'vī-ˌē\ island, largest in independent Samoa

Sa·van·nah \sə-'va-nə\ city & port E Georgia; *pop* 131,510

Sa·voy \sə-'vòi\ *or French* **Sa·voie** \sä-'vwä\ region SE France SW of Switzerland bordering on Italy — **Sa·voy·ard** \sə-'vòi-ˌärd, sa-'vòi-ˌärd, ˌsa-ˌvwä-'yär(d)\ *adj or n*

Sca·fell Pike \ˌskò-'fell\ mountain 3210 ft. (978 m.) NW England; highest in Cumbrian Mountains & in England

Scan·di·na·via \ˌskan-də-'nā-vē-ə, -vyə\ **1** peninsula N Europe occupied by Norway & Sweden **2** Denmark, Norway, Sweden, & sometimes also Iceland & Finland — **Scan·di·na·vian** \ˌskan-də-'nā-vē-ən, -vyən\ *adj or n*

Scar·bor·ough \'skär-ˌbər-ō\ former city Canada in SE Ontario; now part of Toronto

Schel·de \'skel-də\ *or* **Scheldt** \'skelt\ river 270 mi. (434 km.) long W Europe flowing from N France through Belgium into North Sea in Netherlands

Schuyl·kill \'skü-kᵊl, 'skül-ˌkil\ river 131 mi. (211 km.) long SE Pennsylvania flowing SE into the Delaware River at Philadelphia

Scil·ly, Isles of \'si-lē\ island group SW England off Land's End; *pop* 2900

Sco·tia \'skō-shə\ SCOTLAND — the Medieval Latin name

Scot·land \'skät-lənd\ *or Latin* **Cal·e·do·nia** \ˌka-lə-'dō-nyə, -nē-ə\ country N Great Britain; a division of United Kingdom; ✳, Edinburgh; *pop* 5,062,011

Scotts·dale \'skäts-ˌdāl\ city SW *cen* Arizona E of Phoenix; *pop* 202,705

Scyth·ia \'si-thē-ə, -thē-\ ancient area of Europe & Asia N & NE of Black Sea & E of Aral Sea — **Scyth·i·an** \'si-thē-ən, -ˌthē-\ *adj or n*

Se·at·tle \sē-'a-tᵊl\ city & port W Washington; *pop* 563,374

Seine \'sān, 'sen\ river 480 mi. (772 km.) long N France flowing NW into English Channel

Sel·kirk \'sel-ˌkərk\ range of the Rocky Mountains SE British Columbia, Canada; highest peak, 11,555 ft. (3522 m.)

Se·ma·rang \sə-'mär-ˌäṇ\ city Indonesia in *cen* Java; *pop* 1,250,971

Sen·dai \(ˌ)sen-'dī\ city Japan in NE Honshu; *pop* 1,008,130

Sen·e·ca Falls \'se-ni-kə\ village W *cen* New York; *pop* 6861

Sen·e·gal \ˌse-ni-'gòl, -'gäl, 'se-ni-ˌ\ **1** river 1015 mi. (1633 km.) long W Africa flowing W into the North Atlantic **2** country W Africa; ✳, Dakar; *pop* 7,899,000 — **Sen·e·ga·lese** \ˌse-ni-gə-'lēz, -'lēs\ *adj or n*

Seoul \'sōl\ city, ✳ of South Korea; *pop* 9,853,972

Ser·bia \'sər-bē-ə\ region in the Balkans comprising a federated republic of Serbia and Montenegro; *pop* 9,823,000

Serbia and Montenegro *formerly* **Yugoslavia** country S Europe on Balkan Peninsula; ✳, Belgrade; *pop* 10,561,000

Ser·en·ge·ti Plain \ˌser-ən-'ge-tē\ area N Tanzania

Seven Hills the seven hills upon and about which was built the city of Rome, Italy

Sev·ern \'se-vərn\ river 210 mi. (338 km.) long Wales & England flowing from E *cen* Wales into Bristol Channel

Se·ville \sə-'vil\ *or Spanish* **Se·vi·lla** \sā-'vē-(ˌ)yä\ city SW Spain; *pop* 684,633

Sew·ard Peninsula \'sü-ərd\ peninsula 180 mi. (290 km.) long W Alaska projecting into Bering Sea

Sey·chelles \sā-'shel(z)\ islands W Indian Ocean NE of Madagascar; country; ✳, Victoria; *pop* 72,700 — **Sey·chel·lois** \ˌsā-shəl-'wä, -ˌshel-\ *n*

Shang·hai \shaṇ-'hī\ municipality & port E China; *pop* 7,469,509

Shan·non \'sha-nən\ river 230 mi. (370 km.) long W Ireland flowing S & W into the North Atlantic

Sharon, Plain of \'sher-ən\ region Israel on the coast

Shas·ta, Mount \'shas-tə\ mountain 14,162 ft. (4316 m.) N California in Cascade Range

Shatt al Ar·ab \ˌshat-al-'a-rəb\ river 120 mi. (193 km.) long SE Iraq formed by flowing together of Euphrates & Tigris rivers and flowing SE into Persian Gulf

Shef·field \'she-ˌfēld\ city N England; *pop* 499,700

Shen·an·do·ah \ˌshe-nən-'dō-ə, ˌsha-nə-'dō-ə\ valley Virginia between the Allegheny & Blue Ridge mountains

Shen·yang \'shən-'yäṇ\ *or traditionally* **Muk·den** \'múk-dən, 'mək-; múk-'den\ city NE China; chief city of Manchuria; *pop* 3,603,712

Sher·brooke \'shər-ˌbrúk\ city Quebec, Canada E of Montreal; *pop* 75,916

Sher·wood Forest \'shər-ˌwúd\ ancient royal forest *cen* England

Shet·land \'shet-lənd\ islands N Scotland NE of the Orkneys; *pop* 22,270

Shi·jia·zhuang *or* **Shih–chia–chuang** \'shir-'jyä-'jwäṇ, 'shē-\ city NE China; *pop* 1,068,439

Shi·ko·ku \shē-'kō-(ˌ)kü\ island S Japan E of Kyushu; *pop* 4,195,106

Shi·raz \shi-'räz, -'raz\ city SW *cen* Iran; *pop* 848,289

Shreve·port \'shrēv-ˌpòrt\ city NW Louisiana on Red River; *pop* 200,145

Shrews·bury \'sh(r)üz-ˌber-ē, -b(ə-)rē\ town W England; *pop* 31,640

Shrop·shire \'shräp-shər, -ˌshir\ *or 1974–80* **Sal·op** \'sal-əp\ county W England bordering on Wales

Shu·ma·gin \'shü-mə-gən\ islands SW Alaska S of Alaska Peninsula

Siam — see THAILAND

Siam, Gulf of — see THAILAND, GULF OF

Si·be·ria \sī-'bir-ē-ə\ region N Asia in Russia between the Urals & the North Pacific — **Si·be·ri·an** \-ən\ *adj or n*

Sic·i·ly \'si-s(ə-)lē\ *or Italian* **Si·ci·lia** \sē-'chēl-yä\ island S

Italy SW of toe of peninsula of Italy; ✳, Palermo; *pop* 5,076,700 — **Si·cil·ian** \sə-'sil-yən\ *adj or n*

Si·er·ra Le·one \sē-,er-ə-lē-'ōn, ,sir-ə-, -lē-'ō-nē\ country W Africa on the North Atlantic; ✳, Freetown; *pop* 4,491,000 — **Si·er·ra Le·on·ean** \-'ō-nē-ən\ *adj or n*

Si·er·ra Ma·dre \sē-,er-ə-'mä-drā, 'syer-ä-'mä-thrā\ mountain system Mexico including **Sierra Madre Oc·ci·den·tal** \,äk-sə-,den-'täl, ,ōk-sē-,then-'täl\ range W of the *cen* plateau, **Sierra Madre Ori·en·tal** \,ór-ē-,en-'täl\ range E of the plateau, & **Sierra del Sur** \'sùr, 'sür\ range to the S

Sierra Ne·va·da \nə-'va-də, -'vä-\ **1** mountain range E California & W Nevada — see WHITNEY, MOUNT **2** mountain range S Spain

Sik·kim \'si-kəm, -,kim\ former country SE Asia on S slope of the Himalayas between Nepal & Bhutan; part of India (country); *pop* 406,457

Si·le·sia \sī-'lē-zh(ē-)ə, sə-, -sh(ē-)ə\ region E *cen* Europe in valley of the upper Oder; formerly chiefly in Germany now chiefly in E Czech Republic & SW Poland — **Si·le·sian** \-zh(ē-)ən, -sh(ē-)ən\ *adj or n*

Silk Road *or* **Silk Route** ancient trade route that extended from China to the Mediterranean

Sim·coe, Lake \'sim-(,)kō\ lake Canada in SE Ontario

Si·mi Valley \sē-'mē\ city SW California W of Los Angeles; *pop* 111,351

Sim·plon Pass \'sim-,plän\ mountain pass 6590 ft. (2009 m.) between Switzerland & Italy

Si·nai \'sī-,nī\ **1** mountain on Sinai Peninsula where according to the Bible the Law was given to Moses **2** peninsula extension of continent of Asia NE Egypt between Red Sea & the Mediterranean

Sin·ga·pore \'siŋ-ə-,pór\ **1** island off S end of Malay Peninsula; country; *pop* 4,163,700 **2** city, its ✳; *pop* 206,500 — **Sin·ga·por·ean** \,siŋ-ə-'pór-ē-ən\ *adj or n*

Sinkiang Uighur — see XINJIANG UYGUR

Sioux Falls \'sü\ city SE South Dakota; largest in state; *pop* 123,975

Skag·ge·rak \'ska-gə-,rak\ arm of North Sea between S Norway & N Denmark

Skop·je \'skó-pye, -pyə\ city, ✳ of independent Macedonia; *pop* 563,301

Sla·vo·nia \slə-'vō-nē-ə, -nyə\ region E Croatia — **Sla·vo·ni·an** \-nē-ən, -nyən\ *adj or n*

Slo·va·kia \slō-'vä-kē-ə, -'va-\ country *cen* Europe; ✳, Bratislava; *pop* 5,379,455

Slo·ve·nia \slō-'vē-nē-ə, -nyə\ country S Europe; ✳, Ljubljana; *pop* 1,975,164

Smyrna — see IZMIR

Snake \'snāk\ river NW U.S. flowing from NW Wyoming into the Columbia in SE Washington

Snow·don \'snō-dᵊn\ massif 3560 ft. (1085 m.) in **Snow·do·nia** \snō-'dō-nē-ə, -nyə\ (mountainous district) NW Wales; highest point in Wales

So·ci·e·ty \sə-'sī-ə-tē\ islands South Pacific; belonging to France; chief island, Tahiti; *pop* 162,573

So·fia \'sō-fē-ə, 'só-, sō-'\ city, ✳ of Bulgaria; *pop* 1,141,142

So·ho \'sō-,hō\ district of *cen* London, England

So·li·hull \,sō-li-'həl\ city *cen* England; *pop* 194,100

Sol·o·mon \'sä-lə-mən\ **1** islands W Pacific E of New Guinea divided between Papua New Guinea & independent Solomon Islands **2** sea, arm of Coral Sea W of the Solomons

Solomon Islands country, SW Pacific E of New Guinea; ✳, Honiara (on Guadalcanal); *pop* 349,000

So·ma·lia \sō-'mä-lē-ə, sə-, -'mäl-yə\ country E Africa on Gulf of Aden & Indian Ocean; ✳, Mogadishu; *pop* 8,050,000 — **So·ma·li·an** \-'mä-lē-ən, -'mäl-yən\ *adj or n*

So·ma·li·land \sō-'mä-lē-,land, sə-\ region E Africa consisting of Somalia, Djibouti, & part of E Ethiopia — **So·ma·li** \sō-'mä-lē, sə-\ *n*

Som·er·set \'sə-mər-,set, -sət\ *or* **Som·er·set·shire** \-,shir, -shər\ county SW England

So·nor·an \sə-'nór-ən\ *or* **So·no·ra** \sə-'nór-ə\ desert SW U.S. & NW Mexico

Soo Canals — see SAULT SAINTE MARIE CANALS

South island S New Zealand; *pop* 906,756

South Africa, Republic of *formerly* **Union of South Africa** country S Africa; administrative ✳, Pretoria; legislative ✳, Cape Town; judicial ✳, Bloemfontein; *pop* 30,193,000 — **South African** *adj or n*

South America continent of Western Hemisphere SE of North America and chiefly S of the Equator — **South American** *adj or n*

South·amp·ton \saù-'tham(p)-tən, saùth-'ham(p)-\ city S England; *pop* 194,400

South Australia state S Australia; ✳, Adelaide; *pop* 1,462,900 — **South Australian** *adj or n*

South Bend \'bend\ city N Indiana; *pop* 107,789

South Cape *or* **South Point** — see KA LAE

South Car·o·li·na \,ker(-ə)-'lī-nə, ,ka-rə-\ state SE U.S.; ✳, Columbia; *pop* 4,012,012 — **South Car·o·lin·i·an** \-'li-nē-ən, -'li-nyən\ *adj or n*

South China Sea — see CHINA

South Da·ko·ta \də-'kō-tə\ state NW *cen* U.S.; ✳, Pierre; *pop* 754,844 — **South Da·ko·tan** \-'kō-tᵊn\ *adj or n*

South·end–on–Sea \,saù-,thend-,ón-'sē, -ón-\ seaside resort SE England E of London; *pop* 153,700

Southern Alps mountain range New Zealand in W South Island extending almost the length of the island

Southern Hemisphere the half of the earth that lies S of the Equator

South Georgia island S Atlantic E of Tierra del Fuego; administered by United Kingdom

South Korea *or* **Republic of South Korea** country S half of Korean Peninsula in E Asia; ✳, Seoul; *pop* 45,985,289

South Seas the areas of the Atlantic, Indian, & Pacific oceans in the Southern Hemisphere

South Shields \'shēldz\ seaport N England; *pop* 87,203

South Vietnam — see VIETNAM

South·wark \'sə-thərk, 'saùth-wərk\ borough of S Greater London, England; *pop* 196,500

South–West Africa — see NAMIBIA

South Yorkshire metropolitan county N England; *pop* 1,248,500

Soviet Central Asia portion of *cen* & SW Asia formerly belonging to U.S.S.R. and including the former soviet socialist republics of present-day Kyrgyzstan, Tajikistan, Uzbekistan & sometimes Kazakhstan

Soviet Union — see UNION OF SOVIET SOCIALIST REPUBLICS

So·we·to \sō-'wā-tō, -'we-, -tü\ residential area NE Republic of South Africa adjoining SW Johannesburg

Spain \'spān\ country SW Europe on Iberian Peninsula; ✳, Madrid; *pop* 39,141,000

Spanish America 1 the Spanish-speaking countries of America **2** the parts of America settled and formerly governed by the Spanish

Spanish Guinea — see EQUATORIAL GUINEA

Spanish Sahara — see WESTERN SAHARA

Spar·ta \'spär-tə\ ancient city S Greece in Peloponnese; ✳ of Laconia

Spo·kane \spō-'kan\ city E Washington; *pop* 195,629

Spring·field \'spriŋ-,fēld\ **1** city, ✳ of Illinois; *pop* 111,454 **2** city SW Massachusetts; *pop* 152,082 **3** city SW Missouri; *pop* 151,580

Sri Lan·ka \(,)srē-'läŋ-kə, (,)shrē-, -'laŋ-\ *formerly* **Cey·lon** \si-'län, sā-\ country having the same boundaries as island of Ceylon; ✳, Colombo; *pop* 17,829,500 — **Sri Lan·kan** \-'läŋ-kən, -'laŋ-\ *adj or n*

Sri·na·gar \srē-'nə-gər\ city N India; *pop* 894,940

Staf·ford \'sta-fərd\ town W *cen* England; *pop* 117,000

Staf·ford·shire \'sta-fərd-,shir, -shər\ *or* **Stafford** county W *cen* England

Staked Plain — see LLANO ESTACADO

Stam·ford \'stam-fərd\ city SW Connecticut; *pop* 117,083

Stan·ley \'stan-lē\ town, ✳ of Falkland Islands; *pop* 1559

Stat·en Island \'sta-tᵊn\ **1** island SE New York SW of mouth of the Hudson **2** *formerly* **Rich·mond** \'rich-mənd\ borough of New York City including Staten Island; *pop* 443,728

Ster·ling Heights \'stər-liŋ\ city SE Michigan; *pop* 124,471

Stir·ling \'stər-liŋ\ town *cen* Scotland; *pop* 38,638

Stock·holm \'stäk-,hō(l)m\ city, ✳ of Sweden; *pop* 758,148

Stock·port \'stäk-,pórt\ town NW England; *pop* 276,800

Stock·ton \'stäk-tən\ city *cen* California; *pop* 243,771

Stoke–on–Trent \'stōk-,än-'trent, -,ón-\ city *cen* England; *pop* 244,800

Stone·henge \'stōn-ˌhenj, (ˌ)stōn-'\ prehistoric assemblage of megaliths S England in Wiltshire on Salisbury Plain

Stone Mountain mountain 1686 ft. (514 m.) NW Georgia E of Atlanta

Stor·no·way \'stȯr-nə-ˌwā\ seaport NW Scotland; chief town of Lewis with Harris Island; *pop* 8660

Stra·bane \strə-'ban\ district W Northern Ireland; *pop* 35,668

Strath·clyde \strath-'klīd\ former region SW Scotland; included Glasgow

Strom·bo·li \'sträm-bō-(ˌ)lē\ volcano 2500 ft. (758 m.) Italy on **Stromboli Island** in Tyrrhenian Sea

Stutt·gart \'shtu̇t-ˌgärt, 'stu̇t-, 'stət-\ city SW Germany; *pop* 591,946

Styx \'stiks\ chief river of the underworld in Greek mythology

Süchow — see XUZHOU

Su·cre \'sü-(ˌ)krā\ city, constitutional ✳ of Bolivia; *pop* 130,952

Su·dan \sü-'dan, -'dän\ **1** region N Africa S of the Sahara between the Atlantic & the upper Nile **2** country NE Africa S of Egypt; ✳, Khartoum; *pop* 25,000,000 — **Su·da·nese** \ˌsüd-ᵊn-'ēz, -'ēs\ *adj or n*

Sud·bury \'səd-ˌber-ē, -b(ə-)rē\ city SE Ontario, Canada; *pop* 155,219

Su·ez, Gulf of \sü-'ez, 'sü-ˌez\ arm of Red Sea

Suez, Isthmus of isthmus NE Egypt between Mediterranean & Red seas connecting Africa & Asia

Suez Canal canal 100 mi. (161 km.) long NE Egypt across the Isthmus of Suez

Suf·folk \'sə-fək\ county E England on North Sea

Sui·sun Bay \sə-'sün\ inlet of San Francisco Bay, W *cen* California

Su·la·we·si \ˌsü-lä-'wä-sē\ island Indonesia E of Borneo; *pop* 12,520,711

Su·lu \'sü-(ˌ)lü\ **1** archipelago SW Philippines SW of Mindanao **2** sea W Philippines

Su·ma·tra \sü-'mä-trə\ island W Indonesia S of Malay Peninsula — **Su·ma·tran** \-trən\ *adj or n*

Su·mer \'sü-mər\ the S division of ancient Babylonia — **Su·me·ri·an** \sü-'mer-ē-ən, -'mir-\ *adj or n*

Sun·belt \'sən-ˌbelt\ region S & SW U.S.

Sun·da \'sün-də, 'sən-\ strait between Java & Sumatra

Sun·der·land \'sən-dər-lənd\ seaport N England; *pop* 286,800

Sun·ny·vale \'sə-nē-ˌvāl\ city W California; *pop* 131,760

Sun Valley resort center *cen* Idaho

Su·pe·ri·or, Lake \su̇-'pir-ē-ər\ lake E *cen* North America in U.S. & Canada; largest of the Great Lakes

Su·ra·ba·ya \ˌsu̇r-ə-'bī-ə\ city Indonesia in NE Java; *pop* 2,483,871

Su·ri·na·me \ˌsu̇r-ə-'nä-mə\ country N South America between Guyana & French Guiana; ✳, Paramaribo; *pop* 403,000 — **Su·ri·nam·er** \'su̇r-ə-ˌnä-mər, ˌsu̇r-ə-'nä-\ *n* — **Su·ri·nam·ese** \ˌsu̇r-ə-nə-'mēz, -'mēs\ *adj or n*

Sur·rey \'sər-ē, 'sə-rē\ city Canada in SW British Columbia; *pop* 347,825

Sut·ton \'sə-tᵊn\ borough of S Greater London, England; *pop* 164,300

Su·va \'sü-və\ city & port, ✳ of Fiji on Viti Levu Island; *pop* 63,628

Su·wan·nee \sə-'wä-nē, 'swä-\ river 250 mi. (400 km.) SE U.S. flowing SW into Gulf of Mexico

Sverdlovsk — see YEKATERINBURG

Swan·sea \'swän-zē\ city & port SE Wales; *pop* 182,100

Swa·zi·land \'swä-zē-ˌland\ country SE Africa between Republic of South Africa & Mozambique; ✳, Mbabane; *pop* 929,718 — **Swa·zi** \'swä-zē\ *adj or n*

Swe·den \'swēd-ᵊn\ country N Europe on Scandinavia (peninsula) bordering on Baltic Sea; ✳, Stockholm; *pop* 8,940,788

Swit·zer·land \'swit-sər-lənd\ country W Europe in the Alps; ✳, Bern; *pop* 6,996,000

Syd·ney \'sid-nē\ city SE Australia, ✳ of New South Wales; metropolitan area *pop* 3,097,956

Syr·a·cuse \'sir-ə-ˌkyüs, -ˌkyüz\ city *cen* New York; *pop* 147,306

Syr·ia \'sir-ē-ə\ **1** ancient region SW Asia bordering on the Mediterranean **2** country S of Turkey; ✳, Damascus; *pop* 13,398,000 — **Syr·i·an** \'sir-ē-ən\ *adj or n*

Syrian Desert desert region between Mediterranean coast & the Euphrates in N Saudi Arabia, SE Syria, W Iraq, & NE Jordan

Table Bay harbor of Cape Town, Republic of South Africa

Ta·briz \tə-'brēz\ city NW Iran; *pop* 971,482

Ta·co·ma \tə-'kō-mə\ city & port W Washington S of Seattle; *pop* 193,556

Tae·gu \'tā-gü, 'dā-\ or **Dae·gu** \'dā-\ city SE South Korea; *pop* 2,473,990

Tae·jon \'tā-'jən, 'dā-\ or **Dae·jeon** \'dā-\ city *cen* South Korea NW of Taegu; *pop* 1,365,961

Ta·gus \'tā-gəs\ or *Spanish* **Ta·jo** \'tä-(ˌ)hō\ or *Portuguese* **Te·jo** \'tä-(ˌ)zhü\ river 626 mi. (1007 km.) long Spain & Portugal flowing W into the North Atlantic

Ta·hi·ti \tə-'hē-tē\ island South Pacific in Society Islands; *pop* 131,309

Tai·chung \'tī-'chu̇ŋ\ city W Taiwan; *pop* 779,370

T'ai·nan \'tī-'nän\ city SW Taiwan; *pop* 702,237

Tai·pei \'tī-'pā, -'bā\ city, ✳ of (Nationalist) China in N Taiwan; *pop* 2,651,419

Tai·wan \'tī-'wän\ *formerly* **For·mo·sa** \fȯr-'mō-sə, fər-, -zə\ **1** island China off SE coast of mainland; seat of government of (Nationalist) Republic of China; ✳, Taipei; *pop* 20,926,000 **2** strait between Taiwan & mainland of China connecting East China & South China seas — **Tai·wan·ese** \ˌtī-wə-'nēz, -'nēs\ *adj or n*

Tai·yuan \'tī-'ywen, -'ywän\ city N China; *pop* 1,533,884

Ta·jik·i·stan \tä-ji-ki-'stan, tə-, -ˌjē-, -'stän\ country W *cen* Asia bordering on China & Afghanistan; ✳, Dushanbe; *pop* 5,705,000

Ta·kli·ma·kan or **Ta·kla Ma·kan** \ˌtä-klə-mə-'kän\ desert W China

Ta–lien — see DALIAN

Tal·la·has·see \ˌta-lə-'ha-sē\ city, ✳ of Florida; *pop* 150,624

Tal·linn \'ta-lən, 'tä-\ city, ✳ of Estonia; *pop* 398,434

Tam·pa \'tam-pə\ city W Florida on **Tampa Bay** (inlet of Gulf of Mexico); *pop* 303,447

Tan·gan·yi·ka \ˌtaŋ-gə-'nyē-kə, ˌtaŋ-gə-, -'nē-\ former country E Africa S of Kenya; now part of Tanzania

Tanganyika, Lake lake E Africa between Tanzania & Democratic Republic of the Congo

Tang·shan \'däŋ-'shän, 'täŋ-\ city NE China; *pop* 1,044,194

Tan·za·nia \ˌtan-zə-'nē-ə, -ˌtän-\ country E Africa on Indian Ocean, including Zanzibar; designated ✳, Dodoma; seat of government, Dar es Salaam; *pop* 26,542,000 — **Tan·za·ni·an** \-'nē-ən\ *adj or n*

Ta·ra·wa \tə-'rä-wə, 'ta-rə-ˌwä\ island *cen* Pacific, contains ✳ of Kiribati; *pop* 28,802

Tar·ry·town \'ta-rē-ˌtȧu̇n\ village SE New York; *pop* 11,090

Tar·sus \'tär-səs\ ancient city of S Asia Minor; now a city in S Turkey

Tash·kent \tash-'kent, täsh-\ city, ✳ of Uzbekistan; *pop* 2,073,000

Tas·ma·nia \taz-'mā-nē-ə, -nyə\ or *earlier* **Van Die·men's Land** \van-'dē-mənz-\ island SE Australia S of Victoria; a state; ✳, Hobart; *pop* 471,400 — **Tas·ma·nian** \taz-'mā-nē-ən, -nyən\ *adj or n*

Tas·man Sea \'taz-mən\ the part of the South Pacific between SE Australia & New Zealand

Ta·try \'tä-trē\ or **Ta·tra** \'tä-trə\ mountains N Slovakia & S Poland in *cen* Carpathian Mountains

Taun·ton \'tȯn-tᵊn, 'tän-\ town SW England; *pop* 35,326

Tbi·li·si \tə-'bē-lə-sē, tə-bə-'lē-sē\ or **Tif·lis** \'ti-fləs, tə-'flēs\ city, ✳ of Republic of Georgia; *pop* 1,260,000

Te·gu·ci·gal·pa \tə-ˌgü-sə-'gal-pə, tä-ˌgü-sē-'gäl-pä\ city, ✳ of Honduras; *pop* 608,100

Teh·ran \ˌtā-(ə-)'ran, te-'ran, -'rän\ city, ✳ of Iran; at foot of S slope of Elburz Mountains; *pop* 6,042,584

Tel Aviv \ˌtel-ə-'vēv\ city W Israel on the Mediterranean; *pop* 353,200

Tem·pe \tem-'pē\ city S *cen* Arizona; *pop* 158,625

Ten·nes·see \ˌte-nə-'sē, 'te-nə-ˌ\ **1** river 652 mi. (1049 km.) long in Tennessee, N Alabama, & W Kentucky **2** state E *cen* U.S.; ✳, Nashville; *pop* 5,689,283 — **Ten·nes·se·an** or **Ten·nes·see·an** \ˌte-nə-'sē-ən\ *adj or n*

Te·noch·ti·tlan \tā-ˌnóch-tēt-ˈlän\ ancient name of Mexico City

Tex·as \ˈtek-səs, -siz\ state S U.S.; ✳, Austin; *pop* 20,851,820 — **Tex·an** \-sən\ *adj or n*

Texas Panhandle the NW projection of land in Texas

Thai·land \ˈtī-ˌland, -lənd\ *formerly* **Si·am** \sī-ˈam\ country SE Asia on Gulf of Thailand; ✳, Bangkok; *pop* 60,617,200 — **Thai·land·er** \-ˌlan-dər, -lən-\ *n*

Thailand, Gulf of *formerly* **Gulf of Siam** arm of South China Sea between Indochina & Malay Peninsula

Thames \ˈtemz\ river over 200 mi. (322 km.) long S England flowing E from the Cotswolds into the North Sea

Thar \ˈtär\ desert E Pakistan & NW India (country) E of Indus River

Thebes \ˈthēbz\ **1** *or* **The·bae** \ˈthē-ˌbē\ ancient city S Egypt on the Nile **2** ancient city E Greece NNW of Athens — **The·ban** \ˈthē-bən\ *adj or n*

Thes·sa·lo·ní·ki \ˌthe-sä-lō-ˈnē-kē\ city N Greece; *pop* 402,443

Thim·phu \tim-ˈpü\ city, ✳ of Bhutan; *pop* 45,000

Thousand Islands island group Canada & U.S. in the Saint Lawrence River in Ontario & New York

Thousand Oaks city SW California W of Los Angeles; *pop* 117,005

Thrace \ˈthrās\ *or ancient* **Thra·cia** \ˈthrā-sh(ē-)ə\ region SE Europe in Balkan Peninsula N of the Aegean now divided between Greece & Turkey; in ancient times extended N to the Danube — **Thra·cian** \ˈthrā-shən\ *adj or n*

Thunder Bay city SW Ontario, Canada on Lake Superior; *pop* 109,016

Tian·jin \ˈtyän-ˈjin\ *or* **Tien·tsin** \ˈtyen-ˈtsin, ˈtin-\ city NE China SE of Beijing; *pop* 7,764,141

Tian Shan *or* **Tien Shan** \ˈtyen-ˈshän, -ˈshan\ mountain system *cen* Asia extending NE from Pamirs

Ti·ber \ˈtī-bər\ *or Italian* **Te·ve·re** \ˈtā-vä-rā\ river 252 mi. (405 km.) long *cen* Italy flowing through Rome into Tyrrhenian Sea

Tiberias, Lake — see GALILEE, SEA OF

Ti·bes·ti \tə-ˈbes-tē\ mountains N *cen* Africa in *cen* Sahara in NW Chad; highest 11,204 ft. (3415 m.)

Ti·bet \tə-ˈbet\ *or* **Xi·zang** \ˈshēd-ˈzän\ region SW China on high plateau at average altitude 16,000 ft. (4877 m.) N of the Himalayas; ✳, Lhasa; *pop* 2,196,010

Tier·ra del Fue·go \tē-ˈer-ə-(ˌ)del-fü-ˈā-(ˌ)gō, ˈtyer-ä-(ˌ)thel-ˈfwä-gō\ **1** island group off S South America **2** chief island of the group; divided between Argentina & Chile

Tiflis — see TBILISI

Ti·gris \ˈtī-grəs\ river 1180 mi. (1899 km.) long Turkey & Iraq flowing SSE and uniting with the Euphrates to form the Shatt al Arab

Ti·jua·na \ˌtē-ə-ˈwä-nə, tē-ˈhwä-nä\ city NW Mexico on the U.S. border; *pop* 991,592

Tim·buk·tu \ˌtim-ˌbək-ˈtü, tim-ˈbək-(ˌ)tü\ *or* **Tom·bouc·tou** \tōⁿ-bük-ˈtü\ town Mali near Niger River; *pop* 31,925

Ti·mor \ˈtē-ˌmór, tē-ˈ\ island S Malay archipelago SE of Sulawesi; W half part of Indonesia, E half independent East Timor

Ti·ra·ne *or* **Ti·ra·na** \ti-ˈrä-nə, tē-\ city, ✳ of Albania; *pop* 519,720

Ti·rol *or* **Ty·rol** \tə-ˈrōl\ *or Italian* **Ti·ro·lo** \tē-ˈrò-(ˌ)lō\ region in E Alps in W Austria & NE Italy — **Ti·ro·le·an** \tə-ˈrō-lē-ən, ti-\ *or* **Tir·o·lese** \ˌtir-ə-ˈlēz, ˌtē-rə-, -ˈlēs\ *adj or n*

Ti·ti·ca·ca, Lake \ˌti-ti-ˈkä-kä, ˌtē-tē-\ lake on Bolivia–Peru boundary at altitude of 12,500 ft. (3810 m.)

To·ba·go \tə-ˈbā-(ˌ)gō\ island West Indies NE of Trinidad; part of independent Trinidad and Tobago; *pop* 54,084 — **To·ba·go·ni·an** \ˌtō-bə-ˈgō-nē-ən, -nyən\ *n*

To·go \ˈtō-(ˌ)gō\ country W Africa on Gulf of Guinea; ✳, Lomé; *pop* 3,810,000 — **To·go·lese** \ˌtō-gə-ˈlēz, -ˈlēs\ *adj or n*

To·kyo \ˈtō-kē-ō, -ˌkyō\ city, ✳ of Japan in SE Honshu on Tokyo Bay; *pop* 12,064,101 — **To·kyo·ite** \ˈtō-kē-(ˌ)ō-ˌīt\ *n*

To·le·do \tə-ˈlē-(ˌ)dō, -ˈlē-də\ city NW Ohio; *pop* 313,619

Tol'·yat·ti \tól-ˈyä-tē\ city W Russia; NW of Samara; *pop* 666,000

Ton·ga \ˈtäŋ-gə, ˈtäŋ-ə, ˈtóŋ-ä\ islands SW Pacific E of Fiji Islands; country; ✳, Nukualofa; *pop* 101,002 — **Ton·gan** \-(g)ən\ *adj or n*

Tonkin, Gulf of \ˈtäŋ-kən\ arm of South China Sea E of N Vietnam

To·pe·ka \tə-ˈpē-kə\ city, ✳ of Kansas; *pop* 122,377

Tor·bay \(ˌ)tór-ˈbā\ urban area SW England; *pop* 122,500

To·ron·to \tə-ˈrän-(ˌ)tō, -ˈrän-tə\ city, ✳ of Ontario, Canada; *pop* 2,481,494

Tor·rance \ˈtór-ən(t)s, ˈtär-\ city SW California; *pop* 137,946

Tor·res \ˈtór-əs\ strait between New Guinea & Cape York Peninsula, Australia

Tou·louse \tü-ˈlüz\ city SW France; *pop* 390,301

Tower Hamlets borough of E Greater London, England; *pop* 153,500

Trans·vaal \tran(t)s-ˈväl, tranz-\ former province NE Republic of South Africa

Tran·syl·va·nia \ˌtran(t)-səl-ˈvā-nyə, -nē-ə\ region W Romania — **Tran·syl·va·nian** \-nyən, -nē-ən\ *adj or n*

Transylvanian Alps a S extension of Carpathian Mountains in *cen* Romania

Tren·ton \ˈtren-tᵊn\ city, ✳ of New Jersey; *pop* 85,403

Trin·i·dad \ˈtri-nə-ˌdad\ island West Indies off NE coast of Venezuela; with Tobago forms the independent country of **Trinidad and Tobago**; ✳, Port of Spain; *pop* 1,262,386 — **Trin·i·da·di·an** \ˌtri-nə-ˈdā-dē-ən, -ˈda-\ *adj or n*

Trip·o·li \ˈtri-pə-lē\ **1** city & port NW Lebanon; *pop* 127,611 **2** city & port, ✳ of Libya; *pop* 591,062

Tris·tan da Cu·nha \ˌtris-tən-də-ˈkü-nə, -nyə\ island South Atlantic, chief of the Tristan da Cunha Islands (part of British colony of Saint Helena); *pop* 296

Tri·van·drum \tri-ˈvan-drəm\ city S India; *pop* 744,739

Tro·bri·and \ˈtrō-brē-ˌänd, -ˌand\ islands SW Pacific in Solomon Sea belonging to Papua New Guinea

Trond·heim \ˈträn-ˌhām\ city & port *cen* Norway; *pop* 137,346

Trow·bridge \ˈtrō-(ˌ)brij\ town S England; *pop* 22,984

Troy \ˈtrói\ *or* **Il·i·um** \ˈi-lē-əm\ *or* **Tro·ja** \ˈtrō-jə, -yə\ ancient city NW Asia Minor SW of the Dardanelles

Truk — see CHUUK

Tru·ro \ˈtrúr-(ˌ)ō\ city SW England; *pop* 16,277

Tsinan — see JINAN

Tsingtao — see QINGDAO

Tuc·son \ˈtü-ˌsän\ city SE Arizona; *pop* 486,699

Tu·la \ˈtü-lä\ city W Russia S of Moscow; *pop* 541,000

Tul·sa \ˈtəl-sə\ city NE Oklahoma; *pop* 393,049

Tu·nis \ˈtü-nəs, ˈtyü-\ city, ✳ of Tunisia; *pop* 620,149

Tu·ni·sia \tü-ˈnē-zh(ē-)ə, tyü-, -ˈni-\ country N Africa on the Mediterranean E of Algeria; ✳, Tunis; *pop* 9,673,600 — **Tu·ni·sian** \-zh(ē-)ən\ *adj or n*

Tu·rin \ˈtúr-ən, ˈtyúr-\ city NW Italy on the Po; *pop* 900,987

Tur·kana, Lake \tər-ˈka-nə\ *or* **Lake Ru·dolf** \ˈrü-ˌdólf, -ˌdälf\ lake N Kenya in Great Rift Valley

Tur·key \ˈtər-kē\ country W Asia & SE Europe between Mediterranean & Black seas; ✳, Ankara; *pop* 50,664,458 — **Turk** \ˈtərk\ *n*

Turk·men·i·stan \(ˌ)tərk-ˌme-nə-ˈstan, -ˈstän\ country *cen* Asia; ✳, Ashkhabad; *pop* 3,958,000 — **Turk·me·ni·an** \ˌtərk-ˈmē-nē-ən\ *adj*

Turks and Cai·cos \ˈtərks-ənd-ˈkā-kəs, -ˌkōs\ two groups of islands West Indies at SE end of the Bahamas; a British colony; *pop* 12,350

Tu·tu·ila \ˌtü-tü-ˈwē-lä\ island South Pacific, chief of American Samoa group

Tu·va·lu \tü-ˈvä-(ˌ)lü, -ˈvär-(ˌ)ü\ *formerly* **El·lice** \ˈe-lis\ islands W Pacific N of Fiji; country; ✳, Funafuti; *pop* 9700 — see GILBERT AND ELLICE ISLANDS

Tyne and Wear \ˈtīn-ənd-ˈwir\ metropolitan county N England

Tyre \ˈtī(-ə)r\ ancient city, ✳ of Phoenicia; now a town of S Lebanon — **Tyr·i·an** \ˈtir-ē-ən\ *adj or n*

Tyrol — see TIROL — **Ty·ro·le·an** \tə-ˈrō-lē-ən, tī-\ *adj or n* — **Ty·ro·lese** \ˌtir-ə-ˈlēz, ˌtī-rə-, -ˈlēs\ *adj or n*

Tyr·rhe·ni·an Sea \tə-ˈrē-nē-ən\ the part of the Mediterranean SW of Italy, N of Sicily, & E of Sardinia & Corsica

Ufa \ü-ˈfä\ city W Russia NE of Samara; *pop* 1,097,000

Ugan·da \ü-ˈgän-də, yü-, -ˈgan-\ country E Africa N of Lake Victoria; ✳, Kampala; *pop* 24,551,021 — **Ugan·dan** \-dən\ *adj or n*

Ukraine \yü-ˈkrān, ˈyü-ˌ\ country E Europe on N coast of

Black Sea; ✻, Kiev; *pop* 52,344,000 — **Ukrai·ni·an** \yü-ˈkrā-nē-ən\ *adj or n*

Ulaan·baa·tar *or* **Ulan Ba·tor** \ˌü-ˌlän-ˈbä-ˌtòr\ city, ✻ of Mongolia; *pop* 548,400

Ul·san \ˈül-ˈsän\ city SE South Korea; *pop* 1,012,110

Ul·ster \ˈəl-stər\ **1** region N Ireland (island) consisting of Northern Ireland & N Ireland (country) **2** province N Ireland (country); *pop* 246,714 **3** NORTHERN IRELAND

Um·bria \ˈəm-brē-ə\ region *cen* Italy in the Apennines; *pop* 840,482

Un·ga·va \ˌən-ˈga-və\ **1** bay, inlet of Hudson Strait NE Canada **2** peninsula region NE Canada in N Quebec

Union of South Africa — see SOUTH AFRICA, REPUBLIC OF

Union of Soviet Socialist Republics *or* **U.S.S.R.** *or* **Soviet Union** country 1922–91 E Europe & N Asia; former union of 15 republics comprising present-day countries of Armenia, Azerbaijan, Belarus, Estonia, Georgia, Kazakhstan, Kyrgyzstan, Latvia, Lithuania, Moldova, Russia, Tajikistan, Turkmenistan, Ukraine, & Uzbekistan

United Arab Emir·ates \ˈe-mə-rət, -ˌrāts\ country E Arabia on Persian Gulf; composed of seven emirates; ✻, Abu Dhabi; *pop* 1,986,000

United Kingdom *or in full* **United Kingdom of Great Britain and Northern Ireland** country W Europe in British Isles consisting of England, Scotland, Wales, Northern Ireland, Channel Islands, & Isle of Man; ✻, London; *pop* 58,789,194

United Nations international territory; a small area in New York City in E *cen* Manhattan; seat of permanent headquarters of a political organization established in 1945

United States of America *or* **United States** country North America bordering on Atlantic, Pacific, & Arctic oceans & including Hawaii; ✻, Washington; *pop* 281,421,906

Upper Volta — see BURKINA FASO — **Upper Vol·tan** \ˈväl-tᵊn, ˈvòl-, ˈvòl-\ *adj or n*

Ural \ˈyùr-əl\ **1** mountains Russia & Kazakhstan extending about 1640 mi. (2640 km.); usually thought of as dividing line between Europe & Asia; highest about 6214 ft. (1894 m.) **2** river over 1500 mi. (2414 km.) long Russia & Kazakhstan flowing from S end of Ural Mountains into Caspian Sea

Uru·guay \ˈùr-ə-ˌgwī, ˈyùr-\ **1** river about 1000 mi. (1609 km.) long SE South America **2** country SE South America; ✻, Montevideo; *pop* 3,149,000 — **Uru·guay·an** \ˌùr-ə-ˈgwī-ən, ˌyùr-\ *adj or n*

Ürüm·qi \ˈ ̇e-ˈrüm-ˈchē\ *or* **Urum·chi** \u-ˈrüm-chē, ˌùr-əm-\ city NW China; *pop* 1,046,898

Us·pa·lla·ta \ˌüs-pä-ˈyä-tä, -ˈzhä-\ mountain pass S South America in the Andes between Argentina & Chile

Ustinov — see IZHEVSK

Utah \ˈyü-ˌtò, -ˌtä\ state W U.S.; ✻, Salt Lake City; *pop* 2,233,169 — **Utah·an** \-ˌtò(-ə)n, -ˌtä(-ə)n\ *adj or n* — **Utahn** \-ˌtò(-ə)n, -ˌtä(-ə)n\ *n*

Uz·bek·i·stan \(ˌ)ùz-ˌbe-ki-ˈstan, ˌəz-, -ˈstän\ country W *cen* Asia between Aral Sea & Afghanistan; ✻, Tashkent; *pop* 21,179,000

Va·duz \vä-ˈdüts\ town, ✻ of Liechtenstein; *pop* 4949

Val·dez \val-ˈdēz\ city & port S Alaska; *pop* 4036

Va·len·cia \və-ˈlen(t)-sh(ē-)ə, -sē-ə\ **1** region & ancient kingdom E Spain **2** city, its ✻, on the Mediterranean; *pop* 738,441

Val·le·jo \və-ˈlā-(ˌ)ō\ city W California; *pop* 116,760

Valley Forge locality SE Pennsylvania

Val·let·ta \və-ˈle-tə\ city, ✻ of Malta; *pop* 9210

Van·cou·ver \van-ˈkü-vər\ **1** city SW Washington on Columbia River opposite Portland, Oregon; *pop* 143,560 **2** island W Canada in SW British Columbia **3** city & port SW British Columbia, Canada; *pop* 545,671

Van Diemen's Land — see TASMANIA

Van·u·atu \ˌvan-wä-ˈtü, ˌvän-\ *formerly* **New Heb·ri·des** \ˈhe-brə-ˌdēz\ islands SW Pacific W of Fiji; country; ✻, Port-Vila; *pop* 142,419

Va·ra·na·si \və-ˈrä-nə-sē\ city N India; *pop* 1,100,748

Vat·i·can City \ˈva-ti-kən\ independent state within Rome, Italy; *pop* 911

Ven·e·zu·e·la \ˌve-nə-ˈzwā-lə, -zə-ˈwā-; ˌbā-nā-ˈswä-lä\

country N South America; ✻, Caracas; *pop* 20,609,000 — **Ven·e·zu·e·lan** \-lən\ *adj or n*

Ven·ice \ˈve-nəs\ *or Italian* **Ve·ne·zia** \ve-ˈnet-sē-ä\ city N Italy on islands in Lagoon of Venice; *pop* 275,368 — **Ve·ne·tian** \və-ˈnē-shən\ *adj or n*

Ven·tu·ra \ven-ˈtùr-ə, -ˈtyùr-\ city & port SW California; *pop* 100,916

Ve·ra·cruz \ˌver-ə-ˈkrüz, -ˈkrüs\ city E Mexico; metropolitan area *pop* 560,200

Ver·mont \vər-ˈmänt\ state NE U.S.; ✻, Montpelier; *pop* 608,827 — **Ver·mont·er** \-ˈmän-tər\ *n*

Ve·ro·na \ve-ˈrō-nä\ city N Italy W of Venice; *pop* 257,477

Ver·sailles \(ˌ)vər-ˈsī, ver-\ city N France, WSW suburb of Paris; *pop* 91,029

Ve·su·vi·us \və-ˈsü-vē-əs\ volcano about 4190 ft. (1277 m.) S Italy near Bay of Naples

Vicks·burg \ˈviks-ˌbərg\ city W Mississippi; *pop* 26,407

Vic·to·ria \vik-ˈtòr-ē-ə\ **1** city, ✻ of British Columbia, Canada on Vancouver Island; *pop* 74,125 **2** island N Canada in Arctic Archipelago **3** state SE Australia; ✻, Melbourne; *pop* 4,244,221 **4** city & port, Hong Kong; *pop* 1,026,870 **5** seaport, ✻ of Seychelles; *pop* 28,000 — **Vic·to·ri·an** \vik-ˈtòr-ē-ən\ *adj or n*

Victoria, Lake lake E Africa in Tanzania, Kenya, & Uganda

Victoria Falls waterfall 355 ft. (108 m.) S Africa in the Zambezi on border between Zambia & Zimbabwe

Vi·en·na \vē-ˈe-nə\ *or German* **Wien** \ˈvēn\ city, ✻ of Austria on the Danube; *pop* 1,550,123 — **Vi·en·nese** \ˌvē-ə-ˈnēz, -ˈnēs\ *adj or n*

Vien·tiane \(ˌ)vyen-ˈtyän\ city, ✻ of Laos; *pop* 132,253

Vie·ques \vē-ˈā-kās\ island Puerto Rico off E end of main island

Viet·nam \vē-ˈet-ˈnäm, vyet-, ˌvē-ət-, vēt-, -ˈnam\ country SE Asia in Indochina; ✻, Hanoi; divided 1954–75 into the independent states of **North Vietnam** (✻, Hanoi) & **South Vietnam** (✻, Saigon); *pop* 79,727,400 — **Viet·nam·ese** \vē-ˌet-nə-ˈmēz, ˌvyet-, ˌvē-ət-, ˌvēt-, -na-, -nä-, -ˈmēs\ *adj or n*

Vila — see PORT-VILA

Vi·la No·va de Ga·ia \ˈvē-lə-ˈnò-və-dē-ˈgī-ə\ city NW Portugal; *pop* 288,749

Vil·ni·us \ˈvil-nē-əs\ city, ✻ of Lithuania; *pop* 542,287

Vin·land \ˈvin-lənd\ a portion of the coast of North America visited & so called by Norse voyagers about 1000 A.D.; thought to be located along the North Atlantic in what is now E or NE Canada

Vir·gin·ia \vər-ˈji-nyə, -ji-nē-ə\ state E U.S.; ✻, Richmond; *pop* 7,078,515 — **Vir·gin·ian** \-nyən, -nē-ən\ *adj or n*

Virginia Beach city SE Virginia; *pop* 425,257

Virginia City locality W Nevada

Virgin Islands island group West Indies E of Puerto Rico — see BRITISH VIRGIN ISLANDS; VIRGIN ISLANDS OF THE UNITED STATES

Virgin Islands of the United States the W islands of the Virgin Islands; U.S. territory; ✻, Charlotte Amalie (on Saint Thomas); *pop* 108,612

Vi·sa·yan \və-ˈsī-ən\ islands *cen* Philippines

Vish·a·kha·pat·nam \vi-ˌshä-kə-ˈpət-nəm\ *or* **Vis·a·kha·pat·nam** \vi-ˌsä-\ city E India; *pop* 969,608

Vis·tu·la \ˈvis-chə-lə, ˈvish-chə-, ˈvis-tə-\ river over 660 mi. (1062 km.) long Poland flowing N from the Carpathians

Vi·ti Le·vu \ˌvē-tē-ˈle-(ˌ)vü\ island SW Pacific; largest of the Fiji group

Vlad·i·vos·tok \ˌvla-də-və-ˈstäk, -ˈväs-ˌtäk\ city & port SE Russia on Sea of Japan; *pop* 648,000

Vol·ga \ˈväl-gə, ˈvòl-, ˈvōl-\ river about 2300 mi. (3700 km.) long W Russia; longest river in Europe

Vol·go·grad \ˈväl-gə-ˌgrad, ˈvòl-, ˈvōl-, -ˌgrät\ city S Russia in Europe, on the Volga; *pop* 1,006,000

Vol·ta \ˈväl-tə, ˈvòl-, ˈvōl-\ river about 300 mi. (485 km.) long Ghana flowing from **Lake Volta** (reservoir) into Gulf of Guinea

Vo·ro·nezh \və-ˈrò-nish\ city S *cen* Russia in Europe; *pop* 902,000

Vosges \ˈvōzh\ mountains NE France on W side of Rhine valley; highest 4672 ft. (1424 m.)

Wa·co \ˈwā-(ˌ)kō\ city *cen* Texas; *pop* 113,726

DICTIONARY

Wad·den·zee \ˌvä-dᵊn-ˈzā\ inlet of the North Sea N Netherlands

Wake \ˈwāk\ island North Pacific N of Marshall Islands; U.S. territory

Wake·field \ˈwāk-ˌfēld\ city N England; *pop* 60,540

Wa·la·chia *or* **Wal·la·chia** \wä-ˈlā-kē-ə\ region S Romania between Transylvanian Alps & the Danube

Wales \ˈwālz\ *or Welsh* **Cym·ru** \ˈkəm-ˌrē\ principality SW Great Britain; a division of United Kingdom; ✳, Cardiff; *pop* 2,903,085

Wal·lo·nia \wä-ˈlō-nē-ə\ semiautonomous region S Belgium; *pop* 3,358,560

Wal·sall \ˈwȯl-ˌsȯl, -səl\ town W *cen* England; *pop* 255,600

Wal·tham Forest \ˈwȯl-thəm\ borough of NE Greater London, England; *pop* 203,400

Wands·worth \ˈwän(d)z-ˌwərth\ borough of SW Greater London, England; *pop* 237,500

War·ley \ˈwȯr-lē\ town W *cen* England; *pop* 152,455

War·ren \ˈwȯr-lē\ city SE Michigan; *pop* 138,247

War·saw \ˈwȯr-ˌsȯ\ *or Polish* **War·sza·wa** \vär-ˈshä-vä\ city, ✳ of Poland; *pop* 1,655,063

War·wick \ˈwär-ik\ town *cen* England; *pop* 21,936

War·wick·shire \ˈwär-ik-ˌshir, -shər\ *or* **Warwick** county *cen* England

Wa·satch \ˈwȯ-ˌsach\ range of the Rockies SE Idaho & N *cen* Utah; highest Mount Timpanogos 12,008 ft. (3660 m.), in Utah

Wash·ing·ton \ˈwȯ-shiŋ-tən, ˈwä-\ **1** state NW U.S.; ✳, Olympia; *pop* 5,894,121 **2** city, ✳ of U.S.; having the same boundaries as District of Columbia; *pop* 572,059 — **Wash·ing·to·nian** \ˌwȯ-shiŋ-ˈtō-nē-ən, ˌwä-, -nyən\ *adj or n*

Washington, Mount mountain 6288 ft. (1916 m.) N New Hampshire; highest in White Mountains

Wa·ter·bury \ˈwȯ-tə(r)-ˌber-ē, ˈwä-\ city W *cen* Connecticut; *pop* 107,271

Wa·ver·ley \ˈwā-vər-lē\ municipality SE Australia in E New South Wales; *pop* 59,095

Wei·mar Republic \ˈvī-ˌmär, ˈwī-\ the German republic 1919–33

Wel·land \ˈwe-lənd\ canal 27 mi. (44 km.) long SE Ontario connecting Lake Erie & Lake Ontario

Wel·ling·ton \ˈwe-liŋ-tən\ city, ✳ of New Zealand; urban area *pop* 339,747

Wes·sex \ˈwe-siks\ ancient kingdom S England

West Bank area Middle East W of Jordan River; occupied by Israel since 1967 with parts having been transferred to Palestinian administration since 1993

West Brom·wich \ˈbrä-mich\ town W *cen* England; *pop* 154,930

West Co·vi·na \kō-ˈvē-nə\ city SW California; *pop* 105,080

Western Australia state W Australia; ✳, Perth; *pop* 1,676,400 — **Western Australian** *adj or n*

Western Cape province SW Republic of South Africa; *pop* 3,635,000

Western Ghats — see GHATS

Western Hemisphere the half of the earth lying W of the Atlantic Ocean & comprising North America, South America, & surrounding waters

Western Isles English name for the administrative area of W Scotland consisting of the Outer Hebrides

Western Sahara *formerly* **Spanish Sahara** territory NW Africa; occupied by Morocco

Western Samoa — see SAMOA

West Germany — see GERMANY

West Indies islands lying between SE North America & N South America & consisting of the Greater Antilles, Lesser Antilles, & Bahamas — **West Indian** *adj or n*

West Midlands metropolitan county W *cen* England; includes Birmingham

West·min·ster \ˈwes(t)-ˌmin(t)-stər\ city N *cen* Colorado NW of Denver; *pop* 100,940

West Pakistan the former W division of Pakistan now having the same boundaries as Pakistan

West Papua *or formerly* **Iri·an Ja·ya** \ˌir-ē-ˌän-ˈjī-ä\ *or* **West Irian** territory of Indonesia consisting of the W half of New Guinea; *pop* 1,648,708

West·pha·lia \west-ˈfāl-yə, -ˈfā-lē-ə\ region W Germany E

of the Rhine — **West·pha·lian** \west-ˈfāl-yən, -ˈfā-lē-ən\ *adj or n*

West Point U.S. military post SE New York

West Quod·dy Head \ˈkwä-dē\ cape; most easterly point of Maine & of the Lower 48

West Sus·sex \ˈsə-siks\ county SE England

West Valley City city N Utah S of Salt Lake City; *pop* 108,896

West Virginia state E U.S.; ✳, Charleston; *pop* 1,808,344 — **West Virginian** *adj or n*

West York·shire metropolitan county NW England; includes Wakefield

White sea NW Russia in Europe

White·horse \ˈhwīt-ˌhȯrs, ˈwīt-\ city, ✳ of Yukon Territory, Canada; *pop* 19,058

White Mountains mountains N New Hampshire in the Appalachians — see WASHINGTON, MOUNT

Whit·ney, Mount \ˈhwit-nē, ˈwit-\ mountain 14,495 ft. (4418 m.) SE *cen* California in Sierra Nevada; highest in U.S. outside of Alaska

Wich·i·ta \ˈwi-chə-ˌtȯ\ city S Kansas; *pop* 344,284

Wichita Falls city N Texas; *pop* 104,197

Wien — see VIENNA

Wight, Isle of — see ISLE OF WIGHT

Wil·lem·stad \ˈvi-ləm-ˌstät\ city, ✳ of Netherlands Antilles; *pop* 43,547

Wil·liams·burg \ˈwil-yəmz-ˌbərg\ city SE Virginia; *pop* 11,998

Wil·ming·ton \ˈwil-miŋ-tən\ city N Delaware; largest in state; *pop* 72,664

Wilt·shire \ˈwilt-ˌshir, -shər\ county S England

Win·ches·ter \ˈwin-ˌches-tər, -chəs-tər\ city S England; *pop* 30,642

Win·der·mere \ˈwin-də(r)-ˌmir\ lake NW England in Lake District

Wind·hoek \ˈvint-ˌhůk\ city, ✳ of Namibia; *pop* 144,558

Wind·sor \ˈwin-zər\ city S Ontario, Canada on Detroit River; *pop* 208,402

Wind·ward Islands \ˈwind-wərd\ islands West Indies in the S Lesser Antilles extending S from Martinique but not including Barbados, Tobago, or Trinidad

Win·ni·peg \ˈwi-nə-ˌpeg\ city, ✳ of Manitoba, Canada; *pop* 619,544

Winnipeg, Lake lake S *cen* Manitoba, Canada

Win·ni·pe·sau·kee, Lake \ˌwi-nə-pə-ˈsȯ-kē\ lake *cen* New Hampshire

Win·ston–Sa·lem \ˌwin(t)-stən-ˈsā-ləm\ city N *cen* North Carolina; *pop* 185,776

Wis·con·sin \wi-ˈskän(t)-sən\ state N *cen* U.S.; ✳, Madison; *pop* 5,363,675 — **Wis·con·sin·ite** \-sə-ˌnīt\ *n*

Wit·wa·ters·rand \ˈwit-ˌwȯ-tərz-ˌrand, -ˌwä-, -ˌränd, -ˌränt\ *or* **Rand** ridge of gold-bearing rock NE Republic of South Africa

Wol·lon·gong \ˈwù-lən-ˌgäŋ, -ˌgȯŋ\ city SE Australia in E New South Wales S of Sydney; *pop* 211,417

Wol·ver·hamp·ton \ˌwùl-vər-ˈham(p)-tən\ town W *cen* England NW of Birmingham; *pop* 236,582

Worces·ter \ˈwùs-tər\ city E *cen* Massachusetts; *pop* 172,648

Wran·gell, Mount \ˈraŋ-gəl\ volcano 14,163 ft. (4317 m.) S Alaska in **Wrangell Mountains**

Wro·claw \ˈvrȯt-ˌswäf, -ˌsläv\ city SW Poland in Silesia; *pop* 642,334

Wu·han \ˈwü-ˈhän\ city E *cen* China; *pop* 3,284,229

Wu·xi *or* **Wu–hsi** \ˈwü-ˈshē\ city E China; *pop* 826,833

Wy·o·ming \wī-ˈō-miŋ\ state NW U.S.; ✳, Cheyenne; *pop* 493,782 — **Wy·o·ming·ite** \-miŋ-ˌīt\ *n*

Xi'·an *or* **Hsi–an** \ˈshē-ˈän\ city E *cen* China; *pop* 1,959,044

Xianggang — see HONG KONG

Xin·jiang Uy·gur *or* **Sin·kiang Ui·ghur** \ˈshin-ˈjyäŋ-ˈwē-gər\ region W China between the Kunlun & Altai mountains; *pop* 15,155,778

Xizang — see TIBET

Xu·zhou \ˈshü-ˈjō\ *or* **Sü·chow** \ˈshü-ˈjō, ˈsü-\ city E China; *pop* 805,695

Yak·i·ma \ˈya-kə-ˌmȯ\ city S *cen* Washington; *pop* 71,845

Ya·lu \ˈyä-(ˌ)lü\ river 500 mi. (804 km.) long SE Manchuria & North Korea

Ya·mous·sou·kro \ˌyä-mə-ˈsü-krō\ town, official ✳ of
Ivory Coast; *pop* 110,000

Yan·gon \ˌyän-ˈgōn\ *formerly* **Ran·goon** \ran-ˈgün, raŋ-\
city, ✳ of Myanmar; *pop* 1,717,649

Yangtze — see CHANG

Yaoun·dé \ˌyaün-ˈdā\ city, ✳ of Cameroon; *pop* 649,000

Yap \ˈyap, ˈyäp\ island W Pacific in the W Carolines

Ya·ren \ˈyä-ˌrən\ town, ✳ of Nauru; *pop* 1100

Ya·ro·slavl \ˌyär-ə-ˈslä-vᵊl\ city *cen* Russia in Europe, NE
of Moscow; *pop* 637,000

Yaz·oo \ya-ˈzü, ˈya-(ˌ)zü\ river W *cen* Mississippi

Ye·ka·te·rin·burg \yi-ˈka-tə-rən-ˌbərg, yi-ˌkä-ti-rēm-ˈbůrk\
formerly **Sverd·lovsk** \sverd-ˈlófsk\ city W Russia, in *cen*
Ural Mountains; *pop* 1,371,000

Yellow **1** — see HUANG **2** sea, section of East China
Sea between N China, North Korea, & South Korea

Yel·low·knife \ˈye-lō-ˌnīf\ town, ✳ of Northwest Territories, Canada; *pop* 16,541

Ye·men \ˈye-mən\ country S Arabia bordering on Red Sea
& Gulf of Aden; ✳, Sanaa; *pop* 12,961,000 — **Ye·me·ni**
\ˈye-mə-nē\ *adj or n* — **Ye·men·ite** \-mə-ˌnīt\ *adj or n*

Ye·ni·sey *or* **Ye·ni·sei** \ˌyi-ni-ˈsā\ river over 2500 mi. (4022
km.) long *cen* Russia, flowing N into Arctic Ocean

Ye·re·van \ˌyer-ə-ˈvän\ city, ✳ of Armenia; *pop* 1,199,000

Yo·ko·ha·ma \ˌyō-kō-ˈhä-mä\ city Japan in SE Honshu on
Tokyo Bay S of Tokyo; *pop* 3,426,651

Yon·kers \ˈyäŋ-kərz\ city SE New York N of New York
City; *pop* 196,086

York \ˈyórk\ city N England; *pop* 100,600

York, Cape cape NE Australia in Queensland at N tip of
Cape York Peninsula

York·shire \-ˌshir, -shər\ former county N England

Yo·sem·i·te Falls \yō-ˈse-mə-tē\ waterfall E California in
Yosemite Valley; includes two falls, the upper 1430 ft.
(436 m.) & the lower 320 ft. (98 m.)

Youngs·town \ˈyəŋz-ˌtaün\ city NE Ohio; *pop* 82,026

Yu·ca·tán \ˌyü-kə-ˈtan, -kä-ˈtän\ peninsula SE Mexico & N
Central America including Belize & N Guatemala

Yu·go·sla·via \ˌyü-gō-ˈslä-vē-ə, ˌyü-gə-\ **1** former country S Europe including Serbia, Montenegro, Slovenia,
Croatia, Bosnia and Herzegovina, & Macedonia; ✳, Belgrade **2** — see SERBIA AND MONTENEGRO — **Yu·go·**
slav \ˌyü-gō-ˈsläv, -ˈslav; ˈyü-gō-ˌ\ *or* **Yu·go·sla·vi·an** \ˌyü-
gō-ˈslä-vē-ən, -gə-\ *adj or n*

Yu·kon \ˈyü-ˌkän\ **1** river 1979 mi. (3185 km.) long NW
Canada & Alaska flowing into Bering Sea **2** *or* **Yukon**
Territory territory NW Canada; ✳, Whitehorse; *pop*
29,885

Yu·ma \ˈyü-mə\ city SW corner of Arizona on the Colorado; *pop* 77,515

Za·greb \ˈzä-ˌgreb\ city, ✳ of Croatia; *pop* 779,145

Zaire \zä-ˈir\ **1** river in Africa — see CONGO 1 **2** country in Africa — see CONGO 2 — **Zair·ean** *or* **Zair·ian** \zä-
ˈir-ē-ən\ *adj or n*

Zam·be·zi *or* **Zam·be·si** \zam-ˈbē-zē, zäm-ˈbä-zē\ river
about 1700 mi. (2735 km.) long SE Africa flowing from
NW Zambia into Mozambique Channel

Zam·bia \ˈzam-bē-ə\ *formerly* **Northern Rhodesia** country S Africa N of the Zambezi; ✳, Lusaka; *pop* 9,132,000
— **Zam·bi·an** \ˈzam-bē-ən\ *adj or n*

Zan·zi·bar \ˈzan-zə-ˌbär\ island Tanzania off NE Tanganyika coast; united 1964 with Tanganyika forming Tanzania

Za·po·rizh·zhya *or* **Za·po·ro·zh'ye** \ˌzä-pə-ˈrēzh-zhyə\ city
SE Ukraine; *pop* 897,000

Zhang·jia·kou \ˈjäŋ-ˈjyä-ˈkō\ *or* **Kal·gan** \ˈkal-ˈgan\ city
NE China NW of Beijing; *pop* 529,136

Zhdanov — see MARIUPOL

Zheng·zhou *or* **Cheng–chou** \ˈjəŋ-ˈjō\ city NE *cen* China;
pop 1,159,679

Zim·ba·bwe \zim-ˈbä-bwē, -(ˌ)bwä\ *formerly* **Rhodesia**
country S Africa S of Zambezi River; ✳, Harare; *pop*
7,550,000 — **Zim·ba·bwe·an** \-ən\ *adj or n*

Zui·der Zee \ˌzī-dər-ˈzā, -ˈzē\ — see IJSSELMEER

Zu·lu·land \ˈzü-(ˌ)lü-ˌland\ territory E Republic of South
Africa on Indian Ocean

Zu·rich \ˈzůr-ik\ city N Switzerland; *pop* 340,873

A HANDBOOK OF STYLE

PUNCTUATION

Punctuation marks are used in written English to separate groups of words for meaning and emphasis; to convey an idea of the variations of pitch, volume, pauses, and intonation of the spoken language; and to help avoid ambiguity. The uses of the standard punctuation marks are discussed and illustrated in the following pages. For an explanation of the punctuation marks used in the entries in this dictionary, see the Explanatory Notes in the front of the book.

APOSTROPHE '

1. Indicates the possessive of nouns and indefinite pronouns. The possessive of singular nouns and some plural nouns is formed by adding -'s. The possessive of plural nouns ending in an *s* or *z* sound is usually formed by adding only an apostrophe; the possessive of irregular plurals is formed by adding -'s.

the boy's mother   birds' migrations

Douglas's crimes   the Stevenses' house

anyone's guess   people's opinions

Degas's drawings   children's laughter

2. Marks the omission of letters in contracted words.

didn't   they're   she'd

3. Marks the omission of digits in numerals.

class of '03   in the '90s

4. Often forms plurals of letters, figures, abbreviations, symbols, and words referred to as words.

dot your *i*'s and cross your *t*'s

three 8's   *or*   three 8s

these Ph.D.'s   *or*   these Ph.D.s

used &'s instead of *and*'s

BRACKETS [ ]

1. Enclose editorial comments or clarifications inserted into quoted material.

His embarrassment had peaked [sic] her curiosity.

2. Enclose insertions that supply missing letters or that alter the form of the original word.

His letter continues, "If D[eutsch] won't take the manuscript, perhaps someone at Faber will."

He dryly observed that they bought the stock because "they want[ed] to see themselves getting richer."

3. Function as parentheses within parentheses.

Posner's recent essays (like his earlier *Law and Literature* [1988]) bear this out.

COLON :

1. Introduces an amplifying word, phrase, or clause that acts as an appositive.

That year Handley's old obsession was replaced with a new one: jazz.

The issue comes down to this: Will we offer a reduced curriculum, or will we simply cancel the program?

2. Introduces a list or series.

Three abstained: Britain, France, and Belgium.

3. Introduces a clause or phrase that explains, illustrates, amplifies, or restates what has gone before.

Dawn was breaking: the distant peaks were already glowing with the sun's first rays.

4. Introduces lengthy quoted material set off from the rest of the text by indentation but not by quotation marks. It may also be used before a quotation enclosed by quotation marks in running text.

The *Rumpole* series has been well described as follows:

Rumpled, disreputable, curmudgeonly barrister Horace Rumpole often wins cases despite the disdain of his more aristocratic colleagues. Fond of cheap wine ("Château Thames Embankment") and. . . .

The inscription reads: "Here lies one whose name was writ in water."

5. Separates elements in bibliographic publication data and page references, in biblical citations, and in formulas used to express time and ratios.

Boston: Houghton Mifflin, 1997

Scientific American 240 (Jan.):122-33

John 4:10　　　　8:30 a.m.　　　　a ratio of 3:5

6. Separates titles and subtitles.

Southwest Stories: Tales from the Desert

7. Follows the salutation in formal correspondence.

Dear Judge Wright:　　Ladies and Gentlemen:

8. Follows headings in memorandums and business letters.

TO:　　　　　　　　Reference:

9. Is placed outside quotation marks and parentheses when it punctuates the larger sentence.

The problem becomes most acute in "Black Rose and Destroying Angel": plot simply ceases to exist.

COMMA　,

1. Separates main clauses joined by a coordinating conjunction (such as *and, but, or, nor, so*), and occasionally short parallel clauses not joined by conjunctions.

She knew very little about the new system, and he volunteered nothing.

The trial lasted for nine months, but the jury took only four hours to reach its verdict.

She came, she saw, she conquered.

2. Sets off adverbial clauses and phrases that begin or interrupt a sentence. If the sentence can be easily read without a comma, the comma may be omitted.

Having agreed to disagree, they turned to other matters.

The report, after being read aloud, was put up for consideration.

In January the roof fell in.

As cars age they depreciate.

3. Sets off transitional words and phrases (such as *indeed, however*) and words that introduce examples (such as *namely, for example*).

Indeed, no one seemed to have heard of him.

They concluded, however, that it was meaningless.

Three have complied, namely, Togo, Benin, and Ghana.

4. Sets off contrasting expressions within a sentence.

This project will take six months, not six weeks.

5. Separates words, phrases, or clauses in a series. Many writers omit the comma before the last item in a series whenever this would not result in ambiguity.

Men, women[,] and children crowded aboard the train.

Her job required her to pack quickly, to travel often[,] and to have no personal life.

He came down the steps as reporters shouted questions, flashbulbs popped[,] and the crowd pushed closer.

6. Separates two or more adjectives that modify a noun. It is not used between two adjectives when the first modifies the combination of the second plus the noun it modifies.

in a calm, reflective manner

the harsh, damp, piercing wind

the lone bald eagle　　　　a good used car

7. Sets off a nonrestrictive (nonessential) word, phrase, or clause that is in apposition to a preceding or following noun.

We visited Verdun, site of the famous battle.

A cherished landmark, the Hotel Sandburg was spared.

Its author, Maria Olevsky, was an expert diver.

8. Separates a direct quotation from a phrase identifying its source or speaker. The comma is omitted when the quotation ends with a question mark or exclamation point, and usually omitted when the quoted phrase itself is the subject or object of the larger sentence.

She answered, "I'm leaving."

"I suspect," Bob observed, "we'll be hearing more."

"How about another round?" Elaine piped up.

"The network is down" was the reply she feared.

9. Sets off words in direct address and mild interjections.

The facts, my fellow Americans, are very different.

This is our final notice, Mr. Sutton.

Ah, the mosaics in Ravenna are matchless.

10. Precedes a tag question.

That's obvious, isn't it?

11. Indicates the omission of a word or phrase used in a parallel construction earlier in the sentence. In short sentences, the comma may be omitted.

Eight councillors cast their votes for O'Reilly; six, for Mendez.

Seven voted in favor, three against.

12. Is used to avoid ambiguity that might arise from adjacent words.

Under Mr. James, Madison High School flourished.

13. Groups numerals into units of three to separate thousands, millions, and so on. It is not used in street addresses, page numbers, and four-digit years.

2,000 case histories	12537 Wilshire Blvd.
a fee of $12,500	page 1415
numbering 3,450,000	in 3000 B.C.

14. Separates a surname from a following title or degree, and often from the abbreviations *Jr.* and *Sr.*

Sandra H. Cobb, Vice President

Lee Herman Melville, M.D.

Douglas Fairbanks, Jr. *or* Douglas Fairbanks Jr.

15. Sets off elements of an address (except for zip codes) and full dates. When only the month and year are given, the comma is usually omitted.

Write to Bureau of the Census, Washington, DC 20233.

In Reno, Nevada, their luck ran out.

On July 26, 2000, the court issued its opinion.

October 1929 brought an end to all that.

16. Follows the salutation in informal correspondence and follows the complimentary close in a letter.

Dear Aunt Sarah,   Sincerely yours,

DASH —

1. Marks an abrupt change or break in the structure of a sentence.

The students seemed happy enough with the new plan, but the alumni—there was the problem

2. Is used in place of commas or parentheses to emphasize parenthetical or amplifying material. In general, no punctuation immediately precedes an opening dash or immediately follows a closing dash.

It will prevent corporations—large and small—from buying influence with campaign contributions.

3. Introduces defining phrases and lists.

The motion was then tabled—that is, removed indefinitely from consideration.

Davis was a leading innovator in at least three styles—bebop, cool jazz, and jazz-rock fusion.

4. Often precedes the attribution of a quotation, either immediately after the quotation or on the next line.

Only the sign is for sale. —Søren Kierkegaard

or

Only the sign is for sale.

—Søren Kierkegaard

5. Sets off an interrupting clause or phrase. An exclamation point or question mark may immediately precede a dash.

If we don't succeed—and the critics say we won't—then the whole project is in jeopardy.

His hobby was getting on people's nerves—especially mine!—and he was very good at it.

ELLIPSIS ...

1. Indicates the omission of one or more words within a quoted sentence. Omission of a word or phrase is indicated by three ellipsis points. If an entire sentence or more is omitted, the end punctuation of the preceding sentence (including a period) is followed by three ellipsis points. Punctuation used in the original that falls on either side of the ellipsis is often omitted; however, it may be re-

tained, especially if this helps clarify the sentence structure. (The second and third examples below are shortened versions of the first.)

> Is it so bad, then, to be misunderstood? Pythagoras was misunderstood, and Socrates, and Jesus, and Luther, and Copernicus, and Galileo, and Newton, and every pure and wise spirit that ever took flesh. To be great is to be misunderstood.—Emerson

> Is it so bad, then, to be misunderstood? Pythagoras was misunderstood, and Socrates, and Jesus, . . . and every pure and wise spirit that ever took flesh.

> Is it so bad, then, to be misunderstood? . . . To be great is to be misunderstood.

2. Indicates that one or more lines have been omitted from a poem. The row of ellipsis points usually matches the length of the line above.

> When I heard the learned astronomer,
> . . . .
> How soon unaccountable I became tired and sick,
> Til rising and gliding out I wandered off by myself,

3. Indicates faltering speech or an unfinished sentence in dialogue.

> "I mean . . . " he stammered, "like . . . How?"

EXCLAMATION POINT !

1. Ends an emphatic phrase, sentence, or interjection.

> Without a trace!

> There is no alternative!

> Encore!

2. Is placed within brackets, dashes, parentheses, and quotation marks when it punctuates only the enclosed material. It is placed outside them when it punctuates the entire sentence. If it falls where a comma could also go, the comma is dropped.

> All of this proves—at long last!—that we were right from the start.

> Somehow the dog got the gate open (for the third time!) and ran into the street.

> He sprang to his feet and shouted "Point of order!"

> At this rate, the national anthem will soon be replaced by "You Are My Sunshine"!

> "Absolutely not!" he snapped.

> They wouldn't dare! she told herself over and over.

HYPHEN -

1. Is often used to link elements in compound words. Consult the dictionary in doubtful cases.

> secretary-treasurer　　　spin-off
>
> cost-effective　　　light-year
>
> middle-of-the-road　　president-elect

2. Is used to separate a prefix, suffix, or combining form from an existing word if the base word is capitalized, and often when the base word is more than two syllables long, or when identical letters would otherwise be adjacent to each other. Consult the dictionary in doubtful cases.

> pre-Victorian　　　wall-like
>
> industry-wide　　　co-opted
>
> recession-proof　　anti-inflationary

3. Is used in compound nouns containing a particle (usually a preposition or adverb).

> on-ramp　　　falling-out
>
> runner-up　　　right-of-way

4. Is used in most compound modifiers when placed before the noun.

> the fresh-cut grass　　a made-up excuse
>
> her gray-green eyes　　the well-worded statement

5. Is used with the first of two prefixes or modifiers forming a compound with the same base word.

> pre- and postoperative care
>
> anti- or pro-Revolutionary sympathies
>
> early- and mid-20th-century painters

6. Is used with written-out numbers, both cardinal and ordinal, between 21 and 99.

> forty-one years old　　his forty-first birthday
>
> one hundred forty-one

7. Is used in a written-out fraction employed as a modifier. A fraction used as a noun is often left open.

> a one-half share
>
> three fifths of the vote *or* three-fifths of the vote
>
> one one-hundredth of an inch

8. Is used between numbers and dates with the meaning "(up) to and including." In typeset material the hyphen is replaced by the longer en dash.

pages 128–34

the years 1995–99

9. Is used as the equivalent of *to, and,* or *versus* to indicate linkage or opposition. In typeset material the longer en dash is used.

the New York–Paris flight

the Lincoln–Douglas debates

a final score of 7–2.

10. Marks an end-of-line division of a word.

Stanley's search came to an end at Lake Tanganyika, in the Arab settlement of Ujiji.

PARENTHESES ( )

1. Enclose phrases and clauses that provide examples, explanations, or supplementary facts.

Nominations for principal officers (president, vice president, treasurer, and secretary) were approved.

Four computers (all outdated models) were replaced.

Although we liked Mille Fiori (their risotto was the best), we hadn't been there in several months.

2. Enclose numerals that confirm a spelled-out number in a business or legal context.

Delivery will be made in thirty (30) days.

The fee is four thousand dollars ($4,000.00).

3. Enclose numbers or letters indicating individual items in a series within a sentence.

Sentences can be classified as (1) simple, (2) multiple or compound, and (3) complex.

4. Enclose abbreviations that follow their spelled-out forms, or spelled-out forms that follow their abbreviations.

the Food and Drug Administration (FDA)

the ABA (American Booksellers Association)

5. Indicate alternative terms.

Please sign and return the enclosed form(s).

6. Often enclose cross-references and bibliographic references, as well as publishing data in bibliographic citations.

Specialized services are also available (see list below).

The diagram (Fig. 3) illustrates the action of the pump.

Subsequent studies (Braxton 1998; Roh and Weinglass 2002) have confirmed these findings.

3. See Stendhal, *Love* (New York: Penguin, 1975), 342.

7. Are used with other punctuation marks as follows: If an independent sentence is enclosed in parentheses, its first word is capitalized and a period is placed inside the parentheses. If the parenthetical expression occurs within a sentence, it is uncapitalized unless it is a quotation, and does not end with a period but may end with an exclamation point, a question mark, or quotation marks. No punctuation immediately precedes an opening parenthesis within a sentence; if punctuation is required, it follows the closing parenthesis.

The discussion was held in the boardroom. (The results are still confidential.)

This short section (musicians would call it the *bridge*) has the song's most distinctive harmonies.

The background music is always Bach (does the chairman have such good taste?).

He was distraught ("It's my whole career!") and refused to see anyone.

I'll get back to you tomorrow (Friday), when I have more details.

PERIOD .

1. Ends a sentence or a sentence fragment that is neither a question nor an exclamation. Only one period ends a sentence.

She asked if we were swing dancers.

Give it your best.

Unlikely. In fact, inconceivable.

She liked best the sentence that read "Leda Rubin has made the impossible possible."

2. Follows most abbreviations and some contractions.

Calif.	e.g.	Dr.
Sept.	p.m.	Jr.
etc.	dept.	Assn.
Ph.D. *or* PhD		C.E.O. *or* CEO

3. Is used with a person's initials.

F. Scott Fitzgerald   J. B. S. Haldane

4. Follows numerals and letters when used without parentheses in outlines and vertical lists.

I. Objectives
  A. Economy
    1. Low initial cost
    2. Low maintenance cost
  B. Ease of operation

QUESTION MARK   ?

1. Ends a direct question.

"When do they arrive?" she asked.

Was anyone seen in the area after 10 p.m.?

2. Ends a question that forms part of a sentence, but does not follow an indirect question.

What was her motive? you may be asking.

I naturally wondered, Will it really work?

He asked when the club normally closed.

3. Indicates uncertainty about a fact.

Geoffrey Chaucer, English poet (1342?–1400)

4. Is used with other punctuation marks exactly like the exclamation point (see p. 1606).

QUOTATION MARKS, DOUBLE   " "

1. Enclose direct quotations but not indirect quotations.

"I'm leaving," she whispered. "This could last forever."

She whispered that she was leaving.

He asked, "What went wrong?"

The question is, What went wrong?

2. Enclose words or phrases borrowed from others, and words of obvious informality.

They required a "biodata summary"—that is, a résumé.

He called himself "emperor," but he was really just a dictator.

They were afraid the patient had "stroked out"—had had a cerebrovascular accident.

3. Enclose titles of poems, short stories, essays, articles in periodicals, chapters of books, and episodes of radio and television programs.

the article "After the Genocide" in the *New Yorker*

"The Death of the Hired Man" by Robert Frost

Poe's "The Murders in the Rue Morgue"

John Barth's essay "The Literature of Exhaustion"

The Jungle Book's ninth chapter, "Rikki-tikki-tavi"

M*A*S*H's finale, "Goodbye, Farewell and Amen"

4. Enclose lines of poetry run in with the text.

When Gilbert advised, "Stick close to your desks and never go to sea, / And you all may be rulers of the Queen's Navee!" this latest appointee was obviously paying attention.

5. Are used with other punctuation marks as follows: A period or comma is placed within the quotation marks. A colon or semicolon is placed outside them. A dash, question mark, or exclamation point is placed inside the quotation marks when it punctuates the quoted matter only, but outside when it punctuates the whole sentence.

He smiled and said, "I'm happy for you."

"Too easy," she shot back.

There was only one real "issue": noise.

She spoke of her "little cottage in the country"; she might better have called it a mansion.

"I can't see how—" he started to say.

Saturdays there were dances—"sock hops"—in the gym.

He asked, "When did she leave?"

What is the meaning of "the open door"?

She collapsed in her seat with a stunned "Good grief!"

Save us from his "mercy"!

QUOTATION MARKS, SINGLE   ' '

1. Enclose quoted material within quoted material.

"I distinctly heard him say, 'Don't be late,' and then I heard the door close."

This analysis is indebted to Del Banco's "Elizabeth Bishop's 'Insomnia': An Inverted View."

2. In British usage, may enclose quoted material, in which case a quotation within a quotation is set off by double quotation marks.

'I distinctly heard him say, "Don't be late," and then I heard the door close.'

SEMICOLON ;

1. Separates related independent clauses joined without a coordinating conjunction.

> Cream the butter and sugar; add the eggs and beat well.

> The river overflowed its banks; roads vanished; freshly plowed fields turned into lakes.

2. Joins two clauses when the second includes a conjunctive adverb (such as *however, indeed, thus*) or a phrase that acts like one (such as *in that case, as a result, on the other hand*).

> It won't be easy to sort out the facts; a decision must be made, however.

> The case could take years; as a result, many plaintiffs will accept settlements.

3. Is often used before introductory expressions such as *for example, that is,* and *namely*.

> We were fairly successful; that is, we made our deadlines and met our budget.

4. Separates phrases or items in a series when they contain commas.

> The assets include $22 million in land, buildings, and equipment; $34 million in cash and investments; and $8 million in inventory.

> The Pissarro exhibition will travel to Washington, D.C.; Manchester, N.H.; Portland, Ore.; and Oakland, Cal.

> The votes against were: Precinct 1, 418; Precinct 2, 332; Precinct 3, 256.

5. Is placed outside quotation marks and parentheses.

> They again demanded "complete autonomy"; the demand was again rejected.

> She found him urbane and entertaining (if somewhat overbearing); he found her charmingly ingenuous.

SLASH /

1. Separates alternatives, usually representing the words *or* or *and/or*.

> alumni/ae   his/her

2. Replaces the word *to* or *and* in some compound terms and ranges.

> 1998/99 *or* 1998–99

> the May/June issue *or* the May–June issue

3. Separates lines of poetry that are run in with the text. A space usually precedes and follows the slash.

> In Pope's words: "'Tis with our judgments as our watches, none / Go just alike, yet each believes his own."

4. Separates the elements in a numerical date, and numerators and denominators in fractions.

> on 9/11/01   a 7/8-mile course

5. Represents the word *per* or *to* when used between units of measure or the terms of a ratio.

> 400,000 tons/year   price/earnings ratio
> 29 mi/gal   20/20 vision

6. Punctuates some abbreviations.

> w/o [*for* without]   I/O [*for* input/output]
> c/o [*for* care of]   P/E [*for* price/earnings]

7. Punctuates Internet addresses.

> http://unabridged.Merriam-Webster.com/

FOREIGN MARKS

1. Guillemets « » often enclose quotations in French and other European languages.

> Marie Antoinette est censée dire «qu'ils mangent de la brioche».

2. Spanish exclamation points ¡ ! are used in pairs to enclose an exclamatory sentence in Spanish writing.

> ¡Qué buen día!

3. Spanish question marks ¿ ? are used in pairs to enclose an interrogatory sentence in Spanish writing.

> ¿Qué es esto?

CAPITALS AND ITALICS

Words and phrases are capitalized or italicized to indicate that they have a special significance in particular contexts. The following rules and examples describe the most common uses of capitals and italics.

BEGINNINGS

1. The first word of a sentence or sentence fragment is capitalized.

The play lasted nearly three hours.

So many people, so many opinions.

Bravo!

2. The first word of a sentence contained within parentheses is capitalized. However, a parenthetical sentence within another sentence is not capitalized unless it is a complete quoted sentence.

No one answered the telephone. (They were probably on vacation.)

Having waited in line for an hour (why do we do these things?), we finally left.

After some initial defensiveness ("Was it my fault?"), he gradually got over it.

3. The first word of a direct quotation is capitalized. However, if the quotation is interrupted in mid-sentence, the second part does not begin with a capital. When a quotation is syntactically dependent on the sentence in which it occurs, it usually does not begin with a capital.

Hart repeated, "We have no budget for new computers."

"We have no budget for new computers," repeated Hart, "but we may next year."

Hart made it clear that "we have no budget for new computers."

4. The first word of a sentence within a sentence that is not a direct quotation is usually capitalized. Examples include mottoes and rules, unspoken or imaginary dialogue, and direct questions.

You know the saying "Fools rush in where angels fear to tread."

The first rule is, When in doubt, spell it out.

My first thought was, How can I avoid this assignment?

The question is, When can we go?

5. The first word following a colon is usually lowercased, even when it begins a complete sentence. However, when the sentence introduced is lengthy and distinctly separate from the preceding clause, it is often capitalized.

The advantage of this system is clear: it's inexpensive.

The situation is critical: This company cannot hope to recoup the fourth-quarter losses that were sustained in five operating divisions.

6. The first word of a line of poetry is traditionally capitalized. However, in modern poetry the line beginnings are often lowercased. The poem's original capitalization should always be retained.

The best lack all conviction, while the worst
Are full of passionate intensity.
                                        —W. B. Yeats

    If tributes cannot
be implicit
give me diatribes and the fragrance of iodine,
the corn oak acorn grown in Spain. . .
                                        —Marianne Moore

7. The first words of items in vertical lists are usually capitalized. However, numbered phrases within a sentence are lowercased.

The English peerage consists of five ranks:
  1. Duke (Duchess)
  2. Marquess (Marchioness)
  3. Earl (Countess)
  4. Viscount (Viscountess)
  5. Baron (Baroness)

Among the fastest animals are (1) the cheetah, clocked at 70 mph; (2) the pronghorn, at 61 mph; (3) the lion, at 50 mph; (4) the quarter horse, at 47 mph; and (5) the elk, at 45 mph.

8. The first word in an outline heading is capitalized.

  I. Prose texts
    A. Typeface
      1. Alphabets
      2. Characteristics
    B. Type page and trim size

9. The first word and courtesy titles of the salutation of a letter and the first word of a complimentary close are capitalized.

Dear Sir or Madam: Sincerely yours,

To whom it may concern: Love,

PROPER NOUNS AND ADJECTIVES

Awards and Prizes

1. Names of awards and prizes are capitalized. Words and phrases that are not actually part of the award's name are lowercased.

Academy Award	Rhodes Scholarship
Nobel Prize in medicine	Rhodes scholar

Derivatives of Proper Nouns

2. Derivatives of proper nouns are capitalized when used in their primary sense. If the derived term has taken on a specialized meaning, it is often lowercased. Consult the dictionary when in doubt.

Roman sculpture	chinaware
Edwardian era	Hodgkin's disease
french fries	quixotic

Geographical References

3. Terms that identify divisions of the earth's surface and distinct regions, places, or districts are capitalized, as are derivative nouns and adjectives.

Tropic of Cancer	the Highlands
Asia Minor	Highland attitudes
the Great Lakes	Burgundy
Arnhem Land	Burgundians

4. Popular names of localities are capitalized.

the Left Bank	the Sunbelt
Little Italy	the Loop

5. Words designating global, national, regional, or local political divisions are capitalized when they are essential elements of specific names. They are usually lowercased when they precede a proper noun or are not part of a specific name.

the Roman Empire	New York City
the fall of the empire	the city of New York

6. Generic geographical terms (such as *lake, mountain*) are capitalized if they are part of a proper noun.

Lake Tanganyika	Atlas Mountains
Yosemite Valley	Mount Everest

7. Generic geographical terms preceding two or more names are usually capitalized.

Lakes Huron and Erie

Mounts McKinley, Whitney, and Shasta

8. Generic terms that are not used as part of a single proper noun are not capitalized. These include plural terms that follow two or more proper nouns, and terms that are used descriptively or alone.

Maine and Oak streets

the Oder and Nysa rivers

the Pacific coast of Mexico

the river delta

9. Compass points are capitalized when they refer to a geographical region or form part of a place-name or street name. They are lowercased when they refer to a simple direction.

the Southwest	East Coast
North Pole	north of the Rio Grande
West 12th Street	went west on 12th Street

10. Nouns and adjectives that are derived from compass points and that designate or refer to a specific geographical region are usually capitalized.

Easterners	Southern hospitality
Northern Europeans	Southwestern recipes

11. Names of streets, monuments, parks, landmarks, and other public places are capitalized. Generic terms (such as *street, park, bridge*) are lowercased when used alone.

State Street	the Plaza Hotel
Golden Gate Bridge	back to the hotel

Governmental and Judicial Bodies

12. Full names of legislative, executive, and administrative bodies are capitalized, as are easily recognizable short forms of these names. However, nonspecific noun and adjective references to them are usually lowercased.

United States Congress

Congress

congressional hearings

Federal Trade Commission

a federal agency

13. Full names of high courts are capitalized. Short forms of such names are usually lowercased, as are names of city and county courts. However, both the full and short names of the U.S. Supreme Court are capitalized.

International Court of Justice

the state supreme court

Springfield municipal court

small-claims court

the Supreme Court of the United States

the Court

Historical Periods and Events

14. Names of some historical and cultural periods and movements are capitalized. When in doubt, consult a dictionary or encyclopedia.

Bronze Age	Third Reich
the Renaissance	Victorian era
Fifth Republic	Age of Pericles
Prohibition	the atomic age

15. Names of conferences, councils, and specific historical, cultural, and sporting events are capitalized.

Yalta Conference	San Francisco Earthquake
Council of Trent	Cannes Film Festival
Boston Tea Party	World Cup

16. Full names of specific treaties, laws, and acts are capitalized.

Treaty of Versailles	First Amendment rights
the Bill of Rights	Clean Air Act of 1990

Legal Cases

17. Names of the plaintiff and defendant in legal case titles are italicized, as are short forms of case titles. The *v.* (for *versus*) may be roman or italic. When the party involved rather than the case itself is being discussed, the reference is not italicized.

Smith et al. v. [*or* v.] *Jones*

a quick decision in the *Jones* case

She covered the Lemuel Jones trial for the newspaper.

Military Units

18. Full titles of branches and units of the U.S. armed forces are capitalized, as are standard short forms. However, the plurals of *army, navy, air force,* and *coast guard* are lowercased.

U.S. Marine Corps	the Third Army
the Marines	allied armies

Organizations

19. Names of organizations, corporations, and institutions are capitalized, as are derivative terms to designate their members. However, common nouns occurring after the names of two or more organizations are lowercased.

the Rotary Club	AT&T Corporation
all Rotarians	League of Women Voters
University of Wisconsin	
Yale and Harvard universities	

20. Words such as *agency, department, division, group,* or *office* that designate corporate and orga-

nizational units are capitalized only as part of a specific proper noun.

manager of the Sales Division of K2 Outfitters

a memo to the sales divisions of both companies

People

21. Names and initials of persons are capitalized. If a name is hyphenated, both elements are capitalized. Particles forming the initial elements of surnames (such as *de, della, du, la, ten, ter, van,* and *von*) may or may not be capitalized, depending on the practice of the individual. The prefixes *Mac, Mc,* and *O'* are always capitalized.

Cecil Day-Lewis	Martin Van Buren
Cecil B. DeMille	Wernher von Braun
Agnes de Mille	Archibald MacLeish
W. E. B. DuBois	Sean O'Casey

22. Titles preceding the name of a person and epithets or nicknames used instead of a name are capitalized. However, titles used alone or as part of a phrase following a name are usually lowercased.

President Lincoln

Honest Abe

King Henry VIII

Henry VIII, king of England

Logex Corp.'s president

23. Words of family relationship preceding or used in place of a person's name are capitalized; otherwise they are lowercased.

Uncle Fred	Mother's birthday
Cousin Julia	my mother's birthday

24. Words designating languages, nationalities, peoples, races, religious groups, and tribes are capitalized. Designations based on skin color are usually lowercased.

Spanish	Iroquois
Spaniards	Asians
Muslims	blacks and whites

Personifications

25. Abstract concepts or qualities are capitalized when they are personified.

as Autumn paints each leaf in fiery colors

the statue of Justice with her scales

Religious Terms

26. Words designating the supreme being are capitalized. Plural references to deities are lowercased.

Allah	the Almighty
Brahma	in the eyes of God
Jehovah	the angry gods

27. Personal pronouns referring to the supreme being are often capitalized in religious writing.

God made His presence known

28. Traditional designations of apostles, prophets, and saints are capitalized.

the Madonna	the Twelve
the Prophet	St. John of the Cross
Moses the Lawgiver	John the Baptist

29. Names of religions, denominations, creeds and confessions, and religious orders are capitalized, as are derivatives of these names.

Judaism	Apostles' Creed
Islam	a Buddhist
Eastern Orthodox	Society of Jesus
Church of England	Jesuit teachers

30. Full names of specific places of worship are capitalized, but terms such as *church, synagogue,* and *mosque* are lowercased when used alone.

Hunt Memorial Church	the Blue Mosque
Beth Israel Synagogue	the mosque's minaret

31. Names of the Bible and other sacred works, their books and parts, and versions or editions of them are capitalized but not italicized. Adjectives derived from such names are capitalized except for the words *biblical* and *scriptural.*

Bible	Talmud
the Scriptures	Bhagavad Gita
Old Testament	Revised Standard Version
Koran *also* Quran *or* Qur'an	
Koranic *also* Quranic *or* Qur'anic	

Scientific Terms

32. Names of planets and their satellites, stars, constellations, and other specific celestial objects are capitalized. However, the words *sun, earth,* and *moon* are usually lowercased unless they occur with other astronomical names.

Jupiter	Halley's comet
Ganymede	Mars, Venus, and Earth
the North Star	life on earth
Ursa Major	the new moon

33. New Latin genus names in zoology and botany are capitalized and italicized. The second term in binomial scientific names, identifying the species, is lowercased and italicized, as are the names of races, varieties, or subspecies.

the California condor (*Gymnogyps californianus*)

a common buttercup (*Ranunculus acris*)

the Florida panther (*Felis concolor coryi*)

34. In zoology and botany, New Latin names of all groups above genus (such as class or family) are capitalized but not italicized. Their derivative nouns and adjectives are lowercased.

the class Gastropoda	the order Diptera
gastropod	dipteran flies
the family Ascaridae	Bryophyta
ascarid	bryophytic

35. Names of geological time divisions are capitalized. The generic terms that follow them are lowercased.

Mesozoic era	Paleocene epoch
Quaternary period	the Upper Cretaceous

Time Periods and Dates

36. Names of days of the week, months, and holidays and holy days are capitalized. Names of the seasons are lowercased.

Tuesday	Veterans Day	Easter
January	Yom Kippur	winter

Titles of Works

37. Words in titles of books, magazines, newspapers, plays, movies, long poems, and works of art such as paintings and sculpture are capitalized except for internal articles, coordinating conjunctions, prepositions, and the *to* of infinitives. Prepositions of four or more letters are often capitalized. The entire title is italicized. (Titles of articles in periodicals, short poems, short stories, essays, lectures, chapters of books, and episodes of radio and television programs are similarly capitalized but enclosed in quotation marks rather than italicized; see examples at "Quotation Marks, Double" on p. 647.)

Of Mice and Men	*Lawrence of Arabia*
Publishers Weekly	Eliot's *The Waste Land*
USA Today	Monet's *Water-Lily Pool*
Miller's *The Crucible*	Rodin's *Thinker*

38. Titles of long musical compositions are usually capitalized and italicized; the titles of songs and short compositions are capitalized and enclosed in quotation marks, as are the popular names of longer works. The titles of compositions identified

by their musical forms (such as *quartet, sonata, concerto*) are capitalized only, as are movements.

Mozart's *The Magic Flute*

Loesser's *Guys and Dolls*

"My Funny Valentine"

Beethoven's "Für Elise"

the "Moonlight" Sonata

his Violin Concerto in D

Quartet in D, Op. 64, No. 5

the Adagietto movement

39. Common titles of book sections (such as *chapter, preface, index*) are usually capitalized only when they refer to a section of the same book in which the reference appears.

See the Appendix for further information.

In a long introduction, the author explained her goals.

40. Nouns used with numbers or letters to designate major reference headings in books or periodicals are usually capitalized. Nouns designating minor elements are usually lowercased.

in Volume 5   see page 101

of Chapter 2   at paragraph 6.1

in Table 3   in line 8

Trademarks

41. Registered trademarks, service marks, and brand names are capitalized.

Coke	Kleenex	Xerox
Walkman	Band-Aid	Prozac
Levi's	Jacuzzi	Express Mail

Transportation

42. Names of ships, airplanes, and space vehicles are capitalized and italicized. The designations *USS, SS,* and *HMS* are not italicized.

HMS *Bounty*   *Challenger*

Spirit of St. Louis   *Apollo 13*

43. Names of train lines, types of aircraft, and space programs are capitalized but not italicized.

Metroliner   Concorde

Boeing 727   Pathfinder Program

OTHER STYLING CONVENTIONS

44. Italics are used to emphasize or draw attention to words in a sentence.

Students must notify the dean's office *in writing* of any added or dropped courses.

She was not *the* star, merely *a* star.

45. Italics are often used for letters referred to as letters, words referred to as words, and numerals referred to as numerals.

The *g* in *align* is silent.

Purists still insist that *data* is a plural noun.

The first *2* and the last *0* are barely legible.

46. Unfamiliar words or words having a specialized meaning are italicized when first introduced and defined in a text, but not subsequently.

In the *direct-to-consumer* transaction, the publisher markets directly to the individual by mail.

Vitiligo is a condition in which skin pigment cells stop making pigment. Treatment for vitiligo includes . . .

47. Foreign words and phrases that have not been fully adopted into English are italicized. In general, any word that appears in the main A-Z vocabulary of this dictionary does not need to be italicized.

At the club such behavior was distinctly *mal vu*.

The prix fixe lunch was $25.

DICTIONARY

DOCUMENTATION OF SOURCES

Writers are often required to specify the source of a quotation or piece of information borrowed from another work. Though formal documentation is omitted from popular writing, where quotations or information sources are acknowledged only casually (e.g., "As Stephen Hawking observed in his *Brief History of Time,* . . ."), the systematic use of notes, references, and bibliographies is required in most serious nonfiction and all scholarly writing, in which such documentation is an important indicator of the quality of the writer's research.

Footnotes, which are placed at the bottom of a page, and *endnotes,* which are placed at the end of an article, chapter, or book, have been the preferred form of documentation in serious works intended for a wide general readership and traditionally also in scholarly works in the humanities. Numbers within the text refer the reader to the footnotes or endnotes, which contain full bibliographical information on the works cited.

In scholarly works in the social and natural sciences, and increasingly in the humanities as well, *parenthetical references*—very brief references enclosed in parentheses within the actual text—refer the reader to a list of sources at the end. In works that employ parenthetical references, footnotes or endnotes may be used to provide ancillary information.

Regardless of which system is used, most carefully documented works include a *bibliography* or *list of sources* at the end.

The following paragraphs discuss and illustrate standard styles for references, notes, and bibliographic entries in scholarly fields. Fuller treatment can be found in *Merriam-Webster's Manual for Writers and Editors, The Chicago Manual of Style,* Kate Turabian's *Manual for Writers of Term Papers, Theses, and Dissertations,* the *MLA Handbook for Writers of Research Papers* (for the humanities), the *Publication Manual of the American Psychological Association* (for the social sciences), and *Scientific Style and Format* (for the natural sciences). However, the most efficient way to master the standard documentation style employed in any given discipline may be simply to study the citations in one of its leading journals.

FOOTNOTES AND ENDNOTES

Footnotes and endnotes are indicated by superscript numerals, usually placed immediately after the borrowed text. In an article, the numbering is consecutive throughout; in a book, it starts over with each new chapter. The notes themselves begin with numbers (either superscript, or now more commonly, full size with a period) that correspond to the superscript reference numbers in the text. Word-processing programs have greatly simplified the placement and numbering of footnotes and endnotes.

The first thirteen examples below (each of which is keyed to an item in the "Bibliographies" section at the end) illustrate the style to be used for the first reference to a book (nos. 1–9) or article (nos. 10–13). For journals, the abbreviations *vol.* and *no.* are now usually omitted. The reference normally ends with a page reference, though the abbreviations *p.* and *pp.* are usually omitted. In typescript, underlining may be used in place of italics. Any element of the reference that appears in the text itself (e.g., the author's name) can be omitted from the note. Note that citations of online sources (nos. 14–15) replace any physical place of publication with an Internet address, and end with the date on which the user consulted the source. An example of a substantive note (a note providing information other than straight bibliographical data) is also included (no. 16). Subsequent references to a book or article (nos. 17–18) generally consist of only the author's name and the new page reference; a shortened version of the work's title may be added to distinguish two or more cited works by the same author.

One author	1. Elizabeth Bishop, *The Complete Poems: 1927–79* (New York: Farrar, Straus & Giroux, 1983), 46.
Two or more authors	2. John S. Kenyon and Thomas A. Knott, *A Pronouncing Dictionary of American English* (Springfield, Mass.: Merriam-Webster, 1953), xv.
	3. Randolph Quirk et al., *A Comprehensive Grammar of the English Language* (London: Longman, 1985), 135.
Edition and/or translation	4. Arthur S. Banks and Thomas C. Muller, eds., *Political Handbook of the World: 2000–2002* (Binghamton, N.Y.: CSA Publications, 2003), 719–22.
	5. Simone de Beauvoir, *The Second Sex,* trans. and ed. H. M. Parshley (New York: Knopf, 1953; Vintage, 1989), 446.
Second or later edition	6. Albert Hourani and Malise Ruthven, *A History of the Arab Peoples,* 2d ed. (Belknap–Harvard Univ. Press, 2003), 66.

Article in a collection

7. Chester Himes, "Headwaiter," in *Calling the Wind,* ed. Clarence Major (New York: HarperCollins, 1993), 83.

Work in two or more volumes

8. Frederic G. Cassidy and Joan Houston Hall, eds., *Dictionary of American Regional English* (Belknap–Harvard Univ. Press, 1985–), 3:447.

Corporate author

9. *Who's Who in America: 2003* (New Providence, N.J.: Marquis Who's Who, 2002), 1:995.

Monthly magazine

10. Vannevar Bush, "As We May Think," *Atlantic Monthly,* July 1945, 101–8.

Weekly magazine

11. Christopher Hitchens, review of *C. L. R. James* by Farrukh Dhondy, *Times Literary Supplement,* 18 Jan. 2002, 34.

Journal paginated consecutively through-out annual volume

12. Lawrence M. Davis, Charles L. Houck, and Clive Upton, "'Sett Out Verry Eairly Wensdy': The Spelling and Grammar in the Lewis and Clark Journals," *American Speech* 75 (Summer 2000): 138.

Newspaper

13. Carol Kaesuk Yoon, "Scientists Say Orangutans Can Exhibit 'Culture,'" *New York Times,* 3 Jan. 2003, A14.

Electronic source

14. Jim Marchand, "Translating Crescentia," 27 Dec. 2002, Medieval Texts Discussion List ⟨http://listserv.uiuc.edu/wa.cgi?A2=ind0212&L=medtextl &P=20109⟩ (10 Jan. 2003).

15. John Rothgeb, "The Tristan Chord: Identity and Origin," *Music Theory Online,* 1.1 (Jan. 1995), ⟨http://www.societymusictheory.org/mto/issues/ mto.95.1.1/mto.95.1.1.rothgeb.art⟩ (12 June 1999).

Substantive note

16. Both "globalization" and "global village" date at least from the 1960s, with Zbigniew Brzezinski and Marshall McLuhan emphasizing respectively the universal status of the North American model of modernity and the technological convergence of the world. See Mattelart, 115.

Subsequent reference

17. Quirk et al., 106.

18. Beauvoir, *Second Sex,* 251.

PARENTHETICAL REFERENCES

Parenthetical references, though not used in works intended for a wide audience, are standard in scholarly works in the social sciences and natural sciences, and are increasingly being used in the humanities as well. These highly abbreviated references are embedded within the text itself and direct the reader to the more complete source information given in a bibliography at the end.

In the natural sciences, parenthetical references include only the author's last name and the year of publication ("author-date style," or "name-year style"). In the social sciences, writers use either the author-date style or an alternative style that also includes a page reference ("author-date-page style"). In the humanities, a page reference normally takes the place of the year of publication ("author-page style"). To distinguish two works published in the same year, the date may be followed by a lowercase letter—"(Chavis 1999a)," "(Chavis 1999b)." To distinguish among cited works by the same author, a shortened form of the work's title may be added—"(Faulkner, *Absalom* 220)," "(Faulkner, *Intruder* 151)."

The examples below illustrate the use of parenthetical references in, respectively, the natural sciences, the social sciences, and the humanities.

A historical assessment of many small, isolated populations found that every group with fewer than 50 individuals became extinct within 50 years (Berger 1990).

The land in West Africa was quite difficult to settle, and the mortality rate during the passage was "shockingly high" (Schick 1980, 27).

García Lorca critics have pointed out that, although Pepe sets the action of *La casa de Bernarda Alba* in motion, he never appears onstage (Gabriele 388; Urrea 51).

As with footnotes and endnotes, any information evident from the textual context—name, date, or title—is omitted from the reference. As a result, many references in the social sciences and humanities consist simply of page numbers.

References to electronic sources, which usually lack page references, may instead use paragraph numbers, if provided—"(Mather ¶ 16)"—or the number of the paragraph under a given heading within the article—"(Ortiz & Lane, Conclusions, para. 4)."

DICTIONARY

OTHER SYSTEMS

A newer style of citation, now often used in the natural sciences, is the *citation-sequence system*. Every source is given a number corresponding to the order of its first appearance in the article, and every later citation of that source employs the same number. The numbers themselves are either set in the main text as superscripts or are shown full-size in parentheses or brackets. There is usually no bibliography. The excerpt below (in which the source with the lower number had first appeared earlier in the article) is followed by the corresponding entries in the article's list of sources, in a style employing minimal punctuation and italicization.

The relation between bone mass and breast cancer may also involve endogenous androgens, which are determinants of bone mass[100] and which have also been associated with the risk of breast cancer.[21]

21. Zhang Y, Kiel DP, Kreger BE, et al. Bone mass and the risk of breast cancer among postmenopausal women. N Engl J Med 1997;336:611–7.

100. Buchanan JR, Myers C, Lloyd T, Leuenberger P, Demers LM. Determinants of peak trabecular bone density in women: the role of androgens, estrogen, and exercise. J Bone Miner Res 1988;3:673–80.

Another newer system, sometimes used when the intended audience includes both general readers and scholars, is the *white-copy system,* which provides endnotes but omits any reference to them at all on the text pages. The general reader can thus completely ignore the documentation, while the scholar can check sources at will. The excerpt is followed by its corresponding endnotes.

Aiken was on his way out of the flat when Ezra asked him if there was nobody genuinely *modern* he could recommend? Maybe someone at Harvard, 'something DIFFERENT'? Aiken thought for a moment, and answered: 'Oh well, there is Eliot.' Ezra asked who Eliot was, and was told: 'A guy at Harvard doing funny stuff.' Actually, added Aiken, Eliot was in England at the moment, so Ezra could meet him if he wanted to. Ezra told Aiken to arrange it.

257 'something DIFFERENT', PH 21 Dec '56. 'Oh well', Doob 128. 'A guy', Lyndall Gordon, *Eliot's Early Years,* Oxford University Press, 1977, 66.

The style of white-copy endnotes continues to vary widely from publication to publication. Here the abbreviations "PH" (indicating an unpublished collection of letters) and "Doob" (indicating a book) are explained in the book's bibliographic appendix; the third item, not being one of the book's important sources, is omitted from the appendix and instead given its full citation here.

BIBLIOGRAPHIES

A bibliography is usually provided at the end of any properly documented work (except those using the citation-sequence style). In works that rely on parenthetical references, a bibliography is essential, since the full citations are given nowhere else. In works that rely on footnotes or endnotes, the bibliography generally simply provides a convenient listing, alphabetized by the author's last name, of the bibliographic information that first appeared in the notes. Bibliography entries differ from notes chiefly in their punctuation. They include all the information in a full footnote or endnote except specific page references; however, when a journal article or a piece in a collection is being cited, the entry provides the range of pages for the entire article or piece.

The following bibliographies illustrate standard styles employed in, respectively, the humanities and the social and natural sciences. These differ principally in four respects: in the sciences, (1) the author's first and middle names are abbreviated, often without periods, (2) the date directly follows the author's name, (3) all words in book and article titles are lowercased except the first word, the first word of any subtitle, and proper nouns and adjectives, and (4) article titles are not enclosed in quotation marks. Also, in many scientific publications today, book and journal titles are not italicized. In journal citations, the abbreviations *vol.* and *no.* are generally omitted; the issue number either appears in parentheses or is omitted altogether, since pagination alone is sufficient to identify the issue when pagination is continuous throughout the volume. The titles of scientific journals are usually given in standard abbreviated forms.

Humanities

Banks, A. S., and Thomas C. Muller, eds. *Political Handbook of the World: 2000–2002*. Binghamton, N.Y.: CSA Publications, 2003.

Beauvoir, Simone de. *The Second Sex*. Trans. and ed. H. M. Parshley. New York: Alfred A. Knopf, 1953. Reprint: New York: Vintage, 1989.

Bishop, Elizabeth. *The Complete Poems: 1927–79*. New York: Farrar, Straus & Giroux, 1983.

Bush, Vannevar. "As We May Think." *Atlantic Monthly*. July 1945: 101–8.

Cassidy, Frederic G., and Joan Houston Hall, eds. *Dictionary of American Regional English*. 4 vols. to date. Cambridge, Mass.: Belknap–Harvard Univ. Press, 1985–.

Davis, Lawrence M., Charles L. Houck, and Clive Upton. "'Sett Out Verry Eairly Wensdy': The Spelling and Grammar in the Lewis and Clark Journals." *American Speech* 75 (Summer 2000): 137–148.

Himes, Chester. "Headwaiter." In Clarence Major, ed., *Calling the Wind*. New York: HarperCollins, 1993: 79–93.

Hitchens, Christopher. Review of *C. L. R. James,* by Farrukh Dhondy. *Times Literary Supplement*. 18 Jan. 2002: 34.

Hourani, Albert, and Malise Ruthven. *A History of the Arab Peoples*. 2d ed. Cambridge, Mass.: Belknap—Harvard Univ. Press, 2003.

Kenyon, John S., and Thomas A. Knott. *A Pronouncing Dictionary of American English*. Springfield, Mass.: Merriam-Webster, 1953.

Marchand, Jim. "Translating Crescentia." Medieval Texts Discussion List. 27 Dec. 2002. ⟨http://listserv.uiuc.edu/wa.cgi?A2=ind0212&L=medtextl&P=20109⟩ (10 Jan. 2003).

Quirk, Randolph, et al. *A Comprehensive Grammar of the English Language*. London: Longman, 1985.

Rothgeb, John. "The Tristan Chord: Identity and Origin." *Music Theory Online* 1.1 (Jan. 1995). ⟨http://societymusictheory.org/mto/issues/mto.95.1.1/mto.95.1.1.rothgeb.art⟩ (12 June 1999).

Who's Who in America: 2003. 3 vols. New Providence, N.J.: Marquis Who's Who, 2002.

Yoon, Carol Kaesuk. "Scientists Say Orangutans Can Exhibit 'Culture.'" *New York Times*. 3 Jan. 2003: A14.

Sciences

American Ornithologists' Union. 1998. *The A.O.U. checklist of North American birds*. 7th ed. Washington, D.C.: American Ornithologists' Union.

Borio, L., et al. 2001. Death due to bioterrorism-related inhalational anthrax. *JAMA* 286:2554–59.

Charney, R., and A. Lytchak. 2001. Metric characterizations of spherical and Euclidean buildings. *Geom. and Topol.* 5, paper 17: 521–550. ⟨http://www.maths.warwick.ac.uk/gt/GTVol5/paper17.abs.html⟩ (8 Aug. 2002).

Gould, S.J., and N. Eldredge. 1977. Punctuated equilibria: The tempo and mode of evolution reconsidered. *Paleobiology* 3: 115–151.

Hölldobler, B., and E.O. Wilson. 1990. *The ants*. Cambridge, Mass.: Belknap–Harvard Univ. Press.

Mayr, E. 1982. Processes of speciation in animals. In: C. Barigozzi, ed. *Mechanisms of speciation*. New York: Alan R. Liss. 1–19.

McGraw-Hill yearbook of science and technology: 2003. 2003. New York: McGraw-Hill.

Nowak, R.M. 1999. *Walker's mammals of the world*. 6th ed. 2 vols. Baltimore: Johns Hopkins Univ. Press.

DICTIONARY

BASIC ENGLISH GRAMMAR

The essence of the English language is the sentence. A sentence is a gammatically self-contained group of words that expresses a statement, a question, a command, a wish, or an exclamation. It is composed of a *subject*, about which something is said, and a *predicate*, which expresses what is said about the subject. The subject can be a single noun, a noun phrase, such as "*the strong wind*," or a noun clause, such as "*what he decides* is important to all of us." The predicate can be a single verb, a verb phrase, such as "*will be going*," a verb and all its modifiers, such as "*will be going as soon as the bus arrives*," or a verb and its complements, such as "*gave his client the bad news.*"

In English, word order is important. The subject usually comes first, but not necessarily:

An amusement park is across the river.
Across the river is *an amusement park*.
Is *an amusement park* across the river?

The grammar of English is concerned with the structure of these elements that make up a sentence. Every word in a sentence can be classified as a particular part of speech (*noun, verb, adjective,* etc.), according to its function in the sentence. The major parts of speech are briefly discussed in the following guide to basic English grammar.

THE ADJECTIVE

The adjective gives information about a noun or pronoun, such as what kind

the *black* cat
a *joyful* occasion

or which one

a *first* draft
that suggestion

or how many

ten players
few new ideas.

The adjective usually precedes the noun it modifies, but some adjectives can also follow certain verbs:

the house is *white* (→ *white* house)
the speeches seemed *long* (→ *long* speeches)
the chair felt *comfortable* (→ *comfortable* chair)
the tree grew *tall* (→ *tall* tree)

A few adjectives will follow their nouns, but usually only in set phrases:

court-martial
secretary-general

POSITIVE, COMPARATIVE, AND SUPERLATIVE DEGREES OF ADJECTIVES

The positive degree is the basic form of the adjective. It gives basic information about the noun without reference to anything else (a *white* house). The comparative degree relates a noun to another—as having more or less of some quality (this house is *whiter* than that); the superlative degree relates the noun to all others of its class (this is the *whitest* house in the neighborhood).

When the adjective consists of a single syllable, the suffix *-er* is added to form the comparative degree, and the suffix *-est* is added to form the superlative degree. When the adjective consists of two syllables, the suffixes are often used to form the comparative (as *gentler*) and superlative (as *gentlest*), but the adverbs *more/less* can also be used to form the comparative (as *more skillful* and *less skillful*), and likewise, the adverbs *most/least* can be used to form the superlative (as *most skillful* and *least skillful*). For adjectives of more than two syllables, the adverbs are usually used to form the comparative and superlative forms (as *more fortunate, most fortunate*).

There are a few adjectives that have unique comparative and superlative forms:

Positive	Comparative	Superlative
good	better	best
bad	worse	worst
some	more	most
little (amount)	less	least
but		
little (size)	littler	littlest

There are a few adjectives that have no comparative or superlative forms:

an *utter* failure
the *principal* objections

DEMONSTRATIVE ADJECTIVES

The demonstrative adjectives *this* and *that* are used to point out the one person or thing referred to (as "not *this* coat but *that* one"). The plural forms are *these* and *those*, respectively.

These books are mine and *those* books are yours.

DESCRIPTIVE ADJECTIVES

A descriptive adjective describes or indicates a quality, type, or condition:

a *fascinating* conversation
a *positive* attitude
a *fast* computer

INDEFINITE ADJECTIVES

An indefinite adjective is used to designate unspecified person(s) or thing(s):

some children
other projects
any book

INTERROGATIVE ADJECTIVES

An interrogative adjective is used to form a question:

Whose office is this?
Which book do you want?

THE NOUN USED AS ADJECTIVE

A noun sometimes serves to modify another noun and thus functions as an adjective:

the *Vietnam* War
word processing

POSSESSIVE ADJECTIVES

The possessive form of a personal pronoun is called a *possessive adjective*. Following is a list of possessive adjectives and a few examples of how they are used:

Singular	Plural
my	our
your	your
his/her/its	their

Where's *my* magazine?
Your cab is here.
They can read *his* story.
It was *her* idea.
The box and *its* contents were inspected.
She's *our* mother.
Your photos are ready.
We paid for *their* tickets.

PREDICATE ADJECTIVES

A predicate adjective modifies the subject of a linking verb, such as *be*, *become*, *feel*, *taste*, *smell*, or *seem*:

He is *lucky*.
She became *angry*.
They are *happy* with the outcome.
The milk smells *bad*.
The student seems *lonely*.

PROPER ADJECTIVES

A proper adjective is derived from a proper noun and is capitalized:

Victorian furniture
a *Chinese* custom
a *Shakespearean* scholar

THE ADVERB

Adverbs, whether single words or phrases, usually give information about the verbs, such as *when*

We arrived *yesterday*
He woke up *late*

or *where*

I found them *at the restaurant*
He spent time *in [the] hospital*

or *how*

They arose *quickly*
She worked *hard*

Most single-word adverbs end in *-ly* and are formed by adding the suffix *-ly* to an adjective:

mad → *madly*
wonderful → *wonderfully*

When the adjective ends in *-y*, the adverb is formed by changing *-y* to *-i* and adding the suffix *-ly*:

happy → *happily*
dainty → *daintily*

When the adjective ends in *-ic*, the adverb is formed by adding the suffix *-ally*:

basic → *basically*
numeric → *numerically*

When an adjective ends in *-ly*, the adverb retains the same spelling:

a *daily* routine (adjective)
she calls her mother *daily* (adverb)
an *early* meeting (adjective)
the show started *early* (adverb)

Also, there are adverbs that do not end in *-ly*, for example:

again   *now*   *soon*
too   *there*   *how*

POSITIVE, COMPARATIVE, AND SUPERLATIVE DEGREES OF ADVERBS

Adverbs, like adjectives, can have three degrees of comparison: the *positive* form exists without reference to anything else; the *comparative* degree relates to another—as being more or less of the adverb quality; and *superlative* relates to all members of a class. As a general rule, a single-syllable adverb ends in *-er* when it is comparative (as *faster*) and in *-est* when it is superlative (as *fastest*). For adverbs of three or more syllables, the comparative and superlative degrees are formed by using the adverbs *more/less* and *most/least*. The comparative and superlative degrees of an adverb of two syllables are formed by following either one of these methods:

Positive	Comparative	Superlative
early	earlier	earliest
easy	easier	easiest
nearly	more nearly	most nearly
quickly	more quickly	most quickly
satisfactorily	less satisfactorily	least satisfactorily

Some adverbs, such as *only*, *quite*, and *very*, have no comparative or superlative forms.

INTENSIVE ADVERBS

Intensive adverbs, such as *just* and *only*, are usually used only to emphasize other words. The emphasis varies according to the placement of the adverb within the sentence:

He **just** nodded to me as he passed.
He nodded to me **just** as he passed.
I **only** wanted to speak with you.
I wanted to speak **only** with you.

INTERROGATIVE ADVERBS

Interrogative adverbs, such as *when*, *where*, and *why*, are used chiefly to introduce questions:

When will he return?
Where is the remote control?
Why did you hide it?

THE ARTICLE

Articles, sometimes called "determiners," are elements of a noun phrase that indicate whether the noun is "definite," that is, a specific individual, or "indefinite," that is, very general in nature.

THE DEFINITE ARTICLE

There is only one form of the definite article: *the*.

The boys were expelled.
It was **the** best movie I have seen.

THE INDEFINITE ARTICLE

The indefinite article *a* is used with every noun or abbreviation beginning with either a consonant or the sound of a consonant:

a door	*a* union	*a* one-way street
a B.A. degree	*a* hat	*a* U.S. Senator

The indefinite article *an* is used with every noun or abbreviation that begins with a vowel sound, whether or not the first letter of the noun or abbreviation is a vowel or consonant:

an icicle	*an* MP
an honor	*an* FAQ

DICTIONARY

When the first syllable of a noun is not stressed or has only a slight stress, the article *a* is frequently used:

a historian   *a* heroic attempt   *a* hilarious performance

However, the article *an* is sometimes used in these cases:

an historian   *an* heroic attempt   *an* hilarious performance

Both forms are acceptable.

THE CONJUNCTION

There are three main types of conjunctions: *coordinating conjunctions*, *correlative conjunctions*, and *subordinating conjunctions*.

COORDINATING CONJUNCTIONS

Coordinating conjunctions, such as *and*, *but*, *for*, *or*, *nor*, *so*, and *yet*, are used to connect grammatical elements of the same type. These elements may be words, phrases, clauses, or complete sentences. Coordinating conjunctions are used to connect similar elements, to make exclusions or contrasts, to indicate an alternative, to indicate a cause, or to specify a result:

connecting similar elements:	She ordered pencils, pens, ***and*** erasers.
exclusion or contrast:	He is a brilliant ***but*** arrogant man.
	They offered a promising plan, ***but*** it had not yet been tested.
alternative:	She can wait here ***or*** go on ahead.
cause:	The report is useless, ***for*** its information is no longer current.
result:	His diction is excellent, ***so*** every word is clear.

CORRELATIVE CONJUNCTIONS

Correlative conjunctions are used in groups of two to connect choices or elements of the same grammatical type:

Both Rita ***and*** Jane attended the conference.
Either you go ***or*** you stay.
He had ***neither*** looks ***nor*** wit.

SUBORDINATING CONJUNCTIONS

Subordinating conjunctions are used to connect a subordinate clause to an independent clause. These conjunctions express cause, condition or concession, manner, intention or result, time, place, or circumstance, as well as a possibility.

cause:	***Because*** she learns quickly, she is doing well in her new job.
condition or concession:	Don't call ***unless*** you are coming.
manner:	We'll do it ***however*** you tell us.
intention or result:	They burned all the bridges ***so*** that the enemy could not use them.
time:	She kept the meeting to a minimum ***when*** she could.
place:	***Wherever*** he goes, he is welcomed with open arms.

THE NOUN

BASIC USES

The noun may be a single word or a phrase (noun phrase). The noun phrase may consist of an article and/or adjectives and/or prepositional phrases. The noun can function as subject of a sentence, object of a verb, object of a preposition, predicate nominative, complement of an object, in apposition, and in direct discourse:

subject:	*The office* was quiet.
	The house with the green shutters was for sale.
direct object of a verb:	He locked *the office*.
indirect object of a verb:	He gave *his client* the papers.
object of a preposition:	The business was in *bankruptcy*.
	The file is in *the office*.
predicate nominative:	Ms. Adams is *the managing partner*.
complement of an object:	They made Ms. Adams *managing partner*.
in apposition:	Ms. Adams, *the managing partner*, wrote that memo.
in direct discourse:	*Ms. Adams*, may I present Mr. Wilson.

Nouns are often classified as to whether they are proper nouns—capitalized—(*Eiffel Tower*, *White House*) or common nouns (*tower*, *house*), abstract nouns (*honor*, *love*) or concrete nouns (*desk*, *flower*) or collective nouns (*team*, *government*). American English typically uses a singular verb with a collective noun (the team *is*), while British English typically uses a plural verb (the government *are*).

Most nouns are neuter, showing no distinction as to whether having a masculine or feminine reference. However, a few nouns ending in *-ess* (as *empress*, *hostess*) are feminine in gender, and some others have a specific gender. For example: *husband*, *wife*, *father*, *mother*, *brother*, *sister*. The names of certain animals also have a specific gender, for example, *bull/cow*, *stag/doe*. When it is necessary to specify the gender of a neuter noun, the noun is usually modified with words like *male*, *female*, *man*, *woman* (a *male* parrot, *women* painters).

THE NOUN AS ADJECTIVE

The noun has the function of an adjective when it precedes another noun:

olive oil	*business* management
emergency room	*dog* house

THE FORMATION OF THE PLURAL

The plural of most nouns is formed by adding the suffix *-s* to the singular noun:

book → *books*   *cat* → *cats*

When the singular noun ends in *-s*, *-x*, *-z*, *-ch*, or *-sh*, the suffix *-es* is added to the singular:

cross → *crosses*   *fox* → *foxes*
witch → *witches*   *wish* → *wishes*

For a singular noun ending in *-z*, the last letter is doubled before adding the suffix *-es*:

whiz → *whizzes*   *quiz* → *quizzes*

For a singular noun ending in *-y* preceded by a consonant, the *-y* changes to *-i* and the suffix *-es* is added:

fairy → *fairies*   *pony* → *ponies*   *guppy* → *guppies*

For a singular noun ending in *-y* preceded by a vowel, the *-y* usually does not change when the suffix *-s* is added:

boy → *boys*   *attorney* → *attorneys*

Some words that end in *-uy* sometimes change the *-y* to *-i*:

guy → *guys*   *soliloquy* → *soliloquies*

There are a few nouns that do not always change in the plural:

fish → *fish* (or *fishes* when referring to more than one species)
caribou → *caribou* (sometimes *caribous*)
moose → *moose*

There are also some nouns that have a unique plural:

foot → *feet*   *mouse* → *mice*   *knife* → *knives*

THE POSSESSIVE CASE

The possessive case of most singular nouns is formed by adding an apostrophe followed by an -*s*:

Jackie's passport   This hat is **Billy's**

For plural nouns ending in -*s*, only the apostrophe is added:

the **neighbors'** dog   both **boys'** behavior

Proper nouns that end in -*s* often present a special case:

Mr. Douglas's car   **Socrates'** teachings

THE PREPOSITION

The preposition is used with an object (a noun, pronoun, or the equivalent of a noun) to form a phrase that functions generally as an adjective or an adverb.

The man **in the car** is his father. (adjective)
The river winds **through the valley**. (adverb)
I like **to watch sports**. (infinitive phrase used as a noun)

There are two types of prepositions: the simple preposition, which consists of a single word (for example, *against*, *from*, *near*, *of*, *on*, *out*, *in*) and the compound preposition, which consists of more than one element (for example, *according to*, *on account of*, *because of*, *in spite of*).

THE CONJUNCTION VS. THE PREPOSITION

The words *after*, *before*, *but*, *for*, and *since* can be used as prepositions or conjunctions. Their part of speech is determined by their function in the sentence. Conjunctions are usually used to connect two elements of the same grammatical type, while prepositions are followed by an object to form a phrase.

conjunction:	The playful **but** thoughtful youngsters did well in school. (**but** connects two adjectives)
preposition:	I was left with nothing **but** hope. (**but** followed by an object)
conjunction:	The device conserves fuel, **for** it is battery-powered. (**for** connects two clauses)
preposition:	The device conserves fuel **for** better mileage. (**for** followed by an object)

PLACE IN THE SENTENCE

A preposition comes in front of a noun or a pronoun (*under* the desk, *beside* them), after an adjective (antagonistic *to*, insufficient *for*, symbolic *of*), or after a verb as a particle (take *over*, put *on*, come *across*). The preposition may end a sentence, especially if it is a verb particle.

What does this all **add up to**?
After Amy left, Sandra **took over**.

THE PRONOUN

Pronouns are often said to stand in place of the noun or noun phrase in a sentence. Usually, the pronoun stands for something previously specified or generally understood.

Pronouns have the following characteristics: *case* (nominative, possessive, or objective); *number* (singular or plural); *person* (first, second, or third); and *gender* (masculine, feminine, or neuter). Pronouns can be classed in seven main categories, each having a specific function.

DEMONSTRATIVE PRONOUNS

The words *this*, *that*, *these*, and *those* are considered as pronouns when they function as nouns. (They are classed as demonstrative adjectives when they modify a noun.) The demonstrative pronoun designates a person or thing in order to distinguish it from another person or thing:

This is the one I want.
I was happy about *that*.
These are the best designs.
I picked *those* as the prettiest flowers.

The demonstrative pronoun also serves to distinguish a person or thing nearby from one that is farther away (*this* is my desk; *that* is yours).

INDEFINITE PRONOUNS

Indefinite pronouns are used to designate a person or thing of which the identity is unknown or is not immediately evident. The indefinite pronouns include the following:

all	either	none	another	everybody	no one
any	everyone	one	anybody	everything	other(s)
anyone	few	several	anything	many	some
both	much	somebody	each	neither	someone
each one	nobody	something			

The indefinite pronoun and the verb that follows it should agree in number. The following pronouns are used with a singular verb: *another, anything, each one, everything, much, nobody, no one, other, someone, something*:

Much is being done.   **No one** wants to go.

The indefinite pronouns *both, few, many,* and *several* are used with plural verbs:

Many are called; **few** are chosen.

Certain pronouns, such as *all, any, none,* and *some*, sometimes present difficulties, since they can be used with a singular or a plural verb. As a general rule, a pronoun that is used with a noun that cannot be counted requires a singular verb, while a pronoun that is used with a noun that can be counted requires a plural verb.

with an uncountable noun:	All of the property is affected.
	None of the soup was spilled.
	Some of the money was spent.
with a countable noun:	All of my shoes are black.
	None of the clerks were available.
	Some of your friends were here.

INTERROGATIVE PRONOUNS

The interrogative pronouns *what, which, who, whom,* and *whose*, as well as those bound with the word *-ever* (*whatever, whichever,* etc.) are used to introduce a direct or an indirect question:

Who is she?	He asked me **who** she was.
Whoever can that be?	We wondered **whoever** that could be.

PERSONAL PRONOUNS

The personal pronoun reflects the person, number, and gender of the being or the thing it represents. Each category is made up of distinct personal pronouns:

Person	Nominative	Possessive	Objective
First (sing.)	I	my, mine	me
(pl.)	we	our, ours	us
Second (sing.)	you	your, yours	you
(pl.)	you	your, yours	you
Third (sing.)	he	his	him
	she	her, hers	her
	it	its	it
(pl.)	they	their, theirs	them

RECIPROCAL PRONOUNS

The reciprocal pronouns *each other* and *one another* indicate a mutual action or relationship:

Jim and Andy saw *each other* at the party.
They do not quarrel with *one another*.

The reciprocal pronoun is also used as a possessive:

The two companies depend on *each other's* success.
The members enjoyed *one another's* company.

REFLEXIVE PRONOUNS

Reflexive pronouns are formed from the personal pronouns *him*, *her*, *it*, *my*, *our*, *them*, and *your*, to which the combining form *-self* or *-selves* is added. The reflexive pronoun is usually used to express a reflexive action or to emphasize the subject of a sentence, clause, or phrase:

She dressed *herself*.
He asked *himself* if it was worth it.
I *myself* am not involved.
They wanted to do it *themselves*.

RELATIVE PRONOUNS

The relative pronouns are *who*, *whom*, *whose*, *which*, and *that*, as well as the compounds formed by adding the ending *-ever*. These pronouns are used to introduce subordinate clauses that function as a noun or an adjective.

a man *who* sought success
a woman *whom* we can trust
an author *whose* first novel was a success
a move *which* was unforeseen
a boy *that* behaves well
give it to *whomever* you wish
whoever thought of it
pick *whichever* you want

In certain cases the relative pronoun may be omitted:

The man [*whom*] I was talking to is the senator.

THE VERB

Verbs have essentially three classes: ordinary verbs of action, such as *go*, auxiliary verbs, like *can* and *shall*, and fundamental verbs like *be*, *have*, and *do*, which can function as both ordinary verbs and as auxiliaries.

The verb has the following characteristics: *inflection* (for example, helps, helping, helped), *person* (first, second, third), *number* (singular, plural), *tense* (present, past, future), *aspect* (categories of time other than the simple tenses of present, past, future), *voice* (active, passive), and *mood* (indicative, subjunctive, and imperative).

INFLECTION

Regular verbs have three inflections that are formed by adding the suffixes *-s* or *-es*, *-ed*, and *-ing* (for example, *asks*, *asked*, *asking*) Most of the irregular verbs have four inflections (for example, *sees*, *saw*, *seen*, *seeing*). The verb *be* has seven inflections: *is*, *am*, *are*, *was*, *were*, *being*, *been*).

Verbs ending in silent *-e* in general keep the *-e* when a consonantal suffix (such as *-s*) is added to the word, but the *-e* is dropped when the suffix begins with a vowel (such as *-ed*, *-ing*):

arrange; *arranges*; *arranged*; *arranging*
hope; *hopes*; *hoped*; *hoping*

However, certain verbs keep the -*e* in order to avoid confusion with another verb:

> *dye* (color); *dyes*; *dyed*; *dyeing*
> *but*
> *die* (cease to live); *dies*; *died*; *dying*
> *singe* (burn); *singes*; *singed*; *singeing*
> *but*
> *sing* (produce music); *sings*; *sang*; *singing*

If a single-syllable verb ends in a single consonant preceded by a single vowel, the final consonant is often doubled before the addition of -*ed* or -*ing*:

> *brag*; *brags*; *bragged*; *bragging*
> *grip*; *grips*; *gripped*; *gripping*

When a multi-syllable verb ends in the same way, and the last syllable is stressed, the final consonant is also doubled:

> *commit*; *commits*; *committed*; *committing*
> *occur*; *occurs*; *occurred*; *occurring*

It frequently happens that a verb ending in -*y* preceded by a consonant changes -*y* to -*i*, except when the suffix is -*ing*:

> *carry*; *carries*; *carried*; *carrying*
> *study*; *studies*; *studied*; *studying*

When a verb ends in -*c*, a -*k* is added to inflections if the suffix begins with -*e* or -*i*:

> *mimic*; *mimics*; *mimicked*; *mimicking*
> *traffic*; *traffics*; *trafficked*; *trafficking*

TENSE AND ASPECT

The present and past tenses are generally formed as a single word:

> I *do*, I *did*
> we *write*, we *wrote*

The future tense is conjugated with the auxiliary verbs *shall* or *will* and the present or progressive forms:

> I *shall do* it.
> We *will come* tomorrow.
> I *shall be leaving* tomorrow.

Aspect concerns the tense of the verb other than the present, the past, or the future. Aspect has four forms: the *progressive*, the *present perfect*, the *past perfect*, and the *future perfect*.
The *progressive* is used to express an ongoing action that takes place in the present, past, or future:

> He *is reading* the paper at the moment.
> I *was studying* for the test.
> I *will be going* to India.

The *present perfect* tense is used to express an action done in the past but which may be continuing in the present, or to express an action that occurred at an indefinite moment in the past. It is conjugated with the auxiliary verbs *has* or *have* and the past participle:

> She *has written* many books.
> They *have regretted* their mistake.

The *past perfect* expresses a completed action that occurred before another action in the past. It is conjugated with the auxiliary verb *had* and the past participle:

> She *had written* several books previously.
> We *had left* the house before they arrived.

The *future perfect* tense indicates that a future action will take place before another action or occurrence still to come. It is conjugated with the auxiliary verbs *will* or *shall* and *have* and the past participle:

> We *will have finished* the project by then.
> They *will have gone* before we will arrive.

VOICE

The *active* voice indicates that the subject of the sentence is the doer of the action of the verb; the *passive* voice, consisting of a form of the verb *be* and a past participle, indicates that the subject of the sentence is the object of the action:

Active voice:	His colleagues *respect* him.
Passive voice:	He *was respected* by his colleagues.

MOOD

There are three moods: the *indicative*, the *subjunctive*, and the *imperative*. The *indicative* is used to indicate a fact or to ask a question:

He *is* here.
Is he here?

The *subjunctive* is used to express a condition contrary to fact, especially in clauses introduced by *if*, and after the verb *wish*:

If she *were* there, she could answer that.
I wish he *were* here.

The *subjunctive* is also used in clauses beginning with the word *that* following verbs that request, demand, or recommend:

They asked that the books *be* returned.
She insisted that the door *remain* open.
The law required that he *report* his earnings.

The imperative is used to express a command or a demand:

Come here!
Pay attention!

TRANSITIVE AND INTRANSITIVE VERBS

A transitive verb takes a direct object:

She *sold* her car.

An intransitive verb has no direct object:

He *talked* all day.

ENGLISH WORD ROOTS

The capitalized word elements here are the ancient roots of the derived modern English words that appear in italics in the discussion and following in boldface.

AB/ABS comes to us from Latin, and means "from," "away," or "off." *Abuse* is the use of something in the wrong way. To *abduct* is to "lead away from" or kidnap. *Aberrant* behavior is behavior that "wanders away from" what is usually acceptable. But there are so many words that include these roots, it would be *absurd* to try to list them all here. **abscond, abstemious, abstraction, abstruse**

AM/IM comes from the Latin word *amor,* "love." *Amiable* means "friendly or good-natured," and *amigo* is Spanish for "friend." **amicable, enamored, inimical, paramour**

AMBI/AMPHI means "on both sides" or "around"; *ambi-* comes from Latin and *amphi-* from Greek. An *ambidextrous* person can use the right and the left hand equally well. An *amphibian,* such as a frog or salamander, is able to live both on land and in the water. **ambient, ambiguous, ambivalent, amphitheater**

ANIM comes from Latin *anima,* meaning "breath" or "soul," and it generally describes something that is alive or lively. An *animal* is a living, breathing thing. *Animism* is the belief that all things have a spirit and an awareness. **animated, animosity, inanimate, magnanimous**

ANN/ENN comes from Latin *annus* and means "year." An *annual* event occurs yearly. A wedding or birthday *anniversary* is an example, although the older you get the more frequent they seem to be. **annuity, millennium, perennial, superannuated**

ANT/ANTI is opposite to or opposes something else. An *antiseptic* or an *antibiotic* fights germs; an *anticlimax* is the opposite of a climax; an *antidote* is given against a poison; and an *antacid* fights acid in the stomach. Be careful not to confuse *anti-* with *ante-,* meaning "before": *antebellum* means "before a war," not "opposed to war." **antagonist, antigen, antipathy, antithesis**

ANTE is Latin for "before" or "in front of." *Antediluvian,* a word describing something very old or outdated, literally means "before the flood"— that is, the flood described in the Bible. *Antebellum* literally means "before the war," usually the American Civil War. **antechamber, antedate, ante meridiem, anterior**

ANTHROP comes from the Greek word for "human being." An *anthropomorphic* god, such as Zeus or Athena, basically looks and acts like a human. **anthropoid, anthropology, misanthropic, philanthropy**

ART comes from the Latin word for "skill." Until a few centuries ago, almost no one made a strong distinction between skilled craftsmanship and what we would call "art." *Art* could also mean simply "cleverness." The result is that this root appears in some words where we might not expect it. **artful, artifact, artifice, artisan**

AUD, from the Latin verb *audire,* is the root that has to do with hearing. What is *audible* is hearable, and an *audience* is a group of people that listen, sometimes in an *auditorium.* **audition, auditor, auditory, inaudible**

BELL comes from a Latin word meaning "war." Bellona was the little-known Roman goddess of war; her husband, Mars, was the god of war. **antebellum, bellicose, belligerence, rebellion**

BI means "two" or "double." A *bicycle* has two wheels; *binoculars* consist of two little telescopes; *bigamy* is marriage to two people at once. A road through the middle of a neighborhood *bisects* it into two pieces. **biennial, binary, bipartisan, bipolar**

BIO comes from the Greek word for "life." It forms the base for many English words: a *biosphere* is a body of life forms in an environment; *biology* is the study of all living forms and life processes; and *biotechnology* uses the knowledge acquired through biology. **biodegradable, bionic, biopsy, symbiosis**

CAD/CID/CAS all come from the same Latin verb, *cadere,* meaning "to fall, fall down, drop," or from the related noun *casus,* "fall or chance." An *accident* happens to you out of the blue. By *coincidence,* things fall together in a pattern. *Casual* dress is what you put on almost by chance. **cadaver, casualty, decadent, recidivism**

CANT, from the Latin verbs *canere* and *cantare,* meaning "sing," produces several words that come directly from Latin, and others that come by way of French and add an *h* to the root: for example, *chant* and *chantey.* **cantata, cantor, descant, incantation**

CAP/CEP comes from *capere,* the Latin verb meaning "take, seize." *Capture,* which is what a *captor* does to a *captive,* has the same meaning. *Captivate* once meant literally "capture," but now means only to capture mentally through charm or appeal. In some other English words this root produces, its meaning is harder to find. **incipient, perceptible, reception, susceptible**

CAPIT, from the Latin word for "head," *caput,* turns up in some pretty important places. The *captain* of a ship is the head of the whole operation; the *capital* of a state or country is the seat of government, where the head of state is located. A *capital* letter stands head and shoulders above a lowercase letter, as well as at the head of a sentence. **capitalism, capitulate, decapitate, recapitulate**

CARN comes from *caro,* the Latin word for "flesh," and words including this root usually refer to flesh in some form. The word *carnivore,* for example, means "an eater of meat." **carnage, carnal, carnival, incarnation**

CATA comes from Greek *kata,* one of whose meanings was "down." A *catalogue* is a list of items put down on paper. A *catapult* is an ancient military weapon for hurling missiles down on one's enemies. **cataclysm, catalyst, cataract, catatonic**

CED/CESS, from the Latin verb *cedere,* meaning "to go" or "to proceed," produces many English words, from *procession,* meaning something that goes forward, to *recession,* which is a moving back or away. **accede, antecedent, concession, precedent**

CENT means "one hundred," from Latin *centum.* The dollar is made up of a hundred *cents;* other monetary systems use *centavos* or *centimes* as the smallest coin. A *centipede* has what appears to be a hundred pairs of legs, though the actual number varies greatly. But there really are a hundred years in a *century.* **centenary, centigrade, centimeter, centurion**

CENTR/CENTER comes from Greek *kentron* and Latin *centrum,* meaning "sharp point" or "exact middle of a circle." A *centrifuge* is a spinning machine that throws things outward from the *center;* the apparent force that pushes them outward is called *centrifugal* force. **concentrate, eccentric, egocentric, epicenter**

CHRON comes from the Greek word for "time." A *chronicle* records the events of a particular time. A *chronometer* is a device for measuring time, usually one that's more accurate (and more expensive) than an ordinary watch or clock. **anachronism, chronic, chronology, synchronous**

CIRCU/CIRCUM means "around" in Latin. So *circumnavigate* is "to navigate around," often describing a trip around the world, and *circumambulate* means "to walk around." A *circuit* can be a tour around an area or territory, or the complete path of an electric current. **circuitous, circumference, circumspect, circumvent**

CIS comes from the Latin verb meaning "to cut, cut down, or slay." An *incisor* is one of the big front biting teeth; beavers and woodchucks have especially large ones. A *decision* "cuts off" previous discussion and uncertainty. **concise, excise, incisive, precision**

CLAM/CLAIM comes from the Latin verb *cla-*

mare, meaning "to shout or cry out." An *exclamation* is a cry of shock, joy, or surprise. A *proclamation* is read loudly enough so that all can hear its important message. **acclamation, clamor, declaim, reclamation**

CLUD/CLUS, from Latin *claudere,* "to close," appears in *include,* which originally meant "to shut up or enclose" and now means "to contain." *Exclude,* its opposite, means "to expel or keep out"—that is, to close the door to something. **occlusion, preclude, recluse, seclusion**

COD/CODI comes from Latin *codex,* meaning "trunk of a tree" or "document written on wooden tablets." A *code* can be either a set of laws or a system of symbols used to write messages. To *encode* a message is to write it in code. A genetic code, transmitted by genes, is a set of instructions for everything from blood type to eye color. **codex, codicil, codify, decode**

COGN comes from the Latin verb *cognoscere,* "to get to know." We may *recognize* ("know again") the root in some words, but in *quaint* and *acquaint* French has altered it beyond *recognition.* **cognitive, cognizance, cognoscente, incognito**

CONTRA is the Latin equivalent of *anti-* and it too means essentially "against" or "contrary to" or "in contrast to." *Contrary* itself comes directly from this prefix and means simply "opposite" or "opposed." A *contrast* "stands against" something else to which it is compared. *Contrapuntal* music sets one melody against another and produces harmony, which no one is opposed to. **contraband, contradict, contraindication, contravene**

CORD, from the Latin word for "heart," turns up in many common English words. For example, the word *concord* (which includes the prefix *con-,* "with") means literally that one heart is *with* another heart, and thus that they are in agreement. So *discord* (with its prefix *dis-,* "apart") means "disagreement" or "conflict." **accord, concordance, cordial, discordant**

CORP comes from *corpus,* the Latin word for "body." A *corporation* is one kind of body, a *corpse* is another, and a *corps,* such as the Marine Corps, is yet another. **corporal, corporeal, corpulent, incorporate**

COSM, from the Greek word meaning both "ornament" and "order," gives us two different groups of words. *Cosmetics* are the stuff we use to ornament our faces. The "order" meaning combines with the Greek belief that the universe was an orderly place, so words in this group relate to the universe and the worlds within it. *Cosmonaut,* for instance, is the word for a space traveler from the former Soviet Union. **cosmogony, cosmology, cosmopolitan, cosmos**

CRAC/CRAT comes from a Greek word meaning "power." Attached to another root, it indicates which group holds the power. With *demos,* the Greek word for "people," it forms *democracy,* a form of government in which the people rule. In a *meritocracy,* people earn power by their own merit. A *theocracy,* from Greek *theos,* "god," is government based on divine guidance. **aristocrat, autocratic, bureaucrat, plutocracy**

CRE/CRET comes from the Latin verb *crescere,* which means both "to come into being" and "to grow." A *crescendo* in music occurs when the music is growing louder, a *decrescendo* when it is growing softer. **accretion, crescent, excrescence, increment**

CRED comes from *credere,* the Latin verb meaning "to believe." If something is *credible* it is believable, and if it is *incredible* it is almost unbelievable. We have a good *credit* rating when institutions believe in our ability to repay a loan, and we carry *credentials* so that others will believe we are who we say we are. **credence, creditable, credulity, creed**

CRIT comes from a Greek verb that means "to judge" or "to decide." A film *critic* judges a movie and tells us what is good or bad about it. Her *critical* opinion may convince us not to go, or we may overlook any negative *criticism* and see it anyway. **criterion, critique, diacritic, hypercritical**

CRYPT comes from a Greek verb meaning "to hide." *Cryptography* is the practice of putting a message into code—that is, hiding its meaning in a secret language. A medical term beginning with *crypto-* means there is something hidden about the condition. **apocryphal, crypt, cryptic, cryptogram**

CUMB/CUB can be traced to the Latin verbs *cubare,* "to lie," and *-cumbere,* "to lie down." A *cubicle* was originally a small room for sleeping that was separated from a larger room, though now it can be any small area set off by partitions, as in an office. An *incubus* is an evil spirit that was once believed to seek out women in order to "lie on" them in their sleep. **incubate, incumbent, recumbent, succumb**

CUR, from the Latin verb *curare,* means basically "care for." Our verb *cure* comes from this root, as do *manicure* ("care of the hands") and *pedicure* ("care of the feet"). **curative, curator, procure, sinecure**

CURR/CURS comes from *currere,* the Latin verb meaning "to run." Although the sense of speed may be lacking from words based on this root, the sense of movement remains. *Current,* for instance, refers to running water in a stream or river. And an *excursion* is a trip from one place to another. **concurrent, cursory, discursive, precursor**

DE/DIV comes from two related Roman words, *deus,* "god," and *divus,* "divine." *Deism,* a philosophy that teaches natural religion, emphasizes morality, and denies that the creator god interferes with the laws of the universe, was the basic faith of many of America's Founding Fathers. **deity, divination, divine, divinity**

DEC comes from both Greek and Latin and means "ten." A *decade* lasts for ten years, and the *decimal* system is based on 10. **decalogue, decathlon, decibel, decimate**

DEMI/HEMI/SEMI all mean "half." *Hemi-* comes from Greek, *semi-* from Latin, and *demi-* from French. A *hemisphere* is half a sphere. A *demitasse* (the word comes directly from French) is a dainty after-dinner coffee cup, half the size of a regular cup. And a *semicircle* is half a circle. **demigod, demimonde, semiconductor, semisweet**

DEMO comes from the Greek word meaning "people." A *demagogue* leads the people, usually into trouble, by lying and appealing to their prejudices. **demographic, demotic, endemic, pandemic**

DI/DU, the Greek and Latin prefixes meaning "two," show up in both technical and nontechnical terms. A *duel* is a battle between two people. A *duet* is music for a *duo,* or a pair of musicians. If you have *dual* citizenship, you belong to two countries at once. Most birds are *dimorphic,* with feathers of one color for males and another color for females. **dichotomy, diploma, duplex, duplicity**

DIC, from *dicere,* the Latin word meaning "to speak," says a lot. A *contradiction* (with the prefix *contra-,* "against") speaks against or denies something. A *dictionary* is a treasury of words. And *diction* is another word for speech. **edict, interdiction, jurisdiction, malediction**

DIS comes from Latin, where it means "apart." In English, its meanings have increased to include "do the opposite of" (as in *disestablish*), "deprive of" (as in *disfranchise*), "exclude or expel from" (*disbar*), "the opposite or absence of" (*disaffection*), and "not" (*disagreeable*). The original meaning can still be seen in a word like *dissipate,* which means "to break up and scatter." **diffraction, disseminate, dissension, dissipate**

DOC/DOCT comes from the Latin *docere,* which means "to teach." A *doctor* is a highly educated person capable of instructing others in the *doctrines,* or basic principles, of his or her field— which is not necessarily medicine. **docile, doctrinaire, doctrine, indoctrinate**

DOM comes from Latin *domus,* "house," or *dominus,* "master," or the verb *domare,* "to tame or subdue." A *domain* is the area where a person has authority or is *dominant.* Unfortunately, dominant people can also be *domineering,* seeing themselves as the masters of those they live and work with. **domicile, domination, dominion, predominant**

DUC, from the Latin verb *ducere,* "to lead," shows up constantly in English. *Duke* means basically "leader." The Italian dictator Mussolini was known simply as "Il Duce." But such words as *produce* and *reduce* also contain the root, even though their meanings show it less clearly. **conducive, deduction, induce, seduction**

DYNA/DYNAM comes from a Greek verb that means "to be able" or "to have power." *Dynamite* has enough power to blow up the hardest granite bedrock. An instrument that measures force is called a *dynamometer.* **dynamic, dynamo, dynasty, hydrodynamic**

EP/EPI comes from Greek and means variously "upon," "besides," "attached to," "over," "outer," or "after." An *epicenter* is the portion of the earth's surface directly over the focus of an earthquake. The *epidermis* is the outer layer of the skin, overlying the inner layer or "dermis." **ephemeral, epitaph, epithet, epoch**

ERR, from the Latin verb *errare,* means "to wander" or "to stray." This root is easily seen in the word *error,* which means a wandering or straying from what is correct or true. We also use the word *erratum* to mean "a mistake" in a book or other printed material; its plural is *errata,* and the *errata* page is the book page that lists mistakes found too late to correct before publication. **aberrant, errant, erratic, erroneous**

EU comes from the Greek word for "well"; in English words it can also mean "good" or "true." A person delivering a *eulogy* is full of good words, or praise, for the honoree. *Euthanasia* is regarded as a way of providing a hopelessly sick or injured person a "good" or easy death. **eugenic, euphemism, euphoria, evangelism**

EV comes from Latin *aevum,* "age" or "lifetime." This root occurs in only a few English words, but it is related to Greek *aion,* "age," from which we get the English word *eon,* meaning a very long period of time. **coeval, longevity, medieval, primeval**

EXTRA places words outside or beyond their usual or routine territory. *Extraterrestrial* affairs take place beyond the earth. Something *extravagant,* such as an *extravaganza,* goes beyond the limits of reason or necessity. And of course *extra* itself is a word, a shortening of *extraordinary,* "beyond the ordinary." **extracurricular, extramarital, extraneous, extrapolate**

FAC/FEC/FIC comes from the Latin verb *facere,* meaning "to make or do." Thus, a *benefactor* is someone who does good. To *manufacture* is to make, usually in a *factory.* **confection, facile, olfactory, proficient**

FER, from the Latin verb *ferre,* means "to carry." If you *refer* to an incident in your past, you "carry back" to that time. And *transfer* means "to carry across." **confer, deferential, fertile, proliferate**

FID comes from *fides,* the Latin word for "faith." *Fidelity* is another word for "faithfulness." *Confidence* is having faith in someone or something.

And an *infidel* is someone who lacks a particular kind of religious faith. **affidavit, diffident, fiduciary, perfidy**

FIG comes from the Latin verb *fingere,* which means "to shape or mold," and the related noun *figura,* meaning "a form or shape." A *transfiguration* changes the shape or appearance or nature of something. A *disfiguring* injury changes the shape of part of the body. **configuration, effigy, figment, figurative**

FIN comes from the Latin word for "end" or "boundary." *Final* describes last things, and a *finale* or a *finish* is an ending. But its meaning is harder to trace in some of the other English words derived from it. **affinity, definitive, finite, infinitesimal**

FLECT/FLEX comes from *flectere,* the Latin verb meaning "to bend." Things that are *flexible* can be bent. When light is *reflected,* it is bent and bounces back to us. **circumflex, deflect, genuflect, inflection**

FLU comes from the Latin verb *fluere,* "to flow." A *flume* is a narrow gorge with a stream flowing through it. A *fluent* speaker is one from whom words *flow* easily. Originally, *influence* referred to an invisible *fluid* that was believed to flow from the stars and to affect the actions of humans. **affluence, effluent, fluctuation, mellifluous**

FORM is a Latin root meaning "shape" or "form." Marching in *formation* is marching in ordered patterns. A *formula* is a standard form for expressing information, such as a recipe or a rule written in mathematical symbols. **conform, formality, format, formative**

FRAG/FRACT comes from the Latin verb *frangere,* "to break or shatter." A *fraction* is one of the pieces into which a whole can be broken; recipes typically call for *fractional* parts of a stick of butter or a cup of flour. The dinnerware on which food is served is often *fragile* or easily broken. **fractious, fragmentary, infraction, refraction**

FUG comes from the Latin verb *fugere,* meaning "to flee or escape." A *refugee* flees from some threat or danger to a *refuge,* which is a place that provides shelter and safety. **centrifugal, fugitive, fugue, subterfuge**

FUND/FUS, from the Latin verb *fundere,* "to pour out" or "to melt," pours forth English words. A *fuse* depends on melting metal to break an overloaded circuit. A *refund* pours money back into your pocket. *Confusion* results when so many things are poured together that they can't be sorted out. **diffuse, effusive, profusion, suffuse**

FUNG/FUNCT comes from the Latin verb *fungi,* "to perform, carry out, or undergo." A car that is *functional* is able to perform its *function* of providing transportation. A functional illiterate is a person who lacks the skills necessary to carry out the ordinary tasks of reading and writing required by day-to-day life. **defunct, functionary, malfunction, perfunctory**

GEN *generates* many English words. Their basic meaning is "come into being" or "be born." The root occurs in *gene*, the most fundamental of biological architects, and in *genealogy*, the study of family roots. **carcinogenic, congenial, generic, indigenous**

GRAD comes from Latin *gradus*, "step" or "degree." A *grade* is a step up or down on a scale of some kind. A *gradual* change takes place in small steps. The *gradient* of a steep slope might be 45 *degrees*. **degrade, gradation, graduate, retrograde**

GRAT comes from *gratus*, the Latin word meaning "pleasing, welcome, or agreeable," or from *gratia*, meaning "grace, agreeableness, or pleasantness." A meal that is served *graciously* will be received with *gratitude* by *grateful* diners, unless they want to risk being called *ingrates*. **congratulate, gratuitous, gratuity, ingratiate**

GRAV comes from the Latin word meaning "heavy, weighty, serious." Thus, a *grave* matter is serious and important. **aggravate, gravid, gravitate, gravity**

GREG comes from Latin *grex*, "herd" or "flock." Bees, wolves, people—any creatures that like to live together in flocks or herds—are *gregarious* animals. People who greatly enjoy companionship, who are happiest when part of a rowdy herd, are highly gregarious. **aggregate, congregation, egregious, segregate**

HABIT/HIBIT comes from Latin *habere*, "to have" or "to hold." A *habit*, bad or good, has a hold on you. To *prohibit* is to "hold back" or prevent. **exhibitionist, habitual, inhibit, prohibition**

HER/HES, from the Latin verb *haerere*, means "to stick." This has produced words with two kinds of meaning. A word such as *adhesive* means basically "sticking," whereas a word such as *hesitate* means more or less "stuck in one place." **adherent, cohesion, incoherent, inherent**

HOM/HOMO comes from *homos*, the Greek word for "same." In an English word it can mean "one and the same" or "similar" or "alike." A *homograph* is one of two or more words spelled alike but different in meaning or derivation or pronunciation. A *homosexual* is a person who exhibits sexual desire toward others of the same sex. **homogeneous, homologous, homonym, homophone**

HOSP/HOST comes from a Latin word meaning "host." *Hospitality* is what a good *host* or *hostess* offers to a guest. A *hospital* was once a house for religious pilgrims and other travelers or a home for the aged. **hospice, hostage, hostel, inhospitable**

HYDR flows from the Greek word for "water." In the Northwest, rushing rivers provide an abun-

dance of *hydrodynamic* power to convert to electricity. "Water" can also be found in the lovely flower called *hydrangea*: its seed capsules resemble ancient Greek water vessels. **dehydrate, hydraulic, hydroelectric, hydroponics**

HYPER is a Greek prefix that means "above or beyond it all." To be *hypercritical* or *hypersensitive* is to be critical or sensitive above and beyond what is normal. **hyperactive, hyperbole, hypertension, hyperventilate**

HYPO/HYP as a prefix can mean variously "under," "beneath," "down," or "below normal." Many *hypo-* words are medical. A *hypodermic* needle injects medication under the skin. *Hypoglycemia*, low blood sugar, is an unhealthy condition. **hypochondriac, hypocrisy, hypothetical, hypothyroidism**

JAC/JEC comes from *jacere*, the Latin verb meaning "throw" or "hurl." To *reject* something is to throw (or push) it back. To *eject* something is to throw (or drive) it out. To *object* is to throw something in the way of something else. **adjacent, conjecture, dejected, trajectory**

JUR comes from the Latin verb *jurare*, "to swear or take an oath," and the noun *jur-*, "right or law." A *jury*, made up of *jurors*, makes judgments based on the law. A personal *injury* caused by another person is "not right." **abjure, jurisprudence, objurgate, perjury**

LAT comes from a Latin verb that means "to carry or bear." From this root come *relation* and *relative*, a person you are *related* to, whether you like it or not. You might be *elated*, or "carried away by joy," to get free tickets to a rock concert, but your elderly relative might not share your *elation*. **collate, correlate, prelate, relativity**

LEV comes from the Latin adjective *levis*, meaning "light," and the verb *levare*, meaning "to raise or lighten." *Levitation* is the magician's trick in which a body seems to rise into the air by itself. And a *lever* is a bar used to lift something by means of *leverage*. **alleviate, elevate, leavening, levity**

LOCU/LOQU comes from the Latin verb *loqui*, "to talk." An *eloquent* preacher speaks fluently, forcefully, and expressively. A dummy's words come out of a *ventriloquist's* mouth. **circumlocution, colloquial, elocution, loquacious**

LOG, from the Greek word *logos*, meaning "word, speech, reason," is found particularly in English words that end in *-logy* and *-logue*. The ending *-logy* often means "the study of": *biology* is the study of life, and *anthropology* is the study of humans. The ending *-logue* usually indicates a type of discussion: *dialogue* is conversation between two people or groups, and an *epilogue* is an author's last words on a subject. **eulogy, genealogy, monologue, neologism**

LUC comes from the Latin noun *lux*, "light," and the verb *lucere*, "to shine or glitter." *Lucid* prose is clear in meaning, as if light were shining through it. *Lucifer,* a name for the devil, means "Light-bearer," the name he had before he fell from heaven. **elucidate, lucent, lucubration, translucent**

LUD/LUS comes from Latin *ludere,* "to play," and *ludum,* "play" or "game." An *interlude* thus is something "between games" (*inter-* meaning "between"). A *delusion* or an *illusion* plays tricks on a person. **allude, collusion, ludicrous, prelude**

MAL as a combining form means "bad." *Malpractice* is bad medical practice. A *malady* is a bad condition—a disease or illness—of the body or mind. *Malodorous* things smell bad. And a *malefactor* is someone guilty of bad deeds. **malevolent, malicious, malign, malnourished**

MAND/MEND comes from *mandare,* Latin for "entrust" or "order." A *command* and a *commandment* are both orders. A *commando* unit carries out orders for special military actions. A *recommendation* may entrust, praise, or advise. **commendation, mandate, mandatory, remand**

MAR, from the Latin word *mare,* meaning "sea," brings its salty tang to English in words like *marine,* "having to do with the sea," and *submarine,* "under the sea." **aquamarine, marina, mariner, maritime**

MATR/METR comes from the Greek and Latin words for "mother." A *matron* is a mature woman with children; *matrimony* is marriage itself, traditionally a first step toward motherhood; and a *matrix* is something in which something else is embedded or takes form, the way a baby takes form inside the mother. **maternity, matriarch, matriculate, metropolitan**

MENS comes from the Latin noun *mensura,* "measure," and the verb *metiri,* "to measure." **commensurate, dimension, immensity, mensurable**

METR comes to us from Greek by way of Latin; in both languages it refers to "measure." A *thermometer* measures heat; a *perimeter* is the measure around something; and things that are *isometric* are equal in measure. **metric, odometer, symmetrical, tachometer**

MIT/MIS, from the Latin verb *mittere,* "to send," appears in such English words as *missionary, missile,* and *emit.* A missionary is sent out to convert others to a new faith; a missile is sent to explode on some far spot; and to emit is to send something out. **emissary, manumission, missive, remittance**

MONI comes from the Latin verb *monere,* "to warn" or "to remind." Warning and reminding often are rather similar, since some reminders warn against the consequences of forgetting. **admonish, monitor, monitory, premonition**

MONO is Greek for "one" or "only." So a *monorail* is a railroad that has only one rail, a *monotonous* voice seems to have only one tone, and a *monopoly* puts all ownership in the hands of a single company, eliminating any competition. **monogamous, monograph, monolithic, monotheism**

MOR/MORT comes from the Latin noun *mors* (stem *mort-*), meaning "death," and verb *mori,* meaning "to die." A *mortuary* is a place where dead bodies are kept until burial. A *postmortem* examination is one conducted on a recently dead body. And a *memento mori* (a Latin phrase meaning literally "Remember that you must die") is a reminder of death; the death's head carved onto an old gravestone is an example. **immortality, moribund, mortician, mortify**

MORPH comes from the Greek word for "shape." *Morph* is itself an English word with a brand-new meaning; by morphing, filmmakers can now alter photographic images or shapes digitally, making them move or transform themselves in astonishing ways. **amorphous, anthropomorphic, metamorphosis, morphology**

MUT comes from the Latin *mutare,* "to change." Plenty of science-fiction movies have been made on the subject of weird *mutations,* changes in normal people or animals that end up causing no end of death and destruction. More often than not, it is some mysterious or alien force that causes the unfortunate victim to *mutate.* **commutation, immutable, permutation, transmute**

NASC/NAT/NAI comes from the Latin verb *nasci,* meaning "to be born." Words that have come directly from Latin carry the root *nasc-* or *nat-,* but those that took a detour through French bear a telltale *nai-* —words like *renaissance,* "rebirth," or *naive,* "unsophisticated." **cognate, innate, nascent, native**

NEC/NIC/NOX, from the Latin nouns *nex* (stem *nec-*) and *noxa,* have to do with violent death. These roots are related to Greek *nekros,* "corpse," found in such words as *necrology,* "a list of the recently dead," and *necromancy,* "the art of conjuring up spirits of the dead." **internecine, necrosis, noxious, pernicious**

NEG and its variants *nec-* and *ne-* are the prefixes of denial or refusal in Latin. The Latin verb *negare,* "to say no," is the source of our English verb *negate.* A *negative* is something that denies, contradicts, refuses, or reverses. **abnegation, negligible, renegade, renege**

NOM comes from the Latin word for "name." A *nominee* is "named"—or *nominated*—to run for or serve in office. A *binomial* ("two names") is the scientific name for a species; the domestic cat, for example, has the binomial *Felis catus.* A *polynomial,* with "many names," is an algebraic equation involving several terms. **ignominious, misnomer, nomenclature, nominal**

PAN comes from Greek with its spelling and meaning intact. It simply means "all" in Greek; as an English prefix it can also mean "completely," "whole," or "general." A *panoramic* view is a complete view in every direction. *Panchromatic* film is sensitive to the reflected light of all colors in the spectrum. *Pantheism* is the worship of all gods. A *pantheon* is a temple dedicated to all the gods of a particular religion. **panacea, pandemonium, panegyric, panoply**

PARA can mean "beside": *parallel* lines run beside each other. It can mean "beyond or outside": *paranoid,* in which *para-* combines with the Greek word *nous,* "mind," means a little outside of one's mind. Finally, *para-* can mean "associated with, especially as an assistant": *paramedics* and *paralegals* assist doctors and lawyers, and a *paramilitary* force assists regular military forces. **paradigm, paradox, paragon, parameter**

PART, from the Latin word *pars,* meaning "part," comes into English most obviously in our word *part* but also in words like *apartment, compartment,* and *particle,* all of which are parts of a larger whole. **impart, impartial, participle, partisan**

PATER/PATR, from both the Greek and the Latin word for "father," is the source of many English words. A *patriarchy* is a society or institution in which ultimate authority rests with the father or with the men of the family. A *patron* is one who assumes a fatherly role toward an institution or project, typically giving moral and financial support. **expatriate, paternal, patrician, patrimony**

PED comes from the Greek word for "child." It is like the PED that means "foot." The two usually aren't hard to tell apart—but don't mistake a *pediatrician* for a *podiatrist.* **encyclopedic, orthpedics, pedagogy, pediatrics**

PED comes from the Latin word *pes,* closely related to the Greek roots *pod* and *pous,* meaning "foot." From *ped-* we get *pedicure,* "care of the feet, toes, and toenails." From *pod-* we get *podiatrist,* "a foot doctor." **expedient, expedite, impediment, pedestrian**

PEL/PULS comes from the Latin verb *pellere,* meaning "to move or drive." A *propeller* moves an airplane forward. When soldiers *repel* an enemy charge, they drive it back. And to *dispel* something is to drive it away. **compel, expel, impel, repulsion**

PEN/PUN comes from the Latin words *poena,* "penalty," and *poenire* or *punire,* "to punish." From them come such English words as *penalty* and *repentance*; when a penalty is given to someone, it is expected that he or she will be moved to repentance. **impunity, penal, penance, punitive**

PEND/PENS, meaning "to hang, weigh, or cause to hang down," comes from the Latin verb *pen-*

dere. We find it in English in words like *pensive,* meaning "thoughtful," and *appendix,* that useless and sometimes troublesome piece that hangs from the intestine. **appendage, expend, propensity, suspend**

PER, a Latin prefix that generally means "through," "throughout," or "thoroughly," has been a thoroughly useful root throughout its history and through all its many meanings. The "through" and "throughout" meanings are seen in *perforate,* "to bore through," *perennial,* "throughout the years," and *permanent,* "remaining throughout." And the "thoroughly" sense shows up in *persuade,* for "thoroughly advise," and *perverted,* "thoroughly turned around." **percolate, peremptory, permeate, persevere**

PERI usually means "going around something." With a *periscope,* you can see around corners. *Peristalsis* is the bodily function that moves food around the intestines; without it, digestion would grind to a halt. The moon's *perigee* is the point in its orbit where it is closest to the earth. The point in the earth's orbit around the sun that brings it closest to the sun is its *perihelion.* **perimeter, periodontal, peripatetic, peripheral**

PHAN/PHEN, from the Greek verbs that mean "to appear or seem" or "to present to the mind," has to do with the way things seem or appear rather than the way they really are. From these roots come words such as *fanciful* and *fantasy,* in which the imagination plays an important part. **diaphanous, phantasm, phantasmagoria, phenomenon**

PHIL comes from the Greek word meaning "love." In *philosophy,* it is joined with *sophia,* "wisdom," so philosophy means literally "love of wisdom." When joined with *biblio-,* "book," the result is *bibliophile,* or "lover of books." *Philadelphia,* containing the Greek word *adelphos,* "brother," is the city of "brotherly love." **philanthropy, philatelist, philology, philter**

PHON is a Greek root meaning "sound," "voice," or "speech." It is similar to the Latin *voc* in meaning but typically means only "sound" when used in such words as *telephone* ("far sound"), *microphone* ("small sound"), or *xylophone* ("wood sound"). **cacophony, phonetic, polyphonic, symphony**

PHOS/PHOT comes from the Greek word for "light." *Phos* can be seen in the word *phosphorus,* which refers generally to anything that glows in the dark and also to a particular glowing chemical element. *Phot,* the more familiar root, appears in words like *photography,* which is the use of light to create an image on film or paper. **phosphorescent, photogenic, photon, photosynthesis**

PLE comes from a Latin word meaning "to fill." It can be seen in the word *complete,* meaning "possessing all necessary parts." A *supplement* is an addition that makes something fuller. **complement, deplete, implement, replete**

PLIC comes from the Latin verb *plicare,* "to fold." A *complicated* subject has many folds or wrinkles. A person who is *implicated* in a crime is "wrapped up" in it somehow. The person's involvement may become *explicit*—"unwrapped" or revealed—when the details of the crime unfold. **complicity, explicate, implicit, replicate**

POLIS/POLIT comes from the Greek word for "city." "City-states" operated much like separate nations in ancient Greece, so all their *politics* was local, like all their public *policy.* **acropolis, cosmopolitan, megalopolis, politic**

POLY comes from *polys,* the Greek word for "many." *Polysyllabic* words are words of many syllables. *Polygamy* is marriage in which one has many spouses, or at least more than the legal limit of one. A *polygraph* is an instrument for recording variations in many different bodily pulsations simultaneously to reveal whether someone is lying. **polyglot, polyhedron, polymer, polyphony**

PON/POS, from the Latin verb *ponere,* means "put" or "place." You *expose* film by "placing it out" in the light. You *oppose* an *opponent* by "putting yourself against" him or her. You *postpone* a trip by "placing it after" its original date. **component, disposition, repository, superimpose**

POPUL comes from the Latin word meaning "people," and in fact forms the basis of the word *people* itself. *Popular* means not only "liked by many people" but also "relating to the general public." The *population* is the people of an area. **populace, populist, populous, vox populi**

POST comes from a Latin word meaning "after" or "behind." A *postscript* is a note that comes after an otherwise completed letter, usually as an afterthought. *Postpartum* refers to the period following childbirth and all of its related events and complications. To *postdate* a check is to give it a date after the day when it was written. **posterior, posterity, posthumous, postmortem**

PRE, one of the most common of all English *prefixes,* comes from *prae,* the Latin word meaning "before" or "in front of." A television program *precedes* another by coming on the air earlier. You make a *prediction* by saying something will happen before it occurs. A person who *presumes* to know makes an assumption before he or she has all the facts. Someone with a *prejudice* against a class of people has formed an opinion of individuals before having met them. **precept, precocious, predispose, prerequisite**

PRIM comes from *primus,* the Latin word for "first." Something that is *primary* is first in time, development, rank, or importance. A *primer* is a book of first instructions on a subject. A *primate* is a bishop or archbishop of the first rank. Some-

thing *primitive* is in its first stage of development. **primal, primeval, primogeniture, primordial**

PRO comes from Latin, where it means "before," "forward," or "for." As a prefix, it can also mean "earlier than," "front," or "in front of." A lifetime of anger or bitterness can *proceed,* or "come forth," from an unhappy childhood. An ambitious army officer expects to be *promoted,* or "moved forward," rapidly. Those who *provide* for the future by laying away money are "looking ahead." **procrastinate, prodigious, progress, propitious**

PROB/PROV comes from Latin words meaning "good, honest" and "show to be good, prove." *Probate* court is where the genuineness of the wills of deceased people must be *proved.* **approbation, disprove, probity, reprobate**

PROPER/PROPR come from the Latin word *proprius,* meaning "own." A *proprietor* is an owner. *Property* is what he or she owns. **appropriate, expropriate, proprietary, propriety**

PROT/PROTO comes from Greek and has the basic meaning "first in time" or "first formed." *Protozoans* are one-celled animals, such as amoebas and paramecia, that are among the most basic members of the biological kingdom. A *proton* is an elementary particle that, along with neutrons, can be found in all atomic nuclei. **protagonist, protocol, protoplasm, prototype**

PUNG/PUNCT comes from the Latin verb *pungere,* meaning "to prick or stab," and the noun *punctum,* meaning "point." A period is a form of *punctuation* that is literally a point. A *punctured* tire, pricked by a sharp point, can make it hard to be *punctual*—that is, to arrive "on the dot" or at a precise point in time. **compunction, expunge, punctilious, pungent**

PURG comes from the Latin verb *purgare,* "to clean or cleanse." An *unexpurgated* version of Ovid's *Metamorphoses* has not been cleansed of its vulgar or "dirty" sections. *Purging* literature of passages that might harm youthful readers has kept many an editor occupied; even in ancient times, some of Ovid's poetry was carefully *purged.* **expurgate, purgation, purgative, purgatory**

PUT, from the Latin verb *putare,* meaning "to think, consider, or reckon," has come into English in a variety of forms. A *reputation,* for example, is what others think of you; a *deputy* is someone "considered as" the person who appointed him or her. **disputatious, impute, putative, reputed**

QUADR/QUART means "four" and comes from Latin *quadr-,* "four," "fourth" and *quartus,* "fourth." In English, a *quart* is one-fourth of a gallon, just as a *quarter* is one-fourth of a dollar. A *quadrangle* has four sides but is not necessarily square; a *quadrant* is one of four equal parts. **quadrennial, quadrille, quadruple, quartet**

QUINT comes from the Latin word meaning "fifth." A *quintessence* is literally the "fifth essence," the fifth and highest element of ancient and medieval philosophy, which was supposed to be in the celestial bodies. **quintessential, quintet, quintuplet**

QUIS is derived from the Latin verb *quaerere,* meaning "to seek or obtain." You can see it in our word *acquisitive,* which means "having a strong wish to possess things." The roots *quir* and *ques* are also derived from this word and give us words such as *inquiry,* "a search or request for information," and *question,* "something asked." **acquisitive, inquisition, perquisite, requisition**

RECT comes from the Latin word *rectus,* which means "straight" or "right." A *rectangle* is a four-sided figure whose parallel, straight sides meet at right angles. *Rectus,* short for Latin *rectus musculus,* may refer to any of several straight muscles, such as those of the abdomen. To *correct* something is to make it right. **rectify, rectilinear, rectitude, rector**

RETRO means "back," "behind," or "backward" in Latin. A *retrospective* is a "looking back" at events from the past. **retroactive, retrofit, retrograde, retrogress**

ROG comes from *rogare,* the Latin verb meaning "to ask." The ancient Romans also used this word to mean "to propose," thinking perhaps that when we propose an idea, we are actually asking someone to consider it. So *interrogate* means "to question systematically," and a *surrogate* (for example, a surrogate mother) is a substitute, someone who is proposed to stand in for another. **abrogate, arrogate, derogatory, prerogative**

SACR/SANCT, meaning "holy," comes from the Latin words *sacer,* "holy," and *sancire,* "to make holy." A *sacrament* such as the bread and wine of Christian communion is a way of receiving holy grace. The person who receives it is *sanctified* or "made holy" by it; this holiness or *sanctity* is believed to result from God's grace. **sacrilege, sacrosanct, sanction, sanctuary**

SCAND/SCEND comes from the Latin verb *scandere,* "to climb." *Ascend,* "go up," and *descend,* "go down," are the most familiar of the English words it has produced. **ascendancy, condescend, descendant, transcend**

SCI comes from the Latin verb *scire,* "to know" or "to understand." This root appears in the word *science,* which refers to factual knowledge, and in *conscience,* which refers to moral knowledge. And to be *conscious* is to be in a state where you are able to know or understand. **conscientious, omniscience, prescient, unconscionable**

SCRIB/SCRIP comes from the Latin verb *scribere,* "to write." *Scribble* is a word meaning to write or draw carelessly. A written work that hasn't been published is a *manuscript.* To *describe* is to picture something in words. **circumscribe, conscription, inscription, proscribe**

SECU/SEQU comes from the Latin verb *sequi,* meaning "to follow." A *sequel* follows the original novel, film, or television show. The *second* follows the first. But a *non sequitur* is a conclusion that does "not follow" from what was said before. **consequential, execute, obsequious, sequential**

SERV means "to be subject to." A *servant* is the person who *serves* you with meals and provides other necessary *services.* A tennis or volleyball *serve* puts the ball in play much as a servant puts food on the table. **serviceable, servile, servitude, subservient**

SIGN comes from the Latin noun *signum,* "sign or mark." An architect's *design* marks out the pattern for a building; if the owner *designates* that design as the one he wants, he so indicates by putting a *signature,* his own special mark, on an agreement. **assignation, resign, signatory, signet**

SOLV/SOLU comes from the Latin verb *solvere,* "to loosen, free, release." The number of English words that have been spawned by this root is seemingly without end. For example, to *solve* a problem—that is, to find its *solution*—is to free up a situation, and a *solvent dissolves* and releases oil or paint. **absolve, dissolution, resolve, soluble**

SON is the Latin root meaning "sound," as in our word *sonata,* meaning a kind of music usually played by one or two instruments, and *sonorous,* usually meaning "full, loud, or rich in sound." **assonance, dissonant, resonance, sonic**

SOPH is a Greek root from the word meaning "wise" or "wisdom." In our language, the root often appears in words where the "wise" is of the "wiseguy" variety. But in words such as *philosophy* we see a more respectful attitude toward wisdom. **sophisticated, sophistry, sophomoric, theosophy**

SPHER comes from the Greek word for "ball," and it appears in words for things that have something round about them. A ball is itself a *sphere.* The *stratosphere* and the *ionosphere* are parts of the *atmosphere* that encircles the earth. **biosphere, hemisphere, spherical, troposphere**

SPIC/SPEC comes from the Latin verb *specere* or *spicere,* meaning "to look at or behold." Closely related is the root *specta-,* which produces such words as *spectator, spectacles,* and *spectacular.* **auspicious, conspicuous, introspection, perspicacious**

STRU/STRUCT comes from the Latin verb *struere,* meaning "to put together," "to put in order," and "to build or devise." A *structure* is something *constructed,* "built" or "put together"; *instructions* tell how the pieces should be

DICTIONARY

arranged. Something that *obstructs* is "built up in the way." **construe, destructive, infrastructure, instrumental**

SUB means "under," as in *subway, submarine,* and *substandard.* A *subject* is a person who is under the authority of another. The word *subscribe* once meant "to write one's name underneath," and *subscription* was the act of signing at the end of a document or agreement. **subconscious, subjugate, subliminal, subversion**

TANG/TACT comes from the Latin verb *tangere,* "to touch." A person who shows *tact* has a delicate touch when it comes to dealing with other people. To make *contact* is to touch or "get in touch." **intact, tactile, tangential, tangible**

TELE has as its basic meanings "distant" or "at a distance." A *telescope* looks at faraway objects, a *telephoto* lens on a camera magnifies distant objects for a photograph, and a *television,* for better or worse, allows us to watch things taking place far away. **telecommunication, telegenic, telemetry, telepathic**

TEMPER comes from the Latin verb *temperare,* "to moderate or keep within limits" or "to mix." It comes into English in words like *temperature. Tempered* (as in tempered steel) means "hardened by reheating and cooling in oil or water." *Tempered* enthusiasm, similarly, is enthusiasm that has cooled a bit. **intemperate, temper, tempera, temperance**

TEMPOR comes from Latin *tempus,* meaning "time." The Latin phrase *tempus fugit* means "time flies," an observation that somehow seems more true during summer vacation than in the dead of winter. A *temporary* repair is meant to last only a short time. The *tempo,* or speed, of a country-and-western ballad is usually different from that of a heavy metal song. **contemporary, extemporaneous, temporal, temporize**

TEN/TIN, from the Latin verb *tenere* and the related word *tenax,* basically means "hold" or "hold on to." A *tenant* is the "holder" of an apartment, house, or land, but not necessarily the owner. A *lieutenant* governor may "hold the position" or "serve in lieu" of the governor when necessary. **abstinence, sustenance, tenable, tenacious**

TEND/TENT, from Latin *tendere,* meaning "to stretch, extend, or spread," can be seen most simply in the English word *tent,* meaning "a piece of material stretched or extended over a frame." It can also be seen in the word *extend,* which means "to stretch forth or stretch out," and in *tendon,* the word for a tough band of tissue that stretches from a muscle to a bone. **contentious, distend, portend, tendentious**

TERM/TERMIN comes from the Latin verb *terminare,* "to limit, bound, or set limits to," or the related noun *terminus,* a "limit or boundary." In English, those boundaries or limits tend to be final: to *terminate* a sentence or a meeting or a

ballgame means to end it, and a *term* goes on for a given amount of time and then ends. **coterminous, indeterminate, interminable, terminal**

TERR comes from Latin *terra,* "earth." *Terra firma* is a Latin phrase that means "firm ground" as opposed to the swaying seas; a *terrace* is a leveled area along a sloping hill; the French call potatoes *pommes de terre,* literally "apples of the earth"; *territory* is a specific piece of land. **parterre, subterranean, terrarium, terrestrial**

THE comes from the Greek word meaning "god." *Theology* is the study of gods or religion. *Monotheism* is the worship of a single god; someone who is *polytheistic,* however, worships many gods. **apotheosis, atheistic, pantheistic, theocracy**

THERM/THERMO comes from the Greek word meaning "heat." A *thermometer* measures the amount of warmth in a body, the air, or an oven; a *thermostat* makes sure the temperature stays at the same level. In a *thermodynamic* process, heat affects the behavior of atoms, particles, or molecules. **thermal, thermocline, thermocouple, thermonuclear**

TOP comes from *topos,* the Greek word for "place." A *topic* is the subject of a paper or discussion. Its root originally meant "commonplace"—that is, a common subject. **isotope, topical, topography, utopia**

TORS/TORT comes from two forms of the Latin verb *torquere,* meaning "to twist" or "to wind" or "to wrench." A sideshow *contortionist* twists his or her body into bizarre shapes. This may appear to be a form of *torture,* which itself often involves a merciless wrenching and twisting of the body. **extort, torsion, tort, tortuous**

TRACT comes from *trahere,* the Latin verb meaning "drag or draw." Something *attractive* draws us toward it. A *tractor* drags other vehicles behind it, with the help of the *traction* of its wheels. **detract, intractable, protracted, retraction**

TRANS comes from Latin to indicate movement "through, across, or beyond" something. *Translation* carries the meaning from one language to another. A television signal is sent or *transmitted* through the air (or a cable) to your set. When making your way through a city on public *transportation,* you may have to *transfer* from one bus or subway across to another. **transcendent, transfiguration, transfuse, transient**

TRI means "three," whether derived from Greek or Latin. A *tricycle* has three wheels. A *triangle* has three sides and three angles. And a *triumvirate* is a board or government of three people. **triceratops, trident, trilogy, trinity**

TURB comes from the Latin verb *turbare,* "to throw into disorder," and the noun *turba,* "crowd" or "confusion." A *disturbance,* for example, confuses and upsets normal order or routine. **perturb, turbid, turbine, turbulent**

TUT/TUI, from the Latin verb *tueri,* originally meant "to look at," but the English meaning of the root gradually came to be "to guide, guard, or teach." A *tutor* guides a student through a subject, saving the most careful tutoring for the most difficult areas. **intuition, tuition, tutelage, tutorial**

UMBR, from Latin *umbra,* "shadow," is a shady customer. The familiar *umbrella,* with its ending meaning "little," casts a "little shadow" to keep off the sun or the rain. **adumbrate, penumbra, umber, umbrage**

UND comes into English from the Latin words *unda,* "wave," and *undare,* "to rise in waves," "to surge or flood." *Undulations* are waves or wavelike things or motions. To *undulate* is to rise and fall in a wavelike way. **abundant, inundate, redundancy, undulant**

UNI comes from the Latin word for "one." A *uniform* is a single design worn by everyone. A *united* group has one single opinion or forms a single *unit.* A *unicorn* is a mythical animal with one horn; a *unicycle* has only one wheel. **unicameral, unilateral, unison, unitarian**

UT/US comes from the Latin verb *uti,* "to use, make use of, employ," and the related adjective *utilis,* "useful, fit." It is *used* in such words as *abuse,* "improper use," and *reuse,* "to use again." **usufruct, usury, utilitarian, utility**

VEN/VENT comes from *venire,* the Latin verb meaning "come." To *intervene* in a case or an argument is to "come between" the two opponents. An *avenue* is a street, or originally an access road by which to "come toward" something. Groups "come together" at a *convention.* **advent, provenance, venturesome, venue**

VER comes from the Latin word for "truth." A *verdict* in a trial is "the truth spoken." But a just verdict may depend on the *veracity,* or "truthfulness," of the witnesses. **aver, verify, verisimilitude, verity**

VERB comes from Latin *verbum,* meaning "word." A *verb*—or action word—appears in some form in every complete sentence. To express something *verbally*—or to *verbalize* something—is to say it or write it. **proverb, verbatim, verbiage, verbose**

VERT/VERS, from the Latin verb *vertere,* means "to turn" or "to turn around." An *advertisement* turns your attention to a product or service. *Vertigo* is the dizziness that results from turning too rapidly or that makes you feel as if everything else is turning. **avert, divert, perverse, versatile**

VEST comes from the Latin verb *vestire,* "to clothe" or "to dress," and the related noun *vestis,* "clothing" or "garment." *Vest* is the shortest English word we have from this root, and is the name of a rather small piece of clothing. **divest, investiture, transvestite, travesty**

VID/VIS comes from the Latin verb *videre,* and appears in words having to do with seeing and sight. A *videotape* is a collection of *visual* images—that is, images *visible* to our eyes. But this root does not always involve eyes. To *envision* something, for instance, is to see it with your imagination. **revise, visage, visionary, visitation**

VINC/VICT comes from the Latin verb *vincere,* which means "to conquer" or "to overcome." The *victor* defeats an enemy, whether on a battlefield or a football field. To *convince* someone that you're right is a *victory* of another kind. **conviction, evince, invincible, victorious**

VIR is Latin for "man." A *virtue* is a good quality—originally, the kind of quality an ideal man possessed. And *virtuous* behavior is morally excellent. All in all, the Romans seemed to believe that being a man was a good thing. **triumvirate, virago, virility, virtuosity**

VIV comes from *vivere,* the Latin verb meaning "to live or be alive." A *survivor* has lived through something terrible. A *revival* brings something back to life, whether an old film, interest in a long-dead novelist, or the religious faith of a group. **convivial, revivify, vivacious, vivisection**

VOC/VOK, from the Latin noun *vox* and the verb *vocare,* has to do with speaking and calling and the use of the voice. So a *vocation* is a calling to a type of work; an *evocative* sight or smell calls forth memories and feelings; and a *vocal* ensemble is a singing group. **equivocate, irrevocable, provoke, vociferous**

VOLU/VOLV comes from the Latin verb *volvere,* meaning "to roll, wind, turn around, or twist around." From this source come words like *volume,* which was originally the name of a scroll or roll of papyrus, and *revolve,* which simply means "turn in circles." **convoluted, devolution, evolution, voluble**

VOR, from the Latin verb *vorare,* means "to eat." The ending *-ivorous* shows up in words that refer to eaters of certain kinds of food. Some *-ivorous* words such as *insectivorous* are easy to understand at a glance. **carnivorous, herbivorous, omnivorous, voracious**

IRREGULAR ENGLISH VERBS

Regular English verbs, like *call* or *trust*, have a predictable pattern in the past tense and past participle forms (referred to as the principal parts). They form the past and past participle by the addition of *-ed* to the infinitive form. Sometimes the ending results in an added syllable (*trusted* \'trəst-əd\) and sometimes not (*called* \'kȯld\).

Verbs are also considered regular if the final consonant is doubled by the addition of the *-ed* (*abet, abetted, abetted*) or if the final *-e* is dropped in adding the *-ed* ending (*die, died, died*).

Verbs are irregular if the past or past participle have a different pattern from the simple addition of *-ed* (*swim, swam, swum*) or if either or both forms have a variant form in addition to the *-ed*, (*saw, sawed, sawed* or *sawn*). Often this variant form is one in which the *-ed* has been changed to *-t*—which represents a typical pronunciation—(*burn, burned* or *burnt*).

Below is a list of irregular English verbs, showing the past tense and past participle forms, along with any variant forms.

INFINITIVE FORM	PAST TENSE	PAST PARTICIPLE
arise	arose	arisen
awake	awoke	awoken
	also awaked	*or* awaked
		also awoke
be	was, were	been
bear	bore	borne
		also born
beat	beat	beaten
		or beat
become	became	become
befall	befell	befallen
begin	began	begun
behold	beheld	beheld
bend	bent	bent
beseech	besought	besought
	or beseeched	*or* beseeched
beset	beset	beset
bet	bet	bet
	also betted	*also* betted
bid	bade	bidden
	or bid	*or* bid
		also bade
bind	bound	bound
bite	bit	bitten
		also bit
bleed	bled	bled
blow	blew	blown
break	broke	broken
breed	bred	bred
bring	brought	brought
build	built	built
burn	burned	burned
	or burnt	*or* burnt
burst	burst	burst
	also bursted	*also* bursted
buy	bought	bought
can (auxiliary verb)	could	—
cast	cast	cast
catch	caught	caught
choose	chose	chosen
cling	clung	clung
come	came	come
cost	cost	cost

INFINITIVE FORM	PAST TENSE	PAST PARTICIPLE
creep	crept	crept
cut	cut	cut
deal	dealt	dealt
dig	dug	dug
do	did	done
draw	drew	drawn
dream	dreamed *or* dreamt	dreamed *or* dreamt
drink	drank	drunk *or* drank
drive	drove	driven
dwell	dwelt *or* dwelled	dwelt *or* dwelled
eat	ate	eaten
fall	fell	fallen
feed	fed	fed
feel	felt	felt
fight	fought	fought
find	found	found
flee	fled	fled
fling	flung	flung
fly	flew	flown
forbid	forbade *also* forbad	forbidden
forecast	forecast *also* forecasted	forecast *also* forecasted
forego	forewent	foregone
foresee	foresaw	foreseen
foretell	foretold	foretold
forget	forgot	forgotten *or* forgot
forgive	forgave	forgiven
forsake	forsook	forsaken
freeze	froze	frozen
get	got	got *or* gotten
give	gave	given
go	went	gone
grind	ground	ground
grow	grew	grown
hang	hung *also* hanged	hung *also* hanged
have	had	had
hear	heard	heard
hide	hid	hidden *or* hid
hit	hit	hit
hold	held	held
hurt	hurt	hurt
keep	kept	kept
kneel	knelt *or* kneeled	knelt *or* kneeled
know	knew	known
lay	laid	laid
lead	led	led
lean	leaned *also* leant	leaned
leap	leapt *or* leaped	leapt *or* leaped
leave	left	left

INFINITIVE FORM	PAST TENSE	PAST PARTICIPLE
lend	lent	lent
let	let	let
lie (to recline)	lay	lain
light	lit	lit
	or lighted	*or* lighted
lose	lost	lost
make	made	made
may	might	—
mean	meant	meant
meet	met	met
mow	mowed	mowed
		or mown
pay	paid	paid
put	put	put
quit	quit	quit
	also quitted	*also* quitted
read	read	read
rend	rent	rent
rid	rid	rid
	also ridded	*also* ridded
ride	rode	ridden
ring (to sound)	rang	rung
rise	rose	risen
run	ran	run
saw	sawed	sawed
		or sawn
say	said	said
see	saw	seen
seek	sought	sought
sell	sold	sold
send	sent	sent
set	set	set
shake	shook	shaken
shall (auxiliary verb)	should	—
shear	sheared	sheared
		or shorn
shed	shed	shed
shine	shone	shone
	or shined	*or* shined
shoot	shot	shot
show	showed	shown
		or showed
shrink	shrank	shrunk
	or shrunk	*or* shrunken
shut	shut	shut
sing	sang	sung
	or sung	
sink	sank	sunk
	or sunk	
sit	sat	sat
slay	slew	slain
sleep	slept	slept
slide	slid	slid
sling	slung	slung
smell	smelled	smelled
	or smelt	*or* smelt
sow	sowed	sown
		or sowed
speak	spoke	spoken

INFINITIVE FORM	PAST TENSE	PAST PARTICIPLE
speed	sped *or* speeded	sped *or* speeded
spell	spelled	spelled
spend	spent	spent
spill	spilled *also* spilt	spilled *also* spilt
spin	spun	spun
spit (to eject saliva)	spit *or* spat	spit *or* spat
split	split	split
spoil	spoiled *or* spoilt	spoiled *or* spoilt
spread	spread	spread
spring	sprang *or* sprung	sprung
stand	stood	stood
steal	stole	stolen
stick	stuck	stuck
sting	stung	stung
stink	stank *or* stunk	stunk
stride	strode	stridden
strike	struck	struck *also* stricken
swear	swore	sworn
sweep	swept	swept
swell	swelled	swelled *or* swollen
swim	swam	swum
swing	swung	swung
take	took	taken
teach	taught	taught
tear (to rip)	tore	torn
tell	told	told
think	thought	thought
throw	threw	thrown
thrust	thrust	thrust
tread	trod	trodden *or* trod
wake	woke *also* waked	woken *also* waked *or* woke
waylay	waylaid	waylaid
wear	wore	worn
weave	wove *or* weaved	woven *or* weaved
wed	wedded *also* wed	wedded *also* wed
weep	wept	wept
will (auxiliary verb)	would	—
win	won	won
wind (to encircle)	wound *also* winded	wound *also* winded
withdraw	withdrew	withdrawn
withhold	withheld	withheld
withstand	withstood	withstood
wring	wrung	wrung
write	wrote	written *also* writ

DICTIONARY

CONFUSED & MISUSED WORDS

This section contains words that are similar or identical in sound but that are quite different in meaning. They are often confused, and use of the wrong one in English context can sometimes lead to embarrassing mistakes.

a/an *A* is used before a word beginning with a consonant or consonant sound ("a door," "a one-time deal"). *An* is usually used before a word beginning with a vowel or vowel sound ("an operation"). *A* is usually used before *h* when the *h* is pronounced ("a headache"); *an* is used if the *h* is not pronounced ("an honor").

accept/except The verb *accept* means "to agree to, receive" ("accept a gift"). *Except* most often means "not including" ("will visit all national parks except the Grand Canyon").

adapt/adopt The verb *adapt* means "to change or modify" ("adapt to the warmer climate"); the verb *adopt* means "to take as one's own" ("adopt a child").

affect/effect The verb *affect* means to "cause a change in something" ("rain affects plant growth"); the noun *effect* means "the result" ("the effect of rain on plant growth").

ain't *Ain't* is used by some people in informal speech to mean "are not," "is not," or "am not," among other things. Because "ain't" is considered very informal it is not generally used in formal speech or in writing.

aisle/isle *Aisle* means "a walkway between seats"; *isle* is a poetic word meaning "island."

a lot, allot *A lot*, meaning "a great number," is spelled as two words; it is sometimes written incorrectly as *alot*. *Allot* is a verb meaning "to give out in portions" ("alloted one hour for the project").

an See *a/an*.

apt See *liable/likely/apt*.

as . . . as Is it more correct to say "she is as smart as I" or "she is as smart as me"? Actually, both ways are correct. In comparisons with "as . . . as," it's acceptable to use either subject pronouns (like "I," "you," "he," "she," "it," "we," and "they") or object pronouns (like "me," "you," "him," "her," "it," "us," and "them") after the second *as*. However, subject pronouns are more formal, so you may want to use subject pronouns in your comparisons when you are speaking formally or writing.

as/like Sometimes *as* is used with the same meaning as *like* ("do as I do"), ("do like I do"). At other times, *as* means "in the role of" ("acted as a substitute teacher").

as well as When *as well as* is used in a comparison, the pronoun following the second *as* is usually in the subject form ("she can spell as well as I [can]," not "she can spell as well as me"). (For a list of subject pronouns, see *as . . . as*.)

aural/oral *Aural* and *oral* are sometimes pronounced the same, but they have different meanings. *Aural* means "of or relating to the ear or sense of hearing." It comes from the Latin word for "ear." *Oral* means "of, relating to, given by, or near the mouth," and comes from a Latin word for "mouth." (See also *verbal/oral*.)

bare/bear *Bare* means "without clothes or a covering" ("bare feet"); *bear* means "to carry."

bazaar/bizarre *Bazaar* is a fair or an exhibition of things for sale; *bizarre* means *weird*.

beside/besides *Beside* generally means "next to or at the side of" something; *besides* means "in addition to."

born/borne *Born* is having come into life; *borne* means "carried."

bring/take *Bring* usually means "to carry to a closer place"; *take*, "to carry to a farther place."

can/may *Can* usually means "to be able to or know how to" ("they can read and write"); *may* means "to have permission to" ("may I go?"). In casual conversation, *can* also means "to have permission to" ("can I go?"), but *may* is used instead in more formal speech or in writing.

canvas/canvass *Canvas* is a cloth; *canvass* means to ask people's opinions.

capital/capitol *Capital* is the place or city of government; *capitol* is the building of government.

cereal/serial *Cereal* is a breakfast food; *serial* is a story presented in parts.

colonel/kernel *Colonel* is a military rank; *kernel* is a part of a seed.

compliment/complement A *compliment* is a nice thing to say; a *complement* is something that completes.

council/counsel A *council* is a group of people meeting; *counsel* is advice.

country/county *Country* is a nation; *county* is a small, local government area.

data This was originally a plural form, but today it is used as both a singular and a plural noun.

desert/dessert *Desert* (with one *s*) is a dry, barren place; *dessert* is a sweet eaten after a meal.

die/dye To *die* is to cease to live; to *dye* is to change the color of.

dived/dove Both spellings are common as a past tense of the verb *dive* ("she dived into the pool," "she dove into the pool").

effect See *affect/effect*.

except See *accept/except*.

farther/further *Farther* usually refers to distance ("he ran farther than I did"). *Further* refers to degree or extent ("she further explained the situation")

flammable/inflammable Both words mean "capable of catching fire," but *inflammable* is also sometimes used to mean "excitable."

forth/fourth *Forth* means "forward"; *fourth* means "number four in a sequence."

further See *farther/further*.

good/well To *feel good* generally means "to be in good health and good spirits." *To feel well* usually means "to be healthy."

half/half a/a half a The *l* in *half* is silent—it is used in writing, but it is not pronounced. *Half* is often used with the word *a*, which can either come before *half* or after it ("ate a half sandwich," "ate half a sandwich"). In casual speech, *a half a* is sometimes used ("ate a half a sandwich"), but it is avoided in more formal speech and in writing.

hanged/hung Both *hanged* and *hung* are used as the past tense of the verb *to hang*. *Hanged* is used when referring to execution by hanging; *hung* is used in all other senses.

hardy/hearty *Hardy* (suggestive of *hard*) means "strong"; *hearty* (suggestive of *heart*) means "friendly, enthusiastic."

isle See *aisle/isle*.

its/it's *Its* means "of or relating to it or itself" ("the dog wagged its tail"). *It's* is a contraction of *it is* ("it's polite to say *thank you* ").

kernel See *colonel/kernel*.

later/latter *Later* is the comparative form of *late*; it means "after a given time" ("they started later than they had intended"). *Latter* is an adjective that refers to the second of two things mentioned, or the last one of a sequence ("of the two choices, the latter is preferred").

lay/lie *Lay* means "to put (something) down"; *lie* means "to put one's body in a flat position."

lead/led These two words are pronounced the same, but have different meanings. *Lead* is a metal; *led* is the past tense of the verb *to lead*.

less/fewer *Less* is usually used with things that cannot be counted ("there is less sunshine today") and *fewer* with things that can be counted ("there are fewer people today").

liable/likely/apt All three words mean the same thing, but *likely* and *apt* are more often used in situations that could have a positive or neutral outcome ("she's apt to burst out laughing," "they'll likely visit today"). *Liable* is usually used where there is a possibility of a negative outcome ("you're liable to get hurt").

lie See *lay/lie*.

like See *as/like*.

liter/litter A *liter* is a unit of measurement; *litter* is a messy collection of things.

loose/lose *Loose* means "not tight"; *lose* means "to misplace or fail to win."

marital/martial *Marital* has to do with marriage; *martial* has to do with the military.

may See *can/may*.

moral/morale *Moral* has to do with high ideals ("a person of good moral character"); *morale* is the state of feelings of a person or group ("after the victory, morale was high").

naval/navel *Naval* has to do with a navy; a *navel* is a belly button.

no way *No way* is an expression meaning "no" or "not at all." It is used in everyday speech, but is usually considered too casual for formal speech and writing.

oral See *verbal/oral* and *aural/oral*.

peace See *piece/peace*.

pedal/peddle *Pedal* means "to use or work the pedals of something" ("pedal a bicycle"). *Peddle* means "to sell from house to house."

piece/peace A *piece* is a portion of something ("a piece of cake"); *peace* is the freedom from war or fighting.

precede/proceed *Precede* means "to go ahead of or come before"; *proceed* means "to start or move forward."

principle/principal A *principle* is a rule or guiding truth; *principal* is "the main one"—as an adjective or a noun: "the principal meal of the day," "the head of a school is a principal." It may help you to remember that *principle* and *rule* end with the same two letters.

serial See *cereal/serial*.

set/sit The verb *set* means "to rest on eggs to hatch them"; *sit* means "to rest on the part of the body where the hips and legs join."

stationary/stationery Something that is *stationary* stands still; *stationery* is paper that is used for writing letters. It's easy to tell these two words apart if you remember that *stationery* and *letter* are both spelled with *er*.

take See *bring/take*.

than/then *Than* is a conjunction used to indicate a comparison ("better than that"); *then* means "at that time" ("then we went home").

there/their *There* points to a place ("there it is"); *their* refers to "what belongs to them" ("this is their house").

to/too/two *To* implies a direction ("went to the store"). *Too* means "also," "very," or "excessively" ("brought a pen and pencil too," "not too difficult," "too much"). *Two* is the number 2.

used to/use to The phrases *used to* and *use to* are often confused since they have the same pronunciation. *Used to* is correct in most instances ("we used to go to the lake every summer," "I used to know that"). But when it follows *did* or *didn't*, the correct spelling is *use to* ("that didn't use to be a problem").

verbal/oral Both *verbal* and *oral* are sometimes used to mean "spoken rather than written" ("a verbal agreement," "an oral agreement"). *Verbal* can also mean "of, relating to, or formed by a verb," or "of, relating to, or consisting of words." (For more about *oral*, see *aural/oral*.)

want See *won't/want*.

were/we're *Were* is a past tense verb form of *be* ("they were very young"); *we're* is a contraction of *we are* ("we're glad to see you").

who/whom *Who* is used as the subject of a clause (where one would use *he, she,* or *they*). *Whom* is used as the object of a clause (where one would use *him, her,* or *them*), and often follows prepositions like *to, for, from,* or *with*. Subject: "Who is coming to the party?" "He is coming to the party." Object: "John is coming with whom?" "John is coming with them."

who's/whose The word *who's* is a contraction of *who is* ("who's there?"); *whose* is an adjective indicating ownership or quality ("whose book is this?").

won't/want *Won't* is a contraction of *will not* ("I won't go"); *want* is a verb meaning "to need or desire" ("do you want some cake?").

Xmas *Xmas* is a shortened form of the word *Christmas*; the *X* comes a Greek letter, which is the first letter of the Greek word for *Christ*. *Xmas* is used in very casual writing, but it is inappropriate for formal writing.

your/you're *Your* is an adjective meaning "that which belongs to you" ("is that your sister?"). *You're* is a contraction of *you are* ("you're going, aren't you?").

UNITED STATES

© 2005 Encyclopædia Britannica, Inc.

WORLD

NORTH AMERICA

© 2005 Encyclopædia Britannica, Inc.

ATLANTIC OCEAN

Tropic of Cancer

Equator

BERMUDA (U.K.)
Hamilton

VIRGIN ISLANDS (U.S.)
BRITISH VIRGIN ISLANDS (U.K.)
ANGUILLA (U.K.)
ANTIGUA AND BARBUDA
GUADELOUPE (Fr.)
DOMINICA
MARTINIQUE (Fr.)
ST. LUCIA
ST. VINCENT AND THE GRENADINES
BARBADOS
GRENADA
Port-of-Spain
TRINIDAD AND TOBAGO

LESSER ANTILLES

ARUBA (Neth.)
NETHERLANDS ANTILLES (Neth.)

SARGASSO SEA

TURKS AND CAICOS
Grand Turk (Cockburn Town)

DOMINICAN REPUBLIC
SANTO DOMINGO
San Juan
PUERTO RICO (U.S.)

HAITI
Port-au-Prince

GREATER ANTILLES

CARIBBEAN SEA

THE BAHAMAS
Nassau

CUBA
HAVANA

Miami

Jacksonville

NEW YORK CITY
Baltimore PHILADELPHIA
Washington, D.C.
Chesapeake Bay

Cleveland
CHICAGO DETROIT
Columbus
Lake Erie
Ohio
Indianapolis
Nashville
Memphis
Atlanta
Chattahoochee
Savannah
Mt. Mitchell 2037 m
APPALACHIAN MOUNTAINS
PIEDMONT
Kentucky Lake
Tennessee
Tombigbee

St. Louis
Mississippi
Lake of the Ozarks
OZARK PLATEAU

Missouri
Platte
Arkansas
Red
Colorado

UNITED STATES

DALLAS
HOUSTON
San Antonio
Brazos
Rio Grande
Pecos

MONTERREY

Denver
Pikes Peak 4301 m

N. Platte

ROCKY MOUNTAINS

El Paso
Ciudad Juárez

Phoenix
GREAT BASIN
Gila
Lake Powell
Grand Canyon
Glen Canyon Dam
Hoover Dam
Lake Mead
PAINTED DESERT
COLORADO PLATEAU

DEATH VALLEY
SIERRA NEVADA
Mojave Desert
SONORAN DESERT
Salton Sea
California Aqueduct

San Francisco
San Jose
LOS ANGELES
SAN DIEGO

Gulf of California
BAJA CALIFORNIA
Sebastián Vizcaíno Bay

REVILLAGIGEDO ISLANDS

Acapulco
SIERRA MADRE DEL SUR
MEXICO CITY
Ixtaccíhuatl 5286 m
Popocatépetl 5452 m
GUADALAJARA
Colima Volcano 3820 m
Lake Chapala
SIERRA MADRE OCCIDENTAL
MEXICO
MEXICAN PLATEAU
SIERRA MADRE ORIENTAL
MESA DEL NORTE
CENTRAL MESA
Cerro Nevado 4340 m
MESA DEL SUR
MARÍAS ISLANDS
Fuerte
Conchos
Nazas
BOLSÓN DE MAPIMÍ
CHIHUAHUAN DESERT

Rio Grande

Gulf of Mexico

Bay of Campeche
Laguna de Términos
COASTAL LOWLAND
Laguna de Tamiahua

YUCATÁN PENINSULA

BELIZE
Belmopan
Guatemala City
GUATEMALA
Tajumulco 4220 m
ISTHMUS OF TEHUANTEPEC
Gulf of Tehuantepec

HONDURAS
Tegucigalpa
San Salvador
EL SALVADOR
Gulf of Fonseca
San Miguel
MOSQUITO COAST
NICARAGUA
Managua
Lake Managua
Lake Nicaragua

COSTA RICA
San José
Mount Chirripó 3819 m

PANAMA
Panama City
Panama Canal

Yucatan Channel
Yucatan Basin

Cayman Trench
CAYMAN ISLANDS (U.K.)
George Town
Kingston
JAMAICA

Scale 1:33,296,000

550 mi
500
450
400
350
300
250
200
150
100
50
0

800 km
700
600
500
400
300
200
100
0

Chamberlin Trimetric

BERING SEA

ALASKA
Nunivak Island
Bristol Bay

Pavlof Volcano 2714 m
Shishaldin Volcano 2857 m

ALEUTIAN ISLANDS

PRIBILOF ISLANDS

Attu Island

Legend

MEXICO CITY — Cities over 1,000,000
Washington, D.C. — Cities 500,000 to 1,000,000
Ottawa — Cities 100,000 to 500,000
Port-of-Spain — Cities 50,000 to 100,000
Belmopan — Cities under 50,000

⊛ Capital symbols
▪ City symbols

Canals
Aqueducts
Dams
Intermittent rivers
Waterfalls
Reefs
Glaciers
Salt lakes
Swamps
Sand areas

CANADA

© 2005 Encyclopædia Britannica, Inc.

Legend

PUEBLA Cities over 1,000,000
Acapulco Cities 500,000 to 1,000,000
La Paz Cities 100,000 to 500,000
Guaymas Cities 50,000 to 100,000
Taxco Cities under 50,000

⊛ ★ Capital symbols
■ ● City symbols
● Points of interest
⊢ Dams
Intermittent rivers
Salt lakes
National Parks
Aboriginal lands
Swamps
Sand areas

*1 AGUASCALIENTES
2 DISTRITO FEDERAL
3 MORELOS
4 QUERÉTARO
5 TLAXCALA

Scale 1: 13,573,000
Lambert Conformal Conic

REVILLAGIGEDO ISLANDS

N

THE CARIBBEAN

CENTRAL AMERICA

SOUTH AMERICA

SOUTH AMERICA

Scale 1: 21,611,000

Lambert Azimuthal Equal-Area

© 2005 Encyclopædia Britannica, Inc.

Legend

Symbol	Description
	Lava
	Sand areas
	Swamps
▽	National Parks
	Intermittent rivers
	Dams
◉	Oases
✗	Passes
☐	Points of interest
■ ●	City symbols
✹ ★	Capital symbols

Cities under 50,000	Barbacena
Cacoupé	Cities 50,000 to 100,000
Natal	Cities 100,000 to 500,000
La Paz	Cities 500,000 to 1,000,000
SALVADOR	Cities over 1,000,000

N

ATLANTIC OCEAN

Equator

Tropic of Capricorn

MONTEVIDEO

COSTA ATLANTICA NATIONAL MONUMENT

RIO GRANDE DO SUL · PORTO ALEGRE · Pelotas · Rio Grande

SANTA CATARINA · Florianópolis · Joinville · Blumenau

Curitiba · PARANÁ · Londrina · Maringá

SÃO PAULO · Santo André · Santos · Campinas · Guarulhos · São Gonçalo · NOVA IGUAÇU · Duque de Caxias · RIO DE JANEIRO · Niterói

BELO HORIZONTE · Uberlândia · Uberaba · Divinópolis

MINAS GERAIS · Goiânia · GOIÁS · Brasília · DISTRITO FEDERAL

MATO GROSSO DO SUL · Campo Grande · MATO GROSSO · PLATEAU

BRAZILIAN HIGHLANDS

SALVADOR · Feira de Santana · BAHIA · SERGIPE · Aracaju

ALAGOAS · Maceió · PERNAMBUCO · Recife · Olinda · João Pessoa · PARAÍBA · Natal · RIO GRANDE DO NORTE · Mossoró

CEARÁ · Fortaleza · Maranguape

PIAUÍ · Teresina · MARANHÃO · São Luís · Imperatriz

TOCANTINS · PARÁ · Belém · Macapá · AMAPÁ

FRENCH GUIANA (FR) · Cayenne

BOLIVIA

ARGENTINA, CHILE, AND URUGUAY

ECUADOR AND PERU

COLOMBIA AND VENEZUELA

PACIFIC OCEAN

CARIBBEAN SEA

Key to Political Subdivisions

1 DISTRITO FEDERAL
2 CARABOBO
3 YARACUY

CARACAS   Cities over 1,000,000
Valencia   Cities 500,000 to 1,000,000
Valera   Cities 100,000 to 500,000
Girardot   Cities 50,000 to 100,000
Paraguan   Cities under 50,000

⊛ Capital symbols
★ City symbols
□ Points of interest
≈ Bridges
≈ Canals
⊢ Dams
≈ Rapids
     National parks
     Swamps

COLOMBIA

VENEZUELA

ECUADOR

PERU

BRAZIL

GUYANA

UNITED KINGDOM AND IRELAND

EUROPE

SPAIN AND PORTUGAL

© 2005 Encyclopædia Britannica, Inc.

Scale 1: 6,117,000

Albers Conical Equal-Area

0 25 50 75 mi
0 20 40 60 80 100 120 km

ATLANTIC
OCEAN

Bay
of
Biscay

P O R T U G A L

S P A I N

Lisbon

MADRID

Seville

Valencia

BARCELONA

Saragossa

F R A N C E

MEDITERRANEAN
SEA

BALEARIC
ISLANDS

Palma de Majorca

Gulf of
Lion

Gulf of
Valencia

COSTA BRAVA

COSTA DEL SOL

ATLANTIC OCEAN

Scale 1: 9,362,000
Chamberlin Trimetric

0 25 50 75 mi
0 40 80 120 km

CANARY ISLANDS

C A N A R Y   I S L A N D S

MOROCCO
WESTERN
SAHARA

R I F   M O U N T A I N S

M O R O C C O

A L G E R I A

Strait of Gibraltar

Tangier

Tlemcen

MADRID Cities over 1,000,000
Seville Cities 500,000 to 1,000,000
Lleida Cities 100,000 to 500,000
Toledo Cities 50,000 to 100,000
Algora Cities under 100,000

★ Capital symbols
■ City symbols
□ Points of interest
✕ Passes
⌐ Dams
⌒ Canals
⌁ Intermittent rivers
▲ National Parks
Swamps

N

FRANCE

ITALY, SLOVENIA, AND CROATIA

SCANDINAVIA

ICELAND

GREENLAND SEA

Denmark Strait
Arctic Circle
Grímsey
Fonfur Point
Rauðarhöfn
Thorshöfn
Bolungavík
Ísafjörður
Húsavík
Siglufjörður
Skagaströnd
Raufarhöfn
JÖKULSÁ CANYON NATIONAL PARK
Vopnafjörður
Þingeyri
VESTFIRÐIR
Sauðárkrókur
Akureyri
Seyðisfjörður
Vatneyri
Holmavík
Blönduós
Hvammstangi
Neskaupstaður
Eskifjörður
Patreksfjörður
Stykkishólmur
Guðlaug Lava Field
Reyðarfjörður
ICELAND
Faskrudsfjordur
Ólafsvík
Grundarfjörður
Djúpivogur
Faxa Bay
Mount Snæfell 1833 m
HÖFUÐBORGARSVÆÐI
Vatna Glacier
SKAFTAFELL NATIONAL PARK
Borgarnes
Mount Hvannadal 2119 m
Reykjavík
ÞINGVELLIR NAT'L PARK
Keflavík
Selfoss
Hella
Hekla Volcano 1491 m
Ingólfs Headland
SUÐURNES
64°N
REYKJANES PENINSULA
Hvolsvöllur
Heimaey
Vík
Scale 1: 9,367,000
ATLANTIC   OCEAN
Surtsey
0 20 40 60 80 100 mi
0 50 100 150 km
Lambert Conformal Conic
23°W   20°W

NORWEGIAN SEA

Legend

ST. PETERSBURG — Cities over 1,000,000
Stockholm — Cities 500,000 to 1,000,000
Helsinki — Cities 100,000 to 500,000
Kotka — Cities 50,000 to 100,000
Notodden — Cities under 50,000

⊛ ★ — Capital symbols
■ ● — City symbols
⋈ — Bridges
‥‥‥ — Canals
〰 — Waterfalls
〰 — Rapids
◎ — Glaciers
△ — National parks
— Swamps
— Sand areas
— Lava

WESTERN AND CENTRAL EUROPE

TURKEY

Bursa
Xalovia
Inegol
Orhangazi
Balıkesir
Bandırma
Manisa
IZMIR
Aydın
Denizli

Sea of Marmara

Gallipoli
Çanakkale
Dardanelles

MOUNT ATHOS
MONASTIC REPUBLIC

Mount Athos
2033 m

NORTHERN
SPORADES

AEGEAN
SEA

DODECANESE

Rhodes

Karpathos Island

SEA OF CRETE

Iráklion
Crete
SAMARIA
NATIONAL PARK

Thessaloníki
CHALCIDICE
Gulf of PENINSULA
Vardar

BALKAN

MOUNT OLYMPUS
NATIONAL PARK

PINDUS MOUNTAINS
PINDUS
NATIONAL PARK
PELOPONNESE

Lárisa
Vólos

PARNASSUS
NATIONAL PARK
Delphi

PARNIS NATIONAL PARK
Athens
Piraeus
SOUNIO
NATIONAL PARK

GREECE

PELOPONNESE
MOUNT OITHA
NATIONAL PARK
MAINA
PENINSULA
TAYGETOS MOUNTAINS

CYCLADES

PRESPA
NATIONAL PARK

VIKOS-AÖOS NATIONAL PARK

AÍNOS NATIONAL PARK

IONIAN SEA

ISLANDS

Corfu Island

Strait of Otranto

Cape Santa Maria di Leuca

SALENTINE PENINSULA
Lecce
Brindisi
Taranto
Gulf of Taranto
POLLINO NATURE PARK

ITALY

Potenza
LUCANIAN
APENNINES
LA SÍLA MTS
CALABRIAN APENNINES
Catanzaro
Cosenza
Crotone

Reggio di Calabria
Strait of Messina

Salerno
Gulf of Salerno
Torre del Greco

TYRRHENIAN
SEA

EOLIE AND LIPARI ISLANDS

Messina
Catania
Gulf of Catania
NEBRODI MOUNTAINS
Caltanissetta
IBLEI MOUNTAINS
Ragusa
Sicily
Syracuse

MALTA
Valletta

LIBYA

AL-AKHDAR MOUNTAINS
Darnah
Al-Bayda

MEDITERRANEAN SEA

N

Scale 1: 5,913,000

Albers

100 mi
150 km

© 2005 Encyclopædia Britannica, Inc.

SOFIA Cities over 1,000,000
Sarajevo Cities 500,000 to 1,000,000
Tiranë Cities 100,000 to 500,000
Nikea Cities 50,000 to 100,000
Tecuci Cities under 50,000

⊛ Capital symbols
■ City symbols
¤ Points of interest
Bridges
Canals
Dams
Intermittent rivers
National parks
Swamps
Sand areas

RUSSIA AND KAZAKSTAN

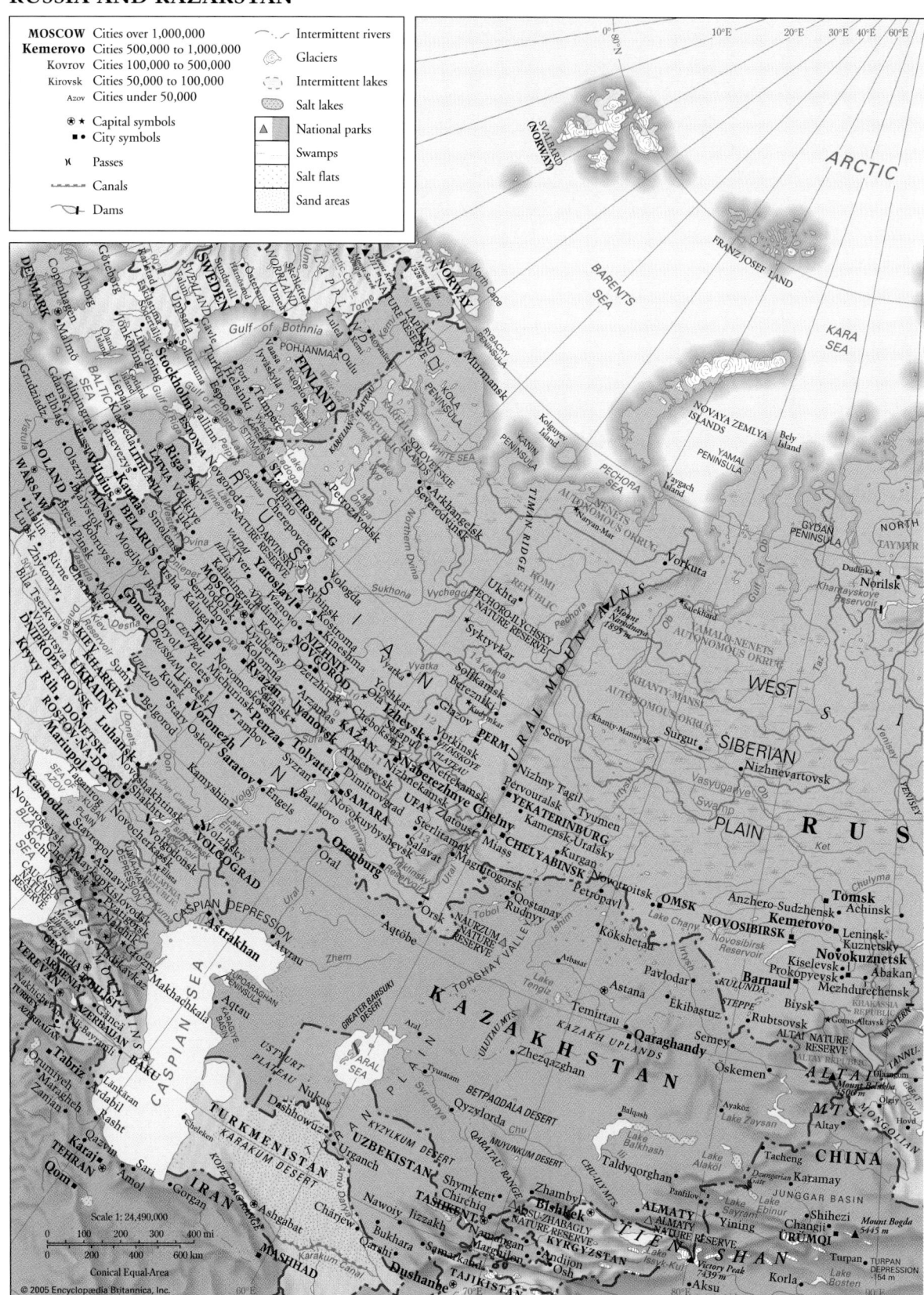

MOSCOW	Cities over 1,000,000
Kemerovo	Cities 500,000 to 1,000,000
Kovrov	Cities 100,000 to 500,000
Kirovsk	Cities 50,000 to 100,000
Azov	Cities under 50,000

⊛ ★ Capital symbols
■ ● City symbols
) (Passes
Canals
Dams

Intermittent rivers
Glaciers
Intermittent lakes
Salt lakes
National parks
Swamps
Salt flats
Sand areas

Scale 1: 24,490,000

0   100   200   300   400 mi

0   200   400   600 km

Conical Equal-Area

© 2005 Encyclopædia Britannica, Inc.

Key to Political subdivision names (shown by number on map):

1 ADYGEA REPUBLIC
2 KARACHAY-CHERKESSIA REPUBLIC
3 KABARDINO-BALKARIA REPUBLIC
4 NORTH OSSETIA (ALANIA) REPUBLIC
5 CHECHNIA REPUBLIC
6 DAGESTAN REPUBLIC
7 INGUSHETIA REPUBLIC
8 MORDVINIA REPUBLIC
9 CHUVASHIA REPUBLIC
10 MARI EL REPUBLIC
11 TATARSTAN REPUBLIC
12 UDMURTIA REPUBLIC
13 BASHKORTOSTAN REPUBLIC
14 KOMI-PERMYAK AUTONOMOUS OKRUG
15 UST-ORDA BURYAT AUTONOMOUS OKRUG
16 AGA-BURYAT AUTONOMOUS OKRUG

EASTERN EUROPE

CENTRAL ASIA

ASIA

ARCTIC OCEAN

FRANZ JOSEF LAND ISLANDS
SEVERNAYA ZEMLYA ISLANDS
Cape Chelyuskin

NOVAYA ZEMLYA ISLANDS
KARA SEA
TAIMYR PENINSULA
LAPTEV SEA

Scale 1: 42,683,000
0 100   300   500   700 mi
0 200 400 600 800 1000 km
Bonne

NORTH SIBERIAN LOWLAND

YAMAL PENINSULA

Mount Narodnaya 1895 m

WEST
SIBERIAN
PLATEAU

CENTRAL

Lower Tunguska

Angara

Lake Baikal

R U S S I A

❋MOSCOW

YEKATERINBURG
CHELYABINSK NOVOSIBIRSK
OMSK Novokuznetsk
Astana ● Barnaul
Qaraghandy ●

Tomsk
Kemerovo Krasnoyarsk
Irkutsk

SIBERIAN
PLAIN

SAYAN MTS.

Yenisey

K A Z A K H S T A N

URAL MOUNTAINS

CASPIAN DEPRESSION
KUMA-MANYCH DEPRESSION
SEA OF AZOV

BLACK SEA

Cape Baba
Bursa ISTANBUL
IZMIR ANKARA
T U R K E Y GEORGIA ❋ T'BILISI
Konya YEREVAN
Adana ARMENIA AZERBAIJAN
TAURUS MTS.

Mount Elbrus 5642 m
CAUCASUS MTS.

CASPIAN SEA

ARAL SEA

Syr Darya

Lake Balkhash

Mount Yovoy 4374 m

MONGOLIA

ALTAI MOUNTAINS

Victory Peak 7439 m

ÜRÜMQI

GOBI DESERT

ALMATY
Bishkek
TASHKENT KYRGYZSTAN
TIEN SHAN

Lop Nor

MEDITERRANEAN SEA
LEBANON SYRIA
BEIRUT ALEPPO Mosul
ISRAEL Hims Kirkuk
Jerusalem DAMASCUS BAGHDAD Bakhtaran
JORDAN AMMAN IRAQ
AN-NAFUD DESERT
Basra
KUWAIT
Kuwait

Gaziantep
Tabriz
TEHRAN
Qom
Zagros Mts.
Ahvaz
Esfahan
IRAN
Shiraz

UZBEKISTAN
TURKMENISTAN
KARAKUM DEPRESSION
Ashgabat
KARAKUM DESERT
Kara-Kum Canal
Mount Damavand 5671 m
ELBURZ MTS.

TAJIKISTAN
Dushanbe
Communism Peak 7495 m
PAMIRS
MASHHAD

HINDU KUSH MTS.
KABUL
AFGHANISTAN
Peshawar
Islamabad

TAKLA MAKAN DESERT
KUNLUN MOUNTAINS
Xining

K2 8611 m
KARAKORAM RANGE
KASHMIR
Srinagar
Nanga Parbat 8126 m

PLATEAU OF TIBET

SAUDI
ARABIA
RIYADH
Manama
BAHRAIN
QATAR
Abu Dhabi
UNITED ARAB EMIRATES
Muscat
OMAN

ARABIAN
PENINSULA

JIDDAH
Mecca

RED SEA

Persian Gulf
Gulf of Oman
MAKRAN MTS.
OMAN

FAISALABAD LAHORE Amritsar
Multan LUDHIANA
Chandigarh
PAKISTAN DELHI Meerut
THAR DESERT New Delhi JAIPUR
Hyderabad Jodhpur Agra
KARACHI Kota Gwalior
Sutlej

Mount Manaslu 8163 m Mount Everest 8850 m
NEPAL
Kathmandu BHUTAN
Thimphu
KANPUR Patna Guwahati
LUCKNOW Ganges
Allahabad Varanasi BANGLADESH
Brahmaputra
DHAKA

H I M A L A Y A S

RUB' AL-KHALI DESERT

Mount An-Nabi Shu'ayb 3660 m
Sanaa
YEMEN

ARABIAN
SEA

Gulf of Aden

Socotra Island (YEMEN)

AHMADABAD BHOPAL
Rajkot Narmada
SURAT VADODARA Jabalpur
Nashik INDORE
I N D I A NAGPUR CALCUTTA
Ranchi
Howrah
KOLKATA
Mandalay

Chittagong
MYANMAR
Mount Inthanon 2581 m

MUMBAI (BOMBAY) PUNE
Sholapur
HYDERABAD
Hubli-Dharwad Vishakhapatnam
Vijayawada
DECCAN PLATEAU
WESTERN GHATS
EASTERN GHATS
Krishna
Godavari

Bay of Bengal

YANGÓN

LAKSHADWEEP ISLANDS (INDIA)
BANGALORE
Coimbatore
CHENNAI (MADRAS)
ANDAMAN ISLANDS (INDIA)
ANDAMAN SEA

Anai Peak 2695 m
Kochi Madurai
Thiruvananthapuram
SRI LANKA
NICOBAR ISLANDS (INDIA)

Colombo

INDIAN OCEAN

Male
MALDIVES

ASIA

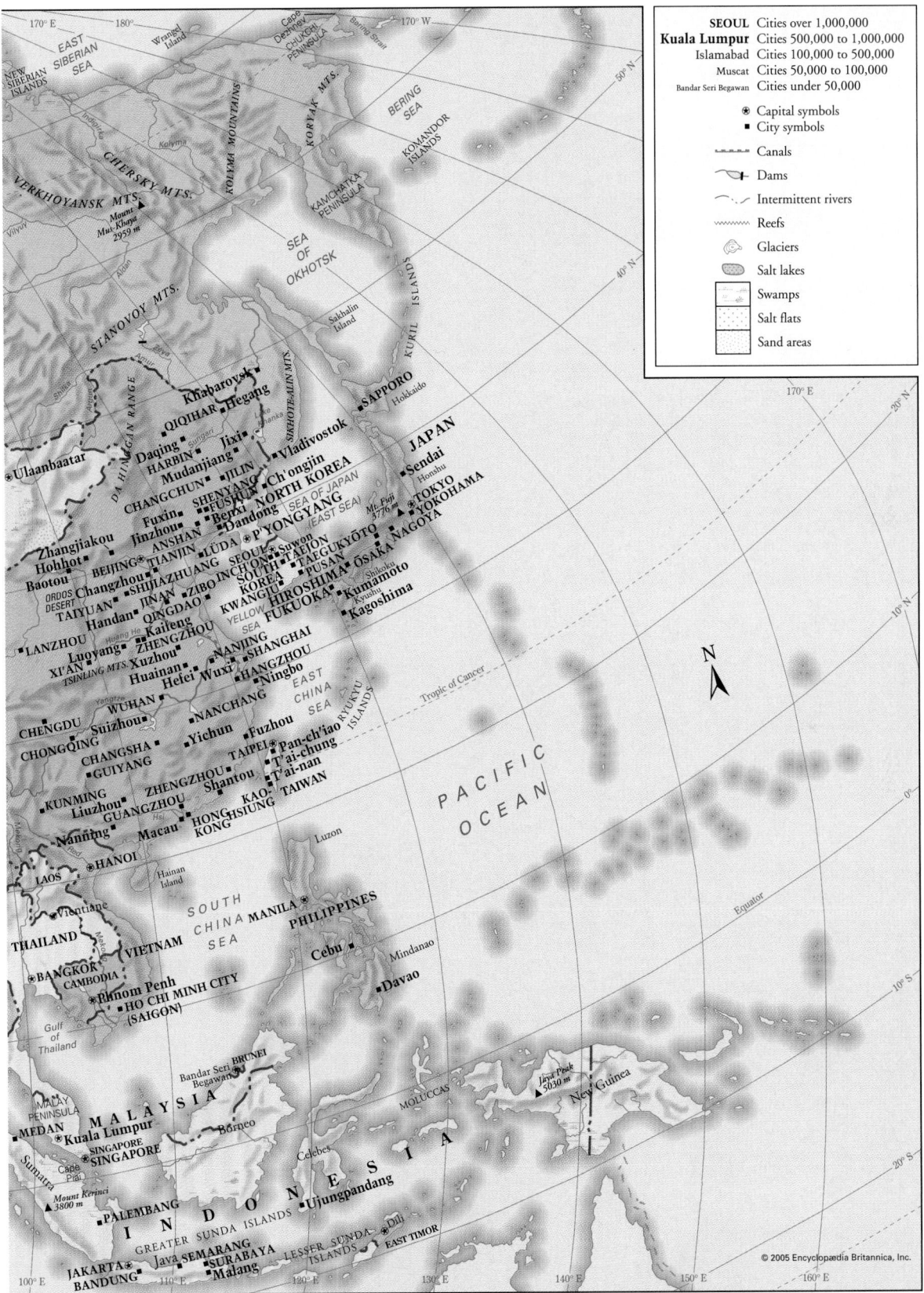

Legend:

SEOUL Cities over 1,000,000
Kuala Lumpur Cities 500,000 to 1,000,000
Islamabad Cities 100,000 to 500,000
Muscat Cities 50,000 to 100,000
Bandar Seri Begawan Cities under 50,000

⊛ Capital symbols
■ City symbols
Canals
Dams
Intermittent rivers
Reefs
Glaciers
Salt lakes
Swamps
Salt flats
Sand areas

N

EAST SIBERIAN SEA
NEW SIBERIAN ISLANDS
Wrangel Island
Cape Dezhnyov
CHUKCHI PENINSULA
Bering Strait
VERKHOYANSK MTS.
Mount Mus-Khaya 2959 m
CHERSKY MTS.
KOLYMA MOUNTAINS
Kolyma
Indigirka
Vilyuy
Aldan
Lena
STANOVOY MTS.
KORYAK MTS.
BERING SEA
KOMANDOR ISLANDS
KAMCHATKA PENINSULA
SEA OF OKHOTSK
Sakhalin Island
SIKHOTE-ALIN MTS.
Amur
Shilka
DA HINGGAN RANGE
KURIL ISLANDS

Ulaanbaatar ⊛
Khabarovsk ■
QIQIHAR ■ Hegang ■
Daqing ■ Jixi ■
HARBIN ■ Vladivostok ■
Mudanjiang ■
CHANGCHUN ■ JILIN ■
SHENYANG ■ Ch'ŏngjin ■
Fuxin ■ FUSHUN ■ NORTH KOREA
Jinzhou ■ Benxi ■ Dandong
ANSHAN ■ P'YONGYANG ⊛
Zhangjiakou ■ LÜDA ■
Hohhot ■ SEA OF JAPAN (EAST SEA)
Baotou ■ BEIJING ⊛ TIANJIN ■
ORDOS DESERT
Changzhou ■ SHIJIAZHUANG ■ Suwon SEOUL ⊛ INCH'ŎN
TAIYUAN ■ ZIBO TAEJŎN
Handan ■ JINAN ■ SOUTH KOREA
QINGDAO ■ KWANGJU PUSAN
LANZHOU ■ Kaifeng ■ YELLOW SEA
Luoyang ■ ZHENGZHOU ■
XI'AN ■ Xuzhou ■ NANJING ■ SHANGHAI
TSINLING MTS. Hefei ■ Wuxi ■ HANGZHOU ■
Huainan ■ Ningbo ■
Huang Ho
Yangtze
WUHAN ■
CHENGDU ■ Suizhou ■ NANCHANG ■
CHONGQING ■ Yichun ■ Fuzhou ■
CHANGSHA ■
GUIYANG ■ ZHENGZHOU ■ TAIPEI ■ Pan-ch'iao
Shantou ■ T'ai-chung ■
KUNMING ■ T'ai-nan
Liuzhou ■ ZHENGZHOU KAO- TAIWAN
GUANGZHOU ■ HSIUNG
Nanning ■ Macau HONG KONG
Xi
LAOS ■ HANOI ⊛
Hainan Island
Vientiane ⊛
THAILAND
Mekong
VIETNAM
BANGKOK ⊛
CAMBODIA
Phnom Penh ⊛ HO CHI MINH CITY (SAIGON)
Gulf of Thailand

JAPAN
SAPPORO ■
Hokkaido
Sendai ■ Honshu
TOKYO ⊛ YOKOHAMA
Mt. Fuji 3776 m
KYŌTO ■ NAGOYA ■
OSAKA ■
HIROSHIMA ■ Shikoku
FUKUOKA ■ Kyushu
Kumamoto ■
Kagoshima ■
RYUKYU ISLANDS

YELLOW SEA
EAST CHINA SEA
Tropic of Cancer

PACIFIC OCEAN

Luzon
SOUTH CHINA SEA
MANILA ⊛ PHILIPPINES
Cebu ■
Mindanao
Davao ■
Equator

BRUNEI
Bandar Seri Begawan ⊛
Borneo
MOLUCCAS
Jaya Peak 5030 m
New Guinea

MALAY PENINSULA
MEDAN ■
Kuala Lumpur ⊛
SINGAPORE ⊛
Cape Piai
Sumatra
Mount Kerinci 3800 m
PALEMBANG ■
Celebes
I N D O N E S I A
GREATER SUNDA ISLANDS
Ujungpandang ■
Dili ■ EAST TIMOR
LESSER SUNDA ISLANDS
JAKARTA ⊛ Java SEMARANG ■ SURABAYA ■
BANDUNG ■ Malang ■

170° E 180° 170° W 50° N 40° N 20° N 10° N 0° 10° S 20° S
160° E 150° E 140° E 130° E 120° E 110° E 100° E

CHINA, MONGOLIA, KOREA, AND JAPAN

© 2005 Encyclopædia Britannica, Inc.

CHINA, MONGOLIA, KOREA, AND JAPAN

Scale 1: 18,257,000

0	100	200	300 mi
0	50	150	250	350	450 km

Conical Equal-Area

SEOUL Cities over 1,000,000
Jinzhou Cities 500,000 to 1,000,000
Hitachi Cities 100,000 to 500,000
Tunxi Cities 50,000 to 100,000
Hondo Cities under 50,000

⊛ ★ Capital symbols
■ • City symbols
⊡ Points of interest
〰 Great Wall
⋉ Passes
⸺ Canals
⬐ Dams
⌁ Intermittent rivers
🌀 Glaciers
🗺 Salt lakes
▲ National parks
🏞 Swamps
⠿ Sand areas

SOUTHEASTERN ASIA

© 2005 Encyclopædia Britannica, Inc.

SOUTHEASTERN ASIA

MANILA	Cities over 1,000,000
Malang	Cities 500,000 to 1,000,000
Seremban	Cities 100,000 to 500,000
Soc Trang	Cities 50,000 to 100,000
Tenasserim	Cities under 50,000
⊛	Capital symbols
■•	City symbols
⊡	Points of interest
Ⴟ	Passes
⌐⌐⌐	Canals
	Dams
	Intermittent rivers
wwwww	Reefs
	Glaciers
▲	National parks
	Swamps

Scale 1: 21,022,000

0   50   150   250   350 mi

0   50 150 250 350 450 550 km

Oblique Mercator

INDIA

MADRAS	Cities over 1,000,000
Srinagar	Cities 500,000 to 1,000,000
Chandrapur	Cities 100,000 to 500,000
Jogighopa	Cities 50,000 to 100,000
Dwarka	Cities under 50,000

⊗ ★ Capital symbols
▪ ▪ City symbols
◻ Points of interest
Canals

Intermittent rivers
Reefs
Glaciers
Salt lakes
National parks
Swamps
Sand areas

Scale 1: 18,315,000

0 50 100 150 200 250 mi

0 100 200 300 400 km

Transverse Mercator

© 2005 Encyclopædia Britannica, Inc.

Persian Gulf

CASPIAN SEA

BLACK SEA

MEDITERRANEAN SEA

BULGARIA

RUSSIA

GEORGIA

ARMENIA

AZERBAIJAN

TURKEY

IRAN

IRAQ

SYRIA

LEBANON

ISRAEL

JORDAN

SAUDI ARABIA

EGYPT

KUWAIT

CYPRUS

TURKISH REPUBLIC OF NORTHERN CYPRUS
(Recognized by Turkey only)

REPUBLIC OF CYPRUS

SINAI PENINSULA

GREATER CAUCASUS

LESSER CAUCASUS

PONTIC MOUNTAINS

TAURUS MOUNTAINS

ANATOLIAN PLATEAU

ARMENIAN HIGHLAND

KURDISTAN MOUNTAINS

MESOPOTAMIA

SYRIAN DESERT

AL-HIJARAH DESERT

AN-NAFUD DESERT

TEHRAN, Qom, Karaj, Ahvaz, Kuwait, Hawalli, Basra, Baghdad, ALEPPO, DAMASCUS, BEIRUT, Tripoli, AMMAN, Jerusalem, Tel Aviv-Jaffa, CAIRO, ANKARA, ISTANBUL, Bursa, IZMIR, Konya, Adana, BAKU, TBILISI, YEREVAN, Tabriz, Mosul, Kirkuk

Scale 1:10,079,000
Lambert Equal-Area

0 25 50 75 100 125 150 mi
0 25 50 75 100 125 150 175 225 275 km

© 2005 Encyclopædia Britannica, Inc.

CAIRO   Cities over 1,000,000
Tripoli Cities 500,000 to 1,000,000
Batman   Cities 100,000 to 500,000
Zugdidi Cities 50,000 to 100,000
al-Fayâh Cities under 50,000
         ✯ Capital symbols
         ● City symbols
         ___ Canals
         Intermittent rivers
         Intermittent lakes
         Salt lakes
         National Parks
         Swamps
         Salt flats
         Sand areas
         ▲ Lava

AFRICA

AFRICA

INDIAN OCEAN

SEYCHELLES

COMOROS

Mayotte (Fr.)

MADAGASCAR

Antananarivo

Mauritius Island (not shown), located about 500 miles east of Madagascar.

Réunion Island (not shown), located about 450 miles east of Madagascar.

Scale 1: 30,860,000

0   100   200   300   400   500 mi
0   200   400   600   800 km
Robinson

Mozambique Channel

DAR ES SALAAM

Kilimanjaro 5895 m

RWANDA

BURUNDI

Bujumbura

TANZANIA

EAST

Ruvuma

Rufiji

Lake Rukwa

Lake Nyasa

Lake Tanganyika

Lake Malawi

MALAWI

Lilongwe

MOZAMBIQUE

MITUMBA MOUNTAINS

Point Barra

DEMOCRATIC REPUBLIC OF THE CONGO

Lubumbashi

Kolwezi

Mbuji-Mayi

ZAMBIA

Lusaka

Lake Bangweulu

Lake Mweru

Lake Kariba

Cabora Bassa

Zambezi

Harare

ZIMBABWE

Limpopo

Maputo

SWAZILAND

Mbabane

DURBAN

PRETORIA

Johannesburg

Soweto

Maseru

LESOTHO

Mont aux Sources 3299

DRAKENSBERG

Kafue

Victoria Falls

Okavango Swamp

Cuando

BOTSWANA

Gaborone

KALAHARI

Bloemfontein

SOUTH AFRICA

GREAT KAROO

Olifants

Cape Agulhas

Orange

Vaal

Lake Mai-Ndombe

Lake Moero

Brazzaville

KINSHASA

Kwango

Kasai

Congo

Cubango

ANGOLA

Okavango

Cunene

NAMIBIA

Windhoek

NAMIB DESERT

Cape of Good Hope

CAPE TOWN

MOUNTAINS

Pointe-Noire

CABINDA (Angola)

LUANDA

ATLANTIC OCEAN

St. Helena

Ascension

Tropic of Capricorn

© 2005 Encyclopædia Britannica, Inc.

N

Legend

BAGHDAD Cities over 1,000,000
Esfahan Cities 500,000 to 1,000,000
⊛ Capital symbols
▪ City symbols
Dams
Intermittent rivers
Waterfalls
Salt lakes
Swamps
Flooded areas
Salt flats
Sand areas

10° S
20° S
30° S
40° S
50° S

10° W
0°
10° E
20° E
30° E
40° E
50° E

NORTHERN AFRICA

Scale 1: 20,343,000

| 0 | 100 | 200 | 300 mi |
| 0 | 50 | 150 | 250 | 350 | 450 km |

Robinson

© 2005 Encyclopædia Britannica, Inc.

NORTHERN AFRICA

BALKAN PENINSULA
IONIAN SEA
GREECE
Athens
Peristérion
Patrai
Kalámai
Piraeus
Khania
Iráklion
Crete
SEA OF CRETE
CYCLADES
DODECANÈSE
Manisa
Usak
IZMIR
Aydin
Denizli
Antalya
Gulf of Antalya
WESTERN TAURUS MOUNTAINS
ANATOLIAN PLATEAU
Afyon
Isparta
Dinar
Konya
TURKEY
Kayseri
SOUTHEASTERN TAURUS MOUNTAINS
Gaziantep
Adana
Antioch
Idlib
Hamah
Al-Hasakah
ALEPPO
Al-Raqqah
Dayr Al-Zawr
Mosul
Kirkuk
IRAQ
BAGHDAD
Karbala
Mount Unayzah 951
SYRIAN DESERT
AL-HIJARAH DESERT
CYPRUS
Nicosia
Tripoli
LEBANON
BEIRUT
Sidon
Tel Aviv-Jaffa
Jerusalem
Damietta
Port Said
Al-Mahallah
Al-Kubra
Al-Mansurah
Al-Zaqaziq
Banha
Hims
SYRIA
DAMASCUS
Al-Zarqa'
AMMAN
JORDAN
ISRAEL
Al-Ramadi
Euphrates
Tigris
Sakakah
Al-Jawf
AN-NAFUD DESERT
Buraydah
MEDITERRANEAN SEA
Banghazi
Gulf of Sidra
Tobruk
Marsa Matruh
ALEXANDRIA
Damanhur
Tanta
Jirja
Shibin al-Kawm
Suez
CAIRO
AL-JIZAH
Al-Fayyum
Bani Suwayf
SINAI PENINSULA
Mount Ramn 1754 m
Mount Lawz 2580 m
Mount Catherine 2642m
Mount Dabbagh 2350 m
Mount Shayb al-Banat 2187m
Zaltan
Al-Jaghbub Oasis
Al-Bahriyah Oasis
Al-Farafirah Oasis
Al-Minya
WESTERN DESERT
Mallawi
Asyut
Al-Dakhilah Oasis
Sawhaj
Akhmim
Al-Khariah
Al-Kharijah Oases
Qina
Luxor
Thebes
ARABIAN DESERT
Nile
Red Sea
Mount Radwa 1814 m
Banas Point
Medina
Rahat Lava Field
Khaybar Lava Field
Tazirbu
EGYPT
Dunqul Oasis
Aswan
Aswan High Dam
Lake Nasser
Mount Babayn 1104m
LIBYAN DESERT
Bikku Bitti 2267m
Aozou
TIBESTI MOUNTAINS
Mount Koussi 3415m
Largeau
CHAD
ENNEDI PLATEAU
Abéché
Al-Junaynah
Mount Marra 3042m
Nyala
Mongo
Biltine
Al-Fashir
NUBIAN DESERT
Kishb Lava Field
Al-Qadimah
Buraykah
Ustan Hadan Lava Field
SAUDI ARABIA
ARABIAN PENINSULA
JIDDAH
Mecca
Al-Ta'if
RED SEA HILLS
Port Sudan
Oda Mountain 2259m
Al-Ju'avda
Abha
Mount Sawda 2995m
Najran
Sa'dah
Hayjan
TIHAMAH PLAIN
RUB' AL-KHALI DESERT
TUWAYQ MOUNTAINS
Atbarah
Shandi
Khartoum North
Kassala
Omdurman
Khartoum
Wad Madani
Halfa al-Jadidah
Ad-Duwaym
Al-Qadarif
Kusti
An-Nuhud
Al-Ubbayid
Sannar
DINDER NATIONAL PARK
ERITREA
Asmara
Keren
Mitsiwa
Nakfa
Aksum
Adwa
FARASAN ISLANDS
DAHLAK ARCHIPELAGO
Al-Hudaydah
Bayt al-Faqih
Al-Mansuriyah
Zabid
Mocha
Al-Sha't
San'a'
YEMEN
Mount an-Nabi Shu'ayb 3660 m
RAMLAT AS-SAB'ATAYN DESERT
Mitn'ar
MAHRAT MOUNTAINS
HADHRAMAUT
Al-Mukalla
Ghayl Ba-Wazir
Al-Shihr
Balhaf
Qana
Ahwar
Zinjibar
Madinat Al Sha't
Ta'izz
Aden
Mount Mousa 2028m
DJIBOUTI
Djibouti
Gulf of Aden
Cape Gwardafuy
Boossaaso
Mekele
Mount Ras Dejen 4620m
Gonder
Maychew
Dese
Lalibela
YANGUDI RASSA NATIONAL PARK
Assab
THE SUDAN
Wadi Al-Malik
Wadi Al-Ghazal
Al-Qash
Al-Ghazal
Malakal
Lake Tana
Bahir Dar
Debre Markos
ETHIOPIAN PLATEAU
Blue Nile
Dire Dawa
Harer
Berbera
Mount Surud Cad 2407m
Hargeysa
NUGAALEED VALLEY
MANOVO-GOUNDA-SAINT FLORIS NATIONAL PARK
RADOM NATIONAL PARK
Birao
Mount Abourassein 1113m
MANDA NAT'L PARK
Sarh
BAMINGUI-BANGORAN NATIONAL PARK
BONGOS MASSIF
Mouka
Waw
ZEMONGO FAUNAL RESERVE
IRONSTONE PLATEAU
Kaga Bandoro
Bria
Bossembélé
Bambari
CENTRAL AFRICAN REPUBLIC
Obo
Bangui
Mbaïki
Zongo
Mbandaka
Boende
Bousso
Mokaye
Gemena
Buta
Bumba
Kisangani
Yanganbi
Impfondo
CONGO BASIN
DEMOCRATIC REPUBLIC OF THE CONGO
Lake Mai-Ndombe
Kutu
Bandundu
Congo
Ubangi
Uele
Isiro
Watsa
Beni
Butembo
Ubundu
MAIKO NATIONAL PARK
Bukavu
KAHUZI-BIEGA NATIONAL PARK
SALONGA NATIONAL PARK
Lolle
Lomami
Luluaba
ADDIS ABABA
Dembidolo
Gore
Debre Zeyit
Akaki
Nazret
Jima
GAMBELLA NATIONAL PARK
Kibre Mengist
Yirga Alem
BALE MOUNTAINS NATIONAL PARK
Mount Batu 4307m
Mount Gara Muleta 3381m
Mount Gnge 4200m
OGADEN
ETHIOPIA
Hobyo
OMO NATIONAL PARK
MAGO NATIONAL PARK
BOMA NATIONAL PARK
SOUTHERN NATIONAL PARK
Yambio
Yei
Juba
Mount Kinyeti 3187m
GARAMBA NATIONAL PARK
Gulu
Adwar
Gode
SIBILOI NATIONAL PARK
Lake Rudolf
Lake Albert
MURCHISON FALLS NATIONAL PARK
Lake Kyoga
UGANDA
Kampala
QUEEN ELIZABETH NATIONAL PARK
Mount Elgon 4321m
Margherita Peak 5119 m
RWANDA
Kigali
Eldoret
Kisumu
Nakuru
KENYA
Mount Kenya 5199m
NAIROBI
Machakos
Meru
Isiolo
Nanyuki
Wajir
MARSABIT NATIONAL RESERVE
Mandera
Beledweyne
Buulobarde
SOMALIA
Baydhabo
Baardheere
Jawhar
Mogadishu
Marka
Baraawe
INDIAN OCEAN
EASTERN RIFT VALLEY
WESTERN RIFT VALLEY
Lake Victoria
Bukoba
Mwanza
BURUNDI
Bujumbura
TANZANIA
SERENGETI NATIONAL PARK
SERENGETI PLAIN
Kilimanjaro 5895m
Lake Kyoga
SOUTH KITUI NATIONAL RESERVE
TSAVO NATIONAL PARK
LAG BADANA NATIONAL PARK
Kismaayo
Jamaame
Lamu
Malindi
Jubba
Shabeelle
BENADIR
HAWD
Eyl

SOUTHERN AFRICA

ATLANTIC OCEAN

Gulf of Guinea

CONGO BASIN

DURBAN Cities over 1,000,000
Harare Cities 500,000 to 1,000,000
Gaborone Cities 100,000 to 500,000
Inhambane Cities 50,000 to 100,000
Hopetown Cities under 50,000

⊛ Capital symbols
■ • City symbols
⌂ Points of interest
Dams
Intermittent rivers
Waterfalls
Reefs
Salt lakes
▲ National parks
Swamps
Flooded areas
Salt flats
Sand areas

© 2005 Encyclopædia Britannica, Inc.

SOUTHERN AFRICA

INDIAN OCEAN

THE SUDAN

ETHIOPIA

SOMALIA

Mogadishu

UGANDA

KENYA

Kampala

NAIROBI

RWANDA

Kigali

BURUNDI

Bujumbura

TANZANIA

DAR ES SALAAM

Zanzibar

Mombasa

Tanga

AMIRANTE ISLES

SEYCHELLES

Victoria
Mahé

ALDABRA ISLANDS

COSMOLEDO GROUP

FARQUHAR GROUP

ILES GLORIEUSES (Fr.)

COMOROS

Moroni

Mayotte (Fr.)

Dzaouvdzi

Cape Bobaomby
Antsiranana

Nosy-Be

Maromokotro Peak 2876 m

MASOALA PENINSULA

Tromelin (Fr.)

Bay of Antongila

MALAWI

Lilongwe

Lusaka

Harare

ZIMBABWE

MOZAMBIQUE

Mahajanga

MADAGASCAR

Antananarivo

Tsiafajavona Peak 2642 m

Toamasina

MAURITIUS

Port Louis

St.-Denis

Réunion (Fr.)

Rodrigues (Mauritius)

Fianarantsoa

Boby Peak 2658 m

Toliara

ANDROY PLATEAU

MAHAFALY PLATEAU

Tôlanaro

Tropic of Capricorn

Maputo

SWAZILAND

KRUGER NATIONAL PARK

DURBAN

Pietermaritzburg

Scale 1: 20,125,000

0   100   200   300 mi

0   50 150 250 350 450 km

Robinson

30° E   40° E   50° E   60° E

0°

10° S

20° S

30° S

ARABIAN PENINSULA

© 2005 Encyclopædia Britannica, Inc.

AUSTRALIA AND NEW ZEALAND

OCEANIA

BRISBANE Cities over 1,000,000
Canberra Cities 500,000 to 1,000,000
Port Moresby Cities 100,000 to 500,000
Suva Cities 50,000 to 100,000
Manuro Cities under 50,000
⊛ Capital symbols
■ • City symbols

Scale 1: 50,660,000
250 500 750 mi
250 500 750 1000 km
Miller

N

NORTH PACIFIC OCEAN

SOUTH PACIFIC OCEAN

Philippine Sea

Arafura Sea

Coral Sea

Solomon Sea

Tasman Sea

Bass Strait

Gulf of Carpentaria

HAWAIIAN ISLANDS (U.S.)
Honolulu
Kauai
Oahu
Maui
Hawaii
Midway Is.

Johnston Atoll (U.S.)

MARQUESAS IS.
TUAMOTU ARCHIPELAGO
FRENCH POLYNESIA (FR.)
Papeete
Tahiti
SOCIETY IS.
Iro Maia
Rapa
AUSTRAL ISLANDS

PITCAIRN (U.K.)
Pitcairn

LINE IS.
Kiritimati (Christmas I.)
Teraina
Tabuaeran

COOK ISLANDS (N.Z.)
Rarotonga
Mangaia

KIRIBATI
Kanton Atoll
PHOENIX ISLANDS

TOKELAU (N.Z.)
AMERICAN SAMOA (U.S.)
Pago Pago
NIUE (N.Z.)

SAMOA
Apia
TONGA
Nuku'alofa

WALLIS AND FUTUNA (FR.)

FIJI
Suva
Lautoka
Viti Levu
Vanua Levu
Rotuma

TUVALU
Funafuti
GILBERT IS.
Tarawa (Bairiki)
Banaba

NAURU

MARSHALL ISLANDS
Majuro
Kwajalein
Kosrae I.

NORTHERN MARIANA ISLANDS (U.S.)
Saipan
Tinian
Rota
Guam (U.S.)

FEDERATED STATES OF MICRONESIA
TRUK IS.
Pohnpei
Pohnpei
CAROLINE ISLANDS
Yap

PALAU
Koror

WAKE I. (U.S.)
Eniwetak
SENYAVIN IS.
Palikir

SOLOMON ISLANDS
Honiara
Guadalcanal
SANTA CRUZ IS.

VANUATU
Espiritu Santo
Luganville
Vila
Port Vila

NEW CALEDONIA (FR.)
Nouméa
Dumbéa

Norfolk I. (N.Z.)

KERMADEC IS. (N.Z.)

NEW ZEALAND
Auckland
Manukau
North I.
Hamilton
Tauranga
Gisborne
Napier
Hastings
Palmerston North
Wanganui
New Plymouth
Whangarei
Te Kao
Kaikohe
East Coast Bays
Nelson
Wellington

Lord Howe I. (N.Z.)

PAPUA NEW GUINEA
Port Moresby
Wewak
Madang
Lae
Goroka
Mount Hagen
New Britain
New Ireland
Rabaul
Bougainville
Hula

INDONESIA
Jayapura
Manokwari
Mamberamo
Fakfak
Biak
Sorong
Manus
Kepulauan Aru

AUSTRALIA
BRISBANE
Gold Coast
SYDNEY
Newcastle
Wollongong
Canberra
MELBOURNE
ADELAIDE
Cairns
Townsville
Mackay
Rockhampton
Gladstone
Bundaberg
Maryborough
Toowoomba
Lismore
Coffs Harbour
Port Macquarie
Gosford
Tamworth
Dubbo
Orange
Bathurst
Broken Hill
Mildura
Wagga Wagga
Albury-Wodonga
Shepparton
Bendigo
Ballarat
Geelong
Warrnambool
Mount Gambier
Portland
Port Augusta
Port Pirie
Whyalla
Ceduna
Kangaroo Island
Burnie
Devonport
Launceston
Flinders Island
King I.
Alice Springs
Tennant Creek
Daly Waters
Mount Isa
Cloncurry
Winton
Longreach
Leigh Creek
Coober Pedy
Charleville
Roma
Bourke
Cobar
Moree
Goondiwindi

CAPE YORK PENINSULA
GREAT DIVIDING RANGE
GREY RANGE
FLINDERS RANGES
GREAT ARTESIAN BASIN
Murray
Darling

Tropic of Capricorn
Equator
Tropic of Cancer

THESAURUS

PREFACE

This thesaurus is specially designed for those who want to enlarge their vocabularies and learn more about the rich variety of the English language. We hope and expect that users will readily turn to a dictionary whenever they need a better understanding of the meaning of any word used in the thesaurus.

In creating this thesaurus, the editors have drawn on years of experience with a thesaurus format that is at once easy to use, broad in its scope, and especially helpful to the user in the selection of the right word. We also believe that this thesaurus will prove to be highly useful as a vocabulary builder. We have parted ways with the more traditional approach of presenting long, undifferentiated lists of words that are tied to some topic or intellectual concept. Instead, we present a strictly alphabetical ordering of entries. These entries consist of lists of words that are centered on a specific—and specified—meaning. Main entries consist of lists of synonyms and related words, as well as antonyms and near antonyms whenever applicable. Phrases and idioms that function as synonyms are occasionally offered as well.

The purpose of the differentiated lists is to accommodate the various purposes for which a thesaurus is used. People use a thesaurus generally because they are dissatisfied with the word they already have in mind. They want a different word. The question is: how different?

If users of this thesaurus are trying to avoid a boring repetition of the same word, or are seeking to vary and enrich their vocabulary, then they will wish to select from the list of synonyms a word that shares the same basic meaning as the one they already have but differs from it in suggestion and tone. If they are seeking a word that is different from but still related to what they already have, then they will want to scan the lists of related words for a rewarding journey through the variety of possibilities that English offers.

If users are seeking a word that is to some degree opposite in meaning to what they have, then they will want to consult the lists of antonyms or near antonyms. By specifying the meaning under consideration, and by making distinctions between words that are truly synonymous and those that are only somewhat synonymous, we hope that we have given users the guidance they desire. We believe that this system minimizes the need to guess and to grope.

What makes this thesaurus unique is the content of the separate entries for each and every word appearing in the lists of synonyms. Since a user's search for the right word may start anywhere, the thesaurus is arranged so that any member of a synonym group can serve as the starting point. An entry for a listed synonym consists of a restatement of the meaning common to all the members of the group. A user who happens to use a particular synonym as a starting point should follow the cross-reference to the main entry for the complete listing of synonyms, related words, and any antonyms or near antonyms.

The thesaurus format is intended to encourage and facilitate users in finding the right word, which results in writing of greater precision and clarity. The word *thesaurus* literally means "treasury" in Latin, and we hope that the treasure trove of words contained in these pages will enhance the user's interest in and appreciation of the English language. We urge all users to read carefully the following sections entitled Introduction and Using Your Thesaurus in order to make the most of what the book has to offer. The Introduction contains an informative discussion of what distinguishes a synonym from a related word, an antonym from a near antonym. The section Using Your Thesaurus explains in detail the organization of the thesaurus and discusses the differences between the two basic types of entries. Study of this section is especially important.

THESAURUS

The editor has been ably assisted in its composition by the editors Rose Martino Bigelow, Daniel B. Brandon, Adam Groff, Kory L. Stamper, and Deanna Stathis. The entire project was supervised by Madeline L. Novak, and Robert D. Copeland served as editor in charge of production. Stephen J. Perrault devised ways to facilitate the creation of the manuscript electronically. The difficult task of cross-referencing the text was accomplished by Christopher Chapin Connor and Allison S. Crawford. Credit for proofreading the text goes to Ilya A. Davidovich, Donna L. Rickerby, Maria Sansalone, Adrienne M. Scholz, Peter A. Sokolowski, Emily A. Vezina, and Judy Yeh. Michael D. Roundy acted as a consultant on miscellaneous scientific questions. Finally, John M. Morse, Merriam-Webster's President and Publisher, must be acknowledged and thanked for his unfailing support for this thesaurus.

Michael G. Belanger,
Editor

INTRODUCTION

Synonyms

The English language contains a wealth of words, and perhaps no other language has as many synonyms as English. Synonyms give color, precision, and variety to a person's writing, breaking up the dullness that can come from too many overused words.

So, just what are synonyms? Put simply, synonyms are words that mean the same thing. Words that are only somewhat similar in meaning—but do not mean the same thing—are not true synonyms. They are merely related words, and they belong in a different category. In this thesaurus a word is classified as a synonym if and only if it shares with another word at least one basic meaning.

Here's an example of how we arrived at a basic meaning shared by one group of words. The word *freight* can be defined as "goods or cargo carried by ship, train, truck, or airplane." We can break up the definition like this:

$$\left.\begin{matrix} \text{goods} \\ \\ \text{cargo} \end{matrix}\right\} \text{carried by} \left\{\begin{matrix} \text{ship} \\ \text{train} \\ \\ \text{truck} \\ \text{airplane} \end{matrix}\right.$$

Since a person using *freight* as the starting point in his or her search for the right word is probably dissatisfied with that term, the word that he or she is seeking will most likely come under a broader or more basic meaning. We can phrase that more basic meaning as: "a mass or quantity of something taken up and carried, conveyed, or transported." The list of synonyms for *freight*—*burden, cargo, draft, haul, lading, load, loading, payload, weight*—can all be said to share this basic meaning.

If a word is more limited in scope than the basic meaning given at a main entry, then it cannot be regarded as a synonym. Hence, *truckload*, which refers specifically to the load carried by a truck, cannot be a synonym of *freight* and the other members of *freight's* synonym group. Likewise, the words *mass* and *quantity* cannot themselves be regarded as synonyms because the notion of being carried, conveyed, or transported is not an essential part of their meaning.

Related Words

Oftentimes thesaurus users are not looking for something that means exactly the same as the word they already have. To help in this situation, this thesaurus includes lists of related words, which are words whose meanings are close enough to the synonymy group to be of interest to the user. These related words do not qualify as synonyms because they have meanings that differ from the basic meaning shared by the synonymy group in some significant way.

For example, the word *funny* has the meaning of "causing or intended to cause laughter." A person who is making "funny faces" is causing, or at least trying to cause, others to laugh. *Witty*, which is certainly closely related to *funny*, has a slightly different meaning: "given to or marked by mature intelligent humor." A witty person is someone who has a habit of making clever remarks that display a grown-up sense of humor. Thus, *funny* and *witty* are related, but the words are not synonymous. Because of the close relationship between two words like *funny* and *witty*, all of the words listed as synonyms at *witty* are given as related words at *funny*.

The lists of related words at a main entry in the thesaurus may be likened to the hyperlinks that connect one Web site to another on the Internet. Following the links between Web sites often takes one to new and unexpected places. Thesaurus users are encouraged to go from one related entry to another in their search for just the right word.

Some words are not true synonyms of anything, but because they are so fundamentally useful, they have been included in this thesaurus among the lists of related words and in places where they are likely to be most helpful. For example, the word *ballast*, which refers to any type of "heavy material used to make a ship steady," is too narrow in meaning to have any synonyms of its own. It is related to the more general term *load*, however, and so, fittingly, it is included as a related word at the entry for *load*.

Antonyms

An antonym is a word whose meaning is directly opposite to another word's meaning. In this thesaurus, an antonym is a word that has a meaning that completely cancels out another word's meaning. *Short* and *tall* are complete opposites. Something cannot be both short and tall at the same time, and both words suggest about the same degree of difference from the norm or average in height. *Good* and *evil* are another pair of exact opposites. Logically, something cannot be both *good* and *evil* in the same way and at the same time.

Words that are only opposite in some aspect of their meaning cannot be said to be true antonyms. For example, *sad*, which means "causing unhappiness," is not a true antonym of *funny*, which means "causing or intended to cause laughter." The opposite of unhappiness is happiness, and so the opposite of sad is happy. There are things, like a frowning clown, that can be both funny and sad, so these words can't be antonyms. Pairs of words like *sad* and *funny* are better regarded as near antonyms.

Near Antonyms

Near antonyms are words that do not qualify as antonyms under the strict definition used for this thesaurus but that clearly have meanings in marked contrast with the members of a synonym group. For example, *afraid* is not so exactly opposite to *courageous* as *cowardly* is, but *afraid* and *courageous* certainly have markedly contrasting meanings and so are considered near antonyms. And just as a user may not be seeking a word that is exactly synonymous with another, he or she may likewise not be seeking a word that is exactly opposite. The user may simply want a word that lies somewhere on the opposite side of the range of meaning.

Phrases

This thesaurus also includes phrases that, taken as a whole, are synonymous with individual words. Within this category are some words that are commonly used in combination with one another but are not necessarily included as entry words in most dictionaries. Some of these fixed phrases represent virtually the only way in which the word is used in contemporary English. For example, *in jeopardy* appears as a synonymous phrase at *liable* because a person exposed to something dangerous or undesirable is a person in jeopardy. The word *jeopardy* is generally only used in the phrase *in jeopardy*.

Idioms constitute the other major class of word combinations that are entered under the heading of Phrases. Idioms are phrases that have a special meaning that is different from the literal meaning that a person would get if adding together the individual meanings of the components of the phrase. For example, the phrase *make good* is virtually meaningless if one attempts to piece together the literal meanings of *make* and *good*. As a fixed phrase, however, *make good* means "to reach a desired level of accomplishment" and is a synonym of *succeed*.

What this thesaurus does not enter are phrases that are simple restatements of the basic meaning shared by the members of the synonym group. The verb *remark*, for example, might be defined as "to express as an opinion." Such rewordings of a basic definition have no place in a thesaurus because they contribute nothing useful to the user's vocabulary.

Choosing the Right Word—Using Your Dictionary

Even after you have mastered all of these categories, deciding which word in a thesaurus entry is best for your purposes is not always easy. The basic meaning shared by the members of a synonym group cannot tell you everything you need to know in order to choose the word that best suits your needs.

Something that is "very pleasing to look at" can be described as *attractive, beauteous, beautiful, bonny, comely, cute, fair, gorgeous, handsome, knockout, lovely, pretty, ravishing, sightly, stunning,* or *taking*, but which word is best for describing a sunset? A city? Should you use *knockout* to describe a cathedral or *ravishing* for a sports car?

If after reviewing the synonyms, you decide that you still have not found the right word, then you have the list of related words to consider:

> **related words** alluring, appealing, charming, delightful, eye-catching, glamorous (*also* glamourous), prepossessing; elegant, exquisite, glorious, resplendent, splendid, statuesque, sublime, superb; flawless, perfect, radiant; dainty, delicate; personable, presentable

Now you have 38 words that mean the same thing or nearly the same thing as *beautiful*. Here's where you need a good dictionary. You can consult the dictionary to get a precise definition of any word in the lists, and perhaps an example of its use. You should always use this thesaurus along with a good dictionary.

EXPLANATORY NOTES

Every user of this thesaurus should read this section of the book carefully in order to use it effectively.

A thesaurus consists mostly of lists of words, and it is often difficult to know which word is best for a particular purpose. Because the English language has so many different ways of combining words with different shades of meaning, you should always use this thesaurus along with a reliable dictionary.

ENTRY ORDER

The first word of a thesaurus entry is called a **headword.** Headwords are printed in boldface type and are in alphabetical order. Alphabetization is by first letter, then second letter, and so on, regardless of any spaces or hyphens that may appear in them:

make *vb*
make–believe *adj*
make out *vb*

make over *vb*
Maker *n*
makeshift *adj*

When a headword contains a numeral, the numeral is alphabetized as though it were a spelled-out word:

anywise *adv*
A1 *adj*
apace *adv*

Homographs are words that are spelled the same, but each is a different part of speech or has a different etymology (word origin). Homographs that are different parts of speech are separate headwords:

hail *n* 1 a heavy fall of objects
hail *vb* 1 to declare enthusiastic approval of

Homographs that have a different etymology, even when they are the same part of speech, are entered as separate headwords. Those that are the same part of speech are grouped together and numbered in sequence:

¹**list** *n* a record of a series of items (as names or titles) usually arranged according to some system
²**list** *n* the act of positioning or an instance of being positioned at an angle
³**list** *n* a long narrow piece of material
¹**list** *vb* 1 to make a list of
²**list** *vb* to set or cause to be at an angle

Verbs that are used in combination with a preposition or an adverb are entered with the verb in boldface type followed by the preposition or adverb in parentheses in lightface type. Such combinations immediately follow the base verb in alphabetical order:

go *vb*
go (for) *vb*
go (on) *vb*
go (to) *vb*

When main entries are compound words, a closed form is entered before a hyphenated form and a hyphenated form is entered before a form that contains spaces:

nosedive *n*
nose–dive *vb*

open–air *adj*
open air *n*

PLURAL NOUNS

Some nouns are always pluralized when they are used a certain way. When there are no thesaurus entries which include the singular form of a such a noun, the plural form is given as the headword:

leavings *n pl* a remaining group or portion — see REMAINDER 1

When a noun is usually, but not always, used in plural form in a certain sense, the singular form is the headword, and the plural follows the label *usually*:

habiliment *n usually* **habiliments** *pl* covering for the human body — see CLOTHING

Such nouns are followed by *s* in parentheses in the synonym list:

clothing *n* covering for the human body

synonyms apparel, attire, clothes, dress, duds, habiliment(s), rags, raiment, togs, wear

When a noun is used in the singular form in one sense and in the plural form in another, the singular form is given as the headword. The plural form is indicated at the individual sense or senses:

provision *n* 1 something upon which the carrying out of an agreement or offer depends — see CONDITION 2 **2 provisions** *pl* substances intended to be eaten — see FOOD

THESAURUS

VARIANTS

An alternate spelling or form of a headword is called a **variant**. Variants are shown in boldface after the headword and are preceded by *or* or *also*. The label *or* means that the variant is as common or nearly as common as the headword. The headword is usually the form that comes first alphabetically:

egotistic *or* **egotistical** *adj*
lighted *or* **lit** *adj*
OK *or* **okay** *vb*

However, if one of the spellings or forms is used slightly more frequently, the more common one is entered first even though it may not fall first alphabetically:

gizmo *or* **gismo** *n*

A variant that is preceded by the label *also* is not as common as the headword:

among *also* **amongst** *prep*
facade *also* **façade** *n*
naught *also* **nought** *n*

When two variants are separated from the headword by *also* but from each other by *or*, it means that they are both less common than the headword:

bogey *also* **bogy** *or* **bogie** *n*

Variants are also given in the word lists:

zero *n* the numerical symbol 0 or the absence of number or quantity represented by it ⟨anything multiplied by *zero* comes out to zero⟩
synonyms aught, cipher, goose egg, naught (*or* nought), nil, nothing, oh, zilch, zip

PARTS OF SPEECH

Every headword is followed by a part-of-speech label. The abbreviations for the parts of speech are *adj* (adjective), *adv* (adverb), *conj* (conjunction), *interj* (interjection), *n* (noun), *prep* (preposition), *pron* (pronoun), and *vb* (verb).

KINDS OF ENTRIES

There are two kinds of entries: main entries and secondary entries. Every headword with its part-of-speech label is followed by either one or more main entries, one or more secondary entries, or a combination of the two. If there is more than one entry, each one begins on a new line introduced by a boldface sense number. Main entries come first. A **main entry** consists of the meaning shared by the members of the synonym group, a verbal illustration, and lists of synonyms as well as any related words, phrases, near antonyms, and antonyms:

eagerness *n* urgent desire or interest
synonyms appetite, ardor, avidity, desirousness, enthusiasm, excitement, hunger, impatience, keenness, thirst
related words alacrity, quickness; ambition, gusto, zest
near antonyms unconcern; aloofness, detachment; impassivity, languor
antonyms apathy, indifference

A **secondary entry** has the same shared meaning that is shown at the main entry. The secondary entry does not contain lists of synonyms, antonyms, related words, phrases, or near antonyms. Instead, at the end of the entry, there is a direction to "see" the appropriate main entry at another headword. Secondary entries follow any main entries at a headword:

gain *vb* **1** to increase in
synonyms build (up), gather, grow (in), pick up
. . .
2 to receive as return for effort — see EARN 1
3 to become healthy and strong again after illness or weakness — see CONVALESCE

fade *vb* **1** to cease to be visible — see DISAPPEAR
2 to make white or whiter by removing color — see WHITEN

CROSS-REFERENCES

The direction at the end of every secondary entry to see another entry is called a **cross-reference**. The cross-reference tells you where the main entry for a word's synonym group is located. No matter which member of a synonym group you used to begin your search, you can always find your way to the entry that has the lists of all the synonyms and any related words, phrases, near antonyms, or antonyms. If there is more than one sense at the headword referred to in the cross-reference, the cross-reference will also include a sense number. If the headword has more than one numbered homograph, the cross-reference will send you to the right homograph number as well:

pain *vb* to feel or cause physical pain — see HURT 1

ranking *n* **1** a scheme of rank or order — see ³SCALE 1

If a headword appears as more than one part of speech, the cross-reference is sending you to the same part of speech as the word you looked up. The cross-reference in the **ranking** example above

tells you that the main entry where you will find *ranking* as a member of the synonym group with the shared meaning "a scheme of rank or order" is at sense 1 of the noun entry ³**scale**:

³scale *n* **1** a scheme of rank or order ⟨how would you rate your experience on a *scale* of one to ten?⟩
synonyms graduation, ladder, ordering, ranking

SPECIAL USAGE LABELS

You will find special usage labels in italics after a headword whenever they apply. The labels are *chiefly British, British, chiefly Scottish, Scottish, Australian, chiefly dialect, chiefly Southern & Midland*, and *slang*.

These labels are placed directly after the part-of-speech label when the word has only one sense or when the label applies to all the senses:

afore *prep, chiefly dialect* **1**
bairn *n, chiefly Scottish*
bobby *n, British*
dis *vb, slang* **1**

The label comes after the sense number when

the word has more than one sense and the label applies only to that sense:

jack *n* **1** *slang* something (as pieces of stamped metal or printed paper) customarily and legally used as a medium of exchange, a measure of value, or a means of payment — see MONEY

Special usage labels also appear in the word lists:

before *prep* **1** earlier than ⟨since I'm a faster runner, I got there *before* him⟩
synonyms afore [*chiefly dialect*], ahead of, ere, of, previous to, prior to, to

SHARED MEANING

The shared meaning follows the sense number when there is more than one sense and the part-of-speech label when there is only one sense. It is a meaning shared equally by the headword and the other members of the synonym group. This shared meaning is the "thing" that is referred to when we say that two or more words "mean the same thing" and thus are synonyms.

Sometimes there are words in parentheses within a shared meaning:

district *n* an area (as of a city) set apart for some purpose or having some special feature ⟨Independence Hall in Philadelphia's historic *district*⟩

synonyms neighborhood, quarter, section
related words belt, zone; department, . . .

In the shared meaning at **district**, the words in parentheses indicate that *district, neighborhood, quarter*, and *section* are synonyms when they refer to an area of a city or something like that, and that the words in the related words list also refer specifically to this type of area.

For information regarding the use and purpose of parentheses around certain words in entries for verbs, read below.

SOME NOTES ABOUT VERBS

A boldface verb headword followed by a light-face word in parentheses tells you to use the parenthetical word with the verb:

comply (with) *vb* **1** to act according to the commands of
hold off (on) *vb* to assign to a later time
knock (about) *vb* to move about from place to place aimlessly

If there are two words inside the parentheses and they are separated by *or*, then either word can be used with the verb:

fit (in *or* into) *vb* to put among or between others

These verbs appear in the synonym lists followed by their customary adverb or preposition in parentheses. These entries are treated this way in the thesaurus because such verb combinations are not the usual form of dictionary entries, but it is only when the verb is used with the adverb or preposition that it matches the shared meaning of its synonym group.

When the meaning of a verb requires a direct object, all of the words in the synonym list take a direct object. If a verb does not take an object, none of the synonyms will take an object.

THESAURUS

VERBAL ILLUSTRATIONS

Every main entry in this thesaurus shows an example of typical use. The **verbal illustration**, as it is called, follows the shared meaning, is enclosed in angle brackets, and italicizes the synonym:

fight *vb* **1** to oppose (someone) in physical conflict ⟨a proud people who have fiercely *fought* all invaders of their homeland⟩
rich *adj* **1** having goods, property, or money in abundance ⟨Tanya's dad works as a chauffeur for the *richest* man in town, a big oil baron⟩

Words in parentheses after a boldface headword are italicized in the verbal illustration:

stick *vb* **1** to hold to something firmly as if by adhesion ⟨these magnets are strong enough to *stick* well to the refrigerator⟩

Some verbal illustrations in the thesaurus are complete sentences and others are only sentence fragments. Though it may look a little odd, for the sake of consistency, all verbal illustrations in this thesaurus begin with a lowercase letter unless the initial word is normally capitalized. Question marks and exclamation points are used when appropriate at the end of a verbal illustration, but otherwise no ending punctuation is used.

A WORD ABOUT SYNONYMS

If a word is used as the defining term in a shared meaning, it will not be listed as one of the synonyms. Since words can only be defined in terms of other words, the result of this restriction is that some terms that might be rightly regarded as synonyms do not appear in the synonym lists. Here is an example:

go *vb* . . . **2** to leave a place often for another

synonyms begone, clear out, depart, exit, get, get off, move, pull (out), quit, sally (forth), shove (off), take off, walk out

Leave, used as the defining term, could be considered another synonym, but it is not entered as such in this thesaurus because it has been used as a defining term.

RELATED WORDS

You will see that in most cases there are more related words than synonyms. That is because there is much more flexibility in choosing words for these lists. They do not have to match the shared meaning: they only need to relate to some aspect of it. Related words are often divided into subgroups separated by a semicolon. Words within each subgroup are generally closer in meaning to each other than to the members of the following subgroups. The subgroups tend to be presented in order of most relevant to least relevant.

object *n* **1** something material that can be perceived by the senses
synonyms thing
related words article, item, piece; being, entity, substance; commodity, good, ware; accessory, accompaniment; bauble, curio, knickknack, spangle, token, trinket

PHRASES

Listed in alphabetical order after the heading **phrases** at some of the main entries are expressions that are synonymous with the headword and the other members of the synonym group. Although they have essentially the same meaning as the synonyms, these phrases tend to be used only

in certain ways, and you should be careful about substituting one of them for a word in the synonym list. Since phrases are not entered as headwords in the thesaurus, they do not come with verbal illustrations. It's a good idea to look them up in a dictionary before considering them.

NEAR ANTONYMS

Just as related words are not exact synonyms, near antonyms are not exact antonyms. Not every synonym group has near antonyms. As is the case with related words, when there are near antonyms, they are often divided into subgroups separated by a semicolon, with the members of each subgroup listed alphabetically.

have *vb* **1** to keep, control, or experience as one's own

synonyms command, enjoy, hold, occupy, own, possess, retain
related words keep, reserve, withhold; bear, carry; boast, show off, sport
near antonyms abandon, cede, disclaim, disown, hand over, relinquish, renounce, surrender, yield; discard, dump; decline, reject, repudiate, spurn; need, require
antonyms lack, want

ANTONYMS

The words in the antonym lists are the exact opposites of the headword and the words in the synonym lists. Not every synonym group has antonyms, and antonym lists tend to be shorter than near antonym lists. Antonyms are listed alphabetically, just as synonyms are. They appear as boldface headwords at their own alphabetical places in the thesaurus only if they are part of a synonym group elsewhere.

Ordinarily, all the words in an antonym list are synonyms of each other. Sometimes, however, a semicolon in an antonym list divides words which, while they are exact opposites of the words in the synonym group, are not synonyms of each other.

Here is an example:

present *adj* **1** existing or in progress right now
   synonyms current, extant, ongoing, present-day
   antonyms ago, past; future

The opposite of "existing or in progress right now" is "*not* existing or in progress right now." All three of the words in the antonyms list fit that meaning. *Ago* and *past*, separated by a comma, are synonyms of each other; they both can mean "earlier than the present time." But *ago* and *past* are not synonyms of *future*, which means, of course, "occurring at a later time."

A NOTE ABOUT THE LISTS: WORD DUPLICATION

No word appears in more than one list at any single main entry. Some words have slight variations in meaning. If they are used one way, they are synonymous with a headword; if they are used another way, they are merely closely related. To avoid confusion, such words have been entered in a main entry's synonym list only. For example, *nice* is in the synonym list at *pleasant* where the shared meaning is "giving pleasure or contentment to the mind or senses." *Nice* is also in the synonym list at *amiable*, where the shared meaning is "having an easygoing and pleasing manner especially in social situations." If you go back to *pleasant*, you will find *amiable* among the related words. So it would stand to reason that *nice*, having the same meaning as *amiable*, would also be entered in the

related word list at *pleasant*. Since it's already in the synonym list, however, it was left out of the related words.

Some words can have two meanings that are opposite of each other—or nearly so. *Nervy* can mean both "fearless" and "fearful, timid." Thus, at the thesaurus entry for *bold*, where the shared meaning is "inclined or willing to take risks," *nervy* might qualify as both a synonym and an antonym (or near antonym). And, indeed, *nervy* appears as a synonym, along with *adventuresome*, *adventurous*, *audacious*, *daring*, *dashing*, *emboldened*, *enterprising*, *gutsy*, *hardy*, *nerved*, *venturesome*, and *venturous*. Although the near antonym list contains *fearful* and *timid* as expected, *nervy* is left off the list. Again, this is to avoid confusion.

GUIDE WORDS

The two boldface words separated by a dot at the top of each page are **guide words**, and they show the alphabetical range of entries on the page. You can use them to find a word more quickly.

The first guide word is the headword of the first entry beginning on that page, and the second guide is the headword of the last entry on the page.

THESAURUS

aback *adv* without warning — see UNAWARES

abaft *adv* near, toward, or in the stern of a ship or the tail of an aircraft — see AFT

abaft *prep* at, to, or toward the rear of — see BEHIND 1

abandon *n* carefree freedom from constraint ⟨added spices to the stew with complete *abandon*⟩
synonyms abandonment, ease, lightheartedness, naturalness, spontaneity, unrestraint
related words ardor, enthusiasm, exuberance, fervor, spirit, warmth, zeal; carelessness, heedlessness, impulsiveness, indiscretion, insouciance, recklessness, thoughtlessness; excess, excessiveness, immoderacy, incontinence, indulgence, intemperance, licentiousness, permissiveness, wantonness, wildness
near antonyms embarrassment, reserve, reticence, self-consciousness, uneasiness; inhibition, repression, self-restraint, suppression; carefulness, discreetness, discretion, heedfulness; discipline, self-control, self-discipline, willpower
antonyms constraint, restraint

abandon *vb* to cause to remain behind — see LEAVE 1

abandoned *adj* left unoccupied or unused ⟨Marlene avoided walking past the *abandoned* house, with its broken windows and sagging porch⟩
synonyms derelict, deserted, disused, forgotten, forsaken, rejected, vacated
related words ignored, neglected, unattended, untended; castaway, cast-off, discarded, jettisoned, junked; desolate, godforsaken, miserable, shabby, wretched; empty, idle, vacant
near antonyms reclaimed, recovered, redeemed, rescued, retrieved, salvaged, saved; reconditioned, rehabilitated, restored; repeopled

abandonment *n* 1 carefree freedom from constraint — see ABANDON
2 the act of abandoning — see DERELICTION 1

abase *vb* 1 to lower in character or dignity — see DEBASE 1
2 to reduce to a lower standing in one's own eyes or in others' eyes — see HUMBLE 1

abash *vb* to throw into a state of self-conscious distress — see EMBARRASS 1

abashment *n* the emotional state of being made self-consciously uncomfortable — see EMBARRASSMENT 1

abate *vb* 1 to grow less in scope or intensity especially gradually — see DECREASE 2
2 to make smaller in amount, volume, or extent — see DECREASE 1

abatement *n* 1 something that is or may be subtracted — see DEDUCTION 1
2 the amount by which something is lessened — see DECREASE

abbey *n* a residence for men under religious vows — see MONASTERY

abbreviate *vb* to make less in extent or duration — see SHORTEN

abbreviation *n* a shortened version of a written work — see ABRIDGMENT

abdicate *vb* to give up (as a position of authority) formally ⟨the revolutionary government forced Nicholas II to *abdicate* the Russian throne⟩
synonyms abnegate, cede, relinquish, renounce, resign, step down (from), surrender
related words abjure, deny, disavow, disclaim, disown, waive; forsake, give up, hand over, yield; abandon, desert, quit, vacate
near antonyms appropriate, arrogate, assume, claim, confiscate; seize, take over, usurp, wrest; defend, guard, protect, safeguard, secure

abdomen *n* the part of the body between the chest and the pelvis — see STOMACH

abduct *vb* to carry a person away by unlawful force or against his or her will — see KIDNAP

aberrant *adj* 1 being out of the ordinary — see EXCEPTIONAL
2 departing from some accepted standard of what is normal — see DEVIANT

aberration *n* a serious mental disorder that prevents one from living a safe and normal life — see INSANITY 1

abet *vb* 1 to cause or encourage the development of — see INCITE 1
2 to provide (someone) with what is useful or necessary to achieve an end — see HELP 1

abettor *also* **abetter** *n* 1 one associated with another in wrongdoing — see ACCOMPLICE
2 someone associated with another to give assistance or moral support — see ALLY

abeyance *n* a state of temporary inactivity ⟨our weekend plans were held in *abeyance* until we could get a weather forecast⟩
synonyms doldrums, dormancy, latency, quiescence, suspense, suspension
related words inaction, inertia, inertness, motionlessness; impasse, standstill; coma, hibernation, hypnosis, repose, rest, sleep, slumber, torpor; recession, remission; idleness
near antonyms recommencement, renewal, resumption, resuscitation
antonyms continuance, continuation

abhor *vb* to dislike strongly — see HATE

abhorrence *n* something or someone that is hated — see HATE 2
2 a very strong dislike — see HATE 1

abhorrent *adj* causing intense displeasure, disgust, or resentment — see OFFENSIVE 1

abide *vb* 1 to continue to be in a place for a significant amount of time — see STAY 1
2 to have a home — see LIVE 1
3 to put up with (something painful or difficult) — see BEAR 2
4 to remain indefinitely in existence or in the same state — see CONTINUE 1

ability *n* the physical or mental power to do something ⟨as a result of the accident he lost the *ability* to walk⟩
synonyms capability, capacity, competence, competency, faculty
related words aptitude, aptness, endowment, facility, gift, knack, talent; adroitness, deftness, dexterity, prowess, skill; gray matter, instinct, intelligence, reason, understanding; potency, staying power, stuff; adequacy, effectiveness, effectualness, fitness, form, influence, resourcefulness, usefulness; means, resources, wherewithal
near antonyms helplessness, impotence, paralysis, powerlessness, weakness; defectiveness, deficien-

cy, inadequacy, ineffectiveness, ineffectualness, uselessness; debilitation, disablement, impairment, incapacitation

antonyms disability, inability, incapability, incapacity, incompetence, incompetency, ineptitude, ineptness

abjure *vb* to solemnly or formally reject or go back on (as something formerly adhered to) ⟨*abjured* some long-held beliefs when she converted to another religion⟩

synonyms recant, renounce, retract, take back, unsay, withdraw

related words contradict, deny, disavow, disclaim, disown, gainsay, negate, negative, repudiate; abandon, abnegate, forsake, give up, relinquish, spurn, surrender; controvert, disagree (with), disprove, dispute, rebut, refute; back down, back off, backtrack; disallow, recall, renege, revoke

near antonyms acknowledge, admit, affirm, assert, avow, claim, contend, declare, maintain, proclaim, profess, state; back, confirm, defend, endorse (*also* indorse), espouse, maintain, support, uphold; accept, adopt, embrace

antonyms adhere (to)

ablaze *adj* **1** being on fire ⟨the entire block was *ablaze* by the time fire fighters arrived⟩

synonyms afire, aflame, blazing, burning, combusting, fiery, flaming, ignited, inflamed, kindled, lighted (*or* lit)

related words aglow, alight, flaring, flickering, glowing, live, smoldering; broiling, hot, piping hot, red-hot, roasting, scalding, scorching, searing, sizzling; burnt, charred, incinerated, scorched, seared, singed

near antonyms choked, damped, dead, doused, extinguished, quenched, smothered, snuffed (out), stamped (out), suffocated

2 filled with much light — see BRIGHT 2

able *adj* having the required skills for an acceptable level of performance — see COMPETENT

able–bodied *adj* enjoying health and vigor — see HEALTHY 1

ably *adv* in a skillful or expert manner — see WELL 3

abnegate *vb* to give up (as a position of authority) formally — see ABDICATE

abnegation *n* the act or practice of giving up or rejecting something once enjoyed or desired — see RENUNCIATION

abnormal *adj* **1** being out of the ordinary — see EXCEPTIONAL

2 departing from some accepted standard of what is normal — see DEVIANT

abnormality *n* a person, thing, or event that is not normal — see FREAK 1

abode *n* the place where one lives — see HOME 1

abolish *vb* to put an end to by formal action ⟨the U.S. *abolished* slavery by constitutional amendment on December 6, 1865⟩

synonyms abrogate, annul, cancel, dissolve, invalidate, negate, nullify, quash, repeal, rescind, void

related words countermand, override, overrule, overturn, veto; retract, reverse, revoke, suspend, withdraw; ban, enjoin, forbid, outlaw, prohibit; disallow, dismiss, reject; eliminate, eradicate, erase, liquidate, remove, throw out, write off

phrases do away with

near antonyms establish, found, institute; formalize, legalize, legitimate, legitimize, validate; pass;

ratify; allow, approve, authorize, clear, endorse (*also* indorse), permit, sanction, warrant; command, decree, mandate, prescribe, order

abominable *adj* causing intense displeasure, disgust, or resentment — see OFFENSIVE 1

abominate *vb* to dislike strongly — see HATE

abomination *n* something or someone that is hated — see HATE 2

2 a very strong dislike — see HATE 1

aboriginal *adj* belonging to a particular place by birth or origin — see NATIVE 1

abort *vb* to put an end to (something planned or previously agreed to) — see CANCEL 1

abortion *n* the act of putting an end to something planned or previously agreed to — see CANCELLATION

abortive *adj* producing no results — see FUTILE

abounding *adj* possessing or covered with great numbers or amounts of something specified — see RIFE

about *adv* **1** on all sides or in every direction — see AROUND 1

2 toward the opposite direction — see AROUND 2

3 very close to but not completely — see ALMOST

about *prep* **1** having to do with ⟨a story *about* a young man who goes off to war⟩

synonyms apropos of, concerning, of, on, regarding, respecting, toward (*or* towards)

related words as to, over

phrases as regards

2 close to — see AROUND 1

3 in random positions within the boundaries of — see AROUND 2

above *prep* higher than ⟨one minute our kite was *above* the telephone wires; the next minute it was tangled in them⟩

synonyms over

related words atop

near antonyms underneath

antonyms below, beneath, under

above *adv* to or in a higher place ⟨we eventually got used to the planes constantly flying *above*⟩

synonyms aloft, over, overhead, skyward

near antonyms underneath

antonyms below, beneath, under

abrade *vb* **1** to damage or diminish by continued friction ⟨ropes *abraded* by the rocks were a huge danger to the climbers⟩

synonyms chafe, erode, fray, fret, gall, rub, wear

related words file, gnaw, grate, graze, grind, nibble, rasp, sandblast, sandpaper, scour, scrape, scuff, shave; erase, reduce, rub out, wear out, wipe (away); bite, break down, break up, chew, corrode, decompose, disintegrate, dissolve, eat; hone, sharpen, whet

2 to make sore by continued rubbing — see CHAFE 1

3 to damage by rubbing against a sharp or rough surface — see SCRAPE 2

abreast *adj* having information especially as a result of study or experience — see FAMILIAR 2

abridge *vb* to make less in extent or duration — see SHORTEN

abridgment *or* **abridgement** *n* a shortened version of a written work ⟨this Italian-English pocket dictionary is an *abridgment* of the hardback edition⟩

synonyms abbreviation, condensation, digest

related words abstract, brief, outline, overview, précis, recap, recapitulation, résumé (*or* resume *also* resumé), review, sketch, sum, summariza-

tion, summary, summation, survey, syllabus, synopsis, wrap-up
near antonyms amplification, elaboration, enlargement, expansion
abrogate *vb* to put an end to by formal action — see ABOLISH
abrupt *adj* **1** being or characterized by direct, brief, and potentially rude speech or manner — see BLUNT 1
2 having an incline approaching the perpendicular — see STEEP 1
abruptly *adv* with great suddenness — see SHORT
abscond *vb* to get free from a dangerous or confining situation — see ESCAPE 1
absence *n* **1** a state of being without something necessary, desirable, or useful — see NEED 1
2 the fact or state of being absent — see LACK 1
absent *adj* **1** not at a certain place ⟨three students were *absent* because of the flu⟩
synonyms away, missing, out
related words AWOL, truant; departed, gone, retired; abroad, vacationing
near antonyms accompanying, attending, participating
antonyms here, present
2 not present or in evidence ⟨the usual stir of activity was *absent* in the city due to the report of an escaped lion from the zoo⟩
synonyms lacking, missing, nonexistent, wanting
related words dead, departed, extinct, lost, perished, vanished; defunct, done, expired, finished, lapsed, obsolete, over, passé; inadequate, insufficient, rare, scarce, sparse, uncommon
near antonyms active, alive, animate, living, thriving; current, going, prevailing, uncanceled; common, prevalent; apparent, conspicuous, evident, obvious, plain
antonyms existent, present
3 lost in thought and unaware of one's surroundings or actions — see ABSENTMINDED 1
absentminded *adj* **1** lost in thought and unaware of one's surroundings or actions ⟨the grieving woman was so *absentminded* that she left her key in the lock after opening the door⟩
synonyms absent, abstracted, preoccupied
related words absorbed, daydreaming, distracted, dreaming, dreamy, engrossed, faraway, intent, pensive, rapt; heedless, inattentive, insensible, oblivious, unaware, unconscious, unheeding, unknowing, unmindful, unobservant, unobserving, unperceiving, unperceptive, unseeing, unthinking, unwary, unwitting, vacant; befogged, befuddled, bemused, bewildered, confused, dazed, flighty, foggy, forgetful, forgetting, hazy, muddled, scatterbrained, unfocused
near antonyms alive, attentive, aware, conscious, heedful, mindful, observant, observing, openeyed, sharp, vigilant, wary, watchful, wide-awake; clearheaded, unconfused
antonyms alert
2 inclined to forget what one has learned or to do what one should — see FORGETFUL
absolute *adj* **1** exercising power or authority without interference by others ⟨the *absolute* monarchy of Russia ended when Czar Nicholas II promised to share power with a legislative body⟩
synonyms autocratic, despotic, dictatorial, tyrannical (*also* tyrannic), tyrannous
related words authoritarian, totalitarian; arbitrary, high-handed, magisterial; domineering, im-

perious, masterful; all-powerful, almighty, omnipotent; autonomous, self-governing, sovereign; unconditional, unlimited
near antonyms circumscribed, restrained, restricted; constitutional, lawful
antonyms limited
2 having no exceptions or restrictions ⟨ironing is an *absolute* bore⟩ ⟨I want the *absolute* truth⟩
synonyms all-out, arrant, categorical (*also* categoric), complete, consummate, dead, downright, flat, out-and-out, outright, perfect, profound, pure, regular, sheer, simple, stark, thorough, thoroughgoing, total, unadulterated, unalloyed, unconditional, unequivocal, unmitigated, unqualified, utter
related words authentic, classic, genuine, real, veritable; constant, endless, eternal, perpetual, undying, unremitting; extreme, rank, unrestricted; confirmed, habitual, hopeless, inveterate; deadly, extraordinary, frightful, horrible, huge, main, superlative, supreme, surpassing, terrible, terrific
near antonyms doubtful, dubious, equivocal, qualified, questionable, restricted, uncertain
3 being entirely without fault or flaw — see PERFECT 1
4 free from added matter — see PURE 1
5 serving to put an end to all debate or questioning — see CONCLUSIVE 1
absolution *n* release from the guilt or penalty of an offense — see PARDON
absolve *vb* to free from a charge of wrongdoing — see EXCULPATE
absorb *vb* **1** to take in (something liquid) through small openings ⟨most of the spilled water was *absorbed* by the tablecloth⟩
synonyms drink, imbibe, soak (up), sponge, suck (up)
related words gulp, guzzle, quaff, sip, slurp, swallow, swig, swill
2 to hold the attention of — see ENGAGE 1
absorbed *adj* having the mind fixed on something — see ATTENTIVE
absorbing *adj* holding the attention or provoking interest — see INTERESTING
absorption *n* a focusing of the mind on something — see ATTENTION 1
abstain (from) *vb* to resist the temptation of — see FORBEAR
abstract *adj* **1** dealing with or expressing a quality or idea ⟨the book deals with *abstract* matters such as honesty and integrity on the job as well as practical subjects such as asking for a raise⟩
synonyms conceptual, theoretical (*also* theoretic)
related words conjectural, hypothetical, speculative; intellectual, mental, spiritual; ethereal, immaterial, incorporeal, insubstantial, metaphysical, nonmaterial, nonphysical, unsubstantial; impalpable, imperceptible, insensible, intangible, invisible; impractical, romantic, transcendent, transcendental, unreal, utopian, visionary
near antonyms material, physical; appreciable, detectable, discernable, noticeable, observable, palpable, perceptible, sensible, substantial, tangible, visible; defined, definite, distinct; actual, factual, real
antonyms concrete
2 using elements of form (as color, line, or texture) with little or no attempt at creating a realistic picture ⟨Cubism is a style of *abstract* art in

which natural forms are broken up into geometric shapes⟩

synonyms nonrealistic

related words impressionist, impressionistic; symbolist, symbolistic

near antonyms lifelike, natural

antonyms realistic, representational

abstract *n* a short statement of the main points — see SUMMARY

abstract *vb* to make into a short statement of the main points (as of a report) — see SUMMARIZE

abstracted *adj* lost in thought and unaware of one's surroundings or actions — see ABSENT-MINDED 1

abstruse *adj* difficult for one of ordinary knowledge or intelligence to understand — see PROFOUND 1

absurd *adj* 1 conceived or made without regard for reason or reality — see FANTASTIC 1

2 showing or marked by a lack of good sense or judgment — see FOOLISH 1

3 so foolish or pointless as to be worthy of scornful laughter — see RIDICULOUS 1

absurdity *n* 1 a foolish act or idea — see FOLLY 1

2 lack of good sense or judgment — see FOOLISHNESS 1

abundance *n* 1 a considerable amount — see LOT 2

2 an amount or supply more than sufficient to meet one's needs — see PLENTY 1

abundant *adj* being more than enough without being excessive — see PLENTIFUL

abuse *n* 1 harsh insulting language ⟨spectators hurled *abuse* at the visiting team⟩

synonyms fulmination, invective, vitriol, vituperation

related words blasphemy, curse, execration, imprecation, malediction, profanity; epithet, insult, put-down, slur; expletive, swearword; aspersion, bad-mouthing, belittlement, disparagement, revilement, vilification; castigation, chastisement, criticism, excoriation, opprobrium, rebuke, reprimand, reproof; broadside, diatribe, harangue, polemic, tirade

near antonyms acclaim, applause, commendation, praise; compliments, congratulations, endearments, felicitations; adulation, blarney, flattery, overpraise, soft soap

2 incorrect or improper use — see MISUSE

abuse *vb* 1 to inflict physical or emotional harm upon ⟨if you *abuse* your pet, he will always have an ugly disposition⟩

synonyms ill-treat, ill-use, maltreat, manhandle, mishandle, mistreat, misuse

related words molest, outrage, violate; harass, harm, hurt, injure, oppress, persecute, torment, torture, victimize, wrong

near antonyms care (for), cherish, foster, nurture; baby, cater (to), coddle, favor, gratify, humor, indulge, mollycoddle, pamper, spoil

2 to criticize harshly and usually publicly — see ATTACK 2

3 to put to a bad or improper use — see MISAPPLY

4 to take unfair advantage of — see EXPLOIT 1

abut *vb* to be adjacent to — see ADJOIN 1

abutting *adj* having a border in common — see ADJACENT

abysmal *adj* extending far downward or inward — see DEEP 1

abyss *n* an immeasurable depth or space ⟨looking

down at the dark ocean from the ship's rail, Malcolm felt as though he was staring into an *abyss*⟩

synonyms chasm, gulf

related words cleft, crevasse, crevice, fissure; cavern, hole, hollow, pit; breadth, expanse, extent, reach, spread, stretch; emptiness, nothingness, vacuity, vacuum, void

academic *adj* of or relating to schooling or learning especially at an advanced level ⟨"If you spent more time in *academic* pursuits and less time in social ones, you could easily make good grades," the dean told Valerie⟩

synonyms educational, scholarly, scholastic

related words bookish, pedantic, professorial; curricular; educative, instructive; collegiate, graduate, postgraduate

near antonyms extracurricular; noncollegiate

antonyms nonacademic, unacademic

academy *n* a place or establishment for teaching and learning — see SCHOOL

accelerate *vb* to cause to move or proceed fast or faster — see HURRY 1

accent *n* a special notice or importance given to something — see EMPHASIS 1

accent *vb* to indicate the importance of by giving prominent display — see EMPHASIZE

accentuate *vb* to indicate the importance of by giving prominent display — see EMPHASIZE

accentuation *n* a special notice or importance given to something — see EMPHASIS 1

accept *vb* 1 to agree to receive whether willingly or reluctantly — see TAKE 2

2 to have a favorable opinion of — see APPROVE (OF)

3 to regard as right or true — see BELIEVE 1

4 to take to or upon oneself — see ASSUME 1

acceptability *n* the quality or state of meeting one's needs adequately — see SUFFICIENCY

acceptable *adj* of a level of quality that meets one's needs or standards — see ADEQUATE

acceptably *adv* in a satisfactory way — see WELL 1

accepting *adj* showing or expressing acceptance or approval — see POSITIVE

access *n* the means or right of entering or participating in — see ENTRANCE 1

access *vb* to go or come in or into — see ENTER 1

accessible *adj* 1 possible to get — see AVAILABLE 1

2 situated within easy reach — see CONVENIENT

accessory *adj* available to supply something extra when needed — see AUXILIARY

accessory *n* 1 something that is not necessary in itself but adds to the convenience or performance of the main piece of equipment ⟨bought a new car with lots of high-tech *accessories*⟩

synonyms accoutrement (*or* accouterment), adjunct, appendage, attachment

related words accompaniment, additive, complement, supplement; auxiliary, subsidiary; amenity, extra, filler, frill, incidental, luxury, nonessential, nonnecessity; equipment, furnishings, paraphernalia, trappings; adornment, decoration, embellishment, enhancement, garnish, ornament, trim

near antonyms essential, necessity, requirement, requisite

2 one associated with another in wrongdoing — see ACCOMPLICE

accident *n* 1 a chance and usually sudden event bringing loss or injury ⟨was involved in an *accident* on her way home from work⟩

synonyms casualty, mischance, mishap

related words calamity, cataclysm, catastrophe, cropper, deathblow, disaster, tragedy; bummer, knock, misadventure, misfortune; collision, crack-up, crash, smashup, wreck

near antonyms boon, break, fluke, godsend, miracle, strike, windfall; fortune, luck, serendipity

2 the uncertain course of events — see CHANCE 1

accidental *adj* happening by chance ⟨finding the gold was all the more remarkable because its discovery was entirely *accidental*⟩

synonyms casual, chance, fluky, fortuitous, inadvertent, incidental, unintended, unintentional, unplanned, unpremeditated, unwitting

related words coincidental; freak, odd; aimless, arbitrary, desultory, haphazard, random; uncertain, unexpected, unforeseeable, unforeseen; coerced, forced, involuntary; unconscious, unexpected, unprompted

near antonyms certain, destined, expected, fixed, foreordained, foreseeable, foreseen, inevitable, predestined, predetermined, predictable, preordained, prescribed, sure; conscious, freewill, knowing, unforced, voluntary, volunteer, willful (*or* wilful)

antonyms deliberate, intended, intentional, planned, premeditated

acclaim *n* public acknowledgment or admiration for an achievement — see GLORY 1

acclaim *vb* to declare enthusiastic approval of ⟨she was *acclaimed* by the critics for her realistic acting⟩

synonyms applaud, cheer, crack up, hail, laud, praise, salute, tout

related words ballyhoo; approve, commend, endorse (*also* indorse), favor, recommend, support; celebrate, emblazon, eulogize, extol (*also* extoll), glorify, sing; adulate, flatter, overpraise; deify, idolize

near antonyms belittle, disparage, put down; blame, censure, reprehend, reprobate; admonish, chide, criticize, rebuke, reprimand, reproach, reprove; castigate, excoriate, lambaste

antonyms knock, pan, slam

acclamation *n* enthusiastic and usually public expression of approval — see APPLAUSE

acclimate *vb* to change (something) so as to make it suitable for a new use or situation — see ADAPT

acclimatize *vb* to change (something) so as to make it suitable for a new use or situation — see ADAPT

accolade *n* **1** a formal expression of praise — see ENCOMIUM

2 public acknowledgment or admiration for an achievement — see GLORY 1

accommodate *vb* **1** to make or have room for ⟨the back seat *accommodates* three people comfortably⟩

synonyms fit, hold, take

related words carry, contain, seat; enclose (*also* inclose), encompass; harbor, house

2 to bring to a state free of conflicts, inconsistencies, or differences — see HARMONIZE 2

3 to change (something) so as to make it suitable for a new use or situation — see ADAPT

4 to do a service or favor for — see OBLIGE 1

5 to provide with living quarters or shelter — see HOUSE 1

accommodation *n* the act or practice of each side giving up something in order to reach an agreement — see CONCESSION 1

accompaniment *n* something that is found along with something else ⟨the sound of crickets was the perfect *accompaniment* to our summer evenings on the porch⟩

synonyms companion, concomitant

related words accessory, adjunct, appendage; complement, supplement; counterpart, fellow, mate; consequence, corollary, follow-up; fixings, trimmings

accompany *vb* to go along with in order to provide assistance, protection, or companionship ⟨children must be *accompanied* by a parent at all times⟩

synonyms attend, chaperone (*or* chaperon), convoy, escort, squire

related words associate, consort, pal (around), team (up); defend, guard, protect; bring, conduct, guide, lead, pilot, see, steer, usher; follow, shadow, tag, tag along, tail; hang (around), hover (over)

near antonyms abandon, desert, ditch, dump, forsake

accompanying *adj* present at the same time and place — see COINCIDENT

accomplice *n* one associated with another in wrongdoing ⟨the thief and his *accomplices* were eventually caught and brought to justice⟩

synonyms abettor (*also* abetter), accessory, cohort, confederate

related words collaborator, collaborationist, informant, informer; companion, comrade, crony, henchman, partner; conspirator, plotter, traitor; gangster, mobster, racketeer

accomplish *vb* to carry through (as a process) to completion — see PERFORM 1

accomplished *adj* having or showing exceptional knowledge, experience, or skill in a field of endeavor — see PROFICIENT

accomplishment *n* **1** a successful result brought about by hard work ⟨Jared's biggest *accomplishment* this week was finishing his art project⟩

synonyms achievement, attainment, coup, success, triumph

related words blockbuster, hit, jackpot, megahit, smash, winner; conquest, gain, victory, win; acquirement, skill; deed, feat, performance; completion, consummation, culmination, execution, fruition, fulfillment, implementation, realization

phrases a feather in one's cap

near antonyms botch, mess, muddle, shambles; bummer, bust, catastrophe, debacle (*also* débâcle), dud, failure, fiasco, fizzle, flop, washout; disappointment, letdown, loss, setback

2 the doing of an action — see COMMISSION 2

3 the state of being actual or complete — see FRUITION

accord *n* **1** a formal agreement between two or more nations or peoples — see TREATY

2 a state of consistency — see CONFORMITY 1

3 an arrangement about action to be taken — see AGREEMENT 2

4 the act or fact of being of one opinion about something — see AGREEMENT 1

5 the act or power of making one's own choices or decisions — see FREE WILL

accord *vb* **1** to be in agreement on every point — see CHECK 1

2 to give the ownership or benefit of (something) formally or publicly — see CONFER 1

accordance *n* a state of consistency — see CONFORMITY 1

accordingly *adv* for this or that reason — see THEREFORE

account *n* **1** a relating of events usually in the order in which they happened ⟨newspaper reporters must strive to provide an accurate *account* of what happened⟩

synonyms chronicle, history, narrative, record, report, story

related words version; deposition, documentation, testament, testimonial, testimony, witness; annals, diary, journal, log, logbook, memoir; anecdote, tale, yarn; epic, saga; recital, recitation

2 a record of goods sold or services performed together with the costs due — see ¹BILL 1

3 a sum of money set aside for a particular purpose — see FUND 1

4 the capacity for being useful for some purpose — see USE 2

5 the relative usefulness or importance of something as judged by specific qualities — see WORTH 1

account *vb* to think of in a particular way — see CONSIDER 1

account (for) *vb* to give the reason for or cause of — see EXPLAIN 2

accountable *adj* being the one who must meet an obligation or suffer the consequences for failing to do so — see RESPONSIBLE 1

accoutre *or* **accouter** *vb* to provide (someone) with what is needed for a task or activity — see FURNISH 1

accoutrement *or* **accouterment** *n* **1** something that is not necessary in itself but adds to the convenience or performance of the main piece of equipment — see ACCESSORY 1

2 **accoutrements** *or* **accouterments** *pl* items needed for the performance of a task or activity — see EQUIPMENT

accredit *vb* **1** to explain (something) as being the result of something else — see CREDIT 1

2 to give official or legal power to — see AUTHORIZE 1

accreditation *n* the granting of power to perform various acts or duties — see COMMISSION 1

accretion *n* something added (as by growth) — see INCREASE 1

accrual *n* something added (as by growth) — see INCREASE 1

accumulate *vb* **1** to become greater in extent, volume, amount, or number — see INCREASE 2

2 to bring together in one body or place — see GATHER 1

3 to gradually form into a layer, pile, or mass — see COLLECT 2

accumulating *n* the act or process of becoming greater in number — see MULTIPLICATION

accumulation *n* **1** a mass or quantity that has piled up or that has been gathered ⟨a vast *accumulation* of evidence about the dangers of smoking⟩

synonyms assemblage, collection, gathering

related words agglomerate, assortment, conglomerate, conglomeration, hodgepodge, hotchpotch, jumble, medley, mélange, mishmash, mix, mixture, motley, potpourri; agglomeration, clutter, hash, heap, litter, mass, pile; aggregate, aggregation, sum, totality; cache, fund, hoard, inventory, nest egg, reserve, stock, stockpile, store, supply

2 the act or process of becoming greater in number — see MULTIPLICATION

accuracy *n* the quality or state of being very accurate — see PRECISION

accurate *adj* **1** being in agreement with the truth or a fact or a standard — see CORRECT 1

2 following an original exactly — see FAITHFUL 2

3 meeting the highest standard of accuracy — see PRECISE 1

accuse *vb* to make a claim of wrongdoing against ⟨she was *accused* of cheating on the test⟩

synonyms charge, impeach, incriminate, indict

related words blame, castigate, censure, condemn, criticize, damn, denounce, fault, impugn, reproach, reprobate; chide, rebuke, reprove, tax; arraign, book, cite, summon; prosecute, sue, try; frame, implicate, inform (against), report; recriminate, retaliate

near antonyms advocate, champion, defend; excuse, forgive, justify, pardon, remit, shrive

antonyms absolve, acquit, clear, exculpate, exonerate, vindicate

accustomed *adj* being in the habit or custom ⟨Josh felt uncomfortably full, as he was not *accustomed* to eating so much⟩

synonyms given, habituated, used, wont

related words apt, inclined, liable, prone; hardened, inured; experienced, practiced (*or* practised), seasoned, veteran; addicted, hooked

near antonyms averse, disinclined, opposed; inexperienced, new, unseasoned

antonyms unaccustomed, unused

ace *adj* having or showing exceptional knowledge, experience, or skill in a field of endeavor — see PROFICIENT 1

ace *n* **1** a person with a high level of knowledge or skill in a field — see EXPERT

2 a very small amount — see PARTICLE 1

3 a very small distance or degree — see HAIR 1

ache *n* a sharp unpleasant sensation usually felt in some specific part of the body — see PAIN 1

ache *vb* to feel or cause physical pain — see HURT 1

ache (for) *vb* to have an earnest wish to own or enjoy — see DESIRE

achievable *adj* capable of being done or carried out — see POSSIBLE 1

achieve *vb* **1** to obtain (as a goal) through effort ⟨finally *achieved* stardom⟩

synonyms attain, hit, make, score, win

related words acquire, capture, carry, draw, garner, get, land, make, obtain, procure, realize, secure; amount (to), approach, equal, match, measure up (to), meet, rival, tie, touch; beat, excel, outdo, surpass, top

near antonyms fall short (of); fail (at); lose

2 to carry through (as a process) to completion — see PERFORM 1

achievement *n* **1** a successful result brought about by hard work — see ACCOMPLISHMENT 1

2 the doing of an action — see COMMISSION 2

3 the state of being actual or complete — see FRUITION

aching *adj* causing or feeling bodily pain — see PAINFUL 1

acid *adj* causing or characterized by the one of the four basic taste sensations that is produced chiefly by acids — see SOUR 1

acidic *adj* causing or characterized by the one of the four basic taste sensations that is produced chiefly by acids — see SOUR 1

acidity *n* **1** a harsh or sharp quality — see EDGE 1

2 biting sharpness of feeling or expression — see ACRIMONY 1

acidness *n* biting sharpness of feeling or expression — see ACRIMONY 1

acknowledge *vb* to accept the truth or existence of (something) usually reluctantly — see ADMIT

acknowledgment *also* **acknowledgement** *n* **1** a formal recognition of an achievement or praiseworthy deed — see COMMENDATION 1

2 an open declaration of something (as a fault or the commission of an offense) about oneself — see CONFESSION

acme *n* the highest part or point — see HEIGHT 1

acoustic *or* **acoustical** *adj* of, relating to, or experienced through the sense of hearing — see AUDITORY

acquaint *vb* **1** to impart knowledge of a new thing or situation to ⟨Mr. King spent the first week of class *acquainting* everyone with the new computers⟩

synonyms familiarize, initiate, introduce, orient, orientate

related words apprise, brief, clue (in), fill in, inform; educate, enlighten, ground, instruct, school, train; expose, present, subject; advise, tell, tip off, warn, wise up

2 to give information to — see ENLIGHTEN 1

3 to make (one person) known (to another) socially — see INTRODUCE 1

acquaintance *n* knowledge gained by personal experience ⟨Tiffany's *acquaintance* with cows is limited to a visit to a petting zoo when she was three⟩

synonyms cognizance, familiarity

related words association, experience, exposure, intimacy, involvement; initiation, introduction; awareness, comprehension, conception, inkling, notion, understanding; education, enlightenment, grounding, information, instruction, learning, schooling, training

near antonyms callowness, greenness, ignorance, inexperience

antonyms unfamiliarity

acquainted *adj* having information especially as a result of study or experience — see FAMILIAR 2

acquiescent *adj* receiving or enduring without offering resistance — see PASSIVE

acquirable *adj* possible to get — see AVAILABLE 1

acquire *vb* **1** to come to have gradually — see DEVELOP 2

2 to receive as return for effort — see EARN 1

acquisitive *adj* having or marked by an eager and often selfish desire especially for material possessions — see GREEDY 1

acquisitiveness *n* an intense selfish desire for wealth or possessions — see GREED

acquit *vb* **1** to free from a charge of wrongdoing — see EXCULPATE

2 to manage the actions of (oneself) in a particular way — see BEHAVE

acrid *adj* **1** having or showing deep-seated resentment — see BITTER 1

2 marked by the use of wit that is intended to cause hurt feelings — see SARCASTIC

acridness *n* **1** a harsh or sharp quality — see EDGE 1

2 biting sharpness of feeling or expression — see ACRIMONY 1

acrimonious *adj* having or showing deep-seated resentment — see BITTER 1

acrimoniousness *n* a harsh or sharp quality — see EDGE 1

acrimony *n* **1** biting sharpness of feeling or expression ⟨she responded with such *acrimony* that he never brought the subject up again⟩

synonyms acidity, acidness, acridness, asperity, bitterness, cattiness, tartness, virulence, vitriol

related words gruffness, harshness, hostility, relentlessness, severity, sternness, vehemence; coldness, crossness, discourteousness, iciness, impoliteness, incivility, nastiness, rudeness, sourness, surliness, ungraciousness; anger, animosity, bile, jaundice, malevolence, malice, rancor, scorn, spite, spleen, venom; jealousy, pique, resentment

near antonyms civility, cordiality, courtesy, diplomacy, geniality, graciousness, politeness, tactfulness; compassion, softness, sweetness, sympathy, tenderness, warmth; oiliness, smoothness, suaveness, unctuousness, urbanity

2 a harsh or sharp quality — see EDGE 1

across *adv* from one side to the other of an intervening space — see OVER 1

across *prep* to the opposite side of ⟨we swam *across* the lake and visited the other summer camp⟩

synonyms athwart, over, through

related words around, round; beyond, past

act *n* **1** a display of emotion or behavior that is insincere or intended to deceive — see MASQUERADE

2 a rule of conduct or action laid down by a governing authority and especially a legislator — see LAW 1

3 something done by someone — see ACTION 1

act *vb* **1** to present a portrayal or performance of ⟨a very talented student *acted* the part of Tiny Tim in our production of *A Christmas Carol*⟩

synonyms impersonate, perform, play, portray

related words depict, dramatize, enact, pantomime, render, represent, role-play, take on; overact, underplay; ape, clown, ham, imitate, masquerade, mime, mimic, pose (as); star (in)

2 to produce a desired effect ⟨the painkiller *acted* quickly⟩

synonyms operate, perform, take, work

related words behave, react, respond; affect, influence, sway; pan out, redound, result

phrases take effect

near antonyms backfire; fizzle

3 to give the impression of being — see SEEM

4 to have a certain purpose — see FUNCTION

act (toward) *vb* to behave toward in a stated way — see TREAT 1

action *n* **1** something done by someone ⟨judge people by their *actions*, not by their words⟩

synonyms act, deed, doing, exploit, feat, thing

related words accomplishment, achievement, attainment; adventure, experience; enterprise, initiative, undertaking; handiwork, performance, work; stunt, trick; activity, dealing; maneuver, measure, move, operation, procedure, proceeding, step, tactic

2 a court case for enforcing a right or claim — see LAWSUIT

3 active fighting during the course of a war — see COMBAT 1

4 **actions** *pl* the way or manner in which one conducts oneself — see BEHAVIOR

activate *vb* to cause to function ⟨the thermostat is

THESAURUS

set to *activate* the heating system only when the temperature drops below 65 degrees⟩

synonyms actuate, crank (up), drive, move, propel, run, set off, spark, start, touch off, trigger, turn on

related words charge, electrify, energize, fire, fuel, generate, power, push; discharge, launch, release, switch, trip; reactivate, recharge; arouse, excite, stimulate, vitalize; incite, instigate, provoke, quicken, stir up; accelerate, catalyze, speed up, step up

near antonyms arrest, brake, chock, cut off, draw up, halt, jam, stall, stick, stop; decelerate, repress, slow, stunt, suppress

antonyms cut, deactivate, kill, shut off, turn off

active *adj* **1** being in effective operation ⟨the abandoned factory had not been *active* for years⟩

synonyms alive, functional, functioning, going, living, on, operating, operational, operative, running, working

related words effective, effectual; employable, operable, usable, viable, workable; performing, producing, productive, serving, useful, yielding; astir, bustling, busy, dynamic, flourishing, humming, roaring, thriving

phrases in commission

near antonyms deactivated, decommissioned; ineffective, ineffectual, useless; inoperable, unusable, unworkable; arrested, asleep, dormant, fallow, idle, inert, latent, lifeless, nonproductive, quiescent, sleepy, stagnating, unproductive, vegetating

antonyms broken, dead, inactive, inoperative, nonfunctional, nonfunctioning, nonoperating

2 having much high-spirited energy and movement — see LIVELY 1

3 involved in often constant activity — see BUSY 1

activity *n* energetic movement of the body for the sake of physical fitness — see EXERCISE 1

actor *n* one who acts professionally (as in a play, movie, or television show) ⟨my sister went to drama school to become an *actor*⟩

synonyms impersonator, mummer, player, trouper

related words barnstormer, entertainer, performer; actress, starlet; lead, leading lady, leading man, star; monologuist (*or* monologist); prima donna, scene-stealer, understudy; comedian, tragedian; ape, aper, ham, imitator, impressionist, masquerader, mime, mimic, pantomime, pantomimist, poser; buffoon, clown, harlequin, stooge, zany

actual *adj* existing in fact and not merely as a possibility ⟨the *actual* outcome of the election was quite different from what everybody expected⟩

synonyms concrete, existent, factual, real, true, very

related words attested, authenticated, confirmed, demonstrated, established, proven, substantiated, validated, verified; incontestable, incontrovertible, indisputable, indubitable, inescapable, irrefutable, undeniable, unquestionable; believable, convincing, literal, realistic, unmistakable, verifiable; authentic, bona fide, genuine, real-life; absolute, certain, final, hard, palpable, positive, substantial, tangible; authoritative, certifiable, certified

near antonyms alleged, assumed, reputed, supposed; conceived, envisaged, imagined, pictured, visualized; chimerical, fabled, fanciful, fictional,

fictitious, legendary, illusory; fabricated, fake, imaginary, invented, made-up, make-believe, pretend, romantic; abstract, unreal

antonyms conjectural, hypothetical, ideal, nonexistent, possible, potential, theoretical (*also* theoretic)

actuality *n* **1** the fact of being or of being real — see EXISTENCE

2 the quality of being actual — see FACT 1

3 the state of being actual or complete — see FRUITION

actually *adv* **1** to tell the truth ⟨*actually*, I'd rather spend the evening at home⟩

synonyms forsooth, frankly, honestly, really, truly, truthfully, verily

related words absolutely, certainly, indisputably, indubitably, positively, realistically, undoubtedly, unquestionably, veritably

phrases in point of fact, in reality, in truth

2 in actual fact — see VERY 2

actuate *vb* **1** to cause to function — see ACTIVATE

2 to set or keep in motion — see MOVE 2

act up *vb* **1** to behave badly — see MISBEHAVE

2 to engage in attention-getting playful or boisterous behavior — see CUT UP

acute *adj* **1** able to sense slight impressions or differences ⟨dogs, with their *acute* sense of smell, are used for finding toxic substances undetectable by humans⟩

synonyms delicate, keen, perceptive, sensitive, sharp

related words accurate, clear, discerning, fine, good, piercing, precise, quick, receptive, sensible, subtle; hypersensitive, oversensitive, supersensitive

near antonyms bad, deadened, dimmed, dull, dulled, fading; dead, imperceptive, insensible, insensitive, numb; imprecise, inaccurate

2 needing immediate attention ⟨famine caused by an *acute* shortage of grain⟩

synonyms critical, crying, dire, imperative, imperious, instant, pressing, urgent

related words compelling, demanding, extreme, immediate, insistent, intense, overriding; crucial, desperate, grave, life-and-death, serious, severe, vital; dangerous, explosive, hazardous, perilous, precarious, unstable

near antonyms incidental, low-pressure, minor, negligible, trivial, unimportant; nonthreatening, safe, stable

antonyms noncritical, nonurgent

3 causing intense mental or physical distress — see SHARP 2

4 having a high musical pitch or range — see SHRILL

acuteness *n* a harsh or sharp quality — see EDGE 1

ad *n* a published statement informing the public of a matter of general interest — see ANNOUNCEMENT

adage *n* an often stated observation regarding something from common experience — see SAYING

adamant *adj* sticking to an opinion, purpose, or course of action in spite of reason, arguments, or persuasion — see OBSTINATE

adamantine *adj* sticking to an opinion, purpose, or course of action in spite of reason, arguments, or persuasion — see OBSTINATE

adapt *vb* to change (something) so as to make it

suitable for a new use or situation ⟨it always takes freshmen a little while to *adapt* themselves to high school⟩
synonyms acclimate, acclimatize, accommodate, adjust, condition, conform, fit, shape
related words readapt, readjust; customize, tailor; attune, harmonize, reconcile, suit, tune; establish, root, settle; acquaint, familiarize, orient, orientate; equip, prepare, prime, rehearse; harden, inure, season, toughen; alter, convert, make over, modify, redo, refashion, refit, remake, remodel, revamp, revise, rework, transform

adaptable *adj* **1** able to do many different kinds of things — see VERSATILE
2 capable of being readily changed — see FLEXIBLE 1

add *vb* **1** to join (something) to a mass, quantity, or number so as to bring about an overall increase ⟨the band recently *added* a saxophonist and a keyboard player to its ranks⟩ ⟨*add* another cup of flour to the mixture⟩
synonyms adjoin, annex, append, tack (on)
related words affix, attach, fasten, fix, graft, hitch, tie; infuse, inject, insert, introduce
near antonyms detach, disconnect, disjoin, separate, unfasten; amputate, cut, excise, lop off, sever
antonyms deduct, remove, subtract, take
2 to combine (numbers) into a single sum ⟨when she *added* all the phone charges she discovered an error in her bill⟩
synonyms foot (up), sum, total
related words calculate, cast, cipher, compute, figure, reckon, tally; count, enumerate, number

add (to) *vb* to make greater in size, amount, or number — see INCREASE 1

added *adj* resulting in an increase in amount or number — see ADDITIONAL

addendum *n* something added (as by growth) — see INCREASE 1

addict *n* **1** a person who regularly uses drugs especially illegally — see DOPER
2 a person with a strong and habitual liking for something — see FAN

addition *n* **1** a smaller structure added to a main building — see ANNEX
2 something added (as by growth) — see INCREASE 1
3 the act or process of becoming greater in number — see MULTIPLICATION

additional *adj* resulting in an increase in amount or number ⟨there turned out to be *additional* reasons for her absence besides those she had given⟩
synonyms added, another, else, farther, further, more, other
related words accessory, collateral, extraneous, side, supplemental, supplementary; fresh, new; extra, plus, spare, surplus
near antonyms fewer, less

additionally *adv* in addition to what has been said — see MORE 1

additive *adj* produced by a series of additions of identical or similar things — see CUMULATIVE

addle *vb* to throw into a state of mental uncertainty — see CONFUSE 1

addled *adj* having undergone organic breakdown — see ROTTEN 1

address *n* a usually formal discourse delivered to an audience — see SPEECH 1

address *vb* to occupy (oneself) diligently or with close attention — see APPLY 2

adduce *vb* to give as an example — see QUOTE 1

add up (to) *vb* **1** to be the same in meaning or effect — see AMOUNT (TO) 2
2 to have a total of — see AMOUNT (TO) 1

adept *adj* having or showing exceptional knowledge, experience, or skill in a field of endeavor — see PROFICIENT

adept *n* a person with a high level of knowledge or skill in a field — see EXPERT

adeptly *adv* in a skillful or expert manner — see WELL 3

adeptness *n* subtle or imaginative ability in inventing, devising, or executing something — see SKILL 1

adequacy *n* the quality or state of meeting one's needs adequately — see SUFFICIENCY

adequate *adj* of a level of quality that meets one's needs or standards ⟨this old computer is probably *adequate* if you just want to type a book report⟩
synonyms acceptable, all right, decent, fine, OK (*or* okay), passable, respectable, satisfactory, tolerable
related words agreeable, bearable, endurable, sufferable; average, fair, mediocre, middling, minimal, unexceptional; appropriate, correct, due, fitting, good, meet, proper, right, seemly, suitable, useful, worthy; gratifying, satisfying
near antonyms disreputable, improper, indecent, objectionable, unfit, unsuitable, unworthy, useless; bad, defective, faulty, imperfect, incomplete, lamentable, pitiful; dissatisfying, unsatisfying; insufficient, meager, mean, miserly, niggardly, poor, scanty, shabby, short, skimpy, spare, stingy; insufferable, intolerable, unbearable, unendurable; exceptional, exquisite, extreme, first-class, matchless, maximized, maximum, optimal, optimum, peerless, preeminent, superior, supreme, unmatched, unparalleled, unsurpassed
antonyms deficient, inadequate, lacking, unacceptable, unsatisfactory, wanting

adequately *adv* **1** in a satisfactory way — see WELL 1
2 in or to a degree or quantity that meets one's requirements or satisfaction — see ENOUGH 1

adhere *vb* to hold to something firmly as if by adhesion — see STICK 1

adhere (to) *vb* to give steadfast support to ⟨our coach *adheres to* the belief that we can win this game if we just have a positive attitude⟩
synonyms cling (to), hew (to), keep (to), stick (to *or* with)
related words cleave (to), hang on (to); back, confirm, defend, endorse (*also* indorse), espouse, support, uphold; accept, adopt, cherish, cultivate, embrace, follow, foster, heed
phrases abide by, live up to, stand by
near antonyms abandon, desert, forsake, give up, relinquish, spurn, surrender; abjure, disavow, disclaim, disown, recall, recant, reconsider, renege, renounce, retract, revoke, take back, unsay, withdraw
antonyms defect (from)

adherence *n* a physical sticking to as if by glue — see ADHESION

adherent *n* one who follows the opinions or teachings of another — see FOLLOWER

adhesion *n* a physical sticking to as if by glue

⟨mom prefers photo albums that keep the pictures in place by *adhesion* to the pages⟩

synonyms adherence, bonding

related words agglutination, clumping, cohesion; adhesiveness, attachment, cohesiveness, tenacity; cementing, glueing

adhesive *adj* being of such a thick consistency as to readily cling to objects upon contact — see STICKY 1

adhesive *n* a substance used to stick things together — see GLUE

adieu *n* an expression of good wishes at parting — see GOOD-BYE

adipose *adj* containing animal fat especially in unusual amounts — see FATTY

adiposity *n* the condition of having an excess of body fat — see CORPULENCE

adjacent *adj* having a border in common ⟨Crystal's house is *adjacent* to a wooded park⟩

synonyms abutting, adjoining, bordering, contiguous, flanking, fringing, joining, juxtaposed, skirting, touching, verging

related words close, closest, immediate, near, nearest, nearby, neighboring, next, next-door, nigh; attached, communicating, connecting, interconnecting, linked; bounding, embracing, encircling, enclosing, fencing, rimming, surrounding; marginal, peripheral, tangent, tangential

near antonyms apart, detached, free-standing, removed, separate, unattached, unconnected, unlinked; away, distant, far, far-off, farthest, remote; discontinuous, noncontinuous

antonyms nonadjacent

adjoin *vb* 1 to be adjacent to ⟨Colleen, whose bedroom *adjoins* her little brother's room, sometimes hears him talking in his sleep⟩

synonyms abut, border (on), flank, fringe, join, skirt, touch, verge (on)

related words attach (to), communicate (with), connect (with), link (with); bound, embrace, encircle, enclose (*also* inclose), fence, line, rim, surround; contact, converge, meet, neighbor

2 to join (something) to a mass, quantity, or number so as to bring about an overall increase — see ADD 1

adjoining *adj* having a border in common — see ADJACENT

adjourn *vb* to bring to a formal close for a period of time ⟨the meeting was *adjourned* by the chairperson until further notice⟩

synonyms recess, suspend

related words break off, discontinue, intermit, interrupt; defer, hold off, postpone, put off, reserve, shelve, table; abort, call off, cancel, dissolve, terminate; break up, close, conclude, wind up, wrap up

near antonyms inaugurate, launch, open; carry on, continue, draw out, extend, proceed, prolong; renew, reopen, resume; convene, convoke

adjudge *vb* to give an opinion about (something at issue or in dispute) — see JUDGE 1

adjudicate *vb* to give an opinion about (something at issue or in dispute) — see JUDGE 1

adjunct *n* something that is not necessary in itself but adds to the convenience or performance of the main piece of equipment — see ACCESSORY 1

adjure *vb* to issue orders to (someone) by right of authority — see COMMAND 1

adjust *vb* to change (something) so as to make it suitable for a new use or situation — see ADAPT

adjustable *adj* capable of being readily changed — see FLEXIBLE 1

adjutant *n* a person who helps a more skilled person — see HELPER

ad-lib *adj* made or done without previous thought or preparation — see EXTEMPORANEOUS

ad-lib *vb* to perform, make, or do without preparation — see IMPROVISE

administer *vb* 1 to give out (something) in appropriate amounts or to appropriate individuals ⟨the principal *administers* discipline fairly when students break the rules⟩

synonyms allocate, apportion, deal (out), dispense, distribute, dole (out), mete (out), parcel (out), portion, prorate

related words allot, allow, appropriate, assign, dish (out), divide, measure (out), ration, redistribute, split; bestow, disburse, furnish, issue, provide, share, supply; circulate, disperse, disseminate, scatter, spread; chip in, contribute, donate, pledge

near antonyms begrudge, deny, deprive (of), pinch, refuse, skimp, stint, withhold

2 to carry out effectively — see ENFORCE

3 to look after and make decisions about — see CONDUCT 1

administration *n* 1 lawful control over the affairs of a political unit (as a nation) — see RULE 2

2 the act or activity of looking after and making decisions about something — see CONDUCT 1

administrative *adj* suited for or relating to the directing of things — see EXECUTIVE

administrator *n* a person who manages or directs — see EXECUTIVE

admirable *adj* deserving of high regard or great approval ⟨it's *admirable* the way Kory helps her grandmother with chores and errands every Saturday⟩

synonyms commendable, creditable, laudable, meritorious, praiseworthy

related words awesome, distinctive, distinguished, excellent, honorable, noteworthy, noticeable, outstanding, reputable, worthy; invaluable, precious, priceless, valuable; delightful, enjoyable, pleasing, satisfying

near antonyms contemptible, deplorable, infamous, notorious, sorry, unlikable, unworthy, worthless; disgraceful, dishonorable, disreputable, low, mean, scandalous, seamy, shady, shameful, shocking, sordid, unsavory

antonyms censurable, discreditable, reprehensible

admiration *n* 1 a feeling of great approval and liking ⟨my *admiration* for Yoko increased when I discovered she had learned English only since coming to the U.S.⟩

synonyms appreciation, esteem, estimation, favor, regard, respect

related words acclamation, adoration, approbation, deference, homage, honor, praise, reverence, veneration, worship; delight, enjoyment, fancy; amazement, awe, wonder, wonderment

near antonyms condemnation, disapproval, disdain, opprobrium, scorn; disappointment, discontent, disenchantment, disgruntlement, disillusionment, displeasure, indignation, unhappiness; aversion, contempt, disgust, dislike, disregard, distaste

antonyms disfavor

2 the rapt attention and deep emotion caused by the sight of something extraordinary — see WONDER 2

admire *vb* to think very highly or favorably of ⟨I *admire* the way you handled such a touchy situation⟩

synonyms appreciate, esteem, regard, respect

related words acclaim, accredit, applaud, approve, commend, compliment, credit, praise; delight (in), drink (in), enjoy, relish, revel (in), savor; dig, fancy, favor, groove (on), like, love, adore, deify, idolize, revere, reverence, venerate, worship; cherish, prize, treasure, value

phrases set store by (*or* on)

near antonyms condemn, decry, deplore, disapprove, discount, discountenance, disdain, disfavor, dislike, dismiss, disregard, frown (on), scorn

admiring *adj* expressing approval — see FAVORABLE 1

admissible *adj* that may be permitted — see PERMISSIBLE

admission *n* 1 an open declaration of something (as a fault or the commission of an offense) about oneself — see CONFESSION

2 the means or right of entering or participating in — see ENTRANCE 1

admit *vb* to accept the truth or existence of (something) usually reluctantly ⟨Eliza readily *admitted* she hadn't read the assignment⟩ ⟨you can't bring yourself to *admit* your mistakes⟩

synonyms acknowledge, agree, allow, concede, confess, grant, own (up)

related words disburden, unburden, unload; affirm, avow, confirm, profess; accept, recognize, yield; announce, break, broadcast, communicate, declare, disclose, divulge, impart, publish, reveal, spill, tell, unveil; betray, blab, expose, give away, inform, leak, rat, squeal, talk, tattle, tip off, warn, wise up; breathe, whisper

near antonyms disallow, disavow, disclaim, disown; contradict, dispute, gainsay, negate, negative; rebut, refute, reject, repudiate; conceal, cover (up), hide, obscure, veil

antonyms deny

admittance *n* the means or right of entering or participating in — see ENTRANCE 1

admixture *n* a distinct entity formed by the combining of two or more different things — see BLEND

admonish *vb* to criticize (someone) usually gently so as to correct a fault — see REBUKE 1

admonishing *adj* serving as or offering a warning — see CAUTIONARY

admonition *n* the act or an instance of telling beforehand of danger or risk — see WARNING 1

admonitory *adj* serving as or offering a warning — see CAUTIONARY

adolescent *adj* 1 being in the early stage of life, growth, or development — see YOUNG

2 having or showing the annoying qualities (as silliness) associated with children — see CHILDISH

3 lacking in adult experience or maturity — see CALLOW

adopt *vb* to take for one's own use (something originated by another) ⟨the family *adopted* the American tradition of having turkey for Thanksgiving after they moved to the U.S.⟩

synonyms borrow, embrace, take up

related words domesticate, naturalize; appropriate, arrogate, take over, usurp; absorb, assimilate, incorporate; cherish, prize, treasure; cultivate, follow, heed, honor; use, utilize; bring up, foster,

nurture, raise, rear; affect, assume, copy, imitate, pretend, put on, simulate

near antonyms abandon, forsake, give up, relinquish, surrender; abjure, abnegate, disown; reject, renounce, repudiate, spurn; discard, jettison, junk, throw away, throw out

adorable *adj* having qualities that tend to make one loved — see LOVABLE

adore *vb* 1 to feel passion, devotion, or tenderness for — see LOVE 2

2 to love or admire too much — see IDOLIZE

3 to offer honor or respect to (someone) as a divine power — see WORSHIP 1

4 to take pleasure in — see ENJOY 1

adoring *adj* 1 feeling or showing love — see LOVING

2 reflecting great admiration or devotion — see WORSHIPFUL

adorn *vb* to make more attractive by adding something that is beautiful or becoming — see DECORATE

adorning *adj* serving to add beauty — see DECORATIVE

adornment *n* something that decorates or beautifies — see DECORATION 1

adroit *adj* accomplished with trained ability — see SKILLFUL

adroitness *n* 1 mental skill or quickness — see DEXTERITY 1

2 subtle or imaginative ability in inventing, devising, or executing something — see SKILL 1

adulate *vb* 1 to love or admire too much — see IDOLIZE

2 to praise too much — see FLATTER 1

adulation *n* 1 excessive admiration of or devotion to a person — see WORSHIP

2 excessive praise — see FLATTERY

adulatory *adj* 1 overly or insincerely flattering — see FULSOME

2 reflecting great admiration or devotion — see WORSHIPFUL

adult *adj* fully grown or developed — see MATURE 1

adult *n* a fully grown person ⟨at the beach, the *adults* sat under broad umbrellas while the children splashed in the water⟩

synonyms grown-up

related words ancient, elder, graybeard, oldster, old-timer, senior, senior citizen

near antonyms kid, moppet, tad, toddler, tot, tyke; baby, infant; adolescent, juvenile, minor, youngster, youth; preteen, teenager, teenybopper

antonyms child

adulterant *n* something that is or that makes impure — see IMPURITY

adulterate *vb* to alter (something) for the worse with the addition of foreign or lower-grade substances ⟨the company was fined for *adulterating* its "all beef" frankfurters with cereal⟩

synonyms dilute, thin, water (down), weaken

related words befoul, contaminate, corrupt, defile, dirty, foul, infect, poison, pollute, soil, spoil, sully, taint; cheapen, debase, degrade; manipulate, misrepresent, tamper (with); counterfeit, fake, falsify, fudge; doctor, spike

near antonyms fertilize, lard; augment, supplement; clarify, clean, cleanse, distill, filter, flush, leach, pasteurize, purge, purify, refine; better, enhance, improve

antonyms enrich, fortify, richen, strengthen

THESAURUS

adulterated *adj* containing foreign or lower-grade substances — see IMPURE

adulthood *n* the state of being fully grown or developed — see MATURITY

advance *n* **1** forward movement in time or place ⟨during her long convalescence, Penny was barely aware of the *advance* of the seasons⟩
synonyms advancement, furtherance, going, headway, march, onrush, passage, process, procession, progress, progression
related words current, drift, flow, flux, stream, way; advent, approach, arrival, coming, nearing; bound, jump, leap, step, stride; impetus, momentum
near antonyms backwash, ebb, reflux; retraction, retreat, return, reversal, reverse; about-face, turnabout, turnaround
antonyms recession, regression, retrogression
2 an instance of notable progress in the development of knowledge, technology, or skill ⟨with her new violin teacher, Nadia has made noticeable *advances* in her technique in just a few weeks⟩
synonyms advancement, breakthrough, enhancement, improvement, refinement
related words amelioration, boost, heightening, increase, melioration, strengthening, upgrade, uplift, upswing, uptrend, upturn; betterment, evolution, maturation, perfection, ripening; civilization, edification, education, enlightenment; renaissance, renascence, revival; discovery, find, windfall; innovation, invention
near antonyms breakdown, collapse, crash; hindrance, impediment, stumbling block; decline, decrease, deterioration, diminishment, failing, flagging, languishment, lapse, lessening, reduction, sinking, slowing, weakening, worsening; detriment, disablement, drawback, glitch, impairment, shortcoming
antonyms setback

advance *vb* **1** to give to another for temporary use with the understanding that it or a like thing will be returned — see LEND
2 to help the growth or development of — see FOSTER 1
3 to move forward along a course — see GO 1
4 to move higher in rank or position — see PROMOTE 1
5 to set before the mind for consideration — see PROPOSE 1
6 to move closer to — see COME 1

advanced *adj* **1** being far along in development ⟨an *advanced* civilization, among the first anywhere to use the plow, developed on the banks of the Nile River thousands of years ago⟩
synonyms developed, evolved, high, higher, improved, progressive, refined
related words full-blown, full-fledged, full-grown, full-scale; aged, grown, mature, matured, perfected, ripe, ripened; civilized, educated, enhanced, enlightened; contemporary, latest, modern, newest, newfangled, new-fashioned, novel, recent, up-to-date; early, precocious
near antonyms green, immature, underdeveloped, undersized, underweight, unripe, unripened; uncivilized, uneducated; early, primeval, primordial; antediluvian, antiquated, Neanderthal, oldfangled, old-fashioned
antonyms backward, low, lower, nonprogressive, primitive, retarded, rudimentary, undeveloped

2 being at a higher level than average — see HIGH 2

advancement *n* **1** a raising or a state of being raised to a higher rank or position ⟨Paul's rapid *advancement* in the company came as no surprise to those who knew he was the president's nephew⟩
synonyms ascent, elevation, preferment, promotion, rise, upgrade
related words aggrandizement, ennoblement, exaltation, glorification
near antonyms deposition, dethronement, dismissal, expulsion, impeachment, ouster, overthrow, removal, suspension, unmaking, unseating; downfall, fall
antonyms abasement, demotion, downgrade, reduction
2 an instance of notable progress in the development of knowledge, technology, or skill — see ADVANCE 2
3 forward movement in time or place — see ADVANCE 1

advantage *n* **1** the more favorable condition or position in a competition ⟨your experience volunteering at the hospital will put you at an *advantage* when you're applying for a job there⟩
synonyms better, drop, edge, jump, upper hand, vantage
related words allowance, head start, lead, margin, odds, start; ascendancy, command, dominance, mastery, predominance, superiority, supremacy, transcendence; favoritism, nepotism, precedence, preference, privilege, seniority; break, foothold, opportunity
near antonyms detriment, drawback, penalty, stranglehold; disparity, imbalance, inequality, unevenness; disability, impairment, shortcoming
antonyms disadvantage, handicap, liability
2 a thing that helps — see HELP 2

advantageous *adj* conferring benefits; promoting or contributing to personal or social well-being — see BENEFICIAL

advent *n* the act of coming upon a scene — see ARRIVAL

adventitious *adj* not being a vital part of or belonging to something — see EXTRINSIC

adventure *n* an exciting or noteworthy event that one experiences firsthand ⟨our quiet hike turned into quite an *adventure* when we encountered a bear and her cub⟩
synonyms experience, happening, time
related words escapade, lark; act, action, deed, doing, exploit; episode, occasion; baptism, ordeal, test, trial, tribulation; enterprise, risk, venture; expedition, exploration, feat, mission, performance, quest, stunt
near antonyms bore, bummer, bust, drag

adventure *vb* to place in danger — see ENDANGER

adventuresome *adj* inclined or willing to take risks — see BOLD 1

adventurous *adj* inclined or willing to take risks — see BOLD 1

adversary *n* **1** one that is hostile toward another — see ENEMY
2 one that takes a position opposite another in a competition or conflict — see OPPONENT 1

adverse *adj* **1** opposed to one's interests ⟨all the *adverse* publicity really caused the movie star's popularity to suffer⟩
synonyms counter, disadvantageous, hostile, in-

imical, negative, prejudicial, unfavorable, unfriendly, unsympathetic

related words bad, baleful, baneful, evil; damaging, deleterious, destructive, detrimental, fatal, harmful, hurtful, injurious, lethal, murderous, poisonous, ruinous, threatening, troublesome, unhealthy, wounding; dangerous, hazardous, imperiling, jeopardizing, parlous, perilous, risky, unsafe; defamatory, detractive, offensive, scathing, slanderous; antagonistic, antipathetic, inhospitable, intolerant, uncongenial, uncooperative; competing, conflicting, counteracting, countering, opposing, resistant, resisting

near antonyms beneficial, good, helpful, propitious, useful; harmless, innocent, innocuous, inoffensive, nondestructive, nonfatal, nonlethal, nonthreatening; unresisting, unresistant; tolerant, understanding; agreeable, affable, amiable, amicable, benign, benignant, congenial, cordial, complying, friendly, hospitable

antonyms advantageous, favorable, friendly, positive, supportive, sympathetic, well-disposed

2 causing or capable of causing harm — see HARMFUL

adversity *n* **1** bad luck or an example of this — see MISFORTUNE

2 something that is a cause for suffering or special effort especially in the attainment of a goal — see DIFFICULTY 1

advert (to) *vb* to make reference to or speak about briefly but specifically — see MENTION 1

advertise *vb* to make known openly or publicly — see ANNOUNCE

advertisement *n* a published statement informing the public of a matter of general interest — see ANNOUNCEMENT

advice *n* an opinion suggesting a wise or proper course of action ⟨Stephanie got some good *advice* from the vet about dealing with her dog's habit of chasing cars⟩

synonyms counsel, guidance

related words recommendation, suggestion; hint, pointer, tip; data, feedback, information; answer, solution; advisement, consideration, thought; admonishment, admonition, caution, cautioning, expostulation, remonstration, urging, warning; judgment (*or* judgement), observation, verdict; assistance, briefing, coaching, direction, instruction, mentoring, priming, prompting, teaching, tutoring; interference, kibitzing, meddling; moralizing, pontificating, preaching; exhortation, lecture, lesson, sermon, speech

advisable *adj* suitable for bringing about a desired result under the circumstances — see EXPEDIENT

advise *vb* **1** to give advice to ⟨a popular guidance counselor who has been *advising* students about their college plans for two decades⟩

synonyms counsel

related words admonish, caution, warn; brief, clue (in), fill in, inform, wise (up); coach, direct, lead, guide, instruct, mentor, teach, tutor; acquaint, apprise, familiarize; convince, encourage, induce, persuade, talk (into); beg, exhort, implore, prevail (upon), urge; propose, recommend, suggest

2 to put forward as one's choice for a wise or proper course of action ⟨she *advised* calling ahead for a reservation at the new restaurant⟩

synonyms counsel, recommend, suggest

related words advocate, back, favor, support; exhort, urge; advance, propose, submit

3 to exchange viewpoints or seek advice for the purpose of finding a solution to a problem — see CONFER 2

4 to give information to — see ENLIGHTEN 1

advised *adj* decided on as a result of careful thought — see DELIBERATE 1

adviser *or* **advisor** *n* a person who gives advice especially professionally — see CONSULTANT

advocate *n* **1** a person who actively supports or favors a cause — see EXPONENT

2 a person whose profession is to conduct lawsuits for clients or to advise about legal rights and obligations — see LAWYER

advocate *vb* to promote the interests or cause of — see SUPPORT 1

aegis *n* means or method of defending — see DEFENSE 1

aeon *or* **eon** *n* a long or seemingly long period of time — see AGE 2

aerodrome *n, British* a place from which aircraft operate that usually has paved runways and a terminal — see AIRPORT

affability *n* the state or quality of having a pleasant or agreeable manner in socializing with others — see AMIABILITY 1

affable *adj* **1** having a relaxed, casual manner — see EASYGOING 1

2 having an easygoing and pleasing manner especially in social situations — see AMIABLE

3 showing a natural kindness and courtesy especially in social situations — see GRACIOUS 1

affair *n* **1** a brief romantic relationship ⟨an *affair* between two teenagers spending the summer at the same beach resort⟩

synonyms love affair, romance

related words amour, intrigue; attachment, infatuation; entanglement, fling, flirtation; liaison, passion

2 a social gathering — see PARTY 1

3 something produced by physical or intellectual effort — see PRODUCT 1

4 something that happens — see EVENT 1

5 something to be dealt with — see MATTER 2

¹affect *vb* **1** to act upon (a person or a person's feelings) so as to cause a response ⟨Gary claims that scary movies don't *affect* him in the least⟩

synonyms impact, impress, influence, move, strike, sway, tell (on), touch

related words bias, color; inspire, stir; carry, engage, interest, involve, penetrate, pierce; afflict, agitate, bother, discomfort, discompose, disquiet, distress, disturb, fluster, harass, harry, perturb, pester, plague, smite, strain, stress, trouble, try, upset, worry, wring; allure, attract, bewitch, captivate, charm, dazzle, enchant

phrases get to

near antonyms bore, jade, pall, tire, weary

2 to be the business or affair of — see CONCERN 2

²affect *vb* to present a false appearance of — see FEIGN

affectation *n* the quality or state of appearing or trying to appear more important or more valuable than is the case — see PRETENSE 1

affected *adj* **1** lacking in natural or spontaneous quality — see ARTIFICIAL 1

2 self-consciously trying to present an appearance of grandeur or importance — see PRETENTIOUS 1

affectedness *n* the quality or state of appearing or trying to appear more important or more valuable than is the case — see PRETENSE 1

affecting *adj* having the power to affect the feelings or sympathies — see MOVING

¹**affection** *n* a feeling of strong or constant regard for and dedication to someone — see LOVE 1

²**affection** *n* an abnormal state that disrupts a plant's or animal's normal bodily functioning — see DISEASE

affectionate *adj* feeling or showing love — see LOVING

affianced *adj* pledged in marriage — see ENGAGED

affiliate *n* a local unit of an organization — see CHAPTER

affiliated *adj* having a close connection like that between family members — see RELATED

affiliation *n* the state of having shared interests or efforts (as in social or business matters) — see ASSOCIATION 1

affirm *vb* 1 to state as a fact usually forcefully — see CLAIM 1
2 to state clearly and strongly — see ASSERT 1

affirmation *n* a solemn and often public declaration of the truth or existence of something — see PROTESTATION

affirmative *adj* showing or expressing acceptance or approval — see POSITIVE

affix *vb* to cause (something) to hold to another — see FASTEN 1

afflict *vb* to cause persistent suffering to ⟨the South was *afflicted* by a severe drought⟩ ⟨he's been *afflicted* by nightmares ever since the accident⟩
synonyms agonize, bedevil, curse, harrow, martyr, persecute, plague, rack, torment, torture
related words assail, attack, beset, set upon; badger, dog, hound, ride; agitate, annoy, bother, distress, disturb, harass, harry, irk, molest, pester; discomfort, discompose, disquiet, fluster, perturb, strain, stress, trouble, try, upset, vex, worry; crush, oppress, overpower, overwhelm, smite, strike, tyrannize; pain, prick, stab, sting, wring
near antonyms abet, aid, assist, help; deliver, release, relieve, reprieve; comfort, console, solace, soothe, succor

afflicting *adj* hard to accept or bear especially emotionally — see BITTER 2

affliction *n* 1 a state of great suffering of body or mind — see DISTRESS 1
2 deep sadness especially for the loss of someone or something loved — see SORROW

affluent *adj* having goods, property, or money in abundance — see RICH 1

affray *n* a rough and often noisy fight usually involving several people — see BRAWL 1

affright *vb* to strike with fear — see FRIGHTEN

affrighted *adj* filled with fear or dread — see AFRAID 1

affront *n* an act or expression showing scorn and usually intended to hurt another's feelings — see INSULT

affront *vb* to cause hurt feelings or deep resentment in — see INSULT

aficionado *n* a person with a strong and habitual liking for something — see FAN

afield *adv* off the desired or intended path or course — see WRONG 1

afire *adj* being on fire — see ABLAZE 1

aflame *adj* being on fire — see ABLAZE 1

aflutter *adj* feeling or showing uncomfortable feelings of uncertainty — see NERVOUS 1

afoot *adj* being in progress or development — see ONGOING 1

afore *adv, chiefly dialect* so as to precede something in order of time — see AHEAD 1

afore *prep, chiefly dialect* 1 earlier than — see BEFORE 1
2 preceding in space — see BEFORE 2

afraid *adj* 1 filled with fear or dread ⟨Melissa is *afraid* of flying, so she takes a train from Boston to visit her brother in Chicago⟩
synonyms affrighted, aghast, alarmed, fearful, frightened, horrified, scared, spooked, terrified, terrorized
related words fainthearted, fearsome, shrinking, shy, timid, timorous, tremulous; agitated, anxious, apprehensive, disconcerted, disquieted, disturbed, jittery, jumpy, nervous, panicky, perturbed, skittish, uneasy, upset, worried; appalled, dismayed, shocked, startled; cowed, daunted, intimidated, unnerved; coward, cowardly, craven, gutless, lily-livered, pusillanimous; careful, cautious, heedful, prudent, unadventurous, wary
near antonyms adventuresome, adventurous, audacious, bold, daredevil, daring, dashing, gutsy, plucky, spirited, spunky, venturesome, venturous; brave, courageous, gallant, hardy, heroic, intrepid, lionhearted, manful, stalwart, stout, stouthearted, valiant, valorous; assured, collected, composed, confident, cool, sanguine, sure, unperturbed; dauntless, resolute, undaunted
antonyms fearless, unafraid
2 having doubts about the wisdom of doing something — see HESITANT

afresh *adv* yet another time — see AGAIN 1

aft *adv* near, toward, or in the stern of a ship or the tail of an aircraft ⟨after transferring the controls to the copilot, the captain went *aft* to see what the disturbance was⟩
synonyms abaft, astern
related words after, back, backward, behind, posteriorly, rearward (*also* rearwards), rearwardly
near antonyms anteriorly; ahead, before
antonyms fore, forward

after *adj* being, occurring, or carried out at a time after something else — see SUBSEQUENT

after *adv* following in time or place ⟨upon seeing *The Nutcracker* for the first time, and for a long time *after*, Irma wanted to play the part of the Mouse King⟩
synonyms afterward (*or* afterwards), later, subsequently, thereafter
related words next; by and by, hereafter, presently, since, soon, then, thereupon
near antonyms antecedently, formerly; heretofore, theretofore
antonyms afore [*chiefly dialect*], before, beforehand, earlier, previously

after *prep* subsequent to in time or order ⟨the high school band came right *after* the mayor in the parade⟩
synonyms behind, following
related words next; since
near antonyms of, to, toward (*or* towards)
antonyms afore [*chiefly dialect*], ahead of, before, ere, previous to, prior to

aftereffect *n* a condition or occurrence traceable to a cause — see EFFECT 1

afterlife *n* unending existence after death — see ETERNITY 2

aftermath *n* a condition or occurrence traceable to a cause — see EFFECT 1

afterward *or* **afterwards** *adv* following in time or place — see AFTER

again *adv* **1** yet another time ⟨now I have to mop the floor *again* because you didn't wipe your feet⟩
synonyms afresh, anew, over
related words always, constantly, continuously, endlessly, ever, evermore, perpetually; frequently, often; recurrently, repeatedly; freshly, newly
near antonyms ne'er, never
antonyms nevermore
2 in addition to what has been said — see MORE 1
3 just the opposite being true — see CONTRARI-WISE

against *prep* in or into contact with ⟨he leaned *against* the fence and it collapsed⟩ ⟨unwittingly rubbed his leg *against* some poison ivy⟩
synonyms on, upon
related words alongside, next, next to

agape *adj* having or showing signs of eagerly awaiting something — see EXPECTANT 1

age *n* **1** an extent of time associated with a particular person or thing ⟨the Bronze *Age* marks the beginning of the use of metal by ancient peoples⟩
synonyms day, epoch, era, period, time
related words cycle, generation, year; span, spell, stretch, while
2 a long or seemingly long period of time ⟨it took *ages* for the clerk to ring up three items⟩
synonyms aeon (*or* eon), cycle, eternity
related words infinity; lifetime
near antonyms flash, instant, jiffy, minute, moment, second, trice, twinkle, twinkling, wink; microsecond, nanosecond

age *vb* to become mature — see MATURE

aged *adj* **1** being of advanced years and especially past middle age — see ELDERLY
2 dating or surviving from the distant past — see ANCIENT 1

agency *n* something used to achieve an end — see AGENT 1

agenda *n* a listing of things to be presented or considered (as at a concert or play) — see PRO-GRAM 1

agent *n* **1** something used to achieve an end ⟨the whitening *agent* in the detergent is chlorine bleach⟩ ⟨the Church has been the traditional *agent* for social justice in impoverished countries⟩
synonyms agency, instrument, instrumentality, machinery, means, medium, organ, vehicle
related words determinant, expedient, factor, influence, ingredient, mechanism, tool; activator, catalyst, driver, energizer, executor, generator, instigator, launcher, mover, power, stimulus, trigger
2 a person who acts or does business for another ⟨the sports *agent* negotiated a record-breaking contract for the baseball player⟩
synonyms attorney, commissary, delegate, deputy, envoy, factor, procurator, proxy, representative
related words ambassador, emissary, foreign minister, legate, minister; alternate, backup, pinch hitter, relief, replacement, stand-in, sub, substitute, surrogate, understudy; informer, operative, spy; broker, distributor, manager; arbiter, arbitrator, go-between, intercessor, intermediary, interposer, liaison, mediator, middleman; mouthpiece, spokesperson

age–old *adj* dating or surviving from the distant past — see ANCIENT 1

agglomerate *vb* to form into a round compact mass — see WAD

aggrandize *vb* **1** to enhance the status of — see EXALT
2 to make greater in size, amount, or number — see INCREASE 1

aggravate *vb* to disturb the peace of mind of (someone) especially by repeated disagreeable acts — see IRRITATE 1

aggravating *adj* **1** causing annoyance — see ANNOYING

aggravation *n* **1** something that is a source of irritation — see ANNOYANCE 3
2 the act of making unwelcome intrusions upon another — see ANNOYANCE 1
3 the feeling of impatience or anger caused by another's repeated disagreeable acts — see ANNOYANCE 2

aggregate *n* a complete amount of something — see WHOLE

aggression *n* **1** an inclination to fight or quarrel — see BELLIGERENCE
2 the act or action of setting upon with force or violence — see ATTACK 1

aggressive *adj* **1** having or showing a bold forcefulness in the pursuit of a goal ⟨if you don't take a more *aggressive* approach to this yard pretty soon, the weeds are going to take over completely⟩
synonyms ambitious, assertive, enterprising, fierce, go-getting, high-pressure, in-your-face, militant, self-assertive
related words dynamic, energetic, gung ho, hustling, scrappy, strenuous, vigorous; emphatic, obtrusive; adventuresome, adventurous, venturesome, venturous; audacious, bold, brash, brassy, cheeky, cocksure, cocky, confident, determined, forward, impudent, insolent, overconfident, presumptuous, unapologetic, unsubdued, unyielding; dominating, domineering, imperious, lordly, magisterial, overbearing
near antonyms easygoing, laid-back, relaxed; acquiescent, compliant, deferential, resigned, submissive, yielding; cowering, cringing, groveling (*or* grovelling), shrinking; bashful, diffident, meek, mousy (*or* mousey), overmodest, passive, quiet, reserved, retiring, shy, subdued, timid, unobtrusive
antonyms low-pressure, unaggressive, unambitious, unassertive, unenterprising
2 feeling or displaying eagerness to fight — see BELLIGERENT
3 marked by or uttered with forcefulness — see EMPHATIC 1

aggressiveness *n* **1** readiness to engage in daring or difficult activity — see ENTERPRISE 2
2 the quality or state of being forceful (as in expression) — see VEHEMENCE 1
3 an inclination to fight or quarrel — see BELLIGERENCE

aggressor *n* one that starts armed conflict against another especially without reasonable cause ⟨the countries formed an alliance to deter potential *aggressors*⟩
synonyms invader, raider
related words initiator, instigator; ambuscader, assailant, attacker, pillager, plunderer; hawk, militarist, warmonger; belligerent, combatant
near antonyms defender; dove, pacifist, peacemaker; nonbelligerent

THESAURUS

aggrieved *adj* having a feeling that one has been wronged or thwarted in one's ambitions — see DISCONTENTED

aghast *adj* filled with fear or dread — see AFRAID 1

agile *adj* moving easily — see GRACEFUL 1

agility *n* ease and grace in physical activity — see DEXTERITY 2

aging *adj* being of advanced years and especially past middle age — see ELDERLY

agitate *vb* **1** to cause (as a liquid) to move about in a circle especially repeatedly — see STIR 1
2 to trouble the mind of; to make uneasy — see DISTURB 1
3 to make a series of small irregular or violent movements — see SHAKE 1

agitated *adj* **1** being in a state of increased activity or agitation — see FEVERISH 1
2 feeling overwhelming fear or worry — see FRANTIC 1

agitating *adj* marked by or causing agitation or uncomfortable feelings — see NERVOUS 2

agitation *n* **1** a state of wildly excited activity or emotion — see FRENZY
2 an uneasy state of mind usually over the possibility of an anticipated misfortune or trouble — see ANXIETY 1

agitator *n* a person who stirs up public feelings especially of discontent ⟨a political *agitator* who led an unsuccessful revolt against the government⟩
synonyms demagogue (*also* demagog), exciter, firebrand, fomenter, incendiary, inciter, instigator, rabble-rouser
related words demonstrator, marcher, objector, picketer, protester (*or* protestor); advocate, champion, exponent, persuader, promoter, proponent, reformer, supporter; alarmist, extremist, insurgent, insurrectionist, radical, rebel, revolter, revolutionary, revolutionist, subversive, troublemaker

aglow *adj* having or being an outward sign of good feelings (as of love, confidence, or happiness) — see RADIANT 1

agog *adj* **1** having or showing signs of eagerly awaiting something — see EXPECTANT 1
2 showing urgent desire or interest — see EAGER

agonize *vb* **1** to cause persistent suffering to — see AFFLICT
2 to feel deep sadness or mental pain — see GRIEVE

agonizing *adj* **1** hard to accept or bear especially emotionally — see BITTER 2
2 intensely or unbearably painful — see EXCRUCIATING 1
3 causing intense mental or physical distress — see SHARP 2

agonizingly *adv* with feelings of bitterness or grief — see HARD 2

agony *n* **1** a situation or state that causes great suffering and unhappiness — see HELL 2
2 a state of great suffering of body or mind — see DISTRESS 1
3 a sudden intense expression of strong feeling — see OUTBURST 1

agrarian *adj* engaged in or concerned with agriculture — see AGRICULTURAL

agree *vb* **1** to have or come to the same opinion or point of view ⟨since we couldn't *agree*, we tossed a coin to decide the matter⟩
synonyms coincide, concur
related words accede (to), accept, acquiesce, assent (to), comply (with), consent (to), go (by), subscribe; affiliate, ally, associate, unite; collaborate, cooperate, get along
phrases see eye to eye
near antonyms clash, collide, conflict; bicker, counter, dispute, dissent, diverge, fall out, object, oppose, protest, quarrel, resist, rival; dissociate, separate, split
antonyms differ, disagree
2 to accept the truth or existence of (something) usually reluctantly — see ADMIT
3 to be in agreement on every point — see CHECK 1
4 to form a pleasing relationship — see HARMONIZE 1

agreeable *adj* **1** being to one's liking — see SATISFACTORY 1
2 giving pleasure or contentment to the mind or senses — see PLEASANT
3 having an easygoing and pleasing manner especially in social situations — see AMIABLE
4 having or marked by agreement in feeling or action — see HARMONIOUS 3

agreeableness *n* the state or quality of having a pleasant or agreeable manner in socializing with others — see AMIABILITY 1

agreeably *adv* in a pleasing way — see WELL 5

agreement *n* **1** the act or fact of being of one opinion about something ⟨I only had the energy to nod in *agreement* when Cheryl said we'd never worked so hard in all our lives⟩
synonyms accord, concurrence, consensus, unanimity, unison
related words accession, assent, consent; acceptance, acquiescence, compliance, concession, conformity; approbation, approval, favor; alliance, collaboration, collusion, complicity, conspiracy; concord, consonance, harmony, oneness, solidarity, understanding, union; empathy, rapport, sympathy
near antonyms conflict, discord, dissension; opposition, resistance; disapprobation, disapproval, disfavor
antonyms disagreement, dissent
2 an arrangement about action to be taken ⟨we finally reached an *agreement* regarding a fair division of the housework⟩
synonyms accord, bargain, compact, contract, convention, covenant, deal, pact, settlement, understanding
related words charter, treaty; pledge, promise; alliance, association, league, partnership; acceptance, approval, assent, concurrence, consent, OK (*or* okay)
3 a state of consistency — see CONFORMITY 1

agricultural *adj* engaged in or concerned with agriculture ⟨he grew up in an *agricultural* community⟩
synonyms agrarian, farming
related words pastoral, rural
near antonyms metropolitan, urban; industrial, industrialized
antonyms nonagricultural

agriculture *n* the science or occupation of cultivating the soil, producing crops, and raising livestock ⟨the forest was cut down, and the land given over to *agriculture*⟩
synonyms farming, husbandry
related words agronomy; animal husbandry

agriculturist *or* **agriculturalist** *n* a person who cultivates the land and grows crops on it — see FARMER

agronomist *n* a person who cultivates the land and grows crops on it — see FARMER

aground *adj* resting on the shore or bottom of a body of water ⟨the villagers came to stare at the foreign ship that was *aground* on their beach and at the strangely dressed sailors on board⟩
synonyms beached, grounded, stranded
related words landed; alongshore
near antonyms offshore
antonyms afloat

ah *interj* how surprising, doubtful, or unbelievable — see NO

aha *interj* how surprising, doubtful, or unbelievable — see NO

ahead *adv* **1** so as to precede something in order of time ⟨we were cautioned not to fill out any of the test answers *ahead* of time⟩ ⟨call *ahead* for reservations⟩
synonyms afore [*chiefly dialect*], antecedently, anteriorly, before, beforehand, previously
related words formerly
phrases in advance
near antonyms behind, by and by, next, presently, subsequently
antonyms after, afterward (*or* afterwards), later

2 toward a point ahead in space or time — see ONWARD 1

3 toward or at a point lying in advance in space or time — see ALONG

ahead of *prep* **1** earlier than — see BEFORE 1

2 preceding in space — see BEFORE 2

aid *n* **1** a person who helps a more skilled person — see HELPER

2 a thing that helps — see HELP 2

3 an act or instance of helping — see HELP 1

aid *vb* to provide (someone) with what is useful or necessary to achieve an end — see HELP 1

aide *n* a person who helps a more skilled person — see HELPER

ailing *adj* **1** chronically or repeatedly suffering from poor health — see SICKLY 1

2 temporarily suffering from a disorder of the body — see SICK 1

ailment *n* an abnormal state that disrupts a plant's or animal's normal bodily functioning — see DISEASE

aim *n* something that one hopes or intends to accomplish — see GOAL

aim *vb* **1** to point or turn (something) toward a target or goal ⟨the anti-drug campaign was *aimed* primarily at preteens⟩
synonyms bend, cast, direct, head, level, set, train
related words bear, face; concentrate, focus; incline, orient, steer
near antonyms avert, curve, deflect, detour, divert, rechannel, shunt, sidetrack

2 to have in mind as a purpose or goal — see INTEND

aimless *adj* lacking a definite plan, purpose, or pattern — see RANDOM

aimlessly *adv* without definite aim, direction, rule, or method — see HIT OR MISS

air *n* **1** a rhythmic series of musical tones arranged to give a pleasing effect — see MELODY

2 a slight or gentle movement of air — see BREEZE 1

3 a special quality or impression associated with something — see AURA

4 **airs** *pl* a display of emotion or behavior that is insincere or intended to deceive — see MASQUERADE

air *vb* to make known (as an idea, emotion, or opinion) — see EXPRESS 1

airdrome *n* a place from which aircraft operate that usually has paved runways and a terminal — see AIRPORT

airfield *n* a place from which aircraft operate that usually has paved runways and a terminal — see AIRPORT

airman *n* one who flies or is qualified to fly an aircraft or spacecraft — see PILOT

airport *n* a place from which aircraft operate that usually has paved runways and a terminal ⟨the *airport* nearest us has plane service on only one major airline⟩
synonyms aerodrome [*British*], airdrome, airfield
related words air base, heliport; airstrip, landing field, landing strip, runway; launchpad, pad

airy *adj* **1** resembling air in lightness ⟨Aunt Helen's lemon pies are famous for their *airy* meringues⟩
synonyms ethereal, fluffy, gossamer, gossamery, light
related words dainty, delicate, downy, feathery, flimsy, insubstantial, tender, wispy; buoyant, lighter-than-air, lightweight, rarefied, unsubstantial, weightless
near antonyms firm, solid, substantial; bulky, burdensome, cumbersome, hefty, hulking, lumpish, ponderous, unwieldy, weighty
antonyms heavy, leaden

2 having little weight — see ¹LIGHT 1

3 located at a greater height than average or usual — see HIGH 3

akin *adj* **1** having a close connection like that between family members — see RELATED

2 having qualities in common — see ALIKE

alacritous *adj* having or showing the ability to respond without delay or hesitation — see QUICK 1

alacrity *n* cheerful readiness to do something ⟨having just acquired his driver's license that morning, Sam agreed with *alacrity* to drive his cousin to the airport⟩
synonyms amenability, gameness, goodwill, willingness
related words celebrity, quickness, rapidity, speed, speediness, swiftness; dispatch, promptitude, promptness; ardor, avidity, eagerness, enthusiasm, exuberance, fervor, gusto, keenness, relish, zeal, zest; agreeableness, geniality, good-naturedness, heartiness, warmth; open-mindedness, receptivity, responsiveness
near antonyms leisureliness, pokiness, slowness, sluggishness; apathy, disinterestedness, halfheartedness, indifference, lukewarmness, perfunctoriness; delay, dilatoriness, doubt, equivocation, hesitance, hesitancy, hesitation, reluctance, reservation, uncertainty, vacillation; disinclination, indisposition, recalcitrance, resistance, unwillingness; antipathy, averseness, aversion

à la mode *also* **a la mode** *adj* being in the latest or current fashion — see STYLISH

alarm *n* **1** suspicion or fear of future harm or misfortune — see APPREHENSION 1

2 the act or an instance of telling beforehand of danger or risk — see WARNING 1

3 the emotion experienced in the presence or threat of danger — see FEAR

alarm *vb* to strike with fear — see FRIGHTEN

alarmed *adj* filled with fear or dread — see AFRAID 1

alarming *adj* causing fear — see FEARFUL 1

albeit *conj* in spite of the fact that — see ALTHOUGH

album *n* a collection of writings — see ANTHOLOGY

alcohol *n* a fermented or distilled beverage that can make a person drunk ⟨once he joined the swim team, Sergei never again touched *alcohol*⟩
synonyms booze, drink, grog, intoxicant, liquor, moonshine, spirits
related words ale, beer, mead, sake (*or* saki), table wine, wine; brandy, gin, mescal, rum, tequila, vodka, whiskey (*or* whisky)

alcove *n* a hollowed-out space in a wall — see NICHE 1

alert *adj* **1** paying close attention usually for the purpose of anticipating approaching danger or opportunity ⟨Susan needed to stay *alert* throughout the train ride so as not to miss her stop⟩
synonyms attentive, awake, open-eyed, vigilant, watchful, wide-awake
related words alive, aware, conscious, sensitive; heedful, mindful, observant, observing, sharp, sharp-eyed; sleepless, wakeful; careful, cautious, chary, wary; prepared, ready
phrases on guard, on the alert
near antonyms absent, absentminded, absorbed, abstracted, daydreaming, dazed, distracted, dreaming, dreamy, engrossed, faraway, insensible, oblivious, preoccupied; asleep, sleeping, unaware, unconscious, unknowing, unperceiving, unseeing, unwitting; careless, heedless, inattentive, unheeding, unmindful, unobservant, unobserving, unthinking, unwary; unprepared, unready
2 having or showing a close attentiveness to avoiding danger or trouble — see CAREFUL 1
3 having or showing quickness of mind — see INTELLIGENT 1
4 having or showing the ability to respond without delay or hesitation — see QUICK 1

alert *n* the act or an instance of telling beforehand of danger or risk — see WARNING 1

alert *vb* to give notice to beforehand especially of danger or risk — see WARN

alertness *n* **1** a close attentiveness to avoiding danger — see CAUTION 1
2 the act or state of being constantly attentive and responsive to signs of opportunity, activity, or danger — see VIGILANCE

alias *n* **1** a descriptive or familiar name given instead of or in addition to the one belonging to an individual — see NICKNAME
2 a fictitious or assumed name — see PSEUDONYM

alibi *n* an explanation that frees one from fault or blame — see EXCUSE

alien *adj* **1** being, relating to, or characteristic of a country other than one's own — see FOREIGN 1
2 not being a vital part of or belonging to something — see EXTRINSIC

alienate *vb* **1** to cause to change from friendly or loving to unfriendly or uncaring — see ESTRANGE
2 to give over the legal possession or ownership of — see TRANSFER 1

alienation *n* the loss of friendship or affection — see ESTRANGEMENT

alight *adj* filled with much light — see BRIGHT 2

alight *vb* to come to rest after descending from the air ⟨a flock of eight swans circled above, then *alighted* on the pond⟩
synonyms land, light, perch, roost, settle, touch down
related words belly-land, crash-land
near antonyms arise, ascend, climb, rise; float, fly, glide, plane, soar, wing; hang, hover
antonyms take off

alike *adj* having qualities in common ⟨all the houses in the neighborhood are *alike* in that they all have a one-car garage and a fenced-in backyard⟩
synonyms akin, analogous, comparable, correspondent, corresponding, like, matching, parallel, resembling, similar, such, suchlike
related words commensurate, proportionate; tantamount, virtual; allied, kindred, related; approaching, approximating, close, coextensive, coincident, conformable, conforming, consistent, consonant, equal, equivalent, identical, indistinguishable, interchangeable, same, selfsame, synonymous, twin; homogeneous, unchanging, uniform, unvaried, unvarying
phrases on the order of
near antonyms disparate, distinct, distinguishable; variable, varied, varying; imprecise, inaccurate, inexact; unallied, unconnected, unrelated
antonyms different, dissimilar, diverse, unlike

alike *adv* in like manner — see ALSO 1

alikeness *n* the quality or state of having many qualities in common — see SIMILARITY 1

alive *adj* **1** having or showing life ⟨after crashing into the plate glass window the little bird was not only still *alive*, it seemed merely dazed⟩
synonyms animate, breathing, live, living
related words active, animated, dynamic, lively, thriving, vibrant, vital, vivacious; current, existent, existing, extant, going, prevailing, surviving
near antonyms dying, fading, moribund; stillborn; absent, extinct, fallen, finished, gone, lapsed, lost, nonexistent, perished, terminated, vanished, wiped out; barren, desert
antonyms breathless, dead, deceased, defunct, departed, expired, inanimate, lifeless, nonliving
2 marked by much life, movement, or activity ⟨the mall was *alive* with holiday shoppers⟩
synonyms animated, astir, bustling, busy, buzzing, flourishing, humming, lively, thriving, vibrant
related words abounding, crowded, overflowing, populous, swarming, teeming, thronging
antonyms asleep, dead, inactive, lifeless, sleepy
3 being in effective operation — see ACTIVE 1
4 having being at the present time — see EXTANT 1
5 having specified facts or feelings actively impressed on the mind — see CONSCIOUS

all *adj* not divided or scattered among several areas of interest or concern — see WHOLE 1

all *adv* **1** to a full extent or degree — see FULLY 1
2 for each one — see APIECE

all *pron* every person — see EVERYBODY

Allah *n* the being worshipped as the creator and ruler of the universe — see DEITY 2

all–around *also* **all-round** *adj* **1** not limited or specialized in application or purpose — see GENERAL 4
2 relating to the main elements and not to specific details — see GENERAL 2
3 able to do many different kinds of things — see VERSATILE

allay *vb* **1** to free from distress or disturbance — see CALM 1

2 to make more bearable or less severe — see HELP 2

allege *vb* to state as a fact usually forcefully — see CLAIM 1

allegiance *n* adherence to something to which one is bound by a pledge or duty — see FIDELITY

allegory *n* a story intended to teach a basic truth or moral about life ⟨Dr. Seuss's story "The Sneetches" is an *allegory* about tolerance for people's differences⟩

synonyms fable, parable

related words morality play; legend, myth, narrative, tale

allergic *adj* having a natural dislike for something — see ANTIPATHETIC

allergy *n* a strong feeling of not liking or approving — see DISLIKE 1

alleviate *vb* to make more bearable or less severe — see HELP 2

alleviation *n* reduction of or freedom from pain — see EASE 1

alliance *n* **1** a formal agreement between two or more nations or peoples — see TREATY

2 an association of persons, parties, or states for mutual assistance and protection — see CONFEDERACY

3 the state of having shared interests or efforts (as in social or business matters) — see ASSOCIATION 1

allied *adj* having a close connection like that between family members — see RELATED

all–important *adj* impossible to do without — see ESSENTIAL 1

allocate *vb* **1** to give as a share or portion — see ALLOT

2 to give out (something) in appropriate amounts or to appropriate individuals — see ADMINISTER 1

3 to keep or intend for a special purpose — see DEVOTE 1

allocation *n* **1** a sum of money allotted for a specific use by official or formal action — see APPROPRIATION

2 the act or process of giving out something to each member of a group — see DISTRIBUTION 1

allot *vb* to give as a share or portion ⟨each speaker was *allotted* five minutes to present his or her opinion in the debate⟩

synonyms allocate, allow, apportion, assign, ration

related words deal, dispense, distribute, divide, dole (out), measure, mete (out), parcel (out), portion, prorate, reserve; accord, award, grant; chip in, contribute, donate

near antonyms begrudge, deny, deprive (of); keep, retain, stint, withhold; appropriate, arrogate, confiscate

allotment *n* **1** a sum of money allotted for a specific use by official or formal action — see APPROPRIATION

2 something belonging to, due to, or contributed by an individual member of a group — see SHARE 1

all–out *adj* **1** having no exceptions or restrictions — see ABSOLUTE 2

2 trying all possibilities — see EXHAUSTIVE

all out *adv* with all power or resources being used — see FULL BLAST

all over *adv* in every place or in all places — see EVERYWHERE

allow *vb* **1** to give permission for or to approve of ⟨flash photography is not *allowed* inside the church⟩

synonyms have, permit, suffer

related words authorize, commission, license (*also* licence); accede (to), acquiesce, agree (to), assent (to), consent (to), OK (*or* okay), warrant; accord, concede, grant, sanction, vouchsafe; admit, brook, condone, countenance, endure, support, tolerate

near antonyms hinder, impede, obstruct; censure, disallow, disapprove, deny, interdict, refuse, reject, revoke, suppress, withhold; deplore, discountenance, dislike, disfavor, frown (at *or* on); check, curb, repress, restrain

antonyms ban, enjoin, forbid, prohibit, proscribe, veto

2 to give permission to ⟨Cindy's parents sometimes *allow* her to take the bus by herself downtown⟩

synonyms let, permit, suffer

related words authorize, commission, empower, license (*also* licence); approve, endorse (*also* indorse), sanction; free, liberate, release; cater (to), give in (to), humor, indulge

near antonyms deter, discourage; bar, block, constrain, curb, frustrate, hold back, impede, inhibit, obstruct, prevent

antonyms enjoin, forbid, prohibit

3 to accept the truth or existence of (something) usually reluctantly — see ADMIT

4 to give as a share or portion — see ALLOT

5 to make able or possible — see ENABLE 1

allowable *adj* that may be permitted — see PERMISSIBLE

allowance *n* **1** something belonging to, due to, or contributed by an individual member of a group — see SHARE 1

2 the approval by someone in authority for the doing of something — see PERMISSION

alloyed *adj* containing foreign or lower-grade substances — see IMPURE

all–powerful *adj* having unlimited power or authority — see OMNIPOTENT

all–purpose *adj* not limited or specialized in application or purpose — see GENERAL 4

all right *adj* **1** being to one's liking — see SATISFACTORY 1

2 not exposed to the threat of loss or injury — see SAFE 1

3 of a level of quality that meets one's needs or standards — see ADEQUATE

all right *adv* **1** in a satisfactory way — see WELL 1

2 used to express agreement — see YES

allude *vb* to convey an idea indirectly — see HINT

allure *n* the power of irresistible attraction — see CHARM 2

allure *vb* **1** to attract or delight as if by magic — see CHARM 1

2 to lead away from a usual or proper course by offering some pleasure or advantage — see LURE

allurement *n* **1** something that persuades one to perform an action for pleasure or gain — see LURE 1

2 the act or pressure of giving in to a desire especially when ill-advised — see TEMPTATION 1

alluring *adj* having an often mysterious or magical power to attract — see FASCINATING 1

THESAURUS

ally *n* someone associated with another to give assistance or moral support ⟨in trying to convince his parents to send him to soccer camp, Toby had a real *ally* in his coach⟩

synonyms abettor (*also* abetter), backer, confederate, supporter, sympathizer

related words well-wisher; accessory, accomplice, collaborationist, collaborator; adjunct, assistant, coadjutor, helper; associate, cohort, colleague, fellow, partner; buddy, chum, companion, comrade, confidant, crony, familiar, friend, intimate, mate, pal

near antonyms belittler, detractor; adversary, enemy, foe, opponent

ally *vb* to form or enter into an association that furthers the interests of its members ⟨the area's small grape growers have *allied* and formed a cooperative that will help them get the best prices⟩

synonyms associate, band, club, confederate, conjoin, cooperate, federate, league, unite

related words collaborate, gang (up), team (up); incorporate, organize, unionize; affiliate; amalgamate, combine, conglomerate, consolidate, converge, group, join, merge; knot, link, tie, wed

near antonyms detach, disengage, dissolve, disunite, divorce, part, segregate, separate, sever, split, sunder; alienate, estrange, fall out

antonyms break up, disband

almighty *adj* having unlimited power or authority — see OMNIPOTENT

Almighty *n* the being worshipped as the creator and ruler of the universe — see DEITY 2

almost *adv* very close to but not completely ⟨we were *almost* finished with dinner when Uncle Richard showed up⟩ ⟨there was *almost* enough seats for everybody on the bus⟩

synonyms about, more or less, most, much, near, nearly, next to, nigh, practically, some, virtually, well-nigh

related words appreciably, by and large, chiefly, largely, mainly, mostly; partially, partly, somewhat

phrases as good as

near antonyms absolutely, altogether, completely, entirely, fully, plumb [*chiefly dialect*], quite, thoroughly; totally, utterly, wholly; barely, hardly, scarcely

alms *n* a gift of money or its equivalent to a charity, humanitarian cause, or public institution — see CONTRIBUTION

almsgiving *n* the giving of necessities and especially money to the needy — see CHARITY 1

aloft *adv* to or in a higher place — see ABOVE

alone *adj* 1 not being in the company of others ⟨no one realized Jeff was *alone* in his room so they all left for the movies without him⟩

synonyms lone, lonely, lonesome, solitary, solo, unaccompanied

related words unattended, unchaperoned; forlorn, friendless; cloistered, insulated, isolated, remote, retired, secluded, withdrawn; quarantined, segregated, separated, sequestered; separate, unattached, unconnected, unlinked; detached, disconnected, disjointed, dissociated, disunited, divided, fractionated; abandoned, adrift, deserted, desolate, forgotten, forsaken, lorn, neglected

near antonyms attended, chaperoned, escorted; adjacent, adjoining, communicating, contiguous, neighboring, next-door; attached, connected, coupled, linked

antonyms accompanied

2 being the one or ones of a class with no other members — see ONLY 2

alone *adv* 1 without aid or support ⟨Rebecca managed to find her way home *alone*⟩

synonyms independently, single-handedly, singly, solely, unaided, unassisted

related words individually, separately

phrases by oneself

near antonyms collectively, conjointly, cooperatively, jointly, mutually, together; en masse

2 for nothing other than — see SOLELY 1

along *adv* toward or at a point lying in advance in space or time ⟨traffic was inching *along* at a snail's pace⟩ ⟨work on the project is moving right *along*⟩

synonyms ahead, forth, forward, on, onward (*also* onwards)

related words before

near antonyms back, backward (*or* backwards), behind, rearward (*or* rearwards)

aloof *adj* having or showing a lack of friendliness or interest in others — see COOL 1

aloud *adv* with one's normal voice speaking the words ⟨Mr. Gripp likes to call on the sleepiest-looking students to read *aloud* from the textbook⟩

synonyms audibly, out, out loud

related words clearly, discernibly, distinctly, distinguishably, perceptibly, plainly; blatantly, boisterously, clamorously, loudly, lustily, mightily, noisily, resoundingly, stridently, thunderously, uproariously, vociferously

near antonyms faintly, feebly, low, noiselessly, quietly, softly

antonyms inaudibly, silently, soundlessly

alp *n* an elevation of land higher than a hill — see MOUNTAIN 1

alpha *n* the point at which something begins — see BEGINNING

alright *adj* 1 being to one's liking — see SATISFACTORY 1

2 not exposed to the threat of loss or injury — see SAFE 1

alright *adv* used to express agreement — see YES

also *adv* 1 in like manner ⟨we stayed at an historic London hotel, the same establishment that had *also* welcomed our grandparents many years ago⟩

synonyms alike, correspondingly, likewise, similarly, so

related words equally, equivalently, identically

near antonyms contrarily, conversely, inversely, oppositely, vice versa; diversely, unequally, variously

antonyms differently, dissimilarly, otherwise

2 in addition to what has been said — see MORE 1

alter *vb* 1 to make different in some way — see CHANGE 1

2 to remove the sex organs of — see NEUTER

alterable *adj* capable of being readily changed — see FLEXIBLE 1

alteration *n* the act, process, or result of making different — see CHANGE

altercation *n* an often noisy or angry expression of differing opinions — see ARGUMENT 1

alternative *n* the power, right, or opportunity to choose — see CHOICE 1

although *also* **altho** *conj* in spite of the fact that ⟨*although* I've been to his house several times, I still can't remember how to get there⟩

synonyms albeit, howbeit, though, when, while, whilst [*chiefly British*]

related words but, whereas

altitude *n* **1** the distance of something or someone from bottom to top — see HEIGHT 3
2 the most extreme or advanced point — see HEIGHT 2
3 *usually* **altitudes** *pl* an area of high ground — see HEIGHT 4

altogether *adv* **1** for the most part — see CHIEFLY 1
2 to a full extent or degree — see FULLY 1

altruistic *adj* having or showing a concern for the welfare of others — see CHARITABLE 1

always *adv* **1** on every relevant occasion ⟨Aunt Trina *always* insists we stay for dinner⟩
synonyms consistently, constantly, continually, ever, forever, incessantly, invariably, perpetually, unfailingly
related words commonly, frequently, oft, often, oftentimes (*or* ofttimes), recurrently, repeatedly; continuously, steadily, uninterruptedly; dependably, normally, ordinarily, regularly, routinely, typically, usually; inevitably; eternally, everlastingly
near antonyms intermittently, occasionally, periodically, sometimes, sporadically; infrequently, rarely, seldom, unusually
antonyms ne'er, never
2 for all time — see EVER 1

amalgam *n* a distinct entity formed by the combining of two or more different things — see BLEND

amalgamate *vb* **1** to mix thoroughly so that the things mixed cannot be recognized — see BLEND 1
2 to turn into a single mass that is more or less the same throughout — see BLEND 1

amalgamated *adj* made from the joining of two or more parts or elements — see COMPOSITE

amalgamation *n* a distinct entity formed by the combining of two or more different things — see BLEND

amass *vb* to bring together in one body or place — see GATHER 1

amateur *adj* lacking or showing a lack of expert skill — see AMATEURISH

amateur *n* a person who regularly or occasionally engages in an activity without being or becoming an expert at it ⟨a homemade doghouse that looked like it was built by an *amateur* who hadn't mastered basic carpentry⟩
synonyms dabbler, dilettante, potterer, putterer
related words apprentice, trainee; beginner, freshman, greenhorn, learner, neophyte, newcomer, novice, rookie, tenderfoot, tyro; hobbyist, tinkerer, trifler; layman, nonprofessional
near antonyms authority, pro, professional; maestro, virtuoso, whiz, wizard; artisan, artist, craftsman, workman; initiate, journeyman; specialist, technician; old hand, old-timer, vet, veteran
antonyms ace, adept, crackerjack, expert, master, past master

amateurish *adj* lacking or showing a lack of expert skill ⟨that's an *amateurish* wallpapering job—the pattern doesn't match at the seams⟩
synonyms amateur, dilettante, inexperienced, inexpert, nonprofessional, unprofessional, unskilled, unskillful
related words primitive, self-taught, uninitiated, unprepared, unqualified, unschooled, untaught, untrained, untutored; clumsy, crude, defective, faulty, flawed, unfinished, unpolished; beginning, green, new, raw, unpracticed, unseasoned, un-

tested, untried; incapable, incompetent, unable, unfit, ungifted, untalented
near antonyms able, accomplished, capable, competent, dexterous (*also* dextrous), gifted, proficient, skilled, skillful, talented; experienced, practiced (*or* practised), seasoned, veteran; educated, fitted, initiated, knowledgeable, prepared, qualified, schooled, taught, trained, tutored, versed; all-around (*also* all-round), versatile, well-rounded; finished, polished
antonyms ace, adept, consummate, crackerjack, expert, master, masterful, masterly, professional, virtuoso

amatory *adj* of, relating to, or expressing sexual attraction — see EROTIC

amaze *vb* to make a strong impression on (someone) with something unexpected — see SURPRISE 1

amazed *adj* **1** affected with sudden and great wonder or surprise — see THUNDERSTRUCK
2 filled with amazement or wonder — see OPEN-MOUTHED

amazement *n* **1** the rapt attention and deep emotion caused by the sight of something extraordinary — see WONDER 1
2 the state of being strongly impressed by something unexpected or unusual — see SURPRISE 2

amazing *adj* **1** causing a strong emotional reaction because unexpected — see SURPRISING 1
2 causing wonder or astonishment — see MARVELOUS 1

ambassador *n* a person sent on a mission to represent another ⟨a beloved entertainer who has often been sent abroad by the president as his country's goodwill *ambassador*⟩
synonyms delegate, emissary, envoy, minister, legate, representative
related words agent, attaché, consul, deputy, diplomat, foreign minister, nuncio, procurator, proxy; apostle, evangelist, missionary; deputation, detachment, legation; courier, messenger; mouthpiece, spokesperson

ambiguity *n* the quality or state of having a veiled or uncertain meaning — see OBSCURITY 1

ambiguous *adj* having an often intentionally veiled or uncertain meaning — see OBSCURE 1

ambiguousness *n* the quality or state of having a veiled or uncertain meaning — see OBSCURITY 1

ambition *n* **1** eager desire for personal advancement ⟨"Talent without *ambition* will not make you a star," McKenzie's dance instructor liked to remind her⟩
synonyms aspiration, go-getting
related words determination, diligence, drive, energy, enterprise, go, hustle, industry, initiative, motivation, push; opportunism; aggression, assertiveness, daring, spirit; ardor, avidity, eagerness, keenness, passion; avarice, greed
near antonyms apathy, indifference, unconcern; idleness, indolence, inertia, laziness, lethargy, shiftlessness, sloth
2 readiness to engage in daring or difficult activity — see ENTERPRISE 2
3 something that one hopes or intends to accomplish — see GOAL

ambitious *adj* **1** having a strong desire for personal advancement ⟨an *ambitious* child actor and his even more ambitious mother, who will do anything to get him in commercials⟩
synonyms aspiring, go-getting, self-seeking

related words determined, diligent, driving, dynamic, enterprising, gung ho, hustling, industrious, motivated, scrappy, venturesome, venturous; animated, lively, spirited; ardent, avid, eager, energetic, impassioned, keen, raring, vigorous; aggressive, assertive, opportunistic, pushy, self-assertive

near antonyms apathetic, disinterested, indifferent, uneager, unenthusiastic, unexcited, uninterested; casual, easygoing, lackadaisical; halfhearted, lukewarm, tepid; lazy, lethargic, listless, shiftless, sluggish, spiritless; unaggressive, unassertive

2 having or showing a bold forcefulness in the pursuit of a goal — see AGGRESSIVE 1

ambrosial *adj* **1** having a pleasant smell — see FRAGRANT

2 very pleasing to the sense of taste — see DELICIOUS 1

ambuscade *n* a scheme in which hidden persons wait to attack by surprise — see AMBUSH 1

ambush *n* **1** a scheme in which hidden persons wait to attack by surprise ⟨revolutionaries laid an *ambush* for the king along the route his carriage would travel⟩

synonyms ambuscade, surprise, trap

related words assault, attack, charge, sally; capture, entrapment, snare; hunting, stalking

2 a device or scheme for capturing another by surprise — see TRAP 1

ambush *vb* to lie in wait for and attack by surprise ⟨the king's enemies planned to *ambush* the royal coach on the way to Paris and capture the king⟩

synonyms surprise, waylay

related words assail, assault, attack, storm, strike; jump, pounce (on), tackle; charge, sally; capture, ensnare, entrap, net, snare, trap; hunt, prey (on *or* upon), stalk

phrases lay for

ameliorate *vb* to make better — see IMPROVE

amenability *n* **1** a desire or disposition to please — see COMPLAISANCE

2 cheerful readiness to do something — see ALACRITY

amenable *adj* **1** having a desire or inclination (as for a specified course of action) — see WILLING 1

2 readily giving in to the command or authority of another — see OBEDIENT

amend *vb* **1** to make better — see IMPROVE

2 to remove errors, defects, deficiencies, or deviations from — see CORRECT 1

amendment *n* a change designed to correct or improve a written work — see CORRECTION 1

amenity *n* **1** an act or utterance that is a customary show of good manners — see CIVILITY 1

2 something adding to pleasure or comfort but not absolutely necessary — see LUXURY 1

3 something that adds to one's ease — see COMFORT 2

4 the state or quality of having a pleasant or agreeable manner in socializing with others — see AMIABILITY 1

American Indian *n* a member of any of the native peoples of the western hemisphere usually not including the Eskimos ⟨Jeremy's great-grandfather was an *American Indian*, a member of the Shoshones⟩

synonyms Amerindian (*also* Amerind), Indian, Native American

related words mestizo

Amerindian *also* **Amerind** *n* a member of any of the native peoples of the western hemisphere usually not including the Eskimos — see AMERICAN INDIAN

amiability *n* **1** the state or quality of having a pleasant or agreeable manner in socializing with others ⟨the waitress's *amiability* is what makes eating at the diner so much fun⟩

synonyms affability, agreeableness, amenity, amiableness, geniality, good-naturedness, good-temperedness, graciousness, niceness, pleasantness, sweetness

related words amenability, complaisance; amicability, amity, cordiality, friendliness; benignity, gentleness, kindness; cheerfulness, cheeriness, sunniness; civility, comity, considerateness, consideration, courteousness, courtesy, politeness, thoughtfulness; attractiveness, delightfulness, enjoyableness

near antonyms boorishness, discourtesy, impoliteness, incivility, rudeness, ungraciousness; biliousness, cantankerousness, churlishness, crankiness, fussiness, grouchiness, grumpiness, irascibility, irritability, peevishness, petulance, testiness; contentiousness, contrariness, orneriness, querulousness; hostility, unfriendliness

antonyms disagreeableness, unpleasantness

2 a desire or disposition to please — see COMPLAISANCE

amiable *adj* having an easygoing and pleasing manner especially in social situations ⟨the owner of the inn is an *amiable*, talkative widow who treats guests like family⟩

synonyms affable, agreeable, genial, good-natured, good-tempered, gracious, nice, sweet, well-disposed

related words amicable, cordial, friendly, neighborly; benign, gentle, kind; cheerful, cheery, sunny; companionable, sociable; civil, considerate, courteous, polite, thoughtful; accommodating, amenable, obliging; attractive, delightful, enjoyable

near antonyms boorish, discourteous, ill-mannered, impolite, inconsiderate, rude, surly, uncivil, unmannerly; bearish, bilious, cantankerous, choleric, churlish, crabby, cranky, dyspeptic, fussy, grouchy, grumpy, ill-humored, irascible, irritable, peevish, petulant, quick-tempered, snappish, testy, touchy; argumentative, contentious, contrary, ornery, querulous; unappealing, unattractive

antonyms disagreeable, ill-natured, ill-tempered, ungracious, unpleasant

amiableness *n* the state or quality of having a pleasant or agreeable manner in socializing with others — see AMIABILITY 1

amicable *adj* **1** having or marked by agreement in feeling or action — see HARMONIOUS 3

2 having or showing kindly feeling and sincere interest — see FRIENDLY 1

amid *or* **amidst** *prep* in or into the middle of — see AMONG

amiss *adv* **1** in a mistaken or inappropriate way — see WRONGLY

2 off the desired or intended path or course — see WRONG 1

amity *n* kindly concern, interest, or support — see GOODWILL 1

ammunition *n* means or method of defending — see DEFENSE 1

amnesty *n* release from the guilt or penalty of an offense — see PARDON

amok *or* **amuck** *adv* in a confused and reckless manner — see HELTER-SKELTER 1

among *also* **amongst** *prep* in or into the middle of ⟨a gull landed *among* the burgers-and-fries eaters at the outdoor snack bar, clearly looking for handouts⟩
synonyms amid (*or* amidst), mid, midst, through
related words between, betwixt
phrases in the thick of
near antonyms from, out of

amorous *adj* of, relating to, or expressing sexual attraction — see EROTIC

amorphous *adj* having no definite or recognizable form — see FORMLESS

amount *n* a given or particular mass or aggregate of matter ⟨is this small *amount* of food supposed to feed the whole hockey team?⟩
synonyms measure, quantity, volume
related words body, portion; many, number

amount (to) *vb* 1 to have a total of ⟨the expenses of the trip *amounted to* nearly double what we'd budgeted for⟩
synonyms add up (to), come (to), number, sum (to *or* into), total
related words average, equal, measure, reach; aggregate, comprise
2 to be the same in meaning or effect ⟨it makes no difference whether you're going to the game or to the movies, for it *amounts to* your unavailability for babysitting⟩
synonyms add up (to), come (to), correspond (to), equal
related words approach, match, measure (up), meet, rival, touch; connote, denote, express, import, mean, signify, smack (of), spell, suggest

ample *adj* 1 being more than enough without being excessive — see PLENTIFUL
2 more than adequate or average in capacity — see SPACIOUS

amplify *vb* 1 to express more fully and in greater detail — see EXPAND 1
2 to make greater in size, amount, or number — see INCREASE 1
3 to make markedly greater in measure or degree — see INTENSIFY

amplitude *n* an area over which activity, capacity, or influence extends — see RANGE 2

amulet *n* something worn or kept to bring good luck or keep away evil — see CHARM 1

amuse *vb* to cause (someone) to pass the time agreeably occupied ⟨Christie *amused* her four-year-old sister at the family reunion by showing her off to all the relatives⟩
synonyms disport, divert, entertain, regale
related words absorb, busy, distract, engage, engross, immerse, interest, involve, occupy; beguile, bewitch, captivate, charm, delight, enchant, enthrall (*or* enthral), fascinate; grip, hypnotize, intrigue, mesmerize; coddle, gratify, humor, indulge, mollycoddle, pamper, please, pleasure, spoil; appease, comfort, conciliate, console, content, mollify, oblige, pacify, placate, propitiate, soothe
near antonyms bore, jade; drain, enervate, exhaust, fatigue, tire, wear, wear out, weary; aggravate, annoy, bother, bug, chafe, disturb, exasperate, fret, gall, grate, harass, harry, irk, nettle, peeve, perturb, pester, pique, upset, vex

amusement *n* the act or activity of providing pleasure or amusement especially for the public — see ENTERTAINMENT 1

amusing *adj* providing amusement or enjoyment — see FUN

analgesic *n* something (as a drug) that relieves pain — see PAINKILLER

analogous *adj* having qualities in common — see ALIKE

analysis *n* 1 the separation and identification of the parts of a whole ⟨investigators took the mysterious powder to the lab for *analysis*⟩
synonyms anatomizing, assay, breakdown, dissection
related words assessment, evaluation, examination, inspection, investigation, scrutiny; arrangement, assortment, cataloging (*or* cataloguing), categorization, classification, codification, indexing; enumeration, inventory, itemization, tabulation; division, reduction, segmentation, separation, subdivision
near antonyms agglomeration, aggregation, amalgamation, assimilation, coalescence, conglomeration, consolidation, integration, synthesis, unification
2 a series of explanations or observations on something (as an event) — see COMMENTARY

analytic *or* **analytical** *adj* according to the rules of logic — see LOGICAL 1

analyze *vb* to identify and examine the basic elements or parts of (something) especially for discovering interrelationships ⟨*analyze* the park's ecosystem before deciding whether hunting should be allowed⟩
synonyms anatomize, assay, break down, dissect
related words assess, evaluate, examine, inspect, investigate, scrutinize; arrange, assort, catalog (*or* catalogue), categorize, classify, codify, diagram, index, order, schematize, sort, tabulate; divide, reduce, segment, separate, subdivide
near antonyms agglomerate, aggregate, amalgamate, assimilate, coalesce, conglomerate, consolidate, integrate, synthesize, unify

anarchic *adj* not restrained by or under the control of legal authority — see LAWLESS

anarchy *n* a state in which there is widespread wrongdoing and disregard for rules and authority ⟨the *anarchy* that the country experienced after the dictator drained the treasury and fled the country⟩
synonyms lawlessness, misrule
related words commotion, tumult, uproar; chaos, confusion, disarray, disorder, disorderliness, disorganization; disruption, disturbance, havoc, riot, strife, turbulence, turmoil, unrest, upheaval; mutiny, rebellion, revolution, uprising; criminality, outlawry
near antonyms law, lawfulness, legality, legitimacy, rule; calmness, harmony, order, orderliness, peace, peacefulness, quiet, tranquillity (*or* tranquility)

anathema *n* 1 a prayer that harm will come to someone — see CURSE 1
2 something or someone that is hated — see HATE 2

anatomize *vb* to identify and examine the basic elements or parts of (something) especially for discovering interrelationships — see ANALYZE

anatomizing *n* the separation and identification of the parts of a whole — see ANALYSIS 1

ancestor *n* **1** a person who is several generations earlier in an individual's line of descent ⟨Bridie's Irish *ancestors* immigrated to the United States in the 19th century during the Great Potato Famine⟩

synonyms father, forebear (*also* forbear), forefather, grandfather

related words grandmother, matriarch, patriarch; ancestry, antecedents

near antonyms children, issue, offspring, posterity, progeny, seed; heir, inheritor, son, successor

antonyms descendant (*or* descendent)

2 something belonging to an earlier time from which something else was later developed ⟨pinball machines—the *ancestors* of today's video games—go back to the 19th century⟩

synonyms antecedent, foregoer, forerunner, precursor, predecessor

related words archetype, model, original, prototype; father, mother

near antonyms by-product, derivative, offshoot, outgrowth, spin-off; daughter, son

antonyms descendant (*or* descendent)

ancestry *n* the line of ancestors from whom a person is descended ⟨a Cambodian immigrant who can trace her Khmer *ancestry* as far back as the 16th century⟩

synonyms birth, blood, bloodline, breeding, descent, extraction, family tree, genealogy, line, lineage, origin, parentage, pedigree, stock, strain

related words heredity, succession; family, house; kin, kindred, relations, relatives; race

near antonyms offspring; child, heir, inheritor, son, successor

antonyms issue, posterity, progeny, seed

anchor *n* one who reads and introduces news reports on a news program — see ANCHORPERSON

anchor *vb* **1** to put securely in place or in a desired position — see FASTEN 2

2 to stop at or near a place along the shore — see LAND 1

anchorage *n* a part of a body of water protected and deep enough to be a place of safety for ships — see HARBOR 1

anchorite *n* a person who lives away from others — see RECLUSE

anchorperson *n* one who reads and introduces news reports on a news program ⟨the new *anchorperson* did an admirable job of dealing with the late-breaking news story⟩

synonyms anchor

related words anchorman, anchorwoman; broadcaster, newscaster, telecaster; correspondent, interviewer, reporter; journalist, newsman

ancient *adj* **1** dating or surviving from the distant past ⟨Rome's *ancient* ruins are carefully preserved in the midst of the bustle of the modern city⟩

synonyms aged, age-old, antediluvian, antique, dateless, hoar, hoary, old, venerable

related words aging, mature; antiquated, obsolete, outmoded, out-of-date, passé; old-fashioned, old-time, old-world; durable, enduring, lasting, long-lived, permanent; ageless, hallowed, time-honored, timeless, time-tested, traditional, tried, tried-and-true; classic, classical; prehistoric, primeval, primordial

near antonyms fresh, young, youthful; contemporary, current, latest, mod, novel, present-day, ultramodern; untested, untried; brand-new, unused, unworn

antonyms modern, new, recent

2 being of advanced years and especially past middle age — see ELDERLY

3 relating to or occurring near the beginning of a process, series, or time period — see EARLY 1

ancient *n* a person of advanced years — see SENIOR CITIZEN

anecdote *n* a brief account of something interesting that happened especially to one personally — see STORY 2

anesthetic *n* something (as a drug) that relieves pain — see PAINKILLER

anew *adv* yet another time — see AGAIN 1

angel *n* **1** an innocent or gentle person — see LAMB

2 one that announces or indicates the later arrival of another — see FORERUNNER 1

anger *n* an intense emotional state of displeasure with someone or something ⟨Dave stifled his *anger* when the kids on the bus made fun of him⟩

synonyms angriness, furor, fury, indignation, irateness, ire, outrage, rage, spleen, wrath, wrathfulness

related words aggravation, annoyance, exasperation, irritation, vexation; animosity, antagonism, antipathy, bile, bitterness, contempt, enmity, grudge, hostility, rancor; envy, jaundice, jealousy, pique, resentment; malevolence, malice, spite, venom, virulence, vitriol; belligerence, contentiousness, contrariness, disputatiousness, orneriness, pugnacity, querulousness; blowup, flare-up, outburst; dander, dudgeon, huff, pet, rise, ruffle, temper; delirium, heat, passion, warmth

near antonyms calmness, forbearance, patience

antonyms delight, pleasure

anger *vb* to make angry ⟨it's virtually impossible to *anger* Mrs. Peterson—she's the most easygoing person I've ever known⟩

synonyms antagonize, enrage, incense, inflame, infuriate, madden, outrage, rankle, rile, roil

related words affront, aggravate, annoy, cross, exasperate, get, irritate, nettle, offend, peeve, pique, provoke, put out, ruffle, vex; embitter, envenom

phrases get one's goat, rub the wrong way

near antonyms allay, assuage, relieve; comfort, console, soothe; appease, conciliate, mollify, pacify, placate; calm, lull, quiet, settle; beguile, bewitch, captivate, charm, disarm, enchant

antonyms delight, gratify, please

angered *adj* feeling or showing anger — see ANGRY

angle *n* **1** a certain way in which something appears or may be regarded — see ASPECT 1

2 a way of looking at or thinking about something — see POINT OF VIEW

3 something that curves or is curved — see BEND 1

angle *vb* to set or cause to be at an angle — see LEAN 1

angling *n* the act of positioning or an instance of being positioned at an angle — see TILT

angriness *n* an intense emotional state of displeasure with someone or something — see ANGER

angry *adj* feeling or showing anger ⟨my sister gets really *angry* and practically throws a tantrum if her soccer team loses⟩

synonyms angered, apoplectic, enraged, foaming, fuming, furious, incensed, indignant, inflamed, infuriated, irate, ireful, mad, outraged, rabid, riled, roiled, shirty [*chiefly British*], sore, steaming, wrathful, wroth

related words ranting, raving, stormy; bristling, burning, cross, huffy, livid, seething, smoldering, worked up, wrought (up); acrid, acrimonious, antagonistic, antipathetic, bitter, embittered, inimical, malevolent, piqued, rancorous, resentful, spiteful, vindictive, virulent; antisocial, cold, cool, disagreeable, disapproving, distant, frigid, icy, ill-tempered, sulky, unfriendly, unpleasant; aggravated, annoyed, bearish, bilious, cantankerous, choleric, churlish, crabby, cranky, dyspeptic, exasperated, fretful, fussy, grouchy, grumpy, ill-humored, irascible, irritable, peevish, perturbed, petulant, put out, quick-tempered, snappish, testy, touchy; argumentative, belligerent, contentious, contrary, disputatious, ornery, pugnacious, quarrelsome, querulous
near antonyms accepting, accommodating, obliging; agreeable, amenable, complaisant; amicable, cordial, friendly; content, happy, satisfied; empathetic, sympathetic, tolerant, understanding; calm, pacific, peaceable, placid, serene, tranquil; affable, amiable, easygoing, genial, good-natured, good-tempered, kind, pleasant, sweet
antonyms delighted, pleased

anguish *n* **1** a state of great suffering of body or mind — see DISTRESS 1
2 deep sadness especially for the loss of someone or something loved — see SORROW

anguished *adj* expressing or suggesting mourning — see MOURNFUL 1

animal *adj* of or relating to the human body — see PHYSICAL 1

animal *n* one of the lower animals as distinguished from human beings ⟨we saw a lot of *animals* at the wildlife refuge—cranes, alligators, deer, a fox, even an armadillo⟩
synonyms beast, brute, creature, critter
related words varmint, vermin; biped, quadruped; carnivore, herbivore, insectivore; invertebrate, vertebrate

animate *adj* **1** having much high-spirited energy and movement — see LIVELY 1
2 having or showing life — see ALIVE 1

animate *vb* to give life, vigor, or spirit to ⟨Mr. Clark *animates* history for his sixth graders by frequently showing up for class dressed like some famous historical figure⟩
synonyms brace, energize, enliven, fire, invigorate, jazz (up), liven (up), pep (up), quicken, stimulate, vitalize, vivify
related words arouse, awake, awaken, raise, rouse, stir, wake (up); activate, actuate, drive, impel, motivate, move, propel; charge, electrify, galvanize; excite, ferment, foment, incite, inflame, instigate, kindle, provoke, set off, spark, trigger, turn on, whip (up); abet, boost, buoy, cheer, embolden, fortify, hearten, inspire, lift, rally, steel, strengthen; reactivate, reanimate, reawake, reawaken, recharge, recreate, reenergize, refresh, regenerate, rejuvenate, rekindle, renew, resurrect, resuscitate, revitalize, revive
near antonyms burn out, debilitate, do in, drain, enervate, enfeeble, exhaust, fag, fatigue, sap, tucker (out), undermine, weaken, wear, wear out; check, curb, inhibit, jade, quell, quench, repress, restrain, slow, still, stunt, suppress; daunt, demoralize, discourage, dishearten, dispirit
antonyms damp, dampen, deaden, dull

animated *adj* **1** having much high-spirited energy and movement — see LIVELY 1

2 marked by much life, movement, or activity — see ALIVE 2

animatedly *adv* in a quick and spirited manner — see GAILY 2

animately *adv* in a quick and spirited manner — see GAILY 2

animation *n* the quality or state of having abundant or intense activity — see VITALITY 1

animosity *n* a deep-seated ill will — see ENMITY

annalist *n* a student or writer of history — see HISTORIAN

annals *n pl* an account of important events in the order in which they happened — see HISTORY 1

annex *n* a smaller structure added to a main building ⟨a new *annex* that will serve as the permanent home for the school library⟩
synonyms addition, extension, penthouse
related words arm, ell, wing

annex *vb* to join (something) to a mass, quantity, or number so as to bring about an overall increase — see ADD 1

annihilate *vb* **1** to destroy all traces of ⟨the family's attempts to *annihilate* the roach population in their apartment had met with little success⟩
synonyms blot out, efface, eradicate, expunge, exterminate, extirpate, liquidate, obliterate, root (out), rub out, snuff (out), stamp (out), wipe out
related words decimate, demolish, destroy, devastate; dismantle, flatten, mow (down), raze, tear down; ruin, total, waste, wreck; blast, blow up, dash, dynamite, smash; atomize, consume, devour, dissolve, fragment, powder, pulverize, shatter, splinter; doom, finish, kill, terminate, zap; cancel, cut, discard, ditch, eject, excise, expel, jettison, oust, throw out
near antonyms conserve, preserve, protect, save; build, construct, create, fabricate, fashion, forge, form, frame, make, manufacture, shape; fix, mend, patch, rebuild, recondition, reconstruct, renew, renovate, repair, restore, revamp
2 to bring to a complete end the physical soundness, existence, or usefulness of — see DESTROY 1

annihilation *n* the state or fact of being rendered nonexistent, physically unsound, or useless — see DESTRUCTION

announce *vb* to make known openly or publicly ⟨Jeannie *announced* to everyone within hearing distance that she didn't care if she failed the test⟩
synonyms advertise, blaze, broadcast, declare, enunciate, placard, post, proclaim, promulgate, publicize, publish, sound
related words advise, apprise, inform, notify; communicate, impart, intimate; disclose, divulge, report, reveal; disseminate, spread
near antonyms conceal, hush (up), silence, suppress, withhold; recall, recant, retract, revoke

announcement *n* a published statement informing the public of a matter of general interest ⟨an *announcement* was in today's paper regarding the merger of the two banks⟩
synonyms ad, advertisement, bulletin, notice, notification, posting, release
related words broadside, circular, flier (*or* flyer), handbill, handout; bill, billboard, placard, poster, sign; broadcast, newscast, telecast; advertising, commercial, message, spot, word; communication, dispatch, report; ballyhoo, boost, buildup, campaign, plug, promotion, propaganda, publicity

annoy *vb* to disturb the peace of mind of (someone) especially by repeated disagreeable acts — see IRRITATE 1

annoyance *n* 1 the act of making unwelcome intrusions upon another ⟨they have an unlisted number in the hopes that it will reduce the constant *annoyance* by telephone salespeople⟩
synonyms aggravation, bedevilment, bothering, bugging, disturbance, harassment, harrying, pestering, teasing, vexation
related words molestation, offense (*or* offence), persecution, provocation, torment, torture
2 the feeling of impatience or anger caused by another's repeated disagreeable acts ⟨Carlene made known her *annoyance* at having to pick up her sister's dirty clothes⟩
synonyms aggravation, bother, exasperation, frustration, irritation, vexation
related words agitation, anger, angriness, discomfort, displeasure, distress, disturbance, indignation, irateness, ire, outrage, perturbation, resentment; dander, dudgeon, huff, peeve, pet, pique, umbrage, upset
near antonyms delight, pleasure
3 something that is a source of irritation ⟨flashing ads, visual clutter, and other *annoyances* that are the price for free information on the Internet⟩
synonyms aggravation, bother, exasperation, frustration, hassle, headache, inconvenience, irritant, nuisance, peeve, pest, problem, thorn
related words affront, insult, offense; upset, worry; affliction, cross, curse, menace, plague; plight, predicament, trial, tribulation; annoyer, disturber, offender
near antonyms delight, joy, pleasure
4 one who is obnoxiously annoying — see NUISANCE 1

annoyer *n* one who is obnoxiously annoying — see NUISANCE 1

annoying *adj* causing annoyance ⟨Sheldon has the *annoying* habit of eating all the pickles and leaving a jar full of pickle juice in the refrigerator⟩
synonyms aggravating, bothersome, disturbing, exasperating, frustrating, galling, irksome, irritating, maddening, nettling, peeving, pesty, rankling, riling, vexatious, vexing
related words burdensome, discomforting, displeasing, disquieting, distressing, importunate, inconveniencing; angering, enraging, infuriating; mischievous, offensive, pesky, troublesome, upsetting; stressful, tiresome, troubling, trying, worrisome
near antonyms delightful, pleasing

annuity *n* a sum of money allotted for a specific use by official or formal action — see APPROPRIATION

annul *vb* 1 to balance with an equal force so as to make ineffective — see OFFSET
2 to put an end to by formal action — see ABOLISH

anoint *vb* to rub an oily or sticky substance over — see SMEAR 1

anomalous *adj* departing from some accepted standard of what is normal — see DEVIANT

anomaly *n* a person, thing, or event that is not normal — see FREAK 1

anon *adv* at or within a short time — see SHORTLY 2

anonymity *n* the quality or state of being mostly or completely unknown — see OBSCURITY 2

anonymous *adj* 1 known but not named — see CERTAIN 1

2 not named or identified by a name — see NAMELESS 1
3 not widely known — see OBSCURE 2

another *adj* resulting in an increase in amount or number — see ADDITIONAL

answer *n* 1 something spoken or written in reaction especially to a question ⟨the standard *answer* of "Nothing" when asked, "What did you do in school today?"⟩
synonyms comeback, rejoinder, reply, response, retort, return
related words banter, persiflage, repartee; acknowledgment (*also* acknowledgement), comment, communication, correspondence, feedback, observation, reaction, remark; defense, explanation, justification, rebuttal, refutation
near antonyms challenge, cross-examination, grilling, interrogation, quiz; poll, questionnaire, survey
antonyms inquiry, query, question
2 something attained by mental effort and especially by computation ⟨the *answers* to the odd-numbered problems are at the back of the book⟩
synonyms result, solution
related words conclusion, determination, explanation, finding; clue, key

answer *vb* 1 to speak or write in reaction to a question or to another reaction ⟨Ryan didn't *answer* right away when Mrs. Jacobs asked him where he'd been for the last three hours⟩
synonyms rejoin, reply, respond, retort, return
related words acknowledge, comment, communicate, correspond, react, remark; explain, rebut, refute
near antonyms challenge, cross-examine, examine, grill, interrogate, pump, quiz; poll, query, survey
antonyms inquire, question
2 to be in agreement on every point — see CHECK 1
3 to do what is required by the terms of — see FULFILL 1
4 to find an answer for through reasoning — see SOLVE

answerable *adj* 1 being the one who must meet an obligation or suffer the consequences for failing to do so — see RESPONSIBLE 1
2 capable of having the reason for or cause of determined — see SOLVABLE

antagonism *n* a deep-seated ill will — see ENMITY

antagonist *n* 1 one that is hostile toward another — see ENEMY
2 one that takes a position opposite another in a competition or conflict — see OPPONENT 1

antagonistic *adj* marked by opposition or ill will — see HOSTILE 1

antagonize *vb* 1 to implant bitter feelings in — see EMBITTER
2 to make angry — see ANGER

antecedent *adj* going before another in time or order — see PREVIOUS

antecedent *n* 1 someone or something responsible for a result — see CAUSE 1
2 something belonging to an earlier time from which something else was later developed — see ANCESTOR 2

antecedently *adv* so as to precede something in order of time — see AHEAD 1

antedate *vb* to go or come before in time — see PRECEDE

antediluvian *adj* dating or surviving from the distant past — see ANCIENT 1

antediluvian *n* a person with old-fashioned ideas — see FOGY

anterior *adj* going before another in time or order — see PREVIOUS

anteriorly *adv* so as to precede something in order of time — see AHEAD 1

anthem *n* a religious song — see HYMN

anthology *n* a collection of writings ⟨an *anthology* of American short stories⟩
synonyms album, compilation, miscellany
related words archives; digest

antic *adj* **1** causing or intended to cause laughter — see FUNNY 1
2 given to good-natured joking or teasing — see PLAYFUL

antic *n* a playful or mischievous act intended as a joke — see PRANK

anticipate *vb* **1** to believe in the future occurrence of (something) — see EXPECT
2 to realize or know about beforehand — see FORESEE

anticipated *adj* being in accordance with the prescribed, normal, or logical course of events — see DUE 2

anticipatory *adj* having or showing signs of eagerly awaiting something — see EXPECTANT 1

antipathetic *adj* having a natural dislike for something ⟨a series of adventure books that turned boys who had been *antipathetic* to reading into avid readers⟩
synonyms allergic, averse
related words disinclined, loath (*or* loth), reluctant, unwilling; adverse, antagonistic, hostile, intolerant, negative, opposed, opposing, resistant, resisting, uncongenial, unfriendly, unsympathetic; disgusted, nauseated, repelled, repulsed, revolted, shocked, squeamish, turned off
near antonyms friendly, sympathetic, tolerant, understanding; admiring, appreciative, charmed, delighted, fond, pleased, tickled

antipathy *n* **1** a deep-seated ill will — see ENMITY
2 something or someone that is hated — see HATE 2

antipodal *adj* being as different as possible — see OPPOSITE

antipode *n* something that is as different as possible from something else — see OPPOSITE

antipodean *adj* being as different as possible — see OPPOSITE

antiquated *adj* having passed its time of use or usefulness — see OBSOLETE

antique *adj* **1** dating or surviving from the distant past — see ANCIENT 1
2 pleasantly reminiscent of an earlier time — see OLD-FASHIONED 1

antique *n* something belonging to or surviving from an earlier period ⟨Shamika's house is filled with *antiques*, including a collection of 19th-century African masks⟩
synonyms relic
related words artifact, fossil; antiquities, ruins; remains, remnant, trace, vestige

antisocial *adj* having or showing a lack of friendliness or interest in others — see COOL 1

antithesis *n* something that is as different as possible from something else — see OPPOSITE

antithetical *adj* being as different as possible — see OPPOSITE

anxiety *n* **1** an uneasy state of mind usually over the possibility of an anticipated misfortune or trouble ⟨Dorothy's *anxiety* about her brother's operation kept her awake all night⟩
synonyms agitation, anxiousness, apprehension, apprehensiveness, care, concern, disquiet, nervousness, perturbation, solicitude, uneasiness, worry
related words strain, stress, tension; alarm, anguish, consternation, desperation, desperateness, discomfort, discomposure, dismay, distraction, distress, disturbance, edginess, jitters, jumpiness; fear, fearfulness, torment, upset, vexation; doubt, dread, foreboding, incertitude, misgiving, presentiment, suspense, uncertainty
near antonyms calm, calmness, content, contentment, ease, peace, placidity, quiet, quietude, serenity, tranquillity (*or* tranquility); comfort, consolation, relief, solace
2 the emotion experienced in the presence or threat of danger — see FEAR

anxious *adj* **1** feeling or showing uncomfortable feelings of uncertainty — see NERVOUS 1
2 marked by or causing agitation or uncomfortable feelings — see NERVOUS 2
3 showing urgent desire or interest — see EAGER

anxiousness *n* an uneasy state of mind usually over the possibility of an anticipated misfortune or trouble — see ANXIETY 1

any *adj* being one of a group — see EACH

anyhow *adv* **1** in spite of everything — see REGARDLESS
2 without definite aim, direction, rule, or method — see HIT OR MISS

anymore *adv* at the present time — see NOW 1

anyway *adv* **1** in spite of everything — see REGARDLESS
2 without definite aim, direction, rule, or method — see HIT OR MISS

anywise *adv* **1** in any way or respect — see AT ALL
2 without definite aim, direction, rule, or method — see HIT OR MISS

A1 *adj* of the very best kind — see EXCELLENT

apace *adv* with great speed — see FAST 1

apart *adv* into parts or to pieces ⟨the fancy new adjustable rake came *apart* the first time Chad tried to use it⟩
synonyms asunder, piecemeal
antonyms together

apartment *n* **1** a room or set of rooms in a private house or a block used as a separate dwelling place ⟨a spacious six-room *apartment* that occupies the entire upper floor of a two-family house⟩
synonyms flat, lodgings, suite, tenement
related words condominium, duplex, penthouse, salon, studio, triplex; apartment house, tenement house, walk-up
2 an area within a building that has been set apart from surrounding space by a wall — see ROOM 2

apathetic *adj* **1** having or showing a lack of interest or concern — see INDIFFERENT 1
2 not feeling or showing emotion — see IMPASSIVE 1

apathy *n* **1** a lack of emotion or emotional expressiveness ⟨the *apathy* of the people of that war-torn country comes from their having seen too many horrors⟩
synonyms impassivity, insensibility, numbness, phlegm
related words callousness, coldness, coolness,

hardheartedness, hardness, heartlessness, insensitivity, obduracy; blankness, deadness, emptiness, vacancy; aloofness, detachment, indifference, unconcern; stiffness, woodenness

near antonyms compassion, empathy, pity, sympathy; responsiveness, sensitivity; solicitude, tenderness, understanding, warmth; histrionics, hysteria, hysterics, melodrama

antonyms emotion, feeling, sensibility

2 lack of interest or concern — see INDIFFERENCE

ape *vb* to use (someone or something) as the model for one's speech, mannerisms, or behavior — see IMITATE 1

aper *n* a person who adopts the appearance or behavior of another especially in an obvious way — see COPYCAT

aperture *n* a place in a surface allowing passage into or through a thing — see HOLE 1

apex *n* **1** the highest part or point — see HEIGHT 1
2 the last and usually sharp or tapering part of something long and narrow — see POINT 2

aphorism *n* **1** an idea or statement about all of the members of a group or all the instances of a situation — see GENERALIZATION
2 an often stated observation regarding something from common experience — see SAYING

aphoristic *adj* marked by the use of few words to convey much information or meaning — see CONCISE

apiece *adv* for each one ⟨when you figure that it comes to six dollars *apiece*, it's too much to pay for used CDs⟩

synonyms all, each, per capita

related words apart, independently, individually, respectively, separately, singly

near antonyms altogether, collectively, together

apish *adj* using or marked by the use of something else as a basis or model — see IMITATIVE

aplomb *n* **1** evenness of emotions or temper — see EQUANIMITY
2 great faith in oneself or one's abilities — see CONFIDENCE 1

apologetic *adj* feeling sorrow for a wrong that one has done — see CONTRITE 1

apoplectic *adj* feeling or showing anger — see ANGRY

apostate *n* one who betrays a trust or an allegiance — see TRAITOR

apostle *n* a person who actively supports or favors a cause — see EXPONENT

apothecary *n* a person who prepares drugs according to a doctor's prescription — see DRUGGIST

appall *vb* to cause an often unpleasant surprise for — see SHOCK 1

appalling *adj* **1** causing intense displeasure, disgust, or resentment — see OFFENSIVE 1
2 extremely disturbing or repellent — see HORRIBLE 1

appanage *n* **1** something granted as a special favor — see PRIVILEGE
2 something to which one has a just claim — see RIGHT 1

apparatus *n* items needed for the performance of a task or activity — see EQUIPMENT

apparel *n* covering for the human body — see CLOTHING

apparel *vb* to outfit with clothes and especially fine or special clothes — see CLOTHE 1

apparent *adj* **1** appearing to be true on the basis of evidence that may or may not be confirmed ⟨at the start of the investigation, the *apparent* cause of the plane crash was mechanical failure⟩

synonyms assumed, evident, ostensible, presumed, reputed, seeming, supposed

related words external, outward, visible; conceivable, plausible; likely, probable; clear, distinct, manifest, obvious, plain; deceptive, delusive, delusory, illusive, illusory, imaginary; misleading, specious; fake, faked, feigned, phony (*also* phoney), pretended, pseudo, put-on; alleged, professed, purported, so-called

near antonyms authenticated, confirmed, corroborated, established, real, substantiated, valid, validated, verified

2 capable of being seen — see VISIBLE

3 not subject to misinterpretation or more than one interpretation — see CLEAR 2

apparently *adv* to all outward appearances ⟨*apparently*, Phil didn't know the cake was for the raffle, since he helped himself to a piece⟩

synonyms evidently, ostensibly, presumably, seemingly, supposedly

related words externally, outwardly, visibly; believably, credibly; maybe, mayhap, perchance, perhaps, possibly, professedly; allegedly, reputedly; clearly, distinctly, obviously, plainly; assuredly, positively, surely

near antonyms implausibly, impossibly, improbably, incredibly

apparition *n* the soul of a dead person thought of especially as appearing to living people — see GHOST

appeal *n* **1** an earnest request — see PLEA 1
2 the power of irresistible attraction — see CHARM 2

appeal (to) *vb* to make a request to (someone) in an earnest or urgent manner — see BEG

appealing *adj* having an often mysterious or magical power to attract — see FASCINATING 1

appear *vb* **1** to come into view ⟨a police car *appeared* just as Michael ran a red light⟩

synonyms come out, materialize, show up, turn up

related words reappear, resurface; bulk, loom; arrive, come; dawn, debut; arise, break, break out, emanate, erupt, issue, rise, spring (up), surface; happen, occur

near antonyms depart, leave, retire, withdraw

antonyms clear, disappear, dissolve, evanesce, evaporate, fade, go (away), melt (away), vanish

2 to give the impression of being — see SEEM

appearance *n* **1** the outward form of someone or something especially as indicative of a quality ⟨the dignified *appearance* of this church leader⟩ ⟨the country club's manicured lawns and well-groomed *appearance* in general⟩

synonyms aspect, look, mien, presence

related words air, attitude, bearing, behavior, comportment, demeanor, deportment, manner, poise, pose; carriage, posture, stance; color, complexion; countenance, face, features, physiognomy, visage

2 outward and often deceptive indication ⟨can't you at least give the *appearance* of listening to what I say?⟩

synonyms face, guise, name, semblance, show

related words affectation, display, fiction, imposture, make-believe, pose, pretense (*or* pretence),

simulation; cloak, disguise, exterior, facade (*also* façade), front, mask, masquerade, shell, surface
3 the act of coming upon a scene — see ARRIVAL

appease *vb* to lessen the anger or agitation of — see PACIFY

appeasing *adj* tending to lessen or avoid conflict or hostility — see PACIFIC 1

appellation *n* a word or combination of words by which a person or thing is regularly known — see NAME 1

append *vb* to join (something) to a mass, quantity, or number so as to bring about an overall increase — see ADD 1

appendage *n* something that is not necessary in itself but adds to the convenience or performance of the main piece of equipment — see ACCESSORY 1

appertain *vb* **1** to be the property of a person or group of persons — see BELONG 2
2 to have a relation or connection — see APPLY 1

appetite *n* **1** a need or desire for food — see HUNGER 1
2 a strong wish for something — see DESIRE
3 positive regard for something — see LIKING
4 urgent desire or interest — see EAGERNESS

appetizing *adj* very pleasing to the sense of taste — see DELICIOUS 1

applaud *vb* to declare enthusiastic approval of — see ACCLAIM

applauding *adj* expressing approval — see FAVORABLE 1

applause *n* enthusiastic and usually public expression of approval ⟨a design for a memorial for the victims of the attack that has received nothing but *applause* from officials, commentators, and the general public⟩
synonyms acclamation, cheering, cheers, ovation, plaudit(s), rave(s)
related words clapping; bravo, hallelujah, hosanna; acclaim, accolade, citation, commendation, compliment, encomium, eulogy, homage, paean, panegyric, salutation, tribute
near antonyms boo, hiss, hoot, jeer, raspberry, smirk, sneer, snicker, snigger, snort, whistle; gibe (*or* jibe), put-down, taunt
antonyms booing, hissing

appliance *n* an interesting and often novel device with a practical use — see GADGET

applicability *n* the fact or state of being pertinent — see PERTINENCE

applicable *adj* **1** capable of being put to use or account — see PRACTICAL 1
2 having to do with the matter at hand — see PERTINENT
3 meeting the requirements of a purpose or situation — see FIT 1

applicant *n* one who seeks an office, honor, position, or award — see CANDIDATE

application *n* the act or practice of employing something for a particular purpose — see USE 1

apply *vb* **1** to have a relation or connection ⟨does your rule about calling home *apply* to me as well?⟩
synonyms appertain, bear, pertain, refer, relate
related words affect, concern, interest, involve, touch; associate, connect, couple, interrelate, link, tie in; deal (with), treat
phrases have to do with
2 to occupy (oneself) diligently or with close attention ⟨Sam *applied* himself to writing thank-

you letters to everyone who'd helped sponsor him for the jamboree⟩
synonyms address, bend, buckle, devote, give
related words readdress, reapply; knuckle down, set (to), settle (down); busy, commit, concern, engage, involve; exert, exhaust, put out, spend, strain, stress, tax, trouble, wear out; carry on, pitch in, plunge (in); grind, hump, hustle, peg (away), plod, plow, plug (away), work
near antonyms dally, dawdle, dillydally, fiddle, fool (around), idle, mess (around), monkey (around), play, potter, putter, trifle
3 to put a layer of on a surface — see SPREAD 2
4 to put into action or service — see USE 1
5 to bring to bear especially forcefully or effectively — see EXERT
6 to carry out effectively — see ENFORCE

appoint *vb* **1** to decide upon (the time or date for an event) usually from a position of authority ⟨at the *appointed* hour we were in our places⟩
synonyms designate, fix, name, set
related words adopt, assign, choose, determine, establish, opt (for), pick, pin down, prefer, select, settle, single (out), specify; arrange, coordinate, orchestrate; advertise, announce, declare, publish
2 to pick (someone) by one's authority for a specific position or duty ⟨Igor was *appointed* hall monitor for May⟩
synonyms assign, attach, commission, constitute, designate, detail, name
related words authorize, delegate, depute, deputize; inaugurate, induct, install, instate, ordain, invest; crown, enthrone, throne; choose, elect, handpick, nominate, select, single (out), vote (in)
near antonyms depose, dethrone, displace, eject, oust, overthrow, remove, throw out, uncrown, unmake
antonyms discharge, dismiss, expel, fire

appointment *n* **1** the state or fact of being chosen for a position or duty ⟨the *appointment* of the mayor's husband to the Board of Health came as a surprise⟩
synonyms assignment, commission, designation
related words billet, job, office, place, position, situation, spot, station; authorization, delegation, deputation, placement, ranking; induction, installation, installment (*or* instalment), instating, investiture, investment, ordination; choosing, election, nomination, picking, selection, singling out
near antonyms deposition, dethronement, ejection, ouster, overthrow, rejection, removal
antonyms discharge, dismissal, expulsion, firing
2 an agreement to be present at a specified time and place — see ENGAGEMENT 2
3 an assignment at which one regularly works for pay — see JOB 1
4 appointments *pl* the movable articles in a room — see FURNITURE

apportion *vb* **1** to give as a share or portion — see ALLOT
2 to give out (something) in appropriate amounts or to appropriate individuals — see ADMINISTER 1

apportionment *n* the act or process of giving out something to each member of a group — see DISTRIBUTION 1

apposite *adj* having to do with the matter at hand — see PERTINENT

appraisal *n* **1** an opinion on the nature, character, or quality of something — see ESTIMATION 1

THESAURUS

2 the act of placing a value on the nature, character, or quality of something — see ESTIMATE 1

appraise *vb* to make an approximate or tentative judgment regarding — see ESTIMATE 1

appraisement *n* **1** an opinion on the nature, character, or quality of something — see ESTIMATION 1

2 the act of placing a value on the nature, character, or quality of something — see ESTIMATE 1

appreciable *adj* able to be perceived by a sense or by the mind — see PERCEPTIBLE

appreciate *vb* **1** to become greater in extent, volume, amount, or number — see INCREASE 2

2 to hold dear — see LOVE 1

3 to recognize the meaning of — see COMPREHEND 1

4 to think very highly or favorably of — see ADMIRE

appreciation *n* **1** a feeling of great approval and liking — see ADMIRATION 1

2 acknowledgment of having received something good from another — see THANKS

3 the knowledge gained from the process of coming to know or understand something — see COMPREHENSION

appreciative *adj* **1** expressing approval — see FAVORABLE 1

2 feeling or expressing gratitude — see GRATEFUL 1

appreciativeness *n* acknowledgment of having received something good from another — see THANKS

apprehend *vb* **1** to recognize the meaning of — see COMPREHEND 1

2 to take or keep under one's control by authority of law — see ARREST 1

apprehended *adj* taken and held prisoner — see CAPTIVE

apprehension *n* **1** suspicion or fear of future harm or misfortune ⟨Erica entered the dark cave with a great deal of *apprehension*⟩
synonyms alarm, apprehensiveness, dread, foreboding, misgiving
related words agitation, anxiousness, concern, disquiet, distress, disturbance, fearfulness, perturbation, solicitude, uneasiness; scruple, worry; doubt, incertitude, suspense, uncertainty, wariness; defeatism, pessimism; foreknowledge, premonition, presage, presentiment
near antonyms anticipation, excitement, hope, hopefulness; confidence, optimism, sanguinity

2 the act of taking or holding under one's control by authority of law — see ARREST

3 the emotion experienced in the presence or threat of danger — see FEAR

4 an uneasy state of mind usually over the possibility of an anticipated misfortune or trouble — see ANXIETY 1

5 the knowledge gained from the process of coming to know or understand something — see COMPREHENSION

apprehensiveness *n* **1** an uneasy state of mind usually over the possibility of an anticipated misfortune or trouble — see ANXIETY 1

2 suspicion or fear of future harm or misfortune — see APPREHENSION 1

apprentice *n* a person who helps a more skilled person — see HELPER

apprise *vb* to give information to — see ENLIGHTEN 1

approach *n* **1** an established course for traveling from one place to another — see PASSAGE 1

2 the means or procedure for doing something — see METHOD

approach *vb* **1** to come near or nearer ⟨The parade's *approaching* ! I can hear the band playing!⟩
synonyms close, draw on, near
related words arrive, attain, come, gain, hit, land, make, reach, show up, turn up; adjoin, border, touch, verge
near antonyms clear out, depart, exit, go, leave, light out, pull (out), quit, remove, run away, shove (off), take off, walk out
antonyms back (up *or* away), recede, retire, retreat, withdraw

2 to move closer to — see COME 1

3 to come near or nearer to in character or quality — see APPROXIMATE

approaching *adj* being soon to appear or take place — see FORTHCOMING

approbation *n* an acceptance of something as satisfactory — see APPROVAL 1

appropriate *adj* meeting the requirements of a purpose or situation — see FIT 1

appropriate *vb* **1** to take or make use of without authority or right ⟨archaeologists once *appropriated* artifacts excavated at ancient African sites for their museums in Europe⟩
synonyms arrogate, commandeer, preempt, usurp
related words annex, claim, confiscate, expropriate, preoccupy, sequester; grab, grasp, seize, snatch, steal, take over, wrench, wrest; encroach, infringe, invade, trespass

2 to take (something) without right and with an intent to keep — see STEAL 1

appropriately *adv* in a manner suitable for the occasion or purpose — see PROPERLY

appropriateness *n* the quality or state of being especially suitable or fitting ⟨Mrs. Bryce-Jones remarked on the *appropriateness* of window boxes on the cottage, noting they gave it a quaint, cheerful look⟩
synonyms aptness, felicitousness, fitness, fittingness, rightness, seemliness, suitability, suitableness
related words agreeableness, compatibility, congruity, harmoniousness; applicability, bearing, connection, materiality, pertinence, relevance; acceptability, adequacy, adequateness, satisfactoriness, serviceableness, usefulness
near antonyms inapplicability, irrelevance; meaninglessness, pointlessness; incompatibility, incongruity
antonyms inappropriateness, inaptness, infelicity, unfitness

appropriation *n* a sum of money allotted for a specific use by official or formal action ⟨the National Park Service received an increased *appropriation* for wildlife management⟩
synonyms allocation, allotment, annuity, grant, subsidy
related words advance, allowance, benefit, endowment, fund, stipend, trust

approval *n* an acceptance of something as satisfactory ⟨Does this dress I bought for the wedding meet with your *approval* ?⟩
synonyms approbation, blessing, favor, imprimatur, OK (*or* okay)
related words backing, endorsement, sanction,

support; benediction, goodwill; agreement, assent, concurrence, consent; countenance, liking, satisfaction

near antonyms refusal, rejection, repudiation; dislike, dissatisfaction; censure, condemnation, criticism, denunciation, deprecation, depreciation, disparagement, opprobrium, reprehension, reproach, reprobation

antonyms disapprobation, disapproval, disfavor

approve *vb* to give official acceptance of something as satisfactory ⟨as soon as the pond project was *approved*, the bulldozers were at the site⟩

synonyms authorize, clear, OK (*or* okay), ratify, sanction, warrant

related words accept, acknowledge, affirm, confirm; accredit, certify, endorse (*also* indorse), validate; initial, sign; allow, license (*or* licence), permit; reapprove

near antonyms ban, enjoin, forbid, interdict, prohibit; disregard, ignore, neglect, overlook; rebuff, rebut, refuse, spurn

antonyms decline, deny, disallow, disapprove, negative, reject, turn down

approve (of) *vb* to have a favorable opinion of ⟨Mrs. Pinkerton doesn't *approve of* people who stand in the "12 items or less" lane with 13 items⟩

synonyms accept, care (for), countenance, favor, OK (*or* okay), subscribe (to)

related words acclaim, applaud, laud, praise, salute; back (up), stand by, support, sustain, uphold; bear, endure, tolerate; assent (to), concur (with), consent (to); commend, recommend; enjoy, like

phrases go for, hold with

near antonyms censure, condemn, criticize, damn, denounce, deprecate, depreciate, disparage, reprehend, reprobate; detest, dislike, hate, loathe; object (to), oppose

antonyms disapprove (of), discountenance, disfavor, frown (on *or* upon)

approving *adj* **1** expressing approval — see FAVORABLE 1

2 showing or expressing acceptance or approval — see POSITIVE

approximate *adj* being such only when compared to something else — see COMPARATIVE

approximate *vb* to come near or nearer to in character or quality ⟨Rob's violin performance last night didn't even *approximate* what he's really capable of when he's not feeling sick⟩

synonyms approach, compare (with), measure up (to), stack up (against *or* with)

related words add up (to), amount (to), come (to); duplicate, equal, match; mirror, parallel, reflect; border (on), touch (on), verge (on)

apropos *adj* having to do with the matter at hand — see PERTINENT

apropos of *prep* having to do with — see ABOUT 1

apt *adj* **1** having a tendency to be or act in a certain way — see PRONE 1

2 meeting the requirements of a purpose or situation — see FIT 1

aptitude *n* a special and usually inborn ability — see TALENT

aptness *n* **1** an established pattern of behavior — see TENDENCY 1

2 the quality or state of being especially suitable or fitting — see APPROPRIATENESS

aquatic *adj* living, lying, or occurring below the surface of the water — see UNDERWATER

aqueduct *n* an open man-made passageway for water — see CHANNEL 1

arbiter *n* one who works with opposing sides in order to bring about an agreement — see MEDIATOR

arbitrary *adj* **1** having or showing a tendency to force one's will on others without any regard to fairness or necessity ⟨an *arbitrary* piano teacher who makes all her students do the same exercises over and over again⟩

synonyms dictatorial, high-handed, imperious, peremptory, willful (*or* wilful)

related words arrogant, commanding, demanding, dominant, domineering, haughty, imperative, lordly, masterful, overbearing, presumptuous; authoritarian, autocratic, despotic, totalitarian, tyrannical (*also* tyrannic), tyrannous; capricious, changeable, erratic, mercurial, whimsical; biased, inequitable, partisan, prejudiced, unequal, unfair, unjust, unreasonable; unconscionable, unethical, unprincipled, unscrupulous

near antonyms balanced, disinterested, dispassionate, equal, equitable, evenhanded, fair, impartial, just, nonpartisan, objective; rational, reasonable, understanding; unbiased, unprejudiced; ethical, honorable, irreproachable, law-abiding, moral, principled, unimpeachable

2 lacking a definite plan, purpose, or pattern — see RANDOM

arbitrate *vb* to give an opinion about (something at issue or in dispute) — see JUDGE 1

arbitrator *n* one who works with opposing sides in order to bring about an agreement — see MEDIATOR

arc *n* something that curves or is curved — see BEND 1

arc *vb* to turn away from a straight line or course — see CURVE 1

arch *adj* **1** coming before all others in importance — see FOREMOST 1

2 displaying or marked by rude boldness — see NERVY 1

arch *n* something that curves or is curved — see BEND 1

arch *vb* **1** to cause to turn away from a straight line — see BEND 1

2 to turn away from a straight line or course — see CURVE 1

archaic *adj* having passed its time of use or usefulness — see OBSOLETE

archetypal *adj* **1** constituting, serving as, or worthy of being a pattern to be imitated — see MODEL

2 having or showing the qualities associated with the members of a particular group or kind — see TYPICAL 1

archetype *n* something from which copies are made — see ORIGINAL

archive *n* a place where books, periodicals, and records are kept for use but not for sale — see LIBRARY

arctic *adj* having a low or subnormal temperature — see COLD 1

ardent *adj* **1** having or expressing great depth of feeling — see FERVENT

2 showing urgent desire or interest — see EAGER

ardor *n* **1** depth of feeling ⟨candidates for citizenship reciting the oath of allegiance to the United States with all the *ardor* that they could muster⟩

synonyms emotion, fervency, fervidness, fervor, heat, intensity, passion, vehemence, warmth

THESAURUS

related words histrionics, mawkishness, melodrama, sappiness, sentimentality; eagerness, earnestness, enthusiasm, excitement, gusto, zest; fanaticism, fever, fire, hot-bloodedness, infatuation, mania, obsession, zeal; compassion, responsiveness, sympathy, tenderness

near antonyms aloofness, calmness, coldness, collectedness, composure, coolness, detachedness, dryness, phlegm, reserve, reservedness, reticence, taciturnity; apathy, indifference, unconcern; stiffness, woodenness

antonyms impassivity

2 urgent desire or interest — see EAGERNESS

arduous *adj* **1** requiring considerable physical or mental effort — see HARD 2

2 requiring much time, effort, or careful attention — see DEMANDING 1

arduously *adv* with great effort or determination — see HARD 1

area *n* **1** a part or portion having no fixed boundaries — see REGION 1

2 a region of activity, knowledge, or influence — see FIELD 2

arena *n* **1** a large room or building for enclosed public gatherings — see HALL 3

2 a region of activity, knowledge, or influence — see FIELD 2

argot *n* the special terms or expressions of a particular group or field — see TERMINOLOGY

argue *vb* **1** to state (something) as a reason in support of or against something under consideration ⟨Luis *argued* that a bake sale would make a lot less money than a car wash⟩

synonyms assert, contend, maintain, plead, reason

related words claim, insist; affirm, aver, avouch, avow; advance, offer, propose, submit; advise, counsel, recommend, suggest, urge; convince, persuade; advocate, champion, espouse, support; explain, justify, rationalize; consider, debate, discuss; counter, disprove, rebut, refute

2 to express different opinions about something often angrily ⟨Francesca didn't *argue* with her little brother the whole time they were at Walt Disney World⟩

synonyms bicker, brawl, dispute, fall out, fight, hassle, quarrel, row, scrap, spat, squabble, wrangle

related words challenge, dare, defy; clash, contend, contest; cavil, fuss, nitpick, quibble; consider, debate, discuss; kick, object, protest

phrases bandy words, fall foul

near antonyms coexist, get along; accept, agree, assent, concur, consent

3 to cause (someone) to agree with a belief or course of action by using arguments or earnest requests — see PERSUADE

4 to talk about (an issue) usually from various points of view and for the purpose of arriving at a decision or opinion — see DISCUSS

arguer *n* a person who takes part in a dispute — see DISPUTANT

argument *n* **1** an often noisy or angry expression of differing opinions ⟨the couple's *arguments* were often loud enough to be heard all over the neighborhood⟩

synonyms altercation, bicker, brawl, cross fire, disagreement, dispute, falling-out, fight, hassle, misunderstanding, quarrel, row, scrap, spat, squabble, tiff, wrangle

related words clash, run-in, skirmish, tussle; feud, vendetta; attack, contention, dissension; controversy, debate; fuss, objection, protest, protestation; affray, feud, fisticuffs, fracas, fray, free-for-all, melee

2 a statement given to explain a belief or act — see REASON 1

3 an exchange of views for the purpose of exploring a subject or deciding an issue — see DISCUSSION 1

4 an idea or opinion that is put forth in a discussion or debate — see CONTENTION

argumentative *adj* **1** given to arguing ⟨Ryan's *argumentative* nature is such that he's always insisting he didn't make the fouls that the referee calls⟩

synonyms contentious, disputatious, quarrelsome, scrappy

related words bellicose, belligerent, combative, pugnacious, truculent; balky, contrary, ornery, perverse, restive, wayward; disobedient, froward, insubordinate, intractable, recalcitrant, refractory; hardheaded, headstrong, mulish, obdurate, obstinate, pigheaded, resistant, self-willed, stubborn, unbending, uncompromising, uncooperative, unreasonable, unyielding, willful (*or* wilful)

near antonyms acquiescent, agreeable, amenable, complaisant, compliant, complying, conciliatory, cooperative, obliging; docile, obedient, submissive, tractable

2 feeling or displaying eagerness to fight — see BELLIGERENT

arid *adj* marked by little or no precipitation or humidity — see DRY 1

arise *vb* **1** to leave one's bed ⟨the travelers *arose* before dawn and were on their way as the sun came up⟩

synonyms get up, rise, uprise

related words arouse, awake, awaken, bestir, stir, wake

near antonyms doze, drop (off), nap, nod, sleep, slumber; bunk, perch, roost, settle; couch, lie (down), recline

antonyms bed (down), retire, turn in

2 to come to one's attention especially gradually or unexpectedly ⟨note in your report any problems that *arise* while you are conducting the experiment⟩

synonyms crop (up), emerge, materialize, spring (up), surface

related words appear, come out, show up, turn up; chance, come, come about, fall out, go (on), go off, hap, happen, occur, pass, transpire; interfere, interpose, intervene, intrude

3 to come into existence — see BEGIN 2

4 to move or extend upward — see ASCEND

aristocracy *n* the highest class in a society ⟨at one time in China only the *aristocracy* could own land⟩

synonyms gentry, upper class, upper crust

related words elect, elite, establishment, gentlefolk, jet set, nobility, quality, royalty, society

near antonyms commoners, (the) crowd, (the) masses, peasantry, peonage, (the) people, plebeians, (the) populace, (the) public, rank and file; bourgeoisie, middle class, working class; dregs, (the) herd, (the) mob, rabble, riffraff, scum, trash

antonyms proletarians, proletariat

aristocrat *n* a man of high birth or social position — see GENTLEMAN 1

aristocratic *adj* of high birth, rank, or station — see NOBLE 1

arithmetic *n* the act or process of performing mathematical operations to find a value — see CALCULATION

¹**arm** *n* a portable weapon from which a shot is discharged by gunpowder — see GUN 1

²**arm** *n* 1 an area of land that juts out into a body of water — see ²CAPE

2 the right or means to command or control others — see POWER 1

armada *n* a group of vehicles traveling together or under one management — see FLEET

armed forces *n pl* the combined army, air force, and navy of a nation ⟨our nation's *armed forces* are stationed throughout the world⟩
synonyms military, service, troops
related words GI's (*or* GIs), men-at-arms, rank and file, servicemen, servicewomen, soldiers, soldiery; militia, reserves; armor, defense
near antonyms civilians, noncombatants

armistice *n* a temporary stopping of fighting — see TRUCE

armor *n* 1 means or method of defending — see DEFENSE 1

2 something that encloses another thing especially to protect it — see ¹CASE

armory *n* a place where military arms are stored ⟨the soldier was sent to the *armory* to get a replacement weapon for the one that had been stolen⟩
synonyms arsenal, depot, dump, magazine
related words fort, fortress, stronghold; repository, storehouse, warehouse

army *n* 1 a large body of men and women organized for land warfare ⟨In 218 B.C., Hannibal marched into Italy with an *army* of 26,000, and even a few elephants, after crossing the Alps⟩
synonyms battalion, host, legion
related words infantry, ranks, regulars, soldiers, troops, troopers

2 a great number of persons or things gathered together — see CROWD 1

aroma *n* a sweet or pleasant smell — see FRAGRANCE

aromatic *adj* having a pleasant smell — see FRAGRANT

around *adv* 1 on all sides or in every direction ⟨he looked *around*⟩ ⟨butterflies were flying all *around*⟩
synonyms about, round
related words all over, everyplace, everywhere; abroad, afloat, hereabouts (*or* hereabout)

2 toward the opposite direction ⟨she turned *around* and saw him⟩
synonyms about, back, round
related words backward (*or* backwards), behind, down, downward, rearward (*or* rearwards); across, athwart, counter, counterclockwise

3 at, within, or to a short distance or time — see NEAR 1

4 from beginning to end — see THROUGH 1

around *prep* 1 close to ⟨I wouldn't stand *around* those rocks—there could be snakes under them⟩
synonyms about, by, near, next to
related words alongside, beside; across, along, at; circa

2 in random positions within the boundaries of ⟨huge, strangely shaped rocks were scattered *around* the canyon floor⟩

synonyms about, over, round, through, throughout
related words on

arouse *vb* 1 to cause to stop sleeping — see WAKE 1

2 to cease to be asleep — see WAKE 2

3 to rouse to strong feeling or action — see PROVOKE 1

arrange *vb* 1 to come to an agreement or decision concerning the details of ⟨*arrange* a time for the meeting⟩ ⟨*arrange* money matters for your trip⟩
synonyms decide, fix, set, settle
related words agree, contract, pledge, promise; draft, frame, hammer (out), intrigue, lay out, maneuver, map (out), plan, program, schematize, scheme, shape, square away, work out; affirm, approve, authorize, clear, confirm, OK (*or* okay), sanction, warrant; close, complete, conclude, end, finalize, finish, round (off *or* out), wind up, wrap up; bargain, chaffer, deal, dicker, haggle, horse-trade, negotiate
phrases dispose of

2 to put into a particular arrangement — see ORDER 1

3 to bring about through discussion and compromise — see NEGOTIATE 1

4 to work out the details of (something) in advance — see PLAN 1

arrangement *n* 1 a method worked out in advance for achieving some objective — see PLAN 1

2 the way in which something is sized, arranged, or organized — see FORMAT 1

3 the way in which the elements of something (as a work of art) are arranged — see COMPOSITION 3

4 the way objects in space or events in time are arranged or follow one another — see ORDER 1

arrant *adj* having no exceptions or restrictions — see ABSOLUTE 2

array *n* 1 a number of things considered as a unit — see GROUP 1

2 a usually small number of persons considered as a unit — see GROUP 2

3 dressy clothing — see FINERY

4 the way objects in space or events in time are arranged or follow one another — see ORDER 1

array *vb* 1 to make more attractive by adding something that is beautiful or becoming — see DECORATE

2 to outfit with clothes and especially fine or special clothes — see CLOTHE 1

3 to put into a particular arrangement — see ORDER 1

arrest *n* the act of taking or holding under one's control by authority of law ⟨there have been only two *arrests* for driving while intoxicated in the county in the last six months⟩
synonyms apprehension, pinch
related words bust [*slang*], raid; capture, entrapment, seizure; captivity, confinement, detention, enchainment, immurement, imprisonment, incarceration, restraint
near antonyms emancipation, liberation, release
antonyms discharge

arrest *vb* 1 to take or keep under one's control by authority of law ⟨the inept robber was promptly *arrested* by the off-duty policeman he had tried to hold up⟩
synonyms apprehend, bust [*slang*], nab, pick up, pinch, restrain, seize
related words bag, capture, catch, collar, get, grab, grapple, hook, land, nail, snare, snatch,

THESAURUS

trap; confine, detain, hold, immure, imprison, incarcerate, intern, jail, lock (up); bind, enchain, fetter, handcuff, manacle, shackle, trammel
near antonyms emancipate, free, liberate, loose, loosen, release, spring; unbind, unchain
antonyms discharge
2 to bring (something) to a standstill — see ¹HALT 1
3 to hold the attention of as if by a spell — see ENTHRALL 1
arrested *adj* taken and held prisoner — see CAPTIVE
arresting *adj* **1** holding the attention or provoking interest — see INTERESTING
2 likely to attract attention — see NOTICEABLE
arrival *n* the act of coming upon a scene ⟨spring's late *arrival* meant we were still skiing in mid-April⟩ ⟨the groom blamed his belated *arrival* for the wedding on a huge traffic snarl⟩
synonyms advent, appearance
related words approach, entrance, ingress; beginning, birth, commencement, dawn, dawning, debut, genesis, inception, morning, onset, start
near antonyms dissipation, dissolution, evaporation, fading, melting, passing, vanishing; clearing out, egress, exit, exiting, leaving, retirement, withdrawal
antonyms departing, departure, disappearance, going
arrive *vb* to get to a destination — see COME 2
arrogance *n* an exaggerated sense of one's importance that shows itself in the making of excessive or unjustified claims ⟨in his *arrogance* the president of the club made all the arrangements for the annual banquet without consulting the members⟩
synonyms haughtiness, imperiousness, loftiness, lordliness, masterfulness, peremptoriness, pompousness, presumptuousness, pretense (*or* pretence), pretension, pretentiousness, self-importance, superciliousness, superiority
related words authoritativeness, bossiness, dominance, high-handedness; condescension, disdain, scorn; snobbery, snobbishness, snobbism, snootiness; cheek, cheekiness, impertinence, impudence, sauciness; boastfulness, bombast, braggadocio, swagger, vaingloriousness, vainglory; cockiness, complacence, conceit, egoism, egotism, pride, pridefulness, self-centeredness, self-conceit, self-satisfaction, smugness, vanity
near antonyms bashfulness, demureness, retiringness, shyness; diffidence, self-doubt, timidity; meekness, passiveness, passivity, submissiveness; quietness, reserve, reservedness
antonyms humility, modesty
arrogant *adj* having a feeling of superiority that shows itself in an overbearing attitude ⟨the *arrogant* young lawyer elbowed his way to the head of the line of customers, declaring that he was too busy to wait like everybody else⟩
synonyms cavalier, haughty, highfalutin, high-handed, high-hat, imperious, important, lofty, lordly, masterful, overweening, peremptory, pompous, presumptuous, pretentious, supercilious, superior, uppish, uppity
related words authoritarian, bossy, dominant, dominating, domineering, magisterial, pontificating; condescending, disdainful, patronizing; impertinent, impudent, saucy; snobbish, snobby, snooty; boastful, bombastic, braggart, bragging, cocky, swaggering, vain, vainglorious; compla-

cent, conceited, egocentric, egoistic, egotistic (*or* egotistical), prideful, proud, self-centered, self-conceited, self-satisfied, smug, stuck-up
near antonyms bashful, cowering, cringing, demure, diffident, mousy (*or* mousey), overmodest, self-doubting, shrinking, shy, subdued, timid; acquiescent, compliant, deferential, meek, passive, submissive, unaggressive, unassertive, unassuming, unobtrusive, yielding; quiet, reserved, retiring
antonyms humble, modest
arrogate *vb* to take or make use of without authority or right — see APPROPRIATE 1
arsenal *n* a place where military arms are stored — see ARMORY
arsonist *n* a person who deliberately and unlawfully sets fire to a building or other property ⟨they finally caught the *arsonist*, but only after he'd set fire to four barns⟩
synonyms firebug, incendiary
related words igniter (*or* ignitor)
art *n* subtle or imaginative ability in inventing, devising, or executing something — see SKILL 1
artery *n* a passage cleared for public vehicular travel — see WAY 1
artful *adj* **1** clever at attaining one's ends by indirect and often deceptive means ⟨the lawyer, by her *artful* questioning, got the witness to admit he had been lying⟩
synonyms beguiling, cagey (*also* cagy), crafty, cunning, devious, foxy, guileful, slick, sly, subtle, wily
related words astute, cute, facile, glib, sharp, shrewd; crooked, deceitful, deceptive, dishonest, insidious, insinuating, Machiavellian, shady, shifty, slippery, sneaky, treacherous, tricky, underhand, underhanded, unscrupulous; backhanded, double-dealing, hypocritical, insincere, mealy-mouthed, smooth-tongued, two-faced; circuitous, circular, roundabout; clandestine, concealed, covert, furtive, hugger-mugger, secret, stealthy, surreptitious, undercover; calculating, designing, scheming, plotting
near antonyms obvious, open, patent, plain, public, unconcealed; aboveboard, candid, direct, forthright, frank, honest, natural, outspoken, plainspoken, real, simple, sincere, straightforward, unaffected, unpretending
antonyms artless, guileless, ingenuous
2 showing a use of the imagination and creativity especially in inventing — see CLEVER 1
3 accomplished with trained ability — see SKILLFUL
artfulness *n* **1** skill in achieving one's ends through indirect, subtle, or underhanded means — see CUNNING 1
2 subtle or imaginative ability in inventing, devising, or executing something — see SKILL 1
article *n* a short piece of writing typically expressing a point of view — see ESSAY 1
articulate *adj* able to express oneself clearly and well ⟨the television crew covering the science fair were looking for photogenic and *articulate* students to explain their projects on the air⟩
synonyms eloquent, fluent, well-spoken
related words facile, glib, smooth-tongued, voluble; expressive, outspoken, verbal, vocal; blabby, chatty, garrulous, loquacious, talkative, verbose; unfaltering, unhesitating
near antonyms faltering, halting, hesitant, maun-

dering, mumbling, muttering, sputtering, stammering, stumbling, stuttering; mute, speechless, tongue-tied, voiceless
antonyms inarticulate
articulate *vb* **1** to utter clearly and distinctly ⟨uses a very measured tone and *articulates* every syllable when issuing scoldings⟩
synonyms enunciate
related words express, pronounce, say, verbalize, vocalize, voice; speak out, speak up
near antonyms falter, grunt, halt, hesitate, maunder, sputter, stammer, stumble, stutter; mouth, mumble, murmur, mutter, whisper
2 to convey in appropriate or telling terms — see PHRASE
3 to express (a thought or emotion) in words — see SAY 1
articulateness *n* the art or power of speaking or writing in a forceful and convincing way — see ELOQUENCE
articulation *n* **1** an act, process, or means of putting something into words — see EXPRESSION 1
2 the clear and accurate pronunciation of words especially in public speaking — see DICTION 1
artifice *n* **1** a clever often underhanded means to achieve an end — see TRICK 1
2 skill in achieving one's ends through indirect, subtle, or underhanded means — see CUNNING 1
3 subtle or imaginative ability in inventing, devising, or executing something — see SKILL 1
4 the inclination or practice of misleading others through lies or trickery — see DECEIT
5 the use of clever underhanded actions to achieve an end — see TRICKERY
artificer *n* a person whose occupation requires skill with the hands — see ARTISAN
artificial *adj* **1** lacking in natural or spontaneous quality ⟨the beauty-pageant contestants' *artificial* smiles looked like they were glued on their faces⟩
synonyms affected, assumed, bogus, contrived, factitious, fake, false, feigned, forced, mechanical, mock, phony (*also* phoney), pretended, pseudo, put-on, sham, simulated, spurious, strained, unnatural
related words automatic, canned, concocted, fabricated, labored, manufactured, unauthentic, unreal, unrealistic; empty, facile, hollow, hypocritical, insincere, left-handed; exaggerated, histrionic, melodramatic, overacted, overdone, theatrical; cute, cutesy, goody-goody, mincing, overrefined, simpering; conventional, formal, impersonal, inflexible, rigid, stiff, stylized, wooden; artful, calculated, conscious, cultivated, deliberate, premeditated, studied
near antonyms authentic, bona fide, real, realistic, true; honest, ingenuous, sincere, unpretending; easy, effortless, smooth; extemporaneous, impromptu, impulsive, instinctive, unconscious, unprompted, unrehearsed
antonyms artless, genuine, natural, spontaneous, unaffected, unfeigned, unforced
2 not being or expressing what one appears to be or express — see INSINCERE
3 being such in appearance only and made with or manufactured from usually cheaper materials — see IMITATION
artillery *n* large firearms (as cannon or rockets) ⟨during the *artillery* attack families hid in their cellars⟩
synonyms guns, ordnance

related words ammunition, armament, arms, munitions, weaponry, weapons
artisan *n* a person whose occupation requires skill with the hands ⟨we visited a re-created 19th-century New England village that features an array of *artisans* —a cooper, a carpenter, a blacksmith, a potter, a glassblower⟩
synonyms artificer, craftsman, handicrafter, tradesman
related words artist, maker; journeyman, master; mechanic, smith, technician, wright; handyman
artist *n* a person with a high level of knowledge or skill in a field — see EXPERT
artistic *adj* of or relating to the fine arts — see CULTURAL
artistry *n* subtle or imaginative ability in inventing, devising, or executing something — see SKILL 1
artless *adj* **1** free from any intent to deceive or impress others — see GUILELESS
2 hastily or roughly constructed — see RUDE 1
artlessly *adv* without any attempt to impress by deception or exaggeration — see NATURALLY 3
artlessness *n* the quality or state of being simple and sincere — see NAÏVETÉ 1
as *conj* for the reason that — see SINCE
ascend *vb* to move or extend upward ⟨the path *ascended* so steeply at one point that we had to scramble up on our hands and knees⟩
synonyms arise, climb, lift, mount, rise, soar, up, uprise, upsweep, upturn
related words boost, elevate, raise, uplift, upraise; take off, zoom; crest, scale, surmount, top
near antonyms dive, nose-dive, plummet, plunge, sink, slide
antonyms decline, descend, dip, drop, fall (off)
ascendancy *n* controlling power or influence over others — see SUPREMACY 1
ascension *n* the act or an instance of rising or climbing up — see ASCENT 1
ascent *n* **1** the act or an instance of rising or climbing up ⟨our plane broke through some heavy low clouds during its *ascent* and leveled off once we were above them⟩
synonyms ascension, climb, rise, rising, soar
related words boost, hike, increase, raise; elevation, levitation, lift-off, raising, takeoff; heave, upheaval, uplifting, upraising, upsurge, upsweep, upswing, uptrend, upturn, upwelling
near antonyms dive, nosedive, plop, plummeting, plunge, sinking; decline, decrease
antonyms descent, dip, drop, fall
2 an upward slope ⟨we'd reached the final *ascent* of the trail to the summit⟩
synonyms rise, upgrade
related words grade, incline; climb, hump, mound, ridge, swell
near antonyms basin, depression, hollow
antonyms declension, decline, declivity, descent, downgrade
3 a raising or a state of being raised to a higher rank or position — see ADVANCEMENT 1
ascertain *vb* **1** to come to an awareness — see DISCOVER 1
2 to come upon after searching, study, or effort — see FIND 1
ascribe *vb* to explain (something) as being the result of something else — see CREDIT 1
aseptic *adj* free from filth, infection, or dangers to health — see SANITARY
ashamed *adj* suffering from or expressive of a feel-

ing of responsibility for wrongdoing — see GUILTY 2

ashen *adj* lacking a healthy skin color — see PALE 2

ashes *n pl* the portion or bits of something left over or behind after it has been destroyed — see REMAINS 1

ashy *adj* lacking a healthy skin color — see PALE 2

aside from *prep* not including — see EXCEPT

as if *conj* the way it would be or one would do if ⟨she looked *as if* she wanted to ask one more question before we left⟩
synonyms as though, like

asinine *adj* showing or marked by a lack of good sense or judgment — see FOOLISH 1

asininity *n* **1** a foolish act or idea — see FOLLY 1
2 lack of good sense or judgment — see FOOLISHNESS 1

ask *vb* **1** to put a question or questions to ⟨my grandfather *asked* me all about my trip⟩
synonyms inquire (of), interrogate, query, question, quiz
related words cross-examine, examine, grill, pump; poll, survey
near antonyms rejoin, retort; comment, observe, remark
antonyms answer, reply, respond
2 to make a request of ⟨*ask* the sales clerk for assistance⟩
synonyms request, solicit
related words appeal (to), beg, beseech, entreat, implore, importune, invoke, petition, pray, supplicate; demand, enjoin, exact, press, require
phrases call on (*or* upon)
3 to set or receive as a price — see CHARGE 1

ask (for) *vb* **1** to make a request for ⟨don't be afraid to *ask for* help if you need it⟩
synonyms call (for), plead (for), quest, request, seek, solicit, sue (for)
related words apply (for), beg (for), clamor (for), urge; demand, enjoin, exact, insist (on), require, requisition
2 to act so as to make (something) more likely — see COURT 1
3 to give a request or demand for — see ORDER 2

askance *adv* with distrust ⟨we looked *askance* at the dealer's assertion that the car had never been in an accident⟩
synonyms distrustfully, doubtfully, doubtingly, dubiously, mistrustfully, skeptically, suspiciously
related words hesitantly, hesitatingly, incredulously, questioningly, quizzically, unbelievingly; charily, guardedly, warily; captiously, critically, cynically, deprecatingly, disapprovingly, disparagingly, negatively, reproachfully, unfavorably; anxiously, apprehensively, uncomfortably, uneasily
phrases with a grain of salt
near antonyms approvingly, favorably, positively; confidently, sanguinely; credulously, uncritically
antonyms trustfully, trustingly

askew *adj* inclined or twisted to one side — see AWRY

aslant *adj* inclined or twisted to one side — see AWRY

asleep *adj* **1** being in a state of suspended consciousness ⟨Paul was *asleep* when the earthquake struck⟩
synonyms dormant, dozing, napping, resting, sleeping, slumbering
related words drowsy, nodding, sleepy, slumber-

ous (*or* slumbrous), somnolent; dreaming, reposing; hypnotized, mesmerized, semiconscious
near antonyms aware, conscious; sleepless; aroused, astir, up
antonyms awake, wakeful, wide-awake
2 lacking in sensation or feeling — see NUMB

aspect *n* **1** a certain way in which something appears or may be regarded ⟨depending on what *aspect* of college life you consider most important, there are several colleges which might be good for you⟩
synonyms angle, facet, hand, phase, side
related words air, appearance, character, color, complexion, condition, face, look, semblance, shape, state, visage; period, stage, step; point of view, position, posture, stance, standpoint, view, viewpoint; interpretation, reading, rendering, translation, version; article, case, component, count, detail, element, factor, instance, item, matter, part, particular, point, regard, respect
2 the outward form of someone or something especially as indicative of a quality — see APPEARANCE 1

asperity *n* **1** a harsh or sharp quality — see EDGE 1
2 biting sharpness of feeling or expression — see ACRIMONY 1
3 something that is a cause for suffering or special effort especially in the attainment of a goal — see DIFFICULTY 1

asperse *vb* to make untrue and harmful statements about — see SLANDER

aspersing *n* the making of false statements that damage another's reputation — see SLANDER

aspirant *n* one who seeks an office, honor, position, or award — see CANDIDATE

aspiration *n* **1** eager desire for personal advancement — see AMBITION 1
2 something that one hopes or intends to accomplish — see GOAL

aspire *vb* to have in mind as a purpose or goal — see INTEND

aspiring *adj* having a strong desire for personal advancement — see AMBITIOUS 1

ass *n* a sturdy and patient domestic mammal that is used especially to carry things — see DONKEY 1

assail *vb* **1** to criticize harshly and usually publicly — see ATTACK 2
2 to take sudden, violent action against — see ATTACK 1

assassin *n* a person who kills another person ⟨shot down by an unknown *assassin*⟩
synonyms killer, murderer
related words butcher, executioner, slaughterer, slayer

assault *n* the act or action of setting upon with force or violence — see ATTACK 1

assault *vb* to take sudden, violent action against — see ATTACK 1

assay *n* the separation and identification of the parts of a whole — see ANALYSIS 1

assay *vb* **1** to identify and examine the basic elements or parts of (something) especially for discovering interrelationships — see ANALYZE
2 to make an effort to do — see ATTEMPT

assemblage *n* **1** a body of people come together in one place — see GATHERING 1
2 a mass or quantity that has piled up or that has been gathered — see ACCUMULATION 1

3 a number of things considered as a unit — see GROUP 1

4 an organized group of objects acquired and maintained for study, exhibition, or personal pleasure — see COLLECTION 1

assemble *vb* **1** to come together into one body or place ⟨the graduates were told to *assemble* in the cafeteria an hour before the ceremony⟩

synonyms cluster, collect, concentrate, conglomerate, congregate, convene, converge, forgather (*or* foregather), gather, meet, rendezvous

related words affiliate, ally, associate, band (together), club, collaborate, confederate, conjoin, consolidate, consort, cooperate, couple, federate, gang (up), join, merge, unite

near antonyms depart, leave, take off; disjoin, dissociate, disunite

antonyms break up, disband, disperse, split up

2 to form by putting together parts or materials — see BUILD

3 to bring together in assembly by or as if by command — see CONVOKE

4 to bring together in one body or place — see GATHER 1

assembly *n* **1** a body of people come together in one place — see GATHERING 1

2 a body of persons gathered for religious worship — see CONGREGATION 1

3 a coming together of a number of persons for a specified purpose — see MEETING 1

assert *vb* **1** to state clearly and strongly ⟨Mrs. Cartwright is never afraid to *assert* her allegiance to flag and country⟩

synonyms affirm, aver, avouch, avow, declare, lay down, profess

related words advance, advertise, boost, plug, promote, publicize; announce, blaze, call, proclaim, pronounce, say; accent, accentuate, emphasize, stress, underline, underscore; advocate, champion, defend, espouse, support, uphold; assure, convince, persuade; explain, justify, rationalize

near antonyms minimize, understate; disregard, ignore, neglect, overlook

2 to state (something) as a reason in support of or against something under consideration — see ARGUE 1

3 to state as a fact usually forcefully — see CLAIM 1

assertion *n* **1** a solemn and often public declaration of the truth or existence of something — see PROTESTATION

2 an idea or opinion that is put forth in a discussion or debate — see CONTENTION

assertive *adj* **1** having or showing a bold forcefulness in the pursuit of a goal — see AGGRESSIVE 1

2 marked by or uttered with forcefulness — see EMPHATIC 1

assertiveness *n* the quality or state of being forceful (as in expression) — see VEHEMENCE 1

assess *vb* **1** to establish or apply as a charge or penalty — see IMPOSE

2 to make an approximate or tentative judgment regarding — see ESTIMATE 1

assessment *n* **1** a charge usually of money collected by the government from people or businesses for public use — see TAX

2 an opinion on the nature, character, or quality of something — see ESTIMATION 1

3 the act of placing a value on the nature, character, or quality of something — see ESTIMATE 1

assets *n pl* the total of one's money and property — see WEALTH 1

assiduity *n* attentive and persistent effort — see DILIGENCE

assiduous *adj* involved in often constant activity — see BUSY 1

assiduously *adv* with great effort or determination — see HARD 1

assiduousness *n* attentive and persistent effort — see DILIGENCE

assign *vb* **1** to give a task, duty, or responsibility to — see ENTRUST 1

2 to give as a share or portion — see ALLOT

3 to give over the legal possession or ownership of — see TRANSFER 1

4 to pick (someone) by one's authority for a specific position or duty — see APPOINT 2

assignment *n* **1** a piece of work that needs to be done regularly — see CHORE 1

2 a specific task with which a person or group is charged — see MISSION

3 something assigned to be read or studied — see LESSON

4 the state or fact of being chosen for a position or duty — see APPOINTMENT 1

assimilate *vb* to make a part of a body or system — see EMBODY 1

assist *n* an act or instance of helping — see HELP 1

assist *vb* to provide (someone) with what is useful or necessary to achieve an end — see HELP 1

assistance *n* an act or instance of helping — see HELP 1

assistant *n* a person who helps a more skilled person — see HELPER

associate *n* **1** a person frequently seen in the company of another ⟨after he took up skateboarding, Michael gained a whole new set of *associates*⟩

synonyms cohort, companion, comrade, crony, fellow, hobnobber, mate

related words colleague, coworker, equal, peer, workmate; accomplice, affiliate, ally, collaborator, confederate, partner; buddy, chum, confidant, familiar, friend, hearty, intimate, pal; compatriot, countryman; classmate, housemate, messmate, playmate, roommate, schoolmate, shipmate, teammate; attendant, escort; hanger-on, leech, parasite

2 a fellow worker — see COLLEAGUE

associate *vb* **1** to come or be together as friends ⟨a boy who would *associate* only with other hardcore basketball fans⟩

synonyms chum, consort, fraternize, hang around, hobnob, pal (around)

related words affiliate, ally, attach, band, bond, club, collaborate, collude, confederate, conjoin, connect, cooperate, couple, gang, get along, group, hook, interrelate, join, knot, league, link, mingle, mix, rally, relate, side, socialize, team, tie, wed

phrases rub elbows (with), rub shoulders (with), take up with

near antonyms avoid, cold-shoulder, shun, snub; alienate, estrange; break up, disband, disperse, split up; disjoin, dissociate, disunite, divorce, sever, split, sunder

2 to think of (something) in combination ⟨Kelly *associates* getting shots with ice cream cones, her treat every time she goes to the doctor⟩

synonyms connect, correlate, identify, link, relate

THESAURUS

related words compare, equate, liken; group, join, lump (together), tie (together)

near antonyms contrast, differentiate, discriminate, distinguish, separate, set off

3 to come together to form a single unit — see UNITE 1

4 to form or enter into an association that furthers the interests of its members — see ALLY

5 to take part in social activities — see SOCIALIZE

association *n* **1** the state of having shared interests or efforts (as in social or business matters) ⟨Rita was honored for her long *association* with the Montgomery Benevolent Society⟩

synonyms affiliation, alliance, collaboration, confederation, connection, cooperation, hookup, liaison, linkup, partnership, relation, relationship, tie-up, union

related words business, dealings, interaction; exchange, interconnection, interrelation, mutualism, reciprocity, symbiosis; incorporation, integration, merger, unification; affinity, attachment, closeness, intimacy, rapport, sympathy; kinship, oneness, solidarity, togetherness, unity; companionship, company, fellowship

near antonyms breakup, dissolution, disunion; division, parting, separation, severance, split; alienation, divorce, estrangement

antonyms dissociation

2 a group of persons formally joined together for some common interest ⟨all *associations* meeting on school property must be registered with and approved by the principal's office⟩

synonyms brotherhood, club, college, congress, council, fellowship, fraternity, guild (*also* gild), institute, institution, junto, league, order, organization, society, sodality

related words collective, commune, community, cooperative; alliance, bloc, coalition, partnership; body, group; circle, clan, clique, coterie, lot, set; crew, outfit, party, squad, team; branch, chapter, local; faithful, fold, membership; sisterhood, sorority; cabal, confederacy, conspiracy; band, gang, ring; cartel, combine, syndicate

3 the fact or state of having something in common — see CONNECTION 1

assort *vb* to arrange or assign according to type — see CLASSIFY 1

assorted *adj* consisting of many things of different sorts — see MISCELLANEOUS

assortment *n* **1** an unorganized collection or mixture of various things — see MISCELLANY 1

2 the quality or state of being composed of many different elements or types — see VARIETY 1

assuage *vb* **1** to make more bearable or less severe — see HELP 2

2 to put a complete end to (a physical need or desire) — see SATISFY 1

assume *vb* **1** to take to or upon oneself ⟨Josh promised to *assume* responsibility for any damage to the flower beds caused by the volleyball game in the backyard⟩

synonyms accept, bear, shoulder, take over, undertake

related words adopt, embrace; back, endorse (*also* indorse), espouse, stand by, support, uphold; accede, acquiesce, agree, assent, consent

near antonyms abjure, recant, renounce, retract, take back; decline, refuse, reject, spurn, turn down; abstain, forbear, refrain; avoid, bypass, detour

antonyms disavow, disclaim, disown, repudiate

2 to take as true or as a fact without actual proof ⟨everyone *assumed*, wrongly, that someone else was bringing dessert⟩

synonyms postulate, premise, presume, presuppose, suppose

related words accept, believe, credit, swallow; conclude, deduce, gather, judge, infer, take; conjecture, figure, guess, reckon [*chiefly dialect*], surmise, suspect, think; conceive, dream, fancy, imagine, perceive, preconceive; hypothesize, speculate, theorize; affirm, allege, assert, aver, avouch, avow, claim, contend, declare, insist, maintain, profess

phrases take for granted

near antonyms challenge, disbelieve, discount, discredit, dispute, distrust, doubt, mistrust, question, suspect, wonder (about); deny, disavow, disclaim, disown, reject, repudiate; confute, disprove, rebut, refute

3 to form an opinion from little or no evidence — see GUESS 1

4 to present a false appearance of — see FEIGN

assumed *adj* **1** appearing to be true on the basis of evidence that may or may not be confirmed — see APPARENT 1

2 lacking in natural or spontaneous quality — see ARTIFICIAL 1

assumption *n* something taken as being true or factual and used as a starting point for a course of action or reasoning ⟨the widespread *assumption* that violent entertainment leads to violent behavior in children⟩ ⟨your argument is faulty because it's based on erroneous *assumptions*⟩

synonyms postulate, premise, presumption, presupposition, supposition

related words hypothesis, proposition, theory, thesis; axiom, truism, verity; belief, canon, doctrine, dogma, gospel, law; precept, principle, rule, standard, tenet; basis, foundation, ground; conclusion, deduction, inference; affirmation, assertion, avouchment, declaration

assurance *n* **1** a state of mind in which one is free from doubt — see CONFIDENCE 1

2 great faith in oneself or one's abilities — see CONFIDENCE 1

assure *vb* **1** to ease the grief or distress of — see COMFORT 1

2 to make sure, certain, or safe — see ENSURE

assured *adj* **1** having or showing a mind free from doubt — see CERTAIN 2

2 having or showing great faith in oneself or one's abilities — see CONFIDENT 1

assuredly *adv* without any question — see INDEED 1

assuredness *n* a state of mind in which one is free from doubt — see CONFIDENCE 2

astern *adv* near, toward, or in the stern of a ship or the tail of an aircraft — see AFT

as though *conj* the way it would be or one would do if — see AS IF

astir *adj* marked by much life, movement, or activity — see ALIVE 2

astonish *vb* to make a strong impression on (someone) with something unexpected — see SURPRISE 1

astonished *adj* **1** affected with sudden and great wonder or surprise — see THUNDERSTRUCK

2 filled with amazement or wonder — see OPENMOUTHED

astonishing *adj* **1** causing a strong emotional reaction because unexpected — see SURPRISING 1
2 causing wonder or astonishment — see MARVELOUS 1
astonishment *n* **1** the rapt attention and deep emotion caused by the sight of something extraordinary — see WONDER 2
2 the state of being strongly impressed by something unexpected or unusual — see SURPRISE 2
astound *vb* to make a strong impression on (someone) with something unexpected — see SURPRISE 1
astounded *adj* **1** affected with sudden and great wonder or surprise — see THUNDERSTRUCK
2 filled with amazement or wonder — see OPENMOUTHED
astounding *adj* **1** causing a strong emotional reaction because unexpected — see SURPRISING 1
2 causing wonder or astonishment — see MARVELOUS 1
astral *adj* of or relating to the stars — see STELLAR 1
astray *adv* off the desired or intended path or course — see WRONG 1
astronomical *also* **astronomic** *adj* unusually large — see HUGE
astronomically *adv* to a large extent or degree — see GREATLY 2
astute *adj* having or showing a practical cleverness or judgment — see SHREWD
asunder *adv* into parts or to pieces — see APART
as well as *prep* in addition to — see BESIDES 1
asylum *n* **1** a place where insane people are cared for — see MADHOUSE 1
2 something (as a building) that offers cover from the weather or protection from danger — see SHELTER
at all *adv* in any way or respect ⟨Ted wasn't *at all* pleased with the way his mother's birthday cake came out⟩
synonyms anywise, ever, half
related words somehow, someway; remotely
phrases by any means
athirst *adj* showing urgent desire or interest — see EAGER
athwart *adv* in a line or direction running from corner to corner — see CROSSWISE
athwart *prep* to the opposite side of — see ACROSS
atmosphere *n* **1** a special quality or impression associated with something — see AURA
2 the circumstances, conditions, or objects by which one is surrounded — see ENVIRONMENT
atom *n* a very small piece — see BIT 1
atomic *adj* very small in size — see TINY
atomize *vb* to reduce to fine particles — see POWDER
atone (for) *vb* to make up for (an offense) — see EXPIATE
atrocious *adj* **1** extremely disturbing or repellent — see HORRIBLE 1
2 extremely unsatisfactory — see WRETCHED 1
atrociousness *n* **1** the quality of inspiring intense dread or dismay — see HORROR 1
2 the state or quality of being utterly evil — see ENORMITY 1
atrocity *n* **1** the quality of inspiring intense dread or dismay — see HORROR 1
2 the state or quality of being utterly evil — see ENORMITY 1

attach *vb* **1** to cause (something) to hold to another — see FASTEN 1
2 to pick (someone) by one's authority for a specific position or duty — see APPOINT 2
attached *adj* having a liking or affection — see FOND 1
attachment *n* **1** a feeling of strong or constant regard for and dedication to someone — see LOVE 1
2 something that is not necessary in itself but adds to the convenience or performance of the main piece of equipment — see ACCESSORY 1
attack *n* **1** the act or action of setting upon with force or violence ⟨The USS Constitution was nicknamed "Old Ironsides" after its oaken hull successfully withstood a British *attack*⟩
synonyms aggression, assault, blitzkrieg, charge, descent, offense (*or* offence), offensive, onset, onslaught, raid, rush, strike
related words ambuscade, ambush; counterattack, counteroffensive, sally, sortie; foray, incursion, invasion; pillage, ravage, sack; air raid, blitz, bombardment; siege, storm
near antonyms defense, defensive, guard, shield; opposition, resistance; protection, security, shelter
2 a sudden experiencing of a physical or mental disorder ⟨malaria is characterized by periodic *attacks* of chills and fever⟩
synonyms bout, case, fit, seizure, siege, spell
related words recurrence, relapse; brainstorm, convulsion, pang, paroxysm, spasm, throe; breakdown, collapse, prostration
near antonyms arrest, relief, remission
attack *vb* **1** to take sudden, violent action against ⟨my dog unexpectedly *attacked* the mailman, sinking his teeth into the startled man's leg⟩
synonyms assail, assault, beset, charge, descend (on *or* upon), jump (on), pounce (on *or* upon), raid, rush, storm, strike
related words gang (up on), mob, swarm; mug, rob; ambuscade, ambush, surprise, waylay; blitz, bomb, bombard; beleaguer, besiege; harry, loot, pillage, plunder, ravage, sack; foray, invade, overrun
phrases fly at, give it to, go at, set upon
near antonyms cover, defend, guard, protect, secure, shield
2 to criticize harshly and usually publicly ⟨the mayor and all his aides were *attacked* mercilessly in the press when the scandal erupted⟩
synonyms abuse, assail, belabor, blast, castigate, excoriate, jump (on), lambaste (*or* lambast), scathe, slam, vituperate
related words berate, harangue, harass, harry, revile, scold; blaspheme, curse, execrate, imprecate, profane; affront, insult, slur; asperse, bad-mouth, belittle, disparage, put down; libel, slander, traduce; chastise, chide, criticize, rebuke, reprimand, reproof; fulminate, lash (out)
near antonyms acclaim, commend, compliment, laud, praise
3 to start work on energetically ⟨Courtney *attacked* the huge mess in her room with determination and enthusiasm⟩
synonyms tackle, wade (into)
related words address, approach, face; buckle (down to), concentrate (on), focus (on), knuckle down (to), zero in (on); fall (to), pitch in, plunge (in), settle (down); pursue, take up, undertake
phrases go at, have at, sail into

near antonyms avoid, evade, shun; dally, dawdle, dillydally, fiddle, fool, idle, lag, mess, monkey, play, poke, potter, putter, trifle

attain *vb* **1** to obtain (as a goal) through effort — see ACHIEVE 1

2 to receive as return for effort — see EARN 1

attainable *adj* **1** capable of being done or carried out — see POSSIBLE 1

2 possible to get — see AVAILABLE 1

attainment *n* **1** a successful result brought about by hard work — see ACCOMPLISHMENT 1

2 the state of being actual or complete — see FRUITION

attempt *n* an effort to do or accomplish something ⟨it took several *attempts* before we made good ice cream with an old-fashioned hand-cranked ice cream freezer⟩

synonyms crack, endeavor, essay, fling, go, pass, shot, stab, trial, try, whack

related words bid, striving, struggle, throes, undertaking; trial and error

attempt *vb* to make an effort to do ⟨after *attempting*— and failing—to start the lawn mower on my own, I finally succeeded with Dad's help⟩ ⟨don't even *attempt* walking on your broken foot⟩

synonyms assay, endeavor, essay, seek, strive, try

related words fight, strain, struggle, toil, trouble, work; aim, aspire, hope; assume, take up, undertake

phrases have a go at

near antonyms drop, give up, quit

attend *vb* **1** to go along with in order to provide assistance, protection, or companionship — see AC-COMPANY

2 to pay attention especially through the act of hearing — see LISTEN

3 to take charge of especially on behalf of another — see ²TEND 1

attendant *adj* **1** coming as a result — see RESULT-ANT

2 present at the same time and place — see COIN-CIDENT

attendant *n* one that accompanies another for protection, guidance, or as a courtesy — see ES-CORT

attending *adj* **1** being within the confines of a specified place — see PRESENT 2

2 present at the same time and place — see COIN-CIDENT

attention *n* **1** a focusing of the mind on something ⟨I need your full *attention* right now⟩

synonyms absorption, concentration, engrossment, enthrallment, immersion

related words fixation, obsession, preoccupation; alertness, application, awareness, consciousness, consideration, heedfulness, intentness, raptness

near antonyms absence, absentmindedness, abstractedness, abstraction, detachment, distraction, obliviousness, remoteness, unawareness, unconsciousness, withdrawal; disinterest, indifference, mindlessness, unconcern; befuddlement, bemusement, bewilderment, confusion

antonyms inattention

2 a state of being aware ⟨several mothers brought to the committee's *attention* the deplorable condition of the playground⟩

synonyms awareness, cognizance, ear, eye, heed, notice, observance, observation

related words advisement, care, concern, consideration, regard, watch; apprehension, discern-

ment, grasp, mind, perception, recognition, thought, understanding

near antonyms disregard, neglect, obliviousness, unawareness

attentive *adj* **1** having the mind fixed on something ⟨Susan became particularly *attentive* when the sportscaster turned to field hockey, her favorite sport⟩

synonyms absorbed, engrossed, enthralled, focused (*also* focussed), immersed, intent, observant, rapt

related words interested, intrigued, involved; hypnotized, mesmerized; alert, alive, conscious, open-eyed, watchful, wide-awake

near antonyms daydreaming, dreamy, faraway, foggy, hazy, oblivious, preoccupied, remote; apathetic, disinterested, uninterested

antonyms absent, absentminded, abstracted, distracted, inattentive, unabsorbed, unfocused (*also* unfocussed), unobservant

2 given to or made with heedful anticipation of the needs and happiness of others — see THOUGHTFUL 1

3 paying close attention usually for the purpose of anticipating approaching danger or opportunity — see ALERT 1

attentiveness *n* the act or state of being constantly attentive and responsive to signs of opportunity, activity, or danger — see VIGILANCE

attest *vb* **1** to declare (something) to be true or genuine — see CERTIFY 1

2 to make a solemn declaration under oath for the purpose of establishing a fact — see TESTIFY

attestation *n* something presented in support of the truth or accuracy of a claim — see PROOF

attire *n* covering for the human body — see CLOTHING

attire *vb* to outfit with clothes and especially fine or special clothes — see CLOTHE 1

attorney *n* **1** a person who acts or does business for another — see AGENT 2

2 a person whose profession is to conduct lawsuits for clients or to advise about legal rights and obligations — see LAWYER

attraction *n* something that attracts interest — see MAGNET

attractive *adj* **1** having an often mysterious or magical power to attract — see FASCINATING 1

2 very pleasing to look at — see BEAUTIFUL

attractiveness *n* **1** the power of irresistible attraction — see CHARM 2

2 the qualities in a person or thing that as a whole give pleasure to the senses — see BEAUTY 1

attribute *n* something that sets apart an individual from others of the same kind — see CHARACTER-ISTIC

attribute *vb* to explain (something) as being the result of something else — see CREDIT 1

attrition *n* a gradual weakening, loss, or destruction — see CORROSION

atypical *adj* **1** being out of the ordinary — see EX-CEPTIONAL

2 departing from some accepted standard of what is normal — see DEVIANT

audacious *adj* inclined or willing to take risks — see BOLD 1

audacity *n* shameless boldness — see EFFRONTERY

audibly *adv* with one's normal voice speaking the words — see ALOUD

audit *n* a close look at or over someone or something in order to judge condition — see INSPECTION

audit *vb* to look over closely (as for judging quality or condition) — see INSPECT

auditorium *n* a large room or building for enclosed public gatherings — see HALL 3

auditory *adj* of, relating to, or experienced through the sense of hearing ⟨I have a bad *auditory* memory—unless I see a word in writing, and not just hear it, I forget it easily⟩
synonyms acoustic (*or* acoustical), aural, auricular
related words audible, clear, discernible, distinct, distinguishable, heard, perceptible
near antonyms faint, feeble, imperceptible, inaudible, indistinguishable, indistinct; low, noiseless, quiet, silent, soft, soundless

aught *n* the numerical symbol 0 or the absence of number or quantity represented by it — see ZERO 1

augment *vb* to make greater in size, amount, or number — see INCREASE 1

augmentation *n* something added (as by growth) — see INCREASE 1

augur *n* one who predicts future events or developments — see PROPHET

augur *vb* 1 to show signs of a favorable or successful outcome — see BODE
2 to tell of or describe beforehand — see FORETELL

auguring *n* a declaration that something will happen in the future — see PREDICTION

augury *n* something believed to be a sign or warning of a future event — see OMEN

august *adj* 1 having or showing a serious and reserved manner — see DIGNIFIED
2 large and impressive in size, grandeur, extent, or conception — see GRAND 1

augustness *n* 1 a dignified bearing or appearance befitting royalty — see MAJESTY 1
2 impressiveness of beauty on a large scale — see MAGNIFICENCE

auld lang syne *n* the events or experience of former times — see PAST

aura *n* a special quality or impression associated with something ⟨the monastery perched high on a mountaintop had an *aura* of unreality and mystery about it⟩
synonyms air, atmosphere, climate, flavor, mood, note, temper
related words feel, feeling, sensation, sense, spirit; attribute, character, characteristic, image, mark, notion, peculiarity, picture, property, trait; color, illusion, overtone, semblance, suggestion, tone

aural *adj* of, relating to, or experienced through the sense of hearing — see AUDITORY

au revoir *n* an expression of good wishes at parting — see GOOD-BYE

auricular *adj* of, relating to, or experienced through the sense of hearing — see AUDITORY

aurora *n* the first appearance of light in the morning or the time of its appearance — see DAWN 1

auspice *n* something believed to be a sign or warning of a future event — see OMEN

auspicious *adj* 1 having qualities which inspire hope — see HOPEFUL 1
2 pointing toward a happy outcome — see FAVORABLE 2

austere *adj* 1 given to exacting standards of discipline and self-restraint — see SEVERE 1

2 harsh and threatening in manner or appearance — see GRIM 1

authentic *adj* 1 being exactly as appears or as claimed ⟨found an *authentic* Native American arrowhead⟩
synonyms bona fide, genuine, real, right, true
related words actual, historical, original; lawful, legal, legitimate; identifiable, recognizable, verifiable; proven, substantiated, validated, verified; incontestable, incontrovertible, indisputable, indubitable, irrefutable, undeniable, undoubted, unmistakable, unquestionable; veritable, very; accurate, correct, proper; pure, unadulterated, unalloyed
near antonyms artificial, factitious, imitation, man-made, simulated, synthetic, unnatural; concocted, fabricated, manufactured; deceptive, delusive, delusory, misleading; unauthenticated, unverified
antonyms bogus, counterfeit, fake, false, mock, phony (*also* phoney), pseudo, sham, spurious, unauthentic, unreal
2 following an original exactly — see FAITHFUL 2

authentically *adv* in actual fact — see VERY 2

authenticate *vb* to declare (something) to be true or genuine — see CERTIFY 1

author *n* 1 a person who creates a written work ⟨a brilliant novel by a first-time *author*⟩
synonyms penman, writer
related words coauthor, ghostwriter, hack, scribbler; autobiographer, biographer; novelist; essayist, pamphleteer; dramatist, playwright, scenarist, screenwriter, scriptwriter; bard, poet, rhymer (*or* rimer); columnist, journalist, newspaperman, reporter, sportswriter
2 a person who establishes a whole new field of endeavor — see FATHER 2

author *vb* to compose and set down on paper the words of — see WRITE 1

authoritarian *adj* 1 fond of ordering people around — see BOSSY
2 given to exacting standards of discipline and self-restraint — see SEVERE 1

authoritative *adj* 1 being the most accurate and apparently thorough — see DEFINITIVE 1
2 having power over the minds or behavior of others — see INFLUENTIAL 1

authority *n* 1 a person with a high level of knowledge or skill in a field — see EXPERT
2 lawful control over the affairs of a political unit (as a nation) — see RULE 2
3 the power to direct the thinking or behavior of others usually indirectly — see INFLUENCE 1
4 the right or means to command or control others — see POWER 1

authorization *n* 1 the approval by someone in authority for the doing of something — see PERMISSION
2 the granting of power to perform various acts or duties — see COMMISSION 1
3 the right to act or move freely — see FREEDOM 2

authorize *vb* 1 to give official or legal power to ⟨only the school nurse is *authorized* to give any necessary shots⟩
synonyms accredit, certify, commission, empower, enable, invest, license (*or* licence), qualify
related words approve, clear, endorse (*also* indorse), OK (*or* okay), sanction; affirm, confirm, validate; inaugurate, induct, initiate, install, in-

state, swear in; allow, let, permit; enfranchise, entitle, privilege

near antonyms ban, bar, block, constrain, deny, disallow, disbar, discourage, disenfranchise, disfranchise, disqualify, exclude, hinder, hold back, impede, inhibit, obstruct, prevent, shut out, stop; enjoin, forbid, interdict, outlaw, prohibit, proscribe, veto

2 to give a right to — see ENTITLE 1

3 to give official acceptance of something as satisfactory — see APPROVE

authorized *adj* ordered or allowed by those in authority — see OFFICIAL

auto *n* a self-propelled passenger vehicle on wheels — see CAR

autocracy *n* a system of government in which the ruler has unlimited power — see DESPOTISM

autocrat *n* **1** a person who uses power or authority in a cruel, unjust, or harmful way — see DESPOT

2 one who rules over a people with a sole, supreme, and usually hereditary authority — see MONARCH

autocratic *adj* **1** exercising power or authority without interference by others — see ABSOLUTE 1

2 fond of ordering people around — see BOSSY

autograph *vb* to write one's name on (as a document) — see SIGN

automated *adj* designed to replace or decrease human labor and especially physical labor — see LABORSAVING

automatic *adj* **1** done instantly and without conscious thought or decision ⟨Carl's *automatic* use of the brakes prevented a serious accident⟩

synonyms instinctive, instinctual, involuntary, mechanical, spontaneous

related words conditioned, natural, reactive, reflex, simple, subliminal, unconscious, unforced; blind, inadvertent, unintended, unintentional, unwilling, unwitting; abrupt, quick, ready, sudden; ad-lib, extemporaneous, extempore, impromptu, improvised, offhand, offhanded, snap, spur-of-the-moment, unconsidered, unplanned, unpremeditated, unprepared, unprompted, unreasoned, unrehearsed, unstudied; casual, chance, chancy, haphazard, hasty, hit-or-miss, impetuous, impulsive, perfunctory, random, rash

near antonyms calculated, conscious, cultivated, deliberate, designed, intended, intentional, predetermined, prepared, projected, refined, rehearsed, volitional, voluntary, willed, willful (*or* wilful); advised, aforethought, careful, considered, foresighted, forethoughtful, measured, meticulous, reasoned, studied, thoughtful

2 designed to replace or decrease human labor and especially physical labor — see LABORSAVING

automobile *n* a self-propelled passenger vehicle on wheels — see CAR

automobile *vb* to travel by a motorized vehicle — see DRIVE 2

automobilist *n* a person who travels by automobile — see MOTORIST

autonomous *adj* not being under the rule or control of another — see FREE 1

autonomy *n* the state of being free from the control or power of another — see FREEDOM 1

autopsy *n* examination of a dead body especially to find out the cause of death ⟨the *autopsy* revealed an advanced stage of cancer⟩

synonyms postmortem, postmortem examination

related words dissection

near antonyms biopsy, vivisection

auxiliary *adj* available to supply something extra when needed ⟨the auditorium has an *auxiliary* cooling system used only on particularly sweltering days⟩

synonyms accessory, peripheral, supplemental, supplementary

related words backup, makeshift, substitute; added, additional, another, further; complementary, contributory; assistant, assisting, helping, supportive, tributary; secondary, subordinate, subservient, subsidiary; dispensable, excess, nonessential, superfluous, surplus, unessential

near antonyms basic, fundamental, primary, prime; all-important, essential, imperative, indispensable, integral, necessary, needed, needful, required, requisite, vital

antonyms chief, main, principal

avail *n* the capacity for being useful for some purpose — see USE 2

avail *vb* to provide with something useful or desirable — see BENEFIT

available *adj* **1** possible to get ⟨the nursery's orchids are *available* by mail order only⟩ ⟨fare information is readily *available* by using the toll-free number⟩

synonyms accessible, acquirable, attainable, obtainable, procurable

related words purchasable, rentable; furnished, provided, supplied; common, omnipresent, prevalent, ubiquitous, universal, widespread; free, free-for-all, open, public, unrestricted

phrases on hand

near antonyms limited, off-limits, restricted; deficient, lacking, missing, rare, scarce, uncommon

antonyms inaccessible, unattainable, unavailable, unobtainable

2 capable of or suitable for being used for a particular purpose — see USABLE 1

avarice *n* an intense selfish desire for wealth or possessions — see GREED

avaricious *adj* having or marked by an eager and often selfish desire especially for material possessions — see GREEDY 1

avariciousness *n* an intense selfish desire for wealth or possessions — see GREED

avenge *vb* to punish in kind the wrongdoer responsible for ⟨a play about a prince who struggles to *avenge* his father's death⟩

synonyms requite, retaliate, revenge

related words castigate, fix, get, penalize, punish, scourge; chasten, chastise, correct, discipline; redress, right; compensate, pay (back), recompense, repay

phrases get even (for)

near antonyms absolve, condone, excuse, forgive, pardon, remit

avenger *n* one who inflicts punishment in return for an injury or offense — see NEMESIS 1

avenue *n* **1** a passage cleared for public vehicular travel — see WAY 1

2 an established course for traveling from one place to another — see PASSAGE 1

aver *vb* **1** to state as a fact usually forcefully — see CLAIM 1

2 to state clearly and strongly — see ASSERT 1

average *adj* **1** being about midway between extremes of amount or size — see MIDDLE 2

2 being of the type that is encountered in the normal course of events — see ORDINARY 1

3 having or showing the qualities associated with the members of a particular group or kind — see TYPICAL 1

average *n* what is typical of a group, class, or series ⟨my cat's a cut above the *average* when it comes to being a finicky eater⟩

synonyms norm, normal, par, standard

related words golden mean, mean, median, middle; commonplace, ordinary, rule, run, status quo, usual; exemplar, representative

near antonyms abnormality, anomaly, deviation, exception, rarity

averse *adj* having a natural dislike for something — see ANTIPATHETIC

averseness *n* a strong feeling of not liking or approving — see DISLIKE 1

aversion *n* **1** a dislike so strong as to cause stomach upset or queasiness — see DISGUST

2 a strong feeling of not liking or approving — see DISLIKE 1

3 something or someone that is hated — see HATE 2

avert *vb* to keep from happening by taking action in advance — see PREVENT

averting *n* the act or practice of keeping something from happening — see PREVENTION

aviator *n* one who flies or is qualified to fly an aircraft or spacecraft — see PILOT

avid *adj* **1** having or marked by an eager and often selfish desire especially for material possessions — see GREEDY 1

2 showing urgent desire or interest — see EAGER

avidity *n* **1** an intense selfish desire for wealth or possessions — see GREED

2 urgent desire or interest — see EAGERNESS

avoid *vb* to get or keep away from (as a responsibility) through cleverness or trickery — see ESCAPE 2

avoidance *n* the act or a means of getting or keeping away from something undesirable — see ESCAPE 2

avoirdupois *n* the state or quality of being heavy — see WEIGHTINESS 1

avouch *vb* **1** to declare (something) to be true or genuine — see CERTIFY 1

2 to state as a fact usually forcefully — see CLAIM 1

3 to state clearly and strongly — see ASSERT 1

avouchment *n* a solemn and often public declaration of the truth or existence of something — see PROTESTATION

avow *vb* **1** to state as a fact usually forcefully — see CLAIM 1

2 to state clearly and strongly — see ASSERT 1

avowal *n* **1** a solemn and often public declaration of the truth or existence of something — see PROTESTATION

2 an open declaration of something (as a fault or the commission of an offense) about oneself — see CONFESSION

await *vb* **1** to believe in the future occurrence of (something) — see EXPECT

2 to remain in place in readiness or expectation of something — see WAIT

awaited *adj* being in accordance with the prescribed, normal, or logical course of events — see DUE 2

awake *adj* **1** not sleeping or able to sleep — see WAKEFUL

2 paying close attention usually for the purpose of anticipating approaching danger or opportunity — see ALERT 1

awake *vb* **1** to cause to stop sleeping — see WAKE 1

2 to cease to be asleep — see WAKE 2

awaken *vb* **1** to cause to stop sleeping — see WAKE 1

2 to cease to be asleep — see WAKE 2

award *n* something given in recognition of achievement ⟨Faye received the highest *award* in the 16 and under category for her poem⟩

synonyms decoration, distinction, honor, plume, premium, prize

related words badge, crown, cup, laurel, medal, order, ribbon, trophy; accolade, applause, bravo, encomium, eulogy, hallelujah, homage, paean, panegyric, plaudit, tribute; citation, commendation, compliment

award *vb* **1** to give something as a token of gratitude or admiration for a service or achievement — see REWARD

2 to give the ownership or benefit of (something) formally or publicly — see CONFER 1

aware *adj* having specified facts or feelings actively impressed on the mind — see CONSCIOUS

awareness *n* a state of being aware — see ATTENTION 2

awash *adj* containing, covered with, or thoroughly penetrated by water — see WET

away *adj* **1** not close in time or space — see DISTANT 1

2 not at a certain place — see ABSENT 1

away *adv* from this or that place ⟨don't walk *away* while I'm still talking to you⟩

synonyms hence, off

related words apart, aside, elsewhere; abroad, afar, afield, astray

awe *n* the rapt attention and deep emotion caused by the sight of something extraordinary — see WONDER 2

awed *adj* filled with amazement or wonder — see OPENMOUTHED

awesome *adj* causing wonder or astonishment — see MARVELOUS 1

awestruck *adj* **1** affected with sudden and great wonder or surprise — see THUNDERSTRUCK

2 filled with amazement or wonder — see OPENMOUTHED

awful *adj* **1** causing intense displeasure, disgust, or resentment — see OFFENSIVE 1

2 causing wonder or astonishment — see MARVELOUS 1

3 extremely disturbing or repellent — see HORRIBLE 1

4 extremely unsatisfactory — see WRETCHED 1

awful *adv* to a great degree — see VERY 1

awfully *adv* to a great degree — see VERY 1

awfulness *n* the quality of inspiring intense dread or dismay — see HORROR 1

awkward *adj* **1** lacking social grace and assurance ⟨preteens feeling *awkward* at their first formal dance⟩

synonyms clumsy, gauche, graceless, inelegant, roughhewn, stiff, stilted, uncomfortable, uneasy, ungraceful, wooden

related words gawky, lubberly, ungainly; boorish, clownish, uncouth; abashed, discomfited, discomforted, discomposed, disconcerted, discountenanced, embarrassed; agitated, bothered, chagrined, dismayed, disquieted, distressed, disturbed, fazed, flustered, jittery, jumpy, mortified, nervous, nonplussed (*also* nonplused), perturbed, rattled, unhinged, unsettled, upset; diffident, insecure, meek, modest, self-doubting, timid, unassertive, unassuming, unpretentious

near antonyms assured, calm, collected, composed, confident, cool, placid, poised, serene, secure, self-assured, self-confident, self-possessed, tranquil, undisturbed, unperturbed

antonyms graceful, suave, urbane

2 showing or marked by a lack of skill and tact (as in dealing with a situation) ⟨her *awkward* handling of the seating arrangements at the wedding reception resulted in many hurt feelings⟩

synonyms botched, bungling, clumsy, fumbled, inept, inexpert, maladroit

related words amateur, amateurish, crude, green, incompetent, ineffectual, inefficient, inexperienced, unpolished, unprofessional, unskilled, unskillful; careless, sloppy, tacky, tactless, undiplomatic; ill-advised, ineffective, ineffectual, misdirected, misguided

near antonyms able, accomplished, adept, capable, clever, competent, consummate, crackerjack, expert, masterful, masterly, polished, professional, proficient, skilled, skillful, talented; diplomatic, easy, effortless, gracious, smooth, tactful

antonyms adroit, deft, dexterous (*also* dextrous), facile

3 causing embarrassment ⟨the *awkward* situation of having to listen in as your teacher talks about you to your parents⟩

synonyms discomfiting, disconcerting, disturbing, embarrassing, flustering, uncomfortable

related words confusing, difficult, disagreeable, impossible, inconvenient, intolerable, troublesome, unpleasant, unwieldy; debasing, degrading, demeaning, humbling, humiliating, mortifying

near antonyms agreeable, comfortable, convenient, pleasing

4 causing difficulty, discomfort, or annoyance — see INCONVENIENT 1

5 difficult to use or operate especially because of size, weight, or design — see CUMBERSOME

6 lacking in physical ease and grace in movement or in the use of the hands — see CLUMSY 1

awning *n* a raised covering over something for decoration or protection — see CANOPY

awry *adj* inclined or twisted to one side ⟨the shutters that still remained on the run-down old house were all *awry*⟩

synonyms askew, aslant, cockeyed, crooked, listing, lopsided, oblique, skewed, slanted, slanting, slantwise, tilted, tipping, uneven

related words asymmetrical (*or* asymmetric), unbalanced, unsymmetrical; contorted, disordered, distorted, irregular

near antonyms ordered, orderly, regular, uniform; balanced, symmetrical (*or* symmetric)

antonyms even, level, straight

awry *adv* off the desired or intended path or course — see WRONG 1

¹aye *also* **ay** *adv* for all time — see EVER 1

²aye *also* **ay** *adv* used to express agreement — see YES

B

babble *n* unintelligible or meaningless talk — see GIBBERISH

babble *vb* **1** to speak rapidly, inarticulately, and usually unintelligibly ⟨in such a rush to tell us the news that she just *babbled*⟩

synonyms chatter, drivel, gabble, gibber, jabber, prattle, sputter

related words gab, jaw, patter, prate, rattle, run on; maunder, mouth, mumble, murmur, mutter; stammer, stutter; chat, converse, palaver, rap, visit; discourse; screech, shout, shriek

near antonyms articulate, enunciate, pronounce

2 to engage in casual or rambling conversation — see CHAT

babbler *n* a person who talks constantly — see CHATTERBOX

babe *n* a recently born person — see BABY

babel *n* a place of uproar or confusion — see MADHOUSE 2

babushka *n* a scarf worn on the head — see BANDANNA

baby *n* a recently born person ⟨the *baby* is just learning to sit up, so be careful⟩

synonyms babe, child, infant, newborn

related words cherub; foundling, nursling, suckling; papoose; kid, moppet, toddler, tot, tyke; boy, nipper, tad; juvenile, minor, youngster, youth; brat, imp, squirt, urchin, whippersnapper; girl, hoyden, tomboy

phrases babe in arms

near antonyms adult, grown-up; elder, graybeard, oldster, old-timer, senior citizen

baby *vb* to treat with great or excessive care ⟨he *babied* his car, faithfully washing it every week⟩

synonyms coddle, dandle, mollycoddle, nurse, pamper, spoil

related words cater (to), humor, indulge; gratify, mother, oblige, please, satisfy

near antonyms control, discipline, restrain; oppress; neglect, overlook, slight

antonyms abuse, ill-treat, ill-use, maltreat, mishandle, mistreat, misuse

babyish *adj* having or showing the annoying qualities (as silliness) associated with children — see CHILDISH

babysitter *n* a girl or woman employed to care for a young child or children — see NURSE

back *adj* being at or in the part of something opposite the front part ⟨she carried all the presents in the *back* door, as the children were playing in the front yard⟩

synonyms hind, hindmost, posterior, rear, rearward

antonyms anterior, fore, forward, front

back *adv* toward the opposite direction — see AROUND 2

back *vb* **1** to promote the interests or cause of — see SUPPORT 1

2 to provide (someone) with what is useful or necessary to achieve an end — see HELP 1

back away *vb* to move back or away (as from something difficult, dangerous, or disagreeable) — see RETREAT 1

backbone *n* **1** a column of bones supporting the trunk of a vertebrate animal — see SPINE

2 the strength of mind that enables a person to endure pain or hardship — see FORTITUDE

back down *vb* to break a promise or agreement — see RENEGE

backdrop *n* the physical conditions or features that form the setting against which something is viewed — see BACKGROUND 1

backer *n* **1** a person who actively supports or favors a cause — see EXPONENT

2 a person who takes the responsibility for some other person or thing — see SPONSOR

3 someone associated with another to give assistance or moral support — see ALLY

background *n* **1** the physical conditions or features that form the setting against which something is viewed ⟨they got married on a mountain top with the sunset as *background*⟩
synonyms backdrop, ground
related words scene, scenery, set, stage; environment, milieu, setting, surroundings
near antonyms foreground; center, focal point, focus, heart

2 the place and time in which the action for a portion of a dramatic work (as a movie) is set — see SCENE 1

backhanded *adj* not being or expressing what one appears to be or express — see INSINCERE

backing *n* an act or instance of helping — see HELP 1

back of *prep* at, to, or toward the rear of — see BEHIND 1

back off *vb* to break a promise or agreement — see RENEGE

backpack *n* a soft-sided case designed for carrying belongings especially on the back — see PACK 1

backside *n* the part of the body upon which someone sits — see BUTTOCKS

backslider *n* a person who has sunk below the normal moral standard — see DEGENERATE

backstage *adj or adv* off or away from the part of the stage visible to the audience — see OFFSTAGE

back talk *n* disrespectful or argumentative talk given in response to a command or request ⟨his mother sent him to his room because of his constant *back talk*⟩
synonyms cheek, impertinence, impudence, insolence, sass, sauce
related words comeback, rejoinder, retort, riposte, wisecrack; discourtesy, disrespect, impoliteness, rudeness, tactlessness; audaciousness, audacity, boldness, brazenness; coarseness, crassness, crudity, vulgarity; abruptness, bluffness, bluntness, brusqueness, crossness, curtness, gruffness, surliness
near antonyms civility, cordiality, courtesy, diplomacy, politeness, tactfulness; consideration, gallantry, gentility, graciousness, smoothness, suaveness; deference, respect; affability

backup *adj* taking the place of one that came before — see NEW 1

backup *n* a person or thing that takes the place of another — see SUBSTITUTE

backward *adj* directed, turned, or done toward the back ⟨a *backward* turn on ice skates is hard to learn, because you can't see where you're going⟩
synonyms rearward, retrograde
related words reversed; hind, posterior, rear
near antonyms forward

backwater *n* a rural region that forms the edge of the settled or developed part of a country — see FRONTIER 2

backwoods *n* a rural region that forms the edge of the settled or developed part of a country — see FRONTIER 2

bad *adj* **1** falling short of a standard ⟨a *bad* first attempt at making meat loaf resulted in a soggy inedible mess⟩
synonyms deficient, inferior, lousy, off, poor, punk, rotten, substandard, unacceptable, ungodly, unsatisfactory, wanting, wretched, wrong
related words defective, faulty, flawed; execrable, lesser, low-grade, mediocre, reprehensible, second-rate, unspeakable; bum, useless, valueless, worthless; inadequate, insufficient, lacking; astray; scurrilous, villainous
phrases below (*or* under) par
near antonyms choice, excellent, exceptional, first-class, first-rate, premium, prime, superior; adequate, sufficient
antonyms acceptable, satisfactory

2 not conforming to a high moral standard; morally unacceptable ⟨stealing is just plain *bad*⟩
synonyms black, evil, immoral, iniquitous, nefarious, rotten, sinful, unethical, unrighteous, unsavory, vicious, vile, villainous, wicked, wrong
related words base, contemptible, despicable, dirty, disreputable, evil-minded, ignoble, ill, infernal, low, mean; atrocious, cruel, nasty; blamable, blameworthy, censurable, reprehensible; corrupt, debased, debauched, degenerate, depraved, dissolute, libertine, loose, perverted, reprobate; banned, barred, condemned, discouraged, forbidden, interdicted, outlawed, prohibited, proscribed, unauthorized, unclean; disallowed; execrable, lousy, miserable, wretched; erring, fallen, unprincipled, unscrupulous; improper, incorrect, indecent, indecorous, unbecoming
near antonyms high-minded, honest, honorable, law-abiding, legitimate, principled, reputable, right-minded, scrupulous, straight, upright; allowed, authorized, legal, licensed, permissible, permitted; approved, endorsed, sanctioned; abetted, encouraged, promoted, supported; clean, correct, decent, decorous, exemplary, proper, seemly; blameless, commendable, creditable, guiltless; chaste, immaculate, innocent, irreproachable, lily-white, perfect, pure, spotless
antonyms good, ethical, moral, right, righteous, virtuous

3 causing or capable of causing harm — see HARMFUL

4 engaging in or marked by childish misbehavior — see NAUGHTY

5 feeling unhappiness — see SAD 1

6 having a fault — see FAULTY

7 having undergone organic breakdown — see ROTTEN 1

8 not giving pleasure to the mind or senses — see UNPLEASANT

9 of low quality — see CHEAP 2

10 temporarily suffering from a disorder of the body — see SICK 1

bad *n* that which is morally unacceptable — see EVIL

badly *adv* in an unsatisfactory way ⟨I'm afraid you performed quite *badly* in our last rehearsal⟩

synonyms inadequately, poorly, unacceptably, unsatisfactorily

related words rottenly; intolerably, unbearably; inappropriately, incorrectly, indecently, rakishly, unsuitably; naughtily

near antonyms appropriately, congruously, correctly, decently, decorously, felicitously, fittingly, genteelly, rightly, seemly, suitably

antonyms acceptably, adequately, all right, fine, good, palatably, passably, so-so, tolerably

bad–mouth *vb* to express scornfully one's low opinion of — see DECRY 1

badness *n* the state or quality of being utterly evil — see ENORMITY 1

baffle *vb* **1** to prevent from achieving a goal — see FRUSTRATE

2 to throw into a state of mental uncertainty — see CONFUSE 1

bafflement *n* a state of mental uncertainty — see CONFUSION 1

bag *n* **1** a container made of a flexible material (as paper or plastic) ⟨she carries her towel and other supplies to the beach in a bright, colorful *bag* slung over her arm⟩

synonyms poke [*chiefly Southern & Midland*], pouch, sack

related words carryall, portmanteau, traveling bag; bundle, pack, package, packet, parcel; backpack, duffel bag, haversack, knapsack, rucksack; handbag, pocketbook, purse, tote bag

2 a container for carrying money and small personal items — see PURSE

bag *vb* **1** to extend outward beyond a usual point — see BULGE

2 to take physical control or possession of (something) suddenly or forcibly — see CATCH 1

bail out *vb* to remove from danger or harm — see SAVE 2

bairn *n, chiefly Scottish* a young person who is between infancy and adulthood — see CHILD 1

bait *n* **1** something used to attract animals to a hook or into a trap ⟨cheese is the traditional *bait* for trapping mice⟩

synonyms decoy, lure

related words ambush, trap; hook, snare, troll; appeal, attraction, call, draw, incentive, pull; enticement, seduction, temptation

near antonyms repellent

2 something that persuades one to perform an action for pleasure or gain — see LURE 1

bait *vb* to attack repeatedly with mean put-downs or insults — see TEASE 2

baiter *n* **1** a person who causes repeated emotional pain, distress, or annoyance to another — see TORMENTOR

2 one that tries to get a person to give in to a desire — see TEMPTER

balance *n* **1** a condition in which opposing forces are equal to one another ⟨in order to determine the weight of that beaker, you need to get the two pans of the scale in perfect *balance*⟩

synonyms equilibrium, equipoise, poise

related words counterbalance, counterpoise; firmness, fixedness, security, stability, steadiness

near antonyms changeability, fluctuation, inconstancy, insecurity, instability, mutability, precariousness, shakiness, unsteadiness, volatility

antonyms imbalance

2 a balanced, pleasing, or suitable arrangement of parts — see HARMONY 1

3 a device for measuring weight — see ¹SCALE

4 a force or influence that makes an opposing force ineffective or less effective — see COUNTERBALANCE

5 a remaining group or portion — see REMAINDER 1

balance *vb* to make equal in amount, degree, or status — see EQUALIZE

balanced *adj* **1** having full use of one's mind and control over one's actions — see SANE

2 having the parts agreeably related — see HARMONIOUS 2

bald *adj* **1** lacking a usual or natural covering — see NAKED 2

2 free from all additions or embellishment — see PLAIN 1

baleful *adj* **1** being or showing a sign of evil or calamity to come — see OMINOUS

2 causing or capable of causing harm — see HARMFUL

3 likely to cause or capable of causing death — see DEADLY

balk *vb* to prevent from achieving a goal — see FRUSTRATE

balky *adj* given to resisting authority or another's control — see DISOBEDIENT

¹ball *n* **1** a more or less round body or mass ⟨the little rubber *ball* used in racquetball⟩ ⟨a *ball* of string⟩

synonyms globe, orb, sphere

related words egg, oval; circle, ring, round; chunk, clump, gob, hunk, lump, nugget, wad

near antonyms block, cube, rectangle, square

2 a usually round or cone-shaped little piece of lead made to be fired from a firearm — see BULLET

²ball *n* a social gathering for dancing — see DANCE

ball *vb* to form into a round compact mass — see WAD

ballad *n* a short musical composition for the human voice often with instrumental accompaniment — see SONG 1

balloon *vb* **1** to become greater in extent, volume, amount, or number — see INCREASE 2

2 to extend outward beyond a usual point — see BULGE

ballot *n* a piece of paper indicating a person's preferences in an election ⟨we collected all of the *ballots* from the students voting for class president⟩

synonyms vote

related words aye (*also* ay), nay, no, yea; blackball; referendum; ticket

ballyhoo *n* newsworthy information released to the media that is designed to gain public attention or support for a person, business, or cause — see PUBLICITY

ballyhoo *vb* **1** to praise or publicize lavishly and often excessively — see TOUT 1

2 to provide publicity for — see PUBLICIZE 1

balminess *n* lack of good sense or judgment — see FOOLISHNESS 1

balmy *adj* **1** having or showing a very abnormal or sick state of mind — see INSANE 1

2 marked by temperatures that are neither too high nor too low — see CLEMENT

3 not harsh or stern especially in manner, nature, or effect — see GENTLE 1

4 showing or marked by a lack of good sense or judgment — see FOOLISH 1

balustrade *n* a protective barrier consisting of a horizontal bar and its supports — see RAILING

ban *n* an order that something not be done or used — see PROHIBITION 2

ban *vb* **1** to order not to do or use or to be done or used — see FORBID

2 to prevent the participation or inclusion of — see EXCLUDE

banal *adj* **1** lacking in qualities that make for spirit and character — see WISHY-WASHY 1

2 used or heard so often as to be dull — see STALE

banality *n* an idea or expression that has been used by many people — see COMMONPLACE

bananas *adj* having or showing a very abnormal or sick state of mind — see INSANE 1

¹**band** *n* **1** a circular strip — see RING 2

2 something that physically prevents free movement — see BOND 1

3 a line or long narrow section differing in color from the background — see STRIPE

²**band** *n* **1** a usually large group of musicians playing together ⟨that traveling *band* needs to find a new singer⟩

synonyms orchestra, philharmonic, symphony, symphony orchestra

related words brass band; brasses, strings, woodwinds; combo, ensemble, group; company, troupe; duo, octet, quartet (*also* quartette), quintet, septet (*also* septette), sextet, trio

2 a group of people working together on a task — see GANG 1

band *vb* **1** to encircle or bind with or as if with a belt — see GIRD 1

2 to form or enter into an association that furthers the interests of its members — see ALLY

3 to gather into a tight mass by means of a line or cord — see TIE 1

4 to make stripes on — see STRIPE

bandage *vb* to cover with a bandage ⟨her mother always *bandages* her scraped knees very carefully⟩

synonyms bind, dress

related words care (for), doctor, medicate, minister (to), nurse, treat; mend, heal

bandanna *or* **bandana** *n* a scarf worn on the head ⟨she uses her colorful print *bandanna* to keep the hair out of her eyes⟩

synonyms babushka, handkerchief, kerchief, mantilla

related words shawl

bandwagon *n* a series of activities undertaken to achieve a goal — see CAMPAIGN

bandy *vb* to talk about (an issue) usually from various points of view and for the purpose of arriving at a decision or opinion — see DISCUSS

bane *n* a substance that by chemical action can kill or injure a living thing — see POISON

baneful *adj* causing or capable of causing harm — see HARMFUL

bang *n* **1** a hard strike with a part of the body or an instrument — see ¹BLOW

2 a loud explosive sound — see CLAP 1

3 a pleasurably intense stimulation of the feelings — see THRILL

bang *vb* **1** to come into usually forceful contact with something — see HIT 2

2 to deliver a blow to (someone or something) usually in a strong vigorous manner — see HIT 1

3 to shove into a closed position with force and noise — see SLAM 1

bangle *n* an ornament worn on a chain around the neck or wrist — see PENDANT

bang–up *adj* of the very best kind — see EXCELLENT

banish *vb* **1** to force to leave a country ⟨in the old days, criminals were sometimes *banished*⟩

synonyms deport, displace, exile, expatriate, transport

related words dismiss, eject, eliminate, evict, exclude, expel, oust, throw out; excommunicate, ostracize, reject, repudiate, spurn; dispossess

near antonyms naturalize, repatriate; accept, admit, receive, take in; entertain, harbor, house, shelter

2 to drive or force out — see EJECT 1

banishment *n* the forced removal from a homeland — see EXILE 1

banister *n* a protective barrier consisting of a horizontal bar and its supports — see RAILING

¹**bank** *n* **1** a number of things considered as a unit — see GROUP 1

2 a series of people or things arranged side by side — see ROW 1

²**bank** *n* a pile or ridge of granular matter (as sand or snow) ⟨he likes to play on the *bank* of dirt the construction workers left⟩

synonyms bar, drift, mound

related words snowbank, snowdrift; embankment, sandbar; heap, hill, mass, mountain, stack

bank *vb* **1** to form into a pile or ridge of earth — see MOUND 1

2 to put in an account — see DEPOSIT 1

bank note *n* a piece of printed paper used as money — see ¹BILL 2

bankroll *n* available money — see FUND 2

bankrupt *vb* to cause to lose one's fortune and become unable to pay one's debts — see RUIN 1

banned *adj* that may not be permitted — see IMPERMISSIBLE

banner *adj* of the very best kind — see EXCELLENT

banner *n* a piece of cloth with a special design that is used as an emblem or for signaling — see FLAG 1

banning *n* the act of ordering that something not be done or used — see PROHIBITION 1

banquet *n* a large fancy meal often accompanied by ceremony or entertainment — see FEAST

banquet *vb* to entertain with a fancy meal — see FEAST

bantam *adj* of a size that is less than average — see SMALL 1

banter *n* good-natured teasing or exchanging of clever remarks ⟨those particular students are known for their brilliant and witty *banter* at lunchtime⟩

synonyms chaff, give-and-take, jesting, joshing, persiflage, raillery, repartee

related words barb, crack, dig, gag, jest, joke, quip, sally, wisecrack, witticism; facetiousness, humorousness; fooling, kidding, mocking, razzing, ribbing, ridiculing; humor, wit, wordplay; chatter, chitchat, gossip, small talk

THESAURUS

banter *vb* to make jokes — see JOKE

bantering *adj* marked by or expressive of mild or good-natured teasing — see QUIZZICAL

baptism *n* the process or an instance of being formally placed in an office or organization — see INSTALLATION 1

baptize *vb* **1** to give a name to — see NAME 1
2 to put into an office or welcome into an organization with special ceremonies — see INSTALL 1

bar *n* **1** a straight piece (as of wood or metal) that is longer than it is wide ⟨all of the prison's windows are partially covered with steel *bars*⟩
synonyms billet, rod
related words beam, board; band, strip; ingot, slab, stick
2 a line or long narrow section differing in color from the background — see STRIPE
3 a pile or ridge of granular matter (as sand or snow) — see ²BANK
4 a place of business where alcoholic beverages are sold to be consumed on the premises — see BARROOM
5 an assembly of persons for the administration of justice — see COURT 3
6 something that makes movement or progress more difficult — see ENCUMBRANCE

bar *prep* not including — see EXCEPT

bar *vb* **1** to make stripes on — see STRIPE
2 to order not to do or use or to be done or used — see FORBID
3 to prevent the participation or inclusion of — see EXCLUDE

barb *n* an act or expression showing scorn and usually intended to hurt another's feelings — see INSULT

barbarian *n* an uncivilized person — see HEATHEN 2

barbaric *adj* having or showing the desire to inflict severe pain and suffering on others — see CRUEL 1

barbarity *n* the willful infliction of pain and suffering on others — see CRUELTY

barbarous *adj* **1** having or showing the desire to inflict severe pain and suffering on others — see CRUEL 1
2 not civilized — see SAVAGE 1

bard *n* a person who writes poetry — see POET

bare *adj* **1** being this and no more — see MERE
2 free from all additions or embellishment — see PLAIN 1
3 lacking a usual or natural covering — see NAKED 2
4 lacking or shed of clothing — see NAKED 1
5 lacking contents that could or should be present — see EMPTY 1

bare *vb* to make known (as information previously kept secret) — see REVEAL 1

barely *adv* by a very small margin — see JUST 2

bareness *n* the quality or state of being empty — see VACANCY 2

bargain *n* **1** something bought or offered for sale at a desirable price ⟨those shoes were a *bargain* because the store was going out of business⟩
synonyms buy, steal
related words markdown; bonus, freebie, gift, giveaway, premium, present; sale; boon, windfall
near antonyms overcharge, rip-off; markup; extravagance, luxury
2 an arrangement about action to be taken — see AGREEMENT 2

bargain *vb* to talk over or dispute the terms of a purchase ⟨they *bargained* with the car salesman for half an hour before settling on a price⟩
synonyms chaffer, deal, dicker, haggle, horse-trade, negotiate, palter
related words argue, bicker, clash, quibble, squabble, wrangle; comparison shop, shop (around); barter, exchange, trade; hawk, peddle; buy, purchase

barge *vb* to move heavily or clumsily — see LUMBER 1

bark *n* a boat equipped with one or more sails — see SAILBOAT

¹bark *vb* to remove the natural covering of — see PEEL

²bark *vb* to speak sharply or irritably — see SNAP 1

baron *n* a person of rank, power, or influence in a particular field — see MAGNATE

baronial *adj* large and impressive in size, grandeur, extent, or conception — see GRAND 1

barrage *n* a rapid or overwhelming outpouring of many things at once ⟨the teacher's rapid-fire *barrage* of homework assignments went by too fast for me to write them all down⟩
synonyms bombardment, cannonade, fusillade, hail, salvo, shower, storm, volley
related words broadside, burst, deluge, flood, flood tide, flush, gush, inundation, outburst, outflow, outpouring, overflow, spate, surge, torrent; current, river, stream, tide; excess, glut, overabundance, overage, overkill, overmuch, oversupply, superabundance, superfluity, surfeit, surplus
near antonyms dribble, drip, trickle

barred *adj* **1** having stripes — see STRIPED
2 that may not be permitted — see IMPERMISSIBLE

barrel *n* **1** a considerable amount — see LOT 2
2 a metal container in the shape of a cylinder — see CAN
3 an enclosed wooden vessel for holding beverages — see CASK

barrel *vb* to proceed or move quickly — see HURRY 2

barren *adj* **1** producing inferior or only a small amount of vegetation ⟨if tobacco fields aren't allowed to lie idle once every few years, they will become *barren*⟩
synonyms impoverished, infertile, poor, stark, unproductive, waste
related words bleak, dead, desolate, inhospitable, lifeless; bankrupted, consumed, debilitated, depleted, diminished, drained, dried up, enfeebled, exhausted, expended, lessened, reduced, spent, used up; arid, desert, dry
near antonyms arable, tillable; green, verdant
antonyms fertile, fruitful, lush, luxuriant, productive, rich
2 not able to produce fruit or offspring — see STERILE 1

barren *n* land that is uninhabited or not fit for crops — see WASTELAND

barricade *n* a physical object that blocks the way — see BARRIER

barrier *n* a physical object that blocks the way ⟨there was a big *barrier* plastered with signs saying "Keep Out" around the trash compactor⟩
synonyms barricade, fence, hedge, wall
related words bar, encumbrance, handicap, hindrance, hurdle, impediment, obstacle, obstruc-

tion, roadblock, stop; fetter, hobble, manacle, shackle; constraint, curb, restraint, snag

near antonyms door, doorway, entrance, entry, entryway, gate, portal

barring *n* the act of ordering that something not be done or used — see PROHIBITION 1

barring *prep* not including — see EXCEPT

barroom *n* a place of business where alcoholic beverages are sold to be consumed on the premises ⟨her mother didn't like her even to walk past the *barroom* because she was worried that there might be drunk people inside⟩

synonyms bar, café (*also* cafe), groggery, grogshop, pub, public house [*chiefly British*], saloon, tavern

related words cabaret, dive, joint, nightclub, roadhouse, speakeasy; package store

barter *n* a giving or taking of one thing of value in return for another — see EXCHANGE 1

base *adj* not following or in accordance with standards of honor and decency — see IGNOBLE 2

base *n* **1** an immaterial thing upon which something else rests ⟨the firm belief that complete trust between husband and wife is the *base* of any successful marriage⟩

synonyms basis, bedrock, cornerstone, footing, foundation, ground, groundwork, keystone, underpinning

related words buttress, framework, prop, substructure, support; assumption, justification, premise, presumption, presupposition, theory, thesis, warrant; center, core, eye, focus, heart, hub, nucleus, seat; essence, quintessence, soul

2 a place from which an advance (as for military operations) is made ⟨the Army's *base* of attack was kept top secret until the battle began⟩

synonyms bridgehead, foothold

related words beachhead, center, front, headquarters; bastion, fastness, fortress, stronghold

3 a thing or place that is of greatest importance to an activity or interest — see CENTER 1

4 the lowest part, place, or point — see BOTTOM 3

5 the place from which a commander runs operations — see COMMAND 3

base *vb* to find a basis ⟨she *based* her argument against the death penalty on careful research⟩

synonyms ground, predicate, rest

related words establish, found; assume, postulate, premise, presume, presuppose, suppose

baseborn *adj* **1** belonging to the class of people of low social or economic rank — see IGNOBLE 1

2 born to a father and mother who are not married — see ILLEGITIMATE 1

basement *n* a room or set of rooms below the surface of the ground — see CELLAR

bash *vb* **1** to come into usually forceful contact with something — see HIT 2

2 to deliver a blow to (someone or something) usually in a strong vigorous manner — see HIT 1

3 to strike repeatedly — see BEAT 1

bashful *adj* not comfortable around people — see SHY 2

basic *adj* of or relating to the simplest facts or theories of a subject — see ELEMENTARY

basically *adv* for the most part — see CHIEFLY

basics *n pl* general or basic truths on which other truths or theories can be based — see PRINCIPLES 1

basis *n* an immaterial thing upon which something else rests — see BASE 1

bask *vb* to refrain from labor or exertion — see REST 1

bass *adj* having a low musical pitch or range — see DEEP 2

bastard *adj* born to a father and mother who are not married — see ILLEGITIMATE 1

bastion *n* a structure or place from which one can resist attack — see FORT

bat *n* **1** a hard strike with a part of the body or an instrument — see ¹BLOW

2 a heavy rigid stick used as a weapon or for punishment — see CLUB 1

bat *vb* **1** to deliver a blow to (someone or something) usually in a strong vigorous manner — see HIT 1

2 to strike repeatedly — see BEAT 1

batch *n* **1** a number of things considered as a unit — see GROUP 1

2 a usually small number of persons considered as a unit — see GROUP 2

bath *n* a room furnished with a fixture for flushing body waste — see TOILET

bathe *vb* to make wet — see WET

bathed *adj* containing, covered with, or thoroughly penetrated by water — see WET

bathroom *n* a room furnished with a fixture for flushing body waste — see TOILET

battalion *n* a large body of men and women organized for land warfare — see ARMY 1

batter *vb* to strike repeatedly — see BEAT 1

battery *n* **1** a number of things considered as a unit — see GROUP 1

2 a usually small number of persons considered as a unit — see GROUP 2

battle *n* **1** a forceful effort to reach a goal or objective — see STRUGGLE 1

2 a physical dispute between opposing individuals or groups — see FIGHT 1

3 active fighting during the course of a war — see COMBAT 1

4 an earnest effort for superiority or victory over another — see CONTEST 1

battle *vb* **1** to engage in a contest — see COMPETE

2 to enter into contest or conflict with — see ENGAGE 2

3 to oppose (someone) in physical conflict — see FIGHT 1

4 to strive to reduce or eliminate — see FIGHT 2

batty *adj* having or showing a very abnormal or sick state of mind — see INSANE 1

bauble *n* a small object displayed for its attractiveness or interest — see KNICKKNACK

bawdiness *n* the quality or state of being obscene — see OBSCENITY 1

bawdy *adj* **1** depicting or referring to sexual matters in a way that is unacceptable in polite society — see OBSCENE 1

2 hinting at or intended to call to mind matters regarded as indecent — see SUGGESTIVE 1

bawl *vb* **1** to shed tears often while making meaningless sounds as a sign of pain or distress — see CRY 1

2 to speak so as to be heard at a distance — see CALL 1

bay *n* **1** a part of a body of water that extends beyond the general shoreline — see GULF 1

2 one of the parts into which an enclosed space is divided — see COMPARTMENT

bay *vb* to make a long loud mournful sound — see HOWL 1

THESAURUS

bazaar *n* an establishment where goods are sold to consumers — see SHOP 1

be *vb* 1 to have life ⟨stories that begin with the familiar line "once upon a time there *was* a beautiful maiden"⟩

synonyms breathe, exist, live, subsist

related words abide, continue, endure, last, lead, persist, survive; move; flourish, prosper, thrive

near antonyms disappear, evaporate, vanish; cease, end, stop

antonyms depart, die, expire, pass away, perish, succumb

2 to occupy a place or location — see STAND 1

3 to take or have a certain position within a group arranged in vertical classes — see RANK 1

4 to take place — see HAPPEN

be (to) *vb* to behave toward in a stated way — see TREAT 1

beach *n* the usually sandy or gravelly land bordering a body of water ⟨she loves walking along the *beach*, looking for shells that the waves cast up⟩

synonyms shore, strand

related words seaboard, seacoast, seashore, seaside; coast, coastline, shoreline; waterfront; bank, riverbank, riverside; esplanade; littoral

beached *adj* resting on the shore or bottom of a body of water — see AGROUND

beacon *n* something that provides illumination — see LIGHT 2

beak *n* the jaws of a bird together with their hornlike covering ⟨the bird cracked the walnut shell with its *beak* and ate its nut⟩

synonyms bill, nib

related words mouth; muzzle; mandible, maw, maxilla

beam *n* a narrow sharply defined line of light radiating from an object — see SHAFT 1

beam *vb* 1 to emit rays of light — see SHINE 1

2 to express an emotion (as amusement) by curving the lips upward — see SMILE 1

beaming *adj* 1 giving off or reflecting much light — see BRIGHT 1

2 having or being an outward sign of good feelings (as of love, confidence, or happiness) — see RADIANT 1

bear *n* an irritable and complaining person — see GROUCH

bear *vb* 1 to bring forth from the womb ⟨luckily, she turned out to be able to *bear* children after all⟩

synonyms drop, have, produce

related words deliver; create; breed, multiply, propagate, reproduce, spawn; beget, father, generate, get, mother, sire

phrases to give birth to

near antonyms abort, lose, miscarry

2 to put up with (something painful or difficult) ⟨I can't *bear* having to eat my vegetables in order to have ice cream⟩

synonyms abide, brook, countenance, endure, meet, stand, stick out, stomach, support, sustain, take, tolerate

related words accept, allow, permit, suffer, swallow; acquiesce, agree (with *or* to), assent (to), capitulate, consent (to), respect, submit (to), yield (to)

near antonyms decline, dismiss, refuse, reject, repudiate, spurn, turn down; combat, contest, fight, oppose, resist; avoid, bypass, circumvent, dodge, elude, escape, evade, miss; abstain, forbear, refrain

3 to have a relation or connection — see APPLY 1

4 to go on a specified course or in a certain direction — see HEAD 1

5 to hold up or serve as a foundation for — see SUPPORT 3

6 to keep in one's mind or heart — see HARBOR 1

7 to manage the actions of (oneself) in a particular way — see BEHAVE

8 to support and take from one place to another — see CARRY 1

9 to take to or upon oneself — see ASSUME 1

10 to wear or have on one's person — see CARRY 2

bearable *adj* capable of being endured ⟨the pain from a sprained ankle is annoying but *bearable*⟩

synonyms endurable, sufferable, supportable, sustainable, tolerable

related words livable (*also* liveable); acceptable, allowable, reasonable

near antonyms agonizing, appalling, awful, bad, cruel, dire, dreadful, excruciating, ghastly, harrowing, harsh, horrible, nasty, painful, rotten, terrible, tormenting, torturous, unfortunate, vicious, vile, wretched; unacceptable; acute, extreme, intense, piercing

antonyms insufferable, insupportable, intolerable, unbearable, unendurable, unsupportable

beard *vb* to oppose (something hostile or dangerous) with firmness or courage — see FACE 2

bear down on *vb* to push steadily against with some force — see PRESS 1

bearing *n* 1 the fact or state of being pertinent — see PERTINENCE

2 the fact or state of having something in common — see CONNECTION 1

3 the way or manner in which one conducts oneself — see BEHAVIOR

bearish *adj* having or showing a habitually bad temper — see ILL-TEMPERED

bear out *vb* to give evidence or testimony to the truth or factualness of — see CONFIRM

beast *n* 1 a mean, evil, or unprincipled person — see VILLAIN

2 a person whose behavior is offensive to others — see JERK 1

3 one of the lower animals as distinguished from human beings — see ANIMAL

beastly *adv* to a great degree — see VERY 1

beat *adj* depleted in strength, energy, or freshness — see WEARY 1

beat *n* 1 a hard strike with a part of the body or an instrument — see ¹BLOW

2 a rhythmic expanding and contracting — see PULSATION

3 the recurrent pattern formed by a series of sounds having a regular rise and fall in intensity — see RHYTHM

beat *vb* 1 to strike repeatedly ⟨they attacked and *beat* him, but fortunately he'll be fine⟩

synonyms bash, bat, batter, belt, bludgeon, buffet, bung (up), club, drub, flog, hammer, hide, lace, lambaste (*or* lambast), lick, maul, pelt, pommel, pound, pummel, thrash, thump, wallop, whale, whip

related words assail, attack, box, bust, cane, chop, clobber, clout, crack, cudgel, cuff, hit, horsewhip, knock, lam, lash, lay on, paste, punch, slap, smack, smash, sock, spank, swat, swipe, thwack, whack; gore, lacerate, wound; maim, mangle, mutilate

2 to achieve a victory over ⟨she always *beats* everyone at checkers, but she's not as good at chess⟩
synonyms best, clobber, conquer, crush, defeat, drub, lick, master, overbear, overcome, overmatch, prevail (over), rout, skunk, subdue, surmount, thrash, trim, triumph (over), trounce, wallop, whip, win (against), worst
related words nose out; excel, flourish, score, succeed; overpower, overthrow, subjugate, vanquish; exceed, outdo, surpass
phrases get around, get the better of
near antonyms fail
antonyms lose (to)
3 to be greater, better, or stronger than — see SURPASS 1
4 to expand and contract in a rhythmic manner — see PULSATE
5 to move or cause to move with a striking motion — see FLAP
6 to prevent from achieving a goal — see FRUSTRATE
7 to shape with a hammer — see HAMMER 1
8 to shine with a bright harsh light — see GLARE 1
9 to strike or cause to strike lightly and usually rhythmically — see ¹TAP
beater *n* one that defeats an enemy or opponent — see VICTOR 1
beating *n* failure to win a contest — see DEFEAT 1
beau *n* a male romantic companion — see BOYFRIEND
beau ideal *n* **1** someone of such unequaled perfection as to deserve imitation — see IDEAL 1
2 the most perfect type or example — see QUINTESSENCE 1
beauteous *adj* very pleasing to look at — see BEAUTIFUL
beauteousness *n* the qualities in a person or thing that as a whole give pleasure to the senses — see BEAUTY 1
beautiful *adj* very pleasing to look at ⟨a strikingly *beautiful* child who is being eagerly pursued by all the modeling agencies⟩
synonyms attractive, beauteous, bonny [*chiefly British*], comely, cute, fair, gorgeous, handsome, knockout, lovely, pretty, ravishing, sightly, stunning, taking
related words alluring, appealing, charming, delightful, eye-catching, glamorous (*also* glamourous), prepossessing; elegant, exquisite, glorious, resplendent, splendid, statuesque, sublime, superb; flawless, perfect, radiant; dainty, delicate; personable, presentable
near antonyms abhorrent, abominable, bad, disagreeable, disgusting, dreadful, foul, frightful, ghastly, hideous, horrible, loathsome, nasty, nauseating, objectionable, offensive, repellent, repugnant, repulsive, revolting, shocking, sickening, terrible; unappealing, unappetizing, unpleasant, unpleasing, unprepossessing
antonyms homely, ill-favored, plain, ugly, unattractive, unbeautiful, unhandsome, unlovely, unpretty, unsightly
beautify *vb* to make more attractive by adding something that is beautiful or becoming — see DECORATE
beautifying *adj* serving to add beauty — see DECORATIVE
beauty *n* **1** the qualities in a person or thing that as

a whole give pleasure to the senses ⟨her *beauty* was enough to take your breath away⟩
synonyms attractiveness, beauteousness, comeliness, cuteness, fairness, gorgeousness, handsomeness, looks, loveliness, prettiness
related words allure, appeal, attraction, glamour (*also* glamor); charm, elegance, exquisiteness, flawlessness, gloriousness, perfection, radiance, resplendence; desirability, desirableness
near antonyms dreadfulness, foulness, ghastliness, grotesqueness, hideousness, loathsomeness, nastiness, offensiveness, repellency, repulsiveness, unattractiveness; blemish, flaw, imperfection
antonyms homeliness, plainness, ugliness, unsightliness
2 a lovely woman ⟨she was quite a *beauty* in her younger days⟩
synonyms eyeful, goddess, knockout, stunner
related words belle, charmer, honey
near antonyms hag, horror, witch
3 something very good of its kind — see JIM-DANDY
because *conj* for the reason that — see SINCE
because of *prep* as the result of ⟨I was late for school *because of* the snowstorm, which made driving very hazardous⟩
synonyms due to, owing to, through, with
beckon *vb* to direct or notify by a movement or gesture — see MOTION
becloud *vb* **1** to make (something) unclear to the understanding — see CONFUSE 2
2 to make dark, dim, or indistinct — see CLOUD 1
beclouded *adj* **1** covered over by clouds — see OVERCAST
2 filled with or dimmed by fine particles (as of dust or water) in suspension — see HAZY 1
become *vb* to eventually have as a state or quality ⟨many people *became* sick with the flu⟩ ⟨with autumn the days *become* crisper and breezier⟩
synonyms come, get, go, grow, run, turn, wax
related words alter, change, metamorphose, modify, mutate, transfigure, transform, transmute
near antonyms abide, be, continue, linger, remain, stay
becoming *adj* meeting the requirements of a purpose or situation — see FIT 1
bed *n* **1** a place set aside for sleeping ⟨the sofa in the living room will be your *bed* for the night⟩
synonyms bunk, pad, sack
related words bedstead, mattress, pallet; cot, couch, daybed, feather bed, four-poster, hammock, sofa, sofa bed, studio couch, trundle bed, water bed; bassinet, cradle, crib
2 the surface upon which a body of water lies — see BOTTOM 2
bed *vb* to go to one's bed in order to sleep ⟨the campers all *bedded* down for the night around 9 pm⟩
synonyms retire, turn in
related words bunk, perch, roost, settle; doze, drop (off), nap, nod, sleep, slumber, snooze; couch, lie (down), recline
near antonyms arouse, awake, awaken, rouse, wake, waken; bestir, stir, wake; reawake, reawaken; shift, stir
antonyms arise, get up, rise, uprise
bedaub *vb* to rub an oily or sticky substance over — see SMEAR 1
bedazzle *vb* to overpower with light — see DAZZLE

THESAURUS

bedazzling *adj* giving off or reflecting much light — see BRIGHT 1

bedeck *vb* to make more attractive by adding something that is beautiful or becoming — see DECORATE

bedevil *vb* to cause persistent suffering to — see AFFLICT

bedevilment *n* the act of making unwelcome intrusions upon another — see ANNOYANCE 1

bedim *vb* to make dark, dim, or indistinct — see CLOUD 1

bedizen *vb* to make more attractive by adding something that is beautiful or becoming — see DECORATE

bedizened *adj* elaborately and often excessively decorated — see ORNATE

bedlam *n* a place of uproar or confusion — see MADHOUSE 2

bedrock *n* an immaterial thing upon which something else rests — see BASE 1

bedspread *n* a decorative cloth used as a top covering for a bed — see COUNTERPANE

beef *n* an expression of dissatisfaction, pain, or resentment — see COMPLAINT 1

beef *vb* to express dissatisfaction, pain, or resentment usually tiresomely — see COMPLAIN

beef (up) *vb* **1** to increase the ability of (as a muscle) to exert physical force — see STRENGTHEN 1

2 to make markedly greater in measure or degree — see INTENSIFY

beefy *adj* strongly and heavily built — see ¹HUSKY

beetle *vb* to extend outward beyond a usual point — see BULGE

befall *vb* to take place — see HAPPEN

befit *vb* to be fitting or proper — see DO 1

befitting *adj* meeting the requirements of a purpose or situation — see FIT 1

befog *vb* **1** to make (something) unclear to the understanding — see CONFUSE 2

2 to make dark, dim, or indistinct — see CLOUD 1

3 to throw into a state of mental uncertainty — see CONFUSE 1

befogged *adj* filled with or dimmed by fine particles (as of dust or water) in suspension — see HAZY 1

before *adv* so as to precede something in order of time — see AHEAD 1

before *prep* **1** earlier than ⟨since I'm a faster runner, I got there *before* him⟩

synonyms afore [*chiefly dialect*], ahead of, ere, of, previous to, prior to, to

related words till, until, up to

phrases in advance of

near antonyms next, next to, since

antonyms after, following

2 preceding in space ⟨the children always insisted on running *before* their parents⟩

synonyms afore [*chiefly dialect*], ahead of

related words against

phrases in advance of, in front of

antonyms after, following

beforehand *adv* **1** before the usual or expected time — see EARLY

2 so as to precede something in order of time — see AHEAD 1

befoul *vb* **1** to make dirty — see DIRTY

2 to make unfit for use by the addition of something harmful or undesirable — see CONTAMINATE

befuddle *vb* to throw into a state of mental uncertainty — see CONFUSE 1

befuddled *adj* suffering from mental confusion — see DIZZY 2

befuddlement *n* a state of mental uncertainty — see CONFUSION 1

beg *vb* to make a request to (someone) in an earnest or urgent manner ⟨she *begged* her mother to let her go on the Girl Scout camporee⟩

synonyms appeal (to), beseech, conjure, entreat, implore, importune, petition, plead (to), pray, solicit, supplicate

related words mooch, sponge; ask, desire, invoke, request, sue; claim, coerce, command, compel, demand, force, insist, require

phrases call on (*or* call upon)

near antonyms hint, imply, intimate, suggest; appease, conciliate, gratify, mollify, oblige, pacify, placate, please, satisfy; comfort, console, content, quiet

beget *vb* to become the father of — see FATHER

begetter *n* a person who establishes a whole new field of endeavor — see FATHER 2

beggar *n* a person who lives by public begging ⟨the poor *beggars* that are such a common sight in underdeveloped countries⟩

synonyms mendicant, panhandler

related words bum, drifter, hobo, tramp, vagabond, vagrant; pauper; hanger-on, leech, moocher, parasite, sponge, sponger; dependent; deadbeat, derelict, idler, ne'er-do-well

beggared *adj* lacking money or material possessions — see POOR 1

beggary *n* the state of lacking sufficient money or material possessions — see POVERTY 1

begin *vb* **1** to take the first step in (a process or course of action) ⟨she *began* walking to school⟩

synonyms commence, embark (on *or* upon), enter (into *or* upon), get off, kick off, launch, open, start, strike (into)

related words create, generate, inaugurate, initiate, innovate, invent, originate; adopt, embrace, take on, take up; establish, father, found, institute, organize, pioneer, set up, spawn

phrases get to, set about

near antonyms cease, desist, discontinue, halt, lay off, quit, stop; close, complete; abandon, forsake, leave; abolish, demolish, destroy, exterminate, extinguish, phase out

antonyms conclude, end, finish, terminate

2 to come into existence ⟨the storm *began* late in the day and lasted all night⟩

synonyms arise, commence, dawn, form, materialize, originate, set in, spring, start

related words be, breathe, exist, live, subsist; appear, arrive, emerge; continue, endure, last, persist, survive

near antonyms conclude, desist, discontinue, finish, halt, quit, terminate; disappear, dissolve, evaporate, vanish; depart, die, expire, pass away, perish

antonyms cease, end, stop

beginner *n* a person who is just starting out in a field of activity ⟨although he is only a *beginner* at swimming, he is making excellent progress⟩

synonyms colt, fledgling, freshman, greenhorn, neophyte, newcomer, novice, recruit, rookie, tenderfoot, tyro

related words apprentice, cub; boot, novitiate;

amateur, dilettante; learner, student, trainee; candidate, entrant, probationer
near antonyms expert, master, pro, professional
antonyms old hand, old-timer, vet, veteran

beginning *n* the point at which something begins ⟨the actual *beginning* of the universe is still under debate, with some scientists believing in the big bang theory⟩
synonyms alpha, birth, commencement, dawn, genesis, inception, incipiency, launch, morning, onset, outset, start, threshold
related words creation, inauguration, initiation, institution, origination; cradle, fountainhead, origin, root, source, spring, well, wellspring; dawning, opening; appearance, arrival, emergence; infancy
near antonyms cessation, closing, closure, completion, finale, finish, period, stop, termination, windup
antonyms close, conclusion, end, ending

begone *vb* to leave a place often for another — see GO 2

begrime *vb* to make dirty — see DIRTY

beguile *vb* **1** to attract or delight as if by magic — see CHARM 1
2 to cause to believe what is untrue — see DECEIVE
3 to lead away from a usual or proper course by offering some pleasure or advantage — see LURE

beguiling *adj* **1** clever at attaining one's ends by indirect and often deceptive means — see ARTFUL 1
2 tending or having power to deceive — see DECEPTIVE 1

behave *vb* to manage the actions of (oneself) in a particular way ⟨if she *behaves* herself properly and sits quietly during church, she will get ice cream afterward⟩
synonyms acquit, bear, comport, conduct, demean, deport, quit
related words check, collect, compose, constrain, contain, control, curb, handle, inhibit, quiet, repress, restrain; moderate, modulate, temper; act, impersonate, play
near antonyms act up, carry on, cut up, misbehave, misconduct

behavior *n* the way or manner in which one conducts oneself ⟨he promised to be on his best *behavior* for the party⟩
synonyms actions, bearing, comportment, conduct, demeanor, deportment
related words etiquette, form, manners, mores, proprieties; amenity, civility, courtesy, decorum, politeness; air, attitude, carriage, poise, pose, posture, presence; aspect, look, mien; formality, protocol, rules; custom, habit, pattern, practice (*also* practise), trick, wont; convention, fashion, form, mode, style; affectation, attribute, characteristic, mark, trait; distinctiveness, oddity, peculiarity, singularity, strangeness, uniqueness, weirdness

behead *vb* to cut off the head of — see DECAPITATE

behemoth *n* something that is unusually large and powerful — see GIANT

behest *n* a statement of what to do that must be obeyed by those concerned — see COMMAND 1

behind *adj* not arriving, occurring, or settled at the due, usual, or proper time — see LATE 1

behind *prep* **1** at, to, or toward the rear of ⟨she preferred to be *behind* the lead hikers, who were always too much in a rush to enjoy the scenery⟩

synonyms abaft, back of
near antonyms ahead of
antonyms before, in front of
2 subsequent to in time or order — see AFTER

behindhand *adj* not arriving, occurring, or settled at the due, usual, or proper time — see LATE 1

behold *vb* to make note of (something) through the use of one's eyes — see SEE 1

being *n* **1** a member of the human race — see HUMAN
2 one that has a real and independent existence — see ENTITY

belabor *vb* to criticize harshly and usually publicly — see ATTACK 2

belated *adj* not arriving, occurring, or settled at the due, usual, or proper time — see LATE 1

belatedness *n* the quality or state of being late — see LATENESS

belch *vb* to throw out or off (something from within) often violently — see ERUPT 1

beldam *or* **beldame** *n* a mean or ugly old woman — see CRONE

beleaguer *vb* to surround (as a fortified place) with armed forces for the purpose of capturing or preventing commerce and communication — see BESIEGE

belie *vb* **1** to give a false idea of ⟨his bright smile *belied* his actual mood, which was really one of great sadness⟩
synonyms misrepresent
related words contradict; camouflage, cloak, conceal, counterfeit, disguise, hide, mask, obscure; color, deceive, distort, falsify, garble, mislead, twist; dissemble, feign, pretend
near antonyms bare, demonstrate, disclose, discover, exhibit, expose, evince, reveal; flaunt, parade, show off
antonyms betray, represent
2 to prove to be false — see DISPROVE

belief *n* **1** mental conviction of the truth of some statement or the reality of some being or phenomenon ⟨a *belief* in unicorns led him to look for them every time he walked through the woods⟩
synonyms credence, credit, faith
related words axiom, law, precept, principle, tenet; assurance, certainty, certitude, conviction, positiveness, sureness; confidence, dependance, reliance, trust; hope; doctrine, dogma, philosophy; dogmatism, fanaticism, insistence
near antonyms distrust, mistrust, skepticism, suspicion, uncertainty
antonyms disbelief, discredit, doubt, unbelief
2 an idea that is believed to be true or valid without positive knowledge — see OPINION 1

believable *adj* worthy of being accepted as true or reasonable ⟨she had a *believable* story for why her homework was late, so she didn't receive any punishment⟩
synonyms credible, likely, plausible, probable
related words acceptable, conceivable, imaginable, possible, practical, reasonable; dependable, reliable, trustworthy
near antonyms absurd, doubtful, dubious, fantastic, flimsy, outlandish, preposterous, questionable, ridiculous; impossible, inconceivable, unimaginable, unthinkable; skeptical, suspect, suspicious, uncertain, unsure; hopeless, unworkable, useless
antonyms far-fetched, implausible, improbable, incredible, unbelievable, unlikely

THESAURUS

believe *vb* **1** to regard as right or true ⟨the teacher *believed* the student's explanation that the assignment was late because she was sick, even though she didn't bring in a note from the doctor⟩
synonyms accept, credit, swallow, trust
related words account, accredit, understand; assume, presume, suppose; conclude, deduce, infer
phrases set store by (*or* on)
near antonyms distrust, doubt, mistrust, question, suspect; challenge, dispute
antonyms disbelieve, discredit, reject
2 to have as an opinion ⟨he *believed* that his favorite tennis player was the best in the world⟩
synonyms consider, deem, feel, figure, guess, hold, imagine, reckon [*chiefly dialect*], suppose, think
related words esteem, regard, view; accept, conceive, perceive; depend, rely, trust; assume, presume, presuppose; conclude, deduce, infer
near antonyms distrust, doubt, mistrust, question, suspect; disbelieve, discredit, reject
belittle *vb* to express scornfully one's low opinion of — see DECRY 1
belittlement *n* the act of making a person or a thing seem little or unimportant — see DEPRECIATION
belittling *adj* intended to make a person or thing seem of little importance or value — see DEROGATORY
bellicose *adj* feeling or displaying eagerness to fight — see BELLIGERENT
bellicosity *n* an inclination to fight or quarrel — see BELLIGERENCE
belligerence *n* an inclination to fight or quarrel ⟨among the Native American tribes of the Colonial period, the Iroquois were known for their *belligerence*⟩
synonyms aggression, aggressiveness, bellicosity, combativeness, contentiousness, disputatiousness, fight, militancy, pugnacity, scrappiness, truculence
related words antagonism, fierceness, hostility, unfriendliness; acidity, biliousness, crabbiness, crankiness, crossness, disagreeableness, fretfulness, grouchiness, grumpiness, huffiness, irascibility, irritability, irritableness, orneriness, peevishness, pettishness, petulance, querulousness, rudeness, surliness, testiness, waspishness
phrases chip on one's shoulder
near antonyms affability, amiability, amicability, benevolence, complaisance, cordiality, friendliness, geniality, graciousness, pleasantness, sociability; gentleness, kindliness, mildness
antonyms pacifism
belligerent *adj* feeling or displaying eagerness to fight ⟨the coach became quite *belligerent* and spit on an umpire after being thrown out of the game⟩
synonyms aggressive, argumentative, bellicose, combative, contentious, discordant, disputatious, gladiatorial, militant, pugnacious, quarrelsome, scrappy, truculent, warlike
related words antagonistic, fierce, hostile, hot-tempered; acidic, bearish, bilious, choleric, crabby, cranky, cross, disagreeable, dyspeptic, fretful, grouchy, grumpy, huffy, ill-humored, ill-natured, ill-tempered, irascible, irritable, ornery, peevish, pettish, petulant, querulous, rude, snappish, snappy, surly, testy, touchy, ugly, waspish; battling, fighting, warring
phrases on the warpath

near antonyms affable, amiable, amicable, benevolent, complaisant, conciliatory, cordial, easygoing, friendly, genial, good-natured, good-tempered, gracious, ingratiating, obliging, pleasant, sociable; calm, quiet, relaxed, serene, tranquil; benign, gentle, kindly, mild
antonyms nonbelligerent, pacific, peaceable, peaceful
bellow *vb* to make a long loud deep noise or cry — see ROAR
belly *n* the part of the body between the chest and the pelvis — see STOMACH
belly *vb* to extend outward beyond a usual point — see BULGE
bellyache *n* abdominal pain especially when focused in the digestive organs — see STOMACHACHE
bellyache *vb* to express dissatisfaction, pain, or resentment usually tiresomely — see COMPLAIN
belong *vb* **1** to have or be in a usual or proper place ⟨your shoes *belong* in the closet, not out on the floor where people will trip on them⟩
synonyms go
related words place, stay; fit (in)
2 to be the property of a person or group of persons ⟨those textbooks *belong* to the school system, and you have to give them back at the end of the year⟩
synonyms appertain, pertain
related words have, hold, own, possess
belongings *n pl* transportable items that one owns — see POSSESSION 2
beloved *adj* granted special treatment or attention — see DARLING 1
beloved *n* a person with whom one is in love — see SWEETHEART
below *adv* **1** in or to a lower place ⟨he climbed *below* to fix the engine⟩
synonyms beneath, under, underneath
related words beside, near, nearby
near antonyms aloft, overhead
antonyms up
2 toward or in a lower position — see DOWN
below *prep* in a lower position than ⟨she sat *below* everyone else, on the floor⟩
synonyms beneath, under
related words underneath
antonyms above, over
¹**belt** *n* a hard strike with a part of the body or an instrument — see ¹BLOW
²**belt** *n* a strip of flexible material (as leather) worn around the waist ⟨he loves his fancily decorated *belt*, but only gets to wear it on special occasions⟩
synonyms cincture, cummerbund, girdle, sash
related words band, waistband; circle, loop, ribbon, ring; baldric, bandolier (*or* bandoleer)
2 a broad geographical area — see REGION 2
belt *vb* **1** to deliver a blow to (someone or something) usually in a strong vigorous manner — see HIT 1
2 to encircle or bind with or as if with a belt — see GIRD 1
3 to strike repeatedly — see BEAT 1
bemoan *vb* **1** to feel or express sorrow for — see LAMENT 1
2 to feel sorry or dissatisfied about — see REGRET
bemoaning *adj* expressing or suggesting mourning — see MOURNFUL 1
bemuse *vb* to throw into a state of mental uncertainty — see CONFUSE 1

bench *n* a public official having authority to decide questions of law — see JUDGE 1

benchmark *n* something set up as an example against which others of the same type are compared — see STANDARD 1

bend *n* **1** something that curves or is curved ⟨it's hard to see around that *bend* in the road, so be careful⟩
synonyms angle, arc, arch, bow, crook, curvature, curve, turn, wind
related words kink, warp; circle, ring, ringlet, round; coil, curl, curlicue (*also* curlycue), flexure, fold, loop, spiral, swirl, twist; decline, inclination, incline, slope; corner, turnoff
antonyms straight line
2 the act of positioning or an instance of being positioned at an angle — see TILT

bend *vb* **1** to cause to turn away from a straight line ⟨she *bent* the knife when she got it stuck in the drawer⟩
synonyms arch, crook, curve, hook, swerve
related words arc, bow, round; deflect, divert; entwine, kink, swirl, turn, twine, twist, veer, warp; coil, curl, loop, spiral; dent, dimple; meander, weave, wind; decline, incline, slope
antonyms straighten, unbend, uncurl
2 to occupy (oneself) diligently or with close attention — see APPLY 2
3 to point or turn (something) toward a target or goal — see AIM 1
4 to turn away from a straight line or course — see CURVE 1

bending *adj* marked by a long series of irregular curves — see CROOKED 1

beneath *adv* in or to a lower place — see BELOW 1

beneath *prep* in a lower position than — see BELOW

benediction *n* a prayer calling for divine care, protection, or favor — see BLESSING 1

benefaction *n* a gift of money or its equivalent to a charity, humanitarian cause, or public institution — see CONTRIBUTION

benefactor *n* one that helps another with gifts or money ⟨an anonymous *benefactor* gave our school a dozen new computers⟩
synonyms donator, donor, patron
related words almsgiver, philanthropist; contributor, giver; subscriber, supporter, helper

beneficence *n* a gift of money or its equivalent to a charity, humanitarian cause, or public institution — see CONTRIBUTION

beneficent *adj* **1** having or marked by sympathy and consideration for others — see HUMANE 1
2 having or showing a concern for the welfare of others — see CHARITABLE 1

beneficial *adj* conferring benefits; promoting or contributing to personal or social well-being ⟨tutoring can often be as *beneficial* and rewarding for the tutor as for the student receiving the help⟩
synonyms advantageous, favorable, helpful, profitable, salutary
related words gratifying, rewarding, satisfying; promising, propitious; advisable, desirable, healthful, healthy, salubrious, wholesome
near antonyms bad, damaging, deleterious, harmful, injurious, unfavorable, unhelpful
antonyms disadvantageous, unfavorable, unhelpful

benefit *n* **1** a thing that helps — see HELP 2

2 something that provides happiness or does good for a person or thing — see BLESSING 2

benefit *vb* to provide with something useful or desirable ⟨his summer job *benefited* him in two ways: by giving him spending money and by offering some work experience⟩
synonyms avail, profit, serve
related words succeed, work (for); aid, assist, help, improve; content, delight, gladden, gratify, please, satisfy; bless
near antonyms hinder, impede; damage, harm, hurt, impair, injure; afflict, distress, upset

benevolence *n* kindly concern, interest, or support — see GOODWILL 1

benevolent *adj* **1** having or marked by sympathy and consideration for others — see HUMANE 1
2 having or showing a concern for the welfare of others — see CHARITABLE 1

benighted *adj* lacking in education or the knowledge gained from books — see IGNORANT 1

benign *adj* not harsh or stern especially in manner, nature, or effect — see GENTLE 1

benignant *adj* having or marked by sympathy and consideration for others — see HUMANE 1

benison *n* a prayer calling for divine care, protection, or favor — see BLESSING 1

bent *n* a habitual attraction to some activity or thing — see INCLINATION 1

bent (on *or* upon) *adj* fully committed to achieving a goal — see DETERMINED

benumb *vb* to reduce or weaken in strength or feeling — see DULL 1

benumbed *adj* lacking in sensation or feeling — see NUMB

bequeath *vb* to give by means of a will — see LEAVE 2

bequest *n* something that is or may be inherited — see INHERITANCE

berate *vb* to criticize (someone) severely or angrily especially for personal failings — see SCOLD

bereaved *adj* suffering the death of a loved one ⟨the *bereaved* parents cried often in the first year⟩
synonyms bereft
related words orphaned, widowed; distressed, grieving, melancholy, miserable, mournful, mourning, sad, sorrowing, suffering, unhappy, upset; bemoaning, crying, lamenting, wailing, weeping

bereft *adj* **1** suffering the death of a loved one — see BEREAVED
2 utterly lacking in something needed, wanted, or expected — see DEVOID 1

berserk *adv* in a confused and reckless manner — see HELTER-SKELTER 1

berth *n* an assignment at which one regularly works for pay — see JOB 1

beseech *vb* to make a request to (someone) in an earnest or urgent manner — see BEG

beseeching *adj* asking humbly — see SUPPLIANT

beset *vb* to take sudden, violent action against — see ATTACK 1

beside *prep* **1** in addition to — see BESIDES 1
2 not including — see EXCEPT

besides *adv* in addition to what has been said — see MORE 1

besides *prep* **1** in addition to ⟨*besides* me, there are five people working on this project⟩
synonyms as well as, beside, over and above
related words plus; including
phrases along with, together with

THESAURUS

near antonyms except (*also* excepting); less, minus
2 not including — see EXCEPT

besiege *vb* to surround (as a fortified place) with armed forces for the purpose of capturing or preventing commerce and communication ⟨the army *besieged* the fort for six months before it finally surrendered⟩
synonyms beleaguer, blockade, invest
related words barricade, block, cut off, dam, encircle; assail, assault, attack, beset; confine, insulate, isolate, quarantine
phrases lay siege to
near antonyms emancipate, free, liberate, release, rescue

besmear *vb* to rub an oily or sticky substance over — see SMEAR 1

besmirch *vb* to make dirty — see DIRTY 1

besmirched *adj* not clean — see DIRTY 1

bespatter *vb* to wet or soil by striking with something liquid or mushy — see SPLASH 2

bespeak *vb* **1** to arrange to have something (as a hotel room) held for one's future use — see RESERVE 1
2 to make known (something abstract) through outward signs — see SHOW 2

best *n* **1** dressy clothing — see FINERY
2 individuals carefully selected as being the best of a class — see ELITE

best *vb* to achieve a victory over — see BEAT 2

bestow *vb* to make a present of — see GIVE 1

bestowal *n* something given to someone without expectation of a return — see GIFT 1

bestrew *vb* to cover by or as if by scattering something over or on — see SCATTER 2

bet *n* the money or things risked on the outcome of an uncertain event ⟨she offered the *bet* of a free lunch if her team won the World Series⟩
synonyms stake, wager
related words collateral; jackpot, kitty, pot

bet *vb* to risk (something) on the outcome of an uncertain event ⟨he *bet* a month's allowance on the World Series⟩
synonyms gamble, go, lay, stake, wager
related words bid, offer; adventure, chance, hazard, speculate, venture; endanger, imperil, jeopardize

bête noire *n* **1** something or someone that causes fear or dread especially without reason — see BOGEY 1
2 something or someone that is hated — see HATE 2

betide *vb* to take place — see HAPPEN

betray *vb* **1** to be unfaithful or disloyal to ⟨childhood friends of movie stars often *betray* them by telling their secrets to the supermarket tabloids⟩
synonyms cross, double-cross, sell (out)
related words give away; inform (on), rat (on), snitch (on), split (on) [*British*], tell (on)
phrases go back on
near antonyms defend, guard, protect, safeguard, save, shield
2 to make known (something abstract) through outward signs — see SHOW 2

betrayal *n* the act or fact of violating the trust or confidence of another ⟨the terrible *betrayal* of having her best friend reveal her confidences to others⟩
synonyms disloyalty, double cross, faithlessness, falseness, falsity, infidelity, perfidy, sellout, treachery, treason, unfaithfulness

related words abandonment, desertion; deceit, deception, double-dealing, duplicity, guile; fraud, informing, lying, snitching, talebearing, trickery
near antonyms dependability, reliability, trustworthiness; allegiance, devotion, faithfulness, fealty, fidelity, loyalty, staunchness, steadfastness; defense, protection, safeguard, shield

betrayer *n* **1** a person who provides secret information about another's wrongdoing — see INFORMER
2 one who betrays a trust or an allegiance — see TRAITOR

betrothal *n* the act or state of being engaged to be married — see ENGAGEMENT 1

betrothed *adj* pledged in marriage — see ENGAGED

betrothed *n* the person to whom one is engaged to be married ⟨he gazed lovingly at his *betrothed* throughout dinner⟩
synonyms fiancé, fiancée, intended
related words admirer, beau, beloved, boyfriend, darling, dear, favorite, fellow, flame, girlfriend, honey, love, lover, steady, swain, sweet, sweetheart, valentine; bride, groom

better *adv* to a greater or higher extent — see MORE 2

better *n* **1** one who is above another in rank, station, or office — see SUPERIOR
2 the more favorable condition or position in a competition — see ADVANTAGE 1

better *vb* **1** to be greater, better, or stronger than — see SURPASS 1
2 to make better — see IMPROVE

bettor *or* **better** *n* one that bets (as on the outcome of a contest or sports event) ⟨*bettors* on the horse race have to place their bets at least 20 minutes before the start of the race⟩
synonyms gambler, wagerer
related words dicer; speculator

beverage *n* a liquid suitable for drinking — see DRINK 1

bewail *vb* to feel or express sorrow for — see LAMENT 1

bewailing *adj* expressing or suggesting mourning — see MOURNFUL 1

beware (of) *vb* to be cautious of or on guard against ⟨*beware of* that parrot because it bites⟩
synonyms guard (against), mind, watch out (for)
related words attend, heed, mark, note, notice; behold, discern, observe, perceive, see, watch
phrases be on the lookout for, look out for
near antonyms discount, disregard, ignore, miss, overlook

bewilder *vb* to throw into a state of mental uncertainty — see CONFUSE 1

bewildered *adj* suffering from mental confusion — see DIZZY 2

bewilderment *n* a state of mental uncertainty — see CONFUSION 1

bewitch *vb* **1** to cast a spell on ⟨a wicked fairy *bewitched* Sleeping Beauty so that she would sleep for a hundred years⟩
synonyms charm, enchant, hex, spell
related words curse, jinx, possess; attract, beguile, captivate, fascinate, mesmerize, spellbind; entice, lure, seduce, tempt
near antonyms bless
2 to attract or delight as if by magic — see CHARM 1

bewitched *adj* being or appearing to be under a magic spell — see ENCHANTED

bewitching *adj* having an often mysterious or magical power to attract — see FASCINATING 1

bewitchment *n* **1** a spoken word or set of words believed to have magic power — see SPELL 1

2 the power to control natural forces through supernatural means — see MAGIC 1

beyond *adv* at or to a greater distance or more advanced point — see FARTHER

beyond *prep* **1** on or to the farther side of ⟨the arrow flew *beyond* the fence and in the woods⟩

synonyms over, past

related words outside

near antonyms inside

2 out of the reach or sphere of ⟨although the school can keep you from screaming during school hours, making someone be quiet after school is *beyond* their authority⟩

synonyms outside, outside of, without

related words except (*also* excepting)

near antonyms inside

antonyms within

bias *n* an attitude that always favors one way of feeling or acting especially without considering any other possibilities ⟨he had a powerful *bias* towards doing all math problems by the same method, regardless of the problem⟩

synonyms favor, one-sidedness, partiality, partisanship, prejudice

related words favoritism, nepotism; bent, inclination, leaning, penchant, predilection, predisposition, proclivity, propensity, tendency; preconception, prejudgment

near antonyms calm, detachment, dispassion, indifference; aversion, dislike, distaste

antonyms impartiality, neutrality, objectivity, open-mindedness

bias *vb* to cause to have often negative opinions formed without sufficient knowledge — see PREJUDICE

biased *adj* inclined to favor one side over another — see PARTIAL 1

Bible *n* a book made up of the writings accepted by Christians as coming from God ⟨she received a lovely *Bible* as a First Communion gift⟩

synonyms Book, Good Book, Holy Writ, Scripture

bicker *n* an often noisy or angry expression of differing opinions — see ARGUMENT 1

bicker *vb* to express different opinions about something often angrily — see ARGUE 2

bid *vb* to issue orders to (someone) by right of authority — see COMMAND 1

bide *vb* to remain in place in readiness or expectation of something — see WAIT

big *adj* **1** having great meaning or lasting effect — see IMPORTANT 1

2 of a size greater than average of its kind — see LARGE

bight *n* a part of a body of water that extends beyond the general shoreline — see GULF 1

bigness *n* the quality or state of being large in size — see LARGENESS

bigoted *adj* unwilling to grant other people social rights or to accept other viewpoints — see INTOLERANT 2

bilious *adj* having or showing a habitually bad temper — see ILL-TEMPERED

biliousness *n* readiness to show annoyance or impatience — see PETULANCE

¹**bill** *n* **1** a record of goods sold or services performed together with the costs due ⟨luckily, the amount due on our electric *bill* wasn't too high this month, because we finally convinced everyone to stop wasting electricity⟩

synonyms account, check, invoice, statement, tab

related words receipt, reckoning; document, record; charge, cost, expense, fee, price, rate, toll; score, tally

2 a piece of printed paper used as money ⟨the United States twenty-dollar *bill* has a picture of Andrew Jackson on the front⟩

synonyms bank note, greenback, note

related words paper money, scrip; buck, dollar; cash, chips, currency, dough, legal tender, lucre, money, pelf; check, draft, money order

3 a sheet bearing an announcement for posting in a public place — see POSTER

4 the amount owed at a bar or restaurant or the slip of paper stating the amount — see CHECK 1

²**bill** *n* **1** the jaws of a bird together with their hornlike covering — see BEAK

2 the projecting front part of a hat or cap — see VISOR

¹**billet** *n* a straight piece (as of wood or metal) that is longer than it is wide — see BAR 1

²**billet** *n* an assignment at which one regularly works for pay — see JOB 1

billet *vb* to provide with living quarters or shelter — see HOUSE 1

bill of fare *n* a list of foods served at or available for a meal — see MENU 1

billow *n* a moving ridge on the surface of water — see WAVE

billow *vb* to extend outward beyond a usual point — see BULGE

billy *n* a heavy rigid stick used as a weapon or for punishment — see CLUB 1

binary *adj* consisting of two members or parts that are usually joined — see DOUBLE 1

bind *vb* **1** to confine or restrain with or as if with chains ⟨prisons tend to *bind* convicted criminals for transport⟩ ⟨Angie feels *bound* to her boyfriend by love and loyalty⟩

synonyms chain, enchain, fetter, handcuff, manacle, shackle, trammel

related words lash, pinion, secure, tie, truss; attach, fasten, join, link; confine, constrain, curb, hamper, hinder, limit, restrict; entangle, tangle

near antonyms emancipate, free, liberate, loose, release, rescue; undo, unfasten, untangle, untie; detach, disengage

antonyms unbind, unfetter

2 to cover with a bandage — see BANDAGE

3 to gather into a tight mass by means of a line or cord — see TIE 1

binge *n* a time or instance of carefree fun — see FLING 1

biography *n* a history of a person's life ⟨an unauthorized *biography* of the actor made him very unhappy⟩

synonyms life, memoir

related words autobiography; chronicle, history, past, story; obituary; character sketch

bipartite *adj* consisting of two members or parts that are usually joined — see DOUBLE 1

birch *vb* to strike repeatedly with something long and thin or flexible — see WHIP 1

bird *n* a member of the human race — see HUMAN

birdman *n* one who flies or is qualified to fly an aircraft or spacecraft — see PILOT

THESAURUS

bird's–eye *adj* relating to the main elements and not to specific details — see GENERAL 2

birth *n* **1** the act or instance of being born ⟨biology class will be showing a movie of the *birth* of kittens⟩
synonyms nativity
related words creation, genesis, origination, rise; bearing, childbearing, labor, parturition; begetting, breeding, fathering, generation, mothering, reproduction, siring, spawning; fatherhood, maternity, motherhood, parenthood, paternity
near antonyms abortion, miscarriage
2 the line of ancestors from whom a person is descended — see ANCESTRY
3 the point at which something begins — see BEGINNING

birthright *n* **1** something that is or may be inherited — see INHERITANCE
2 something to which one has a just claim — see RIGHT 1

bisect *vb* to divide by passing through or across — see INTERSECT

bit *n* **1** a very small piece ⟨she left only a *bit* of the broccoli on her plate, so she was allowed to have dessert⟩
synonyms atom, crumb, fleck, flyspeck, grain, granule, molecule, morsel, mote, nubbin, particle, patch, scrap, scruple, snippet, speck, tittle
related words ace, dab, glimmer, hint, hoot, iota, jot, lick, little, mite, modicum, ounce, peanuts, pinch, ray, shade, shred, smidgen (*also* smidgeon *or* smidgin), spot, strain, streak, suspicion, taste, touch, trace, whisper, whit; dash, driblet, drop; fragment, part, portion, section; bite, mouthful, nibble; handful, scattering, smattering, sprinkling; dose, shot; damn, darn; chip, flake, shard, shiver, sliver, splinter; clipping, paring, shaving; smithereens
near antonyms chunk, gob, lump, hunk, slab; abundance, barrel, bucket, bushel, deal, heaps, loads, mass, mountain, much, peck, pile, plenty, pot, profusion, quantity, raft, scads, stack, volume, wad, wealth
2 a broken or irregular part of something that often remains incomplete — see FRAGMENT
3 a very small amount — see PARTICLE 1
4 an indefinite but usually short period of time — see WHILE 1

bite *n* **1** a harsh or sharp quality — see EDGE 1
2 a small piece or quantity of food — see MORSEL 1
3 an uncomfortable degree of coolness — see CHILL

bite (at) *vb* to consume or wear away gradually — see EAT 2

bite (on) *vb* to crush or grind with the teeth ⟨she likes to *bite on* her pencils when she thinks hard⟩
synonyms champ, chew, chomp (on), crunch (on), gnaw (on), masticate, nibble
related words lap, lick, munch; consume, ingest, eat, swallow; bolt, devour, gobble (up *or* down), gorge, gulp, scarf, scoff, snack, wolf; peck (at), pick (at)

biting *adj* **1** causing intense discomfort to one's skin — see CUTTING 1
2 causing intense mental or physical distress — see SHARP 2
3 marked by the use of wit that is intended to cause hurt feelings — see SARCASTIC

bitter *adj* **1** having or showing deep-seated resentment ⟨a *bitter* attitude about always having to work on Saturday⟩ ⟨she's still *bitter* about the way her boyfriend broke up with her⟩
synonyms acrid, acrimonious, embittered, hard, rancorous, resentful, sore
related words disaffected, discontented, disgruntled, malcontent; contemptuous, cynical, disdainful, scornful; angry, cruel, harsh, irritated, mad, rough, savage, vicious; acid, caustic, cutting, mordant, sarcastic, trenchant
near antonyms caring, forgiving, gentle, kind, loving, sweet, sympathetic, tender, warm, warm-hearted
2 hard to accept or bear especially emotionally ⟨discovering that he had been cut from the team was a *bitter* disappointment⟩
synonyms afflicting, agonizing, cruel, excruciating, galling, grievous, harrowing, harsh, heart-rending, hurtful, painful, tormenting, tortuous
related words insufferable, insupportable, intolerable, unacceptable, unbearable, unendurable, unsupportable; appalling, awful, bad, dire, dreadful, ghastly, horrible, miserable, nasty, rotten, terrible, vile, wretched; acute, extreme, intense, piercing
near antonyms bearable, endurable, supportable, sustainable, tolerable; livable (*also* liveable), sufferable, survivable; acceptable, allowable, reasonable
antonyms gratifying, pleasing, sweet
3 causing intense discomfort to one's skin — see CUTTING 1
4 difficult to endure — see HARSH 1
5 having a low or subnormal temperature — see COLD 1
6 uncomfortably cool — see CHILLY 1

bitterly *adv* with feelings of bitterness or grief — see HARD 2

bitterness *n* **1** a deep-seated ill will — see ENMITY
2 a harsh or sharp quality — see EDGE 1
3 an uncomfortable degree of coolness — see CHILL
4 biting sharpness of feeling or expression — see ACRIMONY 1

bitty *adj* very small in size — see TINY

bivouac *n* a place where a group of people live for a short time in tents or cabins — see CAMP 1

bivouac *vb* to live in a camp or the outdoors — see CAMP

bizarre *adj* **1** conceived or made without regard for reason or reality — see FANTASTIC 1
2 different from the ordinary in a way that causes curiosity or suspicion — see ODD 2

blab *vb* **1** to engage in casual or rambling conversation — see CHAT
2 to relate sometimes questionable or secret information of a personal nature — see GOSSIP

blabber *n* **1** a person who talks constantly — see CHATTERBOX
2 unintelligible or meaningless talk — see GIBBERISH

black *adj* **1** having the color of soot or coal ⟨a little *black* dress blends into the night very well⟩
synonyms ebony, pitch-black, pitch-dark, pitchy, raven, sable
related words dark, dusky, inky; blackish, brunet (*or* brunette)
near antonyms bright, brilliant, light, pale
antonyms white
2 causing or marked by an atmosphere lacking in cheer — see GLOOMY 1

3 not conforming to a high moral standard; morally unacceptable — see BAD 2

black art *n* the power to control natural forces through supernatural means — see MAGIC 1

blackball *vb* to reject by or as if by a vote — see NEGATIVE 1

blacken *vb* **1** to make dirty — see DIRTY

2 to make untrue and harmful statements about — see SLANDER

3 to make dark, dim, or indistinct — see CLOUD 1

blackened *adj* not clean — see DIRTY 1

blackening *n* the making of false statements that damage another's reputation — see SLANDER

black magic *n* the power to control natural forces through supernatural means — see MAGIC 1

blackmailer *n* a person who gets money from another by using force or threats — see RACKETEER

blackness *n* a time or place of little or no light — see DARK 1

blackout *n* a temporary or permanent state of unconsciousness — see FAINT

black out *vb* to lose consciousness — see FAINT

blade *n* **1** a hand weapon with a length of metal sharpened on one or both sides and usually tapered to a sharp point — see SWORD

2 an instrument with a sharp edge for cutting — see KNIFE

blamable *adj* **1** deserving reproach or blame — see BLAMEWORTHY

2 responsible for a wrong — see GUILTY 1

blame *n* **1** responsibility for wrongdoing or failure ⟨willingly accepted the *blame* for not seeing that the kitchen was properly cleaned⟩

synonyms culpability, fault, guilt, rap

related words regret, remorse, self-reproach, shame; accountability, liability; complicity; blameworthiness, reprehensibleness, sinfulness; censure, condemnation, denunciation

near antonyms acclaim, plaudits, praise; achievement, success

antonyms blamelessness, faultlessness, guiltlessness, innocence

2 the state of being held as the cause of something that needs to be set right — see RESPONSIBILITY 1

blame *vb* to express one's unfavorable opinion of the worth or quality of — see CRITICIZE

blameless *adj* free from guilt or blame — see INNOCENT 1

blamelessness *n* the quality or state of being free from guilt or blame — see INNOCENCE 1

blameworthy *adj* deserving reproach or blame ⟨copying another student's work was certainly a *blameworthy* act⟩

synonyms blamable, censurable, culpable, reprehensible, reproachable

related words bad, guilty, sinful, wicked; foolish, irresponsible, reckless; chargeable, impeachable, indictable, punishable; criminal, illegal, illicit, unlawful; illegitimate, improper, wrongful

phrases at fault

near antonyms flawless, perfect, pure; guiltless, innocent

antonyms blameless, faultless, impeccable, irreproachable

blanch *vb* to make white or whiter by removing color — see WHITEN

blanched *adj* lacking a healthy skin color — see PALE 2

bland *adj* not harsh or stern especially in manner, nature, or effect — see GENTLE 1

blandish *vb* to get (someone) to do something by gentle urging, special attention, or flattery — see COAX

blank *adj* **1** not expressing any emotion ⟨the teacher knew no one was paying attention when she looked out and saw all those *blank* faces⟩

synonyms deadpan, expressionless, impassive, inexpressive, stolid, vacant

related words dull, empty, vacuous, vapid; enigmatic (*also* enigmatical), impenetrable, inscrutable, mysterious; dead, inactive, quiescent, sleepy, sluggish; indolent, languorous, lazy, lethargic, listless; motionless, static, still, wooden; reserved, restrained, reticent, taciturn; aloof, apathetic, detached, indifferent, phlegmatic; cold, cool

near antonyms active, alive, animated, bright, busy, dynamic, effervescent, energetic, expansive, exuberant, lively, vigorous, vital, vivacious; eloquent, revealing, revelatory, significant, vivid; emotional, melodramatic, theatrical, unreserved, unrestrained

antonyms demonstrative, expressive

2 lacking contents that could or should be present — see EMPTY 1

blank *n* **1** a piece of paper with information written or to be written on it — see FORM 2

2 empty space — see VACANCY 1

blanket *adj* belonging or relating to the whole — see GENERAL 1

blanket *vb* **1** to form a layer over — see COVER 2

2 to keep secret or shut off from view — see ¹HIDE 2

blankness *n* empty space — see VACANCY 1

blaring *adj* marked by a high volume of sound — see LOUD 1

blarney *n* excessive praise — see FLATTERY

blarney *vb* **1** to get (someone) to do something by gentle urging, special attention, or flattery — see COAX

2 to praise too much — see FLATTER 1

blaspheme *vb* to use offensive or indecent language — see SWEAR 1

blasphemous *adj* not showing proper reverence for the holy or sacred — see IRREVERENT

blasphemy *n* an act of great disrespect shown to God or to sacred ideas, people, or things ⟨in the 17th century the Quakers were persecuted for beliefs and practices that older churches regarded as *blasphemies*⟩

synonyms defilement, desecration, impiety, irreverence, sacrilege

related words cursing, profanity, swearing; affront, insult; violation; contamination, corruption, debasement, pollution; sin, trespass

near antonyms consecration, purification, sanctification; reverence, veneration

antonyms adoration, glorification, worship

blast *n* **1** a loud explosive sound — see CLAP 1

2 a sudden brief rush of wind — see GUST 1

3 the act or an instance of exploding — see EXPLOSION 1

blast *vb* **1** to cause to break open or into pieces by or as if by an explosive ⟨the highway engineers will have to *blast* that hill in order to put a road through it⟩

synonyms blow up, burst, demolish, explode, pop, shatter, smash

related words dynamite; annihilate, decimate, destroy; ruin, wreck; detonate, discharge; fragment, splinter

THESAURUS

near antonyms collapse, implode

2 to cause (a projectile) to be driven forward with force — see SHOOT 1

3 to cause a weapon to release a missile with great force — see SHOOT 2

4 to criticize harshly and usually publicly — see ATTACK 2

blasting *adj* marked by a high volume of sound — see LOUD 1

blasting *n* a directed propelling of a missile by a firearm or artillery piece — see SHOT

blatant *adj* **1** engaging in or marked by loud and insistent cries especially of protest — see VOCIFEROUS

2 very noticeable especially for being incorrect or bad — see EGREGIOUS

blaze *n* the steady giving off of the form of radiation that makes vision possible — see LIGHT 1

blaze *vb* **1** to be on fire especially brightly — see BURN 1

2 to make known openly or publicly — see ANNOUNCE

3 to shine with a bright harsh light — see GLARE 1

blazing *adj* **1** being on fire — see ABLAZE 1

2 having or expressing great depth of feeling — see FERVENT

bleach *vb* to make white or whiter by removing color — see WHITEN

bleak *adj* **1** causing or marked by an atmosphere lacking in cheer — see GLOOMY 1

2 marked by wet and windy conditions — see FOUL 1

3 uncomfortably cool — see CHILLY 1

bleakness *n* an uncomfortable degree of coolness — see CHILL

bleary *adj* not seen or understood clearly — see FAINT 1

bleed *vb* **1** to feel deep sadness or mental pain — see GRIEVE

2 to flow forth slowly through small openings — see EXUDE

3 to remove (liquid) gradually or completely — see DRAIN 1

4 to rob by the use of trickery or threats — see FLEECE

bleed (for) *vb* to have sympathy for — see PITY

blemish *n* something that spoils the appearance or completeness of a thing ⟨a slight *blemish* on the mirror was the only break in the gleaming surface⟩

synonyms defect, deformity, disfigurement, fault, flaw, imperfection, mark, pockmark, scar

related words abnormality, distortion, irregularity, malformation; bug, glitch, kink; blot, blotch, spot, stain; failing, vice, weakness

near antonyms adornment, decoration, embellishment, enhancement, ornament

blemish *vb* **1** to affect slightly with something morally bad or undesirable — see TAINT 1

2 to reduce the soundness, effectiveness, or perfection of — see DAMAGE 1

¹**blench** *vb* to draw back in fear, pain, or disgust — see FLINCH

²**blench** *vb* to make white or whiter by removing color — see WHITEN

blend *n* a distinct entity formed by the combining of two or more different things ⟨that fabric is a cotton and polyester *blend*, so it shouldn't shrink as much as pure cotton⟩

synonyms admixture, amalgam, amalgamation, combination, composite, compound, fusion, intermixture, mix, mixture

related words coalescence, concoction, incorporation, intermingling, mingling; assortment, hash, hodgepodge, hotchpotch, jumble, medley, mélange, mishmash, motley, patchwork, potpourri, variety; accumulation, aggregation, conglomeration

near antonyms component, constituent, element, ingredient

blend *vb* **1** to turn into a single mass that is more or less the same throughout ⟨she *blended* the ingredients for the brownies very thoroughly to eliminate lumps in the batter⟩

synonyms amalgamate, combine, commingle, fuse, incorporate, integrate, intermingle, intermix, merge, mingle, mix

related words fold, mix, stir, toss; coalesce, combine, compound, conjoin, join, link, unite

near antonyms cleave, disjoin, disunite, divide, divorce, part, rupture, sever, sunder; disperse, dissolve, scatter; detach, disengage, split

antonyms break down, break up, separate

2 to form a pleasing relationship — see HARMONIZE 1

bless *vb* **1** to make holy through prayers or ritual ⟨the priest *blessed* the water, thus allowing it to be used as holy water for various rites⟩

synonyms consecrate, hallow, sanctify

related words cleanse, purify; commit, dedicate, devote; reconsecrate

near antonyms defile, desecrate, profane; dirty, foul, pollute, soil, taint; curse, damn, execrate; cast out, condemn, damn, punish

2 to proclaim the glory of — see PRAISE 1

blessed *adj* **1** of, relating to, or being God — see HOLY 3

2 set apart or worthy of veneration by association with God — see HOLY 2

blessedness *n* **1** a feeling or state of well-being and contentment — see HAPPINESS 1

2 the quality or state of being spiritually pure or virtuous — see HOLINESS

blessing *n* **1** a prayer calling for divine care, protection, or favor ⟨that rabbi also always ends the service with a short *blessing*⟩

synonyms benediction, benison

related words Godspeed; appeal, entreaty, grace, invocation, orison, petition, plea, prayer, supplication; sanctification

antonyms anathema, curse, execration, imprecation, malediction

2 something that provides happiness or does good for a person or thing ⟨finding money on the sidewalk just when he needed to buy new sneakers was an unexpected *blessing*⟩

synonyms benefit, boon, felicity, godsend, good, manna, windfall

related words bonus, extra, lagniappe; advantage, aid, assistance, gift, help, relief, support; comfort, consolation, solace; delight, joy, pleasure

near antonyms hex, hoodoo, jinx; bother, irritant, nuisance, pest

antonyms affliction, bane, curse, evil, plague, scourge

3 an acceptance of something as satisfactory — see APPROVAL 1

4 the act of making something holy through religious ritual — see CONSECRATION

blind *adj* lacking the power of sight ⟨our old *blind* cat kept walking into walls and furniture⟩
synonyms eyeless, sightless, stone blind
related words unobservant, unobserving; blinded, purblind
near antonyms observant, observing
antonyms sighted
blind *vb* to overpower with light — see DAZZLE
blink *vb* 1 to shine with light at regular intervals ⟨she loves to sit in the dark and watch the lights on the Christmas tree *blink* in ever-changing patterns⟩
synonyms flash, twinkle, wink
related words flicker, glance, glimmer, glint, glisten, glister, glitter, scintillate, shimmer, sparkle; beam, gleam, irradiate, radiate
2 to rapidly open and close one's eyes — see WINK 1
bliss *n* a feeling or state of well-being and contentment — see HAPPINESS 1
blissful *adj* experiencing pleasure, satisfaction, or delight — see GLAD 1
blissfulness *n* a feeling or state of well-being and contentment — see HAPPINESS 1
blithe *adj* 1 having or showing a good mood or disposition — see CHEERFUL 1
2 indicative of or marked by high spirits or good humor — see MERRY
blithesome *adj* 1 having or showing a good mood or disposition — see CHEERFUL 1
2 indicative of or marked by high spirits or good humor — see MERRY
blitz *vb* to use bombs or artillery against — see BOMBARD
blitzkrieg *n* the act or action of setting upon with force or violence — see ATTACK 1
blob *n* 1 a small uneven mass — see LUMP 1
2 the quantity of fluid that falls naturally in one rounded mass — see DROP 1
bloc *n* 1 a group of people acting together within a larger group — see FACTION
2 an association of persons, parties, or states for mutual assistance and protection — see CONFEDERACY
block *n* 1 a number of things considered as a unit — see GROUP 1
2 something that makes movement or progress more difficult — see ENCUMBRANCE
block *vb* 1 to close up so that no empty spaces remain — see FILL 2
2 to prevent passage through — see CLOG 1
blockade *n* the cutting off of an area by military means to stop the flow of people or supplies ⟨it was the *blockade* of all the enemy's major ports that finally won the war⟩
synonyms investment, siege
related words encompassment, encirclement; confinement, insulation, isolation, quarantine, seclusion, segregation, sequestration; incarceration, internment
near antonyms emancipation, freedom, liberation, release, rescue
blockade *vb* to surround (as a fortified place) with armed forces for the purpose of capturing or preventing commerce and communication — see BESIEGE
blockbuster *n* 1 a person or thing that is successful — see HIT 1
2 something that is unusually large and powerful — see GIANT

blockhead *n* a stupid person — see IDIOT
bloke *n, chiefly British* an adult male human being — see MAN 1
blond *or* **blonde** *adj* of a pale yellow or yellowish brown color ⟨the little boy's *blond* hair darkened to brown as he grew older⟩
synonyms fair, flaxen, golden, sandy, straw, tawny
related words gold, light, white
near antonyms brunet (*or* brunette), dark, swarthy; black, ebony, raven
antonyms dark
blood *n* 1 a group of persons who come from the same ancestor — see FAMILY 1
2 the line of ancestors from whom a person is descended — see ANCESTRY
bloodline *n* the line of ancestors from whom a person is descended — see ANCESTRY
bloodstained *adj* containing, smeared, or stained with blood — see BLOODY 1
bloodthirsty *adj* eager for or marked by the shedding of blood, extreme violence, or killing ⟨the Goths were a wild and *bloodthirsty* people⟩
synonyms bloody, homicidal, murdering, murderous, sanguinary, sanguine
related words barbaric, barbarous, cruel, heartless, inhumane, sadistic, savage, vicious, wanton; antagonistic, fierce, gladiatorial, hostile; aggressive, assertive, bellicose, belligerent, combative, contentious, discordant, pugnacious, quarrelsome, scrappy, truculent, violent; merciless, pitiless, ruthless; fell, ferocious, grim; despiteful, hateful, malevolent, malicious, malign, malignant, mean, nasty, spiteful; destructive, devastating, ruinous
near antonyms appeasing, conciliatory, disarming, dovish, mollifying, pacific, pacifying, peaceable, peaceful, peacemaking, placating, propitiatory; unaggressive, unassertive; benign, benignant, compassionate, good-hearted, humane, kind, kindhearted, sympathetic, tenderhearted; tender, warm, warmhearted; clement, lenient, merciful; affable, amiable, amicable, benevolent, gentle, kindly; submissive, surrendering, yielding
bloody *adj* 1 containing, smeared, or stained with blood ⟨after the fight, her shirt was all *bloody*⟩
synonyms bloodstained, gory
related words carmine, crimson, red, ruby, sanguine; bloodthirsty, sanguinary
2 eager for or marked by the shedding of blood, extreme violence, or killing — see BLOODTHIRSTY
bloom *n* 1 a state or time of great activity, thriving, or achievement ⟨a handsome young man in the full *bloom* of youth⟩
synonyms blossom, flower, flush, heyday, prime
related words acme, apex, climax, meridian, peak, pinnacle, summit, zenith; glory, grandeur, splendor; haleness, heartiness; energy, force, potency, power, vigor
near antonyms decline; bottom, nadir; feebleness, fragility, frailty, weakness; illness, infirmity, sickness; shriveling, wilting, withering
2 a rosy appearance of the cheeks ⟨after a snowball fight, she came inside with a *bloom*⟩
synonyms blush, flush
related words brightness, brilliance, glow; pinkness, rosiness
3 the usually showy plant part that produces seeds — see FLOWER 1

bloom *vb* **1** to produce flowers ⟨forsythias only *bloom* at the beginning of spring⟩
synonyms blossom, blow, burgeon, flower, unfold
related words leaf, leave; bud; open
near antonyms dry (up), fade, shrivel, wilt, wither; die, drop, expire, perish
2 to develop a rosy facial color (as from excitement or embarrassment) — see BLUSH

blooming *adj* having a healthy reddish skin tone — see RUDDY

blossom *n* **1** a state or time of great activity, thriving, or achievement — see BLOOM 1
2 the usually showy plant part that produces seeds — see FLOWER 1

blossom *vb* to produce flowers — see BLOOM

blot *n* a mark of guilt or disgrace — see STAIN 1

blotch *n* a small area that is different (as in color) from the main part — see SPOT 1

blotch *vb* **1** to mark with blotches especially of different colors or shades — see MOTTLE 1
2 to mark with small spots especially unevenly — see SPOT

blotched *adj* having blotches of two or more colors — see PIED

blot out *vb* **1** to destroy all traces of — see ANNIHILATE 1
2 to keep secret or shut off from view — see ¹HIDE 2

¹**blow** *n* a hard strike with a part of the body or an instrument ⟨he was dizzy for the rest of the day after the *blow* to his head⟩
synonyms bang, bat, beat, belt, bop, box, buffet, bust, chop, clap, clip, clout, crack, cuff, hit, hook, knock, lick, pound, punch, rap, slam, slap, slug, smack, smash, sock, spank, stroke, swat, swipe, thud, thump, thwack, wallop, whack
related words flick, jab, poke, roundhouse, stab; beating, battering, bludgeoning, clobbering, drubbing, hammering, lambasting, licking, pasting, pounding, pummeling, thrashing; flogging, walloping, whipping

²**blow** *n* a sudden brief rush of wind — see GUST 1

¹**blow** *vb* **1** to breathe hard, quickly, or with difficulty — see GASP
2 to use up carelessly — see WASTE 1

²**blow** *vb* to produce flowers — see BLOOM

blow (out) *vb* to let or force out of the lungs — see EXHALE 1

blowout *n* a social gathering — see PARTY 1

blowup *n* an outburst or display of excited anger — see TANTRUM

blow up *vb* **1** to become very angry ⟨she *blew up* at everybody after a very long and very bad day⟩
synonyms flare (up), flip
related words fulminate, rant, vituperate; bristle, burn, foam, fume, rage, seethe; burst, explode; enrage, incense, inflame, infuriate, madden; aggravate, anger, annoy, bother, bug, displease, distress, exasperate, gall, get, irk, irritate, nettle, peeve, pique, provoke, put out, rile, vex; agitate, disturb, perturb, upset
phrases fly into a rage, fly off the handle, forget oneself, lose one's temper
near antonyms appease, conciliate, mollify, pacify, placate; comfort, console, quiet, soothe
antonyms calm (down)
2 to break open or into pieces usually because of internal pressure — see EXPLODE 1
3 to cause to break open or into pieces by or as if by an explosive — see BLAST 1

blowy *adj* marked by strong wind or more wind than usual — see WINDY 1

blubber *vb* to shed tears often while making meaningless sounds as a sign of pain or distress — see CRY 1

bludgeon *n* a heavy rigid stick used as a weapon or for punishment — see CLUB 1

bludgeon *vb* **1** to deliver a blow to (someone or something) usually in a strong vigorous manner — see HIT 1
2 to strike repeatedly — see BEAT 1

blue *adj* feeling unhappiness — see SAD 1

blue *n* **1** the expanse of air surrounding the earth — see SKY
2 the whole body of salt water that covers nearly three-fourths of the earth — see OCEAN

blueprint *n* a method worked out in advance for achieving some objective — see PLAN 1

blueprint *vb* to work out the details of (something) in advance — see PLAN 1

blues *n pl* a state or spell of low spirits — see SADNESS

bluff *adj* being or characterized by direct, brief, and potentially rude speech or manner — see BLUNT 1

bluff *n* a steep wall of rock, earth, or ice — see CLIFF

bluff *vb* to cause to believe what is untrue — see DECEIVE

blunder *n* an unintentional departure from truth or accuracy — see ERROR 1

blunt *adj* **1** being or characterized by direct, brief, and potentially rude speech or manner ⟨he values honesty and is quite *blunt* about telling people their flaws⟩
synonyms abrupt, bluff, brusque, crusty, curt, downright, snippy
related words gruff, rough, short; hearty, honest, sincere; candid, direct, forthright, foursquare, frank, free-spoken, open, outspoken, plain, plainspoken, straightforward; discourteous, disrespectful, impertinent, impolite, inconsiderate, rude, tactless, undiplomatic; closemouthed, laconic, reserved, reticent, terse, tight-lipped; artless, earnest, sincere; coarse, crass, crude, low, uncouth, vulgar
near antonyms civil, considerate, courteous, diplomatic, gracious, polite, politic, smooth, suave, tactful; loquacious, talkative, voluble; long-winded, prolix, verbose; courtly, cultivated, gallant, genteel, polished, refined
antonyms circuitous, mealymouthed
2 lacking sharpness of edge or point — see DULL 1

blunt *vb* to reduce or weaken in strength or feeling — see DULL 1

blunted *adj* lacking sharpness of edge or point — see DULL 1

blur *vb* **1** to make (something) unclear to the understanding — see CONFUSE 2
2 to make dark, dim, or indistinct — see CLOUD 1

blurt (out) *vb* to utter with a sudden burst of strong feeling — see EXCLAIM

blush *n* a rosy appearance of the cheeks — see BLOOM 2

blush *vb* to develop a rosy facial color (as from excitement or embarrassment) ⟨she *blushed* when she realized she had walked into the boys' bathroom by mistake⟩

synonyms bloom, color, crimson, flush, glow, redden

related words rouge; abash, chagrin, discomfit, disconcert, embarrass, faze, humiliate, mortify

bluster *n* **1** boastful speech or writing — see BOMBAST 1

2 loud, confused, and usually unharmonious sound — see NOISE 1

bluster *vb* to talk loudly and wildly — see RANT

blustery *adj* marked by strong wind or more wind than usual — see WINDY 1

board *n* a leg-mounted piece of furniture with a broad flat top designed for the serving of food — see TABLE 1

board *vb* **1** to provide food or meals for — see FEED 1

2 to provide with living quarters or shelter — see HOUSE 1

boarder *n* one who rents a room or apartment in another's house — see TENANT

boast *n* an asset that brings praise or renown — see GLORY 2

boast *vb* to praise or express pride in one's own possessions, qualities, or accomplishments often to excess ⟨he *boasted* that he was the best hockey goalie in the whole school⟩

synonyms brag, crow, swagger

related words puff (up); pride; gush; exult, glory, rejoice; brandish, display, exhibit, expose, flaunt, parade, show off; magnify, maximize

near antonyms bad-mouth, belittle, decry, deprecate, depreciate, diminish, discount, disparage, minimize; bemoan, lament, mourn, regret

boat *n* **1** a small buoyant structure for travel on water ⟨paddling the little *boat* across the lake is great exercise, but tiring⟩

synonyms bottom, craft, vessel, watercraft

related words canoe, catamaran, catboat, cockleshell, coracle, dinghy, dory, dugout, flatboat, float, gig, gondola, houseboat, ironclad, kayak, launch, life boat, longboat, motorboat, outrigger, pirogue, pontoon, punt, raft, rowboat, sail, sampan, scow, scull, shallop, shell, sloop, tender, umiak; bark, brig, brigantine, caravel, clipper, galleon, galley, junk, ketch, pinnace, sailboat, schooner, ship, square-rigger, windjammer, xebec, yacht; corvette, cutter, destroyer, fireship, flagship, gunboat, landing craft, privateer, torpedo boat, warship; argosy, barge, coaster, collier, containership, ferryboat, icebreaker, lighter, lightship, liner, merchantman, merchant ship, packet, revenuer, riverboat, showboat, steamboat, steamer, supertanker, taxi, towboat, trader, tugboat; sealer, shrimper, trawler, whaler; derelict, hulk, tub; air-cushion vehicle, hovercraft; hydrofoil, hydroplane

2 a large craft for travel by water — see SHIP

boat *vb* to travel on water in a vessel — see SAIL 1

¹bob *vb* to make (as hair) shorter with or as if with the use of shears — see CLIP

²bob *vb* to make short up-and-down movements — see NOD

bobble *vb* **1** to make or do (something) in a clumsy or unskillful way — see BOTCH

2 to make short up-and-down movements — see NOD

bobby *n, British* a member of a force charged with law enforcement at the local level — see OFFICER 1

bobby–soxer *n* a young usually unmarried woman — see GIRL 1

bode *vb* to show signs of a favorable or successful outcome ⟨her natural gift for reading *boded* well for her future in school⟩

synonyms augur, forebode (*also* forbode), promise

related words forecast, foretell, predict, presage, prognosticate, prophesy; forewarn, warn; anticipate, divine, foreknow, foresee; foreshadow, portend, prefigure; allude, connote, hint, imply, insinuate, intimate, suggest

phrases bid fair, give promise of

bodiless *adj* not composed of matter — see IMMATERIAL 1

bodily *adj* of or relating to the human body — see PHYSICAL 1

boding *n* something believed to be a sign or warning of a future event — see OMEN

body *n* **1** the main or greater part of something as distinguished from its appendages ⟨the *body* of the novel was quite good, even if the beginning was a bit slow⟩

synonyms bulk, core, generality, main, mass, staple, weight

related words majority; aggregate, amount, entirety, sum, sum total, total, totality, whole; bottom, essence, essentiality, marrow, nature, quintessence, soul, stuff, substance; center, heart, hub, middle, nucleus, seat; affair, argument, burden, crux, focus, gist, kernel, nub, pitch, point, purport; matter, motif, subject, text, theme, topic

near antonyms accessory, adjunct, appendage, extension, offshoot; component, constituent, element, ingredient; division, part, piece, section, segment; angle, aspect, facet, feature, quality, side

2 a distinct and separate portion of matter ⟨the Atlantic is a gigantic *body* of water⟩

synonyms mass

related words aggregate, amount, bulk, quantity, volume; item, object, thing; material, stuff, substance; entirety, totality, whole

3 a group of people acting together within a larger group — see FACTION

4 a group of people sharing a common interest and relating together socially — see GANG 2

5 a member of the human race — see HUMAN

6 a usually small number of persons considered as a unit — see GROUP 2

bog *n* spongy land saturated or partially covered with water — see SWAMP

bog (down) *vb* to place in conflict or difficulties — see EMBROIL

bogey *also* **bogy** *or* **bogie** *n* **1** something or someone that causes fear or dread especially without reason ⟨math and math tests have long been *bogeys* for many students⟩

synonyms bête noire, bugaboo, bugbear, hobgoblin, ogre

related words apparition, ghost, phantasm, phantom, poltergeist, shade, specter (*or* spectre), spirit, spook, wraith; banshee, bogeyman, demon, devil, fiend, imp, incubus; fright, horror, monster, monstrosity, terror; bane, curse, plague, scourge, torment; abomination, anathema

2 the soul of a dead person thought of especially as appearing to living people — see GHOST

bogus *adj* **1** being such in appearance only and made with or manufactured from usually cheaper materials — see IMITATION

2 being such in appearance only and made or manufactured with the intention of committing fraud — see COUNTERFEIT

3 lacking in natural or spontaneous quality — see ARTIFICIAL 1

bohemian *n* a person who does not conform to generally accepted standards or customs — see NONCONFORMIST 1

boil *vb* **1** to be excited or emotionally stirred up with anger ⟨she was *boiling* at the thought of her so-called best friend trying to steal her boyfriend⟩
synonyms burn, fume, rage, seethe, steam
related words fulminate, rant, rave; smolder; bristle, flare (up); chafe, fret, stew; agitate, convulse, shake; disturb, perturb, upset

2 to cook in a liquid heated to the point that it gives off steam ⟨*boil* the potatoes very well before you try to mash them⟩
synonyms coddle, parboil, poach, simmer, stew
related words scald; braise, fricassee, pressure-cook, steam; reboil

3 to be in a state of violent rolling motion — see SEETHE 1

boisterous *adj* being rough or noisy in a high-spirited way ⟨the fans at the baseball game became particularly *boisterous* after the home run⟩
synonyms knockabout, rambunctious, raucous, rowdy
related words rampageous, riotous, stormy, tempestuous, turbulent, violent; disorderly, raffish, ruffianly; headstrong, intractable, obstreperous, recalcitrant, uncontrollable, uncontrolled, undisciplined, ungovernable, uninhibited, unmanageable, unruly, wild, willful (*or* wilful); bubbly, buoyant, effervescent, exuberant, high-spirited, impassioned, lively, passionate, sprightly, vivacious; clamorous, loudmouthed, noisy, strident, vociferous; howling, screaming, yelling
near antonyms sedate, sober, solemn, somber (*or* sombre), staid; decorous, dignified, proper, seemly; calm, hushed, noiseless, peaceful, placid, quiet, restrained, serene, silent, soundless, tranquil; collected, composed, constrained, controlled, imperturbable, inhibited, repressed, self-controlled, unflappable, unruffled; moderate, reasonable, subdued, temperate; impassive, phlegmatic, stoic (*or* stoical), stolid; depressed; aloof, detached, indifferent
antonyms orderly

bold *adj* **1** inclined or willing to take risks ⟨our youngest brother was the *boldest* one in the family, instantly taking to everything from skiing to skateboarding⟩
synonyms adventuresome, adventurous, audacious, daring, dashing, emboldened, enterprising, gutsy, hardy, nerved, nervy, venturesome, venturous
related words brash, daredevil, foolhardy, heedless, hotheaded, impetuous, imprudent, impulsive, incautious, madcap, overbold, overconfident, rash, reckless, spirited, thoughtless, wild; brave, courageous, dauntless, fearless, gallant, greathearted, heroic, intrepid, lionhearted, stalwart, stout, stouthearted, unafraid, undaunted, valiant, valorous; gritty, plucky, spirited, spunky; hasty, headlong, precipitate; absurd, asinine, balmy, brainless, crazy, foolish, half-witted, harebrained, insane, lunatic, mad, nutty, scatterbrained, silly, wacky, witless; unnecessary; dumb, idiotic, moronic, stupid; irrational, unreasonable

near antonyms chickenhearted, coward, cowardly, craven, lily-livered, pusillanimous, shy, timid, timorous; careful, cautious, heedful, prudent, wary; overcareful, overcautious; affrighted, afraid, alarmed, fainthearted, fearful, frightened, horrified, scared, shocked, spooked, startled, terrified, terrorized; unnerved; calm, cool, levelheaded, rational, reasonable, sage, sane, sensible, sound, wise; appalled, concerned, dismayed, upset, worried
antonyms unadventurous, unenterprising

2 displaying or marked by rude boldness — see NERVY 1

3 likely to attract attention — see NOTICEABLE

4 showing a lack of proper social reserve or modesty — see PRESUMPTUOUS 1

5 having an incline approaching the perpendicular — see STEEP 1

bold–faced *adj* displaying or marked by rude boldness — see NERVY 1

bolster *vb* to hold up or serve as a foundation for — see SUPPORT 3

bolt *n* something that makes a strong impression because it is so unexpected — see SURPRISE 1

bolt *vb* **1** to move suddenly and sharply (as in surprise) — see START 1

2 to proceed or move quickly — see HURRY 2

3 to hasten away from something dangerous or frightening — see RUN 2

4 to utter with a sudden burst of strong feeling — see EXCLAIM

bomb *vb* to use bombs or artillery against — see BOMBARD

bombard *vb* to use bombs or artillery against ⟨the Allies *bombarded* Germany for a great many months during World War II⟩
synonyms blitz, bomb, shell
related words rake, strafe; assail, assault, attack, devastate, hit, pound, ravage, strike

bombardment *n* a rapid or overwhelming outpouring of many things at once — see BARRAGE

bombast *n* **1** boastful speech or writing ⟨filling a speech with *bombast* about one's unique qualifications for student council is usually a bad idea⟩
synonyms bluster, brag, braggadocio, gas, grandiloquence, hot air, rant
related words rhapsody, rhetoric; babble, blab, chatter, drivel, gabble, gibber, jabber, prattle; jawing, patter, prating, yammering; egotism, self-conceit, self-importance

2 language that is impressive-sounding but not meaningful or sincere — see RHETORIC 1

bombastic *adj* marked by the use of impressive-sounding but mostly meaningless words and phrases — see RHETORICAL

bombshell *n* something that makes a strong impression because it is so unexpected — see SURPRISE 1

bona fide *adj* being exactly as appears or as claimed — see AUTHENTIC 1

bond *n* **1** something that physically prevents free movement ⟨before they could release the captive, they had to undo a number of *bonds*⟩
synonyms band, bracelet, chain, fetter, handcuff(s), irons, ligature, manacle, shackle
related words confinement, constraint, curb, hamper, hindrance, restraint, restriction; entanglement, net, trammel, trap; collar, straitjacket (*also* straightjacket); hobble, tie

2 a uniting or binding force or influence ⟨the

bond of love between them was so strong that even death could not break it⟩

synonyms cement, knot, ligature, link, tie

related words attachment, connection, entanglement, fastening, joint, linkage; affection, fondness, sympathy; fetter, handcuff, manacle, shackle, trammel; constraint, curb, hampering, limit, limitation, restraint, restriction

near antonyms detaching, disengaging, parting, separation; unbinding, unfastening, unfettering, untying; emancipation, freedom, liberation, release

3 a formal agreement to fulfill an obligation — see GUARANTEE 1

bondage *n* the state of being a slave — see SLAVERY 1

bonding *n* a physical sticking to as if by glue — see ADHESION

bondman *n* a person who is considered the property of another person — see SLAVE 1

bondsman *n* a person who is considered the property of another person — see SLAVE 1

bone *n, usually* **bones** *pl* a small cube marked on each side with one to six spots and usually played in pairs in various games — see DIE

bone (up) *vb* to use the mind to acquire knowledge — see STUDY 1

bonny *adj, chiefly British* very pleasing to look at — see BEAUTIFUL

bonus *n* something given in addition to what is ordinarily expected or owed ⟨this job offers a nice Christmas *bonus* in addition to the salary⟩

synonyms dividend, extra, gratuity, gravy, lagniappe, perquisite, tip

related words fillip; bestowal, presentation; benefaction, benevolence, bounty, charity, generosity, largess (*or* largesse), philanthropy; contribution, donation, gift, offering, present; grant, subsidy; boon, manna, windfall; favor, freebie (*or* freebee), giveaway, premium; award, prize, reward; fringe benefit

bon voyage *n* an expression of good wishes at parting — see GOOD-BYE

boo *n* a vocal sound made to express scorn or disapproval — see CATCALL

booby *n* a person who lacks good sense or judgment — see FOOL 1

boobytrap *vb* to place hidden explosive devices in or under — see MINE

booby trap *n* **1** a usually concealed explosive device designed to go off when disturbed ⟨luckily, the bomb squad didn't find any *booby traps*⟩

synonyms mine

related words bomb, explosive; pitfall, snare, trap; ambush

2 a danger or difficulty that is hidden or not easily recognized — see PITFALL 1

book *n* **1** a set of printed sheets of paper bound together between covers and forming a work of fiction or nonfiction ⟨I bought another new *book* yesterday, and I can't wait to read it⟩

synonyms tome, volume

related words hardback, paperback, pocket book; folio, quarto; guidebook, handbook, manual; catalog (*or* catalogue), dictionary, encyclopedia; booklet, brochure, circular, flier (*or* flyer), folder, leaflet, magazine, pamphlet, program; textbook, tract, treatise; novel, novelette, pulp

2 *cap* a book made up of the writings accepted by Christians as coming from God — see BIBLE

book *vb* to arrange to have something (as a hotel room) held for one's future use — see RESERVE 1

bookish *adj* suggestive of the vocabulary used in books ⟨*fealty* is a *bookish* synonym for *loyalty*⟩

synonyms erudite, learned, literary

related words academic, pedantic, scholastic; highbrow, intellectual; educated, schooled; formal

near antonyms chatty, conversational; familiar, informal; slangy

antonyms colloquial, nonliterary

booklet *n* a short printed publication with no cover or with a paper cover — see PAMPHLET

bookworm *n* a person slavishly devoted to intellectual or academic pursuits — see NERD

boom *n* a loud explosive sound — see CLAP 1

boom *vb* to make a long loud deep noise or cry — see ROAR

booming *adj* **1** marked by a high volume of sound — see LOUD 1

2 marked by vigorous growth and well-being especially economically — see PROSPEROUS 1

boon *adj* likely to seek or enjoy the company of others — see CONVIVIAL

boon *n* **1** a thing that helps — see HELP 2

2 an act of kind assistance — see FAVOR 1

3 something granted as a special favor — see PRIVILEGE

4 something that provides happiness or does good for a person or thing — see BLESSING 2

boor *n* a person whose behavior is offensive to others — see JERK 1

boorish *adj* having or showing crudely insensitive or impolite manners — see CLOWNISH

boost *n* **1** an act or instance of helping — see HELP 1

2 something added (as by growth) — see INCREASE 1

3 something that arouses action or activity — see IMPULSE

boost *vb* **1** to lift with effort — see HEAVE 1

2 to make greater in size, amount, or number — see INCREASE 1

3 to make markedly greater in measure or degree — see INTENSIFY

4 to move from a lower to a higher place or position — see RAISE 1

5 to provide publicity for — see PUBLICIZE 1

booster *n* a person who actively supports or favors a cause — see EXPONENT

boot (out) *vb* to drive or force out — see EJECT 1

bootleg *n* illegally produced liquor — see MOONSHINE 1

bootless *adj* producing no results — see FUTILE

booty *n* valuables stolen or taken by force — see LOOT

booze *n* a fermented or distilled beverage that can make a person drunk — see ALCOHOL

bop *n* a hard strike with a part of the body or an instrument — see ¹BLOW

bop *vb* to deliver a blow to (someone or something) usually in a strong vigorous manner — see HIT 1

border *n* **1** the line or relatively narrow space that marks the outer limit of something ⟨a rug with a fancily embroidered *border*⟩

synonyms bound, boundary, brim, circumference, compass, confines, edge, end, fringe, margin, perimeter, periphery, rim, skirt, verge

related words crest, hem, lip; ceiling, maximum;

THESAURUS

demarcation, extent, limitation, measure, restriction, termination; borderland, frontier, march, pale

near antonyms center; inner, inside, interior

2 a region along the dividing line between two countries — see FRONTIER 1

border *vb* to serve as a border for ⟨that velvet *bordered* the sleeves on this shirt, until it fell off⟩

synonyms bound, fringe, margin, rim, skirt

related words edge, hem, trim; circumscribe, define, delineate, demarcate, frame, outline; circle, compass, encircle, girdle, girth, loop, ring, round, surround; check, confine, control, curb, limit, restrain, restrict

border (on) *vb* **1** to come very close to being ⟨that comment *borders on* insubordination, and you should be more careful in the future⟩

synonyms verge (on)

related words approach, near; appear, look, resemble, seem, suggest

2 to be adjacent to — see ADJOIN 1

bordering *adj* having a border in common — see ADJACENT

borderland *n* a region along the dividing line between two countries — see FRONTIER 1

bore *n* someone or something boring — see DRAG 1

¹**bore** *vb* to make a hole or series of holes in — see PERFORATE

²**bore** *vb* to make weary and restless by being dull or monotonous ⟨the teacher's lifeless and unimaginative teaching style *bored* the students to death⟩

synonyms jade, tire, weary

related words pall; drain, enervate, exhaust, fatigue, wear, wear out; debilitate, disable, enfeeble; deject, demoralize, discourage, dishearten, dispirit

phrases put to sleep

near antonyms animate, energize, enliven, excite, galvanize, invigorate, stimulate, vitalize; amuse, entertain; allure, attract, beguile, bewitch, captivate, charm, enchant, enthrall (*or* enthral), fascinate, hypnotize, mesmerize, preoccupy; busy, immerse, involve, occupy; rally, rouse, stir

antonyms absorb, engage, engross, grip, interest, intrigue

bored *adj* having one's patience, interest, or pleasure exhausted — see WEARY 2

boredom *n* the state of being bored ⟨she spends that whole class in a state of complete *boredom*, waiting for lunch⟩

synonyms doldrums, ennui, listlessness, restlessness, tedium, tiredness, weariness

related words cheerlessness, dispiritedness, joylessness, melancholy; languor, lassitude, lethargy, lifelessness, torpor; dullness (*also* dulness), monotonousness, monotony, sameness; apathy, indifference, unconcern

near antonyms beguilement, bewitchment, captivation, enchantment, fascination; absorption, engagement, engrossment, immersion, involvement; animation, enlivenment, excitement, invigoration, stimulation; amusement, entertainment

boring *adj* causing weariness, restlessness, or lack of interest ⟨I wish this book weren't so *boring;* I keep falling asleep whenever I try to read it⟩

synonyms drab, dreary, dry, dull, flat, heavy, humdrum, jading, leaden, monotonous, pedestri-

an, ponderous, stodgy, stuffy, stupid, tame, tedious, tiresome, tiring, unanimated, uninteresting, wearisome, weary, wearying

related words undramatic, unentertaining, uneventful, unexciting, uninspiring, unnewsworthy, unrewarding, unsatisfying, unsensational, unspectacular; annoying, bothersome, irksome, irritating; drudging, palling; draining, enervating, exhausting, fatiguing, wearing; debilitating, enfeebling; demoralizing, discouraging, disheartening, dispiriting; common, commonplace, ordinary, stale, unexceptional; lumbering, plodding, slow

near antonyms amazing, astonishing, astounding, awesome, eye-opening, fabulous, marvelous (*or* marvellous), sensational, spectacular, surprising, wonderful, wondrous; animating, energizing, enlivening, exciting, galvanizing, invigorating, stimulating; amusing, diverting, entertaining; alluring, attracting, attractive, beguiling, bewitching, captivating, charming, enchanting, enthralling, entrancing, fascinating; mesmerizing

antonyms absorbing, engaging, engrossing, gripping, interesting, intriguing, involving

born *adj* **1** being such from birth or by nature — see NATURAL 1

2 belonging to a particular place by birth or origin — see NATIVE 1

borrow *vb* to take for one's own use (something originated by another) — see ADOPT

bosom *adj* closely acquainted — see FAMILIAR 1

boss *adj, slang* of the very best kind — see EXCELLENT

boss *n* the person (as an employer or supervisor) who tells people and especially workers what to do ⟨every morning the *boss* hands out a list of top-priority tasks⟩

synonyms captain, chief, foreman, head, headman, helmsman, kingpin, leader, master, taskmaster

related words administrator, commander, director, executive, general, manager, overseer, principal, standard-bearer, straw boss, superintendent, superior, supervisor; dominator, lord, overlord, potentate, ruler; figurehead; slave driver; baron, czar (*also* tsar *or* tzar), king, magnate, mogul, president, prince

near antonyms dependent, inferior, secondary, subject, subordinate, underling

boss *vb* **1** to be in charge of ⟨she *bossed* that project for years, until she was promoted again⟩

synonyms captain, head, oversee, superintend, supervise

related words command, control, direct, guide, manage, order, run, shepherd, show, steer; quarterback; administer; monitor; govern, reign, rule

2 to exercise authority or power over — see GOVERN 1

3 to serve as leader of — see LEAD 2

boss (around) *vb* to issue orders to (someone) by right of authority — see COMMAND 1

bossy *adj* fond of ordering people around ⟨I don't want to work with him because he's so *bossy* and always runs roughshod over me⟩

synonyms authoritarian, autocratic, despotic, dictatorial, domineering, imperious, masterful, overbearing, peremptory, tyrannical (*also* tyrannic), tyrannous

related words arrogant, disdainful, haughty, lofty, lordly, proud, supercilious, superior; commanding, dictating; arbitrary, high-handed, imperial; authoritative, directorial, magisterial; aggressive, assertive, self-assertive; conceited, narcissistic, pompous, vain; all-powerful, almighty, omnipotent; firm, stern

near antonyms humble, meek, modest, unassuming; amenable, docile, obedient, tractable; indecisive, irresolute; acquiescent, compliant, passive, resigned, submissive, yielding

botch *vb* to make or do (something) in a clumsy or unskillful way ⟨the first time we tried to make a cake, we *botched* the job completely⟩

synonyms bobble, bungle, butcher, flub, foozle, foul up, fumble, louse up, mangle, mess (up), muff, murder

related words blunder, goof (up), gum (up); blemish, blight, damage, flaw, harm, hurt, impair, injure, mar, mutilate, ruin, spoil, vitiate; destroy, wreck; mishandle, mismanage

near antonyms ameliorate, better, enhance, help, improve, meliorate, rectify, refine, reform, remedy

botched *adj* showing or marked by a lack of skill and tact (as in dealing with a situation) — see AWKWARD 2

bother *n* **1** a state of noisy, confused activity — see COMMOTION

2 one who is obnoxiously annoying — see NUISANCE 1

3 something that is a source of irritation — see ANNOYANCE 3

4 the feeling of impatience or anger caused by another's repeated disagreeable acts — see ANNOYANCE 2

bother *vb* **1** to thrust oneself upon (another) without invitation ⟨I am never going to get this work done if people don't stop wandering into the room and *bothering* me⟩

synonyms bug, chivy, disturb, intrude (upon), pester

related words inconvenience, trouble; aggravate, anger, annoy, bedevil, devil, exasperate, fret, gall, get, gnaw, hassle, irritate, nettle, peeve, pique, put out, rile, torment, vex, worry; beleaguer, beset, besiege; distress, plague; afflict, harass, torment; grate, inflame, provoke; enrage, incense, inflame, infuriate, madden; agitate, perturb

near antonyms ignore, leave; appease, conciliate, mollify, oblige, placate; delight, gladden, gratify, please, satisfy; comfort, console, content

2 to disturb the peace of mind of (someone) especially by repeated disagreeable acts — see IRRITATE 1

3 to experience concern or anxiety — see WORRY 1

4 to trouble the mind of; to make uneasy — see DISTURB 1

bothering *n* the act of making unwelcome intrusions upon another — see ANNOYANCE 1

bothersome *adj* causing annoyance — see ANNOYING

bottom *n* **1** the side or part facing downward from something ⟨that side of the shelf is supposed to be the *bottom*, so turn it over before you assemble the bookcase⟩

synonyms underbelly, underbody, underside, undersurface

related words belly, sole; base, floor, foot, ground, seat, underpinning

near antonyms acme, apex, crest, crown, height,

peak, pinnacle, roof, summit; cusp, head, point, tip

antonyms face, top

2 the surface upon which a body of water lies ⟨my missing fishing pole is probably lying on the *bottom* of the lake⟩

synonyms bed, floor

related words riverbed; base, basement, foundation, ground

near antonyms surface

3 the lowest part, place, or point ⟨sliding all the way to the *bottom* of the snow-covered slope⟩

synonyms base, foot, rock bottom

related words basis, bed, bedrock, foundation, ground, groundwork, keystone, seat, underpinning

near antonyms acme, apex, climax, crest, face, height, peak, pinnacle, summit, tip-top, zenith

antonyms head, top

4 the part of the body upon which someone sits — see BUTTOCKS

5 a small buoyant structure for travel on water — see BOAT 1

bottomless *adj* extending far downward or inward — see DEEP 1

bough *n* a major outgrowth from the main stem of a woody plant — see BRANCH 1

boulevard *n* a passage cleared for public vehicular travel — see WAY 1

bounce *n* active strength of body or mind — see VIGOR

bounce *vb* **1** to drive or force out — see EJECT 1

2 to strike and fly off at an angle — see GLANCE 1

bouncing *adj* **1** enjoying health and vigor — see HEALTHY 1

2 having much high-spirited energy and movement — see LIVELY 1

bound *adj* fully committed to achieving a goal — see DETERMINED 1

¹**bound** *n* **1** a real or imaginary point beyond which a person or thing cannot go — see LIMIT

2 the line or relatively narrow space that marks the outer limit of something — see BORDER 1

²**bound** *n* an act of leaping into the air — see JUMP 1

¹**bound** *vb* **1** to mark the limits of — see LIMIT 2

2 to serve as a border for — see BORDER

²**bound** *vb* **1** to move with a light bouncing step — see SKIP 1

2 to propel oneself upward or forward into the air — see JUMP 1

boundary *n* **1** a real or imaginary point beyond which a person or thing cannot go — see LIMIT

2 the line or relatively narrow space that marks the outer limit of something — see BORDER 1

bounded *adj* having distinct or certain limits — see LIMITED 1

boundless *adj* being or seeming to be without limits — see INFINITE

bounteous *adj* giving or sharing in abundance and without hesitation — see GENEROUS 1

bountiful *adj* **1** being more than enough without being excessive — see PLENTIFUL

2 giving or sharing in abundance and without hesitation — see GENEROUS 1

bountifully *adv* in a generous manner — see WELL 2

bountifulness *n* the quality or state of being generous — see LIBERALITY

THESAURUS

bounty *n* **1** something offered or given in return for a service performed — see REWARD

2 the quality or state of being generous — see LIBERALITY

bouquet *n* **1** a bunch of flowers ⟨I bought my mother a nice *bouquet* for her birthday⟩
synonyms nosegay, posy
related words boutonniere, corsage; arrangement; garland, lei

2 a sweet or pleasant smell — see FRAGRANCE

bout *n* **1** a competitive encounter between individuals or groups carried on for amusement, exercise, or in pursuit of a prize — see GAME 1

2 a sudden experiencing of a physical or mental disorder — see ATTACK 2

bow *n* something that curves or is curved — see BEND 1

¹**bow** *vb* **1** to cease resistance (as to another's arguments, demands, or control) — see YIELD 3

2 to give up and cease resistance (as to a liking, temptation, or habit) — see YIELD 1

²**bow** *vb* to turn away from a straight line or course — see CURVE 1

bowed *adj* bending downward or forward — see NODDING

bowing *adj* bending downward or forward — see NODDING

bowl *n* a large usually roofless building for sporting events with tiers of seats for spectators — see STADIUM

bowl *vb* **1** to move or proceed smoothly and readily — see FLOW 2

2 to proceed or move quickly — see HURRY 2

bowl (down *or* over) *vb* to strike (someone) so forcefully as to cause a fall — see FELL 1

bowl (over) *vb* **1** to cause an often unpleasant surprise for — see SHOCK 1

2 to make a strong impression on (someone) with something unexpected — see SURPRISE 1

bowled over *adj* affected with sudden and great wonder or surprise — see THUNDERSTRUCK

¹**box** *n* a covered rectangular container for storing or transporting things — see CHEST

²**box** *n* a hard strike with a part of the body or an instrument — see ¹BLOW

boxer *n* one that engages in the sport of fighting with the fists ⟨that *boxer* is quite famous for being the youngest heavyweight champion ever⟩
synonyms fighter, prizefighter, pugilist
related words bantamweight, featherweight, flyweight, heavyweight, light heavyweight, lightweight, middleweight, welterweight

boy *n* a male person who has not yet reached adulthood ⟨a giggling little *boy* ran by⟩
synonyms lad, laddie, nipper, shaver, sonny, stripling, tad, youth
related words adolescent, juvenile, kid, minor, moppet, teenager, youngster; brat, gamin, hobbledehoy, imp, squirt, urchin, whippersnapper; schoolboy

boyfriend *n* a male romantic companion ⟨her *boyfriend* always brings her flowers for Valentine's Day⟩
synonyms beau, fellow, man, swain
related words admirer, crush, steady; gallant, suitor, wooer; beloved, darling, dear, favorite, flame, honey, love, lover, sweet, sweetheart, valentine; date, escort; groom, husband; fiancé, intended

brace *n* **1** something that holds up or serves as a foundation for something else — see SUPPORT 1

2 two things of the same or similar kind that match or are considered together — see PAIR

brace *vb* **1** to give life, vigor, or spirit to — see ANIMATE

2 to hold up or serve as a foundation for — see SUPPORT 3

3 to prepare (oneself) mentally or emotionally — see FORTIFY 1

bracelet *n* something that physically prevents free movement — see BOND 1

bracing *adj* having a renewing effect on the state of the body or mind — see TONIC

bracket *n* one of the units into which a whole is divided on the basis of a common characteristic — see CLASS 2

bracket *vb* to describe as similar — see COMPARE 1

brag *n* boastful speech or writing — see BOMBAST 1

brag *vb* to praise or express pride in one's own possessions, qualities, or accomplishments often to excess — see BOAST

braggadocio *n* boastful speech or writing — see BOMBAST 1

braid *n* a length of something formed of three or more strands woven together ⟨until she was fifteen, she had a *braid* that reached to her knees⟩
synonyms lace, lacing, plait
related words rickrack (*or* ricrac), stripe; pigtail

braid *vb* to form into a braid ⟨they taught each other how to *braid* yarn into bracelets⟩
synonyms plait, pleat
related words interlace, interweave, weave

brain *n* **1** a very smart person — see GENIUS 1

2 *often* **brains** *pl* the ability to learn and understand or to deal with problems — see INTELLIGENCE 1

brainless *adj* **1** not having or showing an ability to absorb ideas readily — see STUPID 1

2 showing or marked by a lack of good sense or judgment — see FOOLISH 1

brainlessness *n* **1** lack of good sense or judgment — see FOOLISHNESS 1

2 the quality or state of lacking intelligence or quickness of mind — see STUPIDITY 1

brainstorm *vb* to engage in an exchange of information or ideas — see COMMUNICATE 2

brainy *adj* having or showing quickness of mind — see INTELLIGENT 1

brake *n* a thick patch of shrubbery, small trees, or underbrush — see THICKET

brake *vb* to cause to move or proceed at a less rapid pace — see SLOW 1

braking *n* a usually gradual decrease in the pace or level of activity of something — see SLOWDOWN

brambly *adj* likely to cause a scratch — see SCRATCHY 1

branch *n* **1** a major outgrowth from the main stem of a woody plant ⟨I loved climbing among the *branches* of that old tree⟩
synonyms bough, limb
related words offshoot, outgrowth, shoot; spray, sprig, twig

2 a local unit of an organization — see CHAPTER

branch *vb* to extend outwards from or as if from a central point — see RADIATE 1

branch (out) *vb* to go or move in different directions from a central point — see SEPARATE 2

brand *n* **1** a device (as a word) identifying the maker of a piece of merchandise and legally reserved for the exclusive use of that person or company — see TRADEMARK 1

2 a mark of guilt or disgrace — see STAIN 1

brand–new *adj* **1** being in an original and unused or unspoiled state — see FRESH 1

2 recently made and never used before — see NEW 3

brash *adj* **1** displaying or marked by rude boldness — see NERVY 1

2 foolishly adventurous or bold — see FOOL-HARDY 1

brashness *n* shameless boldness — see EFFRON-TERY

brass *n* shameless boldness — see EFFRONTERY

brassiness *n* shameless boldness — see EFFRON-TERY

brassy *adj* displaying or marked by rude boldness — see NERVY 1

brave *adj* feeling or displaying no fear by temperament ⟨the *brave* little boy sat still for the flu shot⟩

synonyms courageous, dauntless, doughty, fearless, gallant, greathearted, heroic, intrepid, lionhearted, manful, stalwart, stout, stouthearted, undaunted, valiant, valorous

related words determined, firm, game, plucky, resolute, undeterred, undismayed, unflinching, unswerving; mettlesome, spirited, spunky; adventuresome, adventurous, audacious, bold, daring, dashing, gutsy, hardy, venturesome, venturous; crazy, foolish, half-witted, insane, lunatic, mad, nutty; brash, brazen, daredevil, foolhardy, heedless, hotheaded, impetuous, imprudent, impulsive, incautious, madcap, overbold, overconfident, rash, reckless, thoughtless, wild; hasty, headlong, precipitate; comforted, emboldened, encouraged, heartened, reassured, unafraid

near antonyms mousy (*or* mousey), scary, shy, skittish, timid, timorous; anxious, apprehensive, nervous; careful, cautious, heedful, prudent, unadventurous; afraid, agitated, disconcerted, disquieted, disturbed, frightened, horrified, panicked, perturbed, scared, shocked, spooked, startled, terrified, terrorized, unnerved, upset; appalled, concerned, dismayed, worried

antonyms chicken, chickenhearted, coward, cowardly, craven, fainthearted, fearful, lily-livered, pusillanimous, timorous

brave *vb* to oppose (something hostile or dangerous) with firmness or courage — see FACE 2

bravery *n* **1** dressy clothing — see FINERY

2 strength of mind to carry on in spite of danger — see COURAGE

brawl *n* **1** a rough and often noisy fight usually involving several people ⟨they were thrown out of the party after starting a *brawl*⟩

synonyms affray, fracas, fray, free-for-all, melee, row, ruckus, ruction

related words battle, clash, combat, conflict, contest, fight, fisticuffs, scrap, scrimmage, scuffle, struggle, tussle; horseplay, roughhousing; altercation, argument, dispute, quarrel, spat, squabble, tiff, wrangle

2 an often noisy or angry expression of differing opinions — see ARGUMENT 1

brawl *vb* to express different opinions about something often angrily — see ARGUE 2

brawn *n* muscular strength — see MUSCLE 1

brawny *adj* **1** having muscles capable of exerting great physical force — see STRONG 1

2 marked by a well-developed musculature — see MUSCULAR 1

3 strongly and heavily built — see ¹HUSKY

brazen *adj* displaying or marked by rude boldness — see NERVY 1

brazen *vb* to oppose (something hostile or dangerous) with firmness or courage — see FACE 2

brazenness *n* shameless boldness — see EFFRONTERY

breach *n* **1** a failure to uphold the requirements of law, duty, or obligation ⟨the president's deliberate misstatements were widely seen as a *breach* of the public trust⟩

synonyms infraction, infringement, transgression, trespass, violation

related words offense, sin, wrong; disregard, forgetting, ignoring, nonobservance, overlooking; delinquency, dereliction, neglect; intrusion, invasion

near antonyms respecting, upholding

antonyms nonviolation, observance

2 a breaking of a moral or legal code — see OFFENSE 1

3 an open space in a barrier (as a wall or hedge) — see GAP 1

breach *vb* to fail to keep — see VIOLATE 1

bread *n* **1** *slang* something (as pieces of stamped metal or printed paper) customarily and legally used as a medium of exchange, a measure of value, or a means of payment — see MONEY

2 substances intended to be eaten — see FOOD

breadbasket *n, slang* the part of the body between the chest and the pelvis — see STOMACH

breadth *n* **1** a wide space or area — see EXPANSE

2 an area over which activity, capacity, or influence extends — see RANGE 2

break *n* **1** a momentary halt in an activity — see PAUSE

2 a period during which the usual routine of school or work is suspended — see VACATION

3 an open space in a barrier (as a wall or hedge) — see GAP 1

break *vb* **1** to cause to separate into pieces usually suddenly or forcibly ⟨I hated admitting to Mom that I had *broken* her favorite glass vase⟩

synonyms bust, fracture, fragment

related words blast, blow up, burst, detonate, explode; pop, shatter, shiver, smash; sliver, splinter, split; collapse, implode; demolish, destroy, ruin, wreck

near antonyms fix, heal, mend, patch, rebuild, reconstruct, repair

2 to bring (as an action or operation) to an immediate end — see STOP 1

3 to bring to a lower grade or rank — see DEMOTE

4 to change (as a secret message) from code into ordinary language — see DECODE

5 to come to a temporary halt in one's activity — see PAUSE

6 to cut into and turn over the sod of (a piece of land) using a bladed implement — see PLOW 1

7 to fail to keep — see VIOLATE 1

8 to find an answer for through reasoning — see SOLVE

9 to reduce the soundness, effectiveness, or perfection of — see DAMAGE 1

10 to stop functioning — see FAIL 1

11 to hasten away from something dangerous or frightening — see RUN 2

THESAURUS

breakable *adj* easily broken — see FRAGILE 1

breakdown *n* **1** the process by which dead organic matter separates into simpler substances — see CORRUPTION 1

2 the separation and identification of the parts of a whole — see ANALYSIS 1

break down *vb* **1** to arrange or assign according to type — see CLASSIFY 1

2 to go through decomposition — see DECAY 1

3 to identify and examine the basic elements or parts of (something) especially for discovering interrelationships — see ANALYZE 1

4 to stop functioning — see FAIL 1

5 to yield to mental or emotional stress — see CRACK 2

break in *vb* **1** to enter a house or building by force usually with illegal intent ⟨the burglars *broke in* by smashing a window⟩

synonyms burglarize

related words invade, trespass; hold up, loot, plunder, rip off, rob, stick up; ransack, rifle; despoil, devastate, maraud, pillage, ravage, sack

2 to cause a disruption in a conversation or discussion — see INTERRUPT

breakneck *adj* moving, proceeding, or acting with great speed — see FAST 1

break off *vb* **1** to bring (as an action or operation) to an immediate end — see STOP 1

2 to come to an end — see CEASE 1

break out *vb* to develop suddenly and violently — see ERUPT 2

breakthrough *n* an instance of notable progress in the development of knowledge, technology, or skill — see ADVANCE 2

breakup *n* the act or process of a whole separating into two or more parts or pieces — see SEPARATION 1

break up *vb* **1** to cease to exist or cause to cease to exist as a group or organization — see DISBAND 1

2 to come to an end — see CEASE 1

3 to set or force apart — see SEPARATE 1

breast *n* the seat of one's deepest thoughts and emotions — see CORE 1

breast *vb* to oppose (something hostile or dangerous) with firmness or courage — see FACE 2

breath *n* **1** a momentary halt in an activity — see PAUSE

2 a slight or gentle movement of air — see BREEZE 1

breathe *vb* **1** to inhale and exhale air ⟨sometimes it gets so hot in here that it's hard to even *breathe*⟩

synonyms respire

related words expire, inspire; gasp, huff, pant, puff, wheeze; sniff, snore, snort, snuffle; yawn

near antonyms asphyxiate, choke, gag, smother, suffocate; garrotte (*or* garotte), stifle, strangle, throttle

2 to have life — see BE 1

breathe (out) *vb* to let or force out of the lungs — see EXHALE 1

breather *n* a momentary halt in an activity — see PAUSE

breathing *adj* having or showing life — see ALIVE 1

breathless *adj* **1** lacking fresh air — see STUFFY 1

2 moving, proceeding, or acting with great speed — see FAST 1

3 no longer living — see DEAD 1

breathtaking *adj* causing great emotional or mental stimulation — see EXCITING 1

breech *n* **1** the part of the body upon which someone sits — see BUTTOCKS

2 breeches *pl* an outer garment covering each leg separately from waist to ankle — see PANTS

breed *n* a number of persons or things that are grouped together because they have something in common — see SORT 1

breed *vb* **1** to bring forth offspring — see PROCREATE

2 to bring to maturity through care and education — see BRING UP 1

breeding *n* the line of ancestors from whom a person is descended — see ANCESTRY

breeze *n* **1** a slight or gentle movement of air ⟨a warm spring *breeze* ruffled our hair⟩

synonyms air, breath, puff, waft, zephyr

related words draft, whiff; land breeze, sea breeze; blast, blow, flurry, gale, northeaster, norther, northwester, southeaster, southwester, westerly, wind; squall, tempest, tornado, windstorm; airflow

near antonyms calm

2 something that is easy to do — see CINCH

breeze *vb* **1** to move or proceed smoothly and readily — see FLOW 2

2 to proceed or move quickly — see HURRY 2

breezy *adj* **1** having a relaxed, casual manner — see EASYGOING 1

2 marked by strong wind or more wind than usual — see WINDY 1

brevity *n* **1** the condition of being short ⟨the best quality a graduation speech can have is *brevity*⟩

synonyms briefness, conciseness, shortness

related words abbreviation, abridgment (*or* abridgement), compression, condensation, contraction, curtailment; decreasing, diminishing, lessening, reducing, shortening, shrinking; abruptness, brusqueness, curtness; pithiness, succinctness, terseness; littleness, minuteness, smallness, tininess

near antonyms extensiveness; elongating, elongation, extending, extension, prolongation, prolonging, protraction, stretching; expansion, growth, spread; diffuseness, prolixity, talkativeness, verboseness, volubility, wordiness; bigness, bulkiness, greatness, heftiness, largeness

antonyms lengthiness

2 the quality or state of being marked by or using only few words to convey much meaning — see SUCCINCTNESS

brew *vb* to be about to happen — see LOOM

bribable *adj* open to improper influence and especially bribery — see VENAL

bribe *n* something given or promised in order to improperly influence a person's conduct or decision ⟨that judge refused a huge *bribe* to dismiss the charges against the wealthy defendant⟩

synonyms fix, sop

related words incentive, incitement, motivation, spur, stimulation, stimulus; boost, goad, inducement; allurement, bait, enticement, lure, temptation; flattery, persuasion; decoy, snare, trap

bribe *vb* to influence someone with a bribe ⟨meat inspectors were *bribed*, and the contaminated beef was sold to the public⟩

synonyms have, square

related words fix, tamper (with); corrupt, debase, defile, dishonor, taint; allure, bait, entice, lure, tempt; motivate, provoke, spur, stimulate; goad, induce; flatter, persuade; snare, trap

bridal *n* a ceremony in which two people are united in matrimony — see WEDDING

bridgehead *n* a place from which an advance (as for military operations) is made — see BASE 2

bridle *vb* to keep from exceeding a desirable degree or level (as of expression) — see CONTROL 1

brief *adj* **1** marked by the use of few words to convey much information or meaning — see CONCISE

2 not lasting for a considerable time — see SHORT 2

brief *vb* to give information to — see ENLIGHTEN 1

briefly *adv* in a few words — see SHORTLY 1

briefness *n* **1** the condition of being short — see BREVITY 1

2 the quality or state of being marked by or using only few words to convey much meaning — see SUCCINCTNESS

brig *n* a place of confinement for persons held in lawful custody — see JAIL

bright *adj* **1** giving off or reflecting much light ⟨in the desert the sun was so *bright* that it hurt my eyes⟩ ⟨the moon is *bright* tonight⟩

synonyms beaming, bedazzling, brilliant, dazzling, effulgent, glowing, incandescent, lambent, lucent, lucid, luminous, lustrous, radiant, refulgent, shining, shiny

related words blazing, burning, combusting, fiery, flaming; agleam, aglitter, blinding, flaring, flashing, flickering, glaring, gleaming, glimmering, glinting, glistening, glittering, scintillating, shimmering, sparkling, twinkling; burnished, polished; sunny

near antonyms blackened, dark, darkened, darkish, darkling, darksome, dimmed, dusky, gloomy, murky, obscure, obscured, pitch-black, pitch-dark, somber (*or* sombre), sunless; cloudy, shadowy, shady; gray (*also* grey), leaden, pale

antonyms dim, dull, lackluster

2 filled with much light ⟨the display windows of department stores are especially *bright* at Christmastime⟩

synonyms ablaze, alight, brightened, illuminated, illumined, light, lighted (*or* lit)

related words floodlit (*or* floodlighted), highlighted, spotlighted (*or* spotlit); kindled, ignited

near antonyms gloomy, somber, sunless; cloudy, murky, obscured, shadowy; gray (*also* grey), leaden, pale

antonyms blackened, dark, darkened, darkish, darkling, dimmed, dusky, pitch-black, pitch-dark

3 having or showing a good mood or disposition — see CHEERFUL 1

4 having or showing quickness of mind — see INTELLIGENT 1

5 having qualities which inspire hope — see HOPEFUL 1

6 pointing toward a happy outcome — see FAVORABLE 2

7 serving to lift one's spirits — see CHEERFUL 2

brighten *vb* to become glad or hopeful — see CHEER (UP) 1

brightened *adj* filled with much light — see BRIGHT 2

brightness *n* the quality or state of having or giving off light — see BRILLIANCE 1

brilliance *n* **1** the quality or state of having or giving off light ⟨the *brilliance* of the flash from the camera was so intense that I was blinded for a moment afterwards⟩

synonyms brightness, brilliancy, dazzle, effulgence, illumination, lightness, lucidity, luminosity, radiance, refulgence, splendor

related words blaze, flare, flicker, light; fluorescence, incandescence, luminescence; burnish, gloss, luster, polish, sheen, shine; fire, flame, glare, glow; flash, gleam, glimmer, glint, glisten, glitter, scintillation, shimmer, sparkle, twinkle

near antonyms dimness, dullness (*also* dulness), gloominess, somberness; cloudiness, haziness, murkiness, obscurity; colorlessness, grayness, paleness

antonyms blackness, dark, darkness, duskiness

2 impressiveness of beauty on a large scale — see MAGNIFICENCE

brilliancy *n* the quality or state of having or giving off light — see BRILLIANCE 1

brilliant *adj* **1** giving off or reflecting much light — see BRIGHT 1

2 having or showing quickness of mind — see INTELLIGENT 1

brilliant *n* a usually valuable stone cut and polished for ornament — see GEM 1

brim *n* **1** the line or relatively narrow space that marks the outer limit of something — see BORDER 1

2 the projecting front part of a hat or cap — see VISOR

brimful *adj* containing or seeming to contain the greatest quantity or number possible — see FULL 1

brimming *adj* containing or seeming to contain the greatest quantity or number possible — see FULL 1

brine *n* the whole body of salt water that covers nearly three-fourths of the earth — see OCEAN

bring *vb* to have a price of — see COST

bring about *vb* to be the cause of (a situation, action, or state of mind) — see EFFECT

bring up *vb* **1** to bring to maturity through care and education ⟨it takes an immense commitment and a lot of love to *bring up* a child properly⟩

synonyms breed, foster, raise, rear

related words father, mother; attend, care (for), cultivate, mind, minister (to), nurse, nurture, watch; discipline, educate, instruct, mentor, school, teach, train, tutor; edify, enlighten, indoctrinate; feed, nourish, provide (for), supply; advance, forward, further, promote; prepare; direct, guide, lead, shepherd, show

near antonyms abuse, ill-treat, ill-use, maltreat, mishandle, mistreat; ignore, neglect; harm, hurt, injure

2 to present or bring forward for discussion — see INTRODUCE 2

brininess *n* the quality or state of being salty — see SALTINESS

briny *adj* of, relating to, or containing salt — see SALTY 1

brisk *adj* **1** having much high-spirited energy and movement — see LIVELY 1

2 moving, proceeding, or acting with great speed — see FAST 1

briskly *adv* with great speed — see FAST 1

briskness *n* the quality or state of having abundant or intense activity — see VITALITY 1

bristle *vb* to express one's anger usually violently — see RAGE 1

bristly *adj* covered with or as if with hair — see HAIRY 1

brittle *adj* having a texture that readily breaks into little pieces under pressure — see CRISP 1

broach *vb* **1** to penetrate the surface (as of water) from below ⟨the immense whales *broaching* was a magnificent sight⟩
synonyms surface
related words break, emerge, rise
near antonyms dive, drop, founder, plunge, sink, submerge, submerse
2 to present or bring forward for discussion — see INTRODUCE 2

broad *adj* **1** having a greater than usual measure across — see WIDE 1
2 having considerable extent — see EXTENSIVE
3 not subject to misinterpretation or more than one interpretation — see CLEAR 2
4 relating to the main elements and not to specific details — see GENERAL 2

broadcast *vb* **1** to cause to be known over a considerable area or by many people — see SPREAD 1
2 to make known openly or publicly — see ANNOUNCE

broadly *adv* to a large extent or degree — see GREATLY 2

broad–minded *adj* **1** not bound by traditional ways or beliefs — see LIBERAL 1
2 willing to consider new or different ideas — see OPEN-MINDED 1

broadside *adv* with one side faced forward — see SIDEWAYS

brochure *n* a short printed publication with no cover or with a paper cover — see PAMPHLET

broiling *adj* having a notably high temperature — see HOT 1

broke *adj* lacking money or material possessions — see POOR 1

broken *adj* **1** having an uneven edge or outline — see RAGGED 1
2 not having a level or smooth surface — see UNEVEN 1

brokenhearted *adj* feeling unhappiness — see SAD 1

brood *vb* to cover and warm eggs to hatch them — see SET 1

brook *n* a natural body of running water smaller than a river — see CREEK 1

brook *vb* to put up with (something painful or difficult) — see BEAR 2

brooklet *n* a natural body of running water smaller than a river — see CREEK 1

brotherhood *n* **1** a group of persons formally joined together for some common interest — see ASSOCIATION 2
2 the body of people in a profession or field of activity — see CORPS

brotherly *adj* of, relating to, or befitting brothers — see FRATERNAL

browbeat *vb* to make timid or fearful by or as if by threats — see INTIMIDATE

brownie *n* an imaginary being usually having a small human form and magical powers — see FAIRY

browse *vb* **1** to feed on grass or herbs — see GRAZE
2 to take a quick or hasty look — see ¹GLANCE 2

bruise *n* a bodily injury in which small blood vessels are broken but the overlying skin is not — see CONTUSION

bruit (about) *vb* to make (as a piece of information) the subject of common talk without any authority or confirmation of accuracy — see RUMOR

brush *n* a brief clash between enemies or rivals — see ENCOUNTER

brush *vb* to pass lightly across or touch gently especially in passing ⟨spiderwebs *brushed* her cheek as she walked through the basement⟩
synonyms graze, kiss, nudge, shave, skim
related words bump, contact, scrape, strike, sweep, swipe, touch; bounce, carom, glance, rebound, ricochet, sideswipe, skip; caress, cuddle, fondle, pet, stroke
near antonyms clash, collide, hit, knock, punch, slap, smack, smash, thwack, whack

brush (aside *or* off) *vb* to overlook or dismiss as of little importance — see EXCUSE 1

brush–off *n* treatment that is deliberately unfriendly — see COLD SHOULDER

brushwood *n* a thick patch of shrubbery, small trees, or underbrush — see THICKET

brusque *adj* being or characterized by direct, brief, and potentially rude speech or manner — see BLUNT 1

brutal *adj* **1** difficult to endure — see HARSH 1
2 having or showing the desire to inflict severe pain and suffering on others — see CRUEL 1

brutality *n* the willful infliction of pain and suffering on others — see CRUELTY

brute *n* **1** one of the lower animals as distinguished from human beings — see ANIMAL
2 a mean, evil, or unprincipled person — see VILLAIN

bubble *vb* to flow in a broken irregular stream — see GURGLE

bubbly *adj* joyously unrestrained — see EXUBERANT

buccaneer *n* someone who engages in robbery of ships at sea — see PIRATE

buck *n* **1** a man extremely interested in his clothing and personal appearance — see DANDY 1
2 an adult male human being — see MAN 1

buck *vb* **1** to move or cause to move with a sharp quick motion — see JERK 1
2 to refuse to give in to — see RESIST

buckaroo *n* a hired hand who tends cattle or horses at a ranch or on the range — see COWBOY

bucket *n* **1** a considerable amount — see LOT 2
2 a round container that is open at the top and outfitted with a handle — see PAIL

buckle *vb* to occupy (oneself) diligently or with close attention — see APPLY 2

bucolic *adj* of, relating to, associated with, or typical of open areas with few buildings or people — see RURAL

buddy *n* a person who has a strong liking for and trust in another — see FRIEND 1

budge *vb* **1** to cease resistance (as to another's arguments, demands, or control) — see YIELD 3
2 to change one's position — see MOVE 3
3 to change the place or position of — see MOVE 1

budget *n* **1** a sum of money set aside for a particular purpose — see FUND 1
2 the number of individuals or amount of something available at any given time — see SUPPLY

buff *n* a person with a strong and habitual liking for something — see FAN

buff *vb* **1** to make smooth by friction — see GRIND 1
2 to make smooth or glossy usually by repeatedly applying surface pressure — see POLISH

buffed *adj* having a shiny surface or finish — see GLOSSY

buffer *n* something that serves as a protective barrier — see CUSHION

buffer *vb* to lessen the shock of — see CUSHION

¹**buffet** *n* a hard strike with a part of the body or an instrument — see ¹BLOW

²**buffet** *n* a storage case typically having doors and shelves — see CABINET

buffet *vb* to strike repeatedly — see BEAT 1

buffoon *n* a comically dressed performer (as at a circus) who entertains with playful tricks and ridiculous behavior — see CLOWN 1

bug *n* **1** a person with a strong and habitual liking for something — see FAN

2 an abnormal state that disrupts a plant's or animal's normal bodily functioning — see DISEASE

bug *vb* **1** to attack repeatedly with mean put-downs or insults — see TEASE 2

2 to disturb the peace of mind of (someone) especially by repeated disagreeable acts — see IRRITATE 1

3 to thrust oneself upon (another) without invitation — see BOTHER 1

bugaboo *n* something or someone that causes fear or dread especially without reason — see BOGEY 1

bugbear *n* something or someone that causes fear or dread especially without reason — see BOGEY 1

bugging *n* the act of making unwelcome intrusions upon another — see ANNOYANCE

build *n* the type of body that a person has — see PHYSIQUE

build *vb* to form by putting together parts or materials ⟨he spent hours *building* a model airplane from a kit⟩
synonyms assemble, construct, erect, fabricate, make, make up, piece, put up, raise, rear, set up
related words fashion, forge, frame, manufacture, mold, produce, shape; prefabricate; begin, coin, create, generate, inaugurate, initiate, innovate, invent, originate; constitute, establish, father, found, institute, organize; conceive, concoct, contrive, cook up, design, devise, imagine, think (up); rebuild; rig up
phrases put together
near antonyms dismember; demolish, destroy, devastate, flatten, pulverize, raze, ruin, shatter, smash, wreck; blow up, explode
antonyms disassemble, dismantle, take down

build (up) *vb* **1** to become greater in extent, volume, amount, or number — see INCREASE 2

2 to increase in — see GAIN 1

3 to produce or bring about especially by long or repeated effort — see HAMMER (OUT)

building *n* something built as a dwelling, shelter, or place for human activity ⟨English class will be in that big stone *building* over there⟩
synonyms edifice, structure
related words construction, erection; bungalow, cabin, chalet, cottage, house, lodge, summerhouse; hovel, hut, shack, shanty, shed; castle, château, estate, hall, manor, mansion, palace, villa; skyscraper, tower

bulge *n* a part that sticks out from the general mass of something ⟨several *bulges* in the old vinyl flooring in the dingy bathroom⟩
synonyms jut, overhang, projection, protrusion, protuberance
related words dome; blob, bump, knob, lump, nub, swelling; block, piece, portion, section; enlargement, escalation, expansion, increase

near antonyms cavity, crater, hole; basin, dip, valley
antonyms concavity, dent, depression, hollow, indentation, pit

bulge *vb* to extend outward beyond a usual point ⟨the sides of the returning camper's suitcase *bulged* with a month's worth of dirty laundry⟩
synonyms bag, balloon, beetle, belly, billow, jut, overhang, poke, project, protrude, stand out, start, stick out
related words dome; blow up, inflate; distend, expand, swell; mushroom, snowball; elongate, extend, lengthen, stretch
near antonyms compress, condense, constrict, contract, shrink

bulk *n* the main or greater part of something as distinguished from its appendages — see BODY 1

bulkiness *n* the quality or state of being large in size — see LARGENESS

bulky *adj* of a size greater than average of its kind — see LARGE

bull *n, slang* a member of a force charged with law enforcement at the local level — see OFFICER 1

bulldoze *vb* to force one's way — see PRESS 4

bullet *n* a usually round or cone-shaped little piece of lead made to be fired from a firearm ⟨it is possible to make your own *bullets*, but it takes a lot of patience and some extra money⟩
synonyms ball, pellet
related words ammunition, cannonball, cap, cartridge, charge, gunshot, lead, load, missile, pop, projectile, round, shell, shot, slug; twenty-two
near antonyms blank

bulletin *n* a published statement informing the public of a matter of general interest — see ANNOUNCEMENT

bully *n* **1** a person who teases, threatens, or hurts smaller or weaker persons ⟨the *bully* spent most of the afternoon in detention for pushing people down on the playground⟩
synonyms intimidator
related words antagonist, enemy; harrier, nuisance, persecutor, pest, tease, teaser; heckler; goon, hood, hoodlum, punk, rough, roughneck, rowdy, ruffian, thug, tough; cutthroat, felon, gangster, gunman, mobster, racketeer

2 a violent, brutal person who is often a member of an organized gang — see HOODLUM

bully *vb* to make timid or fearful by or as if by threats — see INTIMIDATE

bulwark *n* something that holds up or serves as a foundation for something else — see SUPPORT 1

bum *adj* of low quality — see CHEAP 2

bum *n* a homeless wanderer who may beg or steal for a living — see TRAMP

bummer *n* **1** something (as a situation or event) that is depressing — see DOWNER

2 something that disappoints — see DISAPPOINTMENT 2

3 something that has failed — see FAILURE 3

bump *n* **1** a small rounded mass of swollen tissue ⟨that's a nasty *bump* on your arm where you hit the table⟩
synonyms knot, lump, node, nodule, swelling
related words growth, tumor, wart; hump, hunch; bruise, contusion; blob, chunk, clod, clump, gob, gobbet, hunk, knob, nub, nubble, nugget, wad

2 a forceful coming together of two things — see IMPACT 1

bump *vb* to come into usually forceful contact with something — see HIT 2

bumper *adj* unusually large — see HUGE

bumper *n* something that serves as a protective barrier — see CUSHION

bumpkin *n* an awkward or simple person especially from a small town or the country — see HICK

bumpy *adj* **1** marked by a series of sharp quick motions — see JERKY 1

2 not having a level or smooth surface — see UNEVEN 1

bunch *n* **1** a group of people sharing a common interest and relating together socially — see GANG 2

2 a number of things considered as a unit — see GROUP 1

3 a usually small number of persons considered as a unit — see GROUP 2

bunch *vb* to gather into a closely packed group — see PRESS 3

bundle *n* a wrapped or sealed case containing an item or set of items — see PACKAGE 1

bung *vb* to close up so that no empty spaces remain — see FILL 2

bungle *vb* to make or do (something) in a clumsy or unskillful way — see BOTCH

bungling *adj* showing or marked by a lack of skill and tact (as in dealing with a situation) — see AWKWARD 2

¹bunk *n* a place set aside for sleeping — see BED 1

²bunk *n* **1** language, behavior, or ideas that are absurd and contrary to good sense — see NONSENSE 1

2 unintelligible or meaningless talk — see GIBBERISH

bunk *vb* to provide with living quarters or shelter — see HOUSE 1

buoy (up) *vb* to fill with courage or strength of purpose — see ENCOURAGE 1

buoyant *adj* **1** having or showing a good mood or disposition — see CHEERFUL 1

2 joyously unrestrained — see EXUBERANT

burden *n* **1** a mass or quantity of something taken up and carried, conveyed, or transported — see LOAD 1

2 a part of a song or hymn that is repeated every so often — see CHORUS 2

3 something one must do because of prior agreement — see OBLIGATION

burden *vb* **1** to place a weight or burden on — see LOAD 1

2 to make sad — see DEPRESS 1

burdensome *adj* **1** difficult to endure — see HARSH 1

2 requiring much time, effort, or careful attention — see DEMANDING 1

bureau *n* a large unit of a governmental, business, or educational organization — see DIVISION 2

bureaucrat *n* a worker in a government agency ⟨the *bureaucrats* at the town hall seem to think that we need a building permit to build a tree house⟩

synonyms functionary, public servant

related words clerk, officeholder, official; employee, underling, worker

burg *n* a thickly settled, highly populated area — see CITY

burgeon *vb* **1** to become greater in extent, volume, amount, or number — see INCREASE 2

2 to grow vigorously — see THRIVE 1

3 to produce flowers — see BLOOM

burgher *n* a person who lives in a town on a permanent basis ⟨many of the college students are regarded by the local *burghers* as obnoxious louts⟩

synonyms citizen, townie, villager

related words denizen, dweller, habitant, homeowner, inhabitant, national, native, occupant, resident, resider; town, townsfolk, townspeople; suburbanite, urbanite

near antonyms foreigner, guest, tourist, transient, visitor

burglarize *vb* **1** to enter a house or building by force usually with illegal intent — see BREAK IN 1

2 to remove valuables from (a place) unlawfully — see ROB

burial *n* the act or ceremony of putting a dead body in its final resting place ⟨the children wanted to give the dead bird a proper *burial* in the backyard⟩

synonyms burying, entombing, entombment, interment, interring, sepulture

related words embalmment, funeral

near antonyms cremation

antonyms disinterment, exhumation, unearthing

burlesque *n* a work that imitates and exaggerates another work for comic effect — see PARODY 1

burlesque *vb* to copy or exaggerate (someone or something) in order to make fun of — see MIMIC 1

burly *adj* strongly and heavily built — see ¹HUSKY

burn *vb* **1** to be on fire especially brightly ⟨all evening long we just sat there, contentedly watching the Yule log *burn*⟩

synonyms blaze, combust, flame, glow

related words fire, ignite, kindle; flare (up), light (up); flicker, gutter, waver; bake, broil, char, cook, melt, roast, scorch, swelter; smolder, spark, sputter; beam, brighten, radiate; beat (down), flash, glare, gleam, glimmer, glint, glisten, glitter, scintillate, shimmer, shine, sparkle, twinkle

2 to set (something) on fire ⟨it is not a good idea to try to *burn* old papers in the sink⟩

synonyms fire, ignite, inflame, kindle, light

related words char, scorch; bake, cremate, incinerate, kiln; brighten, illumine, illuminate, irradiate, lighten, radiate; scald, scathe, sear; rekindle, relight

near antonyms choke, smother, suffocate; stamp (out); blacken, darken, dim, dull, obscure

antonyms douse, extinguish, put out, quench, snuff (out)

3 to be excited or emotionally stirred up with anger — see BOIL 1

4 to shine with a bright harsh light — see GLARE 1

burnable *adj* capable of catching or being set on fire — see COMBUSTIBLE

burned–out *or* **burnt–out** *adj* depleted in strength, energy, or freshness — see WEARY 2

burning *adj* **1** being on fire — see ABLAZE 1

2 having a notably high temperature — see HOT 1

3 having or expressing great depth of feeling — see FERVENT

burnish *vb* to make smooth or glossy usually by repeatedly applying surface pressure — see POLISH

burnished *adj* having a shiny surface or finish — see GLOSSY

burnout *n* a complete depletion of energy or strength — see FATIGUE

burn out *vb* to use up all the physical energy of — see EXHAUST 1

burro *n* a sturdy and patient domestic mammal that is used especially to carry things — see DONKEY 1

burrow *n* the shelter or resting place of a wild animal — see DEN 1

burst *n* **1** a sudden and usually temporary growth of activity — see OUTBREAK

2 a sudden intense expression of strong feeling — see OUTBURST 1

burst *vb* **1** to break open or into pieces usually because of internal pressure — see EXPLODE 1

2 to cause to break open or into pieces by or as if by an explosive — see BLAST 1

burst (forth) *vb* to develop suddenly and violently — see ERUPT 2

bursting *adj* containing or seeming to contain the greatest quantity or number possible — see FULL 1

bursting *n* the act or an instance of exploding — see EXPLOSION 1

bury *vb* **1** to place (a dead body) in the earth, a tomb, or the sea ⟨he died on Tuesday and was *buried* on Friday⟩
synonyms entomb, inter
related words enshrine; conceal, cover, ensconce, hide; obscure, shade, shield; cloak, curtain, enshroud, shroud
near antonyms burn, cremate; bare, disclose, discover, display, exhibit, expose, reveal, show
antonyms disinter, exhume, unearth

2 to put into a hiding place — see ¹HIDE 1

burying *n* the act or ceremony of putting a dead body in its final resting place — see BURIAL

bush *n* a rural region that forms the edge of the settled or developed part of a country — see FRONTIER 2

bushed *adj* depleted in strength, energy, or freshness — see WEARY 1

bushel *n* a considerable amount — see LOT 2

business *n* **1** a commercial or industrial activity or organization — see ENTERPRISE 1

2 something to be dealt with — see MATTER 2

3 the buying and selling of goods especially on a large scale and between different places — see COMMERCE

bust *n* **1** a hard strike with a part of the body or an instrument — see ¹BLOW

2 something that has failed — see FAILURE 3

bust *vb* **1** to bring to a lower grade or rank — see DEMOTE

2 to cause to lose one's fortune and become unable to pay one's debts — see RUIN 1

3 to cause to separate into pieces usually suddenly or forcibly — see BREAK 1

4 to deliver a blow to (someone or something) usually in a strong vigorous manner — see HIT 1

5 *slang* to take or keep under one's control by authority of law — see ARREST 1

bustle *n* a state of noisy, confused activity — see COMMOTION

bustling *adj* marked by much life, movement, or activity — see ALIVE 2

busy *adj* **1** involved in often constant activity ⟨the deadline is in two days, so everyone at work has been extremely *busy*⟩
synonyms active, assiduous, diligent, employed, engaged, industrious, laborious, occupied, sedulous, working
related words absorbed, concentrating, engrossed, focused (*also* focussed), immersed, intent, preoccupied; alive, functional, functioning, going, living, operating, operational, operative, running; energetic, vigorous; indefatigable, tireless, untiring
near antonyms asleep, dormant, latent, quiescent, sleepy; inert, passive; dead, dull, slow; inoperative, nonoperating
antonyms idle, inactive, unemployed, unengaged, unoccupied

2 marked by much life, movement, or activity — see ALIVE 2

busy *vb* to hold the attention of — see ENGAGE 1

busybody *n* a person who meddles in the affairs of others ⟨that *busybody* across the street is always telling me how to tend to my own garden⟩
synonyms interferer, interloper, intruder, kibitzer, meddler
related words peeper, peeping Tom, snoop, snooper, spy; blabber, discloser, gossip, gossiper, prattler, revealer, teller; betrayer, talebearer, tattletale; snake, sneak; informer, snitcher, squealer, stool pigeon

but *adv* nothing more than — see JUST 3

but *conj* **1** if it were not for the fact that — see EXCEPT

2 in spite of that — see HOWEVER

but *prep* not including — see EXCEPT

butcher *vb* **1** to kill on a large scale — see MASSACRE

2 to make or do (something) in a clumsy or unskillful way — see BOTCH

butchery *n* the killing of a large number of people — see MASSACRE

¹butt *n* the part of the body upon which someone sits — see BUTTOCKS

²butt *n* **1** a person or thing that is made fun of — see LAUGHINGSTOCK

2 a person or thing that is the object of abuse, criticism, or ridicule — see TARGET 1

butt in *vb* to interest oneself in what is not one's concern — see INTERFERE

buttocks *n pl* the part of the body upon which someone sits ⟨she slipped in the mud puddle and hit the ground square on her *buttocks*⟩
synonyms backside, bottom, breech, butt, fanny, hams, haunches, posterior, rear, rump, seat

buttress *n* **1** something or someone to which one looks for support — see DEPENDENCE 2

2 something that holds up or serves as a foundation for something else — see SUPPORT 1

buttress *vb* to hold up or serve as a foundation for — see SUPPORT 3

buy *n* something bought or offered for sale at a desirable price — see BARGAIN 1

buy *vb* to get possession of (something) by giving money in exchange for ⟨I really want to *buy* that new book, but I don't have enough money right now⟩
synonyms pick up, purchase, take
related words acquire, get, obtain, procure, secure; finance, pay (for), spring (for); barter (for), deal (for), exchange (for), trade (for); bargain (with), chaffer (with), dicker (over), horse-trade (with), negotiate (about), palter (with); bid, offer; rebuy, repurchase

buzz *n* **1** a communication by telephone — see CALL 3

2 a monotonous sound like that of an insect in motion — see HUM

THESAURUS

buzz *vb* to fly, turn, or move rapidly with a fluttering or vibratory sound — see WHIRR

buzzing *adj* marked by much life, movement, or activity — see ALIVE 2

by *adv* at, within, or to a short distance or time — see NEAR 1

by *prep* **1** along the way of ⟨went *by* the woods to get to the summer cottage⟩
synonyms through, via
related words across, along, alongside, beyond, near, nearby, over; below, beneath, under, underneath; outside, past
phrases by way of
2 using the means or agency of ⟨try to convince them *by* reason alone, if possible⟩
synonyms per, through, with

phrases by means of, by (*or* in) virtue of, through the medium of
3 close to — see AROUND 1

by-and-by *n* time that is to come — see FUTURE 1

by and large *adv* for the most part — see CHIEFLY

bygone *adj* no longer existing — see EXTINCT

bylaw *n* a statement spelling out the proper procedure or conduct for an activity — see RULE 1

bypass *vb* to avoid by going around — see DETOUR 1

by-product *n* something that naturally develops or is developed from something else — see DERIVATIVE

byword *n* an often stated observation regarding something from common experience — see SAYING

cab *n* an automobile that carries passengers for a fare usually determined by the distance traveled — see TAXI

cabal *n* a group involved in secret or criminal activities — see RING 1

cabaret *n* a bar or restaurant offering special nighttime entertainment (as music, dancing, or comedy acts) — see NIGHTCLUB

cabin *n* **1** a small, simply constructed, and often temporary dwelling — see SHACK
2 an often small house for recreational or seasonal use — see COTTAGE
3 one of the parts into which an enclosed space is divided — see COMPARTMENT

cabinet *n* a storage case typically having doors and shelves ⟨the most precious knickknacks were kept in a *cabinet* with glass doors⟩
synonyms buffet, closet, cupboard, hutch, locker, sideboard
related words bookcase, secretary; shelving; console

cabinetwork *n* the movable articles in a room — see FURNITURE

cable *n* a length of braided, flexible material that is used for tying or connecting things — see CORD

cache *n* **1** a collection of things kept available for future use or need — see STORE 1
2 a supply stored up and often hidden away — see HOARD 1

cache *vb* **1** to put (something of future use or value) in a safe or secret place — see HOARD
2 to put into a hiding place — see ¹HIDE 1

caching *n* the placing of something out of sight — see CONCEALMENT 1

cackle *n* an explosive sound that is a sign of amusement — see LAUGH 1

cackle *vb* to engage in casual or rambling conversation — see CHAT

cackler *n* a person who talks constantly — see CHATTERBOX

cacophony *n* loud, confused, and usually unharmonious sound — see NOISE 1

cad *n* a person whose behavior is offensive to others — see JERK 1

cadaver *n* a dead body — see CORPSE

cadaverous *adj* **1** lacking a healthy skin color — see PALE 2
2 suffering extreme weight loss as a result of hunger or disease — see EMACIATED

caddy *n* a covered rectangular container for storing or transporting things — see CHEST

cadence *n* the recurrent pattern formed by a series of sounds having a regular rise and fall in intensity — see RHYTHM

cadenced *adj* marked by or occurring with a noticeable regularity in the rise and fall of sound — see RHYTHMIC

café *also* **cafe** *n* **1** a bar or restaurant offering special nighttime entertainment (as music, dancing, or comedy acts) — see NIGHTCLUB
2 a place of business where alcoholic beverages are sold to be consumed on the premises — see BARROOM
3 a public establishment where meals are served to paying customers for consumption on the premises — see RESTAURANT

cage *n* an enclosure with an open framework for keeping animals ⟨the dogs and cats at the animal shelter looked so sad in their *cages*⟩
synonyms coop, corral, pen, pound
related words fence; cote, dovecote, fold; aquarium, terrarium

cage *vb* to close or shut in by or as if by barriers — see ENCLOSE 1

cagey *also* **cagy** *adj* clever at attaining one's ends by indirect and often deceptive means — see ARTFUL 1

caginess *n* skill in achieving one's ends through indirect, subtle, or underhanded means — see CUNNING 1

cajole *vb* to get (someone) to do something by gentle urging, special attention, or flattery — see COAX

cake *n* a small usually rounded mass of minced food that has been fried ⟨the rich, tender *cakes* of crabmeat had been lightly fried⟩
synonyms croquette, cutlet, fritter, patty (*also* pattie)
related words finger, stick

cake *vb* to cover with a hardened layer — see EN-CRUST

calamitous *adj* **1** bringing about ruin or misfortune — see FATAL 1

2 causing or tending to cause destruction — see DESTRUCTIVE 1

calamity *n* a sudden violent event that brings about great loss or destruction — see DISASTER

calculate *vb* **1** to determine (a value) by doing the necessary mathematical operations ⟨the family has been *calculating* what a week at the beach resort would end up costing⟩
synonyms compute, figure, reckon, work out
related words conjecture, estimate, guess, judge, suppose; add up, sum, tally, total; add, cipher, divide, multiply, subtract; calibrate, gauge (*also* gage), measure, scale; ascertain, discover, dope (out), figure out, find out; recompute, refigure

2 to decide the size, amount, number, or distance of (something) without actual measurement — see ESTIMATE 2

3 to work out the details of (something) in advance — see PLAN 1

calculated *adj* decided on as a result of careful thought — see DELIBERATE 1

calculation *n* the act or process of performing mathematical operations to find a value ⟨by my *calculation*, it should take me a month to save up for the sneakers⟩
synonyms arithmetic, ciphering, computation, figures, figuring, reckoning
related words mathematics; addition, division, multiplication, subtraction; appraisal, assessment, estimation, evaluation, judgment (*or* judgement)

calendar *n* a listing of things to be presented or considered (as at a concert or play) — see PROGRAM 1

caliber *or* **calibre** *n* degree of excellence — see QUALITY 1

call *n* **1** a natural vocal sound made by an animal ⟨a ranger who could immediately identify the *call* of every creature in the forest⟩
synonyms cry, note
related words bark, bay, bellow, bleat, bray, caterwaul, caw, cheep, chirp, grunt, hoot, howl, low, meow, moo, neigh, peep, roar, screech, squawk, squeak, squeal, twitter, whinny, yap, yelp, yip, yowl

2 a coming to see another briefly for social or business reasons ⟨we paid a *call* on the new neighbors the day after they moved in⟩
synonyms visit, visitation
related words meeting, rendezvous, tryst; stopover

3 a communication by telephone ⟨give me a *call* as soon as you arrive, so I'll know you got there safely⟩
synonyms buzz, ring
related words callback; toll call; message

4 an act or instance of asking for information — see QUESTION 2

5 an entitlement to something — see CLAIM 1

call *vb* **1** to speak so as to be heard at a distance ⟨we could hear someone *calling* for help from the other side of the wall⟩
synonyms bawl, cry, holler, shout, vociferate, yell
related words bellow, roar; whoop; scream, screech, shriek, shrill, squeak, squeal; caterwaul, howl, wail, yawp (*or* yaup), yowl

near antonyms breathe, mumble, murmur, mutter, whisper

2 to make a telephone call to ⟨use this cell phone to *call* me if there's an emergency⟩
synonyms dial, phone, ring (up) [*chiefly British*], telephone
related words beep, buzz

3 to make a brief visit ⟨the hospital posts the hours during which friends and relatives may *call*⟩
synonyms drop (by *or* in), pop (in), stop (by *or* in), visit
related words barge (in); look up, see; frequent, hang around (in), hang out (at), haunt, resort (to)

4 to put an end to (something planned or previously agreed to) — see CANCEL 1

5 to think of in a particular way — see CONSIDER 1

6 to utter one's distinctive animal sound — see CRY 2

7 to bring together in assembly by or as if by command — see CONVOKE

8 to decide the size, amount, number, or distance of (something) without actual measurement — see ESTIMATE 2

9 to demand or request the presence or service of — see SUMMON 1

10 to give a name to — see NAME 1

call (for) *vb* **1** to ask for (something) earnestly or with authority — see DEMAND 1

2 to make a request for — see ASK (FOR) 1

call (on *or* upon) *vb* to make a social call upon — see VISIT 1

caller *n* a person who visits another — see GUEST 1

calligraphy *n* writing done by hand — see HANDWRITING 2

calling *n* **1** the act of putting an end to something planned or previously agreed to — see CANCELLATION

2 the activity by which one regularly makes a living — see OCCUPATION

calling off *n* the act of putting an end to something planned or previously agreed to — see CANCELLATION

call off *vb* to put an end to (something planned or previously agreed to) — see CANCEL 1

callous *adj* having or showing a lack of sympathy or tender feelings — see HARD 1

callow *adj* lacking in adult experience or maturity ⟨a story about a *callow* youth who learns the value of hard work and self-reliance⟩
synonyms adolescent, green, immature, inexperienced, juvenile, puerile, raw, unfledged, unripe, unripened
related words babyish, childish, infantile; boyish, girlish, maidenly, virginal, youthful; ingenuous, innocent, naive (*or* naïve); unpracticed, unseasoned, untrained, untried
near antonyms advanced, precocious; knowing, sophisticated, worldly-wise
antonyms adult, experienced, grown-up, mature, ripe

calm *adj* **1** free from storms or physical disturbance ⟨after a stormy night of high winds and driving rains, the day dawned on a *calm* sea⟩
synonyms halcyon, hushed, peaceful, placid, quiet, serene, still, stilly, tranquil, untroubled
related words calming, pacific, restful, soothing; inactive, inert, quiescent, reposing, resting; smooth, unruffled; clear, cloudless, fair, rainless, sunny, sunshiny

THESAURUS

near antonyms bleak, cloudy, dirty, foul, nasty, overcast, rainy, raw, rough, squally

antonyms agitated, angry, stormy, turbulent

2 free from emotional or mental agitation ⟨bystanders tried to help the injured person remain *calm* while they waited for the ambulance to arrive⟩

synonyms collected, composed, cool, coolheaded, placid, self-possessed, serene, tranquil, undisturbed, unperturbed, unshaken, untroubled, unworried

related words imperturbable, nerveless, unflappable, unshakable; disciplined, self-contained, self-controlled; affable, breezy, devil-may-care, easygoing, happy-go-lucky, laid-back, low-pressure; carefree, nonchalant, unconcerned; assured, confident, self-assured; aloof, detached, dispassionate, indifferent; impassive, phlegmatic, stolid

near antonyms anxious, bothered, distressed, worried; jittery, jumpy, nervous, skittish, tense; high-strung, uptight

antonyms agitated, discomposed, disturbed, flustered, perturbed, upset

3 free from disturbing noise or uproar — see QUIET 1

calm *n* a state of freedom from storm or disturbance ⟨vacationing city dwellers who are tired of the hustle and bustle enjoy the *calm* of the secluded mountain village⟩

synonyms calmness, hush, peace, peacefulness, placidity, quiet, quietness, quietude, repose, restfulness, sereneness, serenity, still, stillness, tranquillity (*or* tranquility)

related words lull, pause, respite; silence; comity, concord, harmony

near antonyms clamor, din, noise, racket

antonyms bustle, commotion, hubbub, hurly-burly, pandemonium, tumult, turmoil, uproar

calm *vb* **1** to free from distress or disturbance ⟨the president's reassuring words did much to *calm* the public during the national emergency⟩

synonyms allay, compose, quiet, settle, soothe, still, tranquilize (*also* tranquillize)

related words alleviate, assuage, ease, mitigate, relieve; appease, conciliate, mollify, pacify, placate; lull, relax, stupefy

near antonyms aggravate, heighten, intensify; arouse, excite, foment, incite, rouse, stir (up)

antonyms agitate, discompose, disquiet, disturb, perturb, upset

2 to gain emotional or mental control of — see COLLECT 1

calm (down) *vb* to become still and orderly — see QUIET 1

calming *adj* tending to calm the emotions and relieve stress — see SOOTHING 1

calmness *n* **1** a state of freedom from storm or disturbance — see CALM

2 evenness of emotions or temper — see EQUANIMITY

camaraderie *n* the feeling of closeness and friendship that exists between companions — see COMPANIONSHIP

camouflage *n* clothing put on to hide one's true identity or imitate someone or something else — see DISGUISE

camouflage *vb* to change the dress or looks of so as to conceal true identity — see DISGUISE

camp *n* **1** a place where a group of people live for a short time in tents or cabins ⟨the war forced people to flee their homes and to live in crowded *camps* along the border⟩

synonyms bivouac, campground, campsite, encampment

related words barracks; colony, plantation, settlement; shantytown; concentration camp, prison camp

2 a small, simply constructed, and often temporary dwelling — see SHACK

3 an often small house for recreational or seasonal use — see COTTAGE

camp *vb* to live in a camp or the outdoors ⟨rather than stay in motels, my family usually *camps* when we're on vacation⟩

synonyms bivouac, encamp

related words tent; backpack

phrases rough it

campaign *n* a series of activities undertaken to achieve a goal ⟨an all-out *campaign* to bring a minor league baseball team to the city⟩

synonyms bandwagon, cause, crusade, drive, movement

related words attack, march, offensive

campaigner *n* one who seeks an office, honor, position, or award — see CANDIDATE

camper *n* a motor vehicle that is specially equipped for living while traveling ⟨the family loaded up the *camper* and headed off for the tour of several national parks⟩

synonyms caravan, mobile home, motor home, trailer

related words van

campground *n* a place where a group of people live for a short time in tents or cabins — see CAMP 1

campsite *n* a place where a group of people live for a short time in tents or cabins — see CAMP 1

can *vb* **1** to bring (as an action or operation) to an immediate end — see STOP 1

2 to let go from office, service, or employment — see DISMISS 1

can *n* a metal container in the shape of a cylinder ⟨the shelter stores huge *cans* of water for an emergency⟩

synonyms barrel, drum

related words tube; tin

canal *n* an open man-made passageway for water — see CHANNEL 1

cancel *vb* **1** to put an end to (something planned or previously agreed to) ⟨please call to *cancel* your appointment with the dentist if you can't make it⟩

synonyms abort, call, call off, drop, recall, repeal, rescind, revoke

related words abrogate, annul, invalidate, nullify, void, write off; recant, retract, take back, withdraw; countermand, reverse; end, halt, stop, terminate; give up, relinquish, surrender

near antonyms engage, pledge, promise; begin, commence, initiate, start; take on, take up, undertake

antonyms continue, keep

2 to put an end to by formal action — see ABOLISH

3 to show (something written) to be no longer valid by drawing a cross over or a line through it — see X (OUT)

cancel (out) *vb* to balance with an equal force so as to make ineffective — see OFFSET

canceler *or* **canceller** *n* a force or influence that makes an opposing force ineffective or less effective — see COUNTERBALANCE

cancellation *n* the act of putting an end to something planned or previously agreed to ⟨the misbehavior of a few bad apples at the end of the football game resulted in the *cancellation* of the victory party⟩
synonyms abortion, calling, calling off, dropping, recall, repeal, rescission, revocation
related words annulment, invalidation, neutralization, nullification; abolishment, abolition, ending, halting, stopping, termination; giving up, relinquishment, surrender
near antonyms beginning, commencement, initiation; engagement, undertaking
antonyms continuation

candid *adj* free in expressing one's true feelings and opinions — see FRANK

candidate *n* one who seeks an office, honor, position, or award ⟨each *candidate* for student council was allowed to speak at the school assembly⟩
synonyms applicant, aspirant, campaigner, contender, hopeful, prospect, seeker
related words competitor, contestant, entrant; also-ran, dark horse, favorite, finisher, has-been, runner-up; nominee; claimant, pretender
near antonyms incumbent, officeholder; dropout

candor *n* the free expression of one's true feelings and opinions ⟨an interview in which the members of the rock band speak with *candor* about their recent squabbling⟩
synonyms directness, forthrightness, frankness, openheartedness, openness, plainness, straightforwardness
related words earnestness, sincerity, sobriety; artlessness, genuineness, naïveté (*also* naivete), simplicity, unsophistication; bluffness, bluntness, brusqueness; freedom, license (*or* licence), unrestraint
near antonyms inhibition, reserve, restraint; diplomacy, tact
antonyms dissembling, pretense (*or* pretence)

cane *n* a heavy rigid stick used as a weapon or for punishment — see CLUB 1

canine *n* a domestic mammal that is related to the wolves and foxes — see DOG

canniness *n* skill in achieving one's ends through indirect, subtle, or underhanded means — see CUNNING 1

cannonade *n* a rapid or overwhelming outpouring of many things at once — see BARRAGE

canny *adj* having or showing a practical cleverness or judgment — see SHREWD

canon *n* 1 a statement or body of statements concerning faith or morals proclaimed by a church — see DOCTRINE 1
2 a record of a series of items (as names or titles) usually arranged according to some system — see ¹LIST

canonize *vb* 1 to declare to be a saint and worthy of public respect — see SAINT
2 to love or admire too much — see IDOLIZE

canopy *n* a raised covering over something for decoration or protection ⟨trees line both sides of the garden path, with their foliage forming a leafy *canopy* for walkers⟩
synonyms awning, ceiling, roof, tent
related words screen, shade, shelter, shield, sunshade; canvas, fly

¹**cant** *n* the degree to which something rises up from a position level with the horizon — see SLANT
²**cant** *n* 1 the pretending of having virtues, principles, or beliefs that one in fact does not have — see HYPOCRISY
2 the special terms or expressions of a particular group or field — see TERMINOLOGY

cant *vb* to set or cause to be at an angle — see LEAN 1

cantankerous *adj* having or showing a habitually bad temper — see ILL-TEMPERED

canted *adj* running in a slanting direction — see DIAGONAL

canticle *n* a religious song — see HYMN

canvas *n* a picture created with usually oil paint — see PAINTING

canvass *vb* to go around and approach (people) with a request for opinions or information ⟨we *canvassed* people all over town, asking if they would be interested in participating in a recycling program⟩
synonyms poll, solicit, survey
related words interrogate, interview, question; feel (out), sound (out)
near antonyms report

canyon *also* **cañon** *n* a narrow opening between hillsides or mountains that can be used for passage ⟨as the scouts made their way through the *canyon*, they marveled at the sheer walls of rock on both sides⟩
synonyms defile, flume, gap, gorge, gulch, gulf, notch, pass, ravine
related words abyss, chasm, cirque, cleft, crevasse, crevice, fissure; dale, glen, hollow, vale, valley; basin, floodplain, plain; arroyo, coulee, gully, gutter, wash [*Western*]

cap *n* 1 a covering for the head usually having a shaped crown — see HAT
2 a piece placed over an open container to hold in, protect, or conceal its contents — see COVER 1

capability *n* 1 a skill, an ability, or knowledge that makes a person able to do a particular job — see QUALIFICATION 1
2 the physical or mental power to do something — see ABILITY

capable *adj* having the required skills for an acceptable level of performance — see COMPETENT

capably *adv* in a skillful or expert manner — see WELL 3

capacious *adj* more than adequate or average in capacity — see SPACIOUS

capacity *n* 1 the largest number or amount that something can hold ⟨the seating *capacity* of the school auditorium is 800 people⟩
synonyms complement, content
related words area, room, space, volume; fill, load, measure
2 an assignment at which one regularly works for pay — see JOB 1
3 the action for which a person or thing is specially fitted or used or for which a thing exists — see ROLE
4 the physical or mental power to do something — see ABILITY

caparison *n* 1 dressy clothing — see FINERY
2 something that decorates or beautifies — see DECORATION 1

caparison *vb* to outfit with clothes and especially fine or special clothes — see CLOTHE 1

¹**cape** *n* a sleeveless garment worn so as to hang over the shoulders, arms, and back ⟨the mysterious figure wrapped his *cape* tightly around his shoulders⟩

THESAURUS

synonyms cloak, mantle, roquelaure

related words frock, gown, robe; shawl, stole, wrap; poncho, serape (*or* sarape)

²**cape** *n* an area of land that juts out into a body of water ⟨residents fled the *cape* as the hurricane roared up the coast⟩

synonyms arm, headland, peninsula, point, promontory, spit

related words breakwater, jetty

caper *n* a playful or mischievous act intended as a joke — see PRANK

caper *vb* to play and run about happily — see FROLIC 1

capital *adj* of the very best kind — see EXCELLENT

capital *n* **1** a thing or place that is of greatest importance to an activity or interest — see CENTER 1

2 the total of one's money and property — see WEALTH

capitalize *vb* to provide money for — see FINANCE 1

capitalize (on) *vb* to take unfair advantage of — see EXPLOIT 1

capitol *n* the building in which a state legislature meets ⟨the legislators were called to the *capitol* for an emergency session⟩

synonyms state house

related words meetinghouse; chamber, hall

capitulate *vb* **1** to cease resistance (as to another's arguments, demands, or control) — see YIELD 3

2 to yield to the control or power of enemy forces — see FALL 2

capitulating *n* the usually forced yielding of one's person or possessions to the control of another — see SURRENDER

capitulation *n* the usually forced yielding of one's person or possessions to the control of another — see SURRENDER

caprice *n* a sudden impulsive and apparently unmotivated idea or action — see WHIM

capricious *adj* **1** likely to change frequently, suddenly, or unexpectedly — see FICKLE 1

2 prone to sudden illogical changes of mind, ideas, or actions — see WHIMSICAL

capriciousness *n* an inclination to sudden illogical changes of mind, ideas, or actions — see WHIMSICALITY

capsize *vb* to turn on one's side or upside down ⟨a huge wave out of nowhere caused our little sailboat to *capsize*⟩

synonyms overturn, upset

related words invert, topple; keel over; heel, list, tilt; founder, sink, swamp

phrases turn turtle

antonyms right

capsule *n* **1** a small mass containing medicine to be taken orally — see PILL

2 something that encloses another thing especially to protect it — see ¹CASE 1

captain *n* **1** a person in overall command of a ship ⟨the *captain* is responsible for everything that happens to his ship in the course of a voyage⟩

synonyms commander, skipper

related words master; commanding officer; admiral, commodore, vice admiral

2 one in official command especially of a military force or base — see COMMANDER 1

3 the person (as an employer or supervisor) who tells people and especially workers what to do — see BOSS

captain *vb* **1** to be in charge of — see BOSS 1

2 to exercise authority or power over — see GOVERN 1

3 to serve as leader of — see LEAD 2

caption *n* **1** an explanation or description accompanying a pictorial illustration ⟨for the school yearbook, funny *captions* were written for snapshots showing a typical day at school⟩

synonyms legend

related words key; subtitle, translation; motto, tag line

2 a word or series of words often in larger letters placed at the beginning of a passage or at the top of a page in order to introduce or categorize — see HEADING

captious *adj* given to making or expressing unfavorable judgments about things — see CRITICAL 1

captivate *vb* to attract or delight as if by magic — see CHARM 1

captivating *adj* having an often mysterious or magical power to attract — see FASCINATING 1

captivation *n* the power of irresistible attraction — see CHARM 2

captive *adj* taken and held prisoner ⟨the *captive* soldiers were treated humanely by the guards⟩

synonyms apprehended, arrested, captured, caught, imprisoned, incarcerated, interned, jailed

related words bound, enslaved, indentured; subdued, subjugated

near antonyms emancipated, enfranchised, freed, liberated, released

antonyms free

captive *n* one that has been taken and held in confinement ⟨the *captives* in the concentration camp had devised a daring plan of escape⟩

synonyms capture, internee, prisoner

related words convict, jailbird; parolee

near antonyms custodian, guard, guardian, jailer (*or* jailor), keeper, warden

antonyms captor

captivity *n* the act of confining or the state of being confined — see INTERNMENT

capture *n* one that has been taken and held in confinement — see CAPTIVE

capture *vb* **1** to receive as return for effort — see EARN 1

2 to take physical control or possession of (something) suddenly or forcibly — see CATCH 1

captured *adj* taken and held prisoner — see CAPTIVE

car *n* a self-propelled passenger vehicle on wheels ⟨every teenager's dream of getting a driver's license and a first *car*⟩

synonyms auto, automobile, machine, motor, motorcar, motor vehicle

related words bus, coach, minibus; beach buggy, brougham, compact, convertible, coupe, dune buggy, fastback, gas-guzzler, hardtop, hatchback, hot rod, jeep, limousine, roadster, sedan, sports car, station wagon, stock car, subcompact, van; flivver, jalopy

caravan *n* **1** a group of vehicles traveling together or under one management — see FLEET

2 a motor vehicle that is specially equipped for living while traveling — see CAMPER

caravansary *or* **caravanserai** *n* a place that provides rooms and usually a public dining room for overnight guests — see HOTEL

carbon copy *n* **1** something or someone that strongly resembles another — see IMAGE 1

2 something that is made to look exactly like something else — see COPY

carcass *n* a dead body — see CORPSE

card *n* a person (as a writer) noted for or specializing in humor — see HUMORIST

cardinal *adj* coming before all others in importance — see FOREMOST 1

care *n* **1** strict attentiveness to what one is doing ⟨that's an extremely valuable violin, so handle it with *care*⟩
synonyms carefulness, conscientiousness, heed, heedfulness, pains, scrupulousness
related words exactness, meticulousness, particularity, punctiliousness; dutifulness, responsibility; bother, effort, trouble; alertness, vigilance, watchfulness
antonyms carelessness, heedlessness
2 a close attentiveness to avoiding danger — see CAUTION 1
3 an uneasy state of mind usually over the possibility of an anticipated misfortune or trouble — see ANXIETY 1
4 responsibility for the safety and well-being of someone or something — see CUSTODY
5 the duty or function of watching or guarding for the sake of proper direction or control — see SUPERVISION 1

care *vb* to have an interest or concern for ⟨a teacher who *cares* what happens to her students long after they leave her classroom⟩
synonyms mind, watch
related words attend, heed, regard; note, notice, observe; empathize (with), feel (for), sympathize (with)
phrases look out for
near antonyms disregard, ignore, overlook

care (for) *vb* **1** to take charge of especially on behalf of another — see ²TEND 1
2 to attend to the needs and comforts of — see NURSE 1
3 to have a favorable opinion of — see APPROVE (OF)
4 to wish to have — see LIKE 1

careen *vb* **1** to make a series of unsteady side-to-side motions — see ROCK 1
2 to move forward while swaying from side to side — see STAGGER 1

career *vb* to proceed or move quickly — see HURRY 2

carefree *adj* having or showing a lack of concern or seriousness ⟨passengers on a luxury cruise ship enjoying a *carefree* vacation⟩ ⟨*carefree* college students on spring break⟩
synonyms careless, cavalier, devil-may-care, easygoing, gay, happy-go-lucky, insouciant, light-hearted, unconcerned
related words breezy, nonchalant; casual, informal, laid-back, low-pressure, relaxed; heedless, irresponsible, lackadaisical, negligent, reckless
near antonyms earnest, grave, serious, somber (*or* sombre); careful, cautious, heedful, wary; concerned, upset, worried; long-suffering, overburdened, sorrowful
antonyms careworn

careful *adj* **1** having or showing a close attentiveness to avoiding danger or trouble ⟨*careful* drivers slow down on slick or icy roadways⟩
synonyms alert, cautious, circumspect, considerate, gingerly, guarded, heedful, safe, wary
related words attentive, chary, observant, vigilant,

watchful; foresighted, forethoughtful, provident; cagey (*also* cagy), noncommittal; calculating, scheming, shrewd; considerate, thoughtful; deliberate, slow
near antonyms bold, impetuous, rash, reckless; inattentive, unobservant; inconsiderate, thoughtless; lax, neglectful, negligent; imprudent, indiscreet, injudicious
antonyms careless, heedless, incautious, unguarded, unsafe, unwary
2 taking great care and effort — see PAINSTAKING

carefulness *n* **1** a close attentiveness to avoiding danger — see CAUTION 1
2 strict attentiveness to what one is doing — see CARE 1

careless *adj* **1** not paying or showing close attention especially for the purpose of avoiding trouble ⟨a *careless* reporter who often doesn't get his facts straight⟩ ⟨a *careless* mistake that caused the plane to crash⟩
synonyms heedless, incautious, mindless, unguarded, unsafe, unwary
related words bold, impetuous, rash, reckless; inattentive, unobservant; blithe, inconsiderate, thoughtless; absentminded, forgetful, unmindful; lax, neglectful, negligent, remiss; imprudent, indiscreet, injudicious; inadvertent, unintentional, unplanned
near antonyms attentive, chary, observant, vigilant, watchful; foresighted, forethoughtful, provident; calculating, scheming, shrewd; considerate, thoughtful
antonyms alert, cautious, circumspect, gingerly, guarded, heedful, safe, wary
2 failing to give proper care and attention — see NEGLIGENT
3 having or showing a lack of concern or seriousness — see CAREFREE

carelessness *n* failure to take the care that a cautious person usually takes — see NEGLIGENCE 1

caress *vb* to touch or handle in a tender or loving manner — see FONDLE

caretaker *n* a person who takes care of a property sometimes for an absent owner — see CUSTODIAN 1

cargo *n* a mass or quantity of something taken up and carried, conveyed, or transported — see LOAD 1

caricature *n* **1** a poor, insincere, or insulting imitation of something — see MOCKERY 1
2 a work that imitates and exaggerates another work for comic effect — see PARODY 1
3 the representation of something in terms that go beyond the facts — see EXAGGERATION

caricature *vb* to copy or exaggerate (someone or something) in order to make fun of — see MIMIC 1

carnage *n* the killing of a large number of people — see MASSACRE

carnal *adj* **1** having to do with life on earth especially as opposed to that in heaven — see EARTHLY
2 of or relating to the human body — see PHYSICAL 1
3 pleasing to the physical senses — see SENSUAL

carnival *n* a time or program of special events and entertainment in honor of something — see FESTIVAL

carol *n* a religious song — see HYMN

THESAURUS

carol *vb* to produce musical sounds with the voice — see SING 1

caroler *or* **caroller** *n* one who sings — see SINGER

carom *vb* to strike and fly off at an angle — see GLANCE 1

carousal *n* a bout of drinking — see CAROUSE

carouse *n* a bout of drinking ⟨the Old West custom of heading to the saloon at night for a *carouse* and some poker playing⟩
synonyms carousal, drunk, wassail
related words binge, jag, spree; blowout, orgy

carp *vb* **1** to express dissatisfaction, pain, or resentment usually tiresomely — see COMPLAIN
2 to make often peevish criticisms or objections about matters that are minor, unimportant, or irrelevant — see QUIBBLE

carper *n* a person given to harsh judgments and to finding faults — see CRITIC 1

carpet *vb* to form a layer over — see COVER 2

carping *adj* given to making or expressing unfavorable judgments about things — see CRITICAL 1

carriage *n* **1** a horse-drawn wheeled vehicle for carrying passengers ⟨a museum with a large collection of beautiful, old *carriages*⟩
synonyms equipage, rig
related words brougham, buckboard, cab, chaise, coach, hackney, hansom, surrey
2 a general way of holding the body — see POSTURE 1

carry *vb* **1** to support and take from one place to another ⟨each camper must be able to *carry* his or her own backpack⟩
synonyms bear, cart, convey, ferry, haul, lug, pack, tote, transport
related words deliver, hand over, transfer; forward, send, ship, transmit; bring, fetch, take; move, remove, shift
2 to wear or have on one's person ⟨I always *carry* a camera with me so as to never miss a great shot⟩
synonyms bear, pack
related words flaunt, show off, sport; display, exhibit, parade, show
3 to bring before the public in performance or exhibition — see PRESENT 1
4 to have as part of a whole — see INCLUDE
5 to hold up or serve as a foundation for — see SUPPORT 3
6 to receive as return for effort — see EARN 1

carryall *n* a bag carried by hand and designed to hold a traveler's clothing and personal articles — see TRAVELING BAG

carry away *vb* **1** to fill with overwhelming emotion (as wonder or delight) — see ENTRANCE
2 to subject to incapacitating emotional or mental stress — see OVERWHELM 1

carry on *vb* **1** to behave badly — see MISBEHAVE
2 to continue despite difficulties, opposition, or discouragement — see PERSEVERE
3 to look after and make decisions about — see CONDUCT 1

carry out *vb* to carry through (as a process) to completion — see PERFORM 1

cart *n* a wheeled usually horse-drawn vehicle used for hauling ⟨an old *cart* piled up with hay⟩
synonyms wagon, wain
related words barrow, pushcart, wheelbarrow; oxcart

cart *vb* to support and take from one place to another — see CARRY 1

cartel *n* a number of businesses or enterprises united for commercial advantage ⟨a *cartel* of oil-producing nations that controls production and influences prices⟩
synonyms combination, combine, syndicate, trust
related words chain, conglomerate, multinational; association, organization, pool

cartoon *n* **1** a picture using lines to represent the chief features of an object or scene — see DRAWING
2 a series of drawings that tell a story or part of a story — see COMIC STRIP

carve *vb* to create a three-dimensional representation of (something) using solid material — see SCULPT

carve (out) *vb* to produce or bring about especially by long or repeated effort — see HAMMER (OUT)

cascade *n* a fall of water usually from a great height — see WATERFALL

¹case *n* **1** something that encloses another thing especially to protect it ⟨those binoculars come with their own *case*⟩
synonyms armor, capsule, casing, cocoon, cover, covering, housing, husk, jacket, pod, sheath, shell
related words bark, crust; mail, plate, plating, shield; hide, skin; envelope, wrapper; backing, coating, facing
2 a covered rectangular container for storing or transporting things — see CHEST

²case *n* **1** an individual awaiting or under medical care and treatment — see PATIENT
2 one of a group or collection that shows what the whole is like — see EXAMPLE
3 something that actually exists — see FACT 2
4 a statement given to explain a belief or act — see REASON 1
5 a sudden experiencing of a physical or mental disorder — see ATTACK 2
6 something that might happen — see EVENT 2
7 something that requires thought and skill for resolution — see PROBLEM 1

cash *n* something (as pieces of stamped metal or printed paper) customarily and legally used as a medium of exchange, a measure of value, or a means of payment — see MONEY

cashier *vb* to let go from office, service, or employment — see DISMISS 1

cash in (on) *vb* to take unfair advantage of — see EXPLOIT 1

casing *n* something that encloses another thing especially to protect it — see ¹CASE 1

cask *n* an enclosed wooden vessel for holding beverages ⟨*casks* of wine that had been in the castle for many years⟩
synonyms barrel, firkin, hogshead, keg, pipe, puncheon
related words tub, vat; can, drum

casket *n* **1** a box for holding a dead body — see COFFIN
2 a covered rectangular container for storing or transporting things — see CHEST

cast *n* **1** a declaration that something will happen in the future — see PREDICTION
2 a property that becomes apparent when light falls on an object and by which things that are identical in form can be distinguished — see COLOR 1
3 an instance of looking especially briefly — see LOOK 2

4 facial appearance regarded as an indication of mood or feeling — see LOOK 1

5 the outward appearance of something as distinguished from its substance — see FORM 1

cast *vb* **1** to get rid of as useless or unwanted — see DISCARD

2 to point or turn (something) toward a target or goal — see AIM 1

3 to put (something) into proper and usually carefully worked out written form — see COMPOSE 1

4 to send through the air especially with a quick forward motion of the arm — see THROW

cast (off) *vb* to throw or give off — see EMIT 1

cast (out) *vb* to drive or force out — see EJECT 1

cast about (for) *vb* to go in search of — see SEEK 1

cast around (for) *vb* to go in search of — see SEEK 1

castaway *n* one who is cast out or rejected by society — see OUTCAST

caste *n* one of the segments of society into which people are grouped — see CLASS 1

castigate *vb* **1** to criticize (someone) severely or angrily especially for personal failings — see SCOLD

2 to criticize harshly and usually publicly — see ATTACK 2

3 to inflict a penalty on for a fault or crime — see PUNISH

castigating *adj* inflicting, involving, or serving as punishment — see PUNITIVE

castigation *n* suffering, loss, or hardship imposed in response to a crime or offense — see PUNISHMENT

castigator *n* **1** a person given to harsh judgments and to finding faults — see CRITIC 1

2 one who inflicts punishment in return for an injury or offense — see NEMESIS 1

castle *n* a large impressive residence — see MANSION

castoff *n* one who is cast out or rejected by society — see OUTCAST

casual *adj* **1** not designed for special occasions ⟨a restaurant where people in *casual* clothes are always welcome⟩

synonyms everyday, informal, workaday

related words sporty; shabby, sloppy, slovenly, unkempt

near antonyms best, Sunday; chic, elegant, fashionable, smart, stylish; neat, tidy, trim; semiformal

antonyms dressy, formal

2 happening by chance — see ACCIDENTAL

3 having or showing a lack of interest or concern — see INDIFFERENT 1

4 lacking in steadiness or regularity of occurrence — see FITFUL

casualness *n* lack of interest or concern — see INDIFFERENCE

casualty *n* **1** a person or thing harmed, lost, or destroyed ⟨the real *casualties* in the war against drugs are millions of innocent children⟩

synonyms fatality, loss, victim

related words failure, loser

near antonyms gainer, victor, winner

2 a chance and usually sudden event bringing loss or injury — see ACCIDENT 1

cat *n* **1** a small domestic animal known for catching mice ⟨the family's *cat* did a good job of keeping the house and yard free of all rodents⟩

synonyms feline, house cat, kitty, puss, pussy

related words mouser; kit, kitten; tabby, tomcat

2 *slang* an adult male human being — see MAN 1

cataclysm *n* **1** a great flow of water or of something that overwhelms — see FLOOD

2 a sudden violent event that brings about great loss or destruction — see DISASTER

3 a violent disturbance (as of the political or social order) — see CONVULSION

cataclysmal *or* **cataclysmic** *adj* **1** bringing about ruin or misfortune — see FATAL 1

2 causing or tending to cause destruction — see DESTRUCTIVE 1

3 marked by sudden or violent disturbance — see CONVULSIVE

catacomb *n, usually* **catacombs** *pl* an underground burial chamber — see CRYPT

catalog *or* **catalogue** *n* a record of a series of items (as names or titles) usually arranged according to some system — see ¹LIST

catalog *or* **catalogue** *vb* to put (someone or something) on a list — see ¹LIST 2

catamount *n* a large tawny cat of the wild — see COUGAR

catapult *vb* to send through the air especially with a quick forward motion of the arm — see THROW

cataract *n* **1** a fall of water usually from a great height — see WATERFALL

2 a great flow of water or of something that overwhelms — see FLOOD

catastrophe *n* **1** a sudden violent event that brings about great loss or destruction — see DISASTER

2 something that has failed — see FAILURE 3

catastrophic *adj* bringing about ruin or misfortune — see FATAL 1

catcall *n* a vocal sound made to express scorn or disapproval ⟨the band's sloppy playing produced only *catcalls* from the crowd⟩

synonyms boo, hiss, hoot, jeer, raspberry, snort

related words smirk, sneer, snicker, snigger; gibe (*or* jibe), put-down, taunt; whistle

near antonyms applause, clapping

antonyms cheer

catch *n* **1** a danger or difficulty that is hidden or not easily recognized — see PITFALL 1

2 someone or something unusually desirable — see PRIZE 1

3 the total amount collected or obtained especially at one time — see HAUL 1

catch *vb* **1** to take physical control or possession of (something) suddenly or forcibly ⟨we tried to *catch* the kitten before she could sneak out the door⟩

synonyms bag, capture, collar, corral, get, grab, grapple, hook, land, nab, nail, seize, snap (up), snare, snatch, trap

related words lasso, rope; apprehend, arrest, detain; clasp, clutch, grasp, grip, hold, secure; rend, wrest; ensnare, entangle, entrap; abduct, kidnap, spirit (away *or* off)

phrases lay hold of

near antonyms discharge, free, liberate, release; drop, loosen

antonyms miss

2 to become affected with (a disease or disorder) — see CONTRACT 1

3 to bring (something) to a standstill — see ¹HALT 1

4 to put securely in place or in a desired position — see FASTEN 2

5 to recognize the meaning of — see COMPREHEND 1

catching *adj* **1** capable of being passed by physical contact from one person to another — see CONTAGIOUS 1

2 exciting a similar feeling or reaction in others — see CONTAGIOUS 2

catch on *vb* to come to an awareness — see DISCOVER 1

catch on (to) *vb* to recognize the meaning of — see COMPREHEND 1

catch up (with) *vb* to move fast enough to get even with — see OVERTAKE

catchy *adj* **1** likely to attract attention — see NOTICEABLE

2 requiring exceptional skill or caution in performance or handling — see TRICKY

categorical *also* **categoric** *adj* having no exceptions or restrictions — see ABSOLUTE 2

categorize *vb* to arrange or assign according to type — see CLASSIFY 1

category *n* one of the units into which a whole is divided on the basis of a common characteristic — see CLASS 2

cater *vb* to provide food or meals for — see FEED 1

cater (to) *vb* to give in to (a desire) — see INDULGE

catnap *n* a short sleep — see ¹NAP

catnap *vb* **1** be in a state of sleep — see SLEEP 1

2 to sleep lightly or briefly — see NAP 1

catnapping *n* a natural periodic loss of consciousness during which the body restores itself — see SLEEP 1

cattily *adv* in a mean or spiteful manner — see NASTILY

cattiness *n* **1** biting sharpness of feeling or expression — see ACRIMONY 1

2 the desire to cause pain for the satisfaction of doing harm — see MALICE

catty *adj* having or showing a desire to cause someone pain or suffering for the sheer enjoyment of it — see HATEFUL

caught *adj* taken and held prisoner — see CAPTIVE

cause *n* **1** someone or something responsible for a result ⟨the much-debated *causes* of the American Civil War⟩

synonyms antecedent, occasion, reason

related words consideration, determinant, factor; impetus, incentive, inspiration, instigation, stimulus; mother, origin, root, source, spring

near antonyms ramification; denouement, repercussion; conclusion, end; by-product, side effect

antonyms aftereffect, aftermath, consequence, corollary, development, effect, fate, fruit, issue, outcome, outgrowth, product, result, resultant, sequel, sequence, upshot

2 a series of activities undertaken to achieve a goal — see CAMPAIGN

cause *vb* to be the cause of (a situation, action, or state of mind) — see EFFECT

caustic *adj* marked by the use of wit that is intended to cause hurt feelings — see SARCASTIC

caution *n* **1** a close attentiveness to avoiding danger ⟨the extreme *caution* with which the zookeeper handled the snake⟩

synonyms alertness, care, carefulness, cautiousness, circumspection, heedfulness, wariness

related words attentiveness, chariness, vigilance, watchfulness; foresight, foresightedness, providence; calculation, canniness, deliberateness, deliberation, shrewdness

near antonyms abruptness, hastiness, impetuousness, precipitousness, rashness, suddenness; inconsideration, thoughtlessness

antonyms brashness, carelessness, heedlessness, incautiousness, recklessness, unwariness

2 something extraordinary or surprising — see WONDER 1

3 something that tells of approaching danger or risk — see WARNING 2

4 the act or an instance of telling beforehand of danger or risk — see WARNING 1

caution *vb* to give notice to beforehand especially of danger or risk — see WARN

cautionary *adj* serving as or offering a warning ⟨the story of King Midas is a *cautionary* tale about the perils of wishing for something—you just might get it⟩

synonyms admonishing, admonitory, cautioning, warning

related words didactic, moralistic, moralizing; advisory, counseling (*or* counselling); punishing, punitive

cautioning *adj* serving as or offering a warning — see CAUTIONARY

cautious *adj* having or showing a close attentiveness to avoiding danger or trouble — see CAREFUL 1

cautiousness *n* a close attentiveness to avoiding danger — see CAUTION 1

cavalcade *n* **1** a group of vehicles traveling together or under one management — see FLEET

2 a staged presentation often with music that consists of a procession of narrated or enacted scenes — see PAGEANT

cavalier *adj* **1** having a feeling of superiority that shows itself in an overbearing attitude — see ARROGANT

2 having or showing a lack of concern or seriousness — see CAREFREE

cavalier *n* an honorable and courteous man ⟨a novel about the dashing *cavaliers* and gracious ladies of the South before the Civil War⟩

synonyms gentleman

related words knight, prince; blade, buck, dandy, fop, gallant; charmer, smoothy (*or* smoothie); aristocrat, patrician

cave *n* a naturally formed underground chamber with an opening to the surface ⟨Kentucky's Mammoth *Cave* is actually a series of large chambers on five levels⟩

synonyms cavern, grot, grotto

related words abyss, chasm, gulf, hollow; subway, tunnel; excavation, mine, pit, shaft, well; bunker, dugout, foxhole; burrow, covert, den, hole, lair, lodge, shelter

cave (in) *vb* to fall down or in as a result of physical pressure — see COLLAPSE 1

cavern *n* a naturally formed underground chamber with an opening to the surface — see CAVE

cavil *vb* to make often peevish criticisms or objections about matters that are minor, unimportant, or irrelevant — see QUIBBLE

caviler *or* **caviller** *n* a person given to harsh judgments and to finding faults — see CRITIC 1

caviling *or* **cavilling** *adj* given to making or expressing unfavorable judgments about things — see CRITICAL 1

cavity *n* a sunken area forming a separate space — see HOLE 2

cavort *vb* to play and run about happily — see FROLIC 1

cease *vb* **1** to come to an end ⟨the rain finally *ceased*, and we were able to continue the baseball game⟩

synonyms break off, break up, close, conclude, die, discontinue, elapse, end, expire, finish, halt, lapse, leave off, let up, pass, quit, stop, terminate, wind up

related words desist (from), lay off (of), refrain (from); knock off; break down, conk (out), cut out, stall; pause, stay, suspend

near antonyms draw out, extend, prolong, protract

antonyms continue, hang on, persist

2 to bring (as an action or operation) to an immediate end — see STOP 1

cease–fire *n* a temporary stopping of fighting — see TRUCE

ceaseless *adj* **1** going on and on without any interruptions — see CONTINUOUS

2 lasting forever — see EVERLASTING

cede *vb* **1** to give (something) over to the control or possession of another usually under duress — see SURRENDER 1

2 to give over the legal possession or ownership of — see TRANSFER 1

3 to give up (as a position of authority) formally — see ABDICATE

ceiling *n* **1** a real or imaginary point beyond which a person or thing cannot go — see LIMIT

2 a raised covering over something for decoration or protection — see CANOPY

celebrant *n* one who engages in merrymaking especially in honor of a special occasion ⟨all of the *celebrants* at the birthday party received a favor to take home⟩

synonyms celebrator, merrymaker, reveler (*or* reveller), roisterer

related words carouser, wassailer; cutup, skylarker

antonyms killjoy, party pooper

celebrate *vb* to act properly in relation to — see KEEP 1

celebrated *adj* widely known — see FAMOUS

celebration *n* a time or program of special events and entertainment in honor of something — see FESTIVAL

celebrator *n* one who engages in merrymaking especially in honor of a special occasion — see CELEBRANT

celebrity *n* **1** a person who is widely known and usually much talked about ⟨*celebrities* from sports and entertainment attended the opening ceremonies of the Olympic Games⟩

synonyms figure, light, luminary, notable, personage, personality, somebody, standout, star, superstar, VIP

related words favorite, hero, idol; demigod, dignitary, eminence, immortal, pillar, worthy; baron, big shot, bigwig, magnate, mogul, nabob

near antonyms lightweight, mediocrity; has-been

antonyms nobody

2 the fact or state of being known to the public — see FAME

celerity *n* a high rate of movement or performance — see SPEED

celestial *adj* of, relating to, or suggesting heaven ⟨movie scenes depicting life after death are usually accompanied by *celestial* music⟩

synonyms Elysian, empyreal, empyrean, heavenly, supernal

related words ethereal, supernatural, transcendent, transcendental, unearthly, unworldly; angelic, beatific, blissful; Olympian, utopian; cosmic, stellar

near antonyms earthly, mundane, terrestrial, worldly

antonyms hellish, infernal

cell *n* **1** an area within a building that has been set apart from surrounding space by a wall — see ROOM 2

2 one of the parts into which an enclosed space is divided — see COMPARTMENT

cellar *n* a room or set of rooms below the surface of the ground ⟨an amazing variety of interesting things were found in the *cellar* of the old house⟩

synonyms basement

related words bunker, crawlway, foundation, hold

cement *n* **1** a substance used to stick things together — see GLUE

2 a uniting or binding force or influence — see BOND 2

cemetery *n* a piece of land used for burying the dead ⟨many of the soldiers who died in the battle are buried in a *cemetery* nearby⟩

synonyms graveyard, potter's field

related words catacombs, churchyard; crypt, grave, mausoleum, sepulcher (*or* sepulchre), sepulture, tomb, vault

censor *vb* to remove objectionable parts from ⟨the producers were told that they would have to *censor* their movie if they wanted a PG rating⟩

synonyms clean (up), expurgate

related words cleanse, purge, purify; abbreviate, edit, shorten; cut (out), delete, excise, expunge; repress, silence, suppress; censure, condemn, denounce; examine, review, screen, scrutinize

near antonyms approve, authorize, sanction

censurable *adj* **1** deserving reproach or blame — see BLAMEWORTHY

2 provoking or likely to provoke protest — see OBJECTIONABLE

censure *n* an often public or formal expression of disapproval ⟨a rare *censure* of a senator by the full United States Senate for misconduct⟩

synonyms condemnation, denunciation, rebuke, reprimand, reproach, reproof, stricture

related words admonishment, admonition, castigation, chastisement, punishment; belittlement, criticism, deprecation, depreciation, disparagement

near antonyms acclamation, honor, tribute; encomium, eulogy, panegyric, plaudit(s), praise; approval, blessing, sanction

antonyms citation, commendation, endorsement

censure *vb* **1** to express public or formal disapproval of ⟨a vote to *censure* the President for conduct that was unbecoming to his office⟩

synonyms condemn, denounce, rebuke, reprimand, reproach, reprove

related words admonish, castigate, chastise, punish; belittle, criticize, deprecate, depreciate, disparage

near antonyms acclaim, applaud, honor; eulogize, laud, praise; approve, bless, sanction

antonyms cite, commend, endorse (*also* indorse)

2 to declare to be morally wrong or evil — see CONDEMN 1

3 to express one's unfavorable opinion of the worth or quality of — see CRITICIZE

censurer *n* a person given to harsh judgments and to finding faults — see CRITIC 1

center *n* **1** a thing or place that is of greatest importance to an activity or interest ⟨a stretch of coastline that has long been the area's *center* of tourism⟩
synonyms base, capital, core, cynosure, eye, focus, heart, hub, mecca, nucleus, seat
related words focus, headquarters; kernel, nub, pith; deep, thick; essence, quintessence, soul; attraction, lodestone, magnet

2 an area or point that is an equal distance from all points along an edge or outer surface ⟨the *center* of the earth⟩
synonyms core, middle, midpoint, midst
related words inside, interior
antonyms perimeter, periphery

center *vb* to bring (something) to a central point or under a single control — see CENTRALIZE

central *adj* coming before all others in importance — see FOREMOST 1

centralize *vb* to bring (something) to a central point or under a single control ⟨the company decided to *centralize* all of its operations at its Ohio plant⟩
synonyms center, compact, concentrate, consolidate, unify, unite
related words coordinate, harmonize, integrate, orchestrate; blend, coalesce, combine, fuse, incorporate, merge; conjoin, join, link; assemble, collect, gather; reunify, reunite
near antonyms segregate, separate
antonyms decentralize, spread (out)

cerebral *adj* **1** much given to learning and thinking — see INTELLECTUAL 1
2 of or relating to the mind — see MENTAL 1

cerebrum *n* the part of a person that feels, thinks, perceives, wills, and especially reasons — see MIND 1

ceremonial *adj* following or agreeing with established form, custom, or rules — see FORMAL 1

ceremonial *n* an oft-repeated action or series of actions performed in accordance with tradition or a set of rules — see RITE

ceremonious *adj* **1** marked by or showing careful attention to set forms and details ⟨a century ago everyday life was much more *ceremonious* than in our anything-goes era⟩
synonyms correct, decorous, formal, proper, starchy
related words sober, solemn, stately; chivalrous, courtly, gallant; genteel, polished, refined; civil, courteous, polite, red-carpet
near antonyms improper, indecorous, unmannerly; discourteous, impolite, rude
antonyms casual, easygoing, informal, laid-back
2 following or agreeing with established form, custom, or rules — see FORMAL 1

ceremony *n* an oft-repeated action or series of actions performed in accordance with tradition or a set of rules — see RITE

certain *adj* **1** known but not named ⟨a *certain* person told me that today is your birthday⟩
synonyms anonymous, one, some, unidentified, unnamed, unspecified
related words particular, specific
near antonyms known, named, specified

2 having or showing a mind free from doubt ⟨I'm *certain* that they'll arrive on time⟩
synonyms assured, clear, cocksure, confident, doubtless, positive, sanguine, sure
related words self-assured, self-conceited, self-confident; decisive, resolute, unfaltering, unhesitating, unwavering
near antonyms hesitant, indecisive, wavering; diffident, unassuming
antonyms doubtful, dubious, uncertain, unsure
3 having been established and usually not subject to change — see FIXED 1
4 impossible to avoid or evade — see INEVITABLE
5 not likely to fail — see INFALLIBLE 2

certainly *adv* without any question — see INDEED 1

certainty *n* a state of mind in which one is free from doubt — see CONFIDENCE 2

certificate *n* a written or printed paper giving information about or proof of something ⟨a *certificate* will be awarded to each person who completes the course in lifesaving⟩
synonyms document, instrument
related words credentials; diploma, parchment; warrant, writ; warranty; coupon, voucher

certify *vb* **1** to declare (something) to be true or genuine ⟨experts *certified* the letter as indeed having been written by Abraham Lincoln⟩
synonyms attest, authenticate, avouch, testify (to), vouch (for), witness
related words guarantee, warrant; affirm, assert, aver, avow, profess
2 to give official or legal power to — see AUTHORIZE 1

certitude *n* a state of mind in which one is free from doubt — see CONFIDENCE 2

cessation *n* the stopping of a process or activity — see END 1

chafe *vb* **1** to make sore by continued rubbing ⟨ill-fitting boots that had badly *chafed* my heels⟩
synonyms abrade, gall, irritate
related words graze, scrape, scratch; burn, inflame; flay, peel, skin
2 to damage or diminish by continued friction — see ABRADE 1
3 to disturb the peace of mind of (someone) especially by repeated disagreeable acts — see IRRITATE 1

chaff *n* **1** discarded or useless material — see GARBAGE
2 good-natured teasing or exchanging of clever remarks — see BANTER

chaff *vb* to make fun of in a good-natured way — see TEASE 1

chaffer *vb* to talk over or dispute the terms of a purchase — see BARGAIN

chaffing *adj* marked by or expressive of mild or good-natured teasing — see QUIZZICAL

chaffy *adj* having no usefulness — see WORTHLESS

chain *n* **1** a series of things linked together ⟨the *chain* of events that led the American colonies to seek independence from Great Britain⟩
synonyms concatenation, progression, sequence, string, train
related words chain reaction; belt, circle, cycle; continuum, gamut, scale, spectrum; flow, river, stream; file, line, queue, row, succession
2 something that makes movement or progress more difficult — see ENCUMBRANCE

3 something that physically prevents free movement — see BOND 1

chain *vb* **1** to confine or restrain with or as if with chains — see BIND 1

2 to put or bring together so as to form a new and longer whole — see CONNECT 1

chair *n* **1** a person in charge of a meeting ⟨all questions and comments should be directed to the *chair*⟩
synonyms chairman, chairperson, moderator, president, speaker
related words chairwoman
2 the place of leadership or command — see HEAD 2

chairman *n* a person in charge of a meeting — see CHAIR 1

chairperson *n* a person in charge of a meeting — see CHAIR 1

chalet *n* an often small house for recreational or seasonal use — see COTTAGE

challenge *n* a feeling or declaration of disapproval or dissent — see OBJECTION

challenge *vb* **1** to demand proof of the truth or rightness of ⟨don't hesitate to *challenge* any statement that generalizes about people⟩
synonyms contest, dispute, query, question
related words doubt, mistrust; kick (about), object (to), protest; combat, fight, oppose, resist
near antonyms back, defend, support; advocate, champion, promote; abide, endure, stomach, tolerate
antonyms accept, believe, embrace, swallow
2 to invite (someone) to take part in a contest or to perform a feat ⟨I *challenge* you to swim to the other side of the pond⟩
synonyms dare, defy, stump
related words beard, brave, brazen, breast, confront, face, outbrave

challenged *adj* deprived of the power to perform one or more natural bodily activities — see DISABLED

challenger *n* one who strives for the same thing as another — see COMPETITOR

challenging *adj* requiring much time, effort, or careful attention — see DEMANDING 1

chamber *n* **1** an area within a building that has been set apart from surrounding space by a wall — see ROOM 2
2 one of the parts into which an enclosed space is divided — see COMPARTMENT

chamber *vb* to provide with living quarters or shelter — see HOUSE 1

champ *n* the person who comes in first in a competition — see CHAMPION 1

champ *vb* to crush or grind with the teeth — see BITE (ON)

champion *n* **1** the person who comes in first in a competition ⟨the *champion* of the national spelling bee⟩
synonyms champ, victor, winner
related words finalist, semifinalist; medalist, prizewinner; star, superstar
near antonyms loser
2 a person who actively supports or favors a cause — see EXPONENT

champion *vb* to promote the interests or cause of — see SUPPORT 1

championship *n* the position occupied by the one who comes in first in a competition — see CROWN 2

chance *adj* happening by chance — see ACCIDENTAL

chance *n* **1** the uncertain course of events ⟨rather than leave everything to *chance*, let's plan how we're going to spend our time in New York City⟩
synonyms accident, circumstance, hap, hazard, luck
related words fortuitousness, randomness, uncertainty; fluke; destiny, doom, fate, fortune, lot; danger, peril, risk
near antonyms intent, intention, purpose; design, outline, plan, scheme
2 a favorable combination of circumstances, time, and place — see OPPORTUNITY
3 a measure of how often an event will occur instead of another — see PROBABILITY 2
4 a risky undertaking — see GAMBLE

chance *vb* **1** to take a chance on — see RISK 1
2 to take place — see HAPPEN

chance (upon) *vb* **1** to come upon face-to-face or as if face-to-face — see MEET
2 to come upon unexpectedly or by chance — see HAPPEN (ON OR UPON)

change *n* the act, process, or result of making different ⟨the positive *change* in our students' attitude toward people who are somehow different was a long and gradual process⟩
synonyms alteration, difference, modification, redoing, refashioning, remaking, remodeling, revamping, revise, revision, reworking, variation
related words amendment, correction, rectification; conversion, deformation, distortion, metamorphosis, mutation, transfiguration, transformation; fluctuation, oscillation, shift; displacement, replacement, substitution; adjustment, modulation, regulation
antonyms fixation, stabilization

change *vb* **1** to make different in some way ⟨Mother has *changed* the look of our living room more times than we care to remember⟩
synonyms alter, make over, modify, recast, redo, refashion, remake, remodel, revamp, revise, rework, vary
related words deform, metamorphose, mutate; revolutionize, transfigure, transform, transmute; commute, convert, exchange
antonyms fix, freeze, set, stabilize
2 to pass from one form, state, or level to another ⟨the weather in New England is constantly *changing*⟩
synonyms fluctuate, mutate, shift, vary
related words metamorphose, transmute; better, improve; deteriorate, worsen; seesaw, teeter, vacillate, waver
antonyms stabilize
3 to give up (something) and take something else in return ⟨would you mind *changing* your seat so my friends can sit together?⟩
synonyms commute, exchange, shift, substitute, swap, switch, trade
related words interchange; displace, replace, supersede; cede, surrender, yield

changeable *adj* **1** capable of being readily changed — see FLEXIBLE 1
2 likely to change frequently, suddenly, or unexpectedly — see FICKLE 1

changeful *adj* likely to change frequently, suddenly, or unexpectedly — see FICKLE 1

changeless *adj* not undergoing a change in condition — see CONSTANT 1

THESAURUS

changelessness *n* the state of continuing without change — see CONSTANCY 1

changeover *n* a change in form, appearance, or use — see CONVERSION

changing *adj* not staying constant — see UNEVEN 2

channel *n* **1** an open man-made passageway for water ⟨water was drained from the swamp through a specially constructed *channel*⟩
synonyms aqueduct, canal, conduit, flume, raceway, watercourse, waterway
related words millrace, millstream; river, rivulet, stream
2 a narrow body of water between two land masses ⟨the world record for swimming the *channel* between France and Great Britain⟩
synonyms narrows, sound, strait
related words arm, bay, gulf, inlet; roads, roadstead; reach, stretch
3 a direct way of passing along information or supplies — see PIPELINE
4 a long hollow cylinder for carrying a substance (as a liquid or gas) — see PIPE 1

channel *vb* to cause to move to a central point or along a restricted pathway ⟨an athletic youth who *channeled* all of his energy into sports⟩
synonyms channelize, conduct, direct, funnel, pipe, siphon
related words carry, convey, transmit; concentrate, consolidate, focus

channelize *vb* to cause to move to a central point or along a restricted pathway — see CHANNEL

chant *vb* **1** to utter in musical or drawn out tones ⟨the frustrated crowd at the rock concert started to *chant*, "We want the show to start!"⟩
synonyms intone, sing
related words bellow, belt, roar; chime, chorus
2 to produce musical sounds with the voice — see SING 1

chaos *n* a state in which everything is out of order ⟨your room is in such *chaos* that it looks as though a tornado had struck⟩
synonyms confusion, disarrangement, disarray, disorder, disorganization, havoc, hell, jumble, mess, muddle, shambles
related words anarchy, lawlessness, misrule; knot, snarl, tangle; labyrinth, maze, web; maelstrom, storm; clutter, litter, mishmash, shuffle; hodgepodge, medley, miscellany, motley
near antonyms method, pattern, plan, system
antonyms order, orderliness

chaotic *adj* lacking in order, neatness, and often cleanliness — see MESSY

chap *n, chiefly British* an adult male human being — see MAN 1

chaparral *n* a thick patch of shrubbery, small trees, or underbrush — see THICKET

chaperone *or* **chaperon** *vb* to go along with in order to provide assistance, protection, or companionship — see ACCOMPANY

chapter *n* a local unit of an organization ⟨our *chapter* of the 4-H Club came in first in the competition⟩
synonyms affiliate, branch, local
related words arm, division, wing; offshoot; lodge, post

char *vb* to burn on the surface — see SCORCH

character *n* **1** a written or printed mark that is meant to convey information to the reader ⟨the pictorial *characters* of the ancient Egyptians were long a mystery⟩
synonyms sign, symbol
related words cipher, letter, numeral; hieroglyph, pictogram, pictograph; rune
2 a person of odd or whimsical habits — see ECCENTRIC
3 conduct that conforms to an accepted standard of right and wrong — see MORALITY 1
4 overall quality as seen or judged by people in general — see REPUTATION
5 something that sets apart an individual from others of the same kind — see CHARACTERISTIC
6 the set of qualities that make a person different from other people — see INDIVIDUALITY
7 the set of qualities that makes a person, a group of people, or a thing different from others — see NATURE 1

characteristic *adj* **1** serving to identify as belonging to an individual or group ⟨the *characteristic* taste of licorice⟩
synonyms classic, distinct, distinctive, distinguishing, identifying, individual, peculiar, proper, symptomatic, typical
related words idiosyncratic; identifiable, pronounced, unmistakable; general, generic; common, normal, regular, usual; particular, special, specific; archetypal, model, paradigmatic
antonyms atypical, nontypical
2 having or showing the qualities associated with the members of a particular group or kind — see TYPICAL 1

characteristic *n* something that sets apart an individual from others of the same kind ⟨the ability to fashion tools and other *characteristics* that distinguish human beings from other animals⟩
synonyms attribute, character, feature, mark, peculiarity, point, property, quality, trait
related words badge, indication, sign; emblem, symbol, token; excellence, merit, virtue; individuality, singularity, uniqueness

characterize *vb* **1** to point out the chief quality or qualities of an individual or group ⟨how would you *characterize* the mission of this environmental organization?⟩
synonyms define, depict, describe, portray, represent
related words categorize, classify, pigeonhole, type; identify, indicate, name, specify; distinguish, individualize, mark, particularize, stamp
2 to be an important feature of ⟨an unsightly rash *characterizes* chicken pox⟩
synonyms distinguish, mark
related words differentiate; customize, individualize, particularize

characterless *adj* lacking strength of will or character — see WEAK 2

charade *n* a display of emotion or behavior that is insincere or intended to deceive — see MASQUERADE

charge *n* **1** a formal claim of criminal wrongdoing against a person ⟨*charges* of burglary and armed robbery that have yet to be proved⟩
synonyms complaint, count, indictment, rap
related words accusation, allegation; arraignment, impeachment; implication, innuendo, insinuation; censure, condemnation, denunciation; incrimination
2 a specific task with which a person or group is charged — see MISSION
3 a statement of what to do that must be obeyed by those concerned — see COMMAND 1

4 something one must do because of prior agreement — see OBLIGATION

5 the act or action of setting upon with force or violence — see ATTACK 1

6 the amount of money that is demanded as payment for something — see PRICE 1

7 the duty or function of watching or guarding for the sake of proper direction or control — see SUPERVISION 1

charge *vb* **1** to set or receive as a price ⟨any shop would *charge* $100 to repair that thing⟩
synonyms ask, command, demand
related words overcharge, undercharge; bring, fetch, sell (for); discount, mark down, mark up; assess, price, value

2 to establish or apply as a charge or penalty — see IMPOSE

3 to give a task, duty, or responsibility to — see ENTRUST 1

4 to issue orders to (someone) by right of authority — see COMMAND 1

5 to make a claim of wrongdoing against — see ACCUSE

6 to put into (something) as much as can be held or contained — see FILL 1

7 to take sudden, violent action against — see ATTACK 1

charged *adj* having or expressing great depth of feeling — see FERVENT

charisma *n* the power of irresistible attraction — see CHARM 2

charitable *adj* **1** having or showing a concern for the welfare of others ⟨a *charitable* couple who have donated a sizable chunk of their fortune to the local university⟩
synonyms altruistic, beneficent, benevolent, humanitarian, philanthropic
related words selfless, self-sacrificing; bounteous, bountiful, free, freehanded, generous, greathearted, handsome, liberal, magnanimous, munificent, openhanded, openhearted, unselfish, unsparing; compassionate, humane, kind
near antonyms self-indulgent, self-seeking; cheap, closefisted, miserly, niggardly, parsimonious, stingy, tight, tightfisted; hardhearted, pitiless, unfeeling
antonyms self-centered, selfish

2 giving or sharing in abundance and without hesitation — see GENEROUS 1

charity *n* **1** the giving of necessities and especially money to the needy ⟨after amassing a fortune in the computer industry, they devoted themselves to *charity*⟩
synonyms almsgiving, philanthropy
related words altruism, humanitarianism; beneficence, benevolence, goodwill; alms, benefaction, contribution, donation; dole, relief, welfare; endowment, fund, grant, subsidy

2 a gift of money or its equivalent to a charity, humanitarian cause, or public institution — see CONTRIBUTION

3 kind, gentle, or compassionate treatment especially towards someone who is undeserving of it — see MERCY 1

4 the capacity for feeling for another's unhappiness or misfortune — see HEART 1

charlatan *n* one who makes false claims of identity or expertise — see IMPOSTOR

charley horse *n* a painful sudden tightening of a muscle — see CRAMP

charm *n* **1** something worn or kept to bring good luck or keep away evil ⟨an old cap that I use as a *charm* for whenever I play softball⟩
synonyms amulet, fetish (*also* fetich), mascot, mojo, phylactery, talisman
related words emblem, symbol, token, totem
near antonyms curse, hex, spell
antonyms hoodoo, jinx

2 the power of irresistible attraction ⟨a young singer with the kind of *charm* that turns a performer into a star⟩
synonyms allure, appeal, attractiveness, captivation, charisma, enchantment, fascination, glamour (*also* glamor), magic, magnetism, seductiveness, witchery
related words allurement, attraction, call, lure, seduction; agreeableness, delightfulness, desirableness, niceness, pleasantness, sweetness
near antonyms disagreeableness, distastefulness, obnoxiousness, offensiveness, unpleasantness
antonyms repulsion, repulsiveness

3 a spoken word or set of words believed to have magic power — see SPELL 1

4 an ornament worn on a chain around the neck or wrist — see PENDANT

charm *vb* **1** to attract or delight as if by magic ⟨a quaint seaside village that *charms* all who visit it⟩
synonyms allure, beguile, bewitch, captivate, enchant, fascinate, magnetize, wile
related words disarm, draw, entice, lure, pull, seduce, tempt; delight, gratify, please; arrest, enrapture, enthrall (*or* enthral); entrance; appeal (to), interest, intrigue; beckon, court, invite, solicit, woo
near antonyms disgust, offend, repel, revolt; annoy, displease, irk; bore, tire, weary

2 to cast a spell on — see BEWITCH 1

charmed *adj* being or appearing to be under a magic spell — see ENCHANTED

charmer *n* a person skilled in using supernatural forces — see MAGICIAN 1

charming *adj* having an often mysterious or magical power to attract — see FASCINATING 1

chart *n* an illustration of certain features of a geographical area — see MAP

chart *vb* to work out the details of (something) in advance — see PLAN 1

charter *vb* to take or get the temporary use of (something) for a set sum — see HIRE 1

charwoman *n* a female domestic servant — see MAID 1

chase *n* **1** an animal that is hunted or killed — see PREY

2 the act of going after or in the tracks of another — see PURSUIT

chase *vb* **1** to drive or force out — see EJECT 1

2 to go after or on the track of — see FOLLOW 2

3 to seek out (game) for food or sport — see HUNT 1

chasing *n* the act of going after or in the tracks of another — see PURSUIT

chasm *n* an immeasurable depth or space — see ABYSS

chaste *adj* free from any trace of the coarse or indecent ⟨as one would expect, the minister's small talk is always *chaste*, even though he likes a joke as much as the next person⟩
synonyms clean, decent, immaculate, modest, pure
related words spotless, stainless, unblemished, un-

defiled, unsoiled, unspotted, unstained, unsullied, untainted, untarnished; decorous, proper, seemly; cultivated, refined, tasteful; harmless, innocent, innocuous, inoffensive

near antonyms blemished, defiled, soiled, spotted, stained, sullied, tainted, tarnished; improper, indecorous, ribald, unseemly; crude, tacky, tasteless, unrefined

antonyms coarse, dirty, filthy, immodest, impure, indecent, obscene, smutty, unchaste, unclean, vulgar

chastely *adv* with purity of thought and deed — see PURELY

chasten *vb* to inflict a penalty on for a fault or crime — see PUNISH

chasteness *n* the quality or state of being morally pure — see CHASTITY

chastening *adj* inflicting, involving, or serving as punishment — see PUNITIVE

chastise *vb* to inflict a penalty on for a fault or crime — see PUNISH

chastisement *n* suffering, loss, or hardship imposed in response to a crime or offense — see PUNISHMENT

chastiser *n* one who inflicts punishment in return for an injury or offense — see NEMESIS 1

chastising *adj* inflicting, involving, or serving as punishment — see PUNITIVE

chastity *n* the quality or state of being morally pure 〈a saint who is often held up as a model of *chastity*〉

synonyms chasteness, modesty, purity

related words goodness, righteousness, virtuousness; morality, probity, rectitude; decency, decorum, propriety, seemliness

near antonyms badness, evil, sinfulness, unrighteousness, wickedness; impropriety, indecency

antonyms immodesty, impurity, unchastity

chat *n* friendly, informal conversation or an instance of this 〈short *chats* between parents and teachers during the school's open house〉

synonyms chatter, chitchat, gabfest, gossip, palaver, rap, small talk, table talk, talk, tête-à-tête

related words colloquy, conference, discourse, parley, powwow, symposium; debate, dialogue (*or* dialog), exchange, give-and-take

chat *vb* to engage in casual or rambling conversation 〈the coffeehouse is a great place to meet friends and *chat* for hours〉

synonyms babble, blab, cackle, chatter, converse, gab, gabble, gas, jabber, jaw, palaver, patter, prate, prattle, rap, rattle, run on, talk, twitter, visit

related words gossip, tattle; descant, discuss, expatiate

phrases shoot the breeze

chat (with) *vb* to communicate with by means of spoken words — see TALK 1

château *n* a large impressive residence — see MANSION

chattel *n* **1** a person who is considered the property of another person — see SLAVE 1

2 chattels *pl* transportable items that one owns — see POSSESSION 2

chatter *n* friendly, informal conversation or an instance of this — see CHAT

chatter *vb* **1** to engage in casual or rambling conversation — see CHAT

2 to speak rapidly, inarticulately, and usually unintelligibly — see BABBLE 1

chatterbox *n* a person who talks constantly 〈my seat companion was a *chatterbox* who never once shut up during the whole trip〉

synonyms babbler, blabber, cackler, chatterer, conversationalist, gabbler, jabberer, magpie, prattler, talker

related words blabbermouth, gossip, gossiper, talebearer, tattler, tattletale; converser

chatterer *n* a person who talks constantly — see CHATTERBOX

chatty *adj* **1** having the style and content of everyday conversation 〈a time when campers were expected to write a *chatty* letter to their folks every week〉

synonyms colloquial, conversational, gossipy, newsy

related words casual, familiar, informal, intimate; digressive, discursive, rambling; communicative, expansive, garrulous, talkative

near antonyms ceremonious, dignified, elevated, formal, solemn, stately

antonyms bookish, literary

2 fond of talking or conversation — see TALKATIVE

chauvinism *n* excessive favoritism towards one's own country 〈their *chauvinism* blinded them to their country's faults〉

synonyms jingoism, nationalism

related words loyalty, patriotism; xenophobia

near antonyms internationalism

chauvinist *n* one who shows excessive favoritism towards his or her country — see NATIONALIST

cheap *adj* **1** costing little 〈e-mail is so popular because it's a *cheap* way to send messages〉

synonyms cut-rate, inexpensive, low, reasonable

related words moderate, popular; discounted, lowered, reduced; wholesale

near antonyms precious, priceless, valuable; increased, inflated

antonyms costly, dear, expensive, high, premium

2 of low quality 〈a *cheap* sweater that started to unravel almost as soon as I bought it〉

synonyms bad, bum, cheesy, coarse, common, cut-rate, execrable, inferior, junky, lousy, low-grade, mediocre, miserable, poor, rotten, rubbishy, second-rate, shoddy, sleazy, terrible, trashy, trumpery, wretched

related words useless, valueless, worthless; flashy, garish, gaudy, meretricious, showy, tawdry; seedy, shabby, tacky; counterfeit, fake, phony (*also* phoney), sham

near antonyms elegant, handsome, tasteful; handcrafted, polished, refined

antonyms excellent, fine, first-class, first-rate, good, high-grade, superior, top-notch

3 giving or sharing as little as possible — see STINGY 1

cheapen *vb* to lower the price or value of — see DEPRECIATE 1

cheapness *n* the quality of being overly sparing with money — see PARSIMONY

cheapskate *n* a mean grasping person who is usually stingy with money — see MISER

cheat *n* a dishonest person who uses clever means to cheat others out of something of value — see TRICKSTER 1

cheat *vb* **1** to use dishonest methods to achieve a goal 〈students who *cheat* on tests end up never knowing anything〉

synonyms fudge

related words distort, falsify, misrepresent, twist; doctor, fake, tamper (with); color, elaborate, embellish, embroider, exaggerate, magnify, pad, stretch; dodge, evade, hedge

2 to fall short in satisfying the expectation or hope of — see DISAPPOINT

3 to rob by the use of trickery or threats — see FLEECE

cheater *n* a dishonest person who uses clever means to cheat others out of something of value — see TRICKSTER 1

check *n* **1** the amount owed at a bar or restaurant or the slip of paper stating the amount ⟨diners at the fancy restaurant often look shocked when they receive the *check*⟩

synonyms bill, tab

related words invoice, receipt; account, record, statement; charge, fee; score, tally

2 a close look at or over someone or something in order to judge condition — see INSPECTION

3 a record of goods sold or services performed together with the costs due — see ¹BILL 1

4 a small sheet of plastic, paper, or paperboard showing that the bearer has a claim to something (as admittance) — see TICKET 1

5 something that limits one's freedom of action or choice — see RESTRICTION 1

check *vb* **1** to be in agreement on every point ⟨their story of what happened *checks* with the report of the eyewitness⟩

synonyms accord, agree, answer, cohere, coincide, comport, conform, correspond, dovetail, fit, go, harmonize, jibe, square, tally

related words equal, match, parallel

near antonyms contradict, dispute, gainsay; negate, nullify; clash, conflict, jar

antonyms differ (from), disagree (with)

2 to bring (something) to a standstill — see ¹HALT 1

3 to keep from exceeding a desirable degree or level (as of expression) — see CONTROL 1

check (out) *vb* to look over closely (as for judging quality or condition) — see INSPECT

checklist *n* a record of a series of items (as names or titles) usually arranged according to some system — see ¹LIST

checkmate *vb* to prevent from achieving a goal — see FRUSTRATE

checkup *n* a close look at or over someone or something in order to judge condition — see INSPECTION

cheek *n* **1** disrespectful or argumentative talk given in response to a command or request — see BACK TALK

2 shameless boldness — see EFFRONTERY

cheekiness *n* shameless boldness — see EFFRONTERY

cheeky *adj* displaying or marked by rude boldness — see NERVY 1

cheep *vb* to make a short sharp sound like a small bird — see CHIRP

cheer *n* **1** a mood characterized by high spirits and amusement and often accompanied by laughter — see MIRTH

2 a feeling of ease from grief or trouble — see COMFORT 1

3 a state of mind dominated by a particular emotion — see MOOD 1

4 cheers *pl* enthusiastic and usually public expression of approval — see APPLAUSE

cheer *vb* **1** to declare enthusiastic approval of — see ACCLAIM

2 to ease the grief or distress of — see COMFORT 1

cheer (up) *vb* **1** to become glad or hopeful ⟨*cheer up* —things are bound to get better⟩

synonyms brighten, perk (up)

related words rejoice; liven (up), revive; beam, glow, radiate, sparkle; encourage, gladden, hearten

near antonyms despair, despond; brood, fret, mope

antonyms darken, sadden

2 to fill with courage or strength of purpose — see ENCOURAGE 1

cheerful *adj* **1** having or showing a good mood or disposition ⟨a *cheerful* person who is always fun to work with and a pleasure to be around⟩

synonyms blithe, blithesome, bright, buoyant, cheery, chipper, gay, gladsome, lightsome, sunny, upbeat

related words hopeful, optimistic, sanguine; jaunty, lively, perky, sprightly, vivacious; carefree, careless, cavalier, devil-may-care, easygoing, happy-go-lucky, insouciant, lighthearted, unconcerned; boon, jolly, jovial, merry, mirthful; glad, happy, pleased

near antonyms dull, lethargic, listless, sluggish, torpid; blue, dejected, depressed, heavyhearted, melancholy, sorrowful; discontented, disgruntled, unhappy

antonyms dour, gloomy, glum, morose, saturnine, sulky, sullen

2 serving to lift one's spirits ⟨a hospital with sunny, *cheerful* rooms that are designed to make a patient's stay as pleasant as possible⟩

synonyms bright, cheering, cheery, gay, glad

related words gladdening, heartening, heartwarming; gleaming, radiant, sparkling

near antonyms discouraging, disheartening; colorless, drab, dull, lackluster, lusterless

antonyms bleak, cheerless, dark, depressing, dismal, dreary, gloomy, gray (*also* grey)

cheerfully *adv* in a cheerful or happy manner — see GAILY 1

cheerfulness *n* a mood characterized by high spirits and amusement and often accompanied by laughter — see MIRTH

cheeriness *n* a mood characterized by high spirits and amusement and often accompanied by laughter — see MIRTH

cheering *adj* **1** making one feel good inside — see HEARTWARMING

2 serving to lift one's spirits — see CHEERFUL 2

cheering *n* enthusiastic and usually public expression of approval — see APPLAUSE

cheerless *adj* causing or marked by an atmosphere lacking in cheer — see GLOOMY 1

cheery *adj* **1** having or showing a good mood or disposition — see CHEERFUL 1

2 serving to lift one's spirits — see CHEERFUL 2

cheesy *adj* **1** marked by an obvious lack of style or good taste — see TACKY 1

2 of low quality — see CHEAP 2

chef *n* a person who prepares food by some manner of heating — see COOK

cherish *vb* **1** to feel passion, devotion, or tenderness for — see LOVE 2

2 to hold dear — see LOVE 1

3 to keep in one's mind or heart — see HARBOR 1

THESAURUS

cherished *adj* granted special treatment or attention — see DARLING 1

chest *n* a covered rectangular container for storing or transporting things ⟨a *chest* containing almost every tool that the home do-it-yourselfer is likely to need⟩
synonyms box, caddy, case, casket, locker, trunk
related words crate; footlocker; coffer, safe, safe-deposit box, strongbox; coffin; compartment, vault

chesterfield *n* a long upholstered piece of furniture designed for several sitters — see COUCH

chew *vb* to crush or grind with the teeth — see BITE (ON)

chew out *vb* to criticize (someone) severely or angrily especially for personal failings — see SCOLD

chew over *vb* 1 to give serious and careful thought to — see PONDER
2 to talk about (an issue) usually from various points of view and for the purpose of arriving at a decision or opinion — see DISCUSS

chewy *adj* not easily chewed — see TOUGH 1

chic *adj* being in the latest or current fashion — see STYLISH

chicanery *n* the use of clever underhanded actions to achieve an end — see TRICKERY

chick *n, slang* a young usually unmarried woman — see GIRL 1

chicken *adj* having or showing a shameful lack of courage — see COWARDLY

chicken *n* a person who shows a shameful lack of courage in the face of danger — see COWARD

chickenhearted *adj* having or showing a shameful lack of courage — see COWARDLY

chide *vb* to criticize (someone) usually gently so as to correct a fault — see REBUKE 1

chief *adj* 1 coming before all others in importance — see FOREMOST 1
2 highest in rank or authority — see HEAD

chief *n* the person (as an employer or supervisor) who tells people and especially workers what to do — see BOSS

chiefly *adv* for the most part ⟨our video collection consists *chiefly* of comedies, but we have a few horror movies⟩
synonyms altogether, basically, by and large, generally, largely, mainly, mostly, overall, predominantly, primarily, principally, substantially
related words nearly, practically, virtually; approximately, broadly, roughly; commonly, frequently, normally, ordinarily, usually; incompletely, partially, partly
phrases in general, on the whole
near antonyms completely, entirely, fully, totally, wholly; barely, hardly, marginally, minimally, scarcely

child *n* 1 a young person who is between infancy and adulthood ⟨an imaginative animated film that appeals to adults as well as to *children*⟩
synonyms bairn [*chiefly Scottish*], cub, juvenile, kid, youngster, youth
related words adolescent, minor; schoolboy, schoolchild, schoolgirl; moppet, nestling, toddler, tot, tyke; brat, imp, squirt, urchin, whippersnapper; cherub; preteen, subteen, teenager, teenybopper; lad, nipper, shaver, stripling, tad; bobbysoxer, hoyden, tomboy
near antonyms golden-ager, oldster, senior citizen
antonyms adult, grown-up
2 a recently born person — see BABY

childbearing *n* the act or process of giving birth to children — see CHILDBIRTH

childbirth *n* the act or process of giving birth to children ⟨women who choose to undergo *childbirth* without the use of anesthetics and other drugs⟩
synonyms childbearing, delivery, labor, parturition
related words pains; pregnancy; abortion, miscarriage; cesarean section (*also* cesarian section)

childhood *n* the state or time of being a child ⟨enjoy your *childhood* —it won't last forever⟩
synonyms youth
related words boyhood, girlhood; adolescence, minority; immaturity, juvenility; babyhood, infancy
near antonyms majority
antonyms adulthood

childish *adj* having or showing the annoying qualities (as silliness) associated with children ⟨you almost spoiled the ceremony for everyone with your *childish* giggling⟩
synonyms adolescent, babyish, immature, infantile, juvenile, kiddish, puerile
related words boyish, girlish; childlike, innocent, naive (*or* naïve), simple, unsophisticated
near antonyms experienced, sophisticated, worldly-wise
antonyms adult, grown-up, mature

child's play *n* 1 something of little importance — see TRIFLE
2 something that is easy to do — see CINCH

chill *adj* 1 lacking in friendliness or warmth of feeling — see COLD 2
2 uncomfortably cool — see CHILLY 1

chill *n* an uncomfortable degree of coolness ⟨there's a *chill* in the air, so you'd better wear a sweater⟩
synonyms bite, bitterness, bleakness, chilliness, nip, rawness, sharpness
related words briskness, crispness; coldness, frigidity, frigidness, frostiness, iciness; cold, freeze, snap
near antonyms balminess, warmth

chill *vb* to cause to lose heat — see COOL 1

chilliness *n* an uncomfortable degree of coolness — see CHILL

chilling *adj* uncomfortably cool — see CHILLY 1

chilly *adj* 1 uncomfortably cool ⟨those *chilly* nights when a warm fire can be especially comforting⟩
synonyms bitter, bleak, chill, chilling, nippy, raw, sharp
related words brisk, crisp; arctic, cold, freezing, frigid, frosty, icy
near antonyms balmy, warm
2 lacking in friendliness or warmth of feeling — see COLD 2

chime *vb* to make the clear sound heard when metal vibrates — see RING 1

chime *n, usually* **chimes** *pl* a series of short high ringing sounds — see TINKLE

chime in *vb* to cause a disruption in a conversation or discussion — see INTERRUPT

chimera *n* a conception or image created by the imagination and having no objective reality — see FANTASY 1

chimerical *adj* not real and existing only in the imagination — see IMAGINARY

chine *n* a column of bones supporting the trunk of a vertebrate animal — see SPINE

chink *n* an irregular usually narrow break in a surface created by pressure — see CRACK 1

chink *vb* to make a repeated sharp light ringing sound — see JINGLE

chip *n* 1 a small flat piece separated from a whole ⟨wood *chips* were spread over the ground between the plants⟩
synonyms flake, sliver, splint, splinter
related words bit, disk (*or* disc), fragment, particle, scrap, shard; shiver, smithereens; shred, tatter; clipping, paring, shaving, snippet; leaf, sheet, slice; chunk, hunk, lump, slab
2 a V-shaped cut usually on an edge or a surface — see NOTCH 1
3 **chips** *pl* something (as pieces of stamped metal or printed paper) customarily and legally used as a medium of exchange, a measure of value, or a means of payment — see MONEY

chip in *vb* to make a donation as part of a group effort — see CONTRIBUTE 1

chipper *adj* 1 enjoying health and vigor — see HEALTHY 1
2 having or showing a good mood or disposition — see CHEERFUL 1

chirp *vb* to make a short sharp sound like a small bird ⟨the sparrows were *chirping* up a storm in the backyard⟩
synonyms cheep, chirrup, peep, pipe, tweet, twitter
related words cackle, chatter, jabber; sing, trill, warble

chirr *n* a monotonous sound like that of an insect in motion — see HUM

chirrup *vb* to make a short sharp sound like a small bird — see CHIRP

chisel *vb* to rob by the use of trickery or threats — see FLEECE

chitchat *n* friendly, informal conversation or an instance of this — see CHAT

chivalrous *adj* having, characterized by, or arising from a dignified and generous nature — see NOBLE 2

chivy *vb* to thrust oneself upon (another) without invitation — see BOTHER 1

chock–full *or* **chockful** *adj* containing or seeming to contain the greatest quantity or number possible — see FULL 1

choice *adj* having qualities that appeal to a refined taste ⟨*choice* chocolates for which chocolate lovers are willing to pay extra⟩
synonyms dainty, delicate, elegant, exquisite, rare, select
related words elite, exclusive; excellent, outstanding, premium, prime, superior
near antonyms coarse, gross, vulgar; commercial, mass-produced, popular; common, ordinary; average, mediocre, run-of-the-mill, second-rate

choice *n* 1 the power, right, or opportunity to choose ⟨you have no *choice* : you have to go to school⟩
synonyms alternative, discretion, option, pick, preference, way
related words say, voice, vote; inclination, liking, partiality, penchant, predilection, proclivity, propensity, tendency; discernment, judgment (*or* judgement), perspicacity
near antonyms coercion, duress, force; duty, obligation
2 a person or thing that is chosen ⟨my *choice* for best song of all time⟩

synonyms pick, selection
related words favorite, like, liking, preference; elective, option; appointment, designation, nomination; appointee, candidate, nominee
3 individuals carefully selected as being the best of a class — see ELITE
4 the act or power of making one's own choices or decisions — see FREE WILL
5 the act or process of selecting — see SELECTION 1

choir *n* an organized group of singers — see CHORUS 1

choke *vb* 1 to keep (someone) from breathing by exerting pressure on the windpipe ⟨let go of my throat—you're *choking* me!⟩
synonyms garrote (*or* garotte), strangle, throttle
related words asphyxiate, smother, suffocate
near antonyms restore, resuscitate, revive
2 to experience complete or partial blockage of the windpipe ⟨the recommended procedure for helping someone who is *choking*⟩
synonyms gag
related words heave, retch, throw up, vomit; asphyxiate, smother, suffocate
near antonyms breathe, respire
3 to be or cause to be killed by lack of breathable air — see SMOTHER 1
4 to prevent passage through — see CLOG 1

choke (back) *vb* to refrain from openly showing or uttering — see SUPPRESS 2

choker *n* an ornamental chain or string (as of beads) worn around the neck — see NECKLACE

choleric *adj* easily irritated or annoyed — see IRRITABLE

chomp (on) *vb* to crush or grind with the teeth — see BITE (ON)

choose *vb* 1 to decide to accept (someone or something) from a group of possibilities ⟨*choose* a computer that best suits your needs⟩
synonyms cull, elect, handpick, name, opt (for), pick, prefer, select, single (out), take
related words appoint, designate, nominate, tab; accept, adopt, embrace, espouse
near antonyms discard, jettison, throw away, throw out
antonyms decline, refuse, reject, turn down
2 to see fit ⟨you can wear whatever you *choose* to the party⟩
synonyms like, want, will, wish
related words crave, desire, fancy, hanker (for), hunger (for), long (for), yearn (for); decide, determine, resolve
3 to come to a judgment after discussion or consideration — see DECIDE 1

chooser *n* someone with the right or responsibility for making a selection — see SELECTOR

choosing *n* the act or process of selecting — see SELECTION 1

choosy *or* **choosey** *adj* 1 hard to please — see FINICKY
2 tending to select carefully — see SELECTIVE

chop *n* a hard strike with a part of the body or an instrument — see ¹BLOW

chop *vb* to cut into small pieces ⟨*chop* the onions before adding them to the pot⟩
synonyms dice, hash, mince
related words chip, grind, mash, puree, slice

chop (down) *vb* to bring down by cutting — see FELL 2

THESAURUS

choppy *adj* lacking in steadiness or regularity of occurrence — see FITFUL

chorale *n* 1 a religious song — see HYMN
2 an organized group of singers — see CHORUS 1

chore *n* 1 a piece of work that needs to be done regularly ⟨everyone in this household is expected to do weekly *chores*⟩
synonyms assignment, duty, job, stint, task
related words endeavor, enterprise, project, undertaking; care, charge, commission, responsibility; function, mission, office; errand; circuit, round, route
2 a dull, unpleasant, or difficult piece of work ⟨cleaning everything out of the attic was a real *chore*⟩
synonyms headache, labor
related words drudgery, grind; effort, strain, sweat; burden, load, weight; bother, nuisance, trouble
near antonyms breeze, child's play, cinch, duck soup, snap

chortle *n* an explosive sound that is a sign of amusement — see LAUGH 1

chorus *n* 1 an organized group of singers ⟨the annual Christmas program presented by the school's *chorus*⟩
synonyms choir, chorale, glee club
related words ensemble; minstrelsy
2 a part of a song or hymn that is repeated every so often ⟨the whole congregation will join in for the *chorus*⟩
synonyms burden, refrain
related words repeat

chosen *adj* singled out from a number or group as more to one's liking — see SELECT 1

chow *n* 1 food eaten or prepared for eating at one time — see MEAL
2 substances intended to be eaten — see FOOD

christen *vb* to give a name to — see NAME 1

Christian name *n* a name that is placed before one's family name — see FORENAME

Christmastime *n* the season celebrating Christmas — see YULETIDE

chronic *adj* being such by habit and not likely to change — see HABITUAL 1

chronicle *n* 1 a relating of events usually in the order in which they happened — see ACCOUNT 1
2 an account of important events in the order in which they happened — see HISTORY 1

chronicler *n* a student or writer of history — see HISTORIAN

chronometer *n* a device to measure time — see TIMEPIECE

chubbiness *n* the condition of having an excess of body fat — see CORPULENCE

chubby *adj* having an excess of body fat — see FAT 1

chuck *vb* to send through the air especially with a quick forward motion of the arm — see THROW

chuckle *n* an explosive sound that is a sign of amusement — see LAUGH 1

chum *n* a person who has a strong liking for and trust in another — see FRIEND 1

chum *vb* to come or be together as friends — see ASSOCIATE 1

chumminess *n* the state of being in a very personal or private relationship — see FAMILIARITY 1

chummy *adj* closely acquainted — see FAMILIAR 1

chump *n* one who is easily deceived or cheated — see DUPE

chunk *n* a small uneven mass — see LUMP 1

chunky *adj* 1 having small pieces or lumps spread throughout ⟨*chunky* peanut butter adds an interesting layer of texture when paired with jelly⟩
synonyms clumpy, curdy, lumpy, nubbly, nubby
related words ropy, thick, viscous; clabbered [*dialect*], clotted, coagulated, congealed, curdled, gelled, thickened
antonyms smooth
2 being compact and broad in build and often short in stature — see STOCKY
3 having or being of relatively great depth or extent from one surface to its opposite — see THICK 1

church *n* 1 a building for public worship and especially Christian worship ⟨a city that is noted for its many historic *churches*⟩
synonyms kirk [*chiefly Scottish*], tabernacle, temple
related words abbey, bethel, cathedral, chapel, oratory, sanctuary, shrine; meetinghouse; mosque, pagoda, synagogue (*or* synagog)
2 a body of persons gathered for religious worship — see CONGREGATION 1

churchly *adj* of or relating to a church — see ECCLESIASTICAL

churl *n* a person whose behavior is offensive to others — see JERK 1

churlish *adj* having or showing crudely insensitive or impolite manners — see CLOWNISH

churn *vb* 1 to be in a state of violent rolling motion — see SEETHE 1
2 to cause (as a liquid) to move about in a circle especially repeatedly — see STIR 1

chutzpah *also* **chutzpa** *or* **hutzpah** *or* **hutzpa** *n* shameless boldness — see EFFRONTERY

cinch *n* something that is easy to do ⟨the clear instructions made setting up the audiovisual system a *cinch*⟩
synonyms breeze, child's play, duck soup, picnic, pushover, snap
related words nothing; sitting duck
phrases piece of cake
near antonyms bother, nuisance, trouble
antonyms chore, headache, labor

cinch *vb* to make sure, certain, or safe — see ENSURE

cincture *n* a strip of flexible material (as leather) worn around the waist — see ²BELT

cinema *n* 1 the art or business of making a movie — see MOVIE 2
2 a building or part of a building where movies are shown — see THEATER 1

cipher *n* the numerical symbol 0 or the absence of number or quantity represented by it — see ZERO 1

ciphering *n* the act or process of performing mathematical operations to find a value — see CALCULATION

circle *n* 1 something with a perfectly round circumference ⟨a *circle* of columns surrounds the memorial to the fallen heroes⟩
synonyms ring, round
related words circlet; ellipse, loop, oval; ball, globe, orb, sphere
2 a circular strip — see RING 2
3 a group of people sharing a common interest and relating together socially — see GANG 2
4 a series of events or actions that repeat them-

selves regularly and in the same order — see CYCLE 1

circle *vb* **1** to form a circle around — see SURROUND

2 to pass completely around — see ENCIRCLE 1

circuitous *adj* **1** not straightforward or direct — see INDIRECT

2 using or containing more words than necessary to express an idea — see WORDY

circular *adj* not straightforward or direct — see INDIRECT

circular *n* a short printed publication with no cover or with a paper cover — see PAMPHLET

circulate *vb* **1** to cause to be known over a considerable area or by many people — see SPREAD 1

2 to make (as a piece of information) the subject of common talk without any authority or confirmation of accuracy — see RUMOR

circumference *n* **1** the distance around a round body ⟨the *circumference* of the earth at the equator⟩

synonyms girth

related words waistline; equator; diameter, perimeter

2 the line or relatively narrow space that marks the outer limit of something — see BORDER 1

circumlocution *n* the use of too many words to express an idea — see VERBIAGE

circumlocutory *adj* using or containing more words than necessary to express an idea — see WORDY

circumnavigate *vb* to pass completely around — see ENCIRCLE 1

circumscribe *vb* **1** to set bounds or an upper limit for — see LIMIT 1

2 to mark the limits of — see LIMIT 2

circumscribed *adj* having distinct or certain limits — see LIMITED 1

circumspect *adj* having or showing a close attentiveness to avoiding danger or trouble — see CAREFUL 1

circumspection *n* a close attentiveness to avoiding danger — see CAUTION 1

circumstance *n* **1** a state or end that seemingly has been decided beforehand — see FATE 1

2 something that happens — see EVENT 1

3 the uncertain course of events — see CHANCE 1

circumstantial *adj* including many small descriptive features — see DETAILED 1

circumvent *vb* **1** to avoid having to comply with (something) especially through cleverness ⟨students who try to *circumvent* the school's dress code⟩

synonyms dodge, sidestep, skirt

related words avoid, duck, elude, escape, eschew, evade, shake, shun; disobey, disregard, flout, ignore

phrases get around

near antonyms accede (to), acquiesce (to), assent (to)

antonyms comply (with), follow, keep, obey, observe

2 to avoid by going around — see DETOUR 1

circus *n* **1** a large usually roofless building for sporting events with tiers of seats for spectators — see STADIUM

2 a place of uproar or confusion — see MADHOUSE 2

citadel *n* a structure or place from which one can resist attack — see FORT

citation *n* **1** a formal expression of praise — see ENCOMIUM

2 a formal recognition of an achievement or praiseworthy deed — see COMMENDATION 1

3 a passage referred to, repeated, or offered as an example — see QUOTATION

cite *vb* **1** to give as an example — see QUOTE 1

2 to make reference to or speak about briefly but specifically — see MENTION 1

citify *vb* to accustom to the ways of the city ⟨we've become so *citified* that many people have no idea where their food comes from⟩

synonyms urbanize

related words civilize, cultivate

citizen *n* **1** a person who owes allegiance to a government and is protected by it ⟨conscientious *citizens* who regard voting as a duty as well as a right⟩

synonyms national, subject

related words compatriot, countryman; inhabitant, native, nonimmigrant, resident

near antonyms foreigner, stranger; immigrant, nonnative

antonyms alien, noncitizen

2 a person who lives in a town on a permanent basis — see BURGHER

city *n* a thickly settled, highly populated area ⟨commuters who drive every day between their homes in the suburbs and their jobs in the *city*⟩

synonyms burg, megalopolis, metropolis, municipality, town

related words borough; conurbation; urban sprawl; suburbia

civil *adj* **1** of or relating to a nation — see NATIONAL

2 showing consideration, courtesy, and good manners — see POLITE 1

civility *n* **1** an act or utterance that is a customary show of good manners ⟨after the usual *civilities*, the parents and the principal had a serious talk about the boy⟩

synonyms amenity, courtesy, formality, gesture

related words ceremony, observance, rite, ritual; etiquette, manners, proprieties; greetings, regards, respects; favor, grace, kindness

2 speech or behavior that is a sign of good breeding — see POLITENESS

civilization *n* **1** the way people live at a particular time and place ⟨a study unit on the advanced *civilization* created by the Mayas over a thousand years ago⟩

synonyms culture, life, lifestyle, society

related words customs, manners, mores, values; folklore, heritage, tradition

2 a high level of taste and enlightenment as a result of extensive intellectual training and exposure to the arts — see CULTURE 1

civilized *adj* having or showing a taste for the fine arts and gracious living — see CULTIVATED

clack *vb* to make a series of short sharp noises — see RATTLE 1

claim *n* **1** an entitlement to something ⟨I'm announcing my *claim* to that last slice of pizza⟩

synonyms call, pretense (*or* pretence), pretension, right

related words birthright, prerogative; favor, privilege; refusal

2 a legal right to participation in the advantages, profits, and responsibility of something — see INTEREST 1

THESAURUS

3 a solemn and often public declaration of the truth or existence of something — see PROTESTATION

4 something that someone insists upon having — see DEMAND 1

claim *vb* **1** to state as a fact usually forcefully ⟨people who *claim* that they have been kidnapped by aliens from other worlds⟩

synonyms affirm, allege, assert, aver, avouch, avow, contend, declare, insist, maintain, profess, protest, warrant

related words announce, broadcast, proclaim; argue, rationalize, reason; confirm, justify, vindicate; defend, support, uphold

near antonyms disavow, disclaim, disown; challenge, dispute, question; confute, disprove, rebut, refute; contradict

antonyms deny, gainsay

2 to ask for (something) earnestly or with authority — see DEMAND 1

clairvoyance *n* the power of seeing or knowing about things that are not present to the senses ⟨people who claim to have *clairvoyance* are sometimes asked to help locate missing persons⟩

synonyms extrasensory perception, sixth sense

related words foreknowledge, foresight, prescience; telepathy

clamber *vb* to move (as up or over something) often with the help of the hands in holding or pulling — see CLIMB 1

clamor *n* **1** a violent shouting ⟨a *clamor* arose from the crowd as the prisoner was brought forward⟩

synonyms howl, hubbub, hue and cry, hullabaloo, noise, outcry, roar, tumult, uproar

related words clangor, din, jangle, racket

near antonyms mumble, mumbling, murmur, murmuring, rumble, rumbling

2 loud, confused, and usually unharmonious sound — see NOISE 1

clamor (for) *vb* to ask for (something) earnestly or with authority — see DEMAND 1

clamorous *adj* **1** engaging in or marked by loud and insistent cries especially of protest — see VOCIFEROUS

2 full of or characterized by the presence of noise — see NOISY 2

3 marked by a high volume of sound — see LOUD 1

clamp *vb* to put securely in place or in a desired position — see FASTEN 2

clamp down (on) *vb* to put a stop to (something) by the use of force — see QUELL 1

clam up *vb* to stop talking — see SHUT UP

clan *n* **1** a group of people sharing a common interest and relating together socially — see GANG 2

2 a group of persons who come from the same ancestor — see FAMILY 1

clandestine *adj* undertaken or done so as to escape being observed or known by others — see SECRET 1

clang *n* the loud sound made when metal strikes metal ⟨the horseshoe hit the stake with a satisfying *clang*⟩

synonyms clangor, clank, clash

related words chime, dingdong, peel, ring; clink, jangle, jingle, tinkle; clap, clop, crack, crash

clangor *n* **1** loud, confused, and usually unharmonious sound — see NOISE 1

2 the loud sound made when metal strikes metal — see CLANG

clangorous *adj* **1** full of or characterized by the presence of noise — see NOISY 2

2 making loud, confused, and usually unharmonious sounds — see NOISY 1

3 marked by a high volume of sound — see LOUD 1

clank *n* the loud sound made when metal strikes metal — see CLANG

clannish *adj* bound together by feelings of very close association — see CLOSE-KNIT

clap *n* **1** a loud explosive sound ⟨a *clap* of thunder that woke the whole house up⟩

synonyms bang, blast, boom, crack, crash, pop, report, slam, smash, snap, thwack, whack

related words clang, clangor, clank, clash; knock, rap, tap; clamor, howl, hubbub, hue and cry, hullabaloo, outcry, roar, tumult, uproar

2 a hard strike with a part of the body or an instrument — see ¹BLOW

clap *vb* to deliver a blow to (someone or something) usually in a strong vigorous manner — see HIT 1

claptrap *n* **1** language, behavior, or ideas that are absurd and contrary to good sense — see NONSENSE 1

2 unintelligible or meaningless talk — see GIBBERISH

clarification *n* a statement that makes something clear — see EXPLANATION 1

clarify *vb* **1** to remove usually visible impurities from ⟨*clarify* the melted butter by skimming off the milky bits⟩

synonyms clear, distill, filter, purify

related words process, refine; clean, cleanse, purge; extract, leach; screen, sieve, sift

near antonyms cloud, dull, muddy; contaminate, dirty, soil

2 to make plain or understandable — see EXPLAIN 1

clarity *n* **1** the state or quality of being easily seen through ⟨mountain streams with water of incredible *clarity*⟩

synonyms clearness, limpidity, limpidness, transparency

related words lucidity, lucidness, translucency; brightness, brilliance, effulgence, luminosity, luminousness; definition, resolution, sharpness

near antonyms fogginess, haziness, murkiness

antonyms cloudiness, opacity, opaqueness

2 clearness of expression — see SIMPLICITY 2

clash *n* **1** a physical dispute between opposing individuals or groups — see FIGHT 1

2 the loud sound made when metal strikes metal — see CLANG

clash *vb* to be out of harmony or agreement usually noticeably ⟨the colors of your shirt and pants *clash*⟩ ⟨Mom's idea of proper dress often *clashes* with mine⟩

synonyms collide, conflict, jar

related words mismatch; battle, combat, fight, war (against); chafe, gall, grate, jangle; differ, disagree

near antonyms agree, coincide, correspond

antonyms blend, harmonize, match

clash (with) *vb* to oppose (someone) in physical conflict — see FIGHT 1

clashing *adj* not being in agreement or harmony — see INCONSISTENT

clasp *n* the act or manner of holding — see HOLD 1

clasp *vb* **1** to put one's arms around and press tightly — see EMBRACE 1

2 to reach for and take hold of by embracing with the fingers or arms — see TAKE 1

class *n* **1** one of the segments of society into which people are grouped ⟨a politician who appeals to people of every *class*⟩

synonyms caste, estate, folk, order, stratum

related words bracket, echelon, grade, layer, level, tier; place, position, rank, standing, status; grouping, hierarchy, stratification; clan, family, people, race, tribe

2 one of the units into which a whole is divided on the basis of a common characteristic ⟨a new *class* of wireless devices that could be used for Internet access as well as personal communication⟩

synonyms bracket, category, division, family, grade, group, kind, order, rank(s), set, species, type

related words description, feather, ilk, nature, sort; branch, section, subdivision, subgroup, variety; breed, race; classification, heading, label, rubric, title

3 a number of persons or things that are grouped together because they have something in common — see SORT 1

4 a series of lectures on a subject — see COURSE 2

5 degree of excellence — see QUALITY 1

6 dignified or restrained beauty of form, appearance, or style — see ELEGANCE

7 high position within society — see RANK 2

class *vb* to arrange or assign according to type — see CLASSIFY 1

classic *adj* **1** constituting, serving as, or worthy of being a pattern to be imitated — see MODEL

2 of the very best kind — see EXCELLENT

3 serving to identify as belonging to an individual or group — see CHARACTERISTIC 1

classic *n* **1** someone of such unequaled perfection as to deserve imitation — see IDEAL 1

2 something (as a work of art) that is a great achievement and often its creator's greatest achievement — see MASTERPIECE

3 the most perfect type or example — see QUINTESSENCE 1

classical *adj* based on customs usually handed down from a previous generation — see TRADITIONAL 1

classify *vb* **1** to arrange or assign according to type ⟨*classify* the baseball cards in your collection on the basis of rarity⟩

synonyms assort, break down, categorize, class, grade, group, peg, place, range, rank, separate, sort

related words arrange, order, organize, systematize; alphabetize, catalog (*or* catalogue), codify, file, index, list; pigeonhole, shelve; distinguish, identify, recognize; cull, screen, sift, winnow

near antonyms confuse, disarrange, jumble, lump, mix (up), scramble

2 to put into a particular arrangement — see ORDER 1

clatter *n* a state of noisy, confused activity — see COMMOTION

clatter *vb* to make a series of short sharp noises — see RATTLE 1

clattering *adj* full of or characterized by the presence of noise — see NOISY 2

clattery *adj* full of or characterized by the presence of noise — see NOISY 2

clean *adj* **1** free from dirt or stain ⟨although the soccer team always starts out with *clean* uniforms, they don't stay that way for long⟩

synonyms immaculate, spick-and-span (*or* spic-and-span), spotless, stainless, unsoiled, unsullied

related words pure, taintless, undefiled, unpolluted, untainted, wholesome; cleanly, hygienic, sanitary; bleached, cleansed, purified, whitened; milky, snowy, white; flawless, unblemished; bright, shiny, sparkling

near antonyms dingy, greasy, grimy, mucky, muddy; defiled, polluted, tainted; blackened, discolored

antonyms besmirched, dirty, filthy, foul, grubby, soiled, spotted, stained, sullied, unclean

2 following or according to the rules — see FAIR 3

3 free from any trace of the coarse or indecent — see CHASTE

4 trying all possibilities — see EXHAUSTIVE

clean *adv* to a full extent or degree — see FULLY 1

clean *vb* **1** to make clean ⟨we *cleaned* the clothes before donating them to charity⟩

synonyms cleanse

related words decontaminate, purge, purify; disinfect, sanitize; brush, dry-clean, dust, launder, mop, rinse, scour, scrub, sweep, wash, wipe; brighten, deodorize, freshen, spruce (up), sweeten; pick up, straighten (up), tidy

near antonyms begrime, muddy; defile, pollute, taint; blacken, discolor

antonyms besmirch, dirty, foul, soil, spot, stain, sully

2 to take the internal organs out of — see GUT

clean (out) *vb* to make complete use of — see DEPLETE

clean (up) *vb* to remove objectionable parts from — see CENSOR

cleaner *n* a substance used for cleaning ⟨a kitchen shelf loaded with household *cleaners*⟩

synonyms cleanser, detergent, soap

related words disinfectant, purifier, solvent

cleanse *vb* **1** to free from moral guilt or blemish especially ceremonially — see PURIFY 1

2 to make clean — see CLEAN 1

cleanser *n* a substance used for cleaning — see CLEANER

cleansing *n* the act or fact of freeing from sin or moral guilt — see PURIFICATION

clear *adj* **1** easily seen through ⟨the *clear* glass walls of the aquarium's giant ocean tank⟩

synonyms limpid, liquid, lucent, pellucid, transparent

related words colorless, uncolored; lucid, translucent; crystal, crystalline, glassy, sparkling; bright, brilliant, effulgent, luminous

near antonyms foggy, hazy, misty, murky, smoky (*also* smokey)

antonyms cloudy, nontransparent, opaque

2 not subject to misinterpretation or more than one interpretation ⟨the meaning of her broad smile was *clear* to the whole class⟩

synonyms apparent, broad, clear-cut, decided, distinct, evident, lucid, manifest, obvious, open-and-shut, palpable, patent, perspicuous, plain, transparent, unambiguous, unequivocal, unmistakable

related words comprehendible, comprehensible, decipherable, fathomable, graspable, intelligible, knowable, understandable; self-evident, self-explanatory; simple, uncomplicated; overt, undisguised; appreciable, perceptible, recognizable,

THESAURUS

sensible, tangible; discernible, noticeable, observable, visible

near antonyms incomprehensible, unfathomable, unintelligible, unknowable; imperceptible, inappreciable, insensible; delicate, subtle

antonyms dark, enigmatic, indistinct, mysterious, obscure, unclear; ambiguous, equivocal

3 having or showing a mind free from doubt — see CERTAIN 2

4 not stormy or cloudy — see FAIR 1

5 serving to put an end to all debate or questioning — see CONCLUSIVE 1

6 allowing passage without obstruction — see OPEN 1

7 free from guilt or blame — see INNOCENT 2

clear *vb* **1** to rid the surface of (as an area) from things in the way ⟨the early settlers worked hard to *clear* the land for crops⟩

synonyms free, open, unblock

related words ease, facilitate, loosen (up), smooth, unclog, unstop

near antonyms clog, dam, obstruct, plug, stop

antonyms block

2 to set (a person or thing) free of something that encumbers — see RID

3 to give what is owed for — see PAY 2

4 to remove the contents of — see EMPTY

5 to remove usually visible impurities from — see CLARIFY 1

6 to set free from entanglement or difficulty — see EXTRICATE

7 to arrange clear passage of (something) by removing obstructions — see OPEN 2

8 to free from a charge of wrongdoing — see EXCULPATE

9 to give official acceptance of something as satisfactory — see APPROVE

10 to take away from a place or position — see REMOVE 2

clear (up) *vb* to make plain or understandable — see EXPLAIN 1

clearance *n* the approval by someone in authority for the doing of something — see PERMISSION

clear–cut *adj* **1** not subject to misinterpretation or more than one interpretation — see CLEAR 2

2 so clearly expressed as to leave no doubt about the meaning — see EXPLICIT

cleared *adj* allowing passage without obstruction — see OPEN 1

clearheaded *adj* **1** having full use of one's mind and control over one's actions — see SANE

2 not having one's mind affected by alcohol — see SOBER 1

clearing *n* a small area of usually open land — see FIELD 1

clearness *n* the state or quality of being easily seen through — see CLARITY 1

clear out *vb* **1** to cause (members of a group) to move widely apart — see SCATTER 1

2 to get free from a dangerous or confining situation — see ESCAPE 1

3 to leave a place often for another — see GO 2

clear–sighted *adj* **1** having or showing a practical cleverness or judgment — see SHREWD

2 having unusually keen vision — see SHARP-EYED

cleave *vb* to hold to something firmly as if by adhesion — see STICK 1

cleft *n* an irregular usually narrow break in a surface created by pressure — see CRACK 1

clemency *n* kind, gentle, or compassionate treatment especially towards someone who is undeserving of it — see MERCY 1

clement *adj* marked by temperatures that are neither too high nor too low ⟨Hawaii is known for its delightfully *clement* climate⟩

synonyms balmy, equable, gentle, mild, moderate, temperate

related words clear, cloudless, fair, rainless, sunny, sunshiny; calm, halcyon, peaceful, placid, tranquil; delightful, fine, pleasant

near antonyms blustering, blustery, breezy, gusty; foggy, hazy, misty; bleak, cloudy, dirty, foul, nasty, overcast, rainy, raw, rough, squally, stormy, sunless

antonyms harsh, inclement, intemperate, severe

clench *vb* to have or keep in one's hands — see HOLD 1

clergyman *n* a person specially trained and authorized to conduct religious services in a Christian church ⟨a special memorial service that attracted *clergymen* from all over the city⟩

synonyms cleric, deacon, divine, dominie, ecclesiastic, father, minister, padre, parson, preacher, priest, reverend

related words evangelist, missionary; deaconess, priestess; dean, pastor, rector, vicar; chaplain, confessor; canon, curate; friar, mendicant, monastic, monk, religious

antonyms layman

cleric *n* a person specially trained and authorized to conduct religious services in a Christian church — see CLERGYMAN

clerical *adj* of, relating to, or characteristic of the clergy ⟨*clerical* duties such as providing spiritual counseling and leading classes in Bible study⟩

synonyms ministerial, pastoral, priestly, sacerdotal

related words evangelical, missionary; apostolic, canonical, episcopal, papal, patriarchal, pontifical; churchly, ecclesiastical (*or* ecclesiastic); divine, holy, religious, sacramental; rabbinic (*or* rabbinical)

antonyms lay, nonclerical

clerk *n* **1** a person whose job is to keep records ⟨you'll need to get a copy of your birth certificate from the office of the town *clerk*⟩

synonyms register, registrar, scribe

related words archivist, bookkeeper, recorder; annalist, chronicler

2 a person employed to sell goods or services especially in a store — see SALESPERSON

clever *adj* **1** showing a use of the imagination and creativity especially in inventing ⟨an inventor who was constantly coming up with *clever* devices for doing everyday chores⟩

synonyms artful, creative, imaginative, ingenious

related words innovative, novel, original; convenient, handy, practical, useful; complex, sophisticated; adroit, deft, dexterous (*also* dextrous); brainy, intelligent, sharp, smart

near antonyms dull, pedestrian, stodgy

antonyms uncreative, unimaginative

2 having or showing quickness of mind — see INTELLIGENT 1

3 skillful with the hands — see DEXTEROUS 1

4 given to or marked by mature intelligent humor — see WITTY

cleverness *n* **1** mental skill or quickness — see DEXTERITY 1

2 subtle or imaginative ability in inventing, devising, or executing something — see SKILL 1

cliché *n* an idea or expression that has been used by many people — see COMMONPLACE

click *vb* **1** to form a close personal relationship — see COMMUNE

2 to turn out as planned or desired — see SUCCEED 1

client *n* a person who buys a product or uses a service from a business — see CUSTOMER 1

cliff *n* a steep wall of rock, earth, or ice ⟨the *cliff* rises 200 feet from the island's south shore⟩
synonyms bluff, crag, escarpment, palisade, precipice, scarp
related words tor; bulwark, embankment

climate *n* **1** a special quality or impression associated with something — see AURA

2 the circumstances, conditions, or objects by which one is surrounded — see ENVIRONMENT

climax *n* **1** a point in a chain of events at which an important change (as in one's fortunes) occurs — see TURNING POINT

2 the highest part or point — see HEIGHT 1

climax *vb* to bring to a triumphant conclusion — see CROWN

climb *n* the act or an instance of rising or climbing up — see ASCENT 1

climb *vb* **1** to move (as up or over something) often with the help of the hands in holding or pulling ⟨visitors should use caution when *climbing* over the wet rocks along the shore⟩
synonyms clamber, scramble
related words shin, shinny; inch; mount, scale, surmount; claw, struggle

2 to move or extend upward — see ASCEND

clinch *vb* to make final, definite, or beyond dispute ⟨the rain *clinched* the matter: we would have the party indoors⟩
synonyms decide, settle
related words demonstrate, determine, establish, prove, show; clarify, clear (up), illuminate; conclude, end, finish
near antonyms confuse, muddle, muddy

clincher *n* something (as a fact or argument) that is decisive or overwhelming ⟨the fact that the resort had tennis courts was the *clincher* in our deciding to stay there⟩
synonyms crusher, topper
related words deathblow, knockout; coup

cling *vb* to hold to something firmly as if by adhesion — see STICK 1

cling (to) *vb* **1** to give steadfast support to — see ADHERE

2 to have or keep in one's hands — see HOLD 1

clink *vb* to make a repeated sharp light ringing sound — see JINGLE

clip *n* a hard strike with a part of the body or an instrument — see ¹BLOW

clip *vb* to make (as hair) shorter with or as if with the use of shears ⟨toddlers are often fearful the first time they get their hair *clipped*⟩
synonyms bob, crop, curtail, cut, cut back, dock, lop (off), nip, pare, prune, shave, shear, snip, trim
related words manicure, mow; abbreviate, abridge, shorten
near antonyms elongate, extend, lengthen

clique *n* a group of people sharing a common interest and relating together socially — see GANG 2

cloak *n* **1** something that covers or conceals like a piece of cloth ⟨the *cloak* of mystery that surrounds the royal family⟩
synonyms curtain, hood, mantle, mask, shroud, veil
related words cover, screen, shield; facade (*also* façade), face, veneer

2 a sleeveless garment worn so as to hang over the shoulders, arms, and back — see ¹CAPE

cloak *vb* **1** to change the dress or looks of so as to conceal true identity — see DISGUISE

2 to keep secret or shut off from view — see ¹HIDE 2

clobber *vb* **1** to deliver a blow to (someone or something) usually in a strong vigorous manner — see HIT 1

2 to defeat by a large margin — see WHIP 2

3 to achieve a victory over — see BEAT 2

clock *n* a device to measure time — see TIMEPIECE

clod *n* **1** a big clumsy often slow-witted person — see OAF

2 a small uneven mass — see LUMP 1

cloddish *adj* having or showing crudely insensitive or impolite manners — see CLOWNISH

clodhopper *n* an awkward or simple person especially from a small town or the country — see HICK

clog *n* something that makes movement or progress more difficult — see ENCUMBRANCE

clog *vb* **1** to prevent passage through ⟨the discovery that a ton of hair was *clogging* the drain in the tub⟩
synonyms block, choke, close (off), congest, dam, jam, obstruct, plug (up), stop (up), stuff
related words bung, fill, pack; flood, glut, inundate, overwhelm, swamp
near antonyms excavate, hollow (out), scoop (out); empty, lighten
antonyms clear, free, open (up), unclog

2 to create difficulty for the work or activity of — see HAMPER

cloister *n* a residence for men under religious vows — see MONASTERY

cloistered *adj* hidden from view — see SECLUDED

close *adj* **1** having little space between items or parts ⟨the soldiers marched in *close* formation against the enemy⟩
synonyms compact, crowded, dense, jam-packed, packed, serried, thick, tight
related words airtight, snug; compacted, compressed, condensed; firm, hard, solid; impenetrable, impermeable, impervious
near antonyms commodious, roomy, spacious
antonyms loose, uncrowded

2 not being distant in time, space, or significance ⟨my birthday is *close* to Christmas⟩ ⟨a shopping mall that is very *close* to the highway⟩ ⟨these words are *close* synonyms⟩
synonyms immediate, near, nearby, neighboring, next-door, nigh
related words abutting, adjacent, adjoining, bordering, contiguous; approaching, coming, forthcoming, oncoming, upcoming; accessible, convenient, handy
phrases at hand
near antonyms divorced, removed, separated
antonyms away, distant, far, faraway, far-off, remote

3 showing little difference in the standing of the competitors ⟨the election results were so *close* that the votes had to be recounted⟩

THESAURUS

synonyms narrow, nip and tuck, tight
related words crowded

4 closely acquainted — see FAMILIAR 1

5 given to keeping one's activities hidden from public observation or knowledge — see SECRETIVE

6 giving or sharing as little as possible — see STINGY 1

7 lacking fresh air — see STUFFY 1

8 meeting the highest standard of accuracy — see PRECISE 1

close *adv* at, within, or to a short distance or time — see NEAR 1

¹**close** *n* an open space wholly or partly enclosed (as by buildings or walls) — see COURT 2

²**close** *n* **1** the stopping of a process or activity — see END 1

2 the last part of a process or action — see FINALE

close *vb* **1** to position (something) so as to prevent passage through an opening ⟨be sure to *close* the gate when you leave⟩
synonyms shut
related words bar, batten (down), bolt, chain, fasten, latch, lock; plug, seal, stopper; secure; bang, clap, slam
near antonyms unbar, unbolt, unchain, unfasten, unlatch, unlock, unseal
antonyms open

2 to stop the operations of ⟨the merchant will *close* the store if business doesn't improve⟩
synonyms shut
related words phase out, turn off; extinguish, quell, suppress; gag, muzzle, silence; fail, fold
near antonyms build, expand
antonyms open, start

3 to bring (an event) to a natural or appropriate stopping point ⟨we'll *close* the assembly with the singing of our national anthem⟩
synonyms conclude, end, finish, round (off *or* out), terminate, wind up, wrap up
related words climax, crown; complete, consummate, perfect; halt, stop, suspend
antonyms begin, commence, inaugurate, open, start

4 to come to an end — see CEASE 1

5 to come near or nearer — see APPROACH 1

close (off) *vb* to prevent passage through — see CLOG 1

closefisted *adj* giving or sharing as little as possible — see STINGY 1

close–knit *adj* bound together by feelings of very close association ⟨a *close-knit* family that constantly keeps in touch⟩
synonyms clannish
related words bosom, chummy, close, familiar, friendly, intimate, thick; exclusive, snobbish, snobby; forbidding, inhospitable, unfriendly

closely *adv* to a close degree — see NEAR 2

closemouthed *adj* **1** given to keeping one's activities hidden from public observation or knowledge — see SECRETIVE

2 tending not to speak frequently (as by habit or inclination) — see SILENT 2

closeness *n* **1** the practice or habit of keeping secrets or keeping one's affairs secret — see SECRECY

2 the quality of being overly sparing with money — see PARSIMONY

3 the quality or state of being very accurate — see PRECISION

4 the state of being in a very personal or private relationship — see FAMILIARITY 1

5 the state or condition of being near — see PROXIMITY

closer *adj* being the less far of two — see NEAR 1

closet *n* **1** a storage case typically having doors and shelves — see CABINET

2 an area within a building that has been set apart from surrounding space by a wall — see ROOM 2

closet *vb* to close or shut in by or as if by barriers — see ENCLOSE 1

closing *adj* following all others of the same kind in order or time — see LAST

closing *n* the last part of a process or action — see FINALE

closure *n* the stopping of a process or activity — see END 1

clot *vb* to turn from a liquid into a substance resembling jelly — see COAGULATE

cloth *n* a woven or knitted material (as of cotton or nylon) ⟨cotton canvas was the *cloth* traditionally used for a ship's sails⟩
synonyms fabric, textile
related words fiber, thread, yarn

clothe *vb* **1** to outfit with clothes and especially fine or special clothes ⟨they liked to *clothe* the twins in identical outfits just to confuse people⟩
synonyms apparel, array, attire, caparison, costume, deck, dress, garb, garment, gown, invest, rig (out), robe, suit
related words cloak, mantle; drape, swaddle, swathe; accoutre (*or* accouter), equip, furnish, outfit
near antonyms divest, uncover, undrape, unveil
antonyms disrobe, strip, unclothe, undress

2 to convey in appropriate or telling terms — see PHRASE

clothes *n pl* covering for the human body — see CLOTHING

clothing *n* covering for the human body ⟨a store that sells both men's and women's *clothing*⟩
synonyms apparel, attire, clothes, dress, duds, habiliment(s), rags, raiment, togs, wear
related words garment, vestment; array, bravery, finery; tatters; costume, garb, getup, guise, outfit, rig, wardrobe; haberdashery

cloud *vb* **1** to make dark, dim, or indistinct ⟨unfortunately, smog *clouds* the view of the city from the hilltop⟩
synonyms becloud, bedim, befog, blacken, blur, darken, dim, fog, haze, mist, obscure, overcast, overcloud, overshadow, shadow, shroud
related words blot out, conceal, hide, screen, shade; camouflage, cloak, cover, curtain, disguise, mask, veil; distort, falsify, garble, misrepresent
near antonyms expose, reveal, uncover, unveil; clarify, clear, purify; highlight, spotlight
antonyms brighten, illuminate, illumine, light (up), lighten

2 to make (something) unclear to the understanding — see CONFUSE 2

cloudburst *n* a steady falling of water from the sky in significant quantity — see RAIN 1

clouded *adj* **1** covered over by clouds — see OVERCAST

2 filled with or dimmed by fine particles (as of dust or water) in suspension — see HAZY 1

cloudless *adj* not stormy or cloudy — see FAIR 1

cloudy *adj* **1** having visible particles in liquid sus-

pension ⟨the water coming out of the faucet was unusually *cloudy*⟩
synonyms muddy, roiled, turbid
related words dingy, filmy, hazy, unfiltered; inky, murky; nontransparent, opaque
near antonyms clarified, filtered, purified
antonyms clear
2 covered over by clouds — see OVERCAST
3 filled with or dimmed by fine particles (as of dust or water) in suspension — see HAZY 1
clout *n* 1 a hard strike with a part of the body or an instrument — see ¹BLOW
2 the power to direct the thinking or behavior of others usually indirectly — see INFLUENCE 1
clout *vb* to deliver a blow to (someone or something) usually in a strong vigorous manner — see HIT 1
clown *n* 1 a comically dressed performer (as at a circus) who entertains with playful tricks and ridiculous behavior ⟨a *clown* wearing big floppy shoes and a red wig⟩
synonyms buffoon, harlequin, zany
related words cutup, madcap; fool, jester, motley; mime, mummer; comedian, comedienne, comic, joker, jokester, wag
2 a person whose behavior is offensive to others — see JERK 1
clown (around) *vb* to engage in attention-getting playful or boisterous behavior — see CUT UP
clowning *n* wildly playful or mischievous behavior — see HORSEPLAY
clownish *adj* having or showing crudely insensitive or impolite manners ⟨the *clownish* antics of some of the teenagers at the wedding reception⟩
synonyms boorish, churlish, cloddish, loutish, uncouth
related words coarse, ill-bred, uncultivated, unpolished, unrefined; tasteless, vulgar; beastly, bestial; doltish, oafish, stupid; discourteous, impolite, rude, uncivil
antonyms cultivated, polished, refined, well-bred; courtly, genteel, gentlemanly, ladylike; civil, courteous, polite
club *n* 1 a heavy rigid stick used as a weapon or for punishment ⟨hit the prisoner with a *club* if he tries anything funny⟩
synonyms bat, billy, bludgeon, cane, cudgel, nightstick, rod, shillelagh, staff, truncheon
related words blackjack, mace; birch, switch; hammer, mallet, maul; walking stick
2 the meeting place of an organization ⟨the Scouts gather at their *club* every Monday evening⟩
synonyms clubhouse, lodge
related words den, hangout, haunt, hideaway, hideout, lair; camp, headquarters; meetinghouse
3 a group of persons formally joined together for some common interest — see ASSOCIATION 2
club *vb* 1 to form or enter into an association that furthers the interests of its members — see ALLY
2 to strike repeatedly — see BEAT 1
clubhouse *n* the meeting place of an organization — see CLUB 2
clue *n* a slight or indirect pointing to something (as a solution or explanation) — see HINT 1
clue *vb* to give information to — see ENLIGHTEN 1
clump *n* 1 a number of things considered as a unit — see GROUP 1
2 a small uneven mass — see LUMP 1
clump *vb* to move heavily or clumsily — see LUMBER 1

clumpy *adj* having small pieces or lumps spread throughout — see CHUNKY 1
clumsy *adj* 1 lacking in physical ease and grace in movement or in the use of the hands ⟨diamond cutting is no job for a *clumsy* person⟩
synonyms awkward, gawky, graceless, heavy-handed, lubberly, lumbering, lumpish, ungainly, unhandy
related words butterfingered, uncoordinated; oafish; bungling, gauche, inept, inexpert, maladroit, unskilled, unskillful; cumbersome, unwieldy
near antonyms expert, masterly, skilled, skillful; lissome (*also* lissom), lithe, nimble; light, light-footed, surefooted
antonyms deft, dexterous (*also* dextrous), graceful, handy
2 lacking social grace and assurance — see AWKWARD 1
3 showing or marked by a lack of skill and tact (as in dealing with a situation) — see AWKWARD 2
4 difficult to use or operate especially because of size, weight, or design — see CUMBERSOME
5 hastily or roughly constructed — see RUDE 1
cluster *n* 1 a number of things considered as a unit — see GROUP 1
2 a usually small number of persons considered as a unit — see GROUP 2
cluster *vb* 1 to come together into one body or place — see ASSEMBLE 1
2 to gather into a closely packed group — see PRESS 3
clutch *n* 1 a time or state of affairs requiring prompt or decisive action — see EMERGENCY
2 the right or means to command or control others — see POWER 1
clutch *vb* to have or keep in one's hands — see HOLD 1
clutter *n* an unorganized collection or mixture of various things — see MISCELLANY 1
cluttered *adj* lacking in order, neatness, and often cleanliness — see MESSY
coach *n* a person who trains performers or athletes ⟨a *coach* who is highly respected by all of the baseball players⟩
synonyms trainer
related words instructor, teacher; driller, drillmaster; adviser (*or* advisor), counselor (*or* counselor), mentor
coach *vb* to give advice and instruction to (someone) regarding the course or process to be followed — see GUIDE 1
coadjutor *n* a person who helps a more skilled person — see HELPER
coagulate *vb* to turn from a liquid into a substance resembling jelly ⟨the blood *coagulated*, and a scab formed on the wound⟩
synonyms clot, congeal, gel, jell, jelly, set
related words concrete, firm (up), freeze, harden, solidify, stiffen; condense, thicken; curdle, lump (up)
near antonyms deliquesce, flux, fuse, liquefy, melt, thaw
coalesce *vb* to come together to form a single unit — see UNITE 1
coalition *n* 1 a group of people acting together within a larger group — see FACTION
2 an association of persons, parties, or states for mutual assistance and protection — see CONFEDERACY

coarse *adj* **1** made up of large particles ⟨*coarse* rock salt was sprinkled on the icy walkway⟩
synonyms grainy, granular, granulated
related words rough; unfiltered, unrefined; gravelly, gritty, sandy; pebbly, rocky, stony (*also* stoney); lumpy, mealy
near antonyms smooth; filtered, pulverized, refined
antonyms dusty, fine, floury, powdery
2 lacking in refinement or good taste ⟨the hockey player's *coarse* manners turned his date off completely⟩
synonyms common, crass, crude, gross, ill-bred, low, lowbred, lowbrow, raffish, rough, roughhewn, rude, tasteless, uncouth, uncultivated, uncultured, unpolished, unrefined, vulgar
related words boorish, churlish, cloddish, clownish, loutish, ungentlemanly; clumsy, lubberly, lumpish, oafish; inconsiderate, insensitive, thoughtless; countrified (*also* countryfied), provincial, rustic; graceless, inelegant, tacky
near antonyms aristocratic, courtly, patrician; elegant, graceful, gracious; considerate, sensitive, thoughtful; citified, sophisticated, urbane
antonyms cultivated, cultured, genteel, polished, refined, smooth, tasteful, well-bred
3 depicting or referring to sexual matters in a way that is unacceptable in polite society — see OBSCENE 1
4 harsh and dry in sound — see HOARSE
5 not having a level or smooth surface — see UNEVEN 1
6 of low quality — see CHEAP 2
coarseness *n* **1** the quality or state of being obscene — see OBSCENITY 1
2 the quality or state of lacking refinement or good taste — see VULGARITY 1
coast *vb* to move or proceed smoothly and readily — see FLOW 2
coat *n* the hairy covering of a mammal especially when fine, soft, and thick — see FUR 1
coat *vb* to form a layer over — see COVER 2
coax *vb* to get (someone) to do something by gentle urging, special attention, or flattery ⟨trying to *coax* Dad into taking us on a ski trip, we mentioned what a great skier he is⟩
synonyms blandish, blarney, cajole, soft-soap, wheedle
related words adulate, flatter, overpraise; compliment, praise; beguile, charm, woo; beg, importune, urge; bug, nag, pester
near antonyms browbeat, bulldoze, bully, cow, intimidate; coerce, compel, constrain, force, oblige
cobble (together) *vb* to make or assemble roughly or hastily ⟨the stranded hikers *cobbled together* a rickety shelter for the night⟩
synonyms patch (together), throw up
related words dash (off)
phrases knock together
near antonyms craft, handcraft; fashion, forge, hammer (out), pound (out)
¹**cock** *n* a fixture for controlling the flow of a liquid — see FAUCET
²**cock** *n* a quantity of things thrown or stacked on one another — see ¹PILE 1
³**cock** *n* the act of positioning or an instance of being positioned at an angle — see TILT
cock *vb* to set or cause to be at an angle — see LEAN 1
cockcrow *n* the first appearance of light in the morning or the time of its appearance — see DAWN 1
cockeyed *adj* **1** inclined or twisted to one side — see AWRY
2 showing or marked by a lack of good sense or judgment — see FOOLISH 1
cocksure *adj* having or showing a mind free from doubt — see CERTAIN 2
cocky *adj* displaying or marked by rude boldness — see NERVY 1
cocoon *n* something that encloses another thing especially to protect it — see ¹CASE 1
coddle *vb* **1** to cook in a liquid heated to the point that it gives off steam — see BOIL 2
2 to treat with great or excessive care — see BABY
code *n* a collection or system of rules of conduct ⟨Hammurabi was an ancient king of Babylon with a famous *code* of laws⟩
synonyms decalogue, law
related words constitution
codger *n* a person of odd or whimsical habits — see ECCENTRIC
codify *vb* to put into a particular arrangement — see ORDER 1
coequal *adj* resembling another in every respect — see SAME 1
coerce *vb* to cause (a person) to give in to pressure — see FORCE
coerced *adj* not made or done willingly or by choice — see INVOLUNTARY 1
coercion *n* the use of power to impose one's will on another — see FORCE 2
coeval *adj* existing or occurring at the same period of time — see CONTEMPORARY 1
coeval *n* a person who lives at the same time or is about the same age as another — see CONTEMPORARY
coexist *vb* to occur or exist at the same time — see COINCIDE 1
coexistence *n* the occurrence or existence of several things at once — see CONCURRENCE 1
coexistent *adj* **1** existing or occurring at the same period of time — see CONTEMPORARY 1
2 present at the same time and place — see COINCIDENT
coexisting *adj* **1** existing or occurring at the same period of time — see CONTEMPORARY 1
2 present at the same time and place — see COINCIDENT
coextensive *adj* existing or occurring at the same period of time — see CONTEMPORARY 1
coffer *n* a specially reinforced container to keep valuables safe — see SAFE
coffin *n* a box for holding a dead body ⟨*coffins* are said to be the preferred sleeping places of vampires⟩
synonyms casket
related words sarcophagus, vault; urn; sepulcher (*or* sepulchre), sepulture
cogency *n* **1** the capacity to persuade ⟨the *cogency* of Thomas Paine's case for American independence⟩
synonyms effectiveness, force, forcefulness, persuasiveness
related words impact, punch, strength; soundness, validity; pertinence, relevance
near antonyms invalidity, unsoundness; weakness
antonyms ineffectiveness
2 the quality of an utterance that provokes interest and produces an effect — see ¹PUNCH 1

cogent *adj* having the power to persuade ⟨the results of the DNA fingerprinting were the most *cogent* evidence for acquittal⟩
synonyms compelling, conclusive, convincing, decisive, effective, forceful, persuasive, satisfying, strong, telling
related words sound, valid, well-founded; important, significant, weighty; material, pertinent, relevant
near antonyms groundless, invalid, unfounded, unsound; inconsequential, insignificant, unimportant; immaterial, irrelevant
antonyms inconclusive, indecisive, ineffective, unconvincing

cogitate *vb* to give serious and careful thought to — see PONDER

cognizance *n* **1** a state of being aware — see ATTENTION 2
2 knowledge gained by personal experience — see ACQUAINTANCE

cognizant *adj* having specified facts or feelings actively impressed on the mind — see CONSCIOUS

cognomen *n* **1** a descriptive or familiar name given instead of or in addition to the one belonging to an individual — see NICKNAME
2 a word or combination of words by which a person or thing is regularly known — see NAME 1

cohere *vb* to be in agreement on every point — see CHECK 1

coherence *n* a balanced, pleasing, or suitable arrangement of parts — see HARMONY 1

coherent *adj* according to the rules of logic — see LOGICAL 1

cohort *n* **1** a person frequently seen in the company of another — see ASSOCIATE 1
2 one associated with another in wrongdoing — see ACCOMPLICE

coil *vb* to follow a circular or spiral course — see WIND

coiling *adj* turning around an axis like the thread of a screw — see SPIRAL

coinage *n* something (as a device) created for the first time through the use of the imagination — see INVENTION 1

coincide *vb* **1** to occur or exist at the same time ⟨the heaviest snowfall of the season *coincided* with the start of our week-long ski vacation⟩
synonyms coexist, concur
related words chance, happen, transpire
near antonyms antedate, precede, predate; follow, succeed
2 to be in agreement on every point — see CHECK 1
3 to have or come to the same opinion or point of view — see AGREE 1

coincidence *n* the occurrence or existence of several things at once — see CONCURRENCE 1

coincident *adj* present at the same time and place ⟨the hard economic times and the *coincident* increase in crime were a double strain on the city's social services⟩
synonyms accompanying, attendant, attending, coexistent, coexisting, coincidental, concomitant, concurrent
related words contemporaneous, contemporary, simultaneous, synchronous; associated, collateral, connected, linked, related; consequent, resultant, resulting; ensuing, following, subsequent; accidental, casual, chance, fluky, fortuitous, freak, incident, incidental

near antonyms unassociated, unconnected, unrelated

coincidental *adj* present at the same time and place — see COINCIDENT

coincidentally *adv* at one and the same time — see TOGETHER 1

coincidently *adv* at one and the same time — see TOGETHER 1

coitus *n* sexual union involving penetration of the vagina by the penis — see SEXUAL INTERCOURSE

cold *adj* **1** having a low or subnormal temperature ⟨the *cold* climate of the Yukon⟩ ⟨an unusually *cold* spring that was followed by a sweltering summer⟩
synonyms arctic, bitter, cool, coolish, freezing, frigid, frosty, glacial, ice-cold, icy, nipping, nippy, numbing, polar, shivery, snappy, wintry
related words subfreezing, subzero; cutting, keen, penetrating, piercing, sharp; bracing, brisk, crisp, invigorating, rigorous; chilled, cooled, frosted, frozen, iced, refrigerated, unheated
near antonyms lukewarm, tepid; heated, warmed
antonyms broiling, burning, fiery, hot, piping hot, red-hot, roasting, scalding, scorching, searing, sultry, summery, sweltering, torrid, tropical, warm, warming
2 lacking in friendliness or warmth of feeling ⟨the prisoners got only a *cold* stare when they tried to befriend the guard⟩
synonyms chill, chilly, cold-blooded, cool, frigid, frosty, glacial, icy, unfriendly, unsympathetic, wintry
related words hardhearted, heartless, pitiless, uncaring, unfeeling; reserved, soulless, undemonstrative, unemotional, unresponsive; apathetic, indifferent, unenthusiastic, uninterested; aloof, detached, impersonal
near antonyms compassionate, kind, kindhearted; demonstrative, emotional, expressive; eager, enthusiastic, passionate
antonyms cordial, friendly, genial, hearty, sympathetic, warm, warm-blooded, warmhearted
3 having or showing a lack of friendliness or interest in others — see COOL 1
4 having lost consciousness — see UNCONSCIOUS 1

cold *n* a weather condition marked by low temperatures ⟨the *cold* will stay with us for another day, then temperatures should rise⟩
synonyms freeze, snap
related words frost; glaciation, ice age; bite, chill, nip, wintriness
near antonyms heat wave; dog days

cold-blooded *adj* **1** having or showing a lack of sympathy or tender feelings — see HARD 1
2 lacking in friendliness or warmth of feeling — see COLD 2
3 not feeling or showing emotion — see IMPASSIVE 1

cold-shoulder *vb* to deliberately ignore or treat rudely — see SNUB 1

cold shoulder *n* treatment that is deliberately unfriendly ⟨at the party the two former friends gave each other the *cold shoulder*⟩
synonyms brush-off, rebuff, repulse, snub
related words dismissal, rejection; banishment, ostracism
near antonyms welcome

coliseum *n* a large usually roofless building for sporting events with tiers of seats for spectators — see STADIUM

collaborate *vb* to participate or assist in a joint effort to accomplish an end — see COOPERATE 1

collaboration *n* 1 the state of having shared interests or efforts (as in social or business matters) — see ASSOCIATION 1

2 the work and activity of a number of persons who individually contribute toward the efficiency of the whole — see TEAMWORK

collapse *n* 1 a complete depletion of energy or strength — see FATIGUE

2 a falling short of one's goals — see FAILURE 2

collapse *vb* 1 to fall down or in as a result of physical pressure ⟨the motel balcony *collapsed* under the weight of so many people⟩

synonyms cave (in), crumple, give, go, yield

related words deflate, flatten, melt; break, break down, conk (out), crash, die, fail, give out, stall; burst, shatter, smash; crack, pop, snap

phrases give way

near antonyms inflate, rise, swell

2 to be unsuccessful — see FAIL 2

collar *vb* to take physical control or possession of (something) suddenly or forcibly — see CATCH 1

colleague *n* a fellow worker ⟨on her first day at work her *colleagues* went out of their way to make her feel welcome⟩

synonyms associate, coworker

related words equal, fellow, peer; accomplice, ally, cohort, collaborator, confederate, partner; buddy, chum, companion, comrade, crony, pal; compatriot, countryman

collect *vb* 1 to gain emotional or mental control of ⟨applicants should *collect* their thoughts while waiting to be interviewed⟩

synonyms calm, compose, contain, control, recollect, settle

related words allay, lull, quiet, soothe, still, tranquilize (*also* tranquillize)

phrases pull oneself together

2 to gradually form into a layer, pile, or mass ⟨dust has been *collecting* under my bed for years⟩

synonyms accumulate, conglomerate, gather, heap, pile (up)

related words bank, drift, ridge

near antonyms disperse, dissipate, scatter

3 to bring together from several sources into a single volume or list — see COMPILE

4 to bring together in one body or place — see GATHER 1

5 to come together into one body or place — see ASSEMBLE 1

collected *adj* free from emotional or mental agitation — see CALM 2

collection *n* 1 an organized group of objects acquired and maintained for study, exhibition, or personal pleasure ⟨his stamp *collection* has become quite valuable⟩

synonyms assemblage, library

related words cache, hoard, repertory, reserve, stock, stockpile, store, supply; accumulation, gathering, heap, pile; clutter, jumble, litter

2 a mass or quantity that has piled up or that has been gathered — see ACCUMULATION 1

3 a number of things considered as a unit — see GROUP 1

collective *adj* used or done by a number of people as a group ⟨the cleanup of the neighborhood park was a *collective* effort for which many people should be thanked⟩

synonyms combined, common, communal, con-

certed, conjoint, joint, mutual, public, shared, united

related words cooperative, reciprocal, symbiotic; mass, popular; general, generic, universal

near antonyms personal, private; independent, separate; particular, special, specialized

antonyms individual, single, sole

college *n* a group of persons formally joined together for some common interest — see ASSOCIATION 2

collide *vb* 1 to be out of harmony or agreement usually noticeably — see CLASH

2 to come into usually forceful contact with something — see HIT 2

collision *n* 1 a forceful coming together of two things — see IMPACT 1

2 the violent coming together of two bodies into destructive contact — see CRASH 1

colloquial *adj* 1 used in or suitable for speech and not formal writing ⟨the new kid's rudeness soon began—to use a *colloquial* expression—to rub me the wrong way⟩

synonyms conversational, informal, nonliterary, unliterary, vernacular, vulgar

related words dialectal, dialectical, nonstandard, substandard, uneducated; slang, slangy

near antonyms educated, standard; correct, genteel, grammatical, proper

antonyms bookish, formal, learned, literary

2 having the style and content of everyday conversation — see CHATTY 1

colloquy *n* 1 a meeting featuring a group discussion — see FORUM

2 an exchange of views for the purpose of exploring a subject or deciding an issue — see DISCUSSION 1

3 talking or a talk between two or more people — see CONVERSATION

collusion *n* a secret agreement or cooperation between two parties for an illegal or dishonest purpose ⟨there was *collusion* between the two companies to fix prices⟩

synonyms complicity, connivance, conspiracy

related words chicanery, foul play, skulduggery (*or* skullduggery); double-dealing, duplicity; cover-up, frame-up; intrigue, plot, scheme

colonist *n* a person who settles in a new region — see FRONTIERSMAN

colonizer *n* a person who settles in a new region — see FRONTIERSMAN

colony *n* 1 a settlement in a new country or region ⟨the early history of New York City when it was a Dutch *colony*⟩

synonyms plantation

related words outpost; dependency, mandate, possession, protectorate, territory

2 a group of people with a common interest living in one place — see COMMUNITY 2

color *n* 1 a property that becomes apparent when light falls on an object and by which things that are identical in form can be distinguished ⟨a shirt that is available in every *color* of the rainbow⟩

synonyms cast, hue, shade, tinge, tint, tone

related words complementary color, primary color, secondary color; brightness, saturation, value; coloration, coloring

2 a substance used to color other materials — see PIGMENT

3 the hue or appearance of the skin and especially of the face — see COMPLEXION 1

4 colors *pl* a piece of cloth with a special design that is used as an emblem or for signaling — see FLAG 1

color *vb* **1** to give color or a different color to ⟨she's *colored* her hair for so long and so often that no one knows what her natural color is⟩
synonyms dye, paint, stain, tinge, tint
related words brighten, lighten; darken, tone (down); daub
near antonyms blanch, bleach, whiten
antonyms decolorize
2 to add to the interest of by including made-up details — see EMBROIDER
3 to change so much as to create a wrong impression or alter the meaning of — see GARBLE
4 to develop a rosy facial color (as from excitement or embarrassment) — see BLUSH

colorful *adj* marked by a variety of usually vivid colors ⟨the *colorful* robes and blankets of the Native Americans of the Southwest⟩
synonyms motley, multicolored, polychromatic, polychrome, varicolored, variegated
related words brave, bright, brilliant, gay; flashy, garish, gaudy, loud, showy, splashy; deep, rich, unbleached; checkered, dotted, plaid, striped; colored, pigmented; dappled, shaded; marbled, mottled, piebald, pied, pinto; flecked, spotted, streaked; specked, speckled; banded, barred, brindled (*or* brindle)
near antonyms achromatic; bleached, decolorized, faded, washed out; dull, faint, gray (*also* grey), neutral, pale, pallid
antonyms colorless; monochromatic, solid

coloring *n* **1** a substance used to color other materials — see PIGMENT
2 the hue or appearance of the skin and especially of the face — see COMPLEXION 1
3 the representation of something in terms that go beyond the facts — see EXAGGERATION

colorless *adj* lacking an addition of color ⟨since we can't decide what color to paint the doghouse, our latest home project remains *colorless* for the time being⟩
synonyms uncolored, undyed, unpainted, unstained, white
related words clear, limpid, liquid, lucent, pellucid, transparent; bleached, faded, washed; dull, faint, gray (*also* grey), neutral, pale, pallid
near antonyms colorful, multicolored, polychromatic, polychrome, varicolored, variegated
antonyms colored, dyed, painted, stained, tinged, tinted

colossal *adj* unusually large — see HUGE
colossally *adv* to a large extent or degree — see GREATLY 2
colosseum *n* a large usually roofless building for sporting events with tiers of seats for spectators — see STADIUM
colossus *n* something that is unusually large and powerful — see GIANT
colt *n* a person who is just starting out in a field of activity — see BEGINNER
coltish *adj* given to good-natured joking or teasing — see PLAYFUL
column *n* **1** a series of persons or things arranged one behind another — see LINE 1
2 an upright shaft that supports an overhead structure — see PILLAR 1
coma *n* a temporary or permanent state of unconsciousness — see FAINT

comb *vb* to look through (as a place) carefully or thoroughly in an effort to find or discover something — see SEARCH 1
combat *n* **1** active fighting during the course of a war ⟨a soldier who served through the war without actually seeing *combat*⟩
synonyms action, battle
related words attack, fire; hostilities, operations, warfare; duty, service
2 a physical dispute between opposing individuals or groups — see FIGHT 1
3 an earnest effort for superiority or victory over another — see CONTEST 1
combat *vb* **1** to oppose (someone) in physical conflict — see FIGHT 1
2 to strive to reduce or eliminate — see FIGHT 2
combative *adj* feeling or displaying eagerness to fight — see BELLIGERENT
combativeness *n* an inclination to fight or quarrel — see BELLIGERENCE
combination *n* **1** a distinct entity formed by the combining of two or more different things — see BLEND
2 the act or an instance of joining two or more things into one — see UNION 1
3 a number of businesses or enterprises united for commercial advantage — see CARTEL
4 an association of persons, parties, or states for mutual assistance and protection — see CONFEDERACY
combine *n* **1** a number of businesses or enterprises united for commercial advantage — see CARTEL
2 an association of persons, parties, or states for mutual assistance and protection — see CONFEDERACY
combine *vb* **1** to come together to form a single unit — see UNITE 1
2 to turn into a single mass that is more or less the same throughout — see BLEND 1
combined *adj* used or done by a number of people as a group — see COLLECTIVE
combining *n* the act or an instance of joining two or more things into one — see UNION 1
combust *vb* to be on fire especially brightly — see BURN 1
combustible *adj* capable of catching or being set on fire ⟨don't store oily rags and other *combustible* materials in a hot attic⟩
synonyms burnable, flammable, ignitable, inflammable
related words explosive, incendiary
near antonyms nonexplosive
antonyms fireproof, incombustible, noncombustible, nonflammable, noninflammable
combusting *adj* being on fire — see ABLAZE 1
come *vb* **1** to move closer to ⟨*come* here and sit by the fire⟩
synonyms advance, approach, near
related words drop (in), enter, pop (in)
near antonyms depart, exit, leave
antonyms go, retreat, withdraw
2 to get to a destination ⟨when do you think they'll *come*?⟩
synonyms arrive, land, show up, turn up
related words hit, make, reach; pull (in), touch down; debark, disembark; barge (in), breeze (in), burst (in *or* into), waltz (in)
antonyms go

THESAURUS

3 to eventually have as a state or quality — see BECOME

4 to take place — see HAPPEN

come (to) *vb* **1** to have a total of — see AMOUNT (TO) 1

2 to be the same in meaning or effect — see AMOUNT (TO) 2

come about *vb* to take place — see HAPPEN

come around *vb* to gain consciousness again — see COME TO

comeback *n* **1** a quick witty response — see RETORT 1

2 something spoken or written in reaction especially to a question — see ANSWER 1

3 the process or period of gradually regaining one's health and strength — see CONVALESCENCE

comedian *n* a person (as a writer) noted for or specializing in humor — see HUMORIST

comedown *n* a loss of status ⟨after a rapid rise to stardom, the rock band's *comedown* was just as quick⟩

synonyms decline, descent, down, downfall, fall
related words breakdown, collapse, crash, meltdown, ruin, undoing; defeat, disappointment, reversal, setback; bottom, nadir
near antonyms advance, headway, progress; flower, heyday, prime
antonyms aggrandizement, ascent, exaltation, rise, up

come down (with) *vb* to become affected with (a disease or disorder) — see CONTRACT 1

comedy *n* humorous entertainment ⟨presented a night of *comedy* as part of the week-long celebrations⟩

synonyms farce, humor, slapstick
related words burlesque, parody, satire; banter, persiflage, wit; foolery, fun, horseplay, monkeyshines, shenanigans

comeliness *n* the qualities in a person or thing that as a whole give pleasure to the senses — see BEAUTY 1

comely *adj* very pleasing to look at — see BEAUTIFUL

come out *vb* **1** to come to be ⟨in the end everything *came out* OK⟩

synonyms pan out, prove, turn out
related words develop, emerge, evolve, play out, unfold, work out

2 to come into view — see APPEAR 1

3 to become known — see GET OUT 1

come round *vb* to gain consciousness again — see COME TO

come to *vb* to gain consciousness again ⟨after being in a coma for months, the patient suddenly *came to*⟩

synonyms come around, come round, revive
related words pull through, rally, recover; awake, awaken, wake up
near antonyms black out, faint, pass out

comfort *n* **1** a feeling of ease from grief or trouble ⟨the mourners found *comfort* in their pastor's words⟩

synonyms cheer, consolation, relief, solace
related words encouragement, inspiration, uplift; assurance, reassurance; alleviation, assuagement, mitigation; contentment, gladness, happiness; commiseration, empathy, sympathy
near antonyms anguish, distress, heartache, heartbreak, torment, torture

2 something that adds to one's ease ⟨a family campground with all the *comforts* of home⟩

synonyms amenity, convenience, luxury
related words extra; benefit, help, service; delight, indulgence, joy, pleasure
antonyms burden, millstone, weight

3 reduction of or freedom from pain — see EASE 1

4 something adding to pleasure or comfort but not absolutely necessary — see LUXURY 1

comfort *vb* **1** to ease the grief or distress of ⟨the minister did his best to *comfort* the victims of the terrible tornado⟩

synonyms assure, cheer, console, reassure, solace, soothe
related words commiserate, condole, empathize, sympathize; boost, buoy (up), elevate, lift, uplift; allay, alleviate, assuage, relieve; calm, quiet, relax, tranquilize (*also* tranquillize)
near antonyms demoralize, discourage, dishearten; fret, upset, worry; aggravate, intensify, worsen; annoy, irk, irritate; harass, pester
antonyms distress, torment, torture, trouble

2 to fill with courage or strength of purpose — see ENCOURAGE 1

comfortable *adj* **1** providing physical comfort ⟨a large, overstuffed chair that is very *comfortable*⟩

synonyms cozy, cushy, easy, snug, soft
related words relaxing, reposeful, restful; genial, hospitable, inviting, pleasant; commodious, roomy, spacious; homelike, homely, homey
near antonyms hard, harsh, severe; inhospitable, uninviting, unpleasant
antonyms uncomfortable

2 enjoying physical comfort ⟨make yourself *comfortable* in the living room while I fix us some snacks⟩

synonyms cozy, relaxed, snug
related words content, contented, pleased, satisfied; peaceful, resting; easygoing, laid-back; undisturbed, unperturbed, untroubled
phrases at ease, at home
near antonyms discontented, displeased, dissatisfied; agitated, disturbed, perturbed, troubled
antonyms uncomfortable

3 being more than enough without being excessive — see PLENTIFUL

comforting *adj* **1** making one feel good inside — see HEARTWARMING

2 tending to calm the emotions and relieve stress — see SOOTHING 1

comforting *n* the giving of hope and strength in times of grief, distress, or suffering — see CONSOLATION 1

comfortless *adj* **1** causing discomfort — see UNCOMFORTABLE 1

2 causing or marked by an atmosphere lacking in cheer — see GLOOMY 1

comic *adj* causing or intended to cause laughter — see FUNNY 1

comic *n* **1** a person (as a writer) noted for or specializing in humor — see HUMORIST

2 a series of drawings that tell a story or part of a story — see COMIC STRIP

comical *adj* **1** causing or intended to cause laughter — see FUNNY 1

2 so foolish or pointless as to be worthy of scornful laughter — see RIDICULOUS 1

comic strip *n* a series of drawings that tell a story or part of a story ⟨a *comic strip* that is beloved by both children and adults⟩

synonyms cartoon, comic, funny
related words comic book, funny paper(s); animated cartoon, animation; caricature

coming *adj* **1** being soon to appear or take place — see FORTHCOMING
2 being the one that comes immediately after another — see NEXT
3 of a time after the present — see FUTURE

comity *n* peaceful coexistence — see HARMONY 2

command *n* **1** a statement of what to do that must be obeyed by those concerned ⟨the captain's *commands* were followed without question⟩
synonyms behest, charge, commandment, decree, dictate, direction, directive, edict, instruction, order, word
related words demand, requirement; injunction, mandate; law, precept, rule; ordinance, regulation, statute
near antonyms appeal, entreaty, petition, plea, urging; proposal, recommendation, suggestion
2 a highly developed skill in or knowledge of something ⟨a *command* of French that is the result of a year spent in France as an exchange student⟩
synonyms mastership, mastery, proficiency
related words virtuosity; fluency, literacy; experience, expertise, know-how, practice (*also* practise), skill(s); acquaintance, familiarity, intimacy
near antonyms incompetence, incompetency; ignorance, illiteracy, unfamiliarity
3 the place from which a commander runs operations ⟨the general set up his *command* in the old port city⟩
synonyms base, headquarters
related words home, seat
4 a place from which authority is exercised — see SEAT 1
5 the right or means to command or control others — see POWER 1

command *vb* **1** to issue orders to (someone) by right of authority ⟨the general *commanded* the troops to advance⟩
synonyms adjure, bid, boss (around), charge, direct, enjoin, instruct, order, tell
related words ask, petition, request; beg, beseech, entreat; advise, counsel, warn; appoint, assign, authorize, commission; oversee, superintend, supervise; conduct, control, lead, manage; coerce, compel, constrain, force, oblige, require
near antonyms comply (with), follow, keep, observe
antonyms mind, obey
2 to give an order ⟨the governor has *commanded* that all state flags be flown at half-mast⟩
synonyms decree, dictate, direct, ordain, order
related words ask, petition, request; demand, require
phrases call for
3 to ask for (something) earnestly or with authority — see DEMAND 1
4 to exercise authority or power over — see GOVERN 1
5 to keep, control, or experience as one's own — see HAVE 1
6 to look down on — see OVERLOOK 1
7 to serve as leader of — see LEAD 2
8 to set or receive as a price — see CHARGE 1

commandant *n* one in official command especially of a military force or base — see COMMANDER 1

commandeer *vb* **1** to take control of (a vehicle) by force ⟨an airliner *commandeered* by terrorists⟩
synonyms hijack (*also* highjack)
related words appropriate, confiscate, expropriate, seize
2 to take or make use of without authority or right — see APPROPRIATE 1

commander *n* **1** one in official command especially of a military force or base ⟨a surrender of the fort by the *commander* without a single shot having been fired⟩
synonyms captain, commandant, commanding officer
related words commissioned officer
phrases commander in chief
2 a person in overall command of a ship — see CAPTAIN 1

commanding *adj* highest in rank or authority — see HEAD

commanding officer *n* one in official command especially of a military force or base — see COMMANDER 1

commandment *n* a statement of what to do that must be obeyed by those concerned — see COMMAND 1

commemorate *vb* **1** to be a memorial of ⟨a stone obelisk *commemorates* the Battle of Bunker Hill⟩
synonyms memorialize
related words celebrate, keep, observe, remember; enshrine, exalt, glorify, honor; bless, consecrate, sanctify, solemnize
near antonyms disgrace, dishonor
2 to act properly in relation to — see KEEP 1

commemorating *adj* serving to preserve the memory of a person, thing, or an event — see COMMEMORATIVE

commemorative *adj* serving to preserve the memory of a person, thing, or an event ⟨*commemorative* stamps for the stars of American popular music⟩
synonyms commemorating, memorial, memorializing
related words dedicatory, testimonial; enshrining, glorifying, honorary

commemorative *n* something that serves to keep alive the memory of a person or event — see MEMORIAL

commence *vb* **1** to take the first step in (a process or course of action) — see BEGIN 1
2 to come into existence — see BEGIN 2

commencement *n* the point at which something begins — see BEGINNING

commend *vb* to put (something) into the possession or safekeeping of another — see GIVE 2

commendable *adj* deserving of high regard or great approval — see ADMIRABLE

commendation *n* **1** a formal recognition of an achievement or praiseworthy deed ⟨a firefighter who has been awarded several *commendations* for bravery⟩
synonyms acknowledgment (*also* acknowledgement), citation
related words decoration, medal, ribbon; accolade, award, prize, tribute; dedication
2 a formal expression of praise — see ENCOMIUM

commendatory *adj* expressing approval — see FAVORABLE 1

commensurate *adj* corresponding in size, amount, extent, or degree — see PROPORTIONAL

comment *n* **1** a briefly expressed opinion — see REMARK

2 comments *pl* a series of explanations or observations on something (as an event) — see COMMENTARY

comment *vb* to make a statement of one's opinion — see REMARK 1

commentary *n* a series of explanations or observations on something (as an event) ⟨the TV anchors provided a running *commentary* on the parade⟩
synonyms analysis, comment, exposition
related words annotation, explication; note, observation, remark; report, review, write-up

commerce *n* the buying and selling of goods especially on a large scale and between different places ⟨a government agency in charge of regulating interstate *commerce*⟩
synonyms business, marketplace, trade, traffic
related words free trade; dealings, horse-trading; merchandising, retailing, wholesaling; bartering

commercial *adj* fit or likely to be sold especially on a large scale ⟨the *commercial* fare produced by the Hollywood movie studios⟩
synonyms marketable, salable (*or* saleable)
related words mass-produced, wholesale
antonyms noncommercial, nonsalable, uncommercial, unmarketable, unsalable

commingle *vb* to turn into a single mass that is more or less the same throughout — see BLEND 1

commiserate (with) *vb* to have sympathy for — see PITY

commiseration *n* **1** sorrow or the capacity to feel sorrow for another's suffering or misfortune — see SYMPATHY 1
2 the capacity for feeling for another's unhappiness or misfortune — see HEART 1

commissary *n* a person who acts or does business for another — see AGENT 2

commission *n* **1** the granting of power to perform various acts or duties ⟨President Jefferson's *commission* to Lewis and Clark to explore the Louisiana Territory⟩
synonyms accreditation, authorization, delegation, license (*or* licence), mandate
related words commendation, consignment, entrustment; facilitation, fostering, promotion; commanding, directing, ordering
2 the doing of an action ⟨a single burglar was responsible for the *commission* of all the break-ins⟩
synonyms accomplishment, achievement, discharge, enactment, execution, fulfillment, implementation, performance, perpetration
related words dispatch, expedition; administration, direction, handling, management; application, operation, practice (*also* practise)
antonyms nonfulfillment, nonperformance
3 a select group of persons assigned to consider or take action on some matter — see COMMITTEE
4 the state or fact of being chosen for a position or duty — see APPOINTMENT 1

commission *vb* **1** to appoint as one's representative — see DELEGATE 1
2 to give official or legal power to — see AUTHORIZE 1
3 to give a task, duty, or responsibility to — see ENTRUST 1
4 to pick (someone) by one's authority for a specific position or duty — see APPOINT 2

commit *vb* **1** to carry through (as a process) to completion — see PERFORM 1
2 to obligate by prior agreement — see PLEDGE 1

3 to put (something) into the possession or safekeeping of another — see GIVE 2
4 to put in or as if in prison — see IMPRISON

commitment *n* something one must do because of prior agreement — see OBLIGATION

committee *n* a select group of persons assigned to consider or take action on some matter ⟨a *committee* in charge of planning the organization's annual Christmas party⟩
synonyms commission, panel
related words subcommittee; delegation, mission; assembly, body, congress, convocation, council, synod

commodious *adj* more than adequate or average in capacity — see SPACIOUS

commodities *n pl* products that are bought and sold in business — see MERCHANDISE

common *adj* **1** often observed or encountered ⟨horse ranches are a *common* sight in that part of the state⟩
synonyms commonplace, everyday, familiar, frequent, garden, household, ordinary, routine, ubiquitous, usual
related words normal, regular, standard; general, universal; ceaseless, constant, continual, continuous, incessant, unceasing; popular, prevailing, prevalent, rampant; perennial, recurrent, repeated
near antonyms aberrant, abnormal, irregular, unnatural; intermittent, occasional, sporadic
antonyms extraordinary, infrequent, rare, uncommon, unfamiliar, unusual
2 being of the type that is encountered in the normal course of events — see ORDINARY 1
3 belonging or relating to the whole — see GENERAL 1
4 belonging to the class of people of low social or economic rank — see IGNOBLE 1
5 held by or applicable to a majority of the people — see GENERAL 3
6 used or done by a number of people as a group — see COLLECTIVE
7 of average to below average quality — see MEDIOCRE 1
8 of low quality — see CHEAP 2
9 lacking in refinement or good taste — see COARSE 2

commoners *n pl* the body of the community as contrasted with the elite — see MASS 1

commonly *adv* according to the usual course of things — see NATURALLY 2

commonness *n* **1** the fact or state of happening often — see FREQUENCY
2 the quality or state of lacking refinement or good taste — see VULGARITY 1

commonplace *adj* **1** being of the type that is encountered in the normal course of events — see ORDINARY 1
2 often observed or encountered — see COMMON 1
3 used or heard so often as to be dull — see STALE

commonplace *n* an idea or expression that has been used by many people ⟨the familiar summertime *commonplace* that "it's not the heat, it's the humidity"⟩
synonyms banality, cliché, platitude, shibboleth, truism
related words inanity; generality, generalization,

simplification; adage, proverb, saw, saying; old wives' tale, stereotype

near antonyms profundity

commonsense *adj* based on sound reasoning or information — see GOOD 1

common sense *n* the ability to make intelligent decisions especially in everyday matters ⟨*common sense* should tell you not to meet face-to-face with someone who is just an online acquaintance⟩

synonyms discreetness, discretion, horse sense, levelheadedness, prudence, sense, sensibleness, wisdom, wit

related words street smarts; farsightedness, foresight, foresightedness, judgment (*or* judgement); brains, gray matter, intelligence; logicalness, practicality, rationality; discernment, discrimination, insight, sagacity, sapience; acumen, astuteness, keenness, penetration, perspicacity, shrewdness; care, caution, circumspection, precaution, premeditation

near antonyms shortsightedness; brainlessness, foolishness, idiocy, senselessness, stupidity; carelessness, heedlessness

antonyms imprudence, indiscretion

commonwealth *n* a body of people composed of one or more nationalities usually with its own territory and government — see NATION

commotion *n* a state of noisy, confused activity ⟨the *commotion* created when the nation's top rock band arrived in town⟩

synonyms bother, bustle, clatter, disturbance, furor, furore, fuss, hubbub, hullabaloo, hurly-burly, pandemonium, pother, row, ruckus, ruction, rumpus, shindy, squall, stew, stir, storm, to-do, tumult, turmoil, uproar, welter, whirl

related words cacophony, clamor, din, howl, hue and cry, outcry, noise, racket, roar; disorder, unrest, upheaval; eruption, flare-up, flurry, outbreak, outburst; brawl, fracas, fray, hassle, melee, scuffle; dither, fever, fret, lather, tizzy

near antonyms calm, hush, peace, quiet, quietude, rest, stillness, tranquillity (*or* tranquility); order, orderliness

communal *adj* used or done by a number of people as a group — see COLLECTIVE

commune *vb* to form a close personal relationship ⟨after a week in the wilderness, the scouts were really starting to *commune* with nature⟩

synonyms click, relate

related words bond; befriend

communicable *adj* capable of being passed by physical contact from one person to another — see CONTAGIOUS 1

communicate *vb* 1 to cause (something) to pass from one to another ⟨the infected cook unknowingly *communicated* the disease to hundreds of people⟩

synonyms convey, impart, spread, transfer, transfuse, transmit

related words deliver, hand over, surrender, turn over; broadcast, diffuse, disseminate, propagate; contaminate, infect, poison

near antonyms catch, come down (with), contract

2 to engage in an exchange of information or ideas ⟨for decades the two medical centers have been *communicating* about cancer research⟩

synonyms brainstorm, intercommunicate

related words correspond; converse, talk; bond, commune, relate; accost, approach, contact

communicate (with) *vb* to transmit information or requests to — see CONTACT

communication *n* a piece of conveyed information ⟨the latest *communication* from the crew of the space station⟩

synonyms dispatch, message

related words bulletin, communiqué, report; memo, memorandum, notice; epistle, letter, missive, note; electronic mail, e-mail; intelligence, news, tidings, word; command, directive, instruction, order

communion *n* a friendly relationship marked by ready communication and mutual understanding — see RAPPORT

community *n* 1 the people living in a particular area ⟨the whole *community* rallied to the aid of the family who had lost its home⟩

synonyms neighborhood

related words city, commune, town, village; denizens, dwellers, inhabitants, residents; citizenry, culture, people, populace, public, society

2 a group of people with a common interest living in one place ⟨a picturesque seacoast village that is known for its sizable *community* of artists⟩

synonyms colony

related words circle, clique, coterie, set, society; band, company, troop; clan, family

3 a group of people sharing a common interest and relating together socially — see GANG 2

4 the body of people in a profession or field of activity — see CORPS

5 the quality or state of having many qualities in common — see SIMILARITY 1

commutation *n* a giving or taking of one thing of value in return for another — see EXCHANGE 1

commute *vb* to give up (something) and take something else in return — see CHANGE 3

compact *adj* 1 having a consistency that does not easily yield to pressure — see FIRM 2

2 having little space between items or parts — see CLOSE 1

3 marked by the use of few words to convey much information or meaning — see CONCISE

compact *n* 1 a formal agreement between two or more nations or peoples — see TREATY

2 an arrangement about action to be taken — see AGREEMENT 2

compact *vb* 1 to bring (something) to a central point or under a single control — see CENTRALIZE

2 to reduce in size or volume by or as if by pressing parts or members together — see COMPRESS 1

compacting *n* the act or process of reducing the size or volume of something by or as if by pressing — see COMPRESSION

compactly *adv* in a few words — see SHORTLY 1

compactness *n* the quality or state of being marked by or using only few words to convey much meaning — see SUCCINCTNESS

companion *n* 1 a person frequently seen in the company of another — see ASSOCIATE 1

2 one that accompanies another for protection, guidance, or as a courtesy — see ESCORT

3 either of a pair matched in one or more qualities — see MATE 1

4 something that is found along with something else — see ACCOMPANIMENT

companionable *adj* 1 having or showing kindly feeling and sincere interest — see FRIENDLY 1

2 likely to seek or enjoy the company of others — see CONVIVIAL

THESAURUS

companionship *n* the feeling of closeness and friendship that exists between companions ⟨the widow's pet cats provided her with her only *companionship*⟩
synonyms camaraderie, company, comradeship, fellowship, society
related words amity, benevolence, cordiality, friendliness, friendship, goodwill, kindliness; civility, comity, concord, harmony, rapport; charity, generosity; affinity, compassion, empathy, sympathy; chumminess, familiarity, inseparability, intimacy, nearness; affection, devotion, fondness, love
near antonyms forlornness, loneliness, lonesomeness

company *n* **1** an organized group of stage performers ⟨a city that is fortunate enough to have two thriving opera *companies*⟩
synonyms troop, troupe
related words stock company; cast, dramatis personae, ensemble
2 a group of people working together on a task — see GANG 1
3 a commercial or industrial activity or organization — see ENTERPRISE 1
4 the feeling of closeness and friendship that exists between companions — see COMPANIONSHIP

comparable *adj* having qualities in common — see ALIKE

comparative *adj* being such only when compared to something else ⟨if you consider the multimillionaire's yearly income, we're living in *comparative* poverty⟩
synonyms approximate, near, relative
related words alike, comparable, similar; equal, equivalent
near antonyms genuine, real, true
antonyms absolute, complete, downright, out-and-out, outright, perfect, pure, unqualified

compare *vb* **1** to describe as similar ⟨reviews that *compared* the adventure movie to a thrilling ride on a roller coaster⟩
synonyms bracket, equate, liken
related words associate, connect, couple, link; allude, refer, relate; equal, match, parallel
antonyms contrast
2 to regard or represent as equal or comparable — see EQUATE 1

compare (with) *vb* to come near or nearer to in character or quality — see APPROXIMATE

compartment *n* one of the parts into which an enclosed space is divided ⟨a backpack with many handy *compartments* for storing your camping gear⟩
synonyms bay, cabin, cell, chamber, cubicle
related words cubbyhole, pigeonhole, snuggery [*chiefly British*]; alcove, niche, nook, recess; cabinet, drawer; cavity, hole, hollow; booth, crib, stall; crypt, vault

compass *n* **1** an area over which activity, capacity, or influence extends — see RANGE 2
2 the line or relatively narrow space that marks the outer limit of something — see BORDER 1

compass *vb* **1** to carry through (as a process) to completion — see PERFORM 1
2 to pass completely around — see ENCIRCLE 1

compassion *n* **1** sorrow or the capacity to feel sorrow for another's suffering or misfortune — see SYMPATHY 1

2 the capacity for feeling for another's unhappiness or misfortune — see HEART 1

compassionate *adj* **1** having or marked by sympathy and consideration for others — see HUMANE 1
2 having or showing the capacity for sharing the feelings of another — see SYMPATHETIC 1

compatibility *n* peaceful coexistence — see HARMONY 2

compatible *adj* **1** having or marked by agreement in feeling or action — see HARMONIOUS 3
2 not having or showing any apparent conflict — see CONSISTENT

compatriot *n* a person living in or originally from the same country as another ⟨an appeal to all of his *compatriots* to come to their country's aid in its hour of need⟩
synonyms countryman
related words nationalist, patriot; citizen, national, subject; aborigine, native; homeboy, resident
near antonyms alien, foreigner, immigrant, outsider

compel *vb* to cause (a person) to give in to pressure — see FORCE

compelling *adj* having the power to persuade — see COGENT

compendious *adj* **1** covering everything or all important points — see ENCYCLOPEDIC
2 marked by the use of few words to convey much information or meaning — see CONCISE

compensate *vb* **1** to provide (someone) with a just payment for loss or injury ⟨you'll have to *compensate* the neighbors for cutting down their tree⟩
synonyms indemnify, recompense, recoup, remunerate, requite
related words refund, reimburse, repay; redress, remedy, repair; discharge, pay, quit
2 to give (someone) the sum of money owed for goods or services received — see PAY 1

compensate (for) *vb* to balance with an equal force so as to make ineffective — see OFFSET

compensation *n* **1** payment to another for a loss or injury ⟨a warehouse worker who received a large *compensation* for his crippling injury while on the job⟩
synonyms damages, indemnification, indemnity, quittance, recompense, recoupment, redress, remuneration, reparation, requital, restitution, satisfaction
related words amends, atonement, expiation; refund, reimbursement, repayment; adjustment, settlement; punishment, reprisal, retaliation
2 something (as money) that is given or received in return for goods or services — see PAYMENT 2
3 the act of offering money in exchange for goods or services — see PAYMENT 1

compete *vb* to engage in a contest ⟨prizefighters *competing* for the world heavyweight championship⟩
synonyms battle, contend, fight, race, vie
related words challenge, engage, play; jockey, maneuver; go out, try out; train, work

competence *n* the physical or mental power to do something — see ABILITY

competency *n* the physical or mental power to do something — see ABILITY

competent *adj* having the required skills for an acceptable level of performance ⟨any *competent* mechanic should be able to fix that⟩
synonyms able, capable, fit, good, qualified, suitable

related words accomplished, ace, adept, experienced, expert, master, masterful, masterly, practiced (*or* practised), proficient, seasoned, skilled, skillful, veteran; prepared, schooled, trained

near antonyms inexperienced, inexpert, unseasoned, unskilled, unskillful; unprepared, unschooled, untrained; beginning, green, new, raw, untested, untried

antonyms incompetent, inept, poor, unfit, unqualified

competently *adv* in a skillful or expert manner — see WELL 3

competition *n* 1 a competitive encounter between individuals or groups carried on for amusement, exercise, or in pursuit of a prize — see GAME 1
2 one who strives for the same thing as another — see COMPETITOR

competitor *n* one who strives for the same thing as another ⟨the *competitors* for the science award come from the best high schools in the country⟩
synonyms challenger, competition, contender, contestant, rival
related words finalist, semifinalist; entrant, player; adversary, antagonist, opponent

compilation *n* a collection of writings — see ANTHOLOGY

compile *vb* to bring together from several sources into a single volume or list ⟨*compiled* the best short stories ever written into one fat book⟩
synonyms collect
related words edit, redraft, revamp, revise, rework; accumulate, amass, assemble, gather, group

complacence *n* an often unjustified feeling of being pleased with oneself or with one's situation or achievements ⟨the *complacence* of some of the rich kids at the exclusive private school⟩
synonyms complacency, conceit, conceitedness, ego, egotism, pompousness, pride, pridefulness, self-admiration, self-conceit, self-esteem, self-importance, self-satisfaction, smugness, vaingloriousness, vainglory, vainness, vanity
related words assurance, confidence, self-assurance, self-confidence; self-righteousness; arrogance, disdainfulness, haughtiness, imperiousness, lordliness, self-assertion, snobbishness, superciliousness, superiority; overconfidence, presumption; pretense (*or* pretence), pretension, pretentiousness; egoism, self-centeredness, selfishness; self-respect
near antonyms diffidence, self-doubt; altruism, unselfishness; bashfulness, demureness, shyness, timidity, timidness; passiveness, passivity
antonyms humbleness, humility, modesty

complacency *n* an often unjustified feeling of being pleased with oneself or with one's situation or achievements — see COMPLACENCE

complacent *adj* having too high an opinion of oneself — see CONCEITED

complain *vb* to express dissatisfaction, pain, or resentment usually tiresomely ⟨the time-honored tradition of students *complaining* about the food in the cafeteria⟩
synonyms beef, bellyache, carp, crab, croak, fuss, gripe, grouse, growl, grumble, kick, moan, murmur, mutter, repine, squawk, wail, whine, yammer
related words object (to), protest, quarrel (with); cavil, quibble; fret, stew, worry; blubber, cry, sob; bemoan, bewail, deplore, lament

near antonyms accept, bear, countenance, endure, tolerate; applaud, cheer, commend
antonyms rejoice

complainant *n* the person in a legal proceeding who makes a charge of wrongdoing against another ⟨the *complainant* charged that the defendant had broken the ironclad contract that both had signed⟩
synonyms plaintiff, suer
related words accuser; litigant, party, suitor; appellant, petitioner, pleader
near antonyms accused
antonyms defendant

complainer *n* 1 a person who makes frequent complaints usually about little things — see CRYBABY
2 an irritable and complaining person — see GROUCH

complaint *n* 1 an expression of dissatisfaction, pain, or resentment ⟨a warning that if there were any more *complaints*, we were turning around and not going to the beach after all⟩
synonyms beef, fuss, grievance, gripe, grumble, murmur, plaint, squawk
related words challenge, demur, expostulation, kick, objection, protest, quibble, remonstrance
near antonyms commendation, compliment, plaudit; acclaim, applause, praise; approval, endorsement, sanction
2 a feeling or declaration of disapproval or dissent — see OBJECTION
3 a formal claim of criminal wrongdoing against a person — see CHARGE 1
4 an abnormal state that disrupts a plant's or animal's normal bodily functioning — see DISEASE

complaisance *n* a desire or disposition to please ⟨the *complaisance* of his girlfriend is such that she goes along with everything he says⟩
synonyms amenability, amiability, good-naturedness
related words affability, amicability, congeniality, cordiality, friendliness, geniality, sociability; agreeableness, graciousness, pleasantness; kindheartedness, kindliness, warmheartedness; compliance, docility, passivity, submissiveness
near antonyms disagreeableness, sullenness, surliness, ungraciousness; disobedience, intractability, recalcitrance

complement *n* 1 something that serves to complete or make up for a deficiency in something else ⟨with his practicality and her refreshing enthusiasm, they are perfect *complements* to each other⟩
synonyms supplement
related words addendum, addition, appendix; adjunct, annex, appendage, extension; accessory, appliance, attachment; additive, filler
2 the largest number or amount that something can hold — see CAPACITY 1

complement *vb* to serve as a completing element to ⟨this cap *complements* your Boy Scout uniform⟩
synonyms complete, round (off *or* out)
related words finish (off), flesh (out); adorn, beautify, decorate, embellish; better, enhance, improve; constitute, form, make up

complementary *adj* related to each other in such a way that one completes the other ⟨the *complementary* contributions of the cooking and cleanup committees were essential to the success of the church barbecue⟩
synonyms reciprocal, supplementary

related words cooperative, mutual, symbiotic; collective, combined, common, communal, conjoint, joint, shared, united

antonyms noncomplementary, nonreciprocal

complete *adj* **1** not lacking any part or member that properly belongs to it ⟨a *complete* deck of cards⟩

synonyms comprehensive, entire, full, grand, intact, integral, perfect, plenary, total, whole

related words unabridged, uncut, undiminished; all-out, exhaustive, extensive; full-blown, full-fledged, full-scale

near antonyms abbreviated, abridged, cut, diminished, reduced

antonyms imperfect, incomplete, partial

2 brought or having come to an end ⟨your education is never *complete* —there's always something more to learn⟩

synonyms completed, concluded, done, down, ended, finished, over, terminated, through, up

related words accomplished, achieved, attained, compassed, realized; dead, defunct, extinct, obsolete; expired

antonyms continuing, incomplete, ongoing, uncompleted, unfinished

3 covering everything or all important points — see ENCYCLOPEDIC

4 having no exceptions or restrictions — see ABSOLUTE 2

5 trying all possibilities — see EXHAUSTIVE

complete *vb* **1** to bring (something) to a state where nothing remains to be done — see FINISH 1

2 to serve as a completing element to — see COMPLEMENT

completed *adj* brought or having come to an end — see COMPLETE 2

completely *adv* **1** to a full extent or degree — see FULLY 1

2 with attention to all aspects or details — see THOROUGHLY 1

complex *adj* **1** having many parts or aspects that are usually interrelated ⟨this camera is a *complex* instrument that requires careful handling⟩ ⟨*complex* issues regarding free speech and school discipline⟩

synonyms complicated, convoluted, elaborate, intricate, involved, knotty, labyrinthine, sophisticated

related words composite, compound, heterogeneous, mixed, multifarious, varied; challenging, difficult, tough; impenetrable, incomprehensible, inexplicable, unfathomable, unintelligible

near antonyms oversimplified, simplified; homogeneous, uniform, unvaried

antonyms plain, simple, uncomplicated

2 made or done with great care or with much detail — see ELABORATE 1

complex *n* **1** a structure that is designed and built for a particular purpose — see FACILITY

2 something made up of many interdependent or related parts — see SYSTEM 1

complexion *n* **1** the hue or appearance of the skin and especially of the face ⟨a sunscreen for people with very light *complexions*⟩

synonyms color, coloring

related words shade, tint, tone; features, lineaments, looks; countenance, face, visage

2 the set of qualities that makes a person, a group of people, or a thing different from others — see NATURE 1

complexity *n* **1** the state or quality of having many interrelated parts or aspects ⟨the *complexity* of the company's computer system is such that a full-time repairman is needed⟩

synonyms complicatedness, elaborateness, intricacy, involution, sophistication

related words diversity, heterogeneousness; impenetrability, incomprehensibility, inexplicability

near antonyms simplification; homogeneity, uniformity

antonyms plainness, simpleness, simplicity

2 something that makes a situation more complicated or difficult — see COMPLICATION 1

compliance *n* **1** a readiness or willingness to yield to the wishes of others ⟨a strong-willed pop star who is not known for her *compliance*⟩

synonyms compliancy, deference, docility, obedience, submissiveness

related words amenability, amiability, complaisance, good-naturedness; servility, slavishness, subservience, subserviency; conformity; cooperativeness, receptiveness, receptivity; humoring, indulgence; acceptance, acquiescence, assent, consent; capitulation, submission, surrender; affability, amicability, congeniality, cordiality, friendliness, geniality, sociability

near antonyms animosity, antipathy, enmity, hostility, ill will

antonyms defiance, disobedience, intractability, recalcitrance

2 a bending to the authority or control of another — see OBEDIENCE 1

compliancy *n* a readiness or willingness to yield to the wishes of others — see COMPLIANCE 1

compliant *adj* readily giving in to the command or authority of another — see OBEDIENT

complicate *vb* to make complex or difficult ⟨the need to go to both a soccer game and band practice really *complicates* tonight's schedule⟩

synonyms perplex, sophisticate

related words develop, elaborate, expand; intensify, magnify; confound, confuse, mess (up), mix (up), muddle; entangle, snarl, tangle

near antonyms abbreviate, cut, shorten; ease, facilitate; disentangle, straighten (out), untangle; oversimplify

antonyms simplify, streamline

complicated *adj* **1** having many parts or aspects that are usually interrelated — see COMPLEX 1

2 made or done with great care or with much detail — see ELABORATE 1

complicatedness *n* the state or quality of having many interrelated parts or aspects — see COMPLEXITY 1

complication *n* **1** something that makes a situation more complicated or difficult ⟨the food allergies of the guests were just another *complication* for the couple trying to plan their wedding reception⟩

synonyms complexity, difficulty, intricacy

related words aftereffect, ramification, side effect; subtlety, technicality; annoyance, bother, headache, inconvenience, matter, trouble

phrases fly in the ointment

2 an abnormal state that disrupts a plant's or animal's normal bodily functioning — see DISEASE

complicity *n* a secret agreement or cooperation between two parties for an illegal or dishonest purpose — see COLLUSION

compliment *vb* to express to (someone) admiration

for his or her success or good fortune — see CON-GRATULATE

complimentary *adj* **1** expressing approval — see FAVORABLE 1

2 not costing or charging anything — see FREE 4

compliments *n pl* best wishes 〈please extend our *compliments* to the chef for a great meal〉
synonyms congratulations, felicitations, greetings, regards, respects
related words approval, blessing, endorsement; acknowledgment (*also* acknowledgement), citation, commendation; adulation, flattery, praise
near antonyms dig, gibe (*or* jibe), insult, putdown, taunt

comply (with) *vb* **1** to act according to the commands of — see OBEY

2 to do what is required by the terms of — see FULFILL 1

component *n* one of the parts that make up a whole — see ELEMENT 1

comport *vb* **1** to be in agreement on every point — see CHECK 1

2 to manage the actions of (oneself) in a particular way — see BEHAVE

comportment *n* the way or manner in which one conducts oneself — see BEHAVIOR

compose *vb* **1** to put (something) into proper and usually carefully worked out written form 〈the whole class *composed* a request to the governor asking that the endangered species be adopted as the official state animal〉
synonyms cast, craft, draft, draw (up), formulate, frame, prepare
related words fabricate, fashion, form, mold, sculpture, shape; couch, express, phrase, state, verbalize, word; author, pen, write; conceive, concoct, devise; build, construct, make; assemble, compound, piece (together)
phrases put together

2 to be all the substance of — see CONSTITUTE 1

3 to free from distress or disturbance — see CALM 1

4 to gain emotional or mental control of — see COLLECT 1

composed *adj* free from emotional or mental agitation — see CALM 2

composer *n* a person who writes musical compositions 〈a versatile *composer* whose works include operas, symphonies, concertos, and sonatas〉
synonyms musician, songwriter
related words arranger, scorer; librettist

composite *adj* made from the joining of two or more parts or elements 〈the movie's special effects included the use of many *composite* photographs〉
synonyms amalgamated, compound
related words blended, combined, commingled, mingled, mixed; fused, integrated; interlaced, intermixed, intertwined, interwoven
near antonyms uncombined, unmixed
antonyms simple

composite *n* a distinct entity formed by the combining of two or more different things — see BLEND

composition *n* **1** a literary, musical, or artistic production 〈the *compositions* of Michelangelo include the dome of St. Peter's, the ceiling of the Sistine Chapel, and his monumental statue of David〉
synonyms opus, piece, work
related words classic, magnum opus, masterpiece,

pièce de résistance, showpiece; model, outline, sketch; étude

2 a short piece of writing done as a school exercise 〈a teacher who is fond of having her class write *compositions*〉
synonyms paper, theme
related words article, essay, story

3 the way in which the elements of something (as a work of art) are arranged 〈student photographers learn the importance of *composition* in creating striking images〉
synonyms arrangement, configuration, design, form, format, layout, makeup, pattern
related words motif, theme

4 a short piece of writing typically expressing a point of view — see ESSAY 1

composure *n* evenness of emotions or temper — see EQUANIMITY

compound *adj* made from the joining of two or more parts or elements — see COMPOSITE

compound *n* a distinct entity formed by the combining of two or more different things — see BLEND

compound *vb* **1** to make greater in size, amount, or number — see INCREASE 1

2 to put or bring together so as to form a new and longer whole — see CONNECT 1

comprehend *vb* **1** to recognize the meaning of 〈the age at which children can *comprehend* the difference between right and wrong〉
synonyms appreciate, apprehend, catch, catch on (to), dig [*slang*], get, grasp, make, make out, perceive, see, seize, tumble (to), understand
related words absorb, assimilate, digest, take in; know, realize, sense; fathom, penetrate
near antonyms misapprehend, misconstrue, misinterpret, misunderstand
antonyms miss

2 to have a practical understanding of — see KNOW 1

3 to have as part of a whole — see INCLUDE

comprehension *n* the knowledge gained from the process of coming to know or understand something 〈the president's *comprehension* of the current situation in the Middle East〉
synonyms appreciation, apprehension, grasp, grip, perception, understanding
related words absorption, assimilation, uptake; conception, visualization; awareness, consciousness, realization
near antonyms misapprehension, misinterpretation, misunderstanding

comprehensive *adj* **1** covering everything or all important points — see ENCYCLOPEDIC

2 not lacking any part or member that properly belongs to it — see COMPLETE 1

3 trying all possibilities — see EXHAUSTIVE

comprehensively *adv* with attention to all aspects or details — see THOROUGHLY 1

compress *vb* **1** to reduce in size or volume by or as if by pressing parts or members together 〈a science textbook that *compresses* a lot of information about human reproduction into a few short chapters〉
synonyms compact, condense, constrict, contract, squeeze
related words cram, crowd, jam, jam-pack, pack; abbreviate, abridge, curtail, shorten; downsize, shrink; concentrate, consolidate; simplify, streamline; decrease, diminish, lessen

near antonyms disperse, dissipate, scatter; distend, inflate, swell

antonyms expand, open, outspread, outstretch

2 to become smaller in size or volume through the drawing together of particles of matter — see CONTRACT 2

compression *n* the act or process of reducing the size or volume of something by or as if by pressing ⟨the *compression* of a long, complicated story into a two-hour movie is never easy⟩

synonyms compacting, condensation, constriction, contraction, squeezing

related words abbreviation, abridgment (*or* abridgement), curtailment, shortening; concentration, consolidation; simplification, streamlining; decreasing, diminishment, lessening

near antonyms dispersion, dissipation, scattering; distension (*or* distention), inflation, swelling

antonyms expansion

comprise *vb* **1** to be made up of ⟨the mall *comprises* three department stores and eighty smaller shops selling specialized goods⟩

synonyms consist (of), contain

related words embrace, encompass, entail, include, involve, take in; assimilate, embody, incorporate

2 to be all the substance of — see CONSTITUTE 1

compromise *n* the act or practice of each side giving up something in order to reach an agreement — see CONCESSION 1

compromise *vb* to place in danger — see ENDANGER

compulsion *n* the use of power to impose one's will on another — see FORCE 2

compulsive *adj* caused by or suggestive of an irresistible urge ⟨his *compulsive* clowning around can sometimes be annoying⟩

synonyms impulsive, obsessive

related words uncontrollable, irrepressible; automatic, instinctive, involuntary, reflex, spontaneous; conditioned, mechanical; unconscious, unthinking, unwitting

near antonyms unforced, voluntary, willful (*or* wilful); controllable, manageable, resistible

compulsory *adj* forcing one's compliance or participation by or as if by law — see MANDATORY

compunction *n* an uneasy feeling about the rightness of what one is doing or going to do — see QUALM

computation *n* the act or process of performing mathematical operations to find a value — see CALCULATION

compute *vb* to determine (a value) by doing the necessary mathematical operations — see CALCULATE 1

comrade *n* **1** a person frequently seen in the company of another — see ASSOCIATE 1

2 a person who has a strong liking for and trust in another — see FRIEND 1

comradely *adj* having or showing kindly feeling and sincere interest — see FRIENDLY 1

comradeship *n* the feeling of closeness and friendship that exists between companions — see COMPANIONSHIP

con *vb* to commit to memory — see MEMORIZE

concatenate *vb* to put together into a series by means of or as if by means of a thread — see THREAD 2

concatenation *n* a series of things linked together — see CHAIN 1

concave *adj* curved inward — see HOLLOW

concavity *n* a sunken area forming a separate space — see HOLE 2

conceal *vb* **1** to put into a hiding place — see ¹HIDE 1

2 to keep secret or shut off from view — see ¹HIDE 2

concealment *n* **1** the placing of something out of sight ⟨your choice of the oven for the *concealment* of the money was unwise⟩

synonyms caching, hiding, secretion, stashing

related words burial, burying, entombment, interment, interring

near antonyms disinterment, unearthing

antonyms display, exhibition, exposure, parading, showing

2 a place where a person goes to hide — see HIDEOUT

concede *vb* **1** to accept the truth or existence of (something) usually reluctantly — see ADMIT

2 to cease resistance (as to another's arguments, demands, or control) — see YIELD 1

conceit *n* **1** an elaborate or fanciful way of expressing something ⟨the *conceit* that the crowd at the outdoor rock concert was a vast sea of people waving to the beat of the music⟩

synonyms metaphor

related words analogy, circumlocution, euphemism, simile

phrases figure of speech

2 a conception or image created by the imagination and having no objective reality — see FANTASY 1

3 an often unjustified feeling of being pleased with oneself or with one's situation or achievements — see COMPLACENCE

conceited *adj* having too high an opinion of oneself ⟨a *conceited* basketball player who was always too busy even to sign autographs⟩

synonyms complacent, egoistic, egotistic (*or* egotistical), important, overweening, pompous, prideful, proud, self-conceited, self-important, self-satisfied, smug, stuck-up, vain, vainglorious

related words boastful, braggart, bragging; arrogant, cavalier, disdainful, haughty, lordly, self-assertive, snobbish, supercilious, superior, uppity; domineering, high-handed, imperious; highfalutin, pretentious; overconfident, presumptuous; confident, self-assured, self-confident; self-centered, selfish

near antonyms diffident, self-doubting; meek, unassertive; down-to-earth, unassuming, unpretentious; bashful, retiring, shy

antonyms humble, modest

conceitedness *n* an often unjustified feeling of being pleased with oneself or with one's situation or achievements — see COMPLACENCE

conceivably *adv* it is possible — see PERHAPS

conceive *vb* to form a mental picture of — see IMAGINE 1

concentrate *vb* **1** to increase the amount of (a substance in a mixture) by removing other substances ⟨prolonged boiling is required to *concentrate* the sap when making maple syrup⟩

synonyms condense

related words distill (*or* distil), purify, refine; compact, harden, solidify; deepen, enhance, heighten, intensify; evaporate, extract, remove

near antonyms weaken

antonyms dilute, water (down)

2 to fix (as one's attention) steadily toward a central objective ⟨a president who will try to *concentrate* public attention on the problems of inner cities⟩
synonyms fasten, focus, rivet, train
related words aim, direct, level, point, zero (in on); attend, heed, mind
3 to bring (something) to a central point or under a single control — see CENTRALIZE
4 to bring together in one body or place — see GATHER 1
5 to come together into one body or place — see ASSEMBLE 1
concentrated *adj* **1** having an abundance of some characteristic quality (as flavor) — see FULL-BODIED
2 not divided or scattered among several areas of interest or concern — see WHOLE 1
concentration *n* a focusing of the mind on something — see ATTENTION 1
concept *n* something imagined or pictured in the mind — see IDEA
conception *n* something imagined or pictured in the mind — see IDEA
conceptual *adj* dealing with or expressing a quality or idea — see ABSTRACT 1
concern *n* **1** a commercial or industrial activity or organization — see ENTERPRISE 1
2 an uneasy state of mind usually over the possibility of an anticipated misfortune or trouble — see ANXIETY 1
concern *vb* **1** to have (something) as a subject matter ⟨the book *concerns* the challenges faced by children growing up in single-parent households⟩
synonyms cover, deal (with), pertain (to), treat (of)
related words appertain (to), bear (on *or* upon), refer (to), relate (to); allude (to), glance (upon), mention, touch (upon); offer, present; contain, embrace, encompass, entail, include, incorporate
phrases have to do with
near antonyms exclude, omit; disregard, ignore, neglect, overlook, pass over, slight
2 to be the business or affair of ⟨the problems of air and water pollution that *concern* all of us⟩
synonyms affect, involve, touch
related words apply (to), relate (to); embroil, ensnare, entangle, implicate
3 to trouble the mind of; to make uneasy — see DISTURB 1
concerning *prep* having to do with — see ABOUT 1
concert *n* an entertainment featuring singing or the playing of musical instruments ⟨during the summer various groups give *concerts* on the town green⟩
synonyms musicale
related words performance, presentation; recital; hootenanny, jam session, sing, songfest; festival
concert *vb* **1** to bring about through discussion and compromise — see NEGOTIATE 1
2 to participate or assist in a joint effort to accomplish an end — see COOPERATE 1
concerted *adj* used or done by a number of people as a group — see COLLECTIVE
concession *n* **1** the act or practice of each side giving up something in order to reach an agreement ⟨when trying to get a raise in your allowance, it's good to know the art of *concession*⟩
synonyms accommodation, compromise, give-and-take, negotiation

related words arrangement, bargain, deal, understanding; agreement, settlement
2 an open declaration of something (as a fault or the commission of an offense) about oneself — see CONFESSION
3 something granted as a special favor — see PRIVILEGE
conciliate *vb* **1** to bring to a state free of conflicts, inconsistencies, or differences — see HARMONIZE 2
2 to lessen the anger or agitation of — see PACIFY
conciliating *adj* tending to lessen or avoid conflict or hostility — see PACIFIC 1
conciliator *n* one who works with opposing sides in order to bring about an agreement — see MEDIATOR
conciliatory *adj* tending to lessen or avoid conflict or hostility — see PACIFIC 1
concise *adj* marked by the use of few words to convey much information or meaning ⟨a *concise* article on violence in the media that manages to say more than most books on the subject⟩
synonyms aphoristic, brief, compact, compendious, crisp, epigrammatic, laconic, pithy, succinct, summary, terse
related words abrupt, blunt, brusque, curt, short, snippy; abbreviated, abridged, condensed, shortened; meaty, substantial; meaningful, significant
near antonyms redundant, repetitious, tautological; enlarged, expanded, supplemented; embellished, embroidered, exaggerated
antonyms diffuse, long-winded, prolix, rambling, verbose, wordy
concisely *adv* in a few words — see SHORTLY 1
conciseness *n* **1** the condition of being short — see BREVITY 1
2 the quality or state of being marked by or using only few words to convey much meaning — see SUCCINCTNESS
conclude *vb* **1** to bring (an event) to a natural or appropriate stopping point — see CLOSE 3
2 to come to an end — see CEASE 1
3 to bring about through discussion and compromise — see NEGOTIATE 1
4 to come to a judgment after discussion or consideration — see DECIDE 1
5 to form an opinion through reasoning and information — see INFER 1
concluded *adj* brought or having come to an end — see COMPLETE 2
concluding *adj* following all others of the same kind in order or time — see LAST
conclusion *n* **1** an opinion arrived at through a process of reasoning ⟨the detective's *conclusion* that the murderer had to be left-handed⟩
synonyms deduction, determination, inference
related words decision, judgment (*or* judgement), ruling, verdict; conjecture, guess, surmise; assumption, presumption, supposition
2 a position arrived at after consideration — see DECISION 1
3 a condition or occurrence traceable to a cause — see EFFECT 1
4 the last part of a process or action — see FINALE
5 the stopping of a process or activity — see END 1
conclusive *adj* **1** serving to put an end to all debate or questioning ⟨the archeological discovery was *conclusive* proof that the Vikings had indeed settled in North America around 1000 A.D.⟩

synonyms absolute, clear, decisive, definitive
related words incontestable, incontrovertible, indisputable, indubitable, irrefutable, undeniable, unquestionable; unchallenged, uncontested, undisputed; unambiguous, unequivocal; certain, definite, positive, sure
near antonyms debatable, disputable, questionable, refutable; ambiguous, equivocal
antonyms inconclusive, indecisive, unclear
2 having the power to persuade — see COGENT
concoct *vb* to create or think of by clever use of the imagination — see INVENT
concoction *n* something (as a device) created for the first time through the use of the imagination — see INVENTION 1
concomitant *n* something that is found along with something else — see ACCOMPANIMENT
concomitant *adj* present at the same time and place — see COINCIDENT
concord *n* peaceful coexistence — see HARMONY 2
concourse *n* a typically long narrow way connecting parts of a building — see HALL 2
concrete *adj* **1** existing in fact and not merely as a possibility — see ACTUAL
2 relating to or composed of matter — see MATERIAL 1
concrete *vb* to become physically firm or solid — see HARDEN 1
concur *vb* **1** to have or come to the same opinion or point of view — see AGREE 1
2 to occur or exist at the same time — see COINCIDE 1
concurrence *n* **1** the occurrence or existence of several things at once ⟨the *concurrence* of my birthday and the concert by my favorite rock band made my preference for a birthday present pretty obvious⟩
synonyms coexistence, coincidence
related words development, happening, occurrence
2 the act or fact of being of one opinion about something — see AGREEMENT 1
3 the approval by someone in authority for the doing of something — see PERMISSION
concurrent *adj* **1** existing or occurring at the same period of time — see CONTEMPORARY 1
2 present at the same time and place — see COINCIDENT
concurrently *adv* at one and the same time — see TOGETHER 1
concussion *n* a forceful coming together of two things — see IMPACT 1
condemn *vb* **1** to declare to be morally wrong or evil ⟨it is a sign of human progress that slavery, which was once common, is now universally *condemned*⟩
synonyms censure, damn, decry, denounce, execrate, reprehend, reprobate
related words attack, blast, criticize, knock, pan, slam; belittle, deprecate, disparage; doom, sentence; convict; blacklist, excommunicate, ostracize; rebuke, reprimand, reproach; admonish, chide, reprove; berate, lambaste (*or* lambast), scold, upbraid; curse, imprecate; abhor, abominate, detest, hate, loathe, revile
near antonyms approve, endorse (*also* indorse), sanction; eulogize, exalt, extol (*also* extoll), glorify, laud, praise; acclaim, applaud, commend, hail; consecrate, hallow, sanctify; honor, revere, venerate

antonyms bless
2 to express one's unfavorable opinion of the worth or quality of — see CRITICIZE
3 to express public or formal disapproval of — see CENSURE 1
4 to find or pronounce guilty — see CONVICT
5 to impose a judicial punishment on — see SENTENCE
condemnation *n* an often public or formal expression of disapproval — see CENSURE
condensation *n* **1** a shortened version of a written work — see ABRIDGMENT
2 the act or process of reducing the size or volume of something by or as if by pressing — see COMPRESSION
condense *vb* **1** to become smaller in size or volume through the drawing together of particles of matter — see CONTRACT 2
2 to reduce in size or volume by or as if by pressing parts or members together — see COMPRESS 1
3 to increase the amount of (a substance in a mixture) by removing other substances — see CONCENTRATE 1
condensed *adj* not lasting for a considerable time — see SHORT 2
condescend *vb* **1** to descend to a level that is beneath one's dignity ⟨I will not *condescend* to answer the sore loser's charge that I cheated in order to win the race⟩
synonyms deign, stoop
related words debase, degrade, demean, humble, humiliate, lower
near antonyms rise
2 to assume or treat with an air of superiority ⟨wealthy people who tend to be *condescending* toward their poor relations⟩
synonyms lord (it over), patronize
related words cold-shoulder, cut, high-hat, snub
condiment *n* something used to enhance the flavor of cooked or prepared food ⟨the cafeteria's self-serve table has a full array of *condiments*⟩
synonyms seasoning
related words herb, savory, spice; relish, sauce; flavoring
condition *n* **1** a state of being or fitness ⟨a car that was ten years old but in still good *condition*⟩
synonyms estate, fettle, form, kilter, order, repair, shape, trim
related words practice (*also* practise); pass, phase, stage
near antonyms disorder, disrepair
2 something upon which the carrying out of an agreement or offer depends ⟨you'll get a raise in your allowance with the *condition* that you'll do a better job of keeping your room clean⟩
synonyms provision, proviso, qualification, reservation, stipulation
related words strings, terms; prerequisite, requirement, requisite; limitation, modification, restriction; exception, exemption; essential, must, necessity
3 an abnormal state that disrupts a plant's or animal's normal bodily functioning — see DISEASE
4 something necessary, indispensable, or unavoidable — see ESSENTIAL 1
5 something that limits one's freedom of action or choice — see RESTRICTION 1
condition *vb* **1** to bring to a proper or desired state of fitness ⟨the length of time that it takes for runners to *condition* their bodies for a marathon⟩

synonyms season, train

related words fit, prepare, ready; acclimate, acclimatize, break in, orient, orientate; accustom, familiarize, habituate; harden, inure

2 to change (something) so as to make it suitable for a new use or situation — see ADAPT

conditional *adj* determined by something else — see DEPENDENT 2

conditioning *n* energetic movement of the body for the sake of physical fitness — see EXERCISE 1

condole (with) *vb* to have sympathy for — see PITY

condone *vb* to overlook or dismiss as of little importance — see EXCUSE 1

conduct *n* **1** the act or activity of looking after and making decisions about something ⟨the president was happy to leave the *conduct* of foreign affairs to his secretary of state⟩

synonyms administration, control, direction, governance, government, guidance, handling, management, operation, oversight, regulation, running, superintendence, supervision

related words care, custody, guardianship, protection, tutelage; engineering, machination, manipulation

2 the way or manner in which one conducts oneself — see BEHAVIOR

conduct *vb* **1** to look after and make decisions about ⟨the company's president continues to *conduct* the everyday affairs of the software firm he founded many years ago⟩

synonyms administer, carry on, control, direct, govern, guide, handle, manage, operate, oversee, regulate, run, superintend, supervise

related words care (for), keep, mind, tend, watch; lead, pilot, steer; guard, protect, safeguard

2 to cause to move to a central point or along a restricted pathway — see CHANNEL

3 to manage the actions of (oneself) in a particular way — see BEHAVE

4 to point out the way for (someone) especially from a position in front — see LEAD 1

conduit *n* **1** a long hollow cylinder for carrying a substance (as a liquid or gas) — see PIPE 1

2 an open man-made passageway for water — see CHANNEL 1

confection *n* a food having a high sugar content — see SWEET 1

confederacy *n* an association of persons, parties, or states for mutual assistance and protection ⟨a *confederacy* of several small nations who had promised to come to one another's aid if any were attacked⟩

synonyms alliance, bloc, coalition, combination, combine, confederation, federation, league, union

related words cabal, conspiracy, junto; cartel, syndicate, trust; faction, side, wing; association, group, organization; affiliation, cooperative, partnership

confederate *n* **1** one associated with another in wrongdoing — see ACCOMPLICE

2 someone associated with another to give assistance or moral support — see ALLY

confederate *vb* to form or enter into an association that furthers the interests of its members — see ALLY

confederation *n* **1** an association of persons, parties, or states for mutual assistance and protection — see CONFEDERACY

2 the state of having shared interests or efforts (as in social or business matters) — see ASSOCIATION 1

confer *vb* **1** to give the ownership or benefit of (something) formally or publicly ⟨the British monarch continues to *confer* knighthood on those who are outstanding in their fields⟩

synonyms accord, award, grant

related words bestow, contribute, donate, give, present; furnish, provide, supply; extend, offer, proffer; allocate, appropriate, assign

near antonyms rescind, revoke

2 to exchange viewpoints or seek advice for the purpose of finding a solution to a problem ⟨my parents are going to *confer* with a financial advisor about saving for my college education⟩

synonyms advise, consult, counsel, parley, powwow, treat

related words debate, deliberate, discuss, hash (over); coach, guide, tutor; recommend, suggest; direct, refer (to)

conference *n* **1** a body of people come together in one place — see GATHERING 1

2 a coming together of a number of persons for a specified purpose — see MEETING 1

3 a meeting featuring a group discussion — see FORUM

4 an exchange of views for the purpose of exploring a subject or deciding an issue — see DISCUSSION 1

confess *vb* to accept the truth or existence of (something) usually reluctantly — see ADMIT

confession *n* an open declaration of something (as a fault or the commission of an offense) about oneself ⟨a *confession* that he had been lying all along⟩

synonyms acknowledgment (*also* acknowledgement), admission, avowal, concession

related words allowance; betrayal, disclosure, divulgence, revelation; announcement, declaration, proclamation; contrition, regret, remorse, repentance

confidant *n* a person who has a strong liking for and trust in another — see FRIEND 1

confidence *n* **1** great faith in oneself or one's abilities ⟨a lifelong *confidence* that enabled her to achieve great things despite powerful obstacles⟩

synonyms aplomb, assurance, self-assurance, self-confidence, self-esteem

related words cockiness, complacence, complacency, conceit, conceitedness, ego, egotism, overconfidence, pompousness, pride, self-admiration, self-conceit, self-importance, self-satisfaction, smugness, vainglory, vanity; calmness, composure, coolness, equanimity; self-possession

near antonyms apprehension, doubt, misgiving

antonyms diffidence, self-doubt

2 a state of mind in which one is free from doubt ⟨the *confidence* with which the game show contestant answered every question⟩

synonyms assurance, assuredness, certainty, certitude, conviction, positiveness, sureness

related words authoritarianism, dogmatism; decisiveness, firmness, resolution

near antonyms hesitancy, hesitation, indecisiveness, irresolution

antonyms doubt, incertitude, nonconfidence, uncertainty

3 firm belief in the integrity, ability, effectiveness, or genuineness of someone or something — see TRUST 1

THESAURUS

4 information shared only with another or with a select few — see SECRET 1

confidence game *n* a scheme in which the victim is cheated out of his money after first gaining his trust ⟨the old *confidence game* in which the victims are told that they must pay a fee in order to collect their prize money⟩
synonyms hustle, racket, swindle
related words double cross, fix; gyp, rip-off; squeeze; ruse, subterfuge, trick

confidence man *n* a dishonest person who uses clever means to cheat others out of something of value — see TRICKSTER 1

confident *adj* **1** having or showing great faith in oneself or one's abilities ⟨you'll need to be *confident* —even in the face of rejection—if you want to pursue a career in show business⟩
synonyms assured, secure, self-assured, self-confident
related words hopeful, optimistic, rosy, sanguine, upbeat; complacent, conceited, egoistic, egotistic (*or* egotistical), important, overweening, pompous, prideful, proud, self-conceited, self-important, self-satisfied, smug, stuck-up, vain, vainglorious; calm, collected, composed, cool, placid, self-possessed, serene, tranquil, undisturbed, unperturbed
near antonyms meek, timid, unassertive; modest, unassuming, unpretentious; jittery, jumpy, nervous
antonyms diffident, insecure, self-doubting
2 having or showing a mind free from doubt — see CERTAIN 2

confidential *adj* not known or meant to be known by the general populace — see PRIVATE 1

confiding *adj* having or showing trust in another — see TRUSTING 1

configuration *n* **1** the arrangement of parts that gives something its basic form — see FRAME 1
2 the way in which something is sized, arranged, or organized — see FORMAT 1
3 the way in which the elements of something (as a work of art) are arranged — see COMPOSITION 3
4 the outward appearance of something as distinguished from its substance — see FORM 1

confine *vb* **1** to set bounds or an upper limit for — see LIMIT 1
2 to put in or as if in prison — see IMPRISON

confinement *n* **1** the act of confining or the state of being confined — see INTERNMENT
2 the act or practice of keeping something (as an activity) within certain boundaries — see RESTRICTION 2

confines *n pl* **1** a real or imaginary point beyond which a person or thing cannot go — see LIMIT
2 the line or relatively narrow space that marks the outer limit of something — see BORDER 1

confirm *vb* to give evidence or testimony to the truth or factualness of ⟨several eyewitnesses who can *confirm* the youngster's account of what happened⟩
synonyms bear out, corroborate, substantiate, support, validate, verify, vindicate
related words attest, authenticate, avouch, certify, testify (to), vouch (for), witness; guarantee, warrant; affirm, assert, aver, avow, profess
near antonyms contradict, gainsay; deny, disavow, disclaim
antonyms disprove, rebut, refute

confirmable *adj* capable of being proven as true or real — see VERIFIABLE

confirmation *n* something presented in support of the truth or accuracy of a claim — see PROOF

confirmatory *adj* serving to give support to the truth or factualness of something — see CORROBORATIVE

confirmed *adj* **1** being such by habit and not likely to change — see HABITUAL 1
2 firmly established over time — see INVETERATE 1

confirming *adj* serving to give support to the truth or factualness of something — see CORROBORATIVE

confiscate *vb* to take ownership or control of (something) by right of one's authority ⟨anything that might be used as a weapon will be *confiscated* by the security guards⟩
synonyms expropriate, sequester
related words appropriate, arrogate, preempt, usurp; commandeer, seize, take over
near antonyms release, relinquish, surrender, yield

conflagration *n* a destructive burning — see FIRE

conflict *n* **1** a lack of agreement or harmony — see DISCORD
2 a physical dispute between opposing individuals or groups — see FIGHT 1
3 a state of armed violent struggle between states, nations, or groups — see WAR 1
4 an earnest effort for superiority or victory over another — see CONTEST 1

conflict *vb* to be out of harmony or agreement usually noticeably — see CLASH

conflicting *adj* not being in agreement or harmony — see INCONSISTENT

confluence *n* the coming together of two or more things to the same point — see CONVERGENCE

conform *vb* **1** to be in agreement on every point — see CHECK 1
2 to form a pleasing relationship — see HARMONIZE 1
3 to bring to a state free of conflicts, inconsistencies, or differences — see HARMONIZE 2
4 to change (something) so as to make it suitable for a new use or situation — see ADAPT

conform (to) *vb* to act according to the commands of — see OBEY

conformable *adj* readily giving in to the command or authority of another — see OBEDIENT

conformable (to) *adj* not having or showing any apparent conflict — see CONSISTENT

conformation *n* **1** the outward appearance of something as distinguished from its substance — see FORM 1
2 the way in which something is sized, arranged, or organized — see FORMAT 1

conformity *n* **1** a state of consistency ⟨the simple lifestyle of the Amish is in *conformity* with their ascetic religious beliefs⟩
synonyms accord, accordance, agreement, congruity, consonance, harmony, tune
related words assimilation, integration; oneness, solidarity, togetherness; affinity, empathy, sympathy
near antonyms discrepancy, disparity, dissimilarity
antonyms conflict, disagreement
2 a bending to the authority or control of another — see OBEDIENCE 1

confound *vb* **1** to throw into a state of mental uncertainty — see CONFUSE 1

2 to throw into a state of self-conscious distress — see EMBARRASS 1

confront *vb* to oppose (something hostile or dangerous) with firmness or courage — see FACE 2

confrontation *n* an earnest effort for superiority or victory over another — see CONTEST 1

confuse *vb* **1** to throw into a state of mental uncertainty ⟨the similar-sounding words "censure" and "censor" often *confuse* people⟩
synonyms addle, baffle, befog, befuddle, bemuse, bewilder, confound, disorient, muddle, muddy, mystify, perplex, puzzle
related words stick, stump; abash, discomfit, disconcert, discountenance, embarrass, faze, fluster, mortify, nonplus, rattle; agitate, bother, chagrin, discomfort, discompose, dismay, disquiet, distress, disturb, perturb, stun, unhinge, unsettle, upset; deceive, misguide, mislead
near antonyms assure, reassure, satisfy; enlighten, inform

2 to make (something) unclear to the understanding ⟨stop *confusing* the issue with irrelevant facts⟩
synonyms becloud, befog, blur, cloud, fog, muddy
related words complicate, perplex, sophisticate; entangle, snarl, tangle; disorder, jumble, mess (up), mix (up)
near antonyms simplify, streamline; disentangle, straighten (out), untangle
antonyms clarify

3 to throw into a state of self-conscious distress — see EMBARRASS 1

4 to undo the proper order or arrangement of — see DISORDER

confused *adj* **1** lacking in order, neatness, and often cleanliness — see MESSY

2 suffering from mental confusion — see DIZZY 2

confusion *n* **1** a state of mental uncertainty ⟨the farmer's driving directions to the fairground just left us in total *confusion*⟩
synonyms bafflement, befuddlement, bewilderment, distraction, muddle, mystification, perplexity, puzzlement, whirl
related words abashment, discomfiture, embarrassment, fluster, mortification; agitation, chagrin, discomfort, dismay, disquiet, distress, disturbance, perturbation, upset
near antonyms assurance, certainty, certitude, confidence, conviction, positiveness, sureness

2 a state in which everything is out of order — see CHAOS

3 the emotional state of being made self-consciously uncomfortable — see EMBARRASSMENT 1

confute *vb* to prove to be false — see DISPROVE

congeal *vb* **1** to become physically firm or solid — see HARDEN 1

2 to turn from a liquid into a substance resembling jelly — see COAGULATE

congenial *adj* **1** giving pleasure or contentment to the mind or senses — see PLEASANT

2 having or marked by agreement in feeling or action — see HARMONIOUS 3

congenital *adj* being such from birth or by nature — see NATURAL 1

congest *vb* to prevent passage through — see CLOG 1

conglomerate *n* a group of businesses or enterprises under one control ⟨the huge media *con-* glomerate owns TV and radio stations, a cable company, and a movie studio⟩
synonyms empire
related words multinational; cartel, combination, syndicate, trust; chain; association, corporation, organization, pool

conglomerate *vb* **1** to come together into one body or place — see ASSEMBLE 1

2 to gradually form into a layer, pile, or mass — see COLLECT 2

congratulate *vb* to express to (someone) admiration for his or her success or good fortune ⟨let me be the first to *congratulate* you on winning the award⟩
synonyms compliment, felicitate
related words applaud, cheer, commend, hail; extol (*also* extoll), glorify, laud, praise
near antonyms bad-mouth, belittle, decry, disparage, put down; jeer, mock, ridicule, taunt, tease

congratulations *n pl* best wishes — see COMPLIMENTS

congregate *vb* to come together into one body or place — see ASSEMBLE 1

congregation *n* **1** a body of persons gathered for religious worship ⟨the whole *congregation* began to sing with great fervor⟩
synonyms assembly, church
related words laity, parish; communion, denomination, fold, sect

2 a body of people come together in one place — see GATHERING 1

congress *n* **1** the highest lawmaking body of a political unit ⟨the national emergency required a special session of *congress*⟩
synonyms parliament
related words assembly, chamber, council, diet, house, legislature

2 a coming together of a number of persons for a specified purpose — see MEETING 1

3 a group of persons formally joined together for some common interest — see ASSOCIATION 2

congruity *n* a state of consistency — see CONFORMITY 1

congruous *adj* **1** having the parts agreeably related — see HARMONIOUS 2

2 not having or showing any apparent conflict — see CONSISTENT

congruously *adv* in a manner suitable for the occasion or purpose — see PROPERLY

conjectural *adj* existing only as an assumption or speculation — see THEORETICAL 1

conjecture *n* an opinion or judgment based on little or no evidence ⟨the many *conjectures* about the true identity of Jack the Ripper⟩
synonyms guess, supposition, surmise
related words hypothesis, theory, thesis; guesswork, speculation; hunch, intuition; belief, faith

conjecture *vb* **1** to decide the size, amount, number, or distance of (something) without actual measurement — see ESTIMATE 2

2 to form an opinion from little or no evidence — see GUESS 1

conjoin *vb* **1** to come together to form a single unit — see UNITE 1

2 to form or enter into an association that furthers the interests of its members — see ALLY

conjoint *adj* used or done by a number of people as a group — see COLLECTIVE

conjointly *adv* in or by combined action or effort — see TOGETHER 2

conjugal *adj* of or relating to marriage — see MARITAL

conjugate *vb* **1** to come together to form a single unit — see UNITE 1

2 to put or bring together so as to form a new and longer whole — see CONNECT 1

conjunction *n* the coming together of two or more things to the same point — see CONVERGENCE

conjuration *n* a spoken word or set of words believed to have magic power — see SPELL 1

conjure *vb* to make a request to (someone) in an earnest or urgent manner — see BEG

conjure (up) *vb* to call into being through the use of one's inner resources or powers — see SUMMON 2

conjurer *or* **conjuror** *n* **1** a person skilled in using supernatural forces — see MAGICIAN 1

2 one who practices tricks and illusions for entertainment — see MAGICIAN 2

conjuring *n* **1** the power to control natural forces through supernatural means — see MAGIC 1

2 the art or skill of performing tricks or illusions for entertainment — see MAGIC 2

conk (out) *vb* to stop functioning — see FAIL 1

connect *vb* **1** to put or bring together so as to form a new and longer whole ⟨*connect* all the sets of lights and attach them to the branches of the Christmas tree⟩

synonyms chain, compound, conjugate, couple, hitch, hook, join, link, yoke

related words dovetail; concatenate, string; cement, coalesce, combine, fuse, unite

near antonyms divide, part, split

antonyms disconnect, disjoin, separate, unchain, uncouple, unhitch, unlink, unyoke

2 to come together to form a single unit — see UNITE 1

3 to think of (something) in combination — see ASSOCIATE 2

connecting *n* the act or an instance of joining two or more things into one — see UNION 1

connection *n* **1** the fact or state of having something in common ⟨the endless debate about the *connection* between crime and poverty⟩

synonyms association, bearing, kinship, liaison, linkage, relation, relationship

related words correlation, interrelation; materiality, pertinence, relevance; bond, link, tie; affiliation, alliance, union; likeness, resemblance, similarity

2 a place where two or more things are united — see JOINT 1

3 an acquaintance who has influence especially in the business or political world — see CONTACT

4 the act or an instance of joining two or more things into one — see UNION 1

5 the fact or state of being pertinent — see PERTINENCE

6 the state of having shared interests or efforts (as in social or business matters) — see ASSOCIATION 1

connivance *n* a secret agreement or cooperation between two parties for an illegal or dishonest purpose — see COLLUSION

connive *vb* to secretly sympathize with or pretend ignorance of something improper or unlawful ⟨the principal *connived* at all the school absences that were recorded on the day of the city's celebration of its Super Bowl victory⟩

synonyms wink

related words condone, disregard, excuse, ignore, overlook, tolerate

near antonyms disapprove (of), frown (on *or* upon); deny, disallow, refuse

connoisseur *n* a person having a knowledgeable and fine appreciation of the arts ⟨a forthcoming exhibit at the art museum that is eagerly awaited by *connoisseurs* of ancient Greek pottery⟩

synonyms dilettante

related words adept, authority, expert, master; critic, reviewer; amateur, dabbler; collector

near antonyms materialist, philistine

connubial *adj* of or relating to marriage — see MARITAL

conquer *vb* **1** to bring under one's control by force of arms ⟨before his final defeat, Napoleon had managed to *conquer* much of Europe⟩

synonyms dominate, overpower, subdue, subject, subjugate, vanquish

related words beat, crush, defeat, drub, lick, mow (down), rout, smash, thrash, trounce; enslave; break, put down, quell, suppress

near antonyms emancipate, free, liberate, manumit, release

2 to achieve a victory over — see BEAT 2

3 to achieve victory (as in a contest) — see WIN 1

conqueror *n* one that defeats an enemy or opponent — see VICTOR 1

conquest *n* the act or process of bringing someone or something under one's control ⟨the *conquest* of much of North and South America by the Spanish during the 16th century⟩

synonyms dominating, domination, overpowering, subduing, subjecting, subjection, subjugating, subjugation, vanquishing

related words triumph, victory, winning; beating, defeat, drubbing, licking, trouncing; enslavement

near antonyms emancipation, freeing, liberation, manumission, release

conscientious *adj* **1** guided by or in accordance with one's sense of right and wrong ⟨operated on the belief that most people are *conscientious*, the unattended farm stand has a price list and a money drawer for customers to leave payment for their purchases⟩

synonyms ethical, honest, honorable, just, moral, principled, scrupulous

related words good, righteous, upright, virtuous; dutiful, observant, respectful; overconscientious; reliable, trustworthy, trusty

near antonyms unreliable, untrustworthy

antonyms cutthroat, dishonest, dishonorable, immoral, unethical, unjust, unprincipled, unscrupulous

2 taking great care and effort — see PAINSTAKING

conscientiousness *n* strict attentiveness to what one is doing — see CARE 1

conscious *adj* having specified facts or feelings actively impressed on the mind ⟨*conscious* of the fact that my hands were sweating the whole time that I was making my presentation⟩

synonyms alive, aware, cognizant, mindful, sensible, sentient

related words attentive, heedful, observant, regardful, vigilant, watchful

near antonyms inattentive, unheeding, unobservant, unobserving

antonyms insensible, unaware, unconscious, unmindful

consciously *adv* with full awareness of what one is doing — see INTENTIONALLY

conscript *n* a person forced or required to enroll in military service ⟨as the war continued, the body of enlisted soldiers was supplemented by an increasing number of *conscripts*⟩
synonyms draftee, inductee
related words recruit, rookie

conscript *vb* to pick especially for required military service — see DRAFT 1

consecrate *vb* **1** to keep or intend for a special purpose — see DEVOTE 1
2 to make holy through prayers or ritual — see BLESS 1

consecrated *adj* set apart or worthy of veneration by association with God — see HOLY 2

consecration *n* the act of making something holy through religious ritual ⟨the *consecration* of the Host during Communion⟩
synonyms blessing, hallowing, sanctification
related words dedication
near antonyms defilement, desecration, profanation

consecutive *adj* following one after another without others coming in between ⟨the team's winning streak has lasted for seven *consecutive* games⟩
synonyms sequential, succeeding, successional, successive
related words serial; constant, continuous, uninterrupted; ensuing, following, later, next, subsequent

consensus *n* the act or fact of being of one opinion about something — see AGREEMENT 1

consent *n* the approval by someone in authority for the doing of something — see PERMISSION

consequence *n* **1** a condition or occurrence traceable to a cause — see EFFECT 1
2 the quality or state of being important — see IMPORTANCE

consequent *adj* coming as a result — see RESULTANT

consequential *adj* **1** coming as a result — see RESULTANT
2 having great meaning or lasting effect — see IMPORTANT 1

consequently *adv* for this or that reason — see THEREFORE

conservation *n* **1** the careful maintaining and protection of something valuable especially in its natural or original state ⟨everyone has a duty to aid in the *conservation* of our nation's wilderness areas⟩
synonyms preservation
related words care, maintenance, upkeep; salvation, saving; guardianship, protection, safeguarding, safekeeping; economy, husbandry, management
near antonyms neglect, squandering, waste; destruction, ruin; damage, injury
2 the act or activity of keeping something in an existing and usually satisfactory condition — see MAINTENANCE

conservative *adj* **1** tending to favor established ideas, conditions, or institutions ⟨*conservative* baseball fans consider the new ballpark too modern-looking and plain ugly⟩
synonyms old-fashioned, orthodox, reactionary, traditional, unprogressive
related words conventional; faithful, loyal, steadfast, true-blue

near antonyms extremist, radical, revolutionary; nonconformist
antonyms liberal, nonorthodox, nontraditional, progressive, unorthodox
2 not excessively showy — see QUIET 2

conservative *n* a person whose political beliefs are centered on tradition and keeping things the way they are ⟨proposed legislation that was opposed by *conservatives* throughout the state⟩
synonyms reactionary, rightist
related words conformist
near antonyms extremist, radical, revolutionary, revolutionist
antonyms leftist, liberal, progressive

conservatory *n* a glass-enclosed building for growing plants ⟨the college's *conservatory* is entirely devoted to cultivating and displaying orchids⟩
synonyms greenhouse, hothouse
related words cold frame; nursery

conserve *vb* to keep in good condition — see MAINTAIN 1

conserving *n* the act or activity of keeping something in an existing and usually satisfactory condition — see MAINTENANCE

consider *vb* **1** to think of in a particular way ⟨I *consider* him a very good friend⟩
synonyms account, call, count, esteem, hold, rate, reckon, regard, take (for)
related words believe, feel, sense, think; conceive, fancy, imagine
phrases look on (*or* upon)
2 to give serious and careful thought to — see PONDER
3 to have as an opinion — see BELIEVE 2

considerable *adj* **1** sufficiently large in size, amount, or number to merit attention ⟨the *considerable* number of auto accidents that resulted from the surprise snowstorm⟩
synonyms good, goodly, good-sized, healthy, largish, respectable, significant, sizable (*or* sizeable), substantial, tidy
related words big, colossal, enormous, gigantic, great, huge, immense, mammoth
near antonyms piddling, puny, trivial, unimportant; marginal, meager, slight; little, small, tiny
antonyms inconsiderable, insignificant, insubstantial
2 of a size greater than average of its kind — see LARGE

considerably *adv* to a large extent or degree — see GREATLY 2

considerate *adj* **1** given to or made with heedful anticipation of the needs and happiness of others — see THOUGHTFUL 1
2 having or showing a close attentiveness to avoiding danger or trouble — see CAREFUL 1

considerately *adv* with good reason or courtesy — see WELL 4

consideration *n* **1** a careful weighing of the reasons for or against something ⟨after much *consideration* we decided to make an offer on the house⟩
synonyms debate, deliberation, thought
related words cogitation, contemplation, meditation, pondering, rumination; introspection, reflection; agonizing, hesitation, indecision
2 something (as money) that is given or received in return for goods or services — see PAYMENT 2

considered *adj* decided on as a result of careful thought — see DELIBERATE 1

THESAURUS

consign *vb* **1** to cause to go or be taken from one place to another — see SEND

2 to put (something) into the possession or safekeeping of another — see GIVE 2

consist (of) *vb* to be made up of — see COMPRISE 1

consistency *n* the degree to which a fluid can resist flowing ⟨beat the egg whites until they take on the *consistency* of whipped cream⟩

synonyms density, thickness, viscosity

related words compactness, firmness, solidity; ropiness, stickiness

consistent *adj* not having or showing any apparent conflict ⟨the clothes you wear to class must be *consistent* with the school's dress code⟩

synonyms compatible, conformable (to), congruous, consonant, correspondent (with *or* to), harmonious, nonconflicting

related words appropriate, fitting, meet, suitable

phrases of a piece

antonyms conflicting, incompatible, incongruous, inconsistent, inharmonious, unharmonious

consistently *adv* on every relevant occasion — see ALWAYS 1

consolation *n* **1** the giving of hope and strength in times of grief, distress, or suffering ⟨the *consolation* of the grieving family by their pastor⟩

synonyms comforting, consoling, solace, solacing

related words commiseration, condolence, sympathy; counseling (*or* counselling)

2 a feeling of ease from grief or trouble — see COMFORT 1

console *vb* to ease the grief or distress of — see COMFORT 1

consolidate *vb* **1** to bring (something) to a central point or under a single control — see CENTRALIZE

2 to make markedly greater in measure or degree — see INTENSIFY

consolidation *n* the act or an instance of joining two or more things into one — see UNION 1

consoling *n* the giving of hope and strength in times of grief, distress, or suffering — see CONSOLATION 1

consonance *n* **1** a balanced, pleasing, or suitable arrangement of parts — see HARMONY 1

2 a state of consistency — see CONFORMITY 1

consonant *adj* **1** having the parts agreeably related — see HARMONIOUS 2

2 not having or showing any apparent conflict — see CONSISTENT

consort *n* the person to whom another is married — see SPOUSE

consort *vb* to come or be together as friends — see ASSOCIATE 1

conspicuous *adj* **1** likely to attract attention — see NOTICEABLE

2 very noticeable especially for being incorrect or bad — see EGREGIOUS

conspiracy *n* **1** a group involved in secret or criminal activities — see RING 1

2 a secret agreement or cooperation between two parties for an illegal or dishonest purpose — see COLLUSION

3 a secret plan for accomplishing evil or unlawful ends — see PLOT 1

conspire *vb* to engage in a secret plan to accomplish evil or unlawful ends — see PLOT

constable *n* a member of a force charged with law enforcement at the local level — see OFFICER 1

constabulary *n* a body of officers of the law — see POLICE 2

constancy *n* **1** the state of continuing without change ⟨the mistaken notion that there is *constancy* in language—words do indeed change their meanings over time⟩

synonyms changelessness, fixedness, immutability, invariability, stability, steadiness, unchangeableness

related words consistency, regularity, sameness, uniformity; durability, lastingness, permanence

near antonyms inconsistency, irregularity, unevenness; evanescence, impermanence

antonyms changeability, changeableness, instability, mutability, unsteadiness, variability

2 adherence to something to which one is bound by a pledge or duty — see FIDELITY

constant *adj* **1** not undergoing a change in condition ⟨change is the only *constant* thing in the world of fashion⟩

synonyms changeless, stable, stationary, steady, unchanging, unvarying

related words fast, fixed, hard-and-fast, immutable, inflexible, invariable, unalterable, unchangeable; established, set, settled; durable, enduring, lasting, permanent

near antonyms alterable, changeable, flexible, mutable, variable; ephemeral, evanescent, fleeting, momentary, transient, transitory

antonyms changeful, changing, fluctuating, inconstant, unstable, unsteady, varying

2 appearing or occurring repeatedly from time to time — see REGULAR 1

3 firm in one's allegiance to someone or something — see FAITHFUL 1

constantly *adv* **1** many times — see OFTEN

2 on every relevant occasion — see ALWAYS 1

consternation *n* the emotion experienced in the presence or threat of danger — see FEAR

constituent *n* one of the parts that make up a whole — see ELEMENT 1

constitute *vb* **1** to be all the substance of ⟨nine players *constitute* a baseball team⟩

synonyms compose, comprise, form, make up

related words embody, incorporate, integrate; complement, complete, supplement; fill out, flesh (out)

2 to be responsible for the creation and early operation or use of — see FOUND

3 to pick (someone) by one's authority for a specific position or duty — see APPOINT 2

constitution *n* **1** the set of qualities that makes a person, a group of people, or a thing different from others — see NATURE 1

2 the type of body that a person has — see PHYSIQUE

constitutional *n* a relaxed journey on foot for exercise or pleasure — see WALK

constitutionally *adv* by natural character or ability — see NATURALLY 1

constrain *vb* **1** to cause (a person) to give in to pressure — see FORCE

2 to keep from exceeding a desirable degree or level (as of expression) — see CONTROL 1

constraint *n* **1** the checking of one's true feelings and impulses when dealing with others ⟨in civilized society people do not just say or do whatever they feel like—they exercise some *constraint*⟩

synonyms inhibition, repression, reserve, restraint, self-control, self-restraint, suppression *related words* control, discipline, self-denial, self-discipline; composure, self-possession; aloofness, detachedness, distance; bashfulness, modesty, shyness; reticence, silence, taciturnity

near antonyms self-indulgence; bluntness, candor, frankness

2 something that limits one's freedom of action or choice — see RESTRICTION 1

3 the use of power to impose one's will on another — see FORCE 2

constrict *vb* **1** to become smaller in size or volume through the drawing together of particles of matter — see CONTRACT 2

2 to reduce in size or volume by or as if by pressing parts or members together — see COMPRESS 1

constriction *n* the act or process of reducing the size or volume of something by or as if by pressing — see COMPRESSION

construct *vb* to form by putting together parts or materials — see BUILD

construction *n* **1** something put together by arranging or connecting an array of parts ⟨the swing set turned out to be a more complicated *construction* than the "some assembly required" warning suggested⟩

synonyms erection, structure

related words arrangement, assembly; frame, framework, skeleton

2 a statement that makes something clear — see EXPLANATION 1

constructive *adj* having a role in deciding something's final form — see FORMATIVE

construe *vb* to make plain or understandable — see EXPLAIN 1

consult *vb* to exchange viewpoints or seek advice for the purpose of finding a solution to a problem — see CONFER 2

consultant *n* a person who gives advice especially professionally ⟨a *consultant* in public relations to a number of large corporations⟩

synonyms adviser (*or* advisor), counselor (*or* counsellor)

related words authority, expert, professional; confidant

consume *vb* **1** to destroy all trace of ⟨massive fires had *consumed* hundreds of square miles of forest⟩

synonyms devour, eat (up)

related words gut; deplete, exhaust, use up; raze, ruin, waste; annihilate, extinguish

2 to make complete use of — see DEPLETE

3 to take in as food — see EAT 1

consummate *adj* **1** having or showing exceptional knowledge, experience, or skill in a field of endeavor — see PROFICIENT

2 having no exceptions or restrictions — see ABSOLUTE 2

3 of the greatest or highest degree or quantity — see ULTIMATE 1

consummate *vb* to bring (something) to a state where nothing remains to be done — see FINISH 1

consummation *n* **1** the last part of a process or action — see FINALE

2 the state of being actual or complete — see FRUITION

contact *n* an acquaintance who has influence especially in the business or political world ⟨an intern who got her summer job in the governor's office through *contacts*⟩

synonyms connection

related words big shot, bigwig, somebody, VIP; go-between, intermediary, mediator

contact *vb* to transmit information or requests to ⟨you can *contact* me at this number⟩

synonyms communicate (with), reach

related words apprise, fill in, inform, notify; buzz, call, phone, ring [*chiefly British*], telephone

phrases get (*or* keep) in touch with

contagious *adj* **1** capable of being passed by physical contact from one person to another ⟨chicken pox, measles, German measles, and other *contagious* diseases⟩

synonyms catching, communicable, transmittable

related words infectious, infective

near antonyms noninfectious

antonyms noncommunicable

2 exciting a similar feeling or reaction in others ⟨the enthusiasm of the new club members was *contagious*⟩

synonyms catching, infectious, spreading

related words palpable, perceptible, tangible; irresistible, overpowering, overwhelming; fetching, inviting, winning

contain *vb* **1** to have within ⟨the top drawer of the cabinet *contains* my stamp collection⟩

synonyms hold

related words accommodate, fit; encase, enclose (*also* inclose), encompass; harbor, house, lodge, shelter

2 to have as part of a whole — see INCLUDE

3 to be made up of — see COMPRISE 1

4 to gain emotional or mental control of — see COLLECT 1

5 to keep from exceeding a desirable degree or level (as of expression) — see CONTROL 1

container *n* something into which a liquid or smaller objects can be put for storage or transportation ⟨save the plastic *containers* from the deli for other uses⟩

synonyms holder, receptacle, vessel

related words cartridge; bin, box, carton, case, crate; bag, pocket, sack; cooler, warmer

contaminant *n* something that is or that makes impure — see IMPURITY

contaminate *vb* to make unfit for use by the addition of something harmful or undesirable ⟨a supply of drinking water that was *contaminated* by a toxic waste dump⟩

synonyms befoul, defile, foul, poison, pollute, taint

related words infect; besmirch, dirty, soil, sully; corrupt, rot, spoil; adulterate, doctor; dilute, water (down)

near antonyms clean, cleanse, purge; filter; disinfect, sanitize

antonyms decontaminate, purify

contaminated *adj* containing foreign or lower-grade substances — see IMPURE

contemplate *vb* **1** to give serious and careful thought to — see PONDER

2 to have in mind as a purpose or goal — see INTEND

contemplation *n* long or deep thinking about spiritual matters ⟨the decision to enter a monastery and to spend one's life in prayer and *contemplation*⟩

synonyms meditation

related words introspection, reflection, retrospection; cogitation, deliberation, musing, pondering, rumination

contemplative *adj* given to or marked by long, quiet thinking ⟨a *contemplative* person who likes to go on solitary walks⟩ ⟨the *contemplative* life of the monks at the abbey⟩
synonyms meditative, melancholy, pensive, reflective, ruminant, thoughtful
related words introspective, retrospective; earnest, serious, sober, somber (*or* sombre); analytic (*or* analytical), logical, rational; deliberate, purposeful
near antonyms flighty, flippant, frivolous; brainless, mindless, silly, thoughtless, unthinking
antonyms unreflective

contemporaneous *adj* existing or occurring at the same period of time — see CONTEMPORARY 1

contemporaneously *adv* at one and the same time — see TOGETHER 1

contemporary *adj* **1** existing or occurring at the same period of time ⟨the absurd notion that early cave dwellers were *contemporary* with the dinosaurs⟩
synonyms coeval, coexistent, coexisting, coextensive, concurrent, contemporaneous, simultaneous, synchronous
related words accompanying, attendant, attending, coincident, concomitant
antonyms noncontemporary
2 being or involving the latest methods, concepts, information, or styles — see MODERN

contemporary *n* a person who lives at the same time or is about the same age as another ⟨Abraham Lincoln and Charles Darwin were exact *contemporaries*, actually being born on the same day in 1809⟩
synonyms coeval
related words accompaniment, companion, concomitant; equal, peer

contempt *n* open dislike for someone or something considered unworthy of one's concern or respect ⟨my undying *contempt* for people who abuse animals⟩
synonyms despite, despitefulness, disdain, scorn
related words abhorrence, abomination, execration, hate, hatred, loathing; cattiness, hatefulness, invidiousness, malevolence, malice, maliciousness, malignancy, malignity, meanness, spite, spitefulness; aversion, disgust, distaste, horror, odium, repugnance, repulsion, revulsion; animosity, antagonism, antipathy, bitterness, enmity, grudge, hostility, jealousy, pique, resentment; bile, jaundice, rancor, spleen, venom, virulence, vitriol
near antonyms acceptance, tolerance; adoration, veneration, worship; affection, fondness, liking
antonyms admiration, esteem, regard, respect

contemptible *adj* **1** arousing or deserving of one's loathing and disgust ⟨the *contemptible* thieves who stole the Christmas gifts intended for needy children⟩
synonyms despicable, lousy, nasty, pitiable, pitiful, scabby, scummy, scurvy, sorry, wretched
related words abhorrent, abominable, detestable, execrable, hateful, loathsome, odious; disgusting, repugnant, repulsive; disgraceful, dishonorable, shameful; base, ignoble, low, mean; shabby, sordid, squalid, vile; cowardly, craven, dastardly
near antonyms high-minded, honorable, noble, principled; commendable, creditable, laudable, praiseworthy
antonyms admirable

2 deserving pitying scorn (as for inadequacy) — see PITIFUL 1
3 not following or in accordance with standards of honor and decency — see IGNOBLE 2

contemptuous *adj* **1** feeling or showing open dislike for someone or something regarded as undeserving of respect or concern ⟨loutish tourists who are *contemptuous* of the ways and traditions of their host countries⟩
synonyms disdainful, scornful
related words discourteous, disrespectful, impudent, insolent; arrogant, cavalier, high-handed; haughty, lofty, lordly, prideful, sniffish, snobbish, supercilious; pompous, self-important, superior
near antonyms deferential, respectful; accepting, tolerant; courteous, polite
antonyms admiring, appreciative
2 intended to make a person or thing seem of little importance or value — see DEROGATORY

contend *vb* **1** to engage in a contest — see COMPETE
2 to state (something) as a reason in support of or against something under consideration — see ARGUE 1
3 to state as a fact usually forcefully — see CLAIM 1

contend (with) *vb* **1** to deal with (something) usually skillfully or efficiently — see HANDLE 1
2 to strive to reduce or eliminate — see FIGHT 2

contender *n* **1** one who seeks an office, honor, position, or award — see CANDIDATE
2 one who strives for the same thing as another — see COMPETITOR

content *adj* feeling that one's needs or desires have been met ⟨are you *content* with your present allowance?⟩
synonyms contented, gratified, happy, pleased, satisfied
related words delighted, glad, joyful, joyous, jubilant; ecstatic, elated, enraptured, euphoric, overjoyed, rapturous, thrilled; appeased, mollified, pacified, placated
near antonyms disaffected, disgruntled; discouraged, disheartened, dispirited
antonyms discontent, discontented, displeased, dissatisfied, malcontent, unhappy

¹content *n* **1** a major object of interest or concern (as in a discussion or artistic composition) — see MATTER 1
2 the amount of something (as subject matter) included — see COVERAGE
3 the largest number or amount that something can hold — see CAPACITY 1

²content *n* the feeling experienced when one's wishes are met — see PLEASURE 1

content *vb* to give satisfaction to — see PLEASE

contented *adj* feeling that one's needs or desires have been met — see CONTENT

contentedness *n* the feeling experienced when one's wishes are met — see PLEASURE 1

contention *n* an idea or opinion that is put forth in a discussion or debate ⟨my *contention* is that today's lower batting averages are the result of better pitching⟩
synonyms argument, assertion, thesis
related words hypothesis, theory; proposal, proposition; assumption, presupposition, supposition; position, stand

contentious *adj* **1** feeling or displaying eagerness to fight — see BELLIGERENT
2 given to arguing — see ARGUMENTATIVE 1

contentiousness *n* an inclination to fight or quarrel — see BELLIGERENCE

contentment *n* the feeling experienced when one's wishes are met — see PLEASURE 1

contest *n* **1** an earnest effort for superiority or victory over another ⟨the eternal *contest* between the forces of good and the forces of evil⟩
synonyms battle, combat, conflict, confrontation, duel, face-off, rivalry, struggle, tug-of-war, warfare
related words showdown; contention, discord, friction, strife; controversy, debate, disagreement
near antonyms concord, harmony, peace
2 a competitive encounter between individuals or groups carried on for amusement, exercise, or in pursuit of a prize — see GAME 1
3 a physical dispute between opposing individuals or groups — see FIGHT 1

contest *vb* to demand proof of the truth or rightness of — see CHALLENGE 1

contestant *n* one who strives for the same thing as another — see COMPETITOR

contiguity *n* the state or condition of being near — see PROXIMITY

contiguous *adj* having a border in common — see ADJACENT

continent *n* one of the great divisions of land on the globe or the main part of such a division — see MAINLAND

contingency *n* something that might happen — see EVENT 2

contingent *n* a body of persons chosen as representatives of a larger group ⟨our Scout troop sent a large *contingent* to the jamboree⟩
synonyms delegation
related words embassy, legation, mission; crew, detachment, gang, outfit, squad

contingent (on *or* upon) *adj* determined by something else — see DEPENDENT 2

continual *adj* **1** going on and on without any interruptions — see CONTINUOUS
2 occurring or appearing at intervals — see INTERMITTENT 1

continually *adv* **1** many times — see OFTEN
2 on every relevant occasion — see ALWAYS 1

continuance *n* **1** continuing existence — see PERSISTENCE 1
2 uninterrupted or lasting existence — see CONTINUATION

continuation *n* uninterrupted or lasting existence ⟨the *continuation* of high unemployment has cost the government much support⟩
synonyms continuance, duration, endurance, persistence, subsistence
related words elongation, extension, lengthening, prolongation
near antonyms abridgment (*or* abridgement), curtailment, shortening
antonyms ending, termination

continue *vb* **1** to remain indefinitely in existence or in the same state ⟨the heavy snow *continued* throughout the night⟩
synonyms abide, endure, hold (up), hold on, keep up, last, persist, run on
related words linger, remain, stay, stick around, tarry
near antonyms abate, die (down), ebb, let up, moderate, subside, wane
antonyms cease, desist, discontinue, quit, stop

2 to begin again or return to after an interruption — see RESUME

continuous *adj* going on and on without any interruptions ⟨a city that has been under *continuous* bombardment for three days⟩
synonyms ceaseless, continual, incessant, unbroken, unceasing, uninterrupted, unremitting
related words endless, eternal, everlasting, interminable, perpetual, unending; changeless, constant, stable, steady, unchanging, unvarying
near antonyms intermittent, periodic, recurrent, recurring
antonyms noncontinuous

contort *vb* to twist (something) out of a natural or normal shape or condition ⟨the acrobat is able to *contort* his body so that it almost looks like a pretzel⟩
synonyms deform, distort, screw, squinch, warp
related words deface, disfigure; wrench, wrest, wring; coil, curl, twine, wind, wreathe

contortion *n* the twisting of something out of its natural or normal shape or condition ⟨the comedian is renowned for his seemingly endless variety of facial *contortions*⟩
synonyms deformation, distortion, screwing, squinching, warping
related words defacement, disfigurement

contour *n* a line that traces the outer limits of an object or surface — see OUTLINE 1

contract *n* **1** a formal agreement to fulfill an obligation — see GUARANTEE 1
2 an arrangement about action to be taken — see AGREEMENT 2

contract *vb* **1** to become affected with (a disease or disorder) ⟨before vaccines were invented, people lived in fear of *contracting* polio⟩
synonyms catch, come down (with), get, sicken (with), take
related words break out (with); die (from), succumb (to); fail, sink, weaken
near antonyms recover (from), shake (off)
2 to become smaller in size or volume through the drawing together of particles of matter ⟨metal *contracts* at low temperatures⟩
synonyms compress, condense, constrict, shrink
related words collapse, deflate; dry (up), shrivel, wither; decrease, diminish, dwindle, lessen; recede, retreat, withdraw
near antonyms accumulate, grow, increase; balloon, inflate, puff (up)
antonyms expand, swell
3 to reduce in size or volume by or as if by pressing parts or members together — see COMPRESS 1

contraction *n* the act or process of reducing the size or volume of something by or as if by pressing — see COMPRESSION

contradict *vb* **1** to make an assertion that is contrary to one made by (another) ⟨no matter what I say, you always have to *contradict* me⟩
synonyms disagree (with), gainsay
related words challenge, contest, dispute, question; confute, rebut, refute; cross, fight, oppose, resist
near antonyms concur (with); confirm, corroborate, substantiate, verify
antonyms agree (with)
2 to declare not to be true — see DENY 1

contradiction *n* **1** someone or something with qualities or features that seem to conflict with

one another ⟨a loving father as well as a ruthless killer, the gangster is a living *contradiction*⟩
synonyms incongruity, paradox
related words conundrum, enigma, mystery, puzzle, riddle
2 a refusal to confirm the truth of a statement — see DENIAL 2
contradictory *adj* being as different as possible — see OPPOSITE
contraption *n* an interesting and often novel device with a practical use — see GADGET
contrariness *n* refusal to obey — see DISOBEDIENCE
contrariwise *adv* just the opposite being true ⟨the rock singer is hardly a carouser; *contrariwise*, he totally abstains from alcohol⟩
synonyms again, conversely
phrases on the contrary
near antonyms even, indeed, nay, truly, verily, yea
contrary *adj* **1** being as different as possible — see OPPOSITE
2 engaging in or marked by childish misbehavior — see NAUGHTY
3 given to resisting authority or another's control — see DISOBEDIENT
contrary *n* something that is as different as possible from something else — see OPPOSITE
contrast *n* the quality or state of being different — see DIFFERENCE 1
contribute *vb* **1** to make a donation as part of a group effort ⟨would you like to *contribute* to the Thanksgiving fund for needy families?⟩
synonyms chip in, kick in, pitch in
related words bestow, donate, give, present
2 to make a present of — see GIVE 1
contribution *n* a gift of money or its equivalent to a charity, humanitarian cause, or public institution ⟨*contributions* for the victims of the earthquake began pouring in⟩
synonyms alms, benefaction, beneficence, charity, donation, philanthropy
related words offering, tithe; bequest, endowment, legacy; aid, assistance, relief, welfare; grant, subsidy
contrite *adj* **1** feeling sorrow for a wrong that one has done ⟨being *contrite* is not enough to spare you an arrest if you're caught shoplifting⟩
synonyms apologetic, penitent, regretful, remorseful, repentant, rueful, sorry
related words sad, grieving, mournful, sorrowful, woeful
near antonyms merciless, pitiless, ruthless
antonyms impenitent, remorseless, unapologetic, unrepentant
2 suffering from or expressive of a feeling of responsibility for wrongdoing — see GUILTY 2
contriteness *n* a feeling of responsibility for wrongdoing — see GUILT 1
contrition *n* a feeling of responsibility for wrongdoing — see GUILT 1
contrivance *n* **1** an interesting and often novel device with a practical use — see GADGET
2 something (as a device) created for the first time through the use of the imagination — see INVENTION 1
contrive *vb* **1** to create or think of by clever use of the imagination — see INVENT
2 to engage in a secret plan to accomplish evil or unlawful ends — see PLOT

3 to plan out usually with subtle skill or care — see ENGINEER
contrived *adj* lacking in natural or spontaneous quality — see ARTIFICIAL 1
contriver *n* one who creates or introduces something new — see INVENTOR
control *n* **1** a mechanism for adjusting the operation of a device, machine, or system ⟨the *controls* for the player are well marked⟩
synonyms regulator
related words button, dial, key, knob, lever, push button, switch
2 the ability to direct the course of something ⟨after the tail fell off, the plane went out of the pilot's *control*⟩ ⟨firefighters keeping *control* of the blaze⟩
synonyms grasp, hand(s)
related words clutch, grip, hold, mastery; command, dominion, helm; authority, jurisdiction, might, power
3 the act or activity of looking after and making decisions about something — see CONDUCT 1
4 the fact or state of having (something) at one's disposal — see POSSESSION 1
5 the right or means to command or control others — see POWER 1
control *vb* **1** to keep from exceeding a desirable degree or level (as of expression) ⟨you must learn to *control* your temper⟩
synonyms bridle, check, constrain, contain, curb, govern, hold in, inhibit, regulate, rein (in), restrain, tame
related words bottle (up), repress, suppress; arrest, interrupt, stop; block, hinder, impede, obstruct; gag, muzzle, silence
near antonyms liberate, loose, loosen, unleash; air, express, take out, vent
2 to gain emotional or mental control of — see COLLECT 1
3 to exercise authority or power over — see GOVERN 1
4 to look after and make decisions about — see CONDUCT 1
controversy *n* variance of opinion on a matter — see DISAGREEMENT 1
contusion *n* a bodily injury in which small blood vessels are broken but the overlying skin is not ⟨*contusions* occurred as a result of a car accident⟩
synonyms bruise
related words black eye; discoloration
conundrum *n* something hard to understand or explain — see MYSTERY
convalesce *vb* to become healthy and strong again after illness or weakness ⟨the long months that the soldier spent in the hospital slowly *convalescing*⟩
synonyms gain, heal, mend, rally, recover, recuperate, snap back
related words come around, come round, come to, improve, pick up, revive; cheer (up), perk (up); pull through, survive; recruit
near antonyms ail, collapse, come down, sicken; decline, degenerate, deteriorate, fade, fail, languish, sink, waste (away), weaken, wilt, wither, worsen; relapse
convalescence *n* the process or period of gradually regaining one's health and strength ⟨her release from the hospital was followed by a long *convalescence* at home⟩

synonyms comeback, healing, mending, rally, recovery, recuperation, rehabilitation, snapback
related words resuscitation, revival; survival
near antonyms decline, deterioration, failing, languishing, sinking, wasting (away), weakening
convene *vb* **1** to bring together in assembly by or as if by command — see CONVOKE
2 to come together into one body or place — see ASSEMBLE 1
convenience *n* something that adds to one's ease — see COMFORT 2
convenient *adj* situated within easy reach ⟨the shopping mall is *convenient* to all of the area's major highways⟩
synonyms accessible, handy, reachable
related words close, near, nigh; abutting, adjacent, adjoining
near antonyms distant, far, remote
antonyms inaccessible, inconvenient, unhandy, unreachable
convention *n* **1** a coming together of a number of persons for a specified purpose — see MEETING 1
2 a formal agreement between two or more nations or peoples — see TREATY
3 an arrangement about action to be taken — see AGREEMENT 2
4 an inherited or established way of thinking, feeling, or doing — see TRADITION 1
conventional *adj* **1** accepted, used, or practiced by most people — see CURRENT 1
2 based on customs usually handed down from a previous generation — see TRADITIONAL 1
3 following or agreeing with established form, custom, or rules — see FORMAL 1
converge *vb* to come together into one body or place — see ASSEMBLE 1
convergence *n* the coming together of two or more things to the same point ⟨the *convergence* of the city's major arteries on a single rotary⟩
synonyms confluence, conjunction, meeting
related words joining, juncture, merging, union
antonyms divergence
conversant *adj* having information especially as a result of study or experience — see FAMILIAR 2
conversation *n* talking or a talk between two or more people ⟨Thomas Jefferson was celebrated for his brilliant, wide-ranging *conversations* with a host of friends and acquaintances⟩
synonyms colloquy, dialogue (*also* dialog), discourse, discussion, exchange
related words banter, cross fire, give-and-take, repartee; conference, parley, powwow; babble, chat, chatter, chitchat, gabfest, gossip, palaver, prate, prattle, rap, small talk, table talk; roundtable, symposium; debate, deliberation
conversational *adj* **1** fond of talking or conversation — see TALKATIVE
2 having the style and content of everyday conversation — see CHATTY 1
3 used in or suitable for speech and not formal writing — see COLLOQUIAL 1
conversationalist *n* a person who talks constantly — see CHATTERBOX
converse *vb* to engage in casual or rambling conversation — see CHAT
converse (with) *vb* to communicate with by means of spoken words — see TALK (TO)
conversely *adv* just the opposite being true — see CONTRARIWISE
conversion *n* a change in form, appearance, or use

⟨the *conversion* of the spare bedroom into a home office was easily accomplished⟩
synonyms changeover, metamorphosis, transfiguration, transformation
related words shift, transition; adjustment, alteration, modification; redoing, refashioning, remaking, remodeling, revamping, revision, reworking, variation; deformation, disfigurement, distortion, mutation, transmutation; displacement, replacement, substitution, supplantation
convert *n* **1** a person who has recently been persuaded to join a religious sect ⟨the *converts* were the most vocal and fervent worshippers in the church⟩
synonyms proselyte
related words newcomer, novice, recruit
2 one who follows the opinions or teachings of another — see FOLLOWER
convert *vb* **1** to persuade to change to one's religious faith ⟨young missionaries who go door-to-door trying to *convert* people⟩
synonyms proselytize
related words brainwash, influence, sway; propagate
near antonyms dissuade
2 to change in form, appearance, or use ⟨the old factory was *converted* into an apartment building⟩
synonyms make over, metamorphose, transfigure, transform
related words adjust, alter, modify; redo, refashion, remake, remodel, revamp, revise, rework, vary; deform, disfigure, distort, mutate, transmute; displace, replace, substitute, supplant
convey *vb* **1** to cause (something) to pass from one to another — see COMMUNICATE 1
2 to support and take from one place to another — see CARRY 1
conveyance *n* something used to carry goods or passengers ⟨the covered wagon was the major *conveyance* that transported settlers and their belongings across the frontier⟩
synonyms transport, transportation, vehicle
related words carrier, hauler, mover; transit
convict *n* a person convicted as a criminal and serving a prison sentence ⟨a warning that the three escaped *convicts* were armed and dangerous⟩
synonyms jailbird
related words captive, capture, inmate, internee, prisoner
convict *vb* to find or pronounce guilty ⟨an accused person is presumed innocent until *convicted* in a court of law⟩
synonyms condemn
related words censure, denounce, rebuke, reprimand, reproach, reprove; admonish, castigate, chastise; penalize, punish, sentence
near antonyms cite, commend, endorse (*also* indorse); approve, bless, sanction
antonyms absolve, acquit, clear, exonerate, vindicate
conviction *n* **1** a state of mind in which one is free from doubt — see CONFIDENCE 2
2 an idea that is believed to be true or valid without positive knowledge — see OPINION 1
convince *vb* to cause (someone) to agree with a belief or course of action by using arguments or earnest requests — see PERSUADE
convincing *adj* having the power to persuade — see COGENT

THESAURUS

convincing *n* the act of reasoning or pleading with someone to accept a belief or course of action — see PERSUASION 1

convivial *adj* likely to seek or enjoy the company of others ⟨the hiking club attracts a wide range of *convivial* people who share a love of the outdoors⟩
synonyms boon, companionable, extroverted (*also* extraverted), gregarious, outgoing, sociable, social
related words cordial, friendly, hospitable; affable, genial, gracious; animated, lively, sprightly, vivacious; communicative, expansive, garrulous, talkative
near antonyms misanthropic; aloof, reserved, standoffish; reticent, silent, taciturn
antonyms antisocial, introverted, reclusive, unsociable

conviviality *n* **1** joyful or festive activity — see MERRYMAKING
2 the quality or state of being social — see SOCIABILITY

convocation *n* **1** a body of people come together in one place — see GATHERING 1
2 a coming together of a number of persons for a specified purpose — see MEETING 1

convoke *vb* to bring together in assembly by or as if by command ⟨*convoked* the leading experts on juvenile delinquency to study the situation⟩
synonyms assemble, call, convene, muster, summon
related words amass, collect, gather, group, round up
near antonyms break up, dissolve

convoluted *adj* having many parts or aspects that are usually interrelated — see COMPLEX 1

convoy *vb* to go along with in order to provide assistance, protection, or companionship — see ACCOMPANY

convulse *vb* to make a series of small irregular or violent movements — see SHAKE 1

convulsion *n* a violent disturbance (as of the political or social order) ⟨the Russian Revolution was one of the major *convulsions* of the 20th century⟩
synonyms cataclysm, paroxysm, storm, tempest, tumult, upheaval, uproar
related words overthrow, overturn, revolution, subversion, upset; fit, seizure, spasm; eruption, flare-up, outbreak, outburst; commotion, furor, fuss, hubbub, hullabaloo, row, ruckus, stew, turmoil; quaking, rocking, shaking, trembling

convulsive *adj* marked by sudden or violent disturbance ⟨the assassination of Martin Luther King was one of the most *convulsive* events of the 1960s⟩
synonyms cataclysmal (*or* cataclysmic), stormy, tempestuous, tumultuous
related words fitful, spasmodic, sporadic
near antonyms calm, peaceful, serene, tranquil

cook *n* a person who prepares food by some manner of heating ⟨the hearty meals prepared by the *cook* at summer camp⟩
synonyms chef, cooker
related words baker

cook (up) *vb* to create or think of by clever use of the imagination — see INVENT

cooker *n* **1** an appliance that prepares food for consumption by heating it ⟨a portable gas-fired *cooker* that's perfect for camping trips⟩

synonyms cookstove, range
related words broiler, fryer (*also* frier), microwave oven, oven, roaster, rotisserie, stove, toaster, toaster oven
2 a person who prepares food by some manner of heating — see COOK

cookery *n* the art or style of preparing food (as in a specified region) ⟨tacos represented my introduction to Mexican *cookery*⟩
synonyms cooking, cuisine

cooking *n* the art or style of preparing food (as in a specified region) — see COOKERY

cookstove *n* an appliance that prepares food for consumption by heating it — see COOKER 1

cool *adj* **1** having or showing a lack of friendliness or interest in others ⟨the locals were *cool* towards outsiders⟩ ⟨the schoolmaster's *cool* manner did not encourage chitchat⟩
synonyms aloof, antisocial, cold, detached, distant, frosty, remote, standoffish, unsociable
related words introverted, reclusive, reserved, withdrawn; misanthropic; apathetic, indifferent, unconcerned; disinterested, incurious, uninterested; reticent, silent, taciturn; diffident, shy, timid
near antonyms companionable, convivial, extroverted (*also* extraverted), gregarious, outgoing; communicative, expansive, garrulous, talkative
antonyms cordial, friendly, sociable, warm
2 free from emotional or mental agitation — see CALM 2
3 having a low or subnormal temperature — see COLD 1
4 lacking in friendliness or warmth of feeling — see COLD 2

cool *vb* **1** to cause to lose heat ⟨*cool* your drinks in the icy mountain stream⟩
synonyms chill, refrigerate
related words air-condition; freeze, ice, quick-freeze, supercool; air-cool, ventilate
near antonyms bake, boil, broil, steam
antonyms heat, warm
2 to become still and orderly — see QUIET 1

coolheaded *adj* free from emotional or mental agitation — see CALM 2

coolheadedness *n* evenness of emotions or temper — see EQUANIMITY

coolish *adj* having a low or subnormal temperature — see COLD 1

coolness *n* evenness of emotions or temper — see EQUANIMITY

coop *n* an enclosure with an open framework for keeping animals — see CAGE

coop (up) *vb* to close or shut in by or as if by barriers — see ENCLOSE 1

cooperate *vb* **1** to participate or assist in a joint effort to accomplish an end ⟨conservation groups *cooperated* with state authorities to find a humane way to manage the area's overpopulation of deer⟩
synonyms collaborate, concert, join, team (up)
related words connive, conspire; affiliate, ally, associate, band, combine, confederate, league, unite
phrases play ball
2 to form or enter into an association that furthers the interests of its members — see ALLY

cooperation *n* **1** the state of having shared interests or efforts (as in social or business matters) — see ASSOCIATION 1

2 the work and activity of a number of persons who individually contribute toward the efficiency of the whole — see TEAMWORK

coordinate *n* one that is equal to another in status, achievement, or value — see EQUAL

coordinate *vb* **1** to bring to a state free of conflicts, inconsistencies, or differences — see HARMONIZE 2
2 to form a pleasing relationship — see HARMONIZE 1

coordination *n* the work and activity of a number of persons who individually contribute toward the efficiency of the whole — see TEAMWORK

cop *n* a member of a force charged with law enforcement at the local level — see OFFICER 1

copacetic *also* **copasetic** *or* **copesetic** *adj* being to one's liking — see SATISFACTORY 1

cope *vb* to meet one's day-to-day needs — see GET ALONG 1

cope (with) *vb* to deal with (something) usually skillfully or efficiently — see HANDLE 1

copious *adj* pouring forth in great amounts — see PROFUSE

cop–out *n* the act or a means of getting or keeping away from something undesirable — see ESCAPE 2

cop out *vb* to break a promise or agreement — see RENEGE

coppice *n* a thick patch of shrubbery, small trees, or underbrush — see THICKET

copse *n* a thick patch of shrubbery, small trees, or underbrush — see THICKET

copulate *vb* to engage in sexual intercourse ⟨the time of year when deer in the wild are likely to *copulate*⟩
synonyms mate, sleep
related words fornicate

copulating *n* sexual union involving penetration of the vagina by the penis — see SEXUAL INTERCOURSE

copulation *n* sexual union involving penetration of the vagina by the penis — see SEXUAL INTERCOURSE

copy *n* something that is made to look exactly like something else ⟨a *copy* of the famous painting "Washington Crossing the Delaware"⟩
synonyms carbon copy, duplicate, duplication, facsimile, imitation, reduplication, replica, replication, reproduction
related words counterfeit, fake, forgery, phony (*also* phoney), sham; dummy, mock-up, simulation; reconstruction, re-creation; image, likeness, semblance, shadow; impression, imprint, print
antonyms original

copy *vb* **1** to make an exact likeness of ⟨for the movie, set designers *copied* the Oval Office in the White House down to the smallest detail⟩
synonyms duplicate, imitate, reduplicate, replicate, reproduce
related words counterfeit, fake, forge; simulate; reconstruct, re-create
near antonyms create, imagine, initiate, invent
antonyms originate
2 to use (someone or something) as the model for one's speech, mannerisms, or behavior — see IMITATE 1

copycat *n* a person who adopts the appearance or behavior of another especially in an obvious way ⟨every rock singer who makes it big soon has a whole cluster of *copycats*⟩

synonyms aper, copyist, imitator
related words parrot

copyist *n* a person who adopts the appearance or behavior of another especially in an obvious way — see COPYCAT

coquettish *adj* affecting shyness or modesty in order to attract masculine interest — see COY 1

cord *n* a length of braided, flexible material that is used for tying or connecting things ⟨a vacuum cleaner with an extra long *cord*⟩
synonyms cable, lace, lacing, line, rope, string, wire
related words guy, lanyard, stay

cordial *adj* **1** having or showing kindly feeling and sincere interest — see FRIENDLY 1
2 showing a natural kindness and courtesy especially in social situations — see GRACIOUS 1

cordiality *n* kindly concern, interest, or support — see GOODWILL 1

core *n* **1** the seat of one's deepest thoughts and emotions ⟨in my very *core* I knew that an injustice was being committed⟩
synonyms breast, heart, quick, soul
related words conscience, mind
phrases bottom of one's heart
2 a thing or place that is of greatest importance to an activity or interest — see CENTER 1
3 the central part or aspect of something under consideration — see CRUX
4 the main or greater part of something as distinguished from its appendages — see BODY 1
5 an area or point that is an equal distance from all points along an edge or outer surface — see CENTER 2

corker *n* something very good of its kind — see JIM-DANDY

corkscrew *adj* turning around an axis like the thread of a screw — see SPIRAL

corn *n* something (as a work of literature or music) that is too sentimental ⟨a story about a lost puppy that was pure *corn*⟩
synonyms mush, schmaltz (*also* schmalz)
related words claptrap, drivel, rubbish, slush

corner *n* **1** a difficult, puzzling, or embarrassing situation from which there is no easy escape — see PREDICAMENT
2 a place where roads meet — see CROSSROAD 1

cornerstone *n* an immaterial thing upon which something else rests — see BASE 1

cornet *n* something shaped like a hollow cone and used as a container ⟨*cornets* of pastry dough that were baked and later filled with cream⟩
synonyms cornucopia, horn
related words funnel, tube

cornucopia *n* something shaped like a hollow cone and used as a container — see CORNET

corny *adj* appealing to the emotions in an obvious and tiresome way ⟨*corny* violin music during the movie's love scenes⟩
synonyms maudlin, mawkish, mushy, saccharine, sappy, schmaltzy, sentimental, sloppy, sugarcoated, sugary
related words dreamy, moonstruck, nostalgic; flat, insipid, tasteless, vapid, watery
near antonyms unadulterated, unvarnished; cynical, hard-boiled, hardheaded
antonyms unsentimental

corollary *n* a condition or occurrence traceable to a cause — see EFFECT 1

coronet *n* a decorative band or wreath worn about

THESAURUS

the head as a symbol of victory or honor — see CROWN 1

corporal *adj* of or relating to the human body — see PHYSICAL 1

corporeal *adj* of or relating to the human body — see PHYSICAL 1

corps *n* the body of people in a profession or field of activity ⟨a reporter who is widely respected throughout the press *corps*⟩
synonyms brotherhood, community, fellowship, fraternity
related words calling, profession; association, club, federation, guild (*also* gild), organization, society, sodality

corpse *n* a dead body ⟨the discovery of a *corpse* required a call to the police⟩
synonyms cadaver, carcass, remains
related words deceased, decedent

corpulence *n* the condition of having an excess of body fat ⟨the doctor warned that *corpulence* is unhealthy and not just unattractive⟩
synonyms adiposity, chubbiness, fatness, fleshiness, grossness, obesity, plumpness, portliness, pudginess, rotundity
related words bulkiness, heaviness; huskiness, stoutness; brawniness, burliness
near antonyms fitness, trimness; scrawniness, skinniness
antonyms leanness, slenderness, slimness, thinness

corpulent *adj* having an excess of body fat — see FAT 1

corral *n* an enclosure with an open framework for keeping animals — see CAGE

corral *vb* 1 to close or shut in by or as if by barriers — see ENCLOSE 1
2 to take physical control or possession of (something) suddenly or forcibly — see CATCH

correct *adj* 1 being in agreement with the truth or a fact or a standard ⟨a real brainteaser with only one *correct* solution to it⟩
synonyms accurate, exact, precise, proper, right, so, true
related words legitimate, logical, valid; errorless, faultless, flawless, impeccable, letter-perfect, perfect; rigorous, strict, stringent
near antonyms defective, faulty, flawed, imperfect
antonyms false, improper, inaccurate, incorrect, inexact, untrue, wrong
2 following the established traditions of refined society and good taste — see PROPER 1
3 marked by or showing careful attention to set forms and details — see CEREMONIOUS 1

correct *vb* 1 to remove errors, defects, deficiencies, or deviations from ⟨students who never take the time to *correct* their own compositions before handing them in⟩
synonyms amend, debug, emend, rectify, reform, remedy
related words redraft, redraw, restyle, revise, rework, rewrite; redress, right; ameliorate, better, improve; perfect, polish, touch up; fix, mend, repair; adjust, modulate, regulate; alter, change, modify
near antonyms damage, harm, hurt, impair, injure, mar, spoil; aggravate, worsen
2 to balance with an equal force so as to make ineffective — see OFFSET
3 to inflict a penalty on for a fault or crime — see PUNISH

correctable *adj* capable of being corrected — see REMEDIABLE

correcting *adj* inflicting, involving, or serving as punishment — see PUNITIVE

correction *n* 1 a change designed to correct or improve a written work ⟨here's your theme back with the *corrections* marked in blue⟩
synonyms amendment, emendation
related words cut, deletion; addition, amplification, supplement; alteration, modification, revision; improvement, renovation; clarification, explanation, explication
2 suffering, loss, or hardship imposed in response to a crime or offense — see PUNISHMENT

correctional *adj* inflicting, involving, or serving as punishment — see PUNITIVE

corrective *adj* 1 serving to raise or adjust something to some standard or proper condition ⟨eyeglasses are called *corrective* lenses by the department of motor vehicles⟩
synonyms rectifying, remedial, remedying, reformative, reformatory
related words curative, medicinal, therapeutic; reparative, restorative; beneficial, helpful, salutary, wholesome
2 inflicting, involving, or serving as punishment — see PUNITIVE

corrective *n* something that corrects or counteracts something undesirable — see CURE 1

correctly *adv* in a manner suitable for the occasion or purpose — see PROPERLY

correlate *vb* to think of (something) in combination — see ASSOCIATE 2

correspond *vb* 1 to engage in an exchange of written messages ⟨old friends who have been *corresponding* for years⟩
synonyms write
related words communicate, intercommunicate; airmail, e-mail, telegraph; mail, post; answer, reply
2 to be in agreement on every point — see CHECK 1

correspond (to) *vb* 1 to be the exact counterpart of — see MATCH 1
2 to be the same in meaning or effect — see AMOUNT (TO) 2

correspondence *n* 1 a point which two or more things share in common — see SIMILARITY 2
2 the quality or state of having many qualities in common — see SIMILARITY 1

correspondent *n* a person employed by a newspaper, magazine, or radio or television station to gather, write, or report news — see REPORTER

correspondent *adj* having qualities in common — see ALIKE

correspondent (with *or* to) *adj* not having or showing any apparent conflict — see CONSISTENT

corresponding *adj* having qualities in common — see ALIKE

correspondingly *adv* in like manner — see ALSO 1

corridor *n* a typically long narrow way connecting parts of a building — see HALL 2

corroborate *vb* to give evidence or testimony to the truth or factualness of — see CONFIRM

corroborating *adj* serving to give support to the truth or factualness of something — see CORROBORATIVE

corroboration *n* something presented in support of the truth or accuracy of a claim — see PROOF

corroborative *adj* serving to give support to the truth or factualness of something ⟨the results of the DNA fingerprinting was all the *corroborative* evidence the jury needed to convict⟩
synonyms confirmatory, confirming, corroborating, corroboratory, substantiating, supporting, supportive, verifying, vindicating
related words auxiliary, supplementary; beneficial, helpful
near antonyms contradictory, contrary, counter, opposing
antonyms confuting, disproving, refuting

corroboratory *adj* serving to give support to the truth or factualness of something — see CORROBORATIVE

corrode *vb* to consume or wear away gradually — see EAT 2

corrosion *n* a gradual weakening, loss, or destruction ⟨the *corrosion* of family values that is often brought on by great wealth⟩
synonyms attrition, erosion
related words breakdown, decay, decomposition, disintegration, dissolution
near antonyms gain, increase
antonyms buildup

corrupt *adj* having or showing lowered moral character or standards ⟨*corrupt* businessmen who are out to fleece the public⟩ ⟨*corrupt* business practices that should be investigated⟩
synonyms debased, debauched, decadent, degenerate, degraded, demoralized, depraved, dissipated, dissolute, perverse, perverted, reprobate, warped
related words crooked, cutthroat, dishonest, unethical, unprincipled, unscrupulous; contaminated, spoiled, tainted; bad, evil, immoral, iniquitous, nefarious, sinful, vicious, wicked
near antonyms incorruptible, uncorruptible; ethical, honest, principled; good, moral, righteous, virtuous
antonyms uncorrupted

corrupt *vb* 1 to go through decomposition — see DECAY 1
2 to lower in character or dignity — see DEBASE 1

corrupted *adj* having undergone organic breakdown — see ROTTEN 1

corruptible *adj* open to improper influence and especially bribery — see VENAL

corruption *n* 1 the process by which dead organic matter separates into simpler substances ⟨the ancient Egyptians used special preservatives to spare their dead from complete *corruption*⟩
synonyms breakdown, decay, decomposition, putrefaction, rot, spoilage
related words crumbling, disintegration, dissolution; curdling, fermentation, moldering, souring
near antonyms growth, maturation, ripening
2 a sinking to a state of low moral standards and behavior ⟨the *corruption* of the upper classes eventually led to the fall of the Roman empire⟩
synonyms corruptness, debasement, debauchery, decadence, degeneracy, degeneration, degradation, demoralization, depravity, dissipatedness, dissipation, dissoluteness, perversion
related words evil, immorality, nefariousness, sinfulness, wickedness
near antonyms goodness, morality, righteousness, virtue
3 immoral conduct or practices harmful or offensive to society — see VICE 1

corruptness *n* a sinking to a state of low moral standards and behavior — see CORRUPTION 2

corsair *n* someone who engages in robbery of ships at sea — see PIRATE

cortege *also* **cortège** *n* 1 a body of employees or servants who accompany and wait on a person ⟨the movie star's *cortege* included her hair stylist, makeup artist, personal assistant, and press agent⟩
synonyms following, retinue, suite, train
related words crew, personnel, staff; assistant, attendant, helper, retainer
2 a body of individuals moving along in an orderly and often ceremonial way ⟨the funeral *cortege* of mourners stretched for three city blocks⟩
synonyms parade, procession
related words column, line, string, train

cosmetics *n pl* preparations intended to beautify the face or hair — see MAKEUP 1

cosmic *adj* unusually large — see HUGE

cosmopolitan *adj* having a wide and refined knowledge of the world especially from personal experience — see WORLDLY-WISE

cosmopolitan *n* a person with the outlook, experience, and manners thought to be typical of big city dwellers ⟨as someone who had lived in Paris for a year as an exchange student, she seemed very much the *cosmopolitan* to her old classmates⟩
synonyms metropolitan, sophisticate
related words urbanite; worldling
antonyms bumpkin, hick, provincial, rustic, yokel

cosmos *n* the whole body of things observed or assumed — see UNIVERSE

cost *n* 1 a payment made in the course of achieving a result — see EXPENSE
2 the amount of money that is demanded as payment for something — see PRICE 1
3 the loss or penalty involved in achieving a goal — see PRICE 2

cost *vb* to have a price of ⟨the raffle tickets *cost* a dollar each⟩
synonyms bring, fetch, go (for), sell (for)
related words amount (to), come (to), total; command, exact; ask, demand

costly *adj* commanding a large price ⟨running is one sport that does not require a lot of *costly* equipment⟩
synonyms dear, expensive, high, precious, premium, valuable
related words exorbitant, extravagant, overpriced, prohibitive, steep, stiff, unreasonable; invaluable, priceless
near antonyms moderate, reasonable; valueless, worthless; discounted
antonyms cheap, inexpensive

costume *n* 1 clothing chosen as appropriate for a specific situation — see OUTFIT 1
2 clothing put on to hide one's true identity or imitate someone or something else — see DISGUISE

costume *vb* to outfit with clothes and especially fine or special clothes — see CLOTHE 1

coterie *n* a group of people sharing a common interest and relating together socially — see GANG 2

cotillion *n* a social gathering for dancing — see DANCE

cottage *n* an often small house for recreational or seasonal use ⟨for a month every summer we rent a *cottage* on the ocean⟩

THESAURUS

synonyms cabin, camp, chalet, lodge

related words bungalow, cot; hut, shack, shanty

cottony *adj* smooth or delicate in appearance or feel — see SOFT 2

couch *n* a long upholstered piece of furniture designed for several sitters ⟨find yourself a place on the *couch* and make yourself at home⟩

synonyms chesterfield, davenport, divan, lounge, settee, sofa

related words love seat; day bed, sofa bed; bench

couch *vb* to convey in appropriate or telling terms — see PHRASE

cougar *n* a large tawny cat of the wild ⟨in many areas suburban developments have encroached upon the habitat of the *cougar*⟩

synonyms catamount, mountain lion, panther, puma

council *n* **1** a coming together of a number of persons for a specified purpose — see MEETING 1

2 a group of persons formally joined together for some common interest — see ASSOCIATION 2

3 a meeting featuring a group discussion — see FORUM

counsel *n* **1** a person whose profession is to conduct lawsuits for clients or to advise about legal rights and obligations — see LAWYER

2 an opinion suggesting a wise or proper course of action — see ADVICE

counsel *vb* **1** to exchange viewpoints or seek advice for the purpose of finding a solution to a problem — see CONFER 2

2 to give advice and instruction to (someone) regarding the course or process to be followed — see GUIDE 1

3 to give advice to — see ADVISE 1

4 to put forward as one's choice for a wise or proper course of action — see ADVISE 2

counselor *or* **counsellor** *n* **1** a person who gives advice especially professionally — see CONSULTANT

2 a person whose profession is to conduct lawsuits for clients or to advise about legal rights and obligations — see LAWYER

count *n* **1** a total number obtained or recorded by noting each thing as it was being added ⟨my *count* for the number of bird species and subspecies that visited the sanctuary that weekend was 43⟩

synonyms tally

related words score; amount, gross, sum, total, whole

2 a formal claim of criminal wrongdoing against a person — see CHARGE 1

count *vb* **1** to find the sum of (a collection of things) by noting each one as it is being added ⟨*count* the baseball gloves in the storage locker to see if there are enough to go around⟩

synonyms enumerate, number, tell

related words add (up), tally, total; calculate, compute, reckon, table, tabulate; check, mark, tick (off)

2 to be of importance — see MATTER

3 to place reliance or trust — see DEPEND 2

4 to think of in a particular way — see CONSIDER 1

countenance *n* **1** facial appearance regarded as an indication of mood or feeling — see LOOK 1

2 the front part of the head — see FACE 1

countenance *vb* **1** to have a favorable opinion of — see APPROVE (OF)

2 to put up with (something painful or difficult) — see BEAR 2

counter *adj* opposed to one's interests — see ADVERSE 1

counter *vb* to strive to reduce or eliminate — see FIGHT 2

counteract *vb* to balance with an equal force so as to make ineffective — see OFFSET

counteraction *n* a force or influence that makes an opposing force ineffective or less effective — see COUNTERBALANCE

counterattack *n* an attack made to counter an enemy's attack ⟨suddenly the tide of battle turned, and the rebels, who had been falling back, made a furious *counterattack*⟩

synonyms counteroffensive

related words sally, sortie; blitzkrieg, charge; assault, attack, offensive, onslaught

counterbalance *n* a force or influence that makes an opposing force ineffective or less effective ⟨charitable giving is usually a good *counterbalance* to the self-indulgent commercialism of the Christmas season⟩

synonyms balance, canceler (*or* canceller), counteraction, counterpoise, counterweight, equipoise, neutralizer, offset

related words trade-off

counterbalance *vb* to balance with an equal force so as to make ineffective — see OFFSET

counterfeit *adj* being such in appearance only and made or manufactured with the intention of committing fraud ⟨*counterfeit* money that had been passed all over town⟩

synonyms bogus, fake, false, forged, inauthentic, phony (*also* phoney), sham, spurious, unauthentic

related words artificial, factitious, imitation, man-made, mimic, mock, simulated, substitute, synthetic; dummy, nonfunctioning, ornamental; cultured, fabricated, manufactured; deceptive, delusive, misleading

near antonyms natural; actual, true, valid

antonyms authentic, bona fide, genuine, real

counterfeit *n* an imitation that is passed off as genuine — see FAKE 1

counterfeit *vb* **1** to imitate or copy especially in order to deceive — see FAKE 1

2 to present a false appearance of — see FEIGN

counteroffensive *n* an attack made to counter an enemy's attack — see COUNTERATTACK

counterpane *n* a decorative cloth used as a top covering for a bed ⟨a beautiful *counterpane* that was a family heirloom⟩

synonyms bedspread, coverlet, spread

related words comforter, puff, quilt; bedclothes, bedding

counterpart *n* **1** one that is equal to another in status, achievement, or value — see EQUAL

2 something or someone that strongly resembles another — see IMAGE 1

counterpoise *n* a force or influence that makes an opposing force ineffective or less effective — see COUNTERBALANCE

counterpoise *vb* to balance with an equal force so as to make ineffective — see OFFSET

countersign *n* a word or phrase that must be spoken by a person in order to pass a guard — see PASSWORD

counterweight *n* a force or influence that makes an opposing force ineffective or less effective — see COUNTERBALANCE

countless *adj* too many to be counted ⟨I've told you *countless* times not to do that⟩

synonyms innumerable, numberless, uncountable, uncounted, unnumbered, untold
related words endless, infinite, unlimited, vast; many, multitudinous, numerous
near antonyms finite, limited
antonyms countable

count out *vb* to prevent the participation or inclusion of — see EXCLUDE

country *adj* of, relating to, associated with, or typical of open areas with few buildings or people — see RURAL

country *n* **1** the land of one's birth, residence, or citizenship ⟨a great love for my *country*⟩
synonyms fatherland, home, homeland, motherland, sod
related words old country; community, neighborhood
2 the open rural area outside of big towns and cities ⟨out in the *country*, where the air is fresh and the rivers are clean⟩
synonyms countryside, sticks
related words exurbia; backwater, backwoods, bush, frontier, hinterland, up-country; wild, wilderness
near antonyms conurbation, megalopolis, urban sprawl
3 a body of people composed of one or more nationalities usually with its own territory and government — see NATION

countryman *n* **1** a person living in or originally from the same country as another — see COMPATRIOT
2 an awkward or simple person especially from a small town or the country — see HICK

countryseat *n* a large impressive residence — see MANSION

countryside *n* the open rural area outside of big towns and cities — see COUNTRY 2

coup *n* a successful result brought about by hard work — see ACCOMPLISHMENT 1

couple *n* two things of the same or similar kind that match or are considered together — see PAIR

couple *vb* **1** to come together to form a single unit — see UNITE 1
2 to put or bring together so as to form a new and longer whole — see CONNECT 1

coupling *n* **1** a place where two or more things are united — see JOINT 1
2 the act or an instance of joining two or more things into one — see UNION 1

coupon *n* a small sheet of plastic, paper, or paperboard showing that the bearer has a claim to something (as admittance) — see TICKET 1

courage *n* strength of mind to carry on in spite of danger ⟨the moral *courage* to speak out against injustice when no one else will⟩
synonyms bravery, courageousness, daring, dauntlessness, doughtiness, fearlessness, gallantry, greatheartedness, guts, hardihood, heart, heroism, intrepidity, intrepidness, nerve, stoutness, valor
related words backbone, fiber, fortitude, grit, gumption, mettle, pluck, spunk; determination, perseverance, resolution; endurance, stamina, tenacity; audacity, boldness, brazenness, cheek, effrontery, gall, temerity
near antonyms faintheartedness, fearfulness, timidity, timorousness; feebleness, softness, weak-

ness; impotence, ineffectualness; hesitation, indecision, indecisiveness, irresolution
antonyms cowardice, cowardliness, cravenness, dastardliness, spinelessness, yellowness

courageous *adj* feeling or displaying no fear by temperament — see BRAVE

courageousness *n* strength of mind to carry on in spite of danger — see COURAGE

courier *n* one that carries a message or does an errand — see MESSENGER

course *n* **1** a way of acting or proceeding ⟨the president's usual *course* has been to obtain advice from several people and then make up his own mind⟩
synonyms line, policy, procedure, program
related words blueprint, design, plan, scheme, strategy; intent, intention, purpose; approach, direction, path, pathway, tack
2 a series of lectures on a subject ⟨a *course* on American history from the colonial period to the present⟩
synonyms class
related words elective, refresher, seminar; core, curriculum
3 a usually fixed or ordered series of actions or events leading to a result — see PROCESS 1
4 the direction along which something or someone moves — see PATH 1

course *vb* to proceed or move quickly — see HURRY 2

court *n* **1** the residence of a ruler ⟨Hampton *Court* was the residence of King Henry VIII⟩
synonyms palace
related words castle, château, estate, mansion, villa
2 an open space wholly or partly enclosed (as by buildings or walls) ⟨the art museum boasts a glass-sided *court* that is filled with an array of greenery and sculpture⟩
synonyms close, courtyard, enclosure (*also* inclosure), patio, quadrangle, yard
related words place, plaza, square; deck, terrace
3 an assembly of persons for the administration of justice ⟨this *court* is now called to order⟩
synonyms bar, tribunal
related words judiciary; court-martial; inquisition, kangaroo court
4 a public official having authority to decide questions of law — see JUDGE 1

court *vb* **1** to act so as to make (something) more likely ⟨you're *courting* disaster if you keep playing with matches⟩
synonyms ask (for), invite, woo
related words angle (for), fish (for); hunt, search, seek
phrases look for
2 to go on dates that may eventually lead to marriage ⟨they *courted* for a year before getting married⟩
synonyms date
related words romance, spark, woo; escort, see, take out
phrases go steady, make love

courteous *adj* showing consideration, courtesy, and good manners — see POLITE 1

courteously *adv* with good reason or courtesy — see WELL 4

courteousness *n* speech or behavior that is a sign of good breeding — see POLITENESS

THESAURUS

courtesy *n* **1** an act of kind assistance — see FAVOR 1

2 an act or utterance that is a customary show of good manners — see CIVILITY 1

3 speech or behavior that is a sign of good breeding — see POLITENESS

courting *n* the series of social engagements shared by a couple looking to get married — see COURTSHIP

courtship *n* the series of social engagements shared by a couple looking to get married ⟨a long-married couple who look back on their whirlwind *courtship* with fondness and laughter⟩

synonyms courting, dating

related words affair, love affair, romance; betrothal, engagement

courtyard *n* an open space wholly or partly enclosed (as by buildings or walls) — see COURT 2

cove *n* a part of a body of water that extends beyond the general shoreline — see GULF 1

covenant *n* **1** a formal agreement between two or more nations or peoples — see TREATY

2 a formal agreement to fulfill an obligation — see GUARANTEE 1

3 an arrangement about action to be taken — see AGREEMENT 2

covenant *vb* to make a solemn declaration of intent — see PROMISE 1

cover *n* **1** a piece placed over an open container to hold in, protect, or conceal its contents ⟨where's the *cover* for the cookie jar?⟩

synonyms cap, lid, top

related words dome, hood, roof; capsule, case, casing, covering, housing, jacket, sheath, shell

2 means or method of defending — see DEFENSE 1

3 something that encloses another thing especially to protect it — see ¹CASE 1

cover *vb* **1** to serve as a replacement usually for a time only ⟨a friend *covered* for me as a hospital volunteer while my family went on vacation⟩

synonyms fill in, pinch-hit, stand in, sub, substitute, take over

related words understudy; relieve, spell; double (as)

2 to form a layer over ⟨by morning a foot of snow *covered* the ground⟩

synonyms blanket, carpet, coat, overlay, overlie, overspread, sheet

related words enclose (*also* inclose), enshroud, envelop, enwrap, mantle, shawl, shroud, swathe, wrap; cloak, clothe, curtain, veil; circle, encircle, encompass

3 to place a protective layer over ⟨*cover* your skin with sunblock so you won't get sunburned⟩

synonyms screen, shield

related words cloak, clothe, veil; disguise, mask, obscure

near antonyms bare, expose, uncover

4 to have (something) as a subject matter — see CONCERN 1

5 to keep secret or shut off from view — see ¹HIDE 2

6 to make one's way through, across, or over — see TRAVERSE

7 to pay continued close attention to (something) for a particular purpose — see MONITOR

8 to drive danger or attack away from — see DEFEND 1

cover (up) *vb* to keep from being publicly known — see SUPPRESS 1

coverage *n* the amount of something (as subject matter) included ⟨the biographical dictionary's *coverage* is limited to people no longer living⟩

synonyms content

related words compass, gamut, range, scope, sweep; membership, participation

covering *n* something that encloses another thing especially to protect it — see ¹CASE 1

coverlet *n* a decorative cloth used as a top covering for a bed — see COUNTERPANE

covert *adj* **1** hidden from view — see SECLUDED

2 undertaken or done so as to escape being observed or known by others — see SECRET 1

covert *n* **1** a place where a person goes to hide — see HIDEOUT

2 a thick patch of shrubbery, small trees, or underbrush — see THICKET

covet *vb* to have an earnest wish to own or enjoy — see DESIRE

coveting *adj* having or marked by an eager and often selfish desire especially for material possessions — see GREEDY 1

covetous *adj* **1** having or marked by an eager and often selfish desire especially for material possessions — see GREEDY 1

2 having or showing mean resentment of another's possessions or advantages — see ENVIOUS

covetousness *n* **1** a painful awareness of another's possessions or advantages and a desire to have them too — see ENVY

2 an intense selfish desire for wealth or possessions — see GREED

cow *vb* to make timid or fearful by or as if by threats — see INTIMIDATE

coward *n* a person who shows a shameful lack of courage in the face of danger ⟨the soldiers who ran as soon as the first shots were fired were branded as *cowards*⟩

synonyms chicken, craven, dastard, poltroon, recreant, sissy

related words defeatist, quitter; pushover, weakling, wimp; snake, sneak

near antonyms daredevil

antonyms hero, stalwart, valiant

cowardice *n* a shameful lack of courage in the face of danger ⟨the *cowardice* shown by political leaders who were willing to give the Nazis whatever they wanted⟩

synonyms cowardliness, cravenness, dastardliness, spinelessness, yellowness

related words diffidence, faintheartedness, fearfulness, timidity, timorousness; carefulness, cautiousness, wariness; bashfulness, shyness; feebleness, softness, weakness

near antonyms audacity, boldness, brazenness; backbone, fiber, fortitude, grit, gumption, mettle, pluck, spunk; determination, perseverance, resolution; endurance, stamina, tenacity

antonyms bravery, courage, courageousness, daring, dauntlessness, doughtiness, fearlessness, gallantry, greatheartedness, guts, hardihood, heart, heroism, intrepidity, intrepidness, nerve, stoutness, valor

cowardliness *n* a shameful lack of courage in the face of danger — see COWARDICE

cowardly *adj* having or showing a shameful lack of courage ⟨a *cowardly* bully who picks on much smaller kids⟩ ⟨vile charges that were made in a *cowardly*, unsigned letter⟩

synonyms chicken, chickenhearted, craven, dastardly, lily-livered, pusillanimous, recreant, spineless, unheroic, yellow

related words diffident, fainthearted, fearful, timid, timorous; afraid, frightened, scared; careful, cautious, wary; bashful, coy, shy; feeble, soft, weak

near antonyms audacious, bold, brazen, cheeky, nervy; plucky, spirited, spunky; determined, resolute

antonyms brave, courageous, daring, dauntless, doughty, fearless, gallant, greathearted, gutsy, hardy, heroic, intrepid, lionhearted, stalwart, stout, stouthearted, valiant, valorous

cowboy *n* a hired hand who tends cattle or horses at a ranch or on the range ⟨*cowboys* were rounding up the cattle for branding⟩

synonyms buckaroo, cowhand, cowman, cowpoke, cowpuncher

related words cowgirl; gaucho, vaquero; horseman, horsewoman, wrangler; cattleman, rancher; herdsman

cower *vb* to draw back or crouch down in fearful submission ⟨the abused dog always *cowered* in the presence of its master⟩

synonyms cringe, grovel, quail

related words flinch, recoil, shrink, squinch; blanch, blench, whiten; fawn, kowtow, toady

cowhand *n* a hired hand who tends cattle or horses at a ranch or on the range — see COWBOY

cowhide *vb* to strike repeatedly with something long and thin or flexible — see WHIP 1

cowman *n* a hired hand who tends cattle or horses at a ranch or on the range — see COWBOY

coworker *n* a fellow worker — see COLLEAGUE

cowpoke *n* a hired hand who tends cattle or horses at a ranch or on the range — see COWBOY

cowpuncher *n* a hired hand who tends cattle or horses at a ranch or on the range — see COWBOY

coy *adj* 1 affecting shyness or modesty in order to attract masculine interest ⟨not wanting him to know that she was interested in him, she acted very *coy* at the dance⟩

synonyms coquettish, demure, kittenish

related words flirtatious; goody-goody, overmodest, priggish, prim, prudish

2 not comfortable around people — see SHY 2

cozen *vb* 1 to cause to believe what is untrue — see DECEIVE

2 to rob by the use of trickery or threats — see FLEECE

cozener *n* a dishonest person who uses clever means to cheat others out of something of value — see TRICKSTER 1

cozy *adj* 1 enjoying physical comfort — see COMFORTABLE 2

2 providing physical comfort — see COMFORTABLE 1

crab *n* an irritable and complaining person — see GROUCH

crab *vb* to express dissatisfaction, pain, or resentment usually tiresomely — see COMPLAIN

crabby *adj* 1 easily irritated or annoyed — see IRRITABLE

2 given to complaining a lot — see FUSSY 1

crack *adj* having or showing exceptional knowledge, experience, or skill in a field of endeavor — see PROFICIENT

crack *n* 1 an irregular usually narrow break in a surface created by pressure ⟨a pebble struck the car's windshield and left a *crack* in it⟩

synonyms chink, cleft, cranny, crevice, fissure, rift, split

related words craze, hairline; fracture, rupture; breach, gap, opening; cut, gash, incision, slit

2 a hard strike with a part of the body or an instrument — see ¹BLOW

3 a loud explosive sound — see CLAP 1

4 an effort to do or accomplish something — see ATTEMPT

5 something said or done to cause laughter — see JOKE 1

crack *vb* 1 to break suddenly with an explosive sound ⟨the tree branch unexpectedly *cracked* under our weight⟩

synonyms pop, snap

related words crackle, hiss, sizzle, sputter; burst, explode, shatter; clack, click, clatter

2 to yield to mental or emotional stress ⟨after hours of tough questioning the suspect finally *cracked* and blurted out a confession⟩

synonyms break (down), flip, freak (out)

phrases go to pieces

3 to change (as a secret message) from code into ordinary language — see DECODE

4 to deliver a blow to (someone or something) usually in a strong vigorous manner — see HIT 1

5 to find an answer for through reasoning — see SOLVE

crackbrain *n* 1 a person judged to be legally or medically insane — see LUNATIC 1

2 a person of odd or whimsical habits — see ECCENTRIC

crackbrained *adj* having or showing a very abnormal or sick state of mind — see INSANE 1

crack down (on) *vb* to put a stop to (something) by the use of force — see QUELL 1

cracked *adj* having or showing a very abnormal or sick state of mind — see INSANE 1

crackerjack *adj* 1 having or showing exceptional knowledge, experience, or skill in a field of endeavor — see PROFICIENT

2 of the very best kind — see EXCELLENT

crackerjack *n* 1 a person with a high level of knowledge or skill in a field — see EXPERT

2 something very good of its kind — see JIM-DANDY

crackpot *n* a person of odd or whimsical habits — see ECCENTRIC

crack–up *n* the violent coming together of two bodies into destructive contact — see CRASH 1

crack up *vb* 1 to declare enthusiastic approval of — see ACCLAIM

2 to praise or publicize lavishly and often excessively — see TOUT 1

craft *n* 1 an occupation requiring skillful use of the hands ⟨the *craft* of cabinetmaking was much admired in colonial times⟩

synonyms handcraft, handicraft, trade

related words art, skill; calling, occupation, profession, vocation

2 a small buoyant structure for travel on water — see BOAT 1

3 the inclination or practice of misleading others through lies or trickery — see DECEIT

4 skill in achieving one's ends through indirect, subtle, or underhanded means — see CUNNING 1

THESAURUS

5 subtle or imaginative ability in inventing, devising, or executing something — see SKILL 1

craft *vb* to put (something) into proper and usually carefully worked out written form — see COMPOSE 1

craftiness *n* **1** skill in achieving one's ends through indirect, subtle, or underhanded means — see CUNNING 1

2 the inclination or practice of misleading others through lies or trickery — see DECEIT

craftsman *n* a person whose occupation requires skill with the hands — see ARTISAN

crafty *adj* clever at attaining one's ends by indirect and often deceptive means — see ARTFUL 1

crag *n* a steep wall of rock, earth, or ice — see CLIFF

craggy *adj* having an uneven edge or outline — see RAGGED 1

cram *vb* **1** to fit (something) into a tight space — see CROWD 1

2 to put into (something) as much as can be held or contained — see FILL 1

crammed *adj* containing or seeming to contain the greatest quantity or number possible — see FULL 1

cramp *n* a painful sudden tightening of a muscle ⟨I was suddenly awakened by a *cramp* in my leg⟩
synonyms charley horse, crick, spasm
related words contraction, jerk, stitch, twinge, twitch

cramp *vb* to create difficulty for the work or activity of — see HAMPER

crane *vb* to move from a lower to a higher place or position — see RAISE 1

cranium *n* the case of bone that encloses the brain and supports the jaws of vertebrates — see SKULL

crank *n* **1** a person of odd or whimsical habits — see ECCENTRIC

2 an irritable and complaining person — see GROUCH

crank (up) *vb* to cause to function — see ACTIVATE

crankiness *n* readiness to show annoyance or impatience — see PETULANCE

cranky *adj* **1** difficult to use or operate especially because of size, weight, or design — see CUMBERSOME

2 easily irritated or annoyed — see IRRITABLE

3 given to complaining a lot — see FUSSY 1

cranny *n* an irregular usually narrow break in a surface created by pressure — see CRACK 1

crash *n* **1** the violent coming together of two bodies into destructive contact ⟨the fiery *crash* of two jumbo jet airplanes in midair⟩
synonyms collision, crack-up, smash, smashup, wreck
related words accident; demolishment, destruction, ruin

2 a falling short of one's goals — see FAILURE 2

3 a loud explosive sound — see CLAP 1

4 a forceful coming together of two things — see IMPACT 1

crash *vb* **1** to cause to break with violence and much noise — see SMASH 1

2 to come into usually forceful contact with something — see HIT 2

3 to stop functioning — see FAIL 1

crass *adj* lacking in refinement or good taste — see COARSE 2

crassness *n* the quality or state of lacking refinement or good taste — see VULGARITY 1

crave *vb* to have an earnest wish to own or enjoy — see DESIRE

craven *adj* having or showing a shameful lack of courage — see COWARDLY

craven *n* a person who shows a shameful lack of courage in the face of danger — see COWARD

cravenness *n* a shameful lack of courage in the face of danger — see COWARDICE

craving *n* a strong wish for something — see DESIRE

crawl *vb* **1** to move slowly with the body close to the ground ⟨the time we had to *crawl* through a narrow passageway from one cave to another⟩
synonyms creep, grovel, slither, snake, worm, wriggle
related words crouch, squat; slide; edge, inch, nose; skulk, sneak, steal, tiptoe

2 to move slowly ⟨the weekend traffic on the road to the beach just *crawled*⟩
synonyms creep, drag, inch, plod, poke
related words lumber, shamble, shuffle, tramp, trudge
near antonyms float, glide, sail; hurry, tear
antonyms fly, race, speed, whiz (*or* whizz), zip

3 to move or act slowly — see DELAY 1

crawler *n* someone who moves slowly or more slowly than others — see SLOWPOKE

crawling *adj* moving or proceeding at less than the normal, desirable, or required speed — see SLOW 1

craze *n* a practice or interest that is very popular for a short time — see FAD

craze *vb* to cause to go insane or as if insane ⟨soldiers who had been *crazed* by months of combat and chaos in the countryside⟩
synonyms derange, madden, unbalance, unhinge, unstring
related words agitate, bother, confuse, discompose, disquiet, distract, disturb, perturb, unsettle, upset; annoy, irritate, vex
near antonyms calm, quiet, relax, settle, soothe, tranquilize (*or* tranquillize)

crazed *adj* having or showing a very abnormal or sick state of mind — see INSANE 1

craziness *n* lack of good sense or judgment — see FOOLISHNESS 1

crazy *adj* **1** conceived or made without regard for reason or reality — see FANTASTIC 1

2 having or showing a very abnormal or sick state of mind — see INSANE 1

3 showing or marked by a lack of good sense or judgment — see FOOLISH 1

4 showing urgent desire or interest — see EAGER

crazy (about *or* over) *adj* filled with an intense or excessive love for — see ENAMORED (OF)

creak *n* a harsh grating sound — see RASP

creak *vb* to make a short shrill noise — see SQUEAK

cream *n* individuals carefully selected as being the best of a class — see ELITE

crease *n* a small fold in a soft and otherwise smooth surface — see WRINKLE 1

crease *vb* to develop creases or folds — see WRINKLE 1

create *vb* to be the cause of (a situation, action, or state of mind) — see EFFECT

creation *n* **1** something (as a device) created for the first time through the use of the imagination — see INVENTION 1

2 the whole body of things observed or assumed — see UNIVERSE

creative *adj* **1** having the skill and imagination to create new things ⟨Thomas Edison's status as perhaps America's greatest *creative* genius⟩
synonyms imaginative, ingenious, innovative, inventive, original
related words gifted, inspired, talented; resourceful; fecund, fertile, fruitful, productive, prolific
near antonyms imitative, uninspired; infertile, unproductive
antonyms uncreative, unimaginative, unoriginal
2 showing a use of the imagination and creativity especially in inventing — see CLEVER 1
creativeness *n* the skill and imagination to create new things — see CREATIVITY 1
creativity *n* **1** the skill and imagination to create new things ⟨the arts and crafts fair showed the remarkable *creativity* of local artists and artisans⟩
synonyms creativeness, imaginativeness, ingeniousness, ingenuity, invention, inventiveness, originality
related words resourcefulness; fecundity, fertility, fruitfulness, productiveness, productivity; freshness, newness, novelty; genius, inspiration, talent
near antonyms dryness, dullness (*also* dulness)
2 the ability to form mental images of things that either are not physically present or have never been conceived or created by others — see IMAGINATION
creator *n* **1** a person who establishes a whole new field of endeavor — see FATHER 2
2 *cap* the being worshipped as the creator and ruler of the universe — see DEITY 2
creature *n* **1** a member of the human race — see HUMAN
2 one of the lower animals as distinguished from human beings — see ANIMAL
credence *n* **1** firm belief in the integrity, ability, effectiveness, or genuineness of someone or something — see TRUST 1
2 mental conviction of the truth of some statement or the reality of some being or phenomenon — see BELIEF 1
credentials *n pl* a skill, an ability, or knowledge that makes a person able to do a particular job — see QUALIFICATION 1
credible *adj* worthy of being accepted as true or reasonable — see BELIEVABLE
credit *n* **1** the right to take possession of goods before paying for them ⟨because of their reputation for not paying their bills, no store will extend the family *credit*⟩
synonyms trust
related words installment plan, layaway
2 an asset that brings praise or renown — see GLORY 2
3 mental conviction of the truth of some statement or the reality of some being or phenomenon — see BELIEF 1
4 public acknowledgment or admiration for an achievement — see GLORY 1
credit *vb* **1** to explain (something) as being the result of something else ⟨has to *credit* his success in picking winning lottery numbers to pure luck⟩
synonyms accredit, ascribe, attribute, impute
related words blame, pin (on); associate, connect, link
2 to regard as right or true — see BELIEVE 1
creditable *adj* deserving of high regard or great approval — see ADMIRABLE
credo *n* **1** a body of beliefs and practices regarding

the supernatural and the worship of one or more deities — see RELIGION 1
2 the basic beliefs or guiding principles of a person or group — see CREED 1
credulity *n* readiness to believe the claims of others without sufficient evidence ⟨the quack pushing the phony medicine was taking advantage of the *credulity* of people hoping for miracle cures⟩
synonyms credulousness, gullibility, naïveté (*also* naivete)
related words artlessness, simplicity, unsophistication; trust, unwariness
near antonyms sophistication, worldliness; distrust, mistrust, suspicion, wariness; doubt, uncertainty
antonyms incredulity, skepticism
credulousness *n* readiness to believe the claims of others without sufficient evidence — see CREDULITY
creed *n* **1** the basic beliefs or guiding principles of a person or group ⟨central to the *creed* of this organization of medical volunteers is the belief that health care is a basic human right⟩
synonyms credo, doctrine, gospel, ideology, philosophy
related words manifesto
2 a body of beliefs and practices regarding the supernatural and the worship of one or more deities — see RELIGION 1
creek *n* **1** a natural body of running water smaller than a river ⟨the shallow *creek* that runs in back of our house⟩
synonyms brook, brooklet, rill, rivulet, run [*chiefly Midland*], streamlet
related words freshet, runoff; river, stream, watercourse, waterway; canal, millrace, millstream, race
2 *chiefly British* a part of a body of water that extends beyond the general shoreline — see GULF 1
creep *n* a person whose behavior is offensive to others — see JERK 1
creep *vb* **1** to advance gradually beyond the usual or desirable limits — see ENCROACH
2 to move or act slowly — see DELAY 1
3 to move slowly with the body close to the ground — see CRAWL 1
4 to move slowly — see CRAWL 2
creeper *n* someone who moves slowly or more slowly than others — see SLOWPOKE
creeping *adj* moving or proceeding at less than the normal, desirable, or required speed — see SLOW 1
creepy *adj* fearfully and mysteriously strange or fantastic — see EERIE
crest *n* the line formed when two sloping surfaces come together along their topmost edge — see RIDGE
crestfallen *adj* feeling unhappiness — see SAD 1
cretin *n* **1** a person whose behavior is offensive to others — see JERK 1
2 a stupid person — see IDIOT
crevice *n* an irregular usually narrow break in a surface created by pressure — see CRACK 1
crew *n* a group of people working together on a task — see GANG 1
crick *n* a painful sudden tightening of a muscle — see CRAMP
crime *n* **1** activities that are in violation of the laws of the state ⟨a promise by the president to step up the war against *crime*⟩

THESAURUS

synonyms criminality, lawbreaking, lawlessness
related words malfeasance, misconduct; wrongdoing; evil, immorality, sin, wickedness; corruption, depravity; malefaction, misdeed, misdoing, offense (*or* offence), transgression, trespass
2 a regrettable or blameworthy act ⟨it's a *crime* to waste food, so give the rest of the pizza to me⟩
synonyms disgrace, pity, shame, sin
related words outrage, scandal
3 a breaking of a moral or legal code — see OFFENSE 1
4 a cause of shame — see DISGRACE 2
criminal *adj* contrary to or forbidden by law — see ILLEGAL 1
criminal *n* a person who has committed a crime ⟨car thieves, pickpockets, burglars, and other *criminals*⟩
synonyms crook, culprit; felon, lawbreaker, malefactor, offender
related words desperado, outlaw; convict, jailbird; perpetrator; evildoer, sinner, transgressor, trespasser, wrongdoer; gangster, gunman, hoodlum, mobster, racketeer, thug; backslider, relapser, repeater
criminality *n* activities that are in violation of the laws of the state — see CRIME 1
crimp *n* **1** a small fold in a soft and otherwise smooth surface — see WRINKLE 1
2 something that makes movement or progress more difficult — see ENCUMBRANCE
crimson *vb* to develop a rosy facial color (as from excitement or embarrassment) — see BLUSH
cringe *vb* to draw back or crouch down in fearful submission — see COWER
crinkle *n* a small fold in a soft and otherwise smooth surface — see WRINKLE 1
crinkle *vb* **1** to create (as by crushing) an irregular mass of creases in — see CRUMPLE 1
2 to develop creases or folds — see WRINKLE 1
cripple *vb* **1** to cause severe or permanent injury to — see MAIM
2 to reduce the soundness, effectiveness, or perfection of — see DAMAGE 1
3 to render powerless, ineffective, or unable to move — see PARALYZE
crisis *n* a time or state of affairs requiring prompt or decisive action — see EMERGENCY
crisp *adj* **1** having a texture that readily breaks into little pieces under pressure ⟨the bag of *crisp* cookies had a lot of crumbs on the bottom⟩
synonyms brittle, crispy, crumbly, flaky, friable, short
related words crunchy; breakable, delicate, fragile
near antonyms elastic, flexible, pliable, pliant, resilient; strong, sturdy, tough
2 being clean and in good order — see NEAT 1
3 marked by the use of few words to convey much information or meaning — see CONCISE
crisply *adv* in a few words — see SHORTLY 1
crispness *n* the quality or state of being marked by or using only few words to convey much meaning — see SUCCINCTNESS
crispy *adj* having a texture that readily breaks into little pieces under pressure — see CRISP 1
crisscross *vb* to make one's way through, across, or over — see TRAVERSE
criterion *n* something set up as an example against which others of the same type are compared — see STANDARD 1

critic *n* **1** a person given to harsh judgments and to finding faults ⟨the president's hard-core *critics* are going to criticize him no matter what he does⟩
synonyms carper, castigator, caviler (*or* caviller), censurer, faultfinder, nitpicker, railer, scold
related words belittler, derider, detractor; pettifogger, quibbler; complainer, crybaby, fusser, whiner
2 a person who makes or expresses a judgment on the quality of offerings in some field of endeavor ⟨the restaurant *critic* said that the fries at that fast-food outlet were the worst that she had ever eaten⟩
synonyms reviewer
related words analyst, columnist, commentator; appraiser, evaluator, judge
critical *adj* **1** given to making or expressing unfavorable judgments about things ⟨adults tend to be *critical* of teenagers' taste in music and movies⟩
synonyms captious, carping, caviling (*or* cavilling), faultfinding, hypercritical, overcritical
related words discerning, discriminating, judicious; demanding, exacting, fastidious, finicky, fussy, particular
near antonyms undiscerning
antonyms uncritical
2 needing immediate attention — see ACUTE 2
3 of the greatest possible importance — see CRUCIAL
criticism *n* an essay evaluating or analyzing something ⟨every *criticism* of the movie has noted that there are major holes in its plot⟩
synonyms notice, review
related words rave; appraisal, assessment, evaluation; analysis, examination, study
criticize *vb* to express one's unfavorable opinion of the worth or quality of ⟨the students who feel the need to *criticize* every single idea by the principal for improving the school⟩
synonyms blame, censure, condemn, denounce, dis [*slang*], fault, knock, pan, reprehend
related words assail, attack, blast, slam, slash; beef, bellyache, carp, complain, crab, croak, fuss, gripe, grouse, growl, grumble, kick, moan, murmur, mutter, repine, squawk, wail, whine, yammer; admonish, chide, rebuke, reprimand, reproach, reprove; berate, castigate, crucify, excoriate, flay, lambaste (*or* lambast), lash, pillory, scold, upbraid; bad-mouth, belittle, disparage, put down
phrases find fault (with), take to task
near antonyms approve, endorse (*also* indorse), recommend, sanction
antonyms extol (*also* extoll), laud, praise
critter *n* one of the lower animals as distinguished from human beings — see ANIMAL
croak *vb* **1** to express dissatisfaction, pain, or resentment usually tiresomely — see COMPLAIN
2 *slang* to stop living — see DIE 1
3 *slang* to deprive of life — see KILL 1
croaker *n* an irritable and complaining person — see GROUCH
croaking *adj* harsh and dry in sound — see HOARSE
crockery *n* articles made of baked clay ⟨a display of beautifully hand-painted *crockery* on the kitchen countertop⟩
synonyms earthenware, pottery, stoneware
related words ceramics; china, porcelain
crone *n* a mean or ugly old woman ⟨a run-down

house that was inhabited by a cantankerous *crone* who kept to herself⟩

synonyms beldam (*or* beldame), hag, witch

related words grandam (*or* grandame); harpy, shrew, virago

crony *n* **1** a person frequently seen in the company of another — see ASSOCIATE 1

2 a person who has a strong liking for and trust in another — see FRIEND 1

crook *n* **1** a person who has committed a crime — see CRIMINAL

2 something that curves or is curved — see BEND 1

crook *vb* **1** to cause to turn away from a straight line — see BEND 1

2 to turn away from a straight line or course — see CURVE 1

crooked *adj* **1** marked by a long series of irregular curves ⟨a long, *crooked* line of people had formed in front of the ticket booth⟩

synonyms bending, curled, curling, curved, curving, devious, serpentine, sinuous, tortuous, twisted, twisting, winding

related words zigzag, zigzagging; circling, coiled, coiling, corkscrew, looping, spiral, spiraling (*or* spiralling), swirling; circuitous, indirect, roundabout; meandering, rambling, wandering

near antonyms direct, linear

antonyms straight, straightaway

2 given to or marked by cheating and deception — see DISHONEST 2

3 inclined or twisted to one side — see AWRY

4 marked by, based on, or done by the use of dishonest methods to acquire something of value — see FRAUDULENT 1

crookedness *n* the inclination or practice of misleading others through lies or trickery — see DECEIT

crop *n* **1** the quantity of an animal or vegetable product gathered at the end of a season ⟨the wheat *crop* is going to be exceptionally large this year⟩

synonyms harvest

related words return, yield

2 a usually small number of persons considered as a unit — see GROUP 2

crop *vb* **1** to look after or assist the growth of by labor and care — see GROW 1

2 to make (as hair) shorter with or as if with the use of shears — see CLIP

crop (up) *vb* to come to one's attention especially gradually or unexpectedly — see ARISE 2

cropper *n* a falling short of one's goals — see FAILURE 2

croquette *n* a small usually rounded mass of minced food that has been fried — see CAKE

cross *adj* easily irritated or annoyed — see IRRITABLE

cross *n* **1** a test of faith, patience, or strength — see TRIAL 1

2 an offspring of parents with different genes especially when of different races, breeds, species, or genera — see HYBRID

cross *vb* **1** to be unfaithful or disloyal to — see BETRAY 1

2 to divide by passing through or across — see INTERSECT

3 to make one's way through, across, or over — see TRAVERSE

cross (out) *vb* to show (something written) to be no longer valid by drawing a cross over or a line through it — see X (OUT)

crossbred *adj* being offspring produced by parents of different races, breeds, species, or genera — see MIXED 1

crossbreed *n* an offspring of parents with different genes especially when of different races, breeds, species, or genera — see HYBRID

cross fire *n* an often noisy or angry expression of differing opinions — see ARGUMENT 1

crossing *n* **1** a journey over water in a vessel — see SAIL

2 a place where roads meet — see CROSSROAD 1

crossness *n* readiness to show annoyance or impatience — see PETULANCE

crossroad *n* **1** *usually* **crossroads** *pl* a place where roads meet ⟨the fast-food chain has a restaurant at practically every *crossroads*⟩

synonyms corner, crossing, intersection

related words overpass, underpass

2 *usually* **crossroads** *pl* a time or state of affairs requiring prompt or decisive action — see EMERGENCY

cross section *n* a number of things selected from a group to stand for the whole — see SAMPLE 1

crossways *adv* in a line or direction running from corner to corner — see CROSSWISE

crosswise *adv* in a line or direction running from corner to corner ⟨first cut the sandwiches *crosswise* and then trim the crusts⟩

synonyms athwart, crossways, obliquely, transversely

crotchet *n* an odd or peculiar habit — see IDIOSYNCRASY

crotchetiness *n* readiness to show annoyance or impatience — see PETULANCE

crotchety *adj* easily irritated or annoyed — see IRRITABLE

crouch *vb* to lie low with the limbs close to the body ⟨the cat *crouched* in the bushes, waiting for the right moment to pounce on the chipmunk⟩

synonyms huddle, hunch, scrunch, squat, squinch

related words curl up

crow *vb* **1** to feel or express joy or triumph — see EXULT

2 to praise or express pride in one's own possessions, qualities, or accomplishments often to excess — see BOAST

crowd *n* **1** a great number of persons or things gathered together ⟨a huge *crowd* of fans was on hand to greet the returning Super Bowl champions⟩

synonyms army, crush, drove, flock, horde, host, legion, mob, multitude, press, swarm, throng

related words masses, rabble, riffraff; gaggle, herd; heap, mountain, pile

2 a group of people sharing a common interest and relating together socially — see GANG 2

crowd *vb* **1** to fit (something) into a tight space ⟨*crowded* all the boats into the harbor before the storm struck⟩

synonyms cram, jam, ram, sandwich, squeeze, stuff, wedge

related words fill, heap, jam-pack, load, pack

2 to move upon or fill (something) in great numbers ⟨cars *crowded* the roads over the long holiday weekend⟩

synonyms flock, mob, swarm, throng

related words beset, infest, invade, overrun; clog, dam, obstruct, plug (up)

THESAURUS

3 to gather into a closely packed group — see PRESS 3

crowded *adj* **1** containing or seeming to contain the greatest quantity or number possible — see FULL 1

2 having little space between items or parts — see CLOSE 1

crown *n* **1** a decorative band or wreath worn about the head as a symbol of victory or honor ⟨the *crown* of laurel leaves that is traditionally placed on the winner of the marathon⟩
synonyms coronet, diadem
related words tiara; garland, laurel

2 the position occupied by the one who comes in first in a competition ⟨his lifelong dream of someday winning the heavyweight boxing *crown*⟩
synonyms championship, title

3 the highest part or point — see HEIGHT 1

crown *vb* to bring to a triumphant conclusion ⟨the Olympic Games were *crowned* by spectacular closing ceremonies⟩
synonyms climax, culminate
related words complete, conclude, finish, round (off *or* out), terminate, wrap up

crucial *adj* of the greatest possible importance ⟨water is *crucial* to our survival⟩
synonyms critical, key, pivotal, vital
related words decisive, life-and-death; basic, elementary, fundamental; essential, indispensable, necessary, requisite; pressing, urgent
near antonyms inconsequential, insignificant, trivial, unimportant

crucible *n* a test of faith, patience, or strength — see TRIAL 1

crude *adj* **1** being such as found in nature and not altered by processing or refining ⟨a spill of *crude* oil along a coastline is the worst kind of environmental disaster⟩
synonyms native, natural, raw, undressed, unprocessed, unrefined, untreated
related words undeveloped; roughhewn, unfinished, unpolished; unbaked, uncooked; impure, unfiltered, unpurified
phrases in the rough
near antonyms filtered, pure, purified
antonyms dressed, processed, refined, treated

2 belonging to or characteristic of an early level of skill or development — see PRIMITIVE 1

3 depicting or referring to sexual matters in a way that is unacceptable in polite society — see OBSCENE 1

4 lacking in refinement or good taste — see COARSE 2

5 hastily or roughly constructed — see RUDE 1

crudeness *n* **1** the quality or state of being obscene — see OBSCENITY 1

2 the quality or state of lacking refinement or good taste — see VULGARITY 1

cruel *adj* **1** having or showing the desire to inflict severe pain and suffering on others ⟨a *cruel* dictator who tortured anyone who dared to speak out against him⟩ ⟨*cruel* and unusual punishments are forbidden by the U.S. Constitution⟩
synonyms barbaric, barbarous, brutal, heartless, inhumane, sadistic, savage, vicious, wanton
related words cutthroat, merciless, pitiless, ruthless; fell, ferocious, grim; bloodthirsty, murderous, sanguinary, sanguine; catty, despiteful, hateful, malevolent, malicious, malign, malignant, mean, nasty, spiteful

near antonyms tender, warm, warmhearted; charitable, clement, lenient, merciful, pitying; pacific, peaceable, peaceful
antonyms benign, benignant, compassionate, good-hearted, humane, kind, kindhearted, sympathetic, tenderhearted

2 difficult to endure — see HARSH 1

3 hard to accept or bear especially emotionally — see BITTER 2

4 having or showing a desire to cause someone pain or suffering for the sheer enjoyment of it — see HATEFUL

cruelness *n* the willful infliction of pain and suffering on others — see CRUELTY

cruelty *n* the willful infliction of pain and suffering on others ⟨centuries after he ravaged Europe, Attila the Hun remains notorious for his *cruelty*⟩
synonyms barbarity, brutality, cruelness, heartlessness, inhumanity, sadism, savageness, savagery, viciousness, wantonness
related words mercilessness, ruthlessness; ferocity, fierceness; bloodthirstiness, sanguinity; cattiness, despitefulness, hatefulness, malevolence, maliciousness, malignity, meanness, nastiness, spitefulness
near antonyms tenderness, warmheartedness, warmth; clemency, leniency, mercifulness, mercy, pity
antonyms benignity, compassion, good-heartedness, humanity, kindheartedness, kindness, sympathy

cruise *n* a journey over water in a vessel — see SAIL

cruise *vb* to travel on water in a vessel — see SAIL 1

crumb *n* **1** a very small amount — see PARTICLE 1

2 a very small piece — see BIT 1

crumble *vb* to become worse or of less value — see DETERIORATE

crumbly *adj* having a texture that readily breaks into little pieces under pressure — see CRISP 1

crumple *vb* **1** to create (as by crushing) an irregular mass of creases in ⟨*crumpled* the piece of paper and angrily threw it in the wastebasket⟩
synonyms crinkle, rumple, scrunch, wrinkle
related words corrugate, crease, crimp, fold, furrow, pleat; ripple, ruffle; disarrange, jumble, mess (up), muss (up)
antonyms iron out, smooth

2 to fall down or in as a result of physical pressure — see COLLAPSE 1

crunch *n* a time or state of affairs requiring prompt or decisive action — see EMERGENCY

crunch *vb* to press or strike against or together so as to make a scraping sound — see GRIND 2

crunch (on) *vb* to crush or grind with the teeth — see BITE (ON)

crusade *n* a series of activities undertaken to achieve a goal — see CAMPAIGN

crusader *n* one who is intensely or excessively devoted to a cause — see ZEALOT

crush *n* **1** a strong but often short-lived liking for another person ⟨the *crush* that she had on a boy whom she had met over the summer⟩
synonyms infatuation, passion
related words fixation, obsession; affection, devotion, fondness, love; craze, fad, rage, vogue

2 a great number of persons or things gathered together — see CROWD 1

crush *vb* **1** to cause to become a pulpy mass ⟨dark-colored grapes that will be *crushed* to make red wine⟩

synonyms mash, pulp, squash

related words press, squeeze; beat, pound, powder, pulverize

2 to achieve a victory over — see BEAT 2

3 to put a stop to (something) by the use of force — see QUELL 1

4 to reduce to fine particles — see POWDER

5 to subject to incapacitating emotional or mental stress — see OVERWHELM 1

6 to apply external pressure on so as to force out the juice or contents of — see PRESS 2

crusher *n* something (as a fact or argument) that is decisive or overwhelming — see CLINCHER

crusty *adj* being or characterized by direct, brief, and potentially rude speech or manner — see BLUNT 1

crux *n* the central part or aspect of something under consideration ⟨the *crux* of the problem is that the school's current budget is totally inadequate⟩

synonyms core, gist, heart, nub, pith, pivot

related words course, direction, drift, tenor; body, essence, substance

cry *n* **1** a loud vocal expression of strong emotion — see SHOUT

2 a natural vocal sound made by an animal — see CALL 1

3 an attention-getting word or phrase used to publicize something (as a campaign or product) — see SLOGAN

4 an earnest request — see PLEA 1

cry *vb* **1** to shed tears often while making meaningless sounds as a sign of pain or distress ⟨some kids started to *cry* even before the doctor had given them their shot⟩

synonyms bawl, blubber, sob, weep

related words grieve, keen, lament, mourn; howl, scream, squall, wail, yowl; pule, whimper, whine; sniffle, snivel; groan, moan, sigh

2 to utter one's distinctive animal sound ⟨we knew that we were getting very close to the ocean when we could hear sea gulls *crying*⟩

synonyms call, sing

3 to speak so as to be heard at a distance — see CALL 1

cry (out) *vb* to utter with a sudden burst of strong feeling — see EXCLAIM

crybaby *n* a person who makes frequent complaints usually about little things ⟨car trips that were often spoiled by a couple of *crybabies* in the back seat⟩

synonyms complainer, fusser, griper, growler, grumbler, whiner

related words malcontent; carper, critic, faultfinder, nitpicker, squawker; bawler, wailer, weeper

cry down *vb* to express scornfully one's low opinion of — see DECRY 1

crying *adj* needing immediate attention — see ACUTE 2

crypt *n* an underground burial chamber ⟨the old church's *crypt* is the final resting place for the president and his beloved wife⟩

synonyms catacomb(s), vault

related words mausoleum, sepulcher (*or* sepulchre), tomb

cryptic *adj* **1** being beyond one's powers to know, understand, or explain — see MYSTERIOUS 1

2 having an often intentionally veiled or uncertain meaning — see OBSCURE 1

crystallize *vb* to take on a definite form — see FORM 1

cub *n* a young person who is between infancy and adulthood — see CHILD 1

cubicle *n* one of the parts into which an enclosed space is divided — see COMPARTMENT

cuckoo *adj* **1** having or showing a very abnormal or sick state of mind — see INSANE 1

2 showing or marked by a lack of good sense or judgment — see FOOLISH 1

cuddle *vb* **1** to lie close — see NUZZLE

2 to sit or recline comfortably or cozily — see SNUGGLE 1

cudgel *n* a heavy rigid stick used as a weapon or for punishment — see CLUB 1

cue *n* **1** a series of persons or things arranged one behind another — see LINE 1

2 a slight or indirect pointing to something (as a solution or explanation) — see HINT 1

cuff *n* a hard strike with a part of the body or an instrument — see ¹BLOW

cuisine *n* the art or style of preparing food (as in a specified region) — see COOKERY

cull *n* something separated from a group or lot for not being as good as the others ⟨the unbruised apples will be packed in bags, and the *culls* will be used for cider⟩

synonyms discard, reject, rejection

related words second, throwaway

cull *vb* to decide to accept (someone or something) from a group of possibilities — see CHOOSE 1

culminate *vb* to bring to a triumphant conclusion — see CROWN

culmination *n* the highest part or point — see HEIGHT 1

culpability *n* responsibility for wrongdoing or failure — see BLAME 1

culpable *adj* **1** deserving reproach or blame — see BLAMEWORTHY

2 responsible for a wrong — see GUILTY 1

culprit *n* a person who has committed a crime — see CRIMINAL

cult *n* **1** a group of people showing intense devotion to a cause, person, or work (as a film) ⟨long after it had gone off the air, the TV series continued to have a huge *cult*⟩

synonyms following

related words discipleship

2 a body of beliefs and practices regarding the supernatural and the worship of one or more deities — see RELIGION 1

cultivate *vb* **1** to come to have gradually — see DEVELOP 2

2 to help the growth or development of — see FOSTER 1

3 to look after or assist the growth of by labor and care — see GROW 1

4 to work by plowing, sowing, and raising crops on — see FARM

cultivated *adj* having or showing a taste for the fine arts and gracious living ⟨the museum's annual gala for charity usually attracts a *cultivated* crowd⟩

synonyms civilized, cultured, genteel, polished, refined

related words cerebral, highbrow, intellectual; educated, erudite, knowledgeable, learned, literate, scholarly, well-read; civil, courteous, mannerly,

THESAURUS

polite, well-bred; cosmopolitan, sophisticated, urbane

near antonyms ignorant, illiterate, uneducated, unlettered; lowbrow, unintelligent; coarse, ill-bred, ill-mannered; provincial, rustic, unsophisticated; boorish, churlish, cloddish, clownish, crude, uncouth, vulgar

antonyms philistine, uncivilized, uncultured, unpolished, unrefined

cultivation *n* a high level of taste and enlightenment as a result of extensive intellectual training and exposure to the arts — see CULTURE 1

cultivator *n* a person who cultivates the land and grows crops on it — see FARMER

cultural *adj* of or relating to the fine arts ⟨with its many museums, theaters, and opera and ballet companies, the city is a *cultural* paradise⟩

synonyms artistic

related words aesthetic, tasteful

culture *n* **1** a high level of taste and enlightenment as a result of extensive intellectual training and exposure to the arts ⟨because of its wide reputation as a place of *culture*, Boston became known as "the Athens of America"⟩

synonyms civilization, cultivation, polish, refinement

related words education, erudition, learning, literacy, scholarship; sophistication, urbanity; breeding, gentility, manners; class, elegance, grace, taste; civility, courtesy, politeness

near antonyms ignorance, illiteracy; parochialism, provincialism, unsophistication; boorishness, churlishness, clownishness, coarseness, crudeness, vulgarity

antonyms philistinism

2 the way people live at a particular time and place — see CIVILIZATION 1

culture *vb* to look after or assist the growth of by labor and care — see GROW 1

cultured *adj* having or showing a taste for the fine arts and gracious living — see CULTIVATED

cumbersome *adj* difficult to use or operate especially because of size, weight, or design ⟨a long-handled wrench that is too *cumbersome* for tight spots, like under the sink⟩

synonyms awkward, clumsy, cranky, cumbrous, ungainly, unhandy, unwieldy

related words uncontrollable, unmanageable; bulky, heavy, massive; impracticable, impractical

near antonyms functional, practicable, practical, serviceable, useful

antonyms handy

cumbrous *adj* difficult to use or operate especially because of size, weight, or design — see CUMBERSOME

cummerbund *n* a strip of flexible material (as leather) worn around the waist — see ²BELT

cumulative *adj* produced by a series of additions of identical or similar things ⟨a *cumulative* weight gain of 20 pounds over the course of a year⟩

synonyms additive, incremental

related words gradual, step-by-step

cunning *adj* **1** clever at attaining one's ends by indirect and often deceptive means — see ARTFUL 1

2 skillful with the hands — see DEXTEROUS 1

cunning *n* **1** skill in achieving one's ends through indirect, subtle, or underhanded means ⟨the *cunning* with which Tom Sawyer was able to get others to whitewash the fence for him⟩

synonyms artfulness, artifice, caginess, canni-

ness, craft, craftiness, deviousness, foxiness, guile, slickness, slyness, sneakiness, subtleness, subtlety, wiliness

related words calculation, care, design; savvy, sharpness, shrewdness; cleverness, ingeniousness, ingenuity, inventiveness; ease, facility, finesse; deceitfulness, duplicity, shiftiness

2 subtle or imaginative ability in inventing, devising, or executing something — see SKILL 1

3 the inclination or practice of misleading others through lies or trickery — see DECEIT

cup *n* a round vessel equipped with a handle and designed for drinking ⟨a large *cup* that can hold almost a pint of hot chocolate⟩

synonyms mug

related words stein, tankard; demitasse, noggin; teacup

cupboard *n* a storage case typically having doors and shelves — see CABINET

cupidity *n* an intense selfish desire for wealth or possessions — see GREED

cur *n* a person whose behavior is offensive to others — see JERK 1

curb *n* something that limits one's freedom of action or choice — see RESTRICTION 1

curb *vb* to keep from exceeding a desirable degree or level (as of expression) — see CONTROL 1

curdy *adj* having small pieces or lumps spread throughout — see CHUNKY 1

cure *n* **1** something that corrects or counteracts something undesirable ⟨a fun hobby is always a good *cure* for boredom⟩

synonyms corrective, remedy

related words cure-all, elixir, panacea; answer, solution; aid, help, relief, succor; balm, palliative

2 a substance or preparation used to treat disease — see MEDICINE

cure *vb* **1** to bring about recovery from ⟨do you have anything that will *cure* my headache?⟩

synonyms heal, remedy

related words allay, alleviate, assuage, relieve; palliate, salve, soothe; ease, lighten, moderate, temper; doctor, treat

near antonyms aggravate, worsen

2 to restore to a healthy condition — see HEAL 1

cure–all *n* something that cures all ills or problems ⟨raising a young person's self-esteem is not the *cure-all* that some people think⟩

synonyms elixir, panacea

related words corrective, cure, remedy

curio *n* **1** a small object displayed for its attractiveness or interest — see KNICKKNACK

2 something strange or unusual that is an object of interest — see CURIOSITY 2

curiosity *n* **1** an eager desire to find out about things that are often none of one's business ⟨the neighbors' *curiosity* about what we paid for our new car was really offensive⟩

synonyms curiousness, inquisitiveness, nosiness

related words attentiveness, concern, interest, regard; inquiry, interrogation, questioning; intrusiveness, obtrusiveness, officiousness; eavesdropping, rubbernecking

near antonyms apathy, disinterestedness, disregard, indifference, unconcern

2 something strange or unusual that is an object of interest ⟨the museum's *curiosities* include items constructed entirely out of toothpicks⟩

synonyms curio, exotic, oddity, rarity

related words marvel, prodigy, wonder; abnormality, anomaly, freak, monster, monstrosity; malformation, mutant, mutation

3 a small object displayed for its attractiveness or interest — see KNICKKNACK

curious *adj* **1** interested in what is not one's own business ⟨*curious* neighbors peered out of their windows as the new people moved in⟩
synonyms inquisitive, nosy (*or* nosey), prying, snoopy
related words interfering, intrusive, meddlesome, meddling, obtrusive, officious; inquisitional, inquisitorial; concerned, interested
near antonyms apathetic, disinterested, indifferent, unconcerned, uninterested
antonyms incurious, uncurious

2 different from the ordinary in a way that causes curiosity or suspicion — see ODD 2

3 noticeably different from what is generally found or experienced — see UNUSUAL 1

curiousness *n* an eager desire to find out about things that are often none of one's business — see CURIOSITY 1

curl *n* a length of hair that forms a loop or series of loops ⟨a young girl with beautiful golden *curls*⟩
synonyms ringlet
related words kink, wave; lock, tress

curl *vb* to follow a circular or spiral course — see WIND

curled *adj* **1** forming or styled into loops — see CURLY

2 marked by a long series of irregular curves — see CROOKED 1

curling *adj* marked by a long series of irregular curves — see CROOKED 1

curl up *vb* to sit or recline comfortably or cozily — see SNUGGLE 1

curly *adj* forming or styled into loops ⟨the boy's naturally *curly* hair⟩
synonyms curled
related words frizzy, kinky, waved, wavy
near antonyms lank, limp
antonyms straight

curmudgeon *n* an irritable and complaining person — see GROUCH

currency *n* something (as pieces of stamped metal or printed paper) customarily and legally used as a medium of exchange, a measure of value, or a means of payment — see MONEY

current *adj* **1** accepted, used, or practiced by most people ⟨the *current* theories on parenting favor allowing children lots of self-expression⟩
synonyms conventional, customary, going, popular, prevailing, prevalent, standard, stock, usual
related words average, common, everyday, normal, ordinary; regular, routine; ubiquitous, universal, widespread; accustomed, wonted; fashionable, in, modish, stylish
near antonyms abnormal, exceptional, extraordinary, uncommon
antonyms nonstandard, unconventional, unpopular, unusual

2 being or involving the latest methods, concepts, information, or styles — see MODERN

3 existing or in progress right now — see PRESENT 1

current *n* **1** a prevailing or general movement or inclination — see TREND 1

2 noticeable movement of air in a particular direction — see ¹WIND 1

currently *adv* at the present time — see NOW 1

curse *n* **1** a prayer that harm will come to someone ⟨the victim's *curse* that the man who robbed her never receive any pleasure from her money⟩
synonyms anathema, execration, imprecation, malediction
related words censure, condemnation, damnation, denunciation; hex, spell
near antonyms citation, commendation, endorsement
antonyms benediction, benison, blessing

2 a disrespectful or indecent word or expression — see SWEARWORD

curse *vb* **1** to ask a divine power to send harm or evil upon ⟨I *curse* the guy who had the idea of having annoying salespeople call up innocent people to sell them things they don't want⟩
synonyms imprecate
related words condemn, damn, denounce, execrate, reprobate; hex, jinx; fulminate (against), rail (against), revile
near antonyms applaud, commend, congratulate
antonyms bless

2 to cause persistent suffering to — see AFFLICT

3 to use offensive or indecent language — see SWEAR 1

cursorily *adv* with excessive or careless speed — see HASTILY 1

cursory *adj* acting or done with excessive or careless speed — see HASTY 1

curt *adj* being or characterized by direct, brief, and potentially rude speech or manner — see BLUNT 1

curtail *vb* **1** to make (as hair) shorter with or as if with the use of shears — see CLIP

2 to make less in extent or duration — see SHORTEN

curtain *n* **1** something that covers or conceals like a piece of cloth — see CLOAK 1

2 **curtains** *pl* pieces of cloth hung to darken, decorate, or divide a room — see DRAPERY

curtain *vb* to keep secret or shut off from view — see ¹HIDE 2

curvature *n* something that curves or is curved — see BEND 1

curve *n* something that curves or is curved — see BEND 1

curve *vb* **1** to turn away from a straight line or course ⟨after following a straight path most of the way down the mountain, the ski trail abruptly *curves* to the right⟩
synonyms arc, arch, bend, bow, crook, hook, round, sweep, swerve, wheel
related words circle, coil, curl, loop, spiral; turn, twist, wind; deviate, veer
antonyms straighten

2 to cause to turn away from a straight line — see BEND 1

curved *adj* marked by a long series of irregular curves — see CROOKED 1

curving *adj* marked by a long series of irregular curves — see CROOKED 1

cushion *n* something that serves as a protective barrier ⟨used a blanket as a *cushion* between the two tables in the moving van⟩
synonyms buffer, bumper, fender, pad
related words baffle, muffler; padding; safeguard, shield; barricade, cordon

cushion *vb* to lessen the shock of ⟨a substantial nest egg helped to *cushion* the sudden loss of her job⟩

synonyms buffer, gentle, soften

related words baffle, dampen, deaden, dull; moderate, modulate, temper; allay, alleviate, assuage, ease; lighten, mitigate, relieve

near antonyms heighten, intensify, sharpen

cushy *adj* providing physical comfort — see COMFORTABLE 1

cusp *n* the last and usually sharp or tapering part of something long and narrow — see POINT 1

cuss *n* a disrespectful or indecent word or expression — see SWEARWORD

cuss *vb* to use offensive or indecent language — see SWEAR 1

custodian *n* 1 a person who takes care of a property sometimes for an absent owner ⟨the *custodian* made his usual rounds of the building to make sure that everything was OK⟩

synonyms caretaker, guardian, janitor, keeper, warden, watchman

related words curator; sexton; steward

2 a person or group that watches over someone or something — see GUARD 1

3 someone that protects — see PROTECTOR

custody *n* responsibility for the safety and well-being of someone or something ⟨the divorcing parents will share *custody* of the children⟩

synonyms care, guardianship, keeping, safekeeping, trust, ward

related words control, governorship, management, superintendence, supervision

custom *adj* made or fitted to the needs or preferences of a specific customer — see CUSTOM-MADE

custom *n* 1 a usual manner of behaving or doing — see HABIT

2 an inherited or established way of thinking, feeling, or doing — see TRADITION 1

customary *adj* 1 accepted, used, or practiced by most people — see CURRENT 1

2 based on customs usually handed down from a previous generation — see TRADITIONAL 1

customer *n* 1 a person who buys a product or uses a service from a business ⟨the store greatly values its regular *customers*⟩

synonyms client, guest, patron

related words consumer, end user, user; buyer, purchaser; browser, prospect, shopper, window-shopper

near antonyms merchant, seller, vendor (*also* vender)

2 a member of the human race — see HUMAN

customized *adj* made or fitted to the needs or preferences of a specific customer — see CUSTOM-MADE

custom–made *adj* made or fitted to the needs or preferences of a specific customer ⟨an odd-sized window that will require the purchase of *custom-made* curtains⟩

synonyms custom, customized, tailored, tailor-made

related words particular, special, specialized; handcrafted, handmade

antonyms mass-produced, ready-made

cut *n* 1 a piece that has been separated from the whole by cutting ⟨choose *cuts* of meat that have very little visible fat⟩

synonyms cutting, slice

related words chop, cutlet; chunk, hunk, lump; clipping, paring, shaving, snippet; sliver, splinter

2 an individual part of a process, series, or ranking — see DEGREE 1

3 something belonging to, due to, or contributed by an individual member of a group — see SHARE 1

cut *vb* 1 to penetrate with a sharp edge (as a knife) ⟨I *cut* my hand on a piece of broken glass⟩

synonyms gash, incise, rip, slash, slice, slit

related words saw, scissor; cleave, rive, split; pierce, stab; bruise, hack, lacerate, mangle; rend, tear; butcher, carve, dissect; chop, dice, mince; amputate, cut off, sever

2 to fail to attend ⟨a warning that she had been *cutting* too many classes without valid excuses⟩

synonyms miss, skip

related words ignore, neglect, pass over

phrases absent oneself, play hooky

antonyms attend, show up (for)

3 to deliberately ignore or treat rudely — see SNUB 1

4 to make (as hair) shorter with or as if with the use of shears — see CLIP

5 to shorten the standing leafy plant cover of — see MOW 1

cut (across) *vb* to make one's way through, across, or over — see TRAVERSE

cut (down) *vb* to bring down by cutting — see FELL 2

cut (out) *vb* to bring (as an action or operation) to an immediate end — see STOP 1

cut back *vb* 1 to make (as hair) shorter with or as if with the use of shears — see CLIP

2 to make less in extent or duration — see SHORTEN

cute *adj* very pleasing to look at — see BEAUTIFUL

cuteness *n* the qualities in a person or thing that as a whole give pleasure to the senses — see BEAUTY 1

cut in *vb* to cause a disruption in a conversation or discussion — see INTERRUPT

cutlet *n* a small usually rounded mass of minced food that has been fried — see CAKE

cut off *vb* to set or keep apart from others — see ISOLATE

cut out *vb* to stop functioning — see FAIL 1

cut–rate *adj* 1 costing little — see CHEAP 1

2 of low quality — see CHEAP 2

cutter *n* an instrument with a sharp edge for cutting — see KNIFE

cutthroat *adj* not guided by or showing a concern for what is right — see UNPRINCIPLED

cutting *adj* 1 causing intense discomfort to one's skin ⟨a frigid day with a *cutting* wind that made it seem even colder⟩

synonyms biting, bitter, keen, penetrating, piercing, raw, sharp, smarting, stinging

related words brisk, invigorating, nippy, snappy; needlelike, prickly, tingling; caustic, corrosive

near antonyms balmy, gentle, mild, soothing

2 having an edge thin enough to cut or pierce something — see SHARP 1

3 marked by the use of wit that is intended to cause hurt feelings — see SARCASTIC

cutting *n* a piece that has been separated from the whole by cutting — see CUT 1

cut up *vb* to engage in attention-getting playful or boisterous behavior ⟨high-spirited cousins who *cut up* at every family gathering⟩

synonyms act up, clown (around), fool (around),

horse (around), monkey (around), show off, sky-lark

related words carry on, misbehave; roughhouse; caper, cavort, disport, frisk, frolic, gambol, lark, rollick, romp; carouse, revel, wassail

cycle *n* **1** a series of events or actions that repeat themselves regularly and in the same order ⟨the *cycle* of birth, growth, decline, and death that is experienced by all life forms⟩
synonyms circle, round
related words pattern, syndrome; course, development, progression, run; circuit, loop, ring; rotation, revolution, turn; chain, sequence, series, string, succession, train
2 a long or seemingly long period of time — see AGE 2

cynic *n* a person who distrusts other people and believes that everything is done for selfish reasons ⟨a *cynic* who believes that nobody does a good deed without expecting something in return⟩
synonyms misanthrope, pessimist
related words misogynist; doubter, skeptic; belit-

tler, derider, detractor, scoffer; malcontent; defeatist, quitter
near antonyms optimist; idealist; sentimentalist

cynical *adj* having or showing a deep distrust of human beings and their motives ⟨so *cynical* that he can't understand why anyone would volunteer to help out at a homeless shelter⟩
synonyms misanthropic, pessimistic
related words distrustful, mistrustful, skeptical, suspicious; derisive, mocking, sardonic, scornful; defeatist, fatalistic, negative; ironic (*or* ironical), sarcastic; jaded, sophisticated, worldly-wise; hard-bitten, hard-boiled, unsentimental
near antonyms trustful, trusting, unsuspicious; cheerful, optimistic, rose-colored; ingenuous, innocent, naive (*or* naïve), unsophisticated; idealistic, impractical, romantic; maudlin, mushy, saccharine, sappy, sentimental

cynosure *n* a thing or place that is of greatest importance to an activity or interest — see CENTER 1

czar *also* **tsar** *or* **tzar** *n* a person of rank, power, or influence in a particular field — see MAGNATE

D

¹dab *n* a quick thrust — see ¹POKE
²dab *n* a very small amount — see PARTICLE 1
dabbler *n* a person who regularly or occasionally engages in an activity without being or becoming an expert at it — see AMATEUR
dad *n* a male human parent — see FATHER 1
daddy *n* a male human parent — see FATHER 1
daffy *adj* **1** having or showing a very abnormal or sick state of mind — see INSANE 1
2 showing or marked by a lack of good sense or judgment — see FOOLISH 1
daft *adj* **1** having or showing a very abnormal or sick state of mind — see INSANE 1
2 showing or marked by a lack of good sense or judgment — see FOOLISH 1
daftness *n* lack of good sense or judgment — see FOOLISHNESS 1
daily *adj* occurring, done, produced, or appearing every day ⟨they made their *daily* stop at the coffee shop after work to relax before dinner⟩
synonyms day-to-day, diurnal
related words alternate, cyclical, intermittent, periodic, recurrent, recurring, regular; continuous, frequent, incessant
near antonyms nightly, nocturnal; monthly, weekly, yearly; erratic, infrequent, irregular; occasional, spasmodic, sporadic; interrupted
daintiness *n* the state or quality of having a delicate structure — see DELICACY 2
dainty *adj* **1** hard to please — see FINICKY
2 having qualities that appeal to a refined taste — see CHOICE
3 satisfying or pleasing because of fineness or mildness — see DELICATE 1
dainty *n* something that is pleasing to eat because it is rare or a luxury — see DELICACY 1
dais *n* a level usually raised surface — see PLATFORM

dale *n* an area of lowland between hills or mountains — see VALLEY
dalliance *n* activity engaged in to amuse oneself — see PLAY 1
dallier *n* someone who moves slowly or more slowly than others — see SLOWPOKE
dally *vb* **1** to engage in activity for amusement — see PLAY 1
2 to move or act slowly — see DELAY 1
3 to show a liking for someone of the opposite sex just for fun — see FLIRT
4 to spend time doing nothing — see IDLE
dallying *adj* moving or proceeding at less than the normal, desirable, or required speed — see SLOW 1
dam *n* a bank of earth constructed to control water ⟨the river backed up behind the *dam* until it formed a new lake⟩
synonyms dike, embankment, levee
related words breakwater, jetty, seawall; breastwork, bulwark, earthwork, rampart; canal, channel, ditch, gutter, trough; lock; barricade, barrier, block; floodgate, sluice
dam *vb* **1** to prevent passage through — see CLOG 1
2 to close up so that no empty spaces remain — see FILL 2
damage *n* **1** something that causes loss or pain — see INJURY 1
2 damages *pl* a sum of money to be paid as a punishment — see FINE
3 damages *pl* payment to another for a loss or injury — see COMPENSATION 1
damage *vb* **1** to reduce the soundness, effectiveness, or perfection of ⟨the explosion in the sewers *damaged* the entire city's water supply⟩
synonyms blemish, break, cripple, deface, disfig-

THESAURUS

ure, flaw, harm, hurt, impair, injure, mar, spoil, vitiate

related words enfeeble, undermine, weaken; erode, scour, wash out, wear (away); blight, tarnish; dent, dint; botch, gum (up); lacerate, wound; maim, mangle, mutilate, torment, torture; annihilate, crush, dash, decimate, demolish, destroy, devastate, pulverize, raze, ruin, scourge, shatter, smash, tear down, waste, wipe out, wreck

near antonyms cure, heal, help, rectify, remedy; edit, remodel, revise; ameliorate, better, enhance, improve, meliorate

antonyms fix, mend, patch, rebuild, recondition, reconstruct, renovate, repair, revamp

2 to cause bodily damage to — see INJURE 1

damaging *adj* causing or capable of causing harm — see HARMFUL

dame *n* **1** a dignified usually elderly woman of some rank or authority — see MATRIARCH

2 a woman of high birth or social position — see GENTLEWOMAN

damn *vb* **1** to declare to be morally wrong or evil — see CONDEMN 1

2 to impose a judicial punishment on — see SENTENCE

damp *adj* slightly or moderately wet — see MOIST

damp *vb* to reduce or weaken in strength or feeling — see DULL 1

dampen *vb* **1** to make or become slightly or moderately wet — see MOISTEN

2 to reduce or weaken in strength or feeling — see DULL 1

damper *n* a device on a musical instrument that deadens or softens its tone — see MUTE

dampness *n* the amount of water suspended in the air in tiny droplets — see MOISTURE

damsel *n* a young usually unmarried woman — see GIRL 1

dance *n* a social gathering for dancing ⟨who are you taking to the *dance* Saturday night?⟩

synonyms ball, cotillion, formal, hop, prom

related words blowout, celebration, event, festival, festivity, fete (*or* fête), gala, masquerade, mixer, party, reception, shindig, soiree (*or* soirée)

dance *vb* **1** to perform a series of usually rhythmic bodily movements to music ⟨she liked to *dance* to her favorite rock bands⟩

synonyms foot (it), hoof (it), step

related words prance, strut, trip; gavotte, jig, jitterbug, jive, mambo, polka, tango, tap-dance, waltz; tread

2 to make an irregular series of quick, sudden movements — see FLIT

dandle *vb* to treat with great or excessive care — see BABY

dandy *adj* of the very best kind — see EXCELLENT

dandy *n* **1** a man extremely interested in his clothing and personal appearance ⟨that *dandy* was willing to spend all day and hundreds of dollars just to get the perfect pair of shoes⟩

synonyms buck, dude, fop, gallant

related words coxcomb, popinjay; blade, cavalier; swell; clotheshorse

near antonyms slattern, slob, sloven, slut

2 something very good of its kind — see JIM-DANDY

danger *n* **1** the state of not being protected from injury, harm, or evil ⟨he knew he was in *danger* when he received the threatening phone calls at home⟩

synonyms distress, endangerment, imperilment, jeopardy, peril, risk, trouble

related words exposure, liability, vulnerability; precariousness, threat

near antonyms preservation, salvation; defense, protection; exemption, immunity, impunity

antonyms safeness, safety, security

2 something that may cause injury or harm ⟨she was willing to face the *dangers* of the construction site in order to get her Frisbee back⟩

synonyms hazard, menace, peril, pitfall, risk, threat, trouble

related words snare, trap

near antonyms guard, protection, safeguard, shield, ward

dangerous *adj* involving potential loss or injury ⟨the soldiers were commanded to go on a *dangerous* mission behind enemy lines⟩

synonyms grave, grievous, hazardous, jeopardizing, menacing, parlous, perilous, risky, serious, threatening, unhealthy, unsafe, venturesome

related words insecure, precarious, treacherous, uncertain; chance, haphazard, random; distressing, sickening, unpleasant; ugly, wicked; adverse, bad, baleful, baneful, deleterious, detrimental, evil, harmful, hurtful, ill, inimical, injurious, malignant, nasty, noxious, pernicious, pestilent; deadly, deathly, destructive, dire, fatal, fateful, fell, killer, lethal, mortal, murderous

near antonyms advantageous, beneficial, good

antonyms harmless, innocent, innocuous, safe

dangle *vb* to place on an elevated point without support from below — see HANG 1

dangling *adj* extending freely from a support from above — see DEPENDENT 1

dank *adj* slightly or moderately wet — see MOIST

dapper *adj* being strikingly neat and trim in style or appearance — see SMART 1

dapple *n* a small area that is different (as in color) from the main part — see SPOT 1

dapple *vb* to mark with small spots especially unevenly — see SPOT

dappled *also* **dapple** *adj* **1** marked with spots — see SPOTTED 1

2 having blotches of two or more colors — see PIED

dare *vb* **1** to invite (someone) to take part in a contest or to perform a feat — see CHALLENGE 2

2 to oppose (something hostile or dangerous) with firmness or courage — see FACE 2

daredevil *adj* **1** foolishly adventurous or bold — see FOOLHARDY 1

2 having or showing a lack of concern for the consequences of one's actions — see RECKLESS 1

daring *adj* inclined or willing to take risks — see BOLD 1

daring *n* strength of mind to carry on in spite of danger — see COURAGE

dark *adj* **1** being without light or without much light ⟨a *dark* alley that most people wisely avoided⟩

synonyms darkened, darkish, darkling, darksome, dim, dimmed, dusky, gloomy, murky, obscure, obscured, pitch-black, pitch-dark, somber (*or* sombre)

related words moonless, sunless; cloudy, dull, dulled, lackluster; shadowy, shady; gray (*also* grey), leaden, pale

near antonyms beaming, effulgent, glowing, lambent, radiant, shining; glossy, lustrous, shiny *antonyms* bright, brightened, brilliant, illuminated, illumined, light, lighted (*or* lit), lucent, lucid, luminous

2 causing or marked by an atmosphere lacking in cheer — see GLOOMY 1

3 given to keeping one's activities hidden from public observation or knowledge — see SECRETIVE

4 having an often intentionally veiled or uncertain meaning — see OBSCURE 1

5 lacking in education or the knowledge gained from books — see IGNORANT 1

dark *n* **1** a time or place of little or no light ⟨I have a bad habit of running into tables in the *dark*⟩
synonyms blackness, darkness, dusk, gloaming, gloom, murk, night, semidarkness, shade, shadows, twilight, umbra
related words blackout, brownout; shadiness; dullness (*also* dulness), somberness; cloudiness, fogginess, haziness, mistiness, murkiness; dimness, faintness, gloominess, grayness, paleness
near antonyms moonlight, starlight, sunlight; effulgence, radiance, shine, sunshine; incandescence, luminescence, luminosity
antonyms blaze, brightness, brilliance, day, daylight, glare, glow, light, lightness

2 the time from sunset to sunrise when there is no visible sunlight — see NIGHT 1

darken *vb* **1** to take on a gloomy or forbidding look ⟨his face slowly *darkened* as we told him the sad news⟩
synonyms gloom, glower, lower (*also* lour)
related words frown, scowl; glare, stare; brood, mope, pout, sulk; anger, fume, rage, steam; intimidate, menace, threaten
antonyms brighten, cheer (up), lighten, perk (up)

2 to make dark, dim, or indistinct — see CLOUD 1

darkened *adj* being without light or without much light — see DARK 1

darkening *adj* causing or marked by an atmosphere lacking in cheer — see GLOOMY 1

darkish *adj* being without light or without much light — see DARK 1

darkling *adj* **1** being beyond one's powers to know, understand, or explain — see MYSTERIOUS 1

2 being without light or without much light — see DARK 1

3 having an often intentionally veiled or uncertain meaning — see OBSCURE 1

darkness *n* **1** a time or place of little or no light — see DARK 1

2 the quality or state of having a veiled or uncertain meaning — see OBSCURITY 1

3 the time from sunset to sunrise when there is no visible sunlight — see NIGHT 1

darksome *adj* being without light or without much light — see DARK 1

darling *adj* **1** granted special treatment or attention ⟨they poured gifts and affection on their *darling* child⟩
synonyms beloved, cherished, dear, favored, favorite, loved, pet, precious, special, sweet
related words admired, adored, appreciated, esteemed, relished, revered; prized, treasured; preferred
near antonyms despised, detested, disdained, disfavored, disliked, execrated, hated, loathed; abandoned, forgotten, ignored

2 having qualities that tend to make one loved — see LOVABLE

3 giving pleasure or contentment to the mind or senses — see PLEASANT

darling *n* **1** a person or thing that is preferred over others — see FAVORITE

2 a person with whom one is in love — see SWEETHEART

darn *vb* to close up with a series of interlacing stitches — see SEW

dart *n* an act or expression showing scorn and usually intended to hurt another's feelings — see INSULT

dart *vb* to make an irregular series of quick, sudden movements — see FLIT

dash *n* active strength of body or mind — see VIGOR 1

dash *vb* **1** to go at a pace faster than a walk — see RUN 1

2 to proceed or move quickly — see HURRY 2

3 to send through the air especially with a quick forward motion of the arm — see THROW

4 to wet or soil by striking with something liquid or mushy — see SPLASH 2

dashing *adj* inclined or willing to take risks — see BOLD 1

dashingly *adv* **1** in a bright and showy way — see GAILY 3

2 in a strikingly neat and trim manner — see SMARTLY

dastard *n* a person who shows a shameful lack of courage in the face of danger — see COWARD

dastardliness *n* a shameful lack of courage in the face of danger — see COWARDICE

dastardly *adj* having or showing a shameful lack of courage — see COWARDLY

date *n* **1** an agreement to be present at a specified time and place — see ENGAGEMENT 2

2 the period during which something exists, lasts, or is in progress — see DURATION 1

date *vb* **1** to go on a social engagement with ⟨I don't want to *date* him—I'd rather just be friends⟩
synonyms take out
related words accompany, escort, see; court, woo

2 to go on dates that may eventually lead to marriage — see COURT 2

dated *adj* having passed its time of use or usefulness — see OBSOLETE

dateless *adj* **1** dating or surviving from the distant past — see ANCIENT 1

2 lasting forever — see EVERLASTING

dating *n* the series of social engagements shared by a couple looking to get married — see COURTSHIP

datum *n* a single piece of information — see FACT 3

daub *vb* to rub an oily or sticky substance over — see SMEAR 1

daunt *vb* to lessen the courage or confidence of — see DISCOURAGE 1

dauntless *adj* feeling or displaying no fear by temperament — see BRAVE

dauntlessness *n* strength of mind to carry on in spite of danger — see COURAGE

davenport *n* a long upholstered piece of furniture designed for several sitters — see COUCH

dawdle *vb* **1** to move or act slowly — see DELAY 1

2 to spend time doing nothing — see IDLE

dawdler *n* someone who moves slowly or more slowly than others — see SLOWPOKE

dawdling *adj* moving or proceeding at less than the normal, desirable, or required speed — see SLOW 1

THESAURUS

dawn *n* **1** the first appearance of light in the morning or the time of its appearance ⟨we stayed up talking until *dawn*⟩
synonyms aurora, cockcrow, dawning, daybreak, daylight, morn, morning, sunrise, sunup
related words day, daytime, light; twilight; forenoon
near antonyms dark, darkness, night, nighttime; afternoon, dusk, evening, gloaming
antonyms nightfall, sundown, sunset
2 the point at which something begins — see BEGINNING
dawn *vb* to come into existence — see BEGIN 2
dawn (on) *vb* to come into the mind of — see OCCUR (TO)
dawning *n* the first appearance of light in the morning or the time of its appearance — see DAWN 1
day *n* **1** the hours of light between one night and the next ⟨during the *day*, we like to go play ball in the park⟩
synonyms daylight, daytime
related words light, sunlight, sunshine; dawn, dawning, daybreak, morn, morning, sunrise, sunset; dusk, evening, gloaming, nightfall, sundown, twilight
near antonyms dark, darkness
antonyms night, nighttime
2 an extent of time associated with a particular person or thing — see AGE 1
daybreak *n* the first appearance of light in the morning or the time of its appearance — see DAWN 1
daydream *n* a conception or image created by the imagination and having no objective reality — see FANTASY 1
daydreaming *n* the state of being lost in thought — see REVERIE
daylight *n* **1** the first appearance of light in the morning or the time of its appearance — see DAWN 1
2 the hours of light between one night and the next — see DAY 1
daytime *n* the hours of light between one night and the next — see DAY 1
day–to–day *adj* occurring, done, produced, or appearing every day — see DAILY
daze *n* a state of mental confusion — see HAZE 2
daze *vb* **1** to make senseless or dizzy by a blow — see STUN 1
2 to overpower with light — see DAZZLE
dazed *adj* suffering from mental confusion — see DIZZY 2
dazzle *n* the quality or state of having or giving off light — see BRILLIANCE 1
dazzle *vb* to overpower with light ⟨skiers were *dazzled* by the glare off of the slopes of freshly packed snow⟩
synonyms bedazzle, blind, daze
related words confuse, overpower, overwhelm, stun
dazzling *adj* giving off or reflecting much light — see BRIGHT 1
deacon *n* a person specially trained and authorized to conduct religious services in a Christian church — see CLERGYMAN
dead *adj* **1** no longer living ⟨I inherited this heirloom from my *dead* great-grandfather⟩
synonyms breathless, deceased, defunct, departed, fallen, gone, late, lifeless

related words extinct; dying, fading, moribund; stillborn; finished, lapsed, terminated; barren, desert; inanimate, insensate, nonliving, unanimated
phrases bitten the dust, passed away, passed on
near antonyms animate, animated; dynamic, lively, thriving, vibrant, vital, vivacious; active, functioning, operative, running
antonyms alive, breathing, going, living
2 depleted in strength, energy, or freshness — see WEARY 1
3 having no exceptions or restrictions — see ABSOLUTE 2
4 lacking in sensation or feeling — see NUMB
5 no longer existing — see EXTINCT
6 not being in a state of use, activity, or employment — see INACTIVE 2
7 of, relating to, or suggestive of death — see DEATHLY 1
dead *adv* **1** in a direct line or course — see DIRECTLY 1
2 to a full extent or degree — see FULLY 1
deaden *vb* to reduce or weaken in strength or feeling — see DULL 1
dead heat *n* a situation in which neither participant in a contest, competition, or struggle comes out ahead of the other — see TIE 1
deadlock *n* a point in a struggle where neither side is capable of winning or willing to give in — see IMPASSE
deadly *adj* likely to cause or capable of causing death ⟨the doctors were alarmed about the outbreak of the *deadly* new virus⟩
synonyms baleful, deathly, fatal, fell, killer, lethal, mortal, murderous, pestilent, vital
related words baneful, destructive, harmful, noxious, pernicious; poisonous, toxic, virulent; dangerous, grave, grievous, hazardous, jeopardizing, menacing, parlous, perilous, risky, serious, threatening, ugly, unhealthy, unsound; capital; bloody, internecine, sanguinary, sanguine
near antonyms beneficial, restorative; nonpoisonous, nontoxic, safe
antonyms healthful, healthy, nonfatal, nonlethal, wholesome
deadly *adv* to a great degree — see VERY 1
deadness *n* the state of being dead — see DEATH 2
deadpan *adj* not expressing any emotion — see BLANK 1
deadwood *n* discarded or useless material — see GARBAGE
deafening *adj* marked by a high volume of sound — see LOUD 1
¹deal *n* a considerable amount — see LOT 2
²deal *n* **1** an arrangement about action to be taken — see AGREEMENT 2
2 the transfer of ownership of something from one person to another for a price — see SALE
deal *vb* **1** to carry on the business of buying and selling goods or other property — see TRADE 1
2 to talk over or dispute the terms of a purchase — see BARGAIN
deal (in) *vb* to offer for sale to the public — see MARKET
deal (out) *vb* to give out (something) in appropriate amounts or to appropriate individuals — see ADMINISTER 1
deal (with) *vb* **1** to behave toward in a stated way — see TREAT 1

2 to have (something) as a subject matter — see CONCERN 1

dealer *n* **1** a buyer and seller of goods for profit — see MERCHANT

2 the person in a business deal who hands over an item in exchange for money — see VENDOR

dealings *n pl* doings between individuals or groups — see RELATION 1

dean *n* the senior member of a group ⟨the *dean* of the Aspen ski instructors oversaw the training of the rescue team⟩
synonyms elder, elder statesman, senior
related words better, superior
near antonyms inferior, subordinate, underling; beginner, freshman, newcomer, rookie
antonyms baby

dear *adj* **1** commanding a large price — see COSTLY

2 granted special treatment or attention — see DARLING 1

3 having qualities that tend to make one loved — see LOVABLE

dear *n* a person with whom one is in love — see SWEETHEART

dearth *n* **1** a falling short of an essential or desirable amount or number — see DEFICIENCY

2 the fact or state of being absent — see LACK 1

death *n* **1** the permanent stopping of all the vital bodily activities ⟨we were all saddened by the *death* of our teacher⟩
synonyms decease, demise, doom, end, passing, quietus
related words casualty, fatality; martyrdom, self-destruction, suicide; annihilation, destruction, ending, expiration, extermination, ruin
near antonyms existence, life; creation
antonyms birth

2 the state of being dead ⟨*death* is one of the few constants in the universe⟩
synonyms deadness, lifelessness, sleep
antonyms existence, life

3 the act of ceasing to exist ⟨the *death* of the Soviet economic system in the wake of the breakup of the USSR⟩
synonyms demise, expiration, termination
related words dispersion, dissolution; shutdown; decease, doom, end, ending, passing, quietus; suicide; annihilation, destruction, ruin
near antonyms existence
antonyms beginning, creation, start

deathless *adj* lasting forever — see EVERLASTING

deathlike *adj* of, relating to, or suggestive of death — see DEATHLY 1

deathly *adj* **1** of, relating to, or suggestive of death ⟨his *deathly* pallor suggested that any attempt to find a pulse would be futile⟩
synonyms dead, deathlike, mortal
related words ghostly, phantom, spectral; inactive, inert, inoperative, lifeless, quiescent, still; macabre; baleful, fatal, fateful, fell, killer, lethal, murderous, pestilent
near antonyms active, alive, living; animated, energetic, lively, vigorous, vivacious; hale, healthy, hearty, robust, sound

2 likely to cause or capable of causing death — see DEADLY

debacle *also* **débâcle** *n* **1** a sudden violent event that brings about great loss or destruction — see DISASTER

2 something that has failed — see FAILURE 3

debar *vb* to prevent the participation or inclusion of — see EXCLUDE

debark *vb* to go ashore from a ship — see DISEMBARK

debase *vb* **1** to lower in character or dignity ⟨we *debased* ourselves when we cheated on the test⟩
synonyms abase, corrupt, debauch, degrade, demean, deprave, pervert, poison, profane, prostitute, subvert, warp
related words contaminate, pollute, taint; descend; disgrace, humble, humiliate; blemish, damage, deface, destroy, flaw, harm, hurt, impair, mar, ruin, spoil, stain, tarnish, vitiate, wreck; depreciate, downgrade
near antonyms dignify, exalt, honor; amend, improve; cleanse, purify, restore; respect
antonyms elevate, ennoble, uplift

2 to reduce to a lower standing in one's own eyes or in others' eyes — see HUMBLE

debased *adj* having or showing lowered moral character or standards — see CORRUPT

debasement *n* a sinking to a state of low moral standards and behavior — see CORRUPTION 2

debatable *adj* **1** open to question or dispute ⟨it's always *debatable* which college football team is really number one, since there's more than one ranking system⟩
synonyms disputable, doubtable, doubtful, moot, questionable
related words refutable; controversial, debated, disputed; dubious, inconclusive, indecisive, problematic (*also* problematical), uncertain; academic, hypothetical, speculative, theoretical (*also* theoretic); ambiguous, equivocal
near antonyms irrefutable; certain, definite, positive, sure; unambiguous, unequivocal; absolute, clear, conclusive, decisive; uncontested, undisputed
antonyms incontestable, incontrovertible, indisputable, indubitable, undeniable, unquestionable

2 giving good reason for being doubted, questioned, or challenged — see DOUBTFUL 2

debate *n* **1** a careful weighing of the reasons for or against something — see CONSIDERATION 1

2 variance of opinion on a matter — see DISAGREEMENT 1

debate *vb* **1** to give serious and careful thought to — see PONDER

2 to talk about (an issue) usually from various points of view and for the purpose of arriving at a decision or opinion — see DISCUSS

debater *n* a person who takes part in a dispute — see DISPUTANT

debauch *vb* to lower in character or dignity — see DEBASE 1

debauched *adj* having or showing lowered moral character or standards — see CORRUPT

debaucher *n* a person who has sunk below the normal moral standard — see DEGENERATE

debauchery *n* **1** immoral conduct or practices harmful or offensive to society — see VICE 1

2 a sinking to a state of low moral standards and behavior — see CORRUPTION 2

debilitate *vb* to diminish the physical strength of — see WEAKEN 1

debilitated *adj* lacking bodily strength — see WEAK 1

debilitation *n* **1** a gradual sinking and wasting away of mind or body — see DECLINE 1

THESAURUS

2 the quality or state of lacking physical strength or vigor — see WEAKNESS 1

debility *n* the quality or state of lacking physical strength or vigor — see WEAKNESS 1

debonair *adj* having or showing very polished and worldly manners — see SUAVE

debris *n* the portion or bits of something left over or behind after it has been destroyed — see REMAINS 1

debt *n* a breaking of a moral or legal code — see OFFENSE 1

debug *vb* to remove errors, defects, deficiencies, or deviations from — see CORRECT 1

debunk *vb* to reveal the true nature of — see EXPOSE 1

decadence *n* **1** a change to a lower state or level — see DECLINE 2
2 a sinking to a state of low moral standards and behavior — see CORRUPTION 2

decadent *adj* **1** having lost forcefulness, courage, or spirit — see EFFETE 1
2 having or showing lowered moral character or standards — see CORRUPT

decadent *n* a person who has sunk below the normal moral standard — see DEGENERATE

decalogue *n* a collection or system of rules of conduct — see CODE

decamping *n* the act of leaving a place — see DEPARTURE

decampment *n* the act of leaving a place — see DEPARTURE

decapitate *vb* to cut off the head of ⟨he started *decapitating* wildflowers with his walking stick as they strolled through the park⟩
synonyms behead, guillotine
related words prune, shorten, trim; scalp

decay *n* **1** a gradual sinking and wasting away of mind or body — see DECLINE 1
2 the process by which dead organic matter separates into simpler substances — see CORRUPTION 1

decay *vb* **1** to go through decomposition ⟨the logs *decayed* on the rain forest floor⟩ ⟨the atom of plutonium *decayed* in the test chamber⟩
synonyms break down, corrupt, decompose, disintegrate, molder, putrefy, rot, spoil
related words sour, turn; contaminate, defile, pollute, taint; curdle, ferment; crumble, degenerate, deteriorate
phrases go to seed, run to seed
near antonyms develop, grow, mature, ripen; refresh, renew, restore; cleanse, purify; assemble, compose, integrate
2 to become worse or of less value — see DETERIORATE
3 to lose bodily strength or vigor — see WEAKEN 2

decayed *adj* **1** having lost forcefulness, courage, or spirit — see EFFETE 1
2 having undergone organic breakdown — see ROTTEN 1

decaying *n* a gradual sinking and wasting away of mind or body — see DECLINE 1

decease *n* the permanent stopping of all the vital bodily activities — see DEATH 1

decease *vb* to stop living — see DIE 1

deceased *adj* no longer living — see DEAD 1

deceit *n* the inclination or practice of misleading others through lies or trickery ⟨the evil queen in the story was full of *deceit*⟩
synonyms artifice, craft, craftiness, crookedness, cunning, deceitfulness, dishonesty, dissembling, dissimulation, double-dealing, duplicity, fakery, foxiness, guile, wiliness
related words equivocation, prevarication; chicanery, skulduggery (*or* skullduggery), subterfuge, trickery; hypocrisy, insincerity; deviousness, shrewdness; treacherousness, underhandedness, unscrupulousness; covertness, furtiveness, secrecy, shadiness, sneakiness, stealthiness; oiliness, shiftiness, slickness, slipperiness, slyness, smoothness
near antonyms candidness, candor, directness, frankness, ingenuousness, openness, plainness; honesty, probity; reliability, trustworthiness
antonyms artlessness, forthrightness, good faith, guilelessness, sincerity

deceitful *adj* **1** marked by, based on, or done by the use of dishonest methods to acquire something of value — see FRAUDULENT 1
2 tending or having power to deceive — see DECEPTIVE 1

deceitfulness *n* **1** the inclination or practice of misleading others through lies or trickery — see DECEIT
2 the tendency to tell lies — see DISHONESTY 1

deceive *vb* to cause to believe what is untrue ⟨he went to great lengths to *deceive* his younger brother about the nature of his new job at the mall⟩
synonyms beguile, bluff, cozen, delude, dupe, fool, gull, have, hoax, hoodwink, humbug, misguide, misinform, mislead, snow, string along, take in, trick
related words cheat, chisel, defraud, fleece, gyp, hustle, rook, swindle
near antonyms debunk, expose, reveal, show up, uncloak, uncover, unmask; disclose, divulge, tell, unveil; disabuse, disenchant, disillusion; edify, enlighten
antonyms undeceive

deceiving *adj* tending or having power to deceive — see DECEPTIVE 1

decelerate *vb* to cause to move or proceed at a less rapid pace — see SLOW 1

deceleration *n* a usually gradual decrease in the pace or level of activity of something — see SLOWDOWN

decency *n* **1** socially acceptable behavior ⟨the standards of basic *decency* demanded that they help the old lady with her groceries⟩
synonyms decorum, form, propriety
related words civility, courtesy, politeness; dignity, grace, refinement; discretion, prudence; correctness, decorousness, fitness, rightness, seemliness; attention, attentiveness, care, carefulness; goodness, high-mindedness, honesty, morality, probity, rectitude, righteousness, straightness, uprightness, virtue, virtuousness
near antonyms coarseness, crudeness, gracelessness; discourtesy, impoliteness, incivility; imprudence, indiscretion; badness, evil, immorality, wickedness
antonyms impropriety, indecency, indecorum
2 conduct that conforms to an accepted standard of right and wrong — see MORALITY 1

decent *adj* **1** conforming to a high standard of morality or virtue — see GOOD 2
2 following the accepted rules of moral conduct — see HONORABLE 1
3 following the established traditions of refined society and good taste — see PROPER 1

4 free from any trace of the coarse or indecent — see CHASTE

5 of a level of quality that meets one's needs or standards — see ADEQUATE

deceptive *adj* **1** tending or having power to deceive ⟨in his *deceptive* answer about the vehicle's history, the salesman said that the used car had never been hit by another car⟩

synonyms beguiling, deceitful, deceiving, deluding, delusive, delusory, fallacious, false, misleading, specious

related words devious, guileful, shady, shifty, sly, sneaking, sneaky, trick, tricky, underhand, underhanded; inaccurate, incorrect, wrong; bewildering, confounding, distracting, perplexing, puzzling; crooked, dishonest, double-dealing, faithless, fast, fraudulent, knavish, lying, mendacious, untrustworthy, untruthful; insidious, perfidious, treacherous; artificial, backhanded, feigned, hypocritical, insincere, left-handed, two-faced

near antonyms candid, frank, open, plain; clarifying, elucidative, explanatory, illuminating; revealing, revelatory; honest, trustworthy, truthful

antonyms aboveboard, forthright, straightforward

2 given to or marked by cheating and deception — see DISHONEST 2

decide *vb* **1** to come to a judgment after discussion or consideration ⟨they *decided* to go out for pizza after the movie was over⟩

synonyms choose, conclude, determine, figure, opt, resolve

related words decree, rule; cull, elect, handpick, pick, prefer, select, single (out), take

phrases make up one's mind

near antonyms abstain, decline, refuse, reject, turn down; delay, hesitate, stall, temporize; shilly-shally, vacillate, waver

2 to give an opinion about (something at issue or in dispute) — see JUDGE 1

3 to come to an agreement or decision concerning the details of — see ARRANGE 1

4 to make final, definite, or beyond dispute — see CLINCH

decided *adj* not subject to misinterpretation or more than one interpretation — see CLEAR 2

decidedness *n* firm or unwavering adherence to one's purpose — see DETERMINATION 1

decimate *vb* to bring to a complete end the physical soundness, existence, or usefulness of — see DESTROY 1

decimation *n* the state or fact of being rendered nonexistent, physically unsound, or useless — see DESTRUCTION

decipher *vb* to change (as a secret message) from code into ordinary language — see DECODE

decision *n* **1** a position arrived at after consideration ⟨after much deliberation, we made a *decision* about what to have on our pizza⟩

synonyms conclusion, deliverance, determination, diagnosis, judgment (*or* judgement), opinion, resolution, verdict

related words decree, mandate, order; say-so; doom, finding, ruling, sentence; choice, option, selection

near antonyms deadlock, draw, stalemate, stand-off, tie

2 firm or unwavering adherence to one's purpose — see DETERMINATION 1

decisive *adj* **1** fully committed to achieving a goal — see DETERMINED 1

2 having the power to persuade — see COGENT

3 serving to put an end to all debate or questioning — see CONCLUSIVE 1

decisiveness *n* firm or unwavering adherence to one's purpose — see DETERMINATION 1

deck *vb* **1** to make more attractive by adding something that is beautiful or becoming — see DECORATE

2 to outfit with clothes and especially fine or special clothes — see CLOTHE 1

declaim *vb* **1** to give a formal often extended talk on a subject — see TALK 1

2 to talk as if giving an important and formal speech — see ORATE 1

declamation *n* a usually formal discourse delivered to an audience — see SPEECH 1

declaration *n* a solemn and often public declaration of the truth or existence of something — see PROTESTATION

declare *vb* **1** to make known openly or publicly — see ANNOUNCE

2 to state as a fact usually forcefully — see CLAIM 1

3 to state clearly and strongly — see ASSERT 1

declension *n* **1** a gradual sinking and wasting away of mind or body — see DECLINE 1

2 a change to a lower state or level — see DECLINE 2

decline *n* **1** a gradual sinking and wasting away of mind or body ⟨her sad *decline* from a robust athlete to an old woman with arthritis⟩

synonyms debilitation, decay, decaying, declension, degeneration, descent, deterioration, ebbing, enfeeblement, weakening

related words atrophy; exhaustion; drooping, flagging, limping; relapse, setback

near antonyms invigoration, strengthening; progress

antonyms improvement, recovery, revitalization

2 a change to a lower state or level ⟨the *decline* of the Roman Empire⟩

synonyms decadence, declension, degeneracy, degeneration, degradation, descent, deterioration, downfall, downgrade, fall

related words decay, rotting, spoiling; breakup, crumbling, decomposition, disintegration, dissolution; abasement, debasement; depreciation, lessening; decimation, demolishment, demolition, desolation, destruction, havoc, ruin, ruination; abatement, decrease, decrement, de-escalation, deflation, diminishment, diminution, dip, drop, fall, loss, lowering, reduction, sag, shrinkage

near antonyms advancement, development, evolution, growth; blossoming, flourishing, flowering; renewal, restoration, revitalization; heightening; accretion, accrual, addendum, addition, augmentation, boost, enhancement, gain, increase, increment, raise, supplement

antonyms ascent, rise, upswing

3 a loss of status — see COMEDOWN

4 the amount by which something is lessened — see DECREASE

decline *vb* **1** to show unwillingness to accept, do, engage in, or agree to ⟨he *declined* the invitation to the party⟩ ⟨she *declined* to participate in the soccer game⟩

synonyms disapprove, negative, refuse, reject, repudiate, spurn, turn down *related words* overrule, veto; forbid, prohibit, proscribe; dismiss; abstain, forbear, refrain; deny, dispute, gainsay; balk, stick; abjure, renounce; avoid, bypass, detour

near antonyms condone, countenance, swallow, tolerate; adopt, embrace, receive, take; accede, acquiesce, agree, assent, consent; choose, select; espouse, support

antonyms accept, agree (to), approve

2 to be unwilling to grant — see DENY 2

3 to go to a lower level — see DROP 2

4 to become worse or of less value — see DETE-RIORATE

5 to grow less in scope or intensity especially gradually — see DECREASE 2

6 to lead or extend downward — see DESCEND 1

declined *adj* bending downward or forward — see NODDING

declining *adj* bending downward or forward — see NODDING

decode *vb* to change (as a secret message) from code into ordinary language ⟨the agents worked into the night to *decode* the transmission from the enemy spy⟩

synonyms break, crack, decipher

related words render, translate; dope (out), figure out, puzzle (out), solve, unravel, work, work out

antonyms cipher, code, encode

decolorize *vb* to make white or whiter by removing color — see WHITEN

decompose *vb* to go through decomposition — see DECAY 1

decomposed *adj* having undergone organic breakdown — see ROTTEN 1

decomposition *n* the process by which dead organic matter separates into simpler substances — see CORRUPTION 1

decorate *vb* to make more attractive by adding something that is beautiful or becoming ⟨they *decorated* the hallway with paintings and tapestries⟩

synonyms adorn, array, beautify, bedeck, bedizen, deck, do, dress, embellish, enrich, garnish, grace, ornament, trim

related words doll up, dress up, trick (out); brighten, freshen, smarten, spruce (up); boss, chase, emboss; embroider, figure, flounce, fringe, garland, hang, lace, wreathe; gild, paint; redecorate, redo

near antonyms simplify, streamline; bare, denude, dismantle, display, divest, expose, reveal, strip, uncover

antonyms blemish, deface, disfigure, mar, scar, spoil

decoration *n* **1** something that decorates or beautifies ⟨they put lots of *decorations* on and around the Christmas tree⟩

synonyms adornment, caparison, embellishment, frill, garnish, ornament, trim

related words finery, frippery; flounce, flourish, furbelow, ruffle; enhancement, enrichment, improvement; embossment, embroidery, fancywork; gilt, glitter; design, figure, pattern; furnishings, regalia, trappings

near antonyms blemish, defacement, disfigurement, scar; blot, spot, stain

2 something given in recognition of achievement — see AWARD

decorative *adj* serving to add beauty ⟨they planted *decorative* flowers all along the path to the cottage⟩

synonyms adorning, beautifying, embellishing, ornamental

related words alluring, appealing, attractive, charming, delightful, glamorous (*also* glamourous), pleasing, prepossessing; beauteous, beautiful, bonny, comely, fair, gorgeous, handsome, lovely, pretty, stunning; detailed, elaborate, fancy, ornate

antonyms functional, utilitarian

decorous *adj* **1** following the established traditions of refined society and good taste — see PROPER 1

2 marked by or showing careful attention to set forms and details — see CEREMONIOUS 1

decorum *n* socially acceptable behavior — see DECENCY 1

decoy *n* something used to attract animals to a hook or into a trap — see BAIT 1

decoy *vb* to lead away from a usual or proper course by offering some pleasure or advantage — see LURE

decrease *n* the amount by which something is lessened ⟨the average *decrease* in the price of milk was five cents per gallon⟩

synonyms abatement, decline, decrement, diminishment, diminution, drop, fall, loss, reduction, shrinkage

related words deduction, dent, depression; slip, slump; curtailment, cut, cutback

near antonyms accretion, accrual, accumulation, addition, supplement; continuation, extension; upswing, uptrend, upturn

antonyms boost, enlargement, gain, increase, increment, raise, rise

decrease *vb* **1** to make smaller in amount, volume, or extent ⟨they *decreased* the amount of water flowing through the pipes in order to prevent an overflow⟩

synonyms abate, de-escalate, diminish, downsize, dwindle, lessen, lower, reduce

related words compress, condense, constrict, contract; abbreviate, abridge, clip, crop, curtail, cut, cut back, cut down, dock, pare, prune, retrench, shorten, slash, trim, truncate, whittle; deflate, shrink; moderate, modify, modulate, qualify

near antonyms blow up, dilate, distend, inflate, swell; elongate, extend, lengthen, prolong, protract; add (to), complement, supplement; enhance, heighten, intensify

antonyms aggrandize, amplify, augment, boost, enlarge, escalate, expand, increase, raise

2 to grow less in scope or intensity especially gradually ⟨the force of the wind slowly *decreased* until the flowers were standing upright again⟩

synonyms abate, decline, de-escalate, die (down), diminish, dwindle, ebb, fall, lessen, let up, lower, moderate, recede, relent, remit, shrink, subside, taper, taper off, wane

related words compress, condense, constrict, contract; evaporate, fade (away), give out, melt (away), peter (out), vanish; slacken, slow (down); alleviate, ease, relax; flag, sink, weaken; cave (in), collapse, deflate, give out

near antonyms appear, emerge, show up; blow up, distend, elongate, lengthen

antonyms accumulate, balloon, build, burgeon, enlarge, escalate, expand, grow, increase, intensify, mount, mushroom, pick up, rise, snowball, soar, swell, wax

decree *n* **1** a statement of what to do that must be obeyed by those concerned — see COMMAND 1

2 an order publicly issued by an authority — see EDICT 1

decree *vb* to give an order — see COMMAND 2

decrement *n* the amount by which something is lessened — see DECREASE

decry *vb* **1** to express scornfully one's low opinion of ⟨scientists were quick to *decry* the claims of the psychic⟩
synonyms bad-mouth, belittle, cry down, deprecate, depreciate, diminish, discount, disparage, minimize, put down, write off
related words abuse, scold; disapprove (of), dislike; censure, condemn, criticize, denounce, reprehend, reprobate; asperse, defame, malign, slander, traduce, vilify; discredit, disgrace
near antonyms approve, countenance, endorse (*also* indorse), favor, recommend, sanction; commend, compliment, eulogize
antonyms acclaim, applaud, exalt, extol (*also* extoll), glorify, laud, magnify, praise
2 to declare to be morally wrong or evil — see CONDEMN 1

decrying *adj* intended to make a person or thing seem of little importance or value — see DEROGATORY

dedicate *vb* to keep or intend for a special purpose — see DEVOTE 1

dedication *n* adherence to something to which one is bound by a pledge or duty — see FIDELITY

deduce *vb* to form an opinion through reasoning and information — see INFER 1

deducible *adj* being or provable by reasoning in which the conclusion follows necessarily from given information — see DEDUCTIVE

deduct *vb* to take away (an amount or number) from a total — see SUBTRACT

deduction *n* **1** something that is or may be subtracted ⟨contestants get a *deduction* from their scores for every incorrect guess⟩
synonyms abatement, discount, reduction
related words kickback, rebate; dent, depreciation; decline, decrement, diminishment, diminution, drop, fall, loss; forfeit, forfeiture, penalty
near antonyms accretion, accrual, augmentation, boost, gain, increase, increment, raise, rise; appreciation
antonyms accession, addition
2 the act or an instance of taking away from a total — see SUBTRACTION
3 an opinion arrived at through a process of reasoning — see CONCLUSION 1

deductive *adj* being or provable by reasoning in which the conclusion follows necessarily from given information ⟨using *deductive* reasoning we must conclude that since everyone eventually dies, sooner or later it's going to be our turn⟩
synonyms deducible, derivable, inferable, reasoned
related words conjectural, hypothetical, purported, supposed, suppositional; academic, speculative, theoretical (*also* theoretic); logical, rational
near antonyms inducible, inductive; absolute, categorical (*also* categoric), definite, explicit, express; instinctive, intuitive; illogical, irrational

deed *n* **1** an act of notable skill, strength, or cleverness — see FEAT 1
2 something done by someone — see ACTION 1

deed *vb* to give over the legal possession or ownership of — see TRANSFER 1

deem *vb* to have as an opinion — see BELIEVE 2

deep *adj* **1** extending far downward or inward ⟨they dropped their bucket down a *deep* well⟩ ⟨the knife made a *deep* cut into the wood⟩
synonyms abysmal, bottomless
related words abyssal, unfathomable; boundless, endless, immeasurable, inestimable, infinite, limitless, measureless, unlimited, vast
near antonyms depthless, two-dimensional; even, flat, flush, horizontal, level, plane, smooth; confined, finite, limited, measured, restricted
antonyms shallow, shoal, skin-deep, superficial, surface
2 having a low musical pitch or range ⟨the tour guide had a very *deep* voice⟩
synonyms bass, low, throaty
related words gruff, hoarse, husky, rough
near antonyms squeaking, squeaky, squealing, thin; earsplitting, penetrating, piercing, strident; peeping, tinny
antonyms acute, high, high-pitched, piping, sharp, shrill, treble
3 being beyond one's powers to know, understand, or explain — see MYSTERIOUS 1
4 difficult for one of ordinary knowledge or intelligence to understand — see PROFOUND 1
5 having an often intentionally veiled or uncertain meaning — see OBSCURE 1
6 extreme in degree, power, or effect — see INTENSE

deep *n* **1** the most intense or characteristic phase of something — see THICK
2 the whole body of salt water that covers nearly three-fourths of the earth — see OCEAN

deepen *vb* to make markedly greater in measure or degree — see INTENSIFY

deep-rooted *adj* firmly established over time — see INVETERATE 1

deep-seated *adj* firmly established over time — see INVETERATE 1

de-escalate *vb* **1** to make smaller in amount, volume, or extent — see DECREASE 1
2 to grow less in scope or intensity especially gradually — see DECREASE 2

deface *vb* **1** to deliberately cause the damage or destruction of another's property — see VANDALIZE 1
2 to reduce the soundness, effectiveness, or perfection of — see DAMAGE 1

defacement *n* deliberate damaging or destroying of another's property — see VANDALISM

defacer *n* a person who damages or destroys property on purpose — see VANDAL

defamation *n* the making of false statements that damage another's reputation — see SLANDER

defamatory *adj* causing or intended to cause unjust injury to a person's good name — see LIBELOUS

defame *vb* to make untrue and harmful statements about — see SLANDER

defaming *n* the making of false statements that damage another's reputation — see SLANDER

default *n* the nonperformance of an assigned or expected action — see FAILURE 1

defeat *n* **1** failure to win a contest ⟨sore losers griping about their *defeat* in the basketball game earlier that week⟩
synonyms beating, drubbing, licking, loss, overthrow, rout, shellacking, trimming, trouncing, whipping
related words collapse, debacle (*also* débâcle),

failure, fizzle, flop, nonsuccess, setback, upset, washout; lurch, shutout
near antonyms accomplishment, achievement; landslide, sweep
antonyms success, triumph, victory, win
2 a falling short of one's goals — see FAILURE 2
defeat *vb* to achieve a victory over — see BEAT 2
defeatist *adj* emphasizing or expecting the worst — see PESSIMISTIC 1
defeatist *n* one who emphasizes bad aspects or conditions and expects the worst — see PESSIMIST 1
defect *n* something that spoils the appearance or completeness of a thing — see BLEMISH
defect (from) *vb* to leave (a cause or party) often in order to take up another ⟨many soldiers *defected from* the rebel army as soon as they realized the uprising was hopeless⟩
synonyms desert, rat (on)
related words abandon, abdicate, abjure, cut off, disown, forsake, quit, reject, renounce, repudiate, spurn; renege; depart, go, leave, withdraw
phrases go back on, walk out on
near antonyms adhere (to), cling (to), stick (to *or* with); cherish, cultivate, foster
defective *adj* having a fault — see FAULTY
defector *n* a person who abandons a cause or organization usually without right — see RENEGADE
defend *vb* **1** to drive danger or attack away from ⟨a solemn oath to *defend* the country at any cost⟩
synonyms cover, guard, protect, safeguard, screen, secure, shield, ward
related words avert, prevent; fend (off), oppose, resist, withstand; battle, contend, fight, war; conserve, keep, preserve, save; buffer, palisade, picket, wall
phrases look out for, stand up for
near antonyms bombard, storm; beset, besiege, overrun; capitulate, cave, submit, yield
antonyms assail, assault, attack
2 to continue to declare to be true or proper despite opposition or objections — see MAINTAIN 2
defendable *adj* capable of being defended with good reasoning against verbal attack — see TENABLE 2
defender *n* someone that protects — see PROTECTOR
defense *n* **1** means or method of defending ⟨thorns are a rose's *defense* against grazing animals⟩
synonyms aegis, ammunition, armor, cover, guard, protection, safeguard, screen, security, shield, wall, ward
related words arm, armament, munitions, weapon, weaponry; fastness, fort, fortress, palisade, stronghold
near antonyms aggression, assault, attack, offense (*or* offence), offensive
2 an explanation that frees one from fault or blame — see EXCUSE
defenseless *adj* lacking protection from danger or resistance against attack — see HELPLESS 1
defenselessness *n* the quality or state of having little resistance to some outside agent — see SUSCEPTIBILITY
defensible *adj* capable of being defended with good reasoning against verbal attack — see TENABLE 1

defensive *adj* intended to resist or prevent attack or aggression ⟨a *defensive* alliance against the aggressors⟩
synonyms protective, self-protective
related words deterrent, preventive; safe, secure
near antonyms aggressive, bellicose, belligerent, combative, contentious, militant, pugnacious, quarrelsome, scrappy, truculent, warlike
antonyms offensive
defensive *n* a position or readiness to oppose actual or expected attack ⟨their harsh words put him on the *defensive*⟩
synonyms guard
related words alert, watch
antonyms offensive
defer *vb* to assign to a later time — see POSTPONE
deference *n* a readiness or willingness to yield to the wishes of others — see COMPLIANCE 1
deferential *adj* marked by or showing proper regard for another's higher status — see RESPECTFUL
deferentially *adv* in manner showing no signs of pride or self-assertion — see LOWLY
defiance *n* **1** refusal to obey — see DISOBEDIENCE
2 the inclination to resist — see RESISTANCE 1
defiant *adj* given to resisting authority or another's control — see DISOBEDIENT
deficiency *n* a falling short of an essential or desirable amount or number ⟨there was a *deficiency* of fresh food in the house⟩
synonyms dearth, deficit, failure, famine, inadequacy, insufficiency, lack, paucity, poverty, scantiness, scarceness, scarcity, shortage, want
related words absence, omission; meagerness, poorness, skimpiness; necessity, need, privation
near antonyms bountifulness, copiousness; excess, overabundance, oversupply, surfeit, surplus
antonyms abundance, adequacy, amplitude, plenitude, plenty, sufficiency
deficient *adj* **1** lacking some necessary part — see INCOMPLETE
2 falling short of a standard — see BAD 1
3 not coming up to a usual standard or meeting a particular need — see SHORT 3
deficit *n* a falling short of an essential or desirable amount or number — see DEFICIENCY
defile *n* a narrow opening between hillsides or mountains that can be used for passage — see CANYON
defile *vb* **1** to make unfit for use by the addition of something harmful or undesirable — see CONTAMINATE
2 to treat (a sacred place or object) shamefully or with great disrespect — see DESECRATE
defilement *n* **1** an act of great disrespect shown to God or to sacred ideas, people, or things — see BLASPHEMY
2 something that is or that makes impure — see IMPURITY
define *vb* **1** to draw or make apparent the outline of — see OUTLINE 1
2 to mark the limits of — see LIMIT 2
3 to point out the chief quality or qualities of an individual or group — see CHARACTERIZE 1
4 to give the rules about (something) clearly and exactly — see PRESCRIBE
defined *adj* having distinct or certain limits — see LIMITED 1
definite *adj* **1** having distinct or certain limits — see LIMITED 1

2 so clearly expressed as to leave no doubt about the meaning — see EXPLICIT

definitely *adv* without any question — see INDEED 1

definitive *adj* **1** being the most accurate and apparently thorough ⟨the *definitive* work on the attack on Pearl Harbor⟩
synonyms authoritative
related words conclusive, decisive; official; accurate, correct; complete, thorough
2 serving to put an end to all debate or questioning — see CONCLUSIVE 1
3 so clearly expressed as to leave no doubt about the meaning — see EXPLICIT

deflect *vb* to change the course or direction of (something) — see TURN 2

deform *vb* to twist (something) out of a natural or normal shape or condition — see CONTORT

deformation *n* the twisting of something out of its natural or normal shape or condition — see CONTORTION

deformed *adj* badly or imperfectly formed — see MALFORMED

deformity *n* something that spoils the appearance or completeness of a thing — see BLEMISH

defraud *vb* to rob by the use of trickery or threats — see FLEECE

defrauder *n* a dishonest person who uses clever means to cheat others out of something of value — see TRICKSTER 1

defrauding *adj* marked by, based on, or done by the use of dishonest methods to acquire something of value — see FRAUDULENT 1

defrosted *adj* freed from a frozen state by exposure to warmth — see THAWED

deft *adj* skillful with the hands — see DEXTEROUS 1

deftness *n* **1** ease and grace in physical activity — see DEXTERITY 2
2 subtle or imaginative ability in inventing, devising, or executing something — see SKILL 1

defunct *adj* **1** no longer existing — see EXTINCT
2 no longer living — see DEAD 1

defy *vb* **1** to go against the commands, prohibitions, or rules of — see DISOBEY
2 to invite (someone) to take part in a contest or to perform a feat — see CHALLENGE 2
3 to oppose (something hostile or dangerous) with firmness or courage — see FACE 2
4 to refuse to give in to — see RESIST

degeneracy *n* **1** a change to a lower state or level — see DECLINE 2
2 a sinking to a state of low moral standards and behavior — see CORRUPTION 2

degenerate *adj* **1** having lost forcefulness, courage, or spirit — see EFFETE 1
2 having or showing lowered moral character or standards — see CORRUPT

degenerate *n* a person who has sunk below the normal moral standard ⟨the *degenerate* would stop at nothing to get satisfaction⟩
synonyms backslider, debaucher, decadent, libertine, pervert, profligate
related words delinquent, derelict, incorrigible; blackguard, cad, heel, knave, rascal, miscreant, reprobate, rogue, scoundrel, villain; playboy, satyr
near antonyms saint

degenerate *vb* to become worse or of less value — see DETERIORATE

degeneration *n* **1** a change to a lower state or level — see DECLINE 2
2 a gradual sinking and wasting away of mind or body — see DECLINE 1
3 a sinking to a state of low moral standards and behavior — see CORRUPTION 2

degradation *n* **1** a change to a lower state or level — see DECLINE 2
2 a sinking to a state of low moral standards and behavior — see CORRUPTION 2

degrade *vb* **1** to bring to a lower grade or rank — see DEMOTE
2 to lower in character or dignity — see DEBASE 1
3 to reduce to a lower standing in one's own eyes or in others' eyes — see HUMBLE

degraded *adj* having or showing lowered moral character or standards — see CORRUPT

degrading *adj* intended to make a person or thing seem of little importance or value — see DEROGATORY

degree *n* **1** an individual part of a process, series, or ranking ⟨they completed the project by *degrees*⟩
synonyms cut, grade, inch, notch, peg, phase, point, stage, step
related words amount, measure, plane; decrement, increment
2 the placement of someone or something in relation to others in a vertical arrangement — see RANK 1

dehydrate *vb* to make dry — see DRY 1

deification *n* excessive admiration of or devotion to a person — see WORSHIP

deify *vb* **1** to love or admire too much — see IDOLIZE
2 to offer honor or respect to (someone) as a divine power — see WORSHIP 1

deifying *adj* reflecting great admiration or devotion — see WORSHIPFUL

deign *vb* to descend to a level that is beneath one's dignity — see CONDESCEND 1

deity *n* **1** a being having superhuman powers and control over a particular part of life or the world ⟨to the ancient Greeks, Zeus was the *deity* who ruled over the sky and weather, and Poseidon was god of the sea⟩
synonyms divinity, god
related words angel, demigod, demon (*or* daemon), devil, spirit, supernatural
2 *cap* the being worshipped as the creator and ruler of the universe ⟨we prayed to the *Deity* for salvation⟩
synonyms Allah, Almighty, Creator, Divinity, Father, God, Godhead, Jehovah, Lord, Maker, Providence, Supreme Being
3 the quality or state of being divine — see DIVINITY

dejected *adj* feeling unhappiness — see SAD 1

dejection *n* a state or spell of low spirits — see SADNESS

delay *n* an instance or period of being prevented from going about one's business ⟨there was a *delay* for our boarding while the airplane unloaded incoming passengers⟩
synonyms detainment, holdup, wait
related words deferment, postponement; reprieve, respite; hesitation, lag, pause, setback, slowdown
near antonyms haste, rush; dispatch, promptness

delay *vb* **1** to move or act slowly ⟨she told them to stop *delaying* and get to bed⟩

THESAURUS

synonyms crawl, creep, dally, dawdle, dillydally, drag, lag, linger, loiter, poke, tarry

related words hang around, hang out, idle, loaf, loll, lounge; amble, ease, inch, lumber, plod, saunter, shuffle, stagger, stroll; decelerate, slow (down *or* up); filibuster, procrastinate, stall, temporize

phrases mark time

near antonyms bowl, breeze, dart, hump, hurtle, hustle, scramble, stampede; gallop, jog, run, sprint, trot; accelerate, quicken, speed up; catch up, fast-forward, outpace, outrun, outstrip, overtake

antonyms barrel, bolt, career, course, dash, fly, hasten, hotfoot (it), hurry, race, rip, rocket, run, rush, scoot, scud, scurry, speed, tear, whirl, whisk, whiz (*or* whizz), zip

2 to assign to a later time — see POSTPONE

3 to create difficulty for the work or activity of — see HAMPER

delectable *adj* **1** giving pleasure or contentment to the mind or senses — see PLEASANT

2 very pleasing to the sense of taste — see DELICIOUS 1

delectably *adv* in a pleasing way — see WELL 5

delectation *n* **1** a source of great satisfaction — see DELIGHT 1

2 the feeling experienced when one's wishes are met — see PLEASURE 1

delegate *n* **1** a person sent on a mission to represent another — see AMBASSADOR

2 a person who acts or does business for another — see AGENT 2

delegate *vb* **1** to appoint as one's representative ⟨he *delegated* his son to go pick up the tickets for him⟩

synonyms commission, depute, deputize

related words assign, charge; appoint, designate, name, nominate

near antonyms abrogate; abdicate

2 to put (something) into the possession or safekeeping of another — see GIVE 2

delegation *n* **1** a body of persons chosen as representatives of a larger group — see CONTINGENT

2 the granting of power to perform various acts or duties — see COMMISSION 1

delete *vb* to show (something written) to be no longer valid by drawing a cross over or a line through it — see X (OUT)

deleterious *adj* causing or capable of causing harm — see HARMFUL

deletion *n* something left out — see OMISSION

deliberate *adj* **1** decided on as a result of careful thought ⟨the judge made a *deliberate* decision to impose the maximum sentence⟩

synonyms advised, calculated, considered, measured, reasoned, studied, thoughtful, weighed

related words aforethought, premeditated; educated, informed; intentional, purposeful; designed, intended, planned, projected; careful, meticulous; foresighted, forethoughtful, provident, prudent

near antonyms ill-advised; chance, haphazard, hit-or-miss, random; aimless, desultory, purposeless; hasty, hurried, rushed; abrupt, impetuous, sudden; automatic, extemporaneous, impromptu, instinctive, spontaneous

antonyms casual

2 made, given, or done with full awareness of what one is doing — see INTENTIONAL

deliberate *vb* to give serious and careful thought to — see PONDER

deliberately *adv* with full awareness of what one is doing — see INTENTIONALLY

deliberation *n* **1** a careful weighing of the reasons for or against something — see CONSIDERATION 1

2 an exchange of views for the purpose of exploring a subject or deciding an issue — see DISCUSSION 1

delicacy *n* **1** something that is pleasing to eat because it is rare or a luxury ⟨they were given a plate of *delicacies* while they waited for the queen⟩

synonyms dainty, goody, tidbit (*also* titbit), treat

related words morsel; candy, dessert, junket, sweet, sweetmeat

2 the state or quality of having a delicate structure ⟨they marvelled at the *delicacy* of a snowflake⟩

synonyms daintiness, delicateness, exquisiteness, fineness, fragility

related words flimsiness, insubstantiality, wispiness

near antonyms firmness, solidity; strength

antonyms coarseness, crudeness, crudity, roughness, rudeness

3 the tendency to be or state of being squeamish ⟨the urgent need for blood prompted many people to overcome their habitual *delicacy* and become first-time donors⟩

synonyms qualmishness, queasiness, squeamishness

related words daintiness, fastidiousness, finickiness, fussiness

near antonyms boldness

antonyms indelicacy

4 the quality or state of being very accurate — see PRECISION

5 the quality or state of lacking physical strength or vigor — see WEAKNESS 1

delicate *adj* **1** satisfying or pleasing because of fineness or mildness ⟨a heavy sauce would spoil the *delicate* flavor of this fish⟩

synonyms dainty, exquisite, refined, subtle

related words choice, elegant, extraordinary, incomparable, peerless, preeminent, prime, rare, select, superior, superlative, supreme, transcendent, unsurpassed; picked, selected; fine, fragile, frail

near antonyms coarse, crude, rough; common, ordinary; average, fair, indifferent, mediocre, medium, middling, run-of-the-mill, second-rate

antonyms robust, strong, sturdy

2 able to sense slight impressions or differences — see ACUTE 1

3 accomplished with trained ability — see SKILLFUL

4 easily broken — see FRAGILE 1

5 easily injured without careful handling — see TENDER 1

6 hard to please — see FINICKY

7 having qualities that appeal to a refined taste — see CHOICE

8 lacking bodily strength — see WEAK 1

9 made or done with extreme care and accuracy — see FINE 2

10 meeting the highest standard of accuracy — see PRECISE 1

11 not harsh or stern especially in manner, nature, or effect — see GENTLE 1

12 requiring exceptional skill or caution in performance or handling — see TRICKY

delicateness *n* **1** the quality or state of lacking physical strength or vigor — see WEAKNESS 1
2 the state or quality of having a delicate structure — see DELICACY 2

delicious *adj* **1** very pleasing to the sense of taste ⟨the family sat down to a *delicious* Thanksgiving dinner⟩
synonyms ambrosial, appetizing, delectable, flavorful, luscious, palatable, savory, scrumptious, tasty, toothsome, yummy
related words digestible, eatable, edible; delightful, heavenly, pleasing; agreeable, gratifying, pleasant; satisfying; choice, dainty, delicate, exquisite, rare
near antonyms banal, boring, commonplace, tedious; noisome, smelly, stinky; noxious, unwholesome; miserable, wretched; abhorrent, abominable, awful, detestable, disagreeable, disgusting, distasteful, foul, horrid, nauseating, offensive, repellent, repugnant, repulsive, sickening, unpleasant
antonyms flat, flavorless, insipid, stale, tasteless, unappetizing, unpalatable
2 giving pleasure or contentment to the mind or senses — see PLEASANT

deliciously *adv* in a pleasing way — see WELL 5

deliciousness *n* the quality of being delicious ⟨the fancy feast was *deliciousness* itself⟩
synonyms lusciousness, savor, savoriness, tastiness

delight *n* **1** a source of great satisfaction ⟨the school play was a *delight* for the parents⟩
synonyms delectation, gas [*slang*], joy, kick, manna, pleasure, treat
related words amusement, diversion, entertainment, fun, recreation; comfort, relief, solace; gratification, indulgence; ambrosia
2 someone or something that provides amusement or enjoyment — see FUN 1
3 the feeling experienced when one's wishes are met — see PLEASURE 1

delight *vb* **1** to feel or express joy or triumph — see EXULT
2 to give satisfaction to — see PLEASE

delight (in) *vb* to take pleasure in — see ENJOY 1

delighted *adj* experiencing pleasure, satisfaction, or delight — see GLAD 1

delightful *adj* **1** giving pleasure or contentment to the mind or senses — see PLEASANT
2 providing amusement or enjoyment — see FUN

delightfully *adv* in a pleasing way — see WELL 5

delimit *vb* to mark the limits of — see LIMIT 2

delineate *vb* **1** to draw or make apparent the outline of — see OUTLINE 1
2 to give a representation or account of in words — see DESCRIBE

delineated *adj* producing a mental picture through clear and impressive description — see GRAPHIC 1

delineation *n* **1** a picture using lines to represent the chief features of an object or scene — see DRAWING
2 a vivid representation in words of someone or something — see DESCRIPTION 1

delinquency *n* **1** the nonperformance of an assigned or expected action — see FAILURE 1
2 the quality or state of being late — see LATENESS

delinquent *adj* not arriving, occurring, or settled at the due, usual, or proper time — see LATE 1

deliquesce *vb* to go from a solid to a liquid state — see LIQUEFY

delirious *adj* **1** feeling overwhelming fear or worry — see FRANTIC 1
2 marked by great and often stressful excitement or activity — see FURIOUS 1

delirium *n* a state of wildly excited activity or emotion — see FRENZY

deliver *vb* **1** to free from the penalties or consequences of sin — see SAVE 1
2 to remove from danger or harm — see SAVE 2
3 to give (something) over to the control or possession of another usually under duress — see SURRENDER 1
4 to put (something) into the possession of someone for use or consumption — see FURNISH 2
5 to put (something) into the possession or safekeeping of another — see GIVE 2
6 to turn out as planned or desired — see SUCCEED 1

deliverance *n* **1** the saving from danger or evil — see SALVATION
2 a position arrived at after consideration — see DECISION 1

deliverer *n* **1** a person who delivers goods to customers usually over a regular local route — see DELIVERYMAN
2 one that saves from danger or destruction — see SAVIOR

delivery *n* **1** a freeing from an obligation or responsibility — see RELEASE 1
2 the act or process of giving birth to children — see CHILDBIRTH

deliveryman *n* a person who delivers goods to customers usually over a regular local route ⟨the *deliveryman* dropped off a package for us while we were at the store⟩
synonyms deliverer
related words bearer, carrier, courier, go-between, liaison, messenger

delude *vb* to cause to believe what is untrue — see DECEIVE

deluding *adj* tending or having power to deceive — see DECEPTIVE 1

deluge *n* **1** a great flow of water or of something that overwhelms — see FLOOD
2 a steady falling of water from the sky in significant quantity — see RAIN 1

deluge *vb* to cover or become filled with a flood — see FLOOD

delusion *n* a conception or image created by the imagination and having no objective reality — see FANTASY 1

delusive *adj* tending or having power to deceive — see DECEPTIVE 1

delusory *adj* tending or having power to deceive — see DECEPTIVE 1

deluxe *adj* showing obvious signs of wealth and comfort — see LUXURIOUS

delve (into) *vb* to search through or into — see EXPLORE 1

delving *n* a systematic search for the truth or facts about something — see INQUIRY 1

demagogue *also* **demagog** *n* a person who stirs up public feelings especially of discontent — see AGITATOR

demand *n* **1** something that someone insists upon having ⟨the terrorists presented their list of *demands*⟩
synonyms claim, dun, requisition, ultimatum

THESAURUS

related words desire, request, want, wish; drive, need, requirement, stipulation; basic, essential, must; imposition; condition, provision
2 something necessary, indispensable, or unavoidable — see ESSENTIAL 1
demand *vb* **1** to ask for (something) earnestly or with authority ⟨the losing party *demanded* a recount of the votes cast in the election⟩
synonyms call (for), claim, clamor (for), command, enjoin, exact, insist (on), press (for), quest, stipulate (for)
related words ask, plead (for), request, want; cry (for), necessitate, need, require, take, warrant; requisition; impose; badger, dun, hound
near antonyms give up, relinquish, surrender, yield
2 to have as a requirement — see NEED 1
3 to set or receive as a price — see CHARGE 1
demanding *adj* **1** requiring much time, effort, or careful attention ⟨the *demanding* assignment kept them working all night⟩
synonyms arduous, burdensome, challenging, exacting, grueling (*or* gruelling), laborious, onerous, taxing, toilsome
related words difficult, formidable, hard, herculean, rough, rugged, stiff, strenuous, tough; oppressive, trying; rigid, rigorous, severe, stern, strict, stringent
near antonyms easy, effortless, facile, simple, smooth
antonyms light, undemanding
2 hard to please — see FINICKY
3 requiring considerable physical or mental effort — see HARD 2
demarcate *vb* to mark the limits of — see LIMIT 2
demarcation *n* the state of being kept distinct — see SEPARATION 2
¹demean *vb* **1** to lower in character or dignity — see DEBASE 1
2 to reduce to a lower standing in one's own eyes or in others' eyes — see HUMBLE
²demean *vb* to manage the actions of (oneself) in a particular way — see BEHAVE
demeaning *adj* intended to make a person or thing seem of little importance or value — see DEROGATORY
demeanor *n* the way or manner in which one conducts oneself — see BEHAVIOR
demented *adj* having or showing a very abnormal or sick state of mind — see INSANE 1
dementia *n* a serious mental disorder that prevents one from living a safe and normal life — see INSANITY 1
demerit *n* a defect in character — see FAULT 1
demesne *n* **1** a part or portion having no fixed boundaries — see REGION 1
2 a region of activity, knowledge, or influence — see FIELD 1
3 the area around and belonging to a building — see GROUND 1
demilitarization *n* the reduction or elimination of a country's armed forces or weapons — see DISARMAMENT
demilitarize *vb* to reduce the size and strength of the armed forces of — see DISARM 1
demise *n* **1** the permanent stopping of all the vital bodily activities — see DEATH 1
2 the act of ceasing to exist — see DEATH 3
democracy *n* government in which the supreme power is held by the people and used by them di-

rectly or indirectly through representation ⟨under our *democracy* the people have some control over their lives by being able to decide who their political leaders will be⟩
synonyms republic, self-government, self-rule
related words home rule, self-determination; autonomy, sovereignty
near antonyms despotism, dictatorship, monarchy, totalitarianism, tyranny
democratic *adj* of, relating to, or favoring political democracy ⟨the *democratic* system ensured that every citizen's voice was heard⟩
synonyms popular, republican, self-governing, self-ruling
related words representative; libertarian
near antonyms autocratic, despotic, dictatorial, monarchal (*or* monarchial), monarchical (*also* monarchic), tyrannical (*also* tyrannic)
antonyms undemocratic
demolish *vb* **1** to destroy (as a building) completely by knocking down or breaking to pieces ⟨they *demolished* the old warehouse to make room for the new shopping mall⟩
synonyms raze, tear down
related words blow up, dynamite; abolish, annihilate, crack up, crush, dash, decimate, destroy, devastate, devour, dissolve, do in, eradicate, extirpate, finish, flatten, obliterate, overturn, pulverize, ravage, ruin, scourge, smash, total, unmake, waste, wipe out, wreck
near antonyms build, construct, erect, put up, raise; rebuild, renew, renovate, restore; create, fabricate, fashion, forge, form, make, manufacture, shape
2 to bring to a complete end the physical soundness, existence, or usefulness of — see DESTROY 1
3 to cause to break open or into pieces by or as if by an explosive — see BLAST 1
demolishment *n* the state or fact of being rendered nonexistent, physically unsound, or useless — see DESTRUCTION
demolition *n* the state or fact of being rendered nonexistent, physically unsound, or useless — see DESTRUCTION
demon *or* **daemon** *n* an evil spirit ⟨only in rare cases is the ancient rite of exorcism performed to cast out a troublesome *demon*⟩
synonyms devil, fiend, ghoul, imp, incubus
related words apparition, bogey (*also* bogy *or* bogie), familiar, ghost, phantasm, phantom, poltergeist, shade, shadow, specter (*or* spectre), spirit, spook, vision, wraith; brownie, dwarf, elf, faerie (*also* faery), fairy, fay, gnome, goblin, gremlin, hobgoblin, leprechaun, pixie (*also* pixy), puck, sprite, troll; monster, ogre
near antonyms angel
demoniac *also* **demoniacal** *adj* of, relating to, or worthy of an evil spirit — see FIENDISH
demonic *adj* of, relating to, or worthy of an evil spirit — see FIENDISH
demonstrable *adj* capable of being proven as true or real — see VERIFIABLE
demonstrate *vb* **1** to gain full recognition or acceptance of — see ESTABLISH 1
2 to show the existence or truth of by evidence — see PROVE 1
3 to make known (something abstract) through outward signs — see SHOW 2
4 to make plain or understandable — see EXPLAIN 1

5 to show or make clear by using examples — see ILLUSTRATE 1

demonstration *n* **1** a mass meeting for the purpose of displaying or arousing support for a cause or person — see RALLY 2

2 an outward and often exaggerated indication of something abstract (as a feeling) for effect — see SHOW 1

demonstrative *adj* showing feeling freely ⟨my grandmother was always very *demonstrative* when we visited, showering us with hugs and kisses⟩

synonyms effusive, emotional, uninhibited, unreserved, unrestrained

related words dramatic, histrionic, melodramatic, theatrical; gushing, maudlin, mawkish, mushy, schmaltzy, sentimental; communicative, expansive; extroverted (*also* extraverted), outgoing; affectionate, feeling, intense, loving, passionate, sensitive, soulful, warm; blunt, candid, frank, outspoken, plain

near antonyms constrained; quiet, reticent, silent, taciturn; bashful, modest, retiring, shy; introverted, self-directed; aloof, detached, dispassionate, impassive, indifferent, phlegmatic, stolid, unconcerned, unfeeling; chilly, cold, frigid, glacial, hard-boiled, hardhearted, icy, unfriendly

antonyms inhibited, reserved, restrained, undemonstrative, unemotional

demoralization *n* **1** a sinking to a state of low moral standards and behavior — see CORRUPTION 2

2 the state of being discouraged — see DISCOURAGEMENT

demoralize *vb* **1** to deprive of courage or confidence — see UNNERVE 1

2 to lessen the courage or confidence of — see DISCOURAGE 1

demoralized *adj* having or showing lowered moral character or standards — see CORRUPT

demote *vb* to bring to a lower grade or rank ⟨the court-martial's decision was to *demote* the officer responsible for the failed mission⟩

synonyms break, bust, degrade, downgrade, reduce

related words can, dismiss, fire, lay off, sack; abase, debase, demean, humble, humiliate, lower

near antonyms hire

antonyms advance, elevate, promote, raise

demount *vb* to take apart — see DISASSEMBLE

demur *n* a feeling or declaration of disapproval or dissent — see OBJECTION

demur *vb* to present an opposing opinion or argument — see OBJECT

demure *adj* **1** affecting shyness or modesty in order to attract masculine interest — see COY 1

2 not comfortable around people — see SHY 2

3 not having or showing any feelings of superiority, self-assertiveness, or showiness — see HUMBLE 1

demureness *n* the absence of any feelings of being better than others — see HUMILITY

den *n* **1** the shelter or resting place of a wild animal ⟨the foxes hid in their *den* until the bear left the area⟩

synonyms burrow, hole, lair, lodge

related words nest

2 a place where a person goes to hide — see HIDEOUT

denial *n* **1** an unwillingness to grant something asked for ⟨our principal's *denial* of our request to come to school on Halloween dressed in costumes⟩

synonyms disallowance, nay, no, refusal, rejection

related words decline, rebuff, repudiation; negative

near antonyms acceptance, accession, consent, leave, permission, sufferance

antonyms allowance, grant

2 a refusal to confirm the truth of a statement ⟨the senator issued a flat *denial* of the accusation against her⟩

synonyms contradiction, disallowance, disavowal, disclaimer, negation, rejection, repudiation

related words disproof, rebuttal, refutation; negative

near antonyms confession; affirmation, assertion, declaration

antonyms acknowledgment (*also* acknowledgement), admission, avowal, confirmation

denizen *n* one who lives permanently in a place — see INHABITANT

denominate *vb* to give a name to — see NAME 1

denomination *n* a word or combination of words by which a person or thing is regularly known — see NAME 1

denotation *n* **1** a word or combination of words by which a person or thing is regularly known — see NAME 1

2 the idea that is conveyed or intended to be conveyed to the mind by language, symbol, or action — see MEANING 1

denotative *adj* indicating something — see INDICATIVE

denote *vb* to communicate or convey (as an idea) to the mind — see MEAN 1

denoting *adj* indicating something — see INDICATIVE

denounce *vb* **1** to declare to be morally wrong or evil — see CONDEMN 1

2 to express one's unfavorable opinion of the worth or quality of — see CRITICIZE

3 to express public or formal disapproval of — see CENSURE 1

dense *adj* **1** having little space between items or parts — see CLOSE 1

2 not having or showing an ability to absorb ideas readily — see STUPID 1

denseness *n* the quality or state of lacking intelligence or quickness of mind — see STUPIDITY 1

density *n* **1** the degree to which a fluid can resist flowing — see CONSISTENCY

2 the quality or state of lacking intelligence or quickness of mind — see STUPIDITY 1

dent *n* a sunken area forming a separate space — see HOLE 2

dented *adj* curved inward — see HOLLOW

denuded *adj* lacking a usual or natural covering — see NAKED 2

denunciation *n* an often public or formal expression of disapproval — see CENSURE

deny *vb* **1** to declare not to be true ⟨the congressman *denied* all charges of wrongdoing⟩

synonyms contradict, disallow, disavow, disclaim, gainsay, negate, negative, reject, repudiate

related words disown, renounce; challenge, confute, disprove, rebut, refute; disagree (with), dispute

THESAURUS

near antonyms accept, adopt, embrace, espouse; affirm, announce, assert, aver, claim, declare, maintain, profess, submit; authenticate, corroborate, substantiate, validate, verify
antonyms acknowledge, admit, allow, avow, concede, confirm, own
2 to be unwilling to grant ⟨he *denied* access to the top secret files to the nosy reporters⟩
synonyms decline, disallow, refuse, reject, withhold
related words rebuff, repel, spurn; check, constrain, hold, keep, restrain, restrict
near antonyms afford, furnish, give, provide, supply
antonyms allow, concede, grant, let, permit
depart *vb* **1** to leave a place often for another — see GO 2
2 to stop living — see DIE 1
departed *adj* **1** no longer existing — see EXTINCT
2 no longer living — see DEAD 1
departing *n* the act of leaving a place — see DEPARTURE
department *n* **1** a large unit of a governmental, business, or educational organization — see DIVISION 2
2 a region of activity, knowledge, or influence — see FIELD 2
departure *n* the act of leaving a place ⟨his sudden *departure* left them wondering if they'd upset him⟩
synonyms decamping, decampment, departing, exit, exiting, farewell, going, leave-taking, lighting out, parting, quitting, walking out
related words flight, retirement, retreat, running away, withdrawal; emigration, evacuation, exodus; egress; abandonment, forsaking, relinquishment
near antonyms advent, coming; entrance, ingress
antonyms arrival
depend *vb* **1** to be determined by, based on, or subject (to) ⟨whether or not we play baseball will *depend* on how much rain we get⟩
synonyms hang, hinge
related words base, establish, found, rest, stay; ground
2 to place reliance or trust ⟨I know I can always *depend* on you for help when I really need it⟩
synonyms count, lean, reckon, rely
related words commit, confide, entrust, trust
phrases bank on, figure on
near antonyms distrust, mistrust
dependability *n* worthiness as the recipient of another's trust or confidence — see RELIABILITY
dependable *adj* worthy of one's trust ⟨Boy Scouts are supposed to be always *dependable*⟩
synonyms good, reliable, responsible, safe, solid, steady, sure, tried, tried-and-true, true, trustworthy, trusty
related words constant, devoted, faithful, fast, loyal, staunch (*or* stanch), steadfast; honest, sincere, single-minded; infallible, unerring; firm, sound, strong; effective, telling; attested, authenticated, confirmed, proven, valid, validated, verified; blameless, irreproachable, unimpeachable, unquestionable
near antonyms disloyal, faithless, false, unfaithful; deceitful, dishonest; doubtful, dubious, questionable, suspect, uncertain, unsound; hazardous, risky; unauthenticated, unconfirmed, untried, unverified

antonyms irresponsible, undependable, unreliable, untrustworthy
dependence *n* **1** the quality or state of needing something or someone ⟨a baby's total *dependence* upon his or her parents for every one of life's needs⟩
synonyms dependency, reliance
related words reciprocity, relativity; confidence, faith, stock, trust
near antonyms autonomy, sovereignty
antonyms independence, self-reliance
2 something or someone to which one looks for support ⟨ultimately rice became the chief *dependence* in that state⟩
synonyms buttress, mainstay, pillar, reliance, standby, support
related words backbone, spine; crutch, prop, stay
dependency *n* the quality or state of needing something or someone — see DEPENDENCE 1
dependent *adj* **1** extending freely from a support from above ⟨the *dependent* willow branches swayed in the gentle breeze⟩
synonyms dangling, hanging, pendent (*or* pendant), pendulous
2 determined by something else ⟨our going to the movies tonight is *dependent* on whether or not we have any money left after we eat out⟩
synonyms conditional, contingent (on *or* upon), subject (to), tentative
related words liable, open, susceptible; limited, modified, qualified, restricted; doubtful, iffy, problematic (*also* problematical), questionable, uncertain
near antonyms absolute, categorical (*also* categoric), ultimate; basal, basic, fundamental, primary
antonyms independent, unconditional
depict *vb* **1** to give a representation or account of in words — see DESCRIBE 1
2 to point out the chief quality or qualities of an individual or group — see CHARACTERIZE 1
3 to present a picture of — see PICTURE 1
depiction *n* a vivid representation in words of someone or something — see DESCRIPTION 1
deplete *vb* to make complete use of ⟨miners *depleted* the vein of copper ore after months of working⟩
synonyms clean (out), consume, drain, exhaust, expend, spend, use up
related words decrease, diminish, lessen, reduce; eat, use; bankrupt, impoverish; cripple, debilitate, disable, enfeeble, sap, undermine, weaken; dry up, empty; dissipate, squander, waste
near antonyms augment, enlarge, increase; bolster, fortify, reinforce, strengthen; rebuild, repair, restore, revive
antonyms renew, replace
deplorable *adj* of a kind to cause great distress — see REGRETTABLE
deplore *vb* **1** to feel or express sorrow for — see LAMENT 1
2 to feel sorry or dissatisfied about — see REGRET
deploring *adj* expressing or suggesting mourning — see MOURNFUL 1
deport *vb* **1** to force to leave a country — see BANISH 1
2 to manage the actions of (oneself) in a particular way — see BEHAVE
deportation *n* the forced removal from a homeland — see EXILE 1

deportee *n* a person forced to emigrate for political reasons — see ÉMIGRÉ 1

deportment *n* the way or manner in which one conducts oneself — see BEHAVIOR

depose *vb* 1 to remove from a position of prominence or power (as a throne) ⟨they *deposed* the dictator after he had bankrupted the country⟩
synonyms dethrone, oust, uncrown, unmake, unseat, unthrone
related words discharge, dismiss; overthrow, usurp, subvert, topple; eject, throw out
near antonyms inaugurate, induct, install, instate, invest; appoint, designate, elect
antonyms crown, enthrone, throne
2 to make a solemn declaration under oath for the purpose of establishing a fact — see TESTIFY

deposit *n* 1 matter that settles to the bottom of a body of liquid ⟨a *deposit* of silt on the river bed⟩
synonyms deposition, dregs, grounds, precipitate, sediment
related words lees; ooze, sludge; dross, slag, waste
2 a collection of things kept available for future use or need — see STORE 1
3 a sum of money set aside for a particular purpose — see FUND 1

deposit *vb* 1 to put in an account ⟨we *deposited* the check in a bank account⟩
synonyms bank
related words cache, hoard, lay away, reserve, salt away, save, squirrel (away), stash, store, stow; invest
near antonyms remove, take out; disburse, expend, lay out, spend
antonyms withdraw
2 to arrange something in a certain spot or position — see PLACE 1

deposition *n* matter that settles to the bottom of a body of liquid — see DEPOSIT 1

depository *n* a building for storing goods — see STOREHOUSE

depot *n* 1 a building for storing goods — see STOREHOUSE
2 a place where military arms are stored — see ARMORY

deprave *vb* to lower in character or dignity — see DEBASE 1

depraved *adj* having or showing lowered moral character or standards — see CORRUPT

depravedness *n* the state or quality of being utterly evil — see ENORMITY 1

depravity *n* 1 a sinking to a state of low moral standards and behavior — see CORRUPTION 2
2 immoral conduct or practices harmful or offensive to society — see VICE 1
3 the state or quality of being utterly evil — see ENORMITY 1

deprecate *vb* 1 to express scornfully one's low opinion of — see DECRY 1
2 to hold an unfavorable opinion of — see DISAPPROVE

deprecation *n* 1 refusal to accept as right or desirable — see DISAPPROVAL
2 the act of making a person or a thing seem little or unimportant — see DEPRECIATION

depreciate *vb* 1 to lower the price or value of ⟨a faded finish will really *depreciate* your car when you decide to trade it in⟩
synonyms cheapen, depress, mark down, write off
related words underrate, undervalue; abate, abridge, compress, contract, de-escalate, deflate, diminish, dwindle, lessen, lower, moderate, reduce, shrink
near antonyms bloat, blow up, inflate; add, aggrandize, amplify, augment, balloon, boost, dilate, enlarge, escalate, expand, extend, heighten, increase, maximize, raise, swell
antonyms appreciate, mark up
2 to express scornfully one's low opinion of — see DECRY 1

depreciation *n* the act of making a person or a thing seem little or unimportant ⟨the boys' *depreciation* of the girls' basketball victories only showed how jealous they were⟩
synonyms belittlement, deprecation, detraction, diminishment, disparagement, put-down
related words aspersion, backbiting, defamation, libel, slander, vilification; derision, mockery, ridicule; abuse, invective, vituperation; censure, condemnation, denunciation
near antonyms acclaim, praise; approbation, approval, commendation
antonyms aggrandizement, ennoblement, exaltation, glorification, magnification

depreciative *adj* intended to make a person or thing seem of little importance or value — see DEROGATORY

depreciatory *adj* intended to make a person or thing seem of little importance or value — see DEROGATORY

depress *vb* 1 to make sad ⟨the thought of failing the test *depressed* me⟩
synonyms burden, oppress, sadden
related words ail, distress, trouble; afflict, torment, torture; discourage, dishearten, dispirit; bother, disquiet, disturb, perturb, upset
near antonyms animate, enliven, invigorate; comfort, console, solace; excite, inspire, stimulate; elate, exhilarate; encourage, hearten; delight, gratify, please
antonyms brighten, buoy, cheer, gladden
2 to cause to fall intentionally or unintentionally — see DROP 1
3 to lower the price or value of — see DEPRECIATE 1
4 to push steadily against with some force — see PRESS 1

depressed *adj* 1 curved inward — see HOLLOW
2 feeling unhappiness — see SAD 1

depressing *adj* 1 causing or marked by an atmosphere lacking in cheer — see GLOOMY 1
2 causing unhappiness — see SAD 2

depression *n* 1 a period of decreased economic activity ⟨during the 1930s the U.S. suffered a great *depression*⟩
synonyms recession, slump
related words crash, panic; stagnation
near antonyms development, growth; advancement, progress
antonyms boom
2 a state or spell of low spirits — see SADNESS
3 a sunken area forming a separate space — see HOLE 2

deprivation *n* the state of being robbed of something normally enjoyed — see PRIVATION

deprived *adj* kept from having the necessities of life or a healthful environment ⟨*deprived* children growing up in the slums⟩
synonyms disadvantaged, underprivileged
related words impoverished, needy, poor; hapless, ill-fated, ill-starred, unfortunate, unlucky

THESAURUS

near antonyms fortunate, lucky; affluent, rich, wealthy; coddled, indulged, pampered, spoiled
antonyms privileged

depth *n* **1** distance measured from the top to the bottom of something ⟨be sure to check the *depth* of the water before diving off the dock⟩
synonyms drop
related words lowness; draft, sounding
near antonyms shallowness; altitude, elevation, height
2 the quality of being great in extent (as of insight) ⟨the *depth* of the poet's understanding of human nature has given his works a timeless appeal⟩
synonyms profoundness, profundity
related words discernment, sense, wisdom; brain, intellect, intelligence; acuteness, keenness, penetration, sharpness
near antonyms shallowness, superficiality; smattering
3 the most intense or characteristic phase of something — see THICK

depthless *adj* lacking significant physical depth — see SHALLOW 1

depute *vb* to appoint as one's representative — see DELEGATE 1

deputize *vb* to appoint as one's representative — see DELEGATE 1

deputy *n* **1** a person who acts or does business for another — see AGENT 2
2 a person who helps a more skilled person — see HELPER

derange *vb* **1** to cause to go insane or as if insane — see CRAZE
2 to undo the proper order or arrangement of — see DISORDER

deranged *adj* having or showing a very abnormal or sick state of mind — see INSANE 1

derangement *n* **1** a serious mental disorder that prevents one from living a safe and normal life — see INSANITY 1
2 an act or instance of the order of things being disturbed — see UPSET

derelict *adj* **1** failing to give proper care and attention — see NEGLIGENT
2 left unoccupied or unused — see ABANDONED

dereliction *n* **1** the act of abandoning ⟨the family's shameful *dereliction* of their pets at the end of the summer season⟩
synonyms abandonment, desertion, forsaking
related words defection; discard, dumping, jettison
near antonyms retention
antonyms reclamation
2 failure to take the care that a cautious person usually takes — see NEGLIGENCE 1
3 the nonperformance of an assigned or expected action — see FAILURE 1

deride *vb* to make (someone or something) the object of unkind laughter — see RIDICULE

derision *n* the making of unkind jokes as a way of showing one's scorn for someone or something — see RIDICULE

derisive *adj* so foolish or pointless as to be worthy of scornful laughter — see RIDICULOUS 1

derisory *adj* so foolish or pointless as to be worthy of scornful laughter — see RIDICULOUS 1

derivable *adj* being or provable by reasoning in which the conclusion follows necessarily from given information — see DEDUCTIVE

derivative *adj* taken or created from something original or basic — see SECONDARY 1

derivative *n* something that naturally develops or is developed from something else ⟨the whole field of industrial robots is a *derivative* of technology developed for the space program⟩
synonyms by-product, offshoot, outgrowth, spin-off
related words descendant (*or* descendent); aftermath, consequence, result; aftereffect, side effect; copy, duplicate, facsimile, replica, reproduction
near antonyms archetype, original, prototype; antecedent, cause, determinant
antonyms origin, root, source

derogatory *adj* intended to make a person or thing seem of little importance or value ⟨fans made a steady stream of *derogatory* remarks about the players on the visiting team⟩
synonyms belittling, contemptuous, decrying, degrading, demeaning, depreciative, depreciatory, disdainful, disparaging, scornful, slighting, uncomplimentary
related words aspersing, defamatory, detractive, insulting, libelous, maligning, slandering, slanderous, vilifying; abusive, opprobrious, scurrilous; despiteful, malevolent, malicious, spiteful
near antonyms admiring, adulatory, laudatory; appreciative, respectful
antonyms commendatory, complimentary

descant *vb* **1** to give a formal often extended talk on a subject — see TALK 1
2 to produce musical sounds with the voice — see SING 1

descend *vb* **1** to lead or extend downward ⟨the pathway *descends* to the river bank⟩
synonyms decline, dip, drop, fall, plunge
related words cant, incline, lean, list, recline, slant, slope, tilt, tip
near antonyms even, flatten, level, straighten
antonyms ascend, climb, rise
2 to become worse or of less value — see DETERIORATE
3 to go to a lower level — see DROP 2

descend (on *or* upon) *vb* to take sudden, violent action against — see ATTACK 1

descendant *or* **descendent** *adj* bending downward or forward — see NODDING

descending *adj* bending downward or forward — see NODDING

descent *n* **1** the act or process of going to a lower level or altitude ⟨the airplane began its gradual *descent* to the landing field⟩
synonyms dip, dive, down, drop, fall, nosedive, plunge
related words comedown, downfall, downgrade; sinking
near antonyms advance, headway, progress, progression; betterment, improvement
antonyms ascent, climb, rise, upswing, upturn
2 a gradual sinking and wasting away of mind or body — see DECLINE 1
3 a change to a lower state or level — see DECLINE 2
4 a loss of status — see COMEDOWN
5 a sudden attack on and entrance into hostile territory — see RAID 1
6 the act or action of setting upon with force or violence — see ATTACK 1
7 the line of ancestors from whom a person is descended — see ANCESTRY

describe *vb* **1** to give a representation or account of in words ⟨he tried to *describe* the dream he had last night as accurately as he could⟩
synonyms delineate, depict, draw, image, paint, picture, portray, sketch
related words characterize, qualify, represent; demonstrate, illustrate; narrate, recite, recount, relate; display, exhibit, show; hint, suggest; draft, outline
near antonyms color, distort, falsify, garble, misrepresent, pervert, twist, warp
2 to give an oral or written account of in some detail — see TELL 1
3 to point out the chief quality or qualities of an individual or group — see CHARACTERIZE 1
description *n* **1** a vivid representation in words of someone or something ⟨we recognized his cousin from his *description*⟩
synonyms delineation, depiction, picture, portrait, portrayal, sketch
related words account, chronicle, narrative, report, story, tale; demonstration, exemplification, illustration
2 a number of persons or things that are grouped together because they have something in common — see SORT 1
descry *vb* **1** to come upon after searching, study, or effort — see FIND 1
2 to make note of (something) through the use of one's eyes — see SEE 1
desecrate *vb* to treat (a sacred place or object) shamefully or with great disrespect ⟨vandals *desecrated* the cemetery last night with graffiti⟩
synonyms defile, profane, violate
related words blaspheme, curse, swear; befoul, contaminate, foul, pollute; affront, insult, offend; crush, decimate, demolish, destroy, devastate, ravage, raze, ruin, waste, wreck; despoil, loot, pillage, plunder, raid, ransack, rob, sack, spoil, strip
near antonyms bless, consecrate, dedicate, hallow, sanctify; honor, respect; cleanse, purify
desecration *n* an act of great disrespect shown to God or to sacred ideas, people, or things — see BLASPHEMY
¹**desert** *n* land that is uninhabited or not fit for crops — see WASTELAND
²**desert** *n* suffering, loss, or hardship imposed in response to a crime or offense — see PUNISHMENT
desert *vb* **1** to leave (a cause or party) often in order to take up another — see DEFECT
2 to cause to remain behind — see LEAVE 1
deserted *adj* left unoccupied or unused — see ABANDONED
deserter *n* a person who abandons a cause or organization usually without right — see RENEGADE
desertion *n* the act of abandoning — see DERELICTION 1
deserve *vb* to be or make worthy of (as a reward or punishment) — see EARN 2
deserved *adj* being what is called for by accepted standards of right and wrong — see JUST 1
deserving *adj* having sufficient worth or merit to receive one's honor, esteem, or reward — see WORTHY
desex *vb* to remove the sex organs of — see NEUTER
design *n* **1** a method worked out in advance for achieving some objective — see PLAN 1

2 a secret plan for accomplishing evil or unlawful ends — see PLOT 1
3 something that one hopes or intends to accomplish — see GOAL
4 a unit of decoration that is repeated all over something (as a fabric) — see PATTERN 1
5 the way in which the elements of something (as a work of art) are arranged — see COMPOSITION 3
design *vb* **1** to have in mind as a purpose or goal — see INTEND
2 to work out the details of (something) in advance — see PLAN 1
designate *vb* **1** to decide upon (the time or date for an event) usually from a position of authority — see APPOINT 1
2 to pick (someone) by one's authority for a specific position or duty — see APPOINT 2
3 to give a name to — see NAME 1
designation *n* **1** a word or combination of words by which a person or thing is regularly known — see NAME 1
2 the state or fact of being chosen for a position or duty — see APPOINTMENT 1
designedly *adv* with full awareness of what one is doing — see INTENTIONALLY
designer *n* one who creates or introduces something new — see INVENTOR
desirable *adj* suitable for bringing about a desired result under the circumstances — see EXPEDIENT
desire *n* a strong wish for something ⟨a *desire* for adventure and excitement prompted him to travel to Africa⟩
synonyms appetite, craving, drive, hankering, hunger, itch, longing, lust, passion, pining, thirst, urge, yearning, yen
related words compulsion, impulse, urge, will, zeal; liking, love, taste; eagerness, impatience; wish, want; necessity, need, requirement; avarice, cupidity, greed, rapacity
near antonyms abhorrence, aversion, disfavor, disgust, dislike, distaste, hatred, repugnance, repulsion; apathy, indifference, unconcern
desire *vb* to have an earnest wish to own or enjoy ⟨he greatly *desired* a new mountain bike for his next birthday⟩
synonyms ache (for), covet, crave, die (for), hanker (for *or* after), hunger (for), itch (for), long (for), lust (for *or* after), pant (after), pine (for), repine (for), sigh (for), thirst (for), want, wish (for), yearn (for)
related words delight (in), enjoy, fancy, like, relish
near antonyms abhor, abominate, detest, hate, loathe; decline, refuse, reject, spurn
desirous *adj* showing urgent desire or interest — see EAGER
desirousness *n* urgent desire or interest — see EAGERNESS
desist (from) *vb* to bring (as an action or operation) to an immediate end — see STOP 1
desk *n* a large unit of a governmental, business, or educational organization — see DIVISION 2
desolate *adj* **1** causing or marked by an atmosphere lacking in cheer — see GLOOMY 1
2 sad from lack of companionship or separation from others — see LONESOME 1
desolate *vb* to bring to a complete end the physical soundness, existence, or usefulness of — see DESTROY 1
desolation *n* **1** a state or spell of low spirits — see SADNESS

THESAURUS

2 land that is uninhabited or not fit for crops — see WASTELAND

3 the state of being unattended to or not cared for — see NEGLECT 1

4 the state or fact of being rendered nonexistent, physically unsound, or useless — see DESTRUCTION

despair *n* **1** utter loss of hope ⟨the endless drought drove the farmers to *despair*⟩

synonyms desperation, despondency, forlornness, hopelessness

related words blues, depression, dejection, desolation, doldrums, dolor, downheartedness, dumps, gloom, melancholy, mopes, oppression, sadness, sorrow, unhappiness; cynicism, pessimism; acceptance, resignation

near antonyms cheer, cheerfulness, sunniness; optimism

antonyms hope, hopefulness

2 the state of being discouraged — see DISCOURAGEMENT

despair *vb* to lose all hope or confidence ⟨we *despaired* when we saw how little time we had left to complete our project⟩

synonyms despond

related words give up, surrender, yield; darken, sadden; grieve, mourn, sorrow; discourage, dishearten, dispirit

near antonyms assure, encourage, hearten, reassure; hope

antonyms brighten, cheer (up), perk (up)

despairing *adj* emphasizing or expecting the worst — see PESSIMISTIC 1

desperation *n* utter loss of hope — see DESPAIR 1

despicable *adj* **1** arousing or deserving of one's loathing and disgust — see CONTEMPTIBLE 1

2 not following or in accordance with standards of honor and decency — see IGNOBLE 2

3 deserving pitying scorn (as for inadequacy) — see PITIFUL 1

despise *vb* **1** to dislike strongly — see HATE

2 to ignore in a disrespectful manner — see SCORN 2

despite *n* **1** open dislike for someone or something considered unworthy of one's concern or respect — see CONTEMPT

2 the desire to cause pain for the satisfaction of doing harm — see MALICE

despite *prep* without being prevented by ⟨we went to the party *despite* the bad weather outside⟩

synonyms notwithstanding, with

phrases in despite of, in spite of

despiteful *adj* having or showing a desire to cause someone pain or suffering for the sheer enjoyment of it — see HATEFUL

despitefully *adv* in a mean or spiteful manner — see NASTILY

despitefulness *n* open dislike for someone or something considered unworthy of one's concern or respect — see CONTEMPT

despoil *vb* to search through with the intent of committing robbery — see RANSACK 1

despond *vb* to lose all hope or confidence — see DESPAIR

despondency *n* **1** a state or spell of low spirits — see SADNESS

2 the state of being discouraged — see DISCOURAGEMENT

3 utter loss of hope — see DESPAIR 1

despondent *adj* feeling unhappiness — see SAD 1

despot *n* a person who uses power or authority in a cruel, unjust, or harmful way ⟨the *despot* threw anyone who dared to criticize his rule into jail⟩

synonyms autocrat, dictator, oppressor, potentate, tyrant

related words dominator, master, overlord, ruler; king, lord, monarch, prince, queen, sovereign; baron, czar (*also* tsar *or* tzar), magnate, mogul, tycoon; authoritarian, disciplinarian, discipliner, martinet

despotic *adj* **1** exercising power or authority without interference by others — see ABSOLUTE 1

2 fond of ordering people around — see BOSSY

despotism *n* a system of government in which the ruler has unlimited power ⟨by the end of the 20th century many countries around the world had rejected *despotism* in favor of democracy⟩

synonyms autocracy, dictatorship, totalitarianism, tyranny

related words monarchy; authoritarianism, fascism; domination, oppression

near antonyms democracy; freedom; anarchy

destine *vb* to determine the fate of in advance ⟨his extreme height seemed to *destine* him for a career in basketball⟩

synonyms doom, fate, foredoom, foreordain, ordain, predestine, predetermine

related words forecast, foretell, predict, prognosticate, prophesy; preconceive, prejudge; condemn, sentence

destiny *n* a state or end that seemingly has been decided beforehand — see FATE 1

destitute *adj* **1** lacking money or material possessions — see POOR 1

2 utterly lacking in something needed, wanted, or expected — see DEVOID 1

destitution *n* the state of lacking sufficient money or material possessions — see POVERTY 1

destroy *vb* **1** to bring to a complete end the physical soundness, existence, or usefulness of ⟨they practically *destroyed* the safe in order to get at the money inside⟩ ⟨their poor scores on the final exam *destroyed* any chance they might have had to pass the course⟩

synonyms annihilate, decimate, demolish, desolate, devastate, do in, extinguish, pulverize, raze, ruin, shatter, smash, tear down, waste, wreck

related words gut; beat, best, clobber, conquer, crush, defeat, lick, master, overbear, overcome, prevail (over), scotch, subdue, surmount, thrash, triumph (over), win (against); blow up, break, damage, deface, disintegrate, dynamite, mangle, mar, mutilate, spoil, vitiate; erode, scour, wash out, wear (away); dismantle, undo, unmake; blot out, eradicate, exterminate, extirpate, obliterate, remove, rub out, stamp (out), wipe out; despoil, loot, pillage, plunder, ravage, sack, vandalize; assassinate, butcher, cut down, dispatch, execute, kill, massacre, murder, slaughter, slay, zap

near antonyms create, invent; fabricate, fashion, forge, form, make, manufacture, shape; bring about, establish, found, institute, organize; conserve, preserve, protect, save; rebuild, reconstruct, remodel, renovate, restore

antonyms build, construct, erect, put up, raise

2 to bring destruction to (something) through violent action — see RAVAGE

3 to deprive of life — see KILL 1

destruction *n* the state or fact of being rendered nonexistent, physically unsound, or useless ⟨the

violent storm resulted in the *destruction* of their tree house⟩
synonyms annihilation, decimation, demolishment, demolition, desolation, devastation, extermination, extinction, havoc, loss, obliteration, ruin, ruination, wastage, wreckage
related words depredation, despoilment, despoliation; breakup, disintegration, dissolution; assassination, execution, killing, massacre, slaughter
near antonyms conservation, preservation, protection; reconstruction, re-creation, remodeling, renovation, restoration
antonyms building, construction, erection, raising
destructive *adj* **1** causing or tending to cause destruction ⟨the *destructive* storm blew down trees all over town, and blew the roof off our neighbor's house⟩
synonyms calamitous, cataclysmal (*or* cataclysmic), devastating, disastrous, ruinous
related words deadly, fatal, lethal, mortal, vital; deleterious, detrimental, harmful, pernicious
near antonyms preservative, protective; creative, formative; harmless, innocuous, inoffensive, nondestructive; ameliorative, helpful, useful
antonyms constructive
2 bringing about ruin or misfortune — see FATAL 1
desultorily *adv* without definite aim, direction, rule, or method — see HIT OR MISS
desultory *adj* **1** lacking a definite plan, purpose, or pattern — see RANDOM
2 passing from one topic to another — see DISCURSIVE
detached *adj* **1** having or showing a lack of friendliness or interest in others — see COOL 1
2 not physically attached to another unit — see SEPARATE 2
detachment *n* **1** lack of favoritism toward one side or another ⟨the judge showed great *detachment* when deciding the controversial case⟩
synonyms disinterestedness, impartiality, neutrality, objectivity
related words equitableness, fairness; apathy, indifference, unconcern; broad-mindedness, open-mindedness, tolerance
near antonyms chauvinism, nepotism; subjectivity; bent, inclination, leaning, penchant, predilection, predisposition, proclivity, propensity, tendency; preconception, prejudgment
antonyms bias, favor, favoritism, one-sidedness, partiality, partisanship, prejudice
2 a small military unit with a special task or function ⟨the general sent a *detachment* ahead to scout the enemy's position⟩
synonyms detail
related words commando, firing squad, paratroops, patrol, picket; battalion, command, company, corps, division, platoon, regiment, squad, troop, wing
detail *n* **1** a separate part in a list, account, or series — see ITEM 1
2 a single piece of information — see FACT 3
3 a small military unit with a special task or function — see DETACHMENT 2
detail *vb* **1** to assign to a place or position — see ²POST
2 to pick (someone) by one's authority for a specific position or duty — see APPOINT 2
3 to specify one after another — see ENUMERATE 1

detailed *adj* **1** including many small descriptive features ⟨a *detailed* report on all the activities that their Scout troop had been involved in over the past year⟩
synonyms circumstantial, elaborate, full, minute, particularized, thorough
related words enumerated, inventoried, itemized, listed; delineated, specific, specified; abundant, copious; comprehensive, exhausting, exhaustive, thoroughgoing; accurate, exact, precise; complete, entire, replete; distinct, explicit, precise, sharp; inclusive, mapped (out); descriptive, graphic (*also* graphical), picturesque, vivid
near antonyms concise, pithy, short, succinct; abbreviated, abridged, curtailed, cut, pruned, shortened, trimmed; indeterminate, nebulous, nondescript, sketchy, vague; bird's-eye, broad, general, nonspecific, overall, unspecified
antonyms compendious, summary
2 made or done with great care or with much detail — see ELABORATE 1
detailedly *adv* with attention to all aspects or details — see THOROUGHLY 1
detainment *n* an instance or period of being prevented from going about one's business — see DELAY
detect *vb* to come upon after searching, study, or effort — see FIND 1
detectable *adj* able to be perceived by a sense or by the mind — see PERCEPTIBLE
detection *n* the act or process of sighting or learning the existence of something for the first time — see DISCOVERY 1
detective *n* a person whose business is solving crimes and catching criminals or gathering information that is not easy to get ⟨the *detective* tracked the criminals to an abandoned warehouse on the south side of town⟩
synonyms investigator, operative, plainclothesman, shadow, sleuth, tail
related words Federal, G-man, narc (*or* nark) [*slang*]
detector *n* a device that detects some physical quantity and responds usually with a transmitted signal — see SENSOR
deter *vb* to steer (a person) from an activity or course of action — see DISCOURAGE 2
detergent *n* a substance used for cleaning — see CLEANER
deteriorate *vb* to become worse or of less value ⟨the garden slowly *deteriorated* after months of neglect⟩
synonyms crumble, decay, decline, degenerate, descend, ebb, rot, sink, worsen
related words recede, wane; decompose, degrade, disintegrate; sour, spoil; lessen, lower, reduce; debilitate, undermine, weaken
phrases go to pot
near antonyms better, upgrade; enhance, enrich, fortify, heighten, intensify, strengthen; advance, develop, progress
antonyms ameliorate, improve, meliorate
deterioration *n* **1** a gradual sinking and wasting away of mind or body — see DECLINE 1
2 a change to a lower state or level — see DECLINE 2
determinate *adj* **1** having been established and usually not subject to change — see FIXED 1
2 having distinct or certain limits — see LIMITED 1
determination *n* **1** firm or unwavering adherence

THESAURUS

to one's purpose ⟨the *determination* with which the pioneers settled the land despite many hardships and setbacks⟩
synonyms decidedness, decision, decisiveness, firmness, granite, purposefulness, resoluteness, resolution, resolve
related words doggedness, obstinacy, perseverance, persistence, stubbornness, tenaciousness, tenacity; backbone, fortitude, grit, pluck
near antonyms uncertainty
antonyms hesitation, indecision, irresolution, vacillation
2 a position arrived at after consideration — see DECISION 1
3 an opinion arrived at through a process of reasoning — see CONCLUSION 1
determine *vb* **1** to give an opinion about (something at issue or in dispute) — see JUDGE 1
2 to come to a judgment after discussion or consideration — see DECIDE 1
3 to come upon after searching, study, or effort — see FIND 1
determined *adj* **1** fully committed to achieving a goal ⟨his *determined* opponent would not be bluffed or shaken⟩
synonyms bent (on *or* upon), bound, decisive, firm, intent, purposeful, resolute, resolved, set
related words certain, cocksure, positive, sure; earnest, serious; steady, unfaltering, unhesitating, unswerving, unwavering
near antonyms doubtful, dubious, uncertain, unsure
antonyms faltering, hesitant, indecisive, irresolute, undetermined, unresolved, vacillating, wavering
2 showing no signs of slackening or yielding in one's purpose — see UNYIELDING 1
determinedly *adv* with great effort or determination — see HARD 1
deterrent *n* something that makes movement or progress more difficult — see ENCUMBRANCE
detest *vb* to dislike strongly — see HATE
detestable *adj* not following or in accordance with standards of honor and decency — see IGNOBLE 2
dethrone *vb* to remove from a position of prominence or power (as a throne) — see DEPOSE 1
detonate *vb* to break open or into pieces usually because of internal pressure — see EXPLODE 1
detonation *n* the act or an instance of exploding — see EXPLOSION 1
detour *vb* **1** to avoid by going around ⟨we had to *detour* the construction zone in order to get to the stadium⟩
synonyms bypass, circumvent, skirt
related words circumnavigate; avoid, dodge, duck, elude, escape, eschew, evade, shake, shun
near antonyms confront, face, meet; accept, court, embrace, pursue, seek, welcome
2 to change one's course or direction — see TURN 3
detraction *n* the act of making a person or a thing seem little or unimportant — see DEPRECIATION
detriment *n* something that causes loss or pain — see INJURY 1
detrimental *adj* causing or capable of causing harm — see HARMFUL
devastate *vb* **1** to bring destruction to (something) through violent action — see RAVAGE
2 to bring to a complete end the physical soundness, existence, or usefulness of — see DESTROY 1

3 to subject to incapacitating emotional or mental stress — see OVERWHELM 1
devastating *adj* causing or tending to cause destruction — see DESTRUCTIVE 1
devastation *n* the state or fact of being rendered nonexistent, physically unsound, or useless — see DESTRUCTION
develop *vb* **1** to gradually become clearer or more detailed ⟨as the story of the bombing *developed*, the scope of the tragedy became more apparent⟩
synonyms evolve, unfold
related words advance, proceed, progress; mature, ripen; materialize
2 to come to have gradually ⟨they *developed* a taste for green olives⟩
synonyms acquire, cultivate, form
related words gain, get, obtain; achieve, attain, reach; foster, nourish, nurture, promote
antonyms lose
3 to become mature — see MATURE
4 to express more fully and in greater detail — see EXPAND 1
developed *adj* being far along in development — see ADVANCED 1
developer *n* one who creates or introduces something new — see INVENTOR
development *n* **1** the act or process of going from the simple or basic to the complex or advanced ⟨the *development* of an idea into a marketable product⟩
synonyms elaboration, evolution, expansion, growth, progress, progression
related words advancement, betterment, improvement, perfection, refinement; maturation
near antonyms decadence, decay, decaying, declension, decline, degeneration, descent, deterioration, downgrade, ebbing, weakening
antonyms regression, retrogression
2 a condition or occurrence traceable to a cause — see EFFECT 1
3 the process of becoming mature — see MATURATION
deviant *adj* departing from some accepted standard of what is normal ⟨some studies show that many violent criminals begin exhibiting *deviant* behavior in early childhood⟩
synonyms aberrant, abnormal, anomalous, atypical, irregular, unnatural
related words extraordinary, preternatural; rare, uncommon, uncustomary, unusual, unwonted; odd, peculiar, strange, weird
near antonyms common, familiar, ordinary; customary, usual, wonted
antonyms natural, normal, regular, standard, typical
deviant *n* a person who does not conform to generally accepted standards or customs — see NONCONFORMIST 1
deviate *vb* to change one's course or direction — see TURN 3
device *n* **1** a clever often underhanded means to achieve an end — see TRICK 1
2 an article intended for use in work — see IMPLEMENT
3 devices *pl* a habitual attraction to some activity or thing — see INCLINATION 1
devil *n* **1** *cap* the supreme personification of evil often represented as the ruler of Hell ⟨the *Devil* is traditionally seen as a being who relentlessly tempts people to commit evil⟩

synonyms Lucifer, Satan
related words deuce, dickens
phrases Prince of Darkness
2 an evil spirit — see DEMON
3 a member of the human race — see HUMAN
4 an appealingly mischievous person — see SCAMP 1
5 a mean, evil, or unprincipled person — see VILLAIN
devilfish *n* any of several extremely large rays ⟨they saw a *devilfish* when they went scuba diving in the Caribbean, but it swam away quickly⟩
synonyms devil ray, manta, manta ray, sea devil
related words ray, skate
devilish *adj* 1 going beyond a normal or acceptable limit in degree or amount — see EXCESSIVE
2 of, relating to, or worthy of an evil spirit — see FIENDISH
3 tending to or exhibiting reckless playfulness — see MISCHIEVOUS 1
devilishly *adv* beyond a normal or acceptable limit — see TOO 1
devilishness *n* playful, reckless behavior that is not intended to cause serious harm — see MISCHIEF 1
devil–may–care *adj* 1 having a relaxed, casual manner — see EASYGOING 1
2 having or showing a lack of concern or seriousness — see CAREFREE
3 having or showing a lack of concern for the consequences of one's actions — see RECKLESS 1
devilment *n* playful, reckless behavior that is not intended to cause serious harm — see MISCHIEF 1
devil ray *n* any of several extremely large rays — see DEVILFISH
devilry *or* **deviltry** *n* playful, reckless behavior that is not intended to cause serious harm — see MISCHIEF 1
devious *adj* 1 clever at attaining one's ends by indirect and often deceptive means — see ARTFUL 1
2 marked by a long series of irregular curves — see CROOKED 1
deviousness *n* skill in achieving one's ends through indirect, subtle, or underhanded means — see CUNNING 1
devise *vb* to create or think of by clever use of the imagination — see INVENT
deviser *n* one who creates or introduces something new — see INVENTOR
devoid *adj* 1 utterly lacking in something needed, wanted, or expected ⟨the so-called comedy is totally *devoid* of intelligence, originality, and even laughs⟩
synonyms bereft, destitute, void
related words bare, barren, blank, empty, lacking, stark, vacant, wanting; deficient, fragmental, fragmentary, incomplete, partial; absent, missing
near antonyms filled, full; furnished, provided, supplied
antonyms replete
2 lacking contents that could or should be present — see EMPTY 1
devote *vb* 1 to keep or intend for a special purpose ⟨he *devoted* several hours every weekend to playing with his dog⟩
synonyms allocate, consecrate, dedicate, earmark, reserve, save
related words hallow, sanctify; commit, confide, consign, entrust
phrases set apart, set aside

2 to occupy (oneself) diligently or with close attention — see APPLY
devoted *adj* 1 feeling or showing love — see LOVING
2 firm in one's allegiance to someone or something — see FAITHFUL 1
devotedness *n* 1 a feeling of strong or constant regard for and dedication to someone — see LOVE 1
2 adherence to something to which one is bound by a pledge or duty — see FIDELITY
devotee *n* a person with a strong and habitual liking for something — see FAN
devotion *n* 1 a feeling of strong or constant regard for and dedication to someone — see LOVE 1
2 adherence to something to which one is bound by a pledge or duty — see FIDELITY
3 belief and trust in and loyalty to God — see FAITH 1
devotional *adj* of, relating to, or used in the practice or worship services of a religion — see RELIGIOUS 1
devour *vb* to destroy all trace of — see CONSUME 1
devout *adj* showing a devotion to God and to a life of virtue — see HOLY 1
devoutness *n* the quality or state of being spiritually pure or virtuous — see HOLINESS
dexterity *n* 1 mental skill or quickness ⟨the ambassador showed great *dexterity* in his handling of the touchy situation⟩
synonyms adroitness, cleverness, finesse, sleight
related words ability, prowess, talent; competence, efficiency, expertise, know-how, proficiency; ingeniousness, ingenuity, resourcefulness
near antonyms inadequacy, ineptitude, ineptness; slowness, stupidity
2 ease and grace in physical activity ⟨the juggler needed lots of *dexterity* in order to keep all five balls in the air at the same time⟩
synonyms agility, deftness, nimbleness, sleight, spryness
related words coordination
antonyms awkwardness, clumsiness, gawkiness
dexterous *also* **dextrous** *adj* 1 skillful with the hands ⟨the *dexterous* watchmaker was able to repair the tiny gears and parts in the antique watch⟩
synonyms clever, cunning, deft, handy
related words agile, flexible, graceful, limber, lissome (*also* lissom), lithe, nimble, spry; coordinated; adept, competent, expert, masterful, masterly, proficient, skilled, skillful; double-jointed, loose-jointed
near antonyms awkward, bungling, clumsy, fumbling, gawky; uncoordinated; incompetent, inept, maladroit
antonyms butterfingered, heavy-handed, unhandy
2 accomplished with trained ability — see SKILLFUL
diabolical *or* **diabolic** *adj* of, relating to, or worthy of an evil spirit — see FIENDISH
diadem *n* a decorative band or wreath worn about the head as a symbol of victory or honor — see CROWN 1
diagnosis *n* a position arrived at after consideration — see DECISION 1
diagonal *adj* running in a slanting direction ⟨the *diagonal* design ran up the wall all the way from the lower left to the upper right-hand corner⟩
synonyms canted, inclined, leaning, listing,

THESAURUS

oblique, pitched, slanted, slantwise, sloped, sloping, tilted, tilting

near antonyms horizontal, vertical; parallel, perpendicular

diagonal *n* the degree to which something rises up from a position level with the horizon — see SLANT

diagram *n* something that visually explains or decorates a text — see ILLUSTRATION 1

dial *vb* to make a telephone call to — see CALL 2

dialect *n* the special terms or expressions of a particular group or field — see TERMINOLOGY

dialogue *also* **dialog** *n* talking or a talk between two or more people — see CONVERSATION

diametric *or* **diametrical** *adj* being as different as possible — see OPPOSITE

diatribe *n* a long angry speech or scolding — see TIRADE

dice *n* a small cube marked on each side with one to six spots and usually played in pairs in various games — see DIE

dice *vb* to cut into small pieces — see CHOP

dicker *vb* to talk over or dispute the terms of a purchase — see BARGAIN

dictate *n* a statement of what to do that must be obeyed by those concerned — see COMMAND 1

dictate *vb* to give an order — see COMMAND 2

dictator *n* a person who uses power or authority in a cruel, unjust, or harmful way — see DESPOT

dictatorial *adj* **1** exercising power or authority without interference by others — see ABSOLUTE 1
2 fond of ordering people around — see BOSSY
3 having or showing a tendency to force one's will on others without any regard to fairness or necessity — see ARBITRARY 1

dictatorship *n* a system of government in which the ruler has unlimited power — see DESPOTISM

diction *n* **1** the clear and accurate pronunciation of words especially in public speaking ⟨the actors had very good *diction*, clearly speaking every single word of the Shakespearean play that they were performing⟩
synonyms articulation, enunciation
related words elocution; speech, wording
2 the way in which something is put into words — see WORDING

dictionary *n* a reference book giving information about the meanings, pronunciations, uses, and origins of words listed in alphabetical order ⟨try to develop the habit of going to the *dictionary* whenever you encounter an unfamiliar word⟩
synonyms lexicon, wordbook
related words glossary, thesaurus, vocabulary

die *n* a small cube marked on each side with one to six spots and usually played in pairs in various games ⟨he rolled the *die*, hoping for a six⟩
synonyms bone(s), dice

die *vb* **1** to stop living ⟨the king *died* of old age after ruling for many years⟩
synonyms croak [*slang*], decease, depart, expire, pass (on), pass away, perish, succumb
related words disappear, fade
phrases bite the dust
near antonyms be, exist, subsist; flourish, prosper, thrive
antonyms breathe, live
2 to come to an end — see CEASE 1
3 to stop functioning — see FAIL 1

die (down) *vb* to grow less in scope or intensity especially gradually — see DECREASE 2

die (for) *vb* to have an earnest wish to own or enjoy — see DESIRE

differ *vb* **1** to be unlike; to not be the same ⟨my brother and I *differ* in looks⟩
synonyms disagree, vary
related words clash, conflict, jar; distinguish, divide, separate
near antonyms blend, harmonize
antonyms accord, agree, conform, correspond
2 to have a different opinion — see DISAGREE 1

difference *n* **1** the quality or state of being different ⟨there's a great *difference* between claiming to care about the environment and living like you really do⟩
synonyms contrast, disagreement, discrepancy, disparateness, disparity, dissimilarity, distinction, distinctiveness, distinctness, diverseness, diversity, unlikeness
related words deviance, divergence; change, modification, variation; conflict, discord, discordance, dissension, dissent, dissidence, disunity, friction, strife; variability, variance; incompatibility, incongruity, incongruousness; disproportion
near antonyms identicalness, identity; analogy, similitude; accordance, agreement, conformity, congruity, correspondence; equality, equivalence, equivalency; parallelism
antonyms alikeness, community, likeness, resemblance, sameness, similarity
2 variance of opinion on a matter — see DISAGREEMENT 1
3 the act, process, or result of making different — see CHANGE

different *adj* **1** being not of the same kind ⟨apples are *different* from oranges⟩
synonyms disparate, dissimilar, distinct, distinctive, distinguishable, diverse, other, unalike, unlike
related words divers, miscellaneous, several, sundry, variant, varied, various; individual, particular, peculiar, single; unequal; disproportionate
near antonyms identical, selfsame; equal, equivalent, tantamount; akin, analogous, comparable, related; homogeneous, uniform
antonyms alike, indistinguishable, like, parallel, same, similar
2 not the same or shared — see SEPARATE 1

differential *adj* favoring, applying, or being unequal treatment of different classes of people — see DISCRIMINATORY

differentiate *vb* to understand or point out the difference — see DISTINGUISH 1

differently *adv* in a different way — see OTHERWISE

difficult *adj* **1** requiring considerable physical or mental effort — see HARD 2
2 requiring exceptional skill or caution in performance or handling — see TRICKY

difficulty *n* **1** something that is a cause for suffering or special effort especially in the attainment of a goal ⟨the many *difficulties* that he encountered on the road from poor orphan to head of a major corporation⟩
synonyms adversity, asperity, hardness, hardship, rigor
related words discomfort, inconvenience, nuisance; affliction, trial, tribulation; knock, misfortune, mishap, tragedy; bar, catch, check, clog, crimp, embarrassment, handicap, hindrance, hitch, hurdle, impediment, interference, let, man-

acle, obstacle, obstruction, rub, shackle, snag, stop, trammel; block, chain, deterrent, encumbrance, fetter, inhibition; hump

near antonyms advantage, break, opportunity
2 something that makes a situation more complicated or difficult — see COMPLICATION 1

diffident *adj* not comfortable around people — see SHY 2

diffuse *adj* using or containing more words than necessary to express an idea — see WORDY

diffuseness *n* the use of too many words to express an idea — see VERBIAGE

dig *n* **1** a quick thrust — see ¹POKE
2 an act or expression showing scorn and usually intended to hurt another's feelings — see INSULT

dig *vb* **1** to hollow out or form (something) by removing earth ⟨a backhoe *dug* a hole in the backyard to make a swimming pool⟩
synonyms excavate, shovel
related words dredge; burrow, claw, grub; dig in; scoop, spade; delve; mine, quarry
near antonyms fill (in); smooth (out *or* over)
2 to take pleasure in — see ENJOY 1
3 *slang* to recognize the meaning of — see COMPREHEND 1

dig (into) *vb* to search through or into — see EXPLORE 1

dig (through) *vb* to look through (as a place) carefully or thoroughly in an effort to find or discover something — see SEARCH 1

dig (up) *vb* to come upon after searching, study, or effort — see FIND 1

digest *n* **1** a short statement of the main points — see SUMMARY
2 a shortened version of a written work — see ABRIDGMENT

digest *vb* to make into a short statement of the main points (as of a report) — see SUMMARIZE

diggings *n pl* the place where one lives — see HOME 1

digit *n* a character used to represent a mathematical value — see NUMBER

dignified *adj* having or showing a serious and reserved manner ⟨the chief justice of the U.S. Supreme Court is always very *dignified* when swearing in the new president⟩ ⟨*dignified* funeral services for the fallen firemen⟩
synonyms august, imposing, solemn, staid, stately
related words decorous, formal, proper, seemly; grim, sober, somber (*or* sombre); aristocratic, lordly, majestic, noble
near antonyms coarse, crass, crude, improper, indecent, uncouth, unseemly, vulgar
antonyms flighty, frivolous, giddy, goofy, silly, undignified

dignify *vb* to enhance the status of — see EXALT

dignity *n* high position within society — see RANK 2

digression *n* a departure from the subject under consideration — see TANGENT

digressive *adj* passing from one topic to another — see DISCURSIVE

dike *n* **1** a bank of earth constructed to control water — see DAM
2 a long narrow channel dug in the earth — see DITCH

dilapidated *adj* showing signs of advanced wear and tear and neglect — see SHABBY 1

dilapidation *n* the state of being unattended to or not cared for — see NEGLECT 1

dilatory *adj* moving or proceeding at less than the normal, desirable, or required speed — see SLOW 1

dilemma *n* a situation in which one has to choose between two or more equally unsatisfactory choices ⟨they were faced with a *dilemma* : either they could spend the night out in the cold or they could walk back into their house and face their father⟩
synonyms quandary
related words deadlock, halt, impasse, quagmire, stalemate, standoff; knot, problem; difficulty, fix, hole, jam, pickle, pinch, plight, predicament, spot
near antonyms breeze, cinch, duck soup, snap

dilettante *adj* lacking or showing a lack of expert skill — see AMATEURISH

dilettante *n* **1** a person having a knowledgeable and fine appreciation of the arts — see CONNOISSEUR
2 a person who regularly or occasionally engages in an activity without being or becoming an expert at it — see AMATEUR

diligence *n* attentive and persistent effort ⟨through the *diligence* and ingenuity of a single detective, the gang's ringleader was finally caught⟩
synonyms assiduity, assiduousness, industriousness, industry
related words application, concentration; doggedness, perseverance, persistence, tenacity, tirelessness
near antonyms carelessness; idleness, indolence, laziness

diligent *adj* involved in often constant activity — see BUSY 1

diligently *adv* with great effort or determination — see HARD 1

dillydally *vb* **1** to move or act slowly — see DELAY 1
2 to spend time doing nothing — see IDLE

dillydallying *adj* moving or proceeding at less than the normal, desirable, or required speed — see SLOW 1

dilute *adj* **1** not containing very much of some important element — see WEAK 3
2 containing foreign or lower-grade substances — see IMPURE

dilute *vb* to alter (something) for the worse with the addition of foreign or lower-grade substances — see ADULTERATE

diluted *adj* **1** not containing very much of some important element — see WEAK 3
2 containing foreign or lower-grade substances — see IMPURE

dim *adj* **1** being without light or without much light — see DARK 1
2 lacking a surface luster or gloss — see MATTE
3 not seen or understood clearly — see FAINT 1

dim *vb* to make dark, dim, or indistinct — see CLOUD 1

dimension *n* **1** the total amount of measurable space or surface occupied by something — see ¹SIZE
2 dimensions *pl* an area over which activity, capacity, or influence extends — see RANGE 2

diminish *vb* **1** to express scornfully one's low opinion of — see DECRY 1
2 to make smaller in amount, volume, or extent — see DECREASE 1
3 to grow less in scope or intensity especially gradually — see DECREASE 2

diminishment *n* **1** the act of making a person or a

THESAURUS

thing seem little or unimportant — see DEPRECI-ATION

2 the amount by which something is lessened — see DECREASE

diminution *n* the amount by which something is lessened — see DECREASE

diminutive *adj* of a size that is less than average — see SMALL 1

diminutive *n* a living thing much smaller than others of its kind — see DWARF 1

diminutiveness *n* the quality or state of being little in size — see SMALLNESS

dimmed *adj* being without light or without much light — see DARK 1

din *n* loud, confused, and usually unharmonious sound — see NOISE 1

din *vb* to say or state again — see REPEAT 1

dine *vb* **1** to take a meal ⟨they *dined* elegantly at the city's finest restaurant before taking in an opera downtown⟩
synonyms eat, fare, feed
related words banquet, feast, fete (*or* fête); board, mess; breakfast, lunch, sup; picnic
2 to entertain with a fancy meal — see FEAST

diner *n* a public establishment where meals are served to paying customers for consumption on the premises — see RESTAURANT

dinghy *n* a boat equipped with one or more sails — see SAILBOAT

dinginess *n* the state or quality of being dirty — see DIRTINESS 1

dingy *adj* not clean — see DIRTY 1

dinky *adj* of a size that is less than average — see SMALL 1

dinner *n* a large fancy meal often accompanied by ceremony or entertainment — see FEAST

dinnerware *n* dishes used for eating or serving food or drink — see TABLEWARE 2

dinning *adj* making loud, confused, and usually unharmonious sounds — see NOISY 1

dint *n* a sunken area forming a separate space — see HOLE 2

dip *n* the act or process of going to a lower level or altitude — see DESCENT 1

dip *vb* **1** to sink or push (something) briefly into or as if into a liquid ⟨he went to *dip* a paper towel in water and clean off the window⟩ ⟨she *dipped* a hand into her pocket and pulled out a piece of candy⟩
synonyms douse, duck, dunk, immerse, souse, submerge, submerse
related words drench, flood, soak, wet; plunge, thrust
near antonyms pour; fill
2 to lift out with something that holds liquid ⟨they *dipped* water from the bucket to pour into the kettle⟩
synonyms lade, ladle, scoop, spoon
related words bail; deplete, drain, eliminate, exhaust; bleed, draw (off); dish; draw, siphon
near antonyms pour; fill
3 to go to a lower level — see DROP 2
4 to lead or extend downward — see DESCEND 1
5 to take a quick or hasty look — see GLANCE 2

diplomacy *n* the ability to deal with others in touchy situations without offending them — see TACT

diplomatic *adj* having or showing tact — see TACTFUL

dipper *n* a utensil with a bowl and a handle that is used especially in cooking and serving food — see SPOON

dire *adj* **1** being or showing a sign of evil or calamity to come — see OMINOUS
2 causing fear — see FEARFUL
3 needing immediate attention — see ACUTE 2

direct *adj* **1** done or working without something else coming in between ⟨a zoologist whose works are based entirely on her *direct* observation of animals in the wild⟩ ⟨the virus was the *direct* cause of the disease⟩
synonyms firsthand, immediate, primary
related words clinical
antonyms indirect, secondhand
2 free in expressing one's true feelings and opinions — see FRANK
3 going straight to the point clearly and firmly — see STRAIGHTFORWARD 1

direct *adv* in a direct line or course — see DIRECTLY 1

direct *vb* **1** to cause to move to a central point or along a restricted pathway — see CHANNEL
2 to issue orders to (someone) by right of authority — see COMMAND 1
3 to give an order — see COMMAND 2
4 to look after and make decisions about — see CONDUCT 1
5 to point or turn (something) toward a target or goal — see AIM 1
6 to point out the way for (someone) especially from a position in front — see LEAD 1

direction *n* **1** a statement of what to do that must be obeyed by those concerned — see COMMAND 1
2 the act or activity of looking after and making decisions about something — see CONDUCT 1

directive *n* **1** a statement of what to do that must be obeyed by those concerned — see COMMAND 1
2 an order publicly issued by an authority — see EDICT 1
3 a written communication giving information or directions — see MEMORANDUM 1

directly *adv* **1** in a direct line or course ⟨we went *directly* to the school without stopping⟩
synonyms dead, direct, due, plumb, plump, right, straight
phrases as the crow flies
near antonyms circuitously, deviously
antonyms indirectly
2 in an honest and direct manner — see STRAIGHTFORWARD
3 in the same words — see VERBATIM
4 without delay — see IMMEDIATELY

directness *n* the free expression of one's true feelings and opinions — see CANDOR

director *n* a person who manages or directs — see EXECUTIVE

directorial *adj* suited for or relating to the directing of things — see EXECUTIVE

direful *adj* causing fear — see FEARFUL 1

dirge *n* a composition expressing one's grief over a loss — see LAMENT 1

dirt *n* **1** the loose surface material in which plants naturally grow ⟨dig into the *dirt* to a depth of about three inches⟩
synonyms earth, ground, soil
related words clay, duff, dust, gravel, humus, loam, loess, marl, mud, sand, silt, subsoil, topsoil
2 the solid part of our planet's surface as distinguished from the sea and air — see EARTH 2

3 foul matter that mars the purity or cleanliness of something — see FILTH 1

4 the quality or state of being obscene — see OBSCENITY 1

dirtiness *n* **1** the state or quality of being dirty ⟨when the maid arrived, she exclaimed over the *dirtiness* of the china⟩

synonyms dinginess, dustiness, filthiness, foulness, griminess, grubbiness, nastiness, squalidness, uncleanliness, uncleanness

related words impurity; messiness, sloppiness, untidiness; shabbiness; squalor; smuttiness, sootiness

near antonyms purity

antonyms cleanliness, immaculateness, spotlessness

2 the quality or state of being obscene — see OBSCENITY 1

dirty *adj* **1** not clean ⟨after playing in the mud all day, his clothes were very *dirty*⟩

synonyms besmirched, blackened, dingy, dusty, filthy, foul, grimy, grubby, grungy, mucky, muddy, nasty, smutty, soiled, sordid, stained, sullied, unclean, uncleanly

related words contaminated, defiled, impure, polluted, tainted; uncleaned, unsanitary, unsterile, unsterilized, unwashed; discolored; bedraggled, draggled; chaotic, cluttered, confused, disarranged, disarrayed, disheveled (*or* dishevelled), disordered, jumbled, littered, messed, messy, muddled, mussed, mussy, rumpled, scruffy, sloppy, slovenly, unkempt, untidy; shabby, sleazy, squalid; smutty, sooty

near antonyms clear, limpid, pure; cleaned, cleansed, combed, groomed, neat, ordered, orderly, tidy; bleached, purified, whitened; bright, flawless, perfect, shiny, sparkling, unspotted, untouched; taintless, unblemished, undefiled, unpolluted, untainted, wholesome

antonyms clean, cleanly, immaculate, spick-and-span (*or* spic-and-span), spotless, stainless, unsoiled, unstained, unsullied

2 depicting or referring to sexual matters in a way that is unacceptable in polite society — see OBSCENE 1

3 marked by wet and windy conditions — see FOUL 1

4 not being in accordance with the rules or standards of what is fair in sport — see FOUL 2

5 not following or in accordance with standards of honor and decency — see IGNOBLE 2

dirty *vb* to make dirty ⟨she *dirtied* her new shoes when she splashed in the puddle⟩

synonyms befoul, begrime, besmirch, blacken, foul, grime, mire, muddy, smirch, smudge, soil, stain, sully

related words contaminate, defile, pollute, taint; discolor; confuse, disarrange, disarray, dishevel, disorder, jumble, mess, muddle

near antonyms decontaminate, purge, purify; disinfect, sanitize; brush, dry-clean, dust, launder, mop, rinse, scour, scrub, sweep, wash, wipe; brighten, deodorize, freshen, renew, spruce (up); straighten (up), tidy (up)

antonyms clean, cleanse

dis *vb, slang* **1** to cause hurt feelings or deep resentment in — see INSULT

2 to express one's unfavorable opinion of the worth or quality of — see CRITICIZE

disable *vb* **1** to cause severe or permanent injury to — see MAIM

2 to render powerless, ineffective, or unable to move — see PARALYZE

disabled *adj* deprived of the power to perform one or more natural bodily activities ⟨the *disabled* man was unable to climb the stairs without help⟩

synonyms challenged, incapacitated

related words blind, deaf, mute; halt, lame, paralyzed, quadriplegic; immobile, immobilized; ailing, diseased, ill, sick, unfit, unhealthy, unsound, unwell

near antonyms bouncing, chipper, fit, hale, healthy, hearty, robust, sound, well, whole, wholesome

antonyms able-bodied, nondisabled

disabuse *vb* to free from mistaken beliefs or foolish hopes — see DISILLUSION

disadvantage *n* a feature of someone or something that creates difficulty for achieving success ⟨their lack of height was a *disadvantage* on the basketball court⟩

synonyms drawback, handicap, liability, minus, penalty, strike

related words stranglehold; detriment, disability, impairment; failing, shortcoming; bar, catch, check, clog, crimp, embarrassment, hindrance, hitch, hurdle, impediment, interference, let, manacle, obstacle, obstruction, rub, shackle, stop, trammel

near antonyms vantage; head start, jump, lead, margin, start; ascendancy, better, command, control, drop, mastery, predominance, superiority, supremacy, transcendence, upper hand; prerogative, privilege; break, opportunity; aid, assistance, help

antonyms advantage, asset, edge, plus

disadvantaged *adj* kept from having the necessities of life or a healthful environment — see DEPRIVED

disadvantageous *adj* opposed to one's interests — see ADVERSE 1

disaffect *vb* **1** to cause to change from friendly or loving to unfriendly or uncaring — see ESTRANGE

2 to make discontented — see DISCONTENT

disaffection *n* the loss of friendship or affection — see ESTRANGEMENT

disagree *vb* **1** to have a different opinion ⟨she thought we were still headed north on the trail, but I *disagreed*⟩

synonyms differ, dissent

related words clash, collide, conflict, contrast; counter, debate, object, oppose, protest, resist; contest, dispute; argue, bicker, fall out, quarrel

near antonyms accede, accept, acquiesce, comply, consent, subscribe; affiliate, ally, associate, collaborate, collude, compromise, cooperate, get along, side

antonyms agree, assent, concur

2 to be unlike; to not be the same — see DIFFER 1

disagree (with) *vb* to make an assertion that is contrary to one made by (another) — see CONTRADICT 1

disagreeable *adj* **1** having or showing a habitually bad temper — see ILL-TEMPERED

2 not giving pleasure to the mind or senses — see UNPLEASANT

disagreeing *adj* not being in agreement or harmony — see INCONSISTENT

disagreement *n* **1** variance of opinion on a matter ⟨there was some *disagreement* about what the color of the missing sweater actually was⟩
synonyms controversy, debate, difference, disputation, dispute, dissension
related words clash, collision, conflict, contention, discord, strife; discussion; altercation, argument, bicker, falling-out, fight, quarrel
near antonyms acceptance, compliance; concord, peace
antonyms accord, agreement, consensus, harmony, unanimity
2 an often noisy or angry expression of differing opinions — see ARGUMENT 1
3 the quality or state of being different — see DIFFERENCE 1
disallow *vb* **1** to declare not to be true — see DENY 1
2 to be unwilling to grant — see DENY 2
disallowance *n* **1** an unwillingness to grant something asked for — see DENIAL 1
2 a refusal to confirm the truth of a statement — see DENIAL 2
disappear *vb* to cease to be visible ⟨the stranger *disappeared* into the mists, never to be seen again⟩
synonyms dissolve, evanesce, evaporate, fade, flee, go (away), melt, vanish
related words clear, dissipate
near antonyms arrive, break out, come out, emerge, issue, loom, show up
antonyms appear, materialize
disappoint *vb* to fall short in satisfying the expectation or hope of ⟨they were *disappointed* by the outcome of the big game⟩
synonyms cheat, dissatisfy, fail, let down
related words discontent, disgruntle, displease; disenchant, disillusion
near antonyms gladden
antonyms satisfy
disappointment *n* **1** the emotion felt when one's expectations are not met ⟨we felt *disappointment* after failing a test that we thought would be easy⟩
synonyms dismay, dissatisfaction, frustration, letdown
related words disenchantment, disillusionment; blues, dejection, depression, desolateness, desolation, despondency, disconsolateness, distress, doldrums, dolefulness, dolor, downheartedness, dreariness, dumps, gloom, gloominess, joylessness, melancholy, mopes, oppression, sadness, sorrow, unhappiness; alarm, concern, consternation; chagrin, discomfiture
near antonyms bliss, felicity, gladness, happiness, joy
antonyms contentment, gratification, satisfaction
2 something that disappoints ⟨after all the publicity and high expectations, the sequel to the movie blockbuster was a *disappointment*⟩
synonyms bummer, letdown
related words anticlimax, failure, fiasco, fizzle; lemon, loser
near antonyms success, winner; relief
disapprobation *n* refusal to accept as right or desirable — see DISAPPROVAL
disapproval *n* refusal to accept as right or desirable ⟨thus far, every one of her boyfriends has met with her parents' *disapproval*⟩
synonyms deprecation, disapprobation, disfavor, dislike, displeasure
related words blame, censure, criticism, condemnation, denunciation, dressing down, opprobrium, reproach, reprobation; antagonism, antipathy, hostility; belittlement, disparagement, opposition
near antonyms acclaim, commendation, praise; endorsement, sanction; empathy, sympathy
antonyms approbation, approval, favor
disapprove *vb* to show unwillingness to accept, do, engage in, or agree to — see DECLINE 1
disapprove (of) *vb* to hold an unfavorable opinion of ⟨my sister *disapproves of* smoking and refuses to date anyone who thinks it's cool⟩
synonyms deprecate, discountenance, disfavor, dislike, frown (on), reprove
related words blame, censure, condemn, criticize, denounce, reprehend, reprobate; chide, rebuke, reproach, scold
near antonyms endorse (*also* indorse), sanction, support; adore, delight (in), dig, enjoy, fancy, groove (on), love, relish, revel (in)
antonyms approve, favor, like
disarm *vb* **1** to reduce the size and strength of the armed forces of ⟨the defeated nation was *disarmed* so that it would never again be a threat to international order⟩
synonyms demilitarize
related words demobilize
near antonyms equip, mobilize
antonyms arm, militarize
2 to lessen the anger or agitation of — see PACIFY
disarmament *n* the reduction or elimination of a country's armed forces or weapons ⟨the ambassador spoke at length about the possible unilateral *disarmament* of his country⟩
synonyms demilitarization
related words demobilization
near antonyms mobilization
antonyms militarization
disarming *adj* **1** having qualities that tend to make one loved — see LOVABLE
2 likely to win one's affection — see INGRATIATING
3 tending to lessen or avoid conflict or hostility — see PACIFIC 1
disarrange *vb* to undo the proper order or arrangement of — see DISORDER
disarranged *adj* lacking in order, neatness, and often cleanliness — see MESSY
disarrangement *n* a state in which everything is out of order — see CHAOS
disarray *n* a state in which everything is out of order — see CHAOS
disarray *vb* to undo the proper order or arrangement of — see DISORDER
disarrayed *adj* lacking in order, neatness, and often cleanliness — see MESSY
disassemble *vb* to take apart ⟨they had to *disassemble* the television set in order to replace the wiring⟩
synonyms demount, dismantle, dismember, knock down, strike, take down
related words detach, disengage; disconnect, disjoin, disunite, divide, separate
near antonyms build, erect; combine, unite
antonyms assemble, construct, put together
disaster *n* a sudden violent event that brings about great loss or destruction ⟨hurricanes are natural *disasters*⟩

synonyms calamity, cataclysm, catastrophe, debacle (*also* débâcle), tragedy
related words collapse, crash, meltdown; convulsion, paroxysm, upheaval; accident, casualty, fatality; misadventure, mischance, misfortune, mishap, woe; bummer, downer
near antonyms godsend, manna, windfall

disastrous *adj* **1** bringing about ruin or misfortune — see FATAL 1
2 causing or tending to cause destruction — see DESTRUCTIVE 1

disavow *vb* **1** to declare not to be true — see DENY 1
2 to refuse to acknowledge as one's own or as one's responsibility — see DISCLAIM 1

disavowal *n* a refusal to confirm the truth of a statement — see DENIAL 2

disband *vb* **1** to cease to exist or cause to cease to exist as a group or organization ⟨they *disbanded* the committee after the report had been submitted⟩ ⟨the rock group *disbanded* upon finishing the tour⟩
synonyms break up, disperse, dissolve
near antonyms incorporate; consolidate
antonyms band, join, unite
2 to cause (members of a group) to move widely apart — see SCATTER 1

disbandment *n* an act or process in which something scatters or is scattered — see SCATTERING 1

disbelief *n* refusal to accept as true ⟨their story explaining their absence was met with frank *disbelief*⟩
synonyms incredulity, unbelief
related words distrust, doubt, mistrust, skepticism, suspicion, uncertainty; denial, rejection, repudiation
near antonyms acceptance, faith; trust
antonyms belief, credence, credit

disbelieve *vb* to think not to be true or real ⟨many *disbelieved* the medium's claims that she could communicate with the spirits of the dead⟩
synonyms discredit, negate
related words deny, reject, repudiate; distrust, doubt, mistrust, suspect; debunk, disprove; deride, pooh-pooh, scoff (at)
near antonyms trust
antonyms accept, believe, credit, swallow

disbeliever *n* a person who is always ready to doubt or question the truth or existence of something — see SKEPTIC

disbelieving *adj* inclined to doubt or question claims — see SKEPTICAL 1

disburden *vb* **1** to empty or rid of cargo — see UNLOAD 1
2 to set (a person or thing) free of something that encumbers — see RID

disburse *vb* to hand over or use up in payment — see SPEND 1

disbursement *n* **1** a payment made in the course of achieving a result — see EXPENSE
2 the act of offering money in exchange for goods or services — see PAYMENT 1

discard *n* something separated from a group or lot for not being as good as the others — see CULL

discard *vb* to get rid of as useless or unwanted ⟨*discard* an old, torn sweater⟩
synonyms cast, ditch, dump, fling (off *or* away), jettison, junk, lose, reject, scrap, shed, shuck (off), slough (*also* sluff), throw away, throw out, unload

related words abandon, desert, forsake; dismiss; abolish, annihilate, eliminate, eradicate, expunge, exterminate, extinguish, extirpate, liquidate, remove, root (out), stamp (out), wipe out
phrases dispose of, set aside
near antonyms adopt, embrace, take on; employ, use, utilize; hold, hold back, keep, retain

discarding *n* the getting rid of whatever is unwanted or useless — see DISPOSAL 1

discern *vb* **1** to make note of (something) through the use of one's eyes — see SEE 1
2 to understand or point out the difference — see DISTINGUISH 1

discernible *adj* able to be perceived by a sense or by the mind — see PERCEPTIBLE

discerning *adj* having or showing deep understanding and intelligent application of knowledge — see WISE 1

discernment *n* the ability to understand inner qualities or relationships — see WISDOM 1

discharge *n* **1** a directed propelling of a missile by a firearm or artillery piece — see SHOT
2 a freeing from an obligation or responsibility — see RELEASE 1
3 the termination of the employment of an employee or a work force often temporarily — see LAYOFF
4 the doing of an action — see COMMISSION 2

discharge *vb* **1** to cause (a projectile) to be driven forward with force — see SHOOT 1
2 to empty or rid of cargo — see UNLOAD 1
3 to give what is owed for — see PAY 2
4 to set free (as from slavery or confinement) — see FREE 1
5 to throw or give off — see EMIT 1
6 to cause a weapon to release a missile with great force — see SHOOT 2

disciple *n* one who follows the opinions or teachings of another — see FOLLOWER

disciplinary *adj* inflicting, involving, or serving as punishment — see PUNITIVE

discipline *n* **1** a region of activity, knowledge, or influence — see FIELD 2
2 suffering, loss, or hardship imposed in response to a crime or offense — see PUNISHMENT

discipline *vb* to inflict a penalty on for a fault or crime — see PUNISH

disciplining *adj* inflicting, involving, or serving as punishment — see PUNITIVE

disclaim *vb* **1** to refuse to acknowledge as one's own or as one's responsibility ⟨the prisoner *disclaimed* any part in the prank⟩
synonyms disavow, disown, repudiate
related words contradict, deny, disallow, gainsay, negate, negative, refuse, reject; challenge, confute, criticize, disprove, rebut, refute; dispute, question
near antonyms accept, adopt, embrace, espouse; admit, concede, confess, grant; affirm, announce, assert, aver, declare, maintain, profess, submit; authenticate, confirm, corroborate, substantiate, validate, verify
antonyms acknowledge, avow, claim, own, recognize
2 to declare not to be true — see DENY 1

disclaimer *n* a refusal to confirm the truth of a statement — see DENIAL 2

disclose *vb* to make known (as information previously kept secret) — see REVEAL 1

disclosure *n* the act or an instance of making

known something previously unknown or concealed — see REVELATION

disco *n* a bar or restaurant offering special nighttime entertainment (as music, dancing, or comedy acts) — see NIGHTCLUB

discomfit *vb* to throw into a state of self-conscious distress — see EMBARRASS 1

discomfiting *adj* causing embarrassment — see AWKWARD 3

discomfiture *n* the emotional state of being made self-consciously uncomfortable — see EMBARRASSMENT 1

discomfort *vb* to trouble the mind of; to make uneasy — see DISTURB 1

discomforting *adj* 1 causing discomfort — see UNCOMFORTABLE 1
2 causing worry or anxiety — see TROUBLESOME

discommode *vb* to cause discomfort to or trouble for — see INCONVENIENCE

discommoding *adj* causing difficulty, discomfort, or annoyance — see INCONVENIENT 1

discompose *vb* 1 to trouble the mind of; to make uneasy — see DISTURB 1
2 to undo the proper order or arrangement of — see DISORDER

discomposing *adj* causing worry or anxiety — see TROUBLESOME

disconcert *vb* to throw into a state of self-conscious distress — see EMBARRASS 1

disconcerting *adj* causing embarrassment — see AWKWARD 3

disconnect *vb* to set or force apart — see SEPARATE 1

disconnected *adj* 1 not clearly or logically connected — see INCOHERENT 1
2 not physically attached to another unit — see SEPARATE 2

disconsolate *adj* feeling unhappiness — see SAD 1

disconsolateness *n* a state or spell of low spirits — see SADNESS

discontent *adj* having a feeling that one has been wronged or thwarted in one's ambitions — see DISCONTENTED

discontent *n* the condition of being dissatisfied with one's life or situation ⟨the rebels tried to stir up *discontent* among the citizens⟩
synonyms discontentedness, discontentment, disgruntlement, displeasure, dissatisfaction
related words bitterness, resentment; disquiet, perturbation, uneasiness; blues, dejection, depression, desolateness, desolation, despondency, disconsolateness, doldrums, dolefulness, dolor, downheartedness, dreariness, dumps; misery, sadness, sorrow, unhappiness, wretchedness
near antonyms bliss, felicity, gladness, happiness, joy, lightheartedness; elatedness, exultation, jubilation, triumph
antonyms contentedness, contentment, pleasure, satisfaction

discontent *vb* to make discontented ⟨the ongoing lack of decent food *discontented* and demoralized the soldiers in the rebel army⟩
synonyms disaffect, disgruntle, displease, dissatisfy
related words alienate, estrange; agitate, discompose, disquiet, disturb, perturb, upset; annoy, irk, irritate, nettle, peeve; depress, sadden
near antonyms delight, gladden, tickle; calm, soothe, tranquilize (*also* tranquillize)
antonyms content, gratify, please, satisfy

discontented *adj* having a feeling that one has been wronged or thwarted in one's ambitions ⟨he was *discontented* with his small role in the school play⟩
synonyms aggrieved, discontent, disgruntled, displeased, dissatisfied, malcontent
related words disappointed, frustrated, unfulfilled; disquieted, disturbed, perturbed, upset; dejected, depressed, despairing, despondent, disconsolate, doleful, down, downcast, downhearted, forlorn, hangdog, inconsolable, joyless, low-spirited, miserable, mournful, sad, sorrowful, unhappy
near antonyms blissful, delighted, glad, happy, joyful, joyous; elated, exultant, jubilant, triumphant
antonyms content, contented, gratified, pleased, satisfied

discontentedness *n* the condition of being dissatisfied with one's life or situation — see DISCONTENT

discontentment *n* the condition of being dissatisfied with one's life or situation — see DISCONTENT

discontinuance *n* the stopping of a process or activity — see END 1

discontinue *vb* 1 to bring (as an action or operation) to an immediate end — see STOP 1
2 to stop doing (something) permanently — see QUIT 2
3 to come to an end — see CEASE 1

discontinuity *n* 1 an open space in a barrier (as a wall or hedge) — see GAP 1
2 a break in continuity — see GAP 2

discontinuous *adj* lacking in steadiness or regularity of occurrence — see FITFUL

discord *n* a lack of agreement or harmony ⟨the *discord* between the two scout leaders threatened to tear our troop apart⟩
synonyms conflict, discordance, dissension, dissent, dissidence, disunity, friction, schism, strife, variance, war, warfare
related words clash, collision, competition, contention; altercation, argument, bicker, brawl, debate, disagreement, dispute, falling-out, fight, hassle, jar, quarrel, row, run-in, scrap, spat, squabble, tiff, wrangle; incompatibility, incongruity, inconsistency, inconsonance; animosity, antagonism, antipathy, enmity, hostility, ill will, rancor
near antonyms concurrence, cooperation
antonyms accord, agreement, concord, concordance, harmony, peace

discordance *n* 1 a lack of agreement or harmony — see DISCORD
2 loud, confused, and usually unharmonious sound — see NOISE 1

discordant *adj* 1 marked by or producing a harsh combination of sounds — see DISSONANT
2 making loud, confused, and usually unharmonious sounds — see NOISY 1
3 feeling or displaying eagerness to fight — see BELLIGERENT
4 not being in agreement or harmony — see INCONSISTENT

discotheque *n* a bar or restaurant offering special nighttime entertainment (as music, dancing, or comedy acts) — see NIGHTCLUB

discount *n* something that is or may be subtracted — see DEDUCTION 1

discount *vb* to express scornfully one's low opinion of — see DECRY 1

discountenance *vb* **1** to hold an unfavorable opinion of — see DISAPPROVE

2 to throw into a state of self-conscious distress — see EMBARRASS 1

discourage *vb* **1** to lessen the courage or confidence of ⟨I didn't let losing *discourage* me from trying again⟩
synonyms daunt, demoralize, dishearten, dismay, dispirit, unman, unnerve
related words browbeat, bully, cow, intimidate; depress, sadden, weigh; afflict, try; damp, dampen, deaden; distress, trouble; bother, irk, vex, worry; debilitate, enfeeble, undermine, weaken; frighten, horrify, scare
near antonyms buoy (up), cheer, gladden; animate, enliven, invigorate; fortify, reinforce, strengthen; assure, reassure; boost, energize, excite, galvanize, inspire, lift, provoke, quicken, rally, stimulate, stir
antonyms embolden, encourage, hearten, nerve, steel

2 to steer (a person) from an activity or course of action ⟨the higher fines may help *discourage* drivers from speeding on the highway⟩
synonyms deter, dissuade, inhibit
related words divert
near antonyms egg (on), exhort, goad, prod, urge; impel, induce, prompt
antonyms encourage, persuade

discouragement *n* the state of being discouraged ⟨we tried to avoid *discouragement* after failing the test twice⟩
synonyms demoralization, despair, despondency, disheartenment, dismay, dispiritedness
related words blues, dejection, depression, dumps, gloom, melancholy, mopes; defeatism, pessimism, resignation
near antonyms optimism, sanguinity
antonyms encouragement

discourse *n* **1** an exchange of views for the purpose of exploring a subject or deciding an issue — see DISCUSSION 1

2 talking or a talk between two or more people — see CONVERSATION

discourse *vb* **1** to give a formal often extended talk on a subject — see TALK 1

2 to talk as if giving an important and formal speech — see ORATE 1

discourteous *adj* showing a lack of manners or consideration for others — see IMPOLITE

discourteousness *n* rude behavior — see DISCOURTESY

discourtesy *n* rude behavior ⟨the courtiers shuddered at the *discourtesy* shown to the king⟩
synonyms discourteousness, disrespect, impertinence, impoliteness, impudence, incivility, inconsideration, insolence, rudeness, ungraciousness
related words audacity, boldness, brashness, brassiness, sauciness, shamelessness; boorishness, churlishness, clownishness, crudeness, loutishness, vulgarity; abruptness, bluntness, brusqueness, crustiness, curtness, gruffness, sharpness; crabbedness, crossness, disagreeableness, grumpiness, sullenness, surliness; impropriety, inappropriateness, incorrectness, indecency, unfitness, unsuitability; arrogance, conceit, conceitedness, presumption, pretense (*or* pretence), pretension, pretentiousness

near antonyms humility, meekness, modesty; deference, dutifulness, respectfulness, submissiveness; acceptability, appropriateness, correctness, decency, decorousness, fitness, goodness, propriety, respectability, respectableness, rightness, seemliness, suitability, suitableness; affability, cordiality, friendliness, geniality, hospitality; felicitousness, grace, gracefulness
antonyms civility, considerateness, consideration, courtesy, genteelness, gentility, graciousness, politeness, thoughtfulness

discover *vb* **1** to come to an awareness ⟨I was startled to *discover* that my keys were missing⟩
synonyms ascertain, catch on, find out, hear, learn, realize, see
related words hit (on *or* upon), tumble (to); descry, detect, encounter, espy, spot; dope (out), figure out, puzzle (out); discern, note, observe, perceive; divine
near antonyms miss, overlook; disregard, ignore; forget, unlearn; blanket, blot out, cloak, conceal, cover, curtain, enshroud, hide, mask, occult, screen, shroud, veil

2 to come upon after searching, study, or effort — see FIND 1

3 to make known (as information previously kept secret) — see REVEAL 1

discovery *n* **1** the act or process of sighting or learning the existence of something for the first time ⟨the *discovery* of a new species of starfish⟩
synonyms detection, finding, spotting, unearthing
related words disclosure, exposure, revelation, uncovering, unveiling; creation, invention; exploration; rediscovery
near antonyms concealment, hiding

2 something discovered ⟨his many zoological *discoveries* included several species of birds⟩
synonyms find
related words pay dirt, strike, treasure trove; breakthrough

discredit *n* the state of having lost the esteem of others — see DISGRACE 1

discredit *vb* **1** to reduce to a lower standing in one's own eyes or in others' eyes — see HUMBLE

2 to think not to be true or real — see DISBELIEVE

discreditable *adj* not respectable — see DISREPUTABLE

discreet *adj* having or showing good judgment and restraint especially in conduct or speech ⟨he was very *discreet*, only saying what was necessary⟩
synonyms judicious, prudent
related words cautious, chary, circumspect; foresighted, forethoughtful; discerning, discriminating, sage, sane, sapient, sensible, wise; canny, provident; astute, perspicacious, sagacious, shrewd
near antonyms careless, heedless; improvident, shortsighted; foolish, unwise
antonyms imprudent, indiscreet, injudicious

discreetness *n* the ability to make intelligent decisions especially in everyday matters — see COMMON SENSE

discrepancy *n* the quality or state of being different — see DIFFERENCE 1

discrepant *adj* not being in agreement or harmony — see INCONSISTENT

discrete *adj* not physically attached to another unit — see SEPARATE 2

discreteness *n* the state of being kept distinct — see SEPARATION 2

discretion *n* **1** the ability to make intelligent decisions especially in everyday matters — see COMMON SENSE

2 the power, right, or opportunity to choose — see CHOICE 1

discretionary *adj* subject to one's freedom of choice — see OPTIONAL

discriminate *vb* to understand or point out the difference — see DISTINGUISH 1

discriminating *adj* favoring, applying, or being unequal treatment of different classes of people — see DISCRIMINATORY

discrimination *n* the state of being kept distinct — see SEPARATION 2

discriminational *adj* favoring, applying, or being unequal treatment of different classes of people — see DISCRIMINATORY

discriminative *adj* favoring, applying, or being unequal treatment of different classes of people — see DISCRIMINATORY

discriminatory *adj* favoring, applying, or being unequal treatment of different classes of people ⟨a company that was fined for its *discriminatory* practices in the hiring of women⟩
synonyms differential, discriminating, discriminational, discriminative
related words biased, inequitable, partial, partisan, prejudiced, prejudicial, unequal, unfair, unjust
near antonyms equal, equitable, fair, just; impartial, neutral, objective, unbiased, uncolored, unprejudiced
antonyms nondiscriminatory

discursive *adj* passing from one topic to another ⟨the speaker's *discursive* style made it difficult to understand his point⟩
synonyms desultory, digressive, leaping, maundering, rambling
related words circuitous, deviating, devious, roundabout
near antonyms focused (*also* focussed)

discuss *vb* to talk about (an issue) usually from various points of view and for the purpose of arriving at a decision or opinion ⟨we *discussed* the new proposal for the school stadium⟩
synonyms argue, bandy, chew over, debate, dispute, hash (over), moot, talk over
related words descant (on), lecture (on *or* about), speak (about), talk (about); broach, introduce; forge, hammer (out), thrash (out); consider, deliberate, weigh; reason (with)

discussion *n* **1** an exchange of views for the purpose of exploring a subject or deciding an issue ⟨the *discussion* about the club budget went on for hours⟩
synonyms argument, colloquy, conference, deliberation, discourse, give-and-take, parley, talk
related words debate, dialogue (*also* dialog); forum, meeting, powwow, roundtable, seminar, symposium; chat, conversation, rap

2 talking or a talk between two or more people — see CONVERSATION

disdain *n* open dislike for someone or something considered unworthy of one's concern or respect — see CONTEMPT

disdain *vb* to show contempt for — see SCORN 1

disdainful *adj* **1** feeling or showing open dislike for someone or something regarded as undeserving of respect or concern — see CONTEMPTUOUS 1

2 having or displaying feelings of scorn for what is regarded as beneath oneself — see PROUD 1

3 intended to make a person or thing seem of little importance or value — see DEROGATORY

disease *n* an abnormal state that disrupts a plant's or animal's normal bodily functioning ⟨they caught a rare *disease* while they were traveling in Africa and were sick for weeks⟩
synonyms affection, ailment, bug, complaint, complication, condition, disorder, fever, ill, illness, infirmity, malady, sickness, trouble
related words contagion, contagious disease; infection, infectious disease; deficiency disease; attack, bout, fit, spell; debility, decrepitude, feebleness, frailness, lameness, weakness; malaise, matter; pest, pestilence, plague
near antonyms fitness, healthiness, heartiness, robustness, soundness, wholeness, wholesomeness
antonyms health, wellness

disembark *vb* to go ashore from a ship ⟨the cruise passengers *disembarked* as soon as they got to the terminal in Miami⟩
synonyms debark, land
related words beach; anchor, dock, put in
near antonyms board, get (on); weigh (anchor)
antonyms embark

disembowel *vb* to take the internal organs out of — see GUT

disenchant *vb* to free from mistaken beliefs or foolish hopes — see DISILLUSION

disencumber *vb* **1** to empty or rid of cargo — see UNLOAD 1

2 to set (a person or thing) free of something that encumbers — see RID

disencumbered *adj* no longer burdened with something unpleasant or painful — see FREE 2

disengage *vb* to set free from entanglement or difficulty — see EXTRICATE

disentangle *vb* **1** to separate the various strands of — see UNRAVEL 1

2 to set free from entanglement or difficulty — see EXTRICATE

disfavor *n* **1** a strong feeling of not liking or approving — see DISLIKE 1

2 refusal to accept as right or desirable — see DISAPPROVAL

disfavor *vb* **1** to feel dislike for — see DISLIKE 1

2 to hold an unfavorable opinion of — see DISAPPROVE

disfigure *vb* to reduce the soundness, effectiveness, or perfection of — see DAMAGE 1

disfigurement *n* something that spoils the appearance or completeness of a thing — see BLEMISH

disgorge *vb* to throw out or off (something from within) often violently — see ERUPT 1

disgrace *n* **1** the state of having lost the esteem of others ⟨the players who threw the game were in *disgrace* with their schoolmates⟩
synonyms discredit, dishonor, disrepute, ignominy, infamy, odium, opprobrium, reproach, shame
related words contempt, disdain, scorn; deprecation, disapprobation, disapproval, disfavor; abasement, debasement, debasing, degradation, humbling, humiliation; blot, brand, slur, smirch, spot, stain, stigma
near antonyms admiration, regard; awe, fear, reverence; fame, glory, renown, repute
antonyms esteem, honor, respect

2 a cause of shame ⟨the exposure of his criminal activities was a huge *disgrace* for the councilman⟩
synonyms crime, dishonor, reflection, reproach, scandal
related words brand, smirch, spot, stain, stigma
antonyms credit, honor
3 a regrettable or blameworthy act — see CRIME 2
disgrace *vb* to reduce to a lower standing in one's own eyes or in others' eyes — see HUMBLE
disgraceful *adj* not respectable — see DISREPUTABLE
disgruntle *vb* **1** to cause to change from friendly or loving to unfriendly or uncaring — see ESTRANGE
2 to make discontented — see DISCONTENT
disgruntled *adj* having a feeling that one has been wronged or thwarted in one's ambitions — see DISCONTENTED
disgruntlement *n* **1** the condition of being dissatisfied with one's life or situation — see DISCONTENT
2 the loss of friendship or affection — see ESTRANGEMENT
disguise *n* clothing put on to hide one's true identity or imitate someone or something else ⟨Mardi Gras revelers dressed in a colorful array of outlandish *disguises*⟩
synonyms camouflage, costume, guise
related words domino, mask, veil, vizard; dress, getup, outfit, rig; coloring, cosmetic, makeup, paint
disguise *vb* to change the dress or looks of so as to conceal true identity ⟨the spies *disguised* themselves as harmless tourists⟩
synonyms camouflage, cloak, dress up, mask
related words blanket, blot out, conceal, cover, curtain, enshroud, hide, obscure, occult, screen, shroud, veil; affect, assume, counterfeit, dissemble, dissimulate, feign, pose, pretend, sham, simulate
near antonyms display, exhibit, expose, flaunt, parade, show, uncover, unmask; betray, disclose, discover, reveal
disgust *n* a dislike so strong as to cause stomach upset or queasiness ⟨we turned from the grisly scene with *disgust*⟩
synonyms aversion, distaste, loathing, nausea, repugnance, repulsion, revulsion
related words abhorrence, abomination, execration, hate, hatred; disapproval, disfavor, disinclination, dislike, disliking, displeasure
near antonyms appetite, bent, fondness, like, liking, partiality, penchant, predilection, preference, propensity, taste
disgust *vb* to cause to feel disgust ⟨the usual school lunch *disgusted* us, so we started bringing our lunches from home⟩
synonyms nauseate, repel, repulse, revolt, sicken, turn off
related words displease, distress; appall, horrify; affront, insult, offend, outrage, shock
near antonyms attract, charm, entice, tempt; delight, gratify, please, rejoice, tickle
disgusted *adj* filled with disgust — see SICK 2
dish *n* a usually circular utensil for holding something (as food) ⟨we threw all of the ingredients for the salsa into a *dish* and mixed them together⟩
synonyms vessel
related words bowl, casserole, charger, cup, plate, platter, salver, saucer, tray

dishearten *vb* to lessen the courage or confidence of — see DISCOURAGE 1
disheartenment *n* the state of being discouraged — see DISCOURAGEMENT
dishevel *vb* to undo the proper order or arrangement of — see DISORDER
disheveled *or* **dishevelled** *adj* lacking in order, neatness, and often cleanliness — see MESSY
dishonest *adj* **1** telling or containing lies ⟨*dishonest* kids who lie about their ages in order to get into R-rated movies⟩ ⟨*dishonest* statements about the fight in the locker room⟩
synonyms lying, mendacious, untruthful
related words erroneous, fallacious, false, misleading; double-dealing, hypocritical, two-faced
near antonyms candid, open, straightforward; earnest, sincere, true
antonyms honest, truthful, veracious
2 given to or marked by cheating and deception ⟨*dishonest* car dealers who roll back mileage gauges⟩ ⟨*dishonest* business deals that landed him in jail⟩
synonyms crooked, deceptive, fast, fraudulent, shady, sharp, shifty, underhand, underhanded
related words unconscionable, unethical, unprincipled, unscrupulous; deceitful, deceiving, deluding, delusive, delusory; artful, cunning; devious, furtive, sneaking, sneaky, tricky; insidious, perfidious, treacherous
near antonyms conscientious, honorable, just, scrupulous, upright; forthright, straightforward
antonyms aboveboard, honest, straight
3 marked by, based on, or done by the use of dishonest methods to acquire something of value — see FRAUDULENT 1
dishonesty *n* **1** the tendency to tell lies ⟨if you gain a reputation for *dishonesty*, no one will believe you even when you're telling the truth⟩
synonyms deceitfulness, mendacity, untruthfulness
related words artifice, craft, craftiness, crookedness, cunning, deceit, dissembling, dissimulation, double-dealing, duplicity, fakery, foxiness, guile, wiliness; falseness; hypocrisy
near antonyms honor, incorruptibility; candidness, candor, frankness, good faith, sincerity, straightforwardness; dependability, reliability, reliableness, trustworthiness; accuracy, objectivity; authenticity, correctness, genuineness; credibility
antonyms honesty, integrity, probity, truthfulness, veracity, verity
2 the inclination or practice of misleading others through lies or trickery — see DECEIT
dishonor *n* **1** the state of having lost the esteem of others — see DISGRACE 1
2 a cause of shame — see DISGRACE 2
dishonor *vb* to reduce to a lower standing in one's own eyes or in others' eyes — see HUMBLE
dishonorable *adj* **1** not following or in accordance with standards of honor and decency — see IGNOBLE 2
2 not respectable — see DISREPUTABLE
disillusion *vb* to free from mistaken beliefs or foolish hopes ⟨we were *disillusioned* when we saw how the movie star acted in real life⟩
synonyms disabuse, disenchant, undeceive
related words debunk, expose, show up, uncloak, uncover, unmask; disclose, divulge, tell, unveil
near antonyms beguile, bluff, cozen, delude, dupe, fool, gull, hoax, hoodwink, kid, misguide,

misinform, mislead, misrepresent, snow, take in, trick

disinclination *n* **1** a lack of willingness or desire to do or accept something — see RELUCTANCE

2 a strong feeling of not liking or approving — see DISLIKE 1

disinclined *adj* having doubts about the wisdom of doing something — see HESITANT

disintegrate *vb* to go through decomposition — see DECAY 1

disinter *vb* to remove from place of burial — see EXHUME

disinterested *adj* **1** having or showing a lack of interest or concern — see INDIFFERENT 1

2 marked by justice, honesty, and freedom from bias — see FAIR 2

disinterestedness *n* **1** lack of favoritism toward one side or another — see DETACHMENT 1

2 lack of interest or concern — see INDIFFERENCE

disjoin *vb* to set or force apart — see SEPARATE 1

disjoint *vb* to set or force apart — see SEPARATE 1

disjointed *adj* not clearly or logically connected — see INCOHERENT 1

dislike *n* **1** a strong feeling of not liking or approving ⟨we have a strong *dislike* for olives and wouldn't eat them even if we were paid⟩

synonyms allergy, averseness, aversion, disfavor, disinclination, disliking

related words disgust, distaste, loathing, nausea, repugnance, repulsion, revulsion; abomination, antipathy, detestation, hate, hatred; deprecation, disapproval, displeasure, dissatisfaction; jaundice

near antonyms affection, attachment, love; bent, leaning, penchant, predilection, propensity, tendency

antonyms appetite, fondness, like, liking, partiality, preference, taste

2 refusal to accept as right or desirable — see DISAPPROVAL

dislike *vb* **1** to feel dislike for ⟨the two dogs *disliked* each other the first time they met, and never did become friends⟩

synonyms disfavor

related words abhor, abominate, detest, hate, loathe; condemn, despise, scorn; disapprove (of), frown (on *or* upon), object (to)

near antonyms admire, appreciate, cherish, revere, venerate, worship; prize, treasure, value; drink (in), savor; dote (on), idolize; favor, prefer

antonyms adore, cotton (to), delight (in), dig, enjoy, fancy, groove (on), like, love, relish, revel (in)

2 to hold an unfavorable opinion of — see DISAPPROVE

disliking *n* a strong feeling of not liking or approving — see DISLIKE 1

dislocate *vb* **1** to change the place or position of — see MOVE 1

2 to undo the proper order or arrangement of — see DISORDER

dislocation *n* an act or instance of the order of things being disturbed — see UPSET

disloyal *adj* not true in one's allegiance to someone or something — see FAITHLESS

disloyalty *n* **1** lack of faithfulness especially to one's husband or wife — see INFIDELITY 1

2 the act or fact of violating the trust or confidence of another — see BETRAYAL

dismal *adj* **1** causing or marked by an atmosphere lacking in cheer — see GLOOMY 1

2 causing unhappiness — see SAD 2

dismantle *vb* to take apart — see DISASSEMBLE

dismay *n* **1** the emotion felt when one's expectations are not met — see DISAPPOINTMENT 1

2 the state of being discouraged — see DISCOURAGEMENT

dismay *vb* to lessen the courage or confidence of — see DISCOURAGE 1

dismember *vb* to take apart — see DISASSEMBLE

dismiss *vb* **1** to let go from office, service, or employment ⟨the secretary was *dismissed* after it was discovered that she was stealing office supplies⟩

synonyms can, cashier, fire, muster out, remove, retire, sack

related words downsize, furlough, lay off; boot (out), bounce

near antonyms contract, subcontract

antonyms employ, hire

2 to drive or force out — see EJECT 1

dismissal *n* the termination of the employment of an employee or a work force often temporarily — see LAYOFF

disobedience *n* refusal to obey ⟨they gave up on training the dog to fetch because of his constant *disobedience*⟩

synonyms contrariness, defiance, frowardness, insubordination, intractability, rebelliousness, recalcitrance, refractoriness, unruliness, willfulness

related words disrespect, impudence, insolence, rudeness; doggedness, hardheadedness, mulishness, obstinacy, pertinaciousness, pertinacity, perversity, stubbornness; mischievousness, naughtiness

near antonyms agreeability, amiability; slavishness, submissiveness, subservience

antonyms amenability, compliance, docility, obedience

disobedient *adj* given to resisting authority or another's control ⟨the *disobedient* child refused to eat his vegetables⟩

synonyms balky, contrary, defiant, froward, insubordinate, intractable, rebellious, recalcitrant, refractory, restive, ungovernable, unruly, untoward, wayward, willful (*or* wilful)

related words insurgent, mutinous; dogged, hardheaded, headstrong, mulish, obdurate, obstinate, peevish, pertinacious, pigheaded, self-willed, stubborn, unyielding; obstreperous, uncontrollable, unmanageable, wild; perverse, resistant, wrongheaded; bad, disorderly, errant, misbehaving, mischievous, monkeying, monkeyish, naughty; undisciplined; dissident, nonconformist; disrespectful, ill-mannered, ill-natured, impolite, impudent, insolent, ornery, rude, uncouth

near antonyms acquiescent, agreeable, amiable, deferential, obliging; submissive, yielding; behaved, disciplined, well-bred; courteous, polite, respectful; servile, slavish, subservient; decorous, orderly, proper; controllable, governable, manageable

antonyms amenable, compliant, docile, obedient, tractable

disobey *vb* to go against the commands, prohibitions, or rules of ⟨students who *disobey* their teachers and use cell phones in class⟩ ⟨drivers who consistently *disobey* traffic laws⟩

synonyms defy, rebel (against)

related words mutiny (against), revolt (against);

disregard, ignore, tune out; dismiss, flout, pooh-pooh, reject, scoff (at), scorn, shrug off; break, transgress, violate; combat, contest, dispute, fight, oppose, resist, withstand

near antonyms defer (to), serve, submit (to), surrender (to), yield (to); keep, observe; accede (to), acquiesce (to), agree (to), assent (to), comply (with), conform (to), oblige; attend, hear, heed, listen (to), mark, note, notice, regard, watch

antonyms follow, mind, obey

disoblige *vb* to cause discomfort to or trouble for — see INCONVENIENCE

disobliging *adj* causing difficulty, discomfort, or annoyance — see INCONVENIENT 1

disorder *n* **1** a state in which everything is out of order — see CHAOS

2 an abnormal state that disrupts a plant's or animal's normal bodily functioning — see DISEASE

disorder *vb* to undo the proper order or arrangement of ⟨be careful not to *disorder* the carefully arranged contents of the dresser⟩

synonyms confuse, derange, disarrange, disarray, discompose, dishevel, dislocate, disorganize, disrupt, disturb, hash, jumble, mess (up), mix (up), muddle, muss, rumple, scramble, shuffle, tousle, tumble, upset

related words embroil, entangle, snarl, tangle; agitate, stir (up), unsettle

near antonyms align, line, line up; systematize; adjust, fix

antonyms arrange, array, draw up, marshal, order, organize, range, regulate, straighten (up), tidy

disordered *adj* lacking in order, neatness, and often cleanliness — see MESSY

disorderly *adj* **1** not restrained by or under the control of legal authority — see LAWLESS

2 lacking in order, neatness, and often cleanliness — see MESSY

disorganization *n* a state in which everything is out of order — see CHAOS

disorganize *vb* to undo the proper order or arrangement of — see DISORDER

disorient *vb* to throw into a state of mental uncertainty — see CONFUSE 1

disown *vb* to refuse to acknowledge as one's own or as one's responsibility — see DISCLAIM 1

disparage *vb* to express scornfully one's low opinion of — see DECRY 1

disparagement *n* the act of making a person or a thing seem little or unimportant — see DEPRECIATION

disparaging *adj* intended to make a person or thing seem of little importance or value — see DEROGATORY

disparate *adj* being not of the same kind — see DIFFERENT 1

disparateness *n* the quality or state of being different — see DIFFERENCE 1

disparity *n* the quality or state of being different — see DIFFERENCE 1

dispassionate *adj* marked by justice, honesty, and freedom from bias — see FAIR 2

dispatch *n* **1** a message on paper from one person or group to another — see LETTER

2 a piece of conveyed information — see COMMUNICATION

dispatch *vb* **1** to cause to go or be taken from one place to another — see SEND

2 to deprive of life — see KILL 1

3 to put to death deliberately — see MURDER 1

dispel *vb* to cause (members of a group) to move widely apart — see SCATTER 1

dispensable *adj* not needed by the circumstances or to accomplish an end — see UNNECESSARY

dispensation *n* the act or process of giving out something to each member of a group — see DISTRIBUTION 1

dispense *vb* to give out (something) in appropriate amounts or to appropriate individuals — see ADMINISTER 1

dispersal *n* an act or process in which something scatters or is scattered — see SCATTERING 1

disperse *vb* **1** to cause (members of a group) to move widely apart — see SCATTER 1

2 to cease to exist or cause to cease to exist as a group or organization — see DISBAND 1

dispersion *n* an act or process in which something scatters or is scattered — see SCATTERING 1

dispirit *vb* to lessen the courage or confidence of — see DISCOURAGE 1

dispiritedness *n* **1** a state or spell of low spirits — see SADNESS

2 the state of being discouraged — see DISCOURAGEMENT

displace *vb* **1** to change the place or position of — see MOVE 1

2 to force to leave a country — see BANISH 1

3 to take the place of — see REPLACE 1

displacement *n* the forced removal from a homeland — see EXILE 1

display *n* **1** a public showing of objects of interest — see EXHIBITION 1

2 an outward and often exaggerated indication of something abstract (as a feeling) for effect — see SHOW 1

display *vb* **1** to present so as to invite notice or attention — see SHOW 1

2 to make known (something abstract) through outward signs — see SHOW 2

displease *vb* to make discontented — see DISCONTENT

displeased *adj* having a feeling that one has been wronged or thwarted in one's ambitions — see DISCONTENTED

displeasing *adj* not giving pleasure to the mind or senses — see UNPLEASANT

displeasure *n* **1** refusal to accept as right or desirable — see DISAPPROVAL

2 the condition of being dissatisfied with one's life or situation — see DISCONTENT

disport *vb* **1** to cause (someone) to pass the time agreeably occupied — see AMUSE

2 to engage in activity for amusement — see PLAY 1

3 to play and run about happily — see FROLIC 1

4 to present so as to invite notice or attention — see SHOW 1

disposal *n* **1** the getting rid of whatever is unwanted or useless ⟨trash *disposal* is on Wednesday in our neighborhood⟩

synonyms discarding, disposition, dumping, jettison, junking, removal, riddance, scrapping, throwing away

related words clearance, clearing; decimation, demolishment, demolition, destruction

near antonyms accumulation, acquirement, acquisition, collection, deposit

2 the way objects in space or events in time are arranged or follow one another — see ORDER 1

dispose *vb* **1** to arrange something in a certain spot or position — see PLACE 1

2 to put into a particular arrangement — see ORDER 1

disposed *adj* having a desire or inclination (as for a specified course of action) — see WILLING 1

disposition *n* **1** one's characteristic attitude or mood ⟨he had a cheerful *disposition* and was very rarely depressed⟩

synonyms grain, nature, temper, temperament

related words cheer, frame, humor, mode, mood; attitude, outlook, perspective, point of view, standpoint, viewpoint; emotion, feeling, heart, passion, sentiment; strain; belief, conviction, mind, opinion, persuasion; expression, tone, vein; character, individuality, personality; responsiveness, sensibility, sensitiveness, sensitivity

2 a habitual attraction to some activity or thing — see INCLINATION 1

3 the getting rid of whatever is unwanted or useless — see DISPOSAL 1

4 the way objects in space or events in time are arranged or follow one another — see ORDER 1

disprove *vb* to prove to be false ⟨Magellan's circumnavigation of the globe *disproved* any lingering notions that the earth is flat⟩

synonyms belie, confute, rebut, refute

related words overthrow, overturn

phrases give the lie to

near antonyms evidence, show; demonstrate, display, illustrate, manifest; argue, reason

antonyms confirm, prove, verify

disputable *adj* **1** giving good reason for being doubted, questioned, or challenged — see DOUBTFUL

2 open to question or dispute — see DEBATABLE 2

disputant *n* a person who takes part in a dispute ⟨there were only three *disputants* in the argument, but they made enough noise for a dozen⟩

synonyms arguer, debater, disputer, quarreler (*or* quarreller), squabbler, wrangler

related words advocate, defendant, plaintiff, pleader; nitpicker, pettifogger, quibbler

disputation *n* variance of opinion on a matter — see DISAGREEMENT 1

disputatious *adj* **1** feeling or displaying eagerness to fight — see BELLIGERENT

2 given to arguing — see ARGUMENTATIVE 1

disputatiousness *n* an inclination to fight or quarrel — see BELLIGERENCE

dispute *n* **1** variance of opinion on a matter — see DISAGREEMENT 1

2 an often noisy or angry expression of differing opinions — see ARGUMENT 1

dispute *vb* **1** to demand proof of the truth or rightness of — see CHALLENGE 1

2 to express different opinions about something often angrily — see ARGUE 2

3 to talk about (an issue) usually from various points of view and for the purpose of arriving at a decision or opinion — see DISCUSS

disputer *n* a person who takes part in a dispute — see DISPUTANT

disquiet *n* **1** a disturbed or uneasy state — see UNREST

2 an uneasy state of mind usually over the possibility of an anticipated misfortune or trouble — see ANXIETY 1

disquiet *vb* to trouble the mind of; to make uneasy — see DISTURB 1

disquieting *adj* **1** causing worry or anxiety — see TROUBLESOME

2 marked by or causing agitation or uncomfortable feelings — see NERVOUS 2

disregard *n* lack of interest or concern — see INDIFFERENCE

disregard *vb* **1** to ignore in a disrespectful manner — see SCORN 2

2 to fail to give proper attention to — see NEGLECT 1

3 to overlook or dismiss as of little importance — see EXCUSE 1

disrepair *n* the state of being unattended to or not cared for — see NEGLECT 1

disreputable *adj* not respectable ⟨a *disreputable* Internet retailer that had a record of hundreds of complaints for shoddy merchandise and slow refunds⟩

synonyms discreditable, disgraceful, dishonorable, ignominious, infamous, notorious, shameful

related words bad, immoral, seamy, shady, sordid, unethical, unsavory, wicked; base, contemptible, despicable, detestable, dirty, low, mean, vile, wretched

near antonyms ethical, good, moral

antonyms honorable, reputable, respectable

disrepute *n* the state of having lost the esteem of others — see DISGRACE 1

disrespect *n* rude behavior — see DISCOURTESY

disrobe *vb* to remove clothing from — see UNDRESS

disrobed *adj* lacking or shed of clothing — see NAKED 1

disrupt *vb* to undo the proper order or arrangement of — see DISORDER

disruption *n* an act or instance of the order of things being disturbed — see UPSET

dissatisfaction *n* **1** the condition of being dissatisfied with one's life or situation — see DISCONTENT

2 the emotion felt when one's expectations are not met — see DISAPPOINTMENT 1

dissatisfied *adj* having a feeling that one has been wronged or thwarted in one's ambitions — see DISCONTENTED

dissatisfy *vb* **1** to fall short in satisfying the expectation or hope of — see DISAPPOINT

2 to make discontented — see DISCONTENT

dissect *vb* to identify and examine the basic elements or parts of (something) especially for discovering interrelationships — see ANALYZE

dissection *n* the separation and identification of the parts of a whole — see ANALYSIS 1

dissemble *vb* to take on a false or deceptive appearance — see PRETEND 1

dissembling *n* **1** the inclination or practice of misleading others through lies or trickery — see DECEIT

2 the pretending of having virtues, principles, or beliefs that one in fact does not have — see HYPOCRISY

disseminate *vb* to cause to be known over a considerable area or by many people — see SPREAD 1

dissension *n* **1** a lack of agreement or harmony — see DISCORD

2 variance of opinion on a matter — see DISAGREEMENT 1

dissent *n* **1** a lack of agreement or harmony — see DISCORD

2 departure from a generally accepted theory, opinion, or practice — see HERESY

dissent *vb* to have a different opinion — see DISAGREE 1

dissenter *n* a person who believes or teaches something opposed to accepted beliefs — see HERETIC

dissentient *adj* deviating from commonly accepted beliefs or practices — see HERETICAL

dissenting *adj* deviating from commonly accepted beliefs or practices — see HERETICAL

disservice *n* unfair or inadequate treatment of someone or something or an instance of this ⟨you do a great *disservice* to the professionals at the day-care center when you refer to them as "babysitters"⟩
synonyms injury, injustice, raw deal, wrong
related words insult, offense, outrage; complaint, grievance
near antonyms cricket
antonyms justice

dissever *vb* to set or force apart — see SEPARATE 1

dissidence *n* **1** a lack of agreement or harmony — see DISCORD
2 departure from a generally accepted theory, opinion, or practice — see HERESY

dissident *adj* deviating from commonly accepted beliefs or practices — see HERETICAL

dissident *n* a person who believes or teaches something opposed to accepted beliefs — see HERETIC

dissimilar *adj* being not of the same kind — see DIFFERENT 1

dissimilarity *n* the quality or state of being different — see DIFFERENCE 1

dissimulation *n* **1** the inclination or practice of misleading others through lies or trickery — see DECEIT
2 the pretending of having virtues, principles, or beliefs that one in fact does not have — see HYPOCRISY

dissipate *vb* **1** to cause (members of a group) to move widely apart — see SCATTER 1
2 to use up carelessly — see WASTE 1

dissipated *adj* having or showing lowered moral character or standards — see CORRUPT

dissipatedness *n* a sinking to a state of low moral standards and behavior — see CORRUPTION 2

dissipation *n* **1** a sinking to a state of low moral standards and behavior — see CORRUPTION 2
2 an act or process in which something scatters or is scattered — see SCATTERING 1

dissociate *vb* to set or force apart — see SEPARATE 1

dissolute *adj* having or showing lowered moral character or standards — see CORRUPT

dissoluteness *n* a sinking to a state of low moral standards and behavior — see CORRUPTION 2

dissolution *n* the act or process of a whole separating into two or more parts or pieces — see SEPARATION 1

dissolve *vb* **1** to cease to be visible — see DISAPPEAR
2 to cease to exist or cause to cease to exist as a group or organization — see DISBAND 1
3 to put an end to by formal action — see ABOLISH

dissonant *adj* marked by or producing a harsh combination of sounds ⟨a *dissonant* chorus of noises arose from the busy construction site⟩
synonyms discordant, inharmonious, unmelodious, unmusical
related words blaring, clanging, clashing, clattering, grating, harsh, jangling, jarring, metallic, raspy, raucous, scratching, screeching, shrill, squeaky, strident; disagreeable, unpleasant, unpleasing; atonal, off-key
near antonyms dulcet, euphonious, mellifluous, mellow, melodic, sweet, tuneful; resonant, sonorous; quavering, trilling, warbling; agreeable, appealing, pleasant; cadenced, lilting, lyric, lyrical, rhythmic (*or* rhythmical); chordal, harmonic, homophonic, orchestral, polyphonic, symphonic, tonal
antonyms harmonious, harmonizing, melodious, musical

dissuade *vb* to steer (a person) from an activity or course of action — see DISCOURAGE 2

distance *n* the space or amount of space between two points, lines, surfaces, or objects ⟨the *distance* between the earth and the sun is about 93 million miles⟩
synonyms lead, length, remove, spacing, spread, stretch, way
related words altitude, area, breadth, depth, height, rise, space, volume, width; extension, extent; cast, range, reach, scope, shot, sweep, throw; drop, fall, flight, haul; berth, clearance
phrases a far cry

distant *adj* **1** not close in time or space ⟨the *distant* towers were barely visible in the fog⟩
synonyms away, far, faraway, far-off, remote, removed
related words apart, isolated, obscure, outlying, out-of-the-way, retired, secluded, secret, sequestered
near antonyms adjacent, adjoining, contiguous
antonyms close, near, nearby, nigh
2 having or showing a lack of friendliness or interest in others — see COOL 1

distaste *n* a dislike so strong as to cause stomach upset or queasiness — see DISGUST

distasteful *adj* **1** disagreeable or disgusting to the sense of taste ⟨cod-liver oil is so *distasteful* that it's worse than anything it cures⟩
synonyms unappetizing, unpalatable, unsavory
related words abominable, awful, bad, filthy, foul, horrible, loathsome, nasty, nauseating, noisome, obnoxious, offensive, repellent, repugnant, repulsive, revolting, shocking, sickening; bland, flat, flavorless, insipid, savorless, tasteless
near antonyms appealing, attractive, flavorful, piquant, rich
antonyms appetizing, delectable, delicious, palatable, savory, tasty
2 not giving pleasure to the mind or senses — see UNPLEASANT
3 causing intense displeasure, disgust, or resentment — see OFFENSIVE 1

distill *vb* to remove usually visible impurities from — see CLARIFY 1

distinct *adj* **1** being not of the same kind — see DIFFERENT 1
2 not subject to misinterpretation or more than one interpretation — see CLEAR 2
3 of a particular or exact sort — see EXPRESS 1
4 serving to identify as belonging to an individual or group — see CHARACTERISTIC 1

distinction *n* **1** exceptionally high quality — see EXCELLENCE 1

THESAURUS

2 a quality that gives something special worth — see EXCELLENCE 2

3 public acknowledgment or admiration for an achievement — see GLORY 1

4 the fact or state of being above others in rank or importance — see EMINENCE 1

5 something given in recognition of achievement — see AWARD

6 the quality or state of being different — see DIFFERENCE 1

7 the state of being kept distinct — see SEPARATION 2

distinctive *adj* **1** being not of the same kind — see DIFFERENT 1

2 serving to identify as belonging to an individual or group — see CHARACTERISTIC 1

distinctiveness *n* the quality or state of being different — see DIFFERENCE 1

distinctness *n* the quality or state of being different — see DIFFERENCE 1

distinguish *vb* **1** to understand or point out the difference ⟨even at such a young age, he could *distinguish* between right and wrong⟩

synonyms differentiate, discern, discriminate, separate

related words comprehend, grasp, know, understand; divide, part, sever; demarcate, mark (off), set off

near antonyms confound, lump (together), mingle

antonyms confuse, mistake, mix (up)

2 to be an important feature of — see CHARACTERIZE 2

3 to find out or establish the identity of — see IDENTIFY 1

4 to make note of (something) through the use of one's eyes — see SEE 1

distinguishable *adj* **1** able to be perceived by a sense or by the mind — see PERCEPTIBLE

2 being not of the same kind — see DIFFERENT 1

distinguished *adj* standing above others in rank, importance, or achievement — see EMINENT

distinguishing *adj* serving to identify as belonging to an individual or group — see CHARACTERISTIC 1

distort *vb* **1** to change so much as to create a wrong impression or alter the meaning of — see GARBLE

2 to twist (something) out of a natural or normal shape or condition — see CONTORT

distorted *adj* badly or imperfectly formed — see MALFORMED

distortion *n* the twisting of something out of its natural or normal shape or condition — see CONTORTION

distract *vb* **1** to draw the attention or mind to something else ⟨we were *distracted* from our homework by the noise outside⟩

synonyms divert

related words amuse, entertain; stray, wander

near antonyms focus

2 to trouble the mind of; to make uneasy — see DISTURB 1

distraction *n* **1** a state of mental uncertainty — see CONFUSION 1

2 a state of wildly excited activity or emotion — see FRENZY

3 the act or activity of providing pleasure or amusement especially for the public — see ENTERTAINMENT 1

distraught *adj* feeling overwhelming fear or worry — see FRANTIC 1

distress *n* **1** a state of great suffering of body or mind ⟨the upcoming final exam is causing us considerable *distress*⟩ ⟨the survivors were in extreme *distress* after having been stranded on the island for a week with no food⟩

synonyms affliction, agony, anguish, misery, pain, strait(s), torment, torture, tribulation, woe

related words discomfort; cross, crucible, trial; heartbreak, joylessness, sadness, sorrow, unhappiness; emergency, pinch; asperity, difficulty, hardship, rigor; ache, hurt, pang, smarting, soreness, stitch, throe, twinge; danger, jeopardy, trouble

near antonyms comfort, consolation, solace; alleviation, assuagement, ease, relief; peace, security

2 the state of not being protected from injury, harm, or evil — see DANGER 1

distress *vb* to trouble the mind of; to make uneasy — see DISTURB 1

distressful *adj* **1** marked by or causing agitation or uncomfortable feelings — see NERVOUS 2

2 of a kind to cause great distress — see REGRETTABLE

distressing *adj* **1** causing worry or anxiety — see TROUBLESOME

2 of a kind to cause great distress — see REGRETTABLE

3 marked by or causing agitation or uncomfortable feelings — see NERVOUS 2

distribute *vb* to give out (something) in appropriate amounts or to appropriate individuals — see ADMINISTER 1

distribution *n* **1** the act or process of giving out something to each member of a group ⟨we oversaw the *distribution* of medicine to the natives⟩

synonyms allocation, apportionment, dispensation, division, issuance

related words disbursement; reapportionment, redistribution

2 the way objects in space or events in time are arranged or follow one another — see ORDER 1

district *n* an area (as of a city) set apart for some purpose or having some special feature ⟨Independence Hall in Philadelphia's historic *district*⟩

synonyms neighborhood, quarter, section

related words belt, zone; department, division, part; precinct, ward; area, locality, place, region; barrio, enclave, ghetto

distrust *n* a feeling or attitude that one does not know the truth, truthfulness, or trustworthiness of someone or something — see DOUBT

distrust *vb* to have no trust or confidence in ⟨we *distrusted* the stranger when he offered us free candy⟩

synonyms doubt, mistrust, question, suspect

related words disbelieve, discount, discredit, negate

phrases look askance at

near antonyms bank (on *or* upon), count (on *or* upon), depend (on *or* upon), rely (on *or* upon)

antonyms trust

distrustful *adj* **1** inclined to doubt or question claims — see SKEPTICAL 1

2 not feeling sure about the truth, wisdom, or trustworthiness of someone or something — see DOUBTFUL 1

distrustfully *adv* with distrust — see ASKANCE

distrustfulness *n* a feeling or attitude that one

does not know the truth, truthfulness, or trustworthiness of someone or something — see DOUBT

disturb *vb* **1** to trouble the mind of; to make uneasy ⟨all that talk of war *disturbed* us⟩

synonyms agitate, bother, concern, discomfort, discompose, disquiet, distract, distress, exercise, freak (out), perturb, undo, unhinge, unsettle, upset, worry

related words aggravate, anger, annoy, bug, chafe, chivy, exasperate, fret, gall, get, grate, harass, harry, irk, irritate, nettle, peeve, pester, pique, put out, rile, vex; bedevil, haunt, plague; abash, confound, confuse, discomfit, disconcert, discountenance, embarrass, faze, fluster, mortify, nonplus, rattle; daunt, demoralize, discourage, dishearten, dismay, dispirit

near antonyms allay, alleviate, assuage; appease, conciliate, mollify, pacify, placate, propitiate

antonyms calm, compose, quiet, settle, soothe, tranquilize (*also* tranquillize)

2 to change the place or position of — see MOVE 1

3 to undo the proper order or arrangement of — see DISORDER

4 to thrust oneself upon (another) without invitation — see BOTHER 1

5 to cause discomfort to or trouble for — see INCONVENIENCE

disturbance *n* **1** a state of noisy, confused activity — see COMMOTION

2 an act or instance of the order of things being disturbed — see UPSET

3 the act of making unwelcome intrusions upon another — see ANNOYANCE 1

disturbing *adj* **1** causing annoyance — see ANNOYING

2 causing embarrassment — see AWKWARD 3

3 causing worry or anxiety — see TROUBLESOME

4 marked by or causing agitation or uncomfortable feelings — see NERVOUS 2

disunion *n* the act or process of a whole separating into two or more parts or pieces — see SEPARATION 1

disunite *vb* to set or force apart — see SEPARATE 1

disunited *adj* disagreeing with each other — see DIVIDED

disunity *n* a lack of agreement or harmony — see DISCORD

disuse *n* lack of use ⟨the old farmhouse showed signs of *disuse*⟩

synonyms idleness, inactivity

related words abandonment, desertion, neglect; dormancy, latency, quiescence

antonyms use

disused *adj* left unoccupied or unused — see ABANDONED

ditch *n* a long narrow channel dug in the earth ⟨after skidding on the ice, our car went right into the *ditch*⟩

synonyms dike, gutter, trench, trough

related words culvert, drain, draw, gully, ravine; drill, furrow

ditch *vb* to get rid of as useless or unwanted — see DISCARD

dither *n* **1** a state of nervous or irritated concern — see FRET

2 a sense of panic or extreme nervousness — see JITTERS

dithery *adj* feeling or showing uncomfortable feelings of uncertainty — see NERVOUS 1

ditty *n* a short musical composition for the human voice often with instrumental accompaniment — see SONG 1

diurnal *adj* occurring, done, produced, or appearing every day — see DAILY

divan *n* a long upholstered piece of furniture designed for several sitters — see COUCH

dive *n* **1** an act or instance of diving ⟨the penguin took a *dive* off of the ice sheet⟩

synonyms pitch, plunge

related words dip, immersion, submersion; fall, slip, spill, stumble, tumble; descent, drop; belly flop, header, jackknife

near antonyms jump, leap

2 the act or process of going to a lower level or altitude — see DESCENT 1

dive *vb* to cast oneself head first into deep water ⟨we watched her *dive* in after the drowning man⟩

synonyms pitch, plunge, sound

related words dip, immerse, submerge; belly flop

near antonyms surface

diverge *vb* **1** to extend outwards from or as if from a central point — see RADIATE 1

2 to go or move in different directions from a central point — see SEPARATE 2

divergence *n* a movement in different directions away from a common point ⟨a growing *divergence* of opinion about that U.S. president's place in history⟩

synonyms separation

related words difference, disagreement, discrepancy, disparateness, disparity, dissidence, dissimilarity, distinction, distinctiveness, distinctness, diversity, unlikeness

near antonyms accord, agreement; likeness, similarity

antonyms convergence

divers *adj* being of many and various kinds — see MANIFOLD

diverse *adj* being not of the same kind — see DIFFERENT 1

diverseness *n* **1** the quality or state of being composed of many different elements or types — see VARIETY 1

2 the quality or state of being different — see DIFFERENCE 1

diversion *n* **1** someone or something that provides amusement or enjoyment — see FUN 1

2 the act or activity of providing pleasure or amusement especially for the public — see ENTERTAINMENT 1

diversity *n* **1** the quality or state of being composed of many different elements or types — see VARIETY 1

2 the quality or state of being different — see DIFFERENCE 1

divert *vb* **1** to cause (someone) to pass the time agreeably occupied — see AMUSE

2 to change the course or direction of (something) — see TURN 2

3 to draw the attention or mind to something else — see DISTRACT 1

diverting *adj* providing amusement or enjoyment — see FUN

divide *vb* **1** to set or force apart — see SEPARATE 1

2 to go or move in different directions from a central point — see SEPARATE 2

divided *adj* disagreeing with each other ⟨the club members were *divided* on the need for more fundraising⟩

THESAURUS

synonyms disunited, split
phrases at loggerheads, at odds
antonyms undivided, united
dividend *n* something given in addition to what is ordinarily expected or owed — see BONUS
divider *n* something that divides, separates, or marks off — see DIVISION 1
divine *adj* 1 of the very best kind — see EXCELLENT
2 of, relating to, or being God — see HOLY 3
divine *n* a person specially trained and authorized to conduct religious services in a Christian church — see CLERGYMAN
divine *vb* to realize or know about beforehand — see FORESEE
diviner *n* one who predicts future events or developments — see PROPHET
divinity *n* 1 the quality or state of being divine ⟨Henry David Thoreau felt the presence of *divinity* in every part of nature⟩
synonyms deity, godhead, godhood
2 a being having superhuman powers and control over a particular part of life or the world — see DEITY 1
3 *cap* the being worshipped as the creator and ruler of the universe — see DEITY 2
divisible *adj* capable of being split into two or more parts or pieces — see SEPARABLE
division *n* 1 something that divides, separates, or marks off ⟨we poked our heads over the *division* between the yards to see what the fuss was about⟩
synonyms divider, partition
related words barrier, fence, wall; border, boundary, limit
2 a large unit of a governmental, business, or educational organization ⟨the complaints *division* handled all of the calls from the angry townsfolk⟩
synonyms bureau, department, desk, office
3 one of the units into which a whole is divided on the basis of a common characteristic — see CLASS 2
4 the act or process of a whole separating into two or more parts or pieces — see SEPARATION 1
5 the act or process of giving out something to each member of a group — see DISTRIBUTION 1
divorce *vb* to set or force apart — see SEPARATE 1
divulge *vb* to make known (as information previously kept secret) — see REVEAL 1
divulgence *n* the act or an instance of making known something previously unknown or concealed — see REVELATION
dizzy *adj* 1 having a feeling of being whirled about and in danger of falling down ⟨I felt very *dizzy* after I got off of the roller coaster⟩
synonyms giddy, light-headed, reeling, whirling
related words faint, weak; addled, befuddled, confused, dazed
near antonyms clearheaded; stable, steady
2 suffering from mental confusion ⟨he felt *dizzy* from trying to remember all of the dates and names that were sure to be asked on the test⟩
synonyms befuddled, bewildered, confused, dazed, stunned, stupefied
related words senseless, unconscious
phrases at sea
near antonyms alert, conscious
antonyms clearheaded, unconfused
3 moving, proceeding, or acting with great speed — see FAST 1

do *vb* 1 to be fitting or proper ⟨Oh, that outfit just won't *do* for the opera⟩
synonyms befit, fit, go, serve, suit
related words satisfy, suffice; function, work
2 to be enough — see SERVE 2
3 to carry through (as a process) to completion — see PERFORM 1
4 to make more attractive by adding something that is beautiful or becoming — see DECORATE
5 to meet one's day-to-day needs — see GET ALONG 1
doable *adj* capable of being done or carried out — see POSSIBLE 1
docile *adj* readily giving in to the command or authority of another — see OBEDIENT
docility *n* a readiness or willingness to yield to the wishes of others — see COMPLIANCE 1
dock *n* a structure used by boats and ships for taking on or landing cargo and passengers ⟨the boat remained tied up at the *dock* for a week, waiting for the weather to clear⟩
synonyms float, jetty, landing, levee, pier, quay, wharf
related words berth, mooring, slip; dockyard, marina, shipyard
¹**dock** *vb* to make (as hair) shorter with or as if with the use of shears — see CLIP
²**dock** *vb* to stop at or near a place along the shore — see LAND 1
docket *n* a listing of things to be presented or considered (as at a concert or play) — see PROGRAM 1
dockworker *n* one who loads and unloads ships at a port ⟨the *dockworkers* spent all afternoon taking crates off of the ship⟩
synonyms longshoreman, stevedore
doctor *n* a person specially trained in healing human medical disorders ⟨we called a *doctor* as soon as we realized the baby was sick⟩
synonyms medic, physician
related words dermatologist, general practitioner, gynecologist, internist, neurologist, obstetrician, ophthalmologist, orthopedist, pediatrician, specialist, surgeon; intern, resident; nurse, paramedic
doctor *vb* 1 to give medical treatment to ⟨a pledge to *doctor* the burn victims until they were whole again⟩
synonyms treat
related words cure, heal, mend, rehabilitate, remedy; attend, care (for), dose, drug, minister (to), nurse
2 to put into good shape or working order again — see MEND 1
doctrine *n* 1 a statement or body of statements concerning faith or morals proclaimed by a church ⟨the Catholic Church's *doctrine* on the Eucharist⟩
synonyms canon, dogma
related words belief, conviction, tenet; credo, creed, ideology, philosophy, theology; axiom, precept, principle
2 the basic beliefs or guiding principles of a person or group — see CREED 1
document *n* 1 a piece of paper with information written or to be written on it — see FORM 2
2 a written or printed paper giving information about or proof of something — see CERTIFICATE
document *vb* to show the existence or truth of by evidence — see PROVE 1

documentary *adj* restricted to or based on fact — see FACTUAL 1

documentation *n* something presented in support of the truth or accuracy of a claim — see PROOF

dodder *vb* to move forward while swaying from side to side — see STAGGER 1

dodge *n* a clever often underhanded means to achieve an end — see TRICK 1

dodge *vb* 1 to move suddenly aside or to and fro ⟨*dodging* through the crowd on his way to the exit⟩
  synonyms duck, sidestep, zigzag
  related words avoid, elude, escape, evade, parry, shirk, skirt; deflect, turn; slide, slip
  2 to avoid having to comply with (something) especially through cleverness — see CIRCUMVENT 1
  3 to get or keep away from (as a responsibility) through cleverness or trickery — see ESCAPE 2

dodger *n* a dishonest person who uses clever means to cheat others out of something of value — see TRICKSTER 1

dodging *n* the act or a means of getting or keeping away from something undesirable — see ESCAPE 2

dodo *n* 1 a person with old-fashioned ideas — see FOGY
  2 a stupid person — see IDIOT

doff *vb* to rid oneself of (a garment) — see REMOVE 1

dog *n* a domestic mammal that is related to the wolves and foxes ⟨we got a *dog* from the pound to keep as a pet⟩
  synonyms canine, doggy (*or* doggie), hound, pooch
  related words cur, mongrel, mutt; bitch; lapdog, pup, puppy, whelp; bird dog, hunter, police dog, sheepdog, sled dog, watchdog, wolf dog, wolfhound

dog *vb* to go after or on the track of — see FOLLOW 2

dog–eared *adj* showing signs of advanced wear and tear and neglect — see SHABBY 1

dogged *adj* 1 continuing despite difficulties, opposition, or discouragement — see PERSISTENT
  2 sticking to an opinion, purpose, or course of action in spite of reason, arguments, or persuasion — see OBSTINATE
  3 showing no signs of slackening or yielding in one's purpose — see UNYIELDING 1

doggedness *n* a steadfast adherence to an opinion, purpose, or course of action — see OBSTINACY

dogging *n* the act of going after or in the tracks of another — see PURSUIT

doggy *or* **doggie** *n* a domestic mammal that is related to the wolves and foxes — see DOG

dogma *n* a statement or body of statements concerning faith or morals proclaimed by a church — see DOCTRINE 1

do in *vb* 1 to bring to a complete end the physical soundness, existence, or usefulness of — see DESTROY 1
  2 to deprive of life — see KILL 1
  3 to put to death deliberately — see MURDER 1
  4 to use up all the physical energy of — see EXHAUST 1

doing *n* something done by someone — see ACTION 1

doldrums *n pl* 1 a state of temporary inactivity — see ABEYANCE

2 a state or spell of low spirits — see SADNESS
  3 the state of being bored — see BOREDOM

dole (out) *vb* to give out (something) in appropriate amounts or to appropriate individuals — see ADMINISTER 1

doleful *adj* 1 expressing or suggesting mourning — see MOURNFUL 1
  2 feeling unhappiness — see SAD 1

dolefulness *n* deep sadness especially for the loss of someone or something loved — see SORROW

doll *n* 1 a small figure often of a human being used especially as a child's plaything ⟨there was a row of *dolls* along the shelf in the bedroom⟩
  synonyms dolly, puppet
  related words rag doll; figure, figurine; plaything, toy
  2 a young usually unmarried woman — see GIRL 1

doll up *vb* to put on one's best or formal clothes — see DRESS UP

dolly *n* a small figure often of a human being used especially as a child's plaything — see DOLL 1

dolor *n* deep sadness especially for the loss of someone or something loved — see SORROW

dolorous *adj* expressing or suggesting mourning — see MOURNFUL 1

dolt *n* a stupid person — see IDIOT

doltish *adj* not having or showing an ability to absorb ideas readily — see STUPID 1

doltishness *n* the quality or state of lacking intelligence or quickness of mind — see STUPIDITY 1

domain *n* a region of activity, knowledge, or influence — see FIELD 2

domestic *adj* 1 of or relating to a household or family ⟨the surest way to maintain *domestic* peace and harmony is to have everyone pitch in on chores⟩
  synonyms familial, household
  related words homelike, homely, homey; residential
  2 changed from the wild state so as to become useful and obedient to humans — see TAME 1

domestic *n* 1 a female domestic servant — see MAID 1
  2 a person hired to perform household or personal services — see SERVANT

domesticated *adj* changed from the wild state so as to become useful and obedient to humans — see TAME 1

domicile *n* the place where one lives — see HOME 1

domicile *vb* to provide with living quarters or shelter — see HOUSE 1

dominance *n* 1 controlling power or influence over others — see SUPREMACY 1
  2 the fact or state of being above others in rank or importance — see EMINENCE 1

dominant *adj* coming before all others in importance — see FOREMOST 1

dominate *vb* 1 to bring under one's control by force of arms — see CONQUER 1
  2 to look down on — see OVERLOOK 1
  3 to serve as leader of — see LEAD 2

dominating *n* the act or process of bringing someone or something under one's control — see CONQUEST

domination *n* the act or process of bringing someone or something under one's control — see CONQUEST

domineering *adj* fond of ordering people around — see BOSSY

dominie *n* a person specially trained and authorized to conduct religious services in a Christian church — see CLERGYMAN

dominion *n* **1** controlling power or influence over others — see SUPREMACY 1

2 the right or means to command or control others — see POWER 1

don *vb* to place on one's person — see PUT ON 1

donate *vb* to make a present of — see GIVE 1

donation *n* **1** a gift of money or its equivalent to a charity, humanitarian cause, or public institution — see CONTRIBUTION

2 something given to someone without expectation of a return — see GIFT 1

donator *n* one that helps another with gifts or money — see BENEFACTOR

done *adj* brought or having come to an end — see COMPLETE 2

done in *adj* depleted in strength, energy, or freshness — see WEARY 1

donkey *n* **1** a sturdy and patient domestic mammal that is used especially to carry things ⟨we put our bags on the *donkey* and headed down the canyon⟩

synonyms ass, burro, jackass

related words jack, jenny; hinny, mule; pack animal

2 a stupid person — see IDIOT

donor *n* one that helps another with gifts or money — see BENEFACTOR

doom *n* **1** a decision made by a court or tribunal regarding a case it has heard — see SENTENCE

2 a state or end that seemingly has been decided beforehand — see FATE 1

3 the permanent stopping of all the vital bodily activities — see DEATH 1

doom *vb* **1** to determine the fate of in advance — see DESTINE

2 to impose a judicial punishment on — see SENTENCE

door *n* **1** a barrier by which an entry is closed and opened ⟨we locked the *door* to the room so that no one could get in⟩

synonyms gate, hatch, portal

related words Dutch door, French door, lattice, portcullis, postern, trapdoor, wicket

2 the opening through which one can enter or leave a structure ⟨a steady stream of visitors through the front *door*⟩

synonyms doorway, entrance, gate, gateway, way

related words hatch, hatchway

doorkeeper *n* a person who tends a door ⟨the *doorkeeper* held the door open for us so we didn't have to put down our packages⟩

synonyms doorman, gatekeeper, janitor, porter [*chiefly British*]

doorman *n* a person who tends a door — see DOORKEEPER

doorway *n* **1** the means or right of entering or participating in — see ENTRANCE 1

2 the opening through which one can enter or leave a structure — see DOOR 2

dope *n* **1** information not generally available to the public ⟨he gave us the *dope* on the deal taking place that night at the warehouse⟩

synonyms lowdown, scoop, tip

related words dirt, gossip, rumor, story; hint, pointer; information, intelligence, news, tidings, word

2 a stupid person — see IDIOT

dope (out) *vb* to find an answer for through reasoning — see SOLVE

doper *n* a person who regularly uses drugs especially illegally ⟨the *doper* had to go straight, since he couldn't keep a steady job while using drugs⟩

synonyms addict, fiend, junkie (*also* junky), substance abuser, user

related words pothead

dopey *adj* not having or showing an ability to absorb ideas readily — see STUPID 1

dopiness *n* the quality or state of lacking intelligence or quickness of mind — see STUPIDITY 1

dork *n, slang* a stupid person — see IDIOT

dorky *adj, slang* not having or showing an ability to absorb ideas readily — see STUPID 1

dormancy *n* **1** a state of temporary inactivity — see ABEYANCE

2 lack of action or activity — see INACTION

dormant *adj* **1** being in a state of suspended consciousness — see ASLEEP 1

2 not being in a state of use, activity, or employment — see INACTIVE 2

dot *n* a small area that is different (as in color) from the main part — see SPOT 1

dot *vb* **1** to cover by or as if by scattering something over or on — see SCATTER 2

2 to mark with small spots especially unevenly — see SPOT

dote (on) *vb* to love or admire too much — see IDOLIZE

dotted *adj* marked with spots — see SPOTTED 1

dotty *adj* showing or marked by a lack of good sense or judgment — see FOOLISH 1

double *adj* **1** consisting of two members or parts that are usually joined ⟨an egg with a *double* yolk⟩

synonyms binary, bipartite, dual, duplex, twin

related words mated, paired

antonyms single

2 being twice as great or as many ⟨after it was ranked the best in the country, the college had *double* the usual number of applicants⟩

synonyms twofold

double *adv* to two times the amount or degree — see DOUBLY

double *n* something or someone that strongly resembles another — see IMAGE 1

double *vb* **1** to make twice as great or as many ⟨we *doubled* our efforts to find a solution to the problem⟩

synonyms duplicate, redouble

related words compound, multiply; accumulate, balloon, build (up), burgeon, enlarge, escalate, expand, increase, mount, mushroom, proliferate, rise, snowball, swell, wax

2 to lay one part over or against another part of — see FOLD 1

double–cross *vb* to be unfaithful or disloyal to — see BETRAY 1

double cross *n* the act or fact of violating the trust or confidence of another — see BETRAYAL

double–crosser *n* one who betrays a trust or an allegiance — see TRAITOR

double–dealing *adj* **1** marked by, based on, or done by the use of dishonest methods to acquire something of value — see FRAUDULENT 1

2 not being or expressing what one appears to be or express — see INSINCERE

double–dealing *n* the inclination or practice of

misleading others through lies or trickery — see DECEIT

doubly *adv* to two times the amount or degree ⟨we were *doubly* certain of her guilt after we read the article in the newspaper⟩
synonyms double, twice, twofold

doubt *n* a feeling or attitude that one does not know the truth, truthfulness, or trustworthiness of someone or something ⟨from the beginning I had my *doubts* about the new kid in school⟩
synonyms distrust, distrustfulness, incertitude, misgiving, mistrust, mistrustfulness, skepticism, suspicion, uncertainty
related words disbelief, incredulity, unbelief; anxiety, concern; compunction, qualm, scruple
near antonyms credence, faith
antonyms assurance, belief, certainty, certitude, confidence, conviction, sureness, surety, trust

doubt *vb* to have no trust or confidence in — see DISTRUST

doubtable *adj* **1** giving good reason for being doubted, questioned, or challenged — see DOUBTFUL 2
2 open to question or dispute — see DEBATABLE 1

doubter *n* a person who is always ready to doubt or question the truth or existence of something — see SKEPTIC

doubtful *adj* **1** not feeling sure about the truth, wisdom, or trustworthiness of someone or something ⟨he was *doubtful* about the decision to complete the project despite its mounting problems⟩
synonyms distrustful, dubious, mistrustful, skeptical, suspicious, uncertain, unconvinced, undecided, unsettled, unsure
related words diffident, insecure; hesitant, indecisive, irresolute, vacillating, wavering
phrases on the fence
near antonyms assured, confident, sanguine, self-assured; decisive, determined, resolute
antonyms certain, convinced, positive, sure
2 giving good reason for being doubted, questioned, or challenged ⟨the election results were highly *doubtful*, so an investigation was begun⟩
synonyms debatable, disputable, doubtable, dubious, equivocal, fishy, problematic (*also* problematical), questionable, shady, shaky, suspect, suspicious
related words moot; ambiguous, open, unclear; uncertain, undecided, undetermined; far-fetched, flimsy, improbable, unlikely
near antonyms decisive, definitive; clear, obvious, open-and-shut, positive
antonyms certain, incontestable, indisputable, indubitable, sure, undeniable, undoubted, unquestionable
3 not likely to be true or to occur — see IMPROBABLE
4 open to question or dispute — see DEBATABLE 1

doubtfully *adv* with distrust — see ASKANCE
doubting *adj* inclined to doubt or question claims — see SKEPTICAL 1
doubtingly *adv* with distrust — see ASKANCE
doubtless *adj* having or showing a mind free from doubt — see CERTAIN 2
doubtless *adv* **1** without any question — see INDEED 1
2 without much doubt — see PROBABLY
dough *n* something (as pieces of stamped metal or printed paper) customarily and legally used as a

medium of exchange, a measure of value, or a means of payment — see MONEY

doughtiness *n* strength of mind to carry on in spite of danger — see COURAGE
doughty *adj* feeling or displaying no fear by temperament — see BRAVE
dour *adj* harsh and threatening in manner or appearance — see GRIM 1
douse *vb* **1** to cause to cease burning — see EXTINGUISH 1
2 to make wet — see WET
3 to sink or push (something) briefly into or as if into a liquid — see DIP 1
doused *adj* containing, covered with, or thoroughly penetrated by water — see WET
dove *n* **1** a person who opposes war or warlike policies ⟨the *doves* were in favor of using the money to improve the school system instead of the army⟩
synonyms pacifist
related words peacemaker
near antonyms militarist; chauvinist, nationalist
antonyms hawk, jingo, warmonger
2 an innocent or gentle person — see LAMB
dovetail *vb* to be in agreement on every point — see CHECK 1
dowager *n* a dignified usually elderly woman of some rank or authority — see MATRIARCH
dowdily *adv* in a careless or unfashionable manner — see SLOPPILY
dowdy *adj* **1** lacking neatness in dress or person — see SLOPPY 1
2 marked by an obvious lack of style or good taste — see TACKY 1
down *adj* **1** brought or having come to an end — see COMPLETE 2
2 directed down — see DOWNCAST 1
3 feeling unhappiness — see SAD 1
4 temporarily suffering from a disorder of the body — see SICK 1
down *adv* toward or in a lower position ⟨the stairs went *down* to the basement⟩
synonyms below, downward, over
related words facedown; low; downgrade, downhill, downstairs
near antonyms aloft
antonyms up, upward (*or* upwards), upwardly
¹**down** *n* a soft airy substance or covering — see FUZZ
²**down** *n* **1** the act or process of going to a lower level or altitude — see DESCENT 1
2 a loss of status — see COMEDOWN
down *vb* **1** to strike (someone) so forcefully as to cause a fall — see FELL 1
2 to take into the stomach through the mouth and throat — see SWALLOW 1
downcast *adj* **1** directed down ⟨her *downcast* gaze made us realize that she was shy⟩
synonyms down, downward, lowered
near antonyms elevated, lifted, raised, uplifted, upward
2 feeling unhappiness — see SAD 1
downer *n* something (as a situation or event) that is depressing ⟨that math exam was a real *downer*⟩
synonyms bummer
related words bore, drag; accident, fatality, mishap, woe; calamity, catastrophe, debacle (*also* débâcle), misfortune, tragedy
near antonyms pick-me-up

THESAURUS

downfall *n* **1** a change to a lower state or level — see DECLINE 2

2 a loss of status — see COMEDOWN

downgrade *n* a change to a lower state or level — see DECLINE 2

downgrade *vb* to bring to a lower grade or rank — see DEMOTE

downhearted *adj* feeling unhappiness — see SAD 1

downheartedness *n* a state or spell of low spirits — see SADNESS

downpour *n* a steady falling of water from the sky in significant quantity — see RAIN 1

downright *adj* **1** being or characterized by direct, brief, and potentially rude speech or manner — see BLUNT 1

2 having no exceptions or restrictions — see ABSOLUTE 2

downs *n pl* a broad area of level or rolling treeless country — see PLAIN

downsize *vb* to make smaller in amount, volume, or extent — see DECREASE 1

down–to–earth *adj* willing to see things as they really are and deal with them sensibly — see REALISTIC 1

downward *adv* toward or in a lower position — see DOWN

downward *adj* directed down — see DOWNCAST 1

downwind *adj* being in the direction that the wind is blowing ⟨we were *downwind* of the deer, so it couldn't smell us⟩

synonyms leeward

antonyms upwind, windward

downy *adj* smooth or delicate in appearance or feel — see SOFT 2

doze *n* a short sleep — see ¹NAP

doze *vb* **1** to be in a state of sleep — see SLEEP 1

2 to sleep lightly or briefly — see NAP 1

dozer *n* one who sleeps — see SLEEPER

dozing *adj* being in a state of suspended consciousness — see ASLEEP 1

dozing *n* a natural periodic loss of consciousness during which the body restores itself — see SLEEP 1

drab *adj* causing weariness, restlessness, or lack of interest — see BORING

draft *n* **1** a mass or quantity of something taken up and carried, conveyed, or transported — see LOAD 1

2 the portion of a serving of a beverage that is swallowed at one time — see DRINK 2

3 noticeable movement of air in a particular direction — see ¹WIND 1

draft *vb* **1** to pick especially for required military service ⟨my grandfather was *drafted* to fight in the war, even though he didn't want to go⟩

synonyms conscript

related words impress, press; enlist, enroll (*also* enrol); sign up, volunteer

near antonyms discharge

2 to put (something) into proper and usually carefully worked out written form — see COMPOSE 1

draftee *n* a person forced or required to enroll in military service — see CONSCRIPT

drag *n* **1** someone or something boring ⟨that lecture was such a *drag* that half of the audience fell asleep⟩

synonyms bore

related words bummer, downer; pill

near antonyms gas [*slang*]

2 a passage cleared for public vehicular travel — see WAY 1

3 something that makes movement or progress more difficult — see ENCUMBRANCE

4 the portion of a serving of a beverage that is swallowed at one time — see DRINK 2

drag *vb* **1** to cause to follow by applying steady force on — see PULL 1

2 to move or act slowly — see DELAY 1

3 to move slowly — see CRAWL 2

dragger *n* someone who moves slowly or more slowly than others — see SLOWPOKE

dragging *adj* moving or proceeding at less than the normal, desirable, or required speed — see SLOW 1

drain *vb* **1** to remove (liquid) gradually or completely ⟨we *drained* the water from the tank before cleaning it⟩

synonyms bleed, draw (off), pump, siphon, tap

related words milk; suck; clear, empty, evacuate, exhaust, vacate, void

antonyms fill

2 to make complete use of — see DEPLETE

3 to use up all the physical energy of — see EXHAUST 1

drained *adj* depleted in strength, energy, or freshness — see WEARY 1

drainpipe *n* a pipe or channel for carrying off water from a roof — see GUTTER 1

drama *n* **1** the public performance of plays ⟨he has been interested in *drama* from the first time he ever saw a play⟩

synonyms dramatics, stage, theater (*or* theatre), theatricals

related words boards; acting, footlights; entertainment, show business

2 a written work in which the story is told through speech and action that is intended to be acted out on stage — see PLAY 2

dramatic *adj* **1** having the general quality or effect of a stage performance ⟨the basketball player's *dramatic* announcement of his sudden retirement held everybody spellbound⟩

synonyms histrionic, melodramatic, theatrical

related words affected, emotional, sensational

near antonyms matter-of-fact, monotonous

antonyms undramatic, untheatrical

2 given to or marked by attention-getting behavior suggestive of stage acting — see THEATRICAL 1

3 likely to attract attention — see NOTICEABLE

dramatics *n pl* the public performance of plays — see DRAMA 1

dramatization *n* a written work in which the story is told through speech and action that is intended to be acted out on stage — see PLAY 2

drapery *n* pieces of cloth hung to darken, decorate, or divide a room ⟨the *drapery* for the picture window matched the color of the furniture in the center of the room⟩

synonyms curtains, drapes

related words hanging(s), tapestry, window shade

drapes *n pl* pieces of cloth hung to darken, decorate, or divide a room — see DRAPERY

draw *n* **1** a situation in which neither participant in a contest, competition, or struggle comes out ahead of the other — see TIE 1

2 something that attracts interest — see MAGNET

3 the act or an instance of applying force on something so that it moves in the direction of the force — see PULL 1

draw *vb* **1** to cause to follow by applying steady force on — see PULL 1

2 to give a representation or account of in words — see DESCRIBE 1

3 to receive as return for effort — see EARN 1

4 to take away from a place or position — see RE-MOVE 2

5 to take the internal organs out of — see GUT

draw (off) *vb* to remove (liquid) gradually or completely — see DRAIN 1

draw (up) *vb* to put (something) into proper and usually carefully worked out written form — see COMPOSE 1

drawback *n* a feature of someone or something that creates difficulty for achieving success — see DISADVANTAGE

drawing *n* a picture using lines to represent the chief features of an object or scene ⟨he made a *drawing* of the tree in his sketchpad while he was waiting for the bus⟩

synonyms cartoon, delineation, sketch

related words outline, silhouette; caricature, doodle, illustration; depiction, image, likeness, portrait, representation; engraving, etching; blueprint

drawing out *n* the act of making longer — see EXTENSION 1

drawn *adj* stretched with little or no give — see TAUT

draw on *vb* to come near or nearer — see APPROACH 1

draw out *vb* to make longer — see EXTEND 1

draw up *vb* **1** to bring (something) to a standstill — see ¹HALT 1

2 to put into a particular arrangement — see ORDER 1

dread *n* **1** suspicion or fear of future harm or misfortune — see APPREHENSION 1

2 the emotion experienced in the presence or threat of danger — see FEAR

dreadful *adj* **1** causing fear — see FEARFUL 1

2 causing intense displeasure, disgust, or resentment — see OFFENSIVE 1

3 extremely disturbing or repellent — see HORRIBLE 1

dreadfulness *n* the quality of inspiring intense dread or dismay — see HORROR 1

dream *n* **1** a series of often striking pictures created by the imagination during sleep ⟨I had a *dream* last night about flying without any support⟩

synonyms nightmare, vision

related words daydream, pipe dream, reverie (*also* revery); chimera, delusion, fancy, fantasy (*also* phantasy), figment, hallucination, illusion, mirage, phantasm

2 a conception or image created by the imagination and having no objective reality — see FANTASY 1

3 something that one hopes or intends to accomplish — see GOAL

dream *vb* to form a mental picture of — see IMAGINE 1

dreamer *n* one whose conduct is guided more by the image of perfection than by the real world — see IDEALIST

dreamily *adv* in a pleasing way — see WELL 5

dreamy *adj* **1** giving pleasure or contentment to the mind or senses — see PLEASANT

2 tending to calm the emotions and relieve stress — see SOOTHING 1

drear *adj* **1** causing or marked by an atmosphere lacking in cheer — see GLOOMY 1

2 causing unhappiness — see SAD 2

dreariness *n* a state or spell of low spirits — see SADNESS

dreary *adj* **1** causing or marked by an atmosphere lacking in cheer — see GLOOMY 1

2 causing unhappiness — see SAD 2

3 causing weariness, restlessness, or lack of interest — see BORING

dredge *vb* to look through (as a place) carefully or thoroughly in an effort to find or discover something — see SEARCH 1

dregs *n pl* matter that settles to the bottom of a body of liquid — see DEPOSIT 1

drench *vb* **1** to make wet — see WET

2 to wet thoroughly with liquid — see SOAK 1

drenched *adj* containing, covered with, or thoroughly penetrated by water — see WET

dress *adj* relating to or suitable for wearing to an event requiring elegant dress and manners ⟨the naval commander wore his *dress* uniform to the ball⟩

synonyms dressy, formal

related words costume; chic, dapper, fashionable, modish, natty, sharp, smart, stylish; custom-made, fitted, tailored; state

near antonyms street; dowdy, unfashionable, unstylish

antonyms casual, informal, sporty

dress *n* **1** a garment with a joined blouse and skirt for a woman or girl ⟨what a lovely *dress* you're wearing today!⟩

synonyms frock, gown

related words chemise, granny, housedress, jumper, Mother Hubbard, muumuu (*or* mumu), overdress

2 clothing chosen as appropriate for a specific situation — see OUTFIT 1

3 covering for the human body — see CLOTHING

dress *vb* **1** to cover with a bandage — see BANDAGE

2 to make more attractive by adding something that is beautiful or becoming — see DECORATE

3 to make smooth or glossy usually by repeatedly applying surface pressure — see POLISH

4 to outfit with clothes and especially fine or special clothes — see CLOTHE 1

5 to put on one's best or formal clothes — see DRESS UP

dress down *vb* to criticize (someone) severely or angrily especially for personal failings — see SCOLD

dressing *n* **1** a medicated covering used to heal an injury ⟨nurses put a *dressing* over his cuts so they wouldn't get infected⟩

synonyms plaster, poultice

related words balm, cream, liniment, lotion, ointment, salve, unguent

2 a savory fluid food used as a topping or accompaniment to a main dish — see SAUCE 1

dress up *vb* **1** to put on one's best or formal clothes ⟨we always like to *dress up* when going to parties⟩

synonyms doll up, dress

related words apparel, array, attire, bedeck, bedizen, caparison, clothe, costume, deck, garb, garment, invest, rig (out), robe

2 to change the dress or looks of so as to conceal true identity — see DISGUISE

THESAURUS

dressy *adj* relating to or suitable for wearing to an event requiring elegant dress and manners — see DRESS

dribble *vb* **1** to fall or let fall in or as if in drops — see DRIP

2 to flow in a broken irregular stream — see GURGLE

3 to let saliva or some other substance flow from the mouth — see DROOL

driblet *n* **1** a very small amount — see PARTICLE 1

2 the quantity of fluid that falls naturally in one rounded mass — see DROP 1

drift *n* **1** a pile or ridge of granular matter (as sand or snow) — see ²BANK

2 a prevailing or general movement or inclination — see TREND 1

3 the idea that is conveyed or intended to be conveyed to the mind by language, symbol, or action — see MEANING 1

drift *vb* **1** to move or proceed smoothly and readily — see FLOW 2

2 to rest or move along the surface of a liquid or in the air — see FLOAT

drifter *n* a person who roams about without a fixed route or destination — see NOMAD

drill *n* something done over and over in order to develop skill — see EXERCISE 2

¹drill *vb* **1** to make a hole or series of holes in — see PERFORATE

2 to strike with a missile from a gun — see SHOOT 3

²drill *vb* to put or set into the ground to grow — see PLANT

drink *n* **1** a liquid suitable for drinking ⟨we went inside to have a *drink* after mowing the lawn⟩
synonyms beverage, libation, quencher
related words potion; pop, soda, soda pop, soft drink; alcohol, brew, intoxicant, liquor, spirits

2 the portion of a serving of a beverage that is swallowed at one time ⟨the thirsty scout took a long *drink* from his canteen⟩
synonyms draft, drag, gulp, nip, quaff, shot, sip, slug, snort, sup, swallow, swig, swill

3 a fermented or distilled beverage that can make a person drunk — see ALCOHOL

drink *vb* **1** to swallow in liquid form ⟨the doctor wants her to *drink* lots of water before the examination⟩
synonyms gulp, guzzle, imbibe, quaff, sip, slurp, sup, swig, swill, toss (down *or* off)
related words lap, lick; consume, down, mouth (down); tipple; toast, wine

2 to take in (something liquid) through small openings — see ABSORB 1

drinkable *adj* suitable for drinking — see POTABLE

drip *n* the quantity of fluid that falls naturally in one rounded mass — see DROP 1

drip *vb* to fall or let fall in or as if in drops ⟨water from the leaky roof was *dripping* all over the floor⟩ ⟨the cracked bottle *dripped* wine⟩
synonyms dribble, trickle
related words bleed, exude, ooze, seep, weep; discharge

dripping *adj* containing, covered with, or thoroughly penetrated by water — see WET

drive *n* **1** a passage cleared for public vehicular travel — see WAY 1

2 a series of activities undertaken to achieve a goal — see CAMPAIGN

3 a strong wish for something — see DESIRE

4 active strength of body or mind — see VIGOR 1

5 readiness to engage in daring or difficult activity — see ENTERPRISE 2

drive *vb* **1** to urge, push, or force onward ⟨cowboys *drove* the herd of cattle from San Antonio to San Francisco⟩
synonyms herd, punch, run
related words shepherd; wrangle; egg, exhort, goad, prick, prod, spur, urge

2 to travel by a motorized vehicle ⟨I'm going to *drive* across the country—want to come?⟩
synonyms automobile, motor
related words roll, wheel; chauffeur, taxi; ride; drag, race

3 to apply force to (someone or something) so that it moves in front of one — see PUSH 1

4 to cause (a person) to give in to pressure — see FORCE

5 to cause to function — see ACTIVATE

6 to set or keep in motion — see MOVE 2

drivel *n* **1** language, behavior, or ideas that are absurd and contrary to good sense — see NONSENSE 1

2 unintelligible or meaningless talk — see GIBBERISH

drivel *vb* **1** to let saliva or some other substance flow from the mouth — see DROOL

2 to speak rapidly, inarticulately, and usually unintelligibly — see BABBLE 1

driver *n* a person who travels by automobile — see MOTORIST

drizzle *n* a light or fine rain ⟨the intermittent *drizzle* was just heavy enough to spoil all of our outdoor activities⟩
synonyms mist, sprinkle
related words precipitation, rainfall, shower
near antonyms cloudburst, deluge, downpour, storm; rainstorm, thunderstorm; monsoon

droll *adj* causing or intended to cause laughter — see FUNNY 1

drollness *n* the amusing quality or element in something — see HUMOR 1

¹drone *n* a lazy person — see LAZYBONES

²drone *n* a monotonous sound like that of an insect in motion — see HUM

drone *vb* to fly, turn, or move rapidly with a fluttering or vibratory sound — see WHIRR

drool *vb* to let saliva or some other substance flow from the mouth ⟨the dog *drooled* when we put the steak down on the floor⟩
synonyms dribble, drivel, salivate, slaver, slobber
related words water; expectorate, spit; foam, froth; sputter

droop *n* the extent to which something hangs or dips below a straight line — see SAG

droop *vb* **1** to be limp from lack of water or vigor ⟨the flowers *drooped* on their stalks in the blazing sun⟩
synonyms flag, hang, loll, sag, wilt
related words slouch, slump; collapse, drop, fall, sink, subside
near antonyms distend, stiffen; rise, straighten

2 to lose bodily strength or vigor — see WEAKEN 2

drooping *adj* bending downward or forward — see NODDING

droopy *adj* **1** bending downward or forward — see NODDING

2 not stiff in structure — see LIMP 1

3 feeling unhappiness — see SAD 1

drop *n* **1** the quantity of fluid that falls naturally in

one rounded mass ⟨a *drop* of water fell from the leaky faucet every few seconds⟩
synonyms blob, driblet, drip, droplet, glob, globule
related words dewdrop, raindrop, tear; spatter; dribble, trickle
2 distance measured from the top to the bottom of something — see DEPTH 1
3 the act or process of going to a lower level or altitude — see DESCENT 1
4 the amount by which something is lessened — see DECREASE
5 the more favorable condition or position in a competition — see ADVANTAGE 1
drop *vb* **1** to cause to fall intentionally or unintentionally ⟨I *dropped* the fly ball⟩ ⟨*drop* the anchor⟩
synonyms depress, lower
related words flatten, floor, level; bobble, bungle, foozle, fumble; immerse, sink, submerge
antonyms lift, pick up, raise
2 to go to a lower level ⟨although they start out high, prices for home electronics eventually *drop*⟩
synonyms decline, descend, dip, fall, lower, nosedive, plummet, plunge, sink, tumble
related words decrease, diminish, lessen; recede, retreat
antonyms arise, lift, rise, soar
3 to bring (as an action or operation) to an immediate end — see STOP 1
4 to stop doing (something) permanently — see QUIT 2
5 to lead or extend downward — see DESCEND 1
6 to put an end to (something planned or previously agreed to) — see CANCEL 1
7 to bring forth from the womb — see BEAR 1
8 to strike (someone) so forcefully as to cause a fall — see FELL 1
drop (by *or* in) *vb* to make a brief visit — see CALL 3
droplet *n* the quantity of fluid that falls naturally in one rounded mass — see DROP 1
dropping *n* **1** droppings *pl* solid matter discharged from an animal's alimentary canal ⟨the only bad part about owning a rabbit was cleaning the *droppings* out of the cage every night⟩
synonyms dung, excrement, excreta, feces, slops, waste
related words stool; dunghill, guano, manure, muck; spoor; sewage
2 the act of putting an end to something planned or previously agreed to — see CANCELLATION
dross *n* discarded or useless material — see GARBAGE
droughty *adj* marked by little or no precipitation or humidity — see DRY 1
drove *n* **1** a great number of persons or things gathered together — see CROWD 1
2 a group of domestic animals assembled or herded together — see HERD
drown *vb* **1** to cover or become filled with a flood — see FLOOD
2 to wet thoroughly with liquid — see SOAK 1
drowse *n* a short sleep — see ¹NAP
drowse *vb* to sleep lightly or briefly — see NAP 1
drowsiness *n* the quality or state of desiring or needing sleep — see SLEEPINESS
drowsy *adj* **1** desiring or needing sleep — see SLEEPY 1
2 tending to cause sleep — see HYPNOTIC

drub *vb* **1** to strike repeatedly — see BEAT 1
2 to achieve a victory over — see BEAT 2
3 to defeat by a large margin — see WHIP 2
drubbing *n* failure to win a contest — see DEFEAT 1
drudge *n* a person who does very hard or dull work — see SLAVE 2
drudge *vb* to devote serious and sustained effort — see LABOR
drudger *n* a person who does very hard or dull work — see SLAVE 2
drudgery *n* very hard or unpleasant work — see TOIL
drug *n* a substance or preparation used to treat disease — see MEDICINE
druggist *n* a person who prepares drugs according to a doctor's prescription ⟨she got her prescription for antibiotics filled by the *druggist*⟩
synonyms apothecary, pharmacist
related words pharmacologist
drugstore *n* a retail store where medicines and miscellaneous articles are sold ⟨we picked up her medicine and some toothpaste at the *drugstore*⟩
synonyms pharmacy
related words dispensary
drum *n* a metal container in the shape of a cylinder — see CAN
drum *vb* to strike or cause to strike lightly and usually rhythmically — see ¹TAP
drum (out) *vb* to drive or force out — see EJECT 1
drunk *adj* being under the influence of alcohol ⟨several wedding guests who got a little *drunk*⟩
synonyms drunken, high, inebriate, inebriated, intoxicated, loaded [*slang*], soused, tipsy
related words maudlin; befuddled, stupefied; debauched, dissipated, dissolute
near antonyms abstemious, abstinent, temperate; clearheaded, cool, level, steady
antonyms sober
drunk *n* **1** a person who makes a habit of getting drunk ⟨you can't trust anything that old *drunk* says⟩
synonyms drunkard, inebriate, soak, sot, souse, tippler
related words alcoholic, substance abuser; drinker
near antonyms abstainer
2 a bout of drinking — see CAROUSE
drunkard *n* a person who makes a habit of getting drunk — see DRUNK 1
drunken *adj* being under the influence of alcohol — see DRUNK
dry *adj* **1** marked by little or no precipitation or humidity ⟨the *dry* climate of the American Southwest⟩
synonyms arid, droughty, sere, thirsty, waterless
related words baked, dehydrated, parched, sunbaked; rainless
near antonyms drenched, dripping, saturated, soaked, soaking, sodden, sopping, soppy, soused
antonyms damp, dank, humid, moist, wet
2 causing weariness, restlessness, or lack of interest — see BORING
dry *vb* **1** to make dry ⟨they *dried* the grapes to make raisins⟩
synonyms dehydrate, parch, sear
related words dehumidify; evaporate; shrivel, wither
near antonyms deluge, douse, drench, saturate,

soak, sop, souse; damp, dampen, moisten; rehydrate

antonyms hydrate, wet

2 to lose liveliness, force, or freshness — see WITHER

dryad *n* a mythical goddess represented as a young girl and said to live outdoors — see NYMPH 1

dry run *n* a private performance or session in preparation for a public appearance — see REHEARSAL

dual *adj* consisting of two members or parts that are usually joined — see DOUBLE 1

dub *vb* to give a name to — see NAME 1

dubious *adj* **1** giving good reason for being doubted, questioned, or challenged — see DOUBTFUL 2

2 having doubts about the wisdom of doing something — see HESITANT

3 not likely to be true or to occur — see IMPROBABLE

4 not feeling sure about the truth, wisdom, or trustworthiness of someone or something — see DOUBTFUL 1

dubiously *adv* with distrust — see ASKANCE

duck *vb* **1** to get or keep away from (as a responsibility) through cleverness or trickery — see ESCAPE 2

2 to move suddenly aside or to and fro — see DODGE 1

3 to sink or push (something) briefly into or as if into a liquid — see DIP 1

ducking *n* the act or a means of getting or keeping away from something undesirable — see ESCAPE 2

duck soup *n* something that is easy to do — see CINCH

duct *n* a long hollow cylinder for carrying a substance (as a liquid or gas) — see PIPE 1

dud *n* **1** something that has failed — see FAILURE 3

2 duds *pl* covering for the human body — see CLOTHING

dude *n* **1** a man extremely interested in his clothing and personal appearance — see DANDY 1

2 an adult male human being — see MAN 1

dudgeon *n* the feeling of being offended or resentful after a slight or indignity — see PIQUE

due *adj* **1** having reached the date at which payment is required ⟨the loan is *due* next April⟩

synonyms mature

related words delinquent, outstanding, overdue, owed, owing, receivable, unpaid, unsettled; payable

2 being in accordance with the prescribed, normal, or logical course of events ⟨their train is *due* to arrive in half an hour⟩

synonyms anticipated, awaited, expected, scheduled, slated

near antonyms belated, delinquent, dilatory, latish, overdue, tardy

3 being what is called for by accepted standards of right and wrong — see JUST 1

due *adv* in a direct line or course — see DIRECTLY 1

due (to) *adj* coming as a result — see RESULTANT

duel *n* an earnest effort for superiority or victory over another — see CONTEST 1

due to *prep* as the result of — see BECAUSE OF

dull *adj* **1** lacking sharpness of edge or point ⟨the *dull* knife just bounced off the skin of the tomato without cutting it⟩

synonyms blunt, blunted, dulled, obtuse

related words rounded

near antonyms cutting, edged, edgy, ground, honed, stropped; jagged, needlelike, prickly, spiked, spiky, spiny

antonyms keen, pointed, sharp, sharpened, whetted

2 causing weariness, restlessness, or lack of interest — see BORING

3 covered over by clouds — see OVERCAST

4 lacking a surface luster or gloss — see MATTE

5 lacking intensity of color — see PALE 1

6 not having or showing an ability to absorb ideas readily — see STUPID 1

7 not loud in pitch or volume — see SOFT 1

8 slow to move or act — see INACTIVE 1

dull *vb* **1** to reduce or weaken in strength or feeling ⟨the aspirin *dulled* his headache and he was soon feeling better⟩

synonyms benumb, blunt, damp, dampen, deaden, numb

related words muffle, mute, tone (down); decrease, diminish, lessen, let up (on), reduce, subdue; debilitate, enfeeble, weaken; dwindle, recede, subside, taper (off), wane; alleviate, ease, lighten; abate, moderate

near antonyms amplify, beef (up), boost, consolidate, deepen, enhance, heighten, intensify, magnify, redouble, step up, strengthen; animate, arouse, stimulate

antonyms sharpen, whet

2 to make white or lighter by removing color — see WHITEN

dulled *adj* **1** lacking a surface luster or gloss — see MATTE

2 lacking intensity of color — see PALE 1

3 lacking sharpness of edge or point — see DULL 1

dullness *also* **dulness** *n* the quality or state of lacking intelligence or quickness of mind — see STUPIDITY 1

dumb *adj* **1** deliberately refraining from speech — see SILENT 1

2 not having or showing an ability to absorb ideas readily — see STUPID 1

dumbbell *n* a stupid person — see IDIOT

dumbfound *also* **dumfound** *vb* to make a strong impression on (someone) with something unexpected — see SURPRISE 1

dumbfounded *or* **dumfounded** *adj* **1** affected with sudden and great wonder or surprise — see THUNDERSTRUCK

2 filled with amazement or wonder — see OPENMOUTHED

dumbfounding *or* **dumfounding** *adj* causing a strong emotional reaction because unexpected — see SURPRISING 1

dumbness *n* **1** incapacity for or restraint from speaking — see SILENCE 1

2 the quality or state of lacking intelligence or quickness of mind — see STUPIDITY 1

dummy *n* **1** a stupid person — see IDIOT

2 a three-dimensional representation of the human body used especially for displaying clothes — see MANNEQUIN 1

dump *n* **1** a place where discarded materials (as trash) are dumped ⟨all of the used packaging eventually ends up in the *dump*⟩

synonyms landfill, sanitary landfill

related words pigpen, pigsty

2 a place where military arms are stored — see ARMORY

dump *vb* to get rid of as useless or unwanted — see DISCARD

dumping *n* the getting rid of whatever is unwanted or useless — see DISPOSAL 1

dumps *n pl* a state or spell of low spirits — see SADNESS

dumpy *adj* being compact and broad in build and often short in stature — see STOCKY

dun *n* something that someone insists upon having — see DEMAND 1

dunce *n* a stupid person — see IDIOT

dung *n* solid matter discharged from an animal's alimentary canal — see DROPPING 1

dunk *vb* to sink or push (something) briefly into or as if into a liquid — see DIP 1

duo *n* two things of the same or similar kind that match or are considered together — see PAIR

dupe *n* one who is easily deceived or cheated ⟨the swindler was able to escape with all of the *dupe's* money⟩
synonyms chump, gull, pigeon, sap, sucker, tool
related words victim; schlemiel; butt, derision, laughingstock, mark, mock, mockery; booby, dodo, fool, goose, half-wit, jackass, lunatic, monkey, nincompoop, ninny, nitwit, simpleton, turkey; pushover; loser
near antonyms confidence man, shark, sharper, swindler, trickster

dupe *vb* to cause to believe what is untrue — see DECEIVE

duplex *adj* consisting of two members or parts that are usually joined — see DOUBLE 1

duplicate *adj* resembling another in every respect — see SAME 1

duplicate *n* **1** something or someone that strongly resembles another — see IMAGE 1
2 something that is made to look exactly like something else — see COPY 1

duplicate *vb* **1** to make an exact likeness of — see COPY 1
2 to make or do again — see REPEAT 4
3 to make twice as great or as many — see DOUBLE 1

duplication *n* **1** something or someone that strongly resembles another — see IMAGE 1
2 something that is made to look exactly like something else — see COPY
3 the act of saying or doing over again — see REPEAT

duplicity *n* the inclination or practice of misleading others through lies or trickery — see DECEIT

durability *n* continuing existence — see PERSISTENCE 1

duration *n* **1** the period during which something exists, lasts, or is in progress ⟨for the whole *duration* of the speech the bored audience fidgeted⟩
synonyms date, life, life span, lifetime, run, standing, time
related words spell, stretch; span, tenure, term; hitch, tour, turn
2 uninterrupted or lasting existence — see CONTINUATION

duress *n* the use of power to impose one's will on another — see FORCE 2

during *prep* in the course of ⟨we wrote notes *during* the boring lecture⟩
synonyms over, through, throughout

dusk *n* **1** the time from when the sun begins to set to the onset of total darkness ⟨we stopped playing at *dusk*, since it was getting too dark to see the ball⟩
synonyms evening, eventide, gloaming, nightfall, sundown, sunset, twilight
related words dark, darkness, night, nighttime
near antonyms day, daytime, light
antonyms aurora, cockcrow, dawn, dawning, daybreak, daylight, morn, morning, sunrise, sunup
2 a time or place of little or no light — see DARK 1

dusky *adj* being without light or without much light — see DARK 1

dust *n* **1** discarded or useless material — see GARBAGE
2 the solid part of our planet's surface as distinguished from the sea and air — see EARTH 2

dustiness *n* the state or quality of being dirty — see DIRTINESS 1

dusty *adj* **1** consisting of very small particles — see FINE 1
2 not clean — see DIRTY 1

dutiful *adj* marked by or showing proper regard for another's higher status — see RESPECTFUL

duty *n* **1** a charge usually of money collected by the government from people or businesses for public use — see TAX
2 a piece of work that needs to be done regularly — see CHORE 1
3 something one must do because of prior agreement — see OBLIGATION

dwarf *adj* of a size that is less than average — see SMALL 1

dwarf *n* **1** a living thing much smaller than others of its kind ⟨Shetland ponies are the *dwarfs* of the horse world⟩
synonyms diminutive, midget, mite, peewee, pygmy, runt, scrub, shrimp
related words mini, miniature
near antonyms whale
antonyms behemoth, colossus, giant, jumbo, leviathan, mammoth, monster, titan
2 an imaginary being usually having a small human form and magical powers — see FAIRY

dwarf *vb* to hold back the normal growth of — see STUNT

dwarfish *adj* of a size that is less than average — see SMALL 1

dwell *vb* **1** to continue to be in a place for a significant amount of time — see STAY 1
2 to have a home — see LIVE 1

dweller *n* one who lives permanently in a place — see INHABITANT

dwelling *n* the place where one lives — see HOME 1

dwindle *vb* **1** to make smaller in amount, volume, or extent — see DECREASE 1
2 to grow less in scope or intensity especially gradually — see DECREASE 2

dye *n* a substance used to color other materials — see PIGMENT

dye *vb* to give color or a different color to — see COLOR 1

dyestuff *n* a substance used to color other materials — see PIGMENT

dying *adj* nearly dead — see MORIBUND

dynamic *adj* **1** having active strength of body or mind — see VIGOROUS 1
2 marked by or uttered with forcefulness — see EMPHATIC 1

dyspeptic *adj* having or showing a habitually bad temper — see ILL-TEMPERED

THESAURUS

each *adj* being one of a group ⟨*each* park visitor receives a free souvenir⟩
synonyms any, every
related words all; several, various; particular; respective, specific
phrases each and every
each *adv* for each one — see APIECE
eager *adj* showing urgent desire or interest ⟨Tom was *eager* to try out his new pair of skis⟩
synonyms agog, anxious, ardent, athirst, avid, crazy, desirous, enthusiastic, excited, gung ho, hot, hungry, impatient, keen, nuts, raring, solicitous, thirsty, voracious
related words engaged, interested; hung up, obsessed; ambitious, covetous, craving, hankering, longing, pining; restive, restless; disposed, inclined, ready, unreluctant, willing
phrases champing at the bit
near antonyms incurious; unconcerned, uninterested; aloof, detached, disinterested; impassive, stolid; halfhearted, lackadaisical, languid, languorous, spiritless; averse, disinclined, hesitant, loath (*or* loth), reluctant, unwilling
antonyms apathetic, indifferent, uneager
eagerness *n* urgent desire or interest ⟨students with an *eagerness* to learn⟩
synonyms appetite, ardor, avidity, desirousness, enthusiasm, excitement, hunger, impatience, keenness, thirst
related words alacrity, quickness; ambition, gusto, zest
near antonyms unconcern; aloofness, detachment; impassivity, languor
antonyms apathy, indifference
ear *n* a state of being aware — see ATTENTION 2
earliest *adj* coming before all others in time or order — see FIRST 1
early *adj* **1** relating to or occurring near the beginning of a process, series, or time period ⟨*early* birds of the Jurassic period⟩
synonyms ancient, primal, primeval, primitive, primordial
related words aged, antediluvian, antiquated, antique, hoary
near antonyms advanced, complex
antonyms late
2 occurring before the usual or expected time ⟨we had an *early* dinner so as not to miss the concert⟩
synonyms inopportune, precocious, premature, unseasonable, untimely
related words unanticipated, unexpected; abrupt, sudden
near antonyms slow, tardy; anticipated, expected
antonyms late
early *adv* before the usual or expected time ⟨that year spring arrived *early*⟩
synonyms beforehand, inopportunely, precociously, prematurely, unseasonably
related words immediately, promptly, punctually; betimes, seasonably
near antonyms belatedly, tardily
antonyms late
earmark *vb* to keep or intend for a special purpose — see DEVOTE 1
earn *vb* **1** to receive as return for effort ⟨for years I've *earned* pocket money by mowing lawns⟩

synonyms acquire, attain, capture, carry, draw, gain, garner, get, land, make, obtain, procure, realize, secure, win
related words clear, net; accomplish, achieve, notch (up), score; accumulate, draw, rack up; catch, pick up; occupy, take over; reacquire, recapture, regain, remake
phrases come by
near antonyms give up, hand over, part (with), relinquish, surrender, yield
antonyms forfeit, lose
2 to be or make worthy of (as a reward or punishment) ⟨you've *earned* the afternoon off after all that hard work⟩
synonyms deserve, merit, rate
related words entitle, qualify
earnest *adj* not joking or playful in mood or manner — see SERIOUS 1
earnestness *n* a mental state free of jesting or trifling ⟨practiced the art of acting with great *earnestness*⟩
synonyms gravity, intentness, seriousness, soberness, sobriety, solemnity
related words deliberation, determination, firmness, purposefulness, resolve; absorption, attentiveness, concentration, engrossment
near antonyms lightness, shallowness, superficiality; dalliance, dilettantism
antonyms frivolity, levity, lightheartedness
earnings *n pl* **1** an increase usually measured in money that comes from labor, business, or property — see INCOME
2 the amount of money left when expenses are subtracted from the total amount received — see PROFIT 1
earshot *n* range of hearing ⟨babysitters should remain within *earshot* of young children⟩
synonyms hearing, sound
related words volume; distance, sight
earsplitting *adj* marked by a high volume of sound — see LOUD 1
earth *n* **1** the celestial body on which we live ⟨environmentalists who are committed to preserving the *earth*⟩
synonyms globe, planet, world
related words cosmos, creation, universe; orb, sphere; macrocosm, microcosm
2 the solid part of our planet's surface as distinguished from the sea and air ⟨after nearly drowning, I was glad to feel the *earth* under my feet⟩
synonyms dirt, dust, ground, land, soil
related words continent, landmass; island, isthmus, mainland, peninsula
3 the loose surface material in which plants naturally grow — see DIRT 1
earthenware *n* articles made of baked clay — see CROCKERY
earthlike *adj* consisting or suggestive of earth — see EARTHY 1
earthly *adj* having to do with life on earth especially as opposed to that in heaven ⟨a sermon against our obsession with *earthly* pursuits⟩
synonyms carnal, fleshly, material, mundane, temporal, terrestrial, worldly
related words bodily, corporal, corporeal, physical; daily, diurnal; unspiritual

near antonyms celestial, empyreal, empyrean; divine, spiritual, utopian; extraterrestrial
antonyms heavenly, nontemporal
earthquake *n* a shaking of the earth ⟨the San Andreas Fault is notorious for its *earthquakes*⟩
synonyms quake, tremor
related words shock; cataclysm, convulsion, upheaval
earthy *adj* **1** consisting or suggestive of earth ⟨the unmistakably *earthy* aroma of a greenhouse⟩
synonyms earthlike, loamy
related words clayey, dusty, muddy, sandy
2 willing to see things as they really are and deal with them sensibly — see REALISTIC 1
ease *n* **1** reduction of or freedom from pain ⟨the sunburn medication brought me instant *ease*⟩
synonyms alleviation, comfort, relief
related words appeasement, assuagement, decrease, diminishment, moderation, mollification; calming, salving, soothing
near antonyms discomfort, unrest; agony, anguish, pain
2 carefree freedom from constraint — see ABANDON
3 freedom from activity or labor — see ¹REST 1
ease *vb* **1** to free from obstruction or difficulty ⟨measures intended to *ease* the flow of traffic during rush hour⟩
synonyms facilitate, loosen (up), smooth, unclog
related words accelerate, expedite, hasten, speed; advance, further, promote; aid, assist, help, improve
phrases pave the way (for)
near antonyms hinder, impede; retard
antonyms complicate
2 to make less taut — see SLACKEN
3 to make more bearable or less severe — see HELP 2
easily *adv* without difficulty ⟨a skater who *easily* executes even the most difficult jumps⟩
synonyms effortlessly, facilely, fluently, freely, handily, lightly, painlessly, readily, smoothly
related words ably, adeptly, adroitly, competently, dexterously, efficiently, expertly, proficiently, skillfully; instinctively, intuitively, naturally, spontaneously
near antonyms awkwardly, clumsily, gracelessly, ineptly, maladroitly; painfully, painstakingly
antonyms arduously, laboriously
easy *adj* **1** involving minimal difficulty or effort ⟨a minor problem with an *easy* solution⟩
synonyms effortless, facile, fluent, fluid, light, painless, ready, simple, smooth, snap, soft
related words apparent, clear, distinct, evident, manifest, obvious, plain; clear-cut, straightforward, uncomplicated
near antonyms painful, troublesome; abstruse, complex, complicated, intricate, knotty
antonyms arduous, difficult, hard, labored
2 readily taken advantage of ⟨senior citizens who are *easy* prey for scam artists⟩
synonyms exploitable, gullible, naive (*or* naïve), susceptible, trusting
related words credulous, trustful, uncritical, unsuspecting, unsuspicious; artless, simple, unsophisticated
near antonyms critical, cynical, mistrustful, skeptical, suspicious; sophisticated
3 providing physical comfort — see COMFORTABLE 1

easygoing *adj* **1** having a relaxed, casual manner ⟨counselors at the summer camp are pretty *easygoing*⟩
synonyms affable, breezy, devil-may-care, happy-go-lucky, laid-back, low-pressure
related words carefree, lackadaisical, nonchalant, unaffected, unconcerned; familiar, homey, informal; lax, lenient, permissive, soft
near antonyms ceremonious, decorous, formal, rigid, strict
antonyms uptight
2 not bound by rigid standards ⟨boys are pretty *easygoing* about housekeeping⟩
synonyms flexible, lax, loose, relaxed, slack, unrestrained, unrestricted
related words careless, heedless, negligent, slipshod, sloppy, slovenly, unfussy
near antonyms constrained, restrained, restricted, rigid, strict, tight; exact, fussy, meticulous, scrupulous
antonyms rigorous
3 having or showing a lack of concern or seriousness — see CAREFREE
eat *vb* **1** to take in as food ⟨having gone all day without food, we greedily *ate* the hamburgers⟩
synonyms consume, ingest
related words digest, down, mouth (down), swallow; bolt, devour, gobble (up *or* down), gorge, gulp, wolf; chew, gnaw (at *or* on), lap, lick, nibble (on); relish, savor, taste; banquet, dine, feast, gormandize, pig out; dispatch, polish off; breakfast, lunch, sup; munch, snack
2 to consume or wear away gradually ⟨the pot's protective coating was *eaten* away by the acid⟩
synonyms bite (at), corrode, erode, fret
related words break down, break up, decompose, disintegrate, dissolve; destroy, ruin, wreck
3 to take a meal — see DINE 1
eat (up) *vb* to destroy all trace of — see CONSUME 1
eatable *adj* suitable for use as food — see EDIBLE
eatables *n pl* substances intended to be eaten — see FOOD
eavesdrop (on) *vb* to listen to (another in private conversation) ⟨a nosy traveler who likes to *eavesdrop on* his fellow airline passengers⟩
synonyms listen in (on), overhear
related words bug, tap, wiretap; monitor, snoop, spy; hear, hearken
eaves trough *n* a pipe or channel for carrying off water from a roof — see GUTTER 1
ebb *vb* **1** to become worse or of less value — see DETERIORATE
2 to grow less in scope or intensity especially gradually — see DECREASE 2
ebbing *n* a gradual sinking and wasting away of mind or body — see DECLINE 1
ebony *adj* having the color of soot or coal — see BLACK 1
eccentric *n* a person of odd or whimsical habits ⟨an *eccentric* who designed his house to look like a Scottish castle⟩
synonyms character, codger, crackbrain, crackpot, crank, kook, nut, oddball, screwball, weirdo
related words bohemian, maverick, nonconformist; coot, rarity; freak
near antonyms conformer, conformist, follower, sheep
eccentricity *n* an odd or peculiar habit — see IDIOSYNCRASY

ecclesiastic *n* a person specially trained and authorized to conduct religious services in a Christian church — see CLERGYMAN

ecclesiastical *or* **ecclesiastic** *adj* of or relating to a church ⟨*ecclesiastical* laws that have been in existence for centuries⟩

synonyms churchly

related words divine, holy, religious, sacramental; apostolic, canonical, clerical, episcopal, evangelical, ministerial, papal, pastoral, patriarchal, pontifical, priestly, rabbinical, sacerdotal

near antonyms lay, profane, secular, temporal

echo *vb* 1 to continue or be repeated in a series of reflected sound waves — see REVERBERATE

2 to say after another — see REPEAT 3

eclipse *vb* to be greater, better, or stronger than — see SURPASS 1

economical *adj* careful in the management of money or resources — see FRUGAL

economize *vb* to avoid unnecessary waste or expense ⟨in tough times people learn how to *economize*⟩

synonyms save, scrimp, skimp

related words conserve, husband, manage; scrape; cut back, cut down, retrench

near antonyms dissipate, fritter (away), squander, throw away

antonyms waste

economizing *adj* careful in the management of money or resources — see FRUGAL

economy *n* careful management of material resources ⟨people on fixed incomes are used to practicing *economy*⟩

synonyms frugality, husbandry, providence, scrimping, skimping, thrift

related words conservation, saving; miserliness, stinginess; discretion, prudence

near antonyms extravagance, improvidence, lavishness, prodigality, squandering

antonyms wastefulness

ecstasy *n* a state of overwhelming usually pleasurable emotion ⟨actors are typically in *ecstasy* upon winning an Oscar⟩

synonyms elation, euphoria, exhilaration, heaven, intoxication, paradise, rapture, rhapsody, transport

related words exaltation; bliss, blissfulness, delight, enchantment, gladness, happiness, joy, joyfulness, pleasure; reverie, trance; inspiration; fervor, frenzy, madness, passion

near antonyms blues, dejection, despondency, doldrums, downheartedness, dumps, melancholy, mopes

antonyms depression

ecstatic *adj* experiencing or marked by overwhelming usually pleasurable emotion ⟨a football player who was *ecstatic* upon receiving a full athletic scholarship to the college of his choice⟩

synonyms elated, enraptured, entranced, euphoric, exhilarated, intoxicated, rapturous, rhapsodic (*also* rhapsodical)

related words exultant, jubilant, triumphant; enthusiastic, excited, gung ho, thrilled; blissful, delighted, glad, gratified, happy, joyful, joyous, pleased, satisfied, tickled

near antonyms blue, dejected, despondent, disconsolate, disheartened, downhearted, melancholy

antonyms depressed

Eden *n* a place or state of great happiness — see PARADISE 1

edge *n* 1 a harsh or sharp quality ⟨the teacher's voice had a sarcastic *edge* as she welcomed the tardy student to class⟩

synonyms acidity, acridness, acrimoniousness, acrimony, acuteness, asperity, bite, bitterness, harshness, keenness, poignancy, pungency, roughness, sharpness, tartness

related words ginger, punch, spice, tang; severity, shrillness, virulence; pointedness, thorniness

2 the line or relatively narrow space that marks the outer limit of something — see BORDER 1

3 the more favorable condition or position in a competition — see ADVANTAGE 1

edge *vb* to make sharp or sharper — see SHARPEN

edged *adj* having an edge thin enough to cut or pierce something — see SHARP 1

edgewise *adv* with one side faced forward — see SIDEWAYS

edginess *n* a state of nervousness marked by sudden jerky movements — see JUMPINESS

edgy *adj* 1 feeling or showing uncomfortable feelings of uncertainty — see NERVOUS 1

2 having an edge thin enough to cut or pierce something — see SHARP 1

edible *adj* suitable for use as food ⟨*edible* plant products⟩

synonyms eatable, esculent

related words absorbable, chewable, digestible; nourishing, nutritious, nutritive; appetizing, delicious, flavorful, palatable, savory, succulent, tasty, toothsome

near antonyms indigestible, nondigestible

antonyms inedible

edibles *n pl* substances intended to be eaten — see FOOD

edict *n* 1 an order publicly issued by an authority ⟨the school board's *edict* put a new student dress code into effect⟩

synonyms decree, directive, fiat, ruling

related words call, decision, judgment (*or* judgement); announcement, declaration, dictum, manifesto, proclamation, pronouncement; canon, encyclical

2 a statement of what to do that must be obeyed by those concerned — see COMMAND 1

edifice *n* 1 a large, magnificent, or massive building ⟨the U.S. Capitol is one of our nation's most impressive *edifices*⟩

synonyms hall, palace, tower

related words construction, erection, structure; castle, château, estate, manor, mansion, villa; mausoleum, memorial, monument

2 something built as a dwelling, shelter, or place for human activity — see BUILDING

edify *vb* to provide (someone) with moral or spiritual understanding — see ENLIGHTEN 2

edit *vb* to prepare for publication by correcting, rewriting, or updating ⟨the publisher *edited* a new version of its best-selling school dictionary⟩

synonyms redraft, revamp, revise, rework

related words amend, correct, emend, rectify; collect, compile; issue, print, publish

educate *vb* 1 to cause to acquire knowledge or skill in some field — see TEACH

2 to provide (someone) with moral or spiritual understanding — see ENLIGHTEN 2

educated *adj* having or displaying advanced knowledge or education ⟨*educated* people are often more aware and tolerant of cultural and ethnic diversity⟩

synonyms erudite, knowledgeable, learned, literate, scholarly, well-read

related words civilized, cultivated, cultured; cerebral, highbrow, intellectual; polished, refined, well-bred; academic, bookish, didactic, pedantic, professorial; instructed, schooled, skilled, trained; homeschooled, self-educated, self-taught; briefed, enlightened, informed, versed

near antonyms uncivilized, uncultivated, uncultured; lowbrow, unintelligent; ill-bred, unpolished, unrefined; uninformed

antonyms ignorant, illiterate, uneducated

education *n* **1** the act or process of imparting knowledge or skills to another ⟨a teacher who devoted herself to the *education* of children with special needs⟩

synonyms instruction, schooling, teaching, training, tutelage, tutoring

related words coaching, conditioning, cultivation, preparation, readying; development, direction, guidance, nurturance, nurturing; edification, enlightenment, improvement

2 the understanding and information gained from being educated ⟨a person whose extensive *education* was obvious to all who met him⟩

synonyms erudition, knowledge, learnedness, learning, scholarship, science

related words culture, edification, enlightenment; literacy, reading; bookishness, pedantry

near antonyms ignorance, illiteracy

educational *adj* **1** providing useful information or knowledge — see INFORMATIVE

2 of or relating to schooling or learning especially at an advanced level — see ACADEMIC

educative *adj* providing useful information or knowledge — see INFORMATIVE

educator *n* a person whose occupation is to give formal instruction in a school — see TEACHER

educe *vb* to draw out (something hidden, latent, or reserved) ⟨the gift of a puppy finally *educed* a response from the shy boy⟩

synonyms elicit, evoke, raise

related words drag, dredge (up), extort, pull, wangle, wrest, wring; gain, get, obtain, procure, secure; expose, reveal, uncover

near antonyms miss, overlook, pass over

eerie *adj* fearfully and mysteriously strange or fantastic ⟨*eerie* noises would occasionally come from locked rooms in the castle⟩

synonyms creepy, haunting, spooky, uncanny, unearthly, weird

related words ghostly, spectral; odd, strange, uncommon, unusual; preternatural, supernatural; enigmatic (*also* enigmatical), inscrutable, mysterious, puzzling; dreadful, fearsome, horrible, horrifying, terrible, terrifying

near antonyms common, commonplace, everyday, normal, ordinary, usual

efface *vb* to destroy all traces of — see ANNIHILATE 1

effect *n* **1** a condition or occurrence traceable to a cause ⟨better health is always one of the *effects* of improved hygiene⟩

synonyms aftereffect, aftermath, conclusion, consequence, corollary, development, fate, fruit, issue, outcome, outgrowth, product, result, resultant, sequel, sequence, upshot

related words ramification; denouement, repercussion; conclusion, end; by-product, side effect

phrases matter of course

near antonyms consideration, determinant, factor; base, basis, foundation, ground, groundwork

antonyms antecedent, cause, occasion, reason

2 the power to bring about a result on another ⟨religion has a profound *effect* on our lives⟩

synonyms impact, influence, mark, repercussion, sway

related words authority, clout, prestige, weight; command, domination, dominion; consequence, importance, significance

3 effects *pl* transportable items that one owns — see POSSESSION 2

effect *vb* to be the cause of (a situation, action, or state of mind) ⟨classroom discussions designed to *effect* a change in racial attitudes⟩

synonyms bring about, cause, create, effectuate, engender, generate, induce, make, produce, prompt, result (in), spawn, work, yield

related words decide, determine; begin, establish, father, found, inaugurate, initiate, institute, introduce, set, set up; advance, encourage, forward, foster, promote; enact, render, turn out

phrases bring forth, give rise to

near antonyms impede, limit, restrict; dampen, repress, smother, stifle, suppress; arrest, check, curb, restrain, retard; can, kill, snuff (out), still; abolish, demolish, destroy, extinguish, liquidate, quash, quell, quench

effective *adj* **1** producing or capable of producing a desired result ⟨an *effective* treatment of the once-dreaded disease⟩

synonyms effectual, efficacious, efficient, fruitful, potent, productive

related words adequate, capable, competent; adept, expert, masterly, proficient, skilled, skillful; cogent, convincing, killer, sound, striking, telling, valid; active, dynamic; operative, useful, working; feasible, practical, realizable, workable

near antonyms incapable, incompetent, inexpert, unqualified; abortive, bootless, futile, vain; empty, hollow, idle, pointless; inoperative, useless, worthless

antonyms fruitless, ineffective, ineffectual, inefficient, unproductive

2 having the power to persuade — see COGENT

effectiveness *n* **1** the capacity to persuade — see COGENCY 1

2 the power to produce a desired result — see EFFICACY

3 the quality of an utterance that provokes interest and produces an effect — see ¹PUNCH 1

effectual *adj* producing or capable of producing a desired result — see EFFECTIVE 1

effectualness *n* the power to produce a desired result — see EFFICACY

effectuate *vb* to be the cause of (a situation, action, or state of mind) — see EFFECT

effeminate *adj* having or displaying qualities more suitable for women than for men ⟨a comedian deliberately affecting *effeminate* mannerisms⟩

synonyms feminine, girlish, sissy, unmanly, womanish, womanlike, womanly

related words old-maidish, overnice, spinsterish; dandyish, foppish, sappy

antonyms manlike, manly, mannish, masculine

effervescent *adj* joyously unrestrained — see EXUBERANT

effete *adj* **1** having lost forcefulness, courage, or spirit ⟨the soft, *effete* society that marked the final years of the Roman empire⟩
synonyms decadent, decayed, degenerate, overripe, washed-up
related words decaying, declining, dying, failing, waning; soft, weak; dissolute, immoral
2 depleted in strength, energy, or freshness — see WEARY 1
3 lacking bodily strength — see WEAK 1
4 lacking strength of will or character — see WEAK 2

efficacious *adj* producing or capable of producing a desired result — see EFFECTIVE 1

efficaciousness *n* the power to produce a desired result — see EFFICACY

efficacy *n* the power to produce a desired result ⟨questioned the *efficacy* of the alarms in actually preventing auto theft⟩
synonyms effectiveness, effectualness, efficaciousness, efficiency, productiveness
related words ability, capability, capacity; potency, strength
near antonyms inability, inadequacy, incompetence
antonyms ineffectiveness, ineffectualness, inefficiency

efficiency *n* the power to produce a desired result — see EFFICACY

efficient *adj* producing or capable of producing a desired result — see EFFECTIVE 1

effort *n* the active use of energy in producing a result ⟨the finished parade float was well worth the *effort*⟩
synonyms elbow grease, exertion, expenditure, labor, pains, sweat, trouble, while, work
related words drudgery, grind, toil, travail; dint, energy; force, might, muscle, power, puissance; attempt, endeavor, essay
near antonyms adroitness, ease, facility, fluency, smoothness; idleness, inaction, inactivity, indolence, inertia, languor, laziness

effortless *adj* involving minimal difficulty or effort — see EASY 1

effortlessly *adv* without difficulty — see EASILY

effrontery *n* shameless boldness ⟨the little squirt had the *effrontery* to deny eating any cookies, even with the crumbs still on his lips⟩
synonyms audacity, brashness, brass, brassiness, brazenness, cheek, cheekiness, chutzpah (*also* chutzpa *or* hutzpah *or* hutzpa), gall, nerve, nerviness, pertness, presumption, presumptuousness, sauce, sauciness, temerity
related words arrogance, assurance, cockiness, confidence, overconfidence, sanguinity, self-assurance, self-confidence; impertinence, impudence, insolence, rudeness
near antonyms bashfulness, diffidence, hesitancy, modesty, shyness, timidity

effulgence *n* the quality or state of having or giving off light — see BRILLIANCE 1

effulgent *adj* giving off or reflecting much light — see BRIGHT 1

effusive *adj* showing feeling freely — see DEMONSTRATIVE

egg (on) *vb* to try to persuade (someone) through earnest appeals to follow a course of action — see URGE

ego *n* **1** a reasonable or justifiable sense of one's worth or importance — see PRIDE 1

2 an often unjustified feeling of being pleased with oneself or with one's situation or achievements — see COMPLACENCE

egocentric *adj* overly concerned with one's own desires, needs, or interests ⟨the cult attracts *egocentric* people who are preoccupied with reaching their potential as individuals⟩
synonyms egoistic, egotistic (*or* egotistical), self-centered, selfish, self-seeking
related words complacent, conceited, self-conceited, self-directed, self-important, self-indulgent, self-satisfied, smug, vain
near antonyms altruistic, generous, greathearted, magnanimous, self-sacrificing
antonyms selfless

egoism *n* excessive interest in oneself ⟨because of her *egoism*, she never gave a thought to asking how the others felt⟩
synonyms egotism, self-centeredness, self-interest, selfishness, self-regard
related words conceit, self-admiration, self-conceit, self-esteem, self-importance, self-indulgence, self-respect, self-satisfaction, self-sufficiency
near antonyms altruism, generosity, magnanimity, self-sacrifice
antonyms selflessness

egoistic *adj* **1** having too high an opinion of oneself — see CONCEITED
2 overly concerned with one's own desires, needs, or interests — see EGOCENTRIC

egotism *n* **1** an often unjustified feeling of being pleased with oneself or with one's situation or achievements — see COMPLACENCE
2 excessive interest in oneself — see EGOISM

egotistic *or* **egotistical** *adj* **1** having too high an opinion of oneself — see CONCEITED
2 overly concerned with one's own desires, needs, or interests — see EGOCENTRIC

egregious *adj* very noticeable especially for being incorrect or bad ⟨the student's theme was marred by a number of *egregious* errors in spelling⟩
synonyms blatant, conspicuous, flagrant, glaring, gross, obvious, patent, pronounced, rank, striking
related words clear, distinct, evident, notable, outstanding, plain, salient; absolute, arrant, downright, out-and-out, outright, sheer, stark, utter; abominable, atrocious, awful, deplorable, execrable, heinous, monstrous, outrageous, preposterous, shameful, shocking
near antonyms imperceptible, inconspicuous; insignificant, slight, trifling, trivial; concealed, hidden, invisible

egress *n* a place or means of going out — see EXIT 1

ejaculate *vb* to utter with a sudden burst of strong feeling — see EXCLAIM

eject *vb* **1** to drive or force out ⟨we quickly *ejected* the unwanted guest from our party⟩
synonyms banish, boot (out), bounce, cast (out), chase, dismiss, drum (out), expel, extrude, oust, rout, run off, throw out
related words deport, displace, dispossess, evict, exile, expatriate, ostracize, shut out; discharge, fire, sack
phrases send packing
near antonyms accept, admit, receive, take in; welcome; entertain, harbor, house, lodge, shelter
2 to throw out or off (something from within) often violently — see ERUPT 1

eke out *vb* to get with great difficulty ⟨*eked out* a living from the family's small farm⟩

synonyms scrape, scrounge, squeeze, wrest, wring
related words acquire, earn, gain, obtain, procure, secure

elaborate *adj* **1** made or done with great care or with much detail ⟨*elaborate* festivities for the 200th anniversary of the town's founding⟩

synonyms complex, complicated, detailed, fancy, intricate, involved, sophisticated
related words elegant, grand, ornate, magnificent, splendid; extravagant, flamboyant, frilly, grandiose, ostentatious, overwrought; labyrinthine
near antonyms modest, plain, uncomplicated, unsophisticated
antonyms simple

2 including many small descriptive features — see DETAILED 1

3 having many parts or aspects that are usually interrelated — see COMPLEX 1

elaborate (on) *vb* **1** to add to the interest of by including made-up details — see EMBROIDER

2 to express more fully and in greater detail — see EXPAND 1

elaborateness *n* the state or quality of having many interrelated parts or aspects — see COMPLEXITY 1

elaboration *n* **1** the act or process of going from the simple or basic to the complex or advanced — see DEVELOPMENT 1

2 the representation of something in terms that go beyond the facts — see EXAGGERATION

elapse *vb* to come to an end — see CEASE 1

elastic *adj* **1** able to revert to original size and shape after being stretched, squeezed, or twisted ⟨*elastic* rubber bands⟩

synonyms flexible, resilient, rubberlike, rubbery, springy, stretch, stretchable, supple
related words adaptable, ductile, malleable, moldable, plastic, pliable, pliant; limber, lissome (*also* lissom), lithe
near antonyms firm, hard, solid; brittle, crisp, friable
antonyms inelastic, inflexible, nonelastic, rigid, stiff

2 capable of being readily changed — see FLEXIBLE 1

elate *vb* to fill with great joy ⟨the winning of the state basketball championship *elated* the whole student body⟩

synonyms elevate, enrapture, exhilarate, overjoy, transport
related words excite, inspire, stimulate, uplift; delight, gladden, gratify, please
near antonyms demoralize, discourage, dishearten, dispirit; distress, oppress, sadden
antonyms depress

elated *adj* experiencing or marked by overwhelming usually pleasurable emotion — see ECSTATIC

elation *n* a state of overwhelming usually pleasurable emotion — see ECSTASY

elbow *vb* to force one's way — see PRESS 4

elbow grease *n* the active use of energy in producing a result — see EFFORT

elbowroom *n* an extent or area available for or used up by some activity or thing — see ROOM 1

elder *n* **1** a person of advanced years — see SENIOR CITIZEN

2 one who is above another in rank, station, or office — see SUPERIOR

3 one who is older than another — see SENIOR 1

4 the senior member of a group — see DEAN

elderly *adj* being of advanced years and especially past middle age ⟨*elderly* people who stay active are usually the healthiest and the happiest⟩

synonyms aged, aging, ancient, geriatric, long-lived, old, older, senior
related words adult, grown-up, mature, middle-aged; pensioned, retired, superannuated; matriarchal, patriarchal, venerable; doddering, senile, tottery
near antonyms youngish; adolescent, immature, juvenile, puerile
antonyms young, youthful

elder statesman *n* the senior member of a group — see DEAN

elect *adj* singled out from a number or group as more to one's liking — see SELECT 1

elect *n* individuals carefully selected as being the best of a class — see ELITE

elect *vb* to decide to accept (someone or something) from a group of possibilities — see CHOOSE 1

election *n* the act or process of selecting — see SELECTION 1

elective *adj* subject to one's freedom of choice — see OPTIONAL

electric *adj* causing great emotional or mental stimulation — see EXCITING 1

electrify *vb* to cause a pleasurable stimulation of the feelings — see THRILL

electrifying *adj* causing great emotional or mental stimulation — see EXCITING 1

elegance *n* dignified or restrained beauty of form, appearance, or style ⟨the *elegance* of the hotel's French furnishings⟩

synonyms class, elegancy, grace, gracefulness, handsomeness, majesty, refinement, stateliness
related words grandeur, lavishness, luxuriousness, magnificence, ornateness, richness, splendor; artfulness, chic, polish, sophistication, taste, tastefulness; choiceness, classicism, dignity, exquisiteness, restraint, simplicity; affectedness, grandiosity, pretentiousness
near antonyms coarseness, crudeness, flashiness, garishness, gaudiness, gracelessness, grotesqueness, tastelessness, tawdriness

elegancy *n* dignified or restrained beauty of form, appearance, or style — see ELEGANCE

elegant *adj* **1** having or showing elegance ⟨the most *elegant* First Lady in the nation's history⟩ ⟨the bride's *elegant* gown received nothing but praise⟩

synonyms graceful, handsome, majestic, refined, stately, tasteful
related words grand, lavish, luxurious, magnificent, ornate, rich, splendid; artful, genteel, polished, sophisticated; classic, exquisite, restrained, simple; chic, fashionable, posh, smart, stylish; affected, grandiose, pretentious
near antonyms coarse, crude, flashy, garish, gaudy, grotesque, tacky, tawdry
antonyms graceless, inelegant, tasteless, unhandsome

2 having qualities that appeal to a refined taste — see CHOICE

elegiac *adj* causing or marked by an atmosphere lacking in cheer — see GLOOMY 1

elegy *n* a composition expressing one's grief over a loss — see LAMENT 2

THESAURUS

element *n* **1** one of the parts that make up a whole ⟨a free press is an essential *element* of a democracy⟩
synonyms component, constituent, factor, ingredient, member
related words detail, item, particular, point; aspect, characteristic, facet, feature, trait; division, fragment, particle, piece, portion, section, sector, segment
near antonyms aggregate, composite, compound, sum, total, totality
antonyms whole
2 elements *pl* general or basic truths on which other truths or theories can be based — see PRINCIPLES 1

elemental *adj* of or relating to the simplest facts or theories of a subject — see ELEMENTARY

elementary *adj* of or relating to the simplest facts or theories of a subject ⟨students who do not have even an *elementary* knowledge of geography⟩
synonyms basic, elemental, essential, fundamental, rudimentary, underlying
related words primal, primary, prime; primitive; beginning, introductory, preliminary
near antonyms complex, sophisticated; detailed, extensive, intricate
antonyms advanced

elephantine *adj* unusually large — see HUGE

elevate *vb* **1** to fill with great joy — see ELATE
2 to move from a lower to a higher place or position — see RAISE 1
3 to move higher in rank or position — see PROMOTE 1

elevated *adj* **1** being positioned above a surface ⟨an *elevated* monorail that transports visitors all over the theme park⟩
synonyms lifted, raised, uplifted, upraised
related words aerial, suspended; erect, upright
near antonyms low-lying
antonyms sunken
2 very dignified in form, tone, or style ⟨the *elevated* language of Lincoln's Gettysburg Address⟩
synonyms eloquent, formal, high-flown, lofty, majestic, stately, towering
related words bombastic, declamatory, florid, flowery, grandiloquent, highfalutin, pompous, stilted
near antonyms casual, colloquial, conversational, informal, slangy; coarse, crude, indecent, vulgar
antonyms low, undignified
3 being at a higher level than average — see HIGH 2
4 having, characterized by, or arising from a dignified and generous nature — see NOBLE 2
5 located at a greater height than average or usual — see HIGH 3

elevation *n* **1** a raising or a state of being raised to a higher rank or position — see ADVANCEMENT 1
2 an area of high ground — see HEIGHT 4
3 the distance of something or someone from bottom to top — see HEIGHT 3
4 the most extreme or advanced point — see HEIGHT 2

elf *n* an imaginary being usually having a small human form and magical powers — see FAIRY

elfin *adj* having an often mysterious or magical power to attract — see FASCINATING 1

elfish *adj* given to good-natured joking or teasing — see PLAYFUL

elicit *vb* to draw out (something hidden, latent, or reserved) — see EDUCE

eliminate *vb* to prevent the participation or inclusion of — see EXCLUDE

elite *n* individuals carefully selected as being the best of a class ⟨the winners of this science award represent the *elite* of our high schools⟩
synonyms best, choice, cream, elect, fat, flower, pick, prime, upper crust
related words aristocracy, (the) establishment, gentry, nobility, society, (the) top, upper class
phrases cream of the crop
near antonyms commoners, masses, rank and file

elixir *n* something that cures all ills or problems — see CURE-ALL

elliptic *or* **elliptical** *adj* having the shape of an egg — see OVAL

elocution *n* the art of speaking in public eloquently and effectively — see ORATORY 1

elongate *vb* to make longer — see EXTEND 1

elongated *adj* of great extent from end to end — see LONG 1

elongation *n* the act of making longer — see EXTENSION 1

eloquence *n* the art or power of speaking or writing in a forceful and convincing way ⟨the *eloquence* of Martin Luther King's "I Have a Dream" speech⟩
synonyms articulateness, poetry, rhetoric
related words expression, expressiveness; declamation, elocution, oratory; forcefulness, meaningfulness, persuasiveness; ardor, fervor, passion, power

eloquent *adj* **1** able to express oneself clearly and well — see ARTICULATE
2 clearly conveying a special meaning (as one's mood) — see EXPRESSIVE
3 very dignified in form, tone, or style — see ELEVATED 2

else *adj* resulting in an increase in amount or number — see ADDITIONAL

else *adv* in a different way — see OTHERWISE

elucidate *vb* to make plain or understandable — see EXPLAIN 1

elucidation *n* a statement that makes something clear — see EXPLANATION 1

elucidative *adj* serving to explain — see EXPLANATORY

elude *vb* to get or keep away from (as a responsibility) through cleverness or trickery — see ESCAPE 2

eluding *n* the act or a means of getting or keeping away from something undesirable — see ESCAPE 2

elusive *adj* hard to find, capture, or isolate ⟨the giant squid is one of the ocean's most *elusive* inhabitants⟩
synonyms evasive, fugitive, slippery
related words cagey (*also* cagy), shifty; ephemeral, evanescent, fleeting; momentary, passing, short-lived, transitory; unavailable, unobtainable
near antonyms accessible, approachable, attainable, available, obtainable

elvish *adj* tending to or exhibiting reckless playfulness — see MISCHIEVOUS 1

Elysian *adj* of, relating to, or suggesting heaven — see CELESTIAL

Elysium *n* **1** a dwelling place of perfect bliss for the soul after death — see HEAVEN 1

2 a place or state of great happiness — see PARADISE 1

emaciated *adj* suffering extreme weight loss as a result of hunger or disease ⟨the *emaciated* bodies of the survivors of the concentration camps⟩
synonyms cadaverous, gaunt, haggard, skeletal, wasted
related words bony, rawboned, scrawny, skinny, thin; starved, underfed, undernourished; shriveled, withered, wizened
near antonyms beefy, brawny, burly, fit, hale, healthy, hearty, husky; chubby, corpulent, fat, fleshy, heavyset, plump, portly, stocky, thickset

emancipate *vb* to set free (as from slavery or confinement) — see FREE 1

emancipation *n* the act of setting free from slavery — see LIBERATION

emasculate *vb* to deprive of courage or confidence — see UNNERVE 1

embankment *n* a bank of earth constructed to control water — see DAM

embargo *n* an order that something not be done or used — see PROHIBITION 2

embark (on *or* upon) *vb* to take the first step in (a process or course of action) — see BEGIN 1

embarrass *vb* **1** to throw into a state of self-conscious distress ⟨the young soldier was *embarrassed* by the public praise for his heroism⟩
synonyms abash, confound, confuse, discomfit, disconcert, discountenance, faze, fluster, mortify, nonplus, rattle
related words agitate, bother, chagrin, discomfort, discompose, dismay, disquiet, distress, disturb, perturb, unhinge, unsettle, upset; debase, degrade, demean, humble, humiliate
near antonyms calm, comfort, console, relieve, soothe; buoy, cheer, embolden, encourage, hearten; assure, reassure
2 to create difficulty for the work or activity of — see HAMPER

embarrassing *adj* causing embarrassment — see AWKWARD 3

embarrassment *n* **1** the emotional state of being made self-consciously uncomfortable ⟨experienced the great *embarrassment* of tripping while on stage⟩
synonyms abashment, confusion, discomfiture, fluster, mortification
related words agitation, bother, chagrin, discomfort, discomposure, dismay, disquiet, distress, disturbance, perturbation, uneasiness, upset; debasement, degradation, humiliation
near antonyms aplomb, assurance, composure, confidence, coolness, equanimity, poise, self-assurance, self-confidence, self-possession
2 something that makes movement or progress more difficult — see ENCUMBRANCE

embed *also* **imbed** *vb* to set solidly in or as if in surrounding matter — see ENTRENCH

embellish *vb* **1** to add to the interest of by including made-up details — see EMBROIDER
2 to make more attractive by adding something that is beautiful or becoming — see DECORATE

embellishing *adj* serving to add beauty — see DECORATIVE

embellishment *n* **1** something that decorates or beautifies — see DECORATION 1
2 the representation of something in terms that go beyond the facts — see EXAGGERATION

embitter *vb* to implant bitter feelings in ⟨the family refused to allow their collision with a drunk driver *embitter* them⟩
synonyms antagonize, envenom
related words aggravate, anger, enrage, incense, infuriate, madden; alienate, disaffect, disgruntle, estrange; sour
near antonyms endear, ingratiate; appease, assuage, mollify, pacify, placate, propitiate; sweeten

embittered *adj* having or showing deep-seated resentment — see BITTER 1

emblem *n* a device, design, or figure used as an identifying mark ⟨the oil company uses a scallop shell as its *emblem*⟩
synonyms hallmark, logo, symbol, trademark
related words icon, pictograph; badge, coat of arms, crest, insignia; monogram, stamp, token

emblematic *also* **emblematical** *adj* having the function or meaning of a symbol — see SYMBOLIC

embodiment *n* a visible representation of something abstract (as a quality) ⟨Mother Theresa was often regarded as the *embodiment* of selfless devotion to others⟩
synonyms epitome, incarnation, manifestation, personification
related words exemplification, incorporation, substantiation; essence, quintessence; archetype, exemplar, model, paradigm, pattern; acme, apex, culmination, peak, pinnacle, summit, zenith

embody *vb* **1** to make a part of a body or system ⟨concepts of moral behavior that we should *embody* into our daily life⟩
synonyms assimilate, incorporate, integrate
related words amalgamate, blend, combine, commingle, fuse, intermingle, merge, mingle
2 to represent in visible form ⟨George Washington *embodied* so many of the virtues that Americans hold dear⟩
synonyms epitomize, incarnate, manifest, materialize, personalize, personify, substantiate
related words actualize, realize; symbolize; exemplify, illustrate

embolden *vb* to fill with courage or strength of purpose — see ENCOURAGE 1

emboldened *adj* inclined or willing to take risks — see BOLD 1

embosom *vb* to surround or cover closely — see ENFOLD 1

embower *vb* to surround or cover closely — see ENFOLD 1

embrace *vb* **1** to put one's arms around and press tightly ⟨upon being finally reunited, the overjoyed father *embraced* his son⟩
synonyms clasp, enfold, grasp, hug
related words cling, cradle, grab, grip, hold; embosom, encircle, entwine, envelop; fold, lock, twine, wrap; cuddle, fondle, nestle, nuzzle, pat, pet, snuggle, stroke
2 to surround or cover closely — see ENFOLD 1
3 to take for one's own use (something originated by another) — see ADOPT
4 receive or accept gladly or readily — see WELCOME
5 to have as part of a whole — see INCLUDE

embroider *vb* to add to the interest of by including made-up details ⟨Dad likes to *embroider* his fishing stories⟩
synonyms color, elaborate (on), embellish, exaggerate, magnify, pad, stretch
related words amplify, enhance, enlarge (upon),

THESAURUS

expand, flesh (out); fudge, hedge; overdo, overdraw, overemphasize, overplay, overstate; caricature; satirize

near antonyms belittle, minimize, play (down), understate

embroidering *n* the representation of something in terms that go beyond the facts — see EXAGGERATION

embroidery *n* decorative stitching done on cloth with the use of a needle — see NEEDLEWORK

embroil *vb* to place in conflict or difficulties ⟨the town has been *embroiled* in controversy over the building of the huge shopping mall⟩

synonyms bog (down), mire

related words enmesh, ensnare, entangle, entrap, snare, tangle, trap

near antonyms emancipate, free, liberate, release

emend *vb* to remove errors, defects, deficiencies, or deviations from — see CORRECT 1

emendation *n* a change designed to correct or improve a written work — see CORRECTION 1

emerge *vb* to come to one's attention especially gradually or unexpectedly — see ARISE 2

emergency *n* a time or state of affairs requiring prompt or decisive action ⟨an alert, quick-thinking girl who is good to have around in an *emergency*⟩

synonyms clutch, crisis, crossroad(s), crunch, exigency, head, juncture, zero hour

related words contingency, possibility; climax, landmark, milestone, turning point; condition, pass, situation, strait; deadlock, impasse, stalemate; corner, fix, hole, hot water, jam, pinch, predicament, scrape, spot

emigrant *n* one that leaves one place to settle in another ⟨a city teeming with *emigrants* from many lands⟩

synonyms émigré (*also* emigré), immigrant, migrant, settler

related words defector, deportee, evacuee, exile, expatriate, refugee; alien, foreigner, noncitizen, nonnative; colonist, newcomer, squatter

near antonyms aborigine, native; citizen, inhabitant, national, resident

antonyms nonimmigrant

émigré *also* **emigré** *n* 1 a person forced to emigrate for political reasons ⟨the revolution resulted in a flood of *émigrés* into neighboring countries⟩

synonyms deportee, evacuee, exile, expatriate, refugee

related words alien, fugitive; castoff, outcast, pariah; loyalist, patriot

2 one that leaves one place to settle in another — see EMIGRANT

eminence *n* 1 the fact or state of being above others in rank or importance ⟨the *eminence* of the Nobel Prize in the field of awards and prizes⟩

synonyms distinction, dominance, noteworthiness, preeminence, superiority

related words celebrity, fame, famousness, glory, honor, renown, reputation, repute; authority, greatness, influence, power, weight

near antonyms insignificance, unimportance; inferiority, mediocrity; obscurity

2 an area of high ground — see HEIGHT 4

eminent *adj* standing above others in rank, importance, or achievement ⟨many *eminent* surgeons are on the hospital's staff⟩

synonyms distinguished, illustrious, noble, no-

table, noteworthy, outstanding, preeminent, prestigious, signal, star, superior

related words celebrated, famed, famous, glorious, honored, renowned, reputable; infamous, notorious; dominant, paramount, predominant

near antonyms insignificant, minor, unimportant; average, inferior, mediocre; obscure, uncelebrated, unsung

emissary *n* a person sent on a mission to represent another — see AMBASSADOR

emit *vb* 1 to throw or give off ⟨the cabin's chimney *emitted* smoke⟩

synonyms cast (off), discharge, exhale, expel, issue, release, shoot, vent

related words eliminate, evacuate, excrete, exude, ooze, secrete; gush, pour, spew

near antonyms absorb, inhale

2 to send forth using the vocal chords — see UTTER 1

emolument *n* the money paid regularly to a person for labor or services — see WAGE

emotion *n* 1 a subjective response to a person, thing, or situation — see FEELING 1

2 depth of feeling — see ARDOR 1

emotional *adj* 1 having or expressing great depth of feeling — see FERVENT

2 having the power to affect the feelings or sympathies — see MOVING

3 showing feeling freely — see DEMONSTRATIVE

emphasis *n* 1 a special notice or importance given to something ⟨a prep school with a long-established *emphasis* on sports⟩

synonyms accent, accentuation, stress, weight

related words attention, concentration, consideration, heed, note, regard; value, worth; consequence, import, moment, significance; precedence, primacy, priority

near antonyms apathy, disregard, indifference

2 the quality or state of being forceful (as in expression) — see VEHEMENCE 1

emphasize *vb* to indicate the importance of by giving prominent display ⟨supermarket tabloids that *emphasize* sensational news stories⟩

synonyms accent, accentuate, feature, highlight, play (up), point (up), stress, underline, underscore

related words focus, identify, pinpoint, spotlight; advertise, boost, plug, promote, publicize

near antonyms tone (down), understate; belittle, discount, disparage, minimize

antonyms play (down)

emphatic *adj* 1 marked by or uttered with forcefulness ⟨the governor issued an *emphatic* denial of all charges⟩

synonyms aggressive, assertive, dynamic, energetic, forceful, resounding, strenuous, vehement, vigorous

related words decided, insistent, marked, pointed; arresting, compelling, conspicuous, noticeable, striking; absolute, categorical (*also* categoric), clear, plain, unambiguous, unequivocal

near antonyms guarded, mild, weak, wishy-washy; ambiguous, equivocal; understated

antonyms unemphatic

2 likely to attract attention — see NOTICEABLE

empire *n* a group of businesses or enterprises under one control — see CONGLOMERATE

empirical *adj* based on observation or experience ⟨guidelines for raising children that are based on *empirical* evidence⟩

synonyms experimental, objective, observational

related words actual, factual, genuine, hard, real; accepted, established, tried, tried-and-true; indisputable, undeniable; demonstrable, provable, verifiable

near antonyms conjectural, hypothetical, speculative; unproven, unsubstantiated, unverified

antonyms nonempirical, theoretical (*also* theoretic)

employ *n* the state of being provided with a paying job — see HIRE 1

employ *vb* **1** to provide with a paying job ⟨a new factory that will *employ* 500 people⟩

synonyms engage, hire, retain, take on

related words recruit, sign on; keep

near antonyms furlough, lay off

antonyms can, discharge, dismiss, fire, sack

2 to put into action or service — see USE 1

employable *adj* capable of or suitable for being used for a particular purpose — see USABLE 1

employed *adj* involved in often constant activity — see BUSY 1

employee *n* one who works for another for wages or a salary ⟨an employer who was loved and admired by generations of *employees*⟩

synonyms hand, hireling, jobholder, worker

related words assistant, cog, flunky (*also* flunkey), subordinate, underling, yes-man; drudge, grub, laborer, navvy [*chiefly British*], toiler, workingman, workman; associate, colleague, coworker

near antonyms boss, superior, supervisor

antonyms employer

employment *n* **1** the act or practice of employing something for a particular purpose — see USE 1

2 the activity by which one regularly makes a living — see OCCUPATION

3 the state of being provided with a paying job — see HIRE 1

emporium *n* an establishment where goods are sold to consumers — see SHOP 1

empower *vb* to give official or legal power to — see AUTHORIZE 1

emptiness *n* **1** a need or desire for food — see HUNGER 1

2 empty space — see VACANCY 1

3 the quality or state of being empty — see VACANCY 2

empty *adj* **1** lacking contents that could or should be present ⟨the refrigerator is *empty*, so we'll have to eat out⟩

synonyms bare, blank, devoid, stark, vacant, void

related words barren, hollow; available, clear, free, open; unfilled, unfurnished; unattended, uninhabited, unoccupied; abandoned, deserted, emptied, forsaken, vacated; depleted, drained, dry, exhausted

near antonyms complete; replete; furnished, provided, supplied; filled, occupied; flush, overflowing, packed, teeming

antonyms full

2 feeling a desire or need for food — see HUNGRY 1

3 having no meaning — see MEANINGLESS

4 having no usefulness — see WORTHLESS

5 producing no results — see FUTILE

empty *vb* to remove the contents of ⟨*empty* the room before starting to paint the ceiling⟩

synonyms clear, evacuate, vacate, void

related words deplete, drain, eliminate, exhaust; bleed, draw (off); clean, flush, purge, scour, sweep

antonyms fill, load

empyreal *adj* of, relating to, or suggesting heaven — see CELESTIAL

empyrean *adj* of, relating to, or suggesting heaven — see CELESTIAL

emulate *vb* to use (someone or something) as the model for one's speech, mannerisms, or behavior — see IMITATE 1

emulative *adj* using or marked by the use of something else as a basis or model — see IMITATIVE

enable *vb* **1** to make able or possible ⟨my new glasses *enable* me to read⟩

synonyms allow, let, permit

related words fit, prepare, qualify, ready; approve, endorse (*also* indorse), sanction; condition, equip

near antonyms inhibit, preclude; disallow, enjoin, forbid, prohibit

antonyms prevent

2 to give official or legal power to — see AUTHORIZE 1

enact *vb* to put into effect through legislative or authoritative action ⟨Congress *enacts* all laws relating to foreign trade and immigration⟩

synonyms lay down, legislate, make, pass

related words bring about, effect; allow, authorize, permit, sanction; decree, dictate, proclaim; administer, execute; approve, confirm, ratify

near antonyms abolish, abrogate, annul, cancel, invalidate, nullify; overturn, reverse

antonyms repeal, rescind, revoke

enactment *n* **1** a rule of conduct or action laid down by a governing authority and especially a legislator — see LAW 1

2 the doing of an action — see COMMISSION 2

enamored (of) *adj* filled with an intense or excessive love for ⟨many teenage girls became *enamored of* the movie idol for his boyish good looks⟩

synonyms crazy (about *or* over), enraptured (by), infatuated (with), mad (about), nuts (about)

related words hung up, obsessed; foolish, silly, wild; bewitched, captivated, charmed, enchanted, entranced, fascinated

phrases sweet on

near antonyms cool, detached, unimpressed; disenchanted, disillusioned

encamp *vb* **1** to live in a camp or the outdoors — see CAMP

2 to provide with living quarters or shelter — see HOUSE 1

encampment *n* a place where a group of people live for a short time in tents or cabins — see CAMP 1

encapsulate *vb* to make into a short statement of the main points (as of a report) — see SUMMARIZE

encapsulation *n* a short statement of the main points — see SUMMARY

encase *vb* to close or shut in by or as if by barriers — see ENCLOSE 1

enchain *vb* to confine or restrain with or as if with chains — see BIND 1

enchant *vb* **1** to attract or delight as if by magic — see CHARM 1

2 to cast a spell on — see BEWITCH 1

3 to hold the attention of as if by a spell — see ENTHRALL 1

enchanted *adj* being or appearing to be under a magic spell ⟨an *enchanted* isle of the South Pacific⟩

synonyms bewitched, charmed, entranced, magic, magical, spellbound

related words dreamy, fairy, fairylike; fantastic, miraculous, utopian, wondrous; hypnotized, mesmerized; captivated, fascinated

enchanter *n* a person skilled in using supernatural forces — see MAGICIAN 1

enchanting *adj* having an often mysterious or magical power to attract — see FASCINATING 1

enchantment *n* **1** a spoken word or set of words believed to have magic power — see SPELL 1

2 the power of irresistible attraction — see CHARM 2

3 the power to control natural forces through supernatural means — see MAGIC 1

enchantress *n* **1** a woman believed to have often harmful supernatural powers — see WITCH 1

2 a woman whom men find irresistibly attractive — see SIREN

encircle *vb* **1** to pass completely around ⟨communication satellites *encircling* the earth⟩

synonyms circle, circumnavigate, compass, girdle, girth, loop, orbit, ring, round

related words cross, perambulate, traverse

2 to form a circle around — see SURROUND

enclose *also* **inclose** *vb* **1** to close or shut in by or as if by barriers ⟨dogs who spend the day *enclosed* in small cages⟩

synonyms cage, closet, coop (up), corral, encase, envelop, fence (in), hedge, hem, house, immure, pen, wall (in)

related words bound, circumscribe, confine, contain, limit, restrict; encircle, encompass, ring, surround

2 to form a circle around — see SURROUND

3 to surround or cover closely — see ENFOLD 1

enclosure *also* **inclosure** *n* an open space wholly or partly enclosed (as by buildings or walls) — see COURT 2

encomium *n* a formal expression of praise ⟨the *encomiums* bestowed on a teacher at her retirement ceremonies⟩

synonyms accolade, citation, commendation, eulogy, homage, paean, panegyric, salutation, tribute

related words award, decoration, honor, prize; acclaim, acclamation, approval, compliment, recommendation; applause, plaudits; bravo, hallelujah

near antonyms censure, condemnation, denunciation, indictment, rebuke, reprimand, reproof; admonition, correction, lecture, sermon

encompass *vb* **1** to form a circle around — see SURROUND

2 to have as part of a whole — see INCLUDE

3 to surround or cover closely — see ENFOLD 1

encounter *n* a brief clash between enemies or rivals ⟨survived an *encounter* with the school bully at the local park⟩

synonyms brush, hassle, run-in, scrape, skirmish

related words argument, fight, quarrel, row, spat, squabble, tiff; battle, brawl, fray, wrangle

encounter *vb* **1** to come upon face-to-face or as if face-to-face — see MEET 1

2 to come upon unexpectedly or by chance — see HAPPEN (ON *OR* UPON)

3 to enter into contest or conflict with — see ENGAGE 2

encourage *vb* **1** to fill with courage or strength of purpose ⟨a pep talk that *encouraged* the team to get out there and win⟩

synonyms buoy (up), cheer (up), comfort, embolden, hearten, inspire, steel

related words animate, enliven, invigorate; fortify, reinforce, strengthen; assure, reassure; boost, energize, excite, galvanize, provoke, quicken, rally, stimulate, stir

near antonyms demoralize, depress, sadden; debilitate, enfeeble, undermine, weaken

antonyms daunt, discourage, dishearten, dispirit

2 to help the growth or development of — see FOSTER 1

3 to rouse to strong feeling or action — see PROVOKE 1

4 to try to persuade (someone) through earnest appeals to follow a course of action — see URGE

encouragement *n* something that arouses action or activity — see IMPULSE

encouraging *adj* **1** having qualities which inspire hope — see HOPEFUL 1

2 making one feel good inside — see HEARTWARMING

3 pointing toward a happy outcome — see FAVORABLE 2

encroach *vb* to advance gradually beyond the usual or desirable limits ⟨each year the sea continues to *encroach* upon the island's beaches⟩

synonyms creep, inch, worm

related words snake, sneak; entrench (*also* intrench), impinge, infringe, intrude, invade; overpass, overreach, overrun, overshoot, overstep

encrust *also* **incrust** *vb* to cover with a hardened layer ⟨refrigerator shelves that were *encrusted* with the residue of many spills⟩

synonyms cake, rime

related words besmear, coat, smear, spread; cover, daub; coagulate, congeal, harden

encumber *vb* **1** to create difficulty for the work or activity of — see HAMPER

2 to place a weight or burden on — see LOAD 1

encumbrance *n* something that makes movement or progress more difficult ⟨without the *encumbrance* of a heavy backpack, I could sprint along the trail⟩

synonyms bar, block, chain, clog, crimp, deterrent, drag, embarrassment, fetter, handicap, hindrance, hurdle, impediment, inhibition, interference, let, manacle, obstacle, obstruction, shackles, stop, stumbling block, trammel

related words catch, hitch, rub, snag; hobble; arrest, check, constraint, curb, rein, restraint, stop; delay, holdup; burden, load; danger, hazard, peril; adversity, difficulty, disadvantage, hardship

near antonyms catalyst, goad, impetus, incentive, spur, stimulant, stimulus; advantage, edge; break

antonyms aid, assistance, benefit, help

encyclopedic *also* **encyclopaedic** *adj* covering everything or all important points ⟨a tour guide with an *encyclopedic* knowledge of New York City and its people⟩

synonyms compendious, complete, comprehensive, full, global, inclusive, in-depth, omnibus, panoramic, universal

related words broad, catholic, extensive, farreaching, general, overall, sweeping, vast, wide; blanket, indiscriminate, unrestricted

near antonyms circumscribed, limited, narrow, restricted, specialized; exact, precise; individual, singular, specific

end *n* **1** the stopping of a process or activity ⟨the *end* of hostilities brought general rejoicing⟩

synonyms cessation, close, closure, conclusion, discontinuance, ending, expiration, finish, halt,

lapse, shutdown, shutoff, stop, stoppage, surcease, termination
related words abeyance, interruption, moratorium, suspension
near antonyms extension, persistence, prolongation
antonyms continuation
2 a real or imaginary point beyond which a person or thing cannot go — see LIMIT
3 an unused or unwanted piece or item typically of small size or value — see ¹SCRAP 1
4 something that one hopes or intends to accomplish — see GOAL
5 the last and usually sharp or tapering part of something long and narrow — see POINT 2
6 the last part of a process or action — see FINALE
7 the line or relatively narrow space that marks the outer limit of something — see BORDER 1
8 the permanent stopping of all the vital bodily activities — see DEATH 1
end *vb* **1** to bring (an event) to a natural or appropriate stopping point — see CLOSE 3
2 to bring (as an action or operation) to an immediate end — see STOP 1
3 to come to an end — see CEASE 1
endanger *vb* to place in danger ⟨a reckless use of fireworks that *endangered* the lives of many people⟩
synonyms adventure, compromise, gamble (with), hazard, imperil, jeopardize, menace, risk, venture
related words intimidate, threaten; expose; subject; chance, wager
near antonyms guard, protect, shelter, shield; preserve, resume, save
endangered *adj* being in a situation where one is likely to meet with harm — see LIABLE 1
endangerment *n* the state of not being protected from injury, harm, or evil — see DANGER 1
endearing *adj* **1** having qualities that tend to make one loved — see LOVABLE
2 likely to win one's affection — see INGRATIATING
endeavor *n* an effort to do or accomplish something — see ATTEMPT
endeavor *vb* **1** to devote serious and sustained effort — see LABOR
2 to make an effort to do — see ATTEMPT
ended *adj* brought or having come to an end — see COMPLETE 2
endemic *adj* belonging to a particular place by birth or origin — see NATIVE 1
ending *n* **1** the last part of a process or action — see FINALE
2 the stopping of a process or activity — see END 1
endless *adj* **1** being or seeming to be without limits — see INFINITE
2 lasting forever — see EVERLASTING
endorse *also* **indorse** *vb* to promote the interests or cause of — see SUPPORT 1
endow *vb* **1** to furnish with something freely or naturally ⟨a young performer *endowed* with a great singing voice⟩
synonyms endue, invest
related words equip, provide, supply; bestow, confer; accord, award, grant; empower, enable, enhance, enrich, heighten; bless, favor, grace; bequeath, will

near antonyms dispossess, divest, strip; deplete, drain, exhaust; skimp, stint
2 to furnish (as an institution) with a regular source of income ⟨a wealthy businessman who *endowed* several museums⟩
synonyms finance, fund, subsidize
related words establish, found, organize; bequeath, contribute, donate, subscribe, support; award, grant; back, promote, sponsor
near antonyms draw, receive; subsist
3 to provide money for — see FINANCE 1
endowment *n* a special and usually inborn ability — see TALENT
endue *vb* to furnish with something freely or naturally — see ENDOW 1
endurable *adj* capable of being endured — see BEARABLE
endurance *n* **1** continuing existence — see PERSISTENCE 1
2 uninterrupted or lasting existence — see CONTINUATION
endure *vb* **1** to come to a knowledge of (something) by living through it — see EXPERIENCE
2 to put up with (something painful or difficult) — see BEAR 2
3 to remain indefinitely in existence or in the same state — see CONTINUE 1
enemy *n* one that is hostile toward another ⟨a beloved minister with no known *enemies*⟩
synonyms adversary, antagonist, foe, opponent
related words archenemy; (the) opposition; nemesis; bane, bête noire; assailant, attacker, combatant, invader; competitor, emulator, rival
near antonyms ally, collaborator, colleague, confederate, friendly, partner; adherent, disciple, follower; backer, benefactor, supporter
antonyms friend
energetic *adj* **1** having active strength of body or mind — see VIGOROUS 1
2 having much high-spirited energy and movement — see LIVELY 1
3 marked by or uttered with forcefulness — see EMPHATIC 1
energetically *adv* in a vigorous and forceful manner — see HARD 3
energize *vb* to give life, vigor, or spirit to — see ANIMATE
energized *adj* made or become fresh in spirits or vigor — see NEW 4
energy *n* **1** active strength of body or mind — see VIGOR 1
2 something with a usable capacity for doing work — see FUEL
3 the ability to exert effort for the accomplishment of a task — see POWER 2
enervate *vb* to diminish the physical strength of — see WEAKEN 1
enervated *adj* **1** lacking bodily energy or motivation — see LISTLESS
2 lacking bodily strength — see WEAK 1
enfeeble *vb* to diminish the physical strength of — see WEAKEN 1
enfeebled *adj* lacking bodily strength — see WEAK 1
enfeeblement *n* **1** a gradual sinking and wasting away of mind or body — see DECLINE 1
2 the quality or state of lacking physical strength or vigor — see WEAKNESS 1
enfold *vb* **1** to surround or cover closely ⟨darkness began to *enfold* the lonely house on the hill⟩

synonyms embosom, embower, embrace, enclose (*also* inclose), encompass, enshroud, envelop, enwrap, invest, lap, mantle, shroud, swathe, veil, wrap

related words curtain, drape; encase; swaddle; blanket, overlay, overspread; camouflage, cloak, disguise, mask; circle, encircle, encompass

near antonyms bare, denude, expose, strip

2 to put one's arms around and press tightly — see EMBRACE 1

enforce *vb* to carry out effectively ⟨the duty of the police is to *enforce* the law⟩

synonyms administer, apply, execute, implement

related words effect, effectuate; discharge, fulfill (*or* fulfil), render; cite, invoke; enact, legislate; honor, observe; prosecute; promulgate

near antonyms disregard, ignore, neglect

enfranchise *vb* to set free (as from slavery or confinement) — see FREE 1

enfranchisement *n* **1** the act of setting free from slavery — see LIBERATION

2 the right to formally express one's position or will in an election — see VOTE 1

engage *vb* **1** to hold the attention of ⟨the challenging jigsaw puzzle *engaged* us all evening⟩

synonyms absorb, busy, engross, enthrall (*or* enthral), fascinate, grip, immerse, interest, intrigue, involve, occupy

related words allure, attract, bewitch, captivate, charm, enchant; hypnotize, mesmerize; monopolize, preoccupy

near antonyms bore, jade, pall, tire, weary

2 to enter into contest or conflict with ⟨the daring young captain was eager to *engage* the enemy⟩

synonyms battle, encounter, face, meet, take on

related words emulate, rival; contend, fight, oppose

near antonyms elude, escape, evade; retreat

3 to obligate by prior agreement — see PLEDGE 1

4 to provide with a paying job — see EMPLOY 1

5 to take or get the temporary use of (something) for a set sum — see HIRE 1

engaged *adj* **1** involved in often constant activity — see BUSY 1

2 pledged in marriage ⟨the *engaged* couple make a charming pair⟩

synonyms affianced, betrothed

related words committed

antonyms unengaged

engagement *n* **1** the act or state of being engaged to be married ⟨the fun couple recently announced their *engagement*⟩

synonyms betrothal, espousal, troth

antonyms disengagement

2 an agreement to be present at a specified time and place ⟨a lifelong practice of marking all of my *engagements* on a weekly calendar⟩

synonyms appointment, date, rendezvous, tryst

related words arrangement; invitation; interview; get-together, meeting; call, visit; schedule

3 the state of being provided with a paying job — see HIRE 1

engaging *adj* **1** having an often mysterious or magical power to attract — see FASCINATING 1

2 holding the attention or provoking interest — see INTERESTING

engender *vb* to be the cause of (a situation, action, or state of mind) — see EFFECT

engine *n* a device that changes energy into me-

chanical motion ⟨a car with a 200-horsepower *engine*⟩

synonyms machine, motor

related words converter, transformer; appliance, mechanism; equipment; mill

engineer *vb* to plan out usually with subtle skill or care ⟨the mayor *engineered* an agreement to have a major league team play in our city⟩

synonyms contrive, finagle, finesse, frame, machinate, maneuver, manipulate, mastermind, negotiate, wangle

related words intrigue, plot, scheme; connive; concoct, cook (up), hatch; captain, command, conduct, direct, handle, manage, quarterback, run; gerrymander

near antonyms blow, bobble, botch, bungle, butcher, flub, fumble, gum (up), louse up, mangle, mess (up), mishandle, muff

engrave *vb* **1** to cut (as letters or designs) on a hard surface ⟨*engraved* the birth and death dates on the tombstone⟩

synonyms etch, grave, incise, inscribe

related words carve, chisel, sculpt, sculpture; chase; score

2 to produce a vivid impression of ⟨a scar that forever *engraved* the killer's face in the witness's mind⟩

synonyms etch, impress, imprint, ingrain

related words imbue, implant, inculcate, infuse, instill

engross *vb* to hold the attention of — see ENGAGE 1

engrossed *adj* having the mind fixed on something — see ATTENTIVE

engrossing *adj* holding the attention or provoking interest — see INTERESTING

engrossment *n* a focusing of the mind on something — see ATTENTION 1

engulf *vb* to cover or become filled with a flood — see FLOOD

enhance *vb* **1** to make better — see IMPROVE

2 to make markedly greater in measure or degree — see INTENSIFY

enhancement *n* an instance of notable progress in the development of knowledge, technology, or skill — see ADVANCE 2

enigma *n* something hard to understand or explain — see MYSTERY

enigmatic *also* **enigmatical** *adj* **1** being beyond one's powers to know, understand, or explain — see MYSTERIOUS 1

2 having an often intentionally veiled or uncertain meaning — see OBSCURE 1

enjoin *vb* **1** to ask for (something) earnestly or with authority — see DEMAND 1

2 to issue orders to (someone) by right of authority — see COMMAND 1

3 to order not to do or use or to be done or used — see FORBID

enjoining *n* the act of ordering that something not be done or used — see PROHIBITION 1

enjoy *vb* **1** to take pleasure in ⟨TV and videos are OK, but we still *enjoy* seeing movies on the big screen⟩

synonyms adore, delight (in), dig, fancy, groove (on), like, love, relish, revel (in)

related words admire, appreciate, cherish, revere, venerate, worship; prize, treasure, value; devour, drink (in), savor; dote (on), idolize; cotton (to), favor, prefer *phrases* be partial to, get a kick (*or* charge) out of, go for, have a soft spot for, take to

near antonyms abhor, abominate, detest, dislike, hate, loathe; condemn, despise, scorn

2 to keep, control, or experience as one's own — see HAVE 1

enjoyable *adj* **1** giving pleasure or contentment to the mind or senses — see PLEASANT

2 providing amusement or enjoyment — see FUN

enjoyment *n* the feeling experienced when one's wishes are met — see PLEASURE 1

enlarge *vb* **1** to become greater in extent, volume, amount, or number — see INCREASE 2

2 to make greater in size, amount, or number — see INCREASE 1

enlarge (on) *vb* to express more fully and in greater detail — see EXPAND 1

enlighten *vb* **1** to give information to ⟨the lecturer at the planetarium *enlightened* us about the latest astronomical discoveries⟩

synonyms acquaint, advise, apprise, brief, clue, familiarize, fill in, inform, instruct, tell, wise (up)

related words clarify, clear (up), construe, elucidate, explain, explicate, expound, illuminate, illustrate, interpret, spell out; announce, disclose, report; disabuse, disenchant, disillusion

near antonyms misinform, mislead

2 to provide (someone) with moral or spiritual understanding ⟨many people around the world have been *enlightened* by the teachings of Gautama Buddha⟩

synonyms edify, educate, nurture

related words elevate, ennoble, lift, uplift; better, improve, transform; exalt, glorify, transfigure

near antonyms confuse, perplex, puzzle; becloud, cloud, darken, obscure

enlist (in) *vb* to become a member of — see ENTER 2

enliven *vb* to give life, vigor, or spirit to — see ANIMATE

enmesh *vb* to catch or hold as if in a net — see ENTANGLE 2

enmity *n* a deep-seated ill will ⟨*enmity* had existed between the two families for generations⟩

synonyms animosity, antagonism, antipathy, bitterness, gall, grudge, hostility, jaundice, rancor

related words hate, hatred, loathing; vindictiveness, virulence, vitriol; alienation, disaffection, estrangement; abhorrence, aversion, repugnance, repulsion; disgust, horror; conflict, coolness, friction, strain, tension; discord, unfriendliness; malice, malignancy, malignity, spite, spitefulness, venom

near antonyms amiability, amicability, civility, cordiality, friendliness, hospitality, neighborliness; comity, empathy, friendship, goodwill, sympathy, understanding

antonyms amity

ennoble *vb* to enhance the status of — see EXALT

ennui *n* the state of being bored — see BOREDOM

enormity *n* **1** the state or quality of being utterly evil ⟨the *enormity* of the crimes committed by the Nazis⟩

synonyms atrociousness, atrocity, badness, depravedness, depravity, evilness, heinousness, monstrosity, nefariousness, sinfulness, vileness, wickedness

related words accursedness, baseness, devilishness, execrableness, fiendishness, hellishness; corruption, decadence, degeneracy; immorality; infamy, notoriety

near antonyms morality; chasteness, innocence, purity

antonyms goodness, righteousness, virtuousness

2 the quality or state of being very large — see IMMENSITY

enormous *adj* unusually large — see HUGE

enormously *adv* to a large extent or degree — see GREATLY 2

enormousness *n* the quality or state of being very large — see IMMENSITY

enough *adv* **1** in or to a degree or quantity that meets one's requirements or satisfaction ⟨the elevator is big *enough* to hold everyone⟩

synonyms adequately, satisfactorily, sufficiently

related words acceptably, decently, fairly, moderately, passably, tolerably; abundantly, amply; commensurately, proportionately

antonyms inadequately, insufficiently, unsatisfactorily

2 to some degree or extent — see FAIRLY

enrage *vb* to make angry — see ANGER

enraged *adj* feeling or showing anger — see ANGRY

enrapture *vb* **1** to fill with great joy — see ELATE

2 to fill with overwhelming emotion (as wonder or delight) — see ENTRANCE

enraptured *adj* experiencing or marked by overwhelming usually pleasurable emotion — see ECSTATIC

enraptured (by) *adj* filled with an intense or excessive love for — see ENAMORED (OF)

enrich *vb* **1** to make better — see IMPROVE

2 to make more attractive by adding something that is beautiful or becoming — see DECORATE

enroll *also* **enrol** *vb* **1** to enter in a list or roll ⟨the school *enrolls* about 800 students⟩

synonyms inscribe, list, matriculate, register

related words catalog (*or* catalogue), itemize, tabulate, tally; file, index; book, log, post; program, schedule; check in

near antonyms cancel, delete, exclude, expel, expunge, reject; omit, overlook

2 to put (someone or something) on a list — see ¹LIST 2

enroll (in) *vb* to become a member of — see ENTER 2

enrollment *n* the number of individuals registered — see REGISTRATION

ensconce *vb* **1** to establish or place comfortably or snugly ⟨the kids had contentedly *ensconced* themselves on the couch before the TV⟩

synonyms install, lodge, perch, roost, settle

related words curl up; park, plant; anchor, bivouac, camp; burrow; locate, situate

2 to put into a hiding place — see ¹HIDE 1

enshrine *vb* to enhance the status of — see EXALT

enshroud *vb* **1** to keep secret or shut off from view — see ¹HIDE 2

2 to surround or cover closely — see ENFOLD 1

ensign *n* a piece of cloth with a special design that is used as an emblem or for signaling — see FLAG 1

enslavement *n* the state of being a slave — see SLAVERY 1

ensnare *vb* to catch or hold as if in a net — see ENTANGLE 2

ensuing *adj* **1** being the one that comes immediately after another — see NEXT

2 being, occurring, or carried out at a time after something else — see SUBSEQUENT

ensure *vb* to make sure, certain, or safe ⟨regulations that *ensure* the wholesomeness of our food⟩
synonyms assure, cinch, guarantee, guaranty, insure, secure
related words attest, certify, vouch, warrant, witness; pledge, promise, swear
near antonyms enfeeble, undermine, weaken

entail *vb* to have as part of a whole — see INCLUDE

entangle *vb* **1** to twist together into a usually confused mass ⟨in the process of taking down the Christmas tree, we managed to *entangle* the string of lights into a hopeless mess of wires⟩
synonyms interlace, intertwine, interweave, knot, snarl, tangle
related words weave, wind, wreathe; braid, plait
antonyms disentangle
2 to catch or hold as if in a net ⟨the young runaway gradually became *entangled* in a web of lies⟩
synonyms enmesh, ensnare, entrap, mesh, snare, tangle, trap
related words bag, capture, collar; embroil, implicate, involve, mire
near antonyms extricate, untangle; detach, disengage; clear, free, liberate
antonyms disentangle

entanglement *n* something that catches and holds — see WEB 1

enter *vb* **1** to go or come in or into ⟨the hikers *entered* the cave with considerable caution⟩
synonyms access, penetrate, pierce
related words barge (in), breeze (in), burst (in *or* into), waltz (in); drop (in), pop (in)
phrases set foot in, step in
antonyms depart, exit, leave
2 to become a member of ⟨patriotic young men and women *entering* the armed services⟩
synonyms enlist (in), enroll (in), join, sign on (for), sign up (for)
related words reenlist, reenroll, reenter
3 to put (someone or something) on a list — see ¹LIST 2

enter (into *or* upon) *vb* to take the first step in (a process or course of action) — see BEGIN 1

enterprise *n* **1** a commercial or industrial activity or organization ⟨the booming economy witnessed the launch of many small *enterprises*⟩
synonyms business, company, concern, establishment, firm, house, outfit
related words conglomerate, corporation, multinational; association, cartel, chain, combine, syndicate, trust; agency, dealer, outlet
2 readiness to engage in daring or difficult activity ⟨the *enterprise* shown by the early developers and promoters of personal computers⟩
synonyms aggressiveness, ambition, drive, go, hustle, initiative
related words gumption, pluck, snap, spirit, spunk, starch; assertiveness, self-reliance; energy, hardihood, pep, vigor, vitality
near antonyms inactivity, inertia, passivity; diffidence, faintheartedness, timidity; hesitation, reluctance; indolence, laziness, lethargy
3 a risky undertaking — see GAMBLE

enterprising *adj* **1** having or showing a bold forcefulness in the pursuit of a goal — see AGGRESSIVE 1
2 inclined or willing to take risks — see BOLD 1

entertain *vb* **1** to cause (someone) to pass the time agreeably occupied — see AMUSE
2 to give serious and careful thought to — see PONDER
3 to keep in one's mind or heart — see HARBOR 1

entertaining *adj* providing amusement or enjoyment — see FUN

entertainment *n* **1** the act or activity of providing pleasure or amusement especially for the public ⟨a variety show was staged as *entertainment* for the scouts at the jamboree⟩
synonyms amusement, distraction, diversion, recreation
related words show business; delectation, delight, enjoyment, joy, mirth; gratification, relaxation, relief, satisfaction; exhibition, performance, presentation, production, show, spectacle; escapism
2 someone or something that provides amusement or enjoyment — see FUN 1

enthrall *or* **enthral** *vb* **1** to hold the attention of as if by a spell ⟨*enthralled* by the flickering fire in the hearth, we lost all track of time⟩
synonyms arrest, enchant, fascinate, grip, hypnotize, mesmerize, spellbind
related words enrapture, entrance, thrill; beguile, bewitch, charm; absorb, engage, engross, involve
phrases cast a spell on
2 to fill with overwhelming emotion (as wonder or delight) — see ENTRANCE
3 to hold the attention of — see ENGAGE 1

enthralled *adj* having the mind fixed on something — see ATTENTIVE 1

enthralling *adj* holding the attention or provoking interest — see INTERESTING

enthrallment *n* a focusing of the mind on something — see ATTENTION 1

enthuse *vb* to make an exaggerated display of affection or enthusiasm — see GUSH 2

enthusiasm *n* **1** a practice or interest that is very popular for a short time — see FAD
2 urgent desire or interest — see EAGERNESS

enthusiast *n* a person with a strong and habitual liking for something — see FAN

enthusiastic *adj* showing urgent desire or interest — see EAGER

enthusiastically *adv* in an enthusiastic manner — see SKY-HIGH

entice *vb* to lead away from a usual or proper course by offering some pleasure or advantage — see LURE

enticement *n* **1** something that persuades one to perform an action for pleasure or gain — see LURE 1
2 the act or pressure of giving in to a desire especially when ill-advised — see TEMPTATION 1

entire *adj* **1** not divided or scattered among several areas of interest or concern — see WHOLE 1
2 not lacking any part or member that properly belongs to it — see COMPLETE 1

entirely *adv* to a full extent or degree — see FULLY 1

entitle *vb* **1** to give a right to ⟨the card *entitles* my grandmother to the discount for senior citizens⟩
synonyms authorize, qualify
related words empower, enable, license (*also* licence); approve, endorse (*also* indorse); allow, let, permit; certify, ratify, sanction, validate
antonyms disqualify
2 to give a name to — see NAME 1

entity *n* one that has a real and independent exis-

tence ⟨the question of whether extrasensory perception will ever be a scientifically recognized *entity*⟩
synonyms being, individual, object, something, substance, thing
related words body; material, matter, stuff
entomb *vb* to place (a dead body) in the earth, a tomb, or the sea — see BURY 1
entombing *n* the act or ceremony of putting a dead body in its final resting place — see BURIAL
entombment *n* the act or ceremony of putting a dead body in its final resting place — see BURIAL
entrails *n pl* the internal organs of the body — see GUT 1
entrance *n* 1 the means or right of entering or participating in ⟨*entrance* to the club is by invitation only⟩
synonyms access, admission, admittance, doorway, entrée (*or* entree), entry, gateway
related words approval, certification, qualification
2 the opening through which one can enter or leave a structure — see DOOR 2
entrance *vb* to fill with overwhelming emotion (as wonder or delight) ⟨a production of *The Nutcracker* ballet that will *entrance* audiences⟩
synonyms carry away, enrapture, enthrall (*or* enthral), overjoy, ravish, transport
related words delight, gladden, gratify, please, satisfy; bewitch, captivate, charm, enchant, fascinate; elate, excite, exhilarate, stir
entranced *adj* 1 being or appearing to be under a magic spell — see ENCHANTED
2 experiencing or marked by overwhelming usually pleasurable emotion — see ECSTATIC
entrancing *adj* having an often mysterious or magical power to attract — see FASCINATING 1
entrap *vb* to catch or hold as if in a net — see ENTANGLE 2
entreat *vb* to make a request to (someone) in an earnest or urgent manner — see BEG
entreating *adj* asking humbly — see SUPPLIANT
entreaty *n* an earnest request — see PLEA 1
entrée *or* **entree** *n* the means or right of entering or participating in — see ENTRANCE 1
entrench *also* **intrench** *vb* to set solidly in or as if in surrounding matter ⟨a father who *entrenched* in our minds the belief that hard work pays off⟩
synonyms embed (*also* imbed), fix, implant, ingrain, lodge, root
related words imbue, infuse, instill; establish, place, put, settle, stick
near antonyms eliminate, eradicate; eject, expel; detach, disconnect, disengage, remove
antonyms dislodge, root (out), uproot
entrenched *also* **intrenched** *adj* firmly established over time — see INVETERATE 1
entrust *vb* 1 to give a task, duty, or responsibility to ⟨we *entrusted* our financial adviser with the investment of all of our savings⟩
synonyms assign, charge, commission, trust
related words confer, impose; commit, consign, delegate, relegate; allocate, allot; authorize, empower, invest
2 to put (something) into the possession or safekeeping of another — see GIVE 2
entry *n* 1 the entrance room of a building — see HALL 1
2 the means or right of entering or participating in — see ENTRANCE 1

entryway *n* the entrance room of a building — see HALL 1
entwine *vb* to follow a circular or spiral course — see WIND
enumerate *vb* 1 to specify one after another ⟨I proceeded to *enumerate* the reasons why my allowance needed raising⟩
synonyms detail, itemize, list, numerate, rehearse, tick (off)
related words outline; tabulate, tally; catalog (*or* catalogue), inventory; chart, diagram, graph; calculate, compute, estimate, figure, reckon; cite, mention, name
2 to find the sum of (a collection of things) by noting each one as it is being added — see COUNT 1
3 to make a list of — see ¹LIST 1
enunciate *vb* 1 to utter clearly and distinctly — see ARTICULATE 1
2 to make known openly or publicly — see ANNOUNCE
enunciation *n* the clear and accurate pronunciation of words especially in public speaking — see DICTION 1
envelop *vb* 1 to close or shut in by or as if by barriers — see ENCLOSE 1
2 to surround or cover closely — see ENFOLD 1
envenom *vb* to implant bitter feelings in — see EMBITTER
envenomed *adj* containing or contaminated with a substance capable of injuring or killing a living thing — see POISONOUS
envious *adj* having or showing mean resentment of another's possessions or advantages ⟨a family that is *envious* of their neighbors' big house⟩
synonyms covetous, invidious, jaundiced, jealous, resentful
related words begrudging, grudging; avaricious, grasping, greedy; distrustful, suspicious; malicious, petty, spiteful
phrases green with envy
near antonyms generous, kind, kindhearted; altruistic, benevolent, charitable; well-meaning
enviousness *n* a painful awareness of another's possessions or advantages and a desire to have them too — see ENVY
environment *n* the circumstances, conditions, or objects by which one is surrounded ⟨the joys of growing up in the *environment* that a small town offers⟩
synonyms atmosphere, climate, environs, medium, milieu, setting, surroundings
related words backdrop, background, context; element; situation, status; habitat
environs *n pl* 1 the area around a city ⟨the city and its *environs* total about a million in population⟩
synonyms exurbia, outskirts, purlieu, suburbia
related words backwater, backwoods, hinterland
2 the circumstances, conditions, or objects by which one is surrounded — see ENVIRONMENT
envisage *vb* to form a mental picture of — see IMAGINE 1
envoy *n* 1 a person sent on a mission to represent another — see AMBASSADOR
2 a person who acts or does business for another — see AGENT 2
envy *n* a painful awareness of another's possessions or advantages and a desire to have them too ⟨her *envy* of her neighbor's fancy clothes wrecked their friendship⟩

THESAURUS

synonyms covetousness, enviousness, invidiousness, jealousy, resentment

related words animosity, enmity, hatred, ill will; malice, maliciousness, spitefulness

near antonyms benevolence, goodwill, kindness, sympathy

enwrap *vb* to surround or cover closely — see ENFOLD 1

ephemeral *adj* lasting only for a short time — see MOMENTARY

epicure *n* a person with refined tastes in food and wine ⟨Thomas Jefferson was one of America's first great *epicures*⟩

synonyms gourmand, gourmet

related words connoisseur, dilettante; savorer

near antonyms glutton, gorger, hog, trencherman

epigram *n* an often stated observation regarding something from common experience — see SAYING

epigrammatic *adj* marked by the use of few words to convey much information or meaning — see CONCISE

episode *n* something that happens — see EVENT 1

episodic *adj* appearing in parts or numbers that follow regularly — see SERIAL

epistle *n* a message on paper from one person or group to another — see LETTER

epithet *n* 1 a descriptive or familiar name given instead of or in addition to the one belonging to an individual — see NICKNAME

2 an act or expression showing scorn and usually intended to hurt another's feelings — see INSULT

epitome *n* 1 a short statement of the main points — see SUMMARY

2 a visible representation of something abstract (as a quality) — see EMBODIMENT

3 the most perfect type or example — see QUINTESSENCE 1

epitomize *vb* 1 to make into a short statement of the main points (as of a report) — see SUMMARIZE

2 to represent in visible form — see EMBODY 2

epoch *n* an extent of time associated with a particular person or thing — see AGE 1

equable *adj* marked by temperatures that are neither too high nor too low — see CLEMENT

equal *vb* 1 to produce something equal to (as in quality or value) ⟨no one has *equaled* Shakespeare's plays⟩

synonyms match, meet, tie

related words beat, excel, outdo, surpass, top; amount (to), approach, touch; measure (up), rival

2 to be the same in meaning or effect — see AMOUNT (TO) 2

3 to be the exact counterpart of — see MATCH 1

equal *adj* 1 marked by justice, honesty, and freedom from bias — see FAIR 2

2 resembling another in every respect — see SAME 1

equal *n* one that is equal to another in status, achievement, or value ⟨a basketball player who truly has no *equal* in his sport⟩

synonyms coordinate, counterpart, equivalent, fellow, like, match, parallel, peer, rival

related words analogue (*or* analog); double, mate, twin; associate, colleague, companion, partner; competitor

equality *n* the state or fact of being exactly the same in number, amount, status, or quality — see EQUIVALENCE

equalize *vb* to make equal in amount, degree, or status ⟨a plan to *equalize* educational opportunities for all the state's children, rich and poor alike⟩

synonyms balance, equate, even, level

related words accommodate, adjust, compensate, fit; homogenize, normalize, regularize, standardize; democratize

equanimity *n* evenness of emotions or temper ⟨an Olympic diver who always displays remarkable *equanimity* on the platform⟩

synonyms aplomb, calmness, composure, coolheadedness, coolness, imperturbability, placidity, self-possession, serenity, tranquillity (*or* tranquility)

related words assurance, confidence, poise, self-assurance, self-confidence; apathy, detachment, indifference, phlegm

near antonyms alarm, anxiety, apprehension, disquiet; excitability, nervousness; disturbance

antonyms agitation, discomposure, perturbation

equate *vb* 1 to regard or represent as equal or comparable ⟨a value system that *equates* money with success⟩

synonyms compare, liken

related words associate, connect, join, link, match; group, lump (together)

near antonyms differentiate, discriminate, distinguish

2 to describe as similar — see COMPARE 1

3 to make equal in amount, degree, or status — see EQUALIZE

equatorial *adj* being near the equator — see LOW 1

equilibrium *n* a condition in which opposing forces are equal to one another — see BALANCE 1

equine *n* a large hoofed domestic animal that is used for carrying or drawing loads and for riding — see HORSE

equip *vb* 1 to make competent (as by training, skill, or ability) for a particular office or function — see QUALIFY 2

2 to provide (someone) with what is needed for a task or activity — see FURNISH 1

equipage *n* a horse-drawn wheeled vehicle for carrying passengers — see CARRIAGE 1

equipment *n* items needed for the performance of a task or activity ⟨the *equipment* for the polar expedition included ships, instruments, sleds, dogs, and provisions⟩

synonyms accoutrements (*or* accouterments), apparatus, gear, material(s), matériel (*or* materiel), outfit, paraphernalia, tackle

related words accessories, attachments, fittings; baggage, belongings, impedimenta; appliances, facilities, instruments, machinery, tools; apparel, attire, habiliments, raiment, trappings; battery

equipoise *n* 1 a condition in which opposing forces are equal to one another — see BALANCE 1

2 a force or influence that makes an opposing force ineffective or less effective — see COUNTERBALANCE

equitable *adj* marked by justice, honesty, and freedom from bias — see FAIR 2

equity *n* the act or practice of giving to others what is their due — see JUSTICE 1

equivalence *n* the state or fact of being exactly the same in number, amount, status, or quality ⟨moviegoers who mistakenly believe that there is an *equivalence* between the personality of an actor and that of his character⟩

synonyms equality, equivalency, par, parity, sameness

related words compatibility, correlation, correspondence; likeness, similarity; exchangeability, interchangeability

near antonyms difference, discrepancy, disparity, divergence; incompatibility; dissimilarity, unlikeness

antonyms inequality

equivalency *n* the state or fact of being exactly the same in number, amount, status, or quality — see EQUIVALENCE

equivalent *n* one that is equal to another in status, achievement, or value — see EQUAL

equivocal *adj* **1** giving good reason for being doubted, questioned, or challenged — see DOUBTFUL 2

2 having an often intentionally veiled or uncertain meaning — see OBSCURE 1

equivocalness *n* the quality or state of having a veiled or uncertain meaning — see OBSCURITY 1

equivocate *vb* to avoid giving a definite answer or position ⟨the candidate *equivocated* as long as he could on controversial issues⟩

synonyms fudge, hedge, pussyfoot

related words dodge, duck, evade, sidestep, skirt; bypass, circumvent; cavil, quibble

phrases beat around (*or* about) the bush, dance around, hem and haw

equivocation *n* the quality or state of having a veiled or uncertain meaning — see OBSCURITY 1

era *n* an extent of time associated with a particular person or thing — see AGE 1

eradicate *vb* to destroy all traces of — see ANNIHILATE 1

ere *prep* earlier than — see BEFORE 1

erect *adj* rising straight up ⟨a lone tree remained *erect* after the terrible tornado had passed⟩

synonyms perpendicular, plumb, raised, standing, upright, upstanding, vertical

related words elevated, lifted, upended, upraised; freestanding

near antonyms prostrate, supine; hanging, sagging, slanted, slanting

antonyms flat, recumbent

erect *vb* **1** to fix in an upright position ⟨the tribes of the Pacific Northwest *erected* totem poles in front of their dwellings⟩

synonyms pitch, put up, raise, rear, set up, upend, upraise

related words brace, buttress, prop (up), shore (up), support; elevate, hoist, lift

near antonyms demolish, flatten, knock down, level, raze, tear down

2 to form by putting together parts or materials — see BUILD

erection *n* something put together by arranging or connecting an array of parts — see CONSTRUCTION 1

ergo *adv* for this or that reason — see THEREFORE

erode *vb* **1** to consume or wear away gradually — see EAT 2

2 to damage or diminish by continued friction — see ABRADE 1

erosion *n* a gradual weakening, loss, or destruction — see CORROSION

erotic *adj* of, relating to, or expressing sexual attraction ⟨the *erotic* aspects of the story of Beauty and the Beast⟩

synonyms amatory, amorous, sexy

related words carnal, sensual, sensuous; bawdy, lascivious, lewd, lustful, obscene, prurient, spicy

err *vb* to commit an offense — see OFFEND 1

errant *adj* **1** engaging in or marked by childish misbehavior — see NAUGHTY

2 traveling from place to place — see ITINERANT

erratic *adj* **1** lacking a definite plan, purpose, or pattern — see RANDOM

2 lacking in steadiness or regularity of occurrence — see FITFUL

3 not staying constant — see UNEVEN 2

erratically *adv* without definite aim, direction, rule, or method — see HIT OR MISS

erroneous *adj* not being in agreement with what is true — see FALSE 1

erroneously *adv* in a mistaken or inappropriate way — see WRONGLY

erroneousness *n* the quality or state of being false — see FALLACY 2

error *n* **1** an unintentional departure from truth or accuracy ⟨a report on the earthquake contained several unfortunate *errors*⟩

synonyms blunder, fault, flub, fumble, goof, inaccuracy, lapse, miscue, misstep, mistake, oversight, slip, slipup, stumble

related words boner, howler; foul-up, muff; misapprehension, miscalculation, misconception, misjudgment, misstatement, misunderstanding

near antonyms accuracy, correctness, precision

2 a breaking of a moral or legal code — see OFFENSE 1

3 a false idea or belief — see FALLACY 1

erstwhile *adj* having been such at some previous time — see FORMER

erudite *adj* **1** having or displaying advanced knowledge or education — see EDUCATED

2 suggestive of the vocabulary used in books — see BOOKISH

erudition *n* the understanding and information gained from being educated — see EDUCATION 2

erupt *vb* **1** to throw out or off (something from within) often violently ⟨the volcano *erupted* clouds of poisonous gas and tons of hot ash⟩

synonyms belch, disgorge, eject, expel, jet, spew, spout, spurt

related words gush, pour, stream, surge; emanate, issue, spring; discharge, emit, fire; cast, fling, heave, hurl, launch, pitch, toss

near antonyms bottle (up), contain, restrain, shut (in *or* up)

2 to develop suddenly and violently ⟨a fire *erupted*, and flames soon engulfed the room⟩

synonyms break out, burst (forth), explode, flame, flare (up)

related words burgeon, mushroom, snowball; blow up, detonate, touch off

eruption *n* **1** a sudden intense expression of strong feeling — see OUTBURST 1

2 the act or an instance of exploding — see EXPLOSION 1

escalate *vb* **1** to become greater in extent, volume, amount, or number — see INCREASE 2

2 to make greater in size, amount, or number — see INCREASE 1

escalated *adj* being at a higher level than average — see HIGH 2

escapade *n* a playful or mischievous act intended as a joke — see PRANK

escape *n* **1** the act or an instance of getting free

THESAURUS

from danger or confinement ⟨a daring prison *es-cape*⟩
synonyms flight, getaway, lam, slip
related words deliverance, liberation, redemption, release, rescue, salvation
near antonyms imprisonment, incarceration; custody, detention, hold, holding, retention; danger, hazard, jeopardy, peril, risk
2 the act or a means of getting or keeping away from something undesirable ⟨the reading of science fiction novels as an *escape* from boring reality⟩
synonyms avoidance, cop-out, dodging, ducking, eluding, eschewing, evasion, out, shaking, shunning
related words bypassing, circumvention; averting, deflection, prevention
near antonyms abidance, endurance, submission, toleration
escape *vb* **1** to get free from a dangerous or confining situation ⟨everyone managed to *escape* from the burning building in time⟩
synonyms abscond, clear out, flee, fly, get away, get out, lam, run away, run off
related words avoid, elude, evade, lose, shun; decamp, depart, exit, leave; disentangle, extricate; emancipate, free, liberate, redeem, release
phrases fly the coop, free oneself
near antonyms abide, linger, remain, stay, tarry; come back, return
2 to get or keep away from (as a responsibility) through cleverness or trickery ⟨a judge who is very determined not to let criminals *escape* punishment⟩
synonyms avoid, dodge, duck, elude, eschew, evade, shake, shirk, shun
related words miss; avert, deflect, divert, obviate, parry, prevent, ward (off); debar, exclude, preclude; bypass, circumvent, skirt; foil, frustrate, outwit, thwart
phrases get around, have nothing to do with, shy away from, steer clear of
near antonyms accept, court, embrace, pursue, seek, welcome; catch, contract, incur
escarpment *n* a steep wall of rock, earth, or ice — see CLIFF
eschew *vb* to get or keep away from (as a responsibility) through cleverness or trickery — see ESCAPE 2
eschewing *n* the act or a means of getting or keeping away from something undesirable — see ESCAPE 2
escort *n* one that accompanies another for protection, guidance, or as a courtesy ⟨the mayor served as the First Lady's *escort* for her tour of the city⟩
synonyms attendant, companion, guard, guide
related words chaperone (*or* chaperon), squire; shadow, sidekick; conductor, leader, pilot
escort *vb* to go along with in order to provide assistance, protection, or companionship — see ACCOMPANY
esculent *adj* suitable for use as food — see EDIBLE
esoteric *adj* difficult for one of ordinary knowledge or intelligence to understand — see PROFOUND 1
especial *adj* of a particular or exact sort — see EXPRESS 1
especially *adv* to a great degree — see VERY 1
espionage *n* the secret gathering of information on others ⟨the acts of *espionage* on behalf of the

Confederacy carried on by Belle Boyd and Rose Greenhow⟩
synonyms spying
related words dope, goods, lowdown; counterintelligence, intelligence; observation, reconnaissance, surveillance; bugging, eavesdropping, wiretapping
espousal *n* **1** a ceremony in which two people are united in matrimony — see WEDDING
2 the act or state of being engaged to be married — see ENGAGEMENT 1
espouse *vb* **1** to give in marriage — see MARRY 2
2 to take as a spouse — see MARRY 3
esprit *n* active strength of body or mind — see VIGOR 1
espy *vb* to make note of (something) through the use of one's eyes — see SEE 1
essay *n* **1** a short piece of writing typically expressing a point of view ⟨school *essays* on what it means to be a patriot⟩
synonyms article, composition, paper, theme
related words column, commentary, editorial, feature, report, review, write-up; dissertation, thesis; tract, treatise; discourse, discussion, exposition, study
2 an effort to do or accomplish something — see ATTEMPT
essay *vb* to make an effort to do — see ATTEMPT
essence *n* the quality or qualities that make a thing what it is ⟨the belief that power ultimately rests with the people is the very *essence* of democracy⟩
synonyms essentiality, nature, quintessence, soul, stuff, substance
related words heart, spirit; center, core, keynote, marrow, pith, seat; embodiment, epitome, incarnation, manifestation, personification; aspect, attribute, feature, property; gist, kernel, nub
essential *adj* **1** impossible to do without ⟨a well-stocked public library is *essential* for the well-being of a community⟩
synonyms all-important, imperative, indispensable, integral, necessary, needed, needful, required, requisite, vital
related words prerequisite; compulsory, mandatory, obligatory; important, momentous, significant; basic, central, fundamental, key, organic; insistent, persistent, pressing, urgent
near antonyms undesired, unwanted; inconsequential, insignificant, unimportant; excess, extra, superfluous, surplus
antonyms dispensable, needless, nonessential, unnecessary, unneeded
2 of or relating to the simplest facts or theories of a subject — see ELEMENTARY
3 being a part of the innermost nature of a person or thing — see INHERENT
essential *n* **1** something necessary, indispensable, or unavoidable ⟨the *essentials* for success include a willingness to work and the right attitude⟩
synonyms condition, demand, must, necessity, need, requirement, requisite
related words precondition, prerequisite; advantage, edge, plus
near antonyms extra, extravagance, frill, luxury, superfluity
antonyms nonessential, nonnecessity
2 essentials *pl* general or basic truths on which other truths or theories can be based — see PRINCIPLES 1

essentiality *n* the quality or qualities that make a thing what it is — see ESSENCE

establish *vb* **1** to gain full recognition or acceptance of ⟨the teenagers accused of shoplifting were able to *establish* their innocence⟩
synonyms demonstrate, prove, show, substantiate
related words attest, authenticate, bear out, document, evidence, support, sustain, uphold; confirm, corroborate, justify, validate, verify
phrases prove beyond a reasonable doubt
near antonyms confute, discredit, invalidate, rebut, refute
antonyms disprove
2 to show the existence or truth of by evidence — see PROVE 1
3 to be responsible for the creation and early operation or use of — see FOUND

establisher *n* a person who establishes a whole new field of endeavor — see FATHER 2

establishment *n* **1** a building, room, or suite of rooms occupied by a service business — see PLACE 2
2 a commercial or industrial activity or organization — see ENTERPRISE 1
3 a public organization with a particular purpose or function — see INSTITUTION 1
4 a structure that is designed and built for a particular purpose — see FACILITY

estate *n* **1** a large impressive residence — see MANSION
2 a state of being or fitness — see CONDITION 1
3 one of the segments of society into which people are grouped — see CLASS 1

esteem *n* a feeling of great approval and liking — see ADMIRATION 1

esteem *vb* **1** to think of in a particular way — see CONSIDER 1
2 to think very highly or favorably of — see ADMIRE

esteemed *adj* having a good reputation especially in a field of knowledge — see RESPECTABLE 1

estimate *n* **1** the act of placing a value on the nature, character, or quality of something ⟨what we owe our war veterans is beyond *estimate*⟩
synonyms appraisal, appraisement, assessment, estimation, evaluation, reckoning, valuation
related words calculation, computation, measurement
2 an opinion on the nature, character, or quality of something — see ESTIMATION 1

estimate *vb* **1** to make an approximate or tentative judgment regarding ⟨experts *estimated* the value of the painting at a million dollars⟩
synonyms appraise, assess, evaluate, rate, set, value
related words adjudge, deem, judge; ascertain, determine, discover, learn; price, prize; decide, settle; analyze, assay, survey, test; reappraise, reassess, reevaluate, revalue
2 to decide the size, amount, number, or distance of (something) without actual measurement ⟨we *estimated* the snowfall to be about a foot⟩
synonyms calculate, call, conjecture, figure, gauge (*also* gage), guess, judge, make, place, put, reckon, suppose
near antonyms calibrate, measure, scale; compute

estimation *n* **1** an opinion on the nature, character, or quality of something ⟨the teacher's *estimation* of her student's scientific aptitude proved to be

well-founded when he won a national science award⟩
synonyms appraisal, appraisement, assessment, estimate, evaluation, judgment (*or* judgement)
related words impression, notion, perception; confidence, faith, stock, trust
2 the act of placing a value on the nature, character, or quality of something — see ESTIMATE 1
3 a feeling of great approval and liking — see ADMIRATION 1

estrange *vb* to cause to change from friendly or loving to unfriendly or uncaring ⟨Carrie's tendency to tattle *estranged* her classmates⟩
synonyms alienate, disaffect, disgruntle, sour
related words antagonize, embitter, envenom; aggravate, anger, enrage, incense, infuriate, madden; disunite, divide, separate, sever, sunder; disappoint, disenchant, disillusion
near antonyms endear, ingratiate; appease, conciliate, mollify, pacify, propitiate
antonyms reconcile

estrangement *n* the loss of friendship or affection ⟨a silly quarrel that eventually resulted in a complete and lasting *estrangement* between the one-time friends⟩
synonyms alienation, disaffection, disgruntlement, souring
related words antagonism, embitterment, envenoming; aggravation, incensing, infuriation; disunion, division, divorce, schism, separation; disenchantment, disillusionment
near antonyms endearment, ingratiation; appeasement, conciliation, mollification, pacification, propitiation
antonyms reconciliation

estuary *n* a part of a body of water that extends beyond the general shoreline — see GULF 1

etch *vb* **1** to cut (as letters or designs) on a hard surface — see ENGRAVE 1
2 to produce a vivid impression of — see ENGRAVE 2

eternal *adj* lasting forever — see EVERLASTING

eternally *adv* for all time — see EVER 1

eternity *n* **1** endless time ⟨the question whether the universe will end someday or continue to exist in *eternity*⟩
synonyms infinity, perpetuity
related words boundlessness, endlessness, interminableness, permanence, timelessness
2 unending existence after death ⟨a firm belief in the *eternity* of the soul⟩
synonyms afterlife, hereafter, immortality
related words otherworld
phrases life after death
3 a long or seemingly long period of time — see AGE 2

ethereal *adj* resembling air in lightness — see AIRY 1

ethical *adj* **1** conforming to a high standard of morality or virtue — see GOOD 2
2 following the accepted rules of moral conduct — see HONORABLE 1
3 guided by or in accordance with one's sense of right and wrong — see CONSCIENTIOUS 1

ethics *n pl* the code of good conduct for an individual or group ⟨the *ethics* of scouting require scouts to be loyal, clean, and reverent⟩
synonyms morality, morals, principles, standards
related words customs, etiquette, manners, mores; beliefs, dogma, faith, tenets

THESAURUS

ethnic *adj* of, relating to, or reflecting the traits exhibited by a group of people with a common ancestry and culture — see RACIAL

etiquette *n* personal conduct or behavior as evaluated by an accepted standard of appropriateness for a social or professional setting — see MANNER 1

eulogy *n* a formal expression of praise — see ENCOMIUM

euphonious *adj* **1** having a pleasantly flowing quality suggestive of music — see LYRIC 1
2 having a pleasing mixture of notes — see HARMONIOUS 1

euphoria *n* a state of overwhelming usually pleasurable emotion — see ECSTASY

euphoric *adj* experiencing or marked by overwhelming usually pleasurable emotion — see ECSTATIC

evacuate *vb* to remove the contents of — see EMPTY

evacuee *n* a person forced to emigrate for political reasons — see ÉMIGRÉ 1

evade *vb* to get or keep away from (as a responsibility) through cleverness or trickery — see ESCAPE 2

evaluate *vb* to make an approximate or tentative judgment regarding — see ESTIMATE 1

evaluation *n* **1** an opinion on the nature, character, or quality of something — see ESTIMATION 1
2 the act of placing a value on the nature, character, or quality of something — see ESTIMATE 1

evanesce *vb* to cease to be visible — see DISAPPEAR

evanescent *adj* lasting only for a short time — see MOMENTARY

evaporate *vb* to cease to be visible — see DISAPPEAR

evasion *n* the act or a means of getting or keeping away from something undesirable — see ESCAPE 2

evasive *adj* hard to find, capture, or isolate — see ELUSIVE

even *adj* **1** being neither more nor less than a certain amount, number, or extent ⟨the distance to town is an *even* mile⟩
synonyms exact, flat, precise, round
near antonyms approximate, comparative, relative
2 having a surface without bends, breaks, or irregularities — see LEVEL
3 resembling another in every respect — see SAME 1

even *adv* not merely this but also ⟨the blue whale is a huge, *even* awesome animal by any measure⟩
synonyms indeed, nay, truly, verily, yea
related words assuredly, certainly, decidedly, definitely, positively, really, surely, undeniably, unquestionably
phrases in fact, in reality, in truth

even *vb* **1** to make free from breaks, curves, or bumps ⟨*even* the filling before adding the top layer of the cake⟩
synonyms flatten, level, plane, smooth
related words clip, crop, pare, prune, shave, trim; lay, spread; card, comb, rake
near antonyms coarsen, rumple, wrinkle
antonyms rough, roughen
2 to make equal in amount, degree, or status — see EQUALIZE

evening *n* the time from when the sun begins to set to the onset of total darkness — see DUSK 1

event *n* **1** something that happens ⟨dinnertime was devoted to talking over the day's *events*, not to watching television⟩
synonyms affair, circumstance, episode, hap, happening, incident, occasion, occurrence, thing
related words coincidence, fluke, freak; landmark, milestone, page, phenomenon, turning point; adventure, experience; accident, crisis, emergency, juncture; achievement, deed, exploit, feat; news, tidings
2 something that might happen ⟨in the *event* of rain, graduation ceremonies will be held indoors⟩
synonyms case, contingency, eventuality, possibility
related words probability; chance, risk
3 a competitive encounter between individuals or groups carried on for amusement, exercise, or in pursuit of a prize — see GAME 1
4 a social gathering — see PARTY 1

eventful *adj* having great meaning or lasting effect — see IMPORTANT 1

eventide *n* the time from when the sun begins to set to the onset of total darkness — see DUSK 1

eventuality *n* **1** something that can develop or become actual — see POTENTIAL
2 something that might happen — see EVENT 2

eventually *adv* at a later time — see YET 1

ever *adv* **1** for all time ⟨the name of Benedict Arnold will *ever* be linked with treason⟩
synonyms always, aye (*also* ay), eternally, everlastingly, evermore, forever, forevermore, permanently, perpetually
related words enduringly, long, perennially
phrases forever and a day, forever and ever, for good, to (*or* until) the end of time
antonyms never, nevermore
2 in any way or respect — see AT ALL
3 on every relevant occasion — see ALWAYS 1

everlasting *adj* lasting forever ⟨valentines typically express the giver's *everlasting* love and devotion⟩
synonyms ceaseless, dateless, deathless, endless, eternal, immortal, permanent, perpetual, undying, unending
related words durable, enduring, lasting, persistent; imperishable, indestructible; timeless; abiding, steadfast, steady, unfailing, unfaltering
near antonyms ephemeral, evanescent, fleeting, momentary, passing, short-lived, transitory
antonyms impermanent, mortal, temporary

everlastingly *adv* for all time — see EVER 1

evermore *adv* for all time — see EVER 1

every *adj* being one of a group — see EACH

everybody *pron* every person ⟨*everybody* must do what his or her conscience dictates⟩
synonyms all, everyone
phrases each and everyone, one and all
antonyms nobody

everyday *adj* **1** being of the type that is encountered in the normal course of events — see ORDINARY 1
2 having to do with the practical details of regular life — see MUNDANE 1
3 not designed for special occasions — see CASUAL 1
4 often observed or encountered — see COMMON 1

everyone *pron* every person — see EVERYBODY

everyplace *adv* in every place or in all places — see EVERYWHERE

everywhere *adv* in every place or in all places ⟨freedom and happiness are the goals of people *everywhere*⟩
synonyms all over, everyplace, throughout
phrases all over the place (*or* map), far and near, far and wide, high and low, in every corner (*or* quarter)
antonyms nowhere

evidence *n* something presented in support of the truth or accuracy of a claim — see PROOF

evident *adj* 1 appearing to be true on the basis of evidence that may or may not be confirmed — see APPARENT 1
2 not subject to misinterpretation or more than one interpretation — see CLEAR 2

evidently *adv* to all outward appearances — see APPARENTLY

evil *adj* 1 causing or capable of causing harm — see HARMFUL
2 not conforming to a high moral standard; morally unacceptable — see BAD 2

evil *n* that which is morally unacceptable ⟨our free will allows us to choose between good and *evil*⟩
synonyms bad, evildoing, ill, immorality, iniquity, sin, villainy, wrong
related words atrociousness, badness, evilness, heinousness, nefariousness, sinfulness, vileness, wickedness; devilry (*or* deviltry), fiendishness; cancer, decay, rot, squalor; corruption, debauchery, degeneracy, depravity, indecency, perversion; abomination, anathema, taboo (*also* tabu)
near antonyms integrity, probity, rectitude, uprightness; goodness, righteousness, virtuousness
antonyms good, morality, right, virtue

evildoer *n* 1 a person who commits moral wrongs ⟨if good people stand by and do nothing, *evildoers* will triumph⟩
synonyms malefactor, sinner, wrongdoer
related words criminal, crook, felon, lawbreaker, miscreant, reprobate, transgressor, villain
near antonyms angel, saint
2 a mean, evil, or unprincipled person — see VILLAIN

evildoing *n* that which is morally unacceptable — see EVIL

evilness *n* the state or quality of being utterly evil — see ENORMITY 1

evince *vb* to make known (something abstract) through outward signs — see SHOW 2

eviscerate *vb* to take the internal organs out of — see GUT

evocative *adj* provoking a memory or mental association — see SUGGESTIVE 2

evoke *vb* to draw out (something hidden, latent, or reserved) — see EDUCE

evolution *n* the act or process of going from the simple or basic to the complex or advanced — see DEVELOPMENT 1

evolve *vb* to gradually become clearer or more detailed — see DEVELOP 1

evolved *adj* being far along in development — see ADVANCED 1

exact *adj* 1 being in agreement with the truth or a fact or a standard — see CORRECT 1
2 being neither more nor less than a certain amount, number, or extent — see EVEN 1
3 following an original exactly — see FAITHFUL 2
4 made or done with extreme care and accuracy — see FINE 2
5 meeting the highest standard of accuracy — see PRECISE 1

exact *vb* 1 to ask for (something) earnestly or with authority — see DEMAND 1
2 to establish or apply as a charge or penalty — see IMPOSE
3 to get (as money) by the use of force or threats — see EXTORT

exacting *adj* 1 hard to please — see FINICKY
2 not allowing for any exceptions or loosening of standards — see RIGID 1
3 requiring considerable physical or mental effort — see HARD 2
4 requiring much time, effort, or careful attention — see DEMANDING 1

exactitude *n* the quality or state of being very accurate — see PRECISION

exactly *adv* 1 as stated or indicated without the slightest difference ⟨we will meet at *exactly* six o'clock⟩
synonyms just, precisely, right, sharp, smack-dab, squarely
2 in a like manner — see JUST 1
3 in the same words — see VERBATIM
4 without any relaxation of standards or precision — see STRICTLY

exactness *n* the quality or state of being very accurate — see PRECISION

exaggerate *vb* 1 to add to the interest of by including made-up details — see EMBROIDER
2 to describe or express in too strong terms — see OVERSTATE

exaggeration *n* the representation of something in terms that go beyond the facts ⟨their *exaggeration* was such that a rainstorm became a hurricane⟩
synonyms caricature, coloring, elaboration, embellishment, embroidering, hyperbole, magnification, overstatement, padding, stretching
related words amplification, enhancement; fabrication, misrepresentation; fudging, hedging
near antonyms belittlement, disparagement, minimizing
antonyms understatement

exalt *vb* to enhance the status of ⟨popular support and media hype have *exalted* Super Bowl Sunday to the level of a national holiday⟩
synonyms aggrandize, dignify, ennoble, enshrine, glorify, magnify
related words boost, elevate, lift, promote, raise, upgrade, uplift; heighten, intensify; idealize, romanticize, sanitize, sugarcoat; canonize, deify; acclaim, extol (*also* extoll), honor, laud, praise
near antonyms belittle, decry, depreciate, detract, disparage, minimize
antonyms abase, degrade, demean, humble, humiliate

exam *n* a set of questions or problems designed to assess knowledge, skills, or intelligence — see EXAMINATION 1

examination *n* 1 a set of questions or problems designed to assess knowledge, skills, or intelligence ⟨applicants to the prep school are required to take an *examination*⟩
synonyms exam, quiz, test
related words catechism; audition; final; checkup, inspection, review; inquiry, interrogation, investigation, probe, research

2 a systematic search for the truth or facts about something — see INQUIRY 1

3 a close look at or over someone or something in order to judge condition — see INSPECTION

examine *vb* **1** to put a series of questions to ⟨the defense attorney was eager to *examine* her star witness⟩

synonyms grill, interrogate, pump, query, question, quiz

related words debrief; cross-examine; catechize; annoy, harass, hound, pester

phrases give the third degree to

2 to look over closely (as for judging quality or condition) — see INSPECT

example *n* one of a group or collection that shows what the whole is like ⟨a war bonnet that is a fine *example* of Native American handicraft⟩

synonyms case, exemplar, illustration, instance, representative, sample, specimen

related words cross section; evidence, indication, manifestation, sign

phrases case in point

exasperate *vb* to disturb the peace of mind of (someone) especially by repeated disagreeable acts — see IRRITATE 1

exasperating *adj* causing annoyance — see ANNOYING

exasperation *n* **1** something that is a source of irritation — see ANNOYANCE 3

2 the feeling of impatience or anger caused by another's repeated disagreeable acts — see ANNOYANCE 2

excavate *vb* to hollow out or form (something) by removing earth — see DIG 1

exceed *vb* to go beyond the limit of ⟨by resorting to corporal punishment, the teacher had *exceeded* his authority⟩

synonyms overreach, overrun, overshoot, overstep, surpass

related words encroach, entrench (*also* intrench), infringe, invade, trespass; overdo, overuse, overwork

exceedingly *also* **exceeding** *adv* to a great degree — see VERY 1

excel *vb* to be greater, better, or stronger than — see SURPASS 1

excellence *n* **1** exceptionally high quality ⟨the annual awards honor *excellence* in children's literature⟩

synonyms distinction, excellency, greatness, preeminence, superbness, superiority, supremacy

related words faultlessness, flawlessness, impeccability, perfection; goodness, value, worth; consequence, importance, notability

near antonyms averageness, badness, inferiority, mediocrity, ordinariness, worthlessness

2 a quality that gives something special worth ⟨the particular *excellence* of down in clothing and sleeping bags is its lightness⟩

synonyms distinction, excellency, merit, value, virtue

related words advantage, edge, superiority

near antonyms blemish, defect, failing, fault, flaw

antonyms deficiency

excellency *n* **1** a quality that gives something special worth — see EXCELLENCE 2

2 exceptionally high quality — see EXCELLENCE 1

excellent *adj* of the very best kind ⟨fast-food fans rate this chain's fries as *excellent*⟩

synonyms A1, bang-up, banner, boss [*slang*], capital, classic, crackerjack, dandy, divine, fabulous, fine, first-class, first-rate, grand, great, groovy, heavenly, jim-dandy, keen, marvelous (*or* marvellous), mean, neat, nifty, noble, par excellence, prime, sensational, splendid, stellar, sterling, superb, superior, superlative, supernal, swell, terrific, tip-top, top, top-notch, unsurpassed, wonderful

related words acceptable, adequate, all right, decent, good, OK, passable, satisfactory, tolerable; better, exceptional, fancy, high-grade, premium, special

phrases out of sight

near antonyms bad, inferior, low-grade, substandard, unsatisfactory; mediocre, second-class, second-rate; atrocious, execrable, vile, wretched

antonyms poor

except *also* **excepting** *conj* if it were not for the fact that ⟨I'd go, *except* it's too far⟩

synonyms but, only, saving, yet

except *also* **excepting** *prep* not including ⟨the store is open daily *except* Sundays⟩

synonyms aside from, bar, barring, beside, besides, but, except for, excluding, outside, outside of, save, saving

except *vb* to prevent the participation or inclusion of — see EXCLUDE

except for *prep* not including — see EXCEPT

exceptionable *adj* provoking or likely to provoke protest — see OBJECTIONABLE

exceptional *adj* being out of the ordinary ⟨an *exceptional* amount of snow fell in March⟩

synonyms aberrant, abnormal, atypical, extraordinary, freak, odd, peculiar, phenomenal, rare, singular, uncommon, uncustomary, unique, unusual, unwonted

related words conspicuous, notable, noticeable, outstanding, prominent, remarkable, salient, striking; bizarre, deviant, eccentric, outlandish, quaint, strange, weird; incomprehensible, inconceivable, incredible, unimaginable, unthinkable

near antonyms everyday, familiar, frequent

antonyms common, customary, normal, ordinary, typical, unexceptional, usual

excerpt *n* a part taken from a longer work ⟨we'll read an *excerpt* from the novel⟩

synonyms extract, passage

related words snippet; citation, quotation; context; selection

excess *adj* being over what is needed — see SPARE 1

excess *n* the state or an instance of going beyond what is usual, proper, or needed ⟨a new television season with an *excess* of wisecracking teenagers⟩

synonyms fat, overabundance, overage, overflow, overkill, overmuch, oversupply, superabundance, superfluity, surfeit, surplus

related words abundance, bounty, plentitude, plenty, profusion, sufficiency; overproduction, overstock

near antonyms dearth, lack, scarcity

antonyms deficiency, deficit, insufficiency

excessive *adj* going beyond a normal or acceptable limit in degree or amount ⟨nerdy hackers who spend an *excessive* amount of time sitting in front of their computers⟩

synonyms devilish, exorbitant, extravagant, extreme, immoderate, inordinate, lavish, overmuch, overweening, steep, stiff, towering, unconscionable, undue *related words* boundless, endless, immeasurable, infinite, limitless; intolerable, unbearable, unjustifiable, unwarranted; improper, inappropriate, thick, unseemly

near antonyms deficient, inadequate, insufficient; minimal, minimum

antonyms moderate, modest, reasonable, temperate

excessively *adv* beyond a normal or acceptable limit — see TOO 1

exchange *n* **1** a giving or taking of one thing of value in return for another ⟨*exchanges* of commemorative pins are common among Olympic athletes⟩

synonyms barter, commutation, swap, trade, truck

related words replacement, substitution; reciprocation, recompense, requital; bargain, deal, horse trade, negotiation, transaction; bargaining, dealing, dickering, haggling, horse trading; logrolling

2 talking or a talk between two or more people — see CONVERSATION

exchange *vb* to give up (something) and take something else in return — see CHANGE 3

excitable *adj* easily excited by nature ⟨an *excitable* child who needed a stable home life⟩

synonyms flighty, fluttery, high-strung, jittery, jumpy, nervous, skittish, spooky

related words hot-blooded, mercurial, temperamental, unstable, volatile, volcanic; anxious, edgy, jumpy, nervy, tense, uptight; emotional, hypersensitive, intense, sensitive, soulful; dramatic, histrionic, melodramatic; irascible, irritable, prickly, testy, touchy

near antonyms calm, collected, cool, serene, tranquil; easy, easygoing, laid-back, relaxed

antonyms unflappable

excite *vb* **1** to cause a pleasurable stimulation of the feelings — see THRILL

2 to rouse to strong feeling or action — see PROVOKE 1

excited *adj* **1** being in a state of increased activity or agitation — see FEVERISH 1

2 showing urgent desire or interest — see EAGER

excitement *n* **1** something that arouses a strong response from another — see PROVOCATION 1

2 urgent desire or interest — see EAGERNESS

exciter *n* a person who stirs up public feelings especially of discontent — see AGITATOR

exciting *adj* **1** causing great emotional or mental stimulation ⟨an *exciting*, come-from-behind victory for the underdogs in the last game of the World Series⟩

synonyms breathtaking, electric, electrifying, exhilarating, galvanizing, inspiring, rip-roaring, rousing, stimulating, stirring, thrilling

related words arresting, interesting, intriguing, provocative, tantalizing; absorbing, engrossing, gripping, riveting; moving, poignant, touching; enchanting, enthralling, fascinating, spellbinding

near antonyms boring, tedious, tiresome; dreary, dull, humdrum, monotonous, uninteresting

antonyms unexciting

2 serving or likely to arouse a strong reaction — see PROVOCATIVE

exclaim *vb* to utter with a sudden burst of strong feeling ⟨the whole team *exclaimed* with one voice, "We won!"⟩

synonyms blurt (out), bolt, cry (out), ejaculate

related words blunder, leak; bellow, bleat, crow,

holler, hoot, howl, roar, shout, whoop, yowl; interject

exclude *vb* to prevent the participation or inclusion of ⟨troublemakers were *excluded* from the club⟩

synonyms ban, bar, count out, debar, eliminate, except, rule out

related words blackball, blacklist, ostracize; banish, deport, exile, expel, oust, throw out; block, hinder, impede, obstruct; cease, discontinue, halt, suspend; deter, stave off, ward (off)

near antonyms accept, entertain, receive, welcome

antonyms admit, include

excluding *prep* not including — see EXCEPT

exclusive *adj* **1** belonging only to the one person, unit, or group named — see SOLE 1

2 not divided or scattered among several areas of interest or concern — see WHOLE 1

exclusively *adv* for nothing other than — see SOLELY 1

excoriate *vb* to criticize harshly and usually publicly — see ATTACK 2

excrement *n* solid matter discharged from an animal's alimentary canal — see DROPPING 1

excrescence *n* an abnormal mass of tissue — see GROWTH 1

excreta *n pl* solid matter discharged from an animal's alimentary canal — see DROPPING 1

excruciating *adj* **1** intensely or unbearably painful ⟨those who publicly disagreed with the government were subjected to *excruciating* torture⟩

synonyms agonizing, harrowing, racking, tormenting, torturing, torturous

related words acute, exquisite, extreme, fierce, intense, vehement, violent; piercing, sharp, shooting, stabbing, stinging, tearing, tingling

2 causing intense mental or physical distress — see SHARP 2

3 difficult to endure — see HARSH 1

4 hard to accept or bear especially emotionally — see BITTER 2

exculpate *vb* to free from a charge of wrongdoing ⟨I will present evidence that will *exculpate* my client⟩

synonyms absolve, acquit, clear, exonerate, vindicate

related words atone (for), expiate; discharge, liberate, redeem, release, unburden; condone, excuse, forgive, pardon, remit; avenge, redress, revenge

near antonyms accuse, arraign, charge, impeach, indict; convict

antonyms incriminate

excursion *n* **1** a short trip for pleasure ⟨our weekend *excursions* have been to all parts of our home state⟩

synonyms jaunt, junket, outing, sally

related words journey, travel(s); circuit, tour; expedition, odyssey, safari; detour; hike, peregrination, trek, walk; pilgrimage

2 a departure from the subject under consideration — see TANGENT

excursionist *n* a person who travels for pleasure — see TOURIST

excusable *adj* worthy of forgiveness — see VENIAL

excuse *n* an explanation that frees one from fault or blame ⟨a whole evening of must-see TV is no *excuse* for not having your homework done⟩

synonyms alibi, defense, justification, plea, reason

related words guise, pretense (*or* pretence), pretext, rationale, rationalization; cop-out, out; acknowledgment (*also* acknowledgement), apology, atonement, confession

excuse *vb* **1** to overlook or dismiss as of little importance ⟨the student's theme is so good that I'm willing to *excuse* the spelling errors⟩

synonyms brush (aside *or* off), condone, disregard, forgive, gloss (over), gloze (over), ignore, pardon, pass over, remit, shrug off, wink (at)

related words explain, justify, rationalize, whitewash; absolve, acquit, clear, exculpate, exonerate, vindicate

phrases forgive and forget

near antonyms heed, mark, mind, note, object (to)

2 to be an acceptable reason for — see JUSTIFY 1

3 to make (something) seem less bad by offering excuses — see PALLIATE 1

execrable *adj* **1** extremely unsatisfactory — see WRETCHED 1

2 of low quality — see CHEAP 2

execrate *vb* **1** to declare to be morally wrong or evil — see CONDEMN 1

2 to dislike strongly — see HATE

execration *n* **1** a prayer that harm will come to someone — see CURSE 1

2 a very strong dislike — see HATE 1

execute *vb* **1** to carry out effectively — see ENFORCE

2 to carry through (as a process) to completion — see PERFORM 1

3 to put to death deliberately — see MURDER 1

execution *n* the doing of an action — see COMMISSION 2

executive *adj* suited for or relating to the directing of things ⟨the *executive* skills needed to manage a large business office⟩

synonyms administrative, directorial, managerial, supervisory

related words bureaucratic, governmental, ministerial, official, parliamentary; regulatory; authoritarian, despotic, dictatorial

executive *n* a person who manages or directs ⟨a program that teaches company *executives* how to better manage their staffs⟩

synonyms administrator, director, manager, superintendent, supervisor

related words officer, official; commissioner, minister; boss, chief, head, leader, president

exemplar *n* **1** one of a group or collection that shows what the whole is like — see EXAMPLE

2 someone of such unequaled perfection as to deserve imitation — see IDEAL 1

3 the most perfect type or example — see QUINTESSENCE 1

exemplary *adj* constituting, serving as, or worthy of being a pattern to be imitated — see MODEL

exemplify *vb* to show or make clear by using examples — see ILLUSTRATE 1

exemption *n* freedom from punishment, harm, or loss — see IMPUNITY

exercise *n* **1** energetic movement of the body for the sake of physical fitness ⟨the doctor ordered plenty of fresh air and *exercise*⟩

synonyms activity, conditioning, exertion

related words training, warm-up, workout; toning, trimming; aerobics, bodybuilding, calisthenics, isometrics, weight lifting; physical therapy

2 something done over and over in order to develop skill ⟨a young piano student dutifully going through the standard finger *exercises*⟩

synonyms drill, practice (*also* practise), routine, training, workout

related words assignment, homework, lesson

3 the act or practice of employing something for a particular purpose — see USE 1

exercise *vb* **1** to bring to bear especially forcefully or effectively — see EXERT

2 to do over and over so as to become skilled — see PRACTICE

3 to put into action or service — see USE 1

4 to trouble the mind of; to make uneasy — see DISTURB 1

exert *vb* to bring to bear especially forcefully or effectively ⟨parental involvement has been shown to *exert* the most influence over a child's success in school⟩

synonyms apply, exercise, ply, put out, wield

related words employ, use, utilize

exertion *n* **1** energetic movement of the body for the sake of physical fitness — see EXERCISE 1

2 the active use of energy in producing a result — see EFFORT

exfoliate *vb* to cast (a natural bodily covering or appendage) aside — see SHED 1

exhale *vb* **1** to let or force out of the lungs ⟨before answering, the suspect *exhaled* a cloud of cigarette smoke⟩

synonyms blow (out), breathe (out), expire

related words expectorate

antonyms inhale, inspire

2 to throw or give off — see EMIT 1

exhaust *vb* **1** to use up all the physical energy of ⟨the long day at the county fair had *exhausted* everyone⟩

synonyms burn out, do in, drain, fag, fatigue, tire, tucker (out), wash out, wear, wear out, weary

related words debilitate, enervate, enfeeble, sap, waste, weaken

phrases wear to a frazzle

near antonyms activate, energize, invigorate, strengthen, vitalize; relax, rest, unwind

2 to make complete use of — see DEPLETE

exhausted *adj* depleted in strength, energy, or freshness — see WEARY 1

exhaustion *n* a complete depletion of energy or strength — see FATIGUE

exhaustive *adj* trying all possibilities ⟨after an *exhaustive* search of our house, we still hadn't found the cat⟩

synonyms all-out, clean, complete, comprehensive, full-scale, out-and-out, thorough, thoroughgoing, total

related words broad, extensive, far-reaching, in-depth, wide; general, global, inclusive

near antonyms aimless, desultory, haphazard, hit-or-miss, random; cursory, shallow, slipshod, superficial; limited, narrow, restricted

exhaustively *adv* with attention to all aspects or details — see THOROUGHLY 1

exhibit *n* a public showing of objects of interest — see EXHIBITION 1

exhibit *vb* to present so as to invite notice or attention — see SHOW 1

exhibition *n* **1** a public showing of objects of interest ⟨an *exhibition* of valuable and fascinating artifacts from a recovered pirate ship⟩

synonyms display, exhibit, exposition, fair, show
related words demonstration, performance, presentation, production; extravaganza, pageant, spectacle; auction, offering, sale
2 an outward and often exaggerated indication of something abstract (as a feeling) for effect — see SHOW 1
exhilarate *vb* **1** to cause a pleasurable stimulation of the feelings — see THRILL
2 to fill with great joy — see ELATE
exhilarated *adj* experiencing or marked by overwhelming usually pleasurable emotion — see ECSTATIC
exhilarating *adj* causing great emotional or mental stimulation — see EXCITING 1
exhilaration *n* **1** a pleasurably intense stimulation of the feelings — see THRILL
2 a state of overwhelming usually pleasurable emotion — see ECSTASY
exhort *vb* to try to persuade (someone) through earnest appeals to follow a course of action — see URGE
exhume *vb* to remove from place of burial ⟨the remains of John Paul Jones were *exhumed* in Paris and transported with great ceremony to the U.S. Naval Academy⟩
synonyms disinter, unearth
antonyms bury, entomb, inter
exigency *n* a time or state of affairs requiring prompt or decisive action — see EMERGENCY
exile *n* **1** the forced removal from a homeland ⟨the *exile* of French settlers from Nova Scotia resulted in the birth of the Cajun community in the U.S.⟩
synonyms banishment, deportation, displacement, expatriation, expulsion
related words ostracism; extradition; dispersion, scattering; emigration, migration; evacuation
near antonyms repatriation, return; immigration
2 a person forced to emigrate for political reasons — see ÉMIGRÉ 1
exile *vb* to force to leave a country — see BANISH 1
exist *vb* to have life — see BE 1
existence *n* the fact of being or of being real ⟨the *existence* of UFOs is something that people continue to argue about⟩
synonyms actuality, reality, subsistence
related words genuineness, realness; activity, animation, life; currency, presence, prevalence
near antonyms absence, dearth, lack, want
antonyms nonexistence
existent *adj* **1** existing in fact and not merely as a possibility — see ACTUAL
2 having being at the present time — see EXTANT 1
existing *adj* having being at the present time — see EXTANT 1
exit *n* **1** a place or means of going out ⟨all of the building's *exits* were being watched by security guards⟩
synonyms egress, issue, outlet
related words escape, release; opening, passage, vent
near antonyms access, entrée (*or* entree)
antonyms entrance, entry, entryway, ingress
2 the act of leaving a place — see DEPARTURE
exit *vb* to leave a place often for another — see GO 2
exiting *n* the act of leaving a place — see DEPARTURE
exodus *n* a flowing or going out — see OUTFLOW

exonerate *vb* to free from a charge of wrongdoing — see EXCULPATE
exorbitant *adj* going beyond a normal or acceptable limit in degree or amount — see EXCESSIVE
exorbitantly *adv* beyond a normal or acceptable limit — see TOO 1
exotic *adj* excitingly or mysteriously unusual ⟨the dream of someday traveling to *exotic* lands⟩
synonyms fantastic, glamorous (*also* glamourous), marvelous (*or* marvellous), outlandish, romantic, strange
related words colorful, picturesque, quaint; alien, foreign; distant, faraway, remote; alluring, captivating, enchanting, fascinating
exotic *n* something strange or unusual that is an object of interest — see CURIOSITY 2
expand *vb* **1** to express more fully and in greater detail ⟨an article on the First Ladies that the author later *expanded* into a book⟩
synonyms amplify, develop, elaborate (on), enlarge (on)
related words add (to), complement, supplement; discourse, expatiate, ramble, run on
near antonyms compress, contract; outline, summarize, sum up
antonyms abbreviate, abridge, condense, shorten
2 to make greater in size, amount, or number — see INCREASE 1
3 to arrange the parts of (something) over a wider area — see OPEN 3
4 to become greater in extent, volume, amount, or number — see INCREASE 2
expanse *n* a wide space or area ⟨the great explorers who crossed the vast *expanse* of the ocean in small ships⟩
synonyms breadth, extent, reach, spread, stretch
related words domain, field, sphere, territory; compass, range, scope, sweep; gamut, scale, spectrum; depth, emptiness, void; distance, extension, latitude, length, span; amplitude, immensity, magnitude
expansion *n* **1** something added (as by growth) — see INCREASE 1
2 the act or process of going from the simple or basic to the complex or advanced — see DEVELOPMENT 1
expansive *adj* having considerable extent — see EXTENSIVE
expatiate *vb* to give a formal often extended talk on a subject — see TALK 1
expatriate *n* a person forced to emigrate for political reasons — see ÉMIGRÉ 1
expatriate *vb* to force to leave a country — see BANISH 1
expatriation *n* the forced removal from a homeland — see EXILE 1
expect *vb* to believe in the future occurrence of (something) ⟨we *expect* their arrival late this afternoon⟩
synonyms anticipate, await, hope (for), watch (for)
related words bank on, count (on *or* upon), depend (on *or* upon), rely (on *or* upon); envisage, foresee; foretell, predict, prophesy; assume, presume, presuppose; contemplate, eye, view
phrases look for, look forward to
near antonyms doubt, question
expectant *adj* **1** having or showing signs of eagerly awaiting something ⟨*expectant* crowds gathered

at the spot where the President was scheduled to make an appearance⟩

synonyms agape, agog, anticipatory

related words open-eyed, openmouthed; alert, vigilant, watchful; anxious, breathless, eager, enthusiastic, raring; impatient, restive, restless

near antonyms apathetic, indifferent, unconcerned, unimpressed, uninterested, unmoved

2 containing unborn young within the body — see PREGNANT 1

expected *adj* being in accordance with the prescribed, normal, or logical course of events — see DUE 2

expedient *adj* suitable for bringing about a desired result under the circumstances ⟨made the *expedient* decision to sell the land to whomever offered the most money⟩

synonyms advisable, desirable, judicious, politic, prudent, tactical, wise

related words advantageous, beneficial, profitable; useful, utilitarian; feasible, possible, practicable, practical; opportune, seasonable, timely; opportunistic, self-seeking

near antonyms impractical, unfeasible, unprofitable; inopportune, unseasonable, untimely

antonyms imprudent, inadvisable, inexpedient, injudicious, unwise

expedient *n* **1** a temporary replacement — see MAKESHIFT

2 an action planned or taken to achieve a desired result — see MEASURE 1

3 something that one uses to accomplish an end especially when the usual means is not available — see RESOURCE 1

expedition *n* a going from one place to another usually of some distance — see JOURNEY

expeditious *adj* having or showing the ability to respond without delay or hesitation — see QUICK 1

expel *vb* **1** to drive or force out — see EJECT 1

2 to throw or give off — see EMIT 1

3 to throw out or off (something from within) often violently — see ERUPT 1

expend *vb* **1** to hand over or use up in payment — see SPEND 1

2 to make complete use of — see DEPLETE

expenditure *n* **1** a payment made in the course of achieving a result — see EXPENSE

2 the active use of energy in producing a result — see EFFORT

expense *n* a payment made in the course of achieving a result ⟨they spared no *expense* in building the house of their dreams⟩

synonyms cost, disbursement, expenditure, outgo, outlay

related words overhead; outflow; spending money; charge, price, rate, tab, tariff, toll

expensive *adj* commanding a large price — see COSTLY

expensively *adv* in a luxurious manner — see HIGH

experience *n* **1** knowledge gained by actually doing or living through something ⟨the hospital is looking for nurses with operating-room *experience*⟩

synonyms expertise, know-how, proficiency, savvy, skills

related words background; command, mastery; acquaintance, familiarity, intimacy

near antonyms ignorance, unawareness, unfamiliarity

antonyms inexperience

2 an exciting or noteworthy event that one experiences firsthand — see ADVENTURE

experience *vb* to come to a knowledge of (something) by living through it ⟨eventually we all have to *experience* the loss of a loved one⟩

synonyms endure, feel, have, know, see, suffer, sustain, taste, undergo

related words encounter, meet; accept, receive

phrases go through

experienced *adj* having or showing exceptional knowledge, experience, or skill in a field of endeavor — see PROFICIENT

experiment *n* a procedure or operation carried out to resolve an uncertainty ⟨Benjamin Franklin's famous *experiment* in which he flew a kite in a thunderstorm to see if lightning and electricity were identical⟩

synonyms experimentation, test, trial

related words trial and error; dry run, shakedown; exercise, practice (*also* practise), rehearsal, tryout, workout; crucible, ordeal; attempt, effort, try

experimental *adj* **1** made or done as an experiment ⟨an *experimental* procedure for patients suffering from leukemia⟩

synonyms pilot, trial

related words developmental, investigative, preparatory; preliminary, provisional, temporary, tentative; conjectural, hypothetical, speculative, theoretical (*also* theoretic); untested, untried; unproved, unproven

near antonyms accepted, established, standard; tested, tried; advanced, developed; proved, proven; conclusive, decisive, definitive, final, permanent

2 based on observation or experience — see EMPIRICAL

experimentation *n* a procedure or operation carried out to resolve an uncertainty — see EXPERIMENT

expert *adj* **1** accomplished with trained ability — see SKILLFUL

2 having or showing exceptional knowledge, experience, or skill in a field of endeavor — see PROFICIENT

expert *n* a person with a high level of knowledge or skill in a field ⟨*experts* at the crime lab were able to tell the sex, race, and approximate age of the murderer⟩

synonyms ace, adept, artist, authority, crackerjack, maestro, master, past master, scholar, shark, virtuoso, whiz, wizard

related words pro, professional; specialist; addict, aficionado, buff, devotee, enthusiast, fan; craftsman, journeyman; jack-of-all-trades

near antonyms apprentice, beginner, neophyte, novice; dabbler, dilettante; layman, nonprofessional

antonyms amateur

expertise *n* knowledge gained by actually doing or living through something — see EXPERIENCE 1

expertly *adv* in a skillful or expert manner — see WELL 3

expiate *vb* to make up for (an offense) ⟨Yom Kippur is the holy day on which Jews are expected to *expiate* sins committed during the past year⟩

synonyms atone (for)

related words compensate, recompense, reimburse, remunerate, repay; amend, correct, rectify, redress; propitiate

phrases make amends for, make good for

expiration *n* **1** the act of ceasing to exist — see DEATH 3

2 the stopping of a process or activity — see END 1

expire *vb* **1** to come to an end — see CEASE 1

2 to let or force out of the lungs — see EXHALE 1

3 to stop living — see DIE 1

expired *adj* no longer existing — see EXTINCT

explain *vb* **1** to make plain or understandable ⟨write an essay that *explains* the meaning of the poem⟩

synonyms clarify, clear (up), construe, demonstrate, elucidate, explicate, expound, illuminate, illustrate, interpret, spell out

related words decipher, decode; analyze, break down; disentangle, undo, unravel, unscramble, untangle; resolve, solve; define, specify

phrases get across

near antonyms befog, cloud; confound, confuse

antonyms obscure

2 to give the reason for or cause of ⟨can you *explain* your very odd behavior at the wedding reception?⟩

synonyms account (for), explain away, rationalize

related words condone, excuse, forgive, justify; absolve, acquit, exculpate, exonerate, vindicate

explainable *adj* capable of having the reason for or cause of determined — see SOLVABLE

explain away *vb* to give the reason for or cause of — see EXPLAIN 2

explanation *n* **1** a statement that makes something clear ⟨an *explanation* of photosynthesis that the whole class was able to understand⟩

synonyms clarification, construction, elucidation, explication, exposition, illumination, illustration, interpretation

related words paraphrase, restatement, translation; deciphering, decoding; disentanglement, unscrambling; analysis; definition, meaning; demonstration, enactment; justification, rationale, rationalization, reasoning

2 a statement given to explain a belief or act — see REASON 1

explanatory *adj* serving to explain ⟨the *explanatory* section has as its heading "Using Your Dictionary"⟩

synonyms elucidative, expository, illuminative, illustrative, interpretive

related words analytic (*also* analytical), demonstrative, discursive; exculpatory

expletive *n* a disrespectful or indecent word or expression — see SWEARWORD

explicable *adj* capable of having the reason for or cause of determined — see SOLVABLE

explicate *vb* to make plain or understandable — see EXPLAIN 1

explication *n* a statement that makes something clear — see EXPLANATION 1

explicit *adj* so clearly expressed as to leave no doubt about the meaning ⟨*explicit* instructions about what to do in an emergency⟩

synonyms clear-cut, definite, definitive, express, specific, unambiguous, unequivocal

related words avowed, declared, stated; categorical (*also* categoric), complete, comprehensive, exhaustive, full; certain, sure, unmistakable; clear, distinct, lucid; exact, precise; direct, literal, plain, simple, straightforward; comprehensible, intelligible, understandable

near antonyms cryptic, dark, enigmatic (*also* enigmatical), obscure, unclear; imprecise, inaccurate, incorrect, inexact; incomprehensible, unintelligible

antonyms implicit, implied, inferred; ambiguous, circuitous; equivocal, indefinite

explicitness *n* **1** careful thoroughness of detail — see PARTICULARITY 1

2 clearness of expression — see SIMPLICITY 2

explode *vb* **1** to break open or into pieces usually because of internal pressure ⟨the building was wrecked when a powerful bomb *exploded*⟩

synonyms blow up, burst, detonate, go off, pop

related words fragment, shatter, smash, splinter; discharge, fire, shoot; balloon, burgeon, mushroom

near antonyms collapse, fizzle

antonyms implode

2 to cause to break open or into pieces by or as if by an explosive — see BLAST 1

3 to develop suddenly and violently — see ERUPT 2

exploit *n* **1** an act of notable skill, strength, or cleverness — see FEAT 1

2 something done by someone — see ACTION 1

exploit *vb* **1** to take unfair advantage of ⟨a student who *exploits* his friend's good nature by always sponging off him⟩

synonyms abuse, capitalize (on), cash in (on), impose (on *or* upon), play (on *or* upon), use

related words manipulate, mistreat; bleed, cheat, fleece, overcharge, skin, soak, stick; commercialize

2 to control or take advantage of by artful, unfair, or insidious means — see MANIPULATE 1

3 to put into action or service — see USE 1

exploitable *adj* **1** capable of or suitable for being used for a particular purpose — see USABLE 1

2 readily taken advantage of — see EASY 2

exploration *n* a systematic search for the truth or facts about something — see INQUIRY 1

explore *vb* **1** to search through or into ⟨let's *explore* new ways of raising money for the school band⟩

synonyms delve (into), dig (into), inquire (into), investigate, look (into), probe, research

related words examine, inspect, sift, study, view; browse, peruse, scan, skim (through), thumb (through)

2 to go into or range over for purposes of discovery ⟨we must continue to *explore* the depths of the ocean⟩

synonyms hunt, probe, prospect, search

related words reconnoiter (*or* reconnoitre), scout; disclose, discover, reveal, unearth; fathom, plumb, sound

explosion *n* **1** the act or an instance of exploding ⟨the *explosion* of the first atomic bomb at Hiroshima⟩

synonyms blast, bursting, detonation, eruption

related words discharge, firing, shooting; blowout, flare-up; bang, boom, pop

antonyms implosion

2 a sudden intense expression of strong feeling — see OUTBURST 1

3 an outburst or display of excited anger — see TANTRUM

explosive *adj* **1** extreme in degree, power, or effect — see INTENSE

THESAURUS

2 marked by bursts of destructive force or intense activity — see VIOLENT 1

exponent *n* a person who actively supports or favors a cause ⟨*exponents* of space exploration called for more missions to the outer reaches of the solar system⟩

synonyms advocate, apostle, backer, booster, champion, friend, promoter, proponent, supporter

related words loyalist, partisan, stalwart; adherent, cohort, disciple, follower; expounder, interpreter; cheerleader

near antonyms enemy, foe, rival; belittler, critic, faultfinder

antonyms adversary, antagonist, opponent

expose *vb* **1** to reveal the true nature of ⟨a well-researched article that *exposes* the UFO story as a hoax⟩

synonyms debunk, show up, uncloak, uncover, unmask

related words discredit, disprove; disclose, divulge, tell, unveil

near antonyms conceal, hide, secrete

antonyms camouflage, cloak, disguise, mask

2 to make known (as information previously kept secret) — see REVEAL 1

3 to make known (something abstract) through outward signs — see SHOW 2

4 to present so as to invite notice or attention — see SHOW 1

exposed *adj* **1** being in a situation where one is likely to meet with harm — see LIABLE 1

2 lacking a usual or natural covering — see NAKED 2

3 lacking protection from danger or resistance against attack — see HELPLESS 1

exposition *n* **1** a public showing of objects of interest — see EXHIBITION 1

2 a series of explanations or observations on something (as an event) — see COMMENTARY

3 a statement that makes something clear — see EXPLANATION 1

expository *adj* serving to explain — see EXPLANATORY

expostulate (with) *vb* to present an opposing opinion or argument — see OBJECT

expostulation *n* a feeling or declaration of disapproval or dissent — see OBJECTION

exposure *n* **1** the state of being left without shelter or protection against something harmful ⟨some people avoid situations in which there is a high level of *exposure* to germs⟩

synonyms liability, openness, vulnerability

related words susceptibility; defenselessness, helplessness, weakness; danger, jeopardy, peril, risk

near antonyms protection, safeguarding, sheltering, shielding

2 the act or an instance of making known something previously unknown or concealed — see REVELATION

expound *vb* to make plain or understandable — see EXPLAIN 1

express *adj* **1** of a particular or exact sort ⟨a trip to the supermarket with the *express* purpose of buying milk⟩

synonyms distinct, especial, precise, set, special, specific

related words lone, only, separate, single, sole, solitary; distinctive, exclusive, individual, peculiar, unique; limited, restricted; specified

near antonyms general, generic, nonexclusive, universal

antonyms nonspecific

2 so clearly expressed as to leave no doubt about the meaning — see EXPLICIT

express *vb* **1** to make known (as an idea, emotion, or opinion) ⟨in a true democracy, a person can freely *express* his or her views⟩

synonyms air, give, look, sound, state, vent, ventilate, voice

related words advertise, announce, declare, enunciate, proclaim; broadcast, circulate, disseminate, publish; describe, write, write up; sound off, speak out, speak up; chime in; communicate, convey, put across, put over; offer, submit

phrases put forth

near antonyms censor, restrain, restrict

antonyms stifle, suppress

2 to apply external pressure on so as to force out the juice or contents of — see PRESS 2

3 to communicate or convey (as an idea) to the mind — see MEAN 1

4 to convey in appropriate or telling terms — see PHRASE

expression *n* **1** an act, process, or means of putting something into words ⟨the poem is his *expression* of his grief upon the loss of his beloved dog⟩

synonyms articulation, formulation, statement, utterance, voice

related words outlet, vent; observation, reflection, remark, thought; speech, tongue

2 facial appearance regarded as an indication of mood or feeling — see LOOK 1

3 a pronounceable series of letters having a distinct meaning especially in a particular field — see WORD 1

4 a sequence of words having a specific meaning — see PHRASE

expressionless *adj* not expressing any emotion — see BLANK 1

expressive *adj* clearly conveying a special meaning (as one's mood) ⟨the teacher's *expressive* sigh showed that she had heard that excuse many times before⟩

synonyms eloquent, meaning, meaningful, pregnant, revealing, significant, suggestive

related words graphic (*also* graphical), pictorial, vivid; evocative, redolent, reminiscent; sententious, weighty; flavorful, rich

expressway *n* a passage cleared for public vehicular travel — see WAY 1

expropriate *vb* to take ownership or control of (something) by right of one's authority — see CONFISCATE

expulsion *n* the forced removal from a homeland — see EXILE 1

expunge *vb* to destroy all traces of — see ANNIHILATE 1

expurgate *vb* to remove objectionable parts from — see CENSOR

exquisite *adj* **1** extreme in degree, power, or effect — see INTENSE

2 having qualities that appeal to a refined taste — see CHOICE

3 satisfying or pleasing because of fineness or mildness — see DELICATE 1

exquisiteness *n* the state or quality of having a delicate structure — see DELICACY 2

extant *adj* **1** having being at the present time ⟨a

celebrated author who is generally regarded as America's greatest novelist *extant*⟩
synonyms alive, existent, existing, living
related words active, busy, flourishing, functioning, operating, working
near antonyms defunct, destroyed, exterminated; departed, gone, lost; nonexistent; idle, inactive, inert
antonyms dead, extinct
2 existing or in progress right now — see PRESENT 1

extemporaneous *adj* made or done without previous thought or preparation ⟨caught by surprise, I had to make an *extemporaneous* speech at the awards banquet⟩
synonyms ad-lib, extempore, impromptu, improvised, offhand, offhanded, snap, spur-of-the-moment, unconsidered, unplanned, unpremeditated, unprepared, unrehearsed
related words automatic, impulsive, instinctive, involuntary, spontaneous; casual, informal, unauthorized
near antonyms deliberate, intended, intentional
antonyms considered, planned, premeditated, prepared, rehearsed

extempore *adj* made or done without previous thought or preparation — see EXTEMPORANEOUS

extemporize *vb* to perform, make, or do without preparation — see IMPROVISE

extend *vb* **1** to make longer ⟨our guests from out of town *extended* their visit by a week⟩
synonyms draw out, elongate, lengthen, prolong, protract, stretch
related words amplify, enlarge, expand, increase; attenuate, thin
near antonyms decrease, diminish, lessen, reduce; thicken
antonyms abbreviate, abridge, curtail, cut, cut back, shorten
2 to put before another for acceptance or consideration — see OFFER 1
3 to arrange the parts of (something) over a wider area — see OPEN 3
4 to be positioned along a certain course or in a certain direction — see RUN 3
5 to make greater in size, amount, or number — see INCREASE 1

extended *adj* **1** expressing one thing in terms normally used for another — see FIGURATIVE
2 having considerable extent — see EXTENSIVE
3 lasting for a considerable time — see LONG 2
4 of great extent from end to end — see LONG 1

extended family *n* those who live as a family in one house — see HOUSEHOLD

extension *n* **1** the act of making longer ⟨the board's *extension* of the school year drew howls of protest⟩
synonyms drawing out, elongation, lengthening, prolongation, prolonging, stretching
antonyms abbreviation, abridgment (*or* abridgement), curtailment, cutback, shortening
2 a smaller structure added to a main building — see ANNEX

extensive *adj* having considerable extent ⟨a rock hound whose *extensive* reading enables him to identify just about any rock or mineral⟩
synonyms broad, expansive, extended, far-flung, far-reaching, wide, widespread
related words comprehensive, general, global, in-

clusive; boundless, endless, limitless, unlimited; capacious, commodious, roomy, spacious
near antonyms circumscribed, limited, restricted
antonyms narrow

extensively *adv* to a large extent or degree — see GREATLY 2

extent *n* **1** a real or imaginary point beyond which a person or thing cannot go — see LIMIT
2 a wide space or area — see EXPANSE
3 an area over which activity, capacity, or influence extends — see RANGE 2
4 the total amount of measurable space or surface occupied by something — see ¹SIZE

extenuate *vb* to make (something) seem less bad by offering excuses — see PALLIATE 1

exterior *adj* situated on the outside or farther out — see OUTER

exterior *n* an outer part or layer ⟨the *exterior* of the tooth consists of very hard enamel⟩
synonyms face, outside, skin, surface, veneer
related words facade (*also* façade), front, top; cover, covering, facing; appearance, disguise, guise, mask, semblance, show
antonyms inside, interior

exterminate *vb* to destroy all traces of — see ANNIHILATE 1

extermination *n* the state or fact of being rendered nonexistent, physically unsound, or useless — see DESTRUCTION

external *adj* situated on the outside or farther out — see OUTER

extinct *adj* no longer existing ⟨a few overgrown ruins are all that remain of that once mighty but now *extinct* civilization⟩
synonyms bygone, dead, defunct, departed, expired, gone, vanished
related words nonexistent; dying, faded, moribund; collapsed, fallen, overthrown; antiquated, dated, obsolete, passé; finished, lapsed, terminated; lost, missing
near antonyms active, dynamic, thriving, vibrant
antonyms alive, existent, existing, extant, living

extinction *n* the state or fact of being rendered nonexistent, physically unsound, or useless — see DESTRUCTION

extinguish *vb* **1** to cause to cease burning ⟨the fire in the skillet was quickly *extinguished* by slamming the lid on⟩
synonyms douse, put out, quench, snuff (out)
related words choke, smother, suffocate; stamp (out)
antonyms fire, ignite, inflame, kindle
2 to bring to a complete end the physical soundness, existence, or usefulness of — see DESTROY 1

extirpate *vb* to destroy all traces of — see ANNIHILATE 1

extol *also* **extoll** *vb* to proclaim the glory of — see PRAISE 1

extort *vb* to get (as money) by the use of force or threats ⟨a school bully who was used to *extorting* lunch money from weaker kids⟩
synonyms exact, wrest, wring
related words bleed, fleece, gouge, milk, skin, squeeze; cheat, gyp, racketeer, swindle; coerce, compel, force

extortioner *n* a person who gets money from another by using force or threats — see RACKETEER

extortionist *n* a person who gets money from another by using force or threats — see RACKETEER

extra *adj* being over what is needed — see SPARE 1

THESAURUS

extra *adv* to a great degree — see VERY 1

extra *n* **1** an interchangeable part or piece of equipment that is kept on hand for replacement of an original — see SPARE

2 something adding to pleasure or comfort but not absolutely necessary — see LUXURY 1

3 something given in addition to what is ordinarily expected or owed — see BONUS

extract *n* a part taken from a longer work — see EXCERPT

extract *vb* to draw out by force or with effort ⟨*extracted* a splinter from my hand⟩
synonyms prize, pry, pull, root (out), tear (out), uproot, wrest, yank
related words remove, take (out), withdraw
near antonyms implant, insert, install, instill; cram, jam, ram, stuff, wedge

extraction *n* the line of ancestors from whom a person is descended — see ANCESTRY

extraneous *adj* **1** not being a vital part of or belonging to something — see EXTRINSIC

2 not having anything to do with the matter at hand — see IRRELEVANT

extraneousness *n* the quality or state of not having anything to do with the matter at hand — see IRRELEVANCE

extraordinary *adj* **1** being out of the ordinary — see EXCEPTIONAL

2 noticeably different from what is generally found or experienced — see UNUSUAL 1

extrapolate *vb* to form an opinion through reasoning and information — see INFER 1

extrasensory perception *n* the power of seeing or knowing about things that are not present to the senses — see CLAIRVOYANCE

extravagance *n* **1** the quality or fact of being free or wasteful in the expenditure of money ⟨Hollywood stars are famous for the *extravagance* of their parties⟩
synonyms lavishness, prodigality, wastefulness
related words bountifulness, generosity, liberality; improvidence, squandering; indulgence, overindulgence, self-indulgence; excess, immoderacy, overkill
near antonyms austerity, moderation, restraint, temperance
antonyms economy, frugality

2 an instance of spending money or resources without care or restraint — see WASTE 1

extravagant *adj* **1** given to spending money freely or foolishly — see PRODIGAL

2 going beyond a normal or acceptable limit in degree or amount — see EXCESSIVE

extravagantly *adv* in a luxurious manner — see HIGH

extreme *adj* **1** most distant from a center ⟨spacecraft that is specially designed to explore the *extreme* edge of our solar system⟩
synonyms farthermost, farthest, furthermost, furthest, outermost, outmost, remotest, ultimate, utmost
near antonyms intermediate, medial, median, mid, middle, middlemost, midmost
antonyms inmost, innermost, nearest

2 being very far from the center of public opinion ⟨their *extreme* political views attracted only a small band of followers⟩
synonyms extremist, fanatic (*or* fanatical), rabid, radical, revolutionary, revolutionist, ultra

related words subversive, violent, wild; reactionary
near antonyms conservative, moderate, temperate; conventional, orthodox, traditional; liberal, progressive
antonyms middle-of-the-road

3 going beyond a normal or acceptable limit in degree or amount — see EXCESSIVE

extremely *adv* to a great degree — see VERY 1

extremist *adj* being very far from the center of public opinion — see EXTREME 2

extremist *n* a person who favors rapid and sweeping changes especially in laws and methods of government — see RADICAL

extricate *vb* to set free from entanglement or difficulty ⟨you've woven such a web of lies that it's hard to see how you can *extricate* yourself now⟩
synonyms clear, disengage, disentangle, free, liberate, release, untangle
related words deliver, redeem, rescue, save; disburden, disencumber, unburden; unravel, unsnarl, untie, untwine
near antonyms block, hamper, hinder, impede, obstruct; burden, encumber, load, weigh
antonyms embroil, entangle

extrinsic *adj* not being a vital part of or belonging to something ⟨the fact that the ring belonged to your grandmother is *extrinsic* to its value to a jeweler⟩
synonyms adventitious, alien, extraneous, foreign
related words exterior, external, outside; immaterial, inapplicable, insignificant, irrelevant; nonessential, unessential, unnecessary
near antonyms congenital, deep-seated, inborn, inbred; inside, interior, internal; basic, essential, necessary
antonyms inherent, innate, intrinsic

extroverted *also* **extraverted** *adj* likely to seek or enjoy the company of others — see CONVIVIAL

extrude *vb* to drive or force out — see EJECT 1

exuberance *n* the quality or state of having abundant or intense activity — see VITALITY 1

exuberant *adj* joyously unrestrained ⟨*exuberant* crowds rushed to greet the returning national champions in collegiate basketball⟩
synonyms bubbly, buoyant, effervescent, frolicsome, high-spirited, vivacious
related words extroverted (*also* extraverted), outgoing, uninhibited; carefree, insouciant, joyful, lighthearted, lively, sprightly; boisterous, raucous, rollicking, rowdy; giddy, light-headed, silly; ecstatic, euphoric, rapturous; audacious, bold, brash, brazen, impertinent, impudent, insolent, saucy
near antonyms constrained, inhibited, repressed, restrained, subdued; impassive, phlegmatic, stoic (*or* stoical), stolid; depressed, dour, glum, morose, surly
antonyms low-spirited, noneffervescent, sullen

exuberantly *adv* **1** in a quick and spirited manner — see GAILY 2

2 in an enthusiastic manner — see SKY-HIGH

exude *vb* to flow forth slowly through small openings ⟨a sticky resin *exudes* from the bark of the tree⟩
synonyms bleed, ooze, percolate, seep, strain, sweat, weep
related words dribble, drip, trickle; discharge, emit, give off, vent; emanate, flow, spring
near antonyms flood, gush, pour, stream, surge

exult *vb* to feel or express joy or triumph ⟨the winners of the Super Bowl spent the next week *exulting* in their victory⟩
synonyms crow, delight, glory, joy, rejoice, triumph
related words gloat; boast, brag; flaunt, parade, show off, strut, swagger
near antonyms bemoan, bewail, grieve, lament, weep

exultant *adj* having or expressing feelings of joy or triumph ⟨the *exultant* winner of the award for best country artist of the year⟩
synonyms exulting, glorying, jubilant, rejoicing, triumphant
related words ecstatic, elated, euphoric; arrogant, boastful, cocky; conquering, victorious, winning
near antonyms crestfallen, defeated, dejected, depressed, disconsolate, dispirited, downcast

exulting *adj* having or expressing feelings of joy or triumph — see EXULTANT

exurbia *n* the area around a city — see ENVIRONS 1

eye *n* **1** a circular strip — see RING 2
2 a state of being aware — see ATTENTION 2
3 a thing or place that is of greatest importance to an activity or interest — see CENTER 1
4 an idea that is believed to be true or valid without positive knowledge — see OPINION 1

5 an instance of looking especially briefly — see LOOK 2
6 the ability to see — see EYESIGHT

eye *vb* **1** to keep one's eyes on — see WATCH 1
2 to make note of (something) through the use of one's eyes — see SEE 1

eye–catching *adj* likely to attract attention — see NOTICEABLE

eyeful *n* a lovely woman — see BEAUTY 2

eyeglasses *n pl* a pair of lenses set in a frame that is held in place with ear supports and which are usually worn to correct vision — see GLASSES 1

eyeless *adj* lacking the power of sight — see BLIND

eye–opening *adj* **1** causing a strong emotional reaction because unexpected — see SURPRISING 1
2 causing wonder or astonishment — see MARVELOUS 1

eyesight *n* the ability to see ⟨the keen *eyesight* of a bird of prey⟩
synonyms eye, sight, vision
related words myopia, nearsightedness; farsightedness; astigmatism

eyesore *n* something unpleasant to look at ⟨the old abandoned house was a neighborhood *eyesore*⟩
synonyms fright, horror, mess, monstrosity, sight
related words blot, smear, smudge, spot, stain

eyespot *n* a small area that is different (as in color) from the main part — see SPOT 1

fable *n* **1** a story intended to teach a basic truth or moral about life — see ALLEGORY
2 a traditional but unfounded story that gives the reason for a current custom, belief, or fact of nature — see MYTH 1
3 something that is the product of the imagination — see FICTION

fabled *adj* based on, described in, or being a myth — see MYTHICAL 1

fabric *n* a woven or knitted material (as of cotton or nylon) — see CLOTH

fabricate *vb* **1** to bring into being by combining, shaping, or transforming materials — see MAKE 1
2 to create or think of by clever use of the imagination — see INVENT
3 to form by putting together parts or materials — see BUILD
4 to make a statement one knows to be untrue — see LIE 1

fabrication *n* **1** a statement known by its maker to be untrue and made in order to deceive — see LIE
2 something that is the product of the imagination — see FICTION

fabricator *n* a person who tells lies — see LIAR

fabulous *adj* **1** based on, described in, or being a myth — see MYTHICAL 1
2 causing wonder or astonishment — see MARVELOUS 1
3 not real and existing only in the imagination — see IMAGINARY
4 of the very best kind — see EXCELLENT

facade *also* **façade** *n* **1** a forward part or surface — see FRONT 1

2 a display of emotion or behavior that is insincere or intended to deceive — see MASQUERADE

face *n* **1** the front part of the head ⟨the criminal hid his *face* from the news cameras as he slumped into the patrol car⟩
synonyms countenance, kisser [*slang*], mug, puss [*slang*], visage
related words appearance, features, lineaments, looks; expression, physiognomy
2 a forward part or surface — see FRONT 1
3 a twisting of the facial features in disgust or disapproval — see GRIMACE
4 an outer part or layer — see EXTERIOR
5 facial appearance regarded as an indication of mood or feeling — see LOOK 1
6 outward and often deceptive indication — see APPEARANCE 2

face *vb* **1** to stand or sit with the face or front toward ⟨the house *faces* the sparkling blue waters of the Pacific Ocean⟩
synonyms front, look (toward), point (toward)
related words abut, adjoin, border, meet, neighbor, touch; command, dominate, overlook
2 to oppose (something hostile or dangerous) with firmness or courage ⟨movie superheroes who are ever ready to *face* danger without blinking an eye⟩
synonyms beard, brave, brazen, breast, confront, dare, defy, outbrave
related words encounter, meet; accost, approach; repel, resist, withstand; battle, combat, contend (with), fight, oppose, square (off)
phrases stand up to

THESAURUS

near antonyms avoid, eschew, shun; elude, escape, evade

antonyms dodge, duck, shirk, sidestep

3 to cover with something that protects — see SHEATHE

4 to enter into contest or conflict with — see ENGAGE 2

face–off *n* an earnest effort for superiority or victory over another — see CONTEST 1

facet *n* a certain way in which something appears or may be regarded — see ASPECT 1

facetious *adj* **1** given to or marked by mature intelligent humor — see WITTY

2 making light of something usually regarded as serious or sacred — see FLIPPANT

facetiousness *n* a lack of seriousness often at an improper time — see FRIVOLITY 1

face–to–face *adv* in person and usually privately — see TÊTE-À-TÊTE

facile *adj* **1** having or showing a lack of depth of understanding or character — see SUPERFICIAL 2

2 involving minimal difficulty or effort — see EASY 1

facilely *adv* without difficulty — see EASILY

facilitate *vb* to free from obstruction or difficulty — see EASE 1

facility *n* a structure that is designed and built for a particular purpose ⟨the city is known for its outstanding medical *facilities*⟩

synonyms complex, establishment, installation

related words building, edifice; institute, institution; business, company, concern, outfit

facsimile *n* **1** something or someone that strongly resembles another — see IMAGE 1

2 something that is made to look exactly like something else — see COPY

fact *n* **1** the quality of being actual ⟨scientists deal in the realm of *fact*, not speculation⟩

synonyms actuality, factuality, materiality, reality

related words authenticity, genuineness, truth

near antonyms fancy, fantasy (*also* phantasy), fiction; fictitiousness

antonyms unreality

2 something that actually exists ⟨once considered a wild fantasy, the Internet is now a *fact* of everyday life⟩

synonyms case, materiality, reality

related words certainty, inevitability; circumstance, event, occurrence, phenomenon; element, item, particular, thing

near antonyms eventuality, possibility, potentiality, probability

antonyms fantasy (*also* phantasy), fiction, illusion

3 a single piece of information ⟨a book of little-known *facts* about famous people⟩

synonyms datum, detail, nicety, particular, particularity, point

related words article, item; element, ingredient, part; aspect, facet, factor; evidence, exhibit; database, information, knowledge

near antonyms error, fallacy, falsehood, misconception, myth

faction *n* a group of people acting together within a larger group ⟨several *factions* within the environmental movement have joined forces⟩

synonyms bloc, body, coalition, party, sect, set, side, wing

related words crew, gang, pack, team; denomination, persuasion, schism

factitious *adj* **1** being such in appearance only and made with or manufactured from usually cheaper materials — see IMITATION

2 lacking in natural or spontaneous quality — see ARTIFICIAL 1

factor *n* **1** a person who acts or does business for another — see AGENT 2

2 one of the parts that make up a whole — see ELEMENT 1

factory *n* a building or set of buildings for the manufacturing of goods ⟨the new *factory* will create hundreds of much-needed jobs⟩

synonyms manufactory, mill, plant, shop, works, workshop

related words sweatshop; workroom; yard

factual *adj* **1** restricted to or based on fact ⟨a *factual* biography of George Washington that scoffs at the story about the cherry tree⟩

synonyms documentary, hard, historical, literal, matter-of-fact, nonfictional, objective, true

related words actual, authentic, genuine, real; documented, established; reliable, verifiable; demonstrable, provable; incontestable, incontrovertible, indisputable, irrefutable, undeniable, unquestionable; plain, simple, unexaggerated; certain, undoubted

near antonyms hypothetical, speculative, theoretical (*also* theoretic); fabulous, fanciful, imaginary, legendary, mythical (*or* mythic); embroidered, exaggerated

antonyms fictional, fictionalized, fictitious, nondocumentary, nonhistorical

2 existing in fact and not merely as a possibility — see ACTUAL

factuality *n* **1** agreement with fact or reality — see TRUTH

2 the quality of being actual — see FACT 1

faculty *n* **1** a natural ability of the mind or body — see POWER 3

2 a special and usually inborn ability — see TALENT

3 the physical or mental power to do something — see ABILITY

fad *n* a practice or interest that is very popular for a short time ⟨the *fad* for that kind of music had long passed⟩

synonyms craze, enthusiasm, fashion, go, last word, mode, rage, sensation, style, trend, vogue

related words crush, infatuation; fervor, passion; furor, fuss, hullabaloo, to-do, uproar; bandwagon, crusade, cult, movement; novelty, wrinkle; caprice, fancy, whim

near antonyms classic, standard

fade *vb* **1** to cease to be visible — see DISAPPEAR

2 to make white or whiter by removing color — see WHITEN

faded *adj* lacking intensity of color — see PALE 1

faerie *also* **faery** *n* an imaginary being usually having a small human form and magical powers — see FAIRY

fag *n* a person who does very hard or dull work — see SLAVE 2

fag *vb* **1** to devote serious and sustained effort — see LABOR

2 to use up all the physical energy of — see EXHAUST 1

fag end *n* an unused or unwanted piece or item typically of small size or value — see ¹SCRAP 1

fail *vb* **1** to stop functioning ⟨my video camera

failed just as I was about to shoot the big moment⟩

synonyms break, break down, conk (out), crash, cut out, die, give out, stall

related words fizzle, sputter, wheeze; malfunction

antonyms start (up)

2 to be unsuccessful ⟨despite all the publicity, the movie *failed* miserably at the box office⟩

synonyms collapse, flop, flunk, fold, wash out

related words flounder, struggle; decline, slip, slump, wane

phrases fall flat

near antonyms flourish, prosper, thrive

antonyms succeed

3 to fall short in satisfying the expectation or hope of — see DISAPPOINT

4 to lose bodily strength or vigor — see WEAKEN 2

5 to miss the opportunity or obligation — see NEGLECT 3

failing *n* a defect in character — see FAULT 1

failure *n* **1** the nonperformance of an assigned or expected action ⟨your *failure* to check the batteries in the smoke detector could have tragic results⟩

synonyms default, delinquency, dereliction, neglect, negligence, oversight

related words carelessness, heedlessness, laxity

near antonyms compliance, discharge, fulfillment

2 a falling short of one's goals ⟨the *failure* of the school's fund-raising drive was a big disappointment to all⟩

synonyms collapse, crash, cropper, defeat, fizzle, nonsuccess

related words futility, uselessness; ineffectiveness, ineffectualness; deficiency, inadequacy, insufficiency; disappointment, letdown, setback

antonyms accomplishment, achievement, success

3 something that has failed ⟨the students' first attempt to build a homemade rocket was a disappointing *failure*⟩

synonyms bummer, bust, catastrophe, debacle (*also* débâcle), dud, fiasco, fizzle, flop, lemon, loser, turkey, washout

related words also-ran, disappointment, has-been; botch, hash, mess, muddle, shambles

near antonyms corker, crackerjack, dandy, jim-dandy, phenomenon

antonyms blockbuster, hit, smash, success, winner

4 a falling short of an essential or desirable amount or number — see DEFICIENCY

faint *adj* **1** not seen or understood clearly ⟨after wandering in the woods for hours, we had only a *faint* idea of where we were⟩

synonyms bleary, dim, foggy, fuzzy, hazy, indefinite, indistinct, indistinguishable, murky, nebulous, obscure, opaque, shadowy, unclear, undefined, undetermined, vague

related words dark, dusky, gloomy; impalpable, inappreciable, intangible, invisible; incomprehensible, inexplicable, mysterious, puzzling

near antonyms bright, distinct, evident, obvious; certain, firm, strong, sure

antonyms clear, definite

2 lacking bodily strength — see WEAK 1

faint *n* a temporary or permanent state of unconsciousness ⟨shocking news can cause a person to fall into a *faint*⟩

synonyms blackout, coma, insensibility, knockout, swoon

related words daze, stupor, trance; drowsiness, narcosis, sleep, somnolence

faint *vb* to lose consciousness ⟨the kind of person who *faints* at the sight of blood⟩

synonyms black out, pass out, swoon

related words break down, collapse

antonyms come around, come round, come to, revive

fainthearted *adj* easily frightened — see SHY 1

faintheartedness *n* lack of willingness to assert oneself and take risks — see TIMIDITY

faintness *n* the quality or state of lacking physical strength or vigor — see WEAKNESS 1

fair *adj* **1** not stormy or cloudy ⟨we prayed that there would be *fair* weather during our vacation at the beach⟩

synonyms clear, cloudless, sunny, sunshiny, unclouded

related words balmy, clement, gentle, mild, temperate; calm, halcyon, peaceful, placid, tranquil; fine, pleasant

near antonyms harsh, inclement, severe; blustering, blustery, breezy, gusty; foggy, hazy, misty

antonyms bleak, cloudy, dirty, foul, nasty, overcast, rainy, raw, rough, squally, stormy, sunless

2 marked by justice, honesty, and freedom from bias ⟨a commanding officer who enjoyed the respect of his soldiers because his decisions were always *fair*⟩

synonyms disinterested, dispassionate, equal, equitable, impartial, just, nonpartisan, objective, square, unbiased, unprejudiced

related words candid, frank, forthright, open, straightforward; balanced, rational, reasonable

near antonyms deceitful, deceptive, dishonest; arbitrary, unconscionable, unreasonable

antonyms biased, inequitable, partisan, prejudiced, unequal, unjust

3 following or according to the rules ⟨a hockey player who is respected for his *fair* play⟩

synonyms clean, legal, sportsmanlike, sportsmanly

related words just, law-abiding; ethical, moral, principled; honorable, irreproachable, unimpeachable

near antonyms immoral, unethical, unprincipled, unscrupulous

antonyms dirty, foul, nasty, unfair, unsportsmanlike

4 of light complexion ⟨*fair* people tend to sunburn easily⟩

synonyms light

related words ashen, pale, pallid, pasty, peaked, sallow, wan, white

antonyms black, brunet (*or* brunette), dark, swarthy

5 having qualities which inspire hope — see HOPEFUL 1

6 of a pale yellow or yellowish brown color — see BLOND

7 of average to below average quality — see MEDIOCRE 1

8 very pleasing to look at — see BEAUTIFUL

fair *n* a public showing of objects of interest — see EXHIBITION 1

fairly *adv* to some degree or extent ⟨for someone without professional training, she sings *fairly* well⟩

synonyms enough, kind of, like, moderately,

THESAURUS

more or less, pretty, quite, rather, relatively, something, somewhat, sort of
related words acceptably, decently, passably, tolerably
near antonyms awfully, exceedingly (*also* exceeding), exceptionally, extremely, greatly, surpassingly, very

fairness *n* the qualities in a person or thing that as a whole give pleasure to the senses — see BEAUTY 1

fairy *n* an imaginary being usually having a small human form and magical powers ⟨*fairies* are part of the folklore of many countries and cultures⟩
synonyms brownie, dwarf, elf, faerie (*also* faery), fay, gnome, goblin, gremlin, hobgoblin, leprechaun, pixie (*also* pixy), puck, sprite, troll
related words changeling; imp; banshee, ghoul, ogre

fairy tale *n* a statement known by its maker to be untrue and made in order to deceive — see LIE

faith *n* **1** belief and trust in and loyalty to God ⟨a people who are known for their strong and steadfast *faith*⟩
synonyms devotion, piety, religion
related words devoutness, piousness, religiousness; adoration, reverence, veneration, worship
near antonyms disbelief, doubt, unbelief
antonyms atheism, godlessness
2 a body of beliefs and practices regarding the supernatural and the worship of one or more deities — see RELIGION 1
3 adherence to something to which one is bound by a pledge or duty — see FIDELITY
4 firm belief in the integrity, ability, effectiveness, or genuineness of someone or something — see TRUST 1
5 mental conviction of the truth of some statement or the reality of some being or phenomenon — see BELIEF 1

faithful *adj* **1** firm in one's allegiance to someone or something ⟨fans of the Chicago Cubs are famously *faithful*⟩
synonyms constant, devoted, fast, good, loyal, pious, staunch (*or* stanch), steadfast, steady, true, true-blue
related words dependable, dutiful, reliable, tried, trustworthy; unfaltering, unhesitating, unwavering; determined, intent, resolute; confirmed, dyed-in-the-wool, inveterate, sworn; ardent, fervent, fervid, impassioned, passionate
near antonyms undependable, unreliable, untrustworthy; faltering, hesitant, vacillating, wavering; dubious, irresolute, uncertain; apathetic, dispassionate, uninterested
antonyms disloyal, faithless, false, fickle, inconstant, perfidious, recreant, traitorous, treacherous, unfaithful, untrue
2 following an original exactly ⟨a *faithful* filming of Robert Louis Stevenson's novel *Treasure Island*⟩
synonyms accurate, authentic, exact, precise, right, strict, true, veracious
related words lifelike, realistic; careful, conscientious, meticulous, punctilious, scrupulous; authoritative; bona fide, genuine, real
near antonyms careless, slack, slipshod, slovenly
antonyms false, imprecise, inaccurate, inauthentic, inexact, loose, unfaithful

faithfulness *n* adherence to something to which one is bound by a pledge or duty — see FIDELITY

faithless *adj* not true in one's allegiance to someone or something ⟨*faithless* friends who deserted him in his time of need⟩
synonyms disloyal, false, fickle, inconstant, perfidious, recreant, traitorous, treacherous, unfaithful, untrue
related words undependable, unreliable, untrustworthy; faltering, hesitant, vacillating, wavering; dubious, irresolute, uncertain; apathetic, dispassionate, uninterested
near antonyms dependable, reliable, tried, trustworthy; unfaltering, unhesitating, unwavering; determined, intent, resolute; confirmed, dyed-in-the-wool, inveterate, sworn; ardent, fervent, fervid, impassioned, passionate
antonyms constant, devoted, faithful, fast, loyal, staunch (*or* stanch), steadfast, steady, true

faithlessness *n* **1** lack of faithfulness especially to one's husband or wife — see INFIDELITY 1
2 the act or fact of violating the trust or confidence of another — see BETRAYAL

fake *adj* **1** being such in appearance only and made with or manufactured from usually cheaper materials — see IMITATION
2 being such in appearance only and made or manufactured with the intention of committing fraud — see COUNTERFEIT
3 lacking in natural or spontaneous quality — see ARTIFICIAL 1

fake *n* **1** an imitation that is passed off as genuine ⟨experts declared that one of the museum's prized paintings was actually a *fake*⟩
synonyms counterfeit, forgery, hoax, humbug, phony (*also* phoney), sham
related words copy, reproduction; dummy; fraud, imposture, swindle; simulation, synthetic
near antonyms original
2 one who makes false claims of identity or expertise — see IMPOSTOR

fake *vb* **1** to imitate or copy especially in order to deceive ⟨pranksters *faked* giant footprints and then claimed that they had seen Bigfoot⟩
synonyms counterfeit, forge
related words simulate; crib, plagiarize; adulterate, doctor, fudge, juggle, manipulate, tamper (with); concoct, cook (up), fabricate, invent
2 to present a false appearance of — see FEIGN

faker *n* one who makes false claims of identity or expertise — see IMPOSTOR

fakery *n* the inclination or practice of misleading others through lies or trickery — see DECEIT

fall *n* **1** the act of going down from an upright position suddenly and involuntarily ⟨a bad *fall* that resulted in several broken bones⟩
synonyms slip, spill, stumble, tumble
related words header, pratfall; trip; descent, dive, plunge, slide; free-fall
2 a change to a lower state or level — see DECLINE 2
3 a loss of status — see COMEDOWN
4 the act or process of going to a lower level or altitude — see DESCENT 1
5 the amount by which something is lessened — see DECREASE
6 *usually* **falls** *pl* a fall of water usually from a great height — see WATERFALL

fall *vb* **1** to go down from an upright position suddenly and involuntarily ⟨better sand that walkway before somebody *falls* on the ice⟩
synonyms slip, stumble, topple, trip, tumble

related words collapse, crumple, drop, keel over, slump (over); nose-dive, plunge, precipitate
antonyms get up, rise, stand (up), uprise
2 to yield to the control or power of enemy forces ⟨the city *fell* after weeks of merciless bombardment⟩
synonyms capitulate, give up, knuckle under, submit, succumb, surrender
related words bow, buckle, cave (in), collapse; hand over, relinquish, yield; lose; fail, fold
near antonyms fight, oppose, resist, withstand; beat, overcome, win; prevail, triumph
antonyms stand
3 to go to a lower level — see DROP 2
4 to grow less in scope or intensity especially gradually — see DECREASE 2
5 to lead or extend downward — see DESCEND 1
fallacious *adj* **1** not using or following good reasoning — see ILLOGICAL
2 tending or having power to deceive — see DECEPTIVE 1
fallaciousness *n* the quality or state of being false — see FALLACY 2
fallacy *n* **1** a false idea or belief ⟨the once-common *fallacy* that girls just weren't any good at math⟩
synonyms error, falsehood, falsity, illusion, misconception, myth, old wives' tale, untruth
related words superstition; distortion, inaccuracy, misinterpretation, misrepresentation, misstatement, misunderstanding; sophism, sophistry; fib, lie, story, tale
antonyms truth, verity
2 the quality or state of being false ⟨the *fallacy* of the notion of spontaneous generation was demonstrated by the Dutch naturalist Leeuwenhoek⟩
synonyms erroneousness, fallaciousness, falseness, falsity, untruth
related words speciousness, spuriousness; deception, deceptiveness, delusion
near antonyms accuracy, correctness, factualness, genuineness
antonyms truth
fall back *vb* to move back or away (as from something difficult, dangerous, or disagreeable) — see RETREAT 1
fallen *adj* no longer living — see DEAD 1
fall guy *n* a person or thing taking the blame for others — see SCAPEGOAT
falling–out *n* an often noisy or angry expression of differing opinions — see ARGUMENT 1
fall out *vb* to express different opinions about something often angrily — see ARGUE 2
fallow *adj* not being in a state of use, activity, or employment — see INACTIVE 2
false *adj* **1** not being in agreement with what is true ⟨early reports about the explosion contained much *false* information⟩
synonyms erroneous, inaccurate, incorrect, inexact, invalid, off, unsound, untrue, untruthful, wrong
related words specious, spurious; deceptive, delusive, delusory, distorted, fallacious, misleading; amiss, askew, awry; deceitful, dishonest, fraudulent, lying, mendacious, untruthful; unconfirmed, unproven, untested; fabricated, invented, made-up, trumped-up
near antonyms confirmed, demonstrated, established, proven, tested
antonyms accurate, correct, errorless, factual, right, sound, true, valid

2 being such in appearance only and made with or manufactured from usually cheaper materials — see IMITATION
3 being such in appearance only and made or manufactured with the intention of committing fraud — see COUNTERFEIT
4 lacking in natural or spontaneous quality — see ARTIFICIAL 1
5 marked by, based on, or done by the use of dishonest methods to acquire something of value — see FRAUDULENT 1
6 not true in one's allegiance to someone or something — see FAITHLESS
7 tending or having power to deceive — see DECEPTIVE 1
falsehood *n* **1** a false idea or belief — see FALLACY 1
2 a statement known by its maker to be untrue and made in order to deceive — see LIE
falseness *n* **1** lack of faithfulness especially to one's husband or wife — see INFIDELITY 1
2 the act or fact of violating the trust or confidence of another — see BETRAYAL
3 the quality or state of being false — see FALLACY 2
falsify *vb* to change so much as to create a wrong impression or alter the meaning of — see GARBLE
falsity *n* **1** a false idea or belief — see FALLACY 1
2 a statement known by its maker to be untrue and made in order to deceive — see LIE
3 lack of faithfulness especially to one's husband or wife — see INFIDELITY 1
4 the act or fact of violating the trust or confidence of another — see BETRAYAL
5 the quality or state of being false — see FALLACY 2
falter *vb* **1** to show uncertainty about the right course of action — see HESITATE
2 to swing unsteadily back and forth or from side to side — see TEETER 1
faltering *n* the act or an instance of pausing because of uncertainty about the right course of action — see HESITATION
fame *n* the fact or state of being known to the public ⟨many go to Hollywood in search of *fame* and fortune⟩
synonyms celebrity, notoriety, renown
related words infamy; name, report, reputation, repute; cachet, position, prestige, rank, standing, stature; distinction, eminence, glory, greatness, honor, illustriousness, note, preeminence, prominence; acclaim, acknowledgment (*also* acknowledgement), praise, recognition; adoration, idolization
near antonyms disgrace, dishonor, disrepute, ignominy, odium, opprobrium, shame; unimportance
antonyms anonymity, obscurity
famed *adj* widely known — see FAMOUS
familial *adj* of or relating to a household or family — see DOMESTIC 1
familiar *adj* **1** closely acquainted ⟨the little inside jokes that people who have long been *familiar* like to share⟩
synonyms bosom, chummy, close, friendly, intimate, thick
related words affable, boon, companionable, convivial, cordial, genial, gracious, hearty; gregarious, sociable, social; comfortable, cozy, easy, snug; amicable, neighborly; confidential, secre-

tive; affectionate, dear, devoted, fond, loving, warm

near antonyms aloof, cold, cool, reserved, standoffish, unfriendly, unsociable, withdrawn

antonyms distant

2 having information especially as a result of study or experience ⟨book editors who are *familiar* with what is being taught in the schools⟩

synonyms abreast, acquainted, conversant, informed, knowledgeable, up, up-to-date, versed

related words aware, cognizant, conscious, heedful, mindful

phrases in the know

near antonyms unaware, unconscious, unmindful; blind, oblivious, unknowing, unwitting

antonyms ignorant, unacquainted, unfamiliar, uninformed

3 often observed or encountered — see COMMON 1

4 showing a lack of proper social reserve or modesty — see PRESUMPTUOUS 1

familiar *n* a person who has a strong liking for and trust in another — see FRIEND 1

familiarity *n* **1** the state of being in a very personal or private relationship ⟨the elderly couple enjoys a *familiarity* that is the result of many years of happy marriage⟩

synonyms chumminess, closeness, inseparability, intimacy, nearness

related words immediacy; affinity, kinship; commitment, devotion; affection, fondness, love; constancy, faithfulness, fidelity; amity, fellowship, friendship, goodwill; affability, conviviality, cordiality, geniality

near antonyms aloofness, coldness, coolness, reserve

antonyms distance

2 a socially improper or unsuitable act or remark — see IMPROPRIETY 2

3 knowledge gained by personal experience — see ACQUAINTANCE

familiarize *vb* **1** to give information to — see ENLIGHTEN 1

2 to impart knowledge of a new thing or situation to — see ACQUAINT 1

family *n* **1** a group of persons who come from the same ancestor ⟨the Adams *family* made remarkable contributions to American life for more than two centuries⟩

synonyms blood, clan, folks, house, kin, kindred, kinfolk, kinsfolk, line, lineage, people, race, stock, tribe

related words nuclear family; extended family, kith; brood; descendant (*or* descendent), issue, offspring, progeny, scion, seed; clansman, kinsman, kinswoman, relative; dynasty

near antonyms ancestry, birth, descent, extraction, origin, pedigree

2 one of the units into which a whole is divided on the basis of a common characteristic — see CLASS 2

family tree *n* the line of ancestors from whom a person is descended — see ANCESTRY

famine *n* a falling short of an essential or desirable amount or number — see DEFICIENCY

famished *adj* feeling a desire or need for food — see HUNGRY 1

famishment *n* a need or desire for food — see HUNGER 1

famous *adj* widely known ⟨a book about some of the most *famous* people of the last century⟩

synonyms celebrated, famed, noted, notorious, prominent, renowned, star, well-known

related words fabled, fabulous, legendary; infamous; distinguished, eminent, exceptional, great, illustrious, leading, notable, outstanding, prestigious, remarkable; important, significant; favorite, popular, preferred; estimable, honorable, reputable, respectable; formidable, redoubtable

near antonyms insignificant, unimportant; inconspicuous; undistinguished, unexceptional; unpopular

antonyms anonymous, obscure, unknown

fan *n* a person with a strong and habitual liking for something ⟨life-long *fans* of country and western music⟩

synonyms addict, aficionado, buff, bug, devotee, enthusiast, fanatic, fancier, fiend, freak, lover, maniac, nut

related words groupie; admirer, collector, connoisseur, dilettante; authority, expert; cultist, disciple, follower, votary; backer, patron, promoter, supporter; partisan, zealot; booster, rooter, wellwisher; faddist

near antonyms belittler, carper, critic, detractor

fan (out) *vb* **1** to arrange the parts of (something) over a wider area — see OPEN 3

2 to extend outwards from or as if from a central point — see RADIATE 1

fanatic *n* **1** a person with a strong and habitual liking for something — see FAN

2 one who is intensely or excessively devoted to a cause — see ZEALOT

fanatic *or* **fanatical** *adj* being very far from the center of public opinion — see EXTREME 2

fancier *n* a person with a strong and habitual liking for something — see FAN

fanciful *adj* **1** conceived or made without regard for reason or reality — see FANTASTIC 1

2 not real and existing only in the imagination — see IMAGINARY

fancy *adj* made or done with great care or with much detail — see ELABORATE 1

fancy *n* **1** a conception or image created by the imagination and having no objective reality — see FANTASY 1

2 a sudden impulsive and apparently unmotivated idea or action — see WHIM

3 positive regard for something — see LIKING

4 the ability to form mental images of things that either are not physically present or have never been conceived or created by others — see IMAGINATION

fancy *vb* **1** to form a mental picture of — see IMAGINE 1

2 to take pleasure in — see ENJOY 1

fanny *n* the part of the body upon which someone sits — see BUTTOCKS

fantastic *adj* **1** conceived or made without regard for reason or reality ⟨a *fantastic* scheme for getting rich quick⟩

synonyms absurd, bizarre, crazy, fanciful, foolish, insane, nonsensical, preposterous, unreal, wild

related words inconceivable, incredible, unbelievable; extravagant, grotesque; eccentric, odd, peculiar, strange, weird; farcical, laughable, ludicrous, ridiculous

antonyms realistic, reasonable

2 excitingly or mysteriously unusual — see EXOTIC

3 not real and existing only in the imagination — see IMAGINARY

4 too extraordinary or improbable to believe — see INCREDIBLE

fantasy *also* **phantasy** *n* **1** a conception or image created by the imagination and having no objective reality ⟨a constant daydreamer who started to believe his own *fantasies*⟩
synonyms chimera, conceit, daydream, delusion, dream, fancy, figment, hallucination, illusion, phantasm, pipe dream, unreality, vision
related words mirage; brainchild, idea; concoction, fabrication, fiction, invention; envisaging, imaging, visualization
near antonyms actuality, fact, reality

2 the ability to form mental images of things that either are not physically present or have never been conceived or created by others — see IMAGINATION

3 something that is the product of the imagination — see FICTION

far *adj* **1** lasting for a considerable time — see LONG 2

2 not close in time or space — see DISTANT 1

far *adv* to a great degree — see VERY 1

faraway *adj* not close in time or space — see DISTANT 1

farce *n* **1** a poor, insincere, or insulting imitation of something — see MOCKERY 1

2 humorous entertainment — see COMEDY

farcical *adj* **1** causing or intended to cause laughter — see FUNNY 1

2 so foolish or pointless as to be worthy of scornful laughter — see RIDICULOUS 1

fare *n* substances intended to be eaten — see FOOD

fare *vb* **1** to meet one's day-to-day needs — see GET ALONG 1

2 to move forward along a course — see GO 1

3 to take a meal — see DINE 1

farewell *adj* given, taken, or performed at parting — see PARTING 1

farewell *n* **1** an expression of good wishes at parting — see GOOD-BYE

2 the act of leaving a place — see DEPARTURE

3 the act or process of two or more persons going off in different directions — see PARTING

far-fetched *adj* not likely to be true or to occur — see IMPROBABLE

far-flung *adj* having considerable extent — see EXTENSIVE

farm *n* a piece of land and its buildings used to grow crops or raise livestock ⟨a *farm* that has been in the same family for five generations⟩
synonyms farmstead, grange, ranch
related words cropland, farmland, farmyard; farmhouse, homestead, manor, plantation; croft [*chiefly British*], station; garden, orchard

farm *vb* to work by plowing, sowing, and raising crops on ⟨we're planning on *farming* 50 acres the first year⟩
synonyms cultivate, tend, till
related words crop, plant; harvest, reap; harrow, hoe

farmer *n* a person who cultivates the land and grows crops on it ⟨a young *farmer* whose family has been growing wheat for many generations⟩
synonyms agriculturist (*or* agriculturalist), agronomist, cultivator, grower, planter, tiller

related words farmhand, gleaner, harvester, reaper; crofter [*chiefly British*], cropper, sharecropper; homesteader, nester [*West*]; granger; rancher, ranchero, ranchman

farming *adj* engaged in or concerned with agriculture — see AGRICULTURAL

farming *n* the science or occupation of cultivating the soil, producing crops, and raising livestock — see AGRICULTURE

farmstead *n* a piece of land and its buildings used to grow crops or raise livestock — see FARM

far-off *adj* not close in time or space — see DISTANT 1

far-out *adj* different from the ordinary in a way that causes curiosity or suspicion — see ODD 2

far-reaching *adj* having considerable extent — see EXTENSIVE

farsighted *adj* having or showing awareness of and preparation for the future — see FORESIGHTED

farsightedness *n* concern or preparation for the future — see FORESIGHT 2

farther *adj* resulting in an increase in amount or number — see ADDITIONAL

farther *adv* at or to a greater distance or more advanced point ⟨they had traveled *farther* down the Colorado River than any previous explorers⟩
synonyms beyond, further, yon, yonder

farthermost *adj* most distant from a center — see EXTREME 1

farthest *adj* most distant from a center — see EXTREME 1

fascinate *vb* **1** to attract or delight as if by magic — see CHARM 1

2 to hold the attention of as if by a spell — see ENTHRALL 1

3 to hold the attention of — see ENGAGE 1

fascinating *adj* **1** having an often mysterious or magical power to attract ⟨the *fascinating* cities and peoples of central Asia have been intriguing travelers at least since the time of Marco Polo⟩
synonyms alluring, appealing, attractive, bewitching, captivating, charming, elfin, enchanting, engaging, entrancing, fetching, glamorous (*also* glamourous), luring, magnetic, seductive
related words enthralling, gripping, hypnotizing, mesmerizing, riveting, spellbinding; enticing, tantalizing, tempting; exciting, haunting, interesting, intriguing, titillating; beckoning, inviting, winning; darling, delightful, pleasing
near antonyms boring, irksome, tedious, tiresome; abhorrent, distasteful, invidious, loathsome, obnoxious, offensive
antonyms repellant, repelling, repugnant, repulsive, revolting

2 holding the attention or provoking interest — see INTERESTING

fascination *n* the power of irresistible attraction — see CHARM 2

fashion *n* **1** a practice or interest that is very popular for a short time — see FAD

2 a distinctive way of putting ideas into words — see STYLE 1

3 a usual manner of behaving or doing — see HABIT

4 the means or procedure for doing something — see METHOD

fashion *vb* to bring into being by combining, shaping, or transforming materials — see MAKE 1

fashionable *adj* **1** being in the latest or current fashion — see STYLISH

2 enjoying widespread favor or approval — see POPULAR 1

fashionableness *n* the state of enjoying widespread approval — see POPULARITY

fast *adj* **1** moving, proceeding, or acting with great speed ⟨the *fast* pace of construction resulted in our new house being done ahead of schedule⟩
synonyms breakneck, breathless, brisk, dizzy, fleet, fleet-footed, flying, hasty, lightning, nippy, quick, rapid, rapid-fire, rattling, snappy, speedy, swift, whirlwind
related words expeditious, prompt, ready; hurried, quickened; breathtaking; energetic, strenuous, strong, vigorous
near antonyms crawling, dawdling, laggard, lingering, plodding, poky (*or* pokey), slowish, sluggish, unhurried; deliberate, leisurely, measured; dilatory, late
antonyms slow

2 firm in one's allegiance to someone or something — see FAITHFUL 1

3 firmly positioned in place and difficult to dislodge — see TIGHT 2

4 given to or marked by cheating and deception — see DISHONEST 2

5 marked by the ability to withstand stress without structural damage or distortion — see STABLE 1

fast *adv* **1** with great speed ⟨run as *fast* as you can to get help⟩
synonyms apace, briskly, fleetly, full tilt, hastily, posthaste, presto, pronto, quick, quickly, rapidly, snappily, soon, speedily, swift, swiftly
related words immediately, promptly, readily; impetuously, impulsively, rashly, recklessly; abruptly, suddenly; energetically, vigorously
phrases at full tilt, by leaps and bounds, in short order
near antonyms laggardly, lingeringly, ploddingly, sluggishly; deliberately, leisurely
antonyms slow, slowly

2 to a full extent or degree — see FULLY 1

fasten *vb* **1** to cause (something) to hold to another ⟨use this paperclip to *fasten* your picture to the application form⟩
synonyms affix, attach, fix
related words adhere, bolt, clamp, clasp, clinch, clip, glue, hang, harness, lace, lash, latch, nail, paste, pin, rivet, screw, staple, stick, strap, tack, tie, yoke; connect, join, link, unite; reattach, refasten, refix
near antonyms part, separate, sever; loose, loosen
antonyms detach, undo, unfasten

2 to put securely in place or in a desired position ⟨don't forget to *fasten* all the lines on your tent⟩
synonyms anchor, catch, clamp, fix, hitch, moor, secure, set
related words embed (*also* imbed), entrench (*also* intrench), implant, ingrain, lodge, wedge
near antonyms extract, pry, yank
antonyms loose, loosen, unfasten, unloose, unloosen

3 to fix (as one's attention) steadily toward a central objective — see CONCENTRATE 2

fastidious *adj* hard to please — see FINICKY

fastness *n* **1** a high rate of movement or performance — see SPEED

2 a structure or place from which one can resist attack — see FORT

3 adherence to something to which one is bound by a pledge or duty — see FIDELITY

fat *adj* **1** having an excess of body fat ⟨the popular image of Santa Claus as a *fat* man in a red suit⟩
synonyms chubby, corpulent, fleshy, full, gross, obese, overweight, plump, portly, pudgy, roly-poly, rotund, round, tubby
related words beefy, bulky, chunky, heavy, heavy-set, stocky, stout, thick, thickset, weighty; brawny, burly, husky; dumpy, squat, stubby; paunchy, pot-bellied; flabby, soft; buxom
near antonyms angular, bony, gaunt, lank, lanky, rawboned, sinewy, skinny; cadaverous, haggard, skeletal, wasted; puny, scraggy, scrawny, slight; reedy, twiggy, willowy
antonyms lean, slender, slim, spare, thin

2 containing or seeming to contain the greatest quantity or number possible — see FULL 1

3 having a greater than usual measure across — see WIDE 1

4 having or being of relatively great depth or extent from one surface to its opposite — see THICK 1

5 producing abundantly — see FERTILE

6 yielding a profit — see PROFITABLE 1

fat *n* **1** individuals carefully selected as being the best of a class — see ELITE

2 the state or an instance of going beyond what is usual, proper, or needed — see EXCESS

fatal *adj* **1** bringing about ruin or misfortune ⟨I made the *fatal* mistake of sharing my secret with the school's biggest blabbermouth⟩
synonyms calamitous, cataclysmal (*or* cataclysmic), catastrophic, destructive, disastrous, fateful, ruinous, unfortunate
related words hapless, ill-fated, ill-starred, luckless
near antonyms fluky, fortuitous, fortunate, happy, lucky, providential; auspicious, bright, encouraging, golden, heartening, hopeful, promising, propitious

2 likely to cause or capable of causing death — see DEADLY

fatality *n* a person or thing harmed, lost, or destroyed — see CASUALTY 1

fate *n* **1** a state or end that seemingly has been decided beforehand ⟨the belief that it was this country's *fate* to extend from sea to sea⟩
synonyms circumstance, destiny, doom, fortune, lot, portion
related words accident, chance, hazard, luck; predestination; consequence, effect, issue, outcome, result, upshot

2 a condition or occurrence traceable to a cause — see EFFECT 1

fate *vb* to determine the fate of in advance — see DESTINE

fateful *adj* bringing about ruin or misfortune — see FATAL 1

fathead *n* a stupid person — see IDIOT

father *n* **1** a male human parent ⟨the special relationship that exists between *fathers* and sons⟩
synonyms dad, daddy, old man, pa, papa, pop
related words patriarch

2 a person who establishes a whole new field of endeavor ⟨Sir Isaac Newton is regarded by many as the *father* of modern science⟩
synonyms author, begetter, creator, establisher, founder, generator, inaugurator, initiator, instituter (*or* institutor), originator

related words conceiver, contriver, designer, formulator, innovator, inventor, spawner; builder, maker, producer; developer, pioneer, researcher; organizer, promoter; encourager, inspiration, inspirer

near antonyms disciple, follower, supporter

3 a person specially trained and authorized to conduct religious services in a Christian church — see CLERGYMAN

4 a person who is several generations earlier in an individual's line of descent — see ANCESTOR 1

5 *cap* the being worshipped as the creator and ruler of the universe — see DEITY 2

father *vb* to become the father of ⟨Paul Revere somehow found room in his small house for the large family he had *fathered*⟩

synonyms beget, get, sire

related words breed, multiply, procreate, propagate, reproduce, spawn; bear, engender, generate, produce

fatherland *n* the land of one's birth, residence, or citizenship — see COUNTRY 1

fathom *vb* to measure the depth of (as a body of water) typically with a weighted line — see ²SOUND 1

fatigue *n* a complete depletion of energy or strength ⟨the day-long battle against the blaze left firefighters in a state of utter *fatigue*⟩

synonyms burnout, collapse, exhaustion, lassitude, prostration, tiredness, weariness

related words debilitation, enervation, faintness, feebleness, weakness; languor, lethargy, listlessness; sluggishness, slumber, stupor, torpor; apathy, inertia, passivity

near antonyms energy, go, liveliness, pep, vigor, vitality; might, potency, strength

antonyms refreshment, rejuvenation, revitalization

fatigue *vb* to use up all the physical energy of — see EXHAUST 1

fatigued *adj* depleted in strength, energy, or freshness — see WEARY 1

fatness *n* the condition of having an excess of body fat — see CORPULENCE

fatty *adj* containing animal fat especially in unusual amounts ⟨*fatty* ground beef that was the cheapest available⟩

synonyms adipose

related words greasy, oily

near antonyms fibrous, gristly, stringy, tough; nonfat

antonyms lean

fatuity *n* **1** a foolish act or idea — see FOLLY 1

2 lack of good sense or judgment — see FOOLISHNESS 1

3 the quality or state of lacking intelligence or quickness of mind — see STUPIDITY 1

fatuous *adj* **1** not having or showing an ability to absorb ideas readily — see STUPID 1

2 showing or marked by a lack of good sense or judgment — see FOOLISH 1

faucet *n* a fixture for controlling the flow of a liquid ⟨don't forget to turn off the *faucet*⟩

synonyms cock, gate, spigot, stopcock, tap, valve

related words hydrant, spout

fault *n* **1** a defect in character ⟨the common *fault* of being quick to judge others⟩

synonyms demerit, failing, foible, frailty, shortcoming, vice, weakness

related words blot, spot, stain; blemish, deficiency, flaw; Achilles' heel; corruption, depravity, evil, immorality, sinfulness, wickedness

near antonyms excellence, perfection; goodness, integrity, morality, probity, rectitude, righteousness

antonyms merit, virtue

2 an unintentional departure from truth or accuracy — see ERROR 1

3 responsibility for wrongdoing or failure — see BLAME 1

4 something that spoils the appearance or completeness of a thing — see BLEMISH

5 the state of being held as the cause of something that needs to be set right — see RESPONSIBILITY 1

fault *vb* to express one's unfavorable opinion of the worth or quality of — see CRITICIZE

faultfinder *n* a person given to harsh judgments and to finding faults — see CRITIC 1

faultfinding *adj* given to making or expressing unfavorable judgments about things — see CRITICAL 1

faultily *adv* in a mistaken or inappropriate way — see WRONGLY

faultless *adj* **1** being entirely without fault or flaw — see PERFECT 1

2 free from guilt or blame — see INNOCENT 2

faultlessly *adv* without any flaws or errors — see PERFECTLY 1

faultlessness *n* the quality or state of being free from guilt or blame — see INNOCENCE 1

faulty *adj* having a fault ⟨the cause of the plane crash was traced to *faulty* wiring⟩

synonyms bad, defective, flawed, imperfect

related words fallible; blemished, broken, damaged, defaced, disfigured, impaired, injured, marred, spoiled; deficient, inadequate, incomplete, insufficient, wanting

near antonyms complete, entire, intact, whole; undamaged, unimpaired, unspoiled

antonyms faultless, flawless, impeccable, perfect

favor *n* **1** an act of kind assistance ⟨a good and generous friend who is always doing *favors* for others⟩

synonyms boon, courtesy, grace, indulgence, kindness, mercy, service, turn

related words dispensation, waiver; advantage, benefit, blessing, godsend, manna; liberty, license (*or* licence), privilege

near antonyms hindrance, impediment, obstacle

2 a feeling of great approval and liking — see ADMIRATION 1

3 an acceptance of something as satisfactory — see APPROVAL 1

4 an attitude that always favors one way of feeling or acting especially without considering any other possibilities — see BIAS

5 positive regard for something — see LIKING

6 the state of enjoying widespread approval — see POPULARITY

favor *vb* **1** to do a service or favor for — see OBLIGE 1

2 to have a favorable opinion of — see APPROVE (OF)

3 to show partiality toward — see PREFER 1

favorable *adj* **1** expressing approval ⟨*favorable* reviews for the movie were few⟩

synonyms admiring, applauding, appreciative, approving, commendatory, complimentary, friendly, good, positive

related words eulogistic, laudatory, praiseful; respectful, supportive; adulatory, worshipful
near antonyms captious, carping, caviling (*or* cavilling), censuring, hypercritical, overcritical
antonyms adverse, disapproving, negative, unappreciative, uncomplimentary, unfavorable, unfriendly
2 pointing toward a happy outcome ⟨*favorable* conditions for opening a new business⟩
synonyms auspicious, bright, encouraging, golden, heartening, hopeful, promising, propitious
related words fortunate, happy, lucky, providential; advantageous, beneficial, profitable
near antonyms unfortunate, unhappy, unlucky; calamitous, catastrophic, disastrous, fatal, ruinous
antonyms discouraging, disheartening, futureless, hopeless, inauspicious, unfavorable, unpromising
3 conferring benefits; promoting or contributing to personal or social well-being — see BENEFICIAL
4 showing or expressing acceptance or approval — see POSITIVE
favorably *adv* in a pleasing way — see WELL 5
favored *adj* **1** granted special treatment or attention — see DARLING 1
2 singled out from a number or group as more to one's liking — see SELECT 1
favorite *adj* granted special treatment or attention — see DARLING 1
favorite *n* a person or thing that is preferred over others ⟨the youngest child was always Mother's *favorite*⟩
synonyms darling, minion, pet, preference
related words beloved, dear; jewel, prize, treasure
near antonyms abomination, anathema, bête noire, bugbear
fawn *vb* to use flattery or the doing of favors in order to win approval especially from a superior ⟨a student who could not wait to *fawn* over the new teacher⟩
synonyms fuss, kowtow, toady
related words drool, gush, slaver, slobber; endear, ingratiate; court, woo; adulate, idolize, worship; blandish, cajole, coax, flatter, soft-soap; cower, cringe, grovel; abase, debase, demean; defer, submit, yield
phrases curry favor
near antonyms despise, disdain, scorn; gibe (*or* jibe), jeer, scoff; brave, challenge, defy
fawner *n* a person who flatters another in order to get ahead — see SYCOPHANT
fay *adj* given to good-natured joking or teasing — see PLAYFUL
fay *n* an imaginary being usually having a small human form and magical powers — see FAIRY
faze *vb* to throw into a state of self-conscious distress — see EMBARRASS 1
fealty *n* adherence to something to which one is bound by a pledge or duty — see FIDELITY
fear *n* the emotion experienced in the presence or threat of danger ⟨the sight of the headless horseman filled the schoolmaster with *fear*⟩
synonyms alarm, anxiety, apprehension, consternation, dread, fearfulness, fright, horror, panic, terror, trepidation
related words phobia; creeps, jitters, nervousness, willies; pang, qualm, twinge; agitation, discomposure, disquiet, perturbation; concern, dismay,

worry; cowardice, faintheartedness, timidity, timorousness
near antonyms aplomb, assurance, boldness, confidence, self-assurance, self-confidence; courage, dauntlessness, fearlessness, fortitude
fear *vb* to experience concern or anxiety — see WORRY 1
fearful *adj* **1** causing fear ⟨the *fearful* roar of a lion⟩
synonyms alarming, dire, direful, dreadful, fearsome, forbidding, formidable, frightening, frightful, hair-raising, horrendous, horrible, horrifying, intimidating, redoubtable, scary, shocking, terrible, terrifying
related words daunting, disconcerting, discouraging, dismaying, disquieting, distressing, disturbing, perturbing, startling, threatening, troubling, trying; creepy, eerie (*also* eery), weird; ghastly, gruesome, nightmarish
near antonyms comforting, consoling, inviting, reassuring, soothing; nonthreatening
2 easily frightened — see SHY 1
3 extreme in degree, power, or effect — see INTENSE
4 filled with fear or dread — see AFRAID 1
fearfulness *n* the emotion experienced in the presence or threat of danger — see FEAR
fearless *adj* feeling or displaying no fear by temperament — see BRAVE
fearlessness *n* strength of mind to carry on in spite of danger — see COURAGE
fearsome *adj* causing fear — see FEARFUL 1
feasible *adj* capable of being done or carried out — see POSSIBLE 1
feast *n* a large fancy meal often accompanied by ceremony or entertainment ⟨some 90 Native Americans showed up for the *feast* put on by the Pilgrims at Plymouth⟩
synonyms banquet, dinner, feed, spread
related words chow, repast; blowout, festival, fete (*or* fête), gala, party, shindig; festivity; barbecue, clambake, cookout, fry, luau, roast
feast *vb* to entertain with a fancy meal ⟨the returning war heroes were *feasted* all over the country⟩
synonyms banquet, dine, junket, regale
related words cater, feed; fete (*or* fête), honor
feat *n* **1** an act of notable skill, strength, or cleverness ⟨Washington's legendary *feat* of tossing a silver dollar across the Rappahannock River⟩
synonyms deed, exploit, stunt, trick
related words accomplishment, achievement, coup; adventure; performance
2 something done by someone — see ACTION 1
feather *n* **1** a number of persons or things that are grouped together because they have something in common — see SORT 1
2 dressy clothing — see FINERY
featherbrained *adj* lacking in seriousness or maturity — see GIDDY 1
feathery *adj* having little weight — see ¹LIGHT 1
feature *n* something that sets apart an individual from others of the same kind — see CHARACTERISTIC
feature *vb* to indicate the importance of by giving prominent display — see EMPHASIZE
feces *n pl* solid matter discharged from an animal's alimentary canal — see DROPPING 1
fecund *adj* producing abundantly — see FERTILE
fed up *adj* having one's patience, interest, or pleasure exhausted — see WEARY 2

federate *vb* to form or enter into an association that furthers the interests of its members — see ALLY

federation *n* an association of persons, parties, or states for mutual assistance and protection — see CONFEDERACY

fee *n* the amount of money that is demanded as payment for something — see PRICE 1

feeble *adj* lacking bodily strength — see WEAK 1

feebleness *n* the quality or state of lacking physical strength or vigor — see WEAKNESS 1

feed *n* **1** a large fancy meal often accompanied by ceremony or entertainment — see FEAST
2 food eaten or prepared for eating at one time — see MEAL

feed *vb* **1** to provide food or meals for ⟨a charity dedicated to *feeding* the hungry⟩
synonyms board, cater, provision
related words serve, wait; nourish, nurture; banquet, dine, feast, regale; mess
2 to put (something) into the possession of someone for use or consumption — see FURNISH 2
3 to take a meal — see DINE 1

feed (on) *vb* to seize and eat (something) as prey — see PREY

feel *n* an indefinite physical response to a stimulus — see SENSATION 1

feel *vb* **1** to have a vague awareness of ⟨I *feel* trouble brewing in the town⟩
synonyms perceive, scent, see, sense, smell, taste
related words behold, discern, observe, view; ascertain, discover, learn; anticipate, expect, foresee
2 to come into bodily contact with (something) so as to perceive a slight pressure on the skin — see TOUCH 1
3 to come to a knowledge of (something) by living through it — see EXPERIENCE
4 to have as an opinion — see BELIEVE 2
5 to search for something blindly or uncertainly — see GROPE

feel (for) *vb* to have sympathy for — see PITY

feeling *n* **1** a subjective response to a person, thing, or situation ⟨an overall *feeling* of happiness about their new home⟩
synonyms emotion, passion, sentiment
related words impression, perception, sense; attitude, outlook, perspective, viewpoint; belief, opinion, view; responsiveness, sensibility, sensitiveness, sensitivity
2 **feelings** *pl* general emotional condition ⟨a remark that thoughtlessly hurt her *feelings*⟩
synonyms heartstrings, passions, sensibilities
related words cheer, frame, humor, mode, mood, temper
3 an idea that is believed to be true or valid without positive knowledge — see OPINION 1
4 an indefinite physical response to a stimulus — see SENSATION 1
5 sorrow or the capacity to feel sorrow for another's suffering or misfortune — see SYMPATHY 1
6 the capacity for feeling for another's unhappiness or misfortune — see HEART 1

feign *vb* to present a false appearance of ⟨I would never *feign* illness just to get out of a test⟩
synonyms affect, assume, counterfeit, fake, pretend, profess, put on, sham, simulate
related words act, dissemble, impersonate, masquerade; forge, imitate; camouflage, conceal, disguise, mask; bluff, feint; malinger

feigned *adj* **1** lacking in natural or spontaneous quality — see ARTIFICIAL 1
2 not being or expressing what one appears to be or express — see INSINCERE

felicitate *vb* to express to (someone) admiration for his or her success or good fortune — see CONGRATULATE

felicitations *n pl* best wishes — see COMPLIMENTS

felicitous *adj* **1** giving pleasure or contentment to the mind or senses — see PLEASANT
2 meeting the requirements of a purpose or situation — see FIT 1

felicitously *adv* in a pleasing way — see WELL 5

felicitousness *n* the quality or state of being especially suitable or fitting — see APPROPRIATENESS

felicity *n* **1** a feeling or state of well-being and contentment — see HAPPINESS 1
2 something that provides happiness or does good for a person or thing — see BLESSING 2

feline *n* a small domestic animal known for catching mice — see CAT 1

fell *adj* **1** likely to cause or capable of causing death — see DEADLY
2 violently unfriendly or aggressive in disposition — see FIERCE 1

fell *vb* **1** to strike (someone) so forcefully as to cause a fall ⟨a boxer who was often *felled* in the first round⟩
synonyms bowl (down *or* over), down, drop, floor, knock (down *or* over), level
related words hit, jab, poke, punch, smite, sock, strike, whack
2 to bring down by cutting ⟨the settlers began the daunting task of *felling* the mighty trees that blanketed the island⟩
synonyms chop (down), cut (down), hew, mow
related words bulldoze, flatten, level, raze, tear down
3 to deprive of life — see KILL 1

fellow *n* **1** a male romantic companion — see BOYFRIEND
2 a person frequently seen in the company of another — see ASSOCIATE 1
3 an adult male human being — see MAN 1
4 either of a pair matched in one or more qualities — see MATE 1
5 one that is equal to another in status, achievement, or value — see EQUAL

fellowship *n* **1** a friendly relationship marked by ready communication and mutual understanding — see RAPPORT
2 a group of persons formally joined together for some common interest — see ASSOCIATION 2
3 kindly concern, interest, or support — see GOODWILL 1
4 the body of people in a profession or field of activity — see CORPS
5 the feeling of closeness and friendship that exists between companions — see COMPANIONSHIP

female *adj* of, relating to, or marked by qualities traditionally associated with women — see FEMININE 1

female *n* an adult female human being — see WOMAN

feminine *adj* **1** of, relating to, or marked by qualities traditionally associated with women ⟨the *feminine* furnishings suggested that the bedroom was intended for a girl⟩
synonyms female, womanish, womanlike, womanly

THESAURUS

related words effeminate, girlish, sissy, unmanly; ladylike; distaff, petticoat

near antonyms boyish, hoydenish, tomboyish; gentlemanly

antonyms male, manlike, manly, mannish, masculine

2 having or displaying qualities more suitable for women than for men — see EFFEMINATE

fen *n* spongy land saturated or partially covered with water — see SWAMP

fence *n* a physical object that blocks the way — see BARRIER

fence (in) *vb* to close or shut in by or as if by barriers — see ENCLOSE 1

fend (off) *vb* to drive back — see REPEL 1

fender *n* something that serves as a protective barrier — see CUSHION

feral *adj* living outdoors without taming or domestication by humans — see WILD 1

ferment *n* a disturbed or uneasy state — see UNREST

ferment *vb* to cause or encourage the development of — see INCITE 1

ferocious *adj* **1** extreme in degree, power, or effect — see INTENSE

2 marked by bursts of destructive force or intense activity — see VIOLENT 1

3 violently unfriendly or aggressive in disposition — see FIERCE 1

ferry *vb* to support and take from one place to another — see CARRY 1

fertile *adj* producing abundantly ⟨the *fertile* mind of Leonardo da Vinci explored art, architecture, engineering, mathematics, and many other fields⟩

synonyms fat, fecund, fruitful, luxuriant, productive, prolific, rich

related words bearing, producing, yielding; abounding, abundant, bountiful; copious, plenteous, plentiful; blooming, bursting, flourishing, swarming, teeming, thriving; creative, inventive, original

near antonyms meager (*or* meagre), scant, scanty, skimpy, spare, sparse

antonyms barren, infertile, sterile, unfruitful, unproductive

fervency *n* depth of feeling — see ARDOR 1

fervent *adj* having or expressing great depth of feeling ⟨a *fervent* speech that called for tolerance and compassion for those who are different⟩

synonyms ardent, blazing, burning, charged, emotional, fervid, feverish, fiery, flaming, glowing, hot-blooded, impassioned, passionate, red-hot, vehement, warm, warm-blooded

related words gushing, maudlin, mawkish, mushy, sentimental; histrionic, melodramatic; enthusiastic, gung ho, zealous; enamored, infatuated, obsessed

phrases on fire

near antonyms detached, dry, impersonal, objective; reserved, undemonstrative

antonyms cold, cool, dispassionate, impassive, unemotional

fervid *adj* having or expressing great depth of feeling — see FERVENT

fervidness *n* depth of feeling — see ARDOR 1

fervor *n* depth of feeling — see ARDOR 1

festival *n* a time or program of special events and entertainment in honor of something ⟨tourists flock to the town for its annual strawberry *festival*⟩

synonyms carnival, celebration, festivity, fete (*or* fête), fiesta, gala, jubilee

related words jamboree, jollification, merrymaking, revel, revelry; exhibit, exhibition, exposition, fair, show; exercises, honors

festive *adj* indicative of or marked by high spirits or good humor — see MERRY

festivity *n* **1** a mood characterized by high spirits and amusement and often accompanied by laughter — see MIRTH

2 a time or program of special events and entertainment in honor of something — see FESTIVAL

3 joyful or festive activity — see MERRYMAKING

fetch *vb* to have a price of — see COST

fetching *adj* having an often mysterious or magical power to attract — see FASCINATING 1

fetch up *vb* to bring (something) to a standstill — see ¹HALT 1

fete *or* **fête** *vb* to show appreciation, respect, or affection for (someone) with a public celebration — see HONOR

fete *or* **fête** *n* **1** a social gathering — see PARTY 1

2 a time or program of special events and entertainment in honor of something — see FESTIVAL

fetid *adj* having an unpleasant smell — see MALODOROUS

fetish *also* **fetich** *n* **1** something about which one is constantly thinking or concerned — see FIXATION

2 something worn or kept to bring good luck or keep away evil — see CHARM 1

fetter *n* **1** something that limits one's freedom of action or choice — see RESTRICTION 1

2 something that makes movement or progress more difficult — see ENCUMBRANCE

3 something that physically prevents free movement — see BOND 1

fetter *vb* **1** to confine or restrain with or as if with chains — see BIND 1

2 to create difficulty for the work or activity of — see HAMPER

fettle *n* a state of being or fitness — see CONDITION 1

fever *n* an abnormal state that disrupts a plant's or animal's normal bodily functioning — see DISEASE

feverish *adj* **1** being in a state of increased activity or agitation ⟨scary stories that were the product of a *feverish* imagination⟩

synonyms agitated, excited, frenzied, heated, hectic, overactive, overwrought

related words ardent, burning, fervent, fiery, impassioned; high-strung, jittery, jumpy, nervous

phrases keyed up

near antonyms calm, composed, cool, serene, tranquil

2 having or expressing great depth of feeling — see FERVENT

3 marked by great and often stressful excitement or activity — see FURIOUS 1

few *n* a small number ⟨a *few* of the songs on the album are good, but most are forgettable⟩

synonyms handful, scattering, smattering, sprinkle, sprinkling

related words minority

near antonyms majority, most; abundance, excess, plenty, surplus

antonyms army, crowd, flock, horde, host, legion, many, mountain, multitude

fiancé *n* the person to whom one is engaged to be married — see BETROTHED

fiancée *n* the person to whom one is engaged to be married — see BETROTHED

fiasco *n* something that has failed — see FAILURE 3

fiat *n* an order publicly issued by an authority — see EDICT 1

fib *n* a statement known by its maker to be untrue and made in order to deceive — see LIE

fib *vb* to make a statement one knows to be untrue — see LIE 1

fibber *n* a person who tells lies — see LIAR

fiber *n* the strength of mind that enables a person to endure pain or hardship — see FORTITUDE

fibrous *adj* resembling or having the texture of a mass of strings — see STRINGY

fickle *adj* **1** likely to change frequently, suddenly, or unexpectedly ⟨a *fickle* friendship that was on and off over the years⟩
synonyms capricious, changeable, changeful, flickery, fluctuating, fluid, inconstant, mercurial, mutable, temperamental, uncertain, unpredictable, unsettled, unstable, unsteady, variable, volatile
related words aimless, erratic, haphazard, irregular, random; hesitating, shilly-shallying, vacillating, wavering; undependable, unreliable, untrustworthy; adaptable, mobile, protean, versatile
near antonyms equable, even, uniform; abiding, durable, lasting, permanent, persistent; dependable, reliable, trustworthy
antonyms certain, changeless, constant, immutable, invariable, settled, stable, steady, unchangeable
2 not true in one's allegiance to someone or something — see FAITHLESS

fiction *n* something that is the product of the imagination ⟨most stories about famous outlaws of the Old West are *fictions* that have little or nothing to do with fact⟩
synonyms fable, fabrication, fantasy (*also* phantasy), figment, invention
related words anecdote, narrative, novel, story, tale, yarn; falsehood, fib, lie, misrepresentation, untruth
near antonyms actuality, reality
antonyms fact

fictional *adj* not real and existing only in the imagination — see IMAGINARY

fictitious *adj* not real and existing only in the imagination — see IMAGINARY

fiddle *vb* to make jerky or restless movements — see FIDGET

fiddle (around) *vb* to spend time in aimless activity ⟨we spent the snow day just *fiddling around*⟩
synonyms fool (around), mess (around), monkey (around), play, potter (around), putter (around), trifle
related words dally, dawdle, dillydally, hang around, hang out, idle, loaf, loll, lounge; clown (around), horse (around); tinker
near antonyms buckle (down)

fiddle (with) *vb* to handle thoughtlessly, ignorantly, or mischievously — see TAMPER

fiddlesticks *n pl* language, behavior, or ideas that are absurd and contrary to good sense — see NONSENSE 1

fidelity *n* adherence to something to which one is bound by a pledge or duty ⟨they have never wavered in their *fidelity* to the cause of freedom⟩
synonyms allegiance, constancy, dedication, de-

votedness, devotion, faith, faithfulness, fastness, fealty, loyalty, steadfastness
related words affection, attachment, fondness; determination, firmness, resolution; dependability, reliability, trustworthiness
near antonyms alienation, disaffection, estrangement, separation
antonyms disloyalty, faithlessness, falseness, inconstancy, infidelity, perfidiousness, perfidy, treachery

fidget *vb* to make jerky or restless movements ⟨small children are likely to *fidget* in church⟩
synonyms fiddle, jerk, squirm, toss, twitch, wiggle, wriggle, writhe
related words flit, flutter, twitter; quake, quiver, shake, shiver, tremble; pace
near antonyms relax, rest, unwind

fidgets *n pl* a state of nervousness marked by sudden jerky movements — see JUMPINESS

fie *interj* how surprising, doubtful, or unbelievable — see NO

field *n* **1** a small area of usually open land ⟨a *field* that is the frequent site of neighborhood softball games⟩
synonyms clearing, ground, lot, parcel, plat, plot, tract
related words common(s); grass, green, greensward, lawn; glade, grassland, heath, lea, meadow, moor, pasture
2 a region of activity, knowledge, or influence ⟨the first woman to enter the *field* of medicine⟩
synonyms area, arena, demesne, department, discipline, domain, line, province, realm, specialty, sphere
related words study, subject; territory, turf; business, occupation, profession, pursuit, racket, vocation
3 a part or portion having no fixed boundaries — see REGION 1

fiend *n* **1** a mean, evil, or unprincipled person — see VILLAIN
2 a person who regularly uses drugs especially illegally — see DOPER
3 a person with a strong and habitual liking for something — see FAN
4 an evil spirit — see DEMON

fiendish *adj* of, relating to, or worthy of an evil spirit ⟨a *fiendish* delight in playing cruel tricks⟩
synonyms demoniac (*also* demoniacal), demonic, devilish, diabolical (*or* diabolic), satanic
related words hellish, infernal; baleful, evil, sinister; malevolent, malicious, malignant; heinous, monstrous; barbarous, cruel, ferocious, inhuman, savage, vicious
near antonyms celestial, heavenly; beneficent, benevolent, benign, benignant; godly, holy, saintly
antonyms angelic

fierce *adj* **1** violently unfriendly or aggressive in disposition ⟨the Vikings had a well-earned reputation for being *fierce* warriors⟩
synonyms fell, ferocious, grim, savage, vicious
related words bellicose, belligerent, pugnacious, warlike; contentious, quarrelsome, truculent; menacing, threatening; bestial, brute, inhuman, inhumane; barbaric, uncivilized, wild; heartless, implacable, merciless, pitiless, relentless, ruthless, unrelenting, wanton; bloodthirsty, bloody, murderous; rapacious, ravenous, voracious
near antonyms amicable, congenial, friendly; compliant, submissive, tame, unaggressive; com-

passionate, kind, merciful; pacific, peaceable, peaceful; amiable, complaisant, obliging; human, humane; civilized, cultured
antonyms gentle, mild
2 extreme in degree, power, or effect — see INTENSE
3 harsh and threatening in manner or appearance — see GRIM 1
4 having or showing a bold forcefulness in the pursuit of a goal — see AGGRESSIVE 1
5 marked by bursts of destructive force or intense activity — see VIOLENT 1
6 marked by great and often stressful excitement or activity — see FURIOUS 1
fierceness *n* the quality or state of being forceful (as in expression) — see VEHEMENCE 1
fiery *adj* **1** being on fire — see ABLAZE 1
2 having a notably high temperature — see HOT 1
3 having or expressing great depth of feeling — see FERVENT
4 marked by a lively display of strong feeling — see SPIRITED 1
fiesta *n* a time or program of special events and entertainment in honor of something — see FESTIVAL
fight *n* **1** a physical dispute between opposing individuals or groups ⟨a troubled youth who got into one *fight* after another⟩
synonyms battle, clash, combat, conflict, contest, fracas, fray, hassle, scrap, scrimmage, scuffle, skirmish, struggle, tussle
related words pitched battle; brawl, free-for-all, melee; fisticuffs; confrontation, duel, face-off; altercation, argument, disagreement, quarrel, row, wrangle
2 a forceful effort to reach a goal or objective — see STRUGGLE 1
3 an inclination to fight or quarrel — see BELLIGERENCE
4 an often noisy or angry expression of differing opinions — see ARGUMENT 1
fight *vb* **1** to oppose (someone) in physical conflict ⟨a proud people who have fiercely *fought* all invaders of their homeland⟩
synonyms battle, clash, combat, scrimmage (with), skirmish (with), war (against)
related words duel; bash, batter, beat, buffet, hit, punch, slug, strike; box, spar; brawl; grapple, scuffle, tussle, wrestle; bump, collide
phrases fall foul (of)
near antonyms give up, submit, surrender
2 to strive to reduce or eliminate ⟨a civil rights leader who dedicated his life to *fighting* prejudice⟩
synonyms battle, combat, contend (with), counter, oppose
related words baffle, foil, frustrate, resist, thwart, withstand; confront, defy, face, meet
near antonyms abide, bear, endure, suffer; advocate, back, support, uphold
antonyms advance, encourage, foster, further, promote
3 to engage in a contest — see COMPETE
4 to express different opinions about something often angrily — see ARGUE 2
5 to refuse to give in to — see RESIST
fighter *n* **1** a person engaged in military service — see SOLDIER
2 one that engages in the sport of fighting with the fists — see BOXER
figment *n* **1** a conception or image created by the

imagination and having no objective reality — see FANTASY 1
2 something that is the product of the imagination — see FICTION
figurative *adj* expressing one thing in terms normally used for another ⟨the *figurative* meaning of "allergy" is "a feeling of dislike"⟩
synonyms extended, metaphorical
related words allegorical, emblematic (*also* emblematical), symbolic (*also* symbolical); euphemistic
near antonyms nonsymbolic
antonyms literal, nonfigurative
figure *n* **1** a character used to represent a mathematical value — see NUMBER
2 a line that traces the outer limits of an object or surface — see OUTLINE 1
3 a person who is widely known and usually much talked about — see CELEBRITY 1
4 a small statue — see FIGURINE
5 a three-dimensional representation of the human body used especially for displaying clothes — see MANNEQUIN 1
6 a unit of decoration that is repeated all over something (as a fabric) — see PATTERN 1
7 something that visually explains or decorates a text — see ILLUSTRATION 1
8 the amount of money that is demanded as payment for something — see PRICE 1
9 the outward appearance of something as distinguished from its substance — see FORM 1
10 the type of body that a person has — see PHYSIQUE
11 **figures** *pl* the act or process of performing mathematical operations to find a value — see CALCULATION
figure *vb* **1** to come to a judgment after discussion or consideration — see DECIDE 1
2 to decide the size, amount, number, or distance of (something) without actual measurement — see ESTIMATE 2
3 to determine (a value) by doing the necessary mathematical operations — see CALCULATE 1
4 to have as an opinion — see BELIEVE 2
figure out *vb* to find an answer for through reasoning — see SOLVE
figurine *n* a small statue ⟨his collection of *figurines* includes toy soldiers from every war that America has fought⟩
synonyms figure, statuette
related words doll, marionette, puppet; bust, figurehead; carving, model, sculpture; dummy, form, mannequin
antonyms colossus
figuring *n* the act or process of performing mathematical operations to find a value — see CALCULATION
filch *vb* to take (something) without right and with an intent to keep — see STEAL 1
file *n* a series of persons or things arranged one behind another — see LINE 1
¹file *vb* to make smooth by friction — see GRIND 1
²file *vb* to move along with a steady regular step especially in a group — see MARCH 1
fill *n* soft material that is used to fill the hollow parts of something — see FILLING
fill *vb* **1** to put into (something) as much as can be held or contained ⟨*fill* the basket with apples⟩
synonyms charge, cram, heap, jam, jam-pack, load, pack, stuff

related words flood, glut, swamp; crowd, crush, press, ram, shove, squash, squeeze; refill, reload, repack
near antonyms lighten
antonyms empty
2 to close up so that no empty spaces remain ⟨before starting to paint, *fill* all the cracks with putty⟩
synonyms block, bung, dam, pack, plug, stop, stuff
related words choke, clog, obstruct; caulk, chink
near antonyms excavate, hollow (out), scoop (out)
3 to do what is required by the terms of — see FULFILL 1
filled *adj* containing or seeming to contain the greatest quantity or number possible — see FULL 1
filler *n* soft material that is used to fill the hollow parts of something — see FILLING
fill in *vb* **1** to give information to — see ENLIGHTEN 1
2 to serve as a replacement usually for a time only — see COVER 1
filling *n* soft material that is used to fill the hollow parts of something ⟨the *filling* for the parka is goose down⟩
synonyms fill, filler, padding, stuffing
related words interlining, lining, wadding; cushion
film *n* **1** a story told by means of a series of continuously projected pictures and a sound track — see MOVIE 1
2 the art or business of making a movie — see MOVIE 2
filmy *adj* **1** being of a material lacking in sturdiness or substance — see FLIMSY 1
2 very thin and easy to see through — see SHEER 1
filter *vb* **1** to pass through a filter — see STRAIN 2
2 to remove usually visible impurities from — see CLARIFY 1
filth *n* **1** foul matter that mars the purity or cleanliness of something ⟨the *filth* in the restaurant's kitchen was unbelievable⟩
synonyms dirt, grime, muck, smut, soil
related words scum, sewage, slime, sludge, swill; garbage, refuse, trash; soot; dirtiness, filthiness, foulness, griminess, grubbiness, nastiness, squalidness, uncleanliness, uncleanness
near antonyms cleanliness, cleanness
2 the quality or state of being obscene — see OBSCENITY 1
filthiness *n* **1** the quality or state of being obscene — see OBSCENITY 1
2 the state or quality of being dirty — see DIRTINESS 1
filthy *adj* **1** depicting or referring to sexual matters in a way that is unacceptable in polite society — see OBSCENE 1
2 not clean — see DIRTY 1
finagle *vb* to plan out usually with subtle skill or care — see ENGINEER
final *adj* **1** following all others of the same kind in order or time — see LAST
2 having been established and usually not subject to change — see FIXED 1
finale *n* the last part of a process or action ⟨the *finale* to the festivities was a grand display of fireworks⟩
synonyms close, closing, conclusion, consummation, end, ending, finis, finish, windup

related words apex, climax, crescendo, culmination, peak, summit, zenith; aftermath, anticlimax, coda, epilogue, postscript; tag end, tail end
near antonyms introduction, overture, prelude, prologue
antonyms beginning, dawn, opening, start
finalize *vb* to bring (something) to a state where nothing remains to be done — see FINISH 1
finally *adv* at a later time — see YET 1
finance *vb* **1** to provide money for ⟨a local business kindly *financed* the high school band's trip to New York City⟩
synonyms capitalize, endow, fund, stake, subsidize, underwrite
related words grubstake; aid, back, patronize, sponsor, support
2 to furnish (as an institution) with a regular source of income — see ENDOW 2
finances *n pl* available money — see FUND 2
financial *adj* of or relating to money, banking, or investments ⟨the *financial* world was watching the stock market closely⟩
synonyms fiscal, monetary, pecuniary
related words capitalist (or capitalistic), commercial, economic
find *n* something discovered — see DISCOVERY 2
find *vb* **1** to come upon after searching, study, or effort ⟨we finally *found* the information after searching dozens of Internet sites⟩
synonyms ascertain, descry, detect, determine, dig (up), discover, find out, get, hit (on or upon), hunt (down or up), learn, locate, run down, scare up, scout (up), track (down)
related words espy, sight, spot; look for, search (for or out), seek
near antonyms lose, mislay, misplace
antonyms miss, overlook, pass over
2 to come upon unexpectedly or by chance — see HAPPEN (ON OR UPON)
finding *n* **1** a decision made by a court or tribunal regarding a case it has heard — see SENTENCE
2 the act or process of sighting or learning the existence of something for the first time — see DISCOVERY 1
find out *vb* **1** to come to an awareness — see DISCOVER 1
2 to come upon after searching, study, or effort — see FIND 1
fine *adj* **1** consisting of very small particles ⟨the *fine* sand found on the island's beaches⟩
synonyms dusty, floury, powdery
related words smooth; filtered, pulverized, refined
near antonyms rough; unfiltered, unrefined; gravelly, gritty, sandy; pebbly, rocky, stony (also stoney); lumpy, mealy
antonyms coarse, grainy, granular, granulated
2 made or done with extreme care and accuracy ⟨the *fine* distinction between bravery and recklessness⟩
synonyms delicate, exact, hairline, hairsplitting, minute, nice, refined, subtle
related words nitpicking, quibbling; petty, piddling, trifling, trivial; fastidious, finicky, fussy, particular
near antonyms apparent, clear, obvious; broad, indefinite; careless, slapdash, slipshod, sloppy
antonyms coarse, inexact, rough
3 being of less than usual width — see NARROW 1
4 being to one's liking — see SATISFACTORY 1
5 free from added matter — see PURE 1

THESAURUS

6 meeting the highest standard of accuracy — see PRECISE 1

7 of a level of quality that meets one's needs or standards — see ADEQUATE

8 of a size that is less than average — see SMALL 1

9 of the very best kind — see EXCELLENT

fine *adv* in a satisfactory way — see WELL 1

fine *n* a sum of money to be paid as a punishment ⟨a $50 *fine* for speeding⟩

synonyms damages, forfeit, forfeiture, mulct, penalty

related words reparations; award, compensation; indemnity

fine *vb* to establish or apply as a charge or penalty — see IMPOSE

fineness *n* **1** the quality or state of being little in size — see SMALLNESS

2 the quality or state of being very accurate — see PRECISION

3 the state or quality of having a delicate structure — see DELICACY 2

finery *n* dressy clothing ⟨the guests arrived at the wedding in all their *finery*⟩

synonyms array, best, bravery, caparison, feather, frippery, full dress, gaiety (*also* gayety), regalia

related words apparel, attire, costume, duds, raiment

near antonyms rags, tatters

finesse *n* mental skill or quickness — see DEXTERITY 1

finesse *vb* to plan out usually with subtle skill or care — see ENGINEER

finicky *adj* hard to please ⟨cats have a reputation for being *finicky* eaters⟩

synonyms choosy (*or* choosey), dainty, delicate, demanding, exacting, fastidious, fussy, nice, old-maidish, particular, picky

related words discerning, discriminating, insightful, knowledgeable; carping, critical; careful, meticulous, punctilious, scrupulous; queasy (*also* queazy), squeamish; peevish, petulant, prickly, touchy

near antonyms affable, breezy, devil-may-care, happy-go-lucky, laid-back; flexible, lax, loose; lenient, permissive; uncritical

antonyms undemanding, unfussy

finis *n* the last part of a process or action — see FINALE

finish *n* **1** the last part of a process or action — see FINALE

2 the stopping of a process or activity — see END 1

finish *vb* **1** to bring (something) to a state where nothing remains to be done ⟨we should *finish* the painting of the house by tomorrow⟩

synonyms complete, consummate, finalize, perfect

related words follow through, see out, stick out; accomplish, achieve, effect; discharge, execute, fulfill (*or* fulfil), perform; machine, polish, refine, round (off *or* out), shine, touch up

near antonyms abandon, desert, drop, forsake, quit

2 to bring (an event) to a natural or appropriate stopping point — see CLOSE 3

3 to come to an end — see CEASE 1

finished *adj* brought or having come to an end — see COMPLETE 2

finite *adj* **1** having a limit ⟨our nation's natural resources are abundant, but they are also *finite*⟩

synonyms limited

related words confined, restricted; definable, defined, definite, determinate; decided, established, fixed, set; exact, precise, specific

near antonyms unconfined, unrestricted; indefinite, indeterminate, undefinable, undefined

antonyms boundless, infinite, unbounded, unlimited

2 having distinct or certain limits — see LIMITED 1

fire *n* a destructive burning ⟨a number of suspicious *fires* in the neighborhood recently⟩

synonyms conflagration, holocaust, inferno

related words blaze, flare-up; backfire, bonfire, forest fire, wildfire; arson

fire *vb* **1** to cause (a projectile) to be driven forward with force — see SHOOT 1

2 to cause a weapon to release a missile with great force — see SHOOT 2

3 to give life, vigor, or spirit to — see ANIMATE

4 to let go from office, service, or employment — see DISMISS 1

5 to send through the air especially with a quick forward motion of the arm — see THROW

6 to set (something) on fire — see BURN 2

fire (up) *vb* to rouse to strong feeling or action — see PROVOKE 1

firearm *n* a portable weapon from which a shot is discharged by gunpowder — see GUN 1

firebrand *n* a person who stirs up public feelings especially of discontent — see AGITATOR

firebug *n* a person who deliberately and unlawfully sets fire to a building or other property — see ARSONIST

fireproof *adj* incapable of being burned — see INCOMBUSTIBLE

fireside *n* the place where one lives — see HOME 1

fireworks *n pl* an outburst or display of excited anger — see TANTRUM

firing *n* a directed propelling of a missile by a firearm or artillery piece — see SHOT

firkin *n* an enclosed wooden vessel for holding beverages — see CASK

firm *adj* **1** not showing weakness or uncertainty ⟨a friendly fellow with a ready smile and a *firm* handshake⟩

synonyms forceful, hearty, iron, lusty, robust, solid, stout, strong, sturdy, vigorous

related words mighty, powerful, tough, unyielding; animated, energetic, lively, spirited; certain, confident, sanguine, sure

near antonyms feeble, fragile, frail; limp, listless, spiritless

antonyms uncertain, weak

2 having a consistency that does not easily yield to pressure ⟨cold butter that was too *firm* to spread⟩

synonyms compact, hard, rigid, solid, stiff, unyielding

related words case-hardened, compacted, compressed, hardened, indurated, stiffened, tempered; close, dense, heavy, thick, thickset; inelastic, inflexible, ramrod, unbending; compressed, condensed; sturdy, substantial; impenetrable, impermeable, nonporous

near antonyms loose, scattered, thin; bendable, elastic, flexible, malleable, pliable; flaccid, floppy, limp, slack; airy, light; permeable, porous

antonyms flabby, soft, spongy, squashy, squishy

3 firmly positioned in place and difficult to dislodge — see TIGHT 2

4 fully committed to achieving a goal — see DE-TERMINED 1

5 having been established and usually not subject to change — see FIXED 1

6 marked by the ability to withstand stress without structural damage or distortion — see STA-BLE 1

firm *n* a commercial or industrial activity or organization — see ENTERPRISE 1

firm (up) *vb* to become physically firm or solid — see HARDEN 1

firmament *n* the expanse of air surrounding the earth — see SKY

firmly *adv* in a vigorous and forceful manner — see HARD 3

firmness *n* **1** firm or unwavering adherence to one's purpose — see DETERMINATION 1

2 the ability to withstand force or stress without being distorted, dislodged, or damaged — see STABILITY 1

first *adj* **1** coming before all others in time or order ⟨the much-studied *first*—and last—voyage of the *Titanic*⟩

synonyms earliest, inaugural, initial, maiden, original, pioneer, premier

related words ancient, early, primal, primary, primeval, primitive, primordial; antecedent, preceding, previous

near antonyms advanced, late; ensuing, following, subsequent, succeeding

antonyms final, last, terminal, ultimate

2 coming before all others in importance — see FOREMOST 1

3 highest in rank or authority — see HEAD

first *adv* **1** as a substitute — see INSTEAD

2 by choice or preference — see RATHER 1

first–class *adj* of the very best kind — see EXCEL-LENT

firsthand *adj* done or working without something else coming in between — see DIRECT 1

firstly *adv* in the beginning — see ORIGINALLY

first–rate *adj* of the very best kind — see EXCEL-LENT

firth *n* a part of a body of water that extends beyond the general shoreline — see GULF 1

fiscal *adj* of or relating to money, banking, or investments — see FINANCIAL

fish *vb* to search for something blindly or uncertainly — see GROPE

fishy *adj* giving good reason for being doubted, questioned, or challenged — see DOUBTFUL 2

fissure *n* an irregular usually narrow break in a surface created by pressure — see CRACK 1

fit *adj* **1** meeting the requirements of a purpose or situation ⟨clothing that is *fit* for horseback riding⟩

synonyms applicable, appropriate, apt, becoming, befitting, felicitous, fitting, good, happy, meet, proper, right, suitable

related words just, justified, right; needed, required, requisite; able, capable, competent, qualified, trained; acceptable, adequate, decent, satisfactory, tolerable; correct, decorous, respectable, seemly

near antonyms incompetent, unqualified, untrained; inadequate, intolerable, unacceptable, unsatisfactory; incorrect, indecorous, unseemly

antonyms improper, inapplicable, inappropriate, inapt, infelicitous, unhappy, unsuitable, wrong

2 being in a state of fitness for some experience or action — see READY 1

3 capable of or suitable for being used for a particular purpose — see USABLE 1

4 enjoying health and vigor — see HEALTHY 1

5 having the required skills for an acceptable level of performance — see COMPETENT

fit *n* **1** a sudden experiencing of a physical or mental disorder — see ATTACK 2

2 a sudden intense expression of strong feeling — see OUTBURST 1

3 an outburst or display of excited anger — see TANTRUM

fit *vb* **1** to be fitting or proper — see DO 1

2 to be in agreement on every point — see CHECK 1

3 to change (something) so as to make it suitable for a new use or situation — see ADAPT

4 to make competent (as by training, skill, or ability) for a particular office or function — see QUALIFY 2

5 to make or have room for — see ACCOMMO-DATE 1

6 to make ready in advance — see PREPARE 1

fit (in *or* into) *vb* to put among or between others — see INSERT

fit (out) *vb* to provide (someone) with what is needed for a task or activity — see FURNISH 1

fitful *adj* lacking in steadiness or regularity of occurrence ⟨a night of *fitful* sleep did not leave me feeling well rested the next morning⟩

synonyms casual, choppy, discontinuous, erratic, intermittent, irregular, occasional, spasmodic, sporadic, spotty, unsteady

related words convulsive, sudden, violent; broken, disconnected, fragmentary, interrupted; desultory, haphazard, hit-or-miss, random; changing, fluctuating, unstable, varying, wavering; changeable, fickle, variable

near antonyms equable, even, stable, uniform; unchanging, unvarying, unwavering; methodical, orderly, systematic

antonyms constant, continuous, regular, steady

fitness *n* **1** the condition of being sound in body — see HEALTH

2 the quality or state of being especially suitable or fitting — see APPROPRIATENESS

fitting *adj* meeting the requirements of a purpose or situation — see FIT 1

fittingly *adv* in a manner suitable for the occasion or purpose — see PROPERLY

fittingness *n* the quality or state of being especially suitable or fitting — see APPROPRIATENESS

fix *n* **1** a difficult, puzzling, or embarrassing situation from which there is no easy escape — see PREDICAMENT

2 something given or promised in order to improperly influence a person's conduct or decision — see BRIBE

fix *vb* **1** to arrange something in a certain spot or position — see PLACE 1

2 to cause (something) to hold to another — see FASTEN 1

3 to come to an agreement or decision concerning the details of — see ARRANGE 1

4 to decide upon (the time or date for an event) usually from a position of authority — see AP-POINT 1

5 to make ready in advance — see PREPARE 1

6 to put into good shape or working order again — see MEND 1

THESAURUS

7 to put securely in place or in a desired position — see FASTEN 2

8 to set solidly in or as if in surrounding matter — see ENTRENCH

fixable *adj* capable of being corrected — see REMEDIABLE

fixation *n* something about which one is constantly thinking or concerned ⟨their weight is an unfortunate *fixation* for many teenagers⟩

synonyms fetish (*also* fetich), idée fixe, mania, obsession, preoccupation, prepossession

related words complex, hang-up, problem; compulsion, craving, enthusiasm, fascination, infatuation, passion; idiosyncrasy, quirk; penchant, predilection, proclivity

near antonyms apathy, indifference, unconcern

fixed *adj* **1** having been established and usually not subject to change ⟨the baseball card dealer's prices were *fixed*, so bargaining was not an option⟩

synonyms certain, determinate, final, firm, flat, frozen, hard, hard-and-fast, set, settled, stable

related words nonadjustable, nonnegotiable, unchangeable; constant, steady, unchanging, uniform, unwavering; definite, exact, explicit, specific; stated, stipulated

near antonyms adjustable, changeable, negotiable; indefinite, unspecified

2 not capable of changing or being changed — see INFLEXIBLE 1

fixedness *n* the state of continuing without change — see CONSTANCY 1

fizz *n* a sound similar to the speech sound \s\ stretched out — see HISS 1

fizz *vb* to make a sound like that of stretching out the speech sound \s\ — see HISS

fizzle *n* **1** a falling short of one's goals — see FAILURE 2

2 something that has failed — see FAILURE 3

fjord *or* **fiord** *n* a part of a body of water that extends beyond the general shoreline — see GULF 1

flabbergast *vb* to make a strong impression on (someone) with something unexpected — see SURPRISE 1

flabbergasted *adj* **1** affected with sudden and great wonder or surprise — see THUNDERSTRUCK

2 filled with amazement or wonder — see OPEN-MOUTHED

flabbergasting *adj* causing a strong emotional reaction because unexpected — see SURPRISING 1

flabby *adj* giving easily to the touch — see SOFT 3

flaccid *adj* not stiff in structure — see LIMP 1

flag *n* **1** a piece of cloth with a special design that is used as an emblem or for signaling ⟨the *flags* of both countries were prominently displayed at the treaty signing⟩

synonyms banner, colors, ensign, guidon, jack, pennant, pennon, standard, streamer

related words bunting; black flag, Jolly Roger, union jack, white flag; semaphore, signaler; badge, coat of arms, crest, insignia

2 an object intended to give public notice or warning — see SIGNAL 1

¹**flag** *vb* **1** to be limp from lack of water or vigor — see DROOP

2 to lose bodily strength or vigor — see WEAKEN 2

²**flag** *vb* to direct or notify by a movement or gesture — see MOTION

flagellate *vb* to strike repeatedly with something long and thin or flexible — see WHIP 1

flagon *n* a handled container for holding and pouring liquids that usually has a lip or a spout — see PITCHER

flagrant *adj* very noticeable especially for being incorrect or bad — see EGREGIOUS

flail *vb* **1** to move or cause to move with a striking motion — see FLAP

2 to strike repeatedly with something long and thin or flexible — see WHIP 1

flair *n* a special and usually inborn ability — see TALENT

flake *n* a small flat piece separated from a whole — see CHIP 1

flaky *adj* having a texture that readily breaks into little pieces under pressure — see CRISP 1

flamboyance *n* excessive or unnecessary display — see OSTENTATION

flamboyant *adj* **1** likely to attract attention — see NOTICEABLE

2 excessively showy — see GAUDY

flamboyantly *adv* in a bright and showy way — see GAILY 3

flame *n* a person with whom one is in love — see SWEETHEART

flame *vb* **1** to be on fire especially brightly — see BURN 1

2 to develop suddenly and violently — see ERUPT 2

3 to shine with a bright harsh light — see GLARE 1

4 to shoot forth bursts of light — see FLASH 1

flaming *adj* **1** being on fire — see ABLAZE 1

2 having or expressing great depth of feeling — see FERVENT

flammable *adj* capable of catching or being set on fire — see COMBUSTIBLE

flank *n* a place, space, or direction away from or beyond a central point or line — see SIDE 1

flank *vb* to be adjacent to — see ADJOIN 1

flanking *adj* having a border in common — see ADJACENT

flap *vb* to move or cause to move with a striking motion ⟨the stirring sight of a huge flock of geese *flapping* their wings⟩

synonyms beat, flail, flop, flutter, whip

related words bang, batter, buffet, knock, pound, smack, spank, thump; flick, flicker, flit; oscillate, sway, swing; undulate, wave; palpitate, pulse, throb

flapjack *n* a flat cake made from thin batter and cooked on both sides (as on a griddle) — see PANCAKE

flare *n* **1** a sudden and usually temporary growth of activity — see OUTBREAK

2 a sudden intense expression of strong feeling — see OUTBURST 1

3 the steady giving off of the form of radiation that makes vision possible — see LIGHT 1

flare *vb* to shine with a bright harsh light — see GLARE 1

flare (out) *vb* to arrange the parts of (something) over a wider area — see OPEN 3

flare (up) *vb* **1** to become very angry — see BLOW UP

2 to develop suddenly and violently — see ERUPT 2

flare-up *n* **1** a sudden and usually temporary growth of activity — see OUTBREAK

2 a sudden intense expression of strong feeling — see OUTBURST 1

flash *adj* lasting only for a short time — see MOMENTARY

flash *n* **1** a sudden and usually temporary growth of activity — see OUTBREAK

2 a sudden intense expression of strong feeling — see OUTBURST 1

3 a very small space of time — see INSTANT

4 something extraordinary or surprising — see WONDER 1

flash *vb* **1** to shoot forth bursts of light ⟨the actress's diamond necklace *flashed* as she hurried on stage to accept the award⟩

synonyms flame, glance, gleam, glimmer, glint, glisten, glister, glitter, scintillate, shimmer, sparkle, twinkle, wink

related words beam, radiate, shine; bedazzle, blind, daze, dazzle; blaze, burn, flare, glare, glow

2 to present so as to invite notice or attention — see SHOW 1

3 to shine with light at regular intervals — see BLINK 1

flashily *adv* in a bright and showy way — see GAILY 3

flashiness *n* excessive or unnecessary display — see OSTENTATION

flashy *adj* **1** attractively eye-catching in style — see JAZZY 1

2 excessively showy — see GAUDY

flat *adj* **1** being neither more nor less than a certain amount, number, or extent — see EVEN 1

2 causing weariness, restlessness, or lack of interest — see BORING

3 having a surface without bends, breaks, or irregularities — see LEVEL

4 having been established and usually not subject to change — see FIXED 1

5 having no exceptions or restrictions — see ABSOLUTE 2

6 lacking a surface luster or gloss — see MATTE

7 lacking in qualities that make for spirit and character — see WISHY-WASHY 1

8 lacking in taste or flavor — see INSIPID 1

flat *adv* to a full extent or degree — see FULLY 1

flat *n, chiefly British* a room or set of rooms in a private house or a block used as a separate dwelling place — see APARTMENT 1

flatten *vb* to make free from breaks, curves, or bumps — see EVEN 1

flatter *vb* **1** to praise too much ⟨the billionaire had an army of assistants who *flattered* him at every opportunity⟩

synonyms adulate, blarney, overpraise, soft-soap

related words blandish, cajole, coax, wheedle; fawn, kowtow, toady; idolize, worship; eulogize, extol (*also* extoll), laud, praise; applaud, commend, compliment; congratulate, felicitate; drool, gush, slaver, slobber; endear, ingratiate; court, woo

near antonyms bad-mouth, belittle, decry, depreciate, disparage, put down

2 to think highly of (oneself) — see PRIDE

flattery *n* excessive praise ⟨a talk show host who is known for charming her guests with *flattery*⟩

synonyms adulation, blarney, overpraise, soft soap

related words allurements, blandishments, endearments; compliments, congratulations, felicitations, greetings, regards, respects; adoration, idolatry, worship; cajolery, endearment, ingratiation; acclaim, applause, commendation, praise

near antonyms bad-mouthing, belittlement, depreciation, detraction, disparagement, put-down

flatware *n* eating and serving utensils — see TABLEWARE 1

flaunt *vb* to present so as to invite notice or attention — see SHOW 1

flaunting *n* an outward and often exaggerated indication of something abstract (as a feeling) for effect — see SHOW 1

flavor *n* **1** a special quality or impression associated with something — see AURA

2 something (as a spice or herb) that adds an agreeable or interesting taste to food — see SEASONING 1

3 the property of a substance that can be identified by the sense of taste — see TASTE 1

flavor *vb* to make more pleasant to the taste by adding something intensely flavored — see SEASON 1

flavorful *adj* very pleasing to the sense of taste — see DELICIOUS 1

flavoring *n* something (as a spice or herb) that adds an agreeable or interesting taste to food — see SEASONING 1

flavorless *adj* lacking in taste or flavor — see INSIPID 1

flaw *n* something that spoils the appearance or completeness of a thing — see BLEMISH

flaw *vb* to reduce the soundness, effectiveness, or perfection of — see DAMAGE 1

flawed *adj* having a fault — see FAULTY

flawless *adj* being entirely without fault or flaw — see PERFECT 1

flawlessly *adv* without any flaws or errors — see PERFECTLY 1

flaxen *adj* of a pale yellow or yellowish brown color — see BLOND

flay *vb* **1** to criticize (someone) severely or angrily especially for personal failings — see SCOLD

2 to remove the natural covering of — see PEEL

fleck *n* **1** a small area that is different (as in color) from the main part — see SPOT 1

2 a very small piece — see BIT 1

fleck *vb* to mark with small spots especially unevenly — see SPOT

flecked *adj* marked with spots — see SPOTTED 1

fledgling *n* a person who is just starting out in a field of activity — see BEGINNER

flee *vb* **1** to cease to be visible — see DISAPPEAR

2 to get free from a dangerous or confining situation — see ESCAPE 1

3 to hasten away from something dangerous or frightening — see RUN 2

fleece *n* the hairy covering of a mammal especially when fine, soft, and thick — see FUR 1

fleece *vb* to rob by the use of trickery or threats ⟨swindlers who use the telephone to *fleece* senior citizens out of their savings⟩

synonyms bleed, cheat, chisel, cozen, defraud, gyp, hustle, mulct, rook, shortchange, skin, squeeze, stick, sting, swindle, victimize

related words extort, wrench, wrest, wring; gouge, overcharge, soak; exploit, milk; deceive, dupe, fool, gull, trick; rope (in); betray, double-cross

fleecy *adj* covered with or as if with hair — see HAIRY 1

fleet *adj* moving, proceeding, or acting with great speed — see FAST 1

fleet *n* a group of vehicles traveling together or

THESAURUS

under one management ⟨a *fleet* of buses rolling down the highway⟩

synonyms armada, caravan, cavalcade, line, motorcade, train

related words convoy, flotilla, navy; column, cortege (*also* cortège), parade, procession

fleet-footed *adj* moving, proceeding, or acting with great speed — see FAST 1

fleeting *adj* lasting only for a short time — see MOMENTARY

fleetly *adv* with great speed — see FAST 1

fleetness *n* a high rate of movement or performance — see SPEED

flesh *n* animal and especially mammal tissue used as food — see MEAT 1

fleshiness *n* **1** the condition of having an excess of body fat — see CORPULENCE
2 the quality or state of being full of juice — see SUCCULENCE

fleshly *adj* **1** having to do with life on earth especially as opposed to that in heaven — see EARTHLY
2 of or relating to the human body — see PHYSICAL 1
3 pleasing to the physical senses — see SENSUAL

fleshy *adj* **1** full of juice — see JUICY
2 having an excess of body fat — see FAT 1

flexible *adj* **1** capable of being readily changed ⟨fortunately, Mom has a very *flexible* schedule for her office job⟩

synonyms adaptable, adjustable, alterable, changeable, elastic, fluid, malleable, modifiable, variable

related words changing, fluctuating, inconstant, unstable, unsteady, varying

near antonyms constant, stable, steady, unchanging, uniform, unvarying

antonyms established, fixed, immutable, inelastic, inflexible, invariable, nonmalleable, ramrod, set, unalterable, unchangeable
2 not bound by rigid standards — see EASYGOING 2
3 able to bend easily without breaking — see WILLOWY
4 able to revert to original size and shape after being stretched, squeezed, or twisted — see ELASTIC 1

flick *vb* to make an irregular series of quick, sudden movements — see FLIT

flicker *n* a sudden and usually temporary growth of activity — see OUTBREAK

flicker *vb* to make an irregular series of quick, sudden movements — see FLIT

flickery *adj* likely to change frequently, suddenly, or unexpectedly — see FICKLE 1

flier *or* **flyer** *n* **1** a risky undertaking — see GAMBLE
2 one who flies or is qualified to fly an aircraft or spacecraft — see PILOT
3 a short printed publication with no cover or with a paper cover — see PAMPHLET

¹**flight** *n* the act or an instance of getting free from danger or confinement — see ESCAPE 1

²**flight** *n* travel through the air by the use of wings ⟨for centuries people had been fascinated by the *flight* of birds⟩

synonyms flying

related words aviation; aeronautics; ballooning, gliding, skydiving, soaring

flightiness *n* **1** a lack of seriousness often at an improper time — see FRIVOLITY 1

2 a state of nervousness marked by sudden jerky movements — see JUMPINESS

flighty *adj* **1** easily excited by nature — see EXCITABLE
2 lacking in seriousness or maturity — see GIDDY 1

flimsy *adj* **1** being of a material lacking in sturdiness or substance ⟨a *flimsy* scarf that was more for decoration than for warmth⟩

synonyms filmy, gauzy, gossamer, gossamery, insubstantial, unsubstantial

related words dainty, delicate, fine; feeble, fragile, frail; sheer, transparent

near antonyms durable, lasting, tough; coarse, heavy, rough, rude

antonyms sturdy, substantial
2 not likely to be true or to occur — see IMPROBABLE

flinch *vb* to draw back in fear, pain, or disgust ⟨there are some patients who *flinch* at the mere sight of a needle⟩

synonyms blench, quail, recoil, shrink, wince

related words blanch, pale, whiten; quake, quiver, shake, shudder, tremble; crouch, squinch; jerk, start, twitch; recede, retire, retreat, withdraw; falter, hesitate, reel, waver

near antonyms advance, approach, near; confront, challenge, defy, face

fling *n* **1** a time or instance of carefree fun ⟨most families spend Labor Day weekend having one last summer *fling*⟩

synonyms binge, frolic, gambol, lark, revel, rollick, romp, spree

related words caper, escapade, prank; antic, monkeyshine(s), shenanigans; field day; festivity, merriment, merrymaking; enjoyment, indulgence, pleasure, self-indulgence; amusement, diversion, entertainment, recreation
2 an effort to do or accomplish something — see ATTEMPT

fling *vb* to send through the air especially with a quick forward motion of the arm — see THROW

fling (off *or* away) *vb* to get rid of as useless or unwanted — see DISCARD

flinty *adj* **1** given to exacting standards of discipline and self-restraint — see SEVERE 1
2 harsh and threatening in manner or appearance — see GRIM 1

flip *adj* making light of something usually regarded as serious or sacred — see FLIPPANT

flip *vb* **1** to become very angry — see BLOW UP
2 to change the position of (an object) so that the opposite side or end is showing — see REVERSE 2
3 to yield to mental or emotional stress — see CRACK 2

flippancy *n* a lack of seriousness often at an improper time — see FRIVOLITY 1

flippant *adj* making light of something usually regarded as serious or sacred ⟨his *flippant* comment that the poor save on taxes offended many people⟩

synonyms facetious, flip, pert, smart, smart-alecky (*or* smart-aleck)

related words flighty, frivolous; cheeky, cocky, cute, fresh, impertinent, impish, impudent, mischievous, playful, roguish, sassy, saucy, waggish; disrespectful, rude; breezy, casual, glib, inappropriate, thoughtless

near antonyms grave, serious, sober, solemn, somber (*or* sombre)

antonyms earnest, sincere

flirt *vb* to show a liking for someone of the opposite sex just for fun ⟨the servers at that restaurant *flirt* with all the customers⟩

synonyms dally, frivol, trifle

related words josh, kid, put on, razz, rib, tease; fool, lead on, string along; play (with), toy (with)

flit *vb* to make an irregular series of quick, sudden movements ⟨bargain hunters at the flea market *flitted* from table to table like hummingbirds in a garden⟩

synonyms dance, dart, flick, flicker, flutter, zip

related words dash, fly, sail, shoot, speed, sprint, zoom; scamper, scud, scurry, scuttle, skip, skitter; meander, ramble, roam, wander

near antonyms float, hang, hover

float *n* a structure used by boats and ships for taking on or landing cargo and passengers — see DOCK

float *vb* to rest or move along the surface of a liquid or in the air ⟨a canoe *floating* down the river⟩ ⟨particles of dust *floating* in the air⟩

synonyms drift, glide, hang, hover, poise, ride, sail, waft

related words bob, dangle, suspend; buoy; balloon, raft

near antonyms dive, lunge, plunge; dip, immerse, submerge, submerse

antonyms settle, sink

flock *n* **1** a great number of persons or things gathered together — see CROWD 1

2 a group of domestic animals assembled or herded together — see HERD

flock *vb* to move upon or fill (something) in great numbers — see CROWD 2

flog *vb* **1** to strike repeatedly with something long and thin or flexible — see WHIP 1

2 to strike repeatedly — see BEAT 1

flogger *n* a long thin or flexible tool for striking — see WHIP

flood *n* a great flow of water or of something that overwhelms ⟨a *flood* nearly wiped out the town⟩ ⟨a *flood* of messages on my computer⟩

synonyms cataclysm, cataract, deluge, flood tide, inundation, overflow, spate, torrent

related words current, river, stream, tide; discharge, flush, gush, outflow, outpouring; flux, inflow, influx; engulfment, washout; avalanche; cascade, waterfall; excess, glut, overabundance, overage, overkill, overmuch, oversupply, superabundance, superfluity, surfeit, surplus

near antonyms dribble, drip, trickle

antonyms drought

flood *vb* to cover or become filled with a flood ⟨the lowlands were completely *flooded*⟩ ⟨angry calls *flooded* the radio station⟩

synonyms deluge, drown, engulf, inundate, overflow, overwhelm, submerge, submerse, swamp

related words overcome, overrun; flow, flush, gush, pour, sluice, spout, spurt, stream; douse, drench, soak, wet

near antonyms dehydrate, dry, parch

antonyms drain

flood tide *n* a great flow of water or of something that overwhelms — see FLOOD

floor *n* the surface upon which a body of water lies — see BOTTOM 2

floor *vb* **1** to cause an often unpleasant surprise for — see SHOCK 1

2 to make a strong impression on (someone) with something unexpected — see SURPRISE 1

3 to strike (someone) so forcefully as to cause a fall — see FELL 1

4 to subject to incapacitating emotional or mental stress — see OVERWHELM 1

flop *n* something that has failed — see FAILURE 3

flop *vb* **1** to throw or set down clumsily or casually ⟨they *flopped* themselves onto the couch to watch the game⟩ ⟨*flopped* the bag of groceries onto the counter⟩

synonyms plop, plump, plunk

related words fling, heave, sling, toss; ensconce, install, plant, settle

2 to be unsuccessful — see FAIL 2

3 to move or cause to move with a striking motion — see FLAP

floppy *adj* not stiff in structure — see LIMP 1

flora *n* green leaves or plants — see GREENERY 1

floral *adj* of or relating to flowers ⟨wallpaper with a *floral* pattern for the bedroom⟩

synonyms flowered, flowery

related words florid; abloom

florid *adj* **1** elaborately and often excessively decorated — see ORNATE

2 full of fine words and fancy expressions — see FLOWERY 1

3 having a healthy reddish skin tone — see RUDDY

floss *n* a soft airy substance or covering — see FUZZ

flounce *n* a strip of fabric gathered or pleated on one edge and used as trimming — see RUFFLE

flounder *vb* **1** to make progress in a clumsy, struggling manner ⟨unprepared choristers who *floundered* helplessly through the musical number⟩

synonyms limp, lumber, plod, stumble, trudge

related words shamble, shuffle; wallow, welter; falter, lurch, reel, stagger, sway, teeter, totter; blunder, fumble, muddle

near antonyms coast, fly, glide, sail, zip, zoom

2 to move heavily or clumsily — see LUMBER 1

flourish *vb* **1** to grow vigorously — see THRIVE 1

2 to reach a desired level of accomplishment — see SUCCEED 2

flourishing *adj* **1** having attained a desired end or state of good fortune — see SUCCESSFUL 1

2 marked by much life, movement, or activity — see ALIVE 2

3 marked by vigorous growth and well-being especially economically — see PROSPEROUS 1

floury *adj* consisting of very small particles — see FINE 1

flout *vb* to ignore in a disrespectful manner — see SCORN 2

flow *vb* **1** to move in a stream ⟨water was *flowing* over the dam at a tremendous rate⟩

synonyms pour, roll, run, stream

related words arise, emanate, issue, spring; course, race, rush; gush, spout, spurt; deluge, engulf, flood, inundate, overflow, swamp; cascade, dribble, drip, gutter, riffle, ripple, trickle; flush, wash out

near antonyms clot, coagulate, congeal, gel, harden, set

antonyms back up

2 to move or proceed smoothly and readily ⟨as everyone relaxed, the conversation really started to *flow*⟩

synonyms bowl, breeze, coast, drift, glide, roll, sail, skim, slide, slip, stream, sweep, whisk

THESAURUS

related words fly, race, rush, speed
near antonyms limp, lumber, plod, stumble, trudge; shamble, shuffle; stamp, stomp, stump, tramp; labor, toil
antonyms flounder, struggle
flower *n* **1** the usually showy plant part that produces seeds ⟨*flowers* are always a thoughtful gift⟩
synonyms bloom, blossom
related words bud, floret; bouquet, nosegay, posy; arrangement, boutonniere, corsage, garland, lei, spray, wreath
2 a state or time of great activity, thriving, or achievement — see BLOOM 1
3 individuals carefully selected as being the best of a class — see ELITE
flower *vb* to produce flowers — see BLOOM
flowered *adj* of or relating to flowers — see FLORAL
flowery *adj* **1** full of fine words and fancy expressions ⟨the *flowery* verses that always appear on valentines⟩
synonyms florid, grandiloquent, highfalutin, high-flown, high-sounding
related words affected, grandiose, inflated, pompous, pretentious, stilted; excessive, flattering, fulsome; boastful, bombastic; elevated, eloquent, lofty
near antonyms prosaic, unpoetic; bald, direct, matter-of-fact, plain, plainspoken, simple, stark, straightforward, unadorned; natural, unaffected, unpretentious
2 of or relating to flowers — see FLORAL
flowing *adj* capable of moving like a liquid — see FLUID 1
flub *n* an unintentional departure from truth or accuracy — see ERROR 1
flub *vb* to make or do (something) in a clumsy or unskillful way — see BOTCH
fluctuate *vb* to pass from one form, state, or level to another — see CHANGE 2
fluctuating *adj* **1** likely to change frequently, suddenly, or unexpectedly — see FICKLE 1
2 not staying constant — see UNEVEN 2
fluent *adj* **1** able to express oneself clearly and well — see ARTICULATE
2 capable of moving like a liquid — see FLUID 1
3 involving minimal difficulty or effort — see EASY 1
fluently *adv* without difficulty — see EASILY
fluff *n* a soft airy substance or covering — see FUZZ
fluffy *adj* resembling air in lightness — see AIRY 1
fluid *adj* **1** capable of moving like a liquid ⟨warm the jam until it is *fluid*, then spread it over the cake⟩
synonyms flowing, fluent, liquid
related words diluted, thin, watery, weak
near antonyms clotted, coagulated, gelatinous, gelled, jelled, jellied, thick; gluey, glutinous, gooey, gummy, viscous
antonyms hard, solid
2 capable of being readily changed — see FLEXIBLE 1
3 involving minimal difficulty or effort — see EASY 1
4 likely to change frequently, suddenly, or unexpectedly — see FICKLE 1
fluky *adj* **1** coming or happening by good luck especially unexpectedly — see FORTUNATE 1
2 happening by chance — see ACCIDENTAL
flume *n* **1** a narrow opening between hillsides or

mountains that can be used for passage — see CANYON
2 an open man-made passageway for water — see CHANNEL 1
flunk *vb* to be unsuccessful — see FAIL 2
flunky *also* **flunkey** *n* **1** a person hired to perform household or personal services — see SERVANT
2 a person who flatters another in order to get ahead — see SYCOPHANT
fluorescence *n* the steady giving off of the form of radiation that makes vision possible — see LIGHT 1
flurry *n* **1** a sudden and usually temporary growth of activity — see OUTBREAK
2 a sudden brief rush of wind — see GUST 1
flush *adj* **1** having a healthy reddish skin tone — see RUDDY
2 having a surface without bends, breaks, or irregularities — see LEVEL
3 having active strength of body or mind — see VIGOROUS 1
4 having goods, property, or money in abundance — see RICH 1
5 possessing or covered with great numbers or amounts of something specified — see RIFE
flush *n* **1** a rosy appearance of the cheeks — see BLOOM 2
2 a state or time of great activity, thriving, or achievement — see BLOOM 1
3 a sudden intense expression of strong feeling — see OUTBURST 1
flush *vb* **1** to pour liquid over or through in order to cleanse ⟨use this cleaner to *flush* the drain in the sink⟩
synonyms irrigate, rinse, sluice, wash
related words deluge, engulf, flood, inundate, swamp; flow, gush, rush, stream; douche, hose; drench, saturate, soak; douse, slosh, splash
2 to develop a rosy facial color (as from excitement or embarrassment) — see BLUSH
fluster *n* **1** a state of nervous or irritated concern — see FRET
2 the emotional state of being made self-consciously uncomfortable — see EMBARRASSMENT 1
fluster *vb* to throw into a state of self-conscious distress — see EMBARRASS 1
flustering *adj* causing embarrassment — see AWKWARD 3
flutter *n* a sudden and usually temporary growth of activity — see OUTBREAK
flutter *vb* **1** to make an irregular series of quick, sudden movements — see FLIT
2 to move or cause to move with a striking motion — see FLAP
fluttery *adj* easily excited by nature — see EXCITABLE
flux *n* a flowing or coming in — see INFLUX
flux *vb* to go from a solid to a liquid state — see LIQUEFY
fly *vb* **1** to move through the air with or as if with outstretched wings ⟨the Wright brothers realized mankind's age-old wish to *fly*⟩
synonyms glide, plane, soar, wing
related words drift, float, hang, hover, waft; coast, cruise, sail, sweep; dart, flit, flutter; catapult, jet, orbit, rocket
2 to get free from a dangerous or confining situation — see ESCAPE 1
3 to proceed or move quickly — see HURRY 2

4 to hasten away from something dangerous or frightening — see RUN 2

flying *adj* **1** acting or done with excessive or careless speed — see HASTY 1

2 moving, proceeding, or acting with great speed — see FAST 1

flying *n* travel through the air by the use of wings — see ¹FLIGHT

flyspeck *n* a very small piece — see BIT 1

foam *n* a light mass of fine bubbles formed in or on a liquid ⟨a steaming cup of hot cocoa with a sprinkling of marshmallows drifting through the *foam*⟩
   synonyms froth, head, lather, spume, suds, surf
   related words mousse; mist, spindrift, spray; scum

foaming *adj* feeling or showing anger — see ANGRY

foamy *adj* covered with, consisting of, or resembling foam ⟨*foamy* milk shakes⟩
   synonyms frothy, lathery, sudsy
   related words bubbly, effervescent, fizzy, sparkling; soapy

focus *n* a thing or place that is of greatest importance to an activity or interest — see CENTER 1

focus *vb* to fix (as one's attention) steadily toward a central objective — see CONCENTRATE 2

focused *also* **focussed** *adj* **1** having the mind fixed on something — see ATTENTIVE

2 not divided or scattered among several areas of interest or concern — see WHOLE 1

foe *n* one that is hostile toward another — see ENEMY

fog *n* **1** a state of mental confusion — see HAZE 2

2 an atmospheric condition in which suspended particles in the air rob it of its transparency — see HAZE 1

fog *vb* **1** to make (something) unclear to the understanding — see CONFUSE 2

2 to make dark, dim, or indistinct — see CLOUD 1

foggy *adj* **1** filled with or dimmed by fine particles (as of dust or water) in suspension — see HAZY 1

2 not seen or understood clearly — see FAINT 1

fogy *also* **fogey** *n* a person with old-fashioned ideas ⟨old *fogies* who said that rap music would never last⟩
   synonyms antediluvian, dodo, fossil, fuddy-duddy, reactionary, stick-in-the-mud
   related words conservative, rightist, tory; old hand, old-timer, veteran; old maid
   near antonyms liberal, progressive, radical
   antonyms modern

foible *n* a defect in character — see FAULT 1

foil *vb* to prevent from achieving a goal — see FRUSTRATE

foist *vb* to offer (something fake, useless, or inferior) as genuine, useful, or valuable ⟨shopkeepers who *foist* shoddy souvenirs on unsuspecting tourists⟩
   synonyms palm off, pass off
   related words force, impose, inflict; counterfeit, fake, forge; distort, falsify, misrepresent

fold *n* a group of people sharing a common interest and relating together socially — see GANG 2

fold *vb* **1** to lay one part over or against another part of ⟨*fold* the blanket so that it will fit inside the trunk⟩
   synonyms double
   related words overlap, overlay, overlie; collapse, telescope; close, shut
   antonyms extend, open, spread, unfold

2 to be unsuccessful — see FAIL 2

folder *n* a short printed publication with no cover or with a paper cover — see PAMPHLET

foliage *n* green leaves or plants — see GREENERY 1

folk *n* **1** **folks** *pl* a group of persons who come from the same ancestor — see FAMILY 1

2 one of the segments of society into which people are grouped — see CLASS 1

3 **folks** *pl* human beings in general — see PEOPLE 1

folklore *n* the body of customs, beliefs, stories, and sayings associated with a people, thing, or place ⟨the Scottish Highlands are rich in *folklore*⟩
   synonyms legend, lore, myth, mythology, tradition
   related words information, knowledge, wisdom; anecdote, fable, folktale, old wives' tale, tale, yarn

follow *vb* **1** to come after in time ⟨a wrap-up always *follows* the Super Bowl broadcast⟩
   synonyms postdate, succeed, supervene
   related words displace, replace, supersede, supplant; ensue
   antonyms antedate, precede, predate

2 to go after or on the track of ⟨let's *follow* the boys to their hiding place⟩
   synonyms chase, dog, hound, pursue, shadow, tag, tail, trace, track, trail
   related words accompany, chaperone (*or* chaperon), escort; hunt, search (for), seek; eye, observe, watch
   near antonyms head
   antonyms guide, lead, pilot

3 to act according to the commands of — see OBEY

4 to make one's way through, across, or over — see TRAVERSE

5 to take notice of and be guided by — see HEED 1

follower *n* one who follows the opinions or teachings of another ⟨the *followers* of Gandhi have spread his philosophy of nonviolence all over the world⟩
   synonyms adherent, convert, disciple, partisan, pupil, votary
   related words apostle; faithful, loyalist; advocate, backer, champion, supporter; scholar, student; ideologist, sectarian; admirer, cultist, devotee, enthusiast, fan, idolater (*or* idolator), worshipper (*or* worshiper), zealot; flunky (*also* flunkey), hanger-on, henchman, lackey, satellite, stooge, sycophant, toady, yes-man
   near antonyms apostate, defector, renegade, traitor, turncoat
   antonyms leader

following *prep* subsequent to in time or order — see AFTER

following *adj* being the one that comes immediately after another — see NEXT

following *n* **1** a body of employees or servants who accompany and wait on a person — see CORTEGE 1

2 a group of people showing intense devotion to a cause, person, or work (as a film) — see CULT 1

3 the act of going after or in the tracks of another — see PURSUIT

follow through *vb* to carry through (as a process) to completion — see PERFORM 1

folly *n* **1** a foolish act or idea ⟨the American purchase of Alaska was originally considered a grand *folly*⟩

synonyms absurdity, asininity, fatuity, foolery, idiocy, imbecility, inanity, insanity, lunacy, stupidity
related words absurdness, craziness, foolishness, madness, senselessness, witlessness; monkeyshine(s), shenanigans, tomfoolery; drivel, humbug, nonsense, twaddle; blunder, bungle, flub, goof, howler
near antonyms discretion, forethought, prudence, sagacity, wisdom; brainstorm, inspiration
2 lack of good sense or judgment — see FOOLISHNESS 1
3 language, behavior, or ideas that are absurd and contrary to good sense — see NONSENSE 1
foment *vb* to cause or encourage the development of — see INCITE 1
fomenter *n* a person who stirs up public feelings especially of discontent — see AGITATOR
fond *adj* **1** having a liking or affection ⟨even lots of city people are *fond* of country music⟩
synonyms attached, inclined, partial
related words crazy (about *or* over), enamored, enraptured, gone (on), infatuated, mad (about), nuts (about); desirous, eager, enthusiastic, excited, gung ho, keen
near antonyms apathetic, cool, indifferent, uninterested; contemptuous, disdainful, scornful; antagonistic, antipathetic, hostile; alienated, disaffected, disenchanted, estranged
antonyms allergic, averse, disinclined
2 feeling or showing love — see LOVING
fondle *vb* to touch or handle in a tender or loving manner ⟨a cat who enjoys being *fondled* by his loving owners⟩
synonyms caress, love, pat, pet, stroke
related words cuddle, nestle, nose, nuzzle, snuggle; cradle, embrace, enfold, hug; bounce, dandle; knead, massage; baby, coddle, indulge, mollycoddle, pamper, spoil
fondness *n* **1** a feeling of strong or constant regard for and dedication to someone — see LOVE 1
2 positive regard for something — see LIKING
food *n* substances intended to be eaten ⟨a simple, little restaurant with excellent *food*⟩
synonyms bread, chow, eatables, edibles, fare, foodstuffs, grub, meat, provender, provisions, table, viands, victuals, vittles
related words rations; aliment, nutriment; diet, nurture, sustenance; mess, pap; feed, fodder, forage, slop, swill; feast, meal, refreshments, repast, spread; board; dish, plate, serving
near antonyms poison
foodstuffs *n pl* substances intended to be eaten — see FOOD
fool *n* **1** a person who lacks good sense or judgment ⟨only a *fool* would attempt to climb that mountain unprepared⟩
synonyms booby, goose, half-wit, jackass, lunatic, nincompoop, ninny, nitwit, nut, simpleton, turkey, yo-yo
related words daredevil; madman, madwoman; blockhead, cretin, dodo, dolt, dope, dumbbell, dummy, dunce, idiot, imbecile, moron; featherbrain, scatterbrain; butt, dupe, laughingstock, mockery, monkey; chump, loser, schlemiel
near antonyms sage, thinker; brain, genius
2 a person formerly kept in a royal or noble household to amuse with jests and pranks ⟨a king's *fool* could get away with saying things that others in the palace couldn't⟩
synonyms jester, motley

related words buffoon, clown, comedian, comedienne, comic, cutup, harlequin, zany
fool *vb* **1** to cause to believe what is untrue — see DECEIVE
2 to make jokes — see JOKE
fool (around) *vb* **1** to engage in attention-getting playful or boisterous behavior — see CUT UP
2 to spend time in aimless activity — see FIDDLE (AROUND)
fool (with) *vb* to handle thoughtlessly, ignorantly, or mischievously — see TAMPER
foolery *n* **1** a foolish act or idea — see FOLLY 1
2 wildly playful or mischievous behavior — see HORSEPLAY
foolhardy *adj* **1** foolishly adventurous or bold ⟨hikers who were *foolhardy* enough to remain on the summit during a thunderstorm⟩
synonyms brash, daredevil, madcap, overbold, overconfident, reckless
related words adventuresome, adventurous, audacious, bold, daring, venturesome, venturous; brave, courageous, dauntless, fearless, intrepid, lionhearted, stouthearted, undaunted, valiant; hotheaded; impetuous, impulsive, rash; brainless, foolish, harebrained, scatterbrained; careless, heedless, thoughtless; hasty, headlong, precipitate
near antonyms unadventurous, unambitious; fainthearted, timid, timorous; calm, cool, levelheaded, sensible; alert, intelligent, quick-witted, sharp
antonyms careful, cautious, heedful, prudent
2 having or showing a lack of concern for the consequences of one's actions — see RECKLESS 1
fooling *adj* marked by or expressive of mild or good-natured teasing — see QUIZZICAL
foolish *adj* **1** showing or marked by a lack of good sense or judgment ⟨*foolish* people who thought that the world would end in the year 2000⟩ ⟨a *foolish* scheme that was supposed to make us all rich⟩
synonyms absurd, asinine, balmy, brainless, cockeyed, crazy, cuckoo, daffy, daft, dotty, fatuous, harebrained, half-witted, insane, jerky, kooky, loony (*also* looney), lunatic, mad, nonsensical, nutty, preposterous, sappy, screwball, senseless, silly, simpleminded, stupid, unwise, wacky, weak-minded, witless, zany
related words dumb, idiotic, imbecilic, moronic; fallacious, illogical, invalid, irrational, unreasonable; farcical, laughable, ludicrous, ridiculous
near antonyms brainy, bright, clever, intelligent, smart; logical, rational, reasonable, valid
antonyms judicious, prudent, sage, sane, sapient, sensible, sound, wise
2 conceived or made without regard for reason or reality — see FANTASTIC 1
foolishness *n* **1** lack of good sense or judgment ⟨the *foolishness* of going off to search for the fountain of youth⟩
synonyms absurdity, asininity, balminess, brainlessness, craziness, daftness, fatuity, folly, inanity, insanity, lunacy, madness, nonsensicalness, nuttiness, preposterousness, senselessness, silliness, simplicity, wackiness, witlessness, zaniness
related words idiocy, imbecility, stupidity; fallacy, irrationality, unreasonableness; laughableness, ludicrousness, ridiculousness
near antonyms logicalness, rationality, reasonableness, validity
antonyms prudence, sageness, sanity, sapience, sensibleness, soundness, wisdom

2 language, behavior, or ideas that are absurd and contrary to good sense — see NONSENSE 1

3 the quality or state of lacking intelligence or quickness of mind — see STUPIDITY 1

foot *n* the lowest part, place, or point — see BOTTOM 3

foot *vb* to give what is owed for — see PAY 2

foot (it) *vb* **1** to go on foot — see WALK

2 to perform a series of usually rhythmic bodily movements to music — see DANCE 1

foot (up) *vb* to combine (numbers) into a single sum — see ADD 2

foothold *n* a place from which an advance (as for military operations) is made — see BASE 2

footing *n* **1** an immaterial thing upon which something else rests — see BASE 1

2 position with regard to conditions and circumstances — see SITUATION 1

3 the placement of someone or something in relation to others in a vertical arrangement — see RANK 1

footloose *adj* **1** not bound, confined, or detained by force — see FREE 3

2 not held back by rules, duties, or worries — see FREEWHEELING

footpath *n* a rough course or way formed by or as if by repeated footsteps — see TRAIL 1

footprint *n* the mark or impression made by a foot ⟨mysterious *footprints* along the beach⟩

synonyms footstep, step

related words hoofprint; spoor, track; sign, trace, vestige

footstep *n* the mark or impression made by a foot — see FOOTPRINT

foozle *vb* to make or do (something) in a clumsy or unskillful way — see BOTCH

fop *n* a man extremely interested in his clothing and personal appearance — see DANDY 1

for *conj* for the reason that — see SINCE

forage *vb* to feed on grass or herbs — see ¹GRAZE

forage (for) *vb* to go in search of — see SEEK 1

foray *n* a sudden attack on and entrance into hostile territory — see RAID 1

foray (into) *vb* to enter for conquest or plunder — see INVADE

forbear *vb* to resist the temptation of ⟨she's old enough to make her own decisions, so we must *forbear* criticizing her taste in clothes⟩

synonyms abstain (from), forgo (*also* forego), keep (from), refrain (from)

related words avoid, eschew, shun; check, constrain, curb, inhibit; deny, refuse, withhold; buck, combat, fight

near antonyms capitulate, knuckle under, submit, surrender

antonyms give in (to), succumb (to), yield (to)

forbearance *n* the capacity to endure what is difficult or disagreeable without complaining — see PATIENCE

forbearing *adj* accepting pains or hardships calmly or without complaint — see PATIENT 1

forbid *vb* to order not to do or use or to be done or used ⟨smoking is *forbidden* throughout the building⟩ ⟨we *forbid* you to see him⟩

synonyms ban, bar, enjoin, interdict, outlaw, prohibit, proscribe

related words deter, discourage, dissuade; repress, suppress; halt, preclude, prevent, stop; embargo, exclude, rule out, shut out; debar, deprive, disal-

low, reject, veto; check, curb, inhibit, restrain; block, hinder, impede, obstruct

near antonyms approve, endorse (*also* indorse), sanction; authorize, license (*also* licence); abet, encourage, promote, support; bid, command, order; abide, bear, endure, tolerate

antonyms allow, let, permit, suffer

forbidden *adj* that may not be permitted — see IMPERMISSIBLE

forbidding *adj* **1** causing fear — see FEARFUL 1

2 harsh and threatening in manner or appearance — see GRIM 1

forbidding *n* the act of ordering that something not be done or used — see PROHIBITION 1

force *n* **1** a body of persons at work or available for work ⟨the nation's labor *force*⟩

synonyms help, manpower, personnel, pool, staff

related words labor, proletariat, rank and file; band, company, crew, gang, outfit, party, team; employee, helper, hireling, worker

2 the use of power to impose one's will on another ⟨a cruel tyrant who disbanded the parliament and ruled by *force*⟩

synonyms coercion, compulsion, constraint, duress, pressure

related words browbeating, bulldozing, bullying; fear, intimidation, menace, sword, terror, terrorism, threat, violence; might, muscle, strength; hardheadedness, self-will, willfulness; strain, stress

near antonyms agreement, approval, consent, permission; persuasion, reason

3 the ability to exert effort for the accomplishment of a task — see POWER 2

4 the capacity to persuade — see COGENCY 1

5 the quality of an utterance that provokes interest and produces an effect — see ¹PUNCH 1

6 the use of brute strength to cause harm to a person or property — see VIOLENCE

force *vb* to cause (a person) to give in to pressure ⟨*forced* the natives to sell their land⟩ ⟨hunger *forced* the refugees to steal⟩

synonyms coerce, compel, constrain, drive, make, muscle, obligate, oblige, press, pressure

related words browbeat, bulldoze, bully; high-pressure, intimidate, menace, terrorize, threaten

near antonyms allow, let, permit; convince, induce, persuade

forced *adj* **1** forcing one's compliance or participation by or as if by law — see MANDATORY

2 lacking in natural or spontaneous quality — see ARTIFICIAL 1

3 not made or done willingly or by choice — see INVOLUNTARY 1

forceful *adj* **1** having the power to persuade — see COGENT

2 marked by or uttered with forcefulness — see EMPHATIC 1

3 not showing weakness or uncertainty — see FIRM 1

4 having power over the minds or behavior of others — see INFLUENTIAL 1

forcefully *adv* in a vigorous and forceful manner — see HARD 3

forcefulness *n* **1** the capacity to persuade — see COGENCY 1

2 the quality of an utterance that provokes interest and produces an effect — see ¹PUNCH 1

3 the quality or state of being forceful (as in expression) — see VEHEMENCE 1

THESAURUS

forcibly *adv* in a vigorous and forceful manner — see HARD 3

ford *n* a place where a body of water (as a sea or river) is shallow — see SHOAL

forearm *vb* to prepare (oneself) mentally or emotionally — see FORTIFY 1

forebear *also* **forbear** *n* a person who is several generations earlier in an individual's line of descent — see ANCESTOR 1

forebode *also* **forbode** *vb* to show signs of a favorable or successful outcome — see BODE

foreboding *adj* being or showing a sign of evil or calamity to come — see OMINOUS

foreboding *n* **1** a feeling that something bad will happen — see PREMONITION
2 something believed to be a sign or warning of a future event — see OMEN
3 suspicion or fear of future harm or misfortune — see APPREHENSION 1

forecast *n* a declaration that something will happen in the future — see PREDICTION

forecast *vb* to tell of or describe beforehand — see FORETELL

forecaster *n* one who predicts future events or developments — see PROPHET

forecasting *n* a declaration that something will happen in the future — see PREDICTION

foredoom *vb* to determine the fate of in advance — see DESTINE

forefather *n* a person who is several generations earlier in an individual's line of descent — see ANCESTOR 1

forefront *n* the leading or most important part of a movement ⟨a politician who was in the *forefront* of women's rights⟩
synonyms vanguard
related words spearhead
near antonyms rank and file

forego *vb* to go or come before in time — see PRECEDE

foregoer *n* **1** one that announces or indicates the later arrival of another — see FORERUNNER 1
2 something belonging to an earlier time from which something else was later developed — see ANCESTOR 2

foregoing *adj* going before another in time or order — see PREVIOUS

forehanded *adj* having or showing awareness of and preparation for the future — see FORESIGHTED

foreign *adj* **1** being, relating to, or characteristic of a country other than one's own ⟨more Americans should take an interest in *foreign* languages⟩
synonyms alien, nonnative
related words imported, introduced, naturalized, transplanted; international, multicultural, multinational; distant, far-off, overseas, remote; bizarre, exotic, outlandish, strange
near antonyms endemic, local; aboriginal, indigenous
antonyms domestic, native
2 not being a vital part of or belonging to something — see EXTRINSIC

foreigner *n* a person who is not native to or known to a community — see STRANGER

foreknow *vb* to realize or know about beforehand — see FORESEE

foreknowledge *n* the special ability to see or know about events before they actually occur — see FORESIGHT 1

foreman *n* the person (as an employer or supervisor) who tells people and especially workers what to do — see BOSS

foremost *adj* **1** coming before all others in importance ⟨Albert Einstein is regarded by many as the *foremost* figure of the 20th century⟩
synonyms arch, cardinal, central, chief, dominant, first, grand, greatest, highest, key, leading, main, paramount, predominant, preeminent, premier, primary, principal, sovereign, supreme
related words distinguished, eminent, notable, noteworthy, illustrious, outstanding, prestigious, stellar, superior; important, major, momentous, significant; incomparable, matchless, unequaled (*or* unequalled), unparalleled, unsurpassed
near antonyms inconsequential, insignificant, minor, trivial, unimportant; collateral, inferior, secondary, subordinate, subsidiary
antonyms last, least
2 highest in rank or authority — see HEAD

forename *n* a name that is placed before one's family name ⟨a long string of *forenames* was given to the latest addition to the royal family⟩
synonyms Christian name, given name
related words appellation, denomination, designation; epithet, handle, nickname, sobriquet (*also* soubriquet); alias, nom de plume, pen name, pseudonym

forenoon *n* the time from sunrise until noon — see MORNING 1

foreordain *vb* to determine the fate of in advance — see DESTINE

forepart *n* a forward part or surface — see FRONT 1

forerunner *n* **1** one that announces or indicates the later arrival of another ⟨the return of the swallows is traditionally regarded as a *forerunner* of spring⟩
synonyms angel, foregoer, harbinger, herald, precursor
related words foreboder, foreshadower, foretaste, forewarning; advertiser, announcer, crier, proclaimer; courier, messenger, runner; augury, omen, portent, presage; mark, sign, symptom; bellwether
2 something belonging to an earlier time from which something else was later developed — see ANCESTOR 2

foresee *vb* to realize or know about beforehand ⟨a freak accident that no one could possibly have *foreseen*⟩
synonyms anticipate, divine, foreknow
related words augur, forecast, foretell, presage, prognosticate, prophesy; envisage, foreshadow, prefigure, visualize; forewarn; preview; descry, discern, perceive; apprehend, dread, fear

foreseeing *adj* having or showing awareness of and preparation for the future — see FORESIGHTED

foreseer *n* one who predicts future events or developments — see PROPHET

foreshadow *vb* to give a slight indication of beforehand ⟨a series of small tremors that *foreshadowed* the massive earthquake the next day⟩
synonyms prefigure
related words anticipate, foreknow, foresee; forecast, foretell, predict, prognosticate, prophesy; forewarn; augur, bode, forebode (*also* forbode), portend, presage, promise; connote, hint, imply, insinuate, intimate, suggest

foreshadowing *n* something believed to be a sign or warning of a future event — see OMEN

foresight *n* **1** the special ability to see or know about events before they actually occur ⟨a mysterious woman who claims to have the gift of *foresight*⟩
  synonyms foreknowledge, prescience
  related words premonition, presentiment; clairvoyance, extrasensory perception, sixth sense; omniscience; divination
  2 concern or preparation for the future ⟨had the *foresight* to realize the global importance of the Internet⟩
  synonyms farsightedness, foresightedness, forethought, prescience, providence
  related words precaution, premeditation; discretion, insight, prudence, sagacity, wisdom
  near antonyms hindsight
  antonyms improvidence, shortsightedness

foresighted *adj* having or showing awareness of and preparation for the future ⟨the *foresighted* conservationists who worked to create the national park system⟩
  synonyms farsighted, forehanded, foreseeing, forethoughtful, prescient, provident
  related words careful, cautious; insightful, perceptive, prudent, sage, wise
  near antonyms careless, heedless, incautious
  antonyms improvident, shortsighted

foresightedness *n* concern or preparation for the future — see FORESIGHT 2

forest *n* a dense growth of trees and shrubs covering a large area ⟨the endless *forest* that the first European settlers encountered⟩
  synonyms timber, timberland, wood(s), woodland
  related words coppice, copse, grove, scrubland, stand, thicket; greenwood, wildwood; woodlot

forestall *vb* to keep from happening by taking action in advance — see PREVENT

forestallment *n* the act or practice of keeping something from happening — see PREVENTION

foretell *vb* to tell of or describe beforehand ⟨a 16th century astrologer who, some claim, accurately *foretold* 20th century events⟩
  synonyms augur, forecast, predict, presage, prognosticate, prophesy
  related words forewarn; bode, forebode (*also* forbode), portend; anticipate, divine, foreknow, foresee; announce, declare, proclaim
  near antonyms recount, relate, report

foreteller *n* one who predicts future events or developments — see PROPHET

foretelling *n* a declaration that something will happen in the future — see PREDICTION

forethought *n* concern or preparation for the future — see FORESIGHT 2

forethoughtful *adj* having or showing awareness of and preparation for the future — see FORESIGHTED

forever *adv* **1** for all time — see EVER 1
  2 on every relevant occasion — see ALWAYS 1

forevermore *adv* for all time — see EVER 1

forewarn *vb* to give notice to beforehand especially of danger or risk — see WARN

forewarning *n* the act or an instance of telling beforehand of danger or risk — see WARNING 1

foreword *n* a short section (as of a book) that leads to or explains the main part — see INTRODUCTION

forfeit *n* a sum of money to be paid as a punishment — see FINE

forfeiture *n* a sum of money to be paid as a punishment — see FINE

forgather *or* **foregather** *vb* to come together into one body or place — see ASSEMBLE 1

¹**forge** *vb* **1** to imitate or copy especially in order to deceive — see FAKE 1
  2 to produce or bring about especially by long or repeated effort — see HAMMER (OUT)
  3 to shape with a hammer — see HAMMER 1

²**forge** *vb* to move forward along a course — see GO 1

forged *adj* being such in appearance only and made or manufactured with the intention of committing fraud — see COUNTERFEIT

forgery *n* an imitation that is passed off as genuine — see FAKE 1

forget *vb* **1** to be unable to recall or think of ⟨I *forget* exactly on which street that the house is⟩
  synonyms unlearn
  related words lose, miss; blank; disregard, ignore, neglect, overlook
  near antonyms reminisce; remind
  antonyms mind [*chiefly dialect*], recall, recollect, remember
  2 to fail to give proper attention to — see NEGLECT 1
  3 to leave undone or unattended to especially through carelessness — see NEGLECT 2
  4 to miss the opportunity or obligation — see NEGLECT 3

forgetful *adj* inclined to forget what one has learned or to do what one should ⟨we become more *forgetful* as we get older⟩
  synonyms absentminded
  related words absent, abstracted, lost, oblivious, preoccupied, unmindful; amnesiac, senile; lax, neglectful, negligent, remiss, slack; careless, heedless, inconsiderate, thoughtless
  near antonyms alert, keen, sharp; careful, conscientious, heedful, thoughtful
  antonyms retentive

forgetfulness *n* a state of being disregardful or unconscious of one's surroundings, concerns, or obligations — see OBLIVION

forgivable *adj* worthy of forgiveness — see VENIAL

forgive *vb* **1** to cease to have feelings of anger or bitterness toward ⟨it is not easy to *forgive* those who have hurt us⟩
  synonyms pardon
  related words absolve, acquit, clear, exculpate, exonerate, vindicate; remit, shrive; condone, disregard, excuse, ignore, pass over, shrug off
  near antonyms smart; despise, detest, dislike, hate, loathe; avenge, redress, revenge
  antonyms resent
  2 to overlook or dismiss as of little importance — see EXCUSE 1

forgiveness *n* release from the guilt or penalty of an offense — see PARDON

forgo *also* **forego** *vb* to resist the temptation of — see FORBEAR

forgotten *adj* left unoccupied or unused — see ABANDONED

fork *vb* to go or move in different directions from a central point — see SEPARATE 2

forlorn *adj* **1** feeling unhappiness — see SAD 1
  2 sad from lack of companionship or separation from others — see LONESOME 1

forlornness *n* **1** a state or spell of low spirits — see SADNESS
  2 utter loss of hope — see DESPAIR 1

form *n* **1** the outward appearance of something as

distinguished from its substance ⟨carved the block of wood into the *form* of a duck⟩
synonyms cast, configuration, conformation, figure, geometry, shape
related words contour, outline, profile, silhouette; framework, skeleton, situation; arrangement, layout, organization, pattern, plan, setup
near antonyms composition, material, matter, stuff, substance
2 a piece of paper with information written or to be written on it ⟨I filled out all the *forms* for applying to the school⟩
synonyms blank, document, paper
related words instrument, writ
3 personal conduct or behavior as evaluated by an accepted standard of appropriateness for a social or professional setting — see MANNER 1
4 a state of being or fitness — see CONDITION 1
5 a three-dimensional representation of the human body used especially for displaying clothes — see MANNEQUIN 1
6 an oft-repeated action or series of actions performed in accordance with tradition or a set of rules — see RITE
7 socially acceptable behavior — see DECENCY 1
8 the means or procedure for doing something — see METHOD
9 the type of body that a person has — see PHYSIQUE
10 the way in which the elements of something (as a work of art) are arranged — see COMPOSITION 3
form *vb* **1** to take on a definite form ⟨my ideas on the subject are just starting to *form*⟩
synonyms crystallize, jell, shape (up), solidify
related words coalesce, cohere, fuse; combine, connect, join, unite
near antonyms break down, decompose, disintegrate
2 to be all the substance of — see CONSTITUTE 1
3 to bring into being by combining, shaping, or transforming materials — see MAKE 1
4 to come into existence — see BEGIN 2
5 to come to have gradually — see DEVELOP 2
formal *adj* **1** following or agreeing with established form, custom, or rules ⟨a *formal* meeting of the school board⟩ ⟨a *formal* contract that was legally binding⟩
synonyms ceremonial, ceremonious, conventional, orthodox, regular, routine
related words authorized, certified, official; accepted, correct, decorous, proper; formalistic, ritual, ritualistic; methodical, orderly, systematic
near antonyms unauthorized, unofficial; improper, incorrect, indecorous
antonyms informal, irregular, unceremonious, unconventional, unorthodox
2 being something in name or form only — see NOMINAL 1
3 marked by or showing careful attention to set forms and details — see CEREMONIOUS 1
4 relating to or suitable for wearing to an event requiring elegant dress and manners — see DRESS
5 very dignified in form, tone, or style — see ELEVATED 2
formal *n* a social gathering for dancing — see DANCE
formality *n* **1** an act or utterance that is a customary show of good manners — see CIVILITY 1
2 an oft-repeated action or series of actions per-

formed in accordance with tradition or a set of rules — see RITE
formalize *vb* to make agree with a single established standard or model — see STANDARDIZE
format *n* **1** the way in which something is sized, arranged, or organized ⟨the book's *format* is very user-friendly⟩
synonyms arrangement, configuration, conformation, formation, layout, setup
related words design, plan, scheme; composition, constitution, makeup; build, construction, structure
2 the way in which the elements of something (as a work of art) are arranged — see COMPOSITION 3
formation *n* the way in which something is sized, arranged, or organized — see FORMAT 1
formative *adj* having a role in deciding something's final form ⟨a teacher who was a *formative* influence on generations of students⟩
synonyms constructive, productive
related words causal, creative; consequential, influential
antonyms nonconstructive, nonproductive, unproductive
former *adj* having been such at some previous time ⟨the coach is a *former* professional baseball player⟩
synonyms erstwhile, late, old, onetime, past, sometime, whilom
related words bygone, dead, extinct
near antonyms contemporary, current, present; future, prospective
formidable *adj* **1** causing fear — see FEARFUL 1
2 requiring considerable physical or mental effort — see HARD 2
formless *adj* having no definite or recognizable form ⟨a *formless* mass of clay that the potter transformed into an attractive bowl⟩
synonyms amorphous, shapeless, unformed, unshaped, unstructured
related words characterless, featureless, nondescript; chaotic, disorganized, incoherent, unordered, unorganized; fuzzy, hazy, indeterminate, indistinct, obscure, unclear, vague
near antonyms coherent, ordered, organized; clear, definite, distinct
antonyms formed, shaped, structured
formulaic *adj* using or marked by the use of something else as a basis or model — see IMITATIVE
formulate *vb* **1** to convey in appropriate or telling terms — see PHRASE
2 to put (something) into proper and usually carefully worked out written form — see COMPOSE 1
formulation *n* an act, process, or means of putting something into words — see EXPRESSION 1
formulator *n* one who creates or introduces something new — see INVENTOR
forsake *vb* to cause to remain behind — see LEAVE 1
forsaken *adj* left unoccupied or unused — see ABANDONED
forsaking *n* the act of abandoning — see DERELICTION 1
forsooth *adv* **1** to tell the truth — see ACTUALLY 1
2 without any question — see INDEED 1
fort *n* a structure or place from which one can resist attack ⟨a series of *forts* along the frontier⟩
synonyms bastion, citadel, fastness, fortification, fortress, hold, stronghold

related words breastwork, bulwark, parapet, rampart; bunker, dugout

forte *n* something for which a person shows a special talent ⟨doing funny impressions of people has always been my *forte*⟩
synonyms speciality, specialty
related words area, demesne, department, discipline, domain, field, line, province, realm, sphere; element; aptness, bent, faculty, flair, genius, gift, knack, talent

forth *adv* **1** toward a point ahead in space or time — see ONWARD 1
2 toward or at a point lying in advance in space or time — see ALONG

forthcoming *adj* being soon to appear or take place ⟨everyone's excited about the *forthcoming* school vacation⟩
synonyms approaching, coming, imminent, impending, nearing, oncoming, pending, upcoming
related words future; anticipated, awaited, expected, foreseen, predicted
near antonyms bygone, former, past
antonyms late, recent

forthright *adj* **1** free in expressing one's true feelings and opinions — see FRANK
2 going straight to the point clearly and firmly — see STRAIGHTFORWARD 1

forthrightly *adv* in an honest and direct manner — see STRAIGHTFORWARD

forthrightness *n* the free expression of one's true feelings and opinions — see CANDOR

forthwith *adv* without delay — see IMMEDIATELY

fortification *n* a structure or place from which one can resist attack — see FORT

fortify *vb* **1** to prepare (oneself) mentally or emotionally ⟨Kelly *fortified* herself for the basketball tournament with a series of confidence-boosting exercises⟩
synonyms brace, forearm, nerve, ready, steel, strengthen
related words harden, inure, season, toughen; bolster, boost, buoy (up), buttress, prop (up), reinforce, support, sustain; embolden, encourage, hearten; rally, rouse, stir
near antonyms demoralize, discourage, dishearten, unnerve; debilitate, enfeeble, undermine, weaken
2 to increase the ability of (as a muscle) to exert physical force — see STRENGTHEN 1
3 to make able to withstand physical hardship, strain, or exposure — see HARDEN 2

fortitude *n* the strength of mind that enables a person to endure pain or hardship ⟨it was only with the greatest *fortitude* that the Pilgrims were able to survive their first winter in Plymouth⟩
synonyms backbone, fiber, grit, guts, pluck, spunk
related words determination, purposefulness, resoluteness, resolution; bravery, courage, fearlessness, intrepidity; endurance, stamina, tolerance; heart, mettle, spirit; audacity, boldness, brass, cheek, chutzpah (*also* chutzpa *or* hutzpah *or* hutzpa), effrontery, hardihood, nerve, temerity
near antonyms indecisiveness, irresoluteness, irresolution, vacillation; cowardliness, cravenness, faintheartedness, timidity, timorousness
antonyms spinelessness

fortress *n* a structure or place from which one can resist attack — see FORT

fortuitous *adj* **1** coming or happening by good luck especially unexpectedly — see FORTUNATE 1
2 happening by chance — see ACCIDENTAL

fortunate *adj* **1** coming or happening by good luck especially unexpectedly ⟨in a *fortunate* turn of events, the motel had one last vacancy⟩
synonyms fluky, fortuitous, happy, lucky, providential
related words convenient, opportune, seasonable, timely; unexpected, unforeseen, unlooked-for; accidental, chance, coincidental; auspicious, bright, fair, promising, propitious; benign, favorable, golden, good; advantageous, beneficial, profitable
near antonyms inconvenient, inopportune, unseasonable, untimely; anticipated, expected, foreseen; deliberate, intentional, planned; inauspicious, unpromising
antonyms luckless, unfortunate, unhappy, unlucky
2 having good luck — see LUCKY 1

fortunateness *n* success that is partly the result of chance — see LUCK 1

fortune *n* **1** what is going to happen to someone in the time ahead ⟨the telephone psychic proceeded to tell me my *fortune*—at great length⟩
synonyms future
related words circumstance, destiny, doom, lot, portion; futurities, outlook, prospect
near antonyms present
antonyms past
2 a very large amount of money ⟨the billionaire's huge mansion must have cost a *fortune*⟩
synonyms king's ransom, mint, wad
related words heap, pile, pot; bonanza, mine, treasure trove; assets, property, riches, wealth
antonyms mite, pittance
3 a state or end that seemingly has been decided beforehand — see FATE 1
4 success that is partly the result of chance — see LUCK 1
5 the total of one's money and property — see WEALTH 1

fortune–teller *n* one who predicts future events or developments — see PROPHET

forty winks *n pl* a short sleep — see ¹NAP

forum *n* a meeting featuring a group discussion ⟨a public *forum* called to find out how residents felt about a large high school being built in their neighborhood⟩
synonyms colloquy, conference, council, panel, parley, powwow, roundtable, seminar, symposium
related words caucus, town meeting; assembly, conclave, congregation, congress, convention, convocation, synod; debate, deliberation; brainstorming

forward *adv* **1** toward or at a point lying in advance in space or time — see ALONG
2 toward a point ahead in space or time — see ONWARD 1

forward *adj* showing a lack of proper social reserve or modesty — see PRESUMPTUOUS 1

forward *vb* to help the growth or development of — see FOSTER 1

fossil *n* a person with old-fashioned ideas — see FOGY

foster *vb* **1** to help the growth or development of ⟨the head librarian firmly declared that it is indeed the duty of local government to *foster* learning and a love of reading⟩

THESAURUS

synonyms advance, cultivate, encourage, forward, further, nourish, nurture, promote

related words back, champion, support, uphold; endow, finance, fund, patronize, subsidize; abet, aid, assist; advertise, boost, plug, publicize, tout; agitate (for), campaign (for), work (for)

near antonyms forbid, prevent, prohibit; battle, combat, counter, fight, oppose; repress, stifle, suppress; arrest, check, halt, retard

antonyms discourage, frustrate, hinder, inhibit

2 to bring to maturity through care and education — see BRING UP 1

foul *adj* **1** marked by wet and windy conditions ⟨the *foul* weather brought out the windbreakers and rain slickers as everyone braced for a day of rough sailing⟩

synonyms bleak, dirty, inclement, nasty, raw, rough, squally, stormy, tempestuous, turbulent

related words blustering, blustery, breezy, gusty, windblown, windswept; cloudy, overcast, sunless; rainy, snowy; foggy, hazy, misty

near antonyms clear, cloudless, rainless, sunny; balmy, calm, halcyon, peaceful, placid

antonyms clement, fair

2 not being in accordance with the rules or standards of what is fair in sport ⟨an aggressive hockey player who is known for his *foul* play and readiness for a fight⟩

synonyms dirty, illegal, unfair, unsportsmanlike

related words dishonorable, shabby, shameful; ignoble, low, mean, ungentlemanly; immoral, unethical, unjust, unprincipled, unrighteous, unscrupulous

near antonyms just, law-abiding; ethical, moral, principled, righteous; honorable, irreproachable, unimpeachable

antonyms clean, fair, legal, sportsmanlike, sportsmanly

3 causing intense displeasure, disgust, or resentment — see OFFENSIVE 1

4 depicting or referring to sexual matters in a way that is unacceptable in polite society — see OBSCENE 1

5 having an unpleasant smell — see MALODOROUS

6 not clean — see DIRTY 1

foul *vb* **1** to make dirty — see DIRTY 1

2 to make unfit for use by the addition of something harmful or undesirable — see CONTAMINATE

foulness *n* **1** the quality or state of being obscene — see OBSCENITY 1

2 the state or quality of being dirty — see DIRTINESS 1

foul play *n* **1** the intentional and unlawful taking of another person's life — see HOMICIDE

2 the use of brute strength to cause harm to a person or property — see VIOLENCE

foul–up *n* an instance of confusion ⟨there was a *foul-up* with our mail order, and not one item arrived as ordered⟩

synonyms mix-up

related words bobble, botch, bungle, fumble; blunder, error, flub, goof, mistake, slipup; chaos, confusion, disarrangement, disarray, disorder, hash, jumble, mess, muddle, shambles

foul up *vb* to make or do (something) in a clumsy or unskillful way — see BOTCH

found *vb* to be responsible for the creation and early operation or use of ⟨John Harvard did not

actually *found* the university that now bears his name⟩

synonyms constitute, establish, inaugurate, initiate, innovate, institute, introduce, launch, pioneer, set up, start

related words author, father, originate; create, invent, produce; construct, erect, put up; develop, enlarge, expand; endow, finance, fund, subsidize; arrange, organize, systematize

near antonyms abolish, annihilate, annul, nullify; end, finish, stop, terminate

antonyms close (down), phase out, shut (up)

foundation *n* **1** a public organization with a particular purpose or function — see INSTITUTION 1

2 an immaterial thing upon which something else rests — see BASE 1

founder *n* a person who establishes a whole new field of endeavor — see FATHER 2

foursquare *adj* **1** free in expressing one's true feelings and opinions — see FRANK

2 going straight to the point clearly and firmly — see STRAIGHTFORWARD 1

foursquare *adv* in an honest and direct manner — see STRAIGHTFORWARD

fox *vb* to get the better of through cleverness — see OUTWIT

foxiness *n* **1** skill in achieving one's ends through indirect, subtle, or underhanded means — see CUNNING 1

2 the inclination or practice of misleading others through lies or trickery — see DECEIT

foxy *adj* clever at attaining one's ends by indirect and often deceptive means — see ARTFUL 1

foyer *n* **1** a centrally located room in a building that serves as a gathering or waiting area or as a passageway into the interior ⟨theatergoers crowded the *foyer* during the play's intermission⟩

synonyms hall, lobby

related words entry, entryway, hallway, vestibule; concourse, corridor, gallery, passageway; antechamber, anteroom, waiting room

2 the entrance room of a building — see HALL 1

fracas *n* **1** a physical dispute between opposing individuals or groups — see FIGHT 1

2 a rough and often noisy fight usually involving several people — see BRAWL 1

fractionation *n* the act or process of a whole separating into two or more parts or pieces — see SEPARATION 1

fracture *vb* to cause to separate into pieces usually suddenly or forcibly — see BREAK 1

fragile *adj* **1** easily broken ⟨attaching the beautiful but *fragile* ornaments to the Christmas tree is always a touchy operation⟩

synonyms breakable, delicate, frail

related words dainty, fine, gossamer; flimsy, slight, tenuous; brittle, crisp, crumbly, flaky, friable, short; feeble, infirm, weak; inelastic, inflexible, stiff

near antonyms firm, solid, substantial; elastic, flexible, resilient

antonyms nonbreakable, strong, sturdy, tough, unbreakable

2 easily injured without careful handling — see TENDER 1

fragility *n* the state or quality of having a delicate structure — see DELICACY 2

fragment *n* a broken or irregular part of something that often remains incomplete ⟨charred *fragments*

of the exploded rocket were scattered over a huge area of ground⟩
synonyms bit, piece, scrap
related words shred, tatter; end, leftover, remainder, remnant; part, portion, section, segment
fragment *vb* to cause to separate into pieces usually suddenly or forcibly — see BREAK 1
fragmental *adj* lacking some necessary part — see INCOMPLETE
fragmentary *adj* lacking some necessary part — see INCOMPLETE
fragrance *n* a sweet or pleasant smell ⟨the *fragrance* of lilac trees in full bloom⟩
synonyms aroma, bouquet, incense, perfume, redolence, scent, spice
related words odor
antonyms reek, stench, stink
fragrant *adj* having a pleasant smell ⟨the balsam fir is a favorite as a Christmas tree because it is so *fragrant*⟩
synonyms ambrosial, aromatic, perfumed, redolent, savory, scented, sweet
related words flowery, fruity, pungent, spicy; odoriferous, odorous; clean, fresh, pure
near antonyms odorless, unscented; fusty, musty, stale; gamy (*or* gamey)
antonyms fetid, foul, malodorous, noisome, putrid, rancid, rank, reeking, reeky, smelly, stinking, stinky, strong
frail *adj* 1 easily broken — see FRAGILE 1
2 easily injured without careful handling — see TENDER 1
3 lacking bodily strength — see WEAK 1
4 lacking strength of will or character — see WEAK 2
frailness *n* 1 the quality or state of lacking physical strength or vigor — see WEAKNESS 1
2 the quality or state of lacking strength of will or character — see WEAKNESS 2
frailty *n* 1 a defect in character — see FAULT 1
2 the quality or state of lacking physical strength or vigor — see WEAKNESS 1
3 the quality or state of lacking strength of will or character — see WEAKNESS 2
frame *n* 1 the arrangement of parts that gives something its basic form ⟨now that the *frame* has been built, we have a better idea of the size of our new house⟩
synonyms configuration, framework, shell, skeleton, structure
related words lattice, network; contour, figure, outline, profile, shape, silhouette; chassis
2 a state of mind dominated by a particular emotion — see MOOD 1
3 the type of body that a person has — see PHYSIQUE
frame *vb* 1 to bring into being by combining, shaping, or transforming materials — see MAKE 1
2 to plan out usually with subtle skill or care — see ENGINEER
3 to put (something) into proper and usually carefully worked out written form — see COMPOSE 1
4 to work out the details of (something) in advance — see PLAN 1
framework *n* the arrangement of parts that gives something its basic form — see FRAME 1
franchise *n* the right to formally express one's position or will in an election — see VOTE 1
frank *adj* free in expressing one's true feelings and opinions ⟨our ballet teacher is very *frank* about

telling her students whether she thinks they have the talent for a career in dance⟩
synonyms candid, direct, forthright, foursquare, free-spoken, honest, open, openhearted, outspoken, plain, plainspoken, straight, straightforward, unguarded, unreserved
related words artless, earnest, sincere; outgoing, uninhibited, unrestrained; vocal, vociferous; abrupt, bluff, blunt, brusque, curt, gruff, sharp; impolite, inconsiderate, rude, tactless, undiplomatic, unsubtle
near antonyms inhibited, reserved, restrained; close-mouthed, reticent, tight-lipped; ambiguous, circuitous, equivocal, evasive; diplomatic, politic, tactful; civil, considerate, courteous, polite
antonyms dissembling
frankly *adv* to tell the truth — see ACTUALLY 1
frankness *n* the free expression of one's true feelings and opinions — see CANDOR
frantic *adj* 1 feeling overwhelming fear or worry ⟨the *frantic* parents were searching all over the fairgrounds for their lost child⟩
synonyms agitated, delirious, distraught, frenzied, hysterical
related words alarmed, anxious, disquieted, disturbed, troubled, upset, worried, wrought (up); berserk, crazed, demented, deranged, mad, maniacal (*also* maniac); raging, ranting, raving
near antonyms calm, peaceful, serene, tranquil; cool, coolheaded, undisturbed, unperturbed, untroubled
antonyms collected, composed, self-possessed
2 marked by great and often stressful excitement or activity — see FURIOUS 1
frantically *adv* in a confused and reckless manner — see HELTER-SKELTER 1
fraternal *adj* of, relating to, or befitting brothers ⟨there was a *fraternal* bond between the two boys all throughout their school years⟩
synonyms brotherly
related words familial, sisterly; chummy, friendly, neighborly
fraternity *n* 1 a group of persons formally joined together for some common interest — see ASSOCIATION 2
2 the body of people in a profession or field of activity — see CORPS
fraternize *vb* 1 to come or be together as friends — see ASSOCIATE 1
2 to take part in social activities — see SOCIALIZE
fraud *n* one who makes false claims of identity or expertise — see IMPOSTOR
fraudulent *adj* 1 marked by, based on, or done by the use of dishonest methods to acquire something of value ⟨hoping to get millions from the insurance company, the man made the *fraudulent* claim that he had been seriously injured in the accident⟩
synonyms crooked, deceitful, defrauding, dishonest, double-dealing, false
related words deceptive, misleading, specious
near antonyms legitimate, true, valid
antonyms aboveboard, honest, truthful
2 given to or marked by cheating and deception — see DISHONEST 2
fraught *adj* possessing or covered with great numbers or amounts of something specified — see RIFE
fray *n* 1 a forceful effort to reach a goal or objective — see STRUGGLE 1

THESAURUS

2 a physical dispute between opposing individuals or groups — see FIGHT 1

3 a rough and often noisy fight usually involving several people — see BRAWL 1

fray *vb* to damage or diminish by continued friction — see ABRADE 1

frayed *adj* worn or torn into or as if into rags — see RAGGED 2

freak *adj* being out of the ordinary — see EXCEPTIONAL

freak *n* **1** a person, thing, or event that is not normal ⟨that snowstorm in April was a *freak*, since our weather is usually much balmier by then⟩

synonyms abnormality, anomaly, monster, monstrosity

related words malformation, mutant, mutation; character, crackbrain, crackpot, eccentric, kook, oddball, screwball, weirdo; deviant; maverick, nonconformist

near antonyms sample, specimen; standard

antonyms average, norm

2 a person with a strong and habitual liking for something — see FAN

3 a sudden impulsive and apparently unmotivated idea or action — see WHIM

freak (out) *vb* **1** to trouble the mind of; to make uneasy — see DISTURB 1

2 to yield to mental or emotional stress — see CRACK 2

freakish *adj* prone to sudden illogical changes of mind, ideas, or actions — see WHIMSICAL

freakishness *n* an inclination to sudden illogical changes of mind, ideas, or actions — see WHIMSICALITY

freckle *vb* to mark with small spots especially unevenly — see SPOT

freckled *adj* marked with spots — see SPOTTED 1

free *adj* **1** not being under the rule or control of another ⟨the 20th century saw many African countries become *free* after many years of European rule⟩

synonyms autonomous, independent, self-governing, separate, sovereign

related words freeborn; delivered, emancipated, freed, liberated, manumitted, redeemed, released; unconquered, ungoverned, unruled, unsupervised; empowered, enfranchised; democratic, republican

near antonyms captive, conquered, enslaved, subdued, subjugated; inferior, subordinate, subservient

antonyms dependent, subject, unfree

2 no longer burdened with something unpleasant or painful ⟨after our son arrived home safely, we were grateful to be *free* from worry⟩

synonyms disencumbered, quit, unburdened

related words delivered, freed, liberated, released; unhampered, unimpeded

3 not bound, confined, or detained by force ⟨all of the animals in the game preserve are *free* to roam all over its vast area⟩

synonyms footloose, loose, unbound, unconfined, unrestrained

related words escaped; uncaged, unchained, unfettered, unleashed; uncaught; unanchored, unbolted, undone, unfastened, untied; clear, disengaged, unengaged

phrases at large, at liberty

near antonyms caught; caged, chained, leashed; anchored, bolted, fastened, shackled, tied

antonyms bound, confined, restrained, unfree

4 not costing or charging anything ⟨although the museum normally charges admission, on Wednesdays it is *free* to all⟩

synonyms complimentary, gratis, gratuitous

related words nominal; discretionary, freewill, optional, voluntary; honorary, uncompensated, unpaid

near antonyms paid

5 allowing passage without obstruction — see OPEN 1

6 giving or sharing in abundance and without hesitation — see GENEROUS 1

7 not being in a state of use, activity, or employment — see INACTIVE 2

8 showing a lack of proper social reserve or modesty — see PRESUMPTUOUS 1

free *vb* **1** to set free (as from slavery or confinement) ⟨a global crusade to *free* Nelson Mandela from a South African prison had emerged⟩

synonyms discharge, emancipate, enfranchise, liberate, loose, loosen, manumit, release, spring, unbind, uncage, unchain, unfetter

related words bail (out), deliver, parole, ransom, redeem, rescue; disengage, disentangle, extricate

near antonyms manacle, shackle, trammel; immure, imprison, incarcerate, intern, jail; conquer, enslave, subdue, subjugate

antonyms bind, confine, enchain, fetter, restrain

2 to arrange clear passage of (something) by removing obstructions — see OPEN 2

3 to rid the surface of (as an area) from things in the way — see CLEAR 1

4 to set (a person or thing) free of something that encumbers — see RID

5 to set free from entanglement or difficulty — see EXTRICATE

freebie *or* **freebee** *n* something given to someone without expectation of a return — see GIFT 1

freebooter *n* someone who engages in robbery of ships at sea — see PIRATE

freedom *n* **1** the state of being free from the control or power of another ⟨we owe our *freedom* to the untold numbers of soldiers who have fought in our nation's wars since its founding⟩

synonyms autonomy, independence, liberty, self-government, sovereignty

related words emancipation, enfranchisement, liberation, manumission, release

near antonyms captivity, enchainment, enslavement, imprisonment, incarceration, subjugation

antonyms dependence, subjection

2 the right to act or move freely ⟨as special guests of the owners, the youngsters had full *freedom* of the resort and its private beach⟩

synonyms authorization, free hand, latitude, license (*or* licence), run

related words authority, mandate, power; range, room, space

free–for–all *adj* freely available for use or participation by all — see OPEN 2

free–for–all *n* a rough and often noisy fight usually involving several people — see BRAWL 1

free hand *n* the right to act or move freely — see FREEDOM 2

freehanded *adj* giving or sharing in abundance and without hesitation — see GENEROUS 1

freeing *n* the act of setting free from slavery — see LIBERATION

freely *adv* **1** of one's own free will — see VOLUNTARILY

2 without difficulty — see EASILY

free–spoken *adj* free in expressing one's true feelings and opinions — see FRANK

freestanding *adj* not physically attached to another unit — see SEPARATE 2

freeway *n* a passage cleared for public vehicular travel — see WAY 1

freewheeling *adj* not held back by rules, duties, or worries ⟨James Bond has long been the model of the *freewheeling* hero who encounters danger and excitement in every corner of the globe⟩
synonyms footloose
related words easygoing, nonchalant, relaxed; unattached, uncommitted; unbridled, ungoverned, unrestrained; uninhibited, unsuppressed; self-assured, self-confident, self-reliant
near antonyms attached, committed
antonyms tied

freewill *adj* **1** made, given, or done with one's own free will — see INTENTIONAL 1

2 done, made, or given with one's own free will — see VOLUNTARY 1

free will *n* the act or power of making one's own choices or decisions ⟨all of the workers at the homeless shelter are unpaid and are there of their own *free will*⟩
synonyms accord, choice, option, self-determination, volition, will
related words election, preference; inclination, penchant, predilection, predisposition
near antonyms coercion, compulsion, constraint, duress, force

freeze *n* a weather condition marked by low temperatures — see COLD

freeze *vb* to become physically firm or solid — see HARDEN 1

freezing *adj* having a low or subnormal temperature — see COLD 1

freight *n* a mass or quantity of something taken up and carried, conveyed, or transported — see LOAD 1

frenetic *adj* marked by great and often stressful excitement or activity — see FURIOUS 1

frenzied *adj* **1** being in a state of increased activity or agitation — see FEVERISH 1

2 feeling overwhelming fear or worry — see FRANTIC 1

3 marked by great and often stressful excitement or activity — see FURIOUS 1

frenziedly *adv* in a confused and reckless manner — see HELTER-SKELTER 1

frenzy *n* a state of wildly excited activity or emotion ⟨in its *frenzy* to flee the danger the crowd became uncontrollable, and a number of people were trampled to death⟩
synonyms agitation, delirium, distraction, furor, furore, fury, hysteria, rage, rampage, uproar
related words chaos, confusion, disorder, turmoil; clamor, commotion, hubbub, hurly-burly, tumult
near antonyms calm, peacefulness, serenity, tranquillity (*or* tranquility)

frequency *n* the fact or state of happening often ⟨the *frequency* of twins in that family is remarkable⟩
synonyms commonness, prevalence
related words constancy, continualness, regularity; appearance, incidence, occurrence

antonyms infrequency, uncommonness, unusualness

frequent *adj* **1** appearing or occurring repeatedly from time to time — see REGULAR 1

2 often observed or encountered — see COMMON 1

frequent *vb* to go to or spend time in often ⟨like their counterparts elsewhere, the town's teenagers like to *frequent* the local malls⟩
synonyms hang around (in), hang out (at), haunt, resort (to), visit
related words attend, take in; infest, invade, swarm, overrun; drop (in *or* by), pop (in), run (in), stop (in *or* by); sojourn (at), stay (at), stop (over), tarry (in)
near antonyms elude, escape, evade
antonyms avoid, shun

frequenter *n* a person who visits another — see GUEST 1

frequently *adv* many times — see OFTEN

fresh *adj* **1** being in an original and unused or unspoiled state ⟨the restaurant uses only really *fresh* ingredients in all of its dishes⟩
synonyms brand-new, pristine, virgin
related words unaltered, unblemished, unbruised, uncontaminated, undamaged, undefiled, unharmed, unhurt, unimpaired, uninjured, unpolluted, unsoiled, unspoiled, unsullied, untainted, untouched, unused, unworn
near antonyms blemished, bruised, damaged, defiled, harmed, hurt, impaired, injured, soiled, sullied, tainted; faded, shopworn, used, worn; contaminated, polluted, spoiled
antonyms stale

2 displaying or marked by rude boldness — see NERVY 1

3 not known or experienced before — see NEW 2

freshen *vb* to bring back to a former condition or vigor — see RENEW 1

freshened *adj* made or become fresh in spirits or vigor — see NEW 4

freshly *adv* not long ago — see NEWLY

freshman *n* a person who is just starting out in a field of activity — see BEGINNER

freshness *n* the quality or appeal of being new — see NOVELTY 1

fret *n* a state of nervous or irritated concern ⟨one of my customers always gets into a *fret* if I'm so much as 15 minutes late delivering his newspaper⟩
synonyms dither, fluster, fuss, huff, lather, pother, stew, tizzy, twitter
related words dudgeon, pique; alarm, panic; ado, agitation, delirium, distraction, furor, hysteria, uproar; nervous breakdown

fret *vb* **1** to consume or wear away gradually — see EAT 2

2 to damage or diminish by continued friction — see ABRADE 1

3 to experience concern or anxiety — see WORRY 1

friable *adj* having a texture that readily breaks into little pieces under pressure — see CRISP 1

friary *n* a residence for men under religious vows — see MONASTERY

friction *n* a lack of agreement or harmony — see DISCORD

frictionless *adj* having or marked by agreement in feeling or action — see HARMONIOUS 3

friend *n* **1** a person who has a strong liking for and

THESAURUS

trust in another ⟨really close *friends* who like to do everything together and are always sharing secrets⟩
synonyms buddy, chum, comrade, confidant, crony, familiar, intimate, pal
related words acquaintance; associate, cohort, colleague, companion, fellow, hearty, hobnobber, mate, partner, peer; brother, sister; accomplice, ally, collaborator, confederate; benefactor, supporter, sympathizer, well-wisher; friendly
near antonyms adversary, antagonist, opponent, rival; archenemy, nemesis
antonyms enemy, foe
2 a person who actively supports or favors a cause — see EXPONENT
friendliness *n* kindly concern, interest, or support — see GOODWILL 1
friendly *adj* **1** having or showing kindly feeling and sincere interest ⟨all of the kids at Stacy's new school seemed *friendly*⟩ ⟨as a *friendly* gesture, we presented our new neighbors with a plate of homemade cookies⟩
synonyms amicable, companionable, comradely, cordial, genial, hearty, neighborly, warm, warmhearted
related words affable, approachable, gracious; convivial, gregarious, hospitable, sociable, social; jolly, jovial, merry; extroverted (*also* extraverted), outgoing; brotherly, fraternal, sisterly; close, familiar, intimate; affectionate, devoted, loving
near antonyms cold, cool, frigid; bellicose, belligerent, contentious, quarrelsome
antonyms antagonistic, hostile, unfriendly
2 closely acquainted — see FAMILIAR 1
3 expressing approval — see FAVORABLE 1
friendship *n* kindly concern, interest, or support — see GOODWILL 1
fright *n* **1** something unpleasant to look at — see EYESORE
2 the emotion experienced in the presence or threat of danger — see FEAR
frighten *vb* to strike with fear ⟨around the campfire the campers tried to *frighten* one another with ghostly legends and grisly tales⟩
synonyms affright, alarm, horrify, panic, scare, shock, spook, startle, terrify, terrorize
related words appall, dismay; amaze, astound, awe; chill, daunt, demoralize, dispirit, unman, unnerve; discompose, disconcert, disquiet, disturb, perturb, upset
near antonyms cheer, comfort, console, solace, soothe; embolden, encourage, hearten
antonyms reassure
frightened *adj* filled with fear or dread — see AFRAID 1
frightening *adj* causing fear — see FEARFUL 1
frightful *adj* **1** causing fear — see FEARFUL 1
2 extremely disturbing or repellent — see HORRIBLE 1
frightfully *adv* to a great degree — see VERY 1
frightfulness *n* the quality of inspiring intense dread or dismay — see HORROR 1
frigid *adj* **1** having a low or subnormal temperature — see COLD 1
2 lacking in friendliness or warmth of feeling — see COLD 2
frill *n* **1** a strip of fabric gathered or pleated on one edge and used as trimming — see RUFFLE
2 something adding to pleasure or comfort but not absolutely necessary — see LUXURY 1

3 something that decorates or beautifies — see DECORATION 1
fringe *n* the line or relatively narrow space that marks the outer limit of something — see BORDER 1
fringe *vb* **1** to be adjacent to — see ADJOIN 1
2 to serve as a border for — see BORDER
fringing *adj* having a border in common — see ADJACENT
frippery *n* **1** dressy clothing — see FINERY
2 something of little importance — see TRIFLE
frisk *vb* to play and run about happily — see FROLIC 1
friskiness *n* a natural disposition for playful behavior — see PLAYFULNESS
frisky *adj* **1** given to good-natured joking or teasing — see PLAYFUL
2 having much high-spirited energy and movement — see LIVELY 1
fritter *n* a small usually rounded mass of minced food that has been fried — see CAKE
fritter (away) *vb* to use up carelessly — see WASTE 1
frivol *vb* to show a liking for someone of the opposite sex just for fun — see FLIRT
frivolity *n* a lack of seriousness often at an improper time ⟨the boys were scolded for joking during the funeral service, which was hardly the time for *frivolity*⟩
synonyms facetiousness, flightiness, flippancy, frivolousness, levity, light-headedness, lightness
related words cheerfulness, gaiety (*also* gayety), glee, high-spiritedness, lightheartedness, merriment, mirth
near antonyms gloom, melancholy, moroseness, sadness, sullenness
synonyms gravity, intentness, seriousness, soberness, sobriety
frivolous *adj* **1** lacking importance — see UNIMPORTANT
2 lacking in seriousness or maturity — see GIDDY 1
frivolousness *n* a lack of seriousness often at an improper time — see FRIVOLITY 1
frock *n* a garment with a joined blouse and skirt for a woman or girl — see DRESS 1
frolic *n* **1** a playful or mischievous act intended as a joke — see PRANK
2 a time or instance of carefree fun — see FLING 1
3 activity engaged in to amuse oneself — see PLAY 1
frolic *vb* **1** to play and run about happily ⟨scores of swimmers were *frolicking* in the ocean surf along the beach⟩
synonyms caper, cavort, disport, frisk, gambol, lark, rollick, romp, sport
related words bound, leap, skip, spring, tumble; curvet, dance, prance; carouse, revel, roister; carry on, fool (around), horse (around); clown, cut up; joyride, roughhouse, skylark
phrases kick up one's heels
near antonyms mope, stew, sulk
2 to engage in activity for amusement — see PLAY 1
frolicking *n* activity engaged in to amuse oneself — see PLAY 1
frolicsome *adj* **1** given to good-natured joking or teasing — see PLAYFUL
2 joyously unrestrained — see EXUBERANT
front *n* **1** a forward part or surface ⟨the *front* of the

church features a magnificent stained-glass window⟩
synonyms exterior, facade (*also* façade), face, forepart, outside, skin, surface, veneer
near antonyms innards, inside, interior
antonyms back, rear, reverse
2 a display of emotion or behavior that is insincere or intended to deceive — see MASQUERADE
front *vb* to stand or sit with the face or front toward — see FACE 1
frontier *n* **1** a region along the dividing line between two countries ⟨the Apaches were once feared on both sides of the U.S.-Mexico *frontier*⟩
synonyms border, borderland, march
related words no-man's-land
2 a rural region that forms the edge of the settled or developed part of a country ⟨Alaska has been called America's last *frontier*⟩
synonyms backwater, backwoods, bush, hinterland, up-country
related words country, countryside, sticks
frontiersman *n* a person who settles in a new region ⟨the *frontiersmen* were willing to brave harsh living conditions in order to achieve a better life⟩
synonyms colonist, colonizer, homesteader, pioneer, settler
related words explorer, pathfinder, trailblazer
frost *n* a covering of tiny ice crystals on a cold surface ⟨the wintertime routine of scraping the *frost* off the car's windshield every morning⟩
synonyms hoar, hoarfrost, rime
related words frostwork
frosty *adj* **1** having a low or subnormal temperature — see COLD 1
2 having or showing a lack of friendliness or interest in others — see COOL 1
3 lacking in friendliness or warmth of feeling — see COLD 2
froth *n* a light mass of fine bubbles formed in or on a liquid — see FOAM
frothy *adj* covered with, consisting of, or resembling foam — see FOAMY
froward *adj* **1** engaging in or marked by childish misbehavior — see NAUGHTY
2 given to resisting authority or another's control — see DISOBEDIENT
3 given to resisting control or discipline by others — see UNCONTROLLABLE
frowardness *n* refusal to obey — see DISOBEDIENCE
frown *n* a twisting of the facial features in disgust or disapproval — see GRIMACE
frown *vb* to look with anger or disapproval ⟨the principal just stood there and *frowned* at the student who, once again, was in trouble⟩
synonyms glare, gloom, glower, lower (*also* lour), scowl
related words gape, gaze, ogle, stare; grimace, pout; growl, snarl, sneer
phrases look daggers
antonyms beam, smile
frown (on) *vb* to hold an unfavorable opinion of — see DISAPPROVE
frowsy *or* **frowzy** *adj* lacking neatness in dress or person — see SLOPPY 1
frozen *adj* **1** firmly positioned in place and difficult to dislodge — see TIGHT 2
2 having been established and usually not subject to change — see FIXED 1

frugal *adj* careful in the management of money or resources ⟨by being *frugal*, the family is able to stretch its monthly budget⟩
synonyms economical, economizing, provident, scrimping, sparing, thrifty
related words conserving, preserving, saving; forehanded, foresighted, prudent; penny-wise; cheap, close, closefisted, miserly, niggardly, parsimonious, stingy, stinting, tight, tightfisted
near antonyms improvident, shortsighted; freehanded, generous, liberal, openhanded, unsparing; extravagant, indulgent, lavish
antonyms prodigal, wasteful
frugality *n* careful management of material resources — see ECONOMY
fruit *n* **1** a condition or occurrence traceable to a cause — see EFFECT 1
2 something produced by physical or intellectual effort — see PRODUCT 1
fruitful *adj* **1** producing abundantly — see FERTILE
2 producing or capable of producing a desired result — see EFFECTIVE 1
fruition *n* the state of being actual or complete ⟨when she landed the lead in a Broadway play, a lifelong dream was brought to *fruition*⟩
synonyms accomplishment, achievement, actuality, attainment, consummation, fulfillment, realization
antonyms naught (*also* nought), nonfulfillment
fruitless *adj* producing no results — see FUTILE
frustrate *vb* to prevent from achieving a goal ⟨a multitude of conflicting opinions *frustrated* me in my attempt to find a computer that best suits my needs⟩
synonyms baffle, balk, beat, checkmate, foil, thwart
related words bar, block, hinder, impede, obstruct; arrest, check, halt, stop; forestall, obviate, preclude; negate, neutralize, nullify; counteract, offset; conquer, defeat, overcome
near antonyms abet, aid, assist; ease, facilitate, smooth;
antonyms advance, cultivate, encourage, forward, foster, further, nurture, promote
frustrating *adj* causing annoyance — see ANNOYING
frustration *n* **1** something that is a source of irritation — see ANNOYANCE 3
2 the emotion felt when one's expectations are not met — see DISAPPOINTMENT 1
3 the feeling of impatience or anger caused by another's repeated disagreeable acts — see ANNOYANCE 2
fuddy-duddy *n* a person with old-fashioned ideas — see FOGY
fudge *n* **1** language, behavior, or ideas that are absurd and contrary to good sense — see NONSENSE 1
2 unintelligible or meaningless talk — see GIBBERISH
fudge *vb* **1** to avoid giving a definite answer or position — see EQUIVOCATE
2 to use dishonest methods to achieve a goal — see CHEAT 1
fuel *n* something with a usable capacity for doing work ⟨such fossil *fuels* as coal, petroleum, and natural gas⟩
synonyms energy, power
related words kindling, propellant

fugitive *adj* **1** hard to find, capture, or isolate — see ELUSIVE

2 lasting only for a short time — see MOMENTARY

fulfill *or* **fulfil** *vb* **1** to do what is required by the terms of ⟨the football player must remain with the team one more year to *fulfill* his contract⟩

synonyms answer, comply (with), fill, keep, meet, redeem, satisfy

related words complete, conclude, finalize, finish; accomplish, achieve, bring about, bring off, effect; discharge, execute, perform

phrases abide by, make good

near antonyms disregard, ignore, neglect, overlook, slight

antonyms breach, break, violate

2 to carry through (as a process) to completion — see PERFORM 1

fulfilling *adj* making one feel good inside — see HEARTWARMING

fulfillment *n* **1** the doing of an action — see COMMISSION 2

2 the state of being actual or complete — see FRUITION

full *adj* **1** containing or seeming to contain the greatest quantity or number possible ⟨at the start of the game everyone was *full* of energy and hope⟩ ⟨the boy's bedroom is *full* of sports trophies and medals⟩

synonyms brimful, brimming, bursting, chockfull (*or* chockful), crammed, crowded, fat, filled, jammed, jam-packed, loaded, packed, stuffed

related words overcrowded, overfilled, overflowing, overfull, overloaded, overstuffed; abounding, fraught, replete, rife, swarming, teeming

near antonyms deficient, incomplete, insufficient, short; depleted, drained, exhausted

antonyms bare, blank, devoid, empty, stark, vacant, void

2 of the highest degree ⟨even at the age of eighteen he hadn't reached his *full* height⟩ ⟨a boat going at *full* speed⟩

synonyms greatest, maximum, top, topmost, utmost

related words high

near antonyms low

antonyms least, lowest, minimal, minimum

3 having one's appetite completely satisfied ⟨even the heartiest eaters are sure to be *full* when they leave that restaurant⟩

synonyms sated, satiate, satiated, stuffed, surfeited

related words glutted, gorged, overfed, overfull, overstuffed

near antonyms underfed, undernourished

antonyms empty, hungry, starving

4 covering everything or all important points — see ENCYCLOPEDIC

5 having an abundance of some characteristic quality (as flavor) — see FULL-BODIED

6 having an excess of body fat — see FAT 1

7 including many small descriptive features — see DETAILED 1

8 not lacking any part or member that properly belongs to it — see COMPLETE 1

full *adv* **1** to a full extent or degree — see FULLY 1

2 to a great degree — see VERY 1

full *n* a complete amount of something — see WHOLE

full blast *adv* with all power or resources being used ⟨Mom and Dad arrived home to find the stereo going *full blast* and the kitchen a mess⟩

synonyms all out, full steam ahead, full tilt, tooth and nail

related words completely, fully, totally; extremely, utterly

phrases in full career, to the hilt

full-blooded *adj* of unmixed ancestry — see PUREBRED

full-blown *adj* fully grown or developed — see MATURE 1

full-bodied *adj* having an abundance of some characteristic quality (as flavor) ⟨after that huge Sunday brunch, Mom and Dad needed a *full-bodied* coffee⟩

synonyms concentrated, full, potent, rich, robust, strong

related words heavy; straight, undiluted, unmixed

near antonyms diluted, watered (down), watery

antonyms light, mild, thin, weak

full dress *n* dressy clothing — see FINERY

full-fledged *adj* fully grown or developed — see MATURE 1

full-grown *adj* fully grown or developed — see MATURE 1

full-scale *adj* trying all possibilities — see EXHAUSTIVE

full steam ahead *adv* with all power or resources being used — see FULL BLAST

full tilt *adv* **1** with all power or resources being used — see FULL BLAST

2 with great speed — see FAST 1

fully *adv* **1** to a full extent or degree ⟨only with daybreak did we *fully* realize the extent of the damage from the storm⟩

synonyms all, altogether, clean, completely, dead, entirely, fast, flat, full, perfectly, plumb [*chiefly dialect*], quite, thoroughly, totally, utterly, well, wholly

related words absolutely, categorically, unqualifiedly; by and large, chiefly, generally, largely, mainly, more or less, mostly, predominately, primarily, principally

phrases at length, to pieces, to the hilt

near antonyms barely, hardly, just, scarcely

antonyms partially, partly

2 with attention to all aspects or details — see THOROUGHLY 1

fulminate *vb* to talk loudly and wildly — see RANT

fulmination *n* harsh insulting language — see ABUSE 1

fulsome *adj* overly or insincerely flattering ⟨the player's *fulsome* praise for the coach showed just how hard he was trying to be named captain of the team⟩

synonyms adulatory, gushing, unctuous

related words drooling, slavering, slobbering; cloying, sickening; demonstrative, effusive, mushy; hypocritical, insincere, sanctimonious; endearing, ingratiating; extravagant, lavish, unrestrained; abundant, copious, profuse

near antonyms earnest, genuine, heartfelt, sincere, unfeigned

fumble *n* an unintentional departure from truth or accuracy — see ERROR 1

fumble *vb* **1** to make or do (something) in a clumsy or unskillful way — see BOTCH

2 to search for something blindly or uncertainly — see GROPE

fumbled *adj* showing or marked by a lack of skill

and tact (as in dealing with a situation) — see AWKWARD 2

fume *vb* **1** to be excited or emotionally stirred up with anger — see BOIL 1
2 to express one's anger usually violently — see RAGE 1

fuming *adj* feeling or showing anger — see ANGRY

fun *adj* providing amusement or enjoyment ⟨there were so many *fun* things to do at summer camp that I really hated to leave⟩
synonyms amusing, delightful, diverting, enjoyable, entertaining, pleasurable
related words agreeable, beguiling, pleasant; funny, hilarious, humorous; gay, happy, jolly, merry; exciting, stimulating, thrilling
near antonyms disagreeable, unpleasant
antonyms boring, dull

fun *n* **1** someone or something that provides amusement or enjoyment ⟨theme parks with their rides, shows, and games are great *fun* for the whole family⟩
synonyms delight, diversion, entertainment, pleasure, recreation
related words binge, fling, frolic, gambol, lark, revel, rollick, romp, spree; carousing, festivity, gaiety (*also* gayety), hilarity, merrymaking, revelry; picnic; laugh, riot, scream
antonyms bore, bummer, downer, drag
2 an attitude or manner not to be taken seriously ⟨when I said that playing the piano like that could get you arrested, I only said it in *fun*⟩
synonyms game, jest, play, sport
related words facetiousness, flippancy, levity
near antonyms earnestness, gravity, seriousness
antonyms earnest
3 activity engaged in to amuse oneself — see PLAY 1

fun *vb* to make jokes — see JOKE

function *n* **1** a social gathering — see PARTY 1
2 an assignment at which one regularly works for pay — see JOB 1
3 the action for which a person or thing is specially fitted or used or for which a thing exists — see ROLE

function *vb* to have a certain purpose ⟨the heart *functions* as a pump for the blood⟩
synonyms act, perform, serve, work
related words operate, run; control, direct, manage

functional *adj* **1** being in effective operation — see ACTIVE 1
2 capable of being put to use or account — see PRACTICAL 1
3 capable of or suitable for being used for a particular purpose — see USABLE 1

functionary *n* **1** a person who holds a public office — see OFFICIAL
2 a worker in a government agency — see BUREAUCRAT

functioning *adj* being in effective operation — see ACTIVE 1

fund *n* **1** a sum of money set aside for a particular purpose ⟨our club has a *fund* for parties—which we like to have as often as possible⟩
synonyms account, budget, deposit, kitty, nest egg, pool
related words chest, coffer(s); assets, savings, savings account; bankroll, cache, collection, hoard, reserve, treasure; petty cash, pin money, pocket money, spending money

2 funds *pl* available money ⟨my *funds* were a little low, so I asked my favorite lending institution—Dad—for a small advance on my allowance⟩
synonyms bankroll, finances, pocket, resources, wherewithal
related words cash, money; assets, capital, means, wealth; purse, treasury
3 the number of individuals or amount of something available at any given time — see SUPPLY

fund *vb* **1** to furnish (as an institution) with a regular source of income — see ENDOW 2
2 to provide money for — see FINANCE 1

fundamental *adj* of or relating to the simplest facts or theories of a subject — see ELEMENTARY

fundamentals *n pl* general or basic truths on which other truths or theories can be based — see PRINCIPLES 1

funeral *adj* expressing or suggesting mourning — see MOURNFUL 1

funeral director *n* a person who manages funerals and prepares the dead for burial or cremation ⟨the *funeral director* instructed the pallbearers on how to proceed⟩
synonyms mortician, undertaker
related words embalmer

funereal *adj* causing or marked by an atmosphere lacking in cheer — see GLOOMY 1

funnel *vb* to cause to move to a central point or along a restricted pathway — see CHANNEL

funniness *n* the amusing quality or element in something — see HUMOR 1

funning *adj* marked by or expressive of mild or good-natured teasing — see QUIZZICAL

funny *adj* **1** causing or intended to cause laughter ⟨a very *funny* movie that had audiences rolling in the aisles⟩
synonyms antic, comic, comical, droll, farcical, hilarious, humorous, hysterical, laughable, ludicrous, ridiculous, riotous, risible, screaming, sidesplitting, uproarious
related words amusing, diverting, entertaining; clownish, slapstick, zany; facetious, flip, flippant, pert, smart, smart-alecky (*or* smart-aleck); jocular, playful, waggish; priceless, rich, whimsical, witty; gleeful, merry, mirthful
near antonyms grave, serious, sober, solemn, somber (*or* sombre); affecting, moving, poignant, touching, tragic; lachrymose, mournful, sad, tearful
antonyms humorless, lame, uncomic, unfunny
2 different from the ordinary in a way that causes curiosity or suspicion — see ODD 2
3 noticeably different from what is generally found or experienced — see UNUSUAL 1

funny *n* a series of drawings that tell a story or part of a story — see COMIC STRIP

fur *n* **1** the hairy covering of a mammal especially when fine, soft, and thick ⟨the chinchilla is known for its exceptionally soft *fur*⟩
synonyms coat, fleece, hair, pelage, pile, wool
related words hide, pelt, skin
2 a soft airy substance or covering — see FUZZ
3 the outer covering of an animal removed for its commercial value — see HIDE 1

furbelow *n* a strip of fabric gathered or pleated on one edge and used as trimming — see RUFFLE

furious *adj* **1** marked by great and often stressful excitement or activity ⟨everyone worked at a *furious* pace in order to get the float ready for the parade⟩

THESAURUS

synonyms delirious, feverish, fierce, frantic, frenetic, frenzied, mad, rabid, violent, wild
related words concentrated, high-pressured, intense, vehement; excessive, extreme, inordinate; crazy, demented, insane, irrational
near antonyms calm, peaceful, quiet, subdued, tranquil; moderate, reasonable, temperate; casual, easygoing, low-pressure
antonyms relaxed
2 extreme in degree, power, or effect — see INTENSE
3 feeling or showing anger — see ANGRY
4 marked by bursts of destructive force or intense activity — see VIOLENT 1

furlough *n* the termination of the employment of an employee or a work force often temporarily — see LAYOFF

furnish *vb* **1** to provide (someone) with what is needed for a task or activity ⟨the students were *furnished* with brushes, crayons, pencils, and various other art supplies⟩
synonyms accoutre (*or* accouter), equip, fit (out), outfit, rig, supply
related words stock, store; bestow, donate, give, present; deal, dispense, distribute, dole (out); allocate, allot, assign
near antonyms deprive, dispossess, divest, strip
2 to put (something) into the possession of someone for use or consumption ⟨we'll gladly *furnish* the food for any out-of-town guests⟩
synonyms deliver, feed, give, hand, hand over, provide, supply
related words administer, dispense, distribute, dole (out), mete (out), parcel (out); cede, deed, transfer
near antonyms conserve, preserve, save
antonyms hold (back), keep (back), reserve, retain, withhold

furnishings *n pl* the movable articles in a room — see FURNITURE

furniture *n* the movable articles in a room ⟨we bought all new *furniture* for our new house⟩
synonyms appointments, cabinetwork, furnishings, movables (*or* moveables)
related words effects, goods, possessions
near antonyms fixtures

furor *n* **1** a state of noisy, confused activity — see COMMOTION
2 a state of wildly excited activity or emotion — see FRENZY
3 an intense emotional state of displeasure with someone or something — see ANGER

furore *n* **1** a state of noisy, confused activity — see COMMOTION
2 a state of wildly excited activity or emotion — see FRENZY

furrow *n* a small fold in a soft and otherwise smooth surface — see WRINKLE 1

furrow *vb* **1** to cut into and turn over the sod of (a piece of land) using a bladed implement — see PLOW 1
2 to develop creases or folds — see WRINKLE 1

furry *adj* **1** covered with or as if with hair — see HAIRY 1
2 made of or resembling hair — see HAIRY 2

further *adj* resulting in an increase in amount or number — see ADDITIONAL

further *adv* **1** at or to a greater distance or more advanced point — see FARTHER
2 in addition to what has been said — see MORE 1

further *vb* to help the growth or development of — see FOSTER 1

furtherance *n* forward movement in time or place — see ADVANCE 1

furthermore *adv* in addition to what has been said — see MORE 1

furthermost *adj* most distant from a center — see EXTREME 1

furthest *adj* most distant from a center — see EXTREME 1

furtive *adj* **1** given to acting in secret and to concealing one's intentions — see SNEAKY 1
2 undertaken or done so as to escape being observed or known by others — see SECRET 1

fury *n* **1** a bad-tempered scolding woman — see SHREW
2 a state of wildly excited activity or emotion — see FRENZY
3 an intense emotional state of displeasure with someone or something — see ANGER

fuse *vb* **1** to come together to form a single unit — see UNITE 1
2 to go from a solid to a liquid state — see LIQUEFY
3 to turn into a single mass that is more or less the same throughout — see BLEND 1

fusillade *n* a rapid or overwhelming outpouring of many things at once — see BARRAGE

fusion *n* a distinct entity formed by the combining of two or more different things — see BLEND

fuss *n* **1** a feeling or declaration of disapproval or dissent — see OBJECTION
2 a state of nervous or irritated concern — see FRET
3 a state of noisy, confused activity — see COMMOTION
4 an expression of dissatisfaction, pain, or resentment — see COMPLAINT 1

fuss *vb* **1** to express dissatisfaction, pain, or resentment usually tiresomely — see COMPLAIN
2 to make an exaggerated display of affection or enthusiasm — see GUSH 2
3 to make often peevish criticisms or objections about matters that are minor, unimportant, or irrelevant — see QUIBBLE
4 to use flattery or the doing of favors in order to win approval especially from a superior — see FAWN

fusser *n* **1** a person who makes frequent complaints usually about little things — see CRYBABY
2 an irritable and complaining person — see GROUCH

fussy *adj* **1** given to complaining a lot ⟨the kids riding in the back were *fussy* passengers, always asking "Are we there yet?"⟩
synonyms crabby, cranky, grouchy, grumpy, querulous
related words fidgety, restive, restless, squirmy, uneasy; discontented, disgruntled, displeased, dissatisfied; fretful, nervous, worrisome; cantankerous, crotchety, irascible, irritable, ornery
near antonyms amiable, genial, good-humored, good-natured, good-tempered; accommodating, complaisant, obliging; easygoing, laid-back, relaxed
antonyms uncomplaining
2 hard to please — see FINICKY
3 taking great care and effort — see PAINSTAKING

fusty *adj* having an unpleasant smell — see MAL-ODOROUS

futile *adj* producing no results ⟨the prison is so well guarded that all attempts to escape have been *futile*⟩
synonyms abortive, bootless, empty, fruitless, ineffective, ineffectual, unavailing, unproductive, unprofitable, unsuccessful, useless, vain
related words hollow, idle, meaningless, pointless, worthless; hopeless, impossible; inadequate, insufficient
phrases in vain, of no avail
near antonyms meaningful, worthwhile; adequate, sufficient
antonyms effective, effectual, efficacious, efficient, fruitful, productive, profitable, successful

future *adj* of a time after the present ⟨we must preserve our national parks in all their glory so that *future* generations can experience the majesty of nature⟩
synonyms coming, unborn
related words approaching, forthcoming, imminent, impending, nearing, oncoming, pending, upcoming; later, posterior, subsequent; antici-pated, awaited, expected, planned, predicted, projected; eventual, final, last, ultimate
near antonyms ancient, olden
antonyms bygone, past

future *n* **1** time that is to come ⟨in the *future*, there may be medical discoveries that are beyond our fondest dreams⟩
synonyms by-and-by, futurity, hereafter, offing
related words eventuality, finality; posterity
near antonyms yesterday, yesteryear; antiquity, old, yore
antonyms past
2 what is going to happen to someone in the time ahead — see FORTUNE 1

futurist *n* one who predicts future events or developments — see PROPHET

futurity *n* time that is to come — see FUTURE 1

fuzz *n* a soft airy substance or covering ⟨a comfortable old sweater with clumps of *fuzz* all over it⟩
synonyms down, floss, fluff, fur, lint, nap, pile
related words batting

fuzzy *adj* **1** made of or resembling hair — see HAIRY 2
2 not clearly expressed — see VAGUE 1
3 not seen or understood clearly — see FAINT 1

G

gab *vb* to engage in casual or rambling conversation — see CHAT

gabble *n* unintelligible or meaningless talk — see GIBBERISH

gabble *vb* **1** to engage in casual or rambling conversation — see CHAT
2 to speak rapidly, inarticulately, and usually unintelligibly — see BABBLE 1

gabbler *n* a person who talks constantly — see CHATTERBOX

gabby *adj* fond of talking or conversation — see TALKATIVE

gabfest *n* friendly, informal conversation or an instance of this — see CHAT

gad (about) *vb* to move about from place to place aimlessly — see WANDER

gadabout *n* a person who roams about without a fixed route or destination — see NOMAD

gadfly *n* one who is obnoxiously annoying — see NUISANCE 1

gadget *n* an interesting and often novel device with a practical use ⟨she tried out a new *gadget* for weeding the garden⟩
synonyms appliance, contraption, contrivance, gimmick, gizmo (*or* gismo), jigger
related words implement, instrument, tool, utensil; ingenuity, innovation, invention; accessory, adjunct; mechanism, trick

gaffe *n* a socially improper or unsuitable act or remark — see IMPROPRIETY 2

gag *n* something said or done to cause laughter — see JOKE 1

gag *vb* **1** to discharge the contents of the stomach through the mouth — see VOMIT
2 to experience complete or partial blockage of the windpipe — see CHOKE 2

gage *n* something given or held to assure that the giver will keep a promise — see PLEDGE 1

gaiety *also* **gayety** *n* **1** dressy clothing — see FINERY
2 joyful or festive activity — see MERRYMAKING

gaily *also* **gayly** *adv* **1** in a cheerful or happy manner ⟨we sat around the table, *gaily* teasing each other and laughing about the good old days⟩
synonyms cheerfully, happily, heartily, jocosely, jovially, merrily, mirthfully
related words blithely, blithesomely, breezily, brightly, buoyantly; cheerily, gladly, gladsomely, sanguinely, sunnily; good-humoredly, good-naturedly
near antonyms abjectly, dejectedly, despondently, disconsolately, dispiritedly, wretchedly; dolefully, dolorously, forlornly, mournfully, plaintively, sorrowfully; dourly, glumly, sternly, sulkily, sullenly; dismally, drearily, gloomily
antonyms bleakly, cheerlessly, darkly, heavily, miserably, morosely, unhappily
2 in a quick and spirited manner ⟨children *gaily* running to the buses on the last day of school⟩
synonyms animatedly, animately, exuberantly, high-spiritedly, jauntily, pertly, sprightly, trippingly
related words friskily, playfully, skittishly, sportively; briskly, crisply, snappily, springily; breezily, cockishly; allegro
near antonyms idly, indolently, lazily, slothfully; heavily, inactively, listlessly
antonyms dully, inanimately, sluggishly, tardily
3 in a bright and showy way ⟨the Mexican dancers were *gaily* dressed in lavish, bright costumes⟩
synonyms dashingly, flamboyantly, flashily, jauntily, rakishly, swankily

THESAURUS

related words garishly, gaudily, loud, loudly, ostentatiously; fancily, gallantly, ornately; nattily, neatly, smartly; conspicuously, luridly, spectacularly, strikingly; gorgeously, splendidly

near antonyms inconspicuously, unobtrusively, unpretentiously; chastely, demurely, homely, modestly; plainly, simply; colorlessly, dirtily, drably, dully; bleakly, severely, somberly

antonyms conservatively, plain, quietly

gain *n* **1** something added (as by growth) — see INCREASE 1

2 the amount of money left when expenses are subtracted from the total amount received — see PROFIT 1

3 gains *pl* an increase usually measured in money that comes from labor, business, or property — see INCOME

gain *vb* **1** to increase in ⟨as the car coasted downhill, it gradually *gained* speed and momentum⟩

synonyms build (up), gather, grow (in), pick up

related words accrue, accumulate, amass; excite, stimulate; enhance, enrich, maximize; boost, jack (up), mount, step up

near antonyms abate, diminish (in), dip, dwindle, fall (in), lessen, taper, taper off

antonyms decrease (in), lose

2 to receive as return for effort — see EARN 1

3 to become healthy and strong again after illness or weakness — see CONVALESCE

gainful *adj* yielding a profit — see PROFITABLE 1

gainsay *vb* **1** to declare not to be true — see DENY 1

2 to make an assertion that is contrary to one made by (another) — see CONTRADICT 1

gal *n* **1** a woman with whom one is in love — see GIRLFRIEND

2 a young usually unmarried woman — see GIRL 1

gala *n* a time or program of special events and entertainment in honor of something — see FESTIVAL

gale *n* a sudden intense expression of strong feeling — see OUTBURST 1

gall *n* **1** a deep-seated ill will — see ENMITY

2 shameless boldness — see EFFRONTERY

gall *vb* **1** to damage or diminish by continued friction — see ABRADE 1

2 to disturb the peace of mind of (someone) especially by repeated disagreeable acts — see IRRITATE 1

3 to make sore by continued rubbing — see CHAFE 1

gallant *adj* **1** feeling or displaying no fear by temperament — see BRAVE

2 having, characterized by, or arising from a dignified and generous nature — see NOBLE 2

3 large and impressive in size, grandeur, extent, or conception — see GRAND 1

gallant *n* **1** a man extremely interested in his clothing and personal appearance — see DANDY 1

2 a man who courts a woman usually with the goal of marrying her — see SUITOR 1

gallantly *adv* in a manner befitting a person of the highest character and ideals — see GREATLY 1

gallantry *n* strength of mind to carry on in spite of danger — see COURAGE

gallery *n* **1** a building or part of a building in which objects of interest are displayed — see MUSEUM

2 a typically long narrow way connecting parts of a building — see HALL 2

galling *adj* **1** causing annoyance — see ANNOYING

2 hard to accept or bear especially emotionally — see BITTER 2

gallivant *also* **galavant** *vb* to move about from place to place aimlessly — see WANDER

gallivanting *also* **galavanting** *adj* traveling from place to place — see ITINERANT

gallop *vb* to go at a pace faster than a walk — see RUN 1

galore *adj* pouring forth in great amounts — see PROFUSE

galvanize *vb* to cause a pleasurable stimulation of the feelings — see THRILL

galvanizing *adj* causing great emotional or mental stimulation — see EXCITING 1

gamble *n* a risky undertaking ⟨would never take a *gamble* on such a poorly researched business deal⟩

synonyms chance, enterprise, flier (*or* flyer), speculation, venture

related words bet, hazard, stake, wager; liberty; dark horse, long shot, play

gamble *vb* to risk (something) on the outcome of an uncertain event — see BET

gamble (on) *vb* to take a chance on — see RISK 1

gamble (with) *vb* to place in danger — see ENDANGER

gambler *n* one that bets (as on the outcome of a contest or sports event) — see BETTOR

gambol *n* a time or instance of carefree fun — see FLING 1

gambol *vb* to play and run about happily — see FROLIC 1

game *adj* having a desire or inclination (as for a specified course of action) — see WILLING 1

game *n* **1** a competitive encounter between individuals or groups carried on for amusement, exercise, or in pursuit of a prize ⟨decided he would indulge in a friendly basketball *game* with his friends before dinner⟩

synonyms bout, competition, contest, event, match, meet, sweepstakes, tournament, tourney

related words athletics, sport; battle, conflict, scrimmage, skirmish, struggle, tug-of-war, tussle; championship, final, nightcap, play-off, semifinal; derby, field day, open; marathon, race; heat, round, run, set; rally, volley; rubber, runoff, sudden death; dead heat, photo finish, seesaw; classic

2 a method worked out in advance for achieving some objective — see PLAN 1

3 an attitude or manner not to be taken seriously — see FUN 2

gameness *n* cheerful readiness to do something — see ALACRITY

gamut *n* the distance or extent between possible extremes — see RANGE 3

gander *n* an instance of looking especially briefly — see LOOK 2

gang *n* **1** a group of people working together on a task ⟨a *gang* of neighborhood residents spent the weekend cleaning up the park⟩

synonyms band, company, crew, outfit, party, squad, team

related words army, battalion, brigade, corps, troop; force, host, posse, stable, troupe; administration, department, help, personnel, staff

2 a group of people sharing a common interest and relating together socially ⟨the whole *gang* went out for pizza⟩ ⟨the school's computer hackers had their own little *gang*⟩

synonyms body, bunch, circle, clan, clique, community, coterie, crowd, fold, lot, ring, set
related words bevy, covey, flock, herd, horde, mob, swarm, throng; club, college, fellowship, guild (*also* gild), league, organization, society; cohort, pack; camp, faction, sect, side, tribe; mess, squad; brotherhood, fraternity, order, sisterhood, sodality, sorority; commune; alliance, bloc, coalition, confederation, congress, council, federation, union
near antonyms loner; individualist
3 a group involved in secret or criminal activities — see RING 1

gangling *adj* being tall, thin and usually loose-jointed — see LANKY

gangly *adj* being tall, thin and usually loose-jointed — see LANKY

gangster *n* a violent, brutal person who is often a member of an organized gang — see HOODLUM

gaol *n, chiefly British* a place of confinement for persons held in lawful custody — see JAIL

gap *n* **1** an open space in a barrier (as a wall or hedge) ⟨there were several visible *gaps* in the wall where the drywall had pulled away from the wall framing⟩
synonyms breach, break, discontinuity, gulf, hole, interval, opening, rent, rift, separation
related words chink, cleft, crack, cranny, crevice, fissure; notch, slit, slot, split; interspace, pore, space; abyss, aperture, cavity, chasm, gape, orifice; fracture, rupture, severance, sundering
2 a break in continuity ⟨there was a 15-minute *gap* between the two televised sporting events⟩
synonyms discontinuity, hiatus, interim, interlude, intermission, interruption, interval
related words caesura, pause, space; lapse, suspension; lull, recess, respite, rest
near antonyms continuum, run, stretch; procession, progression
antonyms continuation, continuity
3 a narrow opening between hillsides or mountains that can be used for passage — see CANYON

gape *vb* to look long and hard in wonder or surprise ⟨she *gaped* openmouthed at the young man in the mall with purple and green hair⟩
synonyms gawk, gaze, goggle, peer, rubberneck, stare
related words glare, gloat, glower; eye, observe, watch; leer, ogle
near antonyms glance, glimpse, peek, peep; browse, dip (into), scan; blink, wink

garb *n* clothing chosen as appropriate for a specific situation — see OUTFIT 1

garb *vb* to outfit with clothes and especially fine or special clothes — see CLOTHE 1

garbage *n* discarded or useless material ⟨the stray dogs were looking for leftover food in the family's *garbage*⟩
synonyms chaff, deadwood, dross, dust, junk, litter, refuse, riffraff, rubbish, scrap, trash, waste
related words offal, sewage, slop, swill, wash; debris, detritus, rubble, ruins; lumber, odds and ends; flotsam, jetsam; castoff, cull, discard, reject, throwaway; nothing, straw, two bits
near antonyms catch, treasure, treasure trove
antonyms find, prize

garble *vb* to change so much as to create a wrong impression or alter the meaning of ⟨the candidate complained that his views had been deliberately *garbled* by his opponent⟩

synonyms color, distort, falsify, misinterpret, misrepresent, misstate, pervert, twist, warp
related words belie, camouflage, disguise, mask, veil; complicate, confound, confuse, mix up; mystify, obscure, puzzle; equivocate, fib, lie, palter, prevaricate
near antonyms clarify, clear (up), explain, illuminate, illustrate, interpret, spell out; decipher

garden *adj* **1** being of the type that is encountered in the normal course of events — see ORDINARY 1
2 often observed or encountered — see COMMON 1

garish *adj* excessively showy — see GAUDY

garishness *n* excessive or unnecessary display — see OSTENTATION

garment *vb* to outfit with clothes and especially fine or special clothes — see CLOTHE 1

garner *vb* **1** to bring together in one body or place — see GATHER 1
2 to receive as return for effort — see EARN 1

garnish *n* something that decorates or beautifies — see DECORATION 1

garnish *vb* to make more attractive by adding something that is beautiful or becoming — see DECORATE

garrote *or* **garotte** *vb* to keep (someone) from breathing by exerting pressure on the windpipe — see CHOKE 1

garrulous *adj* fond of talking or conversation — see TALKATIVE

gas *n* **1** boastful speech or writing — see BOMBAST 1
2 language that is impressive-sounding but not meaningful or sincere — see RHETORIC 1
3 *slang* a source of great satisfaction — see DELIGHT 1

gas *vb* to engage in casual or rambling conversation — see CHAT

gaseous *adj* marked by the use of impressive-sounding but mostly meaningless words and phrases — see RHETORICAL

gash *n* a long deep cut ⟨got a *gash* in his knee that required four stitches⟩
synonyms incision, laceration, rent, rip, slash, slit, tear
related words abrasion, score, scrape, scratch; injury, wound

gash *vb* to penetrate with a sharp edge (as a knife) — see CUT 1

gasp *vb* to breathe hard, quickly, or with difficulty ⟨the runner was *gasping* by the end of the marathon⟩
synonyms blow, hyperventilate, pant, puff, wheeze
related words choke, gulp, huff; exhale, expire
phrases to be out of breath

gassy *adj* marked by the use of impressive-sounding but mostly meaningless words and phrases — see RHETORICAL

gate *n* **1** a barrier by which an entry is closed and opened — see DOOR 1
2 the opening through which one can enter or leave a structure — see DOOR 2
3 a fixture for controlling the flow of a liquid — see FAUCET

gatekeeper *n* a person who tends a door — see DOORKEEPER

gateway *n* **1** something that allows someone to achieve a desired goal — see PASSPORT

THESAURUS

2 the means or right of entering or participating in — see ENTRANCE 1

3 the opening through which one can enter or leave a structure — see DOOR 2

gather *vb* **1** to bring together in one body or place ⟨he *gathered* the leftovers from the table and gave them to the dog⟩ ⟨let's *gather* the students and have them line up on the playground before going in from recess⟩

synonyms accumulate, amass, assemble, collect, concentrate, garner, group, lump, pick up, round up, scrape (together)

related words agglomerate, aggregate, ball, bunch, cluster, huddle; heap, pile, stack; muster, raise, rally; flock, herd, hive, pack, press, swarm, throng, troop; congregate, forgather (*or* foregather), meet, rendezvous; affiliate, ally, combine, connect, join, link, merge, unite; arrange, organize, systematize; regather, regroup

phrases get together

near antonyms break up, disband, disintegrate, dissolve, separate, sever, split (up); dismiss, send

antonyms dispel, disperse, dissipate, scatter

2 to catch or collect (a crop or natural resource) for human use — see HARVEST

3 to come together into one body or place — see ASSEMBLE 1

4 to form an opinion through reasoning and information — see INFER 1

5 to gradually form into a layer, pile, or mass — see COLLECT 2

6 to increase in — see GAIN 1

gather (up) *vb* to call into being through the use of one's inner resources or powers — see SUMMON 2

gathering *n* **1** a body of people come together in one place ⟨the President spoke before the *gathering* of student leaders⟩

synonyms assemblage, assembly, conference, congregation, convocation, meeting, muster

related words aggregation, collection, conglomeration; company, coterie, gang, pack; caucus, forum, market, panel, rally, symposium, synod; crowd, flock, horde, legion, multitude, press, swarm, throng; crush, mob, rabble

2 a coming together of a number of persons for a specified purpose — see MEETING 1

3 a mass or quantity that has piled up or that has been gathered — see ACCUMULATION 1

gauche *adj* lacking social grace and assurance — see AWKWARD 1

gaud *n* a small object displayed for its attractiveness or interest — see KNICKKNACK

gaudiness *n* excessive or unnecessary display — see OSTENTATION

gaudy *adj* excessively showy ⟨the bright purple sequined miniskirt she wore to the wedding was *gaudy*⟩

synonyms flamboyant, flashy, garish, glitzy, loud, ostentatious, splashy, swank (*or* swanky), tawdry

related words meretricious, pretentious; graceless, inelegant, tacky, tasteless, vulgar; bedizened, extravagant, fancy, florid, glittery, spectacular; lurid, ornate, overdone, overwrought

near antonyms appropriate, fitting, proper; inconspicuous, muted, restrained, subdued, toned (down), unobtrusive; elegant, graceful, tasteful; modest, plain, simple, unpretentious

antonyms conservative, quiet, understated

gauge *also* **gage** *vb* **1** to decide the size, amount, number, or distance of (something) without actual measurement — see ESTIMATE 2

2 to find out the size, extent, or amount of — see MEASURE

gaunt *adj* suffering extreme weight loss as a result of hunger or disease — see EMACIATED

gauntlet *also* **gantlet** *n* a test of faith, patience, or strength — see TRIAL

gauzy *adj* **1** being of a material lacking in sturdiness or substance — see FLIMSY 1

2 very thin and easy to see through — see SHEER 1

gawk *n* a big clumsy often slow-witted person — see OAF

gawk *vb* to look long and hard in wonder or surprise — see GAPE

gawky *adj* lacking in physical ease and grace in movement or in the use of the hands — see CLUMSY 1

gay *adj* **1** having much high-spirited energy and movement — see LIVELY 1

2 having or showing a lack of concern or seriousness — see CAREFREE

3 indicative of or marked by high spirits or good humor — see MERRY

4 having or showing a good mood or disposition — see CHEERFUL 1

5 serving to lift one's spirits — see CHEERFUL 2

gaze *vb* to look long and hard in wonder or surprise — see GAPE

gazette *n* a publication that appears at regular intervals — see JOURNAL

gear *n* items needed for the performance of a task or activity — see EQUIPMENT

gel *vb* to turn from a liquid into a substance resembling jelly — see COAGULATE

gelatinous *adj* being of such a thick consistency as to readily cling to objects upon contact — see STICKY 1

gem *n* **1** a usually valuable stone cut and polished for ornament ⟨a ring set with diamonds and other precious *gems*⟩

synonyms brilliant, gemstone, jewel

related words birthstone; baguette, cameo, scarab, solitaire, teardrop; paste, rhinestone, zircon

near antonyms rough

2 someone or something unusually desirable — see PRIZE 1

gemstone *n* a usually valuable stone cut and polished for ornament — see GEM 1

genealogy *n* the line of ancestors from whom a person is descended — see ANCESTRY

general *adj* **1** belonging or relating to the whole ⟨a *general* increase in postage rates⟩ ⟨there's been a *general* improvement in the economy⟩

synonyms blanket, common, generic, global, overall, universal

related words broad, collective, comprehensive, extensive, pervasive, sweeping, ubiquitous, wholesale, wide, widespread; complete, full, plenary; planetary, worldwide

near antonyms component, constituent; crosssectional, divisional, fragmentary, partial; local, localized, regional, sectional

antonyms individual, particular

2 relating to the main elements and not to specific details ⟨gave the *general* impression of being kindhearted⟩ ⟨a *general* course of study in American history⟩

synonyms all-around (*also* all-round), bird's-eye, broad, nonspecific, overall

related words comprehensive, inclusive; absolute, boundless, expansive, extensive, infinite, panoramic, sweeping, vast, wide; indeterminate, nebulous, nondescript, vague; nonspecific, unlimited, unrestricted, unspecified

near antonyms limited, restricted, specified; distinct, explicit, precise, sharp; comprehensive, elaborate, full, mapped (out), thorough; enumerated, inventoried, itemized, listed; individual, singular; particular, peculiar

antonyms delineated, detailed, particularized, specific

3 held by or applicable to a majority of the people ⟨it was the *general* opinion that the politician was a liar⟩ ⟨the *general* mood of the nation was one of hope and optimism⟩

synonyms common, public, popular, prevailing, vulgar

related words unanimous, universal; pop; everyday, familiar, household, usual, well-known; contemporary, current, present; dominant, predominant, preponderant; characteristic, typical; pandemic, pervasive, prevalent, rife, widespread; communal, shared

near antonyms rare, strange, unknown, unusual; distinctive, especial, idiosyncratic, peculiar, special, unique; individual, separate, singular; nonpublic, personal, private

antonyms uncommon, unpopular

4 not limited or specialized in application or purpose ⟨a new kitchen tool of *general* usefulness⟩

synonyms all-around (*also* all-round), all-purpose, unlimited, unqualified, unrestricted, unspecialized

related words broad, wide; nonspecific, unspecified, vague

near antonyms bounded, circumscribed, confined, definite, demarcated, determinate, finite, qualified

antonyms limited, restricted, specialized, technical

generality *n* **1** an idea or statement about all of the members of a group or all the instances of a situation — see GENERALIZATION

2 the main or greater part of something as distinguished from its appendages — see BODY 1

generalization *n* an idea or statement about all of the members of a group or all the instances of a situation ⟨the *generalization* that children who like violent entertainment grow up to be violent criminals⟩

synonyms aphorism, generality, maxim, stereotype

related words concept, conception, notion; precept, rule, rule of thumb; adage, proverb, saw, saying; cliché, commonplace, platitude, truism; hypothesis, proposition, theory

generally *adv* **1** according to the usual course of things — see NATURALLY 2

2 for the most part — see CHIEFLY

generate *vb* to be the cause of (a situation, action, or state of mind) — see EFFECT

generator *n* a person who establishes a whole new field of endeavor — see FATHER 2

generic *adj* belonging or relating to the whole — see GENERAL 1

generosity *n* the quality or state of being generous — see LIBERALITY

generous *adj* **1** giving or sharing in abundance and without hesitation ⟨a civic leader who is very *generous* with his money and time⟩

synonyms bounteous, bountiful, charitable, free, freehanded, liberal, munificent, openhanded, unselfish, unsparing

related words extravagant, handsome, lavish, profuse, unstinting; altruistic, beneficent, benevolent, hospitable, humanitarian, philanthropic; compassionate, good-hearted, greathearted, kindly, magnanimous, openhearted

near antonyms mean, petty, small; frugal, spare, sparing, thrifty; chary, stinting; acquisitive, avaricious, avid, coveting, covetous, desirous, grasping, hoggish, itchy, mercenary, rapacious; begrudging, envious, grudging, resentful

antonyms cheap, close, closefisted, miserly, niggardly, parsimonious, penurious, selfish, stingy, tight, tightfisted, uncharitable

2 being more than enough without being excessive — see PLENTIFUL

generously *adv* in a generous manner — see WELL 2

genesis *n* the point at which something begins — see BEGINNING

genetic *also* **genetical** *adj* genetically passed or capable of being passed from parent to offspring — see HEREDITARY

genial *adj* **1** having an easygoing and pleasing manner especially in social situations — see AMIABLE

2 having or showing kindly feeling and sincere interest — see FRIENDLY 1

3 showing a natural kindness and courtesy especially in social situations — see GRACIOUS 1

geniality *n* the state or quality of having a pleasant or agreeable manner in socializing with others — see AMIABILITY 1

genius *n* **1** a very smart person ⟨the 16-year-old college graduate was considered to be a *genius*⟩

synonyms brain, intellect, thinker, whiz, wizard

related words egghead, highbrow, intellectual; master, virtuoso; ace, crackerjack, natural; sage, savant

near antonyms ignoramus, illiterate, know-nothing; ass, donkey, fool, jackass; beast, boor, cad, churl, clown, creep, cretin, cur, heel, jerk, louse, lout, skunk, snake, stinker

antonyms blockhead, dodo, dolt, dope, dumbbell, dummy, dunce, fathead, goon, half-wit, idiot, imbecile, knothead, moron, nitwit, numskull (*or* numbskull), pinhead

2 a special and usually inborn ability — see TALENT

3 a habitual attraction to some activity or thing — see INCLINATION 1

4 the set of qualities that makes a person, a group of people, or a thing different from others — see NATURE 1

gent *n* an adult male human being — see MAN 1

genteel *adj* **1** following the established traditions of refined society and good taste — see PROPER 1

2 having or showing a taste for the fine arts and gracious living — see CULTIVATED

3 of high birth, rank, or station — see NOBLE 1

4 showing consideration, courtesy, and good manners — see POLITE 1

gentile *n* a person who does not worship the God of the Bible — see HEATHEN 1

gentility *n* speech or behavior that is a sign of good breeding — see POLITENESS

THESAURUS

gentle *adj* **1** not harsh or stern especially in manner, nature, or effect ⟨use a *gentle* detergent on that delicate silk blouse⟩ ⟨the pastor had a *gentle* disposition that calmed everyone he met⟩

synonyms balmy, benign, bland, delicate, light, mellow, mild, soft, soothing, tender

related words sleek, slick, smooth; calm, pacific, peaceful, placid, quiet, serene, tranquil; clement, compassionate, easy, lenient, merciful; buffering, cushioning, softening

near antonyms exquisite, fierce, intense, powerful, severe; forceful, forcible, savage, violent; roughened, rugged, strong; abrading, irritating, roughening; grim, gruff, rude, stiff; heavy-handed, oppressive, tyrannical (*also* tyrannic)

antonyms abrasive, caustic, coarse, hard, harsh, rough, scathing, stern, ungentle

2 marked by temperatures that are neither too high nor too low — see CLEMENT

3 of high birth, rank, or station — see NOBLE 1

gentle *vb* to lessen the shock of — see CUSHION

gentleman *n* **1** a man of high birth or social position ⟨many of the signers of the Declaration of Independence were *gentlemen* who were risking everything⟩

synonyms aristocrat, grandee, noble, nobleman, patrician

related words squire; cavalier, knight; don, nawab, seigneur, seignior, sheikh (*or* sheik); baron, baronet, count, duke, earl, esquire, lord, marquess, marquis, prince, thane, viscount; czar (*also* tsar *or* tzar), magnate, mogul, nabob; socialite, swell

near antonyms boor, churl, cotter (*or* cottar), fellah, peasant, peon; commoner, plebeian; proletarian; toiler

2 an adult male human being — see MAN 1

3 an honorable and courteous man — see CAVALIER

gentlewoman *n* a woman of high birth or social position ⟨in the 19th century a number of American *gentlewomen* used their wealth and influence to further abolitionism, women's rights, and other worthy causes⟩

synonyms dame, lady, noblewoman

related words ladyship, madam; baroness, countess, duchess, marchioness; czarina (*also* tsarina *or* tzarina), empress, queen; dowager, matriarch, matron, mistress

gentry *n* the highest class in a society — see ARISTOCRACY

genuine *adj* **1** being exactly as appears or as claimed — see AUTHENTIC 1

2 free from any intent to deceive or impress others — see GUILELESS

genuinely *adv* in actual fact — see VERY 2

geometry *n* the outward appearance of something as distinguished from its substance — see FORM 1

geriatric *adj* being of advanced years and especially past middle age — see ELDERLY

germane *adj* having to do with the matter at hand — see PERTINENT

germfree *adj* free from filth, infection, or dangers to health — see SANITARY

gestation *n* the state of containing unborn young within the body — see PREGNANCY

gesticulation *n* a movement of the body or limbs that expresses or emphasizes an idea or feeling — see GESTURE 1

gesture *n* **1** a movement of the body or limbs that expresses or emphasizes an idea or feeling ⟨a teenager who often shrugs her shoulders in a *gesture* of indifference⟩

synonyms gesticulation, pantomime, sign, signal

related words beck, flourish, shrug, wave; body language, posture; indication, motion

2 an act or utterance that is a customary show of good manners — see CIVILITY 1

gesture *vb* to direct or notify by a movement or gesture — see MOTION

get *vb* **1** to acquire complete knowledge, understanding, or skill in — see LEARN 1

2 to become affected with (a disease or disorder) — see CONTRACT 1

3 to become the father of — see FATHER

4 to cause (someone) to agree with a belief or course of action by using arguments or earnest requests — see PERSUADE

5 to come upon after searching, study, or effort — see FIND 1

6 to disturb the peace of mind of (someone) especially by repeated disagreeable acts — see IRRITATE 1

7 to eventually have as a state or quality — see BECOME

8 to receive as return for effort — see EARN 1

9 to recognize the meaning of — see COMPREHEND 1

10 to take physical control or possession of (something) suddenly or forcibly — see CATCH 1

11 to leave a place often for another — see GO 2

get along *vb* **1** to meet one's day-to-day needs ⟨most college students can *get along* with just a few hours of sleep at night⟩

synonyms cope, do, fare, get by, get on, make out, manage, shift

related words carry on, contrive, fend, handle, scrape (by *or* through), survive; eke out, scrape (out), scrounge, squeeze, wrest, wring; afford, swing

phrases make shift

near antonyms collapse, fail, fall short, fizzle, flounder; decline, peter (out), slump, wane; give up

2 to move forward along a course — see GO 1

getaway *n* the act or an instance of getting free from danger or confinement — see ESCAPE 1

get by *vb* to meet one's day-to-day needs — see GET ALONG 1

get off *vb* **1** to leave a place often for another — see GO 2

2 to take the first step in (a process or course of action) — see BEGIN 1

get on *vb* to meet one's day-to-day needs — see GET ALONG 1

get out *vb* **1** to become known ⟨news of the rock star's secret wedding *got out* to the news media⟩

synonyms come out, leak (out), out, spread

related words break, develop, transpire, unfold; circulate, disclose, reveal, spill, tell

near antonyms hush (up), suppress; conceal, disguise, hide, mask; secrete

2 to get free from a dangerous or confining situation — see ESCAPE 1

3 to produce and release for distribution in printed form — see PUBLISH 1

get–together *n* **1** a coming together of a number of persons for a specified purpose — see MEETING 1

2 a social gathering — see PARTY 1

getup *n* clothing chosen as appropriate for a specific situation — see OUTFIT 1

get up *vb* to leave one's bed — see ARISE 1

gewgaw *n* a small object displayed for its attractiveness or interest — see KNICKKNACK

ghastliness *n* the quality of inspiring intense dread or dismay — see HORROR 1

ghastly *adj* extremely disturbing or repellent — see HORRIBLE 1

ghost *n* the soul of a dead person thought of especially as appearing to living people ⟨looked for *ghosts* in the graveyard on Halloween⟩
synonyms apparition, bogey (*also* bogy *or* bogie), phantasm, phantom, poltergeist, shade, shadow, specter (*or* spectre), spirit, spook, vision, wraith
related words banshee, demon (*or* daemon), familiar (*or* familiar spirit), genie, imp, incubus, puck; vampire, zombie

ghoul *n* an evil spirit — see DEMON

giant *adj* unusually large — see HUGE

giant *n* something that is unusually large and powerful ⟨the Great Pyramids of Egypt are *giants*⟩
synonyms behemoth, blockbuster, colossus, jumbo, leviathan, mammoth, monster, titan, whale, whopper
related words amazon; bulk, hulk; heavyweight
near antonyms lightweight, weakling, wimp, wisp; nonentity, twerp, whippersnapper
antonyms dwarf, midget, mini, miniature, peewee, pygmy, runt, shrimp

gibber *vb* to speak rapidly, inarticulately, and usually unintelligibly — see BABBLE 1

gibberish *n* unintelligible or meaningless talk ⟨was so excited he could only talk *gibberish*⟩
synonyms babble, blabber, bunk, claptrap, drivel, fudge, gabble, gobbledygook (*also* gobbledegook), hogwash, jabber, jabberwocky, jazz, moonshine, mumbo jumbo, nonsense, piffle, prattle, rigmarole, rot
related words abracadabra; chatter, clatter, gab, gibber, prate, tattle, twaddle; double-talk, hocuspocus, jive; gas, hot air, wind

gibe *or* **jibe** *vb* to make (someone or something) the object of unkind laughter — see RIDICULE

giddy *adj* **1** lacking in seriousness or maturity ⟨the *giddy* youngsters continued to laugh, joke, and make faces during the ceremonies⟩
synonyms featherbrained, flighty, frivolous, goofy, harebrained, light-headed, puerile, scatterbrained, silly
related words fatuous, foolish, inane, nonsensical, thoughtless, witless; crazy, daffy, daft, exuberant, flippant, fluttery, light, lighthearted, playful; sappy, shallow, superficial
near antonyms grave, melancholy, somber (*or* sombre), thoughtful; dignified, heavy, no-nonsense, sedate, severe, solemn, staid
antonyms earnest, serious, serious-minded, sober
2 having a feeling of being whirled about and in danger of falling down — see DIZZY 1

gift *n* **1** something given to someone without expectation of a return ⟨gave him a *gift* for his birthday⟩
synonyms bestowal, donation, freebie (*or* freebee), giveaway, lagniappe, largess (*or* largesse), present, presentation
related words alms, benefaction, beneficence, benevolence, charity, contribution, dole, generosity, offering, philanthropy; grant, subsidy; remembrance, tribute; bonus, boon, windfall; favor,

valentine; gratuity, tip; award, prize, reward; bequest, legacy; sacrifice
near antonyms advance, loan; bribe, sop
2 a special and usually inborn ability — see TALENT

gigantic *adj* unusually large — see HUGE

giggle *n* an explosive sound that is a sign of amusement — see LAUGH 1

gimmick *n* **1** a clever often underhanded means to achieve an end — see TRICK 1
2 an interesting and often novel device with a practical use — see GADGET

ginger *n* active strength of body or mind — see VIGOR 1

gingerbread *adj* elaborately and often excessively decorated — see ORNATE

gingerly *adj* having or showing a close attentiveness to avoiding danger or trouble — see CAREFUL 1

gingery *adj* **1** having active strength of body or mind — see VIGOROUS 1
2 marked by a lively display of strong feeling — see SPIRITED 1

gird *vb* **1** to encircle or bind with or as if with a belt ⟨for the celebration of the heroes' return, well-wishers *girded* hundreds of trees with yellow ribbons⟩ ⟨she *girded* her waist with a delicate sash⟩
synonyms band, belt, girdle, girt, girth, wrap
related words tie up, truss; circle, loop, wind, wreathe; bandage, swathe; chain, cord, enchain, lash, rope, shackle, tape, wire
near antonyms loose, loosen, unbind, unchain, undo, unfasten, unlash, untie, unwind
antonyms unwrap
2 to gather into a tight mass by means of a line or cord — see TIE 1

girdle *n* a strip of flexible material (as leather) worn around the waist — see ²BELT

girdle *vb* **1** to encircle or bind with or as if with a belt — see GIRD 1
2 to pass completely around — see ENCIRCLE 1

girl *n* **1** a young usually unmarried woman ⟨a book that discusses the special challenges that *girls* face as they enter their teenage years⟩
synonyms bobby-soxer, chick [*slang*], damsel, doll, gal, lass, lassie, mademoiselle, maid, maiden, miss
related words gamine; hoyden, tomboy; hussy; ingenue; belle, deb, debutante, sylph; schoolgirl; teenybopper; senorita (*or* señorita)
2 a woman with whom one is in love — see GIRLFRIEND

girlfriend *n* a woman with whom one is in love ⟨he proposed to his *girlfriend* of seven years⟩
synonyms gal, girl, ladylove
related words mistress; beloved, darling, dear, favorite, flame, honey, love, lover, sweet, sweetheart, valentine

girlish *adj* having or displaying qualities more suitable for women than for men — see EFFEMINATE

girt *vb* to encircle or bind with or as if with a belt — see GIRD 1

girth *n* the distance around a round body — see CIRCUMFERENCE 1

girth *vb* **1** to encircle or bind with or as if with a belt — see GIRD 1
2 to pass completely around — see ENCIRCLE 1

gist *n* the central part or aspect of something under consideration — see CRUX

give *vb* **1** to make a present of ⟨tutors *gave* their time to help students after school⟩
synonyms bestow, contribute, donate, present
related words chip in, kick in, pitch in; award, confer, dole (out); endow; afford, furnish, provide; lavish, regale; aid, assist, benefit, help; administer, dispense, impart, issue, render; extend, offer, pay, proffer, tender; sacrifice
near antonyms hold, keep, pocket, retain, withhold; preserve, save; advance, lend, loan; sell
2 to put (something) into the possession or safekeeping of another ⟨*gave* my camera to my father to hold while I went swimming⟩
synonyms commend, commit, consign, delegate, deliver, entrust, hand over, leave, pass, transfer, transmit, trust, turn over, vest
related words confer, grant; assign, deal (out), dispense, disperse, distribute, divide; release, relinquish, submit, surrender, turn in, yield; bequeath, hand down, will; advance, lend, loan; furnish, supply
near antonyms detain, hold back, reserve, withhold; own, possess; accept, receive, take in; occupy, take, take over
antonyms hold, keep, retain
3 to bring before the public in performance or exhibition — see PRESENT 1
4 to fall down or in as a result of physical pressure — see COLLAPSE 1
5 to hand over or use up in payment — see SPEND 1
6 to make known (as an idea, emotion, or opinion) — see EXPRESS 1
7 to occupy (oneself) diligently or with close attention — see APPLY 2
8 to produce as revenue — see YIELD 2
9 to put (something) into the possession of someone for use or consumption — see FURNISH 2
10 to put before another for acceptance or consideration — see OFFER 1
give–and–take *n* **1** an exchange of views for the purpose of exploring a subject or deciding an issue — see DISCUSSION 1
2 the act or practice of each side giving up something in order to reach an agreement — see CONCESSION 1
3 good-natured teasing or exchanging of clever remarks — see BANTER
giveaway *n* something given to someone without expectation of a return — see GIFT 1
give away *vb* to make known (something abstract) through outward signs — see SHOW 2
give in *vb* **1** to give up and cease resistance (as to a liking, temptation, or habit) — see YIELD 1
2 to cease resistance (as to another's arguments, demands, or control) — see YIELD 3
given *adj* **1** being in the habit or custom — see ACCUSTOMED
2 having a tendency to be or act in a certain way — see PRONE 1
given name *n* a name that is placed before one's family name — see FORENAME
give out *vb* to stop functioning — see FAIL 1
give up *vb* **1** to give (something) over to the control or possession of another usually under duress — see SURRENDER 1
2 to stop doing (something) permanently — see QUIT 2
3 to yield to the control or power of enemy forces — see FALL 2

giving *n* the act of offering money in exchange for goods or services — see PAYMENT 1
gizmo *or* **gismo** *n* an interesting and often novel device with a practical use — see GADGET
glacial *adj* **1** having a low or subnormal temperature — see COLD 1
2 lacking in friendliness or warmth of feeling — see COLD 2
glad *adj* **1** experiencing pleasure, satisfaction, or delight ⟨the husband was *glad* to see his wife again, after so long an absence⟩
synonyms blissful, delighted, gratified, happy, joyful, joyous, pleased, satisfied, tickled
related words beaming, blithe, blithesome, buoyant, cheerful, cheery, gay, gladsome, lighthearted, sunny, upbeat; gleeful, jocund, jolly, jovial, laughing, merry, mirthful, smiling; carried away, ecstatic, elated, enraptured, entranced, euphoric, exhilarated, intoxicated, rapturous, rhapsodic; exuberant, exultant, jubilant, rapt, rejoicing, thrilled; hopeful, optimistic, rosy, sanguine
near antonyms abject, aggrieved, anguished, blue, brokenhearted, dejected, depressed, despondent, disconsolate, disheartened, downcast, downhearted, forlorn, melancholy; doleful, dolorous, lachrymose, mournful, plaintive, sorrowful, sorry, woeful; black, dark, desolate, dispirited, gloomy, glum, gray (*also* grey), grieved, heartbroken, heartsick, miserable, woebegone, wretched
antonyms displeased, joyless, sad, unhappy, unsatisfied
2 having a desire or inclination (as for a specified course of action) — see WILLING 1
3 serving to lift one's spirits — see CHEERFUL 2
gladden *vb* to give satisfaction to — see PLEASE
gladdening *adj* making one feel good inside — see HEARTWARMING
gladiatorial *adj* feeling or displaying eagerness to fight — see BELLIGERENT
gladness *n* **1** a feeling or state of well-being and contentment — see HAPPINESS 1
2 the feeling experienced when one's wishes are met — see PLEASURE 1
gladsome *adj* having or showing a good mood or disposition — see CHEERFUL 1
glamorize *also* **glamourize** *vb* to represent or think of as better than reality — see IDEALIZE
glamorous *also* **glamourous** *adj* **1** excitingly or mysteriously unusual — see EXOTIC
2 having an often mysterious or magical power to attract — see FASCINATING 1
glamour *also* **glamor** *n* the power of irresistible attraction — see CHARM 2
glance *n* an instance of looking especially briefly — see LOOK 2
glance *vb* **1** to strike and fly off at an angle ⟨the basketball *glanced* off the rim⟩ ⟨her wild pitch *glanced* off my shoulder and landed in the dugout⟩
synonyms bounce, carom, rebound, ricochet, skim, skip
related words brush, graze, nudge, shave, sweep; bump, contact, hit, kiss, touch; sideswipe; reflect
2 to take a quick or hasty look ⟨just *glanced* at the instructions before assembling the bike⟩ ⟨*glanced* over his shoulder to see if she was still there⟩
synonyms browse, dip, glimpse, peek, skim
related words peep; blink, squint; look over, scan
near antonyms examine, overlook, oversee, ques-

tion, survey; study, view; peer, pry; gawk, goggle, rubberneck; leer, ogle

antonyms gaze, stare

3 to shoot forth bursts of light — see FLASH 1

glare *n* the steady giving off of the form of radiation that makes vision possible — see LIGHT 1

glare *vb* **1** to shine with a bright harsh light ⟨the spotlight *glared* down on the suspect as the police questioned him relentlessly⟩

synonyms beat, blaze, burn, flame, flare

related words beam, glow, radiate; flash, glance, gleam, glimmer, glint, glisten, glister, glitter, scintillate, shimmer, sparkle, twinkle; bedazzle, blind, daze, dazzle

2 to look with anger or disapproval — see FROWN

glaring *adj* very noticeable especially for being incorrect or bad — see EGREGIOUS

glasses *n pl* a pair of lenses set in a frame that is held in place with ear supports and which are usually worn to correct vision ⟨I'm a little nearsighted, so I'm going to need *glasses*⟩

synonyms eyeglasses, specs, spectacles

related words bifocals; monocle, pince-nez; sunglasses; goggles; contact lens

gleam *n* the steady giving off of the form of radiation that makes vision possible — see LIGHT 1

gleam *vb* to shoot forth bursts of light — see FLASH 1

glee *n* a mood characterized by high spirits and amusement and often accompanied by laughter — see MIRTH

glee club *n* an organized group of singers — see CHORUS 1

gleeful *adj* indicative of or marked by high spirits or good humor — see MERRY

gleefulness *n* a mood characterized by high spirits and amusement and often accompanied by laughter — see MIRTH

glide *vb* **1** to move or proceed smoothly and readily — see FLOW 2

2 to move through the air with or as if with outstretched wings — see FLY 1

3 to rest or move along the surface of a liquid or in the air — see FLOAT

glimmer *n* a very small amount — see PARTICLE 1

glimmer *vb* to shoot forth bursts of light — see FLASH 1

glimpse *n* an instance of looking especially briefly — see LOOK 2

glimpse *vb* to take a quick or hasty look — see GLANCE 2

glint *vb* to shoot forth bursts of light — see FLASH 1

glisten *vb* to shoot forth bursts of light — see FLASH 1

glistening *adj* having a shiny surface or finish — see GLOSSY

glister *vb* to shoot forth bursts of light — see FLASH 1

glitter *vb* to shoot forth bursts of light — see FLASH 1

glitz *n* excessive or unnecessary display — see OSTENTATION

glitzy *adj* excessively showy — see GAUDY

gloaming *n* **1** a time or place of little or no light — see DARK 1

2 the time from when the sun begins to set to the onset of total darkness — see DUSK 1

glob *n* **1** a small uneven mass — see LUMP 1

2 the quantity of fluid that falls naturally in one rounded mass — see DROP 1

global *adj* **1** belonging or relating to the whole — see GENERAL 1

2 covering everything or all important points — see ENCYCLOPEDIC

3 having every part of the surface the same distance from the center — see ROUND 1

globe *n* **1** a more or less round body or mass — see ¹BALL 1

2 the celestial body on which we live — see EARTH 1

globule *n* the quantity of fluid that falls naturally in one rounded mass — see DROP 1

gloom *n* **1** a state or spell of low spirits — see SADNESS

2 a time or place of little or no light — see DARK 1

gloom *vb* **1** to look with anger or disapproval — see FROWN

2 to take on a gloomy or forbidding look — see DARKEN 1

gloominess *n* a state or spell of low spirits — see SADNESS

gloomy *adj* **1** causing or marked by an atmosphere lacking in cheer ⟨the cold rain made for a *gloomy* day⟩

synonyms black, bleak, cheerless, comfortless, dark, darkening, depressing, desolate, dismal, drear, dreary, elegiac, funereal, glum, gray (*also* grey), miserable, morbid, morose, murky, saturnine, sepulchral, somber (*or* sombre), sullen, wretched

related words dejected, depressed, despondent, disconsolate, droopy, inconsolable, low, melancholy, sad, unhappy, woebegone, woeful; discomfiting, discouraging, disheartening, dismaying, dispiriting, distressful, distressing, upsetting; desperate, hopeless, pessimistic; lamentable, lugubrious, mournful, sorrowful; cloudy, colorless, drab, dull; dour, grim, lowering (*also* louring), menacing, negative, oppressive, threatening

near antonyms blithe, blithesome, buoyant, gay, jocund, jolly, joyful, joyous, merry, mirthful; encouraging, hopeful, optimistic; lighthearted, lightsome

antonyms bright, cheerful, cheering, cheery, comforting, cordial, gay, festive, friendly, heartwarming, sunshiny

2 feeling unhappiness — see SAD 1

3 being without light or without much light — see DARK 1

glorify *vb* **1** to enhance the status of — see EXALT

2 to offer honor or respect to (someone) as a divine power — see WORSHIP 1

3 to praise or publicize lavishly and often excessively — see TOUT 1

4 to proclaim the glory of — see PRAISE 1

5 to represent or think of as better than reality — see IDEALIZE

glorious *adj* large and impressive in size, grandeur, extent, or conception — see GRAND 1

gloriously *adv* in a pleasing way — see WELL 5

gloriousness *n* impressiveness of beauty on a large scale — see MAGNIFICENCE

glory *n* **1** public acknowledgment or admiration for an achievement ⟨the drama teacher gave the stage crew all the *glory* for the successful production⟩

synonyms acclaim, accolade, credit, distinction, homage, honor, laurels

related words celebrity, fame, renown, repute; compliment, encomium, eulogy, panegyric, toast, tribute; acclamation, ovation, plaudit, praise, rave, rhapsody; citation, commendation, note, recommendation; elevation, exaltation, glorification

2 an asset that brings praise or renown ⟨the new computer lab was the *glory* of the middle school⟩
synonyms boast, credit, honor, jewel, pride, treasure
related words pièce de résistance, showpiece; attraction, feature, highlight; distinction, excellence, merit, value, virtue
phrases a feather in one's cap
near antonyms disgrace, dishonor; blemish, blot, defect, shame, slur, smirch, smudge, stain, stigma; eyesore, fright, horror, mess
3 impressiveness of beauty on a large scale — see MAGNIFICENCE

glory *vb* to feel or express joy or triumph — see EXULT
glorying *adj* having or expressing feelings of joy or triumph — see EXULTANT
gloss *n* brightness created by light reflected from a surface — see SHINE 1
gloss *vb* to make smooth or glossy usually by repeatedly applying surface pressure — see POLISH
gloss (over) *vb* **1** to make (something) seem less bad by offering excuses — see PALLIATE 1
2 to overlook or dismiss as of little importance — see EXCUSE 1
glossy *adj* having a shiny surface or finish ⟨the *glossy* finish on the gym floor⟩ ⟨a sports car with an interior upholstered with *glossy* leather⟩
synonyms buffed, burnished, glistening, lustrous, polished, rubbed, satin, satiny, sleek
related words silken, silky, slick, slippery; glassy, glazed, lacquered, shellacked, varnished; gleaming, glittering, reflective, shining
near antonyms lackluster
antonyms dim, dull, flat, lusterless, matte (*also* mat *or* matt)
glow *n* the steady giving off of the form of radiation that makes vision possible — see LIGHT 1
glow *vb* **1** to be on fire especially brightly — see BURN 1
2 to develop a rosy facial color (as from excitement or embarrassment) — see BLUSH
glower *vb* **1** to look with anger or disapproval — see FROWN
2 to take on a gloomy or forbidding look — see DARKEN 1
glowing *adj* **1** giving off or reflecting much light — see BRIGHT 1
2 having a healthy reddish skin tone — see RUDDY
3 having or being an outward sign of good feelings (as of love, confidence, or happiness) — see RADIANT 1
4 having or expressing great depth of feeling — see FERVENT
gloze (over) *vb* **1** to make (something) seem less bad by offering excuses — see PALLIATE 1
2 to overlook or dismiss as of little importance — see EXCUSE 1
glue *n* a substance used to stick things together ⟨used *glue* to stick the photo in the album⟩
synonyms adhesive, cement, size
related words epoxy, epoxy resin, library paste, mucilage, superglue; dope, goo, gum

gluey *adj* being of such a thick consistency as to readily cling to objects upon contact — see STICKY 1
glum *adj* **1** causing or marked by an atmosphere lacking in cheer — see GLOOMY 1
2 feeling unhappiness — see SAD 1
3 given to or displaying a resentful silence and often irritability — see SULKY
glut *vb* to fill with food to capacity — see GORGE 1
glutinous *adj* being of such a thick consistency as to readily cling to objects upon contact — see STICKY 1
glutton *n* one who eats greedily or too much ⟨he's such a *glutton* that he ate the whole cake⟩
synonyms gorger, gormandizer, gourmand, hog, overeater, stuffer, swiller
related words feaster, trencherman; muncher; guzzler
near antonyms dieter, nibbler, picker
gluttonous *adj* having a huge appetite — see VORACIOUS 1
gnash *vb* to press or strike against or together so as to make a scraping sound — see GRIND 2
gnaw (on) *vb* to crush or grind with the teeth — see BITE (ON)
gnawer *n* one who is obnoxiously annoying — see NUISANCE 1
gnome *n* an imaginary being usually having a small human form and magical powers — see FAIRY
go *adj* being in a state of fitness for some experience or action — see READY 1
go *n* **1** a practice or interest that is very popular for a short time — see FAD
2 active strength of body or mind — see VIGOR 1
3 an effort to do or accomplish something — see ATTEMPT
4 readiness to engage in daring or difficult activity — see ENTERPRISE 2
go *vb* **1** to move forward along a course ⟨everything is *going* according to our plans⟩
synonyms advance, fare, forge, get along, march, proceed, progress
related words accelerate, fast-forward, speed; approach, near; journey, pass, repair, run, travel, wend; actuate, drive, impel, propel, push; do, go off, take out
phrases gain ground
near antonyms arrest, balk, block, check, detain, halt, hinder, hold back, impede, nip, obstruct, slow (down *or* up), stem; repress, retard, stunt, suppress; delay, interrupt, stall; cramp, hamper, inhibit; cease, let up, pause; regress
antonyms remain, stand, stay, stop
2 to leave a place often for another ⟨will *go* on vacation at the end of the year⟩ ⟨decided it would be better to *go* before she got any angrier⟩
synonyms begone, clear out, depart, exit, get, get off, move, pull (out), quit, sally (forth), shove (off), take off, walk out
related words set out, start, strike out; abscond, decamp, escape, evacuate, flee, fly, get out, run away, scat, scram, skip; go out, light out, step out; abandon, desert, forsake, vacate; emigrate; remove, retire, retreat, withdraw
phrases beat it
near antonyms abide, dwell, lodge, remain, settle, stay, tarry; approach, close, near; hit, land, reach
antonyms arrive, come, show up, turn up
3 to be fitting or proper — see DO 1

4 to be in agreement on every point — see CHECK 1

5 to be positioned along a certain course or in a certain direction — see RUN 3

6 to eventually have as a state or quality — see BECOME

7 to fall down or in as a result of physical pressure — see COLLAPSE 1

8 to have or be in a usual or proper place — see BELONG 1

9 to lose bodily strength or vigor — see WEAKEN 2

10 to make one's way through, across, or over — see TRAVERSE

11 to occur within a continuous range of variation — see RUN 4

12 to risk (something) on the outcome of an uncertain event — see BET

go (for) *vb* to have a price of — see COST

go (on) *vb* to take place — see HAPPEN

go (to) *vb* to use or seek out as a source of aid, relief, or advantage — see RESORT (TO) 1

goad *n* something that arouses action or activity — see IMPULSE

goad *vb* **1** to try to persuade (someone) through earnest appeals to follow a course of action — see URGE

2 to urge or push forward with or as if with a pointed object — see PROD 1

goal *n* something that one hopes or intends to accomplish ⟨graduating from high school with honors is one of my main *goals*⟩

synonyms aim, ambition, aspiration, design, dream, end, intent, intention, mark, meaning, object, objective, plan, pretension, purpose, target, thing

related words plot, project, scheme; desire, hope, wish; destination, terminus

near antonyms means, method, way

goat *n* a person or thing taking the blame for others — see SCAPEGOAT

¹gob *n* **1** a small uneven mass — see LUMP 1

2 gobs *pl* a considerable amount — see LOT 2

²gob *n* one who operates or navigates a seagoing vessel — see SAILOR

gobbet *n* a small uneven mass — see LUMP 1

gobbledygook *also* **gobbledegook** *n* unintelligible or meaningless talk — see GIBBERISH

go–between *n* **1** one that carries a message or does an errand — see MESSENGER

2 one who works with opposing sides in order to bring about an agreement — see MEDIATOR

goblin *n* an imaginary being usually having a small human form and magical powers — see FAIRY

god *n* **1** a being having superhuman powers and control over a particular part of life or the world — see DEITY 1

2 *cap* the being worshipped as the creator and ruler of the universe — see DEITY 2

goddess *n* a lovely woman — see BEAUTY 2

godhead *n* **1** the quality or state of being divine — see DIVINITY

2 *cap* the being worshipped as the creator and ruler of the universe — see DEITY 2

godhood *n* the quality or state of being divine — see DIVINITY

godless *adj* lacking religious emotions, principles, or practices — see IRRELIGIOUS

godlike *adj* of, relating to, or being God — see HOLY 3

godliness *n* the quality or state of being spiritually pure or virtuous — see HOLINESS

godly *adj* showing a devotion to God and to a life of virtue — see HOLY 1

godsend *n* something that provides happiness or does good for a person or thing — see BLESSING 2

Godspeed *n* an expression of good wishes at parting — see GOOD-BYE

go–getter *n* an ambitious person who eagerly goes after what is desired ⟨a *go-getter* with his sights set on the presidency⟩

synonyms hummer, hustler, live wire, powerhouse, rustler, self-starter

related words dasher; doer, enterpriser; he-man

near antonyms dawdler, idler, loafer, lounger, putterer, trifler; goldbrick, malingerer, procrastinator, shirker, slacker; drone, lazybones, sluggard; dallier, laggard, lingerer, loiterer, slowpoke, stick-in-the-mud; ignorer, ne'er-do-well, neglecter; daydreamer, dreamer; dropout, quitter

go–getting *adj* **1** having a strong desire for personal advancement — see AMBITIOUS 1

2 having or showing a bold forcefulness in the pursuit of a goal — see AGGRESSIVE 1

go–getting *n* eager desire for personal advancement — see AMBITION 1

goggle *vb* to look long and hard in wonder or surprise — see GAPE

going *adj* **1** accepted, used, or practiced by most people — see CURRENT 1

2 being in effective operation — see ACTIVE 1

3 having attained a desired end or state of good fortune — see SUCCESSFUL 1

going *n* **1** forward movement in time or place — see ADVANCE 1

2 the act of leaving a place — see DEPARTURE

gold *n* something (as pieces of stamped metal or printed paper) customarily and legally used as a medium of exchange, a measure of value, or a means of payment — see MONEY

goldbrick *n* one who deliberately avoids work or duty — see SLACKER

golden *adj* **1** having qualities which inspire hope — see HOPEFUL 1

2 marked by conspicuously full and rich sounds or tones — see RESONANT

3 marked by vigorous growth and well-being especially economically — see PROSPEROUS 1

4 of a pale yellow or yellowish brown color — see BLOND

5 pointing toward a happy outcome — see FAVORABLE 2

golden–ager *n* a person of advanced years — see SENIOR CITIZEN

golden mean *n* a middle point between extremes — see MEAN 1

gone *adj* **1** no longer existing — see EXTINCT

2 no longer living — see DEAD 1

3 no longer possessed — see LOST

good *adj* **1** based on sound reasoning or information ⟨had enough information to make a *good* assessment of the situation⟩

synonyms commonsense, hard, informed, just, justified, levelheaded, logical, rational, reasonable, reasoned, sensible, sober, solid, valid, wellfounded

related words actual, real, true; certain, sure; certified, validated, verified; confirmed, corroborated, substantiated; cogent, convincing, credible

near antonyms unsubstantiated, unsupported, unwarranted; flimsy, implausible, unconvincing, weak; fallacious, false, misled

antonyms groundless, illogical, invalid, irrational, nonrational, nonsensical, nonvalid, unfounded, ungrounded, uninformed, unjustified, unreasonable, unsound

2 conforming to a high standard of morality or virtue ⟨a *good* person who seldom did wrong⟩ ⟨*good* behavior will earn you the respect of others⟩

synonyms decent, ethical, honest, honorable, just, moral, right, righteous, right-minded, straight, upright, virtuous

related words correct, decorous, proper, seemly; high-minded, noble, principled; commendable, creditable, exemplary, legitimate; esteemed, law-abiding, reputable, respected, upstanding, worthy; blameless, clean, guiltless, immaculate, incorruptible, innocent, inoffensive, irreproachable, unobjectionable; lily-white, pure, scrupulous, spotless, uncorrupted, unerring; goody-goody, moralistic, sanctimonious, self-righteous

near antonyms improper, incorrect, indecorous, naughty, unbecoming, unseemly; corrupt, debased, debauched, degenerate, depraved, dissolute, perverted, reprobate; unprincipled, unscrupulous; atrocious, infamous, villainous; base, low, mean, vicious, vile; blameworthy, objectionable, offensive; iniquitous, nefarious; errant, erring, fallen

antonyms bad, black, dishonest, dishonorable, evil, evil-minded, immoral, indecent, sinful, unethical, unrighteous, wicked, wrong

3 according to the rules of logic — see LOGICAL 1

4 being to one's liking — see SATISFACTORY 1

5 expressing approval — see FAVORABLE 1

6 firm in one's allegiance to someone or something — see FAITHFUL 1

7 giving pleasure or contentment to the mind or senses — see PLEASANT

8 having or showing exceptional knowledge, experience, or skill in a field of endeavor — see PROFICIENT

9 having sufficient worth or merit to receive one's honor, esteem, or reward — see WORTHY

10 having the required skills for an acceptable level of performance — see COMPETENT

11 meeting the requirements of a purpose or situation — see FIT 1

12 showing or expressing acceptance or approval — see POSITIVE

13 sufficiently large in size, amount, or number to merit attention — see CONSIDERABLE 1

14 worthy of one's trust — see DEPENDABLE

good *adv* in a satisfactory way — see WELL 1

good *n* **1** something that provides happiness or does good for a person or thing — see BLESSING 2

2 the state of doing well especially in relation to one's happiness or success — see WELFARE

3 goods *pl* products that are bought and sold in business — see MERCHANDISE

Good Book *n* a book made up of the writings accepted by Christians as coming from God — see BIBLE

good–bye *or* **good–by** *n* an expression of good wishes at parting ⟨said our *good-byes* and headed for home⟩

synonyms adieu, au revoir, bon voyage, farewell, Godspeed

related words leave-taking, send-off

near antonyms greeting(s), salutation, salute; welcome

antonyms hello

good–hearted *adj* having or marked by sympathy and consideration for others — see HUMANE 1

goodly *adj* **1** of a size greater than average of its kind — see LARGE

2 sufficiently large in size, amount, or number to merit attention — see CONSIDERABLE 1

good–natured *adj* having an easygoing and pleasing manner especially in social situations — see AMIABLE

good–naturedness *n* **1** a desire or disposition to please — see COMPLAISANCE

2 the state or quality of having a pleasant or agreeable manner in socializing with others — see AMIABILITY 1

goodness *n* conduct that conforms to an accepted standard of right and wrong — see MORALITY 1

good–sized *adj* **1** of a size greater than average of its kind — see LARGE

2 sufficiently large in size, amount, or number to merit attention — see CONSIDERABLE 1

good–tempered *adj* having an easygoing and pleasing manner especially in social situations — see AMIABLE

good–temperedness *n* the state or quality of having a pleasant or agreeable manner in socializing with others — see AMIABILITY 1

goodwill *n* **1** kindly concern, interest, or support ⟨the long tradition of *goodwill* that exists between the United States and Canada⟩

synonyms amity, benevolence, cordiality, fellowship, friendliness, friendship, kindliness

related words camaraderie, community, companionship, comradeship; civility, comity, concord, harmony, rapport; charity, generosity, neighborliness; affinity, communion, empathy, sympathy, tolerance; altruism, philanthropy, selflessness

near antonyms disfavor, intolerance; animosity, antagonism, antipathy, enmity, hate, hatred, hostility, incivility, malice, rancor

antonyms ill will, malevolence

2 cheerful readiness to do something — see ALACRITY

goody *n* something that is pleasing to eat because it is rare or a luxury — see DELICACY 1

gooey *adj* being of such a thick consistency as to readily cling to objects upon contact — see STICKY 1

goof *n* an unintentional departure from truth or accuracy — see ERROR 1

go off *vb* to break open or into pieces usually because of internal pressure — see EXPLODE 1

goofy *adj* lacking in seriousness or maturity — see GIDDY 1

goon *n* **1** a stupid person — see IDIOT

2 a violent, brutal person who is often a member of an organized gang — see HOODLUM

goose *n* a person who lacks good sense or judgment — see FOOL 1

goose egg *n* the numerical symbol 0 or the absence of number or quantity represented by it — see ZERO 1

go over *vb* to turn out as planned or desired — see SUCCEED 1

gore *vb* to penetrate or hold (something) with a pointed object — see IMPALE

gorge *n* a narrow opening between hillsides or

mountains that can be used for passage — see CANYON

gorge *vb* **1** to fill with food to capacity ⟨they *gorged* themselves on the four pies Aunt Martha brought for Thanksgiving⟩
synonyms glut, sate, stuff, surfeit
related words gobble, gormandize, pig out; gulp, guzzle; cloy, fill; banquet, feast, regale
near antonyms diet, fast
2 to eat greedily or to excess ⟨the kids *gorged* on Halloween candy when they got home from trick-or-treating⟩
synonyms gormandize, overeat, pig out, swill
related words devour, glut, sate, stuff, surfeit, wolf; banquet, feast, regale; bolt, cram, gulp, guzzle
near antonyms nibble, peck, pick, taste

gorgeous *adj* very pleasing to look at — see BEAUTIFUL

gorgeousness *n* the qualities in a person or thing that as a whole give pleasure to the senses — see BEAUTY 1

gorger *n* one who eats greedily or too much — see GLUTTON

gormandize *vb* to eat greedily or to excess — see GORGE 2

gormandizer *n* one who eats greedily or too much — see GLUTTON

gory *adj* containing, smeared, or stained with blood — see BLOODY 1

gospel *n* the basic beliefs or guiding principles of a person or group — see CREED 1

gossamer *adj* **1** being of a material lacking in sturdiness or substance — see FLIMSY 1
2 resembling air in lightness — see AIRY 1
3 very thin and easy to see through — see SHEER 1

gossamery *adj* **1** being of a material lacking in sturdiness or substance — see FLIMSY 1
2 resembling air in lightness — see AIRY 1
3 very thin and easy to see through — see SHEER 1

gossip *n* friendly, informal conversation or an instance of this — see CHAT

gossip *vb* to relate sometimes questionable or secret information of a personal nature ⟨likes to *gossip* with others about our neighbors' arguments⟩
synonyms blab, talk, tattle
related words bandy (about), circulate, noise (about), rumor; disclose, divulge, reveal, tell; hint, imply, insinuate, intimate, let on, suggest; inform, report, snitch, squeal, tip (off); babble, spill; confide
phrases spill the beans
near antonyms clam up, shut up

gossipy *adj* having the style and content of everyday conversation — see CHATTY 1

gouge *vb* to charge (someone) too much for goods or services — see OVERCHARGE 1

gourmand *n* **1** a person with refined tastes in food and wine — see EPICURE
2 one who eats greedily or too much — see GLUTTON

gourmet *n* a person with refined tastes in food and wine — see EPICURE

govern *vb* **1** to exercise authority or power over ⟨the president is elected in order to *govern* the country⟩

synonyms boss, captain, command, control, preside (over), rule
related words conduct, direct, head, lead; administer, manage, oversee, regulate, superintend, supervise; dictate, dominate, domineer, lord (it over), master, oppress, reign (over), tyrannize; conquer, subdue, subjugate
2 to keep from exceeding a desirable degree or level (as of expression) — see CONTROL 1
3 to look after and make decisions about — see CONDUCT 1

governance *n* **1** lawful control over the affairs of a political unit (as a nation) — see RULE 2
2 the act or activity of looking after and making decisions about something — see CONDUCT 1

government *n* **1** lawful control over the affairs of a political unit (as a nation) — see RULE 2
2 the act or activity of looking after and making decisions about something — see CONDUCT 1

gown *n* a garment with a joined blouse and skirt for a woman or girl — see DRESS 1

gown *vb* to outfit with clothes and especially fine or special clothes — see CLOTHE 1

grab *n* an instance of theft — see THEFT 2

grab *vb* to take physical control or possession of (something) suddenly or forcibly — see CATCH 1

grace *n* **1** an act of kind assistance — see FAVOR 1
2 dignified or restrained beauty of form, appearance, or style — see ELEGANCE

grace *vb* to make more attractive by adding something that is beautiful or becoming — see DECORATE

graceful *adj* **1** moving easily ⟨the *graceful* ballerina effortlessly leapt across the dance floor⟩
synonyms agile, light, light-footed, lissome (*also* lissom), lithe, lithesome, nimble, spry
related words flexible, limber, loose-jointed, pliable, pliant, supple; adroit, deft, dexterous (*also* dextrous); fleet-footed, surefooted
near antonyms inflexible, rigid, stiff; bungling, inept, maladroit
antonyms awkward, clumsy, gawky, graceless, lumbering, ungainly, ungraceful
2 having or showing elegance — see ELEGANT 1

gracefulness *n* dignified or restrained beauty of form, appearance, or style — see ELEGANCE

graceless *adj* **1** lacking in physical ease and grace in movement or in the use of the hands — see CLUMSY 1
2 lacking social grace and assurance — see AWKWARD 1
3 not appropriate for a particular occasion or situation — see INAPPROPRIATE

gracious *adj* **1** showing a natural kindness and courtesy especially in social situations ⟨a *gracious* teacher who made the new student feel welcome⟩
synonyms affable, cordial, genial, hospitable, sociable
related words agreeable, amiable, benignant, congenial, convivial, friendly, kind, kindly, neighborly; accommodating, obliging; considerate, courteous, polite, thoughtful; sophisticated, urbane; approachable, attentive, outgoing
near antonyms boorish, churlish; abrupt, blunt, brusque, curt, gruff, sharp, snippy; antisocial, disagreeable, discourteous, ill-mannered, impolite, rude, sullen, surly, uncivil, unfriendly, unkind, unmannerly; crabbed, crabby, cross, crusty, grumpy
antonyms inhospitable, ungracious, unsociable

2 having an easygoing and pleasing manner especially in social situations — see AMIABLE

3 showing consideration, courtesy, and good manners — see POLITE 1

graciousness *n* **1** speech or behavior that is a sign of good breeding — see POLITENESS

2 the state or quality of having a pleasant or agreeable manner in socializing with others — see AMIABILITY 1

gradational *adj* proceeding or changing by steps or degrees — see GRADUAL

gradationally *adv* by small steps or amounts — see GRADUALLY

grade *n* **1** an individual part of a process, series, or ranking — see DEGREE 1

2 degree of excellence — see QUALITY 1

3 one of the units into which a whole is divided on the basis of a common characteristic — see CLASS 2

4 something set up as an example against which others of the same type are compared — see STANDARD 1

5 the degree to which something rises up from a position level with the horizon — see SLANT

grade *vb* **1** to arrange or assign according to type — see CLASSIFY 1

2 to take or have a certain position within a group arranged in vertical classes — see RANK 1

gradient *n* the degree to which something rises up from a position level with the horizon — see SLANT

gradual *adj* proceeding or changing by steps or degrees ⟨a *gradual* drop in gas prices will take place over the next several months⟩

synonyms gradational, incremental, phased, piecemeal, step-by-step

related words progressive, stepped, tapered; imperceptible, inching

near antonyms abrupt, acute, sharp; changeable, dynamic, volatile

antonyms sudden

gradually *adv* by small steps or amounts ⟨*gradually* worked his way down the class roster⟩ ⟨add the sugar to the beaten egg whites *gradually* to make the meringue⟩

synonyms gradationally, little by little, piece by piece, piecemeal

related words hierarchically, increasingly, progressively; fractionally, imperceptibly; slowly

near antonyms acutely, sharply, steeply, unprogressively; hastily, precipitously

antonyms abruptly, suddenly

graduation *n* a scheme of rank or order — see ³SCALE 1

grain *n* **1** a very small piece — see BIT 1

2 one's characteristic attitude or mood — see DISPOSITION 1

grainy *adj* made up of large particles — see COARSE 1

grand *adj* **1** large and impressive in size, grandeur, extent, or conception ⟨the *grand* ceremonies that typically mark the opening of the Olympic Games⟩

synonyms august, baronial, gallant, glorious, grandiose, heroic, imposing, magnificent, majestic, monumental, noble, proud, regal, royal, splendid, stately

related words colossal, monstrous, prodigious, stupendous, tremendous; kingly, lordly, princely, queenly; awesome, awful, cosmic, sublime, won-

drous; formidable, impressive, prepossessing, redoubtable; marvelous (*or* marvellous), superb, terrific, wonderful; extravagant, lavish, luxurious, opulent, sumptuous; gorgeous, resplendent, splendiferous; extraordinary, killer, remarkable, sensational, striking; celestial, divine, heavenly

near antonyms lowly, modest, unprepossessing; average, common, mediocre, ordinary, run-of-the-mill, second-rate; abject, mean, meretricious, shabby, sordid; insignificant, measly, paltry, petty, puny, trifling, trivial

antonyms humble, unheroic, unimposing, unimpressive

2 coming before all others in importance — see FOREMOST 1

3 not lacking any part or member that properly belongs to it — see COMPLETE 1

4 of a size greater than average of its kind — see LARGE

5 of high birth, rank, or station — see NOBLE 1

6 of the very best kind — see EXCELLENT

7 unusually large — see HUGE

grandee *n* a man of high birth or social position — see GENTLEMAN 1

grandeur *n* impressiveness of beauty on a large scale — see MAGNIFICENCE

grandfather *n* a person who is several generations earlier in an individual's line of descent — see ANCESTOR 1

grandiloquence *n* **1** boastful speech or writing — see BOMBAST 1

2 language that is impressive-sounding but not meaningful or sincere — see RHETORIC 1

grandiloquent *adj* **1** full of fine words and fancy expressions — see FLOWERY 1

2 marked by the use of impressive-sounding but mostly meaningless words and phrases — see RHETORICAL

grandiose *adj* **1** large and impressive in size, grandeur, extent, or conception — see GRAND 1

2 self-consciously trying to present an appearance of grandeur or importance — see PRETENTIOUS 1

grandiosity *n* the quality or state of appearing or trying to appear more important or more valuable than is the case — see PRETENSE 1

grandly *adv* **1** in a luxurious manner — see HIGH

2 in a manner befitting a person of the highest character and ideals — see GREATLY 1

grandness *n* **1** impressiveness of beauty on a large scale — see MAGNIFICENCE

2 the quality or state of being large in size — see LARGENESS

grange *n* a piece of land and its buildings used to grow crops or raise livestock — see FARM

granite *n* firm or unwavering adherence to one's purpose — see DETERMINATION 1

grant *n* a sum of money allotted for a specific use by official or formal action — see APPROPRIATION

grant *vb* **1** to accept the truth or existence of (something) usually reluctantly — see ADMIT

2 to give the ownership or benefit of (something) formally or publicly — see CONFER 1

granting *n* the approval by someone in authority for the doing of something — see PERMISSION

granular *adj* made up of large particles — see COARSE 1

granulated *adj* made up of large particles — see COARSE 1

granule *n* a very small piece — see BIT 1

graphic *also* **graphical** *adj* **1** producing a mental picture through clear and impressive description ⟨the report offered many *graphic* details about the huge earthquake that rocked the area⟩
synonyms delineated, pictorial, picturesque, vivid
related words depicted, descriptive, expressive; concrete, explicit, specific; faithful, lifelike, natural, realistic; fresh, incisive, sharp
near antonyms indeterminate, nebulous, obscure, sketchy, unclear, vague; blurry, dark, dim, muddy, murky, shadowy
2 consisting of or relating to pictures — see PICTORIAL 1
graphic *n* something that visually explains or decorates a text — see ILLUSTRATION 1
grapple *n* the act or manner of holding — see HOLD 1
grapple *vb* **1** to seize and attempt to unbalance one another for the purpose of achieving physical mastery — see WRESTLE
2 to take physical control or possession of (something) suddenly or forcibly — see CATCH 1
grapple (with) *vb* to deal with (something) usually skillfully or efficiently — see HANDLE 1
grasp *n* **1** the ability to direct the course of something — see CONTROL 2
2 the act or manner of holding — see HOLD 1
3 the knowledge gained from the process of coming to know or understand something — see COMPREHENSION
grasp *vb* **1** to have a practical understanding of — see KNOW 1
2 to put one's arms around and press tightly — see EMBRACE 1
3 to reach for and take hold of by embracing with the fingers or arms — see TAKE 1
4 to recognize the meaning of — see COMPREHEND 1
grasping *adj* having or marked by an eager and often selfish desire especially for material possessions — see GREEDY 1
grassland *n* a broad area of level or rolling treeless country — see PLAIN
grate *vb* **1** to disturb the peace of mind of (someone) especially by repeated disagreeable acts — see IRRITATE 1
2 to pass roughly and noisily over or against a surface — see SCRAPE 1
3 to press or strike against or together so as to make a scraping sound — see GRIND 2
grateful *adj* **1** feeling or expressing gratitude ⟨was *grateful* for her neighbor's help after she broke her foot⟩
synonyms appreciative, obliged, thankful
related words beholden, indebted; gratified, pleased; thanking
antonyms thankless, unappreciative, ungrateful, unthankful
2 giving pleasure or contentment to the mind or senses — see PLEASANT
gratefulness *n* acknowledgment of having received something good from another — see THANKS
gratification *n* the feeling experienced when one's wishes are met — see PLEASURE 1
gratified *adj* **1** experiencing pleasure, satisfaction, or delight — see GLAD 1
2 feeling that one's needs or desires have been met — see CONTENT

gratify *vb* **1** to give in to (a desire) — see INDULGE
2 to give satisfaction to — see PLEASE
gratifying *adj* **1** giving pleasure or contentment to the mind or senses — see PLEASANT
2 making one feel good inside — see HEARTWARMING
grating *adj* **1** disagreeable to one's aesthetic or artistic sense — see HARSH 2
2 harsh and dry in sound — see HOARSE
gratis *adj* not costing or charging anything — see FREE 4
gratitude *n* acknowledgment of having received something good from another — see THANKS
gratuitous *adj* **1** not costing or charging anything — see FREE 4
2 not needed by the circumstances or to accomplish an end — see UNNECESSARY
gratuity *n* **1** a small sum of money given for a service over and above what is due — see ²TIP 1
2 something given in addition to what is ordinarily expected or owed — see BONUS
grave *adj* **1** having a matter of importance as its topic — see SERIOUS 2
2 involving potential loss or injury — see DANGEROUS
3 not joking or playful in mood or manner — see SERIOUS 1
grave *n* a final resting place for a dead person ⟨put flowers on his mother's *grave*⟩
synonyms sepulcher (*or* sepulchre), sepulture, tomb
related words catacomb, charnel, crypt, mausoleum, vault; cemetery, churchyard, graveyard, potter's field; barrow, mound, tumulus
grave *vb* to cut (as letters or designs) on a hard surface — see ENGRAVE 1
gravel *adj* harsh and dry in sound — see HOARSE
gravelly *adj* harsh and dry in sound — see HOARSE
gravestone *n* a shaped stone laid over or erected near a grave and usually bearing an inscription to identify and preserve the memory of the deceased — see TOMBSTONE
graveyard *n* a piece of land used for burying the dead — see CEMETERY
gravid *adj* containing unborn young within the body — see PREGNANT 1
gravity *n* a mental state free of jesting or trifling — see EARNESTNESS
gravy *n* **1** a savory fluid food used as a topping or accompaniment to a main dish — see SAUCE 1
2 something given in addition to what is ordinarily expected or owed — see BONUS
gray *also* **grey** *adj* **1** of the color gray ⟨the *gray* elephant and the gaudily dressed circus performer created a striking contrast⟩
synonyms grayish, leaden, pewter, silver, silvery, slate, slaty, steely
related words achromatic, neutral; dirty, dull, faded, washed-out; ashen, ashy, chalky, livid, mousy (*or* mousey), pale, white, whitish; chocolate, dun, sandy, sepia; brindled, grizzled, hoar, hoary
near antonyms ablaze, bright, deep, gay, rich; chromatic, colored
2 causing or marked by an atmosphere lacking in cheer — see GLOOMY 1
grayish *adj* of the color gray — see GRAY 1
gray matter *n* the ability to learn and understand or to deal with problems — see INTELLIGENCE 1

¹graze *vb* to feed on grass or herbs ⟨cows *grazing* in the meadow⟩
synonyms browse, forage, pasture
related words eat, feed, nibble

²graze *vb* **1** to damage by rubbing against a sharp or rough surface — see SCRAPE 2
2 to pass lightly across or touch gently especially in passing — see BRUSH

grease *vb* to coat (something) with a slippery substance in order to reduce friction — see LUBRICATE

greased *adj* having or being a surface so smooth as to make sliding or falling likely — see SLICK 1

greasy *adj* having or being a surface so smooth as to make sliding or falling likely — see SLICK 1

great *adj* **1** having or showing exceptional knowledge, experience, or skill in a field of endeavor — see PROFICIENT
2 having, characterized by, or arising from a dignified and generous nature — see NOBLE 2
3 lasting for a considerable time — see LONG 2
4 of a size greater than average of its kind — see LARGE
5 of the very best kind — see EXCELLENT

greatcoat *n* a warm outdoor coat — see OVERCOAT

greatest *adj* **1** coming before all others in importance — see FOREMOST 1
2 of the highest degree — see FULL 2

greathearted *adj* **1** feeling or displaying no fear by temperament — see BRAVE
2 having, characterized by, or arising from a dignified and generous nature — see NOBLE 2

greatheartedness *n* strength of mind to carry on in spite of danger — see COURAGE

greatly *adv* **1** in a manner befitting a person of the highest character and ideals ⟨as commander of the Union army's first black regiment, Robert Gould Shaw died as *greatly* as he had lived⟩
synonyms gallantly, grandly, heroically, high-mindedly, honorably, magnanimously, nobly
related words loftily, venerably; magnificently, majestically
near antonyms abominably, contemptibly, despicably, detestably, hatefully; degenerately
antonyms basely, dishonorably, ignobly
2 to a large extent or degree ⟨Todd has *greatly* increased the scope of his theme on civic responsibility⟩
synonyms astronomically, broadly, colossally, considerably, enormously, extensively, hugely, largely, massively, monstrously, much, sizably, stupendously, tremendously, utterly, vastly
related words appreciably, noticeably, significantly; abundantly, amply, copiously, healthily, plentifully
near antonyms modestly; fractionally; imperceptibly, infinitesimally, insignificantly, invisibly, microscopically, minutely, negligibly; barely, hardly, just, scarcely
antonyms little, slightly
3 to a great degree — see VERY 1

greatness *n* **1** exceptionally high quality — see EXCELLENCE 1
2 the quality or state of being large in size — see LARGENESS

greed *n* an intense selfish desire for wealth or possessions ⟨don't let *greed* for riches control you⟩
synonyms acquisitiveness, avarice, avariciousness, avidity, covetousness, cupidity, greediness, rapaciousness, rapacity

related words materialism, possessiveness; appetite, craving, hankering, hunger, itch, longing, lust, passion, ravenousness, thirst, voracity, yearning, yen
near antonyms contentment, fulfillment, satisfaction; bounteousness, bounty, charity, generosity, generousness, liberality, openhandedness, openheartedness, unselfishness

greediness *n* an intense selfish desire for wealth or possessions — see GREED

greedy *adj* **1** having or marked by an eager and often selfish desire especially for material possessions ⟨a young rocker who was *greedy* for fame and riches⟩ ⟨the *greedy* exploitation of the land by developers⟩
synonyms acquisitive, avaricious, avid, coveting, covetous, grasping, mercenary, rapacious
related words materialistic, philistine; desirous, eager, itchy, miserly; hoggish, piggish, swinish; devouring, gluttonous, gobbling, insatiable, ravenous, unquenchable, voracious; discontent, discontented, malcontent, unquenched, unsatisfied; begrudging, grudging, resentful
near antonyms bounteous, bountiful, charitable, freehanded, generous, greathearted, handsome, liberal, munificent, openhanded, openhearted, unselfish, unsparing; controlled, moderate, restrained, temperate; content, sated, satisfied
2 having a huge appetite — see VORACIOUS 1

green *adj* **1** covered with a thick, healthy natural growth — see LUSH 1
2 lacking in adult experience or maturity — see CALLOW
3 lacking in worldly wisdom or informed judgment — see NAIVE 1
4 lacking the warm skin color indicative of or associated with good health — see SICKLY 2

green *n* green leaves or plants — see GREENERY 1

greenback *n* a piece of printed paper used as money — see ¹BILL 2

greenery *n* green leaves or plants ⟨Scottish highlands covered with lush *greenery*⟩
synonyms flora, foliage, green, herbage, leafage, vegetation, verdure
related words grassland, prairie; underbrush, undergrowth

greenhorn *n* a person who is just starting out in a field of activity — see BEGINNER

greenhouse *n* a glass-enclosed building for growing plants — see CONSERVATORY

greenness *n* the quality or state of being simple and sincere — see NAÏVETÉ 1

greeting *n* **1** an expression of goodwill upon meeting — see HELLO
2 greetings *pl* best wishes — see COMPLIMENT

gregarious *adj* likely to seek or enjoy the company of others — see CONVIVIAL

gregariousness *n* the quality or state of being social — see SOCIABILITY

gremlin *n* an imaginary being usually having a small human form and magical powers — see FAIRY

griddle cake *n* a flat cake made from thin batter and cooked on both sides (as on a griddle) — see PANCAKE

grief *n* deep sadness especially for the loss of someone or something loved — see SORROW

grievance *n* **1** a lingering ill will towards a person for a real or imagined wrong — see GRUDGE 1

2 an expression of dissatisfaction, pain, or resentment — see COMPLAINT 1

grieve *vb* to feel deep sadness or mental pain ⟨*grieved* over the lost cat⟩

synonyms agonize, bleed, hurt, mourn, sorrow, suffer

related words ache, long (for), pine (away); rack, torment, torture; bemoan, bewail, deplore, lament, rue; bawl, cry, groan, howl, keen, moan, take on, wail, weep, yammer

near antonyms beam, cheer, exult, joy, laugh, overjoy, ravish, rejoice; comfort, console

grieve (for) *vb* to feel or express sorrow for — see LAMENT 1

grieving *adj* expressing or suggesting mourning — see MOURNFUL 1

grievous *adj* **1** difficult to endure — see HARSH 1
2 hard to accept or bear especially emotionally — see BITTER 2
3 involving potential loss or injury — see DANGEROUS
4 of a kind to cause great distress — see REGRETTABLE

grievously *adv* with feelings of bitterness or grief — see HARD 2

grill *n* a public establishment where meals are served to paying customers for consumption on the premises — see RESTAURANT

grill *vb* to put a series of questions to — see EXAMINE 1

grim *adj* **1** harsh and threatening in manner or appearance ⟨a *grim* and desolate landscape⟩ ⟨a *grim* and short-tempered shopkeeper who didn't exactly invite friendly conversation⟩

synonyms austere, dour, fierce, flinty, forbidding, gruff, intimidating, lowering (*also* louring), rough, rugged, severe, stark, steely, stern, ungentle

related words bleak, cold, hostile, unfriendly; adamant, determined, firm, resolute, steadfast, unflinching; fixed, hard, immovable, implacable, inflexible, obdurate, rigid, set, stiff, unbending, uncompromising, unyielding; immutable, unchangeable; black, cheerless, dark, gloomy, glum, joyless, moody, morose, sulky, sullen, surly; brooding, grave, melancholy, serious, sober, solemn, somber (*or* sombre), unsmiling, weighty

near antonyms bland, meek, mellow, soft; easy, quiet, tranquil; agreeable, bright, cheerful, inviting, pleasant, pleasing, sweet; glad, happy, lighthearted, merry, mirthful, sunny; featherbrained, flighty, frivolous, giddy, goofy, light-headed, playful

antonyms benign, benignant, gentle, mild, tender
2 difficult to endure — see HARSH 1
3 showing no signs of slackening or yielding in one's purpose — see UNYIELDING 1
4 violently unfriendly or aggressive in disposition — see FIERCE 1

grimace *n* a twisting of the facial features in disgust or disapproval ⟨made a *grimace* when he tasted the medicine⟩

synonyms face, frown, lower (*also* lour), mouth, pout, scowl

related words flinch, squinch, wince; growl, snarl; simper, smirk; scoff, sneer; glare, glower, look, stare

near antonyms grin, smile

grimace *vb* to distort one's face — see MUG 1

grime *n* foul matter that mars the purity or cleanliness of something — see FILTH 1

grime *vb* to make dirty — see DIRTY 1

griminess *n* the state or quality of being dirty — see DIRTINESS 1

grimy *adj* not clean — see DIRTY 1

grin *vb* to express an emotion (as amusement) by curving the lips upward — see SMILE 1

grind *n* **1** a harsh grating sound — see RASP
2 a person slavishly devoted to intellectual or academic pursuits — see NERD
3 very hard or unpleasant work — see TOIL

grind *vb* **1** to make smooth by friction ⟨after they are *ground* and polished, these stones can be used for jewelry⟩

synonyms buff, file, hone, rasp, rub, sand

related words plane, scrape; sandblast, scour; burnish, polish; sharpen, whet; regrind

near antonyms coarsen, roughen
2 to press or strike against or together so as to make a scraping sound ⟨everyone in the car winced when the driver *ground* the gears trying to shift into second⟩

synonyms crunch, gnash, grate, grit, scrape, scrunch

related words creak, groan, rasp, scratch; clash, jangle, jar
3 to make sharp or sharper — see SHARPEN
4 to make smooth or glossy usually by repeatedly applying surface pressure — see POLISH
5 to pass roughly and noisily over or against a surface — see SCRAPE
6 to reduce to fine particles — see POWDER

grind (out) *vb* to produce or bring about especially by long or repeated effort — see HAMMER (OUT)

grinder *n* a large sandwich on a long split roll — see SUBMARINE

grip *n* **1** a bag carried by hand and designed to hold a traveler's clothing and personal articles — see TRAVELING BAG
2 the act or manner of holding — see HOLD 1
3 the knowledge gained from the process of coming to know or understand something — see COMPREHENSION
4 the right or means to command or control others — see POWER 1

grip *vb* **1** to have or keep in one's hands — see HOLD 1
2 to hold the attention of as if by a spell — see ENTHRALL 1
3 to hold the attention of — see ENGAGE 1
4 to reach for and take hold of by embracing with the fingers or arms — see TAKE 1

gripe *n* an expression of dissatisfaction, pain, or resentment — see COMPLAINT 1

gripe *vb* to express dissatisfaction, pain, or resentment usually tiresomely — see COMPLAIN

griper *n* **1** a person who makes frequent complaints usually about little things — see CRYBABY
2 an irritable and complaining person — see GROUCH

gripping *adj* holding the attention or provoking interest — see INTERESTING

grisliness *n* the quality of inspiring intense dread or dismay — see HORROR 1

grisly *adj* extremely disturbing or repellent — see HORRIBLE 1

grit *n* the strength of mind that enables a person to endure pain or hardship — see FORTITUDE

grit *vb* to press or strike against or together so as to make a scraping sound — see GRIND 2

groan *n* **1** a crying out in grief — see LAMENT 1

2 a long low sound indicating pain or grief — see MOAN 1

groan *vb* to utter a moan — see MOAN 1

grog *n* a fermented or distilled beverage that can make a person drunk — see ALCOHOL

groggery *n* a place of business where alcoholic beverages are sold to be consumed on the premises — see BARROOM

grogshop *n* a place of business where alcoholic beverages are sold to be consumed on the premises — see BARROOM

groomed *adj* being clean and in good order — see NEAT 1

groove *n* an established and often automatic or monotonous series of actions followed when engaging in some activity — see ROUTINE 1

groove *vb* to mark with or as if with a line or groove — see SCORE 1

groove (on) *vb* to take pleasure in — see ENJOY 1

groovy *adj* of the very best kind — see EXCELLENT

grope *vb* to search for something blindly or uncertainly ⟨*groped* for her car keys⟩ ⟨*groping* for the right answer⟩

synonyms feel, fish, fumble

related words cast about, hunt, look, reach, seek (out); clutch, grab, scrabble, snatch

gross *adj* **1** depicting or referring to sexual matters in a way that is unacceptable in polite society — see OBSCENE 1

2 having an excess of body fat — see FAT 1

3 lacking in refinement or good taste — see COARSE 2

4 very noticeable especially for being incorrect or bad — see EGREGIOUS

grossness *n* **1** the condition of having an excess of body fat — see CORPULENCE

2 the quality or state of being obscene — see OBSCENITY 1

3 the quality or state of lacking refinement or good taste — see VULGARITY 1

grot *n* a naturally formed underground chamber with an opening to the surface — see CAVE

grotesque *adj* **1** disagreeable to one's aesthetic or artistic sense — see HARSH 2

2 unpleasant to look at — see UGLY 1

grotto *n* a naturally formed underground chamber with an opening to the surface — see CAVE

grouch *n* an irritable and complaining person ⟨an uncle who is a real *grouch* when he's sick⟩

synonyms bear, complainer, crab, crank, croaker, curmudgeon, fusser, griper, grouser, growler, grumbler, grump, murmurer, mutterer, whiner

related words fulminator, malcontent, sorehead; killjoy, party pooper, spoilsport; defeatist, pessimist; faultfinder, kicker, nagger, nitpicker, quibbler

near antonyms optimist; rejoicer

grouchiness *n* readiness to show annoyance or impatience — see PETULANCE

grouchy *adj* **1** easily irritated or annoyed — see IRRITABLE

2 given to complaining a lot — see FUSSY 1

ground *adj* having an edge thin enough to cut or pierce something — see SHARP 1

ground *n* **1** **grounds** *pl* the area around and belonging to a building ⟨an escorted tour of the White House and its surrounding *grounds*⟩

synonyms demesne, park, premises, yard

related words acres, estate, land, lot, parcel, plot,

property, real estate, realty; campus; backyard, churchyard, dooryard, schoolyard

2 **grounds** *pl* matter that settles to the bottom of a body of liquid — see DEPOSIT 1

3 **grounds** *pl* something (as a belief) that serves as the basis for another thing — see REASON 2

4 a small area of usually open land — see FIELD 1

5 an immaterial thing upon which something else rests — see BASE 1

6 the loose surface material in which plants naturally grow — see DIRT 1

7 the physical conditions or features that form the setting against which something is viewed — see BACKGROUND 1

8 the solid part of our planet's surface as distinguished from the sea and air — see EARTH 2

ground *vb* to find a basis — see BASE

grounded *adj* resting on the shore or bottom of a body of water — see AGROUND

groundless *adj* having no basis in reason or fact ⟨please stop making *groundless* accusations against the teachers you dislike⟩ ⟨fears of a strike proved *groundless*⟩

synonyms invalid, nonvalid, unfounded, ungrounded, unreasonable, unsubstantiated, unsupported, unwarranted

related words illogical, irrational, nonlogical, unconscionable, unsound; fallacious, false, misled, wrong; gratuitous, uncalled-for, unnecessary; flimsy, implausible, misleading, specious, unconvincing, unsatisfying, untenable, weak; ill-advised, unreasoned; inconsistent; absurd, asinine, foolish, meaningless, nonsensical, preposterous, senseless, silly; insane, nutty, mad, wacky

near antonyms certified, validated, verified; confirmed, corroborated; informed, logical, rational; commonsense, sane, sensible, sober, wise; actual, genuine, real, true; certain, sure; clear, cogent, compelling, convincing, credible, persuasive, plausible, satisfying, solid

antonyms good, hard, just, justified, reasonable, reasoned, substantiated, valid, well-founded

ground plan *n* a method worked out in advance for achieving some objective — see PLAN 1

ground rule *n* a statement spelling out the proper procedure or conduct for an activity — see RULE 1

groundwork *n* an immaterial thing upon which something else rests — see BASE 1

group *n* **1** a number of things considered as a unit ⟨car buffs stood around admiring a *group* of classic cars in the parking lot⟩

synonyms array, assemblage, bank, batch, battery, block, bunch, clump, cluster, collection, grouping, huddle, knot, lot, package, parcel, passel, set, suite

related words accumulation, aggregate, aggregation, conglomeration; agglomeration, assortment, hodgepodge, jumble, miscellany, mixture, odds and ends, sundries, variety; series, suit

phrases the whole kit and caboodle

near antonyms entity, item, single, unit

2 a usually small number of persons considered as a unit ⟨the next *group* of guests were being seated for dinner⟩

synonyms array, batch, battery, body, bunch, cluster, crop, grouping, huddle, knot, lot, parcel, party, passel

related words assembly, congregation, gathering, organization; circle, clan, clique, coterie, fellow-

ship, gang, ring, set; faction, guild (*also* gild), order, school, sect; brigade, crew, outfit, platoon, posse; alliance, bloc, coalition, confederacy, confederation, federation, league, union; bevy, covey
phrases the whole kit and caboodle
near antonyms individual, single

3 one of the units into which a whole is divided on the basis of a common characteristic — see CLASS 2

group *vb* **1** to arrange or assign according to type — see CLASSIFY 1

2 to bring together in one body or place — see GATHER 1

grouping *n* **1** a number of things considered as a unit — see GROUP 1

2 a usually small number of persons considered as a unit — see GROUP 2

grouse *vb* to express dissatisfaction, pain, or resentment usually tiresomely — see COMPLAIN

grouser *n* an irritable and complaining person — see GROUCH

grovel *vb* **1** to draw back or crouch down in fearful submission — see COWER

2 to move slowly with the body close to the ground — see CRAWL 1

grow *vb* **1** to look after or assist the growth of by labor and care ⟨a dedicated home gardener who *grows* tomatoes in her small garden every summer⟩
synonyms crop, cultivate, culture, promote, raise, rear, tend
related words breed, produce, propagate; plant, sow; gather, glean, harvest, reap; germinate, quicken, root, sprout
near antonyms kill; dig, extirpate, pick, pluck, pull (up), uproot; cut, hay, mow

2 to become mature — see MATURE

3 to eventually have as a state or quality — see BECOME

grow (in) *vb* to increase in — see GAIN 1

grower *n* a person who cultivates the land and grows crops on it — see FARMER

growl *vb* **1** to express dissatisfaction, pain, or resentment usually tiresomely — see COMPLAIN

2 to make a long loud deep noise or cry — see ROAR

3 to make a low heavy rolling sound — see RUMBLE

growler *n* **1** a person who makes frequent complaints usually about little things — see CRYBABY

2 an irritable and complaining person — see GROUCH

grown–up *n* a fully grown person — see ADULT

growth *n* **1** an abnormal mass of tissue ⟨found a *growth* on the dog's neck under her collar⟩
synonyms excrescence, lump, neoplasm, tumor
related words outgrowth; cancer, carcinoma, lymphoma, malignancy, melanoma; cyst, tubercle, wart

2 the act or process of going from the simple or basic to the complex or advanced — see DEVELOPMENT 1

3 the process of becoming mature — see MATURATION

grow up *vb* to become mature — see MATURE

grub *n* substances intended to be eaten — see FOOD

grub *vb* to devote serious and sustained effort — see LABOR

grubber *n* a person who does very hard or dull work — see SLAVE 2

grubbiness *n* the state or quality of being dirty — see DIRTINESS 1

grubby *adj* not clean — see DIRTY 1

grudge *n* **1** a lingering ill will towards a person for a real or imagined wrong ⟨he's had a *grudge* against her ever since she snubbed him at the dance⟩
synonyms grievance, resentment, score
related words condemnation; offense (*or* offence), umbrage; complaint; peeve, pique

2 a deep-seated ill will — see ENMITY

grueling *or* **gruelling** *adj* **1** requiring considerable physical or mental effort — see HARD 2

2 requiring much time, effort, or careful attention — see DEMANDING 1

gruesome *adj* extremely disturbing or repellent — see HORRIBLE 1

gruesomeness *n* the quality of inspiring intense dread or dismay — see HORROR 1

gruff *adj* **1** harsh and dry in sound — see HOARSE

2 harsh and threatening in manner or appearance — see GRIM 1

grumble *n* an expression of dissatisfaction, pain, or resentment — see COMPLAINT 1

grumble *vb* **1** to express dissatisfaction, pain, or resentment usually tiresomely — see COMPLAIN

2 to make a low heavy rolling sound — see RUMBLE

grumbler *n* **1** a person who makes frequent complaints usually about little things — see CRYBABY

2 an irritable and complaining person — see GROUCH

grump *n* an irritable and complaining person — see GROUCH

grumpiness *n* readiness to show annoyance or impatience — see PETULANCE

grumpy *adj* **1** easily irritated or annoyed — see IRRITABLE

2 given to complaining a lot — see FUSSY 1

grungy *adj* **1** not clean — see DIRTY 1

2 showing signs of advanced wear and tear and neglect — see SHABBY 1

grunt *n* speech that is not clear enough to be understood — see MUMBLE

grunt *vb* to speak softly and unclearly — see MUMBLE

grunting *n* speech that is not clear enough to be understood — see MUMBLE

guarantee *n* **1** a formal agreement to fulfill an obligation ⟨the contractors gave us a written *guarantee* that the work on the house would be done by Christmas⟩
synonyms bond, contract, covenant, guaranty, surety, warranty
related words oath, pledge, vow, word; bargain, compact, pact, treaty; assurance, insurance; bail, deposit, pawn, security

2 something given or held to assure that the giver will keep a promise — see PLEDGE 1

guarantee *vb* **1** to assume responsibility for the satisfactory quality or performance of — see WARRANT 1

2 to make sure, certain, or safe — see ENSURE

guarantor *n* a person who takes the responsibility for some other person or thing — see SPONSOR

guaranty *n* **1** a formal agreement to fulfill an obligation — see GUARANTEE 1

2 something given or held to assure that the giver will keep a promise — see PLEDGE 1

THESAURUS

guaranty *vb* to make sure, certain, or safe — see ENSURE

guard *n* **1** a person or group that watches over someone or something ⟨checked in with the security *guard* at the gate⟩
synonyms custodian, guardian, keeper, lookout, picket, sentinel, sentry, warden, warder, watch, watchman
related words observer, patrol, spotter, watchdog; bodyguard, convoy, defender, escort, honor guard
2 a position or readiness to oppose actual or expected attack — see DEFENSIVE
3 a protective device (as on a weapon) to prevent accidental operation — see SAFETY 2
4 means or method of defending — see DEFENSE 1
5 one that accompanies another for protection, guidance, or as a courtesy — see ESCORT
6 someone that protects — see PROTECTOR

guard *vb* to drive danger or attack away from — see DEFEND 1

guard (against) *vb* to be cautious of or on guard against — see BEWARE (OF)

guarded *adj* having or showing a close attentiveness to avoiding danger or trouble — see CAREFUL 1

guardian *n* **1** a person or group that watches over someone or something — see GUARD 1
2 a person who takes care of a property sometimes for an absent owner — see CUSTODIAN 1

guardianship *n* responsibility for the safety and well-being of someone or something — see CUSTODY

guardrail *n* a protective barrier consisting of a horizontal bar and its supports — see RAILING

guardroom *n* a place of confinement for persons held in lawful custody — see JAIL

guess *n* an opinion or judgment based on little or no evidence — see CONJECTURE

guess *vb* **1** to form an opinion from little or no evidence ⟨though she does not speak with an accent, I would still *guess* that she is a foreigner⟩
synonyms assume, conjecture, presume, speculate, suppose, surmise, suspect, suspicion [*chiefly dialect*]
related words conclude, deduce, gather, infer; hypothesize, theorize; believe, conceive, expect, imagine, reckon [*chiefly dialect*], take, think
near antonyms demonstrate, establish, prove; ascertain, determine, find out
2 to decide the size, amount, number, or distance of (something) without actual measurement — see ESTIMATE 2
3 to have as an opinion — see BELIEVE 2

guest *n* **1** a person who visits another ⟨invited the afternoon *guests* to stay for dinner⟩
synonyms caller, frequenter, visitant, visitor
related words company; crasher, hanger-on
near antonyms denizen, dweller, habitant, inhabitant, occupant, resident, resider
2 a person who buys a product or uses a service from a business — see CUSTOMER 1

guffaw *n* an explosive sound that is a sign of amusement — see LAUGH 1

guidance *n* **1** an opinion suggesting a wise or proper course of action — see ADVICE
2 the act or activity of looking after and making decisions about something — see CONDUCT 1
3 the duty or function of watching or guarding

for the sake of proper direction or control — see SUPERVISION 1

guide *n* one that accompanies another for protection, guidance, or as a courtesy — see ESCORT

guide *vb* **1** to give advice and instruction to (someone) regarding the course or process to be followed ⟨the famous chef *guided* her through the creation of the wedding cake, showing her how to ice the layers, fashion the elaborate decorations, and assemble the whole shebang⟩
synonyms coach, counsel, lead, mentor, pilot, shepherd, show, tutor
related words direct, steer; accompany, escort, see; oversee, superintend, supervise; drill, train; brief, enlighten, inform; instruct, school, teach; inculcate, indoctrinate; cultivate, foster, nurture
2 to look after and make decisions about — see CONDUCT 1
3 to point out the way for (someone) especially from a position in front — see LEAD 1

guidon *n* a piece of cloth with a special design that is used as an emblem or for signaling — see FLAG 1

guild *also* **gild** *n* a group of persons formally joined together for some common interest — see ASSOCIATION 2

guile *n* **1** skill in achieving one's ends through indirect, subtle, or underhanded means — see CUNNING 1
2 the inclination or practice of misleading others through lies or trickery — see DECEIT

guileful *adj* clever at attaining one's ends by indirect and often deceptive means — see ARTFUL 1

guileless *adj* free from any intent to deceive or impress others ⟨she was an easy-going, *guileless* young woman who was comfortable just being herself⟩
synonyms artless, genuine, honest, ingenuous, innocent, naive (*or* naïve), natural, real, simple, sincere, true, unaffected, unpretending, unpretentious
related words childlike, impressionable, inexperienced, malleable, persuadable, simpleminded, unsophisticated, unworldly; unforced, unstudied; candid, frank, free, openhearted, plain, plainspoken, single-minded; trustful, trusting
phrases on the level
near antonyms sophisticated, worldly, worldly-wise; crooked, deceitful, deceptive, devious, double-dealing, hypocritical, two-faced; arch, calculating, canny, crafty, cunning, designing, scheming, sharp, shifty, shrewd, slick, slippery, sly, tricky, underhanded, wily; flattering, mealymouthed, smooth, sycophantic, unctuous; feigned, forced, strained
antonyms affected, artful, artificial, assuming, dishonest, dissembling, dissimulating, fake, false, guileful, insincere, phony (*also* phoney), pretentious

guilelessly *adv* without any attempt to impress by deception or exaggeration — see NATURALLY 3

guilelessness *n* the quality or state of being simple and sincere — see NAÏVETÉ 1

guillotine *vb* to cut off the head of — see DECAPITATE

guilt *n* **1** a feeling of responsibility for wrongdoing ⟨he was wracked with *guilt* after he accidentally broke his sister's antique grandfather clock⟩
synonyms contriteness, contrition, penitence, re-

gret, remorse, remorsefulness, repentance, rue, self-reproach, shame
related words compunction, misgiving, qualm, scruple; blame, fault, responsibility; chagrin, embarrassment; anguish, distress, grief, sadness, sorrow
antonyms impenitence, remorselessness
2 responsibility for wrongdoing or failure — see BLAME 1

guiltless *adj* free from guilt or blame — see INNOCENT 2

guiltlessness *n* the quality or state of being free from guilt or blame — see INNOCENCE 1

guilty *adj* **1** responsible for a wrong ⟨he was found *guilty* on all charges brought against him⟩
synonyms blamable, culpable
related words blameworthy, censurable, impeachable, indictable, punishable, reprehensible, reproachable; accused, arraigned, impeached, implicated, indicted; accountable, answerable; condemned, convicted
phrases at fault
near antonyms absolved, acquitted, exonerated, vindicated; faultless, impeccable, irreproachable, unimpeachable
antonyms blameless, guiltless, innocent
2 suffering from or expressive of a feeling of responsibility for wrongdoing ⟨she was burdened with a *guilty* conscience after stealing the newspaper from the newsstand⟩
synonyms ashamed, contrite, hangdog, penitent, remorseful, repentant, shamed, shamefaced
related words apologetic, sorry; regretful, rueful; penitential; blushing, chagrined, embarrassed, sheepish
near antonyms unapologetic; brazen, cheeky, impudent
antonyms impenitent, remorseless, shameless, unashamed, unrepentant

guise *n* **1** a display of emotion or behavior that is insincere or intended to deceive — see MASQUERADE
2 clothing chosen as appropriate for a specific situation — see OUTFIT 1
3 clothing put on to hide one's true identity or imitate someone or something else — see DISGUISE
4 outward and often deceptive indication — see APPEARANCE 2

gulch *n* a narrow opening between hillsides or mountains that can be used for passage — see CANYON

gulf *n* **1** a part of a body of water that extends beyond the general shoreline ⟨dipped our feet in the warm waters of the *gulf*⟩
synonyms bay, bight, cove, creek [*chiefly British*], estuary, firth, fjord (*or* fiord), inlet, loch [*Scottish*]
related words harbor, port, road(s), roadstead; narrow, sound, strait; bayou
2 an immeasurable depth or space — see ABYSS
3 a narrow opening between hillsides or mountains that can be used for passage — see CANYON
4 an open space in a barrier (as a wall or hedge) — see GAP 1

gull *n* one who is easily deceived or cheated — see DUPE

gull *vb* to cause to believe what is untrue — see DECEIVE

gullibility *n* readiness to believe the claims of others without sufficient evidence — see CREDULITY

gullible *adj* readily taken advantage of — see EASY 2

gulp *n* the portion of a serving of a beverage that is swallowed at one time — see DRINK 2

gulp *vb* to swallow in liquid form — see DRINK 1

gummy *adj* being of such a thick consistency as to readily cling to objects upon contact — see STICKY 1

gun *n* **1** a portable weapon from which a shot is discharged by gunpowder ⟨while her father preferred hunting with a crossbow, she preferred a *gun*⟩
synonyms arm, firearm, piece, small arm
related words forty-five (*or* .45), gat [*slang*], handgun, pistol, revolver, rod [*slang*], six-gun, six-shooter, zip gun; blunderbuss, flintlock, harquebus (*or* arquebus), matchlock, musket, muzzleloader, rifle, shotgun; automatic, machine gun, repeater, submachine gun, tommy gun; speargun
2 guns *pl* large firearms (as cannon or rockets) — see ARTILLERY

gun *vb* to strike with a missile from a gun — see SHOOT 3

gung ho *adj* showing urgent desire or interest — see EAGER

gurgle *vb* to flow in a broken irregular stream ⟨the tiny stream *gurgled* down the rocky slope and joined the larger river at the bottom of the hill⟩
synonyms bubble, dribble, lap, plash, ripple, splash, trickle, wash
related words eddy, purl, swirl; swash, swish, whish; drip, drop; gush, jet, rush, spout, spurt, squirt
near antonyms run
antonyms pour, roll, stream

gush *n* **1** a flowing or going out — see OUTFLOW
2 a sudden intense expression of strong feeling — see OUTBURST 1

gush *vb* **1** to flow out in great quantities or with force ⟨the dam cracked and water *gushed* from the break⟩
synonyms jet, pour, rush, spew, spout, spurt, squirt
related words cascade, issue, roll, run, stream; plash, slosh, splash; surge, swell; flush, sluice; deluge, engulf, flood, inundate, overflow, overwhelm, submerge, swamp
near antonyms spatter, sprinkle; exude, leak, ooze, seep, weep
antonyms dribble, drip, drop, trickle
2 to make an exaggerated display of affection or enthusiasm ⟨he *gushed* about his favorite basketball player, calling him "the best there ever was"⟩
synonyms enthuse, fuss, rave, rhapsodize, slobber
related words dote (on), fawn; emote

gushing *adj* **1** overly or insincerely flattering — see FULSOME
2 pouring forth in great amounts — see PROFUSE

gust *n* **1** a sudden brief rush of wind ⟨a *gust* tore her umbrella from her grip and blew it down the street⟩
synonyms blast, blow, flurry, williwaw
related words breeze, zephyr; air, breath, waft; puff, whiff; gale, hurricane, squall, tempest, tornado, windstorm; northeaster, norther, northerly, northwester, southeaster, southwester, westerly
2 a sudden intense expression of strong feeling — see OUTBURST 1

gusty *adj* marked by strong wind or more wind than usual — see WINDY 1

THESAURUS

gut *n* **1 guts** *pl* the internal organs of the body ⟨dissected the frog and looked at its *guts*⟩
synonyms entrails, innards, inside(s), viscera, vitals
related words bowel(s), intestine(s); giblet(s), variety meat
2 guts *pl* strength of mind to carry on in spite of danger — see COURAGE
3 guts *pl* the strength of mind that enables a person to endure pain or hardship — see FORTITUDE
4 the part of the body between the chest and the pelvis — see STOMACH
gut *vb* to take the internal organs out of ⟨you'll need to *gut* the fish and wash it out before you can cook it⟩
synonyms clean, disembowel, draw, eviscerate
related words bone, dress; cut, excise, extract, remove, withdraw; transplant
gutsy *adj* inclined or willing to take risks — see BOLD 1
gutter *n* **1** a pipe or channel for carrying off water from a roof ⟨one of his chores is to clean leaves and sticks out of the *gutters* before winter sets in⟩
synonyms drainpipe, eaves trough, spout, trough, waterspout
related words drain, flume, sluice; conduit, duct
2 a long narrow channel dug in the earth — see DITCH
guy *n* **1** a member of the human race — see HUMAN
2 an adult male human being — see MAN 1
guzzle *vb* to swallow in liquid form — see DRINK 1
gym *n* a building or room used for sports activities and exercising ⟨decided to get up early and go to the *gym* to lift weights⟩
synonyms gymnasium, spa
related words arena, bowl, coliseum, colosseum, stadium
gymnasium *n* a building or room used for sports activities and exercising — see GYM
gyp *vb* to rob by the use of trickery or threats — see FLEECE
gyrate *vb* to move in circles around an axis or center — see SPIN 1
gyration *n* a rapid turning about on an axis or central point — see SPIN 1

habiliment *n, usually* **habiliments** *pl* covering for the human body — see CLOTHING
habit *n* a usual manner of behaving or doing ⟨it was his *habit* to rise early⟩
synonyms custom, fashion, pattern, practice (*also* practise), trick, way, wont
related words addiction; disposition; bent, inclination, proclivity, tendency, turn; convention, form, mode, style; usage; manners, mores; groove, rote, routine, rut; affectation, airs, pose; attribute, characteristic, mark, trait; oddity, peculiarity, quirk, singularity, tic; strangeness, weirdness
habitable *adj* suitable for living in — see LIVABLE
habitant *n* one who lives permanently in a place — see INHABITANT
habitat *n* the place where a plant or animal is usually or naturally found — see HOME 2
habitation *n* the place where one lives — see HOME 1
habitual *adj* **1** being such by habit and not likely to change ⟨Sarah admits she's an *habitual* procrastinator, but she still manages to complete her assignments on time⟩
synonyms chronic, confirmed, inveterate
related words incorrigible, unregenerate; born, natural; persistent, regular, steady, unfailing; addicted; accustomed, habituated, used; deep-rooted, entrenched (*also* intrenched), inbred, inherent, innate
near antonyms unaccustomed, unused; occasional
2 appearing or occurring repeatedly from time to time — see REGULAR 1
habituated *adj* being in the habit or custom — see ACCUSTOMED
hacienda *n* a large impressive residence — see MANSION

¹hack *n* a V-shaped cut usually on an edge or a surface — see NOTCH 1
²hack *n* an automobile that carries passengers for a fare usually determined by the distance traveled — see TAXI
hackney *adj* used or heard so often as to be dull — see STALE
hackneyed *adj* used or heard so often as to be dull — see STALE
hag *n* **1** a mean or ugly old woman — see CRONE
2 a woman believed to have often harmful supernatural powers — see WITCH 1
haggard *adj* suffering extreme weight loss as a result of hunger or disease — see EMACIATED
haggle *vb* to talk over or dispute the terms of a purchase — see BARGAIN
hail *n* **1** a heavy fall of objects — see RAIN 2
2 a rapid or overwhelming outpouring of many things at once — see BARRAGE
hail *vb* **1** to declare enthusiastic approval of — see ACCLAIM
2 to demand or request the presence or service of — see SUMMON 1
hair *n* **1** a very small distance or degree ⟨a race that was won by a *hair*⟩
synonyms ace, hairbreadth (*or* hairsbreadth), inch
related words bit, crumb, jot, mite, particle, smidgen, trace, trifle
2 the hairy covering of a mammal especially when fine, soft, and thick — see FUR 1
hairbreadth *or* **hairsbreadth** *n* a very small distance or degree — see HAIR 1
hairline *adj* **1** being of less than usual width — see NARROW 1
2 made or done with extreme care and accuracy — see FINE 2
3 meeting the highest standard of accuracy — see PRECISE 1

hair–raising *adj* causing fear — see FEARFUL 1

hairsplitting *adj* made or done with extreme care and accuracy — see FINE 2

hairy *adj* **1** covered with or as if with hair ⟨a *hairy* spider⟩
synonyms bristly, fleecy, furry, hirsute, rough, shaggy, unshorn, woolly (*also* wooly)
related words bearded, mustachioed, whiskered; downy, fluffy, fuzzy, nappy
near antonyms beardless, shaved, shaven
antonyms bald, furless, hairless, shorn, smooth
2 made of or resembling hair ⟨enough *hairy* clumps around the house to make another cat⟩ ⟨a *hairy* mass of fiberglass insulation⟩
synonyms furry, fuzzy, rough, shaggy, woolly (*also* wooly)
related words downy, fluffy, nappy

halcyon *adj* free from storms or physical disturbance — see CALM 1

hale *adj* enjoying health and vigor — see HEALTHY 1

hale *vb* to cause to follow by applying steady force on — see PULL 1

half *adv* in any way or respect — see AT ALL

half *n* **1** one of two equal or nearly equal parts ⟨to be fair, we each get *half* the pie⟩
synonyms moiety
related words hemisphere, meridian, semicircle; component, division, fraction, part, piece, portion, section, segment
near antonyms aggregate, whole
2 either of a pair matched in one or more qualities — see MATE 1

halfhearted *adj* showing little or no interest or enthusiasm — see TEPID 1

halfway *adj* **1** lacking some necessary part — see INCOMPLETE
2 occupying a position equally distant from the ends or extremes — see MIDDLE 1

half–wit *n* **1** a person who lacks good sense or judgment — see FOOL 1
2 a stupid person — see IDIOT

half–witted *adj* **1** not having or showing an ability to absorb ideas readily — see STUPID 1
2 showing or marked by a lack of good sense or judgment — see FOOLISH 1

hall *n* **1** the entrance room of a building ⟨the guests hung their coats in the *hall*⟩
synonyms entry, entryway, foyer, lobby, vestibule
related words antechamber, anteroom, waiting room; doorway, entrance, threshold
2 a typically long narrow way connecting parts of a building ⟨the bedroom is at the end of the *hall*⟩
synonyms concourse, corridor, gallery, hallway, passage, passageway
related words arcade, breezeway, cloister
3 a large room or building for enclosed public gatherings ⟨the concert *hall* was full⟩
synonyms arena, auditorium, theater (*or* theatre)
related words amphitheater, hippodrome, house, playhouse; ballroom; lyceum; chamber, senate
4 a centrally located room in a building that serves as a gathering or waiting area or as a passageway into the interior — see FOYER 1
5 a large impressive residence — see MANSION
6 a large, magnificent, or massive building — see EDIFICE 1

hallmark *n* a device, design, or figure used as an identifying mark — see EMBLEM

hallow *vb* to make holy through prayers or ritual — see BLESS 1

hallowed *adj* **1** deserving honor and respect especially by reason of age — see VENERABLE 1
2 set apart or worthy of veneration by association with God — see HOLY 2

hallowing *n* the act of making something holy through religious ritual — see CONSECRATION

hallucination *n* a conception or image created by the imagination and having no objective reality — see FANTASY 1

hallway *n* a typically long narrow way connecting parts of a building — see HALL 2

halt *n* **1** a point in a struggle where neither side is capable of winning or willing to give in — see IMPASSE
2 the stopping of a process or activity — see END 1

¹halt *vb* **1** to bring (something) to a standstill ⟨traffic was *halted* by the parade⟩
synonyms arrest, catch, check, draw up, fetch up, hold up, stall, stay, still, stop
related words balk, block, blockade, dam, detain, hinder, hold, hold back, impede, obstruct, stem; conclude, end, terminate; call, discontinue, suspend; clamp down, rein (in), squash, squelch, stamp, stanch (*also* staunch), stunt, suppress, turn back
near antonyms carry on, continue, follow through, keep on, keep up, run on; advance, fare, move, proceed, progress, wend; actuate, budge, drive, impel, propel, push, stir
2 to bring (as an action or operation) to an immediate end — see STOP 1
3 to come to an end — see CEASE 1

²halt *vb* to walk while favoring one leg — see LIMP 1

hammer *vb* **1** to shape with a hammer ⟨medieval artisans *hammered* brass into bowls and trays which they embossed with elaborate designs⟩
synonyms beat, forge, pound
related words chase, fashion, form, knead, model, mold, work; coin, mint, stamp; carve, chisel, hew, sculpt, sculpture
2 to deliver a blow to (someone or something) usually in a strong vigorous manner — see HIT 1
3 to strike repeatedly — see BEAT 1

hammer (out) *vb* to produce or bring about especially by long or repeated effort ⟨the school committee *hammered out* a new sports-participation policy with input from students, parents, and administrators⟩
synonyms build (up), carve (out), forge, grind (out), work out
related words cobble (together *or* up), create, construct, fabricate, fashion, form, frame, manufacture, model, shape, tailor; conceive, concoct, contrive, cook (up), devise, hatch, invent, originate; bring forth, effect; accomplish, achieve, bring off
near antonyms demolish, destroy, dismantle, raze, tear down; ruin, undo, unmake, wreck

hamper *vb* to create difficulty for the work or activity of ⟨fallen branches *hampered* the hikers as they made their way along the narrow path⟩
synonyms clog, cramp, delay, embarrass, encumber, fetter, handicap, hinder, hobble, hold back, hold up, impede, inhibit, interfere (with), manacle, obstruct, shackle, tie up, trammel
related words arrest, brake, check, constrain, curb, rein, restrain, snag; bind, chain, handcuff, leash, muzzle, strap, tether, tie; barricade, block,

blockade, dam, head (off), plug; balk, choke, hurt, repress, retard, stifle, straiten, strangle, stunt; baffle, foil, frustrate, interrupt, sabotage, thwart; bog (down), confine, hedge (in), hem (in), limit, tie (down)
phrases cramp one's style, give a hard time
near antonyms clear, make way, open, unclog, unplug, unstop; free, liberate, release, untie; loosen, smooth; further, promote
antonyms aid, assist, facilitate, help

hams *n pl* the part of the body upon which someone sits — see BUTTOCKS

hamstring *vb* to render powerless, ineffective, or unable to move — see PARALYZE

hand *n* **1** a certain way in which something appears or may be regarded — see ASPECT 1
2 a place, space, or direction away from or beyond a central point or line — see SIDE 1
3 an arrow-shaped piece on a dial or scale for registering information — see POINTER 1
4 one who works for another for wages or a salary — see EMPLOYEE
5 the form or style of a particular person's writing — see HANDWRITING 1
6 *usually* **hands** *pl* the ability to direct the course of something — see CONTROL 2
7 hands *pl* the fact or state of having (something) at one's disposal — see POSSESSION 1

hand *vb* **1** to put (something) into the possession of someone for use or consumption — see FURNISH 2
2 to shift possession of (something) from one person to another — see PASS 1

handbag *n* **1** a bag carried by hand and designed to hold a traveler's clothing and personal articles — see TRAVELING BAG
2 a container for carrying money and small personal items — see PURSE

handbook *n* a book used for instruction in a subject — see TEXTBOOK

handcraft *n* an occupation requiring skillful use of the hands — see CRAFT 1

handcuff *vb* to confine or restrain with or as if with chains — see BIND 1

handcuff *n usually* **handcuffs** *pl* something that physically prevents free movement — see BOND 1

handful *n* a small number — see FEW

handicap *n* **1** a feature of someone or something that creates difficulty for achieving success — see DISADVANTAGE
2 something that makes movement or progress more difficult — see ENCUMBRANCE

handicap *vb* to create difficulty for the work or activity of — see HAMPER

handicraft *n* an occupation requiring skillful use of the hands — see CRAFT 1

handicrafter *n* a person whose occupation requires skill with the hands — see ARTISAN

handily *adv* without difficulty — see EASILY

handiwork *n* something produced by physical or intellectual effort — see PRODUCT 1

handkerchief *n* a scarf worn on the head — see BANDANNA

handle *n* a word or combination of words by which a person or thing is regularly known — see NAME 1

handle *vb* **1** to deal with (something) usually skillfully or efficiently ⟨as host of a live TV talk show, she must *handle* any situation that comes up⟩

synonyms contend (with), cope (with), grapple (with), manage, maneuver, manipulate, negotiate, swing, treat
related words bring off, carry out, pull, swing; command, direct, guide, steer; control, regulate, run
phrases have a grip on
near antonyms botch, bungle, goof (up), louse up, mess (up)
antonyms fumble, muddle (through)
2 to behave toward in a stated way — see TREAT 1
3 to control the mechanical operation of — see OPERATE 1
4 to look after and make decisions about — see CONDUCT 1

handling *n* the act or activity of looking after and making decisions about something — see CONDUCT 1

hand over *vb* **1** to give (something) over to the control or possession of another usually under duress — see SURRENDER 1
2 to put (something) into the possession of someone for use or consumption — see FURNISH 2
3 to put (something) into the possession or safekeeping of another — see GIVE 2
4 to shift possession of (something) from one person to another — see PASS 1

handpick *vb* to decide to accept (someone or something) from a group of possibilities — see CHOOSE 1

handsome *adj* **1** having or showing elegance — see ELEGANT 1
2 of a size greater than average of its kind — see LARGE
3 very pleasing to look at — see BEAUTIFUL

handsomely *adv* in a generous manner — see WELL 2

handsomeness *n* **1** dignified or restrained beauty of form, appearance, or style — see ELEGANCE
2 the qualities in a person or thing that as a whole give pleasure to the senses — see BEAUTY 1

hand-to-mouth *adj* less plentiful than what is normal, necessary, or desirable — see MEAGER

handwriting *n* **1** the form or style of a particular person's writing ⟨she immediately recognized the *handwriting* on the envelope as that of her old college roommate⟩
synonyms hand, penmanship, script
related words scratch, scrawl, scribble; backhand, print; autograph, signature
2 writing done by hand ⟨most students are taught the value of good *handwriting*⟩
synonyms calligraphy, longhand, manuscript, penmanship, script
related words lettering; shorthand
antonyms print, type

handy *adj* **1** situated within easy reach — see CONVENIENT
2 skillful with the hands — see DEXTEROUS 1

hang *vb* **1** to place on an elevated point without support from below ⟨*hang* your coats on the coat rack in the hall⟩
synonyms dangle, sling, suspend, swing
related words hook, pin, tack; drape, festoon, garland, string; extend (out), jut, project, stick out; overhang, protrude; cascade, depend, fall
2 to be determined by, based on, or subject (to) — see DEPEND 1
3 to be limp from lack of water or vigor — see DROOP 1

4 to rest or move along the surface of a liquid or in the air — see FLOAT

hang (over) *vb* to remain poised to inflict harm, danger, or distress on — see THREATEN

hang around *vb* **1** to come or be together as friends — see ASSOCIATE 1

2 to continue to be in a place for a significant amount of time — see STAY 1

3 to spend time doing nothing — see IDLE

hang around (in) *vb* to go to or spend time in often — see FREQUENT

hang back *vb* to show uncertainty about the right course of action — see HESITATE

hangdog *adj* suffering from or expressive of a feeling of responsibility for wrongdoing — see GUILTY 2

hanger–on *n* a person who is supported or seeks support from another without making an adequate return — see LEECH

hanging *adj* **1** bending downward or forward — see NODDING

2 extending freely from a support from above — see DEPENDENT 1

hang on (to) *vb* **1** to continue to have in one's possession or power — see KEEP 2

2 to have or keep in one's hands — see HOLD 1

hangout *n* a place for spending time or for socializing ⟨Jake's favorite *hangout* is the local community center⟩

synonyms haunt, rendezvous, resort

related words camp, canteen, club, clubhouse, den, harbor, haven, nest, refuge, retreat

hang out *vb* to spend time doing nothing — see IDLE

hang out (at) *vb* to go to or spend time in often — see FREQUENT

hanker (for *or* after) *vb* to have an earnest wish to own or enjoy — see DESIRE

hankering *n* a strong wish for something — see DESIRE

hanky–panky *n* the use of clever underhanded actions to achieve an end — see TRICKERY

hap *n* **1** something that happens — see EVENT 1

2 the uncertain course of events — see CHANCE 1

hap *vb* to take place — see HAPPEN

haphazard *adj* lacking a definite plan, purpose, or pattern — see RANDOM

haphazard *adv* without definite aim, direction, rule, or method — see HIT OR MISS

haphazardly *adv* without definite aim, direction, rule, or method — see HIT OR MISS

hapless *adj* having, prone to, or marked by bad luck — see UNLUCKY

happen *vb* to take place ⟨did anything exciting *happen* over the summer?⟩

synonyms be, befall, betide, chance, come, come about, go (on), hap, occur, pass, transpire

related words arise, crop (up), develop, materialize, spring (up); intervene; fall out, go off, proceed, turn out

phrases come to pass

happen (on *or* upon) *vb* to come upon unexpectedly or by chance ⟨*happened on* the filming of a movie⟩

synonyms chance (upon), encounter, find, hit (upon), meet, stumble (on *or* onto)

related words confront, face; discover, turn up

phrases bump into, come across, run across, run into

happen (upon) *vb* to come upon face-to-face or as if face-to-face — see MEET 1

happening *n* **1** an exciting or noteworthy event that one experiences firsthand — see ADVENTURE

2 something that happens — see EVENT 1

happily *adv* **1** in a cheerful or happy manner — see GAILY 1

2 in a manner suitable for the occasion or purpose — see PROPERLY

happiness *n* **1** a feeling or state of well-being and contentment ⟨Marta's *happiness* was complete when she got her very own horse⟩

synonyms blessedness, bliss, blissfulness, felicity, gladness, joy

related words elatedness, elation, exhilaration, exultation, intoxication; ecstasy, euphoria, heaven, rapture, rapturousness; delectation, delight, enjoyment, pleasure; cheer, cheerfulness, exuberance, gaiety (*also* gayety), gladsomeness, glee, gleefulness, jollity, joyfulness, joyousness, jubilation, lightheartedness; content, contentedness, gratification, satisfaction

near antonyms anguish, desolation, joylessness, sorrow, woe, woefulness; blues, dejection, depression, despondency, disheartenment, dispiritedness, doldrums, downheartedness, gloom, gloominess, melancholy, mournfulness

antonyms misery, sadness, unhappiness, wretchedness

2 the feeling experienced when one's wishes are met — see PLEASURE 1

happy *adj* **1** coming or happening by good luck especially unexpectedly — see FORTUNATE 1

2 experiencing pleasure, satisfaction, or delight — see GLAD 1

3 feeling that one's needs or desires have been met — see CONTENT

4 having good luck — see LUCKY 1

5 meeting the requirements of a purpose or situation — see FIT 1

happy–go–lucky *adj* **1** having a relaxed, casual manner — see EASYGOING 1

2 having or showing a lack of concern or seriousness — see CAREFREE

harangue *n* **1** a long angry speech or scolding — see TIRADE

2 a usually formal discourse delivered to an audience — see SPEECH 1

harangue *vb* **1** to give a formal often extended talk on a subject — see TALK 1

2 to talk as if giving an important and formal speech — see ORATE

harassment *n* the act of making unwelcome intrusions upon another — see ANNOYANCE 1

harbinger *n* one that announces or indicates the later arrival of another — see FORERUNNER 1

harbor *n* **1** a part of a body of water protected and deep enough to be a place of safety for ships ⟨the tanker stayed in Boston *harbor* three days to undergo repairs⟩

synonyms anchorage, harborage, haven, port

related words seaport; arm, bay, bight, cove, creek [*chiefly British*], estuary, firth, fjord (*or* fiord), gulf, inlet, loch [*Scottish*], narrow, roads, roadstead; canal, channel, sound, strait

2 something (as a building) that offers cover from the weather or protection from danger — see SHELTER

harbor *vb* **1** to keep in one's mind or heart ⟨Grand-

THESAURUS

pa *harbored* a grudge against his first boss for nearly 50 years〉
synonyms bear, cherish, entertain, have, hold, nurse
related words cultivate, foster, nurture, sustain, support; carry, keep, maintain, preserve, remember, retain, treasure; cleave (to), cling (to), hang on (to), stick (to)
near antonyms disregard, drop, forget, ignore, neglect, overlook; abjure, decline, deny, disdain, refuse, reject, repudiate, scorn; abandon, desert, discard, forsake, give up, quit, renounce, throw out
2 to provide with living quarters or shelter — see HOUSE 1
3 to be or provide a shelter for — see SHELTER 1
harborage *n* **1** a part of a body of water protected and deep enough to be a place of safety for ships — see HARBOR 1
2 something (as a building) that offers cover from the weather or protection from danger — see SHELTER
hard *adj* **1** having or showing a lack of sympathy or tender feelings 〈a *hard* man, who never had a kind word for anyone〉
synonyms callous, cold-blooded, hard-boiled, hardhearted, heartless, inhuman, inhumane, insensate, insensitive, merciless, obdurate, pitiless, ruthless, soulless, stony (*also* stoney), uncharitable, unfeeling, unmerciful, unsparing, unsympathetic
related words inconsiderate, thoughtless, uncaring, unfriendly, unloving, unthinking; grim, hard-bitten, harsh, heavy-handed, oppressive, rough, severe, stern, tough, ungentle; abusive, acrimonious, disagreeable, hateful, ill-natured, ill-tempered, malevolent, malicious, mean, rancorous, spiteful, surly, virulent; barbarous, bestial, brutal, brutish, cruel, evil-minded, savage, vicious
near antonyms benevolent, benignant, gentle, kind; clement, lenient, mild; cordial, friendly, good-natured, good-tempered, gracious; tolerant, understanding; affectionate, loving
antonyms charitable, compassionate, humane, merciful, sensitive, softhearted, sympathetic, tender, tenderhearted, warm, warmhearted
2 requiring considerable physical or mental effort 〈clearing land is *hard* work〉 〈a *hard* Spanish test〉
synonyms arduous, demanding, difficult, exacting, formidable, grueling (*or* gruelling), herculean, killer, laborious, murderous, rough, severe, stiff, strenuous, tall, toilsome, tough
related words abstract, abstruse, complex, complicated, insoluble, intricate, involved, knotty, problematic (*also* problematical), recondite, serious, spiny, thorny, ticklish, tricky, stubborn; burdensome, exhausting, labored, onerous, oppressive, problem, sore, stressful, taxing, tight, trying, uphill; annoying, bothersome, distressing, irksome, troublesome, vexatious; grievous, grim, heavy, strict, stringent; brutal, cruel, inhuman, painful
near antonyms achievable, clear, doable, elementary, manageable, uncomplicated; comforting, gentle, painless, relaxed, smooth, soothing
antonyms easy, effortless, facile, simple, soft, undemanding
3 able to withstand hardship, strain, or exposure — see HARDY 1
4 based on sound reasoning or information — see GOOD 1

5 difficult to endure — see HARSH 1
6 extreme in degree, power, or effect — see INTENSE
7 given to exacting standards of discipline and self-restraint — see SEVERE 1
8 having a consistency that does not easily yield to pressure — see FIRM 2
9 having been established and usually not subject to change — see FIXED 1
10 having or showing deep-seated resentment — see BITTER 1
11 sticking to an opinion, purpose, or course of action in spite of reason, arguments, or persuasion — see OBSTINATE
12 restricted to or based on fact — see FACTUAL 1
hard *adv* **1** with great effort or determination 〈we took a much-needed break after working *hard* all week〉 〈a *hard*-won victory〉
synonyms arduously, assiduously, determinedly, diligently, hardly, indefatigably, industriously, intensely, intensively, intently, laboriously, mightily, sedulously, slavishly, strenuously, tirelessly
related words actively, animatedly, briskly, busily, dynamically, energetically, feverishly, spiritedly, vehemently, vigorously, zealously; continuously, ploddingly, steadily, unabatedly, unrelentingly, unremittingly; ardently, attentively, conscientiously, earnestly, exhaustively, meticulously, painstakingly, seriously, thoroughly
near antonyms casually, desultorily, indolently, lackadaisically, languidly, lazily, listlessly, shiftlessly, sluggishly, spiritlessly, tiredly, wearily
2 with feelings of bitterness or grief 〈took the news of their grandfather's death *hard*〉
synonyms agonizingly, bitterly, grievously, hardly, mournfully, painfully, regretfully, resentfully, ruefully, sadly, sorely, sorrowfully, unhappily, woefully, wretchedly
related words abjectly, dejectedly, despondently, dispiritedly; blackly, darkly, distressfully, distressingly, forlornly, gloomily, miserably; acutely, harshly, keenly, poignantly, severely, sharply; cruelly, hurtfully, ill, rancorously
near antonyms cheerfully, cheerily, delightedly, gaily (*also* gayly), gleefully, good-naturedly, lightheartedly, merrily; blithely, calmly, casually, dispassionately, easily, indifferently, lightly, nonchalantly, unconcernedly; favorably, well
antonyms gladly, happily, joyfully, joyously
3 in a vigorous and forceful manner 〈Terry hit the ball *hard* and it soared out of bounds〉 〈the wind blew *hard* all day〉
synonyms energetically, firmly, forcefully, forcibly, mightily, powerfully, stiffly, stoutly, strenuously, strongly, sturdily, vigorously
related words robustly, sharply, vehemently, violently; animatedly, briskly, crisply, dynamically, heartily, lustily, snappily, spiritedly, vivaciously; decidedly, determinedly, directly, emphatically, fast, fixedly, intensively, intently, resolutely, rigidly, smartly, solidly, soundly, squarely, steadfastly, steadily, surely; aggressively, assertively, manfully, potently
phrases with might and main
near antonyms delicately, faintly, frailly, shakily; indirectly, languidly, listlessly, spiritlessly; impotently, ineffectively, ineffectually, nervelessly, spinelessly, uncertainly
antonyms feebly, gently, softly, weakly

4 at, within, or to a short distance or time — see NEAR 1

5 in a manner so as to cause loss or suffering — see HARDLY 1

hard–and–fast *adj* **1** having been established and usually not subject to change — see FIXED 1

2 not capable of changing or being changed — see INFLEXIBLE 1

hard–bitten *adj* able to withstand hardship, strain, or exposure — see HARDY 1

hard–boiled *adj* having or showing a lack of sympathy or tender feelings — see HARD 1

hard–core *adj* firmly established over time — see INVETERATE 1

harden *vb* **1** to become physically firm or solid ⟨waited for the bubbly caramel-and-nut sauce to cool and *harden* into peanut brittle⟩

synonyms concrete, congeal, firm (up), freeze, set, solidify

related words cake, callus, encrust (*also* incrust); coagulate, clot, gel, jell, jelly, stiffen, thicken; calcify, crystallize, ossify, petrify; anneal, case harden, temper

near antonyms deliquesce, dissolve, flux, fuse, liquefy, melt, smelt, thaw

antonyms soften

2 to make able to withstand physical hardship, strain, or exposure ⟨pioneer women who had been *hardened* by years of living on the plains⟩

synonyms fortify, inure, season, steel, strengthen, toughen

related words acclimate, acclimatize, adapt, adjust; anneal, temper; invigorate, vitalize; immunize; bolster, boost, brace, buttress, forearm, prop (up), reinforce, support; break in, limber (up), train; accustom, condition, habituate, naturalize

near antonyms emasculate, enervate, enfeeble, exhaust, sap, weaken; cripple, debilitate, incapacitate; sensitize

antonyms soften

3 to increase the ability of (as a muscle) to exert physical force — see STRENGTHEN 1

hardened *adj* **1** able to withstand hardship, strain, or exposure — see HARDY 1

2 sticking to an opinion, purpose, or course of action in spite of reason, arguments, or persuasion — see OBSTINATE

hardheaded *adj* **1** having or showing a practical cleverness or judgment — see SHREWD

2 sticking to an opinion, purpose, or course of action in spite of reason, arguments, or persuasion — see OBSTINATE

3 willing to see things as they really are and deal with them sensibly — see REALISTIC 1

hardheadedness *n* a steadfast adherence to an opinion, purpose, or course of action — see OBSTINACY

hardhearted *adj* **1** having or showing a lack of sympathy or tender feelings — see HARD 1

2 sticking to an opinion, purpose, or course of action in spite of reason, arguments, or persuasion — see OBSTINATE

hardihood *n* **1** active strength of body or mind — see VIGOR 1

2 strength of mind to carry on in spite of danger — see COURAGE

hardly *adv* **1** in a manner so as to cause loss or suffering ⟨the new judge vowed to deal *hardly* with repeat offenders⟩

synonyms hard, harshly, ill, oppressively, roughly, severely, sternly, stiffly

related words callously, cold-bloodedly, hardheartedly, heartlessly, inhumanely, inhumanly, insensately, insensitively, mercilessly, obdurately, pitilessly, ruthlessly, tyrannically, uncharitably, unfeelingly, unmercifully, unsparingly; abusively, brutally, brutishly, savagely, viciously; aggressively, assertively, decidedly, determinedly, firmly, grimly, gruffly, resolutely, strongly, toughly

near antonyms benevolently, benignantly, considerately, cordially, graciously, kindly, lovingly, tenderly; charitably, compassionately, humanely, mercifully, softheartedly, sympathetically, tolerantly, understandingly

antonyms clemently, gently, leniently, lightly, mildly, softly

2 certainly not ⟨it's *hardly* surprising that our team won, considering how weak the opponents were⟩

synonyms no, none, no way, scarcely

related words near, never, nothing, nowhere, nowise

phrases by no means, nothing doing, on no account

near antonyms awful, awfully, enormously, exceedingly (*also* exceeding), extremely, greatly, highly, hugely, immensely, mighty, most, quite, terribly, very; assuredly, clearly, perfectly, plainly, positively, really, truly, unequivocally, unquestionably, utterly; doubtless, more or less, mostly, rather, slightly, somewhat

antonyms absolutely, certainly, completely, definitely, positively, surely

3 by a very small margin — see JUST 2

4 with feelings of bitterness or grief — see HARD 2

5 with great effort or determination — see HARD 1

hardness *n* **1** something that is a cause for suffering or special effort especially in the attainment of a goal — see DIFFICULTY 1

2 the quality or state of being demanding or unyielding (as in discipline or criticism) — see SEVERITY

hardship *n* something that is a cause for suffering or special effort especially in the attainment of a goal — see DIFFICULTY 1

hardy *adj* **1** able to withstand hardship, strain, or exposure ⟨chrysanthemums are *hardy* enough to survive a light frost⟩ ⟨the men and women who settled the West were a *hardy* lot⟩

synonyms hard, hard-bitten, hardened, inured, rugged, stout, strong, sturdy, tough, toughened, vigorous

related words flinty, leathery, resilient, stalwart; durable, enduring, everlasting, immortal, imperishable, lasting, permanent, stable, staunch (*or* stanch), staying, tenacious, unyielding; flourishing, prospering, thriving; able-bodied, brawny, muscular; fit, fortified, hale, healthy, husky, lusty, red-blooded, robust, sound, strapping, virile; annealed, seasoned, tempered

near antonyms emasculated, enervated, enfeebled, exhausted, run-down, sapped, wasted, weakened, worn, worn out; crippled, debilitated, diseased, incapacitated, infirm, unsound; fragile, frail, puny; resistless, sensitive, susceptible, unresistant, vulnerable, yielding; mortal, perishable, temporary, transient

antonyms delicate, nonhardy, soft, tender, weak

2 inclined or willing to take risks — see BOLD 1

THESAURUS

harebrained *adj* **1** lacking in seriousness or maturity — see GIDDY 1

2 showing or marked by a lack of good sense or judgment — see FOOLISH 1

hark *vb* to pay attention especially through the act of hearing — see LISTEN

hark back (to) *vb* to bring back to mind — see REMEMBER

harlequin *n* a comically dressed performer (as at a circus) who entertains with playful tricks and ridiculous behavior — see CLOWN 1

harlot *n* a woman who engages in sexual activities for money — see PROSTITUTE

harlotry *n* the practice of engaging in sexual activities for money — see PROSTITUTION

harm *n* something that causes loss or pain — see INJURY 1

harm *vb* **1** to cause bodily damage to — see INJURE 1

2 to reduce the soundness, effectiveness, or perfection of — see DAMAGE 1

harmful *adj* causing or capable of causing harm ⟨DDT has been proven extremely *harmful* to the environment⟩

synonyms adverse, bad, baleful, baneful, damaging, deleterious, detrimental, evil, hurtful, ill, injurious, mischievous, noxious, pernicious, prejudicial

related words hostile, inimical, unfriendly; contagious, deadly, infectious, pestilent, pestilential, poisonous, venomous; insidious, menacing, ominous, sinister, threatening; dangerous, hazardous, imperiling, jeopardizing, parlous, perilous, risky, unsafe, unsound; nasty, noisome, unhealthful, unhealthy, unwholesome; destructive, fatal, lethal, malignant, ruinous

near antonyms advantageous, beneficial, useful; favorable, good, propitious; curative, healthful, healthy, helpful, palliative, remedial, salubrious, salutary, wholesome; secure, sound; benign, benignant; noncorrosive, nondestructive, nonfatal, noninfectious, nonlethal, nonpoisonous, nonpolluting, nontoxic, nonvenomous

antonyms harmless, innocent, innocuous, inoffensive, safe

harmless *adj* not causing injury or hurt ⟨a perfectly *harmless* little spider⟩

synonyms innocent, innocuous, inoffensive, safe, white

related words healthful, healthy, salubrious, wholesome; benign, benignant; sound, trustworthy; gentle, gracious, mild; nonthreatening, painless, unobjectionable; noncorrosive, nondestructive, nonfatal, noninfectious, nonlethal, nonpoisonous, nonpolluting, nontoxic, nonvenomous

near antonyms poisonous, venomous; menacing, ominous, sinister, threatening; dangerous, hazardous, imperiling, jeopardizing, parlous, perilous, risky, unsafe, unsound; nasty, noisome, unhealthful, unhealthy, unwholesome; offensive, painful, scathing, wounding; deadly, fatal, lethal, ruinous; contaminated, corrosive, malignant, noxious, pestilent, polluted, tainted

antonyms adverse, bad, baleful, baneful, damaging, deleterious, detrimental, evil, harmful, hurtful, ill, injurious, mischievous, noxious, pernicious, prejudicial

harmonious *adj* **1** having a pleasing mixture of notes ⟨the naturally *harmonious* sounds of a forest glen in springtime⟩

synonyms euphonious, harmonizing, melodious, musical, symphonic, tuneful

related words blending, chiming, flowing, mellifluous; dulcet, mellow, melodic, sweet; echoing, resonant, sonorous; quavering, trilling, warbling; agreeable, appealing, pleasant; cadenced, lilting, lyric, lyrical, rhythmic (*or* rhythmical); chordal, harmonic, homophonic, orchestral, polyphonic, tonal

near antonyms blaring, clanging, clashing, clattering, grating, harsh, jangling, jarring, metallic, raspy, raucous, scratching, screeching, shrill, squeaky, strident; disagreeable, unpleasant, unpleasing; atonal, off-key

antonyms discordant, dissonant, inharmonious, unharmonious, unmelodious, unmusical

2 having the parts agreeably related ⟨a *harmonious* arrangement of archways and doorways in the palace courtyard⟩

synonyms balanced, congruous, consonant

related words even, proportioned, regular, symmetrical (*or* symmetric); aesthetic (*or* esthetic), artistic, becoming, elegant, graceful, tasteful; agreeable, felicitous, pleasant, pleasing, satisfying; compatible, coordinated, correspondent, matched, matching

near antonyms asymmetrical, disordered, irregular, skewed, unequal, uneven, unsymmetrical; distasteful, graceless, inartistic, inelegant, tasteless, unaesthetic, unbecoming, ungraceful, unlovely; disagreeable, displeasing, dissatisfying, infelicitous, unfortunate, unpleasant, unsightly; clashing, conflicting, disunited, incompatible, uncoordinated

antonyms incongruous, inharmonious, unbalanced

3 having or marked by agreement in feeling or action ⟨an unusually *harmonious* meeting among the leaders resulted in a quick peace agreement⟩

synonyms agreeable, amicable, compatible, congenial, frictionless, kindred, unanimous, united

related words pacific, peaceable, peaceful; collaborating, cooperative, symbiotic; noncompetitive, nonconflicting, uncompetitive; sympathetic, tolerant, understanding; affable, amiable, cordial, friendly, genial, neighborly; collaborating

near antonyms antagonistic, antipathetic, clashing, conflicting, hostile, inimical, unfriendly; belligerent, contentious, quarrelsome; contradicting, contradictory, contrary, opposing, opposite; competing, competitive, rivaling (*or* rivalling)

antonyms disagreeable, disunited, incompatible, inharmonious, uncongenial

4 not having or showing any apparent conflict — see CONSISTENT

harmonize *vb* **1** to form a pleasing relationship ⟨the color of the walls *harmonized* nicely with the blue tones in the carpet⟩

synonyms agree, blend, conform, coordinate

related words balance, correlate, correspond, dovetail, match; meet, parallel; bond, coalesce, cohere, conjoin, fuse, merge, square, tally

near antonyms contradict, contrast, counter, differ, diverge, jar; cancel (out), counteract, negate, offset

antonyms clash, collide, conflict

2 to bring to a state free of conflicts, inconsistencies, or differences ⟨an attempt to *harmonize* the New Testament version of events with the accounts of the ancient Romans⟩

synonyms accommodate, conciliate, conform, coordinate, key, reconcile
related words adapt, attune, tune; blend, combine, connect, correlate, dovetail, fit, fuse, integrate, join, match, merge, orchestrate, pair, square, suit, synchronize, synthesize, unify, unite; align, arrange, array, balance, equalize, even, order, proportion, regularize, standardize
near antonyms confuse, disarray, disorder, disorganize, disrupt, disturb, skew, upset
antonyms alienate, disjoin
3 to be in agreement on every point — see CHECK 1
harmonizing *adj* having a pleasing mixture of notes — see HARMONIOUS 1
harmony *n* **1** a balanced, pleasing, or suitable arrangement of parts ⟨her face had an angelic *harmony* that fascinated the leading painters of her day⟩
synonyms balance, coherence, consonance, proportion, symmetry, symphony, unity
related words coordination, correlation, correspondence, equalization, equilibrium, evenness, order, orderliness, regularity, uniformity
near antonyms confusion, disorganization, dissonance, disturbance, tension; disconnectedness, disjointedness, incompatibility; irregularity, unevenness
antonyms asymmetry, discordance, disproportion, disunity, imbalance, incoherence
2 peaceful coexistence ⟨Mary Beth was determined to live in *harmony* with her new stepsister⟩
synonyms comity, compatibility, concord, peace
related words amity, congeniality, fellowship, fraternization, friendship; collaboration, reciprocity, symbiosis; consensus, unanimity, unity; affinity, connection, empathy, kinship, oneness, rapport, solidarity, sympathy, understanding; peacefulness, serenity, tranquillity (*or* tranquility)
near antonyms antagonism, antipathy, enmity, hatred, hostility, unfriendliness; alienation, breach, divorce, estrangement, rupture, schism, severance; dissent, dissidence; disturbance, strife, turmoil
antonyms conflict, discord, dissension
3 a state of consistency — see CONFORMITY 1
harness *vb* to put into action or service — see USE 1
harpoon *vb* to penetrate or hold (something) with a pointed object — see IMPALE
harpy *n* a bad-tempered scolding woman — see SHREW
harrow *vb* to cause persistent suffering to — see AFFLICT
harrowing *adj* **1** hard to accept or bear especially emotionally — see BITTER 2
2 intensely or unbearably painful — see EXCRUCIATING 2
harrying *n* the act of making unwelcome intrusions upon another — see ANNOYANCE 1
harsh *adj* **1** difficult to endure ⟨*harsh* conditions in the refugee camp⟩
synonyms bitter, brutal, burdensome, cruel, excruciating, grievous, grim, hard, heavy, inhuman, murderous, onerous, oppressive, rough, rugged, severe, stiff, tough, trying
related words austere, bleak, comfortless, discomforting, forbidding, hostile, inhospitable, Spartan, uncomfortable; biting, inclement, intemperate; rigorous, strict, stringent; agonizing, heartbreak-

ing, heartrending, painful, wretched; crushing, grinding, overwhelming, wearing; insufferable, insupportable, intolerable, unbearable, unendurable; harrowing, tortuous; bad, disagreeable, hostile, unfriendly, unpleasant
near antonyms comfortable, cozy, luxurious, snug; agreeable, friendly, genial, hospitable, pleasant; peaceful, relaxing, reposeful, restful; bearable, endurable, painless, tolerable; balmy, calm, clement, gentle, mild, moderate, temperate
antonyms easy, light, soft
2 disagreeable to one's aesthetic or artistic sense ⟨the *harsh* lighting in the cafeteria makes the food look slightly off-color⟩
synonyms grating, grotesque, jarring, unaesthetic
related words flashy, garish, gaudy, loud, tawdry; tacky, tasteless, vulgar; inartistic, unartistic; artless, clumsy, crude, graceless, inelegant, rude; uncouth, uncultured, unrefined; disgusting, gross, obscene, repugnant, repulsive, ugly; disagreeable, jolting, unpleasant, unpleasing; blaring, clashing, discordant, dissonant, inharmonious, off-key, jangling, raspy, raucous, unharmonious, unmelodious, unmusical; bizarre, kinky, odd, outlandish, shocking
near antonyms artful, artistic; attractive, beautiful, becoming, comely; agreeable, appealing, felicitous, good, harmonious, harmonizing, pleasing, seemly; calming, comforting, soothing; softened, subdued; cultured, elegant, graceful, gracious, polished, refined, tasteful
antonyms aesthetic (*or* esthetic)
3 causing discomfort — see UNCOMFORTABLE 1
4 given to exacting standards of discipline and self-restraint — see SEVERE 1
5 hard to accept or bear especially emotionally — see BITTER 2
harshly *adv* in a manner so as to cause loss or suffering — see HARDLY 1
harshness *n* **1** a harsh or sharp quality — see EDGE 1
2 the quality or state of being demanding or unyielding (as in discipline or criticism) — see SEVERITY
harum–scarum *adv* in a confused and reckless manner — see HELTER-SKELTER 1
harvest *n* the quantity of an animal or vegetable product gathered at the end of a season — see CROP 1
harvest *vb* to catch or collect (a crop or natural resource) for human use ⟨*harvest* salmon from nearby rivers⟩ ⟨every year we *harvest* corn from our own garden⟩
synonyms gather, pick, reap
related words clam, fish, seal, shrimp, whale; accumulate, garner; glean; cut, hay, mow; bag, capture, hunt, net, snare, trap; crop, grow, raise
near antonyms plant, seed, sow
hash *n* an unorganized collection or mixture of various things — see MISCELLANY 1
hash *vb* **1** to cut into small pieces — see CHOP
2 to undo the proper order or arrangement of — see DISORDER
hash (over) *vb* to talk about (an issue) usually from various points of view and for the purpose of arriving at a decision or opinion — see DISCUSS
hassle *n* **1** a brief clash between enemies or rivals — see ENCOUNTER
2 a physical dispute between opposing individuals or groups — see FIGHT 1

THESAURUS

3 an often noisy or angry expression of differing opinions — see ARGUMENT 1

4 something that is a source of irritation — see ANNOYANCE 3

hassle *vb* **1** to attack repeatedly with mean put-downs or insults — see TEASE 2

2 to express different opinions about something often angrily — see ARGUE 2

haste *n* **1** a high rate of movement or performance — see SPEED

2 excited and often showy or disorderly speed — see HURRY 1

hasten *vb* **1** to cause to move or proceed fast or faster — see HURRY 1

2 to proceed or move quickly — see HURRY 2

hastily *adv* **1** with excessive or careless speed ⟨the *hastily* put together report contained a lot of errors⟩

synonyms cursorily, headlong, hotfoot, hurriedly, pell-mell, precipitately, precipitously, rashly

related words headily, hotheadedly, impatiently, impetuously, impulsively, recklessly, thoughtlessly; automatically, glancingly, haphazardly; impromptu, spontaneously; abruptly, suddenly; offhand, offhandedly

phrases on the spur of the moment

near antonyms calculatingly, circumspectly, designedly; falteringly, hesitantly, hesitatingly, tentatively; leisurely, slowly

antonyms deliberately, studiedly

2 with great speed — see FAST 1

hastiness *n* excited and often showy or disorderly speed — see HURRY 1

hasty *adj* **1** acting or done with excessive or careless speed ⟨Anna later regretted her *hasty* decision to sell her car⟩

synonyms cursory, flying, headlong, hurried, pell-mell, precipitate, precipitous, rash, rushed

related words breakneck, breathtaking; headstrong, heady, hotheaded, impatient, impetuous, impulsive, madcap, reckless, unadvised; quick, rapid, speedy, swift; impromptu, makeshift, offhand, offhanded, slap-dash, snap, spontaneous, spur-of-the-moment; abrupt, sudden

near antonyms calculated, calculating, measured; circumspect, foresighted, forethoughtful; drawn-out, extended, long-term, prolonged; faltering, hesitant, hesitating, tentative; dallying, dawdling, laggard, leisurely, poky (*or* pokey), shilly-shallying, slow

antonyms deliberate, unhurried

2 moving, proceeding, or acting with great speed — see FAST 1

hat *n* a covering for the head usually having a shaped crown ⟨Paul brought back warm fur *hats* for everyone from Russia⟩

synonyms cap, headdress, headgear, headpiece, lid [*slang*]

related words beret, biretta, boater, bonnet, bowler, derby, fedora, fez, hard hat, helm, helmet, homburg, hood, leghorn, miter, nightcap, panama, pillbox, poke bonnet, shako, skullcap, sombrero, sou'wester, Stetson, stocking cap, stovepipe, sunbonnet, tam-o'-shanter, top hat, topper, toque, turban; war bonnet; coronet, crown, diadem, headband, tiara; babushka, coif, kerchief, mantilla, scarf, shawl, tallith, veil, wimple

hatch *n* a barrier by which an entry is closed and opened — see DOOR 1

hatch *vb* to cover and warm eggs to hatch them — see SET 1

hate *n* **1** a very strong dislike ⟨*hate* can sometimes be replaced with tolerance when people meet face to face⟩

synonyms abhorrence, abomination, execration, hatred, loathing

related words cattiness, despite, despitefulness, hatefulness, invidiousness, malevolence, malice, maliciousness, malignancy, malignity, meanness, spite, spitefulness; aversion, disgust, distaste, horror, odium, repugnance, repulsion, revulsion; animosity, antagonism, antipathy, bitterness, contempt, disdain, enmity, grudge, hostility, jealousy, pique, resentment, scorn; bile, jaundice, rancor, spleen, venom, virulence, vitriol

near antonyms appetite, inclination, liking; adoration, veneration, worship; acceptance, tolerance; passion, relish, taste

antonyms affection, devotion, fondness, love

2 something or someone that is hated ⟨the Alaska pipeline is a pet *hate* of environmentalists⟩

synonyms abhorrence, abomination, anathema, antipathy, aversion, bête noire

related words dread, hang-up, horror, phobia; bogey (*also* bogy *or* bogie), bugaboo, bugbear; adversary, enemy; annoyance, grievance, hassle, nuisance, peeve

near antonyms beloved, darling, dear, honey; delight, enjoyment, felicity, joy, pleasure; favorite, like, preference; treasure

antonyms love

hate *vb* to dislike strongly ⟨Pete *hated* the farm and dreamed of working in the city⟩

synonyms abhor, abominate, despise, detest, execrate, loathe

related words deplore, deprecate, disapprove (of), discountenance, disdain, disfavor, scorn

phrases have it in for

near antonyms fancy, favor, like, prefer; enjoy, relish; adore, esteem, idolize, revere, venerate, worship; cherish, prize, treasure

antonyms love

hateful *adj* having or showing a desire to cause someone pain or suffering for the sheer enjoyment of it ⟨a *hateful* bully who loved to pick on little kids⟩ ⟨Janet's *hateful* remarks drove Penny to tears⟩

synonyms catty, cruel, despiteful, malevolent, malicious, malign, malignant, mean, nasty, spiteful, virulent

related words devious, scoundrelly, scurvy, snakelike; acrimonious, bitter, envious, jaundiced, jealous, rancorous, resentful; contemptuous, deprecating, disdainful, obnoxious, opprobrious, scornful, snide, unkind, unkindly, unloving; baleful, baneful, evil; harsh, hostile, inimical; acrid, caustic, scathing, venomous

near antonyms compassionate, good, good-hearted, kind, kindhearted, kindly, sympathetic, warm, warmhearted; affable, agreeable, amiable, cordial, friendly, genial, gracious, nice, pleasant; affectionate, amorous, sweet, tender, tenderhearted; altruistic, high-minded, humanitarian, magnanimous, noble, philanthropic

antonyms benevolent, benign, benignant, loving, unmalicious

hatefully *adv* in a mean or spiteful manner — see NASTILY

hatefulness *n* the desire to cause pain for the satisfaction of doing harm — see MALICE

hatred *n* a very strong dislike — see HATE 1

haughtiness *n* an exaggerated sense of one's importance that shows itself in the making of excessive or unjustified claims — see ARROGANCE

haughty *adj* **1** having a feeling of superiority that shows itself in an overbearing attitude — see ARROGANT

2 having or displaying feelings of scorn for what is regarded as beneath oneself — see PROUD 1

haul *n* **1** the total amount collected or obtained especially at one time ⟨the trick-or-treaters showed off their *haul*⟩
synonyms catch, take, yield
related words bag; earnings, gain, gross, income, net, payoff, proceeds, profit, receipts, return, revenue, winnings; booty, loot, plunder, spoils, swag; appropriation, collection
near antonyms deduction, loss, subtraction

2 a mass or quantity of something taken up and carried, conveyed, or transported — see LOAD 1
3 the act or an instance of applying force on something so that it moves in the direction of the force — see PULL 1

haul *vb* **1** to cause to follow by applying steady force on — see PULL 1

2 to support and take from one place to another — see CARRY 1

haunches *n pl* the part of the body upon which someone sits — see BUTTOCKS

haunt *n* a place for spending time or for socializing — see HANGOUT

haunt *vb* to go to or spend time in often — see FREQUENT

haunting *adj* fearfully and mysteriously strange or fantastic — see EERIE

have *vb* **1** to keep, control, or experience as one's own ⟨Aunt Chloe *has* 31 pairs of red shoes⟩
synonyms command, enjoy, hold, occupy, own, possess, retain
related words keep, reserve, withhold; bear, carry; boast, show off, sport
near antonyms abandon, cede, disclaim, disown, hand over, relinquish, renounce, surrender, yield; discard, dump; decline, reject, repudiate, spurn; need, require
antonyms lack, want

2 to agree to receive whether willingly or reluctantly — see TAKE 2
3 to bring forth from the womb — see BEAR 1
4 to cause to believe what is untrue — see DECEIVE
5 to come to a knowledge of (something) by living through it — see EXPERIENCE
6 to give permission for or to approve of — see ALLOW 1
7 to influence someone with a bribe — see BRIBE
8 to keep in one's mind or heart — see HARBOR 1

have (to) *vb* to be under necessity or obligation to — see NEED 2

haven *n* **1** a part of a body of water protected and deep enough to be a place of safety for ships — see HARBOR 1

2 something (as a building) that offers cover from the weather or protection from danger — see SHELTER

havoc *n* **1** a state in which everything is out of order — see CHAOS

2 the state or fact of being rendered nonexistent, physically unsound, or useless — see DESTRUCTION

hawk *n* one who urges or attempts to cause a war — see WARMONGER

hawk *vb* to sell from place to place usually in small quantities — see PEDDLE

hawker *n* one who sells things outdoors — see PEDDLER

hazard *n* **1** something that may cause injury or harm — see DANGER 2

2 the uncertain course of events — see CHANCE 1

hazard *vb* **1** to place in danger — see ENDANGER
2 to take a chance on — see RISK 1

hazardous *adj* involving potential loss or injury — see DANGEROUS

haze *n* **1** an atmospheric condition in which suspended particles in the air rob it of its transparency ⟨Jim could barely make out the tall buildings through the *haze*⟩
synonyms fog, mist, murk, reek, smog, soup
related words cloud, fume, miasma, smoke, steam

2 a state of mental confusion ⟨people wandered around in a *haze* in the days following the earthquake⟩
synonyms daze, fog, muddle, spin
related words reverie, stupor, trance; befuddlement, bewilderment, perplexity, puzzlement; delirium, malaise, paralysis; cloudiness, fogginess
near antonyms alertness, levelheadedness

haze *vb* to make dark, dim, or indistinct — see CLOUD 1

hazed *adj* covered over by clouds — see OVERCAST

hazy *adj* **1** filled with or dimmed by fine particles (as of dust or water) in suspension ⟨*hazy* skies made it dangerous to fly⟩ ⟨the *hazy* sunshine so common in August⟩
synonyms beclouded, befogged, clouded, cloudy, foggy, misty, murky, smoggy, soupy
related words overcast, rainy, stormy, thick; dirty, miry, mucky, muddy, slimy, slushy, turbid; smoky (*also* smokey), sooty; filmy, milky, opaque
near antonyms bright, clean; fair, rainless, sunny, sunshiny; translucent, transparent
antonyms clear, cloudless, limpid, pellucid, unclouded

2 covered over by clouds — see OVERCAST
3 not seen or understood clearly — see FAINT 1

head *adj* highest in rank or authority ⟨Mr. Pendergast, *head* editor at the TV station for 17 years, has hired and fired innumerable staff members⟩
synonyms chief, commanding, first, foremost, high, lead, leading, managing, preeminent, premier, presiding, primary, prime, principal, supreme
related words high-level, senior; controlling, directing, officiating, overseeing, reigning, ruling, supervisory; main, major, paramount, predominant; dominant, grand, superior, topmost, upmost, upper, uppermost
phrases in charge
near antonyms inferior, last, lesser, lower, lowly, second, secondary, subordinate; assistant, assisting, coadjutor, deputy, junior, under

head *n* **1** the upper or front part of the body that contains the brain, the major sense organs, and the mouth ⟨I hit my *head* as I went through the low doorway⟩
synonyms noddle, noggin, pate, poll
related words cranium, crown, scalp, skull

THESAURUS

2 the place of leadership or command ⟨every year a different parent is placed at the *head* of the troop's cookie drive⟩
synonyms chair, headship, helm, rein
related words chieftainship, commandership, directorship; forefront, lead, preferment; chairmanship, deanship, dictatorship, governorship, kingship, mastership, mastery, presidency; superintendency; dominance, dominion, jurisdiction, sovereignty, sway, upper hand; eminence, height, pedestal, pinnacle, seat, throne, top
near antonyms ranks
3 a light mass of fine bubbles formed in or on a liquid — see FOAM
4 a member of the human race — see HUMAN
5 a time or state of affairs requiring prompt or decisive action — see EMERGENCY
6 the beginning part of a stream — see HEADWATER
7 the highest part or point — see HEIGHT 1
8 the normal or healthy condition of the mental abilities — see MIND 2
9 the part of a person that feels, thinks, perceives, wills, and especially reasons — see MIND 1
10 the person (as an employer or supervisor) who tells people and especially workers what to do — see BOSS
head *vb* **1** to go on a specified course or in a certain direction ⟨the migrant workers were *heading* for California for the grape harvest⟩
synonyms bear, make
related words aim, bend, direct, point, turn; put, put out, set forth, set off, set out, strike, take off; face, orient, steer; about-face, back, come about, come round, cut, incline, put about, reverse, swerve, tack, veer, yaw, wheel
2 to be at the front of — see LEAD 3
3 to be in charge of — see BOSS 1
4 to be positioned along a certain course or in a certain direction — see RUN 3
5 to point or turn (something) toward a target or goal — see AIM
6 to serve as leader of — see LEAD 2
headache *n* **1** a dull, unpleasant, or difficult piece of work — see CHORE 2
2 something that is a source of irritation — see ANNOYANCE 3
headdress *n* a covering for the head usually having a shaped crown — see HAT
headgear *n* a covering for the head usually having a shaped crown — see HAT
heading *n* a word or series of words often in larger letters placed at the beginning of a passage or at the top of a page in order to introduce or categorize ⟨Fran found the recipe for turkey gumbo under the *heading* "stews" rather than under "soups"⟩
synonyms caption, headline, rubric, title
related words guide word, legend; greeting, salutation; superscript, superscription; subhead, subheading, subtitle
headland *n* **1** an area of high ground jutting out into a body of water beyond the line of the coast ⟨the lighthouse, situated on a narrow, rocky *headland*, commands an expansive view of the coast⟩
synonyms point, promontory
related words cape, peninsula; breakwater, jetty, levee; spit
2 an area of land that juts out into a body of water — see ²CAPE

headline *n* a word or series of words often in larger letters placed at the beginning of a passage or at the top of a page in order to introduce or categorize — see HEADING
headlong *adj* acting or done with excessive or careless speed — see HASTY 1
headlong *adv* with excessive or careless speed — see HASTILY 1
headman *n* the person (as an employer or supervisor) who tells people and especially workers what to do — see BOSS
headpiece *n* a covering for the head usually having a shaped crown — see HAT
headquarters *n pl* **1** a place from which authority is exercised — see SEAT 1
2 the place from which a commander runs operations — see COMMAND 3
headship *n* **1** the duty or function of watching or guarding for the sake of proper direction or control — see SUPERVISION 1
2 the place of leadership or command — see HEAD 2
headstone *n* a shaped stone laid over or erected near a grave and usually bearing an inscription to identify and preserve the memory of the deceased — see TOMBSTONE
headstrong *adj* **1** given to resisting control or discipline by others — see UNCONTROLLABLE
2 sticking to an opinion, purpose, or course of action in spite of reason, arguments, or persuasion — see OBSTINATE
headwater *n usually* **headwaters** *pl* the beginning part of a stream ⟨the first exploration of the Missouri River from its mouth to its *headwaters* was made by Meriwether Lewis and William Clark in the early 1800s⟩
synonyms head, source
related words fountain, fountainhead, geyser, hot spring, spring, thermal spring, wellspring
headway *n* forward movement in time or place — see ADVANCE 1
heal *vb* **1** to restore to a healthy condition ⟨a low-fat vegetarian diet, moderate exercise, and stress management help *heal* a diseased heart⟩ ⟨*heal* the sick⟩
synonyms cure, mend, rehabilitate
related words attend (to), care (for), doctor, minister (to), nurse, treat; fortify, rejuvenate, renew, resuscitate, revive; alleviate, fix, relieve, remedy, repair
phrases take care of
near antonyms damage, disable, harm, hurt, impair, injure, lacerate, lame, maim, mutilate, wound; afflict, ail, debilitate, enervate, enfeeble, lay up, sap, sicken, waste, weaken
2 to become healthy and strong again after illness or weakness — see CONVALESCE
3 to bring about recovery from — see CURE 1
healing *n* the process or period of gradually regaining one's health and strength — see CONVALESCENCE
health *n* the condition of being sound in body ⟨Sam gradually regained his *health* after a long bout with cholera⟩
synonyms fitness, healthiness, heartiness, robustness, soundness, wellness, wholeness, wholesomeness
related words fettle, shape; cleanliness, hygiene; hardiness, lustiness, ruggedness, stamina, strength, toughness, vigor, vigorousness, vitality;

bloom, flush, flushness; activeness, agility, liveliness, spryness; weal, welfare, well-being
near antonyms debility, decrepitude, feebleness, frailness, infirmity, lameness, weakness; ailment, condition, disease, disorder, malady, trouble
antonyms illness, sickness, unhealthiness, unsoundness

healthful *adj* good for the health ⟨one of the most *healthful* forms of exercise is a brisk walk⟩
synonyms healthy, restorative, salubrious, salutary, wholesome
related words alleviate, corrective, curative, remedial, tonic; advantageous, beneficial, useful; antiseptic, clean, hygienic, sanitary; nonfattening, nonpoisonous, nontoxic
near antonyms deleterious, injurious, pernicious; infectious, poisonous, toxic; insanitary, unhygienic, unsanitary
antonyms insalubrious, noxious, unhealthful, unhealthy, unwholesome

healthiness *n* the condition of being sound in body — see HEALTH

healthy *adj* **1** enjoying health and vigor ⟨always a hard worker, Grandma has remained *healthy* into her eighties⟩
synonyms able-bodied, bouncing, chipper, fit, hale, hearty, robust, sound, well, whole, wholesome
related words hardy, lusty, rugged, stalwart, strong, sturdy, tough; nondisabled, nonhandicapped, uncrippled; active, agile, lively, sprightly, spry, vigorous, vital; blooming, clean-cut, flourishing, flush, thriving; all right, good, right
phrases in fine fettle
near antonyms decrepit, enfeebled, feeble, infirm, run-down, sickened, sickly, weak, weakened, weakly, worn-out; challenged, crippled, debilitated, disabled, incapacitated, lame; delicate, fragile, frail; undernourished; afflicted, troubled; bad, poorly
antonyms ailing, diseased, ill, sick, unfit, unhealthy, unsound, unwell
2 good for the health — see HEALTHFUL
3 sufficiently large in size, amount, or number to merit attention — see CONSIDERABLE 1

heap *n* **1** a considerable amount — see LOT 2
2 a quantity of things thrown or stacked on one another — see ¹PILE 1

heap *vb* **1** to give readily and in large quantities — see RAIN 2
2 to gradually form into a layer, pile, or mass — see COLLECT 2
3 to lay or throw on top of one another — see PILE
4 to put into (something) as much as can be held or contained — see FILL 1

hear *vb* **1** to come to an awareness — see DISCOVER 1
2 to pay attention especially through the act of hearing — see LISTEN

hearing *n* range of hearing — see EARSHOT

hearken *vb* to pay attention especially through the act of hearing — see LISTEN

heart *n* **1** the capacity for feeling for another's unhappiness or misfortune ⟨when her parents refused her request for a puppy, Jessica asked, "Have you no *heart*?"⟩
synonyms charity, commiseration, compassion, feeling, humanity, kindheartedness, kindliness, kindness, mercy, pity, softheartedness, sympathy
related words responsiveness, sensitivity; affec-

tion, love, regard; affinity, empathy, rapport; altruism, benevolence, benignity, generosity, goodwill, humanitarianism, philanthropy
near antonyms callousness, coldness, indifference, unconcern; cruelty, harshness; animosity, antipathy, dislike, hatred, hostility
antonyms hardheartedness, inhumanity, mercilessness
2 the body of knowledge that has been retained in one's mind or the use of it ⟨Dan can recite the entire Declaration of Independence by *heart*⟩
synonyms memory, rote
related words association, conning, memorization
3 a thing or place that is of greatest importance to an activity or interest — see CENTER 1
4 strength of mind to carry on in spite of danger — see COURAGE
5 the central part or aspect of something under consideration — see CRUX
6 the seat of one's deepest thoughts and emotions — see CORE 1

heartache *n* deep sadness especially for the loss of someone or something loved — see SORROW

heartbreak *n* deep sadness especially for the loss of someone or something loved — see SORROW

heartbreaking *adj* **1** causing unhappiness — see SAD 2
2 of a kind to cause great distress — see REGRETTABLE
3 deserving of one's pity — see PATHETIC 1

heartbroken *adj* **1** feeling unhappiness — see SAD 1
2 expressing or suggesting mourning — see MOURNFUL 1

hearten *vb* to fill with courage or strength of purpose — see ENCOURAGE

heartening *adj* **1** having qualities which inspire hope — see HOPEFUL 1
2 making one feel good inside — see HEARTWARMING
3 pointing toward a happy outcome — see FAVORABLE 2

hearth *n* the place where one lives — see HOME 1

hearthstone *n* the place where one lives — see HOME 1

heartily *adv* in a cheerful or happy manner — see GAILY 1

heartiness *n* the condition of being sound in body — see HEALTH

heartless *adj* **1** having or showing a lack of sympathy or tender feelings — see HARD 1
2 having or showing the desire to inflict severe pain and suffering on others — see CRUEL 1

heartlessness *n* the willful infliction of pain and suffering on others — see CRUELTY

heartrending *adj* **1** causing unhappiness — see SAD 2
2 hard to accept or bear especially emotionally — see BITTER 2
3 of a kind to cause great distress — see REGRETTABLE
4 deserving of one's pity — see PATHETIC 1

heartsick *adj* feeling unhappiness — see SAD 1

heartsickness *n* a state or spell of low spirits — see SADNESS

heartsore *adj* feeling unhappiness — see SAD 1

heartstrings *n pl* general emotional condition — see FEELING 2

heartwarming *adj* making one feel good inside ⟨Sarah appreciated the *heartwarming* welcome she received from her relatives in Israel⟩

synonyms cheering, comforting, encouraging, fulfilling, gladdening, gratifying, heartening, rewarding, satisfying

related words affecting, inspiring, moving, poignant, stirring, touching; edifying, elevating, uplifting; sympathetic, tender; kind, kindly, loving, warm; exciting, exhilarating, rousing, stimulating, thrilling; pleasing, welcoming

near antonyms cheerless, depressing, disappointing, discouraging, disgruntling, disheartening, displeasing, dissatisfying, saddening; cold, unfeeling, unfriendly, unkind, unloving, unpleasant

antonyms depressing, discouraging, disheartening, dispiriting

hearty *adj* **1** characterized by unqualified enthusiasm ⟨Frank expressed *hearty* approval of his aunt's suggestion to rendezvous in Tokyo⟩

synonyms wholehearted

related words single-minded; ardent, avid, eager, enthusiastic, excited, exuberant, gung ho, impassioned, keen, raring, vehement, warm, zealous; alacritous, immediate, prompt, ready, willing, unhesitating; animated, energetic, lively, spirited, vigorous; absolute, bona fide, genuine, unaffected, undisguised, unequivocal, unrestrained

near antonyms apathetic, disinterested, indifferent, uninterested; lackadaisical, listless, perfunctory, spiritless, uneager, unenthusiastic, unexcited; equivocal, hesitant, qualified, tentative, uncertain; delayed, dilatory, doubtful, hedging, hesitating; forced, reluctant, resistant, unwilling

antonyms grudging, halfhearted, lukewarm, tepid

2 enjoying health and vigor — see HEALTHY 1

3 having or showing kindly feeling and sincere interest — see FRIENDLY 1

4 not showing weakness or uncertainty — see FIRM 1

heat *n* depth of feeling — see ARDOR 1

heat *vb* to cause to have or give off heat to a moderate degree — see WARM 1

heated *adj* **1** being in a state of increased activity or agitation — see FEVERISH 1

2 having or giving off heat to a moderate degree — see WARM 1

heathen *adj* not civilized — see SAVAGE 1

heathen *n* **1** a person who does not worship the God of the Bible ⟨a missionary sent to distant lands to convert the *heathens*⟩

synonyms gentile, idolater (*or* idolator), pagan

related words atheist, infidel, nonbeliever, non-Christian, unbeliever; polytheist, theist

near antonyms Christian, Jew, Muslim

2 an uncivilized person ⟨European colonizers, who considered the New World peoples to be *heathens*, forced them to conform to European ways⟩

synonyms barbarian, savage

related words Neanderthal, primitive

heathenish *adj* not civilized — see SAVAGE 1

heave *vb* **1** to lift with effort ⟨I *heaved* my duffel bag into the bus's overhead compartment⟩

synonyms boost, heft, hoist, jack (up)

related words elevate, hike, raise, rear, up, uplift, upraise

near antonyms drop, lower; sink, submerge, submerse

2 to discharge the contents of the stomach through the mouth — see VOMIT

3 to move from a lower to a higher place or position — see RAISE 1

4 to send through the air especially with a quick forward motion of the arm — see THROW

heaven *n* **1** a dwelling place of perfect bliss for the soul after death ⟨prayed that the souls of the deceased would go to *heaven*⟩

synonyms Elysium, kingdom come, paradise

related words empyrean; glory; otherworld

phrases on high

near antonyms inferno; limbo, purgatory; hades, netherworld, underworld

antonyms hell, perdition

2 a place or state of great happiness — see PARADISE 1

3 a state of overwhelming usually pleasurable emotion — see ECSTASY

4 *usually* **heavens** *pl* the expanse of air surrounding the earth — see SKY

heavenly *adj* **1** of the very best kind — see EXCELLENT

2 of, relating to, or being God — see HOLY 3

3 of, relating to, or suggesting heaven — see CELESTIAL

4 giving pleasure or contentment to the mind or senses — see PLEASANT

heavily *adv* to a great degree — see VERY 1

heaviness *n* **1** the amount that something weighs — see WEIGHT 1

2 the state or quality of being heavy — see WEIGHTINESS 1

heavy *adj* **1** having great weight ⟨this trunk full of books is much too *heavy* for one person to lift⟩

synonyms hefty, massive, ponderous, weighty

related words burdensome, leaden, lumpish; bulky, elephantine, outsize; overweight, top-heavy; solid, substantial

near antonyms airy, ethereal, feathery, gossamer, gossamery; flimsy, fluffy, insubstantial

antonyms light, lightweight, weightless

2 causing weariness, restlessness, or lack of interest — see BORING

3 containing much seasoning, fat, or sugar — see RICH 2

4 covered over by clouds — see OVERCAST

5 difficult to endure — see HARSH 1

6 extreme in degree, power, or effect — see INTENSE

7 having a matter of importance as its topic — see SERIOUS 2

heavy *n* a mean, evil, or unprincipled person — see VILLAIN

heavy–handed *adj* **1** given to exacting standards of discipline and self-restraint — see SEVERE 1

2 lacking in physical ease and grace in movement or in the use of the hands — see CLUMSY 1

heavyset *adj* being compact and broad in build and often short in stature — see STOCKY

heckle *vb* to attack repeatedly with mean put-downs or insults — see TEASE 2

heckler *n* a person who causes repeated emotional pain, distress, or annoyance to another — see TORMENTOR

hectic *adj* being in a state of increased activity or agitation — see FEVERISH 1

hectically *adv* in a confused and reckless manner — see HELTER-SKELTER 1

hector *vb* to make timid or fearful by or as if by threats — see INTIMIDATE

hedge *n* a physical object that blocks the way — see BARRIER

hedge *vb* **1** to avoid giving a definite answer or position — see EQUIVOCATE

2 to close or shut in by or as if by barriers — see ENCLOSE 1

heed *n* **1** a state of being aware — see ATTENTION 2

2 strict attentiveness to what one is doing — see CARE 1

heed *vb* **1** to take notice of and be guided by ⟨if Paul had *heeded* his brother's advice, he might not have gotten lost⟩

synonyms follow, listen (to), mind, note, observe, regard, watch

related words consider, contemplate, mull, ponder, weigh; comply (with), keep, obey, respect; hark (to), hear, hearken (to); mark, notice, see

near antonyms brush (off), dismiss, pooh-pooh, scorn, shrug off; defy, flout; slight, snub

antonyms disregard, ignore, tune out

2 to pay attention especially through the act of hearing — see LISTEN

heedful *adj* having or showing a close attentiveness to avoiding danger or trouble — see CAREFUL 1

heedfulness *n* **1** a close attentiveness to avoiding danger — see CAUTION 1

2 strict attentiveness to what one is doing — see CARE 1

heedless *adj* not paying or showing close attention especially for the purpose of avoiding trouble — see CARELESS 1

heedlessness *n* failure to take the care that a cautious person usually takes — see NEGLIGENCE 1

heel *n* a person whose behavior is offensive to others — see JERK 1

heel *vb* to set or cause to be at an angle — see LEAN 1

heft *n* the amount that something weighs — see WEIGHT 1

heft *vb* **1** to lift with effort — see HEAVE 1

2 to move from a lower to a higher place or position — see RAISE 1

heftiness *n* **1** the quality or state of being large in size — see LARGENESS

2 the state or quality of being heavy — see WEIGHTINESS 1

hefty *adj* **1** having great weight — see HEAVY 1

2 of a size greater than average of its kind — see LARGE

height *n* **1** the highest part or point ⟨many regard the painting of the Sistine Chapel as the *height* of Michelangelo's career⟩

synonyms acme, apex, climax, crown, culmination, head, high-water mark, meridian, peak, pinnacle, summit, tip-top, top, zenith

related words bloom, flood tide, flower, glory, heyday; high; cap, ceiling, crest, roof; crescendo, extremity, maximum, tip, vertex

near antonyms abyss, base, foot; minimum

antonyms bottom, nadir

2 the most extreme or advanced point ⟨the student's defiant use of a cell phone during class was regarded by the teacher as the *height* of insolence⟩

synonyms depth, extremity, limit

related words consummation, epitome, quintessence, ultimate

3 the distance of something or someone from bottom to top ⟨the average *height* of the players on the volleyball team is well over six feet⟩

synonyms altitude, elevation, stature

related words rise; highness, loftiness, tallness

4 an area of high ground ⟨Gulliver, standing on a *height* near the shore, saw an island suspended above the sea⟩

synonyms altitude(s), elevation, eminence, highland, hill, mound, prominence, rise, upland

related words alp, mount, mountain, peak; butte, mesa, plateau, table, tableland; cliff, crag, precipice, tor; ridge, sierra; dome, sugarloaf; foothill, hillock, knob, knoll; down

near antonyms dale, dell, dingle, glen, hollow, vale, valley; basin, bottom, bottomland, fen, flat, floodplain, plain, tidewater

antonyms lowland

5 the most intense or characteristic phase of something — see THICK

heighten *vb* **1** to make markedly greater in measure or degree — see INTENSIFY

2 to move from a lower to a higher place or position — see RAISE 1

heightened *adj* being at a higher level than average — see HIGH 2

heinousness *n* the state or quality of being utterly evil — see ENORMITY 1

heir *n* a person who has the right to inherit property ⟨upon his death, Mr. Parkworth's property was divided evenly among his *heirs*, four sons and three daughters⟩

synonyms inheritor, legatee

related words claimant; heir apparent, successor; heiress; assignee, beneficiary, grantee; descendant (*or* descendent), scion (*also* cion)

helical *adj* turning around an axis like the thread of a screw — see SPIRAL

hell *n* **1** the place of punishment for the wicked after death ⟨condemned to *hell* for their sins⟩

synonyms perdition

related words inferno; purgatory; hades, netherworld, underworld

near antonyms empyrean; glory

antonyms Elysium, heaven, kingdom come, paradise

2 a situation or state that causes great suffering and unhappiness ⟨picking cotton under the hot summer sun was *hell*⟩

synonyms agony, horror, misery, murder, nightmare, torment, torture

related words cross, ordeal, trial, tribulation; gall, thorn; bummer, downer, drag

near antonyms delight, diversion, entertainment, fun, pleasure, recreation; lark, picnic, riot

antonyms heaven, paradise

3 a place of uproar or confusion — see MADHOUSE 2

4 a state in which everything is out of order — see CHAOS

hellion *n* an appealingly mischievous person — see SCAMP 1

hello *n* an expression of goodwill upon meeting ⟨we said our *hellos* and got right down to business⟩

synonyms greeting, salutation, salute, welcome

related words amenities, civilities, pleasantries; regards, respects, wishes

antonyms adieu, bon voyage, farewell, Godspeed, good-bye (*or* good-by)

helm *n* the place of leadership or command — see HEAD 2

helmsman *n* the person (as an employer or supervisor) who tells people and especially workers what to do — see BOSS

help *n* **1** an act or instance of helping ⟨Andrew didn't get any *help* with his homework⟩

synonyms aid, assist, assistance, backing, boost, lift, support

related words advancement, encouragement, facilitation, forwarding, furtherance, furthering, nurturance; benefaction, patronage, promotion, sponsorship; advice, care, counsel, guidance, mentoring; attendance, attention, service; beneficence, charity, favor, kindness, philanthropy; relief, succor

near antonyms constraint, frustration, inhibition, interference, obstruction, repression, restraint; deterrence, discouragement

antonyms hindrance

2 a thing that helps ⟨the computer is a great *help* for writing reports⟩

synonyms advantage, aid, benefit, boon

related words lift, pick-me-up; support, sustenance; blessing, godsend, windfall; recourse, resort, resource; asset

near antonyms constraint, inhibitor, liability, obstacle, obstruction, restraint, stranglehold

antonyms disadvantage, drawback, hindrance, impediment

3 a body of persons at work or available for work — see FORCE 1

help *vb* **1** to provide (someone) with what is useful or necessary to achieve an end ⟨Mary Beth flew to Chicago to *help* her dad when he moved into an apartment⟩

synonyms abet, aid, assist, back, prop (up), support

related words advance, facilitate, forward, foster, further; champion, endorse (*also* indorse), patronize, promote, sponsor; attend, care (for), comfort, minister (to), succor; bolster, boost, buttress, reinforce; advise, counsel, guide, mentor, nurture; bail out, deliver, rescue, save; embolden, encourage, hearten; benefit, favor, profit, serve

phrases to stand one in good stead

near antonyms balk, bar, block, constrain, hamper, hold back, impede, inhibit, obstruct, restrain, strangle; baffle, foil, frustrate, interfere, oppose, sabotage, thwart; desert, disappoint, fail, let down; discourage, dishearten; repress, retard, stifle, straiten, stunt; damage, harm, hurt, injure

antonyms hinder

2 to make more bearable or less severe ⟨the new ointment didn't *help* Josh's sunburn one bit⟩

synonyms allay, alleviate, assuage, ease, mitigate, mollify, palliate, relieve, soothe

related words abate, lighten, moderate, soften, temper; cure, heal, remedy; amend, correct, emend, fix, mend, rectify, reform, repair; ameliorate, better, enhance, enrich, improve, meliorate, perfect, refine

near antonyms harm, hurt, impair, injure; heighten, intensify, sharpen

antonyms aggravate

3 to keep from happening by taking action in advance — see PREVENT

helper *n* a person who helps a more skilled person ⟨over the summer Chris worked as a carpenter's *helper*⟩

synonyms adjutant, aid, aide, apprentice, assistant, coadjutor, deputy, helpmate, helpmeet, mate, sidekick

related words attendant, handmaiden (*also* handmaid), maid, maidservant, scullion, servant; auxiliary, subordinate, underling; employee, hand, help, hireling, laborer, worker

helpful *adj* conferring benefits; promoting or contributing to personal or social well-being — see BENEFICIAL

helpless *adj* **1** lacking protection from danger or resistance against attack ⟨after the storm we found a *helpless* baby bird that had fallen out of its nest⟩

synonyms defenseless, exposed, susceptible, undefended, unguarded, unprotected, unresistant, unshielded, vulnerable

related words indefensible, untenable; uncovered, unsafe, unsheltered; overcome, preyed (on *or* upon); disarmed, passive, resistless, unarmed; feeble, frail, weak; abandoned, marooned

phrases in the lurch

near antonyms defensible; covered, fortified, safe, secure, screened, sheltered; armed, armored; immune, impenetrable, impregnable, invincible, strong, unassailable, unbeatable, unconquerable

antonyms guarded, invulnerable, protected, resistant, shielded

2 unable to act or achieve one's purpose — see POWERLESS

helpmate *n* **1** a person who helps a more skilled person — see HELPER

2 the female partner in a marriage — see WIFE

helpmeet *n* **1** a person who helps a more skilled person — see HELPER

2 the female partner in a marriage — see WIFE

helter-skelter *adv* **1** in a confused and reckless manner ⟨the sheep ran *helter-skelter* inside their pen when the coyote appeared in their midst⟩

synonyms amok (*or* amuck), berserk, frantically, frenziedly, harum-scarum, hectically, madly, pellmell, wild, wildly

related words agitatedly, confusedly, crazily, desperately, feverishly, skittishly, uncontrollably; heedlessly, hotheadedly, recklessly, wantonly; chaotically, riotously, tumultuously, turbulently; aimlessly, haphazardly, hit-or-miss

near antonyms calmly, collectedly, composedly, coolly, imperturbably, peacefully, placidly, serenely, unconcernedly; meekly, mildly, passively, tamely; methodically, orderly, systematically

2 without definite aim, direction, rule, or method — see HIT OR MISS

hem *vb* to close or shut in by or as if by barriers — see ENCLOSE 1

hence *adv* **1** for this or that reason — see THEREFORE

2 from this or that place — see AWAY

henceforth *adv* from this point on ⟨*henceforth*, there will be no more prolonged coffee breaks⟩

synonyms henceforward, hereafter

henceforward *adv* from this point on — see HENCEFORTH

henpeck *vb* to subject (someone) to constant scoldings and sharp reminders — see NAG

herald *n* one that announces or indicates the later arrival of another — see FORERUNNER 1

herbage *n* green leaves or plants — see GREENERY 1

herculean *adj* **1** requiring considerable physical or mental effort — see HARD 2

2 unusually large — see HUGE

herd *n* **1** a group of domestic animals assembled or

herded together ⟨the great *herds* of cattle that cowboys once drove across the plains⟩
synonyms drove, flock
related words colony, covey, gaggle, pack, school, swarm
2 the body of the community as contrasted with the elite — see MASS 1

herd *vb* to urge, push, or force onward — see DRIVE 1

herder *n* a tender of livestock ⟨the nomadic reindeer *herders* of Siberia live in reindeer-skin tents⟩
synonyms herdsman
related words buckaroo, cowboy, cowgirl, cowhand, cowherd, cowman, cowpoke, cowpuncher, gaucho, ranchero, vaquero; shepherd, sheepherder, shepherdess; goatherd; wrangler; drover

herdsman *n* a tender of livestock — see HERDER

hereafter *adv* from this point on — see HENCE-FORTH

hereafter *n* **1** time that is to come — see FUTURE 1
2 unending existence after death — see ETERNITY 2

hereditary *adj* genetically passed or capable of being passed from parent to offspring ⟨eye and hair color are *hereditary*⟩
synonyms genetic (*also* genetical), heritable, inborn, inheritable, inherited
related words congenital, inbred, inherent, innate, native, natural
near antonyms acquired

heresy *n* departure from a generally accepted theory, opinion, or practice ⟨the *heresy* of asserting that Shakespeare was not a great writer⟩
synonyms dissent, dissidence, heterodoxy, nonconformity
related words error, fallacy, falsehood, misbelief, misconception, myth; apostasy, defection, schism, sectarianism, separatism; deviance, deviation, unconventionality; disagreement, discord, dissension
near antonyms agreement, conformation, conventionality
antonyms conformity, orthodoxy

heretic *n* a person who believes or teaches something opposed to accepted beliefs ⟨Galileo was condemned as a *heretic* for supporting Copernicus's thesis that the earth revolves around the sun and not vice versa⟩
synonyms dissenter, dissident, nonconformist
related words apostate, defector, renegade; schismatic, sectarian, separatist; disbeliever, infidel, unbeliever; bohemian, individualist
near antonyms believer
antonyms conformer, conformist

heretical *adj* deviating from commonly accepted beliefs or practices ⟨the belief that women should be allowed to have careers outside the home was once considered *heretical*⟩
synonyms dissentient, dissenting, dissident, heterodox nonconformist, nonorthodox, unconventional, unorthodox
related words nontraditional; apostate, defecting, renegade; schismatic, sectarian, separatist
antonyms conforming, conformist, conventional, orthodox

heretofore *adv* up to this or that time — see HITH-ERTO

heritable *adj* genetically passed or capable of being passed from parent to offspring — see HEREDITARY

heritage *n* something that is or may be inherited — see INHERITANCE

hermit *n* a person who lives away from others — see RECLUSE

hero *n* a large sandwich on a long split roll — see SUBMARINE

heroic *adj* **1** feeling or displaying no fear by temperament — see BRAVE
2 large and impressive in size, grandeur, extent, or conception — see GRAND 1
3 unusually large — see HUGE

heroically *adv* in a manner befitting a person of the highest character and ideals — see GREATLY 1

heroism *n* strength of mind to carry on in spite of danger — see COURAGE

hesitance *n* **1** a lack of willingness or desire to do or accept something — see RELUCTANCE
2 the act or an instance of pausing because of uncertainty about the right course of action — see HESITATION

hesitancy *n* **1** a lack of willingness or desire to do or accept something — see RELUCTANCE
2 the act or an instance of pausing because of uncertainty about the right course of action — see HESITATION

hesitant *adj* having doubts about the wisdom of doing something ⟨Ivan was *hesitant* about lending CDs to his friends after he'd lost several of them that way⟩
synonyms afraid, disinclined, dubious, indisposed, loath (*or* loth), reluctant
related words uneager, unenthusiastic; averse, unwilling; doubtful, faltering, irresolute, questioning, uncertain, undecided, unsure, vacillating, wobbly; fainthearted, shy, timid
near antonyms eager, enthusiastic, glad, happy, keen; ready, willing; certain, decided, resolute, sure, unquestioning
antonyms disposed, inclined

hesitate *vb* to show uncertainty about the right course of action ⟨Keri didn't *hesitate* before answering the question⟩
synonyms falter, hang back, shilly-shally, stagger, teeter, vacillate, waver, wobble
related words haw, hem; dally, dawdle, delay, linger, procrastinate, pause, wait; back down, chicken (out); consider, debate, deliberate, ponder, weigh; oscillate; equivocate, hedge, pussyfoot
near antonyms budge, stir; advance, continue
antonyms dive (in), plunge (in)

hesitation *n* the act or an instance of pausing because of uncertainty about the right course of action ⟨one moment's *hesitation* on my part, and the elusive butterfly was lost to me forever⟩
synonyms faltering, hesitance, hesitancy, indecision, irresolution, shilly-shallying, vacillation, wavering, wobbling
related words delay, hawing, procrastination, waiting; consideration, debate, deliberation, doubt, incertitude, indetermination, uncertainty; avoidance, equivocation; aversion, disinclination, indisposition, reluctance, unwillingness; faintheartedness, shyness, timidness
near antonyms certainty, certitude, confidence, decisiveness, determination, firmness, resoluteness, resolution, sureness; alacrity, eagerness, readiness

heterodox *adj* deviating from commonly accepted beliefs or practices — see HERETICAL

THESAURUS

heterodoxy *n* departure from a generally accepted theory, opinion, or practice — see HERESY

heterogeneous *adj* consisting of many things of different sorts — see MISCELLANEOUS

het up *adj* feeling or showing uncomfortable feelings of uncertainty — see NERVOUS 1

hew *vb* **1** to bring down by cutting — see FELL 2
2 to hold to something firmly as if by adhesion — see STICK 1

hew (to) *vb* to give steadfast support to — see ADHERE

hex *n* **1** a woman believed to have often harmful supernatural powers — see WITCH 1
2 something that brings bad luck — see JINX

hex *vb* to cast a spell on — see BEWITCH 1

heyday *n* a state or time of great activity, thriving, or achievement — see BLOOM 1

hiatus *n* a break in continuity — see GAP 2

hick *n* an awkward or simple person especially from a small town or the country ⟨city dwellers who looked down on their cousins from northern Maine as *hicks*⟩
synonyms bumpkin, clodhopper, countryman, hillbilly, provincial, rustic, yokel
related words boor, clod, gawk, lout, oaf; greenhorn, tenderfoot; peasant, peon; mountaineer
near antonyms slicker, smoothy (*or* smoothie); suburbanite, urbanite
antonyms cosmopolitan, sophisticate

hide *n* **1** the outer covering of an animal removed for its commercial value ⟨seal *hides* are used by Eskimos to make footwear, boats, shelters, bags, and clothing⟩
synonyms fur, leather, pelt, skin
related words badger, beaver, chamois, chinchilla, ermine, fisher, fox, mink, muskrat, otter, Persian lamb, rabbit, raccoon (*also* racoon), sable, seal, silver fox; bearskin, buckskin, calfskin, coonskin, cowhide, deerskin, doeskin, goatskin, horsehide, kidskin, lambskin, pigskin, rawhide, sealskin, sharkskin, sheepskin, snakeskin; fleece, mouton; alligator; cordovan, morocco, patent leather, suede
2 the hairless natural covering of an animal prepared for use — see LEATHER 1

¹hide *vb* **1** to put into a hiding place ⟨the thief *hid* the stolen jewelry under the floorboards⟩
synonyms bury, cache, conceal, ensconce, secrete
related words hoard, squirrel (away), stash; entomb, inter
near antonyms bare, expose, reveal, show, uncover, unmask, unveil, unwrap; flaunt, parade, show off; disinter, unearth
antonyms display, exhibit
2 to keep secret or shut off from view ⟨he tried to *hide* his criminal past⟩ ⟨she *hid* the cat's litter box behind a screen⟩
synonyms blanket, blot out, cloak, conceal, cover, curtain, enshroud, mask, obscure, occult, screen, shroud, veil
related words camouflage, cover (up), disguise, smother; gild, gloss (over), varnish, whitewash; becloud, bedim, befog, cloud, darken, eclipse, overcast, overshadow, shade
near antonyms bring out, present; clarify, illuminate; advertise, air, broadcast, proclaim, publicize
antonyms bare, disclose, display, divulge, expose, reveal, show, uncloak, uncover, unmask, unveil
3 to strike repeatedly with something long and thin or flexible — see WHIP 1

²hide *vb* to strike repeatedly — see BEAT 1

hideaway *n* a place where a person goes to hide — see HIDEOUT

hideous *adj* **1** causing intense displeasure, disgust, or resentment — see OFFENSIVE 1
2 extremely disturbing or repellent — see HORRIBLE 1
3 unpleasant to look at — see UGLY 1

hideousness *n* the quality of inspiring intense dread or dismay — see HORROR 1

hideout *n* a place where a person goes to hide ⟨they found the stolen jewels under the floorboards in the thief's *hideout*, a cabin deep in the woods⟩
synonyms concealment, covert, den, hideaway, lair, nest
related words blind, cover, nook, recess; hangout, harbor, haunt, haven, refuge, retreat, shelter

hiding *n* the placing of something out of sight — see CONCEALMENT 1

higgledy–piggledy *adj* lacking in order, neatness, and often cleanliness — see MESSY

high *adj* **1** extending to a great distance upward ⟨Mt. Everest is the *highest* mountain in the world⟩
synonyms lofty, tall, towering
related words dominant, dominating, eminent, prominent; elevated, lifted, raised, uplifted, upswept; high-rise, statuesque
near antonyms flat, stubby, stumpy
antonyms low, low-lying, short, squat
2 being at a higher level than average ⟨gasoline prices are *high* right now⟩ ⟨a *high* fever⟩ ⟨people with *high* incomes⟩
synonyms advanced, elevated, escalated, heightened, increased, jacked (up), raised, up
related words extreme, full, maximized, maximum, peaked, sky-high, utmost; inflated, over, overfilled, overflowing, overfull, overlarge, overloaded, oversize (*or* oversized)
near antonyms decreased, depressed, dropped, receded, under
antonyms down, low
3 located at a greater height than average or usual ⟨an eagle's nest *high* on the cliff⟩ ⟨an old house with *high* ceilings⟩
synonyms airy, elevated
related words aerial, ascendant, ascending, soaring; overhead, overlooking, raised, upheld, uplifted, upraised; topmost, upmost, upper, uppermost, upward
near antonyms depressed, descendant (*or* descendent), descending, down, dropped, fallen, grounded, lowered, sunken; lowermost, nethermost, undermost; abreast, even, level
antonyms low, low-lying
4 being far along in development — see ADVANCED 1
5 being under the influence of alcohol — see DRUNK
6 commanding a large price — see COSTLY
7 having, characterized by, or arising from a dignified and generous nature — see NOBLE 2
8 highest in rank or authority — see HEAD

high *n* the expanse of air surrounding the earth — see SKY

high *adv* in a luxurious manner ⟨after he won the lottery Philip lived *high* until all the money was gone⟩
synonyms expensively, extravagantly, grandly,

lavishly, luxuriously, opulently, richly, sumptuously

related words imposingly, impressively, magnificently, splendidly; grandiosely, ostentatiously, pretentiously; affluently, comfortably, fine; immoderately, indulgently, intemperately, prodigally, wantonly, wastefully

near antonyms unassumingly, unpretentiously; cheaply, economically, frugally, inexpensively, meagerly, poorly, skimpily, sparely, sparingly, thriftily; conservatively, moderately, prudently, reasonably, restrainedly, sensibly, temperately

antonyms austerely, humbly, modestly, plainly, simply

highborn *adj* of high birth, rank, or station — see NOBLE 1

highbrow *adj* much given to learning and thinking — see INTELLECTUAL 1

higher *adj* being far along in development — see ADVANCED 1

highest *adj* 1 being at a point or level higher than all others — see TOP 1
2 coming before all others in importance — see FOREMOST 1

highfalutin *adj* 1 full of fine words and fancy expressions — see FLOWERY 1
2 having a feeling of superiority that shows itself in an overbearing attitude — see ARROGANT
3 having or displaying feelings of scorn for what is regarded as beneath oneself — see PROUD 1
4 self-consciously trying to present an appearance of grandeur or importance — see PRETENTIOUS 1

high-flown *adj* 1 full of fine words and fancy expressions — see FLOWERY 1
2 very dignified in form, tone, or style — see ELEVATED 2

high-handed *adj* 1 having a feeling of superiority that shows itself in an overbearing attitude — see ARROGANT
2 having or showing a tendency to force one's will on others without any regard to fairness or necessity — see ARBITRARY 1

high-hat *adj* having a feeling of superiority that shows itself in an overbearing attitude — see ARROGANT

high-hat *vb* to show contempt for — see SCORN 1

high jinks *n pl* wildly playful or mischievous behavior — see HORSEPLAY

highland *n* an area of high ground — see HEIGHT 4

highlight *vb* to indicate the importance of by giving prominent display — see EMPHASIZE

highly *adv* to a great degree — see VERY 1

high-minded *adj* having, characterized by, or arising from a dignified and generous nature — see NOBLE 2

high-mindedly *adv* in a manner befitting a person of the highest character and ideals — see GREATLY 1

high noon *n* the middle of the day — see NOON

high-pitched *adj* having a high musical pitch or range — see SHRILL

high-pressure *adj* having or showing a bold forcefulness in the pursuit of a goal — see AGGRESSIVE 1

highroad *n* a passage cleared for public vehicular travel — see WAY 1

high-sounding *adj* full of fine words and fancy expressions — see FLOWERY 1

high-spirited *adj* 1 joyously unrestrained — see EXUBERANT

2 marked by a lively display of strong feeling — see SPIRITED 1

high-spiritedly *adv* in a quick and spirited manner — see GAILY 2

high-strung *adj* easily excited by nature — see EXCITABLE

high-water mark *n* the highest part or point — see HEIGHT 1

highway *n* a passage cleared for public vehicular travel — see WAY 1

hijack *also* **highjack** *vb* to take control of (a vehicle) by force — see COMMANDEER 1

hike *vb* to move from a lower to a higher place or position — see RAISE 1

hilarious *adj* causing or intended to cause laughter — see FUNNY 1

hilariousness *n* the amusing quality or element in something — see HUMOR 1

hilarity *n* a mood characterized by high spirits and amusement and often accompanied by laughter — see MIRTH

hill *n* 1 a quantity of things thrown or stacked on one another — see ¹PILE 1
2 an area of high ground — see HEIGHT 4

hill *vb* to form into a pile or ridge of earth — see MOUND 1

hillbilly *n* an awkward or simple person especially from a small town or the country — see HICK

hind *adj* being at or in the part of something opposite the front part — see BACK

hinder *vb* to create difficulty for the work or activity of — see HAMPER

hindmost *adj* 1 being at or in the part of something opposite the front part — see BACK
2 following all others of the same kind in order or time — see LAST

hindrance *n* 1 something that makes movement or progress more difficult — see ENCUMBRANCE
2 something that stands in the way of one's progress or achievement — see OBSTACLE 1

hinge *vb* to be determined by, based on, or subject (to) — see DEPEND 1

hint *n* 1 a slight or indirect pointing to something (as a solution or explanation) ⟨can't you give me some *hint* as to where you're taking me?⟩
synonyms clue, cue, indication, inkling, intimation, lead, suggestion
related words breath, flicker, glimmer, glimpse, mention, scent, whiff, wind; hunch, idea, inspiration, notion; allusion, implication, inference, innuendo, insinuation; evidence, mark, overtone, pointer, sign, signal, telltale, token; assistance, nod, prompt, tip, tip-off, wink; feeling, foreboding, intuition, premonition, presentiment, suspicion; augury, foreshadower, foretaste, omen, portent, prefigurement, symptom
near antonyms answer, solution
2 a piece of advice or useful information especially from an expert — see ¹TIP 1
3 a very small amount — see PARTICLE 1

hint *vb* to convey an idea indirectly ⟨Cecilia kept *hinting* that she wanted an invitation to Patty's party⟩
synonyms allude, imply, indicate, infer, insinuate, intimate, suggest
related words advert, mention, point, refer, signal, signify; smack (of), smell (of)
near antonyms announce, declare, proclaim; elucidate, explain, spell out

hinterland *n* a rural region that forms the edge of

the settled or developed part of a country — see FRONTIER 2

hip *adj* having inside information — see WISE 2

hire *n* **1** the state of being provided with a paying job ⟨college graduates seeking *hire* by big corporations⟩
synonyms employ, employment, engagement
related words appointment, assignment, conscription, enlistment, recruitment; incumbency, tenure; occupation, place, position, post, situation, work
near antonyms boot, discharge, dismissal, firing, removal, sack; demotion, suspension; furlough, layoff, leave, liberty, retirement
antonyms joblessness, unemployment
2 the money paid regularly to a person for labor or services — see WAGE

hire *vb* **1** to take or get the temporary use of (something) for a set sum ⟨the Young's *hired* a limousine for their daughter's wedding⟩
synonyms charter, engage, lease, rent
related words sublease, sublet; check out; arrange (for), bespeak, book, contract (for), order, reserve, sign up (for)
2 to provide with a paying job — see EMPLOY 1

hireling *n* one who works for another for wages or a salary — see EMPLOYEE

hirsute *adj* covered with or as if with hair — see HAIRY 1

hiss *n* **1** a sound similar to the speech sound \s\ stretched out ⟨the *hiss* of air escaping from a balloon⟩
synonyms fizz, sizzle, swish, whish, whiz (*or* whizz)
related words wheeze, whistle, whoosh, zip; sibilant
2 a vocal sound made to express scorn or disapproval — see CATCALL

hiss *vb* to make a sound like that of stretching out the speech sound \s\ ⟨the frightened kitten *hissed* at us when we tried to pick it up⟩
synonyms fizz, sizzle, swish, whish, whiz (*or* whizz)
related words wheeze, whistle, whoosh, zip; bubble, effervesce; buzz, drone, hum

historian *n* a student or writer of history ⟨historians are still trying to sort out fact from fiction in the story of Kateri Tekakwitha, the Lily of the Mohawks⟩
synonyms annalist, chronicler
related words autobiographer, biographer; archivist, chronologist, genealogist

historical *adj* restricted to or based on fact — see FACTUAL 1

history *n* **1** an account of important events in the order in which they happened ⟨a *history* of the American civil rights movement during the 1960s⟩
synonyms annals, chronicle, record
related words autobiography, diary, journal, memoir, reminiscence(s); biography, life; epic, legend, narrative, saga, story, tale; archives, documentation, log, register, report; chronology, genealogy
2 a relating of events usually in the order in which they happened — see ACCOUNT 1
3 the events or experience of former times — see PAST

histrionic *adj* **1** given to or marked by attention-getting behavior suggestive of stage acting — see THEATRICAL 1

2 having the general quality or effect of a stage performance — see DRAMATIC 1

hit *n* **1** a person or thing that is successful ⟨the new babysitter turned out to be a great *hit* with the kids⟩
synonyms blockbuster, megahit, smash, success, winner
related words corker, crackerjack, dandy, jim-dandy, pip, prizewinner; gem, jewel, treasure; marvel, phenomenon, sensation, wonder; coup, triumph, victory
near antonyms disappointment, fizzle, lemon, loser
antonyms bummer, bust, catastrophe, debacle (*also* débâcle), dud, failure, fiasco, flop, turkey, washout
2 a hard strike with a part of the body or an instrument — see ¹BLOW

hit *vb* **1** to deliver a blow to (someone or something) usually in a strong vigorous manner ⟨a good carpenter *hits* a nail just two or three times to drive it in⟩
synonyms bang, bash, bat, belt, bludgeon, bop, bust, clap, clobber, clout, crack, hammer, knock, paste, pound, punch, rap, slam, slap, slog, slug, smack, smite, sock, strike, swat, swipe, thump, thwack, wallop, whack, whale, zap
related words batter, beat, buffet, bung, chop, drub, lace, lambaste (*or* lambast), lick, mangle, maul, pelt, pepper, pummel, rough; bunt, flick, stroke, tap; bump, butt, jab, jostle, kick, knee, poke, prod, push, shove, stamp; bowl (over), knock (down); cane, club, cudgel, flail, flog, lash, slash, spear, stab, switch, thrash, whip; brain
2 to come into usually forceful contact with something ⟨when she fell on the ice, she *hit* hard and badly bruised her elbow⟩
synonyms bang, bash, bump, collide, crash, impact, impinge, knock, ram, slam, smash, strike, swipe, thud
related words bounce, carom, glance, rebound, ricochet, skim, skip; contact, land, touch; brush, graze, kiss, nudge, scrape, shave, sweep; bulldoze, jostle, muscle, press, push
near antonyms miss, skirt
3 to obtain (as a goal) through effort — see ACHIEVE 1

hit (on *or* upon) *vb* to come upon after searching, study, or effort — see FIND 1

hit (upon) *vb* to come upon unexpectedly or by chance — see HAPPEN (ON *OR* UPON)

hitch *n* a fixed period of time during which a person holds a job or position — see TERM 1

hitch *vb* **1** to move or cause to move with a sharp quick motion — see JERK 1
2 to put or bring together so as to form a new and longer whole — see CONNECT 1
3 to put securely in place or in a desired position — see FASTEN 2
4 to travel by securing free rides — see HITCHHIKE

hitcher *n* one who hitchhikes — see HITCHHIKER

hitchhike *vb* to travel by securing free rides ⟨Andrew *hitchhiked* from Baltimore to attend his sister's wedding in New Jersey⟩
synonyms hitch, thumb
related words bum; stow away; hijack (*also* highjack)

hitchhiker *n* one who hitchhikes ⟨on the highway

out of town we picked up a *hitchhiker* who was trying to get to his sister's wedding〉
synonyms hitcher
related words stowaway; hijacker

hither *adj* being the less far of two — see NEAR 1

hitherto *adv* up to this or that time 〈at the talent show Kyle revealed his *hitherto* unknown gift for doing impressions〉
synonyms heretofore, theretofore, thus far, yet
related words before, formerly, previously
near antonyms afterward (*or* afterwards), later, subsequently; hereupon, thereupon
antonyms henceforth, henceforward, hereafter, thenceforth, thenceforward (*also* thenceforwards), thereafter

hit–or–miss *adj* lacking a definite plan, purpose, or pattern — see RANDOM

hit or miss *adv* without definite aim, direction, rule, or method 〈Angelo was learning Spanish *hit or miss*, mostly just by hearing his friends speak it〉
synonyms aimlessly, anyhow, anyway, anywise, desultorily, erratically, haphazard, haphazardly, helter-skelter, irregularly, randomly
related words capriciously, carelessly, casually, indiscriminately, informally, offhand, offhandedly, promiscuously, whimsically; accidentally, fortuitously, inadvertently, unconsciously, unintentionally, unwittingly; disconnectedly, disjointedly, fitfully, intermittently, spottily, unpredictably; higgledy-piggledy, topsy-turvy
phrases at random
near antonyms carefully, formally, meticulously, orderly, punctiliously; deliberately, intentionally, purposefully, purposely
antonyms methodically, systematically

hoagie *n* a large sandwich on a long split roll — see SUBMARINE

hoar *adj* dating or surviving from the distant past — see ANCIENT 1

hoar *n* a covering of tiny ice crystals on a cold surface — see FROST

hoard *n* **1** a supply stored up and often hidden away 〈Dad was upset when Mom put his entire *hoard* of empty yogurt containers in the recycling bin〉
synonyms cache, stash, stockpile, store
related words coffers, deposit, funds, nest egg, savings, sinking fund, treasure; inventory, reserve, reservoir, stock; provisions, resources; accumulation, collection; repertory
2 a collection of things kept available for future use or need — see STORE 1

hoard *vb* to put (something of future use or value) in a safe or secret place 〈Dad's been *hoarding* empty yogurt containers all winter, with the intention of using them to start seedlings in the spring〉
synonyms cache, lay away, lay up, put by, salt away, squirrel (away), stash, stockpile, store, stow
related words accumulate, acquire, amass, assemble, collect, concentrate, garner, gather, round up, scrape (together); heap, pile, stack; conserve, husband, preserve; bank, deposit, hold, keep, reserve, retain, save, stock, withhold; conceal, ensconce, secrete
phrases set aside
near antonyms discard, dump, throw away, throw out; consume, squander, use up, waste; hand over, relinquish, surrender; blow, dissipate, fritter

(away), lavish, misspend, run through, spend; deplete, exhaust, expend; dispel, disperse, dissipate, scatter

hoarfrost *n* a covering of tiny ice crystals on a cold surface — see FROST

hoarse *adj* harsh and dry in sound 〈the dying man spoke in a *hoarse* whisper〉
synonyms coarse, croaking, grating, gravel, gravelly, gruff, husky, rasping, raspy, scratchy, throaty
related words guttural; abrasive, cacophonous, discordant, grinding, jarring, rough, scraping, scratching; cawing, raucous, squawking, strident; choked, cracked, strained, strangled
near antonyms gentle, gliding, golden, liquid, mellifluous, mellow, sweet, tender; satiny, silken, smooth, soft, velvety

hoary *adj* dating or surviving from the distant past — see ANCIENT 1

hoax *n* an imitation that is passed off as genuine — see FAKE 1

hoax *vb* to cause to believe what is untrue — see DECEIVE

hoaxer *n* **1** a dishonest person who uses clever means to cheat others out of something of value — see TRICKSTER 1
2 one who makes false claims of identity or expertise — see IMPOSTOR

hob *n* playful, reckless behavior that is not intended to cause serious harm — see MISCHIEF 1

hobble *vb* **1** to create difficulty for the work or activity of — see HAMPER
2 to walk while favoring one leg — see LIMP 1

hobgoblin *n* **1** an imaginary being usually having a small human form and magical powers — see FAIRY
2 something or someone that causes fear or dread especially without reason — see BOGEY 1

hobnob *vb* **1** to come or be together as friends — see ASSOCIATE 1
2 to take part in social activities — see SOCIALIZE

hobnobber *n* a person frequently seen in the company of another — see ASSOCIATE 1

hobo *n* a homeless wanderer who may beg or steal for a living — see TRAMP

hock *vb* to leave as a guarantee of repayment of a loan — see PAWN

hodgepodge *n* an unorganized collection or mixture of various things — see MISCELLANY 1

hog *n* one who eats greedily or too much — see GLUTTON

hoggish *adj* having a huge appetite — see VORACIOUS 1

hogshead *n* an enclosed wooden vessel for holding beverages — see CASK

hogwash *n* **1** language, behavior, or ideas that are absurd and contrary to good sense — see NONSENSE 1
2 unintelligible or meaningless talk — see GIBBERISH

hoist *vb* **1** to lift with effort — see HEAVE 1
2 to move from a lower to a higher place or position — see RAISE 1

hold *n* **1** the act or manner of holding 〈make sure you have a firm *hold* on the chain saw before you turn it on〉
synonyms clasp, grapple, grasp, grip
related words anchorage, leverage, purchase; grab, seizure; foothold, footing, toehold; embrace, hug
near antonyms release, relinquishment

2 a structure or place from which one can resist attack — see FORT

3 the right or means to command or control others — see POWER 1

hold *vb* **1** to have or keep in one's hands ⟨this casserole dish is too hot to *hold,* so grab a potholder⟩

synonyms clench, cling (to), clutch, grip, hang on (to), hold on (to)

related words bear, carry; catch, grapple, nab, seize, snatch, take; feel, finger, handle, paw; clasp, embrace, grasp, hug

near antonyms drop, give, hand, unclasp, unhand; release, relinquish

2 to continue to have in one's possession or power — see KEEP 2

3 to have as an opinion — see BELIEVE 2

4 to have within — see CONTAIN 1

5 to keep in one's mind or heart — see HARBOR 1

6 to keep, control, or experience as one's own — see HAVE 1

7 to make or have room for — see ACCOMMODATE 1

8 to reach for and take hold of by embracing with the fingers or arms — see TAKE 1

9 to think of in a particular way — see CONSIDER 1

hold (up) *vb* **1** to continue to operate or to meet one's needs — see HOLD OUT

2 to remain indefinitely in existence or in the same state — see CONTINUE 1

hold back *vb* to create difficulty for the work or activity of — see HAMPER

holder *n* **1** one who has a legal or rightful claim to ownership — see PROPRIETOR

2 something into which a liquid or smaller objects can be put for storage or transportation — see CONTAINER

hold in *vb* to keep from exceeding a desirable degree or level (as of expression) — see CONTROL 1

holding *n* **1** a decision made by a court or tribunal regarding a case it has heard — see SENTENCE

2 *usually* **holdings** *pl* transportable items that one owns — see POSSESSION 2

hold off (on) *vb* to assign to a later time — see POSTPONE

hold on *vb* **1** to remain indefinitely in existence or in the same state — see CONTINUE 1

2 to remain in place in readiness or expectation of something — see WAIT

hold on (to) *vb* to have or keep in one's hands — see HOLD 1

hold out *vb* to continue to operate or to meet one's needs ⟨we hoped our supply of firewood would *hold out* until power was restored⟩ ⟨luckily, the old outboard motor *held out* till we made it to shore⟩

synonyms hold (up), last, keep up, prevail, survive

related words bear up, carry on, cope, endure, go, hang in, persevere; continue, draw out, hang on, linger, persist, remain, stretch

near antonyms break down, collapse, conk (out), crash, die, expire, stall, stop; run down, wane

antonyms fail, fizzle, give out, go out, peter (out), run out

holdup *n* an instance or period of being prevented from going about one's business — see DELAY

hold up *vb* **1** to assign to a later time — see POSTPONE

2 to bring (something) to a standstill — see ¹HALT 1

3 to create difficulty for the work or activity of — see HAMPER

hole *n* **1** a place in a surface allowing passage into or through a thing ⟨Mark was beside himself after seeing that his little sister had punched *holes* in his homework⟩

synonyms aperture, opening, orifice, perforation

related words chink, cleft, crack, cranny, crevice, cut, breach, break, fissure, gash, notch, rent, rift, rupture, slash, slit, split; gap, slot, space; exit, mouth, outlet, pore, vent; entrance, inlet, intake; pinprick, punch, puncture; armhole, buttonhole, knothole, peephole, pinhole, wormhole

near antonyms fill, filler, filling, patch, plug, seal, stopper; barrier, blockage, obstacle, obstruction

2 a sunken area forming a separate space ⟨Ann dug a *hole* big enough to plant the tree⟩

synonyms cavity, concavity, dent, depression, dint, hollow, indentation, pit, recess

related words burrow, cave, cavern, ditch, excavation, furrow, groove, trench, trough; basin, bowl, valley; alcove, cleft, niche, nook, opening, recess, socket; alveolus, dimple, gouge, notch, impression, pocket; chuckhole, crater, posthole, pothole, sinkhole, wallow, waterhole, well; abyss, chasm, gulf, vacuity, vacuum, void

near antonyms hill, mound, projection, rise; bump, lump, pimple, swell, swelling, tumor

antonyms bulge, convexity, protrusion, protuberance

3 a difficult, puzzling, or embarrassing situation from which there is no easy escape — see PREDICAMENT

4 a dirty or messy place — see PIGPEN

5 an open space in a barrier (as a wall or hedge) — see GAP 1

6 the shelter or resting place of a wild animal — see DEN 1

hole *vb* to make a hole or series of holes in — see PERFORATE

holiday *n, chiefly British* a period during which the usual routine of school or work is suspended — see VACATION

holiday *vb* to take or spend a vacation — see VACATION

holiness *n* the quality or state of being spiritually pure or virtuous ⟨known throughout the world for his *holiness,* the prophet was visited daily by hundreds of pilgrims⟩

synonyms blessedness, devoutness, godliness, piety, piousness, sainthood, saintliness, saintship, sanctity

related words asceticism, devotion, morality, prayerfulness, religiousness, spirituality; righteousness, virtuousness

near antonyms blasphemousness, irreverence, sacrilegiousness; depravity, sinfulness, wickedness

antonyms godlessness, impiety, ungodliness, unholiness

holler *n* a loud vocal expression of strong emotion — see SHOUT

holler *vb* to speak so as to be heard at a distance — see CALL 1

hollow *adj* curved inward ⟨there's a *hollow* spot in the mattress where Jim sleeps⟩

synonyms concave, dented, depressed, indented, recessed, sunken

related words alveolar, cavernous, cuplike, cupped; dimpled, pockmarked; compressed, condensed, contracted, diminished, reduced
near antonyms ballooning, bloated, blown up, bulbous, distended, enlarged, expanded, extended, inflated, jutting, projecting, puffed (up), puffy, risen, swollen; domed, globular, rounded, spherical
antonyms bulging, convex, protruding, protuberant
hollow *n* **1** a sunken area forming a separate space — see HOLE 2
2 an area of lowland between hills or mountains — see VALLEY
holocaust *n* a destructive burning — see FIRE
holy *adj* **1** showing a devotion to God and to a life of virtue ⟨the *holy* monk spent many hours on his knees in prayer⟩
synonyms devout, godly, pious, religious, sainted, saintly
related words ascetic, prayerful, reverent, reverential, spiritual, worshipful; beatified, blessed, canonized, venerable; angelic (*or* angelical), cherubic; chaste, pure, righteous, virtuous
near antonyms blasphemous, desecrating, irreverent, profane, sacrilegious, unspiritual; backsliding, unfaithful; sinful, sinning, wicked
antonyms faithless, godless, impious, irreligious, ungodly, unholy
2 set apart or worthy of veneration by association with God ⟨the Torah contains the *holy* writings of Judaism⟩
synonyms blessed, consecrated, hallowed, sacred, sacrosanct, sanctified
related words adored, enshrined, glorified, revered, venerated, worshipped (*also* worshiped); ceremonial, liturgical, priestly, religious, ritual, spiritual; biblical, scriptural
near antonyms nonreligious, unspiritual; earthly, mundane, secular, temporal, worldly
antonyms unconsecrated, unhallowed, unsanctified
3 of, relating to, or being God ⟨the *Holy* Trinity⟩
synonyms blessed, divine, godlike, heavenly, sacred, supernatural
related words eternal, everlasting, immortal; almighty, omnipotent, omniscient, supreme
near antonyms human, mortal
4 not to be violated, criticized, or tampered with — see SACRED 1
Holy Writ *n* a book made up of the writings accepted by Christians as coming from God — see BIBLE
homage *n* **1** a formal expression of praise — see ENCOMIUM
2 public acknowledgment or admiration for an achievement — see GLORY 1
hombre *n* an adult male human being — see MAN 1
home *n* **1** the place where one lives ⟨as we entered his 34-room mansion, Ernest said, "Welcome to my humble *home*!"⟩
synonyms abode, diggings, domicile, dwelling, fireside, habitation, hearth, hearthstone, house, lodging, pad, place, quarters, residence, roof
related words accommodations, housing, nest, residency, shelter; bungalow, cabin, chalet, cottage; duplex, ranch, split level, town house, tract house, triplex; apartment, apartment house, condominium, flat, tenement, tenement house, walkup; penthouse, salon, suite; barracks, boarding-

house, dorm, dormitory, lodgment (*or* lodgement), lodging house, room(s), rooming house; castle, château, country seat, estate, manor, manor house, mansion, palace, villa; farmhouse, grange, hacienda, homestead, ranch house; houseboat, mobile home, motor home, trailer; hermitage, manse, parsonage, vicarage; hovel, hut, shack
2 the place where a plant or animal is usually or naturally found ⟨the American south, the *home* of the armadillo⟩
synonyms habitat, niche, range, territory
related words element, environment, environs, haunt, locality, milieu, neighborhood, setting, surroundings
3 the land of one's birth, residence, or citizenship — see COUNTRY 1
homeboy *n* a violent, brutal person who is often a member of an organized gang — see HOODLUM
homeland *n* the land of one's birth, residence, or citizenship — see COUNTRY 1
homely *adj* unpleasant to look at — see UGLY 1
homesteader *n* a person who settles in a new region — see FRONTIERSMAN
homicidal *adj* eager for or marked by the shedding of blood, extreme violence, or killing — see BLOODTHIRSTY
homicide *n* the intentional and unlawful taking of another person's life ⟨the missing man was thought to be the victim of a *homicide,* but his body was never found⟩
synonyms foul play, murder, slaying
related words killing, manslaughter; bloodshed, butchery, carnage, decimation, destruction, massacre, slaughter; assassination, execution; euthanasia, mercy killing
homily *n* a public speech usually by a member of the clergy for the purpose of giving moral guidance or uplift — see SERMON
homogenize *vb* to make agree with a single established standard or model — see STANDARDIZE
Homo sapiens *n* the human race — see MANKIND
hone *vb* **1** to make sharp or sharper — see SHARPEN
2 to make smooth by friction — see GRIND 1
honed *adj* having an edge thin enough to cut or pierce something — see SHARP 1
honest *adj* **1** being in the habit of telling the truth — see TRUTHFUL
2 conforming to a high standard of morality or virtue — see GOOD 2
3 following the accepted rules of moral conduct — see HONORABLE 1
4 free from any intent to deceive or impress others — see GUILELESS
5 free in expressing one's true feelings and opinions — see FRANK
6 guided by or in accordance with one's sense of right and wrong — see CONSCIENTIOUS 1
honestly *adv* to tell the truth — see ACTUALLY 1
honesty *n* **1** devotion to telling the truth ⟨George Washington has gone down in history for his *honesty*⟩
synonyms integrity, probity, truthfulness, veracity, verity
related words honor, incorruptibility; candidness, candor, frankness, good faith, sincerity, straightforwardness; dependability, reliability, reliableness, trustworthiness; accuracy, objectivity; authenticity, correctness, genuineness; credibility

THESAURUS

near antonyms deception, dissembling, dissimulation, duplicity, fakery, falseness, falsity, fraudulentness, hypocrisy, insincerity; beguilement, craftiness, cunning, furtiveness, guile, insidiousness, oiliness, slickness, slipperiness, slyness, smoothness, trickery, underhandedness, wiliness; equivocation, prevarication; exaggeration, inaccuracy

antonyms deceit, deceitfulness, dishonesty, lying, mendacity, untruthfulness

2 conduct that conforms to an accepted standard of right and wrong — see MORALITY 1

3 faithfulness to high moral standards — see HONOR 1

honey *n* a person with whom one is in love — see SWEETHEART

honor *n* **1** faithfulness to high moral standards ⟨the mayor, a man of *honor,* never broke a promise to the voters⟩
synonyms honesty, integrity, probity, rectitude, righteousness, uprightness
related words blamelessness, character, conscientiousness, decency, fairness, high-mindedness, incorruptibility, justice, morality, nobility, reputability, respectability, scrupulousness, virtue, virtuousness
near antonyms corruptibility, corruption, corruptness, debasement, decadence, degeneracy, depravity, disgracefulness, disreputableness, dissipation, dissoluteness, looseness, perversion, profligacy, shamelessness, venality; blameworthiness, criminality, crookedness, dishonesty, immorality, unrighteousness, unscrupulousness; knavery, rascality, roguishness; meanness, reprehensibleness, rottenness, sinfulness, vileness, villainy, wretchedness
antonyms baseness, lowness

2 an asset that brings praise or renown — see GLORY 2

3 public acknowledgment or admiration for an achievement — see GLORY 1

4 something given in recognition of achievement — see AWARD

5 something granted as a special favor — see PRIVILEGE

honor *vb* to show appreciation, respect, or affection for (someone) with a public celebration ⟨the newlyweds were *honored* with a dinner given by the bride's grandmother⟩
synonyms fete (*or* fête), recognize
related words acknowledge, cite, commend, compliment, credit, thank; extol (*also* extoll), glorify, laud, praise; acclaim, applaud, cheer, hail, salute; celebrate, commemorate, memorialize, observe; congratulate, felicitate
near antonyms bad-mouth, defame, libel, malign, slander; boo, hiss, hoot, jeer; censure, condemn, damn, denounce, reprobate; mock, put down, ridicule, slight

honorable *adj* **1** following the accepted rules of moral conduct ⟨the only *honorable* thing to do is to admit that you were wrong and apologize⟩
synonyms decent, ethical, honest, just, noble, principled, respectable, righteous, upright, upstanding
related words decorous, proper, seemly; blameless, guiltless, irreproachable, unassailable, unimpeachable; chivalrous, high-minded, right-minded; conscientious, fair, good, incorruptible, moral, reputable, respected, scrupulous, uncorrupted, virtuous
near antonyms bad, blackguardly, corrupt, criminal, crooked, immoral, iniquitous, knavish, mean, rascally, reprehensible, roguish, rotten, scoundrelly, sinful; unfair, unscrupulous, vile, villainous, wicked, wretched; blamable, blameworthy, censurable; debased, debauched, decadent, degenerate, depraved, disgraceful, disreputable, dissipated, dissolute, libertine, loose, perverted, profligate, reprobate, shameful, unscrupulous, venal
antonyms base, dishonest, ignoble, low, unethical, unjust, unprincipled, unrighteous

2 conforming to a high standard of morality or virtue — see GOOD 2

3 guided by or in accordance with one's sense of right and wrong — see CONSCIENTIOUS 1

honorably *adv* in a manner befitting a person of the highest character and ideals — see GREATLY 1

¹hood *n* a violent, brutal person who is often a member of an organized gang — see HOODLUM

²hood *n* something that covers or conceals like a piece of cloth — see CLOAK 1

hoodlum *n* a violent, brutal person who is often a member of an organized gang ⟨a couple of *hoodlums* held up the convenience store⟩
synonyms bully, gangster, goon, homeboy, hood, mobster, mug, punk, roughneck, rowdy, ruffian, thug, tough, toughie
related words cutthroat, scoundrel, villain; assassin, bandit, bravo, brigand, criminal, crook, desperado, felon, gunman, highwayman, lawbreaker, mafioso, outlaw, perpetrator, pickpocket, racketeer, robber, swindler, thief

hoodoo *n* something that brings bad luck — see JINX

hoodwink *vb* to cause to believe what is untrue — see DECEIVE

hoof (it) *vb* **1** to go on foot — see WALK

2 to perform a series of usually rhythmic bodily movements to music — see DANCE 1

hook *n* a hard strike with a part of the body or an instrument — see ¹BLOW

hook *vb* **1** to cause to turn away from a straight line — see BEND 1

2 to put or bring together so as to form a new and longer whole — see CONNECT 1

3 to take (something) without right and with an intent to keep — see STEAL 1

4 to take physical control or possession of (something) suddenly or forcibly — see CATCH 1

5 to turn away from a straight line or course — see CURVE 1

hookup *n* the state of having shared interests or efforts (as in social or business matters) — see ASSOCIATION 1

hoop *n* a circular strip — see RING 2

hoosegow *n* a place of confinement for persons held in lawful custody — see JAIL

hoot *n* **1** a loud vocal expression of strong emotion — see SHOUT

2 a vocal sound made to express scorn or disapproval — see CATCALL

3 the smallest amount or part imaginable — see JOT

hop *n* **1** a social gathering for dancing — see DANCE

2 an act of leaping into the air — see JUMP 1

hop *vb* **1** to move with a light bouncing step — see SKIP 1

2 to propel oneself upward or forward into the air — see JUMP 1

hope (for) *vb* to believe in the future occurrence of (something) — see EXPECT

hopeful *adj* **1** having qualities which inspire hope ⟨economists are offering a *hopeful* forecast for a healthy economy in the coming year⟩

synonyms auspicious, bright, encouraging, fair, golden, heartening, likely, optimistic, promising, propitious, rose-colored, rosy, upbeat

related words cheering, comforting, reassuring; assured, confident, decisive, doubtless, positive, sure, unhesitating; bullish, favorable, good

near antonyms cheerless, comfortless; doubtful, dubious, uncertain; bearish, grim, negative, unfavorable

antonyms bleak, dark, desperate, discouraging, disheartening, dismal, dreary, gloomy, hopeless, inauspicious, pessimistic, unlikely, unpromising

2 pointing toward a happy outcome — see FAVORABLE 2

hopeful *n* one who seeks an office, honor, position, or award — see CANDIDATE

hopeless *adj* **1** not capable of being cured or reformed ⟨a *hopeless* optimist who looked for the good in everyone and everything⟩ ⟨a *hopeless* criminal who spent most of his life in jail⟩

synonyms incorrigible, incurable, irrecoverable, irredeemable, irremediable, irretrievable, unrecoverable, unredeemable

related words irreparable, irreversible; unpromising; impenitent, unreformed, unregenerate, unrepentant

near antonyms reversible; promising; penitent, repentant; repairable, reparable, salvageable

antonyms correctable, curable, reclaimable, recoverable, redeemable, reformable, remediable, retrievable

2 emphasizing or expecting the worst — see PESSIMISTIC 1

3 incapable of being solved or accomplished — see IMPOSSIBLE

hopelessness *n* utter loss of hope — see DESPAIR 1

horde *n* a great number of persons or things gathered together — see CROWD 1

horn *n* something shaped like a hollow cone and used as a container — see CORNET

horrendous *adj* **1** causing fear — see FEARFUL 1

2 causing intense displeasure, disgust, or resentment — see OFFENSIVE 1

3 extremely disturbing or repellent — see HORRIBLE 1

horrible *adj* **1** extremely disturbing or repellent ⟨a *horrible* car accident that left eyewitnesses in a state of shock⟩

synonyms appalling, atrocious, awful, dreadful, frightful, ghastly, grisly, gruesome, hideous, horrendous, horrid, horrifying, lurid, macabre, monstrous, nightmarish, shocking, terrible

related words bloodcurdling, dire, direful, fearful, fearsome, forbidding, formidable, frightening, hair-raising, terrifying; abhorrent, deplorable, disagreeable, disgusting, distasteful, loathsome, nauseating, obnoxious, offensive, repugnant, repulsive, revolting, sickening; abominable, evil, foul, heinous, noxious, odious, unspeakable, vile

near antonyms agreeable, appealing, attractive, enticing, inviting; cheering, comforting, soothing

2 causing fear — see FEARFUL 1

3 causing intense displeasure, disgust, or resentment — see OFFENSIVE 1

horrid *adj* **1** causing intense displeasure, disgust, or resentment — see OFFENSIVE 1

2 extremely disturbing or repellent — see HORRIBLE 1

horridness *n* the quality of inspiring intense dread or dismay — see HORROR 1

horrified *adj* filled with fear or dread — see AFRAID 1

horrify *vb* to strike with fear — see FRIGHTEN

horrifying *adj* **1** causing fear — see FEARFUL 1

2 extremely disturbing or repellent — see HORRIBLE 1

horror *n* **1** the quality of inspiring intense dread or dismay ⟨it's difficult to even begin to comprehend the *horror* of the Holocaust⟩

synonyms atrociousness, atrocity, awfulness, dreadfulness, frightfulness, ghastliness, grisliness, gruesomeness, hideousness, horridness, monstrosity, repulsiveness

related words badness, baseness, diabolicalness, evil, foulness, heinousness, immorality, iniquity, invidiousness, nefariousness, ungodliness, viciousness, vileness, wickedness; accursedness, cursedness, deplorableness, despicableness, detestableness, execrableness, hatefulness, loathsomeness, reprehensibleness; creepiness, eeriness, fearfulness, fearsomeness, ghostliness, scariness; agony, hellishness, misery, torment, torture

near antonyms agreeableness, delightfulness, pleasantness; allurement, appeal, attraction, attractiveness, desirability, desirableness

2 a situation or state that causes great suffering and unhappiness — see HELL 2

3 something unpleasant to look at — see EYESORE

4 the emotion experienced in the presence or threat of danger — see FEAR

horse *n* a large hoofed domestic animal that is used for carrying or drawing loads and for riding ⟨the mounted police stable their *horses* in the city park⟩

synonyms equine, nag, steed

related words colt, filly, foal, gelding, mare, stallion; bronco, mustang, pony; charger, courser, cow pony, mount, palfrey, prancer, quarter horse, racehorse, saddle horse, trotter, war-horse, workhorse; bay, black, buckskin, chestnut, dun, palomino, pinto, roan, sorrel; cob, jade, plug

horse (around) *vb* to engage in attention-getting playful or boisterous behavior — see CUT UP

horseplay *n* wildly playful or mischievous behavior ⟨when he saw us spraying each other with the hose instead of washing the car, Dad yelled, "Cut out the *horseplay*!"⟩

synonyms clowning, foolery, high jinks, horsing (around), monkeying, monkeyshines, roughhouse, roughhousing, shenanigans, skylarking, tomfoolery

related words buffoonery, clownishness, foolishness, funning, jesting, joking, nonsense, waggery; boisterousness, rowdiness; devilry (*or* deviltry), impishness, mischief, mischievousness, prankishness, roguishness, trickery; cavorting, frivolity, frolicking, gamboling (*or* gambolling), merrymaking, playfulness, revelry, roistering, romping, sporting, sportiveness

horse sense *n* the ability to make intelligent decisions especially in everyday matters — see COMMON SENSE

THESAURUS

horse–trade *vb* to talk over or dispute the terms of a purchase — see BARGAIN

horsewhip *vb* to strike repeatedly with something long and thin or flexible — see WHIP 1

horsing (around) *n* wildly playful or mischievous behavior — see HORSEPLAY

hose *n* a close-fitting covering for the foot and leg — see STOCKING

hospice *n* a place that provides rooms and usually a public dining room for overnight guests — see HOTEL

hospitable *adj* showing a natural kindness and courtesy especially in social situations — see GRACIOUS 1

host *n* 1 a great number of persons or things gathered together — see CROWD 1
2 a large body of men and women organized for land warfare — see ARMY 1

hostel *n* a place that provides rooms and usually a public dining room for overnight guests — see HOTEL

hostelry *n* a place that provides rooms and usually a public dining room for overnight guests — see HOTEL

hostile *adj* 1 marked by opposition or ill will ⟨our landlord has a *hostile* attitude toward foreigners and refuses to rent to them⟩
synonyms antagonistic, inhospitable, inimical, jaundiced, negative, unfriendly, unsympathetic
related words adverse, bellicose, belligerent, clashing, conflicting, contentious, contrary, opposed, pugnacious, quarrelsome, resisting; antisocial, cold, cool, disagreeable, disapproving, distant, frigid, icy, biased, prejudiced; discourteous, impolite, rude, surly, uncivil, unfavorable, unkind, unpleasant, unsociable; acrimonious, antipathetic, bitter, hateful, malevolent, opprobrious, rancorous, spiteful, unloving, vindictive, virulent
near antonyms affable, amiable, amicable, companionable, convivial, cordial, civil, genial, gracious, gregarious, neighborly, pleasant, sociable, social, warm; affectionate, devoted, kind, loving, nice, sweet; accepting, agreeable, approving, benign, empathetic, favorable, understanding, warmhearted, welcoming
antonyms friendly, hospitable, sympathetic
2 opposed to one's interests — see ADVERSE 1

hostility *n* 1 a deep-seated ill will — see ENMITY
2 **hostilities** *pl* a state of armed violent struggle between states, nations, or groups — see WAR 1

hot *adj* 1 having a notably high temperature ⟨the casserole, just out of the oven, was too *hot* to eat⟩
synonyms broiling, burning, fiery, piping hot, red-hot, roasting, scalding, scorching, searing, sultry, superheated, sweltering, torrid
related words blazing, glowing, molten, sizzling; heated, overheated, reheated, warmed; snug, toasty, warm; feverish, flushed, inflamed; muggy, steamy, summery, tropical
near antonyms chilly, cool, frosty, nippy, snowy, subzero, wintry; cooled, refrigerated, unheated, unthawed; benumbed, numb, shivering; lukewarm, temperate, tepid
antonyms arctic, chill, chilled, cold, freezing, frigid, frozen, glacial, ice-cold, iced, icy
2 being or involving the latest methods, concepts, information, or styles — see MODERN
3 enjoying widespread favor or approval — see POPULAR 1

4 marked by bursts of destructive force or intense activity — see VIOLENT 1
5 showing urgent desire or interest — see EAGER

hot air *n* 1 boastful speech or writing — see BOMBAST 1
2 language that is impressive-sounding but not meaningful or sincere — see RHETORIC 1

hot–blooded *adj* having or expressing great depth of feeling — see FERVENT

hotcake *n* a flat cake made from thin batter and cooked on both sides (as on a griddle) — see PANCAKE

hotchpotch *n* an unorganized collection or mixture of various things — see MISCELLANY 1

hotel *n* a place that provides rooms and usually a public dining room for overnight guests ⟨for their 50th anniversary they stayed at one of the finest *hotels* in San Francisco⟩
synonyms caravansary (*or* caravanserai), hospice, hostel, hostelry, inn, lodge, public house, tavern
related words bed-and-breakfast; accommodations, lodgings, rest; motel, motor court, resort, spa, youth hostel; camp, campground; bunkhouse, dorm, dormitory; boardinghouse, lodging house, rooming house

hotfoot *adv* with excessive or careless speed — see HASTILY 1

hotfoot (it) *vb* to proceed or move quickly — see HURRY 2

hothouse *n* a glass-enclosed building for growing plants — see CONSERVATORY

hotness *n* the state of enjoying widespread approval — see POPULARITY

hot war *n* a state of armed violent struggle between states, nations, or groups — see WAR 1

hound *n* a domestic mammal that is related to the wolves and foxes — see DOG

hound *vb* 1 to go after or on the track of — see FOLLOW 2
2 to subject (someone) to constant scoldings and sharp reminders — see NAG

hounding *n* the act of going after or in the tracks of another — see PURSUIT

house *n* 1 a commercial or industrial activity or organization — see ENTERPRISE 1
2 a group of persons who come from the same ancestor — see FAMILY 1
3 the place where one lives — see HOME 1
4 those who live as a family in one house — see HOUSEHOLD

house *vb* 1 to provide with living quarters or shelter ⟨some of the freshmen were temporarily *housed* in the gym while the new dorm was being finished⟩
synonyms accommodate, billet, board, bunk, chamber, domicile, encamp, harbor, lodge, put up, quarter, roof, shelter, take in
related words ensconce, home, roost, secure, stable, tent
near antonyms eject, evict
2 to close or shut in by or as if by barriers — see ENCLOSE 1

house cat *n* a small domestic animal known for catching mice — see CAT 1

household *adj* 1 of or relating to a household or family — see DOMESTIC 1
2 often observed or encountered — see COMMON 1

household *n* those who live as a family in one

house ⟨a *household* that consists of a single mom, her two kids, and her widowed mother⟩
synonyms extended family, house, ménage
related words folks, kin, kindred, kinfolk, kinsfolk, kith; brood; nuclear family; clan, community

housekeeper *n* a female domestic servant — see MAID 1

housemaid *n* a female domestic servant — see MAID 1

housing *n* something that encloses another thing especially to protect it — see ¹CASE 1

hovel *n* a small, simply constructed, and often temporary dwelling — see SHACK

hover *vb* to rest or move along the surface of a liquid or in the air — see FLOAT

hover (over) *vb* to remain poised to inflict harm, danger, or distress on — see THREATEN

howbeit *adv* in spite of that — see HOWEVER

howbeit *conj* in spite of the fact that — see ALTHOUGH

however *adv* in spite of that ⟨I'm all out of eggs; *however*, I can still make us a nice breakfast⟩
synonyms howbeit, nevertheless, nonetheless, notwithstanding, still, though, withal, yet
related words after all, anyhow, regardless

howl *n* 1 a crying out in grief — see LAMENT 1
2 a loud vocal expression of strong emotion — see SHOUT
3 a violent shouting — see CLAMOR 1

howl *vb* 1 to make a long loud mournful sound ⟨several coyotes began *howling* close by as the sun went down⟩ ⟨the wind *howled* on the open plain⟩
synonyms bay, keen, wail, yowl
related words bawl, caterwaul, squall, yawp (*or* yaup), yell, yelp
2 to cry out loudly and emotionally — see SCREAM

hoydenish *adj* having qualities or traits that are traditionally considered inappropriate for a girl or woman — see UNFEMININE

hub *n* a thing or place that is of greatest importance to an activity or interest — see CENTER 1

hubbub *n* 1 a state of noisy, confused activity — see COMMOTION
2 a violent shouting — see CLAMOR 1

huckster *n* one who sells things outdoors — see PEDDLER

huddle *n* 1 a coming together of a number of persons for a specified purpose — see MEETING 1
2 a number of things considered as a unit — see GROUP 1
3 a usually small number of persons considered as a unit — see GROUP 2

huddle *vb* 1 to gather into a closely packed group — see PRESS 1
2 to lie low with the limbs close to the body — see CROUCH

hue *n* a property that becomes apparent when light falls on an object and by which things that are identical in form can be distinguished — see COLOR 1

hue and cry *n* a violent shouting — see CLAMOR 1

huff *n* 1 a state of nervous or irritated concern — see FRET
2 an outburst or display of excited anger — see TANTRUM
3 the feeling of being offended or resentful after a slight or indignity — see PIQUE

huffiness *n* readiness to show annoyance or impatience — see PETULANCE

hug *vb* to put one's arms around and press tightly — see EMBRACE 1

huge *adj* unusually large ⟨the old stadium was replaced by a *huge* new one that seats 100,000 spectators⟩
synonyms astronomical (*also* astronomic), bumper, colossal, cosmic, elephantine, enormous, giant, gigantic, grand, herculean, heroic, immense, jumbo, king-size (*or* king-sized), mammoth, massive, monster, monstrous, monumental, mountainous, prodigious, super, titanic, tremendous, vast, vasty, whacking, whopping
related words big, bulky, considerable, extensive, good, goodly, good-sized, great, gross, handsome, hefty, hulking, largish, major, sizable (*or* sizeable), substantial, voluminous; august, formidable, grandiose, imposing, lofty, majestic; cavernous, monolithic, overwhelming, staggering, stupendous, towering; boundless, cosmic, immeasurable, infinite
near antonyms little, petite, pint-size (*or* pint-sized), puny, small, smallish, undersized
antonyms bitty, diminutive, microscopic (*or* microscopical), midget, miniature, minute, pocket, pygmy, teeny, teeny-weeny, tiny, wee

hugely *adv* 1 to a great degree — see VERY 1
2 to a large extent or degree — see GREATLY 2

hugeness *n* the quality or state of being very large — see IMMENSITY

hugger-mugger *adj* 1 lacking in order, neatness, and often cleanliness — see MESSY
2 undertaken or done so as to escape being observed or known by others — see SECRET 1

hulk *n* a big clumsy often slow-witted person — see OAF

hulking *adj* 1 of a size greater than average of its kind — see LARGE
2 strongly and heavily built — see ¹HUSKY

hull *vb* to remove the natural covering of — see PEEL

hullabaloo *n* 1 a state of noisy, confused activity — see COMMOTION
2 a violent shouting — see CLAMOR 1

hum *n* a monotonous sound like that of an insect in motion ⟨we heard the *hum* of an outboard motor and a few minutes later the small craft came into sight⟩
synonyms buzz, chirr, drone, purr, thrum, whir (*also* whirr), whiz (*or* whizz), zoom
related words babble, coo, gurgle, hiss, moan, murmur, rustle, sigh, whisper; whish, zing, zip
near antonyms bawl, howl, roar, scream, screech, shriek

hum *vb* to fly, turn, or move rapidly with a fluttering or vibratory sound — see WHIRR

human *adj* relating to or characteristic of human beings ⟨it's *human* nature to care about what people think of us⟩
synonyms mortal, natural
related words anthropoid, hominid, humanlike, humanoid
near antonyms angelic (*or* angelical), divine, godlike, superhuman, supernatural; immortal, omnipotent, omniscient; animal, beastly, bestial, brute; inhuman, robotic
antonyms nonhuman

human *n* a member of the human race ⟨*humans* are the only mammals not endowed with a natu-

THESAURUS

ral defense against the elements, such as fur or a thick hide⟩

synonyms being, bird, body, creature, customer, devil, guy, head, individual, life, man, mortal, party, person, scout, sort, soul, specimen, thing, wight

related words hominid, homo, humanoid; brother, fellow, fellowman, neighbor; celebrity, personage, personality, self, somebody

near antonyms animal, beast, brute

humane *adj* **1** having or marked by sympathy and consideration for others ⟨*humane* guards who treated the prisoners decently⟩ ⟨the Geneva conventions spelled out standards for *humane* treatment of prisoners of war⟩

synonyms beneficent, benevolent, benignant, compassionate, good-hearted, kind, kindhearted, kindly, softhearted, sympathetic, tender, tenderhearted, warmhearted

related words attentive, considerate, thoughtful; affable, benign, cordial, friendly, gentle, good, good-natured, good-tempered, gracious, mild, nice, pleasant; clement, forbearing, forgiving, lenient, merciful, soft; patient, pitying, tolerant, understanding; altruistic, brotherly, charitable, generous, greathearted, humanitarian, magnanimous, noble, openhearted, philanthropic, unselfish, unsparing

near antonyms merciless, pitiless, ruthless; inconsiderate, insensitive, thoughtless, uncaring, unthinking; grim, hard-boiled, harsh, heavy-handed, severe, stern, tough, unsentimental; hateful, malevolent, malicious, mean, spiteful, virulent

antonyms barbarous, bestial, brutal, brutish, callous, cold-blooded, cruel, hardhearted, heartless, inhuman, inhumane, insensate, savage, unfeeling, unkind, unkindly, unsympathetic

2 having or showing the capacity for sharing the feelings of another — see SYMPATHETIC 1

humanitarian *adj* having or showing a concern for the welfare of others — see CHARITABLE 1

humanity *n* **1** human beings in general — see PEOPLE 1

2 the capacity for feeling for another's unhappiness or misfortune — see HEART 1

3 the human race — see MANKIND

humankind *n* **1** human beings in general — see PEOPLE 1

2 the human race — see MANKIND

humble *adj* **1** not having or showing any feelings of superiority, self-assertiveness, or showiness ⟨a medical scientist who remained remarkably *humble* even after winning the Nobel Prize⟩ ⟨even though she'd been twice proven wrong, Janet's attitude was still far from *humble*⟩

synonyms demure, lowly, meek, modest, retiring, unassuming, unpretentious

related words acquiescent, compliant, deferential, resigned, submissive, unaggressive, unassertive, yielding; cowering, cringing, shrinking; ingenuous, naive (*or* naïve), plain, simple, unaffected; bashful, diffident, mousy (*or* mousey), overmodest, passive, quiet, reserved, shy, subdued, timid, unobtrusive

near antonyms aggressive, assertive, audacious, bold, brash, brassy, cheeky, forward; cocksure, cocky, confident, overconfident, self-confident; egocentric, egoistic, self-centered, self-satisfied; boastful, bombastic, vain, vainglorious; condescending, disdainful, dominant, dominating,

domineering, imperious, lofty, lordly, magisterial, masterful, overbearing, patronizing, pontificating; flamboyant, flaunting, highfalutin, parading, ostentatious, showy

antonyms arrogant, conceited, egotistic (*or* egotistical), haughty, high-hat, pompous, presumptuous, pretentious, prideful, proud, self-assertive, self-conceited, self-important, stuck-up, supercilious, superior

2 belonging to the class of people of low social or economic rank — see IGNOBLE 1

humble *vb* to reduce to a lower standing in one's own eyes or in others' eyes ⟨Philip was utterly *humbled* by a crushing defeat in the first round of the state chess tournament⟩

synonyms abase, debase, degrade, demean, discredit, disgrace, dishonor, humiliate, lower, shame, smirch, take down

related words abash, discomfit, discountenance, embarrass, fluster, mortify; belittle, castigate, criticize, decry, depreciate, detract, disparage, minimize, put down, ridicule; bad-mouth, defame, defile, libel, malign, slander; affront, insult; censure, condemn, damn, denounce, reprobate

near antonyms acclaim, applaud, boast, celebrate, cite, commend, compliment, congratulate, decorate, eulogize, extol (*also* extoll), fete (*or* fête); hail, honor, laud, praise, salute, tout; acknowledge, recognize; highlight, play up, spotlight; dignify, ennoble, enshrine, glorify, magnify; lift, promote, raise, upgrade, uplift

antonyms aggrandize, elevate, exalt

humbleness *n* the absence of any feelings of being better than others — see HUMILITY

humbly *adv* in manner showing no signs of pride or self-assertion — see LOWLY

humbug *n* **1** an imitation that is passed off as genuine — see FAKE 1

2 language, behavior, or ideas that are absurd and contrary to good sense — see NONSENSE 1

3 one who makes false claims of identity or expertise — see IMPOSTOR

humbug *vb* to cause to believe what is untrue — see DECEIVE

humbuggery *n* language, behavior, or ideas that are absurd and contrary to good sense — see NONSENSE 1

humdrum *adj* causing weariness, restlessness, or lack of interest — see BORING

humid *adj* containing or characterized by an uncomfortable amount of moisture ⟨the air was so *humid* that our beach towels hanging on the line never really got dry⟩

synonyms muggy, sticky, sultry

related words summery, sweltering, torrid; semitropical (*also* semitropic), subtropical (*also* subtropic), tropic, tropical; close, heavy, oppressive, smothering, stifling, stuffy, suffocating; clammy, damp, dank, moist; drenched, dripping, soaked, sodden, soggy, sopping, soppy, waterlogged, wet

near antonyms bracing, cool, crisp, fresh, invigorating, refreshing; arid, baked, burned, burnt, dehydrated, desert, droughty, dusty, parched, scorched, seared, semiarid, sere, thirsty

antonyms dry

humidity *n* the amount of water suspended in the air in tiny droplets — see MOISTURE

humiliate *vb* to reduce to a lower standing in one's own eyes or in others' eyes — see HUMBLE

humility *n* the absence of any feelings of being

better than others ⟨displaying genuine *humility*, the peace activist accepted the Nobel Prize on behalf of all who have worked to end the violence⟩
synonyms demureness, humbleness, lowliness, meekness, modesty, retiringness
related words acquiescence, compliance, deference, resignedness, submission, submissiveness; ingenuousness, naïveté (*also* naivete); directness, plainness, simpleness; bashfulness, diffidence, passiveness, passivity, quietness, reserve, reservedness, shyness, timidity, timidness
near antonyms aggressiveness, assertiveness; audaciousness, boldness, brashness, brassiness, cheek, cheekiness, cockiness, forwardness, overconfidence, presumptuousness, temerity; impudence, insolence, nerve; boastfulness, selfcenteredness, self-satisfaction; vanity, vaingloriousness; condescension, disdain, imperiousness, lordliness, masterfulness; flamboyance, ostentation, ostentatiousness, showiness
antonyms arrogance, conceit, egoism, egotism, haughtiness, pompousness, pretense (*or* pretence), pretension, pretentiousness, pride, pridefulness, superciliousness, superiority

hummer *n* an ambitious person who eagerly goes after what is desired — see GO-GETTER

humming *adj* marked by much life, movement, or activity — see ALIVE 2

humor *n* 1 the amusing quality or element in something ⟨Sarah failed to see any *humor* in being chased by the dog, but Tom thought it was quite funny⟩
synonyms drollness, funniness, hilariousness, humorousness, richness
related words amusement, enjoyment, fun, pleasure; absurdity, irony, laughableness, ludicrousness, ridiculousness; burlesque, caricature, comedy, farce, jest, lampoon, parody, satire, slapstick
near antonyms agony, anguish, heartache, misery, sorrow, woe
antonyms pathos
2 humorous entertainment — see COMEDY
3 a state of mind dominated by a particular emotion — see MOOD 1

humor *vb* to give in to (a desire) — see INDULGE

humorist *n* a person (as a writer) noted for or specializing in humor ⟨Mark Twain is perhaps America's most beloved *humorist*⟩
synonyms card, comedian, comic, jester, joker, jokester, wag, wit
related words comedienne, entertainer; banterer, cut up, kidder, practical joker, prankster, teaser, wisecracker; buffoon, clown, fool, harlequin, zany; caricaturist, lampooner, parodist, satirist

humorless *adj* not joking or playful in mood or manner — see SERIOUS 1

humorous *adj* 1 causing or intended to cause laughter — see FUNNY 1
2 given to or marked by mature intelligent humor — see WITTY

humorousness *n* the amusing quality or element in something — see HUMOR 1

hump *vb* 1 to devote serious and sustained effort — see LABOR
2 to proceed or move quickly — see HURRY 2

hunch *vb* to lie low with the limbs close to the body — see CROUCH

hung *also* **hanged** *adj* bending downward or forward — see NODDING

hunger *n* 1 a need or desire for food ⟨no amount of *hunger* would induce me to eat octopus⟩
synonyms appetite, emptiness, famishment
related words rapaciousness, ravenousness, voracity; malnutrition, starvation, undernourishment; craving, sweet tooth; stomach; famine, fast, hunger strike; gluttony, gourmandism, greed, hoggishness
near antonyms fill, fullness, glut, repletion, satiation, satiety, satisfaction
2 a strong wish for something — see DESIRE
3 urgent desire or interest — see EAGERNESS

hunger (for) *vb* to have an earnest wish to own or enjoy — see DESIRE

hungry *adj* 1 feeling a desire or need for food ⟨John was still *hungry* after eating only a muffin for breakfast⟩
synonyms empty, famished, starved, starving
related words rapacious, ravenous, voracious, wolfish; malnourished, underfed, undernourished; gluttonous, gormandizing, greedy, hoggish, insatiable, piggish
near antonyms engorged, glutted, gorged, overfed, overfull, replete, sated, satiated, stuffed, surfeited
antonyms full, satisfied
2 showing urgent desire or interest — see EAGER

hung up *adj* 1 having extreme or relentless concern ⟨Stephanie's parents are already *hung up* about her getting into a good college, and she's only six years old⟩
synonyms obsessed
related words absorbed, anxious, concerned, distracted, engaged, engrossed, full, involved, occupied, prepossessed, preoccupied, worried; ardent, crazy, fervent, fervid, foolish, impassioned, nuts, passionate, silly
near antonyms apathetic, cool, detached, dispassionate, unconcerned, unenthusiastic, uninterested, uninvolved
2 feeling or showing uncomfortable feelings of uncertainty — see NERVOUS 1

hunk *n* a small uneven mass — see LUMP 1

hunt *n* an act or process of looking carefully or thoroughly for someone or something — see SEARCH

hunt *vb* 1 to seek out (game) for food or sport ⟨Indians of the plains *hunted* buffalo for food, clothing, and shelter⟩
synonyms chase, stalk
related words capture, drag, net, snare, trap; ferret, dog, hawk, hound; pursue, run down, track, trail; gun (for), harpoon, kill, shoot; poach
2 to go in search of — see SEEK 1
3 to go into or range over for purposes of discovery — see EXPLORE 2

hunt (down *or* up) *vb* to come upon after searching, study, or effort — see FIND 1

hunt (through) *vb* to look through (as a place) carefully or thoroughly in an effort to find or discover something — see SEARCH 1

hunter *n* a person who hunts game ⟨*hunters* must have a license to shoot deer⟩
synonyms huntsman
related words huntress, sportsman, sportswoman; archer, gunner; falconer, hawker; hunter-gatherer, trapper; poacher

huntsman *n* a person who hunts game — see HUNTER

hurdle *n* something that makes movement or progress more difficult — see ENCUMBRANCE

THESAURUS

hurl *vb* to send through the air especially with a quick forward motion of the arm — see THROW

hurly–burly *n* a state of noisy, confused activity — see COMMOTION

hurried *adj* acting or done with excessive or careless speed — see HASTY 1

hurriedly *adv* with excessive or careless speed — see HASTILY 1

hurry *n* 1 excited and often showy or disorderly speed ⟨after all her *hurry* to get her history report done on time, Elizabeth learned that it wasn't due till the following week⟩
synonyms haste, hastiness, hustle, precipitation, precipitousness, rush
related words bustle, flurry, flutter, scurry, scuttle, stir, whirl; beeline, dash, scramble, stampede; hotheadedness, impetuosity, impetuousness, impulsiveness, rashness; fleetness, quickness, rapidity, rapidness, speed, speediness, swiftness; celerity, dispatch, expeditiousness, promptness
near antonyms dilatoriness, lateness, pokiness, procrastination, slowness; languor, leisureliness, lethargy, sluggishness, torpor; inaction, inactivity, inertia, inertness, quiescence
antonyms deliberateness, deliberation
2 a high rate of movement or performance — see SPEED

hurry *vb* 1 to cause to move or proceed fast or faster ⟨the new nursing staff was *hurried* through the orientation because they were so desperately needed on the ward⟩
synonyms accelerate, hasten, quicken, rush, speed (up), whisk
related words drive, goad, prod, propel, push, race, spur, stir, urge; advance, aid, dispatch, ease, encourage, expedite, facilitate, forward, further
near antonyms delay, hamper, hinder, restrain; brake, check, stay
antonyms decelerate, retard, slow (down)
2 to proceed or move quickly ⟨if we *hurry*, we'll make the four o'clock train⟩
synonyms barrel, bolt, bowl, breeze, career, course, dash, fly, hasten, hotfoot (it), hump, hurtle, hustle, pelt, race, rip, rocket, run, rush, rustle, scoot, scurry, scuttle, shoot, speed, step (along), tear, trot, whirl, whisk, zip, zoom
related words dart, flit, scamper, scud, scuffle; stampede, streak, whiz (*or* whizz); gallop, jog, sprint; accelerate, quicken; catch up, fast-forward, outpace, outrun, outstrip, overtake
phrases shake a leg
near antonyms dally, dawdle, drag, lag, linger, loiter, tarry; amble, lumber, plod, saunter, shuffle, stroll; decelerate, slow (down *or* up)
antonyms crawl, creep, poke

hurt *n* something that causes loss or pain — see INJURY 1

hurt *vb* 1 to feel or cause physical pain ⟨my head *hurts*⟩ ⟨a bad sprain that really *hurts*⟩ ⟨I *hurt* all over⟩
synonyms ache, pain, smart
related words bleed, bite, burn, chafe, cramp, fester, itch, nag, pinch, pound, rack, sting, swell, throb, tingle, twinge; agonize, suffer
2 to reduce the soundness, effectiveness, or perfection of — see DAMAGE 1
3 to cause bodily damage to — see INJURE 1
4 to feel deep sadness or mental pain — see GRIEVE

hurtful *adj* 1 causing or capable of causing harm — see HARMFUL
2 hard to accept or bear especially emotionally — see BITTER 2

hurting *adj* causing or feeling bodily pain — see PAINFUL 1

hurtle *vb* 1 to proceed or move quickly — see HURRY 2
2 to send through the air especially with a quick forward motion of the arm — see THROW

husband *n* the male partner in a marriage ⟨she and her *husband* just celebrated their 50th wedding anniversary⟩
synonyms man, old man
related words consort, mate, partner, spouse; bridegroom, groom; widower

husbandry *n* 1 careful management of material resources — see ECONOMY
2 the science or occupation of cultivating the soil, producing crops, and raising livestock — see AGRICULTURE

hush *n* 1 a state of freedom from storm or disturbance — see CALM
2 the near or complete absence of sound — see SILENCE 2

hush *vb* 1 to become still and orderly — see QUIET 1
2 to stop talking — see SHUT UP
3 to stop the noise or speech of — see SILENCE 1

hush (up) *vb* to keep from being publicly known — see SUPPRESS 1

hushed *adj* 1 free from disturbing noise or uproar — see QUIET 1
2 free from storms or physical disturbance — see CALM 1
3 mostly or entirely without sound — see SILENT 3
4 not known or meant to be known by the general populace — see PRIVATE 1

husk *n* something that encloses another thing especially to protect it — see ¹CASE 1

husk *vb* to remove the natural covering of — see PEEL

¹husky *adj* strongly and heavily built ⟨a *husky* weight lifter⟩
synonyms beefy, brawny, burly, hulking
related words able-bodied, athletic, heavy, hefty, herculean, mighty, muscle-bound, muscular, powerful, robust, rugged, stalwart, strapping, strong, sturdy; chunky, compact, heavyset, solid, squat, squatty, stocky, thickset; dumpy, lumpish, portly, pudgy, stout
near antonyms lean, light, lightweight, slender, slight, slim, svelte, sylphlike, thin, willowy; bony, gangling, gangly, gaunt, gawky, lanky, scrawny, skinny, spare, twiggy; sinewy, spidery, wiry; delicate, emaciated, fragile, frail, puny, weakly

²husky *adj* harsh and dry in sound — see HOARSE

hustle *n* 1 a scheme in which the victim is cheated out of his money after first gaining his trust — see CONFIDENCE GAME
2 excited and often showy or disorderly speed — see HURRY 1
3 readiness to engage in daring or difficult activity — see ENTERPRISE 2

hustle *vb* 1 to devote serious and sustained effort — see LABOR
2 to proceed or move quickly — see HURRY 2
3 to rob by the use of trickery or threats — see FLEECE

hustler *n* an ambitious person who eagerly goes after what is desired — see GO-GETTER

hut *n* a small, simply constructed, and often temporary dwelling — see SHACK

hutch *n* **1** a small, simply constructed, and often temporary dwelling — see SHACK
2 a storage case typically having doors and shelves — see CABINET

hybrid *adj* being offspring produced by parents of different races, breeds, species, or genera — see MIXED 1

hybrid *n* an offspring of parents with different genes especially when of different races, breeds, species, or genera ⟨a tangelo is a *hybrid* of the tangerine and the grapefruit⟩
synonyms cross, crossbreed, mongrel
related words mulatto
near antonyms purebred, thoroughbred

hygienic *adj* free from filth, infection, or dangers to health — see SANITARY

hymn *n* a religious song ⟨our Sunday church services always open with a *hymn*⟩
synonyms anthem, canticle, carol, chorale, psalm, spiritual
related words dirge, lament, requiem, threnody; Gloria Patri, hallelujah, paean; mass, oratorio; processional, recessional

hymnal *n* a book of hymns ⟨*hymnals* are distributed among the congregation before the church service so everyone can join in the singing⟩
synonyms hymnbook, psalmody
related words breviary, missal, Psalter, songster

hymnbook *n* a book of hymns — see HYMNAL

hyperbole *n* the representation of something in terms that go beyond the facts — see EXAGGERATION

hypercritical *adj* given to making or expressing unfavorable judgments about things — see CRITICAL 1

hyperventilate *vb* to breathe hard, quickly, or with difficulty — see GASP

hypnosis *n* the art or act of inducing in a person a sleep-like state during which he or she readily follows suggestions ⟨with *hypnosis* there's some question as to just how involuntary the actions of the hypnotized person really are⟩
synonyms hypnotism, mesmerism
related words bewitchment, enchantment, spellbinding

hypnotic *adj* tending to cause sleep ⟨her eyes soon grew heavy from the *hypnotic* rhythm of the train's wheels⟩
synonyms drowsy, narcotic, opiate, slumberous (*or* slumbrous)

related words depressant, relaxant, sedative, tranquilizing (*also* tranquillizing); calming, lulling, quieting, relaxing, restful, settling, soothing; analgesic, anesthetic, anesthetizing, benumbing, deadening, dulling, numbing; hypnotizing, mesmerizing, stupefying
near antonyms arousing, awakening, energizing, invigorating, rousing, stimulating, wakening, waking
antonyms stimulant

hypnotism *n* the art or act of inducing in a person a sleep-like state during which he or she readily follows suggestions — see HYPNOSIS

hypnotize *vb* to hold the attention of as if by a spell — see ENTHRALL 1

hypocrisy *n* the pretending of having virtues, principles, or beliefs that one in fact does not have ⟨the *hypocrisy* of people who claim to care about the environment but ride around in gas-guzzlers⟩
synonyms cant, dissembling, dissimulation, insincerity, piousness, sanctimoniousness
related words deception, deceptiveness, dishonesty, falsity, pretense, pretension, pretentiousness, self-righteousness, self-satisfaction; duplicity, fakery, falseness, fraudulentness, shamming; artificiality, glibness, oiliness, smoothness, unctuousness
near antonyms candor, honesty, openness, probity, straightforwardness, truthfulness; artlessness, guilelessness, naturalness, unaffectedness
antonyms genuineness, sincerity

hypocritical *adj* not being or expressing what one appears to be or express — see INSINCERE

hypodermic *n* a slender hollow instrument by which material is put into or taken from the body through the skin — see NEEDLE 1

hypodermic needle *n* a slender hollow instrument by which material is put into or taken from the body through the skin — see NEEDLE 1

hypodermic syringe *n* a slender hollow instrument by which material is put into or taken from the body through the skin — see NEEDLE 1

hypothesis *n* an idea that is the starting point for making a case or conducting an investigation — see THEORY

hypothetical *adj* existing only as an assumption or speculation — see THEORETICAL 1

hysteria *n* a state of wildly excited activity or emotion — see FRENZY

hysterical *adj* **1** causing or intended to cause laughter — see FUNNY 1
2 feeling overwhelming fear or worry — see FRANTIC 1

ice–cold *adj* having a low or subnormal temperature — see COLD 1

icy *adj* **1** having a low or subnormal temperature — see COLD 1
2 lacking in friendliness or warmth of feeling — see COLD 2

idea *n* something imagined or pictured in the mind ⟨my *idea* of the perfect vacation spot is an unspoiled beach⟩
synonyms concept, conception, image, impression, notion, picture, thought
related words apprehension, premonition, presentiment; chimera, illusion, phantasm; caprice, conceit, fancy, freak, notion, vagary, whim; observa-

tion, perception, reflection; assumption, belief, conclusion, conviction; conjecture, guess, hunch, hypothesis, speculation, supposition, surmise, theory; brainstorm, inspiration

near antonyms actuality, fact, reality

ideal *adj* being entirely without fault or flaw — see PERFECT 1

ideal *n* **1** someone of such unequaled perfection as to deserve imitation ⟨she's our *ideal* of the concerned, caring physician⟩

synonyms beau ideal, classic, exemplar, model, nonpareil, paragon

related words role model; embodiment, epitome, incarnation, manifestation, personification; archetype, example, paradigm, pattern; guideline, principle, rule; gauge (*also* gage), standard, touchstone; essence, quintessence; acme, apex, culmination, peak, pinnacle, summit, zenith

2 the most perfect type or example — see QUINTESSENCE 1

idealist *n* one whose conduct is guided more by the image of perfection than by the real world ⟨an *idealist* sees the best in everyone, regardless of how they behave⟩

synonyms dreamer, romantic, romanticist, utopian, visionary

related words sentimentalist; daydreamer, optimist, theorist; perfectionist; thinker

near antonyms cynic, defeatist, pessimist

antonyms pragmatist, realist

idealize *vb* to represent or think of as better than reality ⟨he had a tendency to *idealize* his heroes and believe they could do no wrong⟩

synonyms glamorize (*also* glamourize), glorify, romanticize

related words daydream, imagine, romance, theorize, vision; better, perfect

near antonyms blame, condemn, criticize, denounce; worsen

ideally *adv* without any flaws or errors — see PERFECTLY 1

idée fixe *n* something about which one is constantly thinking or concerned — see FIXATION

identical *adj* **1** being one and not another — see SAME 2

2 resembling another in every respect — see SAME 1

identicalness *n* the state of being exactly alike — see IDENTITY 1

identify *vb* **1** to find out or establish the identity of ⟨with a quick look at everyone's tongue, Mom was able to *identify* the person who had sneaked a piece of blueberry pie⟩

synonyms distinguish, pinpoint, single (out)

related words diagnose; determine, find; locate, pick out, place, recognize, spot; check, examine, inspect, investigate, notice, observe, scrutinize; betray, disclose, discover, reveal

near antonyms camouflage, conceal, disguise, hide; counterfeit, feign, sham, simulate

2 to think of (something) in combination — see ASSOCIATE 2

identifying *adj* serving to identify as belonging to an individual or group — see CHARACTERISTIC 1

identity *n* **1** the state of being exactly alike ⟨although the covers of the two paperback editions of the novel are different, there's a complete *identity* in the texts⟩

synonyms identicalness, sameness

related words oneness; homogeneity, homology;

equality, equivalence; accordance, agreement, conformity, congruity, correspondence, likeness, resemblance, similarity

near antonyms alteration, change, modification, variation; distinction, distinctiveness, distinctness, exoticness, individuality, separateness, separation, uniqueness, unusualness; deviance, divergence; variance; incompatibility, incongruity, incongruousness; contrast

antonyms difference, disagreement, discrepancy, disparateness, disparity, dissimilarity, unlikeness

2 the set of qualities that make a person different from other people — see INDIVIDUALITY

ideology *n* the basic beliefs or guiding principles of a person or group — see CREED 1

idiocy *n* a foolish act or idea — see FOLLY 1

idiom *n* a sequence of words having a specific meaning — see PHRASE

idiosyncrasy *n* an odd or peculiar habit ⟨his only *idiosyncrasy* was collecting pencil erasers and making little dolls out of them⟩

synonyms crotchet, eccentricity, mannerism, oddity, peculiarity, quirk, singularity, trick

related words affectation, airs; attribute, characteristic, mark, property, trait; custom, habit, pattern, practice (*also* practise), way, wont; addiction; abnormality, perversion; disposition, genius, leaning, partiality; bent, inclination, penchant, predilection, predisposition, proclivity, propensity, tendency, turn; attitude, character, humor, identity, individuality, nature, personality, temperament

near antonyms conformity, sameness

idiot *n* a stupid person ⟨only an *idiot* would jump off a bridge just because their friends told them to⟩

synonyms blockhead, cretin, dodo, dolt, donkey, dope, dork [*slang*], dumbbell, dummy, dunce, fathead, goon, half-wit, ignoramus, imbecile, jackass, knothead, moron, nincompoop, ninny, nitwit, numskull (*or* numbskull), pinhead, simpleton, stock, turkey

related words booby, fool, goose, loony (*also* looney), lunatic, madman, nut, zany; loser; gawk; featherbrain, scatterbrain; beast, boor, cad, churl, clown, creep, cur, heel, jerk, skunk, snake, stinker, villain

near antonyms egghead, intellectual, sage, thinker

antonyms brain, genius

idle *vb* to spend time doing nothing ⟨she likes to *idle* during the summer even though her parents always tell her to get out and do something⟩

synonyms dally, dawdle, dillydally, hang around, hang out, loaf, loll, lounge

related words fiddle, fool, mess, monkey, play, potter, putter, trifle; estivate, hibernate; lag, linger, loiter, poke, relax, rest, tarry; amble, mosey, saunter, stroll; bum, furlough, goldbrick, malinger

phrases kill time, lie around, mark time, waste time

near antonyms drudge, grind, grub, hump, hustle, labor, moil, peg, plod, plow, plug, slave, sweat, toil, travail, work; apply, buckle (down); exert, put out

idle *adj* **1** not being in a state of use, activity, or employment — see INACTIVE 2

2 not easily aroused to action or work — see LAZY

idleness *n* **1** an inclination not to do work or engage in activities — see LAZINESS

2 lack of action or activity — see INACTION

3 lack of use — see DISUSE

idler *n* a lazy person — see LAZYBONES

idolater *or* **idolator** *n* a person who does not worship the God of the Bible — see HEATHEN 1

idolatry *n* excessive admiration of or devotion to a person — see WORSHIP

idolization *n* excessive admiration of or devotion to a person — see WORSHIP

idolize *vb* to love or admire too much ⟨she *idolized* her big sister⟩

  synonyms adore, adulate, canonize, deify, dote (on), worship

  related words appreciate, cherish, esteem, prize, treasure, value; fancy, favor, like, prefer; regard; respect, revere, venerate; approve, endorse (*also* indorse), support

  near antonyms abhor, abominate, despise, detest, disdain, dislike, hate, loathe; belittle, deprecate, disparage, put down

idolizing *adj* reflecting great admiration or devotion — see WORSHIPFUL

ignitable *adj* capable of catching or being set on fire — see COMBUSTIBLE

ignite *vb* to set (something) on fire — see BURN 2

ignited *adj* being on fire — see ABLAZE 1

ignoble *adj* **1** belonging to the class of people of low social or economic rank ⟨an *ignoble* child cannot grow up to be king⟩

  synonyms baseborn, common, humble, inferior, low, lower-class, lowly, mean, plebeian, proletarian, vulgar

  related words bourgeois, middle-class; peasant, plain, poor, simple, working-class

  near antonyms eminent, illustrious, notable, prominent

  antonyms aristocratic, high, highborn, lofty, noble, wellborn

2 not following or in accordance with standards of honor and decency ⟨cheating on a test is an *ignoble* act and can get you expelled⟩

  synonyms base, contemptible, despicable, detestable, dirty, dishonorable, low, mean, snide, sordid, vile, wretched

  related words bad, black, evil, foul, immoral, iniquitous, wicked, wrong; cruel, nasty, vicious; blamable, blameworthy, censurable, reprehensible; corrupt, debased, debauched, degenerate, depraved, dissolute, perverted; atrocious, villainous; unethical, unprincipled, unscrupulous; discreditable, disgraceful, disreputable, ignominious, shameful

  near antonyms ethical, honest, just, principled, righteous, right-minded, scrupulous; commendable, excellent, exemplary, good, moral, right; decent, proper, reputable, respectable, seemly; blameless, guiltless; incorruptible, irreproachable; uncorrupted, unerring

  antonyms high, high-minded, honorable, lofty, noble, straight, upright, venerable, virtuous

ignominious *adj* not respectable — see DISREPUTABLE

ignominy *n* the state of having lost the esteem of others — see DISGRACE 1

ignoramus *n* a stupid person — see IDIOT

ignorance *n* **1** the state of being unaware or uninformed ⟨*ignorance* of the law is no excuse⟩

  synonyms obliviousness, unawareness, unfamiliarity

  related words callowness, greenness, inexperience, innocence, naïveté (*also* naiveté), rawness, simpleness, unsophistication

  near antonyms experience, know-how; sophistication

  antonyms acquaintance, awareness, familiarity

2 the state of being unlearned ⟨with such vast sums spent on education, the level of *ignorance* among graduating seniors is a national disgrace⟩

  synonyms illiteracy

  related words brainlessness, dumbness, idiocy, imbecility, stupidity; philistinism; foolishness, mindlessness, senselessness, witlessness

  near antonyms education, instruction, training; enlightenment, knowledge; erudition, scholarship

  antonyms learning, literacy

ignorant *adj* **1** lacking in education or the knowledge gained from books ⟨the teacher was committed to educating the children of those poor, *ignorant* farmers⟩

  synonyms benighted, dark, illiterate, nonliterate, simple, uneducated, uninstructed, unlearned, unlettered, unread, unschooled, untaught, untutored

  related words lowbrow, uncultivated, uncultured; callow, green, inexperienced, innocent, naive (*or* naïve); unsophisticated; raw, untrained; brainless, dumb, idiotic, imbecilic, moronic, stupid, witless; foolish, senseless, silly

  near antonyms brilliant, intelligent, smart; experienced, expert, trained; erudite, learned, scholarly; cultivated, cultured, highbrow, intellectual; sophisticated; acquainted, aware, familiar

  antonyms educated, knowledgeable, literate, schooled

2 not informed about or aware of something ⟨he was *ignorant* of their plans⟩

  synonyms oblivious, unacquainted, unaware, unconscious, ungrounded, uninformed, unknowing, unmindful, unwitting

  related words uneducated, unschooled, untaught; absent, absentminded, abstracted, heedless, inattentive

  near antonyms conversant, educated, knowledgeable, schooled, taught; heedful, observant; sensitive, sentient

  antonyms acquainted, aware, cognizant, conscious, conversant, grounded, informed, knowing, mindful, witting

ignore *vb* **1** to fail to give proper attention to — see NEGLECT 1

2 to overlook or dismiss as of little importance — see EXCUSE 1

ilk *n* a number of persons or things that are grouped together because they have something in common — see SORT 1

ill *adj* **1** affected with nausea — see NAUSEOUS

2 causing or capable of causing harm — see HARMFUL

3 temporarily suffering from a disorder of the body — see SICK 1

ill *adv* in a manner so as to cause loss or suffering — see HARDLY 1

ill *n* **1** an abnormal state that disrupts a plant's or animal's normal bodily functioning — see DISEASE

2 that which is morally unacceptable — see EVIL

ill–advised *adj* showing poor judgment especially in personal relationships or social situations — see INDISCREET

THESAURUS

ill–bred *adj* **1** lacking in refinement or good taste — see COARSE 2

2 showing a lack of manners or consideration for others — see IMPOLITE

illegal *adj* **1** contrary to or forbidden by law ⟨it is *illegal* to steal⟩

synonyms criminal, illegitimate, illicit, unlawful, wrongful

related words bad, evil, immoral, shameful, sinful, unethical, wicked, wrong; blamable, blameworthy, censurable, reprehensible; banned, barred, disallowed, discouraged, forbidden, interdicted, outlawed, prohibited, proscribed; unauthorized, unlicensed, unsanctioned; corrupt, unprincipled, unscrupulous, villainous

near antonyms ethical, good, just, principled, right, righteous, virtuous; allowed, permitted; authorized, licensed (*also* licenced); approved, endorsed, sanctioned; abetted, encouraged, promoted, suggested, supported; correct, decent, decorous, proper, seemly

antonyms lawful, legal, legitimate

2 not being in accordance with the rules or standards of what is fair in sport — see FOUL 2

illegitimate *adj* **1** born to a father and mother who are not married ⟨despite being *illegitimate*, Alexander Hamilton rose to greatness⟩

synonyms baseborn, bastard, misbegotten

related words fatherless, motherless; adopted, orphaned

antonyms legitimate

2 contrary to or forbidden by law — see ILLEGAL 1

ill–fated *adj* having, prone to, or marked by bad luck — see UNLUCKY

ill–favored *adj* unpleasant to look at — see UGLY 1

ill–humored *adj* having or showing a habitually bad temper — see ILL-TEMPERED

illicit *adj* contrary to or forbidden by law — see ILLEGAL 1

illimitable *adj* being or seeming to be without limits — see INFINITE

illiteracy *n* the state of being unlearned — see IGNORANCE 2

illiterate *adj* lacking in education or the knowledge gained from books — see IGNORANT 1

ill–mannered *adj* showing a lack of manners or consideration for others — see IMPOLITE

ill–natured *adj* having or showing a habitually bad temper — see ILL-TEMPERED

illness *n* **1** an abnormal state that disrupts a plant's or animal's normal bodily functioning — see DISEASE

2 the condition of not being in good health — see SICKNESS 1

illogical *adj* not using or following good reasoning ⟨the *illogical* claim that playing basketball makes people taller because one sees so many tall players⟩ ⟨*illogical* people are likely to believe every sensational claim on TV⟩

synonyms fallacious, invalid, irrational, nonrational, unreasonable, unreasoning, unsound, weak

related words misleading, specious; ill-advised, unconsidered, unreasoned; inconsistent; absurd, asinine, foolish, meaningless, nonsensical, preposterous, senseless, silly; odd, peculiar, strange, unusual, weird; insane, mad, nutty, wacky; disordered, disorganized, rambling, random; unconvincing, unsatisfying; inexplicable, unaccountable, unexplainable

near antonyms commonsense, sane, sensible, sober, wise; enlightened, informed, just, justified, reasoned; ordered, organized; clear, cogent, compelling, convincing, credible, persuasive, plausible, satisfying, solid; certain, sure, true; confirmed, corroborated, demonstrated, established, substantiated, validated, well-founded

antonyms logical, rational, reasonable, sound, valid

ill–starred *adj* having, prone to, or marked by bad luck — see UNLUCKY

ill–tempered *adj* having or showing a habitually bad temper ⟨an *ill-tempered* cat will scratch⟩

synonyms bearish, bilious, cantankerous, disagreeable, dyspeptic, ill-humored, ill-natured, ornery, splenetic, surly

related words choleric, crabby, cranky, crotchety, fussy, grouchy, grumpy, querulous; irascible, irritable, peevish, petulant, quick-tempered, snappish, testy, touchy; argumentative, contentious, contrary; angry, exasperated, indignant, irate, mad, upset, uptight; depressed, dour, glum, morose, sullen

near antonyms agreeable, amicable, congenial, friendly, pleasant; benign, gentle, kind, nice, sweet; bubbly, cheerful, cheery, effervescent, exuberant, high-spirited, lighthearted, lively, joyful, vivacious; content, glad, happy; calm, placid, serene; long-suffering, patient, tolerant

antonyms amiable, good-natured, good-tempered

ill–treat *vb* to inflict physical or emotional harm upon — see ABUSE 1

illuminate *vb* **1** to supply with light ⟨a floor lamp *illuminates* a living room rather nicely⟩

synonyms illumine, irradiate, light, lighten

related words brighten; beam, beat (down), radiate, shine; floodlight; highlight, spotlight; blaze, burn, fire, flame, glare, glow, ignite, incinerate, kindle; bedazzle, blind, daze, dazzle; gleam, glisten, glitter

near antonyms dim, dull, obscure; cover, shroud, veil; douse, extinguish, put out, quench, snuff (out)

antonyms blacken, darken

2 to make plain or understandable — see EXPLAIN 1

illuminated *adj* filled with much light — see BRIGHT 2

illumination *n* **1** a statement that makes something clear — see EXPLANATION 1

2 the quality or state of having or giving off light — see BRILLIANCE 1

3 the steady giving off of the form of radiation that makes vision possible — see LIGHT 1

illuminative *adj* serving to explain — see EXPLANATORY

illumine *vb* to supply with light — see ILLUMINATE 1

illumined *adj* filled with much light — see BRIGHT 2

ill–use *vb* to inflict physical or emotional harm upon — see ABUSE 1

illusion *n* **1** a conception or image created by the imagination and having no objective reality — see FANTASY 1

2 a false idea or belief — see FALLACY 1

illustrate *vb* **1** to show or make clear by using examples ⟨she *illustrated* her point with a story about her last experiment and the results it provided⟩

synonyms demonstrate, exemplify, instance

related words cite, mention, quote; name, specify; analyze, break down; clarify, clear (up), explain, explicate, expound; edify, elucidate, enlighten; illuminate; construe, interpret; simplify, spell out; detail, enumerate, list

near antonyms becloud, blur, cloud, darken, fog, muddy, obscure; confuse, perplex, puzzle

2 to make plain or understandable — see EXPLAIN 1

illustration *n* **1** something that visually explains or decorates a text ⟨the book on birds had gorgeous *illustrations*⟩

synonyms diagram, figure, graphic, plate

related words drawing, illumination, image, pictogram, pictograph, picture; caption, key, legend; depiction, portrait, portrayal, representation; clarification, elucidation, explanation, explication, exposition

2 a statement that makes something clear — see EXPLANATION 1

3 a two-dimensional design intended to look like a person or thing — see PICTURE 1

4 one of a group or collection that shows what the whole is like — see EXAMPLE

illustrative *adj* serving to explain — see EXPLANATORY

illustrious *adj* standing above others in rank, importance, or achievement — see EMINENT

image *n* **1** something or someone that strongly resembles another ⟨the girl is growing up to be the perfect *image* of her mother⟩

synonyms carbon copy, counterpart, double, duplicate, duplication, facsimile, likeness, match, picture, replica, ringer, spit

related words effigy, portrait, portrayal; companion, counterpart, fellow, mate; equal, equivalent, identical twin; analogue (*or* analog), parallel

near antonyms antithesis, converse, opposite, reverse

2 a two-dimensional design intended to look like a person or thing — see PICTURE 1

3 something imagined or pictured in the mind — see IDEA

image *vb* **1** to present a picture of — see PICTURE 1

2 to give a representation or account of in words — see DESCRIBE 1

3 to reproduce or show (an exact likeness) as a mirror would — see REFLECT

imaginary *adj* not real and existing only in the imagination ⟨his *imaginary* friend had purple hair⟩

synonyms chimerical, fabulous, fanciful, fantastic, fictional, fictitious, imagined, invented, made-up, make-believe, mythical (*or* mythic), phantasmal, phantom, pretend, unreal

related words fabled, legendary, romantic; abstract, hypothetical, theoretical (*also* theoretic); unbelievable, unconvincing, unlikely; conceived, envisaged, pictured, visualized; deceptive, delusional, delusive, hallucinatory, illusory; concocted, fabricated

near antonyms authentic, genuine, true; factual, verifiable, verified; believable, convincing, realistic; corporeal, material, physical, solid, substantial; palpable, tangible

antonyms actual, existent, existing, real

imagination *n* the ability to form mental images of things that either are not physically present or

have never been conceived or created by others ⟨a cartoonist needs a good *imagination* in order to think up and draw interesting cartoons⟩

synonyms creativity, fancy, fantasy (*also* phantasy), imaginativeness, invention, inventiveness

related words brainstorm, brainstorming, inspiration; fecundity, fertility; ingenuity, originality; versatility; chimera, daydream, delusion, dream, figment, hallucination, illusion, mirage, phantasm, pipe dream; envisaging, visualization

near antonyms literalness

imaginative *adj* **1** having the skill and imagination to create new things — see CREATIVE 1

2 showing a use of the imagination and creativity especially in inventing — see CLEVER 1

imaginativeness *n* **1** the ability to form mental images of things that either are not physically present or have never been conceived or created by others — see IMAGINATION

2 the skill and imagination to create new things — see CREATIVITY 1

imagine *vb* **1** to form a mental picture of ⟨she *imagined* meeting the members of her favorite rock band face-to-face⟩

synonyms conceive, dream, envisage, fancy, picture, vision, visualize

related words daydream, stargaze; hallucinate; reflect, relive, reminisce; contemplate, meditate, muse, ponder, ruminate; concoct, fabricate, invent, make up, manufacture, plan, project

2 to have as an opinion — see BELIEVE 2

imagined *adj* not real and existing only in the imagination — see IMAGINARY

imbecile *n* a stupid person — see IDIOT

imbecility *n* a foolish act or idea — see FOLLY 1

imbibe *vb* **1** to swallow in liquid form — see DRINK 1

2 to take in (something liquid) through small openings — see ABSORB 1

imbue *vb* to cause (as a person) to become filled or saturated with a certain quality or principle — see INFUSE

imitate *vb* **1** to use (someone or something) as the model for one's speech, mannerisms, or behavior ⟨teenage boys who *imitate* whichever rock stars are hot⟩

synonyms ape, copy, emulate, mime, mimic

related words burlesque, caricature, lampoon, mock, parody, travesty; impersonate, perform, play; pantomime

2 to copy or exaggerate (someone or something) in order to make fun of — see MIMIC 1

3 to make an exact likeness of — see COPY 1

imitation *adj* being such in appearance only and made with or manufactured from usually cheaper materials ⟨you have to be careful not to buy an *imitation* diamond passed off as the real thing⟩

synonyms artificial, factitious, bogus, fake, false, man-made, mimic, mock, sham, simulated, substitute, synthetic

related words dummy, phony (*also* phoney); cultured, manufactured; unauthentic; adulterated, doctored, fudged, juggled, manipulated, tampered (with); concocted, fabricated; counterfeit, deceptive, forged, fraudulent, misleading; affected, feigned, pseudo, spurious

near antonyms authentic, bona fide, legitimate, true; premium, quality, valuable; pure, unadulterated

antonyms genuine, natural, real

THESAURUS

imitation *n* something that is made to look exactly like something else — see COPY

imitative *adj* using or marked by the use of something else as a basis or model ⟨your writing style tends to be *imitative* of whichever author you've recently read⟩

synonyms apish, emulative, formulaic, mimetic, mimic, slavish, unoriginal

related words copied, cribbed, plagiarized; artificial, bogus, factitious, fake, false, imitation, manmade, mock, sham, simulated, substitute, synthetic; duplicated, photocopied, reduplicated, reproduced, transcribed; backup; counterfeit, deceptive, forged, fraudulent, misleading; uninspired

near antonyms authentic, bona fide, legitimate, true; genuine, natural, real; classic, ideal, model

antonyms archetypal, original

imitator *n* **1** a person who adopts the appearance or behavior of another especially in an obvious way — see COPYCAT

2 a person who imitates another's voice and mannerisms for comic effect — see MIMIC

immaculate *adj* **1** free from any trace of the coarse or indecent — see CHASTE

2 free from dirt or stain — see CLEAN 1

immaterial *adj* **1** not composed of matter ⟨it is only possible to study *immaterial* forces like gravity by observing their effects on the physical world⟩

synonyms bodiless, incorporeal, insubstantial, nonmaterial, nonphysical, spiritual, unsubstantial

related words metaphysical, supernatural; impalpable, insensible, intangible, invisible; airy, diaphanous, ethereal, tenuous, thin, vaporous

near antonyms animal, carnal, fleshly; detectable, discernable, noticeable, observable, palpable, sensible, tangible, visible; bulky, heavy, massive, solid

antonyms bodily, corporeal, material, physical, substantial

2 not having anything to do with the matter at hand — see IRRELEVANT

immature *adj* **1** being in the early stage of life, growth, or development — see YOUNG

2 having or showing the annoying qualities (as silliness) associated with children — see CHILDISH

3 lacking in adult experience or maturity — see CALLOW

immeasurable *adj* being or seeming to be without limits — see INFINITE

immediacy *n* the state or condition of being near — see PROXIMITY

immediate *adj* **1** done or occurring without any noticeable lapse in time — see INSTANTANEOUS

2 done or working without something else coming in between — see DIRECT 1

3 done, carried out, or given without delay — see PROMPT 1

4 not being distant in time, space, or significance — see CLOSE 2

immediately *adv* without delay ⟨if you don't leave *immediately*, you'll be late for school and probably get in trouble⟩

synonyms directly, forthwith, instantly, now, promptly, pronto, right away, right now, straightaway, straightway

related words away, freely; anon, momentarily, shortly, soon; apace, briskly, fast, fleetly, full-tilt, posthaste, quick, quickly, rapidly, readily, snappily, speedily, swift, swiftly; abruptly, presto, suddenly, unexpectedly; hastily, impetuously, impulsively, rashly, recklessly; exactly, opportunely, punctually, seasonably

phrases at once, on the line, on the spot

near antonyms slowly; late, tardily

immense *adj* unusually large — see HUGE

immenseness *n* the quality or state of being very large — see IMMENSITY

immensity *n* the quality or state of being very large ⟨the *immensity* of the mountain was awe-inspiring, especially up close⟩

synonyms enormity, enormousness, hugeness, immenseness, magnitude, massiveness, vastness

related words bigness, extensiveness, greatness, largeness, voluminousness, weightiness; awesomeness, grandness, stupendousness; excessiveness, extravagance, extremeness, immoderacy

near antonyms littleness, puniness, smallness; triviality, unimportance

antonyms diminutiveness, minuteness, tininess

immerse *vb* **1** to hold the attention of — see ENGAGE 1

2 to sink or push (something) briefly into or as if into a liquid — see DIP 1

immersed *adj* having the mind fixed on something — see ATTENTIVE

immersing *adj* holding the attention or provoking interest — see INTERESTING

immersion *n* a focusing of the mind on something — see ATTENTION 1

immigrant *n* one that leaves one place to settle in another — see EMIGRANT

imminent *adj* **1** giving signs of immediate occurrence ⟨a storm is *imminent*, so you should seek shelter now⟩

synonyms impending, pending, threatening

related words approaching, coming, forthcoming, future, near, nearing, oncoming, upcoming; brewing, gathering; likely, possible, probable; inevitable, unavoidable; menacing, ominous, portentous; anticipated, awaited, expected, foreseen, predicted

near antonyms distant, far-off, remote; eventual, ultimate; bygone, former, past; late, recent

2 being soon to appear or take place — see FORTHCOMING

immobile *adj* **1** fixed in a place or position — see STATIONARY 1

2 incapable of moving or being moved — see IMMOVABLE 1

immobilize *vb* to render powerless, ineffective, or unable to move — see PARALYZE

immoderate *adj* going beyond a normal or acceptable limit in degree or amount — see EXCESSIVE

immodest *adj* showing a lack of proper social reserve or modesty — see PRESUMPTUOUS 1

immolate *vb* to give up as an offering to a god — see SACRIFICE

immolation *n* something offered to a god — see SACRIFICE

immoral *adj* **1** not conforming to a high moral standard; morally unacceptable — see BAD 2

2 not guided by or showing a concern for what is right — see UNPRINCIPLED

immorality *n* **1** immoral conduct or practices harmful or offensive to society — see VICE 1

2 that which is morally unacceptable — see EVIL

immortal *adj* lasting forever — see EVERLASTING

immortality *n* unending existence after death — see ETERNITY 2

immortalize *vb* to give eternal or lasting existence to — see PERPETUATE

immovable *adj* **1** incapable of moving or being moved ⟨that boulder is *immovable*, even with a bulldozer⟩

synonyms immobile, irremovable, nonmotile, nonmoving, unbudging, unmovable

related words motionless, moveless, static, stationary, still, unmoving; fast, fixed, rooted, steadfast, stuck, wedged

near antonyms portable, removable, transferable, transportable

antonyms mobile, motile, movable (*or* moveable), moving

2 sticking to an opinion, purpose, or course of action in spite of reason, arguments, or persuasion — see OBSTINATE

immunity *n* freedom from punishment, harm, or loss — see IMPUNITY

immure *vb* **1** to close or shut in by or as if by barriers — see ENCLOSE 1

2 to put in or as if in prison — see IMPRISON

immurement *n* the act of confining or the state of being confined — see INTERNMENT

immutability *n* the state of continuing without change — see CONSTANCY 1

immutable *adj* not capable of changing or being changed — see INFLEXIBLE 1

imp *n* **1** an appealingly mischievous person — see SCAMP 1

2 an evil spirit — see DEMON

impact *n* **1** a forceful coming together of two things ⟨the glass shattered on *impact* with the floor⟩

synonyms bump, collision, concussion, crash, jar, jolt, shock, smash, strike, wallop

related words blow, buffet, hit, knock, punch, rap, slap, thump; bashing, battering, bludgeoning, clobbering, hammering, lambasting, licking, pounding, pummelling, thrashing; contact, encounter, meeting, touch

2 the power to bring about a result on another — see EFFECT 2

3 the quality of an utterance that provokes interest and produces an effect — see ¹PUNCH 1

impact *vb* **1** to act upon (a person or a person's feelings) so as to cause a response — see ¹AFFECT 1

2 to come into usually forceful contact with something — see HIT 2

impair *vb* to reduce the soundness, effectiveness, or perfection of — see DAMAGE 1

impale *vb* to penetrate or hold (something) with a pointed object ⟨*impale* a marshmallow or two on that stick and let's start toasting⟩

synonyms gore, harpoon, lance, pierce, puncture, skewer, spear, spike, stab, stick, transfix

related words spindle; perforate; jab, poke, prick, punch, thrust; cut, knife, slice

impalpable *adj* **1** not capable of being perceived by the sense of touch — see INTANGIBLE

2 not perceptible by a sense or by the mind — see IMPERCEPTIBLE

impart *vb* to cause (something) to pass from one to another — see COMMUNICATE 1

impartial *adj* marked by justice, honesty, and freedom from bias — see FAIR 2

impartiality *n* lack of favoritism toward one side or another — see DETACHMENT 1

impassable *adj* impossible to get through or into — see IMPENETRABLE 1

impasse *n* a point in a struggle where neither side is capable of winning or willing to give in ⟨if we cannot ever agree on which movie to see tonight, we are at an *impasse*⟩

synonyms deadlock, halt, stalemate, standstill

related words dead end; bottleneck, corner, dilemma, fix, hole, jam, pickle, pinch, plight, predicament, quagmire, quandary, spot; difficulty; problem

impassioned *adj* having or expressing great depth of feeling — see FERVENT

impassive *adj* **1** not feeling or showing emotion ⟨she remained *impassive* as they told her the bad news⟩

synonyms apathetic, cold-blooded, phlegmatic, stoic (*or* stoical), stolid, undemonstrative, unemotional

related words cold, cool, dispassionate, unmoved; calm, collected, composed; imperturbable, unflappable; reserved, reticent, taciturn; blank, deadpan, dry, empty, expressionless, inexpressive, vacant, wooden; enigmatic (*also* enigmatical), impenetrable, inscrutable; aloof, detached, unconcerned, unsentimental; impersonal, objective, unresponsive; hardhearted, pitiless, unfeeling; inconsiderate, thoughtless

near antonyms blazing, burning, fiery, flaming, glowing, red-hot; ardent, enthusiastic, gung ho, zealous; gushing, maudlin, mawkish, mushy, sentimental; dramatic, histrionic, melodramatic; compassionate, responsive, sympathetic; reactive, sensitive

antonyms demonstrative, emotional, fervent, fervid, hot-blooded, impassioned, passionate

2 not expressing any emotion — see BLANK 1

impassivity *n* a lack of emotion or emotional expressiveness — see APATHY 1

impatience *n* urgent desire or interest — see EAGERNESS

impatient *adj* **1** showing urgent desire or interest — see EAGER

2 unable or unwilling to endure — see INTOLERANT 1

impeach *vb* to make a claim of wrongdoing against — see ACCUSE

impeccability *n* the quality or state of being free from guilt or blame — see INNOCENCE 1

impeccable *adj* **1** being entirely without fault or flaw — see PERFECT 1

2 free from guilt or blame — see INNOCENT 2

impeccably *adv* without any flaws or errors — see PERFECTLY 1

impecunious *adj* lacking money or material possessions — see POOR 1

impecuniousness *n* the state of lacking sufficient money or material possessions — see POVERTY 1

impede *vb* to create difficulty for the work or activity of — see HAMPER

impediment *n* something that makes movement or progress more difficult — see ENCUMBRANCE

impel *vb* to set or keep in motion — see MOVE 2

impend *vb* to be about to happen — see LOOM

impend (over) *vb* to remain poised to inflict harm, danger, or distress on — see THREATEN

impending *adj* **1** being soon to appear or take place — see FORTHCOMING

2 giving signs of immediate occurrence — see IMMINENT 1

impenetrable *adj* **1** impossible to get through or into ⟨the ancient temple was surrounded by vast stretches of *impenetrable* jungle⟩

synonyms impassable, impermeable, impervious
related words close, compact, dense, thick; compressed, condensed; sturdy, substantial, tough; firm, frozen, hard, solid, stiff; inflexible, rigid, unbending, unyielding
near antonyms soft, squishy; bendable, elastic, flexible, giving, malleable, pliable, yielding; absorbent, porous
antonyms negotiable, passable, penetrable, permeable
2 being beyond one's powers to know, understand, or explain — see MYSTERIOUS 1
3 impossible to understand — see INCOMPREHENSIBLE
4 not allowing penetration (as by gas, liquid, or light) — see TIGHT 1
impenitent *adj* not sorry for having done wrong — see REMORSELESS
imperative *adj* **1** forcing one's compliance or participation by or as if by law — see MANDATORY
2 impossible to do without — see ESSENTIAL 1
3 needing immediate attention — see ACUTE 2
imperceptible *adj* not perceptible by a sense or by the mind ⟨a slight difference in hue between the two glasses that's *imperceptible* unless they're placed side by side⟩
synonyms impalpable, inappreciable, indistinguishable, insensible
related words inaudible, intangible, invisible; inconspicuous, indistinct, unnoticeable, unseeable, unseen; faint, insignificant, slight, trivial; buried, concealed, covert, disguised, hidden, obscure, shrouded, unapparent, vague
near antonyms audible, observable, tangible, visible; clear, conspicuous, evident, eye-catching, manifest, noticeable, obvious, plain, prominent, striking; apparent, distinct, significant, straightforward
antonyms appreciable, discernible, palpable, perceptible, sensible
imperfect *adj* having a fault — see FAULTY
imperfection *n* something that spoils the appearance or completeness of a thing — see BLEMISH
imperil *vb* to place in danger — see ENDANGER
imperilment *n* the state of not being protected from injury, harm, or evil — see DANGER 1
imperious *adj* **1** fond of ordering people around — see BOSSY
2 having a feeling of superiority that shows itself in an overbearing attitude — see ARROGANT
3 having or showing a tendency to force one's will on others without any regard to fairness or necessity — see ARBITRARY 1
4 needing immediate attention — see ACUTE 2
imperiousness *n* an exaggerated sense of one's importance that shows itself in the making of excessive or unjustified claims — see ARROGANCE
imperishable *adj* impossible to destroy — see INDESTRUCTIBLE
impermanent *adj* **1** intended to last, continue, or serve for a limited time — see TEMPORARY 1
2 lasting only for a short time — see MOMENTARY
impermeable *adj* **1** impossible to get through or into — see IMPENETRABLE 1
2 not allowing penetration (as by gas, liquid, or light) — see TIGHT 1
impermissible *adj* that may not be permitted ⟨chewing gum is an *impermissible* activity in school⟩
synonyms banned, barred, forbidden, interdicted, outlawed, prohibited, proscribed, taboo (*also* tabu)
related words intolerable, unacceptable, unbearable, unendurable; illegal, illegitimate, illicit, improper, inappropriate, unadvisable, unauthorized, unlawful, unlicensed, unmentionable; unseemly, unsuitable; objectionable; disallowed, disapproved, discouraged; refused, rejected, revoked, unsanctioned, vetoed; repressed, suppressed; precluded, prevented, stopped; excluded, ruled out, shut out; blocked, hindered, impeded, obstructed
near antonyms acceptable, bearable, endurable, tolerable; accepted, accredited, allowed, appropriate, approved, authorized, certified, endorsed, lawful, legal, legitimate, licensed (*also* licenced), OK (*or* okay), permitted, warranted; accorded, granted, sanctioned, vouchsafed; brooked, condoned, countenanced; encouraged, promoted, supported; commanded, mandatory, ordered, required; proper, seemly, suitable, tolerated, unobjectionable
antonyms allowable, licensable, permissible, permissive, sufferable
impersonate *vb* **1** to pretend to be (what one is not) in appearance or behavior ⟨a school intruder was caught trying to *impersonate* a teacher⟩
synonyms masquerade (as), play, pose (as)
related words ape, copy, imitate, mime, mimic, mock, parody, travesty; act, perform, portray
2 to present a portrayal or performance of — see ACT 1
impersonator *n* **1** a person who imitates another's voice and mannerisms for comic effect — see MIMIC
2 one who acts professionally (as in a play, movie, or television show) — see ACTOR
impertinence *n* **1** disrespectful or argumentative talk given in response to a command or request — see BACK TALK
2 rude behavior — see DISCOURTESY
impertinent *adj* **1** displaying or marked by rude boldness — see NERVY 1
2 showing a lack of manners or consideration for others — see IMPOLITE
imperturbability *n* evenness of emotions or temper — see EQUANIMITY
imperturbable *adj* not easily panicked or upset — see UNFLAPPABLE
impervious *adj* **1** not allowing penetration (as by gas, liquid, or light) — see TIGHT 1
2 impossible to get through or into — see IMPENETRABLE 1
impetus *n* something that arouses action or activity — see IMPULSE
impiety *n* an act of great disrespect shown to God or to sacred ideas, people, or things — see BLASPHEMY
impinge *vb* to come into usually forceful contact with something — see HIT 2
impious *adj* not showing proper reverence for the holy or sacred — see IRREVERENT
impish *adj* tending to or exhibiting reckless playfulness — see MISCHIEVOUS 1
impishness *n* **1** a natural disposition for playful behavior — see PLAYFULNESS
2 playful, reckless behavior that is not intended to cause serious harm — see MISCHIEF 1
implacable *adj* **1** sticking to an opinion, purpose, or course of action in spite of reason, arguments, or persuasion — see OBSTINATE

2 showing no signs of slackening or yielding in one's purpose — see UNYIELDING 1

implant *vb* to set solidly in or as if in surrounding matter — see ENTRENCH

implausible *adj* too extraordinary or improbable to believe — see INCREDIBLE

implement *n* an article intended for use in work ⟨gardening *implements* such as hoes, spades, and pruners⟩
  synonyms device, instrument, tool, utensil
  related words apparatus, appliance, mechanism; contraption, contrivance, gadget, gizmo (*or* gismo), jigger

implement *vb* to carry out effectively — see ENFORCE

implementation *n* the doing of an action — see COMMISSION 2

implicit *adj* understood although not put into words ⟨the *implicit* agreement in the outing club is that every member pays his or her own way on all trips⟩
  synonyms implied, tacit, unexpressed, unspoken, unvoiced, wordless
  related words inferred; unannounced, undeclared, unsaid, untold; hinted, intimated, suggested
  near antonyms apparent, blatant, evident, obvious, plain, straightforward; unambiguous, unequivocal, unmistakable
  antonyms explicit, express, expressed, spoken, stated

implied *adj* understood although not put into words — see IMPLICIT

implore *vb* to make a request to (someone) in an earnest or urgent manner — see BEG

imploring *adj* asking humbly — see SUPPLIANT

imply *vb* to convey an idea indirectly — see HINT

impolite *adj* showing a lack of manners or consideration for others ⟨the librarian was shocked that anyone could be so *impolite* as to continue talking despite repeated warnings to be quiet⟩
  synonyms discourteous, ill-bred, ill-mannered, impertinent, inconsiderate, rude, thoughtless, uncalled-for, uncivil, ungracious, unmannerly
  related words audacious, bold, bold-faced, brash, brassy, disrespectful, impudent, insolent, saucy, shameless; boorish, churlish, clownish, loutish, uncouth, vulgar; undiplomatic, unsportsmanlike; abrupt, blunt, brusque, crusty, curt, gruff, sharp, snippy; antisocial, crabbed, cross, disagreeable, grumpy, sullen, surly; improper, inappropriate, incorrect, indecent, indecorous, unseemly; arrogant, conceited, presumptuous, pretentious
  near antonyms humble, meek, modest, unassertive; deferential, dutiful, respectful, submissive, yielding; acceptable, appropriate, becoming, befitting, correct, decent, decorous, fit, fitting, good, meet, proper, respectable, right, seemly, suitable; affable, cordial, friendly, genial, hospitable, sociable; felicitous, graceful
  antonyms civil, considerate, courteous, genteel, gracious, mannerly, polite, thoughtful, well-bred

impoliteness *n* rude behavior — see DISCOURTESY

import *n* **1** the quality or state of being important — see IMPORTANCE
  2 the idea that is conveyed or intended to be conveyed to the mind by language, symbol, or action — see MEANING 1

import *vb* **1** to be of importance — see MATTER
  2 to communicate or convey (as an idea) to the mind — see MEAN 1

importance *n* the quality or state of being important ⟨a final exam has great *importance*⟩
  synonyms consequence, import, magnitude, moment, significance, weight, weightiness
  related words celebrity, distinction, eminence, fame, note, noteworthiness, notoriety, preeminence, prominence, renown; store, substance, value, worth, worthiness; gravity, seriousness; authority, potency, power; mark, name, report, reputation, repute; cachet, position, prestige, rank, standing, stature; glory, greatness, honor, illustriousness
  near antonyms paltriness, pettiness, worthlessness; disgrace, dishonor, disrepute, ignominy, odium, opprobrium, shame; anonymity; obscurity
  antonyms insignificance, littleness, slightness, smallness, triviality, unimportance

important *adj* **1** having great meaning or lasting effect ⟨the discovery of penicillin was a very *important* event in the history of medicine⟩
  synonyms big, consequential, eventful, major, material, meaningful, momentous, significant, substantial, weighty
  related words decisive, fatal, fateful, strategic; earnest, grave, serious, sincere; distinctive, exceptional, impressive, outstanding, prominent, remarkable; valuable, worthwhile, worthy; distinguished, eminent, great, illustrious, preeminent, prestigious; famous, notorious, renowned; all-important, critical, crucial
  near antonyms inconsiderable, minor, paltry, petty, worthless; anonymous, nameless, obscure, uncelebrated, unknown
  antonyms insignificant, little, minor, slight, small, trivial, unimportant
  2 having great power or influence ⟨Rachel Carson was an *important* figure in the environmental movement⟩
  synonyms influential, mighty, potent, powerful, puissant, significant, strong
  related words high-level, senior, top; able, capable, competent, effective, efficient; authoritarian, autocratic, despotic, dictatorial, magisterial, tyrannical (*also* tyrannic); distinguished, dominant, eminent, famous, great, illustrious, notorious, preeminent, prestigious, renowned; dynamic, energetic, forceful, robust, sturdy, tough, vigorous
  near antonyms feeble, flimsy, frail, infirm; anonymous, obscure; incapable, incompetent, ineffective, inept, unfit, useless
  antonyms impotent, insignificant, little, powerless, unimportant, weak
  3 having a feeling of superiority that shows itself in an overbearing attitude — see ARROGANT
  4 having too high an opinion of oneself — see CONCEITED

importune *vb* to make a request to (someone) in an earnest or urgent manner — see BEG

impose *vb* to establish or apply as a charge or penalty ⟨every town *imposes* a fine for speeding⟩
  synonyms assess, charge, exact, fine, lay, levy, put
  related words dock, mulct, penalize, tax; extort, shake down, wrest, wring; bleed, fleece, gouge, milk, skin, squeeze; coerce, compel, force; inflict, wreak; set; reapply, reimpose, relay
  near antonyms abate, diminish, lessen; forgive, release
  antonyms remit

impose (on *or* upon) *vb* to take unfair advantage of — see EXPLOIT 1

imposing *adj* **1** having or showing a serious and reserved manner — see DIGNIFIED

2 large and impressive in size, grandeur, extent, or conception — see GRAND 1

imposition *n* a charge usually of money collected by the government from people or businesses for public use — see TAX

impossible *adj* incapable of being solved or accomplished ⟨the seemingly *impossible* problem of world hunger⟩ ⟨fitting everything in my backpack seemed an *impossible* task⟩

synonyms hopeless, unachievable, unattainable, unsolvable

related words impracticable, impractical; doubtful, dubious, far-fetched, improbable, unlikely; implausible, inconceivable, incredible, unbelievable, unthinkable; futile, useless; absurd, fantastic, outlandish, preposterous, ridiculous

near antonyms practicable, practical, reasonable; likely, probable; acceptable, believable, conceivable, credible, plausible

antonyms achievable, attainable, doable, feasible, possible, realizable, workable

impost *n* a charge usually of money collected by the government from people or businesses for public use — see TAX

impostor *or* **imposter** *n* one who makes false claims of identity or expertise ⟨the man who claimed to be a prince turned out to be an *impostor*⟩

synonyms charlatan, fake, faker, fraud, hoaxer, humbug, mountebank, phony (*also* phoney), pretender, quack

related words imitator, impersonator, mimic; actor, bluffer, counterfeiter, deceiver, dissembler, duper, feigner, misleader, trickster; poseur

near antonyms adept, expert, master, professional, virtuoso, whiz, wizard

impotence *n* the lack of sufficient ability, power, or means — see INABILITY

impotent *adj* **1** not able to produce fruit or offspring — see STERILE 1

2 unable to act or achieve one's purpose — see POWERLESS

impoverished *adj* **1** lacking money or material possessions — see POOR 1

2 producing inferior or only a small amount of vegetation — see BARREN 1

impoverishment *n* the state of lacking sufficient money or material possessions — see POVERTY 1

impracticable *adj* not capable of being put to use or account — see IMPRACTICAL

impractical *adj* not capable of being put to use or account ⟨the flimsy little toy shovel was cute, but completely *impractical* for digging up tree stumps⟩

synonyms impracticable, inoperable, nonpractical, unusable, unworkable, useless

related words unsuitable; inaccessible, unattainable, unavailable, unobtainable, unreachable; dead, dormant, fallow, free, idle, inactive, inert, inoperative, latent; arrested, interrupted, suspended; unrealistic

near antonyms accessible, available, obtainable, reachable; all-around (*also* all-round), handy; active, alive, busy, employed, functioning, operating, operative, running, working

antonyms applicable, feasible, functional, opera-ble, operational, practicable, practical, usable, useful, workable

imprecate *vb* to ask a divine power to send harm or evil upon — see CURSE 1

imprecation *n* a prayer that harm will come to someone — see CURSE 1

imprecise *adj* not precisely correct — see INEXACT 1

impregnable *adj* incapable of being defeated, overcome, or subdued — see INVINCIBLE

impregnate *vb* to wet thoroughly with liquid — see SOAK 1

impress *n* a perceptible trace left by pressure — see PRINT 1

impress *vb* **1** to act upon (a person or a person's feelings) so as to cause a response — see ¹AFFECT 1

2 to produce a vivid impression of — see ENGRAVE 2

impression *n* **1** a perceptible trace left by pressure — see PRINT 1

2 something imagined or pictured in the mind — see IDEA

impressionist *n* a person who imitates another's voice and mannerisms for comic effect — see MIMIC

impressive *adj* having the power to affect the feelings or sympathies — see MOVING

imprimatur *n* an acceptance of something as satisfactory — see APPROVAL 1

imprint *n* **1** a mark or series of marks left on a surface by something that has passed along it — see TRACK 1

2 a perceptible trace left by pressure — see PRINT 1

imprint *vb* to produce a vivid impression of — see ENGRAVE 2

imprison *vb* to put in or as if in prison ⟨in this society, we try to *imprison* criminals so that they can't do any more harm⟩

synonyms commit, confine, immure, incarcerate, intern, jail, jug, lock (up)

related words constrain, limit, restrain, restrict, shut; apprehend, arrest, capture, catch, detain; impress, shanghai; hold, keep; enslave, subjugate

near antonyms emancipate, manumit

antonyms discharge, free, liberate, release

imprisoned *adj* taken and held prisoner — see CAPTIVE

imprisonment *n* the act of confining or the state of being confined — see INTERNMENT

improbable *adj* not likely to be true or to occur ⟨it is *improbable* that we will be allowed to stay out all night⟩

synonyms doubtful, dubious, far-fetched, flimsy, questionable, unapt, unlikely

related words implausible, impossible, inconceivable, incredible, last, unbelievable, unthinkable; absurd, outlandish, preposterous, ridiculous; outside, remote, slight

near antonyms believable, conceivable, credible, plausible; possible; liable

antonyms likely, probable

impromptu *adj* made or done without previous thought or preparation — see EXTEMPORANEOUS

improper *adj* not appropriate for a particular occasion or situation — see INAPPROPRIATE

improperly *adv* in a mistaken or inappropriate way — see WRONGLY

impropriety *n* **1** the quality or state of not being so-

cially proper ⟨the *impropriety* of the song that the campers sang for the visitors was embarrassing⟩
synonyms inappropriateness, incorrectness, indecency, unfitness
related words coarseness, crudeness; imprudence, indiscretion
near antonyms discretion, prudence; etiquette
antonyms appropriateness, correctness, decency, decorousness, fitness, propriety, rightness, seemliness, suitability
2 a socially improper or unsuitable act or remark ⟨such *improprieties* as asking people how much money they make⟩
synonyms familiarity, gaffe, indiscretion, solecism
related words blunder, error, flub, fumble, goof, lapse, miscue, misstep, mistake, slip, slipup, stumble; discourtesy, incivility, offense (*or* offence); boner, howler, screamer; foul-up, muff; misapprehension, miscalculation, misconception, misjudgment, misstatement, misunderstanding
near antonyms manners, proprieties
antonyms amenity, civility, courtesy, formality, gesture
improve *vb* to make better ⟨a little salt would *improve* this bland food⟩
synonyms ameliorate, amend, better, enhance, enrich, meliorate, perfect, refine
related words correct, emend, rectify, reform, remedy; help; edit, revise; upgrade; fortify, intensify, strengthen; retouch, touch up
near antonyms damage, harm, hurt, impair, injure, spoil, tarnish; blemish, blight, deface, disfigure, flaw, mar; diminish, lessen, lower, reduce
antonyms worsen
improved *adj* being far along in development — see ADVANCED 1
improvement *n* an instance of notable progress in the development of knowledge, technology, or skill — see ADVANCE 2
improvident *adj* not thinking about and providing for the future ⟨the *improvident* view that the wearing away of the ozone layer need not concern us⟩
synonyms myopic, shortsighted
related words careless, heedless, imprudent, incautious, injudicious, unwise; extravagant, prodigal, profligate, spendthrift, thriftless, unthrifty; indulgent, lavish, reckless, wasteful
near antonyms careful, judicious, prudent, sensible, wise; economical, economizing, frugal, scrimping, sparing, thrifty; conserving, preserving, saving
antonyms farsighted, forehanded, foreseeing, foresighted, forethoughtful, provident
improvise *vb* to perform, make, or do without preparation ⟨since the award was a complete surprise, I *improvised* an acceptance speech⟩
synonyms ad-lib, extemporize
related words concoct, contrive, cook (up), devise, hatch, invent, make up, think up; cobble (together *or* up), dash (off)
near antonyms arrange, prepare, ready; consider, contemplate, ponder, study, think; practice (*or* practise), rehearse
improvised *adj* made or done without previous thought or preparation — see EXTEMPORANEOUS
imprudent *adj* showing poor judgment especially in personal relationships or social situations — see INDISCREET

impudence *n* **1** disrespectful or argumentative talk given in response to a command or request — see BACK TALK
2 rude behavior — see DISCOURTESY
impudent *adj* displaying or marked by rude boldness — see NERVY 1
impulse *n* something that arouses action or activity ⟨the new auto factory was just the *impulse* that the local economy needed⟩
synonyms boost, encouragement, goad, impetus, incentive, incitement, instigation, momentum, motivation, provocation, spur, stimulant, stimulus, yeast
related words inducement, invitation; cause, consideration, motive, reason
impulsive *adj* **1** caused by or suggestive of an irresistible urge — see COMPULSIVE
2 prone to sudden illogical changes of mind, ideas, or actions — see WHIMSICAL
impulsiveness *n* an inclination to sudden illogical changes of mind, ideas, or actions — see WHIMSICALITY
impunity *n* freedom from punishment, harm, or loss ⟨she mistakenly believed that she could insult people with *impunity*⟩
synonyms exemption, immunity
related words armor, defense, guard, protection, safeguard, safety, security, shield; buffer, bumper, screen; absolution, absolving, dispensation, forgiveness
near antonyms exposure, liability, susceptibility, vulnerability
impure *adj* containing foreign or lower-grade substances ⟨be careful, because *impure* motor oil can damage your car's engine⟩
synonyms adulterated, alloyed, contaminated, dilute, diluted, polluted, tainted, thinned, weakened
related words befouled, besmirched, corrupted, debased, defiled, dirtied, fouled, soiled, spoiled, sullied; blended, commingled, incorporated, intermingled, intermixed, merged, mingled, mixed; coalesced, combined, compounded; cheapened, doctored
near antonyms clarified, filtered, purified, refined; neat, plain, straight; concentrated, strong; uncombined; pasteurized
antonyms pure, unadulterated, unalloyed, uncontaminated, undiluted, unpolluted, untainted
impurity *n* something that is or that makes impure ⟨*impurities* in the water made it cloudy⟩
synonyms adulterant, contaminant, defilement, pollutant
related words blot, blotch, spot, stain, taint; dirt, filth, grime; blemish, defect, disfigurement, fault, flaw; abnormality, imperfection, irregularity
near antonyms clarifier, filter, purifier, refiner; cleanliness, immaculateness, purity
impute *vb* to explain (something) as being the result of something else — see CREDIT 1
in *adj* **1** being in the latest or current fashion — see STYLISH
2 enjoying widespread favor or approval — see POPULAR 1
in *adv* at, within, or to a short distance or time — see NEAR 1
inability *n* the lack of sufficient ability, power, or means ⟨the apparent *inability* of young children to sit still⟩
synonyms impotence, inadequacy, incapability,

incapacity, incompetence, ineptitude, powerlessness

related words inaptitude; ineffectiveness, ineffectualness, inefficiency

near antonyms aptitude, bent, flair, talent; effectiveness, effectualness, efficaciousness, efficiency; fitness, suitability; power, strength

antonyms ability, adequacy, capability, capacity, competence, potency

inaccessible *adj* hard or impossible to get to or get at ⟨my pen is *inaccessible* now that it's fallen down the crack behind my desk⟩

synonyms inconvenient, unapproachable, unattainable, unavailable, unobtainable, unreachable, untouchable

related words distant, far, faraway, far-off, remote, removed; apart, hidden, isolated, out-of-the-way, secluded

near antonyms close, near, nearby

antonyms accessible, approachable, attainable, convenient, obtainable, reachable

inaccuracy *n* an unintentional departure from truth or accuracy — see ERROR 1

inaccurate *adj* 1 not being in agreement with what is true — see FALSE 1

2 not precisely correct — see INEXACT 1

inaccurately *adv* in a mistaken or inappropriate way — see WRONGLY

inaction *n* lack of action or activity ⟨as a result of the park department's *inaction*, the city's pools are not ready to open for the summer⟩

synonyms dormancy, idleness, inactivity, inertness, nonaction, quiescence

related words indolence, languor, lassitude, laziness, lethargy, listlessness, sleepiness, sloth, sluggishness

near antonyms animateness, briskness, liveliness, sprightliness; business, diligence, employment, industriousness, occupation

antonyms action, activeness, activity

inactive *adj* 1 slow to move or act ⟨it's easiest to catch snakes early in the morning, while they're still cold and *inactive*⟩

synonyms dull, inert, lethargic, quiescent, sleepy, sluggish, torpid

related words apathetic, indolent, languorous, lazy, lazyish, listless, slothful; dormant, inanimate, motionless, sedentary, static, still; dead; dopey, drugged

near antonyms busy, engaged, occupied, working; animated, dynamic, energetic, lively, sprightly, vigorous; assiduous, diligent, hardworking, industrious

antonyms active

2 not being in a state of use, activity, or employment ⟨an *inactive* oil well⟩

synonyms dead, dormant, fallow, free, idle, inert, inoperative, latent, off, vacant

related words arrested, interrupted, suspended; asleep, lifeless, quiescent, sleepy; inoperable, unusable, unworkable, useless; dead, dull, slow

phrases out of commission

near antonyms functional, operable, operational, workable; assiduous, industrious; energetic, vigorous; feasible, practical, usable, useful, viable

antonyms active, alive, busy, employed, functioning, on, operating, operative, running, working

inactivity *n* 1 lack of action or activity — see INACTION

2 lack of use — see DISUSE

inadequacy *n* 1 a falling short of an essential or desirable amount or number — see DEFICIENCY

2 the lack of sufficient ability, power, or means — see INABILITY

inadequate *adj* not coming up to a usual standard or meeting a particular need — see SHORT 3

inadequately *adv* in an unsatisfactory way — see BADLY

inadvertent *adj* happening by chance — see ACCIDENTAL

inadvisable *adj* showing poor judgment especially in personal relationships or social situations — see INDISCREET

inane *adj* having no meaning — see MEANINGLESS

inanity *n* 1 a foolish act or idea — see FOLLY 1

2 lack of good sense or judgment — see FOOLISHNESS 1

inapplicability *n* the quality or state of not having anything to do with the matter at hand — see IRRELEVANCE

inapplicable *adj* not having anything to do with the matter at hand — see IRRELEVANT

inappreciable *adj* not perceptible by a sense or by the mind — see IMPERCEPTIBLE

inappropriate *adj* not appropriate for a particular occasion or situation ⟨a bathing suit is *inappropriate* dress for strolling the streets of this seaside village⟩

synonyms graceless, improper, inapt, incongruous, incorrect, indecorous, inept, infelicitous, unapt, unbecoming, unfit, unhappy, unseemly, unsuitable, wrong

related words inopportune, unfortunate, unseasonable, untimely; immaterial, irrelevant; incompatible, uncongenial, unharmonious; bad, naughty, sinful; blamable, blameworthy, censurable; banned, barred, disallowed; forbidden, interdicted, outlawed, prohibited, proscribed; awkward, gauche, ungraceful; unacceptable, unsatisfactory

near antonyms fortunate, opportune, seasonable, timely; apt, material, relevant; compatible, congenial, harmonious; allowed, authorized, permitted; approved, endorsed, licensed (*also* licenced), sanctioned; abetted, encouraged, promoted, supported; acceptable, adequate, satisfactory; commendable, creditable, exemplary; blameless, irreproachable

antonyms appropriate, becoming, befitting, correct, decorous, felicitous, fit, fitting, genteel, happy, meet, proper, right, seemly, suitable

inappropriately *adv* in a mistaken or inappropriate way — see WRONGLY

inappropriateness *n* 1 the quality or state of being unsuitable or unfitting ⟨I cannot even begin to describe the *inappropriateness* of such language for the dinner table⟩

synonyms inaptness, incorrectness, infelicity, unfitness, wrongness

related words inadmissibility, inapplicability, extraneousness, inadequacy, irrelevance, meaninglessness, pointlessness, senselessness; inauspiciousness, intolerability, undesirability, undesirableness, unsatisfactorability, uselessness

near antonyms admissibility, applicability, bearing, connection, materiality, pertinence, pointedness, relevance

antonyms appropriateness, aptness, correctness, felicitousness, felicity, fitness, fittingness, rightness, seemliness, suitability, suitableness

2 the quality or state of not being socially proper — see IMPROPRIETY 1

inapt *adj* not appropriate for a particular occasion or situation — see INAPPROPRIATE

inaptly *adv* in a mistaken or inappropriate way — see WRONGLY

inaptness *n* the quality or state of being unsuitable or unfitting — see INAPPROPRIATENESS 1

inarticulate *adj* unable to speak — see MUTE 1

inasmuch as *conj* for the reason that — see SINCE

inaugural *adj* coming before all others in time or order — see FIRST 1

inaugural *n* the process or an instance of being formally placed in an office or organization — see INSTALLATION 1

inaugurate *vb* **1** to be responsible for the creation and early operation or use of — see FOUND

2 to put into an office or welcome into an organization with special ceremonies — see INSTALL 1

inauguration *n* the process or an instance of being formally placed in an office or organization — see INSTALLATION 1

inaugurator *n* a person who establishes a whole new field of endeavor — see FATHER 2

inauspicious *adj* being or showing a sign of evil or calamity to come — see OMINOUS

inauthentic *adj* being such in appearance only and made or manufactured with the intention of committing fraud — see COUNTERFEIT

inborn *adj* **1** being a part of the innermost nature of a person or thing — see INHERENT

2 genetically passed or capable of being passed from parent to offspring — see HEREDITARY

inbred *adj* being a part of the innermost nature of a person or thing — see INHERENT

incandescence *n* the steady giving off of the form of radiation that makes vision possible — see LIGHT 1

incandescent *adj* giving off or reflecting much light — see BRIGHT 1

incantation *n* a spoken word or set of words believed to have magic power — see SPELL 1

incapability *n* the lack of sufficient ability, power, or means — see INABILITY

incapable *adj* lacking qualities (as knowledge, skill, or ability) required to do a job — see INCOMPETENT

incapacitate *vb* to render powerless, ineffective, or unable to move — see PARALYZE

incapacitated *adj* deprived of the power to perform one or more natural bodily activities — see DISABLED

incapacity *n* the lack of sufficient ability, power, or means — see INABILITY

incarcerate *vb* to put in or as if in prison — see IMPRISON

incarcerated *adj* taken and held prisoner — see CAPTIVE

incarceration *n* the act of confining or the state of being confined — see INTERNMENT

incarnate *vb* to represent in visible form — see EMBODY 2

incarnation *n* a visible representation of something abstract (as a quality) — see EMBODIMENT

incautious *adj* not paying or showing close attention especially for the purpose of avoiding trouble — see CARELESS 1

incautiousness *n* failure to take the care that a cautious person usually takes — see NEGLIGENCE 1

incendiary *n* **1** a person who deliberately and unlawfully sets fire to a building or other property — see ARSONIST

2 a person who stirs up public feelings especially of discontent — see AGITATOR

incense *n* a sweet or pleasant smell — see FRAGRANCE

incense *vb* to make angry — see ANGER

incensed *adj* feeling or showing anger — see ANGRY

incentive *n* something that arouses action or activity — see IMPULSE

inception *n* the point at which something begins — see BEGINNING

incertitude *n* a feeling or attitude that one does not know the truth, truthfulness, or trustworthiness of someone or something — see DOUBT

incessant *adj* going on and on without any interruptions — see CONTINUOUS

incessantly *adv* on every relevant occasion — see ALWAYS 1

inch *n* **1** a very small distance or degree — see HAIR 1

2 an individual part of a process, series, or ranking — see DEGREE 1

inch *vb* **1** to advance gradually beyond the usual or desirable limits — see ENCROACH

2 to move slowly — see CRAWL 2

incident *n* something that happens — see EVENT 1

incidental *adj* happening by chance — see ACCIDENTAL

incipiency *n* the point at which something begins — see BEGINNING

incise *vb* **1** to cut (as letters or designs) on a hard surface — see ENGRAVE 1

2 to penetrate with a sharp edge (as a knife) — see CUT 1

incision *n* a long deep cut — see GASH

incite *vb* **1** to cause or encourage the development of ⟨the rock band's failure to show up *incited* a riot, as the crowd had waited for hours⟩

synonyms abet, ferment, foment, instigate, provoke, raise, stir (up), whip (up)

related words forward, foster, further, promote, sow, stimulate; set off, trigger; excite, galvanize, inflame, inspire, motivate, rouse; activate, energize, quicken, vitalize

near antonyms check, curb, discourage, inhibit, restrain; calm, soothe, subdue, tranquilize (*also* tranquillize)

2 to rouse to strong feeling or action — see PROVOKE 1

incitement *n* **1** something that arouses a strong response from another — see PROVOCATION 1

2 something that arouses action or activity — see IMPULSE

inciter *n* a person who stirs up public feelings especially of discontent — see AGITATOR

inciting *adj* serving or likely to arouse a strong reaction — see PROVOCATIVE

incivility *n* rude behavior — see DISCOURTESY

inclement *adj* marked by wet and windy conditions — see FOUL 1

inclination *n* **1** a habitual attraction to some activity or thing ⟨her natural *inclination* to help people in need⟩

synonyms bent, devices, disposition, genius, leaning, partiality, penchant, predilection, predisposition, proclivity, propensity, tendency, turn

related words bias, prejudice; aptitude, faculty,

THESAURUS

flair, gift, knack, talent; addiction, fondness, liking; forte, speciality, specialty; convention, custom, habit, pattern, practice (*also* practise), routine, trick, way, wont; oddity, peculiarity, quirk, singularity

near antonyms aversion, dislike, distaste; impartiality, neutrality, objectivity; apathy, disinterestedness, indifference

2 the act of positioning or an instance of being positioned at an angle — see TILT

3 the degree to which something rises up from a position level with the horizon — see SLANT

incline *n* the degree to which something rises up from a position level with the horizon — see SLANT

incline *vb* **1** to set or cause to be at an angle — see LEAN 1

2 to show a liking or proneness (for something) — see LEAN 2

inclined *adj* **1** having a desire or inclination (as for a specified course of action) — see WILLING 1

2 having a liking or affection — see FOND 1

3 having a tendency to be or act in a certain way — see PRONE 1

4 running in a slanting direction — see DIAGONAL

inclining *adj* bending downward or forward — see NODDING

include *vb* to have as part of a whole ⟨the test *included* some hard essay questions⟩

synonyms carry, comprehend, contain, embrace, encompass, entail, involve, number, take in

related words comprise, consist (of); have, hold, own, possess; admit, receive; compose, constitute, form, make; assimilate, embody, incorporate, integrate

near antonyms bar, debar, preclude, prevent, prohibit; deny, refuse, reject; eliminate, except, rule out; lose, mislay, misplace

antonyms exclude, omit

inclusive *adj* covering everything or all important points — see ENCYCLOPEDIC

incognito *adj* not named or identified by a name — see NAMELESS 1

incoherent *adj* **1** not clearly or logically connected ⟨the thriller's *incoherent* plot left movie audiences wondering who did what⟩

synonyms disconnected, disjointed, unconnected

related words baffling, bewildering, confounding, confused, confusing, disordered, disorderly, disorganized, muddled, perplexing, puzzling; disconcerting, frustrating; fallacious, illogical, inconsistent, invalid, irrational, unsound; absurd, asinine, eccentric, foolish, odd, peculiar, strange, unreasonable, unusual, weird; meaningless, nonsensical, nutty, preposterous, ridiculous, senseless, silly; unconvincing, unsatisfying; inexplicable, unaccountable, unexplainable

near antonyms ordered, orderly, organized; logical, rational, reasonable, sensible, solid, sound, valid; cogent, compelling, convincing, persuasive, plausible, satisfying; clear, lucid, perspicuous

antonyms coherent, connected

2 consisting of particles that do not stick together — see LOOSE 2

incombustible *adj* incapable of being burned ⟨we keep our important papers in an *incombustible* safe in the basement⟩

synonyms fireproof, noncombustible, nonflammable, noninflammable, uninflammable

related words nonexplosive

near antonyms ablaze, afire, blazing, burning, fiery; consumable; explosive, incendiary, volcanic

antonyms burnable, combustible, flammable, ignitable, inflammable

income *n* an increase usually measured in money that comes from labor, business, or property ⟨her summer job gave her some extra *income*⟩

synonyms earnings, gain(s), proceeds, profit, return, revenue, yield

related words killing, windfall; salary, tips, wages; capital, finances, funds, money

near antonyms cost, expenditures, expenses, outgo, outlay

incommode *vb* to cause discomfort to or trouble for — see INCONVENIENCE

incommoding *adj* causing difficulty, discomfort, or annoyance — see INCONVENIENT 1

incommunicable *adj* beyond the power to describe — see INDESCRIBABLE

incomparable *adj* having no equal or rival for excellence or desirability — see ONLY 1

incompatible *adj* not being in agreement or harmony — see INCONSISTENT

incompetence *n* the lack of sufficient ability, power, or means — see INABILITY

incompetent *adj* lacking qualities (as knowledge, skill, or ability) required to do a job ⟨an *incompetent* carpenter had built the deck, and the railings were loose already⟩

synonyms incapable, inept, inexpert, unfit, unqualified, unskilled, unskillful

related words ineffective, ineffectual, inefficient; callow, green, inexperienced, raw; unequipped, unprepared, untrained; useless, worthless; ineligible; wanting

near antonyms prepared, ready, trained; experienced, practiced (*or* practised), seasoned, veteran

antonyms able, capable, competent, expert, fit, qualified, skilled, skillful

incomplete *adj* lacking some necessary part ⟨an *incomplete* puzzle that has several pieces missing⟩

synonyms deficient, fragmental, fragmentary, halfway, partial

related words broken, damaged, flawed, impaired, imperfect, injured, marred, spoiled; sketchy, uncompleted, unfinished

near antonyms flawless, perfect, unbroken, undamaged, unimpaired, uninjured, unmarred; completed, finished

antonyms complete, entire, full, intact, whole

incompletely *adv* in some measure or degree — see PARTLY

incomprehensible *adj* impossible to understand ⟨rocket science is *incomprehensible* to most people⟩

synonyms impenetrable, unfathomable, unintelligible

related words abstruse, enigmatic (*also* enigmatical), esoteric, inscrutable, recondite; cryptic, mysterious, obscure; unanswerable, unknowable; baffling, bewildering, confounding, confusing, mystifying, perplexing, puzzling

near antonyms basic, elementary, rudimentary; easy, simple; coherent, connected, ordered, orderly, organized; clear, cogent, compelling, convincing, lucid, perspicuous, plain, straightforward

antonyms fathomable, intelligible, understandable

inconceivable *adj* too extraordinary or improbable to believe — see INCREDIBLE

incongruity *n* someone or something with qualities or features that seem to conflict with one another — see CONTRADICTION 1

incongruous *adj* **1** not appropriate for a particular occasion or situation — see INAPPROPRIATE

2 not being in agreement or harmony — see INCONSISTENT

inconsequential *adj* **1** lacking importance — see UNIMPORTANT

2 so small or unimportant as to warrant little or no attention — see NEGLIGIBLE

inconsiderable *adj* **1** lacking importance — see UNIMPORTANT

2 so small or unimportant as to warrant little or no attention — see NEGLIGIBLE 1

inconsiderate *adj* showing a lack of manners or consideration for others — see IMPOLITE

inconsideration *n* rude behavior — see DISCOURTESY

inconsistent *adj* not being in agreement or harmony ⟨*inconsistent* theories make it difficult to settle on one explanation⟩

synonyms clashing, conflicting, disagreeing, discordant, discrepant, incompatible, incongruous, inharmonious

related words irreconcilable; antagonistic, antithetical, contradictory, contrary, opposing, opposite

near antonyms akin, like, similar

antonyms agreeing, compatible, congruous, consistent, consonant, harmonious, nonconflicting

inconsolable *adj* feeling unhappiness — see SAD 1

inconspicuous *adj* not readily seen or noticed — see UNOBTRUSIVE

inconstancy *n* lack of faithfulness especially to one's husband or wife — see INFIDELITY 1

inconstant *adj* **1** likely to change frequently, suddenly, or unexpectedly — see FICKLE 1

2 not true in one's allegiance to someone or something — see FAITHLESS

incontestable *adj* not capable of being challenged or proved wrong — see IRREFUTABLE

incontestably *adv* without any question — see INDEED 1

incontrovertible *adj* not capable of being challenged or proved wrong — see IRREFUTABLE

incontrovertibly *adv* without any question — see INDEED 1

inconvenience *n* something that is a source of irritation — see ANNOYANCE 3

inconvenience *vb* to cause discomfort to or trouble for ⟨he *inconvenienced* his sister by moving into her tiny apartment⟩

synonyms discommode, disoblige, disturb, incommode, trouble

related words burden, encumber, saddle, weigh; hamper, hamstring, hinder, hobble, impede; aggravate, anger, annoy, bother, bug, exasperate, gall, get, nettle, peeve, pique, put out, rile, vex; grate, inflame, provoke; agitate, perturb, upset

near antonyms aid, assist, help; ease, facilitate; appease, conciliate, mollify, pacify, placate; delight, gladden, gratify, please; comfort, console, content

antonyms accommodate, oblige

inconvenient *adj* **1** causing difficulty, discomfort, or annoyance ⟨the unexpected visitors showed up at an *inconvenient* time⟩

synonyms awkward, discommoding, disobliging, incommoding

related words bothersome, burdensome, onerous, troublesome; annoying, exasperating, irritating

near antonyms acceptable, bearable, tolerable; advantageous, desirable, good, helpful

antonyms convenient

2 hard or impossible to get to or get at — see INACCESSIBLE

incorporate *vb* **1** to make a part of a body or system — see EMBODY 1

2 to turn into a single mass that is more or less the same throughout — see BLEND 1

incorporeal *adj* not composed of matter — see IMMATERIAL 1

incorrect *adj* **1** having an opinion that does not agree with truth or the facts ⟨you're *incorrect* about the date of the final exam—it's next Tuesday, not Wednesday⟩

synonyms mistaken, wrong

related words confused, misguided, misled; erroneous, false; deceived, deluded, tricked

phrases all wet, full of it

near antonyms informed; accurate, exact, precise

antonyms correct, right

2 not appropriate for a particular occasion or situation — see INAPPROPRIATE

3 not being in agreement with what is true — see FALSE 1

incorrectly *adv* in a mistaken or inappropriate way — see WRONGLY

incorrectness *n* **1** the quality or state of being unsuitable or unfitting — see INAPPROPRIATENESS 1

2 the quality or state of not being socially proper — see IMPROPRIETY 1

incorrigible *adj* not capable of being cured or reformed — see HOPELESS 1

increase *n* **1** something added (as by growth) ⟨shortly after he turned 12, he had a sudden height *increase*⟩

synonyms accretion, accrual, addendum, addition, augmentation, boost, expansion, gain, increment, plus, proliferation, raise, rise, supplement

related words accumulation; complement; appendix, continuation, extension, uptrend, upturn; jump

near antonyms deduction

antonyms abatement, decrease, diminishment, lessening, lowering, reduction

2 the act or process of becoming greater in number — see MULTIPLICATION

increase *vb* **1** to make greater in size, amount, or number ⟨if you *increase* the number by two, how much do you have now?⟩

synonyms add (to), aggrandize, amplify, augment, boost, compound, enlarge, escalate, expand, extend, multiply, raise, swell, up

related words skyrocket; blow up, dilate, distend, inflate; elongate, lengthen, prolong, protract; enhance, heighten, intensify, magnify; complement, supplement; beef (up), reinforce, strengthen; maximize; accumulate, amass, collect; follow up, parlay

near antonyms abbreviate, abridge, curtail, shorten; compress, condense, constrict, cut back, retrench

antonyms abate, contract, decrease, diminish, lessen, lower, reduce, subtract (from)

2 to become greater in extent, volume, amount,

THESAURUS

or number ⟨the number of Internet users *increased* rapidly during the 1990s⟩
synonyms accumulate, appreciate, balloon, build (up), burgeon, enlarge, escalate, expand, mount, multiply, mushroom, proliferate, rise, snowball, swell, wax
related words rocket, skyrocket; heighten, intensify; blow up, distend, inflate; crest, peak, surge
antonyms contract, decrease, diminish, lessen, wane

increased *adj* being at a higher level than average — see HIGH 2

incredible *adj* too extraordinary or improbable to believe ⟨she came in on Monday with an *incredible* story about monsters eating her homework⟩
synonyms fantastic, implausible, inconceivable, unbelievable, unconvincing, unimaginable, unthinkable
related words doubtful, dubious, far-fetched, fishy, flimsy, questionable, suspect, unlikely, unreasonable; hopeless, impossible; absurd, outlandish, preposterous, ridiculous; indefensible, insupportable, untenable
near antonyms likely, possible, probable; reasonable
antonyms believable, conceivable, convincing, credible, imaginable, plausible

incredulity *n* refusal to accept as true — see DISBELIEF

incredulous *adj* inclined to doubt or question claims — see SKEPTICAL 1

increment *n* something added (as by growth) — see INCREASE 1

incremental *adj* 1 proceeding or changing by steps or degrees — see GRADUAL
2 produced by a series of additions of identical or similar things — see CUMULATIVE

incriminate *vb* to make a claim of wrongdoing against — see ACCUSE

incubate *vb* to cover and warm eggs to hatch them — see SET 1

incubus *n* an evil spirit — see DEMON

inculcate *vb* to cause (as a person) to become filled or saturated with a certain quality or principle — see INFUSE

incumbent *adj* forcing one's compliance or participation by or as if by law — see MANDATORY

incurable *adj* not capable of being cured or reformed — see HOPELESS 1

incurious *adj* having or showing a lack of interest or concern — see INDIFFERENT 1

incursion *n* a sudden attack on and entrance into hostile territory — see RAID 1

indecency *n* 1 the quality or state of being obscene — see OBSCENITY 1
2 the quality or state of not being socially proper — see IMPROPRIETY 1

indecent *adj* depicting or referring to sexual matters in a way that is unacceptable in polite society — see OBSCENE 1

indecision *n* the act or an instance of pausing because of uncertainty about the right course of action — see HESITATION

indecorous *adj* not appropriate for a particular occasion or situation — see INAPPROPRIATE

indeed *interj* how surprising, doubtful, or unbelievable — see NO

indeed *adv* 1 without any question ⟨I know that you can *indeed* do better than that⟩
synonyms assuredly, certainly, definitely, doubt-

less, forsooth, incontestably, incontrovertibly, indisputably, really, surely, truly, undeniably, undoubtedly, unquestionably
related words conceivably, likely, perhaps, possibly, probably; clearly, obviously, unmistakably
phrases by all means, for sure
2 not merely this but also — see EVEN

indefatigable *adj* showing no signs of weariness even after long hard effort — see TIRELESS

indefatigably *adv* with great effort or determination — see HARD 1

indefensible *adj* too bad to be excused or justified — see INEXCUSABLE

indefinable *adj* beyond the power to describe — see INDESCRIBABLE

indefinite *adj* 1 being or seeming to be without limits — see INFINITE
2 not clearly expressed — see VAGUE 1
3 not seen or understood clearly — see FAINT 1

indelicacy *n* the quality or state of lacking refinement or good taste — see VULGARITY 1

indelicateness *n* the quality or state of lacking refinement or good taste — see VULGARITY 1

indemnification *n* payment to another for a loss or injury — see COMPENSATION 1

indemnify *vb* to provide (someone) with a just payment for loss or injury — see COMPENSATE 1

indemnity *n* payment to another for a loss or injury — see COMPENSATION 1

indentation *n* 1 a sunken area forming a separate space — see HOLE 1
2 a V-shaped cut usually on an edge or a surface — see NOTCH 1

indented *adj* curved inward — see HOLLOW

independence *n* 1 the ability to care for one's self — see SELF-SUFFICIENCY
2 the state of being free from the control or power of another — see FREEDOM 1

independent *adj* 1 able to take care of oneself without outside help — see SELF-SUFFICIENT
2 not being under the rule or control of another — see FREE 1

independently *adv* without aid or support — see ALONE 1

in-depth *adj* covering everything or all important points — see ENCYCLOPEDIC

indescribable *adj* beyond the power to describe ⟨the *indescribable* immensity of Mount Everest⟩
synonyms incommunicable, indefinable, ineffable, inexpressible, nameless, unspeakable, unutterable
related words inconceivable, incredible, unbelievable, unimaginable, unthinkable; characterless, featureless, nondescript
near antonyms conceivable, imaginable, thinkable
antonyms communicable, definable, expressible, speakable

indestructible *adj* impossible to destroy ⟨diamonds are widely considered to be *indestructible*, because they are one of the hardest known substances⟩
synonyms imperishable, inextinguishable
related words incorruptible; deathless, immortal, perpetual, undying; indelible; durable, enduring, lasting, permanent, unbreakable; strong, sturdy, tough
near antonyms mortal; impermanent, transient, transitory; breakable, delicate, flimsy, fragile, frail
antonyms destructible, extinguishable, perishable

index *n* an arrow-shaped piece on a dial or scale for registering information — see POINTER 1

index *vb* to put (someone or something) on a list — see ¹LIST 2

Indian *n* a member of any of the native peoples of the western hemisphere usually not including the Eskimos — see AMERICAN INDIAN

indicate *vb* to convey an idea indirectly — see HINT

indication *n* a slight or indirect pointing to something (as a solution or explanation) — see HINT 1

indicative *adj* indicating something ⟨a wide-eyed look that is *indicative* of his constant curiosity⟩
synonyms denotative, denoting, significant, signifying, telltale
related words alluding, allusive, referring; characteristic, symptomatic; demonstrative, exhibiting, expressive; symbolic (*also* symbolical); connoting, hinting, implying, insinuating, suggestive

indicator *n* an arrow-shaped piece on a dial or scale for registering information — see POINTER 1

indict *vb* to make a claim of wrongdoing against — see ACCUSE

indictment *n* a formal claim of criminal wrongdoing against a person — see CHARGE 1

indifference *n* lack of interest or concern ⟨he felt only *indifference* towards his schoolwork⟩
synonyms apathy, casualness, disinterestedness, disregard, insouciance, nonchalance, unconcern
related words halfheartedness, lukewarmness; carelessness, heedlessness, recklessness, unawareness; lethargy, listlessness; calmness, detachment, dispassion; callousness, hardheartedness, hardness, insensitivity; impassivity, phlegm; aloofness, coldness
near antonyms attentiveness, awareness, conscientiousness, heedfulness; sensitivity, warmheartedness; bias, partiality, prejudice; ardor, fervency, passion, warmth, zeal
antonyms concern, interest, regard

indifferent *adj* 1 having or showing a lack of interest or concern ⟨*indifferent* about the result of the football game⟩
synonyms apathetic, casual, disinterested, incurious, insouciant, nonchalant, perfunctory, unconcerned, uncurious, uninterested
related words halfhearted, lukewarm; aloof, cold, numb, remote, unemotional; calm, detached, dispassionate; careless, heedless, mindless; impassive, phlegmatic, stoic (*or* stoical), stolid; lethargic, listless; unawed, undazzled, unimpressed
near antonyms attentive, aware, conscientious, heedful, mindful; caring, sensitive, warmhearted; ardent, fervent, passionate, warm, zealous
antonyms concerned, interested
2 of average to below average quality — see MEDIOCRE 1

indigence *n* the state of lacking sufficient money or material possessions — see POVERTY 1

indigenous *adj* belonging to a particular place by birth or origin — see NATIVE 1

indigent *adj* lacking money or material possessions — see POOR 1

indignant *adj* feeling or showing anger — see ANGRY

indignation *n* an intense emotional state of displeasure with someone or something — see ANGER

indignity *n* an act or expression showing scorn and usually intended to hurt another's feelings — see INSULT

indirect *adj* not straightforward or direct ⟨the cab driver took a very *indirect* route to the hotel⟩ ⟨a long-winded, *indirect* answer to a very simple question⟩
synonyms circuitous, circular, roundabout
related words crooked, serpentine, sinuous, tortuous, twisting, winding; meandering, rambling, wandering; circumlocutory, long-winded, prolix, verbose; deceitful, deceptive, devious, dishonest, duplicitous, insidious, misleading, sneaky, underhand, underhanded; calculating, crafty, cunning, subtle, tricky
near antonyms candid, forthright, frank, honest, open, plain, unconcealed, undisguised
antonyms direct, straight, straightforward

indiscreet *adj* showing poor judgment especially in personal relationships or social situations ⟨telling a friend's secrets is *indiscreet,* and unkind as well⟩
synonyms ill-advised, imprudent, inadvisable, injudicious, tactless, unadvisable, unwise
related words dumb, idiotic, moronic, stupid; inconsiderate, thoughtless; ill-mannered, improper, inappropriate, indecorous, unbecoming, uncivil, unseemly; foolish, harebrained, nonsensical, preposterous, senseless, silly
near antonyms intelligent, logical, rational, sensible, smart, sound; appropriate, becoming, civil, decorous, proper, seemly; sage, sane, sapient
antonyms advisable, discreet, judicious, prudent, tactful, wise

indiscretion *n* a socially improper or unsuitable act or remark — see IMPROPRIETY 2

indispensable *adj* impossible to do without — see ESSENTIAL 1

indisposed *adj* 1 having doubts about the wisdom of doing something — see HESITANT
2 temporarily suffering from a disorder of the body — see SICK 1

indisposition *n* the condition of not being in good health — see SICKNESS 1

indisputable *adj* not capable of being challenged or proved wrong — see IRREFUTABLE

indisputably *adv* without any question — see INDEED 1

indistinct *adj* not seen or understood clearly — see FAINT 1

indistinguishable *adj* 1 not perceptible by a sense or by the mind — see IMPERCEPTIBLE
2 not seen or understood clearly — see FAINT 1
3 resembling another in every respect — see SAME 1

individual *adj* 1 of, relating to, or belonging to a single person ⟨everyone has his or her own *individual* opinion about the subject, but you will have to work together⟩
synonyms individualized, particular, peculiar, personal, personalized, private, privy, separate, singular, unique
related words characteristic, distinctive, intimate; identifying, idiosyncratic; special, specific; independent, nonconformist, self-directed, self-sufficient; custom, customized, specialized
near antonyms broad, prevailing, prevalent, widespread; common, normal, regular, typical
antonyms general, generic, popular, public, shared, universal
2 not the same or shared — see SEPARATE 1
3 serving to identify as belonging to an individual or group — see CHARACTERISTIC 1

individual *n* **1** a member of the human race — see HUMAN

2 one that has a real and independent existence — see ENTITY

individualist *n* a person who does not conform to generally accepted standards or customs — see NONCONFORMIST 1

individuality *n* the set of qualities that make a person different from other people ⟨her *individuality* showed through in everything she did⟩

synonyms character, identity, personality, selfhood, self-identity

related words distinctiveness, oneness, peculiarity, separateness, singleness, singularity, uniqueness; disposition, humor, nature, temper, temperament; independence

near antonyms conformity, conventionality

individualized *adj* of, relating to, or belonging to a single person — see INDIVIDUAL 1

indoctrinate *vb* to cause to acquire knowledge or skill in some field — see TEACH

indolence *n* an inclination not to do work or engage in activities — see LAZINESS

indolent *adj* not easily aroused to action or work — see LAZY

indomitable *adj* incapable of being defeated, overcome, or subdued — see INVINCIBLE

indubitable *adj* not capable of being challenged or proved wrong — see IRREFUTABLE

induce *vb* **1** to be the cause of (a situation, action, or state of mind) — see EFFECT

2 to cause (someone) to agree with a belief or course of action by using arguments or earnest requests — see PERSUADE

inducement *n* the act of reasoning or pleading with someone to accept a belief or course of action — see PERSUASION 1

inducing *n* the act of reasoning or pleading with someone to accept a belief or course of action — see PERSUASION 1

induct *vb* to put into an office or welcome into an organization with special ceremonies — see INSTALL 1

inductee *n* a person forced or required to enroll in military service — see CONSCRIPT

induction *n* the process or an instance of being formally placed in an office or organization — see INSTALLATION 1

indulge *vb* to give in to (a desire) ⟨the grandparents generally *indulged* the child's wishes⟩

synonyms cater (to), gratify, humor

related words bask, luxuriate, revel, wallow; coddle, mollycoddle, pamper, spoil; delight, please, pleasure; sate, satiate, satisfy

near antonyms bridle, check, constrain, curb, inhibit, restrain, stifle

indulgence *n* **1** an act of kind assistance — see FAVOR 1

2 something adding to pleasure or comfort but not absolutely necessary — see LUXURY 1

industrious *adj* involved in often constant activity — see BUSY 1

industriously *adv* with great effort or determination — see HARD 1

industriousness *n* attentive and persistent effort — see DILIGENCE

industry *n* attentive and persistent effort — see DILIGENCE

inebriate *adj* being under the influence of alcohol — see DRUNK 1

inebriate *n* a person who makes a habit of getting drunk — see DRUNK

inebriated *adj* being under the influence of alcohol — see DRUNK

ineffable *adj* beyond the power to describe — see INDESCRIBABLE

ineffective *adj* **1** not producing the desired result ⟨an *ineffective* effort to move the bookcase⟩

synonyms ineffectual, inefficient, inexpedient

related words abortive, bootless, fruitless, futile, nonproductive, pointless, unavailing, unproductive, unprofitable, unsuccessful, useless, worthless

near antonyms availing, beneficial, helpful, productive, profitable, successful, useful, worthwhile

antonyms effective, effectual, efficacious, efficient, expedient

2 producing no results — see FUTILE

ineffectual *adj* **1** not producing the desired result — see INEFFECTIVE 1

2 producing no results — see FUTILE

inefficient *adj* not producing the desired result — see INEFFECTIVE 1

inelegant *adj* **1** lacking social grace and assurance — see AWKWARD 1

2 marked by an obvious lack of style or good taste — see TACKY 1

inept *adj* **1** lacking qualities (as knowledge, skill, or ability) required to do a job — see INCOMPETENT

2 not appropriate for a particular occasion or situation — see INAPPROPRIATE

3 showing or marked by a lack of skill and tact (as in dealing with a situation) — see AWKWARD 2

ineptitude *n* the lack of sufficient ability, power, or means — see INABILITY

inequity *n* the state of being unfair or unjust — see INJUSTICE 1

inert *adj* **1** not being in a state of use, activity, or employment — see INACTIVE 2

2 slow to move or act — see INACTIVE 1

inertia *n* an inclination not to do work or engage in activities — see LAZINESS

inertness *n* lack of action or activity — see INACTION

inescapable *adj* impossible to avoid or evade — see INEVITABLE

inescapably *adv* because of necessity — see NEEDS

inevitable *adj* impossible to avoid or evade ⟨getting wet is *inevitable* if you are going to try to give your dog a bath⟩

synonyms certain, inescapable, necessary, sure, unavoidable

related words decided, definite, settled; likely, possible, probable; destined, fated, foreordained, predestined, predetermined, preordained; inexorable, relentless, unremitting

phrases in the bag

near antonyms preventable (*also* preventible); doubtful, dubious, questionable, shaky, unclear; undecided, unsettled; undependable, unreliable; improbable, unlikely

antonyms avoidable, escapable, uncertain, unsure

inevitably *adv* because of necessity — see NEEDS

inexact *adj* **1** not precisely correct ⟨a thousand is an *inexact* figure for the number of islands in the St. Lawrence River⟩

synonyms imprecise, inaccurate, loose

related words approximate; erroneous, false, incorrect, off, wrong; general, indefinable, indefinite, indeterminate, indistinct, undefined, undetermined, unsettled, vague; faulty, flawed, mistaken; specious; distorted, fallacious, misleading; doubtful, dubious, questionable, uncertain; inconclusive, indecisive; debatable, disputable; invalidated, unconfirmed, unsubstantiated, unsupported

near antonyms certain, incontestable, indubitable, positive, sure, undeniable, unquestionable; correct, errorless, factual, right, sound, true, valid; clear-cut, decisive, definable, defined, definite; incontrovertible, indisputable, irrefutable; absolute, unqualified; confirmed, corroborated, determined, established, substantiated, supported, validated

antonyms accurate, dead, exact, precise
2 not being in agreement with what is true — see FALSE 1

inexcusable *adj* too bad to be excused or justified ⟨spitting at a teacher is *inexcusable* behavior and will be severely punished⟩
synonyms indefensible, unforgivable, unjustifiable, unpardonable, unwarrantable
related words insufferable, insupportable, intolerable, unbearable, unendurable; abominable, atrocious, heinous, monstrous, outrageous, scandalous, shocking, egregious, flagrant, glaring, gross, rank; unacceptable, untenable; black, evil, iniquitous, vicious, wicked; base, contemptible, deplorable, despicable, dirty, execrable, ignoble, reprobate, vile, wretched; cruel, nasty, blamable, blameworthy, censurable, reprehensible; banned, barred, condemned, disallowed, forbidden, interdicted, outlawed, prohibited, proscribed
near antonyms acceptable, tolerable; authorized, legal, permissible; allowed, permitted, tolerated; approved, endorsed, sanctioned; abetted, encouraged, promoted, supported; ethical, good, moral, virtuous
antonyms defensible, excusable, forgivable, justifiable, pardonable

inexhaustible *adj* showing no signs of weariness even after long hard effort — see TIRELESS

inexpedient *adj* not producing the desired result — see INEFFECTIVE 1

inexpensive *adj* costing little — see CHEAP 1

inexperienced *adj* **1** lacking in adult experience or maturity — see CALLOW
2 lacking or showing a lack of expert skill — see AMATEURISH

inexpert *adj* **1** lacking or showing a lack of expert skill — see AMATEURISH
2 lacking qualities (as knowledge, skill, or ability) required to do a job — see INCOMPETENT
3 showing or marked by a lack of skill and tact (as in dealing with a situation) — see AWKWARD 2

inexplicable *adj* impossible to explain ⟨an *inexplicable* desire for ice cream at two in the morning⟩
synonyms unaccountable, unexplainable
related words indefinable, indescribable, inexpressible; enigmatic (*also* enigmatical), impenetrable, incomprehensible, inscrutable, mysterious, unfathomable, unknowable; irrational, unreasonable, unsound; foolish, mindless, senseless; absurd, odd, peculiar, strange, unusual, weird
near antonyms logical, rational, reasonable, understandable; sane, sensible, wise; compelling, convincing, persuasive, plausible, satisfying; con-

firmed, corroborated, determined, established, explained, substantiated, validated
antonyms accountable, explainable, explicable

inexpressible *adj* beyond the power to describe — see INDESCRIBABLE

inexpressive *adj* not expressing any emotion — see BLANK 1

inextinguishable *adj* impossible to destroy — see INDESTRUCTIBLE

infallible *adj* **1** not being or likely to be wrong ⟨a teacher with an *infallible* memory for names⟩
synonyms unerring, unfailing
related words errorless, faultless, flawless, impeccable; certain, foolproof, perfect, sure; dependable, reliable
near antonyms defective, faulty, flawed, imperfect; undependable, unreliable
antonyms fallible
2 not likely to fail ⟨an *infallible* cure for hiccups⟩
synonyms certain, sure, unfailing
related words dependable, reliable, surefire; deadly, unerring
near antonyms doubtful, questionable, uncertain
antonyms fallible

infamous *adj* not respectable — see DISREPUTABLE

infamy *n* the state of having lost the esteem of others — see DISGRACE 1

infant *n* a recently born person — see BABY

infantile *adj* having or showing the annoying qualities (as silliness) associated with children — see CHILDISH

infatuated (with) *adj* filled with an intense or excessive love for — see ENAMORED (OF)

infatuation *n* a strong but often short-lived liking for another person — see CRUSH 1

infectious *adj* exciting a similar feeling or reaction in others — see CONTAGIOUS 2

infelicitous *adj* not appropriate for a particular occasion or situation — see INAPPROPRIATE

infelicity *n* the quality or state of being unsuitable or unfitting — see INAPPROPRIATENESS 1

infer *vb* **1** to form an opinion through reasoning and information ⟨he *inferred* that she had left because her coat was gone⟩
synonyms conclude, deduce, extrapolate, gather, judge, reason, understand
related words conjecture, guess, speculate, surmise; construe, interpret; contemplate, rationalize, think; ascertain, dope (out), find out
phrases draw a conclusion
2 to convey an idea indirectly — see HINT

inferable *adj* being or provable by reasoning in which the conclusion follows necessarily from given information — see DEDUCTIVE

inference *n* an opinion arrived at through a process of reasoning — see CONCLUSION 1

inferior *adj* **1** situated lower down ⟨creatures that inhabit the dark, *inferior* depths of the ocean⟩
synonyms lower, nether
related words lowest, nethermost; underlying
near antonyms highest, uppermost; overhanging, overhead
antonyms higher, superior, upper
2 of little or less value or merit ⟨a girl who has always felt *inferior* to her older sister⟩
synonyms mean, minor, secondary, second-class, second-rate
related words junior, lesser, lower, petty, smaller, subordinate, under; average, common, fair, mid-

dling, ordinary; amiss, bad, defective, unsatisfactory, wrong; deficient, inadequate, insufficient, unacceptable; littler, slighter, smaller; jerkwater, one-horse, two-bit

near antonyms major, more, primary, senior; choice, exceptional, first-class, first-rate, high-grade, premium, prime; acceptable, adequate, sufficient

antonyms greater, higher, superior

3 belonging to the class of people of low social or economic rank — see IGNOBLE 1

4 falling short of a standard — see BAD 1

5 having not so great importance or rank as another — see LESSER

6 of low quality — see CHEAP 2

inferior *n* one who is of lower rank and typically under the authority of another — see UNDERLING

inferno *n* a destructive burning — see FIRE

infertile *adj* **1** not able to produce fruit or offspring — see STERILE 1

2 producing inferior or only a small amount of vegetation — see BARREN 1

infest *vb* to spread or swarm over in a troublesome manner ⟨called in an exterminator because the house was *infested* with ants⟩

synonyms overrun

related words beset, overspread, overwhelm; abound, crawl, teem; annoy, pester, plague; contaminate, infect

infidelity *n* **1** lack of faithfulness especially to one's husband or wife ⟨*infidelity* can lead to divorce⟩

synonyms disloyalty, faithlessness, falseness, falsity, inconstancy, perfidiousness, perfidy, unfaithfulness

related words adultery; betrayal, double-cross, double-dealing, duplicity, sellout, treachery, treason; deceit, deception, lying

near antonyms staunchness, steadfastness; dependability, reliability; honesty, trustworthiness

antonyms allegiance, constancy, devotedness, devotion, faith, faithfulness, fealty, fidelity, loyalty

2 the act or fact of violating the trust or confidence of another — see BETRAYAL

infiltrate *vb* to introduce in a gradual, secret, or clever way — see INSINUATE

infinite *adj* being or seeming to be without limits ⟨the *infinite* expanse of outer space⟩

synonyms boundless, endless, illimitable, immeasurable, indefinite, limitless, measureless, unbounded, unfathomable, unlimited

related words abysmal, bottomless; countless, incalculable, inestimable, innumerable, unmeasured; inexhaustible; far-flung, immense, vast

near antonyms fathomable, measurable; depthless, shallow, superficial

antonyms bounded, circumscribed, confined, definite, finite, limited, restricted

infinitesimal *adj* very small in size — see TINY

infinity *n* endless time — see ETERNITY 1

infirm *adj* lacking bodily strength — see WEAK 1

infirmity *n* **1** an abnormal state that disrupts a plant's or animal's normal bodily functioning — see DISEASE

2 the quality or state of lacking physical strength or vigor — see WEAKNESS 1

inflame *vb* **1** to make angry — see ANGER

2 to set (something) on fire — see BURN 2

inflamed *adj* **1** being on fire — see ABLAZE 1

2 feeling or showing anger — see ANGRY

inflammable *adj* capable of catching or being set on fire — see COMBUSTIBLE

inflexibility *n* the quality or state of being demanding or unyielding (as in discipline or criticism) — see SEVERITY

inflexible *adj* **1** not capable of changing or being changed ⟨the *inflexible* law of gravity⟩

synonyms fixed, hard-and-fast, immutable, invariable, unalterable, unchangeable

related words changeless, constant, determinate, established, set, settled, stable, steadfast, steady, unaltered, unchanging, unvarying; immovable, unmovable

near antonyms adaptable, adjustable; fickle, fluctuating, inconstant, uncertain, unstable, varying

antonyms alterable, changeable, flexible, mutable, variable

2 incapable of or highly resistant to bending — see STIFF 1

3 not allowing for any exceptions or loosening of standards — see RIGID 1

4 sticking to an opinion, purpose, or course of action in spite of reason, arguments, or persuasion — see OBSTINATE

inflow *n* a flowing or coming in — see INFLUX

influence *n* **1** the power to direct the thinking or behavior of others usually indirectly ⟨a mayor who doesn't hesitate to use her *influence* to get business leaders behind civic improvements⟩

synonyms authority, clout, pull, sway, weight

related words command, dominance, dominion, mastery, predominance, scepter, sovereignty, supremacy; consequence, eminence, importance, moment; impact, impression, mark

near antonyms helplessness, impotence, powerlessness, weakness

2 the power to bring about a result on another — see EFFECT 2

influence *vb* to act upon (a person or a person's feelings) so as to cause a response — see ¹AFFECT 1

influential *adj* **1** having power over the minds or behavior of others ⟨in light of the effect that they have had, religious leaders such as Jesus and Muḥammad must be regarded as among the most *influential* people ever⟩

synonyms authoritative, forceful, weighty

related words controlling, dominating, masterful; dominant, predominant, sovereign, supreme; eminent, important, momentous

near antonyms helpless, impotent, powerless, weak; incapable, unable

2 having great power or influence — see IMPORTANT 2

influx *n* a flowing or coming in ⟨a sudden *influx* of people⟩

synonyms flux, inflow, inrush

related words deluge, flood, flow, inundation, overflow, spate, torrent; rush, stampede; flow, river, stream, tide

near antonyms emigration, exodus, flight

antonyms outflow, outpouring

inform *vb* **1** to give information (as to the authorities) about another's improper or unlawful activities — see SQUEAL 1

2 to give information to — see ENLIGHTEN 1

informal *adj* **1** not rigidly following established form, custom, or rules ⟨an *informal* meeting allowed everyone to get acquainted⟩

synonyms irregular, unceremonious, unconventional, unorthodox
related words unauthorized, unofficial; casual, easygoing, lax, loose, relaxed
near antonyms correct, decorous, proper; constrained, inhibited, restrained, rigid, stiff, stuffy, uptight
antonyms ceremonial, ceremonious, conventional, formal, orthodox, regular, routine
2 not designed for special occasions — see CASUAL 1
3 used in or suitable for speech and not formal writing — see COLLOQUIAL 1
informant *n* a person who provides secret information about another's wrongdoing — see INFORMER
information *n* a report of recent events or facts not previously known — see NEWS
informational *adj* providing useful information or knowledge — see INFORMATIVE
informative *adj* providing useful information or knowledge ⟨some Web sites for family vacation resorts are very *informative* and some are practically useless⟩
synonyms educational, educative, informational, instructional, instructive
related words comprehensive, detailed, full; edifying, elucidative, enlightening, explanatory, illuminating; chatty, gossipy, newsy; availing, beneficial, constructive, helpful, profitable; practical, serviceable, usable, useful, worthwhile
near antonyms impractical, unhelpful, unusable, useless
antonyms uninstructive
informed *adj* **1** based on sound reasoning or information — see GOOD 1
2 having information especially as a result of study or experience — see FAMILIAR 2
informer *n* a person who provides secret information about another's wrongdoing ⟨the *informer* who told the police about that conspiracy angered a lot of dangerous people⟩
synonyms betrayer, informant, snitcher, squealer, stool pigeon, talebearer, tattler, tattletale, telltale
related words collaborator; blabbermouth, gossip, gossiper; snoop, snooper, spy; notifier
infraction *n* a failure to uphold the requirements of law, duty, or obligation — see BREACH 1
infrequent *adj* not often occurring or repeated ⟨a shut-in who made *infrequent* trips to the store⟩
synonyms occasional, rare, sporadic
related words scarce, scattered, uncommon, unique, unusual; choppy, discontinuous, erratic, fitful, intermittent, irregular, spasmodic, spotty, unsteady
near antonyms common, ordinary, routine
antonyms frequent
infrequently *adv* not often — see SELDOM
infringe *vb* to fail to keep — see VIOLATE 1
infringement *n* a failure to uphold the requirements of law, duty, or obligation — see BREACH 1
infuriate *vb* to make angry — see ANGER
infuriated *adj* feeling or showing anger — see ANGRY
infuse *vb* to cause (as a person) to become filled or saturated with a certain quality or principle ⟨parents who *infuse* their children with strong moral values⟩
synonyms imbue, inculcate, ingrain, inoculate, invest, steep, suffuse

related words animate, enliven, invigorate; implant, instill, plant; impregnate, permeate, pervade, saturate; deluge, drown, fill, flood, inundate, overwhelm, submerge
near antonyms deprive, divest, strip; clear, empty; eliminate, remove, take away
ingenious *adj* **1** having the skill and imagination to create new things — see CREATIVE 1
2 showing a use of the imagination and creativity especially in inventing — see CLEVER 1
ingeniousness *n* the skill and imagination to create new things — see CREATIVITY 1
ingenuity *n* the skill and imagination to create new things — see CREATIVITY 1
ingenuous *adj* **1** free from any intent to deceive or impress others — see GUILELESS
2 lacking in worldly wisdom or informed judgment — see NAIVE 1
ingenuously *adv* without any attempt to impress by deception or exaggeration — see NATURALLY 3
ingenuousness *n* the quality or state of being simple and sincere — see NAÏVETÉ 1
ingest *vb* **1** to take in as food — see EAT 1
2 to take into the stomach through the mouth and throat — see SWALLOW 1
ingrain *vb* **1** to cause (as a person) to become filled or saturated with a certain quality or principle — see INFUSE
2 to produce a vivid impression of — see ENGRAVE 2
3 to set solidly in or as if in surrounding matter — see ENTRENCH
ingrained *adj* being a part of the innermost nature of a person or thing — see INHERENT
ingratiating *adj* likely to win one's affection ⟨one of the orphans had a most *ingratiating* smile⟩
synonyms disarming, endearing, winning, winsome
related words adorable, charming, likable, lovable; affecting, poignant, touching; adulatory, deferential, groveling (*or* grovelling), kowtowing, obsequious, servile, sycophantic; drooling, slavering, slobbering; soapy, sugary, unctuous
near antonyms alienating, disaffecting, displeasing; repugnant, repulsive; arrogant, disdainful, haughty, insolent, proud, scornful
ingredient *n* one of the parts that make up a whole — see ELEMENT 1
inhabitable *adj* suitable for living in — see LIVABLE
inhabitant *n* one who lives permanently in a place ⟨the *inhabitants* of the town don't like the tourists⟩
synonyms denizen, dweller, habitant, occupant, resident, resider
related words aborigine, native; citizen, national, subject; colonist, émigré (*also* emigré), migrant, newcomer, settler; burgher, townie, villager
near antonyms alien, foreigner; guest, tourist, visitor; defector, escaper, evacuee, exile, expatriate, refugee
antonyms transient
inharmonious *adj* **1** not being in agreement or harmony — see INCONSISTENT
2 marked by or producing a harsh combination of sounds — see DISSONANT
inherent *adj* being a part of the innermost nature of a person or thing ⟨an *inherent* concept of justice⟩
synonyms essential, inborn, inbred, ingrained, innate, integral, intrinsic, natural

THESAURUS

related words basic, constitutional, elemental, fundamental; congenital, hereditary, inherited, inmost, inner, interior; internal; characteristic, distinctive, peculiar; normal, regular, typical

near antonyms alien, foreign; accidental, coincidental, incidental; acquired; superficial, surface; exterior, external

antonyms adventitious, extraneous, extrinsic

inherently *adv* by natural character or ability — see NATURALLY 1

inheritable *adj* genetically passed or capable of being passed from parent to offspring — see HEREDITARY

inheritance *n* something that is or may be inherited ⟨a sense of humor was her *inheritance* from her mother⟩

synonyms bequest, birthright, heritage, legacy, patrimony

related words heirloom; bestowal, gift, offering, present

inherited *adj* genetically passed or capable of being passed from parent to offspring — see HEREDITARY

inheritor *n* a person who has the right to inherit property — see HEIR

inhibit *vb* 1 to create difficulty for the work or activity of — see HAMPER

2 to keep from exceeding a desirable degree or level (as of expression) — see CONTROL 1

3 to steer (a person) from an activity or course of action — see DISCOURAGE 2

inhibition *n* 1 the checking of one's true feelings and impulses when dealing with others — see CONSTRAINT 1

2 something that makes movement or progress more difficult — see ENCUMBRANCE

inhospitable *adj* marked by opposition or ill will — see HOSTILE 1

inhuman *adj* 1 difficult to endure — see HARSH 1

2 having or showing a lack of sympathy or tender feelings — see HARD 1

inhumane *adj* 1 having or showing a lack of sympathy or tender feelings — see HARD 1

2 having or showing the desire to inflict severe pain and suffering on others — see CRUEL 1

inhumanity *n* the willful infliction of pain and suffering on others — see CRUELTY

inimical *adj* 1 marked by opposition or ill will — see HOSTILE 1

2 opposed to one's interests — see ADVERSE 1

inimitable *adj* having no equal or rival for excellence or desirability — see ONLY 1

iniquitous *adj* not conforming to a high moral standard; morally unacceptable — see BAD 2

iniquity *n* 1 immoral conduct or practices harmful or offensive to society — see VICE 1

2 that which is morally unacceptable — see EVIL

initial *adj* coming before all others in time or order — see FIRST 1

initially *adv* in the beginning — see ORIGINALLY

initiate *vb* 1 to be responsible for the creation and early operation or use of — see FOUND

2 to impart knowledge of a new thing or situation to — see ACQUAINT 1

3 to put into an office or welcome into an organization with special ceremonies — see INSTALL 1

initiation *n* the process or an instance of being formally placed in an office or organization — see INSTALLATION 1

initiative *n* readiness to engage in daring or difficult activity — see ENTERPRISE 2

initiator *n* a person who establishes a whole new field of endeavor — see FATHER 2

inject *vb* to put among or between others — see INSERT

injudicious *adj* showing poor judgment especially in personal relationships or social situations — see INDISCREET

injure *vb* 1 to cause bodily damage to ⟨*injured* himself while skiing⟩

synonyms damage, harm, hurt, wound

related words batter, bruise, contuse, gash, gore, lacerate, scald, scar, scathe, tear; cripple, lame, maim, mangle, mutilate; afflict, torment, torture; lay up; blemish, impair, mar, scrape, spoil

near antonyms cure, fix, heal, mend, remedy

2 to reduce the soundness, effectiveness, or perfection of — see DAMAGE 1

injurious *adj* causing or capable of causing harm — see HARMFUL

injury *n* 1 something that causes loss or pain ⟨the harsh words were the worst *injury*⟩

synonyms damage, detriment, harm, hurt

related words disservice, injustice, outrage, wrong; affront, dart, indignity, insult, offense (*or* offence); crippling, mayhem, mutilation; defacement, disablement, disability, disfigurement; abrasion, bruise, bump, contusion, scald, scar, scathe, scrape, scratch, sear

near antonyms healing, recovery; cure, fix, remedy

2 unfair or inadequate treatment of someone or something or an instance of this — see DISSERVICE

injustice *n* 1 the state of being unfair or unjust ⟨the *injustice* of the coach's accusation that I'd been lazy frustrated and angered me⟩

synonyms inequity, unfairness, unjustness

related words dirtiness, foulness

antonyms equity, fairness, justice

2 unfair or inadequate treatment of someone or something or an instance of this — see DISSERVICE

inkling *n* a slight or indirect pointing to something (as a solution or explanation) — see HINT 1

inlet *n* a part of a body of water that extends beyond the general shoreline — see GULF 1

inn *n* a place that provides rooms and usually a public dining room for overnight guests — see HOTEL

innards *n pl* the internal organs of the body — see GUT 1

innate *adj* being a part of the innermost nature of a person or thing — see INHERENT

innately *adv* by natural character or ability — see NATURALLY 1

inner *adj* 1 situated farther in ⟨an *inner* area of the national park that is some distance from the nearest road⟩

synonyms inside, interior, internal, inward

related words inmost, innermost; central, mid, middle

near antonyms outermost, outmost

antonyms exterior, external, outer, outside, outward

2 of or relating to the mind — see MENTAL 1

innocence *n* 1 the quality or state of being free from guilt or blame ⟨the accused criminal eventually proved her *innocence* and was released⟩

'synonyms blamelessness, faultlessness, guiltlessness, impeccability
related words decency, goodness, honesty, incorruptibility, integrity, righteousness, uprightness, virtuousness; morality, virtue; chastity, purity; harmlessness, inoffensiveness
near antonyms blame, fault, responsibility; corruption, criminality, depravity, evil, immorality, reprehensibleness, sinfulness, wickedness; harmfulness, offensiveness
antonyms blameworthiness, culpability, guilt, guiltiness
2 the quality or state of being simple and sincere — see NAÏVETÉ 1
innocent *adj* **1** free from sin ⟨an *innocent* baby⟩
synonyms pure
related words chaste, moral, virtuous; immaculate, spotless, unblemished, unstained, unsullied; decent, ethical, good, honest, honorable, righteous, upright, virtuous; blameless, guiltless
near antonyms lascivious, lewd, lustful, unchaste; evil, immoral, iniquitous, reprobate, unrighteous, wicked; corrupt, debased, debauched, degenerate, depraved, dissolute, erring, fallen, lost, perverted; condemned, damned
antonyms impure, sinful
2 free from guilt or blame ⟨the robbery suspect was found to be *innocent*⟩
synonyms blameless, clear, faultless, guiltless, impeccable, irreproachable
related words absolved, acquitted, cleared, exonerated, vindicated; ethical, law-abiding, moral, righteous, upright, virtuous
phrases in the clear
near antonyms blamable, blameworthy, censurable, culpable, impeachable, indictable, punishable; accused, impeached, indicted; condemned, convicted; hangdog, shamed, shamefaced
antonyms guilty
3 free from any intent to deceive or impress others — see GUILELESS
4 lacking in worldly wisdom or informed judgment — see NAIVE 1
5 not causing injury or hurt — see HARMLESS
innocent *n* an innocent or gentle person — see LAMB
innocently *adv* **1** without any attempt to impress by deception or exaggeration — see NATURALLY 3
2 with purity of thought and deed — see PURELY
innocuous *adj* not causing injury or hurt — see HARMLESS
innovate *vb* to be responsible for the creation and early operation or use of — see FOUND
innovation *n* something (as a device) created for the first time through the use of the imagination — see INVENTION 1
innovative *adj* having the skill and imagination to create new things — see CREATIVE 1
innovator *n* one who creates or introduces something new — see INVENTOR
innumerable *adj* too many to be counted — see COUNTLESS
inoculate *vb* to cause (as a person) to become filled or saturated with a certain quality or principle — see INFUSE
inoffensive *adj* not causing injury or hurt — see HARMLESS
inoperable *adj* **1** not being in working order ⟨we have several *inoperable* cars on the property⟩

synonyms inoperative, malfunctioning, nonfunctional, nonfunctioning, nonoperating
related words broken; off; deactivated, deadlocked, ineffective, ineffectual, nonproductive, unproductive, unusable, unworkable, useless
phrases on the blink, out of commission
near antonyms effective, effectual, employable, performing, producing, productive, serving, usable, useful, viable, workable
antonyms functional, functioning, operable, operating, operational, operative, running, working
2 not capable of being put to use or account — see IMPRACTICAL
inoperative *adj* **1** not being in a state of use, activity, or employment — see INACTIVE 2
2 not being in working order — see INOPERABLE 1
inopportune *adj* occurring before the usual or expected time — see EARLY 2
inopportunely *adv* before the usual or expected time — see EARLY
inordinate *adj* going beyond a normal or acceptable limit in degree or amount — see EXCESSIVE
inordinately *adv* beyond a normal or acceptable limit — see TOO 1
inquest *n* a systematic search for the truth or facts about something — see INQUIRY 1
inquire (into) *vb* to search through or into — see EXPLORE 1
inquire (of) *vb* to put a question or questions to — see ASK 1
inquiry *n* **1** a systematic search for the truth or facts about something ⟨an *inquiry* into the origins of the universe⟩
synonyms delving, examination, exploration, inquest, inquisition, investigation, probe, probing, research, study
related words quest; audit, check; checkup, diagnosis, inspection; hearing, interrogation, trial; feeler, query, question; poll, questionnaire; challenge, cross-examination, grilling, quiz
2 an act or instance of asking for information — see QUESTION 2
inquisition *n* a systematic search for the truth or facts about something — see INQUIRY 1
inquisitive *adj* interested in what is not one's own business — see CURIOUS 1
inquisitiveness *n* an eager desire to find out about things that are often none of one's business — see CURIOSITY 1
inroad *n* a sudden attack on and entrance into hostile territory — see RAID 1
inrush *n* a flowing or coming in — see INFLUX
insane *adj* **1** having or showing a very abnormal or sick state of mind ⟨only an *insane* person would jump off a skyscraper⟩
synonyms balmy, bananas, batty, crackbrained, cracked, crazed, crazy, cuckoo, daffy, daft, demented, deranged, loco, loony (*also* looney), lunatic, mad, maniacal (*also* maniac), mental, moonstruck, nuts, nutty, screwy, unbalanced, unsound, wacky
related words dotty, off; aberrant, delusional, disordered; eccentric, odd, queer, strange; foolish, senseless, witless; irrational, unreasonable; berserk, delirious; depressed; distraught, frantic, frenzied, hysterical
phrases around the bend, off one's rocker, out of one's head (*or* mind)

near antonyms clear, lucid, rational, reasonable; judicious, sensible, wise; healthy, normal
antonyms balanced, sane, sound

2 conceived or made without regard for reason or reality — see FANTASTIC 1

3 showing or marked by a lack of good sense or judgment — see FOOLISH 1

insanity *n* **1** a serious mental disorder that prevents one from living a safe and normal life ⟨his *insanity* requires that he spend the rest of his life in a mental hospital⟩
synonyms aberration, dementia, derangement, lunacy, madness, mania
related words irrationality, unreasonableness; delirium, frenzy, hysteria; neurosis, psychosis, schizophrenia; delusion, hallucination, obsession, phobia; abnormality, unsoundness
near antonyms lucidity, rationality, reasonableness; normality, soundness
antonyms mind, saneness, sanity

2 a foolish act or idea — see FOLLY 1

3 lack of good sense or judgment — see FOOLISHNESS 1

inscribe *vb* **1** to cut (as letters or designs) on a hard surface — see ENGRAVE 1

2 to enter in a list or roll — see ENROLL 1

3 to put (someone or something) on a list — see ¹LIST 2

inscrutable *adj* **1** being beyond one's powers to know, understand, or explain — see MYSTERIOUS 1

2 having an often intentionally veiled or uncertain meaning — see OBSCURE 1

insecure *adj* not tightly fastened, tied, or stretched — see LOOSE 1

insecurity *n* the quality or state of not being firmly fixed in position — see INSTABILITY

insensate *adj* having or showing a lack of sympathy or tender feelings — see HARD 1

insensibility *n* **1** a lack of emotion or emotional expressiveness — see APATHY 1

2 a temporary or permanent state of unconsciousness — see FAINT

insensible *adj* **1** having lost consciousness — see UNCONSCIOUS 1

2 not perceptible by a sense or by the mind — see IMPERCEPTIBLE

insensitive *adj* **1** having or showing a lack of sympathy or tender feelings — see HARD 1

2 lacking in sensation or feeling — see NUMB

inseparability *n* the state of being in a very personal or private relationship — see FAMILIARITY 1

insert *vb* to put among or between others ⟨*inserted* a book in its proper place on the shelf⟩
synonyms fit (in *or* into), inject, insinuate, interject, interpolate, interpose, introduce
related words inlay, inset, install, weave, work (in); cram, sandwich, shove, thrust, wedge; add, append, attach
near antonyms eject, eliminate, exclude, expel, extract, withdraw; deduct, detach, subtract; reject

inside *adj* **1** not known or meant to be known by the general populace — see PRIVATE 1

2 situated farther in — see INNER 1

inside *n* **1** an interior or internal part ⟨the *inside* of the clock features an amazingly complex mechanism⟩
synonyms interior, within
related words bowels, guts, innards; stuffing; recesses; center, core, heart

near antonyms border, boundary, brim, brink, edge, end, extremity, fringe, limit, lip, margin, perimeter, periphery, rim
antonyms exterior, outside

2 *usually* **insides** *pl* the internal organs of the body — see GUT 1

insight *n* the ability to understand inner qualities or relationships — see WISDOM 1

insightful *adj* having or showing deep understanding and intelligent application of knowledge — see WISE 1

insignificant *adj* **1** lacking importance — see UNIMPORTANT

2 so small or unimportant as to warrant little or no attention — see NEGLIGIBLE 1

insincere *adj* not being or expressing what one appears to be or express ⟨the *insincere* compliments of a spiteful gossip⟩
synonyms artificial, backhanded, double-dealing, feigned, hypocritical, left-handed, mealy, mealy-mouthed, two-faced, unctuous
related words empty, hollow, meaningless; deceitful, devious, dishonest, untruthful; facile, glib, superficial; bogus, counterfeit, fake, false, phony (*also* phoney), sham; facetious, jocular
near antonyms candid, direct, forthright, frank, open, plain, straightforward
antonyms genuine, heartfelt, honest, sincere, unfeigned

insincerity *n* the pretending of having virtues, principles, or beliefs that one in fact does not have — see HYPOCRISY

insinuate *vb* **1** to introduce in a gradual, secret, or clever way ⟨the spy *insinuated* himself into the terrorist organization⟩
synonyms infiltrate, slip, sneak, work (in), worm
related words creep, edge, wiggle; insert, interpolate, interpose, introduce

2 to convey an idea indirectly — see HINT

3 to put among or between others — see INSERT

insipid *adj* **1** lacking in taste or flavor ⟨an apple pie with a mushy, *insipid* filling that strongly resembled soggy cardboard⟩
synonyms flat, flavorless, savorless, tasteless
related words bland, dilute, thin, watery, weak; plain, unflavored
near antonyms disgusting, distasteful, loathsome, sickening, unappetizing, unpalatable; appetizing, delectable, delicious, palatable, toothsome; piquant, seasoned, spicy; flavored; heavy, rich
antonyms flavorful, savory, tasty

2 lacking in qualities that make for spirit and character — see WISHY-WASHY 1

insist *vb* to state as a fact usually forcefully — see CLAIM 1

insist (on) *vb* to ask for (something) earnestly or with authority — see DEMAND 1

insistence *n* a solemn and often public declaration of the truth or existence of something — see PROTESTATION

insistent *adj* continuing despite difficulties, opposition, or discouragement — see PERSISTENT

insolence *n* **1** disrespectful or argumentative talk given in response to a command or request — see BACK TALK

2 rude behavior — see DISCOURTESY

insolent *adj* displaying or marked by rude boldness — see NERVY 1

insouciance *n* lack of interest or concern — see INDIFFERENCE

insouciant *adj* **1** having or showing a lack of concern or seriousness — see CAREFREE

2 having or showing a lack of interest or concern — see INDIFFERENT 1

inspect *vb* to look over closely (as for judging quality or condition) ⟨*inspected* the animal before the show⟩

synonyms audit, check (out), examine, review, scan, scrutinize, survey

related words notice, observe, watch; peruse, pore (over); analyze, dissect; delve (into), explore, investigate, probe, research, study; categorize, classify

phrases go over

near antonyms skim; glance (at *or* over); miss, overlook

inspection *n* a close look at or over someone or something in order to judge condition ⟨a room *inspection* should include looking under the bed⟩

synonyms audit, check, checkup, examination, review, scan, scrutiny, survey

related words analysis, dissection; exploration, investigation, probe, research, study; inquisition, interrogation; perusal; observation, surveillance, watch

inspire *vb* to fill with courage or strength of purpose — see ENCOURAGE 1

inspiring *adj* causing great emotional or mental stimulation — see EXCITING 1

instability *n* the quality or state of not being firmly fixed in position ⟨the *instability* of the bridge became apparent when it suddenly collapsed⟩

synonyms insecurity, precariousness, shakiness, unsteadiness

related words insubstantiality, unsoundness; changeability, inconstancy, mutability

near antonyms firmness, soundness, substantiality

antonyms fixedness, security, stability, steadiness

install *vb* **1** to put into an office or welcome into an organization with special ceremonies ⟨*installed* her as the new principal⟩

synonyms baptize, inaugurate, induct, initiate, instate, invest

related words swear in; accept, admit, receive, take in; enlist, enroll (*also* enrol)

near antonyms can, discharge, fire, terminate; muster out

2 to establish or place comfortably or snugly — see ENSCONCE 1

installation *n* **1** the process or an instance of being formally placed in an office or organization ⟨the *installation* of a new president takes place once every four years⟩

synonyms baptism, inaugural, inauguration, induction, initiation, installment, investiture

related words enlistment, enrollment; promotion

near antonyms discharge, removal

2 a structure that is designed and built for a particular purpose — see FACILITY

installment *n* the process or an instance of being formally placed in an office or organization — see INSTALLATION 1

instance *n* one of a group or collection that shows what the whole is like — see EXAMPLE

instance *vb* **1** to give as an example — see QUOTE 1

2 to make reference to or speak about briefly but specifically — see MENTION 1

3 to show or make clear by using examples — see ILLUSTRATE 1

instant *adj* **1** done or occurring without any noticeable lapse in time — see INSTANTANEOUS

2 needing immediate attention — see ACUTE 2

instant *n* a very small space of time ⟨it all happened in an *instant*⟩

synonyms flash, jiffy, minute, moment, second, shake, split second, trice, twinkle, twinkling, wink

related words microsecond, nanosecond; snatch, spurt

near antonyms aeon (*or* eon), age, eternity; infinity, lifetime

instantaneous *adj* done or occurring without any noticeable lapse in time ⟨the thunder following the lightning was nearly *instantaneous*⟩

synonyms immediate, instant, straightaway

related words summary; fast, hit-and-run, prompt, quick, rapid, speedy, swift

near antonyms dilatory, tardy; slow, sluggish; prolonged, protracted; deferred, delayed

instantly *adv* without delay — see IMMEDIATELY

instate *vb* to put into an office or welcome into an organization with special ceremonies — see INSTALL 1

instead *adv* as a substitute ⟨I was offered a ride, but I chose to walk *instead*⟩

synonyms first, rather

related words alternately, alternatively

instigate *vb* **1** to cause or encourage the development of — see INCITE 1

2 to rouse to strong feeling or action — see PROVOKE 1

instigating *adj* serving or likely to arouse a strong reaction — see PROVOCATIVE

instigation *n* **1** something that arouses a strong response from another — see PROVOCATION 1

2 something that arouses action or activity — see IMPULSE

instigator *n* a person who stirs up public feelings especially of discontent — see AGITATOR

instinctive *adj* done instantly and without conscious thought or decision — see AUTOMATIC 1

instinctual *adj* done instantly and without conscious thought or decision — see AUTOMATIC 1

institute *n* **1** a group of persons formally joined together for some common interest — see ASSOCIATION 2

2 a public organization with a particular purpose or function — see INSTITUTION 1

institute *vb* to be responsible for the creation and early operation or use of — see FOUND

instituter *or* **institutor** *n* a person who establishes a whole new field of endeavor — see FATHER 2

institution *n* **1** a public organization with a particular purpose or function ⟨a charitable *institution* devoted to raising funds to feed the hungry⟩

synonyms establishment, foundation, institute

related words body, collective, group; corporation, enterprise; charity, philanthropy; think tank

2 a group of persons formally joined together for some common interest — see ASSOCIATION 2

instruct *vb* **1** to cause to acquire knowledge or skill in some field — see TEACH

2 to give information to — see ENLIGHTEN 1

3 to issue orders to (someone) by right of authority — see COMMAND 1

instruction *n* **1** a statement of what to do that must be obeyed by those concerned — see COMMAND 1

2 the act or process of imparting knowledge or skills to another — see EDUCATION 1

instructional *adj* providing useful information or knowledge — see INFORMATIVE

instructive *adj* providing useful information or knowledge — see INFORMATIVE

instructor *n* a person whose occupation is to give formal instruction in a school — see TEACHER

instrument *n* **1** a written or printed paper giving information about or proof of something — see CERTIFICATE

2 an article intended for use in work — see IMPLEMENT

3 something used to achieve an end — see AGENT 1

instrumentalist *n* a person who plays a musical instrument — see MUSICIAN 1

instrumentality *n* something used to achieve an end — see AGENT 1

insubordinate *adj* given to resisting authority or another's control — see DISOBEDIENT

insubordination *n* refusal to obey — see DISOBEDIENCE

insubstantial *adj* **1** being of a material lacking in sturdiness or substance — see FLIMSY 1

2 not composed of matter — see IMMATERIAL 1

insufferable *adj* more than can be put up with — see UNBEARABLE

insufficiency *n* a falling short of an essential or desirable amount or number — see DEFICIENCY

insufficient *adj* not coming up to a usual standard or meeting a particular need — see SHORT 3

insular *adj* not broad or open in views or opinions — see NARROW 2

insulate *vb* to set or keep apart from others — see ISOLATE

insulation *n* the state of being alone or kept apart from others — see ISOLATION

insult *n* an act or expression showing scorn and usually intended to hurt another's feelings ⟨yelling an *insult* at the bully was not a very smart thing to do⟩
synonyms affront, barb, dart, dig, epithet, indignity, name, offense (*or* offence), outrage, put-down, sarcasm, slight, slur
related words gibe (*or* jibe), jeer, sneer, taunt; abuse, invective, vituperation; disapproval, opprobrium; disgrace, dishonor, shame; attack, criticism, slam; torment, torture
near antonyms accolade, commendation, compliment; acclaim, applause, praise; adulation, flattery

insult *vb* to cause hurt feelings or deep resentment in ⟨*insulted* the people by saying their home was ugly⟩
synonyms affront, dis [*slang*], offend, outrage, slight, wound
related words cut, snub; displease, distress, disturb, hurt, pain, trouble, upset; jeer, mock, ridicule, sneer (at), taunt; defame, disparage, libel, malign, revile, slander, slur, smear; oppress, persecute, torment, torture
near antonyms acclaim, applaud, approve, hail; commend, compliment, eulogize, praise; adulate, flatter; exalt, glorify, honor; delight, gratify, please, satisfy

insupportable *adj* more than can be put up with — see UNBEARABLE

insure *vb* to make sure, certain, or safe — see ENSURE

insurgency *n* open fighting against authority (as one's own government) — see REBELLION

insurgent *adj* taking part in a rebellion — see REBELLIOUS 1

insurgent *n* a person who rises up against authority — see REBEL

insurmountable *adj* incapable of being defeated, overcome, or subdued — see INVINCIBLE

insurrection *n* open fighting against authority (as one's own government) — see REBELLION

insurrectionary *adj* taking part in a rebellion — see REBELLIOUS 1

insurrectionary *n* a person who rises up against authority — see REBEL

insurrectionist *n* a person who rises up against authority — see REBEL

intact *adj* not lacking any part or member that properly belongs to it — see COMPLETE 1

intangible *adj* not capable of being perceived by the sense of touch ⟨electrical energy is completely *intangible*⟩
synonyms impalpable
related words bodiless, immaterial, incorporeal, insubstantial, unsubstantial; ethereal, spiritual, unreal
near antonyms tactile; corporeal, physical; embodied, material, real, solid, substantial
antonyms palpable, tangible, touchable

integer *n* a character used to represent a mathematical value — see NUMBER

integral *adj* **1** being a part of the innermost nature of a person or thing — see INHERENT

2 impossible to do without — see ESSENTIAL 1

3 not lacking any part or member that properly belongs to it — see COMPLETE 1

integrate *vb* **1** to make a part of a body or system — see EMBODY 1

2 to turn into a single mass that is more or less the same throughout — see BLEND 1

integrity *n* **1** conduct that conforms to an accepted standard of right and wrong — see MORALITY 1

2 devotion to telling the truth — see HONESTY 1

3 faithfulness to high moral standards — see HONOR 1

intellect *n* **1** a very smart person — see GENIUS 1

2 the ability to learn and understand or to deal with problems — see INTELLIGENCE 1

intellectual *adj* **1** much given to learning and thinking ⟨as the daughter of college professors, she's used to being around *intellectual* people⟩
synonyms cerebral, highbrow
related words cultivated, cultured; erudite, learned, literate, scholarly, well-read; academic, bookish, professorial; didactic, pedantic; high-hat, snobbish, snobby, snooty; educated, schooled; brainy, bright, brilliant, clever, intelligent, quick-witted, smart
near antonyms uncultivated, uncultured; ignorant, illiterate, uneducated, unlettered, unread; dumb, foolish, idiotic, moronic, slow, stupid, unintelligent
antonyms lowbrow, nonintellectual

2 of or relating to the mind — see MENTAL 1

intelligence *n* **1** the ability to learn and understand or to deal with problems ⟨high scores on this test supposedly demonstrate great *intelligence*⟩
synonyms brain(s), gray matter, intellect, reason, sense
related words acumen, alertness, astuteness, discernment, insight, judgment (*or* judgement), mentality, perception, perspicacity; sagacity, sapience, wisdom, wit; head, mind, skull

near antonyms denseness, density, doltishness, dopiness, dullness (*also* dulness), dumbness, fatuity, feeblemindedness, foolishness, idiocy, imbecility, senselessness, simpleness, slowness, stupidity

2 a report of recent events or facts not previously known — see NEWS

intelligent *adj* **1** having or showing quickness of mind ⟨the dolphin is considered one of the most *intelligent* animals⟩ ⟨running for help was an *intelligent* response to the emergency⟩

synonyms alert, brainy, bright, brilliant, clever, keen, nimble, quick, quick-witted, sharp, sharp-witted, smart

related words apt, ingenious, resourceful; acute, astute, discerning, insightful, knowing, perceptive, perspicacious, sagacious, sapient, savvy, wise; cerebral, erudite, highbrow, knowledgeable, learned, literate, scholarly, well-read; educated, informed, schooled, skilled, trained; creative, inventive, judicious, prudent, sage, sane, sapient, sensible, sound, wise; crafty, cunning, foxy, shrewd, wily; logical, rational, reasonable

near antonyms retarded; foolish, idiotic, imbecile, imbecilic, moronic, silly, witless; ignorant, illiterate, lowbrow, nonintellectual, unacademic, uneducated, uninformed

antonyms brainless, dense, doltish, dorky, dull, dumb, mindless, obtuse, simple, slow, stupid, thick, unintelligent

2 having the ability to reason — see RATIONAL 1

intemperate *adj* showing no signs of being under control — see RAMPANT 1

intend *vb* to have in mind as a purpose or goal ⟨he *intends* to be the president of a large corporation someday⟩

synonyms aim, aspire, contemplate, design, mean, meditate, plan, propose

related words dream, hope, wish; consider, debate, mull (over), ponder; attempt, endeavor, strive, struggle, try; plot, scheme; accomplish, achieve, effect, execute, perform

phrases figure on

intended *n* the person to whom one is engaged to be married — see BETROTHED

intense *adj* extreme in degree, power, or effect ⟨the *intense* cold of the polar regions⟩

synonyms deep, explosive, exquisite, fearful, ferocious, fierce, furious, hard, heavy, intensive, profound, terrible, vehement, vicious, violent

related words accentuated, aggravated, concentrated, deepened; emphasized, enhanced, heightened, intensified, magnified; stressed; exhaustive, thorough; harsh, rigorous, severe

near antonyms feeble, weak; shallow, superficial; moderated, qualified; alleviated, eased, lightened, toned (down); abated, decreased, diminished, lessened, reduced, subdued

antonyms light, moderate, soft

intensely *adv* with great effort or determination — see HARD 1

intensify *vb* to make markedly greater in measure or degree ⟨*intensified* her efforts to move that bookcase by herself⟩

synonyms amplify, beef (up), boost, consolidate, deepen, enhance, heighten, magnify, redouble, step up, strengthen

related words broaden, enlarge, expand, extend, lengthen; accelerate, hasten, quicken; accentuate, emphasize, stress; augment, reinforce, supple-

ment; maximize; enliven, jazz (up); aggravate, exacerbate

near antonyms decrease, diminish, lessen, let up (on), reduce, subdue, tone (down), weaken; dwindle, recede, subside, taper (off), wane; alleviate, ease, lighten

antonyms abate, moderate

intensity *n* **1** depth of feeling — see ARDOR 1

2 the quality or state of being forceful (as in expression) — see VEHEMENCE 1

intensive *adj* extreme in degree, power, or effect — see INTENSE

intensively *adv* with great effort or determination — see HARD 1

intent *adj* **1** fully committed to achieving a goal — see DETERMINED 1

2 having the mind fixed on something — see ATTENTIVE

intent *n* **1** something that one hopes or intends to accomplish — see GOAL

2 the idea that is conveyed or intended to be conveyed to the mind by language, symbol, or action — see MEANING 1

intention *n* something that one hopes or intends to accomplish — see GOAL

intentional *adj* made, given, or done with full awareness of what one is doing ⟨I'm fairly sure that your "accidental" attack on your sister with a water balloon was really *intentional*⟩

synonyms deliberate, purposeful, willful (*or* wilful)

related words knowing, witting; designed, intended, planned; conscious; advised, calculated, considered, measured, reasoned, studied, thoughtful, weighed; premeditated; discretionary, elective, optional, volunteer

near antonyms inadvertent, unwitting; accidental, chance, haphazard, hit-or-miss, incidental, random; aimless, desultory, purposeless; abrupt, impetuous, sudden; coerced, forced, involuntary; compulsory, mandatory, necessary, nonelective, obligatory, ordered, required; casual; extemporaneous, impromptu, impulsive, instinctive, spontaneous, unforced, unpremeditated

antonyms unintentional

intentionally *adv* with full awareness of what one is doing ⟨the witness *intentionally* gave misleading answers to the questions⟩

synonyms consciously, deliberately, designedly, knowingly, purposefully, purposely, willfully, wittingly

related words calculatingly, studiedly; voluntarily, willingly

phrases on purpose

near antonyms accidentally, incidentally, randomly; involuntarily, unwillingly; impulsively, instinctively, spontaneously

antonyms inadvertently, unconsciously, unintentionally, unknowingly, unwittingly

intently *adv* with great effort or determination — see HARD 1

intentness *n* a mental state free of jesting or trifling — see EARNESTNESS

inter *vb* to place (a dead body) in the earth, a tomb, or the sea — see BURY 1

interaction *n* doings between individuals or groups — see RELATION 1

intercede *vb* to act as a go-between for opposing sides — see INTERVENE

intercessor *n* one who works with opposing sides

THESAURUS

in order to bring about an agreement — see ME-
DIATOR

intercommunicate *vb* to engage in an exchange of
information or ideas — see COMMUNICATE 2

intercourse *n* **1** doings between individuals or
groups — see RELATION 1
2 sexual union involving penetration of the vagina by the penis — see SEXUAL INTERCOURSE

interdict *n* an order that something not be done or
used — see PROHIBITION 2

interdict *vb* to order not to do or use or to be done
or used — see FORBID

interdicted *adj* that may not be permitted — see
IMPERMISSIBLE

interdicting *n* the act of ordering that something
not be done or used — see PROHIBITION 1

interdiction *n* **1** an order that something not be
done or used — see PROHIBITION 2
2 the act of ordering that something not be done
or used — see PROHIBITION 1

interest *n* **1** a legal right to participation in the advantages, profits, and responsibility of something
⟨all of the workers at the food cooperative have
an *interest* in it⟩
synonyms claim, share, stake
related words ownership, part, partnership, possession, title
2 the state of doing well especially in relation to
one's happiness or success — see WELFARE

interest *vb* to hold the attention of — see EN-
GAGE 1

interesting *adj* holding the attention or provoking
interest ⟨the history lecture was so *interesting* that
I didn't fall asleep after all⟩
synonyms absorbing, arresting, engaging, engrossing, enthralling, fascinating, gripping, immersing, intriguing, involving, riveting
related words breathtaking, electric, electrifying,
exciting, exhilarating, galvanizing, inspiring,
rousing, stimulating, stirring, thrilling; provocative, tantalizing; emphatic, showy, splashy, striking; alluring, attractive, bewitching, captivating,
charming, enchanting, spellbinding; hypnotizing,
mesmerizing; curious, odd, unusual, weird; amazing, astonishing, astounding, eye-opening, fabulous, marvelous (*or* marvellous), surprising, wonderful, wondrous; amusing, entertaining
near antonyms tiresome, tiring, wearisome, wearying; unexciting; dreary, humdrum, pedestrian;
demoralizing, discouraging, disheartening, dispiriting
antonyms boring, drab, dry, dull, heavy, monotonous, tedious, uninteresting

interfere *vb* to interest oneself in what is not one's
concern ⟨a strong resentment of outsiders who
interfered with their traditional ways of doing
things⟩
synonyms butt in, intrude, meddle, mess, nose,
obtrude, poke, pry, snoop
related words intercede, interpose, intervene; encroach, infringe, invade, trespass; fiddle, fool,
monkey, play, tamper
near antonyms avoid, eschew, shun; disregard, ignore, neglect, overlook

interfere (with) *vb* to create difficulty for the work
or activity of — see HAMPER

interference *n* something that makes movement or
progress more difficult — see ENCUMBRANCE

interferer *n* a person who meddles in the affairs of
others — see BUSYBODY

interfering *adj* thrusting oneself where one is not
welcome or invited — see INTRUSIVE

interim *adj* intended to last, continue, or serve for
a limited time — see TEMPORARY 1

interim *n* a break in continuity — see GAP 2

interior *adj* situated farther in — see INNER 1

interior *n* an interior or internal part — see IN-
SIDE 1

interject *vb* to put among or between others — see
INSERT

interlace *vb* **1** to cause to twine about one another
— see INTERTWINE 1
2 to scatter or set here and there among other
things — see THREAD 1
3 to twist together into a usually confused mass
— see ENTANGLE 1

interloper *n* a person who meddles in the affairs of
others — see BUSYBODY

interlude *n* a break in continuity — see GAP 2

intermediary *adj* occupying a position equally distant from the ends or extremes — see MIDDLE 1

intermediary *n* one who works with opposing sides
in order to bring about an agreement — see ME-
DIATOR

intermediate *adj* **1** being about midway between
extremes of amount or size — see MIDDLE 2
2 occupying a position equally distant from the
ends or extremes — see MIDDLE 1

interment *n* the act or ceremony of putting a dead
body in its final resting place — see BURIAL

intermingle *vb* to turn into a single mass that is
more or less the same throughout — see BLEND 1

intermission *n* a break in continuity — see GAP 2

intermittent *adj* **1** occurring or appearing at intervals ⟨*intermittent* showers had me opening and
closing my umbrella all day long⟩
synonyms continual, periodic, periodical, recurrent, recurring
related words alternate, alternating, cyclic (*or* cyclical), rhythmic (*or* rhythmical), seasonal, serial;
erratic, fitful, irregular, occasional, spasmodic,
sporadic, spotty, unsteady
near antonyms eternal, everlasting, interminable,
perpetual
antonyms constant, continuous, incessant, unceasing
2 lacking in steadiness or regularity of occurrence
— see FITFUL

intermix *vb* to turn into a single mass that is more
or less the same throughout — see BLEND 1

intermixture *n* a distinct entity formed by the combining of two or more different things — see
BLEND

intern *vb* to put in or as if in prison — see IM-
PRISON

internal *adj* situated farther in — see INNER 1

interned *adj* taken and held prisoner — see CAP-
TIVE

internee *n* one that has been taken and held in
confinement — see CAPTIVE

internment *n* the act of confining or the state of
being confined ⟨the *internment* of Americans of
Japanese descent during World War II is one of
the more shameful chapters in United States his-
tory⟩
synonyms captivity, confinement, immurement,
imprisonment, incarceration
related words bondage, enslavement, servitude;
restraint, restriction; arrest, capture, entrapment;
custody, detainment, detention

near antonyms emancipation, liberation, manumission, redemption, release; freedom, independence, liberty

interpenetrate *vb* to spread throughout — see PERMEATE

interpolate *vb* to put among or between others — see INSERT

interpose *vb* **1** to act as a go-between for opposing sides — see INTERVENE

2 to cause a disruption in a conversation or discussion — see INTERRUPT

3 to put among or between others — see INSERT

interposer *n* one who works with opposing sides in order to bring about an agreement — see MEDIATOR

interpret *vb* to make plain or understandable — see EXPLAIN 1

interpretation *n* a statement that makes something clear — see EXPLANATION 1

interpretive *adj* serving to explain — see EXPLANATORY

interring *n* the act or ceremony of putting a dead body in its final resting place — see BURIAL

interrogate *vb* **1** to put a question or questions to — see ASK 1

2 to put a series of questions to — see EXAMINE 1

interrupt *vb* to cause a disruption in a conversation or discussion ⟨it's rude to *interrupt* when someone is making an important point⟩

synonyms break (in), chime in, cut in, interpose, intrude

related words barge (in), bother; add, chip in, contribute, put in

interruption *n* **1** a break in continuity — see GAP 2

2 a momentary halt in an activity — see PAUSE

intersect *vb* to divide by passing through or across ⟨the highway *intersects* that road⟩

synonyms bisect, cross

related words crisscross

intersection *n* a place where roads meet — see CROSSROAD 1

intersperse *vb* to scatter or set here and there among other things — see THREAD 1

intertwine *vb* **1** to cause to twine about one another ⟨*intertwined* two different colors of yarn⟩

synonyms interlace, interweave, lace

related words blend, fuse, join, link, mix

near antonyms disentangle, uncoil, untangle, untwine, unwind

2 to twist together into a usually confused mass — see ENTANGLE

interval *n* **1** a break in continuity — see GAP 2

2 an open space in a barrier (as a wall or hedge) — see GAP 1

intervene *vb* to act as a go-between for opposing sides ⟨*intervened* in the argument before any real harm was done⟩

synonyms intercede, interpose, mediate

related words butt in, interfere, intrude, meddle, obtrude, pry, snoop; arbitrate, moderate, negotiate; barge (in), bother; break (in), chime in, cut in; infringe, invade, trespass

near antonyms stand by; avoid, eschew, shun; disregard, ignore, overlook

interweave *vb* **1** to cause to twine about one another — see INTERTWINE 1

2 to scatter or set here and there among other things — see THREAD 1

3 to twist together into a usually confused mass — see ENTANGLE 1

intimacy *n* the state of being in a very personal or private relationship — see FAMILIARITY 1

intimate *adj* **1** closely acquainted — see FAMILIAR 1

2 not known or meant to be known by the general populace — see PRIVATE 1

intimate *n* a person who has a strong liking for and trust in another — see FRIEND 1

intimate *vb* to convey an idea indirectly — see HINT

intimation *n* a slight or indirect pointing to something (as a solution or explanation) — see HINT 1

intimidate *vb* to make timid or fearful by or as if by threats ⟨refusing to be *intimidated* by the manager's harsh stare, I demanded my money back⟩

synonyms browbeat, bully, cow, hector

related words affright, alarm, frighten, horrify, scare, shock, spook, startle, terrify; menace, terrorize, threaten; badger, harass, hound; bulldoze, coerce, compel, constrain, dragoon, force, make, oblige, press, pressure; demoralize, unman, unnerve; discompose, disconcert, disquiet, distress, disturb, perturb, upset

near antonyms cheer, comfort, console, reassure, solace, soothe; embolden, encourage, hearten, steel; convince, persuade

intimidating *adj* **1** causing fear — see FEARFUL 1

2 harsh and threatening in manner or appearance — see GRIM 1

intimidator *n* a person who teases, threatens, or hurts smaller or weaker persons — see BULLY 1

intolerable *adj* more than can be put up with — see UNBEARABLE

intolerant *adj* **1** unable or unwilling to endure ⟨*intolerant* of pain⟩

synonyms impatient

related words uncompromising, unforgiving, unyielding; complaining, fussing, griping, grumbling, protesting, squawking, whining

near antonyms accepting, forgiving, long-suffering, resigned, uncomplaining, willing; indulgent

antonyms abiding, enduring, forbearing, patient, tolerant

2 unwilling to grant other people social rights or to accept other viewpoints ⟨*intolerant* people supported racism⟩

synonyms bigoted, narrow, narrow-minded, prejudiced, small-minded

related words conservative, hidebound, old-fashioned, reactionary; insular, parochial, provincial; biased, one-sided, partial, partisan

near antonyms extreme, progressive, radical; impartial, objective, unbiased

antonyms broad-minded, liberal, open-minded, tolerant, unprejudiced

intone *vb* to utter in musical or drawn out tones — see CHANT 1

intoxicant *n* a fermented or distilled beverage that can make a person drunk — see ALCOHOL

intoxicate *vb* to cause a pleasurable stimulation of the feelings — see THRILL

intoxicated *adj* **1** being under the influence of alcohol — see DRUNK

2 experiencing or marked by overwhelming usually pleasurable emotion — see ECSTATIC

intoxication *n* a state of overwhelming usually pleasurable emotion — see ECSTASY

intractability *n* refusal to obey — see DISOBEDIENCE

THESAURUS

intractable *adj* **1** given to resisting authority or another's control — see DISOBEDIENT

2 given to resisting control or discipline by others — see UNCONTROLLABLE

intrepid *adj* feeling or displaying no fear by temperament — see BRAVE

intrepidity *n* strength of mind to carry on in spite of danger — see COURAGE

intrepidness *n* strength of mind to carry on in spite of danger — see COURAGE

intricacy *n* **1** something that makes a situation more complicated or difficult — see COMPLICATION 1

2 the state or quality of having many interrelated parts or aspects — see COMPLEXITY 1

intricate *adj* **1** having many parts or aspects that are usually interrelated — see COMPLEX 1

2 made or done with great care or with much detail — see ELABORATE 1

intrigue *n* a secret plan for accomplishing evil or unlawful ends — see PLOT 1

intrigue *vb* **1** to engage in a secret plan to accomplish evil or unlawful ends — see PLOT

2 to hold the attention of — see ENGAGE 1

intriguing *adj* holding the attention or provoking interest — see INTERESTING

intrinsic *adj* being a part of the innermost nature of a person or thing — see INHERENT

intrinsically *adv* by natural character or ability — see NATURALLY 1

introduce *vb* **1** to make (one person) known (to another) socially ⟨a friend *introduced* him to the woman who later became his wife⟩
synonyms acquaint, present
related words address, greet, hail, meet

2 to present or bring forward for discussion ⟨the moderator *introduced* a new topic for the debate⟩
synonyms bring up, broach, moot, raise
related words allude (to), cite, mention, name, refer (to); offer, propose, suggest; air, express, speak (of), talk (about), vent, ventilate; interject, interrupt; debate, discuss, thrash (out *or* over)
near antonyms censor, hush (up), quiet, silence, suppress

3 to be responsible for the creation and early operation or use of — see FOUND

4 to impart knowledge of a new thing or situation to — see ACQUAINT 1

5 to put among or between others — see INSERT

introducer *n* one who creates or introduces something new — see INVENTOR

introduction *n* a short section (as of a book) that leads to or explains the main part ⟨a famous person wrote the *introduction* to that new textbook⟩
synonyms foreword, preamble, preface, prelude, prologue
related words beginning, commencement, initiation, opening, origin, origination, outset, start
near antonyms postscript; aftermath; cessation, close, closing, conclusion, end, finale, finish, stop, termination
antonyms epilogue

introductory *adj* coming before the main part or item usually to introduce or prepare for what follows — see PRELIMINARY

introverted *adj* not comfortable around people — see SHY 2

intrude *vb* **1** to cause a disruption in a conversation or discussion — see INTERRUPT

2 to interest oneself in what is not one's concern — see INTERFERE

intrude (upon) *vb* to thrust oneself upon (another) without invitation — see BOTHER 1

intruder *n* a person who meddles in the affairs of others — see BUSYBODY

intruding *adj* thrusting oneself where one is not welcome or invited — see INTRUSIVE

intrusive *adj* thrusting oneself where one is not welcome or invited ⟨that *intrusive* neighbor never knocks before coming in⟩
synonyms interfering, intruding, meddlesome, meddling, nosy (*or* nosey), obtrusive, officious, presumptuous, prying, snoopy
related words bold, brazen, impertinent, impudent, insolent, rude; invading, trespassing; curious, inquisitive; annoying, harassing, pestiferous
near antonyms quiet, reserved, reticent, retiring, silent, taciturn, withdrawn; inhibited, restrained, subdued
antonyms unobtrusive

inundate *vb* to cover or become filled with a flood — see FLOOD

inundation *n* a great flow of water or of something that overwhelms — see FLOOD

inure *vb* to make able to withstand physical hardship, strain, or exposure — see HARDEN 2

inured *adj* able to withstand hardship, strain, or exposure — see HARDY 1

invade *vb* to enter for conquest or plunder ⟨a superpower that had a tendency to *invade* and take over smaller and weaker countries⟩
synonyms foray (into), overrun, raid
related words despoil, loot, maraud, pillage, plunder, ravage, sack; conquer, crush, overcome, overpower, overwhelm, subdue, subjugate; assail, assault, attack; battle, combat, fight, war (with); encroach, infringe, trespass; besiege, blockade; occupy
near antonyms defend, guard, protect, shield; oppose, resist, withstand; capitulate (to), cede (to), submit (to), succumb (to), surrender (to), yield (to)

invader *n* one that starts armed conflict against another especially without reasonable cause — see AGGRESSOR

¹invalid *adj* chronically or repeatedly suffering from poor health — see SICKLY 1

²invalid *adj* **1** having no legal or binding force — see NULL 1

2 not being in agreement with what is true — see FALSE 1

3 not using or following good reasoning — see ILLOGICAL

4 having no basis in reason or fact — see GROUNDLESS

invalidate *vb* to put an end to by formal action — see ABOLISH

invariability *n* the state of continuing without change — see CONSTANCY 1

invariable *adj* not capable of changing or being changed — see INFLEXIBLE 1

invariably *adv* on every relevant occasion — see ALWAYS 1

invariant *adj* not varying — see UNIFORM

invasion *n* a sudden attack on and entrance into hostile territory — see RAID 1

invective *n* harsh insulting language — see ABUSE 1

invent *vb* to create or think of by clever use of the imagination ⟨they *invented* an explanation for the

broken vase that would satisfy their grandmother⟩
synonyms concoct, contrive, cook (up), devise, fabricate, make up, manufacture, think (up)
related words coin, contrive, create, design, hatch, produce; daydream, dream, fantasize; conceive, envisage, imagine, picture, visualize
near antonyms copy, duplicate, imitate, mimic, replicate
invented *adj* not real and existing only in the imagination — see IMAGINARY
invention *n* **1** something (as a device) created for the first time through the use of the imagination ⟨his clever *invention* made people's lives easier⟩
synonyms coinage, concoction, contrivance, creation, innovation, wrinkle
related words contraption, device, gadget, gizmo (*or* gismo), novelty; design, product, work; dream, fantasy (*also* phantasy), picture, vision; conception, imagining, origination
near antonyms copy, duplicate, imitation
2 something that is the product of the imagination — see FICTION
3 the ability to form mental images of things that either are not physically present or have never been conceived or created by others — see IMAGINATION
4 the skill and imagination to create new things — see CREATIVITY 1
inventive *adj* having the skill and imagination to create new things — see CREATIVE 1
inventiveness *n* **1** the ability to form mental images of things that either are not physically present or have never been conceived or created by others — see IMAGINATION
2 the skill and imagination to create new things — see CREATIVITY 1
inventor *n* one who creates or introduces something new ⟨the *inventor* of the electric light bulb⟩
synonyms contriver, designer, developer, deviser, formulator, innovator, introducer, originator
related words author, creator, establisher, father, founder, inaugurator, originator; pioneer, researcher; builder, maker, producer; dreamer
near antonyms copier, duplicator, imitator
inventory *vb* to make a list of — see ¹LIST 1
invert *vb* to change the position of (an object) so that the opposite side or end is showing — see REVERSE 2
invertebrate *adj* lacking strength of will or character — see WEAK 2
invest *vb* **1** to cause (as a person) to become filled or saturated with a certain quality or principle — see INFUSE
2 to furnish with something freely or naturally — see ENDOW 1
3 to give official or legal power to — see AUTHORIZE 1
4 to outfit with clothes and especially fine or special clothes — see CLOTHE 1
5 to put into an office or welcome into an organization with special ceremonies — see INSTALL 1
6 to surround (as a fortified place) with armed forces for the purpose of capturing or preventing commerce and communication — see BESIEGE
7 to surround or cover closely — see ENFOLD 1
investigate *vb* to search through or into — see EXPLORE 1
investigation *n* a systematic search for the truth or facts about something — see INQUIRY 1

investigator *n* a person whose business is solving crimes and catching criminals or gathering information that is not easy to get — see DETECTIVE
investiture *n* the process or an instance of being formally placed in an office or organization — see INSTALLATION 1
investment *n* the cutting off of an area by military means to stop the flow of people or supplies — see BLOCKADE
inveterate *adj* **1** firmly established over time ⟨he has an *inveterate* tendency to tell tall tales that began when he was just a little boy⟩
synonyms confirmed, deep-rooted, deep-seated, entrenched (*also* intrenched), hard-core, rooted, settled
related words fixed, immutable, set; implanted, inculcated, instilled; inborn, inbred, inherent, innate, natural; accustomed, chronic, customary, habitual, regular, typical, usual; abiding, enduring, lifelong, persistent, persisting
near antonyms brief, ephemeral, fleeting, impermanent, momentary, short-lived, temporary, transient
2 being such by habit and not likely to change — see HABITUAL 1
invidious *adj* having or showing mean resentment of another's possessions or advantages — see ENVIOUS
invidiousness *n* a painful awareness of another's possessions or advantages and a desire to have them too — see ENVY
invigorate *vb* to give life, vigor, or spirit to — see ANIMATE
invigorated *adj* made or become fresh in spirits or vigor — see NEW 4
invigorating *adj* having a renewing effect on the state of the body or mind — see TONIC
invincible *adj* incapable of being defeated, overcome, or subdued ⟨an *invincible* wrestler who has never lost a match⟩
synonyms impregnable, indomitable, insurmountable, invulnerable, unbeatable, unconquerable
related words inviolable, unassailable, untouchable; armored, defended, guarded, protected, safe, safeguarded, secure, shielded; unbeaten, unconquered, undefeated, unsubdued
near antonyms exposed, imperiled, insecure, liable, open, susceptible, unguarded, unprotected, unsafe, unshielded; defenseless, helpless, powerless, weak
antonyms surmountable, vulnerable
inviolable *adj* not to be violated, criticized, or tampered with — see SACRED 1
invite *vb* to act so as to make (something) more likely — see COURT 1
invoice *n* a record of goods sold or services performed together with the costs due — see ¹BILL 1
involuntary *adj* **1** not made or done willingly or by choice ⟨my long stays on the sidelines during our football games were strictly *involuntary*⟩
synonyms coerced, forced, unintended, unintentional, unwilling
related words accidental, unplanned, unpremeditated; automatic, impulsive, instinctive, spontaneous, unprompted; inadvertent, unconscious, unknowing, unwitting
near antonyms advised, conscious, considered, knowing, planned, premeditated, purposeful; volitional

antonyms deliberate, intentional, unforced, voluntary, willful (*or* wilful), willing

2 done instantly and without conscious thought or decision — see AUTOMATIC 1

3 forcing one's compliance or participation by or as if by law — see MANDATORY

involution *n* the state or quality of having many interrelated parts or aspects — see COMPLEXITY 1

involve *vb* **1** to be the business or affair of — see CONCERN 2

2 to have as part of a whole — see INCLUDE

3 to hold the attention of — see ENGAGE 1

involved *adj* **1** having many parts or aspects that are usually interrelated — see COMPLEX 1

2 made or done with great care or with much detail — see ELABORATE 1

involving *adj* holding the attention or provoking interest — see INTERESTING

invulnerable *adj* incapable of being defeated, overcome, or subdued — see INVINCIBLE

inward *adj* situated farther in — see INNER 1

in–your–face *adj* having or showing a bold forcefulness in the pursuit of a goal — see AGGRESSIVE 1

iota *n* the smallest amount or part imaginable — see JOT

irascibility *n* readiness to show annoyance or impatience — see PETULANCE

irascible *adj* easily irritated or annoyed — see IRRITABLE

irate *adj* feeling or showing anger — see ANGRY

irateness *n* an intense emotional state of displeasure with someone or something — see ANGER

ire *n* an intense emotional state of displeasure with someone or something — see ANGER

ireful *adj* feeling or showing anger — see ANGRY

irk *vb* to disturb the peace of mind of (someone) especially by repeated disagreeable acts — see IRRITATE 1

irksome *adj* causing annoyance — see ANNOYING

iron *adj* not showing weakness or uncertainty — see FIRM 1

irons *n pl* something that physically prevents free movement — see BOND 1

irradiate *vb* to supply with light — see ILLUMINATE 1

irrational *adj* not using or following good reasoning — see ILLOGICAL

irrecoverable *adj* **1** not capable of being cured or reformed — see HOPELESS 1

2 not capable of being repaired, regained, or undone — see IRREPARABLE

irredeemable *adj* **1** not capable of being cured or reformed — see HOPELESS 1

2 not capable of being repaired, regained, or undone — see IRREPARABLE

irrefutable *adj* not capable of being challenged or proved wrong ⟨the *irrefutable* reply of "Because I like it!"⟩

synonyms incontestable, incontrovertible, indisputable, indubitable, unanswerable, undeniable, unquestionable

related words certain, definite, positive, sure; unambiguous, unequivocal; absolute, clear, conclusive, decisive; uncontested, undisputed

near antonyms controversial, debated, disputed; doubtful, dubious, inconclusive, indecisive, uncertain; ambiguous, equivocal

antonyms answerable, debatable, disputable, questionable

irregular *adj* **1** departing from some accepted standard of what is normal — see DEVIANT

2 lacking in steadiness or regularity of occurrence — see FITFUL

3 not having a level or smooth surface — see UNEVEN 1

4 not rigidly following established form, custom, or rules — see INFORMAL 1

5 not staying constant — see UNEVEN 2

irregularly *adv* without definite aim, direction, rule, or method — see HIT OR MISS

irrelevance *n* the quality or state of not having anything to do with the matter at hand ⟨the *irrelevance* of the comment brought conversation to a standstill⟩

synonyms extraneousness, inapplicability

related words inappropriateness, inaptness, unfitness, unsuitability; insignificance, unimportance; pointlessness, uselessness

near antonyms bearing, connection; appropriateness, aptness, fitness, suitability; importance, significance; usefulness

antonyms applicability, materiality, pertinence, relevance

irrelevant *adj* not having anything to do with the matter at hand ⟨*irrelevant* questions that merely disrupted the classroom lesson⟩

synonyms extraneous, immaterial, inapplicable

related words inconsequential, insignificant, unimportant; meaningless, pointless, senseless, useless; inappropriate, inapt, unsuitable

phrases beside the point

near antonyms important, meaningful, significant; sensible, useful; appropriate, apt, fit, suitable

antonyms applicable, apposite, apropos, germane, material, pertinent, relevant

irreligious *adj* lacking religious emotions, principles, or practices ⟨raised in an *irreligious* family where the subject of God was never even discussed⟩

synonyms godless, nonreligious

related words ungodly, unholy; blasphemous, impious, irreverent, sacrilegious; agnostic, atheistic; unconsecrated, unhallowed; profane, secular, worldly

near antonyms devout, godly, holy, pious, prayerful, reverent, worshipful, worshipping (*also* worshiping); sanctimonious

antonyms religious

irremediable *adj* **1** not capable of being cured or reformed — see HOPELESS 1

2 not capable of being repaired, regained, or undone — see IRREPARABLE

irremovable *adj* incapable of moving or being moved — see IMMOVABLE 1

irreparable *adj* not capable of being repaired, regained, or undone ⟨*irreparable* damage to the car⟩

synonyms irrecoverable, irredeemable, irremediable, irretrievable, irreversible, unrecoverable, unredeemable

related words irreplaceable, irrevocable; unredeemed, unrepaired

near antonyms corrected, fixed, recovered, remedied, repaired

antonyms fixable, redeemable, remediable, retrievable

irreproachable *adj* **1** free from guilt or blame — see INNOCENT 2

2 being entirely without fault — see PERFECT 1

irresolution *n* the act or an instance of pausing because of uncertainty about the right course of action — see HESITATION

irresponsible *adj* having or showing a lack of concern for the consequences of one's actions — see RECKLESS 1

irretrievable *adj* **1** not capable of being cured or reformed — see HOPELESS 1

2 not capable of being repaired, regained, or undone — see IRREPARABLE

irreverence *n* an act of great disrespect shown to God or to sacred ideas, people, or things — see BLASPHEMY

irreverent *adj* not showing proper reverence for the holy or sacred ⟨*irreverent* behavior during church services⟩
synonyms blasphemous, impious, profane, sacrilegious
related words agnostic, atheistic; godless, irreligious, nonreligious, secular; ungodly, unholy; unconsecrated, unhallowed, unsanctified
near antonyms devout, godly, holy, prayerful, religious, worshipful, worshipping (*also* worshiping); consecrated, hallowed, sanctified
antonyms pious, reverent

irreversible *adj* not capable of being repaired, regained, or undone — see IRREPARABLE

irrigate *vb* to pour liquid over or through in order to cleanse — see FLUSH 1

irritability *n* readiness to show annoyance or impatience — see PETULANCE

irritable *adj* easily irritated or annoyed ⟨that *irritable* old man always yells at people to stay off of his lawn⟩
synonyms choleric, crabby, cranky, cross, crotchety, grouchy, grumpy, irascible, peevish, perverse, pettish, petulant, quick-tempered, short-tempered, snappish, snappy, snippy, testy, waspish
related words bearish, bilious, cantankerous, disagreeable, dyspeptic, ill-humored, ill-natured, ill-tempered, ornery, surly; sensitive, sulky, thin-skinned, touchy; hot-blooded, passionate
phrases out of sorts
near antonyms affable, cordial, friendly, genial, sociable; amiable, good-natured, good-tempered, well-disposed; carefree, easygoing, relaxed; obliging, patient, tolerant, uncomplaining, understanding

irritableness *n* readiness to show annoyance or impatience — see PETULANCE

irritant *n* something that is a source of irritation — see ANNOYANCE 3

irritate *vb* **1** to disturb the peace of mind of (someone) especially by repeated disagreeable acts ⟨constant chatter *irritated* the student, who was trying to concentrate on a hard assignment⟩
synonyms aggravate, annoy, bother, bug, chafe, exasperate, gall, get, grate, irk, nettle, peeve, persecute, pique, put out, rasp, rile, vex
related words hassle, heckle; nag; inflame, provoke, rouse; bait, harass, harry, pester; anger, enrage, incense, infuriate, madden; agitate, disturb, fret, perturb, upset; affront, insult, offend, outrage
phrases rub the wrong way
near antonyms appease, conciliate, mollify, oblige, pacify, placate, propitiate; delight, gladden, gratify, please, satisfy; comfort, console, content, quiet, soothe
2 to make sore by continued rubbing — see CHAFE 1

irritating *adj* causing annoyance — see ANNOYING

irritation *n* the feeling of impatience or anger caused by another's repeated disagreeable acts — see ANNOYANCE 2

irruption *n* a sudden attack on and entrance into hostile territory — see RAID 1

island *n* a fairly small area of land completely surrounded by water ⟨they're taking a trip to an *island* in Hawaii for vacation⟩
synonyms isle, islet
related words barrier reef, cay, coral reef, key; archipelago, atoll; cape, headland, peninsula, promontory
near antonyms continent, main, mainland

isle *n* a fairly small area of land completely surrounded by water — see ISLAND

islet *n* a fairly small area of land completely surrounded by water — see ISLAND

isolate *vb* to set or keep apart from others ⟨*isolated* her in a corner for a five-minute punishment after she threw a book at her friend⟩
synonyms cut off, insulate, seclude, segregate, separate, sequester
related words quarantine; confine, immure, incarcerate, intern, jail, lock (up), restrain, restrict; detach, disengage, remove; detain, hold, keep
near antonyms associate, connect, join, link, unite; discharge, free, liberate, loose, release
antonyms desegregate, integrate

isolated *adj* hidden from view — see SECLUDED

isolation *n* the state of being alone or kept apart from others ⟨*isolation* always made the sociable child lonely⟩
synonyms insulation, secludedness, seclusion, segregation, separateness, sequestration, solitariness, solitude
related words loneliness, lonesomeness; confinement, incarceration, internment, quarantine; retirement, withdrawal
near antonyms companionship, company

issuance *n* the act or process of giving out something to each member of a group — see DISTRIBUTION 1

issue *n* **1** a condition or occurrence traceable to a cause — see EFFECT 1
2 a place or means of going out — see EXIT 1
3 the descendants of a person, animal, or plant — see OFFSPRING

issue *vb* **1** to produce and release for distribution in printed form — see PUBLISH 1
2 to throw or give off — see EMIT 1

Italian sandwich *n* a large sandwich on a long split roll — see SUBMARINE

itch *n* a strong wish for something — see DESIRE

itch (for) *vb* to have an earnest wish to own or enjoy — see DESIRE

item *n* **1** a separate part in a list, account, or series ⟨she got all the *items* on her grocery list except cereal⟩
synonyms detail, particular, point
related words article, belonging, object, stuff, thing; characteristic, constituent, element, feature; ingredient; division, particle, piece, portion, section, segment
near antonyms aggregate, composite, compound, conglomerate; entirety, sum, total, totality, whole
2 a report of recent events or facts not previously known — see NEWS

THESAURUS

itemize *vb* **1** to make a list of — see ¹LIST 1

2 to specify one after another — see ENUMER-ATE 1

itinerant *adj* traveling from place to place ⟨an *itinerant* musician can see a lot of the world⟩

  synonyms errant, gallivanting (*also* galavanting),

nomad (*or* nomadic), peripatetic, ranging, roaming, roving, vagabond, vagrant, wandering, wayfaring

  related words drifting, footloose, meandering, rambling; sauntering, strolling, traipsing, walking

  near antonyms immobile, settled, stationary

jab *n* a quick thrust — see ¹POKE

jabber *n* unintelligible or meaningless talk — see GIBBERISH

jabber *vb* **1** to engage in casual or rambling conversation — see CHAT

2 to speak rapidly, inarticulately, and usually unintelligibly — see BABBLE 1

jabberer *n* a person who talks constantly — see CHATTERBOX

jabberwocky *n* unintelligible or meaningless talk — see GIBBERISH

jack *n* **1** *slang* something (as pieces of stamped metal or printed paper) customarily and legally used as a medium of exchange, a measure of value, or a means of payment — see MONEY

2 a piece of cloth with a special design that is used as an emblem or for signaling — see FLAG 1

3 an adult male human being — see MAN 1

4 one who operates or navigates a seagoing vessel — see SAILOR

jack (up) *vb* **1** to lift with effort — see HEAVE 1

2 to move from a lower to a higher place or position — see RAISE 1

jackass *n* **1** a person who lacks good sense or judgment — see FOOL 1

2 a stupid person — see IDIOT

3 a sturdy and patient domestic mammal that is used especially to carry things — see DONKEY 1

jacked (up) *adj* being at a higher level than average — see HIGH 2

jacket *n* something that encloses another thing especially to protect it — see ¹CASE 1

jackpot *n* the total of the bets at stake at one time — see POT 1

jack–tar *n* one who operates or navigates a seagoing vessel — see SAILOR

jade *vb* to make weary and restless by being dull or monotonous — see ²BORE

jaded *adj* **1** depleted in strength, energy, or freshness — see WEARY 1

2 having one's patience, interest, or pleasure exhausted — see WEARY 2

jading *adj* causing weariness, restlessness, or lack of interest — see BORING

jagged *adj* **1** having an uneven edge or outline — see RAGGED 1

2 not having a level or smooth surface — see UNEVEN 1

jail *n* a place of confinement for persons held in lawful custody ⟨sentenced to three years in *jail* for his crime⟩

  synonyms brig, gaol [*chiefly British*], guardroom, hoosegow, jug, lockup, pen, penitentiary, prison, stockade

  related words bull pen; concentration camp,

prison camp; dungeon, keep; reformatory, reform school

  near antonyms freedom

jail *vb* to put in or as if in prison — see IMPRISON

jailbird *n* a person convicted as a criminal and serving a prison sentence — see CONVICT

jailed *adj* taken and held prisoner — see CAPTIVE

jam *n* a difficult, puzzling, or embarrassing situation from which there is no easy escape — see PREDICAMENT

jam *vb* **1** to fit (something) into a tight space — see CROWD 1

2 to prevent passage through — see CLOG 1

3 to put into (something) as much as can be held or contained — see FILL 1

jammed *adj* **1** containing or seeming to contain the greatest quantity or number possible — see FULL 1

2 firmly positioned in place and difficult to dislodge — see TIGHT 2

jam–pack *vb* to put into (something) as much as can be held or contained — see FILL 1

jam–packed *adj* **1** containing or seeming to contain the greatest quantity or number possible — see FULL 1

2 having little space between items or parts — see CLOSE 1

janitor *n* **1** a person who takes care of a property sometimes for an absent owner — see CUSTODIAN 1

2 a person who tends a door — see DOORKEEPER

jar *n* **1** a forceful coming together of two things — see IMPACT 1

2 something that makes a strong impression because it is so unexpected — see SURPRISE 1

jar *vb* to be out of harmony or agreement usually noticeably — see CLASH

jargon *n* the special terms or expressions of a particular group or field — see TERMINOLOGY

jarring *adj* disagreeable to one's aesthetic or artistic sense — see HARSH 2

jaundice *n* a deep-seated ill will — see ENMITY

jaundiced *adj* **1** having or showing mean resentment of another's possessions or advantages — see ENVIOUS

2 marked by opposition or ill will — see HOSTILE 1

jaunt *n* a short trip for pleasure — see EXCURSION 1

jauntily *adv* **1** in a bright and showy way — see GAILY 3

2 in a quick and spirited manner — see GAILY 2

jaunty *adj* having much high-spirited energy and movement — see LIVELY 1

javelin *n* a weapon with a long straight handle and sharp head or blade — see SPEAR

jaw *vb* **1** to criticize (someone) severely or angrily especially for personal failings — see SCOLD

2 to engage in casual or rambling conversation — see CHAT

jazz *n* unintelligible or meaningless talk — see GIBBERISH

jazz (up) *vb* to give life, vigor, or spirit to — see ANIMATE

jazziness *n* the quality or state of having abundant or intense activity — see VITALITY 1

jazzy *adj* **1** attractively eye-catching in style ⟨that's a *jazzy* bathing suit, with all those spangles⟩

synonyms flashy, snazzy, splashy

related words cool, hip, neat; à la mode (*also* a la mode), chic, dashing; faddish, fashionable, in, modish, posh, ritzy, sharp, smart, snappy, spruce, stylish; custom, designer; garish, gaudy, loud, rakish, wild

near antonyms classic, elegant, genteel, polished, refined, sophisticated, stately, swank; plain, quiet, restrained, simple, understated

2 having much high-spirited energy and movement — see LIVELY 1

jealous *adj* **1** intolerant of rivalry or unfaithfulness ⟨became *jealous* whenever she paid attention to anyone but him⟩

synonyms possessive

related words controlling, demanding, grasping; covetous, envious, invidious, jaundiced; distrustful, mistrustful, suspicious

phrases green with envy

near antonyms undemanding; tolerant, trustful, trusting, understanding

2 having or showing mean resentment of another's possessions or advantages — see ENVIOUS

jealousy *n* a painful awareness of another's possessions or advantages and a desire to have them too — see ENVY

jeer *n* a vocal sound made to express scorn or disapproval — see CATCALL

jeer *vb* to make (someone or something) the object of unkind laughter — see RIDICULE

Jehovah *n* the being worshipped as the creator and ruler of the universe — see DEITY 2

jell *vb* **1** to take on a definite form — see FORM 1

2 to turn from a liquid into a substance resembling jelly — see COAGULATE

jelly *vb* to turn from a liquid into a substance resembling jelly — see COAGULATE

jeopardize *vb* to place in danger — see ENDANGER

jeopardizing *adj* involving potential loss or injury — see DANGEROUS

jeopardy *n* the state of not being protected from injury, harm, or evil — see DANGER 1

jerk *n* **1** a person whose behavior is offensive to others ⟨his constant rudeness and insensitivity made everyone think he was a real *jerk*⟩

synonyms beast, boor, cad, churl, clown, creep, cretin, cur, heel, joker, louse, lout, skunk, slob, snake, stinker

related words brute, Neanderthal, savage; rascal, rogue, scamp, villain; fool, jackass, nincompoop, nitwit; blockhead, dolt, dope, idiot

near antonyms hero, idol, role model

2 the act or an instance of applying force on something so that it moves in the direction of the force — see PULL 1

jerk *vb* **1** to move or cause to move with a sharp quick motion ⟨I *jerked* to one side to avoid getting hit⟩ ⟨*jerked* the leash to get the dog's attention⟩

synonyms buck, hitch, jolt, twitch, yank

related words bump, jounce, lurch, stagger; jiggle, shake; lug, pull, tug; pluck, tweak; grab, snap, snatch, wrench, wrest, wring

2 to make jerky or restless movements — see FIDGET

jerky *adj* **1** marked by a series of sharp quick motions ⟨made *jerky* progress walking with the new crutches⟩

synonyms bumpy, rough

related words choppy, erratic, fitful, irregular, spasmodic, spastic, unsteady

near antonyms calm, placid, smooth, steady, still

2 showing or marked by a lack of good sense or judgment — see FOOLISH 1

jest *n* **1** an attitude or manner not to be taken seriously — see FUN 2

2 something said or done to cause laughter — see JOKE 1

jest *vb* to make jokes — see JOKE

jester *n* **1** a person (as a writer) noted for or specializing in humor — see HUMORIST

2 a person formerly kept in a royal or noble household to amuse with jests and pranks — see FOOL 2

jesting *adj* marked by or expressive of mild or good-natured teasing — see QUIZZICAL

jesting *n* good-natured teasing or exchanging of clever remarks — see BANTER

jet *vb* **1** to flow out in great quantities or with force — see GUSH 1

2 to throw out or off (something from within) often violently — see ERUPT 1

jettison *n* the getting rid of whatever is unwanted or useless — see DISPOSAL 1

jettison *vb* to get rid of as useless or unwanted — see DISCARD

jetty *n* a structure used by boats and ships for taking on or landing cargo and passengers — see DOCK

jewel *n* **1** a usually valuable stone cut and polished for ornament — see GEM 1

2 an asset that brings praise or renown — see GLORY 2

3 someone or something unusually desirable — see PRIZE 1

jibe *vb* to be in agreement on every point — see CHECK 1

jiffy *n* a very small space of time — see INSTANT

jig *n* a clever often underhanded means to achieve an end — see TRICK 1

jigger *n* an interesting and often novel device with a practical use — see GADGET

jiggling *n* a series of slight movements by a body back and forth or from side to side — see VIBRATION

jim-dandy *adj* of the very best kind — see EXCELLENT

jim-dandy *n* something very good of its kind ⟨the brand new car was a *jim-dandy*⟩

synonyms beauty, corker, crackerjack, dandy, knockout, nifty, pip

related words marvel, wonder; gem, jewel, treasure

near antonyms disappointment, failure, lemon, loser

jimmy *vb* to raise, move, or pull apart with or as if with a lever — see ¹PRY 1

jingle *n* **1** a series of short high ringing sounds — see TINKLE

2 a short musical composition for the human voice often with instrumental accompaniment — see SONG 1

jingle *vb* to make a repeated sharp light ringing sound ⟨the bell on the kitten's collar *jingled* as she walked⟩

synonyms chink, clink, tinkle

related words clack, clang, clank; clatter, rattle; ding, jangle, ping, ring

jingo *n* **1** one who shows excessive favoritism towards his or her country — see NATIONALIST

2 one who urges or attempts to cause a war — see WARMONGER

jingoism *n* excessive favoritism towards one's own country — see CHAUVINISM

jinx *n* something that brings bad luck ⟨believed the broken mirror was a *jinx*⟩

synonyms hex, hoodoo

related words curse, evil eye, spell; augury, omen, portent

near antonyms amulet, charm, talisman

jitters *n pl* a sense of panic or extreme nervousness ⟨always got the *jitters* right before a test⟩

synonyms dither, nerves, shakes, shivers, willies

related words cold sweat, creeps; anxiety, fear, hysteria; frazzle, nervous breakdown

near antonyms aplomb, composure, coolheadedness, equanimity, imperturbability, self-possession

jittery *adj* **1** easily excited by nature — see EXCITABLE

2 feeling or showing uncomfortable feelings of uncertainty — see NERVOUS 1

jive *vb* **1** to make fun of in a good-natured way — see TEASE 1

2 to make jokes — see JOKE

job *n* **1** an assignment at which one regularly works for pay ⟨a high-paying *job* as a banker⟩

synonyms appointment, berth, billet, capacity, function, place, position, post, situation

related words business, employment, occupation, profession; work; office, spot; calling, pursuit, vocation; line, racket; engagement; livelihood, living; assignment, mission, task

near antonyms avocation; joblessness, unemployment

2 a piece of work that needs to be done regularly — see CHORE 1

3 a specific task with which a person or group is charged — see MISSION

4 the action for which a person or thing is specially fitted or used or for which a thing exists — see ROLE

jobholder *n* one who works for another for wages or a salary — see EMPLOYEE

jocose *adj* indicative of or marked by high spirits or good humor — see MERRY

jocosely *adv* in a cheerful or happy manner — see GAILY 1

jocular *adj* given to or marked by mature intelligent humor — see WITTY

jocund *adj* indicative of or marked by high spirits or good humor — see MERRY

jog *vb* **1** to go at a pace faster than a walk — see RUN 1

2 to make short up-and-down movements — see NOD

joggle *vb* to make a series of small irregular or violent movements — see SHAKE 1

join *vb* **1** to be adjacent to — see ADJOIN 1

2 to become a member of — see ENTER 2

3 to come together to form a single unit — see UNITE 1

4 to participate or assist in a joint effort to accomplish an end — see COOPERATE 1

5 to put or bring together so as to form a new and longer whole — see CONNECT 1

joining *adj* having a border in common — see ADJACENT

joint *adj* used or done by a number of people as a group — see COLLECTIVE

joint *n* **1** a place where two or more things are united ⟨the leak was found at a *joint* in the pipe⟩

synonyms connection, coupling, junction, juncture

related words crux, link, tie; interconnection, intersection; abutment, articulation; seam, suture; concourse, confluence, meeting; union

near antonyms crack, separation

2 a building, room, or suite of rooms occupied by a service business — see PLACE 2

jointly *adv* in or by combined action or effort — see TOGETHER 2

joke *n* **1** something said or done to cause laughter ⟨he was known for his hilarious *jokes*⟩

synonyms crack, gag, jest, laugh, pleasantry, quip, sally, waggery, wisecrack, witticism

related words funning, joking, wisecracking; antic, buffoonery, caper, monkeyshine(s), prank; caricature, lampoon, parody, put-on; banter, persiflage, raillery, repartee; facetiousness, funniness, hilariousness, humorousness; barb, humor, wit, wordplay

2 a poor, insincere, or insulting imitation of something — see MOCKERY 1

joke *vb* to make jokes ⟨he was known for his ability to *joke*⟩

synonyms banter, fool, fun, jest, jive, josh, kid, quip, wisecrack

related words chaff, mock, rally, razz, rib, ridicule, tease; caricature, lampoon, parody, satirize; amuse, divert, entertain

joker *n* **1** a person (as a writer) noted for or specializing in humor — see HUMORIST

2 a person whose behavior is offensive to others — see JERK 1

3 an adult male human being — see MAN 1

jokester *n* a person (as a writer) noted for or specializing in humor — see HUMORIST

joking *adj* marked by or expressive of mild or good-natured teasing — see QUIZZICAL

jollification *n* joyful or festive activity — see MERRYMAKING

jollity *n* joyful or festive activity — see MERRYMAKING

jolly *adj* indicative of or marked by high spirits or good humor — see MERRY

jolly *adv* to a great degree — see VERY 1

jolt *n* **1** a forceful coming together of two things — see IMPACT 1

2 something that makes a strong impression because it is so unexpected — see SURPRISE 1

jolt *vb* **1** to make a series of small irregular or violent movements — see SHAKE 1

2 to move or cause to move with a sharp quick motion — see JERK 1

3 to cause an often unpleasant surprise for — see SHOCK 1

josh *vb* **1** to make fun of in a good-natured way — see TEASE 1

2 to make jokes — see JOKE

joshing *adj* marked by or expressive of mild or good-natured teasing — see QUIZZICAL

joshing *n* good-natured teasing or exchanging of clever remarks — see BANTER

jot *n* the smallest amount or part imaginable ⟨it's obvious that he doesn't have a *jot* of interest in history⟩

synonyms hoot, iota, lick, modicum, rap, tittle, whit

related words ace, bit, crumb, dab, driblet, glimmer, hint, little, mite, nip, ounce, peanuts, ray, scruple, shade, shadow, shred, smidgen, snap, speck, spot, sprinkling, strain, streak, suspicion, touch, trace

jot (down) *vb* to make a written note of — see RECORD 1

jounce *vb* **1** to make a series of small irregular or violent movements — see SHAKE 1

2 to make short up-and-down movements — see NOD

journal *n* a publication that appears at regular intervals ⟨a monthly scientific *journal*⟩

synonyms gazette, magazine, newspaper, organ, paper, periodical, review

related words annual, bimonthly, biweekly, daily, monthly, quarterly, semimonthly, semiweekly, weekly, yearbook; broadside, extra, sheet, tabloid

journalist *n* a person employed by a newspaper, magazine, or radio or television station to gather, write, or report news — see REPORTER

journey *n* a going from one place to another usually of some distance ⟨they were hungry and tired after their long *journey*⟩

synonyms expedition, passage, peregrination, travel(s), trek, trip

related words errand, excursion, flight, hop, jaunt, junket, outing, sally, tour; cruise, sail, voyage; drive, ride, spin; odyssey, pilgrimage, progress, quest, safari

journey *vb* to take a trip especially of some distance — see TRAVEL 1

jovial *adj* indicative of or marked by high spirits or good humor — see MERRY

joviality *n* a mood characterized by high spirits and amusement and often accompanied by laughter — see MIRTH

jovially *adv* in a cheerful or happy manner — see GAILY 1

joy *n* **1** a feeling or state of well-being and contentment — see HAPPINESS 1

2 a source of great satisfaction — see DELIGHT 1

joy *vb* to feel or express joy or triumph — see EXULT

joyful *adj* experiencing pleasure, satisfaction, or delight — see GLAD 1

joyless *adj* feeling unhappiness — see SAD 1

joylessness *n* a state or spell of low spirits — see SADNESS

joyous *adj* experiencing pleasure, satisfaction, or delight — see GLAD 1

jubilant *adj* having or expressing feelings of joy or triumph — see EXULTANT

jubilee *n* a time or program of special events and entertainment in honor of something — see FESTIVAL

judge *n* **1** a person who impartially decides or resolves a dispute or controversy ⟨their father always played the role of *judge* when there was a disagreement⟩

synonyms arbiter, arbitrator, referee, umpire

related words justice, magistrate; intermediary, mediator, negotiator, conciliator, go-between, peacemaker, reconciler; decider

2 a public official having authority to decide questions of law ⟨the *judge* gave the defendant a suspended sentence⟩

synonyms bench, court, justice, magistrate

related words justice of the peace

near antonyms claimant, plaintiff; defendant

judge *vb* **1** to give an opinion about (something at issue or in dispute) ⟨the committee will *judge* the case based on the evidence⟩

synonyms adjudge, adjudicate, arbitrate, decide, determine, referee, rule (on), settle, umpire

related words consider, hear, ponder, weigh; size (up); mediate, moderate, negotiate; prosecute, try; find (for *or* against)

near antonyms equivocate, skirt

2 to decide the size, amount, number, or distance of (something) without actual measurement — see ESTIMATE 2

3 to form an opinion through reasoning and information — see INFER 1

judgment *or* **judgement** *n* **1** a decision made by a court or tribunal regarding a case it has heard — see SENTENCE

2 a position arrived at after consideration — see DECISION 1

3 an idea that is believed to be true or valid without positive knowledge — see OPINION 1

4 an opinion on the nature, character, or quality of something — see ESTIMATION 1

judicious *adj* **1** having or showing good judgment and restraint especially in conduct or speech — see DISCREET

2 suitable for bringing about a desired result under the circumstances — see EXPEDIENT

jug *n* **1** a place of confinement for persons held in lawful custody — see JAIL

2 a handled container for holding and pouring liquids that usually has a lip or a spout — see PITCHER

jug *vb* to put in or as if in prison — see IMPRISON

jugglery *n* the use of clever underhanded actions to achieve an end — see TRICKERY

juiciness *n* the quality or state of being full of juice — see SUCCULENCE

juicy *adj* full of juice ⟨she bit into the *juicy* orange⟩

synonyms fleshy, pulpy, succulent

related words sappy, watery

near antonyms dehydrated, dry, withered

jumble *n* **1** a state in which everything is out of order — see CHAOS

2 an unorganized collection or mixture of various things — see MISCELLANY 1

jumble *vb* to undo the proper order or arrangement of — see DISORDER

jumbled *adj* lacking in order, neatness, and often cleanliness — see MESSY

jumbo *adj* unusually large — see HUGE

jumbo *n* something that is unusually large and powerful — see GIANT

jump *n* **1** an act of leaping into the air ⟨her first *jump* from an airplane at the age of 12⟩

synonyms bound, hop, leap, spring, vault

related words bounce, lope, skip; caper, gambol; attack, pounce; dive, pitch, plunge

2 the more favorable condition or position in a competition — see ADVANTAGE 1

jump *vb* **1** to propel oneself upward or forward into the air ⟨*jumped* across the ditch⟩

synonyms bound, hop, leap, spring, vault

related words bounce, hurdle, lope, skip; buck; caper, cavort, frolic, gambol, romp; attack, pounce; shoot, skyrocket

2 to move suddenly and sharply (as in surprise) — see START 1

jump (on) *vb* **1** to take sudden, violent action against — see ATTACK 1

2 to criticize harshly and usually publicly — see ATTACK 2

jumpiness *n* a state of nervousness marked by sudden jerky movements ⟨the police detective interpreted the suspect's *jumpiness* as a sign of guilt⟩

synonyms edginess, fidgets, flightiness, restiveness, skittishness

related words agitation, anxiety, anxiousness, apprehension, apprehensiveness, disquiet, feverishness, nervousness, perturbation, uneasiness, upset, worry; nerves, tenseness, tension; dither, jitters, shakes, shivers, willies

near antonyms confidence, self-assurance, self-confidence, sureness; control, self-control, aplomb, calm, calmness, collectedness, composure, coolheadedness, coolness, ease, easiness, equanimity, imperturbability, self-possession

jumpy *adj* **1** easily excited by nature — see EXCITABLE

2 feeling or showing uncomfortable feelings of uncertainty — see NERVOUS 1

junction *n* **1** a place where two or more things are united — see JOINT 1

2 the act or an instance of joining two or more things into one — see UNION 1

juncture *n* **1** a particular and often important moment in time — see POINT 1

2 a place where two or more things are united — see JOINT 1

3 a time or state of affairs requiring prompt or decisive action — see EMERGENCY

junior *adj* having not so great importance or rank as another — see LESSER

junior *n* one who is of lower rank and typically under the authority of another — see UNDERLING

junk *n* discarded or useless material — see GARBAGE

junk *vb* to get rid of as useless or unwanted — see DISCARD

junket *n* a short trip for pleasure — see EXCURSION 1

junket *vb* to entertain with a fancy meal — see FEAST

junkie *also* **junky** *n* a person who regularly uses drugs especially illegally — see DOPER

junking *n* the getting rid of whatever is unwanted or useless — see DISPOSAL 1

junky *adj* **1** having no usefulness — see WORTHLESS

2 of low quality — see CHEAP 2

junto *n* a group of persons formally joined together for some common interest — see ASSOCIATION 2

jurisdiction *n* lawful control over the affairs of a political unit (as a nation) — see RULE 2

just *adj* **1** being what is called for by accepted standards of right and wrong ⟨a *just* punishment should fit the crime⟩

synonyms deserved, due, merited, right, rightful, warranted

related words applicable, appropriate, apt, fit, fitting, meet, proper, requisite, suitable; lawful, legal; accurate, correct

near antonyms incoherent, irrelevant; improper, inapplicable, inappropriate, inapt, inequitable; arbitrary, despotic

antonyms undeserved, undue, unjust, unwarranted

2 based on sound reasoning or information — see GOOD 1

3 conforming to a high standard of morality or virtue — see GOOD 2

4 following the accepted rules of moral conduct — see HONORABLE 1

5 guided by or in accordance with one's sense of right and wrong — see CONSCIENTIOUS 1

6 marked by justice, honesty, and freedom from bias — see FAIR 2

just *adv* **1** in a like manner ⟨you can do it *just* the way they do⟩

synonyms exactly, precisely

related words as well, dead, even, expressly, perfectly

phrases to a T

near antonyms slightly, somewhat, vaguely

2 by a very small margin ⟨I was *just* over the minimum height requirement for admittance to the amusement park ride⟩

synonyms barely, hardly, marginally, scarcely, slightly

related words minimally, minutely; approximately, more or less, roughly, somewhat

near antonyms definitely, easily, plainly, positively, quite, unquestionably; abundantly, completely, copiously, generously, greatly

antonyms considerably, significantly, substantially, well

3 nothing more than ⟨I was *just* kidding⟩

synonyms but, merely, only, simply

4 as stated or indicated without the slightest difference — see EXACTLY 1

5 for nothing other than — see SOLELY 1

6 not long ago — see NEWLY

justice *n* **1** the act or practice of giving to others what is their due ⟨they felt that *justice* had been done in the case⟩

synonyms equity, right

related words fairness, impartiality; goodness, virtue; honor; decorum

near antonyms bias, partiality, prejudice; corruption, foul play; crime

antonyms inequity, injustice, wrong

2 a public official having authority to decide questions of law — see JUDGE 1

justifiable *adj* capable of being defended with good reasoning against verbal attack — see TENABLE 1

justification *n* an explanation that frees one from fault or blame — see EXCUSE

justified *adj* based on sound reasoning or information — see GOOD 1

justify *vb* **1** to be an acceptable reason for ⟨you seem to think that losing a basketball game *justifies* a temper tantrum⟩

synonyms excuse

related words account (for), explain, rationalize; brush (aside *or* off), condone, disregard, forgive, gloss (over), ignore, pardon, pass over, remit, shrug off, wink (at)

2 to continue to declare to be true or proper despite opposition or objections — see MAINTAIN 2

jut *n* a part that sticks out from the general mass of something — see BULGE

jut *vb* to extend outward beyond a usual point — see BULGE

juvenile *adj* **1** being in the early stage of life, growth, or development — see YOUNG

2 having or showing the annoying qualities (as silliness) associated with children — see CHILDISH

3 lacking in adult experience or maturity — see CALLOW

juvenile *n* a young person who is between infancy and adulthood — see CHILD 1

juxtaposed *adj* having a border in common — see ADJACENT

keelhaul *vb* to criticize (someone) severely or angrily especially for personal failings — see SCOLD

keen *adj* **1** able to sense slight impressions or differences — see ²ACUTE 1

2 causing intense discomfort to one's skin — see CUTTING 1

3 having an edge thin enough to cut or pierce something — see SHARP 1

4 having or showing quickness of mind — see INTELLIGENT 1

5 of the very best kind — see EXCELLENT

6 showing urgent desire or interest — see EAGER

keen *n* a crying out in grief — see LAMENT 1

keen *vb* to make a long loud mournful sound — see HOWL 1

keenness *n* **1** a harsh or sharp quality — see EDGE 1

2 urgent desire or interest — see EAGERNESS

keep *vb* **1** to act properly in relation to ⟨*keep* the Sabbath by not working⟩

synonyms celebrate, commemorate, observe

related words bless, consecrate, sanctify, solemnize; honor, laud, praise; obey, respect, revere, reverence, venerate; remember

phrases live up to

near antonyms disregard, forget, ignore, neglect, overlook

antonyms break, transgress, violate

2 to continue to have in one's possession or power ⟨the money is yours to *keep*⟩ ⟨*keep* my secret and don't tell it to anyone⟩

synonyms hang on (to), hold, reserve, retain, withhold

related words conserve, preserve, save; enjoy, have, own, possess; conduct, control, detain, direct; bear, harbor

near antonyms abandon, cede, yield; contribute, donate, give; discard, dump; decline, reject, repudiate, spurn

antonyms hand over, relinquish, surrender

3 to do what is required by the terms of — see FULFILL 1

4 to place somewhere for safekeeping or ready availability — see STORE 1

keep (from) *vb* to resist the temptation of — see FORBEAR

keep (to) *vb* to give steadfast support to — see ADHERE

keeper *n* **1** a person or group that watches over someone or something — see GUARD 1

2 a person who takes care of a property sometimes for an absent owner — see CUSTODIAN 1

keeping *n* **1** responsibility for the safety and well-being of someone or something — see CUSTODY

2 the fact or state of having (something) at one's disposal — see POSSESSION 1

keepsake *n* something that serves to keep alive the memory of a person or event — see MEMORIAL

keep up *vb* **1** to continue to operate or to meet one's needs — see HOLD OUT

2 to keep in good condition — see MAINTAIN 1

3 to remain indefinitely in existence or in the same state — see CONTINUE 1

keg *n* an enclosed wooden vessel for holding beverages — see CASK

kerchief *n* a scarf worn on the head — see BANDANNA

kerf *n* a V-shaped cut usually on an edge or a surface — see NOTCH 1

key *adj* **1** coming before all others in importance — see FOREMOST 1

2 of the greatest possible importance — see CRUCIAL

key *n* **1** an explanatory list of the symbols on a map or chart — see LEGEND 1

2 something that allows someone to achieve a desired goal — see PASSPORT

key *vb* to bring to a state free of conflicts, inconsistencies, or differences — see HARMONIZE 2

keystone *n* an immaterial thing upon which something else rests — see BASE 1

kibitzer *n* a person who meddles in the affairs of others — see BUSYBODY

kick *n* **1** a pleasurably intense stimulation of the feelings — see THRILL

2 a source of great satisfaction — see DELIGHT 1

3 a feeling or declaration of disapproval or dissent — see OBJECTION

kick *vb* **1** to express dissatisfaction, pain, or resentment usually tiresomely — see COMPLAIN

2 to present an opposing opinion or argument — see OBJECT

kick in *vb* to make a donation as part of a group effort — see CONTRIBUTE 1

kick off *vb* to take the first step in (a process or course of action) — see BEGIN 1

kid *n* a young person who is between infancy and adulthood — see CHILD 1

kid *vb* **1** to make fun of in a good-natured way — see TEASE 1

2 to make jokes — see JOKE

kidding *adj* marked by or expressive of mild or good-natured teasing — see QUIZZICAL

kiddish *adj* having or showing the annoying qualities (as silliness) associated with children — see CHILDISH

kidnap *vb* to carry a person away by unlawful force or against his or her will ⟨the child was *kidnapped* and held for ransom⟩
synonyms abduct
related words impress, shanghai, waylay; snatch, spirit
phrases make away with
near antonyms deliver, ransom, redeem, rescue; restore, return

kill *vb* **1** to deprive of life ⟨the soldier was *killed* in battle⟩
synonyms croak [*slang*], destroy, dispatch, do in, fell, slay
related words annihilate, blot out, butcher, decimate, massacre, slaughter, wipe out; cut down, finish, nip, snuff; assassinate, execute, murder, smite
phrases do away with
near antonyms restore, resurrect, resuscitate, revive; nurture
antonyms animate
2 to reject by or as if by a vote — see NEGATIVE 1
3 to show (something written) to be no longer valid by drawing a cross over or a line through it — see X (OUT)

killer *adj* **1** likely to cause or capable of causing death — see DEADLY
2 requiring considerable physical or mental effort — see HARD 2

killer *n* a person who kills another person — see ASSASSIN

killjoy *n* a person who spoils the pleasure of others ⟨his constant negative attitude made him a real *killjoy* when others were trying to have fun⟩
synonyms party pooper, spoilsport
related words fuddy-duddy, goody-goody, old maid, stick-in-the-mud; defeatist, pessimist; complainer, grouch, sorehead, whiner
near antonyms cutup, live wire; carouser, celebrant, celebrator, merrymaker, reveler (*or* reveller), roisterer; libertine, playboy, rake

kilter *n* a state of being or fitness — see CONDITION 1

kin *n* **1** a group of persons who come from the same ancestor — see FAMILY 1
2 a person connected with another by blood or marriage — see RELATIVE

kind *adj* **1** given to or made with heedful anticipation of the needs and happiness of others — see THOUGHTFUL 1
2 having or marked by sympathy and consideration for others — see HUMANE 1

kind *n* **1** a number of persons or things that are grouped together because they have something in common — see SORT 1
2 one of the units into which a whole is divided on the basis of a common characteristic — see CLASS 2

kindhearted *adj* having or marked by sympathy and consideration for others — see HUMANE 1

kindheartedness *n* the capacity for feeling for another's unhappiness or misfortune — see HEART 1

kindle *vb* to set (something) on fire — see BURN 2

kindled *adj* being on fire — see ABLAZE 1

kindliness *n* **1** kindly concern, interest, or support — see GOODWILL 1

2 the capacity for feeling for another's unhappiness or misfortune — see HEART 1

kindly *adj* having or marked by sympathy and consideration for others — see HUMANE 1

kindly *adv* with good reason or courtesy — see WELL 4

kindness *n* **1** an act of kind assistance — see FAVOR 1
2 the capacity for feeling for another's unhappiness or misfortune — see HEART 1

kind of *adv* to some degree or extent — see FAIRLY

kindred *adj* **1** having a close connection like that between family members — see RELATED
2 having or marked by agreement in feeling or action — see HARMONIOUS 3

kindred *n* a group of persons who come from the same ancestor — see FAMILY 1

kinfolk *n pl* a group of persons who come from the same ancestor — see FAMILY 1

king *n* a person of rank, power, or influence in a particular field — see MAGNATE

kingdom come *n* a dwelling place of perfect bliss for the soul after death — see HEAVEN 1

kingly *adj* fit for or worthy of a royal ruler — see MONARCHICAL

kingpin *n* the person (as an employer or supervisor) who tells people and especially workers what to do — see BOSS

king-size *or* **king-sized** *adj* **1** unusually large — see HUGE
2 of great extent from end to end — see LONG 1

king's ransom *n* a very large amount of money — see FORTUNE 2

kinky *adj* different from the ordinary in a way that causes curiosity or suspicion — see ODD 2

kinsfolk *n pl* a group of persons who come from the same ancestor — see FAMILY 1

kinship *n* the fact or state of having something in common — see CONNECTION 1

kinsman *n* a person connected with another by blood or marriage — see RELATIVE

kirk *n, chiefly Scottish* a building for public worship and especially Christian worship — see CHURCH 1

kiss *vb* **1** to touch one another with the lips as a sign of love ⟨it's traditional for couples to *kiss* under the mistletoe at Christmastime⟩
synonyms make out, pet, smooch
related words smack; caress, fondle, hug; bill, cuddle, nestle, snuggle
2 to pass lightly across or touch gently especially in passing — see BRUSH

kisser *n, slang* **1** the front part of the head — see FACE 1
2 the opening through which food passes into the body of an animal — see MOUTH 1

kittenish *adj* affecting shyness or modesty in order to attract masculine interest — see COY 1

¹**kitty** *n* a small domestic animal known for catching mice — see CAT 1

²**kitty** *n* a sum of money set aside for a particular purpose — see FUND 1

knack *n* a special and usually inborn ability — see TALENT

knapsack *n* a soft-sided case designed for carrying belongings especially on the back — see PACK 1

knave *n* a mean, evil, or unprincipled person — see VILLAIN

knavery *n* playful, reckless behavior that is not intended to cause serious harm — see MISCHIEF 1

knavish *adj* tending to or exhibiting reckless playfulness — see MISCHIEVOUS 1

knell *vb* to make the clear sound heard when metal vibrates — see RING 1

knickknack *n* a small object displayed for its attractiveness or interest ⟨a variety of pretty porcelain *knickknacks* adorned the mantel⟩
synonyms bauble, curio, curiosity, gaud, gewgaw, novelty, ornamental, trinket
related words bric-a-brac, trumpery; trifle; figurine, objet d'art, ornament; souvenir

knife *n* an instrument with a sharp edge for cutting ⟨be careful in using the *knife* to split open the cardboard box⟩
synonyms blade, cutter
related words bayonet, bolo, bowie knife, dagger, dirk, machete, pocketknife, poniard, stiletto, switchblade; saber, steel, sword; scalpel

knob *n* a small uneven mass — see LUMP 1

knock *n* **1** a hard strike with a part of the body or an instrument — see ¹BLOW
2 bad luck or an example of this — see MISFORTUNE

knock *vb* **1** to come into usually forceful contact with something — see HIT 2
2 to deliver a blow to (someone or something) usually in a strong vigorous manner — see HIT 1
3 to express one's unfavorable opinion of the worth or quality of — see CRITICIZE

knock (about) *vb* to move about from place to place aimlessly — see WANDER

knock (down *or* over) *vb* to strike (someone) so forcefully as to cause a fall — see FELL 1

knockabout *adj* being rough or noisy in a high-spirited way — see BOISTEROUS

knock down *vb* to take apart — see DISASSEMBLE

knock off *vb* **1** to bring (as an action or operation) to an immediate end — see STOP 1
2 to stop doing (something) permanently — see QUIT 2

knockout *adj* very pleasing to look at — see BEAUTIFUL

knockout *n* **1** a lovely woman — see BEAUTY 2
2 a temporary or permanent state of unconsciousness — see FAINT
3 something very good of its kind — see JIM-DANDY

knot *n* **1** a number of things considered as a unit — see GROUP 1
2 a small rounded mass of swollen tissue — see BUMP 1
3 a uniting or binding force or influence — see BOND 2
4 a usually small number of persons considered as a unit — see GROUP 2

5 something that requires thought and skill for resolution — see PROBLEM 1

knot *vb* to twist together into a usually confused mass — see ENTANGLE 1

knothead *n* a stupid person — see IDIOT

knotty *adj* **1** having many parts or aspects that are usually interrelated — see COMPLEX 1
2 requiring exceptional skill or caution in performance or handling — see TRICKY

know *vb* **1** to have a practical understanding of ⟨he *knows* several languages⟩
synonyms comprehend, grasp, understand
related words appreciate, apprehend, fathom, perceive; have, possess
near antonyms misapprehend, misconceive, misinterpret, misunderstand
2 to come to a knowledge of (something) by living through it — see EXPERIENCE

know–how *n* knowledge gained by actually doing or living through something — see EXPERIENCE 1

knowing *adj* **1** having inside information — see WISE 2
2 having or showing a practical cleverness or judgment — see SHREWD

knowingly *adv* with full awareness of what one is doing — see INTENTIONALLY

knowledge *n* **1** a body of facts learned by study or experience ⟨the forest ranger shared some of his vast *knowledge* of the woods with us⟩
synonyms lore, science, wisdom
related words information, intelligence, lowdown, news; data, evidence, facts; acquaintance, awareness, familiarity, literacy
near antonyms ignorance, inexperience, unfamiliarity
2 the understanding and information gained from being educated — see EDUCATION 2

knowledgeable *adj* **1** having information especially as a result of study or experience — see FAMILIAR 2
2 having or displaying advanced knowledge or education — see EDUCATED

knuckle under *vb* **1** to cease resistance (as to another's arguments, demands, or control) — see YIELD 3
2 to yield to the control or power of enemy forces — see FALL 2

kook *n* a person of odd or whimsical habits — see ECCENTRIC

kooky *adj* showing or marked by a lack of good sense or judgment — see FOOLISH 1

kowtow *vb* to use flattery or the doing of favors in order to win approval especially from a superior — see FAWN

label *n* a slip (as of paper or cloth) that is attached to something to identify or describe it ⟨on its frame the painting had a *label* with its title and the name of the artist⟩
synonyms marker, tag, ticket
related words caption, legend; brand, emblem, logo, mark, symbol; badge, decal, plaque, seal, stamp, sticker

label *vb* **1** to attach an identifying slip to ⟨he *labeled* all of the poisonous materials with the familiar skull and crossbones⟩
synonyms mark, tag, ticket

THESAURUS

related words caption, earmark, stamp; call, designate, identify, name, tab; brand, stigmatize

2 to give a name to — see NAME 1

labor *n* **1** a dull, unpleasant, or difficult piece of work — see CHORE 2

2 the active use of energy in producing a result — see EFFORT

3 very hard or unpleasant work — see TOIL

4 the act or process of giving birth to children — see CHILDBIRTH

labor *vb* to devote serious and sustained effort ⟨he *labored* most of the evening over the difficult homework assignment⟩

synonyms drudge, endeavor, fag, grub, hump, hustle, moil, peg (away), plod, plow, plug, slave, slog, strain, strive, struggle, sweat, toil, travail, work

related words apply (oneself), attempt, buckle (down), hammer (away), pitch in; attack, drive; essay, try; exercise, exert, overexert, overwork; eke out, grind (out), put out, scratch; trudge, wade; employ, ply, use, utilize, wield

near antonyms break, ease (up), let up, slacken; bum, goldbrick, idle, loaf, lounge, shirk, slack (off); dawdle, poke, tarry; relax, rest; disport, frolic, gambol, play, recreate, rollick, romp, sport

antonyms dabble, fiddle (around), fool (around), mess (around), putter (around)

laborer *n* a person who does very hard or dull work — see SLAVE 2

laborious *adj* **1** involved in often constant activity — see BUSY 1

2 requiring considerable physical or mental effort — see HARD 2

3 requiring much time, effort, or careful attention — see DEMANDING 1

laboriously *adv* with great effort or determination — see HARD 1

laborsaving *adj* designed to replace or decrease human labor and especially physical labor ⟨a new *laborsaving* device let us clean the house in half the time⟩

synonyms automated, automatic, robotic, self-acting

related words mechanical, motorized; computerized; aiding, helping; easing, relieving; timesaving

labyrinth *n* a confusing and complicated arrangement of passages — see MAZE

labyrinthine *adj* having many parts or aspects that are usually interrelated — see COMPLEX 1

lace *n* **1** a length of braided, flexible material that is used for tying or connecting things — see CORD

2 a length of something formed of three or more strands woven together — see BRAID

lace *vb* **1** to cause to twine about one another — see INTERTWINE 1

2 to scatter or set here and there among other things — see THREAD 1

3 to strike repeatedly — see BEAT 1

laceration *n* a long deep cut — see GASH

lachrymose *adj* given to expressing strong emotion (as sorrow) by readily shedding tears — see TEARFUL 1

lacing *n* **1** a length of braided, flexible material that is used for tying or connecting things — see CORD

2 a length of something formed of three or more strands woven together — see BRAID

lack *n* **1** the fact or state of being absent ⟨the *lack*

of news about the fate of the soldiers was frustrating⟩

synonyms absence, dearth, want

related words deficiency, deficit, inadequacy, insufficiency, meagerness, paucity, poverty, scantiness, scarceness, scarcity, shortage, skimpiness; deprivation, loss, necessity, need, needfulness, omission; privation; vacuum, void

near antonyms abundance, amplitude, bounty, plenitude, plenty, wealth; adequacy, sufficiency; excess, overabundance, oversupply, surfeit, surplus; deluge, flood; heap, mountain, peck, pile, pot, quantity, raft, stack, volume, wad; fund, pool, stock, supply; hoard, stockpile

antonyms presence

2 a falling short of an essential or desirable amount or number — see DEFICIENCY

3 a state of being without something necessary, desirable, or useful — see NEED 1

lackadaisical *adj* lacking bodily energy or motivation — see LISTLESS

lackey *n* a person hired to perform household or personal services — see SERVANT

lacking *adj* **1** not coming up to a usual standard or meeting a particular need — see SHORT 3

2 not present or in evidence — see ABSENT 2

laconic *adj* **1** marked by the use of few words to convey much information or meaning — see CONCISE

2 tending not to speak frequently (as by habit or inclination) — see SILENT 2

laconically *adv* in a few words — see SHORTLY 1

lad *n* **1** a male person who has not yet reached adulthood — see BOY

2 an adult male human being — see MAN 1

ladder *n* a scheme of rank or order — see ³SCALE 1

laddie *n* a male person who has not yet reached adulthood — see BOY

lade *vb* **1** to lift out with something that holds liquid — see DIP 2

2 to place a weight or burden on — see LOAD 1

lading *n* a mass or quantity of something taken up and carried, conveyed, or transported — see LOAD 1

ladle *n* a utensil with a bowl and a handle that is used especially in cooking and serving food — see SPOON

ladle *vb* to lift out with something that holds liquid — see DIP 2

lady *n* **1** an adult female human being — see WOMAN

2 the female partner in a marriage — see WIFE

3 a woman of high birth or social position — see GENTLEWOMAN

ladylove *n* a woman with whom one is in love — see GIRLFRIEND

lag *vb* **1** to lose bodily strength or vigor — see WEAKEN 2

2 to move or act slowly — see DELAY 1

laggard *adj* moving or proceeding at less than the normal, desirable, or required speed — see SLOW 1

laggard *n* someone who moves slowly or more slowly than others — see SLOWPOKE

laggardly *adv* at a pace that is less than usual, desirable, or expected — see SLOW

lagger *n* someone who moves slowly or more slowly than others — see SLOWPOKE

lagging *adj* moving or proceeding at less than the normal, desirable, or required speed — see SLOW

lagniappe *n* **1** something given in addition to what is ordinarily expected or owed — see BONUS
2 something given to someone without expectation of a return — see GIFT 1

laid–back *adj* having a relaxed, casual manner — see EASYGOING 1

lair *n* **1** a place where a person goes to hide — see HIDEOUT
2 the shelter or resting place of a wild animal — see DEN 1

lam *n* the act or an instance of getting free from danger or confinement — see ESCAPE 1

lam *vb* to get free from a dangerous or confining situation — see ESCAPE 1

lamb *n* an innocent or gentle person ⟨the new guys at football camp were *lambs* who hardly knew what awaited them⟩
synonyms angel, dove, innocent, sheep
related words fledgling, greenhorn, ingenue (*or* ingénue); cherub, saint; mollycoddle, sissy, softy (*or* softie), weakling, wimp; dupe, pigeon, sap, sucker
near antonyms bully, roughneck, rowdy, tough; beast, boor, cad, churl, clown, creep, cretin, cur, heel, jerk; shark, skunk, snake, stinker; rascal, rogue, scamp, villain
antonyms wolf

lambaste *or* **lambast** *vb* **1** to criticize (someone) severely or angrily especially for personal failings — see SCOLD
2 to criticize harshly and usually publicly — see ATTACK 2
3 to strike repeatedly — see BEAT 1

lambent *adj* giving off or reflecting much light — see BRIGHT 1

lame *vb* to cause severe or permanent injury to — see MAIM

lamella *n* a small thin piece of material that resembles an animal scale — see ²SCALE

lament *n* **1** a crying out in grief ⟨the national *lament* that was heard when President Kennedy was assassinated⟩
synonyms groan, howl, keen, lamentation, moan, plaint, wail
related words grieving, mourning, weeping; regret; complaint, outcry, protest
near antonyms cheering, laughing, smiling
antonyms exultation, rejoicing
2 a composition expressing one's grief over a loss ⟨a poem that is her *lament* for her late grandmother⟩
synonyms dirge, elegy, requiem, threnody
related words taps
near antonyms encomium, eulogy, paean, panegyric

lament *vb* **1** to feel or express sorrow for ⟨she *lamented* the loss of her beloved pet⟩
synonyms bemoan, bewail, deplore, grieve (for), mourn, wail (for)
related words elegize; complain (about), cry (for), groan (about), keen, moan, weep; regret, rue; deprecate, disapprove (of)
near antonyms beam, cheer, laugh, smile; boast, brag, crow
antonyms exult (in), glory (in), rejoice (in)
2 to feel sorry or dissatisfied about — see REGRET

lamentable *adj* **1** expressing or suggesting mourning — see MOURNFUL 1
2 of a kind to cause great distress — see REGRETTABLE

lamentation *n* a crying out in grief — see LAMENT 1

lamina *n* a small thin piece of material that resembles an animal scale — see ²SCALE

lamp *n* something that provides illumination — see LIGHT 2

lampoon *n* a creative work that uses sharp humor to point up the foolishness of a person, institution, or human nature in general — see SATIRE

lance *n* a weapon with a long straight handle and sharp head or blade — see SPEAR

lance *vb* to penetrate or hold (something) with a pointed object — see IMPALE

land *n* **1** a body of people composed of one or more nationalities usually with its own territory and government — see NATION
2 a broad geographical area — see REGION 2
3 the solid part of our planet's surface as distinguished from the sea and air — see EARTH 2

land *vb* **1** to stop at or near a place along the shore ⟨the Pilgrims *landed* at Plymouth after exploring Cape Cod Bay⟩
synonyms anchor, dock
related words moor, tie up; beach, ground; harbor; arrive, reach; debark, disembark
phrases drop anchor, make port
near antonyms embark, launch, sail
2 to get to a destination — see COME 2
3 to go ashore from a ship — see DISEMBARK
4 to come to rest after descending from the air — see ALIGHT
5 to receive as return for effort — see EARN 1
6 to take physical control or possession of (something) suddenly or forcibly — see CATCH 1

landfill *n* a place where discarded materials (as trash) are dumped — see DUMP 1

landing *n* a structure used by boats and ships for taking on or landing cargo and passengers — see DOCK

landlord *n* the owner of land or housing that is rented to another ⟨agreed to pay the *landlord* the rent on the first Monday of each month⟩
synonyms lessor, renter
related words landlady; laird, landholder, landowner; host, proprietor; slumlord
antonyms lessee, lodger, tenant

landmark *n* a point in a chain of events at which an important change (as in one's fortunes) occurs — see TURNING POINT

language *n* **1** the stock of words, pronunciation, and grammar used by a people as their basic means of communication ⟨Great Britain, the United States, Australia, and other countries where English is the dominant *language*⟩
synonyms lingo, mother tongue, speech, tongue, vocabulary
related words argot, cant, dialect, idiom, jargon, parlance, patois, patter, pidgin, slang, vernacular; colloquialism, localism, regionalism; terminology
2 the special terms or expressions of a particular group or field — see TERMINOLOGY
3 the way in which something is put into words — see WORDING

languid *adj* **1** lacking bodily energy or motivation — see LISTLESS
2 lacking bodily strength — see WEAK 1
3 moving or proceeding at less than the normal, desirable, or required speed — see SLOW 1

languish *vb* to lose bodily strength or vigor — see WEAKEN 2

languishing *adj* lacking bodily energy or motivation — see LISTLESS

languor *n* the quality or state of lacking physical strength or vigor — see WEAKNESS 1

languorous *adj* lacking bodily energy or motivation — see LISTLESS

lank *adj* not stiff in structure — see LIMP 1

lanky *adj* being tall, thin and usually loose-jointed ⟨the *lanky* basketball star was great at slam-dunking⟩
synonyms gangling, gangly, rangy, spindling, spindly
related words angular, bony, gaunt, lank, rawboned, scrawny, skinny; lean, slender, slim, spare, thin; racy, reedy, spidery, stringy, twiggy, wiry; spindle-shanked
near antonyms chubby, chunky, heavyset, pudgy, squat, stocky, stout, stubby, stumpy, sturdy, thick-bodied, thickset; muscle-bound

lap *n* a portion of a trip — see LEG 2

¹lap *vb* **1** to flow along or against — see WASH 1
2 to flow in a broken irregular stream — see GURGLE
3 to move with a splashing motion — see SLOSH

²lap *vb* **1** to lie over parts of one another — see OVERLAP
2 to surround or cover closely — see ENFOLD 1

lapping *n* a partial covering of one thing by an adjoining thing — see OVERLAP

lapse *n* **1** a change in status for the worse usually temporarily — see REVERSE 1
2 an unintentional departure from truth or accuracy — see ERROR 1
3 the stopping of a process or activity — see END 1

lapse *vb* to come to an end — see CEASE 1

larceny *n* the unlawful taking and carrying away of property without the consent of its owner — see THEFT 1

large *adj* of a size greater than average of its kind ⟨he was hungry, so he ordered the *large* pizza⟩
synonyms big, bulky, considerable, goodly, good-sized, grand, great, handsome, hefty, hulking, largish, outsize (*also* outsized), oversize (*or* oversized), sizable (*or* sizeable), substantial, tidy, voluminous
related words astronomical (*also* astronomic), bumper, cavernous, colossal, enormous, gigantic, gross, heroic, huge, immense, jumbo, king-size (*or* king-sized), major, mammoth, massive, monolithic, monstrous, monumental, prodigious, staggering, stupendous, super, tremendous, vast, vasty, whacking, whopping; excessive, exorbitant, extravagant, extreme, immoderate, inordinate; abundant, ample, appreciable, copious, plentiful; fat, thick; capacious, commodious, roomy, spacious
near antonyms diminutive, microscopic (*or* microscopical), midget, miniature, minute, pint-size (*or* pint-sized), pocket-size (*also* pocket-sized), pygmy, smallish, teeny, teeny-weeny, tiny, wee; petite, slender, slight, slim, thin
antonyms little, puny, small, undersized

largely *adv* **1** for the most part — see CHIEFLY
2 to a large extent or degree — see GREATLY 2

largeness *n* the quality or state of being large in size ⟨I was impressed by the *largeness* of the portions at the new restaurant⟩
synonyms bigness, bulkiness, grandness, greatness, heftiness, substantiality, voluminousness

related words enormity, enormousness, extensiveness, grossness, healthiness, hugeness, immenseness, immensity, magnitude, massiveness, stupendousness, vastness; excessiveness, extravagance, extremeness, immoderacy; abundance, ampleness, bountifulness, copiousness, liberality; adequacy, sufficiency; weightiness
near antonyms diminutiveness, minuteness, tininess; slightness; meagerness, poorness, scantiness, scarceness, scarcity, skimpiness, slenderness, slimness, spareness, sparseness, stinginess; deficiency, inadequacy
antonyms fineness, littleness, puniness, smallness

largess *or* **largesse** *n* **1** something given to someone without expectation of a return — see GIFT 1
2 the quality or state of being generous — see LIBERALITY

largish *adj* **1** of a size greater than average of its kind — see LARGE
2 sufficiently large in size, amount, or number to merit attention — see CONSIDERABLE 1

lariat *n* a rope or long leather thong with a noose used especially for catching livestock — see LASSO

lark *n* a time or instance of carefree fun — see FLING 1

lark *vb* to play and run about happily — see FROLIC 1

larva *n* a young wingless often wormlike form (as a grub or caterpillar) that hatches from the egg of many insects ⟨the *larva* looked ugly, but it was destined to hatch into a beautiful butterfly⟩
synonyms naiad, nymph

lascivious *adj* **1** depicting or referring to sexual matters in a way that is unacceptable in polite society — see OBSCENE 1
2 having a strong sexual desire — see LUSTFUL

lasciviousness *n* the quality or state of being obscene — see OBSCENITY 1

lash *n* a long thin or flexible tool for striking — see WHIP

lash *vb* to strike repeatedly with something long and thin or flexible — see WHIP 1

lass *n* a young usually unmarried woman — see GIRL 1

lassie *n* a young usually unmarried woman — see GIRL 1

lassitude *n* a complete depletion of energy or strength — see FATIGUE

lasso *n* a rope or long leather thong with a noose used especially for catching livestock ⟨the cowpuncher skillfully tossed the *lasso* around the calf's neck⟩
synonyms lariat, reata, riata

last *adj* following all others of the same kind in order or time ⟨*last* one in the pool is a rotten egg⟩
synonyms closing, concluding, final, hindmost, latest, latter, rearmost, terminal, terminating, ultimate
related words consequent, ensuing, eventual, following, succeeding; conclusive, crowning, decisive, definitive; farthest, furthest, remotest; lowermost, lowest, nethermost; endmost, extreme, outermost, outmost; penultimate
near antonyms eminent, premier, superior
antonyms beginning, earliest, first, inaugural, initial, maiden, opening, original, primary, starting

last *vb* **1** to continue to operate or to meet one's needs — see HOLD OUT

2 to remain indefinitely in existence or in the same state — see CONTINUE 1

last word *n* a practice or interest that is very popular for a short time — see FAD

late *adj* **1** not arriving, occurring, or settled at the due, usual, or proper time ⟨I ran as fast as I could, but was still *late* for class⟩
  synonyms behind, behindhand, belated, delinquent, latish, overdue, tardy
  related words delayed, detained, postponed; dilatory, laggard, slow, sluggish
  near antonyms opportune, seasonable, timely; prompt, punctual
  antonyms early, premature
2 having been such at some previous time — see FORMER
3 no longer living — see DEAD 1

late *adv* not long ago — see NEWLY

lately *adv* not long ago — see NEWLY

latency *n* a state of temporary inactivity — see ABEYANCE

lateness *n* the quality or state of being late ⟨we were unable to get into the movie due to our *lateness* in arriving⟩
  synonyms belatedness, delinquency, tardiness
  related words dilatoriness, sluggishness
  near antonyms promptness, punctuality
  antonyms earliness

latent *adj* not being in a state of use, activity, or employment — see INACTIVE 2

later *adj* being, occurring, or carried out at a time after something else — see SUBSEQUENT

later *adv* following in time or place — see AFTER

lateral *adj* of, relating to, or located on one side — see SIDE

latest *adj* following all others of the same kind in order or time — see LAST

lather *n* **1** a light mass of fine bubbles formed in or on a liquid — see FOAM
2 a state of nervous or irritated concern — see FRET

lathery *adj* covered with, consisting of, or resembling foam — see FOAMY

latish *adj* not arriving, occurring, or settled at the due, usual, or proper time — see LATE 1

latitude *n* the right to act or move freely — see FREEDOM 2

latrine *n* a room furnished with a fixture for flushing body waste — see TOILET

latter *adj* following all others of the same kind in order or time — see LAST

laud *vb* **1** to declare enthusiastic approval of — see ACCLAIM
2 to proclaim the glory of — see PRAISE 1

laudable *adj* deserving of high regard or great approval — see ADMIRABLE

laugh *n* **1** an explosive sound that is a sign of amusement ⟨the child's frown turned into a *laugh* when he saw the clown⟩
  synonyms cackle, chortle, chuckle, giggle, guffaw, laughter, snicker, snigger, titter
  related words crow, whoop; grin, simper, smile, smirk
  near antonyms cry, groan, moan, sob, wail
2 someone or something that is very funny — see SCREAM
3 something said or done to cause laughter — see JOKE 1

laugh *vb* to express scornful amusement by means of facial contortions — see SNEER

laugh (at) *vb* to make (someone or something) the object of unkind laughter — see RIDICULE

laughable *adj* **1** causing or intended to cause laughter — see FUNNY 1
2 so foolish or pointless as to be worthy of scornful laughter — see RIDICULOUS 1

laughing *adj* indicative of or marked by high spirits or good humor — see MERRY

laughingstock *n* a person or thing that is made fun of ⟨his nerdy clothes made him the *laughingstock* of the schoolyard⟩
  synonyms butt, mark, mock, mockery, target
  related words chump, dupe, fall guy, fool, gull, monkey, pigeon, sap, sucker, victim
  near antonyms favorite, darling, pet

laughter *n* an explosive sound that is a sign of amusement — see LAUGH 1

launch *n* **1** a rising from a surface at the start of a flight (as of a rocket) — see LIFT-OFF
2 the point at which something begins — see BEGINNING

launch *vb* **1** to be responsible for the creation and early operation or use of — see FOUND
2 to take the first step in (a process or course of action) — see BEGIN 1
3 to send through the air especially with a quick forward motion of the arm — see THROW

laurels *n pl* public acknowledgment or admiration for an achievement — see GLORY 1

lavaliere *also* **lavalliere** *n* an ornament worn on a chain around the neck or wrist — see PENDANT

lavatory *n* a room furnished with a fixture for flushing body waste — see TOILET

lave *vb* to flow along or against — see WASH 1

lavish *adj* **1** going beyond a normal or acceptable limit in degree or amount — see EXCESSIVE
2 pouring forth in great amounts — see PROFUSE
3 showing obvious signs of wealth and comfort — see LUXURIOUS

lavish *vb* **1** to give readily and in large quantities — see RAIN 2
2 to use up carelessly — see WASTE 1

lavishly *adv* in a luxurious manner — see HIGH

lavishness *n* the quality or fact of being free or wasteful in the expenditure of money — see EXTRAVAGANCE 1

law *n* **1** a rule of conduct or action laid down by a governing authority and especially a legislator ⟨a record number of *laws* were passed in that legislative session⟩
  synonyms act, enactment, ordinance, statute
  related words decree, directive, edict, fiat, ruling; bylaw, regulation, rule; amendment, bill, legislation; common law, martial law; prohibition, restriction; canon, encyclical
2 a collection or system of rules of conduct — see CODE
3 the department of government that keeps order, fights crime, and enforces statutes — see POLICE 1

law–abiding *adj* readily giving in to the command or authority of another — see OBEDIENT

lawbreaker *n* a person who has committed a crime — see CRIMINAL

lawbreaking *adj* not restrained by or under the control of legal authority — see LAWLESS

lawbreaking *n* **1** a breaking of a moral or legal code — see OFFENSE 1
2 activities that are in violation of the laws of the state — see CRIME 1

lawful *adj* permitted by law — see LEGAL 1

lawfulness *n* the quality or state of being legal — see LEGALITY

lawgiver *n* a member of an organized body of persons having the authority to make laws — see LEGISLATOR

lawless *adj* not restrained by or under the control of legal authority ⟨the *lawless* rioters were destroying everything in sight⟩

synonyms anarchic, disorderly, lawbreaking, unruly

related words defiant, insubordinate, mutinous, rebellious, refractory, riotous; undisciplined; criminal, illegal, illegitimate, illicit, unlawful, wrongful

near antonyms lawful, legal, legalized, legitimate

antonyms law-abiding, orderly

lawlessness *n* **1** a state in which there is widespread wrongdoing and disregard for rules and authority — see ANARCHY

2 activities that are in violation of the laws of the state — see CRIME 1

lawmaker *n* a member of an organized body of persons having the authority to make laws — see LEGISLATOR

lawsuit *n* a court case for enforcing a right or claim ⟨she filed a *lawsuit* against the moving company that was responsible for breaking her furniture⟩

synonyms action, proceeding, suit

related words litigation; case, cause, complaint

lawyer *n* a person whose profession is to conduct lawsuits for clients or to advise about legal rights and obligations ⟨their *lawyers* told them that they couldn't use the park for the concert without permission from the city⟩

synonyms advocate, attorney, counsel, counselor (*or* counsellor)

related words pettifogger, shyster; district attorney, prosecutor; solicitor; jurist; lawgiver, lawmaker, legislator, solon

lax *adj* **1** failing to give proper care and attention — see NEGLIGENT

2 not bound by rigid standards — see EASYGOING 2

3 not tightly fastened, tied, or stretched — see LOOSE 1

laxness *n* failure to take the care that a cautious person usually takes — see NEGLIGENCE 1

lay *n* **1** a rhythmic series of musical tones arranged to give a pleasing effect — see MELODY

2 a short musical composition for the human voice often with instrumental accompaniment — see SONG 1

lay *vb* **1** to arrange something in a certain spot or position — see PLACE 1

2 to cause to come to rest at the bottom (as of a liquid) — see SETTLE 1

3 to establish or apply as a charge or penalty — see IMPOSE

4 to make ready in advance — see PREPARE 1

5 to put a layer of on a surface — see SPREAD 2

6 to risk (something) on the outcome of an uncertain event — see BET

lay away *vb* to put (something of future use or value) in a safe or secret place — see HOARD

lay down *vb* **1** to put into effect through legislative or authoritative action — see ENACT

2 to state clearly and strongly — see ASSERT 1

3 to give the rules about (something) clearly and exactly — see PRESCRIBE

layoff *n* the termination of the employment of an employee or a work force often temporarily ⟨many people lost their jobs in the *layoff*⟩

synonyms discharge, dismissal, furlough

related words closing, shutdown; downsizing

lay off *vb* to bring (as an action or operation) to an immediate end — see STOP 1

lay off (of) *vb* to stop doing (something) permanently — see QUIT 2

layout *n* **1** the way in which something is sized, arranged, or organized — see FORMAT 1

2 the way in which the elements of something (as a work of art) are arranged — see COMPOSITION 3

lay out *vb* **1** to hand over or use up in payment — see SPEND 1

2 to work out the details of (something) in advance — see PLAN 1

layover *n* a brief halt in a journey — see STOP 1

lay up *vb* to put (something of future use or value) in a safe or secret place — see HOARD

laziness *n* an inclination not to do work or engage in activities ⟨although she often talks about ambitious household projects, nothing even gets started because of her *laziness*⟩

synonyms idleness, indolence, inertia, shiftlessness, sloth

related words apathy, languor, lassitude, lethargy, listlessness, sluggishness; goldbricking, loafing

near antonyms enterprise, initiative; assiduity, diligence, perseverance; energy, pep, vigor, vim, vitality

antonyms drive, industriousness, industry

lazy *adj* not easily aroused to action or work ⟨the *lazy* dog just wanted to lie on the couch all day and sleep⟩

synonyms idle, indolent, shiftless, slothful

related words apathetic, languorous, lazyish, lethargic, listless, sluggish, torpid

near antonyms ambitious, diligent, enterprising, zealous; dynamic, energetic, exuberant, lively, vigorous

antonyms industrious

lazybones *n pl* a lazy person ⟨he's a *lazybones* who is never willing to do any work⟩

synonyms drone, idler, loafer, slouch, slug, sluggard

related words bum, ne'er-do-well; sleepyhead; dawdler, laggard, putterer, slowpoke, stick-in-the-mud, trifler; goldbrick, malingerer, shirker, slacker; dallier, lingerer, loiterer, lounger, saunterer; delayer, procrastinator; dropout, quitter

near antonyms live wire, powerhouse

antonyms doer, go-getter, hummer, hustler, rustler, self-starter

lea *n* open land over which livestock may roam and feed — see RANGE 1

lead *adj* highest in rank or authority — see HEAD

lead *n* **1** the person who has the most important role in a play, movie, or TV show — see STAR 2

2 the space or amount of space between two points, lines, surfaces, or objects — see DISTANCE

3 a piece of advice or useful information especially from an expert — see ¹TIP 1

4 a slight or indirect pointing to something (as a solution or explanation) — see HINT 1

lead *vb* **1** to point out the way for (someone) especially from a position in front ⟨the tour guide *led* the group through the museum⟩

synonyms conduct, direct, guide, marshal, pilot, route, show, steer, usher

related words precede; accompany, attend, chaperone (*or* chaperon), convoy, escort, see; control, manage

near antonyms dog, hound, shadow, tail, tailgate

antonyms follow, trail

2 to serve as leader of ⟨the honor of *leading* the soccer squad⟩

synonyms boss, captain, command, dominate, head, spearhead

related words control, direct, govern, handle, manage, oversee, regulate, superintend, supervise

near antonyms bow (to), comply (with), defer (to), follow, obey, serve, submit (to), yield (to)

3 to be at the front of ⟨the marching band *led* the parade⟩

synonyms head

related words precede; announce, herald; accompany, attend, escort, usher

near antonyms conclude, end, finish, stop, terminate; tail, tailgate; dog, follow, trail

4 to be positioned along a certain course or in a certain direction — see RUN 3

5 to give advice and instruction to (someone) regarding the course or process to be followed — see GUIDE 1

leaden *adj* **1** causing weariness, restlessness, or lack of interest — see BORING

2 of the color gray — see GRAY 1

leader *n* **1** a long hollow cylinder for carrying a substance (as a liquid or gas) — see PIPE 1

2 the person (as an employer or supervisor) who tells people and especially workers what to do — see BOSS

leading *adj* **1** coming before all others in importance — see FOREMOST 1

2 highest in rank or authority — see HEAD

lead on *vb* to lead away from a usual or proper course by offering some pleasure or advantage — see LURE

leafage *n* green leaves or plants — see GREENERY 1

leaflet *n* a short printed publication with no cover or with a paper cover — see PAMPHLET

leafy *adj* covered with a thick, healthy natural growth — see LUSH 1

league *n* **1** a group of persons formally joined together for some common interest — see ASSOCIATION 2

2 an association of persons, parties, or states for mutual assistance and protection — see CONFEDERACY

league *vb* to form or enter into an association that furthers the interests of its members — see ALLY

leak (out) *vb* to become known — see GET OUT 1

lean *adj* having a noticeably small amount of body fat — see THIN 1

lean *n* the degree to which something rises up from a position level with the horizon — see SLANT

lean *vb* **1** to set or cause to be at an angle ⟨just *lean* the ladder against the tree and climb up it⟩

synonyms angle, cant, cock, heel, incline, list, slant, slope, tilt, tip

related words bank; bend, deviate, swerve, veer; decline, descend, recline, retreat

near antonyms even, flatten, level, straighten

2 to show a liking or proneness (for something) ⟨his diet *leans* toward greasy food⟩

synonyms incline, run, tend, trend

related words go, gravitate; indicate, point, suggest

near antonyms avoid, shun, shy (from *or* away from)

3 to place reliance or trust — see DEPEND 2

lean (toward) *vb* to show partiality toward — see PREFER 1

leaning *adj* running in a slanting direction — see DIAGONAL

leaning *n* **1** a prevailing or general movement or inclination — see TREND 1

2 a habitual attraction to some activity or thing — see INCLINATION 1

leap *n* an act of leaping into the air — see JUMP 1

leap *vb* to propel oneself upward or forward into the air — see JUMP 1

leaping *adj* passing from one topic to another — see DISCURSIVE

learn *vb* **1** to acquire complete knowledge, understanding, or skill in ⟨after months of trying, he finally *learned* the dance steps⟩

synonyms get, master, pick up

related words apprehend, comprehend, grasp, know, understand; absorb, assimilate, digest, imbibe; ascertain, descry, detect, determine, dig up, discern, discover, examine, find out, hear, hit (on *or* upon), run down, scare up, search (for), see, track (down), tumble (to), unearth; major (in), study; memorize

phrases get the hang (*or* knack) of

near antonyms forget, misunderstand; miss, overlook; disregard, ignore, neglect

antonyms unlearn

2 to come to an awareness — see DISCOVER 1

3 to come upon after searching, study, or effort — see FIND 1

4 to commit to memory — see MEMORIZE

learned *adj* **1** having or displaying advanced knowledge or education — see EDUCATED

2 suggestive of the vocabulary used in books — see BOOKISH

learnedness *n* the understanding and information gained from being educated — see EDUCATION 2

learning *n* the understanding and information gained from being educated — see EDUCATION 2

lease *vb* **1** to give the possession and use of (something) in return for periodic payment — see RENT 1

2 to take or get the temporary use of (something) for a set sum — see HIRE 1

least *adj* being the least in amount, number, or size possible — see MINIMAL

leather *n* **1** the hairless natural covering of an animal prepared for use ⟨the company claims to use only the finest *leathers* for its shoes and handbags⟩

synonyms hide, skin

related words coat, fleece, fur, pelt; alligator, buckskin, calfskin, chamois, cordovan, cowhide, deerskin, doeskin, goatskin, horsehide, kid, kidskin, lambskin, morocco, pigskin, seal, sharkskin, sheepskin, snakeskin, suede

2 the outer covering of an animal removed for its commercial value — see HIDE 1

leathery *adj* not easily chewed — see TOUGH 1

leave *n* **1** a period during which the usual routine of school or work is suspended — see VACATION

2 the approval by someone in authority for the doing of something — see PERMISSION

leave *vb* **1** to cause to remain behind ⟨you can

leave your lunch in the refrigerator while we're outside⟩ ⟨lovers who promise never to *leave* one another⟩
synonyms abandon, desert, forsake, maroon, quit
related words discard, ditch, dump, fling, jettison, junk, scrap, shed, shuck (off), throw away, throw out; deliver, give up, hand over, relinquish, surrender, yield; retreat (from), take off (from), vacate, withdraw (from); abjure, cut off, disown, reject, renounce, repudiate, separate (from); sacrifice; distance; disregard, forget, ignore, neglect
phrases walk out on
near antonyms harbor, have, hold, keep, own, possess, reserve, retain, withhold; redeem, rescue, save
antonyms reclaim
2 to give by means of a will ⟨I'm going to *leave* all of my possessions to my children⟩
synonyms bequeath, will
related words deed; hand down, pass (down); devise
3 to give up (a job or office) — see QUIT 1
4 to put (something) into the possession or safekeeping of another — see GIVE 2
leave off *vb* **1** to bring (as an action or operation) to an immediate end — see STOP 1
2 to come to an end — see CEASE 1
leave–taking *n* **1** the act of leaving a place — see DEPARTURE
2 the act or process of two or more persons going off in different directions — see PARTING 1
leavings *n pl* a remaining group or portion — see REMAINDER 1
lecture *vb* **1** to criticize (someone) severely or angrily especially for personal failings — see SCOLD
2 to give a formal often extended talk on a subject — see TALK 1
leech *n* a person who is supported or seeks support from another without making an adequate return ⟨whenever the gang went out for pizza, the *leech* in the group always had an excuse for not paying his fair share⟩
synonyms hanger-on, parasite, sponge, sponger
related words dependent; deadbeat, idler; flunky (*also* flunkey), henchman, lackey, satellite, stooge, sycophant, toady, yes-man; cheapskate, miser, niggard, piker, scrooge, skinflint, tightwad
near antonyms benefactor, philanthropist, supporter
leer (at) *vb* to look at in a flirtatious or desiring way — see OGLE
leery *adj* inclined to doubt or question claims — see SKEPTICAL 1
leeward *adj* being in the direction that the wind is blowing — see DOWNWIND
left *n* a political belief stressing progress, the essential goodness of humankind, and individual freedom — see LIBERALISM
left–handed *adj* not being or expressing what one appears to be or express — see INSINCERE
leftover *n* an unused or unwanted piece or item typically of small size or value — see ¹SCRAP 1
leftovers *n* a remaining group or portion — see REMAINDER 1
leg *n* **1** a lower limb of an animal ⟨he broke his *leg* when he accidentally stepped in that gopher hole⟩
synonyms pin
related words member; foreleg, forelimb; calf, drumstick, shank, shin, thigh

2 a portion of a trip ⟨on the first *leg* of the cruise they went south to the Caribbean⟩
synonyms lap, stage
related words layover, stopover
leg (it) *vb* to go on foot — see WALK
legacy *n* something that is or may be inherited — see INHERITANCE
legal *adj* **1** permitted by law ⟨drinking is only *legal* if you are 21 years old⟩
synonyms lawful, legitimate
related words allowable, authorized, noncriminal, permissible; justifiable, warrantable; regulation, statutory; good, innocent, proper, right
near antonyms bad, corrupt, evil, immoral, iniquitous, reprobate, sinful, wicked, wrong; banned, criminal, forbidden, guilty, outlawed, prohibited, unauthorized, unjust; nonconstitutional, unconstitutional
antonyms illegal, illegitimate, illicit, unlawful, wrongful
2 following or according to the rules — see FAIR 3
legality *n* the quality or state of being legal ⟨the senator questioned the *legality* of the proposed program⟩
synonyms lawfulness, legitimacy
related words rightfulness, rightness; permissibility, permissibleness
near antonyms badness, immorality, iniquity, sinfulness, unjustness, wickedness, wrongness; criminality, unconstitutionality
antonyms illegality, illegitimacy, unlawfulness, wrongfulness
legal tender *n* something (as pieces of stamped metal or printed paper) customarily and legally used as a medium of exchange, a measure of value, or a means of payment — see MONEY
legate *n* a person sent on a mission to represent another — see AMBASSADOR
legatee *n* a person who has the right to inherit property — see HEIR
legend *n* **1** an explanatory list of the symbols on a map or chart ⟨the *legend* indicated that a large circle represented each city, while a small circle stood for a small town⟩
synonyms key
related words scale; caption; guide, table
2 an explanation or description accompanying a pictorial illustration — see CAPTION 1
3 a traditional but unfounded story that gives the reason for a current custom, belief, or fact of nature — see MYTH 1
4 the body of customs, beliefs, stories, and sayings associated with a people, thing, or place — see FOLKLORE
legendary *adj* based on, described in, or being a myth — see MYTHICAL 1
legerdemain *n* **1** the art or skill of performing tricks or illusions for entertainment — see MAGIC 2
2 the use of clever underhanded actions to achieve an end — see TRICKERY
legion *n* **1** a large body of men and women organized for land warfare — see ARMY 1
2 a great number of persons or things gathered together — see CROWD 1
legionary *n* a person engaged in military service — see SOLDIER
legionnaire *n* a person engaged in military service — see SOLDIER

legislate *vb* to put into effect through legislative or authoritative action — see ENACT

legislator *n* a member of an organized body of persons having the authority to make laws ⟨the *legislators* met in an all-night session to hammer out the details of the bill⟩
synonyms lawgiver, lawmaker, solon
related words assemblyman, assemblywoman; congressman, congresswoman; senator

legitimacy *n* the quality or state of being legal — see LEGALITY

legitimate *adj* permitted by law — see LEGAL 1

lei *n* an ornamental chain or string (as of beads) worn around the neck — see NECKLACE

leisure *n* freedom from activity or labor — see ¹REST 1

leisurely *adj* moving or proceeding at less than the normal, desirable, or required speed — see SLOW 1

leisurely *adv* at a pace that is less than usual, desirable, or expected — see SLOW

lemon *n* something that has failed — see FAILURE 3

lend *vb* to give to another for temporary use with the understanding that it or a like thing will be returned ⟨I can *lend* you my copy of the textbook until the weekend⟩ ⟨can you *lend* me five dollars?⟩
synonyms advance, loan
related words furnish, give, grant; lease, let [*chiefly British*], rent
near antonyms receive, take
antonyms borrow

length *n* the space or amount of space between two points, lines, surfaces, or objects — see DISTANCE

lengthen *vb* to make longer — see EXTEND 1

lengthening *n* the act of making longer — see EXTENSION 1

lengthy *adj* 1 of great extent from end to end — see LONG 1
2 lasting for a considerable time — see LONG 2

lenience *n* kind, gentle, or compassionate treatment especially towards someone who is undeserving of it — see MERCY 1

leniency *n* kind, gentle, or compassionate treatment especially towards someone who is undeserving of it — see MERCY 1

lenity *n* kind, gentle, or compassionate treatment especially towards someone who is undeserving of it — see MERCY 1

leprechaun *n* an imaginary being usually having a small human form and magical powers — see FAIRY

less *adj* having not so great importance or rank as another — see LESSER

lessen *vb* 1 to make smaller in amount, volume, or extent — see DECREASE 1
2 to grow less in scope or intensity especially gradually — see DECREASE 2

lesser *adj* having not so great importance or rank as another ⟨it was the *lesser* evil of the two choices⟩
synonyms inferior, junior, less, lower, minor, smaller, subordinate, under
related words little, mean, small; minute, petty; jerkwater, one-horse, second-class, second-rate, two-bit; secondary, subsidiary
near antonyms exceptional, first-class, first-rate
antonyms greater, higher, major, more, primary, prime, senior, superior

lesson *n* something assigned to be read or studied ⟨your *lesson* for tonight will be the chapter on chemical reactions⟩
synonyms assignment, reading
related words homework, schoolwork; lecture; drill, exercise, practice (*also* practise); etude, study

lessor *n* the owner of land or housing that is rented to another — see LANDLORD

let *n* something that makes movement or progress more difficult — see ENCUMBRANCE

let *vb* 1 to give permission to — see ALLOW
2 *chiefly British* to give the possession and use of (something) in return for periodic payment — see RENT 1
3 to make able or possible — see ENABLE 1

letdown *n* 1 the emotion felt when one's expectations are not met — see DISAPPOINTMENT 1
2 something that disappoints — see DISAPPOINTMENT 2

let down *vb* to fall short in satisfying the expectation or hope of — see DISAPPOINT

lethal *adj* likely to cause or capable of causing death — see DEADLY

lethargic *adj* slow to move or act — see INACTIVE 1

let on *vb* to take on a false or deceptive appearance — see PRETEND 1

letter *n* a message on paper from one person or group to another ⟨he wrote her a *letter* every week she was away⟩
synonyms dispatch, epistle, memo, memorandum, missive, note
related words airmail, card, electronic mail, e-mail, junk mail, mail, postal card, postcard; communication, report; encyclical

letter carrier *n* a person who delivers mail — see POSTMAN

letter–perfect *adj* being entirely without fault or flaw — see PERFECT 1

letup *n* a usually gradual decrease in the pace or level of activity of something — see SLOWDOWN

let up *vb* 1 to come to an end — see CEASE 1
2 to grow less in scope or intensity especially gradually — see DECREASE 2

levee *n* 1 a bank of earth constructed to control water — see DAM
2 a structure used by boats and ships for taking on or landing cargo and passengers — see DOCK

level *adj* having a surface without bends, breaks, or irregularities ⟨looked for a *level* place to land the plane⟩
synonyms even, flat, flush, plane, smooth
related words exact, uniform; aligned, regular, true; horizontal, tabular; plumb, straight, vertical
near antonyms inexact, irregular, unaligned; undulating, wavy
antonyms bumpy, coarse, lumpy, rough, uneven

level *n* the placement of someone or something in relation to others in a vertical arrangement — see RANK 1

level *vb* 1 to make equal in amount, degree, or status — see EQUALIZE
2 to make free from breaks, curves, or bumps — see EVEN 1
3 to point or turn (something) toward a target or goal — see AIM 1
4 to strike (someone) so forcefully as to cause a fall — see FELL 1

levelheaded *adj* based on sound reasoning or information — see GOOD 1

THESAURUS

levelheadedness *n* the ability to make intelligent decisions especially in everyday matters — see COMMON SENSE

lever *vb* to raise, move, or pull apart with or as if with a lever — see ¹PRY 1

leviathan *n* something that is unusually large and powerful — see GIANT

levity *n* a lack of seriousness often at an improper time — see FRIVOLITY 1

levy *n* a charge usually of money collected by the government from people or businesses for public use — see TAX

levy *vb* to establish or apply as a charge or penalty — see IMPOSE

lewd *adj* 1 depicting or referring to sexual matters in a way that is unacceptable in polite society — see OBSCENE 1
2 having a strong sexual desire — see LUSTFUL
3 hinting at or intended to call to mind matters regarded as indecent — see SUGGESTIVE 1

lewdness *n* the quality or state of being obscene — see OBSCENITY 1

lexical *adj* of or relating to words or language — see VERBAL 1

lexicon *n* a reference book giving information about the meanings, pronunciations, uses, and origins of words listed in alphabetical order — see DICTIONARY

liability *n* 1 a feature of someone or something that creates difficulty for achieving success — see DISADVANTAGE
2 the state of being held as the cause of something that needs to be set right — see RESPONSIBILITY 1
3 the state of being left without shelter or protection against something harmful — see EXPOSURE 1

liable *adj* 1 being in a situation where one is likely to meet with harm ⟨because of his frail constitution, he's *liable* to diseases⟩
synonyms endangered, exposed, open, sensitive, subject (to), susceptible, vulnerable
related words likely, prone; uncovered, undefended, unguarded, unprotected, unscreened, unsecured, unsheltered, unshielded ·
phrases in jeopardy
near antonyms covered, guarded, protected, safeguarded, screened, secured, sheltered, shielded, warded
antonyms invulnerable, unexposed
2 being the one who must meet an obligation or suffer the consequences for failing to do so — see RESPONSIBLE 1

liaison *n* 1 the fact or state of having something in common — see CONNECTION 1
2 the state of having shared interests or efforts (as in social or business matters) — see ASSOCIATION 1

liar *n* a person who tells lies ⟨she knew he was a *liar* when he started claiming that he was an astronaut⟩
synonyms fabricator, fibber, prevaricator, storyteller
related words defamer, libeler (*or* libeller), slanderer; perjurer; distorter, falsifier, equivocator, palterer; gossip, gossiper, talebearer; charlatan, cheat, cheater, confidence man, counterfeiter, cozener, deceiver, defrauder, dissembler, dissimulator, double-dealer, fraud, hustler, mountebank, pretender
near antonyms square shooter

libation *n* a liquid suitable for drinking — see DRINK 1

libel *n* the making of false statements that damage another's reputation — see SLANDER

libel *vb* to make untrue and harmful statements about — see SLANDER

libeling *n* the making of false statements that damage another's reputation — see SLANDER

libelous *or* **libellous** *adj* causing or intended to cause unjust injury to a person's good name ⟨*libelous* statements about a celebrity for which the tabloid was sued⟩
synonyms defamatory, scandalous, slanderous
related words erroneous, false, inaccurate, incorrect, inexact, invalid, off, unsound, untrue, wrong; depreciative, depreciatory, derogatory, detractive, disparaging, uncomplimentary, unfavorable; invidious, objectionable; maligning, traducing, vilifying; hateful, malevolent, malicious, spiteful
near antonyms appreciative, complimentary, favorable; adulatory, commendatory, eulogistic, laudatory; accurate, correct, errorless, factual, right, sound, true, valid

liberal *adj* 1 not bound by traditional ways or beliefs ⟨parents who take a very *liberal* attitude toward letting their children stay out late⟩
synonyms broad-minded, nonconventional, nonorthodox, nontraditional, open-minded, progressive, radical, unconventional, unorthodox
related words advanced, contemporary, modern; forbearing, indulgent, lenient, permissive, tolerant; extreme; impartial, objective, unbiased
near antonyms hard, rigid, strict; doctrinal, dogmatic; bigoted, intolerant, narrow-minded; reactionary
antonyms conservative, conventional, nonprogressive, old-fashioned, orthodox, traditional
2 being more than enough without being excessive — see PLENTIFUL
3 giving or sharing in abundance and without hesitation — see GENEROUS 1

liberalism *n* a political belief stressing progress, the essential goodness of humankind, and individual freedom ⟨*liberalism* had always claimed to stand for the greatest social good⟩
synonyms left
related words radicalism, socialism
antonyms conservatism, right

liberality *n* the quality or state of being generous ⟨already known for his *liberality*, the billionaire continued to give away record amounts of money⟩
synonyms bountifulness, bounty, generosity, largess (*or* largesse), openhandedness, openheartedness, philanthropy, unselfishness
related words beneficence, charity; kindness; gift, gratuity, lagniappe; tribute; extravagance, improvidence, lavishness, prodigality, wastefulness; spendthrift; dissipating, squandering
near antonyms conserving, economizing, economy, frugality, husbandry, providence, scrimping, skimping, thrift; conservation, saving; husbanding, managing; scraping; cutting back
antonyms cheapness, closeness, meanness, miserliness, parsimony, penuriousness, pinching, stinginess, tightness

liberally *adv* in a generous manner — see WELL 2

liberate *vb* 1 to set free (as from slavery or confinement) — see FREE 1

2 to set free from entanglement or difficulty — see EXTRICATE

liberation *n* the act of setting free from slavery ⟨the *liberation* of the slaves was one of the key results of the Civil War⟩

synonyms emancipation, enfranchisement, freeing, manumission

related words deliverance, redemption, salvation; autonomy, freedom, independence, liberty, self-government, sovereignty

near antonyms bondage, serfdom, servitude, thralldom (*or* thraldom), yoke; captivity, enchainment, imprisonment, incarceration; conquest, subjugation

antonyms enslavement

libertine *n* a person who has sunk below the normal moral standard — see DEGENERATE

liberty *n* the state of being free from the control or power of another — see FREEDOM 1

library *n* **1** a place where books, periodicals, and records are kept for use but not for sale ⟨I went to the *library* to do some research for my report⟩

synonyms archive

related words stacks

2 an organized group of objects acquired and maintained for study, exhibition, or personal pleasure — see COLLECTION 1

licensable *adj* that may be permitted — see PERMISSIBLE

license *also* **licence** *vb* to give official or legal power to — see AUTHORIZE 1

license *or* **licence** *n* **1** the approval by someone in authority for the doing of something — see PERMISSION

2 the granting of power to perform various acts or duties — see COMMISSION 1

3 the right to act or move freely — see FREEDOM 2

licentious *adj* having a strong sexual desire — see LUSTFUL

licentiousness *n* immoral conduct or practices harmful or offensive to society — see VICE 1

lick *n* **1** a hard strike with a part of the body or an instrument — see ¹BLOW

2 a very small amount — see PARTICLE 1

3 the smallest amount or part imaginable — see JOT

lick *vb* **1** to strike repeatedly — see BEAT 1

2 to achieve a victory over — see BEAT 2

licking *n* failure to win a contest — see DEFEAT 1

lid *n* **1** a piece placed over an open container to hold in, protect, or conceal its contents — see COVER 1

2 *slang* a covering for the head usually having a shaped crown — see HAT

lie *n* a statement known by its maker to be untrue and made in order to deceive ⟨he wanted to deny the accusation, but he couldn't tell a *lie*⟩

synonyms fabrication, fairy tale, falsehood, falsity, fib, mendacity, prevarication, story, tale, untruth, whopper

related words distortion, exaggeration, half-truth; ambiguity, equivocation; defamation, libel, slander; perjury; bluff, pose, pretense (*or* pretence); humbug, jive, nonsense; fallacy, misconception, myth; misinformation, misrepresentation, misstatement; deceit, deceitfulness, dishonesty, duplicity, fraudulence

near antonyms fact, truism, verity; honesty, truth-fulness, veracity; authentication, confirmation, substantiation, validation, verification

antonyms truth

lie *vb* **1** to make a statement one knows to be untrue ⟨would I *lie* to you about that?⟩

synonyms fabricate, fib, prevaricate

related words forswear, perjure; equivocate, fudge, palter; beguile, cozen, deceive, delude, dupe, fool, gull, hoax, hoodwink, kid, snow, take in, trick; defame, libel, slander, traduce; falsify, misrepresent, misstate; distort, garble; dissemble, dissimulate; misguide, misinform, mislead

phrases tell stories (*or* tales)

near antonyms assert, swear, testify; authenticate, confirm, substantiate, validate, verify

2 to be positioned along a certain course or in a certain direction — see RUN 3

3 to occupy a place or location — see STAND 1

lie detector *n* an instrument for detecting physical signs of the tension that goes with lying ⟨hooked the suspect up to a *lie detector* before interrogating him about the robbery⟩

synonyms polygraph

life *n* **1** a history of a person's life — see BIOGRAPHY

2 a member of the human race — see HUMAN

3 active strength of body or mind — see VIGOR 1

4 the period during which something exists, lasts, or is in progress — see DURATION 1

5 the way people live at a particular time and place — see CIVILIZATION 1

lifeless *adj* no longer living — see DEAD 1

lifelessness *n* the state of being dead — see DEATH 2

lifelike *adj* closely resembling the object imitated — see NATURAL 2

life span *n* the period during which something exists, lasts, or is in progress — see DURATION 1

lifestyle *n* the way people live at a particular time and place — see CIVILIZATION 1

lifetime *n* the period during which something exists, lasts, or is in progress — see DURATION 1

lift *n* **1** an act or instance of helping — see HELP 1

2 a means of getting to a destination in a vehicle driven by another — see RIDE

lift *vb* **1** to move from a lower to a higher place or position — see RAISE 1

2 to move or extend upward — see ASCEND

lifted *adj* being positioned above a surface — see ELEVATED 1

lift–off *n* a rising from a surface at the start of a flight (as of a rocket) ⟨everyone was quiet in the control room as they waited for *lift-off*⟩

synonyms launch, takeoff

near antonyms crash; splashdown

antonyms landing

ligature *n* **1** something that physically prevents free movement — see BOND 1

2 a uniting or binding force or influence — see BOND 2

¹**light** *adj* **1** having little weight ⟨the suitcase was as *light* as a feather after all the clothes fell out⟩

synonyms airy, feathery, lightweight, underweight, weightless

related words bantam, diminutive, little, minute, small, smallish, puny, tiny, undersized, wee; flimsy, fragile, insubstantial; petite, slender, slight, slim, thin

near antonyms big, considerable, extensive, goodly, good-sized, great, handsome, huge, hulking,

jumbo, king-size (*or* king-sized), large, largish, massive, oversize (*or* oversized), sizable (*or* sizeable), substantial, super, voluminous, whacking; bulky, cumbersome, unwieldy
antonyms heavy, hefty, leaden, overweight, ponderous, weighty
2 involving minimal difficulty or effort — see EASY 1
3 less plentiful than what is normal, necessary, or desirable — see MEAGER
4 moving easily — see GRACEFUL 1
5 not harsh or stern especially in manner, nature, or effect — see GENTLE 1
6 resembling air in lightness — see AIRY 1
²**light** *adj* **1** filled with much light — see BRIGHT 2
2 lacking intensity of color — see PALE 1
3 of light complexion — see FAIR 4
light *n* **1** the steady giving off of the form of radiation that makes vision possible ⟨he read poetry by the *light* of the moon⟩
synonyms blaze, flare, fluorescence, glare, gleam, glow, illumination, incandescence, luminescence, radiance, shine
related words flash, glimmer, glint, glitter, scintillation, shimmer, sparkle, twinkle; daylight, moonlight, sunlight; afterglow, aureole, aurora, beam, ray, shaft, streak, stream; glisten, gloss, luster (*or* lustre), polish, reflection, sheen
near antonyms blackness, dark, darkness, dimness, dusk, duskiness, gloom, night, shadow
2 something that provides illumination ⟨turn off the *light* when you go to bed⟩
synonyms beacon, lamp
related words arc lamp (*also* arc light), candelabra, candelabrum, candle, chandelier, dark lantern, electric, flare, flash, flashbulb, flashcube, flashlight, floodlight, fluorescent lamp, gaslight, headlight, incandescent lamp, klieg light (*or* kleig light), lantern, light bulb, lighthouse, lighting, sconce, spotlight, streetlight
3 a person who is widely known and usually much talked about — see CELEBRITY 1
¹**light** *vb* to come to rest after descending from the air — see ALIGHT
²**light** *vb* **1** to set (something) on fire — see BURN 2
2 to supply with light — see ILLUMINATE 1
lighted *or* **lit** *adj* **1** filled with much light — see BRIGHT 2
2 being on fire — see ABLAZE 1
lighten *vb* to supply with light — see ILLUMINATE 1
light–footed *adj* moving easily — see GRACEFUL 1
light–headed *adj* **1** having a feeling of being whirled about and in danger of falling down — see DIZZY 1
2 lacking in seriousness or maturity — see GIDDY 1
light–headedness *n* a lack of seriousness often at an improper time — see FRIVOLITY 1
lighthearted *adj* having or showing a lack of concern or seriousness — see CAREFREE
lightheartedness *n* carefree freedom from constraint — see ABANDON
lighting out *n* the act of leaving a place — see DEPARTURE
lightly *adv* without difficulty — see EASILY
¹**lightness** *n* **1** the state or quality of having little weight ⟨the first thing I noticed about the little bird was its *lightness*; I could hardly tell I was holding it in my hand⟩
synonyms slightness, weightlessness

related words airiness, delicacy, etherealness; flimsiness, fluffiness, insubstantiality
near antonyms solidity, solidness, substantiality
antonyms heaviness, heftiness, massiveness, ponderousness, weightiness
2 a lack of seriousness often at an improper time — see FRIVOLITY 1
²**lightness** *n* the quality or state of having or giving off light — see BRILLIANCE 1
lightning *adj* moving, proceeding, or acting with great speed — see FAST 1
lightsome *adj* having or showing a good mood or disposition — see CHEERFUL 1
lightweight *adj* having little weight — see ¹LIGHT 1
lightweight *n* a person of no importance or influence — see NOBODY
like *adj* having qualities in common — see ALIKE
like *adv* to some degree or extent — see FAIRLY
like *conj* the way it would be or one would do if — see AS IF
¹**like** *n* **1** a number of persons or things that are grouped together because they have something in common — see SORT 1
2 one that is equal to another in status, achievement, or value — see EQUAL
²**like** *n* positive regard for something — see LIKING
like *vb* **1** to wish to have ⟨I'd *like* another slice of pizza, but I've already eaten more than I should have⟩
synonyms care (for), want
related words adore, delight (in), dig, enjoy, fancy, groove (on), like, love, relish, revel (in); covet, crave, die (for), wish (for), yearn (for)
2 to show partiality toward — see PREFER 1
3 to take pleasure in — see ENJOY 1
4 to see fit — see CHOOSE 2
likelihood *n* the quality or state of being likely to occur — see PROBABILITY 1
likeliness *n* the quality or state of being likely to occur — see PROBABILITY 1
likely *adj* **1** having a high chance of occurring ⟨if you don't do well in school, your *likely* fate is a low-paying job⟩
synonyms probable
related words conceivable, earthly, imaginable, possible, potential; apt, bound, certain, doubtless, inescapable, inevitable, necessary, sure, unavoidable
near antonyms impossible, inconceivable, unimaginable
antonyms doubtful, dubious, improbable, questionable, unlikely
2 having qualities which inspire hope — see HOPEFUL 1
3 worthy of being accepted as true or reasonable — see BELIEVABLE
likely *adv* without much doubt — see PROBABLY
liken *vb* **1** to describe as similar — see COMPARE 1
2 to regard or represent as equal or comparable — see EQUATE 1
likeness *n* **1** a two-dimensional design intended to look like a person or thing — see PICTURE 1
2 something or someone that strongly resembles another — see IMAGE 1
3 the quality or state of having many qualities in common — see SIMILARITY 1
likewise *adv* **1** in addition to what has been said — see MORE 1
2 in like manner — see ALSO 1

liking *n* positive regard for something ⟨I have a *liking* for dark chocolate⟩

synonyms appetite, fancy, favor, fondness, like, love, partiality, preference, relish, shine, taste, use

related words craving, desire, longing, thirst, yen; enthusiasm, interest, passion; bias, prejudice; bent, inclination, leaning, propensity, tendency; weakness

near antonyms apathy, disinclination; indifference, unconcern

antonyms aversion, disfavor, dislike, distaste, hatred, loathing

lily–livered *adj* having or showing a shameful lack of courage — see COWARDLY

limb *n* a major outgrowth from the main stem of a woody plant — see BRANCH 1

limber *adj* able to bend easily without breaking — see WILLOWY

limit *n* a real or imaginary point beyond which a person or thing cannot go ⟨there was no *limit* to the number of challenges they faced⟩

synonyms bound, boundary, ceiling, confines, end, extent, limitation, line, termination

related words extremity, fag end; border, brim, edge, margin, rim, verge; outside; bar, barrier, fence, hedge, restraint, stop, wall

limit *vb* **1** to set bounds or an upper limit for ⟨*limit* the note to a few words⟩

synonyms circumscribe, confine, restrict

related words bar, block, hinder, impede, obstruct; constrict, contract, lessen, narrow, pinch, squeeze, tighten; quell, repress, suppress; number; modify, qualify

near antonyms broaden, expand, widen; overextend, overreach

antonyms exceed

2 to mark the limits of ⟨adjectives *limit* the meanings of nouns⟩

synonyms bound, circumscribe, define, delimit, demarcate, mark (out), terminate

related words control, determine, govern; delineate, describe

limitation *n* **1** a real or imaginary point beyond which a person or thing cannot go — see LIMIT

2 something that limits one's freedom of action or choice — see RESTRICTION 1

3 the act or practice of keeping something (as an activity) within certain boundaries — see RESTRICTION 2

limited *adj* **1** having distinct or certain limits ⟨to avoid overcrowding, the number of tickets to the outdoor concerts is *limited*⟩

synonyms bounded, circumscribed, defined, definite, determinate, finite, measured, narrow, restricted

related words modified, qualified; detailed, exact, precise, specific; confined, constricted, moderate, modest; minute, puny, small, tiny; determined, fixed, settled

near antonyms bottomless, countless, incalculable, inestimable, inexhaustible, innumerable, unfathomable; general, indeterminate, nebulous, vague; enlarged, escalated, expanded; considerable, copious, plentiful; big, bulky, bumper, extensive, goodly, good-sized, great, handsome, hefty, hulking, jumbo, king-size (*or* king-sized), large, largish, oversize (*or* oversized), respectable, sizable (*or* sizeable), substantial, super, vast, voluminous, whacking; epic, grandiose, major; ample,

broad, comprehensive, cosmopolitan, expansive, global, inclusive, universal, whole

antonyms boundless, dimensionless, endless, illimitable, immeasurable, indefinite, infinite, limitless, measureless, unbounded, undefined, unlimited, unmeasured

2 having a limit — see FINITE 1

limitless *adj* being or seeming to be without limits — see INFINITE

limp *adj* **1** not stiff in structure ⟨his broken arm was *limp* as he held it against his side⟩

synonyms droopy, flaccid, floppy, lank, yielding

related words flabby, mushy, semisoft, soft, squashy, squishy; delicate, flimsy, insubstantial; elastic, flexible, lax, loose, pliant, relaxed, resilient, springy, stretchy, supple

near antonyms firm, hard, indurated, solid, sound, strong; brittle, crisp; compact, dense, substantial

antonyms inflexible, resilient, rigid, stiff, sturdy, tense; firm, hard, indurated, solid, sound, strong

2 depleted in strength, energy, or freshness — see WEARY 1

3 lacking bodily energy or motivation — see LISTLESS

limp *vb* **1** to walk while favoring one leg ⟨she *limped* all day after stubbing her toe on the lawn sprinkler⟩

synonyms halt, hobble

related words hitch; blunder, falter, lurch, shuffle, stagger, stumble, teeter, totter, waver, wobble; dodder

near antonyms breeze, glide, sail

antonyms stride

2 to make progress in a clumsy, struggling manner — see FLOUNDER 1

limpid *adj* easily seen through — see CLEAR 1

limpidity *n* the state or quality of being easily seen through — see CLARITY 1

limpidness *n* the state or quality of being easily seen through — see CLARITY 1

line *n* **1** a series of persons or things arranged one behind another ⟨we waited in the *line* for lunch for what seemed like hours⟩

synonyms column, cue, file, queue, range, string, train

related words echelon, rank, row, tier; progression, sequence, succession; array

2 a way of acting or proceeding — see COURSE 1

3 the activity by which one regularly makes a living — see OCCUPATION

4 a region of activity, knowledge, or influence — see FIELD 2

5 a real or imaginary point beyond which a person or thing cannot go — see LIMIT

6 a long hollow cylinder for carrying a substance (as a liquid or gas) — see PIPE 1

7 a length of braided, flexible material that is used for tying or connecting things — see CORD

8 a group of vehicles traveling together or under one management — see FLEET

9 the direction along which something or someone moves — see PATH 1

10 a group of persons who come from the same ancestor — see FAMILY 1

11 the line of ancestors from whom a person is descended — see ANCESTRY

lineage *n* **1** the line of ancestors from whom a person is descended — see ANCESTRY

2 a group of persons who come from the same ancestor — see FAMILY 1

THESAURUS

linear *adj* free from irregularities (as curves, bends, or angles) in course — see STRAIGHT 1

linger *vb* to move or act slowly — see DELAY 1

lingerer *n* someone who moves slowly or more slowly than others — see SLOWPOKE

lingo *n* **1** the stock of words, pronunciation, and grammar used by a people as their basic means of communication — see LANGUAGE 1
2 the special terms or expressions of a particular group or field — see TERMINOLOGY

linguistic *adj* of or relating to words or language — see VERBAL 1

link *n* **1** a rod-shaped portion of seasoned ground meat in a casing — see SAUSAGE
2 a uniting or binding force or influence — see BOND 2

link *vb* **1** to put or bring together so as to form a new and longer whole — see CONNECT 1
2 to think of (something) in combination — see ASSOCIATE 2

link (up) *vb* to come together to form a single unit — see UNITE 1

linkage *n* the fact or state of having something in common — see CONNECTION 1

linking *n* the act or an instance of joining two or more things into one — see UNION 1

linkup *n* the state of having shared interests or efforts (as in social or business matters) — see ASSOCIATION 1

lint *n* a soft airy substance or covering — see FUZZ

lionhearted *adj* feeling or displaying no fear by temperament — see BRAVE

liquefy *vb* to go from a solid to a liquid state ⟨the steel *liquefied* in the intense heat of the forge⟩
synonyms deliquesce, flux, fuse, melt, run, thaw
related words found, gutter, smelt, try; dissolve, render; soften, thin
near antonyms clot, coagulate, congeal, gel, jell, jelly, thicken
antonyms harden, set, solidify

liquid *adj* **1** capable of moving like a liquid — see FLUID 1
2 easily seen through — see CLEAR 1

liquidate *vb* **1** to destroy all traces of — see ANNIHILATE 1
2 to put to death deliberately — see MURDER 1
3 to give what is owed for — see PAY 2

liquor *n* a fermented or distilled beverage that can make a person drunk — see ALCOHOL

lissome *also* **lissom** *adj* **1** moving easily — see GRACEFUL 1
2 able to bend easily without breaking — see WILLOWY

¹list *n* a record of a series of items (as names or titles) usually arranged according to some system ⟨we put eggs, sour cream, tomatoes, roast beef, and cheddar cheese on the shopping *list*⟩
synonyms canon, catalog (*or* catalogue), checklist, listing, menu, register, registry, roll, roster, schedule, table
related words agenda, bibliography, compilation, directory, docket, glossary, index, inventory, manifest, payroll; calendar, chronology, timetable

²list *n* the act of positioning or an instance of being positioned at an angle — see TILT

³list *n* a long narrow piece of material — see STRIP

¹list *vb* **1** to make a list of ⟨he *listed* the people on the team⟩
synonyms enumerate, inventory, itemize, numerate

related words count, mark, number; check (off), tick (off)
2 to put (someone or something) on a list ⟨her number isn't *listed* in the phone book⟩
synonyms catalog (*or* catalogue), enroll (*also* enrol), enter, index, inscribe, put down, record, register, schedule, slate
related words book, file, note; classify, compile, tabulate; reschedule
near antonyms delete
3 to enter in a list or roll — see ENROLL 1
4 to specify one after another — see ENUMERATE 1

²list *vb* to set or cause to be at an angle — see LEAN 1

listen *vb* to pay attention especially through the act of hearing ⟨would you *listen* to what I have to say?⟩
synonyms attend, hark, hear, hearken, heed, mind
phrases prick up one's ears
near antonyms discount, disregard
antonyms ignore, tune out

listen (to) *vb* to take notice of and be guided by — see HEED 1

listen in (on) *vb* to listen to (another in private conversation) — see EAVESDROP (ON)

listing *adj* **1** inclined or twisted to one side — see AWRY
2 running in a slanting direction — see DIAGONAL

listing *n* a record of a series of items (as names or titles) usually arranged according to some system — see ¹LIST

listless *adj* lacking bodily energy or motivation ⟨when I had the flu, I felt *listless* and worn-out⟩
synonyms enervated, lackadaisical, languid, languishing, languorous, limp, spiritless
related words indolent, lazy, slothful; lethargic, logy, sleepy, sluggish, torpid; exhausted, tired, weary; feeble, frail, weak; apathetic, impassive, phlegmatic, stolid; careless, heedless, thoughtless, unwary; inactive, inert
near antonyms active, dynamic, industrious; avid, eager, enthusiastic, keen, lively, vivacious; cheerful, chipper, perky, up; agog, alert, awake, dapper, open-eyed, sleepless, vigilant, watchful, wide-awake
antonyms ambitious, animated, energetic, enterprising, motivated

listlessness *n* the state of being bored — see BOREDOM

literal *adj* restricted to or based on fact — see FACTUAL 1

literary *adj* suggestive of the vocabulary used in books — see BOOKISH

literate *adj* having or displaying advanced knowledge or education — see EDUCATED

lithe *adj* **1** able to bend easily without breaking — see WILLOWY
2 moving easily — see GRACEFUL 1

lithesome *adj* moving easily — see GRACEFUL 1

litter *n* **1** an unorganized collection or mixture of various things — see MISCELLANY 1
2 discarded or useless material — see GARBAGE

littered *adj* lacking in order, neatness, and often cleanliness — see MESSY

little *adj* **1** having relatively little height — see SHORT 1
2 lacking importance — see UNIMPORTANT

3 not broad or open in views or opinions — see NARROW 2

4 not lasting for a considerable time — see SHORT 2

5 of a size that is less than average — see SMALL 1

little *adv* **1** in a very small quantity or degree ⟨we had *little* more than we needed to survive in the wilderness⟩

synonyms negligibly, nominally, slightly

related words meagerly, scantily; barely, hardly, just, marginally, minimally, scarcely

phrases a bit

near antonyms completely, entirely, purely, thoroughly, totally, utterly; eminently, exceptionally; appreciably, discernibly, noticeably, palpably; abundantly, plentifully; generously, handsomely, liberally; astronomically, grandly, hugely, monstrously, monumentally

antonyms awful, awfully, beastly, considerably, deadly, especially, exceedingly (*also* exceeding), extensively, extra, extremely, far, frightfully, full, greatly, heavily, highly, jolly, mightily, mighty, mortally, most, much, particularly, rattling, real, right, significantly, so, something, substantially, super, terribly, too, very, whacking

2 not often — see SELDOM

little *n* a very small amount — see PARTICLE 1

little by little *adv* by small steps or amounts — see GRADUALLY

littleness *n* the quality or state of being little in size — see SMALLNESS

littlest *adj* being the least in amount, number, or size possible — see MINIMAL

livable *also* **liveable** *adj* suitable for living in ⟨after adding some furniture and painting the walls, the apartment was *livable*⟩

synonyms habitable, inhabitable

related words comfortable, cozy, homelike, homey, intimate, snug; deluxe, lavish, luxuriant, luxurious, plush, sumptuous; opulent, palatial, rich; acceptable, bearable, endurable, sufferable, supportable, sustainable, tolerable

near antonyms uncomfortable; humble, Spartan; economical, frugal, spare, thrifty; intolerable, unacceptable, unbearable, unendurable, insupportable

antonyms uninhabitable, unlivable

live *adj* having or showing life — see ALIVE 1

live *vb* **1** to have a home ⟨he *lived* next door to the hospital⟩

synonyms abide, dwell, reside

related words lodge, settle, stay; frequent, hang out (at); haunt; inhabit, occupy; people, populate; lease, rent, sublet, tenant

2 to have life — see BE 1

liveliness *n* the quality or state of having abundant or intense activity — see VITALITY 1

lively *adj* **1** having much high-spirited energy and movement ⟨the *lively* puppy was racing around the dining room floor chasing after people's shoelaces⟩

synonyms active, animate, animated, bouncing, brisk, energetic, frisky, gay, jaunty, jazzy, peppy, perky, pert, racy, snappy, spanking, sparky, spirited, sprightly, springy, vital, vivacious, zippy

related words dapper, dashing, spiffy; agog, alert, awake, open-eyed, up, wide-awake; agile, nimble, spry; bright, buoyant, cheerful, chipper, effervescent, upbeat; eager, enthusiastic, keen; frolic-

some, impish, playful; bubbly, exuberant, high-spirited; high-strung, nervous, skittish

phrases on the go

near antonyms indolent, lazy, unambitious; inert, lethargic, sleepy, sluggish, tired, torpid, weary; apathetic, impassive, phlegmatic, stolid; boring, dull, irksome, tedious

antonyms dead, inactive, inanimate, lackadaisical, languid, languishing, languorous, lifeless, limp, listless, spiritless, unanimated

2 marked by much life, movement, or activity — see ALIVE 2

liven (up) *vb* to give life, vigor, or spirit to — see ANIMATE

livery *n* the distinctive clothing worn by members of a particular group — see UNIFORM

live wire *n* an ambitious person who eagerly goes after what is desired — see GO-GETTER

livid *adj* lacking a healthy skin color — see PALE 2

living *adj* **1** being in effective operation — see ACTIVE 1

2 having being at the present time — see EXTANT 1

3 having or showing life — see ALIVE 1

load *n* **1** a mass or quantity of something taken up and carried, conveyed, or transported ⟨they placed a *load* of grain on the truck going to Florida⟩

synonyms burden, cargo, draft, freight, haul, lading, loading, payload, weight

related words consignment, boatload, carload, shipload, truckload; ballast, deadweight; overload, surcharge; bale, bundle, pack, package, packet, parcel, shipment; manifest; body, bulk, mass

2 loads *pl* a considerable amount — see LOT 2

load *vb* **1** to place a weight or burden on ⟨students complaining that their teachers were *loading* them with work⟩

synonyms burden, encumber, lade, lumber, saddle, weight

related words clog, clutter, fill, heap; press, weigh; strain, tax; overburden, overload, overtax, surcharge; handicap; afflict, oppress

near antonyms alleviate, ease, lighten, relieve

antonyms disencumber, unburden, unload

2 to put into (something) as much as can be held or contained — see FILL 1

loaded *adj* **1** containing or seeming to contain the greatest quantity or number possible — see FULL 1

2 having goods, property, or money in abundance — see RICH 1

3 *slang* being under the influence of alcohol — see DRUNK

loading *n* a mass or quantity of something taken up and carried, conveyed, or transported — see LOAD 1

loaf *vb* to spend time doing nothing — see IDLE

loafer *n* a lazy person — see LAZYBONES

loamy *adj* consisting or suggestive of earth — see EARTHY 1

loan *vb* to give to another for temporary use with the understanding that it or a like thing will be returned — see LEND

loath *or* **loth** *adj* having doubts about the wisdom of doing something — see HESITANT

loathe *vb* to dislike strongly — see HATE

THESAURUS

loathing *n* **1** a dislike so strong as to cause stomach upset or queasiness — see DISGUST

2 a very strong dislike — see HATE 1

loathsome *adj* causing intense displeasure, disgust, or resentment — see OFFENSIVE 1

lob *vb* to send through the air especially with a quick forward motion of the arm — see THROW

lobby *n* **1** a centrally located room in a building that serves as a gathering or waiting area or as a passageway into the interior — see FOYER 1

2 the entrance room of a building — see HALL 1

local *n* a local unit of an organization — see CHAPTER

locale *n* the area or space occupied by or intended for something — see PLACE 1

locality *n* the area or space occupied by or intended for something — see PLACE 1

locate *vb* to come upon after searching, study, or effort — see FIND 1

location *n* the area or space occupied by or intended for something — see PLACE 1

loch *n, Scottish* a part of a body of water that extends beyond the general shoreline — see GULF 1

lock (up) *vb* to put in or as if in prison — see IMPRISON

locker *n* **1** a covered rectangular container for storing or transporting things — see CHEST

2 a storage case typically having doors and shelves — see CABINET

lockup *n* a place of confinement for persons held in lawful custody — see JAIL

loco *adj* having or showing a very abnormal or sick state of mind — see INSANE 1

locus *n* the area or space occupied by or intended for something — see PLACE 1

locution *n* a distinctive way of putting ideas into words — see STYLE 1

lodestone *n* something that attracts interest — see MAGNET

lodge *n* **1** a place that provides rooms and usually a public dining room for overnight guests — see HOTEL

2 an often small house for recreational or seasonal use — see COTTAGE

3 the meeting place of an organization — see CLUB 2

4 the shelter or resting place of a wild animal — see DEN 1

lodge *vb* to provide with living quarters or shelter — see HOUSE 1

2 to establish or place comfortably or snugly — see ENSCONCE 1

3 to set solidly in or as if in surrounding matter — see ENTRENCH

lodged *adj* firmly positioned in place and difficult to dislodge — see TIGHT 2

lodger *n* one who rents a room or apartment in another's house — see TENANT

lodging *n* **1** the place where one lives — see HOME 1

2 lodgings *pl* a room or set of rooms in a private house or a block used as a separate dwelling place — see APARTMENT 1

loft *vb* to send through the air especially with a quick forward motion of the arm — see THROW

loftiest *adj* being at a point or level higher than all others — see TOP 1

loftiness *n* an exaggerated sense of one's importance that shows itself in the making of excessive or unjustified claims — see ARROGANCE

lofty *adj* **1** extending to a great distance upward — see HIGH 1

2 having a feeling of superiority that shows itself in an overbearing attitude — see ARROGANT

3 having or displaying feelings of scorn for what is regarded as beneath oneself — see PROUD 1

4 having, characterized by, or arising from a dignified and generous nature — see NOBLE 2

5 very dignified in form, tone, or style — see ELEVATED 2

log *vb* to make a written note of — see RECORD 1

logger *n* a person whose job is to cut down trees — see LUMBERJACK

logic *n* the thought processes that have been established as leading to valid solutions to problems ⟨I tried to use *logic* to figure out the solution to the puzzle⟩

synonyms reason, reasoning, sense

related words cogency, coherence, rationality, thought; analysis; deduction, induction

near antonyms incoherence, insanity, irrationality

logical *adj* **1** according to the rules of logic ⟨the lawyer won the case with a *logical* argument about the motives of the suspect⟩

synonyms analytic (*or* analytical), coherent, good, rational, reasonable, sensible, sound, valid

related words sane; thoughtful; scientific

near antonyms specious; crazy, insane; senseless, thoughtless

antonyms illogical, incoherent, invalid, irrational, unreasonable, unsound

2 based on sound reasoning or information — see GOOD 1

logo *n* a device, design, or figure used as an identifying mark — see EMBLEM

logy *adj* depleted in strength, energy, or freshness — see WEARY 1

loiter *vb* to move or act slowly — see DELAY 1

loiterer *n* someone who moves slowly or more slowly than others — see SLOWPOKE

loll *vb* **1** to be limp from lack of water or vigor — see DROOP 1

2 to refrain from labor or exertion — see REST 1

3 to spend time doing nothing — see IDLE 1

lone *adj* **1** being the one or ones of a class with no other members — see ONLY 2

2 not being in the company of others — see ALONE 1

lonely *adj* **1** not being in the company of others — see ALONE 1

2 sad from lack of companionship or separation from others — see LONESOME 1

loner *n* a person who does not conform to generally accepted standards or customs — see NONCONFORMIST 1

lonesome *adj* **1** sad from lack of companionship or separation from others ⟨a *lonesome* kitten left at the pound by its owners⟩

synonyms desolate, forlorn, lonely, lorn

related words friendless; abandoned, deserted, forgotten, forsaken, neglected; alone, lone, solitary; only, sole

near antonyms accompanied, attended, escorted

2 not being in the company of others — see ALONE 1

lone wolf *n* a person who does not conform to generally accepted standards or customs — see NONCONFORMIST 1

long *adj* **1** of great extent from end to end ⟨giraffes have *long* necks to help them reach leaves on tall trees⟩

synonyms elongated, extended, king-size (*or* king-sized), lengthy

related words extensive, far-reaching, longish, outstretched; oblong, rectangular; big, considerable, good-sized, hefty, hulking, jumbo, large, largish, oversize (*or* oversized), sizable (*or* sizeable), substantial, super

near antonyms abbreviated, abridged, curtailed, diminished, shortened; diminutive, little, minute, puny, small, smallish, tiny, undersized, wee

antonyms brief, short

2 lasting for a considerable time ⟨summer vacation seemed *long*, but we had to go back to school soon enough⟩

synonyms extended, far, great, lengthy, long-lived, long-range, long-term, marathon

related words endless, everlasting, interminable, persistent; longish, overlong, prolonged, protracted; permanent

near antonyms abrupt, sudden; abbreviated, condensed, curtailed; ephemeral, fleeting, momentary, transient, transitory; impermanent

antonyms brief, short, short-lived, short-range, short-term

long (for) *vb* to have an earnest wish to own or enjoy — see DESIRE

longhand *n* writing done by hand — see HANDWRITING 2

longing *n* a strong wish for something — see DESIRE

long–lived *adj* **1** being of advanced years and especially past middle age — see ELDERLY

2 lasting for a considerable time — see LONG 2

long–range *adj* lasting for a considerable time — see LONG 2

longshoreman *n* one who loads and unloads ships at a port — see DOCKWORKER

long–suffering *adj* accepting pains or hardships calmly or without complaint — see PATIENT 1

long–suffering *n* the capacity to endure what is difficult or disagreeable without complaining — see PATIENCE

long–term *adj* lasting for a considerable time — see LONG 2

long–winded *adj* using or containing more words than necessary to express an idea — see WORDY

long–windedness *n* the use of too many words to express an idea — see VERBIAGE

look *n* **1** facial appearance regarded as an indication of mood or feeling ⟨you should have seen the *look* on your face when we yelled "Surprise!"⟩

synonyms cast, countenance, expression, face, visage

related words frown, grimace, mouth, scowl; air, appearance, aspect, bearing, demeanor, manner, mien

2 an instance of looking especially briefly ⟨she gave the junk mail a quick *look* before throwing it in the garbage pail⟩

synonyms cast, eye, gander, glance, glimpse, peek, peep, regard, sight, view

related words gape, gaze, glare, leer, ogle, stare; squint

3 the outward form of someone or something especially as indicative of a quality — see APPEARANCE 1

4 looks *pl* the qualities in a person or thing that as

a whole give pleasure to the senses — see BEAUTY 1

look *vb* **1** to give the impression of being — see SEEM

2 to make known (as an idea, emotion, or opinion) — see EXPRESS 1

look (at) *vb* to make note of (something) through the use of one's eyes — see SEE 1

look (into) *vb* to search through or into — see EXPLORE 1

look (toward) *vb* to stand or sit with the face or front toward — see FACE 1

looking glass *n* a smooth or polished surface (as of glass) that forms images by reflection — see MIRROR

lookout *n* **1** a high place or structure from which a wide view is possible ⟨we went up to the *lookout* on the top of the hill to watch the fireworks⟩

synonyms observatory, outlook

related words aerie, crow's nest, tower, watchtower

2 all that can be seen from a certain point — see VIEW 1

3 the act or state of being constantly attentive and responsive to signs of opportunity, activity, or danger — see VIGILANCE

4 a person or group that watches over someone or something — see GUARD 1

look up *vb* to go in search of — see SEEK 1

loom *vb* to be about to happen ⟨he could tell that trouble was *looming* when the bullies swaggered into the park⟩

synonyms brew, impend

related words advance, approach, close in, draw on, gather, near; lower (*also* lour), menace, threaten

near antonyms die down, diminish, disappear, dwindle, fade, vanish, wane; fall back, pass, recede, retreat, withdraw

loony *n* a person judged to be legally or medically insane — see LUNATIC 1

loony *also* **looney** *adj* **1** showing or marked by a lack of good sense or judgment — see FOOLISH 1

2 having or showing a very abnormal or sick state of mind — see INSANE 1

loop *n* a circular strip — see RING 2

loop *vb* to pass completely around — see ENCIRCLE 1

loose *adj* **1** not tightly fastened, tied, or stretched ⟨secure your neckerchief with a *loose* knot⟩

synonyms insecure, lax, loosened, relaxed, slack, slackened, unsecured

related words detached, free, unattached, unbound, undone, unfastened, untied; baggy; nonrestrictive

near antonyms constrained, restrained; attached, bound, fastened, tied

antonyms taut, tense, tight

2 consisting of particles that do not stick together ⟨the car wheels slipped on the *loose* gravel in the driveway⟩

synonyms incoherent, unconsolidated

related words nonadhesive; disconnected, disjointed, separate, unconnected; coarse, granular, rough

near antonyms connected, solid; compacted, compressed; adhesive, gluey, sticky

antonyms coherent, compact, dense, packed

3 not bound by rigid standards — see EASYGOING 2

THESAURUS

4 not bound, confined, or detained by force — see FREE 3

5 not precisely correct — see INEXACT 1

loose *vb* **1** to cause (a projectile) to be driven forward with force — see SHOOT 1

2 to find emotional release for — see TAKE OUT 1

3 to set free (as from slavery or confinement) — see FREE 1

4 to set free (from a state of being held in check) — see RELEASE 1

loosen *vb* **1** to make less taut — see SLACKEN

2 to set free (as from slavery or confinement) — see FREE 1

3 to set free (from a state of being held in check) — see RELEASE 1

loosen (up) *vb* to free from obstruction or difficulty — see EASE 1

loosened *adj* not tightly fastened, tied, or stretched — see LOOSE 1

loot *n* valuables stolen or taken by force ⟨the burglar was caught when he stopped to examine the *loot* from the robbery⟩

synonyms booty, plunder, spoil, swag

related words prize; catch, haul, take; pilferage; windfall

loot *vb* to search through with the intent of committing robbery — see RANSACK 1

lop (off) *vb* to make (as hair) shorter with or as if with the use of shears — see CLIP

lope *vb* to move with a light bouncing step — see SKIP 1

lopsided *adj* inclined or twisted to one side — see AWRY

loquacious *adj* fond of talking or conversation — see TALKATIVE

Lord *n* the being worshipped as the creator and ruler of the universe — see DEITY 2

lord (it over) *vb* to assume or treat with an air of superiority — see CONDESCEND 2

lordliness *n* an exaggerated sense of one's importance that shows itself in the making of excessive or unjustified claims — see ARROGANCE

lordly *adj* **1** having a feeling of superiority that shows itself in an overbearing attitude — see ARROGANT

2 having or displaying feelings of scorn for what is regarded as beneath oneself — see PROUD 1

3 having, characterized by, or arising from a dignified and generous nature — see NOBLE 2

lore *n* **1** a body of facts learned by study or experience — see KNOWLEDGE 1

2 the body of customs, beliefs, stories, and sayings associated with a people, thing, or place — see FOLKLORE

lorn *adj* sad from lack of companionship or separation from others — see LONESOME 1

lose *vb* **1** to be unable to find or have at hand ⟨I always *lose* my keys⟩

synonyms mislay, misplace

near antonyms have

antonyms find, locate

2 to get rid of as useless or unwanted — see DISCARD

loser *n* something that has failed — see FAILURE 3

loss *n* **1** the act or an instance of not having or being able to find ⟨he was upset over the *loss* of his bike⟩

synonyms mislaying, misplacement

related words deprivation, dispossession; forfeit, forfeiture, penalty; sacrifice; bereavement

antonyms acquisition, gain

2 a person or thing harmed, lost, or destroyed — see CASUALTY 1

3 failure to win a contest — see DEFEAT 1

4 the amount by which something is lessened — see DECREASE

5 the state of being robbed of something normally enjoyed — see PRIVATION

6 the state or fact of being rendered nonexistent, physically unsound, or useless — see DESTRUCTION

lost *adj* no longer possessed ⟨they searched all over the house for the *lost* keys⟩

synonyms gone, mislaid, misplaced, missing

related words absent, castaway; irrecoverable, irretrievable; forgotten, unknown

near antonyms cherished, protected, treasured

antonyms owned, possessed, retained

lot *n* **1** a small piece of land that is developed or available for development ⟨we often played in the vacant *lot* down at the end of the street⟩

synonyms parcel, plat, plot, property, tract

related words patch; frontage; lease; development; real estate

2 a considerable amount ⟨they needed to do a *lot* of studying for the test⟩

synonyms abundance, barrel, bucket, bushel, deal, gobs, heap, loads, mass, mountain, much, oodles, peck, pile, plenitude, plenty, pot, profusion, quantity, raft, reams, scads, stack, volume, wad, wealth

related words embarrassment, excess, overabundance, overage, overkill, overmuch, oversupply, superabundance, superfluity, surfeit, surplus; deluge, flood, overflow

near antonyms atom, crumb, fragment, grain, iota, jot, modicum, molecule, particle, scrap, shred, tittle, whit; scattering, smattering; drop, morsel, shot; piece, portion, section; absence, dearth, lack, paucity, poverty, scarceness, scarcity, shortage, want; deficiency, deficit, inadequacy, insufficiency, meagerness, scantiness, skimpiness

antonyms ace, bit, dab, driblet, glimmer, hint, lick, little, mite, mouthful, ounce, peanuts, pinch, scruple, smidgen, speck, spot, sprinkling, suspicion, taste, touch, trace

3 a small area of usually open land — see FIELD 1

4 a number of things considered as a unit — see GROUP 1

5 a state or end that seemingly has been decided beforehand — see FATE 1

6 a group of people sharing a common interest and relating together socially — see GANG 2

7 a usually small number of persons considered as a unit — see GROUP 2

loud *adj* **1** marked by a high volume of sound ⟨*loud* music that could be heard all over the neighborhood⟩

synonyms blaring, blasting, booming, clamorous, clangorous, deafening, earsplitting, piercing, resounding, ringing, roaring, sonorous, stentorian, thunderous

related words brazen, dinning, discordant, noisy, obstreperous, raucous, rip-roaring, vociferous; grating, harsh, shrill, strident

near antonyms dead, quiet, silent, still; dreamy, peaceful, restful, soothing, tranquil; softened, toned (down)

antonyms gentle, low, soft

2 excessively showy — see GAUDY

lounge *n* a long upholstered piece of furniture designed for several sitters — see COUCH

lounge *vb* **1** to refrain from labor or exertion — see REST 1

2 to spend time doing nothing — see IDLE

louse *n* a person whose behavior is offensive to others — see JERK 1

louse up *vb* to make or do (something) in a clumsy or unskillful way — see BOTCH

lousy *adj* **1** arousing or deserving of one's loathing and disgust — see CONTEMPTIBLE 1

2 falling short of a standard — see BAD 1

3 extremely unsatisfactory — see WRETCHED 1

4 of low quality — see CHEAP 2

lout *n* **1** a big clumsy often slow-witted person — see OAF

2 a person whose behavior is offensive to others — see JERK 1

loutish *adj* having or showing crudely insensitive or impolite manners — see CLOWNISH

lovable *adj* having qualities that tend to make one loved ⟨she was a *lovable* child, always helpful and kind⟩

synonyms adorable, darling, dear, disarming, endearing, precious, sweet, winning

related words embraceable, kissable; beloved, cherished, treasured; attractive, beautiful, desirable, lovely; captivating, charming, fascinating; admirable, likable (*or* likeable), reputable, respectable; affable, agreeable, cheerful, cordial, friendly, genial, gracious, kind, pleasant; delightful, pleasing

near antonyms unloved; contemptible, disagreeable, disgusting, distasteful, heinous, horrible, offensive, unlikable, unpleasant; frightful, grotesque, hideous, ill-favored, monstrous, ogreish, repellent (*also* repellant), repugnant, repulsive; ugly, unattractive, unsightly, vile

antonyms abhorrent, abominable, detestable, hateful, odious, unlovable

love *n* **1** a feeling of strong or constant regard for and dedication to someone ⟨her *love* for her children was truly selfless⟩

synonyms affection, attachment, devotedness, devotion, fondness, passion

related words appetite, favor, like, liking, partiality, preference, taste; craving, crush, desire, infatuation, longing, lust, yearning; ardor, eagerness, enthusiasm, fervor, zeal; esteem, regard, respect; adoration, idolatry, worship; allegiance, fealty, fidelity, loyalty

near antonyms allergy, animosity, antipathy, aversion, disfavor, dislike; abhorrence, disgust, repugnance, repulsion, revulsion; misanthropy

antonyms abomination, hate, hatred, loathing, rancor

2 a person with whom one is in love — see SWEETHEART

3 positive regard for something — see LIKING

love *vb* **1** to hold dear ⟨patriots who *loved* their country well enough to die for it⟩

synonyms appreciate, cherish, prize, treasure, value

related words delight (in), dig, enjoy, fancy, groove (on), like, relish, revel (in); admire, esteem, regard, respect, revere, reverence, venerate; enshrine, memorialize; adore, dote (on), idolize, worship

phrases set store (by *or* on)

near antonyms undervalue; abhor, abominate, de-

spise, detest, execrate, hate, loathe; disdain, scorn, scout; belittle, decry, deprecate, depreciate, disparage; abandon, forget, neglect

2 to feel passion, devotion, or tenderness for ⟨a husband who *loves* his wife more than anything⟩

synonyms adore, cherish, worship

related words idealize, idolize; revere, reverence, venerate; delight (in), dote (on)

phrases fall for, lose one's heart (to)

near antonyms antagonize, displease; disapprove (of), disfavor, dislike; disgust, repulse, turn off

antonyms abhor, abominate, despise, detest, execrate, hate, loathe

3 to take pleasure in — see ENJOY 1

4 to touch or handle in a tender or loving manner — see FONDLE

love affair *n* a brief romantic relationship — see AFFAIR 1

loved *adj* granted special treatment or attention — see DARLING 1

loveliness *n* the qualities in a person or thing that as a whole give pleasure to the senses — see BEAUTY 1

lovely *adj* very pleasing to look at — see BEAUTIFUL

lover *n* a person with a strong and habitual liking for something — see FAN

loving *adj* feeling or showing love ⟨they were a *loving* family, supporting each other when times were bad⟩

synonyms adoring, affectionate, devoted, fond, tender, tenderhearted

related words caring, compassionate, considerate, cordial, doting, forgiving, friendly, kind, warmhearted; ardent, fervent, impassioned, passionate, warm; amatory, amorous, erotic; enamored, infatuated, lovesick; mushy, romantic, sentimental; brotherly, fatherly, motherly, sisterly

near antonyms aloof, detached, hardhearted, indifferent, pitiless, reserved, uncaring, unfeeling; disaffected, unconcerned, uninvolved; cold, frigid, unfriendly; hard-boiled, unromantic, unsentimental

antonyms unloving

low *adj* **1** being near the equator ⟨we took a cruise to the *low* northern latitudes⟩

synonyms equatorial, tropical

near antonyms temperate

antonyms polar

2 belonging to or characteristic of an early level of skill or development — see PRIMITIVE 1

3 belonging to the class of people of low social or economic rank — see IGNOBLE 1

4 feeling unhappiness — see SAD 1

5 having a low musical pitch or range — see DEEP 2

6 having relatively little height — see SHORT 1

7 lacking bodily strength — see WEAK 1

8 lacking in refinement or good taste — see COARSE 2

9 not following or in accordance with standards of honor and decency — see IGNOBLE 2

10 not loud in pitch or volume — see SOFT 1

11 costing little — see CHEAP 1

lowbred *adj* lacking in refinement or good taste — see COARSE 2

lowbrow *adj* lacking in refinement or good taste — see COARSE 2

lowbrow *n* a person who is chiefly interested in

material comfort and is hostile or indifferent to art and culture — see PHILISTINE

lowdown *n* information not generally available to the public — see DOPE 1

lower *adj* **1** having not so great importance or rank as another — see LESSER

2 situated lower down — see INFERIOR 1

¹**lower** *vb* **1** to cause to fall intentionally or unintentionally — see DROP 1

2 to go to a lower level — see DROP 2

3 to make smaller in amount, volume, or extent — see DECREASE 1

4 to grow less in scope or intensity especially gradually — see DECREASE 2

5 to reduce to a lower standing in one's own eyes or in others' eyes — see HUMBLE

²**lower** *also* **lour** *vb* **1** to take on a gloomy or forbidding look — see DARKEN 1

2 to look with anger or disapproval — see FROWN

lower *also* **lour** *n* a twisting of the facial features in disgust or disapproval — see GRIMACE

lower–class *adj* belonging to the class of people of low social or economic rank — see IGNOBLE 1

lowered *adj* directed down — see DOWNCAST 1

lowering *also* **louring** *adj* **1** covered over by clouds — see OVERCAST

2 harsh and threatening in manner or appearance — see GRIM 1

lowest *adj* being the least in amount, number, or size possible — see MINIMAL

low–grade *adj* of low quality — see CHEAP 2

lowliness *n* the absence of any feelings of being better than others — see HUMILITY

lowly *adj* **1** belonging to the class of people of low social or economic rank — see IGNOBLE 1

2 not having or showing any feelings of superiority, self-assertiveness, or showiness — see HUMBLE 1

lowly *adv* in manner showing no signs of pride or self-assertion ⟨the courtier bowed *lowly* before his king during the ceremony⟩

synonyms deferentially, humbly, meekly, modestly, sheepishly, submissively

related words fearfully, timidly; bashfully, diffidently, shyly; civilly, courteously, politely, respectfully

near antonyms fearlessly; discourteously, disdainfully, disrespectfully, impertinently, rashly, recklessly, saucily; impolitely, impudently, rudely, ungraciously

antonyms arrogantly, audaciously, boldly, brashly, brazenly, contemptuously, haughtily, pridefully, proudly, scornfully, swaggeringly

low–lying *adj* having relatively little height — see SHORT 1

lowness *n* **1** the quality or state of lacking refinement or good taste — see VULGARITY 1

2 the quality or state of lacking physical strength or vigor — see WEAKNESS 1

low–pressure *adj* having a relaxed, casual manner — see EASYGOING 1

low–spirited *adj* feeling unhappiness — see SAD 1

loyal *adj* firm in one's allegiance to someone or something — see FAITHFUL 1

loyalist *n* a person who loves his or her country and supports its interests and policies — see PATRIOT

loyalty *n* adherence to something to which one is bound by a pledge or duty — see FIDELITY

lozenge *n* a small mass containing medicine to be taken orally — see PILL

lubber *n* a big clumsy often slow-witted person — see OAF

lubberly *adj* lacking in physical ease and grace in movement or in the use of the hands — see CLUMSY 1

lubricate *vb* to coat (something) with a slippery substance in order to reduce friction ⟨it's not a good idea to use olive oil to *lubricate* the gears in an appliance⟩

synonyms grease, oil, slick, wax

near antonyms coarsen, rough, roughen

lubricated *adj* having or being a surface so smooth as to make sliding or falling likely — see SLICK 1

lucent *adj* **1** easily seen through — see CLEAR 1

2 giving off or reflecting much light — see BRIGHT 1

lucid *adj* **1** giving off or reflecting much light — see BRIGHT 1

2 having full use of one's mind and control over one's actions — see SANE

3 not subject to misinterpretation or more than one interpretation — see CLEAR 2

lucidity *n* **1** clearness of expression — see SIMPLICITY 2

2 the quality or state of having or giving off light — see BRILLIANCE 1

lucidness *n* clearness of expression — see SIMPLICITY 2

Lucifer *n* the supreme personification of evil often represented as the ruler of Hell — see DEVIL 1

luck *n* **1** success that is partly the result of chance ⟨some people have all the *luck*⟩

synonyms fortunateness, fortune, luckiness

related words break, fluke, godsend, hit, serendipity, strike, windfall; chance, opportunity; coup, stroke

near antonyms knock, misadventure, mishap; adversity, curse, sorrow, tragedy, trouble; calamity, cataclysm, catastrophe, disaster; defeat, failure, fizzle, nonsuccess; accident, casualty; disappointment, letdown, setback; circumstance, destiny, doom, fate, lot, portion

antonyms mischance, misfortune, unluckiness

2 the uncertain course of events — see CHANCE 1

luckiness *n* success that is partly the result of chance — see LUCK 1

luckless *adj* having, prone to, or marked by bad luck — see UNLUCKY

lucky *adj* **1** having good luck ⟨the *lucky* gambler walked out of the casino with $10,000⟩

synonyms fortunate, happy

related words blessed, favored, gifted, privileged; fair, golden, promising

near antonyms cursed, disadvantaged

antonyms hapless, ill-fated, ill-starred, luckless, star-crossed, unfortunate, unhappy, unlucky

2 coming or happening by good luck especially unexpectedly — see FORTUNATE 1

lucrative *adj* yielding a profit — see PROFITABLE 1

lucre *n* **1** something (as pieces of stamped metal or printed paper) customarily and legally used as a medium of exchange, a measure of value, or a means of payment — see MONEY

2 the amount of money left when expenses are subtracted from the total amount received — see PROFIT 1

ludicrous *adj* **1** causing or intended to cause laughter — see FUNNY 1

2 so foolish or pointless as to be worthy of scornful laughter — see RIDICULOUS 1

lug *n* a big clumsy often slow-witted person — see OAF

lug *vb* **1** to cause to follow by applying steady force on — see PULL 1

2 to support and take from one place to another — see CARRY 1

lugubrious *adj* expressing or suggesting mourning — see MOURNFUL 1

lukewarm *adj* **1** having or giving off heat to a moderate degree — see WARM 1

2 showing little or no interest or enthusiasm — see TEPID 1

lukewarmness *n* the quality or state of being moderate in temperature — see WARMTH 1

lull *n* a momentary halt in an activity — see PAUSE

lulling *adj* tending to calm the emotions and relieve stress — see SOOTHING 1

lumber *n* tree logs as prepared for human use — see WOOD

lumber *vb* **1** to move heavily or clumsily ⟨the elephant *lumbered* through the jungle⟩

synonyms barge, clump, flounder, lump, pound, scuff, scuffle, shamble, shuffle, stamp, stomp, stumble, stump, tramp, tromp

related words drag, flop, haul; labor, plod, trudge; careen, lurch, stagger, sway, teeter, totter, waddle, weave, wobble

near antonyms float, hover, waft

antonyms breeze, coast, glide, slide, waltz, whisk

2 to make progress in a clumsy, struggling manner — see FLOUNDER 1

3 to make a low heavy rolling sound — see RUMBLE

4 to place a weight or burden on — see LOAD 1

lumbering *adj* lacking in physical ease and grace in movement or in the use of the hands — see CLUMSY 1

lumberjack *n* a person whose job is to cut down trees ⟨the sawmill gets most of its business from the *lumberjacks* up north⟩

synonyms logger

related words sawyer; forester

luminary *n* **1** a ball-shaped gaseous celestial body that shines by its own light — see STAR 1

2 a person who is widely known and usually much talked about — see CELEBRITY 1

luminescence *n* the steady giving off of the form of radiation that makes vision possible — see LIGHT 1

luminosity *n* the quality or state of having or giving off light — see BRILLIANCE 1

luminous *adj* giving off or reflecting much light — see BRIGHT 1

lump *n* **1** a small uneven mass ⟨she dumped a *lump* of clay on the table and started to sculpt⟩

synonyms blob, chunk, clod, clump, glob, gob, gobbet, hunk, knob, nub, nubble, nugget, wad

related words bead, drop, globule; block, body, bulk; particle, piece, portion; bit, chip, crumb, morsel, scrap

2 a small rounded mass of swollen tissue — see BUMP 1

3 an abnormal mass of tissue — see GROWTH 1

lump *vb* **1** to bring together in one body or place — see GATHER 1

2 to move heavily or clumsily — see LUMBER 1

lumpish *adj* lacking in physical ease and grace in movement or in the use of the hands — see CLUMSY 1

lumpy *adj* **1** having small pieces or lumps spread throughout — see CHUNKY 1

2 not having a level or smooth surface — see UNEVEN 1

lunacy *n* **1** a foolish act or idea — see FOLLY 1

2 a serious mental disorder that prevents one from living a safe and normal life — see INSANITY 1

3 lack of good sense or judgment — see FOOLISHNESS 1

lunatic *adj* **1** having or showing a very abnormal or sick state of mind — see INSANE 1

2 showing or marked by a lack of good sense or judgment — see FOOLISH 1

lunatic *n* **1** a person judged to be legally or medically insane ⟨the *lunatic* was committed to an institution after running naked through the department store⟩

synonyms crackbrain, loony (*also* looney), maniac, neurotic, nut, psychopath, psychotic

related words madman, madwoman; deviant; paranoid, schizophrenic; character, crackpot, crank, eccentric, kook, oddball, screwball; case, patient

2 a person who lacks good sense or judgment — see FOOL 1

lurch *vb* **1** to make a series of unsteady side-to-side motions — see ROCK 1

2 to move forward while swaying from side to side — see STAGGER 1

lure *n* **1** something that persuades one to perform an action for pleasure or gain ⟨the promise of easy money is always the *lure* for some people to take up a life of crime⟩

synonyms allurement, bait, enticement, temptation, turn-on

related words appeal, call; attraction, goad, incentive, inducement, persuasion, seduction, spur; decoy, snare, trap

near antonyms caution, warning

2 something used to attract animals to a hook or into a trap — see BAIT 1

3 the act or pressure of giving in to a desire especially when ill-advised — see TEMPTATION 1

lure *vb* to lead away from a usual or proper course by offering some pleasure or advantage ⟨the hunter *lured* the lion into the open with the antelope carcass⟩

synonyms allure, beguile, decoy, entice, lead on, seduce, tempt

related words inveigle, persuade, rope (in), snow; catch, ensnare, entrap, snare; captivate, charm, enchant

near antonyms caution, ward (off), warn; drive (away *or* off), repulse, turn away

lurid *adj* **1** extremely disturbing or repellent — see HORRIBLE 1

2 lacking a healthy skin color — see PALE 2

3 arousing a strong and usually superficial interest or emotional reaction — see SENSATIONAL 1

luring *adj* having an often mysterious or magical power to attract — see FASCINATING 1

lurk *vb* to move about in a sly or secret manner — see SNEAK 1

lurker *n* someone who acts in a sly and secret manner — see SNEAK

luscious *adj* **1** very pleasing to the sense of taste — see DELICIOUS 1

2 pleasing to the physical senses — see SENSUAL

3 giving pleasure or contentment to the mind or senses — see PLEASANT

THESAURUS

lusciousness *n* the quality of being delicious — see DELICIOUSNESS

lush *adj* **1** covered with a thick healthy natural growth ⟨they loved to go for picnics in the *lush* woodlands⟩

synonyms green, leafy, luxuriant, overgrown, verdant

related words fat, fecund, fertile, fruitful, productive, rich; dense, tangled

near antonyms bleak, depleted, infertile, poor, unproductive; arid, dead, desert, dry, parched

antonyms barren, leafless

2 growing thickly and vigorously — see RANK 1

lust (for *or* after) *vb* to have an earnest wish to own or enjoy — see DESIRE

lust *n* a strong wish for something — see DESIRE

luster *or* **lustre** *n* brightness created by light reflected from a surface — see SHINE 1

lusterless *adj* lacking a surface luster or gloss — see MATTE

lustful *adj* having a strong sexual desire ⟨the *lustful* student was always chasing after girls⟩

synonyms lascivious, lewd, licentious, passionate, wanton

related words prurient; dissipated, dissolute, libertine; corrupt, debauched, depraved, immoral, indecent

near antonyms celibate, chaste, decent, modest, moral, pure, virtuous; monastic, monkish; maidenly, virginal; innocent, lily-white

lustiness *n* the quality or state of having abundant or intense activity — see VITALITY 1

lustrous *adj* **1** giving off or reflecting much light — see BRIGHT 1

2 having a shiny surface or finish — see GLOSSY

lusty *adj* **1** having active strength of body or mind — see VIGOROUS 1

2 not showing weakness or uncertainty — see FIRM 1

luxuriant *adj* **1** covered with a thick, healthy natural growth — see LUSH 1

2 growing thickly and vigorously — see RANK 1

3 producing abundantly — see FERTILE

4 showing obvious signs of wealth and comfort — see LUXURIOUS

luxurious *adj* showing obvious signs of wealth and comfort ⟨the *luxurious* apartment was filled with the latest electronic gadgets and fine works of art⟩

synonyms deluxe, lavish, luxuriant, opulent, palatial, plush, sumptuous

related words costly, expensive; rich; extravagant, grandiose, ostentatious, pretentious, showy; awesome, awful, beautiful, gorgeous, grand, imposing, impressive, magnificent, majestic, splendid, stately; comfortable, cozy, homelike, homey, snug

near antonyms economical, frugal, meager (*or* meagre), spare, thrifty

antonyms ascetic, austere, humble, Spartan

luxuriously *adv* in a luxurious manner — see HIGH

luxury *n* something adding to pleasure or comfort but not absolutely necessary ⟨a private yacht is a *luxury*⟩

synonyms amenity, comfort, extra, frill, indulgence, superfluity

related words extravagance; dainty, delicacy, treat; accessory, option

antonyms basic, essential, fundamental, necessity, requirement

2 something that adds to one's ease — see COMFORT 2

lying *adj* telling or containing lies — see DISHONEST 1

lynx-eyed *adj* having unusually keen vision — see SHARP-EYED

lyric *adj* **1** having a pleasantly flowing quality suggestive of music ⟨they performed a slow, *lyric* dance for the audience⟩

synonyms euphonious, lyrical, mellifluous, mellow, melodic, melodious, musical

related words dulcet, golden, sweet

near antonyms disconnected, staccato; discordant, grating, harsh, jarring, strident

2 having qualities suggestive of poetry — see POETIC

lyric *n* **1** a composition using rhythm and often rhyme to create a lyrical effect — see POEM

2 a short musical composition for the human voice often with instrumental accompaniment — see SONG 1

lyrical *adj* **1** having a pleasantly flowing quality suggestive of music — see LYRIC 1

2 having qualities suggestive of poetry — see POETIC

ma *n* a female human parent — see MOTHER

macabre *adj* extremely disturbing or repellent — see HORRIBLE 1

Machiavellian *adj* not guided by or showing a concern for what is right — see UNPRINCIPLED

machinate *vb* **1** to engage in a secret plan to accomplish evil or unlawful ends — see PLOT

2 to plan out usually with subtle skill or care — see ENGINEER

machination *n* a secret plan for accomplishing evil or unlawful ends — see PLOT 1

machine *n* **1** a device that changes energy into mechanical motion — see ENGINE

2 a self-propelled passenger vehicle on wheels — see CAR

machinery *n* something used to achieve an end — see AGENT 1

mackintosh *or* **macintosh** *n chiefly British* a coat made of water-resistant material — see RAINCOAT

macrocosm *n* the whole body of things observed or assumed — see UNIVERSE

mad *adj* **1** feeling or showing anger — see ANGRY

2 having or showing a very abnormal or sick state of mind — see INSANE 1

3 marked by great and often stressful excitement or activity — see FURIOUS 1

4 showing or marked by a lack of good sense or judgment — see FOOLISH 1

mad (about) *adj* filled with an intense or excessive love for — see ENAMORED (OF)

madcap *adj* foolishly adventurous or bold — see FOOLHARDY 1

madden *vb* **1** to cause to go insane or as if insane — see CRAZE

2 to make angry — see ANGER

maddening *adj* causing annoyance — see ANNOYING

mademoiselle *n* a young usually unmarried woman — see GIRL 1

made–up *adj* not real and existing only in the imagination — see IMAGINARY

madhouse *n* **1** a place where insane people are cared for ⟨it was hard to believe that this place with the bright cheery walls was really a *madhouse*⟩
synonyms asylum
related words institution; hospice, hospital, sanatorium, sanitarium; home

2 a place of uproar or confusion ⟨our house is always a *madhouse* on school mornings, with five kids and two dogs running around⟩
synonyms babel, bedlam, circus, hell
related words commotion, havoc, pandemonium, racket, ruckus, tumult, turmoil; clamor, clatter, din, hubbub, noise; chaos, confusion, disarrangement, disarray, disorder, maelstrom, mess, muss
near antonyms heaven, paradise, utopia; order, orderliness, organization; calm, peace; hush, quiet, silence, soundlessness, stillness

madly *adv* **1** in a confused and reckless manner — see HELTER-SKELTER 1

2 in an enthusiastic manner — see SKY-HIGH

madness *n* **1** a serious mental disorder that prevents one from living a safe and normal life — see INSANITY 1

2 lack of good sense or judgment — see FOOLISHNESS 1

maelstrom *n* water moving rapidly in a circle with a hollow in the center — see WHIRLPOOL

maestro *n* a person with a high level of knowledge or skill in a field — see EXPERT

Mafia *n* a group involved in secret or criminal activities — see RING 1

magazine *n* **1** a building for storing goods — see STOREHOUSE

2 a place where military arms are stored — see ARMORY

3 a publication that appears at regular intervals — see JOURNAL

magic *adj* **1** being or appearing to be under a magic spell — see ENCHANTED

2 having seemingly supernatural qualities or powers — see MYSTIC 1

magic *n* **1** the power to control natural forces through supernatural means ⟨he claimed that he could summon a storm through *magic*⟩
synonyms bewitchment, black art, black magic, conjuring, enchantment, mojo, necromancy, sorcery, voodooism, witchcraft, witchery, wizardry
related words abracadabra, amulet, charm, fetish (*also* fetich), mascot, phylactery, talisman; curse, hex, incantation, jinx, spell; augury, divining, forecasting, foreknowing, foreseeing, foretelling, fortune-telling, predicting, presaging, prognosticating, prophesying, soothsaying; hoodoo, occultism, spiritualism; augur, omen; exorcism; alchemy

near antonyms science

2 the art or skill of performing tricks or illusions for entertainment ⟨they hired someone to do *magic* for their child's tenth birthday party⟩
synonyms conjuring, legerdemain
related words deception, trickery
phrases sleight of hand

3 the power of irresistible attraction — see CHARM 2

magical *adj* **1** being or appearing to be under a magic spell — see ENCHANTED

2 being so extraordinary or abnormal as to suggest powers which violate the laws of nature — see SUPERNATURAL 2

3 having seemingly supernatural qualities or powers — see MYSTIC 1

magician *n* **1** a person skilled in using supernatural forces ⟨the *magician* was able to turn birds purple with a simple spell⟩
synonyms charmer, conjurer (*or* conjuror), enchanter, necromancer, sorcerer, voodoo, witch, wizard
related words enchantress, hag, hex, sorceress, warlock; medicine man; foreseer, fortune-teller, prognosticator, prophesier, prophet, soothsayer; medium; exorcist

2 one who practices tricks and illusions for entertainment ⟨the famous *magician's* best trick was always pulling a rabbit out of a hat⟩
synonyms conjurer (*or* conjuror), prestidigitator, trickster
related words charmer, enchanter, enchantress

magistrate *n* a public official having authority to decide questions of law — see JUDGE 1

magnanimous *adj* having, characterized by, or arising from a dignified and generous nature — see NOBLE 2

magnanimously *adv* in a manner befitting a person of the highest character and ideals — see GREATLY 1

magnate *n* a person of rank, power, or influence in a particular field ⟨the film studio *magnate* had movie stars at his beck and call⟩
synonyms baron, czar (*also* tsar *or* tzar), king, mogul, prince, tycoon
related words big shot, bigwig, figure, nabob, notable, personage, VIP; celebrity, personality, star; moneybags, plutocrat

magnet *n* something that attracts interest ⟨the giant theme park is a *magnet* for tourists to the area⟩
synonyms attraction, draw, lodestone
related words capital, cynosure, mecca; allure, allurement, bait, enticement, fascination, lure, temptation, turn-on; appeal, call; incentive, inducement, persuasion, spur

magnetic *adj* having an often mysterious or magical power to attract — see FASCINATING 1

magnetism *n* the power of irresistible attraction — see CHARM 2

magnetize *vb* to attract or delight as if by magic — see CHARM 1

magnification *n* the representation of something in terms that go beyond the facts — see EXAGGERATION

magnificence *n* impressiveness of beauty on a large scale ⟨the *magnificence* of the great castle hallway is beyond description⟩
synonyms augustness, brilliance, gloriousness, glory, grandeur, grandness, majesty, nobility, no-

bleness, resplendence, splendor, stateliness, stupendousness, sublimeness, superbness

related words awesomeness, marvelousness, wondrousness; lavishness, luxuriance, luxury, opulence, sumptuousness; grandiosity, ostentation, pretentiousness; flashiness, gaudiness, ornateness, showiness; extraordinariness, remarkableness

magnificent *adj* large and impressive in size, grandeur, extent, or conception — see GRAND 1

magnify *vb* **1** to add to the interest of by including made-up details — see EMBROIDER

2 to enhance the status of — see EXALT

3 to make markedly greater in measure or degree — see INTENSIFY

4 to proclaim the glory of — see PRAISE 1

magnitude *n* **1** the quality or state of being important — see IMPORTANCE

2 the quality or state of being very large — see IMMENSITY

3 the total amount of measurable space or surface occupied by something — see ¹SIZE

magnum opus *n* something (as a work of art) that is a great achievement and often its creator's greatest achievement — see MASTERPIECE

magpie *n* a person who talks constantly — see CHATTERBOX

maid *n* **1** a female domestic servant ⟨they hired a *maid* to do the housework after the baby was born⟩

synonyms charwoman, domestic, housekeeper, housemaid, maidservant

related words attendant, chambermaid, handmaiden (*also* handmaid), lady-in-waiting; nursemaid

2 a young usually unmarried woman — see GIRL 1

maiden *adj* **1** coming before all others in time or order — see FIRST 1

2 never having had sexual relations — see VIRGIN 1

maiden *n* a young usually unmarried woman — see GIRL 1

maidservant *n* a female domestic servant — see MAID 1

mail *n* communications or parcels sent or carried through the postal system ⟨whenever they were separated, the lovers always sent each other lots of *mail*⟩

synonyms matter, parcel post, post [*chiefly British*]

related words electronic mail, e-mail; dispatch, epistle, message, missive, note, postcard; airmail, rural free delivery, special delivery; junk mail

mail *vb* to send through the postal system ⟨if you don't *mail* that letter soon, it's going to arrive late⟩

synonyms post

related words airmail; address, consign; direct, dispatch, forward, remit, route, ship, transmit, transport; register

near antonyms receive

mail carrier *n* a person who delivers mail — see POSTMAN

mailman *n* a person who delivers mail — see POSTMAN

maim *vb* to cause severe or permanent injury to ⟨on-the-job accidents *maim* far too many workers every year⟩

synonyms cripple, disable, lame, mutilate

related words dismember, hamstring, hobble; batter, bruise, bung (up), mangle, maul, rough (up);

gore, lacerate, wound; disfigure, scar; break, damage, harm, hurt, impair, injure; bash, beat, belt, bludgeon, buffet, drub, hammer, lace, lambaste (*or* lambast), lick, paste, pelt, pound, pummel, thump; bang, box, hit, punch, slap, smack, smash, sock, spank, swat, swipe, thrash, thwack, whack; flog, lash, wallop, whip; kill, murder; torment, torture

near antonyms cure, heal, remedy; doctor, fix, mend, patch; rebuild, recondition, reconstruct, rejuvenate, renew, renovate, repair, restore

main *adj* coming before all others in importance — see FOREMOST 1

main *n* **1** muscular strength — see MUSCLE 1

2 one of the great divisions of land on the globe or the main part of such a division — see MAINLAND

3 the main or greater part of something as distinguished from its appendages — see BODY 1

mainland *n* one of the great divisions of land on the globe or the main part of such a division ⟨the boat back to the *mainland* leaves once every two days⟩

synonyms continent, main

related words subcontinent, supercontinent

near antonyms island, isle, islet; atoll, barrier reef, cay, coral reef, key; cape, headland, peninsula, promontory

mainly *adv* for the most part — see CHIEFLY

mainstay *n* something or someone to which one looks for support — see DEPENDENCE 2

maintain *vb* **1** to keep in good condition ⟨he repairs and *maintains* antique cars as a hobby⟩

synonyms conserve, keep up, preserve, save

related words support, sustain; care (for), husband, manage; defend, guard, protect, safeguard, screen, shield; cure, fix, heal, remedy; mend, patch, rebuild, reconstruct

near antonyms disregard, ignore, neglect; break, damage, destroy, harm, hurt, impair, injure, ruin, wreck

2 to continue to declare to be true or proper despite opposition or objections ⟨part of debating is learning to *maintain* your position in the face of harsh challenges⟩

synonyms defend, justify, support, uphold

related words advocate, champion, espouse; confirm, vindicate, warrant; affirm, assert, avow, claim, contend, declare, insist, proclaim, profess, state; argue, debate, discuss; emphasize, stress, underline, underscore

near antonyms abandon, forsake, recant, retract, take back, withdraw; controvert, disprove, rebut, refute

3 to pay the living expenses of — see SUPPORT 2

4 to state (something) as a reason in support of or against something under consideration — see ARGUE 1

5 to state as a fact usually forcefully — see CLAIM 1

maintainable *adj* capable of being defended with good reasoning against verbal attack — see TENABLE 1

maintenance *n* the act or activity of keeping something in an existing and usually satisfactory condition ⟨I was hired to perform basic *maintenance* until the property could be sold⟩

synonyms conservation, conserving, preservation, preserving, upkeep

related words support, sustaining; care, guardianship; defense, guarding, protection, safeguarding, safekeeping

near antonyms dereliction, ignoring, neglect; damage, destruction, harm, hurt, injury, ruin

majestic *adj* **1** having or showing elegance — see ELEGANT 1

2 large and impressive in size, grandeur, extent, or conception — see GRAND 1

3 very dignified in form, tone, or style — see ELEVATED 2

majesty *n* **1** a dignified bearing or appearance befitting royalty ⟨even as a child, the princess possessed a certain *majesty* that would later serve her well⟩

synonyms augustness, stateliness

related words high-mindedness, magnanimity, nobility; haughtiness, lordliness, pompousness; dignity, poise; grandeur, grandness, greatness, impressiveness, magnificence, resplendence, splendor

2 dignified or restrained beauty of form, appearance, or style — see ELEGANCE

3 impressiveness of beauty on a large scale — see MAGNIFICENCE

major *adj* having great meaning or lasting effect — see IMPORTANT 1

majority *n* the state of being fully grown or developed — see MATURITY

make *vb* **1** to bring into being by combining, shaping, or transforming materials ⟨will you help me *make* the dough for the cookies?⟩

synonyms fabricate, fashion, form, frame, manufacture, produce

related words assemble, build, construct, erect, make up, put up, raise, rear, structure, throw up; craft, handcraft; forge, mold, shape; prefabricate; create, invent, originate; establish, father, institute, organize; concoct, contrive, cook up, design, devise, imagine, think (up); conceive, envisage, picture, visualize; refashion, remake, remanufacture

phrases put together

near antonyms disassemble, dismantle, take apart; break up, dismember; abolish, annihilate, demolish, destroy, devastate, eradicate, exterminate, extinguish, flatten, pulverize, raze, ruin, shatter, smash, wreck; break, damage, harm, hurt, impair; blow up, explode

2 to obtain (as a goal) through effort — see ACHIEVE 1

3 to be the cause of (a situation, action, or state of mind) — see EFFECT

4 to carry through (as a process) to completion — see PERFORM 1

5 to cause (a person) to give in to pressure — see FORCE

6 to decide the size, amount, number, or distance of (something) without actual measurement — see ESTIMATE 2

7 to form by putting together parts or materials — see BUILD

8 to give the impression of being — see SEEM

9 to go on a specified course or in a certain direction — see HEAD 1

10 to put into effect through legislative or authoritative action — see ENACT

11 to receive as return for effort — see EARN 1

12 to recognize the meaning of — see COMPREHEND 1

make–believe *adj* not real and existing only in the imagination — see IMAGINARY

make out *vb* **1** to meet one's day-to-day needs — see GET ALONG 1

2 to recognize the meaning of — see COMPREHEND 1

3 to touch one another with the lips as a sign of love — see KISS 1

make over *vb* **1** to change in form, appearance, or use — see CONVERT 2

2 to give over the legal possession or ownership of — see TRANSFER 1

3 to make different in some way — see CHANGE 1

Maker *n* the being worshipped as the creator and ruler of the universe — see DEITY 2

makeshift *adj* taking the place of one that came before — see NEW 1

makeshift *n* a temporary replacement ⟨when his belt broke, he used string as a *makeshift* until he could get home to replace it⟩

synonyms expedient, stopgap

related words recourse, refuge, resort; alternate, backup, standby, stand-in, substitute, understudy

near antonyms archetype, original, prototype

makeup *n* **1** preparations intended to beautify the face or hair ⟨she never left the house without applying her *makeup* and arranging her jewelry⟩

synonyms cosmetics, paint

related words greasepaint; camouflage; cold cream, cream, eye shadow, kohl, lipstick, lotion, mascara, oil, powder, rouge, vanishing cream

2 the way in which the elements of something (as a work of art) are arranged — see COMPOSITION 3

make up *vb* **1** to be all the substance of — see CONSTITUTE 1

2 to create or think of by clever use of the imagination — see INVENT

3 to form by putting together parts or materials — see BUILD

make up (for) *vb* to balance with an equal force so as to make ineffective — see OFFSET

making *n* the basic elements from which something can be developed ⟨she had all the *makings* of an excellent leader, but she needed some experience first⟩

synonyms material, raw material, stuff, substance

related words possibility, potential, potentiality; matter

maladroit *adj* showing or marked by a lack of skill and tact (as in dealing with a situation) — see AWKWARD 2

malady *n* an abnormal state that disrupts a plant's or animal's normal bodily functioning — see DISEASE

malcontent *adj* having a feeling that one has been wronged or thwarted in one's ambitions — see DISCONTENTED

male *adj* considered characteristic of or appropriate for men — see MASCULINE

male *n* an adult male human being — see MAN 1

malediction *n* a prayer that harm will come to someone — see CURSE 1

malefaction *n* a breaking of a moral or legal code — see OFFENSE 1

malefactor *n* **1** a person who commits moral wrongs — see EVILDOER 1

2 a person who has committed a crime — see CRIMINAL

malevolence *n* the desire to cause pain for the satisfaction of doing harm — see MALICE

THESAURUS

malevolent *adj* having or showing a desire to cause someone pain or suffering for the sheer enjoyment of it — see HATEFUL

malevolently *adv* in a mean or spiteful manner — see NASTILY

malfeasance *n* improper or illegal behavior — see MISCONDUCT

malformed *adj* badly or imperfectly formed ⟨a clay sculpture of an eagle that was so *malformed* that it looked more like a feathered football⟩
synonyms deformed, distorted, misshapen, monstrous, shapeless
related words defaced, disfigured; aberrant, abnormal, freakish, mutant; asymmetrical (*or* asymmetric), crooked, disproportionate, irregular, lopsided, nonsymmetrical, overbalanced, unbalanced, unequal; horrible, horrific, terrible; ugly, unattractive
near antonyms flawless, perfect
antonyms shapely

malfunctioning *adj* not being in working order — see INOPERABLE 1

malice *n* the desire to cause pain for the satisfaction of doing harm ⟨there was no reason other than pure *malice* to spread such disgusting lies all over school⟩
synonyms cattiness, despite, hatefulness, malevolence, maliciousness, malignancy, malignity, meanness, nastiness, spite, spitefulness, spleen, venom, viciousness
related words abusiveness, cruelty; abhorrence, abomination, execration, hate, hatred, loathing; animosity, antagonism, antipathy, bitterness, enmity, grudge, hostility, ill will, jaundice, rancor, resentment; despicableness, invidiousness; vengefulness, vindictiveness; aversion, disgust, distaste, horror, repugnance, repulsion, revulsion; contempt, disdain; jealousy, pique, resentment, scorn; bile, rancor, virulence, vitriol
near antonyms devotion, love, passion; amiability, amicability, amity, civility, cordiality, friendliness, hospitality; adoration, ardor, infatuation, veneration, worship; affection, charity, kindliness; comity, empathy, friendship, goodwill, sympathy, understanding

malicious *adj* having or showing a desire to cause someone pain or suffering for the sheer enjoyment of it — see HATEFUL

maliciously *adv* in a mean or spiteful manner — see NASTILY

maliciousness *n* the desire to cause pain for the satisfaction of doing harm — see MALICE

malign *adj* having or showing a desire to cause someone pain or suffering for the sheer enjoyment of it — see HATEFUL

malign *vb* to make untrue and harmful statements about — see SLANDER

malignancy *n* the desire to cause pain for the satisfaction of doing harm — see MALICE

malignant *adj* having or showing a desire to cause someone pain or suffering for the sheer enjoyment of it — see HATEFUL

malignantly *adv* in a mean or spiteful manner — see NASTILY

maligning *n* the making of false statements that damage another's reputation — see SLANDER

malignity *n* the desire to cause pain for the satisfaction of doing harm — see MALICE

malleability *n* the quality or state of being easily molded — see PLASTICITY

malleable *adj* **1** capable of being easily molded or modeled — see PLASTIC
2 capable of being readily changed — see FLEXIBLE 1

malodorous *adj* having an unpleasant smell ⟨the garbage became quite *malodorous* after it sat there for two weeks⟩
synonyms fetid, foul, fusty, musty, noisome, rank, reeking, reeky, smelly, stinking, stinky, strong
related words putrid, rancid, stale; bad, disgusting, offensive, repulsive, revolting, vile; decayed, decaying, decomposed, decomposing, rotted, rotten, rotting, spoiled, spoiling; dirty, filthy, nasty, noxious; odoriferous, odorous
near antonyms flowery, fruity, spicy, woodsy
antonyms ambrosial, aromatic, fragrant, perfumed, redolent, savory, scented, sweet

maltreat *vb* **1** to inflict physical or emotional harm upon — see ABUSE 1
2 to abuse physically — see MANHANDLE 1

mama *n* a female human parent — see MOTHER

mammoth *adj* unusually large — see HUGE

mammoth *n* something that is unusually large and powerful — see GIANT

mammy *n* a female human parent — see MOTHER

man *n* **1** an adult male human being ⟨the children always feel better when there's a *man* or a woman around⟩
synonyms bloke [*chiefly British*], buck, cat [*slang*], chap [*chiefly British*], dude, fellow, gent, gentleman, guy, hombre, jack, joker, lad, male
related words master, mister, sir
2 a male romantic companion — see BOYFRIEND
3 a member of the human race — see HUMAN
4 the human race — see MANKIND
5 the male partner in a marriage — see HUSBAND

manacle *n* **1** something that physically prevents free movement — see BOND 1
2 something that makes movement or progress more difficult — see ENCUMBRANCE

manacle *vb* **1** to confine or restrain with or as if with chains — see BIND 1
2 to create difficulty for the work or activity of — see HAMPER

manage *vb* **1** to deal with (something) usually skillfully or efficiently — see HANDLE 1
2 to look after and make decisions about — see CONDUCT 1
3 to meet one's day-to-day needs — see GET ALONG 1

management *n* the act or activity of looking after and making decisions about something — see CONDUCT 1

manager *n* a person who manages or directs — see EXECUTIVE

managerial *adj* suited for or relating to the directing of things — see EXECUTIVE

managing *adj* highest in rank or authority — see HEAD

man–at–arms *n* a person engaged in military service — see SOLDIER

mandate *n* the granting of power to perform various acts or duties — see COMMISSION 1

mandatory *adj* forcing one's compliance or participation by or as if by law ⟨the tests are *mandatory* for all students wishing to graduate⟩
synonyms compulsory, forced, imperative, incumbent, involuntary, necessary, nonelective, obligatory, peremptory, required

related words all-important, essential, indispensable, needed, requisite; insistent, persistent, pressing, urgent; demanded, enforced; coercive

near antonyms chosen, discretionary; dispensable, unnecessary, unneeded, unwanted; inconsequential, insignificant, nonessential, unimportant

antonyms elective, optional, voluntary

maneuver *vb* **1** to deal with (something) usually skillfully or efficiently — see HANDLE 1

2 to plan out usually with subtle skill or care — see ENGINEER

manful *adj* feeling or displaying no fear by temperament — see BRAVE

mangle *vb* to make or do (something) in a clumsy or unskillful way — see BOTCH

mangy *adj* showing signs of advanced wear and tear and neglect — see SHABBY 1

manhandle *vb* **1** to abuse physically ⟨charges that the police *manhandled* peaceful protesters⟩

synonyms maltreat, maul, mishandle, rough (up)

related words abuse, ill-treat, ill-use, mistreat, misuse; roughhouse, wrestle; bash, batter, beat, buffet, drub, lambaste (*or* lambast), lick, pound, pummel, slap, thrash; harm, hurt, injure, wound; oppress, persecute, wrong; ambush, assail, attack; clobber, fight, gang up (on), hit, jump, knock; torment, torture

near antonyms caress, fondle, pet; coddle, mollycoddle, pamper; care (for), foster, nurture

2 to inflict physical or emotional harm upon — see ABUSE 1

manhood *n* the set of qualities considered appropriate for or characteristic of men — see VIRILITY

mania *n* **1** a serious mental disorder that prevents one from living a safe and normal life — see INSANITY 1

2 something about which one is constantly thinking or concerned — see FIXATION

maniac *n* **1** a person judged to be legally or medically insane — see LUNATIC 1

2 a person with a strong and habitual liking for something — see FAN

maniacal *also* **maniac** *adj* having or showing a very abnormal or sick state of mind — see INSANE 1

manifest *adj* not subject to misinterpretation or more than one interpretation — see CLEAR 2

manifest *vb* **1** to make known (something abstract) through outward signs — see SHOW 2

2 to represent in visible form — see EMBODY 2

manifestation *n* a visible representation of something abstract (as a quality) — see EMBODIMENT

manifold *adj* being of many and various kinds ⟨the *manifold* attractions of that state make it an ideal destination for a family vacation⟩

synonyms divers, multifarious, myriad

related words multiform, multiple, multiplex, multitudinous; heterogeneous, miscellaneous, mixed, sundry, various; different, diverse, unlike, varied

near antonyms homogeneous, monolithic, unmixed, unvaried; alike, identical, same; distinct, distinctive, individual, separate; alone, lone, only, sole, solitary; singular, unique

manikin *or* **mannikin** *n* **1** a three-dimensional representation of the human body used especially for displaying clothes — see MANNEQUIN 1

2 a person who poses with or wears merchandise (as clothes) often for pictorial advertising — see MODEL 2

manipulate *vb* **1** to control or take advantage of by artful, unfair, or insidious means ⟨*manipulated* their parents into agreeing to let them stay out later by telling their mother that their father agreed, and vice versa⟩

synonyms exploit, play (upon)

related words engineer, finagle, jockey, maneuver; beguile, bluff, cozen, deceive, delude, dupe, fool, gull, hoax, hoodwink, kid, snow, take in, trick; intrigue, machinate, plot, scheme; arrange, contrive, devise, finesse, mastermind; cheat, chisel, defraud, fleece, gyp, hustle, swindle

2 to deal with (something) usually skillfully or efficiently — see HANDLE 1

3 to plan out usually with subtle skill or care — see ENGINEER

mankind *n* the human race ⟨all of *mankind* stands to gain if world peace is finally achieved⟩

synonyms Homo sapiens, humanity, humankind, man

related words being, body, creature, fellowman, human, individual, mortal, party, person

manlike *adj* **1** considered characteristic of or appropriate for men — see MASCULINE

2 having qualities or traits that are traditionally considered inappropriate for a girl or woman — see UNFEMININE

manliness *n* the set of qualities considered appropriate for or characteristic of men — see VIRILITY

manly *adj* considered characteristic of or appropriate for men — see MASCULINE

man–made *adj* being such in appearance only and made with or manufactured from usually cheaper materials — see IMITATION

manna *n* **1** a source of great satisfaction — see DELIGHT 1

2 something that provides happiness or does good for a person or thing — see BLESSING 2

mannequin *n* **1** a three-dimensional representation of the human body used especially for displaying clothes ⟨the *mannequin* over there looks so real⟩

synonyms dummy, figure, form, manikin (*or* mannikin)

related words doll

2 a person who poses with or wears merchandise (as clothes) often for pictorial advertising — see MODEL 2

manner *n* **1** **manners** *pl* personal conduct or behavior as evaluated by an accepted standard of appropriateness for a social or professional setting ⟨her table *manners* were so impeccable that she even knew how to use all five forks⟩

synonyms etiquette, form, mores, proprieties

related words amenities, civilities, pleasantries; bearing, demeanor, deportment; courtesy, decorum, mannerliness, politeness; formalities, protocol, rules; air, attitude, carriage, poise, polish, pose, posture, presence; custom, habit, pattern, practice (*also* practise), trick, way, wont; convention, fashion, mode, style

2 a distinctive way of putting ideas into words — see STYLE 1

3 a number of persons or things that are grouped together because they have something in common — see SORT 1

4 the means or procedure for doing something — see METHOD

mannerism *n* an odd or peculiar habit — see IDIOSYNCRASY

mannerliness *n* speech or behavior that is a sign of good breeding — see POLITENESS

mannerly *adj* showing consideration, courtesy, and good manners — see POLITE 1

mannish *adj* **1** considered characteristic of or appropriate for men — see MASCULINE
2 having qualities or traits that are traditionally considered inappropriate for a girl or woman — see UNFEMININE

manor *n* a large impressive residence — see MANSION

manor house *n* a large impressive residence — see MANSION

manpower *n* a body of persons at work or available for work — see FORCE 1

mansion *n* a large impressive residence ⟨if I ever win the lottery, I'm going to buy a *mansion* in the mountains⟩
synonyms castle, château, countryseat, estate, hacienda, hall, manor, manor house, palace, villa
related words showplace; abode, domicile, dwelling, habitation, hearth, home, house, lodging(s), pad, place; housing, nest, quarter(s), residency, roof; aerie, penthouse; salon, suite, townhouse

man–size *or* **man–sized** *adj* considered characteristic of or appropriate for men — see MASCULINE

manta *n* any of several extremely large rays — see DEVILFISH

manta ray *n* any of several extremely large rays — see DEVILFISH

mantilla *n* a scarf worn on the head — see BANDANNA

mantle *n* **1** a sleeveless garment worn so as to hang over the shoulders, arms, and back — see ¹CAPE
2 something that covers or conceals like a piece of cloth — see CLOAK 1

mantle *vb* to surround or cover closely — see ENFOLD 1

manual *n* a book used for instruction in a subject — see TEXTBOOK

manufactory *n* a building or set of buildings for the manufacturing of goods — see FACTORY

manufacture *vb* **1** to bring into being by combining, shaping, or transforming materials — see MAKE 1
2 to create or think of by clever use of the imagination — see INVENT

manumission *n* the act of setting free from slavery — see LIBERATION

manumit *vb* to set free (as from slavery or confinement) — see FREE 1

manuscript *n* writing done by hand — see HANDWRITING 2

many *adj* being of a large but indefinite number ⟨a journey of *many* miles begins with a single step⟩
synonyms multiple, multiplex, multitudinous, numerous
related words countless, innumerable, numberless, uncountable, unnumbered, untold; several, some; miscellaneous, mixed, sundry, various; divers, manifold, multifarious, myriad
near antonyms countable, limited
antonyms few

map *n* an illustration of certain features of a geographical area ⟨there is a *map* of the United States on the wall over there⟩
synonyms chart
related words graph, graphic; relief map

map (out) *vb* to work out the details of (something) in advance — see PLAN 1

mar *vb* **1** to affect slightly with something morally bad or undesirable — see TAINT 1
2 to reduce the soundness, effectiveness, or perfection of — see DAMAGE 1

marathon *adj* lasting for a considerable time — see LONG 2

maraud *vb* to search through with the intent of committing robbery — see RANSACK 1

marble *vb* to mark with small spots especially unevenly — see SPOT 1

marbled *adj* having blotches of two or more colors — see PIED

march *n* **1** a region along the dividing line between two countries — see FRONTIER 1
2 forward movement in time or place — see ADVANCE 1

march *vb* **1** to move along with a steady regular step especially in a group ⟨the band had to practice for hours to be able to *march* in perfect step⟩
synonyms file, pace, parade, stride
related words goose-step; perambulate, step, traipse, tread; hike, tramp; lumber, plod, stamp, stomp, stride, trudge
near antonyms amble, meander, ramble, stroll, wander
2 to move forward along a course — see GO 1

margin *n* the line or relatively narrow space that marks the outer limit of something — see BORDER 1

margin *vb* to serve as a border for — see BORDER

marginally *adv* by a very small margin — see JUST 2

marine *adj* **1** of or relating to the sea ⟨he loves collecting little *marine* creatures while at the beach⟩
synonyms maritime, oceanic, pelagic
related words abyssal, deep-sea, deepwater, saltwater; admiralty, nautical, naval; undersea, underwater; hydrographic, oceanographic
2 of or relating to navigation of the sea ⟨a collection of *marine* instruments, including a sextant⟩
synonyms maritime, nautical, navigational
related words admiralty, naval; oceangoing, seafaring, seagoing; hydrographic, oceanographic

mariner *n* one who operates or navigates a seagoing vessel — see SAILOR

marital *adj* of or relating to marriage ⟨neither of them ever forgot their *marital* vows, no matter how hard things sometimes were⟩
synonyms conjugal, connubial, married, matrimonial, nuptial, wedded
related words espoused, matched, mated; bridal; wifely; affianced, betrothed, committed, engaged, pledged, promised

maritime *adj* **1** of or relating to navigation of the sea — see MARINE 2
2 of or relating to the sea — see MARINE 1

mark *n* **1** a person or thing that is made fun of — see LAUGHINGSTOCK
2 a person or thing that is the object of abuse, criticism, or ridicule — see TARGET 1
3 overall quality as seen or judged by people in general — see REPUTATION
4 something set up as an example against which others of the same type are compared — see STANDARD 1
5 something that one hopes or intends to accomplish — see GOAL
6 something that sets apart an individual from others of the same kind — see CHARACTERISTIC

7 something that spoils the appearance or completeness of a thing — see BLEMISH

8 the power to bring about a result on another — see EFFECT 2

mark *vb* **1** to attach an identifying slip to — see LABEL 1

2 to be an important feature of — see CHARACTERIZE 2

3 to make a written note of — see RECORD 1

mark (out) *vb* to mark the limits of — see LIMIT 2

mark down *vb* to lower the price or value of — see DEPRECIATE 1

marked *adj* likely to attract attention — see NOTICEABLE

marker *n* a slip (as of paper or cloth) that is attached to something to identify or describe it — see LABEL

market *vb* to offer for sale to the public ⟨local farmers *market* their garden-fresh produce in roadside stands all over the valley⟩
synonyms deal (in), merchandise, put up, retail, sell, vend
related words wholesale; hawk, peddle; barter, distribute, exchange, export, handle, trade, traffic (in); advertise, ballyhoo, boost, plug, promote, tout; bargain, chaffer, dicker, haggle, horse-trade, palter; auction; provide, supply; keep, stock
antonyms buy, purchase

marketable *adj* **1** fit to be offered for sale ⟨you'll need to clean that car up a bit before it's *marketable*⟩
synonyms salable (*or* saleable)
related words commercial, profitable; costly, fancy, fine, high-grade, precious, premium, prime, valuable; dear, expensive, extravagant
near antonyms damaged, shopworn; cheap, useless, worthless; bad, inferior, low-grade, substandard, unsatisfactory
antonyms nonsalable, unmarketable, unsalable

2 fit or likely to be sold especially on a large scale — see COMMERCIAL

marketplace *n* the buying and selling of goods especially on a large scale and between different places — see COMMERCE

market value *n* the amount of money for which something will find a buyer — see VALUE 1

marksman *n* a person skilled in shooting at a target ⟨only the best *marksmen* can hit the bull's-eye at 500 feet⟩
synonyms sharpshooter, shooter, shot
related words rifleman, trapshooter; gunman, gunner, sniper

maroon *vb* to cause to remain behind — see LEAVE 1

marriage *n* **1** a union representing a special kind of social and legal partnership between two people ⟨some religions consider *marriage* a sacrament⟩
synonyms match, matrimony, wedlock
related words bigamy, monogamy, polygamy; intermarriage, miscegenation, remarriage; attachment, commitment, relationship; betrothal, engagement, espousal, hand, pledge, promise, proposal, troth
near antonyms annulment, divorce, separation

2 a ceremony in which two people are united in matrimony — see WEDDING

married *adj* of or relating to marriage — see MARITAL

marry *vb* **1** to perform the ceremony of marriage for ⟨they chose a very nice priest to *marry* them⟩
synonyms wed
related words match, mate; conjoin, connect, unite; affiance

2 to give in marriage ⟨they worried about the cost of *marrying* off five daughters⟩
synonyms espouse, match, wed
related words commit, engage; affiance, betroth, pledge, promise

3 to take as a spouse ⟨he *married* his girlfriend three years ago, and they've been happy ever since⟩
synonyms espouse, wed
related words affiance, betroth, commit, engage, pledge, promise, propose; remarry
near antonyms separate (from)
antonyms divorce

4 to take a spouse ⟨she had always believed she would never *marry*, but fate proved her wrong⟩
synonyms wed
related words couple, mate; pair off, remarry
phrases tie the knot
near antonyms divorce, separate

5 to come together to form a single unit — see UNITE 1

marsh *n* spongy land saturated or partially covered with water — see SWAMP

marshal *vb* **1** to assemble and make ready for action — see MOBILIZE

2 to point out the way for (someone) especially from a position in front — see LEAD 1

3 to put into a particular arrangement — see ORDER 1

marshaling *or* **marshalling** *n* an act of gathering forces together to renew or attempt an effort — see RALLY 1

marshland *n* spongy land saturated or partially covered with water — see SWAMP

martial *adj* **1** of, relating to, or suitable for war or a warrior ⟨the young recruit looked all grown up in his new *martial* uniform⟩
synonyms military, soldierly
related words aggressive, bellicose, combative, contentious, guerrilla, pugnacious, quarrelsome, scrappy, truculent, warlike; belligerent, militant, warring; antagonistic, argumentative, fierce, gladiatorial, hot-tempered; mercenary
near antonyms civil, civilian, nonmilitary; conciliatory, nonviolent, pacific, peaceable, peaceful; affable, amiable, amicable, benevolent, complaisant, cordial, easygoing, friendly, genial, good-natured, gracious, ingratiating, obliging
antonyms unsoldierly

2 of or relating to the armed services — see MILITARY 1

martyr *vb* to cause persistent suffering to — see AFFLICT

marvel *n* something extraordinary or surprising — see WONDER 1

marveling *or* **marvelling** *adj* filled with amazement or wonder — see OPENMOUTHED

marvelous *or* **marvellous** *adj* **1** causing wonder or astonishment ⟨the sheer immensity of the ancient ruin known as Stonehenge is *marvelous* to behold⟩
synonyms amazing, astonishing, astounding, awesome, awful, eye-opening, fabulous, miraculous, portentous, prodigious, staggering, stunning, stupendous, sublime, surprising, wonderful, wondrous
related words incomprehensible, inconceivable,

THESAURUS

incredible, unbelievable, unimaginable, unthinkable; extraordinary, phenomenal, rare, sensational, spectacular; singular, uncommon, unique, unusual, unwonted; conspicuous, notable, noticeable, outstanding, remarkable; impressive, striking; animating, energizing, enlightening, enlivening, exciting, galvanizing, invigorating, stimulating; alluring, attracting, attractive, beguiling, bewitching, captivating, charming, enchanting, entertaining, enthralling, fascinating, interesting
near antonyms unimpressive, uninspiring, unremarkable; boring, dull, jading, monotonous, tedious, tiring, uninspired, uninteresting, wearisome, weary, wearying; common, customary, mundane, normal, ordinary, typical, unexceptional, usual; draining, enervating, exhausting, fatiguing, wearing; debilitating, enfeebling; demoralizing, discouraging, disheartening, dispiriting
2 excitingly or mysteriously unusual — see EXOTIC
3 of the very best kind — see EXCELLENT
mascot *n* something worn or kept to bring good luck or keep away evil — see CHARM 1
masculine *adj* considered characteristic of or appropriate for men ⟨some people consider chest hair to be a particularly appealing *masculine* trait⟩
synonyms male, manlike, manly, mannish, man-size (*or* man-sized), virile
related words boyish, tomboyish
near antonyms girlish, sissy; feminine, womanish, womanlike, womanly; emasculated, impotent, weakened
antonyms effeminate, unmanly, unmasculine
masculinity *n* the set of qualities considered appropriate for or characteristic of men — see VIRILITY
mash *vb* **1** to apply external pressure on so as to force out the juice or contents of — see PRESS 2
2 to cause to become a pulpy mass — see CRUSH 1
mask *n* **1** a cover or partial cover for the face used to disguise oneself ⟨he loved his gorilla *mask* so much that he even tried to sleep with it on⟩
synonyms vizard
related words camouflage, disguise; bill, cloak, domino, hood, veil, visor (*also* vizor)
2 something that covers or conceals like a piece of cloth — see CLOAK 1
mask *vb* **1** to change the dress or looks of so as to conceal true identity — see DISGUISE
2 to keep secret or shut off from view — see ¹HIDE 2
masquerade *n* a display of emotion or behavior that is insincere or intended to deceive ⟨although she was deeply bored, she maintained a *masquerade* of polite interest as her guest droned on⟩
synonyms act, airs, charade, facade (*also* façade), front, guise, pose, pretense (*or* pretence), put-on, semblance, show
related words appearance, color, gloss; camouflage, cloak, disguise; affectation, deceit, deception, double-dealing, duplicity, fraud, guile; betrayal, double cross, faithlessness, falseness, falsity, infidelity, perfidy, treachery, treason, unfaithfulness; excuse, pretext
near antonyms candor, frankness, openheartedness, sincerity
masquerade (as) *vb* to pretend to be (what one is not) in appearance or behavior — see IMPERSONATE 1

mass *n* **1 masses** *pl* the body of the community as contrasted with the elite ⟨the *masses* demanded the elimination of tax breaks for the rich⟩
synonyms commoners, herd, mob, people, plebeians, populace, rank and file
related words proletariat, rabble, riffraff, scum, trash; bourgeoisie, middle class; public
near antonyms aristocracy, gentry, nobility, upper class, upper crust
antonyms elite
2 a considerable amount — see LOT 2
3 a distinct and separate portion of matter — see BODY 2
4 the main or greater part of something as distinguished from its appendages — see BODY 1
massacre *n* the killing of a large number of people ⟨the infamous *massacre* of more than 200 Sioux at Wounded Knee, South Dakota⟩
synonyms butchery, carnage, slaughter
related words bloodshed, foul play, homicide, killing, manslaughter, murder, slaying; mortality; annihilation, decimation, demolishing, destruction, devastation, eradication, extermination; genocide; assassination, execution
massacre *vb* to kill on a large scale ⟨the country's rival ethnic groups began *massacring* one another⟩
synonyms butcher, mow (down), slaughter
related words assassinate, execute, murder, slay; annihilate, decimate, demolish, destroy, devastate, eradicate, exterminate, waste, wipe out
massive *adj* **1** having great weight — see HEAVY 1
2 unusually large — see HUGE
massively *adv* to a large extent or degree — see GREATLY 2
massiveness *n* **1** the quality or state of being very large — see IMMENSITY
2 the state or quality of being heavy — see WEIGHTINESS 1
mass-produced *adj* made beforehand in large numbers — see READY-MADE
master *adj* having or showing exceptional knowledge, experience, or skill in a field of endeavor — see PROFICIENT
master *n* **1** a person with a high level of knowledge or skill in a field — see EXPERT
2 one that defeats an enemy or opponent — see VICTOR 1
3 the person (as an employer or supervisor) who tells people and especially workers what to do — see BOSS
master *vb* **1** to achieve a victory over — see BEAT 2
2 to acquire complete knowledge, understanding, or skill in — see LEARN 1
masterful *adj* **1** accomplished with trained ability — see SKILLFUL 1
2 fond of ordering people around — see BOSSY
3 having a feeling of superiority that shows itself in an overbearing attitude — see ARROGANT
4 having or showing exceptional knowledge, experience, or skill in a field of endeavor — see PROFICIENT
masterfully *adv* in a skillful or expert manner — see WELL 3
masterfulness *n* **1** subtle or imaginative ability in inventing, devising, or executing something — see SKILL 1
2 an exaggerated sense of one's importance that shows itself in the making of excessive or unjustified claims — see ARROGANCE

masterly *adj* **1** accomplished with trained ability — see SKILLFUL 1

2 having or showing exceptional knowledge, experience, or skill in a field of endeavor — see PROFICIENT

mastermind *vb* to plan out usually with subtle skill or care — see ENGINEER

masterpiece *n* something (as a work of art) that is a great achievement and often its creator's greatest achievement ⟨Michelangelo's frescoes in the Sistine Chapel are often considered to be his *masterpieces*⟩

synonyms classic, magnum opus

related words pièce de résistance, showpiece; blockbuster, success; gem, jewel, prize, treasure

near antonyms debacle (*also* débâcle), disaster, failure, fiasco, fizzle, turkey

mastership *n* a highly developed skill in or knowledge of something — see COMMAND 2

mastery *n* **1** a highly developed skill in or knowledge of something — see COMMAND 2

2 the right or means to command or control others — see POWER 1

masticate *vb* to crush or grind with the teeth — see BITE (ON)

match *n* **1** a competitive encounter between individuals or groups carried on for amusement, exercise, or in pursuit of a prize — see GAME 1

2 a union representing a special kind of social and legal partnership between two people — see MARRIAGE 1

3 either of a pair matched in one or more qualities — see MATE 1

4 one that is equal to another in status, achievement, or value — see EQUAL

5 something or someone that strongly resembles another — see IMAGE 1

match *vb* **1** to be the exact counterpart of ⟨does this handbag's shade of blue *match* my navy blue pants?⟩ ⟨the rare blood type that exactly *matched* that of the transplant recipient⟩

synonyms correspond (to), equal, parallel

related words blend (with), coordinate (with), go (with), harmonize (with); complement, supplement; counterbalance, counterpoise; echo, mirror, repeat; amount (to), approach, near; measure (up), partake (of), rival, suggest

2 to give in marriage — see MARRY 2

3 to produce something equal to (as in quality or value) — see EQUAL 1

matching *adj* having qualities in common — see ALIKE

matchless *adj* having no equal or rival for excellence or desirability — see ONLY 1

mate *n* **1** either of a pair matched in one or more qualities ⟨have you seen the *mate* to this glove anywhere?⟩

synonyms companion, fellow, half, match, twin

related words coordinate; counterpart, equal, equivalent, like, parallel, peer, rival; carbon copy, double, duplicate, identical twin, ringer; analogue (*or* analog), similarity

near antonyms antithesis, converse, opposite, reverse

2 a person frequently seen in the company of another — see ASSOCIATE 1

3 *chiefly British* a person who helps a more skilled person — see HELPER

4 the person to whom another is married — see SPOUSE

mate *vb* to engage in sexual intercourse — see COPULATE

material *adj* **1** relating to or composed of matter ⟨there's no *material* evidence, such as a dead body, that a murder has been committed⟩

synonyms concrete, physical, substantial

related words bodily, carnal, corporal, corporeal, fleshly; appreciable, detectable, discernible, noticeable, observable, palpable, perceptible, sensible, tangible; objective, phenomenal; bulky, heavy, massive, solid, weighty

near antonyms bodiless, disembodied, incorporeal; ethereal, insubstantial, unsubstantial; impalpable, imperceptible, insensible, intangible, invisible, unnoticeable; airy, diaphanous, tenuous, thin, vaporous; metaphysical, spiritual

antonyms immaterial, nonmaterial, nonphysical

2 having great meaning or lasting effect — see IMPORTANT 1

3 having to do with life on earth especially as opposed to that in heaven — see EARTHLY

4 having to do with the matter at hand — see PERTINENT

5 of or relating to the human body — see PHYSICAL 1

material *n* **1** the basic elements from which something can be developed — see MAKING

2 *usually* **materials** *pl* items needed for the performance of a task or activity — see EQUIPMENT

materialist *n* a person who is chiefly interested in material comfort and is hostile or indifferent to art and culture — see PHILISTINE

materiality *n* **1** something that actually exists — see FACT 2

2 the fact or state of being pertinent — see PERTINENCE

3 the quality of being actual — see FACT 1

materialize *vb* **1** to come into existence — see BEGIN 2

2 to come into view — see APPEAR 1

3 to come to one's attention especially gradually or unexpectedly — see ARISE 2

4 to represent in visible form — see EMBODY 2

matériel *or* **materiel** *n* items needed for the performance of a task or activity — see EQUIPMENT

maternal *adj* of, relating to, or characteristic of a mother — see MOTHERLY

maternity *n* motherly character or qualities ⟨she had such *maternity* at such a young age that all her classmates went to her for comfort⟩

synonyms motherliness

related words nurturance; fertility, fruitfulness, productivity, richness

mathematical *adj* meeting the highest standard of accuracy — see PRECISE 1

mating *n* sexual union involving penetration of the vagina by the penis — see SEXUAL INTERCOURSE

matriarch *n* a dignified usually elderly woman of some rank or authority ⟨even though she was 87, the *matriarch* of the family knew everything that was going on⟩

synonyms dame, dowager, matron

related words grandam (*or* grandame); headmistress, mistress; ma, mama, mammy, mom, momma

matriculate *vb* to enter in a list or roll — see ENROLL 1

matrimonial *adj* of or relating to marriage — see MARITAL

matrimony *n* a union representing a special kind of

THESAURUS

social and legal partnership between two people — see MARRIAGE 1

matron *n* a dignified usually elderly woman of some rank or authority — see MATRIARCH

matte *also* **mat** *or* **matt** *adj* lacking a surface luster or gloss ⟨I chose a paint with a *matte* finish so the walls wouldn't be too shiny⟩
synonyms dim, dull, dulled, flat, lusterless
related words tarnished, unpolished; cloudy, dingy, dirty, drab, mousy (*or* mousey), muddy; gray (*also* grey), leaden, pale; dark, darkened, dimmed, dusky, gloomy, murky, obscure, obscured, somber (*or* sombre)
near antonyms buffed, burnished, glazed, lacquered, polished, shellacked, varnished; satin, satiny; silken, silky; slick, slippery; gleaming, glimmering, glinting, glistening, glittering, scintillating, shimmering, shining, sparkling, twinkling; beaming, bedazzling, bright, brightened, brilliant, dazzling, effulgent, lucent, lucid, luminous, radiant, shining
antonyms glossy, lustrous, shiny, sleek

matter *n* **1** a major object of interest or concern (as in a discussion or artistic composition) ⟨that is not relevant to the *matter* under discussion⟩
synonyms content, motif, motive, question, subject, theme, topic
related words idea, point, purpose; issue, problem; body, bulk, burden, core, crux, fundamental, generality, gist, heart, kernel, keynote, main, marrow, mass, nub, nucleus, pith, purport, quick, staple, substance, sum; basis; bottom, essential, essentiality; affair, argument, debate
near antonyms aside, digression, interjection, parenthesis, tangent
2 something to be dealt with ⟨we must take care of this *matter* before it becomes a real problem⟩
synonyms affair, business, thing
related words problem; crisis, crossroad, emergency, exigency, juncture, strait, zero hour; concern, trouble, worry; care, lookout, responsibility; deadlock, impasse, stalemate; corner, fix, hole, hot water, pinch, predicament, scrape, spot
3 communications or parcels sent or carried through the postal system — see MAIL
4 something that requires thought and skill for resolution — see PROBLEM 1

matter *vb* to be of importance ⟨she believes that doing well in school really does *matter*⟩
synonyms count, import, mean, signify, weigh
related words affect, influence, sway; add up (to), amount (to)
phrases carry weight, cut ice

matter–of–fact *adj* **1** restricted to or based on fact — see FACTUAL 1
2 willing to see things as they really are and deal with them sensibly — see REALISTIC 1

maturation *n* the process of becoming mature ⟨a flower's *maturation* from bud to full bloom can take weeks⟩
synonyms development, growth, maturing, ripening
related words blossoming, flourishing, flowering; mellowing, softening
near antonyms decadence, decline, declining, deterioration; fading, shriveling, waning, wilting, withering; death, dying, expiring, perishing; regression, retrogression, reversion

mature *adj* **1** fully grown or developed ⟨I like pears when they're still hard, before they're *mature*⟩
synonyms adult, full-blown, full-fledged, full-grown, matured, ripe, ripened
related words aged, aging (*or* ageing), old; golden, mellow
near antonyms blooming, blossoming, burgeoning, flourishing, flowering; undeveloped, unfinished, unformed
antonyms green, immature, juvenile, unripened, young, youthful
2 having reached the date at which payment is required — see DUE 1

mature *vb* to become mature ⟨a young figure skater whose talent is still *maturing*⟩
synonyms age, develop, grow, grow up, progress, ripen
related words mellow, soften; bloom, blossom, burgeon, flourish, flower; open, unfold; advance, evolve
near antonyms decline, deteriorate; dry, fade, shrivel, wane, wilt, wither; regress, retrogress, revert; backslide, lapse, return

matured *adj* fully grown or developed — see MATURE 1

maturing *n* the process of becoming mature — see MATURATION

maturity *n* the state of being fully grown or developed ⟨people are legally considered to have reached *maturity* at eighteen years old in the United States⟩
synonyms adulthood, majority
related words manhood, womanhood; bloom, flush, heyday, prime; middle age, seniority

maudlin *adj* appealing to the emotions in an obvious and tiresome way — see CORNY

maul *vb* **1** to abuse physically — see MANHANDLE 1
2 to strike repeatedly — see BEAT 1

maunder *vb* **1** to move about from place to place aimlessly — see WANDER
2 to talk at length without sticking to a topic or getting to a point — see RAMBLE 1

maundering *adj* passing from one topic to another — see DISCURSIVE

maverick *n* a person who does not conform to generally accepted standards or customs — see NONCONFORMIST 1

mawkish *adj* appealing to the emotions in an obvious and tiresome way — see CORNY

mawkishness *n* the state or quality of having an excess of tender feelings (as of love, nostalgia, or compassion) — see SENTIMENTALITY

maxim *n* **1** an idea or statement about all of the members of a group or all the instances of a situation — see GENERALIZATION
2 an often stated observation regarding something from common experience — see SAYING

maximum *adj* **1** of the greatest or highest degree or quantity — see ULTIMATE 1
2 of the highest degree — see FULL 2

maximum *n* the greatest amount, number, or part — see MOST

maybe *adv* it is possible — see PERHAPS

mayhap *adv* it is possible — see PERHAPS

maze *n* a confusing and complicated arrangement of passages ⟨the mansion had a beautifully landscaped *maze* constructed of tall cypresses⟩
synonyms labyrinth
related words meander; jungle, quagmire; knot, snarl, tangle, web; entanglement, entrapment, snare, trap

meager *or* **meagre** *adj* less plentiful than what is

normal, necessary, or desirable ⟨ever since he started the diet, his dinners have been more *meager* than he would like⟩
synonyms hand-to-mouth, light, niggardly, poor, scant, scanty, scarce, skimpy, slender, slim, spare, sparse, stingy
related words deficient, inadequate, insufficient; lacking, wanting; bare, mere, minimum; slight, small; barren, infertile, sterile, unfruitful, unproductive
near antonyms adequate, enough, sufficient; fat, fecund, fertile, fruitful, prolific, rich; lavish, luxuriant; blooming, bursting, flourishing, swarming, teeming, thriving
antonyms abundant, ample, bountiful, copious, generous, liberal, plenteous, plentiful
meal *n* food eaten or prepared for eating at one time ⟨all she wants to do is sit quietly after the large Thanksgiving *meal*⟩
synonyms chow, feed, mess, repast, table
related words board; breakfast, buffet, dinner, lunch, luncheon, refreshments, smorgasbord, snack, supper, tea; bite, gulp, morsel, serving, taste; banquet, feast, spread; bake, barbecue, clambake, cookout, fry, luau, picnic, potluck, roast
mealy *adj* not being or expressing what one appears to be or express — see INSINCERE
mealymouthed *adj* not being or expressing what one appears to be or express — see INSINCERE
mean *adj* **1** belonging to the class of people of low social or economic rank — see IGNOBLE 1
2 giving or sharing as little as possible — see STINGY 1
3 having or showing a desire to cause someone pain or suffering for the sheer enjoyment of it — see HATEFUL
4 not following or in accordance with standards of honor and decency — see IGNOBLE 2
5 of little or less value or merit — see INFERIOR 2
6 of the very best kind — see EXCELLENT
7 showing signs of advanced wear and tear and neglect — see SHABBY 1
mean *n* **1** a middle point between extremes ⟨that candidate's moderate views were seen as the *mean* that voters were looking for⟩
synonyms golden mean, medium, middle, midpoint
related words arithmetic mean, average; median, norm, par, standard
near antonyms maximum, minimum
2 means *pl* an action planned or taken to achieve a desired result — see MEASURE 1
3 means *pl* something used to achieve an end — see AGENT 1
4 means *pl* the total of one's money and property — see WEALTH 1
mean *vb* **1** to communicate or convey (as an idea) to the mind ⟨the national anthem *means* various things to various people⟩
synonyms denote, express, import, signify, spell
related words connote, imply, suggest; add up (to), amount (to); hint, insinuate, intimate; embody, epitomize, personify, represent, symbolize; advert, allude (to), mention, refer (to); indicate, point (to), signal; announce, declare; elucidate, explain
2 to be of importance — see MATTER
3 to have in mind as a purpose or goal — see INTEND

meander *vb* to move about from place to place aimlessly — see WANDER
meaning *adj* clearly conveying a special meaning (as one's mood) — see EXPRESSIVE
meaning *n* **1** the idea that is conveyed or intended to be conveyed to the mind by language, symbol, or action ⟨the unmistakable *meaning* of the skier's upraised arms as he finished his spectacular run⟩
synonyms denotation, drift, import, intent, purport, sense, significance, signification
related words connotation; hint, implication, intimation, suggestion; message, tenor, theme; bottom, essence, essentiality, nature, soul, stuff; acceptance, definition; burden, crux, gist; core, heart, kernel, marrow, nub, nucleus, pith, point, quick; matter, motif, motive, subject, topic
2 something that one hopes or intends to accomplish — see GOAL
meaningful *adj* **1** clearly conveying a special meaning (as one's mood) — see EXPRESSIVE
2 having great meaning or lasting effect — see IMPORTANT 1
meaningless *adj* having no meaning ⟨this is an utterly *meaningless* bit of nonsense⟩
synonyms empty, inane, pointless, senseless
related words insignificant, trivial, unimportant; absurd, asinine, balmy, brainless, crazy, daffy, daft, dotty, fatuous, foolish, half-witted, harebrained, insane, jerky, kooky, loony (*also* looney), lunatic, mad, mindless, nonsensical, nutty, preposterous, sappy, silly, unintelligent, unwise, wacky, weak-minded, witless, zany; irrational, unreasonable; aimless, haphazard, purposeless
near antonyms eloquent, expressive, pregnant, revealing, suggestive, telling; logical, rational, reasonable, valid
antonyms meaningful
meanly *adv* in a mean or spiteful manner — see NASTILY
meanness *n* the desire to cause pain for the satisfaction of doing harm — see MALICE
measly *adj* so small or unimportant as to warrant little or no attention — see NEGLIGIBLE 1
measure *n* **1** an action planned or taken to achieve a desired result ⟨such new security *measures* as metal detectors at all the entrances⟩
synonyms expedient, means, move, shift, step
related words act, deed, doing, feat, thing; procedure, proceeding, process; accomplishment, achievement, exploit; activity, affair, business, dealing, enterprise, event; attempt, endeavor, essay, initiative, operation, undertaking; effort, exertion, labor, pains, trouble, work; project, proposal, proposition; makeshift, resort, resource, stopgap
2 a given or particular mass or aggregate of matter — see AMOUNT
3 something set up as an example against which others of the same type are compared — see STANDARD 1
4 the recurrent pattern formed by a series of sounds having a regular rise and fall in intensity — see RHYTHM
5 the total amount of measurable space or surface occupied by something — see ¹SIZE
measure *vb* to find out the size, extent, or amount of ⟨for this experiment, you need to carefully *measure* all the chemicals before you mix them together⟩

synonyms gauge (*also* gage), scale, span

related words weigh; calibrate; lay off, mark (off); calculate, compute, figure, reckon, work out; conjecture, estimate, guess, judge, suppose; add up, sum, tally, total; ascertain, discover, dope (out), figure out, find out

measured *adj* **1** decided on as a result of careful thought — see DELIBERATE 1

2 having distinct or certain limits — see LIMITED 1

3 marked by or occurring with a noticeable regularity in the rise and fall of sound — see RHYTHMIC

measureless *adj* being or seeming to be without limits — see INFINITE

measurement *n* the total amount of measurable space or surface occupied by something — see ¹SIZE

measure up (to) *vb* to come near or nearer to in character or quality — see APPROXIMATE

meat *n* **1** animal and especially mammal tissue used as food 〈we need to go shopping; there's only enough *meat* in the freezer for one more dinner〉

synonyms flesh

related words game, poultry, variety meat

2 substances intended to be eaten — see FOOD

mecca *n* a thing or place that is of greatest importance to an activity or interest — see CENTER 1

mechanical *adj* **1** done instantly and without conscious thought or decision — see AUTOMATIC 1

2 lacking in natural or spontaneous quality — see ARTIFICIAL 1

medal *n* a piece of metal given in honor of a special event, a person, or an achievement 〈the display case held an impressive array of military *medals* from World War II〉

synonyms medallion, order

related words decoration, honor; crown, insignia, laurel, ribbon, title; badge, button, chevron, cockade, color, ensign, rosette; distinction; award, prize, trophy; citation, commendation

medallion *n* a piece of metal given in honor of a special event, a person, or an achievement — see MEDAL

meddle *vb* to interest oneself in what is not one's concern — see INTERFERE

meddler *n* a person who meddles in the affairs of others — see BUSYBODY

meddlesome *adj* thrusting oneself where one is not welcome or invited — see INTRUSIVE

meddling *adj* thrusting oneself where one is not welcome or invited — see INTRUSIVE

medial *adj* occupying a position equally distant from the ends or extremes — see MIDDLE 1

median *adj* **1** being about midway between extremes of amount or size — see MIDDLE 2

2 occupying a position equally distant from the ends or extremes — see MIDDLE 1

mediate *vb* to act as a go-between for opposing sides — see INTERVENE

mediator *n* one who works with opposing sides in order to bring about an agreement 〈if you two cannot resolve this argument on your own, we'll have to bring in a *mediator*〉

synonyms arbiter, arbitrator, conciliator, go-between, intercessor, intermediary, interposer, middleman, peacemaker

related words moderator; bargainer, negotiator; appeaser, pacifier, reconciler; broker; agent, attorney, deputy, factor, procurator, proxy; liaison; ambassador, emissary, envoy, messenger; dele-

gate, representative; busybody, interferer, meddler; judge, referee, umpire; adviser (*or* advisor), counselor

medic *n* a person specially trained in healing human medical disorders — see DOCTOR

medication *n* a substance or preparation used to treat disease — see MEDICINE

medicine *n* a substance or preparation used to treat disease 〈if you don't take all the doses of your *medicine*, you might get sick again〉

synonyms cure, drug, medication, pharmaceutical, physic, remedy, specific

related words botanical, patent medicine, prescription; cordial, tonic; miracle drug, wonder drug; capsule, pill, tablet; injection, shot; liniment, lotion, ointment, potion, poultice, salve; syrup, tincture; antibiotic, antiseptic, serum

mediocre *adj* **1** of average to below average quality 〈your grades are *mediocre* and barely acceptable〉

synonyms common, fair, indifferent, medium, middling, ordinary, passable, run-of-the-mill, second-rate, so-so

related words acceptable, adequate, all right, alright, decent, OK (*or* okay), reasonable, satisfactory, sufficient, sufficing, tolerable; moderate, modest; presentable, respectable; minimal, unexceptional; fine, good, nice

near antonyms distinguished, excellent, exceptional, exquisite, first-class, first-rate, matchless, maximum, optimal, optimum, outstanding, peerless, preeminent, special, superior, supreme, topnotch; unmatched, unparalleled, unsurpassed; deficient, inadequate, insufficient, lacking, unacceptable, unsatisfactory, wanting

2 of low quality — see CHEAP 2

meditate *vb* **1** to give serious and careful thought to — see PONDER

2 to have in mind as a purpose or goal — see INTEND

meditation *n* long or deep thinking about spiritual matters — see CONTEMPLATION

meditative *adj* given to or marked by long, quiet thinking — see CONTEMPLATIVE

medium *adj* **1** being about midway between extremes of amount or size — see MIDDLE 2

2 occupying a position equally distant from the ends or extremes — see MIDDLE 1

3 of average to below average quality — see MEDIOCRE 1

medium *n* **1** a middle point between extremes — see MEAN 1

2 something used to achieve an end — see AGENT 1

3 the circumstances, conditions, or objects by which one is surrounded — see ENVIRONMENT

medley *n* an unorganized collection or mixture of various things — see MISCELLANY 1

meek *adj* not having or showing any feelings of superiority, self-assertiveness, or showiness — see HUMBLE 1

meekly *adv* in manner showing no signs of pride or self-assertion — see LOWLY

meekness *n* the absence of any feelings of being better than others — see HUMILITY

meet *adj* meeting the requirements of a purpose or situation — see FIT 1

meet *n* a competitive encounter between individuals or groups carried on for amusement, exercise, or in pursuit of a prize — see GAME 1

meet *vb* **1** to come upon face-to-face or as if face-to-face ⟨we never once *met* another car on that lonely country road⟩
synonyms chance (upon), encounter, happen (upon), stumble (upon)
related words accost, confront; face, greet, salute; collide (with), crash (into); crisscross, cross, pass; hit (upon), light (upon), tumble (to)
phrases bump into
near antonyms avoid, elude, escape, evade, shun
2 to come together into one body or place — see ASSEMBLE 1
3 to come upon unexpectedly or by chance — see HAPPEN (ON OR UPON)
4 to do what is required by the terms of — see FULFILL 1
5 to enter into contest or conflict with — see ENGAGE 2
6 to produce something equal to (as in quality or value) — see EQUAL 1
7 to put up with (something painful or difficult) — see BEAR 2
meeting *n* **1** a coming together of a number of persons for a specified purpose ⟨there will be another committee *meeting* next week to discuss the parish fair⟩
synonyms assembly, conference, congress, convention, convocation, council, gathering, get-together, huddle, powwow, roundtable, seminar
related words caucus, conclave, synod; demonstration, rally; conversation, dialogue (*also* dialog), discourse, discussion, palaver, talk; negotiation, parley; audience, interview, session
2 a body of people come together in one place — see GATHERING 1
3 the coming together of two or more things to the same point — see CONVERGENCE
meetly *adv* in a manner suitable for the occasion or purpose — see PROPERLY
megahit *n* a person or thing that is successful — see HIT 1
megalopolis *n* a thickly settled, highly populated area — see CITY
melancholy *adj* **1** causing unhappiness — see SAD 2
2 feeling unhappiness — see SAD 1
3 given to or marked by long, quiet thinking — see CONTEMPLATIVE
melancholy *n* a state or spell of low spirits — see SADNESS
mélange *n* an unorganized collection or mixture of various things — see MISCELLANY 1
melee *n* a rough and often noisy fight usually involving several people — see BRAWL 1
meliorate *vb* to make better — see IMPROVE
mellifluous *adj* having a pleasantly flowing quality suggestive of music — see LYRIC 1
mellow *adj* **1** having a pleasantly flowing quality suggestive of music — see LYRIC 1
2 not harsh or stern especially in manner, nature, or effect — see GENTLE 1
melodic *adj* having a pleasantly flowing quality suggestive of music — see LYRIC 1
melodious *adj* **1** having a pleasantly flowing quality suggestive of music — see LYRIC 1
2 having a pleasing mixture of notes — see HARMONIOUS 1
melodramatic *adj* **1** given to or marked by attention-getting behavior suggestive of stage acting — see THEATRICAL 1

2 having the general quality or effect of a stage performance — see DRAMATIC 1
melody *n* a rhythmic series of musical tones arranged to give a pleasing effect ⟨this week, we'll learn to play a more complicated *melody* on the saxophone⟩
synonyms air, lay, song, strain, tune, warble
related words descant; cadence, measure, meter, rhythm; ballad, ditty, hymn, lyric, madrigal
melt *vb* **1** to cease to be visible — see DISAPPEAR
2 to go from a solid to a liquid state — see LIQUEFY
member *n* **1** one of the parts that make up a whole — see ELEMENT 1
2 one of the pieces from which something is designed to be assembled — see PART 1
memento *n* something that serves to keep alive the memory of a person or event — see MEMORIAL
memo *n* **1** a message on paper from one person or group to another — see LETTER
2 a usually brief written reminder — see NOTE 1
3 a written communication giving information or directions — see MEMORANDUM 1
memoir *n* a history of a person's life — see BIOGRAPHY
memorandum *n* **1** a written communication giving information or directions ⟨I'm waiting for the *memorandum* that will explain the new vacation policy⟩
synonyms directive, memo, notice
related words announcement, declaration, proclamation, pronouncement; charge, command, dictate; directions, instructions, orders, word; encyclical, epistle, letter, mail, message, missive, note
2 a message on paper from one person or group to another — see LETTER
3 a usually brief written reminder — see NOTE 1
memorial *adj* serving to preserve the memory of a person, thing, or an event — see COMMEMORATIVE
memorial *n* something that serves to keep alive the memory of a person or event ⟨the Vietnam War *Memorial* is a starkly beautiful testimonial to the bravery of the soldiers who served in Vietnam⟩
synonyms commemorative, keepsake, memento, monument, remembrance, reminder, souvenir, token
related words memorabilia; relic, vestige; cairn, landmark, marker; testimonial, tribute
memorialize *vb* to be a memorial of — see COMMEMORATE 1
memorializing *adj* serving to preserve the memory of a person, thing, or an event — see COMMEMORATIVE
memorize *vb* to commit to memory ⟨everyone has to *memorize* a poem for next week⟩
synonyms con, learn, study
related words recall, recollect, relive, remember, reminisce, retain; accept, apprehend, comprehend, get, grasp, understand; absorb, digest
near antonyms forget; ignore, neglect, overlook
antonyms unlearn
memory *n* **1** the power or process of recalling what has been previously learned or experienced ⟨a photographic *memory* makes taking tests entirely too easy⟩
synonyms mind, recollection, remembrance, reminiscence
related words contemplation, musing, reflection,

retrospection, thinking; awareness, cognizance, consciousness; apprehension, comprehension, understanding

near antonyms forgetfulness

2 a particular act or instance of recalling or the thing remembered ⟨I have only the vaguest *memory* of the family vacation we took the year I turned three⟩

synonyms recall, recollection, remembrance, reminiscence

related words flashback; memento, memorial, reminder, souvenir, token; association

3 the body of knowledge that has been retained in one's mind or the use of it — see HEART 2

menace *n* something that may cause injury or harm — see DANGER 2

menace *vb* **1** to place in danger — see ENDANGER
2 to remain poised to inflict harm, danger, or distress on — see THREATEN

menacing *adj* **1** being or showing a sign of evil or calamity to come — see OMINOUS
2 involving potential loss or injury — see DANGEROUS

ménage *n* those who live as a family in one house — see HOUSEHOLD

mend *vb* **1** to put into good shape or working order again ⟨that shirt will be as good as new when I'm finished *mending* it⟩

synonyms doctor, fix, patch, recondition, renovate, repair, revamp

related words overhaul, rebuild, reconstruct, refurbish; aid, cure, heal, help; condition, prepare, ready; care (for), maintain, service; rejuvenate, renew, restore; adjust, correct, modify, rectify, redress, reform, right; ameliorate, better, improve, meliorate

near antonyms break, damage, harm, hurt, impair, injure, mar, ruin, spoil, wreck; cripple, disable

2 to become healthy and strong again after illness or weakness — see CONVALESCE
3 to restore to a healthy condition — see HEAL 1

mendacious *adj* telling or containing lies — see DISHONEST 1

mendacity *n* **1** a statement known by its maker to be untrue and made in order to deceive — see LIE
2 the tendency to tell lies — see DISHONESTY 1

mendicant *n* a person who lives by public begging — see BEGGAR

mending *n* the process or period of gradually regaining one's health and strength — see CONVALESCENCE

menial *n* a person hired to perform household or personal services — see SERVANT

menstruation *n* an occurrence of menstruating — see PERIOD 1

mental *adj* **1** of or relating to the mind ⟨a funny *mental* image made him laugh out loud⟩

synonyms cerebral, inner, intellectual, psychological (*also* psychologic)

related words cognitive, conscious; psychic (*also* psychical), telepathic; spiritual; alert, brainy, bright, clever, intelligent, quick-witted, rational, reasoning, smart, thinking

near antonyms bodily, carnal, corporal, corporeal, fleshly, physical, somatic

2 having or showing a very abnormal or sick state of mind — see INSANE 1

mention *vb* **1** to make reference to or speak about briefly but specifically ⟨you only *mentioned* in passing some of your accomplishments⟩

synonyms advert (to), cite, instance, name, note, notice, quote, refer (to), specify, touch (on *or* upon)

related words allude (to), hint (at), imply, infer, intimate, suggest; point (out), signal, signify; denominate, designate; indicate; bring up, broach, interject, interpolate, interpose, introduce; infiltrate, insinuate, worm; announce, declare, pronounce; elucidate, explain

near antonyms disregard, ignore, neglect, overlook, pass over, slight

2 to give as an example — see QUOTE 1

mentor *vb* to give advice and instruction to (someone) regarding the course or process to be followed — see GUIDE 1

menu *n* **1** a list of foods served at or available for a meal ⟨the *menu* at the fancy restaurant listed many dishes that I had never heard of⟩

synonyms bill of fare

related words chow, cuisine, fare, grub

2 a record of a series of items (as names or titles) usually arranged according to some system — see ¹LIST

mercenary *adj* having or marked by an eager and often selfish desire especially for material possessions — see GREEDY 1

merchandise *n* products that are bought and sold in business ⟨we stock only the finest-quality *merchandise* in this store⟩

synonyms commodities, goods, wares

related words line; export, import; inventory, staples, stock, stuff

merchandise *vb* to offer for sale to the public — see MARKET

merchandiser *n* **1** a buyer and seller of goods for profit — see MERCHANT
2 the person in a business deal who hands over an item in exchange for money — see VENDOR

merchant *n* a buyer and seller of goods for profit ⟨free trade agreements that are favored by *merchants* on both sides of the border⟩

synonyms dealer, merchandiser, trader, tradesman, trafficker

related words businessman; buyer, purchaser; hawker, peddler (*also* pedlar); retailer, seller, shopkeeper, storekeeper, vendor (*also* vender); jobber, middleman, wholesaler; distributor, provider, supplier

mercifulness *n* kind, gentle, or compassionate treatment especially towards someone who is undeserving of it — see MERCY 1

merciless *adj* having or showing a lack of sympathy or tender feelings — see HARD 1

mercurial *adj* likely to change frequently, suddenly, or unexpectedly — see FICKLE 1

mercy *n* **1** kind, gentle, or compassionate treatment especially towards someone who is undeserving of it ⟨always show your enemies *mercy*, because it makes you a better person⟩

synonyms charity, clemency, lenience, leniency, lenity, mercifulness, quarter

related words humanitarianism, philanthropy; empathy, pity, sympathy, understanding; commiseration, favor, grace; benevolence, care, compassion, gentleness, goodness, goodwill, kindliness, kindness, meekness, mildness, niceness, softness, tenderness; altruism, generosity, magnanimity, nobility; affection, devotion, love, worship

near antonyms reprisal, retaliation, retribution, revenge, vengeance; venom, vindictiveness, virulence, vitriol; brutality, cruelty, savagery, violence; castigation, chastisement, punishment, scolding; abhorrence, abomination, execration, hate, hatred, loathing; cattiness, malevolence, malice, malignity, meanness, spite, spitefulness, spleen; animosity, antagonism, antipathy, bitterness, enmity, grudge, hostility, jealousy, pique, resentment; bile, jaundice, rancor; hatefulness, invidiousness; coarseness, grimness, hardness, harshness, roughness

2 an act of kind assistance — see FAVOR 1

3 the capacity for feeling for another's unhappiness or misfortune — see HEART 1

mere *n, chiefly British* a small often deep body of water — see ¹POOL

mere *adj* being this and no more ⟨the *mere* idea of your traveling alone to Europe is ridiculous⟩
  synonyms bare, very
  related words absolute, sheer, simple, stark, utter; alone, only, singular, sole, solitary, solo, unique

merely *adv* nothing more than — see JUST 3

merge *vb* to turn into a single mass that is more or less the same throughout — see BLEND 1

merging *n* the act or an instance of joining two or more things into one — see UNION 1

meridian *n* the highest part or point — see HEIGHT 1

merit *n* **1** a quality that gives something special worth — see EXCELLENCE 2

2 the relative usefulness or importance of something as judged by specific qualities — see WORTH 1

merit *vb* to be or make worthy of (as a reward or punishment) — see EARN 2

merited *adj* being what is called for by accepted standards of right and wrong — see JUST 1

meritorious *adj* **1** deserving of high regard or great approval — see ADMIRABLE

2 having sufficient worth or merit to receive one's honor, esteem, or reward — see WORTHY

merrily *adv* in a cheerful or happy manner — see GAILY 1

merriment *n* **1** a mood characterized by high spirits and amusement and often accompanied by laughter — see MIRTH

2 joyful or festive activity — see MERRYMAKING

merriness *n* a mood characterized by high spirits and amusement and often accompanied by laughter — see MIRTH

merry *adj* indicative of or marked by high spirits or good humor ⟨Santa Claus has *merry*, twinkling blue eyes⟩
  synonyms blithesome, festive, gay, gleeful, jocose, jocund, jolly, jovial, laughing, mirthful, sunny
  related words amused, beaming, chuckling, giggling, smiling; bright, buoyant, carefree, cheerful, cheery, chipper, lighthearted, lightsome, upbeat; animated, jaunty, lively, perky, sprightly, vivacious; blessed, blissful, delighted, ecstatic, elated, enraptured, entranced, euphoric, exhilarated, exuberant, exultant, gladsome, happy, high, joyful, joyous, jubilant, overjoyed, radiant, rapturous, ravished, thrilled; amusing, facetious, flippant, funny, hilarious, jesting, joking, joshing, playful, witty; careless, cavalier, devil-may-care, easygoing, happy-go-lucky, insouciant, unconcerned; hopeful, optimistic, rosy, sanguine
  near antonyms abject, aggrieved, anguished, blue, brokenhearted, dejected, depressed, despondent,

disconsolate, disheartened, dispirited, downcast, downhearted, forlorn, heartbroken, heartsick, melancholy, sad, sorrowful, unhappy; crying, groaning, moaning, sobbing, wailing; discontented, disgruntled, moody; doleful, dolorous, joyless, lachrymose, mournful, plaintive, sorry, woeful; black, dark, desolate, gloomy, glum, gray (*also* grey); miserable, woebegone, wretched; dull, lethargic, listless, sluggish, torpid

merrymaker *n* one who engages in merrymaking especially in honor of a special occasion — see CELEBRANT

merrymaking *n* joyful or festive activity ⟨Christmas Eve is always an occasion of much *merrymaking* at our home⟩
  synonyms conviviality, festivity, gaiety (*also* gayety), jollification, jollity, merriment, reveling, revelry
  related words carousal, carouse; delight, diversion, entertainment, fun, pleasure, recreation, riot; glee, gleefulness, joviality, merriness, mirth, mirthfulness; carnival, celebration, party, revel; frolicking, gamboling, rollicking, romping; enjoyment, happiness, joy; binge, fling, frolic, gambol, lark, rollick, romp, spree; buffoonery, clownishness, flippancy, frivolity, funning, jesting, jocularity, joking, joshing, levity, lightheartedness, playfulness; zaniness
  near antonyms blackness, darkness, gloominess, glumness, grief, grieving, heartbreak, miserableness, misery, mournfulness, mourning, wretchedness; anguish, dejection, depression, despondence, forlornness, melancholy, sorrow, unhappiness

mesa *n* a broad flat area of elevated land — see PLATEAU

mesh *n* a fabric made of strands loosely twisted, knotted, or woven together at regular intervals — see ¹NET 1

mesh *vb* to catch or hold as if in a net — see ENTANGLE 2

mesmerism *n* the art or act of inducing in a person a sleep-like state during which he or she readily follows suggestions — see HYPNOSIS

mesmerize *vb* to hold the attention of as if by a spell — see ENTHRALL 1

mess *n* **1** a state in which everything is out of order — see CHAOS

2 food eaten or prepared for eating at one time — see MEAL

3 something unpleasant to look at — see EYESORE

mess *vb* to interest oneself in what is not one's concern — see INTERFERE

mess (around) *vb* to spend time in aimless activity — see FIDDLE (AROUND)

mess (up) *vb* **1** to make or do (something) in a clumsy or unskillful way — see BOTCH

2 to undo the proper order or arrangement of — see DISORDER

mess (with) *vb* to handle thoughtlessly, ignorantly, or mischievously — see TAMPER

message *n* a piece of conveyed information — see COMMUNICATION

messed *adj* lacking in order, neatness, and often cleanliness — see MESSY

messenger *n* one that carries a message or does an errand ⟨the *messenger* comes by twice a day to pick up packages⟩
  synonyms courier, go-between, page, runner

THESAURUS

related words forerunner, harbinger, herald; agent, ambassador, delegate, deputy, emissary, envoy, representative; bearer, carrier, deliveryman, letter carrier, mail carrier, mailman

messy *adj* lacking in order, neatness, and often cleanliness ⟨you cannot go out to play until you clean up this *messy* room and put away all your toys⟩
synonyms chaotic, cluttered, confused, disarranged, disarrayed, disheveled (*or* dishevelled), disordered, disorderly, higgledy-piggledy, huggermugger, jumbled, littered, messed, muddled, mussed, mussy, pell-mell, rumpled, sloppy, topsyturvy, tousled, tumbled, unkempt, untidy, upsidedown
related words besmirched, blackened, dingy, dirty, filthy, foul, grimy, grubby, grungy, mucky, nasty, soiled, spotted, squalid, stained, sullied, unclean, uncleanly; dowdy, frowsy (*or* frowzy), slatternly, slovenly, uncombed; wrinkled; contaminated, defiled, polluted, tainted; knotted, snarled, tangled; seedy, shabby, sleazy, sordid; neglected, neglectful, negligent
phrases at sixes and sevens
near antonyms clean, cleaned, cleanly, hygienic, immaculate, sparkling, spick-and-span (*or* spicand-span), spotless, stainless, unsoiled, unsullied; methodical, systematic; careful, fastidious, fussy, meticulous; combed, groomed, manicured; taintless, undefiled, unpolluted, untainted; wholesome
antonyms neat, ordered, orderly, organized, shipshape, snug, tidied, tidy, trim

metamorphose *vb* to change in form, appearance, or use — see CONVERT 2

metamorphosis *n* a change in form, appearance, or use — see CONVERSION

metaphor *n* an elaborate or fanciful way of expressing something — see CONCEIT 1

metaphorical *adj* expressing one thing in terms normally used for another — see FIGURATIVE

metaphysical *adj* of, relating to, or being part of a reality beyond the observable physical universe — see SUPERNATURAL 1

mete (out) *vb* to give out (something) in appropriate amounts or to appropriate individuals — see ADMINISTER 1

meter *n* the recurrent pattern formed by a series of sounds having a regular rise and fall in intensity — see RHYTHM

method *n* the means or procedure for doing something ⟨all experiments must be conducted using the proper scientific *method*⟩
synonyms approach, fashion, form, manner, strategy, style, system, tack, tactics, technique, way
related words mode; blueprint, design, game, ground plan, intrigue, layout, line, plan, plot, program, route, scheme; expedient, move, shift, step; practice (*also* practise), process, routine; project, proposal, proposition; policy

methodical *adj* following a set method, arrangement, or pattern ⟨a *methodical* study plan that included lists of points to memorize⟩
synonyms orderly, organized, regular, systematic, systematized
related words regularized, standardized; accurate, correct, exact, precise; detailed, specific; businesslike
near antonyms chaotic, disordered, disorderly, unordered

antonyms disorganized, haphazard, irregular, unsystematic

meticulous *adj* taking great care and effort — see PAINSTAKING

metric *adj* marked by or occurring with a noticeable regularity in the rise and fall of sound — see RHYTHMIC

metrical *adj* marked by or occurring with a noticeable regularity in the rise and fall of sound — see RHYTHMIC

metropolis *n* a thickly settled, highly populated area — see CITY

metropolitan *n* a person with the outlook, experience, and manners thought to be typical of big city dwellers — see COSMOPOLITAN

mettlesome *adj* marked by a lively display of strong feeling — see SPIRITED 1

mewl *vb* to utter feeble plaintive cries — see WHIMPER

microminiature *adj* very small in size — see TINY

microscopic *also* **microscopical** *adj* very small in size — see TINY

mid *adj* occupying a position equally distant from the ends or extremes — see MIDDLE 1

mid *prep* in or into the middle of — see AMONG

midday *n* the middle of the day — see NOON

middle *adj* **1** occupying a position equally distant from the ends or extremes ⟨you must mark the exact *middle* point of each of these lines in order to solve the problem⟩
synonyms halfway, intermediary, intermediate, medial, median, medium, mid, middlemost, midmost, midway
related words equidistant; central, inmost, inner, innermost, nearest
near antonyms outer, peripheral
antonyms extreme, farthest, farthermost, furthermost, furthest, outermost, outmost, remotest, utmost
2 being about midway between extremes of amount or size ⟨a house that is *middle* -sized for that neighborhood⟩ ⟨a man of *middle* height⟩
synonyms average, intermediate, median, medium, moderate, modest
related words reasonable; common, commonplace, conventional, normal, popular, regular, routine, standard, typical, usual; passable, tolerable
near antonyms excessive, extreme; rare, strange, uncommon, unusual; distinctive, idiosyncratic, special, unique; individual, peculiar, private

middle *n* **1** a middle point between extremes — see MEAN 1
2 an area or point that is an equal distance from all points along an edge or outer surface — see CENTER 2
3 the middle region of the human body — see MIDRIFF
4 the most intense or characteristic phase of something — see THICK

middleman *n* one who works with opposing sides in order to bring about an agreement — see MEDIATOR

middlemost *adj* occupying a position equally distant from the ends or extremes — see MIDDLE 1

middle-of-the-road *adj* avoiding major social change or extreme political ideas — see MODERATE 2

middling *adj* of average to below average quality — see MEDIOCRE 1

midget *n* a living thing much smaller than others of its kind — see DWARF 1

midmost *adj* occupying a position equally distant from the ends or extremes — see MIDDLE 1

midpoint *n* **1** a middle point between extremes — see MEAN 1
2 an area or point that is an equal distance from all points along an edge or outer surface — see CENTER 2

midriff *n* the middle region of the human body ⟨*midriff* -baring tops are popular this summer⟩
synonyms middle, waist, waistline
related words abdomen, torso, trunk

midst *n* **1** an area or point that is an equal distance from all points along an edge or outer surface — see CENTER 2
2 the most intense or characteristic phase of something — see THICK

midst *prep* in or into the middle of — see AMONG

midway *adj* occupying a position equally distant from the ends or extremes — see MIDDLE 1

mien *n* the outward form of someone or something especially as indicative of a quality — see APPEARANCE 1

might *n* the ability to exert effort for the accomplishment of a task — see POWER 2

mightily *adv* **1** to a great degree — see VERY 1
2 with great effort or determination — see HARD 1
3 in a vigorous and forceful manner — see HARD 3

mighty *adj* having great power or influence — see IMPORTANT 2

mighty *adv* to a great degree — see VERY 1

migrant *adj* having a way of life that involves moving from one region to another typically on a seasonal basis — see MIGRATORY

migrant *n* one that leaves one place to settle in another — see EMIGRANT

migratory *adj* having a way of life that involves moving from one region to another typically on a seasonal basis ⟨most of the apple crop is picked by *migratory* workers⟩ ⟨*migratory* birds heading south for the winter⟩
synonyms migrant, mobile
related words errant, itinerant, nomadic, peripatetic, ranging, roaming, roving, traveling (*or* travelling), vagabond, vagrant, wandering, wayfaring; ambulatory, drifting, footloose, gallivanting (*also* galavanting), lingering, meandering, rambling, sauntering, strolling, traipsing, walking
near antonyms immobile, stationary; established, fast, fixed, rooted, set, settled
antonyms nonmigratory, resident

mild *adj* **1** marked by temperatures that are neither too high nor too low — see CLEMENT
2 not harsh or stern especially in manner, nature, or effect — see GENTLE 1

milestone *n* a point in a chain of events at which an important change (as in one's fortunes) occurs — see TURNING POINT

milieu *n* the circumstances, conditions, or objects by which one is surrounded — see ENVIRONMENT

militancy *n* an inclination to fight or quarrel — see BELLIGERENCE

militant *adj* **1** feeling or displaying eagerness to fight — see BELLIGERENT
2 having or showing a bold forcefulness in the pursuit of a goal — see AGGRESSIVE 1

militant *n* one who is intensely or excessively devoted to a cause — see ZEALOT

militarist *n* one who urges or attempts to cause a war — see WARMONGER

military *adj* **1** of or relating to the armed services ⟨the colonel testified that revealing any more information would have required giving away *military* secrets⟩
synonyms martial, service
related words naval; GI, gladiatorial, mercenary, soldierly; aggressive, bellicose, combative, contentious, militant, militaristic, pugnacious, quarrelsome, scrappy, truculent, warlike
near antonyms civilian
antonyms nonmilitary
2 of, relating to, or suitable for war or a warrior — see MARTIAL 1

military *n* the combined army, air force, and navy of a nation — see ARMED FORCES

mill *n* a building or set of buildings for the manufacturing of goods — see FACTORY

mime *n* an actor in a story performed silently and entirely by body movements ⟨that annoying *mime* on the sidewalk is pretending to be in an invisible box again⟩
synonyms mimic, mummer, pantomime, pantomimist
related words entertainer, performer, player, trouper; imitator, impersonator, impressionist

mime *vb* to use (someone or something) as the model for one's speech, mannerisms, or behavior — see IMITATE 1

mimetic *adj* using or marked by the use of something else as a basis or model — see IMITATIVE

mimic *adj* **1** being such in appearance only and made with or manufactured from usually cheaper materials — see IMITATION
2 using or marked by the use of something else as a basis or model — see IMITATIVE

mimic *n* **1** a person who imitates another's voice and mannerisms for comic effect ⟨a gifted *mimic* who can do a terrific imitation of anyone's voice⟩
synonyms imitator, impersonator, impressionist
related words caricaturist, lampooner, mocker, parodist, satirist; mime, mummer, pantomimist; entertainer, performer, player, trouper; parrot
2 an actor in a story performed silently and entirely by body movements — see MIME

mimic *vb* **1** to copy or exaggerate (someone or something) in order to make fun of ⟨the comedian was famous for *mimicking* the President's distinctive lisp⟩
synonyms burlesque, caricature, imitate, mock, parody, take off (on), travesty
related words lampoon, satirize; deride, ridicule; ape, parrot; duplicate, emulate, replicate, reproduce; act, counterfeit, dissemble, fake, feign, pretend, sham, simulate; elaborate, embellish, embroider, exaggerate, magnify, pad, stretch; amplify, enhance, enlarge (upon), expand, flesh (out), overdraw, overstate; mime, pantomime; impersonate, perform, play
2 to use (someone or something) as the model for one's speech, mannerisms, or behavior — see IMITATE 1

mince *vb* to cut into small pieces — see CHOP

mind *vb* **1** to pay attention especially through the act of hearing — see LISTEN
2 *chiefly dialect* to bring back to mind — see REMEMBER

THESAURUS

3 to act according to the commands of — see OBEY

4 to be cautious of or on guard against — see BEWARE (OF)

5 to have an interest or concern for — see CARE

6 to take charge of especially on behalf of another — see ²TEND 1

7 to take notice of and be guided by — see HEED 1

mind *n* **1** the part of a person that feels, thinks, perceives, wills, and especially reasons ⟨scientists still disagree about exactly where the *mind* is located⟩

synonyms cerebrum, head

related words brain, gray matter, intellect, intelligence, reason; acumen, alertness, astuteness, brilliance, insight, judgment (*or* judgement), mentality, perception, perspicacity, sagacity, sapience, wisdom, wit; awareness, cognizance, consciousness, self-awareness, self-consciousness

2 the normal or healthy condition of the mental abilities ⟨everyone used to tease him and tell him he was out of his *mind* when he swore he'd seen a flying saucer⟩

synonyms head, reason, saneness, sanity, wit

related words rationality, reasonableness, sense; health, healthfulness, healthiness, wholesomeness; lucidity, lucidness, normality, soundness; wisdom

near antonyms delusion, hallucination; delirium, frenzy, hysteria

antonyms derangement, insanity, lunacy, madness, mania

3 an idea that is believed to be true or valid without positive knowledge — see OPINION 1

4 the power or process of recalling what has been previously learned or experienced — see MEMORY 1

mindful *adj* having specified facts or feelings actively impressed on the mind — see CONSCIOUS

mindless *adj* **1** not having or showing an ability to absorb ideas readily — see STUPID 1

2 not paying or showing close attention especially for the purpose of avoiding trouble — see CARELESS 1

mindlessness *n* the quality or state of lacking intelligence or quickness of mind — see STUPIDITY 1

mine *n* a usually concealed explosive device designed to go off when disturbed — see BOOBY TRAP 1

mine *vb* to place hidden explosive devices in or under ⟨the troops *mined* the field before they gave it up to the enemy⟩

synonyms boobytrap

related words blow up, bomb; ambush, snare, trap; attack

mingle *vb* **1** to turn into a single mass that is more or less the same throughout — see BLEND 1

2 to take part in social activities — see SOCIALIZE

miniature *adj* very small in size — see TINY

miniature *n* an exact representation of something in greatly reduced size — see MODEL 1

minimal *adj* being the least in amount, number, or size possible ⟨the beached whales were returned to the sea with only *minimal* loss of life⟩

synonyms least, littlest, lowest, minimum, slightest

related words fewer, lesser, low, slight, small, smaller

near antonyms highest

antonyms full, greatest, largest, maximum, top, topmost, utmost

minimize *vb* to express scornfully one's low opinion of — see DECRY 1

minimum *adj* being the least in amount, number, or size possible — see MINIMAL

minion *n* a person or thing that is preferred over others — see FAVORITE

minister *n* **1** a person sent on a mission to represent another — see AMBASSADOR

2 a person specially trained and authorized to conduct religious services in a Christian church — see CLERGYMAN

minister (to) *vb* to attend to the needs and comforts of — see NURSE 1

ministerial *adj* of, relating to, or characteristic of the clergy — see CLERICAL

minor *adj* **1** having not so great importance or rank as another — see LESSER

2 of little or less value or merit — see INFERIOR 2

3 lacking importance — see UNIMPORTANT

minstrel *n* a person who writes poetry — see POET

minstrelsy *n* writing that uses rhythm, vivid language, and often rhyme to provoke an emotional response — see POETRY 1

mint *n* a very large amount of money — see FORTUNE 2

minus *n* a feature of someone or something that creates difficulty for achieving success — see DISADVANTAGE

minus *prep* not having — see WITHOUT 1

minute *adj* **1** including many small descriptive features — see DETAILED 1

2 lacking importance — see UNIMPORTANT

3 so small or unimportant as to warrant little or no attention — see NEGLIGIBLE 1

4 made or done with extreme care and accuracy — see FINE 2

5 very small in size — see TINY

minute *n* a very small space of time — see INSTANT

minutely *adv* with attention to all aspects or details — see THOROUGHLY 1

miracle *n* something extraordinary or surprising — see WONDER 1

miraculous *adj* **1** being so extraordinary or abnormal as to suggest powers which violate the laws of nature — see SUPERNATURAL 2

2 causing wonder or astonishment — see MARVELOUS 1

mire *n* **1** soft wet earth — see MUD

2 spongy land saturated or partially covered with water — see SWAMP

mire *vb* **1** to make dirty — see DIRTY

2 to place in conflict or difficulties — see EMBROIL

mirror *n* a smooth or polished surface (as of glass) that forms images by reflection ⟨breaking a *mirror* is supposed to bring seven years of bad luck⟩

synonyms looking glass

related words pier glass; reflector

mirror *vb* to reproduce or show (an exact likeness) as a mirror would — see REFLECT

mirth *n* a mood characterized by high spirits and amusement and often accompanied by laughter ⟨as charming as your mutual *mirth* is, could you refrain from nudging each other and giggling during class?⟩

synonyms cheer, cheerfulness, cheeriness, festivity, glee, gleefulness, hilarity, joviality, merriment, merriness, mirthfulness

related words frivolity, levity; carnival, gaiety (*also* gayety), jollification, jollity, reveling, revelry; brightness, buoyancy, good-humoredness, good-naturedness, humor, sunniness; insouciance, lightheartedness, playfulness; buffoonery, clownishness, flippancy, funning, jesting, jocularity, joking, joshing; animation, jauntiness, liveliness, perkiness, vivacity; joyfulness, joyousness, jubilance, rejoicing; frolicking, gamboling (*or* gambolling), rollicking, romping

near antonyms blues, dejection, depression, despondence, forlornness, sadness, sorrow, unhappiness; bile, gloom, melancholy, sourness, spleen; earnestness, graveness, gravity, grimness, seriousness, soberness, solemnity; discontent, disgruntlement, moodiness; dolefulness, dolorousness, joylessness, mournfulness, plaintiveness, woe, woefulness; blackness, darkness, gloominess, glumness; desolateness, desolation; heartbreak, miserableness, misery, mourning, wretchedness

mirthful *adj* indicative of or marked by high spirits or good humor — see MERRY

mirthfully *adv* in a cheerful or happy manner — see GAILY 1

mirthfulness *n* a mood characterized by high spirits and amusement and often accompanied by laughter — see MIRTH

miry *adj* full of or covered with soft wet earth — see MUDDY 1

misadventure *n* bad luck or an example of this — see MISFORTUNE

misanthrope *n* a person who distrusts other people and believes that everything is done for selfish reasons — see CYNIC

misanthropic *adj* having or showing a deep distrust of human beings and their motives — see CYNICAL

misapplication *n* incorrect or improper use — see MISUSE

misapply *vb* to put to a bad or improper use ⟨you've *misapplied* the theorem to certain problems that require a different formula⟩ ⟨kids who *misapply* their boundless energy and get into trouble⟩

synonyms abuse, misuse, pervert, profane, prostitute

related words degrade, twist; mismanage; corrupt, debase, desecrate

near antonyms apply, employ, use, utilize; respect

misapprehend *vb* to fail to understand the true or actual meaning of — see MISUNDERSTAND

misapprehension *n* 1 a failure to understand correctly — see MISUNDERSTANDING 1

2 a wrong judgment — see MISTAKE 1

misappropriate *vb* to take (something) without right and with an intent to keep — see STEAL 1

misbegotten *adj* born to a father and mother who are not married — see ILLEGITIMATE 1

misbehave *vb* to behave badly ⟨if the two of you *misbehave* in public like that again, you'll have to go to bed early for a week⟩

synonyms act up, carry on

related words misconduct; disobey; clown (around), cut up, fool (around), horse (around); show off; roughhouse

phrases raise Cain, run riot

near antonyms obey; acquit, act, bear, comport, demean, deport, quit; comply, conform; check, collect, compose, constrain, contain, control, curb, handle, inhibit, move, quiet, repress, restrain

misbehaving *adj* engaging in or marked by childish misbehavior — see NAUGHTY

misbehavior *n* improper or illegal behavior — see MISCONDUCT

miscalculate *vb* to make an incorrect judgment regarding ⟨they *miscalculated* how difficult the long trip would be⟩

synonyms misconceive, misjudge, mistake

related words misconstrue, misinterpret, misunderstand; overestimate, overrate, overvalue; underestimate, underrate, undervalue; miscount

miscarry *vb* to go wrong ⟨the scheme to save the dolphins *miscarried*, and all were lost⟩

synonyms misfire

related words miss; break down, conk (out), crash, die, fail, stall; fizzle, flop, flunk, fold, wash out; flounder, struggle; decline, slip, slump, wane

phrases fall flat, fall short

near antonyms prevail, succeed; flourish, prosper, thrive

miscellaneous *adj* consisting of many things of different sorts ⟨the bottom of the drawer was always a *miscellaneous* accumulation of odds and ends⟩

synonyms assorted, heterogeneous, mixed, motley, patchwork, promiscuous, varied

related words manifold, multifarious; multiple, multiplex, myriad; disparate, divergent, diverse, sundry, various; chaotic, cluttered, confused, disarranged, disarrayed, disheveled (*or* dishevelled), disordered, jumbled, littered, messed, messy, muddled; amalgamated, blended, combined, conglomerated, fused, incorporated, intermingled, intermixed, merged, mingled; unclassified, unsorted

near antonyms monolithic, uniform; alike, identical, like, same; distinct, distinctive, individual, separate

antonyms homogeneous

miscellaneousness *n* the quality or state of being composed of many different elements or types — see VARIETY 1

miscellany *n* 1 an unorganized collection or mixture of various things ⟨the box from the attic contained a *miscellany* of old records, family photo albums, and long-forgotten love letters⟩

synonyms assortment, clutter, hash, hodgepodge, hotchpotch, jumble, litter, medley, mélange, mishmash, motley, muddle, potpourri, rummage, scramble, shuffle, tumble, variety, welter

related words notions, odds and ends, sundries; accumulation, aggregation, conglomeration; catchall, patchwork; admixture, amalgam, blend, combination, composite, compound, fusion, intermixture, mix, mixture; chaos, confusion, disarrangement, disarray, disorder, mess, muddle, shambles; knot, snarl, tangle

phrases odds and ends

2 a collection of writings — see ANTHOLOGY

mischance *n* 1 a chance and usually sudden event bringing loss or injury — see ACCIDENT 1

2 bad luck or an example of this — see MISFORTUNE

mischief *n* 1 playful, reckless behavior that is not intended to cause serious harm ⟨the children claimed that setting off a firecracker was harmless *mischief*, but they got a lecture anyway⟩

synonyms devilishness, devilment, devilry (*or*

deviltry), hob, impishness, knavery, mischievous-ness, rascality, roguishness, shenanigans, wag-gery, wickedness
related words diabolicalness, naughtiness; friski-ness, playfulness, sportiveness; chicanery, hanky-panky, trickery; high jinks, monkeyshines, sky-larking, tomfoolery; antic, caper, practical joke; aggravation, annoyance, exasperation, irritation
near antonyms gravity, seriousness, solemnity
2 a natural disposition for playful behavior — see PLAYFULNESS
3 an appealingly mischievous person — see SCAMP 1

mischievous *adj* **1** tending to or exhibiting reck-less playfulness ⟨the children had been so *mis-chievous* that we had to pay the babysitter extra and then clean up the mess⟩
synonyms devilish, elvish, impish, knavish, pixie-ish, prankish, rascally, roguish, sly, waggish, wicked
related words antic, coltish, frisky, kittenish, play-ful, sportive; gay, happy, lighthearted, whimsical; energetic, lively, spirited, sprightly; artful, cun-ning, tricky; misbehaving, naughty; pestering, ril-ing, teasing
near antonyms grave, grim, sober, solemn, stern
2 engaging in or marked by childish misbehavior — see NAUGHTY
3 causing or capable of causing harm — see HARMFUL

mischievousness *n* **1** a natural disposition for playful behavior — see PLAYFULNESS
2 playful, reckless behavior that is not intended to cause serious harm — see MISCHIEF 1

misconceive *vb* to make an incorrect judgment re-garding — see MISCALCULATE

misconception *n* a false idea or belief — see FAL-LACY 1

misconduct *n* improper or illegal behavior ⟨some rough play got the hockey player fined for *mis-conduct* on the ice⟩
synonyms malfeasance, misbehavior, misdoing, wrongdoing
related words crime, malefaction, misdeed, sin, wrong; malpractice; familiarity, gaffe, impropri-ety, indiscretion; blunder, error, fault, flub, fum-ble, goof, lapse, miscue, misstep, mistake, slip, slipup, stumble

misconduct *vb* to manage badly — see MISMAN-AGE

misconstruction *n* a failure to understand cor-rectly — see MISUNDERSTANDING 1

misconstrue *vb* to fail to understand the true or actual meaning of — see MISUNDERSTAND

misconstruing *n* a failure to understand correctly — see MISUNDERSTANDING 1

miscreant *n* a mean, evil, or unprincipled person — see VILLAIN

miscue *n* an unintentional departure from truth or accuracy — see ERROR 1

misdeed *n* a breaking of a moral or legal code — see OFFENSE 1

misdoing *n* **1** a breaking of a moral or legal code — see OFFENSE 1
2 improper or illegal behavior — see MISCON-DUCT

miser *n* a mean grasping person who is usually stingy with money ⟨the *miser* liked to sit and play with his money⟩

synonyms cheapskate, niggard, piker, scrooge, skinflint, tightwad
related words hoarder, saver
near antonyms prodigal, profligate, spender, spendthrift, squanderer, waster, wastrel

miserable *adj* **1** causing or marked by an atmo-sphere lacking in cheer — see GLOOMY 1
2 feeling unhappiness — see SAD 1
3 of low quality — see CHEAP 2
4 showing signs of advanced wear and tear and neglect — see SHABBY 1
5 deserving of one's pity — see PATHETIC 1

miserliness *n* the quality of being overly sparing with money — see PARSIMONY

misery *n* **1** a situation or state that causes great suffering and unhappiness — see HELL 2
2 a state of great suffering of body or mind — see DISTRESS 1

misfire *vb* to go wrong — see MISCARRY

misfortune *n* bad luck or an example of this ⟨through sheer *misfortune* our car got a flat tire and we were late⟩ ⟨our *misfortunes* of the last year included the loss of a beloved pet⟩
synonyms adversity, knock, misadventure, mis-chance, mishap
related words calamity, cataclysm, catastrophe, disaster; tragedy; affliction, hardship, trial, tribu-lation; distress, misery, suffering, unhappiness; defeat, failure, fizzle, nonsuccess; curse, sorrow, trouble; accident, casualty; disappointment, let-down, setback; circumstance, destiny, doom, fate, lot, portion
near antonyms break, chance, fluke, godsend, hit, opportunity, stroke, windfall; accomplishment, achievement, success
antonyms fortune, luck

misgiving *n* **1** a feeling or attitude that one does not know the truth, truthfulness, or trustworthi-ness of someone or something — see DOUBT
2 an uneasy feeling about the rightness of what one is doing or going to do — see QUALM
3 suspicion or fear of future harm or misfortune — see APPREHENSION 1

misgovern *vb* to manage badly — see MISMANAGE

misguide *vb* to cause to believe what is untrue — see DECEIVE

mishandle *vb* **1** to inflict physical or emotional harm upon — see ABUSE 1
2 to abuse physically — see MANHANDLE 1
3 to manage badly — see MISMANAGE

mishap *n* **1** a chance and usually sudden event bringing loss or injury — see ACCIDENT 1
2 bad luck or an example of this — see MISFOR-TUNE

mishmash *n* an unorganized collection or mixture of various things — see MISCELLANY 1

misinform *vb* to cause to believe what is untrue — see DECEIVE

misinterpret *vb* **1** to change so much as to create a wrong impression or alter the meaning of — see GARBLE
2 to fail to understand the true or actual meaning of — see MISUNDERSTAND

misinterpretation *n* a failure to understand cor-rectly — see MISUNDERSTANDING 1

misjudge *vb* to make an incorrect judgment re-garding — see MISCALCULATE

misjudging *n* a wrong judgment — see MISTAKE 1

misjudgment *n* a wrong judgment — see MIS-TAKE 1

mislaid *adj* no longer possessed — see LOST

mislay *vb* to be unable to find or have at hand — see LOSE 1

mislaying *n* the act or an instance of not having or being able to find — see LOSS 1

mislead *vb* to cause to believe what is untrue — see DECEIVE

misleading *adj* tending or having power to deceive — see DECEPTIVE 1

mismanage *vb* to manage badly ⟨the business was *mismanaged* so seriously that it had to declare bankruptcy⟩
synonyms misconduct, misgovern, mishandle, misrule
related words abuse, ill-treat, ill-use, maltreat, mistreat, misuse; damage, harm, hurt, violate
near antonyms govern, handle, manage, rule; care (for), nurture; aid, help, protect, rescue

misplace *vb* to be unable to find or have at hand — see LOSE 1

misplaced *adj* no longer possessed — see LOST

misplacement *n* the act or an instance of not having or being able to find — see LOSS 1

misread *vb* to fail to understand the true or actual meaning of — see MISUNDERSTAND

misreading *n* a failure to understand correctly — see MISUNDERSTANDING 1

misrepresent *vb* **1** to change so much as to create a wrong impression or alter the meaning of — see GARBLE
2 to give a false idea of — see BELIE 1

misrule *n* a state in which there is widespread wrongdoing and disregard for rules and authority — see ANARCHY

misrule *vb* to manage badly — see MISMANAGE

miss *n* a young usually unmarried woman — see GIRL 1

miss *vb* **1** to fail to attend — see CUT 2
2 to fail to understand the true or actual meaning of — see MISUNDERSTAND

misshapen *adj* badly or imperfectly formed — see MALFORMED

missing *adj* **1** no longer possessed — see LOST
2 not present or in evidence — see ABSENT 2
3 not at a certain place — see ABSENT 1

mission *n* a specific task with which a person or group is charged ⟨your *mission* is to clean up the house before company arrives⟩
synonyms assignment, charge, job, operation, post
related words burden, chore, duty, need, obligation, requirement, responsibility; labor, work; commitment, pledge, promise; appointment, designation, nomination; compulsion, constraint, restraint

missive *n* a message on paper from one person or group to another — see LETTER

misspend *vb* to use up carelessly — see WASTE 1

misstate *vb* to change so much as to create a wrong impression or alter the meaning of — see GARBLE

misstep *n* an unintentional departure from truth or accuracy — see ERROR 1

mist *n* **1** a light or fine rain — see DRIZZLE
2 an atmospheric condition in which suspended particles in the air rob it of its transparency — see HAZE 1

mist *vb* to make dark, dim, or indistinct — see CLOUD 1

mistake *n* **1** a wrong judgment ⟨I made a *mistake*

when I assumed that you were the one who broke the window⟩
synonyms misapprehension, misjudging, misjudgment
related words blunder, error, fault, flub, fumble, goof, inaccuracy, lapse, miscue, misstep, slipup, stumble; foul-up, muff; miscalculation, misstatement; misconception, misconstruction, misconstruing, misinterpretation
2 an unintentional departure from truth or accuracy — see ERROR 1

mistake *vb* **1** to fail to understand the true or actual meaning of — see MISUNDERSTAND
2 to make an incorrect judgment regarding — see MISCALCULATE

mistaken *adj* having an opinion that does not agree with truth or the facts — see INCORRECT 1

mistakenly *adv* in a mistaken or inappropriate way — see WRONGLY

mistreat *vb* to inflict physical or emotional harm upon — see ABUSE 1

mistrust *n* a feeling or attitude that one does not know the truth, truthfulness, or trustworthiness of someone or something — see DOUBT

mistrust *vb* to have no trust or confidence in — see DISTRUST

mistrustful *adj* **1** inclined to doubt or question claims — see SKEPTICAL 1
2 not feeling sure about the truth, wisdom, or trustworthiness of someone or something — see DOUBTFUL 1

mistrustfully *adv* with distrust — see ASKANCE

mistrustfulness *n* a feeling or attitude that one does not know the truth, truthfulness, or trustworthiness of someone or something — see DOUBT

misty *adj* filled with or dimmed by fine particles (as of dust or water) in suspension — see HAZY 1

misunderstand *vb* to fail to understand the true or actual meaning of ⟨you *misunderstood* that poem because you didn't look up the words you didn't know⟩
synonyms misapprehend, misconstrue, misinterpret, misread, miss, mistake
related words misconceive
antonyms apprehend, catch, comprehend, conceive, fathom, grasp, know, make out, penetrate, perceive, savvy, see, seize, take in, understand

misunderstanding *n* **1** a failure to understand correctly ⟨people once thought that there were canals on Mars because of a common *misunderstanding* of a report by an Italian astronomer⟩
synonyms misapprehension, misconstruction, misconstruing, misinterpretation, misreading
related words misconception, mistake
near antonyms appreciation, apprehension, comprehension, conception, grasp, knowledge, perception, understanding; awareness, consciousness, realization
2 an often noisy or angry expression of differing opinions — see ARGUMENT 1

misusage *n* incorrect or improper use — see MISUSE

misuse *n* incorrect or improper use ⟨the warranty for this dryer is null and void if you subject the product to deliberate *misuse*⟩
synonyms abuse, misapplication, misusage, perversion
related words mishandling, mismanagement, mismanaging; maltreatment, mistreatment; damage,

THESAURUS

destruction, ruin, spoiling, wrecking; corruption, debasement, desecration, profanation, prostitution

near antonyms application, employment, use, utilization

misuse *vb* **1** to put to a bad or improper use — see MISAPPLY

2 to inflict physical or emotional harm upon — see ABUSE 1

mite *n* **1** a very small sum of money ⟨I have only a *mite* left to buy lunch for the rest of the week⟩

synonyms peanuts, pittance, shoestring, song

related words petty cash, pin money, pocket money, spending money

near antonyms capital, means, wherewithal; opulence, riches, treasure, wealth; heap, pile, pot; bonanza, mine, treasure trove, treasury

antonyms fortune, king's ransom, mint, wad

2 a living thing much smaller than others of its kind — see DWARF 1

3 a very small amount — see PARTICLE 1

mitigate *vb* to make more bearable or less severe — see HELP 2

mix *n* a distinct entity formed by the combining of two or more different things — see BLEND

mix *vb* **1** to turn into a single mass that is more or less the same throughout — see BLEND 1

2 to take part in social activities — see SOCIALIZE

mix (up) *vb* to undo the proper order or arrangement of — see DISORDER

mixed *adj* **1** being offspring produced by parents of different races, breeds, species, or genera ⟨our *mixed* dog has a greyhound's body but the features of a collie⟩

synonyms crossbred, hybrid, mongrel

related words dihybrid, trihybrid; crossbred, crossed, hybridized, interbred, outcrossed

near antonyms pedigreed; inbred

antonyms full-blooded, purebred, thoroughbred

2 consisting of many things of different sorts — see MISCELLANEOUS

mixture *n* a distinct entity formed by the combining of two or more different things — see BLEND

mix-up *n* an instance of confusion — see FOUL-UP

moan *n* **1** a long low sound indicating pain or grief ⟨she uttered an agonized *moan* and clutched her stomach⟩

synonyms groan, wail

related words blubbering, crying, sniveling, sobbing, weeping, whimpering, whining, yammering; keen, lament; bawl, cry, howl, shriek, squall, whimper, whine, yelp, yowl

near antonyms cackle, chuckle, chortle, giggle, guffaw, laugh, snicker, titter

2 a crying out in grief — see LAMENT 1

moan *vb* **1** to utter a moan ⟨he *moaned* and cried for days after his dog died⟩

synonyms groan, wail

related words cry, blubber, sob, weep; sniff, snivel, whimper, whine; bemoan, bewail, deplore, keen, lament, rue; bleed, grieve, mourn, sorrow, suffer; bawl, howl, shriek, squall, yammer, yelp, yowl

near antonyms cackle, chuckle, chortle, giggle, guffaw, laugh, snicker, titter

2 to express dissatisfaction, pain, or resentment usually tiresomely — see COMPLAIN

mob *n* **1** a great number of persons or things gathered together — see CROWD 1

2 a group involved in secret or criminal activities — see RING 1

3 the body of the community as contrasted with the elite — see MASS 1

mob *vb* to move upon or fill (something) in great numbers — see CROWD 2

mobile *adj* **1** capable of being moved especially with ease — see MOVABLE

2 having a way of life that involves moving from one region to another typically on a seasonal basis — see MIGRATORY

mobile home *n* a motor vehicle that is specially equipped for living while traveling — see CAMPER

mobilization *n* an act of gathering forces together to renew or attempt an effort — see RALLY 1

mobilize *vb* to assemble and make ready for action ⟨we are prepared to *mobilize* the troops on very short notice⟩

synonyms marshal, muster, rally

related words arrange, line up, order, organize; call (up), convene, summon; activate

near antonyms disarrange, disorder, disorganize; deactivate, dismiss

antonyms demobilize

mobster *n* a violent, brutal person who is often a member of an organized gang — see HOODLUM

mock *adj* **1** being similar in appearance only and made with or manufactured from usually cheaper materials — see IMITATION

2 lacking in natural or spontaneous quality — see ARTIFICIAL 1

mock *n* a person or thing that is made fun of — see LAUGHINGSTOCK

mock *vb* **1** to copy or exaggerate (someone or something) in order to make fun of — see MIMIC 1

2 to make (someone or something) the object of unkind laughter — see RIDICULE

mocker *n* a person who causes repeated emotional pain, distress, or annoyance to another — see TORMENTOR

mockery *n* **1** a poor, insincere, or insulting imitation of something ⟨the resort's Old West show for tourists is a *mockery* of Native American culture⟩

synonyms caricature, farce, joke, parody, sham, travesty

related words burlesque, comedy; lampoon, takeoff; counterfeit, fake, feigning, pretense (*or* pretence), simulation

near antonyms homage, tribute

2 a person or thing that is made fun of — see LAUGHINGSTOCK

3 the making of unkind jokes as a way of showing one's scorn for someone or something — see RIDICULE

mod *adj* being or involving the latest methods, concepts, information, or styles — see MODERN

¹mode *n* **1** a distinctive way of putting ideas into words — see STYLE 1

2 a state of mind dominated by a particular emotion — see MOOD 1

²mode *n* a practice or interest that is very popular for a short time — see FAD

model *adj* constituting, serving as, or worthy of being a pattern to be imitated ⟨why can't you be like your sister, who is such a well-behaved *model* child?⟩

synonyms archetypal, classic, exemplary, paradigmatic, quintessential

related words ideal, nonpareil, special, unique; absolute, flawless, impeccable, perfect; bang-up, banner, capital, dandy, fine, first-class, first-rate, grand, great, groovy, jim-dandy, par excellence, prime, superb, superior, superlative, terrific, tip-top, top, top-notch, unsurpassed, wonderful; exceptional, fancy, high-grade

near antonyms bad, poor, substandard, unsatisfactory; atrocious, execrable, wretched; deficient, disappointing, failed, inadequate, inferior, poor; average, normal, ordinary, representative, typical; mediocre, second-class, second-rate

model *n* **1** an exact representation of something in greatly reduced size ⟨the dollhouse was a tiny, perfect *model* of the family's actual house⟩
synonyms miniature
related words copy, duplicate, duplication, imitation, replica, replication, reproduction; dwarf, midget, mini, pygmy
near antonyms archetype, original, prototype; blowup, enlargement
2 a person who poses with or wears merchandise (as clothes) often for pictorial advertising ⟨the most famous *models* can earn thousands of dollars an hour⟩
synonyms manikin, mannequin
related words figure, form; doll, dummy
3 someone of such unequaled perfection as to deserve imitation — see IDEAL 1

moderate *adj* **1** avoiding extremes in behavior or expression ⟨he was only a *moderate* drinker, stopping after a couple of glasses of wine⟩
synonyms temperate
related words controlled, curbed, disciplined, restrained, self-controlled; calculated, deliberate, measured; rational, reasonable; average, mediocre, medium, modest, ordinary, run-of-the-mill, so-so; normal, ordinary, regular, routine, typical, usual
near antonyms excessive, extreme, inordinate, radical; irrational, unreasonable; extremist, fanatic (*or* fanatical), rabid, radical
antonyms immoderate, intemperate
2 avoiding major social change or extreme political ideas ⟨the principal's *moderate* position on cell phones is that students can use them at school but only for emergencies⟩
synonyms middle-of-the-road
related words conventional, orthodox, traditional, rational, reasonable; neutral
near antonyms excessive; conservative, reactionary, rightist; leftist, liberal, progressive; fanatic (*or* fanatical), revolutionary, revolutionist, subversive, violent; agitating, fomenting, incendiary, inciting, instigating, provocative, provoking; rabble-rousing; dissenting
antonyms extremist, radical
3 being about midway between extremes of amount or size — see MIDDLE 2
4 marked by temperatures that are neither too high nor too low — see CLEMENT

moderate *vb* to grow less in scope or intensity especially gradually — see DECREASE 2

moderately *adv* to some degree or extent — see FAIRLY

moderateness *n* an avoidance of extremes in one's actions, beliefs, or habits — see TEMPERANCE

moderation *n* an avoidance of extremes in one's actions, beliefs, or habits — see TEMPERANCE

moderator *n* a person in charge of a meeting — see CHAIR 1

modern *adj* being or involving the latest methods,

concepts, information, or styles ⟨this hairstyle is absolutely the most *modern* fashion out there⟩
synonyms contemporary, current, hot, mod, modernistic, new, newfangled, new-fashioned, present-day, red-hot, space-age, ultramodern, up-to-date
related words fashionable, in, modish, stylish; last, latest; modernized, updated; futuristic, nontraditional
near antonyms anachronistic; aged, age-old, ancient, antediluvian, hoary, old, venerable; bygone, former, late, olden, past; antique, historic, historical; obsolete, outmoded, outworn; old-world; discarded, disused, moth-eaten; forgotten, remote; ageless, dateless, timeless
antonyms antiquated, archaic, dated, fusty, musty, noncontemporary, oldfangled, old-fashioned, old-time, out-of-date, passé

modern *n* a person with very modern ideas ⟨the leaders of the American suffragists were originally regarded by many people as uppity *moderns* who should have stayed in their place⟩
synonyms ultramodernist
related words leftist, liberal, progressive; extremist, radical; bohemian
near antonyms conservative, rightist, Tory; old hand, old-timer, veteran
antonyms antediluvian, dodo, fogy (*also* fogey), fossil, fuddy-duddy, reactionary, stick-in-the-mud

modernistic *adj* being or involving the latest methods, concepts, information, or styles — see MODERN

modest *adj* **1** being about midway between extremes of amount or size — see MIDDLE 2
2 free from any trace of the coarse or indecent — see CHASTE
3 not comfortable around people — see SHY 2
4 not having or showing any feelings of superiority, self-assertiveness, or showiness — see HUMBLE 1

modestly *adv* **1** in manner showing no signs of pride or self-assertion — see LOWLY
2 with purity of thought and deed — see PURELY

modesty *n* **1** the absence of any feelings of being better than others — see HUMILITY
2 the quality or state of being morally pure — see CHASTITY

modicum *n* the smallest amount or part imaginable — see JOT

modifiable *adj* capable of being readily changed — see FLEXIBLE 1

modification *n* the act, process, or result of making different — see CHANGE

modify *vb* **1** to limit the meaning of (as a noun) — see QUALIFY 1
2 to make different in some way — see CHANGE 1

modish *adj* **1** being in the latest or current fashion — see STYLISH
2 enjoying widespread favor or approval — see POPULAR 1

modishness *n* the state of enjoying widespread approval — see POPULARITY

mogul *n* a person of rank, power, or influence in a particular field — see MAGNATE

moiety *n* one of two equal or nearly equal parts — see HALF 1

moil *vb* to devote serious and sustained effort — see LABOR

moist *adj* slightly or moderately wet ⟨luckily, my

THESAURUS

new suede shoes are only a bit *moist* after I accidentally wore them in the rain⟩
synonyms damp, dank
related words dewy; clammy; humid, muggy, sticky; sultry, summery, sweltering, torrid, tropical; dripping, drenched, saturated, soaked, soaking, sodden, soggy, sopping, soppy, steeped, water-logged
near antonyms arid, dry, waterless; baked, burned, burnt, dehydrated, desert, droughty, dusty, parched, scorched, seared, sere

moisten *vb* to make or become slightly or moderately wet ⟨*moisten* the cloth before cleaning with it⟩
synonyms dampen
related words drench, saturate, soak, steep; humidify; dip, immerge, immerse
near antonyms dehumidify, dehydrate, parch, scorch, sear
antonyms dry

moisture *n* the amount of water suspended in the air in tiny droplets ⟨dew is really just *moisture* from the air that condenses and collects when the temperature drops at night⟩
synonyms dampness, humidity
related words mugginess, stickiness, stuffiness; sultriness; clamminess, dankness, sogginess, wetness
near antonyms aridity, dehydration, dryness

mojo *n* **1** something worn or kept to bring good luck or keep away evil — see CHARM 1
2 the power to control natural forces through supernatural means — see MAGIC 1

molder *vb* to go through decomposition — see DECAY 1

molecule *n* a very small piece — see BIT 1

mollify *vb* **1** to lessen the anger or agitation of — see PACIFY
2 to make more bearable or less severe — see HELP 2

mollifying *adj* tending to lessen or avoid conflict or hostility — see PACIFIC 1

mollycoddle *n* a person without strength of character — see WEAKLING 2

mollycoddle *vb* to treat with great or excessive care — see BABY

molt *vb* to cast (a natural bodily covering or appendage) aside — see SHED 1

mom *n* a female human parent — see MOTHER

moment *n* **1** a particular point at which an event takes place — see OCCASION 1
2 the quality or state of being important — see IMPORTANCE
3 a very small space of time — see INSTANT
4 the time currently existing or in progress — see PRESENT 1

momentarily *adv* at or within a short time — see SHORTLY 2

momentary *adj* lasting only for a short time ⟨the pain of the flu shot was only *momentary*⟩
synonyms ephemeral, evanescent, flash, fleeting, fugitive, impermanent, passing, short-lived, temporary, transient, transitory
related words brief, short; acting, interim
near antonyms lifelong
antonyms enduring, eternal, everlasting, lasting, long-lived, permanent, perpetual

momentous *adj* having great meaning or lasting effect — see IMPORTANT 1

momentum *n* something that arouses action or activity — see IMPULSE

momma *n* a female human parent — see MOTHER

monarch *n* one who rules over a people with a sole, supreme, and usually hereditary authority ⟨the ruling *monarch* of Britain at that time was Queen Elizabeth I⟩
synonyms autocrat, ruler, sovereign
related words czar (*also* tsar *or* tzar), emperor, empress, kaiser, king, lord, mogul, prince, queen, satrap, sultan; authoritarian, despot, dictator, overlord, potentate, tyrant; royalty

monarchal *or* **monarchial** *adj* fit for or worthy of a royal ruler — see MONARCHICAL

monarchical *also* **monarchic** *adj* fit for or worthy of a royal ruler ⟨guests who stay in the hotel's most expensive suite live in *monarchical* splendor⟩
synonyms kingly, monarchal (*or* monarchial), princely, queenly, regal, royal
related words aristocratic, baronial, imperial, lordly, noble, patrician

monastery *n* a residence for men under religious vows ⟨Gregory Mendel worked out his concepts of genetics by doing breeding experiments using pea plants in the *monastery's* garden⟩
synonyms abbey, cloister, friary, priory
related words house; convent, nunnery; lamasery

monetary *adj* of or relating to money, banking, or investments — see FINANCIAL

money *n* something (as pieces of stamped metal or printed paper) customarily and legally used as a medium of exchange, a measure of value, or a means of payment ⟨are you sure you have enough *money* to buy all that?⟩
synonyms bread [*slang*], cash, chips, currency, dough, gold, jack [*slang*], legal tender, lucre, pelf, tender, wampum [*slang*]
related words change, coinage, specie; paper money, scrip; banknote, cashier's check, check, draft, money order, note; bill, buck, dollar, greenback; bankroll, capital, finances, funds; mite, pittance; bundle, fortune, king's ransom, mint, wad; abundance, means, opulence, riches, treasure, wealth; resources, wherewithal; pin money, pocket money, spending money

moneyed *or* **monied** *adj* having goods, property, or money in abundance — see RICH 1

mongrel *adj* being offspring produced by parents of different races, breeds, species, or genera — see MIXED 1

mongrel *n* an offspring of parents with different genes especially when of different races, breeds, species, or genera — see HYBRID

monitor *vb* to pay continued close attention to (something) for a particular purpose ⟨police regularly *monitor* that road to record traffic density and catch speeders⟩
synonyms cover, watch
related words eye; behold, look, regard, see; gape, gawk, gaze, glare, goggle, peer, stare; glance, glimpse, peek, peep
phrases keep an eye on

monkey *n* an appealingly mischievous person — see SCAMP 1

monkey (around) *vb* **1** to engage in attention-getting playful or boisterous behavior — see CUT UP
2 to spend time in aimless activity — see FIDDLE (AROUND)

monkey (with) *vb* to handle thoughtlessly, ignorantly, or mischievously — see TAMPER

monkeying *n* wildly playful or mischievous behavior — see HORSEPLAY

monkeyshines *n pl* wildly playful or mischievous behavior — see HORSEPLAY

monochromatic *adj* having or consisting of a single color ⟨although marble and bronze sculptures are *monochromatic*, they can be amazingly lifelike⟩
synonyms solid
related words colored, colorful, pigmented; chromatic
near antonyms dappled (*also* dapple), marbled, shaded; mottled, piebald, pied, pinto; barred, brindled (*or* brindle); checkered, patterned, plaid, striped
antonyms motley, multicolored, polychromatic, varicolored, variegated

monopolize *vb* to have complete control over ⟨it is illegal in the United States to *monopolize* an entire industry or product⟩ ⟨you shouldn't *monopolize* that toy while your friends are waiting to play with it⟩
synonyms sew up
related words corner, hog; absorb, consume, engross; have, hold, own, possess; control, direct, govern, manage, reign (over), rule

monotonous *adj* causing weariness, restlessness, or lack of interest — see BORING

monotonousness *n* a tedious lack of variety — see MONOTONY

monotony *n* a tedious lack of variety ⟨the *monotony* of the cafeteria's selections was almost as bad as the quality⟩
synonyms monotonousness, sameness
related words uniformity; boredom, dullness (*also* dulness), ennui, restlessness, tediousness, tedium, tiresomeness, weariness, wearisomeness
near antonyms diversity, multiplicity, variety; variability, variation; absorption, engagement, engrossment, enthrallment, fascination, grip, interest, intrigue; animation, excitement, invigoration, stimulation

monster *adj* unusually large — see HUGE

monster *n* 1 a strange or horrible and often frightening creature ⟨both children insisted that their parents check under the bed for *monsters* every night⟩
synonyms monstrosity, ogre
related words ogre; bête noire, bogey (*also* bogy *or* bogie), bugaboo, bugbear; banshee, bogeyman, demon (*or* daemon), devil, fiend, fright, imp, incubus; horror, terror; abomination, anathema; abnormality, freak; mutant, mutation
2 a person, thing, or event that is not normal — see FREAK 1
3 a mean, evil, or unprincipled person — see VILLAIN 1
4 something that is unusually large and powerful — see GIANT

monstrosity *n* 1 a person, thing, or event that is not normal — see FREAK 1
2 a strange or horrible and often frightening creature — see MONSTER 1
3 something unpleasant to look at — see EYESORE
4 the quality of inspiring intense dread or dismay — see HORROR 1
5 the state or quality of being utterly evil — see ENORMITY 1

monstrous *adj* 1 badly or imperfectly formed — see MALFORMED

2 extremely disturbing or repellent — see HORRIBLE 1
3 unusually large — see HUGE

monstrously *adv* 1 beyond a normal or acceptable limit — see TOO 1
2 to a large extent or degree — see GREATLY 2

monthlies *n pl* an occurrence of menstruating — see PERIOD 1

monument *n* 1 a shaped stone laid over or erected near a grave and usually bearing an inscription to identify and preserve the memory of the deceased — see TOMBSTONE
2 something that serves to keep alive the memory of a person or event — see MEMORIAL

monumental *adj* 1 large and impressive in size, grandeur, extent, or conception — see GRAND 1
2 unusually large — see HUGE

mooch *vb* to move about from place to place aimlessly — see WANDER

mood *n* 1 a state of mind dominated by a particular emotion ⟨losing my favorite sweater left me in a bad *mood* for the rest of the day⟩
synonyms cheer, frame, humor, mode, spirit, temper
related words attitude, outlook, perspective, standpoint, viewpoint; emotion, feeling, heart, passion, sentiment; strain; belief, conviction, mind, opinion; expression, tone, vein; character, disposition, individuality, personality, temperament; responsiveness, sensibility, sensitiveness, sensitivity
2 a special quality or impression associated with something — see AURA

moody *adj* frequently influenced by moods and especially bad moods ⟨teenagers are often both *moody* and changeable⟩
synonyms temperamental
related words capricious, changeable, changeful, fickle, fluctuating, fluid, inconstant, mercurial, mutable, uncertain, unsettled, unstable, unsteady, variable, volatile, whimsical
near antonyms equable, even; changeless, constant, settled, stable, steady, unchanging

moonshine *n* 1 illegally produced liquor ⟨during Prohibition, *moonshine* and "bathtub gin" were made secretly⟩
synonyms bootleg
related words alcohol, booze, drink, grog, spirits
2 a fermented or distilled beverage that can make a person drunk — see ALCOHOL
3 unintelligible or meaningless talk — see GIBBERISH

moonstruck *adj* having or showing a very abnormal or sick state of mind — see INSANE 1

moor *vb* to put securely in place or in a desired position — see FASTEN 2

moot *adj* open to question or dispute — see DEBATABLE 1

moot *vb* 1 to present or bring forward for discussion — see INTRODUCE 2
2 to talk about (an issue) usually from various points of view and for the purpose of arriving at a decision or opinion — see DISCUSS

mope *vb* 1 to move about from place to place aimlessly — see WANDER
2 to silently go about in a bad mood — see SULK

mopes *n pl* a state or spell of low spirits — see SADNESS

moral *adj* 1 conforming to a high standard of morality or virtue — see GOOD 2

THESAURUS

2 guided by or in accordance with one's sense of right and wrong — see CONSCIENTIOUS 1

moralist *n* a person who is greatly concerned with seemly behavior and morality especially regarding sexual matters — see PRUDE

morality *n* **1** conduct that conforms to an accepted standard of right and wrong ⟨the candidate claimed to be the best choice because of his unswerving *morality*⟩
synonyms character, decency, goodness, honesty, integrity, probity, rectitude, righteousness, uprightness, virtue, virtuousness
related words high-mindedness, honor, incorruptibility; appropriateness, correctness, decorousness, decorum, etiquette, fitness, propriety, seemliness; ethics, morals
near antonyms impropriety, indecency, indiscretion; debauchery, degeneracy, degradation, depravity, perversion; crookedness, dishonesty, underhandedness, unscrupulousness; lowness, meanness, viciousness, vileness; corruption, sin
antonyms badness, evil, immorality, wickedness
2 the code of good conduct for an individual or group — see ETHICS

morally *adv* with purity of thought and deed — see PURELY

morals *n pl* the code of good conduct for an individual or group — see ETHICS

morass *n* spongy land saturated or partially covered with water — see SWAMP

morbid *adj* causing or marked by an atmosphere lacking in cheer — see GLOOMY 1

mordant *adj* marked by the use of wit that is intended to cause hurt feelings — see SARCASTIC

more *adj* resulting in an increase in amount or number — see ADDITIONAL

more *adv* **1** in addition to what has been said ⟨the sci-fi movie was totally unbelievable and, what's *more*, it was boring⟩
synonyms additionally, again, also, besides, further, furthermore, likewise, moreover, then, too, withal, yet
phrases as well, in addition to, to boot
2 to a greater or higher extent ⟨the boxers for this bout are *more* evenly matched than the last two were⟩
synonyms better

more or less *adv* **1** very close to but not completely — see ALMOST
2 to some degree or extent — see FAIRLY

moreover *adv* in addition to what has been said — see MORE 1

mores *n pl* personal conduct or behavior as evaluated by an accepted standard of appropriateness for a social or professional setting — see MANNER 1

moribund *adj* nearly dead ⟨with its run-down look and empty aisles, the business appeared *moribund*⟩
synonyms dying
related words expiring, fading, passing away, sinking; decadent, declining, deteriorating; dead, deceased, defunct, departed, gone, passed away; terminal
near antonyms alive, animate, living; being, breathing, existing, subsisting, surviving; flourishing, prospering, thriving

morn *n* **1** the first appearance of light in the morning or the time of its appearance — see DAWN 1

2 the time from sunrise until noon — see MORNING 1

morning *n* **1** the time from sunrise until noon ⟨I hate getting up in the *morning* to go to school⟩
synonyms forenoon, morn
related words aurora, dawn, dawning, daybreak, daylight; cockcrow, sunrise, sunup; day, daytime, light
near antonyms dark, darkness, night, nighttime, twilight; dusk, evening, nightfall, sundown, sunset; afternoon
2 the first appearance of light in the morning or the time of its appearance — see DAWN 1
3 the point at which something begins — see BEGINNING

moron *n* a stupid person — see IDIOT

morose *adj* causing or marked by an atmosphere lacking in cheer — see GLOOMY 1

morsel *n* **1** a small piece or quantity of food ⟨I suppose you can have dessert, since you only left a couple *morsels* on your plate⟩
synonyms bite, mouthful, nibble, taste, tidbit (*also* titbit)
related words snack; appetizer, hors d'oeuvre; bit, chew, crumb, dab, driblet, hint, lick, nubbin, nugget, pinch, scrap, shred, smidgen (*also* smidgeon *or* smidgin), speck, spot, sprinkling, suspicion, touch, trace; dash, drop; gulp, swallow, swig
2 a very small piece — see BIT 1

mortal *adj* **1** likely to cause or capable of causing death — see DEADLY
2 of, relating to, or suggestive of death — see DEATHLY 1
3 relating to or characteristic of human beings — see HUMAN

mortal *n* a member of the human race — see HUMAN

mortally *adv* to a great degree — see VERY 1

mortician *n* a person who manages funerals and prepares the dead for burial or cremation — see FUNERAL DIRECTOR

mortification *n* the emotional state of being made self-consciously uncomfortable — see EMBARRASSMENT 1

mortify *vb* to throw into a state of self-conscious distress — see EMBARRASS 1

¹most *adv* to a great degree — see VERY 1

²most *adv* very close to but not completely — see ALMOST

most *adj* of the greatest or highest degree or quantity — see ULTIMATE 1

most *n* the greatest amount, number, or part ⟨this room will accommodate 50 people at the *most*⟩
synonyms maximum, outside
related words best, utmost
antonyms least, minimum

mostly *adv* for the most part — see CHIEFLY

mote *n* a very small piece — see BIT 1

moth–eaten *adj* **1** having passed its time of use or usefulness — see OBSOLETE
2 showing signs of advanced wear and tear and neglect — see SHABBY 1
3 used or heard so often as to be dull — see STALE

mother *n* a female human parent ⟨he dreaded telling his *mother* that her favorite figurine had gotten broken⟩
synonyms ma, mama, mammy, mom, momma, mum [*chiefly British*]
related words matriarch, matron

mother *vb* to attend to the needs and comforts of — see NURSE 1

motherland *n* the land of one's birth, residence, or citizenship — see COUNTRY 1

motherliness *n* motherly character or qualities — see MATERNITY

motherly *adj* of, relating to, or characteristic of a mother ⟨she showed a sweet *motherly* tenderness toward the tiny kitten she was taking care of⟩

synonyms maternal

related words parental; female, feminine, womanish, womanlike, womanly; matriarchal, matronly; caring, giving, nurturing

mother tongue *n* the stock of words, pronunciation, and grammar used by a people as their basic means of communication — see LANGUAGE 1

motif *n* **1** a major object of interest or concern (as in a discussion or artistic composition) — see MATTER 1

2 a unit of decoration that is repeated all over something (as a fabric) — see PATTERN 1

motion *n* the act or an instance of changing position — see MOVEMENT 1

motion *vb* to direct or notify by a movement or gesture ⟨the referee *motioned* the team captains to confer with him on the sideline⟩

synonyms beckon, flag, gesture, signal, wave

related words gesticulate, pantomime, sign; signalize; acquaint, advise, inform, relate, tell; flourish, shrug

motionlessly *adv* without motion — see STILL 1

motion picture *n* **1** a story told by means of a series of continuously projected pictures and a sound track — see MOVIE 1

2 motion pictures *pl* the art or business of making a movie — see MOVIE 2

motivation *n* something that arouses action or activity — see IMPULSE

motive *n* **1** a major object of interest or concern (as in a discussion or artistic composition) — see MATTER 1

2 a unit of decoration that is repeated all over something (as a fabric) — see PATTERN 1

3 something (as a belief) that serves as the basis for another thing — see REASON 2

motley *adj* **1** consisting of many things of different sorts — see MISCELLANEOUS

2 marked by a variety of usually vivid colors — see COLORFUL

motley *n* **1** a person formerly kept in a royal or noble household to amuse with jests and pranks — see FOOL 2

2 an unorganized collection or mixture of various things — see MISCELLANY 1

motor *n* **1** a device that changes energy into mechanical motion — see ENGINE

2 a self-propelled passenger vehicle on wheels — see CAR

motor *vb* to travel by a motorized vehicle — see DRIVE 2

motorboat *n* a boat equipped with a motor ⟨*motorboats* are banned on the lake because they are a hazard to swimmers⟩

synonyms powerboat, speedboat

related words cabin cruiser, cruiser, runabout

motorcade *n* a group of vehicles traveling together or under one management — see FLEET

motorcar *n* a self-propelled passenger vehicle on wheels — see CAR

motor home *n* a motor vehicle that is specially equipped for living while traveling — see CAMPER

motorist *n* a person who travels by automobile ⟨environmental organizations suggest that *motorists* get together and carpool to avoid using several cars and adding to pollution⟩

synonyms automobilist, driver

related words operator; chauffeur; carpooler

motor vehicle *n* a self-propelled passenger vehicle on wheels — see CAR

mottle *n* a small area that is different (as in color) from the main part — see SPOT 1

mottle *vb* to mark with small spots especially unevenly — see SPOT

mottled *adj* **1** having blotches of two or more colors — see PIED

2 marked with spots — see SPOTTED 1

mound *n* **1** a pile or ridge of granular matter (as sand or snow) — see ²BANK

2 a quantity of things thrown or stacked on one another — see ¹PILE 1

3 an area of high ground — see HEIGHT 4

mound *vb* **1** to form into a pile or ridge of earth ⟨he likes to sit on the beach and *mound* sand into sand castles⟩

synonyms bank, hill

related words heap, pile, pyramid, stack; embank; bunch, bundle, clump, lump, mass, wad; accumulate, amass, assemble, collect, gather, group

2 to lay or throw on top of one another — see PILE

¹**mount** *n* an elevation of land higher than a hill — see MOUNTAIN 1

²**mount** *n* something that holds up or serves as a foundation for something else — see SUPPORT 1

mount *vb* **1** to become greater in extent, volume, amount, or number — see INCREASE 2

2 to bring before the public in performance or exhibition — see PRESENT 1

3 to move or extend upward — see ASCEND

mountain *n* **1** an elevation of land higher than a hill ⟨my cousin likes to climb *mountains* just because she can⟩

synonyms alp, mount, peak

related words mountain range, seamount; mountaintop, pinnacle, precipice, summit

near antonyms basin, bowl, depression, hollow, vale, valley

2 a considerable amount — see LOT 2

3 a quantity of things thrown or stacked on one another — see ¹PILE 1

mountain lion *n* a large tawny cat of the wild — see COUGAR

mountainous *adj* unusually large — see HUGE

mountebank *n* one who makes false claims of identity or expertise — see IMPOSTOR

mounting *n* something that holds up or serves as a foundation for something else — see SUPPORT 1

mourn *vb* **1** to feel deep sadness or mental pain — see GRIEVE

2 to feel or express sorrow for — see LAMENT 1

mournful *adj* **1** expressing or suggesting mourning ⟨she had such a *mournful* expression that someone teasingly asked if her dog had died⟩

synonyms anguished, bemoaning, bewailing, deploring, doleful, dolorous, funeral, grieving, heartbroken, lamentable, lugubrious, plaintive, regretful, rueful, sorrowful, sorry, wailing, weeping, woeful

related words elegiac, melancholy; dejected, de-

pressed, despondent, disconsolate, dispirited, downcast, downhearted, heartsick, inconsolable; careworn, sad, unhappy, woebegone; bawling, crying, groaning, howling, keening, moaning, yammering; bleeding, suffering; black, bleak, cheerless, comfortless, dark, darkening, desolate, dismal, dreary, funereal, gloomy, glum, gray (also grey), joyless, low, miserable, moody, morbid, morose, pathetic, pessimistic, piteous, saturnine, somber (or sombre), sullen, wretched
near antonyms delighted, exulting, glorying, happy, joyful, rejoicing, triumphant; bright, cheerful, cheering, cheery; laughing, smiling; blithe, blithesome, buoyant, gay, jocund, jolly, joyous, lighthearted, merry, mirthful; encouraging, hopeful, optimistic
2 feeling unhappiness — see SAD 1
mournfully *adv* with feelings of bitterness or grief — see HARD 2
mouse *vb* to move about in a sly or secret manner — see SNEAK 1
mousy *or* **mousey** *adj* easily frightened — see SHY 1
mouth *n* **1** the opening through which food passes into the body of an animal ⟨the baby chicks opened their *mouths* very wide and chirped piteously when their mother came back with worms⟩
synonyms kisser [*slang*], mug
related words countenance, face, puss [*slang*], visage; muzzle; jaws, mandible, maxilla; gullet, maw
2 a twisting of the facial features in disgust or disapproval — see GRIMACE
mouth *vb* to speak softly and unclearly — see MUMBLE
mouth (off) *vb* to talk as if giving an important and formal speech — see ORATE 1
mouthful *n* a small piece or quantity of food — see MORSEL 1
mouthpiece *n* a person who speaks for another or for a group — see SPOKESPERSON
movable *or* **moveable** *adj* capable of being moved especially with ease ⟨any furniture that is not *movable* will be covered with protective cloths by the painters⟩
synonyms mobile, portable
related words adjustable, flexible, modular; removable, transferable, transportable; motile, moving; unsteady, unstable; manageable
near antonyms motionless, moveless, static, stationary, still, stuck, unmoving, wedged; fast, fixed, rooted, steadfast
antonyms immobile, immovable, irremovable, unmovable
movables *or* **moveables** *n pl* **1** the movable articles in a room — see FURNITURE
2 transportable items that one owns — see POSSESSION 2
move *n* **1** an action planned or taken to achieve a desired result — see MEASURE 1
2 the act or an instance of changing position — see MOVEMENT 1
move *vb* **1** to change the place or position of ⟨I need you to *move* all your books off the chair before company gets here⟩
synonyms budge, dislocate, displace, disturb, remove, shift, transfer, transpose
related words bear, carry, convey, drive, haul, transmit, transport; transplant; replace, supersede, supplant; alter, make over, modify, redo, re-

fashion, remake, remodel, revamp, revise, rework, vary
near antonyms fix, freeze, set, stabilize
2 to set or keep in motion ⟨the hands of the wall clock are *moved* by battery⟩
synonyms actuate, drive, impel, propel, work
related words activate, motivate, provoke; abet, ferment, foment, incite, raise, stir (up), whip (up); set off, trigger; excite, galvanize, inflame, inspire, motivate, rouse
near antonyms check, curb, inhibit, restrain
3 to change one's position ⟨don't *move* while I'm trying to draw your portrait⟩
synonyms budge, shift, stir
related words fidget, jiggle, squirm, twitch, wiggle, writhe; rouse
near antonyms remain, stay; stabilize
antonyms freeze
4 to act upon (a person or a person's feelings) so as to cause a response — see ¹AFFECT 1
5 to rouse to strong feeling or action — see PROVOKE 1
6 to cause (someone) to agree with a belief or course of action by using arguments or earnest requests — see PERSUADE
7 to cause to function — see ACTIVATE
8 to leave a place often for another — see GO 2
movement *n* **1** the act or an instance of changing position ⟨a sudden *movement* in the far corner of the room made her turn in that direction⟩
synonyms motion, move, shift, shifting, stir, stirring
related words dislocation, migration, relocation; locomotion, mobility, motility; fiddling, fidgeting, squirming, twitching, wriggling, writhing; flailing, flapping, waving
near antonyms immobility; inertia, inertness, stillness; ending, finish, halt, pause, stop, termination
antonyms motionlessness
2 a series of activities undertaken to achieve a goal — see CAMPAIGN
movie *n* **1** a story told by means of a series of continuously projected pictures and a sound track ⟨there was much excitement when it was announced that the popular children's book would be turned into a *movie*⟩
synonyms film, motion picture, moving picture, picture
related words animated cartoon, cartoon, docudrama, documentary, feature
2 movies *pl* the art or business of making a movie ⟨many a small-town girl has gone to Hollywood, dreaming of making it big in the *movies*⟩
synonyms cinema, film, motion pictures, pictures, screen
related words show business
moving *adj* having the power to affect the feelings or sympathies ⟨he gave a truly *moving* graduation speech that had some graduates in tears⟩
synonyms affecting, emotional, impressive, poignant, stirring, touching
related words eloquent, expressive, meaningful, significant; demonstrative, excitable, feeling, passionate, responsive, sensitive; exciting, provoking, rousing, stimulating; dramatic, histrionic, melodramatic, theatrical
near antonyms cold, cool, detached, dispassionate; deadpan
antonyms unemotional, unimpressive

moving picture *n* a story told by means of a series of continuously projected pictures and a sound track — see MOVIE 1

mow *vb* **1** to shorten the standing leafy plant cover of ⟨you really should *mow* the lawn before it gets much higher⟩
synonyms cut
related words clip, crop, dock, lop, manicure, pare, prune, trim; shave, shear
2 to bring down by cutting — see FELL 2

mow (down) *vb* to kill on a large scale — see MASSACRE

much *adv* **1** to a great degree — see VERY 1
2 to a large extent or degree — see GREATLY 2
3 very close to but not completely — see ALMOST

much *n* a considerable amount — see LOT 2

muck *n* **1** foul matter that mars the purity or cleanliness of something — see FILTH 1
2 soft wet earth — see MUD

mucky *adj* **1** full of or covered with soft wet earth — see MUDDY 1
2 not clean — see DIRTY 1

mud *n* soft wet earth ⟨we cannot play softball today because the field turned to *mud* after last night's heavy rain⟩
synonyms mire, muck, ooze, slime, slop, sludge, slush
related words gumbo, silt; clay, dirt, gravel, humus, loam, sand, soil

muddle *n* **1** a state in which everything is out of order — see CHAOS
2 a state of mental confusion — see HAZE 2
3 a state of mental uncertainty — see CONFUSION 1
4 an unorganized collection or mixture of various things — see MISCELLANY 1

muddle *vb* **1** to throw into a state of mental uncertainty — see CONFUSE 1
2 to undo the proper order or arrangement of — see DISORDER

muddled *adj* lacking in order, neatness, and often cleanliness — see MESSY

muddy *adj* **1** full of or covered with soft wet earth ⟨please do not walk in the house with *muddy* boots on, as you will get the carpet dirty⟩
synonyms miry, mucky, oozy, slimy, sludgy, slushy
related words clayey, loamy, silty; bedraggled; dirty, filthy, foul, grimy, grubby, grungy, impure, squalid, unclean, uncleanly
near antonyms clean, cleanly, immaculate, spotless, unsoiled, unsullied
2 having visible particles in liquid suspension — see CLOUDY 1
3 not clean — see DIRTY 1

muddy *vb* **1** to throw into a state of mental uncertainty — see CONFUSE 1
2 to make (something) unclear to the understanding — see CONFUSE 2
3 to make dirty — see DIRTY

muff *vb* to make or do (something) in a clumsy or unskillful way — see BOTCH

muffle *vb* to deaden the sound of ⟨the walls *muffled* their conversation so that only a low murmur was heard⟩
synonyms mute
related words insulate, soundproof; dampen, mellow, soften, subdue, tone (down); baffle; smother
near antonyms amplify, enhance, heighten, increase, magnify, strengthen

mug *n* **1** a round vessel equipped with a handle and designed for drinking — see CUP
2 a violent, brutal person who is often a member of an organized gang — see HOODLUM
3 the front part of the head — see FACE 1
4 the opening through which food passes into the body of an animal — see MOUTH 1

mug *vb* **1** to distort one's face ⟨every time their picture was snapped, both children *mugged* by sticking out their tongues or scrunching up their faces⟩
synonyms grimace
related words pout; contort, deform, twist, warp; frown, glare, gloom, glower, lower (*also* lour), scowl; gape, gaze, ogle, stare; growl, snarl, sneer; simper, smirk
phrases make faces
near antonyms beam, grin, smile
2 to take a photograph of — see PHOTOGRAPH

muggy *adj* containing or characterized by an uncomfortable amount of moisture — see HUMID

mulct *n* a sum of money to be paid as a punishment — see FINE

mulct *vb* to rob by the use of trickery or threats — see FLEECE

mulish *adj* sticking to an opinion, purpose, or course of action in spite of reason, arguments, or persuasion — see OBSTINATE

mulishness *n* a steadfast adherence to an opinion, purpose, or course of action — see OBSTINACY

mull (over) *vb* to give serious and careful thought to — see PONDER

multicolored *adj* marked by a variety of usually vivid colors — see COLORFUL

multifarious *adj* being of many and various kinds — see MANIFOLD

multiple *adj* being of a large but indefinite number — see MANY

multiplex *adj* being of a large but indefinite number — see MANY

multiplication *n* the act or process of becoming greater in number ⟨there's been a steady *multiplication* in our attic of old video equipment since the revolution in consumer electronics⟩
synonyms accumulating, accumulation, addition, increase, proliferation
related words doubling, quadrupling, tripling; growth, rise, spread; enlargement, escalation, expansion; amplification, distention, inflation; accretion, accrual, augmentation; extension, lengthening
near antonyms compressing, compression, condensation, condensing, constricting, constriction, contracting, contraction, diminishing, diminishment, lessening, lowering, shrinking; retrenching, retrenchment, shortening
antonyms decrease

multiply *vb* **1** to bring forth offspring — see PROCREATE
2 to make greater in size, amount, or number — see INCREASE 1
3 to become greater in extent, volume, amount, or number — see INCREASE 2

multitude *n* a great number of persons or things gathered together — see CROWD 1

multitudinous *adj* being of a large but indefinite number — see MANY

mum *n, chiefly British* a female human parent — see MOTHER

mum *adj* deliberately refraining from speech — see SILENT 1

mumble *n* speech that is not clear enough to be understood ⟨please answer the question without your usual *mumble* and try to use complete sentences⟩
synonyms grunt, grunting, murmur, murmuring, mutter, muttering
related words undertone, whisper; babble, babbling, blab, blabbing, chatter, chattering, drivel, driveling (*or* drivelling), gabble, gabbling, jabber, jabbering, maundering, prattle, prattling, rambling

mumble *vb* to speak softly and unclearly ⟨I can't understand you if you *mumble*⟩
synonyms grunt, mouth, murmur, mutter
related words babble, blab, chatter, drivel, gabble, gibber, jabber, maunder, prattle, ramble; breathe, gasp, pant, whisper
near antonyms articulate, enunciate
antonyms speak out, speak up

mumbo jumbo *n* unintelligible or meaningless talk — see GIBBERISH

mummer *n* **1** an actor in a story performed silently and entirely by body movements — see MIME
2 one who acts professionally (as in a play, movie, or television show) — see ACTOR

mundane *adj* **1** having to do with the practical details of regular life ⟨they didn't want to be bothered with *mundane* concerns like doing the dishes while on vacation⟩
synonyms everyday, prosaic, workaday
related words earthly, temporal, worldly; average, common, commonplace, customary, familiar, garden, normal, ordinary, plain, popular, routine, run-of-the-mill, typical, unexceptional, unremarkable, usual; frequent, habitual, regular; expected, predictable
near antonyms high-minded, lofty, noble, sublime; aberrant, abnormal, atypical; exceptional, extraordinary, odd, peculiar, phenomenal, rare, singular, special, uncommon, uncustomary, unique, unusual, unwonted; bizarre, curious, funny, odd, outlandish, quaint, remarkable, strange, weird
2 having to do with life on earth especially as opposed to that in heaven — see EARTHLY

municipality *n* a thickly settled, highly populated area — see CITY

munificent *adj* giving or sharing in abundance and without hesitation — see GENEROUS 1

munificently *adv* in a generous manner — see WELL 2

murder *n* **1** a situation or state that causes great suffering and unhappiness — see HELL 2
2 the intentional and unlawful taking of another person's life — see HOMICIDE

murder *vb* **1** to put to death deliberately ⟨those people made me so mad I felt like I wanted to *murder* them⟩
synonyms dispatch, do in, execute, liquidate, slay
related words blot out, destroy, fell, kill, smite, zap; assassinate; butcher, massacre, mow (down), slaughter; annihilate, eliminate, eradicate, exterminate, wipe out
phrases do away with
2 to make or do (something) in a clumsy or unskillful way — see BOTCH

murderer *n* a person who kills another person — see ASSASSIN

murdering *adj* eager for or marked by the shedding of blood, extreme violence, or killing — see BLOODTHIRSTY

murderous *adj* **1** difficult to endure — see HARSH 1
2 requiring considerable physical or mental effort — see HARD 2
3 likely to cause or capable of causing death — see DEADLY
4 eager for or marked by the shedding of blood, extreme violence, or killing — see BLOODTHIRSTY

murk *n* **1** a time or place of little or no light — see DARK 1
2 an atmospheric condition in which suspended particles in the air rob it of its transparency — see HAZE 1

murkiness *n* the quality or state of having a veiled or uncertain meaning — see OBSCURITY 1

murky *adj* **1** being without light or without much light — see DARK 1
2 causing or marked by an atmosphere lacking in cheer — see GLOOMY 1
3 filled with or dimmed by fine particles (as of dust or water) in suspension — see HAZY 1
4 having an often intentionally veiled or uncertain meaning — see OBSCURE 1
5 not seen or understood clearly — see FAINT 1

murmur *n* **1** an expression of dissatisfaction, pain, or resentment — see COMPLAINT 1
2 speech that is not clear enough to be understood — see MUMBLE

murmur *vb* **1** to express dissatisfaction, pain, or resentment usually tiresomely — see COMPLAIN
2 to speak softly and unclearly — see MUMBLE

murmurer *n* an irritable and complaining person — see GROUCH

murmuring *n* speech that is not clear enough to be understood — see MUMBLE

muscle *n* **1** muscular strength ⟨I'm going to need someone with real *muscle* to help me move all this furniture⟩
synonyms brawn, main
related words force, might, potency, power, puissance, sinew
near antonyms impotence, weakness
2 the ability to exert effort for the accomplishment of a task — see POWER 2

muscle *vb* **1** to cause (a person) to give in to pressure — see FORCE
2 to force one's way — see PRESS 4

muscular *adj* **1** marked by a well-developed musculature ⟨Olympic runners tend to have very *muscular* legs⟩
synonyms brawny, sinewy
related words wiry; powerful, strong; beefy, burly, hefty, hulking, husky; able-bodied, athletic, herculean, mighty, robust, rugged, stalwart, strapping, sturdy
near antonyms nonathletic; delicate, feeble, fragile, frail, weak, weakly, wimpy; light, lightweight, slight; lean, slender, slim, svelte, sylphlike, thin, willowy; emaciated, gaunt, lank, rawboned, spare
antonyms scrawny, skinny
2 having muscles capable of exerting great physical force — see STRONG 1

museum *n* a building or part of a building in which objects of interest are displayed ⟨we're taking a trip to the *Museum* of Natural History as a special treat for science class⟩
synonyms gallery, salon

related words archives, collection, library; display, exhibition; studio

mush *n* **1** something (as a work of literature or music) that is too sentimental — see CORN

2 the state or quality of having an excess of tender feelings (as of love, nostalgia, or compassion) — see SENTIMENTALITY

mushroom *vb* to become greater in extent, volume, amount, or number — see INCREASE 2

mushy *adj* **1** appealing to the emotions in an obvious and tiresome way — see CORNY

2 giving easily to the touch — see SOFT 3

musical *adj* **1** having a pleasantly flowing quality suggestive of music — see LYRIC 1

2 having a pleasing mixture of notes — see HARMONIOUS 1

musicale *n* an entertainment featuring singing or the playing of musical instruments — see CONCERT

musician *n* **1** a person who plays a musical instrument ⟨the violinist was a famous and exquisitely talented *musician*⟩

synonyms instrumentalist, player

related words artist, performer; maestro, virtuoso; accompanist, recitalist, soloist; accordionist, bassoonist, clarinetist (*or* clarinettist), cornetist (*or* cornettist), drummer, fiddler, flautist, flutist, guitarist, harpist, oboist, organ-grinder, organist, percussionist, pianist, piper, saxophonist, trombonist, trumpeter, violinist

2 a person who writes musical compositions — see COMPOSER

muskeg *n* spongy land saturated or partially covered with water — see SWAMP

muss *vb* to undo the proper order or arrangement of — see DISORDER

mussed *adj* lacking in order, neatness, and often cleanliness — see MESSY

mussy *adj* lacking in order, neatness, and often cleanliness — see MESSY

must *n* something necessary, indispensable, or unavoidable — see ESSENTIAL 1

must *vb* to be under necessity or obligation to — see NEED 2

muster *n* a body of people come together in one place — see GATHERING 1

muster *vb* **1** to assemble and make ready for action — see MOBILIZE

2 to bring together in assembly by or as if by command — see CONVOKE

muster out *vb* to let go from office, service, or employment — see DISMISS 1

musty *adj* **1** having an unpleasant smell — see MALODOROUS

2 used or heard so often as to be dull — see STALE

mutable *adj* likely to change frequently, suddenly, or unexpectedly — see FICKLE 1

mutate *vb* to pass from one form, state, or level to another — see CHANGE 2

mute *adj* **1** unable to speak ⟨the child is both deaf and *mute* because her hearing was lost at birth⟩

synonyms inarticulate, speechless, voiceless

related words tongue-tied; incoherent, incomprehensible; closemouthed, laconic, taciturn, tight-lipped, uncommunicative; mum, nonspeaking, quiet, silent, wordless

near antonyms communicative, gabby, garrulous, loquacious, talkative, talky, vocal; expatiating, speaking out, speaking up; articulating, speaking, talking; articulate, eloquent, fluent, voluble

2 deliberately refraining from speech — see SILENT 1

mute *n* a device on a musical instrument that deadens or softens its tone ⟨I got in trouble for practicing my trumpet at three in the morning when the *mute* fell out, and I woke everyone up⟩

synonyms damper

related words muffler, quieter, softener

mute *vb* **1** to stop the noise or speech of — see SILENCE 1

2 to deaden the sound of — see MUFFLE

muted *adj* **1** mostly or entirely without sound — see SILENT 3

2 not excessively showy — see QUIET 2

muteness *n* incapacity for or restraint from speaking — see SILENCE 1

mutilate *vb* to cause severe or permanent injury to — see MAIM

mutineer *n* a person who rises up against authority — see REBEL

mutinous *adj* taking part in a rebellion — see REBELLIOUS 1

mutiny *n* open fighting against authority (as one's own government) — see REBELLION

mutiny *vb* to rise up against established authority — see REBEL

mutter *n* speech that is not clear enough to be understood — see MUMBLE

mutter *vb* **1** to express dissatisfaction, pain, or resentment usually tiresomely — see COMPLAIN

2 to speak softly and unclearly — see MUMBLE

mutterer *n* an irritable and complaining person — see GROUCH

muttering *n* speech that is not clear enough to be understood — see MUMBLE

mutual *adj* used or done by a number of people as a group — see COLLECTIVE

myopic *adj* **1** able to see near things more clearly than distant ones — see NEARSIGHTED

2 not thinking about and providing for the future — see IMPROVIDENT

myriad *adj* being of many and various kinds — see MANIFOLD

mysterious *adj* **1** being beyond one's powers to know, understand, or explain ⟨the huge stone statues on Easter Island are ancient, *mysterious*, and haunting⟩

synonyms cryptic, darkling, deep, enigmatic (*also* enigmatical), impenetrable, inscrutable, mystic, occult, uncanny

related words dark, murky, obscure, shadowy, vague; ambiguous, equivocal; incomprehensible, unfathomable, unintelligible; inexplicable, unaccountable, unexplainable; unanswerable, unknowable; metaphysical, mystical, supernatural; abstruse, esoteric, recondite; baffling, bewildering, confounding, confusing, mystifying, perplexing, puzzling

near antonyms fathomable, intelligible, understandable; clear, obvious, open-and-shut, plain, straightforward, transparent

2 having an often intentionally veiled or uncertain meaning — see OBSCURE 1

mystery *n* something hard to understand or explain ⟨why my sister dyed her hair bright blue is still a *mystery* to my parents⟩

synonyms conundrum, enigma, mystification, puzzle, puzzlement, riddle, secret

related words brainteaser, challenge, perplexity, poser, problem, stumper

mystic *adj* **1** having seemingly supernatural qualities or powers ⟨the notion that a cat has nine lives is based upon the belief that nine is a *mystic* number⟩
synonyms magic, magical, occult, weird
related words bewitched, enchanted, spellbound; bewitching, charming, conjuring, enchanting, wiling; awesome, extraordinary, marvelous (*or* marvellous), wondrous; divining, forecasting, foreknowing, foreseeing, foretelling, fortune-telling, predicting, presaging, prognosticating, prophesying, soothsaying
near antonyms commonplace, ordinary, unremarkable
2 being beyond one's powers to know, understand, or explain — see MYSTERIOUS 1
3 having an often intentionally veiled or uncertain meaning — see OBSCURE 1
mystification *n* **1** a state of mental uncertainty — see CONFUSION 1
2 something hard to understand or explain — see MYSTERY
mystify *vb* to throw into a state of mental uncertainty — see CONFUSE 1
myth *n* **1** a traditional but unfounded story that gives the reason for a current custom, belief, or fact of nature ⟨according to an ancient Greek *myth*, humans acquired fire from a giant who had stolen it from heaven⟩
synonyms fable, legend
related words allegory, parable; fabrication, fantasy (*also* phantasy), fiction, figment, invention; narrative, saga, story, tale, yarn
2 the body of customs, beliefs, stories, and sayings associated with a people, thing, or place — see FOLKLORE
3 a false idea or belief — see FALLACY 1
mythical *or* **mythic** *adj* **1** based on, described in, or being a myth ⟨for years the Spanish conquistadors searched for the *mythical* El Dorado, a place of unimaginable riches⟩
synonyms fabled, fabulous, legendary
related words famed, romanticized, storied; fabricated, fantastic, fantastical, fictional, fictitious; fanciful; allegorical, mythological
near antonyms actual, real; historical; factual, true
2 not real and existing only in the imagination — see IMAGINARY
mythology *n* the body of customs, beliefs, stories, and sayings associated with a people, thing, or place — see FOLKLORE

nab *vb* **1** to take or keep under one's control by authority of law — see ARREST 1
2 to take physical control or possession of (something) suddenly or forcibly — see CATCH 1
nag *n* a large hoofed domestic animal that is used for carrying or drawing loads and for riding — see HORSE
nag *vb* to subject (someone) to constant scoldings and sharp reminders ⟨she kept *nagging* him to fix the furnace before the weather got any colder⟩
synonyms henpeck, hound, needle
related words carp (at), fuss (about *or* over), nitpick; annoy, badger, bait, bother, bug, chivy, harass, harry, hassle, irk, pester, plague, ride, vex, yap (at); egg, goad, incite, prod, prompt, spur, urge; exhort, insist, press, pressure, push; blandish, cajole, coax, wheedle; beg, importune, plead
near antonyms compliment; commend, laud, praise, recommend, tout; acclaim, applaud, eulogize, extol (*also* extoll)
naiad *n* **1** a mythical goddess represented as a young girl and said to live outdoors — see NYMPH 1
2 a young wingless often wormlike form (as a grub or caterpillar) that hatches from the egg of many insects — see LARVA
nail *vb* to take physical control or possession of (something) suddenly or forcibly — see CATCH 1
naive *or* **naïve** *adj* **1** lacking in worldly wisdom or informed judgment ⟨a first-time buyer who was so *naive* that he believed the salesman and paid good money for the rusty and broken-down car⟩
synonyms green, ingenuous, innocent, simple, simpleminded, uncritical, unknowing, unsophisticated, unsuspecting, unsuspicious, unwary, unworldly, wide-eyed
related words callow, dewy, inexperienced, raw; childlike, idealistic, impractical; believing, credulous, gullible, susceptible, trustful, trusting, unguarded; beguiled, duped, gulled, tricked; careless, heedless
near antonyms critical, doubting, incredulous, skeptical, suspecting, suspicious, unconvinced; careful, cautious, guarded, leery, wary, watchful; down-to-earth, hardheaded, pragmatic (*also* pragmatical), realistic, sober
antonyms cynical, experienced, knowing, sophisticated, worldly, worldly-wise
2 free from any intent to deceive or impress others — see GUILELESS
3 readily taken advantage of — see EASY 2
naively *adv* without any attempt to impress by deception or exaggeration — see NATURALLY 3
naïveté *also* **naivete** *n* **1** the quality or state of being simple and sincere ⟨her *naïveté* led her to leave her new bike outside the mall unchained while she shopped⟩
synonyms artlessness, greenness, guilelessness, ingenuousness, innocence, naturalness, simpleness, simplicity, unsophistication, unworldliness
related words candor, frankness, genuineness, honesty, openness, sincerity, straightforwardness; callowness, childishness, inexperience, rawness; carelessness, heedlessness; ignorance, obliviousness, unawareness; credulity, credulousness, gullibility; idealism, impracticality, optimism
near antonyms affectedness, artificiality, pretentiousness; deviousness, dishonesty, insincerity; disbelief, doubtfulness, incredulity, suspicious-

ness; carefulness, caution, wariness; pessimism, skepticism; maturity
antonyms artfulness, cynicism, sophistication, worldliness
2 readiness to believe the claims of others without sufficient evidence — see CREDULITY
naked *adj* **1** lacking or shed of clothing ⟨had recurrent nightmares about being *naked* in public⟩
synonyms bare, disrobed, nude, stripped, unclad, unclothed, undressed
related words denuded, peeled; raw, stark; unveiled
near antonyms covered, veiled; arrayed, caparisoned, decked (out), rigged (out), tricked (out); vested; decent
antonyms appareled (*or* apparelled), attired, clad, clothed, dressed, garbed, invested, robed, suited
2 lacking a usual or natural covering ⟨the winter trees were *naked* without their colorful fall leaves⟩
synonyms bald, bare, denuded, exposed, open, peeled, stripped, uncovered
related words displayed, revealed; hairless, shaven; disrobed, unclad, unclothed, undressed; skinned; divested; unprotected, unsheltered
near antonyms mantled; overgrown, overrun, overspread; bearded, hairy
antonyms covered
3 free from all additions or embellishment — see PLAIN 1
name *adj* having a good reputation especially in a field of knowledge — see RESPECTABLE 1
name *n* **1** a word or combination of words by which a person or thing is regularly known ⟨introduced himself and then asked what my *name* was⟩
synonyms appellation, cognomen, denomination, denotation, designation, handle, title
related words christian name, forename, given name; family name, maiden name, surname; epithet, nickname, sobriquet (*also* soubriquet); alias, nom de plume, pen name, pseudonym; binomial, vernacular; misnomer; label, trademark
2 an act or expression showing scorn and usually intended to hurt another's feelings — see INSULT
3 outward and often deceptive indication — see APPEARANCE 2
4 overall quality as seen or judged by people in general — see REPUTATION
name *vb* **1** to give a name to ⟨decided to *name* her new puppy "Bubbles"⟩
synonyms baptize, call, christen, denominate, designate, dub, entitle, label, style, term, title
related words denote, specify; miscall, misname; nickname; rename
2 to make reference to or speak about briefly but specifically — see MENTION 1
3 to pick (someone) by one's authority for a specific position or duty — see APPOINT 2
4 to decide to accept (someone or something) from a group of possibilities — see CHOOSE 1
5 to decide upon (the time or date for an event) usually from a position of authority — see APPOINT 1
nameless *adj* **1** not named or identified by a name ⟨the victim of the crime will remain *nameless* to protect his privacy⟩ ⟨*nameless* editors who write TV listings in the newspaper⟩
synonyms anonymous, incognito, unbaptized, unchristened, unidentified, unnamed, untitled

related words unspecified; obscure, uncelebrated, unheard-of, unknown, unnoted, unremarkable
near antonyms denominated, designated, specified; labeled (*or* labelled), tabbed, titled; celebrated, famed, famous, known, notable, noted, noteworthy, remarkable, renowned, well-known
antonyms baptized, christened, dubbed, named, termed
2 beyond the power to describe — see INDESCRIBABLE
3 not widely known — see OBSCURE 2
namer *n* someone with the right or responsibility for making a selection — see SELECTOR
¹nap *n* a short sleep ⟨so tired that she needed to take a refreshing *nap* before soccer practice⟩
synonyms catnap, doze, drowse, forty winks, siesta, snooze, wink
related words repose, rest; slumber; bed
²nap *n* a soft airy substance or covering — see FUZZ
nap *vb* **1** to sleep lightly or briefly ⟨decided to let the kids *nap* for a few more minutes before waking them⟩
synonyms catnap, doze, drowse, slumber, snooze
related words relax, repose, rest; couch, lay, lie, roost; lull
near antonyms arise, arouse, awake, awaken, get up, rise, rouse, uprise, wake (up), waken
2 be in a state of sleep — see SLEEP 1
napping *adj* being in a state of suspended consciousness — see ASLEEP 1
napping *n* a natural periodic loss of consciousness during which the body restores itself — see SLEEP 1
narcotic *adj* **1** tending to calm the emotions and relieve stress — see SOOTHING 1
2 tending to cause sleep — see HYPNOTIC
narrate *vb* to give an oral or written account of in some detail — see TELL 1
narrative *n* **1** a relating of events usually in the order in which they happened — see ACCOUNT 1
2 a work with imaginary characters and events that is shorter and usually less complex than a novel — see STORY 1
narrow *adj* **1** being of less than usual width ⟨found a *narrow* opening in the fence that he was able to squeeze through⟩
synonyms fine, hairline, needlelike, skinny, slender, slim, thin
related words attenuated, elongated, linear; close, compressed, condensed, constricted, contracted, squeezed, tight, tightened; reedy, stalky, stringy, twiggy, wispy; spare
near antonyms chunky, squat, stocky, stumpy, thick, thickset; bulky, massive
antonyms broad, fat, wide
2 not broad or open in views or opinions ⟨a *narrow* person who thought that anyone who owned a television was morally corrupt⟩
synonyms insular, little, parochial, petty, provincial, sectarian, small, small-minded
related words inflexible, obdurate, obstinate, rigid, set, stubborn, unyielding, wrongheaded; bigoted, intolerant, narrow-minded; biased, discriminating, discriminatory, jaundiced, one-sided, partial, partisan, prejudiced; old-fashioned, reactionary, stodgy, straitlaced (*or* straightlaced); dogmatic, opinionated; limited
near antonyms impartial, nonpartisan, objective, unbiased, unprejudiced

THESAURUS

antonyms broad-minded, catholic, cosmopolitan, liberal, open, open-minded, receptive, tolerant

3 having distinct or certain limits — see LIMITED 1

4 showing little difference in the standing of the competitors — see CLOSE 3

5 unwilling to grant other people social rights or to accept other viewpoints — see INTOLERANT 2

narrow–minded *adj* unwilling to grant other people social rights or to accept other viewpoints — see INTOLERANT 2

narrows *n pl* a narrow body of water between two land masses — see CHANNEL 2

nastily *adv* in a mean or spiteful manner ⟨he *nastily* stuck his foot out and tripped the front runner because he couldn't stand to see her win⟩

synonyms cattily, despitefully, hatefully, malevolently, maliciously, malignantly, meanly, spitefully, viciously, villainously, virulently, wickedly

related words contemptuously, deprecatingly, disdainfully, scornfully; acrimoniously, antagonistically, caustically, hostilely, invidiously, obnoxiously, rancorously, venomously; bitterly, enviously, jealously, resentfully; balefully, callously, cruelly, hardheartedly, heartlessly, inhumanely, mercilessly, pitilessly, ruthlessly, soullessly, unfeelingly; disagreeably, ill, ungraciously, unkindly; ill-naturedly, inconsiderately, insensitively, thoughtlessly; diabolically, fiendishly; misanthropically

near antonyms affably, agreeably, amiably, cordially, genially, good-humoredly, good-naturedly, graciously, nicely, pleasantly; altruistically, humanely; considerately, feelingly, lovingly, mercifully, sensitively, softheartedly, solicitously, soulfully, thoughtfully; compassionately, sympathetically; angelically, divinely, sweetly, tenderly

antonyms benevolently, benignantly, good-heartedly, kindheartedly, kindly

nastiness *n* **1** the desire to cause pain for the satisfaction of doing harm — see MALICE

2 the quality or state of being obscene — see OBSCENITY 1

3 the state or quality of being dirty — see DIRTINESS 1

nasty *adj* **1** arousing or deserving of one's loathing and disgust — see CONTEMPTIBLE 1

2 causing intense displeasure, disgust, or resentment — see OFFENSIVE 1

3 causing or feeling bodily pain — see PAINFUL 1

4 depicting or referring to sexual matters in a way that is unacceptable in polite society — see OBSCENE 1

5 having or showing a desire to cause someone pain or suffering for the sheer enjoyment of it — see HATEFUL

6 marked by wet and windy conditions — see FOUL 1

7 not clean — see DIRTY 1

8 not giving pleasure to the mind or senses — see UNPLEASANT

nation *n* a body of people composed of one or more nationalities usually with its own territory and government ⟨the American people became one *nation* when they adopted the Constitution in 1789⟩

synonyms commonwealth, country, land, sovereignty, state

related words city-state; domain, dominion, empire, kingdom, realm, republic; duchy, dukedom, principality, seigniory (*or* seignory), sultanate;

democracy, dictatorship, monarchy, oligarchy, sovereign, theocracy; colony, dependency, province, settlement, soil; fatherland, homeland, motherland; power, superpower

national *adj* of or relating to a nation ⟨played the home team's *national* anthem before the start of the soccer game⟩

synonyms civil, public, state

related words civic, federal, municipal; government, governmental; domestic, internal; democratic, republican; nationwide

near antonyms global, international; alien, external, foreign

antonyms nonnational

national *n* a person who owes allegiance to a government and is protected by it — see CITIZEN 1

nationalism *n* **1** excessive favoritism towards one's own country — see CHAUVINISM

2 love and support for one's country — see PATRIOTISM

nationalist *adj* having or showing love and support for one's country — see PATRIOTIC

nationalist *n* one who shows excessive favoritism towards his or her country ⟨a staunch *nationalist* who favored any policy that would give the country more power in the international arena⟩

synonyms chauvinist, jingo

related words loyalist, patriot; hawk, warmonger

near antonyms internationalist; neutralist

nationalistic *adj* having or showing love and support for one's country — see PATRIOTIC

native *adj* **1** belonging to a particular place by birth or origin ⟨though she now lived in the Northeast, she was a *native* Midwesterner⟩

synonyms aboriginal, born, endemic, indigenous

related words domestic, local; original

near antonyms imported, introduced, transplanted; alien, exotic, foreign, strange; expatriate, immigrant

antonyms nonnative

2 being such as found in nature and not altered by processing or refining — see CRUDE 1

Native American *n* a member of any of the native peoples of the western hemisphere usually not including the Eskimos — see AMERICAN INDIAN

nativity *n* the act or instance of being born — see BIRTH 1

nattily *adv* in a strikingly neat and trim manner — see SMARTLY

natty *adj* being strikingly neat and trim in style or appearance — see SMART 1

natural *adj* **1** being such from birth or by nature ⟨from his first visits to the wading pool, we could tell he loved water and was a *natural* swimmer⟩

synonyms born, congenital

related words chronic, confirmed, habitual, ingrained, inveterate, proper, regular; constitutional, consummate; elemental, elementary, essential, hereditary, inborn, inherent, innate, intimate, intrinsic, native; instinctual, intuitive

near antonyms cultivated, developed, trained; alien, foreign, unnatural

antonyms nonnatural

2 closely resembling the object imitated ⟨the display of stuffed birds and plastic plants actually looked very *natural*⟩

synonyms lifelike, near, realistic

related words alike, like, living, matching; akin, analogous, approximate, comparable, resembling; accurate, close, faithful, true; convincing

near antonyms dissimilar, off, unalike, unlike; incomparable, unmatched; contrasted, contrasting, different, disparate; fake, mock, phony (*also* phoney), sham
antonyms nonnatural, nonrealistic, unrealistic
3 being a part of the innermost nature of a person or thing — see INHERENT
4 being such as found in nature and not altered by processing or refining — see CRUDE 1
5 existing without human habitation or cultivation — see WILD 2
6 free from any intent to deceive or impress others — see GUILELESS
7 relating to or characteristic of human beings — see HUMAN

naturally *adv* **1** by natural character or ability ⟨tour guides who are *naturally* outgoing and can easily approach and converse with strangers⟩
synonyms constitutionally, inherently, innately, intrinsically
related words elementally, essentially, fundamentally; instinctively, intuitively; intimately
near antonyms artificially, unnaturally
2 according to the usual course of things ⟨we *naturally* like to be as comfortable as possible⟩
synonyms commonly, generally, normally, ordinarily, typically, usually
related words customarily, habitually, regularly, routinely; familiarly; conventionally, traditionally
phrases of course
near antonyms oddly, peculiarly, queerly, strangely; anomalously, irregularly; radically
antonyms abnormally, atypically, extraordinarily, uncommonly, unusually
3 without any attempt to impress by deception or exaggeration ⟨he tried to act *naturally* around the girl he had a crush on⟩
synonyms artlessly, guilelessly, ingenuously, innocently, naively, sincerely, unaffectedly, unfeignedly, unpretentiously
related words genuinely, honestly, simply, truly; freely, openheartedly, openly; candidly, frankly, matter-of-factly; informally, relaxedly, unceremoniously
near antonyms artfully, cannily, deceitfully, deceptively, deviously, dishonestly, falsely; archly, calculatingly, craftily, cunningly, furtively, insidiously, sharply, shiftily, slickly, slyly, underhand, underhanded, underhandedly; flatteringly, sycophantically, unctuously
antonyms affectedly, artificially, hypocritically, insincerely, pretentiously, unnaturally

naturalness *n* **1** carefree freedom from constraint — see ABANDON
2 the quality or state of being simple and sincere — see NAÏVETÉ 1

nature *n* **1** the set of qualities that makes a person, a group of people, or a thing different from others ⟨it was the violent *nature* of his stories that got them banned from school libraries⟩ ⟨her *nature* was such that lying was never an option for her⟩ ⟨the stoic *nature* of these people enables them to endure one calamity after another⟩
synonyms character, complexion, constitution, genius, personality, tone
related words distinctiveness, distinctness, individuality, singularity, uniqueness; attribute, characteristic, earmark, feature, flavor, hallmark, mark, point, property, savor, stamp, trait; disposition, grain, sort, temper, temperament; composi-

tion, makeup; essence, essentiality, soul, spirit, stuff, substance; habit, way
2 that part of the physical world that is removed from human habitation ⟨needed to get out of the office and be out in *nature* to clear his head⟩
synonyms open, open air, outdoors, out-of-doors, wild, wilderness
related words backwoods, bush, country, frontier, hinterland, sticks, up-country; outside, without; badland, barren, desert, waste, wasteland
3 a number of persons or things that are grouped together because they have something in common — see SORT 1
4 one's characteristic attitude or mood — see DISPOSITION 1
5 the quality or qualities that make a thing what it is — see ESSENCE
6 the whole body of things observed or assumed — see UNIVERSE

naught *also* **nought** *n* the numerical symbol 0 or the absence of number or quantity represented by it — see ZERO 1

naughty *adj* engaging in or marked by childish misbehavior ⟨told her to act her age and stop throwing temper tantrums like a *naughty* little girl⟩
synonyms bad, contrary, errant, froward, misbehaving, mischievous
related words defiant, disrespectful, ill-mannered, ill-natured, impolite, improper, impudent, indecorous, insolent, rude, uncouth, unmannerly; disobedient, headstrong, intractable, obstreperous, recalcitrant, refractory, transgressing, unruly, untoward, willful (*or* wilful); balky, restive, uncontrollable, ungovernable, wayward, wild; arch, elfish, impish, monkeying, monkeyish, ornery, pixieish, prankish, rascally, roguish, waggish; dissolute, perverse, wrongheaded; disorderly, rowdy, ruffianly; corrupt, evil, wicked; insurgent, mutinous, rebellious; disobliging, inconsiderate, selfish, thoughtless, unkind, unkindly; babyish, childish, immature, infantile, puerile
near antonyms acquiescent, compliant, complying, dutiful, obedient, submissive; clean, correct, decent, decorous, moral, proper, respectable; considerate, courteous, kindly, mannerly, polite, thoughtful; angelic, divine, heavenly; amenable, docile, governable, tractable; amiable, complaisant, good-natured, obliging, pleasant; discreet, modest; grown-up, mature
antonyms behaved, behaving, nice, orderly

nausea *n* **1** a disturbed condition of the stomach in which one feels like vomiting ⟨symptoms include fever accompanied by a loss of appetite and *nausea*⟩
synonyms qualmishness, queasiness, queerness, sickness, squeamishness
related words qualm; airsickness, morning sickness, motion sickness, seasickness
2 a dislike so strong as to cause stomach upset or queasiness — see DISGUST

nauseate *vb* to cause to feel disgust — see DISGUST
nauseated *adj* **1** affected with nausea — see NAUSEOUS
2 filled with disgust — see SICK 2
nauseating *adj* causing intense displeasure, disgust, or resentment — see OFFENSIVE 1
nauseous *adj* affected with nausea ⟨after eating the last four pieces of the two-week-old pizza, he was feeling a little *nauseous*⟩

THESAURUS

synonyms ill, nauseated, qualmish, queasy (*also* queazy), queer, queerish, sick, sickish, squeamish
related words green, peaked, sickly; unsettled, upset, woozy
near antonyms settled; healthy, well
nautical *adj* of or relating to navigation of the sea — see MARINE 2
navigable *adj* capable of being traveled on — see PASSABLE 1
navigate *vb* to travel on water in a vessel — see SAIL 1
navigational *adj* of or relating to navigation of the sea — see MARINE 2
navigator *n* one who operates or navigates a seagoing vessel — see SAILOR
nay *adv* not merely this but also — see EVEN
nay *n* 1 a vote or decision against something — see NO 1
2 an unwillingness to grant something asked for — see DENIAL 1
Neanderthal *adj* not civilized — see SAVAGE 1
near *adj* 1 being the less far of two ⟨grab the comforter from the *near* side of the bed⟩
synonyms closer, hither, nigher, this
related words fore, forward, front, inside
near antonyms distant, remote, remoter; back, outside
antonyms far, farther, further, opposite, other, that
2 being such only when compared to something else — see COMPARATIVE
3 closely resembling the object imitated — see NATURAL 2
4 not being distant in time, space, or significance — see CLOSE 2
near *adv* 1 at, within, or to a short distance or time ⟨the campers were cold, so they moved *nearer* to the campfire⟩ ⟨as summer draws *near*, we usually start planning our annual vacation⟩
synonyms around, by, close, hard, in, nearby, nigh
related words hereabouts (*or* hereabout), thereabouts (*or* thereabout); along, alongside
phrases at close quarters, at hand
2 to a close degree ⟨copy the artist's drawing into your own sketchbook as *near* as you can⟩
synonyms closely, nearly
near antonyms distantly, remotely
3 very close to but not completely — see ALMOST
near *prep* close to — see AROUND 1
near *vb* 1 to come near or nearer — see APPROACH 1
2 to move closer to — see COME 1
nearby *adj* not being distant in time, space, or significance — see CLOSE 2
nearby *adv* at, within, or to a short distance or time — see NEAR 1
nearing *adj* being soon to appear or take place — see FORTHCOMING
nearly *adv* 1 to a close degree — see NEAR 2
2 very close to but not completely — see ALMOST
nearness *n* 1 the state of being in a very personal or private relationship — see FAMILIARITY 1
2 the state or condition of being near — see PROXIMITY
nearsighted *adj* able to see near things more clearly than distant ones ⟨I am a little *nearsighted* and need to wear glasses to drive⟩
synonyms myopic, shortsighted
related words astigmatic
antonyms farsighted

neat *adj* 1 being clean and in good order ⟨keep the kitchen *neat* so the cook doesn't have to work around piles of dirty dishes⟩
synonyms crisp, groomed, orderly, picked up, shipshape, snug, tidied, tidy, trim, uncluttered
related words dapper, natty, prim, saucy, smart, spiffy, spruce; immaculate, spick-and-span (*or* spic-and-span), spotless; rakish, sleek, streamlined, taut; organized, straight, systematic
near antonyms seedy, shabby, slipshod, sloppy; dirty, filthy, foul, nasty, sordid, squalid; frowzy, rumpled, tousled, tumbled; disorganized, unsystematic
antonyms disheveled (*or* dishevelled), disordered, disorderly, messy, mussed, mussy, slovenly, unkempt, untidy
2 free from added matter — see PURE 1
3 of the very best kind — see EXCELLENT
nebulous *adj* 1 having an often intentionally veiled or uncertain meaning — see OBSCURE 1
2 not seen or understood clearly — see FAINT 1
nebulousness *n* the quality or state of having a veiled or uncertain meaning — see OBSCURITY 1
necessarily *adv* because of necessity — see NEEDS
necessary *adj* 1 forcing one's compliance or participation by or as if by law — see MANDATORY
2 impossible to avoid or evade — see INEVITABLE
3 impossible to do without — see ESSENTIAL 1
necessitate *vb* to have as a requirement — see NEED 1
necessity *n* something necessary, indispensable, or unavoidable — see ESSENTIAL 1
necklace *n* an ornamental chain or string (as of beads) worn around the neck ⟨found a lovely *necklace* to match the bracelet and ring her mother had given her⟩
synonyms choker, lei
related words rope, strand; bangle, lavaliere (*also* lavalliere), locket, pendant (*also* pendent)
necromancer *n* a person skilled in using supernatural forces — see MAGICIAN 1
necromancy *n* the power to control natural forces through supernatural means — see MAGIC 1
need *n* 1 a state of being without something necessary, desirable, or useful ⟨when it came time to wrap the presents, he found he was in *need* of adhesive tape⟩
synonyms absence, lack, needfulness, want
related words deficiency, deficit, inadequacy, insufficiency; dearth, meagerness, paucity, poverty, scantiness, scarceness, scarcity, shortage, skimpiness; defect, minus; deprivation, famishment, privation; demand, essential, necessity, requirement, requisite
near antonyms adequacy, enough, sufficiency; fund, pool, stock, supply; excess, fill, overabundance, oversupply, plenty, surfeit, surplus; hoard, stockpile
2 something necessary, indispensable, or unavoidable — see ESSENTIAL 1
3 something one must do because of prior agreement — see OBLIGATION
4 the state of lacking sufficient money or material possessions — see POVERTY 1
need *vb* 1 to have as a requirement ⟨a national crisis that *needs* a strong leader to solve it⟩
synonyms demand, necessitate, require, take, want, warrant

related words entail, involve; ask, beg, claim, clamor (for), cry (for); lack; command, enjoin, exact, insist, press, quest, stipulate
phrases call for
near antonyms own, possess
antonyms have, hold
2 to be under necessity or obligation to ⟨you *need* not stand when she enters the room⟩
synonyms have (to), must, ought (to), shall, should
related words will
needed *adj* impossible to do without — see ESSENTIAL 1
needful *adj* impossible to do without — see ESSENTIAL 1
needfulness *n* a state of being without something necessary, desirable, or useful — see NEED 1
neediness *n* the state of lacking sufficient money or material possessions — see POVERTY 1
needle *n* **1** a slender hollow instrument by which material is put into or taken from the body through the skin ⟨the nurse inserted the *needle* into his vein and collected some blood for testing⟩
synonyms hypodermic, hypodermic needle, hypodermic syringe, syringe
2 an arrow-shaped piece on a dial or scale for registering information — see POINTER 1
needle *vb* **1** to attack repeatedly with mean putdowns or insults — see TEASE 2
2 to subject (someone) to constant scoldings and sharp reminders — see NAG
needlelike *adj* being of less than usual width — see NARROW 1
needler *n* a person who causes repeated emotional pain, distress, or annoyance to another — see TORMENTOR
needless *adj* not needed by the circumstances or to accomplish an end — see UNNECESSARY
needlework *n* decorative stitching done on cloth with the use of a needle ⟨a school outing to the museum to see an exhibition of 18th century *needlework*⟩
synonyms embroidery
related words crewel, cross-stitch, needlepoint; hemstitch, fagoting (*or* faggoting), smocking; fancywork
needs *adv* because of necessity ⟨the dangers of global warming must *needs* be recognized—and recognized soon—by the industrialized nations of the world⟩
synonyms inescapably, inevitably, necessarily, perforce, unavoidably
related words involuntarily
antonyms unnecessarily
needy *adj* lacking money or material possessions — see POOR 1
ne'er *adv* at no time — see NEVER 1
nefarious *adj* not conforming to a high moral standard; morally unacceptable — see BAD 2
nefariousness *n* the state or quality of being utterly evil — see ENORMITY 1
negate *vb* **1** to declare not to be true — see DENY 1
2 to put an end to by formal action — see ABOLISH
3 to think not to be true or real — see DISBELIEVE
negation *n* a refusal to confirm the truth of a statement — see DENIAL 2

negative *adj* **1** marked by opposition or ill will — see HOSTILE 1
2 opposed to one's interests — see ADVERSE 1
negative *n* **1** a vote or decision against something — see NO 1
2 something that is as different as possible from something else — see OPPOSITE
negative *vb* **1** to reject by or as if by a vote ⟨though the rebuttal was very eloquent, he *negatived* it in favor of the first argument⟩ ⟨she *negatived* pizza for dinner, noting that they had already had it for three nights that week⟩
synonyms blackball, kill, veto
related words decline, disallow, disapprove, dismiss, refuse; blacklist
near antonyms admit, allow, approve, assent (to), pass, sanction; elect, support
antonyms confirm, ratify
2 to declare not to be true — see DENY 1
3 to show unwillingness to accept, do, engage in, or agree to — see DECLINE 1
neglect *n* **1** the state of being unattended to or not cared for ⟨the barn sat in *neglect* until it finally fell down⟩
synonyms desolation, dilapidation, disrepair, seediness
related words inattention, negligence; abandonment, desertion; decay, decrepitude, dereliction, deterioration, disintegration, ruin, ruination
near antonyms conservation, preservation
antonyms repair
2 the nonperformance of an assigned or expected action — see FAILURE 1
neglect *vb* **1** to fail to give proper attention to ⟨the news media *neglected* the real issues of the campaign and focused on personalities⟩
synonyms disregard, forget, ignore, overlook, overpass, pass over, slight, slur (over)
related words fail; miss, omit; brush (aside *or* off), reject, shrug off, slough (off); disdain, pooh-pooh, scorn; scant, skimp
near antonyms appreciate, cherish, prize, treasure, value; cultivate, foster, nurse, nurture; pamper; remember; listen (to), watch; follow, mark, note, notice, observe, remark
antonyms attend (to), heed, mind, regard, tend (to)
2 to leave undone or unattended to especially through carelessness ⟨she plays too much and *neglects* her homework⟩ ⟨I've *neglected* my garden, and now it's overgrown with weeds⟩
synonyms forget, shirk
related words slack (off)
near antonyms carry out, do, execute, perform; accomplish, achieve
antonyms attend (to), remember
3 to miss the opportunity or obligation ⟨the job applicant *neglected* to mention his criminal record⟩
synonyms fail, forget, omit
related words disregard, ignore, overlook, overpass, pass over, slight; slide, slip; default; skip
near antonyms heed, mind, remember; keep, observe; carry out, do, execute, perform, practice (*or* practise); discharge, fulfill (*or* fulfil), meet, satisfy; comply (with)
neglected *adj* showing signs of advanced wear and tear and neglect — see SHABBY 1
neglectful *adj* failing to give proper care and attention — see NEGLIGENT

THESAURUS

neglecting *adj* failing to give proper care and attention — see NEGLIGENT

negligence *n* **1** failure to take the care that a cautious person usually takes ⟨exhibiting his usual *negligence*, he failed to set the emergency brake, and the car rolled down the steep hill and crashed into the telephone pole⟩
synonyms carelessness, dereliction, heedlessness, incautiousness, laxness, remissness, slackness
related words foolhardiness, rashness, recklessness, wildness; neglect, omission; delinquency, irresponsibility, malfeasance, malpractice, misconduct; misdirection, mishandling, mismanagement; forgetfulness, inattention, inattentiveness, obliviousness, shortsightedness, unwariness
near antonyms alertness, attention, attentiveness, awareness; circumspection, observance, vigilance, watchfulness; responsibility, responsibleness
antonyms care, carefulness, caution, cautiousness, heedfulness
2 the nonperformance of an assigned or expected action — see FAILURE 1

negligent *adj* failing to give proper care and attention ⟨has been *negligent* in taking care of the neighbor's dog, repeatedly forgetting to feed the poor animal⟩
synonyms careless, derelict, lax, neglectful, neglecting, remiss, slack
related words heedless, incautious, irresponsible, reckless, wild; unguarded, unwary; forgetful; disregardful, disregarding, inattentive, oblivious, thoughtless, unheeding, unmindful, unthinking; apathetic, disinterested, indifferent, unconcerned, uninterested; delinquent; loose
near antonyms meticulous, painstaking, punctilious; cautious, chary, circumspect, gingerly, guarded; alert, heedful, heeding, mindful, observant, regardful, regarding, vigilant, wary, watchful; foresighted, forethoughtful, provident, responsible; thinking, thoughtful; concerned, interested
antonyms attentive, careful, conscientious

negligible *adj* **1** so small or unimportant as to warrant little or no attention ⟨the two cents in change was such a *negligible* sum that she left the store without collecting the pennies from the cashier⟩
synonyms inconsequential, inconsiderable, insignificant, measly, minute, nominal, paltry, petty, picayune, piddling, slight, trifling, trivial
related words inferior, mean; imperceptible, inappreciable; little, puny, tiny; hairsplitting, nitpicking, pettifogging; one-horse, small-fry, two-bit
near antonyms serious, substantial, weighty; eventful, momentous; conspicuous, noteworthy, prominent, outstanding, remarkable, striking; appreciable, discernible, measurable
antonyms big, consequential, considerable, important, material, significant
2 lacking importance — see UNIMPORTANT
3 small in degree — see REMOTE 1

negligibly *adv* in a very small quantity or degree — see LITTLE 1

negotiable *adj* capable of being traveled on — see PASSABLE 1

negotiate *vb* **1** to bring about through discussion and compromise ⟨wanted to *negotiate* a higher salary before she accepted the job offer⟩
synonyms arrange, concert, conclude
related words settle (on *or* upon); bargain, chaffer,

deal, dicker, haggle, horse-trade, palter; agree; contract, covenant; argue, debate, discuss, hammer (out), hash (over), reason, talk, talk over, work out
2 to deal with (something) usually skillfully or efficiently — see HANDLE 1
3 to plan out usually with subtle skill or care — see ENGINEER
4 to talk over or dispute the terms of a purchase — see BARGAIN

negotiation *n* the act or practice of each side giving up something in order to reach an agreement — see CONCESSION 1

neigh *vb* to make the cry typical of a horse ⟨the horses *neighed* when the rider came into the barn⟩
synonyms nicker, whinny

neighborhood *n* **1** an area (as of a city) set apart for some purpose or having some special feature — see DISTRICT
2 the people living in a particular area — see COMMUNITY 1

neighboring *adj* not being distant in time, space, or significance — see CLOSE 2

neighborly *adj* having or showing kindly feeling and sincere interest — see FRIENDLY 1

nemesis *n* **1** one who inflicts punishment in return for an injury or offense ⟨Batman is the Joker's main *nemesis* and always foils his wicked plots⟩
synonyms avenger, castigator, chastiser, punisher, scourge, vigilante
related words revenger; redresser, righter; requiter
near antonyms ransomer, redeemer, vindicator
2 suffering, loss, or hardship imposed in response to a crime or offense — see PUNISHMENT

neophyte *n* a person who is just starting out in a field of activity — see BEGINNER

neoplasm *n* an abnormal mass of tissue — see GROWTH 1

nerd *n* a person slavishly devoted to intellectual or academic pursuits ⟨was such a *nerd* she stayed home from the party to study for the exam on Monday⟩
synonyms bookworm, grind
related words egghead, highbrow, intellectual; brain, genius; scholar
near antonyms slacker, underachiever; lowbrow

nerve *n* **1** shameless boldness — see EFFRONTERY
2 strength of mind to carry on in spite of danger — see COURAGE
3 nerves *pl* a sense of panic or extreme nervousness — see JITTERS

nerve *vb* to prepare (oneself) mentally or emotionally — see FORTIFY 1

nerved *adj* inclined or willing to take risks — see BOLD 1

nerveless *adj* **1** lacking strength of will or character — see WEAK 2
2 not easily panicked or upset — see UNFLAPPABLE

nerviness *n* shameless boldness — see EFFRONTERY

nervous *adj* **1** feeling or showing uncomfortable feelings of uncertainty ⟨he was *nervous* about how he would do at the varsity basketball tryouts⟩
synonyms aflutter, anxious, dithery, edgy, het up, hung up, jittery, jumpy, nervy, perturbed, tense, troubled, uneasy, unquiet, upset, uptight, worried

related words aggrieved, bothered, concerned, disquieted, distraught, distressed, disturbed; apprehensive, foreboding, hesitant, misgiving; fretful, fretting, stewing, vexed; qualmish, qualmy; flustered, twittered, undone, unnerved, unstrung; obsessed, preoccupied, restless; fidgety, flighty, fluttery, high-strung, skittish, spooky

phrases keyed up, on edge, on pins and needles
near antonyms confident, self-assured, self-confident, sure; controlled, self-controlled
antonyms calm, collected, cool, easy, nerveless, relaxed

2 marked by or causing agitation or uncomfortable feelings ⟨a *nervous* silence filled the room as the teacher handed out the graded exams⟩
synonyms agitating, anxious, disquieting, distressful, distressing, disturbing, restless, tense, unnerving, unsettling, worrisome
related words bothersome, troublesome; foreboding, misgiving; discouraging, disheartening, strained; restive, restless, unrestful; awkward, embarrassing
near antonyms restful; pacific
antonyms calming, comfortable, easy, peaceful, quiet, quieting, tranquil

3 easily excited by nature — see EXCITABLE
nervousness *n* an uneasy state of mind usually over the possibility of an anticipated misfortune or trouble — see ANXIETY 1

nervy *adj* **1** displaying or marked by rude boldness ⟨the *nervy* waiter held up the small tip and called out to the departing customers, "Hope it doesn't break the bank!"⟩
synonyms arch, bold, bold-faced, brash, brassy, brazen, cheeky, cocky, fresh, impertinent, impudent, insolent, sassy, saucy
related words assertive, forward, obtrusive; audacious, defiant, disrespectful; shameless, unabashed, unblushing; bluff, blunt, curt; facetious, flip, flippant, pert, smart, smart-alecky (*or* smart-aleck)
near antonyms demure, humble, modest; courteous, genteel, mannerly, polite, proper; deferential, respectful; abashed, ashamed, blushing, embarrassed; gentle, mild; inconspicuous, unobtrusive
antonyms meek, mousy (*or* mousey), retiring, shy, timid

2 feeling or showing uncomfortable feelings of uncertainty — see NERVOUS 1
3 inclined or willing to take risks — see BOLD 1
nest *n* a place where a person goes to hide — see HIDEOUT
nest egg *n* a sum of money set aside for a particular purpose — see FUND 1
nestle *vb* **1** to lie close — see NUZZLE
2 to sit or recline comfortably or cozily — see SNUGGLE 1
¹net *n* **1** a fabric made of strands loosely twisted, knotted, or woven together at regular intervals ⟨the basketball didn't go into the basket, it just hit the *net*⟩
synonyms mesh, netting, network
related words web, webbing; grille (*also* grill), lattice, screen, screening; filigree, lace
2 a device or scheme for capturing another by surprise — see TRAP 1
3 something that catches and holds — see WEB 1
²net *n* the amount of money left when expenses are subtracted from the total amount received — see PROFIT 1

nether *adj* situated lower down — see INFERIOR 1
netting *n* a fabric made of strands loosely twisted, knotted, or woven together at regular intervals — see ¹NET 1
nettle *vb* to disturb the peace of mind of (someone) especially by repeated disagreeable acts — see IRRITATE 1
nettling *adj* causing annoyance — see ANNOYING
network *n* **1** a fabric made of strands loosely twisted, knotted, or woven together at regular intervals — see ¹NET 1
2 something made up of many interdependent or related parts — see SYSTEM 1
neurotic *n* a person judged to be legally or medically insane — see LUNATIC 1
neuter *vb* to remove the sex organs of ⟨Dad agreed to buy us the dog on the condition that we have her *neutered* so she couldn't have puppies⟩
synonyms alter, desex
related words castrate, emasculate, geld; spay; sterilize
neutral *adj* not favoring or joined to either side in a quarrel, contest, or war ⟨Sweden remained *neutral* during World War II, refusing to join either side of the conflict⟩
synonyms nonpartisan, unallied
related words autonomous, independent, sovereign, unaffiliated; nonbelligerent; individualistic; disinterested, evenhanded, fair, impartial, unbiased, uninfluenced, unprejudiced; bipartisan
near antonyms biased, partial, partisan, prejudiced, unfair; affiliated, associated, federated; belligerent
antonyms allied, confederate
neutrality *n* lack of favoritism toward one side or another — see DETACHMENT 1
neutralize *vb* to balance with an equal force so as to make ineffective — see OFFSET
neutralizer *n* a force or influence that makes an opposing force ineffective or less effective — see COUNTERBALANCE
never *adv* **1** at no time ⟨I have *never* been out of the country⟩
synonyms ne'er
related words nevermore; not; infrequently, little, rarely, seldom
near antonyms eternally, everlastingly, evermore, invariably; frequently, often, recurrently, repeatedly
antonyms always, constantly, continuously, endlessly, ever, forever, perpetually
2 not in any degree, way, or under any condition ⟨though she turned down his offer of marriage twice, he was *never* convinced that she did not love him⟩
synonyms no, none, nothing, noway (*or* noways), nowise
related words nowhere near
phrases by no means, in no wise, nothing doing, on no account
near antonyms completely, extremely, full, fully, par excellence, right, very; altogether, exactly; somehow, someway (*also* someways); out
antonyms anyhow, anyway, anywise, at all, ever, half, however
nevertheless *adv* in spite of that — see HOWEVER
new *adj* **1** taking the place of one that came before ⟨after my bike was stolen, my scooter became my *new* mode of transportation⟩
synonyms backup, makeshift, substitute

THESAURUS

related words alternate, alternative; different, other, separate; extra, spare; another, second; utility; successive; equivalent

near antonyms first, former; equal, identical, same; lasting, permanent

antonyms original

2 not known or experienced before ⟨Spanish was a *new* course of study for her⟩ ⟨the Americas were *new* lands for the European explorers⟩

synonyms fresh, novel, original, strange, unaccustomed, unfamiliar, unheard-of, unknown, unprecedented

related words innovative, unique; nontraditional, unconventional, untried, unused, unworn

near antonyms conventional, established, traditional, tried, tried-and-true; derivative, imitative

antonyms familiar, old, time-honored, tired

3 recently made and never used before ⟨that unique scent that is the telltale sign of a *new* car⟩

synonyms brand-new, spick-and-span (*or* spic-and-span), unused

related words clean, fresh, pristine, unspoiled; untouched; newfangled, new-fashioned; natural, raw, virgin, unprocessed, untreated, unworked

near antonyms dirty, soiled, spoiled, stale; aged, beat-up, old, worn

antonyms hand-me-down, second hand, used

4 made or become fresh in spirits or vigor ⟨a little rest made him a *new* man after the exhausting basketball game⟩

synonyms energized, freshened, invigorated, reanimated, recreated, reenergized, refreshed, regenerated, renewed, resuscitated, revived

related words animated, enlivened, exhilarated, jazzed (up); resurrected; rested, untired, unwearied

near antonyms tired, weary; dampened, deadened; emasculated, unmanned; demoralized, disheartened, dispirited

antonyms drained, enervated, exhausted, weakened

5 being or involving the latest methods, concepts, information, or styles — see MODERN

new *adv* not long ago — see NEWLY

newborn *n* a recently born person — see BABY

newcomer *n* a person who is just starting out in a field of activity — see BEGINNER

newfangled *adj* being or involving the latest methods, concepts, information, or styles — see MODERN

new–fashioned *adj* being or involving the latest methods, concepts, information, or styles — see MODERN

newly *adv* not long ago ⟨as soon as he left the room, his dog jumped on the *newly* made bed and rumpled it again⟩

synonyms freshly, just, late, lately, new, now, only, recently

related words latterly

phrases of late

near antonyms ago, before, earlier, early, erstwhile, formerly, previously; heretofore, hitherto

antonyms anciently

newness *n* the quality or appeal of being new — see NOVELTY 1

news *n pl* a report of recent events or facts not previously known ⟨dropped by to give me the latest *news* about her daughter⟩

synonyms information, intelligence, item, story, tidings, word

related words announcement, communication, message; dope, lowdown, scoop, tidbit (*also* titbit), tip; gossip, rumor, tale, tattle; feedback

newspaper *n* a publication that appears at regular intervals — see JOURNAL

newsy *adj* having the style and content of everyday conversation — see CHATTY 1

next *adj* being the one that comes immediately after another ⟨my house is the *next* one⟩ ⟨turn at the *next* street, not this one⟩ ⟨she was *next* in line for concert tickets⟩

synonyms coming, ensuing, following, succeeding

related words consecutive, sequential, successive; posterior, subsequent; immediate; second

phrases on deck

near antonyms anterior, former; past; last

antonyms antecedent, foregoing, precedent, preceding, previous, prior

next–door *adj* not being distant in time, space, or significance — see CLOSE 2

next to *adv* very close to but not completely — see ALMOST

next to *prep* close to — see AROUND 1

nib *n* the jaws of a bird together with their hornlike covering — see BEAK

nibble *n* a small piece or quantity of food — see MORSEL 1

nibble *vb* to crush or grind with the teeth — see BITE (ON)

nice *adj* **1** following the established traditions of refined society and good taste — see PROPER 1

2 giving pleasure or contentment to the mind or senses — see PLEASANT

3 hard to please — see FINICKY

4 having an easygoing and pleasing manner especially in social situations — see AMIABLE

5 made or done with extreme care and accuracy — see FINE 2

nicely *adv* **1** in a pleasing way — see WELL 5

2 in a satisfactory way — see WELL 1

3 with good reason or courtesy — see WELL 4

niceness *n* the state or quality of having a pleasant or agreeable manner in socializing with others — see AMIABILITY 1

nicety *n* a single piece of information — see FACT 3

niche *n* **1** a hollowed-out space in a wall ⟨statues of various saints occupy the *niches* lining the abbey's many corridors⟩

synonyms alcove, nook, recess

related words corner, cranny, cubbyhole; cubicle; dent, indentation

2 the place where a plant or animal is usually or naturally found — see HOME 2

nick *n* a V-shaped cut usually on an edge or a surface — see NOTCH 1

nicker *vb* to make the cry typical of a horse — see NEIGH

nickname *n* a descriptive or familiar name given instead of or in addition to the one belonging to an individual ⟨his wavy hair earned him the *nickname* "Curly" early in life⟩

synonyms alias, cognomen, epithet, sobriquet (*also* soubriquet)

related words appellation, denomination, denotation, designation, handle, label, title; nom de plume, pen name, pseudonym

nifty *adj* of the very best kind — see EXCELLENT

nifty *n* something very good of its kind — see JIM-DANDY

niggard *adj* giving or sharing as little as possible — see STINGY 1

niggard *n* a mean grasping person who is usually stingy with money — see MISER

niggardly *adj* **1** giving or sharing as little as possible — see STINGY 1

2 less plentiful than what is normal, necessary, or desirable — see MEAGER

nigh *adj* not being distant in time, space, or significance — see CLOSE 2

nigh *adv* **1** at, within, or to a short distance or time — see NEAR 1

2 very close to but not completely — see ALMOST

nigher *adj* being the less far of two — see NEAR 1

night *adj* of, relating to, or occurring in the night — see NOCTURNAL

night *n* **1** the time from sunset to sunrise when there is no visible sunlight ⟨loved to sit outside at *night* and watch the stars⟩
synonyms dark, darkness, nighttime
related words dusk, evening, gloaming, nightfall, twilight; midnight
near antonyms dawn, daybreak, forenoon, morning; high noon, midday, noon, noonday, noontide, noontime; afternoon
antonyms day, daytime

2 a time or place of little or no light — see DARK 1

nightclub *n* a bar or restaurant offering special nighttime entertainment (as music, dancing, or comedy acts) ⟨decided to go dancing at a local *nightclub* after the long dinner and movie⟩
synonyms cabaret, café (*also* cafe), disco, discotheque, roadhouse
related words barroom, pub [*chiefly British*], public house [*chiefly British*], saloon, tavern; dive, speakeasy; canteen

nightdress *n* a loose pullover garment worn in bed — see NIGHTGOWN

nightfall *n* the time from when the sun begins to set to the onset of total darkness — see DUSK 1

nightgown *n* a loose pullover garment worn in bed ⟨decided to buy a flannel *nightgown* instead of pajamas⟩
synonyms nightdress, nightshirt
related words nightclothes; pajamas, pj's, pyjamas [*chiefly British*]; nightcap; lingerie

nightly *adj* of, relating to, or occurring in the night — see NOCTURNAL

nightmare *n* **1** a series of often striking pictures created by the imagination during sleep — see DREAM 1

2 a situation or state that causes great suffering and unhappiness — see HELL 2

nightmarish *adj* extremely disturbing or repellent — see HORRIBLE 1

nightshirt *n* a loose pullover garment worn in bed — see NIGHTGOWN

nightstick *n* a heavy rigid stick used as a weapon or for punishment — see CLUB 1

nighttime *adj* of, relating to, or occurring in the night — see NOCTURNAL

nighttime *n* the time from sunset to sunrise when there is no visible sunlight — see NIGHT 1

nil *n* the numerical symbol 0 or the absence of number or quantity represented by it — see ZERO 1

nimble *adj* **1** having or showing quickness of mind — see INTELLIGENT 1

2 moving easily — see GRACEFUL 1

nimbleness *n* ease and grace in physical activity — see DEXTERITY 2

nincompoop *n* **1** a person who lacks good sense or judgment — see FOOL 1

2 a stupid person — see IDIOT

ninny *n* **1** a person who lacks good sense or judgment — see FOOL 1

2 a stupid person — see IDIOT

¹nip *n* **1** a very small amount — see PARTICLE 1

2 an uncomfortable degree of coolness — see CHILL

²nip *n* the portion of a serving of a beverage that is swallowed at one time — see DRINK 2

nip *vb* **1** to make (as hair) shorter with or as if with the use of shears — see CLIP

2 to squeeze tightly between two surfaces, edges, or points — see PINCH

3 to take (something) without right and with an intent to keep — see STEAL 1

nip and tuck *adj* showing little difference in the standing of the competitors — see CLOSE 3

nipper *n* a male person who has not yet reached adulthood — see BOY

nipping *adj* having a low or subnormal temperature — see COLD 1

nippy *adj* **1** having a low or subnormal temperature — see COLD 1

2 having a powerfully stimulating odor or flavor — see SHARP 3

3 moving, proceeding, or acting with great speed — see FAST 1

4 uncomfortably cool — see CHILLY 1

nitpick *vb* to make often peevish criticisms or objections about matters that are minor, unimportant, or irrelevant — see QUIBBLE

nitpicker *n* a person given to harsh judgments and to finding faults — see CRITIC 1

nitwit *n* **1** a person who lacks good sense or judgment — see FOOL 1

2 a stupid person — see IDIOT

no *interj* how surprising, doubtful, or unbelievable ⟨*no*—you can't possibly mean that I failed that test! I studied for days!⟩
synonyms ah, aha, fie, indeed, pshaw, well, what, why
related words gee, ha, hello, hey, lo, oh; fiddlesticks, phooey, pooh; there; oops, ugh; egad, gad, the deuce, the devil, the dickens, zounds

no *adv* **1** not in any degree, way, or under any condition — see NEVER 2

2 certainly not — see HARDLY 2

no *n* **1** a vote or decision against something ⟨though I wanted spaghetti for dinner, the consensus was a decisive *no*⟩
synonyms nay, negative
related words con; blackball, veto; denial, negation, refusal
near antonyms pro; acceptance, approval, grace
antonyms positive, yea, yes

2 an unwillingness to grant something asked for — see DENIAL 1

nobility *n* impressiveness of beauty on a large scale — see MAGNIFICENCE

noble *adj* **1** of high birth, rank, or station ⟨despite his *noble* background, the prince is known for his unpretentious way with common people⟩
synonyms aristocratic, genteel, gentle, grand, highborn, patrician, upper-class, wellborn
related words high, lofty, superior; elevated, ennobled, exalted; gentlemanly, kingly, knightly, lady-

like, lordly, princely, queenly, regal, royal; high-level, senior

near antonyms inferior, knavish; bastard, illegitimate; ordinary, plain; abased, degraded; junior, subordinate

antonyms baseborn, common, humble, ignoble, low, lower-class, lowly, mean, plebeian

2 having, characterized by, or arising from a dignified and generous nature ⟨the factory owner had a kind, *noble* disposition that showed in his unstinting generosity toward the poor⟩ ⟨our country was founded on the *noble* ideas that are put forth in the founding fathers' writings⟩

synonyms chivalrous, elevated, gallant, great, greathearted, high, high-minded, lofty, lordly, magnanimous, sublime

related words ennobled, exalted, glorified; heroic, honorable, venerable, worthy; knightly, princely, regal; moving, inspiring, uplifting; august, magnificent, majestic

near antonyms sordid, squalid, vile, wretched; abominable, contemptible, despicable, detestable, hateful, offensive, repulsive, ugly; dastardly, dirty, lousy, sorry; little, mean, narrow, small-minded; degrading, discreditable, humiliating, ignominious; coarse, crude, vulgar

antonyms base, debased, degenerate, degraded, ignoble, low

3 following the accepted rules of moral conduct — see HONORABLE 1

4 large and impressive in size, grandeur, extent, or conception — see GRAND 1

5 of the very best kind — see EXCELLENT

6 standing above others in rank, importance, or achievement — see EMINENT

noble *n* a man of high birth or social position — see GENTLEMAN 1

nobleman *n* a man of high birth or social position — see GENTLEMAN 1

nobleness *n* impressiveness of beauty on a large scale — see MAGNIFICENCE

noblewoman *n* a woman of high birth or social position — see GENTLEWOMAN

nobly *adv* in a manner befitting a person of the highest character and ideals — see GREATLY 1

nobody *n* a person of no importance or influence ⟨she felt like a *nobody* until she won the National Spelling Bee⟩

synonyms lightweight, nonentity, nothing, shrimp, twerp, whippersnapper, zero, zilch

related words least; inferior, mediocrity, obscurity; figurehead, puppet

near antonyms chief, head, lead, leader; celebrity, luminary, notable, personality, star, superstar; authority, superior; great power, party, power

antonyms big shot, bigwig, eminence, figure, magnate, nabob, personage, somebody, VIP

nobody *pron* no person ⟨there is *nobody* home⟩ ⟨*nobody* wants to clean up that mess⟩

synonyms none, no one

near antonyms anybody, anyone; somebody, someone

antonyms everybody, everyone

nocturnal *adj* of, relating to, or occurring in the night ⟨he bought a new telescope so he could pursue his favorite *nocturnal* hobby of astronomy⟩

synonyms night, nightly, nighttime

related words late; midnight, overnight

near antonyms noon

antonyms daily, diurnal

nod *vb* to make short up-and-down movements ⟨though she couldn't see the rain, she knew it had started because she could see the flowers *nod* as raindrops hit them⟩

synonyms bob, bobble, jog, jounce, pump, seesaw

related words jerk, jiggle, shake, wiggle, wobble; oscillate, rock, sway, swing, undulate; drop, duck

nodding *adj* bending downward or forward ⟨some students, with *nodding* heads, were falling asleep during the boring lecture⟩

synonyms bowed, bowing, declined, declining, descendant (*or* descendent), descending, drooping, droopy, hanging, hung (*also* hanged), inclining, pendulous, sagging, stooping

related words floppy, limp; dangling, falling, pendent (*or* pendant), suspended; dipping, sinking, slumping

near antonyms erect, inflexible, rigid, stiff; elevated, raised, upraised

antonyms unbending, upright

noddle *n* the upper or front part of the body that contains the brain, the major sense organs, and the mouth — see HEAD 1

node *n* a small rounded mass of swollen tissue — see BUMP 1

nodule *n* a small rounded mass of swollen tissue — see BUMP 1

Noel *n* the season celebrating Christmas — see YULETIDE

noggin *n* the upper or front part of the body that contains the brain, the major sense organs, and the mouth — see HEAD 1

no-good *adj* having no usefulness — see WORTHLESS

no-good *n* a mean, evil, or unprincipled person — see VILLAIN

noise *n* **1** loud, confused, and usually unharmonious sound ⟨the blaring *noise* of traffic on Fifth Avenue made casual conversation impossible⟩

synonyms bluster, cacophony, clamor, clangor, din, discordance, racket, roar

related words discord, dissonance; commotion, furor, hubbub, hullabaloo, hurly-burly, rumpus, tumult, uproar; babel; clatter, jangle; bang, blast, boom, clap, crack, crash

near antonyms calm, hush, lull; quietude, serenity, tranquillity (*or* tranquility)

antonyms quiet, silence, still, stillness

2 a violent shouting — see CLAMOR 1

noise (about) *vb* to make (as a piece of information) the subject of common talk without any authority or confirmation of accuracy — see RUMOR

noiseless *adj* mostly or entirely without sound — see SILENT 3

noisome *adj* **1** bad for the well-being of the body — see UNHEALTHY 1

2 causing intense displeasure, disgust, or resentment — see OFFENSIVE 1

3 having an unpleasant smell — see MALODOROUS

noisy *adj* **1** making loud, confused, and usually unharmonious sounds ⟨the *noisy* crowd moved up the street, shouting louder as they went along⟩

synonyms clangorous, dinning, discordant

related words cacophonous, dissonant; resounding, sonorous; clamorous, uproarious; blatant, obstreperous, strident, vociferous; blaring, booming, brassy, brazen, clanging, earsplitting

near antonyms calm, hushed
antonyms noiseless, quiet, silent, soundless, still
2 full of or characterized by the presence of noise ⟨the crowded auditorium was *noisy*, packed with excited theatergoers eager for the show to start⟩ ⟨the manufacturing company was a *noisy* place, so we wore ear protection while we toured⟩
synonyms clamorous, clangorous, clattering, clattery, resounding
related words resonant, sonorous; buzzing, humming, murmuring; blustery, boisterous, raucous, rip-roaring, roaring, roistering, romping, rowdy; tumultuous, uproarious, woolly (*also* wooly); obstreperous, vociferous
near antonyms calm, peaceful, serene, tranquil
antonyms hushed, noiseless, quiet, silent, soundless, stilled, stilly
nomad *or* **nomadic** *adj* traveling from place to place — see ITINERANT
nomad *n* a person who roams about without a fixed route or destination ⟨after college she became quite the *nomad*, backpacking through Europe with no particular destination⟩
synonyms drifter, gadabout, rambler, roamer, rover, stroller, vagabond, wanderer, wayfarer
related words laggard, straggler; lingerer, loiterer, sojourner; bum, hobo, tramp; sightseer, traveler (*or* traveller); transient, vagrant; ambler, saunterer
near antonyms homebody; denizen, dweller, habitant, inhabitant, resident, settler
nominal *adj* **1** being something in name or form only ⟨he was the *nominal* head of state—everyone knew the country was actually run by one of his advisers⟩
synonyms formal, paper, titular
related words so-called; phantom, virtual
near antonyms actual, real, true
2 so small or unimportant as to warrant little or no attention — see NEGLIGIBLE 1
nominally *adv* in a very small quantity or degree — see LITTLE 1
nonaction *n* lack of action or activity — see INACTION
nonbinding *adj* having no legal or binding force — see NULL 1
nonchalance *n* lack of interest or concern — see INDIFFERENCE
nonchalant *adj* having or showing a lack of interest or concern — see INDIFFERENT 1
noncombustible *adj* incapable of being burned — see INCOMBUSTIBLE
nonconflicting *adj* not having or showing any apparent conflict — see CONSISTENT
nonconformist *adj* deviating from commonly accepted beliefs or practices — see HERETICAL
nonconformist *n* **1** a person who does not conform to generally accepted standards or customs ⟨always the *nonconformist*, she insisted on wearing red on St. Patrick's Day and not green like everyone else⟩
synonyms bohemian, deviant, individualist, loner, lone wolf, maverick
related words character, codger, crackbrain, crackpot, crank, eccentric, freak, kook, nut, oddball, screwball, weirdo; misfit, outsider; anomaly
near antonyms adherent, follower, supporter; sheep
antonyms conformer, conformist

2 a person who believes or teaches something opposed to accepted beliefs — see HERETIC
nonconformity *n* departure from a generally accepted theory, opinion, or practice — see HERESY
nonconventional *adj* not bound by traditional ways or beliefs — see LIBERAL 1
none *adv* **1** certainly not — see HARDLY 2
2 not in any degree, way, or under any condition — see NEVER 2
none *pron* no person — see NOBODY
nonelective *adj* forcing one's compliance or participation by or as if by law — see MANDATORY
nonentity *n* a person of no importance or influence — see NOBODY
nonessential *adj* not needed by the circumstances or to accomplish an end — see UNNECESSARY
nonetheless *adv* in spite of that — see HOWEVER
nonexistent *adj* not present or in evidence — see ABSENT 2
nonfictional *adj* restricted to or based on fact — see FACTUAL 1
nonflammable *adj* incapable of being burned — see INCOMBUSTIBLE
nonfunctional *adj* not being in working order — see INOPERABLE 1
nonfunctioning *adj* not being in working order — see INOPERABLE 1
noninflammable *adj* incapable of being burned — see INCOMBUSTIBLE
nonliterary *adj* used in or suitable for speech and not formal writing — see COLLOQUIAL 1
nonliterate *adj* lacking in education or the knowledge gained from books — see IGNORANT 1
nonmaterial *adj* not composed of matter — see IMMATERIAL 1
nonmotile *adj* incapable of moving or being moved — see IMMOVABLE 1
nonmoving *adj* **1** fixed in a place or position — see STATIONARY 1
2 incapable of moving or being moved — see IMMOVABLE 1
nonnative *adj* being, relating to, or characteristic of a country other than one's own — see FOREIGN 1
nonnative *n* a person who is not native to or known to a community — see STRANGER
no-nonsense *adj* not joking or playful in mood or manner — see SERIOUS 1
nonoperating *adj* not being in working order — see INOPERABLE 1
nonorthodox *adj* **1** deviating from commonly accepted beliefs or practices — see HERETICAL
2 not bound by traditional ways or beliefs — see LIBERAL 1
nonpareil *adj* having no equal or rival for excellence or desirability — see ONLY 1
nonpareil *n* someone of such unequaled perfection as to deserve imitation — see IDEAL 1
nonpartisan *adj* **1** marked by justice, honesty, and freedom from bias — see FAIR 2
2 not favoring or joined to either side in a quarrel, contest, or war — see NEUTRAL
nonphysical *adj* not composed of matter — see IMMATERIAL 1
nonplus *vb* to throw into a state of self-conscious distress — see EMBARRASS 1
nonpractical *adj* not capable of being put to use or account — see IMPRACTICAL
nonprofessional *adj* lacking or showing a lack of expert skill — see AMATEURISH

THESAURUS

nonpublic *adj* not known or meant to be known by the general populace — see PRIVATE 1

nonrational *adj* not using or following good reasoning — see ILLOGICAL

nonrealistic *adj* using elements of form (as color, line, or texture) with little or no attempt at creating a realistic picture — see ABSTRACT 2

nonreligious *adj* 1 lacking religious emotions, principles, or practices — see IRRELIGIOUS
2 not involving religion or religious matters — see PROFANE 1

nonresistant *adj* receiving or enduring without offering resistance — see PASSIVE

nonsense *n* 1 language, behavior, or ideas that are absurd and contrary to good sense ⟨told him to stop his mischievous *nonsense* and start behaving properly⟩ ⟨the discussion about building a time machine was complete *nonsense*⟩ ⟨a hundred years ago, the idea that man could walk on the moon was regarded as impractical *nonsense*⟩
synonyms bunk, claptrap, drivel, fiddlesticks, folly, foolishness, fudge, hogwash, humbug, humbuggery, piffle, rot, senselessness, silliness, slush, stupidity, trash
related words absurdity, asininity, fatuity, foolery, idiocy, imbecility, inanity, insanity, lunacy; absurdness, craziness, foolishness, madness, senselessness, witlessness; monkeyshines, shenanigans, tomfoolery; gas, hot air, jazz, moonshine, rigmarole, twaddle; double-talk
near antonyms levelheadedness, rationality, reasonability, reasonableness, sensibleness; common sense, horse sense, sense; discernment, judgment (*or* judgement), wisdom
2 unintelligible or meaningless talk — see GIBBERISH

nonsensical *adj* 1 conceived or made without regard for reason or reality — see FANTASTIC 1
2 showing or marked by a lack of good sense or judgment — see FOOLISH 1

nonsensicalness *n* lack of good sense or judgment — see FOOLISHNESS 1

nonspecific *adj* relating to the main elements and not to specific details — see GENERAL 2

nonsuccess *n* a falling short of one's goals — see FAILURE 2

nontraditional *adj* not bound by traditional ways or beliefs — see LIBERAL 1

nonvalid *adj* 1 having no legal or binding force — see NULL 1
2 having no basis in reason or fact — see GROUNDLESS

nonviolent *adj* not involving violence or force — see PEACEFUL 2

nook *n* a hollowed-out space in a wall — see NICHE 1

noon *n* the middle of the day ⟨we eat a big lunch around *noon* then have dinner in the evening⟩
synonyms high noon, midday, noonday, noontide, noontime
related words forenoon, morning; afternoon, evening

noonday *n* the middle of the day — see NOON

no one *pron* no person — see NOBODY

noontide *n* the middle of the day — see NOON

noontime *n* the middle of the day — see NOON

norm *n* what is typical of a group, class, or series — see AVERAGE

normal *adj* 1 being of the type that is encountered in the normal course of events — see ORDINARY 1
2 having full use of one's mind and control over one's actions — see SANE
3 having or showing the qualities associated with the members of a particular group or kind — see TYPICAL 1

normal *n* what is typical of a group, class, or series — see AVERAGE

normalcy *n* the state or fact of being the way things usually are — see NORMALITY

normality *n* the state or fact of being the way things usually are ⟨the county slowly has returned to *normality* after a week of flash flooding⟩
synonyms normalcy, status quo
related words groove, routine, rut; currency, prevalence; conventionality; orderliness, peace
near antonyms irregularity, uncommonness, unusualness; disorderliness, disruptiveness; disruption, disturbance; anomalousness, deviance; exceptionalness, extraordinariness, noteworthiness, remarkableness; unconventionality
antonyms abnormality

normalize *vb* to make agree with a single established standard or model — see STANDARDIZE

normally *adv* according to the usual course of things — see NATURALLY 2

nose *vb* 1 to become aware of by means of the sense organs in the nose — see SMELL 1
2 to interest oneself in what is not one's concern — see INTERFERE

nosedive *n* the act or process of going to a lower level or altitude — see DESCENT 1

nose–dive *vb* to go to a lower level — see DROP 2

nosegay *n* a bunch of flowers — see BOUQUET 1

nosiness *n* an eager desire to find out about things that are often none of one's business — see CURIOSITY 1

nosy *or* **nosey** *adj* 1 interested in what is not one's own business — see CURIOUS 1
2 thrusting oneself where one is not welcome or invited — see INTRUSIVE

notable *adj* standing above others in rank, importance, or achievement — see EMINENT

notable *n* a person who is widely known and usually much talked about — see CELEBRITY 1

notation *n* a usually brief written reminder — see NOTE 1

notch *n* 1 a V-shaped cut usually on an edge or a surface ⟨lifted up the fence rail and put it in the *notch* cut into the post⟩
synonyms chip, hack, indentation, kerf, nick
related words punch; groove, score; slit, slot
2 a narrow opening between hillsides or mountains that can be used for passage — see CANYON
3 an individual part of a process, series, or ranking — see DEGREE 1

note *n* 1 a usually brief written reminder ⟨I'll make a *note* to myself so I don't forget to pick up some milk on the way home⟩
synonyms memo, memorandum, notation
related words memoir, minutes, report; line; document, writing
2 a message on paper from one person or group to another — see LETTER
3 a natural vocal sound made by an animal — see CALL 1
4 a piece of printed paper used as money — see ¹BILL 2
5 a special quality or impression associated with something — see AURA

6 overall quality as seen or judged by people in general — see REPUTATION

7 a briefly expressed opinion — see REMARK

note *vb* **1** to make a statement of one's opinion — see REMARK 1

2 to make a written note of — see RECORD 1

3 to make note of (something) through the use of one's eyes — see SEE 1

4 to make reference to or speak about briefly but specifically — see MENTION 1

5 to take notice of and be guided by — see HEED 1

noted *adj* widely known — see FAMOUS

notepad *n* a number of sheets of writing paper glued together at one edge — see PAD 1

noteworthiness *n* the fact or state of being above others in rank or importance — see EMINENCE 1

noteworthy *adj* standing above others in rank, importance, or achievement — see EMINENT

nothing *adv* not in any degree, way, or under any condition — see NEVER 2

nothing *n* **1** a person of no importance or influence — see NOBODY

2 something of little importance — see TRIFLE

3 the numerical symbol 0 or the absence of number or quantity represented by it — see ZERO 1

notice *n* **1** a published statement informing the public of a matter of general interest — see ANNOUNCEMENT

2 a state of being aware — see ATTENTION 2

3 a written communication giving information or directions — see MEMORANDUM 1

4 an essay evaluating or analyzing something — see CRITICISM

5 the act or an instance of telling beforehand of danger or risk — see WARNING 1

notice *vb* **1** to make note of (something) through the use of one's eyes — see SEE 1

2 to make reference to or speak about briefly but specifically — see MENTION 1

noticeable *adj* likely to attract attention ⟨the stain on the new carpet was quite *noticeable,* and nothing we did made it any lighter⟩

synonyms arresting, bold, catchy, conspicuous, dramatic, emphatic, eye-catching, flamboyant, marked, prominent, pronounced, remarkable, showy, splashy, striking

related words detectable, discernible, observable, perceptible, visible; outstanding, salient; distinguished, eminent, impressive, notable, noteworthy; highlighted, spotlighted; flagrant, glaring, screaming; flashy, garish, gaudy, glitzy, jazzy, loud, meretricious, swank (*or* swanky), tawdry; high-falutin, ostentatious, pretentious; extravagant, fancy, florid, glittery, spectacular; opulent, ornate, overdone, overwrought; absorbing, engrossing, enthralling, fascinating, interesting, riveting

near antonyms subtle; concealed, hidden, shrouded; dim, faint, obscure; insignificant, undistinguished, unimportant; modest, unaffected, unassuming, unpretentious; conservative, plain, quiet, simple, unaffected, understated; muted, restrained, subdued, subtle, toned-down

antonyms inconspicuous, unemphatic, unnoticeable, unobtrusive, unremarkable

notification *n* a published statement informing the public of a matter of general interest — see ANNOUNCEMENT

notion *n* **1** **notions** *pl* small useful items ⟨the fabric

store had a wide variety of thread, pins, buttons, and other *notions*⟩

synonyms novelties, odds and ends, sundries

related words bauble(s), bric-a-brac, gewgaw(s), knickknack(s), trinket(s); hodgepodge, miscellany, variety

2 a sudden impulsive and apparently unmotivated idea or action — see WHIM

3 an idea that is believed to be true or valid without positive knowledge — see OPINION 1

4 something imagined or pictured in the mind — see IDEA

notoriety *n* the fact or state of being known to the public — see FAME

notorious *adj* **1** not respectable — see DISREPUTABLE

2 widely known — see FAMOUS

notwithstanding *adv* in spite of that — see HOWEVER

notwithstanding *prep* without being prevented by — see DESPITE

nourish *vb* **1** to help the growth or development of — see FOSTER 1

2 to supply with nourishment — see SUSTAIN 1

nourishing *adj* providing the substances necessary for health and bodily growth — see NUTRITIOUS

novel *adj* not known or experienced before — see NEW 2

novelette *n* a work with imaginary characters and events that is shorter and usually less complex than a novel — see STORY 1

novella *n* a work with imaginary characters and events that is shorter and usually less complex than a novel — see STORY 1

novelty *n* **1** the quality or appeal of being new ⟨the *novelty* of having a cat quickly wore off⟩

synonyms freshness, newness, originality

related words strangeness, unfamiliarity, unusualness; progressiveness; up-to-dateness; departure, divergence, innovation, offshoot, shoot

near antonyms banality, commonness, familiarity, staleness

2 novelties *pl* small useful items — see NOTION 1

3 a small object displayed for its attractiveness or interest — see KNICKKNACK

novice *n* a person who is just starting out in a field of activity — see BEGINNER

now *adv* **1** at the present time ⟨that company doesn't make those toys *now* because they are unsafe⟩

synonyms anymore, currently, nowadays, presently, right now, today

related words here

near antonyms away, far, farthest, remotest; heretofore, hitherto, since; ago, previously

antonyms before, formerly, long, once, then

2 not long ago — see NEWLY

3 on some occasions — see SOMETIMES

4 without delay — see IMMEDIATELY

now *conj* for the reason that — see SINCE

now *n* the time currently existing or in progress — see PRESENT 1

nowadays *adv* at the present time — see NOW 1

noway *or* **noways** *adv* not in any degree, way, or under any condition — see NEVER 2

no way *adv* certainly not — see HARDLY 2

nowise *adv* not in any degree, way, or under any condition — see NEVER 2

noxious *adj* **1** bad for the well-being of the body — see UNHEALTHY 1

THESAURUS

2 causing or capable of causing harm — see HARMFUL

nth *adj* of the greatest or highest degree or quantity — see ULTIMATE 1

nub *n* 1 a small uneven mass — see LUMP 1

2 the central part or aspect of something under consideration — see CRUX

nubbin *n* a very small piece — see BIT 1

nubble *n* a small uneven mass — see LUMP 1

nubbly *adj* having small pieces or lumps spread throughout — see CHUNKY 1

nubby *adj* having small pieces or lumps spread throughout — see CHUNKY 1

nucleus *n* a thing or place that is of greatest importance to an activity or interest — see CENTER 1

nude *adj* lacking or shed of clothing — see NAKED 1

nudge *vb* to pass lightly across or touch gently especially in passing — see BRUSH

nugget *n* a small uneven mass — see LUMP 1

nuisance *n* 1 one who is obnoxiously annoying ⟨my little brother was being a *nuisance* by poking and prodding me throughout the long car trip⟩
synonyms annoyance, annoyer, bother, gadfly, gnawer, persecutor, pest, tease, teaser
related words headache; harrier, heckler; hassle, plague; molester, tormentor, torturer
near antonyms charmer, smoothy (*or* smoothie)
2 something that is a source of irritation — see ANNOYANCE 3

null *adj* 1 having no legal or binding force ⟨the contract was *null* because the other person forgot to sign it⟩
synonyms invalid, nonbinding, nonvalid, null and void, void
related words illegal; useless, worthless; ineffective, ineffectual
near antonyms legal; working
antonyms binding, good, valid
2 having no usefulness — see WORTHLESS

null and void *adj* having no legal or binding force — see NULL 1

nullify *vb* to put an end to by formal action — see ABOLISH

numb *adj* lacking in sensation or feeling ⟨I sat in one position too long and now my feet are *numb*⟩
synonyms asleep, benumbed, dead, insensitive, numbed, unfeeling
related words chilled, nipped; anesthetized, deadened, drugged, stupefied; insensible, senseless, unconscious; inanimate, insensate
near antonyms awake
antonyms feeling, sensitive

numb *vb* to reduce or weaken in strength or feeling — see DULL 1

numbed *adj* lacking in sensation or feeling — see NUMB

number *n* a character used to represent a mathematical value ⟨asked him to write out the equation in *numbers*, not letters⟩
synonyms digit, figure, integer, numeral, whole number
related words decimal, fraction; cipher; symbol

number *vb* 1 to find the sum of (a collection of things) by noting each one as it is being added — see COUNT 1

2 to have a total of — see AMOUNT (TO) 1

3 to have as part of a whole — see INCLUDE

numberless *adj* too many to be counted — see COUNTLESS

numbing *adj* having a low or subnormal temperature — see COLD 1

numbness *n* a lack of emotion or emotional expressiveness — see APATHY 1

numeral *n* a character used to represent a mathematical value — see NUMBER

numerate *vb* 1 to make a list of — see ¹LIST 1

2 to specify one after another — see ENUMERATE 1

numerous *adj* being of a large but indefinite number — see MANY

numskull *or* **numbskull** *n* a stupid person — see IDIOT

nuptial *adj* of or relating to marriage — see MARITAL

nuptial *n, usually* **nuptials** *pl* a ceremony in which two people are united in matrimony — see WEDDING

nurse *n* a girl or woman employed to care for a young child or children ⟨sent his little son back to his *nurse* so that he could return to his study to work⟩
synonyms babysitter, nursemaid, nurser, sitter
related words mammy; governess

nurse *vb* 1 to attend to the needs and comforts of ⟨took some time to *nurse* his grandmother, helping her get from one room to the other and making sure she was warm⟩
synonyms care (for), minister (to), mother
related words cure, heal, remedy; doctor, treat; aid, conserve, preserve, provide (for), support; baby, coddle, mollycoddle, pamper, spoil; cater (to), humor; indulge
phrases look after, look out for, look to, see to, take care of
near antonyms brush (aside *or* off), forget, ignore, neglect, overlook, slight
2 to keep in one's mind or heart — see HARBOR 1
3 to treat with great or excessive care — see BABY

nursemaid *n* a girl or woman employed to care for a young child or children — see NURSE

nurser *n* a girl or woman employed to care for a young child or children — see NURSE

nurture *vb* 1 to help the growth or development of — see FOSTER 1

2 to provide (someone) with moral or spiritual understanding — see ENLIGHTEN 2

3 to supply with nourishment — see SUSTAIN 1

nut *n* 1 a person of odd or whimsical habits — see ECCENTRIC

2 a person who lacks good sense or judgment — see FOOL 1

3 a person with a strong and habitual liking for something — see FAN

4 a person judged to be legally or medically insane — see LUNATIC 1

nutrient *adj* providing the substances necessary for health and bodily growth — see NUTRITIOUS

nutritional *adj* providing the substances necessary for health and bodily growth — see NUTRITIOUS

nutritious *adj* providing the substances necessary for health and bodily growth ⟨opted for a *nutritious* snack and bought an apple instead of a candy bar⟩
synonyms nourishing, nutrient, nutritional, nutritive
related words dietary, dietetic; beneficial, healthful, healthy, restorative, salubrious, salutary, wholesome

near antonyms insalubrious, unhealthful, unhealthy, unwholesome
antonyms nonnutritious
nutritive *adj* providing the substances necessary for health and bodily growth — see NUTRITIOUS
nuts *adj* **1** having or showing a very abnormal or sick state of mind — see INSANE 1
2 showing urgent desire or interest — see EAGER
nuts (about) *adj* filled with an intense or excessive love for — see ENAMORED (OF)
nuttiness *n* lack of good sense or judgment — see FOOLISHNESS 1
nutty *adj* **1** having or showing a very abnormal or sick state of mind — see INSANE 1
2 showing or marked by a lack of good sense or judgment — see FOOLISH 1

nuzzle *vb* to lie close ⟨newborn puppies *nuzzling* against their mother to stay warm⟩
synonyms cuddle, nestle, snuggle
related words curl up; crouch, huddle
near antonyms blench, flinch, quail, recoil, shrink, shy, start, wince
nymph *n* **1** a mythical goddess represented as a young girl and said to live outdoors ⟨she bought the book of fairy tales for the beautiful engravings of *nymphs* and fairies featured between the stories⟩
synonyms dryad, naiad, oread
related words mermaid, siren
2 a young wingless often wormlike form (as a grub or caterpillar) that hatches from the egg of many insects — see LARVA

oaf *n* a big clumsy often slow-witted person ⟨it is not polite to call your brother a stupid *oaf*⟩
synonyms clod, gawk, hulk, lout, lubber, lug
related words chump, loser, schlemiel, turkey; ass, blockhead, dolt, donkey, dope, dumbbell, dummy, goon, half-wit, idiot, ignoramus, imbecile, jackass, moron, nincompoop, ninny, nitwit, simpleton; beast, boor, brute, cad, churl, clown, creep, cretin, cur, heel, louse, skunk, snake, stinker, villain; booby, fool, goose, loony (*also* looney), lunatic, madman, nut; featherbrain, scatterbrain; rascal, rogue, scamp
near antonyms brain, genius; egghead, intellectual, sage, thinker
oafish *adj* not having or showing an ability to absorb ideas readily — see STUPID 1
oafishness *n* the quality or state of lacking intelligence or quickness of mind — see STUPIDITY 1
oar *vb* to move a boat by means of oars — see ¹ROW
oarsman *n* a person who drives a boat forward by means of oars ⟨the only *oarsman* in a rowboat designed for two⟩
synonyms rower, sculler
related words coxswain, crewman; puller, sailor
oath *n* a person's solemn declaration that he or she will do or not do something — see PROMISE
obduracy *n* a steadfast adherence to an opinion, purpose, or course of action — see OBSTINACY
obdurate *adj* **1** having or showing a lack of sympathy or tender feelings — see HARD 1
2 sticking to an opinion, purpose, or course of action in spite of reason, arguments, or persuasion — see OBSTINATE
obedience *n* **1** a bending to the authority or control of another ⟨the drill sergeant demanded complete and unquestioning *obedience* from the recruits⟩
synonyms compliance, conformity, observance, submission, subordination
related words acquiescence, agreeability, amenability; docility, submissiveness; capitulation, surrender, yielding; servility, slavishness, subservience; inhibition, repression, restraint, suppression; control, discipline, order

near antonyms contrariness, frowardness, intractability, rebelliousness, recalcitrance, refractoriness; disrespect, impudence, insolence, rudeness; insurgency, insurrection, mutiny, revolt; hardheadedness, mulishness, obstinacy, perversity, stubbornness, willfulness; misbehavior, mischievousness, naughtiness; dissent, dissidence
antonyms disobedience, insubordination, noncompliance, rebelling, rebellion
2 a readiness or willingness to yield to the wishes of others — see COMPLIANCE 1
obedient *adj* readily giving in to the command or authority of another ⟨that boy is so *obedient* that he does everything the first time he is asked⟩
synonyms amenable, compliant, conformable, docile, law-abiding, submissive, tractable
related words acquiescent, agreeable, amiable, obliging; surrendering, yielding; obsequious, servile, slavish, subservient; decorous, disciplined, mannerly, orderly; constrained, curbed, inhibited, repressed, restrained; controllable, governable, manageable; gentle, meek, mild
near antonyms insurgent, mutinous; dogged, hardheaded, headstrong, mulish, obdurate, obstinate, peevish, pigheaded, self-willed, stubborn, unyielding, willful (*or* wilful); obstreperous, restive, uncontrollable, ungovernable, unmanageable, wild; balky, defiant, perverse, resistant, wayward; bad, disorderly, errant, misbehaving, mischievous, naughty; ill-bred, undisciplined; dissident, nonconformist; disrespectful, ill-mannered, impolite, impudent, insolent, rude
antonyms contrary, disobedient, froward, insubordinate, intractable, rebellious, recalcitrant, refractory, unruly
obese *adj* having an excess of body fat — see FAT 1
obesity *n* the condition of having an excess of body fat — see CORPULENCE
obey *vb* to act according to the commands of ⟨it is important to *obey* your teachers immediately in the case of an emergency⟩ ⟨most people *obey* the law and wear their seat belts⟩
synonyms comply (with), conform (to), follow, mind, observe

related words defer (to), submit (to), surrender (to), yield (to); accede (to), acquiesce (to), agree (to), assent (to); attend, hear, heed, listen (to), mark, note, notice, regard, watch

phrases abide by

near antonyms challenge, dare; rebel (against); defy; direct, lead; brush off, disregard, ignore, overlook, overpass, pass over, tune out, wink (at); dismiss, pooh-pooh, shrug off; break, transgress, violate; deride, flout, scorn

antonyms disobey

object *n* **1** something material that can be perceived by the senses ⟨I kept tripping over countless little *objects* scattered about the darkened room⟩

synonyms thing

related words article, item, piece; being, entity, substance; commodity, good, ware; accessory, accompaniment, bauble, curio; knickknack, spangle, token, trinket

2 one that has a real and independent existence — see ENTITY

3 something that one hopes or intends to accomplish — see GOAL

object *vb* to present an opposing opinion or argument ⟨they *objected* to the conductor's insistence that their train tickets were not valid⟩

synonyms demur, expostulate (with), kick, protest, remonstrate (with)

related words cavil, quibble; challenge, dare, defy; conflict (with), debate, dispute, hassle, quarrel, squabble, wrangle; complain, inveigh (against); balk (at), stick (at); censure, criticize, denounce; disobey, rebel (against); demonstrate (against)

phrases take exception

near antonyms approve, sanction; accept; accede (to), acquiesce (to), agree (with), assent (to); comply (with), obey; advocate, champion, defend, maintain, support, sustain, uphold

objection *n* a feeling or declaration of disapproval or dissent ⟨pardon me, but I have an *objection* to any plan that requires staying out all night⟩

synonyms challenge, complaint, demur, expostulation, fuss, protest, question, remonstrance

related words compunction, doubt, misgiving, qualm, scruple; difficulty, misunderstanding; cavil, quibble; argument, conflict, debate, dispute, dissent, hassle, quarrel, squabble; censure, criticism; defiance, disobedience, rebellion

near antonyms willingness; approval, sanction; acceptance, acquiescence, agreement, assent; compliance, obedience

objectionable *adj* provoking or likely to provoke protest ⟨that T-shirt displays *objectionable* images which are not appropriate for school⟩

synonyms censurable, exceptionable, obnoxious, offensive, reprehensible

related words bawdy, coarse, crude, dirty, filthy, foul, gross, indecent, lewd, nasty, obscene, smutty, vulgar; blamable, blameworthy, lascivious, pornographic, ribald, scurrilous; debasing, perverted, profane; racy, salty, suggestive; unacceptable, undesirable, unwanted, unwelcome; abhorrent, disgusting, loathsome, repellent (*also* repellant), repugnant, repulsive, revolting; disagreeable, displeasing, distasteful, unpleasant; bad, execrable, lousy, miserable; atrocious, infamous; indecent, indecorous, unbecoming; earthy, unprintable; naughty, wicked

near antonyms acceptable, agreeable, pleasant,

pleasing, welcome; good; approved, endorsed, sanctioned; abetted, encouraged, promoted, supported; becoming, correct, decent, decorous, exemplary, seemly; blameless, commendable, creditable; immaculate, perfect, pure, spotless

antonyms inoffensive, unobjectionable

objective *adj* **1** based on observation or experience — see EMPIRICAL

2 marked by justice, honesty, and freedom from bias — see FAIR 2

3 restricted to or based on fact — see FACTUAL 1

objective *n* something that one hopes or intends to accomplish — see GOAL

objectivity *n* lack of favoritism toward one side or another — see DETACHMENT 1

obligate *vb* to cause (a person) to give in to pressure — see FORCE

obligation *n* something one must do because of prior agreement ⟨their financial *obligations* keep them from giving to charities as much as they would like⟩

synonyms burden, charge, commitment, duty, need, responsibility

related words pledge, promise; arrangement, prearrangement, setup; compact, contract, covenant, pact; payment, tribute; compulsion, constraint, restraint; must, requirement; coercion, duress, force; appointment, engagement, reservation

near antonyms grace, postponement, stay; discharge, exemption, release, waiver; alternative, choice, option, pick, preference, selection

obligatory *adj* forcing one's compliance or participation by or as if by law — see MANDATORY

oblige *vb* **1** to do a service or favor for ⟨I would appreciate it greatly if you could *oblige* me by bringing a dessert to the party⟩

synonyms accommodate, favor

related words humor, indulge; coddle, mollycoddle, pamper; appease, conciliate, mollify, pacify, placate; delight, gladden, gratify, please, satisfy; abet, aid, assist, help, support; attend, care (for), minister (to), relieve, succor

near antonyms bother, discommode, disturb, incommode, inconvenience, trouble; burden, encumber, saddle, weigh; desert, disappoint, fail, let down; constrain, hamper, hamstring, hinder, hobble, hold back, impede, obstruct, restrain; frustrate, oppose, sabotage, thwart

antonyms disoblige

2 to cause (a person) to give in to pressure — see FORCE

obliged *adj* feeling or expressing gratitude — see GRATEFUL 1

oblique *adj* **1** inclined or twisted to one side — see AWRY

2 running in a slanting direction — see DIAGONAL

obliquely *adv* in a line or direction running from corner to corner — see CROSSWISE

obliterate *vb* to destroy all traces of — see ANNIHILATE 1

obliteration *n* the state or fact of being rendered nonexistent, physically unsound, or useless — see DESTRUCTION

oblivion *n* a state of being disregardful or unconscious of one's surroundings, concerns, or obligations ⟨for two weeks each year the stressed-out couple enjoy the blissful *oblivion* that comes with a vacation at the beach⟩

synonyms forgetfulness, obliviousness

related words ignorance, unawareness, unconsciousness, unfamiliarity

near antonyms memory, recall, recollection, remembrance; alertness, awareness, cognizance, consciousness

oblivious *adj* not informed about or aware of something — see IGNORANT 2

obliviousness *n* **1** a state of being disregardful or unconscious of one's surroundings, concerns, or obligations — see OBLIVION

2 the state of being unaware or uninformed — see IGNORANCE 1

obnoxious *adj* **1** causing intense displeasure, disgust, or resentment — see OFFENSIVE 1

2 provoking or likely to provoke protest — see OBJECTIONABLE

obscene *adj* **1** depicting or referring to sexual matters in a way that is unacceptable in polite society ⟨*obscene* language and artwork is forbidden in this school⟩

synonyms bawdy, coarse, crude, dirty, filthy, foul, gross, indecent, lascivious, lewd, nasty, pornographic, ribald, smutty, unprintable, vulgar, wanton

related words earthy, racy, salty, suggestive; indecorous, unbecoming; debasing, perverted, profane; naughty, wicked; exceptionable, objectionable, unacceptable, undesirable, unwanted, unwelcome; abhorrent, disgusting, loathsome, offensive, repellent (*also* repellant), repugnant, repulsive, revolting; distasteful, obnoxious, unpleasant; blamable, blameworthy, censurable, reprehensible; atrocious, infamous; abusive, scurrilous

near antonyms priggish, prim, prudish, puritanical, straitlaced (*or* straightlaced), Victorian; correct, decorous, genteel, polite, proper, seemly; innocuous, inoffensive; acceptable, agreeable, desirable, pleasant, pleasing, welcome; appropriate, becoming, fit, meet, suitable; immaculate, perfect, pure, spotless; approved, endorsed, sanctioned

antonyms clean, decent

2 causing intense displeasure, disgust, or resentment — see OFFENSIVE 1

obscenity *n* **1** the quality or state of being obscene ⟨the issue of whether *obscenity* is a fundamental part of rap music⟩

synonyms bawdiness, coarseness, crudeness, dirt, dirtiness, filth, filthiness, foulness, grossness, indecency, lasciviousness, lewdness, nastiness, ribaldry, smuttiness, vulgarity

related words raciness, saltiness, suggestiveness; perversion, profanity; naughtiness, wickedness; loathsomeness, offensiveness, repulsiveness; distastefulness, obnoxiousness, unpleasantness

near antonyms priggishness, primness, prudery, prudishness, puritanism; correctness, decency, decorousness, decorum, seemliness; appropriateness, fitness, suitability, suitableness; immaculateness, perfection, purity, spotlessness

2 a disrespectful or indecent word or expression — see SWEARWORD

obscure *adj* **1** having an often intentionally veiled or uncertain meaning ⟨a fantasy writer who likes to put lots of *obscure* references and images in her tales of wizards and warlocks⟩

synonyms ambiguous, cryptic, dark, darkling, deep, enigmatic (*also* enigmatical), equivocal, in-

scrutable, murky, mysterious, mystic, nebulous, occult

related words abstruse, esoteric, recondite; bleary, cloudy, dim, faint, foggy, fuzzy, hazy, indefinite, indistinct, indistinguishable, shadowy, unclear, uncertain, undefined, undetermined, vague; impenetrable, incomprehensible; inexplicable; eerie, uncanny, weird; impalpable, inappreciable, intangible, invisible; unanswerable, unknowable; baffling, bewildering, confounding, confusing, mystifying, perplexing, puzzling, unfathomable; difficult, complex, complicated, obtuse

near antonyms comprehensible, fathomable, intelligible, knowable, understandable; bright, distinct, evident; certain, firm, strong, sure; defined, determined; direct, straightforward; definite, exact, explicit; appreciable, palpable, tangible, visible; blatant, patent, unmistakable

antonyms clear, obvious, plain, unambiguous, unequivocal

2 not widely known ⟨he's an *obscure* artist now, but he's sure to be famous someday⟩

synonyms anonymous, nameless, uncelebrated, unknown, unnoted, unsung

related words insignificant, minor, unimportant; undistinguished, unexceptional; unpopular; faceless

near antonyms fabled, fabulous, legendary; infamous; distinguished, eminent, exceptional, great, illustrious, leading, notable, outstanding, prestigious, remarkable; important, significant; favorite, popular, preferred; estimable, honorable, reputable, respectable; influential, major

antonyms celebrated, famed, famous, noted, notorious, prominent, renowned, well-known

3 being without light or without much light — see DARK 1

4 not seen or understood clearly — see FAINT 1

obscure *vb* **1** to keep secret or shut off from view — see ¹HIDE 2

2 to make dark, dim, or indistinct — see CLOUD 1

obscured *adj* being without light or without much light — see DARK 1

obscurity *n* **1** the quality or state of having a veiled or uncertain meaning ⟨the 16th-century astrologer's predictions are so filled with *obscurity* that people can interpret them any way they want⟩

synonyms ambiguity, ambiguousness, darkness, equivocalness, equivocation, murkiness, nebulousness, opacity

related words cloudiness, dimness, faintness, fogginess, fuzziness, haziness, indefiniteness, indistinctness, uncertainty, vagueness; impenetrability, incomprehensibility; deepness, profoundness; intangibility, invisibility; abstruseness; complexity, complication, difficulty, obtuseness

near antonyms comprehensibility, intelligibility; brightness, distinctness; certainty, surety; definiteness, exactness, explicitness; directness, straightforwardness; palpability, tangibility, visibility

antonyms clarity, clearness, obviousness, plainness

2 the quality or state of being mostly or completely unknown ⟨the singer languished in relative *obscurity* for years before becoming famous⟩

synonyms anonymity

related words oblivion; inconspicuousness, invisibility; insignificance, unimportance; unpopularity *near antonyms* name, report, reputation, repute; popularity; importance, significance; distinction, eminence, glory, greatness, honor, illustriousness, note, preeminence, prominence; cachet, position, prestige, rank, standing, stature; acclaim, acknowledgment (*also* acknowledgement), praise, recognition; adoration, idolization

antonyms celebrity, fame, notoriety, renown

observable *adj* capable of being seen — see VISIBLE

observance *n* **1** an act of following a custom, rule, or law ⟨the *observance* of this family tradition would make your grandmother very happy⟩
synonyms observation
related words attention, heed, notice; respecting, upholding
near antonyms infraction, offense (*or* offence), sin, trespass, wrong; disregard, forgetting, ignoring, neglect, overlooking; delinquency, dereliction
antonyms breach, infringement, nonobservance, transgression, violation
2 an oft-repeated action or series of actions performed in accordance with tradition or a set of rules — see RITE
3 a bending to the authority or control of another — see OBEDIENCE 1
4 a state of being aware — see ATTENTION 2

observation *n* **1** a state of being aware — see ATTENTION 2
2 an act of following a custom, rule, or law — see OBSERVANCE 1

observational *adj* based on observation or experience — see EMPIRICAL

observatory *n* a high place or structure from which a wide view is possible — see LOOKOUT 1

observe *vb* **1** to act according to the commands of — see OBEY
2 to act properly in relation to — see KEEP 1
3 to keep one's eyes on — see WATCH 1
4 to make a statement of one's opinion — see REMARK 1
5 to make note of (something) through the use of one's eyes — see SEE 1
6 to take notice of and be guided by — see HEED 1

obsessed *adj* having extreme or relentless concern — see HUNG UP 1

obsession *n* something about which one is constantly thinking or concerned — see FIXATION

obsessive *adj* caused by or suggestive of an irresistible urge — see COMPULSIVE

obsolete *adj* having passed its time of use or usefulness ⟨the abacus was considered *obsolete* once the electronic calculator was invented⟩
synonyms antiquated, archaic, dated, moth-eaten, outdated, outmoded, out-of-date, outworn, passé
related words aging, obsolescent; discarded, disused, superannuated, worn-out; inoperable, unusable, unworkable, useless; dead, defunct, extinct; dormant, fallow, free, idle, inactive, inert, inoperative, latent; ancient, antediluvian, antique, fusty, musty, old, oldfangled, old-fashioned, old-time, old-world; aged, age-old, hoary, venerable; bygone, erstwhile, former, late, past; historic, historical
near antonyms contemporary, current, mod, modern, new, newfangled, new-fashioned, present-day, recent, ultramodern, up-to-date; fresh;

modernized, refurbished, remodeled, renewed; functional, operable, operational, workable; active, alive, busy, employed, functioning, operating, operative

obstacle *n* something that makes movement or progress more difficult — see ENCUMBRANCE

obstinacy *n* a steadfast adherence to an opinion, purpose, or course of action ⟨the mindless *obstinacy* of those people who continue to insist that the earth is flat⟩
synonyms doggedness, hardheadedness, mulishness, obduracy, peevishness, persistence, pertinaciousness, pertinacity, self-will, stubbornness, tenaciousness, tenacity, willfulness
related words perverseness, perversity, resistance, waywardness, wrongheadedness; hardness, inflexibility, relentlessness, sternness, strictness; certainty, determination, firmness, inexorability, resolve, rigidity, rigidness, steadfastness; contrariness, defiance, disobedience, insubordination, recalcitrance
near antonyms broad-mindedness, open-mindedness, reasonableness, receptivity; acceptance, acquiescence, flexibility, pliability; compliance, docility, obedience; submission, surrender, willingness, yielding; slavishness, subservience

obstinate *adj* sticking to an opinion, purpose, or course of action in spite of reason, arguments, or persuasion ⟨the child was *obstinate* about wanting that specific toy, despite being offered several others⟩
synonyms adamant, adamantine, dogged, hard, hardened, hardheaded, hardhearted, headstrong, immovable, implacable, inflexible, mulish, obdurate, opinionated, ossified, pat, peevish, pertinacious, perverse, pigheaded, rigid, self-willed, stubborn, unbending, uncompromising, unrelenting, unyielding, willful (*or* wilful)
related words hidebound, narrow-minded; resistant, wayward, wrongheaded; persistent, tenacious; iron, relentless; grim, severe, stern, strict; determined, firm, inexorable, resolved, single-minded, steadfast, sure, unflinching; contrary, disobedient, froward, insubordinate, intractable, recalcitrant, refractory, uncooperative, ungovernable, unmanageable, unruly; defiant, insurgent, mutinous; indomitable, invincible, unconquerable; confirmed, inveterate, unregenerate; demanding, exacting
near antonyms docile, law-abiding, obedient, submissive, tractable; accepting, receptive, responsive, willing; governable, manageable, reasonable, temperate; slavish, subservient
antonyms acquiescent, agreeable, amenable, compliant, complying, flexible, pliable, pliant, relenting, yielding

obstreperous *adj* engaging in or marked by loud and insistent cries especially of protest — see VOCIFEROUS

obstruct *vb* **1** to create difficulty for the work or activity of — see HAMPER
2 to prevent passage through — see CLOG 1

obstruction *n* something that makes movement or progress more difficult — see ENCUMBRANCE

obtain *vb* to receive as return for effort — see EARN 1

obtainable *adj* possible to get — see AVAILABLE 1

obtrude *vb* to interest oneself in what is not one's concern — see INTERFERE

obtrusive *adj* thrusting oneself where one is not welcome or invited — see INTRUSIVE

obtuse *adj* **1** lacking sharpness of edge or point — see DULL 1

2 not having or showing an ability to absorb ideas readily — see STUPID 1

obtuseness *n* the quality or state of lacking intelligence or quickness of mind — see STUPIDITY 1

obviate *vb* to keep from happening by taking action in advance — see PREVENT

obviating *n* the act or practice of keeping something from happening — see PREVENTION

obvious *adj* **1** not subject to misinterpretation or more than one interpretation — see CLEAR 2

2 very noticeable especially for being incorrect or bad — see EGREGIOUS

occasion *n* **1** a particular point at which an event takes place ⟨the *occasion* of our last meeting with our old friend was several years ago, unfortunately⟩

  synonyms moment, time

  related words flash, instant, jiffy, minute, second, shake, split second, trice, twinkle, wink; while

2 a favorable combination of circumstances, time, and place — see OPPORTUNITY

3 someone or something responsible for a result — see CAUSE 1

4 something that happens — see EVENT 1

occasional *adj* **1** lacking in steadiness or regularity of occurrence — see FITFUL

2 not often occurring or repeated — see INFREQUENT

occasionally *adv* on some occasions — see SOMETIMES

occult *adj* **1** being beyond one's powers to know, understand, or explain — see MYSTERIOUS 1

2 having an often intentionally veiled or uncertain meaning — see OBSCURE 1

3 having seemingly supernatural qualities or powers — see MYSTIC 1

occult *vb* to keep secret or shut off from view — see ¹HIDE 2

occupant *n* one who lives permanently in a place — see INHABITANT

occupation *n* the activity by which one regularly makes a living ⟨my primary *occupation* is as a stockbroker, but I'm a drummer in a rock band on the weekends⟩

  synonyms calling, employment, line, profession, trade, vocation, work

  related words racket; art, craft, handicraft; appointment, assignment, berth, billet, duty, function, job, office, place, position, post, situation; business, engagement, livelihood, living

  near antonyms avocation, hobby, pursuit

occupied *adj* involved in often constant activity — see BUSY 1

occupy *vb* **1** to hold the attention of — see ENGAGE 1

2 to keep, control, or experience as one's own — see HAVE 1

occur *vb* to take place — see HAPPEN

occur (to) *vb* to come into the mind of ⟨it didn't *occur to* me to ask until much later⟩

  synonyms dawn (on), strike

  related words appear, arrive, come, emerge, materialize; con, learn, memorize; recall, recollect, remember, reminisce

  near antonyms forget, unlearn; disregard, neglect, overlook

occurrence *n* something that happens — see EVENT 1

ocean *n* the whole body of salt water that covers nearly three-fourths of the earth ⟨the Vikings explored the *ocean* in small open boats, beginning in the eighth century⟩

  synonyms blue, brine, deep, sea, seven seas

  related words high seas, main, waters; basin; Davy Jones's locker

oceanic *adj* of or relating to the sea — see MARINE 1

ocular *adj* of, relating to, or used in vision — see VISUAL 1

odd *adj* **1** being one of a pair or set without a corresponding mate ⟨somehow, there's always at least one *odd* sock that comes out of the dryer⟩

  synonyms unmatched, unpaired

  related words alone, lone, only, single, singular, sole, solitary

  antonyms matched, paired

2 different from the ordinary in a way that causes curiosity or suspicion ⟨one girl dyed her hair purple with pink polka dots, which was a rather *odd* effect⟩

  synonyms bizarre, curious, far-out, funny, kinky, outlandish, out-of-the-way, outré, peculiar, quaint, queer, queerish, quirky, remarkable, screwy, strange, wacky, way-out, weird, wild

  related words aberrant, abnormal, atypical, extraordinary, fantastic, flaky, freak, freakish, idiosyncratic, phenomenal, singular, unique, unusual, unwonted; conspicuous, notable, noticeable, outstanding, prominent, salient, striking; atrocious, outrageous, shocking; nonconformist, unconventional, unorthodox; eccentric, idiosyncratic; rare, uncommon, uncustomary; baffling, bewildering, confounding, mystifying, perplexing, puzzling

  near antonyms average, commonplace, everyday, garden, ordinary, prosaic, routine, run-of-the-mill, typical, unexceptional, unremarkable, usual, workaday; conformist, conservative, conventional; expected, familiar, predictable; common, customary, frequent, habitual, regular, wonted

3 being out of the ordinary — see EXCEPTIONAL

4 noticeably different from what is generally found or experienced — see UNUSUAL 1

oddball *n* a person of odd or whimsical habits — see ECCENTRIC

oddity *n* **1** an odd or peculiar habit — see IDIOSYNCRASY

2 something strange or unusual that is an object of interest — see CURIOSITY 2

oddment *n* an unused or unwanted piece or item typically of small size or value — see ¹SCRAP 1

odds *n pl* a measure of how often an event will occur instead of another — see PROBABILITY 2

odds and ends *n pl* **1** small useful items — see NOTION 1

2 a remaining group or portion — see REMAINDER 1

odious *adj* causing intense displeasure, disgust, or resentment — see OFFENSIVE 1

odium *n* the state of having lost the esteem of others — see DISGRACE 1

odor *n* the quality of a thing that makes it perceptible to the sense organs in the nose — see SMELL 1

of *prep* **1** earlier than — see BEFORE 1

2 having to do with — see ABOUT 1

off *adv* from this or that place — see AWAY

off *adj* **1** falling short of a standard — see BAD 1

2 not being in a state of use, activity, or employment — see INACTIVE 2

3 not being in agreement with what is true — see FALSE 1

4 small in degree — see REMOTE 1

offbeat *adj* noticeably different from what is generally found or experienced — see UNUSUAL 1

offend *vb* **1** to commit an offense ⟨since this is the first time you've *offended,* we'll let you off lightly⟩

synonyms err, sin, transgress, trespass

related words breach, break, infringe, violate; backslide, lapse

phrases break the law, fall from grace

near antonyms forgive, justify; repent

2 to cause hurt feelings or deep resentment in — see INSULT

offender *n* a person who has committed a crime — see CRIMINAL

offense *or* **offence** *n* **1** a breaking of a moral or legal code ⟨wartime *offenses* that are crimes against all of humanity⟩

synonyms breach, crime, debt, error, lawbreaking, malefaction, misdeed, misdoing, sin, transgression, trespass, violation, wrongdoing

related words felony, misdemeanor; fault, foible, peccadillo; break, infringement; immorality, iniquity, sinfulness, vice, wickedness; criminality, illegality, lawlessness, unlawfulness

near antonyms blamelessness, faultlessness, guiltlessness, innocence; goodness, morality, righteousness, virtue, virtuousness

2 the act or action of setting upon with force or violence — see ATTACK 1

3 an act or expression showing scorn and usually intended to hurt another's feelings — see INSULT

4 the feeling of being offended or resentful after a slight or indignity — see PIQUE

offensive *adj* **1** causing intense displeasure, disgust, or resentment ⟨I find your disrespectful attitude toward religion very *offensive*⟩ ⟨the smell of rotting food is quite *offensive*⟩

synonyms abhorrent, abominable, appalling, awful, distasteful, dreadful, foul, hideous, horrendous, horrible, horrid, loathsome, nasty, nauseating, noisome, obnoxious, obscene, odious, repellent (*also* repellant), repugnant, repulsive, revolting, scandalous, shocking, sickening, ugly

related words exceptionable, objectionable; disagreeable, unpleasant; contemptible, despicable, detestable, hateful; unhealthy, unwholesome; execrable, lousy, miserable; atrocious, heinous, unspeakable; barbarous, unchristian, uncivilized, ungodly, unholy

near antonyms acceptable, agreeable, attractive, delectable, delightful, desirable, likable (*or* likeable), pleasant, pleasing, welcome; unobjectionable; healthy, wholesome

antonyms inoffensive

2 provoking or likely to provoke protest — see OBJECTIONABLE

offensive *n* the act or action of setting upon with force or violence — see ATTACK 1

offer *n* something which is presented for consideration — see PROPOSAL

offer *vb* **1** to put before another for acceptance or consideration ⟨I *offered* my boss an alternative to the plan that required me to work overtime⟩

synonyms extend, give, proffer, tender

related words pose, propose

near antonyms accept, receive, take; decline, refuse, reject; retract, withdraw; consider, contemplate, mull (over), ponder, study, think (over)

2 to set before the mind for consideration — see PROPOSE 1

3 to bring before the public in performance or exhibition — see PRESENT 1

4 to give up as an offering to a god — see SACRIFICE

offering *n* something offered to a god — see SACRIFICE

offhand *adj* made or done without previous thought or preparation — see EXTEMPORANEOUS

offhanded *adj* made or done without previous thought or preparation — see EXTEMPORANEOUS

office *n* a large unit of a governmental, business, or educational organization — see DIVISION 2

officeholder *n* a person who holds a public office — see OFFICIAL

officer *n* **1** a member of a force charged with law enforcement at the local level ⟨if you are ever lost, find the nearest *officer* and ask for help⟩

synonyms bobby [*British*], bull [*slang*], constable, cop, policeman, police officer

related words patrolman, policewoman; detective, inspector, plainclothesman; marshal, sheriff, trooper; captain, lieutenant, sergeant

2 a person who holds a public office — see OFFICIAL

official *adj* ordered or allowed by those in authority ⟨the *official* languages for those Olympic Games were French and English⟩

synonyms authorized, sanctioned

related words legal, permissible; approved, endorsed; abetted, encouraged, promoted, suggested, supported; certified, licensed (*also* licenced); authoritative, canonical, ex officio; semiofficial

near antonyms illegal, illicit, unlawful; unapproved, unendorsed, unlicensed

antonyms unauthorized, unofficial, unsanctioned

official *n* a person who holds a public office ⟨some of our best public *officials* do their jobs quietly and are never in the news⟩

synonyms functionary, officeholder, officer, public servant

related words bureaucrat; administrator, commissioner, director, executive, manager, superintendent, supervisor; chair, chairman

officious *adj* thrusting oneself where one is not welcome or invited — see INTRUSIVE

offing *n* time that is to come — see FUTURE 1

offset *n* a force or influence that makes an opposing force ineffective or less effective — see COUNTERBALANCE

offset *vb* to balance with an equal force so as to make ineffective ⟨if you get a high grade on this quiz, it will *offset* the D from your last one⟩

synonyms annul, cancel (out), compensate (for), correct, counteract, counterbalance, counterpoise, make up (for), neutralize

related words invalidate, negate, nullify; atone (for); outweigh, redeem; redress, relieve, remedy; override, overrule

offshoot *n* **1** a branch of a main stem especially of a plant ⟨we knew the rose bush had survived the winter when it began producing *offshoots* and turning green again⟩

synonyms outgrowth, shoot

related words excrescence, growth; bough, limb, twig; bud, floret; spray, sprig

2 something that naturally develops or is developed from something else — see DERIVATIVE

offspring *n* the descendants of a person, animal, or plant ⟨the racehorse's *offspring* all proved to be very good racers as well⟩ ⟨the couple celebrated their 50th wedding anniversary surrounded by three generations of *offspring*⟩

synonyms issue, posterity, progeny, seed, spawn
related words brood, hatch, litter, young; child, scion (*also* cion)
near antonyms ancestor, antecedent, forebear (*also* forebear), forefather, parent

offstage *adj or adv* off or away from the part of the stage visible to the audience ⟨please wait until you are *offstage* to start changing costumes⟩

synonyms backstage
related words upstage
phrases behind the scenes

oft *adv* many times — see OFTEN

often *adv* many times ⟨I seem to stumble *often* when I try to walk in high heels⟩

synonyms constantly, continually, frequently, oft, oftentimes (*or* ofttimes), repeatedly
related words always, consistently, continuously, perpetually; afresh, again, anew; commonly, ordinarily, regularly, routinely; intermittently, periodically, recurrently; generally, usually
phrases again and again, over and over, time after time, time and again
near antonyms occasionally, sometimes, sporadically, never; once
antonyms infrequently, rarely, seldom

oftentimes *or* **ofttimes** *adv* many times — see OFTEN

ogle *vb* to look at in a flirtatious or desiring way ⟨I do wish you two would stop *ogling* each other during class⟩

synonyms leer (at)
related words eye, gape, gawk, gaze, glare, goggle, peer, rubberneck, stare

ogre *n* **1** a strange or horrible and often frightening creature — see MONSTER 1

2 something or someone that causes fear or dread especially without reason — see BOGEY 1

oh *n* the numerical symbol 0 or the absence of number or quantity represented by it — see ZERO 1

oil *n* a picture created with usually oil paint — see PAINTING

oil *vb* to coat (something) with a slippery substance in order to reduce friction — see LUBRICATE

oiled *adj* having or being a surface so smooth as to make sliding or falling likely — see SLICK 1

oil painting *n* a picture created with usually oil paint — see PAINTING

oilskin *n* a coat made of water-resistant material — see RAINCOAT

OK *or* **okay** *adj* **1** being to one's liking — see SATISFACTORY 1

2 of a level of quality that meets one's needs or standards — see ADEQUATE

OK *or* **okay** *adv* **1** in a satisfactory way — see WELL 1

2 used to express agreement — see YES

OK *or* **okay** *n* an acceptance of something as satisfactory — see APPROVAL 1

OK *or* **okay** *vb* **1** to give official acceptance of something as satisfactory — see APPROVE

2 to have a favorable opinion of — see APPROVE (OF)

old *adj* **1** being of advanced years and especially past middle age — see ELDERLY

2 dating or surviving from the distant past — see ANCIENT 1

3 having been such at some previous time — see FORMER

older *adj* being of advanced years and especially past middle age — see ELDERLY

oldfangled *adj* pleasantly reminiscent of an earlier time — see OLD-FASHIONED 1

old-fashioned *adj* **1** pleasantly reminiscent of an earlier time ⟨an elegant, *old-fashioned* bun that was held in place with pearl hairpins⟩

synonyms antique, oldfangled, old-time, old-world, quaint
related words antiquated, obsolete; historic, historical, olden, traditional; outdated, outmoded, out-of-date, outworn, passé; dated, fusty, moth-eaten, musty; aged, age-old, ancient, antediluvian, fossilized, hoary, venerable; bygone, erstwhile, former, late, past; forgotten, remote; ageless, dateless; timeless
near antonyms fresh, new, up-to-date; chic, fashionable, smart, stylish; modernized, refurbished, remodeled, renewed
antonyms contemporary, hot, mod, modern, newfangled, new-fashioned, ultramodern

2 tending to favor established ideas, conditions, or institutions — see CONSERVATIVE 1

old hand *n* a person with long experience in a specified area — see VETERAN

old-maidish *adj* hard to please — see FINICKY

old man *n* **1** a male human parent — see FATHER 1

2 the male partner in a marriage — see HUSBAND

oldster *n* a person of advanced years — see SENIOR CITIZEN

old-time *adj* pleasantly reminiscent of an earlier time — see OLD-FASHIONED 1

old-timer *n* **1** a person of advanced years — see SENIOR CITIZEN

2 a person with long experience in a specified area — see VETERAN

old wives' tale *n* a false idea or belief — see FALLACY 1

old-world *adj* pleasantly reminiscent of an earlier time — see OLD-FASHIONED 1

omen *n* something believed to be a sign or warning of a future event ⟨some people believe that a black cat crossing your path is an *omen* that something bad is about to happen to you⟩

synonyms augury, auspice, boding, foreboding, foreshadowing, portent, prefiguring, presage
related words forerunner, harbinger, herald, precursor; foretaste, hint, inkling, intimation, suggestion; forewarning; forecast, foretelling, prediction, prognostication, prophecy; badge, mark, note, token

ominous *adj* being or showing a sign of evil or calamity to come ⟨that comment about downsizing from the company president sounded *ominous*⟩

synonyms baleful, dire, foreboding, inauspicious, menacing, portentous, sinister, threatening
related words black, dark, gloomy; unfavorable, unpromising; ill-fated, ill-starred, star-crossed, unfortunate, unlucky; evil, malign, malignant
near antonyms auspicious, benign, favorable, promising, propitious

omission *n* something left out ⟨the disk contains a selection of deleted scenes, and a couple of the *omissions* greatly add to the intelligibility of the movie's plot⟩
synonyms deletion
related words elimination; blank, skip; lapse, slip; deduction, reduction, subtraction
near antonyms inclusion; accretion, accrual, addendum, addition, augmentation, boost, gain, increase, increment, raise, rise, supplement

omit *vb* to miss the opportunity or obligation — see NEGLECT 3

omnibus *adj* covering everything or all important points — see ENCYCLOPEDIC

omnipotent *adj* having unlimited power or authority ⟨the nearly universal religious belief that God is *omnipotent* and can do anything⟩
synonyms all-powerful, almighty
related words great, sovereign, supreme, towering, transcendent; authoritative, chief, majestic, masterful; mighty, potent, powerful, strong; divine, godlike
near antonyms helpless, impotent, powerless; limited, restricted

omnipresent *adj* present in all places and at all times ⟨seeking some much-needed relief from the *omnipresent* noise of the big city⟩
synonyms ubiquitous, universal
related words boundless, endless, illimitable, immeasurable, indefinite, infinite, limitless, measureless, unbounded, unfathomable, unlimited
near antonyms bounded, circumscribed, confined, finite, limited, restricted

on *adj* being in effective operation — see ACTIVE 1

on *adv* **1** toward a point ahead in space or time — see ONWARD 1
2 toward or at a point lying in advance in space or time — see ALONG

on *prep* **1** having to do with — see ABOUT 1
2 in or into contact with — see AGAINST

oncoming *adj* being soon to appear or take place — see FORTHCOMING

one *adj* known but not named — see CERTAIN 1

one–dimensional *adj* having or showing a lack of depth of understanding or character — see SUPERFICIAL 2

onerous *adj* **1** difficult to endure — see HARSH 1
2 requiring much time, effort, or careful attention — see DEMANDING 1

one–sided *adj* inclined to favor one side over another — see PARTIAL 1

one–sidedness *n* an attitude that always favors one way of feeling or acting especially without considering any other possibilities — see BIAS

onetime *adj* having been such at some previous time — see FORMER

ongoing *adj* **1** being in progress or development ⟨we do seem to be making some headway on that *ongoing* project⟩ ⟨the ever *ongoing* quest for knowledge by men and women of science⟩
synonyms afoot, proceeding, under way
related words functioning, happening, operating, working; afloat, alive, going; advancing, gaining
near antonyms receding, regressing, retrogressing
antonyms arrested, halted, stalled, stopped
2 existing or in progress right now — see PRESENT 1

only *adj* **1** having no equal or rival for excellence or desirability ⟨the *only* way to really appreciate the beauty of the forest is to walk through it⟩

synonyms incomparable, inimitable, matchless, nonpareil, peerless, unequaled (*or* unequalled), unexampled, unmatched, unparalleled, unrivaled (*or* unrivalled), unsurpassable, unsurpassed
related words singular, unique; exceptional, extraordinary, rare, uncommon, unusual; A1, bang-up, banner, boss [*slang*], capital, classic, dandy, excellent, fabulous, fine, first-class, first-rate, grand, great, groovy, jim-dandy, keen, marvelous (*or* marvellous), mean, neat, par excellence, prime, superb, superior, superlative, terrific, tiptop, top-notch; better, preferred; exceptional, fancy, high-grade, special
near antonyms common, everyday, normal, ordinary, usual; inferior, lesser, worse, worst; bad, low, lower; low-grade, substandard, unsatisfactory; mediocre, second-class, second-rate; atrocious, execrable, wretched
2 being the one or ones of a class with no other members ⟨that is the *only* possible right answer⟩ ⟨we were the *only* passengers on the tour bus⟩
synonyms alone, lone, singular, sole, solitary, special, unique
related words solo, unaccompanied, unattended; incomparable, inimitable, matchless, peerless, unequaled (*or* unequalled), unmatched, unparalleled, unrivaled (*or* unrivalled), unsurpassable, unsurpassed; distinct, distinctive, individual, separate
near antonyms manifold, multifarious, myriad; assorted, heterogenous, miscellaneous, mixed, motley

only *adv* **1** for nothing other than — see SOLELY 1
2 not long ago — see NEWLY
3 nothing more than — see JUST 3

only *conj* if it were not for the fact that — see EXCEPT

onrush *n* forward movement in time or place — see ADVANCE 1

onset *n* **1** the act or action of setting upon with force or violence — see ATTACK 1
2 the point at which something begins — see BEGINNING

onslaught *n* the act or action of setting upon with force or violence — see ATTACK 1

onward *also* **onwards** *adv* **1** toward a point ahead in space or time ⟨we must continue to move *onward,* or we will die in this desert⟩
synonyms ahead, forth, forward, on
near antonyms backward
2 toward or at a point lying in advance in space or time — see ALONG

oodles *n* a considerable amount — see LOT 2

ooze *n* soft wet earth — see MUD

ooze *vb* to flow forth slowly through small openings — see EXUDE 1

oozy *adj* full of or covered with soft wet earth — see MUDDY 1

opacity *n* the quality or state of having a veiled or uncertain meaning — see OBSCURITY 1

opaque *adj* not seen or understood clearly — see FAINT 1

open *adj* **1** allowing passage without obstruction ⟨thank you for clearing out the hallway so that it's *open* again⟩
synonyms clear, cleared, free, unclogged, unclosed, unobstructed, unstopped
related words emptied, unoccupied, vacant; exposed, revealed; gaping, wide, yawning; unbarred, unbolted, unclasped, unfastened, unlatched, un-

locked, unsealed; unbuttoned, unclenched, unfolded, unfurled, unzipped
near antonyms constricted, cramped, encumbered, hampered, hindered, impeded, interfered (with), trammeled; barricaded, blockaded, dammed
antonyms blocked, clogged, closed, jammed, obstructed, plugged, shut, stopped, stuffed, uncleared
2 freely available for use or participation by all ⟨the beach's *open* sand castle-building contest that every year attracts competitors of all ages and abilities⟩
synonyms free-for-all, public, unrestricted
related words collective, common, communal, shared; accessible, available, free; unregulated
near antonyms limited; inaccessible, unavailable
antonyms closed, exclusive, off-limits, private, restricted
3 being in a situation where one is likely to meet with harm — see LIABLE 1
4 free in expressing one's true feelings and opinions — see FRANK
5 lacking a usual or natural covering — see NAKED 2
6 not known by only a select few — see PUBLIC 1
7 not yet settled or decided — see PENDING 1
8 willing to consider new or different ideas — see OPEN-MINDED 1
open *n* that part of the physical world that is removed from human habitation — see NATURE 2
open *vb* **1** to change from a closed to an open position ⟨please *open* the door to let the cat out⟩
synonyms unclose
related words unbar, unbolt, unclasp, unfasten, unlatch, unlock; unbutton, unclench, unfold, unfurl, unzip; disengage, release, slip
near antonyms bar, bolt, clasp, fasten, latch, lock; button (up), zip (up)
antonyms close, shut
2 to arrange clear passage of (something) by removing obstructions ⟨we need to *open* this drain that's clogged with hair⟩
synonyms clear, free, unclog, unstop
related words ease, facilitate, loosen (up), smooth
near antonyms constrict, encumber, hamper, hinder, impede, interfere (with), obstruct, trammel; barricade, blockade
antonyms block, clog (up), close, dam (up), plug (up), stop
3 to arrange the parts of (something) over a wider area ⟨when we got too close, the cardinal *opened* its wings and flew to a higher branch⟩
synonyms expand, extend, fan (out), flare (out), spread (out), stretch (out), outspread, outstretch, unfold
related words overspread
near antonyms compact, compress, condense, reduce
antonyms close, contract, fold
4 to rid the surface of (as an area) from things in the way — see CLEAR 1
5 to take the first step in (a process or course of action) — see BEGIN 1
open–air *adj* of, relating to, or held in the open air — see OUTDOORS
open air *n* that part of the physical world that is removed from human habitation — see NATURE 2
open–and–shut *adj* not subject to misinterpreta-

tion or more than one interpretation — see CLEAR 2
open–eyed *adj* paying close attention usually for the purpose of anticipating approaching danger or opportunity — see ALERT 1
openhanded *adj* giving or sharing in abundance and without hesitation — see GENEROUS 1
openhandedness *n* the quality or state of being generous — see LIBERALITY
openhearted *adj* free in expressing one's true feelings and opinions — see FRANK
openheartedness *n* **1** the free expression of one's true feelings and opinions — see CANDOR
2 the quality or state of being generous — see LIBERALITY
opening *n* **1** a favorable combination of circumstances, time, and place — see OPPORTUNITY
2 a place in a surface allowing passage into or through a thing — see HOLE 1
3 an open space in a barrier (as a wall or hedge) — see GAP 1
open–minded *adj* **1** willing to consider new or different ideas ⟨all I ask is that you try to be *open-minded* when we present our suggestions⟩
synonyms broad-minded, open, receptive
related words impartial, neutral, objective, unbiased, unprejudiced; easygoing, tolerant; calm, detached, dispassionate; amenable, compliant; impressionable, suggestible, susceptible; persuadable, persuasible
near antonyms biased, one-sided, partial, partisan, prejudiced; bigoted, intolerant
antonyms narrow-minded
2 not bound by traditional ways or beliefs — see LIBERAL 1
openmouthed *adj* filled with amazement or wonder ⟨I was *openmouthed* at the stunning view from the mountaintop⟩
synonyms amazed, astonished, astounded, awed, awestruck, dumbfounded (*or* dumfounded), flabbergasted, marveling (*or* marvelling), wondering
related words startled, surprised; bemused, bewildered, puzzled; overwhelmed, staggered, stunned, stupefied
near antonyms unimpressed; disinterested, incurious, indifferent, unconcerned, uninterested; dispassionate, emotionless, impassive, unemotional; bored, jaded
openness *n* **1** the free expression of one's true feelings and opinions — see CANDOR
2 the state of being left without shelter or protection against something harmful — see EXPOSURE 1
open sesame *n* something that allows someone to achieve a desired goal — see PASSPORT
operable *adj* capable of or suitable for being used for a particular purpose — see USABLE 1
operate *vb* **1** to control the mechanical operation of ⟨do not *operate* heavy machinery, including cars, after taking this medication⟩
synonyms handle, run, work
related words use; maneuver, manipulate, ply, wield; command, control, direct, drive, guide, pilot, steer
2 to look after and make decisions about — see CONDUCT 1
3 to produce a desired effect — see ACT 2
4 to put into action or service — see USE 1
operating *adj* being in effective operation — see ACTIVE 1

THESAURUS

operation *n* **1** a specific task with which a person or group is charged — see MISSION
2 a usually fixed or ordered series of actions or events leading to a result — see PROCESS 1
3 the act or activity of looking after and making decisions about something — see CONDUCT 1
4 the act or practice of employing something for a particular purpose — see USE 1

operational *adj* being in effective operation — see ACTIVE 1

operative *adj* being in effective operation — see ACTIVE 1

operative *n* **1** a person who tries secretly to obtain information for one country in the territory of another usually unfriendly country — see SPY
2 a person whose business is solving crimes and catching criminals or gathering information that is not easy to get — see DETECTIVE

opiate *adj* tending to cause sleep — see HYPNOTIC

opine *vb* to make a statement of one's opinion — see REMARK 1

opinion *n* **1** an idea that is believed to be true or valid without positive knowledge ⟨my *opinion* is that such interference was unnecessary⟩
synonyms belief, conviction, eye, feeling, judgment (*or* judgement), mind, notion, persuasion, sentiment, verdict, view
related words say; impression, perception, take; attitude; assumption, presumption, presupposition; conclusion, decision, determination; deliverance, esteem, estimate, estimation; credence, credit, faith; concept, conception, idea, thought; position, stand; comment, observation, reflection, remark; conjecture, guess, hunch, hypothesis, surmise, theory; advice, recommendation, suggestion; angle, outlook, perspective, point of view, shoes, slant, standpoint, viewpoint
near antonyms fact, truth
2 a position arrived at after consideration — see DECISION 1

opinionated *adj* sticking to an opinion, purpose, or course of action in spite of reason, arguments, or persuasion — see OBSTINATE

opponent *n* **1** one that takes a position opposite another in a competition or conflict ⟨in martial arts, before the match begins, always bow to your *opponent*⟩
synonyms adversary, antagonist, rival
related words equal, match; enemy, foe; archenemy, nemesis; competitor, contestant; bane, bête noire, curse; assailant, attacker, combatant, invader
near antonyms accomplice, ally, confederate, partner; advocate, champion, exponent, proponent, supporter
2 one that is hostile toward another — see ENEMY

opportune *adj* especially suitable for a certain time — see TIMELY 1

opportunist *n* one who does things only for his own benefit and with little regard for right and wrong — see SELF-SEEKER

opportunity *n* a favorable combination of circumstances, time, and place ⟨this art school could be a wonderful *opportunity* for you to finally develop your talent for painting⟩
synonyms chance, occasion, opening, room
related words break; play, way; juncture, pass

oppose *vb* **1** to refuse to give in to — see RESIST
2 to strive to reduce or eliminate — see FIGHT 2

opposite *adj* being as different as possible ⟨your

suggestion that we hold the meeting at night is precisely *opposite* to our original plan for a nice breakfast⟩
synonyms antipodal, antipodean, antithetical, contradictory, contrary, diametric (*or* diametrical), polar
related words adverse, negative, unfavorable; antagonistic, antipathetic, counter, hostile; converse, inverse, reverse; disparate, dissimilar, divergent, unalike, unlike
near antonyms alike, analogous, like, similar; equivalent, identical, same; synonymous
antonyms noncontradictory

opposite *n* something that is as different as possible from something else ⟨no matter what I say, you insist on the *opposite*⟩
synonyms antipode, antithesis, contrary, negative, reverse
related words negation; antonym; converse, inverse
near antonyms synonym; analogue, counterpart; carbon copy, copy, duplicate, replica

opposition *n* the inclination to resist — see RESISTANCE 1

oppress *vb* **1** to make sad — see DEPRESS 1
2 to subject to incapacitating emotional or mental stress — see OVERWHELM 1

oppression *n* a state or spell of low spirits — see SADNESS

oppressive *adj* difficult to endure — see HARSH 1

oppressively *adv* in a manner so as to cause loss or suffering — see HARDLY 1

oppressor *n* **1** a person who causes repeated emotional pain, distress, or annoyance to another — see TORMENTOR
2 a person who uses power or authority in a cruel, unjust, or harmful way — see DESPOT

opprobrium *n* the state of having lost the esteem of others — see DISGRACE 1

opt *vb* to come to a judgment after discussion or consideration — see DECIDE 1

opt (for) *vb* to decide to accept (someone or something) from a group of possibilities — see CHOOSE 1

optic *adj* of, relating to, or used in vision — see VISUAL 1

optical *adj* of, relating to, or used in vision — see VISUAL 1

optimism *n* an inclination to believe in the most favorable outcome ⟨your perpetual *optimism* even when things look bleak⟩
synonyms sanguinity
related words brightness, cheerfulness, perkiness, sunniness; hope, hopefulness, rosiness; idealism
near antonyms pessimism, skepticism; cynicism; desperation, discouragement, disheartenment, hopelessness; bleakness, cheerlessness, dreariness, gloom, gloominess; pragmatism, realism

optimistic *adj* having qualities which inspire hope — see HOPEFUL 1

option *n* **1** the act or power of making one's own choices or decisions — see FREE WILL
2 the power, right, or opportunity to choose — see CHOICE 1

optional *adj* subject to one's freedom of choice ⟨certain activities are *optional,* and you may choose not to participate if you wish⟩
synonyms discretionary, elective, voluntary
related words alternative, chosen; dispensable, unnecessary, unneeded, unwanted

near antonyms essential, indispensable, necessary, requisite

antonyms compulsory, mandatory, nonelective, obligatory, required

opulence *n* the total of one's money and property — see WEALTH 1

opulent *adj* **1** having goods, property, or money in abundance — see RICH 1

2 showing obvious signs of wealth and comfort — see LUXURIOUS

opulently *adv* in a luxurious manner — see HIGH

opus *n* a literary, musical, or artistic production — see COMPOSITION 1

oral *adj* **1** created by the body's organs of sound — see VOCAL

2 made or carried on through speaking rather than in writing — see VERBAL 2

orate *vb* **1** to talk as if giving an important and formal speech ⟨politicians will *orate* lengthily at any opportunity⟩

synonyms declaim, discourse, harangue, mouth (off)

related words rant, rave; lecture, preach; advertise, announce, broadcast, declare, proclaim, pronounce; speak, talk

2 to give a formal often extended talk on a subject — see TALK 1

oration *n* a usually formal discourse delivered to an audience — see SPEECH 1

oratorical *adj* marked by the use of impressive-sounding but mostly meaningless words and phrases — see RHETORICAL

oratory *n* **1** the art of speaking in public eloquently and effectively ⟨this debate class will teach you all to be skilled at *oratory*⟩

synonyms elocution

related words bombast, grandiloquence; rhetoric; discourse, speech, talk

2 language that is impressive-sounding but not meaningful or sincere — see RHETORIC 1

orb *n* a more or less round body or mass — see ¹BALL 1

orbit *vb* to pass completely around — see ENCIRCLE 1

orchestra *n* a usually large group of musicians playing together — see ²BAND 1

ordain *vb* **1** to determine the fate of in advance — see DESTINE

2 to give an order — see COMMAND 2

ordeal *n* a test of faith, patience, or strength — see TRIAL 1

order *n* **1** the way objects in space or events in time are arranged or follow one another ⟨you always keep your books in perfect alphabetical *order*⟩ ⟨we haven't found out the *order* of the speeches yet⟩

synonyms arrangement, array, disposal, disposition, distribution, ordering, sequence, setup

related words continuity; precedence, priority; chain, progression, succession; series; aligning, alignment, lining up; design, layout, pattern, structure, system

near antonyms confusion, disorder, disorganization, disruption, upset; disconnection, disjointedness

2 a group of persons formally joined together for some common interest — see ASSOCIATION 2

3 a number of persons or things that are grouped together because they have something in common — see SORT 1

4 a piece of metal given in honor of a special event, a person, or an achievement — see MEDAL

5 a state of being or fitness — see CONDITION 1

6 a statement of what to do that must be obeyed by those concerned — see COMMAND 1

7 one of the segments of society into which people are grouped — see CLASS 1

8 one of the units into which a whole is divided on the basis of a common characteristic — see CLASS 2

order *vb* **1** to put into a particular arrangement ⟨I've *ordered* all of my CDs according to type of music⟩ ⟨he likes to *order* his life so that there are few surprises⟩

synonyms arrange, array, classify, codify, dispose, draw up, marshal, organize, range, systematize

related words groom, make up, spruce (up), straighten (up), tidy (up); unscramble; align, line, line up, queue; alphabetize, file; emplace, place, set; display, lay out, map (out)

antonyms derange, disarrange, disarray, disorder, mess (up), muss (up), rumple, upset

2 to give a request or demand for ⟨they *ordered* hamburgers for lunch⟩

synonyms ask (for), request, requisition

related words commission, solicit; charter, hire, license (*also* licence)

phrases call for

3 to give an order — see COMMAND 2

4 to issue orders to (someone) by right of authority — see COMMAND 1

ordering *n* **1** a scheme of rank or order — see ³SCALE 1

2 the way objects in space or events in time are arranged or follow one another — see ORDER 1

orderly *adj* **1** being clean and in good order — see NEAT 1

2 following a set method, arrangement, or pattern — see METHODICAL

ordinance *n* a rule of conduct or action laid down by a governing authority and especially a legislator — see LAW 1

ordinarily *adv* according to the usual course of things — see NATURALLY 2

ordinary *adj* **1** being of the type that is encountered in the normal course of events ⟨it was a perfectly *ordinary* and undistinguished shirt⟩

synonyms average, common, commonplace, everyday, garden, normal, prosaic, routine, run-of-the-mill, standard, unexceptional, unremarkable, usual, workaday

related words regular, typical; familiar, homely, plain, popular, vulgar; natural; customary, wonted; insignificant, trivial, unimportant; customary, frequent, habitual; expected, predictable

near antonyms curious, funny, peculiar, quaint, queer; aberrant, atypical, irregular; rare, scarce; fantastic, phenomenal; bizarre, far-out, outrageous, outré, weird, wild; eccentric, idiosyncratic, nonconformist, unconventional, unorthodox; freak, freakish; conspicuous, notable, outstanding, prominent, salient, signal, striking; singular, unique

antonyms abnormal, exceptional, extraordinary, odd, out-of-the-way, strange, unusual

2 of average to below average quality — see MEDIOCRE 1

3 often observed or encountered — see COMMON 1

ordnance *n* large firearms (as cannon or rockets) — see ARTILLERY

oread *n* a mythical goddess represented as a young girl and said to live outdoors — see NYMPH 1

organ *n* **1** a publication that appears at regular intervals — see JOURNAL

2 something used to achieve an end — see AGENT 1

organization *n* a group of persons formally joined together for some common interest — see ASSOCIATION 2

organize *vb* to put into a particular arrangement — see ORDER 1

organized *adj* following a set method, arrangement, or pattern — see METHODICAL

orient *vb* to impart knowledge of a new thing or situation to — see ACQUAINT 1

orientate *vb* to impart knowledge of a new thing or situation to — see ACQUAINT 1

orifice *n* a place in a surface allowing passage into or through a thing — see HOLE 1

origin *n* the line of ancestors from whom a person is descended — see ANCESTRY

original *adj* **1** coming before all others in time or order — see FIRST 1

2 having the skill and imagination to create new things — see CREATIVE 1

3 not known or experienced before — see NEW 2

original *n* something from which copies are made ⟨please make copies to hand out, but keep the *original*⟩
synonyms archetype, prototype
related words example, paradigm, pattern; beau ideal, exemplar, classic, ideal, model, nonpareil, paragon; blueprint, draft
near antonyms copy, imitation, replica, reproduction; counterfeit, fake, forgery, sham

originality *n* **1** the quality or appeal of being new — see NOVELTY 1

2 the skill and imagination to create new things — see CREATIVITY 1

originally *adv* in the beginning ⟨we *originally* planned to go out tonight, but we changed our minds⟩
synonyms firstly, initially, primarily
related words incipiently; primitively
phrases at first
near antonyms finally, lastly, ultimately

originate *vb* to come into existence — see BEGIN 2

originator *n* **1** one who creates or introduces something new — see INVENTOR

2 a person who establishes a whole new field of endeavor — see FATHER 2

orison *n* an address to God or a deity — see PRAYER 1

ornament *n* something that decorates or beautifies — see DECORATION 1

ornament *vb* to make more attractive by adding something that is beautiful or becoming — see DECORATE

ornamental *adj* serving to add beauty — see DECORATIVE

ornamental *n* a small object displayed for its attractiveness or interest — see KNICKKNACK

ornate *adj* elaborately and often excessively decorated ⟨an *ornate* gambling casino that is designed to look like an Italian palace⟩
synonyms bedizened, florid, gingerbread, overdecorated, overwrought
related words arabesque, baroque, rococo; extravagant, flamboyant, spectacular, splashy; flashy, garish, gaudy, glitzy, loud, ostentatious; pretentious, showy, swank, tawdry; elaborate, extreme; adorned, arrayed, beautified, bedecked, decked, decorated, dressed, embellished, enriched, garnished, ornamented, trimmed; flowery, frilly, lacy; enhanced, heightened, intensified; bossed, chased, emblazoned, embossed, embroidered, flounced, fringed, garlanded, gilded, laced, wreathed
near antonyms bare, denuded, exposed, naked, stripped, uncovered; modest, simple, unassuming, unpretentious; conservative, muted, quiet, restrained, subdued, tasteful, toned-down, understated, unobtrusive
antonyms austere, plain, severe, stark, unadorned

ornery *adj* having or showing a habitually bad temper — see ILL-TEMPERED

orthodox *adj* **1** following or agreeing with established form, custom, or rules — see FORMAL 1

2 tending to favor established ideas, conditions, or institutions — see CONSERVATIVE 1

oscillation *n* a series of slight movements by a body back and forth or from side to side — see VIBRATION

ossified *adj* sticking to an opinion, purpose, or course of action in spite of reason, arguments, or persuasion — see OBSTINATE

ostensible *adj* appearing to be true on the basis of evidence that may or may not be confirmed — see APPARENT 1

ostensibly *adv* to all outward appearances — see APPARENTLY

ostentation *n* excessive or unnecessary display ⟨the sheer *ostentation* of the rock star's mansion was overwhelming⟩
synonyms flamboyance, flashiness, garishness, gaudiness, glitz, ostentatiousness, pretentiousness, showiness, swank
related words extravaganza, pageant, parade, show; dazzle, pageantry, spectacle; adornment, decoration, dressing, embellishment, garnishment, ornamentation, trimming; extravagance, fanciness, luxuriousness, opulence, richness, sumptuousness; loudness, luridness; meretriciousness, tawdriness, vulgarity
near antonyms conservativeness, moderation, modesty, restraint, simplicity, understatement; elegance, gracefulness, tastefulness
antonyms austerity, plainness, severity

ostentatious *adj* **1** excessively showy — see GAUDY

2 self-consciously trying to present an appearance of grandeur or importance — see PRETENTIOUS 1

ostentatiousness *n* excessive or unnecessary display — see OSTENTATION

other *adj* **1** being not of the same kind — see DIFFERENT 1

2 resulting in an increase in amount or number — see ADDITIONAL

other *adv* in a different way — see OTHERWISE

otherwise *adv* in a different way ⟨a serious student who always does his best, for his conscience will not let him do *otherwise*⟩
synonyms differently, else, other
related words diversely, variously
near antonyms similarly
antonyms likewise

ought (to) *vb* to be under necessity or obligation to — see NEED 2

ounce *n* a very small amount — see PARTICLE 1

oust *vb* **1** to drive or force out — see EJECT 1
2 to remove from a position of prominence or power (as a throne) — see DEPOSE 1

out *adv* **1** in or into the open air — see OUTDOORS
2 with one's normal voice speaking the words — see ALOUD

out *adj* not at a certain place — see ABSENT 1

out *n* the act or a means of getting or keeping away from something undesirable — see ESCAPE 2

out *vb* to become known — see GET OUT 1

out–and–out *adj* **1** having no exceptions or restrictions — see ABSOLUTE 2
2 trying all possibilities — see EXHAUSTIVE

outbrave *vb* to oppose (something hostile or dangerous) with firmness or courage — see FACE 2

outbreak *n* a sudden and usually temporary growth of activity ⟨there was an immediate *outbreak* of paper shuffling and a pretense of work when the teacher re-entered the room⟩
synonyms burst, flare, flare-up, flash, flicker, flurry, flutter, outburst, spurt
related words binge, jag, spree; boost, increase, pickup, upswing, upturn; epidemic, eruption, explosion, paroxysm; deluge, flood, rush, spate, surge; commotion, furor, uproar
near antonyms calm, doldrums, slump

outburst *n* **1** a sudden intense expression of strong feeling ⟨when the coach suddenly started crying hysterically, everyone was shocked by the unexpected *outburst*⟩
synonyms agony, burst, eruption, explosion, fit, flare, flare-up, flash, flush, gale, gush, gust, paroxysm, spasm, storm
related words blowup, grouch, rage, tantrum; ecstasy, rapture, transport; delirium, frenzy, furor
2 a sudden and usually temporary growth of activity — see OUTBREAK

outcast *n* one who is cast out or rejected by society ⟨they were convinced that they would become total *outcasts* if they didn't buy the newest fashions⟩
synonyms castaway, castoff, pariah, reject
related words untouchable; outsider; deportee, exile
near antonyms insider

outcome *n* a condition or occurrence traceable to a cause — see EFFECT 1

outcry *n* a violent shouting — see CLAMOR 1

outdated *adj* having passed its time of use or usefulness — see OBSOLETE

outdistance *vb* to be greater, better, or stronger than — see SURPASS 1

outdo *vb* to be greater, better, or stronger than — see SURPASS 1

outdoor *also* **outdoors** *adj* of, relating to, or held in the open air ⟨an *outdoor* picnic is always at the mercy of the weather, of course⟩
synonyms open-air, out-of-door (*or* out-of-doors)
related words airy; exterior, external, outer, outside, outward; outermost, outmost
near antonyms inner, inside, interior, internal, inward; inmost, innermost
antonyms indoor

outdoors *adv* in or into the open air ⟨please wait until you're *outdoors* to run around and scream⟩
synonyms out, outside
related words without
near antonyms in, inside, within
antonyms indoors

outdoors *n* that part of the physical world that is removed from human habitation — see NATURE 2

outer *adj* situated on the outside or farther out ⟨the *outer* edge of the blade of your figure skate always wears out faster than the inner because you use it more⟩
synonyms exterior, external, outside, outward
related words outermost, outlying, outmost; superficial, surface
near antonyms inmost, innermost
antonyms inner, inside, interior, internal, inward

outermost *adj* most distant from a center — see EXTREME 1

outfit *n* **1** clothing chosen as appropriate for a specific situation ⟨you'll need a special *outfit* for the scout troop⟩ ⟨do you want to buy a new *outfit* for the Halloween party?⟩
synonyms costume, dress, garb, getup, guise, togs
related words apparel, attire, clothes, duds, raiment; fashion, mode, style; array, caparison, vestments
2 a commercial or industrial activity or organization — see ENTERPRISE 1
3 a group of people working together on a task — see GANG 1
4 items needed for the performance of a task or activity — see EQUIPMENT
5 the distinctive clothing worn by members of a particular group — see UNIFORM

outfit *vb* to provide (someone) with what is needed for a task or activity — see FURNISH 1

outflow *n* a flowing or going out ⟨there was an immediate *outflow* of students from the door when the bell rang⟩
synonyms exodus, gush, outpouring
related words drain, flow; ebb, reflux; rush, stampede; emigration, flight; discharge, emanation, emission
near antonyms deluge, flood, inundation, overflow, spate, torrent; flow, river, stream, tide
antonyms flux, inflow, influx, inrush

outfox *vb* to get the better of through cleverness — see OUTWIT

outgo *n* a payment made in the course of achieving a result — see EXPENSE

outgoing *adj* likely to seek or enjoy the company of others — see CONVIVIAL

outgrowth *n* **1** a branch of a main stem especially of a plant — see OFFSHOOT 1
2 a condition or occurrence traceable to a cause — see EFFECT 1
3 something that naturally develops or is developed from something else — see DERIVATIVE

outing *n* a short trip for pleasure — see EXCURSION 1

outlander *n* a person who is not native to or known to a community — see STRANGER

outlandish *adj* **1** different from the ordinary in a way that causes curiosity or suspicion — see ODD 2
2 excitingly or mysteriously unusual — see EXOTIC

outlast *vb* to last longer than ⟨I truly hope this car will *outlast* our previous one⟩ ⟨your work will probably *outlast* you⟩
synonyms outlive, outwear
related words survive; outstay; abide (beyond), endure (past), hold (past), hold out (past), last (beyond), persist (beyond); draw out, perpetuate; succeed

outlaw *vb* to order not to do or use or to be done or used — see FORBID

outlawed *adj* that may not be permitted — see IMPERMISSIBLE

outlawing *n* the act of ordering that something not be done or used — see PROHIBITION 1

outlay *n* a payment made in the course of achieving a result — see EXPENSE

outlet *n* a place or means of going out — see EXIT 1

outline *n* 1 a line that traces the outer limits of an object or surface ⟨place your hand on the paper and draw an *outline* around it⟩
synonyms contour, figure, silhouette
related words delineation, sketch; profile, skyline; form, cast, configuration, conformation, geometry, shape; framework, skeleton
2 a short statement of the main points — see SUMMARY

outline *vb* 1 to draw or make apparent the outline of ⟨she carefully *outlined* the tree before she started drawing in the leaves⟩
synonyms define, delineate, silhouette, sketch, trace
related words line; bound, fringe, margin, skirt; edge, hem, rim, trim; frame; circle, compass, encircle, girdle, girth, loop, ring, round, surround; chart, diagram, draw, map (out)
2 to make into a short statement of the main points (as of a report) — see SUMMARIZE

outlive *vb* to last longer than — see OUTLAST

outlook *n* 1 a high place or structure from which a wide view is possible — see LOOKOUT 1
2 a way of looking at or thinking about something — see POINT OF VIEW
3 all that can be seen from a certain point — see VIEW 1

out loud *adv* with one's normal voice speaking the words — see ALOUD

outmaneuver *vb* to get the better of through cleverness — see OUTWIT

outmoded *adj* having passed its time of use or usefulness — see OBSOLETE

outmost *adj* most distant from a center — see EXTREME 1

out-of-date *adj* having passed its time of use or usefulness — see OBSOLETE

out-of-door *or* **out-of-doors** *adj* of, relating to, or held in the open air — see OUTDOORS

out-of-doors *n* that part of the physical world that is removed from human habitation — see NATURE 2

out-of-the-way *adj* different from the ordinary in a way that causes curiosity or suspicion — see ODD 2

outpouring *n* a flowing or going out — see OUTFLOW

output *n* something produced by physical or intellectual effort — see PRODUCT 1

outrage *n* 1 an act or expression showing scorn and usually intended to hurt another's feelings — see INSULT
2 an intense emotional state of displeasure with someone or something — see ANGER

outrage *vb* 1 to cause hurt feelings or deep resentment in — see INSULT
2 to make angry — see ANGER

outraged *adj* feeling or showing anger — see ANGRY

outrank *vb* to be greater in importance than — see OUTWEIGH

outré *adj* different from the ordinary in a way that causes curiosity or suspicion — see ODD 2

outright *adj* having no exceptions or restrictions — see ABSOLUTE 2

outset *n* the point at which something begins — see BEGINNING

outshine *vb* to be greater, better, or stronger than — see SURPASS 1

outside *adj* 1 situated on the outside or farther out — see OUTER
2 small in degree — see REMOTE 1

outside *adv* in or into the open air — see OUTDOORS

outside *n* 1 an outer part or layer — see EXTERIOR
2 the greatest amount, number, or part — see MOST

outside *prep* 1 not including — see EXCEPT
2 out of the reach or sphere of — see BEYOND 2

outside of *prep* 1 not including — see EXCEPT
2 out of the reach or sphere of — see BEYOND 2

outsider *n* a person who is not native to or known to a community — see STRANGER

outsize *also* **outsized** *adj* 1 unusually large — see HUGE
2 of a size greater than average of its kind — see LARGE

outskirts *n pl* the area around a city — see ENVIRONS 1

outsmart *vb* to get the better of through cleverness — see OUTWIT

outspoken *adj* free in expressing one's true feelings and opinions — see FRANK

outspread *vb* to arrange the parts of (something) over a wider area — see OPEN 3

outstanding *adj* 1 not yet paid ⟨there are several *outstanding* bills left, but at least we paid the rest⟩
synonyms overdue, owed, owing, payable, unpaid, unsettled
related words due, mature
near antonyms prepaid
antonyms cleared, liquidated, paid (off *or* up), repaid, settled
2 standing above others in rank, importance, or achievement — see EMINENT

outstretch *vb* to arrange the parts of (something) over a wider area — see OPEN 3

outstrip *vb* to be greater, better, or stronger than — see SURPASS 1

outward *adj* situated on the outside or farther out — see OUTER

outwear *vb* to last longer than — see OUTLAST

outweigh *vb* to be greater in importance than ⟨the need to finish your homework *outweighs* your desire to see your favorite TV show⟩
synonyms outrank, overbalance, overshadow, overweigh
related words count, import, matter, mean, signify, weigh; dwarf; exceed, outstrip, surpass, transcend

outwit *vb* to get the better of through cleverness ⟨a plan to *outwit* their opponents at their own game⟩
synonyms fox, outfox, outsmart, outmaneuver, overreach
related words outguess, second-guess; baffle, balk, circumvent, foil, frustrate, thwart; cozen, deceive, dupe, fool, gull, trick; conquer, defeat, lick, overcome; bar, block, hinder, impede, obstruct

outworn *adj* having passed its time of use or usefulness — see OBSOLETE

oval *adj* having the shape of an egg ⟨the *Oval* Office in the White House⟩
  synonyms elliptic (*or* elliptical), ovate, ovoid
ovate *adj* having the shape of an egg — see OVAL
ovation *n* enthusiastic and usually public expression of approval — see APPLAUSE
over *adj* brought or having come to an end — see COMPLETE 2
over *adv* **1** from one side to the other of an intervening space ⟨let's swim *over* to that island⟩
  synonyms across, through
  related words clear
  2 yet another time — see AGAIN 1
  3 to or in a higher place — see ABOVE
  4 from beginning to end — see THROUGH 1
  5 toward or in a lower position — see DOWN
over *prep* **1** higher than — see ABOVE
  2 in the course of — see DURING
  3 on or to the farther side of — see BEYOND 1
  4 to the opposite side of — see ACROSS
  5 in random positions within the boundaries of — see AROUND 2
overabundance *n* the state or an instance of going beyond what is usual, proper, or needed — see EXCESS
overactive *adj* being in a state of increased activity or agitation — see FEVERISH 1
overage *n* the state or an instance of going beyond what is usual, proper, or needed — see EXCESS
overall *adj* **1** belonging or relating to the whole — see GENERAL 1
  2 relating to the main elements and not to specific details — see GENERAL 2
overall *adv* for the most part — see CHIEFLY
over and above *prep* in addition to — see BESIDES 1
overbalance *vb* to be greater in importance than — see OUTWEIGH
overbear *vb* to achieve a victory over — see BEAT 2
overbearing *adj* fond of ordering people around — see BOSSY
overbold *adj* foolishly adventurous or bold — see FOOLHARDY 1
overburden *vb* to fill or load to excess — see OVERLOAD
overcast *adj* covered over by clouds ⟨the dark, *overcast* sky made the whole day seem depressing⟩
  synonyms beclouded, clouded, cloudy, dull, hazed, hazy, heavy, lowering (*also* louring), overclouded
  related words bedimmed, befogged, blackened, darkened, darksome, dim, dimmed, dulled, dusky, misty, murky, obscure, obscured, overshadowed; sunless; black, bleak, cheerless, dark, desolate, dismal, drear, dreary, funereal, gloomy, glum, gray (*also* grey), somber (*or* sombre), sullen
  near antonyms sunny, sunshiny; brightened, brilliant, dazzling, illuminated, illumined, lighted (*or* lit), lightened, radiant, shiny
  antonyms clear, cloudless
overcast *vb* to make dark, dim, or indistinct — see CLOUD 1
overcharge *vb* **1** to charge (someone) too much for goods or services ⟨I think that store may have *overcharged* us for the shoes, which were supposed to be on sale⟩
  synonyms gouge, soak, sting, surcharge

  related words cheat, defraud, stick; clip, fleece, skin
  antonyms undercharge
  2 to fill or load to excess — see OVERLOAD
overcloud *vb* to make dark, dim, or indistinct — see CLOUD 1
overclouded *adj* covered over by clouds — see OVERCAST
overcoat *n* a warm outdoor coat ⟨put your *overcoat* on—it's freezing out there!⟩
  synonyms greatcoat, surcoat, topcoat
  related words chesterfield, frock coat, mackinaw, ulster; jacket, parka; oilskin, raincoat, sou'wester; wrap
  near antonyms undercoat
overcome *vb* **1** to achieve a victory over — see BEAT 2
  2 to subject to incapacitating emotional or mental stress — see OVERWHELM 1
overconfident *adj* foolishly adventurous or bold — see FOOLHARDY 1
overcritical *adj* given to making or expressing unfavorable judgments about things — see CRITICAL 1
overdecorated *adj* elaborately and often excessively decorated — see ORNATE
overdo *vb* to describe or express in too strong terms — see OVERSTATE
overdraw *vb* to describe or express in too strong terms — see OVERSTATE
overdue *adj* **1** not arriving, or occurring, or settled at the due, usual, or proper time — see LATE 1
  2 not yet paid — see OUTSTANDING 1
overeat *vb* to eat greedily or to excess — see GORGE 2
overeater *n* one who eats greedily or too much — see GLUTTON
overestimate *vb* to place too high a value on ⟨they *overestimated* their ability to do the work on such short notice⟩
  synonyms overrate, overvalue
  related words appreciate, cherish, prize, treasure, value; admire, esteem, regard, respect; adore, idolize, revere, reverence, venerate, worship
  near antonyms belittle, decry, depreciate, disparage; despise, disdain, scorn; abhor, abominate, detest, loathe
  antonyms underestimate, underrate, undervalue
overfamiliar *adj* showing a lack of proper social reserve or modesty — see PRESUMPTUOUS 1
overfill *vb* **1** to fill or load to excess — see OVERLOAD
  2 to flow over the brim or top of — see OVERFLOW 1
overflow *n* **1** a great flow of water or of something that overwhelms — see FLOOD
  2 the state or an instance of going beyond what is usual, proper, or needed — see EXCESS
overflow *vb* **1** to flow over the brim or top of ⟨the tea in the cup *overflowed* onto the saucer⟩
  synonyms overfill, run over
  related words boil over, spill, well (up); flow, flush, gush, pour, sluice, spout, spurt, stream; deluge, drown, engulf, flood, inundate, overwhelm, submerge, submerse, swamp; wash (over); brim, cascade, slop, slosh
  near antonyms recede
  2 to cover or become filled with a flood — see FLOOD

overgrown *adj* covered with a thick, healthy natural growth — see LUSH 1

overhang *n* a part that sticks out from the general mass of something — see BULGE

overhang *vb* **1** to extend outward beyond a usual point — see BULGE
2 to remain poised to inflict harm, danger, or distress on — see THREATEN

overhaul *vb* to move fast enough to get even with — see OVERTAKE

overhead *adv* to or in a higher place — see ABOVE

overhear *vb* to listen to (another in private conversation) — see EAVESDROP (ON)

overjoy *vb* **1** to fill with overwhelming emotion (as wonder or delight) — see ENTRANCE
2 to fill with great joy — see ELATE

overkill *n* the state or an instance of going beyond what is usual, proper, or needed — see EXCESS

overlap *n* a partial covering of one thing by an adjoining thing ⟨the orthodontist will try to fix that *overlap* of two of your upper incisors⟩
synonyms lapping, overlaying, overlying, overspreading
related words shingling

overlap *vb* to lie over parts of one another ⟨there were so many papers on the desk that many of them *overlapped*⟩
synonyms lap, overlay, overlie, overspread
related words shingle

overlay *vb* **1** to form a layer over — see COVER 2
2 to lie over parts of one another — see OVERLAP

overlaying *n* a partial covering of one thing by an adjoining thing — see OVERLAP

overlie *vb* **1** to lie over parts of one another — see OVERLAP
2 to form a layer over — see COVER 2

overload *vb* to fill or load to excess ⟨try not to *overload* your backpack, or you could end up with back problems⟩
synonyms overburden, overcharge, overfill
related words stuff; burden, charge, encumber, lade, load, lumber, saddle, weight
near antonyms lighten, unburden, unload

overlook *vb* **1** to look down on ⟨the fortress *overlooks* the city⟩
synonyms command, dominate
related words face, front
2 to fail to give proper attention to — see NEGLECT 1

overly *adv* beyond a normal or acceptable limit — see TOO 1

overlying *n* a partial covering of one thing by an adjoining thing — see OVERLAP

overmaster *vb* to subject to incapacitating emotional or mental stress — see OVERWHELM 1

overmatch *vb* to achieve a victory over — see BEAT 2

overmuch *adj* going beyond a normal or acceptable limit in degree or amount — see EXCESSIVE

overmuch *adv* beyond a normal or acceptable limit — see TOO 1

overmuch *n* the state or an instance of going beyond what is usual, proper, or needed — see EXCESS

overpass *vb* to fail to give proper attention to — see NEGLECT 1

overpower *vb* **1** to bring under one's control by force of arms — see CONQUER 1
2 to subject to incapacitating emotional or mental stress — see OVERWHELM 1

overpowering *n* the act or process of bringing someone or something under one's control — see CONQUEST

overpraise *n* excessive praise — see FLATTERY

overpraise *vb* to praise too much — see FLATTER 1

overrate *vb* to place too high a value on — see OVERESTIMATE

overreach *vb* **1** to get the better of through cleverness — see OUTWIT
2 to go beyond the limit of — see EXCEED

overripe *adj* having lost forcefulness, courage, or spirit — see EFFETE 1

overrun *vb* **1** to enter for conquest or plunder — see INVADE
2 to go beyond the limit of — see EXCEED
3 to spread or swarm over in a troublesome manner — see INFEST

oversee *vb* **1** to look after and make decisions about — see CONDUCT 1
2 to be in charge of — see BOSS 1
3 to take charge of especially on behalf of another — see ²TEND 1

overshadow *vb* **1** to make dark, dim, or indistinct — see CLOUD 1
2 to be greater in importance than — see OUTWEIGH

overshoot *vb* to go beyond the limit of — see EXCEED

oversight *n* **1** the act or activity of looking after and making decisions about something — see CONDUCT 1
2 an unintentional departure from truth or accuracy — see ERROR 1
3 the duty or function of watching or guarding for the sake of proper direction or control — see SUPERVISION 1
4 the nonperformance of an assigned or expected action — see FAILURE 1

oversize *or* **oversized** *adj* **1** unusually large — see HUGE
2 of a size greater than average of its kind — see LARGE

overspread *vb* **1** to form a layer over — see COVER 2
2 to lie over parts of one another — see OVERLAP

overspreading *n* a partial covering of one thing by an adjoining thing — see OVERLAP

overstate *vb* to describe or express in too strong terms ⟨it appears you've somewhat *overstated* your computer skills, if you can't find the "on" button!⟩
synonyms exaggerate, overdo, overdraw, put on
related words color, elaborate, embellish, embroider, magnify, pad, stretch; fudge, hedge; overemphasize, overplay
near antonyms belittle, minimize, play down
antonyms understate

overstatement *n* the representation of something in terms that go beyond the facts — see EXAGGERATION

overstep *vb* to go beyond the limit of — see EXCEED

oversupply *n* the state or an instance of going beyond what is usual, proper, or needed — see EXCESS

overtake *vb* to move fast enough to get even with ⟨she had to hurry to *overtake* her friends, who had forgotten their umbrellas⟩ ⟨the thunderstorm *overtook* them suddenly⟩

synonyms catch up (with), overhaul
related words chase, pursue; gain, reach; pass, surpass
near antonyms fall short
overthrow *n* failure to win a contest — see DEFEAT 1
overtop *vb* to be greater, better, or stronger than — see SURPASS 1
overturn *vb* to turn on one's side or upside down — see CAPSIZE
overvalue *vb* to place too high a value on — see OVERESTIMATE
overweening *adj* 1 having too high an opinion of oneself — see CONCEITED
2 going beyond a normal or acceptable limit in degree or amount — see EXCESSIVE
3 having a feeling of superiority that shows itself in an overbearing attitude — see ARROGANT
overweigh *vb* to be greater in importance than — see OUTWEIGH
overweight *adj* having an excess of body fat — see FAT 1
overwhelm *vb* 1 to subject to incapacitating emo-

tional or mental stress ⟨just the thought of how much work there is to do *overwhelms* me⟩
synonyms carry away, crush, devastate, floor, oppress, overcome, overmaster, overpower, prostrate, snow under, swamp, whelm
related words deluge, drown; confute, defeat, refute; demoralize, distress, disturb, rock, shatter, stagger, unman, unnerve, upset
2 to cover or become filled with a flood — see FLOOD
overwrought *adj* 1 being in a state of increased activity or agitation — see FEVERISH 1
2 elaborately and often excessively decorated — see ORNATE
ovoid *adj* having the shape of an egg — see OVAL
owed *adj* not yet paid — see OUTSTANDING 1
owing *adj* not yet paid — see OUTSTANDING 1
owing to *prep* as the result of — see BECAUSE OF
own *vb* to keep, control, or experience as one's own — see HAVE 1
own (up) *vb* to accept the truth or existence of (something) usually reluctantly — see ADMIT
owner *n* one who has a legal or rightful claim to ownership — see PROPRIETOR

pa *n* a male human parent — see FATHER 1
pace *vb* to move along with a steady regular step especially in a group — see MARCH 1
pacific *adj* 1 tending to lessen or avoid conflict or hostility ⟨as a *pacific* gesture, we invited our feuding neighbors to our backyard barbecue⟩
synonyms appeasing, conciliating, conciliatory, disarming, mollifying, pacifying, peacemaking, placating, propitiatory
related words endearing, ingratiating; peaceable, peaceful; nonbelligerent, unaggressive, unassertive; calming, comforting, quieting, soothing; obliging, satisfying; affable, amiable, amicable, benevolent, gentle, kind, kindly; submissive, surrendering, yielding
near antonyms aggravating, annoying, exasperating, inflammatory, irritating, nettling, offensive, provocative, provoking, vexing; engaging, incensing, infuriating, maddening; antagonistic, hostile; aggressive, assertive, bellicose, belligerent, combative, contentious, pugnacious, quarrelsome, scrappy, truculent; martial, militant, military, warlike
antonyms antagonizing
2 inclined to live in peace and to avoid war — see PEACEFUL 1
pacifist *n* a person who opposes war or warlike policies — see DOVE 1
pacify *vb* to lessen the anger or agitation of ⟨the only thing that would *pacify* the child and end the tantrum was a new toy⟩
synonyms appease, conciliate, disarm, mollify, placate, propitiate
related words calm, comfort, console, content, quiet, soothe; endear (to), ingratiate; delight, gladden, gratify, please; blarney, flatter, overpraise, soft-soap; assuage, quench, sate, satiate,

satisfy; cater (to), humor, indulge; blandish, cajole, coax, wheedle; coddle, mollycoddle, pamper, spoil
near antonyms aggravate, annoy, bother, bug, chafe, cross, exasperate, gall, get, grate, irk, irritate, nettle, peeve, pique, put out, rankle, rile, roil, ruffle, vex; provoke, rouse; harass, harry, pester; agitate, distress, disturb, fret, perturb, upset; affront, insult, offend
antonyms anger, enrage, incense, infuriate, madden, outrage
pacifying *adj* 1 tending to calm the emotions and relieve stress — see SOOTHING 1
2 tending to lessen or avoid conflict or hostility — see PACIFIC 1
pack *n* 1 a soft-sided case designed for carrying belongings especially on the back ⟨part of basic training is becoming accustomed to taking very long hikes with an eighty-pound *pack*⟩
synonyms backpack, knapsack, rucksack
related words haversack; grip, luggage, suitcase, traveling bag
2 a wrapped or sealed case containing an item or set of items — see PACKAGE 1
pack *vb* 1 to close up so that no empty spaces remain — see FILL 2
2 to put into (something) as much as can be held or contained — see FILL 1
3 to support and take from one place to another — see CARRY 1
4 to wear or have on one's person — see CARRY 2
pack (off) *vb* to cause to go or be taken from one place to another — see SEND
package *n* 1 a wrapped or sealed case containing an item or set of items ⟨Mom needed our help carrying all the *packages* and bags home from the store⟩

synonyms bundle, pack, packet, parcel
related words bag, poke [*chiefly Southern and Midland*], pouch, sack; box, container, crate
2 a number of things considered as a unit — see GROUP 1
packed *adj* **1** containing or seeming to contain the greatest quantity or number possible — see FULL 1
2 having little space between items or parts — see CLOSE 1
packet *n* a wrapped or sealed case containing an item or set of items — see PACKAGE 1
pact *n* **1** a formal agreement between two or more nations or peoples — see TREATY
2 an arrangement about action to be taken — see AGREEMENT 2
pad *n* **1** a number of sheets of writing paper glued together at one edge ⟨we'll need to buy a new *pad* for telephone messages soon⟩
synonyms notepad, tablet
related words album, notebook, scrapbook; booklet, pamphlet
2 a place set aside for sleeping — see BED 1
3 something that serves as a protective barrier — see CUSHION
4 the place where one lives — see HOME 1
pad *vb* **1** to add to the interest of by including made-up details — see EMBROIDER
2 to go on foot — see WALK
padding *n* **1** soft material that is used to fill the hollow parts of something — see FILLING
2 the representation of something in terms that go beyond the facts — see EXAGGERATION
paddle *vb* to move a boat by means of oars — see ¹ROW
padre *n* a person specially trained and authorized to conduct religious services in a Christian church — see CLERGYMAN
paean *n* a formal expression of praise — see ENCOMIUM
pagan *n* a person who does not worship the God of the Bible — see HEATHEN 1
page *n* one that carries a message or does an errand — see MESSENGER
pageant *n* a staged presentation often with music that consists of a procession of narrated or enacted scenes ⟨we always put on a Christmas *pageant* every year⟩
synonyms cavalcade
related words tableau; kaleidoscope, montage, panorama; drama, play; demonstration, performance, presentation, production; exhibition, extravaganza, show, spectacle; parade
pail *n* a round container that is open at the top and outfitted with a handle ⟨fetch me a *pail* full of water, please⟩
synonyms bucket
related words cauldron, kettle, pot; canteen, flagon, jar, jug, pitcher; bail, hod; tank, tub, vat
pain *n* **1** a sharp unpleasant sensation usually felt in some specific part of the body ⟨the child was crying because of a *pain* in her knee⟩
synonyms ache, pang, prick, smart, sting, stitch, throe, tingle, twinge
related words discomfort, distress, soreness, tenderness; agony, anguish, misery, suffering, torment, torture; inflammation, swelling; damage, harm, hurt, injury; backache, bellyache, charley horse, colic, earache, gripe, headache, stomachache, toothache

near antonyms comfort, ease
2 a state of great suffering of body or mind — see DISTRESS 1
3 pains *pl* strict attentiveness to what one is doing — see CARE 1
4 pains *pl* the active use of energy in producing a result — see EFFORT
pain *vb* to feel or cause physical pain — see HURT 1
painful *adj* **1** causing or feeling bodily pain ⟨her broken arm was too *painful* for her to go on the trip⟩
synonyms aching, hurting, nasty, sore
related words damaging, harmful, hurtful, injurious; raw, tender; bleeding, burning, chafing, cramping, festering; itching, nagging, pinching, pricking, prickling, smarting, stinging; inflamed, swollen; threatening, wounding
near antonyms curative, healing, helping, remedial
antonyms painless
2 hard to accept or bear especially emotionally — see BITTER 2
painfully *adv* with feelings of bitterness or grief — see HARD 2
painkiller *n* something (as a drug) that relieves pain ⟨a lot of *painkillers* have turned out to be addictive substances for patients⟩
synonyms analgesic, anesthetic
related words sedative, tranquilizer (*also* tranquilizer); narcotic, opiate
painless *adj* involving minimal difficulty or effort — see EASY 1
painlessly *adv* without difficulty — see EASILY
painstaking *adj* taking great care and effort ⟨she was always *painstaking* about her homework⟩
synonyms careful, conscientious, fussy, meticulous
related words assiduous, diligent, indefatigable, persevering, sedulous; exhaustive, thorough, thoroughgoing; attentive, observant, vigilant, watchful; accurate, precise; critical, demanding, discriminating, exacting, finicky, particular; cautious, chary, circumspect, gingerly, guarded, heedful, wary; deliberate, plodding, slow; studied, thoughtful; all-out, determined, dogged, intensive, tenacious, tireless, zealous
near antonyms cursory; heedless, inattentive, incautious, mindless, unguarded, unsafe, unwary; lax, neglectful, negligent, slipshod, sloppy, slovenly; imprecise; inaccurate, uncritical, undemanding, undiscriminating; bold, impetuous, rash, reckless; apathetic, indifferent, lackadaisical, lazy
antonyms careless
paint *n* preparations intended to beautify the face or hair — see MAKEUP 1
paint *vb* **1** to give a representation or account of in words — see DESCRIBE 1
2 to give color or a different color to — see COLOR 1
painting *n* a picture created with usually oil paint ⟨the Mona Lisa is a beautiful *painting* of a woman with a most mysterious smile⟩
synonyms canvas, oil, oil painting
related words fresco, mural, panorama; cartoon, drawing, etching, pastel, sketch, watercolor, work; masterpiece; pièce de résistance, showpiece
phrases work of art
pair *n* two things of the same or similar kind that match or are considered together ⟨a *pair* of blue

socks⟩ ⟨the cheerleader and the computer nerd make quite a *pair* together⟩
synonyms brace, couple, duo, twain, twosome
related words span, yoke; partnership, team; companion, complement, doublet, fellow, half, match, mate, twin; counterpart, equal, equivalent, like, parallel, peer

pal *n* a person who has a strong liking for and trust in another — see FRIEND 1

pal (around) *vb* to come or be together as friends — see ASSOCIATE 1

palace *n* 1 a large impressive residence — see MANSION
2 a large, magnificent, or massive building — see EDIFICE 1
3 the residence of a ruler — see COURT 1

palatable *adj* 1 being to one's liking — see SATISFACTORY 1
2 giving pleasure or contentment to the mind or senses — see PLEASANT
3 very pleasing to the sense of taste — see DELICIOUS 1

palatial *adj* showing obvious signs of wealth and comfort — see LUXURIOUS

palaver *n* friendly, informal conversation or an instance of this — see CHAT

palaver *vb* to engage in casual or rambling conversation — see CHAT

pale *adj* 1 lacking intensity of color ⟨we chose a very *pale* pink for the walls of the room⟩
synonyms dull, dulled, faded, light, pastel, washed-out
related words flat, lackluster, lusterless, matte (*also* mat *or* matt); dim, faint; dirty, muddy; achromatic, colorless, uncolored, undyed, unpainted, unstained; blanched, bleached, washed, white, whitened; gray (*also* grey), indistinct, neutral
near antonyms bright, brilliant, vibrant, vivid; chromatic, colored, dyed, painted, stained, tinged, tinted; colorful, multicolored, polychromatic, polychrome, varicolored, variegated; flashy, garish, gaudy, loud, showy, splashy
antonyms dark, deep, gay, rich
2 lacking a healthy skin color ⟨after a week with the flu, she was deathly *pale* and noticeably thinner⟩
synonyms ashen, ashy, blanched, cadaverous, livid, lurid, paled, pallid, pasty, peaked, wan
related words sallow, sick, sickly, waxen, waxy; white, whitened; deathlike; anemic, bloodless; untanned
near antonyms blooming, blushing, flushed, glowing, pink
antonyms florid, flush, rubicund, ruddy, sanguine

pale *vb* to make white or whiter by removing color — see WHITEN

paled *adj* lacking a healthy skin color — see PALE 2

palisade *n* a steep wall of rock, earth, or ice — see CLIFF

palliate *vb* 1 to make (something) seem less bad by offering excuses ⟨don't try to *palliate* your constant lying by claiming that everybody lies⟩
synonyms excuse, extenuate, gloss (over), gloze (over), whitewash
related words sugarcoat, varnish; apologize, atone, confess; explain, justify, rationalize; alleviate, lessen, lighten, mitigate, moderate, soften, temper; absolve, acquit, clear, exculpate, exonerate, vindicate

2 to make more bearable or less severe — see HELP 2

pallid *adj* lacking a healthy skin color — see PALE 2

palm off *vb* to offer (something fake, useless, or inferior) as genuine, useful, or valuable — see FOIST

palmy *adj* 1 having attained a desired end or state of good fortune — see SUCCESSFUL 1
2 marked by vigorous growth and well-being especially economically — see PROSPEROUS 1

palpable *adj* 1 able to be perceived by a sense or by the mind — see PERCEPTIBLE
2 capable of being perceived by the sense of touch — see TANGIBLE
3 not subject to misinterpretation or more than one interpretation — see CLEAR 2

palpitate *vb* to expand and contract in a rhythmic manner — see PULSATE

palpitation *n* a rhythmic expanding and contracting — see PULSATION

palsy *n* complete or partial loss of physical function (as motion or sensation) in a part of the body — see PARALYSIS

palter *vb* to talk over or dispute the terms of a purchase — see BARGAIN

paltry *adj* so small or unimportant as to warrant little or no attention — see NEGLIGIBLE 1

pamper *vb* to treat with great or excessive care — see BABY

pamphlet *n* a short printed publication with no cover or with a paper cover ⟨*pamphlets* about common safety precautions that we all can put into use⟩
synonyms booklet, brochure, circular, flier (*or* flyer), folder, leaflet
related words advertisement, catalog (*or* catalogue); tract; paperback, pocket book; guidebook, handbook, instructions, manual

pan *vb* to express one's unfavorable opinion of the worth or quality of — see CRITICIZE

panacea *n* something that cures all ills or problems — see CURE-ALL

pancake *n* a flat cake made from thin batter and cooked on both sides (as on a griddle) ⟨every Sunday morning, we have *pancakes* and bacon for breakfast⟩
synonyms flapjack, griddle cake, hotcake, slapjack
related words crepe (*or* crêpe); waffle

pandemonium *n* a state of noisy, confused activity — see COMMOTION

panegyric *n* a formal expression of praise — see ENCOMIUM

panel *n* 1 a meeting featuring a group discussion — see FORUM
2 a select group of persons assigned to consider or take action on some matter — see COMMITTEE

pang *n* a sharp unpleasant sensation usually felt in some specific part of the body — see PAIN 1

panhandler *n* a person who lives by public begging — see BEGGAR

panic *n* the emotion experienced in the presence or threat of danger — see FEAR

panic *vb* to strike with fear — see FRIGHTEN

panorama *n* all that can be seen from a certain point — see VIEW 1

panoramic *adj* covering everything or all important points — see ENCYCLOPEDIC

pan out *vb* 1 to come to be — see COME OUT 1

2 to turn out as planned or desired — see SUC-CEED 1

pant *vb* to breathe hard, quickly, or with difficulty — see GASP

pant (after) *vb* to have an earnest wish to own or enjoy — see DESIRE

pantaloons *n pl* an outer garment covering each leg separately from waist to ankle — see PANTS

panther *n* a large tawny cat of the wild — see COUGAR

pantomime *n* **1** a movement of the body or limbs that expresses or emphasizes an idea or feeling — see GESTURE 1

2 an actor in a story performed silently and entirely by body movements — see MIME

pantomimist *n* an actor in a story performed silently and entirely by body movements — see MIME

pants *n pl* an outer garment covering each leg separately from waist to ankle ⟨you'll need a nice pair of *pants* for the job interview⟩

synonyms breeches, pantaloons, slacks, trousers
related words corduroys, denims, jeans; hose, legging (*or* leggin), pantsuit

papa *n* a male human parent — see FATHER 1

paper *adj* being something in name or form only — see NOMINAL 1

paper *n* **1** a piece of paper with information written or to be written on it — see FORM 2

2 a publication that appears at regular intervals — see JOURNAL

3 a short piece of writing done as a school exercise — see COMPOSITION 2

4 a short piece of writing typically expressing a point of view — see ESSAY 1

par *n* **1** something set up as an example against which others of the same type are compared — see STANDARD 1

2 the state or fact of being exactly the same in number, amount, status, or quality — see EQUIVALENCE

3 what is typical of a group, class, or series — see AVERAGE

parable *n* a story intended to teach a basic truth or moral about life — see ALLEGORY

parade *n* a body of individuals moving along in an orderly and often ceremonial way — see CORTEGE 2

parade *vb* **1** to move along with a steady regular step especially in a group — see MARCH 1

2 to present so as to invite notice or attention — see SHOW 1

paradigmatic *adj* constituting, serving as, or worthy of being a pattern to be imitated — see MODEL

paradise *n* **1** a place or state of great happiness ⟨Susan's idea of *paradise* was a world where no one had to go to work⟩

synonyms Eden, Elysium, heaven, utopia
related words dreamland, fairyland, promised land, wonderland; bliss, euphoria, gladness, joy
antonyms hell

2 a dwelling place of perfect bliss for the soul after death — see HEAVEN 1

3 a state of overwhelming usually pleasurable emotion — see ECSTASY

paradox *n* someone or something with qualities or features that seem to conflict with one another — see CONTRADICTION 1

paragon *n* someone of such unequaled perfection as to deserve imitation — see IDEAL 1

parallel *adj* having qualities in common — see ALIKE

parallel *n* **1** a point which two or more things share in common — see SIMILARITY 2

2 one that is equal to another in status, achievement, or value — see EQUAL

parallel *vb* to be the exact counterpart of — see MATCH 1

parallelism *n* the quality or state of having many qualities in common — see SIMILARITY 1

paralysis *n* complete or partial loss of physical function (as motion or sensation) in a part of the body ⟨the car accident left one athlete with *paralysis* from the waist down⟩

synonyms palsy
related words cerebral palsy, multiple sclerosis, poliomyelitis; debilitation, debility, decrepitude, enfeeblement, feebleness, frailness, weakness; infirmity, lameness; disability, impairment
near antonyms mobility, motility, sensation

paralytic *adj* affected with paralysis ⟨at first, he would not accept that he was now *paralytic* and needed help⟩

synonyms paralyzed
related words challenged, crippled, disabled, handicapped, maimed, mutilated; hobbled, lame, lamed; impaired, incapacitated; hamstrung; debilitated, decrepit, enfeebled, feeble, infirm, weak, weakened
near antonyms able-bodied

paralyze *vb* to render powerless, ineffective, or unable to move ⟨a blizzard *paralyzed* the city for two days⟩

synonyms cripple, disable, hamstring, immobilize, incapacitate, prostrate
related words attenuate, debilitate, enfeeble, sap, undermine, weaken; hobble, lame; maim, mutilate
near antonyms energize, galvanize, vitalize; fortify, strengthen; empower; refresh, rejuvenate, restore

paralyzed *adj* affected with paralysis — see PARALYTIC

paramount *adj* **1** coming before all others in importance — see FOREMOST 1

2 of the greatest or highest degree or quantity — see ULTIMATE 1

paraphernalia *n* **1** items needed for the performance of a task or activity — see EQUIPMENT

2 transportable items that one owns — see POSSESSION 2

paraphrase *n* an instance of expressing something in different words ⟨your essays on human rights should have some original thought and not be simply a *paraphrase* of what's in the textbook⟩

synonyms rephrasing, restatement, restating, rewording, translating, translation
related words rehash; summary
near antonyms copy, transcript, transcription
antonyms quotation, quote

paraphrase *vb* to express something (as a text or statement) in different words ⟨could you *paraphrase* your diagnosis of my medical condition, using simpler language?⟩

synonyms rephrase, restate, reword, translate
related words summarize
near antonyms repeat; copy, reproduce, transcribe
antonyms quote

parasite *n* a person who is supported or seeks support from another without making an adequate return — see LEECH

parboil *vb* to cook in a liquid heated to the point that it gives off steam — see BOIL 2

parcel *n* **1** a number of things considered as a unit — see GROUP 1

2 a small area of usually open land — see FIELD 1

3 a small piece of land that is developed or available for development — see LOT 1

4 a usually small number of persons considered as a unit — see GROUP 2

5 a wrapped or sealed case containing an item or set of items — see PACKAGE 1

parcel (out) *vb* to give out (something) in appropriate amounts or to appropriate individuals — see ADMINISTER 1

parcel post *n* communications or parcels sent or carried through the postal system — see MAIL

parch *vb* to make dry — see DRY 1

pardon *n* release from the guilt or penalty of an offense ⟨the criminal is hoping for a Presidential *pardon*⟩

synonyms absolution, amnesty, forgiveness, remission, remittal

related words parole; acquittal, exculpation, exoneration, vindication; exemption, immunity, impunity, indemnity; commutation, commuting, reprieve

near antonyms conviction, sentence; assessment, charge, fine, imposition, levying; castigation, chastening, chastisement, condemnation

antonyms penalty, punishment, retribution

pardon *vb* **1** to cease to have feelings of anger or bitterness toward — see FORGIVE 1

2 to overlook or dismiss as of little importance — see EXCUSE 1

pardonable *adj* worthy of forgiveness — see VENIAL

pare *vb* to make (as hair) shorter with or as if with the use of shears — see CLIP

parentage *n* the line of ancestors from whom a person is descended — see ANCESTRY

parenthood *n* the caring for a child by its parents — see PARENTING

parenting *n* the caring for a child by its parents ⟨as the big day approaches, the expectant couple are starting to get worried about their fitness for *parenting*⟩

synonyms parenthood

related words raising, rearing, upbringing; fatherhood, fathering, paternity; maternity, motherhood, mothering

par excellence *adj* of the very best kind — see EXCELLENT

pariah *n* one who is cast out or rejected by society — see OUTCAST

parity *n* the state or fact of being exactly the same in number, amount, status, or quality — see EQUIVALENCE

park *n* the area around and belonging to a building — see GROUND 1

parley *n* **1** a meeting featuring a group discussion — see FORUM

2 an exchange of views for the purpose of exploring a subject or deciding an issue — see DISCUSSION 1

parley *vb* to exchange viewpoints or seek advice for the purpose of finding a solution to a problem — see CONFER 2

parliament *n* the highest lawmaking body of a political unit — see CONGRESS 1

parlor *n* a building, room, or suite of rooms occupied by a service business — see PLACE 2

parlous *adj* involving potential loss or injury — see DANGEROUS

parochial *adj* not broad or open in views or opinions — see NARROW 2

parody *n* **1** a work that imitates and exaggerates another work for comic effect ⟨the musical was a *parody* of *Romeo and Juliet*, with silly songs during the sad scenes⟩

synonyms burlesque, caricature, spoof, takeoff

related words lampoon, mockery, satire, travesty; comedy, farce, sketch, slapstick, squib; distortion, exaggeration; imitation, impersonation, mimicking

near antonyms archetype, original, prototype

2 a poor, insincere, or insulting imitation of something — see MOCKERY 1

parody *vb* to copy or exaggerate (someone or something) in order to make fun of — see MIMIC 1

paroxysm *n* **1** a sudden intense expression of strong feeling — see OUTBURST 1

2 a violent disturbance (as of the political or social order) — see CONVULSION

parrot *vb* to say after another — see REPEAT 3

parsimonious *adj* giving or sharing as little as possible — see STINGY 1

parsimony *n* the quality of being overly sparing with money ⟨her *parsimony* was so extreme that she'd walk five miles to the store to save a few cents on gas⟩

synonyms cheapness, closeness, miserliness, penuriousness, pinching, stinginess, tightness

related words conserving, economizing, economy, frugality, husbandry, providence, scrimping, skimping, thrift; conservation, saving; husbanding, managing

near antonyms extravagance, lavishness; dissipation, improvidence, prodigality, squandering, wastefulness

antonyms generosity, liberality, openhandedness, openheartedness, philanthropy

parson *n* a person specially trained and authorized to conduct religious services in a Christian church — see CLERGYMAN

part *adv* in some measure or degree — see PARTLY

part *n* **1** one of the pieces from which something is designed to be assembled ⟨the model car came in several small *parts* that had to be assembled⟩

synonyms member, partition, portion, section, segment

related words component, constituent, element, factor, ingredient, moiety, parcel; cut, length; bit, fragment, particle, scrap

near antonyms whole; aggregate, composite, compound, sum, total, totality

2 something belonging to, due to, or contributed by an individual member of a group — see SHARE 1

3 the action for which a person or thing is specially fitted or used or for which a thing exists — see ROLE

4 usually **parts** *pl* a broad geographical area — see REGION 2

part *vb* to set or force apart — see SEPARATE 1

partake *vb* to take a share or part ⟨we should all *partake* of this fine meal together⟩

synonyms participate, share

related words endure, experience, feel, see, taste, undergo; encounter, meet; accept, receive

partaker *n* one who takes part in something — see PARTICIPANT

partial *adj* **1** inclined to favor one side over another ⟨that judge is always *partial* to the defense, so be careful⟩
synonyms biased, one-sided, partisan, prejudiced
related words jaundiced, unfriendly, unsympathetic; colored, distorted, misrepresented, warped; convinced, influenced, persuaded, predisposed, prepossessed, swayed; affected, concerned, interested
near antonyms open, open-minded, persuasible, receptive; fair, honest, just, reasonable; bipartisan; autonomous, independent, unallied; aloof, detached, dispassionate, hardheaded, impersonal, objective, unemotional; apathetic, indifferent, unenthusiastic, uninterested
antonyms evenhanded, impartial, neutral, nonpartisan, unbiased, unprejudiced
2 having a liking or affection — see FOND 1
3 lacking some necessary part — see INCOMPLETE

partiality *n* **1** an attitude that always favors one way of feeling or acting especially without considering any other possibilities — see BIAS
2 a habitual attraction to some activity or thing — see INCLINATION 1
3 positive regard for something — see LIKING

partially *adv* in some measure or degree — see PARTLY

participant *n* one who takes part in something ⟨he seemed to be a willing *participant* in the prank⟩
synonyms partaker, participator, party, sharer
related words actor; accessory, aide, assistant, helper; colleague, partner
near antonyms bystander, looker-on, observer, onlooker, spectator, watcher
antonyms nonparticipant

participate *vb* to take a share or part — see PARTAKE

participator *n* one who takes part in something — see PARTICIPANT

particle *n* **1** a very small amount ⟨I did all but a *particle* of my work⟩
synonyms ace, bit, crumb, dab, driblet, glimmer, hint, lick, little, mite, nip, ounce, peanuts, ray, scruple, shade, shadow, shred, smidgen (*also* smidgeon *or* smidgin), snap, spark, speck, spot, sprinkling, strain, streak, suspicion, touch, trace
related words iota, jot, modicum, tittle, whit; atom, dot, fleck, flyspeck, grain, granule, molecule, morsel, mote, nubbin, patch, scrap; dash, drop, pinch; part, portion, section; bite, nibble, taste; handful, scattering, smattering; dose, shot; chip, flake, fragment, shard, shiver, sliver, smithereens, splinter; shred, tatter; clipping, paring, shaving
near antonyms abundance, barrel, bucket, bushel, deal, gobs, heaps, loads, mass, mountain, much, peck, pile, plenty, profusion, quantity, raft, scads, stack, wad, wealth; volume; embarrassment, excess, overabundance, overage, overflow, overkill, overmuch, oversupply, superabundance, superfluity, surfeit, surplus; chunk, hunk, lump, slab
2 a very small piece — see BIT 1

particular *adj* **1** hard to please — see FINICKY
2 of, relating to, or belonging to a single person — see INDIVIDUAL 1
3 tending to select carefully — see SELECTIVE

particular *n* **1** a separate part in a list, account, or series — see ITEM 1
2 a single piece of information — see FACT 3

particularity *n* **1** careful thoroughness of detail ⟨with great *particularity* she described the qualities she's looking for in a boyfriend⟩
synonyms explicitness, specificity
related words attentiveness, care, carefulness, conscientiousness, finickiness, fussiness, meticulousness; alertness, cautiousness, circumspection, heedfulness, safeness; discrimination; accuracy, exactitude, exactness, precision
near antonyms imprecision, inaccuracy, inexactness; indistinctness, vagueness
antonyms generality
2 a single piece of information — see FACT 3

particularized *adj* including many small descriptive features — see DETAILED 1

particularly *adv* to a great degree — see VERY 1

parting *adj* given, taken, or performed at parting ⟨she gave him a *parting* gift to remember her by⟩
synonyms farewell, valedictory
related words final, last, ultimate; departing, leaving

parting *n* **1** the act or process of two or more persons going off in different directions ⟨although their *parting* was sad, they knew they would see each other again⟩
synonyms farewell, leave-taking, separation
related words departure, egress, exit, exiting, exodus, going, leaving, quitting, running away; decampment, flight, withdrawal; abandonment, desertion, forsaking
near antonyms reunion; arrival, greeting, welcome; gathering, joining, meeting
2 the act of leaving a place — see DEPARTURE

partisan *adj* inclined to favor one side over another — see PARTIAL 1

partisan *n* **1** one who follows the opinions or teachings of another — see FOLLOWER
2 one who is intensely or excessively devoted to a cause — see ZEALOT

partisanship *n* an attitude that always favors one way of feeling or acting especially without considering any other possibilities — see BIAS

partition *n* **1** one of the pieces from which something is designed to be assembled — see PART 1
2 something that divides, separates, or marks off — see DIVISION 1
3 the act or process of a whole separating into two or more parts or pieces — see SEPARATION 1

partly *adv* in some measure or degree ⟨you're only *partly* right⟩
synonyms incompletely, part, partially
related words in part
near antonyms absolutely, dead, downright, plain, plumb, utterly
antonyms completely, entirely, totally, wholly

partner *n* the person to whom another is married — see SPOUSE

partnership *n* the state of having shared interests or efforts (as in social or business matters) — see ASSOCIATION 1

parturition *n* the act or process of giving birth to children — see CHILDBIRTH

party *n* **1** a social gathering ⟨we're all invited to the big *party* to celebrate the end of the term⟩
synonyms affair, blowout, event, fete (*or* fête), function, get-together, reception, shindig
related words ball, formal, prom; celebration,

gala, occasion; orgy, saturnalia; benefit, clam-bake, hen party, housewarming, masquerade, mixer, shower, salon, soiree (*or* soirée), stag, tea
2 a group of people acting together within a larger group — see FACTION
3 a group of people working together on a task — see GANG
4 a member of the human race — see HUMAN
5 a usually small number of persons considered as a unit — see GROUP 2
6 one who takes part in something — see PARTICIPANT

party pooper *n* a person who spoils the pleasure of others — see KILLJOY

pass *n* **1** a narrow opening between hillsides or mountains that can be used for passage — see CANYON
2 a passage cleared for public vehicular travel — see WAY 1
3 a small sheet of plastic, paper, or paperboard showing that the bearer has a claim to something (as admittance) — see TICKET 1
4 an effort to do or accomplish something — see ATTEMPT

pass *vb* **1** to shift possession of (something) from one person to another ⟨could you please *pass* me the phone?⟩
synonyms hand, hand over, reach, transfer
related words relay; bear, carry; finger, handle, paw; cede, give, give up, release, relinquish, surrender
2 to come to an end — see CEASE 1
3 to put (something) into the possession or safekeeping of another — see GIVE 2
4 to put into effect through legislative or authoritative action — see ENACT
5 to take place — see HAPPEN

pass (on) *vb* to stop living — see DIE 1

pass (over) *vb* to make one's way through, across, or over — see TRAVERSE

passable *adj* **1** capable of being traveled on ⟨after the snowstorm, the roads might not be *passable* for the morning ride to school⟩
synonyms navigable, negotiable
related words clear, cleared, open, unclogged, unobstructed
near antonyms blocked, choked, clogged, closed, congested, dammed, jammed, obstructed; barricaded, blockaded
antonyms impassable
2 capable of being passed into or through — see PENETRABLE
3 of a level of quality that meets one's needs or standards — see ADEQUATE
4 of average to below average quality — see MEDIOCRE 1

passably *adv* in a satisfactory way — see WELL 1

passage *n* **1** an established course for traveling from one place to another ⟨the long *passage* down the Atlantic seaboard, around Cape Horn, and up the Pacific Coast to California⟩
synonyms approach, avenue, path, route, way
related words bypath, byway, lane; bypass, drive, freeway, highway, road, street, thoroughfare; trace, track, trail; airway; channel, watercourse, waterway; door, doorway, gate, gateway, portal
2 a going from one place to another usually of some distance — see JOURNEY
3 a journey over water in a vessel — see SAIL
4 a part taken from a longer work — see EXCERPT

5 forward movement in time or place — see ADVANCE 1

passageway *n* **1** a passage cleared for public vehicular travel — see WAY 1
2 a typically long narrow way connecting parts of a building — see HALL 2

pass away *vb* to stop living — see DIE 1

passé *adj* having passed its time of use or usefulness — see OBSOLETE

passel *n* **1** a number of things considered as a unit — see GROUP 1
2 a usually small number of persons considered as a unit — see GROUP 2

passing *adj* lasting only for a short time — see MOMENTARY

passing *n* the permanent stopping of all the vital bodily activities — see DEATH 1

passion *n* **1** a feeling of strong or constant regard for and dedication to someone — see LOVE 1
2 a strong but often short-lived liking for another person — see CRUSH 1
3 a strong wish for something — see DESIRE
4 a subjective response to a person, thing, or situation — see FEELING 1
5 depth of feeling — see ARDOR 1
6 passions *pl* general emotional condition — see FEELING 2

passionate *adj* **1** having a strong sexual desire — see LUSTFUL
2 having or expressing great depth of feeling — see FERVENT

passive *adj* receiving or enduring without offering resistance ⟨the student body was surprisingly *passive* about having recess shortened⟩
synonyms acquiescent, nonresistant, resigned, tolerant, tolerating, unresistant, unresisting, yielding
related words forbearing, long-suffering, patient, uncomplaining; agreeable, amenable, compliant, complying, conformist, docile, guidable, law-abiding, obedient, subordinate, tractable, willing; submissive, surrendering; amiable, obliging; slavish, subservient; disciplined, governable, manageable; apathetic, uncaring, unresponsive
near antonyms defiant; contrary, disobedient, insubordinate, insurgent, intractable, mutinous, rebellious, recalcitrant, refractory, uncontrollable, ungovernable, unruly; balky, perverse, wayward, wrongheaded; headstrong, willful (*or* wilful); indomitable; undisciplined, unmanageable; dissident, nonconformist
antonyms protesting, resistant, resisting, unyielding

pass off *vb* to offer (something fake, useless, or inferior) as genuine, useful, or valuable — see FOIST

pass out *vb* to lose consciousness — see FAINT

pass over *vb* **1** to fail to give proper attention to — see NEGLECT 1
2 to overlook or dismiss as of little importance — see EXCUSE 1

passport *n* something that allows someone to achieve a desired goal ⟨meeting that movie director could be your *passport* to a big acting career⟩
synonyms gateway, key, open sesame
related words password; accomplishment, achievement, success; manner, means, method, system, technique, way; blueprint, design, plan, scheme, strategy

password *n* a word or phrase that must be spoken

THESAURUS

by a person in order to pass a guard ⟨the *password* for the dance party will be changed next week⟩
synonyms countersign, watchword
related words shibboleth, sign; signal; hint, indication

past *adj* having been such at some previous time — see FORMER

past *n* the events or experience of former times ⟨we spent a pleasant evening recalling the *past* together⟩
synonyms auld lang syne, history, yesterday, yesteryear, yore
related words bygone; flashback; annals, chronicle, record; memoir; antiquity
near antonyms future, tomorrow; present

past *prep* on or to the farther side of — see BEYOND 1

paste *vb* to deliver a blow to (someone or something) usually in a strong vigorous manner — see HIT 1

pastel *adj* lacking intensity of color — see PALE 1

past master *n* a person with a high level of knowledge or skill in a field — see EXPERT

pastoral *adj* 1 of, relating to, associated with, or typical of open areas with few buildings or people — see RURAL
2 of, relating to, or characteristic of the clergy — see CLERICAL

pasturage *n* open land over which livestock may roam and feed — see RANGE 1

pasture *n* open land over which livestock may roam and feed — see RANGE 1

pasture *vb* to feed on grass or herbs — see ¹GRAZE

pasty *adj* lacking a healthy skin color — see PALE 2

pat *adj* sticking to an opinion, purpose, or course of action in spite of reason, arguments, or persuasion — see OBSTINATE

pat *vb* to touch or handle in a tender or loving manner — see FONDLE

patch *n* 1 a small area that is different (as in color) from the main part — see SPOT 1
2 a very small piece — see BIT 1

patch *vb* to put into good shape or working order again — see MEND 1

patch (together) *vb* to make or assemble roughly or hastily — see COBBLE (TOGETHER)

patchwork *adj* consisting of many things of different sorts — see MISCELLANEOUS

pate *n* the upper or front part of the body that contains the brain, the major sense organs, and the mouth — see HEAD 1

patent *adj* 1 not subject to misinterpretation or more than one interpretation — see CLEAR 2
2 very noticeable especially for being incorrect or bad — see EGREGIOUS

path *n* 1 the direction along which something or someone moves ⟨try to stay out of the *path* of the golf balls while playing⟩ ⟨I tripped over a rock directly in my *path*⟩
synonyms course, line, pathway, route, steps, track, way
related words circle, circuit, loop, orbit; flight path, trajectory; ascent, descent
2 a rough course or way formed by or as if by repeated footsteps — see TRAIL 1
3 an established course for traveling from one place to another — see PASSAGE 1

pathetic *adj* 1 deserving of one's pity ⟨the plight of the homeless family was quite *pathetic*⟩

synonyms heartbreaking, heartrending, miserable, piteous, pitiable, pitiful, poor, rueful, sorry, wretched
related words deplorable, lamentable, regrettable; emotional, impressive, inspiring; affecting, moving, poignant, stirring, touching; awful, horrible, terrible; distressing, disturbing, upsetting; grievous, sad, sorrowful, woeful
near antonyms unimpressive, uninspiring
2 causing unhappiness — see SAD 2

pathway *n* 1 a rough course or way formed by or as if by repeated footsteps — see TRAIL 1
2 the direction along which something or someone moves — see PATH 1

patience *n* the capacity to endure what is difficult or disagreeable without complaining ⟨my mother is endowed with nearly endless *patience*⟩
synonyms forbearance, long-suffering, sufferance, tolerance
related words acquiescence, resignation; passiveness, passivity; amenability, compliance, conformism, docility, obedience, subordination, tractability, willingness; discipline, self-control; submission, submissiveness
near antonyms defiance; contrariness, disobedience, insubordination, intractability, recalcitrance, resistance, willfulness
antonyms impatience

patient *adj* 1 accepting pains or hardships calmly or without complaint ⟨you were very *patient* about having to wait for me for so long⟩
synonyms forbearing, long-suffering, stoic (*or* stoical), tolerant, uncomplaining
related words lenient; acquiescent, passive, resigned, unresistant, unresisting, yielding; agreeable, amenable, compliant, complying, conformist, docile, law-abiding, obedient, submissive, subordinate, tractable, willing; slavish, subservient; amiable, obliging; collected, composed; constrained, contained, curbed, inhibited, repressed, restrained; disciplined, self-contained, self-controlled; apathetic, uncaring, unresponsive
near antonyms bored, tired, weary; defiant, resistant; contrary, disobedient, insubordinate, intractable, rebellious, recalcitrant, refractory, ungovernable, unmanageable, unruly
antonyms complaining, fed up, impatient, protesting
2 continuing despite difficulties, opposition, or discouragement — see PERSISTENT

patient *n* an individual awaiting or under medical care and treatment ⟨the nurse asked the *patient* to change into a paper gown⟩
synonyms case
related words inpatient, outpatient; sufferer, victim; convalescent, nursling

patio *n* an open space wholly or partly enclosed (as by buildings or walls) — see COURT 2

patois *n* the special terms or expressions of a particular group or field — see TERMINOLOGY

patrician *adj* of high birth, rank, or station — see NOBLE 1

patrician *n* a man of high birth or social position — see GENTLEMAN 1

patrimony *n* something that is or may be inherited — see INHERITANCE

patriot *n* a person who loves his or her country and supports its interests and policies ⟨the contention that true *patriots* would be willing to do anything for their country⟩

synonyms loyalist

related words chauvinist; jingoist, nationalist; compatriot, countryman

near antonyms collaborator, quisling, spy, traitor; betrayer, deserter, recreant; renegade

patriotic *adj* having or showing love and support for one's country ⟨hanging a flag outside is a *patriotic* gesture⟩

synonyms nationalist, nationalistic

related words chauvinist; jingoistic; constant, devoted, faithful, loyal, staunch (*or* stanch), steadfast, steady, true; ardent, fervent, fervid, impassioned, passionate

near antonyms traitorous, treasonous; disaffected, disloyal, faithless, false, fickle, inconstant, perfidious, recreant, treacherous, unfaithful

antonyms unpatriotic

patriotism *n* love and support for one's country ⟨her *patriotism* was so great that she quit her job to work for the war effort⟩

synonyms nationalism

related words chauvinism; jingoism; allegiance, constancy, devotion, faithfulness, fealty, loyalty, staunchness, steadfastness; fervency, fervidness, passion

near antonyms desertion, treason; disaffection, disloyalty, faithlessness, falseness, fickleness, inconstancy, perfidiousness, treachery, unfaithfulness

patron *n* **1** a person who buys a product or uses a service from a business — see CUSTOMER 1

2 a person who takes the responsibility for some other person or thing — see SPONSOR

3 one that helps another with gifts or money — see BENEFACTOR

patronize *vb* **1** to assume or treat with an air of superiority — see CONDESCEND 2

2 to promote the interests or cause of — see SUPPORT 1

patter *vb* to engage in casual or rambling conversation — see CHAT

patter *n* the special terms or expressions of a particular group or field — see TERMINOLOGY

pattern *n* **1** a unit of decoration that is repeated all over something (as a fabric) ⟨a quilt with tiny pink roses as the *pattern*⟩

synonyms design, figure, motif, motive

related words device; adornment, caparison, decoration, embellishment, frill, garnish, ornament, trim

2 a usual manner of behaving or doing — see HABIT

3 an established and often automatic or monotonous series of actions followed when engaging in some activity — see ROUTINE 1

4 the way in which the elements of something (as a work of art) are arranged — see COMPOSITION 3

patty *also* **pattie** *n* a small usually rounded mass of minced food that has been fried — see CAKE

paucity *n* a falling short of an essential or desirable amount or number — see DEFICIENCY

paunch *n* an enlarged or bulging abdomen — see POTBELLY

pauperism *n* the state of lacking sufficient money or material possessions — see POVERTY 1

pause *n* a momentary halt in an activity ⟨there was a brief *pause* for applause in her speech⟩

synonyms break, breath, breather, interruption, lull, recess

related words time-out; interim, interlude, intermission, interval, respite, rest; cessation, discontinuance, ending, expiration, finishing, lapse, stopping, termination; abeyance, moratorium, surcease, suspension; discontinuity, gap, hiatus

near antonyms continuation, endurance, persistence, progress, progression; extension, prolongation

pause *vb* to come to a temporary halt in one's activity ⟨he *paused* for a moment to tie his shoe⟩

synonyms break

related words break in, interrupt; cease, discontinue, end, finish, stop, terminate; knock off, lay off, quit; lapse, let up

near antonyms continue, persist; advance, progress; extend, prolong, stretch

pawn *n* **1** one that is or can be used to further the purposes of another ⟨she disliked being a *pawn* in her friends' power games⟩

synonyms puppet, tool

related words chump, dupe, foil, gull, sucker, victim; minion, stooge; yes-man

2 something given or held to assure that the giver will keep a promise — see PLEDGE 1

pawn *vb* to leave as a guarantee of repayment of a loan ⟨he *pawned* his watch in order to pay off his gambling debt⟩

synonyms hock, pledge

related words deposit, mortgage; bond

near antonyms buy (back), redeem, win (back)

pay *n* **1** the money paid regularly to a person for labor or services — see WAGE

2 something (as money) that is given or received in return for goods or services — see PAYMENT 2

pay *vb* **1** to give (someone) the sum of money owed for goods or services received ⟨we need to *pay* the cashier and then we can leave⟩

synonyms compensate, recompense, remunerate

related words reimburse, repay, requite; pay off, pay up, prepay

2 to give what is owed for ⟨you ought to *pay* that bill before it's overdue⟩

synonyms clear, discharge, foot, liquidate, pay off, pay up, quit, recompense, settle, spring (for), stand

antonyms repudiate

3 to hand over or use up in payment — see SPEND 1

4 to produce as revenue — see YIELD 2

payable *adj* not yet paid — see OUTSTANDING 1

paying *adj* yielding a profit — see PROFITABLE 1

paying *n* the act of offering money in exchange for goods or services — see PAYMENT 1

payload *n* a mass or quantity of something taken up and carried, conveyed, or transported — see LOAD 1

payment *n* **1** the act of offering money in exchange for goods or services ⟨they are very prompt in the *payment* of their credit card bills⟩

synonyms compensation, disbursement, giving, paying, remitment, remittance, remuneration

related words rendering, tendering; reimbursement, repayment; paying off, paying up, prepayment; overpayment

near antonyms underpayment

antonyms nonpayment, repudiation

2 something (as money) that is given or received in return for goods or services ⟨their *payment* for mowing the lawn was $20⟩ ⟨we finally mailed our last car *payment* last week⟩

THESAURUS

synonyms compensation, consideration, pay, recompense, remittance, remuneration, requital

related words salary, stipend, wage(s); disbursement, expenditure, outlay; rebate, refund; indemnity, recoupment, redress, reparation, restitution; adjustment, settlement; deposit; reimbursement; repayment; prepayment; overpayment; rent, rental

3 the money paid regularly to a person for labor or services — see WAGE

payoff *n* the amount of money left when expenses are subtracted from the total amount received — see PROFIT 1

pay off *vb* to give what is owed for — see PAY 2

pay up *vb* to give what is owed for — see PAY 2

peace *n* **1** a state without war ⟨after a long and bitter war, the troubled region finally achieved *peace*⟩

synonyms peacefulness

related words accord, amity, concord, harmony; calm, quiet, serenity, tranquillity (*or* tranquility); order, stability; pacification

near antonyms conflict, contention, discord, dissidence, strife, trouble; tumult, turmoil, unrest, upheaval; fighting, warfare; action, battle, combat

antonyms war

2 a state of freedom from storm or disturbance — see CALM

3 peaceful coexistence — see HARMONY 2

peaceable *adj* **1** inclined to live in peace and to avoid war — see PEACEFUL 1

2 not involving violence or force — see PEACEFUL 2

peaceful *adj* **1** inclined to live in peace and to avoid war ⟨a *peaceful* tribe that had quietly inhabited these shores for centuries before the arrival of the Europeans⟩

synonyms pacific, peaceable

related words calm, mild, neutral, quiet, relaxed, serene, tranquil; affable, amiable, amicable, benevolent, gentle, kind, kindly; nonbelligerent, unaggressive; submissive, yielding

near antonyms militaristic; aggressive, bellicose, belligerent, combative, contentious, discordant, pugnacious, quarrelsome, scrappy, truculent; antagonistic, argumentative, fierce, gladiatorial, hostile, hot-tempered

antonyms warlike

2 not involving violence or force ⟨UN officials struggled to find a *peaceful* solution to the troublesome conflict⟩

synonyms nonviolent, peaceable

related words conciliatory, pacific, peacemaking; nonbelligerent, unaggressive, unassertive; appeasing, conciliating, mollifying, pacifying, placating; calming, quieting, soothing

near antonyms armed, martial, militant, military, warlike; aggressive, assertive, bellicose, belligerent, combative, contentious, quarrelsome; antagonistic, argumentative, fierce, gladiatorial, hostile; tempestuous, volcanic

antonyms forced, violent

3 free from disturbing noise or uproar — see QUIET 1

4 free from storms or physical disturbance — see CALM 1

peacefulness *n* **1** a state of freedom from storm or disturbance — see CALM

2 a state without war — see PEACE 1

peacemaker *n* one who works with opposing sides in order to bring about an agreement — see MEDIATOR

peacemaking *adj* tending to lessen or avoid conflict or hostility — see PACIFIC 1

peak *n* **1** an elevation of land higher than a hill — see MOUNTAIN 1

2 the highest part or point — see HEIGHT 1

3 the projecting front part of a hat or cap — see VISOR

peaked *adj* **1** lacking a healthy skin color — see PALE 2

2 tapering to a thin tip — see POINTED 1

3 temporarily suffering from a disorder of the body — see SICK 1

peal *vb* to make the clear sound heard when metal vibrates — see RING 1

peanuts *n pl* **1** a very small amount — see PARTICLE 1

2 a very small sum of money — see MITE 1

pearl *n* someone or something unusually desirable — see PRIZE 1

pebbly *adj* not having a level or smooth surface — see UNEVEN 1

peck *n* a considerable amount — see LOT 2

peculiar *adj* **1** being out of the ordinary — see EXCEPTIONAL

2 different from the ordinary in a way that causes curiosity or suspicion — see ODD 2

3 noticeably different from what is generally found or experienced — see UNUSUAL 1

4 of, relating to, or belonging to a single person — see INDIVIDUAL 1

5 serving to identify as belonging to an individual or group — see CHARACTERISTIC 1

peculiarity *n* **1** an odd or peculiar habit — see IDIOSYNCRASY

2 something that sets apart an individual from others of the same kind — see CHARACTERISTIC

pecuniary *adj* of or relating to money, banking, or investments — see FINANCIAL

pedagogue *n* a person whose occupation is to give formal instruction in a school — see TEACHER

peddle *vb* to sell from place to place usually in small quantities ⟨he traveled around the country *peddling* Bibles⟩

synonyms hawk

related words retail, wholesale; deal (in), distribute, high-pressure, hustle, market, merchandise, trade (in), vend

peddler *also* **pedlar** *n* one who sells things outdoors ⟨the *peddler* on the street corner selling baseball caps⟩

synonyms hawker, huckster

related words dealer, merchandiser, seller, vendor (*also* vender); concessionaire; black marketer, bootlegger, fence, fencer, hustler, smuggler, trader

near antonyms buyer, purchaser; consumer, end user, user

pedestrian *adj* causing weariness, restlessness, or lack of interest — see BORING

pedigree *n* the line of ancestors from whom a person is descended — see ANCESTRY

pedigreed *adj* of unmixed ancestry — see PUREBRED

peek *n* an instance of looking especially briefly — see LOOK 2

peek *vb* to take a quick or hasty look — see GLANCE 2

peel *vb* to remove the natural covering of ⟨she *peeled* an apple with great care⟩
synonyms bark, flay, hull, husk, shell, shuck, skin
related words bare, denude, expose, scale, strip; pare

peel (off) *vb* to rid oneself of (a garment) — see REMOVE 1

peeled *adj* lacking a usual or natural covering — see NAKED 2

peep *n* an instance of looking especially briefly — see LOOK 2

peep *vb* to make a short sharp sound like a small bird — see CHIRP

peer *n* one that is equal to another in status, achievement, or value — see EQUAL

peer *vb* to look long and hard in wonder or surprise — see GAPE

peerless *adj* having no equal or rival for excellence or desirability — see ONLY 1

peeve *n* **1** something that is a source of irritation — see ANNOYANCE 3
2 the feeling of being offended or resentful after a slight or indignity — see PIQUE

peeve *vb* to disturb the peace of mind of (someone) especially by repeated disagreeable acts — see IRRITATE 1

peeving *adj* causing annoyance — see ANNOYING

peevish *adj* **1** easily irritated or annoyed — see IRRITABLE
2 sticking to an opinion, purpose, or course of action in spite of reason, arguments, or persuasion — see OBSTINATE

peevishness *n* **1** a steadfast adherence to an opinion, purpose, or course of action — see OBSTINACY
2 readiness to show annoyance or impatience — see PETULANCE

peewee *n* a living thing much smaller than others of its kind — see DWARF 1

peg *n* an individual part of a process, series, or ranking — see DEGREE 1

peg *vb* **1** to arrange or assign according to type — see CLASSIFY 1
2 to send through the air especially with a quick forward motion of the arm — see THROW

peg (away) *vb* to devote serious and sustained effort — see LABOR

pelage *n* the hairy covering of a mammal especially when fine, soft, and thick — see FUR 1

pelagic *adj* of or relating to the sea — see MARINE 1

pelf *n* something (as pieces of stamped metal or printed paper) customarily and legally used as a medium of exchange, a measure of value, or a means of payment — see MONEY

pellet *n* a usually round or cone-shaped little piece of lead made to be fired from a firearm — see BULLET

pell–mell *adj* **1** acting or done with excessive or careless speed — see HASTY 1
2 lacking in order, neatness, and often cleanliness — see MESSY

pell–mell *adv* **1** in a confused and reckless manner — see HELTER-SKELTER 1
2 with excessive or careless speed — see HASTILY 1

pellucid *adj* easily seen through — see CLEAR 1

pelt *n* the outer covering of an animal removed for its commercial value — see HIDE 1

pelt *vb* **1** to proceed or move quickly — see HURRY 2
2 to send through the air especially with a quick forward motion of the arm — see THROW
3 to strike repeatedly — see BEAT 1

pen *n* **1** a place of confinement for persons held in lawful custody — see JAIL
2 an enclosure with an open framework for keeping animals — see CAGE

pen *vb* **1** to close or shut in by or as if by barriers — see ENCLOSE 1
2 to compose and set down on paper the words of — see WRITE 1

penal *adj* inflicting, involving, or serving as punishment — see PUNITIVE

penalize *vb* to inflict a penalty on for a fault or crime — see PUNISH

penalizing *adj* inflicting, involving, or serving as punishment — see PUNITIVE

penalty *n* **1** a feature of someone or something that creates difficulty for achieving success — see DISADVANTAGE
2 a sum of money to be paid as a punishment — see FINE
3 suffering, loss, or hardship imposed in response to a crime or offense — see PUNISHMENT

penchant *n* a habitual attraction to some activity or thing — see INCLINATION 1

pencil (in) *vb* to compose and set down on paper the words of — see WRITE 1

pendant *also* **pendent** *n* an ornament worn on a chain around the neck or wrist ⟨Navajo necklaces with *pendants* finely crafted in genuine sky-blue turquoise⟩
synonyms bangle, charm, lavalier (*also* lavalliere)
related words locket, teardrop

pendent *or* **pendant** *adj* extending freely from a support from above — see DEPENDENT 1

pending *adj* **1** not yet settled or decided ⟨a decision is *pending* about whether to buy computers or sports equipment with this money⟩
synonyms open, undecided, undetermined, unresolved, unsettled
related words hanging; arguable, debatable, disputable, moot, uncertain, unsure
near antonyms confirmed, established; certain, sure
antonyms decided, determined, resolved, settled
2 being soon to appear or take place — see FORTHCOMING
3 giving signs of immediate occurrence — see IMMINENT 1

pendulous *adj* **1** bending downward or forward — see NODDING
2 extending freely from a support from above — see DEPENDENT 1

penetrable *adj* capable of being passed into or through ⟨unfortunately, our netting proved to be a rather *penetrable* barrier that allowed in our cabin a steady stream of mosquitoes⟩
synonyms passable, permeable, porous
related words absorbent
near antonyms airtight, watertight; close, compact, dense, thick
antonyms impassable, impenetrable, impermeable, impervious, nonporous

penetrate *vb* to go or come in or into — see ENTER 1

penetrating *adj* causing intense discomfort to one's skin — see CUTTING 1

THESAURUS

peninsula *n* an area of land that juts out into a body of water — see ²CAPE

penitence *n* a feeling of responsibility for wrongdoing — see GUILT 1

penitent *adj* **1** feeling sorrow for a wrong that one has done — see CONTRITE 1
2 suffering from or expressive of a feeling of responsibility for wrongdoing — see GUILTY 2

penitentiary *n* a place of confinement for persons held in lawful custody — see JAIL

penman *n* a person who creates a written work — see AUTHOR 1

penmanship *n* **1** the form or style of a particular person's writing — see HANDWRITING 1
2 writing done by hand — see HANDWRITING 2

pennant *n* a piece of cloth with a special design that is used as an emblem or for signaling — see FLAG 1

penniless *adj* lacking money or material possessions — see POOR 1

pennon *n* a piece of cloth with a special design that is used as an emblem or for signaling — see FLAG 1

pensive *adj* given to or marked by long, quiet thinking — see CONTEMPLATIVE

penstock *n* a long hollow cylinder for carrying a substance (as a liquid or gas) — see PIPE 1

penthouse *n* a smaller structure added to a main building — see ANNEX

penumbra *n* partial darkness due to the obstruction of light rays — see SHADE 1

penurious *adj* **1** giving or sharing as little as possible — see STINGY 1
2 lacking money or material possessions — see POOR 1

penuriousness *n* **1** the quality of being overly sparing with money — see PARSIMONY
2 the state of lacking sufficient money or material possessions — see POVERTY 1

penury *n* the state of lacking sufficient money or material possessions — see POVERTY 1

peon *n* a person who does very hard or dull work — see SLAVE 2

people *n pl* **1** human beings in general ⟨despite the horrors she witnessed, Anne Frank never lost her faith in *people*⟩
synonyms folks, humanity, humankind, public, society, world
related words crowd, masses, mob, populace, proletariat, rabble, riffraff
2 the body of the community as contrasted with the elite — see MASS 1
3 a group of persons who come from the same ancestor — see FAMILY 1

pep *n* active strength of body or mind — see VIGOR 1

pep (up) *vb* to give life, vigor, or spirit to — see ANIMATE

pepper *vb* **1** to cover by or as if by scattering something over or on — see SCATTER 2
2 to mark with small spots especially unevenly — see SPOT

peppery *adj* marked by a lively display of strong feeling — see SPIRITED 1

peppiness *n* the quality or state of having abundant or intense activity — see VITALITY 1

peppy *adj* **1** having active strength of body or mind — see VIGOROUS 1
2 having much high-spirited energy and movement — see LIVELY 1

per *prep* using the means or agency of — see BY 2

perambulation *n* a relaxed journey on foot for exercise or pleasure — see WALK

per capita *adv* for each one — see APIECE

perceive *vb* **1** to have a vague awareness of — see FEEL 1
2 to make note of (something) through the use of one's eyes — see SEE 1
3 to recognize the meaning of — see COMPREHEND 1

percentage *n* a measure of how often an event will occur instead of another — see PROBABILITY 2

perceptible *adj* able to be perceived by a sense or by the mind ⟨you should note a *perceptible* temperature change when you add the second element⟩
synonyms appreciable, detectable, discernible, distinguishable, palpable, sensible
related words audible, observable, tangible, visible; clear, conspicuous, evident, eye-catching, manifest, noticeable, obvious, plain, prominent, striking; apparent, distinct, significant, straightforward
near antonyms inaudible, intangible, invisible; inconspicuous, indistinct, unnoticeable; faint, insignificant, slight, trivial; buried, concealed, covert, disguised, hidden, obscure, shrouded, vague
antonyms impalpable, imperceptible, inappreciable, indistinguishable, insensible

perception *n* **1** the ability to understand inner qualities or relationships — see WISDOM 1
2 the knowledge gained from the process of coming to know or understand something — see COMPREHENSION

perceptive *adj* **1** able to sense slight impressions or differences — see ACUTE 1
2 having or showing deep understanding and intelligent application of knowledge — see WISE 1

perceptiveness *n* the ability to understand inner qualities or relationships — see WISDOM 1

perch *vb* **1** to come to rest after descending from the air — see ALIGHT
2 to establish or place comfortably or snugly — see ENSCONCE 1

perchance *adv* it is possible — see PERHAPS

percolate *vb* to flow forth slowly through small openings — see EXUDE

percolate (into) *vb* to spread throughout — see PERMEATE

perdition *n* the place of punishment for the wicked after death — see HELL 1

peregrinate *vb* to take a trip especially of some distance — see TRAVEL 1

peregrination *n* a going from one place to another usually of some distance — see JOURNEY

peremptoriness *n* an exaggerated sense of one's importance that shows itself in the making of excessive or unjustified claims — see ARROGANCE

peremptory *adj* **1** fond of ordering people around — see BOSSY
2 forcing one's compliance or participation by or as if by law — see MANDATORY
3 having a feeling of superiority that shows itself in an overbearing attitude — see ARROGANT
4 having or showing a tendency to force one's will on others without any regard to fairness or necessity — see ARBITRARY 1

perfect *adj* **1** being entirely without fault or flaw ⟨a stunningly *perfect* performance—not the slightest mistake—won her the gold medal in women's figure skating⟩

synonyms absolute, faultless, flawless, ideal, impeccable, irreproachable, letter-perfect, unblemished

related words consummate, expert, masterly; classic, dandy, excellent, fabulous, fine, first-class, first-rate, grand, great, marvelous (*or* marvellous), prime, superb, superior, superlative, terrific, top, top-notch, unsurpassed; completed, finished, perfected, polished; complete, entire, intact, whole; immaculate, unbruised, undamaged, unimpaired, uninjured, unmarred, unspoiled; exceptional, fancy, high-grade, special; accurate, correct, exact, precise; infallible, unerring, unfailing

near antonyms deficient, inadequate, incomplete, insufficient, wanting; unfinished, unpolished; fallible; blemished, blighted, broken, damaged, defaced, disfigured, impaired, injured, marred, spoiled, vitiated; atrocious, execrable, wretched; imprecise, inaccurate, incorrect, inexact, wrong

antonyms bad, censurable, defective, faulty, flawed, imperfect, reproachable

2 having no exceptions or restrictions — see ABSOLUTE 2

3 not lacking any part or member that properly belongs to it — see COMPLETE 1

perfect *vb* **1** to bring (something) to a state where nothing remains to be done — see FINISH 1

2 to make better — see IMPROVE

perfection *n* the most perfect type or example — see QUINTESSENCE 1

perfectly *adv* **1** without any flaws or errors ⟨you did that handspring *perfectly* on your first try⟩

synonyms faultlessly, flawlessly, ideally, impeccably

related words excellently, fabulously, finely, grandly, greatly, marvelously, superbly, superiorly, superlatively, terrifically; exceptionally, fancily, specially

phrases to a nicety, to a T, to a turn

near antonyms deficiently, inadequately, incompletely, insufficiently; fallibly; atrociously, execrably, wretchedly

antonyms badly, defectively, faultily, imperfectly

2 to a full extent or degree — see FULLY 1

perfidious *adj* not true in one's allegiance to someone or something — see FAITHLESS

perfidiousness *n* lack of faithfulness especially to one's husband or wife — see INFIDELITY 1

perfidy *n* **1** lack of faithfulness especially to one's husband or wife — see INFIDELITY 1

2 the act or fact of violating the trust or confidence of another — see BETRAYAL

perforate *vb* to make a hole or series of holes in ⟨he *perforated* the sheet with his pencil and put it in his binder⟩

synonyms bore, drill, hole, pierce, punch, puncture

related words broach, tap; poke, prick; penetrate; burrow (into), excavate, gouge, groove, hollow; break, cut, gash, notch, rend, rupture, slash, slit, split

near antonyms fill, patch, plug, seal

perforation *n* **1** a mark or small hole made by a pointed instrument — see PRICK 1

2 a place in a surface allowing passage into or through a thing — see HOLE 1

perforce *adv* because of necessity — see NEEDS

perform *vb* **1** to carry through (as a process) to completion ⟨she *performed* the task quickly and expertly⟩

synonyms accomplish, achieve, carry out, commit, compass, do, execute, follow through, fulfill (*or* fulfil), make

related words bring about, effect, effectuate, implement; engage (in), practice (*or* practise); work (at); reduplicate, reenact, repeat; actualize, attain, realize; complete, end, finish, wind up

phrases go through

near antonyms fail; skimp, slight, slur

2 to have a certain purpose — see FUNCTION

3 to present a portrayal or performance of — see ACT 1

4 to produce a desired effect — see ACT 2

performance *n* the doing of an action — see COMMISSION 2

perfume *n* a sweet or pleasant smell — see FRAGRANCE

perfume *vb* to fill or infuse with a pleasant odor or odor-releasing substance — see SCENT 1

perfumed *adj* having a pleasant smell — see FRAGRANT

perfunctory *adj* having or showing a lack of interest or concern — see INDIFFERENT 1

perhaps *adv* it is possible ⟨*perhaps* we will not have to take this exam, but I doubt it⟩

synonyms conceivably, maybe, mayhap, perchance, possibly

related words likely, probably; certainly, doubtless, surely, undoubtedly; presumably

peril *n* **1** something that may cause injury or harm — see DANGER 2

2 the state of not being protected from injury, harm, or evil — see DANGER 1

perilous *adj* involving potential loss or injury — see DANGEROUS

perimeter *n* the line or relatively narrow space that marks the outer limit of something — see BORDER 1

period *n* **1** an occurrence of menstruating ⟨girls having their *period* will be excused from gym class⟩

synonyms menstruation, monthlies

related words menses

2 an extent of time associated with a particular person or thing — see AGE 1

periodic *adj* **1** appearing in parts or numbers that follow regularly — see SERIAL

2 appearing or occurring repeatedly from time to time — see REGULAR 1

3 occurring or appearing at intervals — see INTERMITTENT 1

periodical *adj* **1** appearing in parts or numbers that follow regularly — see SERIAL

2 occurring or appearing at intervals — see INTERMITTENT 1

periodical *n* a publication that appears at regular intervals — see JOURNAL

peripatetic *adj* traveling from place to place — see ITINERANT

peripheral *adj* available to supply something extra when needed — see AUXILIARY

periphery *n* the line or relatively narrow space that marks the outer limit of something — see BORDER 1

perish *vb* to stop living — see DIE 1

perk (up) *vb* **1** to become glad or hopeful — see CHEER (UP) 1

THESAURUS

2 to move from a lower to a higher place or position — see RAISE 1

perky *adj* having much high-spirited energy and movement — see LIVELY 1

permanent *adj* lasting forever — see EVERLASTING

permanently *adv* for all time — see EVER 1

permeable *adj* capable of being passed into or through — see PENETRABLE

permeate *vb* to spread throughout ⟨the smell of freshly baked bread *permeated* the house⟩
synonyms interpenetrate, percolate (into), pervade, suffuse, transfuse
related words diffuse (through), impregnate, pass (into), penetrate; fill (up); drench, infuse, saturate, soak, steep; flood, glut

permissible *adj* that may be permitted ⟨fortunately, that is a *permissible* shortcut to the answer⟩
synonyms admissible, allowable, licensable
related words acceptable, bearable, endurable, tolerable; accredited, allowed, authorized, certified, endorsed, licensed (*also* licenced), OK (*or* okay), permitted, sanctioned, warranted; mandatory, ordered, required
near antonyms intolerable, unacceptable, unbearable, unendurable; objectionable; denied, disallowed, refused, rejected, vetoed; repressed, suppressed; outlawed
antonyms banned, barred, forbidden, impermissible, inadmissible, interdicted, prohibited, proscribed

permission *n* the approval by someone in authority for the doing of something ⟨she asked for *permission* to have a piece of candy⟩ ⟨the President granted *permission* for the foreign diplomats to have special quarters⟩
synonyms allowance, authorization, clearance, concurrence, consent, granting, leave, license (*or* licence), sanction, sufferance
related words imprimatur, seal, signature, stamp; accreditation, certification; liberty, pass; concession, patent, permit; acceptance, acquiescence, agreement, assent, OK (*or* okay); accord, grant
near antonyms denial, refusal, rejection, revocation; taboo; injunction, veto; deterrence, discouragement, repression, suppression; ban, embargo, exclusion
antonyms interdiction, prohibition, proscription

permit *vb* **1** to give permission for or to approve of — see ALLOW 1
2 to give permission to — see ALLOW 2
3 to make able or possible — see ENABLE 1

pernicious *adj* causing or capable of causing harm — see HARMFUL

perpendicular *adj* rising straight up — see ERECT

perpetration *n* the doing of an action — see COMMISSION 2

perpetual *adj* lasting forever — see EVERLASTING

perpetually *adv* **1** for all time — see EVER 1
2 on every relevant occasion — see ALWAYS 1

perpetuate *vb* to give eternal or lasting existence to ⟨we hope to *perpetuate* this holiday tradition⟩
synonyms immortalize
related words commemorate, memorialize; celebrate, enshrine, honor; conserve, keep up, maintain, preserve, support, sustain; defend, guard, protect, safeguard
near antonyms extinguish, put out, snuff (out); annihilate, crush, decimate, demolish, destroy,

devastate; eradicate, erase, expunge, extirpate, obliterate, wipe out

perpetuity *n* endless time — see ETERNITY 1

perplex *vb* **1** to make complex or difficult — see COMPLICATE
2 to throw into a state of mental uncertainty — see CONFUSE 1

perplexity *n* a state of mental uncertainty — see CONFUSION 1

perquisite *n* **1** a small sum of money given for a service over and above what is due — see ²TIP 1
2 something given in addition to what is ordinarily expected or owed — see BONUS

persecute *vb* **1** to cause persistent suffering to — see AFFLICT
2 to disturb the peace of mind of (someone) especially by repeated disagreeable acts — see IRRITATE 1

persecutor *n* **1** a person who causes repeated emotional pain, distress, or annoyance to another — see TORMENTOR
2 one who is obnoxiously annoying — see NUISANCE 1

persevere *vb* to continue despite difficulties, opposition, or discouragement ⟨although he was frustrated by the lack of financial resources and support, he *persevered* in his scientific research⟩
synonyms carry on, persist
related words hang on; follow through; knuckle down
phrases hang in there
near antonyms give up, quit, surrender, yield; falter, hesitate, vacillate, waver

persevering *adj* continuing despite difficulties, opposition, or discouragement — see PERSISTENT

persiflage *n* good-natured teasing or exchanging of clever remarks — see BANTER

persist *vb* **1** to continue despite difficulties, opposition, or discouragement — see PERSEVERE
2 to remain indefinitely in existence or in the same state — see CONTINUE 1

persistence *n* **1** continuing existence ⟨the *persistence* of the child's fever made us start to worry⟩
synonyms continuance, durability, endurance
related words longevity, staying power, tenacity; permanence; survival; continuation
near antonyms discontinuance; cessation, desisting, ending, finish, quitting, stop
2 uninterrupted or lasting existence — see CONTINUATION
3 a steadfast adherence to an opinion, purpose, or course of action — see OBSTINACY

persistent *adj* continuing despite difficulties, opposition, or discouragement ⟨although his first attempts were unsuccessful, he was *persistent* in his pursuit of a career in rock music⟩
synonyms dogged, insistent, patient, persevering, pertinacious, tenacious
related words assured, certain, dedicated, determined, firm, intent, positive, resolute, resolved, single-minded, sure; hardheaded, headstrong, mulish, obdurate, obstinate, opinionated, peevish, perverse, pigheaded, self-willed, stubborn, unyielding; unfaltering, unhesitating, unwavering; resistant, wayward, wrongheaded; constant, devoted, faithful, good, loyal, staunch (*or* stanch), steadfast, steady, true; indomitable, unconquerable; hard, inflexible, relentless, stern, unbending, unrelenting, unyielding
near antonyms quitting, surrendering, yielding;

faltering, hesitant, hesitating, irresolute, vacillating, wavering; disloyal, faithless, false, fickle, inconstant, perfidious, traitorous, treacherous

person *n* a member of the human race — see HUMAN

personage *n* a person who is widely known and usually much talked about — see CELEBRITY 1

personal *adj* of, relating to, or belonging to a single person — see INDIVIDUAL 1

personality *n* **1** a person who is widely known and usually much talked about — see CELEBRITY 1
2 the set of qualities that make a person different from other people — see INDIVIDUALITY
3 the set of qualities that makes a person, a group of people, or a thing different from others — see NATURE 1

personalize *vb* to represent in visible form — see EMBODY 2

personalized *adj* of, relating to, or belonging to a single person — see INDIVIDUAL 1

personally *adv* in person and usually privately — see TÊTE-À-TÊTE

personalty *n* transportable items that one owns — see POSSESSION 2

personification *n* a visible representation of something abstract (as a quality) — see EMBODIMENT

personify *vb* to represent in visible form — see EMBODY 2

personnel *n* a body of persons at work or available for work — see FORCE 1

perspective *n* a way of looking at or thinking about something — see POINT OF VIEW

perspicuity *n* clearness of expression — see SIMPLICITY 2

perspicuous *adj* not subject to misinterpretation or more than one interpretation — see CLEAR 2

perspicuousness *n* clearness of expression — see SIMPLICITY 2

persuade *vb* to cause (someone) to agree with a belief or course of action by using arguments or earnest request ⟨she *persuaded* us that she can indeed communicate with the dead⟩ ⟨he *persuaded* his teachers to grant an extension⟩
synonyms argue, convince, get, induce, move, prevail (on *or* upon), satisfy, talk (into), win (over)
related words cajole, coax, exhort, urge; lead on, seduce, snow, tempt; incline, influence, move, prompt, sell, sway; attract, bring, draw, entice, interest; chew over, converse, debate, discuss, dispute, hash (over), moot; reason (with)
near antonyms dissuade

persuading *n* the act of reasoning or pleading with someone to accept a belief or course of action — see PERSUASION 1

persuasion *n* **1** the act of reasoning or pleading with someone to accept a belief or course of action ⟨the suffragists' gradual *persuasion* of the American people that voting rights had to be extended to women⟩
synonyms convincing, inducement, inducing, persuading, suasion
related words cajolery, coaxing, exhortation, urging; seduction, tempting; influencing, prompting, swaying; lobbying, pressuring
2 a body of beliefs and practices regarding the supernatural and the worship of one or more deities — see RELIGION 1
3 an idea that is believed to be true or valid without positive knowledge — see OPINION 1

persuasive *adj* having the power to persuade — see COGENT

persuasiveness *n* the capacity to persuade — see COGENCY 1

pert *adj* **1** having much high-spirited energy and movement — see LIVELY 1
2 making light of something usually regarded as serious or sacred — see FLIPPANT

pertain *vb* **1** to be the property of a person or group of persons — see BELONG 2
2 to have a relation or connection — see APPLY 1

pertain (to) *vb* to have (something) as a subject matter — see CONCERN 1

pertinacious *adj* **1** continuing despite difficulties, opposition, or discouragement — see PERSISTENT
2 sticking to an opinion, purpose, or course of action in spite of reason, arguments, or persuasion — see OBSTINATE

pertinaciousness *n* a steadfast adherence to an opinion, purpose, or course of action — see OBSTINACY

pertinacity *n* a steadfast adherence to an opinion, purpose, or course of action — see OBSTINACY

pertinence *n* the fact or state of being pertinent ⟨job applicants should question the *pertinence* of any questions about their personal lives⟩
synonyms applicability, bearing, connection, materiality, relevance, relevancy
related words appropriateness, aptness, fitness, suitability; importance, significance; usefulness
near antonyms inappropriateness, inaptness, unfitness, unsuitability; insignificance, unimportance; pointlessness, uselessness
antonyms extraneousness, inapplicability, irrelevance

pertinent *adj* having to do with the matter at hand ⟨he impressed the jury with his concise, *pertinent* answers to the attorney's questions⟩
synonyms applicable, apposite, apropos, germane, material, pointed, relative, relevant
related words appropriate, apt, fit, fitting, suitable; important, meaningful, significant; sensible, useful; admissible, allowable
phrases in point, to the point
near antonyms inconsequential, insignificant, unimportant; meaningless, purposeless, senseless, useless; inappropriate, inapt, unsuitable; inadmissible
antonyms extraneous, immaterial, inapplicable, irrelevant, pointless

pertly *adv* in a quick and spirited manner — see GAILY 2

pertness *n* shameless boldness — see EFFRONTERY

perturb *vb* to trouble the mind of; to make uneasy — see DISTURB 1

perturbation *n* an uneasy state of mind usually over the possibility of an anticipated misfortune or trouble — see ANXIETY 1

perturbed *adj* feeling or showing uncomfortable feelings of uncertainty — see NERVOUS 1

perturbing *adj* causing worry or anxiety — see TROUBLESOME

peruse *vb* to go over and mentally take in the content of — see READ

pervade *vb* to spread throughout — see PERMEATE

perverse *adj* **1** easily irritated or annoyed — see IRRITABLE
2 having or showing lowered moral character or standards — see CORRUPT

THESAURUS

3 sticking to an opinion, purpose, or course of action in spite of reason, arguments, or persuasion — see OBSTINATE

perverseness *n* readiness to show annoyance or impatience — see PETULANCE

perversion *n* **1** a sinking to a state of low moral standards and behavior — see CORRUPTION 2
2 incorrect or improper use — see MISUSE

perversity *n* readiness to show annoyance or impatience — see PETULANCE

pervert *n* a person who has sunk below the normal moral standard — see DEGENERATE

pervert *vb* **1** to change so much as to create a wrong impression or alter the meaning of — see GARBLE
2 to lower in character or dignity — see DEBASE 1
3 to put to a bad or improper use — see MISAPPLY

perverted *adj* having or showing lowered moral character or standards — see CORRUPT

pessimist *n* **1** one who emphasizes bad aspects or conditions and expects the worst ⟨she's such a *pessimist* that she's convinced she'll fail every test⟩
synonyms defeatist
related words cynic, fatalist; pragmatist, realist
near antonyms dreamer, idealist, romantic, utopian, visionary; sentimentalist
antonyms optimist
2 a person who distrusts other people and believes that everything is done for selfish reasons — see CYNIC

pessimistic *adj* **1** emphasizing or expecting the worst ⟨with that *pessimistic* attitude, it's no wonder you're depressed⟩
synonyms defeatist, despairing, hopeless
related words cynical, fatalistic; desperate, discouraging, disheartening, inauspicious, unlikely, unpromising; bleak, cheerless, comfortless, dismal, dreary, gloomy; grim; contrary, hostile, negative
near antonyms auspicious, encouraging, fair, heartening, likely, promising, propitious; cheering, comforting, reassuring; favorable, good, positive; idealist, romantic, utopian, visionary
antonyms hopeful, optimistic, rose-colored, rosy, upbeat
2 having or showing a deep distrust of human beings and their motives — see CYNICAL

pest *n* **1** a widespread disease resulting in a high rate of death — see PLAGUE
2 one who is obnoxiously annoying — see NUISANCE 1
3 something that is a source of irritation — see ANNOYANCE 3

pester *vb* to thrust oneself upon (another) without invitation — see BOTHER 1

pestering *n* the act of making unwelcome intrusions upon another — see ANNOYANCE 1

pestilence *n* a widespread disease resulting in a high rate of death — see PLAGUE

pestilent *adj* likely to cause or capable of causing death — see DEADLY

pesty *adj* causing annoyance — see ANNOYING

pet *adj* granted special treatment or attention — see DARLING 1

pet *n* **1** a person or thing that is preferred over others — see FAVORITE
2 a state of resentful silence or irritability — see SULK

pet *vb* **1** to touch or handle in a tender or loving manner — see FONDLE

2 to touch one another with the lips as a sign of love — see KISS 1

petition *n* an earnest request — see PLEA 1

petition *vb* to make a request to (someone) in an earnest or urgent manner — see BEG

petitioner *n* one who asks earnestly for a favor or gift — see SUPPLICANT

pettish *adj* easily irritated or annoyed — see IRRITABLE

pettishness *n* readiness to show annoyance or impatience — see PETULANCE

petty *adj* **1** not broad or open in views or opinions — see NARROW 2
2 so small or unimportant as to warrant little or no attention — see NEGLIGIBLE 1

petulance *n* readiness to show annoyance or impatience ⟨I do not appreciate your *petulance* and eagerness to argue⟩
synonyms biliousness, crankiness, crossness, crotchetiness, grouchiness, grumpiness, huffiness, irascibility, irritability, irritableness, peevishness, perverseness, perversity, pettishness, testiness, waspishness
related words cantankerousness, disagreeableness, dyspepsia, fretfulness, orneriness, sulkiness, surliness; aggression, aggressiveness, bellicosity, belligerence, combativeness, contentiousness, contrariness, disputatiousness, fight, pugnacity, scrappiness, truculence; fussiness, querulousness, rudeness; oversensitiveness, sensitivity; antagonism, fierceness, hostility, unfriendliness; anger, exasperation, rage, wrath; hot-bloodedness, passion
near antonyms forbearance, patience, tolerance, understanding; affability, amicability, cordiality, friendliness, sociability; amiability, good-humoredness, good-naturedness, good-temperedness; coolness, serenity, tranquility; easygoingness, gentleness, kindliness, mildness

petulant *adj* easily irritated or annoyed — see IRRITABLE

pewter *adj* of the color gray — see GRAY 1

phantasm *n* **1** a conception or image created by the imagination and having no objective reality — see FANTASY 1
2 the soul of a dead person thought of especially as appearing to living people — see GHOST

phantasmal *adj* not real and existing only in the imagination — see IMAGINARY

phantom *adj* not real and existing only in the imagination — see IMAGINARY

phantom *n* the soul of a dead person thought of especially as appearing to living people — see GHOST

pharmaceutical *n* a substance or preparation used to treat disease — see MEDICINE

pharmacist *n* a person who prepares drugs according to a doctor's prescription — see DRUGGIST

pharmacy *n* a retail store where medicines and miscellaneous articles are sold — see DRUGSTORE

phase *n* **1** a certain way in which something appears or may be regarded — see ASPECT 1
2 an individual part of a process, series, or ranking — see DEGREE 1

phased *adj* proceeding or changing by steps or degrees — see GRADUAL

phenomenal *adj* **1** being out of the ordinary — see EXCEPTIONAL
2 being so extraordinary or abnormal as to sug-

gest powers which violate the laws of nature — see SUPERNATURAL 2

phenomenon *n* something extraordinary or surprising — see WONDER 1

philanthropic *adj* having or showing a concern for the welfare of others — see CHARITABLE 1

philanthropy *n* **1** a gift of money or its equivalent to a charity, humanitarian cause, or public institution — see CONTRIBUTION

2 the giving of necessities and especially money to the needy — see CHARITY 1

3 the quality or state of being generous — see LIBERALITY

philharmonic *n* a usually large group of musicians playing together — see ²BAND 1

philistine *n* a person who is chiefly interested in material comfort and is hostile or indifferent to art and culture ⟨the town's *philistines* who think that spending on the arts is a waste of taxpayers' money⟩
  synonyms lowbrow, materialist
  related words capitalist, plutocrat; boor, cad, churl, clown, creep, cur, jerk, lout
  near antonyms highbrow; egghead, intellectual, sage, thinker; brain, genius

philosophy *n* the basic beliefs or guiding principles of a person or group — see CREED 1

phlegm *n* a lack of emotion or emotional expressiveness — see APATHY 1

phlegmatic *adj* not feeling or showing emotion — see IMPASSIVE 1

phone *vb* to make a telephone call to — see CALL 2

phony *also* **phoney** *adj* **1** being such in appearance only and made or manufactured with the intention of committing fraud — see COUNTERFEIT

2 lacking in natural or spontaneous quality — see ARTIFICIAL 1

phony *also* **phoney** *n* **1** an imitation that is passed off as genuine — see FAKE 1

2 one who makes false claims of identity or expertise — see IMPOSTOR

photo *n* a picture created from an image recorded on a light-sensitive surface by a camera — see PHOTOGRAPH

photo *vb* to take a photograph of — see PHOTOGRAPH

photograph *n* a picture created from an image recorded on a light-sensitive surface by a camera ⟨the old *photograph* was faded but still clear enough to make out⟩
  synonyms photo, print, shot, snap, snapshot
  related words blowup, close-up, enlargement, still; daguerreotype, monochrome, tintype

photograph *vb* to take a photograph of ⟨we *photographed* the baby birds frequently⟩
  synonyms mug, photo, shoot, snap
  related words image, picture, retake; film, videotape
  phrases capture on film

photographer *n* one who takes photographs ⟨we'll need to choose a *photographer* for the wedding⟩
  synonyms shooter, shutterbug
  related words cinematographer

phrase *n* a sequence of words having a specific meaning ⟨draw a literal representation of the *phrase* "to rain cats and dogs"⟩
  synonyms expression, idiom
  related words cliché; locution, term; epithet, expletive, name; byword, cry, motto, shibboleth, slogan, watchword; archaism, colloquialism, eu-

phemism, modernism, neologism, provincialism, vulgarism
  phrases figure of speech

phrase *vb* to convey in appropriate or telling terms ⟨he had trouble thinking of how to *phrase* his question for the visiting dignitary⟩
  synonyms articulate, clothe, couch, express, formulate, put, say, state, word
  related words craft, frame; hint, imply, insinuate, intimate, suggest; paraphrase, rephrase, restate, reword, summarize, translate; communicate, disclose, speak, tell; describe, render, write up

phraseology *n* **1** a distinctive way of putting ideas into words — see STYLE 1

2 the way in which something is put into words — see WORDING

phrasing *n* the way in which something is put into words — see WORDING

phylactery *n* something worn or kept to bring good luck or keep away evil — see CHARM 1

physic *n* a substance or preparation used to treat disease — see MEDICINE

physical *adj* **1** of or relating to the human body ⟨*physical* sensations such as heat and pain⟩
  synonyms animal, bodily, carnal, corporal, corporeal, fleshly, material, somatic
  related words anatomic (*or* anatomical), physiological; sensual, sensuous; hand-to-hand
  near antonyms intellectual, mental, psychological (*also* psychologic); bodiless, immaterial, incorporeal, spiritual; ethereal, metaphysical, psychic (*also* psychical)
  antonyms nonmaterial, nonphysical

2 relating to or composed of matter — see MATERIAL 1

physician *n* a person specially trained in healing human medical disorders — see DOCTOR

physique *n* the type of body that a person has ⟨she had a well-toned *physique*⟩
  synonyms build, constitution, figure, form, frame, shape
  related words anatomy, structure

picayune *adj* so small or unimportant as to warrant little or no attention — see NEGLIGIBLE 1

pick *n* **1** a person or thing that is chosen — see CHOICE 2

2 individuals carefully selected as being the best of a class — see ELITE

3 the power, right, or opportunity to choose — see CHOICE 1

pick *vb* **1** to catch or collect (a crop or natural resource) for human use — see HARVEST

2 to decide to accept (someone or something) from a group of possibilities — see CHOOSE 1

picked *adj* singled out from a number or group as more to one's liking — see SELECT 1

picked up *adj* being clean and in good order — see NEAT 1

picker *n* someone with the right or responsibility for making a selection — see SELECTOR

picket *n* a person or group that watches over someone or something — see GUARD 1

picking *n* the act or process of selecting — see SELECTION 1

pickle *n* a difficult, puzzling, or embarrassing situation from which there is no easy escape — see PREDICAMENT

pick up *vb* **1** to acquire complete knowledge, understanding, or skill in — see LEARN 1

2 to bring together in one body or place — see GATHER 1

3 to get possession of (something) by giving money in exchange for — see BUY

4 to increase in — see GAIN 1

5 to move from a lower to a higher place or position — see RAISE 1

6 to take or keep under one's control by authority of law — see ARREST 1

picky *adj* **1** hard to please — see FINICKY

2 tending to select carefully — see SELECTIVE

picnic *n* something that is easy to do — see CINCH

pictorial *adj* **1** consisting of or relating to pictures ⟨he's planning to do a primarily *pictorial* report on Africa⟩

synonyms graphic (*also* graphical), visual

related words photographic, video; drawn, painted, represented; illustrative; pictographic

2 producing a mental picture through clear and impressive description — see GRAPHIC 1

picture *n* **1** a two-dimensional design intended to look like a person or thing ⟨she produced a beautiful *picture* of her mother using watercolors⟩

synonyms illustration, image, likeness

related words delineation, depiction, representation; portrait; drawing, finger painting; etching, silhouette, sketch, watercolor; caricature, cartoon, doodle; collage, montage, photograph; hieroglyphic, ideogram; pictograph

2 a story told by means of a series of continuously projected pictures and a sound track — see MOVIE 1

3 a vivid representation in words of someone or something — see DESCRIPTION 1

4 position with regard to conditions and circumstances — see SITUATION 1

5 something or someone that strongly resembles another — see IMAGE 1

6 something imagined or pictured in the mind — see IDEA

7 **pictures** *pl* the art or business of making a movie — see MOVIE 2

picture *vb* **1** to present a picture of ⟨the famous painting that *pictures* the Founding Fathers signing the Declaration of Independence⟩

synonyms depict, image, portray, represent

related words delineate, describe, render; outline, sketch; illustrate, show; caricature

2 to form a mental picture of — see IMAGINE 1

3 to give a representation or account of in words — see DESCRIBE 1

picturesque *adj* producing a mental picture through clear and impressive description — see GRAPHIC 1

piddling *adj* so small or unimportant as to warrant little or no attention — see NEGLIGIBLE 1

piebald *adj* having blotches of two or more colors — see PIED

piece *n* **1** a broken or irregular part of something that often remains incomplete — see FRAGMENT

2 a literary, musical, or artistic production — see COMPOSITION 1

3 a portable weapon from which a shot is discharged by gunpowder — see GUN 1

piece *vb* to form by putting together parts or materials — see BUILD

piece by piece *adv* by small steps or amounts — see GRADUALLY

piecemeal *adj* proceeding or changing by steps or degrees — see GRADUAL

piecemeal *adv* **1** by small steps or amounts — see GRADUALLY

2 into parts or to pieces — see APART

pied *adj* having blotches of two or more colors ⟨although the mother's was pure black, the foal's coat was *pied*⟩

synonyms blotched, dappled (*also* dapple), marbled, mottled, piebald, pinto, splotched, spotted

related words shaded; checkered, motley, multicolored, polychromatic, polychrome, varicolored, variegated; blotted, brindled (*or* brindle), specked, speckled, streaked; colored, colorful, pigmented; dotted, peppered, sprinkled; stippled; discolored, dyed, marked, stained; flecked, streaked; bespattered, spattered

near antonyms monochromatic, solid

pier *n* **1** a structure used by boats and ships for taking on or landing cargo and passengers — see DOCK

2 an upright shaft that supports an overhead structure — see PILLAR 1

pierce *vb* **1** to go or come in or into — see ENTER 1

2 to make a hole or series of holes in — see PERFORATE

3 to penetrate or hold (something) with a pointed object — see IMPALE

piercing *adj* **1** causing intense discomfort to one's skin — see CUTTING 1

2 marked by a high volume of sound — see LOUD 1

piety *n* **1** belief and trust in and loyalty to God — see FAITH 1

2 the quality or state of being spiritually pure or virtuous — see HOLINESS

piffle *n* **1** language, behavior, or ideas that are absurd and contrary to good sense — see NONSENSE 1

2 unintelligible or meaningless talk — see GIBBERISH

pigeon *n* one who is easily deceived or cheated — see DUPE

piggish *adj* having a huge appetite — see VORACIOUS 1

pigheaded *adj* sticking to an opinion, purpose, or course of action in spite of reason, arguments, or persuasion — see OBSTINATE

pigment *n* a substance used to color other materials ⟨I'm running out of the black *pigment*⟩

synonyms color, coloring, dye, dyestuff, stain, tincture

related words cast, hue, shade, tinge, tint, tone

pig out *vb* to eat greedily or to excess — see GORGE 2

pigpen *n* a dirty or messy place ⟨your room is a *pigpen* —so clean it up!⟩

synonyms hole, pigsty, shambles

related words chaos, confusion, disarrangement, disarray, disorder, jumble, mess, muddle; dump; clutter, litter, mishmash

pigsty *n* a dirty or messy place — see PIGPEN

¹pike *n* a passage cleared for public vehicular travel — see WAY 1

²pike *n* a weapon with a long straight handle and sharp head or blade — see SPEAR

³pike *n* the last and usually sharp or tapering part of something long and narrow — see POINT 2

piker *n* a mean grasping person who is usually stingy with money — see MISER

pikestaff *n* a weapon with a long straight handle and sharp head or blade — see SPEAR

pilaster *n* an upright shaft that supports an overhead structure — see PILLAR 1

¹pile *n* **1** a quantity of things thrown or stacked on one another ⟨a large *pile* of newspapers that needed to be disposed of⟩
  synonyms cock, heap, hill, mound, mountain, rick, stack
  related words bank, bar, drift, embankment; pyramid; barrow, cairn, pyre; accumulation, aggregate, assemblage, collection, conglomeration, gathering, grouping, hoard, jumble
  2 a considerable amount — see LOT 2

²pile *n* **1** a soft airy substance or covering — see FUZZ
  2 the hairy covering of a mammal especially when fine, soft, and thick — see FUR 1

pile *vb* to lay or throw on top of one another ⟨*piled* all the clothes on the chair before putting them away⟩
  synonyms heap, mound, stack
  related words bank; layer, pyramid; accumulate, amass, assemble, collect, gather, group, mass; bunch, clump, lump
  antonyms unpile

pile (up) *vb* to gradually form into a layer, pile, or mass — see COLLECT 2

pilfer *vb* to take (something) without right and with an intent to keep — see STEAL 1

pilgrimage *vb* to take a trip especially of some distance — see TRAVEL 1

pill *n* a small mass containing medicine to be taken orally ⟨you'll have to take one of these *pills* every six hours for your flu⟩
  synonyms capsule, lozenge, tablet
  related words drug, medication, pharmaceutical, specific; miracle drug, wonder drug; potion, preparation; dosage, dose, drop, sleeping pill, tranquilizer (*also* tranquilizer)

pillage *vb* to search through with the intent of committing robbery — see RANSACK 1

pillar *n* **1** an upright shaft that supports an overhead structure ⟨the ancient Greek temple boasted graceful marble *pillars* with richly ornamented tops⟩
  synonyms column, pier, pilaster, post, stanchion
  related words caryatid, pedestal; buttress, flying buttress; needle, obelisk
  2 something or someone to which one looks for support — see DEPENDENCE 2

pilot *adj* made or done as an experiment — see EXPERIMENTAL 1

pilot *n* one who flies or is qualified to fly an aircraft or spacecraft ⟨the airline is seeking experienced *pilots* to fly the new airplane⟩
  synonyms airman, aviator, birdman, flier (*or* flyer)
  related words ace, bush pilot, copilot, test pilot

pilot *vb* **1** to give advice and instruction to (someone) regarding the course or process to be followed — see GUIDE 1
  2 to point out the way for (someone) especially from a position in front — see LEAD 1

pin *n* a lower limb of an animal — see LEG 1

pinch *n* an instance of theft — see THEFT 2
  2 the act of taking or holding under one's control by authority of law — see ARREST

pinch *vb* **1** to squeeze tightly between two surfaces, edges, or points ⟨the zipper on those jeans always *pinches* me⟩
  synonyms nip

related words clasp, clutch, grasp, grip
  near antonyms drop, free, loose, loosen, release
  2 to take (something) without right and with an intent to keep — see STEAL 1
  3 to take or keep under one's control by authority of law — see ARREST 1

pincher *n* one who steals — see THIEF

pinch–hit *vb* to serve as a replacement usually for a time only — see COVER 1

pinch hitter *n* a person or thing that takes the place of another — see SUBSTITUTE

pinching *adj* giving or sharing as little as possible — see STINGY 1

pinching *n* the quality of being overly sparing with money — see PARSIMONY

pine (for) *vb* to have an earnest wish to own or enjoy — see DESIRE

pinhead *n* a stupid person — see IDIOT

pinhole *n* a mark or small hole made by a pointed instrument — see PRICK 1

pining *n* a strong wish for something — see DESIRE

pinnacle *n* the highest part or point — see HEIGHT 1

pinpoint *adj* meeting the highest standard of accuracy — see PRECISE 1

pinpoint *vb* to find out or establish the identity of — see IDENTIFY 1

pinprick *n* a mark or small hole made by a pointed instrument — see PRICK 1

pinto *adj* having blotches of two or more colors — see PIED

pint–size *or* **pint–sized** *adj* of a size that is less than average — see SMALL 1

pioneer *adj* coming before all others in time or order — see FIRST 1

pioneer *n* a person who settles in a new region — see FRONTIERSMAN

pioneer *vb* to be responsible for the creation and early operation or use of — see FOUND

pious *adj* **1** firm in one's allegiance to someone or something — see FAITHFUL 1
  2 showing a devotion to God and to a life of virtue — see HOLY 1

piousness *n* **1** the pretending of having virtues, principles, or beliefs that one in fact does not have — see HYPOCRISY
  2 the quality or state of being spiritually pure or virtuous — see HOLINESS

pip *n* something very good of its kind — see JIM-DANDY

pipe *n* **1** a long hollow cylinder for carrying a substance (as a liquid or gas) ⟨the plumber came and fixed the water *pipe* that was leaking⟩
  synonyms channel, conduit, duct, leader, line, penstock, trough, tube
  related words drain, drainpipe, funnel, hydrant, main, smokestack, spout, stovepipe, tile, waterspout; pipeline, piping
  2 an enclosed wooden vessel for holding beverages — see CASK

pipe *vb* **1** to cause to move to a central point or along a restricted pathway — see CHANNEL
  2 to make a short sharp sound like a small bird — see CHIRP

pipe dream *n* a conception or image created by the imagination and having no objective reality — see FANTASY 1

pipeline *n* a direct way of passing along information or supplies ⟨an equipment hauler serves as

the columnist's *pipeline* for gossip about the rock band⟩ ⟨the battle was ultimately lost because the enemy had destroyed our *pipeline* for resupply⟩
synonyms channel
related words conduit; grapevine, outlet; fountainhead, origin, source, wellspring; supplier; connection, contact

piping *adj* having a high musical pitch or range — see SHRILL

piping hot *adj* having a notably high temperature — see HOT 1

piquancy *n* the quality or state of being stimulating to the mind or senses ⟨a talk show host known for the quickness and *piquancy* of his wit⟩ ⟨I appreciated the *piquancy* of the peppers in the sauce⟩
synonyms pungency, zest
related words raciness, spiciness; fieriness, hotness; acuteness, keenness, sharpness; provocativeness; excitement, invigoration, stimulation, thrill; flavor, savor, tastiness
near antonyms flatness, tastelessness; dullness (*also* dulness), monotonousness, predictability, tediousness; blandness, thinness, weakness
antonyms insipidity

piquant *adj* sharp and pleasantly stimulating to the mind or senses ⟨a *piquant* tidbit of information about the new neighbors⟩ ⟨the *piquant* cuisine of India boasts some highly spiced dishes⟩
synonyms pungent, zesty
related words racy, spicy; fiery, hot; acute, keen; biting, bitter, cutting, mordant, trenchant; animating, energizing, enlightening, exciting, galvanizing, invigorating, provocative; appetizing, delectable, delicious, palatable, toothsome; flavorful, savory, tasty; absorbing, engaging, engrossing, enthralling, fascinating, gripping, interesting, intriguing
near antonyms flat, flavorless, savorless, tasteless; banal, boring, dull, monotonous, pedestrian, predictable, tedious, tiring, uninteresting, wearisome, wearying; bland, dilute, thin, watery, weak
antonyms insipid

pique *n* the feeling of being offended or resentful after a slight or indignity ⟨she's still in a *pique* over being snubbed by a so-called friend at the party⟩
synonyms dudgeon, huff, offense (*or* offence), peeve, resentment, umbrage
related words aggravation, anger, annoyance, bother, discomfort, exasperation, frustration, irritation, vexation; agitation, angriness, displeasure, distress, disturbance, indignation, irateness, ire, outrage, perturbation, upset; dander, temper; fit, pet, sulk(s), tantrum, tizzy; affront, insult
near antonyms satisfaction; appeasement, mollification, pacification; delight, pleasure

pique *vb* 1 to disturb the peace of mind of (someone) especially by repeated disagreeable acts — see IRRITATE 1
2 to rouse to strong feeling or action — see PROVOKE 1

piquing *adj* serving or likely to arouse a strong reaction — see PROVOCATIVE

piracy *n* the act or pursuit of robbing ships at sea ⟨many countries have harsh penalties for *piracy* now⟩
synonyms pirating
related words depredation, despoilment, despoliation, looting, marauding, pillaging, plunder, plun-

dering, raiding, robbery; privateering; burglary, housebreaking, stealing, thieving; hijacking (*also* highjacking), rustling

pirate *n* someone who engages in robbery of ships at sea ⟨Sir Francis Drake was a British *pirate* who preyed on Spanish ships with the permission of the British queen⟩
synonyms buccaneer, corsair, freebooter, rover
related words looter, marauder, pillager, plunderer, raider, robber; privateer; burglar, housebreaker, stealer, thief; hijacker, rustler

pirating *n* the act or pursuit of robbing ships at sea — see PIRACY

pirouette *n* a rapid turning about on an axis or central point — see SPIN 1

pirouette *vb* to move in circles around an axis or center — see SPIN 1

pit *n* a sunken area forming a separate space — see HOLE 2

pit–a–pat *vb* to expand and contract in a rhythmic manner — see PULSATE

pitch *n* 1 an act or instance of diving — see DIVE 1
2 the degree to which something rises up from a position level with the horizon — see SLANT

pitch *vb* 1 to fix in an upright position — see ERECT 1
2 to cast oneself head first into deep water — see DIVE
3 to make a series of unsteady side-to-side motions — see ROCK 1
4 to send through the air especially with a quick forward motion of the arm — see THROW

pitch–black *adj* 1 being without light or without much light — see DARK 1
2 having the color of soot or coal — see BLACK 1

pitch–dark *adj* 1 being without light or without much light — see DARK 1
2 having the color of soot or coal — see BLACK 1

pitched *adj* running in a slanting direction — see DIAGONAL

pitcher *n* a handled container for holding and pouring liquids that usually has a lip or a spout ⟨please bring me the *pitcher* full of lemonade from the table⟩
synonyms flagon, jug
related words carafe, decanter; bucket, pail, pot; canteen, cup, flask, mug, stein; barrel, cask, hogshead, pipe, puncheon

pitch in *vb* to make a donation as part of a group effort — see CONTRIBUTE 1

pitchy *adj* having the color of soot or coal — see BLACK 1

piteous *adj* deserving of one's pity — see PATHETIC 1

pitfall *n* 1 a danger or difficulty that is hidden or not easily recognized ⟨buying a house can be full of *pitfalls* for the unwary⟩
synonyms booby trap, catch, snag
related words snare, trap, web; hazard, peril, risk; bombshell, surprise; bait, lure
2 something that may cause injury or harm — see DANGER 2

pith *n* the central part or aspect of something under consideration — see CRUX

pithily *adv* in a few words — see SHORTLY 1

pithiness *n* the quality or state of being marked by or using only few words to convey much meaning — see SUCCINCTNESS

pithy *adj* marked by the use of few words to convey much information or meaning — see CONCISE

pitiable *adj* **1** arousing or deserving of one's loathing and disgust — see CONTEMPTIBLE 1

2 deserving pitying scorn (as for inadequacy) — see PITIFUL 1

3 deserving of one's pity — see PATHETIC 1

pitiful *adj* **1** deserving pitying scorn (as for inadequacy) ⟨that is a *pitiful* attempt at an essay on patriotism; you'll have to do it over⟩

synonyms contemptible, despicable, pitiable, sorry

related words deplorable, discreditable, disgraceful, disreputable, infamous, notorious; abhorrent, abominable, detestable, hateful, odious; bad, inferior, poor; disgusting, dishonorable, shameful; unworthy, worthless; scandalous, shocking, sordid, unsavory

near antonyms admirable, creditable, laudable, meritorious, praiseworthy; notable, noteworthy, noticeable, outstanding, reputable, worthy; excellent; flawless, perfect; honorable, noble; honest, straight

antonyms decent, presentable, respectable

2 arousing or deserving of one's loathing and disgust — see CONTEMPTIBLE 1

3 deserving of one's pity — see PATHETIC 1

pitiless *adj* having or showing a lack of sympathy or tender feelings — see HARD 1

pittance *n* a very small sum of money — see MITE 1

pitter–patter *vb* to expand and contract in a rhythmic manner — see PULSATE

pity *n* **1** a regrettable or blameworthy act — see CRIME 2

2 the capacity for feeling for another's unhappiness or misfortune — see HEART 1

pity *vb* to have sympathy for ⟨I always *pity* the people who have to work in this freezing weather⟩

synonyms bleed (for), commiserate (with), condole (with), feel (for), sympathize (with)

related words care (for); grieve (for), sorrow (for); love; tolerate, understand

near antonyms disregard, ignore, neglect, overlook; dislike, hate, scorn

pivot *n* the central part or aspect of something under consideration — see CRUX

pivot *vb* to move (something) in a curved or circular path on or as if on an axis — see TURN 1

pivotal *adj* of the greatest possible importance — see CRUCIAL

pixie *also* **pixy** *n* an imaginary being usually having a small human form and magical powers — see FAIRY

pixieish *adj* tending to or exhibiting reckless playfulness — see MISCHIEVOUS 1

placard *n* a sheet bearing an announcement for posting in a public place — see POSTER

placard *vb* **1** to affix (as a notice) to or on a suitable place — see ¹POST 1

2 to make known openly or publicly — see ANNOUNCE

placate *vb* to lessen the anger or agitation of — see PACIFY

placating *adj* tending to lessen or avoid conflict or hostility — see PACIFIC 1

place *n* **1** the area or space occupied by or intended for something ⟨the *place* chosen for the picnic⟩ ⟨there's the *place* where I left my umbrella⟩

synonyms locale, locality, location, locus, point, position, site, spot

related words scene; region, section, sector

2 a building, room, or suite of rooms occupied by a service business ⟨we're going to our favorite *place* to eat⟩

synonyms establishment, joint, parlor, salon

related words spot, station; facility, installation; studio; den, dive, hole

3 an assignment at which one regularly works for pay — see JOB 1

4 an extent or area available for or used up by some activity or thing — see ROOM 1

5 the action for which a person or thing is specially fitted or used or for which a thing exists — see ROLE

6 the place where one lives — see HOME 1

7 the placement of someone or something in relation to others in a vertical arrangement — see RANK 1

place *vb* **1** to arrange something in a certain spot or position ⟨he carefully *placed* the flowers in a vase⟩

synonyms deposit, dispose, fix, lay, position, put, set, set up, situate, stick

related words rearrange, reorder; orient; establish, locate, settle; assemble, collect; carry; berth, park; affix, anchor, wedge; lay out, line up, queue, rank; set down

near antonyms relocate, remove, take; banish; displace, replace, supplant

2 to arrange or assign according to type — see CLASSIFY 1

3 to decide the size, amount, number, or distance of (something) without actual measurement — see ESTIMATE 2

4 to take or have a certain position within a group arranged in vertical classes — see RANK 1

placid *adj* **1** free from emotional or mental agitation — see CALM 2

2 free from storms or physical disturbance — see CALM 1

placidity *n* **1** a state of freedom from storm or disturbance — see CALM

2 evenness of emotions or temper — see EQUANIMITY

plague *n* a widespread disease resulting in a high rate of death ⟨the Black Death was a *plague* that killed about one third of Europe's population in the Middle Ages⟩

synonyms pest, pestilence

related words epidemic, pandemic; affection, affliction, contagion, contagious disease, infection, infectious disease, infirmity, malady; curse, scourge

plague *vb* to cause persistent suffering to — see AFFLICT

plain *adj* **1** free from all additions or embellishment ⟨I like my hamburgers *plain*, with no ketchup or relish⟩ ⟨just give us the *plain* facts and none of your snide comments⟩

synonyms bald, bare, naked, simple, unadorned, undecorated, unvarnished

related words chaste, modest; unexaggerated, unsophisticated; denuded, divested, stripped; dry, laconic, terse; unpretentious; austere, bleak, severe, spartan, stark; inconspicuous, muted, restrained, subdued, toned (down), unobtrusive; conservative, quiet, understated

near antonyms flamboyant, flashy, garish, gaudy, glittery, glitzy, loud, ostentatious, showy, splashy, swank (*or* swanky), tawdry; bedizened, florid, lurid, ornate; exaggerated, overdecorated, over-

done, overwrought; baroque, extravagant, rococo; arrayed, bedecked, decked-out, dressed, garnished, trimmed
antonyms adorned, decorated, embellished, fancy, ornamented
2 free from added matter — see PURE 1
3 free in expressing one's true feelings and opinions — see FRANK
4 going straight to the point clearly and firmly — see STRAIGHTFORWARD 1
5 not subject to misinterpretation or more than one interpretation — see CLEAR 2
plain *adv* in an honest and direct manner — see STRAIGHTFORWARD
plain *n* a broad area of level or rolling treeless country ⟨the first settlers in that area lived on the vast *plains* in lonely log cabins⟩
synonyms down, grassland, prairie, savanna (*also* savannah), steppe, tundra, veld (*or* veldt)
related words pampas; floodplain; bottom, bottomland, flat, lowland; plateau, table, tableland, upland
plainclothesman *n* a person whose business is solving crimes and catching criminals or gathering information that is not easy to get — see DETECTIVE
plainly *adv* in an honest and direct manner — see STRAIGHTFORWARD
plainness *n* **1** the free expression of one's true feelings and opinions — see CANDOR
2 the quality or state of having a form or structure of few parts or elements — see SIMPLICITY 1
plainspoken *adj* free in expressing one's true feelings and opinions — see FRANK
plaint *n* **1** a crying out in grief — see LAMENT 1
2 an expression of dissatisfaction, pain, or resentment — see COMPLAINT 1
plaintiff *n* the person in a legal proceeding who makes a charge of wrongdoing against another — see COMPLAINANT
plaintive *adj* expressing or suggesting mourning — see MOURNFUL 1
plait *n* a length of something formed of three or more strands woven together — see BRAID
plait *vb* to form into a braid — see BRAID
plan *n* **1** a method worked out in advance for achieving some objective ⟨there is a contingency *plan* in the office for handling almost any emergency⟩
synonyms arrangement, blueprint, design, game, ground plan, program, project, scheme, strategy, system
related words collusion, conspiracy, plot; maneuver, ruse, stratagem, subterfuge, trick; means, method, tactic, technique, way; conception, idea, proposal; aim, intention, purpose; diagram, formula, layout, map, policy, recipe, setup
2 something that one hopes or intends to accomplish — see GOAL
plan *vb* **1** to work out the details of (something) in advance ⟨we *planned* the school dance down to the smallest detail⟩
synonyms arrange, blueprint, calculate, chart, design, frame, lay out, map (out), project, schematize, scheme (out)
related words conspire, intrigue, machinate; draft, outline, sketch; aim, figure, intend, mean; contemplate, meditate, premeditate
2 to have in mind as a purpose or goal — see INTEND

plane *adj* having a surface without bends, breaks, or irregularities — see LEVEL
plane *vb* **1** to make free from breaks, curves, or bumps — see EVEN 1
2 to move through the air with or as if with outstretched wings — see FLY 1
planet *n* the celestial body on which we live — see EARTH 1
plant *n* a building or set of buildings for the manufacturing of goods — see FACTORY
plant *vb* to put or set into the ground to grow ⟨I'll *plant* the marigold seeds in the spring⟩
synonyms drill, put in, seed, sow
related words bed; replant, transplant; scatter; pot
near antonyms gather, harvest, reap
plantation *n* a settlement in a new country or region — see COLONY 1
planter *n* a person who cultivates the land and grows crops on it — see FARMER
plash *vb* **1** to flow in a broken irregular stream — see GURGLE
2 to move with a splashing motion — see SLOSH
3 to wet or soil by striking with something liquid or mushy — see SPLASH 2
plaster *n* a medicated covering used to heal an injury — see DRESSING 1
plastic *adj* capable of being easily molded or modeled ⟨Silly Putty is famous for being very *plastic*⟩
synonyms malleable
related words adaptable; ductile, pliable, pliant, supple, willowy; elastic, flexible, resilient, workable; bending, giving, tractable, yielding
near antonyms inflexible, rigid, stiff
plasticity *n* the quality or state of being easily molded ⟨we chose that type of clay for its greater *plasticity*⟩
synonyms malleability
related words adaptability; pliability, suppleness; elasticity, flexibility, resilience
near antonyms inflexibility, rigidity, stiffness
plat *n* **1** a small area of usually open land — see FIELD 1
2 a small piece of land that is developed or available for development — see LOT 1
plate *n* **1** a small thin piece of material that resembles an animal scale — see ²SCALE
2 something that visually explains or decorates a text — see ILLUSTRATION 1
plateau *n* a broad flat area of elevated land ⟨Native Americans have inhabited the *plateau* for centuries⟩
synonyms mesa, table, tableland
related words butte, dome, height, highland, upland
platform *n* a level usually raised surface ⟨you'll have to stand up there on the *platform* for your speech⟩
synonyms dais, podium, rostrum, stage, stand
related words altar, pulpit; balcony
platitude *n* an idea or expression that has been used by many people — see COMMONPLACE
plaudit *n* *usually* **plaudits** *pl* enthusiastic and usually public expression of approval — see APPLAUSE
plausible *adj* worthy of being accepted as true or reasonable — see BELIEVABLE
play *n* **1** activity engaged in to amuse oneself ⟨it's such a delight to watch the children in their *play*⟩

synonyms dalliance, frolic, frolicking, fun, recreation, relaxation, rollicking, sport

related words gamboling, romping; amusement, diversion, entertainment; delight, enjoyment, pleasure; friskiness, playfulness, sportiveness, wantonness; devilment, devilry (or deviltry), hob, impishness, mischief, mischievousness, rascality, roguishness, waggery; binge, fling, lark, revel, spree; hilarity, merrymaking, revelry; buffoonery, horseplay, tomfoolery

near antonyms drudgery, labor, work; duty, obligation, responsibility

2 a written work in which the story is told through speech and action that is intended to be acted out on stage ⟨we'll be putting on a school *play* using that stage⟩

synonyms drama, dramatization

related words comedy, melodrama, musical, musical comedy, tragedy, tragicomedy; magnum opus, opus, work; adaptation

3 an attitude or manner not to be taken seriously — see FUN 2

4 the act or practice of employing something for a particular purpose — see USE 1

play *vb* **1** to engage in activity for amusement ⟨you need some time to run and *play* in the yard after that hard work⟩

synonyms dally, disport, frolic, recreate, rollick, sport

related words gambol, romp; dabble, trifle; amuse, divert, entertain; delight, please; dabble, mess (around), putter; bum (around), dawdle, goldbrick, idle, loaf, lounge (around or about), relax, rest, slack (off); jest, joke, tease

near antonyms drudge, labor, plod, plug (away), slave, strain, strive, struggle, sweat, toil, work

2 to present a portrayal or performance of — see ACT 1

3 to pretend to be (what one is not) in appearance or behavior — see IMPERSONATE 1

4 to spend time in aimless activity — see FIDDLE (AROUND)

play (on or upon) *vb* to take unfair advantage of — see EXPLOIT 1

play (up) *vb* to indicate the importance of by giving prominent display — see EMPHASIZE

play (upon) *vb* to control or take advantage of by artful, unfair, or insidious means — see MANIPULATE 1

play (with) *vb* to handle thoughtlessly, ignorantly, or mischievously — see TAMPER

played out *adj* depleted in strength, energy, or freshness — see WEARY 1

player *n* **1** a person who plays a musical instrument — see MUSICIAN 1

2 one who acts professionally (as in a play, movie, or television show) — see ACTOR

playful *adj* given to good-natured joking or teasing ⟨the little girl was lighthearted and *playful*⟩

synonyms antic, coltish, elfish, fay, frisky, frolicsome, rollicking, sportive

related words kittenish; gay, happy, lighthearted, whimsical; energetic, lively, spirited, sprightly; devilish, knavish, rascally; amusing, diverting, enjoyable, entertaining, fun, pleasurable; dabbling, frivolous, trifling; delightful, pleasant, pleasing; jesting, joking, teasing

near antonyms dutiful, responsible; grave, grim, serious, solemn, somber (or sombre), stern, stolid; no-nonsense, priggish, starchy, stuffy; decorous,

formal, proper, sedate, staid; guarded, inhibited, restrained

antonyms earnest, serious-minded, sober

playfulness *n* a natural disposition for playful behavior ⟨the *playfulness* of the kitten can be quite amusing⟩

synonyms friskiness, impishness, mischief, mischievousness, prankishness, sportiveness

related words devilment, devilry (or deviltry), hob, rascality, waggery; devilishness, diabolicalness, knavery; frivolousness; energy, liveliness, sprightliness; gaiety (also gayety), lightheartedness, whimsicality

near antonyms graveness, grimness, seriousness, solemnity, sternness; priggishness, starchiness, stuffiness; constraint, restraint, self-control

antonyms earnestness, soberness

playhouse *n* a building or part of a building where movies are shown — see THEATER 1

plea *n* **1** an earnest request ⟨the student made an impassioned *plea* for more time to finish the test⟩

synonyms appeal, cry, entreaty, petition, prayer, solicitation, suit, supplication

related words application; call, demand, insistence

2 an explanation that frees one from fault or blame — see EXCUSE

plead *vb* to state (something) as a reason in support of or against something under consideration — see ARGUE 1

plead (for) *vb* to make a request for — see ASK (FOR) 1

plead (to) *vb* to make a request to (someone) in an earnest or urgent manner — see BEG

pleader *n* one who asks earnestly for a favor or gift — see SUPPLICANT

pleading *adj* asking humbly — see SUPPLIANT

pleasant *adj* giving pleasure or contentment to the mind or senses ⟨the massage was extremely *pleasant* and relaxing⟩

synonyms agreeable, congenial, darling, delectable, delicious, delightful, dreamy, enjoyable, felicitous, good, grateful, gratifying, heavenly, luscious, nice, palatable, pleasing, pleasurable, satisfying, welcome

related words alluring, attractive, desirable, inviting, tempting; charming, enchanting, fascinating; calming, comforting, soothing; affable, amiable, amusing, cheerful, cheery, genial, goodly, good-natured, gracious, hospitable, kindly, personable; blissful, glad, happy, joyous; elating, exhilarating, intoxicating; ecstatic, euphoric, rapturous

near antonyms abominable, horrid, miserable, wretched; disgusting, distasteful, obnoxious, offensive, repellent (also repellant), repugnant, repulsive; abhorrent, detestable, hateful, odious; boring, commonplace, dull, flat, insipid, irksome, stale, tedious; displeasing, dissatisfying; depressing, disheartening, dismal, dreary, gloomy; black, blue, dejected, depressed, despondent, disconsolate, down, downcast, downhearted, forlorn, hangdog, heartbreaking, heartrending, heartsick, heartsore, inconsolable, joyless, lachrymose, low-spirited, sad, unhappy; bemoaning, bewailing, deploring, doleful, dolorous, grieving, lugubrious, mournful, plaintive, regretful, rueful, sorrowful, wailing, weeping; aggravating, annoying, exasperating, irritating, peeving, perturbing, vexing; forbidding; hostile, intimidating; angering, enraging, incensing, inflaming, infuriating, maddening, out-

THESAURUS

raging, rankling, riling; distressing, disturbing, upsetting

antonyms disagreeable, unpalatable, unpleasant, unwelcome

pleasantly *adv* in a pleasing way — see WELL 5

pleasantness *n* the state or quality of having a pleasant or agreeable manner in socializing with others — see AMIABILITY 1

pleasantry *n* something said or done to cause laughter — see JOKE 1

please *vb* to give satisfaction to ⟨fresh flowers *please* me greatly⟩

synonyms content, delight, gladden, gratify, rejoice, satisfy, suit, warm

related words appease, mollify, pacify, placate, soothe; assuage, quench, sate, satiate; excite, tickle, titillate; overjoy, thrill; calm, comfort; cater (to), humor, indulge; coddle, mollycoddle, pamper, spoil

near antonyms aggravate, annoy, bother, bug, chafe, cross, exasperate, gall, get, grate, irk, irritate, nettle, peeve, perturb, pique, put out, ruffle, vex; anger, enrage, incense, inflame, infuriate, madden, outrage, rankle, rile, roil; provoke, rouse; agitate, distress, disturb, fret, upset; harass, harry, pester; affront, insult, offend

antonyms displease

pleased *adj* 1 experiencing pleasure, satisfaction, or delight — see GLAD 1

2 feeling that one's needs or desires have been met — see CONTENT

pleasing *adj* giving pleasure or contentment to the mind or senses — see PLEASANT

pleasingly *adv* in a pleasing way — see WELL 5

pleasurable *adj* 1 giving pleasure or contentment to the mind or senses — see PLEASANT

2 providing amusement or enjoyment — see FUN

pleasure *n* 1 the feeling experienced when one's wishes are met ⟨nothing gives me more *pleasure* than a hot meal after a long day⟩

synonyms content, contentedness, contentment, delectation, delight, enjoyment, gladness, gratification, happiness, relish, satisfaction

related words bliss, felicity, glee, gleefulness, joy; amusement, diversion, entertainment; elatedness, elation, exhilaration, exultation, intoxication; ecstasy, euphoria, heaven, rapture; cheer, cheerfulness, exuberance, gaiety (*also* gayety), jollity, joyfulness, jubilation; comfort, ease, restfulness

near antonyms misery, sadness, unhappiness, wretchedness; anguish, desolation, joylessness, sorrow, woe; dejection, depression, despondency, dispiritedness, gloom, melancholy; aggravation, annoyance, exasperation, irritation, pique, vexation; anger, fury, rage; agitation, distress, disturbance, upset; discomfort, restlessness, uneasiness

antonyms discontent, discontentedness, discontentment, displeasure, dissatisfaction, unhappiness

2 a source of great satisfaction — see DELIGHT 1

3 someone or something that provides amusement or enjoyment — see FUN 1

pleat *vb* to form into a braid — see BRAID

plebeian *adj* belonging to the class of people of low social or economic rank — see IGNOBLE 1

plebeians *n pl* the body of the community as contrasted with the elite — see MASS 1

pledge *n* 1 something given or held to assure that the giver will keep a promise ⟨I was required to leave my keys as a *pledge* that I would bring the car back⟩

synonyms gage, guarantee, guaranty, pawn, security

related words bail, bond; deposit, down payment; surety, warranty; oath, promise, word; commitment, compact, contract, covenant; recognizance

2 a person's solemn declaration that he or she will do or not do something — see PROMISE

pledge *vb* 1 to obligate by prior agreement ⟨I would love to go to dinner with you, but I've *pledged* myself to a play with my parents that night⟩

synonyms commit, engage, troth

related words affiance, betroth, plight, promise, swear, vow; contract, enlist, enroll (*also* enrol), sign on, sign up

near antonyms renege

2 to leave as a guarantee of repayment of a loan — see PAWN

3 to make a solemn declaration of intent — see PROMISE 1

plenary *adj* not lacking any part or member that properly belongs to it — see COMPLETE 1

plenitude *n* 1 a considerable amount — see LOT 2

2 an amount or supply more than sufficient to meet one's needs — see PLENTY 1

plenteous *adj* being more than enough without being excessive — see PLENTIFUL

plentiful *adj* being more than enough without being excessive ⟨a *plentiful* amount of strawberries that will be more than enough for a couple of pies⟩

synonyms abundant, ample, bountiful, comfortable, generous, liberal, plenteous

related words abounding, overflowing, replete, rich, rife, teeming, wealthy; adequate, enough, sufficient; fat, fecund, fertile, fruitful, prolific; copious, galore, lavish, profuse; luxuriant

near antonyms deficient, inadequate, insufficient, lacking, wanting; meager (*or* meagre), niggardly, stingy; skimpy; least, minimum; light, slight, small; barren, infertile, sterile, unfruitful, unproductive

antonyms bare, minimal, scant

plentitude *n* an amount or supply more than sufficient to meet one's needs — see PLENTY 1

plenty *n* 1 an amount or supply more than sufficient to meet one's needs ⟨you'll have *plenty* of time to do your science project⟩

synonyms abundance, plenitude, plentitude, superabundance, wealth

related words adequacy, competence, competency, enough, sufficiency; amplitude, liberality; excess, overflow, overkill, oversupply, superfluity, surfeit, surplus; fecundity, fertility, fruitfulness, richness; lavishness, luxuriance

near antonyms paucity, poverty, scarcity; barrenness, infertility, sterility

antonyms deficiency, inadequacy, insufficiency

2 a considerable amount — see LOT 2

pliable *adj* able to bend easily without breaking — see WILLOWY

pliant *adj* able to bend easily without breaking — see WILLOWY

plod *vb* 1 to devote serious and sustained effort — see LABOR

2 to make progress in a clumsy, struggling manner — see FLOUNDER 1

3 to move slowly — see CRAWL 2

plop *vb* to throw or set down clumsily or casually — see FLOP 1

plot *n* **1** a secret plan for accomplishing evil or unlawful ends ⟨they uncovered a *plot* to assassinate the President just in time⟩
synonyms conspiracy, design, intrigue, machination, scheme
related words frame-up; manipulation, subterfuge, trickery; artifice, contrivance, maneuver, stratagem, trick; cabal, confederacy, ring; game, gimmick, racket; ground plan, program, strategy, system; collusion, complicity, connivance, conniving
2 a small area of usually open land — see FIELD 1
3 a small piece of land that is developed or available for development — see LOT 1

plot *vb* to engage in a secret plan to accomplish evil or unlawful ends ⟨mobsters were caught *plotting* to take over the company⟩
synonyms conspire, contrive, intrigue, machinate, scheme
related words brew, concoct, cook (up), hatch; connive; engineer, jockey, maneuver, manipulate; design, frame, lay out, map, plan, shape

plow *vb* **1** to cut into and turn over the sod of (a piece of land) using a bladed implement ⟨we'll have to get out there and *plow* and plant both fields before it rains⟩
synonyms break, furrow
related words cultivate, till; fallow; harrow, hoe, rake
2 to devote serious and sustained effort — see LABOR

ploy *n* a clever often underhanded means to achieve an end — see TRICK 1

pluck *n* **1** the act or an instance of applying force on something so that it moves in the direction of the force — see PULL 1
2 the strength of mind that enables a person to endure pain or hardship — see FORTITUDE

plug *vb* **1** to close up so that no empty spaces remain — see FILL 2
2 to devote serious and sustained effort — see LABOR
3 to provide publicity for — see PUBLICIZE 1
4 to strike with a missile from a gun — see SHOOT 3

plug (up) *vb* to prevent passage through — see CLOG 1

plugger *n* a person who does very hard or dull work — see SLAVE 2

plum *n* someone or something unusually desirable — see PRIZE 1

plumb *adj* rising straight up — see ERECT

plumb *adv* **1** in a direct line or course — see DIRECTLY 1
2 *chiefly dialect* to a full extent or degree — see FULLY 1

plumb *vb* to measure the depth of (as a body of water) typically with a weighted line — see ²SOUND 1

plume *n* something given in recognition of achievement — see AWARD

plume *vb* to think highly of (oneself) — see PRIDE

plummet *vb* to go to a lower level — see DROP 2

plump *adj* having an excess of body fat — see FAT 1

plump *adv* in a direct line or course — see DIRECTLY 1

plump *vb* to throw or set down clumsily or casually — see FLOP 1

plumpness *n* the condition of having an excess of body fat — see CORPULENCE

plunder *n* valuables stolen or taken by force — see LOOT

plunder *vb* to search through with the intent of committing robbery — see RANSACK 1

plunge *n* **1** an act or instance of diving — see DIVE 1
2 the act or process of going to a lower level or altitude — see DESCENT 1

plunge *vb* **1** to cast oneself head first into deep water — see DIVE
2 to go to a lower level — see DROP 2
3 to lead or extend downward — see DESCEND 1

plunk *vb* to throw or set down clumsily or casually — see FLOP 1

plus *n* something added (as by growth) — see INCREASE 1

plush *adj* showing obvious signs of wealth and comfort — see LUXURIOUS

ply *vb* to bring to bear especially forcefully or effectively — see EXERT

poach *vb* to cook in a liquid heated to the point that it gives off steam — see BOIL 2

po'boy *also* **poor boy** *n* a large sandwich on a long split roll — see SUBMARINE

pocket *adj* of a size that is less than average — see SMALL 1

pocket *n* available money — see FUND 2

pocket *vb* **1** to refrain from openly showing or uttering — see SUPPRESS 2
2 to take (something) without right and with an intent to keep — see STEAL 1

pocketbook *n* a container for carrying money and small personal items — see PURSE

pocket–size *also* **pocket–sized** *adj* of a size that is less than average — see SMALL 1

pockmark *n* something that spoils the appearance or completeness of a thing — see BLEMISH

pod *n* something that encloses another thing especially to protect it — see ¹CASE 1

podium *n* a level usually raised surface — see PLATFORM

poem *n* a composition using rhythm and often rhyme to create a lyrical effect ⟨your assignment is to write two *poems* about springtime⟩
synonyms lyric, song, verse
related words rhyme (*also* rime); ballad, lay; elegy, English sonnet, epic, epigram, haiku, jingle, lament, limerick, ode, psalm, sonnet; blank verse, free verse, minstrelsy, poesy, poetry

poesy *n* writing that uses rhythm, vivid language, and often rhyme to provoke an emotional response — see POETRY 1

poet *n* a person who writes poetry ⟨Emily Dickinson is famous as the *poet* who rarely left the house but often journeyed to the depths of the human heart⟩
synonyms bard, minstrel, versifier
related words poetess; poet laureate; troubadour; epigrammatist, rhymer, sonneteer

poetic *adj* having qualities suggestive of poetry ⟨your description of the sun setting over the Grand Canyon was a particularly *poetic* piece of writing⟩
synonyms lyric, lyrical, poetical
related words metric, metrical, rhyming, rhythmic (*or* rhythmical); rhapsodic (*also* rhapsodical);

THESAURUS

florid, flowery, grandiloquent, highfalutin, high-flown, ornate; figurative, metaphorical, symbolic (*also* symbolical)

near antonyms factual, literal, matter-of-fact

antonyms prosaic, prose, unpoetic

poetical *adj* having qualities suggestive of poetry — see POETIC

poetry *n* **1** writing that uses rhythm, vivid language, and often rhyme to provoke an emotional response ⟨not all *poetry* has to rhyme⟩

synonyms minstrelsy, poesy, song, verse

related words rhyme (*also* rime); blank verse, free verse

antonyms prose

2 the art or power of speaking or writing in a forceful and convincing way — see ELOQUENCE

poignancy *n* a harsh or sharp quality — see EDGE 1

poignant *adj* having the power to affect the feelings or sympathies — see MOVING

point *n* **1** a particular and often important moment in time ⟨it was at that *point* that I had to stop and check on the experiment⟩

synonyms juncture

related words flash, instant, jiffy, minute, moment, second, shake, split second, trice, twinkle, wink; bit, spell, stretch, while; brink, threshold, verge

2 the last and usually sharp or tapering part of something long and narrow ⟨be careful with the *point* on that umbrella, or you could hurt someone⟩

synonyms apex, cusp, end, pike, tip

related words prong, tine; barb, jag, prickle, snag, spike, sticker

3 a separate part in a list, account, or series — see ITEM 1

4 a single piece of information — see FACT 3

5 a small area that is different (as in color) from the main part — see SPOT 1

6 an area of high ground jutting out into a body of water beyond the line of the coast — see HEADLAND 1

7 an area of land that juts out into a body of water — see ²CAPE

8 an individual part of a process, series, or ranking — see DEGREE 1

9 something that sets apart an individual from others of the same kind — see CHARACTERISTIC

10 the area or space occupied by or intended for something — see PLACE 1

11 the quality of an utterance that provokes interest and produces an effect — see ¹PUNCH 1

point (toward) *vb* to stand or sit with the face or front toward — see FACE 1

point (up) *vb* to indicate the importance of by giving prominent display — see EMPHASIZE

pointed *adj* **1** tapering to a thin tip ⟨the snake plant's long *pointed* leaves make it an easily recognized houseplant⟩

synonyms peaked, sharp, tipped

related words barbed, jagged, pronged, spiky

near antonyms dull, rounded

antonyms blunt

2 having to do with the matter at hand — see PERTINENT

pointer *n* **1** an arrow-shaped piece on a dial or scale for registering information ⟨the *pointer* on my bathroom scale must be stuck—I know I lost weight⟩

synonyms hand, index, indicator, needle

related words dial, face, gauge (*also* gage)

2 a piece of advice or useful information especially from an expert — see ¹TIP 1

pointless *adj* having no meaning — see MEANINGLESS

point of view *n* a way of looking at or thinking about something ⟨who actually has the right to possession of that wilderness area depends on your *point of view*⟩

synonyms angle, outlook, perspective, shoes, slant, standpoint, viewpoint

related words interpretation, spin; belief, conviction, eye, feeling, judgment (*or* judgement), mind, notion, opinion, perception, persuasion, sentiment, verdict, view; impression, take; wavelength; side; attitude, position, posture, stand

poise *n* a condition in which opposing forces are equal to one another — see BALANCE 1

poise *vb* to rest or move along the surface of a liquid or in the air — see FLOAT

poison *adj* containing or contaminated with a substance capable of injuring or killing a living thing — see POISONOUS

poison *n* a substance that by chemical action can kill or injure a living thing ⟨the only way to get rid of rats is to leave out *poison*⟩

synonyms bane, toxin, venom

related words cancer, contagion, disease, virus; fungicide, germicide, herbicide, insecticide

near antonyms antidote, antivenin; cure; cure-all, elixir, panacea

poison *vb* **1** to affect slightly with something morally bad or undesirable — see TAINT 1

2 to make unfit for use by the addition of something harmful or undesirable — see CONTAMINATE

3 to lower in character or dignity — see DEBASE 1

poisoned *adj* containing or contaminated with a substance capable of injuring or killing a living thing — see POISONOUS

poisonous *adj* containing or contaminated with a substance capable of injuring or killing a living thing ⟨some evil person was leaving out *poisonous* meat for neighborhood dogs to eat⟩

synonyms envenomed, poison, poisoned, toxic, venomous

related words contagious, infectious; deleterious, harmful, hurtful, injurious, malignant, noxious, virulent; unhealthful, unhealthy, unwholesome; calamitous, deadly, fatal, lethal, murderous

near antonyms beneficial, curative, healthful, healthy, helpful, palliative, remedial, salubrious, salutary, wholesome; benign, harmless, innocuous, inoffensive; nonfatal, nonlethal

antonyms nonpoisonous, nontoxic, nonvenomous

¹poke *n* a quick thrust ⟨please stop giving the cat *pokes* while it's trying to sleep⟩

synonyms dab, dig, jab

related words punch; stab, stick; push, shove; jam, jerk, jog, nudge

²poke *n* *chiefly Southern & Midland* a container made of a flexible material (as paper or plastic) — see BAG 1

poke *vb* **1** to extend outward beyond a usual point — see BULGE

2 to interest oneself in what is not one's concern — see INTERFERE

3 to move or act slowly — see DELAY 1

4 to move slowly — see CRAWL 2

poking *adj* moving or proceeding at less than the normal, desirable, or required speed — see SLOW 1

poky *or* **pokey** *adj* moving or proceeding at less than the normal, desirable, or required speed — see SLOW 1

polar *adj* **1** being as different as possible — see OPPOSITE

2 having a low or subnormal temperature — see COLD 1

police *n* **1** the department of government that keeps order, fights crime, and enforces statutes ⟨the appearance of a ransom note meant that the teenager's disappearance was now a matter for the *police*⟩
synonyms law
related words judiciary, jurisprudence, justice
2 a body of officers of the law ⟨the National Guard will serve as backup for the metropolitan *police* in the event of violent protests⟩
synonyms constabulary, police force
related words constable, cop, gendarme, officer, policeman, police officer, policewoman, trooper

police force *n* a body of officers of the law — see POLICE 2

policeman *n* a member of a force charged with law enforcement at the local level — see OFFICER 1

police officer *n* a member of a force charged with law enforcement at the local level — see OFFICER 1

policy *n* a way of acting or proceeding — see COURSE 1

polish *n* **1** a high level of taste and enlightenment as a result of extensive intellectual training and exposure to the arts — see CULTURE 1

2 brightness created by light reflected from a surface — see SHINE 1

polish *vb* to make smooth or glossy usually by repeatedly applying surface pressure ⟨you'll need to *polish* your shoes with a clean rag before the performance⟩
synonyms buff, burnish, dress, gloss, grind, rub, shine, smooth
related words sleek, slick; coat, glaze; finish, veneer; brighten; rasp, sand, sandblast, sandpaper, scour, scrape, scrub
near antonyms rough (up), roughen, scuff (up)

polished *adj* **1** having a shiny surface or finish — see GLOSSY

2 having or showing a taste for the fine arts and gracious living — see CULTIVATED

polite *adj* **1** showing consideration, courtesy, and good manners ⟨it's only *polite* to hold the door for the person behind you⟩
synonyms civil, courteous, genteel, gracious, mannerly, well-bred
related words attentive, considerate, thoughtful; chivalrous, courtly, gallant; ceremonial, ceremonious; formal, suave, unctuous, urbane; elegant, refined; deferential, dutiful, respectful, submissive, yielding; acceptable, appropriate, becoming, befitting, correct, decent, decorous, fit, fitting, good, meet, proper, respectable, right, seemly, suitable; affable, cordial, friendly, genial, hospitable, sociable; felicitous, graceful; humble, meek, modest, unassertive
near antonyms heedless, inconsiderate, thoughtless; audacious, bold, bold-faced, brash, brassy, disrespectful, impertinent, impudent, insolent, saucy, shameless; boorish, churlish, clownish, loutish, uncouth, vulgar; casual, informal, unceremonious; improper, inappropriate, incorrect, indecent, indecorous, uncalled-for, unrespectable, unseemly; arrogant, conceited, presumptuous, pretentious
antonyms discourteous, ill-bred, ill-mannered, impolite, inconsiderate, rude, thoughtless, uncivil, ungracious, unmannerly

2 following the established traditions of refined society and good taste — see PROPER 1

politeness *n* speech or behavior that is a sign of good breeding ⟨the little girl's *politeness* greatly impressed her teacher⟩
synonyms civility, courteousness, courtesy, gentility, graciousness, mannerliness
related words attentiveness, consideration, thoughtfulness; ceremonialness, ceremoniousness, ceremony, formality; chivalrousness, chivalry, courtliness, gallantry; breeding, manners; suaveness, unctuousness, urbanity; elegance, refinement; deference, respect; decency, decorousness, decorum, propriety, respectability, seemliness; affability, cordiality, friendliness, geniality, hospitality, sociability; felicitousness, gracefulness; humility, meekness, modesty, shyness
near antonyms audaciousness, audacity, boldness, brashness, brassiness, disrespect, impertinence, impudence, insolence, sauciness, shamelessness; boorishness, churlishness, clownishness, loutishness, vulgarity; casualness, informality; impropriety, inappropriateness, incorrectness, indecency; inconsideration, thoughtlessness; arrogance, conceit, presumption, pretentiousness
antonyms discourteousness, discourtesy, impoliteness, incivility, rudeness, ungraciousness

politic *adj* suitable for bringing about a desired result under the circumstances — see EXPEDIENT

poll *n* the upper or front part of the body that contains the brain, the major sense organs, and the mouth — see HEAD 1

poll *vb* to go around and approach (people) with a request for opinions or information — see CANVASS

pollutant *n* something that is or that makes impure — see IMPURITY

pollute *vb* to make unfit for use by the addition of something harmful or undesirable — see CONTAMINATE

polluted *adj* containing foreign or lower-grade substances — see IMPURE

poltergeist *n* the soul of a dead person thought of especially as appearing to living people — see GHOST

poltroon *n* a person who shows a shameful lack of courage in the face of danger — see COWARD

polychromatic *adj* marked by a variety of usually vivid colors — see COLORFUL

polychrome *adj* marked by a variety of usually vivid colors — see COLORFUL

polygraph *n* an instrument for detecting physical signs of the tension that goes with lying — see LIE DETECTOR

pommel *vb* to strike repeatedly — see BEAT 1

pompous *adj* **1** having a feeling of superiority that shows itself in an overbearing attitude — see ARROGANT

2 having too high an opinion of oneself — see CONCEITED

3 self-consciously trying to present an appearance of grandeur or importance — see PRETENTIOUS 1

THESAURUS

pompousness *n* **1** an exaggerated sense of one's importance that shows itself in the making of excessive or unjustified claims — see ARROGANCE **2** an often unjustified feeling of being pleased with oneself or with one's situation or achievements — see COMPLACENCE

ponder *vb* to give serious and careful thought to ⟨I'm *pondering* whether or not I should join another club⟩
synonyms chew over, cogitate, consider, contemplate, debate, deliberate, entertain, meditate, mull (over), question, ruminate, study, think (about *or* over), weigh
related words muse (upon), reflect (on *or* upon), reminisce; conclude, reason; second-guess, speculate; brood (about *or* over), fret (about *or* over), obsess (about *or* over); believe, conceive, opine; absorb, assimilate, digest, drink (in)
phrases cudgel one's brains
near antonyms disregard, ignore, overlook, slight; dismiss, pooh-pooh (*also* pooh), reject

ponderous *adj* **1** causing weariness, restlessness, or lack of interest — see BORING
2 having great weight — see HEAVY 1

ponderousness *n* the state or quality of being heavy — see WEIGHTINESS 1

pooch *n* a domestic mammal that is related to the wolves and foxes — see DOG

¹**pool** *n* a small often deep body of water ⟨when it rains, that small *pool* grows to almost the size of a lake⟩
synonyms mere [*chiefly British*], puddle
related words basin, hole, sinkhole; swimming pool; lake

²**pool** *n* **1** a body of persons at work or available for work — see FORCE 1
2 the number of individuals or amount of something available at any given time — see SUPPLY
3 a sum of money set aside for a particular purpose — see FUND 1
4 the total of the bets at stake at one time — see POT 1

poor *adj* **1** lacking money or material possessions ⟨every year, we make up a basket of food at Thanksgiving for a *poor* family in the neighborhood⟩
synonyms beggared, broke, destitute, impecunious, impoverished, indigent, needy, penniless, penurious, poverty-stricken, stone-broke
related words deprived, disadvantaged, underprivileged; bankrupt, bankrupted, insolvent; depressed, pinched, reduced, straitened; low, short
phrases hard up
near antonyms comfortable, prosperous
antonyms affluent, flush, moneyed (*or* monied), opulent, rich, wealthy, well-heeled, well-off, well-to-do
2 producing inferior or only a small amount of vegetation — see BARREN 1
3 less plentiful than what is normal, necessary, or desirable — see MEAGER
4 falling short of a standard — see BAD 1
5 of low quality — see CHEAP 2
6 deserving of one's pity — see PATHETIC 1

poorly *adj* temporarily suffering from a disorder of the body — see SICK 1

poorly *adv* in an unsatisfactory way — see BADLY

poorness *n* the state of lacking sufficient money or material possessions — see POVERTY 1

¹**pop** *n* a loud explosive sound — see CLAP 1

²**pop** *n* a male human parent — see FATHER 1

pop *vb* **1** to break open or into pieces usually because of internal pressure — see EXPLODE 1
2 to break suddenly with an explosive sound — see CRACK 1
3 to cause to break open or into pieces by or as if by an explosive — see BLAST 1
4 to strike with a missile from a gun — see SHOOT 3

pop (in) *vb* to make a brief visit — see CALL 3

populace *n* the body of the community as contrasted with the elite — see MASS 1

popular *adj* **1** enjoying widespread favor or approval ⟨bell-bottom jeans were *popular* in the seventies⟩
synonyms fashionable, hot, in, modish, popularized, vogue
related words favorite, preferred; desirable, liked, wanted; celebrated, famed, famous, noted, notorious, prominent, renowned, well-known; fabled, fabulous, legendary; leading, notable, outstanding, remarkable; important, significant
near antonyms washed-up; despised, detested, disliked, hated, rejected; insignificant, unimportant; indistinguished, unexceptional; anonymous, nameless, obscure, unknown; inconspicuous
antonyms out, unpopular
2 accepted, used, or practiced by most people — see CURRENT 1
3 held by or applicable to a majority of the people — see GENERAL 3
4 of, relating to, or favoring political democracy — see DEMOCRATIC

popularity *n* the state of enjoying widespread approval ⟨the sudden *popularity* of low-cut blouses horrified my mother⟩
synonyms fashionableness, favor, hotness, modishness, vogue
related words craze, fad, mode, rage, style, trend; bandwagon; fame, notoriety, prominence, renown; enthusiasm, fervor, passion
near antonyms oblivion, obscurity
antonyms disfavor, unpopularity

popularized *adj* enjoying widespread favor or approval — see POPULAR 1

pore (over) *vb* to go over and mentally take in the content of — see READ

pornographic *adj* depicting or referring to sexual matters in a way that is unacceptable in polite society — see OBSCENE 1

porous *adj* capable of being passed into or through — see PENETRABLE

port *n* a part of a body of water protected and deep enough to be a place of safety for ships — see HARBOR 1

portable *adj* capable of being moved especially with ease — see MOVABLE

portal *n* a barrier by which an entry is closed and opened — see DOOR 1

portent *n* **1** something believed to be a sign or warning of a future event — see OMEN
2 something extraordinary or surprising — see WONDER 1

portentous *adj* **1** being or showing a sign of evil or calamity to come — see OMINOUS
2 causing wonder or astonishment — see MARVELOUS 1

porter *n chiefly British* a person who tends a door — see DOORKEEPER

portion *n* **1** a state or end that seemingly has been decided beforehand — see FATE 1

2 one of the pieces from which something is designed to be assembled — see PART 1

3 something belonging to, due to, or contributed by an individual member of a group — see SHARE 1

portion *vb* to give out (something) in appropriate amounts or to appropriate individuals — see ADMINISTER 1

portliness *n* the condition of having an excess of body fat — see CORPULENCE

portly *adj* having an excess of body fat — see FAT 1

portmanteau *n* a bag carried by hand and designed to hold a traveler's clothing and personal articles — see TRAVELING BAG

portrait *n* a vivid representation in words of someone or something — see DESCRIPTION 1

portray *vb* **1** to give a representation or account of in words — see DESCRIBE 1

2 to point out the chief quality or qualities of an individual or group — see CHARACTERIZE 1

3 to present a picture of — see PICTURE 1

4 to present a portrayal or performance of — see ACT 1

portrayal *n* a vivid representation in words of someone or something — see DESCRIPTION 1

pose *n* a display of emotion or behavior that is insincere or intended to deceive — see MASQUERADE

pose *vb* to set before the mind for consideration — see PROPOSE 1

pose (as) *vb* to pretend to be (what one is not) in appearance or behavior — see IMPERSONATE 1

position *n* **1** an assignment at which one regularly works for pay — see JOB 1

2 the action for which a person or thing is specially fitted or used or for which a thing exists — see ROLE

3 the area or space occupied by or intended for something — see PLACE 1

4 the place where someone is assigned to stand or remain — see STATION 1

5 the placement of someone or something in relation to others in a vertical arrangement — see RANK 1

position *vb* to arrange something in a certain spot or position — see PLACE 1

positive *adj* **1** expressing approval — see FAVORABLE 1

2 having or showing a mind free from doubt — see CERTAIN 2

positiveness *n* a state of mind in which one is free from doubt — see CONFIDENCE 2

possess *vb* to keep, control, or experience as one's own — see HAVE 1

possession *n* **1** the fact or state of having (something) at one's disposal ⟨a student who was found to have several overdue library books in his *possession*⟩

synonyms control, hands, keeping

related words ownership, proprietorship; authority, command, dominion, mastery, power; enjoyment, repossession, retention; claiming, collaring, commandeering, confiscation, procurement

near antonyms dispossession, relinquishment, surrendering, transferal

antonyms nonpossession

2 possessions *pl* transportable items that one

owns ⟨we packed up all of our *possessions* and moved to a new house⟩

synonyms belongings, chattels, effects, holdings, movables (*or* moveables), paraphernalia, personalty, things

related words treasures, valuables; junk, stuff; appointments, fixtures, furnishings; property, tangibles; collateral

near antonyms real estate

possessive *adj* intolerant of rivalry or unfaithfulness — see JEALOUS 1

possessor *n* one who has a legal or rightful claim to ownership — see PROPRIETOR

possibility *n* **1** something that can develop or become actual — see POTENTIAL

2 something that might happen — see EVENT 2

possible *adj* **1** capable of being done or carried out ⟨I think that building the entire set in two days is *possible*, if difficult⟩

synonyms achievable, attainable, doable, feasible, practicable, realizable, viable, workable

related words practical, reasonable, sensible; likely, probable; acceptable, believable, conceivable, creditable, plausible; available, usable

near antonyms impractical, unrealistic; doubtful, dubious, far-fetched, improbable, unlikely; implausible, inconceivable, incredible, unbelievable; futile, useless, vain; absurd, fantastic, outlandish, preposterous, ridiculous; unthinkable

antonyms hopeless, impossible, impracticable, unachievable, unattainable, unworkable

2 existing only as a possibility and not in fact — see POTENTIAL

possibly *adv* it is possible — see PERHAPS

¹post *n chiefly British* communications or parcels sent or carried through the postal system — see MAIL

²post *n* **1** a specific task with which a person or group is charged — see MISSION

2 the place where someone is assigned to stand or remain — see STATION 1

3 an assignment at which one regularly works for pay — see JOB 1

³post *n* an upright shaft that supports an overhead structure — see PILLAR 1

¹post *vb* **1** to affix (as a notice) to or on a suitable place ⟨the student organizations always *post* their announcements on the cafeteria walls⟩

synonyms placard

related words nail, plaster, tack (up); advertise, announce, blaze, broadcast, call, declare, proclaim, promulgate, publicize, publish

near antonyms remove, take down

2 to make known openly or publicly — see ANNOUNCE

²post *vb* to assign to a place or position ⟨the police are planning to *post* an officer outside the hospital room of the witness⟩

synonyms detail, station

related words set; appoint; place, position

³post *vb* to send through the postal system — see MAIL

postdate *vb* to come after in time — see FOLLOW 1

poster *n* a sheet bearing an announcement for posting in a public place ⟨we put up a hundred *posters* announcing the concert⟩

synonyms bill, placard

related words billboard, sign, signboard; broadside, flier (*or* flyer), handbill, handout, playbill;

THESAURUS

ad, advertisement, announcement, bulletin, dispatch, release

posterior *adj* **1** being at or in the part of something opposite the front part — see BACK
2 being, occurring, or carried out at a time after something else — see SUBSEQUENT

posterior *n* the part of the body upon which someone sits — see BUTTOCKS

posterity *n* the descendants of a person, animal, or plant — see OFFSPRING

posthaste *adv* with great speed — see FAST 1

posthumous *adj* occurring after one's death ⟨the soldier was awarded a *posthumous* medal for valor⟩
synonyms postmortem
related words belated, delayed, late

posting *n* a published statement informing the public of a matter of general interest — see ANNOUNCEMENT

postman *n* a person who delivers mail ⟨the *postman* comes at around nine every morning⟩
synonyms letter carrier, mail carrier, mailman
related words messenger; postmaster

postmortem *adj* occurring after one's death — see POSTHUMOUS

postmortem *n* examination of a dead body especially to find out the cause of death — see AUTOPSY

postmortem examination *n* examination of a dead body especially to find out the cause of death — see AUTOPSY

postpone *vb* to assign to a later time ⟨we'll have to *postpone* the decision until we have all the information⟩
synonyms defer, delay, hold off (on), hold up, put off, shelve
related words suspend; hesitate, pause, stay; detain, retard, slow; extend, lengthen, prolong, protract, stretch (out); wait
near antonyms act, deal (with), decide (upon), do, work (on)

postulate *n* something taken as being true or factual and used as a starting point for a course of action or reasoning — see ASSUMPTION

postulate *vb* to take as true or as a fact without actual proof — see ASSUME 2

posture *n* **1** a general way of holding the body ⟨a good upright *posture* will prevent backaches⟩
synonyms carriage, stance
related words attention; body language; pose, seat; bearing, behavior, conduct, demeanor, deportment; air, poise, presence; aspect, look, mien
2 position with regard to conditions and circumstances — see SITUATION 1

posy *n* a bunch of flowers — see BOUQUET 1

pot *n* **1** the total of the bets at stake at one time ⟨everyone got a bit nervous when the *pot* was more than a hundred dollars⟩
synonyms jackpot, pool
related words fund, kitty; bet, stake, wager
2 a considerable amount — see LOT 2

potable *adj* suitable for drinking ⟨around here, the only *potable* water comes from wells⟩
synonyms drinkable
related words clean, fresh, pure, uncontaminated, unpolluted; nonpoisonous
near antonyms contaminated, dirty, foul, polluted; poison, poisonous, toxic; unhealthful, unhealthy, unwholesome
antonyms undrinkable

potbelly *n* an enlarged or bulging abdomen ⟨he began exercising to get rid of his growing *potbelly* and tighten up his stomach⟩
synonyms paunch
related words belly, breadbasket [*slang*], gut, stomach, tummy; chubbiness, corpulence, fat, fatness, fleshiness, obesity, overweight, paunchiness, plumpness, portliness, pudginess; chunkiness, heaviness, stoutness

potency *n* the ability to exert effort for the accomplishment of a task — see POWER 2

potent *adj* **1** having an abundance of some characteristic quality (as flavor) — see FULL-BODIED
2 having great power or influence — see IMPORTANT 2
3 producing or capable of producing a desired result — see EFFECTIVE 1

potentate *n* a person who uses power or authority in a cruel, unjust, or harmful way — see DESPOT

potential *adj* existing only as a possibility and not in fact ⟨I can see a few *potential* problems with getting a puppy, but we'll wait and see if they come up⟩
synonyms possible
related words conceivable, imaginable, plausible, thinkable; likely, probable; conjectural, hypothetical, suppositional, theoretical (*also* theoretic); alleged, assumed, purported, reputed, supposed; achievable, attainable, doable, feasible, practicable, viable, workable
near antonyms authenticated, confirmed, demonstrated, established, proven, substantiated; authentic, bona fide, genuine, true
antonyms actual, existent, factual, real

potential *n* something that can develop or become actual ⟨a time when cloning was merely a *potential* and the stuff of science fiction⟩
synonyms eventuality, possibility, potentiality
related words likelihood, probability; latency
near antonyms actuality, reality; certainty

potentiality *n* something that can develop or become actual — see POTENTIAL

pother *n* **1** a state of nervous or irritated concern — see FRET
2 a state of noisy, confused activity — see COMMOTION

potpourri *n* an unorganized collection or mixture of various things — see MISCELLANY 1

potter (around) *vb* to spend time in aimless activity — see FIDDLE (AROUND)

potterer *n* a person who regularly or occasionally engages in an activity without being or becoming an expert at it — see AMATEUR

potter's field *n* a piece of land used for burying the dead — see CEMETERY

pottery *n* articles made of baked clay — see CROCKERY

pouch *n* a container made of a flexible material (as paper or plastic) — see BAG 1

poultice *n* a medicated covering used to heal an injury — see DRESSING 1

pounce (on *or* upon) *vb* to take sudden, violent action against — see ATTACK 1

pound *n* **1** a hard strike with a part of the body or an instrument — see ¹BLOW
2 an enclosure with an open framework for keeping animals — see CAGE

pound *vb* **1** to move heavily or clumsily — see LUMBER 1

2 to deliver a blow to (someone or something) usually in a strong vigorous manner — see HIT 1

3 to strike repeatedly — see BEAT 1

4 to shape with a hammer — see HAMMER 1

pour *vb* **1** to cause to flow in a stream ⟨she lifted the teakettle and *poured* some hot water through the spout⟩

synonyms stream

related words ladle, spoon; cascade, trickle; deluge, flood, inundate, overflow

2 to move in a stream — see FLOW 1

3 to flow out in great quantities or with force — see GUSH 1

4 to fall as water in a continuous stream of drops from the clouds — see RAIN 1

5 to give readily and in large quantities — see RAIN 2

pouring *adj* marked by or abounding with rain — see RAINY

pout *n* **1** a twisting of the facial features in disgust or disapproval — see GRIMACE

2 pouts *pl* a state of resentful silence or irritability — see SULK

pout *vb* to silently go about in a bad mood — see SULK

pouting *adj* given to or displaying a resentful silence and often irritability — see SULKY

poverty *n* **1** the state of lacking sufficient money or material possessions ⟨he dreamed of finding a good job and working his way out of *poverty* and debt⟩

synonyms beggary, destitution, impecuniousness, impoverishment, indigence, need, neediness, pauperism, penuriousness, penury, poorness, want

related words misery, woe, wretchedness; exigency, necessity; austerity, deprivation, privation; bankruptcy, insolvency; belt-tightening, pinching, straitening

near antonyms luxury, prosperity

antonyms affluence, opulence, richness, wealthiness

2 a falling short of an essential or desirable amount or number — see DEFICIENCY

poverty–stricken *adj* lacking money or material possessions — see POOR 1

powder *vb* to reduce to fine particles ⟨you have to *powder* the antibiotic tablet and mix it with food⟩

synonyms atomize, crush, grind, pulverize

related words grate; crumble, crunch; break, bust, dash, fracture, fragment; shatter, smash, splinter; mill

powdery *adj* consisting of very small particles — see FINE 1

power *n* **1** the right or means to command or control others ⟨the principal has nearly complete *power* over this school⟩

synonyms arm, authority, clutch, command, control, dominion, grip, hold, mastery, sway

related words clout, influence, pull, weight; jurisdiction; direction, management; dominance, predominance, sovereignty, supremacy; prerogative, privilege, right; eminence, importance, moment

near antonyms helplessness, weakness

antonyms impotence, powerlessness

2 the ability to exert effort for the accomplishment of a task ⟨the corporation has the *power* to accomplish almost anything⟩ ⟨you'll need to build a bit more *power* in order to be a star pitcher⟩

synonyms energy, force, might, muscle, potency, puissance, sinew, strength, vigor

related words aptitude, capability, capacity, competence, competency; adequacy, effectiveness, effectualness, usefulness

near antonyms disability, inability, inaptitude, incapability, incapacity, incompetence, incompetency; ineffectiveness, ineffectualness, uselessness; helplessness, paralysis

antonyms impotence, powerlessness, weakness

3 a natural ability of the mind or body ⟨dogs have a very highly developed *power* of smell⟩

synonyms faculty

related words function; capability, capacity; aptitude, endowment, flair, genius, gift, instinct, knack, talent

near antonyms inability, incapability, incapacity; inaptitude, inaptness, ineptness

4 something with a usable capacity for doing work — see FUEL

powerboat *n* a boat equipped with a motor — see MOTORBOAT

powerful *adj* having great power or influence — see IMPORTANT 2

powerfully *adv* in a vigorous and forceful manner — see HARD 3

powerhouse *n* an ambitious person who eagerly goes after what is desired — see GO-GETTER

powerless *adj* unable to act or achieve one's purpose ⟨I wish I could help you, but I am *powerless* in this situation⟩

synonyms helpless, impotent, weak

related words incapable, incompetent, ineffective, ineffectual, inept, unfit, useless; feeble, frail, infirm, passive, spineless, supine, unaggressive

near antonyms able, capable, competent, effective, efficient; authoritarian, autocratic, despotic, dictatorial, magisterial, tyrannical (*also* tyrranic); dominant, dynamic, energetic, forceful, robust, sturdy, tough, vigorous; important, major, significant; high-level, senior, top

antonyms mighty, potent, powerful, puissant, strong

powerlessness *n* the lack of sufficient ability, power, or means — see INABILITY

powwow *n* **1** a coming together of a number of persons for a specified purpose — see MEETING 1

2 a meeting featuring a group discussion — see FORUM

powwow *vb* to exchange viewpoints or seek advice for the purpose of finding a solution to a problem — see CONFER 2

practicable *adj* **1** capable of being done or carried out — see POSSIBLE 1

2 capable of being put to use or account — see PRACTICAL 1

3 capable of or suitable for being used for a particular purpose — see USABLE 1

practical *adj* **1** capable of being put to use or account ⟨a *practical* and simple solution for the town's waste disposal⟩ ⟨she has some *practical* information on sight-seeing in San Francisco⟩

synonyms applicable, functional, practicable, serviceable, usable, useful, workable, working

related words down-to-earth, pragmatic (*also* pragmatical), utilitarian; accessible, available, obtainable, reachable; all-around (*also* all-round), handy; active, alive, busy, employed, functioning, operating, operative

near antonyms abstract, academic, theoretical (*also* theoretic); inaccessible, unattainable, unavailable, unobtainable, unreachable; unsuitable

antonyms impracticable, impractical, unusable, unworkable, useless

2 willing to see things as they really are and deal with them sensibly — see REALISTIC 1

practical joke *n* a playful or mischievous act intended as a joke — see PRANK

practically *adv* very close to but not completely — see ALMOST

practice *also* **practise** *n* **1** a private performance or session in preparation for a public appearance — see REHEARSAL

2 a usual manner of behaving or doing — see HABIT

3 something done over and over in order to develop skill — see EXERCISE 2

practice *or* **practise** *vb* to do over and over so as to become skilled ⟨in order to play the guitar well, you need to *practice* fingering every single day⟩

synonyms exercise, rehearse

related words prepare (for), train (with); drill, repeat; work (at *or* on); review, study

practiced *or* **practised** *adj* **1** having or showing exceptional knowledge, experience, or skill in a field of endeavor — see PROFICIENT

2 accomplished with trained ability — see SKILLFUL

pragmatic *also* **pragmatical** *adj* willing to see things as they really are and deal with them sensibly — see REALISTIC 1

prairie *n* a broad area of level or rolling treeless country — see PLAIN

praise *vb* **1** to proclaim the glory of ⟨hymns that *praise* God⟩

synonyms bless, extol (*also* extoll), glorify, laud, magnify

related words adore, deify, idolize, worship; acclaim, applaud, commend, compliment, hail, salute; celebrate, cheer, eulogize, rhapsodize; cite; flatter; crack up, recommend, tout

near antonyms blame, censure, reprehend, reprobate; criticize, reprove; admonish, chide, rebuke, reprimand, reproach; castigate, lambaste (*or* lambast)

2 to declare enthusiastic approval of — see ACCLAIM

praiseworthy *adj* deserving of high regard or great approval — see ADMIRABLE

prance *vb* to walk with exaggerated arm and leg movements — see STRUT 1

prank *n* a playful or mischievous act intended as a joke ⟨as a *prank*, several students managed to change all the classroom clocks to different times⟩

synonyms antic, caper, escapade, frolic, practical joke, trick

related words skylarking; adventure, experience, game, lark, time; high jinks, horseplay, play, roughhousing, rowdiness; shenanigans, tomfoolery; joking, kidding, teasing; gambit, hoax, maneuver, ploy; deed, feat, mission, performance, stunt; caprice, conceit, fancy, vagary, whim, whimsy; deceit, deception, delusion, fooling, fraud, hoodwinking, ruse, sham, stratagem, subterfuge, trickery, wile

prankish *adj* tending to or exhibiting reckless playfulness — see MISCHIEVOUS 1

prankishness *n* a natural disposition for playful behavior — see PLAYFULNESS

prate *vb* to engage in casual or rambling conversation — see CHAT

prattle *n* unintelligible or meaningless talk — see GIBBERISH

prattle *vb* **1** to engage in casual or rambling conversation — see CHAT

2 to speak rapidly, inarticulately, and usually unintelligibly — see BABBLE 1

prattler *n* a person who talks constantly — see CHATTERBOX

pray *vb* to make a request to (someone) in an earnest or urgent manner — see BEG

prayer *n* **1** an address to God or a deity ⟨he always directed a bedside *prayer* to God before going to sleep⟩

synonyms orison

related words collect, grace, invocation, litany, thanksgiving; evensong, matins, vespers; appeal, begging, beseeching, entreaty, imploring, petition, pleading, request, soliciting, suit, supplication

2 an earnest request — see PLEA 1

prayerful *adj* asking humbly — see SUPPLIANT

preacher *n* a person specially trained and authorized to conduct religious services in a Christian church — see CLERGYMAN

preamble *n* a short section (as of a book) that leads to or explains the main part — see INTRODUCTION

precariousness *n* the quality or state of not being firmly fixed in position — see INSTABILITY

precautionary *adj* concerned with or serving to keep something from happening — see PREVENTIVE

precede *vb* to go or come before in time ⟨there are two speeches which will *precede* yours⟩

synonyms antedate, forego, predate

antonyms follow, succeed

precedence *n* the right to one's attention before other things considered less important — see PRIORITY

precedent *adj* going before another in time or order — see PREVIOUS

preceding *adj* going before another in time or order — see PREVIOUS

preceptor *n* a person whose occupation is to give formal instruction in a school — see TEACHER

precious *adj* **1** commanding a large price — see COSTLY

2 granted special treatment or attention — see DARLING 1

3 having qualities that tend to make one loved — see LOVABLE

precipice *n* a steep wall of rock, earth, or ice — see CLIFF

precipitate *adj* acting or done with excessive or careless speed — see HASTY 1

precipitate *n* matter that settles to the bottom of a body of liquid — see DEPOSIT 1

precipitate *vb* to fall as water in a continuous stream of drops from the clouds — see RAIN 1

precipitately *adv* with excessive or careless speed — see HASTILY 1

precipitating *adj* marked by or abounding with rain — see RAINY

precipitation *n* excited and often showy or disorderly speed — see HURRY 1

precipitous *adj* **1** acting or done with excessive or careless speed — see HASTY 1

2 having an incline approaching the perpendicular — see STEEP 1

precipitously *adv* with excessive or careless speed — see HASTILY 1

precipitousness *n* excited and often showy or disorderly speed — see HURRY 1

précis *n* a short statement of the main points — see SUMMARY

precise *adj* **1** meeting the highest standard of accuracy ⟨a machine which takes very *precise* measurements⟩
synonyms accurate, close, delicate, exact, fine, hairline, mathematical, pinpoint, rigorous
related words correct, right, strict, true; definite, definitive; nice, subtle; careful, fastidious, finicky
near antonyms approximate, round; false, incorrect, untrue, wrong; careless, loose; indefinite, unclear, vague; doubtful, dubious, questionable, unreliable, untrustworthy
antonyms coarse, imprecise, inaccurate, inexact, rough
2 being in agreement with the truth or a fact or a standard — see CORRECT 1
3 being neither more nor less than a certain amount, number, or extent — see EVEN 1
4 following an original exactly — see FAITHFUL 2
5 of a particular or exact sort — see EXPRESS 1

precisely *adv* **1** as stated or indicated without the slightest difference — see EXACTLY 1
2 in a like manner — see JUST 1
3 without any relaxation of standards or precision — see STRICTLY

preciseness *n* the quality or state of being very accurate — see PRECISION

precision *n* the quality or state of being very accurate ⟨the company that measures TV ratings prides itself on the *precision* of its calculations⟩
synonyms accuracy, closeness, delicacy, exactitude, exactness, fineness, preciseness, rigorousness, veracity
related words correctness, rightness, strictness, truth; definiteness, definitiveness; nicety, subtlety; care, carefulness, fastidiousness
near antonyms approximation, roundness; falseness, falsity, incorrectness, wrongness; carelessness, guesswork, looseness; indefiniteness, unclearness, vagueness
antonyms coarseness, impreciseness, imprecision, inaccuracy, inexactness, roughness

preclude *vb* to keep from happening by taking action in advance — see PREVENT

precluding *n* the act or practice of keeping something from happening — see PREVENTION

precocious *adj* occurring before the usual or expected time — see EARLY 2

precociously *adv* before the usual or expected time — see EARLY

preconception *n* an attitude, belief, or impression formed in advance of actual experience of something — see PREPOSSESSION 1

precursor *n* **1** one that announces or indicates the later arrival of another — see FORERUNNER 1
2 something belonging to an earlier time from which something else was later developed — see ANCESTOR 2

predaceous *or* **predacious** *adj* living by killing and eating other animals — see PREDATORY

predate *vb* to go or come before in time — see PRECEDE

predatory *adj* living by killing and eating other animals ⟨hawks are *predatory* and pose a danger to rabbits and other pets⟩
synonyms predaceous (*or* predacious), rapacious

related words carnivorous; aggressive, deadly, ferocious, fierce, savage, violent; untamed, wild
near antonyms herbivorous, vegetarian; gentle, submissive, tame

predecessor *n* something belonging to an earlier time from which something else was later developed — see ANCESTOR 2

predestine *vb* to determine the fate of in advance — see DESTINE

predetermine *vb* to determine the fate of in advance — see DESTINE

predicament *n* a difficult, puzzling, or embarrassing situation from which there is no easy escape ⟨if you had told the truth in the first place, we wouldn't be in this *predicament*⟩
synonyms corner, fix, hole, jam, pickle, spot
related words difficulty, dilemma, hot water, pinch, plight, quagmire, quandary, scrape, trouble; deadlock, halt, impasse, stalemate, standstill; clutch, crisis, crossroad, emergency, exigency, juncture, strait

predicate *vb* to find a basis — see BASE

predict *vb* to tell of or describe beforehand — see FORETELL

predicting *n* a declaration that something will happen in the future — see PREDICTION

prediction *n* a declaration that something will happen in the future ⟨we were all amazed when the fortune-teller's *predictions* turned out to be true⟩
synonyms auguring, cast, forecast, forecasting, foretelling, predicting, presaging, prognosis, prognosticating, prognostication, prophecy, soothsaying
related words augury, omen, portent, sign; anticipation, foreknowledge; foresight; conjecture, guess, surmise

predictive *adj* being a sign of a later course of events — see PROPHETIC

predilection *n* a habitual attraction to some activity or thing — see INCLINATION 1

predisposition *n* a habitual attraction to some activity or thing — see INCLINATION 1

predominance *n* controlling power or influence over others — see SUPREMACY 1

predominant *adj* coming before all others in importance — see FOREMOST 1

predominantly *adv* for the most part — see CHIEFLY

preeminence *n* **1** exceptionally high quality — see EXCELLENCE 1
2 controlling power or influence over others — see SUPREMACY 1
3 the fact or state of being above others in rank or importance — see EMINENCE 1

preeminent *adj* **1** coming before all others in importance — see FOREMOST 1
2 highest in rank or authority — see HEAD
3 standing above others in rank, importance, or achievement — see EMINENT

preempt *vb* to take or make use of without authority or right — see APPROPRIATE 1

preface *n* a short section (as of a book) that leads to or explains the main part — see INTRODUCTION

prefer *vb* **1** to show partiality toward ⟨I generally *prefer* chocolate ice cream over vanilla⟩
synonyms favor, lean (toward), like
related words adore, cotton (to), delight (in), dig, enjoy, fancy, groove (on), relish, revel (in); choose, cull, handpick, name, pick, select, single

THESAURUS

(out), take; covet, crave, desire, want, wish (for); bias, prejudice; incline (towards), tend (to); admire, appreciate, cherish, prize, treasure, value
phrases be partial to
near antonyms disfavor, dislike; abhor, abominate, detest, hate, loathe; decline, refuse, reject, turn down; discard, jettison, throw away, throw out
2 to decide to accept (someone or something) from a group of possibilities — see CHOOSE 1
preferably *adv* by choice or preference — see RATHER 1
preference *n* **1** a person or thing that is preferred over others — see FAVORITE
2 positive regard for something — see LIKING
3 the power, right, or opportunity to choose — see CHOICE 1
preferment *n* a raising or a state of being raised to a higher rank or position — see ADVANCEMENT 1
preferred *adj* singled out from a number or group as more to one's liking — see SELECT 1
prefigure *vb* to give a slight indication of beforehand — see FORESHADOW
prefiguring *n* something believed to be a sign or warning of a future event — see OMEN
pregnancy *n* the state of containing unborn young within the body ⟨an elephant's *pregnancy* can last almost a year⟩
synonyms gestation
related words conception; begetting, breeding, generation, siring, spawning
near antonyms barrenness, infertility
pregnant *adj* **1** containing unborn young within the body ⟨we only realized that our cat had been *pregnant* when she unexpectedly delivered three kittens⟩
synonyms expectant, gravid
related words childbearing; brooding; conceiving, impregnated
phrases with child, with young
near antonyms barren, infertile; aborting, miscarrying; delivered
antonyms nonpregnant
2 clearly conveying a special meaning (as one's mood) — see EXPRESSIVE
prejudgment *n* an attitude, belief, or impression formed in advance of actual experience of something — see PREPOSSESSION 1
prejudice *n* **1** an attitude that always favors one way of feeling or acting especially without considering any other possibilities — see BIAS
2 hatred of or discrimination against a person or persons based on their race — see RACISM 2
prejudice *vb* to cause to have often negative opinions formed without sufficient knowledge ⟨all the bad stories I had heard about that teacher *prejudiced* me against him even before the first class⟩
synonyms bias
related words dispose, incline, predispose; influence, prepossess; convince, persuade, suggest
prejudiced *adj* **1** inclined to favor one side over another — see PARTIAL 1
2 unwilling to grant other people social rights or to accept other viewpoints — see INTOLERANT 2
prejudicial *adj* **1** causing or capable of causing harm — see HARMFUL
2 opposed to one's interests — see ADVERSE 1
preliminary *adj* coming before the main part or item usually to introduce or prepare for what fol-

lows ⟨we need to do some *preliminary* research in order to properly focus the experiment⟩
synonyms introductory, preparatory
related words introducing, prefacing, preparing, readying; premonitory, warning; basic, fundamental; ahead, early, former, preceding, previous, prior
near antonyms after, behind, following, subsequent
prelude *n* a short section (as of a book) that leads to or explains the main part — see INTRODUCTION
premature *adj* occurring before the usual or expected time — see EARLY 2
prematurely *adv* before the usual or expected time — see EARLY
premier *adj* **1** coming before all others in time or order — see FIRST 1
2 highest in rank or authority — see HEAD
3 coming before all others in importance — see FOREMOST 1
premise *n* **1** something taken as being true or factual and used as a starting point for a course of action or reasoning — see ASSUMPTION
2 premises *pl* the area around and belonging to a building — see GROUND 1
premise *vb* to take as true or as a fact without actual proof — see ASSUME 2
premium *adj* commanding a large price — see COSTLY
premium *n* something given in recognition of achievement — see AWARD
premonition *n* a feeling that something bad will happen ⟨she had a *premonition* that her cat would somehow get hurt that day⟩
synonyms foreboding, presage, presentiment
related words anticipation, foreknowledge; insight, intuition; augury, omen, portent, sign; impression, suspicion; anxiety, apprehension, care, concern, disquiet, doubt, dread, fear, misgiving, unease, worry; foresight
preoccupation *n* something about which one is constantly thinking or concerned — see FIXATION
preoccupied *adj* lost in thought and unaware of one's surroundings or actions — see ABSENTMINDED 1
preparatory *adj* coming before the main part or item usually to introduce or prepare for what follows — see PRELIMINARY
prepare *vb* **1** to make ready in advance ⟨I think I *prepared* myself well for this test⟩ ⟨we *prepared* the classroom for the important visitors by getting rid of some unsightly clutter⟩
synonyms fit, fix, lay, ready
related words brace, fortify, steel; batten, gather, gear (up), mount, train; boot (up), prime; arrange, set, spread; arm, equip, furnish, outfit, provide, supply; incline, predispose; draft, draw (up), frame; warm (up)
2 to make competent (as by training, skill, or ability) for a particular office or function — see QUALIFY 2
3 to put (something) into proper and usually carefully worked out written form — see COMPOSE 1
prepared *adj* being in a state of fitness for some experience or action — see READY 1
prepossession *n* **1** an attitude, belief, or impression formed in advance of actual experience of something ⟨the foreign tourists' *prepossessions* about life in the U.S. had been formed by many hours of American TV shows⟩

synonyms preconception, prejudgment
related words bias, prejudice; conjecture, hypothesis, imagining, predetermination, presumption, presupposition, speculation, supposition, theorizing, theory; concept, thought
2 something about which one is constantly thinking or concerned — see FIXATION
preposterous *adj* **1** conceived or made without regard for reason or reality — see FANTASTIC 1
2 showing or marked by a lack of good sense or judgment — see FOOLISH 1
3 so foolish or pointless as to be worthy of scornful laughter — see RIDICULOUS 1
preposterousness *n* lack of good sense or judgment — see FOOLISHNESS 1
prerogative *n* something to which one has a just claim — see RIGHT 1
presage *n* **1** a feeling that something bad will happen — see PREMONITION
2 something believed to be a sign or warning of a future event — see OMEN
presage *vb* to tell of or describe beforehand — see FORETELL
presaging *n* a declaration that something will happen in the future — see PREDICTION
prescience *n* **1** the special ability to see or know about events before they actually occur — see FORESIGHT 1
2 concern or preparation for the future — see FORESIGHT 2
prescient *adj* having or showing awareness of and preparation for the future — see FORESIGHTED
prescribe *vb* to give the rules about (something) clearly and exactly ⟨in chess, you can move the various pieces only in certain *prescribed* ways⟩
synonyms define, lay down, specify
related words decree, dictate, ordain; assign, direct, fix, set, settle; arrange, order; choose, select; adjure, bid, charge, command, enjoin, instruct, tell; conduct, control, lead, manage; coerce, constrain, force; oblige, require
presence *n* **1** a position within view ⟨men should watch their language when in the *presence* of ladies⟩
synonyms sight
related words nearness, proximity
2 the outward form of someone or something especially as indicative of a quality — see APPEARANCE 1
present *adj* **1** existing or in progress right now ⟨I am very busy at the *present* moment⟩
synonyms current, extant, ongoing, present-day
related words contemporary, mod, modern, new, newfangled, new-fashioned, now, recent, red-hot, space-age, ultramodern, up-to-date; being, breathing, existing, living
near antonyms done, ended, finished, over; ancient, antediluvian, antiquated, antique, archaic, dated, fusty, musty, noncontemporary, obsolete, old, oldfangled, old-fashioned, old-time, out-of-date, outworn, passé; bygone, erstwhile, formerly
antonyms ago, past; future
2 being within the confines of a specified place ⟨all of you are required to be *present* for every class⟩
synonyms attending
related words accompanying, observing, participating; available; abounding; latent; breathing, existing, existent, extant, live
phrases in attendance, on hand

near antonyms departed, gone, retired; nonexistent; AWOL, truant; dead, departed, lost, vanished; delayed, late, overdue, tardy
antonyms absent, away, missing, out
present *n* **1** the time currently existing or in progress ⟨I cannot talk to you at *present*, but perhaps in a few minutes⟩
synonyms moment, now, today
related words phase, stage, state; tonight, tomorrow
near antonyms yesterday, yesteryear
antonyms past; future
2 something given to someone without expectation of a return — see GIFT 1
present *vb* **1** to bring before the public in performance or exhibition ⟨we will *present* a performance of *Our Town* this week⟩
synonyms carry, give, mount, offer, stage
related words display, exhibit, show; preview; act, impersonate, perform, play, portray; depict, dramatize, enact, render, represent; extend, proffer, tender
2 to make (one person) known (to another) socially — see INTRODUCE 1
3 to make a present of — see GIVE 1
presentation *n* something given to someone without expectation of a return — see GIFT 1
present–day *adj* **1** being or involving the latest methods, concepts, information, or styles — see MODERN
2 existing or in progress right now — see PRESENT 1
presentiment *n* a feeling that something bad will happen — see PREMONITION
presently *adv* **1** at or within a short time — see SHORTLY 2
2 at the present time — see NOW 1
preservation *n* **1** the act or activity of keeping something in an existing and usually satisfactory condition — see MAINTENANCE
2 the careful maintaining and protection of something valuable especially in its natural or original state — see CONSERVATION 1
preserve *vb* to keep in good condition — see MAINTAIN 1
preserving *n* the act or activity of keeping something in an existing and usually satisfactory condition — see MAINTENANCE
president *n* a person in charge of a meeting — see CHAIR 1
preside (over) *vb* to exercise authority or power over — see GOVERN 1
presiding *adj* highest in rank or authority — see HEAD
press *n* a great number of persons or things gathered together — see CROWD 1
press *vb* **1** to push steadily against with some force ⟨an old doorbell that requires you to *press* the button hard⟩
synonyms bear (down on), depress, shove, weigh (on *or* upon)
related words compress, squash, squeeze; compel, force, pressure; lean (on *or* against), muscle; drive, propel, thrust; compact, constrict, contract, crush, scrunch, wring; cram, jam, jampack, pack, stuff, wedge
2 to apply external pressure on so as to force out the juice or contents of ⟨my family will only drink juice from freshly *pressed* oranges⟩
synonyms crush, express, mash, squeeze

THESAURUS

related words pulp, puree; extract, extrude

3 to gather into a closely packed group ⟨everyone *pressed* around me to see the pictures⟩

synonyms bunch, cluster, crowd, huddle

related words assemble, collect, congregate, flock, gather, herd, swarm, throng; encircle, mob, surround; embrace, hug

4 to force one's way ⟨we continued to *press* deeper and deeper into the tangled rain forest⟩

synonyms bulldoze, elbow, muscle, push

related words jostle; ram, shove, thrust

5 to cause (a person) to give in to pressure — see FORCE

6 to try to persuade (someone) through earnest appeals to follow a course of action — see URGE

press (for) *vb* to ask for (something) earnestly or with authority — see DEMAND 1

pressing *adj* needing immediate attention — see ACUTE 2

pressure *n* **1** the burden on one's emotional or mental well-being created by demands on one's time — see STRESS 1

2 the use of power to impose one's will on another — see FORCE 2

pressure *vb* to cause (a person) to give in to pressure — see FORCE

prestidigitator *n* one who practices tricks and illusions for entertainment — see MAGICIAN 2

prestigious *adj* **1** having a good reputation especially in a field of knowledge — see RESPECTABLE 1

2 standing above others in rank, importance, or achievement — see EMINENT

presto *adv* with great speed — see FAST 1

presumably *adv* **1** to all outward appearances — see APPARENTLY

2 without much doubt — see PROBABLY

presume *vb* **1** to form an opinion from little or no evidence — see GUESS 1

2 to take as true or as a fact without actual proof — see ASSUME 2

presumed *adj* appearing to be true on the basis of evidence that may or may not be confirmed — see APPARENT 1

presuming *adj* showing a lack of proper social reserve or modesty — see PRESUMPTUOUS 1

presumption *n* **1** shameless boldness — see EFFRONTERY

2 something taken as being true or factual and used as a starting point for a course of action or reasoning — see ASSUMPTION

presumptuous *adj* **1** showing a lack of proper social reserve or modesty ⟨it's a little *presumptuous* of you to assume that I'm your new best friend just because I invited you along⟩

synonyms bold, familiar, forward, free, immodest, overfamiliar, presuming

related words arrogant, complacent, conceited, egoistic, egotistic (*or* egotistical), important, overweening, pompous, prideful, proud, self-assertive, self-conceited, self-important, self-satisfied, smug, uppity, vain, vainglorious; cavalier, disdainful, haughty, lordly, pretentious, snobbish, stuck-up, supercilious, superior; audacious, brash, brassy, brazen, fresh, impertinent, impudent, pert, saucy; confident, self-assured, self-confident, sure; boastful, braggart, bragging; domineering, high-handed, imperious; self-centered, selfish

near antonyms humble, meek, unassertive; bashful, retiring, shy; diffident, self-doubting

antonyms modest, unassuming

2 having a feeling of superiority that shows itself in an overbearing attitude — see ARROGANT

3 thrusting oneself where one is not welcome or invited — see INTRUSIVE

presumptuousness *n* **1** an exaggerated sense of one's importance that shows itself in the making of excessive or unjustified claims — see ARROGANCE

2 shameless boldness — see EFFRONTERY

presuppose *vb* to take as true or as a fact without actual proof — see ASSUME 2

presupposition *n* something taken as being true or factual and used as a starting point for a course of action or reasoning — see ASSUMPTION

pretend *adj* not real and existing only in the imagination — see IMAGINARY

pretend *vb* **1** to take on a false or deceptive appearance ⟨I *pretended* that I was scared of the vacuum cleaner⟩

synonyms dissemble, let on

related words act, impersonate, masquerade, play, pose; affect, assume, counterfeit, fake, feign, profess, put on, simulate; camouflage, conceal, disguise, mask; bluff, feint

phrases make a pretense, make a show, make believe, put on an act, put up a front

2 to present a false appearance of — see FEIGN

pretended *adj* lacking in natural or spontaneous quality — see ARTIFICIAL 1

pretender *n* one who makes false claims of identity or expertise — see IMPOSTOR

pretense *or* **pretence** *n* **1** the quality or state of appearing or trying to appear more important or more valuable than is the case ⟨she seemed to be a very down-to-earth woman who was completely free of *pretense*⟩

synonyms affectation, affectedness, grandiosity, pretension, pretentiousness

related words arrogance, complacency, conceit, egotism, pride, self-assertion, self-conceit, self-importance, self-satisfaction, smugness, vaingloriousness, vainglory, vainness, vanity; disdain, haughtiness, lordliness, snobbery, snobbishness, superciliousness, superiority; confidence, presumption, self-assurance, self-confidence, sureness; boastfulness, braggadocio; aggressiveness, assertiveness, audaciousness, boldness, brassiness, cheekiness, cockiness, forwardness, impudence, insolence, rudeness; grandiloquence; flashiness, gaudiness, ostentation, show, showiness

near antonyms demureness, humbleness, humility, meekness, modesty; bashfulness, diffidence, shyness, timidity; naturalness, sincerity

2 a display of emotion or behavior that is insincere or intended to deceive — see MASQUERADE

3 an entitlement to something — see CLAIM 1

4 an exaggerated sense of one's importance that shows itself in the making of excessive or unjustified claims — see ARROGANCE

pretension *n* **1** an entitlement to something — see CLAIM 1

2 an exaggerated sense of one's importance that shows itself in the making of excessive or unjustified claims — see ARROGANCE

3 the quality or state of appearing or trying to appear more important or more valuable than is the case — see PRETENSE 1

4 something that one hopes or intends to accomplish — see GOAL

pretentious *adj* **1** self-consciously trying to present an appearance of grandeur or importance ⟨the *pretentious* hosts served caviar at their party, even though they themselves dislike it⟩
synonyms affected, grandiose, highfalutin, ostentatious, pompous
related words grandiloquent, high-sounding, sententious; arrogant, complacent, conceited, egoistic, egotistic (*or* egotistical), important, overweening, prideful, proud, self-assertive, self-conceited, self-important, self-satisfied, smug, uppity, vain, vainglorious; cavalier, disdainful, haughty, lordly, snobbish, snobby, stuck-up, supercilious, superior; confident, self-assured, self-confident, sure; boastful, braggart, bragging; aggressive, assertive, audacious, bold, brassy, cheeky, cocky, forward, impudent, insolent, rude; flashy, flaunting, gaudy, showy
near antonyms demure, homely, humble, lowly, meek, retiring, unassertive, unassuming; bashful, diffident, mousy (*or* mousey), overmodest, passive, quiet, reserved, shy, timid
antonyms modest, unpretentious
2 having a feeling of superiority that shows itself in an overbearing attitude — see ARROGANT
pretentiousness *n* **1** an exaggerated sense of one's importance that shows itself in the making of excessive or unjustified claims — see ARROGANCE
2 excessive or unnecessary display — see OSTENTATION
3 the quality or state of appearing or trying to appear more important or more valuable than is the case — see PRETENSE 1
preternatural *adj* of, relating to, or being part of a reality beyond the observable physical universe — see SUPERNATURAL 1
prettiness *n* the qualities in a person or thing that as a whole give pleasure to the senses — see BEAUTY 1
pretty *adj* very pleasing to look at — see BEAUTIFUL
pretty *adv* to some degree or extent — see FAIRLY
prevail *vb* **1** to achieve victory (as in a contest) — see WIN 1
2 to continue to operate or to meet one's needs — see HOLD OUT
prevail (on *or* upon) *vb* to cause (someone) to agree with a belief or course of action by using arguments or earnest requests — see PERSUADE
prevail (over) *vb* to achieve a victory over — see BEAT 2
prevailing *adj* **1** accepted, used, or practiced by most people — see CURRENT 1
2 held by or applicable to a majority of the people — see GENERAL 3
prevalence *n* the fact or state of happening often — see FREQUENCY
prevalent *adj* accepted, used, or practiced by most people — see CURRENT 1
prevaricate *vb* to make a statement one knows to be untrue — see LIE 1
prevarication *n* a statement known by its maker to be untrue and made in order to deceive — see LIE
prevaricator *n* a person who tells lies — see LIAR
prevent *vb* to keep from happening by taking action in advance ⟨a lot of problems would have been *prevented* if we'd just prepared better⟩
synonyms avert, forestall, help, obviate, preclude

related words anticipate, provide; negate, neutralize, nullify; avoid, save; baffle, balk, checkmate, deter, foil, frustrate, thwart; bar, block, hamper, hinder, impede, interfere (with), retard, stall; deflect, fend (off), head (off), stave off, stop, ward (off); avoid, circumvent, dodge, elude, escape, evade; forbid, inhibit, prohibit; arrest, check, halt, stop; counteract, offset
near antonyms abet, aid, assist; ease, facilitate, smooth; advance, cultivate, encourage, forward, foster, further, nurture, promote; allow, leave, let, permit
preventative *adj* concerned with or serving to keep something from happening — see PREVENTIVE
prevention *n* the act or practice of keeping something from happening ⟨good crowd control is crucial to the *prevention* of riots⟩
synonyms averting, forestallment, obviating, precluding
related words avoidance, circumvention; negation, neutralization, nullification; baffling, balking, checkmate, debarment, deterrence, foiling, frustration, thwarting; bar, block, hindrance, interference; interdiction, prohibition
near antonyms aid, assistance; facilitation; advancement, cultivation, encouragement, nurture, promotion
preventive *adj* concerned with or serving to keep something from happening ⟨if you start taking this *preventive* medicine now, you may not get sick after all⟩
synonyms precautionary, preventative
related words deterrent, deterring; negating, neutralizing, nullifying; baffling, balking, foiling, frustrating, thwarting; blocking, hampering, hindering, impeding, retardant, stalling
near antonyms abetting, aiding, assisting; easing, facilitating, smoothing; encouraging, forwarding, fostering, furthering, nurturing, promoting
previous *adj* going before another in time or order ⟨the new instructor should consult with the *previous* teacher about the lesson plans⟩ ⟨the *previous* math problem also included a reference to store discounts⟩
synonyms antecedent, anterior, foregoing, precedent, preceding, prior
related words advance, early, premature; earliest, first, inaugural, initial, maiden, original, pioneer; preexisting; introductory, preliminary; erstwhile, former, whilom
near antonyms advanced, late; final, last, terminal, ultimate
antonyms after, ensuing, following, subsequent, succeeding
previously *adv* so as to precede something in order of time — see AHEAD 1
previous to *prep* earlier than — see BEFORE 1
prey *n* an animal that is hunted or killed ⟨rabbits are common *prey* for owls and hawks⟩
synonyms chase, quarry
related words game; kill, victim; creature, critter, beast, brute; target
near antonyms carnivore; chaser, hunter, pursuer; killer, murderer
antonyms predator
prey (on *or* upon) *vb* to seize and eat (something) as prey ⟨a fox has been *preying on* the chickens⟩
synonyms feed (on, upon, *or* off)
related words chase, hunt, pursue; destroy, dispatch, do in, fell, kill, slay

THESAURUS

price *n* **1** the amount of money that is demanded as payment for something ⟨I really wanted to buy that shirt, but the *price* was more money than I had⟩

synonyms charge, cost, fee, figure

related words list price, market value, rate, tariff, unit price; carrying charge, overcharge, surcharge; deduction, discount, markdown, reduction, sale; deposit; down payment; account, bill, check, invoice, tab

2 the loss or penalty involved in achieving a goal ⟨I finished the essay, but the *price* was losing a night's sleep⟩

synonyms cost

related words expense, toll; forfeit, penalty, sacrifice

3 something offered or given in return for a service performed — see REWARD

prick *n* **1** a mark or small hole made by a pointed instrument ⟨the immunization shot left a *prick* on my arm that turned into a bruise⟩

synonyms perforation, pinhole, pinprick, punch, puncture, stab

related words gouge, groove, hollow; break, cut, gash, notch, rupture, slash, slit

2 a sharp unpleasant sensation usually felt in some specific part of the body — see PAIN 1

prickly *adj* likely to cause a scratch — see SCRATCHY 1

pride *n* **1** a reasonable or justifiable sense of one's worth or importance ⟨finishing that survival course gave me a real sense of *pride* and confidence in my abilities⟩

synonyms ego, pridefulness, self-esteem, self-regard, self-respect

related words confidence, self-assurance, self-confidence; dignity, face, honor, prestige

near antonyms disgrace, humiliation, shame; demureness, humbleness, humility, modesty; diffidence, meekness, shyness, timidity, timidness

2 an asset that brings praise or renown — see GLORY 2

3 an often unjustified feeling of being pleased with oneself or with one's situation or achievements — see COMPLACENCE

pride *vb* to think highly of (oneself) ⟨he *prides* himself on the quality of his writing⟩

synonyms flatter, plume

related words boast, brag, vaunt; congratulate, felicitate

prideful *adj* **1** having or displaying feelings of scorn for what is regarded as beneath oneself — see PROUD 1

2 having too high an opinion of oneself — see CONCEITED

pridefulness *n* **1** a reasonable or justifiable sense of one's worth or importance — see PRIDE 1

2 an often unjustified feeling of being pleased with oneself or with one's situation or achievements — see COMPLACENCE

priest *n* a person specially trained and authorized to conduct religious services in a Christian church — see CLERGYMAN

priestly *adj* of, relating to, or characteristic of the clergy — see CLERICAL

prim *adj* given to or marked by very conservative standards regarding personal behavior or morals — see STRAITLACED

primal *adj* relating to or occurring near the begin-

ning of a process, series, or time period — see EARLY 1

primarily *adv* **1** in the beginning — see ORIGINALLY

2 for the most part — see CHIEFLY

primary *adj* **1** coming before all others in importance — see FOREMOST 1

2 done or working without something else coming in between — see DIRECT 1

3 highest in rank or authority — see HEAD

prime *adj* **1** highest in rank or authority — see HEAD

2 of the very best kind — see EXCELLENT

prime *n* **1** a state or time of great activity, thriving, or achievement — see BLOOM 1

2 individuals carefully selected as being the best of a class — see ELITE

primer *n* a book used for instruction in a subject — see TEXTBOOK

primeval *adj* relating to or occurring near the beginning of a process, series, or time period — see EARLY 1

primitive *adj* **1** belonging to or characteristic of an early level of skill or development ⟨*primitive* wooden tools were used before the Iron Age⟩

synonyms crude, low, rude, rudimentary

related words basic, simple, uncomplicated; homely, homespun, unsophisticated; early, primeval, primordial; backward, underdeveloped, undeveloped; aged, ancient, antediluvian, antiquated, antique, dated, fusty, hoary, musty, obsolete, old, oldfangled, old-fashioned, old-time, out-of-date, outworn, passé, past

near antonyms complex, complicated, intricate, involved, sophisticated; full-blown, full-grown, grown, mature, matured, perfected, ripe, ripened; civilized, cultivated, enlightened, refined; contemporary, current, latest, mod, modern, new, newfangled, new-fashioned, novel, now, present-day, space-age, ultramodern, up-to-date

antonyms advanced, developed, evolved, higher

2 relating to or occurring near the beginning of a process, series, or time period — see EARLY 1

primordial *adj* relating to or occurring near the beginning of a process, series, or time period — see EARLY 1

prince *n* a person of rank, power, or influence in a particular field — see MAGNATE

princely *adj* fit for or worthy of a royal ruler — see MONARCHICAL

principal *adj* **1** coming before all others in importance — see FOREMOST 1

2 highest in rank or authority — see HEAD

principal *n* the person who has the most important role in a play, movie, or TV show — see STAR 2

principally *adv* for the most part — see CHIEFLY

principled *adj* **1** following the accepted rules of moral conduct — see HONORABLE 1

2 guided by or in accordance with one's sense of right and wrong — see CONSCIENTIOUS 1

principles *n pl* **1** general or basic truths on which other truths or theories can be based ⟨if you don't learn the *principles* of algebra now, you won't understand much later on⟩

synonyms basics, elements, essentials, fundamentals, rudiments

related words basis, foundation, groundwork; nitty-gritty; belief, canon, doctrine, dogma, faith, philosophy; axiom, law, precept, tenet; rule, standard; theorem *near antonyms* details, trivia

2 the code of good conduct for an individual or group — see ETHICS

print *n* **1** a perceptible trace left by pressure ⟨one telltale sign that I had been napping was the *print* left by the chenille bedspread on my cheek⟩
synonyms impress, impression, imprint, stamp
related words dent, hollow, indentation; mark, sign

2 a picture created from an image recorded on a light-sensitive surface by a camera — see PHOTOGRAPH

print *vb* to produce and release for distribution in printed form — see PUBLISH 1

prior *adj* going before another in time or order — see PREVIOUS

priority *n* the right to one's attention before other things considered less important ⟨the principal has decided to give your request *priority*, so you'll have a meeting early tomorrow morning⟩
synonyms precedence, right-of-way
related words preference; urgency; ascendancy, preeminence, primacy, supremacy; transcendence; order, progression, sequence, succession

prior to *prep* earlier than — see BEFORE 1

priory *n* a residence for men under religious vows — see MONASTERY

prison *n* a place of confinement for persons held in lawful custody — see JAIL

prisoner *n* one that has been taken and held in confinement — see CAPTIVE

pristine *adj* being in an original and unused or unspoiled state — see FRESH 1

private *adj* **1** not known or meant to be known by the general populace ⟨that he is planning to retire is *private* information until he makes a public announcement⟩
synonyms confidential, hushed, inside, intimate, nonpublic, privy, secret
related words classified, top secret; unadvertised, unannounced, undisclosed, unmentioned; clandestine, collusive, conspiratorial, covert; surreptitious, undercover, underhand, underhanded; personal; closeted, concealed, hidden; repressed, silenced, stifled, suppressed
near antonyms well-known; advertised, aired, announced, blazed, broadcast, declared, disclosed, divulged, enunciated, heralded, proclaimed, professed, promulgated, publicized, published, reported, spotlighted; general, popular, prevailing, vulgar; prevalent, rife, widespread; communal, shared
antonyms common, open, public

2 undertaken or done so as to escape being observed or known by others — see SECRET 1

3 of, relating to, or belonging to a single person — see INDIVIDUAL 1

privation *n* the state of being robbed of something normally enjoyed ⟨the constant *privation* of sleep was starting to affect my schoolwork⟩
synonyms deprivation, loss
related words lack, need, want; dispossession; denial, forfeit, forfeiture, penalty, sacrifice; bereavement
near antonyms ownership, possession; accumulation, acquiring, gain

privilege *n* something granted as a special favor ⟨you will have the *privilege* of leading the line today⟩
synonyms appanage, boon, concession, honor

related words courtesy; claim, entitlement, right; birthright; perquisite; prerogative; charter, grant, patent; exemption, immunity, waiver
near antonyms duty, obligation, responsibility

privy *adj* **1** not known or meant to be known by the general populace — see PRIVATE 1

2 undertaken or done so as to escape being observed or known by others — see SECRET 1

3 of, relating to, or belonging to a single person — see INDIVIDUAL 1

prize *n* **1** someone or something unusually desirable ⟨in her parents' view, her current boyfriend is certainly no *prize*⟩
synonyms catch, gem, jewel, pearl, plum, treasure
related words find, godsend, goody, valuable, windfall; booty, loot, spoil; glory, pride; jackpot, treasure trove
near antonyms lemon, loser

2 something given in recognition of achievement — see AWARD

¹prize *vb* **1** to draw out by force or with effort — see EXTRACT

2 to raise, move, or pull apart with or as if with a lever — see ¹PRY 1

²prize *vb* to hold dear — see LOVE 1

prizefighter *n* one that engages in the sport of fighting with the fists — see BOXER

probability *n* **1** the quality or state of being likely to occur ⟨the plot of the movie thriller was exciting and surprising but woefully lacking in *probability*⟩
synonyms likelihood, likeliness
related words credibility, plausibility; liability; feasibility, feasibleness, possibility, potentiality, reasonability, viability
near antonyms doubtfulness, dubiousness; impracticability, impracticality; implausibility, incredibility
antonyms improbability, unlikelihood, unlikeliness

2 a measure of how often an event will occur instead of another ⟨the *probability* of flipping a coin and getting heads fifty times in a row is not good⟩
synonyms chance, odds, percentage
related words outlook, prospect; possibility, potential, potentiality

probable *adj* **1** worthy of being accepted as true or reasonable — see BELIEVABLE

2 having a high chance of occurring — see LIKELY 1

probably *adv* without much doubt ⟨we would *probably* win that bet⟩
synonyms doubtless, likely, presumably
related words mayhap, perchance, perhaps, possibly; conceivably, imaginably, plausibly, practically, reasonably; potentially; assuredly, certainly, clearly, conclusively, decisively, definitely, definitively, indubitably, positively, surely
near antonyms implausibly, inconceivably, incredibly, unbelievably
antonyms improbably

probe *n* a systematic search for the truth or facts about something — see INQUIRY 1

probe *vb* **1** to search through or into — see EXPLORE 1

2 to go into or range over for purposes of discovery — see EXPLORE 2

probing *n* a systematic search for the truth or facts about something — see INQUIRY 1

probity *n* **1** conduct that conforms to an accepted standard of right and wrong — see MORALITY 1
2 devotion to telling the truth — see HONESTY 1
3 faithfulness to high moral standards — see HONOR 1

problem *n* **1** something that requires thought and skill for resolution ⟨the *problem* of world hunger⟩
synonyms case, knot, matter, trouble
related words issue, question; challenge; corner, fix, hole, hot water, jam, pickle, predicament, situation; glitch, hitch, snag; conundrum, enigma, mystery, puzzle, puzzlement, riddle; brainteaser, perplexer, poser, stumper
antonyms answer, solution
2 an interrogative expression often used to test knowledge — see QUESTION 1
3 something that is a source of irritation — see ANNOYANCE 3

problematic *also* **problematical** *adj* **1** requiring exceptional skill or caution in performance or handling — see TRICKY
2 giving good reason for being doubted, questioned, or challenged — see DOUBTFUL 2

procedure *n* **1** a usually fixed or ordered series of actions or events leading to a result — see PROCESS 1
2 a way of acting or proceeding — see COURSE 1

proceed *vb* to move forward along a course — see GO 1

proceed (along) *vb* to make one's way through, across, or over — see TRAVERSE

proceeding *adj* being in progress or development — see ONGOING 1

proceeding *n* **1** a court case for enforcing a right or claim — see LAWSUIT
2 a usually fixed or ordered series of actions or events leading to a result — see PROCESS 1

proceeds *n pl* **1** an increase usually measured in money that comes from labor, business, or property — see INCOME
2 the amount of money left when expenses are subtracted from the total amount received — see PROFIT 1

process *n* **1** a usually fixed or ordered series of actions or events leading to a result ⟨the *process* by which the elastic fibers spun by silkworms is turned into soft, lustrous cloth⟩
synonyms course, operation, procedure, proceeding
related words fashion, manner, method, mode, style, system, technique, way; approach, blueprint, design, game plan, layout, plan, plot, program, scheme, strategy; accomplishment, achievement, attainment, enterprise, performance, undertaking, work; activity, functioning, movement
2 forward movement in time or place — see ADVANCE 1

procession *n* **1** a body of individuals moving along in an orderly and often ceremonial way — see CORTEGE 2
2 forward movement in time or place — see ADVANCE 1

proclaim *vb* to make known openly or publicly — see ANNOUNCE

proclivity *n* a habitual attraction to some activity or thing — see INCLINATION 1

procreate *vb* to bring forth offspring ⟨in life science class we learned how animals *procreate*⟩

synonyms breed, multiply, propagate, reproduce
related words bear, beget, engender, generate, get, mother, parent, produce, sire; hatch, spawn

procurable *adj* possible to get — see AVAILABLE 1

procurator *n* a person who acts or does business for another — see AGENT 2

procure *vb* to receive as return for effort — see EARN 1

prod *vb* **1** to urge or push forward with or as if with a pointed object ⟨my sister keeps *prodding* me with her pencil to move along faster⟩
synonyms goad, spur
related words chuck, jab, jog, nudge, poke; bore, drill, pierce, prick, punch, puncture, stab, stick; drive, propel
2 to try to persuade (someone) through earnest appeals to follow a course of action — see URGE

prodigal *adj* given to spending money freely or foolishly ⟨the *prodigal* child always spent her allowance the minute she got it⟩
synonyms extravagant, profligate, spendthrift, squandering, thriftless, unthrifty, wasteful
related words improvident, myopic, shortsighted; bountiful, generous, lavish, liberal, openhanded, openhearted, philanthropic; careless, heedless, imprudent, incautious, injudicious, unwise; indulgent, reckless, self-indulgent, splurging, wanton
near antonyms cheap, close, mean, miserly, niggardly, parsimonious, penurious, pinching, spare, sparing, stingy, tight, tightfisted; careful, judicious, prudent, sensible, wise; farsighted, forehanded, foresighted, forethoughtful, provident
antonyms conserving, economical, economizing, frugal, scrimping, skimping, thrifty

prodigal *n* someone who carelessly spends money ⟨the million-dollar lottery winner was such a *prodigal* that there was no money left after a few years⟩
synonyms profligate, spender, spendthrift, squanderer, waster, wastrel
near antonyms miser, skinflint, tightwad; conserver, saver
antonyms economizer

prodigality *n* **1** an instance of spending money or resources without care or restraint — see WASTE 1
2 the quality or fact of being free or wasteful in the expenditure of money — see EXTRAVAGANCE 1

prodigious *adj* **1** causing wonder or astonishment — see MARVELOUS 1
2 unusually large — see HUGE

prodigy *n* something extraordinary or surprising — see WONDER 1

produce *n* something produced by physical or intellectual effort — see PRODUCT 1

produce *vb* **1** to be the cause of (a situation, action, or state of mind) — see EFFECT
2 to bring forth from the womb — see BEAR 1
3 to bring into being by combining, shaping, or transforming materials — see MAKE 1

product *n* **1** something produced by physical or intellectual effort ⟨that book is the *product* of years of work⟩ ⟨a rebuilt car which is the *product* of several people's labor⟩
synonyms affair, fruit, handiwork, output, produce, production, thing, work, yield
related words article, commodity, object; goods, line, merchandise, wares; handcraft, handicraft; aftereffect, aftermath, conclusion, consequence,

development, effect, issue, outcome, result, upshot; by-product, derivative, offshoot, outgrowth, residual, side effect, spin-off
2 a condition or occurrence traceable to a cause — see EFFECT 1
production *n* something produced by physical or intellectual effort — see PRODUCT 1
productive *adj* **1** having a role in deciding something's final form — see FORMATIVE
2 producing abundantly — see FERTILE
3 producing or capable of producing a desired result — see EFFECTIVE 1
productiveness *n* the power to produce a desired result — see EFFICACY
profane *adj* **1** not involving religion or religious matters ⟨it was hard to juggle the requirements of church and our more *profane* duties⟩
synonyms secular, temporal
related words atheistic, godless, irreligious, pagan; lay, nonclerical; nondenominational, nonsectarian; earthly, mundane, terrestrial, worldly; material, physical, substantial; bodily, carnal, corporal, fleshly; blasphemous, impious, irreverent, sacrilegious; unconsecrated, unhallowed, unsanctified
near antonyms divine, spiritual; consecrated, hallowed, holy, sanctified; churchly, devout, godly, pious, prayerful, reverent, worshipful; ethereal, insubstantial, metaphysical, unsubstantial; bodiless, immaterial, incorporeal, nonphysical
antonyms religious, sacred
2 not showing proper reverence for the holy or sacred — see IRREVERENT
profane *vb* **1** to lower in character or dignity — see DEBASE 1
2 to put to a bad or improper use — see MISAPPLY
3 to treat (a sacred place or object) shamefully or with great disrespect — see DESECRATE
profess *vb* **1** to present a false appearance of — see FEIGN
2 to state clearly and strongly — see ASSERT 1
3 to state as a fact usually forcefully — see CLAIM 1
profession *n* **1** a solemn and often public declaration of the truth or existence of something — see PROTESTATION
2 the activity by which one regularly makes a living — see OCCUPATION
proffer *n* something which is presented for consideration — see PROPOSAL
proffer *vb* **1** to put before another for acceptance or consideration — see OFFER 1
2 to set before the mind for consideration — see PROPOSE 1
proficiency *n* **1** a highly developed skill in or knowledge of something — see COMMAND 2
2 knowledge gained by actually doing or living through something — see EXPERIENCE 1
proficient *adj* having or showing exceptional knowledge, experience, or skill in a field of endeavor ⟨she is quite *proficient* at computer repair⟩ ⟨a *proficient* rendition of a difficult piano piece⟩
synonyms accomplished, ace, adept, consummate, crack, crackerjack, experienced, expert, good, great, master, masterful, masterly, practiced (*or* practised), skilled, skillful, versed, veteran, virtuoso
related words adroit, clever, deft, dexterous (*also* dextrous), handy; gifted, talented; experienced, polished, refined; effective, effectual, efficient, workmanlike; able, capable, competent, fit, qual-

ified; educated, knowledgeable, schooled, taught, trained, tutored; all-around (*also* all-round), well-rounded; long-term, old
near antonyms incapable, incompetent, inept, unable, unfit, unqualified; artless, crude, rude; ineffective, ineffectual, inefficient; ungifted, untalented; ignorant, unschooled, untaught, untrained, untutored; beginning, green, inexperienced, new, raw, untested, untried; rough, unpolished
antonyms amateur, amateurish, inexperienced, inexpert, unexperienced, unpracticed, unprofessional, unseasoned, unskilled, unskillful
proficiently *adv* in a skillful or expert manner — see WELL 3
profit *n* **1** the amount of money left when expenses are subtracted from the total amount received ⟨after we deducted the cost of sugar, lemons, and paper cups, the *profit* from a day of lemonade sales was about $20⟩
synonyms earnings, gain, lucre, net, payoff, proceeds, return
related words killing, windfall; gross; compensation, emolument, income, pay, payment, remittal, requital, salary, wages; interest, return, yield; (the) black; royalty
near antonyms cost, expenditure, expense, loss, outgo, outlay
2 an increase usually measured in money that comes from labor, business, or property — see INCOME
profit *vb* to provide with something useful or desirable — see BENEFIT
profitable *adj* **1** yielding a profit ⟨selling lemonade turned out to be a *profitable* venture⟩
synonyms fat, gainful, lucrative, paying, remunerative
related words advantageous, beneficial, rewarding, useful, worthwhile
antonyms unprofitable
2 conferring benefits; promoting or contributing to personal or social well-being — see BENEFICIAL
profligate *adj* given to spending money freely or foolishly — see PRODIGAL
profligate *n* **1** someone who carelessly spends money — see PRODIGAL
2 a person who has sunk below the normal moral standard — see DEGENERATE
profound *adj* **1** difficult for one of ordinary knowledge or intelligence to understand ⟨a *profound* observation about good and evil that few listeners fully grasped⟩
synonyms abstruse, deep, esoteric, recondite
related words erudite, learned, scholarly; academic, pedantic; complex, complicated, hard; darkling, enigmatic (*also* enigmatical), inscrutable, mysterious, mystic, uncanny; impenetrable, incomprehensible, unfathomable, unintelligible; ambiguous, cryptic; unanswerable, unknowable; baffling, bewildering, confounding, confusing, mystifying, perplexing, puzzling
near antonyms easy, facile, simple, straightforward; comprehensible, fathomable, intelligible, understandable; clear, obvious, plain
antonyms shallow
2 extreme in degree, power, or effect — see INTENSE
3 having no exceptions or restrictions — see ABSOLUTE 2
profoundness *n* the quality of being great in extent (as of insight) — see DEPTH 2

profundity *n* the quality of being great in extent (as of insight) — see DEPTH 2

profuse *adj* pouring forth in great amounts ⟨we received *profuse* thanks for our efforts⟩ ⟨a *profuse* rush of water from the collapsing dike⟩
synonyms copious, galore, gushing, lavish, riotous
related words abounding, abundant, ample, bounteous, bountiful, liberal, plenteous, plentiful; extravagant, luxuriant; fat, fecund, fertile; free, liberal, munificent, openhanded, unsparing, unstinting; excessive, immoderate; adequate, complete, enough, sufficient
near antonyms meager, niggardly, poor, scant, scanty, spare, sparse, stingy; deficient, inadequate, incomplete, insufficient, lacking, unsatisfactory, wanting; bare, mere, minimal; slight, small
antonyms dribbling, trickling

profusion *n* a considerable amount — see LOT 2

progeny *n* the descendants of a person, animal, or plant — see OFFSPRING

prognosis *n* a declaration that something will happen in the future — see PREDICTION

prognosticate *vb* to tell of or describe beforehand — see FORETELL

prognosticating *n* a declaration that something will happen in the future — see PREDICTION

prognostication *n* a declaration that something will happen in the future — see PREDICTION

prognosticator *n* one who predicts future events or developments — see PROPHET

program *n* **1** a listing of things to be presented or considered (as at a concert or play) ⟨the *program* will tell us the scheduled order of musical numbers⟩
synonyms agenda, calendar, docket, schedule, timetable
related words card, exercises; arrangement, order, organization
2 a method worked out in advance for achieving some objective — see PLAN 1
3 a way of acting or proceeding — see COURSE 1

progress *n* **1** forward movement in time or place — see ADVANCE 1
2 the act or process of going from the simple or basic to the complex or advanced — see DEVELOPMENT 1

progress *vb* **1** to become mature — see MATURE
2 to move forward along a course — see GO 1

progression *n* **1** a series of things linked together — see CHAIN 1
2 forward movement in time or place — see ADVANCE 1
3 the act or process of going from the simple or basic to the complex or advanced — see DEVELOPMENT 1

progressive *adj* **1** being far along in development — see ADVANCED 1
2 not bound by traditional ways or beliefs — see LIBERAL 1

prohibit *vb* to order not to do or use or to be done or used — see FORBID

prohibited *adj* that may not be permitted — see IMPERMISSIBLE

prohibiting *n* the act of ordering that something not be done or used — see PROHIBITION 1

prohibition *n* **1** the act of ordering that something not be done or used ⟨the principal's *prohibition* against the use of cell phones in the school building met with unanimous approval by the teachers⟩
synonyms banning, barring, enjoining, forbidding, interdicting, interdiction, outlawing, prohibiting, proscribing, proscription
related words bidding, charging, decreeing, dictation, direction, instruction; deterrence, discouragement, dissuading; repression, suppression; coercion, compulsion, constraint, force
near antonyms allowance, permission, sufferance, toleration; approval, endorsement; encouragement, promotion, support; compliance, obedience
2 an order that something not be done or used ⟨the school issued a *prohibition* against wearing clothing with obscene and provocative slogans⟩
synonyms ban, embargo, interdict, interdiction, proscription, veto
related words taboo (*also* tabu); injunction; constraint, inhibition, limitation, restraint, restriction; deterrent, discouragement; repression, suppression; prevention; denial, disallowance, negation, refusal, rejection; objection, protest
near antonyms sufferance, tolerance, toleration; allowance, allowing, authorization, consent, granting, leave, letting, license (*or* licence), licensing, permission, permitting, sanctioning; approval, endorsement; enabling, encouragement, facilitation, promotion, support; compliance, obedience; accession, acquiescence, agreement, assent
antonyms prescription

project *n* a method worked out in advance for achieving some objective — see PLAN 1

project *vb* **1** to extend outward beyond a usual point — see BULGE
2 to work out the details of (something) in advance — see PLAN 1

projection *n* a part that sticks out from the general mass of something — see BULGE

proletarian *adj* belonging to the class of people of low social or economic rank — see IGNOBLE 1

proletariat *n* people looked down upon as ignorant and of the lowest class — see RABBLE

proliferate *vb* to become greater in extent, volume, amount, or number — see INCREASE 2

proliferation *n* **1** something added (as by growth) — see INCREASE 1
2 the act or process of becoming greater in number — see MULTIPLICATION

prolific *adj* producing abundantly — see FERTILE

prolix *adj* using or containing more words than necessary to express an idea — see WORDY

prolixity *n* the use of too many words to express an idea — see VERBIAGE

prologue *n* a short section (as of a book) that leads to or explains the main part — see INTRODUCTION

prolong *vb* to make longer — see EXTEND 1

prolongation *n* the act of making longer — see EXTENSION 1

prolonging *n* the act of making longer — see EXTENSION 1

prom *n* a social gathering for dancing — see DANCE

prominence *n* an area of high ground — see HEIGHT 4

prominent *adj* **1** likely to attract attention — see NOTICEABLE
2 widely known — see FAMOUS

promiscuous *adj* consisting of many things of different sorts — see MISCELLANEOUS

promise *n* a person's solemn declaration that he or she will do or not do something ⟨he gave a *promise* that he would arrive on time⟩
synonyms oath, pledge, troth, vow, word
related words appointment, arrangement, commitment, engagement; compact, contract, covenant; assurance, guarantee, guaranty; bail, bond, deposit, gage, pawn, security, token, warranty
promise *vb* **1** to make a solemn declaration of intent ⟨I *promised* not to fight with my sister⟩
synonyms covenant, pledge, swear, vow
related words affiance, betroth, plight, troth; accede, agree, assent, consent; contract, engage, guarantee, undertake; affirm, assert, aver, avouch, avow, declare, insist, warrant
phrases give one's word
2 to show signs of a favorable or successful outcome — see BODE
promising *adj* **1** having qualities which inspire hope — see HOPEFUL 1
2 pointing toward a happy outcome — see FAVORABLE 2
promontory *n* **1** an area of high ground jutting out into a body of water beyond the line of the coast — see HEADLAND 1
2 an area of land that juts out into a body of water — see ²CAPE
promote *vb* **1** to move higher in rank or position ⟨the Navy *promoted* her to captain for her record of outstanding performance⟩
synonyms advance, elevate, raise, upgrade
related words forward, further; aggrandize, boost, heighten, improve, lift, uplift; commission, ennoble, knight; acclaim, applaud, celebrate, cite, commend, compliment, congratulate, decorate; eulogize, extol (*also* extoll), glorify, hail, honor, laud, praise, salute
near antonyms depose, dethrone, dismiss, expel, impeach, oust, overthrow, remove, unmake, unseat; demean, disgrace, dishonor, humble, humiliate, mortify, shame, take down; censure, condemn, damn, denounce, reprobate
antonyms abase, degrade, demote, downgrade, lower, reduce
2 to help the growth or development of — see FOSTER 1
3 to look after or assist the growth of by labor and care — see GROW 1
4 to provide publicity for — see PUBLICIZE 1
promoter *n* a person who actively supports or favors a cause — see EXPONENT
promotion *n* a raising or a state of being raised to a higher rank or position — see ADVANCEMENT 1
prompt *adj* **1** done, carried out, or given without delay ⟨*prompt* treatment of snakebites is always advisable⟩
synonyms immediate, punctual, timely
related words apt, quick, ready, willing; opportune, seasonable; early
near antonyms delinquent, latish, overdue; behind, behindhand, delayed, detained; dilatory, laggard, slow
antonyms belated, late, tardy
2 having or showing the ability to respond without delay or hesitation — see QUICK 1
prompt *vb* **1** to be the cause of (a situation, action, or state of mind) — see EFFECT
2 to try to persuade (someone) through earnest appeals to follow a course of action — see URGE
promptitude *n* the quality or habit of arriving on time ⟨the teacher's *promptitude* was such that you could set your watch by his morning arrival⟩
synonyms promptness, punctuality, timeliness
related words aptness, quickness, readiness, willingness; earliness
near antonyms belatedness, lateness; slowness
antonyms tardiness
promptly *adv* without delay — see IMMEDIATELY
promptness *n* the quality or habit of arriving on time — see PROMPTITUDE
promulgate *vb* to make known openly or publicly — see ANNOUNCE
prone *adj* **1** having a tendency to be or act in a certain way ⟨he was *prone* to emotional outbursts under stress⟩
synonyms apt, given, inclined, tending
related words choosing, preferring; disposed, likely, predisposed, willing
near antonyms averse, disinclined, indisposed, loath (*or* loth), unwilling
2 lying with the face downwards ⟨stretched out *prone* on the bed for a backrub⟩
synonyms prostrate
related words flat, recumbent; reclining, reposing; horizontal
near antonyms erect, raised, standing, upright, upstanding, vertical
antonyms supine
proneness *n* an established pattern of behavior — see TENDENCY 1
pronounced *adj* **1** likely to attract attention — see NOTICEABLE
2 very noticeable especially for being incorrect or bad — see EGREGIOUS
pronto *adv* **1** with great speed — see FAST 1
2 without delay — see IMMEDIATELY
proof *n* something presented in support of the truth or accuracy of a claim ⟨she presented *proof* that she had not cheated⟩
synonyms attestation, confirmation, corroboration, documentation, evidence, substantiation, testament, testimony, validation, witness
related words (the) goods; certificate, document, exhibit; demonstration, illustration; authentication, identification, manifestation, verification
near antonyms rebuttal, refutation; accusation, allegation, charge; assumption, conjecture, guess, presumption, surmise, suspicion
antonyms disproof
prop (up) *vb* **1** to hold up or serve as a foundation for — see SUPPORT 3
2 to provide (someone) with what is useful or necessary to achieve an end — see HELP 1
propagate *vb* **1** to bring forth offspring — see PROCREATE
2 to cause to be known over a considerable area or by many people — see SPREAD 1
propel *vb* **1** to apply force to (someone or something) so that it moves in front of one — see PUSH 1
2 to cause to function — see ACTIVATE
3 to set or keep in motion — see MOVE 2
propensity *n* **1** an established pattern of behavior — see TENDENCY 1
2 a habitual attraction to some activity or thing — see INCLINATION 1
proper *adj* **1** following the established traditions of refined society and good taste ⟨the formal ball called for *proper* attire—tuxedos and full-length gowns only⟩

THESAURUS

synonyms correct, decent, decorous, genteel, nice, polite, respectable, seemly

related words acceptable, adequate, satisfactory, tolerable; dress, dressy, formal; dignified, elegant, gracious; priggish, prim, stuffy; apt, material, relevant; compatible, congenial, harmonious; allowed, authorized, kosher, permitted

near antonyms intolerable, unacceptable, unsatisfactory; casual, grungy, informal; seedy, shabby, tacky; banned, barred, disallowed; forbidden, interdicted, outlawed, prohibited, proscribed; awkward, gauche, ungraceful

antonyms improper, incorrect, indecent, indecorous, unbecoming, unseemly

2 being in agreement with the truth or a fact or a standard — see CORRECT 1

3 marked by or showing careful attention to set forms and details — see CEREMONIOUS 1

4 meeting the requirements of a purpose or situation — see FIT 1

5 serving to identify as belonging to an individual or group — see CHARACTERISTIC 1

properly *adv* in a manner suitable for the occasion or purpose ⟨the scouts were *properly* dressed for a week of camping⟩

synonyms appropriately, congruously, correctly, fittingly, happily, meetly, rightly, suitably

related words well; acceptably, adequately, passably, satisfactorily, tolerably; decently, decorously

near antonyms unacceptably, unsatisfactorily; inopportunely, unfortunately, unseasonably; inaptly, irrelevantly; awkwardly, ungracefully

antonyms improperly, inappropriately, incongruously, incorrectly, unsuitably, wrongly

property *n* **1** a small piece of land that is developed or available for development — see LOT 1

2 something that sets apart an individual from others of the same kind — see CHARACTERISTIC

prophecy *n* a declaration that something will happen in the future — see PREDICTION

prophesier *n* one who predicts future events or developments — see PROPHET

prophesy *vb* to tell of or describe beforehand — see FORETELL

prophet *n* one who predicts future events or developments ⟨a *prophet* who swore he could see wars before they happened⟩

synonyms augur, diviner, forecaster, foreseer, foreteller, fortune-teller, futurist, prognosticator, prophesier, seer, soothsayer

related words prophetess; mystic, oracle; astrologer

prophetic *or* **prophetical** *adj* being a sign of a later course of events ⟨the breaking of the cereal bowl was a *prophetic* start to a day filled with accidents and foul-ups⟩

synonyms predictive

related words baleful, dire, foreboding, menacing, portentous, sinister, threatening; inauspicious, unpromising; oracular; revelatory, telling

near antonyms auspicious, promising, propitious, rosy

propitiate *vb* to lessen the anger or agitation of — see PACIFY

propitiatory *adj* tending to lessen or avoid conflict or hostility — see PACIFIC 1

propitious *adj* **1** having qualities which inspire hope — see HOPEFUL 1

2 pointing toward a happy outcome — see FAVORABLE 2

proponent *n* a person who actively supports or favors a cause — see EXPONENT

proportion *n* **1** a balanced, pleasing, or suitable arrangement of parts — see HARMONY 1

2 something belonging to, due to, or contributed by an individual member of a group — see SHARE 1

3 the relationship in quantity, amount, or size between two or more things — see RATIO

4 the total amount of measurable space or surface occupied by something — see ¹SIZE

proportional *adj* corresponding in size, amount, extent, or degree ⟨each child receives an allowance *proportional* to his or her age and needs⟩

synonyms commensurate, proportionate

related words balanced, symmetrical; correlative, reciprocal; contingent, dependent, relative; akin, comparable, similar

phrases in proportion

near antonyms asymmetrical (*or* asymmetric), distorted, irregular, lopsided, nonsymmetrical, twisted; unsymmetrical; unbalanced

antonyms disproportionate

proportionate *adj* corresponding in size, amount, extent, or degree — see PROPORTIONAL

proposal *n* something which is presented for consideration ⟨the city council is accepting *proposals* for ways to use that land⟩

synonyms offer, proffer, proposition, suggestion

related words feeler, overture; motion; advancement, nomination, recommendation; presentation, submission, tender; arrangement, game, ground plan, layout, line, plan, plot, project, strategy, system; conception, idea, notion, thought

propose *vb* **1** to set before the mind for consideration ⟨he *proposed* that we go for a walk this afternoon⟩

synonyms advance, offer, pose, proffer, propound, suggest, vote

related words move; nominate, recommend; present, submit, tender; file, lay, lodge; arrange, calculate, chart, contrive, cover, frame, map, plan, plot, shape

phrases put forward

2 to have in mind as a purpose or goal — see INTEND

proposition *n* **1** an idea that is the starting point for making a case or conducting an investigation — see THEORY

2 something which is presented for consideration — see PROPOSAL

propound *vb* to set before the mind for consideration — see PROPOSE 1

proprieties *n pl* personal conduct or behavior as evaluated by an accepted standard of appropriateness for a social or professional setting — see MANNER 1

proprietor *n* one who has a legal or rightful claim to ownership ⟨I am the sole *proprietor* of my car⟩

synonyms holder, owner, possessor

related words homeowner, landowner

near antonyms squatter; lessee, renter, tenant

propriety *n* socially acceptable behavior — see DECENCY 1

prorate *vb* to give out (something) in appropriate amounts or to appropriate individuals — see ADMINISTER 1

prosaic *adj* **1** being of the type that is encountered in the normal course of events — see ORDINARY 1

2 having to do with the practical details of regular life — see MUNDANE 1

proscribe *vb* to order not to do or use or to be done or used — see FORBID

proscribed *adj* that may not be permitted — see IMPERMISSIBLE

proscribing *n* the act of ordering that something not be done or used — see PROHIBITION 1

proscription *n* **1** the act of ordering that something not be done or used — see PROHIBITION 1
2 an order that something not be done or used — see PROHIBITION 2

proselyte *n* a person who has recently been persuaded to join a religious sect — see CONVERT 1

proselytize *vb* to persuade to change to one's religious faith — see CONVERT 1

prospect *n* **1** all that can be seen from a certain point — see VIEW 1
2 one who seeks an office, honor, position, or award — see CANDIDATE

prospect *vb* to go into or range over for purposes of discovery — see EXPLORE 2

prosper *vb* **1** to grow vigorously — see THRIVE 1
2 to reach a desired level of accomplishment — see SUCCEED 2

prospering *adj* marked by vigorous growth and well-being especially economically — see PROSPEROUS 1

prosperous *adj* **1** marked by vigorous growth and well-being especially economically ⟨a *prosperous* business that will soon be expanding⟩
synonyms booming, flourishing, golden, palmy, prospering, roaring, successful, thriving
related words affluent, moneyed (*or* monied), opulent, rich, substantial, wealthy, well-heeled, well-off, well-to-do; comfortable
near antonyms declining, dying, failing, floundering, languishing, struggling; bankrupt, bankrupted, insolvent
antonyms unsuccessful
2 having attained a desired end or state of good fortune — see SUCCESSFUL 1
3 growing thickly and vigorously — see RANK 1

prostitute *n* a woman who engages in sexual activities for money ⟨the town was horrified to discover that she had once been a *prostitute*⟩
synonyms harlot, whore
related words coquette, flirt, libertine, siren, tempter, temptress, wench

prostitute *vb* **1** to lower in character or dignity — see DEBASE 1
2 to put to a bad or improper use — see MISAPPLY

prostitution *n* the practice of engaging in sexual activities for money ⟨*prostitution* is illegal in most states⟩
synonyms harlotry

prostrate *adj* **1** depleted in strength, energy, or freshness — see WEARY 1
2 lacking bodily strength — see WEAK 1
3 lying with the face downwards — see PRONE 2

prostrate *vb* **1** to diminish the physical strength of — see WEAKEN 1
2 to render powerless, ineffective, or unable to move — see PARALYZE
3 to subject to incapacitating emotional or mental stress — see OVERWHELM 1

prostrated *adj* lacking bodily strength — see WEAK 1

prostration *n* a complete depletion of energy or strength — see FATIGUE

protean *adj* able to do many different kinds of things — see VERSATILE

protect *vb* to drive danger or attack away from — see DEFEND 1

protection *n* **1** means or method of defending — see DEFENSE 1
2 someone that protects — see PROTECTOR
3 the state of not being exposed to danger — see SAFETY 1

protective *adj* intended to resist or prevent attack or aggression — see DEFENSIVE

protector *n* someone that protects ⟨a bigger girl served as her *protector* against bullies at school⟩
synonyms custodian, defender, guard, protection
related words bodyguard, champion; keeper, lookout, sentinel, sentry, warden, warder, watch, watchdog, watchman; conserver, keeper, preserver, saver

protest *n* a feeling or declaration of disapproval or dissent — see OBJECTION

protest *vb* **1** to state as a fact usually forcefully — see CLAIM 1
2 to present an opposing opinion or argument — see OBJECT

protestation *n* a solemn and often public declaration of the truth or existence of something ⟨the governor went on television to make a passionate *protestation* of his innocence in the bribery scandal⟩
synonyms affirmation, assertion, avouchment, avowal, claim, declaration, insistence, profession
related words announcement, declaration, proclamation, pronouncement; argument, justification, rationalization, reason; confirmation, vindication
near antonyms disclaimer; challenge, dispute, question; confutation, disproof, rebuttal, refutation; contradiction, denial, negation
antonyms disavowal

prototype *n* something from which copies are made — see ORIGINAL

protract *vb* to make longer — see EXTEND 1

protrude *vb* to extend outward beyond a usual point — see BULGE

protrusion *n* a part that sticks out from the general mass of something — see BULGE

protuberance *n* a part that sticks out from the general mass of something — see BULGE

proud *adj* **1** having or displaying feelings of scorn for what is regarded as beneath oneself ⟨the unemployed woman was too *proud* to take a job as a maid⟩
synonyms disdainful, haughty, highfalutin, lofty, lordly, prideful, superior
related words complacent, conceited, egoistic, egotistic (*or* egotistical), important, self-assertive, self-conceited, self-important, self-satisfied, smug, uppity, vain, vainglorious; arrogant, pretentious, snobbish, stuck-up, supercilious; cavalier, overbearing, overweening, peremptory, swaggering; high-sounding, pompous; condescending, patronizing; cocky, overconfident, presumptuous; bloated, boastful, bombastic; audacious, bold, brash, brassy, cheeky, cocksure, forward, impertinent, impudent, saucy; confident, presuming, self-assured, self-confident, sure; domineering, high-handed, imperious; self-centered, selfish; dominating, magisterial, masterful
near antonyms demure, homely, meek, unassuming, unpretentious; bashful, retiring, shy, timid;

diffident, self-doubting; acquiescent, compliant, deferential, resigned, submissive, unassertive, yielding; apologetic, cowering, cringing, shrinking; passive, quiet, reserved, subdued, unobtrusive
antonyms humble, lowly, modest
2 having too high an opinion of oneself — see CONCEITED
3 large and impressive in size, grandeur, extent, or conception — see GRAND 1

provable *adj* capable of being proven as true or real — see VERIFIABLE

prove *vb* **1** to show the existence or truth of by evidence ⟨the prosecutor used DNA evidence to *prove* the defendant's guilt⟩
synonyms demonstrate, document, establish, substantiate, validate
related words back (up), buttress, corroborate; evidence, evince, record, support, witness; adduce, attest, authenticate, certify, identify; confirm, sustain, verify; clinch, nail, settle; depose, testify
near antonyms challenge, dispute, object; allege, assume, conjecture, guess, presume, surmise, suspect
antonyms disprove, rebut, refute
2 to come to be — see COME OUT 1
3 to gain full recognition or acceptance of — see ESTABLISH 1

provender *n* substances intended to be eaten — see FOOD

proverb *n* an often stated observation regarding something from common experience — see SAYING

provide *vb* to put (something) into the possession of someone for use or consumption — see FURNISH 2

provide (for) *vb* to pay the living expenses of — see SUPPORT 2

providence *n* **1** careful management of material resources — see ECONOMY
2 concern or preparation for the future — see FORESIGHT 2
3 *cap* the being worshipped as the creator and ruler of the universe — see DEITY 2

provident *adj* **1** careful in the management of money or resources — see FRUGAL
2 having or showing awareness of and preparation for the future — see FORESIGHTED

providential *adj* coming or happening by good luck especially unexpectedly — see FORTUNATE 1

province *n* a region of activity, knowledge, or influence — see FIELD 2

provincial *adj* not broad or open in views or opinions — see NARROW 2

provincial *n* an awkward or simple person especially from a small town or the country — see HICK

provision *n* **1** something upon which the carrying out of an agreement or offer depends — see CONDITION 2
2 provisions *pl* substances intended to be eaten — see FOOD

provision *vb* to provide food or meals for — see FEED 1

provisional *adj* intended to last, continue, or serve for a limited time — see TEMPORARY 1

proviso *n* something upon which the carrying out of an agreement or offer depends — see CONDITION 2

provocation *n* **1** something that arouses a strong response from another ⟨Dad only gets angry from the greatest of *provocations*⟩

synonyms excitement, incitement, instigation, stimulant, stimulation, stimulus
related words encouragement, goad, incentive, inducement, jog, prod, spur; induction, inspiration, motivation; aggravation, annoyance, bother, exasperation, frustration, hassle, headache, irritant, nuisance, peeve, pest
near antonyms subduing
2 something that arouses action or activity — see IMPULSE

provocative *adj* serving or likely to arouse a strong reaction ⟨a *provocative* editorial that sparked a heated discussion⟩
synonyms exciting, inciting, instigating, piquing, provoking, stimulating
related words explosive, fiery, incendiary, inflammatory, triggering; inducing, inspirational, inspiring, motivating; jeering, taunting, teasing; activating, energizing, galvanizing, quickening, vitalizing; angering, enraging, maddening, upsetting; aggravating, annoying, bothersome, exasperating, galling, irksome, irritating, pesky, vexatious, vexing
near antonyms subduing

provoke *vb* **1** to rouse to strong feeling or action ⟨his teasing finally *provoked* her to anger⟩ ⟨a strong chilling breeze *provoked* the picnickers to move inside⟩
synonyms arouse, encourage, excite, fire (up), incite, instigate, move, pique, stimulate, stir
related words fan, inflame, kindle, trigger; activate, energize, galvanize, induce, inspire, motivate, quicken, vitalize; abet, ferment, foment, raise, whip (up); anger, enrage, madden, upset; jeer, taunt, tease; aggravate, annoy, bother, exasperate, gall, get, irritate, vex
near antonyms calm, soothe, subdue, tranquilize (*also* tranquillize)
2 to cause or encourage the development of — see INCITE 1

provoking *adj* serving or likely to arouse a strong reaction — see PROVOCATIVE

proximity *n* the state or condition of being near ⟨the *proximity* of the curtains to the fireplace was a cause of concern to the safety inspector⟩
synonyms closeness, contiguity, immediacy, nearness
related words abutment, juxtaposition
antonyms distance, remoteness

proxy *n* a person who acts or does business for another — see AGENT 2

prude *n* a person who is greatly concerned with seemly behavior and morality especially regarding sexual matters ⟨it's not true that only a *prude* would object to being pressured for physical intimacy⟩
synonyms moralist, puritan
related words goody-goody; fuddy-duddy, old maid, prig, spoilsport
near antonyms libertarian, libertine

prudence *n* the ability to make intelligent decisions especially in everyday matters — see COMMON SENSE

prudent *adj* **1** having or showing good judgment and restraint especially in conduct or speech — see DISCREET
2 suitable for bringing about a desired result under the circumstances — see EXPEDIENT

prudery *n* a tendency to care a great deal about seemly behavior and morals especially in sexual matters ⟨such *prudery* regarding artistic depictions of the nude has no place on a college campus⟩

synonyms prudishness, puritanism
related words priggishness, primness; morality, virtue
near antonyms libertarianism

prudish *adj* given to or marked by very conservative standards regarding personal behavior or morals — see STRAITLACED

prudishness *n* a tendency to care a great deal about seemly behavior and morals especially in sexual matters — see PRUDERY

prune *vb* to make (as hair) shorter with or as if with the use of shears — see CLIP

¹pry *vb* **1** to raise, move, or pull apart with or as if with a lever ⟨it took some effort to *pry* up the trap door⟩
synonyms jimmy, lever, prize
related words elevate, hoist, lift, uplift; break, break up, detach, disengage, disjoin, divide, part, pull, separate; shift
near antonyms connect, join
2 to draw out by force or with effort — see EXTRACT

²pry *vb* to interest oneself in what is not one's concern — see INTERFERE

prying *adj* **1** interested in what is not one's own business — see CURIOUS 1
2 thrusting oneself where one is not welcome or invited — see INTRUSIVE

psalm *n* a religious song — see HYMN

psalmody *n* a book of hymns — see HYMNAL

pseudo *adj* lacking in natural or spontaneous quality — see ARTIFICIAL 1

pseudonym *n* a fictitious or assumed name ⟨the most notorious serial killer of the 19th century remains known only by the *pseudonym* of Jack the Ripper⟩
synonyms alias
related words nom de plume, pen name; appellation, designation; misnomer; epithet, nickname, sobriquet (*also* soubriquet)

pshaw *interj* how surprising, doubtful, or unbelievable — see NO

psyche *n* an immaterial force within a human being thought to give the body life, energy, and power — see SOUL 1

psychological *also* **psychologic** *adj* of or relating to the mind — see MENTAL 1

psychopath *n* a person judged to be legally or medically insane — see LUNATIC 1

psychotic *n* a person judged to be legally or medically insane — see LUNATIC 1

pub *n* a place of business where alcoholic beverages are sold to be consumed on the premises — see BARROOM

public *adj* **1** not known by only a select few ⟨it was *public* knowledge that they were expecting a baby⟩
synonyms open
related words general, popular; unclassified, well-known; advertised, aired, announced, broadcast, declared, disclosed, divulged, heralded, posted, proclaimed, promulgated, publicized, published, spotlighted; current, prevalent, rife, widespread; communal, shared; reported, reputed, rumored
near antonyms classified; unadvertised, unannounced, undisclosed; clandestine, collusive, conspiratorial, covert; surreptitious, undercover,

underhand, underhanded; intimate, personal; concealed, repressed, reserved, silenced, stifled, suppressed, withheld; recanted, retracted, revoked
antonyms confidential, private, privy, secret
2 freely available for use or participation by all — see OPEN 2
3 of or relating to a nation — see NATIONAL
4 held by or applicable to a majority of the people — see GENERAL 3
5 used or done by a number of people as a group — see COLLECTIVE

public *n* human beings in general — see PEOPLE 1

public house *n* **1** a place that provides rooms and usually a public dining room for overnight guests — see HOTEL
2 *chiefly British* a place of business where alcoholic beverages are sold to be consumed on the premises — see BARROOM

publicity *n* newsworthy information released to the media that is designed to gain public attention or support for a person, business, or cause ⟨an endless flow of *publicity* for our charity event resulted in a great turnout⟩
synonyms ballyhoo
related words ad, advertisement, commercial, message, plug, promotion, spot, word; banner, bill, billboard, placard, poster, sign; advertising, marketing, propaganda; pronouncement, publication, release; broadcast, bulletin, dispatch, newscast, report, story; testimonial, write-up

publicize *vb* **1** to provide publicity for ⟨the movie studios widely *publicized* their summer blockbusters⟩
synonyms ballyhoo, plug, promote, tout
related words advertise; push; acclaim, hail, laud, praise; recommend, review; announce, broadcast, publish
2 to make known openly or publicly — see ANNOUNCE

public servant *n* **1** a person who holds a public office — see OFFICIAL
2 a worker in a government agency — see BUREAUCRAT

publish *vb* **1** to produce and release for distribution in printed form ⟨our local animal shelter *publishes* a newsletter⟩
synonyms get out, issue, print
related words serialize; contribute, edit, syndicate; manufacture, produce; distribute, market
near antonyms censor, suppress
2 to make known openly or publicly — see ANNOUNCE

puck *n* an imaginary being usually having a small human form and magical powers — see FAIRY

puddle *n* a small often deep body of water — see ¹POOL

pudginess *n* the condition of having an excess of body fat — see CORPULENCE

pudgy *adj* having an excess of body fat — see FAT 1

puerile *adj* **1** having or showing the annoying qualities (as silliness) associated with children — see CHILDISH
2 lacking in adult experience or maturity — see CALLOW
3 lacking in seriousness or maturity — see GIDDY 1

puff *n* a slight or gentle movement of air — see BREEZE 1

puff *vb* to breathe hard, quickly, or with difficulty — see GASP

pugilist *n* one that engages in the sport of fighting with the fists — see BOXER

pugnacious *adj* feeling or displaying eagerness to fight — see BELLIGERENT

pugnacity *n* an inclination to fight or quarrel — see BELLIGERENCE

puissance *n* the ability to exert effort for the accomplishment of a task — see POWER 2

puissant *adj* having great power or influence — see IMPORTANT 2

pule *vb* to utter feeble plaintive cries — see WHIMPER

pull *n* **1** the act or an instance of applying force on something so that it moves in the direction of the force ⟨I gave the door such a *pull* that when it suddenly opened, I nearly fell backwards⟩
  synonyms draw, haul, jerk, pluck, tug, wrench, yank
  related words drag, tow; hitch, jerk, twitch; grab, snatch
  near antonyms heave, shove, thrust
  antonyms push
2 the power to direct the thinking or behavior of others usually indirectly — see INFLUENCE 1

pull *vb* **1** to cause to follow by applying steady force on ⟨a team of horses *pulling* a heavy wagon⟩
  synonyms drag, draw, hale, haul, lug, tow, tug
  related words attract; jerk, yank; carry, convey, ferry, move, transport
  near antonyms shove, thrust
  antonyms drive, propel, push
2 to draw out by force or with effort — see EXTRACT
3 to injure by overuse, misuse, or pressure — see STRAIN 1

pull (out) *vb* to leave a place often for another — see GO 2

pulp *vb* to cause to become a pulpy mass — see CRUSH 1

pulpiness *n* the quality or state of being full of juice — see SUCCULENCE

pulpy *adj* **1** full of juice — see JUICY
2 giving easily to the touch — see SOFT 3

pulsate *vb* to expand and contract in a rhythmic manner ⟨the heart muscle *pulsates* regularly to pump blood⟩
  synonyms beat, palpitate, pit-a-pat, pitter-patter, pulse, throb
  related words fluctuate, oscillate, vibrate; quiver, tremble

pulsation *n* a rhythmic expanding and contracting ⟨you should press against the artery in your wrist and count the *pulsations* to calculate your heart rate⟩
  synonyms beat, palpitation, pulse, throb
  related words fluctuation, oscillation, vibration; quiver, tremble, tremor

pulse *n* a rhythmic expanding and contracting — see PULSATION

pulse *vb* to expand and contract in a rhythmic manner — see PULSATE

pulverize *vb* **1** to bring to a complete end the physical soundness, existence, or usefulness of — see DESTROY 1
2 to reduce to fine particles — see POWDER

puma *n* a large tawny cat of the wild — see COUGAR

pummel *vb* to strike repeatedly — see BEAT 1

pump *vb* **1** to make short up-and-down movements — see NOD
2 to put a series of questions to — see EXAMINE 1
3 to remove (liquid) gradually or completely — see DRAIN 1

¹punch *n* **1** the quality of an utterance that provokes interest and produces an effect ⟨the real *punch* of the speech came in its closing lines⟩
  synonyms cogency, effectiveness, force, forcefulness, impact, point
  related words payoff; importance, significance; appeal, attraction, charm, fascination
2 active strength of body or mind — see VIGOR 1
3 a hard strike with a part of the body or an instrument — see ¹BLOW

²punch *n* a mark or small hole made by a pointed instrument — see PRICK 1

punch *vb* **1** to deliver a blow to (someone or something) usually in a strong vigorous manner — see HIT 1
2 to make a hole or series of holes in — see PERFORATE
3 to urge, push, or force onward — see DRIVE 1

puncheon *n* an enclosed wooden vessel for holding beverages — see CASK

punctual *adj* done, carried out, or given without delay — see PROMPT 1

punctuality *n* the quality or habit of arriving on time — see PROMPTITUDE

puncture *n* a mark or small hole made by a pointed instrument — see PRICK 1

puncture *vb* **1** to make a hole or series of holes in — see PERFORATE
2 to penetrate or hold (something) with a pointed object — see IMPALE

pungency *n* **1** a harsh or sharp quality — see EDGE 1
2 the quality or state of being stimulating to the mind or senses — see PIQUANCY

pungent *adj* **1** having a powerfully stimulating odor or flavor — see SHARP 3
2 marked by the use of wit that is intended to cause hurt feelings — see SARCASTIC
3 sharp and pleasantly stimulating to the mind or senses — see PIQUANT

puniness *n* the quality or state of being little in size — see SMALLNESS

punish *vb* to inflict a penalty on for a fault or crime ⟨the child was *punished* for breaking dishes on purpose⟩ ⟨if caught, the thief will be severely *punished*⟩
  synonyms castigate, chasten, chastise, correct, discipline, penalize
  related words assess, charge, dock, fine, impose, levy, mulct; convict, sentence; condemn, damn, denounce; criticize, reprove; wreak
  near antonyms forfeit; get off, ransom, release; commute, reprieve; absolve, acquit, exculpate, exonerate, vindicate
  antonyms excuse, pardon, spare

punisher *n* one who inflicts punishment in return for an injury or offense — see NEMESIS 1

punishment *n* suffering, loss, or hardship imposed in response to a crime or offense ⟨the child's *punishment* was confiscation of his toys for a day⟩
  synonyms castigation, chastisement, correction, desert, discipline, nemesis, penalty, wrath
  related words reprisal, retaliation, retribution, revenge, vengeance; assessment, charge, fine, mulct;

example, sentence; confinement, imprisonment, incarceration; condemnation, damnation, denouncement; criticism, reproof

near antonyms amnesty, indemnity, pardon, parole; acquittal, exculpation, exoneration, vindication; exemption, immunity, impunity; release; commutation, reprieve; absolution, forgiveness, remission, remitment; condonation, disregard, overlooking

punitive *adj* inflicting, involving, or serving as punishment ⟨any misbehavior was immediately met with a *punitive* response⟩ ⟨the company had to pay a million dollars in *punitive* damages⟩

synonyms castigating, chastening, chastising, correcting, correctional, corrective, disciplinary, disciplining, penal, penalizing

related words retaliatory, retributive, retributory, revengeful; vengeful, wrathful

near antonyms compensatory; acquitting, exculpating, exculpatory, exonerating, vindicating; absolving, condoning, pardoning, remitting; commuting, reprieving

punk *adj* **1** falling short of a standard — see BAD 1

2 extremely unsatisfactory — see WRETCHED 1

3 temporarily suffering from a disorder of the body — see SICK 1

punk *n* a violent, brutal person who is often a member of an organized gang — see HOODLUM

puny *adj* of a size that is less than average — see SMALL 1

pupil *n* **1** one who attends a school — see STUDENT

2 one who follows the opinions or teachings of another — see FOLLOWER

puppet *n* **1** a small figure often of a human being used especially as a child's plaything — see DOLL 1

2 one that is or can be used to further the purposes of another — see PAWN 1

purchasable *adj* open to improper influence and especially bribery — see VENAL

purchase *vb* to get possession of (something) by giving money in exchange for — see BUY

pure *adj* **1** free from added matter ⟨I'm allergic to any jewelry that isn't *pure* silver⟩ ⟨the solution must be kept *pure* for the experiment to work⟩

synonyms absolute, fine, neat, plain, purified, refined, straight, unadulterated, unalloyed, undiluted, unmixed

related words clarified, filtered, refined; clean, uncontaminated, uncorrupted, undefiled, unpolluted, untainted; rendered, tried; concentrated, full-bodied, strong; uncombined

near antonyms befouled, besmirched, contaminated, corrupted, debased, defiled, fouled, polluted, soiled, spoiled, sullied, tainted; amalgamated, blended, coalesced, combined, commingled, compounded, incorporated, intermingled, intermixed, merged, mingled; conjoined, fused, joined, linked, united; cheapened, doctored, watered (down)

antonyms adulterated, alloyed, diluted, impure, mixed

2 free from any trace of the coarse or indecent — see CHASTE

3 free from sin — see INNOCENT 1

4 having no exceptions or restrictions — see ABSOLUTE 2

purebred *adj* of unmixed ancestry ⟨that horse is a *purebred* Arabian⟩

synonyms full-blooded, pedigreed, thoroughbred

related words inbred

near antonyms crossbred, crossed, hybridized, interbred, outcrossed

antonyms hybrid, mixed, mongrel

purely *adv* with purity of thought and deed ⟨the devout girl vowed to live her life *purely* and in the service of God⟩

synonyms chastely, innocently; morally, righteously; modestly, virtuously

related words decently, decorously, properly; priggishly, primly, prudishly

near antonyms indecently, obscenely, vulgarly; lasciviously, lewdly, lustfully

antonyms evilly, immorally, impurely, sinfully, wickedly

purge *vb* to free from moral guilt or blemish especially ceremonially — see PURIFY 1

purification *n* the act or fact of freeing from sin or moral guilt ⟨some people must undergo a ritual *purification* after certain activities⟩

synonyms cleansing, sanctification

related words rebirth, regeneration, restoration; grace, redemption, salvation; absolution, forgiveness, remission; acquittal, clearance, clearing, exoneration, vindication; atonement, expiation

near antonyms blasphemy, defilement, desecration, profanation, violation; corruption, debasement, perversion; contamination, pollution, sullying, tarnishing

purified *adj* free from added matter — see PURE 1

purify *vb* **1** to free from moral guilt or blemish especially ceremonially ⟨Catholics go to confession to be *purified*⟩

synonyms cleanse, purge, sanctify

related words amend, improve, refine; heal, regenerate, restore; elevate, ennoble, uplift; absolve, acquit, clear, exonerate, vindicate

near antonyms corrupt, debase, debauch, defile, degrade, demean, deprave, pervert, stain, warp; poison, profane, prostitute; sully, tarnish

2 to remove usually visible impurities from — see CLARIFY 1

puritan *n* a person who is greatly concerned with seemly behavior and morality especially regarding sexual matters — see PRUDE

puritanical *adj* given to or marked by very conservative standards regarding personal behavior or morals — see STRAITLACED

puritanism *n* a tendency to care a great deal about seemly behavior and morals especially in sexual matters — see PRUDERY

purity *n* the quality or state of being morally pure — see CHASTITY

purlieus *n pl* the area around a city — see ENVIRONS 1

purloin *vb* to take (something) without right and with an intent to keep — see STEAL 1

purloiner *n* one who steals — see THIEF

purport *n* the idea that is conveyed or intended to be conveyed to the mind by language, symbol, or action — see MEANING 1

purpose *n* **1** something that one hopes or intends to accomplish — see GOAL

2 the action for which a person or thing is specially fitted or used or for which a thing exists — see ROLE

purposeful *adj* **1** fully committed to achieving a goal — see DETERMINED 1

THESAURUS

2 made, given, or done with full awareness of what one is doing — see INTENTIONAL

purposefully *adv* with full awareness of what one is doing — see INTENTIONALLY

purposefulness *n* firm or unwavering adherence to one's purpose — see DETERMINATION 1

purposely *adv* with full awareness of what one is doing — see INTENTIONALLY

purr *n* a monotonous sound like that of an insect in motion — see HUM

purse *n* a container for carrying money and small personal items ⟨I left my *purse* at home, so I can't buy anything after all⟩
synonyms bag, handbag, pocketbook
related words billfold, wallet; compact, vanity; poke, pouch, sack; backpack, haversack, knapsack, rucksack

pursue *vb* **1** to go after or on the track of — see FOLLOW 2
2 to go in search of — see SEEK 1

pursuing *n* the act of going after or in the tracks of another — see PURSUIT

pursuit *n* the act of going after or in the tracks of another ⟨the constant *pursuit* of the rock band by a horde of screaming fans as they roamed about the city⟩
synonyms chase, chasing, dogging, following, hounding, pursuing, shadowing, tagging, tailing, tracing, tracking, trailing
related words tagging along; path, track, trail; search, seeking

push *vb* **1** to apply force to (someone or something) so that it moves in front of one ⟨I had to *push* my damaged bike all the way home⟩
synonyms drive, propel, shove, thrust
related words impel, move; bear (down), compress, depress, jam, pressure, squash, squeeze, weigh (upon); bulldoze, compel, force, lean (on *or* against), muscle, ram
2 to force one's way — see PRESS 4

pushover *n* something that is easy to do — see CINCH

pusillanimous *adj* having or showing a shameful lack of courage — see COWARDLY

¹puss *n slang* the front part of the head — see FACE 1

²puss *n* a small domestic animal known for catching mice — see CAT 1

pussy *n* a small domestic animal known for catching mice — see CAT 1

pussyfoot *vb* **1** to avoid giving a definite answer or position — see EQUIVOCATE
2 to move about in a sly or secret manner — see SNEAK 1

put *vb* **1** to arrange something in a certain spot or position — see PLACE 1
2 to convey in appropriate or telling terms — see PHRASE
3 to decide the size, amount, number, or distance of (something) without actual measurement — see ESTIMATE 2
4 to establish or apply as a charge or penalty — see IMPOSE

put by *vb* to put (something of future use or value) in a safe or secret place — see HOARD

put–down *n* **1** an act or expression showing scorn and usually intended to hurt another's feelings — see INSULT
2 the act of making a person or a thing seem little or unimportant — see DEPRECIATION

put down *vb* **1** to express scornfully one's low opinion of — see DECRY 1
2 to make a written note of — see RECORD 1
3 to put (someone or something) on a list — see ¹LIST 2
4 to put a stop to (something) by the use of force — see QUELL 1

put in *vb* to put or set into the ground to grow — see PLANT

put off *vb* **1** to assign to a later time — see POSTPONE
2 to rid oneself of (a garment) — see REMOVE 1

put–on *adj* lacking in natural or spontaneous quality — see ARTIFICIAL 1

put–on *n* a display of emotion or behavior that is insincere or intended to deceive — see MASQUERADE

put on *vb* **1** to place on one's person ⟨I *put on* a coat and shoes to go outside⟩
synonyms don, slip (on *or* into), throw (on)
related words apparel, array, attire, bedeck, bedizen, bundle up, caparison, clothe, doll up, dress, garb, rig, robe, suit, trick, uniform; overdress
near antonyms disrobe, strip, undress
antonyms doff, remove, take off
2 to describe or express in too strong terms — see OVERSTATE
3 to present a false appearance of — see FEIGN

put out *vb* **1** to bring to bear especially forcefully or effectively — see EXERT
2 to cause to cease burning — see EXTINGUISH 1
3 to disturb the peace of mind of (someone) especially by repeated disagreeable acts — see IRRITATE 1

putrefaction *n* the process by which dead organic matter separates into simpler substances — see CORRUPTION 1

putrefied *adj* having undergone organic breakdown — see ROTTEN 1

putrefy *vb* to go through decomposition — see DECAY 1

putrid *adj* having undergone organic breakdown — see ROTTEN 1

putter (around) *vb* to spend time in aimless activity — see FIDDLE (AROUND)

putterer *n* a person who regularly or occasionally engages in an activity without being or becoming an expert at it — see AMATEUR

put up *vb* **1** to fix in an upright position — see ERECT 1
2 to form by putting together parts or materials — see BUILD
3 to offer for sale to the public — see MARKET
4 to provide with living quarters or shelter — see HOUSE 1

puzzle *n* something hard to understand or explain — see MYSTERY

puzzle *vb* to throw into a state of mental uncertainty — see CONFUSE 1

puzzle (out) *vb* to find an answer for through reasoning — see SOLVE

puzzlement *n* **1** a state of mental uncertainty — see CONFUSION 1
2 something hard to understand or explain — see MYSTERY

pygmy *adj* of a size that is less than average — see SMALL 1

pygmy *n* a living thing much smaller than others of its kind — see DWARF 1

quack *n* one who makes false claims of identity or expertise — see IMPOSTOR

quadrangle *n* an open space wholly or partly enclosed (as by buildings or walls) — see COURT 2

quaff *n* the portion of a serving of a beverage that is swallowed at one time — see DRINK 2

quaff *vb* to swallow in liquid form — see DRINK 1

quail *vb* **1** to draw back in fear, pain, or disgust — see FLINCH
2 to draw back or crouch down in fearful submission — see COWER

quaint *adj* **1** different from the ordinary in a way that causes curiosity or suspicion — see ODD 2
2 pleasantly reminiscent of an earlier time — see OLD-FASHIONED 1

quake *n* a shaking of the earth — see EARTHQUAKE

quake *vb* to make a series of small irregular or violent movements — see SHAKE 1

quaking *adj* marked by or given to small uncontrollable bodily movements — see SHAKY 1

qualification *n* **1** a skill, an ability, or knowledge that makes a person able to do a particular job ⟨the fashion firm was looking for an applicant who could list superior sewing skills among his or her *qualifications*⟩
synonyms capability, credentials, stuff
related words command, expertise, mastery, proficiency; ability, capacity, competence, competency, facility, faculty; flair, genius, gift, talent; forte, specialty; fitness, suitability, suitableness; makings, potentiality
2 something upon which the carrying out of an agreement or offer depends — see CONDITION 2

qualified *adj* having the required skills for an acceptable level of performance — see COMPETENT

qualify *vb* **1** to limit the meaning of (as a noun) ⟨*qualifying* the noun "adventure" in the title of your story with a descriptive adjective would make it more attention-grabbing⟩
synonyms modify, restrict
related words alter, distort, twist; narrow; compare, conjugate, decline, inflect
near antonyms broaden, expand, widen
2 to make competent (as by training, skill, or ability) for a particular office or function ⟨raising five children has *qualified* her to be an advice columnist on parenting⟩
synonyms equip, fit, prepare, ready, season
related words accustom, adapt, adjust, condition, groom, habituate, shape, tailor, train; authorize, entitle; empower, enable
3 to give a right to — see ENTITLE 1
4 to give official or legal power to — see AUTHORIZE 1

quality *n* **1** degree of excellence ⟨we expect a high *quality* of service in such a fancy restaurant⟩
synonyms caliber (*or* calibre), class, grade, rate
related words hallmark, standard; mark; footing, place, position, rank, standing, stature, status
2 high position within society — see RANK 2
3 something that sets apart an individual from others of the same kind — see CHARACTERISTIC

qualm *n* an uneasy feeling about the rightness of what one is doing or going to do ⟨she had no *qualms* about selling her old term papers to other

students, even though it was against the academic honor code⟩
synonyms compunction, misgiving, scruple
related words conscience; distrust, doubt, mistrust, suspicion, uncertainty; qualmishness, unease, uneasiness; reluctance, unwillingness; demur, objection, protest; guilt, regret, remorse, self-reproach, shame; contrition, penitence, repentance
near antonyms aplomb, assurance, certainty, certitude, confidence, conviction, self-assurance, self-confidence, sureness

qualmish *adj* affected with nausea — see NAUSEOUS

qualmishness *n* **1** a disturbed condition of the stomach in which one feels like vomiting — see NAUSEA 1
2 the tendency to be or state of being squeamish — see DELICACY 3

quandary *n* a situation in which one has to choose between two or more equally unsatisfactory choices — see DILEMMA

quantity *n* **1** a considerable amount — see LOT 2
2 a given or particular mass or aggregate of matter — see AMOUNT

quarrel *n* an often noisy or angry expression of differing opinions — see ARGUMENT 1

quarrel *vb* to express different opinions about something often angrily — see ARGUE 2

quarreler *or* **quarreller** *n* a person who takes part in a dispute — see DISPUTANT

quarrelsome *adj* **1** feeling or displaying eagerness to fight — see BELLIGERENT
2 given to arguing — see ARGUMENTATIVE 1

quarry *n* an animal that is hunted or killed — see PREY

quarter *n* **1** an area (as of a city) set apart for some purpose or having some special feature — see DISTRICT
2 kind, gentle, or compassionate treatment especially towards someone who is undeserving of it — see MERCY 1
3 the place where someone is assigned to stand or remain — see STATION 1
4 quarters *pl* the place where one lives — see HOME 1

quarter *vb* to provide with living quarters or shelter — see HOUSE 1

¹quash *vb* to put a stop to (something) by the use of force — see QUELL 1

²quash *vb* to put an end to by formal action — see ABOLISH

quaver *vb* to sing with the alternation of two musical tones — see WARBLE

quavery *adj* marked by or given to small uncontrollable bodily movements — see SHAKY 1

quay *n* a structure used by boats and ships for taking on or landing cargo and passengers — see DOCK

queasiness *n* **1** a disturbed condition of the stomach in which one feels like vomiting — see NAUSEA 1
2 the tendency to be or state of being squeamish — see DELICACY 3

queasy *also* **queazy** *adj* affected with nausea — see NAUSEOUS

queenly *adj* fit for or worthy of a royal ruler — see MONARCHICAL

queer *adj* **1** affected with nausea — see NAUSEOUS
2 different from the ordinary in a way that causes curiosity or suspicion — see ODD 2
3 noticeably different from what is generally found or experienced — see UNUSUAL 1

queerish *adj* **1** affected with nausea — see NAUSEOUS
2 different from the ordinary in a way that causes curiosity or suspicion — see ODD 2

queerness *n* a disturbed condition of the stomach in which one feels like vomiting — see NAUSEA 1

quell *vb* **1** to put a stop to (something) by the use of force ⟨the National Guard was called in to help *quell* the late-night disturbances downtown⟩
synonyms clamp down (on), crack down (on), crush, put down, quash, repress, silence, snuff (out), squash, squelch, subdue, suppress
related words douse, extinguish, put out, quench; smother, stifle, strangle; annihilate, destroy, smash; exterminate, obliterate, wipe out; conquer, overcome, overwhelm, subjugate, vanquish
near antonyms abet, aid, assist, help, support; incite, instigate, provoke, stir; advance, encourage, foster, further, promote
2 to stop the noise or speech of — see SILENCE 1

quench *vb* **1** to cause to cease burning — see EXTINGUISH 1
2 to put a complete end to (a physical need or desire) — see SATISFY 1

quencher *n* a liquid suitable for drinking — see DRINK 1

querulous *adj* given to complaining a lot — see FUSSY 1

query *n* an act or instance of asking for information — see QUESTION 2

query *vb* **1** to demand proof of the truth or rightness of — see CHALLENGE 1
2 to put a question or questions to — see ASK 1
3 to put a series of questions to — see EXAMINE 1

quest *n* an act or process of looking carefully or thoroughly for someone or something — see SEARCH

quest *vb* **1** to ask for (something) earnestly or with authority — see DEMAND 1
2 to go in search of — see SEEK 1
3 to make a request for — see ASK (FOR) 1

question *n* **1** an interrogative expression often used to test knowledge ⟨because I have missed so many classes, I had a hard time answering every *question* on today's surprise quiz⟩
synonyms problem
related words brainteaser, conundrum, poser, puzzle, quiz, riddle, stickler, stumper
near antonyms answer, response, solution
2 an act or instance of asking for information ⟨after reading the brief statement to the reporters, the lawyer ended the press conference by saying, "No more *questions*, please"⟩ ⟨the dozens of *questions* researched by the reference librarians⟩
synonyms call, inquiry, request, query
related words questionnaire, survey; inquisition, interrogating, interrogation, questioning
3 a feeling or declaration of disapproval or dissent — see OBJECTION
4 a major object of interest or concern (as in a discussion or artistic composition) — see MATTER 1

question *vb* **1** to demand proof of the truth or rightness of — see CHALLENGE 1

2 to give serious and careful thought to — see PONDER
3 to have no trust or confidence in — see DISTRUST
4 to put a question or questions to — see ASK 1
5 to put a series of questions to — see EXAMINE 1

questionable *adj* **1** giving good reason for being doubted, questioned, or challenged — see DOUBTFUL 2
2 not likely to be true or to occur — see IMPROBABLE
3 open to question or dispute — see DEBATABLE 1

questioner *n* a person who is always ready to doubt or question the truth or existence of something — see SKEPTIC

questioning *adj* inclined to doubt or question claims — see SKEPTICAL 1

queue *n* a series of persons or things arranged one behind another — see LINE 1

quibble *vb* to make often peevish criticisms or objections about matters that are minor, unimportant, or irrelevant ⟨he spent the entire evening *quibbling* about the historical inaccuracies in the television series on World War II⟩
synonyms carp, cavil, fuss, nitpick
related words criticize, fault; beef, bellyache, complain, crab, croak, gripe, grouse, growl, grumble, moan, squawk, wail, whine, yammer; murmur, mutter
phrases split hairs
near antonyms applaud, commend, compliment, praise, recommend; approve, back, endorse (*also* indorse), support

quick *adj* **1** having or showing the ability to respond without delay or hesitation ⟨she was a *quick* wit, always ready with a pun or joke when the moment called for one⟩
synonyms alacritous, alert, expeditious, prompt, ready, willing
related words receptive, responsive; immediate, instant, instantaneous, summary; fast, hit-and-run, rapid, speedy, swift; eager, keen, sharp; apt, clever, smart
near antonyms unresponsive; dull, indolent, laggard, lazy, logy, slothful, slow, sluggish, tardy; dormant, idle, inactive, inert
2 having or showing quickness of mind — see INTELLIGENT 1
3 moving, proceeding, or acting with great speed — see FAST 1

quick *adv* with great speed — see FAST 1

quick *n* the seat of one's deepest thoughts and emotions — see CORE 1

quicken *vb* **1** to cause to move or proceed fast or faster — see HURRY 1
2 to give life, vigor, or spirit to — see ANIMATE

quickly *adv* with great speed — see FAST 1

quickness *n* a high rate of movement or performance — see SPEED

quick–tempered *adj* easily irritated or annoyed — see IRRITABLE

quick–witted *adj* having or showing quickness of mind — see INTELLIGENT 1

quiescence *n* **1** a state of temporary inactivity — see ABEYANCE
2 lack of action or activity — see INACTION

quiescent *adj* slow to move or act — see INACTIVE 1

quiet *adj* **1** free from disturbing noise or uproar ⟨left the din of the rock concert and went to a

quiet restaurant where we could hear one another talk⟩
synonyms calm, hushed, peaceful, restful, serene, still, stilly, tranquil
related words noiseless, silent, soundless; speechless, wordless; dead, motionless, quiescent; muffled, muted, quieted
near antonyms crazy, tempestuous, wild
antonyms boisterous, clamorous, clattery, deafening, loud, noisy, raucous, rip-roaring, roistering, romping, rowdy, tumultuous, uproarious, woolly (*also* wooly)
2 not excessively showy ⟨she decided to wear a *quiet* business suit to the interview instead of her blue satin party dress⟩
synonyms conservative, muted, restrained, subdued, toned-down, understated, unpretentious
related words appropriate, fit, fitting, proper, suitable; modest, plain, simple, unadorned; inconspicuous, unobtrusive; tasteful; drab, mousy (*or* mousey); practical, sensible
near antonyms meretricious; graceless, inelegant, tacky, tasteless, vulgar; baroque, fancy, frilly, gilded, ornate, rococo; overdecorated, overdone, overwrought
antonyms flamboyant, flashy, garish, gaudy, glitzy, loud, ostentatious, splashy, swank (*or* swanky), tawdry
3 free from storms or physical disturbance — see CALM 1
4 hidden from view — see SECLUDED
5 mostly or entirely without sound — see SILENT 3
6 not loud in pitch or volume — see SOFT 1
quiet *n* **1** a state of freedom from storm or disturbance — see CALM
2 the near or complete absence of sound — see SILENCE 2
quiet *adv* without motion — see STILL 1
quiet *vb* **1** to become still and orderly ⟨told his rowdy class to *quiet* down during the lesson⟩
synonyms calm (down), cool, hush, settle (down)
related words relax, tranquilize (*also* tranquillize), unwind
near antonyms agitate, discompose, disrupt, disturb, provoke, rile, ruffle, stir; annoy, irritate
antonyms act up, carry on, cut up
2 to free from distress or disturbance — see CALM 1
quiet (down) *vb* to stop talking — see SHUT UP
quieted *adj* mostly or entirely without sound — see SILENT 3
quieting *adj* tending to calm the emotions and relieve stress — see SOOTHING 1
quietly *adv* without motion — see STILL 1
quietness *n* **1** a state of freedom from storm or disturbance — see CALM
2 the near or complete absence of sound — see SILENCE 2
quietude *n* **1** a state of freedom from storm or disturbance — see CALM
2 the near or complete absence of sound — see SILENCE 2
quietus *n* **1** a freeing from an obligation or responsibility — see RELEASE 1
2 the permanent stopping of all the vital bodily activities — see DEATH 1
quintessence *n* **1** the most perfect type or example ⟨the Parthenon in Greece was considered the

quintessence of the perfectly proportioned building⟩
synonyms beau ideal, classic, epitome, exemplar, ideal, perfection
related words archetype, model, prototype; paradigm, standard; nonpareil, paragon; embodiment, incarnation, personification; acme, height, last word, ultimate, zenith
2 the quality or qualities that make a thing what it is — see ESSENCE
quintessential *adj* constituting, serving as, or worthy of being a pattern to be imitated — see MODEL
quip *n* something said or done to cause laughter — see JOKE 1
quip *vb* to make jokes — see JOKE
quirk *n* an odd or peculiar habit — see IDIOSYNCRASY
quirky *adj* different from the ordinary in a way that causes curiosity or suspicion — see ODD 2
quisling *n* one who betrays a trust or an allegiance — see TRAITOR
quit *adj* no longer burdened with something unpleasant or painful — see FREE 2
quit *vb* **1** to give up (a job or office) ⟨decided to *quit* his job at the fast-food restaurant⟩
synonyms leave, resign (from), retire (from), step down (from)
related words abandon, vacate; drop out (of), throw up
phrases give notice
near antonyms hire (out *or* on)
antonyms stay (at)
2 to stop doing (something) permanently ⟨told her it was high time she *quit* smoking⟩
synonyms discontinue, drop, give up, knock off, lay off (of)
related words break off, break up, close, conclude, end, expire, finish; pause, taper off; throw up; cease, desist, leave off
phrases have done (with)
near antonyms go, run on; hang on, hold on, persevere, persist; follow through, see out; resume; preserve, stay
antonyms carry on, continue, keep, keep up, maintain
3 to bring (as an action or operation) to an immediate end — see STOP 1
4 to cause to remain behind — see LEAVE 1
5 to cease resistance (as to another's arguments, demands, or control) — see YIELD 3
6 to come to an end — see CEASE 1
7 to give what is owed for — see PAY 2
8 to leave a place often for another — see GO 2
9 to manage the actions of (oneself) in a particular way — see BEHAVE
quite *adv* **1** to a full extent or degree — see FULLY 1
2 to some degree or extent — see FAIRLY
quittance *n* **1** a freeing from an obligation or responsibility — see RELEASE 1
2 payment to another for a loss or injury — see COMPENSATION 1
quitting *n* the act of leaving a place — see DEPARTURE
quiver *n* an instance of shaking involuntarily with fear or cold — see SHIVER 1
quiver *vb* to make a series of small irregular or violent movements — see SHAKE 1
quivering *n* a series of slight movements by a body

back and forth or from side to side — see VIBRA-TION

quiz *vb* **1** to put a question or questions to — see ASK 1

2 to put a series of questions to — see EXAMINE 1

quiz *n* **1** a person who causes repeated emotional pain, distress, or annoyance to another — see TORMENTOR

2 a set of questions or problems designed to assess knowledge, skills, or intelligence — see EXAMINATION 1

quizzer *n* a person who causes repeated emotional pain, distress, or annoyance to another — see TORMENTOR

quizzical *adj* marked by or expressive of mild or good-natured teasing ⟨my puns are usually greeted with loud *quizzical* groans by my so-called friends⟩

synonyms bantering, chaffing, fooling, funning, jesting, joking, joshing, kidding, rallying, razzing, ribbing

related words bandying, quipping; deriding, derisive, derisory, jeering, mocking, ridiculing, taunting; contemptuous, sarcastic, scornful

quota *n* something belonging to, due to, or contributed by an individual member of a group — see SHARE 1

quotation *n* a passage referred to, repeated, or offered as an example ⟨the beautiful autumn day brought to mind this *quotation* from Thoreau: "So live in each season as it passes; breathe the air, drink the drink, taste the fruit, and resign yourself to the influences of each"⟩

synonyms citation, quote

related words allusion, reference; excerpt, extract; line, part, section

quote *n* a passage referred to, repeated, or offered as an example — see QUOTATION

quote *vb* **1** to give as an example ⟨I could *quote* to you a hundred instances in the past when you've lied to me⟩

synonyms adduce, cite, instance, mention

related words exemplify, represent; illustrate, refer (to); document, substantiate

2 to make reference to or speak about briefly but specifically — see MENTION 1

3 to say after another — see REPEAT 3

R

rabble *n* people looked down upon as ignorant and of the lowest class ⟨the crown prince was reminded that even the *rabble* of the realm deserved his attention and compassion⟩

synonyms proletariat, riffraff, scum, trash

related words dregs; herd, masses, mob, people, populace, public, rank and file; bourgeoisie, middle class, working class

near antonyms elect, establishment; gentlefolk, nobility

antonyms aristocracy, elite, gentry, society, upper class, upper crust

rabble–rouser *n* a person who stirs up public feelings especially of discontent — see AGITATOR

rabid *adj* **1** being very far from the center of public opinion — see EXTREME 2

2 feeling or showing anger — see ANGRY

3 marked by bursts of destructive force or intense activity — see VIOLENT 1

4 marked by great and often stressful excitement or activity — see FURIOUS 1

race *n* a group of persons who come from the same ancestor — see FAMILY 1

race *vb* **1** to engage in a contest — see COMPETE

2 to proceed or move quickly — see HURRY 2

raceway *n* an open man-made passageway for water — see CHANNEL 1

racial *adj* of, relating to, or reflecting the traits exhibited by a group of people with a common ancestry and culture ⟨humanitarian aid workers are often given special training to help them understand the *racial* differences between them and the people they will be serving⟩

synonyms ethnic, tribal

related words familial; folk; kin, kindred; cultural, multicultural, national

racialism *n* **1** the belief that certain races of people

are by birth and nature superior to others — see RACISM 1

2 hatred of or discrimination against a person or persons based on their race — see RACISM 2

racialist *n* a person who believes that one race should control all others — see SUPREMACIST

racism *n* **1** the belief that certain races of people are by birth and nature superior to others ⟨Hitler's declaration of his belief in a "master race" was the first indication of the inherent *racism* of the Nazi movement⟩

synonyms racialism

related words apartheid, segregation; eugenics

near antonyms desegregation, integration

2 hatred of or discrimination against a person or persons based on their race ⟨the 1963 bombing of the Sixteenth Street Baptist Church in Birmingham, Alabama, was one of the most notorious incidents of *racism* that occurred during the civil rights movement of the 1960s⟩

synonyms prejudice, racialism

related words apartheid, jim crow, segregation; bigotry, intolerance, narrow-mindedness, narrowness

racist *n* a person who believes that one race should control all others — see SUPREMACIST

rack *vb* **1** to cause persistent suffering to — see AFFLICT

2 to injure by overuse, misuse, or pressure — see STRAIN 1

racket *n* **1** a scheme in which the victim is cheated out of his money after first gaining his trust — see CONFIDENCE GAME

2 loud, confused, and usually unharmonious sound — see NOISE 1

racketeer *n* a person who gets money from another by using force or threats ⟨the *racketeer* threat-

ened to have his thugs vandalize the shop if the shopkeeper didn't pay him a monthly bribe⟩
synonyms blackmailer, extortioner, extortionist
related words crook, gangster, hoodlum, mafioso, mobster; bully, ruffian, thug; cheat, cheater, chiseler, confidence man, defrauder, double-dealer, gouger, gyp, hustler, profiteer, shark, sharper, swindler
racking *adj* intensely or unbearably painful — see EXCRUCIATING 1
rack up *vb* to gain (as points or runs in a game) as credit towards one's total number of points — see SCORE 2
racy *adj* **1** having much high-spirited energy and movement — see LIVELY 1
2 hinting at or intended to call to mind matters regarded as indecent — see SUGGESTIVE 1
radiance *n* **1** the quality or state of having or giving off light — see BRILLIANCE 1
2 the steady giving off of the form of radiation that makes vision possible — see LIGHT 1
radiant *adj* **1** having or being an outward sign of good feelings (as of love, confidence, or happiness) ⟨left the interview with a *radiant* smile on her face, confident she had gotten the job⟩ ⟨a *radiant* bride⟩
synonyms aglow, beaming, glowing, sunny
related words brilliant, dazzling, effulgent, gleaming, luminous, refulgent, shining, starry; blithe, blithesome, bright, cheerful, cheery, chipper, gay, gladsome, lightsome, merry, mirthful, optimistic, upbeat; jocund, jovial, laughing, smiling; blooming, rosy
near antonyms flat, listless, stoic (*or* stoical), unemotional; dark, darkening, depressing, dismal, gloomy, glum, gray (*also* grey), melancholy, sullen; frowning, glaring, glowering, lowering (*also* louring), scowling
2 giving off or reflecting much light — see BRIGHT 1
radiate *vb* **1** to extend outwards from or as if from a central point ⟨the heat *radiating* from the fire⟩ ⟨the spokes of a bicycle wheel *radiate* from the hub towards the rim⟩
synonyms branch, diverge, fan (out)
related words diffuse, dispel, disperse, dissipate; fork, stem; divide, separate, split; scatter, splay, spread; arise, derive, emanate, flow, issue, proceed, spring
near antonyms approach, close in (on), near; center (on), centralize
antonyms concentrate, converge, focus, funnel, meet
2 to emit rays of light — see SHINE 1
radical *adj* **1** being very far from the center of public opinion — see EXTREME 2
2 not bound by traditional ways or beliefs — see LIBERAL 1
radical *n* a person who favors rapid and sweeping changes especially in laws and methods of government ⟨*radicals* staged large, violent protests in the hopes of toppling the government⟩
synonyms extremist, revolutionary, revolutionist
related words leftist, red; progressive, reformer; anarchist, subversive; agitator, insurgent, insurrectionist, rebel; secessionist, separatist
near antonyms conservative, reactionary, rightist, Tory
antonyms moderate

raffish *adj* lacking in refinement or good taste — see COARSE 2
raffishness *n* the quality or state of lacking refinement or good taste — see VULGARITY 1
raft *n* a considerable amount — see LOT 2
rage *n* **1** a state of wildly excited activity or emotion — see FRENZY
2 an intense emotional state of displeasure with someone or something — see ANGER
3 a practice or interest that is very popular for a short time — see FAD
rage *vb* **1** to express one's anger usually violently ⟨the bad call prompted the coach to *rage* about the refereeing, even throwing his clipboard at one referee⟩
synonyms bristle, fume, storm
related words blow up, flare (up), flip; bluster, carry on, fulminate, rampage, rant, rave, take on; burn, foam, seethe, smolder, steam; chafe, fret, stew
near antonyms allay, appease, pacify, soothe; check, collect, compose, contain, curb, hold in, rein, repress, restrain, smother, subdue, suppress; moderate, tone (down), temper; ease, let up, relax; calm, cool, hush, quell, quiet, settle, still
2 to be excited or emotionally stirred up with anger — see BOIL 1
ragged *adj* **1** having an uneven edge or outline ⟨the Rocky Mountains cut an angular, *ragged* profile against the sky, in contrast to the rounded silhouette of the rolling, green Adirondack Mountains⟩
synonyms broken, craggy, jagged, scraggly, scraggy
related words saw-toothed, serrate, serrated; harsh, rough, rugged; irregular, nonuniform
near antonyms regular, uniform; flat, level, plane
antonyms clean, even, smooth, unbroken
2 worn or torn into or as if into rags ⟨finally convinced her to throw away her favorite pair of jeans, *ragged* from decades of yard work⟩
synonyms frayed, raggedy, ratty, seedy, shabby, tattered, threadbare, worn-out
related words dowdy, scruffy; dingy, faded; shredded; holey, patchy
3 not having a level or smooth surface — see UNEVEN 1
4 wearing torn or worn out clothes — see TATTERED 1
raggedy *adj* **1** wearing torn or worn out clothes — see TATTERED 1
2 worn or torn into or as if into rags — see RAGGED 2
rags *n pl* covering for the human body — see CLOTHING
ragtag *adj* wearing torn or worn out clothes — see TATTERED 1
raid *n* **1** a sudden attack on and entrance into hostile territory ⟨repeated Viking *raids* wore down the defenses of the seaside village⟩
synonyms descent, foray, incursion, inroad, invasion, irruption
related words pillage, plunder; aggression, assault, offense (*or* offence), offensive, onset, onslaught, siege, storm, strike; charge, sally, sortie; ambuscade, ambush, surprise; air raid, blitz, blitzkrieg, bombardment
2 the act or action of setting upon with force or violence — see ATTACK 1
raid *vb* **1** to enter for conquest or plunder — see INVADE

2 to take sudden, violent action against — see AT-TACK 1

raider *n* one that starts armed conflict against another especially without reasonable cause — see AGGRESSOR

rail *n* **1** a protective barrier consisting of a horizontal bar and its supports — see RAILING

2 a roadway overlaid with parallel steel rails over which trains travel — see RAILROAD

rail (at *or* against) *vb* to criticize (someone) severely or angrily especially for personal failings — see SCOLD

railer *n* a person given to harsh judgments and to finding faults — see CRITIC 1

railing *n* a protective barrier consisting of a horizontal bar and its supports ⟨had to put a *railing* on the balcony when the baby started walking⟩

synonyms balustrade, banister, guardrail, rail

related words handrail; taffrail; bar; fender

raillery *n* good-natured teasing or exchanging of clever remarks — see BANTER

railroad *n* a roadway overlaid with parallel steel rails over which trains travel ⟨Grandpa used to walk along the main *railroad* in town to get to school⟩

synonyms rail, railway, road

related words el, elevated, elevated railroad; monorail

railway *n* a roadway overlaid with parallel steel rails over which trains travel — see RAILROAD

raiment *n* covering for the human body — see CLOTHING

rain *n* **1** a steady falling of water from the sky in significant quantity ⟨Mom yelled at us to come in out of the *rain* before we caught cold⟩

synonyms cloudburst, deluge, downpour, rainfall, rainstorm, storm, wet

related words precipitation, shower; thunderstorm

near antonyms drizzle, mist, sprinkle

2 a heavy fall of objects ⟨the Norman invaders fled when the castle's defenders threw a *rain* of stones down upon them⟩

synonyms hail, shower, storm

related words barrage, broadside, cannonade, fusillade, salvo, volley; flood, gush, rush, spate, torrent; eruption, outbreak, outburst

rain *vb* **1** to fall as water in a continuous stream of drops from the clouds ⟨it started *raining* this morning and hasn't let up since⟩

synonyms pour, precipitate, storm

related words shower; hail, squall; deluge, flood

phrases rain cats and dogs

near antonyms drizzle, mist, spit, sprinkle

2 to give readily and in large quantities ⟨she *rained* praise upon her graduating students⟩ ⟨the squadron *rained* bombs on the enemy's fortifications⟩

synonyms heap, lavish, pour, shower

related words gush, stream; flood, inundate, overflow; bombard, hail

near antonyms hold back, keep, reserve, retain, withhold

raincoat *n* a coat made of water-resistant material ⟨grabbed my umbrella and *raincoat* before going out in the thunderstorm⟩

synonyms mackintosh (*or* macintosh) [*chiefly British*], oilskin, slicker, waterproof [*chiefly British*]

related words rainwear; poncho, sou'wester, trench coat

rainfall *n* a steady falling of water from the sky in significant quantity — see RAIN 1

rainstorm *n* a steady falling of water from the sky in significant quantity — see RAIN 1

rainy *adj* marked by or abounding with rain ⟨found that the cold, *rainy* weather made his joints swell and ache⟩

synonyms pouring, precipitating, stormy, wet

related words drizzling, drizzly, misty, spitting, sprinkling

near antonyms dry

raise *n* something added (as by growth) — see INCREASE 1

raise *vb* **1** to move from a lower to a higher place or position ⟨asked the students to *raise* their hands if they knew the answer⟩

synonyms boost, crane, elevate, heave, heft, heighten, hike, hoist, jack (up), lift, perk (up), pick up, up, uphold, uplift, upraise

related words ascend, mount, rise; rear, upend

near antonyms descend, fall, pitch, plunge, slip; bear, depress, press, push; sink, submerge

antonyms drop, lower

2 to bring to maturity through care and education — see BRING UP 1

3 to cause or encourage the development of — see INCITE 1

4 to draw out (something hidden, latent, or reserved) — see EDUCE

5 to fix in an upright position — see ERECT 1

6 to form by putting together parts or materials — see BUILD

7 to look after or assist the growth of by labor and care — see GROW 1

8 to make greater in size, amount, or number — see INCREASE 1

9 to move higher in rank or position — see PROMOTE 1

10 to present or bring forward for discussion — see INTRODUCE 2

raised *adj* **1** being at a higher level than average — see HIGH 2

2 being positioned above a surface — see ELEVATED 1

3 rising straight up — see ERECT

rake *vb* to look through (as a place) carefully or thoroughly in an effort to find or discover something — see SEARCH 1

rakishly *adv* in a bright and showy way — see GAILY 3

rally *n* **1** an act of gathering forces together to renew or attempt an effort ⟨in a last-minute *rally* the Confederates at Bull Run were able to turn a near defeat into an upset victory⟩

synonyms marshaling (*or* marshalling), mobilization, rallying

related words call-up, summons; convening, muster, mustering

2 a mass meeting for the purpose of displaying or arousing support for a cause or person ⟨a huge *rally* for the candidate on the eve of the election⟩

synonyms demonstration

related words assembly, convention, gathering; march; protest, sit-down, sit-down strike, sit-in, strike

3 the process or period of gradually regaining one's health and strength — see CONVALESCENCE

¹**rally** *vb* **1** to assemble and make ready for action — see MOBILIZE

2 to become healthy and strong again after illness or weakness — see CONVALESCE

3 to regain a former or normal state — see RECOVER 2

²**rally** *vb* to make fun of in a good-natured way — see TEASE 1

rallying *n* an act of gathering forces together to renew or attempt an effort — see RALLY 1

rallying *adj* marked by or expressive of mild or good-natured teasing — see QUIZZICAL

ram *vb* **1** to come into usually forceful contact with something — see HIT 2

2 to fit (something) into a tight space — see CROWD 1

ramble *n* a relaxed journey on foot for exercise or pleasure — see WALK

ramble *vb* **1** to talk at length without sticking to a topic or getting to a point ⟨the teenagers sat around the pizza parlor, *rambling* on about dating, homework, movies, and the local football team⟩

synonyms maunder, rattle, run on

related words deviate, digress, stray, wander; sidetrack; blab, chatter, gab, gabble, jabber, patter, prate, prattle

2 to move about from place to place aimlessly — see WANDER

rambler *n* a person who roams about without a fixed route or destination — see NOMAD

rambling *adj* **1** passing from one topic to another — see DISCURSIVE

2 using or containing more words than necessary to express an idea — see WORDY

rambunctious *adj* being rough or noisy in a high-spirited way — see BOISTEROUS

ramify *vb* to set or force apart — see SEPARATE 1

rampage *n* a state of wildly excited activity or emotion — see FRENZY

rampant *adj* **1** showing no signs of being under control ⟨the mayor promised to put a stop to the *rampant* crime that plagued the city⟩

synonyms intemperate, unbridled, unchecked, uncontrolled, uncurbed, ungoverned, unhampered, unhindered, unrestrained

related words uncontrollable, ungovernable; immoderate; riotous, uninhibited, wild

near antonyms moderate, tempered

antonyms checked, controlled, curbed, hampered, hindered, restrained, temperate

2 growing thickly and vigorously — see RANK 1

ramrod *adj* given to exacting standards of discipline and self-restraint — see SEVERE 1

ranch *n* a piece of land and its buildings used to grow crops or raise livestock — see FARM

rancor *n* a deep-seated ill will — see ENMITY

rancorous *adj* having or showing deep-seated resentment — see BITTER 1

random *adj* lacking a definite plan, purpose, or pattern ⟨since we were new in town, our choice of a vet for our dog was entirely *random*⟩

synonyms aimless, arbitrary, desultory, erratic, haphazard, hit-or-miss, scattered, slapdash, stray

related words accidental, casual, chance, fluky, fortuitous, inadvertent, incidental, lucky, unconsidered, unintended, unintentional, unplanned, unpremeditated; irregular, sporadic, spot; objectless, purposeless; indiscriminate, unsystematic; unaimed, undirected

near antonyms established, fixed, regular, set, stable, steady; constant, continuous, even; arranged, managed, orchestrated, ordered, planned; aware, conscious, deliberate, purposeful, thoughtful

antonyms methodical, nonrandom, orderly, systematic

randomly *adv* without definite aim, direction, rule, or method — see HIT OR MISS

range *n* **1** open land over which livestock may roam and feed ⟨knew exactly how many head of cattle were turned out on the *range* that morning to graze⟩

synonyms lea, pasturage, pasture

related words ranch, station; feedlot, stockyard, yard; grassland, pampas, prairie, savanna (*also* savannah), steppe

2 an area over which activity, capacity, or influence extends ⟨didn't know she had such a wide *range* of knowledge until I talked to her⟩

synonyms amplitude, breadth, compass, dimension(s), extent, reach, realm, scope, sweep, width

related words gamut, spectrum, spread; domain, field, sphere; horizon, panorama

3 the distance or extent between possible extremes ⟨an actor who can go through the full *range* of emotion, from joy to sorrow, in mere minutes⟩

synonyms gamut, scale, spectrum, spread, stretch

related words measure, pitch, scale; amplitude, compass, dimension(s), extent, reach, realm, scope, sweep, width

4 a relaxed journey on foot for exercise or pleasure — see WALK

5 a series of persons or things arranged one behind another — see LINE 1

6 an appliance that prepares food for consumption by heating it — see COOKER 1

7 the place where a plant or animal is usually or naturally found — see HOME 2

range *vb* **1** to arrange or assign according to type — see CLASSIFY 1

2 to move about from place to place aimlessly — see WANDER

3 to occur within a continuous range of variation — see RUN 4

4 to put into a particular arrangement — see ORDER 1

ranging *adj* traveling from place to place — see ITINERANT

rangy *adj* being tall, thin and usually loose-jointed — see LANKY

rank *adj* **1** growing thickly and vigorously ⟨covered with trumpet vines so *rank* you couldn't see the trellis beneath them⟩

synonyms lush, luxuriant, prosperous, rampant, weedy

related words lavish, profuse; overgrown, overrun; close, dense, thick

near antonyms dormant; blighted, stunted

antonyms sparse

2 having an unpleasant smell — see MALODOROUS

3 very noticeable especially for being incorrect or bad — see EGREGIOUS

rank *n* **1** the placement of someone or something in relation to others in a vertical arrangement ⟨attained the highest *rank* in Boy Scouting⟩

synonyms degree, footing, level, place, position, ranking, situation, standing, station, status

THESAURUS

related words condition, echelon, estate, order, walk; capacity, function; rating

2 high position within society ⟨was born a woman of *rank* who socialized only with other members of the elite⟩

synonyms class, dignity, quality, standing

related words gentility, gentleness, nobility, nobleness; grandness, highness, loftiness; distinction, precedence, preeminence, primacy; caste, position, station, status; preferment

near antonyms debasement, degradation; subordinateness, subordination; baseness, commonness, inferiority, lowliness, lowness

3 a series of people or things arranged side by side — see ROW 1

4 *usually* **ranks** *pl* one of the units into which a whole is divided on the basis of a common characteristic — see CLASS 2

rank *vb* **1** to take or have a certain position within a group arranged in vertical classes ⟨my favorite pitcher *ranks* first in the league for number of consecutive outs⟩

synonyms be, grade, place, rate

related words seed; count; class, classify, set, sort; install, instate

2 to arrange or assign according to type — see CLASSIFY 1

rank and file *n* the body of the community as contrasted with the elite — see MASS 1

ranking *n* **1** a scheme of rank or order — see ³SCALE 1

2 the placement of someone or something in relation to others in a vertical arrangement — see RANK 1

rankle *vb* to make angry — see ANGER

rankling *adj* causing annoyance — see ANNOYING

ransack *vb* **1** to search through with the intent of committing robbery ⟨it was clear that the thieves who had *ransacked* the museum were professionals—they bypassed most of the exhibits and went straight for the vaults⟩

synonyms despoil, loot, maraud, pillage, plunder, sack, strip

related words burglarize; comb, hunt, rake, rifle, rummage; harry, raid; ravish

2 to look through (as a place) carefully or thoroughly in an effort to find or discover something — see SEARCH 1

ransom *vb* to free from captivity or punishment by paying a price ⟨the prince emptied the treasury to *ransom* his son from the kidnappers⟩

synonyms redeem

related words bail; deliver, rescue, save; emancipate, liberate; recover, regain, retrieve; release; buy; salvage

rant *n* **1** a long angry speech or scolding — see TIRADE

2 boastful speech or writing — see BOMBAST 1

rant *vb* to talk loudly and wildly ⟨when the salesclerk gave him incorrect change, he began *ranting* about the sorry state of math education today⟩

synonyms bluster, fulminate, rave, spout

related words sound off, speak out, speak up; blare, blurt out, bolt; declaim, harangue, mouth, orate, pontificate; carry on, rage, storm, take on

near antonyms grunt, murmur, mutter, slur; breathe, whisper

¹rap *n* **1** a formal claim of criminal wrongdoing against a person — see CHARGE 1

2 a hard strike with a part of the body or an instrument — see ¹BLOW

3 responsibility for wrongdoing or failure — see BLAME 1

²rap *n* friendly, informal conversation or an instance of this — see CHAT

³rap *n* the smallest amount or part imaginable — see JOT

¹rap *vb* to deliver a blow to (someone or something) usually in a strong vigorous manner — see HIT 1

2 to strike or cause to strike lightly and usually rhythmically — see ¹TAP

²rap *vb* to engage in casual or rambling conversation — see CHAT

rapacious *adj* **1** having a huge appetite — see VORACIOUS 1

2 living by killing and eating other animals — see PREDATORY

3 having or marked by an eager and often selfish desire especially for material possessions — see GREEDY 1

rapaciousness *n* an intense selfish desire for wealth or possessions — see GREED

rapacity *n* an intense selfish desire for wealth or possessions — see GREED

rapid *adj* moving, proceeding, or acting with great speed — see FAST 1

rapid–fire *adj* moving, proceeding, or acting with great speed — see FAST 1

rapidity *n* a high rate of movement or performance — see SPEED

rapidly *adv* with great speed — see FAST 1

rapidness *n* a high rate of movement or performance — see SPEED

rapport *n* a friendly relationship marked by ready communication and mutual understanding ⟨his good *rapport* with his students was one of the reasons why the school board named him Teacher of the Year⟩

synonyms communion, fellowship, rapprochement

related words accord, agreement, concord, harmony; oneness, solidarity, togetherness, unity; affinity, empathy, sympathy, understanding; amity, chumminess, companionship, friendship; reciprocity, symbiosis

near antonyms alienation, disaffection, estrangement; coldness, cold shoulder, distance, iciness; animosity, antagonism, enmity, hostility, rancor, spite

rapprochement *n* a friendly relationship marked by ready communication and mutual understanding — see RAPPORT

rapscallion *n* **1** a mean, evil, or unprincipled person — see VILLAIN

2 an appealingly mischievous person — see SCAMP 1

rapt *adj* having the mind fixed on something — see ATTENTIVE

rapture *n* a state of overwhelming usually pleasurable emotion — see ECSTASY

rapturous *adj* experiencing or marked by overwhelming usually pleasurable emotion — see ECSTATIC

rare *adj* **1** being out of the ordinary — see EXCEPTIONAL

2 having qualities that appeal to a refined taste — see CHOICE

3 not often occurring or repeated — see INFREQUENT

4 noticeably different from what is generally found or experienced — see UNUSUAL 1

rarely *adv* not often — see SELDOM

raring *adj* showing urgent desire or interest — see EAGER

rarity *n* something strange or unusual that is an object of interest — see CURIOSITY 2

rascal *n* **1** a mean, evil, or unprincipled person — see VILLAIN
2 an appealingly mischievous person — see SCAMP 1

rascality *n* playful, reckless behavior that is not intended to cause serious harm — see MISCHIEF 1

rascally *adj* tending to or exhibiting reckless playfulness — see MISCHIEVOUS 1

rash *adj* acting or done with excessive or careless speed — see HASTY 1

rashly *adv* with excessive or careless speed — see HASTILY 1

rasp *n* a harsh grating sound ⟨the rusted lock opened with a *rasp*⟩
synonyms creak, grind, scrape, scratch
related words clash, jangle, jar; croak; blast, bleat, bray, screech

rasp *vb* **1** to make smooth by friction — see GRIND 1
2 to pass roughly and noisily over or against a surface — see SCRAPE 1
3 to disturb the peace of mind of (someone) especially by repeated disagreeable acts — see IRRITATE 1

raspberry *n* a vocal sound made to express scorn or disapproval — see CATCALL

rasping *adj* harsh and dry in sound — see HOARSE

raspy *adj* harsh and dry in sound — see HOARSE

rat (on) *vb* to leave (a cause or party) often in order to take up another — see DEFECT

rate *n* **1** degree of excellence — see QUALITY 1
2 the relationship in quantity, amount, or size between two or more things — see RATIO

¹**rate** *vb* **1** to be or make worthy of (as a reward or punishment) — see EARN 2
2 to make an approximate or tentative judgment regarding — see ESTIMATE 1
3 to take or have a certain position within a group arranged in vertical classes — see RANK 1
4 to think of in a particular way — see CONSIDER 1

²**rate** *vb* to criticize (someone) severely or angrily especially for personal failings — see SCOLD

rather *adv* **1** by choice or preference ⟨I would *rather* go to the movies than stay at home⟩
synonyms first, preferably, readily, soon, willingly
related words alternately, alternatively, either, instead; electively, optionally; desirably, gladly, wishfully; voluntarily
near antonyms reluctantly; forcibly, willy-nilly
antonyms involuntarily, unwillingly
2 as a substitute — see INSTEAD
3 to some degree or extent — see FAIRLY

ratify *vb* to give official acceptance of something as satisfactory — see APPROVE

ratio *n* the relationship in quantity, amount, or size between two or more things ⟨the *ratio* of students to teachers in my school is nine to one⟩
synonyms proportion, rate
related words average; frequency; correspondence; percentage
near antonyms disproportion

ration *vb* to give as a share or portion — see ALLOT

rational *adj* **1** having the ability to reason ⟨human beings are *rational* creatures⟩
synonyms intelligent, reasonable, reasoning, thinking
related words analytic (*or* analytical), logical; brainy, cerebral, highbrow, intellectual; cognitive, mental; practical, sane, sensible
near antonyms brainless, mindless, stupid; illogical
antonyms irrational, nonrational, unintelligent, unreasonable, unreasoning, unthinking
2 according to the rules of logic — see LOGICAL 1
3 based on sound reasoning or information — see GOOD 1

rationale *n* a statement given to explain a belief or act — see REASON 1

rationalize *vb* to give the reason for or cause of — see EXPLAIN 2

rattle *vb* **1** to make a series of short sharp noises ⟨the children tromped through the kitchen, making the plates on the shelf *rattle*⟩
synonyms clack, clatter
related words chink, chirp, clank, click, clink; clang, clash, crash; spatter, sputter
2 to engage in casual or rambling conversation — see CHAT
3 to talk at length without sticking to a topic or getting to a point — see RAMBLE 1
4 to throw into a state of self-conscious distress — see EMBARRASS 1

rattling *adj* moving, proceeding, or acting with great speed — see FAST 1

rattling *adv* to a great degree — see VERY 1

ratty *adj* **1** showing signs of advanced wear and tear and neglect — see SHABBY 1
2 worn or torn into or as if into rags — see RAGGED 2

raucous *adj* being rough or noisy in a high-spirited way — see BOISTEROUS

ravage *vb* to bring destruction to (something) through violent action ⟨Hurricane Andrew *ravaged* Louisiana and Florida in 1992, causing $19 billion in damage⟩
synonyms destroy, devastate, ruin, scourge
related words despoil, foray, harry, loot, maraud, pillage, plunder, sack, strip; annihilate, desolate, extirpate, obliterate, smash, waste, wipe out, wreck; decimate, mow; demolish, raze; crush, overpower, overrun, overthrow, overwhelm
near antonyms recondition, recover, redeem, rehabilitate, restore

rave *vb* to make an exaggerated display of affection or enthusiasm — see GUSH 2
2 to talk loudly and wildly — see RANT

rave *n*, *often* **raves** *pl* enthusiastic and usually public expression of approval — see APPLAUSE

ravel (out) *vb* to separate the various strands of — see UNRAVEL 1

raven *adj* having the color of soot or coal — see BLACK 1

ravenous *adj* having a huge appetite — see VORACIOUS 1

ravine *n* a narrow opening between hillsides or mountains that can be used for passage — see CANYON

ravish *vb* to fill with overwhelming emotion (as wonder or delight) — see ENTRANCE

ravishing *adj* very pleasing to look at — see BEAUTIFUL

THESAURUS

raw *adj* **1** not cooked ⟨you should wash your hands after handling *raw* chicken⟩
synonyms uncooked
related words unbaked, unheated; rare; underdone
near antonyms well-done; overdone; baked, boiled, braised, broiled, fried, grilled, heated, roasted, sautéed
antonyms cooked
2 being such as found in nature and not altered by processing or refining — see CRUDE 1
3 lacking in adult experience or maturity — see CALLOW
4 marked by wet and windy conditions — see FOUL 1
5 uncomfortably cool — see CHILLY 1
6 causing intense discomfort to one's skin — see CUTTING 1
raw deal *n* unfair or inadequate treatment of someone or something or an instance of this — see DISSERVICE
rawhide *vb* to strike repeatedly with something long and thin or flexible — see WHIP 1
raw material *n* the basic elements from which something can be developed — see MAKING
rawness *n* an uncomfortable degree of coolness — see CHILL
ray *n* **1** a narrow sharply defined line of light radiating from an object — see SHAFT 1
2 a very small amount — see PARTICLE 1
raze *vb* **1** to bring to a complete end the physical soundness, existence, or usefulness of — see DESTROY 1
2 to destroy (as a building) completely by knocking down or breaking to pieces — see DEMOLISH 1
razz *vb* to make fun of in a good-natured way — see TEASE 1
razzing *adj* marked by or expressive of mild or good-natured teasing — see QUIZZICAL
reach *n* **1** a wide space or area — see EXPANSE
2 an area over which activity, capacity, or influence extends — see RANGE 2
reach *vb* **1** to shift possession of (something) from one person to another — see PASS 1
2 to transmit information or requests to — see CONTACT
reachable *adj* situated within easy reach — see CONVENIENT
reacquire *vb* to get again in one's possession — see RECOVER 1
react *vb* to act or behave in response (as to a stimulus or influence) ⟨it was my first touchdown, and I didn't know how to *react* to the cheers of the crowd⟩
synonyms reply, respond
related words answer, return; retaliate; construe, interpret, read, take, understand
near antonyms act, behave; affect, cause, draw, effect
reaction *n* action or behavior that is done in return to other action or behavior ⟨we were startled by her extreme *reaction* to the bad grade⟩
synonyms reply, response, take
related words answer, return; backlash; rebound; revulsion, rise; jerk, start, twitch
near antonyms action, behavior; cause, effect
reactionary *adj* tending to favor established ideas, conditions, or institutions — see CONSERVATIVE

reactionary *n* **1** a person whose political beliefs are centered on tradition and keeping things the way they are — see CONSERVATIVE 1
2 a person with old-fashioned ideas — see FOGY
read *vb* to go over and mentally take in the content of ⟨he always *reads* the newspaper in the morning as he eats breakfast⟩
synonyms peruse, pore (over)
related words browse, dip (into), leaf (through), scan, skim, thumb (through); slog (through), wade (through); reread; proofread; decipher; review, study; apprehend, comprehend, get, grasp, make, make out, perceive, see, understand
readdress *vb* to consider again especially with the possibility of change or reversal — see RECONSIDER
readily *adv* **1** by choice or preference — see RATHER 1
2 without difficulty — see EASILY
reading *n* something assigned to be read or studied — see LESSON
ready *adj* **1** being in a state of fitness for some experience or action ⟨after studying for a whole month, she felt *ready* for the final exam⟩
synonyms fit, go, prepared, set
related words conditioned, primed; braced, fortified, steeled; qualified, trained
near antonyms unqualified, untrained
antonyms half-cocked, unprepared, unready
2 having a desire or inclination (as for a specified course of action) — see WILLING 1
3 having or showing the ability to respond without delay or hesitation — see QUICK 1
4 involving minimal difficulty or effort — see EASY 1
ready *vb* **1** to make competent (as by training, skill, or ability) for a particular office or function — see QUALIFY 2
2 to make ready in advance — see PREPARE 1
3 to prepare (oneself) mentally or emotionally — see FORTIFY 1
ready–made *adj* made beforehand in large numbers ⟨the store was full of inexpensive *ready-made* clothing⟩
synonyms mass-produced, store
related words ready-to-wear; commercial; prefabricated
near antonyms handcrafted, handmade, homemade; tailored, tailor-made
antonyms custom, custom-made
real *adj* **1** being exactly as appears or as claimed — see AUTHENTIC 1
2 existing in fact and not merely as a possibility — see ACTUAL
3 free from any intent to deceive or impress others — see GUILELESS
real *adv* to a great degree — see VERY 1
realistic *adj* **1** willing to see things as they really are and deal with them sensibly ⟨our guidance counselor encouraged us to be more *realistic* in our job choices, so we reluctantly gave up the idea of becoming professional snake charmers⟩
synonyms down-to-earth, earthy, hardheaded, matter-of-fact, practical, pragmatic (*also* pragmatical)
related words philistine, utilitarian; logical, nononsense, rational, reasonable, sane, sensible, sound; hard-boiled, unromantic, unsentimental; cynical, disillusioned
near antonyms fanciful, fantastic, imaginative; ro-

1195 reality • rebellious

mantic, sentimental; illogical, insane, irrational, unreasonable; theoretical (*also* theoretic)
antonyms idealistic, impractical, unrealistic, utopian, visionary
2 closely resembling the object imitated — see NATURAL 2

reality *n* **1** something that actually exists — see FACT 2
2 the fact of being or of being real — see EXISTENCE
3 the quality of being actual — see FACT 1

realizable *adj* capable of being done or carried out — see POSSIBLE 1

realization *n* the state of being actual or complete — see FRUITION

realize *vb* **1** to come to an awareness — see DISCOVER 1
2 to receive as return for effort — see EARN 1

really *adv* **1** in actual fact — see VERY 2
2 to tell the truth — see ACTUALLY 1
3 without any question — see INDEED 1

realm *n* **1** a region of activity, knowledge, or influence — see FIELD 2
2 an area over which activity, capacity, or influence extends — see RANGE 2

reams *n pl* a considerable amount — see LOT 2

reanalyze *vb* to consider again especially with the possibility of change or reversal — see RECONSIDER

reanimate *vb* to bring back to life, practice, or activity — see REVIVE 1

reanimated *adj* made or become fresh in spirits or vigor — see NEW 4

reanimation *n* the act or an instance of bringing something back to life, public attention, or vigorous activity — see REVIVAL

reap *vb* to catch or collect (a crop or natural resource) for human use — see HARVEST

reappraisal *n* a usually critical look at a past event — see REVIEW 1

rear *adj* being at or in the part of something opposite the front part — see BACK

rear *n* the part of the body upon which someone sits — see BUTTOCKS

rear *vb* **1** to bring to maturity through care and education — see BRING UP 1
2 to fix in an upright position — see ERECT 1
3 to form by putting together parts or materials — see BUILD
4 to look after or assist the growth of by labor and care — see GROW 1

rearmost *adj* following all others of the same kind in order or time — see LAST

rearward *adj* **1** being at or in the part of something opposite the front part — see BACK
2 directed, turned, or done toward the back — see BACKWARD

reason *n* **1** a statement given to explain a belief or act ⟨gave a good *reason* for her seemingly suspicious behavior⟩
synonyms argument, case, explanation, rationale
related words alibi, defense, excuse, justification; appeal, plea; guise, pretense (*or* pretence), pretext, rationalization
2 something (as a belief) that serves as the basis for another thing ⟨a firm belief that we are here on earth to help others is the *reason* for her tireless volunteer work⟩
synonyms grounds, motive, wherefore, why
related words antecedent, cause, occasion

3 an explanation that frees one from fault or blame — see EXCUSE
4 someone or something responsible for a result — see CAUSE 1
5 the ability to learn and understand or to deal with problems — see INTELLIGENCE 1
6 the normal or healthy condition of the mental abilities — see MIND 2
7 the thought processes that have been established as leading to valid solutions to problems — see LOGIC

reason *vb* **1** to form an opinion through reasoning and information — see INFER 1
2 to state (something) as a reason in support of or against something under consideration — see ARGUE 1

reasonable *adj* **1** according to the rules of logic — see LOGICAL 1
2 based on sound reasoning or information — see GOOD 1
3 costing little — see CHEAP 1
4 having the ability to reason — see RATIONAL 1

reasonably *adv* with good reason or courtesy — see WELL 4

reasoned *adj* **1** based on sound reasoning or information — see GOOD 1
2 being or provable by reasoning in which the conclusion follows necessarily from given information — see DEDUCTIVE
3 decided on as a result of careful thought — see DELIBERATE 1

reasoning *adj* having the ability to reason — see RATIONAL 1

reasoning *n* the thought processes that have been established as leading to valid solutions to problems — see LOGIC

reassure *vb* to ease the grief or distress of — see COMFORT 1

reata *n* a rope or long leather thong with a noose used especially for catching livestock — see LASSO

rebel *n* a person who rises up against authority ⟨the *rebel* would not submit peacefully, even after he was captured⟩
synonyms insurgent, insurrectionary, insurrectionist, mutineer, red, revolter, revolutionary, revolutionist, revolutionizer
related words challenger, defier, resister; anarchist; extremist, malcontent, radical
near antonyms loyalist, supporter; counterrevolutionary, counterrevolutionist

rebel *vb* to rise up against established authority ⟨the colonists *rebelled* when the unfair tax was imposed⟩
synonyms mutiny, revolt
related words defy, disobey; revolutionize
near antonyms obey, submit; attend, serve

rebel (against) *vb* to go against the commands, prohibitions, or rules of — see DISOBEY

rebellion *n* open fighting against authority (as one's own government) ⟨the *rebellion* would have failed if not for the aid sent by other countries⟩
synonyms insurgency, insurrection, mutiny, revolt, revolution, uprising
related words coup, coup d'état, overthrow; sedition, treachery, treason; sabotage, subversion
near antonyms counterrevolution

rebellious *adj* **1** taking part in a rebellion ⟨the *rebellious* troops fought a pitched battle with divisions still loyal to the government⟩

THESAURUS

synonyms insurgent, insurrectionary, mutinous, revolutionary
related words seditious, traitorous, treacherous, treasonous
near antonyms loyal; obedient
2 given to resisting authority or another's control — see DISOBEDIENT
rebelliousness *n* refusal to obey — see DISOBEDIENCE
rebirth *n* the act or an instance of bringing something back to life, public attention, or vigorous activity — see REVIVAL
rebound *vb* **1** to regain a former or normal state — see RECOVER 2
2 to strike and fly off at an angle — see GLANCE 1
rebuff *n* treatment that is deliberately unfriendly — see COLD SHOULDER
rebuke *n* an often public or formal expression of disapproval — see CENSURE
rebuke *vb* **1** to criticize (someone) usually gently so as to correct a fault ⟨*rebuked* the toddler for his habit of telling fibs⟩
synonyms admonish, chide, reprimand, reproach, reprove
related words berate, castigate, chew out, dress down, flay, jaw, keelhaul, lambaste (*or* lambast), lecture, rail (at *or* against), scold, score, upbraid; abuse, assail, attack, bad-mouth, blame, blast, censure, condemn, criticize, crucify, denounce, dis [*slang*], excoriate, fault, knock, lash, pan, reprehend, slam; belittle, disparage, mock, put down; ridicule, scoff, scorn
near antonyms approve, endorse (*also* indorse), sanction; extol (*also* extoll), laud, praise
2 to criticize (someone) severely or angrily especially for personal failings — see SCOLD
3 to express public or formal disapproval of — see CENSURE 1
rebut *vb* to prove to be false — see DISPROVE
recalcitrance *n* refusal to obey — see DISOBEDIENCE
recalcitrant *adj* **1** given to resisting authority or another's control — see DISOBEDIENT
2 given to resisting control or discipline by others — see UNCONTROLLABLE
recall *n* **1** a particular act or instance of recalling or the thing remembered — see MEMORY 2
2 the act of putting an end to something planned or previously agreed to — see CANCELLATION
recall *vb* **1** to bring back to mind — see REMEMBER
2 to put an end to (something planned or previously agreed to) — see CANCEL 1
recant *vb* to solemnly or formally reject or go back on (as something formerly adhered to) — see ABJURE
recap *n* a short statement of the main points — see SUMMARY
recap *vb* to make into a short statement of the main points (as of a report) — see SUMMARIZE
recapitulate *vb* to make into a short statement of the main points (as of a report) — see SUMMARIZE
recapitulation *n* a short statement of the main points — see SUMMARY
recapture *vb* to get again in one's possession — see RECOVER 1
recast *vb* to make different in some way — see CHANGE 1

recede *vb* **1** to grow less in scope or intensity especially gradually — see DECREASE 2
2 to move back or away (as from something difficult, dangerous, or disagreeable) — see RETREAT 1
recently *adv* not long ago — see NEWLY
receptacle *n* something into which a liquid or smaller objects can be put for storage or transportation — see CONTAINER
reception *n* a social gathering — see PARTY 1
receptive *adj* willing to consider new or different ideas — see OPEN-MINDED 1
recess *n* **1** a hollowed-out space in a wall — see NICHE 1
2 a period during which the usual routine of school or work is suspended — see VACATION
3 a momentary halt in an activity — see PAUSE
4 a sunken area forming a separate space — see HOLE 2
recess *vb* to bring to a formal close for a period of time — see ADJOURN
recessed *adj* curved inward — see HOLLOW
recession *n* **1** a period of decreased economic activity — see DEPRESSION 1
2 an act of moving away especially from something difficult, dangerous, or disagreeable — see RETREAT 1
reciprocal *adj* related to each other in such a way that one completes the other — see COMPLEMENTARY
recite *vb* **1** to give an oral or written account of in some detail — see TELL 1
2 to give from memory — see REPEAT 2
reckless *adj* **1** having or showing a lack of concern for the consequences of one's actions ⟨the *reckless* skiers were making everyone nervous by schussing down the mountainside at lightning speed⟩
synonyms daredevil, devil-may-care, foolhardy, irresponsible
related words adventurous, bold, daring, venturesome; hasty, headlong, hotheaded, impetuous, precipitate, rash, wild; nonchalant, unconcerned, unworried; careless, heedless, inattentive, incautious, unheeding; inconsiderate, thoughtless, unthinking
near antonyms careful, cautious, circumspect, heedful; overcareful, overcautious, timid
antonyms responsible
2 foolishly adventurous or bold — see FOOLHARDY 1
reckon *vb* **1** to decide the size, amount, number, or distance of (something) without actual measurement — see ESTIMATE 2
2 *chiefly dialect* to have as an opinion — see BELIEVE 2
3 to determine (a value) by doing the necessary mathematical operations — see CALCULATE 1
4 to place reliance or trust — see DEPEND 2
5 to think of in a particular way — see CONSIDER 1
reckoning *n* **1** the act of placing a value on the nature, character, or quality of something — see ESTIMATE 1
2 the act or process of performing mathematical operations to find a value — see CALCULATION
reclaim *vb* **1** to get again in one's possession — see RECOVER 1
2 to make better in behavior or character — see REFORM 1

3 to obtain (a raw material) by separating it from a by-product or waste product — see RECYCLE

reclamation *n* the act or process of getting something back — see RECOVERY 1

recluse *n* a person who lives away from others ⟨he was sick of cities and crowds, so he decided to go live by himself in the woods as a *recluse*⟩
synonyms anchorite, hermit, solitary
related words homebody, shut-in; monk
near antonyms socialite

recognize *vb* to show appreciation, respect, or affection for (someone) with a public celebration — see HONOR

recoil *vb* to draw back in fear, pain, or disgust — see FLINCH

recollect *vb* to bring back to mind — see REMEMBER

re-collect *vb* **1** to gain emotional or mental control of — see COLLECT 1
2 to get again in one's possession — see RECOVER 1

recollection *n* **1** a particular act or instance of recalling or the thing remembered — see MEMORY 2
2 the power or process of recalling what has been previously learned or experienced — see MEMORY 1

recommend *vb* to put forward as one's choice for a wise or proper course of action — see ADVISE 2

recompense *n* **1** payment to another for a loss or injury — see COMPENSATION 1
2 something (as money) that is given or received in return for goods or services — see PAYMENT 2

recompense *vb* **1** to give (someone) the sum of money owed for goods or services received — see PAY 1
2 to give what is owed for — see PAY 2
3 to provide (someone) with a just payment for loss or injury — see COMPENSATE 1

reconceive *vb* to consider again especially with the possibility of change or reversal — see RECONSIDER

reconcile *vb* to bring to a state free of conflicts, inconsistencies, or differences — see HARMONIZE 2

recondite *adj* difficult for one of ordinary knowledge or intelligence to understand — see PROFOUND 1

recondition *vb* to put into good shape or working order again — see MEND 1

reconsider *vb* to consider again especially with the possibility of change or reversal ⟨the new information forced the general to *reconsider* his plan of attack⟩
synonyms readdress, reanalyze, reconceive, reevaluate, reexamine, rethink, review, reweigh
related words reappraise, reassess; amend, correct, emend, rectify, reform, remedy, revise
phrases change one's mind (about), go over, think better of, view in a new light
near antonyms assert, defend, maintain, uphold

reconsideration *n* a usually critical look at a past event — see REVIEW 1

record *n* **1** a relating of events usually in the order in which they happened — see ACCOUNT 1
2 an account of important events in the order in which they happened — see HISTORY 1

record *vb* **1** to make a written note of ⟨the reporter *recorded* the events of the evening in her notebook for later reference⟩
synonyms jot (down), log, mark, note, put down, register, set down

related words chronicle; chalk (up), score; rerecord
2 to put (someone or something) on a list — see ¹LIST 2

recount *vb* to give an oral or written account of in some detail — see TELL 1

recoup *vb* **1** to get again in one's possession — see RECOVER 1
2 to provide (someone) with a just payment for loss or injury — see COMPENSATE 1

recoupment *n* **1** payment to another for a loss or injury — see COMPENSATION 1
2 the act or process of getting something back — see RECOVERY 1

recourse *n* something that one uses to accomplish an end especially when the usual means is not available — see RESOURCE 1

recover *vb* **1** to get again in one's possession ⟨after fishing around in the garbage for ten minutes, I was able to *recover* my lost keys⟩
synonyms reacquire, recapture, reclaim, re-collect, recoup, regain, repossess, retake, retrieve
related words recruit, replenish; redeem, repurchase; rescue
phrases get back
near antonyms lose, mislay, misplace
2 to regain a former or normal state ⟨after a disastrous first half, the team was able to *recover* toward the end of the game and manage a win⟩
synonyms rally, rebound, snap back
related words reanimate, revitalize, revive
phrases make a comeback
near antonyms decline, fail, worsen
3 to become healthy and strong again after illness or weakness — see CONVALESCE
4 to obtain (a raw material) by separating it from a by-product or waste product — see RECYCLE

recovery *n* **1** the act or process of getting something back ⟨the *recovery* of the sunken boat took over a week⟩
synonyms reclamation, recoupment, repossession, retrieval
related words recruitment, replenishment; redemption, rescue
near antonyms loss, misplacement
2 the process or period of gradually regaining one's health and strength — see CONVALESCENCE

recreant *adj* **1** having or showing a shameful lack of courage — see COWARDLY
2 not true in one's allegiance to someone or something — see FAITHLESS

recreant *n* **1** a person who abandons a cause or organization usually without right — see RENEGADE
2 a person who shows a shameful lack of courage in the face of danger — see COWARD
3 one who betrays a trust or an allegiance — see TRAITOR

recreate *vb* **1** to bring back to a former condition or vigor — see RENEW 1
2 to engage in activity for amusement — see PLAY 1

recreated *adj* made or become fresh in spirits or vigor — see NEW 4

recreation *n* **1** activity engaged in to amuse oneself — see PLAY 1
2 someone or something that provides amusement or enjoyment — see FUN 1
3 the act or activity of providing pleasure or

amusement especially for the public — see EN-
TERTAINMENT 1

recruit *n* a person who is just starting out in a field
of activity — see BEGINNER

rectifiable *adj* capable of being corrected — see
REMEDIABLE

rectify *vb* to remove errors, defects, deficiencies,
or deviations from — see CORRECT 1

rectifying *adj* serving to raise or adjust something
to some standard or proper condition — see COR-
RECTIVE 1

rectitude *n* **1** conduct that conforms to an accepted
standard of right and wrong — see MORALITY 1
2 faithfulness to high moral standards — see
HONOR 1

recuperate *vb* to become healthy and strong again
after illness or weakness — see CONVALESCE

recuperation *n* the process or period of gradually
regaining one's health and strength — see CONVA-
LESCENCE

recurrent *adj* occurring or appearing at intervals
— see INTERMITTENT 1

recurring *adj* occurring or appearing at intervals
— see INTERMITTENT 1

recycle *vb* to obtain (a raw material) by separating
it from a by-product or waste product 〈*recycling*
the aluminum from pop cans is environmentally
sound〉
synonyms reclaim, recover
related words reuse; process

red *n* a person who rises up against authority —
see REBEL

red–blooded *adj* having active strength of body or
mind — see VIGOROUS 1

redden *vb* to develop a rosy facial color (as from
excitement or embarrassment) — see BLUSH

redeem *vb* **1** to do what is required by the terms of
— see FULFILL 1
2 to free from captivity or punishment by paying
a price — see RANSOM
3 to free from the penalties or consequences of
sin — see SAVE 1
4 to make better in behavior or character — see
REFORM 1

redeemer *n* one that saves from danger or destruction — see SAVIOR

red–hot *adj* **1** being or involving the latest methods, concepts, information, or styles — see MOD-
ERN
2 having a notably high temperature — see HOT 1
3 having or expressing great depth of feeling —
see FERVENT

redo *vb* **1** to make different in some way — see
CHANGE 1
2 to make or do again — see REPEAT 4

redoing *n* the act, process, or result of making different — see CHANGE

redolence *n* **1** a sweet or pleasant smell — see FRA-
GRANCE
2 the quality of a thing that makes it perceptible
to the sense organs in the nose — see SMELL

redolent *adj* having a pleasant smell — see FRA-
GRANT

redouble *vb* **1** to make markedly greater in measure or degree — see INTENSIFY
2 to make twice as great or as many — see DOU-
BLE 1

redoubtable *adj* causing fear — see FEARFUL 1

redraft *vb* to prepare for publication by correcting,
rewriting, or updating — see EDIT

redress *n* payment to another for a loss or injury
— see COMPENSATION 1

reduce *vb* **1** to bring to a lower grade or rank —
see DEMOTE
2 to make smaller in amount, volume, or extent
— see DECREASE 1

reduction *n* **1** something that is or may be subtracted — see DEDUCTION 1
2 the amount by which something is lessened —
see DECREASE

redundancy *n* the use of too many words to express an idea — see VERBIAGE

reduplicate *vb* **1** to make an exact likeness of —
see COPY 1
2 to make or do again — see REPEAT 4

reduplication *n* **1** something that is made to look
exactly like something else — see COPY
2 the act of saying or doing over again — see RE-
PEAT

reecho *vb* to continue or be repeated in a series of
reflected sound waves — see REVERBERATE

reek *n* **1** a strong unpleasant smell — see STINK
2 an atmospheric condition in which suspended
particles in the air rob it of its transparency — see
HAZE 1

reek *vb* to give off an extremely unpleasant smell
— see STINK

reeking *adj* having an unpleasant smell — see
MALODOROUS

reeky *adj* having an unpleasant smell — see MAL-
ODOROUS

reel *n* a rapid turning about on an axis or central
point — see SPIN 1

reel *vb* **1** to be in a confused state as if from being
twirled around — see SPIN 2
2 to move forward while swaying from side to
side — see STAGGER 1

reeling *adj* having a feeling of being whirled about
and in danger of falling down — see DIZZY 1

reenergized *adj* made or become fresh in spirits or
vigor — see NEW 4

reevaluate *vb* to consider again especially with the
possibility of change or reversal — see RECON-
SIDER

reexamination *n* a usually critical look at a past
event — see REVIEW 1

reexamine *vb* to consider again especially with the
possibility of change or reversal — see RECON-
SIDER

refashion *vb* to make different in some way — see
CHANGE 1

refashioning *n* the act, process, or result of making different — see CHANGE

refer *vb* to have a relation or connection — see
APPLY 1

refer (to) *vb* **1** to make reference to or speak about
briefly but specifically — see MENTION 1
2 to use or seek out as a source of aid, relief, or
advantage — see RESORT (TO) 1

referee *vb* to give an opinion about (something at
issue or in dispute) — see JUDGE 1

reference *n* relation to or concern with something
specified — see RESPECT 1

refine *vb* to make better — see IMPROVE

refined *adj* **1** being far along in development — see
ADVANCED 1
2 free from added matter — see PURE 1
3 having or showing a taste for the fine arts and
gracious living — see CULTIVATED
4 having or showing elegance — see ELEGANT 1

5 made or done with extreme care and accuracy — see FINE 2

6 satisfying or pleasing because of fineness or mildness — see DELICATE 1

refinement *n* **1** an instance of notable progress in the development of knowledge, technology, or skill — see ADVANCE 2

2 a high level of taste and enlightenment as a result of extensive intellectual training and exposure to the arts — see CULTURE 1

3 dignified or restrained beauty of form, appearance, or style — see ELEGANCE

reflect *vb* to reproduce or show (an exact likeness) as a mirror would ⟨her face was *reflected* in the waters of the still pond⟩
synonyms image, mirror
related words copy, duplicate, imitate, reduplicate, repeat, replicate, reproduce

reflection *n* **1** a briefly expressed opinion — see REMARK

2 a cause of shame — see DISGRACE 2

reflective *adj* given to or marked by long, quiet thinking — see CONTEMPLATIVE

reform *vb* **1** to make better in behavior or character ⟨a *reformed* criminal who is now a productive member of society⟩
synonyms reclaim, redeem, rehabilitate
related words amend, improve; cleanse, purify, restore
near antonyms abase, corrupt, debauch, degrade, demean, demoralize, deprave, pervert, poison, profane, prostitute, subvert, warp

2 to remove errors, defects, deficiencies, or deviations from — see CORRECT 1

reformative *adj* serving to raise or adjust something to some standard or proper condition — see CORRECTIVE 1

reformatory *adj* serving to raise or adjust something to some standard or proper condition — see CORRECTIVE 1

refractoriness *n* refusal to obey — see DISOBEDIENCE

refractory *adj* **1** given to resisting authority or another's control — see DISOBEDIENT

2 given to resisting control or discipline by others — see UNCONTROLLABLE

refrain *n* a part of a song or hymn that is repeated every so often — see CHORUS 2

refrain (from) *vb* to resist the temptation of — see FORBEAR

refresh *vb* to bring back to a former condition or vigor — see RENEW 1

refreshed *adj* made or become fresh in spirits or vigor — see NEW 4

refreshen *vb* to bring back to a former condition or vigor — see RENEW 1

refreshing *adj* having a renewing effect on the state of the body or mind — see TONIC

refrigerate *vb* to cause to lose heat — see COOL 1

refuge *n* something (as a building) that offers cover from the weather or protection from danger — see SHELTER

refugee *n* a person forced to emigrate for political reasons — see ÉMIGRÉ 1

refulgence *n* the quality or state of having or giving off light — see BRILLIANCE 1

refulgent *adj* giving off or reflecting much light — see BRIGHT 1

refund *vb* to make a return payment to — see REPAY

refusal *n* an unwillingness to grant something asked for — see DENIAL 1

refuse *n* discarded or useless material — see GARBAGE

refuse *vb* **1** to be unwilling to grant — see DENY 2

2 to show unwillingness to accept, do, engage in, or agree to — see DECLINE 1

refute *vb* to prove to be false — see DISPROVE

regain *vb* to get again in one's possession — see RECOVER 1

regal *adj* **1** fit for or worthy of a royal ruler — see MONARCHICAL

2 large and impressive in size, grandeur, extent, or conception — see GRAND 1

regale *vb* **1** to cause (someone) to pass the time agreeably occupied — see AMUSE

2 to entertain with a fancy meal — see FEAST

regalia *n* dressy clothing — see FINERY

regard *n* **1** a feeling of great approval and liking — see ADMIRATION 1

2 an instance of looking especially briefly — see LOOK 2

3 relation to or concern with something specified — see RESPECT 1

4 regards *pl* best wishes — see COMPLIMENT

regard *vb* **1** to make note of (something) through the use of one's eyes — see SEE 1

2 to take notice of and be guided by — see HEED 1

3 to think of in a particular way — see CONSIDER 1

4 to think very highly or favorably of — see ADMIRE

regardful *adj* marked by or showing proper regard for another's higher status — see RESPECTFUL

regarding *prep* having to do with — see ABOUT 1

regardless *adv* in spite of everything ⟨the weather looked bad, but they were resolved to go on with their picnic *regardless*⟩
synonyms anyhow, anyway
related words nevertheless
phrases in any case, no matter

regenerate *vb* **1** to bring back to a former condition or vigor — see RENEW 1

2 to bring back to life, practice, or activity — see REVIVE 1

regenerated *adj* made or become fresh in spirits or vigor — see NEW 4

regeneration *n* the act or an instance of bringing something back to life, public attention, or vigorous activity — see REVIVAL

regime *also* **régime** *n* lawful control over the affairs of a political unit (as a nation) — see RULE 2

regimen *n* lawful control over the affairs of a political unit (as a nation) — see RULE 2

region *n* **1** a part or portion having no fixed boundaries ⟨if you look in the upper left *region* of the sky, you can see the constellation Orion⟩
synonyms area, demesne, field, zone
related words section; locale, locality, location, locus, place, point, position, site, spot

2 a broad geographical area ⟨corn is mostly grown in the central *regions* of the country⟩
synonyms belt, land, part(s), tract, zone
related words district, territory

¹register *n* a person whose job is to keep records — see CLERK 1

²register *n* a record of a series of items (as names or titles) usually arranged according to some system — see ¹LIST

register *vb* **1** to enter in a list or roll — see EN-
ROLL 1
2 to make a written note of — see RECORD 1
3 to put (someone or something) on a list — see
¹LIST 2

registrar *n* a person whose job is to keep records
— see CLERK 1

registration *n* the number of individuals registered
⟨there was a large *registration* for the popular
swim classes at the community center⟩
synonyms enrollment, registry
related words class

registry *n* **1** a record of a series of items (as names
or titles) usually arranged according to some system — see ¹LIST
2 the number of individuals registered — see
REGISTRATION

regress *vb* to go back to a previous and usually
lower state or level ⟨in extreme circumstances,
people sometimes *regress* to the behavior they exhibited in childhood⟩
synonyms retrogress, revert
related words backslide, lapse, relapse; return
near antonyms grow, mature, ripen
antonyms advance, develop, evolve, progress

regression *n* the act or an instance of going back
to an earlier and lower level especially of intelligence or behavior ⟨the *regression* to really childish behavior that boys often undergo when put in
large groups⟩
synonyms retrogression, reversion
related words backslide, lapse, relapse; return;
nondevelopment
near antonyms growth, maturation, ripening
antonyms advancement, development, evolution,
progression

regret *n* a feeling of responsibility for wrongdoing
— see GUILT 1

regret *vb* to feel sorry or dissatisfied about ⟨we *regret* any inconvenience that we may have caused
you⟩
synonyms bemoan, deplore, lament, repent, rue
related words bewail, grieve (for), mourn, sorrow
(for)

regretful *adj* **1** expressing or suggesting mourning
— see MOURNFUL 1
2 feeling sorrow for a wrong that one has done —
see CONTRITE 1

regretfully *adv* with feelings of bitterness or grief
— see HARD 2

regrettable *adj* of a kind to cause great distress
⟨the explorers forged ahead despite the *regrettable* loss of some of their companions⟩
synonyms deplorable, distressful, distressing,
grievous, heartbreaking, heartrending, lamentable, unfortunate, woeful
related words affecting, moving, poignant, touching; awful, dire, dreadful, fearful, terrible; horrible, horrifying, intolerable, overwhelming, shocking, sickening, unbearable; miserable, pitiful,
wretched; calamitous, disastrous
near antonyms gratifying, pleasing, rewarding,
satisfying; comforting, encouraging, heartening;
cheering, heartwarming, inspiring; fortunate,
happy, lucky

regular *adj* **1** appearing or occurring repeatedly
from time to time ⟨what with one or another of
our pets having problems, we've been *regular* visitors at the animal hospital⟩

synonyms constant, frequent, habitual, periodic,
repeated, steady
related words chronic, confirmed, inveterate; expected, usual
near antonyms unexpected, unusual
antonyms inconstant, infrequent, irregular
2 following a set method, arrangement, or pattern
— see METHODICAL
3 following or agreeing with established form,
custom, or rules — see FORMAL 1
4 having no exceptions or restrictions — see AB-
SOLUTE 2
5 having or showing the qualities associated with
the members of a particular group or kind — see
TYPICAL 1

regular *n* a person engaged in military service —
see SOLDIER

regularize *vb* to make agree with a single established standard or model — see STANDARDIZE

regulate *vb* **1** to keep from exceeding a desirable
degree or level (as of expression) — see CON-
TROL 1
2 to look after and make decisions about — see
CONDUCT 1

regulation *n* **1** a statement spelling out the proper procedure or conduct for an activity — see
RULE 1
2 the act or activity of looking after and making
decisions about something — see CONDUCT 1
3 the duty or function of watching or guarding
for the sake of proper direction or control — see
SUPERVISION 1

regulator *n* a mechanism for adjusting the operation of a device, machine, or system — see CON-
TROL 1

rehabilitate *vb* **1** to make better in behavior or
character — see REFORM 1
2 to restore to a healthy condition — see HEAL 1

rehabilitation *n* the process or period of gradually
regaining one's health and strength — see CONVA-
LESCENCE

rehearsal *n* a private performance or session in
preparation for a public appearance ⟨we made a
few mistakes in *rehearsal*, but we were pretty sure
that we'd be okay on opening night⟩
synonyms dry run, practice (*also* practise), trial
related words dress rehearsal; preview; drill, exercise

rehearse *vb* **1** to do over and over so as to become
skilled — see PRACTICE
2 to give an oral or written account of in some detail — see TELL 1
3 to say or state again — see REPEAT 1
4 to specify one after another — see ENUMER-
ATE 1

reimburse *vb* to make a return payment to — see
REPAY

rein *n* the place of leadership or command — see
HEAD 2

rein (in) *vb* to keep from exceeding a desirable degree or level (as of expression) — see CONTROL 1

reiterate *vb* **1** to make or do again — see REPEAT 4
2 to say or state again — see REPEAT 1

reiteration *n* the act of saying or doing over again
— see REPEAT

reiterative *adj* marked by repetition — see REPET-
ITIVE

reject *n* **1** one who is cast out or rejected by society — see OUTCAST

2 something separated from a group or lot for not being as good as the others — see CULL

reject *vb* **1** to be unwilling to grant — see DENY 2

2 to declare not to be true — see DENY 1

3 to get rid of as useless or unwanted — see DISCARD

4 to show unwillingness to accept, do, engage in, or agree to — see DECLINE 1

rejected *adj* left unoccupied or unused — see ABANDONED

rejection *n* **1** a refusal to confirm the truth of a statement — see DENIAL 2

2 an unwillingness to grant something asked for — see DENIAL 1

3 something separated from a group or lot for not being as good as the others — see CULL

rejoice *vb* **1** to feel or express joy or triumph — see EXULT

2 to give satisfaction to — see PLEASE

rejoicing *adj* having or expressing feelings of joy or triumph — see EXULTANT

rejoin *vb* to speak or write in reaction to a question or to another reaction — see ANSWER 1

rejoinder *n* something spoken or written in reaction especially to a question — see ANSWER 1

rejuvenate *vb* **1** to bring back to a former condition or vigor — see RENEW 1

2 to bring back to life, practice, or activity — see REVIVE 1

rejuvenation *n* the act or an instance of bringing something back to life, public attention, or vigorous activity — see REVIVAL

rekindle *vb* to bring back to life, practice, or activity — see REVIVE 1

relate *vb* **1** to form a close personal relationship — see COMMUNE

2 to give an oral or written account of in some detail — see TELL 1

3 to have a relation or connection — see APPLY 1

4 to think of (something) in combination — see ASSOCIATE 2

related *adj* having a close connection like that between family members ⟨the *related* fields of anthropology and archaeology⟩

synonyms affiliated, akin, allied, kindred

related words associated, connected; alike, analogous, comparable, correspondent, corresponding, like, matching, parallel, resembling, similar, such, suchlike; identical, same; germane, pertinent, relevant

near antonyms different, disparate, dissimilar, distinct, distinctive, distinguishable, diverse, other, unalike, unlike

antonyms unrelated

relation *n* **1** **relations** *pl* doings between individuals or groups ⟨*relations* between the rival newspapers remained friendly despite their competition for the same stories⟩

synonyms dealings, interaction, intercourse

related words interrelationship

2 a person connected with another by blood or marriage — see RELATIVE

3 the fact or state of having something in common — see CONNECTION 1

4 the state of having shared interests or efforts (as in social or business matters) — see ASSOCIATION 1

relationship *n* **1** the fact or state of having something in common — see CONNECTION 1

2 the state of having shared interests or efforts (as in social or business matters) — see ASSOCIATION 1

relative *adj* **1** being such only when compared to something else — see COMPARATIVE

2 having to do with the matter at hand — see PERTINENT

relative *n* a person connected with another by blood or marriage ⟨it's always fun to see all your *relatives* at a big family gathering⟩

synonyms kin, kinsman, relation

related words in-law; kinswoman; blood, clan, family, folk, house, kindred, kinfolk, kinsfolk, line, lineage, people, race, stock, tribe

relatively *adv* to some degree or extent — see FAIRLY

relax *vb* **1** to get rid of nervous tension or anxiety ⟨she took deep breaths to *relax* before going on stage⟩

synonyms unwind

related words loosen (up), unbend; repose, rest; alleviate, comfort, ease, relieve; calm, compose, cool, quiet, settle

antonyms tense (up)

2 to make less taut — see SLACKEN

3 to refrain from labor or exertion — see REST 1

relaxation *n* **1** activity engaged in to amuse oneself — see PLAY 1

2 freedom from activity or labor — see ¹REST 1

relaxed *adj* **1** enjoying physical comfort — see COMFORTABLE 2

2 not bound by rigid standards — see EASYGOING 2

3 not tightly fastened, tied, or stretched — see LOOSE 1

relaxing *adj* tending to calm the emotions and relieve stress — see SOOTHING 1

release *n* **1** a freeing from an obligation or responsibility ⟨after they declared bankruptcy, the bank agreed to a *release* from their debt⟩

synonyms delivery, discharge, quietus, quittance

related words exemption, immunity, waiver

2 a document containing a declaration of an intentional giving up of a right, claim, or privilege — see WAIVER

3 a published statement informing the public of a matter of general interest — see ANNOUNCEMENT

release *vb* **1** to set free (from a state of being held in check) ⟨he *released* his anger with a great yell of frustration⟩

synonyms loose, loosen, uncork, unleash, unlock, unloose, unloosen

related words discharge, emancipate, enfranchise, free, liberate, manumit, spring, unbind, uncage, unchain, unfetter; air, express, vent

near antonyms manacle, shackle, trammel; bind, confine, enchain, fetter

antonyms bridle, check, constrain, contain, control, curb, govern, hold in, inhibit, regulate, rein (in), restrain, tame

2 to find emotional release for — see TAKE OUT 1

3 to set free (as from slavery or confinement) — see FREE 1

4 to set free from entanglement or difficulty — see EXTRICATE

5 to throw or give off — see EMIT 1

relent *vb* to grow less in scope or intensity especially gradually — see DECREASE 2

relentless *adj* showing no signs of slackening or yielding in one's purpose — see UNYIELDING 1

relevance *n* the fact or state of being pertinent —
see PERTINENCE

relevancy *n* the fact or state of being pertinent —
see PERTINENCE

relevant *adj* having to do with the matter at hand
— see PERTINENT

reliability *n* worthiness as the recipient of another's trust or confidence ⟨we never had to question
the *reliability* of the park rangers in an emer-
gency⟩
synonyms dependability, reliableness, solidity,
solidness, sureness, trustworthiness
related words infallibility
near antonyms doubtfulness, dubiousness

reliable *adj* worthy of one's trust — see DEPEND-
ABLE

reliableness *n* worthiness as the recipient of another's trust or confidence — see RELIABILITY

reliance *n* **1** something or someone to which one
looks for support — see DEPENDENCE 2
2 the quality or state of needing something or
someone — see DEPENDENCE 1

relic *n* **1** a tiny often physical indication of something lost or vanished — see VESTIGE
2 something belonging to or surviving from an
earlier period — see ANTIQUE

relief *n* **1** a feeling of ease from grief or trouble —
see COMFORT 1
2 a person or thing that takes the place of another — see SUBSTITUTE
3 reduction of or freedom from pain — see
EASE 1

relieve *vb* **1** to make more bearable or less severe
— see HELP 2
2 to set (a person or thing) free of something that
encumbers — see RID

religion *n* **1** a body of beliefs and practices regarding the supernatural and the worship of one
or more deities ⟨the Jewish *religion* has followers
in many parts of the globe⟩
synonyms credo, creed, cult, faith, persuasion
related words church, communion, denomination, sect; belief, doctrine, dogma, theology;
monotheism, polytheism, theism
near antonyms agnosticism, atheism, secularism
2 belief and trust in and loyalty to God — see
FAITH 1

religious *adj* **1** of, relating to, or used in the practice or worship services of a religion ⟨J.S. Bach
wrote some of the most beautiful *religious* music
in the world⟩
synonyms devotional, sacred, spiritual
related words blessed, consecrated, hallowed,
holy, sacrosanct, sanctified; liturgical, ritual,
sacramental
near antonyms earthly, mundane, worldly; irreligious, semireligious
antonyms nonreligious, profane, secular
2 showing a devotion to God and to a life of
virtue — see HOLY 1

relinquish *vb* **1** to give (something) over to the control or possession of another usually under duress
— see SURRENDER 1
2 to give up (as a position of authority) formally
— see ABDICATE

relinquishment *n* the usually forced yielding of
one's person or possessions to the control of another — see SURRENDER

relish *n* **1** positive regard for something — see LIK-
ING

2 the feeling experienced when one's wishes are
met — see PLEASURE 1

relish *vb* to take pleasure in — see ENJOY 1

reluctance *n* a lack of willingness or desire to do or
accept something ⟨the mice showed an odd *reluctance* to eat the cheese we had put out for them⟩
synonyms disinclination, hesitance, hesitancy, unwillingness
related words faltering, hesitation, indecision, irresolution, shilly-shallying, staggering, vacillation, wavering, wobbling; distrust, distrustfulness,
doubt, incertitude, misgiving, mistrust, mistrustfulness, skepticism, suspicion, uncertainty
near antonyms certainty, certitude, sureness,
surety
antonyms inclination, willingness

reluctant *adj* having doubts about the wisdom of
doing something — see HESITANT

rely *vb* to place reliance or trust — see DEPEND 2

remain *vb* to continue to be in a place for a significant amount of time — see STAY 1

remainder *n* **1** a remaining group or portion ⟨the
remainder of the pills were saved in case they
were needed later⟩
synonyms balance, leavings, leftovers, odds and
ends, remains, remnant, residue, rest
related words fragment, scrap; oddment, scrap-
ing(s), stub, stump; excess, surplus
near antonyms bulk, most
2 an unused or unwanted piece or item typically
of small size or value — see ¹SCRAP 1

remains *n pl* **1** the portion or bits of something left
over or behind after it has been destroyed ⟨the *remains* of the house ripped apart by the tornado
littered the block for weeks afterward⟩
synonyms ashes, debris, residue, rubble, ruins,
wreck, wreckage
related words detritus, flotsam, jetsam; garbage,
refuse, trash
2 a dead body — see CORPSE
3 a remaining group or portion — see REMAIN-
DER 1

remake *vb* **1** to make different in some way — see
CHANGE 1
2 to make or do again — see REPEAT 4

remaking *n* the act, process, or result of making
different — see CHANGE

remark *n* a briefly expressed opinion ⟨the speaker
made some short *remarks* about the new museum
before officially opening the doors to visitors⟩
synonyms comment, note, observation, reflection
related words analysis, commentary, exposition;
annotation; belief, conviction, eye, feeling, judgment (*or* judgement), mind, notion, opinion, persuasion, sentiment, verdict, view

remark *vb* **1** to make a statement of one's opinion
⟨he *remarked* on the attractiveness of the background music in the restaurant⟩
synonyms comment, note, observe, opine
related words articulate, express, say, speak, state,
talk, tell, utter, verbalize, vocalize
2 to make note of (something) through the use of
one's eyes — see SEE 1

remarkable *adj* **1** different from the ordinary in a
way that causes curiosity or suspicion — see
ODD 2
2 likely to attract attention — see NOTICEABLE

remediable *adj* capable of being corrected ⟨the
problems with the local transportation system
were severe but still *remediable*⟩

synonyms correctable, fixable, rectifiable, repairable, reparable

related words amendable, improvable, resolvable; redeemable

near antonyms irredeemable, irretrievable, unrecoverable

antonyms incorrigible, irremediable, irreparable

remedial *adj* serving to raise or adjust something to some standard or proper condition — see CORRECTIVE 1

remedy *n* **1** a substance or preparation used to treat disease — see MEDICINE

2 something that corrects or counteracts something undesirable — see CURE 1

remedy *vb* **1** to bring about recovery from — see CURE 1

2 to remove errors, defects, deficiencies, or deviations from — see CORRECT 1

remedying *adj* serving to raise or adjust something to some standard or proper condition — see CORRECTIVE 1

remember *vb* to bring back to mind ⟨I *remember* the fun we had last summer very clearly, but I can't *remember* anything I learned in school yesterday⟩

synonyms hark back (to), mind [*chiefly dialect*], recall, recollect, reminisce (about), think (of)

related words recapture, recur; educe, elicit, evoke, extract, remind; relive

phrases look back (on *or* upon)

near antonyms disregard, ignore, neglect, overlook; lose, miss; blank (out)

antonyms forget, unlearn

remembrance *n* **1** a particular act or instance of recalling or the thing remembered — see MEMORY 2

2 something that serves to keep alive the memory of a person or event — see MEMORIAL

3 the power or process of recalling what has been previously learned or experienced — see MEMORY 1

reminder *n* something that serves to keep alive the memory of a person or event — see MEMORIAL

reminisce (about) *vb* to bring back to mind — see REMEMBER

reminiscence *n* **1** a particular act or instance of recalling or the thing remembered — see MEMORY 2

2 the power or process of recalling what has been previously learned or experienced — see MEMORY 1

reminiscent *adj* provoking a memory or mental association — see SUGGESTIVE 2

remiss *adj* failing to give proper care and attention — see NEGLIGENT

remission *n* release from the guilt or penalty of an offense — see PARDON

remissness *n* failure to take the care that a cautious person usually takes — see NEGLIGENCE 1

remit *vb* **1** to grow less in scope or intensity especially gradually — see DECREASE 2

2 to overlook or dismiss as of little importance — see EXCUSE 1

remitment *n* the act of offering money in exchange for goods or services — see PAYMENT 1

remittable *adj* worthy of forgiveness — see VENIAL

remittal *n* release from the guilt or penalty of an offense — see PARDON

remittance *n* **1** something (as money) that is given

or received in return for goods or services — see PAYMENT 2

2 the act of offering money in exchange for goods or services — see PAYMENT 1

remnant *n* **1** a remaining group or portion — see REMAINDER 1

2 an unused or unwanted piece or item typically of small size or value — see ¹SCRAP 1

remodel *vb* to make different in some way — see CHANGE 1

remodeling *n* the act, process, or result of making different — see CHANGE

remonstrance *n* a feeling or declaration of disapproval or dissent — see OBJECTION

remonstrate (with) *vb* to present an opposing opinion or argument — see OBJECT

remorse *n* a feeling of responsibility for wrongdoing — see GUILT 1

remorseful *adj* **1** feeling sorrow for a wrong that one has done — see CONTRITE 1

2 suffering from or expressive of a feeling of responsibility for wrongdoing — see GUILTY 2

remorsefulness *n* a feeling of responsibility for wrongdoing — see GUILT 1

remorseless *adj* not sorry for having done wrong ⟨the *remorseless* killer was sentenced to life in prison without chance of parole⟩

synonyms impenitent, unrepentant

related words compassionless, cruel, merciless, pitiless, ruthless, unmerciful; shameless, unashamed

near antonyms ashamed, hangdog, shamed, shamefaced

antonyms contrite, guilty, penitent, regretful, remorseful, repentant, sorry

remote *adj* **1** small in degree ⟨there's a *remote* chance that it'll rain today, so I brought an umbrella⟩

synonyms negligible, off, outside, slight, slim, small

near antonyms great, large; distinct, significant

antonyms good

2 having or showing a lack of friendliness or interest in others — see COOL 1

3 hidden from view — see SECLUDED

4 not close in time or space — see DISTANT 1

remotest *adj* most distant from a center — see EXTREME 1

removal *n* the getting rid of whatever is unwanted or useless — see DISPOSAL 1

remove *n* the space or amount of space between two points, lines, surfaces, or objects — see DISTANCE

remove *vb* **1** to rid oneself of (a garment) ⟨I *removed* my coat as soon as I got inside⟩

synonyms doff, peel (off), put off, take off

related words husk, shed

near antonyms wear

antonyms don, put on, slip (into)

2 to take away from a place or position ⟨he carefully *removed* the old manuscript from the shelf⟩

synonyms clear, draw, withdraw

related words demount, dislodge; abstract, cut, extract, pull; move, shift, transfer

near antonyms mount

antonyms place, put

3 to change the place or position of — see MOVE 1

4 to let go from office, service, or employment — see DISMISS 1

removed *adj* not close in time or space — see DIS-TANT 1

remunerate *vb* **1** to give (someone) the sum of money owed for goods or services received — see PAY 1
2 to provide (someone) with a just payment for loss or injury — see COMPENSATE 1

remuneration *n* **1** the act of offering money in exchange for goods or services — see PAYMENT 1
2 payment to another for a loss or injury — see COMPENSATION 1
3 something (as money) that is given or received in return for goods or services — see PAYMENT 2

remunerative *adj* yielding a profit — see PROFITABLE 1

rend *vb* to cause (something) to separate into jagged pieces by violently pulling at it — see TEAR 1

render *vb* to give (something) over to the control or possession of another usually under duress — see SURRENDER 1

rendezvous *vb* to come together into one body or place — see ASSEMBLE 1

rendezvous *n* **1** a place for spending time or for socializing — see HANGOUT
2 an agreement to be present at a specified time and place — see ENGAGEMENT 2

renegade *n* a person who abandons a cause or organization usually without right ⟨a band of *renegades* who had deserted their infantry units and were making their way to Mexico⟩
synonyms defector, deserter, recreant
related words betrayer, double-crosser, quisling, traitor, turncoat; chicken, coward, craven, dastard, poltroon; defier, insurgent, insurrectionary, insurrectionist, mutineer, rebel, red, revolter, revolutionary, revolutionist, revolutionizer
near antonyms adherent, disciple, follower, zealot
antonyms loyalist

renege *vb* to break a promise or agreement ⟨Dad promised to take me out for ice cream on the weekend, only to *renege* on Saturday morning⟩
synonyms back down, back off, cop out
related words chicken (out); disavow, recall, recant, retract, take back, withdraw
phrases go back on
near antonyms follow through; fulfill (*or* fulfil), honor

renew *vb* **1** to bring back to a former condition or vigor ⟨the trip to New York *renewed* our enthusiasm for travel⟩
synonyms freshen, recreate, refresh, refreshen, regenerate, rejuvenate, restore, revitalize, revive
related words make over, refurbish, rehabilitate, remake, remodel, renovate; refill, replenish, resupply
2 to begin again or return to after an interruption — see RESUME
3 to bring back to life, practice, or activity — see REVIVE 1

renewal *n* the act or an instance of bringing something back to life, public attention, or vigorous activity — see REVIVAL

renewed *adj* made or become fresh in spirits or vigor — see NEW 4

renounce *vb* **1** to give up (as a position of authority) formally — see ABDICATE
2 to solemnly or formally reject or go back on (as something formerly adhered to) — see ABJURE

renouncement *n* the act or practice of giving up or rejecting something once enjoyed or desired — see RENUNCIATION

renovate *vb* to put into good shape or working order again — see MEND 1

renown *n* the fact or state of being known to the public — see FAME

renowned *adj* widely known — see FAMOUS

rent *n* **1** a long deep cut — see GASH
2 an open space in a barrier (as a wall or hedge) — see GAP 1

rent *vb* **1** to give the possession and use of (something) in return for periodic payment ⟨we *rented* the apartment to a college student for $500 a month⟩
synonyms lease, let [*chiefly British*]
related words charter, hire; lodge; sublease, sublet
2 to take or get the temporary use of (something) for a set sum — see HIRE 1

renter *n* **1** one who rents a room or apartment in another's house — see TENANT
2 the owner of land or housing that is rented to another — see LANDLORD

renunciation *n* the act or practice of giving up or rejecting something once enjoyed or desired ⟨his *renunciation* of his smoking habit pleased his whole family⟩
synonyms abnegation, renouncement, repudiation, self-denial
related words denial, refusal; relinquishment, resignation, surrender
near antonyms acceptance; adoption, embrace, espousal
antonyms indulgence, self-indulgence

reopen *vb* to begin again or return to after an interruption — see RESUME

repair *n* a state of being or fitness — see CONDITION 1

repair *vb* to put into good shape or working order again — see MEND 1

repairable *adj* capable of being corrected — see REMEDIABLE

reparable *adj* capable of being corrected — see REMEDIABLE

reparation *n* payment to another for a loss or injury — see COMPENSATION 1

repartee *n* **1** a quick witty response — see RETORT 1
2 good-natured teasing or exchanging of clever remarks — see BANTER

repast *n* food eaten or prepared for eating at one time — see MEAL

repay *vb* to make a return payment to ⟨I *repaid* my friend the twenty dollars he had lent me⟩
synonyms refund, reimburse
related words quit, satisfy, settle
phrases pay back

repeal *n* the act of putting an end to something planned or previously agreed to — see CANCELLATION

repeal *vb* **1** to put an end to (something planned or previously agreed to) — see CANCEL 1
2 to put an end to by formal action — see ABOLISH

repeat *n* the act of saying or doing over again ⟨the news story will be broadcast on the six o'clock show, with a *repeat* on the 11 o'clock newscast⟩
synonyms duplication, reduplication, reiteration, repetition, replication
related words rerun

repeat *vb* **1** to say or state again ⟨I *repeated* the address over and over until I had it memorized⟩
synonyms din, rehearse, reiterate
related words echo, parrot; mouth
2 to give from memory ⟨*repeated* correctly all the verses she had memorized⟩
synonyms recite, say
related words declaim, mouth, orate, speak
near antonyms read
3 to say after another ⟨now *repeat* the oath after me⟩
synonyms echo, parrot, quote
related words mouth; copy, imitate, mimic
4 to make or do again ⟨try not to *repeat* your mistakes⟩
synonyms duplicate, redo, reduplicate, reiterate, remake, replicate
related words renew

repeated *adj* appearing or occurring repeatedly from time to time — see REGULAR 1

repeatedly *adv* many times — see OFTEN

repel *vb* **1** to drive back ⟨the defenders *repelled* the attacking army after several hours of fierce fighting⟩
synonyms fend (off), repulse, stave off
related words hold off, resist, withstand; deflect, ward (off); rebuff, snub, spurn
near antonyms welcome
2 to cause to feel disgust — see DISGUST
3 to refuse to give in to — see RESIST

repelled *adj* filled with disgust — see SICK 2

repellent *also* **repellant** *adj* causing intense displeasure, disgust, or resentment — see OFFENSIVE 1

repent *vb* to feel sorry or dissatisfied about — see REGRET

repentance *n* a feeling of responsibility for wrongdoing — see GUILT 1

repentant *adj* **1** feeling sorrow for a wrong that one has done — see CONTRITE 1
2 suffering from or expressive of a feeling of responsibility for wrongdoing — see GUILTY 2

repercussion *n* the power to bring about a result on another — see EFFECT 2

repetition *n* the act of saying or doing over again — see REPEAT

repetitious *adj* marked by repetition — see REPETITIVE

repetitive *adj* marked by repetition ⟨the *repetitive* lyrics of so many rock songs⟩
synonyms reiterative, repetitious

rephrase *vb* to express something (as a text or statement) in different words — see PARAPHRASE

rephrasing *n* an instance of expressing something in different words — see PARAPHRASE

repine *vb* to express dissatisfaction, pain, or resentment usually tiresomely — see COMPLAIN

repine (for) *vb* to have an earnest wish to own or enjoy — see DESIRE

replace *vb* **1** to take the place of ⟨the old street lights were *replaced* with more energy-efficient models⟩
synonyms displace, substitute, supersede, supplant
related words preempt, usurp
2 to bring, send, or put back to a former or proper place — see RETURN 1

replacement *n* a person or thing that takes the place of another — see SUBSTITUTE

replete *adj* possessing or covered with great numbers or amounts of something specified — see RIFE

replica *n* **1** something or someone that strongly resembles another — see IMAGE 1
2 something that is made to look exactly like something else — see COPY

replicate *vb* **1** to make an exact likeness of — see COPY 1
2 to make or do again — see REPEAT 4

replication *n* **1** something that is made to look exactly like something else — see COPY
2 the act of saying or doing over again — see REPEAT

reply *n* **1** action or behavior that is done in return to other action or behavior — see REACTION
2 something spoken or written in reaction especially to a question — see ANSWER 1

reply *vb* **1** to act or behave in response (as to a stimulus or influence) — see REACT
2 to speak or write in reaction to a question or to another reaction — see ANSWER 1

report *n* **1** a loud explosive sound — see CLAP 1
2 a relating of events usually in the order in which they happened — see ACCOUNT 1
3 overall quality as seen or judged by people in general — see REPUTATION

report *vb* to give an oral or written account of in some detail — see TELL 1

reporter *n* a person employed by a newspaper, magazine, or radio or television station to gather, write, or report news ⟨the *reporter* was careful to ask as many questions as possible without annoying anyone⟩
synonyms correspondent, journalist
related words announcer, broadcaster, newscaster, newsman, newspaperman; anchor, anchorman, anchorperson, anchorwoman, legman; columnist, commentator, copyreader, editor, sportswriter, staffer

repose *n* **1** a natural periodic loss of consciousness during which the body restores itself — see SLEEP 1
2 a state of freedom from storm or disturbance — see CALM
3 freedom from activity or labor — see ¹REST 1

repose *vb* to refrain from labor or exertion — see REST 1

repository *n* a building for storing goods — see STOREHOUSE

repossess *vb* to get again in one's possession — see RECOVER 1

repossession *n* the act or process of getting something back — see RECOVERY 1

reprehend *vb* **1** to declare to be morally wrong or evil — see CONDEMN 1
2 to express one's unfavorable opinion of the worth or quality of — see CRITICIZE

reprehensible *adj* **1** deserving reproach or blame — see BLAMEWORTHY
2 provoking or likely to provoke protest — see OBJECTIONABLE

represent *vb* **1** to point out the chief quality or qualities of an individual or group — see CHARACTERIZE 1
2 to present a picture of — see PICTURE 1
3 to serve as a material counterpart of — see SYMBOLIZE 1

representative *n* **1** a person who acts or does business for another — see AGENT 2

2 a person sent on a mission to represent another — see AMBASSADOR

3 one of a group or collection that shows what the whole is like — see EXAMPLE

representative *adj* **1** having or showing the qualities associated with the members of a particular group or kind — see TYPICAL 1

2 having the function or meaning of a symbol — see SYMBOLIC

repress *vb* **1** to put a stop to (something) by the use of force — see QUELL 1

2 to refrain from openly showing or uttering — see SUPPRESS 2

repression *n* the checking of one's true feelings and impulses when dealing with others — see CONSTRAINT 1

reprimand *n* an often public or formal expression of disapproval — see CENSURE

reprimand *vb* **1** to criticize (someone) severely or angrily especially for personal failings — see SCOLD

2 to criticize (someone) usually gently so as to correct a fault — see REBUKE 1

3 to express public or formal disapproval of — see CENSURE 1

reprisal *n* the act or an instance of paying back an injury with an injury — see REVENGE

reproach *n* **1** a cause of shame — see DISGRACE 2

2 an often public or formal expression of disapproval — see CENSURE

3 the state of having lost the esteem of others — see DISGRACE 1

reproach *vb* **1** to criticize (someone) severely or angrily especially for personal failings — see SCOLD

2 to criticize (someone) usually gently so as to correct a fault — see REBUKE 1

3 to express public or formal disapproval of — see CENSURE 1

reproachable *adj* deserving reproach or blame — see BLAMEWORTHY

reprobate *adj* having or showing lowered moral character or standards — see CORRUPT

reprobate *n* a mean, evil, or unprincipled person — see VILLAIN

reprobate *vb* to declare to be morally wrong or evil — see CONDEMN 1

reproduce *vb* **1** to bring forth offspring — see PROCREATE

2 to make an exact likeness of — see COPY 1

reproduction *n* something that is made to look exactly like something else — see COPY

reproof *n* an often public or formal expression of disapproval — see CENSURE

reprove *vb* **1** to criticize (someone) usually gently so as to correct a fault — see REBUKE 1

2 to express public or formal disapproval of — see CENSURE 1

3 to hold an unfavorable opinion of — see DISAPPROVE

republic *n* government in which the supreme power is held by the people and used by them directly or indirectly through representation — see DEMOCRACY

republican *adj* of, relating to, or favoring political democracy — see DEMOCRATIC

repudiate *vb* **1** to declare not to be true — see DENY 1

2 to refuse to acknowledge as one's own or as one's responsibility — see DISCLAIM 1

3 to show unwillingness to accept, do, engage in, or agree to — see DECLINE 1

repudiation *n* **1** a refusal to confirm the truth of a statement — see DENIAL 2

2 the act or practice of giving up or rejecting something once enjoyed or desired — see RENUNCIATION

repugnance *n* a dislike so strong as to cause stomach upset or queasiness — see DISGUST

repugnant *adj* causing intense displeasure, disgust, or resentment — see OFFENSIVE 1

repulse *n* treatment that is deliberately unfriendly — see COLD SHOULDER

repulse *vb* **1** to cause to feel disgust — see DISGUST

2 to drive back — see REPEL 1

repulsed *adj* filled with disgust — see SICK 2

repulsion *n* a dislike so strong as to cause stomach upset or queasiness — see DISGUST

repulsive *adj* causing intense displeasure, disgust, or resentment — see OFFENSIVE 1

repulsiveness *n* the quality of inspiring intense dread or dismay — see HORROR 1

reputable *adj* having a good reputation especially in a field of knowledge — see RESPECTABLE 1

reputation *n* overall quality as seen or judged by people in general ⟨the college's athletic department has a good *reputation*, but the school's science facilities are a bit lacking⟩

synonyms character, mark, name, note, report, repute

related words credit, honor; celebrity, fame, notoriety, renown

near antonyms infamy

repute *n* overall quality as seen or judged by people in general — see REPUTATION

reputed *adj* **1** appearing to be true on the basis of evidence that may or may not be confirmed — see APPARENT 1

2 having a good reputation especially in a field of knowledge — see RESPECTABLE 1

request *n* an act or instance of asking for information — see QUESTION 2

request *vb* **1** to give a request or demand for — see ORDER 2

2 to make a request for — see ASK (FOR) 1

3 to make a request of — see ASK 2

requiem *n* a composition expressing one's grief over a loss — see LAMENT 2

require *vb* to have as a requirement — see NEED 1

required *adj* **1** forcing one's compliance or participation by or as if by law — see MANDATORY

2 impossible to do without — see ESSENTIAL 1

requirement *n* something necessary, indispensable, or unavoidable — see ESSENTIAL 1

requisite *adj* impossible to do without — see ESSENTIAL 1

requisite *n* something necessary, indispensable, or unavoidable — see ESSENTIAL 1

requisition *n* something that someone insists upon having — see DEMAND 1

requisition *vb* to give a request or demand for — see ORDER 2

requital *n* **1** payment to another for a loss or injury — see COMPENSATION 1

2 something (as money) that is given or received in return for goods or services — see PAYMENT 2

3 the act or an instance of paying back an injury with an injury — see REVENGE

requite *vb* **1** to provide (someone) with a just payment for loss or injury — see COMPENSATE 1

2 to punish in kind the wrongdoer responsible for — see AVENGE

rescind *vb* **1** to put an end to (something planned or previously agreed to) — see CANCEL 1

2 to put an end to by formal action — see ABOLISH

rescission *n* the act of putting an end to something planned or previously agreed to — see CANCELLATION

rescue *vb* to remove from danger or harm — see SAVE 2

rescuer *n* one that saves from danger or destruction — see SAVIOR

research *n* a systematic search for the truth or facts about something — see INQUIRY 1

research *vb* to search through or into — see EXPLORE 1

resemblance *n* **1** a point which two or more things share in common — see SIMILARITY 2

2 the quality or state of having many qualities in common — see SIMILARITY 1

resembling *adj* having qualities in common — see ALIKE

resentful *adj* **1** having or showing deep-seated resentment — see BITTER 1

2 having or showing mean resentment of another's possessions or advantages — see ENVIOUS

resentfully *adv* with feelings of bitterness or grief — see HARD 2

resentment *n* **1** a lingering ill will towards a person for a real or imagined wrong — see GRUDGE 1

2 a painful awareness of another's possessions or advantages and a desire to have them too — see ENVY

3 the feeling of being offended or resentful after a slight or indignity — see PIQUE

reservation *n* something upon which the carrying out of an agreement or offer depends — see CONDITION 2

reserve *n* **1** the checking of one's true feelings and impulses when dealing with others — see CONSTRAINT 1

2 a collection of things kept available for future use or need — see STORE

3 a person or thing that takes the place of another — see SUBSTITUTE

4 an interchangeable part or piece of equipment that is kept on hand for replacement of an original — see SPARE

reserve *vb* **1** to arrange to have something (as a hotel room) held for one's future use ⟨we made sure to *reserve* a kennel for our dog several months before the start of the family vacation⟩
synonyms bespeak, book
related words earmark; contract, engage, retain

2 to continue to have in one's possession or power — see KEEP 2

3 to keep or intend for a special purpose — see DEVOTE 1

reserved *adj* tending not to speak frequently (as by habit or inclination) — see SILENT 2

reside *vb* to have a home — see LIVE 1

residence *n* the place where one lives — see HOME 1

resident *n* one who lives permanently in a place — see INHABITANT

resider *n* one who lives permanently in a place — see INHABITANT

residue *n* **1** the portion or bits of something left

over or behind after it has been destroyed — see REMAINS 1

2 a remaining group or portion — see REMAINDER 1

resign *vb* to give up (as a position of authority) formally — see ABDICATE

resign (from) *vb* to give up (a job or office) — see QUIT 1

resigned *adj* receiving or enduring without offering resistance — see PASSIVE

resilient *adj* able to revert to original size and shape after being stretched, squeezed, or twisted — see ELASTIC 1

resist *vb* to refuse to give in to ⟨it is important to *resist* the temptation to run away from your problems⟩
synonyms buck, defy, fight, oppose, repel, withstand
related words battle, combat, contend (with), counter; contest, dispute; baffle, balk, foil, frustrate, thwart; check, counter, hinder, obstruct, stem
antonyms bow (to), capitulate (to), give in (to), submit (to), succumb (to), surrender (to), yield (to)

resistance *n* **1** the inclination to resist ⟨there was much *resistance* to the idea of removing our baseball caps while eating⟩
synonyms defiance, opposition
related words demur, objection, protest, remonstrance; compunction, misgiving, reservation; disobedience, noncompliance
near antonyms compliance, obedience; acceptance, approval
antonyms acquiescence

2 a secret organization in a conquered country fighting against enemy forces ⟨soldiers from the *resistance* were captured after a short battle outside the foreign ministry⟩
synonyms underground
related words cabal, conspiracy

resolute *adj* fully committed to achieving a goal — see DETERMINED 1

resoluteness *n* firm or unwavering adherence to one's purpose — see DETERMINATION 1

resolution *n* **1** a position arrived at after consideration — see DECISION 1

2 firm or unwavering adherence to one's purpose — see DETERMINATION 1

resolvable *adj* capable of having the reason for or cause of determined — see SOLVABLE

resolve *n* firm or unwavering adherence to one's purpose — see DETERMINATION 1

resolve *vb* **1** to come to a judgment after discussion or consideration — see DECIDE 1

2 to find an answer for through reasoning — see SOLVE

3 to set or force apart — see SEPARATE 1

resolved *adj* fully committed to achieving a goal — see DETERMINED 1

resonant *adj* marked by conspicuously full and rich sounds or tones ⟨the orator's *resonant* voice filled the hall⟩
synonyms golden, resounding, reverberant, reverberating, ringing, round, sonorous, vibrant
related words deep, full, mellifluous, mellow, rich; loud, powerful, stentorian, thundering, thunderous
near antonyms cavernous, hollow; faint, low, murmurous, muted, smothered, soft, weak; thin, tinny

resonate *vb* to continue or be repeated in a series of reflected sound waves — see REVERBERATE

resort (to) *vb* **1** to use or seek out as a source of aid, relief, or advantage ⟨we were so desperate for better grades on our homework that we were forced to *resort to* spending all our evenings at the library⟩
synonyms go (to), refer (to), turn (to)
related words employ, use, utilize; depend (on), rely (on)
phrases fall back on
2 to go to or spend time in often — see FREQUENT

resort *n* **1** a place for spending time or for socializing — see HANGOUT
2 something that one uses to accomplish an end especially when the usual means is not available — see RESOURCE 1

resound *vb* to continue or be repeated in a series of reflected sound waves — see REVERBERATE

resounding *adj* **1** full of or characterized by the presence of noise — see NOISY 2
2 marked by a high volume of sound — see LOUD 1
3 marked by conspicuously full and rich sounds or tones — see RESONANT
4 marked by or uttered with forcefulness — see EMPHATIC 1

resource *n* **1** something that one uses to accomplish an end especially when the usual means is not available ⟨we used every possible *resource* to raise the funds needed to save our town's oldest house⟩
synonyms expedient, recourse, resort
related words hope, opportunity, possibility, relief; makeshift, replacement, stopgap, substitute
2 **resources** *pl* available money — see FUND 2

respect *n* **1** relation to or concern with something specified ⟨with *respect* to your application⟩
synonyms reference, regard
2 a feeling of great approval and liking — see ADMIRATION 1
3 **respects** *pl* best wishes — see COMPLIMENT

respect *vb* to think very highly or favorably of — see ADMIRE

respectable *adj* **1** having a good reputation especially in a field of knowledge ⟨no *respectable* dietician would advise people to eat just one kind of food⟩
synonyms esteemed, name, prestigious, reputable, reputed, respected
related words honorable, worthy; creditable, good, praiseworthy; celebrated, distinguished, famed, famous, honored, illustrious, notable, prominent, renowned, well-known
antonyms disreputable, loose
2 following the accepted rules of moral conduct — see HONORABLE 1
3 following the established traditions of refined society and good taste — see PROPER 1
4 of a level of quality that meets one's needs or standards — see ADEQUATE
5 sufficiently large in size, amount, or number to merit attention — see CONSIDERABLE 1

respected *adj* having a good reputation especially in a field of knowledge — see RESPECTABLE 1

respectful *adj* marked by or showing proper regard for another's higher status ⟨the children were remarkably *respectful* while in the President's office⟩
synonyms deferential, dutiful, regardful
related words reverent, reverential, venerating, worshipful; fawning, groveling (*or* grovelling), obsequious, servile, subservient, sycophantic, toadying; civil, courteous, gracious, polite
near antonyms abusive, insulting, offensive; contemptuous, impudent, irreverent; discourteous, insolent, rude, uncivil
antonyms disrespectful

respecting *prep* having to do with — see ABOUT 1

respective *adj* not the same or shared — see SEPARATE 1

respire *vb* to inhale and exhale air — see BREATHE 1

resplendence *n* impressiveness of beauty on a large scale — see MAGNIFICENCE

respond *vb* **1** to act or behave in response (as to a stimulus or influence) — see REACT
2 to speak or write in reaction to a question or to another reaction — see ANSWER 1

response *n* **1** action or behavior that is done in return to other action or behavior — see REACTION
2 something spoken or written in reaction especially to a question — see ANSWER 1

responsibility *n* **1** the state of being held as the cause of something that needs to be set right ⟨*responsibility* for the accident lies with the driver who was speeding⟩
synonyms blame, fault, liability
related words accountability
2 something one must do because of prior agreement — see OBLIGATION

responsible *adj* **1** being the one who must meet an obligation or suffer the consequences for failing to do so ⟨each student is *responsible* for getting his or her own homework done on time⟩
synonyms accountable, answerable, liable
related words beholden, indebted, obligated, obliged
near antonyms exempt, immune
antonyms irresponsible, unaccountable
2 worthy of one's trust — see DEPENDABLE

¹rest *n* **1** freedom from activity or labor ⟨I'm looking forward to enjoying some *rest* at the end of the school term⟩
synonyms ease, leisure, relaxation, repose
related words catnapping, dozing, napping, resting, sleep, slumber, slumbering, snoozing; quiet, silence, stillness; calm, peace, peacefulness, placidity, restfulness, serenity, tranquillity (*or* tranquility)
near antonyms pressure, strain, stress, tension
antonyms exertion, labor, toil, work
2 a natural periodic loss of consciousness during which the body restores itself — see SLEEP 1

²rest *n* a remaining group or portion — see REMAINDER 1

rest *vb* **1** to refrain from labor or exertion ⟨a beach resort that caters to gung ho exercisers and athletes as well as vacationers who just want to *rest*⟩
synonyms bask, loll, lounge, relax, repose
related words bum, goldbrick, idle, loaf, slack (off)
near antonyms drudge, grub, hump, hustle, labor, moil, peg (away), plod, plow, plug, slave, slog, strain, strive, struggle, sweat, toil, travail, work; exercise, work out
2 be in a state of sleep — see SLEEP 1
3 to find a basis — see BASE

restart *vb* to begin again or return to after an interruption — see RESUME

restate *vb* to express something (as a text or statement) in different words — see PARAPHRASE

restatement *n* an instance of expressing something in different words — see PARAPHRASE

restating *n* an instance of expressing something in different words — see PARAPHRASE

restaurant *n* a public establishment where meals are served to paying customers for consumption on the premises ⟨when we get sick of cooking dinner at home, we like to go out to eat at a nice *restaurant*⟩
synonyms café (*also* cafe), diner, grill
related words cafeteria, coffeehouse, garden, luncheonette, lunchroom, snack bar, tearoom; bar, barroom, inn, tavern

restful *adj* free from disturbing noise or uproar — see QUIET 1

restfulness *n* a state of freedom from storm or disturbance — see CALM

resting *adj* being in a state of suspended consciousness — see ASLEEP 1

resting *n* a natural periodic loss of consciousness during which the body restores itself — see SLEEP 1

restitution *n* payment to another for a loss or injury — see COMPENSATION 1

restive *adj* **1** given to resisting authority or another's control — see DISOBEDIENT
2 lacking or denying rest — see RESTLESS 1

restiveness *n* **1** a disturbed or uneasy state — see UNREST
2 a state of nervousness marked by sudden jerky movements — see JUMPINESS

restless *adj* **1** lacking or denying rest ⟨the worried mother spent a *restless* night, tossing and turning in bed for hours⟩
synonyms restive, uneasy, unquiet, unrestful
related words agitated, distressed, disturbed, perturbed, troubled, unsettled; aflutter, anxious, dithery, edgy, fidgety, het up, hung up, jittery, jumpy, nervous, nervy, tense, upset, uptight, worried
near antonyms calm, easy, peaceful, quiet, relaxing, tranquil
antonyms restful
2 marked by or causing agitation or uncomfortable feelings — see NERVOUS 2

restlessness *n* **1** a disturbed or uneasy state — see UNREST
2 the state of being bored — see BOREDOM

restorative *adj* **1** good for the health — see HEALTHFUL
2 having a renewing effect on the state of the body or mind — see TONIC

restore *vb* **1** to bring back to a former condition or vigor — see RENEW 1
2 to bring, send, or put back to a former or proper place — see RETURN 1

restrain *vb* **1** to keep from exceeding a desirable degree or level (as of expression) — see CONTROL 1
2 to take or keep under one's control by authority of law — see ARREST 1

restrained *adj* not excessively showy — see QUIET 2

restraint *n* **1** the checking of one's true feelings and impulses when dealing with others — see CONSTRAINT 1

2 something that limits one's freedom of action or choice — see RESTRICTION 1
3 the power to control one's actions, impulses, or emotions — see WILL 1

restrict *vb* **1** to set bounds or an upper limit for — see LIMIT 1
2 to limit the meaning of (as a noun) — see QUALIFY 1

restricted *adj* having distinct or certain limits — see LIMITED 1

restriction *n* **1** something that limits one's freedom of action or choice ⟨my parents placed several *restrictions* on the party we were planning⟩
synonyms check, condition, constraint, curb, fetter, limitation, restraint
related words exception, proviso, qualification, reservation, stipulation, strings
near antonyms freedom, latitude
2 the act or practice of keeping something (as an activity) within certain boundaries ⟨the *restriction* of surfing to the southern end of the beach rankled some surfers⟩
synonyms confinement, limitation
related words constraint, restraint; isolation, segregation

rest room *n* a room furnished with a fixture for flushing body waste — see TOILET

result *n* **1** a condition or occurrence traceable to a cause — see EFFECT 1
2 something attained by mental effort and especially by computation — see ANSWER 2

result (in) *vb* to be the cause of (a situation, action, or state of mind) — see EFFECT

resultant *adj* coming as a result ⟨frequent trips to the ice cream parlor and the *resultant* gain in weight were starting to affect my tennis game⟩
synonyms attendant, consequent, consequential, due (to)
related words accompanying, coincident, concomitant
near antonyms causal

resultant *n* a condition or occurrence traceable to a cause — see EFFECT 1

resume *vb* to begin again or return to after an interruption ⟨we *resumed* the game as soon as the rain had passed⟩
synonyms continue, renew, reopen, restart
related words resuscitate, revive
near antonyms complete, conclude, consummate, end, finalize, finish; belay, break, can, cease, check, cut, desist, discontinue, drop, halt, knock off, leave off, quit, scuttle, shut off, stay, stop, terminate

résumé *or* **resume** *also* **resumé** *n* a short statement of the main points — see SUMMARY

resurgence *n* the act or an instance of bringing something back to life, public attention, or vigorous activity — see REVIVAL

resurrect *vb* to bring back to life, practice, or activity — see REVIVE 1

resurrection *n* the act or an instance of bringing something back to life, public attention, or vigorous activity — see REVIVAL

resuscitate *vb* to bring back to life, practice, or activity — see REVIVE 1

resuscitated *adj* made or become fresh in spirits or vigor — see NEW 4

resuscitation *n* the act or an instance of bringing something back to life, public attention, or vigorous activity — see REVIVAL

THESAURUS

retail *vb* to offer for sale to the public — see MAR-
KET

retain *vb* **1** to continue to have in one's possession
or power — see KEEP 2

2 to keep, control, or experience as one's own —
see HAVE 1

3 to provide with a paying job — see EMPLOY 1

retainer *n* a person hired to perform household or
personal services — see SERVANT

retake *vb* to get again in one's possession — see
RECOVER 1

retaliate *vb* to punish in kind the wrongdoer responsible for — see AVENGE

retaliation *n* the act or an instance of paying back
an injury with an injury — see REVENGE

retard *vb* to cause to move or proceed at a less
rapid pace — see SLOW 1

retardation *n* a usually gradual decrease in the
pace or level of activity of something — see
SLOWDOWN

retarding *n* a usually gradual decrease in the pace
or level of activity of something — see SLOW-
DOWN

retch *vb* to discharge the contents of the stomach
through the mouth — see VOMIT

rethink *vb* to consider again especially with the
possibility of change or reversal — see RECON-
SIDER

reticent *adj* **1** given to keeping one's activities hidden from public observation or knowledge — see
SECRETIVE

2 tending not to speak frequently (as by habit or
inclination) — see SILENT 2

retinue *n* a body of employees or servants who accompany and wait on a person — see CORTEGE 1

retire *vb* **1** to go to one's bed in order to sleep —
see BED

2 to let go from office, service, or employment —
see DISMISS 1

3 to move back or away (as from something difficult, dangerous, or disagreeable) — see RE-
TREAT 1

retire (from) *vb* to give up (a job or office) — see
QUIT 1

retired *adj* hidden from view — see SECLUDED

retirement *n* an act of moving away especially
from something difficult, dangerous, or disagreeable — see RETREAT 1

retiring *adj* **1** not comfortable around people —
see SHY 2

2 not having or showing any feelings of superiority, self-assertiveness, or showiness — see HUM-
BLE 1

retiringness *n* the absence of any feelings of being
better than others — see HUMILITY

retort *n* **1** a quick witty response ⟨the clever boy
responded to the bully's threat with a rude
retort⟩

synonyms comeback, repartee, riposte

related words back talk; crack, quip, sally, wisecrack, witticism; cut, insult, put-down

2 something spoken or written in reaction especially to a question — see ANSWER 1

retort *vb* to speak or write in reaction to a question or to another reaction — see ANSWER 1

retract *vb* to solemnly or formally reject or go
back on (as something formerly adhered to) —
see ABJURE

retreat *n* **1** an act of moving away especially from
something difficult, dangerous, or disagreeable

⟨we made a strategic *retreat* when we realized
that we were outnumbered⟩

synonyms recession, retirement, revulsion, withdrawal

related words flinch, recoil, shrinking

antonyms advancement

2 something (as a building) that offers cover from
the weather or protection from danger — see
SHELTER

retreat *vb* **1** to move back or away (as from something difficult, dangerous, or disagreeable) ⟨we
retreated to the safety of the cellar at the first sign
of the tornado⟩

synonyms back (away), fall back, recede, retire,
withdraw

related words flinch, recoil, shrink; chicken (out);
back down, backtrack; abandon, depart, evacuate, go, leave, quit, vacate

phrases give way, lose ground

near antonyms beard, brave, brazen, breast, confront, dare, defy, face, outbrave

antonyms advance

2 to hasten away from something dangerous or
frightening — see RUN 2

retribution *n* the act or an instance of paying back
an injury with an injury — see REVENGE

retrieval *n* the act or process of getting something
back — see RECOVERY 1

retrieve *vb* to get again in one's possession — see
RECOVER 1

retrograde *adj* directed, turned, or done toward
the back — see BACKWARD

retrogress *vb* to go back to a previous and usually
lower state or level — see REGRESS

retrogression *n* the act or an instance of going
back to an earlier and lower level especially of intelligence or behavior — see REGRESSION

retrospect *n* a usually critical look at a past event
— see REVIEW 1

retrospection *n* a usually critical look at a past
event — see REVIEW 1

return *n* **1** something spoken or written in reaction
especially to a question — see ANSWER 1

2 an increase usually measured in money that
comes from labor, business, or property — see
INCOME

3 the amount of money left when expenses are
subtracted from the total amount received — see
PROFIT 1

return *vb* **1** to bring, send, or put back to a former
or proper place ⟨when I'm done reading a book, I
always *return* it to the very shelf I got it from⟩

synonyms replace, restore

near antonyms remove, take

2 to produce as revenue — see YIELD 2

3 to speak or write in reaction to a question or to
another reaction — see ANSWER 1

revamp *vb* **1** to make different in some way — see
CHANGE 1

2 to prepare for publication by correcting, rewriting, or updating — see EDIT

3 to put into good shape or working order again
— see MEND 1

revamping *n* the act, process, or result of making
different — see CHANGE

reveal *vb* **1** to make known (as information previously kept secret) ⟨at the end of the book, the detective *reveals* the identity of the mysterious
stranger⟩

synonyms bare, disclose, discover, divulge, expose, spill, tell, unbosom, uncloak, uncover, unmask, unveil

related words debunk, show up; unclothe, undrape; advertise, announce, blaze, broadcast, declare, placard, post, proclaim, promulgate, publicize, publish, sound; betray, blab, give away, leak, let on; inform, squeal, talk; communicate, impart, relate; acknowledge, admit, avow, concede, confess, own; disinter, unearth

phrases spill the beans (about)

near antonyms camouflage, disguise; gild, gloss (over), varnish, whitewash; becloud, bedim, befog, cloud, darken, eclipse, obscure, overcast, overshadow, shade

antonyms cloak, conceal, cover (up), enshroud, hide, mask, shroud, veil

2 to make known (something abstract) through outward signs — see SHOW 2

revealing *adj* clearly conveying a special meaning (as one's mood) — see EXPRESSIVE

revel *n* a time or instance of carefree fun — see FLING 1

revel (in) *vb* to take pleasure in — see ENJOY 1

revelation *n* the act or an instance of making known something previously unknown or concealed ⟨the *revelation* of the movie star's secret marriage by the tabloids⟩ ⟨a new biography of the former president that contains several shocking *revelations*⟩

synonyms disclosure, divulgence, exposure

related words bombshell, surprise; acknowledgment (*also* acknowledgement), admission, avowal, concession, confession

near antonyms concealment, cover-up

reveler *or* **reveller** *n* one who engages in merrymaking especially in honor of a special occasion — see CELEBRANT

reveling *n* joyful or festive activity — see MERRYMAKING

revelry *n* joyful or festive activity — see MERRYMAKING

revenge *n* the act or an instance of paying back an injury with an injury ⟨my *revenge* on the bully who stole my lunch money was the talk of the whole school⟩

synonyms reprisal, requital, retaliation, retribution, vengeance

related words counter, counterattack, counteroffensive; castigation, chastisement, correction; desert(s), discipline, nemesis, penalty, punishment, wrath; amends, compensation, indemnification, indemnity, quittance, recompense, recoupment, redress, remuneration, reparation(s), restitution

near antonyms clemency, grace, leniency, lenity, mercy; forgiveness, pardon, remission

revenge *vb* to punish in kind the wrongdoer responsible for — see AVENGE

revengeful *adj* likely to seek revenge — see VINDICTIVE

revenue *n* an increase usually measured in money that comes from labor, business, or property — see INCOME

reverberant *adj* marked by conspicuously full and rich sounds or tones — see RESONANT

reverberate *vb* to continue or be repeated in a series of reflected sound waves ⟨a room with nothing but hard surfaces will cause the music from your audio system to *reverberate*⟩

synonyms echo, reecho, resonate, resound, sound

near antonyms damp, dampen, deaden, dull, quiet

reverberating *adj* marked by conspicuously full and rich sounds or tones — see RESONANT

revere *vb* to offer honor or respect to (someone) as a divine power — see WORSHIP 1

revered *adj* deserving honor and respect especially by reason of age — see VENERABLE 1

reverence *vb* to offer honor or respect to (someone) as a divine power — see WORSHIP 1

reverend *adj* deserving honor and respect especially by reason of age — see VENERABLE 1

reverend *n* a person specially trained and authorized to conduct religious services in a Christian church — see CLERGYMAN

reverie *also* **revery** *n* the state of being lost in thought ⟨unfortunately, I was deep in *reverie* when the teacher called my name⟩

synonyms daydreaming, study, trance, woolgathering

related words contemplation, meditation, musing; absentmindedness, absorption, abstraction, preoccupation; chimera, conceit, daydream, delusion, dream, fancy, fantasy (*also* phantasy), figment, hallucination, illusion, phantasm, pipe dream, unreality, vision

reversal *n* a change in status for the worse usually temporarily — see REVERSE 1

reverse *n* **1** a change in status for the worse usually temporarily ⟨the loss of my paper route was just the first of my financial *reverses* since the start of the new year⟩

synonyms lapse, reversal, setback

related words disappointment, frustration, letdown; comedown, decline, descent, down, downfall, fall; turnabout, turnaround; recession, regression, retrogression, reversion; relapse; breakdown, collapse, crash, meltdown, ruin, undoing

near antonyms status quo

2 something that is as different as possible from something else — see OPPOSITE

reverse *vb* **1** to change (as an opinion) to the contrary ⟨the principal refused to *reverse* his decision regarding the use of cellular phones⟩

synonyms switch

related words abrogate, overturn, repeal, rescind, revoke, strike (down); countermand, about-face, backtrack, revert

near antonyms maintain, support, uphold

2 to change the position of (an object) so that the opposite side or end is showing ⟨when one side of the cleaning cloth gets dirty, just *reverse* it⟩ ⟨you can *reverse* the jacket for a whole new look⟩

synonyms flip, invert, turn (over)

related words transpose; exchange, interchange, shift, switch; overturn, upset

reversion *n* the act or an instance of going back to an earlier and lower level especially of intelligence or behavior — see REGRESSION

revert *vb* to go back to a previous and usually lower state or level — see REGRESS

review *n* **1** a usually critical look at a past event ⟨a *review* of yesterday's football game gave us a lot of good ideas on how to improve for the next one⟩

synonyms reappraisal, reconsideration, reexamination, retrospect, retrospection

related words recap, recapitulation, rehash

near antonyms preview

THESAURUS

2 a close look at or over someone or something in order to judge condition — see INSPECTION

3 a publication that appears at regular intervals — see JOURNAL

4 an essay evaluating or analyzing something — see CRITICISM

review *vb* **1** to consider again especially with the possibility of change or reversal — see RECONSIDER

2 to look over closely (as for judging quality or condition) — see INSPECT

reviewer *n* a person who makes or expresses a judgment on the quality of offerings in some field of endeavor — see CRITIC 2

revise *n* the act, process, or result of making different — see CHANGE

revise *vb* **1** to make different in some way — see CHANGE 1

2 to prepare for publication by correcting, rewriting, or updating — see EDIT

revision *n* the act, process, or result of making different — see CHANGE

revitalization *n* the act or an instance of bringing something back to life, public attention, or vigorous activity — see REVIVAL

revitalize *vb* **1** to bring back to a former condition or vigor — see RENEW 1

2 to bring back to life, practice, or activity — see REVIVE 1

revival *n* the act or an instance of bringing something back to life, public attention, or vigorous activity ⟨there was a *revival* of interest in the author's classic horror stories after a film version of his best-known story was released⟩

synonyms reanimation, rebirth, regeneration, rejuvenation, renewal, resurgence, resurrection, resuscitation, revitalization

related words renaissance, renascence; reactivation; rally, recovery, recuperation

near antonyms death, expiration, extinction

revive *vb* **1** to bring back to life, practice, or activity ⟨an effort to *revive* the once-common custom of celebrating May 1 as a springtime festival of games and dances⟩

synonyms reanimate, regenerate, rejuvenate, rekindle, renew, resurrect, resuscitate, revitalize

related words reactivate, restart

near antonyms extinguish, quench, suppress

2 to bring back to a former condition or vigor — see RENEW 1

3 to gain consciousness again — see COME TO

revived *adj* made or become fresh in spirits or vigor — see NEW 4

reviving *adj* having a renewing effect on the state of the body or mind — see TONIC

revocation *n* the act of putting an end to something planned or previously agreed to — see CANCELLATION

revoke *vb* to put an end to (something planned or previously agreed to) — see CANCEL 1

revolt *n* open fighting against authority (as one's own government) — see REBELLION

revolt *vb* **1** to cause to feel disgust — see DISGUST

2 to rise up against established authority — see REBEL

revolted *adj* filled with disgust — see SICK 2

revolter *n* a person who rises up against authority — see REBEL

revolting *adj* causing intense displeasure, disgust, or resentment — see OFFENSIVE 1

revolution *n* **1** a rapid turning about on an axis or central point — see SPIN 1

2 open fighting against authority (as one's own government) — see REBELLION

revolutionary *adj* **1** being very far from the center of public opinion — see EXTREME 2

2 taking part in a rebellion — see REBELLIOUS 1

revolutionary *n* **1** a person who favors rapid and sweeping changes especially in laws and methods of government — see RADICAL

2 a person who rises up against authority — see REBEL

revolutionist *adj* being very far from the center of public opinion — see EXTREME 2

revolutionist *n* **1** a person who favors rapid and sweeping changes especially in laws and methods of government — see RADICAL

2 a person who rises up against authority — see REBEL

revolutionizer *n* a person who rises up against authority — see REBEL

revolve *vb* **1** to move (something) in a curved or circular path on or as if on an axis — see TURN 1

2 to move in circles around an axis or center — see SPIN 1

revulsion *n* **1** a dislike so strong as to cause stomach upset or queasiness — see DISGUST

2 an act of moving away especially from something difficult, dangerous, or disagreeable — see RETREAT 1

reward *n* something offered or given in return for a service performed ⟨there was a *reward* of twenty dollars for the return of her missing cat⟩

synonyms bounty, price

related words bonus, lagniappe, premium; bonanza, jackpot, treasure trove; award, decoration, distinction, honor, plume, premium, prize; gratuity, tip; desert(s), wages

reward *vb* to give something as a token of gratitude or admiration for a service or achievement ⟨the firefighters were *rewarded* by the city for their heroic actions with vacations⟩

synonyms award

related words cite, decorate, honor, remember; compensate, pay, recompense, requite; reimburse, repay; acclaim, applaud, commend, compliment, hail, praise, salute

rewarding *adj* making one feel good inside — see HEARTWARMING

reweigh *vb* to consider again especially with the possibility of change or reversal — see RECONSIDER

reword *vb* to express something (as a text or statement) in different words — see PARAPHRASE

rewording *n* an instance of expressing something in different words — see PARAPHRASE

rework *vb* **1** to make different in some way — see CHANGE 1

2 to prepare for publication by correcting, rewriting, or updating — see EDIT

reworking *n* the act, process, or result of making different — see CHANGE

rhapsodic *also* **rhapsodical** *adj* experiencing or marked by overwhelming usually pleasurable emotion — see ECSTATIC

rhapsodically *adv* in an enthusiastic manner — see SKY-HIGH

rhapsodize *vb* to make an exaggerated display of affection or enthusiasm — see GUSH 2

rhapsody *n* a state of overwhelming usually pleasurable emotion — see ECSTASY

rhetoric *n* **1** language that is impressive-sounding but not meaningful or sincere ⟨the mayor's promise to fight drugs was just *rhetoric*, since there was no money in the city budget for a drug program⟩
synonyms bombast, gas, grandiloquence, hot air, oratory, wind
related words claptrap, drivel, gibberish, hogwash, humbug, jabberwocky, jazz, moonshine, nonsense; affectedness, floweriness, grandiosity, loftiness, pomposity, pretension, pretentiousness; verboseness, verbosity, windiness, wordiness
2 the art or power of speaking or writing in a forceful and convincing way — see ELOQUENCE

rhetorical *adj* marked by the use of impressive-sounding but mostly meaningless words and phrases ⟨an essay on civic duty that was mostly *rhetorical*, full of flowery quotations but providing nothing helpful⟩
synonyms bombastic, gaseous, gassy, grandiloquent, oratorical, windy
related words elevated, florid, flowery, grandiose, highfalutin, high-flown, high-sounding, inflated, lofty, pompous, pretentious, stilted; overdone, verbose, wordy
near antonyms eloquent, well-spoken; bald, direct, matter-of-fact, plain, plainspoken, simple, stark, straightforward, unadorned, unaffected, unpretentious

rhythm *n* the recurrent pattern formed by a series of sounds having a regular rise and fall in intensity ⟨the steady *rhythm* of the rain falling on the roof⟩
synonyms beat, cadence, measure, meter
related words accent, accentuation, emphasis, stress; drum, throb; lilt, movement, sway; hexameter, pentameter, tetrameter, trimeter

rhythmic *or* **rhythmical** *adj* marked by or occurring with a noticeable regularity in the rise and fall of sound ⟨lulled to sleep by the *rhythmic* sound of her mother's voice reading the Bible⟩
synonyms cadenced, measured, metric, metrical
related words even, regular, steady, uniform; lilting, musical, swaying
antonyms unmeasured, unrhythmic

riata *n* a rope or long leather thong with a noose used especially for catching livestock — see LASSO

rib *vb* to make fun of in a good-natured way — see TEASE 1

ribald *adj* **1** depicting or referring to sexual matters in a way that is unacceptable in polite society — see OBSCENE 1
2 hinting at or intended to call to mind matters regarded as indecent — see SUGGESTIVE 1

ribaldry *n* the quality or state of being obscene — see OBSCENITY 1

ribbing *adj* marked by or expressive of mild or good-natured teasing — see QUIZZICAL

ribbon *n* a long narrow piece of material — see STRIP

rich *adj* **1** having goods, property, or money in abundance ⟨Tanya's dad works as chauffeur for the *richest* man in town, a big oil baron⟩
synonyms affluent, flush, loaded, moneyed (*or* monied), opulent, wealthy, well-heeled, well-off, well-to-do
related words comfortable, propertied, prosperous, successful; flourishing, prospering, thriving; advantaged, blessed, privileged
near antonyms deprived, disadvantaged, underprivileged; bankrupt, bankrupted, beggared, broke, indebted, insolvent, pauperized, ruined, stone-broke; depressed, pinched, reduced, straitened; low, short
antonyms destitute, impecunious, impoverished, indigent, needy, penniless, penurious, poor, poverty-stricken
2 containing much seasoning, fat, or sugar ⟨stay away from *rich* foods before you sing tonight⟩
synonyms heavy
related words buttery, fat, fatty, greasy, oily; caloric, calorific, fattening; cloying, filling, overfilling, satiating, sating; spicy, sugary; creamy, sauced
near antonyms natural, plain, simple; unseasoned; diet, nonfattening, slimming; nonfat
antonyms light
3 having an abundance of some characteristic quality (as flavor) — see FULL-BODIED
4 producing abundantly — see FERTILE

riches *n* the total of one's money and property — see WEALTH 1

richly *adv* in a luxurious manner — see HIGH

richness *n* the amusing quality or element in something — see HUMOR 1

rick *n* a quantity of things thrown or stacked on one another — see ¹PILE 1

ricochet *vb* to strike and fly off at an angle — see GLANCE 1

rid *vb* to set (a person or thing) free of something that encumbers ⟨worked two jobs to *rid* himself of debt⟩
synonyms clear, disburden, disencumber, free, relieve, unburden
related words discharge, emancipate, enfranchise, liberate, loose, loosen, manumit, release, spring, unbind, uncage, unchain, unfetter; bail (out), deliver, redeem, rescue; disengage, disentangle, extricate
near antonyms bog (down), fetter, restrain, shackle, subject, weigh (down), weight (down)
antonyms burden, encumber, saddle

riddance *n* the getting rid of whatever is unwanted or useless — see DISPOSAL 1

riddle *n* something hard to understand or explain — see MYSTERY

riddle *vb* to find an answer for through reasoning — see SOLVE

ride *n* a means of getting to a destination in a vehicle driven by another ⟨Laurie sometimes gets a *ride* to school from her neighbor⟩
synonyms lift, transportation
related words drive, spin, turn; joyride; conveyance, passage, transit, transport

ride *vb* **1** to attack repeatedly with mean put-downs or insults — see TEASE 2
2 to make fun of in a good-natured way — see TEASE 1
3 to rest or move along the surface of a liquid or in the air — see FLOAT

ride (out) *vb* to come safely through — see SURVIVE 1

ridge *n* the line formed when two sloping surfaces come together along their topmost edge ⟨pigeons roosting along the *ridge* of the roof⟩
synonyms crest
related words divide; backbone, chine, ridgepole,

THESAURUS

spine; eminence, peak, prominence, promontory, rise

ridicule *n* the making of unkind jokes as a way of showing one's scorn for someone or something ⟨the early efforts by the suffragists to obtain voting rights for women were met with *ridicule*⟩
synonyms derision, mockery
related words contempt, disdain, scorn; belittlement, deprecation, disparagement; insult, putdown; laughter, snickering; burlesque, caricature, mimicry, satire
near antonyms applause, approval, commendation, praise

ridicule *vb* to make (someone or something) the object of unkind laughter ⟨the term "big bang theory" was originally coined to *ridicule* the belief that the universe was created by a giant explosion⟩
synonyms deride, gibe (*or* jibe), jeer, laugh (at), mock, scout
related words scoff (at), scorn, sneer (at); badmouth, belittle, decry, disparage, pooh-pooh (*also* pooh), put down; chaff, jive, josh, kid, quiz, rally, razz, rib, ride, tease; bait, bug, harass, harry, hassle, heckle, needle, pester, target, taunt, torment; ape, burlesque, caricature, imitate, lampoon, mimic, parody, parrot, satirize, take off (on), travesty
phrases make fun of, poke fun at
near antonyms applaud, approve, commend, endorse (*also* indorse), sanction

ridiculer *n* a person who causes repeated emotional pain, distress, or annoyance to another — see TORMENTOR

ridiculous *adj* **1** so foolish or pointless as to be worthy of scornful laughter ⟨a movie thriller with such a *ridiculous* plot that it gets only guffaws from audiences⟩
synonyms absurd, comical, derisive, derisory, farcical, laughable, ludicrous, preposterous, risible, silly
related words asinine, brainless, dumb, fatuous, foolish, half-witted, harebrained, idiotic, imbecilic, inane, jerky, moronic, nonsensical, simpleminded, stupid, unwise, weak-minded, witless; balmy, cockeyed, crazy, cuckoo, daffy, daft, dotty, insane, kooky, loony (*also* looney), lunatic, mad, nutty, screwball, senseless, wacky; fantastic, farfetched, inconceivable, incredible, unbelievable, unreal, unreasonable
near antonyms earnest, serious, solemn; believable, conceivable, credible, logical, rational, realistic, reasonable, sensible
2 causing or intended to cause laughter — see FUNNY 1

rife *adj* possessing or covered with great numbers or amounts of something specified ⟨our school is *rife* with rumors about the incoming principal⟩
synonyms abounding, flush, fraught, replete, swarming, teeming, thick, thronging
related words brimming, bulging, bursting, chock-full (*or* chockful), crammed, crowded, fat, filled, full, jammed, jam-packed, loaded, packed, saturated, stuffed; clogged, congested, overcrowded, overfilled, overflowing, overfull, overloaded, overstuffed, surfeited; alive, animated, astir, bustling, busy, buzzing, humming, lively
near antonyms bare, barren, blank, devoid, empty, stark, vacant, void; depleted, drained, exhausted; deficient, incomplete, insufficient, short

riffraff *n* **1** discarded or useless material — see GARBAGE
2 people looked down upon as ignorant and of the lowest class — see RABBLE

rifle *vb* to look through (as a place) carefully or thoroughly in an effort to find or discover something — see SEARCH 1

rift *n* **1** an irregular usually narrow break in a surface created by pressure — see CRACK 1
2 an open space in a barrier (as a wall or hedge) — see GAP 1

rig *n* a horse-drawn wheeled vehicle for carrying passengers — see CARRIAGE 1

rig *vb* to provide (someone) with what is needed for a task or activity — see FURNISH 1

rig (out) *vb* to outfit with clothes and especially fine or special clothes — see CLOTHE 1

right *adj* **1** following an original exactly — see FAITHFUL 2
2 being exactly as appears or as claimed — see AUTHENTIC 1
3 being in agreement with the truth or a fact or a standard — see CORRECT 1
4 being what is called for by accepted standards of right and wrong — see JUST 1
5 conforming to a high standard of morality or virtue — see GOOD 2
6 free from irregularities (as curves, bends, or angles) in course — see STRAIGHT 1
7 having full use of one's mind and control over one's actions — see SANE
8 meeting the requirements of a purpose or situation — see FIT 1

right *adv* **1** as stated or indicated without the slightest difference — see EXACTLY 1
2 in a direct line or course — see DIRECTLY 1
3 to a great degree — see VERY 1

right *n* **1** something to which one has a just claim ⟨everyone has the *right* to life, liberty, and the pursuit of happiness⟩
synonyms appanage, birthright, prerogative
related words due, entitlement, perquisite, privilege
2 an entitlement to something — see CLAIM 1
3 the act or practice of giving to others what is their due — see JUSTICE 1

right away *adv* without delay — see IMMEDIATELY

righteous *adj* **1** conforming to a high standard of morality or virtue — see GOOD 2
2 following the accepted rules of moral conduct — see HONORABLE 1

righteously *adv* with purity of thought and deed — see PURELY

righteousness *n* **1** conduct that conforms to an accepted standard of right and wrong — see MORALITY 1
2 faithfulness to high moral standards — see HONOR 1

rightful *adj* being what is called for by accepted standards of right and wrong — see JUST 1

rightist *n* a person whose political beliefs are centered on tradition and keeping things the way they are — see CONSERVATIVE

rightly *adv* in a manner suitable for the occasion or purpose — see PROPERLY

right-minded *adj* conforming to a high standard of morality or virtue — see GOOD 2

rightness *n* the quality or state of being especially suitable or fitting — see APPROPRIATENESS

right now *adv* **1** at the present time — see NOW 1
2 without delay — see IMMEDIATELY

right–of–way *n* the right to one's attention before other things considered less important — see PRIORITY

rigid *adj* **1** not allowing for any exceptions or loosening of standards ⟨*rigid* enforcement of drug laws⟩
synonyms exacting, inflexible, rigorous, strict, stringent, uncompromising
related words close, conscientious, scrupulous, undeviating; adamant, adamantine, determined, dogged, firm, relentless, resolved, single-minded, steadfast, stubborn, tenacious, unbending, unflinching; immovable, implacable, unrelenting, unyielding; austere, demanding, flinty, grim, hard, hardened, hardhearted, harsh, ironbound, severe, stern, tough
near antonyms acquiescent, compliant, compromising, pliable, pliant, relenting, yielding; easy, easygoing, gentle, indulgent, kindly, lenient, merciful, mild, pampering, soft, spoiling, tolerant
antonyms flexible, lax, loose, relaxed
2 given to exacting standards of discipline and self-restraint — see SEVERE 1
3 having a consistency that does not easily yield to pressure — see FIRM 2
4 incapable of or highly resistant to bending — see STIFF 1
5 sticking to an opinion, purpose, or course of action in spite of reason, arguments, or persuasion — see OBSTINATE
6 stretched with little or no give — see TAUT

rigidity *n* the quality or state of being demanding or unyielding (as in discipline or criticism) — see SEVERITY

rigidly *adv* without any relaxation of standards or precision — see STRICTLY

rigidness *n* the quality or state of being demanding or unyielding (as in discipline or criticism) — see SEVERITY

rigmarole *n* unintelligible or meaningless talk — see GIBBERISH

rigor *n* something that is a cause for suffering or special effort especially in the attainment of a goal — see DIFFICULTY 1

rigorous *adj* **1** given to exacting standards of discipline and self-restraint — see SEVERE 1
2 meeting the highest standard of accuracy — see PRECISE 1
3 not allowing for any exceptions or loosening of standards — see RIGID 1

rigorously *adv* without any relaxation of standards or precision — see STRICTLY

rigorousness *n* **1** the quality or state of being demanding or unyielding (as in discipline or criticism) — see SEVERITY
2 the quality or state of being very accurate — see PRECISION

rile *vb* to disturb the peace of mind of (someone) especially by repeated disagreeable acts — see IRRITATE 1

rile *vb* to make angry — see ANGER

riled *adj* feeling or showing anger — see ANGRY

riling *adj* causing annoyance — see ANNOYING

rill *n* a natural body of running water smaller than a river — see CREEK 1

rim *n* the line or relatively narrow space that marks the outer limit of something — see BORDER 1

rim *vb* to serve as a border for — see BORDER

rime *n* a covering of tiny ice crystals on a cold surface — see FROST

rime *vb* to cover with a hardened layer — see ENCRUST

ring *n* **1** a group involved in secret or criminal activities ⟨a *ring* of counterfeiters passing phony $20 bills⟩
synonyms cabal, conspiracy, gang, Mafia, mob, syndicate
related words circle, clan, clique, coterie, crowd; junta, oligarchy
2 a circular strip ⟨a metal *ring* encircled the barrel⟩
synonyms band, circle, eye, hoop, loop, round
related words belt, cincture, collar, girdle; wreath; coil, spiral
3 a communication by telephone — see CALL 3
4 a group of people sharing a common interest and relating together socially — see GANG 2
5 something with a perfectly round circumference — see CIRCLE 1

ring *vb* **1** to make the clear sound heard when metal vibrates ⟨I didn't hear the doorbell *ring*⟩
synonyms chime, knell, peal, toll
related words clang, clank, ding, jangle, jingle, ping, tinkle; resound, reverberate
2 to form a circle around — see SURROUND
3 to pass completely around — see ENCIRCLE 1

ring (up) *vb, chiefly British* to make a telephone call to — see CALL 2

ringer *n* something or someone that strongly resembles another — see IMAGE 1

ringing *adj* **1** marked by a high volume of sound — see LOUD 1
2 marked by conspicuously full and rich sounds or tones — see RESONANT

ringlet *n* a length of hair that forms a loop or series of loops — see CURL

rinse *vb* to pour liquid over or through in order to cleanse — see FLUSH 1

riot *n* someone or something that is very funny — see SCREAM

riotous *adj* **1** causing or intended to cause laughter — see FUNNY 1
2 pouring forth in great amounts — see PROFUSE

rip *n* a long deep cut — see GASH

rip *vb* **1** to cause (something) to separate into jagged pieces by violently pulling at it — see TEAR 1
2 to penetrate with a sharp edge (as a knife) — see CUT 1
3 to proceed or move quickly — see HURRY 2
4 to separate or remove by forceful pulling — see TEAR 2

ripe *adj* fully grown or developed — see MATURE 1

ripen *vb* to become mature — see MATURE

ripened *adj* fully grown or developed — see MATURE 1

ripening *n* the process of becoming mature — see MATURATION

rip–off *n* an instance of theft — see THEFT 2

rip off *vb* **1** to remove valuables from (a place) unlawfully — see ROB
2 to take (something) without right and with an intent to keep — see STEAL 1

riposte *n* a quick witty response — see RETORT 1

ripple *vb* to flow in a broken irregular stream — see GURGLE

rip–roaring *adj* causing great emotional or mental stimulation — see EXCITING 1

THESAURUS

rise *n* **1** a raising or a state of being raised to a higher rank or position — see ADVANCEMENT 1

2 an area of high ground — see HEIGHT 4

3 an upward slope — see ASCENT 2

4 something added (as by growth) — see IN-CREASE 1

5 the act or an instance of rising or climbing up — see ASCENT 1

rise *vb* **1** to become greater in extent, volume, amount, or number — see INCREASE 2

2 to leave one's bed — see ARISE 1

3 to move or extend upward — see ASCEND

risible *adj* **1** causing or intended to cause laughter — see FUNNY 1

2 so foolish or pointless as to be worthy of scornful laughter — see RIDICULOUS 1

rising *n* the act or an instance of rising or climbing up — see ASCENT 1

risk *n* **1** something that may cause injury or harm — see DANGER 2

2 the state of not being protected from injury, harm, or evil — see DANGER 1

risk *vb* **1** to take a chance on ⟨Colette didn't want to *risk* running out of film on her trip, so she brought along a dozen rolls⟩

synonyms chance, gamble, (on), hazard, venture

related words brave, challenge, dare, defy, face; compromise, endanger, imperil, jeopardize, menace; expose, subject; bet (on), wager

2 to place in danger — see ENDANGER

risky *adj* involving potential loss or injury — see DANGEROUS

rite *n* an oft-repeated action or series of actions performed in accordance with tradition or a set of rules ⟨the annual summer *rite* of loading up the car for the big family vacation⟩

synonyms ceremonial, ceremony, form, formality, observance, ritual, solemnity

related words amenities, civility, decorum, etiquette, graces, proprieties; convention, custom, habit, manners, mores, practice (*also* practise), standard, tradition, way; celebration, service

ritual *n* an oft-repeated action or series of actions performed in accordance with tradition or a set of rules — see RITE

rival *n* **1** one that is equal to another in status, achievement, or value — see EQUAL

2 one that takes a position opposite another in a competition or conflict — see OPPONENT 1

3 one who strives for the same thing as another — see COMPETITOR

rivalry *n* an earnest effort for superiority or victory over another — see CONTEST 1

rive *vb* to cause (something) to separate into jagged pieces by violently pulling at it — see TEAR 1

rivet *vb* to fix (as one's attention) steadily toward a central objective — see CONCENTRATE 2

riveting *adj* holding the attention or provoking interest — see INTERESTING

rivulet *n* a natural body of running water smaller than a river — see CREEK 1

road *n* **1** a passage cleared for public vehicular travel — see WAY 1

2 a roadway overlaid with parallel steel rails over which trains travel — see RAILROAD

roadhouse *n* a bar or restaurant offering special nighttime entertainment (as music, dancing, or comedy acts) — see NIGHTCLUB

roadway *n* a passage cleared for public vehicular travel — see WAY 1

roam *vb* to move about from place to place aimlessly — see WANDER

roamer *n* a person who roams about without a fixed route or destination — see NOMAD

roaming *adj* traveling from place to place — see ITINERANT

roar *n* **1** a violent shouting — see CLAMOR 1

2 loud, confused, and usually unharmonious sound — see NOISE 1

roar *vb* to make a long loud deep noise or cry ⟨its engine *roared* as the car sped away⟩

synonyms bellow, boom, growl, thunder

related words grumble, roll, rumble; blare, blast, peal, scream, screech, shriek, squall; cry, holler, hoot, shout, whoop, yell; caterwaul, howl, wail, yowl

near antonyms mumble, murmur, mutter, whisper; squeak, whimper

roaring *adj* **1** marked by a high volume of sound — see LOUD 1

2 marked by vigorous growth and well-being especially economically — see PROSPEROUS 1

roast *vb* to make fun of in a good-natured way — see TEASE 1

roasting *adj* having a notably high temperature — see HOT 1

rob *vb* to remove valuables from (a place) unlawfully ⟨in jail for *robbing* a bank⟩

synonyms burglarize, rip off, steal (from)

related words despoil, loot, pillage, plunder, sack, spoil, strip; bleed, break in, cheat, chisel, cozen, defraud, exploit, fleece, gyp, mulct, rook, squeeze, stick, swindle; hold up, mug, stick up

robber *n* one who steals — see THIEF

robbery *n* the unlawful taking and carrying away of property without the consent of its owner — see THEFT 1

robe *vb* to outfit with clothes and especially fine or special clothes — see CLOTHE 1

robotic *adj* designed to replace or decrease human labor and especially physical labor — see LABOR-SAVING

robust *adj* **1** enjoying health and vigor — see HEALTHY 1

2 having active strength of body or mind — see VIGOROUS 1

3 having an abundance of some characteristic quality (as flavor) — see FULL-BODIED

4 not showing weakness or uncertainty — see FIRM 1

robustness *n* **1** the condition of being sound in body — see HEALTH

2 the quality or state of having abundant or intense activity — see VITALITY 1

rock *vb* **1** to make a series of unsteady side-to-side motions ⟨the boat was *rocking* so much that Rosa felt seasick⟩

synonyms careen, lurch, pitch, roll, seesaw, sway, toss, wobble

related words blunder, dodder, falter, flounder, halt, hitch, hobble, jerk, reel, stagger, stumble, teeter, toddle, totter, tumble, waddle, weave; oscillate, undulate, wag, waggle

2 to swing unsteadily back and forth or from side to side — see TEETER 1

rock bottom *n* the lowest part, place, or point — see BOTTOM 3

rocket *vb* **1** to proceed or move quickly — see HURRY 2

2 to rise abruptly and rapidly — see SKYROCKET

rod *n* **1** a heavy rigid stick used as a weapon or for punishment — see CLUB 1
2 a straight piece (as of wood or metal) that is longer than it is wide — see BAR 1

rogue *n* **1** a mean, evil, or unprincipled person — see VILLAIN
2 an appealingly mischievous person — see SCAMP 1

roguish *adj* tending to or exhibiting reckless playfulness — see MISCHIEVOUS 1

roguishness *n* playful, reckless behavior that is not intended to cause serious harm — see MISCHIEF 1

roil *vb* **1** to be in a state of violent rolling motion — see SEETHE 1
2 to make angry — see ANGER

roiled *adj* **1** feeling or showing anger — see ANGRY
2 having visible particles in liquid suspension — see CLOUDY 1

roisterer *n* one who engages in merrymaking especially in honor of a special occasion — see CELEBRANT

role *also* **rôle** *n* the action for which a person or thing is specially fitted or used or for which a thing exists ⟨in science class we're studying the *role* of sunlight in the body's production of vitamin D⟩
synonyms capacity, function, job, part, place, position, purpose, task, work
related words affair, business, concern, involvement, participation; niche, office, post, situation; calling, occupation, pursuit, vocation; activity, assignment, charge, commission, duty, mission, responsibility, service, use

roll *n* **1** a rapid turning about on an axis or central point — see SPIN 1
2 a record of a series of items (as names or titles) usually arranged according to some system — see ¹LIST

roll *vb* **1** to form into a round compact mass — see WAD
2 to make a low heavy rolling sound — see RUMBLE
3 to make a series of unsteady side-to-side motions — see ROCK 1
4 to move (something) in a curved or circular path on or as if on an axis — see TURN 1
5 to move in a stream — see FLOW 1
6 to move in circles around an axis or center — see SPIN 1
7 to move or proceed smoothly and readily — see FLOW 2

rollick *n* a time or instance of carefree fun — see FLING 1

rollick *vb* **1** to engage in activity for amusement — see PLAY 1
2 to play and run about happily — see FROLIC 1

rollicking *adj* given to good-natured joking or teasing — see PLAYFUL

rollicking *n* activity engaged in to amuse oneself — see PLAY 1

roly–poly *adj* having an excess of body fat — see FAT 1

romance *n* a brief romantic relationship — see AFFAIR

romantic *adj* excitingly or mysteriously unusual — see EXOTIC

romantic *n* one whose conduct is guided more by the image of perfection than by the real world — see IDEALIST

romanticist *n* one whose conduct is guided more by the image of perfection than by the real world — see IDEALIST

romanticize *vb* to represent or think of as better than reality — see IDEALIZE

romp *n* a time or instance of carefree fun — see FLING 1

romp *vb* to play and run about happily — see FROLIC 1

roof *n* **1** a raised covering over something for decoration or protection — see CANOPY
2 the place where one lives — see HOME 1

roof *vb* to provide with living quarters or shelter — see HOUSE 1

rook *vb* to rob by the use of trickery or threats — see FLEECE

rookie *n* a person who is just starting out in a field of activity — see BEGINNER

room *n* **1** an extent or area available for or used up by some activity or thing ⟨need more *room* to do a cartwheel⟩ ⟨made *room* for him on the bench⟩
synonyms elbowroom, place, space, way
related words capacity, range, scope; clearance, freedom, latitude, leeway, play
2 an area within a building that has been set apart from surrounding space by a wall ⟨finally had a *room* to himself when his brother went off to college⟩
synonyms apartment, cell, chamber, closet
related words accommodation, berth, booth, cabin, compartment, cubicle
3 a favorable combination of circumstances, time, and place — see OPPORTUNITY

roomer *n* one who rents a room or apartment in another's house — see TENANT

roomy *adj* more than adequate or average in capacity — see SPACIOUS

roost *vb* **1** to come to rest after descending from the air — see ALIGHT
2 to establish or place comfortably or snugly — see ENSCONCE 1

root *vb* to set solidly in or as if in surrounding matter — see ENTRENCH

root (out) *vb* **1** to destroy all traces of — see ANNIHILATE 1
2 to draw out by force or with effort — see EXTRACT

rooted *adj* firmly established over time — see INVETERATE 1

rope *n* a length of braided, flexible material that is used for tying or connecting things — see CORD

ropy *adj* being of a consistency that resists flow — see THICK 2

roquelaure *n* a sleeveless garment worn so as to hang over the shoulders, arms, and back — see ¹CAPE

rose–colored *adj* having qualities which inspire hope — see HOPEFUL 1

roster *n* a record of a series of items (as names or titles) usually arranged according to some system — see ¹LIST

rostrum *n* a level usually raised surface — see PLATFORM

rosy *adj* **1** having a healthy reddish skin tone — see RUDDY
2 having qualities which inspire hope — see HOPEFUL 1

rot *n* **1** language, behavior, or ideas that are absurd and contrary to good sense — see NONSENSE 1

2 the process by which dead organic matter separates into simpler substances — see CORRUPTION 1

3 unintelligible or meaningless talk — see GIBBERISH

rot *vb* **1** to become worse or of less value — see DETERIORATE

2 to go through decomposition — see DECAY 1

rotate *vb* **1** to move (something) in a curved or circular path on or as if on an axis — see TURN 1

2 to move in circles around an axis or center — see SPIN 1

rotation *n* a rapid turning about on an axis or central point — see SPIN 1

rote *n* **1** an established and often automatic or monotonous series of actions followed when engaging in some activity — see ROUTINE 1

2 the body of knowledge that has been retained in one's mind or the use of it — see HEART 2

rotten *adj* **1** having undergone organic breakdown ⟨*rotten*, smelly meat that should have been refrigerated⟩

synonyms addled, bad, corrupted, decayed, decomposed, putrefied, putrid, spoiled

related words curdled, fermented, rancid, sour, soured, turned; contaminated, defiled, fouled, polluted, tainted; corroded, crumbled, degenerated, deteriorated, disintegrated; decaying, decomposing, moldering, moldy, putrefying, rotting

near antonyms fresh, good, preserved; pristine, uncontaminated, undefiled, unpolluted, unspoiled, untainted, untouched

2 falling short of a standard — see BAD 1

3 not conforming to a high moral standard; morally unacceptable — see BAD 2

4 not giving pleasure to the mind or senses — see UNPLEASANT

5 extremely unsatisfactory — see WRETCHED 1

6 of low quality — see CHEAP 2

rotund *adj* having an excess of body fat — see FAT 1

rotundity *n* the condition of having an excess of body fat — see CORPULENCE

rough *adj* **1** covered with or as if with hair — see HAIRY 1

2 marked by bursts of destructive force or intense activity — see VIOLENT 1

3 marked by wet and windy conditions — see FOUL 1

4 not having a level or smooth surface — see UNEVEN 1

5 requiring considerable physical or mental effort — see HARD 2

6 difficult to endure — see HARSH 1

7 harsh and threatening in manner or appearance — see GRIM 1

8 hastily or roughly constructed — see RUDE 1

9 lacking in refinement or good taste — see COARSE 2

10 made of or resembling hair — see HAIRY 2

11 marked by a series of sharp quick motions — see JERKY 1

rough (up) *vb* to abuse physically — see MANHANDLE 1

roughened *adj* not having a level or smooth surface — see UNEVEN 1

roughhewn *adj* **1** hastily or roughly constructed — see RUDE 1

2 lacking in refinement or good taste — see COARSE 2

3 lacking social grace and assurance — see AWKWARD 1

roughhouse *n* wildly playful or mischievous behavior — see HORSEPLAY

roughhousing *n* wildly playful or mischievous behavior — see HORSEPLAY

roughly *adv* in a manner so as to cause loss or suffering — see HARDLY 1

roughneck *n* a violent, brutal person who is often a member of an organized gang — see HOODLUM

roughness *n* **1** a harsh or sharp quality — see EDGE 1

2 the quality or state of lacking refinement or good taste — see VULGARITY 1

round *adj* **1** having every part of the surface the same distance from the center ⟨*round* golf balls⟩ ⟨the earth is not perfectly *round*⟩

synonyms global, spherical

related words annular, circular, disklike (*or* disclike), ringlike; curved, looped, spiral; balled, rotund, rounded, roundish; elliptic (*or* elliptical), oval, ovate, ovoid

2 having an excess of body fat — see FAT 1

3 marked by conspicuously full and rich sounds or tones — see RESONANT

4 being neither more nor less than a certain amount, number, or extent — see EVEN 1

round *adv* **1** from beginning to end — see THROUGH 1

2 on all sides or in every direction — see AROUND 1

3 toward the opposite direction — see AROUND 2

round *n* **1** a circular strip — see RING 2

2 a series of events or actions that repeat themselves regularly and in the same order — see CYCLE 1

3 something with a perfectly round circumference — see CIRCLE 1

round *prep* in random positions within the boundaries of — see AROUND 2

round *vb* **1** to form into a round compact mass — see WAD

2 to pass completely around — see ENCIRCLE 1

3 to turn away from a straight line or course — see CURVE 1

round (off *or* out) *vb* **1** to bring (an event) to a natural or appropriate stopping point — see CLOSE 3

2 to serve as a completing element to — see COMPLEMENT

roundabout *adj* not straightforward or direct — see INDIRECT

roundly *adv* with attention to all aspects or details — see THOROUGHLY 1

roundtable *n* **1** a coming together of a number of persons for a specified purpose — see MEETING 1

2 a meeting featuring a group discussion — see FORUM

roundup *n* a short statement of the main points — see SUMMARY

round up *vb* to bring together in one body or place — see GATHER 1

rouse *vb* **1** to cause to stop sleeping — see WAKE 1

2 to cease to be asleep — see WAKE 2

rousing *adj* causing great emotional or mental stimulation — see EXCITING 1

rout *n* failure to win a contest — see DEFEAT 1

rout *vb* **1** to achieve a victory over — see BEAT 2

2 to defeat by a large margin — see WHIP 2

3 to drive or force out — see EJECT 1

route *n* **1** a passage cleared for public vehicular travel — see WAY 1

2 an established course for traveling from one place to another — see PASSAGE 1

3 the direction along which something or someone moves — see PATH 1

route *vb* to point out the way for (someone) especially from a position in front — see LEAD 1

routine *adj* **1** being of the type that is encountered in the normal course of events — see ORDINARY 1

2 following or agreeing with established form, custom, or rules — see FORMAL 1

3 often observed or encountered — see COMMON 1

routine *n* **1** an established and often automatic or monotonous series of actions followed when engaging in some activity ⟨part of my morning *routine* is drinking a cup of hot chocolate while waiting for the bus⟩

synonyms groove, pattern, rote, rut, treadmill

related words custom, fashion, habit, practice (*also* practise), trick, wont; approach, manner, method, procedure, strategy, style, tack, way; design, plan, program, scheme; convention, policy, tradition

2 something done over and over in order to develop skill — see EXERCISE 2

rove *vb* to move about from place to place aimlessly — see WANDER

rover *n* **1** a person who roams about without a fixed route or destination — see NOMAD

2 someone who engages in robbery of ships at sea — see PIRATE

roving *adj* traveling from place to place — see ITINERANT

row *n* **1** a series of people or things arranged side by side ⟨stood in a *row* to have their picture taken⟩ ⟨three *rows* of eight jelly beans equals 24 jelly beans⟩

synonyms bank, rank

related words chain, column, cue, file, line, procession, queue, string, train; echelon, tier; array, sequence

2 a passage cleared for public vehicular travel — see WAY 1

3 a rough and often noisy fight usually involving several people — see BRAWL 1

4 a state of noisy, confused activity — see COMMOTION

5 an often noisy or angry expression of differing opinions — see ARGUMENT 1

¹row *vb* to move a boat by means of oars ⟨*rowed* around the lake⟩

synonyms oar, paddle, scull

related words canoe; pole, punt

²row *vb* to express different opinions about something often angrily — see ARGUE 2

rowdy *adj* being rough or noisy in a high-spirited way — see BOISTEROUS

rowdy *n* a violent, brutal person who is often a member of an organized gang — see HOODLUM

rower *n* a person who drives a boat forward by means of oars — see OARSMAN

royal *adj* **1** fit for or worthy of a royal ruler — see MONARCHICAL

2 large and impressive in size, grandeur, extent, or conception — see GRAND 1

rub *vb* **1** to damage or diminish by continued friction — see ABRADE 1

2 to make smooth by friction — see GRIND 1

3 to make smooth or glossy usually by repeatedly applying surface pressure — see POLISH

rubbed *adj* having a shiny surface or finish — see GLOSSY

rubberlike *adj* able to revert to original size and shape after being stretched, squeezed, or twisted — see ELASTIC 1

rubberneck *vb* to look long and hard in wonder or surprise — see GAPE

rubbery *adj* able to revert to original size and shape after being stretched, squeezed, or twisted — see ELASTIC 1

rubbish *n* discarded or useless material — see GARBAGE

rubbishy *adj* of low quality — see CHEAP 2

rubble *n* the portion or bits of something left over or behind after it has been destroyed — see REMAINS 1

rubicund *adj* having a healthy reddish skin tone — see RUDDY

rub out *vb* to destroy all traces of — see ANNIHILATE 1

rubric *n* a word or series of words often in larger letters placed at the beginning of a passage or at the top of a page in order to introduce or categorize — see HEADING

rucksack *n* a soft-sided case designed for carrying belongings especially on the back — see PACK 1

ruckus *n* **1** a rough and often noisy fight usually involving several people — see BRAWL 1

2 a state of noisy, confused activity — see COMMOTION

ruction *n* **1** a rough and often noisy fight usually involving several people — see BRAWL 1

2 a state of noisy, confused activity — see COMMOTION

ruddy *adj* having a healthy reddish skin tone ⟨his *ruddy* complexion runs in the family⟩

synonyms blooming, florid, flush, glowing, rosy, rubicund, sanguine

related words bronzed, brown, suntanned, tanned; flushed, pink, pinkish, warm; cherubic

near antonyms ashen, ashy, pale, pallid, pasty, sallow, wan, waxen, waxy; blanched, white, whitened; anemic, peaked, sick, sickly; bloodless, cadaverous, deathlike

rude *adj* **1** hastily or roughly constructed ⟨a *rude* shelter built from unfinished logs by some forgotten pioneer⟩

synonyms artless, clumsy, crude, rough, rough-hewn, unrefined

related words defective, faulty, flawed, imperfect; imprecise, inexact; inartistic, undressed, unfinished, unpolished, unworked; amateur, amateurish, inexpert, unprofessional, unskilled, unskillful; primitive, rudimentary

near antonyms faultless, finished, meticulous, perfected, polished, well-done; adept, adroit, dexterous (*also* dextrous), expert, masterful, masterly, neat, practiced (*or* practised), skillful, workmanlike; artful, artistic, sophisticated; exact, precise

antonyms refined

2 belonging to or characteristic of an early level of skill or development — see PRIMITIVE 1

3 lacking in refinement or good taste — see COARSE 2

4 not civilized — see SAVAGE 1

5 showing a lack of manners or consideration for others — see IMPOLITE

THESAURUS

rudeness *n* **1** rude behavior — see DISCOURTESY
2 the quality or state of lacking refinement or good taste — see VULGARITY 1

rudimentary *adj* **1** belonging to or characteristic of an early level of skill or development — see PRIMITIVE 1
2 of or relating to the simplest facts or theories of a subject — see ELEMENTARY

rudiments *n pl* general or basic truths on which other truths or theories can be based — see PRINCIPLES 1

rue *n* a feeling of responsibility for wrongdoing — see GUILT 1

rue *vb* to feel sorry or dissatisfied about — see REGRET

rueful *adj* **1** expressing or suggesting mourning — see MOURNFUL 1
2 feeling sorrow for a wrong that one has done — see CONTRITE 1
3 deserving of one's pity — see PATHETIC 1

ruefully *adv* with feelings of bitterness or grief — see HARD 2

ruffian *n* a violent, brutal person who is often a member of an organized gang — see HOODLUM

ruffle *n* a strip of fabric gathered or pleated on one edge and used as trimming ⟨likes lace curtains without *ruffles* and chintz curtains with *ruffles*⟩
synonyms flounce, frill, furbelow
related words border, edging, fringe, trim; pleat, ruff; bunting, skirting

rugged *adj* **1** able to withstand hardship, strain, or exposure — see HARDY 1
2 difficult to endure — see HARSH 1
3 harsh and threatening in manner or appearance — see GRIM 1
4 having muscles capable of exerting great physical force — see STRONG 1
5 not having a level or smooth surface — see UNEVEN 1

ruin *n* **1** the state or fact of being rendered nonexistent, physically unsound, or useless — see DESTRUCTION
2 ruins *pl* the portion or bits of something left over or behind after it has been destroyed — see REMAINS 1

ruin *vb* **1** to cause to lose one's fortune and become unable to pay one's debts ⟨*ruined* by the Great Chicago Fire of 1871, the industrialist was forced to sell his mansion and start all over again⟩
synonyms bankrupt, bust
related words beggar, impoverish, pauperize; break, reduce, straiten; clean (out), wipe out
near antonyms enrich, richen
2 to bring destruction to (something) through violent action — see RAVAGE
3 to bring to a complete end the physical soundness, existence, or usefulness of — see DESTROY 1

ruination *n* the state or fact of being rendered nonexistent, physically unsound, or useless — see DESTRUCTION

ruinous *adj* **1** bringing about ruin or misfortune — see FATAL 1
2 causing or tending to cause destruction — see DESTRUCTIVE 1

rule *n* **1** a statement spelling out the proper procedure or conduct for an activity ⟨read the *rules* that are posted before you use the pool⟩
synonyms bylaw, ground rule, regulation
related words code, constitution, decalogue; act, law, ordinance, statute; command, decree, dictate, directive, edict, fiat, order; axiom, fundamental, maxim, precept; moral, principle, value; prohibition, restriction; convention, custom, habit, manners, mores, practice (*also* practise), tradition, way; blueprint, canon, formula, guide, guideline, recipe, standard
2 lawful control over the affairs of a political unit (as a nation) ⟨the years during which Russia was under Communist *rule*⟩
synonyms administration, authority, governance, government, jurisdiction, regime (*also* régime), regimen
related words reign; dominion, power, sovereignty, supremacy, sway; command, leadership; direction, management, regulation, superintendence, supervision; dictatorship, domination, mastery, oppression, subjugation, tyranny

rule *vb* to exercise authority or power over — see GOVERN

rule (on) *vb* to give an opinion about (something at issue or in dispute) — see JUDGE 1

rule out *vb* to prevent the participation or inclusion of — see EXCLUDE

ruler *n* one who rules over a people with a sole, supreme, and usually hereditary authority — see MONARCH

ruling *n* **1** a decision made by a court or tribunal regarding a case it has heard — see SENTENCE
2 an order publicly issued by an authority — see EDICT 1

rumble *vb* to make a low heavy rolling sound ⟨when thunder *rumbled* in the distant sky, we wisely began packing up our stuff⟩
synonyms growl, grumble, lumber, roll
related words boom, drum, thunder

ruminant *adj* given to or marked by long, quiet thinking — see CONTEMPLATIVE

ruminate *vb* to give serious and careful thought to — see PONDER

rummage *n* an unorganized collection or mixture of various things — see MISCELLANY 1

rummage *vb* to look through (as a place) carefully or thoroughly in an effort to find or discover something — see SEARCH 1

rumor *vb* to make (as a piece of information) the subject of common talk without any authority or confirmation of accuracy ⟨for years people have been *rumoring* the principal's imminent retirement⟩
synonyms bruit (about), circulate, noise (about), whisper
related words bandy (about), blab, gossip; disclose, divulge, report, reveal, tell; hint, imply, insinuate, intimate, let on, suggest; broadcast, promulgate, propagate, spread

rump *n* the part of the body upon which someone sits — see BUTTOCKS

rumple *vb* **1** to create (as by crushing) an irregular mass of creases in — see CRUMPLE 1
2 to develop creases or folds — see WRINKLE 1
3 to undo the proper order or arrangement of — see DISORDER

rumpled *adj* lacking in order, neatness, and often cleanliness — see MESSY

rumpus *n* a state of noisy, confused activity — see COMMOTION

run *n* **1** a prevailing or general movement or inclination — see TREND 1
2 *chiefly Midland* a natural body of running water smaller than a river — see CREEK 1

3 the period during which something exists, lasts, or is in progress — see DURATION 1

4 the right to act or move freely — see FREEDOM 2

run *vb* **1** to go at a pace faster than a walk ⟨*ran* all the way to the bus stop, but still missed the bus⟩
synonyms dash, gallop, jog, scamper, sprint, trip, trot
related words bound, canter, leap, lope, skip, spring; foot (it), hoof (it), hotfoot (it), leg (it); nip, race, scuttle, step (along)
near antonyms amble, lumber, plod, saunter, shamble, shuffle, stroll; crawl, creep, poke; plod, trudge; hobble, limp

2 to hasten away from something dangerous or frightening ⟨rather than *run* from a black bear, it's better to hold your ground and make lots of noise⟩
synonyms bolt, break, flee, fly, retreat, run away, run off
related words abscond, clear out, decamp, elope, escape, light out, retreat, scat, scram, skip (out)
phrases beat it, turn tail
near antonyms beard, brave, confront, dare, defy, face

3 to be positioned along a certain course or in a certain direction ⟨the road *runs* along the river for a while⟩
synonyms extend, go, head, lead, lie
related words cross, cut, pass; follow, span, traverse

4 to occur within a continuous range of variation ⟨the electric bill *runs* between 30 and 50 dollars a month⟩
synonyms go, range, vary
related words alternate, move, shift; change, mutate; extend, reach, stretch, sweep

5 to move in a stream — see FLOW 1

6 to proceed or move quickly — see HURRY 2

7 to show a liking or proneness (for something) — see LEAN 2

8 to urge, push, or force onward — see DRIVE 1

9 to control the mechanical operation of — see OPERATE 1

10 to eventually have as a state or quality — see BECOME

11 to go from a solid to a liquid state — see LIQUEFY

12 to look after and make decisions about — see CONDUCT 1

13 to cause to function — see ACTIVATE

run away *vb* **1** to get free from a dangerous or confining situation — see ESCAPE 1

2 to hasten away from something dangerous or frightening — see RUN 2

run–down *adj* **1** showing signs of advanced wear and tear and neglect — see SHABBY 1

2 temporarily suffering from a disorder of the body — see SICK 1

run down *vb* to come upon after searching, study, or effort — see FIND 1

run–in *n* a brief clash between enemies or rivals — see ENCOUNTER

runner *n* one that carries a message or does an errand — see MESSENGER

running *adj* being in effective operation — see ACTIVE 1

running *n* the act or activity of looking after and making decisions about something — see CONDUCT 1

runny *adj* having an overly soft liquid consistency ⟨*runny* scrambled eggs⟩
synonyms soupy, watery
related words flowing, fluid, liquefied; dilute, diluted, thin, thinned, watered (down), weak; slushy, soggy, wet
near antonyms syrupy, viscid, viscous; creamy, heavy, thick, thickened, thickish; gelatinous, gluey, glutinous, gooey, gummy, sticky

run off *vb* **1** to drive or force out — see EJECT 1

2 to get free from a dangerous or confining situation — see ESCAPE 1

3 to hasten away from something dangerous or frightening — see RUN 2

run–of–the–mill *adj* **1** being of the type that is encountered in the normal course of events — see ORDINARY 1

2 of average to below average quality — see MEDIOCRE 1

run on *vb* **1** to engage in casual or rambling conversation — see CHAT

2 to remain indefinitely in existence or in the same state — see CONTINUE 1

3 to talk at length without sticking to a topic or getting to a point — see RAMBLE 1

run over *vb* to flow over the brim or top of — see OVERFLOW 1

runt *n* a living thing much smaller than others of its kind — see DWARF 1

run through *vb* to use up carelessly — see WASTE 1

rural *adj* of, relating to, associated with, or typical of open areas with few buildings or people ⟨grew up in a *rural* community where more than half the people were farmers⟩ ⟨a painter noted for his *rural* landscapes⟩
synonyms bucolic, country, pastoral, rustic
related words countrified (*also* countryfied), provincial; agrarian, agricultural
near antonyms citified, urbanized; metropolitan, municipal; nonagricultural, nonfarm
antonyms urban

rush *n* **1** excited and often showy or disorderly speed — see HURRY 1

2 the act or action of setting upon with force or violence — see ATTACK 1

rush *vb* **1** to cause to move or proceed fast or faster — see HURRY 1

2 to flow out in great quantities or with force — see GUSH 1

3 to proceed or move quickly — see HURRY 2

4 to take sudden, violent action against — see ATTACK 1

rushed *adj* acting or done with excessive or careless speed — see HASTY 1

rustic *adj* of, relating to, associated with, or typical of open areas with few buildings or people — see RURAL

rustic *n* an awkward or simple person especially from a small town or the country — see HICK

rustle *vb* to proceed or move quickly — see HURRY 2

rustler *n* an ambitious person who eagerly goes after what is desired — see GO-GETTER

rut *n* an established and often automatic or monotonous series of actions followed when engaging in some activity — see ROUTINE 1

ruthless *adj* having or showing a lack of sympathy or tender feelings — see HARD 1

sable *adj* having the color of soot or coal — see BLACK 1

saccharine *adj* appealing to the emotions in an obvious and tiresome way — see CORNY

sacerdotal *adj* of, relating to, or characteristic of the clergy — see CLERICAL

sack *n* **1** a container made of a flexible material (as paper or plastic) — see BAG 1
2 a place set aside for sleeping — see BED 1

sack *vb* **1** to let go from office, service, or employment — see DISMISS 1
2 to search through with the intent of committing robbery — see RANSACK 1

sacred *adj* **1** not to be violated, criticized, or tampered with ⟨we took a *sacred* oath not to let anyone find our hideout⟩
synonyms holy, inviolable, sacrosanct, unassailable, untouchable
related words inviolate, pure; privileged, protected, shielded; exempt, immune
near antonyms blasphemous, irreverent, profane
2 of, relating to, or being God — see HOLY 3
3 of, relating to, or used in the practice or worship services of a religion — see RELIGIOUS 1
4 set apart or worthy of veneration by association with God — see HOLY 2

sacrifice *n* something offered to a god ⟨the herders selected their best lamb as a *sacrifice* in order to receive blessings from their god⟩
synonyms immolation, offering, victim
related words holocaust; contribution, donation

sacrifice *vb* to give up as an offering to a god ⟨in the Old Testament Abraham was willing to *sacrifice* even his son to God⟩
synonyms immolate, offer
related words consecrate, dedicate, devote; give, surrender, yield

sacrilege *n* an act of great disrespect shown to God or to sacred ideas, people, or things — see BLASPHEMY

sacrilegious *adj* not showing proper reverence for the holy or sacred — see IRREVERENT

sacristy *n* a room in a church building for sacred furnishings (as vestments) ⟨our choir robes were stored in the *sacristy*⟩
synonyms vestry
related words cloakroom

sacrosanct *adj* **1** not to be violated, criticized, or tampered with — see SACRED 1
2 set apart or worthy of veneration by association with God — see HOLY 2

sad *adj* **1** feeling unhappiness ⟨movies in which the hero dies always make us feel *sad*⟩
synonyms bad, blue, brokenhearted, crestfallen, dejected, depressed, despondent, disconsolate, doleful, down, downcast, downhearted, droopy, forlorn, gloomy, glum, heartbroken, heartsick, heartsore, inconsolable, joyless, low, low-spirited, melancholy, miserable, mournful, saddened, sorrowful, sorry, unhappy, woebegone, woeful, wretched
related words aggrieved, distressed, troubled; despairing, hopeless; disappointed, discouraged, disheartened, dispirited; suicidal; dolorous, lugubrious, plaintive, tearful; regretful, rueful; grieving, wailing, weeping; black, bleak, cheerless, com-

fortless, dark, darkening, depressing, desolate, dismal, drear, dreary, funereal, gray (*also* grey), morbid, morose, murky, saturnine, somber (*or* sombre), sullen
near antonyms ecstatic, elated, enraptured, entranced, euphoric, exhilarated, exuberant, exultant; blithe, blithesome, gay, jocund, jolly, jovial, lightsome, merry, mirthful; excited, thrilled; hopeful, optimistic; encouraged, heartened; animated, jaunty, lively, perky, sprightly, vivacious; content, gratified, pleased, satisfied; beaming, grinning, laughing, smiling; boon, carefree, careless, cavalier, devil-may-care, easygoing, happy-go-lucky, insouciant, lighthearted, unconcerned
antonyms blissful, buoyant, buoyed, cheerful, cheery, chipper, delighted, glad, gladdened, gladsome, gleeful, happy, joyful, joyous, jubilant, sunny, upbeat
2 causing unhappiness ⟨the *sad* news about our uncle's death made my father cry⟩
synonyms depressing, dismal, drear, dreary, heartbreaking, heartrending, melancholy, pathetic, saddening, sorry, tearful, teary
related words discomforting, discomposing, disquieting, distressing, disturbing, perturbing; affecting, moving, poignant, touching; discouraging, disheartening, dispiriting
near antonyms heartening, heartwarming, inspiring, stimulating, stirring, uplifting; agreeable, pleasant, pleasurable; exhilarating, thrilling
antonyms cheering, cheery, glad, happy

sadden *vb* to make sad — see DEPRESS 1

saddened *adj* feeling unhappiness — see SAD 1

saddening *adj* causing unhappiness — see SAD 2

saddle *vb* to place a weight or burden on — see LOAD 1

sadism *n* the willful infliction of pain and suffering on others — see CRUELTY

sadistic *adj* having or showing the desire to inflict severe pain and suffering on others — see CRUEL 1

sadly *adv* with feelings of bitterness or grief — see HARD 2

sadness *n* a state or spell of low spirits ⟨she was filled with *sadness* at the thought of having to leave her family⟩
synonyms blues, dejection, depression, desolation, despondency, disconsolateness, dispiritedness, doldrums, downheartedness, dreariness, dumps, forlornness, gloom, gloominess, heartsickness, joylessness, melancholy, mopes, oppression, unhappiness
related words melancholia, self-pity; anguish, dolor, grief, sorrow; dolefulness, mournfulness, somberness, sorrowfulness, woefulness; agony, distress, pain; misery, woe, wretchedness; discouragement, disheartenment; moodiness; despair, desperation, hopelessness; boredom, ennui, tedium
near antonyms gaiety (*also* gayety), gayness, glee, gleefulness, humor, jollity, joviality, lightheartedness, merriment, mirth, mirthfulness; cheer, cheerfulness, hopefulness, optimism, sunniness; content, contentedness, contentment, satisfaction; delight, gratification
antonyms bliss, blissfulness, ecstasy, elatedness,

elation, euphoria, exhilaration, exuberance, exultation, felicity, gladness, gladsomeness, happiness, heaven, intoxication, joy, joyfulness, joyousness, jubilation, rapture, rapturousness

safe *adj* **1** not exposed to the threat of loss or injury ⟨the minute the rain started, we ran to a place where we were *safe* from getting wet⟩
synonyms all right, alright, secure
related words hale, healthy, intact, sound, well, whole; scatheless, unharmed, unhurt, uninjured, unscathed
near antonyms damaged, harmed, hurt, injured, scathed, wounded
antonyms endangered, imperiled, insecure, liable, threatened, unsafe, vulnerable
2 providing safety ⟨we tried to find a *safe* place to hide the candy⟩
synonyms secure, snug
related words guarding, protecting, safeguarding, sheltering, shielding; defended, guarded, protected, sheltered, shielded; impregnable, inviolable, invulnerable, unassailable, unconquerable
near antonyms undefended, unguarded, unprotected, vulnerable
antonyms dangerous, hazardous, insecure, risky, unsafe
3 having or showing a close attentiveness to avoiding danger or trouble — see CAREFUL 1
4 not causing injury or hurt — see HARMLESS
5 worthy of one's trust — see DEPENDABLE
safe *n* a specially reinforced container to keep valuables safe ⟨the hotel recommended that we keep all our valuables in its *safe* during our stay⟩
synonyms coffer, safe-deposit box, strongbox
related words vault; locker, storeroom, treasury; footlocker, trunk
safe–deposit box *n* a specially reinforced container to keep valuables safe — see SAFE
safeguard *n* means or method of defending — see DEFENSE 1
safeguard *vb* to drive danger or attack away from — see DEFEND 1
safekeeping *n* responsibility for the safety and well-being of someone or something — see CUSTODY
safeness *n* the state of not being exposed to danger — see SAFETY 1
safety *n* **1** the state of not being exposed to danger ⟨we were lucky to make it to *safety* just as the lions broke loose from their cage at the zoo⟩
synonyms protection, safeness, security
related words aegis, defense, guardianship, ward; guard, safeguard, screen, shield; asylum, harbor, haven, refuge, retreat, shelter; inviolability, invulnerability
near antonyms hazard, risk, threat; instability, precariousness
antonyms danger, distress, endangerment, imperilment, jeopardy, peril, trouble
2 a protective device (as on a weapon) to prevent accidental operation ⟨the gun couldn't be fired as long as the *safety* was on⟩
synonyms guard
related words lock
sag *n* the extent to which something hangs or dips below a straight line ⟨if there's too much *sag* in the rod, the curtains will drag on the floor⟩
synonyms droop, slack, slackness
related words laxity, laxness, looseness

near antonyms tautness, tenseness, tension, tightness
sag *vb* **1** to be limp from lack of water or vigor — see DROOP 1
2 to decline gradually from a standard level — see SLIP 1
3 to lose bodily strength or vigor — see WEAKEN 2
sagacious *adj* having or showing deep understanding and intelligent application of knowledge — see WISE 1
sagaciousness *n* the ability to understand inner qualities or relationships — see WISDOM 1
sagacity *n* the ability to understand inner qualities or relationships — see WISDOM 1
sage *adj* having or showing deep understanding and intelligent application of knowledge — see WISE 1
sage *n* a person of deep wisdom or learning ⟨the young prince visited the *sage* to learn the meaning of life⟩
synonyms savant, scholar
related words brain, egghead, genius, highbrow, intellectual, thinker; guru, mahatma; rabbi; master, mentor, teacher
near antonyms blockhead, dodo, dolt, donkey, dope, dumbbell, dunce, fathead, fool, goon, half-wit, idiot, ignoramus, imbecile, jackass, knothead, know-nothing, moron, nincompoop, ninny, nitwit, numskull (*or* numbskull), pinhead, simpleton, stock, turkey
sageness *n* the ability to understand inner qualities or relationships — see WISDOM 1
sagging *adj* bending downward or forward — see NODDING
sail *n* a journey over water in a vessel ⟨we went for a brief *sail* on the bay to relax⟩
synonyms crossing, cruise, passage, voyage
sail *vb* **1** to travel on water in a vessel ⟨I can't *sail* when there's any breeze at all because I get seasick easily⟩
synonyms boat, cruise, navigate, voyage
related words yacht; coast; log
phrases make sail
2 to move or proceed smoothly and readily — see FLOW 2
3 to rest or move along the surface of a liquid or in the air — see FLOAT
sailboat *n* a boat equipped with one or more sails ⟨we were stuck in the *sailboat* for an hour until the wind came up and we could move again⟩
synonyms bark, dinghy, windjammer
related words brigantine, caravel, catboat, clipper, corvette, cutter, frigate, galleon, galley, junk, ketch, lugger, outrigger, pinnace, schooner, shallop, ship, sloop, square-rigger, xebec, yacht, yawl; bottom, craft, vessel
sailor *n* one who operates or navigates a seagoing vessel ⟨the *sailors* were glad to be arriving in port after their long voyage⟩
synonyms gob, jack, jack-tar, mariner, navigator, salt, sea dog, seafarer, seaman, swab, tar
related words crewman, deckhand
saint *vb* to declare to be a saint and worthy of public respect ⟨Brigid of Sweden was *sainted* in October of 1391⟩
synonyms canonize
related words deify, worship; consecrate, hallow, sanctify; beatify, venerate
sainted *adj* showing a devotion to God and to a life of virtue — see HOLY 1

THESAURUS

sainthood *n* the quality or state of being spiritually pure or virtuous — see HOLINESS

saintliness *n* the quality or state of being spiritually pure or virtuous — see HOLINESS

saintly *adj* showing a devotion to God and to a life of virtue — see HOLY 1

saintship *n* the quality or state of being spiritually pure or virtuous — see HOLINESS

salable *or* **saleable** *adj* **1** fit or likely to be sold especially on a large scale — see COMMERCIAL

2 fit to be offered for sale — see MARKETABLE 1

salary *n* the money paid regularly to a person for labor or services — see WAGE

sale *n* the transfer of ownership of something from one person to another for a price ⟨my neighbor tried to make a *sale*, but no one was interested in buying his old car⟩

synonyms deal, trade, transaction

related words auction; haggle, negotiation; bargain, buy; purchase; clearance; fair; garage sale, rummage sale, yard sale

salesclerk *n* a person employed to sell goods or services especially in a store — see SALESPERSON

salesman *n* a person employed to sell goods or services especially in a store — see SALESPERSON

salesperson *n* a person employed to sell goods or services especially in a store ⟨we asked a *salesperson* to see if they had any shoes in the stockroom in our size⟩

synonyms clerk, salesclerk, salesman

related words salespeople; saleswoman

saline *adj* of, relating to, or containing salt — see SALTY 1

salinity *n* the quality or state of being salty — see SALTINESS

saliva *n* the fluid that is secreted into the mouth by certain glands ⟨our mouths filled with *saliva* when we smelled the delicious dinner⟩

synonyms slobber, spit, spittle

related words foam, froth; expectoration, sputum

salivate *vb* to let saliva or some other substance flow from the mouth — see DROOL

sallow *adj* lacking the warm skin color indicative of or associated with good health — see SICKLY 2

sally *n* **1** a short trip for pleasure — see EXCURSION 1

2 something said or done to cause laughter — see JOKE 1

sally (forth) *vb* to leave a place often for another — see GO 2

salon *n* **1** a building or part of a building in which objects of interest are displayed — see MUSEUM

2 a building, room, or suite of rooms occupied by a service business — see PLACE 2

saloon *n* a place of business where alcoholic beverages are sold to be consumed on the premises — see BARROOM

salt *adj* of, relating to, or containing salt — see SALTY 1

salt *n* one who operates or navigates a seagoing vessel — see SAILOR

salt away *vb* to put (something of future use or value) in a safe or secret place — see HOARD

saltiness *n* the quality or state of being salty ⟨the *saltiness* of the pretzels went well with the soda pop we were drinking⟩

synonyms brininess, salinity, saltness

near antonyms purity; sweetness

saltness *n* the quality or state of being salty — see SALTINESS

salty *adj* **1** of, relating to, or containing salt ⟨*salty* sea water is safe to swim in, but you really shouldn't swallow it⟩

synonyms briny, saline, salt

related words brackish

near antonyms sweet; clear, pure

2 hinting at or intended to call to mind matters regarded as indecent — see SUGGESTIVE 1

salubrious *adj* good for the health — see HEALTHFUL

salutary *adj* **1** conferring benefits; promoting or contributing to personal or social well-being — see BENEFICIAL

2 good for the health — see HEALTHFUL

salutation *n* **1** a formal expression of praise — see ENCOMIUM

2 an expression of goodwill upon meeting — see HELLO

salute *n* an expression of goodwill upon meeting — see HELLO

salute *vb* to declare enthusiastic approval of — see ACCLAIM

salvation *n* the saving from danger or evil ⟨we spent the night in the jungle praying for *salvation* from the dangerous animals⟩

synonyms deliverance

related words ransom, recovery, redemption, rescue; extrication; defense, protection, safeguarding; conservation, preservation

salvo *n* a rapid or overwhelming outpouring of many things at once — see BARRAGE

same *adj* **1** resembling another in every respect ⟨I bought the *same* shirt at the mall for five dollars less⟩

synonyms coequal, duplicate, equal, even, identical, indistinguishable

related words akin, alike, analogous, comparable, correspondent, corresponding, equivalent, like, matching, parallel, similar, such, suchlike, tantamount

near antonyms disparate, diverse, varied, various; distinct, distinctive

antonyms different, dissimilar, distinguishable, other, unalike, unlike

2 being one and not another ⟨that's the *same* guy I saw down at the beach yesterday⟩

synonyms identical, selfsame, very

near antonyms disparate, dissimilar, distinct, distinctive, distinguishable, diverse, unalike, unlike, varied, various

antonyms another, different, other

sameness *n* **1** a tedious lack of variety — see MONOTONY

2 the state of being exactly alike — see IDENTITY 1

3 the state or fact of being exactly the same in number, amount, status, or quality — see EQUIVALENCE

sample *n* **1** a number of things selected from a group to stand for the whole ⟨based on a *sample* of the menu items, we decided that this was the best restaurant in town⟩

synonyms cross section

related words case, example, exemplar, illustration, instance, representative, specimen; selection

2 one of a group or collection that shows what the whole is like — see EXAMPLE

sample *vb* to put (something) to a test — see TRY (OUT) 1

sanctification *n* **1** the act of making something

holy through religious ritual — see CONSECRA-
TION

2 the act or fact of freeing from sin or moral guilt
— see PURIFICATION

sanctified *adj* set apart or worthy of veneration by
association with God — see HOLY 2

sanctify *vb* **1** to free from moral guilt or blemish
especially ceremonially — see PURIFY 1

2 to make holy through prayers or ritual — see
BLESS 1

sanctimoniousness *n* the pretending of having
virtues, principles, or beliefs that one in fact does
not have — see HYPOCRISY

sanction *n* the approval by someone in authority
for the doing of something — see PERMISSION

sanction *vb* to give official acceptance of something as satisfactory — see APPROVE

sanctioned *adj* ordered or allowed by those in authority — see OFFICIAL

sanctity *n* the quality or state of being spiritually
pure or virtuous — see HOLINESS

sanctuary *n* **1** a place that is considered sacred (as
within a religion) — see SHRINE

2 something (as a building) that offers cover from
the weather or protection from danger — see
SHELTER

sanctum *n* **1** a place that is considered sacred (as
within a religion) — see SHRINE

2 something (as a building) that offers cover from
the weather or protection from danger — see
SHELTER

sand *vb* to make smooth by friction — see GRIND 1

sandwich *vb* to fit (something) into a tight space
— see CROWD 1

sandy *adj* of a pale yellow or yellowish brown
color — see BLOND

sane *adj* having full use of one's mind and control
over one's actions ⟨the court ruled that the
woman was indeed *sane* when she made out her
will⟩

synonyms balanced, clearheaded, lucid, normal,
right, stable

related words clear, logical, rational, reasonable;
judicious, levelheaded, sensible, wise; healthy,
sound

near antonyms balmy, bananas, batty, crackbrained, cracked, cuckoo, daffy, daft, dotty, loco
[*slang*], loony (*also* looney), moonstruck, nuts,
nutty, off, screwy, wacky; aberrant, disordered;
delusional, neurotic, paranoid, psychotic, schizophrenic; eccentric, odd, queer, strange; foolish, senseless, witless; irrational, unreasonable;
berserk, delirious; depressed, despondent; distraught, frantic, frenzied, hysterical

antonyms crazed, crazy, demented, deranged, insane, lunatic, mad, maniacal (*also* maniac), mental, unbalanced, unsound

saneness *n* the normal or healthy condition of the
mental abilities — see MIND 2

sanguinary *adj* eager for or marked by the shedding of blood, extreme violence, or killing — see
BLOODTHIRSTY

sanguine *adj* **1** eager for or marked by the shedding of blood, extreme violence, or killing — see
BLOODTHIRSTY

2 having a healthy reddish skin tone — see RUDDY

3 having or showing a mind free from doubt —
see CERTAIN 1

sanguinity *n* an inclination to believe in the most
favorable outcome — see OPTIMISM

sanitary *adj* free from filth, infection, or dangers
to health ⟨the nurse made sure that everything in
the room was *sanitary* so that the baby wouldn't
get sick⟩

synonyms aseptic, germfree, hygienic, sterile

related words antibacterial, antibiotic, antiseptic,
germicidal; clean, immaculate, spick-and-span (*or*
spic-and-span), spotless, stainless, unsoiled, unsullied; beneficial, healthful, healthy, restorative,
salubrious, salutary, wholesome

near antonyms pathogenic; bedraggled, besmirched, dingy, dirty, draggled, dusty, filthy,
foul, grimy, grubby, grungy, mucky, muddy,
nasty, soiled, sordid, stained, sullied, unclean, uncleanly; insalubrious, noxious, unhealthful, unhealthy, unwholesome

antonyms insanitary, unhygienic, unsanitary

sanitary landfill *n* a place where discarded materials (as trash) are dumped — see DUMP 1

sanity *n* the normal or healthy condition of the
mental abilities — see MIND 2

sans *prep* not having — see WITHOUT 1

sap *n* **1** active strength of body or mind — see
VIGOR 1

2 one who is easily deceived or cheated — see
DUPE

sap *vb* to diminish the physical strength of — see
WEAKEN 1

sapience *n* the ability to understand inner qualities or relationships — see WISDOM 1

sapient *adj* having or showing deep understanding
and intelligent application of knowledge — see
WISE 1

sapped *adj* lacking bodily strength — see WEAK 1

sappiness *n* the state or quality of having an excess of tender feelings (as of love, nostalgia, or
compassion) — see SENTIMENTALITY

sappy *adj* **1** appealing to the emotions in an obvious and tiresome way — see CORNY

2 showing or marked by a lack of good sense or
judgment — see FOOLISH 1

sarcasm *n* an act or expression showing scorn and
usually intended to hurt another's feelings — see
INSULT

sarcastic *adj* marked by the use of wit that is intended to cause hurt feelings ⟨her *sarcastic* comments that my singing reminded her of the time
her dog was sick⟩

synonyms acrid, biting, caustic, cutting, mordant, pungent, sardonic, satiric (*or* satirical),
scalding, scathing, sharp, smart-alecky (*or* smart-
aleck), tart

related words acid, acidic, cross, sour; incisive,
trenchant; cynical, dry, ironic, wry; facetious,
flippant, tongue-in-cheek; acrimonious, bitter, resentful; harsh, rough, severe, stringent; concise,
crisp, curt, pithy, succinct, terse; backhanded, insincere

near antonyms amusing, droll, merry, playful,
sportive, waggish; gentle, mild; bland; good-humored, good-natured; diplomatic, polite, smooth,
suave, urbane; affable, cordial, genial, gracious

sardonic *adj* marked by the use of wit that is intended to cause hurt feelings — see SARCASTIC

sash *n* a strip of flexible material (as leather) worn
around the waist — see ²BELT

sass *n* disrespectful or argumentative talk given in
response to a command or request — see BACK
TALK

THESAURUS

sassy *adj* displaying or marked by rude boldness — see NERVY 1

Satan *n* the supreme personification of evil often represented as the ruler of Hell — see DEVIL 1

satanic *adj* of, relating to, or worthy of an evil spirit — see FIENDISH

sate *vb* 1 to fill with food to capacity — see GORGE 1

2 to put a complete end to (a physical need or desire) — see SATISFY 1

sated *adj* having one's appetite completely satisfied — see FULL 3

satiate *adj* having one's appetite completely satisfied — see FULL 3

satiate *vb* to put a complete end to (a physical need or desire) — see SATISFY 1

satiated *adj* having one's appetite completely satisfied — see FULL 3

satin *adj* 1 having a shiny surface or finish — see GLOSSY

2 smooth or delicate in appearance or feel — see SOFT 2

satiny *adj* 1 having a shiny surface or finish — see GLOSSY

2 smooth or delicate in appearance or feel — see SOFT 2

satire *n* a creative work that uses sharp humor to point up the foolishness of a person, institution, or human nature in general ⟨a *satire* about the music industry in which a handsome but untalented youth is turned into a rock star⟩

synonyms lampoon

related words burlesque, caricature, parody, spoof, takeoff; comedy, farce, sketch, slapstick, squib; derision, ridicule; mockery, travesty

satiric *or* **satirical** *adj* marked by the use of wit that is intended to cause hurt feelings — see SARCASTIC

satisfaction *n* 1 the feeling experienced when one's wishes are met — see PLEASURE 1

2 payment to another for a loss or injury — see COMPENSATION 1

satisfactorily *adv* 1 in a satisfactory way — see WELL 1

2 in or to a degree or quantity that meets one's requirements or satisfaction — see ENOUGH 1

satisfactoriness *n* the quality or state of meeting one's needs adequately — see SUFFICIENCY

satisfactory *adj* 1 being to one's liking ⟨we found the meal most *satisfactory*⟩

synonyms agreeable, all right, alright, copacetic (*also* copasetic *or* copesetic), fine, good, OK (*or* okay), palatable

related words delectable, delicious, delightful, dreamy, felicitous, gratifying, nice, pleasant, pleasing, scrumptious, welcome; acceptable, adequate, decent, passable, tolerable

antonyms disagreeable, unsatisfactory

2 of a level of quality that meets one's needs or standards — see ADEQUATE

satisfied *adj* 1 experiencing pleasure, satisfaction, or delight — see GLAD 1

2 feeling that one's needs or desires have been met — see CONTENT

satisfy *vb* 1 to put a complete end to (a physical need or desire) ⟨they *satisfied* their hunger after the game with a big pasta dinner⟩

synonyms assuage, quench, sate, satiate

related words cater (to), gratify, indulge; alleviate, lighten, relieve

near antonyms arouse, excite, pique, stimulate; tantalize, tease

2 to cause (someone) to agree with a belief or course of action by using arguments or earnest requests — see PERSUADE

3 to do what is required by the terms of — see FULFILL 1

4 to give satisfaction to — see PLEASE

satisfying *adj* 1 giving pleasure or contentment to the mind or senses — see PLEASANT

2 having the power to persuade — see COGENT

3 making one feel good inside — see HEARTWARMING

satisfyingly *adv* in a pleasing way — see WELL 5

saturate *vb* to wet thoroughly with liquid — see SOAK 1

saturated *adj* containing, covered with, or thoroughly penetrated by water — see WET

saturnine *adj* causing or marked by an atmosphere lacking in cheer — see GLOOMY 1

sauce *n* 1 a savory fluid food used as a topping or accompaniment to a main dish ⟨the chef poured *sauce* over the meat just before he served it⟩

synonyms dressing, gravy

related words condiment, relish, seasoning; fixing(s), garnish, topping; dip, marinade

2 disrespectful or argumentative talk given in response to a command or request — see BACK TALK

3 shameless boldness — see EFFRONTERY

sauciness *n* shameless boldness — see EFFRONTERY

saucy *adj* displaying or marked by rude boldness — see NERVY 1

saunter *n* a relaxed journey on foot for exercise or pleasure — see WALK

sausage *n* a rod-shaped portion of seasoned ground meat in a casing ⟨a couple of *sausages* and eggs make a good breakfast⟩

synonyms link

related words bologna, frankfurter, hot dog, knockwurst, liverwurst, pepperoni, salami, wiener

savage *adj* 1 not civilized ⟨Tarzan is usually portrayed as a noble but *savage* warrior of the jungle⟩

synonyms barbarous, heathen, heathenish, Neanderthal, rude, uncivil, uncivilized, uncultivated, wild

related words coarse, crude, primitive, rough; uncouth, uncultured

near antonyms cultured, enlightened, humane, sophisticated; genteel, polite, refined, urbane, well-bred

antonyms civilized

2 having or showing the desire to inflict severe pain and suffering on others — see CRUEL 1

3 living outdoors without taming or domestication by humans — see WILD 1

4 violently unfriendly or aggressive in disposition — see FIERCE 1

savage *n* 1 a mean, evil, or unprincipled person — see VILLAIN 1

2 an uncivilized person — see HEATHEN 2

savageness *n* the willful infliction of pain and suffering on others — see CRUELTY

savagery *n* the willful infliction of pain and suffering on others — see CRUELTY

savanna *also* **savannah** *n* a broad area of level or rolling treeless country — see PLAIN

savant *n* a person of deep wisdom or learning — see SAGE

save *prep* not including — see EXCEPT

save *vb* **1** to free from the penalties or consequences of sin ⟨the Christian belief that Jesus lived and died to *save* humanity⟩
synonyms deliver, redeem
related words reclaim, reform; forgive, pardon, remit; bless, hallow; consecrate, purify, sanctify
2 to remove from danger or harm ⟨the fire fighter *saved* my brother from the burning building⟩
synonyms bail out, deliver, rescue
related words salvage; emancipate, free, liberate, manumit, release; disentangle, extricate; recover
antonyms compromise, endanger, imperil, jeopardize
3 to avoid unnecessary waste or expense — see ECONOMIZE
4 to keep in good condition — see MAINTAIN 1
5 to keep or intend for a special purpose — see DEVOTE 1

saver *n* one that saves from danger or destruction — see SAVIOR

saving *conj* if it were not for the fact that — see EXCEPT

saving *prep* not including — see EXCEPT

savior *or* **saviour** *n* one that saves from danger or destruction ⟨the policeman proved to be our *savior*, arriving on the scene just as we were about to be mugged⟩
synonyms deliverer, redeemer, rescuer, saver
related words custodian, defender, guard, guardian, keeper, lookout, protector, sentinel, sentry, warden, warder, watch, watchman

savor *n* **1** the property of a substance that can be identified by the sense of taste — see TASTE 1
2 the quality of being delicious — see DELICIOUSNESS

savor *vb* to make more pleasant to the taste by adding something intensely flavored — see SEASON 1

savoriness *n* the quality of being delicious — see DELICIOUSNESS

savorless *adj* lacking in taste or flavor — see INSIPID 1

savory *adj* **1** having a pleasant smell — see FRAGRANT
2 very pleasing to the sense of taste — see DELICIOUS 1

savvy *n* knowledge gained by actually doing or living through something — see EXPERIENCE 1

saw *n* an often stated observation regarding something from common experience — see SAYING

saw-toothed *adj* notched or toothed along the edge — see SERRATED

say *vb* **1** to express (a thought or emotion) in words ⟨why don't you just *say* what's on your mind?⟩
synonyms articulate, speak, state, talk, tell, utter, verbalize, vocalize
related words air, discuss, express, give, look, sound, state, vent, ventilate, voice; advertise, announce, blaze, broadcast, declare, enunciate, proclaim, publicize, publish; affirm, allege, assert, aver, avouch, avow; breathe, drawl, gasp, mouth, murmur, shout, splutter, spout, whisper; couch, formulate, phrase, put, word; comment, remark
phrases put into words
near antonyms stifle, suppress
2 to convey in appropriate or telling terms — see PHRASE

3 to give from memory — see REPEAT 2

say *n* the right to express a wish, choice, or opinion — see VOICE 1

saying *n* an often stated observation regarding something from common experience ⟨there's an old *saying* that you should let sleeping dogs lie⟩
synonyms adage, aphorism, byword, epigram, maxim, proverb, saw
related words cliché, commonplace, platitude; expression, felicity; axiom, motto, precept, truism, truth; observation, reflection, remark

scabby *adj* arousing or deserving of one's loathing and disgust — see CONTEMPTIBLE 1

scads *n pl* a considerable amount — see LOT 2

scalawag *or* **scallywag** *n* a mean, evil, or unprincipled person — see VILLAIN

scalding *adj* **1** having a notably high temperature — see HOT 1
2 marked by the use of wit that is intended to cause hurt feelings — see SARCASTIC

¹scale *n* a device for measuring weight ⟨I hate getting on the bathroom *scale*⟩
synonyms balance
related words gravimeter

²scale *n* a small thin piece of material that resembles an animal scale ⟨*scales* of mica were embedded in the granite⟩
synonyms lamella, lamina, plate
related words chip, flake, sliver, splinter

³scale *n* **1** a scheme of rank or order ⟨a student who scored very highly on a standard intelligence *scale*⟩
synonyms graduation, ladder, ordering, ranking
related words arrangement, array, disposal, disposition, distribution, order, sequence, series
2 the distance or extent between possible extremes — see RANGE 3

scale *vb* to find out the size, extent, or amount of — see MEASURE

scaly *adj* composed of or covered with scales ⟨the snake's *scaly* skin was dry to the touch⟩
synonyms squamous
related words scalelike
near antonyms smooth
antonyms scaleless

scamp *n* **1** an appealingly mischievous person ⟨those little *scamps* are always getting into trouble, but no one has the heart to punish them⟩
synonyms devil, hellion, imp, mischief, monkey, rapscallion, rascal, rogue, urchin
related words cutup, madcap, skylarker; ragamuffin; brat, disrupter, nuisance; juvenile delinquent; gamin, gamine
near antonyms beast, boor, cad, churl, clown, creep, cretin, cur, heel, joker, louse, lout, skunk, snake, stinker; knave, scalawag (*or* scallywag), scoundrel, villain
2 a mean, evil, or unprincipled person — see VILLAIN

scamper *vb* to go at a pace faster than a walk — see RUN 1

scan *n* a close look at or over someone or something in order to judge condition — see INSPECTION

scan *vb* to look over closely (as for judging quality or condition) — see INSPECT

scandal *n* a cause of shame — see DISGRACE 2

scandalous *adj* **1** causing intense displeasure, disgust, or resentment — see OFFENSIVE 1

THESAURUS

2 causing or intended to cause unjust injury to a person's good name — see LIBELOUS

scant *adj* less plentiful than what is normal, necessary, or desirable — see MEAGER

scant *vb* to use or give out in stingy amounts — see SPARE

scantiness *n* a falling short of an essential or desirable amount or number — see DEFICIENCY

scanty *adj* less plentiful than what is normal, necessary, or desirable — see MEAGER

scapegoat *n* a person or thing taking the blame for others ⟨companies often use the economy as a *scapegoat* to avoid taking responsibility for dropping sales⟩
synonyms fall guy, goat, whipping boy
related words victim; butt, dupe, fool, laughingstock, mockery, monkey; excuse

scar *n* something that spoils the appearance or completeness of a thing — see BLEMISH

scarce *adj* **1** less plentiful than what is normal, necessary, or desirable — see MEAGER
2 not coming up to a usual standard or meeting a particular need — see SHORT 3

scarcely *adv* **1** by a very small margin — see JUST 2
2 certainly not — see HARDLY 2

scarceness *n* a falling short of an essential or desirable amount or number — see DEFICIENCY

scarcity *n* a falling short of an essential or desirable amount or number — see DEFICIENCY

scare *vb* to strike with fear — see FRIGHTEN

scared *adj* filled with fear or dread — see AFRAID 1

scare up *vb* to come upon after searching, study, or effort — see FIND 1

scarp *n* a steep wall of rock, earth, or ice — see CLIFF

scary *adj* **1** causing fear — see FEARFUL 1
2 easily frightened — see SHY 1

scathe *vb* to criticize harshly and usually publicly — see ATTACK 2

scathing *adj* marked by the use of wit that is intended to cause hurt feelings — see SARCASTIC

scatter *vb* **1** to cause (members of a group) to move widely apart ⟨the noise of the backfiring car *scattered* the pigeons⟩
synonyms clear out, disband, dispel, disperse, dissipate
related words break up, isolate, part, segregate, separate, split up; diffuse, disseminate, diverge, spread
near antonyms agglutinate, conglomerate; unify, unite
antonyms assemble, cluster, collect, concentrate, congregate, gather
2 to cover by or as if by scattering something over or on ⟨the hillside was *scattered* with wildflowers⟩
synonyms bestrew, dot, pepper, sow, spray, sprinkle, strew
related words blanket, dust; stud; dapple, fleck, speckle, spot, stipple

scatterbrained *adj* lacking in seriousness or maturity — see GIDDY 1

scattered *adj* lacking a definite plan, purpose, or pattern — see RANDOM

scattering *n* **1** an act or process in which something scatters or is scattered ⟨the *scattering* of the protesters suddenly turned violent and chaotic⟩
synonyms disbandment, dispersal, dispersion, dissipation

near antonyms assembly, collection, concentration, gathering
2 a small number — see FEW

scenario *n* the written form of a story prepared for film production — see SCREENPLAY

scene *n* **1** the place and time in which the action for a portion of a dramatic work (as a movie) is set ⟨the first *scene* was the kitchen of a fancy restaurant during dinner⟩
synonyms background, setting
related words backdrop, scenery, set; tableau
2 an outburst or display of excited anger — see TANTRUM
3 position with regard to conditions and circumstances — see SITUATION 1
4 the array of painted backgrounds and furnishings used for a scene in a stage production — see SCENERY

scenery *n* the array of painted backgrounds and furnishings used for a scene in a stage production ⟨the *scenery* in the high school production was all handmade⟩
synonyms scene, set
related words backdrop, drop; background, setting; prop, property

scent *n* **1** a sweet or pleasant smell — see FRAGRANCE
2 the quality of a thing that makes it perceptible to the sense organs in the nose — see SMELL 1

scent *vb* **1** to fill or infuse with a pleasant odor or odor-releasing substance ⟨fancy bars of soap *scented* with lavender⟩
synonyms perfume
near antonyms deodorize
2 to become aware of by means of the sense organs in the nose — see SMELL
3 to have a vague awareness of — see FEEL 1

scented *adj* having a pleasant smell — see FRAGRANT

schedule *n* **1** a listing of things to be presented or considered (as at a concert or play) — see PROGRAM 1
2 a record of a series of items (as names or titles) usually arranged according to some system — see ¹LIST

schedule *vb* to put (someone or something) on a list — see ¹LIST 2

scheduled *adj* being in accordance with the prescribed, normal, or logical course of events — see DUE 2

schematize *vb* to work out the details of (something) in advance — see PLAN 1

scheme *n* **1** a clever often underhanded means to achieve an end — see TRICK 1
2 a secret plan for accomplishing evil or unlawful ends — see PLOT 1
3 a method worked out in advance for achieving some objective — see PLAN 1

scheme *vb* to engage in a secret plan to accomplish evil or unlawful ends — see PLOT

scheme (out) *vb* to work out the details of (something) in advance — see PLAN 1

schism *n* **1** a lack of agreement or harmony — see DISCORD
2 the act or process of a whole separating into two or more parts or pieces — see SEPARATION 1

schmaltz *also* **schmalz** *n* something (as a work of literature or music) that is too sentimental — see CORN

schmaltzy *adj* appealing to the emotions in an obvious and tiresome way — see CORNY

scholar *n* **1** a person of deep wisdom or learning — see SAGE

2 a person with a high level of knowledge or skill in a field — see EXPERT

3 one who attends a school — see STUDENT

scholarly *adj* **1** having or displaying advanced knowledge or education — see EDUCATED

2 of or relating to schooling or learning especially at an advanced level — see ACADEMIC

scholarship *n* the understanding and information gained from being educated — see EDUCATION 2

scholastic *adj* of or relating to schooling or learning especially at an advanced level — see ACADEMIC

school *n* a place or establishment for teaching and learning ⟨one of the first *schools* in the country to admit girls as students⟩

synonyms academy, seminary

related words elementary school, grammar school, high school, junior high school, middle school, preparatory school, public school, secondary school, trade school; Sunday school, yeshiva (*also* yeshivah)

school *vb* to cause to acquire knowledge or skill in some field — see TEACH

schooling *n* the act or process of imparting knowledge or skills to another — see EDUCATION 1

schoolteacher *n* a person whose occupation is to give formal instruction in a school — see TEACHER

science *n* **1** a body of facts learned by study or experience — see KNOWLEDGE 1

2 the understanding and information gained from being educated — see EDUCATION 2

scintillate *vb* **1** to give off sparks — see SPARK 1

2 to shoot forth bursts of light — see FLASH 1

scoffer *n* a person who causes repeated emotional pain, distress, or annoyance to another — see TORMENTOR

scold *n* a person given to harsh judgments and to finding faults — see CRITIC 1

scold *vb* to criticize (someone) severely or angrily especially for personal failings ⟨he *scolded* the kids for not cleaning up the mess they had made in the kitchen⟩

synonyms berate, castigate, chew out, dress down, flay, jaw, keelhaul, lambaste (*or* lambast), lecture, rail (at *or* against), rate, rebuke, reprimand, reproach, score, upbraid

related words admonish, chide, remonstrate (with), reprove; abuse, assail, attack, bad-mouth, blame, blast, censure, condemn, criticize, crucify, denounce, dis [*slang*], excoriate, fault, knock, lash, pan, reprehend, slam; belittle, disparage, mock, put down; ridicule, scoff, scorn

phrases read the riot act (to), take to task

near antonyms approve, endorse (*also* indorse), sanction; extol (*also* extoll), laud, praise

scoop *n* **1** a utensil with a bowl and a handle that is used especially in cooking and serving food — see SPOON

2 information not generally available to the public — see DOPE 1

scoop *vb* to lift out with something that holds liquid — see DIP 2

scoot *vb* to proceed or move quickly — see HURRY 2

scope *n* an area over which activity, capacity, or influence extends — see RANGE 2

scorch *vb* to burn on the surface ⟨the picnickers kept *scorching* their marshmallows, deliberately sticking their skewers into the licking flames of the campfire⟩

synonyms char, sear, singe

related words fire, ignite, inflame, kindle, light; bake, cremate, incinerate; scald, scathe

scorching *adj* having a notably high temperature — see HOT 1

score *n* a lingering ill will towards a person for a real or imagined wrong — see GRUDGE 1

score *vb* **1** to mark with or as if with a line or groove ⟨the glassblower *scored* the glass rod first so that it would break cleanly⟩

synonyms groove, scribe, seam

related words abrade, file, graze, rasp, scarify, scratch

2 to gain (as points or runs in a game) as credit towards one's total number of points ⟨he *scored* the winning goal in the final minute of play⟩

synonyms rack up, tally

related words triumph, win; best, defeat

near antonyms lose

3 to obtain (as a goal) through effort — see ACHIEVE 1

4 to criticize (someone) severely or angrily especially for personal failings — see SCOLD

scorn *n* open dislike for someone or something considered unworthy of one's concern or respect — see CONTEMPT

scorn *vb* **1** to show contempt for ⟨*scorned* the religious traditions of their ancestors⟩

synonyms disdain, high-hat, slight, sniff (at), snub

related words scout; abhor, despise, detest, hate, loathe; disapprove (of), discountenance, disfavor, frown (on *or* upon)

phrases look down on, sneeze at

near antonyms cherish, prize, treasure, value; admire, esteem; revere, venerate, worship; accept, appreciate, approve (of), care (for), countenance, favor, OK (*or* okay), subscribe (to)

antonyms honor, respect

2 to ignore in a disrespectful manner ⟨she *scorned* the suggestions of her classmates for the parade float⟩

synonyms despise, disregard, flout

related words dismiss, forget, ignore, neglect, overlook, overpass, pass over, slight, slur (over)

near antonyms accept, approve; use

scorner *n* a person who causes repeated emotional pain, distress, or annoyance to another — see TORMENTOR

scornful *adj* **1** feeling or showing open dislike for someone or something regarded as undeserving of respect or concern — see CONTEMPTUOUS 1

2 intended to make a person or thing seem of little importance or value — see DEROGATORY

Scot *n* a person born or living in Scotland ⟨my grandfather was a *Scot*, but my grandmother was Welsh⟩

synonyms Scotchman, Scotsman, Scottie

Scotch *adj* of, relating to, or characteristic of the people of Scotland — see SCOTTISH

Scotchman *n* a person born or living in Scotland — see SCOT

Scots *adj* of, relating to, or characteristic of the people of Scotland — see SCOTTISH

Scotsman *n* a person born or living in Scotland — see SCOT

Scottie *n* a person born or living in Scotland — see SCOT

Scottish *adj* of, relating to, or characteristic of the people of Scotland ⟨golf was originally a *Scottish* game⟩
synonyms Scotch, Scots

scoundrel *n* a mean, evil, or unprincipled person — see VILLAIN

scour *vb* to look through (as a place) carefully or thoroughly in an effort to find or discover something — see SEARCH 1

scourge *n* 1 a long thin or flexible tool for striking — see WHIP
2 one who inflicts punishment in return for an injury or offense — see NEMESIS 1

scourge *vb* 1 to bring destruction to (something) through violent action — see RAVAGE
2 to strike repeatedly with something long and thin or flexible — see WHIP 1

scout *n* a member of the human race — see HUMAN

scout *vb* to make (someone or something) the object of unkind laughter — see RIDICULE

scout (up) *vb* to come upon after searching, study, or effort — see FIND 1

scowl *n* a twisting of the facial features in disgust or disapproval — see GRIMACE

scowl *vb* to look with anger or disapproval — see FROWN

scrabble *n* a forceful effort to reach a goal or objective — see STRUGGLE 1

scraggly *adj* having an uneven edge or outline — see RAGGED 1

scraggy *adj* 1 having an uneven edge or outline — see RAGGED 1
2 not having a level or smooth surface — see UNEVEN 1

scramble *n* an unorganized collection or mixture of various things — see MISCELLANY 1

scramble *vb* 1 to move (as up or over something) often with the help of the hands in holding or pulling — see CLIMB 1
2 to undo the proper order or arrangement of — see DISORDER

¹**scrap** *n* 1 an unused or unwanted piece or item typically of small size or value ⟨only a *scrap* of silk was left on the sewing table after they had finished the project⟩
synonyms end, fag end, leftover, oddment, remainder, remnant, stub
related words leavings, odds and ends, remains, residual, residue, scraping(s), stump; balance, rest; chip, flake, fragment, piece, sliver, splinter; ribbon(s), shred, tatter
near antonyms whole
2 a broken or irregular part of something that often remains incomplete — see FRAGMENT
3 a physical dispute between opposing individuals or groups — see FIGHT 1
4 a very small piece — see BIT 1
5 discarded or useless material — see GARBAGE

²**scrap** *n* an often noisy or angry expression of differing opinions — see ARGUMENT 1

¹**scrap** *vb* to express different opinions about something often angrily — see ARGUE 2

²**scrap** *vb* to get rid of as useless or unwanted — see DISCARD

scrape *n* 1 a brief clash between enemies or rivals — see ENCOUNTER
2 a harsh grating sound — see RASP

scrape *vb* 1 to pass roughly and noisily over or against a surface ⟨the rusty old gate *scraped* whenever anyone managed to open it⟩
synonyms grate, grind, rasp, scratch
related words rub; groan, whine
near antonyms glide, skate, slide
2 to damage by rubbing against a sharp or rough surface ⟨she *scraped* her knee when she fell down⟩
synonyms abrade, graze, scratch, scuff
related words bark, skin; chafe, fret, gall; claw, cut, lacerate; bruise, contuse
near antonyms polish, smooth, soften, wax
3 to get with great difficulty — see EKE OUT
4 to press or strike against or together so as to make a scraping sound — see GRIND 2

scrape (together) *vb* to bring together in one body or place — see GATHER 1

scrappiness *n* an inclination to fight or quarrel — see BELLIGERENCE

scrapping *n* the getting rid of whatever is unwanted or useless — see DISPOSAL 1

scrappy *adj* 1 feeling or displaying eagerness to fight — see BELLIGERENT
2 given to arguing — see ARGUMENTATIVE 1

scratch *n* a harsh grating sound — see RASP

scratch *vb* 1 to damage by rubbing against a sharp or rough surface — see SCRAPE 2
2 to pass roughly and noisily over or against a surface — see SCRAPE 1
3 to write or draw hastily or carelessly — see SCRIBBLE

scratch (out) *vb* 1 to compose and set down on paper the words of — see WRITE 1
2 to show (something written) to be no longer valid by drawing a cross over or a line through it — see X (OUT)

scratchy *adj* 1 likely to cause a scratch ⟨*scratchy* shrubbery that's intended to keep kids and pets off the old man's property⟩
synonyms brambly, prickly, thistly, thorny
related words burred; coarse, jagged, rough; irritating, itchy, stinging
near antonyms polished, smooth, soft, soothing; gentle
2 harsh and dry in sound — see HOARSE

scrawl *vb* to write or draw hastily or carelessly — see SCRIBBLE

scream *n* someone or something that is very funny ⟨that new comedy is a *scream*⟩
synonyms laugh, riot
related words howler; crack, gag, jest, joke, pleasantry, quip, sally, waggery, wisecrack, witticism; caution, sight
near antonyms bummer, downer

scream *vb* to cry out loudly and emotionally ⟨we *screamed* when the roller coaster began its thirty foot plunge⟩
synonyms howl, screech, shriek, shrill, squall, squeal, yelp, yell
related words bay, caterwaul, keen, squawk, wail, yawp (*or* yaup), yowl; bawl, call, cry, holler, shout, vociferate
near antonyms murmur, mutter, whisper

screaming *adj* 1 arousing a strong and usually superficial interest or emotional reaction — see SENSATIONAL 1

2 causing or intended to cause laughter — see FUNNY 1

screech *vb* to cry out loudly and emotionally — see SCREAM

screeching *adj* having a high musical pitch or range — see SHRILL

screen *n* **1** the art or business of making a movie — see MOVIE 2

2 means or method of defending — see DEFENSE 1

screen *vb* **1** to drive danger or attack away from — see DEFEND 1

2 to keep secret or shut off from view — see ¹HIDE 2

3 to pass through a filter — see STRAIN 2

4 to place a protective layer over — see COVER 3

screenplay *n* the written form of a story prepared for film production ⟨each actor was given a copy of the *screenplay* to study⟩
synonyms scenario, script
related words story, text

screw *vb* to twist (something) out of a natural or normal shape or condition — see CONTORT

screwball *adj* showing or marked by a lack of good sense or judgment — see FOOLISH 1

screwball *n* a person of odd or whimsical habits — see ECCENTRIC

screwing *n* the twisting of something out of its natural or normal shape or condition — see CONTORTION

screwlike *adj* turning around an axis like the thread of a screw — see SPIRAL

screwy *adj* **1** different from the ordinary in a way that causes curiosity or suspicion — see ODD 2

2 having or showing a very abnormal or sick state of mind — see INSANE 1

scribble *vb* to write or draw hastily or carelessly ⟨she *scribbled* a quick note on the pad by the door before leaving⟩
synonyms scratch, scrawl
related words doodle; jot (down); ink, inscribe, letter, pen, pencil, print, write

scribe *n* a person whose job is to keep records — see CLERK 1

scribe *vb* to mark with or as if with a line or groove — see SCORE 1

scrimmage *n* a physical dispute between opposing individuals or groups — see FIGHT 1

scrimmage (with) *vb* to oppose (someone) in physical conflict — see FIGHT 1

scrimp *vb* to avoid unnecessary waste or expense — see ECONOMIZE

scrimping *adj* careful in the management of money or resources — see FRUGAL

scrimping *n* careful management of material resources — see ECONOMY

script *n* **1** the form or style of a particular person's writing — see HANDWRITING 1

2 the written form of a story prepared for film production — see SCREENPLAY

3 writing done by hand — see HANDWRITING 2

Scripture *n* a book made up of the writings accepted by Christians as coming from God — see BIBLE

scrooge *n* a mean grasping person who is usually stingy with money — see MISER

scrounge *vb* to get with great difficulty — see EKE OUT

scrub *n* a living thing much smaller than others of its kind — see DWARF 1

scruffy *adj* showing signs of advanced wear and tear and neglect — see SHABBY 1

scrumptious *adj* very pleasing to the sense of taste — see DELICIOUS 1

scrunch *vb* **1** to create (as by crushing) an irregular mass of creases in — see CRUMPLE 1

2 to lie low with the limbs close to the body — see CROUCH

3 to press or strike against or together so as to make a scraping sound — see GRIND 2

scruple *n* **1** a very small amount — see PARTICLE 1

2 a very small piece — see BIT 1

3 an uneasy feeling about the rightness of what one is doing or going to do — see QUALM

scrupulous *adj* guided by or in accordance with one's sense of right and wrong — see CONSCIENTIOUS 1

scrupulousness *n* strict attentiveness to what one is doing — see CARE 1

scrutinize *vb* to look over closely (as for judging quality or condition) — see INSPECT

scrutiny *n* a close look at or over someone or something in order to judge condition — see INSPECTION

scuff *vb* **1** to damage by rubbing against a sharp or rough surface — see SCRAPE 2

2 to move heavily or clumsily — see LUMBER 1

scuffle *n* a physical dispute between opposing individuals or groups — see FIGHT 1

scuffle *vb* **1** to move heavily or clumsily — see LUMBER 1

2 to seize and attempt to unbalance one another for the purpose of achieving physical mastery — see WRESTLE

scull *vb* to move a boat by means of oars — see ¹ROW

sculler *n* a person who drives a boat forward by means of oars — see OARSMAN

sculpt *vb* to create a three-dimensional representation of (something) using solid material ⟨I *sculpted* a figure of a giraffe out of clay in art class today⟩
synonyms carve, sculpture
related words chisel, engrave, etch, grave, incise, inscribe; cast, form, model, mold, shape

sculpture *vb* to create a three-dimensional representation of (something) using solid material — see SCULPT

scum *n* people looked down upon as ignorant and of the lowest class — see RABBLE

scummy *adj* arousing or deserving of one's loathing and disgust — see CONTEMPTIBLE 1

scurry *vb* to proceed or move quickly — see HURRY 2

scurvy *adj* arousing or deserving of one's loathing and disgust — see CONTEMPTIBLE 1

scuttle *vb* to proceed or move quickly — see HURRY 2

sea *n* the whole body of salt water that covers nearly three-fourths of the earth — see OCEAN

sea devil *n* any of several extremely large rays — see DEVILFISH

sea dog *n* one who operates or navigates a seagoing vessel — see SAILOR

seafarer *n* one who operates or navigates a seagoing vessel — see SAILOR

seam *vb* to mark with or as if with a line or groove — see SCORE 1

seaman *n* one who operates or navigates a seagoing vessel — see SAILOR

sear *vb* **1** to burn on the surface — see SCORCH
2 to make dry — see DRY 1
search *n* an act or process of looking carefully or thoroughly for someone or something ⟨the *search* for the lost puppy took hours⟩
synonyms hunt, quest
related words chase, pursuit; reconnaissance, scout; canvas, survey; exploration, probe; forage
search *vb* **1** to look through (as a place) carefully or thoroughly in an effort to find or discover something ⟨we *searched* the closet for half an hour until we found the missing shoe⟩
synonyms comb, dig (through), dredge, hunt (through), rake, ransack, rifle, rummage, scour
related words audit, check (out), examine, inspect, investigate, review, scan, scrutinize, survey; ascertain, descry, detect, determine, discover, ferret (out), find, find out, get, hit (on *or* upon), learn, locate, run down, scare up, track (down); explore, probe, prospect, skirmish, snoop; browse, glance (over), look over; peruse, study
near antonyms hide; abandon, lose; ignore, neglect
2 to go into or range over for purposes of discovery — see EXPLORE 2
search (for *or* out) *vb* to go in search of — see SEEK 1
searing *adj* having a notably high temperature — see HOT 1
season *vb* **1** to make more pleasant to the taste by adding something intensely flavored ⟨the chef *seasoned* the vegetables as soon as they came out of the oven⟩
synonyms flavor, savor, spice
related words enhance, enrich, sauce; salt, pepper
2 to bring to a proper or desired state of fitness — see CONDITION 1
3 to make able to withstand physical hardship, strain, or exposure — see HARDEN 2
4 to make competent (as by training, skill, or ability) for a particular office or function — see QUALIFY 2
seasonable *adj* especially suitable for a certain time — see TIMELY 1
seasoning *n* **1** something (as a spice or herb) that adds an agreeable or interesting taste to food ⟨the stew was too bland before they added the *seasoning*⟩
synonyms flavor, flavoring, spice
related words sauce
2 something used to enhance the flavor of cooked or prepared food — see CONDIMENT
seat *n* **1** a place from which authority is exercised ⟨all applications had to be submitted at the county *seat* for proper processing⟩
synonyms command, headquarters
related words center, home; capital
2 the part of the body upon which someone sits — see BUTTOCKS
3 a thing or place that is of greatest importance to an activity or interest — see CENTER 1
seat *vb* to cause to sit down ⟨the usher *seated* them in the third row⟩
synonyms set down, sit
related words ensconce, settle; lay, lie, rest; place, put; recline, repose
seclude *vb* to set or keep apart from others — see ISOLATE
secluded *adj* hidden from view ⟨we stayed in a se-

cluded resort, far away from the regular tourist crowds⟩
synonyms cloistered, covert, isolated, quiet, remote, retired, secret, sheltered
related words lonely, reclusive, solitary; private
near antonyms obvious, visible; exposed
secludedness *n* the state of being alone or kept apart from others — see ISOLATION
seclusion *n* the state of being alone or kept apart from others — see ISOLATION
second *n* a very small space of time — see INSTANT
secondary *adj* **1** taken or created from something original or basic ⟨history textbooks are *secondary* sources for historical information and do not represent original research⟩
synonyms derivative, secondhand
related words unoriginal; consequent, resultant
near antonyms fundamental, nonderivative; first, primary
antonyms basic, original
2 of little or less value or merit — see INFERIOR 2
second-class *adj* of little or less value or merit — see INFERIOR 2
secondhand *adj* taken or created from something original or basic — see SECONDARY 1
second-rate *adj* **1** of average to below average quality — see MEDIOCRE 1
2 of little or less value or merit — see INFERIOR 2
3 of low quality — see CHEAP 2
secrecy *n* the practice or habit of keeping secrets or keeping one's affairs secret ⟨in picking helpers for a surprise party, you'd very much want to choose people known for their *secrecy*⟩
synonyms closeness, secretiveness
related words discreetness, discretion, prudence; circumspection, wariness; reserve, reticence, silence, taciturnity; furtiveness, shiftiness, slyness, sneakiness, underhandedness; concealment, stealth, subterfuge
near antonyms candor, frankness, honesty, openness; imprudence, indiscretion
secret *adj* **1** undertaken or done so as to escape being observed or known by others ⟨a *secret* operation to rescue captive soldiers behind enemy lines⟩
synonyms clandestine, covert, furtive, huggermugger, private, privy, sneak, sneaking, sneaky, stealthy, surreptitious, undercover, underground, underhand, underhanded
related words classified, confidential, restricted, top secret, undisclosed; concealed, hidden, secreted, subterranean, unadvertised, unexposed
near antonyms acknowledged, avowed; aboveboard, straightforward, unconcealed, undisguised; unclassified, unrestricted; clear, evident, manifest, obvious, patent, plain
antonyms open, overt, public
2 working on missions in which one's objectives, activities, or true identity are not publicly revealed ⟨*secret* agents whose wartime exploits were known only by top government officials⟩
synonyms undercover
related words covert, private, secretive, subterranean
near antonyms overt
3 hidden from view — see SECLUDED
4 not known or meant to be known by the general populace — see PRIVATE 1
secret *n* **1** information shared only with another or

with a select few ⟨they're best friends and are constantly sharing *secrets*⟩
synonyms confidence
related words dope, lowdown
near antonyms open secret
2 something hard to understand or explain — see MYSTERY
secrete *vb* to put into a hiding place — see ¹HIDE 1
secretion *n* the placing of something out of sight — see CONCEALMENT 1
secretive *adj* given to keeping one's activities hidden from public observation or knowledge ⟨the intelligence agency remained *secretive* despite the media's demands for more openness in government⟩
synonyms close, closemouthed, dark, reticent, uncommunicative
related words quiet, reserved, silent, taciturn, tight-lipped; discreet, prudent; clandestine, covert, furtive, hugger-mugger, secret, sneak, sneaky, stealthy, surreptitious, undercover, underhand, underhanded
near antonyms candid, frank, honest; blunt, outspoken, tactless
antonyms communicative, open
secretiveness *n* the practice or habit of keeping secrets or keeping one's affairs secret — see SECRECY
sect *n* a group of people acting together within a larger group — see FACTION
sectarian *adj* not broad or open in views or opinions — see NARROW 2
section *n* **1** an area (as of a city) set apart for some purpose or having some special feature — see DISTRICT
2 one of the pieces from which something is designed to be assembled — see PART 1
secular *adj* not involving religion or religious matters — see PROFANE 1
secure *adj* **1** firmly positioned in place and difficult to dislodge — see TIGHT 2
2 having or showing great faith in oneself or one's abilities — see CONFIDENT 1
3 not exposed to the threat of loss or injury — see SAFE 1
4 providing safety — see SAFE 2
secure *vb* **1** to drive danger or attack away from — see DEFEND 1
2 to make sure, certain, or safe — see ENSURE
3 to put securely in place or in a desired position — see FASTEN 2
4 to receive as return for effort — see EARN 1
security *n* **1** means or method of defending — see DEFENSE 1
2 something given or held to assure that the giver will keep a promise — see PLEDGE 1
3 the state of not being exposed to danger — see SAFETY 1
sedate *adj* not joking or playful in mood or manner — see SERIOUS 1
sedative *adj* tending to calm the emotions and relieve stress — see SOOTHING 1
sediment *n* matter that settles to the bottom of a body of liquid — see DEPOSIT 1
sediment *vb* to cause to come to rest at the bottom (as of a liquid) — see SETTLE 1
seduce *vb* to lead away from a usual or proper course by offering some pleasure or advantage — see LURE

seducer *n* one that tries to get a person to give in to a desire — see TEMPTER
seduction *n* the act or pressure of giving in to a desire especially when ill-advised — see TEMPTATION 1
seductive *adj* having an often mysterious or magical power to attract — see FASCINATING 1
seductiveness *n* the power of irresistible attraction — see CHARM 2
seductress *n* a woman whom men find irresistibly attractive — see SIREN
sedulous *adj* involved in often constant activity — see BUSY 1
sedulously *adv* with great effort or determination — see HARD 1
see *vb* **1** to make note of (something) through the use of one's eyes ⟨out of the corner of my eye I *saw* the deer run into the woods⟩
synonyms behold, descry, discern, distinguish, espy, eye, look (at), note, notice, observe, perceive, regard, remark, sight, spy, view, witness
related words identify, make out, pick out; attend (to), consider, heed, mark, mind; study, watch; examine, inspect, scan, scrutinize, survey; glance (at), glimpse, peer (at)
phrases get a load of [*slang*], lay eyes on, set eyes on
near antonyms disregard, ignore, neglect, overpass, pass over; miss, overlook
2 to come to a knowledge of (something) by living through it — see EXPERIENCE
3 to come to an awareness — see DISCOVER 1
4 to have a vague awareness of — see FEEL 1
5 to make a social call upon — see VISIT 1
6 to recognize the meaning of — see COMPREHEND 1
seeable *adj* capable of being seen — see VISIBLE
seed *n* the descendants of a person, animal, or plant — see OFFSPRING
seed *vb* to put or set into the ground to grow — see PLANT
seediness *n* the state of being unattended to or not cared for — see NEGLECT 1
seedy *adj* **1** showing signs of advanced wear and tear and neglect — see SHABBY 1
2 worn or torn into or as if into rags — see RAGGED 2
seeing *conj* for the reason that — see SINCE
seek *vb* **1** to go in search of ⟨the knights of the Round Table fervently *sought* the Holy Grail⟩
synonyms cast about (for), cast around (for), forage (for), hunt, look up, pursue, quest, search (for *or* out)
related words ferret (out), root (out)
phrases look for
near antonyms hide, lose; ignore, neglect
2 to make a request for — see ASK (FOR) 1
3 to make an effort to do — see ATTEMPT
seeker *n* one who seeks an office, honor, position, or award — see CANDIDATE
seem *vb* to give the impression of being ⟨I tried to cheer them up because they *seemed* depressed⟩
synonyms act, appear, look, make, sound
related words dissemble, pretend; resemble, suggest; hint, imply, insinuate
seeming *adj* appearing to be true on the basis of evidence that may or may not be confirmed — see APPARENT 1
seemingly *adv* to all outward appearances — see APPARENTLY

THESAURUS

seemliness *n* the quality or state of being especially suitable or fitting — see APPROPRIATENESS

seemly *adj* following the established traditions of refined society and good taste — see PROPER 1

seep *vb* to flow forth slowly through small openings — see EXUDE

seer *n* one who predicts future events or developments — see PROPHET

seesaw *vb* **1** to make a series of unsteady side-to-side motions — see ROCK 1
2 to make short up-and-down movements — see NOD

seethe *vb* **1** to be in a state of violent rolling motion ⟨the water *seethed* with schools of feeding piranha⟩
synonyms boil, churn, roil
related words reel, spin, swirl, whirl; agitate, stir
near antonyms abate, calm, subside
2 to be excited or emotionally stirred up with anger — see BOIL 1

segment *n* one of the pieces from which something is designed to be assembled — see PART 1

segregate *vb* to set or keep apart from others — see ISOLATE

segregation *n* the state of being alone or kept apart from others — see ISOLATION

seize *vb* **1** to recognize the meaning of — see COMPREHEND 1
2 to take or keep under one's control by authority of law — see ARREST 1
3 to take physical control or possession of (something) suddenly or forcibly — see CATCH 1

seizure *n* a sudden experiencing of a physical or mental disorder — see ATTACK 2

seldom *adv* not often ⟨we *seldom* go to the theater downtown because its prices are so high⟩
synonyms infrequently, little, rarely
related words ne'er, never
phrases hardly ever
near antonyms generally, usually; always, constantly, continuously, endlessly, eternally, ever, everlastingly, evermore, forever, invariably; recurrently, repeatedly
antonyms frequently, often

select *adj* **1** singled out from a number or group as more to one's liking ⟨they use only *select* beans to make their coffee⟩
synonyms chosen, elect, favored, picked, preferred, selected
related words fashionable; exclusive; culled, screened, weeded (out), winnowed (out)
near antonyms average, common, commonplace, ordinary, run-of-the-mill
2 having qualities that appeal to a refined taste — see CHOICE

select *vb* to decide to accept (someone or something) from a group of possibilities — see CHOOSE 1

selected *adj* singled out from a number or group as more to one's liking — see SELECT 1

selecting *n* the act or process of selecting — see SELECTION 1

selection *n* **1** the act or process of selecting ⟨his *selection* of a running mate was a long, tedious affair⟩
synonyms choice, choosing, election, picking, selecting
related words option; appointment, assignment, designation, naming, nomination
2 a person or thing that is chosen — see CHOICE 2

selective *adj* tending to select carefully ⟨we were highly *selective* about the music we listened to while trying out loudspeakers⟩
synonyms choosy (*or* choosey), particular, picky
related words fastidious, finicky, fussy; discerning, discriminating, judicious
near antonyms indiscriminate
antonyms nonselective

selector *n* someone with the right or responsibility for making a selection ⟨the librarians who are the *selectors* of the annual award for best children's book⟩
synonyms chooser, namer, picker
related words elector, voter

self-acting *adj* designed to replace or decrease human labor and especially physical labor — see LABORSAVING

self-admiration *n* an often unjustified feeling of being pleased with oneself or with one's situation or achievements — see COMPLACENCE

self-assertive *adj* having or showing a bold forcefulness in the pursuit of a goal — see AGGRESSIVE 1

self-assurance *n* great faith in oneself or one's abilities — see CONFIDENCE 1

self-assured *adj* having or showing great faith in oneself or one's abilities — see CONFIDENT 1

self-centered *adj* overly concerned with one's own desires, needs, or interests — see EGOCENTRIC

self-centeredness *n* excessive interest in oneself — see EGOISM

self-conceit *n* an often unjustified feeling of being pleased with oneself or with one's situation or achievements — see COMPLACENCE

self-conceited *adj* having too high an opinion of oneself — see CONCEITED

self-confidence *n* great faith in oneself or one's abilities — see CONFIDENCE 1

self-confident *adj* having or showing great faith in oneself or one's abilities — see CONFIDENT 1

self-containment *n* the power to control one's actions, impulses, or emotions — see WILL 1

self-control *n* **1** the power to control one's actions, impulses, or emotions — see WILL 1
2 the checking of one's true feelings and impulses when dealing with others — see CONSTRAINT 1

self-denial *n* the act or practice of giving up or rejecting something once enjoyed or desired — see RENUNCIATION

self-destruction *n* the act of deliberately killing oneself — see SUICIDE

self-determination *n* the act or power of making one's own choices or decisions — see FREE WILL

self-discipline *n* the power to control one's actions, impulses, or emotions — see WILL 1

self-esteem *n* **1** a reasonable or justifiable sense of one's worth or importance — see PRIDE 1
2 an often unjustified feeling of being pleased with oneself or with one's situation or achievements — see COMPLACENCE
3 great faith in oneself or one's abilities — see CONFIDENCE 1

self-governing *adj* **1** not being under the rule or control of another — see FREE 1
2 of, relating to, or favoring political democracy — see DEMOCRATIC

self-government *n* **1** government in which the supreme power is held by the people and used by them directly or indirectly through representation — see DEMOCRACY

2 the power to control one's actions, impulses, or emotions — see WILL 1

3 the state of being free from the control or power of another — see FREEDOM 1

selfhood *n* the set of qualities that make a person different from other people — see INDIVIDUALITY

self–identity *n* the set of qualities that make a person different from other people — see INDIVIDUALITY

self–importance *n* **1** an exaggerated sense of one's importance that shows itself in the making of excessive or unjustified claims — see ARROGANCE

2 an often unjustified feeling of being pleased with oneself or with one's situation or achievements — see COMPLACENCE

self–important *adj* having too high an opinion of oneself — see CONCEITED

self–interest *n* excessive interest in oneself — see EGOISM

selfish *adj* overly concerned with one's own desires, needs, or interests — see EGOCENTRIC

selfishness *n* excessive interest in oneself — see EGOISM

self–possessed *adj* free from emotional or mental agitation — see CALM 2

self–possession *n* **1** evenness of emotions or temper — see EQUANIMITY

2 the power to control one's actions, impulses, or emotions — see WILL 1

self–protective *adj* intended to resist or prevent attack or aggression — see DEFENSIVE

self–regard *n* **1** excessive interest in oneself — see EGOISM

2 a reasonable or justifiable sense of one's worth or importance — see PRIDE 1

self–reliance *n* the ability to care for one's self — see SELF-SUFFICIENCY

self–reliant *adj* able to take care of oneself without outside help — see SELF-SUFFICIENT

self–reproach *n* a feeling of responsibility for wrongdoing — see GUILT 1

self–respect *n* a reasonable or justifiable sense of one's worth or importance — see PRIDE 1

self–restraint *n* **1** the power to control one's actions, impulses, or emotions — see WILL 1

2 the checking of one's true feelings and impulses when dealing with others — see CONSTRAINT 1

self–rule *n* government in which the supreme power is held by the people and used by them directly or indirectly through representation — see DEMOCRACY

self–ruling *adj* of, relating to, or favoring political democracy — see DEMOCRATIC

selfsame *adj* being one and not another — see SAME 2

self–satisfaction *n* an often unjustified feeling of being pleased with oneself or with one's situation or achievements — see COMPLACENCE

self–satisfied *adj* having too high an opinion of oneself — see CONCEITED

self–seeker *n* one who does things only for his own benefit and with little regard for right and wrong ⟨he was accused of being a *self-seeker*, of being nice only to people who could do him favors⟩
synonyms opportunist, temporizer
related words egoist, egotist; conniver, machinator, plotter, schemer

self–seeking *adj* **1** having a strong desire for personal advancement — see AMBITIOUS 1

2 overly concerned with one's own desires, needs, or interests — see EGOCENTRIC

self–starter *n* an ambitious person who eagerly goes after what is desired — see GO-GETTER

self–sufficiency *n* the ability to care for one's self ⟨*self-sufficiency* is a goal that all teenagers should work towards⟩
synonyms independence, self-reliance, self-support
related words autonomy, self-determination; potency, power, resilience, strength
near antonyms helplessness, impotence, inadequacy, weakness
antonyms dependence, reliance

self–sufficient *adj* able to take care of oneself without outside help ⟨the college student worked nights so that he would be *self-sufficient*⟩
synonyms independent, self-reliant, self-supporting
related words potent, powerful, resilient, strong
near antonyms helpless, inadequate, insufficient; impotent, weak
antonyms dependent, reliant

self–support *n* the ability to care for one's self — see SELF-SUFFICIENCY

self–supporting *adj* able to take care of oneself without outside help — see SELF-SUFFICIENT

self–will *n* a steadfast adherence to an opinion, purpose, or course of action — see OBSTINACY

self–willed *adj* sticking to an opinion, purpose, or course of action in spite of reason, arguments, or persuasion — see OBSTINATE

sell *vb* to offer for sale to the public — see MARKET

sell (for) *vb* to have a price of — see COST

sell (out) *vb* to be unfaithful or disloyal to — see BETRAY 1

seller *n* the person in a business deal who hands over an item in exchange for money — see VENDOR

sellout *n* the act or fact of violating the trust or confidence of another — see BETRAYAL

semblance *n* **1** a display of emotion or behavior that is insincere or intended to deceive — see MASQUERADE

2 outward and often deceptive indication — see APPEARANCE 2

semidarkness *n* a time or place of little or no light — see DARK 1

seminar *n* **1** a coming together of a number of persons for a specified purpose — see MEETING 1

2 a meeting featuring a group discussion — see FORUM

seminary *n* a place or establishment for teaching and learning — see SCHOOL

send *vb* to cause to go or be taken from one place to another ⟨they promised to *send* the package in the morning⟩
synonyms consign, pack (off), ship, transfer, transmit, transport
related words convey, deliver, hand over; advance, drop, launch, remit; address, forward; bestow, contribute, donate, give, present
near antonyms acquire, draw, earn, gain, garner, get, obtain, procure, secure
antonyms accept, receive

senior *adj* being of advanced years and especially past middle age — see ELDERLY

senior *n* **1** one who is older than another ⟨since the man next door is my *senior* by a number of years, I always address him as "Mr. Barton"⟩

synonyms elder

related words ancestor, forerunner, predecessor

near antonyms contemporary, peer; descendant (*or* descendent), successor

antonyms junior

2 one who is above another in rank, station, or office — see SUPERIOR

3 the senior member of a group — see DEAN

senior citizen *n* a person of advanced years ⟨more and more *senior citizens* are living active, rewarding lives⟩

synonyms ancient, elder, golden-ager, oldster, old-timer

related words senior; graybeard, patriarch; beldam (*or* beldame), grandam (*or* grandame); adult, grown-up

near antonyms adolescent, minor; child, cub, juvenile, kid

antonyms youngster, youth

sensation *n* **1** an indefinite physical response to a stimulus ⟨we felt just the barest *sensation* of warmth when we leaned against the radiator⟩

synonyms feel, feeling, sense

related words impression, perception; hint, suggestion

2 a practice or interest that is very popular for a short time — see FAD

3 something extraordinary or surprising — see WONDER 1

sensational *adj* **1** arousing a strong and usually superficial interest or emotional reaction ⟨the *sensational* news story caused a stir, but after a few days everyone forgot about it⟩

synonyms lurid, screaming

related words colorful, juicy, racy; dramatic, histrionic, melodramatic, theatrical; coarse, vulgar

near antonyms innocuous, inoffensive; dignified, formal, proper, restrained

2 of or relating to physical sensation or the senses — see SENSORY

3 of the very best kind — see EXCELLENT

sense *n* **1** an indefinite physical response to a stimulus — see SENSATION 1

2 the ability to learn and understand or to deal with problems — see INTELLIGENCE 1

3 the ability to make intelligent decisions especially in everyday matters — see COMMON SENSE

4 the idea that is conveyed or intended to be conveyed to the mind by language, symbol, or action — see MEANING 1

5 the thought processes that have been established as leading to valid solutions to problems — see LOGIC

sense *vb* to have a vague awareness of — see FEEL 1

senseless *adj* **1** having lost consciousness — see UNCONSCIOUS 1

2 having no meaning — see MEANINGLESS

3 not having or showing an ability to absorb ideas readily — see STUPID 1

4 showing or marked by a lack of good sense or judgment — see FOOLISH 1

senselessness *n* **1** lack of good sense or judgment — see FOOLISHNESS 1

2 language, behavior, or ideas that are absurd and contrary to good sense — see NONSENSE 1

3 the quality or state of lacking intelligence or quickness of mind — see STUPIDITY 1

sensibilities *n* general emotional condition — see FEELING 2

sensible *adj* **1** able to be perceived by a sense or by the mind — see PERCEPTIBLE

2 according to the rules of logic — see LOGICAL 1

3 based on sound reasoning or information — see GOOD 1

4 having specified facts or feelings actively impressed on the mind — see CONSCIOUS

sensibleness *n* the ability to make intelligent decisions especially in everyday matters — see COMMON SENSE

sensitive *adj* **1** able to sense slight impressions or differences — see ACUTE 1

2 being in a situation where one is likely to meet with harm — see LIABLE 1

3 easily injured without careful handling — see TENDER 1

4 of or relating to physical sensation or the senses — see SENSORY

sensor *n* a device that detects some physical quantity and responds usually with a transmitted signal ⟨the thief accidentally triggered the motion *sensor*, which alerted the police⟩

synonyms detector

related words eye; electric eye, photoelectric cell; alarm, trigger

sensory *adj* of or relating to physical sensation or the senses ⟨trying to listen to music while watching the TV and eating dinner caused a sort of *sensory* overload⟩

synonyms sensational, sensitive, sensuous

related words afferent, receptive; sensual

near antonyms extrasensory, intuitional

sensual *adj* pleasing to the physical senses ⟨the *sensual* feel of a velvet shirt against the skin⟩

synonyms carnal, fleshly, luscious, sensuous, voluptuous

related words bodily, corporeal; agreeable, delectable, delicious, delightful, dreamy, gratifying, palatable, pleasant, pleasing, pleasurable, scrumptious; epicurean, luxurious, self-indulgent

near antonyms harsh, painful, uncomfortable

sensuous *adj* **1** of or relating to physical sensation or the senses — see SENSORY

2 pleasing to the physical senses — see SENSUAL

sentence *n* a decision made by a court or tribunal regarding a case it has heard ⟨the court-martial pronounced a *sentence* of not guilty on all counts of cowardice⟩

synonyms doom, finding, holding, judgment (*or* judgement), ruling

related words verdict; injunction; decree, edict, order; declaration, deliverance, dictum, pronouncement; conclusion, decision, determination, opinion, resolution; discipline, penalty, punishment

sentence *vb* to impose a judicial punishment on ⟨the judge *sentenced* him to a fine of fifty dollars and time served⟩

synonyms condemn, damn, doom

related words adjudge, judge; castigate, chasten, chastise, correct, discipline, penalize, punish; conclude, decide, determine, find, opine, resolve

sentient *adj* having specified facts or feelings actively impressed on the mind — see CONSCIOUS

sentiment *n* **1** a subjective response to a person, thing, or situation — see FEELING 1

2 an idea that is believed to be true or valid without positive knowledge — see OPINION 1

sentimental *adj* appealing to the emotions in an obvious and tiresome way — see CORNY

sentimentalism *n* the state or quality of having an excess of tender feelings (as of love, nostalgia, or compassion) — see SENTIMENTALITY

sentimentality *n* the state or quality of having an excess of tender feelings (as of love, nostalgia, or compassion) ⟨the *sentimentality* of the story of star-crossed lovers only made it even more popular with moviegoers⟩
   synonyms mawkishness, mush, sappiness, sentimentalism, sloppiness
   related words emotion; sentiment; corn, schmaltz (*also* schmalz)
   near antonyms cynicism, hardheadedness, hardheartedness

sentinel *n* a person or group that watches over someone or something — see GUARD 1

sentry *n* a person or group that watches over someone or something — see GUARD 1

separable *adj* capable of being split into two or more parts or pieces ⟨the outdated belief that the atom is the smallest particle of matter and is not *separable*⟩
   synonyms divisible
   related words detachable
   near antonyms combinable, joinable
   antonyms indivisible, inseparable

separate *adj* **1** not the same or shared ⟨we stayed in *separate* apartments on our vacation⟩
   synonyms different, individual, respective
   related words disparate, dissimilar, distinct, distinctive, distinguishable, diverse, unalike, varied
   near antonyms identical, selfsame, very
   antonyms same
   2 not physically attached to another unit ⟨the housing development has 200 *separate* homes, each with its own enclosed yard⟩
   synonyms detached, disconnected, discrete, freestanding, single, unattached, unconnected
   related words independent, self-contained; individual, private
   antonyms attached, connected, joined
   3 not being under the rule or control of another — see FREE 1
   4 of, relating to, or belonging to a single person — see INDIVIDUAL 1

separate *vb* **1** to set or force apart ⟨we tried to *separate* the gluey pages, but they were stuck tight⟩
   synonyms break up, disconnect, disjoin, disjoint, dissever, dissociate, disunite, divide, divorce, part, ramify, resolve, sever, split, sunder, uncouple, unlink, unyoke
   related words decompose, disassemble, dissolve; bisect, fractionate, halve, quarter, segment, subdivide; break, rend, rip, rupture, tear; cut off, insulate, isolate, seclude, segregate, sequester; detach, disengage, disentangle, untie
   near antonyms assemble, associate, blend, combine, mingle, mix; connect, couple; unify; accumulate, agglutinate, attach, bind, cement, close, fasten, fuse, stick, weld
   antonyms join, link, unify, unite
   2 to go or move in different directions from a central point ⟨the searchers *separated* in order to cover more ground⟩
   synonyms branch (out), diverge, divide, fork
   related words bestrew, broadcast, clear out, disband, dispel, disperse, dissipate, distribute, scatter, sow; distance, recede, retreat

   near antonyms assemble, gather, meet
   antonyms converge, join
   3 to arrange or assign according to type — see CLASSIFY 1
   4 to set or keep apart from others — see ISOLATE
   5 to understand or point out the difference — see DISTINGUISH 1

separateness *n* the state of being alone or kept apart from others — see ISOLATION

separation *n* **1** the act or process of a whole separating into two or more parts or pieces ⟨the *separation* of Czechoslovakia into the Czech Republic and Slovakia⟩
   synonyms breakup, dissolution, disunion, division, fractionation, partition, schism, split
   related words breach, rupture; decomposition, disassembly, segmentation, subdivision; dispersal, scattering; administration, apportionment, distribution; isolation, seclusion, segregation, sequestration
   near antonyms assemblage, association; attachment, connection, link, linkage, linkup; combination, fusion
   antonyms unification, union
   2 the state of being kept distinct ⟨the *separation* of church and state is an important concept in the United States⟩
   synonyms demarcation, discreteness, discrimination, distinction
   related words differentiation
   near antonyms blurring, confusion
   3 a movement in different directions away from a common point — see DIVERGENCE
   4 an open space in a barrier (as a wall or hedge) — see GAP 1
   5 the act or process of two or more persons going off in different directions — see PARTING 1

sepulcher *or* **sepulchre** *n* a final resting place for a dead person — see GRAVE

sepulchral *adj* causing or marked by an atmosphere lacking in cheer — see GLOOMY 1

sepulture *n* **1** a final resting place for a dead person — see GRAVE
   2 the act or ceremony of putting a dead body in its final resting place — see BURIAL

sequel *n* a condition or occurrence traceable to a cause — see EFFECT 1

sequence *n* **1** a condition or occurrence traceable to a cause — see EFFECT 1
   2 a series of things linked together — see CHAIN 1
   3 the way objects in space or events in time are arranged or follow one another — see ORDER 1

sequential *adj* following one after another without others coming in between — see CONSECUTIVE

sequester *vb* **1** to set or keep apart from others — see ISOLATE
   2 to take ownership or control of (something) by right of one's authority — see CONFISCATE

sequestration *n* the state of being alone or kept apart from others — see ISOLATION

sere *adj* marked by little or no precipitation or humidity — see DRY 1

serene *adj* **1** free from disturbing noise or uproar — see QUIET 1
   2 free from emotional or mental agitation — see CALM 2
   3 free from storms or physical disturbance — see CALM 1

sereneness *n* a state of freedom from storm or disturbance — see CALM

THESAURUS

serenity *n* **1** a state of freedom from storm or disturbance — see CALM

2 evenness of emotions or temper — see EQUANIMITY

serial *adj* appearing in parts or numbers that follow regularly ⟨"Uncle Tom's Cabin" first appeared as a *serial* novel from 1851 to 1852⟩
synonyms episodic, periodic, periodical
related words sequential; recurrent, regular

serious *adj* **1** not joking or playful in mood or manner ⟨our parents were quite *serious* when they told us not to stay out too late⟩
synonyms earnest, grave, humorless, no-nonsense, sedate, severe, sober, solemn, staid, uncomic, unfunny, unsmiling, weighty
related words harsh, stern, strict; dignified, distinguished, elevated, serious-minded
near antonyms antic, comic, comical, droll, farcical, funny, hilarious, hysterical, laughable, light, light-headed, ludicrous, ridiculous, risible, riotous, screaming, side-splitting, uproarious; featherbrained, flighty, frivolous, goofy, harebrained, lighthearted, puerile, scatterbrained; absurd, asinine, balmy, brainless, cockeyed, crazy, cuckoo, daffy, daft, dotty, fatuous, foolish, half-witted, insane, jerky, kooky, loony (*also* looney), lunatic, mad, nonsensical, nutty, preposterous, sappy, screwball, senseless, silly, unwise, wacky, weak-minded, witless, zany
antonyms facetious, flip, flippant, humorous, jesting, jocular, joking, playful

2 having a matter of importance as its topic ⟨a very *serious* film that dealt with the aftermath of the Gulf War⟩
synonyms grave, heavy, weighty
related words big, consequential, eventful, important, major, material, meaningful, momentous, significant, substantial
near antonyms insignificant, little, minor, slight, small, trivial, unimportant
antonyms light

3 involving potential loss or injury — see DANGEROUS

seriousness *n* a mental state free of jesting or trifling — see EARNESTNESS

sermon *n* a public speech usually by a member of the clergy for the purpose of giving moral guidance or uplift ⟨a *sermon* whose message was that we should love our neighbors as much as we love ourselves⟩
synonyms homily
related words lecture, speech; lesson

serpent *n* a limbless reptile with a long body — see SNAKE 1

serpentine *adj* marked by a long series of irregular curves — see CROOKED 1

serrate *adj* notched or toothed along the edge — see SERRATED

serrated *adj* notched or toothed along the edge ⟨you should use a *serrated* knife when cutting bread, so you don't squash the loaf⟩
synonyms saw-toothed, serrate
related words wavy
near antonyms flat, smooth

serried *adj* having little space between items or parts — see CLOSE 1

servant *n* a person hired to perform household or personal services ⟨the wealthy family had *servants* to clean and cook for them⟩
synonyms domestic, flunky (*also* flunkey), lackey, menial, retainer, steward
related words butler, footman, groom, houseboy, man, majordomo, manservant, servitor, valet; handmaiden (*also* handmaid), housekeeper, housemaid, lady-in-waiting, maid, maidservant, wench, woman; attendant, follower
near antonyms boss, captain, chief, foreman, head, headman, helmsman, kingpin, leader, taskmaster
antonyms master

serve *vb* **1** to be a servant for ⟨he *served* his master faithfully for twenty years⟩
synonyms slave (for), work (for)
phrases wait on, wait upon

2 to be enough ⟨they made the pasta *serve* for eight guests⟩
synonyms do, suffice
related words answer, suit; assuage, content, quench, sate, satiate, satisfy

3 to be fitting or proper — see DO 1

4 to behave toward in a stated way — see TREAT 1

5 to have a certain purpose — see FUNCTION

6 to provide with something useful or desirable — see BENEFIT

server *n* a person who serves food or drink ⟨we had barely finished ordering when the *server* brought our salads⟩
synonyms waiter
related words waitress; bartender; steward, stewardess

service *adj* of or relating to the armed services — see MILITARY 1

service *n* **1** an act of kind assistance — see FAVOR 1

2 the capacity for being useful for some purpose — see USE 2

3 the combined army, air force, and navy of a nation — see ARMED FORCES

serviceability *n* the capacity for being useful for some purpose — see USE 2

serviceable *adj* **1** capable of being put to use or account — see PRACTICAL 1

2 capable of or suitable for being used for a particular purpose — see USABLE 1

serviceableness *n* the capacity for being useful for some purpose — see USE 2

serviceman *n* a person engaged in military service — see SOLDIER

servility *n* the state of being a slave — see SLAVERY 1

servitude *n* the state of being a slave — see SLAVERY 1

set *adj* **1** being in a state of fitness for some experience or action — see READY 1

2 firmly positioned in place and difficult to dislodge — see TIGHT 2

3 fully committed to achieving a goal — see DETERMINED 1

4 having been established and usually not subject to change — see FIXED 1

5 of a particular or exact sort — see EXPRESS 1

set *n* **1** a group of people acting together within a larger group — see FACTION

2 a group of people sharing a common interest and relating together socially — see GANG 2

3 a number of things considered as a unit — see GROUP 1

4 one of the units into which a whole is divided on the basis of a common characteristic — see CLASS 2

5 the array of painted backgrounds and furnishings used for a scene in a stage production — see SCENERY

set *vb* **1** to cover and warm eggs to hatch them ⟨the hen *set* for days⟩
synonyms brood, hatch, incubate, sit
related words lay, spawn; pip
2 to decide upon (the time or date for an event) usually from a position of authority — see APPOINT 1
3 to make an approximate or tentative judgment regarding — see ESTIMATE 1
4 *chiefly dialect* to rest on the buttocks or haunches — see SIT 1
5 to point or turn (something) toward a target or goal — see AIM 1
6 to come to an agreement or decision concerning the details of — see ARRANGE 1
7 to put securely in place or in a desired position — see FASTEN 2
8 to turn from a liquid into a substance resembling jelly — see COAGULATE
9 to arrange something in a certain spot or position — see PLACE 1
10 to become physically firm or solid — see HARDEN 1

setback *n* a change in status for the worse usually temporarily — see REVERSE 1

set down *vb* **1** to cause to sit down — see SEAT
2 to make a written note of — see RECORD 1

set in *vb* to come into existence — see BEGIN 2

set off *vb* to cause to function — see ACTIVATE

settee *n* a long upholstered piece of furniture designed for several sitters — see COUCH

setting *n* **1** the circumstances, conditions, or objects by which one is surrounded — see ENVIRONMENT
2 the place and time in which the action for a portion of a dramatic work (as a movie) is set — see SCENE 1

settle *vb* **1** to cause to come to rest at the bottom (as of a liquid) ⟨the light rain will *settle* the dust in the air⟩ ⟨careful handling will *settle* the lees in the bottom of the wine bottle⟩
synonyms lay, sediment
related words filter, screen, sieve, sift, strain; resettle
near antonyms disturb, mix, stir
antonyms raise
2 to give an opinion about (something at issue or in dispute) — see JUDGE 1
3 to come to an agreement or decision concerning the details of — see ARRANGE 1
4 to come to rest after descending from the air — see ALIGHT
5 to establish or place comfortably or snugly — see ENSCONCE 1
6 to free from distress or disturbance — see CALM 1
7 to gain emotional or mental control of — see COLLECT 1
8 to give what is owed for — see PAY 2
9 to make final, definite, or beyond dispute — see CLINCH
10 to stop the noise or speech of — see SILENCE 1

settle (down) *vb* to become still and orderly — see QUIET 1

settled *adj* **1** firmly established over time — see INVETERATE 1

2 having been established and usually not subject to change — see FIXED 1

settlement *n* an arrangement about action to be taken — see AGREEMENT 2

settler *n* **1** a person who settles in a new region — see FRONTIERSMAN
2 one that leaves one place to settle in another — see EMIGRANT

setup *n* **1** the way in which something is sized, arranged, or organized — see FORMAT 1
2 the way objects in space or events in time are arranged or follow one another — see ORDER 1

set up *vb* **1** to arrange something in a certain spot or position — see PLACE 1
2 to be responsible for the creation and early operation or use of — see FOUND
3 to fix in an upright position — see ERECT 1
4 to form by putting together parts or materials — see BUILD

seven seas *n pl* the whole body of salt water that covers nearly three-fourths of the earth — see OCEAN

sever *vb* to set or force apart — see SEPARATE 1

severe *adj* **1** given to exacting standards of discipline and self-restraint ⟨a *severe*, uncompromising teacher who locked the classroom door precisely when the bell rang and let no one in afterward⟩
synonyms austere, authoritarian, flinty, hard, harsh, heavy-handed, ramrod, rigid, rigorous, stern, strict
related words demanding, exacting; uncharitable, unforgiving; adamant, adamantine, hardened, hardhearted, immovable, implacable, inflexible, ossified, unbending, uncompromising, unyielding; dour, gruff; ascetic, monastic; browbeating, bullying; determined, firm, resolved, single-minded, steadfast, unflinching; dogged, intractable, obstinate, relentless
near antonyms easy, easygoing, laid-back, undemanding; charitable, kind, merciful, patient, soft, softhearted; accepting, compromising, yielding; responsive, willing; acquiescent, agreeable, amenable, compliant, flexible, pliable, pliant
antonyms forbearing, indulgent, lax, lenient, tolerant
2 harsh and threatening in manner or appearance — see GRIM 1
3 not joking or playful in mood or manner — see SERIOUS 1
4 difficult to endure — see HARSH 1
5 requiring considerable physical or mental effort — see HARD 2

severely *adv* in a manner so as to cause loss or suffering — see HARDLY 1

severity *n* the quality or state of being demanding or unyielding (as in discipline or criticism) ⟨Jane's parents were legendary for the *severity* of their discipline—she never got away with so much as a white lie⟩
synonyms hardness, harshness, inflexibility, rigidity, rigidness, rigorousness, sternness, strictness
related words hardheartedness, implacability, obduracy; dourness, gruffness; asceticism, austerity, monasticism; determination, firmness, resolve, steadfastness; obstinacy, stubbornness
near antonyms forbearance, indulgence, kindness, lenience, patience, softness, tenderness, tolerance; responsiveness, willingness; compliance, pliability
antonyms flexibility, gentleness, laxness, mildness

sew *vb* to close up with a series of interlacing stitches ⟨luckily, Mom was able to *sew* the tear in my pants so skillfully that they looked as good as new⟩
synonyms darn, stitch
related words mend, patch, repair; baste, ease, fell, finish, overcast; crochet, knit, quilt
sew up *vb* to have complete control over — see MONOPOLIZE
sex *n* sexual union involving penetration of the vagina by the penis — see SEXUAL INTERCOURSE
sexual intercourse *n* sexual union involving penetration of the vagina by the penis ⟨many people believe that it's best to wait to experience *sexual intercourse* until you're mature enough to handle it⟩
synonyms coitus, copulating, copulation, intercourse, mating, sex, sexual relations
related words fornication; safe sex; sexuality
phrases making love
sexual relations *n pl* sexual union involving penetration of the vagina by the penis — see SEXUAL INTERCOURSE
sexy *adj* of, relating to, or expressing sexual attraction — see EROTIC
shabby *adj* **1** showing signs of advanced wear and tear and neglect ⟨*shabby* wallpaper that was peeling from the walls⟩
synonyms dilapidated, dog-eared, grungy, mangy, mean, miserable, moth-eaten, neglected, ratty, run-down, scruffy, seedy, tacky, threadbare
related words abandoned, desolate, forlorn; broken-down, decrepit, worn-out; bedraggled, dingy, ragged, tattered; decaying, deteriorated, deteriorating, ramshackle; broken, damaged, destroyed, harmed, hurt, impaired, injured, ruined, wrecked
phrases gone to seed
near antonyms brand-new, fresh, new; cared-for, kept-up, maintained; mended, patched, rebuilt, reconstructed; smart, spiffy, spruce
2 worn or torn into or as if into rags — see RAGGED 2
shack *n* a small, simply constructed, and often temporary dwelling ⟨a farmer's *shack* out in the fields that's used for lambing and as a shelter from storms⟩
synonyms cabin, camp, hovel, hut, hutch, shanty
related words lean-to, shed; cot, cottage, lodge; cabana; bungalow, chalet; hogan, wickiup, wigwam
shackle *n* **1** something that physically prevents free movement — see BOND 1
2 shackles *pl* something that makes movement or progress more difficult — see ENCUMBRANCE
shackle *vb* **1** to confine or restrain with or as if with chains — see BIND 1
2 to create difficulty for the work or activity of — see HAMPER
shade *n* **1** partial darkness due to the obstruction of light rays ⟨it was hard to see in the *shade* after being in the brilliant sunlight⟩ ⟨the trees cast *shade*⟩
synonyms penumbra, shadiness, shadow, umbra
related words blackness, dimness, duskiness, gloominess, murkiness, obscurity, somberness; cloudiness, dullness (*also* dulness)
near antonyms brightness, brilliance, effulgence, illumination, incandescence, light, lightness, lucidity, lucidness, luminosity, radiance
2 a time or place of little or no light — see DARK 1
3 a property that becomes apparent when light falls on an object and by which things that are identical in form can be distinguished — see COLOR 1
4 a very small amount — see PARTICLE 1
5 the soul of a dead person thought of especially as appearing to living people — see GHOST
shade *vb* to shelter (something) from light and heat ⟨the trees *shaded* us quite nicely from the noonday sun⟩
synonyms shadow
related words cloud, darken, dim, dull; canopy, cover, protect, screen
near antonyms illuminate, light, lighten; expose
shaded *adj* protected from the sun's rays — see SHADY 1
shadiness *n* partial darkness due to the obstruction of light rays — see SHADE 1
shadow *n* **1** a person whose business is solving crimes and catching criminals or gathering information that is not easy to get — see DETECTIVE
2 partial darkness due to the obstruction of light rays — see SHADE 1
3 shadows *pl* a time or place of little or no light — see DARK 1
4 a tiny often physical indication of something lost or vanished — see VESTIGE
5 a very small amount — see PARTICLE 1
6 the soul of a dead person thought of especially as appearing to living people — see GHOST
shadow *vb* **1** to go after or on the track of — see FOLLOW 2
2 to make dark, dim, or indistinct — see CLOUD 1
3 to shelter (something) from light and heat — see SHADE
shadowed *adj* protected from the sun's rays — see SHADY 1
shadowing *n* the act of going after or in the tracks of another — see PURSUIT
shadowy *adj* **1** not seen or understood clearly — see FAINT 1
2 protected from the sun's rays — see SHADY 1
shady *adj* **1** protected from the sun's rays ⟨a lovely *shady* spot in the park that was pleasantly cool⟩
synonyms shaded, shadowed, shadowy
related words canopied, covered, sheltered; cloudy; dark, darkened, darkish, darkling, darksome, dim, dimmed, dusky, gloomy, moonless, murky, obscure, obscured, pitch-black, pitch-dark, somber (*or* sombre), sunless
near antonyms bedazzling, bright, brightened, brilliant, dazzling, effulgent, illuminated, illumined, incandescent, light, lighted (*or* lit), lucent, lucid, luminous; beaming, lambent, radiant, shining; lustrous
antonyms sunny
2 given to or marked by cheating and deception — see DISHONEST 2
3 giving good reason for being doubted, questioned, or challenged — see DOUBTFUL 2
4 given to acting in secret and to concealing one's intentions — see SNEAKY 1
shaft *n* **1** a narrow sharply defined line of light radiating from an object ⟨*shafts* of late-afternoon sunlight pierced the blinds and streaked the floor⟩
synonyms beam, ray
related words moonbeam, sunbeam; laser, spotlight
2 a weapon with a long straight handle and sharp head or blade — see SPEAR

shaggy *adj* **1** covered with or as if with hair — see HAIRY 1

2 made of or resembling hair — see HAIRY 2

shake *vb* **1** to make a series of small irregular or violent movements ⟨the bus rattled and *shook* as it barreled down a rutted road⟩

synonyms agitate, convulse, joggle, jolt, jounce, quake, quiver, shudder, vibrate, wobble

related words rock, sway; quaver, shiver, tremble; dodder, waver; flicker, fluctuate, flutter, oscillate, wave; beat, palpitate, pit-a-pat, pitter-patter, pulsate, pulse, throb

2 to get or keep away from (as a responsibility) through cleverness or trickery — see ESCAPE 2

shake *n* **1** a very small space of time — see INSTANT

2 shakes *pl* a sense of panic or extreme nervousness — see JITTERS

shake up *vb* to cause an often unpleasant surprise for — see SHOCK 1

shakiness *n* the quality or state of not being firmly fixed in position — see INSTABILITY

shaking *adj* marked by or given to small uncontrollable bodily movements — see SHAKY 1

shaking *n* **1** a series of slight movements by a body back and forth or from side to side — see VIBRATION

2 the act or a means of getting or keeping away from something undesirable — see ESCAPE 2

shaky *adj* **1** marked by or given to small uncontrollable bodily movements ⟨the old man's hands were so *shaky* that I was afraid he'd drop the glass⟩

synonyms quaking, quavery, shaking, shuddering, shuddery, tottery, trembling, tremulous, wobbling, wobbly

related words shivering, shivery

near antonyms controlled, firm, settled, stable, steady

2 giving good reason for being doubted, questioned, or challenged — see DOUBTFUL 2

shall *vb* to be under necessity or obligation to — see NEED 2

shallow *adj* **1** lacking significant physical depth ⟨the dog quickly dug a *shallow* hole that was barely deep enough to accommodate his bone⟩

synonyms depthless, shoal

related words skin-deep, superficial, surface; fathomable, measurable; finite, limited, measured, restricted; even, flat, flush, horizontal, level, plane, smooth

near antonyms abysmal, abyssal, bottomless, boundless, endless, immeasurable, inestimable, infinite, limitless, measureless, unfathomable, unlimited, vast; navigable

antonyms deep

2 having or showing a lack of depth of understanding or character — see SUPERFICIAL 2

shallow *n, usually* **shallows** *pl* a place where a body of water (as a sea or river) is shallow — see SHOAL

sham *adj* **1** being such in appearance only and made with or manufactured from usually cheaper materials — see IMITATION

2 being such in appearance only and made or manufactured with the intention of committing fraud — see COUNTERFEIT

3 lacking in natural or spontaneous quality — see ARTIFICIAL 1

sham *n* **1** a poor, insincere, or insulting imitation of something — see MOCKERY 1

2 an imitation that is passed off as genuine — see FAKE 1

sham *vb* to present a false appearance of — see FEIGN

shamble *vb* to move heavily or clumsily — see LUMBER 1

shambles *n pl* **1** a dirty or messy place — see PIGPEN

2 a state in which everything is out of order — see CHAOS

shame *n* **1** a feeling of responsibility for wrongdoing — see GUILT 1

2 a regrettable or blameworthy act — see CRIME 2

3 the state of having lost the esteem of others — see DISGRACE 1

shame *vb* to reduce to a lower standing in one's own eyes or in others' eyes — see HUMBLE

shamed *adj* suffering from or expressive of a feeling of responsibility for wrongdoing — see GUILTY 2

shamefaced *adj* suffering from or expressive of a feeling of responsibility for wrongdoing — see GUILTY 2

shameful *adj* not respectable — see DISREPUTABLE

shanty *n* a small, simply constructed, and often temporary dwelling — see SHACK

shape *n* **1** a state of being or fitness — see CONDITION 1

2 the outward appearance of something as distinguished from its substance — see FORM 1

3 the type of body that a person has — see PHYSIQUE

shape *vb* to change (something) so as to make it suitable for a new use or situation — see ADAPT

shape (up) *vb* to take on a definite form — see FORM 1

shapeless *adj* **1** badly or imperfectly formed — see MALFORMED

2 having no definite or recognizable form — see FORMLESS

share *n* **1** something belonging to, due to, or contributed by an individual member of a group ⟨my *share* of the lottery winnings is over a million dollars⟩ ⟨Sue's *share* of the bill comes to $13.44⟩

synonyms allotment, allowance, cut, part, portion, proportion, quota

related words lot, ration; commission, percentage; member, partition, section, segment

near antonyms aggregate, composite, compound, sum, total, totality; whole

2 a legal right to participation in the advantages, profits, and responsibility of something — see INTEREST 1

share *vb* to take a share or part — see PARTAKE

shared *adj* used or done by a number of people as a group — see COLLECTIVE

sharer *n* one who takes part in something — see PARTICIPANT

shark *n* **1** a dishonest person who uses clever means to cheat others out of something of value — see TRICKSTER 1

2 a person with a high level of knowledge or skill in a field — see EXPERT

sharp *adj* **1** having an edge thin enough to cut or pierce something ⟨be careful, as that knife is *sharp* enough to slice off a finger⟩

synonyms cutting, edged, edgy, ground, honed, keen, sharpened, stropped, trenchant, whetted

THESAURUS

related words clawlike; jabbing, jagged, lacerating, piercing, scratching, stabbing
near antonyms rounded, seamless, smooth; soft; even, flat, level, slick
antonyms blunt, blunted, dull, dulled, obtuse

2 causing intense mental or physical distress ⟨sudden *sharp* pains in your right lower belly can be a sign of appendicitis⟩
synonyms acute, agonizing, biting, excruciating, smart, smarting
related words bitter, cutting, keen, penetrating, piercing, raw, stinging; afflicting, distressing, disturbing, upsetting; cruel, grievous, harsh, heartrending, hurtful, lacerating, painful, paralyzing, severe, tormenting, torturous; insufferable, insupportable, intolerable, unacceptable, unbearable, unsupportable; appalling, awful, bad, dire, dreadful, ghastly, horrible, miserable, nasty, rotten, terrible, vile, wretched
near antonyms painless; acceptable, bearable, endurable, supportable, sustainable, tolerable; livable (*also* liveable), sufferable
antonyms dull

3 having a powerfully stimulating odor or flavor ⟨the cheese is so *sharp* that its rank aroma can practically clear a room⟩
synonyms nippy, pungent, strong
related words acid, acidic; acrid, bitter, harsh; piquant, spicy, tart, zesty; putrid, rancid, rank; acute, keen; animating, energizing, exciting, galvanizing, invigorating, provocative; appetizing, delectable, delicious, palatable, toothsome; flavorful, savory, tasty
near antonyms aged, mellow; gentle, soft; flat, flavorless, insipid; savorless, tasteless; dilute, thin, watery, weak
antonyms bland, mild, smooth

4 tapering to a thin tip — see POINTED 1
5 being in the latest or current fashion — see STYLISH
6 being strikingly neat and trim in style or appearance — see SMART 1
7 causing intense discomfort to one's skin — see CUTTING 1
8 given to or marked by cheating and deception — see DISHONEST 2
9 having or showing a practical cleverness or judgment — see SHREWD
10 having or showing quickness of mind — see INTELLIGENT 1
11 marked by the use of wit that is intended to cause hurt feelings — see SARCASTIC
12 able to sense slight impressions or differences — see ACUTE 1
13 uncomfortably cool — see CHILLY 1

sharp *adv* as stated or indicated without the slightest difference — see EXACTLY 1

sharpen *vb* to make sharp or sharper ⟨you need to *sharpen* your penknife's blade frequently in order to be able to whittle properly⟩
synonyms edge, grind, hone, strop, whet
related words file
near antonyms buff, burnish, gloss, polish, round, smooth
antonyms blunt, dull

sharpened *adj* having an edge thin enough to cut or pierce something — see SHARP 1

sharper *n* a dishonest person who uses clever means to cheat others out of something of value — see TRICKSTER 1

sharp–eyed *adj* having unusually keen vision ⟨a very *sharp-eyed* child found the last Easter egg, which was hidden in the flower arrangement⟩
synonyms clear-sighted, lynx-eyed
related words sighted; alert, attentive, aware, observant, observing, vigilant, watchful
near antonyms blind, eyeless, sightless, stone-blind, unseeing; astigmatic, myopic, nearsighted, shortsighted; unobservant, unobserving; purblind

sharply *adv* in a strikingly neat and trim manner — see SMARTLY

sharpness *n* **1** a harsh or sharp quality — see EDGE 1
2 an uncomfortable degree of coolness — see CHILL

sharpshooter *n* a person skilled in shooting at a target — see MARKSMAN

sharp–witted *adj* **1** having or showing a practical cleverness or judgment — see SHREWD
2 having or showing quickness of mind — see INTELLIGENT 1

shatter *vb* **1** to bring to a complete end the physical soundness, existence, or usefulness of — see DESTROY 1
2 to cause to break open or into pieces by or as if by an explosive — see BLAST 1
3 to cause to break with violence and much noise — see SMASH 1

shave *vb* **1** to make (as hair) shorter with or as if with the use of shears — see CLIP
2 to pass lightly across or touch gently especially in passing — see BRUSH

shaver *n* a male person who has not yet reached adulthood — see BOY

shear *vb* to make (as hair) shorter with or as if with the use of shears — see CLIP

sheath *n* something that encloses another thing especially to protect it — see ¹CASE 1

sheathe *vb* to cover with something that protects ⟨sometimes shipbuilders *sheathe* a ship's bottom with copper for extra protection from barnacles and other threats⟩
synonyms face
related words apparel, array, clothe, dress, garb, robe; side, skin; embosom, embower, embrace, encase, enclose (*also* inclose), encompass, enshroud, envelop, enwrap, invest, lap, mantle, shroud, surround, swathe, veil, wrap; blanket, overlay, overspread
near antonyms bare, denude, expose, strip

shed *vb* **1** to cast (a natural bodily covering or appendage) aside ⟨a snake's skin doesn't grow as the snake does, so every so often the snake will *shed* its old skin⟩
synonyms exfoliate, molt, slough (*also* sluff)
related words flake, peel, scale; discard
2 to get rid of as useless or unwanted — see DISCARD

sheen *n* brightness created by light reflected from a surface — see SHINE 1

sheep *n* an innocent or gentle person — see LAMB

sheepish *adj* not comfortable around people — see SHY 2

sheepishly *adv* in manner showing no signs of pride or self-assertion — see LOWLY

sheer *adj* **1** very thin and easy to see through ⟨we had to get window shades because passersby could see right through our *sheer* curtains⟩
synonyms filmy, gauzy, gossamer, gossamery, transparent

related words clear, limpid, liquid, lucent, pellucid; lucid, translucent; dainty, delicate, flimsy, fragile, frail; colorless, uncolored

near antonyms opaque; cloudy, foggy, hazy, misty, murky, smoky (*also* smokey); drab, dull, lackluster, lusterless

2 having no exceptions or restrictions — see ABSOLUTE 2

3 having an incline approaching the perpendicular — see STEEP 1

sheer *vb* **1** to change one's course or direction — see TURN 3

2 to depart abruptly from a straight line or course — see SWERVE 1

sheet *vb* to form a layer over — see COVER 2

shell *n* **1** something that encloses another thing especially to protect it — see ¹CASE 1

2 the arrangement of parts that gives something its basic form — see FRAME 1

shell *vb* **1** to remove the natural covering of — see PEEL

2 to use bombs or artillery against — see BOMBARD

shellacking *n* failure to win a contest — see DEFEAT 1

shell-shocked *adj* suffering from high levels of physical and especially psychological stress — see STRESSED-OUT

shelter *n* something (as a building) that offers cover from the weather or protection from danger ⟨the sudden fierce storm forced us to run to the nearest *shelter*⟩

synonyms asylum, harbor, harborage, haven, refuge, retreat, sanctuary, sanctum

related words anchorage, mooring, port; cover, screen; abode, diggings, domicile, dwelling, habitation, house, housing, lodging, lodgment (*or* lodgement), pad, place, quarters, residence, rest, roof; den, lair, hermitage, hideaway, hideout; fastness, fort, fortress, palisade, stronghold; lean-to, shed, windbreak

shelter *vb* **1** to be or provide a shelter for ⟨the abandoned barn *shelters* a colony of stray cats⟩

synonyms harbor

related words cover, defend, protect, safeguard, screen, shield, ward; domicile, house, place; shade, shadow

near antonyms expose

2 to provide with living quarters or shelter — see HOUSE 1

sheltered *adj* hidden from view — see SECLUDED

shelve *vb* to assign to a later time — see POSTPONE

shenanigans *n pl* **1** playful, reckless behavior that is not intended to cause serious harm — see MISCHIEF 1

2 wildly playful or mischievous behavior — see HORSEPLAY

shepherd *vb* to give advice and instruction to (someone) regarding the course or process to be followed — see GUIDE 1

shibboleth *n* **1** an attention-getting word or phrase used to publicize something (as a campaign or product) — see SLOGAN

2 an idea or expression that has been used by many people — see COMMONPLACE

shield *n* means or method of defending — see DEFENSE 1

shield *vb* **1** to drive danger or attack away from — see DEFEND 1

2 to place a protective layer over — see COVER 3

shift *n* **1** an action planned or taken to achieve a desired result — see MEASURE 1

2 the act or an instance of changing position — see MOVEMENT 1

shift *vb* **1** to change the place or position of — see MOVE 1

2 to change one's position — see MOVE 3

3 to pass from one form, state, or level to another — see CHANGE 2

4 to give up (something) and take something else in return — see CHANGE 3

5 to meet one's day-to-day needs — see GET ALONG 1

shifting *n* the act or an instance of changing position — see MOVEMENT 1

shiftless *adj* not easily aroused to action or work — see LAZY

shiftlessness *n* an inclination not to do work or engage in activities — see LAZINESS

shifty *adj* **1** given to acting in secret and to concealing one's intentions — see SNEAKY 1

2 given to or marked by cheating and deception — see DISHONEST 2

shillelagh *n* a heavy rigid stick used as a weapon or for punishment — see CLUB 1

shilly-shally *vb* to show uncertainty about the right course of action — see HESITATE

shilly-shallying *n* the act or an instance of pausing because of uncertainty about the right course of action — see HESITATION

shimmer *vb* to shoot forth bursts of light — see FLASH 1

shindig *n* a social gathering — see PARTY 1

shindy *n* a state of noisy, confused activity — see COMMOTION

shine *n* **1** brightness created by light reflected from a surface ⟨the troop inspector insisted on nothing less than a dazzling *shine* from every pair of shoes in the line of review⟩

synonyms gloss, luster (*or* lustre), polish, sheen

related words glare, gleam, glimmer, glint, glisten, glow, shimmer; flicker, sparkle, twinkle; illumination, irradiation; iridescence, luminescence; brightness, brilliance, luminosity, radiance; finish, glaze

near antonyms dimness, dinginess, dirtiness, drabness, dullness (*also* dulness), flatness; grayness, paleness; cloudiness, gloom, murkiness, obscurity, somberness

2 the steady giving off of the form of radiation that makes vision possible — see LIGHT 1

3 positive regard for something — see LIKING

shine *vb* **1** to emit rays of light ⟨the sun appears to *shine* particularly brightly in summer because that is when it's closest to the Earth⟩

synonyms beam, radiate

related words blaze, burn, fire, flame, gleam, glimmer, glint, glisten, glitter, glow, shimmer; blink, flare, flash, flicker, scintillate, sparkle, twinkle, wink; beat (down), glare; brighten, illuminate, illumine, irradiate, light, lighten; bedazzle, blind, daze, dazzle

near antonyms blacken, darken; lower (*also* lour)

2 to make smooth or glossy usually by repeatedly applying surface pressure — see POLISH

shining *adj* giving off or reflecting much light — see BRIGHT 1

shiny *adj* giving off or reflecting much light — see BRIGHT 1

ship *n* a large craft for travel by water ⟨we chose

to spend our vacation on a cruise *ship* traveling through the Caribbean⟩

synonyms boat, vessel

related words argosy, containership, corvette, cruiser, cutter, destroyer, ferryboat, flagship, freighter, icebreaker, ironclad, lightship, liner, man-of-war, merchantman, merchant ship, packet, steamer, supertanker, tanker, trader, tramp, transport, warship

ship *vb* to cause to go or be taken from one place to another — see SEND

shippable *adj* capable of being taken from one place to another by public carrier ⟨only boxes of five pounds and under are *shippable* by the postal service⟩

synonyms transferable, transmittable, transportable-

related words addressable

antonyms nontransferable, receivable

shipshape *adj* being clean and in good order — see NEAT 1

shipwreck *n* the destruction or loss of a ship ⟨the *shipwreck* of much of the Spanish Armada ended Spain's plans for invading England⟩

synonyms shipwrecking, wreck, wreckage, wrecking

related words beaching, grounding, stranding; foundering, sinking

near antonyms salvage, salvaging

shipwreck *vb* to cause irreparable damage to (a ship) by running aground or sinking ⟨the helmsman fell asleep at the wheel and *shipwrecked* his yacht on the rocks⟩

synonyms strand, wreck

related words beach; founder, sink

near antonyms salvage

shipwrecking *n* the destruction or loss of a ship — see SHIPWRECK

shirk *vb* **1** to get or keep away from (as a responsibility) through cleverness or trickery — see ESCAPE 2

2 to leave undone or unattended to especially through carelessness — see NEGLECT 2

shirker *n* one who deliberately avoids work or duty — see SLACKER

shirty *adj, chiefly British* feeling or showing anger — see ANGRY

shiver *n* **1** an instance of shaking involuntarily with fear or cold ⟨Joe experienced a sudden *shiver* when confronted with the sight of the dark basement⟩

synonyms quiver, shudder, tremble

related words agitation, convulsing, jolt, quake, shake, tremor, vibration, wobble; fluctuation, flutter, oscillation, wave; beat, palpitation, pulsation, pulse, throb

2 shivers *pl* a sense of panic or extreme nervousness — see JITTERS

shivery *adj* having a low or subnormal temperature — see COLD 1

shoal *adj* lacking significant physical depth — see SHALLOW 1

shoal *n* a place where a body of water (as a sea or river) is shallow ⟨the *shoals* off Nantucket Island are famous as the final resting places of many ill-fated ships⟩

synonyms ford, shallows

related words bank, bar, sandbank, sandbar

near antonyms trench; abyss, deep, depth

shock *n* **1** a forceful coming together of two things — see IMPACT 1

2 the state of being strongly impressed by something unexpected or unusual — see SURPRISE 2

shock *vb* **1** to cause an often unpleasant surprise for ⟨Mom was *shocked* by the terrible news that her cousin had died in an accident⟩ ⟨Jack was *shocked* to find out that his grades were much lower than he realized⟩

synonyms appall, bowl (over), floor, jolt, shake up

related words affright, alarm, dismay, frighten, horrify, panic, scare, spook, startle, terrify, terrorize; disgust, nauseate, repel, revolt, sicken, turn off; displease, offend, outrage, scandalize; amaze, astound, awe; chill, daunt, demoralize, dispirit, unman, unnerve; discompose, disconcert, disquiet, disturb, perturb, unsettle, upset; crush, overpower, overwhelm

phrases knock for a loop

near antonyms cushion; delight, gratify, please, rejoice, tickle; charm, entice, tempt; cheer, comfort, console, solace, soothe; reassure

2 to make a strong impression on (someone) with something unexpected — see SURPRISE 1

3 to strike with fear — see FRIGHTEN

shocked *adj* **1** affected with sudden and great wonder or surprise — see THUNDERSTRUCK

2 filled with disgust — see SICK 2

shocking *adj* **1** causing a strong emotional reaction because unexpected — see SURPRISING 1

2 causing fear — see FEARFUL 1

3 causing intense displeasure, disgust, or resentment — see OFFENSIVE 1

4 extremely disturbing or repellent — see HORRIBLE 1

shoddy *adj* of low quality — see CHEAP 2

shoes *n pl* a way of looking at or thinking about something — see POINT OF VIEW

shoestring *n* a very small sum of money — see MITE 1

shoot *n* a branch of a main stem especially of a plant — see OFFSHOOT 1

shoot *vb* **1** to cause (a projectile) to be driven forward with force ⟨BB guns *shoot* small round metal pellets⟩

synonyms blast, discharge, fire, loose

related words launch, project; blaze (at), snipe (at); cast, catapult, fling, heave, hurl, pelt, pitch, sling, throw, toss

2 to cause a weapon to release a missile with great force ⟨soldiers train extensively to learn to *shoot* accurately and quickly⟩

synonyms blast, discharge, fire

related words blaze, pepper, snipe

3 to strike with a missile from a gun ⟨hunters can *shoot* deer only during the legally specified open season⟩

synonyms drill, gun, plug, pop

related words blaze, pepper; blast (at), fire (at); pick off; overshoot; snipe (at); croak [*slang*], destroy, dispatch, do in, fell, kill, slay; annihilate, blot out, butcher, decimate, massacre, slaughter, wipe out

4 to proceed or move quickly — see HURRY 2

5 to take a photograph of — see PHOTOGRAPH

6 to throw or give off — see EMIT 1

shoot (up) *vb* to rise abruptly and rapidly — see SKYROCKET

shooter *n* **1** a person skilled in shooting at a target — see MARKSMAN

2 one who takes photographs — see PHOTOGRAPHER

shop *n* **1** *also* **shoppe** an establishment where goods are sold to consumers ⟨the only *shop* which carries that game is halfway across the state⟩
synonyms bazaar, emporium, store
related words market, marketplace, outlet, showroom; boutique, department store, dime store, five-and-ten, thrift shop, variety store
2 a building or set of buildings for the manufacturing of goods — see FACTORY

¹shore *n* something that holds up or serves as a foundation for something else — see SUPPORT 1

²shore *n* the usually sandy or gravelly land bordering a body of water — see BEACH

shore (up) *vb* to hold up or serve as a foundation for — see SUPPORT 3

short *adj* **1** having relatively little height ⟨a lot of boys are *shorter* than the girls in middle school, but they quickly catch up by high school⟩
synonyms little, low, low-lying
related words dwarf, dwarfish; petite, slight; diminutive, little, pint-size (*or* pint-sized), small, smallish; bantam, bitty, dinky, miniature, minimized, minute, puny, teeny, teeny-weeny, tiny, undersized, wee; dumpy, flat, scrubby, squat, squatty, stubby, stumpy, stunted
near antonyms elevated, lifted, raised, uplifted, upswept; high-rise, statuesque; gangling, gangly, lanky, rangy
antonyms high, lofty, tall, towering
2 not lasting for a considerable time ⟨fortunately for those of us in the hot sun, the graduation speech was *short* and to the point⟩
synonyms brief, condensed, little
related words abbreviated, abridged, curtailed, cut-back, shortened; compact, condensed; abrupt, sudden; ephemeral, fleeting, momentary, short-lived, transient, transitory; impermanent; compendious, concise, crisp, epigrammatic, laconic, pithy, succinct, summary, terse; short-range, short-term
near antonyms endless, everlasting, interminable, persistent, unending; longish, overlong, prolonged, protracted; permanent; enlarged, expanded, supplemented; long-range, long-term
antonyms extended, great, lengthy, long, long-lived, marathon
3 not coming up to a usual standard or meeting a particular need ⟨regrettably, the art supplies are *short* this year, so you'll have to share⟩
synonyms deficient, inadequate, insufficient, lacking, scarce, shy, wanting
related words hand-to-mouth, light, meager, niggardly, poor, scant, scanty, skimpy, slender, slim, spare, sparse, stingy; bare, mere, minimum; slight, small
near antonyms abundant, ample, bounteous, bountiful, copious, generous, liberal, plenteous, plentiful; enlarged, expanded, supplemented; abounding, overflowing, teeming; lavish, luxuriant, rich; big, considerable, hefty, jumbo, large, largish, oversize (*or* oversized), sizable (*or* sizeable), substantial, super
antonyms adequate, enough, sufficient
4 having a texture that readily breaks into little pieces under pressure — see CRISP 1

short *adv* with great suddenness ⟨the bicyclist ahead of me unexpectedly pulled up *short* and I plowed into him⟩

synonyms abruptly, suddenly
related words quickly; surprisingly, unexpectedly
near antonyms gradually, slowly; hesitantly

shortage *n* a falling short of an essential or desirable amount or number — see DEFICIENCY

shortchange *vb* to rob by the use of trickery or threats — see FLEECE

shortcoming *n* a defect in character — see FAULT 1

shorten *vb* to make less in extent or duration ⟨we decided to *shorten* the distance we had to walk home by cutting across the neighbor's lawn⟩ ⟨if Grandma has to go shopping today, you'll need to *shorten* your visit⟩
synonyms abbreviate, abridge, curtail, cut back
related words digest, summarize; abate, compress, constrict, contract, cut, cut down, pare, prune, trim; decrease, de-escalate, deflate, diminish, dock, dwindle, lessen, lower, moderate, modify, reduce, retrench, shrink, slash, taper
near antonyms enlarge, expand, supplement; add, aggrandize, amplify, augment, balloon, boost, dilate, escalate, heighten, increase, maximize, raise; blow up, distend, inflate, swell
antonyms elongate, extend, lengthen, prolong, protract

short–lived *adj* lasting only for a short time — see MOMENTARY

shortly *adv* **1** in a few words ⟨the sudden closing of the restaurant was announced only with a *shortly* worded sign: "Out of Business"⟩
synonyms briefly, compactly, concisely, crisply, laconically, pithily, succinctly, summarily, tersely
related words aphoristically; exactly, precisely; abruptly, bluntly, brusquely, curtly
phrases in a nutshell
near antonyms redundantly, repetitiously
antonyms diffusely, long-windedly, verbosely, wordily
2 at or within a short time ⟨the test will begin *shortly*, so don't go too far away to find a bathroom⟩
synonyms anon, momentarily, presently, soon
related words directly, forthwith, immediately, instantly, now, promptly, pronto, right away, right now, straightaway
phrases by and by

shortness *n* the condition of being short — see BREVITY 1

shortsighted *adj* **1** able to see near things more clearly than distant ones — see NEARSIGHTED
2 not thinking about and providing for the future — see IMPROVIDENT

short story *n* a work with imaginary characters and events that is shorter and usually less complex than a novel — see STORY 1

short–tempered *adj* easily irritated or annoyed — see IRRITABLE

short–term *adj* intended to last, continue, or serve for a limited time — see TEMPORARY 1

shot *n* **1** a directed propelling of a missile by a firearm or artillery piece ⟨cannon operators often had to use several *shots* to figure out the range of their targets⟩
synonyms blasting, discharge, firing
related words potshot; barrage, bombardment, broadside, burst, cannonade, fusillade, hail, salvo, storm, volley
2 an effort to do or accomplish something — see ATTEMPT

THESAURUS

3 a picture created from an image recorded on a light-sensitive surface by a camera — see PHOTOGRAPH

4 a person skilled in shooting at a target — see MARKSMAN

5 the portion of a serving of a beverage that is swallowed at one time — see DRINK 2

should *vb* to be under necessity or obligation to — see NEED 2

shoulder *vb* to take to or upon oneself — see ASSUME 1

shout *n* a loud vocal expression of strong emotion ⟨Jason gave a sudden *shout* of surprise when the shower abruptly turned ice-cold⟩

synonyms cry, holler, hoot, howl, yell, yowl, whoop

related words scream, screech, shriek, squall, squeak, squeal, yelp; bellow, clamor, roar; caterwaul, wail

near antonyms mumble, murmur, mutter; gasp, whimper, whisper

shout *vb* to speak so as to be heard at a distance — see CALL 1

shove *vb* **1** to apply force to (someone or something) so that it moves in front of one — see PUSH 1

2 to push steadily against with some force — see PRESS 1

shove (off) *vb* to leave a place often for another — see GO 2

shovel *vb* to hollow out or form (something) by removing earth — see DIG 1

show *n* **1** an outward and often exaggerated indication of something abstract (as a feeling) for effect ⟨the children made a *show* of disgust when confronted with asparagus⟩

synonyms demonstration, display, exhibition, flaunting

related words act, pretense (*or* pretence), simulation; affectation, pose, sham; betrayal, disclosure

2 a display of emotion or behavior that is insincere or intended to deceive — see MASQUERADE

3 outward and often deceptive indication — see APPEARANCE 2

4 a public showing of objects of interest — see EXHIBITION 1

show *vb* **1** to present so as to invite notice or attention ⟨Julie made sure she *showed* the test paper with a big A on it to everyone in her family⟩

synonyms display, disport, exhibit, expose, flash, flaunt, parade, show off, sport, strut, unveil

related words brandish, flourish; advertise, air, broadcast, proclaim, publicize; divulge, talk (about), tell (of); bare, discover, reveal, uncloak, uncover

near antonyms camouflage, disguise, mask; conceal, cover, curtain, enshroud, hide, obscure, occult, shroud, veil

2 to make known (something abstract) through outward signs ⟨John's expressive face *shows* his every thought and emotion clearly⟩

synonyms bespeak, betray, demonstrate, display, expose, evince, give away, manifest, reveal

related words bare, disclose, unbosom, uncloak, uncover; advertise, air, broadcast, proclaim, publicize

near antonyms belie, misrepresent; distort, falsify, garble, twist; camouflage, disguise; gild, gloss (over), varnish, whitewash; conceal, counterfeit, cover, hide, mask, obscure, veil

3 to gain full recognition or acceptance of — see ESTABLISH 1

4 to give advice and instruction to (someone) regarding the course or process to be followed — see GUIDE 1

5 to point out the way for (someone) especially from a position in front — see LEAD 1

shower *n* **1** a heavy fall of objects — see RAIN 2

2 a rapid or overwhelming outpouring of many things at once — see BARRAGE

shower *vb* to give readily and in large quantities — see RAIN 2

showiness *n* excessive or unnecessary display — see OSTENTATION

show off *vb* **1** to engage in attention-getting playful or boisterous behavior — see CUT UP

2 to present so as to invite notice or attention — see SHOW 1

show up *vb* **1** to come into view — see APPEAR 1

2 to get to a destination — see COME 2

3 to reveal the true nature of — see EXPOSE 1

showy *adj* likely to attract attention — see NOTICEABLE

shred *n* a very small amount — see PARTICLE 1

shred *vb* to cause (something) to separate into jagged pieces by violently pulling at it — see TEAR 1

shrew *n* a bad-tempered scolding woman ⟨Rip Van Winkle went off into mountains to escape his wife, a *shrew* who made his life miserable⟩

synonyms fury, harpy, termagant, virago

related words carper, castigator, censurer, caviler (*or* caviller), critic, faultfinder, nitpicker, railer, scold; belittler, derider, detractor; pettifogger, quibbler

shrewd *adj* having or showing a practical cleverness or judgment ⟨a *shrewd* used car dealer who knew how to make the best possible deal⟩ ⟨*shrewd* investments that paid off big⟩

synonyms astute, canny, clear-sighted, hardheaded, knowing, sharp, sharp-witted, smart

related words artful, cagey (*also* cagy), crafty, cunning, devious, foxy, guileful, slick, sly, subtle, wily; discerning, insightful, perceptive, perspicacious, sagacious, sage, sapient, wise; experienced, veteran; discriminating, discriminative; agile, alert, brainy, bright, brilliant, clever, intelligent, keen, quick, quick-witted; apt, ingenious, resourceful; informed, knowledgeable, well-read

near antonyms artless, guileless, ingenuous, innocent, naive (*or* naïve); exploitable, gullible; undiscerning, unperceptive, unwise; dense, dull, obtuse; brainless, dumb, feebleminded, simple, slow, stupid, unintelligent, weak-minded; foolish, idiotic, imbecilic, moronic, silly, simple, thoughtless, witless; ignorant, uninformed

antonyms unknowing

shriek *vb* to cry out loudly and emotionally — see SCREAM

shrieking *adj* having a high musical pitch or range — see SHRILL

shrill *adj* having a high musical pitch or range ⟨the *shrill* sound of a policeman's whistle⟩

synonyms acute, high-pitched, piping, screeching, shrieking, squeaking, squeaky, treble, whistling

related words peeping, thin, tinny; piercing, ear-splitting, piercing, penetrating, strident; squealing, whining, yelping

near antonyms gruff

antonyms bass, deep, low, throaty

shrill *vb* to cry out loudly and emotionally — see SCREAM

shrimp *n* **1** a living thing much smaller than others of its kind — see DWARF 1

2 a person of no importance or influence — see NOBODY

shrine *n* a place that is considered sacred (as within a religion) ⟨for centuries pilgrims have traveled to the *shrine* of Saint Thomas à Becket in Canterbury, England⟩

synonyms sanctuary, sanctum

related words reliquary

shrink *vb* **1** to become smaller in size or volume through the drawing together of particles of matter — see CONTRACT 2

2 to draw back in fear, pain, or disgust — see FLINCH

3 to grow less in scope or intensity especially gradually — see DECREASE 2

shrinkage *n* the amount by which something is lessened — see DECREASE

shroud *n* something that covers or conceals like a piece of cloth — see CLOAK 1

shroud *vb* **1** to keep secret or shut off from view — see ¹HIDE 2

2 to make dark, dim, or indistinct — see CLOUD 1

3 to surround or cover closely — see ENFOLD 1

shrug off *vb* to overlook or dismiss as of little importance — see EXCUSE 1

shuck *vb* to remove the natural covering of — see PEEL

shuck (off) *vb* to get rid of as useless or unwanted — see DISCARD

shudder *n* an instance of shaking involuntarily with fear or cold — see SHIVER 1

shudder *vb* to make a series of small irregular or violent movements — see SHAKE 1

shuddering *adj* marked by or given to small uncontrollable bodily movements — see SHAKY 1

shuddering *n* a series of slight movements by a body back and forth or from side to side — see VIBRATION

shuddery *adj* marked by or given to small uncontrollable bodily movements — see SHAKY 1

shuffle *n* an unorganized collection or mixture of various things — see MISCELLANY 1

shuffle *vb* **1** to move heavily or clumsily — see LUMBER 1

2 to undo the proper order or arrangement of — see DISORDER

shun *vb* to get or keep away from (as a responsibility) through cleverness or trickery — see ESCAPE 2

shunning *n* the act or a means of getting or keeping away from something undesirable — see ESCAPE 2

shush *vb* to stop the noise or speech of — see SILENCE 1

shut *vb* **1** to position (something) so as to prevent passage through an opening — see CLOSE 1

2 to stop the operations of — see CLOSE 2

shutdown *n* the stopping of a process or activity — see END 1

shutoff *n* the stopping of a process or activity — see END 1

shut off *vb* to bring (as an action or operation) to an immediate end — see STOP 1

shutterbug *n* one who takes photographs — see PHOTOGRAPHER

shut up *vb* to stop talking ⟨it's not polite to tell your classmates to *shut up*, even if you disagree with them⟩

synonyms clam up, hush, quiet (down)

related words calm (down), cool (down), settle (down); haw, hem

antonyms speak, talk

shy *adj* **1** easily frightened ⟨a *shy* cat who hid under the bed every time she heard any loud noise⟩

synonyms fainthearted, fearful, mousy (*or* mousey), scary, skittish, timid, timorous

related words chicken, chickenhearted, cowardly, craven, dastardly, lily-livered, jittery, jumpy, pusillanimous, spineless, unheroic, yellow; anxious, apprehensive, nervous; afraid, alarmed, horrified, panicked, panicky, scared, shocked, spooked, startled, terrified, terrorized

near antonyms brave, courageous, dauntless, doughty, fearless, gallant, greathearted, heroic, intrepid, lionhearted, stalwart, stout, stouthearted, valiant, valorous; assured, confident, self-assured, self-confident; determined, firm, game, plucky, resolute, unflinching, unswerving; mettlesome, spirited, spunky

antonyms adventuresome, adventurous, audacious, bold, daring, dashing, gutsy, hardy, venturous, venturesome

2 not comfortable around people ⟨a *shy* person who finds talking to anyone but a close friend to be an awkward and unpleasant experience⟩

synonyms bashful, coy, demure, diffident, introverted, modest, retiring, sheepish

related words antisocial, unsociable, unsocial; awkward, embarrassed, self-conscious, unadventurous, unassertive, unenterprising; inhibited, reserved, uneasy, uptight

near antonyms convivial, sociable, social; bold, dashing, forceful; brash, forward, uninhibited, unreserved

antonyms extroverted (*also* extraverted), immodest, outgoing

3 not coming up to a usual standard or meeting a particular need — see SHORT 3

sick *adj* **1** temporarily suffering from a disorder of the body ⟨Jessie was *sick* with a cold on Monday and had to stay home from school⟩

synonyms ailing, bad, down, ill, indisposed, peaked, poorly, punk, run-down, sickened, unhealthy, unsound, unwell

related words nauseated, nauseous, qualmish, queasy (*also* queazy), sickish, squeamish; airsick, carsick, seasick, dizzy, light-hearted, woozy; achy, feverish; diseased, disordered; feeble, frail, infirm, sickly, weak, weakly; afflicted, troubled, challenged, crippled, debilitated, disabled, incapacitated, lame

phrases out of sorts, under the weather

near antonyms cured; better, convalescing, improved, mending, recovering, recuperating, rehabilitated; hardy, hearty, lusty, robust, rugged, stalwart, strong, tough; blooming, bouncing, flourishing, flush, thriving

antonyms chipper, hale, healthful, healthy, sound, well, whole, wholesome

2 filled with disgust ⟨it makes me *sick* to think of someone hurting a helpless animal⟩

synonyms disgusted, nauseated, repelled, repulsed, revolted, shocked, sickened, squeamish

related words angry, displeased, mad, upset

near antonyms delighted, pleased, thrilled; be-

guiled, bewitched, captivated, charmed, enchanted, enthralled, fascinated, mesmerized
3 affected with nausea — see NAUSEOUS
4 having one's patience, interest, or pleasure exhausted — see WEARY 2
sicken *vb* to cause to feel disgust — see DISGUST
sicken (with) *vb* to become affected with (a disease or disorder) — see CONTRACT 1
sickened *adj* **1** temporarily suffering from a disorder of the body — see SICK 1
2 filled with disgust — see SICK 2
sickening *adj* causing intense displeasure, disgust, or resentment — see OFFENSIVE 1
sickish *adj* affected with nausea — see NAUSEOUS
sickly *adj* chronically or repeatedly suffering from poor health ⟨a *sickly* foal that seemed to catch everything that the other horses had⟩
synonyms ailing, invalid, weakly
related words bedridden; delicate, fragile, frail; dying, fading, incurable, moribund; challenged, crippled, debilitated, incapacitated, lame; decrepit, enfeebled, feeble, infirm, weak, weakened, worn-out
near antonyms able-bodied, nondisabled, nonhandicapped
antonyms healthy, well
sickness *n* **1** the condition of not being in good health ⟨Jamie pleaded *sickness* and tried to stay home from school every single time there was a spelling test scheduled⟩
synonyms illness, indisposition, unhealthiness, unsoundness
related words malaise; ailment, condition, disease, disorder, malady, trouble, upset; debility, decrepitude, feebleness, frailness, infirmity, lameness
near antonyms fettle, fitness, shape; hardiness, heartiness, lustiness, robustness, ruggedness, stamina, strength, toughness, vigor, vigorousness, vitality; bloom, flush, flushness; weal, welfare, well-being
antonyms health, healthiness, soundness, wellness, wholeness, wholesomeness
2 an abnormal state that disrupts a plant or animal's normal bodily functioning — see DISEASE 1
3 a disturbed condition of the stomach in which one feels like vomiting — see NAUSEA 1
side *adj* of, relating to, or located on one side ⟨please bring all deliveries to the *side* door⟩
synonyms lateral
related words left, right; one-sided
side *n* **1** a place, space, or direction away from or beyond a central point or line ⟨will everyone who wants to sign up for volleyball please stand off to this *side* of the gym?⟩
synonyms flank, hand
related words direction, face, outside, underpart, underside; lee, leeward, windward; left, right
2 a certain way in which something appears or may be regarded — see ASPECT 1
3 a group of people acting together within a larger group — see FACTION
sideboard *n* a storage case typically having doors and shelves — see CABINET
sidekick *n* a person who helps a more skilled person — see HELPER
side–splitting *adj* causing or intended to cause laughter — see FUNNY 1
sidestep *vb* **1** to avoid having to comply with (something) especially through cleverness — see CIRCUMVENT 1

2 to move suddenly aside or to and fro — see DODGE 1
sideways *adv* with one side faced forward ⟨I had to walk *sideways* to get between the two towering piles of boxes⟩
synonyms broadside, edgewise, sidewise
related words aslant, obliquely, indirectly; laterally, sideward (*or* sidewards)
near antonyms dead, direct, right, straight
sidewise *adv* with one side faced forward — see SIDEWAYS
siege *n* **1** a sudden experiencing of a physical or mental disorder — see ATTACK 2
2 the cutting off of an area by military means to stop the flow of people or supplies — see BLOCKADE
siesta *n* a short sleep — see ¹NAP
sigh *vb* to take in and let out a deep audible breath or to make a similar sound ⟨Mom always used to *sigh* loudly whenever she found a mess on the floor⟩ ⟨a breeze *sighed* through the leaves⟩
synonyms sough
related words gasp, huff, pant, puff, wheeze; breathe, respire; exhale, expire, inhale, inspire; yawn
sigh (for) *vb* to have an earnest wish to own or enjoy — see DESIRE
sight *n* **1** a position within view — see PRESENCE 1
2 an instance of looking especially briefly — see LOOK 2
3 something unpleasant to look at — see EYESORE
4 the ability to see — see EYESIGHT
sight *vb* to make note of (something) through the use of one's eyes — see SEE 1
sightless *adj* lacking the power of sight — see BLIND
sightly *adj* very pleasing to look at — see BEAUTIFUL
sightseer *n* a person who travels for pleasure — see TOURIST
sign *n* **1** a movement of the body or limbs that expresses or emphasizes an idea or feeling — see GESTURE 1
2 a written or printed mark that is meant to convey information to the reader — see CHARACTER 1
sign *vb* to write one's name on (as a document) ⟨you'll have to *sign* the contract for it to be legal⟩
synonyms autograph
related words countersign, endorse (*also* indorse), register, sign on; author, pen, pencil (in), scratch (out), scrawl, scribble, write
signal *adj* standing above others in rank, importance, or achievement — see EMINENT
signal *n* **1** an object intended to give public notice or warning ⟨stop signs are *signals* for vehicles to come to a full stop—not suggestions for slowing down, as some drivers seem to think⟩
synonyms flag, tocsin
2 a movement of the body or limbs that expresses or emphasizes an idea or feeling — see GESTURE 1
signal *vb* to direct or notify by a movement or gesture — see MOTION
significance *n* **1** the idea that is conveyed or intended to be conveyed to the mind by language, symbol, or action — see MEANING 1
2 the quality or state of being important — see IMPORTANCE
significant *adj* **1** clearly conveying a special meaning (as one's mood) — see EXPRESSIVE

2 indicating something — see INDICATIVE

3 having great meaning or lasting effect — see IMPORTANT 1

4 having great power or influence — see IMPORTANT 2

5 sufficiently large in size, amount, or number to merit attention — see CONSIDERABLE 1

signification *n* the idea that is conveyed or intended to be conveyed to the mind by language, symbol, or action — see MEANING 1

signify *vb* **1** to be of importance — see MATTER

2 to communicate or convey (as an idea) to the mind — see MEAN 1

signifying *adj* indicating something — see INDICATIVE

sign on (for) *vb* to become a member of — see ENTER 2

sign up (for) *vb* to become a member of — see ENTER 2

silence *n* **1** incapacity for or restraint from speaking ⟨the teacher expects complete *silence* from everyone during all tests⟩

synonyms dumbness, muteness, speechlessness, stillness

related words inarticulateness, voicelessness; reserve, reticence, reticency, taciturnity

near antonyms communication, speaking, talking; eloquence, fluency, volubility; chattiness, garrulousness, loquaciousness, loquacity, talkativeness; verboseness, verbosity, windiness, wordiness

2 the near or complete absence of sound ⟨the *silence* of the garden was refreshing after the din of the party inside⟩

synonyms hush, quiet, quietness, quietude, still, stillness

related words calm, lull, peacefulness, tranquillity (*or* tranquility)

near antonyms din, clamor, hubbub, racket, tumult, uproar

antonyms noise, sound

silence *vb* **1** to stop the noise or speech of ⟨the instructor quickly *silenced* anyone who tried to interrupt⟩ ⟨we need to have a repairman come and *silence* that door alarm⟩

synonyms hush, mute, quell, settle, shush, still

near antonyms agitate, stir

2 to put a stop to (something) by the use of force — see QUELL 1

silent *adj* **1** deliberately refraining from speech ⟨the *silent* child had to be prompted to say hello⟩

synonyms dumb, mum, mute, speechless, uncommunicative

related words inarticulate, tongue-tied; nonvocal, voiceless

near antonyms articulate, eloquent, fluent, voluble; gabby, garrulous, loquacious, talkative, talky; outspoken, unreserved, vocal

antonyms communicative, speaking, talking

2 tending not to speak frequently (as by habit or inclination) ⟨a naturally *silent* boy, he was often overshadowed by his louder siblings⟩

synonyms closemouthed, laconic, reserved, reticent, taciturn, tight-lipped, uncommunicative

related words inhibited, introverted, restrained; sedate, self-contained, sober, staid

near antonyms free-spoken, outspoken, vocal; blabby, gossipy, talebearing; long-winded, verbose, windy, wordy

antonyms chatty, communicative, conversational, gabby, garrulous, loquacious, talkative, talky, unreserved

3 mostly or entirely without sound ⟨the room was so *silent* that you could have heard a pin drop⟩

synonyms hushed, muted, noiseless, quiet, quieted, soundless, still

related words peaceful, tranquil

antonyms noisy, unquiet

silhouette *n* a line that traces the outer limits of an object or surface — see OUTLINE 1

silhouette *vb* to draw or make apparent the outline of — see OUTLINE 1

silken *adj* smooth or delicate in appearance or feel — see SOFT 2

silky *adj* smooth or delicate in appearance or feel — see SOFT 2

silliness *n* **1** lack of good sense or judgment — see FOOLISHNESS 1

2 language, behavior, or ideas that are absurd and contrary to good sense — see NONSENSE 1

silly *adj* **1** lacking in seriousness or maturity — see GIDDY 1

2 showing or marked by a lack of good sense or judgment — see FOOLISH 1

3 so foolish or pointless as to be worthy of scornful laughter — see RIDICULOUS 1

silver *adj* of the color gray — see GRAY 1

silver *n* eating and serving utensils — see TABLEWARE 1

silverware *n* eating and serving utensils — see TABLEWARE 1

silvery *adj* of the color gray — see GRAY 1

similar *adj* having qualities in common — see ALIKE

similarity *n* **1** the quality or state of having many qualities in common ⟨the *similarity* between the two essays is too great to be coincidental — one student virtually copied the other⟩

synonyms alikeness, community, correspondence, likeness, parallelism, resemblance, similitude

related words analogousness; equivalence, equivalency, parity; identicalness, identity, sameness; correlation, relationship; exchangeability, interchangeability; accordance, agreement, compatibility, conformity, congruity

near antonyms inequality; conflict, disagreement, discrepancy, disparity, variance; incompatibility, incongruity, incongruousness

antonyms dissimilarity, unlikeness

2 a point which two or more things share in common ⟨the only *similarity* between this project and the last one is that both will involve some lab work⟩

synonyms correspondence, parallel, resemblance, similitude

related words counterpart, equal, equivalent

near antonyms difference, discrepancy; deviance, divergence; change, modification, variation

antonyms dissimilarity

similarly *adv* in like manner — see ALSO 1

similitude *n* **1** the quality or state of having many qualities in common — see SIMILARITY 1

2 a point which two or more things share in common — see SIMILARITY 2

simmer *vb* to cook in a liquid heated to the point that it gives off steam — see BOIL 2

simple *adj* **1** free from all additions or embellishment — see PLAIN 1

2 free from any intent to deceive or impress others — see GUILELESS

3 having no exceptions or restrictions — see ABSOLUTE 2

4 involving minimal difficulty or effort — see EASY 1

5 lacking in worldly wisdom or informed judgment — see NAIVE 1

6 lacking in education or the knowledge gained from books — see IGNORANT 1

7 not having or showing an ability to absorb ideas readily — see STUPID 1

simpleminded *adj* **1** lacking in worldly wisdom or informed judgment — see NAIVE 1

2 showing or marked by a lack of good sense or judgment — see FOOLISH 1

simpleness *n* **1** the quality or state of being simple and sincere — see NAÏVETÉ 1

2 the quality or state of lacking intelligence or quickness of mind — see STUPIDITY 1

simpleton *n* **1** a person who lacks good sense or judgment — see FOOL 1

2 a stupid person — see IDIOT

simplicity *n* **1** the quality or state of having a form or structure of few parts or elements ⟨the *simplicity* of this machine should enable everyone to learn how to use it⟩
synonyms plainness, unsophistication
related words homogeneity, unity
antonyms complexity, complication, elaborateness, intricacy, sophistication

2 clearness of expression ⟨the *simplicity* of this poem is beautiful⟩
synonyms clarity, explicitness, lucidity, lucidness, perspicuity, perspicuousness
related words incisiveness, directness, forthrightness, openness, straightforwardness
near antonyms ambiguity, equivocalness; incomprehensibility, unintelligibility; circuitousness, deviousness, indirectness, indistinctness; dimness, disjointedness, incoherence; faintness, fuzziness, muddiness, nebulousness, vagueness
antonyms obscurity

3 lack of good sense or judgment — see FOOLISHNESS 1

4 the quality or state of being simple and sincere — see NAÏVETÉ 1

simplify *vb* to make less complex ⟨you need to *simplify* this process somewhat or you'll never finish it today⟩
synonyms streamline
related words oversimplify; prune, strip (down), trim; purify, refine
near antonyms elaborate
antonyms complicate, perplex, sophisticate

simply *adv* **1** for nothing other than — see SOLELY 1

2 nothing more than — see JUST 3

simulate *vb* to present a false appearance of — see FEIGN

simulated *adj* **1** being such in appearance only and made with or manufactured from usually cheaper materials — see IMITATION

2 lacking in natural or spontaneous quality — see ARTIFICIAL 1

simultaneous *adj* existing or occurring at the same period of time — see CONTEMPORARY 1

simultaneously *adv* at one and the same time — see TOGETHER 1

sin *n* **1** a breaking of a moral or legal code — see OFFENSE 1

2 that which is morally unacceptable — see EVIL

3 immoral conduct or practices harmful or offensive to society — see VICE 1

4 a regrettable or blameworthy act — see CRIME 2

sin *vb* to commit an offense — see OFFEND 1

since *conj* for the reason that ⟨*since* I've done all my chores today, I should be allowed to go out and play⟩
synonyms as, because, for, inasmuch as, now, seeing, whereas
phrases as long as (*or* so long as), in view (*or* light) of the fact

sincere *adj* free from any intent to deceive or impress others — see GUILELESS

sincerely *adv* without any attempt to impress by deception or exaggeration — see NATURALLY 3

sinew *n* the ability to exert effort for the accomplishment of a task — see POWER 2

sinewy *adj* **1** having muscles capable of exerting great physical force — see STRONG 1

2 marked by a well-developed musculature — see MUSCULAR 1

sinful *adj* not conforming to a high moral standard; morally unacceptable — see BAD 2

sinfulness *n* the state or quality of being utterly evil — see ENORMITY 1

sing *vb* **1** to produce musical sounds with the voice ⟨it's relatively rare to find actors who can also *sing* well⟩
synonyms carol, chant, descant, vocalize
related words belt, croon, harmonize, hum, lilt, quaver, scat, sharp, slur, trill, troll, warble, yodel; serenade

2 to utter in musical or drawn out tones — see CHANT 1

3 to utter one's distinctive animal sound — see CRY 2

singe *vb* to burn on the surface — see SCORCH

singer *n* one who sings ⟨a famous opera *singer* will be performing tomorrow⟩
synonyms caroler (*or* caroller), songster, vocalist, vocalizer, voice
related words harmonizer, hummer, warbler, yodeler; serenader; cantor, chorist; songstress

single *adj* **1** not married ⟨there was such a shortage of *single* men in the neighborhood that he had his pick of girlfriends⟩
synonyms unattached, unmarried, unwed
related words fancy-free, footloose; marriageable, unmated, unpaired; divorced, separated
near antonyms mated, paired; affianced, betrothed, committed, engaged, pledged, promised; remarried
antonyms attached, espoused, married, wed

2 belonging only to the one person, unit, or group named — see SOLE 1

3 not physically attached to another unit — see SEPARATE 2

single (out) *vb* **1** to decide to accept (someone or something) from a group of possibilities — see CHOOSE 1

2 to find out or establish the identity of — see IDENTIFY 1

single–handedly *adv* without aid or support — see ALONE 1

singly *adv* without aid or support — see ALONE 1

singular *adj* **1** being out of the ordinary — see EXCEPTIONAL

2 noticeably different from what is generally found or experienced — see UNUSUAL 1

3 of, relating to, or belonging to a single person — see INDIVIDUAL 1

4 being the one or ones of a class with no other members — see ONLY 2

singularity *n* an odd or peculiar habit — see IDIOSYNCRASY

sinister *adj* being or showing a sign of evil or calamity to come — see OMINOUS

sink *vb* **1** to become worse or of less value — see DETERIORATE

2 to go to a lower level — see DROP 2

sinner *n* a person who commits moral wrongs — see EVILDOER 1

sinuous *adj* marked by a long series of irregular curves — see CROOKED 1

sip *n* the portion of a serving of a beverage that is swallowed at one time — see DRINK 2

sip *vb* to swallow in liquid form — see DRINK 1

siphon *vb* **1** to remove (liquid) gradually or completely — see DRAIN 1

2 to cause to move to a central point or along a restricted pathway — see CHANNEL

sire *vb* to become the father of — see FATHER

siren *n* a woman whom men find irresistibly attractive ⟨one of history's most famous *sirens*, Cleopatra charmed both Julius Caesar and Mark Antony⟩
synonyms enchantress, seductress, temptress
related words charmer, seducer

sissy *adj* having or displaying qualities more suitable for women than for men — see EFFEMINATE

sissy *n* a person who shows a shameful lack of courage in the face of danger — see COWARD

sit *vb* **1** to rest on the buttocks or haunches ⟨everybody needs to *sit* down, or no one will be able to see the movie⟩
synonyms set [*chiefly dialect*]
related words perch; lounge, slouch, sprawl, squat, straddle
near antonyms arise, get up, rise, stand

2 to cause to sit down — see SEAT

3 to cover and warm eggs to hatch them — see SET 1

4 to occupy a place or location — see STAND 1

site *n* the area or space occupied by or intended for something — see PLACE 1

sitter *n* a girl or woman employed to care for a young child or children — see NURSE

sitting duck *n* a person or thing that is the object of abuse, criticism, or ridicule — see TARGET 1

situate *vb* to arrange something in a certain spot or position — see PLACE 1

situation *n* **1** position with regard to conditions and circumstances ⟨the school's *situation* is improving with additional financial help⟩
synonyms footing, picture, posture, scene, status
related words rank, standing; place, spot, state; score, status quo

2 an assignment at which one regularly works for pay — see JOB 1

3 the placement of someone or something in relation to others in a vertical arrangement — see RANK 1

sixth sense *n* the power of seeing or knowing about things that are not present to the senses — see CLAIRVOYANCE

sizable *or* **sizeable** *adj* **1** of a size greater than average of its kind — see LARGE

2 sufficiently large in size, amount, or number to merit attention — see CONSIDERABLE 1

sizably *adv* to a large extent or degree — see GREATLY 2

size *n* the total amount of measurable space or surface occupied by something ⟨we worried that the immense *size* of the sofa would make getting it through the doorway impossible⟩
synonyms dimension, extent, magnitude, measure, measurement, proportion
related words area; capaciousness, commodiousness, roominess, spaciousness; ampleness, amplitude, bigness, bulk, bulkiness, enormousness, grandness, greatness, grossness, heftiness, hugeness, immenseness, immensity, largeness, mass, massiveness, monstrousness, stupendousness, tremendousness, vastness, volume, voluminousness

size *n* a substance used to stick things together — see GLUE

sizzle *n* a sound similar to the speech sound \s\ stretched out — see HISS 1

sizzle *vb* to make a sound like that of stretching out the speech sound \s\ — see HISS

skeletal *adj* suffering extreme weight loss as a result of hunger or disease — see EMACIATED

skeleton *n* the arrangement of parts that gives something its basic form — see FRAME 1

skeptic *n* a person who is always ready to doubt or question the truth or existence of something ⟨the demand by *skeptics* that believers in Bigfoot produce some hard evidence of that hairy humanoid⟩
synonyms disbeliever, doubter, questioner, unbeliever
related words cynic, misanthrope, pessimist; derider, ridiculer, scoffer
near antonyms chump, dupe, gull, pigeon, sucker

skeptical *adj* **1** inclined to doubt or question claims ⟨it's good to be *skeptical* about what you see on TV⟩
synonyms disbelieving, distrustful, doubting, incredulous, leery, mistrustful, questioning, suspecting, suspicious, unbelieving
related words paranoid; critical, puzzled, quizzical; careful, cautious, guarded, leery, wary, watchful; cynical, experienced, knowing, sophisticated, worldly, worldly-wise; curious, inquiring, inquisitive, nosy (*or* nosey), snoopy; uncertain, unconvinced, undecided, undetermined, unsettled, unsure; hesitant
near antonyms green, ingenuous, innocent, naive (*or* naïve), simple, simpleminded, unknowing, unsophisticated, unworldly, wide-eyed; certain, confident, positive, sure; callow, inexperienced, raw; childlike, idealistic, impractical; beguiled, deceived, duped, gulled, tricked; careless, heedless, unsuspecting, unsuspicious, unwary
antonyms credulous, gullible, trustful, trusting, uncritical, unquestioning

2 not feeling sure about the truth, wisdom, or trustworthiness of someone or something — see DOUBTFUL 1

skeptically *adv* with distrust — see ASKANCE

skepticism *n* a feeling or attitude that one does not know the truth, truthfulness, or trustworthiness of someone or something — see DOUBT

sketch *n* **1** a picture using lines to represent the chief features of an object or scene — see DRAWING

2 a vivid representation in words of someone or something — see DESCRIPTION 1

THESAURUS

sketch *vb* **1** to draw or make apparent the outline of — see OUTLINE 1

2 to give a representation or account of in words — see DESCRIBE 1

skewed *adj* inclined or twisted to one side — see AWRY

skewer *vb* to penetrate or hold (something) with a pointed object — see IMPALE

skill *n* **1** subtle or imaginative ability in inventing, devising, or executing something ⟨with unbelievable *skill*, the expert in origami transformed a few sheets of paper into a menagerie of exotic animals⟩

synonyms adeptness, adroitness, art, artfulness, artifice, artistry, cleverness, craft, cunning, deftness, masterfulness, skillfulness

related words dexterity, ease, finesse, handiness; experience, expertise, expertness, know-how, proficiency; creativity, ingenuity, inventiveness, knowledge, learning; aptitude, bent, flair, gift, knack, talent

near antonyms amateurishness, awkwardness, clumsiness, crudeness, rudeness; inability, inadequacy, incapability, incapacity, incompetence, ineffectiveness, ineffectualness, inefficiency

antonyms artlessness, ineptitude, ineptness, maladroitness

2 skills *pl* knowledge gained by actually doing or living through something — see EXPERIENCE 1

skilled *adj* having or showing exceptional knowledge, experience, or skill in a field of endeavor — see PROFICIENT

skillful *adj* **1** accomplished with trained ability ⟨the ice skater performed a *skillful* and graceful series of jumps⟩

synonyms adroit, artful, delicate, dexterous (*also* dextrous), expert, masterful, masterly, practiced (*or* practised), virtuoso, workmanlike

related words facile, smooth; artistic, creative, fancy, ingenious, neat; adept, clever, cunning; able, adequate, capable, competent

near antonyms awkward, clumsy, crude; ineffective, ineffectual; incompetent, inept

antonyms amateur, amateurish, artless, rude, unprofessional, unskillful

2 having or showing exceptional knowledge, experience, or skill in a field of endeavor — see PROFICIENT

skillfully *adv* in a skillful or expert manner — see WELL 3

skillfulness *n* subtle or imaginative ability in inventing, devising, or executing something — see SKILL 1

skim *vb* **1** to move or proceed smoothly and readily — see FLOW 2

2 to pass lightly across or touch gently especially in passing — see BRUSH

3 to strike and fly off at an angle — see GLANCE 1

4 to take a quick or hasty look — see GLANCE 2

skimp *vb* to avoid unnecessary waste or expense — see ECONOMIZE

skimp (on) *vb* to use or give out in stingy amounts — see SPARE

skimping *n* careful management of material resources — see ECONOMY

skimpy *adj* less plentiful than what is normal, necessary, or desirable — see MEAGER

skin *n* **1** an outer part or layer — see EXTERIOR

2 the outer covering of an animal removed for its commercial value — see HIDE 1

3 the hairless natural covering of an animal prepared for use — see LEATHER 1

skin *vb* **1** to remove the natural covering of — see PEEL

2 to rob by the use of trickery or threats — see FLEECE

skin–deep *adj* **1** lying on or affecting only the outer layer of something — see SUPERFICIAL 1

2 having or showing a lack of depth of understanding or character — see SUPERFICIAL 2

skinflint *n* a mean grasping person who is usually stingy with money — see MISER

skinny *adj* **1** being of less than usual width — see NARROW 1

2 having a noticeably small amount of body fat — see THIN 1

skip *vb* **1** to move with a light bouncing step ⟨children *skipping* across the playground⟩

synonyms bound, hop, lope, trip

related words caper, frisk, gambol, romp; skim, skitter; jump, leap, vault

near antonyms lumber, plod, trudge

2 to fail to attend — see CUT 2

3 to strike and fly off at an angle — see GLANCE 1

skipper *n* a person in overall command of a ship — see CAPTAIN 1

skirmish *n* **1** a brief clash between enemies or rivals — see ENCOUNTER

2 a physical dispute between opposing individuals or groups — see FIGHT

skirmish (with) *vb* to oppose (someone) in physical conflict — see FIGHT 1

skirt *n* the line or relatively narrow space that marks the outer limit of something — see BORDER 1

skirt *vb* **1** to avoid by going around — see DETOUR 1

2 to avoid having to comply with (something) especially through cleverness — see CIRCUMVENT 1

3 to be adjacent to — see ADJOIN 1

4 to serve as a border for — see BORDER

skirting *adj* having a border in common — see ADJACENT

skittish *adj* **1** easily excited by nature — see EXCITABLE

2 easily frightened — see SHY 1

skittishness *n* a state of nervousness marked by sudden jerky movements — see JUMPINESS

skulk *vb* to move about in a sly or secret manner — see SNEAK 1

skulker *n* someone who acts in a sly and secret manner — see SNEAK

skull *n* the case of bone that encloses the brain and supports the jaws of vertebrates ⟨anthropologists just found the *skull* of a prehistoric man in the desert⟩

synonyms cranium

related words braincase; death's-head; head, noddle, noggin, pate, poll; crown, scalp

skunk *n* a person whose behavior is offensive to others — see JERK 1

skunk *vb* **1** to defeat by a large margin — see WHIP 2

2 to achieve a victory over — see BEAT 2

sky *n* the expanse of air surrounding the earth ⟨the *sky* usually looks deep blue on a bright clear day⟩

synonyms blue, firmament, heaven(s), high

related words horizon, skyline

sky–high *adv* in an enthusiastic manner ⟨some re-

viewers had praised the movie *sky-high*, but we thought that it was just a so-so comedy⟩
synonyms enthusiastically, exuberantly, madly, rhapsodically
related words avidly, eagerly, excitedly, impatiently, keenly; fanatically, rabidly, zealously
near antonyms aloofly, disinterestedly, impassively, incuriously; hesitantly, reluctantly, unwillingly
antonyms apathetically, indifferently, lukewarmly, perfunctorily

skylark *vb* to engage in attention-getting playful or boisterous behavior — see CUT UP

skylarking *n* wildly playful or mischievous behavior — see HORSEPLAY

skyrocket *vb* to rise abruptly and rapidly ⟨the price of candy bars in the vending machine has *skyrocketed* over the past few months⟩
synonyms rocket, shoot (up), soar, zoom
related words accumulate, appreciate, balloon, build (up), burgeon, enlarge, escalate, expand, increase, mount, multiply, mushroom, proliferate, snowball, swell, wax; crest, peak, surge; heighten, intensify
near antonyms collapse, fall; contract, decrease, diminish, drop, lessen, wane
antonyms nose-dive, plummet, plunge, slump, tumble

skyward *adv* to or in a higher place — see ABOVE

slack *adj* **1** failing to give proper care and attention — see NEGLIGENT
2 not bound by rigid standards — see EASYGOING 2
3 not tightly fastened, tied, or stretched — see LOOSE 1

slack *n* **1** the extent to which something hangs or dips below a straight line — see SAG
2 **slacks** *pl* an outer garment covering each leg separately from waist to ankle — see PANTS

slack *vb* to make less taut — see SLACKEN

slacken *vb* to make less taut ⟨you'll need to *slacken* the rope a bit to get it free of that post⟩
synonyms ease, loosen, relax, slack
related words detach, free, unbind, undo, unfasten, untie
near antonyms attach, bind, fasten, tie; constrain, restrain
antonyms strain, stretch, tense, tighten

slackened *adj* not tightly fastened, tied, or stretched — see LOOSE 1

slacker *n* one who deliberately avoids work or duty ⟨there will be no *slackers* tolerated in this group—anyone who doesn't do their share will get booted out⟩
synonyms goldbrick, shirker
related words malingerer; dropout, quitter; drone, idler, lazybones, loafer, slouch, slug, sluggard; dallier, lingerer, loiterer, lounger, saunterer; dawdler, laggard, putterer, slowpoke
near antonyms live wire, powerhouse; doer, gogetter, hummer, hustler, rustler, self-starter

slackness *n* **1** failure to take the care that a cautious person usually takes — see NEGLIGENCE 1
2 the extent to which something hangs or dips below a straight line — see SAG

slam *n* **1** a hard strike with a part of the body or an instrument — see BLOW 1
2 a loud explosive sound — see CLAP 1

slam *vb* **1** to shove into a closed position with force

and noise ⟨the sulky child ran into her room and *slammed* the door loudly⟩
synonyms bang
related words close, shut, stop; bar, batten (down), bolt, chain, fasten, latch, lock, seal, secure
near antonyms open; unbar, unbolt, unfasten, unlatch, unlock, unseal
2 to deliver a blow to (someone or something) usually in a strong vigorous manner — see HIT 1
3 to come into usually forceful contact with something — see HIT 2
4 to criticize harshly and usually publicly — see ATTACK 2

slander *n* the making of false statements that damage another's reputation ⟨unhappy that she hadn't won, the girl resorted to *slander* and claimed that the winner's science project had actually been done by his father⟩
synonyms aspersing, blackening, defamation, defaming, libel, libeling, maligning, smearing, traducing, vilification, vilifying
related words aspersion, innuendo, smear; backbiting, detraction; abuse, invective, vituperation; attack, criticism, censure, denunciation; contempt, disdain, scorn; belittlement, disparagement; cattiness, despite, hatefulness, malevolence, malice, maliciousness, malignancy, malignity, meanness, nastiness, spite, spitefulness, spleen, venom, viciousness
near antonyms acclaim, accolade, applause, commendation, praise; esteem, honor, respect; adulation, flattery; adoration, reverence, veneration, worship

slander *vb* to make untrue and harmful statements about ⟨for some reason, that newspaper seems determined to *slander* one particular celebrity⟩
synonyms asperse, blacken, defame, libel, malign, smear, traduce, vilify
related words belittle, detract, disparage; discredit, disgrace, dishonor, shame; abase, debase, degrade, humble, humiliate; disdain, scorn
near antonyms exalt, glorify, honor; acclaim, applaud, commend, praise; esteem, respect; admire, regard; adore, revere, venerate, worship

slanderous *adj* causing or intended to cause unjust injury to a person's good name — see LIBELOUS

slang *n* the special terms or expressions of a particular group or field — see TERMINOLOGY

slant *n* **1** the degree to which something rises up from a position level with the horizon ⟨the road has just enough of a *slant* to make bicycling up it a little strenuous⟩
synonyms cant, diagonal, grade, gradient, inclination, incline, lean, pitch, slope, tilt, upgrade
related words ascent, bank, climb, rise
near antonyms declension, declination, decline, declivity, descent, dip, downgrade, fall, receding
2 a way of looking at or thinking about something — see POINT OF VIEW

slant *vb* to set or cause to be at an angle — see LEAN 1

slanted *adj* **1** inclined or twisted to one side — see AWRY
2 running in a slanting direction — see DIAGONAL

slanting *adj* inclined or twisted to one side — see AWRY

slantways *adv* so as to slant — see SLANTWISE

THESAURUS

slantwise *adj* **1** inclined or twisted to one side — see AWRY

2 running in a slanting direction — see DIAGONAL

slantwise *adv* so as to slant ⟨be careful not to lay the first boards *slantwise*, or the whole bookcase won't be straight⟩

synonyms slantways

related words down, downward (*or* downwards), up, upward (*or* upwards)

slap *n* a hard strike with a part of the body or an instrument — see ¹BLOW

slap *vb* to deliver a blow to (someone or something) usually in a strong vigorous manner — see HIT 1

slapdash *adj* lacking a definite plan, purpose, or pattern — see RANDOM

slapjack *n* a flat cake made from thin batter and cooked on both sides (as on a griddle) — see PANCAKE

slapstick *n* humorous entertainment — see COMEDY

slash *n* a long deep cut — see GASH

slash *vb* **1** to penetrate with a sharp edge (as a knife) — see CUT 1

2 to strike repeatedly with something long and thin or flexible — see WHIP 1

slate *adj* of the color gray — see GRAY 1

slate *vb* to put (someone or something) on a list — see ¹LIST 2

slated *adj* being in accordance with the prescribed, normal, or logical course of events — see DUE 2

slaty *adj* of the color gray — see GRAY 1

slaughter *n* the killing of a large number of people — see MASSACRE

slaughter *vb* to kill on a large scale — see MASSACRE

slave *n* **1** a person who is considered the property of another person ⟨many American *slaves* reached freedom in the North through the network known as the Underground Railroad⟩

synonyms bondman, bondsman, chattel, thrall

related words helot, serf; attendant, domestic, drudge, lackey, menial, servant

near antonyms freedman; enslaver, slave driver, slaveholder, slaver; master, taskmaster

antonyms freeman

2 a person who does very hard or dull work ⟨unappreciated office *slaves* who perform the necessary but tedious task of filing paperwork⟩

synonyms drudge, drudger, fag, grubber, laborer, peon, plugger, slogger, toiler, worker

related words workhorse; coolie, serf

near antonyms goldbrick, shirker; drone, idler, lazybones, loafer, slouch, slug, sluggard

slave *vb* to devote serious and sustained effort — see LABOR

slave (for) *vb* to be a servant for — see SERVE 1

slave driver *n* a boss who assigns much work — see TASKMASTER 1

slaver *vb* to let saliva or some other substance flow from the mouth — see DROOL

slavery *n* **1** the state of being a slave ⟨a child born into *slavery* was considered simply another addition to the master's wealth and property⟩

synonyms bondage, enslavement, servility, servitude, thrall, thralldom (*or* thraldom), yoke

related words peonage, serfdom; dependence, subjection, subjugation; captivity, enchainment, imprisonment, incarceration

near antonyms emancipation, enfranchisement, liberation, manumission; autonomy, independence, self-government, sovereignty

antonyms freedom, liberty

2 very hard or unpleasant work — see TOIL

slavish *adj* using or marked by the use of something else as a basis or model — see IMITATIVE

slavishly *adv* with great effort or determination — see HARD 1

slay *vb* **1** to deprive of life — see KILL 1

2 to put to death deliberately — see MURDER 1

slaying *n* the intentional and unlawful taking of another person's life — see HOMICIDE

sleazy *adj* of low quality — see CHEAP 2

sleek *adj* having a shiny surface or finish — see GLOSSY

sleep *n* **1** a natural periodic loss of consciousness during which the body restores itself ⟨eight hours of *sleep* or more are necessary for children and teenagers to function⟩

synonyms catnapping, dozing, napping, repose, rest, resting, slumber, slumbering, snoozing

related words catnap, doze, drowse, forty winks, nap, siesta, snooze, wink; oversleeping; dreaming, rapid eye movement

near antonyms insomnia, sleeplessness

antonyms consciousness, wakefulness

2 the state of being dead — see DEATH 2

sleep *vb* **1** be in a state of sleep ⟨the baby *slept* for the entire length of the car trip⟩

synonyms catnap, doze, nap, rest, slumber, snooze

related words drowse (off), nod (off); oversleep; dream, hibernate

near antonyms arise, arouse, awake, rise

2 to engage in sexual intercourse — see COPULATE

sleeper *n* one who sleeps ⟨Joe is a restless *sleeper* who always wakes up with the covers kicked off⟩

synonyms dozer, slumberer

related words nodder

near antonyms insomniac; riser, waker

sleepiness *n* the quality or state of desiring or needing sleep ⟨Sarah suffered such *sleepiness* in class that there were days when she could hardly keep her eyes open⟩

synonyms drowsiness, somnolence

related words lassitude, lethargy, sluggishness, torpor; dozing, resting, sleeping, slumbering; oversleeping

near antonyms awareness, consciousness

antonyms insomnia, sleeplessness, wakefulness

sleeping *adj* being in a state of suspended consciousness — see ASLEEP 1

sleepless *adj* not sleeping or able to sleep — see WAKEFUL

sleepy *adj* **1** desiring or needing sleep ⟨the *sleepy* children were carried up to bed⟩

synonyms drowsy, slumberous (*or* slumbrous), somnolent

related words asleep, dormant, dozing, resting, sleeping, slumbering; nodding, yawning

near antonyms restive, restless, sleepless

antonyms alert, awake, conscious, wakeful, wide-awake

2 slow to move or act — see INACTIVE 1

sleight *n* **1** a clever often underhanded means to achieve an end — see TRICK 1

2 mental skill or quickness — see DEXTERITY 1

3 ease and grace in physical activity — see DEX-
TERITY 2

slender *adj* **1** being of less than usual width — see
NARROW 1

2 having a noticeably small amount of body fat —
see THIN 1

3 less plentiful than what is normal, necessary, or
desirable — see MEAGER

sleuth *n* a person whose business is solving crimes
and catching criminals or gathering information
that is not easy to get — see DETECTIVE

slice *n* a piece that has been separated from the
whole by cutting — see CUT 1

slice *vb* **1** to cut into long slender pieces — see
SLIVER

2 to penetrate with a sharp edge (as a knife) —
see CUT 1

slick *adj* **1** having or being a surface so smooth as
to make sliding or falling likely ⟨roads are often
slick during the first hour of a rainstorm⟩

synonyms greased, greasy, lubricated, oiled,
slicked, slippery, slithery

related words brushed, buffed, burnished,
glossed, ground, polished, rubbed, shined; coated,
glazed, waxed; soapy, waxy; rasped, sandblasted,
sanded, sandpapered, scoured, scraped, scrubbed

near antonyms coarsened, rough, roughened,
scuffed, uneven

2 clever at attaining one's ends by indirect and
often deceptive means — see ARTFUL 1

slick *vb* to coat (something) with a slippery substance in order to reduce friction — see LUBRI-
CATE

slicked *adj* having or being a surface so smooth as
to make sliding or falling likely — see SLICK 1

slicker *n* a coat made of water-resistant material
— see RAINCOAT

slickness *n* skill in achieving one's ends through
indirect, subtle, or underhanded means — see
CUNNING 1

slide *vb* **1** to move about in a sly or secret manner
— see SNEAK 1

2 to move or proceed smoothly and readily — see
FLOW 2

slight *adj* **1** lacking bodily strength — see WEAK 1

2 lacking importance — see UNIMPORTANT

3 of a size that is less than average — see SMALL 1

4 so small or unimportant as to warrant little or
no attention — see NEGLIGIBLE 1

5 small in degree — see REMOTE 1

slight *n* an act or expression showing scorn and
usually intended to hurt another's feelings — see
INSULT

slight *vb* **1** to cause hurt feelings or deep resentment in — see INSULT

2 to deliberately ignore or treat rudely — see
SNUB 1

3 to show contempt for — see SCORN 1

4 to fail to give proper attention to — see NEG-
LECT 1

slightest *adj* being the least in amount, number, or
size possible — see MINIMAL

slighting *adj* intended to make a person or thing
seem of little importance or value — see
DEROGATORY

slightly *adv* **1** by a very small margin — see JUST 2

2 in a very small quantity or degree — see LIT-
TLE 1

slightness *n* **1** the quality or state of being little in
size — see SMALLNESS

2 the state or quality of having little weight — see
[1]LIGHTNESS 1

slim *adj* **1** being of less than usual width — see
NARROW 1

2 having a noticeably small amount of body fat —
see THIN 1

3 less plentiful than what is normal, necessary, or
desirable — see MEAGER

4 small in degree — see REMOTE 1

slime *n* soft wet earth — see MUD

slimy *adj* full of or covered with soft wet earth —
see MUDDY 1

[1]sling *vb* to place on an elevated point without support from below — see HANG 1

[2]sling *vb* to send through the air especially with a
quick forward motion of the arm — see THROW

slink *vb* to move about in a sly or secret manner —
see SNEAK 1

[1]slip *n* a long narrow piece of material — see STRIP

[2]slip *n* **1** an unintentional departure from truth or
accuracy — see ERROR 1

2 the act of going down from an upright position
suddenly and involuntarily — see FALL 1

3 the act or an instance of getting free from danger or confinement — see ESCAPE 1

slip *vb* **1** to decline gradually from a standard level
⟨Susie's grades *slipped* somewhat after she joined
five after-school activities⟩

synonyms sag

related words drop, fall, slump; flag, sink, slack-
en, slow (down), weaken; abate, contract, decrease, de-escalate, die (down), diminish, dwindle, ebb, lessen, let up, lower, moderate, recede,
relent, shrink, subside, taper, taper off, wane

near antonyms rocket, shoot (up), soar; balloon,
burgeon, enlarge, escalate, expand, increase,
mount, multiply, mushroom, proliferate, snowball, swell, wax; crest, peak, surge

2 to go down from an upright position suddenly
and involuntarily — see FALL 1

3 to introduce in a gradual, secret, or clever way
— see INSINUATE

4 to move about in a sly or secret manner — see
SNEAK 1

5 to move or proceed smoothly and readily — see
FLOW 2

slip (on *or* into) *vb* to place on one's person — see
PUT ON 1

slippery *adj* **1** given to acting in secret and to concealing one's intentions — see SNEAKY 1

2 hard to find, capture, or isolate — see ELUSIVE

3 having or being a surface so smooth as to make
sliding or falling likely — see SLICK 1

slipup *n* an unintentional departure from truth or
accuracy — see ERROR 1

slit *n* a long deep cut — see GASH

slit *vb* to penetrate with a sharp edge (as a knife)
— see CUT 1

slither *vb* to move slowly with the body close to the
ground — see CRAWL 1

slithery *adj* having or being a surface so smooth as
to make sliding or falling likely — see SLICK 1

sliver *n* a small flat piece separated from a whole
— see CHIP 1

sliver *vb* to cut into long slender pieces ⟨carefully
slivered the rattan stems into strips for basketry⟩

synonyms slice, splinter

related words chip, chop, dice, hash, mince; saw,
scissor; cleave, rive, split; gash, incise, rip, slash,
slit

slob *n* **1** a dirty or sloppy person ⟨only a *slob* would let his bedroom get so messy that his own mother couldn't remember what the floor looked like⟩
synonyms sloven
related words slattern, slut
near antonyms cleaner
antonyms old maid
2 a person whose behavior is offensive to others — see JERK 1

slobber *n* the fluid that is secreted into the mouth by certain glands — see SALIVA

slobber *vb* **1** to let saliva or some other substance flow from the mouth — see DROOL
2 to make an exaggerated display of affection or enthusiasm — see GUSH 2

slog *vb* **1** to deliver a blow to (someone or something) usually in a strong vigorous manner — see HIT 1
2 to devote serious and sustained effort — see LABOR

slogan *n* an attention-getting word or phrase used to publicize something (as a campaign or product) ⟨within days, virtually everyone was familiar with the newest advertising *slogan* for that brand of soda⟩
synonyms cry, shibboleth, watchword
related words tag line; expression, idiom; cliché; maxim, motto

slogger *n* a person who does very hard or dull work — see SLAVE 2

slop *n* **1** soft wet earth — see MUD
2 **slops** *pl* solid matter discharged from an animal's alimentary canal — see DROPPING 1

slope *n* the degree to which something rises up from a position level with the horizon — see SLANT

slope *vb* to set or cause to be at an angle — see LEAN 1

sloped *adj* running in a slanting direction — see DIAGONAL

sloping *adj* running in a slanting direction — see DIAGONAL

sloppily *adv* in a careless or unfashionable manner ⟨everyone dressed *sloppily* for the task of cleaning out the garage⟩
synonyms dowdily, slovenly, unstylishly
related words slatternly; chaotically, messily, untidily; shabbily, sleazily; dingily, dirtily, filthily, foully, grubbily, nastily
near antonyms neatly, orderly, tidily; fashionably, modishly; carefully, fastidiously, fussily, meticulously; cleanly, immaculately, spotlessly
antonyms nattily, sharply, smartly, sprucely

sloppiness *n* the state or quality of having an excess of tender feelings (as of love, nostalgia, or compassion) — see SENTIMENTALITY

sloppy *adj* **1** lacking neatness in dress or person ⟨a *sloppy* child who always seems to have spilled something on his clothes⟩
synonyms dowdy, frowsy (or frowzy), slovenly, unkempt, untidy
related words slatternly, sluttish; chaotic, cluttered, confused, disarranged, disheveled (or dishevelled), disordered, messed, messy, muddled, mussed, mussy, rumpled, uncombed, wrinkled; shabby, sleazy; besmirched, blackened, dingy, dirty, filthy, foul, grimy, grubby, grungy, mucky, nasty, soiled, spotted, squalid, stained, sullied, unclean, uncleanly
near antonyms chic, fashionable, modish, stylish;

combed, groomed; neat, ordered, orderly, tidy; careful, fastidious, fussy, meticulous; clean, cleaned, cleanly, immaculate, sparkling, spotless, stainless, unsoiled, unsullied
antonyms dapper, dashing, dolled up, sharp, smart, spruce
2 lacking in order, neatness, and often cleanliness — see MESSY
3 appealing to the emotions in an obvious and tiresome way — see CORNY

slosh *vb* to move with a splashing motion ⟨the baby gurgled contentedly as the water *sloshed* gently around him in the bathtub⟩
synonyms lap, plash, splash, swash
related words babble, bubble, gurgle, ripple

sloth *n* an inclination not to do work or engage in activities — see LAZINESS

slothful *adj* not easily aroused to action or work — see LAZY

slouch *n* a lazy person — see LAZYBONES

slough *also* **slue** *n* spongy land saturated or partially covered with water — see SWAMP

slough *also* **sluff** *vb* **1** to cast (a natural bodily covering or appendage) aside — see SHED 1
2 to get rid of as useless or unwanted — see DISCARD

sloven *n* a dirty or sloppy person — see SLOB 1

slovenly *adj* lacking neatness in dress or person — see SLOPPY 1

slovenly *adv* in a careless or unfashionable manner — see SLOPPILY

slow *adj* **1** moving or proceeding at less than the normal, desirable, or required speed ⟨because of the holiday, traffic to the beach was particularly *slow*⟩ ⟨*slow* readers⟩
synonyms crawling, creeping, dallying, dawdling, dilatory, dillydallying, dragging, laggard, lagging, languid, leisurely, poking, poky (or pokey), sluggish, tardy, unhurried
related words deliberate, measured; inactive, inert, lethargic, loafing, lounging; lingering, loitering, tarrying; ambling, inching, plodding, shuffling, strolling; decelerating, slowing; filibustering, procrastinating, stalling
near antonyms expeditious, prompt, ready; accelerated, hastened, quickened; hurried, rushed
antonyms barreling, bolting, breakneck, breathless, brisk, careering, dizzy, fast, fleet, flying, hasty, hurrying, lightning, quick, racing, rapid, rocketing, running, rushing, scooting, scudding, scurrying, snappy, speeding, speedy, swift, whirling, whirlwind, whisking, zipping
2 not having or showing an ability to absorb ideas readily — see STUPID 1

slow *adv* at a pace that is less than usual, desirable, or expected ⟨you need to go *slow* with this experiment, or you'll make mistakes⟩
synonyms laggardly, leisurely, slowly, sluggishly, tardily
related words carefully, cautiously, deliberately, purposefully; ploddingly
near antonyms immediately, posthaste, presto, promptly, pronto, readily, soon; impetuously, impulsively, rashly, recklessly; abruptly, suddenly
antonyms apace, briskly, fast, fleetly, full tilt, hastily, quick, quickly, rapidly, snappily, speedily, swift, swiftly

slow *vb* to cause to move or proceed at a less rapid pace ⟨if you don't *slow* your delivery down a bit, your speech will be over too soon⟩

synonyms brake, decelerate, retard

related words halt, stop; encumber, hamper, handicap, hinder, hobble, hold back, hold up, impede, inhibit, obstruct, tie up; arrest, check, constrain, curb, rein, restrain; baffle, foil, frustrate, sabotage, thwart

near antonyms drive, encourage, goad, propel, push, spur, stir, urge; advance, aid, dispatch, ease, expedite, facilitate, forward, further, help

antonyms accelerate, hasten, hurry, quicken, rush, speed (up), step up

slowdown *n* a usually gradual decrease in the pace or level of activity of something ⟨disease experts are encouraged by the recent *slowdown* in the spread of the virus⟩

synonyms braking, deceleration, letup, retardation, retarding

related words decline, drop, slump; ebb, remission, retreat, wane; flagging, weakening; arrest, check, halt, stoppage; collapse, crash, fall, plunge

antonyms acceleration, hastening, quickening

slowly *adv* at a pace that is less than usual, desirable, or expected — see SLOW

slowness *n* the quality or state of lacking intelligence or quickness of mind — see STUPIDITY 1

slowpoke *n* someone who moves slowly or more slowly than others ⟨quit being such a *slowpoke* this morning, or you'll be late⟩

synonyms crawler, creeper, dallier, dawdler, dragger, laggard, lagger, lingerer, loiterer, snail, stick-in-the-mud, straggler

related words latecomer; drone, idler, lazybones, loafer, lounger, slouch, slug, sluggard; delayer, procrastinator

near antonyms go-getter, hustler, scrambler; hurrier, rusher, speeder

antonyms speedster

sludge *n* soft wet earth — see MUD

sludgy *adj* full of or covered with soft wet earth — see MUDDY 1

¹slug *n* a hard strike with a part of the body or an instrument — see ¹BLOW

²slug *n* 1 a lazy person — see LAZYBONES

2 the portion of a serving of a beverage that is swallowed at one time — see DRINK 2

slug *vb* to deliver a blow to (someone or something) usually in a strong vigorous manner — see HIT 1

sluggard *n* a lazy person — see LAZYBONES

sluggish *adj* 1 moving or proceeding at less than the normal, desirable, or required speed — see SLOW 1

2 slow to move or act — see INACTIVE 1

sluggishly *adv* at a pace that is less than usual, desirable, or expected — see SLOW

sluice *vb* to pour liquid over or through in order to cleanse — see FLUSH 1

slumber *n* a natural periodic loss of consciousness during which the body restores itself — see SLEEP 1

slumber *vb* 1 be in a state of sleep — see SLEEP 1

2 to sleep lightly or briefly — see NAP 1

slumberer *n* one who sleeps — see SLEEPER

slumbering *adj* being in a state of suspended consciousness — see ASLEEP 1

slumbering *n* a natural periodic loss of consciousness during which the body restores itself — see SLEEP 1

slumberous *or* **slumbrous** *adj* 1 desiring or needing sleep — see SLEEPY 1

2 tending to cause sleep — see HYPNOTIC

slump *n* a period of decreased economic activity — see DEPRESSION 1

slur *n* an act or expression showing scorn and usually intended to hurt another's feelings — see INSULT

slur (over) *vb* to fail to give proper attention to — see NEGLECT 1

slurp *vb* to swallow in liquid form — see DRINK 1

slush *n* 1 language, behavior, or ideas that are absurd and contrary to good sense — see NONSENSE 1

2 soft wet earth — see MUD

slushy *adj* full of or covered with soft wet earth — see MUDDY 1

sly *adj* 1 clever at attaining one's ends by indirect and often deceptive means — see ARTFUL 1

2 given to acting in secret and to concealing one's intentions — see SNEAKY 1

3 tending to or exhibiting reckless playfulness — see MISCHIEVOUS 1

slyness *n* skill in achieving one's ends through indirect, subtle, or underhanded means — see CUNNING 1

smack *n* a hard strike with a part of the body or an instrument — see ¹BLOW

smack *vb* to deliver a blow to (someone or something) usually in a strong vigorous manner — see HIT 1

smack–dab *adv* as stated or indicated without the slightest difference — see EXACTLY 1

small *adj* 1 of a size that is less than average ⟨a *small* cat who never weighed more than five pounds⟩

synonyms bantam, diminutive, dinky, dwarf, dwarfish, fine, little, pint-size (*or* pint-sized), pocket, pocket-size (*also* pocket-sized), puny, pygmy, slight, smallish, undersized

related words petite; scrubby, stunted; bitty, inappreciable, infinitesimal, micro, microscopic (*also* microscopical), midget, miniature, miniaturized, minute, teeny, teeny-weeny, tiny, wee; underweight; meager (*or* meagre), niggardly, poor, scant, scanty, scarce, skimpy, slender, slim, spare, sparse, stingy; deficient, inadequate, insufficient, lacking, wanting

near antonyms bulky, hefty, hulking, massive, voluminous; cavernous, colossal, elephantine, enormous, giant, gigantic, gross, Herculean, heroic, huge, immense, jumbo, mammoth, monolithic, monstrous, monumental, prodigious, staggering, stupendous, tremendous, vast; abundant, ample, appreciable, bountiful, copious, generous, healthy, liberal, plenteous, plentiful; fat, thick; broad, wide; boundless, cosmic, immeasurable, infinite; adequate, enough, sufficient

antonyms big, bumper, considerable, goodly, good-sized, grand, great, handsome, king-size (*or* king-sized), large, largish, outsize (*also* outsized), oversize (*or* oversized), sizable (*or* sizeable), substantial, super, whacking, whopping

2 small in degree — see REMOTE 1

3 lacking importance — see UNIMPORTANT

4 not broad or open in views or opinions — see NARROW 2

small arm *n* a portable weapon from which a shot is discharged by gunpowder — see GUN 1

THESAURUS

smaller *adj* having not so great importance or rank as another — see LESSER

small–fry *adj* lacking importance — see UNIMPORTANT

smallish *adj* of a size that is less than average — see SMALL 1

small–minded *adj* 1 unwilling to grant other people social rights or to accept other viewpoints — see INTOLERANT 2
2 not broad or open in views or opinions — see NARROW 2

smallness *n* the quality or state of being little in size ⟨my grandmother was surprised by the *smallness* of the latest electronic devices⟩
synonyms diminutiveness, fineness, littleness, puniness, slightness
related words minuteness, tininess; meagerness, poorness, scantiness, scarceness, scarcity, skimpiness, slenderness, slimness, spareness, sparseness, stinginess; deficiency, inadequacy
near antonyms enormity, enormousness, grossness, hugeness, immenseness, immensity, stupendousness; extensiveness, vastness; excessiveness, extravagance, extremeness, immoderacy; abundance, ampleness, bountifulness, copiousness, healthiness, liberality; adequacy, sufficiency; heaviness, heftiness, weightiness; bulkiness, massiveness, voluminousness
antonyms bigness, grandness, greatness, largeness, magnitude

small talk *n* friendly, informal conversation or an instance of this — see CHAT

smart *adj* 1 being strikingly neat and trim in style or appearance ⟨dressed in their *smart* new uniforms, the cadets proudly paraded around the grounds of the military school⟩
synonyms dapper, natty, sharp, spruce
related words dressy, elegant, formal; neat, orderly, tidy; fashionable, modish, stylish; careful, fastidious, fussy, meticulous; clean, immaculate, spotless
near antonyms messy, untidy; shabby, sleazy; dingy, dirty, filthy, foul, grimy, grubby, nasty; dowdy, inelegant, unfashionable, unstylish
antonyms sloppy, slovenly
2 being in the latest or current fashion — see STYLISH
3 causing intense mental or physical distress — see SHARP 2
4 given to or marked by mature intelligent humor — see WITTY
5 making light of something usually regarded as serious or sacred — see FLIPPANT
6 having or showing a practical cleverness or judgment — see SHREWD
7 having or showing quickness of mind — see INTELLIGENT 1
8 having a wide and refined knowledge of the world especially from personal experience — see WORLDLY-WISE

smart *n* a sharp unpleasant sensation usually felt in some specific part of the body — see PAIN 1

smart *vb* to feel or cause physical pain — see HURT 1

smart aleck *n* a person who likes to show off in a clever but annoying way ⟨some *smart aleck* in the audience kept shouting clever insults at the speaker⟩
synonyms smarty (*or* smartie), wiseacre, wise guy

related words know-it-all; wisecracker; hotshot, show-off

smart–alecky *or* **smart–aleck** *adj* 1 making light of something usually regarded as serious or sacred — see FLIPPANT
2 marked by the use of wit that is intended to cause hurt feelings — see SARCASTIC

smarting *adj* 1 causing intense discomfort to one's skin — see CUTTING 1
2 causing intense mental or physical distress — see SHARP 2

smartly *adv* in a strikingly neat and trim manner ⟨the *smartly* dressed scouts marched at the head of the Memorial Day parade⟩
synonyms dashingly, nattily, sharply, sprucely
related words neatly, orderly, tidily, trimly; elegantly, fashionably, modishly, stylishly, swankily; carefully, fastidiously, fussily, meticulously; cleanly, immaculately, spotlessly
near antonyms dowdily, inelegantly, unstylishly; slatternly; messily, untidily; shabbily, sleazily; dingily, dirtily, filthily, foully, grubbily, nastily
antonyms sloppily, slovenly

smarty *or* **smartie** *n* a person who likes to show off in a clever but annoying way — see SMART ALECK

smash *n* 1 a forceful coming together of two things — see IMPACT 1
2 the violent coming together of two bodies into destructive contact — see CRASH 1
3 a hard strike with a part of the body or an instrument — see ¹BLOW
4 a loud explosive sound — see CLAP 1
5 a person or thing that is successful — see HIT 1

smash *vb* 1 to cause to break with violence and much noise ⟨deliberately *smashed* a glass against the brick fireplace⟩
synonyms crash, shatter
related words bust, fracture, fragment; bash, demolish, destroy, pulverize, ruin, wreck; shiver, splinter, split; crack, crunch, crush, snap
2 to cause to break open or into pieces by or as if by an explosive — see BLAST 1
3 to bring to a complete end the physical soundness, existence, or usefulness of — see DESTROY 1
4 to come into usually forceful contact with something — see HIT 2

smashup *n* the violent coming together of two bodies into destructive contact — see CRASH 1

smattering *n* a small number — see FEW

smear *vb* 1 to rub an oily or sticky substance over ⟨the toddler gleefully *smeared* her hair and face with maple syrup⟩
synonyms anoint, bedaub, besmear, daub
related words coat, paint, plaster; grease, oil; gum, lard, pitch, tar; begrime, besmirch, blacken, dirty, foul, grime, mire, muddy, smirch, smudge, soil, stain, sully
2 to make untrue and harmful statements about — see SLANDER

smearing *n* the making of false statements that damage another's reputation — see SLANDER

smell *n* the quality of a thing that makes it perceptible to the sense organs in the nose ⟨the *smell* of vanilla is supposed to be very soothing⟩
synonyms odor, redolence, scent, sniff
related words whiff; aroma, bouquet, fragrance, perfume; ambrosia, lusciousness, savor, savoriness, spice, tang; acridness, fetidness, foulness, noisomeness, rancidity, rankness, stench, stink; incense, musk

smell *vb* **1** to become aware of by means of the sense organs in the nose ⟨we *smelled* the aroma of freshly baked cookies as soon as we walked in the house⟩
synonyms nose, scent, sniff, whiff
related words breathe, drink (in), inhale
2 to have a vague awareness of — see FEEL 1
smelly *adj* having an unpleasant smell — see MALODOROUS
smidgen *also* **smidgeon** *or* **smidgin** *n* a very small amount — see PARTICLE 1
smile *vb* **1** to express an emotion (as amusement) by curving the lips upward ⟨he *smiled* in pleasure when he saw the giant sign welcoming him home⟩
synonyms beam, grin
related words laugh, simper; smirk, sneer
near antonyms grimace; frown, glare, glower, scowl
2 to express scornful amusement by means of facial contortions — see SNEER
smirch *n* a mark of guilt or disgrace — see STAIN 1
smirch *vb* **1** to make dirty — see DIRTY
2 to reduce to a lower standing in one's own eyes or in others' eyes — see HUMBLE
smite *vb* to deliver a blow to (someone or something) usually in a strong vigorous manner — see HIT 1
smog *n* an atmospheric condition in which suspended particles in the air rob it of its transparency — see HAZE 1
smoggy *adj* filled with or dimmed by fine particles (as of dust or water) in suspension — see HAZY 1
smooch *vb* to touch one another with the lips as a sign of love — see KISS 1
smooth *adj* **1** having or showing very polished and worldly manners — see SUAVE
2 involving minimal difficulty or effort — see EASY 1
3 having a surface without bends, breaks, or irregularities — see LEVEL
smooth *vb* **1** to free from obstruction or difficulty — see EASE 1
2 to make free from breaks, curves, or bumps — see EVEN 1
3 to make smooth or glossy usually by repeatedly applying surface pressure — see POLISH
smoothly *adv* without difficulty — see EASILY
smother *vb* **1** to be or cause to be killed by lack of breathable air ⟨you should never play inside discarded appliances because you could become trapped and *smother*⟩
synonyms choke, stifle, strangle, suffocate
related words garrote (*or* garotte), throttle; asphyxiate; drown
near antonyms breathe, exhale, expire, inhale, inspire
2 to refrain from openly showing or uttering — see SUPPRESS 2
smudge *vb* to make dirty — see DIRTY
smug *adj* having too high an opinion of oneself — see CONCEITED
smugness *n* an often unjustified feeling of being pleased with oneself or with one's situation or achievements — see COMPLACENCE
smut *n* foul matter that mars the purity or cleanliness of something — see FILTH 1
smuttiness *n* the quality or state of being obscene — see OBSCENITY 1
smutty *adj* **1** depicting or referring to sexual mat-

ters in a way that is unacceptable in polite society — see OBSCENE 1
2 not clean — see DIRTY 1
snag *n* a danger or difficulty that is hidden or not easily recognized — see PITFALL 1
snail *n* someone who moves slowly or more slowly than others — see SLOWPOKE
snake *n* **1** a limbless reptile with a long body ⟨*snakes* are cold-blooded, so they regulate their body temperature by alternately basking in sunlight and seeking shade⟩
synonyms serpent, viper
related words adder, anaconda, asp, blacksnake, boa, bull snake, bushmaster, cobra, constrictor, copperhead, coral snake, cottonmouth moccasin, diamondback rattlesnake, fer-de-lance, garter snake, glass snake, gopher snake, green snake, hognose snake, indigo snake, king cobra, king snake, krait, mamba, milk snake, pit viper, puff adder, python, racer, rat snake, rattlesnake, sea serpent, sidewinder, water moccasin, water snake
2 a person whose behavior is offensive to others — see JERK 1
snake *vb* **1** to move about in a sly or secret manner — see SNEAK 1
2 to move slowly with the body close to the ground — see CRAWL 1
snap *adj* **1** involving minimal difficulty or effort — see EASY 1
2 made or done without previous thought or preparation — see EXTEMPORANEOUS
snap *n* **1** a loud explosive sound — see CLAP 1
2 a picture created from an image recorded on a light-sensitive surface by a camera — see PHOTOGRAPH
3 active strength of body or mind — see VIGOR 1
4 a weather condition marked by low temperatures — see COLD
5 a very small amount — see PARTICLE 1
6 something that is easy to do — see CINCH
snap *vb* **1** to speak sharply or irritably ⟨the shopkeeper finally *snapped* at one customer who couldn't seem to make up his mind⟩
synonyms bark, snarl
related words shout, yell; blow up, explode
2 to break suddenly with an explosive sound — see CRACK 1
3 to take a photograph of — see PHOTOGRAPH
snap (up) *vb* to take physical control or possession of (something) suddenly or forcibly — see CATCH 1
snapback *n* the process or period of gradually regaining one's health and strength — see CONVALESCENCE
snap back *vb* **1** to become healthy and strong again after illness or weakness — see CONVALESCE
2 to regain a former or normal state — see RECOVER 2
snappily *adv* with great speed — see FAST 1
snappish *adj* easily irritated or annoyed — see IRRITABLE
snappy *adj* **1** being in the latest or current fashion — see STYLISH
2 easily irritated or annoyed — see IRRITABLE
3 having a low or subnormal temperature — see COLD 1
4 having much high-spirited energy and movement — see LIVELY 1

THESAURUS

5 moving, proceeding, or acting with great speed — see FAST 1

snapshot *n* a picture created from an image recorded on a light-sensitive surface by a camera — see PHOTOGRAPH

snare *n* **1** a device or scheme for capturing another by surprise — see TRAP 1

2 something that catches and holds — see WEB 1

snare *vb* **1** to catch or hold as if in a net — see ENTANGLE 2

2 to take physical control or possession of (something) suddenly or forcibly — see CATCH 1

¹**snarl** *vb* to speak sharply or irritably — see SNAP 1

²**snarl** *vb* to twist together into a usually confused mass — see ENTANGLE 1

snatch *vb* to take physical control or possession of (something) suddenly or forcibly — see CATCH 1

snatching *n* an instance of theft — see THEFT 2

snazzy *adj* attractively eye-catching in style — see JAZZY 1

sneak *adj* undertaken or done so as to escape being observed or known by others — see SECRET 1

sneak *n* someone who acts in a sly and secret manner ⟨"Why, you little *sneak*," Mom exclaimed, "you made my birthday present right under my nose!"⟩
synonyms lurker, skulker
related words skunk, snake; sharper, slicker, swindler; stalker

sneak *vb* **1** to move about in a sly or secret manner ⟨the little kids *sneak* around upstairs when they're supposed to be in bed⟩
synonyms lurk, mouse, pussyfoot, skulk, slide, slink, slip, snake, steal
related words crawl, creep, edge, inch, worm; pad, tiptoe

2 to introduce in a gradual, secret, or clever way — see INSINUATE

sneakiness *n* skill in achieving one's ends through indirect, subtle, or underhanded means — see CUNNING 1

sneaking *adj* **1** given to acting in secret and to concealing one's intentions — see SNEAKY 1

2 undertaken or done so as to escape being observed or known by others — see SECRET 1

sneaky *adj* **1** given to acting in secret and to concealing one's intentions ⟨the *sneaky* little girl was clearly up to something⟩
synonyms furtive, shady, shifty, slippery, sly, sneaking, stealthy
related words devious, guileful; close, close-mouthed, reticent, secretive; clandestine, covert, dark; deceitful, deceiving, deceptive, tricky, underhand, underhanded; crooked, dishonest, double-dealing, two-faced; lying, mendacious, untrustworthy, untruthful; insidious, perfidious, treacherous
near antonyms aboveboard, forthright, straightforward; candid, frank, open, plain; honest, trustworthy, truthful

2 undertaken or done so as to escape being observed or known by others — see SECRET 1

sneer *vb* to express scornful amusement by means of facial contortions ⟨the most popular girl in school *sneered* every time she saw the "nerds"⟩
synonyms laugh, smile, snicker, snigger
related words sniff, snort; catcall, hoot, insult, jeer, mock, ridicule; decry, despise, disdain; scorn

snicker *n* an explosive sound that is a sign of amusement — see LAUGH 1

snicker *vb* to express scornful amusement by means of facial contortions — see SNEER

snide *adj* not following or in accordance with standards of honor and decency — see IGNOBLE 2

sniff *n* the quality of a thing that makes it perceptible to the sense organs in the nose — see SMELL

sniff *vb* to become aware of by means of the sense organs in the nose — see SMELL 1

sniff (at) *vb* to show contempt for — see SCORN 1

snigger *n* an explosive sound that is a sign of amusement — see LAUGH 1

snigger *vb* to express scornful amusement by means of facial contortions — see SNEER

snip *vb* to make (as hair) shorter with or as if with the use of shears — see CLIP

snippet *n* a very small piece — see BIT 1

snippy *adj* **1** being or characterized by direct, brief, and potentially rude speech or manner — see BLUNT 1

2 easily irritated or annoyed — see IRRITABLE

¹**snitch** *vb* to give information (as to the authorities) about another's improper or unlawful activities — see SQUEAL 1

²**snitch** *vb* to take (something) without right and with an intent to keep — see STEAL 1

snitcher *n* a person who provides secret information about another's wrongdoing — see INFORMER

snoop *vb* to interest oneself in what is not one's concern — see INTERFERE

snoopy *adj* **1** interested in what is not one's own business — see CURIOUS 1

2 thrusting oneself where one is not welcome or invited — see INTRUSIVE

snooze *n* a short sleep — see NAP

snooze *vb* **1** be in a state of sleep — see SLEEP 1

2 to sleep lightly or briefly — see ¹NAP 1

snoozing *n* a natural periodic loss of consciousness during which the body restores itself — see SLEEP 1

snort *n* **1** a vocal sound made to express scorn or disapproval — see CATCALL

2 the portion of a serving of a beverage that is swallowed at one time — see DRINK 2

snow *vb* to cause to believe what is untrue — see DECEIVE

snowball *vb* to become greater in extent, volume, amount, or number — see INCREASE 2

snow under *vb* **1** to defeat by a large margin — see WHIP 2

2 to subject to incapacitating emotional or mental stress — see OVERWHELM 1

snub *n* treatment that is deliberately unfriendly — see COLD SHOULDER

snub *vb* **1** to deliberately ignore or treat rudely ⟨the snob in town always *snubbed* anyone she thought was beneath her⟩
synonyms cold-shoulder, cut, slight
related words ostracize; brush (aside *or* off), disdain, rebuff, reject, repulse; disregard, forget, neglect, overlook, overpass, pass over, shrug off

2 to show contempt for — see SCORN 1

snuff (out) *vb* **1** to cause to cease burning — see EXTINGUISH 1

2 to destroy all traces of — see ANNIHILATE 1

3 to put a stop to (something) by the use of force — see QUELL 1

snug *adj* **1** being clean and in good order — see NEAT 1
2 providing physical comfort — see COMFORTABLE 1
3 enjoying physical comfort — see COMFORTABLE 2
4 firmly positioned in place and difficult to dislodge — see TIGHT 2
5 providing safety — see SAFE 2
snug *vb* to sit or recline comfortably or cozily — see SNUGGLE 1
snuggle *vb* **1** to sit or recline comfortably or cozily ⟨it's particularly nice to *snuggle* next to the fire on a snowy day⟩
synonyms cuddle, curl up, nestle, snug
related words huddle
2 to lie close — see NUZZLE
so *adj* being in agreement with the truth or a fact or a standard — see CORRECT 1
so *adv* **1** for this or that reason — see THEREFORE
2 in like manner — see ALSO 1
3 to a great degree — see VERY 1
soak *n* a person who makes a habit of getting drunk — see DRUNK 1
soak *vb* **1** to wet thoroughly with liquid ⟨we ran for home as soon as the rain started, but our clothes still ended up *soaked*⟩
synonyms drench, drown, impregnate, saturate, sop, souse, steep
related words marinate; presoak; dip, immerse, inundate, submerge; bathe, douse, wash, water, wet; infiltrate, penetrate, permeate
near antonyms dehydrate, dry; drain, empty, void
antonyms wring (out)
2 to charge (someone) too much for goods or services — see OVERCHARGE 1
3 to make wet — see WET
soak (up) *vb* to take in (something liquid) through small openings — see ABSORB 1
soaked *adj* containing, covered with, or thoroughly penetrated by water — see WET
soaking *adj* containing, covered with, or thoroughly penetrated by water — see WET
soap *n* a substance used for cleaning — see CLEANER
soar *n* the act or an instance of rising or climbing up — see ASCENT 1
soar *vb* **1** to move or extend upward — see ASCEND
2 to move through the air with or as if with outstretched wings — see FLY 1
3 to rise abruptly and rapidly — see SKYROCKET
sob *vb* to shed tears often while making meaningless sounds as a sign of pain or distress — see CRY 1
sober *adj* **1** not having one's mind affected by alcohol ⟨it's important to stay *sober* if you're going to be driving a car⟩
synonyms clearheaded, straight
related words abstemious, abstinent, dry, temperate
near antonyms alcoholic
antonyms befuddled, dissipated, drunk, drunken, high, inebriate, inebriated, intoxicated, loaded [*slang*], soused, tipsy
2 based on sound reasoning or information — see GOOD 1
3 not joking or playful in mood or manner — see SERIOUS 1
soberness *n* a mental state free of jesting or trifling — see EARNESTNESS

sobriety *n* a mental state free of jesting or trifling — see EARNESTNESS
sobriquet *also* **soubriquet** *n* a descriptive or familiar name given instead of or in addition to the one belonging to an individual — see NICKNAME
sociability *n* the quality or state of being social ⟨her *sociability* was called into question when she said she hated parties⟩
synonyms conviviality, gregariousness
related words amiability, friendliness, neighborliness; camaraderie, companionship, fellowship; boldness, brashness, extroversion (*or* extraversion), forwardness, immodesty
near antonyms bashfulness, coyness, diffidence, shyness, timidity, timidness; introversion; modesty
sociable *adj* **1** likely to seek or enjoy the company of others — see CONVIVIAL
2 showing a natural kindness and courtesy especially in social situations — see GRACIOUS 1
social *adj* likely to seek or enjoy the company of others — see CONVIVIAL
socialize *vb* to take part in social activities ⟨he likes to *socialize* with his coworkers after work ends⟩
synonyms associate, fraternize, hobnob, mingle, mix
phrases rub elbows, rub shoulders
near antonyms avoid, eschew, shun; slight, snub
society *n* **1** a group of persons formally joined together for some common interest — see ASSOCIATION 2
2 human beings in general — see PEOPLE 1
3 the feeling of closeness and friendship that exists between companions — see COMPANIONSHIP
4 the way people live at a particular time and place — see CIVILIZATION 1
sock *n* **1** a close-fitting covering for the foot and leg — see STOCKING
2 a hard strike with a part of the body or an instrument — see ¹BLOW
sock *vb* to deliver a blow to (someone or something) usually in a strong vigorous manner — see HIT 1
sod *n* the land of one's birth, residence, or citizenship — see COUNTRY 1
sodality *n* a group of persons formally joined together for some common interest — see ASSOCIATION 2
sodden *adj* containing, covered with, or thoroughly penetrated by water — see WET
sofa *n* a long upholstered piece of furniture designed for several sitters — see COUCH
soft *adj* **1** not loud in pitch or volume ⟨*soft* music played in the background while we ate⟩
synonyms dull, low, quiet
related words dead, silent, still; dreamy, peaceful, restful, soothing, tranquil; muffled, muted, softened, toned (down)
near antonyms brazen, dinning, discordant, noisy, obstreperous, raucous, rip-roaring, vociferous; grating, harsh, shrill, strident
antonyms blaring, blasting, booming, clamorous, clangorous, deafening, earsplitting, loud, piercing, resounding, ringing, roaring, sonorous, stentorian, thunderous
2 smooth or delicate in appearance or feel ⟨I like this sweater the best because it is so *soft* and comfortable⟩

synonyms cottony, downy, satin, satiny, silken, silky, velvety
related words creamy; delicate, fine, slick, smooth
near antonyms bumpy, lumpy, pebbly; broken, jagged, ragged, rugged; grainy, granular, gritty
antonyms coarse, harsh, rough, scratchy
3 giving easily to the touch ⟨*soft* mattresses make it very easy to fall asleep, but they have a tendency to get lumpy⟩
synonyms flabby, mushy, pulpy, spongy, squashy, squishy
related words unhardened; doughy, fleshy; droopy, flaccid, floppy, lank, limp, slack, yielding; compressible, malleable, pliable, pliant, workable
near antonyms inflexible, resilient, rigid, stiff, tense; resistant, sound, strong, sturdy, tough, unyielding; hardened, indurated, tempered
antonyms firm, hard, solid
4 involving minimal difficulty or effort — see EASY 1
5 lacking bodily strength — see WEAK 1
6 lacking strength of will or character — see WEAK 2
7 not harsh or stern especially in manner, nature, or effect — see GENTLE 1
8 providing physical comfort — see COMFORTABLE 1
soften *vb* **1** to diminish the physical strength of — see WEAKEN 1
2 to lessen the shock of — see CUSHION
softened *adj* lacking bodily strength — see WEAK 1
softhearted *adj* having or marked by sympathy and consideration for others — see HUMANE 1
softheartedness *n* the capacity for feeling for another's unhappiness or misfortune — see HEART 1
softness *n* the quality or state of lacking strength of will or character — see WEAKNESS 2
soft–soap *vb* **1** to get (someone) to do something by gentle urging, special attention, or flattery — see COAX
2 to praise too much — see FLATTER 1
soft soap *n* excessive praise — see FLATTERY
softy *or* **softie** *n* a person lacking in physical strength — see WEAKLING 1
soggy *adj* containing, covered with, or thoroughly penetrated by water — see WET
soil *n* **1** foul matter that mars the purity or cleanliness of something — see FILTH 1
2 the loose surface material in which plants naturally grow — see DIRT 1
3 the solid part of our planet's surface as distinguished from the sea and air — see EARTH 2
soil *vb* to make dirty — see DIRTY
soiled *adj* not clean — see DIRTY 1
sojourn *n* a temporary residing as another's guest — see VISIT 1
sojourn *vb* to reside as a temporary guest — see VISIT 2
solace *n* **1** a feeling of ease from grief or trouble — see COMFORT 1
2 the giving of hope and strength in times of grief, distress, or suffering — see CONSOLATION 1
solace *vb* to ease the grief or distress of — see COMFORT 1
solacing *n* the giving of hope and strength in times of grief, distress, or suffering — see CONSOLATION 1
solar plexus *n* the part of the body between the chest and the pelvis — see STOMACH
soldier *n* a person engaged in military service ⟨one

of the goals of war is to keep as many *soldiers* as possible from being killed⟩
synonyms fighter, legionary, legionnaire, man-at-arms, regular, serviceman, warrior
related words servicewoman; cavalier, cuirassier, dragoon, trooper; dogface, doughboy, footman, foot soldier, infantryman; commando, marine, ranger; artilleryman, musketeer, rifleman; archer, lancer, spearman; Confederate, Continental, Federal, GI, guardsman, Rough Rider; guerilla, irregular, partisan; combatant, noncombatant; mercenary, soldier of fortune; veteran, war-horse; conscript, draftee, recruit; reservist
antonyms civilian
soldierly *adj* of, relating to, or suitable for war or a warrior — see MARTIAL 1
sole *adj* **1** belonging only to the one person, unit, or group named ⟨the landowner has *sole* rights to the property, so he can do whatever he wants to with it⟩
synonyms exclusive, single, unshared
related words proprietary
near antonyms joint, mutual, shared
antonyms nonexclusive
2 being the one or ones of a class with no other members — see ONLY 2
solecism *n* a socially improper or unsuitable act or remark — see IMPROPRIETY 2
solely *adv* **1** for nothing other than ⟨I fight *solely* for my country, not for money!⟩
synonyms alone, exclusively, just, only, simply
related words mainly, mostly, primarily
near antonyms additionally, also, likewise
2 without aid or support — see ALONE 1
solemn *adj* **1** having or showing a serious and reserved manner — see DIGNIFIED
2 not joking or playful in mood or manner — see SERIOUS 1
solemnity *n* **1** a mental state free of jesting or trifling — see EARNESTNESS
2 an oft-repeated action or series of actions performed in accordance with tradition or a set of rules — see RITE
solicit *vb* **1** to go around and approach (people) with a request for opinions or information — see CANVASS
2 to make a request for — see ASK (FOR) 1
3 to make a request of — see ASK 2
4 to make a request to (someone) in an earnest or urgent manner — see BEG
solicitation *n* an earnest request — see PLEA 1
soliciting *adj* asking humbly — see SUPPLIANT
solicitor *n* **1** one that tries to get a person to give in to a desire — see TEMPTER
2 one who asks earnestly for a favor or gift — see SUPPLICANT
solicitous *adj* **1** given to or made with heedful anticipation of the needs and happiness of others — see THOUGHTFUL 1
2 showing urgent desire or interest — see EAGER
solicitude *n* an uneasy state of mind usually over the possibility of an anticipated misfortune or trouble — see ANXIETY 1
solid *adj* **1** based on sound reasoning or information — see GOOD 1
2 having a consistency that does not easily yield to pressure — see FIRM 2
3 having or consisting of a single color — see MONOCHROMATIC

4 not showing weakness or uncertainty — see FIRM 1

5 worthy of one's trust — see DEPENDABLE

solidify *vb* **1** to become physically firm or solid — see HARDEN 1

2 to take on a definite form — see FORM 1

solidity *n* worthiness as the recipient of another's trust or confidence — see RELIABILITY

solidness *n* worthiness as the recipient of another's trust or confidence — see RELIABILITY

solitariness *n* the state of being alone or kept apart from others — see ISOLATION

solitary *adj* **1** being the one or ones of a class with no other members — see ONLY 2

2 not being in the company of others — see ALONE 1

solitary *n* a person who lives away from others — see RECLUSE

solitude *n* the state of being alone or kept apart from others — see ISOLATION

solo *adj* not being in the company of others — see ALONE 1

solon *n* a member of an organized body of persons having the authority to make laws — see LEGISLATOR

soluble *adj* capable of having the reason for or cause of determined — see SOLVABLE

solution *n* something attained by mental effort and especially by computation — see ANSWER 2

solvable *adj* capable of having the reason for or cause of determined ⟨I'm sure that the mystery of what happened to the missing pizza is *solvable*⟩
synonyms answerable, explainable, explicable, resolvable, soluble
related words analyzable, decipherable; feasible, workable
near antonyms impossible
antonyms inexplicable, insoluble, unexplainable, unsolvable

solve *vb* to find an answer for through reasoning ⟨it took me half an hour to *solve* the logic puzzle⟩
synonyms answer, break, crack, dope (out), figure out, puzzle (out), resolve, riddle, unravel, work, work out
related words clear (up), iron out, straighten (out), unscramble, untangle, untie; divine, guess; decipher, decode

somatic *adj* of or relating to the human body — see PHYSICAL 1

somber *or* **sombre** *adj* **1** being without light or without much light — see DARK 1

2 causing or marked by an atmosphere lacking in cheer — see GLOOMY 1

some *adj* known but not named — see CERTAIN 1

some *adv* very close to but not completely — see ALMOST

somebody *n* a person who is widely known and usually much talked about — see CELEBRITY 1

someday *adv* at a later time — see YET 1

something *adv* **1** to a great degree — see VERY 1

2 to some degree or extent — see FAIRLY

something *n* one that has a real and independent existence — see ENTITY

sometime *adj* having been such at some previous time — see FORMER

sometime *adv* at a later time — see YET 1

sometimes *adv* on some occasions ⟨*sometimes* I like to go skiing, and *sometimes* I prefer to stay inside where it's warm⟩
synonyms now, occasionally

related words intermittently, periodically; infrequently, rarely, seldom; irregularly, sporadically
phrases at times, from time to time, now and then, once in a while
near antonyms frequently, often, oftentimes (*or* ofttimes); commonly, ordinarily, regularly, usually; always, constantly, invariably; continually, continuously, incessantly, perpetually, unceasingly, uninterruptedly; endlessly, ever, interminably

somewhat *adv* to some degree or extent — see FAIRLY

somnolence *n* the quality or state of desiring or needing sleep — see SLEEPINESS

somnolent *adj* desiring or needing sleep — see SLEEPY 1

song *n* **1** a short musical composition for the human voice often with instrumental accompaniment ⟨she sang a short *song* for the talent show⟩
synonyms ballad, ditty, jingle, lay, lyric, vocal
related words anthem, canticle, carol, chorale, hymn, noel, psalm, spiritual; dirge, lament, requiem, threnody; hallelujah, paean; aria, barcarole (*or* barcarolle), blues, cantata, chantey (*or* chanty), chorus, croon, descant, glee, lullaby, madrigal, motet, part-song, pop, rocker, round, roundelay, serenade, troll

2 a composition using rhythm and often rhyme to create a lyrical effect — see POEM

3 a rhythmic series of musical tones arranged to give a pleasing effect — see MELODY

4 a very small sum of money — see MITE 1

5 writing that uses rhythm, vivid language, and often rhyme to provoke an emotional response — see POETRY 1

songster *n* one who sings — see SINGER

songwriter *n* a person who writes musical compositions — see COMPOSER

sonny *n* a male person who has not yet reached adulthood — see BOY

sonorous *adj* **1** marked by a high volume of sound — see LOUD 1

2 marked by conspicuously full and rich sounds or tones — see RESONANT

soon *adv* **1** at or within a short time — see SHORTLY 2

2 by choice or preference — see RATHER 1

3 with great speed — see FAST 1

soothe *vb* **1** to ease the grief or distress of — see COMFORT 1

2 to free from distress or disturbance — see CALM 1

3 to make more bearable or less severe — see HELP 2

soothing *adj* **1** tending to calm the emotions and relieve stress ⟨the *soothing* music eventually put the entire yoga class in the proper mood⟩
synonyms calming, comforting, dreamy, lulling, narcotic, pacifying, quieting, relaxing, sedative, tranquilizing (*also* tranquillizing)
related words hypnotic, opiate; anesthetic, deadening, depressant, numbing
near antonyms energizing, invigorating, stimulant, stimulating; aggravating, annoying, bothersome, exasperating, galling, grating, irksome, irritating, troublesome, vexing

2 not harsh or stern especially in manner, nature, or effect — see GENTLE 1

soothsayer *n* one who predicts future events or developments — see PROPHET

THESAURUS

soothsaying *n* a declaration that something will happen in the future — see PREDICTION

sop *n* something given or promised in order to improperly influence a person's conduct or decision — see BRIBE

sop *vb* to wet thoroughly with liquid — see SOAK 1

sophisticate *n* a person with the outlook, experience, and manners thought to be typical of big city dwellers — see COSMOPOLITAN

sophisticate *vb* to make complex or difficult — see COMPLICATE

sophisticated *adj* **1** having a wide and refined knowledge of the world especially from personal experience — see WORLDLY-WISE
2 having many parts or aspects that are usually interrelated — see COMPLEX 1
3 having or showing very polished and worldly manners — see SUAVE
4 made or done with great care or with much detail — see ELABORATE 1

sophistication *n* the state or quality of having many interrelated parts or aspects — see COMPLEXITY 1

soppy *adj* containing, covered with, or thoroughly penetrated by water — see WET

sorcerer *n* a person skilled in using supernatural forces — see MAGICIAN 1

sorceress *n* a woman believed to have often harmful supernatural powers — see WITCH 1

sorcery *n* the power to control natural forces through supernatural means — see MAGIC 1

sordid *adj* **1** not clean — see DIRTY 1
2 not following or in accordance with standards of honor and decency — see IGNOBLE 2

sore *adj* **1** causing or feeling bodily pain — see PAINFUL 1
2 feeling or showing anger — see ANGRY
3 having or showing deep-seated resentment — see BITTER 1

sorely *adv* with feelings of bitterness or grief — see HARD 2

sorriness *n* deep sadness especially for the loss of someone or something loved — see SORROW

sorrow *n* deep sadness especially for the loss of someone or something loved ⟨he felt great *sorrow* at the loss of his beloved pet⟩
synonyms affliction, anguish, dolefulness, dolor, grief, heartache, heartbreak, sorriness, woe
related words agony, distress, pain, suffering, torment; blues, dejection, depression, desolateness, desolation, despondency, disconsolateness, dispiritedness, distress, doldrums, downheartedness, dreariness, dumps, forlornness, gloom, gloominess, heartsickness, joylessness, melancholy, miserableness, misery, mopes, oppression, sadness, unhappiness, wretchedness; regret, remorse, rue
near antonyms gaiety (*also* gayety), gayness, humor, jollity, joviality, lightheartedness, merriment, merrymaking, mirth, mirthfulness; hopefulness, optimism; enjoyment; content, contentedness
antonyms blessedness, bliss, blissfulness, cheer, cheerfulness, cheeriness, delight, ecstasy, elatedness, elation, euphoria, exhilaration, exuberance, exultation, gladness, gladsomeness, glee, gleefulness, happiness, joy, joyfulness, joyousness, jubilation, pleasure, rapture, rapturousness

sorrow *vb* to feel deep sadness or mental pain — see GRIEVE

sorrowful *adj* **1** expressing or suggesting mourning — see MOURNFUL 1
2 feeling unhappiness — see SAD 1

sorrowfully *adv* with feelings of bitterness or grief — see HARD 2

sorry *adj* **1** arousing or deserving of one's loathing and disgust — see CONTEMPTIBLE 1
2 causing unhappiness — see SAD 2
3 deserving pitying scorn (as for inadequacy) — see PITIFUL 1
4 feeling sorrow for a wrong that one has done — see CONTRITE 1
5 feeling unhappiness — see SAD 1
6 expressing or suggesting mourning — see MOURNING 1
7 deserving of one's pity — see PATHETIC 1

sort *n* **1** a number of persons or things that are grouped together because they have something in common ⟨I prefer jackets with zippers to the *sort* that close with buttons⟩
synonyms breed, class, description, feather, ilk, kind, like, manner, nature, order, type
related words model; sample, specimen; bracket, category, division, family, grade, group, lot, persuasion, rank(s), set
2 a member of the human race — see HUMAN

sort *vb* to arrange or assign according to type — see CLASSIFY 1

sort of *adv* to some degree or extent — see FAIRLY

so–so *adj* of average to below average quality — see MEDIOCRE 1

so–so *adv* in a satisfactory way — see WELL 1

sot *n* a person who makes a habit of getting drunk — see DRUNK 1

sough *vb* to take in and let out a deep audible breath or to make a similar sound — see SIGH

soul *n* **1** an immaterial force within a human being thought to give the body life, energy, and power ⟨many religions teach that the *soul* is immortal⟩
synonyms psyche, spirit
related words life, vitality
near antonyms body, flesh
2 a member of the human race — see HUMAN
3 the quality or qualities that make a thing what it is — see ESSENCE
4 the seat of one's deepest thoughts and emotions — see CORE 1

soulless *adj* having or showing a lack of sympathy or tender feelings — see HARD 1

sound *adj* **1** according to the rules of logic — see LOGICAL 1
2 enjoying health and vigor — see HEALTHY 1
3 marked by the ability to withstand stress without structural damage or distortion — see STABLE 1

sound *n* **1** a narrow body of water between two land masses — see CHANNEL 2
2 range of hearing — see EARSHOT

¹sound *vb* **1** to continue or be repeated in a series of reflected sound waves — see REVERBERATE
2 to give the impression of being — see SEEM
3 to make known (as an idea, emotion, or opinion) — see EXPRESS 1
4 to make known openly or publicly — see ANNOUNCE

²sound *vb* **1** to measure the depth of (as a body of water) typically with a weighted line ⟨the pilot *sounded* the river to make sure we weren't in any danger of running aground⟩
synonyms fathom, plumb

related words gauge (*also* gage), measure, scale
2 to cast oneself head first into deep water — see DIVE

soundless *adj* mostly or entirely without sound — see SILENT 3

soundness *n* **1** the ability to withstand force or stress without being distorted, dislodged, or damaged — see STABILITY 1
2 the condition of being sound in body — see HEALTH

sound off *vb* to voice one's opinions freely with force — see SPEAK UP

soup *n* an atmospheric condition in which suspended particles in the air rob it of its transparency — see HAZE 1

soupy *adj* **1** filled with or dimmed by fine particles (as of dust or water) in suspension — see HAZY 1
2 having an overly soft liquid consistency — see RUNNY

sour *adj* **1** causing or characterized by the one of the four basic taste sensations that is produced chiefly by acids ⟨the *sour* candy made our mouths all wrinkly inside⟩
synonyms acid, acidic, tart, vinegary
related words dry, soured, unsweetened; pungent, sharp, tangy; astringent, puckery; acetic; hyperacid
near antonyms sweet; bland, smooth
2 not giving pleasure to the mind or senses — see UNPLEASANT

sour *vb* to cause to change from friendly or loving to unfriendly or uncaring — see ESTRANGE

source *n* the beginning part of a stream — see HEADWATER

souring *n* the loss of friendship or affection — see ESTRANGEMENT

souse *n* a person who makes a habit of getting drunk — see DRUNK 1

souse *vb* **1** to make wet — see WET
2 to sink or push (something) briefly into or as if into a liquid — see DIP 1
3 to wet thoroughly with liquid — see SOAK 1

soused *adj* **1** being under the influence of alcohol — see DRUNK
2 containing, covered with, or thoroughly penetrated by water — see WET

souvenir *n* something that serves to keep alive the memory of a person or event — see MEMORIAL

sovereign *adj* **1** coming before all others in importance — see FOREMOST 1
2 not being under the rule or control of another — see FREE 1

sovereign *n* one who rules over a people with a sole, supreme, and usually hereditary authority — see MONARCH

sovereignty *n* **1** the state of being free from the control or power of another — see FREEDOM 1
2 a body of people composed of one or more nationalities usually with its own territory and government — see NATION

sow *vb* **1** to cover by or as if by scattering something over or on — see SCATTER 2
2 to put or set into the ground to grow — see PLANT

spa *n* a building or room used for sports activities and exercising — see GYM

space *n* **1** an extent or area available for or used up by some activity or thing — see ROOM 1
2 an indefinite but usually short period of time — see WHILE 1

space–age *adj* being or involving the latest methods, concepts, information, or styles — see MODERN

spacing *n* the space or amount of space between two points, lines, surfaces, or objects — see DISTANCE

spacious *adj* more than adequate or average in capacity ⟨almost all of the guests were able to fit into the *spacious* living room⟩
synonyms ample, capacious, commodious, roomy
related words broad, wide; big, bulky, considerable, generous, goodly, good-sized, grand, great, handsome, hefty, hulking, king-size (*or* king-sized), large, largish, outsize (*also* outsized), oversize (*or* oversized), sizable (*or* sizeable), substantial, super, voluminous; enormous, immense, vast; expansive, extended, extensive; boundless, limitless, unbounded
near antonyms confined, cramped, limited, narrow, restricted; small, snug, tight, tiny

span *vb* to find out the size, extent, or amount of — see MEASURE

spank *n* a hard strike with a part of the body or an instrument — see ¹BLOW

spanking *adj* having much high-spirited energy and movement — see LIVELY 1

spare *adj* **1** being over what is needed ⟨I had some *spare* time to kill, so I cleaned up my room a bit⟩
synonyms excess, extra, superfluous, supernumerary, surplus
related words accessory, additional, supplemental, supplementary; dispensable, extraneous, gratuitous, needless, nonessential, unessential, unnecessary, unneeded, unwanted
near antonyms inadequate, insufficient, meager, scant, scanty, scarce, short, sparse
2 giving or sharing as little as possible — see STINGY 1
3 having a noticeably small amount of body fat — see THIN 1
4 less plentiful than what is normal, necessary, or desirable — see MEAGER

spare *n* an interchangeable part or piece of equipment that is kept on hand for replacement of an original ⟨first we took the burnt light bulb out, and then we replaced it with the *spare*⟩
synonyms extra, reserve
related words backup, substitute; stock; copy, double, duplicate, replacement
near antonyms archetype, original

spare *vb* to use or give out in stingy amounts ⟨I'll have a banana split and don't *spare* the whipped cream⟩
synonyms scant, skimp (on), stint (on)
related words dole (out), mete (out), portion (out), ration (out); pinch, shortchange
near antonyms lavish, rain

sparing *adj* **1** careful in the management of money or resources — see FRUGAL
2 giving or sharing as little as possible — see STINGY 1

spark *n* a very small amount — see PARTICLE 1

spark *vb* **1** to give off sparks ⟨the broken radio *sparked* and smoked the instant it was plugged in⟩
synonyms scintillate, sparkle
related words flash; burn
2 to cause to function — see ACTIVATE

sparkle *vb* **1** to give off sparks — see SPARK 1
2 to shoot forth bursts of light — see FLASH 1

sparky *adj* having much high-spirited energy and movement — see LIVELY 1

sparse *adj* less plentiful than what is normal, necessary, or desirable — see MEAGER

spasm *n* 1 a painful sudden tightening of a muscle — see CRAMP

2 a sudden intense expression of strong feeling — see OUTBURST 1

spasmodic *adj* lacking in steadiness or regularity of occurrence — see FITFUL

spat *n* an often noisy or angry expression of differing opinions — see ARGUMENT 1

spat *vb* to express different opinions about something often angrily — see ARGUE 2

spate *n* a great flow of water or of something that overwhelms — see FLOOD

spatter *vb* 1 to cause (something liquid or mushy) to move along in sheets — see SPLASH 1

2 to wet or soil by striking with something liquid or mushy — see SPLASH 2

spawn *n* the descendants of a person, animal, or plant — see OFFSPRING

spawn *vb* to be the cause of (a situation, action, or state of mind) — see EFFECT

speak *vb* 1 to express (a thought or emotion) in words — see SAY 1

2 to give a formal often extended talk on a subject — see TALK 1

speak (to *or* with) *vb* to communicate with by means of spoken words — see TALK 1

speaker *n* 1 a person in charge of a meeting — see CHAIR 1

2 a person who speaks for another or for a group — see SPOKESPERSON

speak out *vb* to voice one's opinions freely with force — see SPEAK UP

speak up *vb* to voice one's opinions freely with force ⟨she's never been afraid to *speak up* in class⟩

synonyms sound off, speak out, spout (off)

related words bawl, call, cry, holler, shout, sing (out), vociferate, yell; articulate, enunciate

phrases speak one's mind

near antonyms hush, suppress; quiet

spear *n* a weapon with a long straight handle and sharp head or blade ⟨the Roman gladiator thrust his *spear* triumphantly into the lion's side⟩

synonyms javelin, lance, pike, pikestaff, shaft

related words dart, spike; gaff, halberd, harpoon, trident

spear *vb* to penetrate or hold (something) with a pointed object — see IMPALE

spearhead *vb* to serve as leader of — see LEAD 2

special *adj* 1 being the one or ones of a class with no other members — see ONLY 2

2 granted special treatment or attention — see DARLING 1

3 of a particular or exact sort — see EXPRESS 1

speciality *n* something for which a person shows a special talent — see FORTE

specialized *adj* used by or intended for experts in a particular field of knowledge — see TECHNICAL

specialty *n* 1 a region of activity, knowledge, or influence — see FIELD 2

2 something for which a person shows a special talent — see FORTE

species *n* one of the units into which a whole is divided on the basis of a common characteristic — see CLASS 2

specific *adj* 1 of a particular or exact sort — see EXPRESS 1

2 so clearly expressed as to leave no doubt about the meaning — see EXPLICIT

specific *n* a substance or preparation used to treat disease — see MEDICINE

specificity *n* careful thoroughness of detail — see PARTICULARITY 1

specify *vb* 1 to give the rules about (something) clearly and exactly — see PRESCRIBE

2 to make reference to or speak about briefly but specifically — see MENTION 1

specimen *n* 1 a member of the human race — see HUMAN

2 one of a group or collection that shows what the whole is like — see EXAMPLE

specious *adj* tending or having power to deceive — see DECEPTIVE 1

speck *n* 1 a small area that is different (as in color) from the main part — see SPOT 1

2 a very small amount — see PARTICLE 1

3 a very small piece — see BIT 1

speck *vb* to mark with small spots especially unevenly — see SPOT

speckle *n* a small area that is different (as in color) from the main part — see SPOT 1

speckle *vb* to mark with small spots especially unevenly — see SPOT

speckled *adj* marked with spots — see SPOTTED 1

specs *n pl* a pair of lenses set in a frame that is held in place with ear supports and which are usually worn to correct vision — see GLASSES 1

spectacles *n pl* a pair of lenses set in a frame that is held in place with ear supports and which are usually worn to correct vision — see GLASSES 1

specter *or* **spectre** *n* the soul of a dead person thought of especially as appearing to living people — see GHOST

spectrum *n* the distance or extent between possible extremes — see RANGE 3

speculate *vb* to form an opinion from little or no evidence — see GUESS 1

speculation *n* a risky undertaking — see GAMBLE

speculative *adj* existing only as an assumption or speculation — see THEORETICAL 1

speech *n* 1 a usually formal discourse delivered to an audience ⟨the guest of honor gave a short *speech* in appreciation of the award⟩

synonyms address, declamation, harangue, oration, talk

related words diatribe, rant, tirade; eulogy, panegyric, tribute; keynote address, lecture; homily, sermon; monologue, soliloquy; pitch, presentation, spiel

2 the stock of words, pronunciation, and grammar used by a people as their basic means of communication — see LANGUAGE 1

speechless *adj* 1 deliberately refraining from speech — see SILENT 1

2 unable to speak — see MUTE 1

speechlessness *n* incapacity for or restraint from speaking — see SILENCE 1

speed *n* a high rate of movement or performance ⟨we did our homework with as much *speed* as possible so we could go to the movies⟩

synonyms celerity, fastness, fleetness, haste, hurry, quickness, rapidity, rapidness, speediness, swiftness, velocity

related words clip, pace, rate, tempo; drive, hustle; acceleration, rush; dispatch, expedition, expeditiousness, promptness

near antonyms languidness, languor, leisureliness,

lethargy, torpor; reluctance; deliberateness, deliberation
antonyms slowness, sluggishness
speed *vb* to proceed or move quickly — see HURRY 2
speed (up) *vb* to cause to move or proceed fast or faster — see HURRY 1
speedboat *n* a boat equipped with a motor — see MOTORBOAT
speedily *adv* with great speed — see FAST 1
speediness *n* a high rate of movement or performance — see SPEED
speedy *adj* moving, proceeding, or acting with great speed — see FAST 1
spell *n* 1 a spoken word or set of words believed to have magic power ⟨the witch cast a *spell* that turned the prince into a toad⟩
synonyms bewitchment, charm, conjuration, enchantment, incantation
related words curse, hex, jinx; black magic, conjuring, magic, mojo, necromancy, sorcery, voodooism, witchcraft, witchery, wizardry
2 a sudden experiencing of a physical or mental disorder — see ATTACK 2
3 an indefinite but usually short period of time — see WHILE 1
spell *vb* 1 to cast a spell on — see BEWITCH 1
2 to communicate or convey (as an idea) to the mind — see MEAN 1
spellbind *vb* to hold the attention of as if by a spell — see ENTHRALL 1
spellbound *adj* being or appearing to be under a magic spell — see ENCHANTED
spell out *vb* to make plain or understandable — see EXPLAIN 1
spend *vb* 1 to hand over or use up in payment ⟨I always end up *spending* too much money at the mall⟩
synonyms disburse, expend, give, lay out, pay
related words lavish, rain; blow; squander, waste
near antonyms cache, hoard, save; acquire, earn, make
2 to make complete use of — see DEPLETE
3 to use up carelessly — see WASTE 1
spender *n* someone who carelessly spends money — see PRODIGAL
spendthrift *adj* given to spending money freely or foolishly — see PRODIGAL
spendthrift *n* someone who carelessly spends money — see PRODIGAL
spent *adj* depleted in strength, energy, or freshness — see WEARY 1
spew *vb* 1 to flow out in great quantities or with force — see GUSH 1
2 to throw out or off (something from within) often violently — see ERUPT 1
sphere *n* 1 a more or less round body or mass — see ¹BALL 1
2 a region of activity, knowledge, or influence — see FIELD 2
spherical *adj* having every part of the surface the same distance from the center — see ROUND 1
spice *n* 1 a sweet or pleasant smell — see FRAGRANCE
2 something (as a spice or herb) that adds an agreeable or interesting taste to food — see SEASONING 2
spice *vb* to make more pleasant to the taste by adding something intensely flavored — see SEASON 1

spick–and–span *or* **spic–and–span** *adj* 1 free from dirt or stain — see CLEAN 1
2 recently made and never used before — see NEW 3
spicy *adj* hinting at or intended to call to mind matters regarded as indecent — see SUGGESTIVE 1
spigot *n* a fixture for controlling the flow of a liquid — see FAUCET
spike *vb* to penetrate or hold (something) with a pointed object — see IMPALE
spill *n* the act of going down from an upright position suddenly and involuntarily — see FALL 1
spill *vb* to make known (as information previously kept secret) — see REVEAL 1
spin *n* 1 a rapid turning about on an axis or central point ⟨the ice skater moved into a tight *spin* at the end of her routine⟩
synonyms gyration, pirouette, reel, revolution, roll, rotation, twirl, wheel, whirl
related words circuit, circulation; coil, curl, curve, spiral, twist; circle, orbit; eddy, swirl
2 a state of mental confusion — see HAZE 2
spin *vb* 1 to move in circles around an axis or center ⟨after *spinning* around three times blindfolded, I tried to pin the tail on the donkey and almost fell over⟩
synonyms gyrate, pirouette, revolve, roll, rotate, turn, twirl, wheel, whirl
related words coil, curl, curve, round, spiral, twine, twist, wind; circle, orbit
2 to be in a confused state as if from being twirled around ⟨my head *spun* as I contemplated all the possible problems this could cause⟩
synonyms reel, swim, whirl
near antonyms calm, collect; settle, steady
3 to move (something) in a curved or circular path on or as if on an axis — see TURN 1
spinal column *n* a column of bones supporting the trunk of a vertebrate animal — see SPINE
spindling *adj* being tall, thin and usually loose-jointed — see LANKY
spindly *adj* being tall, thin and usually loose-jointed — see LANKY
spine *n* a column of bones supporting the trunk of a vertebrate animal ⟨he hurt his *spine* in the accident, but the doctor says he'll be walking again in no time⟩
synonyms backbone, chine, spinal column, vertebral column
related words back, spinal cord, vertebra
spineless *adj* 1 lacking strength of will or character — see WEAK 2
2 having or showing a shameful lack of courage — see COWARDLY
spinelessness *n* 1 the quality or state of lacking strength of will or character — see WEAKNESS 2
2 a shameful lack of courage in the face of danger — see COWARDICE
spin–off *n* something that naturally develops or is developed from something else — see DERIVATIVE
spiny *adj* requiring exceptional skill or caution in performance or handling — see TRICKY
spiral *adj* turning around an axis like the thread of a screw ⟨a *spiral* staircase takes visitors up into the Statue of Liberty⟩
synonyms coiling, corkscrew, helical, screwlike, winding
related words curving, curling, twisting
near antonyms lineal, linear, straight

spiral *vb* to follow a circular or spiral course — see WIND

spirit *n* **1** an immaterial force within a human being thought to give the body life, energy, and power — see SOUL 1

2 a state of mind dominated by a particular emotion — see MOOD 1

3 the soul of a dead person thought of especially as appearing to living people — see GHOST

4 **spirits** *pl* a fermented or distilled beverage that can make a person drunk — see ALCOHOL

spirited *adj* **1** marked by a lively display of strong feeling ⟨the town meeting featured a *spirited* debate about the proposed ban on skateboarding in the plaza downtown⟩

synonyms fiery, gingery, high-spirited, mettlesome, peppery, spunky

related words animate, animated, bouncing, bouncy, brisk, energetic, frisky, jaunty, jazzy, peppy, perky, pert, racy, snappy, spanking, sparky, sprightly, springy, vital, vivacious, zippy; ardent, fervent, impassioned, passionate

near antonyms boring, dull, lifeless

antonyms spiritless

2 having much high-spirited energy and movement — see LIVELY 1

spiritless *adj* lacking bodily energy or motivation — see LISTLESS

spiritual *adj* **1** not composed of matter — see IMMATERIAL 1

2 of, relating to, or used in the practice or worship services of a religion — see RELIGIOUS 1

spiritual *n* a religious song — see HYMN

¹**spit** *n* an area of land that juts out into a body of water — see ²CAPE

²**spit** *n* **1** something or someone that strongly resembles another — see IMAGE 1

2 the fluid that is secreted into the mouth by certain glands — see SALIVA

spite *n* the desire to cause pain for the satisfaction of doing harm — see MALICE

spiteful *adj* having or showing a desire to cause someone pain or suffering for the sheer enjoyment of it — see HATEFUL

spitefully *adv* in a mean or spiteful manner — see NASTILY

spitefulness *n* the desire to cause pain for the satisfaction of doing harm — see MALICE

spittle *n* the fluid that is secreted into the mouth by certain glands — see SALIVA

spit up *vb* to discharge the contents of the stomach through the mouth — see VOMIT

splash *vb* **1** to cause (something liquid or mushy) to move along in sheets ⟨I always *splash* water at my sister when we go to the pool⟩

synonyms spatter

related words dabble, lap, plash, wash

2 to wet or soil by striking with something liquid or mushy ⟨the bus *splashed* us as it passed⟩

synonyms bespatter, dash, plash, spatter, splatter

related words drench, drown, impregnate, saturate, soak, sop, souse, steep; bathe, douse, wash, water, wet; throw; spray; slop, sprinkle; squirt

3 to flow along or against — see WASH 1

4 to flow in a broken irregular stream — see GURGLE

5 to move with a splashing motion — see SLOSH

splashy *adj* **1** likely to attract attention — see NOTICEABLE

2 attractively eye-catching in style — see JAZZY 1

3 excessively showy — see GAUDY

splatter *vb* to wet or soil by striking with something liquid or mushy — see SPLASH 2

spleen *n* **1** an intense emotional state of displeasure with someone or something — see ANGER

2 the desire to cause pain for the satisfaction of doing harm — see MALICE

splendid *adj* **1** large and impressive in size, grandeur, extent, or conception — see GRAND 1

2 of the very best kind — see EXCELLENT

splendidly *adv* in a pleasing way — see WELL 5

splendor *n* **1** impressiveness of beauty on a large scale — see MAGNIFICENCE

2 the quality or state of having or giving off light — see BRILLIANCE 1

splenetic *adj* having or showing a habitually bad temper — see ILL-TEMPERED

splint *n* a small flat piece separated from a whole — see CHIP 1

splinter *n* a small flat piece separated from a whole — see CHIP 1

splinter *vb* to cut into long slender pieces — see SLIVER

split *adj* disagreeing with each other — see DIVIDED

split *n* **1** an irregular usually narrow break in a surface created by pressure — see CRACK 1

2 the act or process of a whole separating into two or more parts or pieces — see SEPARATION 1

split *vb* to set or force apart — see SEPARATE 1

split second *n* a very small space of time — see INSTANT

splotch *n* a small area that is different (as in color) from the main part — see SPOT 1

splotch *vb* to mark with small spots especially unevenly — see SPOT

splotched *adj* having blotches of two or more colors — see PIED

splotchy *adj* marked with spots — see SPOTTED 1

spoil *n* valuables stolen or taken by force — see LOOT

spoil *vb* **1** to affect slightly with something morally bad or undesirable — see TAINT 1

2 to go through decomposition — see DECAY 1

3 to reduce the soundness, effectiveness, or perfection of — see DAMAGE 1

4 to treat with great or excessive care — see BABY

spoilage *n* the process by which dead organic matter separates into simpler substances — see CORRUPTION 1

spoiled *adj* having undergone organic breakdown — see ROTTEN 1

spoilsport *n* a person who spoils the pleasure of others — see KILLJOY

spoken *adj* made or carried on through speaking rather than in writing — see VERBAL 2

spokesman *n* a person who speaks for another or for a group — see SPOKESPERSON

spokesperson *n* a person who speaks for another or for a group ⟨the *spokesperson* for the protesting students presented their demands to the principal⟩

synonyms mouthpiece, speaker, spokesman

related words spokeswoman; sayer, talker; agent, delegate, deputy, representative

sponge *n* a person who is supported or seeks support from another without making an adequate return — see LEECH

sponge *vb* to take in (something liquid) through small openings — see ABSORB 1

sponger *n* a person who is supported or seeks support from another without making an adequate return — see LEECH

spongy *adj* giving easily to the touch — see SOFT 3

sponsor *n* a person who takes the responsibility for some other person or thing ⟨you need a *sponsor* to recommend you in order to get into the exclusive country club⟩
synonyms backer, guarantor, patron, surety
related words chaperone (*or* chaperon); advocate, champion, supporter; benefactor; coach, mentor, teacher

spontaneity *n* carefree freedom from constraint — see ABANDON

spontaneous *adj* done instantly and without conscious thought or decision — see AUTOMATIC 1

spoof *n* a work that imitates and exaggerates another work for comic effect — see PARODY 1

spook *n* **1** a person who tries secretly to obtain information for one country in the territory of another usually unfriendly country — see SPY
2 the soul of a dead person thought of especially as appearing to living people — see GHOST

spook *vb* to strike with fear — see FRIGHTEN

spooked *adj* filled with fear or dread — see AFRAID 1

spooky *adj* **1** easily excited by nature — see EXCITABLE
2 fearfully and mysteriously strange or fantastic — see EERIE

spoon *n* a utensil with a bowl and a handle that is used especially in cooking and serving food ⟨it's easier to eat soup with a *spoon* than with a fork⟩
synonyms dipper, ladle, scoop
related words skimmer

spoon *vb* to lift out with something that holds liquid — see DIP 2

sporadic *adj* **1** lacking in steadiness or regularity of occurrence — see FITFUL
2 not often occurring or repeated — see INFREQUENT

sport *n* **1** activity engaged in to amuse oneself — see PLAY 1
2 an attitude or manner not to be taken seriously — see FUN 2

sport *vb* **1** to engage in activity for amusement — see PLAY 1
2 to play and run about happily — see FROLIC 1
3 to present so as to invite notice or attention — see SHOW 1

sportive *adj* given to good-natured joking or teasing — see PLAYFUL

sportiveness *n* a natural disposition for playful behavior — see PLAYFULNESS

sportsmanlike *adj* following or according to the rules — see FAIR 3

sportsmanly *adj* following or according to the rules — see FAIR 3

spot *n* **1** a small area that is different (as in color) from the main part ⟨in summer the white coat of the snow leopard is studded with brownish black *spots*⟩
synonyms blotch, dapple, dot, eyespot, fleck, mottle, patch, point, speck, speckle, splotch
related words birthmark, freckle, mole; blot, mark, smear, smudge, stain; spatter, splash
2 a difficult, puzzling, or embarrassing situation

from which there is no easy escape — see PREDICAMENT
3 a mark of guilt or disgrace — see STAIN 1
4 a very small amount — see PARTICLE 1
5 the area or space occupied by or intended for something — see PLACE 1

spot *vb* to mark with small spots especially unevenly ⟨to give the effect of sunlight on water, the artist *spotted* the lake in his painting with flecks of gold paint⟩
synonyms blotch, dapple, dot, fleck, freckle, marble, mottle, pepper, speck, speckle, splotch, sprinkle, stipple
related words blot, dye, stain; streak, stripe; intersperse, stud; bespatter, spatter

spotless *adj* free from dirt or stain — see CLEAN 1

spotted *adj* **1** marked with spots ⟨the *spotted* tablecloth clashed with the stripes on the wallpaper⟩
synonyms dappled (*also* dapple), dotted, flecked, freckled, mottled, speckled, splotchy, spotty, stippled, variegated
related words spangled; marbled, moiré (*or* moire), veined; motley, multicolored; piebald, roan
near antonyms solid
2 having blotches of two or more colors — see PIED

spotting *n* the act or process of sighting or learning the existence of something for the first time — see DISCOVERY 1

spotty *adj* **1** lacking in steadiness or regularity of occurrence — see FITFUL
2 marked with spots — see SPOTTED 1

spouse *n* the person to whom another is married ⟨employees and their *spouses* are covered by the health plan⟩
synonyms consort, mate, partner
related words husband, man, old man; lady, wife
near antonyms single; bachelor; maid, maiden, spinster

spout *n* a pipe or channel for carrying off water from a roof — see GUTTER 1

spout *vb* **1** to flow out in great quantities or with force — see GUSH 1
2 to talk loudly and wildly — see RANT
3 to throw out or off (something from within) often violently — see ERUPT 1

spout (off) *vb* to voice one's opinions freely with force — see SPEAK UP

spray *vb* to cover by or as if by scattering something over or on — see SCATTER 2

spread *n* **1** a decorative cloth used as a top covering for a bed — see COUNTERPANE
2 a large fancy meal often accompanied by ceremony or entertainment — see FEAST
3 a wide space or area — see EXPANSE
4 the distance or extent between possible extremes — see RANGE 3
5 the space or amount of space between two points, lines, surfaces, or objects — see DISTANCE

spread *vb* **1** to cause to be known over a considerable area or by many people ⟨*spread* the news!⟩
synonyms broadcast, circulate, disseminate, propagate
related words radiate, sprawl; diffuse, dispense, disperse, dissipate, scatter, sow; communicate, pass (on), transmit
near antonyms conceal, hide, hold (in), secrete; contain, limit, restrict
2 to put a layer of on a surface ⟨we *spread* the fer-

tilizer over the lawn evenly until it was fully covered⟩

synonyms apply, lay

related words dab, daub, plaster, smear; blanket, carpet, coat, cover, layer, overlay, overlie, overspread, sheet, surface

near antonyms peel, strip, uncover

3 to become known — see GET OUT 1

4 to cause (something) to pass from one to another — see COMMUNICATE 1

spread (out) *vb* to arrange the parts of (something) over a wider area — see OPEN 3

spreading *adj* exciting a similar feeling or reaction in others — see CONTAGIOUS 2

spree *n* a time or instance of carefree fun — see FLING 1

sprightliness *n* the quality or state of having abundant or intense activity — see VITALITY 1

sprightly *adv* in a quick and spirited manner — see GAILY 2

sprightly *adj* having much high-spirited energy and movement — see LIVELY 1

spring *n* an act of leaping into the air — see JUMP 1

spring *vb* **1** to come into existence — see BEGIN 2

2 to propel oneself upward or forward into the air — see JUMP 1

3 to set free (as from slavery or confinement) — see FREE 1

spring (for) *vb* to give what is owed for — see PAY 2

spring (up) *vb* to come to one's attention especially gradually or unexpectedly — see ARISE 2

springy *adj* **1** able to revert to original size and shape after being stretched, squeezed, or twisted — see ELASTIC 1

2 having much high-spirited energy and movement — see LIVELY 1

sprinkle *n* **1** a light or fine rain — see DRIZZLE

2 a small number — see FEW

sprinkle *vb* **1** to cover by or as if by scattering something over or on — see SCATTER 2

2 to mark with small spots especially unevenly — see SPOT

sprinkling *n* **1** a small number — see FEW

2 a very small amount — see PARTICLE 1

sprint *vb* to go at a pace faster than a walk — see RUN 1

sprite *n* an imaginary being usually having a small human form and magical powers — see FAIRY

spruce *adj* being strikingly neat and trim in style or appearance — see SMART 1

sprucely *adv* in a strikingly neat and trim manner — see SMARTLY

spry *adj* moving easily — see GRACEFUL 1

spryness *n* ease and grace in physical activity — see DEXTERITY 2

spume *n* a light mass of fine bubbles formed in or on a liquid — see FOAM

spunk *n* the strength of mind that enables a person to endure pain or hardship — see FORTITUDE

spunky *adj* marked by a lively display of strong feeling — see SPIRITED 1

spur *n* something that arouses action or activity — see IMPULSE

spur *vb* to urge or push forward with or as if with a pointed object — see PROD 1

spurious *adj* **1** being such in appearance only and made or manufactured with the intention of committing fraud — see COUNTERFEIT

2 lacking in natural or spontaneous quality — see ARTIFICIAL 1

spurn *vb* to show unwillingness to accept, do, engage in, or agree to — see DECLINE 1

spur–of–the–moment *adj* made or done without previous thought or preparation — see EXTEMPORANEOUS

spurt *n* a sudden and usually temporary growth of activity — see OUTBREAK

spurt *vb* **1** to flow out in great quantities or with force — see GUSH 1

2 to throw out or off (something from within) often violently — see ERUPT 1

sputter *vb* to speak rapidly, inarticulately, and usually unintelligibly — see BABBLE 1

spy *n* a person who tries secretly to obtain information for one country in the territory of another usually unfriendly country ⟨the government *spy* risked his life every day to get vital information back to his country⟩

synonyms operative, spook

related words counterspy, shadow

phrases secret agent, undercover agent

spy *vb* to make note of (something) through the use of one's eyes — see SEE 1

spying *n* the secret gathering of information on others — see ESPIONAGE

squabble *n* an often noisy or angry expression of differing opinions — see ARGUMENT 1

squabble *vb* to express different opinions about something often angrily — see ARGUE 2

squabbler *n* a person who takes part in a dispute — see DISPUTANT

squad *n* a group of people working together on a task — see GANG 1

squalidness *n* the state or quality of being dirty — see DIRTINESS 1

squall *n* **1** a disturbance of the atmosphere accompanied by wind and often by precipitation (as rain or snow) — see STORM 1

2 a state of noisy, confused activity — see COMMOTION

squall *vb* to cry out loudly and emotionally — see SCREAM

squally *adj* marked by wet and windy conditions — see FOUL 1

squamous *adj* composed of or covered with scales — see SCALY

squander *vb* to use up carelessly — see WASTE 1

squanderer *n* someone who carelessly spends money — see PRODIGAL

squandering *adj* given to spending money freely or foolishly — see PRODIGAL

square *adj* marked by justice, honesty, and freedom from bias — see FAIR 2

square *vb* **1** to be in agreement on every point — see CHECK 1

2 to influence someone with a bribe — see BRIBE

squarely *adv* as stated or indicated without the slightest difference — see EXACTLY 1

squash *vb* **1** to cause to become a pulpy mass — see CRUSH 1

2 to put a stop to (something) by the use of force — see QUELL 1

squashy *adj* giving easily to the touch — see SOFT 3

squat *adj* being compact and broad in build and often short in stature — see STOCKY

squat *vb* to lie low with the limbs close to the body — see CROUCH

squatty *adj* being compact and broad in build and often short in stature — see STOCKY

squawk *n* an expression of dissatisfaction, pain, or resentment — see COMPLAINT 1

squawk *vb* to express dissatisfaction, pain, or resentment usually tiresomely — see COMPLAIN

squeak *vb* to make a short shrill noise ⟨a loose board that *squeaked* every time we walked on the floor⟩

synonyms creak

related words cheep, peep; scream, screech, shriek, shrill, sing, squeal, yelp, yip

squeaking *adj* having a high musical pitch or range — see SHRILL

squeaky *adj* having a high musical pitch or range — see SHRILL

squeal *vb* **1** to give information (as to the authorities) about another's improper or unlawful activities ⟨as soon as the stool pigeon got to the police station, he *squealed* to the police about the whole smuggling operation⟩

synonyms inform, snitch, talk, tell

related words betray, give away, rat (on), turn in; blab, tattle; tip (off)

2 to cry out loudly and emotionally — see SCREAM

squealer *n* a person who provides secret information about another's wrongdoing — see INFORMER

squeamish *adj* **1** affected with nausea — see NAUSEOUS

2 filled with disgust — see SICK 2

squeamishness *n* **1** a disturbed condition of the stomach in which one feels like vomiting — see NAUSEA 1

2 the tendency to be or state of being squeamish — see DELICACY 3

squeeze *vb* **1** to apply external pressure on so as to force out the juice or contents of — see PRESS 2

2 to fit (something) into a tight space — see CROWD 1

3 to get with great difficulty — see EKE OUT

4 to reduce in size or volume by or as if by pressing parts or members together — see COMPRESS 1

5 to rob by the use of trickery or threats — see FLEECE

squeezing *n* the act or process of reducing the size or volume of something by or as if by pressing — see COMPRESSION

squelch *vb* to put a stop to (something) by the use of force — see QUELL 1

squinch *vb* **1** to lie low with the limbs close to the body — see CROUCH

2 to twist (something) out of a natural or normal shape or condition — see CONTORT

squinching *n* the twisting of something out of its natural or normal shape or condition — see CONTORTION

squire *vb* to go along with in order to provide assistance, protection, or companionship — see ACCOMPANY

squirm *vb* to make jerky or restless movements — see FIDGET

squirrel (away) *vb* to put (something of future use or value) in a safe or secret place — see HOARD

squirt *vb* to flow out in great quantities or with force — see GUSH 1

squishy *adj* giving easily to the touch — see SOFT 3

stab *n* **1** a mark or small hole made by a pointed instrument — see PRICK 1

2 an effort to do or accomplish something — see ATTEMPT

stab *vb* to penetrate or hold (something) with a pointed object — see IMPALE

stability *n* **1** the ability to withstand force or stress without being distorted, dislodged, or damaged ⟨the bridge was designed with such great *stability* that it supposedly will not collapse even under the harshest weather conditions⟩

synonyms firmness, soundness, steadiness, strength, sturdiness

related words dependability, durability, reliability; solidity, solidness; cohesion, toughness

near antonyms insecurity, weakness

antonyms instability, unsoundness, unsteadiness

2 the state of continuing without change — see CONSTANCY 1

stable *adj* **1** marked by the ability to withstand stress without structural damage or distortion ⟨the tower was *stable* enough to withstand the strongest winds without collapsing⟩

synonyms fast, firm, sound, stalwart, strong, sturdy

related words dependable, durable, reliable; solid; cohesive, tough

near antonyms insecure, weak

antonyms unsound, unstable, unsteady

2 having been established and usually not subject to change — see FIXED 1

3 having full use of one's mind and control over one's actions — see SANE

4 not undergoing a change in condition — see CONSTANT 1

stack *n* **1** a considerable amount — see LOT 2

2 a quantity of things thrown or stacked on one another — see ¹PILE 1

stack *vb* to lay or throw on top of one another — see PILE

stack up (against *or* with) *vb* to come near or nearer to in character or quality — see APPROXIMATE

stadium *n* a large usually roofless building for sporting events with tiers of seats for spectators ⟨the football game will be held at the new *stadium*, which seats 100,000 people⟩

synonyms bowl, circus, coliseum, colosseum

related words gym, gymnasium, spa; arena, hippodrome

staff *n* **1** a body of persons at work or available for work — see FORCE 1

2 a heavy rigid stick used as a weapon or for punishment — see CLUB 1

stage *n* **1** a level usually raised surface — see PLATFORM

2 a portion of a trip — see LEG 2

3 an individual part of a process, series, or ranking — see DEGREE 1

4 the public performance of plays — see DRAMA 1

stage *vb* to bring before the public in performance or exhibition — see PRESENT 1

stagger *vb* **1** to move forward while swaying from side to side ⟨I was so tired last night that I just *staggered* upstairs to bed without eating dinner⟩

synonyms careen, dodder, lurch, reel, teeter, totter, waddle

related words rock, sway, weave, wobble; clump, flounder, lumber, lump, pound, scuff, scuffle, shamble, shuffle, stamp, stomp, stumble, tramp, tromp

2 to show uncertainty about the right course of action — see HESITATE

staggering *adj* causing wonder or astonishment — see MARVELOUS 1

staid *adj* **1** not joking or playful in mood or manner — see SERIOUS 1

2 having or showing a serious and reserved manner — see DIGNIFIED

stain *n* **1** a mark of guilt or disgrace ⟨the *stain* of this cowardly act would haunt him for the rest of his career⟩
synonyms blot, brand, smirch, spot, stigma, taint
related words discredit, disgrace, dishonor, disrepute, guilt, ignominy, infamy, odium, opprobrium, reproach, shame
near antonyms award, credit, honor
2 a substance used to color other materials — see PIGMENT

stain *vb* **1** to affect slightly with something morally bad or undesirable — see TAINT 1

2 to give color or a different color to — see COLOR 1

3 to make dirty — see DIRTY

stained *adj* not clean — see DIRTY 1

stainless *adj* free from dirt or stain — see CLEAN 1

stake *n* **1** a legal right to participation in the advantages, profits, and responsibility of something — see INTEREST 1

2 the money or thing risked on the outcome of an uncertain event — see BET

stake *vb* **1** to provide money for — see FINANCE 1

2 to risk (something) on the outcome of an uncertain event — see BET

stale *adj* used or heard so often as to be dull ⟨viewers were bored by the *stale* story lines of the new crop of sitcoms⟩
synonyms banal, commonplace, hackney, hackneyed, moth-eaten, musty, stereotyped, threadbare, tired, trite
related words canned, unimaginative, uninspired, unoriginal; normal, ordinary, rote, routine, standard, stock, typical, usual; boring, drab, dreary, dry, dull, flat, heavy, humdrum, jading, leaden, monotonous, pedestrian, ponderous, prosaic, tame, tedious, tiresome, tiring, unanimated, undramatic, uninteresting, vapid, wearisome, weary, wearying; corny, maudlin, mawkish, mushy, saccharine, sappy, schmaltzy, sentimental, sloppy, sugarcoated, sugary
near antonyms animating, energizing, enlivening, exciting, galvanizing, invigorating, stimulating; absorbing, engaging, engrossing, gripping, interesting, intriguing, involving; atypical, extraordinary, uncommon, unusual
antonyms fresh, new, original

stalemate *n* **1** a point in a struggle where neither side is capable of winning or willing to give in — see IMPASSE

2 a situation in which neither participant in a contest, competition, or struggle comes out ahead of the other — see TIE 1

stalk *vb* **1** to seek out (game) for food or sport — see HUNT 1

2 to walk with exaggerated arm and leg movements — see STRUT 1

stall *vb* **1** to bring (something) to a standstill — see ¹HALT 1

2 to stop functioning — see FAIL 1

stalwart *adj* **1** feeling or displaying no fear by temperament — see BRAVE

2 having muscles capable of exerting great physical force — see STRONG 1

3 marked by the ability to withstand stress without structural damage or distortion — see STABLE 1

stamp *n* a perceptible trace left by pressure — see PRINT 1

stamp *vb* **1** to move heavily or clumsily — see LUMBER 1

2 to tread on heavily so as to crush or injure — see TRAMPLE

stamp (out) *vb* to destroy all traces of — see ANNIHILATE 1

stance *n* a general way of holding the body — see POSTURE 1

stanchion *n* an upright shaft that supports an overhead structure — see PILLAR 1

stand *n* a level usually raised surface — see PLATFORM

stand *vb* **1** to occupy a place or location ⟨the monument *stands* in the middle of the town plaza⟩
synonyms be, lie, sit
related words command, overlook; remain, rest, stay; await, wait; post, station
2 to put up with (something painful or difficult) — see BEAR 2
3 to give what is owed for — see PAY 2

standard *adj* **1** accepted, used, or practiced by most people — see CURRENT 1

2 being of the type that is encountered in the normal course of events — see ORDINARY 1

3 having or showing the qualities associated with the members of a particular group or kind — see TYPICAL 1

standard *n* **1** something set up as an example against which others of the same type are compared ⟨the animation in that movie set the *standard* against which all later animated cartoons were judged⟩
synonyms benchmark, criterion, grade, mark, measure, par, touchstone, yardstick
related words rule; case, example, instance; acme, apex, meridian, peak, pinnacle, summit, zenith
near antonyms aberration, abnormality, deviation
2 a piece of cloth with a special design that is used as an emblem or for signaling — see FLAG 1
3 what is typical of a group, class, or series — see AVERAGE
4 **standards** *pl* the code of good conduct for an individual or group — see ETHICS

standardize *vb* to make agree with a single established standard or model ⟨the plan is to *standardize* the test for reading comprehension so that we can see how students across the state compare⟩
synonyms formalize, homogenize, normalize, regularize
related words codify, organize, systematize; average, equalize, even; accredit, certify; control, govern, regulate; coordinate, harmonize, integrate, reconcile, synthesize
near antonyms customize, individualize, tailor

standby *n* something or someone to which one looks for support — see DEPENDENCE 2

stand-in *n* a person or thing that takes the place of another — see SUBSTITUTE

stand in *vb* to serve as a replacement usually for a time only — see COVER 1

standing *adj* **1** fixed in a place or position — see STATIONARY 1

2 rising straight up — see ERECT

standing *n* 1 high position within society — see RANK 2

2 the period during which something exists, lasts, or is in progress — see DURATION 1

3 the placement of someone or something in relation to others in a vertical arrangement — see RANK 1

standoff *n* a situation in which neither participant in a contest, competition, or struggle comes out ahead of the other — see TIE 1

standoffish *adj* having or showing a lack of friendliness or interest in others — see COOL 1

standout *n* a person who is widely known and usually much talked about — see CELEBRITY 1

stand out *vb* to extend outward beyond a usual point — see BULGE

standpoint *n* a way of looking at or thinking about something — see POINT OF VIEW

standstill *n* a point in a struggle where neither side is capable of winning or willing to give in — see IMPASSE

staple *n* the main or greater part of something as distinguished from its appendages — see BODY 1

star *adj* 1 of or relating to the stars — see STELLAR 1

2 standing above others in rank, importance, or achievement — see EMINENT

3 widely known — see FAMOUS

star *n* 1 a ball-shaped gaseous celestial body that shines by its own light ⟨it's difficult to see the *stars* at night in the middle of the city because of all the streetlights⟩

synonyms luminary, sun

related words constellation; dwarf, fixed star, giant star, lodestar (*also* loadstar), neutron star, nova, red giant, supernova, variable star, white dwarf

2 the person who has the most important role in a play, movie, or TV show ⟨when the *star* of the school play came down with the flu on opening night, her understudy got to go on⟩

synonyms lead, principal

related words leading lady, leading man; superstar; ingenue (*or* ingénue), starlet

near antonyms extra, supernumerary

3 a person who is widely known and usually much talked about — see CELEBRITY 1

starch *n* active strength of body or mind — see VIGOR 1

starchy *adj* marked by or showing careful attention to set forms and details — see CEREMONIOUS 1

star–crossed *adj* having, prone to, or marked by bad luck — see UNLUCKY

stare *vb* to look long and hard in wonder or surprise — see GAPE

stark *adj* 1 harsh and threatening in manner or appearance — see GRIM 1

2 having no exceptions or restrictions — see ABSOLUTE 2

3 lacking contents that could or should be present — see EMPTY 1

4 producing inferior or only a small amount of vegetation — see BARREN 1

starry *adj* of or relating to the stars — see STELLAR 1

start *n* the point at which something begins — see BEGINNING

start *vb* 1 to move suddenly and sharply (as in surprise) ⟨I *started* from my chair when I heard the sudden scream⟩

synonyms bolt, jump, startle

related words jerk, twitch; flinch, recoil; bound, leap, spring; react, respond

2 to be responsible for the creation and early operation or use of — see FOUND

3 to cause to function — see ACTIVATE

4 to come into existence — see BEGIN 2

5 to extend outward beyond a usual point — see BULGE

6 to take the first step in (a process or course of action) — see BEGIN 1

startle *vb* 1 to make a strong impression on (someone) with something unexpected — see SURPRISE 1

2 to move suddenly and sharply (as in surprise) — see START 1

3 to strike with fear — see FRIGHTEN

startling *adj* causing a strong emotional reaction because unexpected — see SURPRISING 1

starved *adj* feeling a desire or need for food — see HUNGRY 1

starving *adj* feeling a desire or need for food — see HUNGRY 1

stash *n* a supply stored up and often hidden away — see HOARD 1

stash *vb* to put (something of future use or value) in a safe or secret place — see HOARD

stashing *n* the placing of something out of sight — see CONCEALMENT 1

state *adj* of or relating to a nation — see NATIONAL

state *n* a body of people composed of one or more nationalities usually with its own territory and government — see NATION

state *vb* 1 to convey in appropriate or telling terms — see PHRASE

2 to express (a thought or emotion) in words — see SAY 1

3 to make known (as an idea, emotion, or opinion) — see EXPRESS 1

state house *n* the building in which a state legislature meets — see CAPITOL

stateliness *n* 1 a dignified bearing or appearance befitting royalty — see MAJESTY 1

2 dignified or restrained beauty of form, appearance, or style — see ELEGANCE

3 impressiveness of beauty on a large scale — see MAGNIFICENCE

stately *adj* 1 having or showing a serious and reserved manner — see DIGNIFIED

2 having or showing elegance — see ELEGANT 1

3 large and impressive in size, grandeur, extent, or conception — see GRAND 1

4 very dignified in form, tone, or style — see ELEVATED 2

statement *n* 1 a record of goods sold or services performed together with the costs due — see ¹BILL 1

2 an act, process, or means of putting something into words — see EXPRESSION 1

3 something that is said — see WORD 2

static *adj* fixed in a place or position — see STATIONARY 1

station *n* 1 the place where someone is assigned to stand or remain ⟨the soldiers remained at their *station* even though a huge enemy force was approaching⟩

synonyms position, post, quarter

THESAURUS

related words assignment, detail

2 a regular stopping place ⟨the historic house was once a *station* on the Underground Railroad, the network that helped slaves reach freedom in the North⟩

synonyms stop, way station

related words depot, terminal; layover, stopover

3 the placement of someone or something in relation to others in a vertical arrangement — see RANK 1

station *vb* to assign to a place or position — see ²POST

stationary *adj* **1** fixed in a place or position ⟨a *stationary* bicycle is good for exercise, but you won't enjoy the scenery very much⟩

synonyms immobile, nonmoving, standing, static

related words immovable, irremovable, nonmotile, unmovable; frozen, motionless, stagnant, still, unbudging

near antonyms motile

antonyms mobile, movable (*or* moveable), moving, nonstationary

2 not undergoing a change in condition — see CONSTANT 1

statuette *n* a small statue — see FIGURINE

stature *n* the distance of something or someone from bottom to top — see HEIGHT 3

status *n* **1** position with regard to conditions and circumstances — see SITUATION 1

2 the placement of someone or something in relation to others in a vertical arrangement — see RANK 1

status quo *n* the state or fact of being the way things usually are — see NORMALITY

statute *n* a rule of conduct or action laid down by a governing authority and especially a legislator — see LAW 1

staunch *or* **stanch** *adj* firm in one's allegiance to someone or something — see FAITHFUL 1

stave off *vb* to drive back — see REPEL 1

¹stay *n* a temporary residing as another's guest — see VISIT 1

²stay *n* something that holds up or serves as a foundation for something else — see SUPPORT 1

stay *vb* **1** to continue to be in a place for a significant amount of time ⟨let's *stay* inside this pavilion until it stops raining⟩

synonyms abide, dwell, hang around, remain, stick around, tarry

related words await, hang on, hold on, wait; dally, linger, loiter; keep

antonyms go, leave, quit

2 to bring (something) to a standstill — see ¹HALT 1

3 to hold up or serve as a foundation for — see SUPPORT 3

4 to remain in place in readiness or expectation of something — see WAIT

5 to reside as a temporary guest — see VISIT 2

steadfast *adj* firm in one's allegiance to someone or something — see FAITHFUL 1

steadfastness *n* adherence to something to which one is bound by a pledge or duty — see FIDELITY

steadiness *n* **1** the ability to withstand force or stress without being distorted, dislodged, or damaged — see STABILITY 1

2 the state of continuing without change — see CONSTANCY 1

steady *adj* **1** firm in one's allegiance to someone or something — see FAITHFUL 1

2 appearing or occurring repeatedly from time to time — see REGULAR 1

3 not undergoing a change in condition — see CONSTANT 1

4 not varying — see UNIFORM

5 worthy of one's trust — see DEPENDABLE

steal *n* something bought or offered for sale at a desirable price — see BARGAIN 1

steal *vb* **1** to take (something) without right and with an intent to keep ⟨the guy who tried to *steal* my car was sentenced to a year in jail⟩

synonyms appropriate, filch, hook, misappropriate, nip, pilfer, pinch, pocket, purloin, rip off, snitch, swipe, thieve

related words burglarize, fleece, rob; loot, pillage, plunder, sack; hijack (*or* highjack); pick, rifle; poach, rustle, shoplift; collar, grab, grasp, nail, seize, snatch, take; mooch, sponge; abduct, kidnap, shanghai, spirit

phrases make away with, run off with, walk off with

near antonyms buy, purchase; bestow, contribute, donate, give, present

2 to move about in a sly or secret manner — see SNEAK 1

steal (from) *vb* to remove valuables from (a place) unlawfully — see ROB

stealer *n* one who steals — see THIEF

stealing *n* the unlawful taking and carrying away of property without the consent of its owner — see THEFT 1

stealthy *adj* **1** given to acting in secret and to concealing one's intentions — see SNEAKY 1

2 undertaken or done so as to escape being observed or known by others — see SECRET 1

steam *vb* to be excited or emotionally stirred up with anger — see BOIL 1

steaming *adj* feeling or showing anger — see ANGRY

steed *n* a large hoofed domestic animal that is used for carrying or drawing loads and for riding — see HORSE

steel *n* a hand weapon with a length of metal sharpened on one or both sides and usually tapered to a sharp point — see SWORD

steel *vb* **1** to fill with courage or strength of purpose — see ENCOURAGE 1

2 to make able to withstand physical hardship, strain, or exposure — see HARDEN 2

3 to prepare (oneself) mentally or emotionally — see FORTIFY 1

steely *adj* **1** harsh and threatening in manner or appearance — see GRIM 1

2 of the color gray — see GRAY 1

steep *adj* **1** having an incline approaching the perpendicular ⟨a very *steep* rock face that was nearly impossible to climb⟩

synonyms abrupt, bold, precipitous, sheer

related words perpendicular, plumb, straight, vertical; craggy, hilly, mountainous, scarped; angled, canted, cocked, heeled, inclined, listed, slanted, sloped, tilted, tipped

near antonyms gentle, gradual, moderate; even, flat, flush, horizontal, level, plane, smooth, unruffled, unwrinkled

antonyms easy

2 going beyond a normal or acceptable limit in degree or amount — see EXCESSIVE

steep *vb* **1** to cause (as a person) to become filled or saturated with a certain quality or principle — see INFUSE

2 to wet thoroughly with liquid — see SOAK 1

steer *vb* to point out the way for (someone) especially from a position in front — see LEAD 1

stellar *adj* **1** of or relating to the stars ⟨humankind's dream of *stellar* navigation is hampered by the vast distances between the stars, even in our own galaxy⟩
synonyms astral, star, starry
related words celestial, empyrean, heavenly; astronomical (*also* astronomic), astrophysical; astronautic (*or* astronautical); starlike, star-spangled

2 of the very best kind — see EXCELLENT

stench *n* a strong unpleasant smell — see STINK

stentorian *adj* marked by a high volume of sound — see LOUD 1

step *n* **1** an action planned or taken to achieve a desired result — see MEASURE 1

2 an individual part of a process, series, or ranking — see DEGREE 1

3 the mark or impression made by a foot — see FOOTPRINT

4 steps *pl* the direction along which something or someone moves — see PATH 1

step *vb* **1** to go on foot — see WALK

2 to perform a series of usually rhythmic bodily movements to music — see DANCE 1

step (along) *vb* to proceed or move quickly — see HURRY 2

step–by–step *adj* proceeding or changing by steps or degrees — see GRADUAL

step down (from) *vb* **1** to give up (a job or office) — see QUIT 1

2 to give up (as a position of authority) formally — see ABDICATE

steppe *n* a broad area of level or rolling treeless country — see PLAIN

step up *vb* to make markedly greater in measure or degree — see INTENSIFY

stereotype *n* an idea or statement about all of the members of a group or all the instances of a situation — see GENERALIZATION

stereotyped *adj* used or heard so often as to be dull — see STALE

sterile *adj* **1** not able to produce fruit or offspring ⟨*sterile* couples sometimes choose to adopt needy children⟩ ⟨the apple tree turned out to be *sterile*, never yielding a crop of apples⟩
synonyms barren, impotent, infertile, unfruitful
related words altered, desexed, neutered, sterilized; castrated, emasculated, gelded; spayed; fruitless, unproductive
near antonyms fecund, luxuriant, productive, prolific; enriched, fertilized, rich; impregnated, pregnant; potent; bearing, producing, yielding; blooming, bursting, flourishing, swarming, teeming
antonyms fat, fertile, fruitful

2 free from filth, infection, or dangers to health — see SANITARY

sterling *adj* of the very best kind — see EXCELLENT

stern *adj* **1** given to exacting standards of discipline and self-restraint — see SEVERE 1

2 harsh and threatening in manner or appearance — see GRIM 1

sternly *adv* in a manner so as to cause loss or suffering — see HARDLY 1

sternness *n* the quality or state of being demanding or unyielding (as in discipline or criticism) — see SEVERITY

stevedore *n* one who loads and unloads ships at a port — see DOCKWORKER

stew *n* **1** a state of nervous or irritated concern — see FRET

2 a state of noisy, confused activity — see COMMOTION

stew *vb* **1** to cook in a liquid heated to the point that it gives off steam — see BOIL 2

2 to experience concern or anxiety — see WORRY 1

steward *n* a person hired to perform household or personal services — see SERVANT

stick *vb* **1** to hold to something firmly as if by adhesion ⟨those magnets are strong enough to *stick* well to the refrigerator⟩
synonyms adhere, cleave, cling, hew
related words bind, cohere, fasten, fuse, glue, unite
near antonyms loosen; drop, fall

2 to arrange something in a certain spot or position — see PLACE 1

3 to penetrate or hold (something) with a pointed object — see IMPALE

4 to rob by the use of trickery or threats — see FLEECE

stick (to *or* with) *vb* to give steadfast support to — see ADHERE

stick around *vb* to continue to be in a place for a significant amount of time — see STAY 1

stick–in–the–mud *n* **1** a person with old-fashioned ideas — see FOGY

2 someone who moves slowly or more slowly than others — see SLOWPOKE

stick out *vb* **1** to extend outward beyond a usual point — see BULGE

2 to put up with (something painful or difficult) — see BEAR 2

sticks *n pl* the open rural area outside of big towns and cities — see COUNTRY 2

sticky *adj* **1** being of such a thick consistency as to readily cling to objects upon contact ⟨the *sticky* maple syrup was a mess to clean up⟩
synonyms adhesive, gelatinous, gluey, glutinous, gooey, gummy, viscid, viscous
related words ropy, tacky; adherent, tenacious
antonyms nonadhesive, nonviscous

2 containing or characterized by an uncomfortable amount of moisture — see HUMID

stiff *adj* **1** incapable of or highly resistant to bending ⟨use a *stiff* piece of paper for the project⟩
synonyms inflexible, rigid, stiffened, unyielding
related words inelastic; firm, hard, solid, sound, strong; brittle, crisp; compact, dense, substantial; arthritic, rheumatic; nonelastic, nonmalleable
near antonyms elastic, resilient, springy, stretchy, workable; malleable; droopy, flabby, flaccid, mushy, semisoft, soft, squashy, squishy; lank, limber, limp, lissome (*also* lissom), lithe, willowy
antonyms flexible, floppy, pliable, pliant, supple, yielding

2 difficult to endure — see HARSH 1

3 going beyond a normal or acceptable limit in degree or amount — see EXCESSIVE

4 having a consistency that does not easily yield to pressure — see FIRM 2

5 lacking social grace and assurance — see AWKWARD 1

THESAURUS

6 requiring considerable physical or mental effort — see HARD 2

stiffened *adj* incapable of or highly resistant to bending — see STIFF 1

stiffly *adv* **1** in a manner so as to cause loss or suffering — see HARDLY 1

2 in a vigorous and forceful manner — see HARD 3

stifle *vb* **1** to be or cause to be killed by lack of breathable air — see SMOTHER 1

2 to refrain from openly showing or uttering — see SUPPRESS 2

stifling *adj* lacking fresh air — see STUFFY 1

stigma *n* a mark of guilt or disgrace — see STAIN 1

still *adj* **1** free from disturbing noise or uproar — see QUIET 1

2 free from storms or physical disturbance — see CALM 1

3 mostly or entirely without sound — see SILENT 3

still *adv* **1** without motion ⟨now, you have to sit very *still* while the hairdresser cuts your hair⟩
synonyms motionlessly, quiet, quietly
related words immovably; inactively
near antonyms movably

2 in spite of that — see HOWEVER

still *n* **1** a state of freedom from storm or disturbance — see CALM

2 the near or complete absence of sound — see SILENCE 2

still *vb* **1** to bring (something) to a standstill — see ¹HALT 1

2 to free from distress or disturbance — see CALM 1

3 to stop the noise or speech of — see SILENCE 1

stillness *n* **1** a state of freedom from storm or disturbance — see CALM

2 incapacity for or restraint from speaking — see SILENCE 1

3 the near or complete absence of sound — see SILENCE 2

stilly *adj* **1** free from disturbing noise or uproar — see QUIET 1

2 free from storms or physical disturbance — see CALM 1

stilted *adj* lacking social grace and assurance — see AWKWARD 1

stimulant *n* **1** something that arouses a strong response from another — see PROVOCATION 1

2 something that arouses action or activity — see IMPULSE

stimulate *vb* **1** to give life, vigor, or spirit to — see ANIMATE

2 to rouse to strong feeling or action — see PROVOKE 1

stimulating *adj* **1** causing great emotional or mental stimulation — see EXCITING 1

2 having a renewing effect on the state of the body or mind — see TONIC

3 serving or likely to arouse a strong reaction — see PROVOCATIVE

stimulation *n* something that arouses a strong response from another — see PROVOCATION 1

stimulative *adj* having a renewing effect on the state of the body or mind — see TONIC

stimulus *n* **1** something that arouses a strong response from another — see PROVOCATION 1

2 something that arouses action or activity — see IMPULSE

sting *n* a sharp unpleasant sensation usually felt in some specific part of the body — see PAIN 1

sting *vb* **1** to charge (someone) too much for goods or services — see OVERCHARGE 1

2 to rob by the use of trickery or threats — see FLEECE

stinginess *n* the quality of being overly sparing with money — see PARSIMONY

stinging *adj* causing intense discomfort to one's skin — see CUTTING 1

stingy *adj* **1** giving or sharing as little as possible ⟨until his redemption, Ebenezer Scrooge is the classic example of a very *stingy*, heartless miser⟩
synonyms cheap, close, closefisted, mean, niggard, niggardly, parsimonious, penurious, pinching, spare, sparing, stinting, tight, tightfisted, uncharitable
related words careful, chary, conserving, economical, economizing, frugal, saving, scrimping, skimping, thrifty; acquisitive, avaricious, avid, coveting, covetous, desirous, grasping, greedy, hoggish, itchy, mercenary, rapacious, selfish, shabby, small, sordid; begrudging, envious, grudging, resentful; inhospitable
near antonyms altruistic, selfless, unselfish; extravagant, free, handsome, lavish, profuse; beneficent, benevolent, hospitable, humanitarian, philanthropic; compassionate, good-hearted, greathearted, kindly, magnanimous, openhearted; thriftless, unthrifty; dissipating, frittering, prodigal, profligate, spendthrift, splurging, squandering, wasteful, wasting
antonyms bounteous, bountiful, charitable, freehanded, generous, liberal, munificent, openhanded, unsparing, unstinting

2 less plentiful than what is normal, necessary, or desirable — see MEAGER

stink *n* a strong unpleasant smell ⟨the *stink* of burned plastic lingered in the kitchen for days after we accidentally melted a spatula on the stove⟩
synonyms reek, stench
related words acridness, fetidness, foulness, fustiness, malodorousness, mustiness, rancidity, rankness, staleness; badness, vileness; dirt, dirtiness, filth, filthiness, nastiness; odor, redolence, scent, sniff
near antonyms floweriness, lusciousness, savoriness, spiciness, sweetness; bouquet; ambrosia
antonyms aroma, fragrance, perfume

stink *vb* to give off an extremely unpleasant smell ⟨the dog *stinks* because she tangled with a skunk again⟩
synonyms reek
related words exhale, savor, smell; decay, decompose, rot, spoil; disgust, offend, repulse, revolt

stinker *n* a person whose behavior is offensive to others — see JERK 1

stinking *adj* having an unpleasant smell — see MALODOROUS

stinky *adj* having an unpleasant smell — see MALODOROUS

stint *n* **1** a fixed period of time during which a person holds a job or position — see TERM 1

2 a piece of work that needs to be done regularly — see CHORE 1

stint (on) *vb* to use or give out in stingy amounts — see SPARE

stinting *adj* giving or sharing as little as possible — see STINGY 1

stipend *n* the money paid regularly to a person for labor or services — see WAGE

stipple *vb* to mark with small spots especially unevenly — see SPOT

stippled *adj* marked with spots — see SPOTTED 1

stipulate (for) *vb* to ask for (something) earnestly or with authority — see DEMAND 1

stipulation *n* something upon which the carrying out of an agreement or offer depends — see CONDITION 2

stir *n* **1** a state of noisy, confused activity — see COMMOTION

2 the act or an instance of changing position — see MOVEMENT 1

stir *vb* **1** to cause (as a liquid) to move about in a circle especially repeatedly ⟨the recipe says to *stir* the mixture carefully until it's properly blended⟩
synonyms agitate, churn, swirl, whirl
related words beat, paddle, whip, whisk; reel, shake, wheel

2 to change one's position — see MOVE 3

3 to rouse to strong feeling or action — see PROVOKE 1

stir (up) *vb* to cause or encourage the development of — see INCITE 1

stirring *adj* **1** causing great emotional or mental stimulation — see EXCITING 1

2 having the power to affect the feelings or sympathies — see MOVING

stirring *n* the act or an instance of changing position — see MOVEMENT 1

stitch *n* a sharp unpleasant sensation usually felt in some specific part of the body — see PAIN 1

stitch *vb* to close up with a series of interlacing stitches — see SEW

stock *adj* accepted, used, or practiced by most people — see CURRENT 1

stock *n* **1** a group of persons who come from the same ancestor — see FAMILY 1

2 a stupid person — see IDIOT

3 firm belief in the integrity, ability, effectiveness, or genuineness of someone or something — see TRUST 1

4 the line of ancestors from whom a person is descended — see ANCESTRY

stockade *n* a place of confinement for persons held in lawful custody — see JAIL

stocking *n* a close-fitting covering for the foot and leg ⟨be sure to wear your thick wool *stockings* if it's cold today⟩
synonyms hose, sock
related words hosiery; anklet, bobby socks, bootee

stockpile *n* a supply stored up and often hidden away — see HOARD 1

stockpile *vb* to put (something of future use or value) in a safe or secret place — see HOARD

stocky *adj* being compact and broad in build and often short in stature ⟨he was a tough, *stocky* little boy, muscular and solid⟩
synonyms chunky, dumpy, heavyset, squat, squatty, stout, stubby, stumpy, thickset
related words beefy, brawny, bulky, burly, husky, sturdy, thick, thickish, weighty; chubby, corpulent, fat, fleshy, full, gross, heavy, obese, overweight, plump, portly, pudgy, roly-poly, rotund, round, tubby; paunchy, potbellied; flabby, soft
near antonyms delicate, fragile, frail, puny; lean, skinny, slender, slim, spare, thin; angular, bony, gaunt, lank, lanky, rawboned, sinewy; scraggy,

scrawny, slight; anorexic, cadaverous, emaciated, haggard, skeletal, wasted; spindly, twiggy, waspish, weedy, willowy, wiry

stodgy *adj* causing weariness, restlessness, or lack of interest — see BORING

stoic *or* **stoical** *adj* **1** accepting pains or hardships calmly or without complaint — see PATIENT 1

2 not feeling or showing emotion — see IMPASSIVE 1

stolid *adj* **1** not expressing any emotion — see BLANK 1

2 not feeling or showing emotion — see IMPASSIVE 1

stomach *n* the part of the body between the chest and the pelvis ⟨please don't lean on my *stomach* —I just had a big meal⟩
synonyms abdomen, belly, breadbasket [*slang*], gut, solar plexus, tummy
related words middle, midriff, waist; paunch, potbelly; thorax

stomach *vb* to put up with (something painful or difficult) — see BEAR 2

stomachache *n* abdominal pain especially when focused in the digestive organs ⟨you can stay home from school tomorrow if you still have a *stomachache*⟩
synonyms bellyache
related words colic, cramps

stomp *vb* **1** to move heavily or clumsily — see LUMBER 1

2 to tread on heavily so as to crush or injure — see TRAMPLE

stone blind *adj* lacking the power of sight — see BLIND

stone–broke *adj* lacking money or material possessions — see POOR 1

stoneware *n* articles made of baked clay — see CROCKERY

stony *also* **stoney** *adj* having or showing a lack of sympathy or tender feelings — see HARD 1

stool pigeon *n* a person who provides secret information about another's wrongdoing — see INFORMER

stoop *vb* to descend to a level that is beneath one's dignity — see CONDESCEND 1

stooping *adj* bending downward or forward — see NODDING

stop *n* **1** a brief halt in a journey ⟨our guide called for a *stop* at the trail hut to eat and rest a bit⟩
synonyms layover, stopover
related words break, pause, rest

2 a regular stopping place — see STATION 2

3 something that makes movement or progress more difficult — see ENCUMBRANCE

4 the stopping of a process or activity — see END 1

stop *vb* **1** to bring (as an action or operation) to an immediate end ⟨please *stop* that running in the library⟩
synonyms break, break off, can, cease, cut (out), desist (from), discontinue, drop, end, halt, knock off, lay off, leave off, quit, shut off
related words complete, conclude, finish; close (down); deactivate; block, blockade, dam, delay, detain, hinder, hold, hold back, impede, obstruct, stem; call, suspend; arrest, brake, check, clamp down, rein (in), squash, squelch, stamp, stanch (*also* staunch), stunt, suppress, turn back; pause, stay, suspend; abolish, abort, annul, demolish, destroy, dissolve, kill, ruin, scuttle, snuff

phrases have done with, put the kibosh on

near antonyms carry on, continue, follow through, keep up, run on; advance, proceed, progress; actuate, drive, impel, propel, stir

2 to bring (something) to a standstill — see ¹HALT 1

3 to close up so that no empty spaces remain — see FILL 2

4 to come to an end — see CEASE 1

stop (by *or* in) *vb* to make a brief visit — see CALL 3

stop (up) *vb* to prevent passage through — see CLOG 1

stopcock *n* a fixture for controlling the flow of a liquid — see FAUCET

stopgap *n* a temporary replacement — see MAKESHIFT

stopover *n* a brief halt in a journey — see STOP 1

stoppage *n* the stopping of a process or activity — see END 1

storage *n* a building for storing goods — see STOREHOUSE

store *adj* made beforehand in large numbers — see READY-MADE

store *n* **1** a collection of things kept available for future use or need ⟨Dad has a *store* of funny stories for when conversation lags at company parties⟩

synonyms cache, deposit, hoard, reserve

related words budget, fund, nest egg, pool, reservoir, stock, stockpile, supply; accumulation, assemblage, collection, gathering

2 a supply stored up and often hidden away — see HOARD 1

3 an establishment where goods are sold to consumers — see SHOP 1

store *vb* **1** to place somewhere for safekeeping or ready availability ⟨we decided to *store* the lawn mower in the shed instead of the garage⟩

synonyms keep, stow

related words garage, house; file, pack, shelve

2 to put (something of future use or value) in a safe or secret place — see HOARD

storehouse *n* a building for storing goods ⟨the company has a large *storehouse* filled with lumber for manufacturing its line of furniture⟩

synonyms depository, depot, magazine, repository, storage, stowage, warehouse

related words cache, stockroom, storeroom; bank, bin, container, locker, safe-deposit box, strongbox; arsenal, dump

storm *n* **1** a disturbance of the atmosphere accompanied by wind and often by precipitation (as rain or snow) ⟨a winter *storm* bringing about six inches of snow⟩

synonyms squall, tempest

related words blizzard, hail storm, ice storm, northeaster, norther, rainstorm, sandstorm, snowstorm, southeaster, southwester, thunderstorm, windstorm; cyclone, hurricane, typhoon

2 a heavy fall of objects — see RAIN 2

3 a rapid or overwhelming outpouring of many things at once — see BARRAGE

4 a state of noisy, confused activity — see COMMOTION

5 a steady falling of water from the sky in significant quantity — see RAIN 1

6 a sudden intense expression of strong feeling — see OUTBURST 1

7 a violent disturbance (as of the political or social order) — see CONVULSION

storm *vb* **1** to express one's anger usually violently — see RAGE 1

2 to fall as water in a continuous stream of drops from the clouds — see RAIN 1

3 to take sudden, violent action against — see ATTACK 1

stormy *adj* **1** marked by bursts of destructive force or intense activity — see VIOLENT 1

2 marked by or abounding with rain — see RAINY

3 marked by sudden or violent disturbance — see CONVULSIVE

4 marked by turmoil or disturbance especially of natural elements — see WILD 3

5 marked by wet and windy conditions — see FOUL 1

story *n* **1** a work with imaginary characters and events that is shorter and usually less complex than a novel ⟨if you go right to bed, Daddy will read a *story* to you⟩

synonyms narrative, novelette, novella, short story, tale, yarn

related words exemplum, fable, parable; anecdote, joke; fairy tale, folktale, legend, myth, romance; account, annals, chronicle, history, record, report

2 a brief account of something interesting that happened especially to one personally ⟨Grandpa is always telling *stories* about what it was like growing up on a farm⟩

synonyms anecdote, tale, yarn

related words episode, event, happening, incident, occurrence; recital, recitation

3 a report of recent events or facts not previously known — see NEWS

4 a relating of events usually in the order in which they happened — see ACCOUNT 1

5 a rumor or report of a personal or sensational nature — see TALE 1

6 a statement known by its maker to be untrue and made in order to deceive — see LIE

storyteller *n* a person who tells lies — see LIAR

stout *adj* **1** able to withstand hardship, strain, or exposure — see HARDY 1

2 being compact and broad in build and often short in stature — see STOCKY

3 feeling or displaying no fear by temperament — see BRAVE

4 having muscles capable of exerting great physical force — see STRONG 1

5 not showing weakness or uncertainty — see FIRM 1

stouthearted *adj* feeling or displaying no fear by temperament — see BRAVE

stoutly *adv* in a vigorous and forceful manner — see HARD 3

stoutness *n* strength of mind to carry on in spite of danger — see COURAGE

stow *vb* **1** to place somewhere for safekeeping or ready availability — see STORE 1

2 to put (something of future use or value) in a safe or secret place — see HOARD

stowage *n* a building for storing goods — see STOREHOUSE

straggler *n* someone who moves slowly or more slowly than others — see SLOWPOKE

straight *adj* **1** free from irregularities (as curves, bends, or angles) in course ⟨in the wide, open spaces of the West some rural roads are incredibly *straight*⟩

synonyms linear, right, straightaway, straightforward

related words unbent, uncurled, untwisted; direct, undeviating, unswerving

near antonyms bowed, rounded; entwined, kinked, swirled, turned, turning, twined, twining, twisted, twisting, veering, warped; bending, coiled, coiling, corkscrew, curled, curling, curved, curving, looped, looping, spiral, spiraling (*or* spiralling), winding; meandering, weaving; devious, serpentine, sinuous, zigzag, zigzagging

antonyms crooked

2 conforming to a high standard of morality or virtue — see GOOD 2

3 free from added matter — see PURE 1

4 free in expressing one's true feelings and opinions — see FRANK

5 going straight to the point clearly and firmly — see STRAIGHTFORWARD 1

6 not having one's mind affected by alcohol — see SOBER 1

straight *adv* **1** in a direct line or course — see DIRECTLY 1

2 in an honest and direct manner — see STRAIGHTFORWARD

straightaway *adj* **1** done or occurring without any noticeable lapse in time — see INSTANTANEOUS

2 free from irregularities (as curves, bends, or angles) in course — see STRAIGHT 1

straightaway *adv* without delay — see IMMEDIATELY

straighten *vb* to cause to follow a line that is without bends or curls ⟨*straighten* that extension cord—it should be just long enough to reach the wall outlet⟩

synonyms unbend, uncurl

related words uncoil, unwind; disentangle, untangle, untwine, untwist

near antonyms arc, bend, bow, hook, round; entwine, kink, swirl, turn, twine, twist; coil, loop, spiral, wind

antonyms bend, crook, curl, curve

straightforward *also* **straightforwards** *adv* in an honest and direct manner ⟨she finally told him *straightforward* that she wasn't interested in a date⟩

synonyms directly, forthrightly, foursquare, plain, plainly, straight, straightforwardly

related words candidly, frankly, honestly, openheartedly, openly, unguardedly, unreservedly; artlessly, earnestly, sincerely; abruptly, bluntly, brusquely, curtly, gruffly, sharply; impolitely, inconsiderately, rudely, tactlessly; truthfully, veraciously

near antonyms long-windedly, verbosely, wordily; civilly, courteously, diplomatically, politely, tactfully; deceitfully, mendaciously, untruthfully; erroneously, fallaciously, falsely, hypocritically, insincerely; ambiguously, circuitously, equivocally, evasively, indirectly

straightforward *adj* **1** going straight to the point clearly and firmly ⟨a *straightforward* account of the football game with no digressions or personal comments⟩

synonyms direct, forthright, foursquare, plain, straight

related words aboveboard, candid, frank, free-spoken, honest, open, openhearted, outspoken, plainspoken, unguarded, unreserved; artless, earnest, sincere; uninhibited, unrestrained;

abrupt, bluff, blunt, brusque, curt, gruff, sharp; impolite, inconsiderate, rude, tactless, undiplomatic; true, truthful, veracious

near antonyms circumlocutory, long-winded, prolix, verbose, wordy; inhibited, reserved, restrained; civil, courteous, polite, tactful; deceitful, lying, mendacious, untruthful; erroneous, fallacious, false; ambiguous, equivocal, evasive, misleading; double-dealing, hypocritical, two-faced

antonyms circuitous, indirect, roundabout

2 free from irregularities (as curves, bends, or angles) in course — see STRAIGHT 1

3 free in expressing one's true feelings and opinions — see FRANK

straightforwardly *adv* in an honest and direct manner — see STRAIGHTFORWARD

straightforwardness *n* the free expression of one's true feelings and opinions — see CANDOR

straightway *adv* without delay — see IMMEDIATELY

¹**strain** *n* **1** the line of ancestors from whom a person is descended — see ANCESTRY

2 a rhythmic series of musical tones arranged to give a pleasing effect — see MELODY

3 a very small amount — see PARTICLE 1

²**strain** *n* the burden on one's emotional or mental well-being created by demands on one's time — see STRESS 1

strain *vb* **1** to injure by overuse, misuse, or pressure ⟨in order to lift something heavy, squat down and lift with your legs, or you'll *strain* your back⟩

synonyms pull, rack, stretch, wrench

related words fray, tax, weaken; damage, harm, hurt, impair, wound; batter, bruise, tear; cripple, lame, mangle, mutilate

2 to pass through a filter ⟨better *strain* that coffee carefully to get all the grounds out⟩

synonyms filter, screen

related words percolate; refilter

3 to devote serious and sustained effort — see LABOR

4 to flow forth slowly through small openings — see EXUDE

5 to subject (a personal quality or faculty) to often excessive stress — see TRY (OUT) 2

strained *adj* lacking in natural or spontaneous quality — see ARTIFICIAL 1

strait *n* **1** a narrow body of water between two land masses — see CHANNEL 2

2 *often* **straits** *pl* a state of great suffering of body or mind — see DISTRESS 1

straitlaced *or* **straightlaced** *adj* given to or marked by very conservative standards regarding personal behavior or morals ⟨a very *straitlaced* old lady who believed women shouldn't even show a bare ankle in public⟩

synonyms prim, prudish, puritanical

related words priggish, staid, stuffy; genteel, proper, refined; decent, honest, moral, right, righteous, upright, virtuous

near antonyms liberated, permissive; bad, immoral, improper, indecent, lax, loose, wicked; debauched, degenerate, degraded, depraved, perverted

strand *n* the usually sandy or gravelly land bordering a body of water — see BEACH

strand *vb* to cause irreparable damage to (a ship) by running aground or sinking — see SHIPWRECK

stranded *adj* resting on the shore or bottom of a body of water — see AGROUND

THESAURUS

strange *adj* **1** different from the ordinary in a way that causes curiosity or suspicion — see ODD 2
2 excitingly or mysteriously unusual — see EXOTIC
3 not known or experienced before — see NEW 2
4 noticeably different from what is generally found or experienced — see UNUSUAL 1
stranger *n* a person who is not native to or known to a community ⟨the people of the island are quick to make *strangers* feel at home⟩
synonyms foreigner, nonnative, outlander, outsider
related words alien; outcast, pariah; drifter, transient, wanderer
near antonyms buddy, chum, comrade, confidant, crony, familiar, friend, intimate, pal; acquaintance, associate, cohort, colleague, companion, fellow, hearty, hobnobber, mate, partner, peer; adversary, antagonist, enemy, foe, opponent, rival; archenemy, nemesis; citizen, inhabitant, resident
antonyms native
strangle *vb* **1** to be or cause to be killed by lack of breathable air — see SMOTHER 1
2 to keep (someone) from breathing by exerting pressure on the windpipe — see CHOKE 1
3 to refrain from openly showing or uttering — see SUPPRESS 2
stratagem *n* a clever often underhanded means to achieve an end — see TRICK 1
strategy *n* **1** a method worked out in advance for achieving some objective — see PLAN 1
2 the means or procedure for doing something — see METHOD
stratum *n* one of the segments of society into which people are grouped — see CLASS 1
straw *adj* of a pale yellow or yellowish brown color — see BLOND
stray *adj* lacking a definite plan, purpose, or pattern — see RANDOM
streak *n* **1** a line or long narrow section differing in color from the background — see STRIPE
2 a very small amount — see PARTICLE 1
streak *vb* to make stripes on — see STRIPE
streaked *adj* having stripes — see STRIPED
stream *vb* **1** to cause to flow in a stream — see POUR 1
2 to move in a stream — see FLOW 1
3 to move or proceed smoothly and readily — see FLOW 2
streamer *n* a piece of cloth with a special design that is used as an emblem or for signaling — see FLAG 1
streamlet *n* a natural body of running water smaller than a river — see CREEK 1
streamline *vb* to make less complex — see SIMPLIFY
street *n* a passage cleared for public vehicular travel — see WAY 1
strength *n* **1** the ability to exert effort for the accomplishment of a task — see POWER 2
2 the ability to withstand force or stress without being distorted, dislodged, or damaged — see STABILITY 1
strengthen *vb* **1** to increase the ability of (as a muscle) to exert physical force ⟨lifting weights every day will eventually *strengthen* your muscles⟩ ⟨the Army makes new recruits run for miles in order to *strengthen* them⟩
synonyms beef (up), fortify, harden, toughen

related words anneal, temper; firm (up), tone (up); energize, invigorate, vitalize; restrengthen
near antonyms cripple, incapacitate, paralyze; damage, harm, hurt, impair, injure; break down, wear out; sap, undermine
antonyms debilitate, enervate, enfeeble, weaken
2 to make able to withstand physical hardship, strain, or exposure — see HARDEN 2
3 to make markedly greater in measure or degree — see INTENSIFY
4 to prepare (oneself) mentally or emotionally — see FORTIFY 1
strenuous *adj* **1** marked by or uttered with forcefulness — see EMPHATIC 1
2 requiring considerable physical or mental effort — see HARD 2
strenuously *adv* **1** in a vigorous and forceful manner — see HARD 3
2 with great effort or determination — see HARD 1
stress *n* **1** the burden on one's emotional or mental well-being created by demands on one's time ⟨with a full-time job and her college courses, the young woman is under a lot of *stress* right now⟩
synonyms pressure, strain, tension
related words load, weight; anxiety, concern, uneasiness, worry; aggravation, anger, annoyance, exasperation, irritation, persecution, trouble
near antonyms comfort, consolation
2 a special notice or importance given to something — see EMPHASIS 1
stress *vb* to indicate the importance of by giving prominent display — see EMPHASIZE
stressed–out *adj* suffering from high levels of physical and especially psychological stress ⟨I'm becoming *stressed-out* from trying to keep up with the demands of my school work and the grueling workouts for the football team⟩
synonyms shell-shocked
related words burned-out (*or* burnt-out), exhausted, tired, worn-out; undone, unmanned, unnerved, unstrung; edgy, nervous, tense, uneasy; agitated, disturbed, perturbed, troubled, upset; aggravated, angry, annoyed, exasperated, irritated
near antonyms relaxed, rested
stretch *adj* able to revert to original size and shape after being stretched, squeezed, or twisted — see ELASTIC 1
stretch *n* **1** a wide space or area — see EXPANSE
2 an indefinite but usually short period of time — see WHILE 1
3 the distance or extent between possible extremes — see RANGE 3
4 the space or amount of space between two points, lines, surfaces, or objects — see DISTANCE
stretch *vb* **1** to add to the interest of by including made-up details — see EMBROIDER
2 to injure by overuse, misuse, or pressure — see STRAIN 1
3 to make longer — see EXTEND 1
4 to subject (a personal quality or faculty) to often excessive stress — see TRY (OUT) 2
stretch (out) *vb* to arrange the parts of (something) over a wider area — see OPEN 3
stretchable *adj* able to revert to original size and shape after being stretched, squeezed, or twisted — see ELASTIC 1
stretching *n* **1** the act of making longer — see EXTENSION 1
2 the representation of something in terms that go beyond the facts — see EXAGGERATION

strew *vb* to cover by or as if by scattering something over or on — see SCATTER 2

strict *adj* **1** following an original exactly — see FAITHFUL 2

2 given to exacting standards of discipline and self-restraint — see SEVERE 1

3 not allowing for any exceptions or loosening of standards — see RIGID 1

strictly *adv* without any relaxation of standards or precision ⟨*strictly* speaking, Columbus did not discover America—the people living there had long known about it⟩ ⟨the rules must be *strictly* obeyed⟩

synonyms exactly, precisely, rigidly, rigorously

related words carefully, conscientiously, meticulously, scrupulously

antonyms imprecisely, inexactly, loosely

strictness *n* the quality or state of being demanding or unyielding (as in discipline or criticism) — see SEVERITY

stricture *n* an often public or formal expression of disapproval — see CENSURE

stride *vb* to move along with a steady regular step especially in a group — see MARCH 1

strife *n* a lack of agreement or harmony — see DISCORD

strike *n* **1** a work stoppage by a body of workers intended to force an employer to meet their demands ⟨the nurses will go on *strike* tomorrow unless they're finally given a pay raise⟩

synonyms walkout

related words shutdown, shutoff, sit-down, slowdown; lockout

2 the act or action of setting upon with force or violence — see ATTACK 1

3 a feature of someone or something that creates difficulty for achieving success — see DISADVANTAGE

4 a forceful coming together of two things — see IMPACT 1

strike *vb* **1** to refuse to work in order to force an employer to meet demands ⟨the union is calling for its members to *strike* until the mining company agrees to meet safety standards⟩

synonyms walk out

related words knock off, lay off; leave, quit, resign; decamp, depart, exit, go, leave, light out, part

2 to act upon (a person or a person's feelings) so as to cause a response — see ¹AFFECT 1

3 to come into the mind of — see OCCUR (TO)

4 to come into usually forceful contact with something — see HIT 2

5 to deliver a blow to (someone or something) usually in a strong vigorous manner — see HIT 1

6 to take apart — see DISASSEMBLE

7 to take sudden, violent action against — see ATTACK 1

strike (into) *vb* to take the first step in (a process or course of action) — see BEGIN 1

strike (out) *vb* to show (something written) to be no longer valid by drawing a cross over or a line through it — see X (OUT)

striking *adj* **1** likely to attract attention — see NOTICEABLE

2 very noticeable especially for being incorrect or bad — see EGREGIOUS

string *n* **1** a length of braided, flexible material that is used for tying or connecting things — see CORD

2 a series of persons or things arranged one behind another — see LINE 1

3 a series of things linked together — see CHAIN 1

string *vb* to put together into a series by means of or as if by means of a thread — see THREAD 2

string along *vb* to cause to believe what is untrue — see DECEIVE

stringent *adj* not allowing for any exceptions or loosening of standards — see RIGID 1

stringy *adj* resembling or having the texture of a mass of strings ⟨*stringy* hair that clearly needed a good washing⟩

synonyms fibrous

related words knotty, ropy, thready; sinewy, wiry

strip *n* a long narrow piece of material ⟨now tear the paper into *strips* and fold them up carefully⟩

synonyms list, ribbon, slip

related words band, bandage, belt, binding, strap, swath, tape

strip *vb* **1** to remove clothing from — see UNDRESS

2 to search through with the intent of committing robbery — see RANSACK 1

stripe *n* a line or long narrow section differing in color from the background ⟨the United States flag has seven red *stripes*⟩

synonyms band, bar, streak

related words blaze, crossbar, pinstripe

stripe *vb* to make stripes on ⟨the children carefully *striped* the paper with red and blue paint⟩

synonyms band, bar, streak

related words blaze

striped *adj* having stripes ⟨the zebra is a black-and-white *striped* animal⟩

synonyms barred, streaked

related words corded, tabby

stripling *n* a male person who has not yet reached adulthood — see BOY

stripped *adj* **1** lacking a usual or natural covering — see NAKED 2

2 lacking or shed of clothing — see NAKED 1

strive *vb* **1** to devote serious and sustained effort — see LABOR

2 to make an effort to do — see ATTEMPT

stroke *n* a hard strike with a part of the body or an instrument — see ¹BLOW

stroke *vb* to touch or handle in a tender or loving manner — see FONDLE

stroke (out) *vb* to show (something written) to be no longer valid by drawing a cross over or a line through it — see X (OUT)

stroll *n* a relaxed journey on foot for exercise or pleasure — see WALK

stroller *n* a person who roams about without a fixed route or destination — see NOMAD

strong *adj* **1** having muscles capable of exerting great physical force ⟨I need some *strong* people to help me move furniture⟩

synonyms brawny, muscular, rugged, sinewy, stalwart, stout

related words forceful, mighty, potent, powerful, puissant; able-bodied, athletic, fit, trim; beefy, burly, husky, strapping; masculine, virile; hard, inured, strengthened, sturdy, tough, toughened; energetic, energized, invigorated, lusty, red-blooded, robust, vigorous, vitalized; hale, healthy, hearty, sound

near antonyms challenged, disabled, incapacitated, paralyzed; impotent, powerless; puny, slight, small, unfit, unhealthy

antonyms delicate, feeble, frail, weak, wimpy

THESAURUS

2 able to withstand hardship, strain, or exposure — see HARDY 1

3 having a powerfully stimulating odor or flavor — see SHARP 3

4 having an abundance of some characteristic quality (as flavor) — see FULL-BODIED

5 having an unpleasant smell — see MALODOROUS

6 having great power or influence — see IMPORTANT 2

7 having the power to persuade — see COGENT

8 marked by the ability to withstand stress without structural damage or distortion — see STABLE 1

9 not showing weakness or uncertainty — see FIRM 1

strongbox *n* a specially reinforced container to keep valuables safe — see SAFE

stronghold *n* a structure or place from which one can resist attack — see FORT

strongly *adv* in a vigorous and forceful manner — see HARD 3

strop *vb* to make sharp or sharper — see SHARPEN

stropped *adj* having an edge thin enough to cut or pierce something — see SHARP 1

structure *n* **1** something built as a dwelling, shelter, or place for human activity — see BUILDING

2 something put together by arranging or connecting an array of parts — see CONSTRUCTION 1

3 the arrangement of parts that gives something its basic form — see FRAME 1

struggle *n* **1** a forceful effort to reach a goal or objective ⟨a physically challenged child's determined *struggle* to make straight A's in school⟩

synonyms battle, fight, fray, scrabble

related words effort, exertion, labor, pains, trouble, work; drudgery, grind, sweat, toil, travail; combat, conflict, contest, strife, tussle, war, warfare; attempt, endeavor, essay, try

2 a physical dispute between opposing individuals or groups — see FIGHT 1

3 an earnest effort for superiority or victory over another — see CONTEST 1

struggle *vb* to devote serious and sustained effort — see LABOR

strut *vb* **1** to walk with exaggerated arm and leg movements ⟨the toy soldiers in the Christmas pageant *strutted* stiffly across the stage⟩

synonyms prance, stalk, swagger

related words flounce, mince, traipse; pussyfoot, tiptoe; parade, promenade; pad, step, tread; pace, stride; lumber, lurch, pound, shamble, shuffle, stagger

2 to present so as to invite notice or attention — see SHOW 1

stub *n* an unused or unwanted piece or item typically of small size or value — see ¹SCRAP 1

stubborn *adj* sticking to an opinion, purpose, or course of action in spite of reason, arguments, or persuasion — see OBSTINATE

stubbornness *n* a steadfast adherence to an opinion, purpose, or course of action — see OBSTINACY

stubby *adj* being compact and broad in build and often short in stature — see STOCKY

stuck *adj* firmly positioned in place and difficult to dislodge — see TIGHT 2

stuck–up *adj* having too high an opinion of oneself — see CONCEITED

student *n* one who attends a school ⟨a straight-A *student* at the local high school⟩

synonyms pupil, scholar

related words schoolboy, schoolchild, schoolgirl; schoolfellow, schoolmate; collegian, postgraduate, undergraduate; freshman, junior, senior, sophomore; underclassman, upperclassman

studied *adj* decided on as a result of careful thought — see DELIBERATE 1

study *n* **1** a systematic search for the truth or facts about something — see INQUIRY 1

2 the state of being lost in thought — see REVERIE

study *vb* **1** to use the mind to acquire knowledge ⟨you'll have to *study* hard and learn all about the Revolutionary War in order to pass the history test⟩

synonyms bone (up)

related words cram; analyze, deduce, find out; learn, read; research, restudy

phrases go over, go through

2 to commit to memory — see MEMORIZE

3 to give serious and careful thought to — see PONDER

stuff *n* **1** a skill, an ability, or knowledge that makes a person able to do a particular job — see QUALIFICATION 1

2 the basic elements from which something can be developed — see MAKING

3 the quality or qualities that make a thing what it is — see ESSENCE

stuff *vb* **1** to close up so that no empty spaces remain — see FILL 2

2 to fill with food to capacity — see GORGE 1

3 to fit (something) into a tight space — see CROWD 1

4 to prevent passage through — see CLOG 1

5 to put into (something) as much as can be held or contained — see FILL 1

stuffed *adj* **1** containing or seeming to contain the greatest quantity or number possible — see FULL 1

2 having one's appetite completely satisfied — see FULL 3

stuffer *n* one who eats greedily or too much — see GLUTTON

stuffing *n* soft material that is used to fill the hollow parts of something — see FILLING

stuffy *adj* **1** lacking fresh air ⟨the house was so *stuffy* after being closed up for a month⟩

synonyms breathless, close, stifling, suffocating

related words airless, unventilated; heavy, oppressive, thick

near antonyms bracing, brisk, invigorating, refreshed, sweet; ventilated

antonyms airy, breezy

2 causing weariness, restlessness, or lack of interest — see BORING

stumble *n* **1** an unintentional departure from truth or accuracy — see ERROR 1

2 the act of going down from an upright position suddenly and involuntarily — see FALL 1

stumble *vb* **1** to go down from an upright position suddenly and involuntarily — see FALL 1

2 to make progress in a clumsy, struggling manner — see FLOUNDER 1

3 to move heavily or clumsily — see LUMBER 1

stumble (on *or* onto) *vb* to come upon unexpectedly or by chance — see HAPPEN (ON *OR* UPON)

stumble (upon) *vb* to come upon face-to-face or as if face-to-face — see MEET 1

stumbling block *n* something that makes progress

or movement more difficult — see ENCUM-BRANCE

stump *vb* **1** to move heavily or clumsily — see LUMBER 1

2 to invite (someone) to take part in a contest or to perform a feat — see CHALLENGE 2

stumpy *adj* being compact and broad in build and often short in stature — see STOCKY

stun *vb* **1** to make senseless or dizzy by a blow ⟨a powerful uppercut to the jaw *stunned* the boxer and sent him crashing to the canvas⟩

synonyms daze

related words deaden, knock out, paralyze; benumb, numb, stupefy; bowl (over), knock (down)

phrases knock for a loop

2 to make a strong impression on (someone) with something unexpected — see SURPRISE 1

stunned *adj* **1** affected with sudden and great wonder or surprise — see THUNDERSTRUCK

2 suffering from mental confusion — see DIZZY 2

stunner *n* **1** a lovely woman — see BEAUTY 2

2 something that makes a strong impression because it is so unexpected — see SURPRISE 1

stunning *adj* **1** causing a strong emotional reaction because unexpected — see SURPRISING 1

2 causing wonder or astonishment — see MARVELOUS 1

3 very pleasing to look at — see BEAUTIFUL

stunt *n* an act of notable skill, strength, or cleverness — see FEAT 1

stunt *vb* to hold back the normal growth of ⟨unfortunately, an unusually dry summer seems to have permanently *stunted* the tree⟩

synonyms dwarf, suppress

related words arrest, catch, check, halt, hold up, stall, stay, still, stop; balk, block, hold back, impede, obstruct, stem

near antonyms advance, boost, encourage, forward, promote

stupefied *adj* **1** affected with sudden and great wonder or surprise — see THUNDERSTRUCK

2 suffering from mental confusion — see DIZZY 2

stupefy *vb* to make a strong impression on (someone) with something unexpected — see SURPRISE 1

stupefying *adj* causing a strong emotional reaction because unexpected — see SURPRISING 1

stupendous *adj* causing wonder or astonishment — see MARVELOUS 1

stupendously *adv* to a large extent or degree — see GREATLY 2

stupendousness *n* impressiveness of beauty on a large scale — see MAGNIFICENCE

stupid *adj* **1** not having or showing an ability to absorb ideas readily ⟨it's not nice to constantly call your brother *stupid* and ugly⟩ ⟨don't ask *stupid* questions⟩

synonyms brainless, dense, doltish, dopey, dorky [*slang*], dull, dumb, fatuous, half-witted, mindless, oafish, obtuse, senseless, simple, slow, thick, thickheaded, unintelligent, vacuous, weak-minded, witless

related words feebleminded, retarded, simpleminded; foolish, idiotic, imbecile, imbecilic, moronic; ignorant, illiterate, lowbrow, uneducated, uninformed, untaught, unthinking; absurd, asinine, balmy, cockeyed, crazy, cuckoo, daffy, daft, dotty, harebrained, insane, kooky, loony (*also* looney), lunatic, mad, nonsensical, nutty, preposterous, sappy, screwball, silly, unwise, wacky,

zany; fallacious, illogical, invalid, irrational, unreasonable

near antonyms ingenious, resourceful; acute, astute, discerning, insightful, keen, knowing, perceptive, perspicacious, sagacious, sage, sapient, savvy, wise; cerebral, erudite, highbrow, intellectual, knowledgeable, learned, literate, scholarly, thinking, well-read; educated, informed, schooled, skilled, trained; crafty, cunning, foxy, shrewd, wily; judicious, prudent, sane, sensible, sound; logical, rational, reasonable, valid

antonyms apt, brainy, bright, brilliant, clever, intelligent, keen, nimble, quick, quick-witted, sharp, sharp-witted, smart

2 causing weariness, restlessness, or lack of interest — see BORING

3 showing or marked by a lack of good sense or judgment — see FOOLISH 1

stupidity *n* **1** the quality or state of lacking intelligence or quickness of mind ⟨the *stupidity* of the dialogue between the two romantic leads had movie audiences giggling uncontrollably⟩

synonyms brainlessness, denseness, density, doltishness, dopiness, dullness (*also* dulness), dumbness, fatuity, foolishness, mindlessness, oafishness, obtuseness, senselessness, simpleness, slowness, stupidness, vacuity, witlessness

related words absurdity, asininity, balminess, craziness, daftness, folly, idiocy, inanity, insanity, lunacy, madness, nonsensicalness, nuttiness, preposterousness, silliness, simplicity, wackiness, zaniness; fallacy, irrationality, unreasonableness

near antonyms acumen, alertness, astuteness, discernment, insight, judgment (*or* judgement), perception, perspicacity; sagacity, sageness, sapience, wisdom, wit; logicalness, rationality, reasonableness, soundness, validity

antonyms braininess, brightness, brilliance, cleverness, intelligence, keenness, quickness, quickwittedness, sharpness, smartness

2 a foolish act or idea — see FOLLY 1

3 language, behavior, or ideas that are absurd and contrary to good sense — see NONSENSE 1

stupidness *n* the quality or state of lacking intelligence or quickness of mind — see STUPIDITY 1

sturdily *adv* in a vigorous and forceful manner — see HARD 3

sturdiness *n* the ability to withstand force or stress without being distorted, dislodged, or damaged — see STABILITY 1

sturdy *adj* **1** able to withstand hardship, strain, or exposure — see HARDY 1

2 marked by the ability to withstand stress without structural damage or distortion — see STABLE 1

3 not showing weakness or uncertainty — see FIRM 1

style *n* **1** a distinctive way of putting ideas into words ⟨I correctly identified the quotation because I recognized Mark Twain's inimitable *style*⟩

synonyms fashion, locution, manner, mode, phraseology, tone, vein

related words delivery, elocution; archaism, colloquialism, regionalism; acceptation, connotation, denotation, idiom

2 the means or procedure for doing something — see METHOD

3 a practice or interest that is very popular for a short time — see FAD

style *vb* to give a name to — see NAME 1

THESAURUS

styleless *adj* marked by an obvious lack of style or good taste — see TACKY 1

stylish *adj* being in the latest or current fashion ⟨a pretty, *stylish* dress⟩
synonyms à la mode (*also* a la mode), chic, fashionable, in, modish, sharp, smart, snappy
related words dapper, dashing, natty, rakish, spiffy, spruce; posh, ritzy, swank (*or* swanky); elegant, graceful, handsome, majestic, refined, sophisticated, stately, tasteful, understated; dandyish, dudish, foppish; classic, exquisite, quiet, restrained, simple; affected, grandiose, pretentious
near antonyms tacky, unattractive, unbecoming; graceless, inelegant, tasteless, unhandsome; frowsy (*or* frowzy), sloppy, slovenly, unkempt, untidy; disheveled (*or* dishevelled), messy, mussy, rumpled, wrinkled; shabby, sleazy
antonyms dowdy, outmoded, styleless, unfashionable, unstylish

suasion *n* the act of reasoning or pleading with someone to accept a belief or course of action — see PERSUASION 1

suave *adj* having or showing very polished and worldly manners ⟨the *suave* gentleman was a great favorite of the elegant ladies who attended parties at the embassy⟩
synonyms debonair, smooth, sophisticated, urbane
related words glib, slick, unctuous; civilized, cultivated, cultured, graceful, poised, polished, refined; cosmopolitan, smart, worldly-wise; experienced, knowing, practiced (*or* practised), schooled, seasoned; amiable, appealing, attractive; assured, calm, collected, composed, confident, cool, placid, secure, self-assured, self-confident, self-possessed, serene, tranquil, undisturbed, unperturbed
near antonyms awkward, clumsy, gauche, graceless, stiff, stilted, uncomfortable, uneasy, ungraceful, wooden; callow, green, inexperienced, raw; parochial, provincial, roughhewn, rustic; inelegant, philistine, uncivilized, uncultured, unrefined; unsophisticated, unworldly; gawky, lubberly, stodgy, ungainly; diffident, insecure
antonyms boorish, churlish, clownish, loutish, uncouth

¹sub *n* a large sandwich on a long split roll — see SUBMARINE

²sub *n* a person or thing that takes the place of another — see SUBSTITUTE

sub *vb* to serve as a replacement usually for a time only — see COVER 1

subdue *vb* **1** to achieve a victory over — see BEAT 2
2 to bring under one's control by force of arms — see CONQUER 1
3 to put a stop to (something) by the use of force — see QUELL 1

subdued *adj* not excessively showy — see QUIET 2

subduer *n* one that defeats an enemy or opponent — see VICTOR 1

subduing *n* the act or process of bringing someone or something under one's control — see CONQUEST

subject *n* **1** a major object of interest or concern (as in a discussion or artistic composition) — see MATTER 1
2 a person who owes allegiance to a government and is protected by it — see CITIZEN 1

subject *vb* to bring under one's control by force of arms — see CONQUER 1

subject (to) *adj* **1** determined by something else — see DEPENDENT 2
2 being in a situation where one is likely to meet with harm — see LIABLE 1

subjecting *n* the act or process of bringing someone or something under one's control — see CONQUEST

subjection *n* the act or process of bringing someone or something under one's control — see CONQUEST

subjugate *vb* to bring under one's control by force of arms — see CONQUER 1

subjugating *n* the act or process of bringing someone or something under one's control — see CONQUEST

subjugation *n* the act or process of bringing someone or something under one's control — see CONQUEST

sublime *adj* **1** causing wonder or astonishment — see MARVELOUS 1
2 having, characterized by, or arising from a dignified and generous nature — see NOBLE 2

sublimeness *n* impressiveness of beauty on a large scale — see MAGNIFICENCE

submarine *adj* living, lying, or occurring below the surface of the water — see UNDERWATER

submarine *n* a large sandwich on a long split roll ⟨always orders a roast beef *submarine* with the works⟩
synonyms grinder, hero, hoagie, Italian sandwich, po'boy (*also* poor boy), sub

submerge *vb* **1** to cover or become filled with a flood — see FLOOD
2 to sink or push (something) briefly into or as if into a liquid — see DIP 1

submerged *adj* living, lying, or occurring below the surface of the water — see UNDERWATER

submerse *vb* **1** to cover or become filled with a flood — see FLOOD
2 to sink or push (something) briefly into or as if into a liquid — see DIP 1

submission *n* **1** a bending to the authority or control of another — see OBEDIENCE 1
2 the usually forced yielding of one's person or possessions to the control of another — see SURRENDER

submissive *adj* readily giving in to the command or authority of another — see OBEDIENT

submissively *adv* in manner showing no signs of pride or self-assertion — see LOWLY

submissiveness *n* a readiness or willingness to yield to the wishes of others — see COMPLIANCE 1

submit *vb* **1** to cease resistance (as to another's arguments, demands, or control) — see YIELD 3
2 to give up and cease resistance (as to a liking, temptation, or habit) — see YIELD 1
3 to yield to the control or power of enemy forces — see FALL 2

submitting *n* the usually forced yielding of one's person or possessions to the control of another — see SURRENDER

subordinate *adj* having not so great importance or rank as another — see LESSER

subordinate *n* one who is of lower rank and typically under the authority of another — see UNDERLING

subordination *n* a bending to the authority or control of another — see OBEDIENCE 1

subpoena *n* a written notice ordering a person to appear in court — see SUMMONS

subscribe (to) *vb* to have a favorable opinion of — see APPROVE (OF)

subsequent *adj* being, occurring, or carried out at a time after something else ⟨I'll do the first problem as an example, but all *subsequent* efforts must be done on your own⟩

synonyms after, ensuing, later, posterior

related words behind, belated, delayed, late, slow; eventual, last, ultimate; following

near antonyms advance, early, premature

antonyms antecedent, anterior, fore, precedent, preceding, previous, prior

subsequently *adv* following in time or place — see AFTER

subside *vb* to grow less in scope or intensity especially gradually — see DECREASE 2

subsidize *vb* 1 to furnish (as an institution) with a regular source of income — see ENDOW 2

2 to provide money for — see FINANCE 1

subsidy *n* a sum of money allotted for a specific use by official or formal action — see APPROPRIATION

subsist *vb* to have life — see BE 1

subsistence *n* 1 the fact of being or of being real — see EXISTENCE

2 uninterrupted or lasting existence — see CONTINUATION

substance *n* 1 the basic elements from which something can be developed — see MAKING

2 the quality or qualities that make a thing what it is — see ESSENCE

3 the total of one's money and property — see WEALTH 1

4 one that has a real and independent existence — see ENTITY

substance abuser *n* a person who regularly uses drugs especially illegally — see DOPER

substandard *adj* falling short of a standard — see BAD 1

substantial *adj* 1 having great meaning or lasting effect — see IMPORTANT 1

2 of a size greater than average of its kind — see LARGE

3 relating to or composed of matter — see MATERIAL 1

4 sufficiently large in size, amount, or number to merit attention — see CONSIDERABLE 1

substantiality *n* the quality or state of being large in size — see LARGENESS

substantially *adv* for the most part — see CHIEFLY

substantiate *vb* 1 to gain full recognition or acceptance of — see ESTABLISH 1

2 to give evidence or testimony to the truth or factualness of — see CONFIRM

3 to represent in visible form — see EMBODY 2

4 to show the existence or truth of by evidence — see PROVE 1

substantiating *adj* serving to give support to the truth or factualness of something — see CORROBORATIVE

substantiation *n* something presented in support of the truth or accuracy of a claim — see PROOF

substitute *adj* 1 being such in appearance only and made with or manufactured from usually cheaper materials — see IMITATION

2 taking the place of one that came before — see NEW 1

substitute *n* a person or thing that takes the place of another ⟨you'll be getting a *substitute* until your regular teacher is feeling better⟩ ⟨if you like, you can use nuts as a *substitute* for coconut in that recipe⟩

synonyms backup, pinch hitter, relief, replacement, reserve, stand-in, sub

related words alternate, understudy; apology, makeshift, stopgap; agent, attorney, commissary, delegate, deputy, envoy, factor, procurator, proxy, representative, surrogate; assistant, second

substitute *vb* 1 to give up (something) and take something else in return — see CHANGE 3

2 to serve as a replacement usually for a time only — see COVER 1

3 to take the place of — see REPLACE 1

subterfuge *n* the use of clever underhanded actions to achieve an end — see TRICKERY

subtle *adj* 1 clever at attaining one's ends by indirect and often deceptive means — see ARTFUL 1

2 made or done with extreme care and accuracy — see FINE 2

3 satisfying or pleasing because of fineness or mildness — see DELICATE 1

subtleness *n* skill in achieving one's ends through indirect, subtle, or underhanded means — see CUNNING 1

subtlety *n* skill in achieving one's ends through indirect, subtle, or underhanded means — see CUNNING 1

subtract *vb* to take away (an amount or number) from a total ⟨if you *subtract* 10 from 23, you get 13⟩ ⟨you can *subtract* the time you spent daydreaming from your total homework time⟩

synonyms deduct, take off

related words decrease, diminish, discount, downsize, lessen, lower, reduce; abbreviate, abridge, clip, crop, curtail, cut, cut back, cut down, dock, pare, prune, retrench, shorten, slash, trim, truncate, whittle

near antonyms adjoin, annex, append, tack (on); add (to), complement, supplement; enhance, heighten, intensify; aggrandize, amplify, augment, boost, enlarge, escalate, expand, increase, raise

antonyms add

subtraction *n* the act or an instance of taking away from a total ⟨the dog was responsible for the unexplained *subtraction* in the number of potato chips on my sister's plate⟩

synonyms deduction

related words discount; abatement, decline, decrement, diminishment, diminution, drop, fall, loss, reduction, shrinkage; curtailment, cut, cutback

near antonyms boost, enlargement, gain, increase, increment, raise, rise; accretion, accrual, accumulation, addendum, appendix, supplement

antonyms addition

suburbia *n* the area around a city — see ENVIRONS 1

subvert *vb* to lower in character or dignity — see DEBASE 1

succeed *vb* 1 to turn out as planned or desired ⟨the advertising campaign that finally *succeeded* used humor to sell the product⟩

synonyms click, deliver, go over, pan out, work out

related words catch on; flourish, prosper, thrive

phrases catch fire

near antonyms languish; flounder, struggle; decline, slip, slump, wane

THESAURUS

antonyms collapse, fail, flop, flunk, fold, wash out

2 to reach a desired level of accomplishment ⟨if you want to *succeed* in show business, you have to feel comfortable in front of an audience⟩

synonyms flourish, prosper, thrive

related words prevail, triumph, win

phrases get ahead, make good, make it

near antonyms flounder, struggle

antonyms fail

3 to come after in time — see FOLLOW 1

succeeding *adj* **1** being the one that comes immediately after another — see NEXT

2 following one after another without others coming in between — see CONSECUTIVE

success *n* **1** a person or thing that is successful — see HIT 1

2 a successful result brought about by hard work — see ACCOMPLISHMENT 1

successful *adj* **1** having attained a desired end or state of good fortune ⟨the family runs several *successful* restaurants⟩

synonyms flourishing, going, palmy, prosperous, thriving, triumphant

related words coming, promising; booming, growing, roaring, robust

near antonyms futureless, hopeless, inauspicious, no-good; collapsing, failing, flopping, flunking, folding, washing-out; declining, slipping, slumping, waning; bankrupt, destroyed, ruined, wrecked

antonyms failed, unsuccessful

2 marked by vigorous growth and well-being especially economically — see PROSPEROUS 1

successional *adj* following one after another without others coming in between — see CONSECUTIVE

successive *adj* following one after another without others coming in between — see CONSECUTIVE

succinct *adj* marked by the use of few words to convey much information or meaning — see CONCISE

succinctly *adv* in a few words — see SHORTLY 1

succinctness *n* the quality or state of being marked by or using only few words to convey much meaning ⟨Caesar's observation, "I came, I saw, I conquered," is famous for its *succinctness*⟩

synonyms brevity, briefness, compactness, conciseness, crispness, pithiness, terseness

related words abruptness, bluntness, brusqueness, curtness, shortness

near antonyms redundancy, repetitiousness

antonyms diffuseness, long-windedness, prolixity, verbosity, wordiness

succulence *n* the quality or state of being full of juice ⟨the *succulence* of the apple was such that the first bite sent juice running down my chin⟩

synonyms fleshiness, juiciness, pulpiness

related words sap, sappiness

succulent *adj* full of juice — see JUICY

succumb *vb* **1** to cease resistance (as to another's arguments, demands, or control) — see YIELD 3

2 to give up and cease resistance (as to a liking, temptation, or habit) — see YIELD 1

3 to stop living — see DIE 1

4 to yield to the control or power of enemy forces — see FALL 2

such *adj* having qualities in common — see ALIKE

suchlike *adj* having qualities in common — see ALIKE

suck (up) *vb* to take in (something liquid) through small openings — see ABSORB 1

sucker *n* one who is easily deceived or cheated — see DUPE

suddenly *adv* **1** with great suddenness — see SHORT

2 without warning — see UNAWARES

suds *n* a light mass of fine bubbles formed in or on a liquid — see FOAM

sudsy *adj* covered with, consisting of, or resembling foam — see FOAMY

sue (for) *vb* to make a request for — see ASK (FOR)

suer *n* the person in a legal proceeding who makes a charge of wrongdoing against another — see COMPLAINANT

suffer *vb* **1** to give permission to — see ALLOW 2

2 to come to a knowledge of (something) by living through it — see EXPERIENCE

3 to feel deep sadness or mental pain — see GRIEVE

4 to give permission for or to approve of — see ALLOW 1

sufferable *adj* capable of being endured — see BEARABLE

sufferance *n* **1** the approval by someone in authority for the doing of something — see PERMISSION

2 the capacity to endure what is difficult or disagreeable without complaining — see PATIENCE

suffice *vb* to be enough — see SERVE 2

sufficiency *n* the quality or state of meeting one's needs adequately ⟨the *sufficiency* of the portions is such that you will leave the restaurant with a full stomach but without doggie bags⟩

synonyms acceptability, adequacy, satisfactoriness

related words appropriateness, correctness, fitness, goodness, properness, rightness, seemliness, suitability, suitableness; bountifulness, copiousness; excess, overabundance, oversupply, surfeit, surplus; abundance, amplitude, plenitude, plenty

near antonyms lack, want; dearth, shortage; meagerness, paucity, poorness, poverty, rareness, rarity, scantiness, scarceness, scarcity, skimpiness; necessity, need, privation

antonyms inadequacy, insufficiency

sufficiently *adv* in or to a degree or quantity that meets one's requirements or satisfaction — see ENOUGH 1

suffocate *vb* to be or cause to be killed by lack of breathable air — see SMOTHER 1

suffocating *adj* lacking fresh air — see STUFFY 1

suffrage *n* the right to formally express one's position or will in an election — see VOTE 1

suffuse *vb* **1** to cause (as a person) to become filled or saturated with a certain quality or principle — see INFUSE

2 to spread throughout — see PERMEATE

sugarcoated *adj* appealing to the emotions in an obvious and tiresome way — see CORNY

sugary *adj* appealing to the emotions in an obvious and tiresome way — see CORNY

suggest *vb* **1** to convey an idea indirectly — see HINT

2 to put forward as one's choice for a wise or proper course of action — see ADVISE 2

3 to set before the mind for consideration — see PROPOSE 1

suggestion *n* **1** a slight or indirect pointing to

something (as a solution or explanation) — see HINT 1

2 something which is presented for consideration — see PROPOSAL

suggestive *adj* **1** hinting at or intended to call to mind matters regarded as indecent ⟨making *suggestive* remarks to one's classmates will not be tolerated⟩

synonyms bawdy, lewd, racy, ribald, salty, spicy

related words leering; coarse, crude, earthy, foul, gross; dirty, filthy, lascivious, nasty, obscene, pornographic, smutty, unprintable, vulgar; indecorous, unbecoming; naughty, wicked; exceptionable, objectionable, unacceptable, undesirable, unwanted, unwelcome

near antonyms clean, decent; innocuous, inoffensive; priggish, prim, prudish, puritanical, straitlaced (*or* straightlaced), Victorian; correct, decorous, genteel, polite, proper, seemly; acceptable, agreeable, desirable, pleasant, pleasing, welcome; appropriate, becoming, fit, meet, suitable; immaculate, pure, spotless

2 provoking a memory or mental association ⟨a haunting and *suggestive* song about a long-lost love⟩

synonyms evocative, reminiscent

related words eloquent, expressive, meaningful, significant; affecting, emotional, moving, poignant, stirring, touching; exciting, provocative, provoking, rousing, stimulating

3 clearly conveying a special meaning (as one's mood) — see EXPRESSIVE

suicide *n* the act of deliberately killing oneself ⟨teenagers are more prone to *suicide* because they mistakenly believe their troubles are insurmountable⟩

synonyms self-destruction

related words martyrdom; foul play, homicide, murder, slaying; killing, manslaughter; assassination, execution; euthanasia, mercy killing

suit *n* **1** a court case for enforcing a right or claim — see LAWSUIT

2 an earnest request — see PLEA 1

suit *vb* **1** to be fitting or proper — see DO 1

2 to give satisfaction to — see PLEASE

3 to outfit with clothes and especially fine or special clothes — see CLOTHE 1

suitability *n* the quality or state of being especially suitable or fitting — see APPROPRIATENESS

suitable *adj* **1** having the required skills for an acceptable level of performance — see COMPETENT

2 meeting the requirements of a purpose or situation — see FIT 1

suitableness *n* the quality or state of being especially suitable or fitting — see APPROPRIATENESS

suitably *adv* in a manner suitable for the occasion or purpose — see PROPERLY

suitcase *n* a bag carried by hand and designed to hold a traveler's clothing and personal articles — see TRAVELING BAG

suite *n* **1** a body of employees or servants who accompany and wait on a person — see CORTEGE 1

2 a number of things considered as a unit — see GROUP 1

3 a room or set of rooms in a private house or a block used as a separate dwelling place — see APARTMENT 1

suitor *n* **1** a man who courts a woman usually with the goal of marrying her ⟨my sister finally married her *suitor* of six years on Sunday⟩

synonyms gallant, swain, wooer

related words beau, boyfriend, fellow, man; admirer, crush, steady; beloved, darling, dear, favorite, flame, honey, love, lover, sweet, sweetheart, valentine; date, escort; fiancé, intended

2 one who asks earnestly for a favor or gift — see SUPPLICANT

sulk *n* a state of resentful silence or irritability ⟨a child sitting in a *sulk* over a minor disagreement⟩

synonyms pet, pouts, sulkiness, sullenness

related words blues, dumps, mopes; surliness; biliousness, crankiness, crossness, crotchetiness, grouchiness, grumpiness, irascibility, irritability, peevishness, perverseness, perversity, pettishness, petulance, testiness, waspishness; cantankerousness, disagreeableness, orneriness

near antonyms sociability; cheerfulness, gaiety (*also* gayety), gladsomeness, good-humoredness, high-spiritedness, lightheartedness, perkiness

sulk *vb* to silently go about in a bad mood ⟨the toddler *sulked* all day whenever he didn't get his way⟩

synonyms mope, pout

related words brood, dwell (on), mull (over), muse (over), ponder; frown, glower, lower (*also* lour), scowl; carry on, take on

sulkiness *n* a state of resentful silence or irritability — see SULK

sulky *adj* given to or displaying a resentful silence and often irritability ⟨our teenage daughter turns *sulky* if we refuse to let her borrow the car⟩

synonyms glum, pouting, sullen, surly

related words dour, gloomy, morose; choleric, crabby, cranky, cross, crotchety, grouchy, grumpy, irascible, irritable, peevish, perverse, pettish, petulant, quick-tempered, short-tempered, snappy, snippy, testy, waspish; brooding, moping; bearish, bilious, cantankerous, disagreeable, dyspeptic, ill-humored, ill-natured, ill-tempered, ornery; sensitive, temperamental, thin-skinned, touchy

near antonyms sociable; cheerful, cheery, gladsome, good-humored, good-natured, perky

sullen *adj* **1** causing or marked by an atmosphere lacking in cheer — see GLOOMY 1

2 given to or displaying a resentful silence and often irritability — see SULKY

sullenness *n* a state of resentful silence or irritability — see SULK

sullied *adj* not clean — see DIRTY 1

sully *vb* to make dirty — see DIRTY

sultry *adj* **1** containing or characterized by an uncomfortable amount of moisture — see HUMID

2 having a notably high temperature — see HOT 1

sum *n* **1** a complete amount of something — see WHOLE

2 a short statement of the main points — see SUMMARY

sum *vb* to combine (numbers) into a single sum — see ADD 2

sum (to *or* into) *vb* to have a total of — see AMOUNT (TO) 1

summarily *adv* in a few words — see SHORTLY 1

summarization *n* a short statement of the main points — see SUMMARY

summarize *vb* to make into a short statement of the main points (as of a report) ⟨the closing minute of the newscast *summarizes* the main story of the day⟩

synonyms abstract, digest, encapsulate, epitomize, outline, recap, recapitulate, sum up, wrap up

related words abridge, condense, curtail, shorten; downsize, shrink; concentrate, consolidate; simplify, streamline

near antonyms amplify, elaborate (on *or* upon), enlarge (on *or* upon), expand

summary *adj* marked by the use of few words to convey much information or meaning — see CONCISE

summary *n* a short statement of the main points ⟨many book reports choose to begin with a *summary* of the book⟩

synonyms abstract, digest, encapsulation, epitome, outline, précis, recap, recapitulation, résumé (*or* resume *also* resumé), roundup, sum, summarization, synopsis

related words abbreviation, abridgment (*or* abridgement), condensation, curtailment, shortening; brief; rundown; simplification, streamlining

near antonyms amplification, enlargement, expansion

summation *n* a complete amount of something — see WHOLE

summit *n* the highest part or point — see HEIGHT 1

summon *vb* 1 to demand or request the presence or service of ⟨without explanation, the principal *summoned* me to his office⟩

synonyms call, hail

related words cite, subpoena; assemble, convene, convoke, muster; ask, bid, invite; command, order, request, requisition; beckon, demand, invoke

phrases send for

near antonyms dismiss, send (away), turn away

2 to call into being through the use of one's inner resources or powers ⟨managed to *summon* a bright smile despite the gloomy day⟩

synonyms conjure (up), gather (up)

related words educe, elicit, evoke, raise

3 to bring together in assembly by or as if by command — see CONVOKE

summons *n* a written notice ordering a person to appear in court ⟨if you ignore a court *summons*, you will be fined⟩

synonyms subpoena

related words warrant, writ

sumptuous *adj* showing obvious signs of wealth and comfort — see LUXURIOUS

sumptuously *adv* in a luxurious manner — see HIGH

sum up *vb* to make into a short statement of the main points (as of a report) — see SUMMARIZE

sun *n* 1 the light given off by the star around which the planet Earth revolves ⟨be sure to wear sunscreen if you plan to spend more than a few minutes in the *sun*⟩

synonyms sunlight, sunshine

related words sunburst; daylight

near antonyms cloudiness; penumbra, shade, shadiness, shadow, umbra

2 a ball-shaped gaseous celestial body that shines by its own light — see STAR 1

sunder *vb* to set or force apart — see SEPARATE 1

sundown *n* the time from when the sun begins to set to the onset of total darkness — see DUSK 1

sundowner *n, Australian* a homeless wanderer who may beg or steal for a living — see TRAMP

sundries *n pl* small useful items — see NOTION 1

sunken *adj* 1 curved inward — see HOLLOW

2 living, lying, or occurring below the surface of the water — see UNDERWATER

sunlight *n* the light given off by the star around which the planet Earth revolves — see SUN 1

sunny *adj* 1 having or being an outward sign of good feelings (as of love, confidence, or happiness) — see RADIANT 1

2 having or showing a good mood or disposition — see CHEERFUL 1

3 indicative of or marked by high spirits or good humor — see MERRY

4 not stormy or cloudy — see FAIR 1

sunrise *n* the first appearance of light in the morning or the time of its appearance — see DAWN 1

sunset *n* the time from when the sun begins to set to the onset of total darkness — see DUSK 1

sunshine *n* the light given off by the star around which the planet Earth revolves — see SUN 1

sunshiny *adj* not stormy or cloudy — see FAIR 1

sunup *n* the first appearance of light in the morning or the time of its appearance — see DAWN 1

sup *n* the portion of a serving of a beverage that is swallowed at one time — see DRINK 2

sup *vb* to swallow in liquid form — see DRINK 1

super *adj* unusually large — see HUGE

super *adv* to a great degree — see VERY 1

superabundance *n* 1 an amount or supply more than sufficient to meet one's needs — see PLENTY 1

2 the state or an instance of going beyond what is usual, proper, or needed — see EXCESS

superb *adj* of the very best kind — see EXCELLENT

superbness *n* 1 exceptionally high quality — see EXCELLENCE 1

2 impressiveness of beauty on a large scale — see MAGNIFICENCE

supercilious *adj* having a feeling of superiority that shows itself in an overbearing attitude — see ARROGANT

superciliousness *n* an exaggerated sense of one's importance that shows itself in the making of excessive or unjustified claims — see ARROGANCE

superficial *adj* 1 lying on or affecting only the outer layer of something ⟨a *superficial* scratch that barely even broke the skin⟩

synonyms skin-deep, surface

related words depthless, shallow, shoal; two-dimensional

near antonyms deep, deep-rooted, deep-seated; subcutaneous, subterranean

2 having or showing a lack of depth of understanding or character ⟨a *superficial* analysis of how movie and video violence affects young people⟩

synonyms facile, one-dimensional, shallow, skin-deep

related words cursory, hasty, sketchy; aimless, desultory, haphazard, hit-or-miss, random; limited, narrow, restricted

near antonyms discerning, penetrating; definitive, hard; broad, complete, comprehensive, exhaustive, extensive, far-reaching, wide; general, global, inclusive; detailed, in-depth; critical

antonyms deep, profound

superfluity *n* 1 something adding to pleasure or comfort but not absolutely necessary — see LUXURY 1

2 the state or an instance of going beyond what is usual, proper, or needed — see EXCESS

superfluous *adj* being over what is needed — see SPARE 1

superheated *adj* having a notably high temperature — see HOT 1

superhuman *adj* **1** being so extraordinary or abnormal as to suggest powers which violate the laws of nature — see SUPERNATURAL 2
2 of, relating to, or being part of a reality beyond the observable physical universe — see SUPERNATURAL 1

superintend *vb* **1** to be in charge of — see BOSS 1
2 to look after and make decisions about — see CONDUCT 1
3 to take charge of especially on behalf of another — see ²TEND 1

superintendence *n* **1** the act or activity of looking after and making decisions about something — see CONDUCT 1
2 the duty or function of watching or guarding for the sake of proper direction or control — see SUPERVISION 1

superintendency *n* the duty or function of watching or guarding for the sake of proper direction or control — see SUPERVISION 1

superintendent *n* a person who manages or directs — see EXECUTIVE

superior *adj* **1** having a feeling of superiority that shows itself in an overbearing attitude — see ARROGANT
2 having or displaying feelings of scorn for what is regarded as beneath oneself — see PROUD 1
3 of the very best kind — see EXCELLENT
4 standing above others in rank, importance, or achievement — see EMINENT

superior *n* one who is above another in rank, station, or office ⟨if a customer is rude to you, report it to your *superior* and they'll handle it⟩
synonyms better, elder, senior
related words boss, chief, head, leader, master
near antonyms assistant, deputy
antonyms inferior, subordinate, underling

superiority *n* **1** an exaggerated sense of one's importance that shows itself in the making of excessive or unjustified claims — see ARROGANCE
2 exceptionally high quality — see EXCELLENCE 1
3 the fact or state of being above others in rank or importance — see EMINENCE 1

superlative *adj* of the very best kind — see EXCELLENT

supernal *adj* **1** of the very best kind — see EXCELLENT
2 of, relating to, or suggesting heaven — see CELESTIAL

supernatural *adj* **1** of, relating to, or being part of a reality beyond the observable physical universe ⟨Susie believes in ghosts, guardian angels, and other *supernatural* beings⟩
synonyms metaphysical, preternatural, superhuman, unearthly
related words occult; extrasensory; celestial, divine, heavenly
antonyms natural
2 being so extraordinary or abnormal as to suggest powers which violate the laws of nature ⟨he seems to read books with *supernatural* speed⟩
synonyms magical, miraculous, phenomenal, superhuman, uncanny, unearthly
related words bizarre, curious, far-out, funny, kinky, outlandish, out-of-the-way, outrageous, outré, peculiar, quaint, queer, queerish, quirky,

remarkable, screwy, strange, wacky, way-out, weird, wild; baffling, bewildering, confounding, mystifying, perplexing, puzzling, shocking; aberrant, abnormal, atypical, extraordinary, fantastic, flaky, freak, freakish, idiosyncratic, rare, singular, uncommon, unique, unusual, unwonted; unconventional, uncustomary, unorthodox; conspicuous, notable, noticeable, outstanding, prominent, salient, striking
near antonyms average, commonplace, everyday, garden, ordinary, prosaic, routine, run-of-the-mill, typical, unexceptional, unremarkable, usual, workaday; expected, familiar, predictable; common, customary, frequent, habitual, regular, wonted
3 of, relating to, or being God — see HOLY 3

supernumerary *adj* being over what is needed — see SPARE 1

supersede *vb* to take the place of — see REPLACE 1

superstar *n* a person who is widely known and usually much talked about — see CELEBRITY 1

supervene *vb* to come after in time — see FOLLOW 1

supervise *vb* **1** to be in charge of — see BOSS 1
2 to look after and make decisions about — see CONDUCT 1
3 to take charge of especially on behalf of another — see ²TEND 1

supervision *n* **1** the duty or function of watching or guarding for the sake of proper direction or control ⟨our French teacher has *supervision* of all activities of the French Club⟩
synonyms care, charge, guidance, headship, oversight, regulation, superintendence, superintendency
related words monitoring, observing; administration, control, direction, management, running; leadership, piloting, shepherding, steering; government, reign, rule; aegis, guardianship, protection, tutelage
2 the act or activity of looking after and making decisions about something — see CONDUCT 1

supervisor *n* a person who manages or directs — see EXECUTIVE

supervisory *adj* suited for or relating to the directing of things — see EXECUTIVE

supplant *vb* to take the place of — see REPLACE 1

supple *adj* **1** able to bend easily without breaking — see WILLOWY
2 able to revert to original size and shape after being stretched, squeezed, or twisted — see ELASTIC 1

supplement *n* **1** something added (as by growth) — see INCREASE 1
2 something that serves to complete or make up for a deficiency in something else — see COMPLEMENT 1

supplemental *adj* available to supply something extra when needed — see AUXILIARY

supplementary *adj* **1** available to supply something extra when needed — see AUXILIARY
2 related to each other in such a way that one completes the other — see COMPLEMENTARY

suppliant *adj* asking humbly ⟨the *suppliant* student pleaded for a second chance⟩
synonyms beseeching, entreating, imploring, pleading, prayerful, soliciting, supplicant, supplicating
related words importunate, insistent, persistent

THESAURUS

suppliant *n* one who asks earnestly for a favor or gift — see SUPPLICANT

supplicant *adj* asking humbly — see SUPPLIANT

supplicant *n* one who asks earnestly for a favor or gift ⟨the new governor soon had to deal with a long line of *supplicants* asking for jobs and other political favors⟩

synonyms petitioner, pleader, solicitor, suitor, suppliant

related words beggar, mendicant, panhandler; asker, requester, suer

supplicate *vb* to make a request to (someone) in an earnest or urgent manner — see BEG

supplicating *adj* asking humbly — see SUPPLIANT

supplication *n* an earnest request — see PLEA 1

supply *n* the number of individuals or amount of something available at any given time ⟨the *supply* of grown-ups willing to coach soccer seems to be shrinking⟩

synonyms budget, fund, pool

related words reserve, reservoir, resource; cache, hoard, stockpile; refill, renewal, replacement; kitty, nest egg, pot, purse; source, well, wellspring

supply *vb* **1** to provide (someone) with what is needed for a task or activity — see FURNISH 1

2 to put (something) into the possession of someone for use or consumption — see FURNISH 2

support *n* **1** something that holds up or serves as a foundation for something else ⟨if you don't add a couple more *supports* to that tower of blocks, it's going to fall down⟩

synonyms brace, bulwark, buttress, mount, mounting, shore, stay, underpinning

related words column, pedestal, pilaster, pillar; arch, bracket, cantilever; crutch, mainstay, peg, post, stake, stanchion, stand, stilt, truss; base, foundation, frame

2 an act or instance of helping — see HELP 1

3 something or someone to which one looks for support — see DEPENDENCE 2

support *vb* **1** to promote the interests or cause of ⟨my parents *support* the local schools both by volunteering and by fiercely opposing funding cuts at town meetings⟩

synonyms advocate, back, champion, endorse (*also* indorse), patronize

related words adopt, embrace, espouse; abet, aid, assist, prop (up), second; bolster, boost, buttress, reinforce; bail out, deliver, rescue, save

phrases stand up for

near antonyms baffle, foil, frustrate, interfere, oppose, sabotage, thwart; desert, disappoint, fail, let down

2 to pay the living expenses of ⟨a young widow *supporting* a sick mother as well as two small children on a teacher's salary⟩

synonyms maintain, provide (for)

related words finance, fund, stake

phrases foot the bills for, take care of

3 to hold up or serve as a foundation for ⟨pillars *supporting* the bridge⟩

synonyms bear, bolster, brace, buttress, carry, prop (up), shore (up), stay, underpin, uphold

related words steady, truss, underlie

4 to continue to declare to be true or proper despite opposition or objections — see MAINTAIN 2

5 to give evidence or testimony to the truth or factualness of — see CONFIRM

6 to provide (someone) with what is useful or necessary to achieve an end — see HELP 1

7 to put up with (something painful or difficult) — see BEAR 2

supportable *adj* **1** capable of being defended with good reasoning against verbal attack — see TENABLE 1

2 capable of being endured — see BEARABLE

3 capable of being proven as true or real — see VERIFIABLE

supporter *n* **1** a person who actively supports or favors a cause — see EXPONENT

2 someone associated with another to give assistance or moral support — see ALLY

supporting *adj* serving to give support to the truth or factualness of something — see CORROBORATIVE

supportive *adj* serving to give support to the truth or factualness of something — see CORROBORATIVE

suppose *vb* **1** to decide the size, amount, number, or distance of (something) without actual measurement — see ESTIMATE 2

2 to form an opinion from little or no evidence — see GUESS 1

3 to have as an opinion — see BELIEVE 2

4 to take as true or as a fact without actual proof — see ASSUME 2

supposed *adj* appearing to be true on the basis of evidence that may or may not be confirmed — see APPARENT 1

supposedly *adv* to all outward appearances — see APPARENTLY

supposition *n* **1** an idea that is the starting point for making a case or conducting an investigation — see THEORY

2 an opinion or judgment based on little or no evidence — see CONJECTURE

3 something taken as being true or factual and used as a starting point for a course of action or reasoning — see ASSUMPTION

suppositional *adj* existing only as an assumption or speculation — see THEORETICAL 1

suppress *vb* **1** to keep from being publicly known ⟨the government tried to *suppress* the truth about that incident⟩

synonyms cover (up), hush (up)

related words censor, silence; repress, smother, squash, squelch, stifle

phrases keep a lid on

near antonyms debunk, expose, reveal, show up, uncloak, uncover, unmask; disclose, divulge, tell, unveil; broadcast, circulate, publish, spread; describe, narrate, recite, recount, rehearse, relate, report

2 to refrain from openly showing or uttering ⟨he managed to *suppress* a scream at the sight of the dead body⟩ ⟨*suppressed* her anger⟩

synonyms choke (back), pocket, repress, smother, stifle, strangle, swallow

related words control, govern, handle, manage; bridle, check, curb, hold back, quell; bottle up, contain, hold in; muffle, squelch

near antonyms loose, release, take out, unleash, vent

3 to hold back the normal growth of — see STUNT

4 to put a stop to (something) by the use of force — see QUELL 1

suppression *n* the checking of one's true feelings and impulses when dealing with others — see CONSTRAINT 1

supremacist *n* a person who believes that one race

should control all others ⟨white *supremacists* were arrested for painting racial slurs on a church⟩
synonyms racialist, racist
related words segregationist; bigot

supremacy *n* **1** controlling power or influence over others ⟨the Roman empire had *supremacy* over the entire Mediterranean world⟩
synonyms ascendancy, dominance, dominion, predominance, preeminence
related words primacy, superiority; lordship, scepter, sovereignty; arm, authority, clutch, command, control, grip, hold, mastery, sway; takeover; direction, jurisdiction, management; clout, pull, weight; eminence, importance, moment; prerogative, privilege, right
near antonyms helplessness, weakness; impotence, powerlessness
2 exceptionally high quality — see EXCELLENCE 1

supreme *adj* **1** highest in rank or authority — see HEAD
2 coming before all others in importance — see FOREMOST 1
3 of the greatest or highest degree or quantity — see ULTIMATE 1

Supreme Being *n* the being worshipped as the creator and ruler of the universe — see DEITY 2

surcease *n* the stopping of a process or activity — see END 1

surcharge *vb* to charge (someone) too much for goods or services — see OVERCHARGE 1

surcoat *n* a warm outdoor coat — see OVERCOAT

sure *adj* **1** having or showing a mind free from doubt — see CERTAIN 2
2 impossible to avoid or evade — see INEVITABLE
3 not likely to fail — see INFALLIBLE 2
4 worthy of one's trust — see DEPENDABLE

surely *adv* without any question — see INDEED 1

sureness *n* **1** a state of mind in which one is free from doubt — see CONFIDENCE 2
2 worthiness as the recipient of another's trust or confidence — see RELIABILITY

surety *n* **1** a formal agreement to fulfill an obligation — see GUARANTEE 1
2 a person who takes the responsibility for some other person or thing — see SPONSOR

surf *n* a light mass of fine bubbles formed in or on a liquid — see FOAM

surface *adj* lying on or affecting only the outer layer of something — see SUPERFICIAL 1

surface *n* an outer part or layer — see EXTERIOR

surface *vb* **1** to come to one's attention especially gradually or unexpectedly — see ARISE 2
2 to penetrate the surface (as of water) from below — see BROACH 1

surfeit *n* the state or an instance of going beyond what is usual, proper, or needed — see EXCESS

surfeit *vb* to fill with food to capacity — see GORGE 1

surfeited *adj* having one's appetite completely satisfied — see FULL 3

surge *n* a moving ridge on the surface of water — see WAVE

surly *adj* **1** given to or displaying a resentful silence and often irritability — see SULKY
2 having or showing a habitually bad temper — see ILL-TEMPERED

surmise *n* an opinion or judgment based on little or no evidence — see CONJECTURE

surmise *vb* to form an opinion from little or no evidence — see GUESS 1

surmount *vb* to achieve a victory over — see BEAT 2

surpass *vb* **1** to be greater, better, or stronger than ⟨she always tried to *surpass* her older brother at anything he did⟩
synonyms beat, better, eclipse, excel, outdistance, outdo, outshine, outstrip, overtop, top, transcend
related words exceed, outpace, outrun, overpass; best, clobber, conquer, crush, defeat, drub, lick, master, overcome, overmatch, prevail (over), rout, skunk, subdue, surmount, thrash, trim, triumph (over), trounce, wallop, whip, win (against), worst; outweigh, overbear, overshadow
phrases go one better
near antonyms lose (to)
2 to go beyond the limit of — see EXCEED

surplus *adj* being over what is needed — see SPARE 1

surplus *n* the state or an instance of going beyond what is usual, proper, or needed — see EXCESS

surprise *also* **surprize** *vb* **1** to make a strong impression on (someone) with something unexpected ⟨I was very *surprised* when my parents offered to pay for guitar lessons⟩
synonyms amaze, astonish, astound, bowl (over), dumbfound (*also* dumfound), flabbergast, floor, shock, startle, stun, stupefy
related words befuddle, bewilder, confound, confuse, discomfit, disconcert, dismay, muddle, nonplus, perplex
phrases knock for a loop, take aback, take by surprise
2 to lie in wait for and attack by surprise — see AMBUSH

surprise *n* **1** something that makes a strong impression because it is so unexpected ⟨the birthday party was such a complete *surprise* that Jane was speechless for a moment⟩
synonyms bolt, bombshell, jar, jolt, stunner
related words shock, thunderclap; revelation, shocker
2 the state of being strongly impressed by something unexpected or unusual ⟨Danny stared in utter *surprise* at the deer in his living room⟩
synonyms amazement, astonishment, shock
related words awe, wonder, wonderment; startle; bewilderment, confusion, discomfiture, dismay
3 a scheme in which hidden persons wait to attack by surprise — see AMBUSH 1

surprising *adj* **1** causing a strong emotional reaction because unexpected ⟨the *surprising* news that they were going to have a baby had them rushing to buy nursery furniture⟩
synonyms amazing, astonishing, astounding, dumbfounding (*or* dumfounding), eye-opening, flabbergasting, shocking, startling, stunning, stupefying
related words unannounced, unanticipated, unexpected, unforeseen; awesome, awful, breathtaking, fabulous, marvelous (*or* marvellous), miraculous, portentous, prodigious, staggering, stupendous, sublime, wonderful, wondrous; extraordinary, phenomenal, rare, sensational, spectacular; befuddling, bewildering, confounding, confusing, discomfiting, disconcerting, dismaying, muddling, nonplussing, perplexing; incomprehensible, inconceivable, incredible, unbelievable, unimaginable, unthinkable; singular, uncommon, unique, unusual, unwonted; conspic-

uous, notable, noticeable, outstanding, remarkable; impressive, striking

near antonyms common, customary, mundane, normal, ordinary, typical, unexceptional, unremarkable, usual

2 causing wonder or astonishment — see MARVELOUS 1

surrender *n* the usually forced yielding of one's person or possessions to the control of another ⟨the police demanded the *surrender* of all hostages as a condition for allowing the hijackers safe passage out of the country⟩

synonyms capitulating, capitulation, relinquishment, submission, submitting

related words acceptance, acquiescence, concession; compromise; appeasement, conciliation; capture, fall

near antonyms resistance

surrender *vb* **1** to give (something) over to the control or possession of another usually under duress ⟨Annie *surrendered* the doll to her mother after a brief struggle⟩ ⟨the commander *surrendered* the garrison without having fired a single shot⟩

synonyms cede, deliver, give up, hand over, relinquish, render, turn over, yield

related words commit, consign, entrust; waive; renounce, resign; abandon, desert, discard, forsake, shed

near antonyms keep, retain, withhold

2 to cease resistance (as to another's arguments, demands, or control) — see YIELD 3

3 to give up (as a position of authority) formally — see ABDICATE

4 to give up and cease resistance (as to a liking, temptation, or habit) — see YIELD 1

5 to yield to the control or power of enemy forces — see FALL 2

surreptitious *adj* undertaken or done so as to escape being observed or known by others — see SECRET 1

surround *vb* to form a circle around ⟨she was *surrounded* by cheering fans within moments of scoring the winning goal⟩

synonyms circle, encircle, enclose (*also* inclose), encompass, ring

related words fence (in), hem (in), wall; besiege, entrench (*also* intrench), invest

surroundings *n pl* the circumstances, conditions, or objects by which one is surrounded — see ENVIRONMENT

surveillance *n* the act or state of being constantly attentive and responsive to signs of opportunity, activity, or danger — see VIGILANCE

survey *n* a close look at or over someone or something in order to judge condition — see INSPECTION

survey *vb* **1** to go around and approach (people) with a request for opinions or information — see CANVASS

2 to look over closely (as for judging quality or condition) — see INSPECT

survive *vb* **1** to come safely through ⟨the cat miraculously *survived* a two-story fall⟩

synonyms ride (out), weather

related words outlast, outlive; pull through; abide, continue, endure, hang on, last, lead, persist; be, breathe, exist, live, subsist; flourish, prosper, thrive

near antonyms croak [*slang*], decease, depart, die,

expire, pass (on), pass away, perish, succumb; disappear, evaporate, fade, vanish; cease, end, stop

2 to continue to operate or to meet one's needs — see HOLD OUT

susceptibility *n* the quality or state of having little resistance to some outside agent ⟨Carol's unfortunate *susceptibility* to viruses meant she was nearly always sick⟩ ⟨Stephen had a well-known *susceptibility* to anyone with a pathetic story⟩

synonyms defenselessness, vulnerability, weakness

related words helplessness, powerlessness; passiveness, passivity; feebleness, frailness; exposure, liability, openness, sensitivity; receptiveness, receptivity; easiness, gullibility, näiveté (*also* naivete); credulity, credulousness

near antonyms immunity; impenetrability, indomitability, indomitableness, invincibility

antonyms invulnerability

susceptible *adj* **1** being in a situation where one is likely to meet with harm — see LIABLE 1

2 lacking protection from danger or resistance against attack — see HELPLESS 1

3 readily taken advantage of — see EASY 2

suspect *adj* giving good reason for being doubted, questioned, or challenged — see DOUBTFUL 2

suspect *vb* **1** to form an opinion from little or no evidence — see GUESS 1

2 to have no trust or confidence in — see DISTRUST

suspecting *adj* inclined to doubt or question claims — see SKEPTICAL 1

suspend *vb* **1** to bring to a formal close for a period of time — see ADJOURN

2 to place on an elevated point without support from below — see HANG 1

suspense *n* a state of temporary inactivity — see ABEYANCE

suspension *n* a state of temporary inactivity — see ABEYANCE

suspicion *vb, chiefly dialect* to form an opinion from little or no evidence — see GUESS 1

suspicion *n* **1** a feeling or attitude that one does not know the truth, truthfulness, or trustworthiness of someone or something — see DOUBT

2 a very small amount — see PARTICLE 1

suspicious *adj* **1** giving good reason for being doubted, questioned, or challenged — see DOUBTFUL 2

2 inclined to doubt or question claims — see SKEPTICAL 1

3 not feeling sure about the truth, wisdom, or trustworthiness of someone or something — see DOUBTFUL 1

suspiciously *adv* with distrust — see ASKANCE

sustain *vb* **1** to supply with nourishment ⟨a granola bar will *sustain* you long enough to last until lunch⟩

synonyms nourish, nurture

related words sate, satiate, satisfy; cloy, fill, surfeit; fortify, strengthen; feed; board, cater, provision

2 to come to a knowledge of (something) by living through it — see EXPERIENCE

3 to put up with (something painful or difficult) — see BEAR 2

sustainable *adj* **1** capable of being defended with good reasoning against verbal attack — see TENABLE 1

2 capable of being proven as true or real — see VERIFIABLE

3 capable of being endured — see BEARABLE

swab *n* one who operates or navigates a seagoing vessel — see SAILOR

swag *n* valuables stolen or taken by force — see LOOT

swagger *vb* **1** to praise or express pride in one's own possessions, qualities, or accomplishments often to excess — see BOAST

2 to walk with exaggerated arm and leg movements — see STRUT 1

swain *n* **1** a male romantic companion — see BOYFRIEND

2 a man who courts a woman usually with the goal of marrying her — see SUITOR 1

swallow *n* the portion of a serving of a beverage that is swallowed at one time — see DRINK 2

swallow *vb* **1** to take into the stomach through the mouth and throat ⟨try not to *swallow* the toothpaste, because it's not good for you⟩
  synonyms down, ingest
  related words drink, imbibe, sip; bolt, devour, gobble (up *or* down), gulp; consume, eat, mouth (down); gorge, scarf, scoff, wolf; chew, gnaw (at *or* on), lap, lick, nibble (on); dispatch, polish off
2 to refrain from openly showing or uttering — see SUPPRESS 2
3 to regard as right or true — see BELIEVE 1

swamp *n* spongy land saturated or partially covered with water ⟨be careful in the *swamp*, because alligators sometimes lurk there⟩
  synonyms bog, fen, marsh, marshland, mire, morass, muskeg, slough (*also* slue), swampland
  related words quagmire; muck, mud, ooze, slime, slop, sludge, slush

swamp *vb* **1** to cover or become filled with a flood — see FLOOD
2 to subject to incapacitating emotional or mental stress — see OVERWHELM 1

swampland *n* spongy land saturated or partially covered with water — see SWAMP

swank *or* **swanky** *adj* excessively showy — see GAUDY

swank *n* excessive or unnecessary display — see OSTENTATION

swankily *adv* in a bright and showy way — see GAILY 3

swap *n* a giving or taking of one thing of value in return for another — see EXCHANGE 1

swap *vb* to give up (something) and take something else in return — see CHANGE 3

swarm *n* a great number of persons or things gathered together — see CROWD 1

swarm *vb* to move upon or fill (something) in great numbers — see CROWD 2

swarming *adj* possessing or covered with great numbers or amounts of something specified — see RIFE

swash *vb* to move with a splashing motion — see SLOSH

swat *n* a hard strike with a part of the body or an instrument — see ¹BLOW

swat *vb* to deliver a blow to (someone or something) usually in a strong vigorous manner — see HIT 1

swathe *vb* to surround or cover closely — see ENFOLD 1

sway *n* **1** the power to bring about a result on another — see EFFECT 2

2 the power to direct the thinking or behavior of others usually indirectly — see INFLUENCE 1

3 the right or means to command or control others — see POWER 1

sway *vb* **1** to act upon (a person or a person's feelings) so as to cause a response — see ¹AFFECT 1
2 to make a series of unsteady side-to-side motions — see ROCK 1

swear *vb* **1** to use offensive or indecent language ⟨you're not allowed to *swear* in this house⟩
  synonyms blaspheme, curse, cuss
  related words confound, damn, execrate, imprecate; fulminate, rail, rant
2 to make a solemn declaration of intent — see PROMISE 1
3 to make a solemn declaration under oath for the purpose of establishing a fact — see TESTIFY

swearword *n* a disrespectful or indecent word or expression ⟨this is a list of *swearwords* that will not be permitted in my classroom⟩
  synonyms curse, cuss, expletive, obscenity, vulgarism
  related words profanity; execration, imprecation, malediction; epithet, name; oath

sweat *n* **1** the active use of energy in producing a result — see EFFORT
2 very hard or unpleasant work — see TOIL

sweat *vb* **1** to devote serious and sustained effort — see LABOR
2 to experience concern or anxiety — see WORRY 1
3 to work hard and long — see TOIL
4 to flow forth slowly through small openings — see EXUDE

sweep *n* an area over which activity, capacity, or influence extends — see RANGE 2

sweep *vb* **1** to move or proceed smoothly and readily — see FLOW 2
2 to turn away from a straight line or course — see CURVE 1

sweepstakes *n pl* a competitive encounter between individuals or groups carried on for amusement, exercise, or in pursuit of a prize — see GAME 1

sweet *adj* **1** granted special treatment or attention — see DARLING 1
2 having a pleasant smell — see FRAGRANT
3 having an easygoing and pleasing manner especially in social situations — see AMIABLE
4 having qualities that tend to make one loved — see LOVABLE

sweet *n* **1** a food having a high sugar content ⟨remember to brush your teeth after eating *sweets*⟩
  synonyms confection, sweetmeat
  related words confectionery; candy, dessert, pastry
2 a person with whom one is in love — see SWEETHEART

sweetheart *n* a person with whom one is in love ⟨I married my high-school *sweetheart* as soon as we both finished college⟩
  synonyms beloved, darling, dear, flame, honey, love, sweet
  related words beau, boyfriend, fellow, lover, man, swain; gal, girl, girlfriend, ladylove, mistress; date, escort; gallant, suitor, wooer; groom, husband; fiancé, intended; admirer, crush, steady

sweetmeat *n* a food having a high sugar content — see SWEET 1

sweetness *n* the state or quality of having a pleasant or agreeable manner in socializing with others — see AMIABILITY 1

swell *adj* of the very best kind — see EXCELLENT

swell *n* a moving ridge on the surface of water — see WAVE

swell *vb* **1** to become greater in extent, volume, amount, or number — see INCREASE 2

2 to make greater in size, amount, or number — see INCREASE 1

swelling *n* a small rounded mass of swollen tissue — see BUMP 1

sweltering *adj* having a notably high temperature — see HOT 1

swerve *vb* **1** to depart abruptly from a straight line or course ⟨the car *swerved* sharply to avoid the squirrel in the road⟩
synonyms sheer, veer, yaw
related words skew, slew (*also* slue); arc, arch, bend, bow, crook, curve, hook, round, sweep, wheel; circle, coil, curl, loop, spiral; turn, twist, wind; deviate, stray, wander, waver
antonyms straighten

2 to turn away from a straight line or course — see CURVE 1

3 to cause to turn away from a straight line — see BEND 1

swift *adj* moving, proceeding, or acting with great speed — see FAST 1

swift *adv* with great speed — see FAST 1

swiftly *adv* with great speed — see FAST 1

swiftness *n* a high rate of movement or performance — see SPEED

swig *n* the portion of a serving of a beverage that is swallowed at one time — see DRINK 2

swig *vb* to swallow in liquid form — see DRINK 1

swill *n* the portion of a serving of a beverage that is swallowed at one time — see DRINK 2

swill *vb* **1** to eat greedily or to excess — see GORGE 2

2 to swallow in liquid form — see DRINK 1

swiller *n* one who eats greedily or too much — see GLUTTON

swim *vb* to be in a confused state as if from being twirled around — see SPIN 2

swimmingly *adv* in a pleasing way — see WELL 5

swindle *n* a scheme in which the victim is cheated out of his money after first gaining his trust — see CONFIDENCE GAME

swindle *vb* to rob by the use of trickery or threats — see FLEECE

swindler *n* a dishonest person who uses clever means to cheat others out of something of value — see TRICKSTER 1

swing *vb* **1** to change one's course or direction — see TURN 3

2 to change the course or direction of (something) — see TURN 2

3 to deal with (something) usually skillfully or efficiently — see HANDLE 1

4 to move (something) in a curved or circular path on or as if on an axis — see TURN 1

5 to place on an elevated point without support from below — see HANG 1

swipe *n* a hard strike with a part of the body or an instrument — see ¹BLOW

swipe *vb* **1** to come into usually forceful contact with something — see HIT 2

2 to deliver a blow to (someone or something) usually in a strong vigorous manner — see HIT 1

3 to take (something) without right and with an intent to keep — see STEAL 1

swiping *n* an instance of theft — see THEFT 2

swirl *vb* **1** to cause (as a liquid) to move about in a circle especially repeatedly — see STIR 1

2 to move (something) in a curved or circular path on or as if on an axis — see TURN 1

swish *n* a sound similar to the speech sound \s\ stretched out — see HISS 1

swish *vb* to make a sound like that of stretching out the speech sound \s\ — see HISS

switch *n* **1** a long thin or flexible tool for striking — see WHIP

2 a quick jerky movement from side to side or up and down — see WAG 1

switch *vb* **1** to give up (something) and take something else in return — see CHANGE 3

2 to move from side to side or up and down with quick jerky motions — see WAG

3 to strike repeatedly with something long and thin or flexible — see WHIP 1

4 to change (as an opinion) to the contrary — see REVERSE 1

swoon *n* a temporary or permanent state of unconsciousness — see FAINT

swoon *vb* to lose consciousness — see FAINT

sword *n* a hand weapon with a length of metal sharpened on one or both sides and usually tapered to a sharp point ⟨once upon a time dueling with *swords* was the gentlemanly way to settle a point of honor⟩
synonyms blade, steel
related words broadsword, cutlass, rapier, saber (*or* sabre), scimitar

sycophant *n* a person who flatters another in order to get ahead ⟨my teacher isn't fooled by the class *sycophants*, who are always telling her what a wonderful teacher she is⟩
synonyms fawner, flunky (*also* flunkey), toady
related words yes-man; hanger-on, leech, parasite, sponge, sponger; henchman, lackey, minion, satellite, slave, stooge; admirer, cultist, devotee, enthusiast, fan, groveler (*or* groveller), idolater (*or* idolator), worshipper (*or* worshiper), zealot; adherent, convert, disciple, follower, partisan, pupil, votary

symbol *n* **1** a device, design, or figure used as an identifying mark — see EMBLEM

2 a written or printed mark that is meant to convey information to the reader — see CHARACTER 1

symbolic *also* **symbolical** *adj* having the function or meaning of a symbol ⟨the teddy bear in the story was intended to be *symbolic* of a mother's love⟩
synonyms emblematic (*also* emblematical), representative
related words figurative, metaphorical; allegorical
antonyms nonsymbolic

symbolize *vb* to serve as a material counterpart of ⟨the flag *symbolizes* our country⟩
synonyms represent
related words embody, epitomize, incarnate, manifest, materialize, personalize, personify; exemplify, illustrate
phrases stand for

symmetry *n* a balanced, pleasing, or suitable arrangement of parts — see HARMONY 1

sympathetic *adj* **1** having or showing the capacity for sharing the feelings of another ⟨a *sympathetic* smile⟩ ⟨Jane was always a *sympathetic* listener⟩

synonyms compassionate, humane, understanding

related words gentle, sensitive, softhearted, tender, tenderhearted, warm, warmhearted; benevolent, benignant, charitable, kind; clement, lenient, merciful; cordial, friendly, good-natured, good-tempered, gracious; affectionate, loving

near antonyms inconsiderate, insensitive, thoughtless, unthinking; uncaring, unloving; merciless, pitiless, ruthless; grim, hard-bitten, hard-boiled, harsh, oppressive, rough, severe, stern, tough, ungentle; abusive, acrimonious, disagreeable, hateful, ill-natured, ill-tempered, malevolent, malicious, mean, rancorous, spiteful, surly, virulent

antonyms callous, cold-blooded, hardhearted, heartless, inhuman, inhumane, unfeeling, unsympathetic

2 having or marked by sympathy and consideration for others — see HUMANE 1

sympathize (with) *vb* to have sympathy for — see PITY

sympathizer *n* someone associated with another to give assistance or moral support — see ALLY

sympathy *n* **1** sorrow or the capacity to feel sorrow for another's suffering or misfortune ⟨although I'd never lost a relative, I felt great *sympathy* for the classmate whose grandfather died⟩

synonyms commiseration, compassion, feeling

related words condolence, regret; humanity, kindheartedness, kindliness, kindness, mercy, pity, softheartedness; affinity, empathy, rapport, sensitivity; altruism, benevolence, benignity, charity, generosity, goodwill, humanitarianism, philanthropy

near antonyms indifference, insensitivity, unconcern; cruelty, harshness; animosity, antipathy, dislike, hatred, hostility

antonyms callousness, hardheartedness, heartlessness

2 the capacity for feeling for another's unhappiness or misfortune — see HEART 1

symphonic *adj* having a pleasing mixture of notes — see HARMONIOUS 1

symphony *n* **1** a balanced, pleasing, or suitable arrangement of parts — see HARMONY 1

2 a usually large group of musicians playing together — see ²BAND 1

symphony orchestra *n* a usually large group of musicians playing together — see ²BAND 1

symposium *n* a meeting featuring a group discussion — see FORUM

symptomatic *adj* serving to identify as belonging to an individual or group — see CHARACTERISTIC 1

synchronous *adj* existing or occurring at the same period of time — see CONTEMPORARY 1

syndicate *n* **1** a group involved in secret or criminal activities — see RING 1

2 a number of businesses or enterprises united for commercial advantage — see CARTEL

synopsis *n* a short statement of the main points — see SUMMARY

synthetic *adj* being such in appearance only and made with or manufactured from usually cheaper materials — see IMITATION

syringe *n* a slender hollow instrument by which material is put into or taken from the body through the skin — see NEEDLE 1

syrupy *adj* being of a consistency that resists flow — see THICK 2

system *n* **1** something made up of many interdependent or related parts ⟨the national highway *system* allows travel from one end of the country to the other⟩ ⟨the democratic *system* of checks and balances in government⟩

synonyms complex, network

related words interlacement, Internet, net, web; aggregate, conglomerate, totality, whole

2 a method worked out in advance for achieving some objective — see PLAN 1

3 the means or procedure for doing something — see METHOD

systematic *adj* following a set method, arrangement, or pattern — see METHODICAL

systematize *vb* to put into a particular arrangement — see ORDER 1

systematized *adj* following a set method, arrangement, or pattern — see METHODICAL

tab *n* **1** a record of goods sold or services performed together with the costs due — see ¹BILL 1

2 the amount owed at a bar or restaurant or the slip of paper stating the amount — see CHECK 1

tabernacle *n* a building for public worship and especially Christian worship — see CHURCH 1

table *n* **1** a leg-mounted piece of furniture with a broad flat top designed for the serving of food ⟨we sat at the kitchen *table*, playing cards for hours on end⟩

synonyms board

related words coffee table, refectory table; bar, counter; buffet, sideboard

2 food eaten or prepared for eating at one time — see MEAL

3 a broad flat area of elevated land — see PLATEAU

4 a record of a series of items (as names or titles) usually arranged according to some system — see ¹LIST

5 substances intended to be eaten — see FOOD

tableland *n* a broad flat area of elevated land — see PLATEAU

tablet *n* **1** a number of sheets of writing paper glued together at one edge — see PAD 1

2 a small mass containing medicine to be taken orally — see PILL

table talk *n* friendly, informal conversation or an instance of this — see CHAT

tableware *n* **1** eating and serving utensils ⟨we ran short of *tableware*, so Emily went next door and borrowed some forks and knives⟩

synonyms flatware, silver, silverware

related words place setting, setting; silver plate;

THESAURUS

cutlery; chopstick, fork, knife, spoon, tablespoon, teaspoon

2 dishes used for eating or serving food or drink ⟨Betty would take out her good *tableware* only on special occasions, as when the mayor came to dinner⟩

synonyms dinnerware

related words setting; china, chinaware, crockery, earthenware, porcelain, pottery, stoneware, ware; crystal, glassware; plate, saucer; cup, glass, goblet, mug, teacup; bowl, casserole, charger, platter, tureen

taboo *also* **tabu** *adj* that may not be permitted — see IMPERMISSIBLE

tacit *adj* understood although not put into words — see IMPLICIT

taciturn *adj* tending not to speak frequently (as by habit or inclination) — see SILENT 2

tack *n* the means or procedure for doing something — see METHOD

tack (on) *vb* to join (something) to a mass, quantity, or number so as to bring about an overall increase — see ADD 1

tackle *n* items needed for the performance of a task or activity — see EQUIPMENT

tackle *vb* to start work on energetically — see ATTACK 3

tacky *adj* **1** marked by an obvious lack of style or good taste ⟨it was *tacky* to wear sneakers, but Tracey's dress shoes hurt her feet⟩ ⟨*tacky* plastic flowers⟩

synonyms cheesy, dowdy, inelegant, styleless, tasteless, trashy, unfashionable, unstylish

related words inappropriate, incorrect, unbecoming, unseemly, unsuitable, wrong; outmoded, out-of-date, passé; coarse, crude, unrefined, vulgar; cheap, common, inferior, junky, lousy, low-grade, second-rate, shoddy, sleazy, tawdry; gaudy, loud, ostentatious, overdone, showy, splashy

near antonyms appropriate, becoming, correct, fitting, proper, right, seemly, suitable; genteel, handsome, neat, quiet, refined, understated; contemporary, modern, up-to-date

antonyms elegant, fashionable, modish, ritzy, smart, stylish, tasteful

2 showing signs of advanced wear and tear and neglect — see SHABBY 1

tact *n* the ability to deal with others in touchy situations without offending them ⟨with supreme *tact*, Isabel suggested to her neighbor that her flower garden was probably not the best place for his dog to use as a bathroom⟩

synonyms diplomacy, tactfulness

related words considerateness, consideration, courtesy, delicacy, graciousness, thoughtfulness; civility, etiquette, mannerliness, manners, politeness; charm, gallantry, gentility, grace, gracefulness, suaveness, suavity; adroitness, deftness, dexterity, finesse; deference, regard, respect

near antonyms discourteousness, discourtesy, inconsiderateness, inconsideration, indelicacy, thoughtlessness, ungraciousness, unthoughtfulness; impoliteness, incivility; boorishness, brashness, brassiness, loutishness; awkwardness, gaucheness, gracelessness, maladroitness; disregard, disrespect, impertinence, impudence, insolence, rudeness

antonyms tactlessness

tactful *adj* having or showing tact ⟨Allie tried to be

tactful when asked to comment on the short story that a classmate had written⟩

synonyms diplomatic

related words considerate, courteous, delicate, gracious, thoughtful; civil, mannerly, polite; charming, gallant, genteel, suave; deferential, regardful, respectful

near antonyms discourteous, inconsiderate, indelicate, thoughtless, ungracious, unthoughtful; ill-bred, ill-mannered, impolite, uncivil, unmannerly; boorish, brash, brassy, loutish; disregardful, disrespectful, impertinent, impudent, insolent, rude

antonyms tactless, undiplomatic

tactfulness *n* the ability to deal with others in touchy situations without offending them — see TACT

tactical *adj* suitable for bringing about a desired result under the circumstances — see EXPEDIENT

tactics *n pl* the means or procedure for doing something — see METHOD

tactless *adj* showing poor judgment especially in personal relationships or social situations — see INDISCREET

tad *n* a male person who has not yet reached adulthood — see BOY

tag *n* a slip (as of paper or cloth) that is attached to something to identify or describe it — see LABEL

tag *vb* **1** to attach an identifying slip to — see LABEL 1

2 to go after or on the track of — see FOLLOW 2

tagging *n* the act of going after or in the tracks of another — see PURSUIT

tail *n* a person whose business is solving crimes and catching criminals or gathering information that is not easy to get — see DETECTIVE

tail *vb* to go after or on the track of — see FOLLOW 2

tailing *n* the act of going after or in the tracks of another — see PURSUIT

tailored *adj* made or fitted to the needs or preferences of a specific customer — see CUSTOM-MADE

tailor–made *adj* made or fitted to the needs or preferences of a specific customer — see CUSTOM-MADE

taint *n* a mark of guilt or disgrace — see STAIN 1

taint *vb* **1** to affect slightly with something morally bad or undesirable ⟨criticism of her sister's singing that was *tainted* by envy⟩ ⟨a tendency toward conceitedness *taints* that athlete's status as a role model⟩

synonyms blemish, mar, poison, spoil, stain, tarnish, touch, vitiate

related words besmear, besmirch, blacken, cloud, dirty, discolor, smear, smirch, smudge, smut, soil, sully, tar; color, distort, twist; damage, deface, flaw, harm, hurt, impair; destroy, ruin, wreck

near antonyms cleanse, purify; elevate, ennoble, uplift

2 to make unfit for use by the addition of something harmful or undesirable — see CONTAMINATE

tainted *adj* containing foreign or lower-grade substances — see IMPURE

take *n* **1** action or behavior that is done in return to other action or behavior — see REACTION

2 the total amount collected or obtained especially at one time — see HAUL 1

take *vb* **1** to reach for and take hold of by embrac-

ing with the fingers or arms ⟨*take* my hand, or we'll get separated in this crowd⟩
synonyms clasp, grasp, grip, hold
related words clench, cling (to), clutch, hang on (to), hold on (to); catch, nab, seize, snatch
phrases lay hold of
near antonyms discharge, drop, free, liberate, release; give, hand, relinquish, unhand
2 to agree to receive whether willingly or reluctantly ⟨will you *take* that call?⟩ ⟨*took* a cut in pay⟩
synonyms accept, have
related words accede (to), assent (to), concede (to), consent (to), OK (*or* okay); acquiesce (to), bow (to), capitulate (to), give in (to), submit (to), succumb (to), surrender (to), yield (to); bear, endure, shoulder, tolerate, swallow; adopt, embrace, welcome
near antonyms dissent (to), object (to), oppose, protest; hold off, resist, withstand
antonyms decline, refuse, reject, spurn, turn down
3 to become affected with (a disease or disorder) — see CONTRACT 1
4 to decide to accept (someone or something) from a group of possibilities — see CHOOSE 1
5 to get possession of (something) by giving money in exchange for — see BUY
6 to have as a requirement — see NEED 1
7 to make or have room for — see ACCOMMODATE 1
8 to produce a desired effect — see ACT 2
9 to put up with (something painful or difficult) — see BEAR 2
take (for) *vb* to think of in a particular way — see CONSIDER 1
take back *vb* to solemnly or formally reject or go back on (as something formerly adhered to) — see ABJURE
take down *vb* **1** to reduce to a lower standing in one's own eyes or in others' eyes — see HUMBLE
2 to take apart — see DISASSEMBLE
take in *vb* **1** to cause to believe what is untrue — see DECEIVE
2 to have as part of a whole — see INCLUDE
3 to provide with living quarters or shelter — see HOUSE 1
takeoff *n* **1** a rising from a surface at the start of a flight (as of a rocket) — see LIFT-OFF
2 a work that imitates and exaggerates another work for comic effect — see PARODY 1
take off *vb* **1** to leave a place often for another — see GO 2
2 to rid oneself of (a garment) — see REMOVE 1
3 to take away (an amount or number) from a total — see SUBTRACT
take off (on) *vb* to copy or exaggerate (someone or something) in order to make fun of — see MIMIC 1
take on *vb* **1** to enter into contest or conflict with — see ENGAGE 2
2 to provide with a paying job — see EMPLOY 1
take out *vb* **1** to find emotional release for ⟨*took out* his frustrations by splitting a cord of firewood⟩
synonyms loose, release, unleash, vent
phrases give way (to)
near antonyms control, govern, handle, manage; bridle, check, contain, curb, hold back, hold in, quell, restrain, smother; allay, lull, quiet, soothe,

still; choke, inhibit, muffle, pocket, repress, stifle, strangle, swallow
antonyms bottle (up), repress, suppress
2 to go on a social engagement with — see DATE 1
take over *vb* **1** to serve as a replacement usually for a time only — see COVER 1
2 to take to or upon oneself — see ASSUME 1
take up *vb* to take for one's own use (something originated by another) — see ADOPT
taking *adj* very pleasing to look at — see BEAUTIFUL
tale *n* **1** a rumor or report of a personal or sensational nature ⟨don't believe the *tales* you hear about our neighbor's kid⟩
synonyms story, whisper
related words dirt, gossip, scuttlebutt, talebearing, talk, tattle; defamation, libel, slander; hearsay; fabrication, fairy tale, falsehood, falsity, fib, lie
2 a brief account of something interesting that happened especially to one personally — see STORY 2
3 a statement known by its maker to be untrue and made in order to deceive — see LIE
4 a work with imaginary characters and events that is shorter and usually less complex than a novel — see STORY 1
talebearer *n* a person who provides secret information about another's wrongdoing — see INFORMER
talent *n* a special and usually inborn ability ⟨Liza's musical *talent* was already apparent by the time she was five⟩ ⟨Jim's *talent* for coming up with really funny answers⟩
synonyms aptitude, endowment, faculty, flair, genius, gift, knack
related words bent, inclination, leaning, partiality, penchant, predilection, predisposition, proclivity, propensity, turn; ear, eye, head, mind, nose; feel, hang, instinct, touch, way; capability, competence, facility, proficiency, skill; capacity, power, potential
near antonyms disability, handicap, inability, incapacity; shortcoming, weakness
talisman *n* something worn or kept to bring good luck or keep away evil — see CHARM 1
talk *n* **1** a usually formal discourse delivered to an audience — see SPEECH 1
2 an exchange of views for the purpose of exploring a subject or deciding an issue — see DISCUSSION 1
3 friendly, informal conversation or an instance of this — see CHAT
talk *vb* **1** to give a formal often extended talk on a subject ⟨detective Connolly often *talks* at school assemblies about safety⟩
synonyms declaim, descant, discourse, expatiate, harangue, lecture, orate, speak
related words recite, soliloquize; mouth, spout; filibuster; stump; eulogize
phrases hold forth, take the floor
2 to engage in casual or rambling conversation — see CHAT
3 to express (a thought or emotion) in words — see SAY 1
4 to give information (as to the authorities) about another's improper or unlawful activities — see SQUEAL 1
5 to relate sometimes questionable or secret information of a personal nature — see GOSSIP
talk (into) *vb* to cause (someone) to agree with a

belief or course of action by using arguments or earnest request — see PERSUADE 1

talk (to) *vb* to communicate with by means of spoken words 〈Patty had never *talked to* a real live cowboy before〉
synonyms chat (with), converse (with), speak (to *or* with)
related words accost, address, greet, hail, herald; inform, notify, tell
phrases engage in conversation

talkative *adj* fond of talking or conversation 〈a *talkative* outgoing tour guide showed our school group around the city〉
synonyms chatty, conversational, gabby, garrulous, loquacious, talky
related words communicative, expansive; demonstrative, effusive, gushing; outspoken, unreserved, vocal; articulate, fluent, glib, voluble; blabby, gossipy, talebearing; long-winded, prolix, verbose, windy, wordy; extroverted (*also* extraverted), gregarious, outgoing, sociable
near antonyms quiet, shy; mum, mute, silent, speechless, tongue-tied, wordless; evasive, nonvocal, secretive, self-contained, uncommunicative; aloof, introverted, unsociable, withdrawn
antonyms closemouthed, laconic, reserved, reticent, taciturn, tight-lipped

talker *n* a person who talks constantly — see CHATTERBOX

talk over *vb* to talk about (an issue) usually from various points of view and for the purpose of arriving at a decision or opinion — see DISCUSS

talky *adj* fond of talking or conversation — see TALKATIVE

tall *adj* **1** extending to a great distance upward — see HIGH 1
2 requiring considerable physical or mental effort — see HARD 2

tally *n* a total number obtained or recorded by noting each thing as it was being added — see COUNT 1

tally *vb* **1** to be in agreement on every point — see CHECK 1
2 to gain (as points or runs in a game) as credit towards one's total number of points — see SCORE 2

tame *adj* **1** changed from the wild state so as to become useful and obedient to humans 〈every evening, a Canada goose is at the food trough with our *tame* geese〉
synonyms domestic, domesticated, tamed
related words broken, housebroken, trained; docile, gentle
near antonyms unbroken, untrained
antonyms feral, nondomesticated, undomesticated, untamed, wild
2 causing weariness, restlessness, or lack of interest — see BORING

tame *vb* to keep from exceeding a desirable degree or level (as of expression) — see CONTROL 1

tamed *adj* changed from the wild state so as to become useful and obedient to humans — see TAME 1

tamper (with) *vb* to handle thoughtlessly, ignorantly, or mischievously 〈someone has *tampered with* my computer files〉
synonyms fiddle (with), fool (with), mess (with), monkey (with), play (with), tinker (with)
related words alter, doctor, manhandle, manipulate, misuse; butt in, interfere, intrude, meddle

tan *vb* to strike repeatedly with something long and thin or flexible — see WHIP 1

tangent *n* a departure from the subject under consideration 〈in the middle of her description of her dog's symptoms, she went off on a *tangent* about its cute behavior〉
synonyms digression, excursion
related words aside, parenthesis; rambling; circuitousness, circularity, circumlocution

tangible *adj* capable of being perceived by the sense of touch 〈a firm belief in the existence of the soul, even though it is not at all *tangible*〉
synonyms palpable, touchable
related words tactile; corporeal, physical; actual, concrete, embodied, existent, material, real, substantial; discernible, observable, perceptible, sensible
near antonyms bodiless, immaterial, incorporeal, insubstantial, nonmaterial, nonphysical, unsubstantial; abstract, ethereal, spiritual, unreal
antonyms impalpable, intangible

tangle *vb* **1** to catch or hold as if in a net — see ENTANGLE 2
2 to twist together into a usually confused mass — see ENTANGLE 1

tantrum *n* an outburst or display of excited anger 〈had a *tantrum* when he found his little sister using his model paints〉
synonyms blowup, explosion, fireworks, fit, huff, scene
related words eruption, flare-up, outburst, storm, uproar; agitation, delirium, distraction, frenzy, furor, furore, fury, hysteria, rage, rampage, uproar; convulsion(s), paroxysm, seizure, spasm, upheaval; reaction, rise; dander, temper; pet, pouts, sulk(s)

tap *n* a fixture for controlling the flow of a liquid — see FAUCET

¹tap *vb* to strike or cause to strike lightly and usually rhythmically 〈*tapped* her foot in time to the music〉 〈kept *tapping* the desk with his pencil〉
synonyms beat, drum, rap, thrum
related words bang, hammer, hit, knock, pound, thud, thump, thwack, whack; chink, clatter, clink, ping; pat; chuck, clap, flick, tip

²tap *vb* to remove (liquid) gradually or completely — see DRAIN 1

taper *vb* to grow less in scope or intensity especially gradually — see DECREASE 2

taper off *vb* to grow less in scope or intensity especially gradually — see DECREASE 2

tar *n* one who operates or navigates a seagoing vessel — see SAILOR

tardily *adv* at a pace that is less than usual, desirable, or expected — see SLOW

tardiness *n* the quality or state of being late — see LATENESS

tardy *adj* **1** moving or proceeding at less than the normal, desirable, or required speed — see SLOW 1
2 not arriving, occurring, or settled at the due, usual, or proper time — see LATE 1

target *n* **1** a person or thing that is the object of abuse, criticism, or ridicule 〈Cinderella became the *target* of her stepsisters' envy〉
synonyms butt, mark, sitting duck, victim
related words laughingstock, mockery; fall guy, goat, scapegoat, whipping boy
near antonyms gossip, gossiper, talebearer, tattler, tattletale, troublemaker; defamer, libeler (*or* li-

beller), traducer; baiter, heckler, needler, ribber, taunter, teaser, tormentor; derider, insulter, mocker, ridiculer, scoffer, scorner; caricaturist, lampooner, parodist, satirist

2 a person or thing that is made fun of — see LAUGHINGSTOCK

3 something that one hopes or intends to accomplish — see GOAL

tarnish *vb* to affect slightly with something morally bad or undesirable — see TAINT 1

tarry *vb* **1** to continue to be in a place for a significant amount of time — see STAY 1

2 to move or act slowly — see DELAY 1

3 to reside as a temporary guest — see VISIT 2

tart *adj* **1** causing or characterized by the one of the four basic taste sensations that is produced chiefly by acids — see SOUR 1

2 marked by the use of wit that is intended to cause hurt feelings — see SARCASTIC

tartness *n* **1** a harsh or sharp quality — see EDGE 1

2 biting sharpness of feeling or expression — see ACRIMONY 1

task *n* **1** a piece of work that needs to be done regularly — see CHORE 1

2 the action for which a person or thing is specially fitted or used or for which a thing exists — see ROLE

taskmaster *n* **1** a boss who assigns much work ⟨pitiless *taskmaster* that he was, Ebenezer Scrooge only reluctantly let his ill-paid clerk have Christmas day off⟩

synonyms slave driver

related words enslaver; authoritarian, disciplinarian, discipliner, martinet, stickler; despot, dictator, oppressor, tyrant; dominator, overlord

2 the person (as an employer or supervisor) who tells people and especially workers what to do — see BOSS

taste *n* **1** the property of a substance that can be identified by the sense of taste ⟨Nora can't stand the *taste* of cherry-flavored cough syrup⟩

synonyms flavor, savor

related words relish, smack, tang; savoriness, tastiness; aftertaste

2 a small piece or quantity of food — see MORSEL 1

3 positive regard for something — see LIKING

taste *vb* **1** to come to a knowledge of (something) by living through it — see EXPERIENCE

2 to have a vague awareness of — see FEEL 1

tasteful *adj* having or showing elegance — see ELEGANT 1

tasteless *adj* **1** lacking in refinement or good taste — see COARSE 2

2 lacking in taste or flavor — see INSIPID 1

3 marked by an obvious lack of style or good taste — see TACKY 1

tastelessness *n* the quality or state of lacking refinement or good taste — see VULGARITY 1

tastiness *n* the quality of being delicious — see DELICIOUSNESS

tasty *adj* very pleasing to the sense of taste — see DELICIOUS 1

tatter *vb* to cause (something) to separate into jagged pieces by violently pulling at it — see TEAR 1

tattered *adj* **1** wearing torn or worn out clothes ⟨arrived at the refugee camp *tattered* and exhausted⟩

synonyms ragged, raggedy, ragtag

related words bedraggled, scruffy, shabby, threadbare

near antonyms decked (out), dolled up, dressed up; spiffy

2 worn or torn into or as if into rags — see RAGGED 2

tattle *vb* to relate sometimes questionable or secret information of a personal nature — see GOSSIP

tattler *n* a person who provides secret information about another's wrongdoing — see INFORMER

tattletale *n* a person who provides secret information about another's wrongdoing — see INFORMER

taunt *vb* to attack repeatedly with mean put-downs or insults — see TEASE 2

taunter *n* a person who causes repeated emotional pain, distress, or annoyance to another — see TORMENTOR

taut *adj* stretched with little or no give ⟨a *taut* clothesline⟩

synonyms drawn, rigid, tense, tight

related words firm, inflexible, stiff, tightened, unrelaxed, unyielding

near antonyms drooping, droopy, flaccid, floppy, hanging, lank, limp, loosened, relaxed, slackened, yielding

antonyms lax, loose, slack

tavern *n* **1** a place of business where alcoholic beverages are sold to be consumed on the premises — see BARROOM

2 a place that provides rooms and usually a public dining room for overnight guests — see HOTEL

tawdry *adj* excessively showy — see GAUDY

tawny *adj* of a pale yellow or yellowish brown color — see BLOND

tax *n* a charge usually of money collected by the government from people or businesses for public use ⟨the state sales *tax* boosted the final cost of my new computer⟩

synonyms assessment, duty, imposition, impost, levy

related words custom(s), excise, income tax, poll tax, sales tax, tariff, toll, tribute, withholding tax; surcharge, surtax; revenue

tax *vb* to subject (a personal quality or faculty) to often excessive stress — see TRY (OUT) 2

taxi *n* an automobile that carries passengers for a fare usually determined by the distance traveled — see TAXI

taxicab *n* an automobile that carries passengers for a fare usually determined by the distance traveled ⟨took a *taxicab* to the airport⟩

synonyms cab, hack, taxi

related words hackney; limousine; rickshaw (*also* ricksha)

taxing *adj* requiring much time, effort, or careful attention — see DEMANDING 1

teach *vb* to cause to acquire knowledge or skill in some field ⟨*taught* us about the basics of organic gardening⟩

synonyms educate, indoctrinate, instruct, school, train, tutor

related words coach, mentor, drill, fit, ground, prepare, prime, qualify; direct, guide, lead, rear; catechize, lecture, moralize, preach; implant, inculcate, instill (*also* instil); homeschool; edify, enlighten; brief, familiarize, impart (to), inform, verse; initiate, introduce, show; reeducate, retrain

teacher *n* a person whose occupation is to give formal instruction in a school ⟨a young man who ardently wants to become a *teacher* and teach first grade⟩

synonyms educator, instructor, pedagogue, preceptor, schoolteacher

related words headmaster, master, schoolmaster; headmistress, schoolmarm (*or* schoolma'am), schoolmistress; coach, guide, guru, trainer; mentor, tutor; drillmaster; dean, don, professor; pedant; governess, homeschooler; catechist, lecturer, moralizer, preacher

teaching *n* the act or process of imparting knowledge or skills to another — see EDUCATION 1

team *n* a group of people working together on a task — see GANG 1

team (up) *vb* to participate or assist in a joint effort to accomplish an end — see COOPERATE 1

teamwork *n* the work and activity of a number of persons who individually contribute toward the efficiency of the whole ⟨it takes *teamwork* to pull off a successful fund-raiser⟩

synonyms collaboration, cooperation, coordination

related words fellowship, partnership; community, mutualism, symbiosis; synergism; communion, oneness, solidarity, togetherness, unity

tear *n* a long deep cut — see GASH

tear *vb* 1 to cause (something) to separate into jagged pieces by violently pulling at it ⟨angrily *tore* the letter to shreds⟩

synonyms rend, rip, rive, shred, tatter

related words break, cleave, rupture, split; cut, gash, incise, lacerate, slash; butcher, dismember, dissect, hack, mangle

2 to separate or remove by forceful pulling ⟨*tore* the book from his hand⟩

synonyms rip, wrench, wrest, yank

related words grab, nab, seize, snap (up), snatch; lop (off), nip, jerk; amputate, cut (off), dissever, sever; force, pry

near antonyms reattach

3 to proceed or move quickly — see HURRY 2

tear (out) *vb* to draw out by force or with effort — see EXTRACT

tear down *vb* 1 to bring to a complete end the physical soundness, existence, or usefulness of — see DESTROY 1

2 to destroy (as a building) completely by knocking down or breaking to pieces — see DEMOLISH 1

tearful *adj* 1 given to expressing strong emotion (as sorrow) by readily shedding tears ⟨a *tearful* woman who can be counted on to cry at every wedding, anniversary, and funeral⟩

synonyms lachrymose, teary

related words emotional; maudlin, mawkish, sentimental; bawling, blubbering, crying, keening, sniffling, sniveling, sobbing, wailing, weeping, whimpering; bemoaning, bewailing; doleful, dolorous, grieving, mournful, plaintive; funereal, gloomy, lugubrious; brokenhearted, sad, sorrowful, woeful

near antonyms grinning, laughing, smiling; blithe, blithesome, cheerful, cheery, gay, happy, lighthearted, lightsome, merry, mirthful, sunny

2 causing unhappiness — see SAD 2

teary *adj* 1 causing unhappiness — see SAD 2

2 given to expressing strong emotion (as sorrow) by readily shedding tears — see TEARFUL 1

tease *n* 1 a person who causes repeated emotional

pain, distress, or annoyance to another — see TORMENTOR

2 one who is obnoxiously annoying — see NUISANCE 1

tease *vb* 1 to make fun of in a good-natured way ⟨Hilary liked to *tease* her twin brother about his girlfriend⟩

synonyms chaff, jive, josh, kid, rally, razz, rib, ride, roast

related words banter, joke; fool, fun, string along; jest, quip, wisecrack

2 to attack repeatedly with mean put-downs or insults ⟨some of the boys *teased* Michael because his parents were hog farmers⟩

synonyms bait, bug, hassle, heckle, needle, ride, taunt

related words haze; gibe (*or* jibe), mock, ridicule; annoy, bother, chafe, fret, nag, nettle, irritate, gall, get, gnaw (at), pester, trouble, vex; aggravate, exasperate, goad, test, try; aggrieve, agitate, bedevil, beleaguer, discomfort, disturb, perturb; badger, dog, hound; browbeat, bully, hector; harass, harry, persecute, plague, terrorize, torment, torture

phrases pick on

teaser *n* 1 a person who causes repeated emotional pain, distress, or annoyance to another — see TORMENTOR

2 one who is obnoxiously annoying — see NUISANCE 1

teasing *n* the act of making unwelcome intrusions upon another — see ANNOYANCE 1

technical *adj* used by or intended for experts in a particular field of knowledge ⟨although the owner's manual for the receiver was supposedly written for the average consumer, it's filled with *technical* language⟩

synonyms specialized

related words esoteric, especial, exclusive, limited, narrow, peculiar, restricted, special, specific, unique; authoritative, expert, professional, specialist (*or* specialistic)

near antonyms common, generalized, generic, nonexclusive, nonspecific, ordinary, universal; inexpert, lay, nonprofessional, unprofessional

antonyms general, nonspecialized, nontechnical

technique *n* the means or procedure for doing something — see METHOD

tedious *adj* causing weariness, restlessness, or lack of interest — see BORING

tedium *n* the state of being bored — see BOREDOM

teeming *adj* possessing or covered with great numbers or amounts of something specified — see RIFE

teeny *adj* very small in size — see TINY

teeny-weeny *adj* very small in size — see TINY

teeter *vb* 1 to swing unsteadily back and forth or from side to side ⟨*teetered* at the edge of the pool⟩

synonyms falter, rock, totter, waver, wobble

related words flounder, lurch, stumble, toddle; quaver, tremble; career, reel, stagger, weave

2 to move forward while swaying from side to side — see STAGGER 1

3 to show uncertainty about the right course of action — see HESITATE

telephone *vb* to make a telephone call to — see CALL 2

tell *vb* 1 to give an oral or written account of in some detail ⟨*told* the story of how they had met⟩

synonyms describe, narrate, recite, recount, rehearse, relate, report

related words deliver, give, state, utter, voice; detail, enumerate, itemize, particularize; disclose, divulge, reveal; delineate, depict, express, render, sketch

2 to express (a thought or emotion) in words — see SAY 1

3 to find the sum of (a collection of things) by noting each one as it is being added — see COUNT 1

4 to give information (as to the authorities) about another's improper or unlawful activities — see SQUEAL 1

5 to give information to — see ENLIGHTEN 1

6 to issue orders to (someone) by right of authority — see COMMAND 1

7 to make known (as information previously kept secret) — see REVEAL 1

tell (on) *vb* to act upon (a person or a person's feelings) so as to cause a response — see ¹AFFECT 1

telling *adj* having the power to persuade — see COGENT

telltale *adj* indicating something — see INDICATIVE

telltale *n* a person who provides secret information about another's wrongdoing — see INFORMER

temerity *n* shameless boldness — see EFFRONTERY

temperance *n* an avoidance of extremes in one's actions, beliefs, or habits ⟨Mr. Grindell attributes his ripe old age to *temperance* in all things, especially eating and drinking⟩

synonyms moderateness, moderation, temperateness

related words constraint, control, discipline, restraint, self-control, self-discipline; asceticism, austerity, frugality, mortification, sacrifice, self-denial, self-deprivation; abnegation, abstention, avoidance, eschewal, forbearance; modesty, rationality, reasonableness; abstinence, soberness, sobriety

near antonyms excess, superfluity; extremeness, extremity; unconstraint, unrestraint; extremism, radicalness; irrationality, unreasonableness

antonyms excessiveness, immoderacy, intemperance, intemperateness

temper *n* **1** a special quality or impression associated with something — see AURA

2 a state of mind dominated by a particular emotion — see MOOD 1

3 one's characteristic attitude or mood — see DISPOSITION 1

temperament *n* one's characteristic attitude or mood — see DISPOSITION 1

temperamental *adj* **1** frequently influenced by moods and especially bad moods — see MOODY

2 likely to change frequently, suddenly, or unexpectedly — see FICKLE 1

temperate *adj* **1** avoiding extremes in behavior or expression — see MODERATE 1

2 marked by temperatures that are neither too high nor too low — see CLEMENT

temperateness *n* an avoidance of extremes in one's actions, beliefs, or habits — see TEMPERANCE

tempest *n* **1** a disturbance of the atmosphere accompanied by wind and often by precipitation (as rain or snow) — see STORM 1

2 a violent disturbance (as of the political or social order) — see CONVULSION

tempestuous *adj* **1** marked by bursts of destructive force or intense activity — see VIOLENT 1

2 marked by sudden or violent disturbance — see CONVULSIVE

3 marked by turmoil or disturbance especially of natural elements — see WILD 3

4 marked by wet and windy conditions — see FOUL 1

temple *n* a building for public worship and especially Christian worship — see CHURCH 1

temporal *adj* **1** having to do with life on earth especially as opposed to that in heaven — see EARTHLY

2 not involving religion or religious matters — see PROFANE 1

temporary *adj* **1** intended to last, continue, or serve for a limited time ⟨summer workers look for *temporary* accommodations in private homes⟩ ⟨a *temporary* cook until a permanent replacement can be found⟩

synonyms impermanent, interim, provisional, short-term

related words acting; alternate, proxy, substitute; expedient, improvised, makeshift; intermediary, intermediate, transitional; ephemeral, short-lived, transitory; conditional, contingent, limited, qualified, short-range, tentative; replaceable, terminable

near antonyms final, fixed, set, settled; unconditional, unlimited, unqualified; extended, lasting, long-range, standing; dateless, endless, enduring, eternal, everlasting, perpetual, timeless, unending

antonyms long-term, permanent

2 lasting only for a short time — see MOMENTARY

temporizer *n* one who does things only for his own benefit and with little regard for right and wrong — see SELF-SEEKER

tempt *vb* to lead away from a usual or proper course by offering some pleasure or advantage — see LURE

temptation *n* **1** the act or pressure of giving in to a desire especially when ill-advised ⟨resisted the *temptation* to go sailing and did his chores instead⟩

synonyms allurement, enticement, lure, seduction

related words appeal, attraction; beckoning, invitation; inducement, influence, persuasion, power, sway

2 something that persuades one to perform an action for pleasure or gain — see LURE 1

tempter *n* one that tries to get a person to give in to a desire ⟨there is no greater *tempter* to put off studying than my dog when he wants to play⟩

synonyms baiter, seducer, solicitor

related words enchantress, siren, temptress; briber, inducer, persuader; corrupter (*or* corruptor), debaucher, undoer

temptress *n* a woman whom men find irresistibly attractive — see SIREN

tenable *adj* **1** capable of being defended against physical attack ⟨the soldiers' encampment on the open plain was not *tenable*, so they retreated to higher ground⟩

synonyms defensible

related words defended, guarded, protected, safeguarded, secure, secured, shielded; impregnable, indomitable, invincible, inviolable, invulnerable, unassailable, unbeatable, unconquerable, untouchable

near antonyms assailable, exposed, insecure, li-

able, open, susceptible, undefended, unguarded, unprotected, unsecured, unshielded; defenseless, helpless, powerless, vulnerable, weak
antonyms indefensible, untenable
2 capable of being defended with good reasoning against verbal attack ⟨the *tenable* theory that a giant meteor strike set off a chain of events resulting in the demise of the dinosaurs⟩
synonyms defendable, defensible, justifiable, maintainable, supportable, sustainable
related words rational, reasonable, sensible; acceptable, admissible, allowable, exceptional, legitimate, passable, unobjectionable, viable, warrantable; confirmable, provable, verifiable; explainable, explicable
near antonyms absurd, irrational, ridiculous; extreme, outrageous, unreasonable; groundless, objectionable, unacceptable, unfounded; inexplicable, unexplainable
antonyms indefensible, insupportable, unjustifiable, untenable
tenacious *adj* continuing despite difficulties, opposition, or discouragement — see PERSISTENT
tenaciousness *n* a steadfast adherence to an opinion, purpose, or course of action — see OBSTINACY
tenacity *n* a steadfast adherence to an opinion, purpose, or course of action — see OBSTINACY
tenant *n* one who rents a room or apartment in another's house ⟨the laundry in the basement is for *tenants* only⟩
synonyms boarder, lodger, renter, roomer
related words roommate; guest, visitor; occupant, resident, resider
near antonyms landholder, landowner, proprietor; landlady; slumlord; host, innkeeper
antonyms landlord
¹**tend** *vb* to show a liking or proneness (for something) — see LEAN 2
²**tend** *vb* **1** to take charge of especially on behalf of another ⟨*tend* the store while I run an errand⟩
synonyms attend, care (for), mind, oversee, superintend, supervise
related words direct, manage; guard, patrol, protect, safeguard; baby, baby-sit, chaperone (*or* chaperon), mother, shepherd
phrases look after, see to
near antonyms abandon, disregard, forget, ignore, neglect
2 to look after or assist the growth of by labor and care — see GROW 1
3 to work by plowing, sowing, and raising crops on — see FARM
tendency *n* **1** an established pattern of behavior ⟨a *tendency* to drop things⟩ ⟨a *tendency* to make snap judgements⟩
synonyms aptness, proneness, propensity, way
related words bent, disposition, inclination, leaning, penchant, predilection, predisposition, proclivity; custom, habit, pattern, practice (*also* practise), routine, wont; oddity, peculiarity, quirk, singularity, trick
near antonyms averseness, disinclination, indisposition
2 a prevailing or general movement or inclination — see TREND 1
3 a habitual attraction to some activity or thing — see INCLINATION 1
tender *adj* **1** easily injured without careful handling ⟨a *tender* wound⟩ ⟨*tender* plants that cannot

take the cold⟩ ⟨*tender* pride that got bruised when his girlfriend dumped him⟩
synonyms delicate, fragile, frail, sensitive
related words breakable, brittle; flimsy, puny, soft, weak; nonhardy, perishable, resistless, susceptible, unresistant, vulnerable, yielding
near antonyms durable, firm, flinty, hard, hardy, resistant, robust, rugged, solid, sound, stiff, stout, strong, sturdy, substantial; nonbreakable, unbreakable; hardened, inured, strengthened, tempered, toughened
antonyms tough
2 feeling or showing love — see LOVING
3 having or marked by sympathy and consideration for others — see HUMANE 1
4 lacking bodily strength — see WEAK 1
5 not harsh or stern especially in manner, nature, or effect — see GENTLE 1
tender *n* something (as pieces of stamped metal or printed paper) customarily and legally used as a medium of exchange, a measure of value, or a means of payment — see MONEY
tender *vb* to put before another for acceptance or consideration — see OFFER 1
tenderfoot *n* a person who is just starting out in a field of activity — see BEGINNER
tenderhearted *adj* **1** feeling or showing love — see LOVING
2 having or marked by sympathy and consideration for others — see HUMANE 1
tending *adj* having a tendency to be or act in a certain way — see PRONE 1
tenement *n* a room or set of rooms in a private house or a block used as a separate dwelling place — see APARTMENT 1
tense *adj* **1** feeling or showing uncomfortable feelings of uncertainty — see NERVOUS 1
2 marked by or causing agitation or uncomfortable feelings — see NERVOUS 2
3 stretched with little or no give — see TAUT
tension *n* the burden on one's emotional or mental well-being created by demands on one's time — see STRESS 1
tent *n* a raised covering over something for decoration or protection — see CANOPY
tentative *adj* determined by something else — see DEPENDENT 2
tenure *n* a fixed period of time during which a person holds a job or position — see TERM 1
tepid *adj* **1** showing little or no interest or enthusiasm ⟨the proposed table tennis club met with only a *tepid* response⟩
synonyms halfhearted, lukewarm, uneager, unenthusiastic
related words apathetic, disinterested, dispassionate, indifferent, neutral, uncaring, uninterested; lackadaisical, languid, listless, perfunctory, undemonstrative, unemotional, unresponsive; unfeeling, unsympathetic; chill, chilly, cold, cool, frigid, frosty, glacial, icy, unfriendly, wintry
near antonyms agog, ardent, avid, exuberant, gung ho, impassioned, raring; engaged, engrossed, interested; ready, willing; cordial, friendly, genial, warmhearted
antonyms eager, enthusiastic, hearty, keen, passionate, warm, wholehearted
2 having or giving off heat to a moderate degree — see WARM 1
term *n* **1** a fixed period of time during which a per-

son holds a job or position ⟨elected for a two-year *term* as mayor⟩

synonyms hitch, stint, tenure, tour

related words shift, watch; go, turn; duration, standing, time; cycle, span, spell, stretch; life, life span, lifetime

2 a pronounceable series of letters having a distinct meaning especially in a particular field — see WORD 1

term *vb* to give a name to — see NAME 1

termagant *n* a bad-tempered scolding woman — see SHREW

terminal *adj* following all others of the same kind in order or time — see LAST

terminate *vb* **1** to bring (an event) to a natural or appropriate stopping point — see CLOSE 3

2 to come to an end — see CEASE 1

3 to mark the limits of — see LIMIT 2

terminated *adj* brought or having come to an end — see COMPLETE 2

terminating *adj* following all others of the same kind in order or time — see LAST

termination *n* **1** a real or imaginary point beyond which a person or thing cannot go — see LIMIT

2 the act of ceasing to exist — see DEATH 3

3 the stopping of a process or activity — see END 1

terminology *n* the special terms or expressions of a particular group or field ⟨the *terminology* favored by sportscasters⟩ ⟨medical *terminology* that can be hard for the patient to understand⟩

synonyms argot, cant, dialect, jargon, language, lingo, patois, patter, slang, vocabulary

related words colloquialism, idiom, localism, parlance, pidgin, provincialism, regionalism, speech, vernacular; journalese

terrestrial *adj* having to do with life on earth especially as opposed to that in heaven — see EARTHLY

terrible *adj* **1** causing fear — see FEARFUL 1

2 extreme in degree, power, or effect — see INTENSE

3 extremely disturbing or repellent — see HORRIBLE 1

4 extremely unsatisfactory — see WRETCHED 1

5 of low quality — see CHEAP 2

terribly *adv* to a great degree — see VERY 1

terrific *adj* of the very best kind — see EXCELLENT

terrified *adj* filled with fear or dread — see AFRAID 1

terrify *vb* to strike with fear — see FRIGHTEN

terrifying *adj* causing fear — see FEARFUL 1

territory *n* the place where a plant or animal is usually or naturally found — see HOME 2

terror *n* the emotion experienced in the presence or threat of danger — see FEAR

terrorize *vb* to strike with fear — see FRIGHTEN

terrorized *adj* filled with fear or dread — see AFRAID 1

terse *adj* marked by the use of few words to convey much information or meaning — see CONCISE

tersely *adv* in a few words — see SHORTLY 1

terseness *n* the quality or state of being marked by or using only few words to convey much meaning — see SUCCINCTNESS

test *n* **1** a procedure or operation carried out to resolve an uncertainty — see EXPERIMENT

2 a set of questions or problems designed to assess knowledge, skills, or intelligence — see EXAMINATION 1

test *vb* **1** to put (something) to a test — see TRY (OUT) 1

2 to subject (a personal quality or faculty) to often excessive stress — see TRY (OUT) 2

testament *n* something presented in support of the truth or accuracy of a claim — see PROOF

testify *vb* to make a solemn declaration under oath for the purpose of establishing a fact ⟨Mrs. Pattle was called to *testify* against the man whom she saw stealing her neighbor's car⟩

synonyms attest, depose, swear, witness

related words vouch; vow, promise

phrases bear witness

testify (to) *vb* to declare (something) to be true or genuine — see CERTIFY 1

testimony *n* something presented in support of the truth or accuracy of a claim — see PROOF

testiness *n* readiness to show annoyance or impatience — see PETULANCE

testy *adj* easily irritated or annoyed — see IRRITABLE

tête-à-tête *adv* in person and usually privately ⟨met *tête-à-tête* with the student's parents to discuss his disciplinary problems in class⟩

synonyms face-to-face, personally

related words familiarly, intimately; confidentially, secretly; directly, immediately

phrases in private

near antonyms distantly, indirectly; openly, publicly

tête-à-tête *n* friendly, informal conversation or an instance of this — see CHAT

text *n* a book used for instruction in a subject — see TEXTBOOK

textbook *n* a book used for instruction in a subject ⟨new, up-to-date middle school science *textbooks*⟩

synonyms handbook, manual, primer, text

related words schoolbook; grammar, reader, speller; tract, treatise; dictionary, lexicon, vocabulary, wordbook; encyclopedia, reference; bible, guide, guidebook

textile *n* a woven or knitted material (as of cotton or nylon) — see CLOTH

thankful *adj* feeling or expressing gratitude — see GRATEFUL 1

thankfulness *n* acknowledgment of having received something good from another — see THANKS

thankless *adj* not showing gratitude ⟨a *thankless* guest who complained that my home cooking was not to her liking⟩

synonyms unappreciative, ungrateful

related words rude, thoughtless, ungracious

near antonyms beholden, indebted; gratified, pleased; courteous, gracious, thoughtful

antonyms appreciative, grateful, obliged, thankful

2 not likely to be appreciated by those who benefit ⟨the *thankless* job of cleaning up after a party⟩

synonyms unappreciated

related words uncredited, underrated, undervalued, unnoticed, unrecognized, unrewarded, unsung, unvalued

near antonyms credited, esteemed, honored, prized, recognized, regarded, rewarded, valued; creditable, meritorious, praiseworthy

antonyms appreciated, thanked

THESAURUS

thanks *n pl* acknowledgment of having received something good from another ⟨to express our *thanks*, we'd like to present you with this plaque⟩
synonyms appreciation, appreciativeness, gratefulness, gratitude, thankfulness
related words thanksgiving; gratification, indebtedness, satisfaction; acknowledgment (*also* acknowledgement), recognition, tribute
antonyms ingratitude, thanklessness, ungratefulness

thaw *vb* to go from a solid to a liquid state — see LIQUEFY

thawed *adj* freed from a frozen state by exposure to warmth ⟨recommends cooking *thawed* fish within 24 hours⟩
synonyms defrosted, unfrozen
related words liquefied, melted, molten; deiced; heated, warmed
near antonyms chilled, iced, refrigerated; quick-frozen, refrozen, supercooled; congealed, glaciated, semisolid; frostbitten, frosty, icy
antonyms frozen, unthawed

theater *or* **theatre** *n* **1** a building or part of a building where movies are shown ⟨there's still one *theater* in town that shows movies for two dollars⟩
synonyms cinema, playhouse
related words nickelodeon; multiplex; drive-in
2 the public performance of plays — see DRAMA 1
3 a large room or building for enclosed public gatherings — see HALL 3

theatrical *adj* **1** given to or marked by attention-getting behavior suggestive of stage acting ⟨after stepping out of their hired limousine, the prom couple made a *theatrical* entrance in their evening clothes⟩
synonyms dramatic, histrionic, melodramatic
related words overacted, overdone, sensational, staged; conspicuous, elaborate, flamboyant, grandiose, ostentatious, showy; affected, artificial, exaggerated, formal, mannered, pretentious, self-conscious, studied, unnatural
near antonyms nondramatic, nontheatrical, unaffected, underplayed, unpretentious; muted, restrained, subdued, toned (down); conservative, discreet, inconspicuous; modest, quiet, plain, simple
antonyms undramatic, untheatrical
2 having the general quality or effect of a stage performance — see DRAMATIC 1

theatricals *n pl* the public performance of plays — see DRAMA 1

theft *n* **1** the unlawful taking and carrying away of property without the consent of its owner ⟨*theft* has never been a big problem at our school⟩
synonyms larceny, robbery, stealing, thievery
related words burglary, housebreaking; embezzlement, embezzling, graft, misappropriation; filching, pilfering, purloining, shoplifting; abduction, hijacking, kidnapping, shanghaiing; despoilment, despoliation, looting, pillage, plundering, rapine; poaching, rustling, smuggling; banditry, piracy
2 an instance of theft ⟨the police found the stolen car an hour after the *theft* was reported⟩
synonyms grab, pinch, rip-off, snatching, swiping
related words burglary, holdup, mugging, stickup; confidence game, con game

theme *n* **1** a major object of interest or concern (as in a discussion or artistic composition) — see MATTER 1

2 a short piece of writing done as a school exercise — see COMPOSITION 2
3 a short piece of writing typically expressing a point of view — see ESSAY 1

then *adv* in addition to what has been said — see MORE 1

theoretical *also* **theoretic** *adj* **1** existing only as an assumption or speculation ⟨the merits of the new testing procedures are purely *theoretical*, since no one has ever used them before⟩
synonyms conjectural, hypothetical, speculative, suppositional
related words alleged, assumed, presumed, presupposed, proposed, supposed, unproved, unproven, untested; academic, debatable, moot; abstract, conceptual, intellectual; nonclinical, nonpractical; nonempirical
near antonyms clinical, practical; concrete, defined, definite, distinct; attested, authenticated, confirmed, demonstrated, established, proven, substantiated, tested, time-tested, validated, verified; empirical (*also* empiric), observational
antonyms actual, factual, real
2 dealing with or expressing a quality or idea — see ABSTRACT 1

theory *n* an idea that is the starting point for making a case or conducting an investigation ⟨set out to prove her *theory* that people can't really taste any difference between colas, so they buy according to the product's image⟩
synonyms hypothesis, proposition, supposition
related words assumption, concession, premise, presumption, presupposition; generalization, guess, guesswork, inference, speculation, surmise; proffer, proposal, suggestion; feeling, hunch, impression, inkling, notion, suspicion; abstraction, concept, conception
near antonyms assurance, certainty, fact, knowledge

thereafter *adv* following in time or place — see AFTER

therefore *adv* for this or that reason ⟨it's snowing hard; *therefore* I think we should stay home⟩
synonyms accordingly, consequently, ergo, hence, so, thereupon, thus, wherefore

theretofore *adv* up to this or that time — see HITHERTO

thereupon *adv* for this or that reason — see THEREFORE

thesis *n* an idea or opinion that is put forth in a discussion or debate — see CONTENTION

thick *adj* **1** having or being of relatively great depth or extent from one surface to its opposite ⟨a *thick* board was laid across the pit⟩
synonyms chunky, fat
related words bulky, dense, hefty, thickish; broad, deep, wide
near antonyms narrow, shallow
antonyms skinny, slender, slim, thin
2 being of a consistency that resists flow ⟨*thick* maple syrup for pancakes⟩
synonyms ropy, syrupy, viscid, viscous
related words creamy, heavy, slushy, thickened, thickish, turbid, undiluted; gluey, glutinous, sticky; gelatinous, gooey, gummy, jellylike; concentrated, condensed
near antonyms flowing, fluid; dilute, diluted, liquid, watered (down), weak
antonyms runny, soupy, thin, watery
3 closely acquainted — see FAMILIAR 1

4 having a greater than usual measure across — see WIDE 1

5 having little space between items or parts — see CLOSE 1

6 not having or showing an ability to absorb ideas readily — see STUPID 1

7 possessing or covered with great numbers or amounts of something specified — see RIFE

thick *n* the most intense or characteristic phase of something ⟨in the *thick* of winter many Northerners are dreaming of tropical islands⟩
synonyms deep, depth, height, middle, midst
related words center, heart

thicket *n* a thick patch of shrubbery, small trees, or underbrush ⟨flushed a pheasant from a *thicket* of willows⟩
synonyms brake, brushwood, chaparral, coppice, copse, covert
related words canebrake; brush, bush, scrub, scrubland; bramble, jungle, tangle; grove, hedge, stand, woodlot; forest, greenwood, wildwood, wood, woodland

thickheaded *adj* not having or showing an ability to absorb ideas readily — see STUPID 1

thickness *n* the degree to which a fluid can resist flowing — see CONSISTENCY

thickset *adj* being compact and broad in build and often short in stature — see STOCKY

thief *n* one who steals ⟨sentenced the *thief* who stole Mrs. Stuckey's rosebushes to 30 hours of community service in the municipal rose garden⟩
synonyms pincher, purloiner, robber, stealer
related words burglar, housebreaker; embezzler, grafter; kleptomaniac; pickpocket, pilferer, rifler, shoplifter; abductor, hijacker, kidnapper, skyjacker; despoiler, looter, plunderer, ransacker, ravisher; poacher, rustler, smuggler; bandit, highwayman, pirate; grabber, mugger

thieve *vb* to take (something) without right and with an intent to keep — see STEAL 1

thievery *n* the unlawful taking and carrying away of property without the consent of its owner — see THEFT 1

thin *adj* **1** having a noticeably small amount of body fat ⟨after her bout with pneumonia, she looked *thinner*⟩
synonyms lean, skinny, slender, slim, spare
related words angular, bony, rawboned, scraggy, scrawny, sinewy; lank, lanky, rangy, reedy, spindling, spindly, twiggy, waspish, weedy, willowy, wiry; anorexic, cadaverous, emaciated, gaunt, haggard, pinched, skeletal, wasted, wizened; puny, meager (*or* meagre), slight
near antonyms beefy, bulky, chunky, fleshy, heavy, heavyset, stocky, stout, thick, thickset, weighty; brawny, burly, husky; dumpy, pudgy, roly-poly, squat, stubby; paunchy, potbellied; flabby, soft; buxom; fleshed-out, full, round
antonyms chubby, corpulent, fat, gross, obese, overweight, plump, portly, rotund, tubby

2 being of less than usual width — see NARROW 1

3 not containing very much of some important element — see WEAK 3

thin *vb* to alter (something) for the worse with the addition of foreign or lower-grade substances — see ADULTERATE

thing *n* **1** a member of the human race — see HUMAN

2 one that has a real and independent existence — see ENTITY

3 something done by someone — see ACTION 1

4 something material that can be perceived by the senses — see OBJECT 1

5 something produced by physical or intellectual effort — see PRODUCT 1

6 something that happens — see EVENT 1

7 something that one hopes or intends to accomplish — see GOAL

8 something to be dealt with — see MATTER 2

9 things *pl* transportable items that one owns — see POSSESSION 2

think *vb* to have as an opinion — see BELIEVE 2

think (about *or* over) *vb* to give serious and careful thought to — see PONDER

think (of) *vb* to bring back to mind — see REMEMBER

think (up) *vb* to create or think of by clever use of the imagination — see INVENT

thinker *n* a very smart person — see GENIUS 1

thinking *adj* having the ability to reason — see RATIONAL 1

thinned *adj* **1** containing foreign or lower-grade substances — see IMPURE

2 not containing very much of some important element — see WEAK 3

thirst *n* **1** a strong wish for something — see DESIRE

2 urgent desire or interest — see EAGERNESS

thirst (for) *vb* to have an earnest wish to own or enjoy — see DESIRE

thirsty *adj* **1** marked by little or no precipitation or humidity — see DRY 1

2 showing urgent desire or interest — see EAGER

this *adj* being the less far of two — see NEAR 1

thistly *adj* likely to cause a scratch — see SCRATCHY 1

thorn *n* something that is a source of irritation — see ANNOYANCE 3

thorny *adj* **1** likely to cause a scratch — see SCRATCHY 1

2 requiring exceptional skill or caution in performance or handling — see TRICKY

thorough *adj* **1** having no exceptions or restrictions — see ABSOLUTE 2

2 including many small descriptive features — see DETAILED 1

3 trying all possibilities — see EXHAUSTIVE

thoroughbred *adj* of unmixed ancestry — see PUREBRED

thoroughfare *n* a passage cleared for public vehicular travel — see WAY 1

thoroughgoing *adj* **1** having no exceptions or restrictions — see ABSOLUTE 2

2 trying all possibilities — see EXHAUSTIVE

thoroughly *adv* **1** with attention to all aspects or details ⟨they searched the grounds *thoroughly* for any sign of the intruder⟩
synonyms completely, comprehensively, detailedly, exhaustively, fully, minutely, roundly, totally
related words all-out, full blast, intensively; broadly, extensively, generally, globally, widely; conclusively, consummately, definitely, perfectly
phrases in detail
near antonyms aimlessly, desultorily, haphazardly, hit-or-miss, randomly; cursorily, imperfectly, inadequately, narrowly, shallowly, sketchily, summarily, superficially; indeterminately, nebulously, vaguely

2 to a full extent or degree — see FULLY 1

THESAURUS

though *conj* in spite of the fact that — see AL-THOUGH

though *adv* in spite of that — see HOWEVER

thought *n* **1** a careful weighing of the reasons for or against something — see CONSIDERATION 1
2 something imagined or pictured in the mind — see IDEA

thoughtful *adj* **1** given to or made with heedful anticipation of the needs and happiness of others ⟨a *thoughtful* offer to watch the neighbors' children on moving day⟩ ⟨a *thoughtful* aunt who never forgets the birthday of a niece or nephew⟩
synonyms attentive, considerate, kind, solicitous
related words brotherly, good, good-hearted, helpful, hospitable, kindhearted, kindly, neighborly, nice; caring, compassionate, sympathetic, tender; chivalrous, courteous, courtly, gallant, gracious, polite; diplomatic, tactful; deferential, dutiful, obliging, regardful, respectful; altruistic, beneficent, benevolent, benignant, humane, selfless, unselfish; charitable, generous, magnanimous
near antonyms inattentive, uncaring, unheeding; inhospitable, unkind, unkindly, unneighborly; ill-bred, ill-mannered, impolite, rude, uncivil, uncourteous, unmannerly; unhelpful, unobliging; malevolent, malicious, mean, spiteful
antonyms heedless, inconsiderate, thoughtless, unthinking
2 decided on as a result of careful thought — see DELIBERATE 1
3 given to or marked by long, quiet thinking — see CONTEMPLATIVE

thoughtfully *adv* with good reason or courtesy — see WELL 4

thoughtless *adj* showing a lack of manners or consideration for others — see IMPOLITE

thrall *n* **1** a person who is considered the property of another person — see SLAVE 1
2 the state of being a slave — see SLAVERY 1

thralldom *or* **thraldom** *n* the state of being a slave — see SLAVERY 1

thrash *vb* **1** to achieve a victory over — see BEAT 2
2 to defeat by a large margin — see WHIP 2
3 to strike repeatedly with something long and thin or flexible — see WHIP 1
4 to strike repeatedly — see BEAT 1

thread *vb* **1** to scatter or set here and there among other things ⟨this history book *threads* excerpts from the diaries of pioneer women into its account of the settlement of the West⟩
synonyms interlace, intersperse, interweave, lace, weave, wreathe
related words insert, intermingle, mingle, mix; alternate, juxtapose; amalgamate, assimilate, blend, combine, commingle, embody, fuse, incorporate, integrate, merge
2 to put together into a series by means of or as if by means of a thread ⟨the reporter *threaded* his newspaper articles about the basketball team into a book that was essentially a chronicle of their championship season⟩
synonyms concatenate, string
related words chain, connect, join, link, unite; interlace, intersperse, intertwine, interweave, lace, weave, wreathe

threadbare *adj* **1** showing signs of advanced wear and tear and neglect — see SHABBY 1
2 used or heard so often as to be dull — see STALE
3 worn or torn into or as if into rags — see RAGGED 2

threat *n* something that may cause injury or harm — see DANGER 2

threaten *vb* to remain poised to inflict harm, danger, or distress on ⟨unless the home fans' unacceptable behavior and name-calling stops, the possibility of expulsion from the league *threatens* the school's basketball team⟩
synonyms hang (over), hover (over), impend (over), menace, overhang
related words endanger, hazard, imperil, jeopardize

threatening *adj* **1** giving signs of immediate occurrence — see IMMINENT 1
2 being or showing a sign of evil or calamity to come — see OMINOUS
3 involving potential loss or injury — see DANGEROUS

threefold *adj* having three units or parts — see TRIPLE

threesome *n* a group of three ⟨the *threesome* from Crystal Falls—Jocelyn, Katie, and Lynn—missed their plane and joined up with the rest of the group the next day⟩
synonyms triad, trinity, trio, triple, triplet, triumvirate
related words trilogy; triplicate; triplex

threnody *n* a composition expressing one's grief over a loss — see LAMENT 2

threshold *n* the point at which something begins — see BEGINNING

thrift *n* careful management of material resources — see ECONOMY

thriftless *adj* given to spending money freely or foolishly — see PRODIGAL

thrifty *adj* careful in the management of money or resources — see FRUGAL

thrill *n* a pleasurably intense stimulation of the feelings ⟨everyone gets a real *thrill* out of the Independence Day fireworks⟩
synonyms bang, exhilaration, kick, titillation
related words arousal, electrification, intoxication, stimulation; jolt, shock, surprise; delectation, delight, enjoyment, joy, lift, pleasure; amusement, diversion, entertainment, fun, treat

thrill *vb* to cause a pleasurable stimulation of the feelings ⟨was *thrilled* by the news of Betsy's promotion⟩
synonyms electrify, excite, exhilarate, galvanize, intoxicate, titillate, turn on
related words arouse, incite, inspire, provoke, stimulate; bewitch, captivate, charm, delight, enchant, enthrall (*or* enthral), hypnotize, mesmerize, rivet, spellbind; interest, intrigue, tantalize
near antonyms bore, jade, pall, tire, weary; deject, demoralize, discourage, dishearten, dispirit

thrilling *adj* causing great emotional or mental stimulation — see EXCITING 1

thrive *vb* **1** to grow vigorously ⟨these plants *thrive* with relatively little sunlight⟩
synonyms burgeon, flourish, prosper
related words luxuriate, overgrow, proliferate, shoot up; germinate, root, sprout; bloom, flower, fruit, produce, propagate, regenerate, seed
2 to reach a desired level of accomplishment — see SUCCEED 2

thriving *adj* **1** having attained a desired end or state of good fortune — see SUCCESSFUL 1
2 marked by much life, movement, or activity — see ALIVE 2

3 marked by vigorous growth and well-being especially economically — see PROSPEROUS 1

throaty *adj* **1** harsh and dry in sound — see HOARSE

2 having a low musical pitch or range — see DEEP 2

throb *n* a rhythmic expanding and contracting — see PULSATION

throb *vb* to expand and contract in a rhythmic manner — see PULSATE

throe *n* a sharp unpleasant sensation usually felt in some specific part of the body — see PAIN 1

throng *n* a great number of persons or things gathered together — see CROWD 1

throng *vb* to move upon or fill (something) in great numbers — see CROWD 2

thronging *adj* possessing or covered with great numbers or amounts of something specified — see RIFE

throttle *vb* to keep (someone) from breathing by exerting pressure on the windpipe — see CHOKE 1

through *adv* **1** from beginning to end ⟨read the letter *through* twice⟩ ⟨never once missed class the whole year *through*⟩
synonyms around, over, round, throughout
2 from one side to the other of an intervening space — see OVER 1

through *prep* **1** in or into the middle of — see AMONG
2 in random positions within the boundaries of — see AROUND 2
3 in the course of — see DURING
4 to the opposite side of — see ACROSS
5 along the way of — see BY 1
6 as the result of — see BECAUSE OF
7 using the means or agency of — see BY 2

through *adj* brought or having come to an end — see COMPLETE 2

throughout *prep* **1** in random positions within the boundaries of — see AROUND 2
2 in the course of — see DURING

throughout *adv* **1** from beginning to end — see THROUGH 1
2 in every place or in all places — see EVERYWHERE

throw *vb* to send through the air especially with a quick forward motion of the arm ⟨*threw* a life preserver to the drowning man⟩
synonyms cast, catapult, chuck, dash, fire, fling, heave, hurl, hurtle, launch, lob, loft, peg, pelt, pitch, sling, toss
related words bowl, flip, hook, pass, roll, shoot; buck, eject, impel, precipitate, project, propel, rifle, thrust

throw (on) *vb* to place on one's person — see PUT ON 1

throw away *vb* **1** to get rid of as useless or unwanted — see DISCARD
2 to use up carelessly — see WASTE 1

throwing away *n* the getting rid of whatever is unwanted or useless — see DISPOSAL 1

throw out *vb* **1** to drive or force out — see EJECT 1
2 to get rid of as useless or unwanted — see DISCARD

throw up *vb* **1** to discharge the contents of the stomach through the mouth — see VOMIT
2 to make or assemble roughly or hastily — see COBBLE (TOGETHER)

thrum *n* a monotonous sound like that of an insect in motion — see HUM

thrum *vb* to strike or cause to strike lightly and usually rhythmically — see ¹TAP

thrust *vb* to apply force to (someone or something) so that it moves in front of one — see PUSH 1

thud *n* a hard strike with a part of the body or an instrument — see ¹BLOW

thud *vb* to come into usually forceful contact with something — see HIT 2

thug *n* a violent, brutal person who is often a member of an organized gang — see HOODLUM

thumb *vb* to travel by securing free rides — see HITCHHIKE

thump *n* a hard strike with a part of the body or an instrument — see ¹BLOW

thump *vb* **1** to deliver a blow to (someone or something) usually in a strong vigorous manner — see HIT 1
2 to strike repeatedly — see BEAT 1

thunder *vb* to make a long loud deep noise or cry — see ROAR

thunderous *adj* marked by a high volume of sound — see LOUD 1

thunderstruck *adj* affected with sudden and great wonder or surprise ⟨Colin was *thunderstruck* when his parents told him he was adopted⟩
synonyms amazed, astonished, astounded, awestruck, bowled over, dumbfounded (*or* dumfounded), flabbergasted, shocked, stunned, stupefied
related words startled, surprised; aghast, appalled, dismayed, horrified; bewildered, confused, dazed, overwhelmed; agape, awed, awesome, openmouthed, wide-eyed, widemouthed
near antonyms casual, nonchalant, unruffled
antonyms unawed

thus *adv* for this or that reason — see THEREFORE

thus far *adv* up to this or that time — see HITHERTO

thwack *n* **1** a hard strike with a part of the body or an instrument — see ¹BLOW
2 a loud explosive sound — see CLAP 1

thwack *vb* to deliver a blow to (someone or something) usually in a strong vigorous manner — see HIT 1

thwart *vb* to prevent from achieving a goal — see FRUSTRATE

tick (off) *vb* to specify one after another — see ENUMERATE 1

ticket *n* **1** a small sheet of plastic, paper, or paperboard showing that the bearer has a claim to something (as admittance) ⟨only people with *tickets* will be allowed past the front gates⟩
synonyms check, coupon, pass
related words certificate, note, token, voucher
2 a slip (as of paper or cloth) that is attached to something to identify or describe it — see LABEL

ticket *vb* to attach an identifying slip to — see LABEL 1

tickled *adj* experiencing pleasure, satisfaction, or delight — see GLAD 1

ticklish *adj* requiring exceptional skill or caution in performance or handling — see TRICKY

tidbit *also* **titbit** *n* **1** something that is pleasing to eat because it is rare or a luxury — see DELICACY 1
2 a small piece or quantity of food — see MORSEL 1

tide *n* a prevailing or general movement or inclination — see TREND 1

tidied *adj* being clean and in good order — see NEAT 1

tidings *n pl* a report of recent events or facts not previously known — see NEWS

tidy *adj* **1** being clean and in good order — see NEAT 1

2 of a size greater than average of its kind — see LARGE

3 sufficiently large in size, amount, or number to merit attention — see CONSIDERABLE 1

tie *n* **1** a situation in which neither participant in a contest, competition, or struggle comes out ahead of the other ⟨the competition for first place in the dessert division ended in a *tie* between the chocolate pecan pie and the walnut fudge tart⟩
synonyms dead heat, draw, stalemate, standoff
related words deadlock, impasse; photo finish; toss-up
2 a uniting or binding force or influence — see BOND 2

tie *vb* **1** to gather into a tight mass by means of a line or cord ⟨*tied* the newspapers into a bundle⟩
synonyms band, bind, gird, truss
related words cinch, cord, rope, strap, thread, wire; lash, leash, tether; interlace, intertwine, interweave, lace; entangle, knot, snarl, tangle, twist; coil, wind
near antonyms undo, unfasten, unlace, unlash, unloose, unloosen, unthread; unleash, untether; disentangle, uncoil, untangle, untwine, untwist, unwind
antonyms unbind, untie
2 to produce something equal to (as in quality or value) — see EQUAL 1

tie–up *n* the state of having shared interests or efforts (as in social or business matters) — see ASSOCIATION 1

tie up *vb* to create difficulty for the work or activity of — see HAMPER

tiff *n* an often noisy or angry expression of differing opinions — see ARGUMENT 1

tight *adj* **1** not allowing penetration (as by gas, liquid, or light) ⟨a *tight* hull that was no match for an iceberg⟩
synonyms impenetrable, impermeable, impervious
related words close, compact, dense, snug, thick; airtight, hermetic, watertight; lightproof, soundproof, waterproof
near antonyms absorbent, leaky, porous, unsealed
antonyms penetrable, permeable
2 firmly positioned in place and difficult to dislodge ⟨a *tight* screw that won't come loose⟩ ⟨a jar with a *tight* lid⟩
synonyms fast, firm, frozen, jammed, lodged, secure, set, snug, stuck, wedged
related words bonded, cemented, glued; anchored, clamped; embedded, entrenched (*also* intrenched), implanted; attached, bound, fastened, secured; immovable, unyielding
near antonyms detached, dislodged, freed, loosened, unattached, unbound, undone, unfastened, unsecured; movable (*or* moveable), yielding
antonyms insecure, loose
3 giving or sharing as little as possible — see STINGY 1
4 having little space between items or parts — see CLOSE 1
5 showing little difference in the standing of the competitors — see CLOSE 3
6 stretched with little or no give — see TAUT

tightfisted *adj* giving or sharing as little as possible — see STINGY 1

tight–lipped *adj* tending not to speak frequently (as by habit or inclination) — see SILENT 2

tightness *n* the quality of being overly sparing with money — see PARSIMONY

tightwad *n* a mean grasping person who is usually stingy with money — see MISER

till *vb* to work by plowing, sowing, and raising crops on — see FARM

tiller *n* a person who cultivates the land and grows crops on it — see FARMER

tilt *n* the act of positioning or an instance of being positioned at an angle ⟨indicated her approval with a slight forward *tilt* of her head⟩
synonyms angling, bend, cock, inclination, list, tip
related words turn, twist, veer; bow, dip, nod

tilt *vb* to set or cause to be at an angle — see LEAN 1

tilted *adj* **1** inclined or twisted to one side — see AWRY
2 running in a slanting direction — see DIAGONAL

tilting *adj* running in a slanting direction — see DIAGONAL

timber *n* **1** a dense growth of trees and shrubs covering a large area — see FOREST
2 tree logs as prepared for human use — see WOOD

timberland *n* a dense growth of trees and shrubs covering a large area — see FOREST

time *n* **1** a particular point at which an event takes place — see OCCASION 1
2 an exciting or noteworthy event that one experiences firsthand — see ADVENTURE
3 an extent of time associated with a particular person or thing — see AGE 1
4 the period during which something exists, lasts, or is in progress — see DURATION 1

timeliness *n* the quality or habit of arriving on time — see PROMPTITUDE

timely *adj* **1** especially suitable for a certain time ⟨a *timely* invitation to lunch that came just as I was starting to feel hungry⟩
synonyms opportune, seasonable
related words appropriate, apt, fit, fitting, meet, pat, proper, relevant, suitable; fortunate, lucky, propitious; anticipated, expected; prompt, punctual, undelayed
near antonyms improper, inappropriate, irrelevant, unfit, unsuitable; unfortunate, unlucky; behind, behindhand, belated, delayed, delinquent, late, latish, overdue, postponed, slow, tardy; anticipatory, early, precocious, premature; abrupt, sudden, unanticipated, unexpected
antonyms inopportune, unseasonable, untimely
2 done, carried out, or given without delay — see PROMPT 1

timepiece *n* a device to measure time ⟨the only *timepiece* she used at the cabin was a garden sundial⟩
synonyms chronometer, clock, timer
related words alarm clock, atomic clock, cuckoo clock, grandfather clock, time clock; hourglass, sandglass, sundial, water clock; chronograph, stopwatch, watch

timer *n* a device to measure time — see TIMEPIECE

timetable *n* a listing of things to be presented or

considered (as at a concert or play) — see PRO-GRAM 1

timid *adj* easily frightened — see SHY 1

timidity *n* lack of willingness to assert oneself and take risks ⟨none of the scouts showed the least *timidity* about rappeling down the cliff⟩
synonyms faintheartedness, timidness, timorousness
related words bashfulness, constraint, embarrassment, inhibition, restraint, shyness, skittishness; hesitation, indecision, indecisiveness, irresoluteness, irresolution; alarm, anxiety, apprehension, concern, discomposure, dismay, fear, panic, upset, worry; cowardice, cowardliness, cravenness, spinelessness, yellowness
near antonyms assurance, confidence, self-assurance, self-confidence; composure, coolness, insouciance, nonchalance, unconcern; backbone, decisiveness, determination, fiber, firmness, fortitude, gameness, grit, gumption, mettle, resoluteness, resolution, spunk; bravery, courage, courageousness, daring, dauntlessness, doughtiness, fearlessness, intrepidity, intrepidness
antonyms audaciousness, audacity, boldness, guts, nerve

timidness *n* lack of willingness to assert oneself and take risks — see TIMIDITY

timorous *adj* easily frightened — see SHY 1

timorousness *n* lack of willingness to assert oneself and take risks — see TIMIDITY

tincture *n* a substance used to color other materials — see PIGMENT

tinge *n* a property that becomes apparent when light falls on an object and by which things that are identical in form can be distinguished — see COLOR 1

tinge *vb* to give color or a different color to — see COLOR 1

tingle *n* a sharp unpleasant sensation usually felt in some specific part of the body — see PAIN 1

tinker (with) *vb* to handle thoughtlessly, ignorantly, or mischievously — see TAMPER

tinkle *n* a series of short high ringing sounds ⟨Mrs. Mouse ignored the warning *tinkle* of the cat's bell, and now her children are orphans⟩
synonyms chime(s), jingle, tintinnabulation
related words clatter, jangle, rattle; chink, clang, clank, clink, dingdong, ping, ring, toll; chirr, ripple, trill, warble

tinkle *vb* to make a repeated sharp light ringing sound — see JINGLE

tint *vb* to give color or a different color to — see COLOR 1

tint *n* a property that becomes apparent when light falls on an object and by which things that are identical in form can be distinguished — see COLOR 1

tintinnabulation *n* a series of short high ringing sounds — see TINKLE

tiny *adj* very small in size ⟨the forest ranger showed us how every square foot of forest is alive with *tiny* creatures⟩
synonyms atomic, bitty, infinitesimal, microminiature, microscopic (*also* microscopical), miniature, minute, teeny, teeny-weeny, wee
related words diminutive, dwarf, little, midget, model, petite, pocket, pocket-size (*also* pocketsized), pygmy, small, smallish; dinky, dwarfish, insignificant, pint-size (*or* pint-sized), puny, scrubby, undersized

near antonyms big, bulky, bumper, considerable, extensive, good, goodly, good-sized, grand, great, gross, handsome, hefty, hulking, jumbo, king-size (*or* king-sized), large, largish, major, outsize (*also* outsized), oversize (*or* oversized), sizable (*or* sizeable), substantial, super, whacking, whopping; formidable, grandiose, imposing, lofty, majestic, monolithic, staggering, stupendous, towering; boundless, cavernous, immeasurable, infinite, vast, vasty, voluminous
antonyms astronomical (*also* astronomic), colossal, cosmic, elephantine, enormous, giant, gigantic, herculean, heroic, huge, immense, mammoth, massive, monster, monstrous, monumental, mountainous, prodigious, titanic, tremendous

¹**tip** *n* **1** a piece of advice or useful information especially from an expert ⟨got some *tips* from a horticulturist on how to get my violets to bloom⟩
synonyms hint, lead, pointer
related words advice, advisement, assistance, counsel, guidance, recommendation, suggestion; caution, cautioning, sign, signal, telltale, tip-off, warning; brief, direction, feedback, instruction, observation; prompt, reminder, urging; answer, clue, solution
2 information not generally available to the public — see DOPE 1

²**tip** *n* **1** a small sum of money given for a service over and above what is due ⟨gave our waiter an extra large *tip* for such fantastic service⟩
synonyms gratuity, perquisite
related words donation, gift, lagniappe, largess (*or* largesse), present; bonus, favor, reward; contribution, offering
2 something given in addition to what is ordinarily expected or owed — see BONUS

³**tip** *n* the act of positioning or an instance of being positioned at an angle — see TILT

⁴**tip** *n* the last and usually sharp or tapering part of something long and narrow — see POINT 2

tip *vb* to set or cause to be at an angle — see LEAN 1

tipped *adj* tapering to a thin tip — see POINTED 1

tipping *adj* inclined or twisted to one side — see AWRY

tippler *n* a person who makes a habit of getting drunk — see DRUNK 1

tipsy *adj* being under the influence of alcohol — see DRUNK

tip–top *adj* of the very best kind — see EXCELLENT

tip–top *n* the highest part or point — see HEIGHT 1

tirade *n* a long angry speech or scolding ⟨after the inspection by the health department, Jay had to listen to his boss's *tirade* about keeping the restaurant's kitchen cleaner⟩
synonyms diatribe, harangue, rant
related words assault, attack, invective, lambasting, lashing, tongue-lashing, vituperation; berating, chewing out, rebuke, reprimand, reproach, reproof; abuse, castigation, censure, condemnation, criticism, denunciation; belittlement, deprecation, depreciation, disparagement, dissing; excoriation, execration, revilement; admonishment, admonition, lecture, sermon
near antonyms encomium, eulogy, panegyric, rhapsody, tribute; acclaim, acclamation, accolade, citation, homage, honor, praise; approval, blessing, commendation, endorsement, sanction; ovation, plaudit, rave

THESAURUS

tire *vb* **1** to diminish the physical strength of — see WEAKEN 1

2 to make weary and restless by being dull or monotonous — see ²BORE

3 to use up all the physical energy of — see EXHAUST 1

tired *adj* **1** depleted in strength, energy, or freshness — see WEARY 1

2 having one's patience, interest, or pleasure exhausted — see WEARY 2

3 used or heard so often as to be dull — see STALE

tiredness *n* **1** a complete depletion of energy or strength — see FATIGUE

2 the state of being bored — see BOREDOM

tireless *adj* showing no signs of weariness even after long hard effort ⟨a *tireless* advocate for human rights⟩

synonyms indefatigable, inexhaustible, unflagging, untiring, unwearying, weariless

related words assiduous, conscientious, diligent, meticulous, painstaking, sedulous; determined, dogged, patient, persevering, persistent, pertinacious, plodding, relentless, steadfast, steady, stubborn, tenacious, unabating, unfailing, unfaltering, unflinching, unrelenting, unremitting, unwavering; active, busy, dynamic, energetic, feverish, spirited, vigorous; hard, industrious, intense, laborious, slavish, strenuous

near antonyms indolent, lackadaisical, laggard, lazy, listless, shiftless, slothful, sluggish; apathetic, casual, desultory, languid, spiritless; beat, broken, burned-out (*or* burnt-out), done in, drained, enervated, jaded, overtaxed, overworked, played out, sapped, spent, tuckered (out), wearied, worn-out

tirelessly *adv* with great effort or determination — see HARD 1

tiresome *adj* causing weariness, restlessness, or lack of interest — see BORING

tiring *adj* causing weariness, restlessness, or lack of interest — see BORING

titan *n* something that is unusually large and powerful — see GIANT

titanic *adj* unusually large — see HUGE

titillate *vb* to cause a pleasurable stimulation of the feelings — see THRILL

titillation *n* a pleasurably intense stimulation of the feelings — see THRILL

title *n* **1** a word or combination of words by which a person or thing is regularly known — see NAME 1

2 a word or series of words often in larger letters placed at the beginning of a passage or at the top of a page in order to introduce or categorize — see HEADING

3 the position occupied by the one who comes in first in a competition — see CROWN 2

title *vb* to give a name to — see NAME 1

titter *n* an explosive sound that is a sign of amusement — see LAUGH 1

tittle *n* **1** a very small piece — see BIT 1

2 the smallest amount or part imaginable — see JOT

titular *adj* being something in name or form only — see NOMINAL 1

tizzy *n* a state of nervous or irritated concern — see FRET

to *prep* earlier than — see BEFORE 1

toady *n* a person who flatters another in order to get ahead — see SYCOPHANT

toady *vb* to use flattery or the doing of favors in order to win approval especially from a superior — see FAWN

toast *vb* to cause to have or give off heat to a moderate degree — see WARM 1

toasty *adj* having or giving off heat to a moderate degree — see WARM 1

tocsin *n* **1** an object intended to give public notice or warning — see SIGNAL 1

2 something that tells of approaching danger or risk — see WARNING 2

today *adv* at the present time — see NOW 1

today *n* the time currently existing or in progress — see PRESENT 1

to–do *n* a state of noisy, confused activity — see COMMOTION

together *adv* **1** at one and the same time ⟨the two packages, although sent on different days, arrived *together*⟩

synonyms coincidentally, coincidently, concurrently, contemporaneously, simultaneously

related words close, immediately, narrowly, near

phrases at once

near antonyms apart, independently, individually, singly; consecutively, successively

antonyms separately

2 in or by combined action or effort ⟨working *together*, we can get this project done on time⟩

synonyms conjointly, jointly

related words collectively, mutually, reciprocally, unanimously, unitedly; cooperatively, symbiotically

phrases in concert

antonyms apart, independently, individually, separately, severally, singly, unilaterally

togs *n pl* **1** clothing chosen as appropriate for a specific situation — see OUTFIT 1

2 covering for the human body — see CLOTHING

toil *n* very hard or unpleasant work ⟨after years of *toil* in a sweatshop, Kim was finally able to start her own dressmaking business⟩

synonyms drudgery, grind, labor, slavery, sweat, travail

related words effort, exertion, pains, struggle, trouble; chore, duty, job, obligation, responsibility; routine, tedium, treadmill

near antonyms ease, leisure, relaxation, repose, rest; amusement, diversion, entertainment, recreation, sport; idleness, inactivity, inertia, inertness

antonyms fun, play

toil *vb* to devote serious and sustained effort — see LABOR

toiler *n* a person who does very hard or dull work — see SLAVE 2

toilet *n* a room furnished with a fixture for flushing body waste ⟨we were directed to the *toilets* in the church basement⟩

synonyms bath, bathroom, latrine, lavatory, rest room, washroom, water closet

related words commode; outhouse, privy

toilsome *adj* **1** requiring considerable physical or mental effort — see HARD 2

2 requiring much time, effort, or careful attention — see DEMANDING 1

token *n* something that serves to keep alive the memory of a person or event — see MEMORIAL

tolerable *adj* **1** capable of being endured — see BEARABLE

2 of a level of quality that meets one's needs or standards — see ADEQUATE

tolerably *adv* in a satisfactory way — see WELL 1

tolerance *n* the capacity to endure what is difficult or disagreeable without complaining — see PATIENCE

tolerant *adj* **1** accepting pains or hardships calmly or without complaint — see PATIENT 1

2 receiving or enduring without offering resistance — see PASSIVE

tolerate *vb* to put up with (something painful or difficult) — see BEAR 2

tolerating *adj* receiving or enduring without offering resistance — see PASSIVE

toll *vb* to make the clear sound heard when metal vibrates — see RING 1

tomb *n* a final resting place for a dead person — see GRAVE

tomboyish *adj* having qualities or traits that are traditionally considered inappropriate for a girl or woman — see UNFEMININE

tombstone *n* a shaped stone laid over or erected near a grave and usually bearing an inscription to identify and preserve the memory of the deceased ⟨the many *tombstones* marking the graves of children in the old cemetery reveal the harshness of pioneer life⟩
synonyms gravestone, headstone, monument
related words cross, marker, plaque, stone, table, tablet; monolith, obelisk, pillar; memorial, shrine

tome *n* a set of printed sheets of paper bound together between covers and forming a work of fiction or nonfiction — see BOOK 1

tomfoolery *n* wildly playful or mischievous behavior — see HORSEPLAY

tone *n* **1** a distinctive way of putting ideas into words — see STYLE 1

2 a property that becomes apparent when light falls on an object and by which things that are identical in form can be distinguished — see COLOR 1

3 the set of qualities that makes a person, a group of people, or a thing different from others — see NATURE 1

toned–down *adj* not excessively showy — see QUIET 2

tongue *n* the stock of words, pronunciation, and grammar used by a people as their basic means of communication — see LANGUAGE 1

tonic *adj* having a renewing effect on the state of the body or mind ⟨breathe in clear *tonic* mountain air⟩ ⟨never underestimate the *tonic* power of humor on a sick person⟩
synonyms bracing, invigorating, refreshing, restorative, reviving, stimulating, stimulative, vitalizing
related words conditioning, strengthening; animating, exhilarating, exhilarative, quickening, sharp; corrective, curative, curing, medicinal, rectifying, reformative, reformatory, remedial, remedying, reparative, therapeutic; beneficial, healthful, healthy, helpful, salubrious, salutary, wholesome
near antonyms deadening, debilitating, enervating, enfeebling, exhausting, numbing, sapping, weakening

too *adv* **1** beyond a normal or acceptable limit ⟨Ryan thought the test was *too* hard, but, on the other hand, he hadn't studied for it⟩
synonyms devilishly, excessively, exorbitantly, inordinately, monstrously, overly, overmuch, unacceptably, unduly
related words extravagantly, immoderately, intemperately; extortionately, inexcusably, intolerably, unbearably, unconscionably, unreasonably; improperly, inappropriately; abnormally, extraordinarily, freakishly, singularly, uncommonly, uncustomarily, unusually; astronomically, considerably, eminently, especially, exceedingly, exceptionally, extensively, extra, extremely, incredibly, remarkably, significantly, substantially, super, very, whacking
phrases to a fault
near antonyms acceptably, moderately, modestly, reasonably, temperately; barely, hardly, just, marginally, minimally, scarcely
antonyms deficiently, inadequately, insufficiently

2 in addition to what has been said — see MORE 1

3 to a great degree — see VERY 1

tool *n* **1** an article intended for use in work — see IMPLEMENT

2 one that is or can be used to further the purposes of another — see PAWN 1

3 one who is easily deceived or cheated — see DUPE

tooth and nail *adv* with all power or resources being used — see FULL BLAST

toothsome *adj* very pleasing to the sense of taste — see DELICIOUS 1

top *adj* **1** being at a point or level higher than all others ⟨an office in the *top* story of the building⟩ ⟨the *top* student in our graduating class⟩
synonyms highest, loftiest, topmost, upmost, uppermost
related words higher, loftier, upper; maximized, maximum, peaked, utmost; chief, first, foremost, head, leading, predominant, preeminent, premier, principal; dominant, dominating, eminent, prominent, towering; elevated, escalated, heightened, jacked (up), lifted, raised, uplifted, upraised
near antonyms below, lower, under; low, lowered, low-lying, sunken
antonyms lowermost, lowest, nethermost, undermost

2 of the greatest or highest degree or quantity — see ULTIMATE 1

3 of the highest degree — see FULL 2

4 of the very best kind — see EXCELLENT

top *n* **1** a piece placed over an open container to hold in, protect, or conceal its contents — see COVER 1

2 the highest part or point — see HEIGHT 1

top *vb* to be greater, better, or stronger than — see SURPASS 1

topcoat *n* a warm outdoor coat — see OVERCOAT

topic *n* a major object of interest or concern (as in a discussion or artistic composition) — see MATTER 1

topmost *adj* **1** being at a point or level higher than all others — see TOP 1

2 of the highest degree — see FULL 2

top–notch *adj* of the very best kind — see EXCELLENT

topper *n* something (as a fact or argument) that is decisive or overwhelming — see CLINCHER

topple *vb* to go down from an upright position suddenly and involuntarily — see FALL 1

topsy–turvy *adj* lacking in order, neatness, and often cleanliness — see MESSY

torment *n* **1** a situation or state that causes great suffering and unhappiness — see HELL 2

2 a state of great suffering of body or mind — see DISTRESS 1

THESAURUS

torment *vb* to cause persistent suffering to — see AFFLICT

tormenting *adj* **1** hard to accept or bear especially emotionally — see BITTER 2
2 intensely or unbearably painful — see EXCRUCIATING 1

tormentor *n* a person who causes repeated emotional pain, distress, or annoyance to another ⟨Phillip was relieved when his *tormentor* moved away, and he no longer had to take pains to avoid the bully⟩
synonyms baiter, heckler, mocker, needler, oppressor, persecutor, quiz, quizzer, ridiculer, scoffer, scorner, taunter, tease, teaser, torturer
related words belittler, derider, detractor, insulter; smart aleck, smarty (*or* smartie), wiseacre, wiseguy; lampooner, satirist; accuser, blamer, troublemaker; assailant, attacker, molester; bother, disturber, pest
near antonyms defender, deliverer, protector, rescuer, saviour; comforter, consoler, solace, soother, succorer

torpid *adj* **1** lacking bodily strength — see WEAK 1
2 slow to move or act — see INACTIVE 1

torrent *n* a great flow of water or of something that overwhelms — see FLOOD

torrid *adj* having a notably high temperature — see HOT 1

tortuous *adj* marked by a long series of irregular curves — see CROOKED 1

torture *n* **1** a situation or state that causes great suffering and unhappiness — see HELL 2
2 a state of great suffering of body or mind — see DISTRESS 1

torture *vb* to cause persistent suffering to — see AFFLICT

torturer *n* a person who causes repeated emotional pain, distress, or annoyance to another — see TORMENTOR

torturing *adj* intensely or unbearably painful — see EXCRUCIATING 1

torturous *adj* intensely or unbearably painful — see EXCRUCIATING 1

toss *vb* **1** to make a series of unsteady side-to-side motions — see ROCK 1
2 to make jerky or restless movements — see FIDGET
3 to send through the air especially with a quick forward motion of the arm — see THROW

toss (down *or* off) *vb* to swallow in liquid form — see DRINK 1

total *adj* **1** having no exceptions or restrictions — see ABSOLUTE 2
2 not lacking any part or member that properly belongs to it — see COMPLETE 1
3 trying all possibilities — see EXHAUSTIVE

total *n* a complete amount of something — see WHOLE

total *vb* **1** to have a total of — see AMOUNT (TO) 1
2 to combine (numbers) into a single sum — see ADD 2

totalitarianism *n* a system of government in which the ruler has unlimited power — see DESPOTISM

totality *n* a complete amount of something — see WHOLE

totally *adv* **1** to a full extent or degree — see FULLY 1
2 with attention to all aspects or details — see THOROUGHLY 1

tote *vb* to support and take from one place to another — see CARRY 1

totter *vb* **1** to move forward while swaying from side to side — see STAGGER 1
2 to swing unsteadily back and forth or from side to side — see TEETER 1

tottery *adj* marked by or given to small uncontrollable bodily movements — see SHAKY 1

touch *n* a very small amount — see PARTICLE 1

touch *vb* **1** to come into bodily contact with (something) so as to perceive a slight pressure on the skin ⟨be careful not to *touch* this pan—it's still hot⟩
synonyms feel
related words caress, embrace, finger, fondle, hug, paw, rub, stroke; brush, graze; clasp, clench, cling (to), clutch, grasp, grip, handle, hold, palm; chuck, clap, dab, flick, pat, tag, tap, tip; hit, knock, pound, rap, whack
2 to act upon (a person or a person's feelings) so as to cause a response — see ¹AFFECT 1
3 to affect slightly with something morally bad or undesirable — see TAINT 1
4 to be adjacent to — see ADJOIN 1
5 to be the business or affair of — see CONCERN 2

touch (on *or* upon) *vb* to make reference to or speak about briefly but specifically — see MENTION 1

touchable *adj* capable of being perceived by the sense of touch — see TANGIBLE

touch down *vb* to come to rest after descending from the air — see ALIGHT

touching *adj* **1** having a border in common — see ADJACENT
2 having the power to affect the feelings or sympathies — see MOVING

touch off *vb* to cause to function — see ACTIVATE

touchstone *n* something set up as an example against which others of the same type are compared — see STANDARD 1

touchy *adj* requiring exceptional skill or caution in performance or handling — see TRICKY

tough *adj* **1** not easily chewed ⟨her steak was so *tough* that she suggested the waiter use it as a hockey puck⟩
synonyms chewy, leathery
related words fibrous, gristly, sinewy, stringy; brittle, crunchy, hard
near antonyms mushy, soft
antonyms tender
2 able to withstand hardship, strain, or exposure — see HARDY 1
3 difficult to endure — see HARSH 1
4 requiring considerable physical or mental effort — see HARD 2
5 requiring exceptional skill or caution in performance or handling — see TRICKY

tough *n* a violent, brutal person who is often a member of an organized gang — see HOODLUM

toughen *vb* **1** to increase the ability of (as a muscle) to exert physical force — see STRENGTHEN 1
2 to make able to withstand physical hardship, strain, or exposure — see HARDEN 2

toughened *adj* able to withstand hardship, strain, or exposure — see HARDY 1

toughie *n* a violent, brutal person who is often a member of an organized gang — see HOODLUM

tour *n* a fixed period of time during which a person holds a job or position — see TERM 1

tour *vb* to take a trip especially of some distance — see TRAVEL 1

tourist *n* a person who travels for pleasure ⟨*tourists* from all over like to take pictures of the alligators in the bayou⟩
synonyms excursionist, sightseer, traveler (*or* traveller), tripper [*chiefly British*]
related words holidayer, vacationer, vacationist; guest, visitor; transient; journeyer, pilgrim, wayfarer

tournament *n* a competitive encounter between individuals or groups carried on for amusement, exercise, or in pursuit of a prize — see GAME 1

tourney *n* a competitive encounter between individuals or groups carried on for amusement, exercise, or in pursuit of a prize — see GAME 1

tousle *vb* to undo the proper order or arrangement of — see DISORDER

tousled *adj* lacking in order, neatness, and often cleanliness — see MESSY

tout *vb* 1 to praise or publicize lavishly and often excessively ⟨a new cleaning agent *touted* as the only product a homeowner needs for all his or her cleaning chores⟩
synonyms ballyhoo, crack up, glorify, trumpet
related words advance, advertise, announce, boost, herald, offer, plug, promote, publicize; assert, aver, claim, declare, lay down, make out, proclaim, pronounce
2 to declare enthusiastic approval of — see ACCLAIM
3 to provide publicity for — see PUBLICIZE 1

tow *vb* to cause to follow by applying steady force on — see PULL 1

toward *or* **towards** *prep* having to do with — see ABOUT 1

tower *n* a large, magnificent, or massive building — see EDIFICE 1

towering *adj* 1 extending to a great distance upward — see HIGH 1
2 going beyond a normal or acceptable limit in degree or amount — see EXCESSIVE
3 very dignified in form, tone, or style — see ELEVATED 2

town *n* a thickly settled, highly populated area — see CITY

townie *n* a person who lives in a town on a permanent basis — see BURGHER

toxic *adj* containing or contaminated with a substance capable of injuring or killing a living thing — see POISONOUS

toxin *n* a substance that by chemical action can kill or injure a living thing — see POISON

trace *n* 1 a mark or series of marks left on a surface by something that has passed along it — see TRACK 1
2 a passage cleared for public vehicular travel — see WAY 1
3 a rough course or way formed by or as if by repeated footsteps — see TRAIL 1
4 a tiny often physical indication of something lost or vanished — see VESTIGE
5 a very small amount — see PARTICLE 1

trace *vb* 1 to draw or make apparent the outline of — see OUTLINE 1
2 to go after or on the track of — see FOLLOW 2

tracing *n* the act of going after or in the tracks of another — see PURSUIT

track *n* 1 a mark or series of marks left on a sur-

face by something that has passed along it ⟨a muddy *track* across the kitchen floor⟩
synonyms imprint, trace, trail
related words footprint, footstep, path, print, step, tread; artifact, evidence, leavings, mark, relic, remainder, remain(s), reminder, remnant, residual, residue, sign, spoor, telltale, token, vestige; clue, cue, hint, indication, inkling, intimation, suggestion; scent, shadow, whiff
2 a rough course or way formed by or as if by repeated footsteps — see TRAIL 1
3 the direction along which something or someone moves — see PATH 1

track *vb* to go after or on the track of — see FOLLOW 2

track (down) *vb* to come upon after searching, study, or effort — see FIND 1

tracking *n* the act of going after or in the tracks of another — see PURSUIT

tract *n* 1 a broad geographical area — see REGION 2
2 a small area of usually open land — see FIELD 1
3 a small piece of land that is developed or available for development — see LOT 1

tractable *adj* readily giving in to the command or authority of another — see OBEDIENT

trade *n* 1 a giving or taking of one thing of value in return for another — see EXCHANGE 1
2 an occupation requiring skillful use of the hands — see CRAFT 1
3 the activity by which one regularly makes a living — see OCCUPATION
4 the buying and selling of goods especially on a large scale and between different places — see COMMERCE
5 the transfer of ownership of something from one person to another for a price — see SALE

trade *vb* 1 to carry on the business of buying and selling goods or other property ⟨the U.S. agreed to *trade* with China⟩
synonyms deal, traffic
related words bargain, barter, horse-trade, negotiate, transact; auction, exchange, merchandise, rebuy, resell, swap; buy, purchase; distribute, market, peddle, retail, sell, supply, vend, wholesale; bootleg, fence, smuggle; corner, monopolize, undersell; invest, speculate
near antonyms boycott
2 to give up (something) and take something else in return — see CHANGE 3

trademark *n* 1 a device (as a word) identifying the maker of a piece of merchandise and legally reserved for the exclusive use of that person or company ⟨*Kleenex* is a *trademark* for a cleansing tissue⟩
synonyms brand
related words hallmark, imprint, label, logo, mark, name, service mark, stamp; copyright, patent
2 a device, design, or figure used as an identifying mark — see EMBLEM

trader *n* a buyer and seller of goods for profit — see MERCHANT

tradesman *n* 1 a buyer and seller of goods for profit — see MERCHANT
2 a person whose occupation requires skill with the hands — see ARTISAN

tradition *n* 1 an inherited or established way of thinking, feeling, or doing ⟨the town *tradition* of having the oldest resident ride at the head of the parade⟩

synonyms convention, custom

related words ethic, form, mode, mores, norm, values; birthright, inheritance, legacy; folklore, lore, superstition; culture, heritage, lifestyle

2 the body of customs, beliefs, stories, and sayings associated with a people, thing, or place — see FOLKLORE

traditional *adj* **1** based on customs usually handed down from a previous generation ⟨Ruben had a *traditional* Passover meal at his grandparents' house⟩

synonyms classical, conventional, customary

related words authentic, established, fixed, historical; common, habitual, orthodox, usual; ancestral, historic, old-time, old-world; aged, age-old, ancient, hoary, old, venerable; ageless, dateless, immemorial, timeless

near antonyms contemporary, current, modern, modernized, new, present-day, updated, up-to-date; futuristic, hot, latest, mod, modernistic, newfangled, new-fashioned, red-hot, space-age, ultramodern; nonconformist, nonorthodox, original, progressive, revolutionary, unorthodox, unusual

antonyms nontraditional, unconventional, uncustomary

2 tending to favor established ideas, conditions, or institutions — see CONSERVATIVE 1

traduce *vb* to make untrue and harmful statements about — see SLANDER

traducing *n* the making of false statements that damage another's reputation — see SLANDER

traffic *n* the buying and selling of goods especially on a large scale and between different places — see COMMERCE

traffic *vb* to carry on the business of buying and selling goods or other property — see TRADE 1

trafficker *n* a buyer and seller of goods for profit — see MERCHANT

tragedy *n* a sudden violent event that brings about great loss or destruction — see DISASTER

trail *n* **1** a rough course or way formed by or as if by repeated footsteps ⟨took a *trail* through the woods to get to the main road⟩

synonyms footpath, path, pathway, trace, track

related words bridle path; towpath; bypath, byroad, byway, passageway, walkway; detour, shortcut; course, passage, road, route, run, runway, way

2 a mark or series of marks left on a surface by something that has passed along it — see TRACK 1

trail *vb* to go after or on the track of — see FOLLOW 2

trailer *n* a motor vehicle that is specially equipped for living while traveling — see CAMPER

trailing *n* the act of going after or in the tracks of another — see PURSUIT

train *n* **1** a body of employees or servants who accompany and wait on a person — see CORTEGE 1

2 a group of vehicles traveling together or under one management — see FLEET

3 a series of persons or things arranged one behind another — see LINE 1

4 a series of things linked together — see CHAIN 1

train *vb* **1** to bring to a proper or desired state of fitness — see CONDITION 1

2 to cause to acquire knowledge or skill in some field — see TEACH

3 to fix (as one's attention) steadily toward a central objective — see CONCENTRATE 2

4 to point or turn (something) toward a target or goal — see AIM 1

trainer *n* a person who trains performers or athletes — see COACH

training *n* **1** something done over and over in order to develop skill — see EXERCISE 2

2 the act or process of imparting knowledge or skills to another — see EDUCATION 1

traipse *vb* **1** to go on foot — see WALK

2 to move about from place to place aimlessly — see WANDER

trait *n* something that sets apart an individual from others of the same kind — see CHARACTERISTIC

traitor *n* one who betrays a trust or an allegiance ⟨accused by her family of being a *traitor* when she sold their traditionally animal-friendly business to a competitor known to use animals for testing its products⟩

synonyms apostate, betrayer, double-crosser, quisling, recreant, turncoat

related words collaborationist, collaborator, subversive; conspirator, intriguer, plotter, schemer; defector, deserter, renegade; blabbermouth, gossip, gossiper, informant, informer, rat, snitcher, talebearer, talker, tattler, tattletale

traitorous *adj* not true in one's allegiance to someone or something — see FAITHLESS

trammel *n* something that makes movement or progress more difficult — see ENCUMBRANCE

trammel *vb* **1** to confine or restrain with or as if with chains — see BIND 1

2 to create difficulty for the work or activity of — see HAMPER

tramp *n* a homeless wanderer who may beg or steal for a living ⟨the police encouraged the *tramps* who were sleeping in the park to spend the bitterly cold night in the homeless shelter⟩

synonyms bum, hobo, sundowner [*Australian*], vagabond, vagrant

related words drifter, roamer, transient; beggar, derelict; dodger, malingerer, shirker, slacker; gamine, ragamuffin, urchin, waif

tramp *vb* **1** to move heavily or clumsily — see LUMBER 1

2 to tread on heavily so as to crush or injure — see TRAMPLE

trample *vb* to tread on heavily so as to crush or injure ⟨Isabel looked out her window and beheld the neighbor's Labrador retriever *trampling* her begonias⟩

synonyms stamp, stomp, tramp, tromp

related words override, run down, run over, step (on); mash, smash, squash; boot, kick

trance *n* the state of being lost in thought — see REVERIE

tranquil *adj* **1** free from disturbing noise or uproar — see QUIET 1

2 free from emotional or mental agitation — see CALM 2

3 free from storms or physical disturbance — see CALM 1

tranquilize *also* **tranquillize** *vb* to free from distress or disturbance — see CALM 1

tranquilizing *also* **tranquillizing** *adj* tending to calm the emotions and relieve stress — see SOOTHING 1

tranquillity *or* **tranquility** *n* **1** a state of freedom from storm or disturbance — see CALM

2 evenness of emotions or temper — see EQUANIMITY

transaction *n* the transfer of ownership of something from one person to another for a price — see SALE

transcend *vb* to be greater, better, or stronger than — see SURPASS 1

transfer *vb* **1** to give over the legal possession or ownership of ⟨Claire's grandfather agreed to *transfer* certain stocks to her when she turned 18⟩
synonyms alienate, assign, cede, deed, make over
related words bequeath, hand down, leave, pass down, will; bestow, confer, contribute, deliver, donate, grant, hand over, move, pass, present, release, relinquish, surrender, turn in, turn over, transmit, vest, yield; consign, entrust, trust; lease, lend, loan, rent
2 to cause (something) to pass from one to another — see COMMUNICATE 1
3 to cause to go or be taken from one place to another — see SEND
4 to change the place or position of — see MOVE 1
5 to put (something) into the possession or safekeeping of another — see GIVE 2
6 to shift possession of (something) from one person to another — see PASS 1

transferable *adj* capable of being taken from one place to another by public carrier — see SHIPPABLE

transfiguration *n* a change in form, appearance, or use — see CONVERSION

transfigure *vb* to change in form, appearance, or use — see CONVERT 2

transfix *vb* to penetrate or hold (something) with a pointed object — see IMPALE

transform *vb* to change in form, appearance, or use — see CONVERT 2

transformation *n* a change in form, appearance, or use — see CONVERSION

transfuse *vb* **1** to cause (something) to pass from one to another — see COMMUNICATE 1
2 to spread throughout — see PERMEATE

transgress *vb* **1** to commit an offense — see OFFEND 1
2 to fail to keep — see VIOLATE 1

transgression *n* **1** a breaking of a moral or legal code — see OFFENSE 1
2 a failure to uphold the requirements of law, duty, or obligation — see BREACH 1

transient *adj* lasting only for a short time — see MOMENTARY

transitory *adj* lasting only for a short time — see MOMENTARY

translate *vb* to express something (as a text or statement) in different words — see PARAPHRASE

translating *n* an instance of expressing something in different words — see PARAPHRASE

translation *n* an instance of expressing something in different words — see PARAPHRASE

transmit *vb* **1** to cause (something) to pass from one to another — see COMMUNICATE 1
2 to cause to go or be taken from one place to another — see SEND
3 to put (something) into the possession or safekeeping of another — see GIVE 2

transmittable *adj* **1** capable of being passed by physical contact from one person to another — see CONTAGIOUS 1
2 capable of being taken from one place to another by public carrier — see SHIPPABLE

transparency *n* the state or quality of being easily seen through — see CLARITY 1

transparent *adj* **1** easily seen through — see CLEAR 1
2 not subject to misinterpretation or more than one interpretation — see CLEAR 2
3 very thin and easy to see through — see SHEER 1

transpire *vb* to take place — see HAPPEN

transport *n* **1** a state of overwhelming usually pleasurable emotion — see ECSTASY
2 something used to carry goods or passengers — see CONVEYANCE

transport *vb* **1** to cause to go or be taken from one place to another — see SEND
2 to fill with great joy — see ELATE
3 to fill with overwhelming emotion (as wonder or delight) — see ENTRANCE
4 to force to leave a country — see BANISH 1
5 to support and take from one place to another — see CARRY 1

transportable *adj* capable of being taken from one place to another by public carrier — see SHIPPABLE

transportation *n* **1** a means of getting to a destination in a vehicle driven by another — see RIDE
2 something used to carry goods or passengers — see CONVEYANCE

transpose *vb* to change the place or position of — see MOVE 1

transversely *adv* in a line or direction running from corner to corner — see CROSSWISE

trap *n* **1** a device or scheme for capturing another by surprise ⟨undercover agents devised a *trap* to catch the counterfeiters⟩ ⟨a bear *trap*⟩
synonyms ambush, net, snare, web
related words entanglement, entrapment; booby trap, catch, hazard, pitfall, snag; deception, ploy, ruse, subterfuge, trick
2 a scheme in which hidden persons wait to attack by surprise — see AMBUSH 1

trap *vb* **1** to catch or hold as if in a net — see ENTANGLE 2
2 to take physical control or possession of (something) suddenly or forcibly — see CATCH 1

trash *n* **1** discarded or useless material — see GARBAGE
2 language, behavior, or ideas that are absurd and contrary to good sense — see NONSENSE 1
3 people looked down upon as ignorant and of the lowest class — see RABBLE

trashy *adj* **1** marked by an obvious lack of style or good taste — see TACKY 1
2 of low quality — see CHEAP 2

travail *n* very hard or unpleasant work — see TOIL

travail *vb* to devote serious and sustained effort — see LABOR

travel *vb* **1** to take a trip especially of some distance ⟨loves to *travel* and has been to 34 countries⟩
synonyms journey, peregrinate, pilgrimage, tour, trek, voyage
related words gallivant (*also* galavant), hop, jaunt, knock (about), ramble, roam, rove, traipse, wander; cruise, drive, fly, jet, motor, navigate, sail
2 to make one's way through, across, or over — see TRAVERSE

travel *n, often* **travels** *pl* a going from one place to another usually of some distance — see JOURNEY

traveler *or* **traveller** *n* a person who travels for pleasure — see TOURIST

traveling bag *n* a bag carried by hand and designed to hold a traveler's clothing and personal articles ⟨*traveling bags* made of lightweight but tough fabrics⟩
synonyms carryall, grip, handbag, portmanteau, suitcase
related words carpetbag, duffel bag, kit; backpack, haversack, knapsack, rucksack; attaché case, valise; baggage, bags, luggage

traverse *vb* to make one's way through, across, or over ⟨Julie watched the spider *traverse* the entire wall from floor to ceiling⟩
synonyms cover, crisscross, cross, cut (across), follow, go, pass (over), proceed (along), travel
related words hike, tread, walk; ride

travesty *n* a poor, insincere, or insulting imitation of something — see MOCKERY 1

travesty *vb* to copy or exaggerate (someone or something) in order to make fun of — see MIMIC 1

treacherous *adj* not true in one's allegiance to someone or something — see FAITHLESS

treachery *n* the act or fact of violating the trust or confidence of another — see BETRAYAL

tread *vb* to go on foot — see WALK

treadmill *n* an established and often automatic or monotonous series of actions followed when engaging in some activity — see ROUTINE 1

treason *n* the act or fact of violating the trust or confidence of another — see BETRAYAL

treasure *n* **1** an asset that brings praise or renown — see GLORY 2
2 someone or something unusually desirable — see PRIZE 1

treasure *vb* to hold dear — see LOVE 1

treat *n* **1** a source of great satisfaction — see DELIGHT 1
2 something that is pleasing to eat because it is rare or a luxury — see DELICACY 1

treat *vb* **1** to behave toward in a stated way ⟨she tries to *treat* all of her students fairly and equally, regardless of her personal feelings toward them⟩
synonyms act (toward), be (to), deal (with), handle, serve, use
related words consider, regard; react (to), respond (to)
2 to deal with (something) usually skillfully or efficiently — see HANDLE 1
3 to exchange viewpoints or seek advice for the purpose of finding a solution to a problem — see CONFER 2
4 to give medical treatment to — see DOCTOR 1

treat (of) *vb* to have (something) as a subject matter — see CONCERN 1

treaty *n* a formal agreement between two or more nations or peoples ⟨in accordance with a *treaty* between the United States and the tribes of the Pacific Northwest, commercial fishing of certain kinds of salmon is limited to Native Americans⟩
synonyms accord, alliance, compact, convention, covenant, pact
related words bargain, charter, contract, deal, settlement, understanding

treble *adj* **1** having a high musical pitch or range — see SHRILL
2 having three units or parts — see TRIPLE

trek *n* a going from one place to another usually of some distance — see JOURNEY

trek *vb* to take a trip especially of some distance — see TRAVEL 1

tremble *n* an instance of shaking involuntarily with fear or cold — see SHIVER 1

trembling *adj* marked by or given to small uncontrollable bodily movements — see SHAKY 1

trembling *n* a series of slight movements by a body back and forth or from side to side — see VIBRATION

tremendous *adj* unusually large — see HUGE

tremendously *adv* to a large extent or degree — see GREATLY 2

tremor *n* a shaking of the earth — see EARTHQUAKE

tremulous *adj* marked by or given to small uncontrollable bodily movements — see SHAKY 1

trench *n* a long narrow channel dug in the earth — see DITCH

trenchant *adj* having an edge thin enough to cut or pierce something — see SHARP 1

trend *n* **1** a prevailing or general movement or inclination ⟨according to the survey, there's a growing *trend* for companies to run their own day-care centers for the benefit of employees⟩
synonyms current, drift, leaning, run, tendency, tide, wind
related words curve, shift, swing, turn; custom, habit, propensity, tenor, way
2 a practice or interest that is very popular for a short time — see FAD

trend *vb* to show a liking or proneness (for something) — see LEAN 2

trepidation *n* the emotion experienced in the presence or threat of danger — see FEAR

trespass *n* **1** a breaking of a moral or legal code — see OFFENSE 1
2 a failure to uphold the requirements of law, duty, or obligation — see BREACH 1

trespass *vb* to commit an offense — see OFFEND 1

triad *n* a group of three — see THREESOME

triadic *adj* having three units or parts — see TRIPLE

trial *adj* made or done as an experiment — see EXPERIMENTAL 1

trial *n* **1** a test of faith, patience, or strength ⟨Nancy found living with her cousin a real *trial* and couldn't wait for the summer to end⟩
synonyms cross, crucible, gauntlet (*also* gantlet), ordeal
related words adversity, affliction, asperity, misfortune, mishap, privation, tragedy, tribulation, trouble, vicissitude, woe; challenge, complication, difficulty, grief, hardship, rigor; annoyance, discomfort, inconvenience, nuisance
2 a private performance or session in preparation for a public appearance — see REHEARSAL
3 a procedure or operation carried out to resolve an uncertainty — see EXPERIMENT
4 an effort to do or accomplish something — see ATTEMPT

tribal *adj* of, relating to, or reflecting the traits exhibited by a group of people with a common ancestry and culture — see RACIAL

tribe *n* a group of persons who come from the same ancestor — see FAMILY 1

tribulation *n* a state of great suffering of body or mind — see DISTRESS 1

tribunal *n* an assembly of persons for the administration of justice — see COURT 3

tribute *n* a formal expression of praise — see ENCOMIUM

trice *n* a very small space of time — see INSTANT

trick *n* **1** a clever often underhanded means to

achieve an end ⟨used every *trick* in the book to get out of appearing in the fashion show featuring clothes for teens⟩
synonyms artifice, device, dodge, gimmick, jig, ploy, scheme, sleight, stratagem, wile
related words bluff, deception, feint; fraud, hoax, swindle
2 a playful or mischievous act intended as a joke — see PRANK
3 a usual manner of behaving or doing — see HABIT
4 an act of notable skill, strength, or cleverness — see FEAT 1
5 an odd or peculiar habit — see IDIOSYNCRASY
trick *vb* to cause to believe what is untrue — see DECEIVE
trickery *n* the use of clever underhanded actions to achieve an end ⟨Delia resorted to *trickery*—even loading up the fishing equipment—to induce her dog into the car for his vet appointment⟩
synonyms artifice, chicanery, hanky-panky, jugglery, legerdemain, subterfuge, wile
related words artfulness, caginess, craftiness, cunning, deviousness, foxiness, shadiness, sharpness, shiftiness, slickness, slipperiness, slyness, sneakiness, treachery, underhandedness, wiliness; deceit, deceitfulness, deception, deceptiveness, dishonesty, dissimulation, double-dealing, duplicity, guile, hypocrisy, insincerity; fakery, humbuggery, imposture, quackery; design, plotting, scheming, secrecy, stealth
trickle *vb* **1** to fall or let fall in or as if in drops — see DRIP
2 to flow in a broken irregular stream — see GURGLE
trickster *n* **1** a dishonest person who uses clever means to cheat others out of something of value ⟨a heartless *trickster* swindled the elderly woman out of her life savings⟩
synonyms cheat, cheater, confidence man, cozener, defrauder, dodger, hoaxer, shark, sharper, swindler
related words double-crosser, double-dealer; bluffer, charlatan, fake, faker, humbug, imposter, mountebank, pretender, quack; adventurer, fox, knave, prankster, rascal, rogue; slicker, smoothy (*or* smoothie); plotter, schemer, sneak
2 one who practices tricks and illusions for entertainment — see MAGICIAN 2
tricky *adj* requiring exceptional skill or caution in performance or handling ⟨a *tricky* musical passage for the woodwind section⟩
synonyms catchy, delicate, difficult, knotty, problematic (*also* problematical), spiny, thorny, ticklish, touchy, tough
related words abstract, abstruse, complex, complicated, hard, intricate, involved, recondite; stubborn, troublesome, vexatious, vexing; burdensome, demanding, discommoding, exacting, importunate, inconvenient, onerous, oppressive, painful
near antonyms easy, manageable, painless, straightforward, uncomplicated, undemanding, untroublesome
tried *adj* worthy of one's trust — see DEPENDABLE
tried–and–true *adj* worthy of one's trust — see DEPENDABLE
trifle *n* something of little importance ⟨let us not speak of *trifles* when our nation may be going to war⟩

synonyms child's play, frippery, nothing, triviality
related words naught, nothingness, smoke, zero; molehill, peanuts, pittance, song, straw, two bits; nonsense, trivia
trifle *vb* **1** to show a liking for someone of the opposite sex just for fun — see FLIRT
2 to spend time in aimless activity — see FIDDLE (AROUND)
trifling *adj* **1** lacking importance — see UNIMPORTANT
2 so small or unimportant as to warrant little or no attention — see NEGLIGIBLE 1
trigger *vb* to cause to function — see ACTIVATE
trill *vb* to sing with the alternation of two musical tones — see WARBLE
trim *adj* being clean and in good order — see NEAT 1
trim *n* **1** a state of being or fitness — see CONDITION 1
2 something that decorates or beautifies — see DECORATION 1
trim *vb* **1** to achieve a victory over — see BEAT 2
2 to defeat by a large margin — see WHIP 2
3 to make (as hair) shorter with or as if with the use of shears — see CLIP
4 to make more attractive by adding something that is beautiful or becoming — see DECORATE
trimmer *n* one that defeats an enemy or opponent — see VICTOR 1
trimming *n* failure to win a contest — see DEFEAT 1
trinity *n* a group of three — see THREESOME
trinket *n* a small object displayed for its attractiveness or interest — see KNICKKNACK
trio *n* a group of three — see THREESOME
trip *n* a going from one place to another usually of some distance — see JOURNEY
trip *vb* **1** to go at a pace faster than a walk — see RUN 1
2 to go down from an upright position suddenly and involuntarily — see FALL 1
3 to move with a light bouncing step — see SKIP 1
tripartite *adj* having three units or parts — see TRIPLE
triple *adj* having three units or parts ⟨a *triple* scoop of chocolate ice cream⟩
synonyms threefold, treble, triadic, tripartite, triplex
related words triplicate
triple *n* a group of three — see THREESOME
triplet *n* a group of three — see THREESOME
triplex *adj* having three units or parts — see TRIPLE
tripper *n, chiefly British* a person who travels for pleasure — see TOURIST
trippingly *adv* in a quick and spirited manner — see GAILY 2
trite *adj* used or heard so often as to be dull — see STALE
triumph *n* **1** a successful result brought about by hard work — see ACCOMPLISHMENT 1
2 an instance of defeating an enemy or opponent — see VICTORY
triumph *vb* **1** to achieve victory (as in a contest) — see WIN 1
2 to feel or express joy or triumph — see EXULT
triumph (over) *vb* to achieve a victory over — see BEAT 2
triumphant *adj* **1** having attained a desired end or state of good fortune — see SUCCESSFUL 1

THESAURUS

2 having or expressing feelings of joy or triumph — see EXULTANT

triumvirate *n* a group of three — see THREESOME

trivial *adj* 1 lacking importance — see UNIMPORTANT

2 so small or unimportant as to warrant little or no attention — see NEGLIGIBLE 1

triviality *n* something of little importance — see TRIFLE

troll *n* an imaginary being usually having a small human form and magical powers — see FAIRY

tromp *vb* 1 to move heavily or clumsily — see LUMBER 1

2 to tread on heavily so as to crush or injure — see TRAMPLE

troop *n* 1 an organized group of stage performers — see COMPANY 1

2 **troops** *pl* the combined army, air force, and navy of a nation — see ARMED FORCES

tropical *adj* being near the equator — see LOW 1

trot *vb* 1 to go at a pace faster than a walk — see RUN 1

2 to proceed or move quickly — see HURRY 2

troth *n* 1 a person's solemn declaration that he or she will do or not do something — see PROMISE

2 the act or state of being engaged to be married — see ENGAGEMENT 1

troth *vb* to obligate by prior agreement — see PLEDGE 1

trouble *n* 1 an abnormal state that disrupts a plant's or animal's normal bodily functioning — see DISEASE

2 something that may cause injury or harm — see DANGER 2

3 something that requires thought and skill for resolution — see PROBLEM 1

4 the active use of energy in producing a result — see EFFORT

5 the state of not being protected from injury, harm, or evil — see DANGER 1

trouble *vb* 1 to experience concern or anxiety — see WORRY 1

2 to cause discomfort to or trouble for — see INCONVENIENCE

troubled *adj* feeling or showing uncomfortable feelings of uncertainty — see NERVOUS 1

troublesome *adj* causing worry or anxiety ⟨the *troublesome* news that there will be more cuts in the school budget⟩

synonyms discomforting, discomposing, disquieting, distressing, disturbing, perturbing, troubling, troublous, unsettling, upsetting, worrisome

related words daunting, demoralizing, discomfiting, disconcerting, discouraging, disheartening, dismaying, dispiriting

near antonyms calming, quieting, settling, soothing

antonyms reassuring, untroublesome

troubling *adj* causing worry or anxiety — see TROUBLESOME

troublous *adj* causing worry or anxiety — see TROUBLESOME

trough *n* 1 a long hollow cylinder for carrying a substance (as a liquid or gas) — see PIPE 1

2 a long narrow channel dug in the earth — see DITCH

3 a pipe or channel for carrying off water from a roof — see GUTTER 1

trounce *vb* 1 to achieve a victory over — see BEAT 2

2 to defeat by a large margin — see WHIP 2

trouncing *n* failure to win a contest — see DEFEAT 1

troupe *n* an organized group of stage performers — see COMPANY 1

trouper *n* one who acts professionally (as in a play, movie, or television show) — see ACTOR

trousers *n pl* an outer garment covering each leg separately from waist to ankle — see PANTS

truce *n* a temporary stopping of fighting ⟨both sides agreed to a 24-hour *truce* beginning at midnight on Christmas Eve⟩

synonyms armistice, cease-fire

related words accord, reconciliation; peace, peacetime

truck *n* a giving or taking of one thing of value in return for another — see EXCHANGE 1

truculence *n* an inclination to fight or quarrel — see BELLIGERENCE

truculent *adj* feeling or displaying eagerness to fight — see BELLIGERENT

trudge *vb* to make progress in a clumsy, struggling manner — see FLOUNDER 1

true *adj* 1 being exactly as appears or as claimed — see AUTHENTIC 1

2 being in agreement with the truth or a fact or a standard — see CORRECT 1

3 existing in fact and not merely as a possibility — see ACTUAL

4 firm in one's allegiance to someone or something — see FAITHFUL 1

5 following an original exactly — see FAITHFUL 2

6 free from any intent to deceive or impress others — see GUILELESS

7 restricted to or based on fact — see FACTUAL 1

8 worthy of one's trust — see DEPENDABLE

true–blue *adj* firm in one's allegiance to someone or something — see FAITHFUL 1

truism *n* an idea or expression that has been used by many people — see COMMONPLACE

truly *adv* 1 not merely this but also — see EVEN

2 to tell the truth — see ACTUALLY 1

3 without any question — see INDEED 1

trumpery *adj* of low quality — see CHEAP 2

trumpet *vb* to praise or publicize lavishly and often excessively — see TOUT 1

truncheon *n* a heavy rigid stick used as a weapon or for punishment — see CLUB 1

trunk *n* a covered rectangular container for storing or transporting things — see CHEST

truss *vb* to gather into a tight mass by means of a line or cord — see TIE 1

trust *n* 1 firm belief in the integrity, ability, effectiveness, or genuineness of someone or something ⟨a relationship of mutual *trust* between lawyer and client⟩

synonyms confidence, credence, faith, stock

related words acceptance, assurance, assuredness, certainty, certitude, conviction, positiveness, sureness; credit, dependence, hope, reliance

near antonyms disbelief, incredulity, unbelief; doubt, dubiousness, incertitude, nonconfidence, skepticism, suspicion, uncertainty

antonyms distrust, mistrust

2 a number of businesses or enterprises united for commercial advantage — see CARTEL

3 responsibility for the safety and well-being of someone or something — see CUSTODY

4 the right to take possession of goods before paying for them — see CREDIT 1

trust *vb* **1** to give a task, duty, or responsibility to — see ENTRUST 1

2 to put (something) into the possession or safe-keeping of another — see GIVE 2

3 to regard as right or true — see BELIEVE 1

trustful *adj* having or showing trust in another — see TRUSTING 1

trusting *adj* **1** having or showing trust in another ⟨Delia couldn't look into her dog's *trusting* eyes as she drove him to the vet⟩

synonyms confiding, trustful

related words artless, childlike, credulous, guileless, gullible, innocent, naive (*also* naïve), simple, unsophisticated; dependent, hopeful, reliant; accepting, believing, certain, confident, convinced, overconfident, secure, sure, unquestioning, unsuspecting, unsuspicious, unwary

near antonyms disbelieving, incredulous, unbelieving, unconvinced, unpersuaded; hesitant, leery, oversuspicious, skeptical, suspicious, uncertain, unsure, wary

antonyms distrustful, doubtful, doubting, mistrustful

2 readily taken advantage of — see EASY 2

trustworthiness *n* worthiness as the recipient of another's trust or confidence — see RELIABILITY

trustworthy *adj* worthy of one's trust — see DEPENDABLE

trusty *adj* worthy of one's trust — see DEPENDABLE

truth *n* agreement with fact or reality ⟨there is no *truth* to her accusation that Emory cheated on the test⟩

synonyms factuality, verity

related words accuracy, actuality, authenticity, correctness; credibility, honesty, trustworthiness, truthfulness, veracity; dependability, reliability

near antonyms erroneousness, fallaciousness, fallacy; falsehood, fiction, inaccuracy, incorrectness; deceit, dishonesty, mendacity, untruthfulness

antonyms falseness, falsity, untruth

truthful *adj* being in the habit of telling the truth ⟨a *truthful* youngster who wouldn't just make up a story like that⟩

synonyms honest, veracious

related words candid, frank, open, plainspoken; believable, credible, veritable, true; conscientious, moral, principled, scrupulous; dependable, reliable, trustworthy, trusty

near antonyms fallacious, false, untrue; unbelievable, undependable, unreliable, untrustworthy; bluffing, dissembling, dissimulating, duplicitous, equivocating, hypocritical, insincere, posing, pretending; artful, deceitful, deceptive, devious, slick, slippery, sly, sneaky, treacherous, tricky, underhanded, wily

antonyms dishonest, fibbing, lying, mendacious, prevaricating, untruthful

truthfully *adv* to tell the truth — see ACTUALLY 1

truthfulness *n* devotion to telling the truth — see HONESTY 1

try *n* an effort to do or accomplish something — see ATTEMPT

try *vb* to make an effort to do — see ATTEMPT

try (out) *vb* **1** to put (something) to a test ⟨want to *try out* my new skateboard?⟩ ⟨*tried* his skill at archery⟩

synonyms sample, test

related words check out, examine, experiment (with), explore, feel (out), research

2 to subject (a personal quality or faculty) to often excessive stress ⟨you're *trying* my patience⟩

synonyms strain, stretch, tax, test

related words demand, exact, importune, press, pressure, push; aggravate, agitate, exasperate, get (to), gnaw (at), grate, harass, harry, hassle, irk, irritate, pain, pester

trying *adj* difficult to endure — see HARSH 1

tryst *n* an agreement to be present at a specified time and place — see ENGAGEMENT 2

tubby *adj* having an excess of body fat — see FAT 1

tube *n* a long hollow cylinder for carrying a substance (as a liquid or gas) — see PIPE 1

tucker (out) *vb* to use up all the physical energy of — see EXHAUST 1

tuckered (out) *adj* depleted in strength, energy, or freshness — see WEARY 1

tug *n* the act or an instance of applying force on something so that it moves in the direction of the force — see PULL 1

tug *vb* to cause to follow by applying steady force on — see PULL 1

tug-of-war *n* an earnest effort for superiority or victory over another — see CONTEST 1

tumble *n* **1** an unorganized collection or mixture of various things — see MISCELLANY 1

2 the act of going down from an upright position suddenly and involuntarily — see FALL 1

tumble *vb* **1** to go down from an upright position suddenly and involuntarily — see FALL 1

2 to go to a lower level — see DROP 2

3 to undo the proper order or arrangement of — see DISORDER

tumble (to) *vb* to recognize the meaning of — see COMPREHEND 1

tumbled *adj* lacking in order, neatness, and often cleanliness — see MESSY

tummy *n* the part of the body between the chest and the pelvis — see STOMACH

tumor *n* an abnormal mass of tissue — see GROWTH 1

tumult *n* **1** a state of noisy, confused activity — see COMMOTION

2 a violent disturbance (as of the political or social order) — see CONVULSION

3 a violent shouting — see CLAMOR 1

tumultuous *adj* **1** marked by sudden or violent disturbance — see CONVULSIVE

2 marked by turmoil or disturbance especially of natural elements — see WILD 3

tundra *n* a broad area of level or rolling treeless country — see PLAIN

tune *n* **1** a rhythmic series of musical tones arranged to give a pleasing effect — see MELODY

2 a state of consistency — see CONFORMITY 1

tuneful *adj* having a pleasing mixture of notes — see HARMONIOUS 1

turbid *adj* having visible particles in liquid suspension — see CLOUDY 1

turbulent *adj* **1** marked by bursts of destructive force or intense activity — see VIOLENT 1

2 marked by turmoil or disturbance especially of natural elements — see WILD 3

3 marked by wet and windy conditions — see FOUL 1

turkey *n* **1** a person who lacks good sense or judgment — see FOOL 1

2 a stupid person — see IDIOT

3 something that has failed — see FAILURE 3

THESAURUS

turmoil *n* **1** a disturbed or uneasy state — see UNREST

2 a state of noisy, confused activity — see COMMOTION

turn *n* **1** a relaxed journey on foot for exercise or pleasure — see WALK

2 an act of kind assistance — see FAVOR 1

3 a habitual attraction to some activity or thing — see INCLINATION 1

4 something that curves or is curved — see BEND 1

turn *vb* **1** to move (something) in a curved or circular path on or as if on an axis ⟨*turned* the doorknob as quietly as possible⟩

synonyms pivot, revolve, roll, rotate, spin, swing, swirl, twirl, twist, wheel, whirl

related words screw, unscrew; twiddle; crank, reel, wind; circulate

2 to change the course or direction of (something) ⟨the dog *turned* the stampeding flock of sheep around⟩ ⟨he *turned* his cart uphill⟩

synonyms deflect, divert, swing, veer, wheel, whip

related words avert, move, rechannel, shift, shunt, sidetrack, switch, transfer; swivel, twist, whirl, zigzag; bend, curve, sway; reverse, turn back

3 to change one's course or direction ⟨we *turned* left at the light⟩ ⟨the storm unexpectedly *turned* south and missed our area⟩

synonyms detour, deviate, sheer, swing, turn off, veer

related words tack, zigzag; double (back), turn back

4 to eventually have as a state or quality — see BECOME

5 to move in circles around an axis or center — see SPIN 1

turn (over) *vb* to change the position of (an object) so that the opposite side or end is showing — see REVERSE 2

turn (to) *vb* to use or seek out as a source of aid, relief, or advantage — see RESORT (TO) 1

turncoat *n* one who betrays a trust or an allegiance — see TRAITOR

turn down *vb* to show unwillingness to accept, do, engage in, or agree to — see DECLINE 1

turn in *vb* to go to one's bed in order to sleep — see BED

turning point *n* a point in a chain of events at which an important change (as in one's fortunes) occurs ⟨the *turning point* came when Victor finally admitted he was a werewolf⟩

synonyms climax, landmark, milestone

related words break, clincher, highlight; conversion, metamorphosis, transfiguration, transformation, turnabout, turnaround; clutch, crisis, crossroad(s), crunch, emergency, exigency, head, juncture, zero hour

turn off *vb* **1** to cause to feel disgust — see DISGUST

2 to change one's course or direction — see TURN 3

turn–on *n* something that persuades one to perform an action for pleasure or gain — see LURE 1

turn on *vb* **1** to cause a pleasurable stimulation of the feelings — see THRILL

2 to cause to function — see ACTIVATE

turn out *vb* to come to be — see COME OUT 1

turn over *vb* **1** to give (something) over to the control or possession of another usually under duress — see SURRENDER 1

2 to put (something) into the possession or safekeeping of another — see GIVE 2

turnpike *n* a passage cleared for public vehicular travel — see WAY 1

turn up *vb* **1** to come into view — see APPEAR 1

2 to get to a destination — see COME 2

tussle *n* a physical dispute between opposing individuals or groups — see FIGHT 1

tussle *vb* to seize and attempt to unbalance one another for the purpose of achieving physical mastery — see WRESTLE

tutelage *n* the act or process of imparting knowledge or skills to another — see EDUCATION 1

tutor *vb* **1** to cause to acquire knowledge or skill in some field — see TEACH

2 to give advice and instruction to (someone) regarding the course or process to be followed — see GUIDE 1

tutoring *n* the act or process of imparting knowledge or skills to another — see EDUCATION 1

twain *n* two things of the same or similar kind that match or are considered together — see PAIR

tweet *vb* to make a short sharp sound like a small bird — see CHIRP

twerp *n* a person of no importance or influence — see NOBODY

twice *adv* to two times the amount or degree — see DOUBLY

twilight *n* **1** a time or place of little or no light — see DARK 1

2 the time from when the sun begins to set to the onset of total darkness — see DUSK 1

twin *adj* consisting of two members or parts that are usually joined — see DOUBLE 1

twin *n* either of a pair matched in one or more qualities — see MATE 1

twine *vb* to follow a circular or spiral course — see WIND

twinge *n* a sharp unpleasant sensation usually felt in some specific part of the body — see PAIN 1

twinkle *n* a very small space of time — see INSTANT

twinkle *vb* **1** to shine with light at regular intervals — see BLINK 1

2 to shoot forth bursts of light — see FLASH 1

twinkling *n* a very small space of time — see INSTANT

twirl *n* a rapid turning about on an axis or central point — see SPIN 1

twirl *vb* **1** to move (something) in a curved or circular path on or as if on an axis — see TURN 1

2 to move in circles around an axis or center — see SPIN 1

twist *n* a forceful rotating or pulling motion for the purpose of dislodging something — see WRENCH 1

twist *vb* **1** to change so much as to create a wrong impression or alter the meaning of — see GARBLE

2 to follow a circular or spiral course — see WIND

3 to move (something) in a curved or circular path on or as if on an axis — see TURN 1

4 to move by or as if by a forceful rotation — see WRENCH 1

twisted *adj* marked by a long series of irregular curves — see CROOKED 1

twisting *adj* marked by a long series of irregular curves — see CROOKED 1

twisting *n* a forceful rotating or pulling motion for the purpose of dislodging something — see WRENCH 1

twitch *vb* **1** to make jerky or restless movements — see FIDGET

2 to move or cause to move with a sharp quick motion — see JERK 1

twitching *n* a series of slight movements by a body back and forth or from side to side — see VIBRATION

twitter *n* a state of nervous or irritated concern — see FRET

twitter *vb* **1** to engage in casual or rambling conversation — see CHAT

2 to make a short sharp sound like a small bird — see CHIRP

two–faced *adj* not being or expressing what one appears to be or express — see INSINCERE

twofold *adj* being twice as great or as many — see DOUBLE 2

twosome *n* two things of the same or similar kind that match or are considered together — see PAIR

tycoon *n* a person of rank, power, or influence in a particular field — see MAGNATE

type *n* **1** a number of persons or things that are grouped together because they have something in common — see SORT 1

2 one of the units into which a whole is divided on the basis of a common characteristic — see CLASS 2

typical *adj* **1** having or showing the qualities associated with the members of a particular group or kind ⟨*typical* behavior for a two-year-old⟩
synonyms archetypal, average, characteristic, normal, regular, representative, standard
related words common, conventional, customary, ordinary, usual, wonted; expected, familiar, habitual, predictable, routine, unexceptional, unremarkable; predominant, preponderant
near antonyms uncommon, unconventional, uncustomary, unusual, unwonted; distinctive, especial, exceptional, extraordinary, infrequent, noteworthy, rare, remarkable, singular, special, unexpected, unfamiliar, unique, unpredictable; eccentric, idiosyncratic, nonconformist, peculiar; unknown, unorthodox; curious, funny, odd, queer, strange; bizarre, fantastic, far-out, freak, freakish, out-of-the-way, outrageous, outré, unnatural, weird, wild
antonyms aberrant, abnormal, anomalous, atypical, deviant, irregular, nonrepresentative, nontypical

2 serving to identify as belonging to an individual or group — see CHARACTERISTIC 1

typically *adv* according to the usual course of things — see NATURALLY 2

tyrannical *also* **tyrannic** *adj* **1** exercising power or authority without interference by others — see ABSOLUTE 1

2 fond of ordering people around — see BOSSY

tyrannous *adj* **1** exercising power or authority without interference by others — see ABSOLUTE 1

2 fond of ordering people around — see BOSSY

tyranny *n* a system of government in which the ruler has unlimited power — see DESPOTISM

tyrant *n* a person who uses power or authority in a cruel, unjust, or harmful way — see DESPOT

tyro *n* a person who is just starting out in a field of activity — see BEGINNER

U

ubiquitous *adj* **1** often observed or encountered — see COMMON 1

2 present in all places and at all times — see OMNIPRESENT

ugly *adj* **1** unpleasant to look at ⟨her first attempt at painting was pretty *ugly* —a portrait of her sister that was not at all flattering⟩
synonyms grotesque, hideous, homely, ill-favored, unappealing, unattractive, unbeautiful, unhandsome, unlovely, unpleasing, unpretty, unsightly, vile
related words disgusting, repugnant, repulsive, revolting; unimposing, unprepossessing, unimpressive; plain, unaesthetic, unbecoming, unshapely
near antonyms becoming, bonny [*chiefly British*], cute, shapely; imposing, impressive, prepossessing
antonyms attractive, beauteous, beautiful, comely, cute, fair, gorgeous, handsome, lovely, pretty, stunning, taking

2 causing intense displeasure, disgust, or resentment — see OFFENSIVE 1

ultimate *adj* **1** of the greatest or highest degree or quantity ⟨the *ultimate* speed yet attained by a land-based vehicle⟩
synonyms consummate, maximum, most, nth, paramount, supreme, top, utmost, uttermost
related words unequaled (*or* unequalled), unmatched, unparalleled, unrivaled (*or* unrivalled), unsurpassed; topmost, upmost, uppermost
near antonyms littlest, smallest; lowest
antonyms least, minimal, minimum

2 following all others of the same kind in order or time — see LAST

3 most distant from a center — see EXTREME 1

ultimately *adv* at a later time — see YET 1

ultimatum *n* something that someone insists upon having — see DEMAND 1

ultra *adj* being very far from the center of public opinion — see EXTREME 2

ultramodern *adj* being or involving the latest methods, concepts, information, or styles — see MODERN

ultramodernist *n* a person with very modern ideas — see MODERN

umbra *n* **1** a time or place of little or no light — see DARK 1

2 partial darkness due to the obstruction of light rays — see SHADE 1

umbrage *n* the feeling of being offended or resentful after a slight or indignity — see PIQUE

umpire *vb* to give an opinion about (something at issue or in dispute) — see JUDGE 1

unabashed *adj* not embarrassed or ashamed ⟨*unabashed* by their booing and hissing, he continued with his performance⟩

THESAURUS

synonyms unashamed, unblushing, unembarrassed

related words prideful, proud; bold, brassy, brazen, impudent, insolent, saucy, shameless; unapologetic, undaunted, undeterred, undismayed; unblinking, unflinching, unshrinking

near antonyms discomfited, disconcerted, nonplussed (*also* nonplused)

antonyms abashed, ashamed, embarrassed, shamefaced, sheepish

unacceptable *adj* falling short of a standard — see BAD 1

unacceptably *adv* **1** beyond a normal or acceptable limit — see TOO 1
2 in an unsatisfactory way — see BADLY

unacclimated *adj* not having acquired a habit or tolerance — see UNUSED 1

unaccompanied *adj* not being in the company of others — see ALONE 1

unaccountable *adj* impossible to explain — see INEXPLICABLE

unaccustomed *adj* **1** not having acquired a habit or tolerance — see UNUSED 1
2 not known or experienced before — see NEW 2
3 noticeably different from what is generally found or experienced — see UNUSUAL 1

unachievable *adj* incapable of being solved or accomplished — see IMPOSSIBLE

unacquainted *adj* not informed about or aware of something — see IGNORANT 2

unadapted *adj* not having acquired a habit or tolerance — see UNUSED 1

unadjusted *adj* not having acquired a habit or tolerance — see UNUSED 1

unadorned *adj* free from all additions or embellishment — see PLAIN 1

unadulterated *adj* **1** free from added matter — see PURE 1
2 having no exceptions or restrictions — see ABSOLUTE 2

unadvisable *adj* showing poor judgment especially in personal relationships or social situations — see INDISCREET

unaesthetic *adj* disagreeable to one's aesthetic or artistic sense — see HARSH 2

unaffected *adj* free from any intent to deceive or impress others — see GUILELESS

unaffectedly *adv* without any attempt to impress by deception or exaggeration — see NATURALLY 3

unaided *adv* without aid or support — see ALONE 1

unalike *adj* being not of the same kind — see DIFFERENT 1

unallied *adj* not favoring or joined to either side in a quarrel, contest, or war — see NEUTRAL

unalloyed *adj* **1** free from added matter — see PURE 1
2 having no exceptions or restrictions — see ABSOLUTE 2

unalterable *adj* not capable of changing or being changed — see INFLEXIBLE 1

unambiguous *adj* **1** not subject to misinterpretation or more than one interpretation — see CLEAR 2
2 so clearly expressed as to leave no doubt about the meaning — see EXPLICIT

unanimated *adj* causing weariness, restlessness, or lack of interest — see BORING

unanimity *n* the act or fact of being of one opinion about something — see AGREEMENT 1

unanimous *adj* having or marked by agreement in feeling or action — see HARMONIOUS 3

unanswerable *adj* not capable of being challenged or proved wrong — see IRREFUTABLE

unanticipated *adj* not expected — see UNEXPECTED

unappealing *adj* unpleasant to look at — see UGLY 1

unappeasable *adj* showing no signs of slackening or yielding in one's purpose — see UNYIELDING 1

unappetizing *adj* disagreeable or disgusting to the sense of taste — see DISTASTEFUL 1

unappreciated *adj* not likely to be appreciated by those who benefit — see THANKLESS 2

unappreciative *adj* not showing gratitude — see THANKLESS 1

unapproachable *adj* hard or impossible to get to or get at — see INACCESSIBLE

unapt *adj* **1** not appropriate for a particular occasion or situation — see INAPPROPRIATE
2 not likely to be true or to occur — see IMPROBABLE

unashamed *adj* not embarrassed or ashamed — see UNABASHED

unasked *adj* not searched or asked for — see UNSOUGHT

unassailable *adj* not to be violated, criticized, or tampered with — see SACRED 1

unassisted *adv* without aid or support — see ALONE 1

unassuming *adj* not having or showing any feelings of superiority, self-assertiveness, or showiness — see HUMBLE 1

unattached *adj* **1** not married — see SINGLE 1
2 not physically attached to another unit — see SEPARATE 2

unattainable *adj* **1** hard or impossible to get to or get at — see INACCESSIBLE
2 incapable of being solved or accomplished — see IMPOSSIBLE

unattractive *adj* unpleasant to look at — see UGLY 1

unauthentic *adj* being such in appearance only and made or manufactured with the intention of committing fraud — see COUNTERFEIT

unavailable *adj* hard or impossible to get to or get at — see INACCESSIBLE

unavailing *adj* producing no results — see FUTILE

unavoidable *adj* impossible to avoid or evade — see INEVITABLE

unavoidably *adv* because of necessity — see NEEDS

unaware *adj* not informed about or aware of something — see IGNORANT 2

unaware *adv* without warning — see UNAWARES

unawareness *n* the state of being unaware or uninformed — see IGNORANCE 1

unawares *adv* without warning ⟨the thunderstorm caught us *unawares*, and we scrambled to get off the ridge as lightning started to flash⟩
synonyms aback, suddenly, unaware, unexpectedly
related words abruptly, short
phrases all of a sudden
near antonyms slowly; obviously

unbalance *vb* to cause to go insane or as if insane — see CRAZE

unbalanced *adj* **1** having or showing a very abnormal or sick state of mind — see INSANE 1

2 not being in or able to maintain a state of balance — see UNSTABLE 1

unbaptized *adj* not named or identified by a name — see NAMELESS 1

unbearable *adj* more than can be put up with ⟨this heat is *unbearable* —when are we going to get air-conditioning?⟩
synonyms insufferable, insupportable, intolerable, unendurable, unsupportable
related words unacceptable; crushing, overwhelming; comfortless, harsh, painful, uncomfortable
near antonyms acceptable; adequate
antonyms endurable, sufferable, supportable, tolerable

unbeatable *adj* incapable of being defeated, overcome, or subdued — see INVINCIBLE

unbeautiful *adj* unpleasant to look at — see UGLY 1

unbecoming *adj* not appropriate for a particular occasion or situation — see INAPPROPRIATE

unbeknownst *also* **unbeknown** *adj* happening or existing without one's knowledge — see UNKNOWN 1

unbelief *n* refusal to accept as true — see DISBELIEF

unbelievable *adj* too extraordinary or improbable to believe — see INCREDIBLE

unbeliever *n* a person who is always ready to doubt or question the truth or existence of something — see SKEPTIC

unbelieving *adj* inclined to doubt or question claims — see SKEPTICAL

unbend *vb* to cause to follow a line that is without bends or curls — see STRAIGHTEN

unbending *adj* sticking to an opinion, purpose, or course of action in spite of reason, arguments, or persuasion — see OBSTINATE

unbiased *adj* marked by justice, honesty, and freedom from bias — see FAIR 2

unbidden *also* **unbid** *adj* not searched or asked for — see UNSOUGHT

unbind *vb* **1** to disengage the knotted parts of — see UNTIE
2 to set free (as from slavery or confinement) — see FREE 1

unblemished *adj* being entirely without fault or flaw — see PERFECT 1

unblock *vb* to rid the surface of (as an area) from things in the way — see CLEAR 1

unblushing *adj* not embarrassed or ashamed — see UNABASHED

unborn *adj* of a time after the present — see FUTURE

unbosom *vb* to make known (as information previously kept secret) — see REVEAL 1

unbound *adj* not bound, confined, or detained by force — see FREE 3

unbounded *adj* being or seeming to be without limits — see INFINITE

unbraid *vb* to separate the various strands of — see UNRAVEL 1

unbridled *adj* showing no signs of being under control — see RAMPANT 1

unbroken *adj* **1** going on and on without any interruptions — see CONTINUOUS
2 living outdoors without taming or domestication by humans — see WILD 1

unbudging *adj* incapable of moving or being moved — see IMMOVABLE 1

unburden *vb* **1** to empty or rid of cargo — see UNLOAD 1
2 to set (a person or thing) free of something that encumbers — see RID

unburdened *adj* no longer burdened with something unpleasant or painful — see FREE 2

uncage *vb* to set free (as from slavery or confinement) — see FREE 1

uncalled–for *adj* **1** not needed by the circumstances or to accomplish an end — see UNNECESSARY
2 showing a lack of manners or consideration for others — see IMPOLITE

uncanny *adj* **1** being beyond one's powers to know, understand, or explain — see MYSTERIOUS 1
2 being so extraordinary or abnormal as to suggest powers which violate the laws of nature — see SUPERNATURAL 2
3 fearfully and mysteriously strange or fantastic — see EERIE

uncataloged *adj* not appearing on a list — see UNLISTED

unceasing *adj* going on and on without any interruptions — see CONTINUOUS

uncelebrated *adj* not widely known — see OBSCURE 2

unceremonious *adj* not rigidly following established form, custom, or rules — see INFORMAL 1

uncertain *adj* **1** likely to change frequently, suddenly, or unexpectedly — see FICKLE 1
2 not feeling sure about the truth, wisdom, or trustworthiness of someone or something — see DOUBTFUL 1

uncertainty *n* a feeling or attitude that one does not know the truth, truthfulness, or trustworthiness of someone or something — see DOUBT

unchain *vb* to set free (as from slavery or confinement) — see FREE 1

unchangeable *adj* not capable of changing or being changed — see INFLEXIBLE 1

unchangeableness *n* the state of continuing without change — see CONSTANCY 1

unchanging *adj* **1** not undergoing a change in condition — see CONSTANT 1
2 not varying — see UNIFORM

uncharitable *adj* **1** giving or sharing as little as possible — see STINGY 1
2 having or showing a lack of sympathy or tender feelings — see HARD 1

unchecked *adj* showing no signs of being under control — see RAMPANT 1

unchristened *adj* not named or identified by a name — see NAMELESS 1

uncivil *adj* **1** not civilized — see SAVAGE 1
2 showing a lack of manners or consideration for others — see IMPOLITE

uncivilized *adj* not civilized — see SAVAGE

unclad *adj* lacking or shed of clothing — see NAKED 1

unclean *adj* not clean — see DIRTY 1

uncleanliness *n* the state or quality of being dirty — see DIRTINESS 1

uncleanly *adj* not clean — see DIRTY 1

uncleanness *n* the state or quality of being dirty — see DIRTINESS 1

unclear *adj* **1** not clearly expressed — see VAGUE 1
2 not seen or understood clearly — see FAINT 1

uncloak *vb* **1** to make known (as information previously kept secret) — see REVEAL 1
2 to reveal the true nature of — see EXPOSE 1

THESAURUS

unclog *vb* **1** to arrange clear passage of (something) by removing obstructions — see OPEN 2
2 to free from obstruction or difficulty — see EASE 1

unclogged *adj* allowing passage without obstruction — see OPEN 1

unclose *vb* to change from a closed to an open position — see OPEN 1

unclosed *adj* allowing passage without obstruction — see OPEN 1

unclothe *vb* to remove clothing from — see UNDRESS

unclothed *adj* lacking or shed of clothing — see NAKED 1

unclouded *adj* not stormy or cloudy — see FAIR 1

uncluttered *adj* being clean and in good order — see NEAT 1

uncolored *adj* lacking an addition of color — see COLORLESS

uncomfortable *adj* **1** causing discomfort ⟨unfortunately, dressing up for the dance meant wearing an *uncomfortable* shirt⟩
synonyms comfortless, discomforting, harsh
related words aching, hurting, nasty, painful, sore; distressing, disturbing, upsetting; awkward, cumbersome, inconvenient, ungainly; uneasy
near antonyms easy, soothing; cozy, snug
antonyms comfortable
2 causing embarrassment — see AWKWARD 3
3 lacking social grace and assurance — see AWKWARD 1

uncomic *adj* not joking or playful in mood or manner — see SERIOUS 1

uncommon *adj* **1** being out of the ordinary — see EXCEPTIONAL
2 noticeably different from what is generally found or experienced — see UNUSUAL 1

uncommunicative *adj* **1** deliberately refraining from speech — see SILENT 1
2 given to keeping one's activities hidden from public observation or knowledge — see SECRETIVE
3 tending not to speak frequently (as by habit or inclination) — see SILENT 2

uncomplaining *adj* accepting pains or hardships calmly or without complaint — see PATIENT 1

uncomplimentary *adj* intended to make a person or thing seem of little importance or value — see DEROGATORY

uncompromising *adj* **1** not allowing for any exceptions or loosening of standards — see RIGID 1
2 sticking to an opinion, purpose, or course of action in spite of reason, arguments, or persuasion — see OBSTINATE

unconcern *n* lack of interest or concern — see INDIFFERENCE

unconcerned *adj* **1** having or showing a lack of concern or seriousness — see CAREFREE
2 having or showing a lack of interest or concern — see INDIFFERENT 1

unconditional *adj* having no exceptions or restrictions — see ABSOLUTE 2

unconfined *adj* not bound, confined, or detained by force — see FREE 3

uncongenial *adj* not giving pleasure to the mind or senses — see UNPLEASANT

unconnected *adj* **1** not clearly or logically connected — see INCOHERENT 1
2 not physically attached to another unit — see SEPARATE 2

unconquerable *adj* incapable of being defeated, overcome, or subdued — see INVINCIBLE

unconscionable *adj* **1** going beyond a normal or acceptable limit in degree or amount — see EXCESSIVE
2 not guided by or showing a concern for what is right — see UNPRINCIPLED

unconscious *adj* **1** having lost consciousness ⟨the guard was knocked *unconscious* by a blow to the head⟩
synonyms cold, insensible, senseless
related words semiconscious; anesthetized
near antonyms alert, awake, aware, up
antonyms conscious
2 not informed about or aware of something — see IGNORANT 2

unconsidered *adj* made or done without previous thought or preparation — see EXTEMPORANEOUS

unconsolidated *adj* consisting of particles that do not stick together — see LOOSE 2

uncontrollable *adj* given to resisting control or discipline by others ⟨the *uncontrollable* child kept throwing tantrums in public and creating scenes⟩
synonyms froward, headstrong, intractable, recalcitrant, refractory, ungovernable, unmanageable, unruly, untoward, wayward, willful (*or* wilful)
related words contrary, incorrigible, obstinate, perverse, self-willed, stubborn; undisciplined, unpunished; uncontrolled, ungoverned, wild; boisterous, rambunctious, rowdy; disobedient, insubordinate, rebellious; misbehaving, naughty
phrases out of hand
near antonyms docile, obedient, well-behaved; compliant, submissive, yielding
antonyms controllable, governable, tractable

uncontrolled *adj* showing no signs of being under control — see RAMPANT 1

unconventional *adj* **1** deviating from commonly accepted beliefs or practices — see HERETICAL
2 not bound by traditional ways or beliefs — see LIBERAL 1
3 not rigidly following established form, custom, or rules — see INFORMAL 1

unconvinced *adj* not feeling sure about the truth, wisdom, or trustworthiness of someone or something — see DOUBTFUL 1

unconvincing *adj* too extraordinary or improbable to believe — see INCREDIBLE

uncooked *adj* not cooked — see RAW 1

uncordial *adj* lacking in friendliness or warmth of feeling — see COLD 2

uncork *vb* to set free (from a state of being held in check) — see RELEASE 1

uncountable *adj* too many to be counted — see COUNTLESS

uncounted *adj* too many to be counted — see COUNTLESS

uncouple *vb* to set or force apart — see SEPARATE 1

uncouth *adj* **1** having or showing crudely insensitive or impolite manners — see CLOWNISH
2 lacking in refinement or good taste — see COARSE 2

uncover *vb* **1** to make known (as information previously kept secret) — see REVEAL 1
2 to reveal the true nature of — see EXPOSE 1

uncovered *adj* lacking a usual or natural covering — see NAKED 2

uncritical *adj* lacking in worldly wisdom or informed judgment — see NAIVE 1

uncrown *vb* to remove from a position of prominence or power (as a throne) — see DEPOSE 1

unctuous *adj* **1** not being or expressing what one appears to be or express — see INSINCERE

2 overly or insincerely flattering — see FULSOME

uncultivated *adj* **1** existing without human habitation or cultivation — see WILD 2

2 lacking in refinement or good taste — see COARSE 2

3 not civilized — see SAVAGE 1

uncultured *adj* lacking in refinement or good taste — see COARSE 2

uncurbed *adj* showing no signs of being under control — see RAMPANT 1

uncurious *adj* having or showing a lack of interest or concern — see INDIFFERENT 1

uncurl *vb* to cause to follow a line that is without bends or curls — see STRAIGHTEN

uncustomary *adj* **1** being out of the ordinary — see EXCEPTIONAL

2 noticeably different from what is generally found or experienced — see UNUSUAL 1

undaunted *adj* feeling or displaying no fear by temperament — see BRAVE

undeceive *vb* to free from mistaken beliefs or foolish hopes — see DISILLUSION

undecided *adj* **1** not yet settled or decided — see PENDING 1

2 not feeling sure about the truth, wisdom, or trustworthiness of someone or something — see DOUBTFUL 1

undecorated *adj* free from all additions or embellishment — see PLAIN 1

undefended *adj* lacking protection from danger or resistance against attack — see HELPLESS 1

undefined *adj* not seen or understood clearly — see FAINT 1

undemonstrative *adj* not feeling or showing emotion — see IMPASSIVE 1

undeniable *adj* not capable of being challenged or proved wrong — see IRREFUTABLE

undeniably *adv* without any question — see INDEED 1

under *adj* having not so great importance or rank as another — see LESSER

under *adv* in or to a lower place — see BELOW 1

under *prep* in a lower position than — see BELOW

underbelly *n* the side or part facing downward from something — see BOTTOM 1

underbody *n* the side or part facing downward from something — see BOTTOM 1

underclothes *n pl* clothing intended to be worn underneath other clothing — see UNDERWEAR

underclothing *n* clothing intended to be worn underneath other clothing — see UNDERWEAR

undercover *adj* **1** undertaken or done so as to escape being observed or known by others — see SECRET 1

2 working on missions in which one's objectives, activities, or true identity are not publicly revealed — see SECRET 2

undergarments *n pl* clothing intended to be worn underneath other clothing — see UNDERWEAR

undergo *vb* to come to a knowledge of (something) by living through it — see EXPERIENCE

underground *adj* undertaken or done so as to escape being observed or known by others — see SECRET 1

underground *n* a secret organization in a conquered country fighting against enemy forces — see RESISTANCE 2

underhand *adj* **1** given to or marked by cheating and deception — see DISHONEST 2

2 undertaken or done so as to escape being observed or known by others — see SECRET 1

underhanded *adj* **1** given to or marked by cheating and deception — see DISHONEST 2

2 undertaken or done so as to escape being observed or known by others — see SECRET 1

underline *vb* to indicate the importance of by giving prominent display — see EMPHASIZE

underling *n* one who is of lower rank and typically under the authority of another ⟨he instructed his *underlings* to carry out the order immediately⟩

synonyms inferior, junior, subordinate

related words attendant, follower, retainer; domestic, menial, steward; flunky (*also* flunkey), henchman, lackey, minion; adjutant, aid, aide, assistant, coadjutor, deputy, second; helpmate, helpmeet, mate, sidekick

near antonyms boss, captain, chief, foreman, head, headman, helmsman, kingpin, leader, master, taskmaster

antonyms senior, superior

underlying *adj* of or relating to the simplest facts or theories of a subject — see ELEMENTARY

underneath *adv* in or to a lower place — see BELOW 1

underpin *vb* to hold up or serve as a foundation for — see SUPPORT 3

underpinning *n* **1** an immaterial thing upon which something else rests — see BASE 1

2 something that holds up or serves as a foundation for something else — see SUPPORT 1

underprivileged *adj* kept from having the necessities of life or a healthful environment — see DEPRIVED

underscore *vb* to indicate the importance of by giving prominent display — see EMPHASIZE

underside *n* the side or part facing downward from something — see BOTTOM 1

undersized *adj* of a size that is less than average — see SMALL 1

understand *vb* **1** to form an opinion through reasoning and information — see INFER 1

2 to have a practical understanding of — see KNOW 1

3 to recognize the meaning of — see COMPREHEND 1

understanding *adj* having or showing the capacity for sharing the feelings of another — see SYMPATHETIC 1

understanding *n* **1** an arrangement about action to be taken — see AGREEMENT 2

2 the knowledge gained from the process of coming to know or understand something — see COMPREHENSION

understated *adj* not excessively showy — see QUIET 2

undersurface *n* the side or part facing downward from something — see BOTTOM 1

undertake *vb* to take to or upon oneself — see ASSUME 1

undertaker *n* a person who manages funerals and prepares the dead for burial or cremation — see FUNERAL DIRECTOR

underwater *adj* living, lying, or occurring below the surface of the water ⟨*underwater* plants don't require as much light to grow as surface plants⟩ ⟨*underwater* exploring takes a long time because you can't move quickly⟩

synonyms aquatic, submarine, submerged, sunken

related words oceanic; abysmal, abyssal, deep, deep-sea, deepwater

under way *adj* being in progress or development — see ONGOING 1

underwear *n* clothing intended to be worn underneath other clothing ⟨*underwear* has got to be the most boring thing that one could ever receive as a birthday present!⟩

synonyms underclothes, underclothing, undergarments, undies

related words lingerie; pantie (*or* panty), slip, underskirt; briefs, drawers, long johns, pants, shorts, underdrawers, underpants, undershirt, union suit; nightdress, nightgown, nightshirt, pajamas, pj's

near antonyms outerwear

underweight *adj* having little weight — see ¹LIGHT 1

underwrite *vb* to provide money for — see FINANCE 1

undesired *adj* not searched or asked for — see UNSOUGHT

undetermined *adj* **1** not seen or understood clearly — see FAINT 1

2 not yet settled or decided — see PENDING 1

undeviating *adj* not varying — see UNIFORM

undies *n pl* clothing intended to be worn underneath other clothing — see UNDERWEAR

undiluted *adj* free from added matter — see PURE 1

undisturbed *adj* free from emotional or mental agitation — see CALM 2

undivided *adj* not divided or scattered among several areas of interest or concern — see WHOLE 1

undo *vb* **1** to deprive of courage or confidence — see UNNERVE 1

2 to disengage the knotted parts of — see UNTIE

3 to trouble the mind of; to make uneasy — see DISTURB 1

undomesticated *adj* living outdoors without taming or domestication by humans — see WILD 1

undoubtedly *adv* without any question — see INDEED 1

undress *vb* to remove clothing from ⟨Mom *undressed* the mud-covered little toddler and plopped her in the bath⟩

synonyms disrobe, strip, unclothe

related words bare, denude, divest, expose, uncover, undrape, unveil; bark, flay, peel, skin

near antonyms apparel, array, attire, caparison, clothe, costume, cover, deck, dress, feather, garb, garment, invest, rig (out), vest; cloak, mantle; drape, swaddle, swathe; accoutre (*or* accouter), equip, furnish, outfit

antonyms dress, gown, robe

undressed *adj* **1** being such as found in nature and not altered by processing or refining — see CRUDE 1

2 lacking or shed of clothing — see NAKED 1

undue *adj* going beyond a normal or acceptable limit in degree or amount — see EXCESSIVE 1

unduly *adv* beyond a normal or acceptable limit — see TOO 1

undyed *adj* lacking an addition of color — see COLORLESS

undying *adj* lasting forever — see EVERLASTING

uneager *adj* showing little or no interest or enthusiasm — see TEPID 1

unearth *vb* to remove from place of burial — see EXHUME

unearthing *n* the act or process of sighting or learning the existence of something for the first time — see DISCOVERY 1

unearthly *adj* **1** being so extraordinary or abnormal as to suggest powers which violate the laws of nature — see SUPERNATURAL 2

2 fearfully and mysteriously strange or fantastic — see EERIE

3 of, relating to, or being part of a reality beyond the observable physical universe — see SUPERNATURAL 1

uneasiness *n* **1** a disturbed or uneasy state — see UNREST

2 an uneasy state of mind usually over the possibility of an anticipated misfortune or trouble — see ANXIETY 1

uneasy *adj* **1** feeling or showing uncomfortable feelings of uncertainty — see NERVOUS 1

2 lacking or denying rest — see RESTLESS 1

3 lacking social grace and assurance — see AWKWARD 1

uneducated *adj* lacking in education or the knowledge gained from books — see IGNORANT 1

unembarrassed *adj* not embarrassed or ashamed — see UNABASHED

unemotional *adj* not feeling or showing emotion — see IMPASSIVE 1

unending *adj* lasting forever — see EVERLASTING

unendurable *adj* more than can be put up with — see UNBEARABLE

unenjoyable *adj* not giving pleasure to the mind or senses — see UNPLEASANT

unenthusiastic *adj* showing little or no interest or enthusiasm — see TEPID 1

unequal *adj* not staying constant — see UNEVEN 2

unequaled *or* **unequalled** *adj* having no equal or rival for excellence or desirability — see ONLY 1

unequivocal *adj* **1** having no exceptions or restrictions — see ABSOLUTE 2

2 not subject to misinterpretation or more than one interpretation — see CLEAR 2

3 so clearly expressed as to leave no doubt about the meaning — see EXPLICIT

unerring *adj* not being or likely to be wrong — see INFALLIBLE 1

unessential *adj* not needed by the circumstances or to accomplish an end — see UNNECESSARY

unethical *adj* **1** not conforming to a high moral standard; morally unacceptable — see BAD 2

2 not guided by or showing a concern for what is right — see UNPRINCIPLED

uneven *adj* **1** not having a level or smooth surface ⟨we had to plane and sand down the *uneven* wooden board before we could paint it⟩

synonyms broken, bumpy, coarse, irregular, jagged, lumpy, pebbly, ragged, rough, roughened, rugged, scraggy

related words lopsided, unbalanced; inexact, irregular, unaligned; rutted, rutty, undulating, wavy; burred, harsh, nubbly, nubby, scraggly, scratchy; nonuniform

near antonyms exact, uniform; aligned, regular, true; horizontal, tabular; plumb, straight, vertical; flush

antonyms even, flat, level, plane, smooth

2 not staying constant ⟨the level of attendance at the ball park has been very *uneven* this season⟩
synonyms changing, erratic, fluctuating, irregular, unequal, unstable, unsteady, varying
related words capricious, changeable, changeful, choppy, fickle, fluid, inconsistent, inconstant, mercurial, mutable, uncertain, unsettled, variable, volatile
antonyms changeless, constant, stable, steady, unchanging, unvarying
3 inclined or twisted to one side — see AWRY
unexampled *adj* having no equal or rival for excellence or desirability — see ONLY 1
unexceptional *adj* being of the type that is encountered in the normal course of events — see ORDINARY 1
unexpected *adj* not expected ⟨the pop quiz was *unexpected*, but fortunately I was prepared⟩
synonyms unanticipated, unforeseen, unlooked-for
related words unintended, unplanned; improbable, unlikely; startling, surprising
near antonyms predicted, prophesied
antonyms anticipated, expected, foreseen
unexpectedly *adv* without warning — see UNAWARES
unexplainable *adj* impossible to explain — see INEXPLICABLE
unexpressed *adj* understood although not put into words — see IMPLICIT
unfailing *adj* **1** not being or likely to be wrong — see INFALLIBLE 1
2 not likely to fail — see INFALLIBLE 2
unfailingly *adv* on every relevant occasion — see ALWAYS 1
unfair *adj* not being in accordance with the rules or standards of what is fair in sport — see FOUL 2
unfairness *n* the state of being unfair or unjust — see INJUSTICE 1
unfaithful *adj* not true in one's allegiance to someone or something — see FAITHLESS
unfaithfulness *n* **1** lack of faithfulness especially to one's husband or wife — see INFIDELITY 1
2 the act or fact of violating the trust or confidence of another — see BETRAYAL
unfamiliar *adj* not known or experienced before — see NEW 2
unfamiliarity *n* the state of being unaware or uninformed — see IGNORANCE 1
unfashionable *adj* marked by an obvious lack of style or good taste — see TACKY 1
unfasten *vb* to disengage the knotted parts of — see UNTIE
unfathomable *adj* **1** being or seeming to be without limits — see INFINITE
2 impossible to understand — see INCOMPREHENSIBLE
unfavorable *adj* opposed to one's interests — see ADVERSE 1
unfeeling *adj* **1** having or showing a lack of sympathy or tender feelings — see HARD 1
2 lacking in sensation or feeling — see NUMB
unfeignedly *adv* without any attempt to impress by deception or exaggeration — see NATURALLY 3
unfeminine *adj* having qualities or traits that are traditionally considered inappropriate for a girl or woman ⟨in bygone days pants were considered *unfeminine*, and even women bicycling were expected to wear skirts⟩

synonyms hoydenish, manlike, mannish, tomboyish, unladylike, unwomanly
related words gentlemanly, male, manly, masculine
near antonyms effeminate, girlish, sissy, unmanly, unmasculine, womanish, womanlike; distaff, petticoat
antonyms female, feminine, ladylike, womanly
unfetter *vb* to set free (as from slavery or confinement) — see FREE 1
unfit *adj* **1** lacking qualities (as knowledge, skill, or ability) required to do a job — see INCOMPETENT
2 not appropriate for a particular occasion or situation — see INAPPROPRIATE
unfitness *n* **1** the quality or state of being unsuitable or unfitting — see INAPPROPRIATENESS 1
2 the quality or state of not being socially proper — see IMPROPRIETY 1
unflagging *adj* showing no signs of weariness even after long hard effort — see TIRELESS
unflappable *adj* not easily panicked or upset ⟨the *unflappable* teacher never even blinked when the wall map came crashing down⟩
synonyms imperturbable, nerveless, unshakable
related words calm, collected, composed, cool, coolheaded, nonchalant, placid, self-possessed, serene, tranquil, undisturbed, unperturbed, unruffled, unshaken, untroubled, unworried
near antonyms panicky; aflutter, anxious, dithery, edgy, het up, hung up, jittery, jumpy, nervous, nervy, perturbed, shaky, tense, troubled, uneasy, upset, uptight, worried
antonyms perturbable, shakable
unfledged *adj* lacking in adult experience or maturity — see CALLOW
unflinching *adj* showing no signs of slackening or yielding in one's purpose — see UNYIELDING 1
unfold *vb* **1** to arrange the parts of (something) over a wider area — see OPEN 3
2 to gradually become clearer or more detailed — see DEVELOP 1
3 to produce flowers — see BLOOM
unforced *adj* done, made, or given with one's own free will — see VOLUNTARY 1
unforeseen *adj* not expected — see UNEXPECTED
unforgivable *adj* too bad to be excused or justified — see INEXCUSABLE
unformed *adj* having no definite or recognizable form — see FORMLESS
unfortunate *adj* **1** bringing about ruin or misfortune — see FATAL 1
2 having, prone to, or marked by bad luck — see UNLUCKY
3 of a kind to cause great distress — see REGRETTABLE
unfounded *adj* having no basis in reason or fact — see GROUNDLESS
unfriendly *adj* **1** lacking in friendliness or warmth of feeling — see COLD 2
2 marked by opposition or ill will — see HOSTILE 1
3 opposed to one's interests — see ADVERSE 1
unfrozen *adj* freed from a frozen state by exposure to warmth — see THAWED
unfruitful *adj* not able to produce fruit or offspring — see STERILE 1
unfunny *adj* not joking or playful in mood or manner — see SERIOUS 1
ungainly *adj* **1** difficult to use or operate especial-

THESAURUS

ly because of size, weight, or design — see CUM-
BERSOME

2 lacking in physical ease and grace in movement
or in the use of the hands — see CLUMSY 1

ungentle *adj* harsh and threatening in manner or
appearance — see GRIM 1

ungodly *adj* falling short of a standard — see
BAD 1

ungovernable *adj* **1** given to resisting authority or
another's control — see DISOBEDIENT

2 given to resisting control or discipline by others
— see UNCONTROLLABLE

ungoverned *adj* showing no signs of being under
control — see RAMPANT 1

ungraceful *adj* lacking social grace and assurance
— see AWKWARD 1

ungracious *adj* showing a lack of manners or consideration for others — see IMPOLITE

ungraciousness *n* rude behavior — see DISCOUR-
TESY

ungrateful *adj* not showing gratitude — see
THANKLESS 1

ungrounded *adj* **1** having no basis in reason or fact
— see GROUNDLESS

2 not informed about or aware of something —
see IGNORANT 2

unguarded *adj* **1** free in expressing one's true feelings and opinions — see FRANK

2 lacking protection from danger or resistance
against attack — see HELPLESS 1

3 not paying or showing close attention especially
for the purpose of avoiding trouble — see CARE-
LESS 1

unhampered *adj* showing no signs of being under
control — see RAMPANT 1

unhandsome *adj* unpleasant to look at — see
UGLY 1

unhandy *adj* **1** difficult to use or operate especially because of size, weight, or design — see CUM-
BERSOME

2 lacking in physical ease and grace in movement
or in the use of the hands — see CLUMSY 1

unhappily *adv* with feelings of bitterness or grief
— see HARD 2

unhappiness *n* a state or spell of low spirits — see
SADNESS

unhappy *adj* **1** feeling unhappiness — see SAD 1

2 having, prone to, or marked by bad luck — see
UNLUCKY

3 not appropriate for a particular occasion or situation — see INAPPROPRIATE

unhealthful *adj* bad for the well-being of the body
— see UNHEALTHY 1

unhealthiness *n* the condition of not being in
good health — see SICKNESS 1

unhealthy *adj* **1** bad for the well-being of the body
⟨we knew that the junk food at the carnival was
unhealthy, but it tasted so good!⟩

synonyms noisome, noxious, unhealthful, unwholesome

related words insanitary, unhygienic, unsanitary;
nonnutritious; poisonous, toxic; fatal, lethal, mortal

near antonyms hygienic, sanitary; nutritious

antonyms healthful, healthy

2 involving potential loss or injury — see DAN-
GEROUS

3 temporarily suffering from a disorder of the
body — see SICK 1

unheard–of *adj* not known or experienced before
— see NEW 2

unheroic *adj* having or showing a shameful lack of
courage — see COWARDLY

unhindered *adj* showing no signs of being under
control — see RAMPANT 1

unhinge *vb* **1** to cause to go insane or as if insane
— see CRAZE

2 to trouble the mind of; to make uneasy — see
DISTURB 1

unhurried *adj* moving or proceeding at less than
the normal, desirable, or required speed — see
SLOW 1

unidentified *adj* **1** known but not named — see
CERTAIN 1

2 not named or identified by a name — see
NAMELESS 1

unification *n* the act or an instance of joining two
or more things into one — see UNION 1

uniform *adj* not varying ⟨with flat-screen TVs, picture sharpness is *uniform* over the entire screen,
even in the corners⟩

synonyms invariant, steady, unchanging, undeviating, unvarying, unwavering

related words immutable, invariable, unalterable,
unchangeable

antonyms changing, deviating, varying

uniform *n* the distinctive clothing worn by members of a particular group ⟨the band *uniform* was
brown with red and white stripes⟩

synonyms livery, outfit

related words fatigues, full dress, regimentals;
costume, finery, regalia

unify *vb* **1** to bring (something) to a central point
or under a single control — see CENTRALIZE

2 to come together to form a single unit — see
UNITE 1

unimaginable *adj* too extraordinary or improbable
to believe — see INCREDIBLE

unimportant *adj* lacking importance ⟨we figured
that the details were *unimportant* as long as we
got the basic design correct⟩

synonyms frivolous, inconsequential, inconsiderable, insignificant, little, minor, minute, negligible, slight, small, small-fry, trifling, trivial

related words jerkwater, one-horse; paltry, petty,
worthless; anonymous, nameless, obscure, uncelebrated, unknown

near antonyms decisive, fatal, fateful; distinctive,
exceptional, impressive, outstanding, prominent,
remarkable; valuable, worthwhile, worthy; distinguished, eminent, great, illustrious, preeminent,
prestigious; famous, notorious, renowned; all-important, basic, essential, fundamental

antonyms big, consequential, eventful, important,
major, material, meaningful, momentous, significant, substantial, weighty

uninflammable *adj* incapable of being burned —
see INCOMBUSTIBLE

uninformed *adj* not informed about or aware of
something — see IGNORANT 2

uninhibited *adj* showing feeling freely — see
DEMONSTRATIVE

uninstructed *adj* lacking in education or the
knowledge gained from books — see IGNORANT 1

unintelligent *adj* not having or showing an ability
to absorb ideas readily — see STUPID 1

unintelligible *adj* impossible to understand — see
INCOMPREHENSIBLE

unintended *adj* **1** happening by chance — see ACCIDENTAL

2 not made or done willingly or by choice — see INVOLUNTARY 1

unintentional *adj* **1** happening by chance — see ACCIDENTAL

2 not made or done willingly or by choice — see INVOLUNTARY 1

uninterested *adj* having or showing a lack of interest or concern — see INDIFFERENT 1

uninteresting *adj* causing weariness, restlessness, or lack of interest — see BORING

uninterrupted *adj* going on and on without any interruptions — see CONTINUOUS

uninvited *adj* not searched or asked for — see UNSOUGHT

union *n* **1** the act or an instance of joining two or more things into one ⟨the *union* of East Germany and West Germany that became possible after the fall of communism⟩

synonyms combination, combining, connecting, connection, consolidation, coupling, junction, linking, merging, unification

related words amalgamation, blend, commingling, compounding, fusion, intermingling, intermixture, mingling, mix, mixture; reunification, reunion

near antonyms detachment, divorcement, separation, severance

antonyms breakup, disconnection, dissolution, disunion, division, parting, partition, schism, split

2 an association of persons, parties, or states for mutual assistance and protection — see CONFEDERACY

3 the state of having shared interests or efforts (as in social or business matters) — see ASSOCIATION 1

unique *adj* **1** of, relating to, or belonging to a single person — see INDIVIDUAL 1

2 being out of the ordinary — see EXCEPTIONAL

3 being the one or ones of a class with no other members — see ONLY 2

4 noticeably different from what is generally found or experienced — see UNUSUAL 1

unison *n* the act or fact of being of one opinion about something — see AGREEMENT 1

unite *vb* **1** to come together to form a single unit ⟨using the microscope, we watched the water droplets *unite* into a single pool⟩

synonyms associate, coalesce, combine, conjoin, conjugate, connect, couple, fuse, join, link (up), marry, unify

related words mate, yoke; ally, confederate, league; chain, compound, hitch, hook; congregate, gather, meet; recombine, rejoin, reunify, reunite

near antonyms detach, disconnect, disjoin, disjoint, dissociate, disunite, divide, divorce, fractionate, isolate, resolve, uncouple, unyoke; disband, disperse, scatter

antonyms break up, dissever, part, section, separate, sever, split, sunder, unlink

2 to bring (something) to a central point or under a single control — see CENTRALIZE

3 to form or enter into an association that furthers the interests of its members — see ALLY

united *adj* **1** having or marked by agreement in feeling or action — see HARMONIOUS 3

2 used or done by a number of people as a group — see COLLECTIVE

unity *n* a balanced, pleasing, or suitable arrangement of parts — see HARMONY 1

universal *adj* **1** able to do many different kinds of things — see VERSATILE

2 belonging or relating to the whole — see GENERAL 1

3 covering everything or all important points — see ENCYCLOPEDIC

4 present in all places and at all times — see OMNIPRESENT

universe *n* the whole body of things observed or assumed ⟨the theory that the *universe* is constantly expanding⟩

synonyms cosmos, creation, macrocosm, nature, world

related words existence, reality

near antonyms nothingness, void

unjustifiable *adj* too bad to be excused or justified — see INEXCUSABLE

unjustness *n* the state of being unfair or unjust — see INJUSTICE 1

unkempt *adj* **1** lacking in order, neatness, and often cleanliness — see MESSY

2 lacking neatness in dress or person — see SLOPPY 1

unknowing *adj* **1** lacking in worldly wisdom or informed judgment — see NAIVE 1

2 not informed about or aware of something — see IGNORANT 2

unknown *adj* **1** happening or existing without one's knowledge ⟨*unknown* to me was the fact that while I was out, my family was hurriedly preparing a surprise birthday party⟩

synonyms unbeknownst (*also* unbeknown)

related words unperceived, unrecognized, unsuspected; unaware, unconscious, unmindful; unknowing, unsuspecting, unwitting; ignorant, unacquainted, unfamiliar

2 not known or experienced before — see NEW 2

3 not widely known — see OBSCURE 2

unlade *vb* to empty or rid of cargo — see UNLOAD 1

unladylike *adj* having qualities or traits that are traditionally considered inappropriate for a girl or woman — see UNFEMININE

unlash *vb* to disengage the knotted parts of — see UNTIE

unlawful *adj* contrary to or forbidden by law — see ILLEGAL 1

unlearn *vb* to be unable to recall or think of — see FORGET 1

unlearned *adj* lacking in education or the knowledge gained from books — see IGNORANT 1

unleash *vb* **1** to set free (from a state of being held in check) — see RELEASE 1

2 to find emotional release for — see TAKE OUT 1

unlettered *adj* lacking in education or the knowledge gained from books — see IGNORANT 1

unlike *adj* being not of the same kind — see DIFFERENT 1

unlikely *adj* not likely to be true or to occur — see IMPROBABLE

unlikeness *n* the quality or state of being different — see DIFFERENCE 1

unlimited *adj* **1** being or seeming to be without limits — see INFINITE

2 not limited or specialized in application or purpose — see GENERAL 4

unlink *vb* to set or force apart — see SEPARATE 1

unlisted *adj* not appearing on a list ⟨she kept her

THESAURUS

phone number *unlisted* so as to reduce the number of unwanted calls⟩

synonyms uncataloged, unrecorded, unregistered

related words unwritten; unidentified, unspecified; undisclosed, unknown, unrevealed

antonyms cataloged (*or* catalogued), listed, recorded, registered

unliterary *adj* used in or suitable for speech and not formal writing — see COLLOQUIAL 1

unload *vb* 1 to empty or rid of cargo ⟨the dockworkers *unloaded* the ship⟩

synonyms disburden, discharge, disencumber, unburden, unlade, unpack

related words free, lighten, relieve; clear, empty, evacuate, vacate, void

near antonyms charge, cram, fill, heap, jam, jam-pack, stuff

antonyms load, pack

2 to get rid of as useless or unwanted — see DISCARD

unlock *vb* to set free (from a state of being held in check) — see RELEASE 1

unlooked–for *adj* not expected — see UNEXPECTED

unloose *vb* to set free (from a state of being held in check) — see RELEASE 1

unloosen *vb* to set free (from a state of being held in check) — see RELEASE 1

unlovely *adj* 1 not giving pleasure to the mind or senses — see UNPLEASANT

2 unpleasant to look at — see UGLY 1

unlucky *adj* having, prone to, or marked by bad luck ⟨the *unlucky* campers had rain all week⟩ ⟨I'm so *unlucky* I don't bother to play the lottery⟩ ⟨an *unlucky* throw of the dice⟩

synonyms hapless, ill-fated, ill-starred, luckless, star-crossed, unfortunate, unhappy

related words adverse, ill, inauspicious, unfavorable, unpromising, untoward; calamitous, catastrophic, disastrous; damned, doomed, tragic

near antonyms blessed, favored, gifted, privileged; auspicious, fair, favorable, golden, promising, propitious

antonyms fortunate, happy, lucky

unmake *vb* to remove from a position of prominence or power (as a throne) — see DEPOSE 1

unman *vb* 1 to deprive of courage or confidence — see UNNERVE 1

2 to lessen the courage or confidence of — see DISCOURAGE 1

unmanageable *adj* given to resisting control or discipline by others — see UNCONTROLLABLE

unmanly *adj* having or displaying qualities more suitable for women than for men — see EFFEMINATE

unmannerly *adj* showing a lack of manners or consideration for others — see IMPOLITE

unmarried *adj* not married — see SINGLE 1

unmask *vb* 1 to make known (as information previously kept secret) — see REVEAL 1

2 to reveal the true nature of — see EXPOSE 1

unmatched *adj* 1 being one of a pair or set without a corresponding mate — see ODD 1

2 having no equal or rival for excellence or desirability — see ONLY 1

unmelodious *adj* marked by or producing a harsh combination of sounds — see DISSONANT

unmerciful *adj* having or showing a lack of sympathy or tender feelings — see HARD 1

unmindful *adj* not informed about or aware of something — see IGNORANT 2

unmistakable *adj* not subject to misinterpretation or more than one interpretation — see CLEAR 2

unmitigated *adj* having no exceptions or restrictions — see ABSOLUTE 2

unmixed *adj* free from added matter — see PURE 1

unmoral *adj* not guided by or showing a concern for what is right — see UNPRINCIPLED

unmovable *adj* incapable of moving or being moved — see IMMOVABLE 1

unmusical *adj* marked by or producing a harsh combination of sounds — see DISSONANT

unnamed *adj* 1 known but not named — see CERTAIN 1

2 not named or identified by a name — see NAMELESS 1

unnatural *adj* 1 departing from some accepted standard of what is normal — see DEVIANT

2 lacking in natural or spontaneous quality — see ARTIFICIAL 1

unnecessary *adj* not needed by the circumstances or to accomplish an end ⟨a hair dryer was an *unnecessary* item on a trip to the desert⟩

synonyms dispensable, gratuitous, needless, nonessential, uncalled-for, unessential, unwarranted

related words discretionary, elective, optional; extra, extraneous, irrelevant, redundant, superfluous

near antonyms all-important, crucial, important, vital; imperative, pressing, urgent

antonyms essential, indispensable, necessary, needed, needful, required

unnerve *vb* 1 to deprive of courage or confidence ⟨the riding accident so *unnerved* me that for a while I was afraid to get back on a horse⟩

synonyms demoralize, emasculate, undo, unman, unstring

related words debilitate, enervate, enfeeble, weaken; prostrate, sap, soften, tire, waste; frighten, scare, terrify, terrorize; daunt, discourage, dishearten, dismay, dispirit; craze, derange, madden, unbalance, unhinge; discompose, disquiet, disturb, faze, perturb, unsettle, upset

near antonyms fortify, strengthen; embolden, encourage, hearten

antonyms nerve

2 to lessen the courage or confidence of — see DISCOURAGE 1

unnerving *adj* marked by or causing agitation or uncomfortable feelings — see NERVOUS 2

unnoted *adj* not widely known — see OBSCURE 2

unnoticeable *adj* not readily seen or noticed — see UNOBTRUSIVE

unnumbered *adj* too many to be counted — see COUNTLESS

unobstructed *adj* allowing passage without obstruction — see OPEN 1

unobtainable *adj* hard or impossible to get to or get at — see INACCESSIBLE

unobtrusive *adj* not readily seen or noticed ⟨the notice that an 18% tip would be automatically added was so *unobtrusive* we almost didn't see it at the bottom of the menu⟩

synonyms inconspicuous, unnoticeable

related words unnoticed; impalpable, imperceptible, inappreciable, indistinguishable, insensible; faint, indistinct, obscure; concealed, hidden

near antonyms arresting, eye-catching, showy, striking; apparent, blatant, clear, distinct, evident, manifest, obvious, plain, unmistakable
antonyms conspicous, noticeable

unoriginal *adj* using or marked by the use of something else as a basis or model — see IMITATIVE

unorthodox *adj* **1** deviating from commonly accepted beliefs or practices — see HERETICAL
2 not bound by traditional ways or beliefs — see LIBERAL 1
3 not rigidly following established form, custom, or rules — see INFORMAL 1

unpack *vb* to empty or rid of cargo — see UNLOAD 1

unpaid *adj* not yet paid — see OUTSTANDING 1

unpainted *adj* lacking an addition of color — see COLORLESS

unpaired *adj* being one of a pair or set without a corresponding mate — see ODD 1

unpalatable *adj* disagreeable or disgusting to the sense of taste — see DISTASTEFUL 1

unparalleled *adj* having no equal or rival for excellence or desirability — see ONLY 1

unpardonable *adj* too bad to be excused or justified — see INEXCUSABLE

unperturbed *adj* free from emotional or mental agitation — see CALM 2

unplanned *adj* **1** happening by chance — see ACCIDENTAL
2 made or done without previous thought or preparation — see EXTEMPORANEOUS

unpleasant *adj* not giving pleasure to the mind or senses ⟨the burnt pot roast had a very *unpleasant* odor⟩
synonyms bad, disagreeable, displeasing, distasteful, nasty, rotten, sour, uncongenial, unlovely, unpleasing, unsatisfying, unwelcome
related words abhorrent, abominable, appalling, awful, beastly, disgusting, dreadful, foul, hideous, horrendous, horrible, horrid, invidious, loathsome, nauseating, noisome, obnoxious, obscene, odious, repellent (*also* repellant), repugnant, repulsive, revolting, scandalous, shocking, sickening, ugly, villainous; annoying, galling, irritating, vexing
near antonyms delectable, delicious, delightful, dreamy, felicitous; affable, amiable, friendly, genial, good-natured, good-tempered, gracious, sweet, well-disposed
antonyms agreeable, congenial, good, grateful, gratifying, nice, palatable, pleasant, pleasing, pleasurable, satisfying, welcome

unpleasing *adj* **1** not giving pleasure to the mind or senses — see UNPLEASANT
2 unpleasant to look at — see UGLY 1

unpolished *adj* lacking in refinement or good taste — see COARSE 2

unprecedented *adj* not known or experienced before — see NEW 2

unpredictable *adj* likely to change frequently, suddenly, or unexpectedly — see FICKLE 1

unprejudiced *adj* marked by justice, honesty, and freedom from bias — see FAIR 2

unpremeditated *adj* **1** happening by chance — see ACCIDENTAL
2 made or done without previous thought or preparation — see EXTEMPORANEOUS

unprepared *adj* made or done without previous thought or preparation — see EXTEMPORANEOUS

unpretending *adj* free from any intent to deceive or impress others — see GUILELESS

unpretentious *adj* **1** free from any intent to deceive or impress others — see GUILELESS
2 not excessively showy — see QUIET 2
3 not having or showing any feelings of superiority, self-assertiveness, or showiness — see HUMBLE 1

unpretentiously *adv* without any attempt to impress by deception or exaggeration — see NATURALLY 3

unpretty *adj* unpleasant to look at — see UGLY 1

unprincipled *adj* not guided by or showing a concern for what is right ⟨the *unprincipled* businessman made a lot of money—and didn't care how he made it⟩
synonyms cutthroat, immoral, Machiavellian, unconscionable, unethical, unmoral, unscrupulous
related words calculating, intriguing, opportunistic, scheming; merciless, pitiless, remorseless, ruthless; crooked, deceitful, dishonest; corrupt, debased, debauched, decadent, degenerate, degraded, demoralized, depraved, dissipated
near antonyms good, just, noble, righteous, virtuous
antonyms ethical, moral, principled, scrupulous

unprintable *adj* depicting or referring to sexual matters in a way that is unacceptable in polite society — see OBSCENE 1

unprocessed *adj* being such as found in nature and not altered by processing or refining — see CRUDE 1

unproductive *adj* **1** producing inferior or only a small amount of vegetation — see BARREN 1
2 producing no results — see FUTILE

unprofessional *adj* lacking or showing a lack of expert skill — see AMATEURISH

unprofitable *adj* producing no results — see FUTILE

unprogressive *adj* tending to favor established ideas, conditions, or institutions — see CONSERVATIVE 1

unprotected *adj* lacking protection from danger or resistance against attack — see HELPLESS 1

unqualified *adj* **1** having no exceptions or restrictions — see ABSOLUTE 2
2 lacking qualities (as knowledge, skill, or ability) required to do a job — see INCOMPETENT
3 not limited or specialized in application or purpose — see GENERAL 4

unquestionable *adj* not capable of being challenged or proved wrong — see IRREFUTABLE

unquestionably *adv* without any question — see INDEED 1

unquiet *adj* **1** feeling or showing uncomfortable feelings of uncertainty — see NERVOUS 1
2 lacking or denying rest — see RESTLESS 1

unravel *vb* **1** to separate the various strands of ⟨it took us forever to *unravel* the jumbled mass of Christmas tree lights⟩
synonyms disentangle, ravel (out), unbraid, unsnarl, untangle, untwine, untwist
related words smooth, straighten (out); undo, unlace, unstring, unthread, untie, unwind
near antonyms braid, knot, lace, tie, wind
antonyms entangle, snarl, tangle
2 to find an answer for through reasoning — see SOLVE

unreachable *adj* hard or impossible to get to or get at — see INACCESSIBLE

THESAURUS

unread *adj* lacking in education or the knowledge gained from books — see IGNORANT 1

unreal *adj* 1 conceived or made without regard for reason or reality — see FANTASTIC 1

2 not real and existing only in the imagination — see IMAGINARY

unreality *n* a conception or image created by the imagination and having no objective reality — see FANTASY 1

unreasonable *adj* 1 having no basis in reason or fact — see GROUNDLESS

2 not using or following good reasoning — see ILLOGICAL

unreasoning *adj* not using or following good reasoning — see ILLOGICAL

unrecorded *adj* not appearing on a list — see UNLISTED

unrecoverable *adj* 1 not capable of being cured or reformed — see HOPELESS 1

2 not capable of being repaired, regained, or undone — see IRREPARABLE

unredeemable *adj* 1 not capable of being cured or reformed — see HOPELESS 1

2 not capable of being repaired, regained, or undone — see IRREPARABLE

unrefined *adj* 1 being such as found in nature and not altered by processing or refining — see CRUDE 1

2 hastily or roughly constructed — see RUDE 1

3 lacking in refinement or good taste — see COARSE 2

unregistered *adj* not appearing on a list — see UNLISTED

unrehearsed *adj* made or done without previous thought or preparation — see EXTEMPORANEOUS

unrelenting *adj* 1 sticking to an opinion, purpose, or course of action in spite of reason, arguments, or persuasion — see OBSTINATE

2 showing no signs of slackening or yielding in one's purpose — see UNYIELDING 1

unremarkable *adj* being of the type that is encountered in the normal course of events — see ORDINARY 1

unremitting *adj* going on and on without any interruptions — see CONTINUOUS

unrepentant *adj* not sorry for having done wrong — see REMORSELESS

unreserved *adj* 1 free in expressing one's true feelings and opinions — see FRANK

2 showing feeling freely — see DEMONSTRATIVE

unresistant *adj* 1 lacking protection from danger or resistance against attack — see HELPLESS 1

2 receiving or enduring without offering resistance — see PASSIVE

unresisting *adj* receiving or enduring without offering resistance — see PASSIVE

unresolved *adj* not yet settled or decided — see PENDING 1

unrest *n* a disturbed or uneasy state ⟨*unrest* gripped the city as the people nervously awaited the expected bombardment⟩ ⟨his stomach *unrest* was just a sign of stage fright⟩

synonyms disquiet, ferment, restiveness, restlessness, turmoil, uneasiness

related words fidgets; agitation, commotion, confusion, tumult, turbulence, upheaval; anarchy, chaos, disorder

near antonyms order, orderliness

antonyms calm, ease, peace, quiet

unrestful *adj* lacking or denying rest — see RESTLESS 1

unrestrained *adj* 1 not bound by rigid standards — see EASYGOING 2

2 not bound, confined, or detained by force — see FREE 3

3 showing feeling freely — see DEMONSTRATIVE

4 showing no signs of being under control — see RAMPANT 1

unrestraint *n* carefree freedom from constraint — see ABANDON

unrestricted *adj* 1 freely available for use or participation by all — see OPEN 2

2 not bound by rigid standards — see EASYGOING 2

3 not limited or specialized in application or purpose — see GENERAL 4

unrighteous *adj* not conforming to a high moral standard; morally unacceptable — see BAD 2

unripe *adj* lacking in adult experience or maturity — see CALLOW

unripened *adj* lacking in adult experience or maturity — see CALLOW

unrivaled *or* **unrivalled** *adj* having no equal or rival for excellence or desirability — see ONLY 1

unruliness *n* refusal to obey — see DISOBEDIENCE

unruly *adj* 1 given to resisting authority or another's control — see DISOBEDIENT

2 given to resisting control or discipline by others — see UNCONTROLLABLE

3 not restrained by or under the control of legal authority — see LAWLESS

unsafe *adj* 1 involving potential loss or injury — see DANGEROUS

2 not paying or showing close attention especially for the purpose of avoiding trouble — see CARELESS 1

unsatisfactorily *adv* in an unsatisfactory way — see BADLY

unsatisfactory *adj* falling short of a standard — see BAD 1

unsatisfying *adj* not giving pleasure to the mind or senses — see UNPLEASANT

unsavory *adj* 1 disagreeable or disgusting to the sense of taste — see DISTASTEFUL 1

2 not conforming to a high moral standard; morally unacceptable — see BAD 2

unsay *vb* to solemnly or formally reject or go back on (as something formerly adhered to) — see ABJURE

unschooled *adj* lacking in education or the knowledge gained from books — see IGNORANT 1

unscrupulous *adj* not guided by or showing a concern for what is right — see UNPRINCIPLED

unseasonable *adj* occurring before the usual or expected time — see EARLY 2

unseasonably *adv* before the usual or expected time — see EARLY

unseat *vb* to remove from a position of prominence or power (as a throne) — see DEPOSE 1

unsecured *adj* not tightly fastened, tied, or stretched — see LOOSE 1

unseemly *adj* not appropriate for a particular occasion or situation — see INAPPROPRIATE

unselfish *adj* giving or sharing in abundance and without hesitation — see GENEROUS 1

unselfishness *n* the quality or state of being generous — see LIBERALITY

unsettle *vb* to trouble the mind of; to make uneasy — see DISTURB 1

unsettled *adj* **1** likely to change frequently, suddenly, or unexpectedly — see FICKLE 1
2 not yet paid — see OUTSTANDING 1
3 not yet settled or decided — see PENDING 1
4 not feeling sure about the truth, wisdom, or trustworthiness of someone or something — see DOUBTFUL 1

unsettling *adj* **1** causing worry or anxiety — see TROUBLESOME
2 marked by or causing agitation or uncomfortable feelings — see NERVOUS 2

unshakable *adj* not easily panicked or upset — see UNFLAPPABLE

unshaken *adj* free from emotional or mental agitation — see CALM 2

unshaped *adj* having no definite or recognizable form — see FORMLESS

unshared *adj* belonging only to the one person, unit, or group named — see SOLE 1

unshielded *adj* lacking protection from danger or resistance against attack — see HELPLESS 1

unshorn *adj* covered with or as if with hair — see HAIRY 1

unsightly *adj* unpleasant to look at — see UGLY 1

unskilled *adj* **1** lacking or showing a lack of expert skill — see AMATEURISH
2 lacking qualities (as knowledge, skill, or ability) required to do a job — see INCOMPETENT

unskillful *adj* **1** lacking qualities (as knowledge, skill, or ability) required to do a job — see INCOMPETENT
2 lacking or showing a lack of expert skill — see AMATEURISH

unsmiling *adj* not joking or playful in mood or manner — see SERIOUS 1

unsnarl *vb* to separate the various strands of — see UNRAVEL 1

unsociable *adj* having or showing a lack of friendliness or interest in others — see COOL 1

unsoiled *adj* free from dirt or stain — see CLEAN 1

unsolicited *adj* not searched or asked for — see UNSOUGHT

unsolvable *adj* incapable of being solved or accomplished — see IMPOSSIBLE

unsophisticated *adj* lacking in worldly wisdom or informed judgment — see NAIVE 1

unsophistication *n* **1** the quality or state of being simple and sincere — see NAÏVETÉ 1
2 the quality or state of having a form or structure of few parts or elements — see SIMPLICITY 1

unsought *adj* not searched or asked for ⟨the meddling neighbor insisted on giving us *unsought* advice⟩
synonyms unasked, unbidden (*also* unbid), undesired, uninvited, unsolicited, unwanted, unwelcome
related words objectionable, offensive, unacceptable, undesirable; uncalled-for, unnecessary
near antonyms necessary, needed, required
antonyms desired, solicited, wanted, welcome

unsound *adj* **1** having or showing a very abnormal or sick state of mind — see INSANE 1
2 not being in agreement with what is true — see FALSE 1
3 not using or following good reasoning — see ILLOGICAL
4 temporarily suffering from a disorder of the body — see SICK 1

unsoundness *n* the condition of not being in good health — see SICKNESS 1

unsparing *adj* **1** giving or sharing in abundance and without hesitation — see GENEROUS 1
2 having or showing a lack of sympathy or tender feelings — see HARD 1

unspeakable *adj* beyond the power to describe — see INDESCRIBABLE

unspecialized *adj* not limited or specialized in application or purpose — see GENERAL 4

unspecified *adj* known but not named — see CERTAIN 1

unspoken *adj* understood although not put into words — see IMPLICIT

unsportsmanlike *adj* not being in accordance with the rules or standards of what is fair in sport — see FOUL 2

unstable *adj* **1** not being in or able to maintain a state of balance ⟨when we put the books down on the *unstable* desk, the whole stack went crashing to the floor⟩
synonyms unbalanced, unsteady
related words rickety, shaky, tottery, wobbly; cockeyed, lopsided, uneven
near antonyms even, level, straight; sound, sturdy, substantial
antonyms balanced, stable, steady
2 likely to change frequently, suddenly, or unexpectedly — see FICKLE 1
3 not staying constant — see UNEVEN 2

unstained *adj* lacking an addition of color — see COLORLESS

unsteadiness *n* the quality or state of not being firmly fixed in position — see INSTABILITY

unsteady *adj* **1** lacking in steadiness or regularity of occurrence — see FITFUL
2 likely to change frequently, suddenly, or unexpectedly — see FICKLE 1
3 not being in or able to maintain a state of balance — see UNSTABLE 1
4 not staying constant — see UNEVEN 2

unstop *vb* to arrange clear passage of (something) by removing obstructions — see OPEN 2

unstopped *adj* allowing passage without obstruction — see OPEN 1

unstring *vb* **1** to cause to go insane or as if insane — see CRAZE
2 to deprive of courage or confidence — see UNNERVE 1

unstructured *adj* having no definite or recognizable form — see FORMLESS

unstylish *adj* marked by an obvious lack of style or good taste — see TACKY 1

unstylishly *adv* in a careless or unfashionable manner — see SLOPPILY

unsubstantial *adj* **1** not composed of matter — see IMMATERIAL 1
2 being of a material lacking in sturdiness or substance — see FLIMSY 1
3 lacking bodily strength — see WEAK 1

unsubstantiated *adj* having no basis in reason or fact — see GROUNDLESS

unsuccessful *adj* producing no results — see FUTILE

unsuitable *adj* not appropriate for a particular occasion or situation — see INAPPROPRIATE

unsuitably *adv* in a mistaken or inappropriate way — see WRONGLY

unsullied *adj* free from dirt or stain — see CLEAN 1

unsung *adj* not widely known — see OBSCURE 2

unsupportable *adj* more than can be put up with — see UNBEARABLE

THESAURUS

unsupported *adj* having no basis in reason or fact — see GROUNDLESS

unsure *adj* not feeling sure about the truth, wisdom, or trustworthiness of someone or something — see DOUBTFUL 1

unsurpassable *adj* having no equal or rival for excellence or desirability — see ONLY 1

unsurpassed *adj* **1** having no equal or rival for excellence or desirability — see ONLY 1

2 of the very best kind — see EXCELLENT

unsuspecting *adj* lacking in worldly wisdom or informed judgment — see NAIVE 1

unsuspicious *adj* lacking in worldly wisdom or informed judgment — see NAIVE 1

unsympathetic *adj* **1** having or showing a lack of sympathy or tender feelings — see HARD 1

2 lacking in friendliness or warmth of feeling — see COLD 2

3 marked by opposition or ill will — see HOSTILE 1

4 opposed to one's interests — see ADVERSE 1

untamed *adj* **1** existing without human habitation or cultivation — see WILD 2

2 living outdoors without taming or domestication by humans — see WILD 1

untangle *vb* **1** to separate the various strands of — see UNRAVEL 1

2 to set free from entanglement or difficulty — see EXTRICATE

untaught *adj* lacking in education or the knowledge gained from books — see IGNORANT 1

unthinkable *adj* too extraordinary or improbable to believe — see INCREDIBLE

unthrifty *adj* given to spending money freely or foolishly — see PRODIGAL

unthrone *vb* to remove from a position of prominence or power (as a throne) — see DEPOSE 1

untidy *adj* **1** lacking in order, neatness, and often cleanliness — see MESSY

2 lacking neatness in dress or person — see SLOPPY 1

untie *vb* to disengage the knotted parts of ⟨she always made sure to *untie* her shoelaces before removing her shoes⟩
synonyms unbind, undo, unfasten, unlash
related words unbraid, unlace; disentangle, ravel, unbraid, unravel, unsnarl, untangle, unwind; loose, loosen
near antonyms braid, interlace, interweave, lace, wind; entangle, snarl, tangle
antonyms bind, fasten, knot, lash, tie

untimely *adj* occurring before the usual or expected time — see EARLY 2

untiring *adj* showing no signs of weariness even after long hard effort — see TIRELESS

untitled *adj* not named or identified by a name — see NAMELESS 1

untold *adj* too many to be counted — see COUNTLESS

untouchable *adj* **1** hard or impossible to get to or get at — see INACCESSIBLE

2 not to be violated, criticized, or tampered with — see SACRED 1

untoward *adj* **1** given to resisting authority or another's control — see DISOBEDIENT

2 given to resisting control or discipline by others — see UNCONTROLLABLE

untreated *adj* being such as found in nature and not altered by processing or refining — see CRUDE 1

untroubled *adj* **1** free from emotional or mental agitation — see CALM 2

2 free from storms or physical disturbance — see CALM 1

untrue *adj* **1** not being in agreement with what is true — see FALSE 1

2 not true in one's allegiance to someone or something — see FAITHLESS

untruth *n* **1** a false idea or belief — see FALLACY 1

2 a statement known by its maker to be untrue and made in order to deceive — see LIE

3 the quality or state of being false — see FALLACY 2

untruthful *adj* **1** not being in agreement with what is true — see FALSE 1

2 telling or containing lies — see DISHONEST 1

untruthfulness *n* the tendency to tell lies — see DISHONESTY 1

untutored *adj* lacking in education or the knowledge gained from books — see IGNORANT 1

untwine *vb* to separate the various strands of — see UNRAVEL 1

untwist *vb* to separate the various strands of — see UNRAVEL 1

unusable *adj* not capable of being put to use or account — see IMPRACTICAL

unused *adj* **1** not having acquired a habit or tolerance ⟨while in Mexico we tried to stay out of the sun because we were simply *unused* to the tropical heat⟩
synonyms unacclimated, unaccustomed, unadapted, unadjusted
related words unhardened, unseasoned
near antonyms unaffected, uninfluenced
antonyms acclimated, accustomed, adapted, adjusted, habituated, used

2 recently made and never used before — see NEW 3

unusual *adj* **1** noticeably different from what is generally found or experienced ⟨finding some *unusual* shells by the high-tide mark, we brought them home for our collection⟩
synonyms curious, extraordinary, funny, odd, offbeat, peculiar, queer, rare, singular, strange, unaccustomed, uncommon, uncustomary, unique, weird
related words bizarre, eccentric, far-out, outlandish, outré, way-out; aberrant, abnormal, atypical, exceptional, irregular; newsworthy, notable, noteworthy, noticeable, particular, remarkable, special
near antonyms unexceptional; expected, predictable; familiar, normal, regular, typical
antonyms common, ordinary, usual

2 being out of the ordinary — see EXCEPTIONAL

unutterable *adj* beyond the power to describe — see INDESCRIBABLE

unvarnished *adj* free from all additions or embellishment — see PLAIN 1

unvarying *adj* **1** not undergoing a change in condition — see CONSTANT 1

2 not varying — see UNIFORM

unveil *vb* **1** to make known (as information previously kept secret) — see REVEAL 1

2 to present so as to invite notice or attention — see SHOW 1

unvoiced *adj* understood although not put into words — see IMPLICIT

unwanted *adj* not searched or asked for — see UNSOUGHT

unwarrantable *adj* too bad to be excused or justified — see INEXCUSABLE

unwarranted *adj* **1** not needed by the circumstances or to accomplish an end — see UNNECESSARY

2 having no basis in reason or fact — see GROUNDLESS

unwary *adj* **1** lacking in worldly wisdom or informed judgment — see NAIVE 1

2 not paying or showing close attention especially for the purpose of avoiding trouble — see CARELESS 1

unwavering *adj* not varying — see UNIFORM

unwearying *adj* showing no signs of weariness even after long hard effort — see TIRELESS

unwed *adj* not married — see SINGLE 1

unwelcome *adj* **1** not giving pleasure to the mind or senses — see UNPLEASANT

2 not searched or asked for — see UNSOUGHT

unwell *adj* temporarily suffering from a disorder of the body — see SICK 1

unwholesome *adj* bad for the well-being of the body — see UNHEALTHY 1

unwieldy *adj* difficult to use or operate especially because of size, weight, or design — see CUMBERSOME

unwilling *adj* not made or done willingly or by choice — see INVOLUNTARY 1

unwillingness *n* a lack of willingness or desire to do or accept something — see RELUCTANCE

unwind *vb* to get rid of nervous tension or anxiety — see RELAX 1

unwise *adj* **1** showing or marked by a lack of good sense or judgment — see FOOLISH 1

2 showing poor judgment especially in personal relationships or social situations — see INDISCREET

unwitting *adj* **1** happening by chance — see ACCIDENTAL

2 not informed about or aware of something — see IGNORANT 2

unwomanly *adj* having qualities or traits that are traditionally considered inappropriate for a girl or woman — see UNFEMININE

unwonted *adj* being out of the ordinary — see EXCEPTIONAL

unworkable *adj* not capable of being put to use or account — see IMPRACTICAL

unworldliness *n* the quality or state of being simple and sincere — see NAÏVETÉ 1

unworldly *adj* lacking in worldly wisdom or informed judgment — see NAIVE 1

unworried *adj* free from emotional or mental agitation — see CALM 2

unwritten *adj* made or carried on through speaking rather than in writing — see VERBAL 2

unyielding *adj* **1** showing no signs of slackening or yielding in one's purpose ⟨the pioneers faced the challenge of settling the frontier with *unyielding* courage⟩

synonyms determined, dogged, grim, implacable, relentless, unappeasable, unflinching, unrelenting

related words hardheaded, headstrong, mulish, obdurate, opinionated, peevish, pertinacious, perverse, pigheaded, self-willed, stubborn, uncooperative, willful (*or* wilful); merciless, ruthless, unforgiving

near antonyms slackening, softening, yielding; impotent, invertebrate, slack, spineless, weak

2 having a consistency that does not easily yield to pressure — see FIRM 2

3 incapable of or highly resistant to bending — see STIFF 1

4 sticking to an opinion, purpose, or course of action in spite of reason, arguments, or persuasion — see OBSTINATE

unyoke *vb* to set or force apart — see SEPARATE 1

up *adj* **1** being at a higher level than average — see HIGH 2

2 brought or having come to an end — see COMPLETE 2

3 having information especially as a result of study or experience — see FAMILIAR 2

up *vb* **1** to make greater in size, amount, or number — see INCREASE 1

2 to move from a lower to a higher place or position — see RAISE 1

3 to move or extend upward — see ASCEND

upbeat *adj* **1** having or showing a good mood or disposition — see CHEERFUL 1

2 having qualities which inspire hope — see HOPEFUL 1

upbraid *vb* to criticize (someone) severely or angrily especially for personal failings — see SCOLD

upcoming *adj* being soon to appear or take place — see FORTHCOMING

up–country *n* a rural region that forms the edge of the settled or developed part of a country — see FRONTIER 2

upend *vb* to fix in an upright position — see ERECT 1

upgrade *n* **1** an upward slope — see ASCENT 2

2 a raising or a state of being raised to a higher rank or position — see ADVANCEMENT 2

3 the degree to which something rises up from a position level with the horizon — see SLANT

upgrade *vb* to move higher in rank or position — see PROMOTE 1

upheaval *n* a violent disturbance (as of the political or social order) — see CONVULSION

uphold *vb* **1** to continue to declare to be true or proper despite opposition or objections — see MAINTAIN 2

2 to hold up or serve as a foundation for — see SUPPORT 3

3 to move from a lower to a higher place or position — see RAISE 1

upkeep *n* the act or activity of keeping something in an existing and usually satisfactory condition — see MAINTENANCE

upland *n* an area of high ground — see HEIGHT 4

uplift *vb* to move from a lower to a higher place or position — see RAISE 1

uplifted *adj* being positioned above a surface — see ELEVATED 1

upmost *adj* being at a point or level higher than all others — see TOP 1

upon *prep* in or into contact with — see AGAINST

upper–class *adj* of high birth, rank, or station — see NOBLE 1

upper class *n* the highest class in a society — see ARISTROCRACY

upper crust *n* **1** individuals carefully selected as being the best of a class — see ELITE

2 the highest class in a society — see ARISTROCRACY

upper hand *n* the more favorable condition or position in a competition — see ADVANTAGE 1

THESAURUS

uppermost *adj* being at a point or level higher than all others — see TOP 1

uppish *adj* having a feeling of superiority that shows itself in an overbearing attitude — see ARROGANT

uppity *adj* having a feeling of superiority that shows itself in an overbearing attitude — see ARROGANT

upraise *vb* **1** to move from a lower to a higher place or position — see RAISE 1
2 to fix in an upright position — see ERECT 1

upraised *adj* being positioned above a surface — see ELEVATED 1

upright *adj* **1** conforming to a high standard of morality or virtue — see GOOD 2
2 following the accepted rules of moral conduct — see HONORABLE 1
3 rising straight up — see ERECT

uprightness *n* **1** conduct that conforms to an accepted standard of right and wrong — see MORALITY 1
2 faithfulness to high moral standards — see HONOR 1

uprise *vb* **1** to leave one's bed — see ARISE 1
2 to move or extend upward — see ASCEND

uprising *n* open fighting against authority (as one's own government) — see REBELLION

uproar *n* **1** a state of noisy, confused activity — see COMMOTION
2 a state of wildly excited activity or emotion — see FRENZY
3 a violent disturbance (as of the political or social order) — see CONVULSION
4 a violent shouting — see CLAMOR 1

uproarious *adj* causing or intended to cause laughter — see FUNNY 1

uproot *vb* to draw out by force or with effort — see EXTRACT

upset *adj* feeling or showing uncomfortable feelings of uncertainty — see NERVOUS 1

upset *n* an act or instance of the order of things being disturbed ⟨the move to a new town is just the latest in a series of *upsets* for my family over the last year⟩
synonyms derangement, dislocation, disruption, disturbance
related words convulsion, revolution, upheaval

upset *vb* **1** to trouble the mind of; to make uneasy — see DISTURB 1
2 to turn on one's side or upside down — see CAPSIZE
3 to undo the proper order or arrangement of — see DISORDER

upsetting *adj* causing worry or anxiety — see TROUBLESOME

upshot *n* a condition or occurrence traceable to a cause — see EFFECT 1

upside–down *adj* lacking in order, neatness, and often cleanliness — see MESSY

upstanding *adj* **1** following the accepted rules of moral conduct — see HONORABLE 1
2 rising straight up — see ERECT

upsweep *vb* to move or extend upward — see ASCEND

uptight *adj* feeling or showing uncomfortable feelings of uncertainty — see NERVOUS 1

up–to–date *adj* **1** being or involving the latest methods, concepts, information, or styles — see MODERN

2 having information especially as a result of study or experience — see FAMILIAR 2

upturn *vb* to move or extend upward — see ASCEND

urbane *adj* having or showing very polished and worldly manners — see SUAVE

urbanize *vb* to accustom to the ways of the city — see CITIFY

urchin *n* an appealingly mischievous person — see SCAMP 1

urge *n* a strong wish for something — see DESIRE

urge *vb* to try to persuade (someone) through earnest appeals to follow a course of action ⟨our teacher *urged* us to do a good job on the assignment⟩
synonyms egg (on), encourage, exhort, goad, press, prod, prompt
related words drive, propel, spur, stimulate; hurry, hustle, push, rush; beseech, implore, importune; blandish, cajole, coax, soft-soap, wheedle; high-pressure, nag, needle, pressure; foment, incite, instigate, provoke, stir (up)
near antonyms deter, discourage, dissuade; brake, check, constrain, curb, hold back, inhibit, restrain

urgent *adj* needing immediate attention — see ACUTE 2

usable *adj* **1** capable of or suitable for being used for a particular purpose ⟨although the spade was *usable* as a snow shovel, it didn't do a very good job⟩
synonyms available, employable, exploitable, fit, functional, operable, practicable, serviceable, useful
related words applicable, relevant; doable, feasible; reusable
near antonyms outdated, outmoded
antonyms impracticable, inoperable, nonfunctional, unavailable, unemployable, unusable
2 capable of being put to use or account — see PRACTICAL 1

usage *n* the act or practice of employing something for a particular purpose — see USE 1

use *n* **1** the act or practice of employing something for a particular purpose ⟨the *use* of boom boxes was strictly prohibited in the park⟩
synonyms application, employment, exercise, operation, play, usage
related words exertion; reuse
near antonyms disuse
2 the capacity for being useful for some purpose ⟨the broken grill wasn't going to be of much *use* in cooking the hamburgers⟩
synonyms account, avail, service, serviceability, serviceableness, usefulness, utility
related words advantage, benefit, gain; aid, assistance, help; applicability, appropriateness, fitness, relevance; profit, value, worth
near antonyms inapplicability, inappropriateness
antonyms uselessness, worthlessness
3 positive regard for something — see LIKING

use *vb* **1** to put into action or service ⟨I think I'm going to need to *use* the large hammer for this project⟩
synonyms apply, employ, exercise, exploit, harness, operate, utilize
related words handle, manipulate, wield; direct, run, work; recycle, reuse
phrases draw on (*or* upon), make use of
near antonyms ignore, neglect; misapply, misuse

2 to behave toward in a stated way — see TREAT 1

3 to take unfair advantage of — see EXPLOIT 1

used *adj* being in the habit or custom — see AC-CUSTOMED

useful *adj* **1** capable of being put to use or account — see PRACTICAL 1

2 capable of or suitable for being used for a particular purpose — see USABLE 1

usefulness *n* the capacity for being useful for some purpose — see USE 2

useless *adj* **1** not capable of being put to use or account — see IMPRACTICAL

2 producing no results — see FUTILE

user *n* a person who regularly uses drugs especially illegally — see DOPER

use up *vb* to make complete use of — see DE-PLETE

usher *vb* to point out the way for (someone) especially from a position in front — see LEAD 1

usual *adj* **1** accepted, used, or practiced by most people — see CURRENT 1

2 being of the type that is encountered in the normal course of events — see ORDINARY 1

3 often observed or encountered — see COM-MON 1

usually *adv* according to the usual course of things — see NATURALLY 2

usurp *vb* to take or make use of without authority or right — see APPROPRIATE 1

utensil *n* an article intended for use in work — see IMPLEMENT

utility *n* the capacity for being useful for some purpose — see USE 2

utilize *vb* to put into action or service — see USE 1

utmost *adj* **1** most distant from a center — see EX-TREME 1

2 of the greatest or highest degree or quantity — see ULTIMATE 1

3 of the highest degree — see FULL 2

utopia *n* a place or state of great happiness — see PARADISE 1

utopian *n* one whose conduct is guided more by the image of perfection than by the real world — see IDEALIST

utter *adj* having no exceptions or restrictions — see ABSOLUTE 2

utter *vb* **1** to send forth using the vocal chords ⟨she tried not to *utter* a sound as the doctor gave her a flu shot⟩

synonyms emit

related words blurt (out), ejaculate, exclaim; gasp, groan, heave, hoot, moan, pant, quaver, snarl, sob, sputter, squawk, squeak, squeal, stammer, stutter, whimper, yowl; mouth, whisper

2 to express (a thought or emotion) in words — see SAY 1

utterance *n* **1** an act, process, or means of putting something into words — see EXPRESSION 1

2 something that is said — see WORD 2

uttered *adj* created by the body's organs of sound — see VOCAL

utterly *adv* **1** to a full extent or degree — see FULLY 1

2 to a large extent or degree — see GREATLY 2

uttermost *adj* of the greatest or highest degree or quantity — see ULTIMATE 1

vacancy *n* **1** empty space ⟨the vast *vacancy* that exists between our solar system and the nearest star having its own orbiting planets⟩

synonyms blank, blankness, emptiness, vacuity, void

related words nothingness; vacuum; bareness, barrenness, bleakness, desolateness, hollowness

near antonyms fullness, repleteness

2 the quality or state of being empty ⟨the *vacancy* of the cavernous gymnasium was eerily apparent to me as I shot baskets alone⟩

synonyms bareness, emptiness, vacuity

related words hollowness; blankness, vacuum, void; barrenness, bleakness, desolateness; availability, clearness, openness; depletion, dryness, exhaustion

near antonyms completeness; abundance, fatness, repleteness

antonyms fullness

vacant *adj* **1** lacking contents that could or should be present — see EMPTY 1

2 not being in a state of use, activity, or employment — see INACTIVE 2

3 not expressing any emotion — see BLANK 1

vacate *vb* to remove the contents of — see EM-PTY

vacated *adj* left unoccupied or unused — see ABANDONED

vacation *n* a period during which the usual routine of school or work is suspended ⟨we take a *vacation* at the beach for a week every year⟩

synonyms break, holiday [*chiefly British*], leave, recess

related words furlough, liberty; breather, relaxation, respite, rest; interim, intermission, interval; feast, holy day, legal holiday; honeymoon; idling, loafing, lounging, slacking off

near antonyms routine, work

vacation *vb* to take or spend a vacation ⟨Sue is hoping to *vacation* in Spain this summer⟩

synonyms holiday

related words escape, get away; break, ease up, let up, relax, rest; bum, goldbrick, idle, loaf, lounge, slack off

near antonyms drudge, endeavor, grub, hump, hustle, labor, moil, peg (away), plod, plow, plug, slave, slog, strain, strive, struggle, sweat, toil, travail, work

vacillate *vb* to show uncertainty about the right course of action — see HESITATE

vacillation *n* the act or an instance of pausing because of uncertainty about the right course of action — see HESITATION

vacuity *n* **1** empty space — see VACANCY 1

2 the quality or state of being empty — see VA-CANCY 2

THESAURUS

3 the quality or state of lacking intelligence or quickness of mind — see STUPIDITY 1

vacuous *adj* not having or showing an ability to absorb ideas readily — see STUPID 1

vagabond *adj* traveling from place to place — see ITINERANT

vagabond *n* **1** a homeless wanderer who may beg or steal for a living — see TRAMP

2 a person who roams about without a fixed route or destination — see NOMAD

vagary *n* a sudden impulsive and apparently un-motivated idea or action — see WHIM

vagrant *adj* traveling from place to place — see ITINERANT

vagrant *n* a homeless wanderer who may beg or steal for a living — see TRAMP

vague *adj* **1** not clearly expressed ⟨Johnny gave as *vague* a reply to the test question as he could, hoping for partial credit⟩
synonyms fuzzy, indefinite, unclear
related words ambiguous, cryptic, dark, enigmatic (*also* enigmatical), equivocal, murky, nebulous, obscure, unintelligible; bleary, dim, faint, foggy, hazy, indeterminate, indistinguishable, uncertain, undefinable, undefined, undetermined; inexplicable, inscrutable, mysterious; baffling, bewildering, confounding, confusing, mystifying, perplexing, puzzling, unfathomable
near antonyms candid, direct, forthright, foursquare, frank, honest, open, openhearted, outspoken, plainspoken, straight, straightforward, unguarded; obvious, plain, unambiguous, understandable, unequivocal; comprehensible, fathomable, intelligible; defined, distinct; blatant, patent, unmistakable
antonyms clear, definite, explicit, specific

2 not seen or understood clearly — see FAINT 1

vain *adj* **1** having too high an opinion of oneself — see CONCEITED

2 producing no results — see FUTILE

vainglorious *adj* having too high an opinion of oneself — see CONCEITED

vaingloriousness *n* an often unjustified feeling of being pleased with oneself or with one's situation or achievements — see COMPLACENCE

vainglory *n* an often unjustified feeling of being pleased with oneself or with one's situation or achievements — see COMPLACENCE

vainness *n* an often unjustified feeling of being pleased with oneself or with one's situation or achievements — see COMPLACENCE

vale *n* an area of lowland between hills or mountains — see VALLEY

valedictory *adj* given, taken, or performed at parting — see PARTING

valiant *adj* feeling or displaying no fear by temperament — see BRAVE

valid *adj* **1** according to the rules of logic — see LOGICAL 1

2 based on sound reasoning or information — see GOOD 1

validate *vb* **1** to give evidence or testimony to the truth or factualness of — see CONFIRM

2 to show the existence or truth of by evidence — see PROVE 1

validation *n* something presented in support of the truth or accuracy of a claim — see PROOF

valley *n* an area of lowland between hills or mountains ⟨the *valley* will be the first to flood if the river rises⟩

synonyms dale, hollow, vale
related words canyon, dell, depression, dingle, glen, ravine, rift valley; basin, bowl
near antonyms alp, mount, peak; mountain range; mountaintop, pinnacle, precipice, summit

valor *n* strength of mind to carry on in spite of danger — see COURAGE

valorous *adj* feeling or displaying no fear by temperament — see BRAVE

valuable *adj* commanding a large price — see COSTLY

valuation *n* **1** the act of placing a value on the nature, character, or quality of something — see ESTIMATE 1

2 the amount of money for which something will find a buyer — see VALUE 1

3 the relative usefulness or importance of something as judged by specific qualities — see WORTH 1

value *n* **1** the amount of money for which something will find a buyer ⟨the real *value* of that house is close to a million dollars⟩
synonyms market value, valuation, worth
related words charge, cost, fee, figure, price; appraisal, assessment, estimate, estimation, evaluation; face value, list price, unit price

2 a quality that gives something special worth — see EXCELLENCE 2

3 the relative usefulness or importance of something as judged by specific qualities — see WORTH 1

value *vb* **1** to hold dear — see LOVE 1

2 to make an approximate or tentative judgment regarding — see ESTIMATE 1

valueless *adj* having no usefulness — see WORTHLESS

valve *n* a fixture for controlling the flow of a liquid — see FAUCET

vandal *n* a person who damages or destroys property on purpose ⟨a group of *vandals* broke into school and painted graffiti on the walls⟩
synonyms defacer
related words demolisher, desecrater (*or* desecrator), despoiler, destroyer, dynamiter, ravager, ruiner, saboteur, wrecker; looter, pillager, plunderer, spoiler
near antonyms conserver, preserver, protector, saver

vandalism *n* deliberate damaging or destroying of another's property ⟨anyone guilty of *vandalism* to school property will be expelled⟩
synonyms defacement
related words demolishing, demolishment, desecrating, desecration, despoiling, despoilment, destruction, ravaging, ruin, ruination, wrecking; sabotage; looting, pillaging, plunder, plundering, sacking
near antonyms conservation, preservation, protection, saving

vandalize *vb* to deliberately cause the damage or destruction of another's property ⟨he decided to *vandalize* the store because the owner had kicked him out⟩
synonyms deface
related words desecrate, violate; break, damage, despoil, harm, hurt, impair, mar, shatter, spoil; demolish, destroy, devastate, ravage, raze, ruin, scourge, smash, tear down, waste, wipe out, wreck; sabotage; loot, pillage, plunder, sack

near antonyms conserve, preserve, protect, save; build, rebuild

vanguard *n* the leading or most important part of a movement — see FOREFRONT

vanish *vb* to cease to be visible — see DISAPPEAR

vanished *adj* no longer existing — see EXTINCT

vanity *n* an often unjustified feeling of being pleased with oneself or with one's situation or achievements — see COMPLACENCE

vanquish *vb* to bring under one's control by force of arms — see CONQUER 1

vanquisher *n* one that defeats an enemy or opponent — see VICTOR 1

vanquishing *n* the act or process of bringing someone or something under one's control — see CONQUEST

vantage *n* the more favorable condition or position in a competition — see ADVANTAGE 1

variable *adj* **1** capable of being readily changed — see FLEXIBLE 1
2 likely to change frequently, suddenly, or unexpectedly — see FICKLE 1

variance *n* a lack of agreement or harmony — see DISCORD

variation *n* the act, process, or result of making different — see CHANGE

varicolored *adj* marked by a variety of usually vivid colors — see COLORFUL

varied *adj* consisting of many things of different sorts — see MISCELLANEOUS

variegated *adj* **1** marked by a variety of usually vivid colors — see COLORFUL
2 marked with spots — see SPOTTED 1

variety *n* **1** the quality or state of being composed of many different elements or types ⟨the sheer *variety* of the city's ethnic restaurants was dazzling⟩
synonyms assortment, diverseness, diversity, miscellaneousness, variousness
related words heterogeneousness; disparateness, disparity, dissimilarity, distinction, distinctiveness, distinctness, unlikeness
near antonyms homogeneity, likeness, sameness, similarity; fewness, paucity
2 an unorganized collection or mixture of various things — see MISCELLANY 1

variousness *n* the quality or state of being composed of many different elements or types — see VARIETY 1

varlet *n* a mean, evil, or unprincipled person — see VILLAIN

vary *vb* **1** to be unlike; to not be the same — see DIFFER 1
2 to make different in some way — see CHANGE 1
3 to occur within a continuous range of variation — see RUN 4
4 to pass from one form, state, or level to another — see CHANGE 2

varying *adj* not staying constant — see UNEVEN 2

vast *adj* unusually large — see HUGE

vastly *adv* to a large extent or degree — see GREATLY 2

vastness *n* the quality or state of being very large — see IMMENSITY

vasty *adj* unusually large — see HUGE

¹**vault** *n* an underground burial chamber — see CRYPT

²**vault** *n* an act of leaping into the air — see JUMP 1

vault *vb* to propel oneself upward or forward into the air — see JUMP 1

veer *vb* **1** to change one's course or direction — see TURN 3
2 to change the course or direction of (something) — see TURN 2
3 to depart abruptly from a straight line or course — see SWERVE 1

vegetation *n* green leaves or plants — see GREENERY 1

vehemence *n* **1** the quality or state of being forceful (as in expression) ⟨the *vehemence* in her voice when she said that she never gossiped surprised me⟩
synonyms aggressiveness, assertiveness, emphasis, fierceness, forcefulness, intensity, vigorousness
related words potency, power, strength; eloquence; fervency, insistence, passion, warmth; absoluteness, clearness, incisiveness, plainness
near antonyms ambiguity, equivocation
antonyms feebleness, mildness, weakness
2 depth of feeling — see ARDOR 1

vehement *adj* **1** marked by or uttered with forcefulness — see EMPHATIC 1
2 extreme in degree, power, or effect — see INTENSE
3 having or expressing great depth of feeling — see FERVENT

vehicle *n* **1** something used to achieve an end — see AGENT 1
2 something used to carry goods or passengers — see CONVEYANCE

veil *n* something that covers or conceals like a piece of cloth — see CLOAK 1

veil *vb* **1** to keep secret or shut off from view — see ¹HIDE 2
2 to surround or cover closely — see ENFOLD 1

vein *n* a distinctive way of putting ideas into words — see STYLE 1

veld *or* **veldt** *n* a broad area of level or rolling treeless country — see PLAIN

velocity *n* a high rate of movement or performance — see SPEED

velvety *adj* smooth or delicate in appearance or feel — see SOFT 2

venal *adj* open to improper influence and especially bribery ⟨that judge is known for being *venal* and easily bought⟩
synonyms bribable, corruptible, purchasable
related words hack, mercenary; crooked, cutthroat, dishonest, unethical, unprincipled, unscrupulous; corrupt, debased, debauched, degenerate, degraded, demoralized, depraved, dissipated, dissolute, perverse, perverted, warped; bad, evil, immoral, iniquitous, nefarious, sinful, vicious, wicked
near antonyms ethical, honest, principled; good, moral, righteous, virtuous
antonyms incorruptible, uncorruptible

vend *vb* to offer for sale to the public — see MARKET

vendor *also* **vender** *n* the person in a business deal who hands over an item in exchange for money ⟨we're thinking of making a deal with that other software *vendor*⟩
synonyms dealer, merchandiser, seller
related words auctioneer, concessionaire; blackmarketer, bootlegger, fence, fencer, hustler, smuggler, trader; distributor, retailer; sacrificer; wholesaler; hawker, huckster, peddler (*also* pedlar); salesclerk, salesman, salesperson, saleswom-

THESAURUS

an; exporter, handler; bargainer, haggler, horse trader, palterer
near antonyms consumer, end user, user
antonyms buyer, purchaser
veneer *n* an outer part or layer — see EXTERIOR
venerable *adj* **1** deserving honor and respect especially by reason of age ⟨the *venerable* old man was a cherished source of advice and wisdom for the villagers⟩
synonyms hallowed, revered, reverend, venerated
related words honorable, reputable, respectable; honored, respected, reverenced; admirable, estimable, redoubtable; good, moral, righteous
near antonyms bad, discreditable, disgraceful, dishonorable, disreputable, ignominious, infamous, loose, notorious, shameful; immoral, seamy, shady, sordid, unsavory, vile, wicked; base, contemptible, despicable, detestable, dirty, low, mean, wretched
2 dating or surviving from the distant past — see ANCIENT 1
venerate *vb* to offer honor or respect to (someone) as a divine power — see WORSHIP 1
venerated *adj* deserving honor and respect especially by reason of age — see VENERABLE 1
vengeance *n* the act or an instance of paying back an injury with an injury — see REVENGE
vengeful *adj* likely to seek revenge — see VINDICTIVE
venial *adj* worthy of forgiveness ⟨stealing pencils is a *venial* offense⟩
synonyms excusable, forgivable, pardonable, remittable
related words justifiable, redeemable; allowable; insignificant, minor, trifling, trivial; harmless, tolerable
near antonyms abominable, criminal, damning, evil, heinous; sinful, vile, wicked
antonyms inexcusable, mortal, unforgivable, unpardonable
venom *n* **1** a substance that by chemical action can kill or injure a living thing — see POISON
2 the desire to cause pain for the satisfaction of doing harm — see MALICE
venomous *adj* containing or contaminated with a substance capable of injuring or killing a living thing — see POISONOUS
vent *vb* **1** to find emotional release for — see TAKE OUT 1
2 to make known (as an idea, emotion, or opinion) — see EXPRESS 1
3 to throw or give off — see EMIT 1
ventilate *vb* to make known (as an idea, emotion, or opinion) — see EXPRESS 1
venture *n* a risky undertaking — see GAMBLE
venture *vb* **1** to place in danger — see ENDANGER
2 to take a chance on — see RISK 1
venturesome *adj* **1** inclined or willing to take risks — see BOLD 1
2 involving potential loss or injury — see DANGEROUS
venturous *adj* inclined or willing to take risks — see BOLD 1
veracious *adj* **1** being in the habit of telling the truth — see TRUTHFUL
2 following an original exactly — see FAITHFUL 2
veracity *n* **1** devotion to telling the truth — see HONESTY 1
2 the quality or state of being very accurate — see PRECISION

verbal *adj* **1** of or relating to words or language ⟨the child didn't yet have the *verbal* skills needed to tell the doctor about the pain he was experiencing⟩
synonyms lexical, linguistic
related words communicative, conversational
2 made or carried on through speaking rather than in writing ⟨a *verbal* agreement carries less force than a written contract⟩
synonyms oral, spoken, unwritten
related words implicit, informal; articulated, verbalized; given, pronounced, said, sounded, stated, told, voiced
near antonyms explicit, formal
antonyms written
verbalize *vb* to express (a thought or emotion) in words — see SAY 1
verbatim *adv* in the same words ⟨you can't just copy the encyclopedia article *verbatim* for your report—that's plagiarism⟩
synonyms directly, exactly
related words accurately, precisely; identically; literally
phrases word for word
near antonyms basically, essentially; carelessly, freely, imprecisely, inaccurately, loosely
antonyms inexactly
verbiage *n* the use of too many words to express an idea ⟨teachers loathe the *verbiage* that students resort to in order to pad a paper⟩
synonyms circumlocution, diffuseness, long-windedness, prolixity, redundancy, verboseness, verbosity, windiness, wordiness
related words circuitousness, circularity; tautology; reiteration, repetition, repetitiousness; embellishment, embroidering, exaggeration, hyperbole
near antonyms brevity, briefness, compactness, conciseness, crispness, pithiness, succinctness, terseness
verbose *adj* using or containing more words than necessary to express an idea — see WORDY
verboseness *n* the use of too many words to express an idea — see VERBIAGE
verbosity *n* the use of too many words to express an idea — see VERBIAGE
verdant *adj* covered with a thick, healthy natural growth — see LUSH 1
verdict *n* **1** a position arrived at after consideration — see DECISION 1
2 an idea that is believed to be true or valid without positive knowledge — see OPINION 1
verdure *n* green leaves or plants — see GREENERY 1
verge (on) *vb* **1** to be adjacent to — see ADJOIN 1
2 to come very close to being — see BORDER (ON)
verge *n* the line or relatively narrow space that marks the outer limit of something — see BORDER 1
verging *adj* having a border in common — see ADJACENT
verifiable *adj* capable of being proven as true or real ⟨we're not sure whether that's a *verifiable* hypothesis⟩ ⟨you need a *verifiable* note from your doctor to be excused from gym class⟩
synonyms confirmable, demonstrable, provable, supportable, sustainable
related words certifiable, documentable, warrantable; excusable, justifiable; alleged, assumed,

conjectured, guessed, presumed, surmised, suspected

near antonyms debatable, disputable, refutable

antonyms insupportable, unsupportable

verify *vb* to give evidence or testimony to the truth or factualness of — see CONFIRM

verifying *adj* serving to give support to the truth or factualness of something — see CORROBORATIVE

verily *adv* **1** to tell the truth — see ACTUALLY 1

2 not merely this but also — see EVEN

veritably *adv* in actual fact — see VERY 2

verity *n* **1** agreement with fact or reality — see TRUTH

2 devotion to telling the truth — see HONESTY 1

vernacular *adj* used in or suitable for speech and not formal writing — see COLLOQUIAL 1

versatile *adj* able to do many different kinds of things ⟨a *versatile* baseball player can play any position⟩ ⟨this tool is *versatile* enough to serve as a wrench or pliers⟩

synonyms adaptable, all-around (*also* all-round), protean, universal

related words multipurpose; well-rounded; able, ace, adept, experienced, expert, masterful, skilled, skillful; adjustable, alterable, changeable, elastic, flexible, fluid, malleable, modifiable, variable

near antonyms limited; amateur, inexperienced

verse *n* **1** a composition using rhythm and often rhyme to create a lyrical effect — see POEM

2 writing that uses rhythm, vivid language, and often rhyme to provoke an emotional response — see POETRY 1

versed *adj* **1** having information especially as a result of study or experience — see FAMILIAR 2

2 having or showing exceptional knowledge, experience, or skill in a field of endeavor — see PROFICIENT

versifier *n* a person who writes poetry — see POET

vertebral column *n* a column of bones supporting the trunk of a vertebrate animal — see SPINE

vertical *adj* rising straight up — see ERECT

verve *adj* active strength of body or mind — see VIGOR 1

very *adj* **1** being one and not another — see SAME 2

2 being this and no more — see MERE

3 existing in fact and not merely as a possibility — see ACTUAL

very *adv* **1** to a great degree ⟨that was a *very* brave thing to do⟩

synonyms awful, awfully, beastly, deadly, especially, exceedingly (*also* exceeding), extra, extremely, far, frightfully, full, greatly, heavily, highly, hugely, jolly, mightily, mighty, mortally, most, much, particularly, rattling, real, right, so, something, super, terribly, too, whacking

related words completely, entirely, purely, thoroughly, totally, utterly; eminently, exceptionally; considerably, extensively, significantly, substantially; appreciably, discernibly, noticeably, palpably; abundantly, plentifully; astronomically, grandly, monstrously, monumentally

phrases by far, far and away, good and, in particular

near antonyms meagerly, scantily; barely, hardly, just, marginally, minimally, scarcely

antonyms little, negligibly, nominally, slightly

2 in actual fact ⟨the *very* same thing happened to me⟩

synonyms actually, authentically, genuinely, really, veritably

related words accurately, exactly, just, precisely, right, sharp, smack-dab, squarely; almost, nearly, practically; literally, truly

phrases in truth

near antonyms apparently, ostensibly, outwardly, seemingly

antonyms professedly, supposedly

vessel *n* **1** a large craft for travel by water — see SHIP

2 a small buoyant structure for travel on water — see BOAT 1

3 a usually circular utensil for holding something (as food) — see DISH

4 something into which a liquid or smaller objects can be put for storage or transportation — see CONTAINER

vest *vb* to put (something) into the possession or safekeeping of another — see GIVE 2

vestibule *n* the entrance room of a building — see HALL 1

vestige *n* a tiny often physical indication of something lost or vanished ⟨a few strange words carved on a tree were the only *vestige* of the lost colony of Roanoke⟩

synonyms relic, shadow, trace

related words memento, remembrance, reminder; artifact; afterimage, aftertaste; balance, oddment, remainder, remnant, scrap, scraping(s); leavings, remains, residual, residue, rest

vestry *n* a room in a church building for sacred furnishings (as vestments) — see SACRISTY

vet *n* a person with long experience in a specified area — see VETERAN

veteran *adj* having or showing exceptional knowledge, experience, or skill in a field of endeavor — see PROFICIENT

veteran *n* a person with long experience in a specified area ⟨as a *veteran* of politics, she is often consulted by eager young hopefuls⟩

synonyms old hand, old-timer, vet

related words war-horse; expert, master, pro, professional

near antonyms apprentice, cub; boot, novitiate; amateur, dilettante; learner, student, trainee; candidate, entrant, probationer

antonyms beginner, colt, fledgling, freshman, greenhorn, neophyte, newcomer, novice, recruit, rookie, tenderfoot, tyro

veto *n* an order that something not be done or used — see PROHIBITION 2

veto *vb* to reject by or as if by a vote — see NEGATIVE 1

vex *vb* to disturb the peace of mind of (someone) especially by repeated disagreeable acts — see IRRITATE 1

vexation *n* **1** the act of making unwelcome intrusions upon another — see ANNOYANCE 1

2 the feeling of impatience or anger caused by another's repeated disagreeable acts — see ANNOYANCE 2

vexatious *adj* causing annoyance — see ANNOYING

vexing *adj* causing annoyance — see ANNOYING

via *prep* along the way of — see BY 1

viable *adj* capable of being done or carried out — see POSSIBLE 1

viands *n pl* substances intended to be eaten — see FOOD

vibrancy *n* the quality or state of having abundant or intense activity — see VITALITY 1

THESAURUS

vibrant *adj* **1** marked by much life, movement, or activity — see ALIVE 2

2 marked by conspicuously full and rich sounds or tones — see RESONANT

vibrate *vb* to make a series of small irregular or violent movements — see SHAKE 1

vibration *n* a series of slight movements by a body back and forth or from side to side ⟨the *vibration* of the floor caused by thundering feet in the hallway⟩

synonyms jiggling, oscillation, quivering, shaking, shuddering, trembling, twitching

related words jiggle, palpitation, shake, shudder, tremor, twitch

vice *n* **1** immoral conduct or practices harmful or offensive to society ⟨that section of the city is legendary for crime and *vice*⟩

synonyms corruption, debauchery, depravity, immorality, iniquity, licentiousness, sin

related words bad, badness, blackness, evil, evildoing, ill, wickedness, wrong, villainy; atrociousness, evilness, heinousness, nefariousness, sinfulness, unscrupulousness, viciousness, vileness; devilry (*or* deviltry), fiendishness; corruptness, debasement, degeneracy, degeneration, depravedness, dissolution; indecency, lasciviousness, lewdness, looseness, perversion; abomination, anathema, taboo (*also* tabu); criminality, reprehensibleness; baseness, despicableness, dirtiness, lowness, meanness; lousiness, miserableness, wretchedness

near antonyms good, right; honesty, honor, integrity, legitimacy, probity, rectitude, scrupulousness, uprightness; goodness, righteousness, virtuousness; blamelessness; chastity, innocence, perfection, pureness, purity, spotlessness; cleanness, correctness, decency, decorousness, propriety, rightness, seemliness

antonyms morality, virtue

2 a defect in character — see FAULT 1

vicious *adj* **1** extreme in degree, power, or effect — see INTENSE

2 having or showing the desire to inflict severe pain and suffering on others — see CRUEL 1

3 not conforming to a high moral standard; morally unacceptable — see BAD 2

4 violently unfriendly or aggressive in disposition — see FIERCE 1

viciously *adv* in a mean or spiteful manner — see NASTILY

viciousness *n* **1** the desire to cause pain for the satisfaction of doing harm — see MALICE

2 the willful infliction of pain and suffering on others — see CRUELTY

victim *n* **1** a person or thing harmed, lost, or destroyed — see CASUALTY 1

2 a person or thing that is the object of abuse, criticism, or ridicule — see TARGET 1

3 something offered to a god — see SACRIFICE

victimize *vb* to rob by the use of trickery or threats — see FLEECE

victor *n* **1** one that defeats an enemy or opponent ⟨the computer is usually the *victor* in a chess match against a human opponent⟩

synonyms beater, conqueror, master, subduer, trimmer, vanquisher, whipper, winner

related words champion, finalist; ruler, subjugator

near antonyms pushover, quitter; failure, flop, washout

antonyms loser

2 the person who comes in first in a competition — see CHAMPION 1

victory *n* an instance of defeating an enemy or opponent ⟨with great effort, our team managed an upset *victory* in the final moments⟩

synonyms triumph, win

related words conquest, mastery, subjugation, vanquishing; landslide, shutout, sweep; success; takeover

near antonyms upset; collapse, debacle (*also* débâcle), failure, fizzle, flop, folding, nonsuccess, washout; decline, slip, slump, wane; lurch, setback

antonyms beating, defeat, licking, loss, overthrow, rout, shellacking, trimming, whipping

victuals *n pl* substances intended to be eaten — see FOOD

vie *vb* to engage in a contest — see COMPETE

view *n* **1** all that can be seen from a certain point ⟨the *view* of the mountains from the inn's porch is spectacular⟩

synonyms lookout, outlook, panorama, prospect, vista

related words landscape, scene, scenery; ken, sight

2 an idea that is believed to be true or valid without positive knowledge — see OPINION 1

3 an instance of looking especially briefly — see LOOK 2

view *vb* to make note of (something) through the use of one's eyes — see SEE 1

viewpoint *n* a way of looking at or thinking about something — see POINT OF VIEW

vigilance *n* the act or state of being constantly attentive and responsive to signs of opportunity, activity, or danger ⟨eternal *vigilance* is the price of freedom⟩

synonyms alertness, attentiveness, lookout, surveillance, watch, watchfulness

related words aliveness, awareness, consciousness, sensitivity; heedfulness, observance, observation; sleeplessness, wakefulness; care, carefulness, caution, chariness, wariness; preparation, readiness

near antonyms absentmindedness, absorption, abstraction, daydreaming, daze, distraction; engrossment, obliviousness, preoccupation; unawareness, unconsciousness; carelessness, heedlessness, inattention, inattentiveness; unwariness

vigilant *adj* paying close attention usually for the purpose of anticipating approaching danger or opportunity — see ALERT 1

vigilante *n* one who inflicts punishment in return for an injury or offense — see NEMESIS 1

vigor *n* **1** active strength of body or mind ⟨she was picked for the soccer team because of her *vigor* and enthusiasm⟩

synonyms bounce, dash, drive, energy, esprit, ginger, go, hardihood, life, pep, punch, sap, snap, starch, verve, vim, vitality, zing, zip

related words animation, briskness, jauntiness, liveliness, spiritedness, sprightliness, vivaciousness, vivacity; ardor, fervor, fire, passion, zeal; main, might, muscle, potency, power, puissance, strength; brawniness, fitness, hardiness, huskiness, virility; haleness, health, healthiness, soundness, wellness

near antonyms indolence, laziness; debilitation, debility, delicacy, delicateness, disablement, enfeeblement, faintness, feebleness, frailness, frailty, impotence, infirmity, powerlessness, puniness, slightness, softness, tenderness, weakness; enervation, exhaustion, prostration

antonyms lethargy, listlessness, sluggishness

2 the ability to exert effort for the accomplishment of a task — see POWER 2

vigorous *adj* **1** having active strength of body or mind ⟨he remains healthy and *vigorous* despite being over eighty years old⟩

synonyms dynamic, energetic, flush, gingery, lusty, peppy, red-blooded, robust, vital

related words animated, lively, spirited, sprightly, vivacious; energized, enlivened, invigorated, vitalized; firm, fortified, mettlesome, mighty, powerful, puissant, strong; refreshed, rejuvenated, revitalized; able-bodied, beefy, brawny, fit, fortified, hardy, husky, rugged, stalwart, stout, strapping, sturdy, tough; hale, healthy, sound; capable, competent

near antonyms delicate, effete, enervated, faint, feeble, frail, infirm, weak, weakened; impotent, powerless, prostrate, prostrated, sapped, tired; indolent, lackadaisical, languid, lazy; invertebrate, nerveless, soft, spineless, wimpy; ill, unhealthy, unsound, unwell; broken-down, debilitated, decrepit, disabled, wasted, worn-out

antonyms lethargic, listless, sluggish, torpid

2 able to withstand hardship, strain, or exposure — see HARDY 1

3 marked by or uttered with forcefulness — see EMPHATIC 1

4 not showing weakness or uncertainty — see FIRM 1

vigorously *adv* in a vigorous and forceful manner — see HARD 3

vigorousness *n* the quality or state of being forceful (as in expression) — see VEHEMENCE 1

vile *adj* **1** not conforming to a high moral standard; morally unacceptable — see BAD 2

2 not following or in accordance with standards of honor and decency — see IGNOBLE 2

3 unpleasant to look at — see UGLY 1

vileness *n* the state or quality of being utterly evil — see ENORMITY 1

vilification *n* the making of false statements that damage another's reputation — see SLANDER

vilify *vb* to make untrue and harmful statements about — see SLANDER

vilifying *n* the making of false statements that damage another's reputation — see SLANDER

villa *n* a large impressive residence — see MANSION

villager *n* a person who lives in a town on a permanent basis — see BURGHER

villain *n* a mean, evil, or unprincipled person ⟨only a heartless *villain* would kidnap a baby for ransom⟩

synonyms beast, brute, devil, evildoer, fiend, heavy, knave, miscreant, monster, no-good, rapscallion, rascal, reprobate, rogue, savage, scalawag (*or* scallywag), scamp, scoundrel, varlet, wretch

related words blackguard; criminal, crook, culprit, felon, lawbreaker, malefactor, offender, transgressor; perpetrator, sinner, trespasser, wrongdoer; cad, heel; bravo, desperado, outlaw, convict, jailbird; assassin, cutthroat, gangster, gunman, hoodlum, racketeer, ruffian, thug; ne'er-do-well, trash

near antonyms angel, saint; hero

villainous *adj* not conforming to a high moral standard; morally unacceptable — see BAD 2

villainously *adv* in a mean or spiteful manner — see NASTILY

villainy *n* that which is morally unacceptable — see EVIL

vim *n* active strength of body or mind — see VIGOR 1

vindicate *vb* **1** to free from a charge of wrongdoing — see EXCULPATE

2 to give evidence or testimony to the truth or factualness of — see CONFIRM

vindicating *adj* serving to give support to the truth or factualness of something — see CORROBORATIVE

vindictive *adj* likely to seek revenge ⟨be careful not to annoy the *vindictive* old woman who lives down the street⟩

synonyms revengeful, vengeful

related words avenging; resentful, uncharitable, unforgiving; catty, cruel, despiteful, hateful, malevolent, malicious, malign, malignant, mean, nasty, sadistic, spiteful, vicious, virulent; grim, implacable, merciless, relentless, unrelenting; baleful, baneful, evil; harsh, hostile, inimical

near antonyms charitable, forgiving, merciful, relenting; benevolent, benign, benignant, loving; brotherly, compassionate, good, good-hearted, kind, kindhearted, kindly, sympathetic, warm, warmhearted; altruistic, humane, humanitarian, philanthropic; sweet, tender, tenderhearted; high-minded, magnanimous, noble

vinegary *adj* causing or characterized by the one of the four basic taste sensations that is produced chiefly by acids — see SOUR 1

violate *vb* **1** to fail to keep ⟨you *violated* the school rule against swearing at sporting events⟩

synonyms breach, break, infringe, transgress

related words disobey, rebel; brush off, disregard, ignore, overlook, overpass, pass over, tune out, wink (at); dismiss, pooh-pooh (*also* pooh), scorn, shrug off; defy, resist, withstand

near antonyms defer (to), serve, submit (to), surrender (to), yield (to); attend, hear, heed, listen (to), mark, note, notice, regard, watch

antonyms comply (with), conform (to), follow, mind, obey, observe

2 to treat (a sacred place or object) shamefully or with great disrespect — see DESECRATE

violation *n* **1** a breaking of a moral or legal code — see OFFENSE 1

2 a failure to uphold the requirements of law, duty, or obligation — see BREACH 1

violence *n* the use of brute strength to cause harm to a person or property ⟨the police believe that the woman died of natural causes rather than as a result of *violence*⟩

synonyms force, foul play

related words coercion, compulsion, constraint, duress, pressure; damage, detriment, harm, hurt, impairment, injury; crippling, maiming, mayhem, mutilation; assault, attack, bashing, battering, battery, batting, beating, belting, bludgeoning, buffeting, clubbing, drubbing, flogging, hammering, lacing, licking, mauling, pelting, pommeling, pounding, pummeling, thrashing, thumping, walloping, whaling, whipping; onslaught, outbreak, outrage, paroxysm, rampage, revolt, riot, shock, terror, threat, turbulence, upheaval, uproar; browbeating, bulldozing, bullying

near antonyms pacifism

antonyms nonviolence

violent *adj* **1** marked by bursts of destructive force or intense activity ⟨a *violent* fight that left several people badly hurt⟩
synonyms explosive, ferocious, fierce, furious, hot, rabid, rough, stormy, tempestuous, turbulent, volcanic
related words brutal, savage, vicious; antagonistic, hostile; aggressive, assertive, bellicose, belligerent, combative, contentious, gladiatorial, quarrelsome; frantic, frenzied, mad; destructive, ruinous
near antonyms calm, pacific, serene, tranquil; nonbelligerent, unaggressive, unassertive
antonyms nonviolent, peaceable, peaceful
2 extreme in degree, power, or effect — see INTENSE
3 marked by great and often stressful excitement or activity — see FURIOUS 1
VIP *n* a person who is widely known and usually much talked about — see CELEBRITY 1
viper *n* a limbless reptile with a long body — see SNAKE 1
virago *n* a bad-tempered scolding woman — see SHREW
virgin *adj* **1** never having had sexual relations ⟨*virgin* boys are sometimes unfairly teased⟩
synonyms maiden, virginal
related words chaste, modest, pure; innocent, untouched; abstinent, celibate; unmarried, unwed
2 being in an original and unused or unspoiled state — see FRESH 1
virginal *adj* never having had sexual relations — see VIRGIN 1
virile *adj* considered characteristic of or appropriate for men — see MASCULINE
virility *n* the set of qualities considered appropriate for or characteristic of men ⟨many cultures value *virility* as a sign of power⟩
synonyms manhood, manliness, masculinity
related words maleness; boyishness, mannishness, tomboyishness
near antonyms girlishness; femaleness; girlhood, maidenhood
antonyms femininity
virtually *adv* very close to but not completely — see ALMOST
virtue *n* **1** a quality that gives something special worth — see EXCELLENCE 2
2 conduct that conforms to an accepted standard of right and wrong — see MORALITY 1
virtuoso *adj* **1** accomplished with trained ability — see SKILLFUL
2 having or showing exceptional knowledge, experience, or skill in a field of endeavor — see PROFICIENT
virtuoso *n* a person with a high level of knowledge or skill in a field — see EXPERT
virtuous *adj* conforming to a high standard of morality or virtue — see GOOD 2
virtuously *adv* with purity of thought and deed — see PURELY
virtuousness *n* conduct that conforms to an accepted standard of right and wrong — see MORALITY 1
virulence *n* biting sharpness of feeling or expression — see ACRIMONY 1
virulent *adj* having or showing a desire to cause someone pain or suffering for the sheer enjoyment of it — see HATEFUL
virulently *adv* in a mean or spiteful manner — see NASTILY

visage *n* **1** facial appearance regarded as an indication of mood or feeling — see LOOK 1
2 the front part of the head — see FACE 1
viscera *n pl* the internal organs of the body — see GUT 1
viscid *adj* **1** being of a consistency that resists flow — see THICK 2
2 being of such a thick consistency as to readily cling to objects upon contact — see STICKY 1
viscosity *n* the degree to which a fluid can resist flowing — see CONSISTENCY
viscous *adj* **1** being of a consistency that resists flow — see THICK 2
2 being of such a thick consistency as to readily cling to objects upon contact — see STICKY 1
visible *adj* capable of being seen ⟨the *visible* light spectrum runs from red to violet⟩
synonyms apparent, observable, seeable, visual
related words external, outer, outward; detectable, discernible, noticeable, perceptible; clear, conspicuous, evident, eye-catching, manifest, obvious, plain, prominent, striking
near antonyms disappeared, dissolved, evanesced, evaporated, melted, vanished; imperceptible, inconspicuous, indistinct, unnoticeable; faint, insignificant, slight, vague; buried, concealed, covert, disguised, hidden, latent, obscure, shrouded
antonyms invisible, unseeable
vision *n* **1** a conception or image created by the imagination and having no objective reality — see FANTASY 1
2 a series of often striking pictures created by the imagination during sleep — see DREAM 1
3 the ability to see — see EYESIGHT
4 the soul of a dead person thought of especially as appearing to living people — see GHOST
vision *vb* to form a mental picture of — see IMAGINE 1
visionary *n* one whose conduct is guided more by the image of perfection than by the real world — see IDEALIST
visit *n* **1** a temporary residing as another's guest ⟨my aunt always looks forward to her week-long annual *visit* with her mother⟩
synonyms sojourn, stay
related words field trip; layover, stopover
2 a coming to see another briefly for social or business reasons — see CALL 2
visit *vb* **1** to make a social call upon ⟨the club ladies make a point of *visiting* everyone who moves into the neighborhood⟩
synonyms call (on *or* upon), see
related words look up, seek (out); frequent, hang out (at), haunt
phrases drop in on
near antonyms brush (off), cold-shoulder, ignore, snub
2 to reside as a temporary guest ⟨Johnny loves it when his friend Susie comes to *visit* for a month every summer⟩
synonyms sojourn, stay, tarry
related words frequent, hang out (at), haunt; inhabit, occupy
near antonyms abide, dwell, live, reside
3 to engage in casual or rambling conversation — see CHAT
4 to go to or spend time in often — see FREQUENT
5 to make a brief visit — see CALL 3
visitant *n* a person who visits another — see GUEST

visitation *n* a coming to see another briefly for social or business reasons — see CALL 2

visitor *n* a person who visits another — see GUEST 1

visor *also* **vizor** *n* the projecting front part of a hat or cap ⟨the *visor* of her baseball cap shades her eyes nicely⟩
synonyms bill, brim, peak
related words shade

vista *n* all that can be seen from a certain point — see VIEW 1

visual *adj* 1 of, relating to, or used in vision ⟨the eyes are the primary *visual* organs in humans⟩
synonyms ocular, optic, optical
related words seeing, sighted; focusing
antonyms nonvisual
2 capable of being seen — see VISIBLE
3 consisting of or relating to pictures — see PICTORIAL 1

visualize *vb* to form a mental picture of — see IMAGINE 1

vital *adj* 1 having active strength of body or mind — see VIGOROUS 1
2 having much high-spirited energy and movement — see LIVELY 1
3 impossible to do without — see ESSENTIAL 1
4 likely to cause or capable of causing death — see DEADLY
5 of the greatest possible importance — see CRUCIAL

vitality *n* 1 the quality or state of having abundant or intense activity ⟨a city known for the *vitality* of its entertainment and sports scenes⟩
synonyms animation, briskness, exuberance, jazziness, liveliness, lustiness, peppiness, robustness, sprightliness, vibrancy
related words buoyancy, jauntiness, springiness; brightness, cheer, cheerfulness, effervescence, vivacity, vivaciousness; eagerness, enthusiasm, keenness, spiritedness; friskiness, impishness, pertness, playfulness
near antonyms indolence, laziness; languor, lethargy, limpness, listlessness, sleepiness, sluggishness, torpor, weariness; apathy, impassivity; dullness (*or* dulness), tediousness, tedium
antonyms inactivity, lifelessness
2 active strength of body or mind — see VIGOR 1

vitalize *vb* to give life, vigor, or spirit to — see ANIMATE

vitalizing *adj* having a renewing effect on the state of the body or mind — see TONIC

vitals *n pl* the internal organs of the body — see GUT 1

vitiate *vb* 1 to affect slightly with something morally bad or undesirable — see TAINT 1
2 to reduce the soundness, effectiveness, or perfection of — see DAMAGE 1

vitriol *n* 1 biting sharpness of feeling or expression — see ACRIMONY 1
2 harsh insulting language — see ABUSE 1

vittles *n pl* substances intended to be eaten — see FOOD

vituperate *vb* to criticize harshly and usually publicly — see ATTACK 2

vituperation *n* harsh insulting language — see ABUSE 1

vivacious *adj* 1 having much high-spirited energy and movement — see LIVELY 1
2 joyously unrestrained — see EXUBERANT

vivid *adj* producing a mental picture through clear and impressive description — see GRAPHIC 1

vivify *vb* to give life, vigor, or spirit to — see ANIMATE

vizard *n* a cover or partial cover for the face used to disguise oneself — see MASK 1

vocabulary *n* 1 the special terms or expressions of a particular group or field — see TERMINOLOGY
2 the stock of words, pronunciation, and grammar used by a people as their basic means of communication — see LANGUAGE 1

vocal *adj* created by the body's organs of sound ⟨our cat is given to making strange *vocal* noises in the dead of night⟩
synonyms oral, uttered, voiced
related words articulate, articulated, spoken; breathed, drawled, gasped, mouthed, mumbled, murmured, muttered, shouted, spluttered, sputtered, whispered
near antonyms inarticulate; mute, quiet, silent; unexpressed, unspoken, unuttered, unvoiced
antonyms nonvocal

vocal *n* a short musical composition for the human voice often with instrumental accompaniment — see SONG 1

vocalist *n* one who sings — see SINGER

vocalize *vb* 1 to express (a thought or emotion) in words — see SAY 1
2 to produce musical sounds with the voice — see SING 1

vocalizer *n* one who sings — see SINGER

vocation *n* the activity by which one regularly makes a living — see OCCUPATION

vociferate *vb* to speak so as to be heard at a distance — see CALL 1

vociferous *adj* engaging in or marked by loud and insistent cries especially of protest ⟨*vociferous* opponents of the bill protested angrily outside the chambers of the legislature⟩
synonyms blatant, clamorous, obstreperous
related words clangorous, dinning, discordant, noisy; loudmouthed, outspoken, vocal; boisterous, rowdy, uproarious; cacophonous, dissonant, shrill, strident; blaring, booming, brassy, brazen
near antonyms noiseless, quiet, silent, soundless, still; calm, hushed, subdued

vogue *adj* enjoying widespread favor or approval — see POPULAR 1

vogue *n* 1 a practice or interest that is very popular for a short time — see FAD
2 the state of enjoying widespread approval — see POPULARITY

voice *n* 1 the right to express a wish, choice, or opinion ⟨everyone will have a *voice* in the decision of where to go for our field trip⟩
synonyms say, vote
related words part, role, share; enfranchisement, franchise, suffrage; judgment (*or* judgement), say-so; belief, conviction, opinion, sentiment, view
2 an act, process, or means of putting something into words — see EXPRESSION 1
3 one who sings — see SINGER

voice *vb* to make known (as an idea, emotion, or opinion) — see EXPRESS 1

voiced *adj* created by the body's organs of sound — see VOCAL

voiceless *adj* unable to speak — see MUTE 1

void *vb* to put an end to by formal action — see ABOLISH

void *adj* 1 having no legal or binding force — see NULL 1

THESAURUS

2 lacking contents that could or should be present — see EMPTY 1

3 utterly lacking in something needed, wanted, or expected — see DEVOID 1

void *n* empty space — see VACANCY 1

void *vb* to remove the contents of — see EMPTY

volatile *adj* likely to change frequently, suddenly, or unexpectedly — see FICKLE 1

volcanic *adj* marked by bursts of destructive force or intense activity — see VIOLENT 1

volition *n* the act or power of making one's own choices or decisions — see FREE WILL

volley *n* a rapid or overwhelming outpouring of many things at once — see BARRAGE

volume *n* **1** a considerable amount — see LOT 2

2 a given or particular mass or aggregate of matter — see AMOUNT

3 a set of printed sheets of paper bound together between covers and forming a work of fiction or nonfiction — see BOOK 1

voluminous *adj* of a size greater than average of its kind — see LARGE

voluminousness *n* the quality or state of being large in size — see LARGENESS

voluntarily *adv* of one's own free will ⟨you took part in this *voluntarily*, so you have no cause to complain⟩
synonyms freely, willingly
related words consciously, knowingly, wittingly
phrases of one's own accord
near antonyms unconsciously, unknowingly, unwittingly
antonyms involuntarily, unwillingly

voluntary *adj* **1** done, made, or given with one's own free will ⟨a *voluntary* contribution to the school's fund-raising drive⟩
synonyms freewill, unforced, volunteer, willing
related words discretionary, elective, nonobligatory, optional; impulsive, instinctive, spontaneous, unforced, unpremeditated; conscious, deliberate, intentional, knowing, willful (*or* wilful)
near antonyms compulsory, mandatory, necessary, nonelective, obligatory, ordered, required
antonyms coerced, forced, involuntary
2 subject to one's freedom of choice — see OPTIONAL

volunteer *adj* done, made, or given with one's own free will — see VOLUNTARY 1

voluptuous *adj* pleasing to the physical senses — see SENSUAL

vomit *vb* to discharge the contents of the stomach through the mouth ⟨the children with the flu *vomited* every time they tried to eat something⟩
synonyms gag, heave, retch, spit up, throw up
related words disgorge, regurgitate; eject, expel, spew

voodoo *n* a person skilled in using supernatural forces — see MAGICIAN 1

voodooism *n* the power to control natural forces through supernatural means — see MAGIC 1

voracious *adj* **1** having a huge appetite ⟨it seemed like the *voracious* kitten was eating her weight in food every day⟩
synonyms gluttonous, greedy, hoggish, piggish, rapacious, ravenous
related words hearty, wolfish; devouring, gobbling, gorging, gormandizing, insatiable, unquenchable; empty, famished, hungry, starved, starving; malnourished, underfed, undernourished

near antonyms full, content, sated, satisfied
2 showing urgent desire or interest — see EAGER

vortex *n* water moving rapidly in a circle with a hollow in the center — see WHIRLPOOL

votary *n* one who follows the opinions or teachings of another — see FOLLOWER

vote *n* **1** the right to formally express one's position or will in an election ⟨in the United States, women were granted the *vote* by the Nineteenth Amendment in 1920⟩
synonyms enfranchisement, franchise, suffrage
related words say, voice
antonyms disenfranchisement
2 a piece of paper indicating a person's preferences in an election — see BALLOT
3 the right to express a wish, choice, or opinion — see VOICE 1

vote *vb* to set before the mind for consideration — see PROPOSE 1

vouch (for)*vb* to declare (something) to be true or genuine — see CERTIFY 1

vow *n* a person's solemn declaration that he or she will do or not do something — see PROMISE

vow *vb* to make a solemn declaration of intent — see PROMISE 1

voyage *n* a journey over water in a vessel — see SAIL

voyage *vb* **1** to take a trip especially of some distance — see TRAVEL 1
2 to travel on water in a vessel — see SAIL 1

vulgar *adj* **1** belonging to the class of people of low social or economic rank — see IGNOBLE 1
2 depicting or referring to sexual matters in a way that is unacceptable in polite society — see OBSCENE 1
3 held by or applicable to a majority of the people — see GENERAL 3
4 lacking in refinement or good taste — see COARSE 2
5 used in or suitable for speech and not formal writing — see COLLOQUIAL 1

vulgarism *n* a disrespectful or indecent word or expression — see SWEARWORD

vulgarity *n* **1** the quality or state of lacking refinement or good taste ⟨our cousins' general *vulgarity* and poor manners irritate my mother⟩
synonyms coarseness, commonness, crassness, crudeness, grossness, indelicacy, indelicateness, lowness, raffishness, roughness, rudeness, tastelessness
related words boorishness, churlishness, clownishness, loutishness; insensitivity, thoughtlessness; gracelessness, tackiness
near antonyms courtliness; elegance, grace, graciousness; consideration, sensitivity, thoughtfulness
antonyms cultivation, gentility, polish, refinement, tastefulness
2 the quality or state of being obscene — see OBSCENITY 1

vulnerability *n* **1** the quality or state of having little resistance to some outside agent — see SUSCEPTIBILITY
2 the state of being left without shelter or protection against something harmful — see EXPOSURE 1

vulnerable *adj* **1** being in a situation where one is likely to meet with harm — see LIABLE 1
2 lacking protection from danger or resistance against attack — see HELPLESS 1

wackiness *n* lack of good sense or judgment — see FOOLISHNESS 1

wacky *adj* **1** different from the ordinary in a way that causes curiosity or suspicion — see ODD 2

2 having or showing a very abnormal or sick state of mind — see INSANE 1

3 showing or marked by a lack of good sense or judgment — see FOOLISH 1

wad *n* **1** a considerable amount — see LOT 2

2 a small uneven mass — see LUMP 1

3 a very large amount of money — see FORTUNE 2

wad *vb* to form into a round compact mass ⟨she *wadded* up the paper and threw it in the wastebasket⟩

synonyms agglomerate, ball, roll, round

related words clump, lump; bead

near antonyms open, spread, unfold

antonyms unroll

waddle *vb* to move forward while swaying from side to side — see STAGGER 1

wade (into) *vb* to start work on energetically — see ATTACK 3

waft *n* a slight or gentle movement of air — see BREEZE 1

waft *vb* to rest or move along the surface of a liquid or in the air — see FLOAT

wag *n* **1** a quick jerky movement from side to side or up and down ⟨the dog gave its tail a single *wag* before it flopped back down⟩

synonyms switch, waggle

related words oscillation, swing; flap, flutter, wave; jerk, shake, twitch, wiggle

2 a person (as a writer) noted for or specializing in humor — see HUMORIST

wag *vb* to move from side to side or up and down with quick jerky motions ⟨the cat's tail *wagged* back and forth in annoyance⟩

synonyms switch, waggle

related words oscillate, swing; beat, flail, flap, flop, whip; flick, flicker, flutter, wave; jerk, shake, twitch, wiggle

wage *n, often* **wages** *pl* the money paid regularly to a person for labor or services ⟨the *wage* you earn is more than enough to support us comfortably⟩

synonyms emolument, hire, pay, payment, salary, stipend

related words minimum wage, take-home pay; compensation, recompense, remittance, remuneration, requital, return; check, commission, paycheck; recoupment, redress, reparation, restitution; reimbursement, repayment; profit, takings, yield

wager *n* the money or thing risked on the outcome of an uncertain event — see BET

wager *vb* to risk (something) on the outcome of an uncertain event — see BET

wagerer *n* one that bets (as on the outcome of a contest or sports event) — see BETTOR

waggery *n* **1** playful, reckless behavior that is not intended to cause serious harm — see MISCHIEF 1

2 something said or done to cause laughter — see JOKE 1

waggish *adj* tending to or exhibiting reckless playfulness — see MISCHIEVOUS 1

waggle *n* a quick jerky movement from side to side or up and down — see WAG 1

waggle *vb* to move from side to side or up and down with quick jerky motions — see WAG

wagon *n* a wheeled usually horse-drawn vehicle used for hauling — see CART

wail *n* **1** a crying out in grief — see LAMENT 1

2 a long low sound indicating pain or grief — see MOAN 1

wail *vb* **1** to express dissatisfaction, pain, or resentment usually tiresomely — see COMPLAIN

2 to make a long loud mournful sound — see HOWL 1

3 to utter a moan — see MOAN 1

wail (for) *vb* to feel or express sorrow for — see LAMENT 1

wailing *adj* expressing or suggesting mourning — see MOURNFUL 1

wain *n* a wheeled usually horse-drawn vehicle used for hauling — see CART

waist *n* the middle region of the human body — see MIDRIFF

waistline *n* the middle region of the human body — see MIDRIFF

wait *n* an instance or period of being prevented from going about one's business — see DELAY

wait *vb* to remain in place in readiness or expectation of something ⟨hurry up, as your sisters are already at the door *waiting* for you⟩

synonyms await, bide, hold on, stay

related words hang around, linger, stick around; anticipate, expect

phrases bide one's time

waiter *n* a person who serves food or drink — see SERVER

waiver *n* a document containing a declaration of an intentional giving up of a right, claim, or privilege ⟨before the hospital will treat you, you have to sign a *waiver* in which you give up your right to sue⟩

synonyms release

related words dispensation, exemption; abdication, relinquishment, renouncement; renunciation, surrender

wake *vb* **1** to cause to stop sleeping ⟨my banging around in the kitchen *woke* the cat⟩

synonyms arouse, awake, awaken, rouse, waken

related words raise, revive; reawake, reawaken; agitate, disturb, excite, provoke, stimulate, stir

near antonyms hypnotize, mesmerize; lay (down)

antonyms lull

2 to cease to be asleep ⟨I *woke* with a start when the door slammed⟩

synonyms arouse, awake, awaken, rouse, waken

related words arise, get up, rise, uprise; watch; revive; reawake, reawaken; shift, stir

near antonyms catnap, doze, drop (off), nap, nod, sleep, slumber, snooze; bed (down), couch, retire, turn in; oversleep

wakeful *adj* not sleeping or able to sleep ⟨the mother remained *wakeful* until her child returned home⟩

synonyms awake, sleepless, wide-awake

related words aroused, awakened, roused, wakened; aware, conscious; revived; reawakened

near antonyms drowsy, nodding, sleepy, slumberous, somnolent; dreaming; hypnotized, mesmerized

antonyms asleep, dormant, dozing, napping, resting, sleeping, slumbering

waken *vb* **1** to cause to stop sleeping — see WAKE 1
2 to cease to be asleep — see WAKE 2

walk *n* a relaxed journey on foot for exercise or pleasure ⟨we went for a long *walk* outside because it was such a nice night⟩
synonyms constitutional, perambulation, ramble, range, saunter, stroll, turn
related words parade, promenade; expedition, hike, march, peregrination, tramp, travel, trek, trip; excursion, jaunt, junket, outing, sally, spin, tour; pilgrimage, progress, safari

walk *vb* to go on foot ⟨I *walked* slowly to school⟩
synonyms foot (it), hoof (it), leg (it), pad, step, traipse, tread
related words parade, promenade; march, pace, stride; hike, peregrinate, trek; amble, perambulate, ramble, saunter, stroll, wander; clump, stomp, stump, tramp, tromp; plod, trudge; hobble, limp; mince, prance, pussyfoot, tiptoe; stalk, strut, swagger; lumber, lurch, pound, shamble, shuffle, stagger; nip, trip, trot

walking out *n* the act of leaving a place — see DEPARTURE

walkout *n* a work stoppage by a body of workers intended to force an employer to meet their demands — see STRIKE 1

walk out *vb* **1** to leave a place often for another — see GO 2
2 to refuse to work in order to force an employer to meet demands — see STRIKE 1

wall *n* **1** a physical object that blocks the way — see BARRIER
2 means or method of defending — see DEFENSE 1

wall (in) *vb* to close or shut in by or as if by barriers — see ENCLOSE 1

wallop *n* **1** a forceful coming together of two things — see IMPACT 1
2 a hard strike with a part of the body or an instrument — see ¹BLOW

wallop *vb* **1** to strike repeatedly — see BEAT 1
2 to achieve a victory over — see BEAT 2
3 to defeat by a large margin — see WHIP 2
4 to deliver a blow to (someone or something) usually in a strong vigorous manner — see HIT 1

wampum *n slang* something (as pieces of stamped metal or printed paper) customarily and legally used as a medium of exchange, a measure of value, or a means of payment — see MONEY

wan *adj* lacking a healthy skin color — see PALE 2

wander *vb* to move about from place to place aimlessly ⟨we just went outside and *wandered* around until it was time to go⟩
synonyms gad (about), gallivant (*also* galavant), knock (about), maunder, meander, mooch, mope, ramble, range, roam, rove, traipse
related words amble, saunter, stroll; bum, hobo; straggle, stray; prowl, tramp, travel

wanderer *n* a person who roams about without a fixed route or destination — see NOMAD

wandering *adj* traveling from place to place — see ITINERANT

wane *vb* to grow less in scope or intensity especially gradually — see DECREASE 2

wangle *vb* to plan out usually with subtle skill or care — see ENGINEER

want *n* **1** the fact or state of being absent — see LACK 1
2 a falling short of an essential or desirable amount or number — see DEFICIENCY
3 a state of being without something necessary, desirable, or useful — see NEED 1
4 the state of lacking sufficient money or material possessions — see POVERTY 1

want *vb* **1** to have an earnest wish to own or enjoy — see DESIRE
2 to have as a requirement — see NEED 1
3 to see fit — see CHOOSE 2
4 to wish to have — see LIKE 1

wanting *adj* **1** falling short of a standard — see BAD 1
2 not coming up to a usual standard or meeting a particular need — see SHORT 3
3 not present or in evidence — see ABSENT 2

wanting *prep* not having — see WITHOUT 1

wanton *adj* **1** depicting or referring to sexual matters in a way that is unacceptable in polite society — see OBSCENE 1
2 having a strong sexual desire — see LUSTFUL
3 having or showing the desire to inflict severe pain and suffering on others — see CRUEL 1

wantonness *n* the willful infliction of pain and suffering on others — see CRUELTY

war *n* **1** a state of armed violent struggle between states, nations, or groups ⟨the United States declared *war* on Japan after the bombing of Pearl Harbor⟩
synonyms conflict, hostilities, hot war
related words civil war, cold war, holy war, limited war, world war; action, battle, engagement; combat, fighting, warfare; belligerency; wartime
near antonyms demilitarization, demobilization, disarmament; pacification; cease-fire, truce; calm, peacefulness, tranquility
antonyms peace
2 a lack of agreement or harmony — see DISCORD

war (against) *vb* to oppose (someone) in physical conflict — see FIGHT 1

warble *n* a rhythmic series of musical tones arranged to give a pleasing effect — see MELODY

warble *vb* to sing with the alternation of two musical tones ⟨the skylark *warbled* prettily outside our window⟩
synonyms quaver, trill
related words slur; yodel; belt, carol, chant, chorus, croon, descant, harmonize, troll, vocalize; lilt, scat

ward *n* **1** means or method of defending — see DEFENSE 1
2 responsibility for the safety and well-being of someone or something — see CUSTODY

ward *vb* to drive danger or attack away from — see DEFEND 1

warden *n* **1** a person or group that watches over someone or something — see GUARD 1
2 a person who takes care of a property sometimes for an absent owner — see CUSTODIAN 1

warder *n* a person or group that watches over someone or something — see GUARD 1

warehouse *n* a building for storing goods — see STOREHOUSE

wares *n pl* products that are bought and sold in business — see MERCHANDISE

warfare *n* **1** a lack of agreement or harmony — see DISCORD

2 an earnest effort for superiority or victory over another — see CONTEST 1

wariness *n* a close attentiveness to avoiding danger — see CAUTION 1

warlike *adj* feeling or displaying eagerness to fight — see BELLIGERENT

warm *adj* **1** having or giving off heat to a moderate degree ⟨the pan was still *warm*, but no longer too hot to touch⟩
synonyms heated, lukewarm, tepid, toasty, warmed
related words thawed; broiling, burning, fiery, hot, piping hot, red-hot, roasting, scalding, scorching, searing, sultry, sweltering, torrid; overheated, roasted, superheated, sweltering; blazing, glowing, molten, sizzling; reheated
near antonyms arctic, bitter, bleak, chill, chilly, cold, freezing, frigid, frosty, glacial, ice-cold, iced, icy, nippy, polar, raw, sharp, snappy, snowy, subfreezing, subzero, wintry; unthawed; frosted; benumbed, nipped, numb
antonyms chilled, cool, cooled, refrigerated, unheated
2 having or expressing great depth of feeling — see FERVENT
3 having or showing kindly feeling and sincere interest — see FRIENDLY 1
4 showing or expressing acceptance or approval — see POSITIVE

warm *vb* **1** to cause to have or give off heat to a moderate degree ⟨you'll need to *warm* the food in the microwave⟩
synonyms heat, toast
related words overheat, superheat; reheat; burn, char, fire, scald, scorch, sear
near antonyms freeze, frost, ice
antonyms chill, cool, refrigerate
2 to give satisfaction to — see PLEASE

warm-blooded *adj* having or expressing great depth of feeling — see FERVENT

warmed *adj* having or giving off heat to a moderate degree — see WARM 1

warmhearted *adj* **1** having or marked by sympathy and consideration for others — see HUMANE 1
2 having or showing kindly feeling and sincere interest — see FRIENDLY 1

warmness *n* the quality or state of being moderate in temperature — see WARMTH 1

warmonger *n* one who urges or attempts to cause a war ⟨fortunately, the *warmongers* met with overwhelming opposition⟩
synonyms hawk, jingo, militarist
related words agitator, firebrand, fomenter, instigator, rabble-rouser; belligerent, combatant, militant; chauvinist
near antonyms peacemaker
antonyms dove, pacifist

warmth *n* **1** the quality or state of being moderate in temperature ⟨the cozy *warmth* of the inn's parlor was a welcome relief from the wintry weather outside⟩
synonyms lukewarmness, warmness
related words glow, radiance; heat, hotness, sultriness, stuffiness
near antonyms bitterness, bleakness, cold, coldness, frigidity, frostiness, iciness, rawness, sharpness; frost
antonyms chill, chilliness, coolness
2 depth of feeling — see ARDOR 1

warn *vb* to give notice to beforehand especially of danger or risk ⟨Dad *warned* us that if we continued playing so rough, someone was sure to get hurt⟩
synonyms alert, caution, forewarn
related words augur, forecast, foretell, predict, presage, prognosticate, prophesy; advise, apprise, inform, notify; admonish; bode, forebode, portend
near antonyms imperil, risk

warning *adj* serving as or offering a warning — see CAUTIONARY

warning *n* **1** the act or an instance of telling beforehand of danger or risk ⟨she delivered a strict *warning* that anyone who was caught cheating would get expelled⟩
synonyms admonition, alarm, alert, caution, forewarning, notice
related words auguring, augury, forecasting, foretelling, predicting, prediction, presaging, prognosticating, prophecy, prophesying; apprising, informing, notification, notifying; advice, counsel, guidance, recommendation, suggestion; announcement, declaration
2 something that tells of approaching danger or risk ⟨the ominously darkening sky was a *warning* that a tornado was approaching⟩
synonyms caution, tocsin
related words omen, portent; notification; buoy, knell, sign, signal; foretaste, foretoken; announcement, declaration

warp *vb* **1** to change so much as to create a wrong impression or alter the meaning of — see GARBLE
2 to lower in character or dignity — see DEBASE 1
3 to twist (something) out of a natural or normal shape or condition — see CONTORT

warped *adj* having or showing lowered moral character or standards — see CORRUPT

warping *n* the twisting of something out of its natural or normal shape or condition — see CONTORTION

warrant *vb* **1** to assume responsibility for the satisfactory quality or performance of ⟨the computer company unconditionally *warrants* all of its products for one full year⟩
synonyms guarantee
related words attest, authenticate, avouch, certify, testify (to), vouch (for), witness; assure, bond, contract, covenant; pledge, plight, swear, vow; adhere, assert, declare, insist; insure
2 to give official acceptance of something as satisfactory — see APPROVE
3 to have as a requirement — see NEED 1
4 to state as a fact usually forcefully — see CLAIM 1

warranted *adj* being what is called for by accepted standards of right and wrong — see JUST 1

warranty *n* a formal agreement to fulfill an obligation — see GUARANTEE 1

warrior *n* a person engaged in military service — see SOLDIER

wary *adj* having or showing a close attentiveness to avoiding danger or trouble — see CAREFUL 1

wash *vb* **1** to flow along or against ⟨crystal-clear waters gently *wash* the island's unspoiled beaches⟩
synonyms lap, lave, splash
related words gurgle, ripple, slosh
2 to flow in a broken irregular stream — see GURGLE
3 to make wet — see WET

4 to pour liquid over or through in order to cleanse — see FLUSH 1

washed *adj* containing, covered with, or thoroughly penetrated by water — see WET

washed–out *adj* lacking intensity of color — see PALE 1

washed–up *adj* having lost forcefulness, courage, or spirit — see EFFETE 1

washout *n* something that has failed — see FAILURE 3

wash out *vb* **1** to be unsuccessful — see FAIL 2

2 to make white or whiter by removing color — see WHITEN

3 to use up all the physical energy of — see EXHAUST 1

washroom *n* a room furnished with a fixture for flushing body waste — see TOILET

waspish *adj* easily irritated or annoyed — see IRRITABLE

waspishness *n* readiness to show annoyance or impatience — see PETULANCE

wassail *n* a bout of drinking — see CAROUSE

wastage *n* the state or fact of being rendered nonexistent, physically unsound, or useless — see DESTRUCTION

waste *adj* producing inferior or only a small amount of vegetation — see BARREN 1

waste *n* **1** an instance of spending money or resources without care or restraint ⟨it seems like a *waste* to spend my entire paycheck on a bigger TV⟩

synonyms extravagance, prodigality

related words indulgence, luxury, splurge; loss, wastage; generosity, liberality, openhandedness, profligacy; improvidence, shortsightedness; overindulgence, self-indulgence; excess, immoderacy, overkill; carelessness, heedlessness, imprudence, incautiousness; recklessness

near antonyms necessity; economizing, economy, frugality, saving, scrimping, skimping; austerity, moderation, restraint, temperance, temperateness

2 discarded or useless material — see GARBAGE

3 land that is uninhabited or not fit for crops — see WASTELAND

4 solid matter discharged from an animal's alimentary canal — see DROPPING 1

waste *vb* **1** to use up carelessly ⟨he *wasted* most of his allowance by buying comic books⟩

synonyms blow, dissipate, fritter (away), lavish, misspend, run through, spend, squander, throw away

related words splurge; consume, deplete, exhaust, impoverish; indulge, overindulge; disburse, expend, lay out

near antonyms economize, scrimp, skimp; preserve, protect, save; hoard, lay up

antonyms conserve

2 to bring to a complete end the physical soundness, existence, or usefulness of — see DESTROY 1

3 to diminish the physical strength of — see WEAKEN 1

waste (away) *vb* to lose bodily strength or vigor — see WEAKEN 2

wasted *adj* **1** lacking bodily strength — see WEAK 1

2 suffering extreme weight loss as a result of hunger or disease — see EMACIATED

wasteful *adj* given to spending money freely or foolishly — see PRODIGAL

wastefulness *n* the quality or fact of being free or

wasteful in the expenditure of money — see EXTRAVAGANCE 1

wasteland *n* land that is uninhabited or not fit for crops ⟨with proper irrigation and fertilizer, they turned the desert *wasteland* into a fertile plain⟩

synonyms barren, desert, desolation, waste

related words badland; bush, brush; dust bowl; hinterland, upland; open, open air, outdoors, out-of-doors; nature, wild, wilderness

waster *n* someone who carelessly spends money — see PRODIGAL

wastrel *n* someone who carelessly spends money — see PRODIGAL

watch *n* **1** a person or group that watches over someone or something — see GUARD 1

2 the act or state of being constantly attentive and responsive to signs of activity, opportunity, or danger — see VIGILANCE

watch *vb* **1** to keep one's eyes on ⟨I turned my head to continue *watching* the bird as it flew away⟩

synonyms eye, observe

related words behold, look, regard, see, view; gape, gawk, gaze, glare, goggle, peer, rubberneck, stare; guard, wake, ward; monitor, read; spy; glance, glimpse, peek, peep

near antonyms blink, wink

2 to take notice of and be guided by — see HEED 1

3 to pay continued close attention to (something) for a particular purpose — see MONITOR

4 to have an interest or concern for — see CARE

watch (for) *vb* to believe in the future occurrence of (something) — see EXPECT

watchful *adj* paying close attention usually for the purpose of anticipating approaching danger or opportunity — see ALERT 1

watchfulness *n* the act or state of being constantly attentive and responsive to signs of opportunity, activity, or danger — see VIGILANCE

watchman *n* **1** a person or group that watches over someone or something — see GUARD 1

2 a person who takes care of a property sometimes for an absent owner — see CUSTODIAN 1

watch out (for) *vb* to be cautious of or on guard against — see BEWARE (OF)

watchword *n* **1** a word or phrase that must be spoken by a person in order to pass a guard — see PASSWORD

2 an attention-getting word or phrase used to publicize something (as a campaign or product) — see SLOGAN

water *vb* to make wet — see WET

water (down) *vb* to alter (something) for the worse with the addition of foreign or lower-grade substances — see ADULTERATE

water closet *n* a room furnished with a fixture for flushing body waste — see TOILET

watercourse *n* an open man-made passageway for water — see CHANNEL 1

watercraft *n* a small buoyant structure for travel on water — see BOAT 1

watered *adj* containing, covered with, or thoroughly penetrated by water — see WET

waterfall *n* a fall of water usually from a great height ⟨I used to like to throw sticks in the stream and watch them go over the *waterfall*⟩

synonyms cascade, cataract, fall(s)

related words rapid(s), white water; eddy, riffle; undertow, vortex, whirlpool

waterless *adj* marked by little or no precipitation or humidity — see DRY 1

waterlogged *adj* containing, covered with, or thoroughly penetrated by water — see WET

waterproof *n chiefly British* a coat made of water-resistant material — see RAINCOAT

waterproof *adj* made of or treated with material that does not allow water to penetrate ⟨luckily, my backpack is *waterproof*, so my notes didn't get wet⟩

synonyms waterproofed, watertight

related words rainproof; water-repellent, water-resistant; nonabsorbent, nonporous

near antonyms absorbent, porous

waterproofed *adj* made of or treated with material that does not allow water to penetrate — see WATERPROOF

waterspout *n* a pipe or channel for carrying off water from a roof — see GUTTER 1

watertight *adj* made of or treated with material that does not allow water to penetrate — see WATERPROOF

waterway *n* an open man-made passageway for water — see CHANNEL 1

watery *adj* 1 containing, covered with, or thoroughly penetrated by water — see WET

2 having an overly soft liquid consistency — see RUNNY

3 not containing very much of some important element — see WEAK 3

wave *n* a moving ridge on the surface of water ⟨the toddler was almost knocked down by the *waves* created by the speedboat⟩

synonyms billow, surge, swell

related words sea(s); breaker, whitecap; curl; comber, roller; eddy, riffle, ripple, wavelet; tidal wave, tsunami; undertow, vortex, whirlpool

wave *vb* to direct or notify by a movement or gesture — see MOTION

waver *vb* 1 to show uncertainty about the right course of action — see HESITATE

2 to swing unsteadily back and forth or from side to side — see TEETER 1

wavering *n* the act or an instance of pausing because of uncertainty about the right course of action — see HESITATION

wax *vb* 1 to become greater in extent, volume, amount, or number — see INCREASE 2

2 to coat (something) with a slippery substance in order to reduce friction — see LUBRICATE

3 to eventually have as a state or quality — see BECOME

way *n* 1 a passage cleared for public vehicular travel ⟨the town honored the local sports hero by naming after him a short *way* connecting two shopping centers⟩

synonyms artery, avenue, boulevard, drag, drive, expressway, freeway, highroad, highway, pass, passageway, pike, road, roadway, route, row, street, thoroughfare, trace, turnpike

related words causeway; alley, alleyway, bystreet, byway, catwalk, court, lane, place; approach, concourse, path, walkway; access; dead end; aisle, corridor, course, line; track, trail; channel; corduroy, tarmac; crossroad; bypass, overpass, underpass; cloverleaf, rotary

2 a usual manner of behaving or doing — see HABIT

3 an established course for traveling from one place to another — see PASSAGE 1

4 an established pattern of behavior — see TENDENCY 1

5 an extent or area available for or used up by some activity or thing — see ROOM 1

6 the direction along which something or someone moves — see PATH 1

7 the means or procedure for doing something — see METHOD

8 the opening through which one can enter or leave a structure — see DOOR 2

9 the power, right, or opportunity to choose — see CHOICE 1

10 the space or amount of space between two points, lines, surfaces, or objects — see DISTANCE

wayfarer *n* a person who roams about without a fixed route or destination — see NOMAD

wayfaring *adj* traveling from place to place — see ITINERANT

waylay *vb* to lie in wait for and attack by surprise — see AMBUSH

way–out *adj* different from the ordinary in a way that causes curiosity or suspicion — see ODD 2

way station *n* a regular stopping place — see STATION 2

wayward *adj* 1 given to resisting authority or another's control — see DISOBEDIENT

2 given to resisting control or discipline by others — see UNCONTROLLABLE

weak *adj* 1 lacking bodily strength ⟨the little boy was simply too *weak* to lift the box⟩

synonyms debilitated, delicate, effete, enervated, enfeebled, faint, feeble, frail, infirm, languid, low, prostrate, prostrated, sapped, slight, soft, softened, tender, torpid, unsubstantial, wasted, weakened, wimpy

related words challenged, disabled, incapacitated; paralyzed; broken-down, decrepit, worn out; impotent, powerless, puny; breakable, flimsy, fragile; dizzy, groggy, rocky, unsteady, woozy; exhausted, tired, weary; damaged, harmed, hurt, impaired, injured; resistless, susceptible, unresistant, vulnerable, yielding

near antonyms able-bodied, athletic, beefy, brawny, fit, husky, muscular, sinewy, strapping, virile; hard, hardy, lusty, robust, sturdy, tough; fortified, hardened, inured, strengthened, toughened; energetic, energized, invigorated, vigorous, vitalized; hale, healthy, sound; capable, competent; convalescing, recovering, recuperating

antonyms mighty, powerful, rugged, stalwart, stout, strong

2 lacking strength of will or character ⟨the opinion that overweight people are just *weak* individuals who easily give in to temptation⟩

synonyms characterless, effete, frail, invertebrate, nerveless, soft, spineless, weakened, wimpy, wishy-washy

related words forceless, ineffective, ineffectual; impotent, powerless; emasculated, unnerved; pliable, submissive; corrupt, unprincipled, unscrupulous, villainous; cowardly, craven, lily-livered

near antonyms ethical, good, moral, principled, right, righteous, upright, virtuous; determined, mettlesome, resolute; courageous, stalwart, stouthearted

antonyms backboned, firm, strong, tough

3 not containing very much of some important element ⟨the coffee came out too *weak* because I didn't put enough ground beans in⟩

synonyms dilute, diluted, thin, thinned, watery, weakened

related words adulterated, watered (down)

near antonyms enriched, fortified; concentrated, condensed, evaporated

antonyms full-bodied, rich, strong

4 not using or following good reasoning — see ILLOGICAL

5 unable to act or achieve one's purpose — see POWERLESS

weaken *vb* **1** to diminish the physical strength of ⟨several days of hardship in the desert had *weakened* them⟩

synonyms debilitate, enervate, enfeeble, prostrate, sap, soften, tire, waste

related words cripple, disable, incapacitate; deplete, depress, exhaust, impoverish, unman, wash out; damage, harm, hurt, impair, injure; break down, wear out; paralyze

near antonyms energize, invigorate, vitalize; harden, season, toughen

antonyms beef (up), fortify, recruit, strengthen

2 to lose bodily strength or vigor ⟨the bodybuilder *weakened* once she eased off on her workouts⟩

synonyms decay, droop, fail, flag, go, lag, languish, sag, waste (away), wilt

related words break down, wear out; yield

near antonyms convalesce, recover, recuperate; gain

2 to alter (something) for the worse with the addition of foreign or lower-grade substances — see ADULTERATE

weakened *adj* **1** containing foreign or lower-grade substances — see IMPURE

2 lacking bodily strength — see WEAK 1

3 lacking strength of will or character — see WEAK 2

4 not containing very much of some important element — see WEAK 3

weakening *n* a gradual sinking and wasting away of mind or body — see DECLINE 1

weakling *n* **1** a person lacking in physical strength ⟨he was a *weakling* until high school, when he started working out to put on muscle⟩

synonyms softy (*or* softie), wimp

related words pushover, sissy

antonyms powerhouse

2 a person without strength of character ⟨only a *weakling* would be willing to lie to save himself from punishment⟩

synonyms mollycoddle, wimp

related words coward, mouse

antonyms stalwart

weakly *adj* chronically or repeatedly suffering from poor health — see SICKLY 1

weak–minded *adj* **1** not having or showing an ability to absorb ideas readily — see STUPID 1

2 showing or marked by a lack of good sense or judgment — see FOOLISH 1

weakness *n* **1** the quality or state of lacking physical strength or vigor ⟨the flu left me with such *weakness* that I could hardly stand⟩

synonyms debilitation, debility, delicacy, delicateness, enfeeblement, faintness, feebleness, frailness, frailty, infirmity, languor, lowness

related words decay, decrepitude; breakdown, collapse, exhaustion, nervous breakdown, prostration; defenselessness, helplessness; softness, tenderness; disablement, incapacitation; damage, harm, hurt, impairment, injury

near antonyms energy, vitality; brawniness, fitness, huskiness, virility; hardness, ruggedness, stoutness, sturdiness, toughness; haleness, health, healthiness, soundness

antonyms hardihood, hardiness, robustness, strength, vigor

2 the quality or state of lacking strength of will or character ⟨in a moment of *weakness* he shoplifted the comic book⟩

synonyms frailness, frailty, softness, spinelessness

related words collapse; failing, flaw, foibles, peccadillo; evil, immorality, wickedness; corruption, corruptness

near antonyms discipline, self-discipline; goodness, morality, rightness, righteousness, uprightness, virtuousness

antonyms backbone, firmness, fortitude, mettle, resoluteness, strength

3 a defect in character — see FAULT 1

4 the quality or state of having little resistance to some outside agent — see SUSCEPTIBILITY

weal *n* the state of doing well especially in relation to one's happiness or success — see WELFARE

wealth *n* **1** the total of one's money and property ⟨her *wealth* increased to the point where she could afford several luxurious homes⟩

synonyms assets, capital, fortune, means, opulence, riches, substance, wherewithal

related words belongings, chattels, effects, holdings, paraphernalia, possessions, things; finances, money; king's ransom, mint, wad; abundance, affluence, prosperity, success; treasure, valuables; accession, acquisition, personalty, property; nest egg, reserve, resources, savings, treasury; collateral; heap, pile, pot; bonanza, mine, treasure trove

near antonyms debts, liabilities; indebtedness

2 a considerable amount — see LOT 2

3 an amount or supply more than sufficient to meet one's needs — see PLENTY 1

wealthy *adj* having goods, property, or money in abundance — see RICH 1

wear *n* **1** the result of long and hard use ⟨after several years, the carpet was finally showing *wear*⟩

synonyms wear and tear

related words abrasion, corrosion, erosion, erasure; decomposition, disintegration

near antonyms fixing, mending, patching, rebuilding, reconditioning, reconstruction, renovation, repair, revamping

2 covering for the human body — see CLOTHING

wear *vb* **1** to use up all the physical energy of — see EXHAUST 1

2 to damage or diminish by continued friction — see ABRADE 1

wear and tear *n* the result of long and hard use — see WEAR 1

wearied *adj* **1** depleted in strength, energy, or freshness — see WEARY 1

2 having one's patience, interest, or pleasure exhausted — see WEARY 2

weariless *adj* showing no signs of weariness even after long hard effort — see TIRELESS

weariness *n* **1** a complete depletion of energy or strength — see FATIGUE

2 the state of being bored — see BOREDOM

wearisome *adj* causing weariness, restlessness, or lack of interest — see BORING

wear out *vb* to use up all the physical energy of — see EXHAUST 1

weary *adj* **1** depleted in strength, energy, or freshness ⟨I am just too *weary* to do any more work tonight⟩

synonyms beat, burned-out (*or* burnt-out), bushed, dead, done in, drained, effete, exhausted, fatigued, jaded, limp, logy, played out, prostrate, spent, tired, tuckered (out), wearied, worn, worn-out

related words overtaxed, overworked; run-down; debilitated, enervated, enfeebled, sapped, weakened

phrases worn to a frazzle

near antonyms refreshed, rejuvenated, relaxed, rested, revitalized; active, energetic, invigorated, strengthened, strong, tireless, vitalized

antonyms untired

2 having one's patience, interest, or pleasure exhausted ⟨I am totally *weary* of this constant bickering⟩

synonyms bored, fed up, jaded, sick, tired, wearied

related words apathetic, disinterested, uninterested; glutted, sated, satiated, surfeited; dejected, demoralized, discouraged, disheartened, dispirited; beat, burned-out (*or* burnt-out), bushed, done in, drained, enervated, exhausted, fatigued, limp, played out, tuckered, worn-out; annoyed, frustrated, irritated; disgusted, nauseated, repulsed

near antonyms animated, energized, enlivened, excited, galvanized, invigorated, stimulated, vitalized; amused, entertained; beguiled, bewitched, captivated, charmed, enchanted, enthralled, fascinated, hypnotized, mesmerized; delighted, pleased, thrilled

antonyms absorbed, engaged, engrossed, gripped, interested, intrigued

3 causing weariness, restlessness, or lack of interest — see BORING

weary *vb* **1** to make weary and restless by being dull or monotonous — see ²BORE

2 to use up all the physical energy of — see EXHAUST 1

wearying *adj* causing weariness, restlessness, or lack of interest — see BORING

weather *vb* to come safely through — see SURVIVE 1

weave *vb* to scatter or set here and there among other things — see THREAD 1

web *n* **1** something that catches and holds ⟨he was caught in the *web* of branches⟩ ⟨she was trapped by her own *web* of lies⟩

synonyms entanglement, net, snare

related words mesh, trap; knot, snarl, tangle; labyrinth, maze; cobweb, spiderweb

2 a device or scheme for capturing another by surprise — see TRAP 1

wed *vb* **1** to give in marriage — see MARRY 2

2 to perform the ceremony of marriage for — see MARRY 1

3 to take a spouse — see MARRY 4

4 to take as a spouse — see MARRY 3

wedded *adj* of or relating to marriage — see MARITAL

wedding *n* a ceremony in which two people are united in matrimony ⟨they chose to have the *wedding* outdoors in the spring⟩

synonyms bridal, espousal, marriage, nuptial(s)

related words match, matrimony, wedlock; reception; engagement, hand, pledge, promise, proposal, troth

wedge *vb* to fit (something) into a tight space — see CROWD 1

wedged *adj* firmly positioned in place and difficult to dislodge — see TIGHT 2

wedlock *n* a union representing a special kind of social and legal partnership between two people — see MARRIAGE 1

wee *adj* very small in size — see TINY

weedy *adj* growing thickly and vigorously — see RANK 1

weep *vb* **1** to flow forth slowly through small openings — see EXUDE

2 to shed tears often while making meaningless sounds as a sign of pain or distress — see CRY 1

weeping *adj* expressing or suggesting mourning — see MOURNFUL 1

weigh *vb* **1** to be of importance — see MATTER

2 to give serious and careful thought to — see PONDER

weigh (on *or* upon) *vb* to push steadily against with some force — see PRESS 1

weighed *adj* decided on as a result of careful thought — see DELIBERATE 1

weight *n* **1** the amount that something weighs ⟨I'm not allowed to lift anything with a *weight* of over ten pounds⟩

synonyms heaviness, heft

related words mass; tonnage; deadweight; heftiness, massiveness, ponderousness, weightiness; solidity, solidness, substantiality; burdensomeness, cumbersomeness

2 the quality or state of being important — see IMPORTANCE

3 a mass or quantity of something taken up and carried, conveyed, or transported — see LOAD 1

4 a special notice or importance given to something — see EMPHASIS 1

5 the main or greater part of something as distinguished from its appendages — see BODY 1

6 the power to direct the thinking or behavior of others usually indirectly — see INFLUENCE 1

weight *vb* to place a weight or burden on — see LOAD 1

weightiness *n* **1** the state or quality of being heavy ⟨the *weightiness* of the bookcase made it difficult to move⟩

synonyms avoirdupois, heaviness, heftiness, massiveness, ponderousness

related words overweight; solidity, solidness, substantiality; bulk, bulkiness, hugeness; burdensomeness, cumbersomeness

near antonyms airiness, delicacy, etherealness; flimsiness, fluffiness, insubstantiality, slightness

antonyms lightness, weightlessness

2 the quality or state of being important — see IMPORTANCE

weightless *adj* having little weight — see ¹LIGHT 1

weightlessness *n* the state or quality of having little weight — see ¹LIGHTNESS 1

weighty *adj* **1** having a matter of importance as its topic — see SERIOUS 2

2 having great meaning or lasting effect — see IMPORTANT 1

3 having great weight — see HEAVY 1

4 not joking or playful in mood or manner — see SERIOUS 1

5 having power over the minds or behavior of others — see INFLUENTIAL 1

weird *adj* **1** different from the ordinary in a way that causes curiosity or suspicion — see ODD 2

THESAURUS

2 fearfully and mysteriously strange or fantastic — see EERIE

3 having seemingly supernatural qualities or powers — see MYSTIC 1

4 noticeably different from what is generally found or experienced — see UNUSUAL 1

weirdo *n* a person of odd or whimsical habits — see ECCENTRIC

welcome *adj* giving pleasure or contentment to the mind or senses — see PLEASANT

welcome *n* an expression of goodwill upon meeting — see HELLO

welcome *vb* receive or accept gladly or readily ⟨the eager recruits *welcomed* every new project with which they were presented⟩
synonyms embrace
related words adopt, espouse, take up; greet, hail; enjoy, like, prefer; choose, cull, decide (on), elect, handpick, name, opt (for), pick, select, single (out), take
near antonyms decline, refuse, reject, turn down

welfare *n* the state of doing well especially in relation to one's happiness or success ⟨the social worker was pleased at the improvement in the child's *welfare*⟩
synonyms good, interest, weal, well-being
related words prosperity, success, successfulness; fitness, health, healthiness, robustness, soundness, wellness, wholeness, wholesomeness; bliss, felicity, happiness, joy; advantage, benefit, gain, sake; content, contentedness, gratification, satisfaction
near antonyms unhealthiness, unsoundness; misery, sadness, unhappiness, wretchedness

well *adv* **1** in a satisfactory way ⟨our current system for dividing household chores works *well*, so let's keep it⟩
synonyms acceptably, adequately, all right, fine, good, nicely, OK (*or* okay), passably, satisfactorily, so-so, tolerably
related words appropriately, congruously, correctly, decently, decorously, felicitously, fittingly, meetly, rightly, seemly, suitably
near antonyms unbearably; inappropriately, incorrectly, indecently, unsuitably
antonyms bad, badly, inadequately, intolerably, poorly, unacceptably, unsatisfactorily

2 in a generous manner ⟨the warm and gracious couple always treat overnight guests *well*⟩
synonyms bountifully, generously, handsomely, liberally, munificently
related words considerately, courteously, hospitably, kindly, nicely, reasonably, thoughtfully; affably, amiably, cheerfully, cheerily, genially, good-naturedly, graciously
near antonyms contemptuously, disdainfully, rudely, scornfully; obnoxiously, provocatively; coldly, coolly, frigidly, hostilely; angrily, belligerently
antonyms stingily

3 in a skillful or expert manner ⟨she plays the piano very *well*⟩
synonyms ably, adeptly, capably, competently, expertly, masterfully, proficiently, skillfully
related words aptly; adroitly, deftly, dexterously
near antonyms inaptly
antonyms incapably, incompetently, inefficiently, ineptly, inexpertly, poorly, unskillfully

4 with good reason or courtesy ⟨we cannot *well* get out of going to your cousin's wedding⟩

synonyms considerately, courteously, kindly, nicely, reasonably, thoughtfully
related words pleasantly; excusably, justifiably
near antonyms contemptuously, disdainfully, rudely, scornfully

5 in a pleasing way ⟨the day went *well*, despite the rough beginning⟩
synonyms agreeably, delectably, deliciously, delightfully, dreamily, favorably, felicitously, gloriously, nicely, pleasantly, pleasingly, satisfyingly, splendidly, swimmingly
related words finely, grandly; advantageously, helpfully; fortunately, happily, luckily; prosperously, successfully
antonyms badly

6 to a full extent or degree — see FULLY 1

well *adj* enjoying health and vigor — see HEALTHY 1

well *interj* how surprising, doubtful, or unbelievable — see NO

well–being *n* the state of doing well especially in relation to one's happiness or success — see WELFARE

wellborn *adj* of high birth, rank, or station — see NOBLE 1

well–bred *adj* showing consideration, courtesy, and good manners — see POLITE 1

well–disposed *adj* having an easygoing and pleasing manner especially in social situations — see AMIABLE

well–founded *adj* based on sound reasoning or information — see GOOD 1

well–heeled *adj* having goods, property, or money in abundance — see RICH 1

well–known *adj* widely known — see FAMOUS

wellness *n* the condition of being sound in body — see HEALTH

well–nigh *adv* very close to but not completely — see ALMOST

well–off *adj* having goods, property, or money in abundance — see RICH 1

well–read *adj* having or displaying advanced knowledge or education — see EDUCATED

well–spoken *adj* able to express oneself clearly and well — see ARTICULATE

well–to–do *adj* having goods, property, or money in abundance — see RICH 1

welter *n* **1** a state of noisy, confused activity — see COMMOTION

2 an unorganized collection or mixture of various things — see MISCELLANY 1

wet *adj* containing, covered with, or thoroughly penetrated by water ⟨I left the car windows open while it rained, and the seats got all *wet*⟩
synonyms awash, bathed, doused, drenched, dripping, saturated, soaked, soaking, sodden, soggy, soppy, soused, washed, watered, waterlogged, watery
related words deluged, drowned, flooded, inundated, overflowed; submerged, swamped; hydrated; dipped, dunked, splashed; aqueous; steeped; flushed, irrigated, laved, rinsed, sluiced; clammy, damp, dank, humid, moist
near antonyms waterproof, water-resistant, water-repellent, watertight; baked, dehydrated, freeze-dried; droughty, parched, sere, sunbaked, thirsty; wrung
antonyms arid, dry, unwatered, waterless

2 marked by or abounding with rain — see RAINY

wet *n* a steady falling of water from the sky in significant quantity — see RAIN 1

wet *vb* to make wet ⟨you need to *wet* your hair thoroughly first⟩
synonyms bathe, douse, drench, soak, souse, wash, water
related words damp, dampen, humidify, hydrate, moisten; deluge, drown, flood, inundate, overflow; submerge, swamp; splash; impregnate, saturate, steep; flush, irrigate, lave, rinse, sluice; dip, dunk
near antonyms bake, dehydrate, evaporate, freeze-dry, parch; wring; dehumidify
antonyms dry

whack *n* 1 an effort to do or accomplish something — see ATTEMPT
2 a hard strike with a part of the body or an instrument — see ¹BLOW
3 a loud explosive sound — see CLAP 1

whack *vb* to deliver a blow to (someone or something) usually in a strong vigorous manner — see HIT 1

whacking *adj* unusually large — see HUGE

whacking *adv* to a great degree — see VERY 1

whale *n* something that is unusually large and powerful — see GIANT

whale *vb* 1 to deliver a blow to (someone or something) usually in a strong vigorous manner — see HIT 1
2 to strike repeatedly with something long and thin or flexible — see WHIP 1
3 to strike repeatedly — see BEAT 1

wharf *n* a structure used by boats and ships for taking on or landing cargo and passengers — see DOCK

what *interj* how surprising, doubtful, or unbelievable — see NO

wheedle *vb* to get (someone) to do something by gentle urging, special attention, or flattery — see COAX

wheel *n* a rapid turning about on an axis or central point — see SPIN 1

wheel *vb* 1 to change the course or direction of (something) — see TURN 2
2 to move (something) in a curved or circular path on or as if on an axis — see TURN 1
3 to move in circles around an axis or center — see SPIN 1
4 to turn away from a straight line or course — see CURVE 1

wheeze *vb* to breathe hard, quickly, or with difficulty — see GASP

whelm *vb* to subject to incapacitating emotional or mental stress — see OVERWHELM 1

when *conj* in spite of the fact that — see ALTHOUGH

where *adv* at, in, or to what place ⟨*where* will you be tonight?⟩
synonyms whereabouts (*also* whereabout), whither
related words wherever

whereabouts *also* **whereabout** *adv* at, in, or to what place — see WHERE

whereas *conj* for the reason that — see SINCE

wherefore *adv* for this or that reason — see THEREFORE

wherefore *n* something (as a belief) that serves as the basis for another thing — see REASON 2

wherewithal *n* 1 available money — see FUND 2

2 the total of one's money and property — see WEALTH 1

whet *vb* to make sharp or sharper — see SHARPEN

whetted *adj* having an edge thin enough to cut or pierce something — see SHARP 1

whiff *vb* to become aware of by means of the sense organs in the nose — see SMELL 1

while *conj* in spite of the fact that — see ALTHOUGH

while *n* 1 an indefinite but usually short period of time ⟨we stayed at school for a *while* longer⟩
synonyms bit, space, spell, stretch
related words lapse; season, span; day, epoch, era; flash, instant, jiffy, minute, moment, second, shake, spurt, trice, twinkle, twinkling, wink; aeon (*or* eon), age, eternity; interim, interlude, intermission, interval
2 the active use of energy in producing a result — see EFFORT

whilom *adj* having been such at some previous time — see FORMER

whilst *conj chiefly British* in spite of the fact that — see ALTHOUGH

whim *n* a sudden impulsive and apparently unmotivated idea or action ⟨on a *whim*, we stopped at the roadside stand to get ice cream⟩
synonyms caprice, fancy, freak, notion, vagary, whimsy (*also* whimsey)
related words capriciousness, freakishness, whimsicality; conceit; concept, conception, image, impression, picture, thought; brainstorm, inspiration

whimper *vb* to utter feeble plaintive cries ⟨the dog *whimpered* to be let in⟩
synonyms mewl, pule
related words fuss, snivel, snuffle, whine; bawl, cry, weep; peep, squeak; yelp; mumble, murmur, mutter
near antonyms scream, screech, shriek, squeal; howl, squall, wail, yowl; call, caterwaul, squawk; bellow, roar

whimsical *adj* prone to sudden illogical changes of mind, ideas, or actions ⟨it's hard to make plans with my *whimsical* best friend⟩
synonyms capricious, freakish, impulsive
related words mercurial, moody, temperamental, volatile; eccentric, flaky, quirky; arbitrary, erratic, fickle, inconstant, irregular, willful (*or* wilful); impractical, quixotic, romantic
near antonyms equable; levelheaded, logical, practical, reasonable, sensible; fast, fixed, hard-and-fast, immutable, inflexible, invariable, unalterable, unchangeable; changeless, constant, established, set, settled, stable, steadfast, steady, unchanging, unvarying

whimsicality *n* an inclination to sudden illogical changes of mind, ideas, or actions ⟨her *whimsicality* made her unpredictable⟩
synonyms capriciousness, freakishness, impulsiveness
related words moodiness, volatility; eccentricity, flakiness; changeability, unpredictability; arbitrariness, fickleness, inconstancy, irregularity, willfulness; changeability, flexibility, mutability, variability
near antonyms levelheadedness, practicality, reasonableness; fastness, fixedness, immutability, inflexibility, invariability; changelessness, constancy, stability, steadfastness, steadiness

whimsy *also* **whimsey** *n* a sudden impulsive and

apparently unmotivated idea or action — see WHIM

whine *vb* to express dissatisfaction, pain, or resentment usually tiresomely — see COMPLAIN

whiner *n* **1** a person who makes frequent complaints usually about little things — see CRYBABY
2 an irritable and complaining person — see GROUCH

whinny *vb* to make the cry typical of a horse — see NEIGH

whip *n* a long thin or flexible tool for striking ⟨please do not use your belt as a *whip*⟩
synonyms flogger, lash, scourge, switch
related words blacksnake, cat-o'-nine-tails, cowhide, crop, knout, quirt, rawhide, strap; cane, club, cudgel, flail; stripe

whip *vb* **1** to strike repeatedly with something long and thin or flexible ⟨*whipped* the animal when it did not move fast enough to please him⟩
synonyms birch, cowhide, flagellate, flail, flog, hide, horsewhip, lash, rawhide, scourge, slash, switch, tan, thrash, whale
related words cane, club, cudgel; stripe; bang, bop, box, bust, clap, clip, clobber, clout, crack, cuff, hit, knock, lam, paste, punch, slap, slug, smack, smite, sock, spank, swat, swipe, thwack, wallop, whack; bash, batter, belt, bludgeon, buffet, bung, drub, hammer, lace, lambaste (*or* lambast), lick, mangle, maul, pelt, pound, pummel, rough, thump
2 to defeat by a large margin ⟨we *whipped* them 13-0 in the last game⟩
synonyms clobber, drub, rout, skunk, snow under, thrash, trim, trounce, wallop
related words beat, best, conquer, hurdle, lick, master, overbear, overcome, overmatch, prevail (over), subdue, surmount, throw, triumph (over), win (against), worst; crush, overpower, overthrow, subjugate, vanquish; exceed, outdo, surpass
3 to achieve a victory over — see BEAT 2
4 to change the course or direction of (something) — see TURN 2
5 to move or cause to move with a striking motion — see FLAP
6 to strike repeatedly — see BEAT 1

whip (up) *vb* to cause or encourage the development of — see INCITE 1

whipper *n* one that defeats an enemy or opponent — see VICTOR 1

whippersnapper *n* a person of no importance or influence — see NOBODY

whipping *n* failure to win a contest — see DEFEAT 1

whipping boy *n* a person or thing taking the blame for others — see SCAPEGOAT

whir *also* **whirr** *vb* to fly, turn, or move rapidly with a fluttering or vibratory sound ⟨the hummingbird *whirred* as it hovered over a flower⟩ ⟨our tires *whirred* as we traveled over the rough road⟩
synonyms buzz, drone, hum, whish, whiz (*or* whizz), zip, zoom
related words thrum; hiss, murmur, purr, rustle, sigh, whisper

whir *n* a monotonous sound like that of an insect in motion — see HUM

whirl *n* **1** a rapid turning about on an axis or central point — see SPIN 1
2 a state of mental uncertainty — see CONFUSION 1

3 a state of noisy, confused activity — see COMMOTION

whirl *vb* **1** to cause (as a liquid) to move about in a circle especially repeatedly — see STIR 1
2 to move (something) in a curved or circular path on or as if on an axis — see TURN 1
3 to move in circles around an axis or center — see SPIN 1
4 to proceed or move quickly — see HURRY 2
5 to be in a confused state as if from being twirled around — see SPIN 1

whirling *adj* having a feeling of being whirled about and in danger of falling down — see DIZZY 1

whirlpool *n* water moving rapidly in a circle with a hollow in the center ⟨in *The Odyssey*, Ulysses is trapped between the six-headed monster Scylla and Charybdis, a deadly *whirlpool* that threatens to suck his ship down⟩
synonyms maelstrom, vortex
related words eddy, swirl, whirl

whirlwind *adj* moving, proceeding, or acting with great speed — see FAST 1

whish *n* a sound similar to the speech sound \s\ stretched out — see HISS 1

whish *vb* **1** to fly, turn, or move rapidly with a fluttering or vibratory sound — see WHIRR
2 to make a sound like that of stretching out the speech sound \s\ — see HISS

whisk *vb* **1** to cause to move or proceed fast or faster — see HURRY 1
2 to move or proceed smoothly and readily — see FLOW 2
3 to proceed or move quickly — see HURRY 2

whisper *n* a rumor or report of a personal or sensational nature — see TALE 1

whisper *vb* to make (as a piece of information) the subject of common talk without any authority or confirmation of accuracy — see RUMOR

whistling *adj* having a high musical pitch or range — see SHRILL

whit *n* the smallest amount or part imaginable — see JOT

white *adj* **1** lacking an addition of color — see COLORLESS
2 not causing injury or hurt — see HARMLESS

whiten *vb* to make white or whiter by removing color ⟨years of sunlight had almost completely *whitened* the flag⟩
synonyms blanch, bleach, blench, decolorize, dull, fade, pale, wash out
related words brighten, lighten; dim, matte (*also* mat *or* matt); whitewash; frost, silver
near antonyms blacken; blotch, discolor, mottle, shade, splotch, spot, tarnish; color, dye, paint, stain, tinge, tint; burnish, polish, shine
antonyms darken, deepen

whitewash *vb* to make (something) seem less bad by offering excuses — see PALLIATE 1

whither *adv* at, in, or to what place — see WHERE

¹**whiz** *or* **whizz** *n* **1** a sound similar to the speech sound \s\ stretched out — see HISS 1
2 a monotonous sound like that of an insect in motion — see HUM

²**whiz** *n* **1** a person with a high level of knowledge or skill in a field — see EXPERT
2 a very smart person — see GENIUS 1

whiz *or* **whizz** *vb* **1** to make a sound like that of stretching out the speech sound \s\ — see HISS
2 to fly, turn, or move rapidly with a fluttering or vibratory sound — see WHIRR

whole *adj* **1** not divided or scattered among several areas of interest or concern ⟨you'll need to put your *whole* effort into this project⟩
synonyms all, concentrated, entire, exclusive, focused (*also* focussed), undivided
related words absolute, complete, full, thorough, total; comprehensive, intact, integral, perfect
near antonyms deficient, fragmental, fragmentary, incomplete, partial
antonyms diffuse, divided, scattered
2 enjoying health and vigor — see HEALTHY 1
3 not lacking any part or member that properly belongs to it — see COMPLETE 1
whole *n* a complete amount of something ⟨the landlord eventually refunded the *whole* of our deposit⟩
synonyms aggregate, full, sum, summation, total, totality
related words gross; completeness, comprehensiveness, entirety; bulk, lion's share, mass
phrases the whole kit and kaboodle, the whole shebang
near antonyms net
wholehearted *adj* characterized by unqualified enthusiasm — see HEARTY 1
wholeness *n* the condition of being sound in body — see HEALTH
whole number *n* a character used to represent a mathematical value — see NUMBER
wholesome *adj* **1** enjoying health and vigor — see HEALTHY 1
2 good for the health — see HEALTHFUL
wholesomeness *n* the condition of being sound in body — see HEALTH
wholly *adv* to a full extent or degree — see FULLY 1
whoop *n* a loud vocal expression of strong emotion — see SHOUT
whopper *n* **1** a statement known by its maker to be untrue and made in order to deceive — see LIE
2 something that is unusually large and powerful — see GIANT
whopping *adj* unusually large — see HUGE
whore *n* a woman who engages in sexual activities for money — see PROSTITUTE
why *interj* how surprising, doubtful, or unbelievable — see NO
why *n* something (as a belief) that serves as the basis for another thing — see REASON 2
wicked *adj* **1** not conforming to a high moral standard; morally unacceptable — see BAD 2
2 tending to or exhibiting reckless playfulness — see MISCHIEVOUS 1
wickedly *adv* in a mean or spiteful manner — see NASTILY
wickedness *n* **1** playful, reckless behavior that is not intended to cause serious harm — see MISCHIEF 1
2 the state or quality of being utterly evil — see ENORMITY 1
wide *adj* **1** having a greater than usual measure across ⟨the river was so *wide* that it was impossible to cross it in less than a day⟩
synonyms broad, fat, thick
related words expansive, extensive; commodious, roomy, spacious
near antonyms fine, hairlike; elongated; needlelike; close, compressed, condensed, constricted, contracted, squeezed, tight, tightened

antonyms narrow, skinny, slender, slim, thin
2 having considerable extent — see EXTENSIVE
wide–awake *adj* **1** not sleeping or able to sleep — see WAKEFUL
2 paying close attention usually for the purpose of anticipating approaching danger or opportunity — see ALERT 1
wide–eyed *adj* lacking in worldly wisdom or informed judgment — see NAIVE 1
widespread *adj* having considerable extent — see EXTENSIVE
width *n* an area over which activity, capacity, or influence extends — see RANGE 2
wield *vb* to bring to bear especially forcefully or effectively — see EXERT
wife *n* the female partner in a marriage ⟨a husband and *wife* who treat each other as equals in their marriage⟩
synonyms helpmate, helpmeet, lady
related words bride; consort, mate, partner, spouse; dowager, matron; homemaker, housewife
wiggle *vb* to make jerky or restless movements — see FIDGET
wight *n* a member of the human race — see HUMAN
wild *adj* **1** living outdoors without taming or domestication by humans ⟨*wild* animals can be shy or aggressive when confronted by humans⟩
synonyms feral, savage, unbroken, undomesticated, untamed
related words uncontrolled, unsubdued; bestial, brutal, brute; barbarous, uncivilized
near antonyms controlled, subdued; housebroken, trained; civilized, socialized
antonyms broken, busted, domestic, domesticated, tame, tamed
2 existing without human habitation or cultivation ⟨that land has been completely *wild* since the owners abandoned it⟩
synonyms natural, uncultivated, untamed
related words native; uninhabited; overgrown, untended; waste; undeveloped
near antonyms inhabited; developed
antonyms cultivated, tamed
3 marked by turmoil or disturbance especially of natural elements ⟨a *wild* night, full of wind and rain⟩
synonyms stormy, tempestuous, tumultuous, turbulent
related words blustery, rough, violent; brutal, harsh, severe; unsettled
near antonyms calm, halcyon, peaceful, placid, quiet, serene, tranquil
4 conceived or made without regard for reason or reality — see FANTASTIC 1
5 different from the ordinary in a way that causes curiosity or suspicion — see ODD 2
6 marked by great and often stressful excitement or activity — see FURIOUS 1
7 not civilized — see SAVAGE 1
wild *adv* in a confused and reckless manner — see HELTER-SKELTER 1
wild *n* that part of the physical world that is removed from human habitation — see NATURE 2
wilderness *n* that part of the physical world that is removed from human habitation — see NATURE 2
wildly *adv* in a confused and reckless manner — see HELTER-SKELTER 1

THESAURUS

wile *n* **1** a clever often underhanded means to achieve an end — see TRICK 1
2 the use of clever underhanded actions to achieve an end — see TRICKERY
wile *vb* to attract or delight as if by magic — see CHARM 1
wiliness *n* **1** skill in achieving one's ends through indirect, subtle, or underhanded means — see CUNNING 1
2 the inclination or practice of misleading others through lies or trickery — see DECEIT
will *n* **1** the power to control one's actions, impulses, or emotions ⟨she kept her face still by sheer force of *will*⟩
synonyms restraint, self-containment, self-control, self-discipline, self-government, self-possession, self-restraint, willpower
related words self-denial; moderation, temperance; determination, nerve; command, control, discipline, mastery; aplomb, assurance, composure, confidence, coolness, equanimity, poise, self-confidence; discretion
near antonyms gratification, indulgence, self-indulgence; immoderacy, intemperance, overindulgence; demerit, failing, fault, feebleness, foible, frailty, shortcoming, vice, weakness
2 the act or power of making one's own choices or decisions — see FREE WILL
will *vb* **1** to give by means of a will — see LEAVE 2
2 to see fit — see CHOOSE 2
willful *or* **wilful** *adj* **1** given to resisting authority or another's control — see DISOBEDIENT
2 given to resisting control or discipline by others — see UNCONTROLLABLE
3 having or showing a tendency to force one's will on others without any regard to fairness or necessity — see ARBITRARY 1
4 made, given, or done with full awareness of what one is doing — see INTENTIONAL
5 sticking to an opinion, purpose, or course of action in spite of reason, arguments, or persuasion — see OBSTINATE
willfully *adv* with full awareness of what one is doing — see INTENTIONALLY
willfulness *n* **1** a steadfast adherence to an opinion, purpose, or course of action — see OBSTINACY
2 refusal to obey — see DISOBEDIENCE
willies *n pl* a sense of panic or extreme nervousness — see JITTERS
willing *adj* **1** having a desire or inclination (as for a specified course of action) ⟨I'm a little confused, but perfectly *willing* to do as you ask⟩
synonyms amenable, disposed, game, glad, inclined, ready
related words predisposed; agreeable, compliant, obedient, submissive; favorable, receptive; prepared, prompt, quick, responsive, swift
near antonyms averse, loath, reluctant
antonyms disinclined, unwilling
2 having or showing the ability to respond without delay or hesitation — see QUICK 1
3 done, made, or given with one's own free will — see VOLUNTARY 1
willingly *adv* **1** by choice or preference — see RATHER 1
2 of one's own free will — see VOLUNTARILY
willingness *n* cheerful readiness to do something — see ALACRITY

williwaw *n* a sudden brief rush of wind — see GUST 1
willowy *adj* able to bend easily without breaking ⟨the rattan's stems are split into *willowy* staves that are woven together to produce exquisite baskets⟩
synonyms flexible, limber, lissome (*also* lissom), lithe, pliable, pliant, supple
related words adaptable, ductile, elastic, fluid, malleable, modifiable, plastic, variable, yielding; flaccid, floppy
near antonyms inelastic, nonmalleable, unyielding; breakable, brittle, fragile
antonyms inflexible, rigid, stiff
willpower *n* the power to control one's actions, impulses, or emotions — see WILL 1
wilt *vb* **1** to be limp from lack of water or vigor — see DROOP 1
2 to lose bodily strength or vigor — see WEAKEN 2
3 to lose liveliness, force, or freshness — see WITHER
wily *adj* clever at attaining one's ends by indirect and often deceptive means — see ARTFUL 1
wimp *n* **1** a person lacking in physical strength — see WEAKLING 1
2 a person without strength of character — see WEAKLING 2
wimpy *adj* **1** lacking bodily strength — see WEAK 1
2 lacking strength of will or character — see WEAK 2
win *n* an instance of defeating an enemy or opponent — see VICTORY
win *vb* **1** to achieve victory (as in a contest) ⟨the kind of person who always has to *win* —even if the game is just for fun⟩
synonyms conquer, prevail, triumph
related words overcome, sweep; squeak, squeeze; contend, vie; succeed
phrases carry the day
near antonyms collapse, fail, flop, fold, wash out; flounder, struggle; decline, slip, slump, wane
antonyms lose
2 to receive as return for effort — see EARN 1
3 to obtain (as a goal) through effort — see ACHIEVE 1
win (against) *vb* to achieve a victory over — see BEAT 2
win (over) *vb* to cause (someone) to agree with a belief or course of action by using arguments or earnest requests — see PERSUADE
wince *vb* to draw back in fear, pain, or disgust — see FLINCH
¹**wind** *n* **1** noticeable movement of air in a particular direction ⟨there's a *wind* coming from underneath the front door⟩
synonyms current, draft
related words blast, blow, flurry, gale, gust, head wind, squall, tail wind, tempest, tornado, windstorm; breath, breeze, puff, waft, zephyr
2 a prevailing or general movement or inclination — see TREND 1
3 language that is impressive-sounding but not meaningful or sincere — see RHETORIC 1
²**wind** *n* something that curves or is curved — see BEND 1
wind *vb* to follow a circular or spiral course ⟨flowering vines *wind* around the porch's graceful columns⟩
synonyms coil, curl, entwine, spiral, twine, twist
related words arc, arch, bend, crook, curve, hook,

sweep, swerve, turn, veer, wheel; swirl, whirl; circle, encircle, loop, interlace, intertwine, lace; bow, bulge; meander, weave, zigzag
near antonyms straighten

windfall *n* something that provides happiness or does good for a person or thing — see BLESSING 2

windiness *n* the use of too many words to express an idea — see VERBIAGE

winding *adj* **1** marked by a long series of irregular curves — see CROOKED 1
2 turning around an axis like the thread of a screw — see SPIRAL

windjammer *n* a boat equipped with one or more sails — see SAILBOAT

windup *n* the last part of a process or action — see FINALE

wind up *vb* **1** to bring (an event) to a natural or appropriate stopping point — see CLOSE 3
2 to come to an end — see CEASE 1

windy *adj* **1** marked by strong wind or more wind than usual ⟨one particularly *windy* day should shake the last of the autumn leaves from the trees⟩
synonyms blowy, blustery, breezy, gusty
related words drafty; stormy, tempestuous
near antonyms breathless, calm, motionless, still
2 marked by the use of impressive-sounding but mostly meaningless words and phrases — see RHETORICAL
3 using or containing more words than necessary to express an idea — see WORDY

wing *n* a group of people acting together within a larger group — see FACTION

wing *vb* to move through the air with or as if with outstretched wings — see FLY 1

wink *n* **1** a short sleep — see ¹NAP
2 a very small space of time — see INSTANT

wink *vb* **1** to rapidly open and close one's eyes ⟨she *winked* several times to get the dust and grit out of her eyes⟩
synonyms blink
related words bat, flutter; squint
2 to shine with light at regular intervals — see BLINK 1
3 to shoot forth bursts of light — see FLASH 1
4 to secretly sympathize with or pretend ignorance of something improper or unlawful — see CONNIVE

wink (at) *vb* to overlook or dismiss as of little importance — see EXCUSE 1

winner *n* **1** a person or thing that is successful — see HIT 1
2 one that defeats an enemy or opponent — see VICTOR 1
3 the person who comes in first in a competition — see CHAMPION 1

winning *adj* **1** having qualities that tend to make one loved — see LOVABLE
2 likely to win one's affection — see INGRATIATING

winsome *adj* likely to win one's affection — see INGRATIATING

wintry *adj* **1** having a low or subnormal temperature — see COLD 1
2 lacking in friendliness or warmth of feeling — see COLD 2

wipe out *vb* to destroy all traces of — see ANNIHILATE 1

wire *n* a length of braided, flexible material that is used for tying or connecting things — see CORD

wisdom *n* **1** the ability to understand inner qualities or relationships ⟨with age and experience comes *wisdom* —hopefully⟩ ⟨neither book learning nor simple intelligence should be confused with *wisdom*⟩
synonyms discernment, insight, perception, perceptiveness, sagaciousness, sagacity, sageness, sapience
related words acuity, acumen, astuteness, penetration, perspicacity, sensitivity, understanding; appreciation, apprehension, comprehension, grasp; braininess, brain(s), brightness, brilliance, canniness, cleverness, gray matter, intellect, intelligence, judgment (*or* judgement), mentality, power, reason, sense, smartness, wit; discrimination, judiciousness, prudence, sanity; logic, rationality
near antonyms density, dullness (*or* dulness), obtuseness; brainlessness, folly, foolishness, idiocy, imbecility, mindlessness, silliness, simpleness, stupidity, witlessness; illogic, irrationality, unreasonableness, unsoundness; craziness, insanity, lunacy, madness; preposterousness, senselessness, silliness, zaniness
2 a body of facts learned by study or experience — see KNOWLEDGE 1
3 the ability to make intelligent decisions especially in everyday matters — see COMMON SENSE

wise *adj* **1** having or showing deep understanding and intelligent application of knowledge ⟨a respected and *wise* old judge famous for her sensible rulings⟩
synonyms discerning, insightful, perceptive, sagacious, sage, sapient
related words acute, perspicacious; experienced; discriminating, discriminative; brainy, brilliant, bright, clever, intelligent, keen, nimble, quick, quick-witted, smart; cerebral, erudite, knowledgeable, learned, literate, scholarly; astute, sharp, shrewd; contemplative, reflective, thoughtful
near antonyms dense, dull, obtuse; brainless, dumb, feebleminded, foolish, idiotic, imbecilic, moronic, silly, simple, slow, stupid, thoughtless, unintelligent, witless; undiscriminating
antonyms undiscerning, unperceptive, unwise
2 having inside information ⟨they fooled everyone else, but I'd heard them talking and was *wise* to their true intentions⟩
synonyms hip, knowing
related words alerted, aware, clued, forewarned, informed, prepared, ready, warned; observant, observing, sharp, sharp-eyed; alert, attentive, open-eyed, vigilant, watchful
phrases in the know
near antonyms oblivious, unaware, unconscious, uninformed, unperceiving, unseeing, unwitting; heedless, unmindful, unobservant, unobserving; unprepared, unready, unwary
antonyms unknowing
3 suitable for bringing about a desired result under the circumstances — see EXPEDIENT

wise (up) *vb* to give information to — see ENLIGHTEN 1

wiseacre *n* a person who likes to show off in a clever but annoying way — see SMART ALECK

wisecrack *n* something said or done to cause laughter — see JOKE 1

wisecrack *vb* to make jokes — see JOKE

wise guy *n* a person who likes to show off in a clever but annoying way — see SMART ALECK

wish *vb* to see fit — see CHOOSE 2

wish (for) *vb* to have an earnest wish to own or enjoy — see DESIRE

wishy–washy *adj* **1** lacking in qualities that make for spirit and character ⟨this story is too *wishy-washy*; you need to add some verve to it⟩

synonyms banal, flat, insipid

related words unentertaining, unexciting, uninspiring, unrewarding, unsatisfying; bland, boring, drab, dreary, dry, dull, heavy, humdrum, jading, leaden, monotonous, pedestrian, ponderous, tedious, tiresome, tiring, uninteresting, wearisome, weary, wearying; inane; innocuous, inoffensive; mild, soft, subdued, tame, weak; common, commonplace, ordinary, stale, unexceptional

near antonyms piquant, poignant, pungent, racy, spicy; meaty, substantial; entertaining, exciting, galvanizing, inspiring, invigorating, thrilling

2 lacking strength of will or character — see WEAK 2

wit *n* **1** a person (as a writer) noted for or specializing in humor — see HUMORIST

2 the ability to make intelligent decisions especially in everyday matters — see COMMON SENSE

3 the normal or healthy condition of the mental abilities — see MIND 2

witch *n* **1** a woman believed to have often harmful supernatural powers ⟨in the old days women were sometimes accused of being *witches* and using evil magic to make the crops fail or an animal die suddenly⟩

synonyms enchantress, hag, hex, sorceress

related words charmer, conjuror (*or* conjurer), enchanter, necromancer, voodoo; magician, sorcerer, warlock, wizard

2 a mean or ugly old woman — see CRONE

3 a person skilled in using supernatural forces — see MAGICIAN 1

witchcraft *n* the power to control natural forces through supernatural means — see MAGIC 1

witchery *n* **1** the power of irresistible attraction — see CHARM 2

2 the power to control natural forces through supernatural means — see MAGIC 1

with *prep* **1** as the result of — see BECAUSE OF

2 using the means or agency of — see BY 2

3 without being prevented by — see DESPITE

withal *adv* **1** in addition to what has been said — see MORE 1

2 in spite of that — see HOWEVER

withdraw *vb* **1** to move back or away (as from something difficult, dangerous, or disagreeable) — see RETREAT 1

2 to solemnly or formally reject or go back on (as something formerly adhered to) — see ABJURE

3 to take away from a place or position — see REMOVE 2

withdrawal *n* an act of moving away especially from something difficult, dangerous, or disagreeable — see RETREAT 1

wither *vb* to lose liveliness, force, or freshness ⟨shortly after the moon landing, interest in the space program *withered*⟩ ⟨the old man seemed to *wither* suddenly when he turned eighty⟩

synonyms dry, wilt

related words mummify, shrivel, wizen; decline, fade, wane; decrease, diminish, lessen

near antonyms freshen, revive; flourish, prosper,
thrive; develop, grow, increase, wax; crest, peak, surge

withhold *vb* **1** to be unwilling to grant — see DENY 2

2 to continue to have in one's possession or power — see KEEP 2

within *n* an interior or internal part — see INSIDE 1

without *prep* **1** not having ⟨spent two days *without* food⟩

synonyms minus, sans, wanting

2 out of the reach or sphere of — see BEYOND 2

withstand *vb* to refuse to give in to — see RESIST

witless *adj* **1** not having or showing an ability to absorb ideas readily — see STUPID 1

2 showing or marked by a lack of good sense or judgment — see FOOLISH 1

witlessness *n* **1** lack of good sense or judgment — see FOOLISHNESS 1

2 the quality or state of lacking intelligence or quickness of mind — see STUPIDITY 1

witness *n* something presented in support of the truth or accuracy of a claim — see PROOF

witness *vb* **1** to declare (something) to be true or genuine — see CERTIFY 1

2 to make note of (something) through the use of one's eyes — see SEE 1

3 to make a solemn declaration under oath for the purpose of establishing a fact — see TESTIFY

witticism *n* something said or done to cause laughter — see JOKE 1

wittingly *adv* with full awareness of what one is doing — see INTENTIONALLY

witty *adj* given to or marked by mature intelligent humor ⟨Susan is popular because she is so *witty* and fun-loving⟩ ⟨he's well-known for his *witty* retorts⟩

synonyms clever, facetious, humorous, jocular, smart

related words cerebral, highbrow, intellectual; bantering, frivolous, jesting, joking, joshing, teasing; antic, comic, comical, droll, farcical, funny, hysterical, laughable, ludicrous, ridiculous, riotous, risible, rollicking, screaming, side-splitting, uproarious; amusing, diverting, entertaining; mischievous, playful, prankish; jocose, jocund, jolly, jovial, laughing, merry, mirthful, sunny; scintillating, sparkling; flip, flippant, pert, smart-alecky (*or* smart-aleck); whimsical

near antonyms brainless, lowbrow, stupid, witless; corny, hackneyed, lame; humorless, uncomic, unfunny; earnest, grave, serious, sober, solemn, somber (*or* sombre); doleful, dolorous, lachrymose, plaintive, weary, tearful, woeful

wizard *n* **1** a person skilled in using supernatural forces — see MAGICIAN 1

2 a person with a high level of knowledge or skill in a field — see EXPERT

3 a very smart person — see GENIUS 1

wizardry *n* the power to control natural forces through supernatural means — see MAGIC 1

wobble *vb* **1** to make a series of small irregular or violent movements — see SHAKE 1

2 to make a series of unsteady side-to-side motions — see ROCK 1

3 to show uncertainty about the right course of action — see HESITATE

4 to swing unsteadily back and forth or from side to side — see TEETER 1

wobbling *adj* marked by or given to small uncontrollable bodily movements — see SHAKY 1

wobbling *n* the act or an instance of pausing because of uncertainty about the right course of action — see HESITATION

wobbly *adj* marked by or given to small uncontrollable bodily movements — see SHAKY 1

woe *n* **1** a state of great suffering of body or mind — see DISTRESS 1

2 deep sadness especially for the loss of someone or something loved — see SORROW

woebegone *adj* feeling unhappiness — see SAD 1

woeful *adj* **1** expressing or suggesting mourning — see MOURNFUL 1

2 feeling unhappiness — see SAD 1

3 of a kind to cause great distress — see REGRETTABLE

woefully *adv* with feelings of bitterness or grief — see HARD 2

woman *n* an adult female human being ⟨for a while, the toddler called every *woman* "mama"⟩

synonyms female, lady

related words dame, gentlewoman; madam, madame, senora (*or* señora); beauty, belle, chick [*slang*], damsel, doll, gal, girl, ingenue (*or* ingénue), lass, lassie, mademoiselle, maid, maiden, miss, senorita (*or* señorita)

womanish *adj* **1** having or displaying qualities more suitable for women than for men — see EFFEMINATE

2 of, relating to, or marked by qualities traditionally associated with women — see FEMININE 1

womanlike *adj* **1** having or displaying qualities more suitable for women than for men — see EFFEMINATE

2 of, relating to, or marked by qualities traditionally associated with women — see FEMININE 1

womanly *adj* **1** having or displaying qualities more suitable for women than for men — see EFFEMINATE

2 of, relating to, or marked by qualities traditionally associated with women — see FEMININE 1

wonder *n* **1** something extraordinary or surprising ⟨the cunningly crafted miniature of our house is a *wonder*, perfect in every detail⟩

synonyms caution, flash, marvel, miracle, phenomenon, portent, prodigy, sensation

related words curiosity, sight, spectacle; apparition, appearance

2 the rapt attention and deep emotion caused by the sight of something extraordinary ⟨when we first saw the pyramids of Egypt, we gazed with openmouthed *wonder*⟩

synonyms admiration, amazement, astonishment, awe, wonderment

related words dread; fear; respect, reverence, veneration; curiosity, interest; shock, surprise; disbelief, incomprehension, incredulity; beguilement, bewitchment, captivation, enchantment, fascination; animation, enlightenment, enlivenment, excitement, invigoration, stimulation; absorption, engagement, engrossment, enthrallment, immersion, involvement

near antonyms apathy, disinterest, incuriosity, indifference, unconcern; boredom, doldrums, ennui, listlessness, restlessness, tedium, tiredness, weariness; cheerlessness, dispiritedness, joylessness, melancholy

wonderful *adj* **1** causing wonder or astonishment — see MARVELOUS 1

2 of the very best kind — see EXCELLENT

wondering *adj* filled with amazement or wonder — see OPENMOUTHED

wonderment *n* the rapt attention and deep emotion caused by the sight of something extraordinary — see WONDER 2

wondrous *adj* causing wonder or astonishment — see MARVELOUS 1

wont *adj* being in the habit or custom — see ACCUSTOMED

wont *n* a usual manner of behaving or doing — see HABIT

woo *vb* to act so as to make (something) more likely — see COURT 1

wood *n* tree logs as prepared for human use ⟨a huge load of *wood* outside the furniture maker's factory⟩

synonyms lumber, timber

related words beam, brace, pile, post, ridgepole, sill, splint, stake, stave, stick; bar, billet, block; cordwood, firewood

wood *n*, *often* **woods** *pl* a dense growth of trees and shrubs covering a large area — see FOREST

wooden *adj* lacking social grace and assurance — see AWKWARD 1

woodland *n* a dense growth of trees and shrubs covering a large area — see FOREST

wooer *n* a man who courts a woman usually with the goal of marrying her — see SUITOR 1

wool *n* the hairy covering of a mammal especially when fine, soft, and thick — see FUR 1

woolgathering *n* the state of being lost in thought — see REVERIE

woolly *also* **wooly** *adj* **1** made of or resembling hair — see HAIRY 2

2 covered with or as if with hair — see HAIRY 1

word *n* **1** a pronounceable series of letters having a distinct meaning especially in a particular field ⟨my doctor used all of these medical *words* that I didn't understand⟩

synonyms expression, term

related words linguistic form, monosyllable, morpheme; collocation, idiom, locution, phrase; archaism, coinage, colloquialism, euphemism, loan word, modernism, neologism

2 something that is said ⟨people who believe that the Bible is the literal *word* of God⟩

synonyms statement, utterance

related words communication, message; announcement, declamation, declaration, manifesto, proclamation, pronouncement

3 a report of recent events or facts not previously known — see NEWS

4 a person's solemn declaration that he or she will do or not do something — see PROMISE

5 a statement of what to do that must be obeyed by those concerned — see COMMAND 1

word *vb* to convey in appropriate or telling terms — see PHRASE

wordbook *n* a reference book giving information about the meanings, pronunciations, uses, and origins of words listed in alphabetical order — see DICTIONARY

wordiness *n* the use of too many words to express an idea — see VERBIAGE

wording *n* the way in which something is put into words ⟨it's important to get the *wording* of this law precisely correct⟩

synonyms diction, language, phraseology, phrasing

related words expression, formulation, locution;

THESAURUS

enunciation, phrase, speech, style, utterance, voice

wordless *adj* understood although not put into words — see IMPLICIT

wordy *adj* using or containing more words than necessary to express an idea ⟨your paper is two pages too long—it doesn't need to be so *wordy*⟩
synonyms circuitous, circumlocutory, diffuse, long-winded, prolix, rambling, verbose, windy
related words chatty, communicative, conversational, gabby, garrulous, loquacious, talkative, talky, voluble; redundant, repetitious, tautological; embellished, embroidered, exaggerated; bombastic, grandiloquent, highfalutin
near antonyms brief, short; aphoristic, epigrammatic, sententious; compendious, summary; abbreviated, abridged, condensed, shortened; abrupt, blunt, brusque, curt, laconic, snippy
antonyms compact, concise, crisp, pithy, succinct, terse

work *n* 1 a literary, musical, or artistic production — see COMPOSITION 1
2 something produced by physical or intellectual effort — see PRODUCT 1
3 the action for which a person or thing is specially fitted or used or for which a thing exists — see ROLE
4 the active use of energy in producing a result — see EFFORT
5 the activity by which one regularly makes a living — see OCCUPATION
6 works *pl* a building or set of buildings for the manufacturing of goods — see FACTORY

work *vb* 1 to be the cause of (a situation, action, or state of mind) — see EFFECT
2 to find an answer for through reasoning — see SOLVE
3 to have a certain purpose — see FUNCTION
4 to produce a desired effect — see ACT 2
5 to set or keep in motion — see MOVE 2
6 to control the mechanical operation of — see OPERATE 1
7 to devote serious and sustained effort — see LABOR

work (for) *vb* to be a servant for — see SERVE 1
work (in) *vb* to introduce in a gradual, secret, or clever way — see INSINUATE

workable *adj* 1 capable of being done or carried out — see POSSIBLE 1
2 capable of being put to use or account — see PRACTICAL 1

workaday *adj* 1 being of the type that is encountered in the normal course of events — see ORDINARY 1
2 having to do with the practical details of regular life — see MUNDANE 1
3 not designed for special occasions — see CASUAL 1

worker *n* 1 a person who does very hard or dull work — see SLAVE 2
2 one who works for another for wages or a salary — see EMPLOYEE

working *adj* 1 being in effective operation — see ACTIVE 1
2 capable of being put to use or account — see PRACTICAL 1
3 involved in often constant activity — see BUSY 1

workmanlike *adj* accomplished with trained ability — see SKILLFUL 1

workout *n* something done over and over in order to develop skill — see EXERCISE 2

work out *vb* 1 to find an answer for through reasoning — see SOLVE
2 to produce or bring about especially by long or repeated effort — see HAMMER (OUT)
3 to turn out as planned or desired — see SUCCEED 1
4 to determine (a value) by doing the necessary mathematical operations — see CALCULATE 1

workshop *n* a building or set of buildings for the manufacturing of goods — see FACTORY

world *n* 1 human beings in general — see PEOPLE 1
2 the celestial body on which we live — see EARTH 1
3 the whole body of things observed or assumed — see UNIVERSE

worldly *adj* 1 having a wide and refined knowledge of the world especially from personal experience — see WORLDLY-WISE
2 having to do with life on earth especially as opposed to that in heaven — see EARTHLY

worldly–wise *adj* having a wide and refined knowledge of the world especially from personal experience ⟨having followed their father on his military assignments all over the world, the Johnson kids have become very *worldly-wise*⟩
synonyms cosmopolitan, smart, sophisticated, worldly
related words suave, urbane; civilized, cultivated, cultured, polished, refined; experienced, knowing, practiced, schooled, seasoned; bored, cynical, jaded, skeptical; down-to-earth, pragmatic (*also* pragmatical), realistic, sober
near antonyms callow, green, inexperienced, raw; parochial, provincial, rustic; philistine, uncivilized, uncultured, unrefined; childlike, simple, simpleminded; idealistic, impractical; uncritical, unknowing
antonyms ingenuous, innocent, naive (*or* naïve), unsophisticated, unworldly, wide-eyed

worm *vb* 1 to advance gradually beyond the usual or desirable limits — see ENCROACH
2 to introduce in a gradual, secret, or clever way — see INSINUATE
3 to move slowly with the body close to the ground — see CRAWL 1

worn *adj* depleted in strength, energy, or freshness — see WEARY 1

worn–out *adj* 1 depleted in strength, energy, or freshness — see WEARY 1
2 worn or torn into or as if into rags — see RAGGED 2

worried *adj* feeling or showing uncomfortable feelings of uncertainty — see NERVOUS 1

worrisome *adj* 1 causing worry or anxiety — see TROUBLESOME
2 marked by or causing agitation or uncomfortable feelings — see NERVOUS 2

worry *n* an uneasy state of mind usually over the possibility of an anticipated misfortune or trouble — see ANXIETY 1

worry *vb* 1 to experience concern or anxiety ⟨they *worried* for days about the upcoming exam⟩
synonyms bother, fear, fret, stew, sweat, trouble
related words agonize; long, pine, yearn; chafe; despair
phrases care a hang, give a hang
near antonyms accept; abide, bear, endure, stick out, stomach, sustain, take, tolerate

2 to trouble the mind of; to make uneasy — see DISTURB 1

worsen *vb* to become worse or of less value — see DETERIORATE

worship *n* excessive admiration of or devotion to a person ⟨his *worship* of his big brother meant that he'd go to any extreme for his idol⟩
synonyms adulation, deification, idolatry, idolization, worshipping (*also* worshiping)
related words adoration, deference, glorification, reverence, veneration; idealization, romanticization; affection, fancy, favor, fondness, like, liking, love; appreciation, esteem, regard, respect; approval
near antonyms condemnation, disapproval, disfavor, dislike, dismissal, disregard, hatred, loathing, scorn

worship *vb* **1** to offer honor or respect to (someone) as a divine power ⟨the ancient Greeks *worshipped* many different gods⟩
synonyms adore, deify, glorify, revere, reverence, venerate
related words admire, honor, love, regard, respect; dignify, exalt, magnify; extol (*also* extoll), laud, praise; delight, gratify, please, satisfy
near antonyms blaspheme, desecrate, profane, violate; affront, dishonor, disrespect, insult, offend, outrage, pique, ridicule, scorn, slight; displease; defame, disparage, libel, malign, slander, slur, smear
2 to feel passion, devotion, or tenderness for — see LOVE 2
3 to love or admire too much — see IDOLIZE

worshipful *adj* reflecting great admiration or devotion ⟨a movie fan's *worshipful* stare upon finally meeting her idol⟩ ⟨a teacher surrounded by *worshipful* little children⟩
synonyms adoring, adulatory, deifying, idolizing, worshipping (*also* worshiping)
related words glorifying, reverential, venerating; affectionate, fond, loving; appreciative, deferential, respectful; approving
near antonyms condemning, contemptuous, disapproving, hateful, loathing, scornful

worshipping *also* **worshiping** *n* excessive admiration of or devotion to a person — see WORSHIP

worshipping *also* **worshiping** *adj* reflecting great admiration or devotion — see WORSHIPFUL

worst *vb* to achieve a victory over — see BEAT 2

worth *n* **1** the relative usefulness or importance of something as judged by specific qualities ⟨money alone cannot determine the true *worth* of some things⟩
synonyms account, merit, valuation, value
related words assessment, estimation, evaluation; excellence, greatness, perfection; consequence, importance, significance, weight; desirability
near antonyms emptiness, worthlessness; baseness, cheapness, inferiority, meanness, paltriness, pettiness, poorness; deficiency, inadequacy, insufficiency, unacceptability
2 the amount of money for which something will find a buyer — see VALUE 1

worthless *adj* having no usefulness ⟨that expensive toy is *worthless* now that it's broken⟩
synonyms chaffy, empty, no-good, junky, null, valueless
related words base, cheap, inferior, lousy, low-grade, second-rate; bad, defective, flawed, imper-

fect, substandard, unsatisfactory; deficient, inadequate, insufficient, unacceptable
near antonyms invaluable, precious, priceless; cherished, esteemed, prized, treasured; choice, exceptional, fancy, high-grade, special
antonyms useful, valuable, worthy

worthy *adj* having sufficient worth or merit to receive one's honor, esteem, or reward ⟨made charitable contributions to the American Red Cross and other *worthy* causes⟩ ⟨a *worthy* opponent in a tennis match⟩
synonyms deserving, good, meritorious
related words admirable, commendable, creditable, laudable, praiseworthy; invaluable, priceless; cherished, prized, treasured; choice, excellent, exceptional, fancy, high-grade, primary, prime, special
near antonyms base, cheap, inferior, second-rate, substandard; bad, defective, flawed, imperfect; deficient, inadequate, insufficient, unacceptable, unsatisfactory
antonyms no-good, undeserving, valueless, worthless

wound *vb* **1** to cause bodily damage to — see INJURE 1
2 to cause hurt feelings or deep resentment in — see INSULT

wraith *n* the soul of a dead person thought of especially as appearing to living people — see GHOST

wrangle *n* an often noisy or angry expression of differing opinions — see ARGUMENT 1

wrangle *vb* to express different opinions about something often angrily — see ARGUE 2

wrangler *n* a person who takes part in a dispute — see DISPUTANT

wrap *vb* **1** to encircle or bind with or as if with a belt — see GIRD 1
2 to surround or cover closely — see ENFOLD 1

wrap up *vb* **1** to bring (an event) to a natural or appropriate stopping point — see CLOSE 3
2 to make into a short statement of the main points (as of a report) — see SUMMARIZE 1

wrath *n* **1** an intense emotional state of displeasure with someone or something — see ANGER
2 suffering, loss, or hardship imposed in response to a crime or offense — see PUNISHMENT

wrathful *adj* feeling or showing anger — see ANGRY

wrathfulness *n* an intense emotional state of displeasure with someone or something — see ANGER

wreathe *vb* to scatter or set here and there among other things — see THREAD 1

wreck *n* **1** the portion or bits of something left over or behind after it has been destroyed — see REMAINS 1
2 the destruction or loss of a ship — see SHIPWRECK
3 the violent coming together of two bodies into destructive contact — see CRASH 1

wreck *vb* **1** to cause irreparable damage to (a ship) by running aground or sinking — see SHIPWRECK
2 to bring to a complete end the physical soundness, existence, or usefulness of — see DESTROY 1

wreckage *n* **1** the state or fact of being rendered nonexistent, physically unsound, or useless — see DESTRUCTION
2 the portion or bits of something left over or behind after it has been destroyed — see REMAINS 1

3 the destruction or loss of a ship — see SHIP-WRECK

wrecking *n* the destruction or loss of a ship — see SHIPWRECK

wrench *n* **1** a forceful rotating or pulling motion for the purpose of dislodging something ⟨a sharp *wrench* only served to lodge the bent nail more securely into the wood⟩
synonyms twist, twisting, wrenching, wresting, wringing
related words draft, draw, extraction, pull, tug, yank; dislocation, displacement
2 the act or an instance of applying force on something so that it moves in the direction of the force — see PULL 1

wrench *vb* **1** to move by or as if by a forceful rotation ⟨with one last sharp yank, he *wrenched* the cap off the medicine bottle⟩
synonyms twist, wrest, wring
related words draw, dredge (up), extract, jerk, lug, pluck, pull, tug, tweak, yank; jimmy, lever, pry; budge, dislocate, displace, disturb, remove; shift, transfer, transpose
2 to injure by overuse, misuse, or pressure — see STRAIN 1
3 to separate or remove by forceful pulling — see TEAR 2

wrenching *n* a forceful rotating or pulling motion for the purpose of dislodging something — see WRENCH 1

wrest *vb* **1** to draw out by force or with effort — see EXTRACT 1
2 to get (as money) by the use of force or threats — see EXTORT
3 to get with great difficulty — see EKE OUT
4 to move by or as if by a forceful rotation — see WRENCH 1
5 to separate or remove by forceful pulling — see TEAR 2

wresting *n* a forceful rotating or pulling motion for the purpose of dislodging something — see WRENCH 1

wrestle *vb* to seize and attempt to unbalance one another for the purpose of achieving physical mastery ⟨the sisters *wrestled* on the floor over the last cookie⟩
synonyms grapple, scuffle, tussle
related words battle, clash (with), combat, contend, fight, war (against); duel, bash, batter, beat, buffet, hit, punch, slug, strike; box, spar; brawl, skirmish

wretch *n* a mean, evil, or unprincipled person — see VILLAIN

wretched *adj* **1** extremely unsatisfactory ⟨this paper is simply *wretched* —you'll have to rewrite it⟩
synonyms atrocious, awful, execrable, lousy, punk, rotten, terrible
related words bad, deficient, inferior, off, poor, substandard, unsatisfactory, wanting; contemptible, miserable, shameful; defective, faulty, flawed; low-grade, mediocre, reprehensible, second-rate; bum, useless, valueless, worthless; inadequate, insufficient, lacking; abominable, odious, vile
near antonyms choice, excellent, exceptional, first-class, first-rate, premium, prime, superior; adequate, sufficient; acceptable, satisfactory
antonyms great, marvelous (*or* marvellous), wonderful

2 arousing or deserving of one's loathing and disgust — see CONTEMPTIBLE 1
3 causing or marked by an atmosphere lacking in cheer — see GLOOMY 1
4 falling short of a standard — see BAD 1
5 feeling unhappiness — see SAD 1
6 not following or in accordance with standards of honor and decency — see IGNOBLE 2
7 of low quality — see CHEAP 2
8 deserving of one's pity — see PATHETIC 1

wretchedly *adv* with feelings of bitterness or grief — see HARD 2

wriggle *vb* **1** to make jerky or restless movements — see FIDGET
2 to move slowly with the body close to the ground — see CRAWL 1

wring *vb* **1** to get (as money) by the use of force or threats — see EXTORT
2 to get with great difficulty — see EKE OUT
3 to move by or as if by a forceful rotation — see WRENCH 1

wringing *n* a forceful rotating or pulling motion for the purpose of dislodging something — see WRENCH 1

wrinkle *n* **1** a small fold in a soft and otherwise smooth surface ⟨the old woman's face creased into *wrinkles* as she smiled⟩ ⟨the curtains cascaded onto the floor in ripples and *wrinkles*⟩
synonyms crease, crimp, crinkle, furrow
related words corrugation, layer, loop, plait, pleat, ply, pucker, seam, tuck; crow's-foot
2 something (as a device) created for the first time through the use of the imagination — see INVENTION 1

wrinkle *vb* **1** to develop creases or folds ⟨if you don't fold clothes promptly after drying, they'll *wrinkle*⟩
synonyms crease, crinkle, furrow, rumple
related words collapse, crumple, double, fold
2 to create (as by crushing) an irregular mass of creases in — see CRUMPLE 1

write *vb* **1** to compose and set down on paper the words of ⟨*write* a theme in which you name your choice for the most important person in human history⟩
synonyms author, pen, pencil (in), scratch (out)
related words cast, compose, craft, draft, draw (up), formulate, frame, prepare; recast, redraft, revise, rewrite; letter, print, type, typewrite; record, take down, transcribe; autograph, register, sign; couch, express, phrase, put, word
2 to engage in an exchange of written messages — see CORRESPOND 1

writer *n* a person who creates a written work — see AUTHOR 1

write off *vb* **1** to express scornfully one's low opinion of — see DECRY 1
2 to lower the price or value of — see DEPRECIATE 1

writhe *vb* to make jerky or restless movements — see FIDGET

wrong *adj* **1** falling short of a standard — see BAD 1
2 having an opinion that does not agree with truth or the facts — see INCORRECT 1
3 not appropriate for a particular occasion or situation — see INAPPROPRIATE
4 not being in agreement with what is true — see FALSE 1
5 not conforming to a high moral standard; morally unacceptable — see BAD 2

wrong *adv* off the desired or intended path or course ⟨all of our carefully laid plans went *wrong*⟩
synonyms afield, amiss, astray, awry
related words badly; faultily, improperly, inappropriately, incorrectly, mistakenly, wrongly; inadequately, insufficiently
near antonyms perfectly; auspiciously, favorably, promisingly; correctly, properly, rightly; appropriately, fittingly, suitably
antonyms aright, right, well

wrong *n* **1** that which is morally unacceptable — see EVIL
2 unfair or inadequate treatment of someone or something or an instance of this — see DISSERVICE

wrongdoer *n* a person who commits moral wrongs — see EVILDOER 1

wrongdoing *n* **1** a breaking of a moral or legal code — see OFFENSE 1
2 improper or illegal behavior — see MISCONDUCT

wrongful *adj* contrary to or forbidden by law — see ILLEGAL 1

wrongly *adv* in a mistaken or inappropriate way ⟨you have *wrongly* interpreted this passage in the Bible⟩
synonyms amiss, erroneously, faultily, improperly, inaccurately, inappropriately, inaptly, incorrectly, mistakenly
related words fallibly, imperfectly; extraneously, irrelevantly, meaninglessly, pointlessly, senselessly; inadequately, insufficiently; undesirably, unsatisfactorily; foolishly, unwisely
near antonyms infallibly, perfectly; meaningfully, pertinently, relevantly, sensibly; acceptably, adequately, satisfactorily, sufficiently; prudently, sagely, wisely
antonyms appropriately, aptly, correctly, fittingly, properly, right, rightly, suitably

wrongness *n* the quality or state of being unsuitable or unfitting — see INAPPROPRIATENESS 1

wroth *adj* feeling or showing anger — see ANGRY

X (out) *vb* to show (something written) to be no longer valid by drawing a cross over or a line through it ⟨*x out* the names of the people who have already left⟩

synonyms cancel, cross (out), delete, kill, scratch (out), strike (out), stroke (out)
related words blot out, efface, erase, expunge, obliterate, rub out, wipe out; cut, excise, remove

yammer *vb* to express dissatisfaction, pain, or resentment usually tiresomely — see COMPLAIN

yank *n* the act or an instance of applying force on something so that it moves in the direction of the force — see PULL 1

yank *vb* **1** to move or cause to move with a sharp quick motion — see JERK 1
2 to draw out by force or with effort — see EXTRACT
3 to separate or remove by forceful pulling — see TEAR 2

yard *n* **1** an open space wholly or partly enclosed (as by buildings or walls) — see COURT 2
2 the area around and belonging to a building — see GROUND 1

yardstick *n* something set up as an example against which others of the same type are compared — see STANDARD 1

yarn *n* **1** a brief account of something interesting that happened especially to one personally — see STORY 2
2 a work with imaginary characters and events that is shorter and usually less complex than a novel — see STORY 1

yaw *vb* to depart abruptly from a straight line or course — see SWERVE 1

yea *adv* **1** not merely this but also — see EVEN
2 used to express agreement — see YES

yeah *adv* used to express agreement — see YES

yearn (for) *vb* to have an earnest wish to own or enjoy — see DESIRE

yearning *n* a strong wish for something — see DESIRE

yeast *n* something that arouses action or activity — see IMPULSE

yell *n* a loud vocal expression of strong emotion — see SHOUT

yell *vb* **1** to cry out loudly and emotionally — see SCREAM
2 to speak so as to be heard at a distance — see CALL 1

yellow *adj* having or showing a shameful lack of courage — see COWARDLY

yellowness *n* a shameful lack of courage in the face of danger — see COWARDICE

yelp *vb* to cry out loudly and emotionally — see SCREAM

yen *n* a strong wish for something — see DESIRE

yes *adv* used to express agreement ⟨*yes*, I'll be ready for the test tomorrow⟩
synonyms all right, alright, aye (*also* ay), OK (*or* okay), yea, yeah

related words certainly, indeed, indisputably, undoubtedly, unquestionably
antonyms nay, no, no way

yesterday *n* the events or experience of former times — see PAST

yesteryear *n* the events or experience of former times — see PAST

yet *adv* 1 at a later time ⟨we may *yet* figure it out⟩
synonyms eventually, finally, someday, sometime, ultimately
phrases at last, at length, at long last
near antonyms ne'er, never, nevermore
2 in addition to what has been said — see MORE 1
3 in spite of that — see HOWEVER
4 up to this or that time — see HITHERTO

yet *conj* if it were not for the fact that — see EXCEPT

yield *n* 1 an increase usually measured in money that comes from labor, business, or property — see INCOME
2 something produced by physical or intellectual effort — see PRODUCT 1
3 the total amount collected or obtained especially at one time — see HAUL 1

yield *vb* 1 to give up and cease resistance (as to a liking, temptation, or habit) ⟨I finally *yielded* to temptation and had a bowl of ice cream⟩
synonyms bow, give in, submit, succumb, surrender
related words gratify, indulge, wallow; acquiesce (to), concede (to)
near antonyms battle, breast, combat, confront, counter, defy, face, meet, object, oppose, repel; thwart, withstand
antonyms hold off, resist
2 to produce as revenue ⟨I expect that stock to *yield* at least 14% profit this year⟩
synonyms give, pay, return
related words bring in, produce; afford, furnish, provide, supply
3 to cease resistance (as to another's arguments, demands, or control) ⟨after insisting that her answer was not incorrect, Mary *yielded* when her teacher threatened her with detention⟩
synonyms bow, budge, capitulate, concede, give in, knuckle under, quit, submit, succumb, surrender
related words acquiesce
near antonyms contend, fight
antonyms resist
4 to be the cause of (a situation, action, or state of mind) — see EFFECT
5 to fall down or in as a result of physical pressure — see COLLAPSE 1
6 to give (something) over to the control or possession of another usually under duress — see SURRENDER 1

yielding *adj* 1 receiving or enduring without offering resistance — see PASSIVE
2 not stiff in structure — see LIMP 1

yoke *n* the state of being a slave — see SLAVERY 1

yoke *vb* to put or bring together so as to form a new and longer whole — see CONNECT 1

yokel *n* an awkward or simple person especially from a small town or the country — see HICK

yon *adv* at or to a greater distance or more advanced point — see FARTHER

yonder *adv* at or to a greater distance or more advanced point — see FARTHER

yore *n* the events or experience of former times — see PAST

young *adj* being in the early stage of life, growth, or development ⟨a *young* cat requires more food than an older one⟩ ⟨a *young* tree that will eventually reach 50 feet tall⟩
synonyms adolescent, immature, juvenile, youngish, youthful
related words minor, underage; embryonic; callow, green, inexperienced, puerile, raw; babyish, childish, childlike, infantile; undeveloped, unfinished, unfledged, unformed, unripe, unripened; blooming, blossoming, burgeoning, flourishing, flowering
near antonyms aged, aging, elderly, old; fullblown, full-fledged; golden, mellow, ripe, ripened
antonyms adult, full-grown, mature, matured

youngish *adj* being in the early stage of life, growth, or development — see YOUNG

youngster *n* a young person who is between infancy and adulthood — see CHILD 1

youth *n* 1 a male person who has not yet reached adulthood — see BOY
2 a young person who is between infancy and adulthood — see CHILD 1
3 the state or time of being a child — see CHILDHOOD

youthful *adj* being in the early stage of life, growth, or development — see YOUNG

yowl *n* a loud vocal expression of strong emotion — see SHOUT

yowl *vb* to make a long loud mournful sound — see HOWL 1

yo–yo *n* a person who lacks good sense or judgment — see FOOL 1

yuletide *n* the season celebrating Christmas ⟨these days, as far as the stores are concerned, *yuletide* starts in September⟩
synonyms Christmastime, Noel
related words Advent; Christmas, nativity, Xmas, yule

yummy *adj* very pleasing to the sense of taste — see DELICIOUS 1

Z

zaniness *n* lack of good sense or judgment — see FOOLISHNESS 1

zany *adj* showing or marked by a lack of good sense or judgment — see FOOLISH 1

zany *n* a comically dressed performer (as at a circus) who entertains with playful tricks and ridiculous behavior — see CLOWN 1

zap *vb* to deliver a blow to (someone or something) usually in a strong vigorous manner — see HIT 1

zealot *n* one who is intensely or excessively devoted to a cause ⟨some people called John a *zealot* because he was always crusading for human rights⟩
synonyms crusader, fanatic, militant, partisan
related words activist; dreamer, visionary; cultist, disciple, follower, idolizer, votary; addict, aficionado, buff, bug, devotee, enthusiast, fan, fancier, fiend, freak, lover, maniac, nut; backer, patron, promoter, supporter; booster, rooter, well-wisher; faddist
near antonyms dabbler, dilettante

zenith *n* the highest part or point — see HEIGHT 1

zephyr *n* a slight or gentle movement of air — see BREEZE 1

zero *n* **1** the numerical symbol 0 or the absence of number or quantity represented by it ⟨anything multiplied by *zero* comes out to zero⟩
synonyms aught, cipher, goose egg, naught (*also* nought), nil, nothing, oh, zilch, zip
related words blank, void
2 a person of no importance or influence — see NOBODY

zero hour *n* a time or state of affairs requiring prompt or decisive action — see EMERGENCY

zest *n* the quality or state of being stimulating to the mind or senses — see PIQUANCY

zesty *adj* sharp and pleasantly stimulating to the mind or senses — see PIQUANT

zigzag *vb* to move suddenly aside or to and fro — see DODGE 1

zilch *n* **1** a person of no importance or influence — see NOBODY
2 the numerical symbol 0 or the absence of number or quantity represented by it — see ZERO 1

zing *n* active strength of body or mind — see VIGOR 1

zip *n* **1** active strength of body or mind — see VIGOR 1
2 the numerical symbol 0 or the absence of number or quantity represented by it — see ZERO 1

zip *vb* **1** to fly, turn, or move rapidly with a fluttering or vibratory sound — see WHIRR
2 to make an irregular series of quick, sudden movements — see FLIT
3 to proceed or move quickly — see HURRY 2

zippy *adj* having much high-spirited energy and movement — see LIVELY 1

zone *n* **1** a broad geographical area — see RE-GION 2
2 a part or portion having no fixed boundaries — see REGION 1

zoom *n* a monotonous sound like that of an insect in motion — see HUM

zoom *vb* **1** to fly, turn, or move rapidly with a fluttering or vibratory sound — see WHIRR
2 to proceed or move quickly — see HURRY 2
3 to rise abruptly and rapidly — see SKYROCKET

THESAURUS